Who Was Who in American History–Science and Technology®

A Component of
Who's Who in American History

MARQUIS
Who's Who

Marquis Who's Who, Inc.
200 East Ohio Street
Chicago, Illinois 60611 U.S.A.

7698

Copyright 1976 by Marquis Who's Who, Inc. All rights reserved. No part of this publication may be reproduced, stored in a retrieval system, or transmitted, in any form or by any means, electronic, mechanical, photocopying, or otherwise, without the prior written permission of the publisher, except in a magazine or newspaper article referring to a specific listee.

STATE BOARD FOR
TECHNICAL AND
COMPREHENSIVE EDUCATION
Beaufort TEC
Library

Library of Congress Catalog Card Number 76-5763
International Standard Book Number 0-8379-3601-2

Distributed in the United Kingdom by
George Prior Associated Publishers
Rugby Chambers, 2 Rugby Street
London WC1N 3QU

Manufactured in the United States of America by
Kingsport Press, Inc., Kingsport, Tennessee 37662

Table of Contents

Preface

"Be there a thousand lives, My great curiosity has stomach for 'em all." In the two hundred years since James Boswell thus expressed his "great curiosity," our interest in biography has remained insatiable.

Today's increased demand among researchers for biographical reference books, in addition to the desire of Marquis Who's Who, Inc. to contribute to the commemoration of our nation's Bicentennial, has made possible both the growth of the Who's Who in American History series and the appearance now of WHO WAS WHO IN AMERICAN HISTORY – ARTS AND LETTERS, WHO WAS WHO IN AMERICAN HISTORY – THE MILITARY, and WHO WAS WHO IN AMERICAN HISTORY – SCIENCE AND TECHNOLOGY.

Who's Who in America, the major component of the Who's Who in American History series, has advanced the highest standards of biographical compilation throughout its more than three-quarters of a century of continuous publication, while the WHO WAS WHO IN AMERICA books have sought to reflect the history and genealogical heritage of America.

Basically, however, the WAS books (to use the shortened form by which they are perhaps better known) inherited those unique characteristics that made *Who's Who in America* an internationally respected reference book and a household word here in the country of its origin.

Sketches in each WAS volume, for example, have not only been prepared from information supplied by the biographees themselves, but have been approved personally — and frequently revised — before being printed in a Marquis publication during the subject's lifetime. As with all WAS volumes, many of these sketches have been scrutinized and revised by relatives or legal representatives of the deceased biographee. Except for the resulting changes, and those occasional variations interjected by the compilers, the WAS biographies are printed precisely as they last appeared during the subject's lifetime. As a result, many contain personal data unavailable elsewhere. The preface to the first volume of *Who's Who in America* selected this fact as one of that volume's outstanding characteristics, and stated: "The book is autobiographical, the data having been obtained from first hand." It follows that WHO WAS WHO IN AMERICAN HISTORY – ARTS AND LETTERS, WHO WAS WHO IN AMERICAN HISTORY – THE MILITARY and WHO WAS WHO IN AMERICAN HISTORY – SCIENCE AND TECHNOLOGY are autobiographical to a distinctive degree. In that respect, they are unique among American biographical directories. And although condensed to the concise style that Marquis Who's Who, Inc. has made famous, their sketches contain all essential facts.

There results far more than a biographical directory of some 90,000 deceased American notables within the covers of the WAS volumes. WHO WAS WHO IN AMERICA is a vital portion of American history from the early days of the colonies to mid-1973. It is authentic history. It is the autobiography of America.

Table of Abbreviations

The following abbreviations are frequently used in this book:

*Following a sketch signifies that the published biography could not be verified.

††Non-current sketches of WHO'S WHO IN AMERICA biographees who were born 95 or more years ago (see Preface for explanation).

A.A., Associate in Arts.
A.A.A., Agricultural Adjustment Administration; Anti-Aircraft Artillery.
A.A.A.S., American Association for the Advancement of Science.
AAC, Army Air Corps.
a.a.g., asst. adjutant general.
AAF, Army Air Forces.
A. and M., Agricultural and Mechanical.
A.A.H.P.E.R., American Association for Health, Physical Education and Recreation.
A.A.O.N.M.S., Ancient Arabic Order of the Nobles of the Mystic Shrine.
A.A.S.R., Ancient Accepted Scottish Rite (Masonic).
A.B.C.F.M., American Board of Commissioners for Foreign Missions (Congregational).
A.B. (also **B.A.**), Bachelor of Arts.
A.,B.& C. R.R., Atlanta, Birmingham & Coast R.R.
ABC, American Broadcasting Company.
AC, Air Corps.
acad., academy; academic.
A.C.L. R.R., Atlantic Coast Line R.R.
A.C.P., American College of Physicians.
A.C.S., American College of Surgeons.
actg., acting.
a.d.c., aide-de-camp.
add., additional.
adj., adjutant; adjunct.
adj. gen., adjutant general.
adm., admiral.
adminstr., administrator.
adminstrn., administration.
adminstrv., administrative.
adv., advocate; advisory.
advt., advertising.
A.E., Agricultural Engineer.
AEC, Atomic Energy Commission.
A.E. and P., Ambassador Extraordinary and Plenipotentiary.
AEF, American Expeditionary Forces.
aero., aeronautics, aeronautical.
AFB, Air Force Base.
A.F.D., Doctor of Fine Arts.
A.F. and A.M., Ancient Free and Accepted Masons.
AFL (or **A.F. of L.**), American Federation of Labor.
A.F.T.R.A., American Federation TV and Radio Artists.
agr., agriculture.
agrl., agricultural.
agt., agent.
Agy., Agency.
a.i., ad interim.
A.I.A., American Institute of architects.
AID, Agency for International Development.
A.I.M., American Institute of Management.
AK—Alaska
AL—Alabama
Ala., Alabama
A.L.A., American Library Association.
Am., American, America.
A.M. (also **M.A.**), Master of Arts.
A.M.A., American Medical Association.
A.M.E., African Methodist Episcopal.
Am. Inst. E.E., American Institute of Electrical Engineers.
Am. Soc. C.E., American Society of Civil Engineers.
Am. Soc. M.E., American Society of Mechanical Emgineers.
A.N.A., Associate National Academician.
anat., anatomical.
ann., annual.
ANTA, American National theatre and Academy.
anthrop., anthropological.
antiq., antiquarian.
A.O.H., Ancient Order of Hibernians.
A.P., Associated Press.
appmnt., appointment.
apptd., appointed.
apt., apartment.
a.q.m., assistant quartermaster.
AR—Arkansas
A.R.C., American Red Cross.
archeol., archeological.
archtl., architectural.
Ark., Arkansas
Ariz.—Arizona.
Arts D., Doctor of Arts.
arty., artillery.
AS, Air Service.
A.S.C.A.P., American Society of Composers, Authors and Publishers.
ASF, Air Service Force.
assn., association.
asso., associate; associated.
asst., assistant.
astron., astronomical.
astrophys., astrophysical.
A.T.S.C., Air Technical Service Command.
A.,T.& S.F. Ry., Atchison, Topeka & Santa Fe Ry.
Atty., attorney.
AUS, Army of the United States.
Aux., Auxiliary.
Av., Avenue.
AZ—Arizona

b., born.
B., Bachelor.
B.A. (ALSO **A.B.**), Bachelor of Arts.
B.A.A.S., British Association for the Advancement of Science.
B.Agr., Bachelor of Agriculture.
Balt., Baltimore.
Bapt., Baptist.
B.Arch., Bachelor of Architecture.
B.& A. R.R., Boston & Albany R. R.
B.A.S. (or **B.S.A.**), Bachelor of Agricultural Science.
batn., batin., batt., battalion.
B.B.A., Bachelor of Business Administration.
BBC, British Broadcasting Company.
B.C., British Columbia.
B.C.E., Bachelor of Civil Engineering.
B.Chir., Bachelor of Surgery.
B.C.L., Bachelor of Civil Law.
B.C.S., Bachelor of Commercial Science.
bd., board.
B.D., Bachelor of Divinity.
B.DI., Bachelor of Didactics.
B.E. (or **Ed.B.**), Bachelor of Education.
B.E.E., Bachelor of Electrical Engineering.
BEF, British Expeditionary Force.
bet., between.
B.F.A., Bachelor of fine Arts.
bibl., bibilcal.
bibliog., bibliographical.
biog., biographical.
biol., biological.
B.J., Bachelor of Journalism.
Bklyn., Brooklyn.
B.L. (or **Litt.B.**), Bachelor of Letters.
Bldg., building.
blk., block.
B.L.S., Bachelor of Library Science.
Blvd., Boulevard.
B.& M. R.R., Boston & Marine R.R.
Bn. (or **Batn.**), Battalion.
B.O. (or **O.B.**), Bachelor of Oratory.
B.& O. R.R., Baltimore & Ohio R.R.
bot., botanical.
B.P., Bachelor of Painting.
B.P.E., Bachelor of Physical Education.
B.P.O.E., Benevolent and Protective Order of Elks.
B.Pd. (or **Pd.B.**, or **Py.B.**), Bachelor of Pedagogy.
Br., branch.
B.R.E., Bachelor of Religious Education.
brig., brigadier, brigade.
brig. gen., brigadier general.
Brit., British; Britannica.
Bro., Brother.
B., R. & P. Ry., Buffalo, Rochester & Pittsburg Ry.
B.S. (also **S.B.** or **ScB.**), Bachelor of Science.
B.S. in Ry. M.E., Bachelor in Railway Mechanical Engineering.
B.S.A., Bachelor of Agricultural Science.
B.S.D., Bachelor of Didactic Science.
B.S.T., Bachelor of Sacred Theology.
B.Th., Bachelor of Theology.
bull., bulletin.
bur., bureau.
bus., business.
B.W.I., British West Indies.

CA—California
C.A., Central America.
CAA, Civil Aeronautics Adminstrn.
CAB, Civil Aeronautics Board.
CAC, Coast Artillery Corps.
Cal., California.
Can., Canada.
Cantab., of or pertaining to Cambridge University, Eng.
capt., captain.
C. & A. R.R., Chicago & Alton R.R., now Alton Ry. Co.
Cath., Catholic.

cav., cavalry.
CBI, China - Burma - India theater of operations.
C.,B.& Q. R.R., Chicago, Burlington & Quincy R.R. Co.
CBS, Columbia Broadcasting System
CCC. Commodity Credit Corporation.
C.,C.,C.& St.L. Ry., Cleveland, Cincinnati. Chicago & St. Louis Ry.
C.E., Civil Engineer (degree), Corps of Engineers.
CEF, Canadian Expeditionary Forces.
C.& E.I. R.R., Chicago & Eastern Illinois R.R.
C.G.W. R.R., Chicago Great Western Railway.
ch., church.
Ch.D., Doctor of Chemistry.
chem., chemical.
Chem.E., Chemical Engineer.
Chgo., Chicago.
Chirurg., Chirurgical.
chmn., chairman.
chpt., chapter.
Cia, (Spanish), Company.
CIA, Central Intelligence Agency.
CIC, Counter Intelligence Corps.
C., I.&L. Ry., Chicago, indianapolis & Louisville Railway.
Cin., Cincinnati.
CIO, Congress of Industrial Organizations.
civ., civil.
Cleve., Cleveland.
climatol., climatological.
clin., clinical.
clk., clerk.
C.L.S.C., Chautauqua Literary and Scientific Circle.
C.L.U., Certified Life Underwriter.
C.M., Master in Surgery.
C. M., St.P.&P.R.R., Chicago, Milwaukee, St. Paul & Pacific R.R. Co.
C. N. Ry., Canadian Northern Ry.
C.& N.-W. Ry., Chicago & Northwestern Railway.
CO—Colorado
Co., Company;
C. of C.. Chamber of Commerce.
C.O.F., Catholic Order of Foresters.
C. of Ga. Ry., Central of Georgia Ry.
col., colonel.
coll., college
Colo., Colorado
com., committee.
comd., commanded.
comdg., commanding.
comdr., commander.
comdt., commandant.
commd., commissioned.
comml., commercial.
commn., commission.
commr., commissioner.
Com. Sub., Commissary of Subsistence.
condr., conductor.
conf., conference.
confed., confederate.
Congl., Congregational; Congressional.
Conglist., Congregationalist.
CONN—Connecticut.
cons., consulting, consultant.
consol., consolidated.
constl., constitutional.
constn., constitution.
constrn., construction.
contbd., contributed.
contbg., contributing.
contbn., contribution.
contbr., contributor.
conv., convention.
coop. (or **co-op.**), cooperative.
corp., corporation.
corr., correspondent; corresponding, correspondence.
C & O. Ry., Chesapeake & Ohio Ry. Co.
C.P.A., Certified Public Accountant.
C.P.C.U., Chartered Property and Casualty Underwriter.
C.P.H., Certificate of Public Health.
cpl. (or **corpl.**), corporal.
C.P. Ry., Canadian Pacific Ry. Co.
C. R.I.& P. Ry., Chicago, Rock Island & Pacific Ry. Co.
C.R.R. of N.J., Central Railroad Co. of New Jersey.
C.S., Christian Science.
C.S. Army, Confederate State Army.
C.S.B., Bachelor of Christian Science.
C.S.D., Doctor of Christian Science.
C.S.N., Confederate States Navy.
C.& S. Ry. Co., Colorado & Southern Ry. Co.
C.,St.P.,M.&O. Ry., Chicago, St. Paul, Minneapolis & Omaha Ry. Co.
Ct., Court.
C.T., Candidate in Theology.
CT—Connecticut.
c.Vt. Ry., Central Vermont Ry.
C.& W.I. R.R., Chicago & Western Indiana R.R. Co.
CWS, Chemical Warfare Service.
cycle., cyclopedia.
C.Z., Canal Zone.

d. (also dau.), daughter.
D., Doctor.
D. Agr., Doctor of Agriculture.
D.A.R., Daughters of the American Revolution.
D.A.V., Disabled American Veterans.
D.C., District of Columbia.-D.C.
D.C.L., Doctor of Civil Law.
D.C.S., Doctor of Commercial Science
D.D., Doctor of Divinity.
D.D.S., Doctor of Dental Surgery.
DE—Delaware.
dec., deceased.
Def., Defense.
deg., degree.
Del., Delaware.
del., delegate.
Dem., Democratic.
D.Eng. (also **Dr. Engring.**, or **e.d.** Doctor of Engineering.
denom., denominational.
dep., deputy.
dept., department.
dermatol., determatological.
desc., descendant.
devel., development.
D.F.C., Distinguished Flying Cross.
D.H.L., Doctor of Hebrew Literature.
D.& H. R.R., Delaware & Hudson R.R. Co.
dir., director.
disch., discharged.
dist., district.
distbg., distributing.
distbn., distribution.
distbr., distributor.
div., division; divinity; divorce proceedings.
D.Litt., Doctor of Literature.
D.,L.& W.R.R., Delaware Lackawanna & Western R.R. co.
D.M.D., Doctor of Medical Dentistry.
D.M.S., Doctor of Medical Science.
D.O., Doctor of Osteopathy.
DPA. Defense Production Administration.
D.P.H. (also **Dr.P.H.**), Diploma in Public Health or Doctor of Public Health or Doctor of Public Hygiene.
Dr., Doctor, Drive.
D.R., Daughters of the Revolution.
D.R.E., Doctor of Religious Education.
D.& R.G.W. R.R. Co., Denver & Rio Grande Western R.R. Co.
D.Sc. (or **Sc. D.**). Doctor of Science.
D.S.C., Distinguished Service Cross.
D.S.M., Distinguished Service Medal.
D.S.T., Doctor of Sacred Theology.
D.T.M., Doctor of Tropical Medicine.
D.V.M., Doctor of Veterinary Medicine.
D.V.S., Doctor of Veterinary Surgery.

E., East.
E. AND P., Extraordinary and Plenipotentiary.
ECA, Economic Cooperation Administration.
eccles., ecclesiastical.
ecol., ecological.
econ., economic.
ECOSOC, Economic and Social Council of UN.
ed., educated.
E.D. (also **D.Eng., or Dr.Engring.**), Doctor of Engineering.
Ed.B., Bachelor of Education.
Ed.D., Doctor of Education.
edit., edition.
Ed.M. (or **M.Ed.**), Master of Education.
edn., education.
ednl., educational.
E.E., Electrical Engineer.
E.E. and M. P., Envoy Extraordinary and Minister Plenipotentiary.
Egyptol., Egyptological.
elec., electrical.
electrochem., electrochemical.
electrophys., electrophysical.
E. M., Engineer of Mines.
ency., encyclopedia.
Eng., England.
engr., engineer.
engring., engineering.
entomol., entomological.
e.s., eldest son.
E.S.M.W.T.P., Engring. Science and Management War Training Program.
ethnol., ethnological.
ETO, European Theater of Operations.
Evang., Evangelical.

exam., examination; examining.
exc., executive.
exhbn., exhibition.
expdn., expedition.
expn., exposition.
expt., experiment.
exptl., experimental.

F., Fellow.
F.A., Field Artillery.
FAA, Federal Aviation Agency.
F.A.C.P., Fellow American College of Physicians.
F.A.C.S., Fellow American College of Surgeons.
FAO, Food and Agriculture Organization.
FBI, Federal Bureau of Investigation.
FCA, Farm Credit Administration.
FCC, Federal Communications Commission.
FCDA, Federal Civil Defense Administration.
FDA, Food and Drug Administration.
FDIA, Federal Deposit Insurance Administration.
F.E., Forest Engineer.
Fed., Federal.
Fedn., Federation.
Fgn., Foreign.
FHA, Federal Housing Administration.
FL—Florida.
Fla., Florida.
FOA, Foreign Operations Administration.
Found., Foundation.
frat., fraternity.
F.R.C.P., Fellow Royal College of Physicians (England).
F.R.C.S., Fellow Royal College of Surgeons (England).
frt., Freight.
FSA, Federal Security Agency.
Ft., Fort.
FTC, Federal Trade Commission.

G.-1 (or other number), Division of General Staff.
gastroent., gastroenterological.
GA—Georgia.
Ga., Georgia.
G.A.R., Grand Army of the Republic.
GATT, General Agreement on Tariffs and Trade.
G.,C.& S.F. Ry., Gulf, Colorado & Santa Fe Ry. Co.
G.D., Graduate in Divinity.
g.d., granddaughter.
gen., general.
geneal., genealogical.
geod., geodetic.
geog., gecgraphical; geographic.
geol., geological.
geophys., geophysical.
g.g.d., great granddaughter.
g.g.s., great grandson.
G.H.Q., General Headquarters.
G.,M.& N. R.R., Gulf, Mobile & Northern R.R. Co.
G., M.& O. R.R., Gulf, Mobile & Ohio R.R. Co.
G.N. Ry., Great Northern Ry. Co.
gov., governor.
govt., government.
govtl., governmental.
grad., graduated; graduate.
g.s., grandson.
Gt., Great.
G.T. Ry., Grand Trunk Ry. System.
GU—Guam.
G.W. Ry. of Can., Great Western Ry. of Canada.
gynecol., gynecological.

Hdqrs., Headquarters.
H.G., Home Guard.
H.H.D., Doctor of Humanities.
HHFA, Housing and Home Finance Agency.
H.I., Hawaiian Islands.
HI—Hawaii.
hist., historical.
H.M., Master of Humanics.
HOLC, Home Owners Loan Corporation.
homeo., homeopathic.
hon., honorary; honorable.
Ho. of Reps., House of Representatives.
hort., horticultural.
hosp., hospital.
Hts., Heights.
H.Ty. (or **H.T.**), Hawaiian Territory.
Hwy., Highway.
Hydrog., hydrographic.

IA— Iowa.
Ia., Iowa.
IAEA, International Atomic Energy Agency.
IBM, International Business Machines Corporation.
ICA, International Cooperation Administration.
ICC, Interstate Commerce Commission.
I.C.R.R., Illinois Central R.R. System.
ID—Idaho.
Ida., Idaho.
I.E.E.E., Institute of Electrical and Electronics Engineers.
IFC, International Finance Corp.
I.G.N. R.R., International - Great Northern R.R.
IGY, International Geophysical Year.
IL—Illinois.
Ill., Illinois.
ILO, International Labor Organization.
Illus., Illustrated.
IMF, International Monetary Fund.
IN— Indiana.
Inc., Incorporated.
Ind., Indiana, Independent.
Indpls., Indianapolis.
Indsl., Industrial.
inf., infantry.
ins., insurance.
insp., inspector.
inst., institute.
instl., institutional.
instn., institution.
instr., instructor.
instrn., instruction.
internat., international.
intro., introduction.
I.O.B.B., Independent Order of B'nai B'rith.
I.O.G.T., Independent Order of Good Templars.
I.O.O.F., Independent Order of Odd Fellows.
I.R.E., Institute of Radio Engineers.

J.B., Jurum Baccalaureus.
J.C.B., Juris Canonici Bachelor.
J.C.L., Juris Canonici Lector.
J.D., Doctor of Jurisprudence.
j.g., junior grade.
jour., journal.
jr., junior.
J.S.D., Doctor of Juristic Science.
Jud., Judicial.
J.U.D., Juris Utriusque Doctor: Doctor of Both (Canon and Civil) Laws.

Kan.—Kansas.
K.C., Knight of Columbus.
K.C.C.H., Knight Commander of Court of Honor.
K.P., Knight of Pythias.
K.N.S. Ry., Kansas City Southern Ry.
KS—Kansas.
KY—Kentucky.
Ky., Kentucky.

lab., laboratory.
lang., language.
laryngol., laryngological.
lectr., lecturer.
L.H.D., Doctor of Letters of Humanity.
L.I., Long Island.
lieut., lieutenant.
L.I. R.R., Long Island R.R. Co.
lit., literary; literature.
Lit. Hum., Literae Humanores (classics Oxford U., Eng.).
Litt.B. (or **B.L.**). Bachelor of Letters.
Litt.D., Doctor of Letters.
LL.B., Bachelor of Laws.
LL.D., Doctor of Laws.
LL.M. (or **ML.**). Master of Laws.
L.& N. R.R., Louisville & Nashville R.R.
L.O.M., Loyal Order of Moose.
L.R.C.P., Licentiate Royal Coll. Physicians.
L.R.C.S., Licentiate Royal Coll. Surgeons.
L.S., Library Science.
L.S.A., Licentiate Society of Apothecaries.
L.S.& M. S. Ry., Lake Shore & Michigan Southern Ry.
lt. or **(lieut.)**, lieutenant.
Ltd., Limited.
Luth., Lutheran.
L.V. R.R., Lehigh Valley R.R. co.

m., marriage ceremony.
M.A. (OR **A.M.**), Master of Arts.
mag., magazine.
M.Agr., Master of Agriculture.
maj., major.
Man., Manitoba.
M.Arch., Master in Architecture.
Mass., Massachusetts.
Math., mathematical.
M.B., Bachelor of Medicine.
M.B.A., Master of Business Administration.

MBS, Mutual Broadcasting System.
M.C., Medical Corps.
M.C.S., Master of Commercial Science.
mcht., merchant.
M.C. R.R., Michigan Central R.R.
Md., Maryland
MD—Maryland
M.D., Doctor of Medicine.
M.Di., Master of Didactics.
M.Dip., Master in Diplomacy.
mdse., merchandise.
M.D.V., Doctor of Veterinary Medicine.
Me., Maine.
ME—Maine.
M.E., Mechanical Engineer.
mech., mechanical.
M.E. Ch., Methodist Episcopal Church.
M.Ed., Master of Education.
med., medical.
Med. O.R.C., Medical Officers' Reserve Corps.
Med. R.C., Medical Reserve Corps.
M.E.E., Master of Electrical Engineering.
mem., member.
Meml. (or **Mem.**), Memorial.
merc., mercantile.
met., metropolitan.
metall., metallurgical.
Met.E., Metallurgical Engineer.
meteorol., meteorological.
Meth., Methodist.
metrol., metrological.
M.F., Master of Forestry.
M.F.A., Master of Fine Arts.
mfg., manufacturing.
mfr., manufacturer.
mgmt., management.
mgr., manager.
M.H.A., Master of Hospital Administration.
M.I., Military Intelligence.
MI—Michigan.
Mich., Michigan.
micros., microscopical.
mil., military.
Milw., Milwaukee.
Mineral., mineralogical.
Minn., Minnesota.
Miss., Mississippi.
M.-K.-I. R.R., Missouri - Kansas-Texas R.R. Co.
M.L. (or **LL. M.**), Master of Laws.
M.Litt., Master of Literature.
Mlle., Mademoiselle (Miss).
M.L.S., Master of Library Science.
Mme., Madame.
M.M.E., Master of Mechanical Engineering.
MN—Minnesota.
mng., managing.
Moblzn., Mobilization.
Mont., Montana.
M.P., Member of Parliament.
Mpls., Minneapolis.
M.P. R.R., Missouri Pacific R.R.
M.Pd., Master of Pedagogy.
M.P.E., Master of Physical Education.
M.P.L., Master of Patent Law.
M.R.C.P., Member Royal College of Physicians.
M.R.C.S., Member Royal College of Surgeons.
M.R.E., Master of Religious Education.
MS—Mississippi.
M.S. (or **M.Sc.**). Master of Science.
M.S.F., Master of Science of Forestry.
M.S.T., Master of Sacred Theology.
M.& St. L. R.R., Minneapolis & St. Louis R.R. Co.
M.,St.P.& S.S.M. Ry., Minneapolis, St. Paul & Sault Ste. Marie Ry.
M.S.W., Master of Social Work.
MT—Montana.
Mt., Mount.
mtn., mountain.
M.T.O.U.S.A., Mediterranean Theater of Operations, U.S. Army.
mus., museum; musical.
Mus.B., Bachelor of Music.
Mus.D. (or **Mus. Doc.**), Doctor of Music.
Mus. M., Master of Music.
Mut., Mutual.
M.V.M., Massachusetts Volunteer Militia.
M.W.A., Modern Woodmen of America.
mycol., mycological.

N., North.
N.A., National Academician; North America; National Army.
N.A.A.C.P., National Association for the Advancement of Colored People.
NACA, National Advisory Committee for Aeronautics.
N.A.D., National Academy of Design.
N.A.M., National Association of Manufacturers.
NASA, Nátional Aeronautics and Space Administration.
nat., national.
NATO, North Atlantic Treaty Organization.
N.A.T.O.U.S.A., North African Theater of Operations, U.S. Army.
nav., navigation.
NB—Nebraska.
N.B., New Brunswick.
NBC, National Broadcasting Co.
NC—North Carolina.
N.,C.& St.L. Ry., Nashville, Chattanooga & St. Louis Ry.
NDCR, National Defense Research Committee.
N.E., Northeast; New England.
N.E.A., National Education Association.
Neb., Nebraska.
neurol., neurological.
Nev., Nevada.
New Eng., New England.
N.G., National Guard.
N.G.S.N.Y., National Guard State of New York.
N.H., New Hanpshire.
NH—New Hampshire.
NIH, National Institutes of Health.
N.J., New Jersey.
NJ—New Jersey
NLRB, National Labor Relations Board.
N.Ph.D., Doctor Natural Philosophy.
N.P. Ry., Northern Pacific Ry.
No., Northern.
NPA, National Production Authority.
nr., near.
NRA, National Recovery Administration.
NRC, National Research Council.
N.S., Nova Scotia.
NSC, National Security Council.
NSF, National Science Foundation.
NSRB, National Security Resources Board.
N.T., New Testament.
numis., numismatic.
N.W., Northwest
N.& W. Ry., Norfolk & Western Ry.
NV—Nevada.
N.Y., New York.
NY—New York.
N.Y.C., New York City.
N.Y. Central R.R. (or **N.Y.C. R.R.**), New York Central Railroad Company.
N.Y.,C.& St.L. R.R., New York, Chicago & St. Louis R.R. Co.
N.Y., N.H.& H. R.R., New York, New Haven & Hartford R.R. Co.
N.Y.,O.& W. Ry., New York, Ontario & Western Ry.

O—Ohio.
OAS, Organization of American States.
O.B., Bachelor of Oratory.
obs., observatory.
obstet., obstetrical.
OCDM, Office of Civil and Defense Mobilization.
ODM, Office of Defense Mobilization.
OECD, organization European Cooperation and Development.
OEEC, Organization European Economic Cooperation.
O.E.S., Order of the Eastern Star.
ofcl., Official.
OH—Ohio.
OK—Oklahoma.
Okla., Oklahoma.
Ont., Ontario.
OPA, Office of Price Administration.
opthal., ophthalmological.
OPM, Office of Production management.
OPS, Office of Price Stabilization.
O.Q.M.G., Office of Quartermaster General.
O.R.C., Officers' Reserve Corps.
orch., orchestra.
OR—Oregon.
Ore., Oregon.
orgn., organization.
ornithol., ornithological.
O.S.B., Order of Saint Benedict.
O.S.L. R.R., Oregon Short Line R.R.
OSRD, Office of Scientific Research and Development.
OSS, Office of Strategic Services.
osteo, osteopathic.
O.T., Old Testament.
O.T.C., Officers' Training Camp.
otol., otological.
O.T.S., Officers' Training School.
O.U.A.M., Order United American Mechanics.
OWI, Office of War Information.
O.-W.R.R.& N. Co., Oregon-Washington R.R. & Navigation Co.
Oxon., Of or pertaining to Oxford University, Eng.

PA—Pennsylvania
Pa., Pennsylvania
Pa. R.R., Pennsylvania R.R.
paleontol., paleontological.
pass., passenger.
path., pathological.
Pd.B. (or **B.Pd.**, or **Py.B.**), Bachelor of Pedagogy.
Pd.D., Doctor of Pedagogy.
Pd.M., master of Pedagogy.
P.E., Protestant Episcopal.
Pe.B., Bachelor of Pediatrics.
P.E.I., Prince Edward Island.
P.E.M., Poets, Playwrights, Editors, Essayists and Novelists (Internat. Assn.).
penol., penological.
pfc., private first class.
PHA, Public Housing Administration.
pharm., pharmaceutical.
Pharm.D., Doctor of Pharmacy.
Pharm.M., Master of Pharmacy.
Ph.B., Bachelor of Philosophy.
Ph.C., Pharmaceutical Chemist.
Ph.D., Doctor of Philosophy.
Ph.G., Graduate in Pharmacy.
Phila., Philadelphia.
philol., philological.
philes., philosophical.
photog., photographic.
phys., physical.
Phys. and Surg., Physicians and Surgeons (college at Columbia University).
Physiol., physiological.
P.I., Philippine Islands.
Pitts., Pittsburg.
Pkwy., Parkway.
Pl., Place.
P.& L.E. R.R., Pittsburgh & Lake Erie R.R.
P.M., Paymaster.
P.M. R.R., Pere Marquette R.R. Co.
polit., political.
poly., polytechnic.
pomol., pomological.
P.Q., Province of Quebec.
P.R., Puerto Rico.
prep., preparatory.
pres., president.
Presbyn., Presbyterian.
presdl., presidential.
prin., principal.
Proc., Proceedings.
prod., produced (play production).
prodn., production.
prof., professor.
profl. professional.
Prog., Progressive.
propr., proprietor.
pros. atty., prosecuting attorney.
pro tem, pro tempore (for the time being).
psychiat., psychiatrical; psychiatric,
psychol., psychological.
P.T.A., parent-Teacher Association.
PTO, Pacific Theatre of Operations.
pub., public; publisher; publishing; published.
publ., publication.
pvt., private.
PWA, Public Works Administration.
Py. B., Bachelor of Pedagogy.

q.m., quartermaster.
Q.M.C., Quartermaster Corps.
q.m. gen., quartermaster general.
Q.M.O.R.C., Quartermaster Officers' Reserve Corps.
quar., quarterly.
Que., Quebec (province).
q.v., quod vide (which see).

radiol., radiological.
R.A.F., Royal Air Force.
R.A.M., Royal Arch Mason.
R.C., Roman Catholic; Reserve Corps.
RCA, Radio Corporation of America.
RCAF, Royal Canadian Air Force.
R.C.S., Revenue Cutter Service.
Rd., Road.
R.D., Rural Delivery.
R.E., Reformed Episcopal.
rec., recording.
Ref., Reformed.
Regt., Regiment.
regtl., regimental.
rehab., rehabilitation.
Rep., Republican.
rep., representative.
Res., Reserve.
ret., retired.
Rev., Reverend, Review.
rev., revised.
RFC, Reconstruction Finance Corporation.
R.F.D., Rural Free Delivery.
rhinol., rhinological.
RI—Rhode Island
R.I., Rhode Island
R.N., Registered Nurse.
rontgenal., rontgenological.
R.O.S.C., Reserve Officers' Sanitary Corps.
R.O.T.C., Reserve Officers' Training Corps.
R.P., Reformed Presbyterian.
R.P.D., Rerum Politicarum Doctor (Doctor Political Science).
R.R., Railroad.
R.T.C., Reserve Training Corps.
Ry., Railway.

s., son.
S., South.
S.A., South America.
S.A. (Spanish) Sociedad Anonima, (French) Société Anonyme.
SAC, Strategic Air Command.
S.A.L. Ry., Seaboard Air Line Ry.
san., sanitary.
S.A.R., Sons of the Am. Revolution.
Sask., Saskatchewan.
S.A.T.C., Students' Army Training Corps.
Sat.Eve.Post, Saturday Evening Post.
Savs., Savings.
S.B. (also **B.S. or Sc.B.**), Bachelor of Science.
SC—South Carolina.
S.C., South Carolina; San. Corps.
SCAP, Supreme Command Allies Pacific.
Sc.D. (or **D.Sc.**), Doctor of Science.
S.C.D., Doctor of Commercial Science.
sch., school.
sci., science; scientific.
S.C.V., Sons of Confederate Veterans.
SD— South Dakota.
S.D., South Dakota.
S.E., Southeast.
SEATO, Southeast Asia Treaty Organization.
SEC, Securities and Exchange Commission.
sec., secretary.
sect., section.
seismol., seismological.
Sem., Seminary.
sgt. (or **sergt.**), sergeant.
SHAEF, Supreme Headquarters, Allied Expeditionary Forces.
SHAPE, Supreme Headquarters Allied Powers in Europe.
S.I., Staten Island.
S.J., Society of Jesus (Jesuit).
S.J.D., Doctor Juristic Science.
S.M., Master of Science.
So., Southern.
soc., society.
social., sociological.
sos, Services of Supply.
S. of V., Sons of Veterans.
S.P. Co., Southern Pacific Co.
spl., special.
splty., specialty.
Sq., Square.
S.R.C., Signal Reserve Corps.
sr., senior.
S.R., Sons of the Revolution.
S.S., Steamship.
SSS, Selective Service System.
St., Saint; Street.
Sta., station.
statis., statistical.
Stblzn., Stabilization.
S.T.B., Bachelor of Sacred Theology.
S.T.D., Doctor of Sacred Theology.
S.T.L., Licentiate in Sacred Theology; Lector of Sacred Theology.
St.L.-S.F. R.R., St. Louis - San Francisco Ry. Co.
supr., supervisor.
supt., superintendent.
surg., surgical.
S.W., Southwest.

T.A.P.P.I., Technical Association Pulp and Paper Industry.
T. and S., Trust and Savings.
Tb (or **TB**), tuberculosis.
Tchrs., Teachers.
tech., technical; technology.
technol., technological.
Tel.&Tel., Telephone and Telegraph.
temp., temporary.
Tenn., Tennessee.
Tex., Texas.
T.H. (or **H.T.**), Territory of Hawaii.
Th.D., Doctor of Theology.
ThM., Master of Theology.
theol., theological.
TN—Tennessee.
Tng., Training.
topog., topographical.
T.P.A., Travelers Protective Assn.
T.&P. Ry., Texas & Pacific Ry. Co.
trans., transactions; transferred.
Transl., translation; translations.
transp., transportation.

treas., treasurer.
TV, television.
TX—Texas.
TVA, Tennessee Valley Authority.
Twp., Township.
Ty. (or **Ter.**), Territory.
Typog., typographical.

U. (or **Univ.**), University.
UAR, United Arab Republic.
UAW, United Automobile Workers.
U.B., United Brethren in Christ.
U.C.V., United Confederate Veterans.
U.D.C., United Daughters of the Confederacy.
U.K., United Kingdom.
UN, United Nations.
UNESCO, United Nations Educational Scientific and Cultural Organization.
UNICEF, United Nations International Childrens Emergency Fund.
UNRRA, United Nations Relief and Rehabilitation Administration.
U.P., United Presbyterian.
U.P. R.R., Union Pacific R.R.
urol., urological.
U.S., United States.
U.S.A., United States of America.
USAAF, United States Army Air Force.
USAC, United States Air Corps.
USAF, United States Air Force.
USCG, United States Coast Guard.
U.S.C.T., U.S. Colored Troops.
USES, United States Employment Service.
USIA, United States Information Agency.
USIS, United States Information Service.
USMC, United States Marine Corps.
USMHS, United States Marine Hospital Service.
USN, United States Navy.
USNA, United States National Army.
U.S.N.G., United States National Guard.
U.S.O., United Service Organizations.
USNG, United States National Guard.
USNRF, United States Naval Reserve Force.
USPHS, United States Public Health Service.
U.S.R., U.S. Reserve.
U.S.R.C.S., U.S. Revenue Cutter Service.
U.S.S., United States Ship.
USSR, Union of Soviet Socialist Republics.
U.S.V., United States Volunteers.
UT—Utah.

v., vice.
VA—Virginia.
Va., Virginia.
VA, Veterans Administration.
vet., veteran; veterinary.
V.F.W., Veterans of Foreign Wars.
V.I., Virgin Islands.
VI—Virgin Islands.
vice pres. (or **v.p.**,), vice president.
vis., visiting.
vol., volunteer; volume.
vs., versus (against).
VT—Vermont.
Vt., Vermont.

W., West.
WA—Washington (state).
WAC, Women's Army Corps.
Wash., Washington (state).
WAVES, Womens Reserve. U.S. Naval Reserve.
W.C.T.U., Women's Christian Temperance Union.
WHO, World Health Organization.
W.I., West Indies.
WI—Wisconsin.
Wis., Wisconsin.
W.& L.E. Ry., Wheeling & Lake Erie Ry. Co.
WPA, Works Progress Administration.
WPB, War Production Board.
W.P. R.R. Co., Western Pacific R.R. Co.
WSB, Wage Stabilization Board.
WV—West Virginia.
W. Va., West Virginia.

YMCA, Young Men's Christian Association.
YMHA, Young Men's Hebrew Association.
YM and YWHA, Young Men's and Young Women's Hebrew Association.
Y.& M.V. R.R., Yazoo & Mississippi Valley R.R.
yrs., years.
YWCA, Young Women's Christian Association.

zoöl., zoölogical.

ALPHABETICAL PRACTICES

Names are arranged alphabetically according to the surnames, and under identical surnames according to the first given name. If both surname and first given name are identical, names are arranged alphabetically according to the second given name. Where full names are identical, they are arranged in order of age—those of the elder being put first.

Surnames, beginning with De, Des, Du, etc., however capitalized or spaced, are recorded with the prefix preceding the surname and arranged alphabetically under the letter D.

Surnames beginning with Mac are arranged alphabetically under M. This likewise holds for names beginning with Mc; that is, all names beginning Mc will be found in alphabetical order after those beginning Mac.

Surnames beginning with Saint or St. all appear after names that would begin Sains, and such surnames are arranged according to the second part of the name, e.g., St. Clair would come before Saint Dennis.

Surnames beginning with prefix Van are arranged alphabetically under letter V.

Surnames containing the prefix Von or von are usually arranged alphabetically under letter V; any exceptions are noted by cross references (Von Kleinsmid, Rufus Bernhard; see Kleinsmid, Rufus Bernhard von).

Compound hyphenated surnames are arranged according to the first member of the compound.

Compound unhyphenated surnames common in Spanish are not rearranged but are treated as hyphenated names.

Since Chinese names have the family name first, they are so arranged, but without comma between family name and given name (as Lin Yutang).

Parentheses used in connection with a name indicate which part of the full name is usually deleted in common usage. Hence Abbott, W(illiam) Lewis indicates that the usual form of the given name is W. Lewis. In alphabetizing this type, the parentheses are not considered. However if the name is recorded Abbott, (William) Lewis, signifying that the entire name William is not commonly used, the alphabetizing would be arranged as though the name were Abbott, Lewis.

Who Was Who in American History-Science and Technology

AANDAHL, FRED GEORGE, asst. sec. of interior, gov. N.D.; b. Litchville, N.D., Apr. 9, 1897; s. Sam J. and Mamie C. (Lawry) A.; A.B., U. N.D., 1921; m. Luella Brekke, June 28, 1926; children—Mamie Louise, Margaret Winnifred, Marilyn Jean. Engaged in farming in N.D., 1921 and since 1927; supt. school, Litchville, 1922-27; state senator, N.D., 1931, 39, 41; gov. of N.D., 1944-51; asst. sec. for water and power devel., Dept. Interior, 1953-60. Mem. Svea Sch. Bd., 15 yrs.; mem. U.S. House of Reps. from N.D., 1951-52. Dir. N.D. Winter Show, an agrl. fair. Mem. Sigma Alpha Epsilon, Delta Sigma Rho. Republican. Modern Woodman. Home: Litchville, N.D. Died Apr. 7, 1966; buried Valley City, N.D.

AARON, CHARLES DETTIE, physician; b. Lockport, N.Y., May 8, 1866; s. Abraham Higham and Hanna (Barnett) A.; M.D., U. of Buffalo, N.Y., 1891; Sc.D., Heidelberg U., 1910; m. Winifred Comstock, June 23, 1902; 1 dau., Josephine Comstock. Began practice of medicine at Detroit, 1891; city physician, 1893-95; became prof. gastroenterology and dietetics, Wayne U. Coll. of Medicine, 1905, now emeritus; cons. gastroenterologist to Harper, Receiving, Tuberculosis, Shurly and Alexander Blaine hosps. Fellow West London Medico-Chirurg. Soc. (Eng.), Am. Coll. Physicians, Am. Therapeutic Soc.; mem. A.M.A., Mich. State Med. Soc., Wayne County Med. Soc., Detroit Acad. Medicine (ex-pres.), Am. Gastroenterol. Assn. (founder and sec. 14 yrs.), Northern Tri-State Med. Soc. (ex-pres.), Mich. Authors' Assn., Mich. Acad. Science, Arts and Letters, Am. Med. Editors' and Authors' Assn., Assn. for the Study of Internal Secretions, Am. Congress Internal Medicine; hon. mem. Jackson Co. Med. Soc., Kalamazoo Acad. Medicine, Eugene Field Soc.; mem. Phi Rho Sigma, Alpha Omega Alpha. Republican. Mason. Author: Diseases of the Stomach, 1911; Diseases of the Digestive Organs, 1915, 4th edit., 1927; also chapter on Dietetic Treatment of Disease (Oxford Index of Therapeutics), 1921, and many scientific papers in various foreign and American jours. Translator (from the German): Examination of the Feces by Means of the Test-Died, 1906, 2d edit., 1909. Home: 748 Seminole Av. Office: 76 Adams Av., W., Detroit MI

ABBE, CLEVELAND, meteorologist; b. at New York, N.Y., Dec. 3, 1838; s. George Waldo and Charlotte (Colgate) A.; brother of Robert A. (q.v.); A.B., Coll. City of N.Y., 1857, A.M., 1860, Ph.D., 1891; S.B., Harvard, 1864; LL.D., U. of Mich., 1888, U. of Glasgow, 1896; tutor, Trinity Ch. Grammar Sch., New York, 1857-58; studied astronomy with Brünnow, of Ann Arbor, Mich., 1858-59, under B.A. Gould, Cambridge, Mass., 1860-64; m. Frances Martha Neal, May 10, 1870 (died July 24, 1908); 2d, Margaret A. Percival, Apr. 12, 1909; children—Cleveland A., Jr., William and Truman A. Asst. prof. Mich. Agrl. Coll., 1859; tutor, U. of Mich., 1859-60; aid in U.S. Coast and Geod. Survey, 1860-64; guest at Nicholas Central Obs., Poulkova, nr. St. Petersburg, Russia, 1864-66; aid U.S. Naval Obs., 1867-68; dir. Cincinnati Obs., 1868-73. On Sept. 1, 1869, inaugurated daily weather report for Cincinnati Chamber of Commerce, which at once led U.S. Govt. to take up similar work; became widely known as "Old Probs"; meteorologist in the U.S. Signal Service, 1871-91, U.S. Weather Bureau 1891—; editor Monthly Weather Review, 1873 and 1892-1915; editor Bulletin Mount Weather Observatory, 1909-13; prof. meteorology, Columbian (now George Washington) U., 1886-1905; lecturer on meteorology, Johns Hopkins, 1896-1914. Mem. Nat. Acad. Sciences. Author: Report on the Total Solar Eclipse of July 29, 1878, 1881; Report on Standard Time, 1879, which started the agitation that resulted in the modern standard hour meridians from Greenwich; Meteorological Apparatus and Methods, 1887; Preliminary Studies in Storm and Weather Prediction, 1889; The Mechanics of the Earth's Atmosphere, Vol. I, 1891, Vol. II, 1909; The Altitude of the Aurora, 1896; Physical Basis of Long-Range Forecasting, 1902. Died Oct. 28, 1916.

ABBE, CLEVELAND, JR., geographer; b. Washington, D.C., Mar. 25, 1872; s. Cleveland and Frances Martha (Neal) A.; A.B., Harvard, 1894, A.M., 1896; Ph.D., Johns Hopkins, 1898; student, geography Imperial U., Vienna, 1901-03; m. Frieda Dauer, Apr. 12, 1903; children—Ernest Cleveland, Elfriede Martha. Inst. physiography, Corcoran Scientific Sch., Columbia, 1894-97; asst. Md. Geol. Survey, 1896-1901; prof. geology and biology, Western Md. Coll., 1898-99; acting prof. natural sciences Winthrop Normal and Industrial Coll., S.C., 1899-1901; aid U.S. Weather Bureau, 1906-08; research observer, U.S. Weather Bureau, 1906-08; asst. editor Monthly Weather Review, 1908-10, and 1914-16, editor, 1916-18; meteorologist, 1914-18; asst. in library U.S. Weather Bur., 1910-13. Asso. editor in charge Scientific Am. Supplement, New York, May-Oct., 1919; asst. editor Engring. and Mining Jour., New York, 1919-21; asst. prof. Coll. of City of N.Y., 1921-25; editor of volumes of Geo. F. Baker Non-resident Lectureship in Chemistry at Cornell U., 1930—. Home: Ithaca, N.Y. Died Apr. 18, 1934.

ABBE, ROBERT, surgeon; b. New York, N.Y., April 13, 1851; s. George Waldo and Charlotte (Colgate) A.; brother of Cleveland A.; A.B., Coll. City of N.Y., 1870; M.D., College Phys. and Surg. (Columbia), 1874; m. Mrs. Catherine Armory Palmer, Nov. 14, 1891. Instr. English, drawing and geometry, Coll. City of N.Y., 1870-72; attending surgeon out-patient dept., N.Y. Hosp., 1877-84; prof. didactic surgery, Woman's Med. Coll., 2 yrs.; surgeon to St. Luke's Hosp. 1884—, N.Y. Cancer Hosp., 1893—; attending surgeon N.Y. Babies' Hosp., 1892-97; prof. surgery, N.Y. Post-Grad. Med. Sch., 1889-97. Died Mar. 7, 1928.

ABBE, TRUMAN, surgeon; b. Washington, Nov. 1, 1873; s. Cleveland and Frances Martha (Neal) A.; A.B., Harvard, 1895; M.D., Coll. Physicians and Surgeons (Columbia), 1899; U. Berlin Med. Sch., 1899-1900; surg. intern Mt. Sinai Hosp., N.Y., 1900-02; intern N.Y. Lying-in Hosp., 1902; m. Ethel Whipple Brown, Apr. 22, 1905; children—Truman Waldo, Petrena, Gilbert, Margaret, William Whipple. Instr. in physics, 1902-04, physiology, 1902-05, surgery, 1903-05, Georgetown U.; instr. physiology, 1905-10, surgery, 1909-25, George Washington U.; anesthetist Columbia Hosp. George Washington U.; anesthetist Columbia Hosp. for Women, 1906-16; surgeon in charge Garfield for Women, 1906-16; surgeon in charge Garfield Surg. Dispensary, 1906-10; asso. surgeon, Columbia Hosp. for Women, 1916-26, asso. radiologist, 1916-46; prof. of Roentgenology, George Washington U., 1917-19. Awarded silver medal, Jamestown Expn., 1907, for demonstration of application of radium to medicine. Mem. A.M.A., Dist. Columbia Med. Soc.; hon. fellow Wash. Gynecol. Soc., Phi Chi. Unitarian. Club: Harvard. Author: Robert Colgate the Immigrant, a geneology of the New York Colgates (with Hubert A. Howson), 1942; also articles on radium, cancer, surgery. Editor: Vol. III, Medical Jurisprudence by Wharton and Stilles, 1905. Home: 7308 Radcliffe Dr., College Park, Md. Died May 2, 1955.

ABBIATI, F. ALEXANDER, (ab-e-a'te), chem. exec.; b. Barre, Vt., Dec. 30, 1904; s. Charles and Regina (Comolli) A.; B.S., U. N.H., 1927; m. Virginia M. McCrillis, Sept. 21, 1929; children—Melvin A., M. Virginia. Asst. sales mgr. Merrimac div. Monsanto Chem. Co., Everett, Mass., 1927-38, plastics div., Springfield, Mass., 1938-39, asst. gen. mgr. sales, 1939-44, gen. mgr. sales, 1944-47, asst. gen. mgr., 1947-50, gen. mgr. since 1950, v.p. Monsanto Chem. Co. since 1951; pres. Shawinigan Resins Corp.; dir. Union Trust Co.; corporator Hampden Savs. Bank. Dir. Future Springfield; mem. adv. com. Salvation Army, Springfield. Trustee Proctor Acad., Andover, N.H. Mem. Mfg. Chemists Assn., Employers Assn. Western Mass. (dir.), Am. Chem. Soc., Soc. Plastics Industry, Springfield C. of C. (dir.). Clubs: Colony (Springfield, Mass.); Metropolitan (N.Y. City); Longmeadow (Mass.) Country. Home: 130 Ellington St., Longmeadow. Office: Monsanto Chemical Co., Plastics Div., Springfield 2, Mass. Died Aug. 13, 1952; buried Longmeadow (Mass.) Cemetery.

ABBOT, FREDERIC VAUGHAN, army officer, b. Cambridge, Mass., Mar. 4, 1858; s. Henry Larcom and Mary Susan (Everett) A.; grad. Flushing (L.I.) Inst. 1873; grad. U.S. Mil. Acad., 1879; m. Sara Julie Dehon, Oct. 15, 1885; children—Marion Beatrice, Elinor Russell, Henry Dehon. Second lt. engr. corps, June 13, 1879; advanced through grades to col., June 24, 1909, brig. gen. N.A., Aug. 5, 1917. Survey of boundary line bet. Md. and Va., 1883-84; asst. to chief of engrs. U.S. Army, Aug. 12, 1900-10; charge defensive works southern and eastern entrances to N.Y. Harbor, and of river and harbor works, 2d N.Y. Dist., Apr. 30, 1915-Oct. 15, 1917; prin. asst. to chief of engrs. U.S. Army and comdg. officer, post of Washington Barracks, 1917; acting chief of engrs., U.S. Army, 1918-19; retired May 10, 1920. Home: Washington, D.C. Died Sept. 26, 1928.

ABBOTT, AMOS, congressman; b. Andover, Mass., Sept. 10, 1786; attended Bradford Acad. Became a mcht.; hwy. surveyor, 1812, 14, 16; town clk., 1822, 26, 28; town treas., 1824-29; mem. sch. com., 1828-29, 30; a founder Boston Portland R.R. (now Boston & Me. R.R.), 1833, dir., 1833-41; mem. Mass. Ho. of Reps., 1835, 36, 37, 43, mem. Mass. Senate, 1840-42; mem. U.S. Ho. of Reps. (Whig) from Mass., 28th-30th congresses, 1843-49. Died Andover, Nov. 2, 1868; buried South Parish Cemetery.

ABBOTT, ARTHUR VAUGHAN, Civil mech. and elec. engr., author; b. New York, N.Y., 1854; mem. Am. Inst. Mining Engrs., 1882—; mem. Am. Inst. Elec. Engrs. (v.p., 1902); was chief engr. Chicago Telephone Co., engr. Westinghouse, Church, Kerr & Co., 1902—. Author Electrical Transmission of Energy; The Evolution of a Switchboard; History and Use of Testing Machines; Treatise on Fuel. Home: New York, N.Y. Died 1906.

ABBOTT, CHARLES CONRAD, naturalist; b. Trenton, N.J., June 4, 1843; s. Timothy and Susan (Conrad) A.; M.D., U. of Pa., 1865; m. Julia Boggs Olden, Feb. 13, 1867. Made large collection of archaeol. specimens, now in Peabody Mus., Cambridge, Mass., where he was asst., 1876-89. Demonstrated existence of man in Delaware River Valley during glacial and subsequent prehistoric periods. Made 2d large archaeological collection of Del. Valley for Princeton, 1901-07. Author: The Stone Age in New Jersey, 1876; Primitive Industry, 1881; A Naturalist's Rambles About Home, 1884; Upland and Meadow, 1886; Wasteland Wanderings, 1887; Days Out of Doors, 1889; Outings at Odd Times, 1890; Recent Rambles, 1892; Travels in a Treetop, 1894; The Birds About Us, 1894; Notes of the Night, 1895; A Colonial Wooing (novel), 1895; Birdland Echoes, 1896; When the Century Was New (novel) 1897; The Freedom of the Fields, 1898; Clear Skies and Cloudy, 1899; In Nature's Realm, 1900; Archealogia Explorations in the Valley of the Delaware, 1894; Rambles of an Idler, 1906; Archaeologia Nova Caesarea, 1907, 1908, 1909; Ten Years' Diggings in Lanâpè Land, 1912. Home: Bristol, Pa. Died July 27, 1919.

ABBOTT, CLINTON GILBERT, museum dir., ornithologist; b. Liverpool, Eng., Apr. 17, 1881 (parents U.S. citizens); s. Lewis Lowe and Grace (Van Dusen) A.; came to U.S., 1897; A.B. Columbia, 1903, student Cornell U., 1914-15; m. Dorothy Clarke, May 18, 1915; children—Dorothea Van Dusen (Mrs. Hal G. Evarts, Jr.), Lois Virginia (Mrs. Peter D. Whitney), Lucia Grace. Lecturer on ornithology and travel, Bd. of Edn., N.Y.; confidential sec. and editor, Conservation Comm., State of N.Y., 1918-21; in charge pub. edn., San Diego Natural History Museum, 1921-22, dir. since 1922. Trustee, The Bishop's Sch., La Jolla, Calif. Fellow San Diego Soc. Natural History (pres. 1923-25); mem. Linnaean Soc., N.Y. (sec. 1904-10, v.p. 1910-14), Am. Ornithologists' Union, Cooper Ornith. Club (pres. south div. 1934), Am. Soc. Mammalogists, Western Soc. Naturalists, National Audubon Soc., Internat. Com. for Wildlife Protection, Alpha Delta Phi, Phi Beta Kappa. Clubs: Univ. (San Diego); La Jolla Beach and Tennis. Author: The Home Life of the Osprey, 1911. Contbr. to sci. journs. Home: 129 W. Palm St. Address: Natural History Museum, Balboa Park, San Diego, Calif. Died Mar. 5, 1946.

ABBOTT, EDVILLE GERHARDT, orthopedic surgeon; b. Hancock, Me., Nov. 6, 1871; s. Alonzo and Maria B. (Mercer) A.; grad. E. Me. Conf. Sem., Bucksports, Me., 1889; M.D., Bowdoin, 1898, A.B., 1906, A.M., 1908, Sc.D., 1914; Sc.D., Colby, 1925; studied Friedrich Wilhelm Universität, Berlin, 1900-01; also in Vienna, Paris, Göttingen and London; m. Sara Sargent, Mar. 14, 1893. Surgeon in chief, Children's Hosp., Portland, Me. Mem. bd. dirs. Nat. Bank of Commerce, Portland. Author: Treatment of Scoliosis (trans. foreign langs.) Home: Portland, Me. Died Aug. 27, 1938.

ABBOTT, FRANK, dentist, educator; b. Shapleigh, Me., Sept. 5, 1836; studied dentistry with Dr. J.E. Ostrander, Onedia, N.Y., 1855; M.D., U. City N.Y., 1871; m. Catharine Ann Cuyler, 3 children. Practised dentistry, Johnstown, N.Y., 1858; served as 1st lt. 115th N.Y. Volunteer Inf., U.S. Army, Civil War, captured at Harper's Ferry, 1862, exchanged, returned to practice dentistry; moved to N.Y.C., 1863; became clin. lectr. N.Y. Coll. of Dentistry, 1866, prof. operative dentistry, 1868, dean, 1869-97, failed in attempts to establish chairs of pathology and bacteriology (with his son as incumbent) and substitution of new charter for the act of incorporation of U. State N.Y., 1894-95; pres. Am. Dental Assn., 1888; pres. Nat. Assn. Dental Faculties, 1895. Author: Dental Pathology and Practice (textbook), 1896. Died Apr. 20, 1897.

ABBOTT, FREDERICK WALLACE, physician; b. Dover, N.H., Mar. 5, 1861; s. Sylvester and Elizabeth Graves (Wortman) A.; A.B., U. of America, 1883; attended Med. Sch. of Me. (mem. dept. Bowdoin Coll.), 1884, 1885; M.D., Eclectic Med. Coll. of Me., 1886; H.F.B.S., 1893; A.M., Taylor U, 1901; Ph.D., Nat. Normal U., 1901; LL.D., Potomac U., 1905; F.S.Sc. (London), 1908; F.S.P. (Eng.), 1914; F.B.P.C. (Eng.), 1915; F.P.C. (London), 1916; D.P.H., Eclectic Med. U., Kansas City, Mo., 1917; m. Sylvina Apphia Emery, Sept. 2, 1886. Practiced in Taunton, Mass., 1886—; lecturer on physiology and hygiene in Merrimack County Acad., 1892; asso. editor Mass. Med. Jour., 1894-1904, Am. Med. Jour., 1906—; senior censor Eclectic Med. Coll. of City of New York; prof. eugenics, Eclectic Med. U., Kansas City, Mo., 1913—; prof. med. history and of med. ethics, Middlesex, Coll. Medicine amd Surgery, and consulting physician at Middlesex Hosp., 1916—. Pres. Mass. Eclectic Med. Soc., 1894, N.E. Eclectic Med. Assn., 1900, Am. Eclectic Materia Medica Assn., 1905-07, Boston Dist. Eclectic Med. Soc., 1910; v.p. Am. Anti-Tuberculosis League, 1907. Academician of Toulouse, France; life-mem. and medalist of the 1st class (gold) Italian Acad. Physics and Chemistry; chmn. bd. of trustees and sec.-treas. Alumnal Soc., Potomac U. Democrat. Author: Limitation of the Family, 1891; The Education of Youth Upon Matters Sexual, 1895. Home: Taunton, Mass. Died June 19, 1919.

ABBOTT, GEORGE ALONZO, prof. chemistry; b. Alma, Marion Co., Ill., July 7, 1874; s. John Baughman and Harriet (Stuart) A.; B.S., De Pauw U., 1895, M.A., 1896; Ph.D. in Chemistry, Mass. Inst. Tech., 1908; m. Ruth Ware, of Minneapolis, Minn., June 15, 1910; children—Marion Ware, Stuart Ware. Served as instr. in chemistry, high schs., Evansville (Ind.), Duluth (Minn.), Manual Tr. High Sch., Indianapolis; was Austin fellow and research asst., Mass. Inst. Tech., also fellow U. of Chicago; asst. prof. organic and industrial chemistry, N. Dak. State Coll., 1908-10; prof. chemistry and head of chemistry dept., U. of N. Dak., since 1910, also chmn. grad. dept.; exchange lecturer U. of Manitoba, 1912. Consulting chemist and court expert. Del. 8th Internat. Congress of Applied Chemistry, New York, 1922. Mem. Am. Chem. Soc., N. Dak. Acad. Science (sec.), Am. Assn. Univ. Profs., N.E.A., Delta Kappa Epsilon, Phi Beta Kappa, Sigma Xi; fellow Ind. Acad. Science. Republican. Methodist. Clubs: Fortnightly, Franklin, Commercial, Kiwanis Internat. (lt. gov.; dist. gov. Minn. and Dakotas). Contbr. to chem. jours.; contbg. editor Jour. of Chem. Edn. Home: Grand Forks ND

ABBOTT, HORACE, iron mfr.; b. Sudbury, Mass., July 29, 1806; s. Alpheus and Lydia (Fay) A.; m. Charlotte Hapgood, 1830, 7 children. Owner Canton Iron Works, Balt., specialized in prodn. wrought iron shafts, cranks, axles and other equipment for steamboats, railroads; constructed a rolling-mill capable of turning out the largest rolled plate in the U.S., 1850, other mills erected 1857, 59, 61; made armor plates for the Monitor and for nearly all vessels of Monitor class constructed on the Atlantic Coast; elected pres. Abbott Iron Co., 1865; a founder Balt. 1st Nat. Bank; dir. 2d Nat. Bank, Balt. Copper Co., Union R.R. of Balt. Died Aug. 8, 1887

ABBOTT, JACOB, educator, writer; b. Hallowell, Me., Nov. 14, 1803; s. Jacob II and Betsey Abbot; grad. Bowdoin Coll., 1820; studied theology Andover (Me.) Sem., 1821-22, 24; m. Harriet Vaughan, May 18, 1829; m. 2d, Mrs. Mary Dana Woodbury, 1853; at least 1 son, Edward. Tchr., Portland (Me. Acad. (Henry Wadsworth Longfellow was one of his pupils), 1820-21; tchr., Beverly, Mass., 1823; tutor Amherst Coll., 1824-25, prof. mathematics and natural philosophy, 1825; licensed to preach by Hampshire Assn., Congregationalist Ch., 1826; moved to Boston, 1828; founder, prin. Mt. Vernon Sch. (one of earliest schs. for young women, largely self-governing), 1828-33; minister Eliot Congregational Ch., Roxbury, Mass., 1834-35; founder (with his brothers) Abbott's Instn., N.Y.C., 1843-51, Mt. Vernon Sch. for Boys, 1845-58; sole author of 180 volumes, joint author of 31 vols.; books include: The Young Christian (1st important work), 1832; The Corner Stone (became subject of controversy because of emphasis on Unitarianism, changed wording in later edits. to clarify meanings), 1834; Rollo series (stories for elementary instrn. of children), 28 vols., begun 1834. Died Farmington, Me., Oct. 31, 1879.

ABBOTT, JOEL, congressman; b. Fairfield, Conn., Mar. 17, 1776; studied medicine under father in Fairfield. Began practice medicine in Washington, Ga., 1794; held several local offices; mem. Ga. Ho. of Reps., 1809, twice re-elected; mem. U. S. Ho. of Reps. (Democrat) from Ga., 15th-18th congresses, 1817-25; del. to conv. in Phila. which met to prepare 1st Nat. Pharmacopoeia, 1820. Died Washington, Ga., Nov. 19, 1826; buried Rest Haven Cemetery.

ABBOTT, SAMUEL WARREN, M.D., sec. Mass. State Bd. of Health, 1886—; b. Woburn, Mass., June 12, 1837; grad. Harvard Med. School, 1862; asst. surgeon, U.S. Navy, 1861-64, resigned; asst. surgeon and surgeon 1st Mass. cav., 1864-65; coroner, Middlesex County, Mass., 1872-77; med. examiner, same, 1877-84; practiced medicine at Woburn, 1865-69; later at Wakefield. Author of The Past and Present Condition of Public Hygiene and State Medicine in the United States, 1900 (U.S. Commrs. Paris Expn.). Home: Newton Centre, Mass. Died 1904.

ABBOTT, WALLACE CALVIN, physician, editor; b. Bridgewater, Vt., Oct. 12,1857; s. Luther and Wealtha (Barrows) A.; Randolph (Vt.) State Normal Sch.; St. Johnsbury (Vt.) Coll.; Dartmouth Coll.; M.D., U. of Mich., 1885; m. Clara Ingraham, Aug. 10, 1886. Settled in Chicago, 1886, and engaged in gen. practice; established The Abbott Alkaloidal Co., now The Abbott Laboratories; mng. editor Am. Jour. Clin. Medicine. Republican. Methodist. Clubs: Hamilton, Press, Chicago Advertising, Union League, Author: (with W.F. Waugh) Text-Book of Alkaloidal Practice. Home: Chicago, Ill. Died July 4, 1921.

ABBOTT, WILLIAM HAWKINS, oil producer; b. Middlebury, Conn., Oct. 27, 1819; s. David and Hannah (Hawkins) A.; m. Jane Wheeler, Sept. 1845. Clk., gen. store, Watertown, Conn., circa 1837-44; moved to Newton Falls, O., entered gen. merc. bus., 1845; partner in store Bronson & Abbott, 1846-47, sole owner, 1848-62, also in real estate bus., 1848-62; became interested in oil (discovered in Pa. circa 1860), leased farm where well was being drilled; went to N.Y. (after well produced oil), sold 200 barrels oil at 35 cents per gallon to Schieffelin Bros. (marked beginning of oil trade); a builder of 1st refinery at Titusville, Pa., 1861; moved to Titusville, 1862, brought in coal for domestic use (1st retail coal bus.); engaged in coal mining, 1865; organized co., built Titusville and Pitt-Hole plank road at cost of $200,000, 1865; formed (with Henery Harley) Pa. Transp. Co. (1st Oil pipe-line consolidation), 1867; helped revive interest in Union & Titusville R.R. Co., 1870 (opened 1871); pres. Citizens Bank of Titusville. Died Jan. 8, 1901

ABBOTT, WILLIAM LAMONT, engineer; b. Whiteside County, Illinois, February 14, 1861; s. Asa M. and Sarah (Sperry) A.; M.E., University of Illinois, 1884; m. Carrie Entwhistle, Sept. 14, 1887; children—Arthur William, Helen (Mrs. O.C.F. Randolph, dec.), Robert Edward, Josephine Ellenor, Dorothy Caroline (Mrs. Leonard Knopf). Machinist and draftsman in Chicago, 1884-87; president National Electric Construction Co., 1887-94; chief engineer, power house, Chicago Edison Co., 1894-99; chief operating engr. same, 1899-1935; retired; later with Otto Randolph, Inc., gen. contractors. Fellow Am. Inst. Elec. Engrs.; hon. mem. Am. Soc. Mech. Engrs. (pres. 1926), Western Soc. Engrs. (pres. 1907). Trustee U. of Ill., 1904-23 (pres. bd 14 yrs.), Republican. Clubs: Chicago Athletic, Engineers, University. Hon. LL.D. from U. of Ill., 1929. Recipient Washington Award from 4 nat. engrng. socs. and Western Soc. Engrs., 1942. Home: 3500 Sheridan Rd. Office: 20 N. Wacker Dr., Chicago IL

ABEL, JOHN JACOB, pharmacologist; b. Cleveland, O., May 19, 1857; s. George M. and Mary (Becker) A.; Ph.B., U. of Mich., 1883, A.M., 1903, Sc.D., 1912; Sc.D., U. of Pittsburgh, 1915; LL.D., U. of Cambridge, Eng., 1920; Sc.D., Harvard, 1925, Yale U., 1927; hon. M.D., John Casmir U., Lwow, Poland, John Hopkins, 1883-84; student of chemistry and medicine at Leipzig, Strassburg, Heidelberg, Vienna, Berne, Würsburg and Berlin, 1884-91; M.D., Strassburg, 1888; m. Mary W. Hinman, July 10, 1883. Lecturer and prof. materia medica amd therapeutics, U. of Mich., 1891-93; prof. pharmacology John Hopkins, 1893-1932; prof. emeritus pharmacology, and dir. of Laboratory for Endocrine Research, 1932—. Editor Jour. of Pharmacology and Exptl. Therapeutics, 1909-32. Awarded Research Corporation prize 1925; first award of lectureship of Kober Foundation, Am. Assn. Physicians, 1925; Willard Gibbs medal, Chicago sect. Am. Chem. Soc., 1926; gold medal, Soc. of Apothecaries, London, 1928; Philip A. Conné medal, New York Chemists' Club, 1932; Kober medal awarded, 1934. Home: Baltimore, Md. Died May 26, 1938.

ABELL, ARUNAH SHEPHERDSON, journalist; b. East Providence, R.I., Aug. 10, 1806; s. Caleb and Elona (Shepherdson) A.; m. Mary Fox, 1838, 8 children. Apprenticed by his father to Providence Patriot, 1822; started Public Ledger, Phila., 1836; issued 1st number Balt. Sun, 1837, continued as sole propr., 1868; established daily pony express from New Orleans, 1847; 1st to use telegraphy to transmit news, 1st to buy Hoe cylinder press. Died Balt., Apr. 19, 1888.

ABELL, IRVIN, surgeon; b. Lebanon, Ky., Sept. 13, 1876; s. Irvin and Sarah Silesia (Rogers) A.; A.M., St. Mary's Coll., St. Mary, Ky., 1894; M.D., Louisville Med. Coll., 1897; studied in U. of Berlin, Bermany, 1898; Sc.D., U. of Louisville, 1937; D.Sc., Georgetown U., 1939, Manhattan Coll., N.Y. City, 1939; LL.D., Marquette U., Milwaukee, 1939; Sc.D., U. of Ky., 1942; LL.D., U. of Cincinnati, 1943; m. Carrie Harting, Oct. 19, 1907; children—Irvin, William, Rogers (dec.), Spalding. Practiced in Louisville, Ky., since 1900; prof. surgery, U. of Louisville, 1904-47; visiting surgeon, Louisville Public Hosp., St. Joseph Infirmary; cons. surgeon, Children's Free Hosp., Kosair Hosp. for Crippled Children; dir. Commonwealth Life Ins. Co., Citizens Fidelity Bank and Trust Co. Awarded Laetare medal by U. of Notre Dame, 1938. Trustee University of Louisville. Fellow American College of Surgeons, American Surgical Assn.; hon. fellow Royal Co-lege of Surgeons, Eng., 1947; member A.M.A. (pres. 1938-39), Ky. State Med. Assn. (pres. 1927), Jefferson Co. Med. Soc., Southern Med. Assn. (pres. 1933), Southern Surg. Assn. (pres. 1926), Am. Urol. Assn., Am. Gastroenter-] ological Assn. (pres. 1939-40), Am. Coll. Surgeons (pres. 1945-46), Assn. Mil. Surgs. (pres. 1945-46), Southeastern Surg. Congress (pres. 1937), Phi Chi, Alpha Omega Alpha, Phi Kappa Phi. Catholic. Clubs: Pendennis, Louisville Country; Army and Navy Country (Washington, D.C.). Home: 1433 S. Third St., Louisville 8 Office: 321 W. Broadway, Louisville 2, Ky. Died Aug. 28, 1949.

ABERNATHY, CHESS, JR., aerospace co. exec.; b. Gastonia, N.C., Mar. 2, 1912; s. Chess and Myra (Herman) A.; A.B., Emory U., 1934; postgrad. U. Mich., 1939, Pub. Relations Soc. Am. Inst., Cornell U., 1962; m. Martha Virginia McDonald, Sept. 24, 1937; children—Martha Virginia, Margaret Louise. Editor in chief Cobb County Times, Marietta, Ga., 1934-40; alumni sec., editor, then alumni dir. Emory U., Atlanta, 1940-50; pres. Brumby Inc., Times-Jour., Inc., Marietta, Ga., 1950-52; pub. relations coordinator Lockheed-Ga. Co., Marietta, 1953-58, pub. information mgr., 1958-69. Instr. journalism Emory U., 1940-43, Ga. State Coll., 1955-56. Mem. regional expansion council U.S. Dept. Commerce. Dir. Met. Atlanta Community Services, Cobb County Emergency Aid Assn.; bd. dirs. Cobb YMCA; alumni council Emory U. Served to capt. AUS, 1942-45; maj. Res. Decorated Legion of Merit. Recipient honor award Emory U., 1950; Rosenwald fellow, 1939-40. Mem. Pub. Relations Soc. Am. Cobb County C. of C., Assn. U.S. Army, Navy League, Army Aviation Assn. Am., Sigma Alpha Epsilon, Sigma Delta Chi. Methodist. Home: Marietta GA Died May 3, 1969.

ABERNATHY, MILTON AUBREY, gas exec.; b. Whitney, Tex., Dec. 11, 1892; s. William Harvel and Minnie Annetta (Overton) A.; B.S., Texas A. and M. Coll., 1916; m. Ernestine Olivia Faulk, Oct. 16, 1923. Various positions r.r. maintenance, location, constrn., 1916-20; engr. Magnolia Petroleum Co., Dallas, 1920-24; supt. Magnolia Gas Co., Dallas, 1924-30; gen. supt. transmission United Gas Pub. Service Co., Houston, 1930-37; v.p., dir. United Gas Pipe Line Co. since 1937, United Gas Corp. since 1947; dir. Union Producing Co., Shreveport, La., since 1947, v.p. since 1952. Mem. gas. industry adv. council, oil and gas div. U.S. Dept. of Interior. Mem. bd. nat., so. YMCA's. Trustee Tex. A. and M. Coll. Research Found., Centenary Coll. Served as lt., 315th C.E., World War I. Mem. Am. (director), So. gas assns., Am. Petroleum Inst., Mid-Continent Oil and Gas Assn. Methodist. Clubs: Engineers (N.Y. City); Country, Petroleum, Rotary (Shreveport); Petroleum (New Orleans). Home: 555 Southfield Rd. Office: United Gas Bldg., Shreveport, La. Died Nov. 2, 1955; buried Forest Park Cemetery, Shreveport.

ABERT, JAMES WILLIAM, topog. artist; b. Nov. 18, 1820. Mt. Holly, N.J.; grad. U.S. Mil. Acad., 1842. Served with Topog. Engrs. Corps, U.S. Army; made several expdns. into West, illustrated reports of expdns. with sketches; asst. in drawing U.S. Mil. Acad., 1848-50; engaged in improvement of Western rivers, circa 1850-60; served with Union Army during Civil War, wounded, ret. as col., 1864; became prof. mathematics and drawing U. Mo. after Civil War; his original watercolors are now privately owned. Died 1871.

ABERT, JOHN JAMES, topog. engr.; b. Shepherdstown, Va., Sept. 17, 1788; s. John and Margarita (Meng) A.; grad. U.S. Mil. Acad., 1811; m. Ellen Matlack Stretch, Jan. 5, 1812, 6 children including James William, Silvanus Thayer, William Stretch. Asst. to chief clk. War Office, 1811-14; admitted to D.C. bar, 1813; volunteer in D.C. Militia, 1814; served in battle of Bladensburg; apptd. maj. Topog. Engrs., U.S. Army, 1814; assisted in geodetic surveys Atlantic coast, 1816-18; made topog. surveys for river and harbor improvements, canals and defense; brevetted lt. col., 1824; in charge of Topog. Bur., War Dept., 1829-31, chief Topog. Bur. (after its creation as separate br. of War Dept.), 1831, 34-61; commr. for Indian affairs, 1832-34; promoted to col. when Topog. Engrs. became a staff corps of army, 1838; founder, dir. Nat. Inst. Sci., Washington, D.C.; mem. Geog. Soc. of Paris; mem. bd. visitors U.S. Mil. Acad., 1842. Died Washington, Jan. 27, 1863

ABRAHAM, HERBERT, corp. official; b. N.Y.C., July 9, 1883; Samuel and Rosalie (Strauss) chemistry, Columbia, 1903; m. Dorothy Jacoby, Dec. 15, 1915; children—George, Amy, Robin, Jane. With Ruberoid Co. since 1903, beginning as chemist, pres., chmn. bd., 1924-53, chmn. bd., 1954-59, chmn. exec. com., 1959-61, hon. chmn. bd., 1959-67. Chmn. Code Authority, Asphalt Shingle and Roofing Industry, 1932; pres. Asphalt Roofing Industry Bur., 1919, 1932-38,

1944-45. Served on War Industries Board, Washington, D.C., 1917-18. Mem. Am. Chem. Soc., Am. Soc. Testing Materials, Soc. Chem. Industry (Eng.). Mason. Author: Asphalts and Allied Substances, 1918, 6th edit., 1960. Clubs: Engineers, Chemists (N.Y.C.). Contbr. articles to scientific jours. Home: 1100 Park Av., N.Y.C. Office: 500 5th Av., N.Y.C. Died Apr. 4, 1967.

ABRAMS, ALBERT, physician; b. San Francisco, Dec. 8, 1863; s. Marcus amd Rachel (Leavey) A.; M.D., U. of Heidelberg, 1882; A.M., Portland U., 1892 (LL.D); post-grad. courses, London, Berlin, Vienna, Paris; m. Jeanne Roth, Nov. 25, 1897; 2d, Blanche Schwabacher, Sept. 28, 1915. Prof. pathology, Cooper Med. Coll., 1893-98; pres. Emanuel Polyclinic, 1904—. Author: Synopsis of Morbid Renal Secretions, 1892; Manual of Clinical Diagnosis, 1894; Consumption-Its Causes and Prevention, 1895; Scattered Leaves of a Physician's Diary, 1900, Diseases of Heart, 1901; Nervous Breakdown, 1901; Hygiene, in A System of Physiologic Therapeutics, 1901; Diseases of the Lung, 1905; Self-Poisoning; Diagnostic Therapeutics, 1909; Spinal Therapeutics, 1909; Spondylotherapy, in Reference Handbook Medical Sciences, 1917. Discoverer Abram's Reflexes and Electronic Reactions of Abrams. Home: San Francisco, Calif. Died Jan. 13, 1924.

ABRAMS, BENJAMIN, radio and phonograph exec.; b. Rumania; ed. in Europe and U.S. First invested in small phonograph assembly business; became distbr. Emerson Phonograph Co., later purchasing the co. (including manufacture of records); now chmn. chief exec. officer Emerson Radio and Phonograph Corp., Jersey City, pioneered in production of small radios, also in combination radio and phonograph design, and design and prodn. television receivers; mem. bd. Nestle Le Mur. Co. Trustee Long Island U.; dir. Weizmann Inst. Sc. Mem. bd. dirs. Better Bus. Bur. N.Y.C., mem. industry adv. com. Munitions Bd.; mem. com. Joint Electronics Industry Commn.; mem. bd. dirs. Radio-Television Mfrs. Assn. Reorgn. Com. Mem. bd. trustees Bklyn. Hebrew Orphan Asylum, Fedn. Jewish Philanthropies. Chmn. Greater N.Y. Com. for State of Israel Bond Issue; mem. bd. United service for New Americans Joint Distbn. Com. Address: Emerson Radio and Phonograph Corp., 14th & Coles Sts., Jersey City. Died June 23, 1967.

ABRAMS, LEROY, botanist; b. Sheffield, Ia., Oct. 1, 1874; s. James DeWitt and Almina Barbara (Shoudy) A.; student U. of Southern Calif., 1895-96; Stanford, 1896-99, and 1900-04, A.B., 1899, A.M., 1902; studied Columbia, 1904-05, Ph.D., 1910; m. Letitia Patterson (A.B., Stanford, 1901), Mar. 29, 1909. Acting prof. botany, U. of Ida., 1899-1900; asst. in botany, Stanford, 1900-02, instr., 1902-04; fellow Columbia U., 1904-05; asst. curator of plants, Nat. Museum, 1905-06; asst. prof. botany, 1906-12, asso. prof., 1912-20, prof. Stanford U., 1920-40, emeritus, 1940—; acting asso. prof. botany, U. of Calif., 1915. Fellow A.A.A.S., Calif. Acad. Sci., Am. Acad. Arts and Science; mem. Am. Bot. Soc., Calif. Bot. Soc., Sigma Xi. Author: Flora of Los Angeles and Vicinity, 1904, 11, 17; Illustrated Flora of the Pacific State, 1923, 41, 44, also bulletin, A Phytogeographical and Taxonomic Study of the Southern California Trees and Shrubs, 1910; etc. Home: Stanford University, CA

ABT, ISAAC ARTHUR, pediatrist; b. Wilmington, Ill., Dec. 18, 1867; s. Levi and Henrietta (Hart) A.; completed preliminary med. course Johns Hopkins, 1889; M.D., Chicago Med. Coll., 1891; interne Michael Reese Hosp., Chicago, 1891-93; post-grad. work in Vienna and Berlin, 1893-94; Sc.D., Northwestern U., 1931; m. Lena Rosenberg, Aug. 20, 1897; children—Arthur F., Lawrence E. Prof. diseases of children Northwestern U. Woman's Med. Sch., 1897-1901; asso. prof. diseases of children Rush Med. Coll., 1902-08; professor diseases of children Northwestern University Medical School, 1909-42, professor emeritus, 1942—; cons. physician diseases of children at Children's Memorial Hosp., Sarah Morris Children's Hosp., St. Luke's Hosp.; was attending physician diseases of children Passavant Hosp. Honorary mem. Deutsche Gesellschaft für Kinderheilkunde; mem. Am. Pediatric Soc. (pres. 1926-27), Am. Acad. Pediatrics (pres. 1930-31), A.M.A., Chicago Med. Soc. (pres. 1927), Chicago Pediatric Soc., Central States Pediatric Soc., Am. Assn. Teachers of Diseases of Children (pres. 1922), Children's Hosp. Assn. of American, Washington Med. and Surg. Soc. (hon.), Alpha Omega Alpha (hon. Minnesota Chapter). Distinguished Service Award, A.M.A., 1948, Chevalier of Legion of Honor (France). Clubs: City, Ill. Athletic (Chicago). Author: The Baby's Food, 1917, The Baby Doctor, 1944. Editor vol. on Pediatrics in the Practical Medicine Series; also editor, A System of Pediatrics. Has written many monographs on subjects relating to diseases of children. Home: 4747 S. Kenwood Av., Chgo. 15. Office: 104 S. Michigan Av., Chgo. Died Nov. 22, 1955; buried Rosehill Cemetery, Chgo.

ACHESON, ALBERT ROBERT, mech. and elec. engr. b. Riverton, New Zealand, Oct. 12, 1882; s. Robert amd Annie (Sinclair) A.; B.S.C. in M.E., 1905, B.E., in E.E., 1906, Canterbury, Coll. (New Zealand U.); m. Pansy Kate Shaw, July 1, 1909; children—Cedric Robert, Mildred Frances(Mrs. Raymond Ames), Dorothy Violet, Douglas Frank. In employ New Zealand Government railways, summers, 1901-04; with Westinghouse Air Brake Co., Addington, New Zealand, 1904-05; with Wellington & Manwatu Ry. Co., 1905-06; with Westinghouse Electric & Mfg. Co., Pittsburgh, 1906-08; prof. mech. engring. and head of dept. of mech. engring., Coll. of Applied Science, Syracuse U., 1908—; industrial engr. with Westinghouse Electric & Mfg. Co., summer of 1910; operating engr. in charge 6000 h.p. boiler room, Utica & Mohawk Valley Ry. Co., Utica, N.Y., summer of 1911; cons. engr. Bur. of Gas and Electricity, Syracuse, 1914-19; gen. cons. engring. practice, 1919—. Home: Syracuse, N.Y. Died Feb. 25, 1941.

ACHESON, ALEXANDER MAHON, civil engr.; b. Washington, Pa., July 20, 1858; s. James C. and Mary E. (Mahon) A.; student Washington and Jefferson Coll., 1876-79; m. Alice Hanna, of Denison, Tex., Dec. 6, 1893. Began as rodman, N.Y., L.E. & Western Rd., 1880; levelman N.Y., West Shore & Buffalo R.R., 1881-83; transitman P. R.R., 1883-85; r.r. surveys, 1885-87; asst. engr. St. Paul, Minneapolis & Manitoba Ry., 1887-89; asst. engr., 1889-1900, resident engr., at Dallas, Tex., 1900-06, div. supt., 1906—, M.K. & T. Ry. of Tex. Home: Trinity, Texas.

ACHESON, EDWARD GOODRICH, inventor; b. Washington, Pa., Mar. 9, 1856; s. William amd Sarah D. (Ruplé) A.; acad. edn. Bellefonte, Pa.: hon. Sc.D., U. of Pittsburgh, 1909; m. Margaret Maher, 1884; children—Veronica Belle, Edward Goodrich, Raymond Maher (dec.), Sarah Ruth, George Wilson, John Huyler, Margaret Irene, Jean Ellen (dec.), Howard Archibald. Asst. to Thomas A. Edison, 1880-81. Inventor of carborundum, siloxicon, Egypttianized clay, Aquadag, Oildag, and a method of making graphite. Awarded Rumford medal of Am. Acad. of Arts and Sciences, 1908; Perkin Research medal, 1910; grand prix, Paris Expn., 1900, St. Louis Expn., 1904. Officer Royal Order of the Polar Star (Sweden). Hon. mem. Russian Imperial Tech. Soc., Swedish Tech. Soc.; was pres. Electrochem soc.; v.p. Am. Inst. Chem. Engrs., E.E. Donor of $25,000, 1928, to Electrochem. Soc., to establish Edward Goodrich Acheson biennial prize; recieved Acheson medal from Electrochem. Soc., 1929. Died July 6, 1931.

ACHESON, WILLIAM MCCARTHY, civil engr.; born Cohoes, N.Y., July 16, 1878; s. James Francis and Mary (McCarthy) A.; prep. edn., Troy (N.Y.) Acad.; student Rensselaer Poly. Inst., 1895-98, also Union U., Royal Engrs. Sch., Chatham, Eng. 1917; hon. E.D., Syracuse U., 1927; m. Inger Thira Miller, Apr. 25, 1908; children—Margaret Miller, Thomas Temple. Began in water works dept., Troy, N.Y.; in Isthmian Canal Service, Panama, 1904-10; supervising engr. with contractor, later div. engr. N.Y. State Highway Dept., Buffalo, same, Syracuse Div., 1915-16; chief engr. Crescent Portland Cement Co., 1916-17; div. engr., Bur. of Highways and Bur. of Canals, N.Y. State Dept. Pub. Works, 1923-27, in charge div. engring., later chief engr., 1927—; lecturer on engring., Syracuse U., 1922—. Served as capt., later maj. engrs. U.S. Army, assigned to staff of chief of roads and railroads, 1917, chief of road service, 1918; maj. Engr. R.C., 1919, lt. col., 1920. Mem. Nat. Research Council. Citation from Gen. Pershing and Maj. Gen. Langfitt, chief of engrs., World War. Republican. Catholic. Consultant on pub. works to Republic of Cuba. Home: Syracuse, N.Y. Died Jan. 25, 1930.

ACKER, CHARLES ERNEST, inventor, mfr. b. Bourbon, Ind., Mar. 19, 1868; s. William James and Mercia (Grant) A.; Ph.B., Cornell, 1888; m. Alice Reynolds Beal, Apr. 26, 1892. Elec. engr., Chicago, 1888-93; originator of the Acker process of mfr. caustic soda by electrolysis of molten salt, and built works at Niagara Falls; originator chem. and electrochem. processes; granted many patents. Awarded Elliott Cresson gold medal by Franklin Inst.; also awarded other medals. Home: Ossining N.Y. Died Oct. 18, 1920.

ACKERMAN, NATHAN WARD, psychiatrist, educator; b. Russia, Nov. 22, 1908; s. David and Bertha (Greenberg) A.; came to U.S., 1912, naturalized, 1920; B.A., Columbia, 1929, M.D., 1933; m. Gwendolyn Hill, Oct. 10, 1937; children—Jeanne (Mrs. Barry Curnan), Deborah. Intern Montefiore Hosp., N.Y.C., 1933-34; resident Menninger Clinic and Sanitorium, Topeka, 1935-36; mem. psychiat. staff Menninger Clinic, 1936-37; chief psychiatrist Jewish Bd. Guardians, N.Y.C., 1937-51; dir. Child Devel. Center, N.Y.C., 1946-51, Family Mental Health Clinic, Jewish Family Service, N.Y.C., 1957-66, profl. program Family Inst., N.Y.C., 1960-71; clin. prof. psychiatry Columbia Coll. Phys. and Surg. 1957-71; vis. prof. Tulane U., 1956, U. N.C., 1960; vis lectr. Albert Einstein Med Coll., 1962-71; lectr. Columbia Sch. Social Work, 1946-64. Recipient Adolph Meyer award Assn. Improvement Mental Health, 1959; Wilfred Hulse award Eastern Group Psychotherapy Psychotherapy Assn., 1965. Diplomate Am. Bd. Psychiatry and Neurology. Fellow N.Y. Acad. Medicine, Am. Psychiat. Assn., Am. Orthopsychiat. Assn., Acad. Psychoanalysis, Am. Acad. Child Psychiatry; mem. Assn. Psychoanalytic medicine (pres. 1957-59), Am. Psychopath. Assn., Group for Advancement Psychiatry, N.Y. Council Child Psychiatry, N.Y. Soc. Clin. Psychiatry, Am. Psychoanalytic Assn., Am. Group Therapy Assn., Mexican Psychoanalytic Assn. (hon.), Assn. Applied Psychoanalysis (hon.). Author: (with others) Personality and Arterial Hypertension, 1945; (with M. Jahoda) Antisemitism and Emotional Disorder, 1950; The Psychodynamics of Family Life, 1958; Treating the Troubled Family, 1966; also articles. Editor: Exploring the Base of Family Therapy, 1961; Expanding the Theory and Practice of Family Therapy, 1967; Family Process, 1970; also others. Editor: Family Therapy in Transition, 1970. Home: New York City NY Died June 12, 1971; buried Westchester Hills Cemetery, Hastings-on-Hudson NY

ACREE, SOLOMON FARLEY, chemist; b. McGregor, Tex., Dec. 18, 1875; s. George Wren and Elizabeth Virginia (Grimes) A.; B.S., U. Tex., 1896, M.S., 1897; Ph.D., C. Chgo., 1902; grad. study U. Berlin, 1903-04; Johnston scholar Johns Hopkins, 1904-06; m. Ruby Jarvis Tiller, May 1, 1917; children—Ruby Jane de Haven, George Wren. Asst. in chemistry U. Tex., 1896-97; fellow and asst. in chemistry U. Chgo., 1898-1901; asst. prof. chemistry U. Utah, 1901-04; asst. and asso. prof. Johns Hopkins, 1906-14; prof. Forest chemistry U. Wis., 1914-17, prof. and chief of chem. sect., Forest Products Lab., 1914-17; prof. forest chemistry Syracuse U., 1917-19; v.p. Internat. Chem. Products Co. and pres. Grahame Chem. Co., 1920-24; prof. physical organic chemistry, George Washington U., 1924-26; prin. chemist U.S. Bur. Standards, Washington, 1927—, chief of sect. Fiber Structures and Hydrogen Ion Measurements, 1931—. Fellow A.A.A.S., Texas Acad. Science, Chemical Soc. (London); mem. Am. Chem. Soc., German Chem. Soc., Phi Beta Kappa, Sigma Xi. Baptist. Writer of Graphs and Theory of Errors, Physical Organic Chemistry, Reactions of Ions and Molecules (in mimeographed form). Contbr. to Jour. Am. Chem. Soc., Am. Chem. Jour., Jour. Physical Chemistry, Science, Jour. Chem. Soc., Eerichte Chemische Gesellschaft, etc. Research on utilization of agrl. and lumber waste; pH standards; etc. Home: 3259 R St. N.W., Washington 7. Office: Bureau of Standards, Washington. Died Oct. 23, 1957.

ACUFF, HERBERT, surgeon; b. Washburn, Tenn., Aug. 22, 1886; s. Joel and Sarah A.; Pharm.G., Ky. Sch. of Pharmacy, 1911; M.D., U. of Louisville Med. Sch., 1911; Honoris Causa, U. of Argentina; m. Lola Pruden, Oct. 20, 1915; 1 dau., Betty Rose (Mrs. Lawrence Barker). In practice at Knoxville, Tenn.; chief of staff, St. Mary's Memorial Hospital; vis. surg. East Tenn. Bapt. Hosp., Knoxville General Hospital, Fort Sanders Hospital, cons. surgeon and chmn. operating com., Beverly Hills Sanatorium; chief cons. surgeon of Pruden Coal & Coke Co., surgeon, Southern Ry. System; pres. and surg. dir. surgery, Acuff Clinic. Served as maj., Med. Corps, U.S. Army, World War I. Mem. Tenn. Hosp. Licensing Bd.; sec. Internat. Bd. Cancerology. Life fellow Am. Coll. Surgeons, Southeastern Surg. Congress (pres., 1947-48), Internat. Coll. Surgeons (treas., 1946-48; pres. U.S. Chapt., 1946-48; founder fellow Qualification Bd. since 1947; pres. since 1950); hon. fellow Med. and Surg. Society of Sao Paulo, Brazil, Surg. Soc. of Rome, Italy, Piemontese Soc. of Torino, Italy; mem. Am. Goiter Assn., American Coll. Chest Physicians (asso.), Am. Cancer Soc. (bd. dirs., 1945-46; bd. dirs. and service dir., Tenn. div. since 1945), World Med. Assn. (mem. bd. dirs., U.S. Com., Inc.), Knoxville Acad. Medicine (pres. 1945-46), Am. Assn. Ry. Surgeons. Clubs: Civitan (internat. pres. 1926-27), Cherokee Country. Contbr. papers to med. lit. on surg. subjects. Home: 632 Cherokee Blvd. Office: 514 Church Av., Knoxville, Tenn. Died Nov. 2, 1951.

ADAIR, FRED LYMAN, obstetrician, gynecologist; b. Anamosa, Ia., July 28, 1877; s. Lyman Joseph and Sarah Jennings (Porter) A.; B.S., U. of Minn., 1898; M.D., Rush Med. Coll. (U. of Chicago), 1901; M.A., U. of Minn.; m. Myrtle May Ingalls, Nov. 18, 1911; children—Agnes Jennings Kuhn, Robert Chamberlain, Richard Porter. Intern Michael Reese Hosp., Chicago, 1901-03; gen. practice, 1903-08; became connected with U. of Minn., 1905; studied in Berlin, 1908-09; specialized in obstetrics and gynecology since 1909; prof. obstetrics and gynecology, U. of Minn., 1926-29; chmn. dept. and emeritus prof. obstetrics and gynecology Univ. of Chicago since 1929; former chief of service Chicago Lying-in Hosp.; consultant Children's Bur., U.S. Dept. of Labor; chmn. Joint Maternal Welfare Comm. Cook County; former chief maternal and child division Ill. Department Public Health. Was maj. Minn. N.G.; physician with Red Cross in France, Belgium, World War I. Chmn. Com. on Prenatal Care, Hoover Conf. on Child Health and Protection; chmn. Am. Com. on Maternal Welfare, Inc.; chmn. 1st, 2d, 3d, 4th Am. Congress on Obstet. and Gynecology. Mem. Am. Medical Assn. (past pres. and sec. section on obstetrics and gynecology), Minn Academy Medicine, Central Assn. Obstetricians and Gynecologists, Am. Gynecological Soc. (past treas. and pres.), Chicago Gynecological Soc. (past pres.), Am. Board Obstetrics and Gynecology (past vice-pres.), American College of Surgeons, Illinois Medical Society, Sigma Xi, Delta Upsilon, Nu Sigma Nu. Past pres. Fedn. Obstetric & Gynecologic Soc. Awarded Croix Civique (Belgium). Club: Cosmos. Author: (with Stieglitz) Obstetric Medicine: (with Potter) Fetal and Neonatal Death, 1940; also textbooks on obstetrics and gynecology.

Home: Box 340, Chesterton, Ind. Office: 24 W. Ohio St., Chicago 10 IL

ADAMS, BENJAMIN CULLEN, utilities exec.; b. Madison, Wis., Apr. 1, 1880; s. Henry Cullen and Anna Berkeley (Norton) A.; B.S. in Elec. engring. U. Wis., 1903; m. Rachel Lloyd Nicholson, June 3, 1908; children—Florence (Mrs. Robt. H. McDonnell), Benjamin Cullen. Tester electric meters, later supt. distbn. Madison (Wis.) Gas & Electric Light Co., 1903-06; supt., later gen. mgr. Lincoln (Neb.) Gas & Electric Light Co., 1906-13; v.p., gen. mgr. Spokane (Wash.) Gas & Fuel Co., Eng. in Brazil, 1914-15; v.p., gen. mgr. Montgomery (Ala.) Light & Water Power Co., 1915-16, Empire Dist. Electric Co., Joplin, Mo., 1916-20, St. Joseph (Mo.) Ry., Light, Heat and Power Co., 1920-22, Toledo Edison Company; pres. Community Traction Co. 1922-25; v.p., gen. mgr. Gas Service Co., Kansas City, Mo., 1925-40, pres., gen. mgr., dir. 1940; exec. v.p., dir. Kansas City (Mo.) Gas Co., 1925-40, pres., 1940-47; exec. v.p., dir. Wyandotte County Gas Co., 1925-40, pres., 1940-47; Kansas City Gas Co. and Wyandotte Gas Co. merged with Gas Service Co. 1947-56; chmn. bd., 1956—; dir. Commerce Trust Co., Mo. Mem. bd. govs. Am. Royal Live Stock and Horse Show; mem. bd. dirs. A.R.C.; trustee Midwest Research Inst. Mem. Am. Gas Assn. (dir.). Clubs: Kansas City, Kansas City Country, Mission Hills Country, University, Saddle & Sirloin, River (Kansas City, Mo.); Tennis, Racquet, Committee of Twenty-Five (Palm Springs, Cal.). Home: 420 E. Armour. Office: Scarritt Bldg., Kansas City, Mo. Died Oct. 14, 1959; buried Mt. Moriah Cemetery, Kansas City, Mo.

ADAMS, CHARLES, diplomat; b. Pomerania, Germany, Dec. 19, 1845; s. Karl Heinrich and Maria J. (Markman) Schwanbeck (dropped last name circa 1870); m. Margaret Thompson Phelps, circa 1870. Fought in Civil War; apptd. brig. gen. Colo. Militia, 1870; Ute Indian agt. until 1874; post office insp., 1874, 82-85; U.S. minister to Bolivia, 1880-82; U.S. arbitrator for Bolivia and Chile War confs., Arica, Bolivia. Engaged in glass manufacture, mining, mineral water devel. Died Denver, Colo., Aug. 19, 1895.

ADAMS, CHARLES BAKER, naturalist; b. Dorchester, Mass., Jan. 11, 1814; s. Charles J. Adams; grad. Amherst, 1834; m. Mary Holmes, Feb. 1839. Asst. in Geol. Survey of N.Y., 1836; tutor, lectr. geology Amherst, 1837, prof. natural history Middlebury (Vt.) Coll., 1838-47; state geologist Vt., 1845-48. Died Jan. 18, 1853.

ADAMS, CHARLES CHRISTOPHER, ecologist; b. Clinton, Ill., July 23, 1873; s. William Henry Harrison and Hannah Westfall (Concklin) A.; B.S., Ill. Wesleyan U., 1895; M.S., Harvard, 1899, Ph.D., U. Chgo., 1908; Sc.D., Ill. Wesleyan U., 1920; m. Alice Luthera Norton, Oct. 3, 1908 (dec. Sept. 1, 1931); 1 dau., Harriet Dyer. Asst. in biology Ill. Wesleyan U., 1895-96; asst. entomologist Ill. State Lab. of Natural History, 1896-98; curator U. Museum, U. Mich., 1903-06; dir. Cin. Soc. Natural History, 1906-07; asso., animal ecology U. Ill., 1908-14; asst. prof. forest zoology N.Y. State Coll. Forestry, Syracuse U., 1914-16, prof. 1916; dir. Roosevelt Wild Life Forest Expt. Sta., 1919-26; N.Y. State Mus., 1926-43, retired. Mem. Am. Soc. Naturalists, Assn. Am. Geographers, Ecol. Soc. Am., A.A.A.S., History Sci. Soc., Sigma Xi. Author: Guide to the Study of Animal Ecology, 1913. Contbr. sci. mags. and reviews. Address: 149 Manning Blvd., Albany 3, N.Y. Died May 22, 1955; buried Burlington, Wis.

ADAMS, CHARLES CLOSSON, telegraph official; b. Freeport, Pa., Aug. 15, 1858; s. Alexander Ainsworth and Isabella (Thompson) A.; ed. pub. schs., Pittsburgh, and Sharpsburg (Pa.) Acad.; m. Elizabeth K. Spillin, Feb. 15, 1896. Telegraph operator in oil regions and Pittsburgh, 1874-80; with Associated Press, Ft. Wayne, Ind.; removed to N.Y. City and entered employ of Western Union Telegraph Co.; later became mgr. Pittsburgh Office Mut. Union Telegraph Co.; apptd. mgr. Phila. office, Postal Telegraph Co., 1884, dist. supt., 1886, gen. supt. Southern div., 1902, second v.p. since 1904; v.p. Brooklyn Dist. Telegraph Co.; dir. North Am. Telegraph Co. Clubs: Rockaway Hunting (Lawrence, L.I.), Union League (New York). Home: Lawrence, L.I. Office: 253 Broadway, New York. Died Mar. 30, 1938.

ADAMS, CLARENCE RAYMOND, mathematician; b. Cranston, R.I., Apr. 10, 1898; s. Clarence Warren and Leola Sarah (Ranney) A.; A.B., Brown U., 1918, M.S., 1920, A.M., Harvard, 1921, Ph.D., 1922; Sheldon traveling fellow of Harvard at U. Rome (Italy), 1922-23, and U. Göttingen (Germany), 1923; m. Rachel Blodgett, Aug. 17, 1922. Instr. math. Brown U., 1918-20, 23-25, asst. prof., 1925-28, asso., 1928-36, prof., 1936-65, prof. emeritus, 1965—, chmn. dept., 1942-60. Served in SATC, Brown U., 1918. Fellow Am. Acad. Arts and Scis.; mem. Am. Math. Soc. (v.p. 1939-40), Math. Assn. Am. (bd. govs. 1948-50), Am. Assn. U. Profs. council (1942-44), A.A.A.S., Royal Instn. Gt. Britain, R.I. Hist. Soc., Soc. of Colonial Wars, Phi Beta Kappa, Sigma Xi, Alpha Tau Omega. Republican. Baptist. Clubs: Providence Art; Faculty (Brown U.). Contbr. math. articles to profl. jours. Home: 60 Intervale Road, Providence 02906. Died Oct. 15, 1965; buried Swan Point Cemetery, Providence.

ADAMS, COMFORT AVERY, electrical engr.; b. Cleveland, Nov. 1, 1868; s. Comfort Avery and Katherine Emily (Peticolas) A.; S.B., Case Sch. of Applied Science, Cleveland, 1890, E.E., 1905, Dr. Engring., 1925; hon. Dr. Engring., Lehigh U., 1938; student mathematics and physics, Harvard, 1891-93; m. Elizabeth Challis Parsons, June 21, 1894; children—John, Clayton Comfort. Asst. in physics, Case School of Applied Science, 1886-90; designing engr., 1890-91; instr., 1891-95, asst. prof., 1896-1905, prof. elec. engring., 1906-16, Lawrence prof. of engring., Harvard U., 1914-36, Gordon McKay prof. of elec. engring., 1935-36, emeritus since 1936; dean Harvard Engring. Sch., 1919; chmn. div. engring. Nat. Research Council, 1919-21; consulting engr. for Am. Tool & Machine Co., Boston, 1905-30, The Okonite Co. since 1915, Okonite Callender Cable Co. since 1925, Babcock and Wilcox Co. since 1926, General Electric Co., 1927-32, The Budd Company, 1934-47. Member International Jury of Awards (department electricity), St. Louis Expn., 1904. Unitarian. Fellow Am. Acad. Arts and Sciences, Am. Inst. Elec. Engrs. (pres. 1918-19), Am. Soc. Mech. Engrs., A.A.A.S.; mem. Nat. Acad. of Sciences, Instn. Elec. Engrs., Societe Francaise 'des Electricienes, Am. Soc. C.E., Soc. Promotion Engring. Edn., Am. Physical Soc., Am. Welding Soc. (pres. 1919-20), American Bureau Welding (dir. 1919-36), Engineering Foundation (hon. chmn. welding research council since 1949), American Engineering Standards Committee (chairman 1918-20). Mem. John Fritz Medal Bd. of Award (pres. 1922), Edison Medal Bd. of Award (chmn. 1920). Chmn. Gen. Engring. Com. of Council Nat. Defense, during war period, also as chmn. Welding Com. of Emergency Fleet Corp. Clubs: Engineers (Philadelphia) (New York); Cedarbrook Country. Author: Dynamo Design Schedules; also articles on kindred subjects. Received 1st award of Miller medal, "for conspicuous contributions to the art of welding," 1929; Lamme medal from Am. Inst. E.E. for contributions to theory and design of alternating current elec. machinery and to electric welding, 1940. Edison Medal 1956 by Am. Inst. E.E. Home: 417 W. Price St., Phila. 44. Died Feb. 21, 1958

ADAMS, CUYLER, mining engr.; b. Canton, Ill., Aug. 20, 1852, but reared in N.Y.; s. Herman Cuyler and Frances M. (Burr) A.; ed. tutors, pvt. schs. and Poughkeepsie Mil. Inst., N.Y.; m. Virginia B., d. Col. J. B. Culver, Oct. 20, 1881; children—Culver (dec.), Francis Salisbury (dec.), Robert M. Went to Minn., 1870, for the N.P. Ry. on dock constrn.; lager bonanza farmer in Stutsman County, N.D., and exploring and developing mining properties in western Ont.; discovered by magnetic observation and developed the Cuyuna Iron Range in Minn.; built Cuyuna Iron Range Ry., of which was pres. and gen. mgr.; pres. Biwanago Mining Co., Cuyuna Northern Ry. Co. Republican. Episcopalian. Home: Duluth, Minn. Died Nov. 29, 1932.

ADAMS, CYRUS CORNELIUS, geographer; b. Naperville, Ill., Jan. 7, 1849; s. Cyrus and Cornelia (Stevens) A.; A.B., U. of Chicago, 1876; m. Mrs. Blanche C. Dodge, Aug. 17, 1877; children—Jessie, Ernest. First pres., dept. of geography, Brooklyn Inst. of Arts and Sciences; journalist, Chicago and New York, 1874-03; geog. writer on New York Sun, 1884-06; editor Bull. Am. Geog. Soc., 1908-15. Pres. Assn. Am. Geographers, 1906. Author: Commercial Geography for High Schools, 1901; Elementary Commercial Geography, 1902. Wrote: David Livingstone, African Development (in Vol. XIV, Beacon Lights of History), 1902. Home: Jewett, N.Y. Died May 4, 1928.

ADAMS, DANIEL, physician, author; b. Townsend, Mass., Sept. 29, 1773; s. Daniel and Lydia (Taylor) A.; grad. Dartmouth, 1797, B.M., 1799, M.D., 1799; m. Nancy Mulliken, Aug. 17, 1800. Practiced medicine, Leominster, Mass.; delivered eulogy for George Washington at meml. service in Leominster, 1800; published with Salmon Wilder weekly newspaper Telescope, Mass., 1800-02; moved to Boston, circa 1805, taught at pvt. sch.; edited Med. and Agrl. Register (monthly periodical); moved to Mt. Vernon, N.H., 1813, again moved to Keene, N.H., 1846. Author: The Scholar's Arithmetic, 1801; The Understanding Reader of Knowledge before Oratory, 1805; Geography, or a Description of the World, 1814, 2d edit., 1816; The Monitorial Reader, 1841; Primary Arithmetic, 1848; Bookkeeping, 1849. Died Keene, June 8, 1864.

ADAMS, DUDLEY, W., horticulturist, granger; b. Winchendon, Mass., Nov. 30, 1831; s. Joseph Boynton and Hannah (Whitney) A. Tchr. in Mass.; one of 1st settlers of Waukon, Ia., 1852; county assessor, Ia., 1852-62; established Iron Clad Nursery, 1856, one of best tree nurseries in that area; mem. Nat. Grange of Patrons of Husbandry, master, 1873; father of 1st attempt to pass railroad freight legislation; aided in framing proposals for forbidding discrimination in fixing rates introduced into Congress 1873-74, called unconstl. at that time, but passed as constl. in Ia., stimulated nat. and state railroad regulation; moved to Fla., 1875, promoted horticulture; organized and pres. Fla. Hort. Soc. Died Feb. 13, 1897.

ADAMS, EBENEZER, educator; b. Oct. 22, 1765; s. Ephraim and Rebecca (Locke) A.; grad. Dartmouth, 1791; m. Alice Frink, July 9, 1795, 5 children; m. 2d, Beulah Minot, May 17, 1807, 2 children. Became preceptor acad., Leicester, Mass., 1792; 1st prof. mathematics and natural philosophy Phillips Exeter Acad.; prof. langs. Dartmouth, 1809-33; pres. Bible Soc. of N.H. Died Aug. 15, 1841.

ADAMS, FRANK, irrigation economist; b. Chicago, Ill., Sept. 19, 1875; s. Edward Francis and Delia Ray (Cooper) A.; prep. edn., Cogswell Polytechnic Coll., San Francisco, and Belmont (Calif.) Prep. Sch.; A.B., Stanford, 1901; A.M., U. of Neb., 1906; LL.D., University of California, 1947; m. Amy Belle Hill, June 20, 1906; children—Helen (Mrs. Percy M. Barr), Francis Edward, David Hill, Thomas Cooper. Professor of irrigation, College of Agriculture, University of Calif., 1916-45, emeritus since Sept. 19, 1945; also irrigation economist in California Agricultural Experimental Station. Successively, 1900-06, and 1910-39, agt. and expert, irrigation asst., irrigation engr., irrigation mgr. and collaborator in irrigation investigations, U.S. Dept. Agr.; cons. engr. U.S. Bur. of Reclamation, 1926-40; consulting engineer, International Water Commission, United States and Mexico, 1928-30. Served with Army Ednl. Corps, in France, Apr.-June 1919. Mem. Advisory Commn. on Agrl. Colonization in Palestine, May-Nov. 1927; chmn. Calif. Econ. Research Council, 1930-32; consultant Nat. Resources Com. Rio Grande Joint Investigation, 1935-38. Fellow Am. Society of Agricultural Engrs.; mem. Western Farm Econ. Assn., Am. Geophysical Union, Tau Beta Pi. Awarded John Deere Gold Medal by Am. Society Agrl. Engrs., 1947. Decorated Officier du Merite Agricole. Republican. Conglist. Clubs: Faculty, Commonwealth. Author of numerous repts. and articles pertaining to irrigation, agriculture, etc. Home: 1831 San Juan Av., Berkeley 7 CA

ADAMS, FREDERICK W., physician; b. Pawlet, Vt., 1786; grad. Dartmouth, 1822; married twice; at least 1 child. Practiced medicine in vicinity of Barton, Vt., 1822-36; attended med. lectures, Phila., 1835-36; practiced medicine, Montpelier, Vt., 1836-58; made violins as an avocation. Author works on theology including: Theological Criticism; or, Hints of the Philosophy of Man and Nature, 1843. Died Montpelier, Dec. 17, 1858.

ADAMS, GEORGE EDWARD, agronomist; b. North Kingstown, R.I., May 12, 1874; s. George L. and Annie (Gould) A.; B.S., R.I. State Coll., Kingston, R.I., 1894; grad. student, Cornell U., Ithaca, N.Y., 1899-1900; Master in Agr., Rhode Island State Coll., 1916; m. Oct. 20, 1903, Mary Gates Schermerhorn, of Malden, Mass. Asst. horticulturist, 1895-1901, asso. in agronomy, 1901-08, horticulturist, 1908-12, R.I. Expt. Sta.; chief agrl. dept., 1907-12, prof. of agronomy, 1907-38, R.I. State Coll., also dean sch. of agr. and home economics and dir. agrl. expt. sta. and extension service, emeritus since 1938. State statistical agt. R.I. for Bur. Statistics, U.S. Dept. Agr., 1901-14. Fellow A.A.A.S.; member American Breeders' Assn., Am. Soc. Agronomy, Mass. Hort. Soc., Phi Kappa Phi, Alpha Zeta. Mason, Grange. Home: Kingston RI

ADAMS, GEORGE IRVING, geologist; b. Lena, Ill., Aug. 17, 1870; s. Howard Brooks and Ruth Ann (Harris) A.; grad. Kan. State Normal Sch., 1889; A.B., U. of Kan., 1893, A.M., 1895; Sc.D., Princeton, 1896; student U. of Munich and Yale U.; m. Bertha Barin, 1914. Instr. natural sciences, Kan. State Normal Sch., 1893-94; asst. geologist Univ. Geol. Survey of Kan., 1894-97; field asst. U.S. Geol. Survey 1898-99, asst. geologist, 1900-04; chief hydrologist Cuerpo de Ingenieros de Minas del Peru, 1904-06; mine examinations, S. America, 1906-07; geologist Div. of Mines, Bur. of Science, P.I., 1908-10; prof. geology and mining, Pei Yang U., 1915-20; prof. geology and mineralogy, U. of Ala., 1920—; geologist Geol. Survey of Ala., 1927—. Home: Tuscaloosa,

ADAMS, HARRIET CHALMERS, explorer, lecturer; b. Stockton, Calif.; d. Alexander and Frances (Wilkins) Chalmers; ed. pvt. tutors; m. Franklin Pierce Adams, Oct. 5, 1899. Traveled through Mexico and became student of Latin Am. affairs, 1900; began 3 yrs'. journey through Central and S. America, Jan., 1903; lecturing and writing in U.S. upon S.A., Mar. 1906—. Crossed Haiti in saddle, 1910, returning with 8 Solendon, classified among rarest known animals; followed the trail of Columbus through the Old and the New World, 1912; traveled through Phillippines, 1913; from Siberia to Sumatra, studying ancient races allied with earliest American peoples, 1913-14; war corr. at tje French front, 1916; visited every Indian tribe in U.S.; in S. America, 1919-20; research worl in Spain and Spanish Africa, 1923-24, in Spain and Portugual, 1926-27, in Libya and Near East, 1929, in Ethiopia, Egypt amd Palestine, 1930, in Italy and Spain, 1931, in Near East, North Africa, Spain and Portugual, 1933, in the Balkans, 1934-36. Pres. Internat. Soc. of Woman Geographers, 1925-33, hon. pres. 1933—. Died July 17, 1937.

ADAMS, HENRY FOSTER, psychologist; b. Oak Park, Ill., Nov. 11, 1882; s. Samuel Hawley (D.D.) and Mary H. (Dunbar; M.D.) A.; student Cazenovia (N.Y.)

Sem., 1897-99, Erasmus Hall High Sch., Brooklyn, 1899-1901; Ph.B., Wesleyan U., 1905; Ph.D., U. of Chicago, 1910; m. Susan Hitch, Aug. 24, 1915; 1 son, Henry Hitch. Reporter, N.Y. Morning Sun, 1905-06; with Chicago Screw Co., 1906-07; asst. U. of Chicago, 1910-11; mem. faculty, U. of Mich., 1911-73, prof. of psychology, 1927-53, prof. emeritus, 1953-73. Fellow A.A.A.S.; mem. Am. Psychol. Assn. (life), Michigan Acad. Sci., Sigma Xi, Psi Upsilon. Club: Research (U. of Mich.). Author: Autokinetic Sensation, Psychol. Monographs, 1912; Advertising and Its Mental Laws, 1916; The Ways of the Mind, 1925; series of popular articles on aspects of psychology, Scribner's mag., 1920-21. Contbr. articles on psychology in profl. publs. Home: Ann Arbor MI Died Feb. 16, 1973.

ADAMS, ISAAC, inventor, mfr.; b. Rochester, N.H. Aug. 16, 1802; s. Benjamin and Elizabeth (Horne) A. Invented Adams Power Press the leading machine used in book binding, 1836-1900), 1827; formed firm I. & S. Adams, 1836. Died July 19, 1883.

ADAMS, JOHN EMERY, geologist; b. Solon, Ia., June 5, 1899; s. Harry Delvie and Virginia (Bacon) A.; B.A., U. of Ia., 1922, M.S., 1923; grad. study, U. of Chicago, 1923-24, U. of Wis., 1925, U. of Tex., 1926-27; m. Margaret MacLaughlin, July 25, 1926; 1 dau., Mary Ann (Mrs. A.B. Plunkett). Began career as geologist at the Roxana Petroleum Corp., St. Louis, 1923; biology instr., Tex. A. and M. Coll., 1925-26; asso. Texas Bur. of Econ. Geology, Austin, Tex., 1926-27; geologist, later sr. geologist Cal. Co. and Standard Oil Co. of Tex., 1927-64; geological consultant, Midland, Texas, 1964-70. Mem. Am. Geophys. Union, Am. Assn. Petroleum Geologists (hon. mem.; pres. 1953), Geol. Soc. Am. (councilor, 1945-47), Soc. Econ. Paleontol. and Mineralogy, West Tex. Geol. Soc. (hon. life mem.; v.p. 1931, pres. 1940), Soc. Ind. Earth Scientists, Soc. Econ. Paleontologists and Mineralogists (hon. life), Sigma Xi. Unitarian. Interested in geology of Southwestern history. Home: Midland TX Died Sept. 29, 1970; buried Resthaven Meml. Park, Midland TX

ADAMS, JOHN WILLIAM, veterinary surgeon; b. Middleton, Miss., Nov. 8, 1862; s. Rev. John Charles and Helen Marr (Doty) A.; grad. U. of Minn., 1886; taught Shattuck Mil. School, Faribault, Minn.; V.M.D., U. of Pa., 1892; m. Mary, d. Dr. O. B. Adams, Dec. 28, 1893; children—Alice Naomi, Helen Janet. Veterinary practitioner, 1892—; asst. prof., 1893-96, prof. veterinary surgery and obstetrics, 1896—, U. of Pa. Republican. Episcopalian. Author: Text-Book on Horse-Shoeing, 1898; Disease of the Horse's Foot, 1903; Horse-Shoeing, 1903; A Movable School of Horse-Shoeing, 1907. Home: Swarthmore, Pa. Died Oct. 22, 1926.

ADAMS, JOSEPH ALEXANDER, engraver; b. New Germantown, N.J., 1803. Apprentice in printing bus.; work had appeared in Treasury of Knowledge, Cottage Bible, by 1833; engraved "Last Arrow" for N.Y. Mirror, 1837; engraved sixteen hundred illustrations for Harper's Illuminated Bible, published 1843, said to have been 1st electrotyper in Am., made improvements in process. Died N.J., Sept. 11, 1880.

ADAMS, JULIUS WALKER, civil engr; b. Boston Mass., Oct. 12, 1812; entered U.S. Mil. Acad., 1830, but did not graduate; engaged in engring. work, 1832-60; col. 67th N.Y. vols. in Civil war; wounded at Fair Oaks; became chief engr. city works, Brooklyn, N.Y. Has been pres. Am. Soc. Civ. Engrs. Cons. engr. to dept. of pub. works, N.Y. Home: Brooklyn, N.Y. Died 1899.

ADAMS, LEVERETT ALLEN, prof. zoology; b. Lawrence, Kan., Sept. 23, 1877; s. James W. and Mary Jane (Pierson) A.; B.A., U. of Kan., 1903, M.A., 1906; PhD., Columbia U., 1914; m. Mary Louise Moss, Nov. 27, 1917; children—Leverett Allen, Virginia Louise, Mary Ladd. Mus. asst. U. of Kan., 1903-06; asst. prof. biology, State Teachers Coll., Greeley, Colo., 1906-14, head dept. biology, 1914-22; asst. prof. zool., U. of Ill., 1922-35, asso. prof., 1935-38; prof. zool. and curator Museum of Natural History, U. of Ill., 1938-48; now emeritus prof. Zool., emeritus curator, Museum Natural History. Fellow A.A.A.S.; mem. Soc. Ichthyologists and Herpetologists, Soc. of Zoologists, Asso. of Museums, Midwest Museums Asso., Acacia, Sigma Xi, Beta Theta Pi. Republican. Conglist. Author: Necturus, 1926; Introduction to Vertebrates, 1933; Adams and Eddy-Comparative Anatomy, 1949. Contbr. to jours. Home: 401 Vermont St., Urbana IL

ADAMS, NUMA POMPILIUS GARFIELD, medical dean; b. Delaphane, Va., Feb. 26, 1885; A.B., Howard U., 1911; A.M., Columbia, 1912; M.D., Rush Med. Coll., Chicago, 1924; A.B., Dartmouth Coll., 1937; student Mass. Inst. Tech.,; m. Osceola Marie Macarthy, 1915; 1 son, Charles Macarthy. Teacher of chemistry, Howard U., 1912-19; began practice of medicine at Chicago; practice in Washington, D.C., since 1929; now dean school of medicine, Howard U. Mem. bd. of dirs. Tuberculosis Assn. of D.C.; mem. advisory health council of Washington Council on Social Agencies. Fellow A.A.A.S.; mem. Nat. Med. Assn., Cook County (Ill.) Physicians Assn. Contrbr. to med. jours. Home: 341 Bryant St. N.W. Office: Howard Univ., Washington, D.C. Died Aug. 29, 1940.

ADAMS, OSCAR SHERMAN, mathematician; b. nr. Mt. Vernon, O., Jan. 9, 1874; s. David W. and Louisa (McElroy) A.; B.S., 1st honors, Kenyon Coll., 1896 (valedictorian), A.M., 1915, Sc.D., 1922; m. Mary Edna Fuller, June 20, 1900 (dec.); children—Catherine Fuller, Jane Elizabeth, George David; m. 2d, Mrs. Pauline Gleeson Pealer; 1 dau., Carola Ann. Supt. schs., Centerburg, Ohio, 1899-1903; Dover, Ohio, 1903-05, Rock Creek, 1905-06; prin. Madison Twp. High School, North Madison, O., 1906-10; goedetic computer and mathematician, U.S. Coast and Geodetic Survey, 1910-44. Served in Co. L. 4th O. Vol. Inf., Spanish-Am. War, Puerto Rico Campaign; 1st lt. Engr. O.R.C., 1917. Mem. Math. Assn. Am. (pres. Md.-Va.-D.C. sect. 1921-22), Washington Philos Soc. (rec. sec. 1929-30, v.p. 1931-32, pres. 1933), Washington Acad. Scis. (sec. 1938-39), Grange, Am. Geophys. Union, Phi Beta Kappa, Sigma Xi (sec. of D.C. Chapter, 1937-39). Methodist. Author: Application of Least Squares to Adjustment of Triangulation, 1915; General Theory of Lambert Projection, 1918; General Theory of Polyconic Projections, 1919; Latitude Developments, 1921; Elements of Map Projection (with Chas. H. Deetz), 1921; Radio-Compass Bearings, 1921; Elliptic Functions Applied to Conformal World Maps, 1925; Tables for Albers Projection, 1927; The Bowie Method of Triangulation Adjustment, 1930. Co-Author: Manual of Plane Coordinate Computation, 1935; Manual of Traverse Computation on the Lambert Grid, 1935; Manual of Traverse Computation on the Transverse Mercator Grid, 1935. Compiler: Triangulation in Colorado, 1930; Triangulation in North Carolina, 1935. Home: Route 3, Mt. Vernon, O. 43050. Died Mar. 5, 1962; buried Arlington Nat. Cemetery, Va.

ADAMS, OTTO VINCENT, engring. educator; b. Cadiz, O., Sept. 6, 1884; s. McNary Francis and Elizabeth (Cope) A.; B.S. in Civil and Irrigation Engring., Colo. State Coll. of Agr. and Mechanics, 1918; M.S.E., University of Mich., 1924; D.Sc., Colorado A. and M. Coll., 1945 m. Elsie M. Mathias, Dec. 22, 1909 (dec., 1945); m. 2d, Ada Vivian Johnson, Aug., 1947. Surveyor, Fort Collins, Colo., 1905-06; field asst., U.S. Reclamation Service, Mitchell, Neb., 1906-07, jr. engr., 1907-08; private practice of civil engring., Monte Vista, Colo., 1908-16; drainage engr. U.S. Dept. of Agr., Fort Collins, 1918; asst. commr. of works, Fort Collins., 1918; testing engr. and asso. prof. of civil engring., Colo. State Coll. of Agr. and Mechanics, 1919-27; asso. prof. of civil engring., Tex. Tech. Coll., Lubbock, Tex., 1927-32, prof. of civil engring., 1932-55, retired, dean engineering, 1932-49. Chmn. Northwest Texas Com. on Engineering, Science and Management War Training Asso. member Am. Soc. C.E. (v.p. Tex. sect.); mem. Soc. for Promotion Engring. Edn., South Plains Ret. Tchrs. Assn. (1st pres.), Lubbock Tech. Club, Tau, Beta Pi, Phi Kappa Phi. Presbyn. (elder emeritus). Mason (32 degree), Tex. Lodge Research (charter). Club: Kiwanis. Home: Lubbock TX Died Oct. 17, 1971; buried Lubbock TX

ADAMS, PARMENIO, congressman; b. Hartford, Conn., Sept. 9, 1776; attended common schs. Moved to Phelps Corners, Batavia, Genesee County (now Attica, Wyoming County), N.Y., 1806; served with N.Y. Militia, 1806-16, as lt. light inf., capt. Grenadiers, 2d and 1st maj., div. insp. Inf.; served as maj. and commandant N.Y. Volunteers, in War of 1812; sheriff of Genesee County, 1815-16, 18-21; engaged in agrl. pursuits, also as constrn. contractor on Erie Canal; mem. U.S. Ho. of Reps. from N.Y. (contested election), 18th, 19th congresses, Jan. 7, 1824-27. Died Alexander, N.Y., Feb. 19, 1832.

ADAMS, PORTER (HARTWELL), educator; b. at Andover, Mass., Aug. 10, 1894; s. Charles Albert and Jeannie Hortense (Porter) A.; prep. edn. Stone Sch. and Chauncy Hall Sch., Boston; student U. of Redlands, Calif., Mass. Inst. Tech.; hon. M.Sc., Norwich U., 1933, Sc.D., 1935; m. 2d, Sue Shorter, July 27, 1931. With Cooper Aircraft Co., Bridgeport, Conn., 1915; associated with Donald Douglass on first porposed world flight, 1916; development work, 1920-22. Intelligence and communications officer, U.S. Navy, Rockland, Me., and Boston, 1917-18; aide to comdg. officer, Naval Air Sta., Chatham, Mass., 1918-19; lt. comdr. U.S.N.R., retired. Executor and trustee of various estates; pres. of Norwich U., Dec. 1933-June 1939, now pres. emeritus. Pres. Village Soc. of Thetford, Vt., since 1929; mem. Thetford Water Bd.; mem. Thetford Bd. of Selectmen, 1933-36; mem. Vt. Ho. of Reps., 1933-34; mem. Vt. Chamber of Commerce. Chmn. exec. com. Nat. Aeronautic Assn., 1922-26 and since 1928, pres. 1926-28; chmn. Municipal Air Bd., Boston, since 1922; Vt. airport supervisor for aeronautics branch, Dept. of Commerce and Civil Works Adminstrn.; dir. Miniature Aircraft Tournament under Playground Recreation Assn. America, Nat. Glider Assn.; v.p. Internat. Air Congress, Rome, Italy, 1927; tech. adviser for Am. Delegation, Internat. Civil Aeronatuics Conf., Washington, 1928; mem. Fed. Bd. of Maps and Surveys; mem. Am. Olympic ,Com., 1928; chmn. First Intercollegiate Aeronatuical Conf., Yale U., 1928; chmn. aviation med. sec., First Nat. Aeronatuical Safety Conf., 1928; chmn. first aviation com., Am. Legion, Dept. of Mass.; mem. advisory council on student flying activities, Mass. Inst. Tech.,; mem. special com. on Aeronautical Research in Ednl. Instns. of Nat. Advisory Com. for Aeronautics; mem. New Eng. Planning Com. of Nat. Resources Bd., also chmn. aviation com.; chmn. Aero Com. of A.L. Dept., Vt., 1935; Vt. chmn. for Navy Day, 1933-40; apptd. by gov. chmn. Vt. Aviation Commn. for term, 1936-40. Mem. Vt. advisory bd. for N.Y. World's Fair. Trustee Norwich U.; elected chmn. spl. com. of trustees to administer James Jackson Cabot professorship of air traffic regulation and air transportation, and also appointed first James Jackson Cabot prof. of air traffic regulation and air transportation at Norwich Univ., Aug. 1935; trustee Thetford Acad.; v.p. Vt. Boy Scouts. Fellow A.A.A.S.; mem. Inst. of Aeronautical Sciences, Am. Soc. M.E. (exec. Inst. of Aronautical Sciences, Am. Soc. M.E. (exec. com., aeronatuics sect.), Navy League of U.S., Soc. Automotive Engrs., Am. Acad. Air Law, Vt. Hist. Soc., Vt. Soc. Engrs., U.S. Naval Inst., Naval Order of U.S., lMil. Order of World War, Nat. Grange (7th degree), Newcomen Soc., New Eng. Railroad Club, Pi Gamma Mu, Epsilon Tau Sigma; also hon. mem. foreign aeronautical socs. Conglist. Clubs: Metropolitan, Aero (trustee), Army and Navy (Washington); St. Botolph, Wardroom, Engineers, Aero Club of lMass. (dir., ex-vice pres.), Aero Club of New England (dir., ex-pres.), Woodland Country (Boston); University (Boston and Northfield, Vt.); Newcomen Soc. (England). Contbr. to periodicals on subject of aviation. Inventor of aeroplane brakes, 1916, Adams type of wind tunnel balance for aerodynamical research, 1933, Adams system of combustion for steam submarines, aircraft tanks, etc. Home: "Aero Acres" Thetford, Vt. Address: Norwich University, Northfield, Vt. Died Dec. 5, 1945.

ADAMS, ROGER, educator; b. Boston, Jan. 2, 1889; s. Austin Winslow and Lydia (Curtis) A.; A.B., Harvard, 1909, A.M., 1910, Ph.D., 1912, D.Sc., 1945; D.Sc., Bklyn. Poly. Inst., 1935, Northwestern U., 1942, U. Rochester, 1943, U. Pa., 1947, Yale, 1948, Drexel Institute of Tech., 1955, University Ill., 1957. U. Bridgeport, 1960; LL.D., U. Mich., 1954; student U. Berlin. 1912-13, Kaiser Wilhelm Inst., 1913; m. Lucile Wheeler, Aug. 29, 1918; 1 dau., Lucile. Instr. organic chemistry Harvard U. and Radcliffe Coll., 1913-16: asst. prof. U. Ill., 1916-19, prof., 1919-57, head dept. chemistry and chemical engineering, 1926-54, research professor, 1954-57, emeritus prof., 1957-71. Dir. Champaign Nat. Bank. Mem. Ill. Bd. Natural Resources and Conservation, from 1942; mem. Nat. Inventors Council, 1945-63; dir. Council for Agrl. and Chemurgic Research, Nat. Sci. Found., 1954-60; mem. NDRC, 1941-46, scientific adviser to U.S. Deputy Military Governor Germany, 1945; chmn. sci. adv. com. U.S. Mil. Govt. Japan, 1947; mem. sci. adv. mission Japan, 1948. Trustee Battelle Meml. Inst., Sloan-Kettering Inst. Cancer Research; mem. bd. overseers Harvard, 1950-52. Commd. maj. CWS, 1918. Recipient (medals) Nichols, 1927, Gibbs, 1936. Cresson, 1944, Davy, 1945, Richards, 1946, Priestley, 1946, Hofmann, 1953, Midwest, 1953, Perkin, 1954, Parsons, 1958, Franklin, 1960, Am. Inst. Chemists, 1964, Nat. Medal of Sci., 1964; John R. Kuebler award, 1966; also the Northwestern University Centennial award, 1951. Decorated Medal for Merit (U.S.); hon. commander of civil div. Order Brit. Empire. Fellow A.A.A.S. (chmn. sect. C 1927, exec. com. 1941-45, 47-51, pres. 1950), Am. Inst. Chemists, Soc. Chem. Industry, Harvey Soc., German Chem. Soc.; mem. Internat. Union Pure and Applied Chemistry (v.p. 1951-55), Am. Chem. Soc. (dir. 1930-35, pres. 1935, chmn. bd. 1944-50), Am. Acad. Arts and Scis., Am. Philos. Soc., Nat. Acad. Scis. (council 1931-37, 59-62, chmn. chem. sect. 1938-41, fgn. sec. 1950-54); hon. mem. Chem. Soc. London, Societe Chimique de France, Polish, Swiss, Spanish, Japanese, Argentine chem. socs. Conglist. Author articles organic chemistry. Editor, Organic Reactions, 1941-68. Home: Urbana IL Died July 6, 1971; buried Mt. Hope Cemetery, Urbana IL

ADAMS, ROMANZO, sociologist; b. Bloomingdale, Wis., Mar. 22, 1868; s. Mighill Dustin and Catherine (Wolfe) A.; M.Di., Ia. State Teachers' Coll., Cedar Falls, Ia., 1892; Ph.B., U. of Mich., 1897, Ph.M., 1898; Ph.D., U. of Chicago, 1904; m. Nellie Cronk, Sept. 16, 1902; 1 dau., Katharine. Prin. pub. schs., Ireton, Ia., 1892-94; prof. economics and sociology, Western Coll., Toledo, Ia., 1898-1900; prof. edn. and sociology, 1902-11, prof. economics and sociology, U. of Nev., 1911-20, U. of Hawaii since 1920. Mem. Inst. of Pacific Relations. Methodist. Author: Taxation in Nevada, 1918; Statistical Studies of the Japanese in Hawaii, 1923; The Peoples of Hawaii-A Statistical Study, 1925. Home: 2315 Liloa Rise, Honolulu, Hawaii. Died Sept. 10, 1942/

ADAMS, WALTER SYDNEY, astronomer; b. Antioch, North Syria, Dec. 20, 1876; s. Lucien Harper and Dora (Francis) A.; A.B., Dartmouth, 1898; D.Sc., 1913; A.M., U. Chgo., 1900, U. Munich, 1901; LL.D., Pomona, 1926; D.Sc., Columbia, 1926, U. So. Cal., 1930, U. Chgo., 1945, Princeton, 1947; m. Lillian M. Wickham, June 2, 1910 (died 1920); m. 2d, Adeline L. Miller, June 15, 1922; children—Edmund Miller, John Francis. Asst. 1901-03, instr. 1903-04, Yerkes Obs., Asst. astronomer, 1904-09, astronomer, 1909—, acting dir., 1910-11, asst. dir., 1913-23, dir., 1923-46, Mt. Wilson Obs. of Carnegie Instn., Pasadena, Cal., research asso., 1946-47. Mem. Am. Astron. Soc. (pres. 1931-34), Astron. Soc. Pacific (pres. 1923), Royal Acad. Sciences of Upsala, Astron. Union (v.p. 1935-38), Am. Philos.

Soc.; fgn. mem. Royal Society of London, Royal Astronomical Society (London), Institute of France (Acad. of Sciences), Royal Swedish Acad. of Scis. Gold medal Royal Astron. Soc., 1917, Draper medal Nat. Acad. Sciences, 1918; Janssen medal, Societe Astronomique de France, 1926; Bruce medal, Astron. Soc. Pacific, 1928; Janssen medal, Paris Acad. of Sciences, 1935. Clubs: Athenaeum, Twilight. Writer numerous papers on solar and stellar spectroscopy, radial velocities and distances of stars. Home: 873 N. Hill Av., Pasadena 7, Cal. Died May 11, 1956; buried Derry, N.H.

ADAMS, WILLIAM MILTON, plastic surgeon; b. Ripley, Miss., Apr. 26, 1905; s. Dr. R. M. and Patty Etter (Murray) A.; B.S., U. Miss., 1928; M.D., Tulane, 1930; m. Catherine Taylor, May 22, 1934; children—William Milton, Robert Franklin, Ann Taylor, Catherine Sue. Intern N.Y. Post Grad. Hosp., N.Y. City, 1931-32; asso. prof. surgery U. Tenn., 1951—, chief plastic surgery dept. U. Tenn., John Gaston Hosp., 1935—; chief staff, 1948; senior attending plastic surgery Bapt. Meml., John Gaston, Meth., St. Joseph's hosps.; chief cons. plastic surgery Kennedy V.A., U.S. Marine hosps. Mem. Examining Bd. Plastic Surgery, 1947—. Diplomate Am. Bd. Plastic Surgery. Fellow Internat. Coll. Surgeons, A.C.S.; mem. Am. Soc. Plastic and Reconstructive Surgery (pres. 1954; asso. editor Jour.), Am., Brit. assns. plastic surgeons, American Association Surgery Trauma, Am. Med. Assn., Southern, Tenn., Shelby Co., Memphis med. assns., Southeastern Surg. Congress, Southwestern Surg. Assn., Memphis Surg. Soc., La.-Miss. Ophthal. and Otolaryngol. Soc. (hon. mem.). Clubs: Rotary, Memphis Country (Memphis). Contributor articles medical journals. Home: 689 East Drive, Memphis 2. Office: 1073 Madison St., Memphis 3. Died Apr. 4, 1957; buried Memorial Park, Memphis.

ADDIS, THOMAS, prof. medicine; b. Edinburgh, Scotland, July 27, 1881; s. Thomas Chalmers and Cornelia Beers (Campbell) A.; came to U.S., 1911, naturalized, 1917; M.B., Ch.B., U. of Edinburgh, 1905, M.D., 1908; m. Elesa Bolton Bolton Partridge, 1913; children—Elesa Campbell, Jean Thorburn. Prof. medicine Stanford U. Med. Sch. since 1911. Mem. Nat. Acad. of Science. Author: Glomerular Nephritis, 1948. Contbr. to scientific mags. Home: 1109 Alta Loma Rd., Los Angeles 46. Address: Inst. for Medical Research, 4751 Fountain Av., Los Angeles 27. Died June 4, 1949.

ADDISON, WILLIAM H(ENRY) F(ITZGERALD), anatomist; b. Whitby, Ont., Can., Apr. 23, 1880; s. John Hardill and Harriet Matilda (Rowe) A.; B.A., U. Toronto, 1902, M.B., 1905, M.D., 1917; studied in Europe 7 summers; Madrid, spring of 1928 with Ramón y Cajal, spring of 1934 with Rio Hortega; m. Elenaor Corkhill Adams, Dec. 25, 1905 (died Dec. 19, 1948); 1 dau., Agnes Eleanor (Mrs. John M. Gilchrist). Demonstrator, histology and embryology U. Pa., 1905-12, asst. prof., 1912-19, prof., 1919-48, prof. emeritus, 1948—. Fellow A.A.A.S., Coll. of Physicians of Phila.; mem. Am. Assn. Anatomists, Am. Soc. Naturalists, Phila. Zoöl. Soc., Phila. Acad. Nat. Scis., Phila. Pathol. Soc., Marine Biol. Lab. (Woods Hole, Mass.), Am. Physiol. Soc., Sigma Xi, Phi Beta Pi. Episcopalian. Editor: Villiger's Brain and Spinal Cord; Piersol's Normal Histology; Contbr. chapters in McClung's Microscopic Technique and in Griffith and Farris' The Rate in Laboratory Investigation; papers in sci. jours. on the microscopic structure of tissues and organs, including the brain. Home: 286 E. Sidney Av., Mt. Vernon, N.Y. 10553. Office: Univ. of Pa. School of Medicine, Phila. 4. Died Feb. 24, 1963: buried Union Cemetery, Oshawa, Ont., Can.

ADGATE, FREDERICK WHITNEY, consulting engr.; b. Keeseville, N.Y., June 5, i868; s. George and Martha (Whitney) A.; student Kan. State Agrl. Coll., 3 yrs.; m. Dolly May Triplett, June 21, 1904; children—George, Dorothy. Engr. and supt. various cos. until 1902; with The Foundation Co., Chicago, Ill., since its organization, 1902, successively as engr., supt., asst. western mgr. and mgr.; has built numerous large bridges, power plants, mining shafts, foundations, etc.; v.p. and dir. Money Corp.; dir. Service Oil Co., Charlton Fur Corp. In charge ship building and dry dock during World War. Republican. Episcopalian. Mason. Home: Wheaton, Ill. Died Oct. 23, 1934.

ADKINS, HOMER (BURTON), univ. prof.; b. Newport, Washington County, O., Jan. 16, 1892; s. Alvin and Emily (Middleswart) A.; B.Sc., Denison Univ., 1915, D.Sc., 1938; M.A., Ohio State U., 1916, Ph.D., 1918; m. Louise Spivey, Feb. 21, 1917; children—Dorothea, Nancy, Roger. Began as instr. chemistry, Ohio State U., 1918; asst. prof. organic chemistry, U. of Wis., 1919-24, asso. prof., 1924-28, prof. since 1928. Mem. division 9, National Defense Research Com. Awarded Medal for Merit. Mem. Nat. Acad. of Scis. Am. Chem. Soc. (past chmn. organic div.), A.A.A.S., Chemical Society (London), Phi Beta Kappa, Phi Delta Theta, Phi Lambda Upsilon, Alpha Chi Sigma, Sigma Xi. Author: Practice of Organic chemistry, 1925; Elementary Organic Chemistry, 1928; Reactions of Hydrogen, 1937; also about 160 scientific papers. Mem. bd. editors, Organic Chemistry, 1938; Organic Syntheses (annual vols.) and Organic Reactions. Home: 2103 Rowley Av., Madison, Wis. Died Aug. 10, 1949; buried Forest Hills, Madison.

ADKINS, JOHN SCUDDER, architect; b. St. Louis, Mo.; s. Silas and Maria G. (Morgan) A.; ed. tech. div. Washington U. Sch. of Fine Arts; m. Olive Bridgeman, Oct. 5, 1898; children—Marcia Lee (Mrs. Ralph Ingalsbe Finn), Eleanor Pelton (Mrs. Stanford Church Richmond). Designer, Barnett, Haynes & Barnett, later with Shepley, Rutan & Coolidge, St. Louis; began practice as architect, 1900. Architect: Clinton County Court House, Wilmington, O.; Scioto County Court House, Portsmouth, O.; City Hall, Norwood. O.; Governor's Mansion, Frankfort, Ky.; Second Nat. Bank, Oakley Bank Bldg., Cincinnati Gymnasium and Athletic Club and Grace Episcopal Ch., Cincinnati; First and Merchants Nat. Bank, Middleton, O.; Kanawha Nat. Bank, Charleston, W. Va.; Audubon Bldg., New Orleans: First Bapt. Ch. Lexington, Ky.; Nurses Home, Muncie, Ind. Mem. City Planning Comm., Cincinnati. Episcopalian. Mason. Home: Vernon Manor, Cincinnati, O. Deceased.

ADLER, ALFRED, psychologist; b. Vienna, Austria, Feb. 7, 1870; s. Leopold and Pauline Adler; M.D., Vienna U., 1895; LL.D.; m. Raissa Epstein, 1898; 1 son, 3 daus. Worked in Vienna Gen. Hosp. and Polyclinic, 1895-97; gen. med. practitioner, nerve specialist, Vienna, 1897-1927; organized (with others) Child Guidance Centres to prevent neurosis and delinquency in childhood, at 30 schs. in Vienna, from 1912; founded Jour. Individual Psychology, 1914; attached to Austrian Army, Vienna, also Cracow, 1914-18; lectr. Pedagogical Inst. City of Vienna, 1924; lectr. Columbia U., N.Y.C., 1927, later at Med. Centre, N.Y.C.; clin. dir. Mariahilfer Ambulatorium, Vienna, 1928; became vis. prof. med. psychology, cons. psychologist L.I. Coll. Medicine, 1932; founded Jour. Individual Psychology in U.S.A., 1935. Author: Individual Psychology; Practice and Theory of Individual Psychology, 1920, transl., 1927; The Science of Living, 1929; Education of children, 1930; The Pattern of Life, 1930; What Life Should Mean to You, 1931; Social Interest: a Challenge to Mankind, 1937; Understanding Human Nature, transl. 1946; Problem Child, transl. 1963; The Education of the Indivdual; also numerous books in German on individual psychology, edn., religion, homosexuality. Founder sci. of individual psychology. Died May 28, 1937.

ADLER, DANKMAR, architect; b. Langsfeld, Saxe Weimar, July 3, 1844; ed. public schools; studied architecture, Detroit and Chicago, 1857-62; m. Dila d. Abraham Kohn, of Chicago, June 25, 1872. Served 1862-65, Bat. M 1st Ill. Artillery. Began practice of architecture in Chicago, 1869; with A. J. Kinney, 1869-71; with Edward Burling, 1871-78; with Louis H. Sullivan, 1881-95; architect of Unity Ch., Grace M.E., and 1st M.E. Chs., Sinai, Zion, Anshe, Maariv and Isiah synagogues, Central Music Hall, McVicker's Theatre, The Auditorium, Stock Exchange bldg. and Schiller bldg., Chicago; Pueblo (Colo.) Opera House; Union Trust, Wainwright and St. Nicholas Hotel bldgs., St. Louis; Guaranty bldg., Buffalo, N.Y.; I.C. R.R. passenger station, New Orleans; asso. architect Carnegie Music Hall, New York, etc. Home: Chicago, Ill. Died 1900.

ADLER, DAVID, architect; b. Milw., Jan. 3, 1883; s. Isaac and Therese (Hyman) A.; student Lawrenceville (N.J.) Sch., 1898-1900; A.B., Princeton, 1904; student Ecole des Beaux Arts, Paris, 1906-11; m. Katherine Keith, June 1, 1916. Began practice of architecture with Henry Corwith Dangier, Chgo., 1912; partner firm David Adler & Robert Work, Inc., 1917-28, alone, 1928—. Trustee Art Inst., Chgo. Fellow A.I.A.; mem. Nat. Inst. Arts and Letters. Home: Libertyville, Ill. Office: 220 S. Michigan Av., Chgo. Died Sept. 27, 1949.

ADLER, HERMAN MORRIS, psychiatrist; b. New York, N.Y., Oct. 10, 1876; s. Isaac and Frieda (Grumbacher) A.; A.B., Harvard, 1897; A.M., M.D., Columbia, 1901; m. Frances Porter, Mar. 17, 1917; 1 dau., Frances Porter, Asst. prof. psychiatry, Harvard Med. Sch., 1912-17; was chief of staff, Boston Psychopathic Hosp.; removed to Chicago, 1916, to make a study of facilities in Cook County for detection and care of mental diseases and mental deficiency, under auspices of Rockefeller Foundation and Nat. Com. Mental Hygiene. Apptd. by Judge Scully, 1917, to make survey of Cook County's psychopathic cases and to act as med. adviser to county bd.; apptd. state criminologist of Ill. by Gov. Lowden, June 30, 1917; dir. Juvenile Psychopathic Inst., Feb. 10, 1917—. Maj. Med. Corps, U.S. Army, July 1918-Mar. 1919; spl. duty in disciplinary psychiatry at mil. prisons; prof. criminology and head of dept. of social hygiene, med. jurisprudence and criminology, Med. Coll. U. of Ill., 1919-28; prof. psychiatry, U. of Calif., 1930—: also advisor Calif. Dept. of Instns. Dir. Behavior Research Fund, 1926—; mem. Harvard Survey of Crime and Law; consultant to Nat. Commn. on Law Observance and Enforcement. Author of section on Medical Science and Criminal Justice, in Criminal Justice Survey of the Cleveland Foundation, 1921. Home: Berkeley, Calif. Deceased.

ADRAIN, ROBERT, mathematician, educator; b. Carrickfergus, Ireland, Sept. 30, 1775; m. Ann Pollock, 1 child. Came to Am., 1789; prof. natural philosophy and mathematics Queens Coll. (now Rutgers U.), New Brunswick, N.J., 1809-12, 26; prof. Columbia, N.Y.C., 1813-25; prof. mathematics U. Pa., 1827-34, vice provost, 1828-34; considered one of most brilliant mathematicians of his time in Am.; founder journals Analyst, or Mathematical Companion, 1808, The Mathematical Diary, 1825-33. Died New Brunswick, Aug. 10, 1843.

ADRIANCE, JOHN SABIN, chemist; b. New York, Feb. 18, 1861; s. John and Lucy Whitman (Sabin) A.; A.B., Williams Coll., 1882, A.M., Ph.D.; unmarried. Professionally engaged as chemist from graduation; chemist for Wacker Gordon Laboratory, New York; prof. chemistry and toxicology, New York Homoe. Med. Coll. Fellow London Chem. Soc., A.A.A.S.; mem. Am. Chem. Soc., Soc. Chem. Industry, S.R. Congregationalist. Republican. Club: Union League. Author: Chemical Calculations (4 edits.), 1886-1904. Residence: 105 E. 38th St., New York.

ADSON, ALFRED WASHINGTON, surgeon; b. Terril, Ia., Mar. 13, 1887; s. Martin and Anna (Bergeson) A.; B.Sc., U. of Neb., 1912, A.M., 1918; M.D., U. of Pa., 1914; M.S. in surgery, U. of Minn., 1918; hon. D.Sc., U. of Neb., 1948, St. Olaf Coll.; m. Lora G. Smith, Aug. 3, 1911; children—William Walter, Mary Louise, Martin Alfred. Successively fellow in surgery, Mayo Clinic, 1st asst., jr. surgeon, neurol. surgeon, chief neurol. surgeon; now senior neuro-surgeon professor neuro-surgery Mayo Foundation Grad. Sch. of U. of Minn. Colonel Med. R.C., United States Army. Mem. Minn. State Board of Med. Examiners since 1929, pres., 2 years. Mem. Medical Council of the Veterans Administration, Council on Medical Service and Public Relations of A.M.A., adv. com. Med. Unit of Div. of Social Welfare of Minn., Dept. of Social Security; mem. Commn. on Associated Med. Care Plans; chmn. Minn. State Med. Service Com.; pres. Northwest National Conference. Fellow American College of Surgeons; member A.M.A., American Surg. Assn., American Neurol. Assn., American Neurosurgical Assn. (pres. 1932), Internat. Neurol. Assn., Internat. Congress of Surgeons, Western Surg. Assn. (v.p. 1936), Minn. State Med. Assn. (pres. 1937; del. to A.M.A.), Am. Bd. Neurol. Surgery (chmn.), Minn. Soc. of Neurology and Psychiatry (pres. 1943), also numerous local, state and district medical societies, Phi Rho Sigma, Sigma Xi, Alpha Omega Alpha. Republican (chmn. co. com.). Mason (32 deg., K.T., Shriner). Clubs: University, Golf. Contbr. more than 242 articles to med. jours. in development and improvement of surg. technique in removal of brain and spinal cord tumors; development of operations for treatment of glossopharyngeal neuralgia, cervical ribs, Reynaud's disease, Hirschsprung's disease and essential hypertension. Home: 831 9th Av. S.W., Rochester, Minn. Died Nov. 12, 1951.

ADULM, JOHN viticulturiest; b. York, Pa., Apr. 29, 1759; m. Margaret Adlum, 1813. Commd. maj. Provisional Army; brig. gen. Pa. Militia; asso. judge Lycoming County (Pa.), 1795-98; established exptl. farm and nursery, Georgetown, D.C., studied about 30 native varieties of grapes, also wine-making processes; introduced and propagated Catawba grape; among 1st to urge fed. aid to agrl. research; climbing fumitory plant Adlumia named in his honor. Author: A Memoir on the Cultivation of the Vine in America and the Best Mode of Making Wine, 1823; Adlum on Making Wine, 1826. Died "Vineyard" nr. Georgetown, Mar. 1, 1836.

AEBERSOLD, PAUL C(LARENCE), biophysicist; b. Fresno, Cal., July 7, 1910; s. Paul and Dora (Houck) A.; A.B. cum laude, Stanford, 1932; M.A., U. of Cal., 1934, Ph.D., 1938; m. Florence Katherine Martinson, July 7, 1942; children—Paul Martin, Alice Constance, Mickie Claire. Research in nuclear physics, radiology and biomedical physics. Radiation Lab., U. Cal. at Berkeley, and Med. Sch., San Francisco, 1932-43; research and adminstrn. Atomic Energy (Manhattan) Project, Oak Ridge, Tenn., and Los Alamos, N.M., 1942-46; dir. isotopes div. AEC, Oak Ridge, 1947-57, asst. dir. for isotopes and radiation Div. of Civilian Application, 1957, Office of Indsl. Devel., 1958; dir. Office of Isotopes Devel., AEC, Washington, 1958—, chmn. AEC adv. com. on istope and radiation devel. Mem. com. on nuclear sci. NRC; mem. on safe handling of radioisotopes Nat. Com. Radiation Protection. U.S. del. 4th Inter-Am. Congress Radiology, Mexico D.F., 1952; tech. adviser U.S. delegation UN Conf. on Peaceful Uses of Atomic Energy, Geneva, 1955; mem. Atoms for Peace Mission to S.A., 1956; U.S. del. 5th Internat. Electronic and Nuclear Congress and Expn., Rome, 1958. Diplomate in radiol. physics Am. Bd. Radiology. Fellow Am. Phys. Soc., A.A.A.S., N.Y. Acad. Sci., Sigma Xi, Am. Coll. Radiology (asso.); mem. Radiol. Soc. N.A., Am. Radium Soc., Rocky Mountain Radiol. Soc. (hon.), Am. Assn. Cancer Research, Radiation Research Soc., Am. Nuclear Soc. (chmn. isotopes and radiation div. 1960-61, dir. 1961—), Soc. Nuclear Medicine, Phi Beta Kappa. Home: 4811 Grantham Av., Chevy Chase, Md. Died May 29, 1967.

AGAR, WILLIAM MACDONOUGH, geologist, author; b. N.Y. City, Feb. 14, 1894; s. John Giraud and Agnes Louise (Macdonough) A.; grad. The Newman Sch., Lakewood, N.J., 1912; B.S., Princeton, 1916; A.M., 1920, Ph.D., 1922; D.Sc. (honorary), Long Island

Univ., 1967; m. Alida Stewart Carter, May 6, 1922 (dec. Mar. 1970); children—Alida Marie, Sylvia Carter, Catherine Macdonough, John Herbert Michael. Geologist Anaconda Copper Co., Butte, Mont., 1922-23; instr. in geology, Yale, 1923-26, asst. prof., 1926-28; asst. prof. of geology, Columbia, 1928-35; headmaster and trustee The Newman Sch., Lakewood, N.J., 1935-40; visiting lecturer in geology, Columbia U., 1940-41; sr. geol., U.S. Geol. Survey, 1942-45, gen. publicity (writing, radio) with Fight For Freedom, Inc., 1940-41; chmn. bd. Freedom House; with Dept. Public Information, United Nations, 1946-56; chmn. Met. region. American Assn. for the UN, 1956-59, chairman of the advisory committee, 1959, 60; chmn. Hampton chpt. A.R.C., 1960-63, treas. Southampton dist., from 1964; chmn. exec. council Southampton Coll.; chmn. Coll. Com. Eastern L.I., 1962-63. Author and lectr. Served as sous chef Service Sanitaire (Etats) Unis No. 16 (Am. Field Service), 1917; 1st lt. Air Service (pilot), U.S. Army, with A.E.F., 1917-18. Decorated Croix de Guerre (France). Mem. Geol. Soc. Am. Democrat. Roman Catholic. Club: Southampton (N.Y.). Contbr. articles on geology to tech. jours. Formerly mem. editorial advisor bd. and contributor articles and revs. to The Commonweal. Home: Southhampton NY Died June 10, 1972; buried Southampton NY

AGASSIZ, ALEXANDER (EMMANUEL RODOLPHE), naturalist; b. Neuchatel, Switzerland, Dec. 17, 1835; s. Professor Jean Louis Rodolphe and Cecile (Braun) A.; came to U.S., 1849; A.B., Harvard, 1855; B.S., Lawrence Scientific Sch., 1857; LL.D., Harvard, 1885, St. Andrew's, 1901; Sc.D., U. of Cambridge, 1887, Bologna, 1888; m. Anna Russell, Nov. 13, 1860. Asst. on U.S. Coast Survey in Calif., 1859; asst. in zoälogy, Mus. Comparative Zoölogy, Harvard, 1860-65; developed and was supt. 1865-69, Calumet & Hecla copper mines, Lake Superior; dir. Anderson Sch. of Natural History on Penjkese Island, 1874; mem. expdn. to S. America, 1875, where inspected copper mines of Peru and Chili and made surveys of Lake Titicaca; curator Mus. Comparative Soölogy, 1874-85, dir. same, 1902—; has made gifts to the museums aggregating over $1,000,000; also valuable W. Indian, Central, S. America and Pacific zoöl. collection, 1898. Assisted Sir Charles Wyville Thomson in classifying the collections of the expdn. of the Challenger in her voyage of 68,900 miles of deep-sea exploration, 1872-76; spent winters 1876-81 in deep-sea dredging in W. Indies on board U.S. Coast Survey steamer Blake; in charge of expdn. to the Sandwich Islands, the West Indies, the Fiji Islands, the Great Basin Reef of Australia; in charge of expdn. of U.S.S. Albatross to the Panamic regions and Galapagos, to the central Pacific and to eastern Pacific. Overseer, 1873-78 and 1885, fellow, 1878-84 and 1886-90, Harvard. Knight Order of Merit (Prussia), 1902; Officer Legion of Honor (France), 1896. Pres. Nat. Acad. of Sciences; pres. Am. Acad. Arts amd Sciences, 1898. Author: Seaside Studies in Natural History (with Mrs. Elizabeth Cabot Agassiz), 1865; Marine Animals of Massachussetts Bay, 1871; Exploration of Lake Titicaca; Three Cruises of the Blake; Revision of the Echini; Coral Reefs of Florida, Bahamas, Bermudas, W. Indies, of the Pacific, of the Maldives; Panamic Deep Sea Echini; Hawaiian Echini, Embryological Memoirs on Fishes, Worms, Echinoderms, etc. Home: Cambridge, Mass. Died 1910.

AGASSIZ, ELIZABETH CABOT, author; b. Boston Mass., d. Thomas Greaves Cary; m. late Prof. Louis Agassiz; accompanied her husband to Brazil, 1865-66 and on Hassler expdn., 1871-72; was associated with him in many of his studies and writings; has taken active part in promoting the welfare of Radcliffe Coll., formerly the Harvard "Annex." Author: Seaside Studies in Natural History (with her son, Alexander Agassiz); Life of Louis Agassiz. Home: Cambridge, Mass. Died 1907.

AGASSIZ, GEORGE RUSSELL, trustee; b. Nahant, Mass., July 21, 1862; s. Alexander and Anna (Russell) A.; LL.D., Harvard U., 1938; m. Mabel Simpkins, June 27, 1902. Dir. Calumet and Hech Mining Co. since 1933; former pres. Harvard Bd. of Overseers. Fellow Am. Acad.; mem. Mass. Historical Soc. (past. pres.), Harvard Alumni Assn. Faculty Museum Comparative Zoology (Harvard). Author: Letters and Recollections of Alexander Agassiz, 1913; Meade's Headquarters, 1927. Contbr. articles to jours. Home: Dedham, Mass. Office: 14 Ashburton Place, Boston. Died Feb. 5, 1951.

AGASSIZ, JEAN LOUIS RODOLPHE, zoologist; b. Motier-en-Vuly, Canton Fribourg, Switzerland, May 28, 1807; attended Coll. Lausanne (France), 1822-24, U. Zurich (Germany), 1824-26, U. Heidelberg (Germany), 1826-27; M.D., U. Munich (Germany); 1827; Ph. D., U. Erlangen (Germany), 1829; m. Cecile Braun, Oct. 1833; children—Alexander, Ida, Pauline; m. 2d, Elizabeth Cabot Cary, 1850. Conducted zool. research under French naturalist Cuvier, Paris, 1831-32; prof. natural history U. Neuchatel (Switzerland), 1832-46; established Hotel des Neuchatelois for glacier study; came to Am., 1846, toured East Coast delivering lectures in comparative embryology; went on scientific cruise along Mass. coast, 1847; prof. zoology and geology Lawrence Scientific Sch., Harvard, 1848-73; made exploration cruise of Fla. coral reefs, 1851; curator of mus. of comparative zoology, Cambridge, Mass., 1859-73; became naturalized Am. citizen, 1861; collected specimens for Cambridge Mus. in Brazil, 1863; non-resident prof. natural history Cornell U., Ithaca, N.Y., 1868; made scientific voyage around Cape Horn aboard Hassler, 1871-72; established Anderson Sch. of Natural History, Penikese Island, Buzzard's Bay, 1873. Author: The Fishes of Brazil, 1829; Recherches sur les Poissons (foundation of our present knowledge of fish), 1833-44; History of the Fresh Water Fishes of Central Europe, 1839-42; Etudes sur les Glaciers, 1840; Etudes Critiques sur les Mollusque fossilin, 1840-45; Nomenclator Zoologicus, 1842-46; Monograph on the Fossil Fishes of the Old Red or Devonian of the British Isles, 1844-45; Systeme Glaciare, 1846; Nouvelles etudes et experiences sur les Glaciers actuels, 1847; Contributions to the Natural History of the United States (contained Essay on Classification), 1857. Died Cambridge, Mass., Dec. 14, 1873; buried Mt. Auburn Cemetery, Cambridge.

AGEE, ALVA, agrl. educator; b. Cheshire, O., Oct. 1, 1858; s. Jesse Thornhill and Lydia (Mauck) A.; ed. Marietta Coll. to close of sophomore yr.; M.S., Univ. of Wooster, O.; M.S., Princeton, 1922; m. Louise Grace Hibbs, Oct. 6, 1887. Prof. in charge agrl. extension, Pa. State Coll., 1907-12; in charge agrl. extension and prof. soil fertility, Rutgers Coll., 1912-18. Asso. editor Nat. Stockman and Farmer; contbr. to agrl. periodicals since 1890; lecturer on agrl. topics since 1891. Mem. Delta Upsilon, Alpha Zeta, Phi Kappa Phi. Author: Essentials of Soil Fertility; Crops and Methods for Soil Improvement; Right Use of Lime in Soil Improvement; First Steps in Farming. Sec. Agr., N.J. State Dept. of Agr., Trenton, 1916-25. Address: 1835 Altura Pl., San Diego, Calif. Died Dec. 10, 1943.

AGERSBORG, H(ELMER) P(ARELI DE WOLD) K(JERSCHOW), author, biologist; b. Gjersvik Rodoy, Nordre Helgeland, Norway, Oct. 26, 1881; s. Albert Martin Petersen (de Tonder) and Hansine Marie Zahl (de Mechlenborg) A.; came to U.S. 1906, naturalized, 1928; student Seattle Seminary, 1908-12; B.S., M.S., U. of Wash., 1916; student Univ. of Oslo, and Akademisk Borger, Norway, 1917; M.A., Columbia, 1920; Ph.D., U. of Ill., 1923; m. Jennie Elizabeth Dunbar, July 28, 1926; children—James Albert Zahl, Helmer Pareli Kjerschow, Jr. Investigator, tchr., demonstrator in biology, zoology, anatomy at various colls., labs. and for surveys, 1913-24; Wheeler prof. biology, head dept. James Millikin U., 1924-28; aquatic biologist Ill. Dept. Conservation, 1928-29; prof. biology Shepherd Coll., 1929-30; prof. biology, head dept. Atlantic U., 1930-32; spl.cons. biologist N.H. Planning Bd., 1932-34; sr. wild life technician state park div. Emergency Conservation Works, Nat. Park Service, 1934-35, chief biologist, 1935-37; traveling lectr. conservation land and water resources, 1937—; prof. biology McKindree Coll., 1943-46; prof. biology and embryology, dir. research Des Moines Sill Coll. Osteopathy and Surgery, 1947-49; founder, 1949, and since dir. Agersborg Biol. Lab. Fellow A.A.A.S., Ia. Acad. Sci.; mem. Nat. Assn. Biology Tchrs., Nat. Wildlife Fedn., Am. Soc. Zoologists, Frat. Order Sons of Norway Eugene Field Hon. Lit. Soc., N.Y. Acad. Scis., Internat. League of Norsemen, Sigma Xi, Sigma Zeta. Presbyn. Mason; mem. Eastern Star. Author: Nature Lore, 6 vols.; An Angle of American Way of Life: Memoirs; (with Embrik Strand) International Entomological-Arachnological Dictionary. Contbr. articles in field to mags., newspapers. Address: 1212 N. Maple St., Centralia, Ill. Died Jan. 14, 1960; buried Hillcrest Meml. Park, Marion Coounty, Ill.

AGG, THOMAS RADFORD, highway engring.; b. Fairfield, Ia., May 17, 1878; s. Henry and Sarah Jane (Tansey) A.; B.S. in E.E., Ia. State Coll., Ames, Ia., 1905, C.E., 1914; m. Lois Woodman, Dec. 27, 1906; children—Muriel Lois, Alice Jane, Instr. in theoretical mechanics, U. of Ill., 1905-08; road engr. Ill. Highway Dept., summers, 1906, 1907, and full time 1908-13; prof. highway engring., Ia. State Coll., 1913-30, asst. dean of engring., 1930-32, dean of engring. and idr. Engring. Expt. Sta., 1930-46; resident prof. highway engring. since July 1946, also cons. practice. Developed outstanding instrn. and research in ghiway engring. at Ia. State Coll. Entered Engeering Offics Training Camp, May 1917; and 98th Engineers. Received Geroge S. Bartlett award for outstanding contribution to highway progress, 1936. Member American Society Civil Engrs. (dir. Dist. 16, 1938-40); (v.p. Zone 3, 1943-44), Am. Soc. for Testing Materials, Soc. for Promotion Engrings. Edn., Iowa Engring. Soc., Newcomen Soc., Tau Beta Pi, Sigma Xi, Phi Kappa Phi, Acacia. Republican. Episcopalian. Mason (32 deg.). Mem. Rotary Internat. Author: Construction of Roads and Pavements, 1916, 5th edit., 1939; American Rural Highways, 1920; (with Dr. John E. Brindley) Higway Adminstration and Finance, 1927; (with W. L. Foster) Preparation of Engineering Reports, 1935; (with Anson Marston) Engineering Reports, 1935; (with Anson Marston) Engineering Valuation, 1936. Home: 325 Pearson Av., Ames, Ia. Died May 7, 1947.

AGNEW, CORNELIUS REA, ophthalmologist, med. organizer; b. N.Y.C., Aug. 8, 1830; s. William and Elizabeth (Thompson) A.; grad. Columbia, 1849, M.D., 1852; m. Mary Nash, 1856. Began practice of medicine, 1854; surgeon Eye and Ear Infirmary, N.Y.C., 1855-64; surgeon gen. N.Y. Militia, 1858; med. dir. N.Y. State Hosp. for Volunteers during Civil War; an organizer U.S. Sanitary Comm.; organizer Sch. of Mines, Columbia, 1864, an ophthalmic clinic at Coll. Physicians and Surgeons (of Columbia), Bklyn. Eye and Ear Hosp., Manhattan Eye and Ear Hosp.; prof. diseases of the eye and ear Coll. Physicians and Surgeons, 1869-88. Died N.Y.C., Apr. 18, 1888.

AGNEW, DAVID HAYES, surgeon, educator; b. Lancaster County, Pa., Nov. 24, 1818; s. Robert and Mrs. (Henderson) A.; grad. med. dept. U. Pa., 1838; m. Margaret Irwin, 1841. A founder Irwin & Agnew Iron Foundry, 1846; bought, revived Phila. Sch. Anatomy, 1852-62; surgeon Phila. Hosp., 1854, Wills Eye Hosp., 1863, Pa. Hosp., 1865, Orthopedic Hosp., 1867; became asst. prof. surgery U. Pa., 1854, prof. clin. surgery, 1870; prof. surgery, 1871-89, prof. emeritus, 1889; pres. Phila. Coll. of Physicians, 1889; chief cons. to Pres. Garfield when he was shot by Guiteau, 1881; one of his classes painted by Thomas Eakins. Author: Treatise on the Principles and the Practice of Surgery, 3 vols., 1878-83. Died Phila., Mar. 22, 1892.

AGNEW, P(AUL) G(OUGH), engineer; b. Hillsdale Co., Mich., July 3, 1881; s. Allen and Rhoda Ann (Mason) A.; B.L., Hillsdale Coll., 1901; A.M., U. of Mich., 1902; Ph.D., Johns Hopkins, 1911; m. Ethna Mercedes Heebner, Sept. 27, 1911. Instr. physics, high schs., Monroe and Pontiac, Mich., 1902-05; physicist Bur. Standards, 1906-19, v.p., sec. Am. Standards Assn., 1920-47, consultant to the association, 1948-51, awarded Standards medal, 1951. Mem. Am. Ins. E.E., A.A.A.S., Washington Acad. Scis. Clubs: Cosmos (Washington, D.C.); Town Hall (New York). Author of papers on physics, elec. engring. and standardization. Home: 325 E. 72nd St., N.Y. City. Died Jan. 9, 1954.

AGRAMONT, ARISTIDES, bacteriologist; b. Camagüey, Cuba, June 3, 1869; s. Dr. Edward and Mathilde (Simoni) A.; brought to U.S., in infancy; student Coll. City of New York, 1885-87; M.D., Coll. Physicians and Surgeons (Columbia), 1892 (Harsen prize); M.B., Havana U., 1899, M.D., 1900; (Sc.D., Columbia U., New York, 1914); m. Frances Pierra, Apr. 17, 1895. Practiced, New York; asst. surgeon U.S. Army, May, 1898-Oct., 1902; mem. U.S. Army bd. that discovered, 1901, transmission of yellow fever by mosquitoes; chmn. Bd. of Infectious Disease and mem. Nat. Bd. of Health, Republic of Cuba; prof. bacteriology and exptl. pathology, U. of Havana, 1900—. Mem. AM. Acad. Sciences. Home: Havana, Cuba. Died Aug. 19, 1931.

AHALT, ARTHUR M(ONTRAVILLE), agril. educator; b. Monesson, Pa., Jluy 8, 1907; s. Alonza Joshua and Hattie Mozell (Flook) A.; B.S. (first honors), U. of Md., 1931; M.S., Pa. State Univ., 1937; student part time George Washington U., 1943-46; m. Mary Jane Ziegler, Mar. 29, 1935; children—Mary Jane, Arthur Montraville. Teacher vocational agr., Dorchester County, Md., 1931-34, Frederick County, Md., 1934-39; mem. faculty, U. of Md. since Sept. 1939, prof. and head agr. edn. since 1947, part time teaching in agrl. edn. as asst. prof. and asso. prof. agrl. edn. and part time research worker in agr. economics, Agr. Expt. Sta., as asst. prof. and asso. prof. agr. economics, 1939-47. Cons. specialist in agricultural education Inter-American Seminar in Vocational Education, U. of Maryland, 1952. Mem. Am. Assn. Univ. Profs., Future Farmers of Am. (hon.), N.E.A., Am. Vocational Assn., Nat. Vocational Agr. Teachers Assn., Am. Assn. Adult Edn., Md. Vocational Assn. (bd. dirs., 1947-55), Md. Vocational Agr. Teachers Assn. (sec.-treasurer 1935-36, pres., 1936-37), Md. State Teachers Assn., Phi Kappa Phi, Alpha Gamma Rho, Alpha Tau Alpha, Kappa Phi Kappa. Mem. Grange (local master, 1937-39). Lutheran. Author expt. sta. bulletins; contbr. numerous articles in Vocational Agricultural Education. Home: 7007 Rhode Island Av., College Park 1, Md. Died Sept. 12, 1958; buried Lutheran Cemetery, Middletown, Md.

AIKEN, GAYLE, homoe. physician; b. Charleston, S.C., Oct. 16, 1859; s. Col. Hugh Kerr and Mary Reese (Gayle) A.; A.B., U. of South, 1878; M.D., Med. Dept., Tulane U., 1891; M.D., Hahnemann Med. Coll., Chicago, 1892; m. Ada Holcombe, of New Orleans, June 6, 1882. Practiced, New Orleans, 1891—; mem. Homoe. State Bd. Med. Examiners. Mem. Am. Inst. Homoeopathy. Democrat. Episcopalian. Home: Warwick Manor. Office: Macheca Bldg., New Orleans.

AIKEN, WILLIAM MARTIN, architect; b. Charleston, S.C., April 1, 1855; s. Joseph Daniel and Ellen Daniel (Martin) A.;attended U. of the South, 1872-74; taught in same, 1874; taught in high school, Charleston,1874-76; spl. course in architecture, Mass. Inst. Tech., 1877-79; student in office of H. H. Richardson, 1880-83 and W. R. Emerson, 1883-85, Boston; in office James W. McLaughlin, Cincinnati, 1885-86; practiced architecture, Cincinnati, 1886-95; taught in Cincinnati Art Acad., 1894-95; supervising architect U.S. Treasury Dept., 1895-97, and designed Govt. expn. bldgs., Atlanta 1895, Nashville 1897, and Omaha 1898, also mint , bldgs. at Phila. and Denver, and numerous postoffices and custom-house bldgs.; in practice, New York, with Bruce Price, 1897-1901; taught in Columbia, 1899; cons. architect for Borough of Manhattan, 1901-03. Fellow Am. Inst. Architects.

Collaborator with Russell Sturgis: Dictionary of Architecture. Home: New York, N.Y. Died 1908.

AIME, VALCOUR, sugar planter; b. St. Charles Parish, La., 1798; s. Francois and Miss (Fortier) A.; m. Josephine Roman. Owner St. James Plantation (9,500 acres), contained 1st sugar refinery in U.S.; a leader in agrl. and mech. improvements in sugar prodn. for over 50 years; contbr. to chs. of his parish, also New Orleans; contbr. to Jefferson Coll. Died St. James Plantation, La.; Dec. 31, 1867; buried Little Grave Yard, St. James Ch.

AIRD, ALEXANDER N(EILSON), industrialist; b. Jersey City, Sept. 7, 1903; s. Alexander and Grace (Smith) A.; M.E., Cornell U., 1927; m. Ola E. Odendhal, Sept. 15, 1946; children—Alexander N., Douglas B. With Revere Copper & Grass, Inc., 1927—, successively mech. engr., mech. supt., chief engr., works mgr., v.p., 1953—. Mem. Saint Andrews Soc., Alpha Chi Rho. Republican. Clubs: Baltimore Country, Merchants, Cornell. Home: 1208 Robin Hood Circle, Towson, Md. Office: 1301 Wicomico St., Balt. 30. Died Sept. 7, 1958.

AIREY, JOHN, engineer; b. Leeds, Eng., Apr. 23, 1885; s. Fred and Elizabeth (Simms) A.; Whitworth Sch. 1909; A.R.C. Sc., Royal Coll. Sch., London, Eng., 1909; D.I.C., City & Guilds Tech. Inst., London, 1910; hon. B.Sc., London Univ., 1910; m. Ethel Mary Nunn, Sept. 16, 1911; children—Ethel Maude (Mrs. O. Willard Hoffman), Iris (Mrs. Gregory Stephan Timoshenko), George Vernon, John. Apprentice, machine shop, Bradford, 1902-06; engineer, Maschinenfabrik Oerlikon, Switzerland, 1910-11; instr., later asst. prof., U. of Mich., 1912-16; inspector British Munition Commn., U.S.A., 1916-17; master mechanic, R.V. Wagner Ordnance Co., Moline, Ill., 1917-19; prof. U. of Mich., 1919-22; gen. mgr. King-Seeley corp., Ann Arbor, Mich., 1922, v.p. 1923, pres. 1937, chmn. bd., 1947-52; bd. dirs. Ann Arbor Bank (Mich.). Member of the advisory com. R.F.C., Detroit, 1934-50; bus. adv. com. Pres. Council Econ. Advisors, 1947-52. Mem. Automotive Parts Mfrs. Assn. (dir. 1943-48, pres. 1947-48). National Association of Manufacturers (dir. 1943-49, exec. com. 1947-49, chmn. committees, price control termination 1945-46, economic policy 1948, federal tax 1949), American Society M.E. (life), Sigma Xi. Republican. Mason. Clubs: Detroit (Detroit); Ann Arbor Golf and Outing (Ann Arbor). Home: 2125 Brockman Blvd., Ann Arbor, Mich. Office: 1st National Bldg., Ann Arbor. Died Dec. 6, 1962; buried Forest Hill Cemetery, Ann Arbor, Mich.

AITKEN, ROBERT, printer, publisher, engraver; b. Dalkeith, Scotland, 1734. Bookseller, Phila., 1769, 71; publisher The Pennsylvania Magazine, 1775-76; published New Testament, 1777, 1778, 1779, 1781; printed 1st Am. Bible, 1782. Died Phila., July 15, 1802.

AITKEN, ROBERT GRANT, astronomer; b. Jackson, Calif., Dec. 31, 1864; s. Robert and Wilhelmina (Depinau) A.; A.B., Williams Coll., 1887, A.M., 1892; hon. Sc.D., U. of the Pacific, 1903, Williams Coll., 1917, U. of Ariz., 1923; LL.D., U. of Calif., 1935; m. Jessie L. Thomas, June 19, 1888; children—Wilhelmine, Robert Thomas, Malcolm Darroch, Douglas Carryl. Instr. mathematics, Livermore Coll., 1888-91; prof. mathematics and astronomy, U. of Pacific, 1891-95; astronomer at Lick Obs., 1895-1935, asso. dir., 1923-30, dir., 1930-35, emeritus dir. and astronomer since 1935. Discovered 3,100 double stars since 1899. Lalande prize, Acad. of Sciences of France, 1906, for double star discoveries; Bruce gold medal "for distinguished services to astronomy," 1926; gold medal of Royal Astron. Soc., 1932. George Darwin lecturer, Royal Astron. Soc., 1932. Lecturer astronomy, U. of Calif., summers, 1908-09, 1913, 1919; mem. Lick Obs. Eclipse Expdn. to Flint Island, 1908. Mem. Phi Beta Kappa, Sigma Xi, Nat. Acad. Sciences (chmn. sect. of astronomy, 1929-32), Am. Philos. Soc., Am. Astron. Soc. (v.p., 1929-31, pres. 1937-40), Internat. Astron. Union (chmn. double star commn., 1918-28), Astron. Soc. Pacific; fellow A.A.A.S. (pres. Pacific div., 1925-36; v.p. sect. D, 1926-27), Calif. Acad. Science; fgn. asso. Royal Astronomical Soc. Editor Publs. Astronomical Society Pacific, 1897-1908 and 1911-1942. Official delegate U.S.A. to Fifth Pacific Science Congress, Victoria, B.C., 1933. Author: Publs. Lick Obs., vol. XII, 1914; The Binary Stars, 1918, 2d edit., 1935; New General Catalogue of Double Stars within 120 deg. of the North Pole, 1932. Editor and contbr. Adolfo Stahl Lectures in Astronomy, 1919. Contbr. astron. and other scientific jours. Address: 1109 Spruce St., Berkeley 7, Calif. Died Oct. 29, 1951; buried Oakland, Calif.

AKELEY, CARL ETHAN, taxidermist, inventor; b. Orleans Co., N.Y., May 19, 1864; s. Daniel Webster and Julia M. (Glidden) A.; ed. State Normal Sch. Brockport, N.Y.; m. 2d, Mary L. Jobe, Oct. 18, 1924. With Field Mus., Chicago, 1895-1909, Am. Mus. Natural History, New York, 1909—. Served as cons. engr., div. of investigation, research and development, Engr. Dept., U.S. Army, also as spl. asst. concrete dept. Emergency Fleet Corp.; inventor of cement gun, Akeley Camera, etc.; medalist Franklin Inst. Big game hunter; made four trips to Africa for studying and collection of big game. Republican. Author: In Brightest Africa, 1923. Died Nov. 17, 1926.

AKELEY, MARY L. JOBE (MRS. CARL AKELEY), explorer, lectr., educator, author; b. Tappan, Ohio; d. Richard Watson and Sarah Jane (Pittis) Jobe; Ph.D., Scio (O.) Coll.; postgrad. Bryn Mawr Coll., Columbia U. (M.A.); Litt.D., Mt. Union Coll., 1930; m. Carl Ethan Akeley, 1924 (died Belgian Congo, 1926). Tchr. Am. history, Hunter Coll.; founder and owner Camp Mystic, summer outdoor training camp for girls, Mystic Conn. Exploration of Northern Canadian Rockies headwaters of Fraser and Wapiti rivers, and first partial ascent of Mt. Sir Alexander; one of highest peaks in Canadian Rockies named Mt. Jobe in recognition of her explorations; with Am. Museum of Natural History expdn. to Africa, 1926-27, in charge of expdn. after death of husband; apptd. adviser in Akeley Africian Hall work of Am. Museum Natural History, 1926, also became mem. Trustees' com. on African Hall and African Collections, 1938; guest of Belgian Nat. Parks Mission to Belgian Congo to study wildlife therein, 1947. Decorated Cross of Knight of Order of Crown (Belgium). Fellow Am. Geog. Soc., Royal Geog. Soc.; mem. A.A.A.S., Am. Assn. Univ. Women, Canadian Geog. Soc., Am. Game Protective Assn., Am. Soc. Mammalogists, Nat. Inst. Social Sciences, Woman's Roosevelt Memorial Assn. (life), English-Speaking Union, Soc. for Preservation of Fauna of Empire (British); sec. am. Com. for Scientific Research in Parc National Albert, Belgian Cong. Unitarian. Clubs: Town Hall and Bryn Mawr (N.Y.); American Alpine Club, Alpine Club of Can., Club Alpin Francais, Camp Fire (Chicago, hon.). Expdn. to S. Africa, Swaziland and Portuguese E. Africa, making survey of wild life and native customs, 1935-36, Canoe River, B.C., 1938; made survey of Canadian women's war effort and study of Alaskan defense including Kodiak Island, 1941; expdn. South, East and Central Africa and Belgian Congo, 1952; lectr. on Africa and Canada. Author: Congo Eden, 1950; also book revs. N.Y. Times, 1940-50, Saturday Review Lit., 1950, Yale Review, 1940-41. Home: "Great Hill," Mystic, Conn. Office: Am. Mus. of Nat. History, N.Y.C. Died July 1966.

AKERMAN, JOHN D., prof. of aeronautical engring.; b. Mitau, Courland, Latvia (then Russia), Apr. 24, 1897; s. David D. and Elizabeth J. (Ravovski) A.; grad. Aeronautical Sch., Imperial Tech. Inst., Moscow, 1917; student French aeronautical schs. at Avord, Pau, Cozeaux, 1917; B.S. in Aeronautics, U. of Mich., 1925, grad. student, 1927; m. Florence N. Simons, June 18, 1927. Came to U.S., 1918, naturalized, 1925. Engr. Stout-Ford All-Metal Aircraft, Detroit, Mich., 1925-27; designer Guggenheim Aeronautical Lab., U. of Mich., 1927-28; chief engr. in charge of design and construction all-metal transport sea and land planes, Hamilton Metalplane Co., Milwaukee, 1927-28, chief engr., developing New Pinto, low wing, monoplane and Mohawk-twin motored, low wing cabin plane capable of sustaining flight on one engine, Mohawk Aircraft Corp., Minneapolis, 1928-29; asso. prof. of aeronautical engring., U. of Minn., 1929-30, prof. and head of dept. 1931-59, in charge U. Minn. Supersonic Labs., Rosemont, Minn., from 1946; cons. Madaras Rotor Power Plant, charge design and supervision of constrn. of exptl. rotar, 1933; con. for Porterfield Aircraft & Engring. Corp., Kansas City, Missouri, Boeing Aircraft Corp., Seattle, Wash., 1940, Strato Equipment Co., Minneapolis, Minn., 1940-45; for Minneapolis Honeywell Regulator Co., 1942; official investigator Nat. Defense Research Council, 1942; commr. of Aeronautics for Minn., 1934-37; A.A.F. tech. representative in Europe, summer, 1945. Served as 2d lt. Engring. Corps (Aviation), Imperial Russian Army, 1916; pilote de chasse, French Army, 1917. Mem. Nat. Aeronautics Assn. (gov., Minn. 1939); Soc. for Promotion Engring. Edn., Am. Assn. Univ. Profs., Iota Alpha; Fellow Inst. of Aeronautical Sciences (mem. advisory board); fellow Royal Aero. Soc. (London), Sigma Xi, Tau Omega. Lutheran. Clubs: U. of Minn. Flying; Engineers (Minneapolis); University (St. Paul). Contbr. articles on aeronautical engineering, liquid oxygen use and the stratosphere to jours. Inventor Polio-traciatomy collar. Home: Minneapolis MN Died Jan. 8, 1972; buried Crystal Cemetery, Minneapolis MN

ALBEE, FRED HOUDLETT surgeon; b. Alna, Me., Apr. 13, 1876; s. F. Huysen and Charlotte Mary (Houdlett) A.; A.B., Bowdoin, 1899; M.D., Harvard, 1903; traveled and studies in Europe; Sc.D., U. of Vt., 1916, Bowdoin Coll., 1917; LL.D., Colby, 1930; hon. Sc.D., Rutgers U., 1940; m. Louella May Berry, Feb. 2, 1907; 1 son, Fred H. Formerly prof. orthopedic surgery, N.Y. Post-Grad. Med. Sch. and dir. of the dept.; prof. orthopedic surgery, U. of Vt. Coll. of Medicine; cons. surgeon to 24 hospitals. Col. Med. R.C., 1917; cons. surgeon Pa. R.R. System and Seaboard Air Line; consultant in orthopedics, Byrd Antarctic Expdn.; founder and med. dir. Fla. Med. Center, Venice, Fla.; editor in chief Rehabilitation Rev.; chmn. N.J. Rehabilitation Commn.; formerly dir. U.S. Army Gen. Hosp. No. 3; mem. advisory orthopedic council to surgeon general U.S. Army. Grand Office Crown of Roumania; Comdr. Order of Carlos P. Findlay of Cuba; Comdr. Order of Isabella Catolica (Spain); Comdr. Order of Merit (Hungary); Chevalier of the Legion of Honor (France); Cavaliere Order of the Crown (Taly); Comdr. Order of Liberatador (Venezuela); Grand Officer Order of Southern Cross (Brazil); Officer Ordem Nacional do Cruziere do Sul (Brazil). Life mem. Congressional Country Club; founding fellow and gov. Am. Coll. Surgeons; hon. fellow Royal Soc. Medicine (Great Britain); founder Internat. Soc. of Orthopedic Surgery; ex-pres. Assn. Surgeons of Pa. R.R., Am. Orthopedic Assn., Am. Acad. of Orthopedic Surgeons, Pan-Am. Med. Assn.; hon. mem. Leningrad Soc. of Orthopedic Surgeons; hon. foreign mem. Brazilian Coll. of Surgeons; mem. A.M.A., Mil. Order Foreign Wars. S.A.R., Sons of Revolution, Kappa Sigma, Phi Chi. Methodist. Clubs: International Medical, New York Athletic, Interuban Orthopedic, Harvard, Colonia Country (pres. 1914-15), Barnegat Hunting and Fishing (dir.). Author: Bone Graft Surgery, 1915; Orthopedic and Reconstructional Surgery, 1919; Injuries and Diseases of the Hip, 1937; Bone Graft Surgery in Disease, Injury and Deformity, 1940; also author numerous pamphlets on surg. subjects. Demonstrated original surg. methods of bone grafting in Germany, England and France, 1914, also in mil. hosps. of France, 1916; official rep. of Med. Corps U.S. Army, to Inter-Allied Congress, Rome, Paris and Bologna, 1919; opening address Surg. Congress of France, Paris, 1922, 29; rep. U.S. Army at Netherland Orthopedic Congress, Amsterdam, 1923; hon. Am. pres. Internat. Congress for Industrial Accidents and Diseases, Amsterdam, 1925, Budapest, 1927. Author: A Surgeon's Fight to Rebuild Men, 1943. Home: Colonia, N.J.; and Venice, Fla. Office: 57 W. 57th St., New York, N.Y. Died Feb. 15, 1945. *

ALBERT A(BRAHAM) ADRIAN, educator; b. Chicago, Ill., Nov. 9, 1905; s. Elias Albert and Fannie (Fradkin) A.; B.S., U. of Chicago, 1926, M.S., 1927, Ph.D., 1928; LL.D. (honorary), Notre Dame, 1965; Sc.D. (honorary), Yeshira University, 1968; L.H.D., U. Ill., Chgo., 1971; m. to Frieda Davis, December 18, 1927; children—Alan Davis, Roy M. (dec.), Nancy Elizabeth Fellow Nat. Research Council, Princeton, N.J., and Chicago, 1928-29; instr. in mathematics, Columbia U., 1929-31; asst. prof. mathematics, U. of Chicago, 1931-36; associate professor mathematics, 1936-41, prof. mathematics, 1941-72, chmn. dept., 1958-62, dean, division of physical sciences, 1962-71, Eliakim Hastings Moore Distinguished Service Prof., 1960; asso. dir. applied math. group Northwestern U., 1945-46; with Institute for Advanced Study, Princeton, 1933-34; visiting professor University of Brazil, Rio de Janeiro U. Buenos Aires, 1947, U. So. Cal., 1950; Yale, 1956-57, U. Cal. at Los Angeles, 1958; cons. Nat. Security Agy., Dept. Def., IBM Corp., U.S. Office Edn., 1963-66, Inst. for Defense Analyses. Member of the com. div. math., phys., engring. scis. Nat. Sci. Found., 1952-54; mem. gen. scis. panel Dept. of Def.; chmn. div. math. NRC, 1952-55; chairman sect. math. Nat. Acad. Scis., 1958-61; dir. communications research div. Inst. for Defense Analyses, 1961-62, trustee, until 1972; trustee Inst. for advanced Study. Recipient Cole prize for outstanding research in algebra, 1939. Fellow of American Academy Arts and Scis., member National Academy Science, Am. Math. Soc. (pres. 1965-66), Internat. Math. Union (v.p.), Math. Assn. Am., Acad. Scis. Buenos Aires, Brazilian Acad. of Sciences (corr. mem.), Phi Beta Kappa, Sigma Xi. Club: Quadrangle (Chicago). Author: Modern Higher Algebra, 1936; Structure of Algebras, 1939; Introduction to Algebraic Theories, 1940; College Algebra, 1941; Solid Analytic Geometry, 1947; Fundamental Concepts of Higher Algebra, 1957; (with R. Sandler) An Introduction to Finite Projective Planes, 1968; Tensor Products of Quaternion Algebras, 1972. Editor Bull. of Am. Math. Soc., 1939-43. Transactions of Am. Math. Soc., 1943-49. Colloguum Publs., 1951-57. Mathematical Surveys 1941-45. Home: Chicago IL Died June 6, 1972; buried Chicago IL

ALBERT, CALVIN DODGE, mech. engr.; b. White Haven, Pa., Nov. 17, 1876; s. Frank Henry and Ella (Wood) A.; Poly. Inst., Brooklyn, 1896-97; Media (Pa.) Acad., 1897-98; M.E. Cornell U., 1902; m. Claudia Louise Agnew, July 5, 1905. In charge machinery design, Columbia Iron Works, St. Clair, Mich., 1902-03; designer Great Lakes Engring. Works, Detroit, 1903-04; with Cornell U. since 1904, prof. mach. design 1916-44, also head department of machine design, professor emeritus since July 1944. With U.S. Shipping Board Emergency Fleet Corporation, June 1917-Aug. 1919; chief supervising insp. Middle Atlantic Dist., later chief insp., sr. engr. and exec. asst., in charge tech. dept. steel ship constrn. Mem. Am. Soc. M.E., Am. Gear Mfrs. Assn., Sigma Xi. Co-Author: Kinematics of Machinery. Author: Machine Design Drawing Room Problems. Home: 205 Eddy St., Ithaca NY

ALBERT, HENRY, pathologist, bacteriologist; b. Wolcott, Scott County, Ia., Oct. 11, 1878; s. Fred and Catharina (Stiefel) A.; B.S., State U. of Ia. 1900, M.S., 1902, M.D., 1902; studied U. of Austria, 1902; m. Edith Whiteis, June 10, 1905. Instr. pathology and bacteriology, 1902-03, prof. and head of dept., 1903-22, State U. of Ia. Dir. labs. Ia. State Bd. of Health, 1903-22; dir. Hygienic Lab., U. of Nev., 1922—; commr. Ia. State Dept. of Health, 1926—. Republican. Lutheran. Home: Des Moines, Ia. Died Apr. 6, 1930.

ALBERTS, JOSEPH ORTAN, veterinarian; b. Urbana, Ill., Nov. 12, 1907; s. Wiley Dayton and Justine Adeline (Berhm) A.; B.S., U. Ill., 1934, M.S., 1935, Ph.D., 1949; V.M.D., U. Pa., 1943; m. Edna Patricia Murphy, Feb. 18, 1933; children—Jeffrey Stephen, Jo

Elaine. Bacteriologist Ill. Dept. Pub. Health, 1935-39; asst. animal pathology and hygiene U. Ill., 1939-40, prof. pathology and hygiene Coll. Vet. Medicine, 1944—, head dept. vet. patholog. and hygiene, 1954—, asst. dean coll., 1964—; sr. mem. U. Ill. Center zoonoses research. Fellow Am. Acad. Microbiology; mem. Am., Ill. veterinary med. assns., A.A.A.S., N.Y. Acad. Scis., Sigma Xi, Phi Sigma, Phi Zeta, Omega Tau Sigma. Contbr. profl. jours. on microbiology and pathology. Home: Bayles Lake, Loda, Ill. Died Oct. 3, 1967; buried Woodlawn, Urbana, Ill.

ALBERTSON, ABRAHAM HORACE, architect; b. Hope, N.J., Apr. 14, 1872; s. Edward Horace and Victoria (Newman) A.; Ph.B. in Architecture, Columbia, 1895; m. Clara D. Fox, Feb. 6, 1915 (dec.); m. 2d, Elizabeth G. Henry, Nov. 26, 1946. Began practice in N.Y.C., 1895, Duluth, 1905, Seattle, 1907; asso. firm Howells & Stokes until 1917, Howells & Albertson until 1919; cons. architect, Port Commn., City of Seattle, Med. Dental Bldg., U.S. Bur. Edn., etc. Prin. works: U.S. war housing project, Bremerton, for Dept. Labor; Becker Bldg., Aberdeen; Security Bldg., Olympia; Municipal Bldg., Everett; Orthopedic Hosp. bldgs., No. Life Tower, Met. Group Office Bldgs., St. Joseph's Ch., YMCA Bldg., Law Sch. Bldg. and Infirmary Hosp. of U. of Wash., others (all Seattle). Served as cpl. N.Y. Vol. Inf., Spanish-Santiago. Chmn. Seattle Bldg. Code Commn., 1922; mem. Fed. Fair Rentals Commn., 1917-19; vice chmn. State Emergency Pub. Works Bd.; chmn. Bi-State Fed. Hist. Monuments Survey; state archtl. advisor Home Owners Loan Corp.; state chief architect FHA, 1934-49. Hon. citation Pan Am. Congress Architects, 1940. Fellow A.I.A. (ex-dir.); Architects (Wash. chpt.). Home: 508 34th Av., Seattle 22. Died Apr. 18, 1964.

ALBRIGHT, WILLIAM FOXWELL, orientalist; b. Coquimbo, Chile, May 24, 1891; s. Rev. Wilbur Finley and Zephine Viola (Foxwell) A.; A.B., Upper Ia. U., 1912, Ph.D., Johns Hopkins University, Baltimore, 1916, LL.D. (honorary), 1964; Litt.D. (hon.) Upper Ia., 1922, Yale, 1951, Georgetown U., 1952, U. Dublin, 1953, Loyola College, Balt., 1958; Loyola University, Chicago, 1960, Lake Erie College, 1966; D.H.L., Jewish Theol. Sem. in America, Jewish Inst. Religion, 1936, Hebrew Union Coll., 1948, Coll. Jewish Studies, Chgo., 1950; Th.D., U. Utrecht (Netherlands), 1936, U. Uppsala (Sweden), 1952; D. hon. caus., U. Oslo (Norway) 1946; LL.D., Boston Coll., 1947, U. St. Andrews, Scotland, 1949, Franklin and Marshall Coll., 1953; D.Phil., Hebrew U., Jerusalem, 1957; D.C.L., Pace Coll., 1957; Pd.D., La Salle Coll., 1958; Litt.D., Harvard U., 1962; L.H.D., Manhattan Coll., 1961, Colby Coll., 1966, Dropsie College, 1967, Yeshiva, Univ., 1969; H.H.D., Wayne State University, 1961, Brigham Young U., 1962; m. Ruth Norton, August 31, 1921; children—Paul N., Hugh N., Stephen Foxwell, David Foxwell. Acting dir. Am. Sch. Oriental Research, Jerusalem, 1920-21, dir. 1921-29, 33-36; W. W. Spence prof. Semitic langs. Johns Hopkins, 1929-58, emeritus, 1958-71; research prof. Jewish Theol. Sem. Am., 1957-59; dir. archeol. expdn., Palestine, 1922-34, mem. U. Cal. African Expdn., Sinai, 1947-48; chief archeologist S. Arabian Expdn., Am. Found. Study Man, 1950-51; pres. Palestine Oriental Soc., 1921-22, 34-35; Am. mem. consultative com., Internat. Congress Orientalists, 1931-48; pres. Am. Oriental Soc., 1935-36; 1st v.p. Am. Schs. of Oriental Research. from 1937. Mem. Am. Council of Learned Societies (vice chairman of the council 1939, recipient 10,000 prize 1961), Am. Philos. Soc. (v.p. 1956-59), Archeol. Inst. Am. (v.p., 1949) Soc. Bibl. Lit. (pres. 1939), Linguistic Soc. Am. (v.p. 1941), Internat. Orgn. Old Testament Scholars, (pres. 1956-59), Nat. Acad. Scis., Royal Danish, Flemish & Irish Acads.; corr. mem. Institut de France & Austrian Acad. Scis.; fellow Am. Acad. Arts & Scis., German Archeol. Inst.; hon. or corr. mem. many other tech. profl. socs. Author over 800 publs. on archeol., Bibl. and oriental subjects, including: The Excavation of Tell Beit Mirsim, 1932-43; From the Stone Age to Christianity, 1940; Archaeology of Palestine, 1949; History, Archaeology and Christian Humanism, 1964; Yahweh and The Gods of Canaan, 1968. Sr. editor: Anchor Bible, from 1956. Home: Baltimore MD Died Sept. 19, 1971.

ALCOCK, NATHANIEL GRAHAM, (awl'kok), urologist; b. 1881; B.S., Northwestern U., 1907, M.S., 1908, M.D., 1912. With State U. of Ia., 1915—, prof. and head dept. of genito-urinary surgery, 1923—. Mem. A.M.A., Am. Assn. Genito-Urinary Surgeons, Am. Urol. Assn., others. Home: 430 E. Brown St. Office: 105 E. Iowa Av., Iowa City, Ia. Died 1953.

ALCOTT, WILLIAM ANDRUS, educator; b. Wolcott, Conn., Aug. 6, 1798; attended Yale Med. m. Phebe Bronson, 1836, 2 children. Taught sch., Litchfield and Hartford counties, Conn., 1816-20; in charge of Central Sch., Bristol, Conn., 1824-25; taught sch. privately most of his life; editor Juvenile Rambler, 1832-33, Parley's Mag., 1833-37. Author 108 volumes on gen. edn., phys. edn., health, other subjects, including: Confessions of a Schoolmaster, 1829; Lectures for the Fireside, 1852; The Home Book of Life and Health, 1856; Forty Years in the Wilderness of Pills and Powders, 1859. Died Newton, Mass., Mar. 29, 1859; buried Newton.

ALDEN, CHARLES HENRY, architect; b. Hingham, Mass., Sept. 27, 1867; s. Charles Henry and Katharine Russell (Lincoln) A.; student U. Minn., 1884-87; B.S. in Architecture, Mass. Inst. Tech., 1890. Began practice in Boston, 1897; with Howard and Galloway, supervising architects Alaska Yukon Pacific Expn. and U. Wash., 1906-09; in charge specifications and archtl. dept., div. of works Panama-Pacific Expn., 1913-15; practiced in Seattle, 1909—; lectr. on architecture U. Wash. Mem. Mass. N.G., 1891-1900; commd. capt., O.R.C., U.S. Army, 1917; apptd. supply officer, 311th Sanitary Train, 86th Div., later asst. depot q.m., Boston, 1917; asst. q.m. 6th A.C., 1918; adj. 122d Engrs. supply officer and asst. to engr. officer in charge constrn., Am. Embarkation Center, Le Mans, France, 1918-19; maj. to col. Q.M. Res. Corps, 1919-31. Mem. Seattle Zoning Commn., Building Code Revision Commn., Seattle City Planning Commn. (chmn. zoning commn.), King County Planning Commn., 1939; state chmn. Pub. Works of Art Project, 1933-34; mem. Com. on City and Local Planning of Wash. Planning Council, 1934; chmn. planning com. Assn. of Wash. Cities, 1940; trustee Seattle Traffic and Safety Council, 1937. Engr. Seattle Municipal Def. Commn. Fellow A.I.A. (pres. Wash. chpt.); mem. Fine Arts Soc. of Seattle (pres.), Pacific N.W. Acad. Arts, Mil. Order Loyal Legion, Municipal League of Seattle (dir.), Chi Psi. Episcopalian. Clubs: University, Cosmos. Home: University Club, 1004 Boren Av. Office: Arcade Bldg., Seattle. Died 1951.

ALDEN, EBENEZER, physician; b. Randolph, Mass., May 17, 1788; s. Dr. Ebenezer and Sarah (Bass) A.; grad. Harvard, 1808; M.B., Dartmouth Med. Sch., 1811; M.D., U. Pa., 1812; m. Anne Kimball, 1818, 6 children. Practiced medicine, Randolph, 70 years; mem. Mass. Med. Soc. Author: Historical Sketch of the Origin and Progress of the Massachusetts Medical Society, 1838; The Early History of the Medical Profession in the Country of Norfolk, Mass., 1853; Memorial of the Descendants of the Hon. John Alden, 1867; The Medical Uses of Alcohol (read before Mass. Temperance Assn.), 1868. Died Randolph, Jan. 26, 1881.

ALDEN, WILLIAM CLINTON, geologist; b. Mitchell, Ia., Sept. 27, 1871; s. Benjamin Dorr and Lydia Martin (Waterman) A.; A.B., Cornell Coll., 1893; A.M., U. Chgo., 1898, Ph.D., 1903; m. Bess Mae Hollabaugh, Dec. 27, 1898 (dec. Jan. 9, 1934); children—John Herbert, Leland Milton, Elizabeth Lydia (dec.), Helen Hollabaugh. Asst. prin. High Sch., Parker, S.D., 1893-94; prin. sch., Centerville, S.D., 1894-95; spl. field asst. U.S. Geol. Survey, 1898-1901, asst. geologist, 1901-10, geologist since 1910, in charge glacial geology since 1912, sr. geologist, 1928-42, ret. Sept. 1942. Mem. Geol. Soc. Am., Geol. Soc. Washington, Phi Beta Kappa. Republican. Presbyn. Part Author: Gaines and Elkland-Tioga Folios; Geography of Chicago and Its Environs; The Iowan Drift, a Review of the Evidences of the Iowan State of Glaciation. Author: Chicago and Milwaukee Folios; Quaternary Geology of S.E. Wisconsin; Physical Features of Central Massachusetts; Delavan Lobe of Lake Michigan Glacier; Drumlins of S.E. Wisconsin; Physiography and Glacial Geology of Eastern Montana and Adjacent Areas; also bulls. articles. Home: 5313 Broad Branch Road N.W. Washington, D.C. Died Apr. 11, 1959; buried Fort Lincoln Cemetery, Washington.

ALDER, KURT, scientist; b. Germany, 1902; s. Joseph and Maria (Lammel) A.; student U. Berlin, 1922; Ph.D., Kiel U., 1922-26; M.D. (hon.), Cologne U., 1950; Dr. E. h., der Universitat Salamanca, 1954. Extraordinary professor Christian Albrechts U., Kiel, Germany, 1934-36; research lab. staff Bayer Dye Works, Leverkusen, 1936-40; prof. chemistry Cologne U. since 1940, dean faculty of philosophy, 1949-50, engaged in organic research since 1926. Awarded Nobel prize for chemistry (with Diels), 1950. Hon. mem. Real Sociedad Espagñola de Fisica y Quimica (Madrid), Censejo Superior de Investigationes Cientificas (Madrid). Home: Köln, Zülpicherstr. 47. Office: Chemisches Instut der Universitat Cologne, Cologne, Germany. Died June 20, 1958.

ALDERSON, VICTOR CLIFTON, cons. mining engr., educator; b. Plymouth, Mass., June 4, 1862; s. Andrew P. and Sarah P. (Sears) A.; A.B., Harvard, summa cum laude, 1885; (D.Sc., Armour Inst. of Tech., 1903, Beloit Coll., 1903; D.Eng., Colorado School of Mines, 1939; m. Harriet En. Thomas, July 3, 1888 (dec.). Supt. schools, Bublin, Ind., 1885-87; teacher Englewood High Sch., Chicago, 1887-93; prof. mathematics, 1893-98, dean, 1898-1900, acting pres., 1900-01, dean 1901-03, Armour Inst. of Tech., Chicago; pres. Colo. Sch. of Mines, July, 1903-13; pres. Winnemucca (Nev.) Mountain Mining Co., 1913-15; cons. mining engr., 1915-17; again pres. Colo. School of Mines, Golden, 1917-25; cons. mining engr., specialty oil shale, since, 1925. Fellow A.A.A.S.; mem. Am. Inst. Mining Engrs., Am. Social Science Assn., Soc. Colonial Wars, Soc. Mayflower Descendants, Intr. Petroleum Technologists (London), Phi Beta Kappa, etc. Writer on scientfic and math. subjects and tech. edn. Author: Oil Shale Industry, 1920. Home: La Jolla, Calif. Deid Feb. 25, 1946.

ALDRICH, CHARLES ANDERSON, pediatrician; b. Plymouth, Mass., Mar. 4, 1888; s. David E. and Laura Linwood (Perkins) A.; B.S., Northwestern U., 1914, M.D., 1915; grad. student Harvard, 1921; m. Mary McCague, Oct. 3, 1916; children—Robert A., Cynthia, Stephen. Engaged in practice of medicine since 1915; intern N.Y. Nursery and Child's Hosp., 1915; intern Evanston (Ill.) Hosp., 1915-16, attending roentgenologist and jr. attending physician in medicine, 1916-21, attending physician in medicine, 1916-21, attending pediatrist newly born service, 1930-36, asso. physician and chmn. pediatric dept., 1936-42 asst. attending physician Children's Memorial Hosp., Chicago, 1921-22, asso. attending physician, 1922-41; chief of staff, 1941-44; cons. pediatrist, Municipal Tuberculosis Sanitarium, 1925-27; cons. physician on staff Chicago Nursery : and Half-Orphan Asylum, 1941-44; asso. inpediatrics, Northwestern U. Med. Sch., 1934-35, asst. prof. 1935-36, professor of pediatrics, 1941-44; prof. pediatrics, Mayo Foundation Grad. Sch., U. of Minn., since 1944; mem. sect. on pediatrics, Mayo Clinic, since 1944. Director Rochester Child Health Project, 1944. Member White House Conf. on Children in a Democracy. Mem. com. Elizabeth McCormick Child Research Grant 1941-44. Trustee Ill. Children's Home Aid Society, 1941-44. Mem. Ednl. Council. Winnetka Pub. Schs.; member sch. bd.; mem. bd. North Shore Country Day Sch. Mem. Northwester Pediatric Soc., Minn. Mental Hygiene Soc. (mem. bd. dirs.), National Research Council (com. on child development, etc.); member A.M.A. (mem. adv. bd. med. splty.), Am. Acad. Pediatrics (mem. com. on metnal health since 1940), Am. Board Pediatrics, Inc. (sec.-treas. 1934-44, pres. 1945-47), Nat. Assn. for Nursery Edn., Soc. Research in Child Development; mem. (hon.) National Committee on Mental Hygiene, Northwest Pediatric Soc., Omaha Mid-West Clin. Soc.; sec. Am. com. Internat. Pediatric Congress in London (Eng.), 1933. Conglist. Author: Cultivating the Child's Appetitie, 1927; Babies Are Human Beings (with Mary M. Aldrich), 1938 (English reprint, Understand Your Baby, 1939); Feeding Our Old Fashioned Children (with Mary M. Aldrich), 1941. Contbr. numerous professional articles and bollk revs. to med. periodicals. Clubs: Billings (pres.); University (Rochester). Home: 626 Fifth St., S.W. Office: Mayo Clinic, 102 Second Av. S.W., Rochester, Minn. Died Oct. 5, 1949.

ALDRICH, CHILSON DARRAGH, architect, writer; b. Detroit, Mich., Mar. 25, 1876; s. Charles Whipple and Julia Louesa (Saunders) A.; prep. edn., pub. schs.; spl. student U. of Minn.; m. Clara Chapline Thomas, Apr. 18, 1914. Began practice at Minneapolis, 1900; designer of residences until 1916; builder of cantonments, World War; designer and builder of log cabins, camps and vacation homes since 1918. Built replica of pioneer cabin for Minn. State Hist. Soc. Member same soc. Republican. Episcopalian. Clubs: Friars, Six O'clock, Hennepin County Sportsman's. Author: The Real Log Cabin, 1929. Contbr. to House and Garden, Country Life in America, etc. Home-Studio: 701 Kenwood Parkway, Minneapolis, Minn: (country) Pals' Cove, Grand Marais, Minn. Died July 13, 1948.

ALDRICH, JOHN entomologist; b. Olmsted Co., Minn., Jan. 28, 1866; s. Levi O. and Mary M. (Moore) A.; B.S., S.D. State Coll., 1888, M.S., 1891; studied entomology, etc., U. of Minn., Mich. Agrl. Coll., and U. of Kan., M.S., 1893; Ph.D., Leland Stanford Jr. U., 1906; m. Ellen J. Roe, Jan. 3, 1893 (died 1897); 1 son, Spencer (dec.); m. 2d, Della Smith, June 28, 1905. Prof. zoology and entomologist of Expt. Sta., 1893-1905; prof. biology, 1905-13, U. of Ida.; entomol. asst., U.S. Dept. of Agr., 1913-19; asso. curator of insects, 1919—, U.S. Nat. Museum. Mason. Unitarian. Democrat. Author: Catalogue of North American Diptera, 1905; Sarcophaga and Allies. 1916. Editor, Thomas Say Foundation. Home: Washington, D.C. Died May 27, 1934.

ALDRICH, LOYAL BLAINE, obs. dir.; b. Milw., Nov. 20, 1884; s. Lafayette and Isabelle (Hay) A.; A.B., U. Wis., 1907, M.A., 1909; m. Elizabeth Stanley, 1919 (dec. Sept. 17, 1941); children—Stanley, Lafayette; m. 2d, Sara Grace Smith, Dec. 1943. Bolometric asst. Astrophys. Obs., Smithsonian Instn., 1909-30, asst. dir., 1930-45, dir. since 1945; dir. Smithsonian eclipse expdn., June, 1918; dir. solar sta., Montezuma (Chili), 1922-25. Co-authro: Annals of Astrophysical Observatory; Vols. III-IV, articles in Smithsonian Misc. Collection. Developed melikeron, pvranometer, others, for measurement nocturnal radiation, sky brightness. Mem. Optical Soc. Am., Am. Geophys. Union, Internat. Meteorol. Orgn., Phi Beta Kappa. Co-author: Annals of Astrophysical Observatory, vols. III-VII. Home: 1642 Jonquil St., Washington. Died Feb. 11, 1965.

ALDRICH, WILLIAM SLEEPER, educator; b. Phila., Mar. 3, 1863; s. George Wells and Sallie Edith (Sleeper) A.; grad. U.S. Naval Acad., 1883; M.E., Stevens Inst. Tech., 1884; m. Mary Lavinia Purdy, of Phila., July 1, 1886. Asst. Boys' High Sch., Reading, Pa., 1885-87, Central Manual Training Sch., Phila., 1887-89; instr. drawing, 1889-91, asso. in mech. engring., 1891-92, Johns Hopkins; prof. mech. Engring. and dir. mechanic arts, W.Va. U., 1893-99; prof. and head dept. elec. engring., U. of Ill., 1899-1901; dir. Thomas S. Clarkson Memorial School of Technology,

1901-11; U.S. Reclamation Service, Shoshone Project, Powell, Wyo., 1911-13; acting prof. elec. and mech. engring., U. of Ariz., 1913-14. Passed asst. engr. (with relative rank of lt. USN), attached to the U.S.S. Vulcan, with Admiral Sampson's fleet in Cuban Waters, May 12-Oct. 18, 1898. Fellow A.A.A.S.; mem. Am. Inst. Elec. Engrs., Am. Soc. Mech. Engrs., Soc. Promotion Engring. Edn. Contbr. papers to engring. and scientific societies and tech. press. Author: Notes on Building Construction and Architecture (with William H. Browne, Jr.); Manual for Electrical Engineering Laboratory. Address: Tucson, Arizona.

ALDRICH, WILLIAM TRUMAN, architect; b. Washington, Feb. 16, 1880; B.S., Mass. Inst. Tech., 1901; diploma Ecole des Beaux Arts, Paris, 1909. With Carrere & Hastings, N.Y.C., 1909-11; partner Bellows & Aldrich, Boston 1911-23; practice William T. Aldrich, Boston, 1923-66; prin. works include R.I. Sch. Design, Providence, 1926, Art. Mus., Worcester, Mass., 1932, Am. Mil. Cemetery, St. James France, residence H. Cabot Lodge, Beverly, Mass.; cons. architect John Hancock Life Ins. Co. Housing Project, 1950; instr. Sch. Arch., Harvard, 1920, R.I. Sch. Design, 1922, Mus. Sch. Fine Arts, Boston, 1936. Mem. plan bd. Town of Brookline, Mass., 1940-43; exec. Am. Battle Monuments Commn., 1955. Served as capt. U.S. Army, 1918-19. Fellow A.I.A.; mem. Nat. Acad. Design. Address: 30 Ipswich St., Boston. Died June 1966.

ALDRIDGE, WALTER HULL, mining engr.; b. Bklyn., Sept. 8, 1867; s. Volney and Harriet Elizabeth (Hull) A.; E.M., Sch. of Mines, Columbia U., 1887 (hon Sc.D., 1929); m. Maude Miller, Mar. 18, 1914. Assayer, chemist and metallurgist, Colo. Smelting Co., Pueblo, until 1892; mgr. United Smelting & Refining Co., Mont., 1892-97; in charge mining and metall. work Canadian Pacific Ry., 1897-1911; mng. dir. Consol. Mining and Smelting Co. of Can.; was at various times mng. dir. Inspiration Copper Co.; pres. Magma Copper Co.; v.p. Mines Co. of America; pres. Tex. Gulf Sulphur Co., 1918-51, chmn. bd., 1951-57, chmn. emeritus, dir., 1957—. Recipient John Fritz medal for 1949. Mem. Am. Inst. Mining and Metall. Engrs., Mining and Metall. Soc. America, Am. Electrochem. Soc., Canadian Inst. Mining Engrs., Instn. Mining and Metallurgy (London), Newcomen Soc. England. Republican. Episcopalian. Clubs: Union League, Down Town, Columbia University, Apawamis, Shenorock Shore. Home: 71 E. 71st N.Y.C. Office: 75 E. 45th St., N.Y.C. 17. Died Aug. 1959.

ALEXANDER, EDWARD PORTER, engr.; b. Washington, Ga., May 26, 1835; s. Adam Leopold and Sarah Gilbert A.; grad. U.S. Mil. Acad., 1857; m. Bettie Mason, 1860; 2d, Mary L., d. Augustine S. Mason, of Hagerstown, Md., Oct. 1, 1901. Apptd. 2d U.S. engr. corps; resigned, 1861; entered C.S.A. and served through war; was brig.-gen. and chief of arty., Longstreet's Corps. at Appomattox, 1865; prof. of mathematics and engring., U. of S.C., 1866-70; gen. mgr. and pres. of various railroads (including L.&N., Central of Ga., Ga. R.R. & Bank Co.), 1871-92; capitol commr., State of Ga., 1883-88; mem. bds. on navigation of Columbia River, Ore., and on ship canal between Chesapeke and Deleware bays, 1892-94; govt. dir. U. P. R.R. Co., 1895-97; arbitrator boundary survey between Costa Rica and Nicaragua. Rice planter on South Island, Georgetown, S.C. Author: Railway Practice; Military Memoirs of a Confederate. Home: Savannah, Ga. Died 1910.

ALEXANDER, FRANZ, psychoanalist, psychiatrist; b. Budapest, Hungary, Jan. 22, 1891; s. Bernard and Regina (Brossler) A.; B.A., Humanistic Gymnasium, Budapest, 1908; M.D., U. of Budapest, 1913; m. Anita Venier, Mar. 7, 1921; children—Sylvia, Kiki (Francesca). Came to U.S., 1930, naturalized citizen, 1938. Research asso, in physiology, Inst. for Exptl. Pathology, U. of Budapest, 1910-13; research asso. in bacteriology, Inst. for Hygiene, same, 1913-14; head bacteriol. field lab. and malaria station of Austro-Hungarian Army with rank of 1st lt., 1914-18; research and clin. asso. in psychiatry and neurology, Neuropsychiatric Clinic, U. of Budapest, 1918-19; postgrad. work Psychiatric Hosp. (Charite), U. of Berlin, 1920-21; clin. asso. and lecturer in psychoanalysis, Inst. for Psychoanalysis, Berlin, 1921-30; visting prof. psychoanalysis, U. of Chicago, 1930-31; research asso. in criminology, Judge Baker Foundation, Boston, 1931-32; teacher and research work and dir. Chicago Inst. for Psychoanalysis since 1932; asso. prof. psychiatry U. Ill., 1938-43, prof. psychiatry, 1943-56; attending physician Cook County Psychopathic Hospital, 1838-56; now clinical professor of psychology University Southern California, also chief of staff, Psychiatric Dept., Mt. Sinai Hospital director of Psychiatric and Psychosomatic Research Institute at Mt. Sinai Hospital, Los Angeles; consultant Nat. Adv. Mental Health Council, 1947-49; chmn. sect. on psychotherapy, psychoanalysis and psychosomatic medicine Congres Internat. de Psychiatrie, Paris, 1950; mem. Nat. Research Council Com. on Rheumatic Diseases, 1948—. Ford Found. Fellow Center for Advanced Study in Behavioral Scis., Stanford, Cal., 1955. Recipient Samuel Ruben award for outstanding achievement in mental health, 1958; Semmelweis medal for basic and lasting contbns. in field exptl. and clin. psychiatry Am.-Hungarian Med. Assn., 1959. Roman Catholic. Clubs: Tavern (Chgo.); Tamarisk Country (Cal.); Racquet (Palm Springs, California). Author numerous books including: Psychosomatic Medicine, Fundamentals of Psychoanalysis, 1950; The History of Psychiatry. Co-editor: Dynamic Psychiatry, 1952; also Psychosomatic Medicine. Pub: Psychoanalysis and Psychotherapy, 1956. Contbr. articles medical jours. Home: 1011 Cielo Dr., Palm Springs, Cal. Office: Mt. Sinai Hosp., 8720 Beverly Blvd., Los Angeles 48. Died Mar. 8, 1964.

ALEXANDER, JAMES WADDELL, II, mathematician; b. Sea Bright, N.J., Sept. 19, 1888; s. John White and Elizabeth A. Alexander; B.S., Princeton, 1910, M.A. (Gordon Macdonald fellow), 1911, Ph.D., 1915, D.Sc., 1947; student U. Paris, U. Bologna; m. Natalie Levitzkaja, Jan. 11, 1918; children—Irina, John. Instr., Princeton U., 1911-12, 15-16, asst. prof., 1920-26, asso. prof., 1926-28, prof., 1928-33, prof. Inst. for Advanced Study, 1933-51; Rouse Ball lectr. Cambridge (Eng.) U., 1936; a founder of modern topology. Served with tech. staff, ordnance dept. U.S. Army, overseas, 1917-18; ret. as capt.; mem. N.J. Nat. Guard. Recipient Bocher prize Am. Math Soc., 1928. Mem. Nat. Acad. Sciences, Am. Philos. Soc., Am. Math. Soc., Math. Assn. Am., A.A.A.S., Phi Beta Kappa. Clubs: American Alpine; Quadrangle; Nassau. Contbr. articles math. publs. Home: Princeton NJ Died Sept. 23, 1971.

ALEXANDER, JEROME, chemist; b. New York, N.Y., Dec. 21, 1876; s. Isaac and Annie Josephine Lewis (Jackson) A.; B.S., Coll. City of New York, 1896, M.Sc., 1899; m. Gertrude Eleanor Hammerslough, Apr. 9, 1903 (died Dec. 25, 1945); children—Dr. Eleanor Gertrude Jackson, Mrs. Dorothy Alexander Livingston (dec.). Consulting chemist and chem. engr. Past chmn. spl. com. on colloids of Nat. Research Council. Fellow A.A.A.S., Am. Inst. Chemists (hon. mem.); mem. Am. Inst. Chem. Engrs. (hon.), Am. Chem. Soc., Assn. Cons. Chemists and Chem. Engrs., Soc. de Chimie Industrielle (hon. sec. Am. sect.; hon. mem. parent société), American Genetics Association, N.Y. Micros. Soc., Sons of Confed. Vets. (historian), Phi Beta Kappa Associates (dir.) Phi Beta Kappa (past president N. Y. Alumni), Pi Gamma Mu, Pi Lambda Phi, Tau Beta Pi (hon.). Decorated Officer de l'Instruction Publique (France), 1931, also Chevalier de la Légion d'Honneur, 1936; Townsend Harris Medal, 1943. Mason. Clubs: Chemists (New York); Authors' (London). Author: Colloid Chemistry, 1919, and subsequent editions: Glue and Gelatin (American Chemical Soc. monograph), 1923; also chapters on "Glue and Gelatin" and "Colloid Chemistry" Rogers' Industrial Chemistry, 1942; chapter on "Albuminoids or Seleroproteins," in Allen's Commercial Organic Analysis, 1913 and 1931; chapter on "Colloid Chemistry" in Liddell's Handbook for Chemical Engineers, 1920; Colloid Chemistry, Theoretical and Applied (in collaboration with about 450 men of all nations). Volume I, 1926, II, 1928, III, 1931, IV, 1932, V, 1944, VI, 1946, VII, 1950, volume VIII in preparation; (verses "Essences from Life's Alembic" and "Retorts from a Chemist's Laboratory," 1941; Tribute to Gertrude, 1946; "Life-Its Nature and Origin," 1948 Translator: Colloids and the Ultramicroscope, by Prof. Dr. Richard Zsigmondy, 1909. Pioneer worker with the ultramicroscope in America; specialist in colloid chem. and its scientific and indsl. applications. Address: 390 Riverside Dr., N.Y.C. 25. Died Jan. 18, 1959.

ALEXANDER, JOHN surgeon; b. Phila., Pa., Feb. 24, 1891; s. Lucien Hugh and Mazie (Just) A.; student Episcopal Acad., Phila., 1903-04, Chestnut Hill Acad., 1904-08; B.S., U. of Pa., 1912, M.A., 1913, M.D., 1916 (hon. Sc.D., 1940); m. Emma Ward Woolfolk, July 11, 1936. Formerly mem. surg. and teaching staff U. of Pa.; now prof. surgery, U. of Mich.; surg. in charge sect. thoracic surg., U. of Mich. Hosp.; chief surg., Mich. State Sanatorium; cons. thoracic surg., various sanatoria and hosps. Surg. with French Army; lt. U.S.M.C., World War I. Awarded Samuel D. Gross prize of Phila. Acad. Surgery, 1925; Henry Russell award, U. of Mich., 1930; Trudeau medal, Nat. Tuberculosis Assn., 1941. Henry Russel lectureship, U. of Mich., 1944. Fellow Am. Coll. Surgeons; mem. Am. Surg. Assn., Soc. of Thoracic Surgery of Great Britain and Ire. (hon.). Sociedad de Argentina de Cirujanos (hon.); Societe Belge de Chirurgie (hon.); Sociedad Paraguaya de Tisiologia (hon.); Sociedad de Tisiologia de Cordoba, Argentina (corr.); Tuberculosis Assn. of India (corr.); Detroit Heart Club; Am. Trudeau Soc. (pres. elect, 1946), Am. Bd. Surg. (founders' group), Soc. of Clin. Surg., Internat. Soc. of Surgery, Am. Assn. for Thoracic Surg. (p. 1935), Detroit Acad. of Surgery (hon.), Central Surg. Assn. (founders' group), A.M.A., Mich. State Med. Soc. (chmn. sect. on surgery, 1932). Mich. Tuberculosis Assn. (dir. 1941-44, v.p. 1945), Mich. Trudeau Soc., Alpha Omega Alpha, Alpha Mu Pi Omega, Nu Sigma Nu (hon.), Sigma Xi, Phi Kappa Phi, Delta Tau Delta. Republican. Presbyterian. Author: The Surgery of Pulmonary Tuberculosis, 1925; The Collapse Therapy of Pulmonary Tuberculosis, 1937; also articles on thoracic surgery. Mem. adv. editorial bd. Journal of Thoracic Surgery. Home: 788 Arlington Blvd. Office: U. of Mich. Hospital, Ann Arbor. Died July 16, 1954; buried Forest Hills Cemetery.

ALEXANDER, JOHN BREVARD, physician; b. Mecklenburg Co., N.C., May 27, 1834; s. R. E. and Abigail Bain (Caldwell) A.; grad. Davidson College, N.C., 1852; S.C. Medical College, 1855; m. May 18, 1858, Annie Lowrie. Served in C.S.A. as private, 1861-62, surgeon, 1862-65; resumed practice after war. Has a daughter, Annie Lowrie Alexander, M.D. (Woman's College, Phila., 1884), who was the first woman in any of the Southern states to graduate in medicine. State senator, 1897; Populist-Democrat. Author: Hopewell Section, 1898 L11; History of Mecklenburg County, 1902 L11. Address: Charlotte, N.C.

ALEXANDER, JOHN HENRY, scientist; b. Annapolis, Md., June 26, 1812; s. William and Mary (Stockett) A.; ed. St. John's Coll., 1826; m. Margaret Hammer, 1836, 6 children. Apptd. state topog. engr. Md., 1834; a founder Georges Creek Coal & Iron Co., pres., 1836-45; published A Universal Dictionary of Weights and Measures, Ancient and Modern, 1850; incorporator Nat. Acad. Sci. Died Balt., Mar. 2, 1867.

ALEXANDER, MAGNUS WASHINGTON, engineering; b. New York, Feb. 1870; s. Alexander M. and M. (Jelenkiewicz) A.; studied mech., metall. and elec. engring. at Austrian univers., in Wien, 1889, Leoben, 1891, Gratz, 1892; hon. M.S., Trinity Coll.; married. Began as engineer with largest Austrian iron and steel co.; designer and engr. with Westeon Elec. Instrument Co., 1893-94 and with Westinghouse Electric & Mfg. Co., 1893-99; chief designer and engr. Siemens & Halske Electric Co. of America, 1899-1900; engr. in charge of designing, 1900-18, cons. engr. on economic issues, 1918-1922, Gen. Electric Co. Pres. Nat. Indsl. Conf. Bd. from its orgn., May 1916. Home: New York, N.Y. Died Sept. 10, 1932.

ALEXANDER, NATHANIEL, state gov., congressman; b. nr. Concord, Mecklenburg County, N.C., Mar. 5, 1756; grad. Princeton, 1776; studied medicine and surgery. Served as surgeon during Revoluntionary War, 1778-82; practiced medicine, High Hills of Santee, S.C., after war; continued practice later in Charlotte, N.C.; mem. N.C. House of Commons, 1797, N.C. Senate, 1801, 02; mem. U.S. Ho. of Reps. from N.C., 8th-9th congresses, 1803-Nov. 1805; resigned to become gov. N.C., 1805-07. Died Salisbury, N.C., Mar. 7, 1808; buried Old Cemetery, Charlotte.

ALEXANDER, STEPHEN, astronomer; b. Schenectady, N.Y., Sept. 1, 1806; s. Alexander and Maria A.; grad. Union Coll., 1824; attended Princeton Theol. Sem., 1832. LL.D. (hon.), Columbia, 1852; m. Louisa Meads, Oct. 3, 1826; m. 2d, Caroline Foreman, Jan. 2, 1850; 5 children. Tutor in mathematics Coll. of N.J. (now Princeton), 1832, prof. astronomy, 1840, prof. mathematics, 1845-54, prof. astronomy, mechanics, 1855-78; head expdn. to observe solar eclipse, Labrador, 1860. An original mem. Nat. Acad. Scis., 1862; mem. Am. Philos. Soc., Am. Acad. Arts and Scis., A.A.A.S. (pres. 1859). Died June 25, 1883.

ALEXANDER, WILLIAM HENRY, sr. meteorologist; b. Greenville, Tex., Jan. 10, 1867; s. Thomas Carroll and Martha Ann (Banta) A.; A.B., Sam Houston State Normal Coll., 1887, U. of Va., 1892; m. Mary P. Clonts, Aug. 29, 1894; children—Ralph Clonts (capt. U.S. Navy), Ryllis Clair (wife of Omar P. Goslin). Teacher high sch., Decatur, Tex., 1887-90; prof., Latin and Greek, N.W. Tex. Bapt. Coll., Decatur, 1892-94; prof. physics, Henry Coll., Campbell, Tex., 1894-98; observer and meteorologist U.S. Weather Bur., 1898-1937; now retired; climatologist for State of Md., 1913-16, for Ohio 1916-37. Fellow A.A.A.S., Am. Meteorol. Soc., Ohio Acad. Science (ex-pres., sec. 1923-1941). Mem. Columbus Geneal. Soc. (pres. 1930-35), Fed. Business Assn. of Columbus (ex-pres.), S.A.R. (state pres. 1937), Sigma Xi. Baptist. Mason (32 deg.). Club: Faculty (Ohio State U.). Author: Climatological History of Ohio; Fifty Stories About the Weather (manuscript form). Contbr. to scientific publs. Home: Normandie Hotel Columbus OH

ALEXIS, ALGERT DANIEL, cons. civil engr., ret. naval officer; b. Minersville, Pa., June 25, 1897; s. William V. and Helen (Kell) A.; C.E., Lafayette Coll., Easton, Pa., 1919, D.Sc.; m. Mabel Lewis Glenn, Apr. 13, 1927; children—Algert D., Jr., Donald Glenn, Diane. Apptd. lt. (j.g.), C.E.C., U.S. Navy, 1921, and advanced through grades to rear adm., 1950; at N.Y. Naval Shipyard, 1921-22, Third Naval Dist. Hdqrs., N.Y.C., 1922-24, Naval Base, Norfolk, 1924-25; treaty engr., Republic of Haiti, 1925-29; at 11th Naval Dist., San Diego, Cal., 1929-34; Island Engr., Am. Samoa, 1934-35; at Naval Shipyard and Dist. Hdqrs., Charleston, S.C., 1935-40; resident officer in charge constrn., 12th Naval Dist., San Francisco, 1940-41; officer in charge of constrn. Naval Dry Dock & Supply Depot, Bayonne, N.J., 1941-42; officer in charge constrn.; also dir. Alaska div., Bur. of Yards and Docks, 1942-44; officer in charge, Advance Base Depot, Port Huenema, Cal., 1944-45; staff comdr. Service Force, Pacific staging for invasion of Japan, 1945; public works officer 5th Naval Dist., 1948-50; dir. Atlantic div., Bur. of Yards and Docks, N.Y.C.; 1950-54, ret. USN, 1954; now cons. civil engr.; ret. Rear Adm. Civil Engr. Corps, USN; now v.p., cons. civil engr. Hill & Hill, Inc. Decorated Navy Commendation medal with ribbon,

Am. Def., Am. campaign, Asiatic-Pacific and Victory World War II medals (U.S.), Medal of Honor and Merit (Rep. of Haiti). Mem. Am. Soc. C.E., Soc. Am. Mil. Engrs., Naval Order of U.S., Naval Hist. Foundation, U.S. Naval Order of U.S., Naval Inst., Tau Beta Pi, Sigma Nu. Episcopalian. Mason. Office: Hill & Hill Inc., North at Elm, Westfield, N.J. Died June 12, 1967.

ALEY, JUDSON, educator; b. Coal City, Ind., May 11,1863; s. Jesse J. and Paulina (Moyer) A.; B.S., Valparaiso (Ind.) Coll., 1882; A.B., Indiana U., 1888, A.M., 1890; Stanford U., 1894-95; Ph.D, U. of Pa., 1897; LL.D., Franklin Coll., 1909; LL.D., U. of Pa., 1917, Butler Coll., 1922; m. Nellie Archer, Aug. 28, 1884; children—Bruce (dec.), Maxwell. Taught country schs., 1877-81, Coal City graded sch., 1881-82; prin. Spencer (Ind.) High Sch., 1882-85, 1886-87; instructor mathematics, Indiana Univ., 1887-88; prof. mathematics, Vincennes U., 1888-91, Ind. U., 1891-1909; supt. pub. instrn. of Ind., Mar. 1909-Nov. 12, 1910; pres. U. of Me., 1910-1921; pres. Butler U., 1921-31, emeritus. Acting asst. prof. mathematics, Stanford, 1894-95; was math. editor Inland Educator and Educator-Journal; editor-in-chief and pres. Educator-Journal, Aug. 1, 1903-Aug. 1, 1912. Trustee N.E.A., 1911-17 and pres. 1916-17; sec. Nat. Council Edn., 1911-13 and pres. 1913-16. Member Disciples Ch. Mason (33 degree). Democrat. Author: The Geometry of the Triangle, 1897; Graphs, 1900; Revision of Cook and Cropsy Arithmetics (with O. L. Kelso), 1904; The Essentials of Alegbra (with David Andrew Rothrock), 1904; Supplementary Problems in Algebra (with same); Story of Indiana (with Max Aley), 1912. Home: Indianapolis, Ind. Died Nov. 18, 1935.

ALFORD, LEON PRATT, engineer, editor; b. Simsbury, Conn., Jan. 3, 1877; Emerson and Sarah Merriam (Pratt) A.; B.S. in Electrical Engineering, Worcester Poly. Institute, 1896, M.E., 1905, Dr. of Engineering, 1932; m. Grace A. Hutchins, January 1, 1900; 1 son, Ralph I. Shop foreman McKay Metallic Fastening Assn., Boston, 1896-97, McKay-Bigelow Heeling Assn., 1897-99; production supt. McKay Shoe Machinery Co., 1899-1902; mech. engr. United Shoe Machinery Co., Boston, 1902-07; engring. editor American Machinist, 1907-11, editor in chief, 1911-17; editor Industrial Management, 1917-20, Management Engineering, New York, 1921-23, Mfg. Industries, 1923-28; v.p. Ronald Press Co., 1928-34; asst. engr. in charge mfg. costs, Federal Communications Commn., 1935-37; prof. Adminstrative engring., New York Univ., since 1937. Past v.p. and mem. research coms. American Engring. Council which produced repts. on Waste in Industry, Twelve-Hour-Shieft in Industry, Safety and Production in Industry and Tech. Changes in Mfg. Industries. Fellow Am. Soc. Mech. Engrs. (ex.-v.p.), Inst. of Management (ex.-pres.); mem. Institut Scientifique d'Organisation et de Gestion, Nat. Association Cost Accountants, Sigma Xi. Melville Gold Medalist, 1927; Gantt Gold Medalist, 1931. Methodist. Club: Engineers, Author: Bearings and Their Lubrication, 1912; Laws of Management, 1928; Life of Henry Laurence Gantt, 1934. Editor: Artillery and Artillery Ammunition, 1917; Management's Handbook, 1924; Cost and Production Handbook, 1934; Principles of Industrial Management, 1940. Home: 9 Mountain Av. N., Montclair, N.J. Office: New York University, University Heights, New York, N.Y. Died Jan. 2, 1942.

ALGER, CYRUS, iron-master, inventor; b. West Bridgewater, Mass., Nov. 11, 1781; s. Abiezer and Hepsibah (Keith) A.; m. Lucy Willis, 1804, 7 children; m. 2d, Mary Pillsbury, 1833. Established iron foundry, 1809; designed 1st cylinder stoves 1822; contbr. rapid devel. of South Boston; alderman South Boston, 1824-27; formed So. Boston Iron Co., 1827; his shop turned out 1st gun ever rifled, 1834; Cyrus Alger Primary Sch. named after him, 1881; considered one of outstanding metallurgists of his time. Died Boston, Feb. 4, 1856.

ALINSKY, SAUL DAVID, sociologist; b. Chgo., Jan. 30, 1909; s. Benjamin and Sarah (Tannenbaum) A.; Ph.B., U. Chgo., 1930, postgrad. Grad. Sch., 1930-32; LL.D., Saint Procopius Coll., 1958; m. Helene Simon, June 9, 1932 (dec.); children—Kathryn, David; m. 2d, Jean Graham, May 15, 1952 (div. 1969). Sociologist, Inst. for Juvenile Research, Chgo., 1931-36, 36-39; mem. state prison classification bd., div. criminology Ill. State Penitentiary System, Joliet, 1933-36; co-founder Back of Yards Neighborhood Council, Chgo.; exec. dir. Indsl. Areas Found. and Tng. Inst., 1969-72. Vis. prof. Vassar Coll., 1969, Antioch Coll., 1970. Will D. Wood fellow Amherst Coll., 1969. Recipient award for social justice Cath. Youth Orgn. Am., 1950. Mem. Authors League Am. Author: Reveille for Radicals, 1946, 70; John L. Lewis, a Biography, 1949, 70; (with Marion K. Sanders) The Professional Radical, 1970; Rules for Radicals, 1971. Contbr. numerous articles to sociol., psychol. and ednl. publs. Office: Chicago IL Died June 12, 1972.

ALLAIRE, JAMES PETER, master mechanic, steam engine builder; b. 1785; m. Frances Roe; m. 2d, Calicia Tompkins. Began as brass founder, N.Y.C., 1813; founder Allaire Works (1st steam engine works in N.Y.), 1815, Howell Works, 1831; built 1st compound-type engine for marine purposes; built 1st house designed as tenement, N.Y.C., 1833. Died May 20, 1858.

ALLARDICE, ROBERT EDGAR, mathematician; b. Edinburgh, Scotland, Mar. 2, 1862; s. John amd Isabella Edgar (Laing) A.; A.M., U. of Edinburgh, 1882, post-grad., 1882-84; unmarried. Asst. prof. mathematics, U. of Edinburgh, 1882-92; prof. mathematics, Leland Stanford Jr. U., 1892—. Home: Stanford University, Calif. Died 1928.

ALLEE, WARDER CLYDE, (al-le'), zoologist; b. nr. Bloomingdale, Ind., June 5, 1885; s. John Wesley and Mary Emily (Newlin) A.; S.B., Earlham Coll., Ind., 1908, LL.D., 1940; S.M. U. of Chicago, 1910, Ph.D., 1912; m. Marjorie Hill, Sept. 4, 1912 (dec. 1945); children—Warder (dec.), Barbara Elliott, Mary Newlin; married 2d, Ann Silver, June 26, 1953. Assistant in zoölogy, University of Chicago, 1910-12; instr. in botany, U. of Ill., 1912-13, in zoölogy Williams Coll., 1913-14; asst. prof. zoölogy Okla. U., 1914-15; prof. biology, Lake Forest Coll., 1915-21; asst. prof. zoölogy, 1921, asso. prof., 1923, prof., 1928-50, U. of Chicago, prof. of zoology emeritus since 1950, dean in the colleges, 1925-27; head professor biology University of Florida, 1950-55; instructor Marine Biol. Lab., Woods Hole, Mass., summers 1914-21, invertebrate course, 1918-21; lecturer in zoölogy, U. of Calif., winter 1923; prof. zoölogy, Nat. Summer Sch., Logan, Utah, 1924-26. Alumni trustee, Earlham Coll., 1925-39; trustee Marine Biol. Lab. since 1932. Fellow Am. Assn. Advancement Sci. (v.p. 1942), Am. Soc. Entomologists, Am. Acad. Arts and Scis.; mem. Am. Soc. Zoologists (pres. 1936), Nat. Acad. Sci., Ecol. Soc. Am. (pres. 1929), Am. Soc. Naturalists, Gamma Alpha, Phi Beta Kappa, Sigma Xi, Soc. Friends. Club: Quadrangle. Author: Animal Aggregations, 1931; Animal Life and Social Growth, 1932; The Social Life of Animals, 1938; Cooperation among Animals, with Human Implications, 1951. Co-author: Jungle Island (with Marjorie Hill Allee), 1925; Nature of the World and Man, 1926; The World and Man, 1937; Ecological Animal Geography, 1937; A Laboratory Introduction to Animal Ecology and Taxonomy, 1939; Principles of Animal Ecology, 1949. Managing editor Physiological Zoology, 1930-55. Chmn. com. on revision of Zoological articles, Encyclopedia Britannica, 1944-50. Contributor technical articles to professional journals. Home: 1080 S.W. 11th Terrace, Gainesville, Fla. Died Mar. 18, 1955.

ALLEFONSCE, JEAN, explorer; b. Saintonge, France, circa 1482. Chief pilot for Roverval on journey at Am., Apr.-June 1542; explored for Western Passage along St. Lawrence River; made maps of coasts which appeared in Cosmographie, 1545. Author: Voyages Avantureaux, published posthumously, 1559. Died reef of Rochelle, Bay of Biscay, France, circa 1557.

ALLEMAN, GELLERT, chemist; b. Littletown, Pa., July 23, 1871; s. Monroe John and Elizabeth (Gilfillan) A.; B.S., Pa. Coll. (Gettysburg), 1893, Sc.D., 1925; Ph.D., John Hopkins, 1897; u. of Berlin, 1911-12; m. Katharine Constable Spencer, July 7, 1902; children—Gellert Spencer, Robert Gilfillan. Instr. chemistry, U. of Me., 1897-98, Washington U., St. Louis, 1898-1902; prof. chemistry, Swarthmore Coll. since 1902, on leave of absence since 1928, prof. emeritus since 1936. Mem. advisory board Chemical Warfare Service. Fellow Soc. of Chem. Industry (London), A.A.A.S., Chem. Soc. (London), Deutsche Chemische Gesellschaft; mem. Am. Chem. Soc., Am. Electrochem. Soc., Franklin Inst. (bd. mgrs.; v.p.). Club: Chemists (New York). Visited various European universities, 1927-28. Home: Wallingford, Pa. Died Sept. 6, 1946; buried at Media, Pa.

ALLEN, ALEXANDER JOHN, research physicist, educator; b. Glenwood Springs, Colo., Oct. 4, 1900; s. Alexander and Leah (Blotiaux) A.; A.B., U. Colo., 1923; Master Arts, New York University, 1926, Ph.D., 1928; m. Elinor Hale Waterhouse, Feb. 29, 1956. Engineer with the Mountain States Telephone Company, Denver, 1923-24; grad. fellow, N.Y. Univ., 1924-26, instr. in physics, 1926-28, research fellow, 1928-29, at Bartol Found., 1929-30; research physicist, U. Pa. Sch. Medicine, 1930-35, Biochem. Research Found., Franklin Inst., 1935-39; asso. prof. physics, U. Pittsburgh, 1939-41, Westinghouse prof. engring. and physics, and dir. Sarah Mellon Scaife Radiation Lab. 1944-68; staff mem. and research asso. Mass. Inst. Tech. Radiation Lab., 1941-44; asst. dir., Biochem. Research Found., Delaware, 1944; prof. physics, chmn. grad. study com. Centro Tecnico de Aeronautica, Departmento de Fisica, Sao Jose dos Campos, S. Paulo, Brazil, 1960-62. Consultant Atomic Energy Commn.; director of Navy "Precision Scattering of Nuclear Particles" Contract; council rep. of U. of Pittsburgh for Argonne Nat. Labs. Fellow Am. Physical Soc.; mem. Am. Assn. U. Profs., Eta Kappa Nu, Sigma Xi. Club: University. Home: Pittsburgh PA Died June 7, 1968; buried Eagle CO

ALLEN, ANDREWS, engr.; b. Madison, Wis., Jan. 11, 1870; s. Prof. William Francis and Margaret Loring (Andrews) A.; B.S. in C.E., U. of Wis., 1891. C.E., 1893; m. Margaret Isabel Thomas, Oct. 9, 1894 (divorced1915); m. 2d, Elizabeth Emerson Cooke, Jan. 15, 1916; children—Andrews, Katharine Elisabeth, Francis J. and Henry (both adopted). With U.S. Geol. Survey in Upper Mich., 1891; draftsman and asst. engr., Edge Moor Bridge Works, 1891-991 contracting engr., Wis. Bridge & Iron Co., 1899-1911; pres. Allen & Garcia Co., 1911—. Mason (K.T., Shriner). Home: Glencoe, Ill. Died Mar. 21, 1931.

ALLEN, ANTHONY BENEZET, farmer; b. Hampshire County, Mass., June 24, 1802; s. Samuel and Ruth (Falley) A.; m. Mary E. Butterworth, 1852. Moved to Buffalo (N.Y.) to farm and breed livestock, 1833; visited Eng. to study livestock, 1841; founder, co-editor (with brother Richard L.) Am. Agriculturist, 1842-56; formed (with Richard) farm machinery bus. A.B. Allen & Co., 1847; toured Europe studying farming methods, 1867; purchased farm on Toms River, Ocean County, N.J., 1870. Died Jan. 12, 1892.

ALLEN, ARTHUR AUGUSTUS, ornithology; b. Buffalo, Dec. 28, 1885; s. Daniel Williams and Anna (Moore) A.; A.B., Cornell U., 1907, M.A., 1908, Ph.D., 1911; m. Elsa Guerdrum, Aug. 17, 1913; children—Constance, Glen Olaf, Phebe Laura, David Guerdrum, Prudence Lloyd. Asst., later instr. in zoölogy Cornell U., 1906-15, asst. prof. ornithology, 1915-25, prof. since 1925; explorer, lectr. ornithol. fields since 1912. Ornithol. expdns. to Colombia, 1912, Labrador, 1918, 1945; Hudson Bay, 1934, 1944; Europe, 1938, Panama, 1944-45; O.S.R.D. project on jungle acoustics, for War Dept. Mex., 1946, Alaska, 1948. Fellow Am. Orinthol. Union; mem. Wilson Ornithol. Club; mem. Cooper Ornithol. Club. Am. Soc. Mammalogists, Am. Soc. Naturalists, Wildlife Soc. (pres. 1938), Sigma Xi, Gamma Alpha. In charge ruffed grouse investigations Am. Game Assn.; discoverer method rearing ruffed grouse in captivity. Awarded Outdoor Life medal, 1924, for research on ruffed grouse. Nat. Geog. Soc. Burr prize, 1948. Republican. Author: The Book of Bird Life, 1930, Laboratory Notebook for Ornithology (with Fuertes and Pirnie), 1926; American Bird Biographies, 1934; The Book of Birds (with others). 1938; The Golden Plover and Other Birds, 1939; American Bird Songs and Voices of the Night, albums of phonograph records (with P. P. Kellogg), 1942 and 1948. Contbr. articles on birds to encys., sci. jours., Nat. Geog. Mag., others. Home: 208 Kline Rd., Ithaca, N.Y. Died Jan. 17, 1964.

ALLEN, ARTHUR WATTS, chem. and metall. engr.; b. Devon. Eng., Feb. 22, 1879; s. Joseph and Eliza Reeves (Stevens) A.; B.A., St. John's Coll., Cambridge, Eng., 1902, M.A., 1910; m. Margaret Benyon Brown, Nov. 5, 1907; children—Clement Harold, Margarita Frances, Vivien Mary. Biol. research in New Guinea, 1902-04, with Sir H. Wickham; design, erection, mgmt. chem., metall. and oredressing plants in Australia, Mexico, Uruguay, Africa and Argentina, 1904-16; studied nitrate industry in Chile, 1916; pvt. practice and metall. editor Engring. and Mining Jour., N.Y., 1917-19; developed nitrate process in Chile, 1919-20; asso. editor, Mining and Sci. Press, San Francisco, 1921-22; asst. editor Engring. and Mining Jour.-Press, N.Y., 1922-26; asst. editor, Chem. and Metall. Engring., N.Y., 1923-62; tech. adviser to Gibbs & Co., Chile, Argentina 1926-27, founder, exec. editor, Food Industries, N.Y., 1927-33, Engring. and Mining World, 1930-31, Met. and Min. Markets, 1930-33; prof. work in Eng., 1934; Western U.S., 1935-36; Chile and Ecuador, 1936-37; Japan, China, P.I., 1937; Peru, 1938; Costa Rica, 1939-43; Brit. Guiana, 1943; prin. economist, fgn. minerals div. U.S. Bur. Mines, Washington, 1943-45; archivist, editor. Inter-Am. Inst. Agrl. Scis., Turrialba, Costa Rica, 1947-50; tech. adviser Inst. Inter-Am. Affairs, San José, since 1950. Author: Mill and Cyanide Handbook, 1916; Handbook of Ore Dressing, 1920; Recovery of Nitrate from Chilean Caliche, 1921. Editor 3d edit. Julian & Smart's Cyaniding Gold and Silver Ores. 1922. Contbr. to trans. Linnean Soc., Instn. Mining & Met., Am. Inst. Min. and Metall. Engrs., Electro-chem. Soc., Am. Inst. Chem. Engrs. Address: Apartado 1714, San José, Costa Rica. Died May 1966.

ALLEN, ARTHUR WILBURN, surgeon; b. McKinney, Ky., Nov. 30, 1887; s. James Hayden and Emma (Arthur) A.; A.B., Georgetown Coll., 1909, D.Sc. (hon.), 1943; M.D., Johns Hopkins, 1913; D.Sc. (hon.), Harvard, 1952; m. Vida Weddle, July 9, 1913; 1 son, Arthur Wilburn, Jr. Chief east surg. service Mass. Gen. Hosp., 1936-48, cons. in surgery, 1948—; lectr. surgery Harvard Med. Sch., 1936-48. Served as capt. M.C., U.S. Army, 1917-19. Diplomate Am. Bd. Surgery. Fellow A.C.S. (pres. 1947-48, chmn. bd. regents 1948-51), Royal Coll. Surgeons Eng. and Edinburgh (hon.), Royal Soc. Medicine Eng. (hon.); mem. Am. Acad. Arts and Scis., Am., So., New Eng. surg. assns., Pan-Pacific (pres. 1954—), Eastern (hon., 1954—), N.E., Boston (pres. 1942-44) surg. socs., A.M.A., Boston Med. Library (pres. 1953—), Soc. Clin. Surgery, Mass. Med. Soc. (pres. 1949-50). Republican. Mason. Clubs: Harvard, Somerset, Tavern (Boston); The Country (Brookline). Home: 191 Commonwealth Av. Office: 266 Beacon St., Boston. Died Boston Mar. 18, 1958; buried West Boxford, Mass.

ALLEN, CALVIN FRANCIS (C. FRANK), engineer; b. Roxbury (Boston), Mass., July 10, 1851; s. Calvin and Ann Priscilla (Watson) A.; grad. Roxbury Latin Sch., 1868; S.B., Massachusetts Inst. Tech., 1872; Eng. D.,

Northeastern Univ., 1938; m. Caroline Elizabeth Hadley, June 21, 1888; children—Mildred, Margaret, Frances (dec.). Asst. engr. water works or sewers, Providence, R.I., and Newton, Mass., 1872-78; asst. engr. A., T. & S.F.R.R., 1878-85 (except 1 yr. chief engr. water works at Las Vegas, N.M.); asst. prof. 1887, later asso. prof. and prof. railroad engring., Mass. Inst. of Tech.; retired under Carnegie Foundation, 1916 (prof. emeritus). Admitted to N.M. bar, 1885, Mass. bar, 1901; city atty., Socorro, N.M. 1886; mem. sch. com., Sharon, Mass., 1892-95 (chmn. pres.), Am. Soc. Civil Engrs., Mass. Highway Assn. (ex-pres.), New Eng. R.R. Club (ex-pres.); mem. Am. Ry. Engring. Assn. (life), Soc. Prom. Engring. Edn. (ex-sec., ex-pres.), Technology Club (ex-sec.); mem. com. on pub. utilities Boston Chamber of Commerce (but not a mem. of the Chamber). Has been member Publ. Com., Technology Review; also of Jour. of Mass. Highway Assn. Unitarian. Republican. Author: Railroad Curves and Earthwork, 1889; Tables for Earthwork Computation, 1893; Field and Office Tables, 1903; Business Law for Engineers, 1917. Administration, Sept. 1-Dec. 31, 1918. Mem. Advisory Zoning Commn. for Boston, 1922-23. Home: West Roxbury, Mass. Died June 6, 1948.

ALLEN, CHARLES ELMER, botanist; b. Horicon, Wis., Oct. 4, 1872; s. Charles and Eliza (North) A.; B.S., U. Wis., 1899, Ph.D., 1904; Sc.D., U. Chgo., 1941; m. Genevieve Sylvester, June 20, 1902; children—Edith (Mrs. C. R. Slater), Harold Sylvester, Charles Rittenhouse. Ct. reporter, 1890-1901; instr. botany U. Wis., 1901-04, asst. prof., 1904-07, asso. prof., 1907-09, prof., 1909-43, emeritus prof., 1943—; research asst. Carnegie Inst. of Washington, at Univ. of Bonn, 1904-05; vis. prof. Columbia U., 1924. Mem. NRC, 1925-31, chmn. div. biology and agr., 1929-30. Fellow A.A.A.S. (v.p. and chmn. Sect. G 1928); mem. Nat. Acad. Sciences, Am. Society Naturalists (pres. 1936), Genetics Soc. Am., Am. Genetic Assn., Am. Microscopic Soc. (pres. 1921), Wis. Acad. Sci. Arts and Letters (pres. 1930-33), Hist. Soc. Wis., Am. Assn. U., Profs., Delta Upsilon, Phi Beta Kappa, Sigma Xi, Phi Sigma. Author: A Textbook of Botany (with Edward M. Gilbert), 1917; A Textbook of General Botany (with Gilbert M. Smith and others), 1924, 4th ed., 1942. Editor-in-chief Wis. Alumni Mag., 1899-04, Am. Jour. of Botany, 1918-26. Contbr. to scientific publs. Home: 2014 Chamberlin Av., Madison 4, Wis. Died June 24, 1954.

ALLEN, CHARLES METCALF, hydraulic engr.; b. Walpole, Mass., Dec. 12, 1871; s. Melzar Waterman and Martha (Metcalf) A.; B.S., Worcester Poly. Inst., 1894, M.S., 1899, hon. D.Eng., 1929; m. Eva May Taylor, Mar. 27, 1907; children—Virginia, Lucian Taylor, Jeannette. Instr. exptl., mech. and hydraulic engring., Worcester Poly. Inst., 1894-1906; prof. hydraulic engring., 1906-45; prof. emeritus, hydraulic engring., 1945—; dir. Alden Hydraulic Lab., also practicing engr. Mem. A.A.A.S., Am. Soc. M.E., Am. Soc. C.E., Soc. Soc. Promotion Engring. Edn., Boston Soc. C.E. Republican. Conglist. Clubs: Worcester, Rotary (Worcester). Home: 1 Lincoln Av., Holden, Mass. Died Aug. 15, 1950; buried Maple Grove Cemetery, Walpole, Mass.

ALLEN, CHARLES MORSE, chemist; b. Farmington, Me., Apr. 6, 1859; s. Charles F. (D.D.) and Ruth Sibley (Morse) A.; U. of Me., 1878-9; A.B., Wesleyan U.,-Conn., 1882, A.M., 1886; Dresden Polytechnic and Zürich Polytechnic, 1896-1897; m. Carol Shepard, Aug. 2, 1888. Instr. chemistry, Wyoming Sem., Kingston, Pa., 1882-9; instr. chemistry, Pratt Inst., 1889-98, head of dept. of chemistry, 1898. Mem. Am. Chem. Soc., New York Chem. Teachers' Club, Phi Nu Theta, Phi Beta Kappa. Methodist. Author: Laboratory Notes on General Chemistry; Quantitative Chemical Analysis. Home: 226 Willoughby Av., Brooklyn. Died Apr. 3, 1942.

ALLEN, CHARLES RICKETSON, vocational edn.; b. New Bedford, Mass., Aug. 6, 1862; s. John A. P. and Abbie (Chaddock) A.; B.S., Mass. Inst. Tech., 1885; studied Johns Hopkins, 1893; M.A., Harvard, 1903; D.Sc., Stout Inst., Menomonie, Wis., 1927; m. Lissa H. Hall, June 28, 1889. Teacher high sch., New Bedford, 1886-1909; in charge development of vocational training, New Bedford, 1906-11, dir. New Bedford Independent Industrial Sch. last 2 yrs.; agt. for industrial training, Mass. Bd. of Edn., 1911-17; asst. supt. training and supt. of instr. training, Emergency Fleet Corpn., 1917-18; staff Fed. Bd. Vocational Edn., Washington, Nov. 19i8-19; dir. of training, C. of C., Niagara Falls, N.Y., 1920-21; spl. agt. Fed. Bd. Vocational Edn., 1921; dir. indsl. training service, Dunwoody Inst., Minneapolis, 1922-24; editor and ednl. cons. Fed. Bd. Vocational Edn. since 1924. Mem. Nat. Soc. Vocational Edn., Am. Management Assn., The Civil Legion; hon. mem. Boston Soc. Civil Engrs, Author: Laboratory Manual of Physics, 1890; The Instructor, The Man and The Job, 1919; The Foreman and His Job, 1921; (with C. A. Prosser) Vocational Education in a Democracy; Have We Kept the Faith? 1929; (with J. C. Wright) The Supervision of Vocational Education, 1926; The Adminstration of Vocational Education, 1927; Efficiency in Education, 1928; Efficiency in Vocational Education, 1929; (with H. A. Tiemon) Managing Minds, 1932; also a number of articles and publs. of the Federal Bd. of Vocational. Education and the Dept. of the Interior. Office: Washington. Died July 6, 1938.

ALLEN CHARLES WARRENNE, physician; b. Flemington, N.J., Dec. 4, 1854; s. George Anderson and Mary (Bonnell) A.; early edn. Lycée Imperial, Nantes, France; grad. Exeter Acad., 1875, med. sept. Columbia Coll. (Phys. & Surg.), New York, 1878; post-grad. studies univs. of Vienna and Paris; m. Grace Lawrence Boardman (dec.). Prof. dermatology, N.Y. Post-Grad. Med. Sch. and Hosp.; cons. surgeon in various hosps. Author: Practitioners' Manual, 1899; Handy Book of Medical Progress, 1899; Radiotherapy, Photography, Radium and High Frequency Currents, 1904. Home: New York, N.Y. Deceased.

ALLEN, CLAXTON EDMONDS, electrical engr.; b. Seven Islands, Va., Feb. 4, 1881; s. George Hunt and Mollie (Edmonds) A.; grad. high sch., Covington, Va., 1897; B.S. in E.E., Va. Poly. Inst., 1901; m. Lydia Ann Kimbrough, Apr. 7, 1908 (deceased 1943); children—Claxton Edmonds, Lydia Ann (Mrs. IIA. I. A. Long). Electrical apprentice with General Electric Co., Lynn, Mass., 1901-03, designing engr. and research work, Lynn, 1903-07, commercial engr. and instr. of salesmen, at Schenectady, N.Y., 1907-09; with Westinghouse Electric & Mfg. Co., successively mgr. transformer dept., at East Pittsburgh, Aug.-Nov. 1909, asst. mgr. and mgr. supply dept., N.Y.C., until 1914, mgr. supply and Central Sta. depts., Chgo., 1914-22, dist. mgr., St. Louis, 1922-30, v.p. charge merchandising, 1930-47; vice president Comml. Electric Supply Co.; dir. Electric Appliance Co., Columbia Electric Co. Dept. fuel administrator of Ill., World War. Fellow Am. Inst. E.E.; mem. Electric Light Assn., St. Louis Elec. Bd. of Trade (pres.). Episcopalian. Clubs: Noonday, Bellerive Country, Racquet; University (Pitts.). Inventor: Original distributed core transformer; maximum demand electric meter; electric relay. Home: 4626 Maryland Av. Office: 411 N. 7th St., St. Louis. Deceased.

ALLEN, DUFF S(HEDERIC), surgeon; b. Lebanon, Mo., July 3, 1895; s. William Thomas and Mary Elizabeth (Casey) A.; grad. Druy Acad., Springfield, Mo., 1913; student Washington U., 1913-15, M.D., 1919; m. Mildred Lucille Burns, 1926. House physician St. Luke's Hosp., 1919; asst. in surgery Washington U., 1921-24, instr. in surgery, 1924-26, asst. prof., 1926—; resident surgeon Barnes Hosp., 1923-24, now asst. surgeon; asst. surgeon St. Louis Maternity Hosp.; vis. surgeon and chief of unit St. Louis City Hosp. Editor Washington U. Med. Alumnus, 1924; asso. editor Journal of Thoracic Surgery, Diplomate Am. Bd. Surgery. Mem. Phi Beta Pi (nat. pres.). Republican. Catholic. Worked out surg. procedure for reconstruction of the esophagus; devised needle which reduces time required for an operation 5 minutes; devised first method for doing operations inside a living heart under direct vision. Contbr. studies on goitre and on the etiology of empyema and abscess of the lung and the mechanism of secretion of the gastric juice and method of absorption of egg white from gastro-intestinal tract. Address: 10 Oakleigh Lane, St. Louis. Died Dec. 7, 1958; buried Calvary Cemetery, St. Louis.

ALLEN, EDGAR, prof. anatomy; b. Canon City, Colo., 1892; s. Asa and Edith (Day) A.; Ph.B., Brown U., 1915, A.M., 1916, Arnold fellow, 1916-17, Ph.D., 1921, Sc.D., 1936; m. lMarion Robins Pfeiffer, June 26, 1918; children—Frances Isabelle, Marjorie Eleanor. Asst. in biology, Brown U., 1913-15, asst. in embryology and neurology, 1915-17; investigator, U.S. Bur. Fisheries, Woods Hole, Mass., summer 1919, Fairport, Ia., summer 1922; instr. and asso. in anatomy, Washington U. Sch. of Medicine, 1919-23; prof. anatomy, Univ. of Mo, since 1923, also dean med. sch., 1929-33; prof. anatomy, Yale U. Sch. of Medicine since 1933. Served as pvt., later 2d lt. U.S. Army, May 1917-Feb. 1919. Mem. A.A.A.S., Assn. Anatomists, A.M.A., Soc. Study Internal Secretions, Soc. Zoölogists, Phi Gamma Delta, Phi Beta Pi. Contbr. to Am. Jour. Anatomy, Anat. Record, Am. Jour. Physiology, Jour. A.M.A., Endocrinology, Am. Naturalist, Biol. Bull., Embryology, etc. Home: 472 Whitney Av., New Haven, Conn. Died Feb. 3, 1943.

ALLEN, EDGAR VAN NUYS, physician; b. Cozad, Neb., June 22, 1900; s. Charles Edgar and Sue (Morrow) A.; B.Sc.,, U. of Neb., 1923, M.A., 1923, M.D., 1925, Doctor of Science (honorary) 1952; M.Sc., Univ. of Minnesota, 1933; student of medicine, Germany and England, 1929-30; m. Margaret Wise, Nov. 23, 1929; children—Katherine Lee, Charles van Nuys, David Wise. Fellow and first asst. in medicine, Mayo Foundation, U. of Minn., Rochester, Minn., 1925-29; fellow Nat. Research Council, studying in Germany and Eng., 1929-30; consultant in medicine, Mayo Clinic since 1930, also chief of sect. div. medicine, 1935-47 (on mil. leave of absence from both positions, 1942-46); sr. cons. med. since 1948; instr., U. of Minn., Rochester, Minn., 1931-34, asst. prof. 1934-37, asso. prof., 1937, prof. med. since 1947. Served in S.A.T.C., 1918; commissioned lieut. col. Med. Corps, Army of U.S., Aug. 1942, promoted col., Feb. 1944; med. consultant 7th Service Command, 1942-46. Awarded Legion of Merit, 1946; Gold Heart award, Am. Heart Assn., 1959, Albert Lasker award, 1960, Distinguished Service medal, 1957. Diplomate of the American Board of Internal Medicine; Am. Bd. Cardiovascular. Diseases. Member American College of Physicians, A.M.A. (member Ho. Dels. 1942-60); member American Soc. Clin. Investigation, Central Soc. Clin. Research, (pres. 1948), Am. Heart Assn. (dir., pres. 1956-57), Assn. American Physicians, Minn. Society Internal Med., Minn. Med. Assn., Soc. Med. Cons. for World War II, Alpha Omega Alpha, Sigma Xi, Phi Chi. Republican. Presbyterian. Author: Thromboangitis Obliterans (with George E. Brown), 1928; Periopheral Vascular Diseases (with N. W. Barker and E. A. Hines, Jr.), 1946; also numerous sci. articles. Home: 1121 Plummer Circle. Office: Mayo Clinic, Rochester, Minn. Died June 14, 1961; buried Mankato, Minn.

ALLEN, EDWARD BARTLETT, physician; b. Killingly, Conn., July 27, 1888; s. Jude L. and Martha F. (Bartlett) A.; A.B., A.M., Brown U., 1911; M.D., Harvard, 1915; m. Ethel Dasie Skinner, June 15, 1918 (dec. Feb. 26, 1960; 1 dau., Elizabeth Skinner. Asst. pathologist, clinican Danvers State Hosp., 1915; intern Boston City Hosp., 1915-17; physician Cheney Bros. Med. Dept., 1917-18, supt., 1919-24; orthopedist Base Hosp. 80, Beaune, France, 1918-19; asst. psychiatrist Evacuation Hosp. 14 and 16, Coblenz, Germany, 1919; attending staff Manchester (Conn.) Meml. Hosp., 1920-24; attending psychiatrist Payne Whitney Clinic, 1932-54; asst. resident physician to sr. asst. psychiatrist Westchester div. N.Y. Hosp., 1924-56; instr. psychiatry Cornell U. Med. Coll., 1933-54; asso. prof. psychology 1st Inst. Podiatry, L.D. Med. Coll., 1948; cons. geriatrics and psychiatry Augusta (Me.) State Hosp., 1956-57; part-time psychiatrist Manhattan State Hosp., 1957-61. Discussion leader sect. on health maintenance and rehab. Nat. Conf. on Aging, Washington, 1950; mem. adult edn. adv. council White Plains Pub. Schs.; exec. com. Westchester Com. on Alcoholism; cons. White Plains br. Mental Health Assn. Westchester. Diplomate in psychiatry Am. Bd. Psychiatry and Neurology. Mem. Old Guard of White Plains, Am. Psychopathol. Assn., Am. Psychiat. Assn., Am. Geriatrics Soc. (sec., bd. dirs., past pres., mem. editorial bd. Jour.), N.Y. Psychiat. Soc. (pres.), Med. Soc. N.Y. (life), Med. Soc. Westchester (hon. life), N.Y. State Westchester acads. medicine, Harvard Med. Soc. N.Y., Acad. Religion and Mental Health Club: Brown U. (N.Y.C.). Contbr. chpt. on alcoholism Progress in Neurology and Psychiatry, 1916. Contbr. articles med. jours. Home: 21 Greenridge Av., White Plains, N.Y. Office: 1405 Coliseum, 10 Columbus Circle, N.Y.C. 19. Died Oxt. 8, 1964; buried Grove Street Cemetery, Putnam, Conn.

ALLEN, EDWARD TYSON, ret. forester; b. New Haven, Dec. 26, 1875; s. Oscar Dana and Fidella Roberts (Totman) A.; student pvt. schs.; m. Matilda Price Riley, Oct. 20, 1902 (died 1927); children—Olmsted Tyson (Mrs. Donald Plimpton Abott), Barbara (Mrs. Robert E. Burns); m. 2d, Mildred Grudolf-Smith, Feb. 18, 1928. Forest ranger, 1898; entered Bur. Forestry, U.S. Dept. Agr., 1899; Cal. state forester, 1905-06; in U.S. Forest Service, 1906-09, charge establishment and adminstrn. nat. forests in far west; organized, 1909, and managed Western Forestry and Conservation Assn., an alliance of all pvt., state and fed. forest agencies in Mont., Ida., and Pacific Coast states; counsel to Nat. Lumber Mfrs. Assn. for many yrs., also to U.S. Treasury Dept., FTC, Dept. Interior, Dept. Agr., ret. from active service, 1932. Was specialist on forest econs., taxation and preservation. Charter mem. Soc. Am. Foresters. Author many articles for popular, sci. and trade mags.; manuals for field officers and briefs for lawyers and legislators. Home: Otis, Ore. Died 1942.

ALLEN EDWIN WEST, chemist; b. Amherst, Mass., Oct. 28, 1864; s. Lysander H. and Mary M. (Bullard) A.; grad. Mass. Agrl. Coll., 1885; B.S., Boston Univ., 1885; Ph.D., U. of Göttingen, 1890; LL.D., U. of Mo., 1929; m. Estelle Standish (dec.), Dorothy Helen. Entered service of U.S. Dept. of Agr., Aug. 11, 1890; asst. dir., 1893-1915, then chief Office of Expt. Stas.; asso. editor to 1895, editor in chief to 1924, Experiment Station Record, also asst. dir. of scientific work. Exec. sec. of Commn. on Country Life, 1908. Contbr. to the Am. and Internat. Yearbooks; editor agr. and agrl. chemistry of New Internatl. Ency. Editor Jour. Agrl. Research, 1926—. Home: Washington, D.C. Died 1929.

ALLEN, EUGENE THOMAS, geochemist; b. Athol. Mass., Apr. 2, 1864; s. Frederic and Harriet Augusta (Thomas) A.; A.bB., Amherst, 1887; Ph.D., Johns Hopkins, 1892; postgrad. Harvard, 1893-95; m. Harriet E. Doughty, Aug. 26, 1896. Acting prof. chemistry, U. Colo., 1892-93; prof. chemistry, Sch. of Miles, U. Mo., 1895-1901; chem. geologist U.S. Geol. Survey, 1901-06; chemist Geophys. Lab., Carnegie Inst., Washington, D.C., 1907-32. Mem. Nat. Acad. Scis., Geol. Soc. Am., Geol. Soc. Boston, Delta Kappa Epsilon. Club: Cosmos, Contbr. to sci. jours. Researches chiefly in geochemistry, mineral chemistry and volcanology. Author: Isomorphism and Thermal Properties of the Feldspars, 1905; The Volcanic Activity and Hot Springs of Lassen Peak, 1925; The Steam Wells and other Thermal Activity of the Geysers of California, 1927; Hot Springs of Yellowstone National Park, 1935-all with Dr. A. L. Day. Died July 17, 1964.

ALLEN, GLOVER MORRILL, naturalist; b. Walpole, N.H., Feb. 8, 1879; s. Rev. Nathaniel Glover and Harriet Ann (Schouler) A.; A.B., Harvard, 1901, Sarah Moody Cushing, June 26, 1911; 1 dau., Elizabeth Cushing (Mrs. Arthur Gilman). Librarian, Boston Society Natural History, 1901-27; curator of mammals, Mus. Comparative Zoölogy, Harvard, 1907; lecturer on zoölogy, 1924, professor 1938, Harvard. Mem. expdns. to Bahama Islands, 1904, British E. Africa, 1909, Grenada, B.W.I., 1910, Sudan, 1912, Liberia, 1926, Brazil, 1929. Republican. Episcopalian. Fellow A.A.A.S., Am. Ornithologists' Union, Harvard Travelers' Club; mem. Boston Soc. of Natural History, Nuttall Ornithol. Club, Phi Beta Kappa, Sigma Xi. Author: The Birds of Massachusetts (with R. H. Howe, Jr.), 1901; Birds and Their Attributes, 1925; Bats, 1939; numerous paper chiefly on mammals and birds. Home: 25 Garden St. Office: Museum of Comparative Zoölogy, Cambridge, Mass. Died Feb. 14, 1942.

ALLEN GRANT, author; b. Kingston, Ont., Feb. 24, 1848; ed. U.S., France and England; grad. Merton Coll., Oxford; is a writer upon evolution, and also a novelist. Author: Physiological Aesthetics; Charles Darwin; The Evolutionist at Large; The Color Sense; Phillistia; Babylon; Colin Clout's Calendar; The Color of Flowers; Flowers and Their Pedigrees; For Mamie's Sake In All Shades; The Beckoning Hand; The Devil's Die; This Mortal Coil; White Man's Foot; Force and Energy; The Tents of Shem; The Women Who Did; Post-Prandial Philosophy; Strange Stories; Anglo-Saxon Britian; The British Barbarians; Science in Arcady; Historical Guides to Paris, Florence, and Belgium; The Evolution of the Idea of God; etc. Died 1899.

ALLEN, HARRIS CAMPBELL, architect; b. Rutland, Vt., Nov. 22, 1876; s. Charles Linnacus and Gertrude Margaret (Lyon) A.; B.A., Stanford U., 1897; student U. of Calif., 1897-98. Draftsman, 1898-1908; architect, 1908-17 and since 1919; editor Pacific Coast Architect, 1919-29, Calif. Arts and Architecture, 1929-34, Bulletin of State Assn. of Calif. Architects, 1934-42; zone architect Zone 5, Federal Housing Adminstrn., 1938-41; architectural examiner Federal Housing Adminstrn., War and Veterans Housing, 1941-45. Served as capt. U.S. Air Service, 1917-19. Fellow Am. Inst. Architects (v.p. No. Calif. Chapter 1925-27, pres. 1927-29, dir. 1922-25 and 1929-32); mem. State Assn. of Calif. Architects (pres. 1933, dir. 1930-32 and 1934-36), San Francisco Soc. Architects (pres. 1933-38), Am. Legion of Calif. (chmn. aviation com. 1921-25), Sons of the American Revolution, Nat. Aeronautic Assn., Phi Kappa Psi. Republican. Episcopalian. Mason (Shriner). Club: Bohemian (San Francisco). Contbr. to professional jours. Address: Bohemian Club San Francisco

ALLEN, HARRISON, anatomist, physician; b. Phila., Apr. 17, 1841; s. Samuel and Elizabeth (Thomas) A.; M.D., U. Pa., 1861; m. Julia A. Colton, Dec. 1869. Asst. surgeon U.S. Army, 1862, brevetted maj., 1865; prof. zoology, comparative anatomy Auxiliary Faculty Medicine, U. Pa., 1865-97; prof. anatomy and surgery Pa. Dental Coll., 1866-68. Fellow Coll. Physicians of Phila.; mem. Path. Soc., Am. Laryngol. Assn. (a founder). Author: Monograph of the Bats of North America, 1864; System of Anatomy, 1884. Died Phila., Nov. 14, 1897.

ALLEN, HORATIO, civil engr., inventor; b. Schenectady, N.Y., May 10, 1802; s. Dr. Benjamin and Mary (Benedict) A.; A.B., Columbia, 1823; m. Mary Moncrief Simons, 1834, 4 children. Chief engr. S.C. R.R. Co., 1829; asst. prin. engr. Croton Aqueduct, 1838; cons. engr. N.Y. & Erie R.R. Co.; a propr. Novelty Iron Works, 1842; pres. Erie R.R., 1843; cons. engr. constrn. Bklyn. Bridge, also Panama R.R., 1870. An organizer N.Y. Gallery Art; pres. Am. Soc. C.E., 1872; a founder Union League Club, N.Y.C. Died South Orange, N.J., Dec. 31, 1899.

ALLEN, JEREMIAH MERVIN, engr.; b. Enfield, Conn., May 18, 1833; s. Jeremiah V. and Emily (Pease) A.; m. Harriet S. Griswold, 1856. Taught sch., Longmeadow, Mass., 1861-65; with ins. co., Hartford, Conn., 1865-67; pres. of firm which insured against damage to steam-boilers, 1867-1903; trustee Hartford Theol. Sem.; pres. YMCA, 1 term. Died Dec. 29, 1903.

ALLEN, JOEL ASAPH, curator; b. Springfield, Mass., July 19, 1838; s. Joel and Harriet (Trumbull) A.; studied at Wilbraham Acad.; then studied zoölogy under Agassiz, Lawrence Scientific Sch., Harvard; (hon. Ph.D., Ind. U., 1886); m. Mary Manning Cleveland, Oct. 6, 1874 (died Apr. 17, 1789); 2d, Susan A. Taft, of Cornwall-on-Hudson, N.Y., Apr. 27, 1886. Lecturer, 1871-73, asst. in ornithology, Mus. Comparative Zoölogy, 1871-85, Harvard; curator mammalogy and ornithology, Am. Mus. Natural History, New York, 1885—. Editor Bull. Nuttall Ornithol. Club, 1876-83, The Auk (ornithol. quarterly-, 1884-1912, Bulletin and Memoirs, Am. Mus. Natural History, 1889-1917. Awarded Walker Grand Prize, 1903. Mem. Nat. Acad. Sciences, Am. Ornithologists Union (1st pres.). Fellow Am. Acad. Arts and Sciences. Author: History of North American Pinnipeds; Monographs of North American Rodentia (with Elliott Coues); Mammals of Patagonia, Belgian Congo, etc. Home: New York, N.Y. Died Aug. 29, 1921.

ALLEN, JOHN, dentist, inventor; b. Broome County, N.Y., Nov. 4, 1810; s. Nirum Allen. M.D., Cincinnati Med. Coll.; studied dentistry under Dr. James Harris, Chillicothe, O.; m. Charlotte Dana, 1835, 1 son, Charles; m. 2d, Mrs. Cornelia Reeder, 1 dau. Practiced dentistry primarily in N.Y.C.; devised new denture; recipient gold medal from Am. Soc. Dental Surgeons for devising method of restoring facial contours which fell in due to previous denture practices, 1845; granted patent for new denture method, 1851; made false teeth of porcelain with platinum base instead of gold (enabled him to devise continous gum to prevent oral fluids from entering into crevices of teeth); involved in much litigation over invention with Dr. William Hunter. Mem. Am. Soc. Dental Surgeons; a founder Ohio Coll. Dental Surgery, 1845, N.Y. Coll. Dentistry, 1865. Died Plainfield, N.J., Mar. 8, 1892.

ALLEN, JOHN F., inventor; b. Eng., 1829. Came to Am., 1841; engr. aboard ship Curlew in Long Island Sound, invented new form of high speed valve motion; became engr. for Henry A. Burr, felt-hat body mfr., N.Y.C., 1860; formed (with Charles Porter, inventor of engine governor) Porter-Allen Co., produced Porter-Allen engine (pioneer high-speed steam engine); invented inclined tube vertical water-tube boiler; opened his own shop, Mott Haven, N.Y.; inventor of 2 pneumatic riveting systems (1 by percussion, 1 by pressure). Died N.Y.C., Oct. 4, 1900.

ALLEN, KENNETH, civil engr.; b. New Bedford, Mass., Apr. 6, 1857; s. Edward Augustus Holyoke and Eugenia Sophia (Teulon) A.; grad. West Newton (Mass.) English and Classical Sch., 1874; C.E., Rensselaer Poly Inst., 1879; m. Rose Whitmore Switzer, Sept. 11, 1886; children—Edward Switzer, Harold Ames, Russell (dec.), Frances Eleanor. In ry. engring. work in the West, 1879-83; asst. engr., water dept., Phila. 1883-86; mem. Breithaupt & Allen cons. engrs., and later supt. of constrn. for City of Kansas City, Mo., 1886-90; engr. in charge topog. survey of Connellsville coke region for H. C. Frick Coke Co., 1890-93; asst. engr. in charge pub. work, Yonkers, 1893-95; prin. asst. engr., Baltimore Sewerage Commn., 1895-99; mem. Hill, Quick & Allen, engrs. Baltimore 1899-1902; engr. and supt. water dept., Atlantic City, N.J., 1902-06; div. engr., Baltimore Sewerage Commn., 1906-08; engr. Met. Sewerage Commn., New York, 1908-14; engr. Bur. of Sewer Plan, New York, 1915-16; engr. sewage disposal, and then sanitary engr. Bd. Estimate and Apportionment of New York, 1916-30; sanitary engr. Sanitation Commn., New York, 1930—. Dist. engr. U.S. Housing Corp., Washington, until armistice. Pres. N.Y. State Sewage Works Assn. Democrat. Unitarian. Home: White Plains, N.Y. Died Sept. 7, 1930.

ALLEN, LEWIS GEORGE, physician and surgeon; b. Lenexa, Kan., Oct. 19, 1891; s. George and Adda May (Calvin) A.; A.B., U. of Kan., 1915, IM.D., 1917; student U.S. Army Sch. of Mil. Roentgenology, 1917-18; m. Pauline Sams McLaughlin, June 2, 1920; children—Lewis George, Jr., William R. Interne, Royal Victoria Hosp., Montreal, Can., 1917; in practice as physician, specializing in radiology, Kansas City, Kan., since 1920; with Sch. of Medcine, U. of Kan., since 1924, prof. clin. roentgenology since 1938; radiologist Providence Hosp. since 1920, St. Margaret's Hosp. since 1920, Bethany Hosp. since 1927. Certified by Am. Bd. Radiology, 1934. Trustee Group Hosp. Service, Inc., Surgical Care, Inc., Boylan Research Fund, Wyandotte County Tuberculosis Assn. Fellow A.C.P., Am. Coll. Radiology (mem. commn. on education), Kansas City Academy Medicine; mem. A.M.A., Kan. and Wyandotte County med. socs., Kansas City Southwest Clin. Soc. (pres. 1939), Radiol. Soc. of N.A. (pres. 1945), Am. Roentgen Ray Soc. Home: 1051 Kimball Ave. Office: 907 N. 7th St., Kansas City, Kan. Died May 28, 1948.

ALLEN, NATHAN, physician; b. Princeton, Mass., Apr. 25, 1813; s. Moses and Methitable (Oliver) A.; grad. Amherst Coll., 1836; M.D., U. Pa., 1841; m. Sarah H. Spaulding, Sept. 24, 1841; m. 2d, Annie A. Waters, May 20, 1857. Editor, Am. Phrenol. Journal and Miscellany, 1839-42; practiced medicine, Lowell, Mass., 1841-89. Author: The Intermarriage of Relations, 1869; Physical Degeneracy, 1870; The Treatment of the Insane, 1876. Died Lowell, Jan. 1, 1889.

ALLEN, PHILIP, mfr., senator, gov. R.I.; b. Providence, R.I., Sept. 1, 1785; s. Capt. Zachariah and Nancy (Crawford) A.; grad. R.I. Coll. (now Brown U.), 1803; m. Phoebe Aborn, Jan. 1814, 11 children. Constructed 1st steam engine ever built in Providence; mem. R.I. Ho. of Reps. from Providence, 1819-21; pres. R.I. br. U.S. Bank, 1827-36; gov. R.I. (Democrat), 1851-53; mem. U.S. Senate from R.I., 1853-59, chmn. com. on agr. Died Providence, Dec. 16, 1865; buried North Burial Ground Providence.

ALLEN, RICHARD LAMB, argiculturist; b. Westfield, Mass., Oct. 30, 1803; s. Samuel and Ruth (Falley) A.; m. Sally O. Lyman, Dec. 30, 1834. Owner (with brother Anthony B.) farm, Buffalo, N.Y.; founded Am. Agriculturist, N.Y.C., 1842, co-editor, 1849-56; formed (with brother) A.B. Allen & Co., farm machinery bus. Author: A Brief Compend of American Agriculture, 1846. Died Stockholm, Sweden, Sept. 22, 1869.

ALLEN, ROBERT PORTER, biologist; b. South Williamsport, Pa., Apr. 24, 1905; s. Robert Fleming and Edith (Bennington) A.; student Lafayette Coll., 1923-25, Cornell U., 1925; m. Evelyn Sedgwick, Jan. 14, 1933; children—Robert Fleming II, Alice. Librarian, staff asst. Nat. Audubon Soc., 1930-33, sanctuary dir., 1934-38, research asso., 1939-53, research dir., 1954-60. Served with AUS, 1942-46. Recipient Pa. Ambassador award, 1952, Nash conservation award, 1955; John Burroughs medal, 1958. Fellow Am. Ornithologists Union (Brewster award 1957); mem. Wilson Ornithol. Club, Soc. for Protection Flamingo in Bahamas, Sociedad Cubana para la Proteccion y Conservacion de la Naturaleza. Democrat. Author: (monographs) The Roseate Spoonbill, 1942, The Whooping Crane, 1952, The Flamingos, 1956; (books) The Flame Birds, 1947, On The Trail of Vanishing Birds, 1957; Birds of Caribbean, 1961. Home: Tavernier, Fla. Died June 28, 1963.

ALLEN, ROLLAND CRATEN, geologist; b. Richmond, Ind., May 24, 1881; s. George DeBolt and Florence (Brown) A.; B.A., U. of Wis., 1905 (science medal for grad. thesis), M.A., 1908; studied U. of Mich., 1901-10; D.E., Rensselaer Polytechnic Inst., 1939; m. Martha Hill, Nov. 30, 1910; children—Jean, Craten, George, Joseph, James. Teacher of Science, high sch., Plymouth, Wis., 1903-04; instr. economic geology, U. of Mich., 1908-09; state geologist of Mich., 1909-19; also special lecturer in economic geology and ore deposits, U. of Mich., 1909-14; commr. mineral statistics of Mich., 1911-19, also appraiser of mines, 1913-19; adviser to Mich. Securities Commn., and valuation engr. mines, oil and gas wells, lands and timber; cons. practics; mem. Federal Excess Profits Tax Bd., 1918-19; exam. and valuation of zinc mines in Okla., 1919; resigned as state geologist of Mich., Aug. 1919; pres. Am. Inst. of Mining and Metall. Engrs., 1937; consultatn for ferrous minerals and alloys, Office of Production Management, 1941; deputy chief Iron and Steel Branch, W.P.B., 1941-42, vice chairman Metals and Minerals, 1945; president Lake Superior Iron Ore Assn.; vice-pres., gen. mgr. of mines of Oglebay, Norton & Co.; pres. Reserve Mining Co., The Saginaw Dock and Terminal Co.; dir. Montreal Mining Co., Castile Mining Co., Bristol Mining Co., Brule Smokeless Coal Co., Ferro Engring. Co., Bristol Holding Co. vice-pres. and dir. Toledo, Lorain and Fairport Dock Co. Trustee Battelle Memorial Inst. Mem. A.A.A.S., Am. Assn. Economic Geologists, Am. Iron and Steel Inst., Geol. Soc. America. Mining and Metall. Soc., Sigma Xi, Alpha Chi Sigma. Republican. Mason. Club: Union (Cleveland, O.). Author of various repts., brochures and articles on geol. subjects. Home: Hudson, O. Office: Hanna Bldg., Cleveland, O. Died July 18, 1948; buried at Hudson, O.

ALLEN, SAMUEL JAMES MCINTOSH, prof. physics; b. Maitland, N.S., Can., Oct. 5, 1877; s. Capt. James McIntyre and Elizabeth (Lawrence) A.; B.Sc., McGill U., Montreal, P.Q., 1900, M.Sc., 1901; Ph.D., Johns Hopkins, 1906; m. Eva Blanche Sircom, of Halifax, N.S., Aug., 1910; children—James Sircom, Samuel Stephen, George Churchill, John Edward, Florence Elizabeth. Demonstrator in physics, McGill U., 1900-03; fellow Johns Hopkins, 1903-04; with U. of Cincinnati since 1906, now prof. physics. Research asso. dept. terrestrial magnetism and electricity, Carnegie Instn., Washington, D.C., 1924. Naturalized citizen of U.S., 1917. Fellow Am. Physical Soc., Ohio Acad. Science; mem. Phi Beta Kappa. Episcopalian. Clubs: Faculty, Ohio River Launch. Mem., and ex-commodore, Chester (N.S.) Yacht Club. Contbr. numerous papers on researches in X-ray, radio-activity, and kindred subjects. Research physicist with Liebel Flarzeim Co.; developed "Kuprox." Home: 2316 Auburn Crest Av., Cincinnati OH*

ALLEN, WILLIAM FITCH, educator; b. Oneonta, N.Y., Nov. 11, 1875; s. Horace Hews and Frances (Fitch) A.; student Cornell U., 1896-98; A.B., Stanford, 1900, A.M., 1902; Ph.D., U. Minn., 1915; Sc.D., U. Ore., 1945; m. Augusta Annette Nahl, Sept. 11, 1908; 1 son, Horace Hews. Research asst. to Mr. Edward P. Allis, Pacific Grove, Cal., 1901-06, to Jacques Loeb, Monterey, Cal., 1906-10; instr. zoology, U. Ill., 1910-11; instr. anatomy, U. Minn., 1911-16; prof. anatomy, head dept., U. Ore., 1916-46; prof. emeritus, 1946—. Mem. Wash., N.Y. acads. sci., Am. Assn. Anatomists, Am. Physiol. Soc., Anatomischen Gesellschaft Soc. Exptl. Biology and Medicine, A.A.A.S., Sigma Xi. Author many publs. on anatomy and physiology of nervous, blood and lymphatic systems. Home: 3947 S.E. Salmon St., Portland 15, Ore. Died Mar. 11, 1951; buried Portland Crematorium and Mausoleum.

ALLEN, WILLIAM HENRY, coll. pres.; b. Readfield (now Manchester), Me., Mar. 27, 1808; s. Jonathan and Thankful (Longley) A.; grad. Bowdoin Coll. 1833; m. Martha Richardson; 2d, Ellen Honora; 3d, Mary Frances Quincy; 4th, Anna Gamwill. Prof. chemistry and natural history Dickinson Coll., 1836-46, prof. philosophy and English lit., 1846-49; pres. Girard Coll., 1849-62, 67-82, Pa. Agrl. Coll., 1865-67. Pres. Am. Bible Soc., 1872. Died Phila., Aug. 29, 1882.

ALLEN, WILLIAM RAY, educator; b. Ossian, Ind., Mar. 8, 1885; s. Elza and Ellen (Chupp) A.; A.B., Ind. U., 1913, A.M., 1914; student Cornell, 1916-17; Ph.D.,

Ind. U., 1920; m. Lura Belle Devin, June 14, 1922; children—Martha Jane (Mrs. W. B. Jackson), Barbara Janet, Ellen Claire. Newspaper, advt. work, 1903-07; tchr., prin. Hartford City, Ind., 1907-12; asst. Carnegie Sta. Exptl. Evol., Cold Spring Harbor, L.I., N.Y., 1914; instr. zoology, Kan. State Coll., 1914-16; asst. biology, Cornell U., 1916-17; instr. Ind. U., 1918-19; traveling fellow, U. Ill., Peru, Bolivia, Chile, 1918-19, Ind. U., 1920-21; asst. prof. zoology, Municipal U. Akron, 1921-22; asst. prof. zoology, U. Ky., 1922-25, asso. prof., 1925-30, prof., 1930—, head dept., 1948-50. Mem. Am. Soc. Zoologists, Am. Ecol. Soc., Am. Microscop. Soc., Am. Soc. Ichtyologists and Herpetologist, Am. Fishery Soc., Am. Soc. Limnologists, Oceanographers, Am. Assn. U. Profs., Ind., Ky. Acads. Sci., Phi Beta Kappa (sec., pres. Ky. chpt.), Sigma Xi (treas., v.p., pres. Ky. chpt.). Author: Fishes of Western South America, 1942 (with C.H. Eigenmann); Nature Sketch Book, 1935; Laboratory Guide to Zoology, 1916. Editor: Genera Insectorum, Family Membracidae, Genera Insectorum, 1951. Home: 417 Clifton Av., Lexington, Ky. Died Apr. 7, 1955; buried Oak Lawn Cemetery, Ossian, Ind.

ALLEN, WYETH, educator; b. Milw., July 28, 1893; s. Stanton and Maria (McLaren) A.; B.Mech. Engring., U. Mich., 1915, D.Engring., 1953; m. Lillian Carnegie, Apr. 20, 1918; children—Stanton, Richard Crafts, Jean Carnegie. Foreman, Pfeiffer & Smith, 1915-16; works mgr. Allen-Bradley Co., 1916-21; resident engr. William Baum & Co., 1921-25; cons. management engr., 1925-48; exec. v.p. Globe-Union, Inc., 1948-49; pres., 1949-55; pres. Centralah Canada, Ltd., 1953-55; cons. mgmt. engring., 1955; prof. indsl. engring., chmn. depts. indsl. engring. and mech. engring. U. Mich., 1955-63; dir. Clinton Engines Corp. Prin. contract rep. ICA, Waseda U. (Tokyo, Japan) U. Mich., 1955-73. Vice pres. Am. Humanics Found.; trustee Found. Allergic Diseases. Mem. Acad. of Mgmt., 1956-73; panel mem. Am. Arbitration Assn., 1957-73. Pres. United Fund Ann Arbor, Barton Hills Assn.; dir. Ann Arbor Community Welfare Council; vice chmn. region 7, hon. life mem. exec. bd. Boy Scouts America. Mem. Am. Inst. Indsl. Engrs., Inst. Mgmt. Engrs., Am. Soc. M.E., A.A.A.S., Soc. Engring. Edn., Am. Soc. Advancement Mgmt., Am. Ordnance Assn., Navy League, U. Mich. Alumni Assn. (life dir.), Inst. Mgmt. Scis., Mil. Operations Research Society America, Sigma Xi, Delta Phi, Tau Beta Pi, Alpha Tau Sigma, Pi Tau Theta. Clubs: University, Rotary; Raquet; Barton Hills Country. Home: Ann Arbor MI Died May 2, 1973.

ALLEN, ZACHARIAH, scientist, inventor; b. Providence, R.I., Sept. 15, 1795; s. Zachariah and Anne (Crawford) A.; grad. Brown U., 1813; m. Eliza Arnold, 1817. Admitted to R.I. bar, 1815; constructed 1st central furnace system for heating houses by hot air, 1821; mem. Town Council of Providence, 1822; inventor automatic steam-engine cut off, 1834; founder Mfrs. Mut. Fire Ins. Co., 1835. Died Providence, Mar. 17, 1882.

ALLEY, JOHN BASSETT, congressman, businessman; b. Lynn, Mass., Jan. 7, 1817; attended common schs. Apprenticed to shoemaker, 1831-36; moved to Cincinnati, 1836, freighted mdse. up and down Mississippi River; entered shoe mfg. bus., Lynn, Mass., 1838; established hide and leather house, Boston, 1847; mem. 1st bd. alderman, Lynn, 1850; mem. Gov.'s Council, 1847-51; mem. Mass. Senate, 1852; mem. Mass. Constl. Conv., 1853; mem. U.S. Ho. of Reps. (Republican) from Mass., 36-39th congresses, 1859-67; became connected with Union Pacific R.R.; ret. from bus., 1886; took European trip. Died West Newton, Mass., Jan. 19, 1896; buried Pine Grove Cemetery, Lynn.

ALLING, ARTHUR NATHANIEL, ophthalmologist; b. New Haven, Conn., July 1, 1862; s. George and Mary (Alverson) A.; A.B., Yale, 1886; Sheffield Scientific Sch. (Yale), 1886-87; M.D., Coll. Phys. and Surg. (Columbia), 1891; m. Francella Walker, Oct. 27, 1887; 1 dau., Helen Frances. Practiciing New Haven, Conn., since 1893; asst. surgeon to N.Y. Ophthalmic and Aural Hosp., 1897-1901; lecturer opthalmology , 1893-94, instr. 1894-1902, prof., 1902-38, emeritus since 1938, Yale; chief of eye clinic, New Haven Dispensary since 1896; ophthalmic surgeon, New Haven Hosp., 1905-38, cons. ophthalmic surgeon since 1938; cons. ophthalmologist, Meridian Hosp. Mem. Am. Opthal. Soc., N.Y. Ophthal. Soc., City County and State Med. Socs., Phi Beta Kappa, fellow N.Y. Acad. Medicine, Am. Coll. Surgeons, A.M.A. Republican. Clubs: Graduate, New Haven Lawn, Yale Faculty. Author: Diseases of the Eye, 1905; Ocular Theapeutics, 1923. Home: 190 St. Ronan St. Office: 257 Church St., New Haven Conn. Died Mar. 15, 1949.

ALLING, HAROLD LATTIMORE, geologist; b. Rochester, N.Y., Feb. 7, 1888; s. Joseph Tilden and Rose (Lattimore) A.; B.S., U. of Rochester, 1915; A.M., Columbia, 1917, Ph.D., 1920; m. Merle Kolb, Aug. 23, 1922; children-Joanna Tilden (Mrs. James D. Secrest), Rosamond Lattimore (Mrs. Philip J. Secrest), Norman Larrabee. Geologist, N.Y. State Museum, 1917-20; instr. geology, U. of Rochester, 1920-23, asst. prof., 1923-24, prof., 1924-53, now prof. emeritus. Dir. Alling & Corry Co., 1938-45. Sec. Rochester Acad. Sci., 1920-21; chmn. Feldspar Com. of Natural Research Council, 1927-32; dir. Ward's Natural Sci. Establishment, 1931-40. Trustee Nat. Sci. Assn. of the Catskills, 1945-49. Fellow A.A.A.S., Mineral. Soc. Am. (v.p. 1936), Geological Soc. of Am.; mem. Seismol. Soc. Am., Soc. Econ. Geol., Am. Geophys. Union, Soc. Econ. Paleontologists and Mineralogists. N.Y. State Geol. Assn. (pres. 1932, 41), Am. Inst. Mining Metallurgical and Petroleum Engineers, The Geochemical Society, Psi Upsilon, Sigma Xi. Republican. Presbyn. Author: Interpretative Petrology of the Igneous Rocks, 1936; An Orientation in Science (with others), 1938; The Adirondack Magnetite Deposits, Chapter in Ore Deposits, as Related to Structural Features, 1942. Contbr. geol. papers to Journal Geology, Am. Jour. Science, Am. Mineralogist, etc. Has written many papers and articles on geol. subjects. Home: 155 W. Jefferson Rd., Pittsford, N.Y. Died July 27, 1960.

ALLIOT, HECTOR, archeologist; b. Chateau des Forestiers, Gironde, France, Nov. 20, 1862; s. Jehan Hector and Lelia (Boymier) A.; ed. Lycée Bordeaux; Acad. of Medicine, Sch. of Tech., Montpelier (France); A.B., U. of France; D.Sc., U. of Lombardy; m. Laurena Moore, Aug. 20, 1893. Associated with Farah Pasha in explorations at Tyre, Asia Minor, 1891; dir. Cliff Dwellers exploration, Chicago Expn., 1893; prof. art history, U. of Southern Calif., 1908-19; dir. Southwest Mus., Nov. 1, 1909—. Trustee Los Angeles Sch. of Art and Design; v.p. Southern Calis. Acad. Sciences; sec. Los Angeles Soc. Archaeol. Inst. America; sec.-treas. Hispanic Soc. of Calif. Officer d'Académie, 1907; Knight Comdr. O. of M. (P.M.), 1910; officer de l'Instruction Publique, 1913. Deviser of Metrical Color Standard, Marine Colormeter, 1910; del. Internat. Congress Geog., Rome, 1911. Author: Bibliography of Arizona. Home: Los Angeles, Calif. Died Feb. 15, 1919.

ALLIS, EDWARD PHELPS, mfr.; b. Casenovia, N.Y., May 12, 1824; s. Jere and Mary (White) A.; grad. Union Coll., Schenectady, N.Y., 1845; m. Margaret Watson, 1848, 12 children. Built and operated tanneries, Two Rivers, Wis., 1846-54; banker and realtor, 1854-61; established Reliance Iron Works, Milw., 1861, expanded to largest indsl. plant in Midwest, produced machinery for flour mill roller process, also Corliss engine; unsuccessful candidate for gov. Wis., 1877. Died Milw., Apr. 1, 1889.

ALLIS, EDWARD PHELPS, JR.; scientist; b. Milwaukee, Sept., 14, 1851; s. Edward Phelps and Margaret Maria (Watson) A.; C.E., Delaware Lit. Inst., Franklin (N.Y., 1867; Antioch, (O.) Coll., 1867-68, Mass. Inst. Tech., 1868-71; LL.D., U. of Wis., 1903; asso. in zoölogy, Harvard U. Mus., 1911; M.D., U. of Gröningen, 1914; m. Amédine Sgrèna, of Paris, France, Oct. 28, 1896 (died 1905); children—Maude, William Phelps. Mem. Edward P. Allis & Co., Milwaukee, 1871-89, v.p. since 1889. Established the Lake (now Allis Research) Lab., 1887; removed it to Mentone, France, 1890, and since conducted spl. research in vertebrate morphology. Was editor, with Dr. Charles Otis Whitman, Journal of Morphology, from 1887, mem. editorial bd., 1908-11. Fellow A.A.A.S., N.Y. Acad. Science, Zoöl. Soc., Linnean Soc., Soc. of Arts, Royal Micros. Soc., Royal Metrol. Soc. (London) Anat. Soc. Great Britain and Ireland, North British Acad.; mem. Assn. Am. Anatomists, Am. Soc. Naturalists, Boston Soc. Natural History, Am. Geog. Soc., Ecol. Soc. America, Am. Soc. Mammalogists, Founders and Patriots of America, Inst. Francais Aux E'ats-Unis Société Astronomique de France, Sociétz Meteo rologique de France, Nat. Economic League, Am. Bison Soc., Soc. Am. Mil. Engrs., Am. Micros. Soc., Am. Genetic Assn., British Inst. of Philos. Studies, Priz Lallemand, Paris (with title Laureat de l'Institut); Palmes Paris (with title officer d'Academie); Chevalier de la Légion d'Honneur, France; etc. Clubs: University (Madison, Wis.), Authors', Royal Societies (London). Home: Palais de Carnoles, Mentone, France.

ALLISON, JAMES BOYD, educator; b. Punxsutawney, Pa., Jan. 28, 1901; s. James Boyd and Elizabeth (Robinson) A.; B.S., Pa. State U., 1923; Ph.D., Ia. State Coll., 1927; m. Dorothy Lewis, Dec. 31, 1926; children—Marjorie (wife of Dr. Arthur Marshall Smith), Dorothy (Mrs. D. Jeffrey Bostock). Asst. Ia. State Coll., 1923-26, indsl. fellow, 1926-27; instr. biochemistry Rutgers U., 1927-29, asst. prof., 1929-41, asso. prof., 1941-45, prof. physiology and biochemistry, 1945—, dir. Bur. Biol. Research, 1944-64; director of the research council, 1959—; lecturer physiology College Phys. and Surg., Columbia, 1943-45. Liaison, sci. adv. bd. Q.M. Food and Container Inst., 1948, chmn. subcom. nutrition Q.M. Inst., 1954—; chmn. com. amino acids Food and Nutrition Bd., 1954; com. protein requirements FAO, 1955; mem. food nutrition bd. NRC, 1956; mem.-at-large Council of Gordon Research Conf., 1956; tech. adv. com. Instituto de Nutricion de Centro America y Panama, 1956. Mem. bd. health, Highland Park, N.J., 1955. Trustee Middlesex Gen. Hosp., New Brunswick, N.J. Mem. Am. Assn. Cancer Research, Am. Chem. Soc., A.A.A.S., Soc. Exptl. Biol. and Medicine, N.Y. Acad. Sci. (pres. 1962), Am. Inst. Chemists (chmn. N.J., 1953-54), Am. Society Biological Chemists, American Institute Nutrition (treasurer 1959-62), Sigma Xi, Phi Beta Kappa, Phi Lambda Upsilon, Alpha Zeta, Phi Kappa Phi, Gamma Sigma Delta. Presbyn. (elder, trustee). Rotarian (pres. New Brunswick 1953-54). Mem. editorial bd. Jour. Nutrition, 1952-56. Home: 409 Grant Av., Highland Park, N.J. Office: Bureau of Biological Research, Rutgers U., New Brunswick, N.J. Died Sept. 25, 1964; buried Circle Hill Cemetery, Punxsutawney, Pa.

ALLISON, NATHANIEL, surgeon; b. St. Louis, Mo., May 22, 1876; s. James W. and Addie (Schultz) A.; Harvard Coll., 1900; M.D., Harvard Medical Sch., 1901; m. Marion Aldrich, 1909. Practiced at St. Louis, 1903-23; formerly asso. surgeon St. Louis Children's Hosp. and Barnes Hosp.; dean and prof. orthopedic surgery, Washington U., 1919-23; later prof. orthopedic surgery, Harvard Med. Sch.; became prof. surgery U. of Chicago, in charge Div. Orthopedic Surgery; was chief of orthopedic service, Mass. Gen. Hosp., Boston; chief surgeon N.E. Peabody Home for Crippled Children. Fellow Am. Acad. Arts and Letters. Awarded D.S.M. for services as chief of orthopedic surgery, First Army, A.E.F., 1917-19. Presbyn. Home: Chicago, Ill. Died Aug. 30, 1931.

ALLISON, RICHARD, army med. officer; b. nr. Goshen, Orange County, N.Y., 1757. Surgeon's mate 5th Pa. Regiment, Continental Army, 1778-83; transferred to 1st Pa. Regiment, 1783; surgeon's mate 1st Inf. Regt., U.S. Army, 1784-88, promoted regtl. surgeon, 1788; stationed at Ft. Bibiography; went to Europe, 1888; works include: campaigns under Gen. Josiah Harmar and Gen. Arthur St. Clair; apptd. surgeon to Legion of U.S., 1792, honorably discharged when Legion dissolved, 1796; practiced medicine, Cincinnati, 1796-1816. Died Cincinnati, Mar. 22, 1816; buried Wesleyan Cemetery, Cumminsville, O.

ALLISON, SAMUEL KING, educator; b. Chgo., Nov. 13, 1900; s. Samuel Buell and Caroline (King) A.; Ph.D., U. Chgo., 1923; m. Helen Catherine Campbell, May 28, 1928; children—Samuel Campbell, Catherine King (Mrs. David Marshall). Fellow NRC, Harvard, 1923-25, Carnegie Found., 1925-26, U. Cal., 1926-30; with U. Chgo., since 1930. Cons., Nat. Def. Research Com. 1940-41; Uranium Com., O.S.R.D., 1941-42; dir. chem. div., Metall. Lab., U. of Chicago, 1942-43; dir. Metall. Lab. U. Chgo., 1943-44; chmn. tech. and scheduling com. Los Alamos Project, 1944-45; dir. Inst. for Nuclear Studies, 1946-57; prof. physics U. Chgo., 1943—, Frank P. Hixon distinguished service prof., 19S9; dir. Farrington Mfg. Co. Chmn. nuclear sci. com. NRC, 1960—. Fellow Am. Phys. Soc.; mem. Nat. Acad. Scis. (chmn. phys. sect.), Awarded Medal for Merit, Maj. General Leslie R. Groves, at U. Chgo., with citation from Pres. Truman, Jan. 12, 1946; Commendador en el Orden Alfonso El Sabio, 1960. Club: Quadrangle. Author: (with A. H. Compton) X-Rays in Theory and Experiment, 1935. Address: Enrico Ferm Institute for Nuclear Studies, U. Chgo., Chgo. Died Sept. 15, 1965.

ALLPORT, GORDON WILLARD, psychologist; b. Montezuma, Ind., Nov. 11, 1897; s. John Edwards and Nellie Edith (Wise) A.; A.B., Harvard, 1919, A.M., 1921, Ph.D., 1922; grad. work U. of Berlin and U. of Hamburg, 1922-23, Cambridge U., 1923-24; L.H.D. (hon.), Boston U., 1958; Ohio Wesleyan U., 1962; D.Sc., Colby Coll., 1964; D.Litt. (hon.), Durham U. (Eng.), 1965; m. Ada Lufkin Gould, June 30, 1925; 1 son, Robert Bradlee. Instr. in English, Robert Coll., Istanbul, Turkey, 1919-20; instr. in social ethics, Harvard U., 1924-26; asst. prof. in psychology, Dartmouth Coll., 1926-30; asst. prof. psychology, Harvard U., 1930-36, asso. prof., 1937, prof. psychology since 1942. Mem. S.A.T.C. Past mem. nat. com. for UNESCO. Pres. Edn. Exchange Greater Boston; past dir. Nat. Opinion Research Center; past mem. Social Sci. Research and Nat. Research Councils. Recipient Gold Medal award Am. Psychol. Found., 1963. Hon. fellow Brit. Pyschol. Soc.; hon. mem. Spanish, Italian psychological societies, Deutsche Gesellschaft fur Psychologie, Österreichische Arztegesellschaft fur Psuchotherapie; mem. Am. (mem. council 1936-38; pres. 1939), Eastern (pres. 1943) psychol. assns., Phi Beta Kappa. Episcopalian. Clubs: Faculty, Harvard of N.Y. Author: Studies in Expressive Movement (with P. E. Vernon), 1933; The Psychology of Radio (with H. Cantril), 1935; Trait-Names: A Psycho-lexical study with H. S. Odbert), 1936; Personality—a Psychological Interpretation, 1937; Psychology of Rumor (with L. Postman), 1947; The Individual and His Religion, 1950; The Nature of Personality, 1950; The Nature of Prejudice, 1954; Becoming: Basic Considerations for a Psychology of Personality, 1955; Personality and Social Encounter, 1960; Pattern and Growth of Personality, 1961; Letters From Jenny, 1965. Editor Jour. Abnormal and Social Psychology, 1937-49. Home: 386 School St., Watertown 72, Mass. Office: Harvard U., Cambridge, Mass. Died. Oct. 1967.

ALLSTON, ROBERT FRANCIS WITHERS, planter, gov. S.C.; b. All Saints Parish, S.C., Apr. 21, 1801; s. Benjamin and Charlotte Anne (Allston) A.; grad. U.S. Mil. Acad., 1821; m. Adele Petigru, 1832. Planter, All Saints Parish; surveyor gen. S.C., 1823-77; elected to lower house S.C. Gen. Assembly, 1826-32; del. to Nashville Conv., 1850; mem. S.C. Senate, 1834-56, speaker, 1847-56; gov. S.C., 1856-58. Author: Introduction and Planting of Rice in South Carolina, 1843. Died Georgetown, S.C., Apr. 7, 1864.

STATE BOARD FOR TECHNICAL AND COMPREHENSIVE EDUCATION
7698
Beaufort TEC

ALMERT, HAROLD, consulting engr.; b. Chicago, June 2, 1876; s. Andrew and Wilhelmina (Walhstrom) A.; ed. in engring., in Chicago, 8 yrs., law, 3 yrs., accounting, 2 yrs.; m. Anita C. Tiedeman, of Chicago, Dec. 28, 1907; children—John Gordon, Jane Louise. Consulting engring. practice in Chicago since 1909; tech. counsel to a number of the largest utilities and industrial companies, including Commonwealth Edison Co., Pub. Service Co. of Northern Ill. (Chicago), Washington Ry. & Electric Co., Potomac Electric Power Co. (Washington), etc.; with staff has constructed or appraised over $1,000,000,000 worth of public utility and industrial plants and approved the issue of over $500,000,000 par value of securities. Developed a chem. treatment for improvement of pig iron and gray foundry iron; invented device for converting hard coal burners to soft coal heaters, soot destroyer, etc. Patentee of the Almert Central Home Service plan. Dir. of conservation U.S. Fuel Administration for Ill., during the war. Mem. Am. Assn. Engrs. (ex-pres.), Am. Soc. C.E., Western Soc. Engrs., Am. Soc. M.E., Am. Inst. E.E., Nat. Elec. Light Assn., Am. Gas Assn. Republican. Clubs: Electric, Lincoln Park Gun, The Indians, South Shore Country, Midday (Chicago); Engineers' (New York). Home: 119 E. 84th St., New York NY

ALPERS, WILLIAM CHARLES, chemist; b. Harburg, Germany, July 7, 1851; s. Julius and Elise (Nonnenkamp) A.;B.Sc., Poly. Inst. Hanover, Germany; studied U. of Göttingen; came to America, 1872; D.Sc., New York U., 1890; m. Bertha Guder, Oct. 29, 1885 (dec.); m. 2d, Miss M. Van Damm, 1910. Pahrmicist Bayónne, N.J., 1879-97; conductor Merck's Chem. and Bacteriol. Lab., 1897-99; pres. Alpers Chem. Co., 1901—. Alpers Pharmacy, 1902. Dean Sch. of Pharmacy, Western Reserve U., 1913—. Mem. N.J. State Bd. Pharmacy, 1893-97. Author: The Pharmicist at Work; The Medicinal Plants of Staten Island. Home: Cleveland, O. Died 1917.

ALSBERG, C(ARL) LUCAS, biochemist; b. New York, N.Y., Apr. 2, 1877; s. Meinhard and Bertha (Baruch) A.; A.B., Columbia, 1896, A.M., 1900; M.D., Coll. of Phys. and Surg. (Columbia), 1900; univs. of Strassburg and Berlin, Germany, 1900-03; m. Emma B. Peebles. Asst. in physiol. chem., 1902-05, instr. in biol. chem., 1905-08, Harvard; chem. biologist Bur. Chem., 1912-21, U.S. Dept. Agr.; dir. Stanford Food Research Inst., 1921-37, consultant, 1937—; dean of grad. study Stanford, 1927-33; dir. Giannini Foundation of Agrl. Economics, U. of California. Investigator U.S. Bureau of Fisheries, 1906-08. Home: Berkeley, Calif. Died Nov. 1, 1940.

ALSOP, GEORGE, author; b. Eng., 1638. Came to Am., 1658. Author: A Character of the Province of Mary-Land, wherein is Described in four distinct Parts, (Viz.) I. The Scituation, and plenty of the Province. II. The Laws, Customs, and natural Demeanor of the Inhabitant. III. The worst and best Usage of a Mary-Land Servant, opened in view. IV The Traffique and vendable Commodities of the Country. Also a small Treatise on the wilde and naked Indians (of Susquehanokes) of Mary-Land, their Customs, Manners, Absurdities & Religion. Together with a Collection of Historical Letters, 1666.

ALTER, DAVID, inventor; b. Westmoreland County, Pa., Dec. 3, 1807; s. John and Eleanor (Sheetz) A.; grad. Reformed Med. Coll., N.Y.C., 1831; m. Laura Rowley, 1832; m. 2d, Elizabeth A. Rowley, 1844; 11 children. Invented an electric clock, model of electric locomotive; invented elec. telegraph, 1836; discovered method of purifying bromine, method of obtaining coal oil from coal, 2d law of spectrum analysis (various elemental gases have spectra peculiar to themselves). Died Sept. 18, 1881.

ALTER, DINSMORE, astronomer; b. Colfax, Wash., Mar. 28, 1888; s. Joseph and Jeannette (Copley) A.; B.S., Westminster Coll., New Wilmington, Pa., 1909; M.S., U. of Pittsburgh, 1910; Ph.D., U. of Calf., 1916; D.Sc., Monmouth Coll., 1941; m. Ada McClelland, Dec. 26, 1910; children—Helen Jeannette, Dinsmore (dec.). Instr. and adj. prof. physics and astronomy, U. of Ala., 1911-14; instr. astronomy, U. of Calif., 1914-17; asst. prof. of astronomy, U. of Kan., 1917-19, asso. prof., 1919-24, prof., 1924-36; dir. Griffith Observatory, Los Angeles, 1935-58, dir. emeritus, 1958. Served to maj. C.A., U.S. Army, World War I; col. T.C. Reserve; on active service, col. T.C., A.U.S., 1942-1947, World War II. Fellow, Royal Astron. Soc., Am. Meteorol. Soc. (v.p. 1926-27), American Geophysical Union, Institute of Math. Statistics, British Astron. Assn., Astron. Soc. of Pacific, A.A.A.S., American Astronomical Society American Legion, Forty and Eight, Sigma Xi. Democrat. United Presbyn. Contbr. to Lick Obs. bulls., Astron. Jour., numerous others. Known for original research in meteorol. periodicities and math. methods pertaining to same. John Simon Guggenheim memorial fellow in England for statistical research on rainfall, 1929-30. Home: Berkeley CA Died Sept. 1968.

ALTON, CHARLES DE LANCEY, physician; b. Kenosha, Wis., May 9, 1845; s. Conde R. and Carolan Esther (Turner) A.; ed. Woodstock Acad., Conn., 1863; Phillips Exeter Acad., 1864-65; civil engr., 1867-74; M.D., Bellevue Hosp. Med. Coll. (New York U.), 1875; interne Charity Hosp., Jersey City, N.J., 1875-76; m. Jane Gray Skinner, Sept. 3, 1878 (died Apr. 24, 1882); 2d, Minnie Moore Clarke, June 25, 1885. Med. referee for U.S. of Conn. Mut. Life Ins. Co. since 1878. Treas. 10 yrs. Hartford Med. Soc.; mem. Conn. State Med. Soc., A.M.A., Am. Climatol. Assn. of Life Ins. Med. Directors, etc. Has written: The Therapeutic Value of Mountain Forests, 1895; State Sanatoria for Tuberculosis Patients, 1900; Prophylaxis in Tuberculosis, 1905. Address: Elizabeth Park, N., Hartford, Conn.

ALVORD, CORYDON ALEXIS printer; b. Winchester, Conn., May 12, 1813; s. John and Experience 1836, 10 children. Printing apprentice, Hartford, Conn., then opened own shop, N.Y.C., 1845, specialized in unusual and illustration printing, such as facsimiles of old books and newspapers; printed Thomas Daring's Recollection of the Jersey Prison-Ship, 1865, James Parton's Life and Times of Benjamin Franklin, 1865, Greene Halleck's Fanny: A Poem, 1866; moved to Hartford, 1867, continued bus. in N.Y.C.; merged with other printing firms to form N.Y. Printing Co., 1871, City of N.Y. confiscated co. for associations with "Tweed Ring," 1871. Author: Genealogy of the Descendants of Alexander Alvord, published posthumously, 1908. Died Hartford, Nov. 28, 1874.

ALVORD, HENRY ELIJAH, organized 1895, and from then chief Dairy Div., U.S. Dept. of Agr.; b. Greenfield, Mass., Mar. 11, 1844; s. late Hon. Daniel Wells A.; s. studied at Norwich Univ. (B.S., 1863; C.E., LL.D); served as private U.S.V., 1862, to maj. 2d Mass. cav., 186S; capt. regular army, 1886-72; m. Martha Scott Swink, Sept. 6, 1866. Farmed and taught agr. Va., N.Y., Mass., Md. amd N.H.; prof. agr. Mass. Agrl. Coll., 1885-87; pres. Md. Agrl. Coll., 1887-92; pres. Assn. of Am. Agrl. colleges and Expt. Stations, 1894-95; mem. Internat. Jury (and v.p. class 40), Universal Expn., Paris, 1900; mem. Standing Commn. for Internat. Agrl. Congress. Author: Am. chapters of "Dairy Farming," 1881. Home: Lewinsville, Fairfax County, Va. Died 1904.

ALVORD, JOHN WATSON, engineer; b. Newton Centre, Mass., Jan. 25, 1861; s. Rev. John Watson and Myrtilla Mead (Peck) A.; ed. Howard U. Prep. Sch., 1873-74, J. W. Hunt's Normal Sch., Washington 1874-77 (hon. C.E., U. of Wis., 1913); m. Helen C. Cornell, Sept. 4, 1889 (died 1926); m. 2d, Lucy B. Pitkin, Apr. 12, 1927. Asst. engr. constrn. Hyde Park and Lake View pumping stas., Chicago water works, 1880-84; city engr. Lake View (Chicago), 1884-88; town engr., Cicero, Ill., 1889-90; chief engr. surveys Chicago Exposition, 1890-93, medal as one of 70 designers; also chief engineer Hygeia Water Co., 1891-92; consulting engr. since 1894, to over 300 municipalities on sewerage works, water supply, sewage disposal, water power, appraisal bds., etc., among these Ill. and Mich. Canal, 1897-1901, City of Columbus, O., 1898, Dubuque Water Co., 1897, Gen. Electric Co., Des Moines, Ia., 1904, U.S. Steel Corp., Gary, Ind., 1907, City of Grand Rapids, Mich., and Des Moines (Ia.) Water Co., 1907, Milwaukee, 1910, Merriam Commn., Chicago, 1910: flood commn., Dayton, 1913, Columbus, 1913; Citizens' Terminal Plan Com., 1914, Ill. State Bd. of Natural Resources and Conservation, 1918. Supervising engr. Camp Grant (Ill.), Camp La Cruses, P.R.; cons. engr. Gt. Lakes Naval Tr. Sta. and chief engr. U.S. Housing Corp., 1917-19. Pres. Am. Water Works Assn., 1910; hon. mem. Am. Soc. C.E. (dir. 1918), Ill. Soc. Engrs. (pres. 1904-06), N.E. Water Works Association, Wester Soc. Engrs. (pres. 1910; Washington award for 1929); fellow A.A.A.S.; mem. Ill. Soc. S.A.R., Soc. Mayflower Descendants. Clubs: Engineers', Union League. Author: Relief from Floods, 1918. Office: Civic Opera Bldg., Chicago, Ill. Died July 31, 1943.

ALWAY, FREDERICK JAMES, chemist; b. Rockford, Ont., Can., May 28, 1874; s. Frederick and Rachel (Mason) A.; B.A., U. of Toronto, 1894 (D.Sc., 1927); Ph.D., Heidelberg U., 1897; m. Eva M. Cook, 1898; children—Mrs. Filomena Erica Robinson, Lazelle Martha and Leonore Katherine (twins), Mrs. Fredrica Jane Bull, Robert Hamilton. Prof. chemistry, Neb. Wesleyan U., 1898-1906; prof. agrl. chemistry, U. of Neb., 1906-13; prof. soil chemistry and chief div. of soils, U. of Minn., 1913-42; prof. emeritus since 1942. Fellow A.A.A.S.; mem. Am. Chem. Soc., Am. Soc. Agronomy, Soil Science Soc. America, Sigma Xi; corr. mem. Swedish Peat Soc. Baptist. Author numerous papers on organic and soil chemistry and soil physics. Home: 1386 Grantham Av., St Paul MN

ALWOOD, WILLIAM BRADFORD, Horticulturist; b. Delta, O., Aug. 11, 1859; s. David William and Ann Eliza (Bradley) A.; student Ohio State U., 1882-85, Columbian (now George Washington) U., 1886-88, Royal Pomol. Sch., Germany, 1900-01, Inst. Pasteur, Paris, 1907; m. Seffie S. Gantz, Mar. 6, 1884; children—Hubert Jackson, Helen Anna, Nellie Sarah, Mabel Seffie, William Bradford (dec.), Lewis Gantz (dec.), Esther (dec.), Richard Olney. Taught country sch., 1879-81; supt. Ohio Agrl. Expt. Sta., 1882-86; spl. agt. U.S. Dept. Agr., 1886-88; vice-dir. Va. Agrl. Expt. Sta., 1888-1904; conducted investigations in horticulture and mycology, 1888-1904; porf. horticulture and allied subjects, Va. Poly. Inst., 1891-1904; in charge investigations on fermentation of fruit products for Bur. of Chemistry, U.S. Dept. of Agr., 1900-06; enological chemist, 1907-14; fruit grower, 1914. V.p. Internat. Congress on Agrl. Edn., Paris, 1900; mem. Internat. Jury of Awards, St. Louis Expn., 1904; del. U.S. Dept. Agr. to Internat. Congress on Viticulture, Frances, 1907, and v.p.; pres. Internat. Congress Viticulture, San Francisco, 1915. Awarded Gold Medal and Commemorative Medal, St. Louis Expn., 1904; decorated by French Govt, with Corss, Officier du Mérite Agricole, 1907; silver medal and diploma, Nat. Agrl. Soc., France. Fellow A.A.A.S., Royal Hort. Soc., Great Britain; mem. Permanent Internat. Commn. on Viticulture, Nat. Council of Horticulture, 1907, Société des Chemistes Experts de France; mem. nat. council Nat. Econ. League, Presbyterian. Mason. Author many pamphlets and bulls, on hort. subjects and the chem. composition of apples and grapes, and composition of wines and ciders fermented with pure yeasts. Awarded certificate Meritorious Services to Agriculture by Va. Poly. Inst., 1923. Address: Greenwood, Va. Died Apr. 13, 1946.

AMBERG, EMIL otologist; b. at Santa Fe, New Mexico, May 1, 1868; s. Jacob and Minna (Loewenbein) A.; grad. Real Gymnasium, Elberfield, Germany, 1887, Gymnasium, Arnsberg, 1888, U. of Heidelberg, 1894; post grad. work Berlin and Vienna; m. Cecile Siegel, Nov. 16, 1909; children—Robert Siegel, Blanche Adele (Mrs. Edward T. Kelley, Jr.). Intern Mass. Charitable Eye and Ear Infirmary, Boston, 1896-97; practiced in Detroit since 1898; med. adv. bd. North End Clinic; assistant clinical professor of rhinology, laryngology and otology, Detroit Medical College (now Wayne U. Medical Sch.), 1913-14; aurist School of the Deaf; consulting otologist Grace Hospital; cons. otologist Harper Hospital. Formerly sec. of committee on interstate reciprocity, Nat. Conf. State Med. Examining and Licensing Bds.; Fellow A.A.A.S., Am. Coll. Surgeons; mem. A.M.A., Am. Otol. Soc., Acad. Ophthalmology and Otolaryngology (life), Mich. State, Wayne County med. socs., Detroit Soc. for Better Hearing (editor official publication The Rainbow), American Hearing Society, Detroit Philos. Society, Detroit Philos. Society, Detroit Otolaryngol. Soc., (ex-pres.), The Factfinders. Inventor of various surg. devices; extensive contbr. on med. and reform subjects. Home: 1244 Boston Blvd., W., Detroit 2, Mich. Died Apr. 12, 1948.

AMDUR, ISADORE, univ. prof; b. Pittsburgh, Pa., Jan. 24, 1910; s. Benjamin and Mollie (Silberblatt) A.; B.S., U. of Pittsburgh, 1930, M.S., 1930, Ph.D., 1932; m. Alice Pauline Steiner, June 16, 1935; children—Stephen Benjamin, Nicholas John. Special lecturer U. of Pittsburgh, summer, 1932; nat. research fellow in chemistry, Mass. Inst. of Tech., 1932-34, instr., 1934-40, asst. prof., 1940-45, asso. prof., 1945-51, prof. phys. chemistry, 1951-70; vis. scientist U.S.-Japan Coop. Program sponsored by National Science Foundation, Kyoto University, 1965-66. Honorary president International Committee of High and Intermediate Energy Molecular Beams; chmn. local organizing com. VI Internat. Conf. on Physics Electronic and Atomic Collisions, 1969, mem. exec. com. for VII Conf. John Simon Guggenheim Meml. Fellow, 1955-56. Fellow Am. Phys. Soc.; mem. Am. Chem. Soc., A.A.A.S., Am. Acad. Arts and Scis. (recording sec., 1946-47, mem. council 1948-52). Sigma Xi, Phi Lambda Upsilon, Pi Lambda Phi, Phi Beta Kappa. Author: (with Gordon G. Hammes) Chemical Kinetics, 1966. Contbr. articles to sci. journals. Home: Belmont MA Died June 3, 1970.

AMEND, BERNHARD GOTTWALD, chemist; mem. firm of Eimer & Amend; v.p. German Exchange Bank; mem. N.Y. Acad. Sciences; N.Y. chpt. Am. Chem. Soc., N.Y. Mineralogical Club, Am. Chem. Soc. Residence: 120 E. 19th St. Office: 211 3d Ave., N.Y.C. Died 1917.

AMES, ADELBERT, JR., educator; b. Lowell, Mass., Aug. 19, 1880; s. Adelbert and Blanche (Butler) A.; student Phillips Andover Acad., 1896-98; A.B., Harvard, 1903, LL.B., 1906; hon. A.M., Dartmouth, 1921, LL.D., 1955; m. Fanny Vose Hazen, Jan. 3, 1920; children—Adelbert 3d, Priscilla Vose. Admitted to Mass. bar, 1906, practiced law, 1906-10; studied art and painted, 1910-14; research fellow Clark U., Worcester, Mass., 1914-17; research prof. dept. research in physiological optics Dartmouth, 1919-46; research prof. Dartmouth Eye Inst., 1946—; research dir. Inst. Asso. Research, Princeton. Served as aerial observer, U.S. Army, 1917-19. Recipient Edgar D. Tillyer medal Optical Soc. Am., 1955. Mem. Acad. Arts and Scis., Optical Soc. Am. Address: Rope Ferry Rd., Hanover, N.H. Died July 3, 1955.

AMES, EDGAR, shipbuilder; b. St. Louis, Mo., Feb. 26, 1868; s. Edgar and Lucy V. (Semple) A.; A.B., Yale, 1890; m. Anne Shaw Sheldon, July 6, 1909. Engaged in harbor improvements, Seattle, 1895-1915; pres. Ames Shipbuilding & Drydock Co., 1916—, Seattle Contract Co. Built 25 steel ships (223,000 tons dead-weight), for Govt. during World War. Republican. Episcopalian. Home: 932 13th Av., N. Office: 3200 26th Av., S.W., Seattle, Wash. Died June 28, 1944.

AMES, JAMES TYLER, mfr.; b. Lowell, Mass., May 13, 1810; s. Nathan Peabody and Phoebe (Tyler) A.; M.A. (hon.), Amherst Coll., 1863; m. Ellen Huse, 1839

3 children. Mechanic in his father's factory, Lowell, before 1829; moved (with entire family) to Chicopee Falls, Mass., 1829; formed (with brother Nathan P. Ames, Jr.) Ames Mfg. Co., specializing in cutlery and tools, 1834, expanded into mfg. of brass cannon, then became 1st sword co. in U.S.; became head of co. after death of brother, 1847-74, expanded co.'s operations, began manufacture of cotton-machinery, lathes, planes, turbine water wheels, 1849; manufactured Eldredge Sewing Machine and 1st Victor and Eagle bicycles; expanded operations to include bronze castings, before Civil War; casted Crawford Doors on East wing U.S. Capitol Bldg., statue of Washington in Boston Public Gardens, Minute Man at Concord, Mass., Lincoln Monument at Springfield, Ill.; manufactured munitions (1 of North's largest factories) during Civil War; manufactured sabers for Turkey during Russo-Turkish War, for France during Franco-Prussian War; invented (with Gen. James of Providence, R.I.) cannon-ball which necessitated rifled cannon, also invented machinery for manufacture of rifled canon. Died Feb. 16, 1883.

AMES, JOSEPH SWEETMAN, physicist; b. Manchester, Vt., July 3, 1864; s. Dr. George Lapham and Elizabeth (Bacon) A.; A.B., Johns Hopkins, 1886, fellow, 1887-88, Ph.D., 1890; LL.D., Washington Coll., 1907, U. of Pa., 1933; Johns Hopkins, 1936; m. Mrs. Mary B. (Williams) Harrison, Sept. 14, 1899 (died 1931). Asst. in physics, 1888-91, asso., 1891-93, asso. prof., 1893-99, prof. physics, 1899-1926, dir. Phsyical Lab., 1901-26, provost, 1926-29, pres., 1929-35, pres. emeritus since 1935, Johns Hopkins U. Hon. mem. Royal Instn. Great Britain; fellow Am. Acad. Arts and Sciences; mem. Nat. Acad. Sciences, Am. Phys. Soc. Mem. Nat. Advisory Com. for Aeronautics since 1917 (chmn. 1927-39); chairman foreign service committee of Nat. Research Council which visited France and Eng. in May and June, 1917, to study origin and development of scientific activities in connection with warfare. Home: 2 Charlcote Pl., Guklford, Baltimore, Md. Died June 24, 1943. *

AMES, NATHAN PEABODY, mfr.; b. Chelmsford, Mass., Sept. 1, 1803; s. Nathan Peabody and Phoebe (Tyler) A.; m. Mary Bailey, no children. Learned mechanic's trade in father's cutlery shop, Chelmsford, before 1829, inherited bus., 1829, (with brother) moved factory to Dwight Mill Bldg., Chicopee Falls, Mass., 1829-33; contbd. half of his savings to aid building of 3d Congregational Ch. of Chicopee, Mass., 1834; organized Ames Mfg. Co., Chicopee, 1834, specialized in cutlery and tools; began manufacture of brass cannon, leather belting, bells, turbine water-wheels, 1836; with boom of textile industry in New Eng., produced every type of cotton machinery; invented rotary bell-clapper; commd. by U.S. Ordnance Dept. to study arsenals and gun factories in Europe, 1840. Died Chicopee, Apr. 3, 1847.

AMES, OAKES, manufacturer, congressman; born Easton, Massachusetts, on January 10, 1804; son of Oliver and Susannah (Angier) Ames; m. Evelyn Gilmore. Controlled Oliver Ames & Sons, shovel co., 1844; dir. Emigrant Aid Co. during Kan. troubles, 1858; mem. Exec. Council Mass., 1860; mem. U.S. Ho. of Reps. from Mass., 38th-42d congresses, 1863-73; partially controlled Credit Mobilier Co., 1865; sold shares to congressmen to forestall investigation of doubtful affairs of constrn. of Union Pacific R.R., 1867-68; exposed 1872, publicly censured by vote of U.S. Congress, 1873. Died North Easton, Mass., May 8, 1873; buried Unity Cemetery, North Easton.

AMES, OAKES, botanist, trustee; b. North Easton, Mass., Sept. 26, 1874; s. Gov. Oliver and Anna Coffin Ray A.; A.B., Harvard, 1898, A.M., 1899; Sc.D., Washington U., 1938; m. Blanche Ames, May 15, 1900; children—Pauline, Oliver, Amyas, Evelyn. Asst. in botany, Harvard, 1898-1900, instr., 1900-10; asst. dir. Bot. Garden of Harvard, 1899-1900, dir. from 1901-22; apptd. asst. prof. botany, Harvard, 1915, prof. botany, 1926-32, Arnold prof. botany, 1932-35, research prof. botany, 1935-41, research prof. botany, emeritus, 1941—, curator Bot. Mus., Harvard, 1923-27; supr. Bot. Mus., Arnold Arboretum, Atkins Inst. Arnold Arboretum, Cuba (Harvard), 1927-35; dir. Bot. Mus., 1936-45, asso. dir., 1945—, also chmn. Council Bot. Collections, Harvard, 1926-35; dir. 1st Nat. Bank of Easton. Awarded gold medal for eminent service to orchidology, Am. Orchid Soc., 1924; Centennial medal for same, Mass. Hort. Soc., 1929; George Robert White medal of honor for eminent service in horticulture, 1935. Fellow A.A.A.S., Linnaean Soc. London, Am. Acad. Arts and Scis., Am. Orchid Soc. (v.p.); mem. Am. Soc. Naturalists, N.Y. Acad. Scis., Nat. Inst. Social Scis., N.E. Bot. Club, Mass. Horticultural Soc., Boston Soc. Natural History, Washington Acad. Scis., Biol. Soc. Washington, Assn. Internat. des Botanistes, Orchid Circle of Ceylon, Canal Zone Orchid Soc. (hon. pres.), Sigma Xi, Unitarian. Club: Harvard. Author numerous papers mainly dealing with orchids, in botany periodicals, and contbrs. on orchid flora of Fla., serial work entitled "Orchidaceae" (7 vols.); also Enumeration of the Orchids of the U.S., Can., Economic Annuals and Human Cultures, 1939. Home: "Borderland," North Easton, Mass.; and Ormond, Fla. Office: 81 Ames Bldg., Boston. Died Apr. 28, 1950; buried North Easton, Mass.

AMES, OLIVER, mfr., railroad ofcl.; b. Plymouth, Mass., Nov. 5, 1807; s. Oliver and Susannah (Angier) A.; ed. Franklin Acad. of North Andover; m. Sarah Lothrop, children—Helen, Frederick L. Mem. Mass. Senate, 1852-54, 58-60; engaged in building Easton Branch R.R., 1855; acting pres. Union Pacific R.R., 1866-68, pres., 1868-71; not involved in scandals of Credit Mobilier (which financed Union Pacific R.R.); trustee Taunton Insane Asylum; dir. Atlantic & Pacific R.R., Kansas Pacific R.R., Denver Pacific R.R., v.p. Mass. Total Abstinence Soc. Died Mar. 9, 1877.

AMMANN, OTHMAR HERMANN, civil engr.; b. Schaffhausen, Switzerland, Mar. 26, 1879; s. Emmanuel and Emilie Rosa (Labhardt) A.; C.E., Swiss Fed. Poly. Inst., Zurich, 1902, Dr. Tech. Scis., 1930; Dr. Engring., N.Y.U., 1931, Bklyn. Poly. Inst., 1956; Sc.M., Yale, 1932; Dr. Engring., Pa. Mil. Coll., 1934; Sc.D., Columbia, N.Y.C., 1941, Fordham U., 1964; m. Lilly Selma Wehrli, July 24, 1905 (dec. 1933); children—Werner, George Andrew, Margaret; m. 2d, Klary Vogt Noetzli, 1935. Came to U.S., 1904, naturalized, 1924. Investigation, design and bldg. of bridges, others, Europe, U.S., 1902-23; asst. chief engr. on design and constrn. Hell Gate Bridge, N.Y.C., 1912-18; cons. engr., N.Y.C., 1923-25; chief engr. bridges, 1925-30, chief engr. Port of N.Y. Authority, 1930-39, in gen. charge planning and constrn. Outerbridge Crossing and Goethals Bridge across Arthur Kill, arch bridge across Kill van Kull at Bayonne, N.J., George Washington Bridge and Lincoln Tunnel across Hudson River at N.Y., other projects; mem. bd. engrs. in charge Golden Gate Bridge, San Francisco, 1929-36; chief engr. Triborough Bridge. Authority in charge planning and constrn. Triborough Bridge and Bronx-Whitestone Bridge, both across East River, N.Y.C., 1934-39; cons. engr., N.Y.C., 1939-46; partner Ammann & Whitney, cons. engrs., 1946—; prin. projects include Verrazono-Narrows Bridge, Throgs Neck Bridge, N.Y., Walt Whitman Bridge, Phila., N.J., Conn. turnpikes Dulles Internat. Airport, Washington, 600 foot radio telescope for USN. Fellow N.Y. Acad. Scis.; mem. Am. Soc. C.E. (hon.), Swiss Soc. Architects and Engrs. (hon.), Am. Inst. Cons. Engrs. (award merit 1965), Am. Ry. Engring. Assn., Am. Soc. Testing Materials, Inst. Civil Engrs. Gt. Britain. Awarded Thomas Fitch Rowland prize, 1918, Ernest E. Howard award Am. Soc. C.E., Nat. Medal of Sci., Howard S. Cullman Distinguished Service medal, 1964; Engr. of Year award N.Y. State Soc. Profl. Engrs., 1965; numerous other awards. Club: Engineers. Home: Kenilworth Rd., Rye, N.Y. Died Sept. 22, 1965.

AMMEN, DANIEL, naval officer; b. Ohio, May 16, 1819; s. David and Sally (Houtz) A.; m. Mary Jackson; m. 2d, Zoe Atocha, Apr. 11, 1866; 5 children. Commd. midshipman U.S. Navy, advanced through grades to rear adm.; in charge of Bur. Yards and Docks, Bur. Navigation; sec. Isthmian Canal Commn., 1872-76; fought in battles of Port Royal (1861), Ft. McAllister (1863), Ft. Fisher (1864); ret. as rear adm., 1878. Author: The Atlantic Coast, 1883: The Old Navy and the New, 1891. Died July 11, 1898.

AMOUR, ALLISON VINCENT, plant and archaeol. research; b. Chicago, Ill., Mar. 18, 1863; s. George and Barbara (Allison) A.; grad. Harvard Sch., Chicago, 1880; B.A., Yale, 1884; m. Anne Louise Kelley, Dec. 10, 1885 (died 1890). Conducted 8 voyages for plant research, U.S. Dept. Agr., also several voyages in archaeol. research. Vol. aid (temp. service) Naval Intelligences, World War. Awarded Meyer medal by Am. Genetic Assn. for plant exploration. Republican. Home: New York, N.Y. Died Mar. 6, 1941.

ANAST, JAMES LOUIS, engineering executive; born Columbus, O., May 27, 1918; s. Louis D. and Kally (Drosos) A.; B.E.E., Ohio State U., 1940; m. Marie Ellen Pirpiris, Apr. 25, 1946; 1 son, Louis J. Research engr. U.S. Air Force, 1946-49, chief engr. All Weather Flying Center, 1949-52; dir. missile intelligence Hdqrs. USAFE, 1952-53; chief systems engr. Air Navigation Development Bd., 1954-55; tech. asst. to spl. asst. to Pres. for aviation planning, 1955-56; tech. dir. Airways Modernization Bd., 1957-58; v.p. tech. planning Lear, Inc., 1958, pres. 1959; dir. Bur. Research and Devel., Fed. Aviation Agy., 1959-61; director of European operations for Ling Temco Vought Corporation, 1961—. Served from pvt. to lt. col., AUS, 1940-46, 1952-53. Decorated Air Medal. Mem. Sigma Epsilon Phi. Mem. Greek Orthodox Ch. Developed 1st translantic automatic flight system, 1947. Home: 15 Rue Vineuse, Paris, France. Died Aug. 6, 1964; buried Cabourg, Calvados, France.

ANDEREGG, FREDERICK, prof. mathematics; b. Meiringen, Switzerland, June 11, 1852; s. Andrew and Magdelena (Otth) A.; brought to America, 1862; A.B., Oberlin Coll., 1885; A.M., 1889; A.M., Harvard, 1889; studied U. of Berne, Switzerland, 1903-04; m. Anna E. Krebs (died 1879); m. 2d. Mary Osband Swift. Prof. mathematics. Oberlin Coll., 1890-1920. Conglist. Joint Author: Anderegg and Roe's Trigonometry, 1896, rev. edit., 1913. Home: Oberlin, O. Died Oct. 9, 1922.

ANDERS, JAMES MESCHTER, M.D.; b. Fairview, Village, lMontgomery County, Pa., July 22, 1854; s. Samuel Drescher and Christina (Meschter) A.; ed. acad. dept. pf a theol. sem. at Wadsworth, O.; Ph.D., U. of Pa., M.D., 1877; m. Margaret Wunderlich, Apr. 30, 1902. Visiting phys., P.E. Hosp., 1878-92;was mem. visiting med. staff Phila. Hosp., many years, later mem. med. advisory board; prof. medicine, Medico-Chirurg. Coll., 1892-1918; prof. medicine and clin. medicine, Medico-Chirurg Coll., Grad. Sch. U. of Pa., Phila., 1917-28, emeritus; phys. Medico-Chirurg. Hosp.; cons. mem. Bd. of Health, Phila. Pres. bd. trustees Perkiomen School; mem. bd. dirs. Ursinis College; mem. bd. mgrs. City Parks Assn., Phila. Hosp. (v.p.), Medico-Chirurg, and Graduate hosps.; chmn. Better Homes Committee, Phila. Author: House Plants as Sanitary Agents, 1887; Principles and Practice of Medicine, 14 editions, 1897-1917; Text-Book of Medical Diagnosis (with L. Napolean Boston), 1909; Meditations on Verse, 1934. Officier de l'Instruction Publique, 1912; Chevalier Legion of Honor (France), 1923. Home: Philadelphia, Pa. Died Aug. 29, 1936.

ANDERSEN, BJORN, chem. engr.; b. Norway, June 29, 1897; s. Elling and Auguste Petrea (Lorensen) A.; B.S., Norway Inst. Tech., 1918, M.S., Chem.E., 1920, research fellow, 1920-23; m. Ingeborg Solberg, Mar. 27, 1924; children—Bjorn Andreas, Thor Bjorn, Erik Bjorn, Nils Olav, Lars Rolf. Came to U.S., 1924, naturalized, 1930. Asst. prof. Norway Inst. Tech., 1921-24, chief chemist Norway Inst. Testing Materials, 1920-22; research chemist Guggenheim Bros. Research Labs., N.Y.C., 1924-26, mgr. research, 1926-28; research asso. Celluloid Corp., 1928-30, technical dir., 1930-41; dir. research, tech. dir. plastic div. Celanese Corp. Am., 1941-47, dir. research Celanese Corp. Am., 1947-51, v.p., tech. dir. 1951-55, v.p., gen. mgr. Plastics div., Celanese Corp., 1955-59; vice president Celanese Devel. Company, 1959-62. Mem. Princeton adv. council Plastics Program, 1954-62, chmn., 1959-62; del. U.S. Dept. Commerce Trade Missions, Australia, 1961, Burma, 1962, Finland, 1964, Bulgaria-Hungary, 1966. Decorated Liberty Cross (Norway), 1947. Mem. Soc. Chem. Industry, Soc. Plastics Industry, Am. Soc. Testing Materials, Am. Inst. Chem. Engrs., Am. Chem. Soc., Am. Inst. Chemists, Am. Electrochem. Soc., N.Y. Acad. Scis., Plastic Pioneers Assn., A.A.A.S., Indsl. Research Inst. Clubs: Chemist (N.Y.), Appalachian, Maplewood Country. Author sci. articles. Holder 30 patents. Home: Maplewood NJ Died Sept. 27, 1971; buried Greenwood Cemetery, Brielle NJ

ANDERSON, ALEXANDER, engraver; b. N.Y.C., Apr. 21, 1775; s. John and Mary A.; medical degree, 1796; m. Ann Van Vleck, Apr. 1797. Became 1st wood engraver in Am., 1794; produced wood and copper plate engravings for leading mags. and book publishers, 1794-1868; mem. Acad. Fine Arts, N.A.D. Died Jersey City, N.J., Jan. 17, 1870.

ANDERSON, ALEXANDER PIERCE, botanical and chem. research; b. Red Wing, Minn., Nov. 22, 1862; s. John and Britta M. (Gustafsdotter) A.; B.S., U. of Minn., 1894, M.S., 1895; Ph.D., U. of Munich, 1897; m. Lydia Johnson, Aug. 11, 1898; children—Leonard A. (dec.), Louise A. (Mrs. R. M. Sargent), John P. Lydia Elizabeth (Mrs. R. F. Hedin), Jean M. (Mrs. F. G. Chesley). Was botanist Clemson Coll., S.C., 1896-99; asst. prof. botany, U. of Minn., 1899-1900; curator herbarium Columbia U., 1901. Made over 15,000 expts. with cereal grains and starch, 1901-36; inventor new processes of treating cereal grains and starch materials, including puffed rice, puffed wheat, Quaker Crackels and similar products. Awarded Charles Reid Barnes hon. life membership by Am. Soc. pLant Physiologists, 1937. Fellow A.A.A.S.; mem. Am. Forestry Assn., Minn. Acad. Science, Minn. Hist. Soc., Geol. Soc. Minn. Address: Laboratory, Red Wing, Minn. Died May 7, 1943.

ANDERSON, EDGAR, botanist; b. Forestville, N.Y., Nov. 9, 1897; s. Anson Crosby and Inez (Shannon) A.; B.S., Mich. State Coll., 1918; M.S., Sc.D., Harvard, 1922; m. Dorothy Moore, June 21, 1923 (dec. 1971); 1 dau., Phoebe. Asst. in genetics Harvard, 1920-22; geneticist Mo. Botanical Garden, and asst. prof. botany, Washington Univ. (St. Louis), 1922-30, asso. prof., 1930-31, prof. from 1935; arborist Arnold Arboretum of Harvard Univ., 1931-35; Engelman prof. of botany Washington Univ., 1937-69; asst. dir. Mo. Bot. Garden, 1952-54, dir., 1954-56, curator useful plants, 1957-69; vis. prof. biology, Stanford U., 1952, vis. fellow mathematics, Princeton, 1957. Mem. U.S. Naval Res. Force, 1918-19. Fellow Nat. Research Council, 1929-30 (England); Guggenheim fellow (California and Mexico, 1943-44; Guggenheim Sr. fellow, 1957-69; fellow Center for Advanced Study in Behavorial Sciences, 1959-60. Decorated Order of the Yugoslavian Crown; Darwin Wallace silver medal, 1958; gold medal Men's Garden Clubs American, 1958, Federated Garden Clubs, 1959. Mem. Sigma Xi, Society American Naturalists, Herb Society America, Bot. Soc. Am. Author: Introgressive Hybridization Plants, Man and Life. Discoverer introgression; research on origin and evolution of maize. Home: St Louis MO Died June 18, 1969.

ANDERSON, ERNEST, ret. educator; b. Kaufman, Tex., Feb. 1, 1881; s. William Robert and Emily (Muckleroy) A.; A.B., Trinity Univ., 1902; B.S., Univ. of Tex., 1903, M.S., 1905; Ph.D., Univ. of Chicago, 1909; m. Lillian Hilliard, Dec. 25, 1907; children—William Ernest, Frank Hilliard. Research asst., Univ. of Chicago, 1909-12; prof. chemistry, Mass. State Coll., 1912-17, Univ. of South Africa, Pretoria, 1917-20, Univ. of Neb., 1920-23; prof. chemistry and head dept., U. Ariz., 1923-52, ret. 1952; temp. asso., Carnegie Inst., Palo Alto, California, summers, 1932036; research asso., institute of Paper Chemistry, summers, 1941-48. Mem. Phi Beta Kappa, Sigma Xi, Phi Kappa Phi, Protestant. Contributor research articles on sugars and related carbohydrates to chem. jours. Home: 1930 E. Hawthorne St., Tucson, Ariz. Office: Dept. of Chemistry, Univ. of Arizona, Tucson. Died Feb. 19, 1954; buried South Lawn Meml. Park.

ANDERSON, HAROLD V(ICTOR), educator; b. Manistique, Mich., Apr. 4, 1890; s. Johannes and Anna Christine (Nelson) A.; B.Chem. E., U. Mich., 1912; M.S., Lehigh U., 1925; postgrad. U. Ill., 1928-29; m. Judith Botvidson, Aug. 1915 (dec. Jan. 1944); 1 son, Frank John; m. 2d, Eleanor Blanche Aldridge, June 28, 1947. Chemist, Dixie Portland Cement Co., Richard City, Tenn., 1914-18, Air Nitrates Corp., Muscle Shoals, Ala., 1918; instr. chemistry Lehigh U., Bethlehem, Pa., 1918-21, asst. prof., 1921-30, asso. prof., 1930-41, prof. chemistry since 1941; tech. rep. and dir. research on project sponsored by OSRD through Nat. Def. Research Com. at Lehigh U., 1941-46. Mem. bd. sch. dirs. and sec., Salisbury Twp., Lehigh County, Pa., 1937-49. Mem. Am. Chem. Soc., Am. Crystallographic Assn., Alpha Chi Sigma, Phi Eta Sigma, Kappa Sigma, Sigma Xi. Republican. Lutheran. Author: Qualitative Analysis (with T. H. Hazlehurst), 1941; Chemical Calculations (with J. S. Long), 1924, 5th rev. edit., 1948. Home: Uplands, Route 60, Allentown, Pa. Office: Chemistry Bldg., Lehigh University, Bethlehem, Pa. Died Dec. 18, 1965.

ANDERSON, HENRY CLAY, prof. and dean engring.; b. Morganfield Ky., Bec. 4, 1872; s. John Gerry amd Sophia F. (Cromwell) A.;prep. edn., Morganfield Acad. and Acad. of Ky. State Coll., Lexington, Ky.; B.M.E., U. of Ky., 1897; s. Sara Graham Simrall, Aug. 19, 1903 (died Jan. 1920); children—Henry Clay (dec.), Ellen Harrison, John Gerry. Asst. master mechanic, C.,N.O. & T.P. Ry., Chattanooga, Tenn., 1897-1900; with U. of Mich. as instr. in mech. engring., 1900-03, asst. prof., 1903-06, jr. prof. steam power engring., 1912-17, prof. mech. engring. and head of dept., 1917-39, dir. student-alumni relations, 1933-39, dean Coll. of Engring., 1937-39, also consulting practice, appraisal of steam and electric rys., etc., and spl. engring. investigations. Democrat. Episcopalian. Mason. Home: Ann Arbor, Mich. Died Oct. 14, 1939.

ANDERSON, HENRY JAMES, educator; b. N.Y.C., Feb. 6, 1799; grad. Columbia, 1818; grad. Coll. Physicians and Surgeons, N.Y.C., 1823. Prof. Mathematics and astronomy Columbia, 1825-50, became trustee, 1851, prof. emeritus mathematics and astronomy, 1866; went to Europe, circa 1850, converted to Catholicism, geologist for Dead Sea expdn. while travelling in Holy Land; one of pilgrims who travelled to Lourdes (France), received by Pope Pius IX, 1874; mem. Am. scientific expdn. to observe patterns of planet Venus; served as pres. St. Vincent de Paul Soc., N.Y.C.; an orginator Catholic Union, N.Y.C.; a founder Cath. Protectory, Westchester, N.Y.; visited India, stricken with fatal disease. Died Lahore, Northern Hindustan, India, Oct. 19, 1875.

ANDERSON, JOHN AUGUST, astronomer; b. Rollag, Minn., Aug. 7, 1876; s. Brede and Ellen Martha (Berg) A.; Concordia Coll., Moorhead, Minn., 1891-93; State Normal Sch., Moorhead, 1893-94; B.S., Valparaiso Coll., 1900; Ph.D., Johns Hopkins, 1907; m. Josephine Virginia Barron, June 9, 1909. Asso. prof. astronomy, Johns Hopkins, 1908-16; physicist at Mount Wilson (Cal.) Obs., 1916-43, retired 1949; exec. officer Obs. Council, Cal. Inst. Tech., 1928—. Asso. editor Am. Optical Journal. Mem. Optical Soc., Am. Astron. Soc., Am. Seismol. Soc., A.A.A.S., Am. Phys. Soc., Am. Chem. Soc., Nat. Acad. of Sciences. Phi Beta Kappa. Club: University. Author: Absorption Spectra of Solutions (with H. C. Jones), 1908. Received Howard N. Pitt's gold medal, Franklin Inst., 1924. Home: 978 E. Poppyfields Dr., Altadena, Cal. Died Dec. 1959.

ANDERSON, JOHN EDWARD, psychology; b. Laramie, Wyo., June 13, 1893; s. John August and Julia (Wilhelmson) A.; A.B., U. Wyo., 1914, LL.D., 1942; A.M., Harvard, 1915, Ph.D., 1917; m. Dorothea Lynde, Dec. 3, 1918; children—Frances Julia (Mrs. Louis J. Moran), John Lynde, Richard Davis, Theodore Robert, Dorothea Jean (Mrs. Martin A. Antman). Inst. psychology, Yale, 1917, 1919-21, asst. prof., 1921-25; prof. psychology Inst. Chiid Devel., U. Minn., 1925-61, dir. Inst., 1925-54, emeritus 1961—; vis. prof. U. Chgo., U. Cal. at Los Angeles, summers 1939, 49. Chmn. sect. child welfare Minn. Def. Council 1951-45. Served as 1st lt. U.S. Army, chief psychol. examiner, sr. instr. Sch. Mil. Psychology, Camp Greenleaf, 1917-19. Chmn. com. on edn. and tng. infant and presch. child, White House Conf. on Child Health and Protection, 1929-31; mem. White House Conf. on Children and Youth, 1940, 1950; NRC (chmn. com. on child devel. 1928-32; mem. div. anthropology and psychology, 1931-34, 1943-46); mem. Social Sci. Research Council, 1929-32; chmn. Com. on Exceptional Child, Nat. Congress Parents and Tchrs., 1937-43, Nat. Conf. on Aging, 1950, Minn. Commn. on Aging 1951-53 (chmn. com. on Living Arrangements); mem. nat. adv. com. for 1960 White House Conf. on Aging, chmn. com. on research in pyschol. and social scis. Fellow A.A.A.S. (sec. psychol. sect. 1929-33, v.p. 1934); mem. Soc. for Exptl. Biology and Medicine, Am. Psychol. Assn. (sec., 1923-25; mem. council, 1926-28, 1934-37; pres. 1942-43; pres. div. on Childhood and Adolescence, 1946-47, pres. div. Maturity and Old Age, 1955-56), Tenn. Psychol. Assn., Sr. Neighbors Chattanooga (mem. Minn. Acad. Sic. (v.p. 1944-45), Gerontol. Soc., Phi Beta Kappa, Sigma Xi, Phi Delta Kappa, Delta Sigma Rho, Sigma Alpha Epsilon. Club: Campus. Author numerous books, 1927—, also editor. Editor: Psychological Aspects of Aging, 1956. Asso. editor Gerontologist, 1961—. Home: Wideview, Route 4, Chattanooga 9. Died May 10, 1966.

ANDERSON, JOHN FRANCIS, bridge builder; b. Jemshog, Sweden, Dec. 30, 1848; s. Anders Anderson Thore and Ingar Suneson; self ed.; m. Cecelia Anderson, of Scania, Sweden, May 19, 1880. Came to America as a sailor, 1869; assisted in constrn. of bridge across Mo. River for U.P. Ry., 1870; built river piers for South St. Bridge, Phila., 1872; foundations for Iron Mountain Ry. bridge over Ark. River, at Little Rock, 1873; employed be govt. of Venezuela, 1876; engaged on bridge work in Eng., 1876-79; supt. Hudson River Tunnel, between New York and Jersey City, 1879-82; built bridge over Atchfalaya River, La., for Tex. Pacific Ry., 1882-84; mem. Anderson & Barr, 1884-95. Inventor and owner of patents for aerial bridges and the pilot system of tunneling. Decorated Merit of Military, Spain; Knight Comdr. Order of Vasa, Sweden. Home: San Diego, Calif. Died Jan. 23, 1927.

ANDERSON, JOHN WILL, mfr., inventor; b. Woodland, Ill., Oct. 23, 1883; s. John Will and Mary Belle (Warren) A.; ed. pub. schs.; m. Reba McLeish, Oct. 3, 1906; 1 dau., Mary Ellen Duffy. Organizer, pres. and gen. mgr., The Anderson Co., mfg. automotive products, 1918—, also Productive Inventions, Inc., devel., patent holding and licensing, 1952—, now merged with The Anderson Co.; founder Anco Bldg. Corp., 1947, since pres. Dir. Am. Fair Trade Council, 1938-59, pres., 1944-59; pres. Quality Brands Assos. of Am., Inc., 1959—; pres. Nat. Patent Council, 1945—; co-founder Automotive Council for War Prond., Detroit, Mich., 1942 (mem. bd. dirs.; sec.; chmn. mil. replacement parts governing bd.; mem. public relations com.). Former mem. adv. coms. WPB, OPA, Dept. State, Washington; mem. Patent Office adv. com. Sec. Commerce, Washington. Mem. Motor and Equipment Mfrs. Assn. (chmn. policy com. 1937—, dir. 4 terms, pres. 1942-44), Soc. Automotive Engrs., Ind. Mfrs. Assn. (past dir.) Republican. Methodist. Clubs: Recess, Detroit, Athletic (Detroit); Advertising (N.Y.C.); Gary (Ind.) Country; Phoenix Country; Automobile Old Timers (life mem.); Executives (Chgo.); Columbia Country (Chevy Chase, Md.); Key Largo Anglers (Fla.). Contbr. paper, addresses, radio, TV discussions to nat. orgns. Home: 405 S. Huntington St., Gary. Office: care The Anderson Co., Cary, 40, Ind. Died Sept. 28, 1967.

ANDERSON, JOSEPH REID, iron mfr.; b. Fincastle, Va., Feb. 6, 1813; s. William and Anna (Thomas) A.; grad. U.S. Mil. Acad. 1836; m. Sally Archer, 1837, 5 children; m. 3d Mary Pegram. Chief engr. Valley Turnpike Co. (Va.), 1838-41; became owner Tredegar Iron Co., 1848, shop produced majority of shot, rails and irons products of South during Civil War; mem. Va. Ho. of Dels., 1852-55; commd. brig. gen. Confederate States Army, 1861; fought in Peninsula Campaign, 1862; elected pres. Richmond (Va.) C. of C., 1874; mem. Common Council of Richmond. Died Isles of Shoals, N.H., Sept. 7, 1892.

ANDERSON, PAUL LEWIS, photog. expert; b. Trenton, N.J., Oct. 8, 1880; s. Edward Johnson and Belle (Lewis) A.; E.E., Lehigh U., 1901; m. Mary Lyon Green, Aug. 22, 1910; children—Priscilla, Ruth. With Westinghouse Electric & Mfg. Co., Pitts., 1901; engring. and testing depts., Sprague Electric Co., Watsessing, N.J., 1902-04; engring. dept. N.Y. Telephone Co., 1904-07; a founder and mem. Struss-Anderson Labs., mfrs. "Kalogen" (photog. developer), of which was originator. Has exhibited photographs in leading cities of Am., also London, Hamburg and Budapest. Mem. Orange Camera Club (pres. 1938-40). Author's League Am. Author: Pictorial Landscape Photography, 1914; Pictorial Photography, Its Principles and Practice, 1917; The Fine Art of Photography, 1919; The Cub Arrives, 1927; Half-Pint Shannon, 1928; With the Eagles, 1929; A Slave of Catiline, 1930; For Freedom and for Gaul, 1931; The Knights of St. John, 1932; Swords in the North, 1935; Pugnax the Gladiator, 1939; The Technique of Pictorial Photography, 1939. Contbr. short stories to mags. Home: 27 Hillside Av., Short Hills, N.J. Died Sept. 15, 1956.

ANDERSON, ROBERT EARLE, naval architect, writer; b. Trenton, N.J., Feb. 18, 1881; s. Robert Morris and Frances (Baily) A.; C.E., Princeton U., 1903; student naval architecture, U. Glasgow, 1903-04; m. Emily Hays Farr, June 6, 1906; children—Edith (Mrs. Harold E. Smith), Helen (Mrs. James B. Daly), Robert Earle. Began as naval architect, 1904; with U.S. Navy Dept., Bur. Constrn. and Repair, 1904-13; asst. to mng. dir. Lake Torpedo Boat Co., 1913-14; gen. mgr. Augusta-Savannah Nav. Co., 1914-15; successivley asst. to gen. supt., indsl. engr., comptroller, treas., and v.p. in charge finance Winchester Repeating Arms Co., 1915-24, also officer or dir. various subsidiaries and pres. Barney & Berry, Ind., sec. and treas. Winchester Co. and v.p. Simmons Hardware Co., comptroller, later gen. supt. and treas. R. Hoe & Co., N.Y.C., 1924-26; comptroller, later treas. and in gen. charge contracts, bus. relations, etc., Elec. Research Products, Inc. and officer various subsidiary cos., 1927-35; pres. Exhibitors Reliance Corp.; financial v.p. Paramount Picutures, Inc., and officer various subsidiary cos., 1935-36; in private cons. practice, 1937; dir. finance U.S. Maritime Commn., 1938-64; mem. adv. bd. Columbus Circle Br., Mfrs. Trust Co. N.Y. Fellow Am. Geog. Soc.; mem. Princeton Engring. Assn. (ex-pres.), Soc. Colonial Wars, Soc. Naval Architects and Marine Engrs., Am. Acad. Polit. and Social Sci., (asso.) U.S. Naval Inst., Propeller Club, Port of N.Y., Phi Beta Kappa. Republican. Presbyn. (elder). Author: General Specifications for Building Ships of the United States Navy, 1908; The Merchant Marine and World Frontiers, 1945; Liberia, America's African Friend, 1952; numerous articles in tech. and bus. periodicals. Inventor of cage mast used on U.S. battleships. Home: 11 Sussex Av., Chatham, N.J. Died Winston-Salem, N.C., Mar. 1967.

ANDERSON, ROBERT VAN VLECK, geologist; b. Galesburg, Ill., Apr. 18, 1884; s. Melville Best (LL.D.) and Charlena (van Vleck) A.; B.A., Stanford University, 1906; married Gracella Rountree, Mar. 1923; children—Robert Playfair, Patricia Sage (Mrs. John Loveland Armstrong), Gracella Gurnee. Geological and Zoölogical work, Japan, 1905; assistant in investigations of Calif. earthquake for Carnegie Inst., 1906; geologic aid, asst. geologist and geologist, U.S. Geol. Survey, 1906-13; made investigations of geol. and petroleum resources of Calif., and was member Oil Land Classification Board; as cons. geologist visited many parts of world since 1911; geologist for S. Pearson & Son, Ltd., London, Eng., 1913-18; representative of U.S. War Trade Bd. in Sweden; Am. delegate on Inter-Allied Trade Com., Stockholm, 1918-19; dir. Whitehall Petroleum Corp., Ltd., London, 1919-23; chief geologist, 1923-26. Engaged in indepndent scientific work, 1927-34. Collaborateur, Service de la Carte Geologique de l'Algérie, 1930-32; research in Algeria under grant from Geol. Soc. America, 1933; with Socony Vacuum Oil Co., Inc., 1934-44; research associate, Stanford Univ., since 1945. Fellow Geological Society of America (chmn. Cordilleran sect. 1928), Calif. Acad. Sciences; mem. Paleontol. Soc. America, Assn. Am. Geographers, Soc. Econ. Geologists, Archaeol. Inst. America, Am. Assn. Petroleum Geologists, Société Géologique de Francé, Sigma Xi. Unitarian. Author: Geology in Coastal Atlas of Western Algeria; also various reports pub. by U.S. Govt., and other scientific papers. Home: 1140 Hamilton Av., Palo Alto, Calif. Address: Dept. of Geology, Stanford University, Stanford P.O., Calif. Died June 6, 1949.

ANDERSON, RUDOLPH JOHN, biochemist; b. Härna, Sweden, Sept. 13, 1879; s. Anders and Johanna (Johanson) A.; came to U.S., 1893; Ph.G., New Orleans Coll. of Pharmacy, 1903; B.S. Tulane U., 1906; grad. work, 1906-07; grad. work, Upsala U., Sweden, 1909-10, Berlin U., 1910-11, 14, Univ. Coll., London, 1914-15; Ph.D., Cornell University 1919; hon. M.D., Lund University, Sweden, 1947; m. Clara Tillinghast, Jan. 3, 1920. Asso. in chemistry, N.Y. Agrl. Expt. Sta., Geneva, N.Y., 1911; biochemist same, 1919; chief in research biochemistry, also prof., Cornell U., 1920-27; prof. chemistry, Yale U. 1927-48; fellow Calhoun College. Mem. editorial board Jour. of Biol. Chemistry; mem. board of scientific advisors, The Jane Coffin Childs Memorial Fund for Medical Research. Served as captain San. Corps, U.S.A., 1917-19; sr. instr. Sch. of Nutrition, Camp Greenleaf, Ga., July-Dec. 1918; maj. San. Res. Corps since 1921. Awarded Trudeau Medal, 1948. Fellow A.A.A.S.; mem. Am. Chem. Soc., Trudeau Soc. (hon.), Am. Soc. of Biological Chemists (v.p., 1939-40; pres., 1941-43), Soc. for Exptl. Biology and Medicine, National Academy of Science, Sigma Xi. Republican. Specializing in chem. problems dealing with plant products having biol. significance and in the chemistry of bacteria. Contbr. to Jour. Biol. Chemistry. Jour. Am. Chem. Soc., etc. Home: 101 Cottage St., New Haven, Conn; also Nut Plains Rd., Guilford, Conn. Died Apr. 6, 1916; buried Brookside Cemetery, Englewood, N.J.

ANDERSON, RUDOLPH MARTIN, zoologist, govt. official, writer; b. near Decorah, Ia., June 30, 1876; s. John Emanuel and Martha Ann (Johnson) A.; Ph.D., U. of Ia., 1903, Ph.D., 1906; m. Mae Belle Allstrand, Jan. 22, 1913 (dec. Mar. 1960); children—Dorothy, Mary, Isabel. Asst. in zoology, asst. curator Mus. Natural History, U. Ia., 1902-06; instr. and asst. comdt. Blees

Mil. Acad., Macon, Mo., 1906-08; field agt., asst. in mammalogy and explorer, Am. Mus. Nat. History, New York, 1908-13; zoologist Geol. Survey of Can., Ottawa, Can., 1913-20; chief of div. of biology National Museum of Canada, 1920-46, hon. curator in mammalogy since 1946. Active in biol. and anthropol. exploration, Arctic Alaska. Yukon, Ty., and Northwest Territories, Can., 1908-12; chief of southern party Canadian Arctic Expdn., 1913-16; gen. editor sci. reports of expdn. since 1919; investigated 28 provisional wildlife sanctuaries in Prairie provinces, Nat. Parks Bur., 1918-19; naturalist on Canadian Arctic expdn. to Greenland and Canadian Arctic Archipelago, 1928; Columbia and Kootenay valleys, Southern B.C., and Nat. Parks, 1938-39. Served with Co. I, 52d Iowa Infantry, Inf., Spanish-Am. War, 1898; 54th Inf., N.G. of Ia., 1900-06; staff capt., N.G. of Mo., 1906-08. Awarded Spanish-Am. War medal, expert rifleman medal with bars; King Am. War medal, expert rifleman medal with bars; King George VI Coronation medal. Knight Officer International Order, St. Hubert, 1951. Mem. adv. bd. on wild life protection, Can., 1917-46; mem. library com. of Geol. Survey and Nat. Mus. of Can., also Northern adv. bd. and interdeptl. reindeer com. Fellow Royal Soc. of Can.; mem. Wildlife Soc., Biol. Soc. of Washington, D.C., (hon.) Ornithologische Verein zu Dresden, (corr.) Zool. Soc. (London), La Société Provancher d'histoire naturelle du Can., Am. Soc. Mammalogists (charter mem. 1919; bd. dirs. 26 yrs.; vice pres. 1946), Am. Ornithol. Union (asso. 1906, mem. since 1914), Am. Soc. Ichthyologists and Herpetologists (bd. govs. since 1946), Pacific Northwest Bird and Mammal Soc., Ottawa Field-Nat. Club. Wilson Ornithol. Club, Cooper Ornithol. Club of Calif., Sigma Xi, Sigma Alpha Epsilon. Mason. Author: Birds of Iowa, 1907; Methods of Collecting and Preserving Vertebrae Animals, (bull.), 1932, revised edit., 1948; Catalogue of Can. Recent Mammals (bull.), 1947. Asst. editor Can. Naturalist since 1917. Contbr. numerous papers in sci. jours. and govt. reports. Hon. mem. Arctic Inst. N.A., 1956. Home: 58 Driveway. Office: National Museum of Canada, Ottawa, Ont., Can. Died June 21, 1961; buried Beechwood Cemetery, Ottawa, Ont., Can.

ANDERSON, VICTOR VANCE, M.D., psychiatrist; b. Barbourville, Ky., Dec. 26, 1879; s. William Ballinger and Flora (Herndon) A.; A.B., Union Coll., Barbourville, 1898; M.D., U. of Louisville, 1903; A.M., Harvard, 1916; LL.D., Union Coll., Barbourville, Ky., 1935; m. Clara Beaumont, 1906 (died 1928); 1 dau., Pauline; m. 2d, Margaret Cavender, 1930. In practice, Lynchburg, Va., 1904-11; research at Harvard, 1911-12; physician Psychopathic Hosp., Boston, 1912-13; psychiatrist and med. dir. Municipal Court, Boston, 1913-18; scientific advisor N.Y. Prison Com., 1918-19; asso. med. dir. Nat. Com. for Mental Hygiene, 1919-24; psychiatrist and dir. of med. research, R. H. Macy & Co., 1924-30; dir. Anderson Sch., Staatsburg, New York. Directed work of National Com. for Mental Hygiene in orgn. and demonstration of child guidance clinics throughout U.S.; directed and wrote official reports of mental deficiency surveys of Ga., W.Va. and Wis., mental hygiene surveys of Md., S.C., Ky., Mo. and City of Cincinnati, study of criminal and delinquency problems in St. Louis and study of jails in N.Y. state. Fellow American Academy of Child Psychiatry; member Am. Psychiatric Assn., Nat. Com. for Mental Hygiene, A.M.A., N.E.A., Progressive Edn. Assn., Am. Orthopsychiatric Assn., Am. Psychopathological Assn., N.Y. State Med. Soc., N.Y. Neurol. Soc., N.Y. Psychiatric Assn. Author: Psychiatry in Industry, 1929; Psychiatry in Education, 1932; also Selecting Executives; The Problem Employee: A Psychiatric Guide for Employment; Psychiatry in College; Pupil Guidance; Intergration of Psychiatry with Education. Home: The Anderson School, Staatsburgh, N.Y. Died July 26, 1960.

ANDERSON, WINSLOW, surgeon; collegiate edn.; M.D., U. of Calif., 1884; L.R.C.P., M.R.C.P., London, 1891; M.R.C.S., . Eng.l 1891; L.S.A., London, 1891; m. Bertha Lillian Collins, Mar. 1890. Pres. and prof. gynecology and abdominal surgery, Coll. Phys. and Surg., San Francisco, 1896-1911; emeritus; surgeon-in-chief to St. Winifred's Hosp., San Francisco, 1899—, to Sierra Ry. Co., 1904—; abdominal surgeon and gynecologist to San Francisco Hosp. Mem. State Bd. Health, Calif., 1893-97, 1900-03; ex-mem. Bd. Med. Examiners, State of Calif.; surgeon-gen. N.G. Calif., 1900-04, 1907-11. Editor Pacific Med. Jour., 1890—. Author: Mineral Springs and Health Resorts of California; also articles on diseases of the lungs, in 20th Century Practice of Medicine. Home: San Francisco, Calif. Died May 8, 1917.

ANDRE, FLOYD, coll. dean; b. New Sharon, Ia., Sept. 13, 1909; s. Graham and Alice (Fox) A.; B.S. in Agronomy, Ia. State Coll., 1931; M.S. in Entomology, 1933, Ph.D., 1936; m. Hazel May Beck, June 22, 1935 (dec. Apr. 1956); children—Jacqueline, Alice, Richard Graham; m. 2d, Avis Lovell, Nov. 12, 1970. Asst. Ia. State Coll., 1932-34, instr. entomology and zoology, 1936-38, asst. entomologist, expt. sta., 1934-38, asso. entomologist Bur. Entomology and Plant Quarantine, U.S. Dept. Agr., 1938-40, entomologist and expt. sta. adminstr. Office Expt. Stations, 1940-43, sr. entomologist and expt. sta. adminstr., 1943-46; prof. econ. entomology U. Wis., also asst. dir. state agr. expt. sta., 1946-48, asst. dean Coll. of Agr., asst. dir. state agr. expt. sta. and agr. extension service, 1948-49; dean of agr. Ia. State U. and dir. Coll. Agr., 1949-72. Dir. Union Story Trust & Savs. Bank. Adviser on agrl. edn. to Argentina, 1960, 61 Paraguay, 1964, Brazil, 1964, 65, 67. Mem. Entomol. Soc. Am., Assn. Econ. Entomologists, Biol. Soc. Washington, Phi Kappa Phi, Alpha Zeta, Sigma Xi, Gamma Delta. Presbyn. Author of articles and bulls. on agrl. and entomol. subjects. One of the world's leading collectors of thrips. Home: Ames IA Died Jan. 18, 1972; buried Iowa State Univ. Cemetery.

ANDREA, FRANK A. D., radio, TV mfr.; b. Salerno, Italy, 1889; came to U.S., 1890, naturalized; student Mechanics Inst.; m. Concetta Ambrose. Exptl. radio staff Frederick Pierce Co., 1913; prodn. mgr. radio plant, Lee de Forest until 1919; founder Fada Co., 1920, propr., 1920-32; devel. five inch TV set, 1937; now pres., treas., dir. Andrea Radio Corp. Address: Andrea Radio Corp., 27-01 Bridge Plaza North, L.I. City, N.Y. Died Dec. 22, 1965.

ANDRESEN, ALBERT FREDERICK RUGER, physician, educator; b. Bklyn., Sept. 11, 1885; s. John H. and Emma (Ruger) A.; M.D., Long Island Coll. Hosp., 1907; children—Dorothy Marie (Mrs. John E. Standard), Marjorie Alberta (Mrs. Richard G. McManus), Albert Frederick Ruger (M.D.). Intern Bklyn. Hosp., 1907-09; asst. gastroenterologic clinic, under Dr. A. Albu, Berlin, Germany, 1909; mem. med. clinic Bklyn. Hosp. and Meth. Episcopal Hosp. dispensaries, 1909-12; attending gastroenterologist Bklyn. Hosp. Dispensary, 1912-19; asst. gastroenterologist Polhemus Meml. Clinc, 1910-15, dir. gastroenterologic clinic, 1919-51; cons. gastroenterologist Bushwick Hosp., 1913-17; asst. physician Bklyn. Hosp., 1915-19; attending gastroenterologist Polyclinic Hosp., N.Y.C., 1919-20; attending physician gastroenterology Long Island Coll. Hosp., 1919—, instr. anatomy, 1909-11, gastroenterology, 1910-15; clin. prof. medicine Long Island Coll. Medicine, 1919-39, prof. clin. medicine, 1939-50; prof. gastroenterology N.Y. Polyclinic Med. Sch. and Hosp., 1925-26; clin. prof. medicine State U. of N.Y., State U. Med. Center at N.Y.C., Coll. Medicine, 1950-51, clin. prof. medicine emeritus, 1952—; cons. medicine St. Peter's Hosp.; postgrad. tchr. gastroenterology under auspices Kings County and N.Y. State med. socs., 1930—; cons. medicine Flushing Hosp., 1930—; area cons. gastroenterology VA. Recipient alumni medal for distinguished service to Am. medicine State U. N.Y. Coll. Madison, 1952; Julius Friendenwald medal for outstanding achievement in gastroenterology Am. Gastroent. Assn., 1954. Diplomate Am. Bd. Internal Medicine; mem. Internat. Soc. Internal Medicine, World Med. Assn. (dir.), Nat. Soc. Med. Research A.M.A., Am. Gastroenterol. Assn. (past pres.), Am. Cancer Soc., Am. Proctologic Soc. (hon. asso.), Med. Library Assn., Bklyn. Inst. Arts and Scis., Friend Bklyn. Pub. Library, Bklyn. Mus., Am. Mus. Natural History, Alpha Omega Alpha, Alpha Kappa Kappa (life). Author articles med. jours., 1910—; also chpts. or part chpts. in med. works, among latest Peptic Ulcer in General Practice, 1951; also monograph, Office Gastroenterology, 1958. Address: 88 6th Av., Bklyn. 17. Died Jan. 26, 1961.

ANDREWS, CLAYTON FARRINGTON, surgeon; b. St. Paul, Neb., Jan. 4, 1891; s. Ernest Irving and Pearl Josephine (Waite) A.; Ph.G., Creighton Coll. Pharmacy, Omaha, 1909; postgrad. U. Neb., 1910-12; M.D., U. Pa., 1916; M.S. in Surgery, Mayo Clinic and Post Grad. Sch., U. Minn., 1923; m. Mildred Rae Wells, Aug. 28, 1919; 1 son, David Irving. Began practice surgery, 1923; attending surgeon Lincoln Gen. and Bryan Meml. hosps. Chmn. med. sect. Neb. Civilian Def. Com. Served as 1st lt. M.C., U.S. Army, 1917-19; comdr. M.C. USNR (ret.). Treas. Neb. Med. Found.; mem. Exec. Council, Order of de Molay. Fellow A.C.S., Ex-residents Assn. of Mayo Clinic; Diplomate Am. Bd. Surgery; mem. A.M.A., Neb. State Med. Soc. (past pres.), Lancaster County Med. Soc. (past pres.), S.A. R., Delta Upsilon (past pres.), Phi Rho Sigma. Republican. Ch. of Holy Trinity (sr. warden emeritus). Mason (33 deg., K.T., Shriner; Past Protentate Sesstoris Temple; pres. Central States Shrine Assn., 1946; imperial potentate 1959-60). Clubs: Country (pres. 1938), University, Polemic (Lincoln); Newcomen Society (Eng.). Contbr. surg. articles to various, med. jours. Home: 2626 S. 24th St., Lincoln 2, Neb. Died Mar. 27, 1964.

ANDREWS, DANIEL MARSHALL, civil engr.; b. Americus, Ga., Oct. 24, 1853; s. Judge Garnett and Annulet (Ball) A.; bro. of Eliza Frances A.; U. of Ga. Sch. of Civ. Engring., 1872-74 inclusive (graduation prevented by illness); m. Adeline Van Court, Apr. 20, 1897. In ry. engring., Ga. and S.C., 1881-84; asst. engr., U.S. Engr. Dept. on river and harbor improvement, Ga., Ala. and Fla., 1884—. Episcopalian. Home: Rome, Ga. Died June 28, 1917.

ANDREWS, EDMUND, surgeon; b. Putney, Vt., April 22, 1824 grad. Univ. of Mich., 1849; M.D. and A.M., 1852 (LL.D., 1880); m. E. Eliza Taylor, Apr. 13, 1852; m. 2d, Mrs. Frances M. Barrett, Apr. 25, 1877. Demonstrator and prof. med. dept. same, 1852-56; surgeon 1st. Regt. Ill. Light Art,; surgeon-in-chief Camp Douglas, Civil war; since then in practice in Chicago; was instr. in human and comparative anatomy, Rush Med. Coll.; a founder and prof. surgery, Chicago Med. Coll. (now med. dept. Northwestern Univ.); was surgeon-in-chief Mercy Hospital. Home: Chicago, Ill. Died 1904.

ANDREWS, ETHAN ALLEN, biologist; b. New York, Sept. 10, 1859; s. Horace and Julia Russell (Johnson) A.; Ph.B., Yale, 1881; grad. student Yale and Polytechnicum, Hanover; fellow Johns Hopkins, 1884-86, Ph.D., 1887; m. Sara Gwendolen Foulke, of Phila., Mar. 17, 1894; children—Ethan Allen, John Hare Powel, Julia Gwenllian De Veau. Asst. U.S. Fish Commn., 1879-81; asst., 1887-92, asso. prof. biology, 1892-1908; prof. zoölogy since 1908, Johns Hopkins. Mem. Soc. Am. Zoölogists (pres., 1904), etc. Has written biol. papers in various jours. Home: 107 E. Lake Av., Baltimore, Md.

ANDREWS, HIRAM BERTRAND, civil engr.; b. Stetson, Me., Oct. 7, 1867; s. Eben and Francena L. (Hurd) A.; ed. pub. schs. Stetson, Me., and Wayland, Mass.; grad. Univ. of Me., 1888; m. Somerville, Mass., May 30, 1890, Anna May Bailey. Asst. in office of Edw. A. Buss, mill engr., Boston, 1889-90; with West End St. Ry., Boston, and Boston Elevated Ry., 1890-1904, last 8 yrs. as asst. engr. surface lines; engr. for Simpson Bros. Corp. since Dec., 1904, contractors for reinforced concrete constrn. Mem. Am. Soc. Civ. Engrs. Republican. Author: Handbook for Street Railway Engineers, 1902 W9. Residence: Melrose, Mass. Office: 166 Devonshire St., Boston.

ANDREWS, JOSEPH, engraver; b. Hingham, Mass., circa 1805; s. Ephraim and Lucy (Lane) A.; married twice. Apprenticed to engraver Abel Bowen, Boston, 1821; mem. Carter, Andrews & Co., Lancaster, Mass., 1827; studied under Joseph Goodyear, London, Eng., 1835; went to Paris, France, engraved head of Benjamin Franklin for Works of Franklin (edited by Jared Sparks); visited Europe, 1840-42; engraved 6 plates for Galerie Historique de Versailles under patronage of Louis Philippe, Paris; began engraving of Duke of Urbino (Titian), Florence, Italy; returned to Paris, 1853; engraved Plymouth Rock 1620 (after painting by Peter Frederick Rothermale); other works include; portrait of George Washington (from painting by Gilbert Stuart), Oliver Wolcott, John Quincy Adams, Zachary Taylor, Jared Sparks (from portrait by Gilbert Stuart), Crossing the Ford (after painting by Alvan Fisher), The Panther Scene (after painting by George Loring Brow), Bargaining for a House (after painting by William S. Mount). Died Hingham, May 7, 1873.

ANDREWS, JUSTIN M(EREDITH), pub. health scientist and adminstrn.; b. Providence, Aug. 28, 1902; s. Clark Willett and Annie F. (Bliven) A.; Ph.B. cum laude, Brown U., 1923; Sc.D., Johns Hopkins 1926, LL.D., 1951; m. Arline S. Anderson, Sept. 24, 1927 (div.); children—Donald C., Theodore H.; m. 2d, Jean Simone Grant, Apr. 6, 1957; 1 stepson, Richard W. Grant. Instr. Johns Hopkins Sch. Hygiene and Pub. Health, 1926-27, asso. protozoology, 1927-30, asso. prof. protozoology, 1931-38; spl. mem. Rockefeller Found., 1929; vis. prof. parasitology U. Philippines, Manila, 1930-31; dir. div. malaria and hookworm service, Ga. Dept. Pub. Health, Atlanta, 1941-42, 1938-42; sr. zoologist U.S.P.H.S., Atlanta, 1941-42, dir., profl. functions, office Malaria control in war areas, 1946, dep. officer in charge, 1946-51, officer in charge communicable disease center, 1952, asst. surgeon gen., Bur. State Services, USPHS, 1953-57; dir. Nat. Inst. of Allergy and Infectious Disease, Nat. Insts. of Health, Bethesda, Md., 1957—. Cons. amebiasis, Fresnillo, Mex., 1931, malaria Venezuela, 1947, Iran, 1948, enteric infections Armed Forces Epidemiol. Bd., Europe and N. Africa, 1956; cons. med. adv. council Iran Found., 1953—; mem. Armed Forces Epidemiol. Bd. Commn. Enteric Infections, 1953—; mem. adv. com. malaria eradication PanAm. San. Bur., 1955—; mem. expert panel on malaria AID; mem. psittacosis bd. Surgeon Gen. Pub. Health Service; dir. Gorgas Meml. Inst.; lectr. Harvard Med. Sch., Tulane Med. Sch., Emory U., Army and Navy Med. Grad. Schs. Served from maj. to col., AUS, 1942-46. Awarded Legion of Merit, 1944; Le Prince award Am. Soc. Tropical Medicine and Hygiene, 1960. Mem. bd. of editors Pub. Health Reports, 1952-55; editorial com. protozoologic mem. Journal Parsitology, 1949-53, editorial bd. Journal Nat. Malaria Soc., 1942-44, expert adv. panels on malaria and insecticides World Health Orgn., 1956—, mem. nat. citizens com.; med. dir. Allergy bound. Am. Fellow Am. Pub. Health Assn. (governing council 1954—), A.A.A.S., Am. Acad. Microbiology, Royal Soc. Tropical Med. and Hygiene; mem. Am. Epdiemiol. Soc., Assn. Mil. Surgeons, Am. Acad. Tropical Med. (council 1947-51, treas. 1952-53), Am. Soc. Tropical Med. and Hygiene (pres. 1957), Am. Soc. Parasitologists (pres. 1961), Helminthological Soc. Washington, D.C. Pub. Health Assn., Belgian Soc. Tropical Med., Mexican Soc. Parasitology, Tropical Med. Assn. Wash. (pres. 1955-56), Sigma Xi. Author: Problems and Methods of Research in Protozoology (with Robert Hegner), 1930. Contbr. to profl. publs. numerous articles on epidemiologic phases of protozoan diseases. Home: 8 North Dr., Bethesda 14. Office: Nat. Inst. of Allergy and Infectious Diseases, Nat. Insts. of Health, Bethesda, Md. Died June 29, 1967.

ANDREWS, LAUNCELOT (WINCHESTER), chemist; b. London, Can., June 13, 1856; s. Alfred A. and Louisa (Jones) A.; Ph.B., Yale, 1875; A.M., Ph.D., Göttingen, 1882; grad. course in philosophy, history, etc., Harvard; m. Anna Ritter Lane, 1883. Taught high sch., Springfield, Mass., 1876-77; practiced as analytical chemist, Springfield, 1878-82; prof. chemistry, Ia. State Coll. of Agr., 1884-85; prof. chemistry, State U. of Ia., 1885-1904; research and cons. chemist to Mallinckrodt Chem. Works, St. Louis, 1904-10; special investigator on canning, U.S. Dept. of Agr., 1913-14; research chemist to Victor Chem. Works, Chicago, 1915-21. Author: An Introduction to the Study of Qualitative Analysis, 1891; etc. Home: Williamstown, Mass. Died 1938.

ANDREWS, ROBERT ROBBINS, dental surgeon; b. Boston, Mass., Aug. 7, 1844; s. Thomas Jefferson and Jerusha (Baker) A.; ed. pub. shcs.; D.D.S., Boston Dental Coll., 1875; (hon. A.M., Dartmouth, 1892); m. Mary Emily Leseur, Sept. 14, 1870. Served 2 yrs. in Civil War, pvt. to lt. and adj., 47th and 60th M.V.M. Dental surgeon, Cambridge, 1869—; prof. histology, Boston Dental Coll. (trustee); trustee Tufts Coll. Awarded Jarvie gold medal, N.Y. State Dental Soc., May 3, 1911, "for distinguished services to the Science and art of dentistry." Author: Embriology of the Dental Tissues, 1900; Kirk's American System of Dentistry, 1900; writer of numerous papers on dental histology. Home: Cambridge, Mass. Died Jan. 1921.

ANDREWS, ROY CHAPMAN, zoologist, explorer; b. Beloit, Wis., Jan. 26, 1884; s. Charles E. and Cora M. (Chapman) A.; grad. Beloit Coll. Acad., 1902; B.A., Beloit Coll., 1906, hon. Sc.D., 1928; M.A., Columbia, 1913; hon. Sc.D., Brown U., 1926; m. Yvette Borup; children—George Borup, Roy Kevin; m. 2d, Wilhelmina Christmas, Feb. 21, 1935. Dir. Am. Museum of Natural History, retired Jan. 1, 1942, appointed honorary director, Expedition to Alaska, 1908; collected white whales Saquenay River, 1909; special naturalist U.S.S. Albatross, on voyage to Dutch East Indies, Borneo, Celebes, 1909-10; explored N. Korea, 1911-12; with Borden Alaska Expdn., 1913; specialized in study of whales and other water mammals until 1914; leader Asiatic expdns. of Am. Mus. Natural History, 1st expdn., Tibet frontier, S.W. China and Burma, 1916, 17, 2d expdn., N. China and Outer Mongolia, 1919; 3d expedn., Central Asia, 1921-32, Opened the Gobi Desert to use of motor cars for commercial purposes; mapped much new area in the Gobi Desert; made first accurate general map of Mongolia; discovered many geological strata previously unknown; discovered some the richest fossil fields in the world; also first dinosaur eggs, skulls and parts of the skeleton of the Baluchitherium, and many other fossil mammals and reptiles previously unknown to science. The researches proved Central Asia to be one of the chief centers of the origin and distribution of the world's reptillian and mammalian life. Served in Intelligence Service, U.S., 1918. Awarded Elisha Kent Kane gold medal, Phila. Geog. Soc., 1931; Explorers' Club medal, 1932, Charles P. Daly gold medal, Am. Geog. Soc., 1936; Vega gold medal, Royal Swedish Anthropol. and Geog. Soc., 1937; Loczy medal, Hungarian Geog. Soc., 1937; Silver Buffalo Award, Nat. Council, Boy Scouts Am., 1952. Hon. Mem. Am. Mus. of Natural History (New York); fellow Nat. Geog. Soc., A.A.A.S., N.Y. Acad. Sciences, Am. Geog. Soc., N.Y. Zool. Soc.; mem. Am. Philos. Soc. of Phila., Sigma Chi (awarded Significant medal), Phi Beta Kappa. Mem. numerous other scientific soc. U.S. and fgn. Mem. coll. electors Hall of Fame, N.Y.U. Clubs: Ends of the Earth, Angler's (N.Y.C.); Wilderness (Philadelphia); Wayfarer's (Chicago); Explorers' (pres. 1931-35), Doolittle, Boone and Crockett; Peking (Peking). Author many scientific papers, mag. articles, 22 books on exploration, adventure, popular science; among books are: On the Trail of Ancient Man, The New Conquest of Central Asia, Under a Lucky Star, Meet Your Ancestors, Heart of Asia, Beyond Adventure, All About Dinosaurs, All about Whales, Quest of the Snow Leopard. Home: Pondwood Far, Colebrook, Conn. Office: American Museum of Natural History, N.Y.C. 24. Died Mar. 12, 1960. Cremated.

ANDREWS, W(ILLIAM) EARLE, cons. engr.; b. Hampton, Va., Nov. 17, 1899; s. Marcus Peyton and Emma (Smith) A.; student Coll. of William and Mary; m. Mary Taylor Johnson, Oct. 7, 1926; 1 dau., Martha J.; m. 2d, Elizabeth Goodwin, Oct. 22, 1964. Apprentice, draftsman M. P. Andrews & Co., to 1921; draftsman, surveyor, insp. Va. State Hwy. Commn., 1921-22, 24; res. engr. Sam L. Matz Coal Corp., 1922-24; engr.-supt. M. T.McArthur Constrn. Co., 1925-27; dep. chief engr. L.I. State Park Commn. in charge design and constrn. state parks and pkwys. on L.I. including Jones Beach; dep. chief engr. Jones Beach Pkwy. Authority, Bethpage State Park Authority; dir. Jones Beach State Park during initial operation, 1927-34; chief engr.-gen. supt. N.Y.C. Park Dept. during reorgn. under Commr. Robert Moses, chief engr.-gen. mgr. Henry Hudson Pkwy. Authority, also Marine Pkwy. Authority, 1934-36; gen. mgr. and cons. engr. N.Y. World's Fair, 1936-40; cons. in pvt. practice since 1938; designed maj. pkwys. and expressways, beach and park devels.; plans for municipal pub. works in some of largest cities in U.S.; dir. N.Y. Community Trust; partner Andrews & Clark, N.Y.C., 1949—; cons. engr. U.N. Site Improvement; mem. bd. design Bklyn. War Meml.; cons. on Pub. Works for Com. on Orgn. of Exec. Br. Fed. Govt.; cons. N.Y. World's Fair, 1964-65; cons. Temp. State Commn. on Protection and Preservation of Atlantic Shore Front. Bd. mgrs. N.Y. Bot. Gardens. Exec. bd. Greater N.Y. council Boy Scouts. Served as seaman USN, World War I. Mem. Am. Soc. C.E., N.Y. Soc. Profl. Engrs., Theta Delta Chi. Clubs: Brook, Deepdale (L.I.) Golf; Church (N.Y.C.). Home: 116 E. 68th St., N.Y.C. 21. Died Oct. 6, 1965; buried Richmond, Va.

ANDREWS, WILLIAM SYMES, electrical engr.; b. Saltford, Somersetshire, Eng., Sept. 10, 1847; s. Bailey Symes and Selina (Chesterton) A.; ed. pvt. sch., Bath, and bus. coll., Beckington, Eng.; came to America, 1875; m. Emma J. Marden, Jan. 1, 1891. With Edison at Menlo Park, N.J., 1879-81; supt. of testing, Edison Machine Wks. New York, 1881-83; chief elec. engr., Edison Electric Constrn. Co., 1883-86; gen. supt. Marr Constrn. Co., 1886-88; v.p., sec. and treas., Leonard & Izard Co., Chicago, 1888-89; supt. United Edison Mfg. Co., New York, 1889-91; tech. asst. Edison Gen. Electric Co., New York, 1891-92; supt. Peterboro Wks. Canada Gen. Elec. Co., Canada, 1892-93; sec. and gen. mgr. Edison Electric Illuminating Co., Lancaster, Pa., 1893-94; with Gen. Electric Co., in various capacities from 1894, then sons. engineer. Republican. Episcopalian. Home: Schenectady, N.Y. Died July 1, 1929.

ANGAS, W(ILLIAM) MACK, civil engr.; b. Great Burdon, Eng., July 5, 1892; s. William Moore and Elizabeth (Mack) A.; came to U.S., 1895, naturalized, 1917; student Chestnut Hill Acad., Phila., 1911-13; B.S., Mass. Inst. Tech., 1917; m. Elizabeth Abbie Gale, Dec. 26, 1917 (dec. 1952); children—Elizabeth Gale (Mrs. W.T. Hardaker), Mary Mack (Mrs. Arnold Dreyer, Jr.), Jean Moore (Mrs. Willard Starks), Frances Louise (Mrs. Fred Weaver), and Roberta Martin (Mrs. George B. Douglas); m. 2d, Katherine Tracy L'Engle, July 27, 1954. Instr. in nav., tng. officers for merchant service, Shipping Bd., Boston and Baltimore, 1917; commd. lt. (j.g.), Civil Engr. Corps, U.S. Navy, 1918, and advanced through the grades to rear adm., 1948; pub. works officer in charge constrn. work, Naval Air Sta., Pensacola, Fla., 1929-32, Navy Yard, Charleston, S.C., 1938-42, N.Y. Naval Shipyard (Brooklyn Navy Yard), 1942-43; joined staff comdr., 7th Fleet, Southwest Pacific area, 1943; officer in charge 3d Naval Constrn., Brigade and comdr. Constrn. Forces, 7th Fleet, in charge Seabees. Southwest Pacific Area, 1944-45; superintending civil engr. with consulting supervisory responsibility Bureau of Yards and Docks constrn. on East Coast 1945-48; dir., Atlantic Div., Bur. of Yards and Docks, with additional duty on staff of Comdr. in Chief, U.S. Atlantic Fleet and on staff of Comdr. Eastern Sea Frontier, Mar. 1948-May 1950, ret. from active duty in navy with rank of vice admiral; apptd. chmn. civil engring. Princeton U.; cons. to State N.J. on beach erosion problems. Awarded Wason medal by Am. Concrete Inst., 1944; commended by sec. of navy for duty at N.Y. Naval Shipyard. Decorated Legion of Merit. Am. Soc. C.E., Am. Concrete Inst., N.J. Soc. Profl. Engrs., Theta Chi. Episcopalian. Clubs: N.Y. Yacht (N.Y.C.); Nassau. Author: Rivalry on the Atlantic, 1939. Contbr. tech. and semi-tech. articles to various tech. and boating publs. Home: 59 Coll. Rd. W., Princeton, N.J. Died Dec. 12, 1960; buried Arlington Nat. Cemetery, Ft. Myer, Va.

ANGELL, JAMES ROWLAND, educator, psychologist; b. Burlington, Vt., May 8, 1869; s. Dr. James Burrill and Sarah Swope (Caswell) A.; bro. of Alexis Caswell Angell; A.B., U. of Mich., 1890, A.M., 1891; A.M., Harvard, 1892; Litt.D., U. of Vt., 1915; LL.D., Yale, Harvard, Princeton, Columbia, Chicago, Union, Cincinnati, McGill, Wesleyan (Conn.), Brown, Middlebury, Ill. Coll., U. of Mich., Wabash, U. of Calif., New York U., Williams Coll., Dartmouth Coll., Rutgers, University of Pennsylvania, Pennsylvania Military College, and hon. Ph.D., Rensselaer Polytech.; univs. of Berlin and Halle, 1893; traveled and studied at Vienna, Paris, Leipzig, etc.; m. Marion Isabel Watrous, Dec. 18, 1894 (died June 23, 1931); children—James Waterhouse, Marion Waterhouse, Caswell (Mrs. William Rockefeller McAlpin); m. 2d, Mrs. Katharine Cramer Woodman, Aug. 2, 1932. Instr. philosophy, Univ. of Minn., 1893; asst. prof. psychology and dir. psychol. lab., 1894-1901, asso. prof., 1901-05; prof. and head of dept., 1905-19, sr. dean, 1908-11, dean univ. faculties, 1911-19, acting pres., 1918-19, U. of Chicago; pres. Carnegie Corporation, 1920-21; president Yale University, 1921-37; ednl. counselor Nat. Broadcasting Co. since 1937. Exchange prof., The Sorbonne, Paris, 1914. Lecturer Univ. of California Wellesley Coll., Columbia U., Stanford U., etc.; Ichabod Spencer lecturer, Union U. Mem. psychology com. of Nat. Research Council; mem. com. of the adj. gen.'s office on classification of personnel in the Army, 1917-18; advisory mem. com. on edn. and spl. training, 1918; chmn. Nat. Research Council, 1919-20; dir. New York Life Ins. Co., Nat. Broadcasting Co.; vice-pres. Nat. Com. for Mental Hygiene, Internat. Com. for Mental Hygiene. Decorated Chevalier Legion of Honor, 1930, Officer, 1931; Grand Officer of the Order of the Crown of Italy, 1935; Chinese Blue Grand Cordon Order of the Jade, 1937; gold medal Nat. Inst. Social Science, 1937. Trustee Am. Museum Natural History since 1937; curator STephens Coll., 1937; dir. Museum of Sicence and Industry, 1941; director Hall of Fame 1944. Fellow American Academy Arts and Sciences; mem. American Psychological Assn. (pres. 1906), Am. Philos. Soc., Nat. Acad. Sciences, Conn. Soc. of Cincinnati, Berzelius and Aurclian socs., English-Speaking Union (nat. pres. since June 1939), Phi Beta Kappa, Sigma Xi, Delta Kappa Epsilon, Kappa Delta Pi; hon. mem. British Psychol. Soc. Clubs: Graduate (New Haven, Conn.); Yale, University (Boston); Century, Yale (New York); Cosmos (Washington, D.C.); Univeristy (Chicago). Author: Psychology (4th edit.), 1908. Chapters from Modern Psychology, 1911; Introduction to Psychology, 1913; American Education, 1937; also many articles in scientific jours. Editor of Psychological Monographs, 1912-22. Home: 155 Blake Road, Hamden, Conn. Died Mar. 3, 1949.

ANGELL, WILLIAM GORHAM, inventor; b. Providence, R.I., Nov. 21, 1811; s. Enos and Catherine (Gorham) A.; m. Ann R. Stewart, 2 children including Edwin. Partner in reed-making firm, circa 1832; experimented in making iron screws for woodwork; agt., mgr. Eagle Screw Co., 1838; invented screw superior to that of English models which were flooding Am. market; became pres., mgr. Am. Screw Co., (merger of Eagle Screw Co. and New Eng. Co.), 1858; also draftsman, architect and builder. Died May 13, 1870.

ANGIER, WALTER EUGENE, civil engr.; b. Fitzwilliam, N. H., May 18, 1863; s. Phillip Doddridge and Sarah Arabella (Reed) A.; B.S., N.H. Coll. Agr. and Mechanic Arts, 1885; C.E., Dartmouth, 1887; m. Mary Elizabeth Powell, 1889; children—Philip Powell, Mary Estelle, Robert Mitchell. Began practice at Forst Madison, Ia., 1887; moved to Chicago, Ill., 1892; mem. Modjeski & Angier, 1910-27. retired, 1927. Democratic. Baptist. Home: Wheaton, Ill. Died Dec. 20, 1928.

ANGLE, EDWARD HARTLEY, orthodontist; b. Herrick, Bradford County, Pa., June 1, 1855; s. Philip Casebeer and Isabel (Erskine) A.; ed. high sch., Canton, Pa.; grad. Pa. Coll. Dental Surgery, Phila. 1878; M.D., Marion Sims Coll. of Medicine, St. Louis, 1897; Sc.D., U. of Pa., 1915; m. Anna Hopkins, June 27, 1908; 1 dau., Florence Isabel. Began practice of dentistry at Towanda. Pa., 1878; prof. orthdontia, U. of Minn., 1887-92, Northwestern U., 1892-98, Marion Sims Coll. of Medicine, 1896-99, med. dept. Washington U., 1897-99; founder, 1900, and first pres. Angle Sch. of Orthodontia, St. Louis, also of Angle Coll. of Orthodontia and Infirmary, Pasadena, Calif., 1917. Established orthodontia as a speciality and was the first orthodontic specialist; made 40 orthodontic inventions, granted 43 patents. Presbyn. Author: Malocclusion of the Teeth, 1887 (8 edits.) Home: Pasadena, Calif. Died Aug. 11, 1930.

ANGLE, GLENN D(ALE), mech. engr.; b. Imlay City, Mich., Jan. 5, 1891; s. Vernon E. and Mary Edith (O'Neil) A.; student U. of Mich., 1911-13; hon. M.E., Lawrence Inst. of Tech., Highland Park, Mich; m. Eleanor B. Grantham, Sept. 6, 1916; 1 son, John Grantham. Chief draftsman Welch Motor Car Co., 1909-11, Dort Motor Car Co., 1916; designer Curtiss Aeroplane & Motor Corp., 1917; charge of engine design, U.S. Army Air Corps, 1918-24; vice-pres. and chief engr. LeBlond Aircraft Engine Corp., Cincinnati, O., 1928-31; prof. mech. engring., Lawrence Inst. of Tech., 1934-39; pres. Angle Engineering Sales Corp. Associate fellow Inst. Aeronautical Sciences; hon. mem. Eugene Field Soc.; mem. Alpha Tau Omega, Author: Airplane Engine Ency., 1921; Engine Dynamics and Crankshaft Design, 1925; Aerosphere, 1939, 41, 42, 43; Aircraft Engine Design. Contbr. Aero Digest (formerly tech. editor), Popular Aviation, Automotive Industries, Aviation, Sportsman Pilot. Address: Brooklyn MI Died Jan. 26, 1966;buried St. Michael and All Angels Cemetery, Cambridge Junction MI

ANNAND, PERCY NICOL, entomologist; b. Telluride, Colo., Nov. 16, 1898; s. James and Indiana (Nicol) Annand; student Colo. Coll., 1916-17; B.S., Colo. State Coll., 1920, D.Sc., 1945; A.M., Stanford, 1922, Ph.D., 1928; m. Ruth E. Lovett, Sept. 20, 1921; children—Richard Jay, Doris Marye. Asst. entomologist Great Western Sugar Co., Longmont, Colo., 1920-21; asst. in instrn., Stanford, 1921-22; head dept. biology, San Mateo Jr. Coll., 1922-29; asso. entomologist U.S. Bur. Entomology and Plant Quarantine, 1929-30, charge research on sugar beet insects, 1930-32, asst. chief Div. of Truck Crop Insect Investigation, 1932-34, chief Div. Cereal and Forage Insect Investigation, 1934-36, asst. chief Bur. Entomology and Plant Quarantine, charge research, 1936-41, chief of bur., 1941—. Fellow A.A.A.S., Am. Entomol. Soc., Am. Assoc. Econ. Entomologist (pres. 1943), Entomol. Soc. Wash. (pres. 1944), Nat. Research Council, Sigma Xi, Alpha Zeta, Sigma Chi, Pi Kappa Delta. Conglist. Clubs: Cosmos (Washington); Washington Golf and Country (Arlington, Va.). Contbr. tech. jours. Home: 4247 Vacation Lane, Arlington, Va. Office: Dept. of Agriculture, Washington. Died Mar. 29, 1950.

ANSHEN, S. ROBERT, architect; b. Revere, Mass., Jan. 29, 1910; s. Louis J and Sarah (Jaffe) A.; B.Arch., U. Pa., 1935, M.Arch., 1963; divorced;

children—Haven, John. Designer, Clarence Tantau, 1938-39; partner Anshen & Allen, architects, San Francisco, 1940-41, 45-64; draftsman Joslyn & Ryan, 1941-43; tech. dir. Housing Authority City of Vallejo, 1943-45; lectr. U. Cal. at Berkeley, 1952-53; projects include numerous devel. houses and pvt. residences, bldgs., also Coast Counties Gas & Electric Co., Taylor Instruments Co., Chapel of Holy Cross, Sedona, Ariz., Diamond House, Squaw Valley, home on Yankee Point, Carmel, Cal., Internat. Bldg., San Francisco, Chemistry Complex U. Cal. at Berkeley, Master plan U. Cal. at Santa Cruz, Natural Scis. Bldg. U. Cal. at Santa Cruz, Lawrence Meml. Hall Sci. U. Cal. at Berkeley, labs. for NASA, Bank of Cal. Office Bldg., San Francisco. Recipient numerous awards A.I.A., Sunset mag., Nat. Assn. Home Builders, Am. Inst. Steel Constrn., Church Archtl. Guild Am., House and Home, Life mag., Parents mag.; award U. Cal. Lawrence Meml. Hall of Sci. competition, 1962. Fellow A.I.A. Clubs: World Trade, Commonwealth (San Francisco). Home: Mill Valley CA Died May 26, 1964; buried Ferncliff Cemetery, Hartsdale NY

ANSLOW, GLADYS AMELIA, educator; b. Springfield, Mass., May 22, 1892; d. John and Ella (Leonard) Anslow; A.B., Smith Coll., 1914, A.M., 1917, Dr. of Sci. (honorary), 1950; postgrad. U. Chgo., 1921; Ph.D., Yale 1924; research fellow, University of Calif., 1938-39. Demonstrator in physics, Smith Coll., 1914-15, asst., 1915-18, instr., 1918-24, asst. prof., 1924-30, asso. prof., 1930-36, prof. physics 1936-60, research prof., 1960—, Nat. Sci. Found. grantee, 1958—, dir. grad. sch., 1940-58; special consultant, office of field service, Office of Scientific Research and Development, 1944-45. Vice president New England Conference on Graduate Edn., 1946-47; dir. of contract with Office of Naval Research, U.S. Navy, 1948-58. Awarded President's Certificate of merit, 1948. Fellow A.A.A.S., American Academy of Arts and Sciences, American Physical Soc. (vice chmn. New England section 1941-42, chmn. 1942-44); mem. Am. Physics Teachers Assn. (mem. exec. com. 1943-44; asso. editor Am. Jour. of Physics 1935-38), Am. Optical Society, Nat. Federation of Business and Profl. Women, American Assn. Univ. Profs., Am. Assn. Univ. Women (2d v.p. Mass. State Division, 1946-48), Phi Beta Kappa, Sigma Xi. Republican. Unitarian. Researches in nuclear physics, electron collisions, absorption spectra, biological effects of radiation. Contbr. of tech. articles to sci. jours. Home: Northampton MA Died Mar. 31, 1969.

ANTES, JOHN, musician, missionary; b. Montgomery County, Pa., Mar. 14, 1740; ed. Moravian boys' sch., Bethlehem, Pa. Made perhaps the 1st violin, viola and cello in Am.; went to Europe to serve Moravian Ch., also working as watchmaker in Germany; later ordained to Moravian ministry, became 1st Am. missionary in Egypt, was tortured and imprisoned by Turkish bey; composed 3 string trios while recovering in Cairo; settled in Eng., pub. trios there between 1783 and 1790, giving authorship as Giovanni A-T-S, Dillettante (sic) Americano; also composed anthems, motets, chorales, arias; devised mechanism for better violin tuning, improvements for violin bow and keyboard hammer, machine to turn pages of mus. scores. Regarded as 1st important Am. composer of chamber music; influenced primarily by Haydn, also by Handel, Graun, Hasse. Died Bristol, Eng., Dec. 17, 1811.

ANTHONY GARDNER CHACE, coll. dean; b. Providence, R.I., Apr. 24, 1856; s. David Chace and Sarah Clark (Carpenter) A.; ed. English and Classical Sch., Providence; spl. course in engring. Brown U. and Tufts, 1875-78; hon. A.M., 1889, Sc.D., 1905, Tufts; m. Susan Pearson, June 25, 1879. (died 1917); 1 son, Charles Pearson; m. 2d, Ella M. Taylor, April, 1921. Practiced engineering 1878-85; dir. mech. dept., R.I. School of Design, 1886; founded R.I. Tech. Drawing Sch., 1887; dean Bromfield-Pearson Sch. and prof. drawing, Tufts Coll., 1893-1927; dean Engring. Sch., 1898-1927, Tufts Coll. (emeritus). Author: Elements of Mechanical Drawing, 1893; Machine Drawing, 1893; Essentials of Gearing, 1897; Descriptive Geometry (with G. F. Ashley), 1909; An Introduction to the Graphic Language, 1921. Home: New Rochelle, N.Y. Died Nov. 23, 1937.

ANTHONY, JOHN GOULD, zoologist; b. Providence, R.I., May 17, 1804; s. Joseph and Mary (Gould) parents to Cincinnati, 1816, engaged in bus., until 1851; became interested in natural history, collected mollusks in Ohio River; corresponded with mollusk collectors and students in East and Europe, including Louis Agassiz and S.S. Holderman, from 1835; toured Ky., Tenn., Ga. for health reasons, also to collect mollusks, 1853; apptd. by Agassiz in charge of mollusk collection Mus. of Comparative Zoology, Cambridge, Mass., 1863; mem. scientific staff on expdn. to Brazil, 1865; spent later years in classifying and arranging collections at Cambridge, also gathering data on family history. Author papers: "Two Species of Fossil Asterias in the Blue Limestone of Cincinnati", 1846, "Descriptions of New Species of American Fluviate Gasteropods," 1861, "Description of a New Species of Shells," 1865. Died Cambridge, Oct. 16, 1877.

APPLE, ANDREW THOMAS GEIGER, astronomer; b. Hamburg, Pa., Mar. 5, 1858; s. Rev. Dr. Joseph Henry and Elizabeth Ann (Geiger) A.; A.B., Franklin and Marshall Coll., 1878, A.M., 1881; m. Ada Krebs, Sept. 4, 1884 (died 1910). Prof. natural science, Palatinate Coll., Myerstown, Pa., 1880-83; ordained ministry Ref. Ch. in U.S., 1883; pastor in Bedford County, Pa., Catawissa, Bedford, and Washington, D.C., until 1907; prof. mathematics and astronomy and dir. Daniel Scholl Obs. of Franklin and Marshall Coll., 1907—. Made observations of total eclipse of the sun, in connection with Franklin and Marshall expdn., Centerville, Va., May, 1900. Frequent contrb. to scientific and popular mags, and to encys. Home: Lancaster, Pa. Died Feb. 15, 1918.

APPLEBY, WILLIAM REMSEN, metallurgist; b. Hoboken N.J., Feb. 11, 1865; s. J. Charles and Julia M. (Curtis) A.; A.B., Williams, 1886, A.M., 1893; student Columbia Sch. of Mines, 1886-87; m. Elizabeth Y., d. Thomas McDonald Waller, Nov. 21, 1889. Asst. analytical and pharm. chemist, N.Y. Coll. of Pharmacy, 1888-89; prof. mining and metallurgy, 1890-91, prof. metallurgy and dean Sch. of Mines, 1891-1935, emeritus, U. of Minn. In charge of party examining coal and iron properties and operations of the South Manchurian Ry., in Manchuria, 1921. Home: Newton Centre (Boston), Mass. Died Apr. 8, 1941.

APPLEMAN, CHARLES ORVILLE, plant physiologist; b. Millville, Pa., Dec. 6, 1878; s. Emanuel L. and Elizabeth Jane (Gillespie) A.; B.P., Bloomsburg (Pa.) State Normal Sch., 1898; Ph.B., Dickinson Coll., 1903; Ph.D., U. Chgo., 1910; m. Emma Frances Reeme, June 9, 1904; 1 dau., Katharine Reeme. Prof. biology, Lombard Coll., Galesburg, Ill., 1904-08; plant physiologist Md. Agrl. Expt. Sta., since 1910; prof. plant physiology, U. Md., since 1917, also chmn. botany, dean emeritus grad. sch. Fellow A.A.A.S.; mem. Am. Bot. Soc., Am. Soc. Plant Physiologists (pres. 1933), Washington Acad. Scis., Am. Soc. Naturalists, Phi Delta Theta, Phi Beta Kappa, Sigma Xi, Alpha Zeta, Phi Kappa Phi. Author numerous articles and bulls. relating to plant life. Home: College Park, Md. Died July 28, 1964; buried Fort Lincoln Cemetery, Washington.

APPLETON, EDWARD VICTOR, scientist; b. Bradford, Eng., Sept. 6, 1892; s. Peter and Mary (Wilcock) A.; ed. Hanson High Sch., Bradford, Eng.; M.A., St. Johns Coll., Cambridge; hon. S.C.D., Oxford, Leeds, Brussels, Cambridge, Syndey; LL.D. (honorary), Aberdeen, Birmingham, London, Glasglow, St. Andrew's; married Jessie Longson, 1915; children—Margery (wife of Rev. W. M. Lamont), Rosalind Isabel (Mrs. Michael.Collins); m. 2d, Helen Lennie, 1965. Wheatstone prof. physics King's Coll., London, 1924-36; Jacksonian prof., nat. philosophy, U. of Cambridge, 1936-39; sec., Dept. of Sci. and Indsl. Research, 1939-49; principal and vice chancellor Edinburgh U. since 1949. Commd. capt., served in World War I, Royal Engrs. Awarded: Knight Grand Cross Order of the British Empire, Knight Commander of the Bath. Fellow of the Royal Society; mem. of Royal Inst. of Brit. Architects (hon.). Recipient Liebmann Meml. Prize and medal of honor Am. I.R.E.; Hughes Medal of Royal Soc.; Faraday Medal, Inst. of Elec. Engrs., United States Medal of merit, Nobel Prize, 1947. Mem. Am. Inst. of Radio Engrs., the Newcomen Soc., Am. Acad. Arts and Sci., Instn. of Elec. Engrs., Internat. Sci. Radio Union (hon. pres.). Home: Abden House, Edinburgh, Scotland, Office: Old College, The University, Edinburgh, Scotland. Died Apr. 21, 1965; buried Morningside Cemetery, Belhaven Terrace, Edinburgh, Scotland.

APPLETON, JOHN HOWARD, chemist; b.Portland, Me., Feb. 3, 1844; s. Elisha Williams and Martha Wylly (Hyde) A.; Ph.B, Brown, 1863, A.M., 1869, Sc.D., 1900; m. Louise Mumford Day, Feb. 24, 1875; children—Ruth (Mrs. George Albert Goulding), Everard, William Day (dec.), alice, Paul, Marguerite. Asst. instr. and instr. analytical chemistry, 1863-68, prof. chemistry applied to arts, 1868-72, prof. chemistry, 1872-1914, emeritus, Brown. State sealer weights and measures many yrs.; was chemist R.I. State Bd. Agr., and Providence Water Works; mem. U.S. Mint Commn., 1891. Author: The Young Chemist, 1878; Short Course in Qualitative Analysis, 1878; Quantitative Analysis, 1881; Laboratory Year-Book, 1883-92; Beginner's Hand-Book of Chemistry, 1884; Advanced Quantitative Analysis, 1889; Medical Chemistry, 1889; Lessons in Chemical Philosophy, 1890; Metals of the Chemist, 1891; Carbon Compounds, 1892; Chemistry of Non-metals, 1897; Easy experiments of Organic Chemistry, 1898. Home: Providence, R.I. Died Feb. 18, 1930.

APPLETON, NATHAN, cotton mfr., congressman; b. New Ipswich, N.H., Oct. 6, 1779; s. Rev. Isaac and Mary (Adams) A.; m. Maria Gold, 1806, m. 2d, Harriet Sumner, 1833; 7 children including Frances Elizabeth. A founder Waltham Cotton Factory (Mass.), operating 1st loom used in U.S., 1813; developed cotton producing centers Waltham and Lawrence, Mass., also Manchester, N.H.; a founder city of Lowell (Mass.); mem. Mass. legislature, 1815, 16, 21, 23, 24, 27; mem. U.S. Ho. of Reps. from Mass., 22d, 27th congresses, 1831-33, 42; active Mass. Hist. Soc.; an organizer Boston Athenaeum; mem. Acad. Arts and Sci. Author: Remarks on Currency and Banking, 1841. Died Boston, July 14, 1861; buried Mt. Auburn Cemetery, Cambridge, Mass.

ARBUCKLE, HOWARD BELL, chemist; b. near Lewisburg, W. Va., Oct. 5, 1870; s. John David Arbuckle and Elizabeth (Van Lear) A.; B.A., with first honor, Hampden-Sidney Coll., 1889, M.A., 1890; spl. student in chemistry, U. of Va., 1894-96; Ph.D., in Chemistry from Johns Hopkins University, 1898; m. Ida Meginniss, June 4, 1896; children—Howard Bell, Adele Taylor (Mrs. Donald Rohl). Fellowship at Hampden-Sidney Coll., 1889-90; prof. ancient langs., Seminary West of Suwanee (foundation for U. of Fla.), 1891-94; teacher, and prof. Agnes Scott Inst. (later coll.), Decatur, Ga., 1898-1912; prof. chemistry, Davidson (N.C.) Coll., since 1913. A founder of Continental Dorset Club for registry of pure bred Dorset Sheep; contbg. editor Am. Sheep Breeder, 1900-20; founder Edgewood Stock Farm and brought over selected importation of sheep from Eng., 1904. Pres. N.C. Jersey Breeders Assn., 1930. Mem. Am. Red Poll Breeders Assn., Am. Aberdeen-Angus Breeders Assn., Continetnal Dorset Clu (a founder), Am. Chem. Soc. (founder and ex-pres. Ga. sect., ex-pres. N.C. sect.), N.C. Acad. Science (pres. 1925), Pi Kappa Alpha (councilor princeps, 1900-05; grand councilor, 1913-33), Gamma Sigma Epsilon (honorary chemical; grand chancellor 1920-28), Phi Beta Kappa, Omicron Delta Kappa, Scabbard and Blade, Presbyterian. Clubs: Kenmore Golf (founder ; pres. 1925-30), Symposium (Atlanta, Ga.). Author: Redetmination of the Atomic Weight of Zinc and Cadmium, 1898; Laboratory Manual in Household Chemistry, 1912; The Life and Habits of the Honey Bee, 1925. Contbr. numerous articles to chem. lit. and agrl. jours. Researches in corn proteins and cellulose products; discovered pyrolen. Home: Davidson, N.C.; (summer) "Maplemont" Maxwelton Greebrier County, W.Va. Died July 19, 1945. *

ARCHER, PETER mathematician; b. Buffalo, Apr. 22, 1873; A.B., Canisius Coll., Buffalo, 1892; specialized in Greek and Latin classics Campion Coll., Prairie du Chien, Wis., 1894-96; Ph.D., Ignatius Coll., Valkenberg, Holland, 1899, D.D., 1908; studied astronomy and math. U. Vienna, 1911-12, U. Berlin, 1912-14. Joined Soc. of Jesus, 1892; prof. Latin, Greek and Math. Canisius Coll., 1899-1904; spiritual dir. Jesuit faculty at coll., 1937-58; ordained priest Roman Catholic Ch., 1907; prof. Latin, Greek, math., 1908-11, astronomy, math., 1914-25, Georgetown U., also dir. Georgetown Obs.; prof. math. Boston Coll., 1925; treas. Canisius High Sch., 1926-37. Author: The Christian Calendar and the Gregorian Reform, 1941. Address: St. Andrew on Hudson, Poughkeepsie, N.Y. 12601. Died July 22, 1962.

ARCHIBALD, RAYMOND CLARE, mathematician; b. Colchester County, N.S., Can., Oct. 7, 1875; s. Abram Newcomb and Mary (Mellish) A.; B.A., U. of Mt. Allison Coll., N.B., 1894, LL.D., 1923; Harvard, 1895-98; B.A., 1896, M.A., 1897; U. of Berlin, 1898-99; U. of Strassburg, 1899-1900, Ph.D., 1900; Sorbonne, Paris, France, 1909-10; U. of Rome, 1922; hon. doctor, U. of Padua, 1922; unmarried. Prof. mathemetics, librarian, head violin dept. Mt. Allison Ladies' Coll., Sackville, N.B., 1900-07; prof. mathematics Acadia U., Wolfville, N.S., 1907-08; instr. mathematics, 1908-11, asst. prof., 1911-17, asso. prof. 1917-23, prof. 1923-43; prof. emeritus since 1943, Brown University; lecturer University of California 1924, Harvard, 1931, Columbia, 1939-40. Del. to congress univs. of Brit. Empire, London, 1912; del. to celebration 700th anniversary of founding U. of Padua, 1922; rep. for U.S. and Can. of Euler Commn. of Swiss Society of Naturalists, 1922-39; del. to opening of Gennadius Library (Athens), 1926; mem. Am. sect. Internat. Math. Union (mem. Internat. Com. on Bibliography 1924-28). Methodist. Fellow Am. Acad. Arts and Sciences, A.A.A.S. (sec. sect. A, 1925-27, v.p. and chmn. 1928; v.p. and chmn. sect. L 1937); mem. Div. of Phys. Sciences, National Research Council, 1928-31, 1940-43 and 1944-47, chmn. Internat. Com. on Math. Tables and Other Aids to Computation, 1939-50; fgn. fellow Masarykova Akademie Prace (Czecho-Slovakia), Sovietatea de Stiinte of Clju (Rumania); hon. mem. Polish Math. Soc., Math. Assn. (Eng.), Phi Beta Kappa (Harvard Cahpter); mem. Sigma Xi, London Math. Soc., Deutsche Mathematiker Vereinigung, Edinburgh Math. Soc., Unione Matematica Italiana, Am. Math. Soc. (council, 1918-41; librarian, 1921-41; trustee 1923), Math. Assn. America (pres. 1922, trustee, 1923-30), History of Science Soc. (council 1924-40, mem. com. on publs., 1923-30), Founder Mary Mellish and Archibald Mem. Library English and Am. Poetry and Mt. Allison U., Sackville, New Brunswick, Can., 1905-55. Author: The Cardioid and Some of Its Related Curves, 1900; Bibliography of Life and Works of Simon Newcomb, 1905, 24; Carlyle's First Love, Margaret Gordon, Lady Bannerman, 1910; Mathematical Instruction in France, 1910; Euclid's Book on Divisions of Figures with a Restoration, 1915; The Training of Teachers of Mathematics for the Secondary Schools of the Countries Represented in the International Commision on the Teaching of Mathematics, 1918; Benjamin Peirce (1809-1880), 1925; Bibliography of Babylonian and Egyptian Mathematics, 1927-29; Klein's Famous Problems of Elementary Geometry, rev.

edit., 1930; Outline of the History of Mathematics, 1932, 6th edit., 1949. The Scientific Achievements of Nathaniel Bowditch, 1937; Semicentennial History American Mathematical Soc., 1888-1938, 1938; Fifty Mathematical Table-Makers, 1948; articles in Encyclopedia Britannica, 1929, Dictionary of Am. Biography, 1929-36, 1942; Historical Notes on the Education of Women at Mount Allison University, 1854-1954, 1954. Editor: with Introduction and notes of an English transl. of J. Steiner's, Geometrical Constructions with a Ruler—Given a Fixed Circle, 1949; asso. editor of the Bulletin of American Math. Society, 1914-20, of American Math. Monthly, 1917-18; editor in chief latter, 1919-21; Revue Semestrielle des Publications Mathematiques, 1921-34, of Isis since 1924, Scripta Mathematica since 1932; founder, editor Math. Tables and Aids to Computation (quar.), 1943-49. Extensive contbr. to math. jours. and revs. Address: 392 Benefit St., Providence. Died July 26, 1955; buried Halifax, N.S.

ARCTOWSKI, HENRYK, scientist, explorer; b. Warsaw, Poland, July 15, 1871; studied chemistry and geology univs. of Paris, Liege and Zurich, 1888-96; British Mus., London, 1896-7; Ph.D., U. Lemberg, 1912; m. Arian Jane Addy, Mar. 28, 1900. In charge phys. observations, Belgian Antarctic Expdn., 1897-9; discovered and studied geology of Antarctic Andes and established the first complete record of meteorol. observations made in south polar regions; afterwards assisted at Royal Ob. of Belgium until coming to America, 1909; visited Spitzbergen, 1910; chief of science div. N.Y. Pub. Library, May, 1911-19. Sec. for meteorology Belgian Astron. Soc.; mem. Belgica Commn.; Internat. Polar Conf.; fellow Royal Geog. Soc. (London), A.A.A.S., N.Y. Acad. Sciences, Assn. Am. Geographers; mem. Nat. Inst. Social Sciences; corr. mem. Belgian Geol. and Geog. socs. Knight of Order of Leopole; medals and hon. distinctions from Belgian Royal Acad., City of Antwerp, Geog. Soc., London, etc. Author: Die Antarktischen Eisverhaltnisse, 1903; L'Enchainement des Variations Climatiques, 1909; Study of the Changes in the Distribution of Temperature, 1916; also reports pub. by the Belgian Govt. and contbr. to Am. and European scientific jours. Prepared for Am. Delegation to Peace Conf. 14 reports on the geog., mineral resources, ethnography, demography, agr. and industry of Poland and many maps; in Poland with Inter-Allied Commn., Feb.-Mar. 1919. Address: 1 Livingston Av., Yonkers, N.Y. Died Feb. 21, 1958.

ARENBERG, ALBERT LEE, illumination engr.; b. Des Moines, Ia., Nov. 16, 1891; s. Max and Augusta (Kawin) A.; B.S., Ill. Inst. Tech., 1913, E.E., 1917; m. Claire Strauss, June 2, 1923; children—Ann (Mrs. Walter Fuld Gips, Jr.), Henry X., Jane (Mrs. David Eiseman III). Manager lighting division of the Central Electric Company, 1913-24; pres. New England Mills, jobber electric, automotive radio supplies, 1924-29; pres., dir. Harrison Wholesale Co., 1929-62, chmn. bd., 1962-69; pres., chief engr. Luminator Inc., Chgo., 1929-62, chmn. bd., 1962-69; pres. Luminator-Harrison, Inc., Chgo., 1950-62, chmn. bd. 1962-67, chairman of the exec. committee, 1967-69. Mem. Am. Inst. E.E., Western Soc. Engrs., Illuminating Engring. Soc., Am. Transit Assn. Clubs: The Arts, Lake Shore Country, Mid-Am. (Chgo.). Home: Highland Park IL Died Oct. 31, 1969; buried Chicago IL

ARENS, EGMONT, indsl. designer; b. Cleve., Dec. 15, 1889; s. Franz Xavier and Emma (Huegel) A.; student U. N.M., 1911-14, U. Chgo., 1915-16; m. Mathilde Zwilling, July 1952; 1 dau. by previous marriage—Patricia (Mrs. Edward Cummings). Sports editor Albuquerque Tribune-Citizen, 1916-17; owner Washington Sq. Bookshop, 1917; founder Flying Stag Press, 1918-27; printer, pub., editor Playboy mag., 1919-25; art editor Vanity Fair, 1922-23; mng. editor Creative Arts, 192S-27; owner, designer Panglo Lamps, 1927-29; founder, dir. indsl. styling div. Calkins & Holden, 1929-35; pvt. practice indsl. designing, N.Y.C., 1935-62; chmn. bd. Egmont Arens-DeRaffel, Inc., N.Y.C., 1962—; design counsel various nat. corps. Mgr. Peoples Symphony Concerts, N.Y.C., 1917-20, dir., 1920—. Mem. adv. com. Pratt Inst. Art Sch., 1952—; mem. planning com. Center for Graphic Industries, N.Y. U., 1946—. Fellow Soc. Indsl. Designers (pres. 1949-50), Package Designers Council; mem. Am. Union Decorative Artists and Craftsmen (pres. 1929), Soc. Plastics Industry, Inter-Soc. Color Council, Carnegie Printers Alumni (hon.). Club: Huntington (L.I.) Yacht. Author: Consumer Engineering (with Roy Sheldon), 1932. Contbr. articles periodicals and jours. U.S. Del. Internat. Trade Fair, Liege, Belgium, 1955. Home: 16 Blair Dr., Huntington, L.I., N.Y. 11743. Office: 305 E. 40th St., N.Y.C. 16. Died Oct. 1966.

ARENTS, ALBERT, mining engr.; b. Clausthal, Germany, Mar. 14, 1840; grad. Sch. of Mines, Clausthal, 1858; studied at U. of Berlin, Germany, 2 yrs.; widower. Came to U.S., 1865, under engagement to treat lead ores in Hampden Co., Mass.; has practiced in West since 1866; introduced the rectangular large-sized lead-furnaces with boshes at Eureka, Nev., which are the type now used by lead-smelters of U.S.; invented and patented modern "leadwell" or "siphon-tap" for lead blast furnaces. Mem. Am. Soc. Mining Engrs. Address: Alameda, California.

ARENTZ, FREDERIC C. H., engr., contractor; b. Norway, May 6, 1862; s. Peter N. and Trine (Hansen) A.; C.E., Tech. Sch., Throndhjem, 1880; m. Lillian Murfitt, of Evansville, Ind., Jan. 24, 1894; 1 dau., Elizabeth M. Came to U.S., 1881, naturalized citizen, 1886. In employ bridge mfrs. and contractors until 1889; contracting engr. Milwaukee Bridge & Iron Co., 1889-93; chief engr. Lafayette Bridge Co., 1893-1901; engr. in charge highway dept. Am. Bridge Co., 1901-02; chief engr. Joliet Bridge & Iron Co., 1902-08; contr. and engr. on own account since 1908. Mem. Am. Soc. C.E., Western Soc. Engrs., Joliet Chamber of Commerce. Republican. Universalist. Mason (K.T.), Home: 627 Western Ave. Office: Young Bldg., Joliet, Ill.

ARGYLE, WILLIAM ROBERTSON, refinery exec.; b. Spanish Fork, Utah, June 18, 1891; s. Ben and Jane (Robertson) A.; B.S., U. of Utah, 1915; m. Rose Cease, Dec. 24, 1920; children—Jane, Ann, Rosemary. Prin. of pub. high sch., Spanish Fork, Utah, 1915; asst. physicist U.S. Bur. of Mines, 1918-20; fuel engr. Sinclair Refining Co., 1920-25, supt. Marcushook (Pa.) Refinery, 1925-43, asst. gen. mgr., 1945-48, v.p. charge mfg., 1948-56; cons. oil and gas div. U.S. Dept. of Interior, 1956-57; pres. Commerce Oil Refining Co., N.Y.C., 1957—; asso. dir. refining Petroleum Adminstrn. for War, 1943-45. Republican. Presbyn. Clubs: Union League (Phila.); Manursing Island (Rye, N.Y.); Scarsdale (N.Y.) Golf; Aronomink Golf. Home: Leedom Dr., R.D. 1. Media, Pa. Office: 136 E. 57th St., N.Y.C. Died June 1964.

ARMSTRONG, CHARLES, U.S. Public Health Service; b. Alliance, O., Sept. 25, 1886; s. Theodore and Emma Maria (Bertolette) A.; B.S., Mt. Union Coll., 1910, Sc.D., 1933; M.D., Johns Hopkins, 1915; m. Elizabeth Alberta Rich, June 21, 1920; 1 dau., Mary Emma. Interne New Haven (Conn.) Gen. Hosp., 1915-16; asst. surgeon U.S. Pub. Health Service, 1916, passed asst. surgeon, 1920, surgeon, 1924, sr. surgeon, 1936; med. dir., 1942; investigator Nat. Inst. of Health, chief div. infectious diseases. Extension research in botulism, influenza, syphilis, tetanus following vaccination, milk-borne epidemics, dengue, enceopalitsi, psittacosis, poliomeyelitis, choriomeningltis, etc. Med. officer in charge U.S.S. Seneca, World War. Mem. Sigma Alpha Epsilon. Author various pub. health reports. Home: 7005 Meadow Lane, Chevy Chase 15, Md. Retired 1950. Died June 22, 1967

ARMSTRONG, DONALD BUDD, physician; b. Bangor, Pa., Dec. 19, 1886; s. Elmer R. and Sarah (Budd) A.; Ph.B., Lafayette Coll., 1908, D.Sc., 1923; M.D., Columbia, 1912, M.A., 1912; M.S., Mass. Inst. Tech., 1913; m. Eunice Burton, Sept. 19, 1913; children—Donald, Stewart, Lincoln, Burton. Supt. Bur. Pub. Health and Hygiene and dir. Dept. of Social Welfare, N.Y. A.I.C.P., 1913-16, also chmn. sanitary com. Dept. of Health adv. Council, chmn. Dept. of Street Cleaning adv. Council, chmn. com. on block recreation of Recreation Alliance—all N.Y.C.; exec. officer Framingham (Mass.) Community Health and Tb Demonstration, Nat. Tb Assn., exec. officer Nat. Health Council (Washington, N.Y.); lectr. pub. health, N.Y. U., and Columbia; sec. tech. bd. and mem. adv. council Milbank Meml. Fund; 2d v.p. Met. Life Ins. Co., in charge of health and welfare work of policy holders; mem. Presidents Nat. Nutrition Conf. for Defense; mem. bd. cons. N.Y. State Dept. Health; mem. mng. com. Life Ins. Adjustment Bur.; dir. N.Y. Tb. and Health Assn.; former chmn. home safety com. and v.p. Nat. Safety Council; former mem. N.Y. State Com. on Prevention of Diphtheria, U.S.P.H.S., N.Y. State and N.Y.C. Pneumonia Control commns.; chmn. Med. Information Bur., mem. council N.Y. Acad. Medicine; mem. com. on cardivascular disease in industry, N.Y. Heart Assn.; dir. Am. Social Hygiene Assn.; mem. Tb and exec. coms. N.Y. State Charities Aid Assn.; vice chmn. Com. on N.Y. State Tb Control Project, from 1941; former bd. govs. Am. Pub. Health Assn.; bd. dirs. N.Y.C. Cancer Com.; vice chmn. gen. adv. com. Nat. Found. for Infantile Paralysis; bd. dirs. and v.p. Greater N.Y. Safety Council; bd. trustees Am. Mus. Safety; mem. exec. com., dir. and ex-pres. Nat. Health Council; mem. nat. adv. council, Cleve. Health Mus.; ex-pres. N.Y.C. Pub. Health Assn.; mem. hygiene reference bd. Life Extension Examiners; former mem. bd. dirs., War Community Service; mem. Nursing Procurement and Assignment Com., W.M.C.; adv. com. N.Y.C. Dept. of Health. Directed establishment of the first pub. laundry in N.Y.C.; investigated relation of flies to infant mortality; developed plans for Framingham Demonstration and program for Nat. Health Council, Diplomate Am. Bd. Preventive Medicine and Pub. Health, Fellow Am. Pub. Health Assn. (former chmn. com. on accident prevention), A.M.A.; mem. N.Y. State and N.Y. County med. socs., N.Y. Acad. Med., Nat. Tb Assn., Nat. Com. for Mental Hygiene, A.A.A.S., Chi Phi, Alpha Omega Alpha, Delta Omega, Omega Club. Author: Popular Encyclopedia of Health (with Lee K. Frankel and G. M. Fox), 1926; What to Do Till the Doctor Comes (with Grace T. Hallock), 1943; also numerous monographs and pamphlets on med. topics. Home: Scarborough NY Died Aug. 1968.

ARMSTRONG, EDWIN H(OWARD), elec. engr.; b. New York, N.Y., Dec. 18, 1890; s. John and Emily Gertrude (Smith) A.; E.E., Columbia, 1913, Sc.D., 1929; Sc.D., Muhlenberg College, 1941; married Marian MacInnis, Dec. 1, 1923. Assistant in dept. elec. engring., Columbia, 1913-14; asso. with Prof. Michael I. Pupin in research, Marcellus Hartley Research Lab., at Columbia U., 1914-35; prof. of elec. engring., Columbia, since 1934. Served as capt. and major, Signal Corps, with A.E.F., 1917-19. Chevalier, Legion d'honneur, 1919. Awards: Medal of Honor, Inst. of Radio Engrs., 1917; Egleston medal, Columbia U., 1939; "Modern Pioneer" plaque, Nat. Assn. Mfrs., 1940; Holley medal, Am. Soc. Mech. Engrs., 1940; Franklin medal, Franklin Inst., 1941; John Scott medal, Bd. of City Trusts, City of Phila., 1941; Edison medal, Am. Inst. of Elec. Engrs., 1943; award to be known as Armstrong Medal, established by Radio Club of America, 1935; Medal for Merit, 1947; Washington award for 1951 Western Soc. Engrs. Mem. Inst. Radio Engrs. Rep. Presbyn. Contributor to tech. jours. Inventions: regenerative circuit, 1912; superheterodyne, 1918; super-regenerative circuit, 1920; method of eliminating static in radio by means of frequency modulation, 1939. Home: 435 E. 52d St., N.Y. City. Died Feb. 1, 1954; buried Locust Grove Cemetery, Merrimack, Mass.

ARMSTRONG, GEORGE SIMPSON, cons. engr.; b. Brooklyn, Apr. 19, 1886; s. George Simpson and Lucy (Fisher) A.; B.S., N.Y. Univ., 1908, C.E., 1909, M.E., 1913; m. Dorothy Chace Miller, Sept. 22, 1917; 1 son, John C. Employee constrn. dept., Thompson Starrett Constrn. Co., 1908-09; Alphons Custodis Chimney Co., 1909-10; mem. metall. staff Carpenter Steel Co., 1910-12; staff engr. indsl. engrs., Suffern & Son, 1912-14; staff engr. and sr. supervising engr., Miller, Franklin, Basset & Co., 1914-18; independent practice, cons. indsl. engr., 1918-21; asst. v.p. Nat. City. Co., in charge indsl. investigation Nat. City Co. and Nat. City Bank, 1921-32; pres. indsl. engrs. and management consultants, George S. Armstrong & Co., N.Y.C., 1932—. Trustee Robert Coll. Istanbul, Turkey, 1942-58. Pres. Am. Inst. Cons. Engrs., 1947; pres. Assn. Cons. Management Engrs., 1941-42; mem. Am. Soc. M.E., Am. Inst. Mining and Metall. Engrs., Soc. Automotive Engrs., Newcomen Soc. of N.Am., Chaplain Soc. of Can. S.R., Royal Soc. for Encouragement Arts, Mfr. and Commerce (London), indsl. mem. Inst. Aeronautical Science; mem. Com. for Econ. Development (trustee), Zeta Psi (pres., 1937-38), Tau Beta Pi. Clubs: Chemists, Wall Street, Century Association, Canadian (N.Y.C.); Riverside (Connecticut) Yacht. Author: Essentials of Industrial Costing, 1921; An Engineering Interpretation of the Economic and Financial Aspects of American Industry (series), 1940-55; An Engineer in Wall Street, 1962. Home: Gilliam Lane, Riverside, Conn. Office: 551 Fifth Av., N.Y.C. 17. Died Sept. 12, 1962.

ARMSTRONG, LYNDON KING, mining engr.; b. Mukwonago, Wis., Sept. 26, 1859; s. John Adams and Laura V. (Hlllenback) A.; ed. common and high schs., Fairmont, Minn.; m. Charlotte J. Grandy, 1884 (died 1890); 1 son, Halbert; m. 2d, Lulu E. Hyat, Nov. 21, 1896; children—Helen M., L. Maian. In Black Hills, later Mont., 1877-81; chemist and pharmacist in Dak. Ty., 1882-90; mining and cons. practice Spokane, Wash., since 1890; mgr. Armstrong Syndicate. Life mem. Nat. Resources Assn. (pres. 1930-36); fellow A.A.A.S.; mem. Am. Inst. Mining and Metall. Engrs. (life), also Columbia sect. Am. Inst. Mining Engrs. (sec.-treas. 1912-39), Mineral Soc. America, Electrochem. Soc. (chmn. power com. 1934-39), Canadian Inst. Mining and Metallurgy (life); hon. mem. West Coast Mineral Assn., Ass. Engrs. of Spokane; founder and hon. mem. Northwest Mining Assn.; founder mem. Northwest Scientific Assn. (pres. 1927, trustee 1928); life mem. Eastern Wash. Hist. Soc.; asso. mem. Sigma Gamma Epsilon. Protestant. Consecutively editor, asso. editor and mem. editorial bd. Northwest Science. Home: W. 2103 17th Av. Office: Peyton Bldg., Spokane, Wash. Died June 21, 1942.

ARN, WILLIAM GODFREY, civil engr.; b. Terre Haute, Ind., Feb. 7, 1877; s. Godfrey and Elizabeth (Van Brunt) A.; B.S. in C.E., Rose Poly. Inst., Terre Haute, Ind., 1897; unmarried. With L. & N. R.R. Co., 1897-1906, as rodman, masonry insp., building insp., asst. engr. and roadmaster; engr. and supt. Southern Bitulithic Co., Nashville, Tenn., 1906; with I.C.R.R. Co., 1907-17, and since 1919 as asst. div. engr., asst. engr., roadmaster, asst. engr. maintenance of way and asst. chief engr., Chicago Terminal Improvement. Served in U.S. Army, May 8, 1917-June 1, 1919; capt., maj. and lt. col. 13th Engrs.; with A.E.F., in France; now lt. col. engrs., O.R.C. Mem. Am. Soc. C.E., Am. Ry. Engring. Assn., Western Soc. Engrs., Soc. Am. Mil. Engrs., A.A.A.S., Am. Legion, Mil. Order World War, Maintenance of Way Club of Chicago. Citation by Gen. Pershing. Republican. Methodist. Mason (32 deg., Shriner). Clubs: University, Engineers', Prairie, Sojourners, Adventurers', Cambridge, Lincolnshire Country. Home: 5202 Cornell Av. Office: I.C.R.R. Station, Chicago IL

ARNETT, D(AVID) W(ESLEY), biologist; b. Carthage, N.C., Mar. 18, 1882; s. Allen and Mary Jane (Fry) A.; A.B., Wake Forest Coll., 1913, A.M., 1914; postgrad. U. Colo., summer 1922, U. Tex., summers 1926, 38; m. Charlotte Watkins, Dec. 22, 1908; 1 son, Joseph Hoyland. Ordained Bapt. minister; faculty Hardin-Simmons U., Abilene, Tex., 1914-53, prof. of biology since 1914, chmn. dept. 1946-53. Mem.

A.A.A.S. Tex. Acad. Sci. Democrat. Baptist. Home: Abilene, Tex. 79603. Died May 21, 1957.

ARNOLD, AZA, inventor, patent atty.; b. Smithfield, R.I., Oct. 4, 1788; s. Benjamin and Isabel (Greene) A.; m. Abigail Dennis, July 28, 1815. As youth learned carpenter's and machinist's trades; worked in mfg. plant of Samuel Slater, Pawtucket, R.I., 1808; operated (with Larned Pritcher and P. Hovey) machine shop, Pawtucket until 1819; opened cotton mill, Great Falls, N.H., 1819; went back to R.I. few years later (North Providence), made machine for mfg. textile machinery; obtained patent for roving machine for spinning cotton, 1823, introduced into England, 1825, brought law suits because of infringement of patent rights (new code of patents laws passed largely because of his suits, 1836, however he received no compensation); operated Mulhausen Print Works, Phila., 1838-50; patent atty., Washington, D.C., circa 1850-65; invented self-raking and self-setting saw for sawing machines (his last invention, patented 1856). Died 1856.

ARNOLD, BION JOSEPH, electrical engr.; b. Casnovia, near Grand Rapids, Mich., Aug. 14, 1861; s. Joseph and Geraldine (Reynolds) A.; U. of Neb., 1879-80; B.S., Hillsdale (Mich.) Coll., 1884, M.S., 1887; grad. course Cornell, 1888-89; E.E., U. of Neb., 1897; hon. M.Ph., Hillsdale, 1889, hon. diploma, 1903; D.Sc., Armour Inst., 1907; D.Eng., U. of Neb., 1911; m. Carrie Estelle Berry, Jan. 14, 1886 (dec.); m. 2d, Mrs. Margaret Latimer Fonda, Dec. 22, 1909. Chief designer, Ia. Iron Works, Dubuque; mech. engr. C.G.W. Ry.; later cons. engr. for Chicago office Gen. Electric Co.; independent cons. engr. since 1893. Designed and built Intramural Ry., Chicago Expn.; cons. elec. engr. Chicago & Milwaukee Elec. Ry., Chicago Bd. of Trade, C., B. & Q. R.R., Grand Trunk Ry. on electrification of St. Clair tunnel; cons. engr. Wis. State Ry. Commn., 1905-07; devised plan for electrically operating trains of N.Y. Central R.R. in and out of New York, and mem. Electric Traction Commrs. engaged in carrying on the work; mem. electric traction com. Erie R.R., 1900-04; cons. engr. for city of Chicago to revise street ry. systems of city, 1902; chief engr. rebuilding Chicago traction system at cos approx. $140,000,000, and chmn. bd. supervising engrs. same since 1907; cons. engr. Pub. Service Commn., 1st Dist., N.Y., matters connected with subway and st. ry. properties, New York; chief subway engr. city of Chicago and cons. engr. on traction matters for cities of Pittsburgh, 1910, Providence, Los Angeles, San Francisco, 1911, Toronto and Cincinnati, 1912; appraised properties of Seattle Electric Co., Puget Sound Elevtric Ry. Co., Southern Calif. Edison Co., Los Angeles, 1911; Chicago Telephone Company's System, 1911; Internat. Ry. Co., Buffalo, N.Y., 1911; Met. St. Ry. System of Kansas City, Toronto St. Ry., and Lincoln (Neb.) Tel. & Tel. Co., 1913; Mountain State Tel. & Tel. Co., Denver, 1914; Denver Tramway Co., 1915; Brooklyn R.T. Co. surface lines, 1917-18. Chosen by the Citizens' Terminal Plan Com. of Chicago to review plans submitted by Pa. Ry. Co. and others for terminals and to recommend a comprehensive system of steam ry. terminals for city; mem. of Chicago Ry. Terminal Commn. until 1921; mem. Traction and Subway Commn., 1916-17; retained by Mass. Pub. Service Commn. to report on rys. and by Bay State Ry. Co., Boston, 1916-17; adviser to Des Moines, Omaha, Winnipeg, Sacramento, New Orleans, Detroit, Harrisburg, Rochester, Syracuse, Jersey City, Toronto, etc. Pres. The Arnold Engineering Co. Inventor of combined direct-connected machines, a magnetic clutch, storage battery improvements, and new systems and devices for elec. rys.; pioneer in alternating current, direct current and in single phase electric traction systems. Mem. Naval Consulting Board; chairman com. Am. Inst. Elec. Engrs. on Nat. Reserve Corps Civilian Engrs., 1915. Commd. maj. Engr. R.C., Jan. 23, 1917; transferred to regular army, Dec. 14, 1917, with rank lt. col., Aviation Sect., Signal Corps; assigned to equipment div. production sect. of aircraft, Washington, D.C., and continued to act in advisory capacity to Army and Navy; made 2 surveys of aircraft production, and report on aluminum situation; had control for 5 mos. previous to armistice over development and production of aerial torpedoes; hon. discharged Feb. 6, 1919; commd. maj. Aviation Sect., O.R.C., Mar. 28, 1919, col. Air Service U.S. Army Sept. 13, 1919, col. Aux. Corps. Aug. 14, 1925; col. Inactive Reserve since 1929. Trustee Hillsdale Coll.; mem. bd. mgrs. Lewis Inst.; trustee Illinois Inst. of Technology since 1940. Pres. Am. Inst. E.E., 1903-04, elected hon. mem., 1937, was also del. for Inst. at Internat. Elec. Congress, 1900; pres. Western Soc. Engrs., 1906-07, elected hon. mem., 1927, and received Washington Award, 1929, "for devoted, unselfish and preeminent service in advancing human progress"; member A.A.A.S. (vice pres.), American Soc. Promotion Engring. Edn.; 1st v.p. and chmn. exec. com. Internat. Elec. Congress, St. Louis, 1904; chmn. com. Internat. Elec. Congress, St. Louis, 1904; chmn. com. on award Anthony N. Brady medals of N.Y. Mus. Safety; chmn. Am. Committee on Electrolysis; mem. of Inventors Guild, Aero Club of Ill. (past pres.), N.Y. Elec. Soc., Mil. Order World War (comdr. Chicago chapter, 1932-33, state comdr. for Engineers' (New York); Union League, South Shore, Commerical, Engineers, Army and Navy (pres. 1926-27). Home: 4713 Kimbark Av. Office: 231 S. LaSalle St., Chicago, Ill. Died Jan. 29, 1942.

ARNOLD, ERNST HERMANN, M.D.; b. Erfurt, Germany, Feb. 11, 1865; s. Johann Bruno and Ernestine (Orzakowsky) A.; ed. Realgymnasium, Halle, to 1883; grad. Normal Sch. of Gymnastics, Milwaukee, Wis., 1888; M.D., Yale, 1894; univs. of Halle and Leipzig, 1895, courses in surgery and orthopaedics; m. Marie Nagel, Mar. 1889; children—Marie Ernestine, Hermann Bruno. Chief, New Haven Orthopaedic Dispensary; orthopaedic surgeon to Griffin Hosp., Derby Conn., and Grace Hosp., New Haven; late instr. orthopaedic surgery, Yale; dir. New Haven Normal Sch. of Gymnastics. Pres. Anderson Gymnasium Co.; Arnold Coll. for Hygiene and Phys. Edn.; formerly asso. editor Mind and Body. Author: Elementary Apparatus Work, 1896; Manual of School Gymnastics, 1898; Gymnasium Tactics, 1899; Gymnastic Games, 1900; Tactics of the Rank, 1914; Tactics of the Body of Ranks, 1922. Home: New Haven, Conn. Died Mar. 1929.

ARNOLD, HAROLD DEFOREST, physicist; b. Woodstock, Conn., Sept. 3, 1883; s. Calvin and Audra Elizabeth (Allen) A.; Ph.B., Wesleyan U., 1906, M.S., 1907, D.Sc. 1930; fellow in physics U. of Chicago, 1907-09, Ph.D, 1911; m. Leila Stone Beeman, Sept. 3, 1908; children—Audra Elizabeth, Dorothy Edith. Asst. in physics, Wesleyan U., 1906-07; prof. physics, Mt. Allison U., Sackville, N.B., Can., 1909-10; research engr., Western Electric Co., N.Y. City, 1911-24; dir. research Bell Telephone Labs., N.Y. City, 1925—. Capt. Signal Corps, U.S.R., 1917. Recieved John Scott medal and award, 1928, for development of 3-electrode high vacuum therionie tube. Methodist. Home: Summit, N.J. Died July i0, 1933.

ARNOLD, HORACE DAVID, physician; b. Boston, Nov. 4, 1862; s. George Jerome and Anna Elizabeth (Bullard) A.; A.B., Harvard, 1885, M.D., 1889; m. Ida P. Lane, June 8, 1892. House officer Boston City Hosp., Boston Lying-in Hosp., 1889-90; asst. supt. Boston Dispensary and Boston City Hosp.; instr., later prof. clin. medicine, Tufts Coll. Med. Sch., 1912-16, dir. same, 1916. Mem. Nat. Bd. Med. Examiners, 1915. Major, Med. R.C., Apr. 11, 1917. Mem. A.M.A. (chmn. council on med. edn., 1917), Mass. Med. Soc., Am. Climatol. Assn., Boston Soc. for Med. Improvement, Boston Soc. Med. Sciences, etc. Mason, Clubs: Union, Harvard (Boston). Home: 427 Beacon St. Office: 520 Commonwealth Av., Boston, Died Apr., 1935.

ARNOLD, LLOYD, educator; b. Kinmundy, Ill., July 8, 1888; s. James Asbury and Emma Frances (Holt) A.; A.B., Tex. Christian U., 1908, A.M., 1918; M.D., Vanderbilt, 1919; postgrad. chemistry and biology Univs. Munich, Göttingen, Tuebingen, 1911-14; m. Hildred Schoonover, Mar. 1, 1915; children—Lloyd, James. Asst. in anatomy Tulane U., 1908-10, research asst. in physiology, 1915-16; dir. lab. City Hosp., Nashville, 1919-20; asst. in medicine Vanderbilt Med. Sch., 1919-20; asst. prof. bacteriology Loyola U. Sch. of Medicine, Chgo., 1921-22, prof. pathology, bacteriology and preventive medicine 1922-25; dir. lab. Mercy Hosp.; pathologist Misericordia 1921-25; prof. bacteriology and preventive medicine U. Ill. Coll. Medicine, 1925-42; bacteriologist Ill. Dept. Pub. Health, 1927-38; mem. Chgo. Bd. Health 1938-42; pvt. cons. for sanitation and pub. health problems, 1942-63. Mem. A.M.A., Ill., Chgo. med. socs., Am. Soc. Bacteriologists, Am. Assn. Immunologists, Am. Pub. Health Assn. Republican. Methodist. Clubs: Quadrangle, Union League. Died Dec. 25, 1963; buried Kinmundy, Ill.

ARNSTEIN, HENRY, chem. and mech. engr.; b. N.Y. City, Nov. 10, 1886; s. Adolph and Rose (Markstein) A.; A.M., U. of Budapest, 1906; Sc.D., U. of Berlin, 1908; D.Eng., U. of Heidelberg, 1910; m. Nettie Becker, June 3, 1917; children—Burnerd, Lawrence Hugo, J. Robert. Began with Krupp's Essen, Germany, 1908; chief chemist and plant mgr. Fleischmann Yeast Co. and Am. Diamalt Co., 1913-19; cons. engr., San Francisco, 1919-21; cons. chemist and industrial engr., Philadelphia, 1921—; pres. Farm Products Chem. Co. of America. Special tech. adviser to govts. of Cuba, Argentine, Brazil, Columbia and Peru. With Chem. Warfare Service, World War. Contbr. many papers to trade and tech. publs.; many of his works pub. by Cuban govt. Spl. research on industrial fermentation and distillation, particularly the production of yeast and alcohol; developer of process for production of fuel alcohol from waste products. Recieved first prizes from Uruguayan govt. in world-wide competition for best and most practical engineering project dealing woth utilization of surplus agrl. crops and establishment of industries. Home: Philadelphia, Pa. Died July 24, 1935.

ARNY, HENRY VINECOME, pharmaceutical chemist; b. Phila., Feb. 28, 1868; s. Louis Christian and Sarah (Shinn) A.; Ph.G., Phila. Coll. Pharmacy, 1889; studied U. of Berlin, 1893-94, U. of Göttingen, 1892-93, 1894-96, Ph.D., 1896; m. Katharine Moody Smith, Apr. 22, 1903; children—Robert Allen, Sarah Elizabeth, Malcolm Moody, Francis Vinacomb. Prof. pharmacy and dean Coll. of Pharmacy, Western Reserve U., Cleveland, 1897-1911; prof. chemistry, 1911-37, dean, 1930-37, Coll, of Pharmacy, Columbia Univ., now retired. Editor of The Druggists' Circular, 1914-15, Year Book, Am. Pharm. Assn., 1916-22; technical editor of American Druggist, 1928-1936. Remington medalist, 1922; Ebert medalist, 1924. Mem. com. of revision U.S. Pharmacopoeia, com. of revision Nat. Formulary; pres. Am. Conf. of Pharm. Faculties, 1915-16; mem. exec. com. Am. Metric Assn., 1916-20; chmn. Nat. Conf. on Pharm. Research, 1922-29; fellow Chem. Soc. (Eng.); mem. Am. Pharm. Assn. Inst.; hon. mem. German Pharm. Soc. (Berlin), Pharm. Soc. of Great Britain. Democrat. Episcopalian. Club: Columbia Faculty (New York). Author: Principles of Pharmacy, 1909, 4th edit., 1936. Home: 135 Watchung Av., Upper Montclair, N.J. Died Nov. 3, 1943.

ARTHUR, JOSEPH CHARLES, botanist; b. Lowville, N.Y., Jan 11, 1850; s. Charles and Ann (Allen) A.; B.S. Ia. State Coll 1872, M.S., 1877; student Johns Hopkins, 1879, Harvard, 1879, U. of Bonn, 1896; Sc.D., Cornell, 1886; LL.D., State U. of Ia., 1916; Sc.D., Ia. State Coll., 1920; Sc.D., Purdue, 1931; m. Emily Stiles Potter, June 12, 1901. Instr. botany, Univ. of Wis., 1879-81, U. of Minn., 1882; botanist, Expt. Sta., Geneva, N.Y., 1884-87; prof. botany, Purdue, 1887; prof. vegetable physiology and pathology, and botanist, Ind. Expt. Sta., 1888-1915; prof. emeritus, Purdue, since 1915. Speaker Internat. Congress Arts and Sciences, St. Louis, 1904; del. Internat. Bot. Congress, 1905, 10, 30. Fellow A.A.A.S. (sec. sect. F. 1886, asst. gen. sec., 1887, v.p., 1895); mem. Bot. Soc. Am. (twice pres.), Torrey Bot. Club, Deutsche Botanische Gesellschaft, Ind. Acad. Science (pres. 1902), Soc. Promotion Agrl. Science, Am. Acad. Arts and Sciences, Ia. Acad. Science, Phila. Acad. Science, Am. Philos. Soc., Am. Assn. Univ. Profs., Am. Soc. Naturalists, Mycol.Soc. Am., Am. Phytopathol. Soc. (past pres.). Author: Handbook of Plant Dissection (with C. R. Barnes and J. M. Coulter), 1886; Living Plants and Their Properties (with Daniel Trembly MacDougal), 1898; Uredinales, in N. Am. Flora, 1907-29; The Plant Rusts (with others), 1929; Manual of the Rusts in United States and Canada, 1934. Home: Lafayette, Ind. Died Apr. 20, 1942.

ARTOM, CAMILIO, biochemist, educator; b. Asti, Italy, June 5, 1893; s. Vittorio and Gemma (Pugliese) A.; M.D., U. Padua, Italy, 1917, Ph.D. in Physiology, U. Messina, 1923; Ph.D. in Biochemistry, U. Palermo, 1926; m. Bianca M. Ara; July 28, 1928; 1 son, George Victor. Came to U.S., 1939, naturalized, 1946. Instr. physiology U. Messina, Italy, 1920-25; guest investigator dept. biochemistry U. Frankfurt, Germany, 1921, dept. physiology U. Amsterdam, 1924; asst. prof. physiology U. Palermo, Italy, 1925-27, asso. prof. biochemistry, 1927-30, prof., head dept. physiology, 1935-38; Rockefeller Found. fellow dept. physiology U. Naples, Italy, 1927; prof., head dept. physiology, U. Cagliari, Italy, 1930-35; prof. biochemistry Sch. Med. Scis., Wake Forest Coll., 1939-41, prof., head dept. biochemistry Bowman Gray Sch. Medicine, 1941-63, prof. emeritus, 1963-69; cons. Oak Ridge Nuclear Studies. Decorated Italian War Cross, Rumanian War Cross. Fellow A.A.A.S.; mem. Am. Soc. Biol. Chemists, Soc. Exptl. Biology and Medicine, Am. Chem. Soc., Societe de Chimie Biologique (Paris), Societa Italiana di Biologia Sperimentale (Italy). Club: Torch (Winston-Salem). Editor: Archives Intern Physiology (Belgium), Enzymologia (Netherlands). Home: Winston-Salem NC Died Feb. 3, 1970; buried Asti Italy

ASHE, WILLIAM FRANCIS, JR., physician, educator; b. Braddock, Pa., Dec. 14, 1909; s. William Francis and Catherine Nancy (Euwer) A.; A.B., Oberlin Coll., 1932; M.D., Western Res. U., 1936; m. Kathleen Terry Little, Dec. 24, 1945; children—James Allyn, Nancy E., Sarah A., Susan K., Carl Francis, Lynn Terry. Intern. U. Hosp., Cleve., 1936-38; resident U. Cin. Coll. Medicine, 1937-40; research in indsl. medicine Kettering Lab. Applied Physiology, Cin., 1940-42; dir. Inst. Indsl. Medicine, U. Cin. Coll. Medicine, 1946-50; chief internal med. dept. Holzer Clinic and Hosp., Gallipolis, O., 1950-54; prof., chmn. dept. preventive medicine Ohio State U. Coll. Medicine, 1954—; cons. on thermal environmental problems in industry to Govt. India; med. cons. VA Hosp., Dayton O.; vis. staff U. Hosps., Columbus. Dir. nutrition survey Armed Forces, Spain, 1958, Chile, 1960. Served from capt. to lt. col. M.C. AUS, 1942-46. Decorated Order al Merito Bernardo O'Higgins (Chile). Diplomate Am. Bd. Preventive Medicine in occupational medicine, 1955. Fellow, A.C.P., A.A.A.S., Am. Coll. Preventive Medicine, Am. Acad. Occupational Medicine, Aerospace Med. Assn.; mem. A.M.A., Am. Pub. Health Assn. Home: 2006 Collingswood Rd., Columbus 21, O. Died Feb. 27, 1966; buried Union Cemetery, Columbus.

ASHFORD, BAILEY KELLY, med. officer; b. Washington, D.C., Sept. 18, 1873; s. Francis Asbury (M.D.) and Isabella Walker (Kelly) A.; grad. Washington High Sch., 1891; Columbian (now George Washington) U., 1 yr.; M.D., Georgetown U. Med. Sch., 1896; grad. Army Med. Sch., 1898; Sc.D., Georgetown, 1911, Columbia Univ., 1933, U. of Puerto Rico, 1933; hon. M.D., U. of Egypt, 1932; m. Maria Asuncion Lopez, June 24, 1899; children—Mahlon, Gloria Maria, Margarita. Resident phys. Children's Hosp., Washington, D.C., 1895-96; apptd. 1st lt. U.S. Army, Nov. 6, 1897; promoted through grades to col., May 15, 1917. Served with mil. expdn. to P.R., July 1898; and in Battle if Hormigueros, Aug. 13, 1898; div. surgeon 1st Div., June-Oct. 1917; in charge battle training of med. officers, Zone of Armies, A.E.F., Nov. 1917-Nov. 1918; battle clasps for Aisne-Marne and Argonne-Meuse. In

1899 determined cause of the anemia of agrl. class of Puerto Rico, later popularized as "hookworm disease"; founded, 1904, P.R. Anemia Commn., which began first campaign against disease in Western Hemisphere. Del. from U.S. to Internat. Cong. Indsl. and Alimentary Hygiene, Brussels, 1910; mem. med. commn. to Brazil, Rockefeller Foundation, 1916; del. from U.S. to Internat. Cong. of Tropical Medicine and Hygiene, Cairo, 1928. Prof. tropical medicine and mycology Columbia U., collaborating with Sch. of Tropical Medicine (Puerto Rico). Hon. ,e,. and pres. Am. Soc. Tropical Medicine, Puerto Rico Med. Assn.; fellow Am. Coll. Physicians, Am. Coll. Surgeons. Awarded D.S.M. (U.S.); Companion of St. Michael and St. George (Eng.); Grand Cordon, officer 1st class, Order of the Nile. Author: Anemia in Porto Rico, 1904; Uncinariasis in Porto Rico, (with Gutierrez), 1911; also The Organization and Administration of the Medical Department in the Zone of the Armies (Keen's Surgery, Vol. VII); Sprue (Tice's Loose-leaf Medicine), 1931; A Soldier in Science, 1934. Home: San Juan, P.R. Died Nov. 1, 1934.

ASHLEY, GEORGE HALL, geologist; b. Rochester, N.Y., Aug. 9, 1866; s. Roscoe B. and Anna (Hall) A.; M.E., Cornell Univ., 1890, A.M., 1892; Ph.D., Stanford Univ., 1894; Sc.D., Lehigh U., 1937; m. Mary E. Martin, July 11, 1895; children—Carlyle, Jr., Dorothy (Mrs. R.H. Ross). Paleontologist, Rochester, N.Y., 1889-91; asst. geologist, Geol. Survey of Ark., 1891-93; teaching in Calif., 1894-96; asst. state geologist of Ind., 1896-1900; prof. biology and geology and curator of museum, Coll. of Charleston, S.C., 1900-03; prof. pharmacognosy, Med. Coll. State of S.C., 1901-03; asst. geologist, 1901-05, geologist, 1905-12, administrative geologist, 1912-19, U.S. Geol. Survey; state geologist of Pennsylvania, 1919-46; consulting mining geologist since 1946. Acting prof. geology, Vanderbilt U., 1917. Fellow A.A.A.S.; Fellow Geological Soc. of Am., Pa. Acad. Scis., Am. Inst. Mining and Metall. Engrs.; mem. Coal Mining Inst. America, Soc. Econ. Geol. (pres. 1948); hon. mem. Tenn. Acad., Ind. Acad. Science, S.C. Pharm. Assn.; ex-pres. Internat. Assn. of Torch Clubs. Author of numerous geol. reports and articles in lit. and tech. jours. Home: 3037 N. Front St., Harrisburg, Pa. Died May 28, 1951.

ASHMEAD, ISAAC, printer; b. Germantown, Pa., Dec. 22, 1790; s. Jacob and Mary (Noglee) A.; m. Belina Farren, 1828. Served in War of 1812; apprentice to printer William Bradford, Phila.; founded Sunday and Adult Sch. Union (later Am. Sunday Sch. Union), 1819, printer for the Union; established printing business in Phila., 1821, 1st to introduce composition roller and hydraulic press for smooth-pressing wet sheets; 1st in Phila. to use power printing press; mgr. Phila. Inst. for Apprentics. Died Phila., Mar. 1, 1870.

ASHMEAD, WILLIAM HARRIS, asst. curator, div. insects, U.S. Nat. Museum, 1897—; b. Phila., Pa., Sept. 19, 1855; s. Capt. Albert S. amd Elizabeth (Graham) A.; A.M., Fla. Agrl. Coll., 1901; D.Sc., Western Univ. of Pa., 1901; m. Harriet Holmes 1878. Was with J. B. Lippincott Co., Phila.; with brother became pub. agrl. books, agrl. weekly, and daily, Jacksonville, Fla., 1876; edited scientific dept. of weekly, devoting self chiefly to investigation injurious insects; spl. field entomologist, U.S. Dept. Agr., 1887;entomologist State Agrl. Coll., Lake City, Fla., 1888; asst. entomologist and investigator, U.S. Dept. Agr., 1889; spl. studies in Berlin, winter 1889-90; returned to Dept. Agr. Author: Orange Insects (treatise on beneficial and injurious insects in Fla.), 1880 A7. Wrote: Monograph of the North American Proctotryphidae; also 250 contributions to jours. Home: Washington, D.C. Died 1908.

ASHTON, WILLIAM, civil engr.; b. at Salem, N.Y., Feb. 2, 1860; s. Michael Kerr and Jeannette (McNab) A.; ed. Washington Acad., Salem, N.Y.; m. Ella E. Thompson, of Howells, N.Y., Oct., 1893. Chainman to asst. engr. on different rys., 1881-87; div. engr. U.P. R.R., Denver, 1887-1900; resident engr., 1900-04, chief engr., May 1, 1904-June 1, 1911, Ore. Short Line R.R., with jurisdiction over S.P. lines east of Sparks, Nev.; consulting engr. Utah Light & Ry. Co., Mar. 1, 1907-June 1, 1911; consulting engr., Salt Lake City, since June 1, 1911. Mem. Am. Soc. C.E., Nat. Geog. Soc. Address: Salt Lake City, Utah.

ASKENSTEDT, FRITZ CONRAD, physician; b. Venersborg, Sweden, Jan. 18, 1865; s. Frederik and Eleonore M. (Hjorthen) A.; ed. pvt. schs., Sweden; came to America, 1884; M.D., Pulte Med. Coll., Cincinnati, 1889; post-grad. work Charité Hosp., Berlin, Germany, and Serafimerlazarettet, Stockholm, Sweden, 1900; James Mackenzie's Inst. for Clin. Research, St. Andrews, Scotland, and Nat. Hosp. for Diseases of Heart, London, 1920; m. Lillian S. Bryan, M.D., May 10, 1904. Prof. pathology, Southwestern Homeo. Med. Coll., 1896-1910, phys. diagnosis and diseases of chest, 1899-1910, registrar, nosis and diseases of chest, 1899-1910, registrar, 1906-10; visiting phys., Louisville City Hosp., 1900-11. Fellow A.M.A.; mem. Am. Inst. Homeopathy, Ky. Homeo. Med. Soc. (pres. 1906-07), Ky. State Med. Assn., Falls Cities Homeo. Med. Soc. (pres., 1906-07), Southern Homeo. Assn.; hon. mem. bd. for life, Scandinavian Assn. of Louisville, Devised quantitative tests for indican and glycuronates in urine. Address: 1210 4th Av., Louisville, Ky. Died June 16, 1943.

ASTON, JAMES, metall. engr.; b. Bury, Eng., June 14, 1876; s. Thomas and Mary (Marsden) A.; B.S. in E.E., U. of Wis., 1898, Ch.E., 1912. D.Sc. (hon.), 1933; m. Ellen Gertrude Felsen, Jan. 11, 1902; children-Alice Marsden (Mrs. Wm. Schellhammer), Ruth (Mrs. Ruth Wright). Brought to U.S., 1879, naturalized, 1906. In steel and foundry business, 1898-1908; research on iron alloys, U. of Wis., 1908-12; prof. metallurgy, U. of Cincinnati, 1912-15; metall. engr. U.S. Bureau of Mines, 1915-16; metallurgist A. M. Byers Co., Pittsburgh, 1916-26; prof. mining and metallurgy and head dept., Carnegie Inst. Tech., 1926-35; also cons. metallurgist, A. M. Byers Co. since 1926. Inventor of process for mfr. of wrought iron, displacing hand pubbling. Awarded Robert W. Hunt medal, Am. Inst. Mining and Metall. Engrs. Mem. Engrs. Soc. of Western Pa., Am. Soc. for Metals, British Iron and Steel Inst., Am. Iron and Steel Inst., Am. Inst. Mining and Metall Engrs., Am. Soc. for Testing Materials, Sigma Xi, Tau Beta Pi, Alpha Chi Sigma, Phi Lambda Upsilon. Mason. Club: University, Shannopin Country (Pittsburgh). Co-author: Johnson's Materials of Construction. Home: 7315 Perrysville Av., Ben Avon, Pittsburgh, Pa. Died Sept. 27, 1962.

ATKINS, HARRY THOMAS, physician; b. Cin., Jan. 13, 1910; s. Frank Pearce and Louise (Isham) A.; M.D., U. Cin., 1937; m. Nina Augusta Anderson, Oct. 7, 1944; children—John Anderson, Thomas Pearce. Intern Cin. Gen. Hosp., 1936-37, asst. resident obstetrics, 1937-38, resident obstetrics, 1938-39, later cons.; resident in surgery Christ Hosp., Cin., mem. staff, 1946-52; house surgeon Free Hosp. for Women, Brookline, Mass., 1940-41; mem. staffs Bethesda Hosp., Cin., 1946-52, Ft. Hamilton Hosp., Mercy Hosp., Hamilton, O., 1952-60. Instr. obstetrics, U. Cin. Served to comdr. M.C., USNR, 1941-46. Diplomate Am. Bd. Obstetrics and Gynecology. Fellow Am. Coll. Obstetrics and Gynecology; mem. A.M.A., Gyro Internat., Alpha Kappa Kappa. Republican. Presbyn. Home: Cincinnati OH Died Nov. 21, 1970; buried Spring Grove Cemetery, Cincinnati OH

ATKINS, JEARUM, inventor; b. Vt., flourished 1840-80. Millwright, nr. Chgo., circa 1840; inventor of the self-rake which was added to the reaper and imitated motion of human arms, patented 1852; reaper with his attachment manufactured by J. S. Wright, Chgo., 1853-56.

ATKINSON, DONALD TAYLOR, physician; b. Shemogwe, New Brunswick, Can., May 31, 1874; s. Joseph Silliker and Elizabeth (Grant) A.; M.D., Hosp. Coll. of Medicine, Louisville, Kyl, 1902; K.K. Allgemeines Krankenhaus, Vienna, Austria, 1906-07; student Royal London (Eng.) Ophthal. Hosp., 1907; Sc.D., Center College, Danville, Ky., 1944; LL.D., honoris causa, Huron (S.D.) College, 1945; m. Wanda Wiley, 1937. Became naturalized U.S. citizen, 1916. Engaged in practice of medicine at San Antonio, Tex., since 1902; mem. staff of Nix Hospital, Santa Rosa Infirmary, Medical and Surgical Hosp., San Antonio; specialist in diseases of eye; senior partner Atkinson & DeGasperi; asso. editor Eye, Ear, Nose and Throat Jour.; editor ophthalmic dept. Texas Med. News, 1905-09. Awarded Patronis Medal Award, U. Florence, 1951; selected outstanding author of yr., 10th annual Writers Roundup, Theta Sigma Phi, 1958. Fellow of the American College of Surgeons, Am. Acad. Ophthalmology and Otolaryngology, Royal Acad. Medicine (Ireland), Internat. Coll. Surgeons (Geneva, member of the adv. bd., school surgical history), National Surgical Soc. of Italy, 1951; mem. Am. Med. Editors and Authors Assn., A.A.A.S., Am. Med. Assn. of Vienna (life), Am. Southern, Bexar County and Tex. State Med. assns., Nat. Tuberculosis, Am. Genetic and Am. Social Hygiene assns., Nat. Soc. Arts and Letters, Nat. Assn. Authors and Journalists, The River Art Group. Republican. Club: Oak Hills Country. Author: Social Travesties, 1912; A Treatise on Cataract, 1913; Great Medical Innovations, 1915; External Diseases of the Eye, 1934, 2d edit., 1936; The Problem of the Secondary Cataract, 1934; Magic Myth and Medicine (World Publishers), 1936; The Ocular Fundus in Diagnosis and Treatment, 1937, many scientific essays including The Artificial Pupil in the Restoration of Vision. Art collaborator Southall's Introduction to Physiological Optics; Rea's System of Neuro Ophthalmology; Texas Surgeon (autobiography), 1958. Illustrates his technical books himself; reproductions of his illustrations in several med. books. Originator of Atkinson trocheo laryngoscope Home: Rt. 11, Box 121. Office: 827 Medical Arts Bldg., San Antonio, Tex. Died Mar. 20, 1959; buried Grove Hill Meml. Park Cemetery, Dallas.

ATKINSON, GEORGE FRANCIS, botanist; b. Raisinville, Monroe Co., Mich., Jan. 26, 1854; s. Joseph and Josephine (Fish) A.; student Olivet Coll,m 1878-83; Ph.B., Cornell, 1885; m. Lizzie S. Kerr, Aug., 1888. Asst. prof. entomology and gen. zoölogy, 1885-86. asso. prof., 1886-88, U. of N.C.; prof. botany and zoölogy, U. of S.C., and botanist of exptl. sta., 1888-89; prof. biology, Ala. Poly Inst. and Agrl. and Mech. Coll. pf Ala., and biologist of exptl. sta., 1889-92; asst. prof. cryptogamic botany and head dept. botany, 1896—; Cornell U. Asso. editor The Botanical Gazette, 1896-98. Author: Biology of Ferns, 1894; Elementary Botany, 1898; Lessons in Botany, 1900; Studies of American Fungi, 1900; Mushrooms, Edible, Poisonous, Etc., 1903; First Studies on Plant Life, 1904; College Text-Book of Botany (enlargement of Elementary Botany), 1905. Contbr. to botan. jours. Home: Ithaca, N.Y. Died Nov. 14, 1918.

ATKINSON, RALPH WALDO, elec. engr.; b. Smithland, Ia., June 16, 1887; s. Walter Edward and Dessa Flora (Waterman) A.; grad. high sch., Carroll, Ia., 1901; B.S. in E.E., Ia. State Coll., 1906, E.E., 1911; m. Elsie Lee Mercer, June 1, 1916; children—Alice Lee (Mrs. Norman Morash), George Mercer. Assistant to chief engineer, Standard Underground Cable Company (a division of General Cable Company), 1908-23, chief elec. engr., 1923-29; dir. high voltage research General Cable Corp. since 1929, chief research engineer, 1944-52, director research, 1952-54, consulting engineer, 1954—; guest prof. elec. engring. Bihar Inst. Tech., India, 1956-60. Director Westfield Y.M.C.A., First Meth. Ch. of Westfield. Awarded Marston medal Ia. State Coll., 1951. Fellow Am. Inst. E.E. (mem. bd. examiners), A.A.A.S.; asso. Instn. E.E. (British); mem. Inst. Metals (England), Am. Standards Association (chmn. tech., com. on standards and definitions, com. C8 on wires and cables). Republican. Mason. Clubs: Engineers (N.Y.C.); Rotary (Sindri, India). Contbr. jours. Inventor methods of manufacturing, testing, terminating and jointing high voltage electric cables. A scientific observer at the Bikini atomic tests. Home: 206 Watchung Fork, Westfield, N.J. Office: Gen. Cable Corp., Bayonne, N.J. Died May 17, 1961; buried Alpine Cemetery, Perth Amboy, N.J.

ATKINSON, THOMAS WILSON, educator; b. Spalding Co., Ga., Nov. 28, 1867; s. James Archibald and Rebekah Catherine (Wilson) A.; B.S., La. State U., 1891. C.E., 1892; grad. student Johns Hopkins, 1894-95; Cornell U., 1896-97; m. Marie Antoinette Bilger, July 27, 1898. Instr., prep.dept., La. State U., 1891-94, asst. prof. physics and mechanics, 1895-96, prof. mechanics and drawing, 1897-99, prof. physics and mechanics 1899-1906, prof. physics and elec. engring., 1906-07, prof. elec. engring. amd dean Coll. of Engring., 1907-27, dir. Engring. Expt. Sta., 1923-27, acting pres., 1927-29, pres., 1929-31. Dir. vocational training U.S. Soldiers, La. State U., June-Nov. 1918. Democrat. Episcopalian. Home: Baton Rouge, La. Died Dec. 25, 1933.

ATKINSON, WILLIAM BIDDLE (BITTLE), physician; b. Haverford Township, Delaware Co., Pa., June 21, 1832; grad. Phila. Central High School, 1850 (A. M., 1855); Jefferson Med. Coll., 1853. Has been editor of several med. jours.; lecturer on diseases of Children, Jefferson Med. Coll.; prof. sanitary science and pediatrics, Medico-Chirurg. Coll., Phila.; permanent sec. Am. Med. Assn., 1864-99; permanent sec. Med. Soc., State of Pa., 1862-97; has been pres. Phila. Co. Med. Soc.; member several learned socs.; married. Author: Hints in the Obstetric Procedure, 1879; Therapeutics of Gynecology and Obstetrics, 1881; Physicians and Surgeons of the United States, 1879; all O1; also many monographs on medical subjects. Address: 864 East Chelten Av., Germantown, Philadelphia.

ATKINSON, WILLIAM BROCKLISS, anatomist, clergyman; b. N.Y.C., Feb. 26, 1918; s. William Edmunds and Ethel Mae (Carstang) A.; B.S., U. Va., 1938, M.S., 1940; Ph.D., Yale, 1943; m. Barbara Uhl, June 16, 1943; children—William Eugene, Pamela Jane. Asst. biology U. Va., 1938-40; asst. anatomy Yale, 1941-43; instr. anatomy Columbia, 1943-47, asst. prof., 1947-49; histochemist Army Chem. Corps Research and Devel. Dept., 1949-50; asso. prof. anatomy U. Cin., 1950-58; prof. anatomy, chmn. dept. U. Louisville, 1958—; sci. asso. Roscoe B. Jackson Meml. Lab., 1953—. Ordained deacon P.E. Ch., 1954, priest, 1956; deacon charge Ch. of Good Shepherd, Norwood O., 1954-55, curate, 1955-58; priest charge Ch. St. Simon of Cyrene, Lincoln Heights, O., 1957-58; curate Grace Ch., Louisville, 1958-60. Asso. Christ the King Found., 1959—. Mem. Am. Assn. Anatomists, Am. Assn. U. Profs., Endocrine Soc., Histochem. Soc., Ky. Acad. Sci., Soc. Exptl. Biology and Medicine, Sigma Xi, Sigma Alpha Epsilon. Author numerous sci. articles. Home: 3002 Tremont Dr., Louisville 5. Died Mar. 4, 1961; buried N.Y.C.

ATKINSON, WILLIAM SACKSTON, scientific illustrator; b. Cazenovia, N.Y., Sept. 17, 1864; s. James and Mary (Peck) A.; student Cazenovia Sem.; A.B., Stanford U., 1899; unmarried. With Stanford U. since 1896; specializes in zoöl. and bot. drawing, restoration of fossil fishes of Calif. Miocene. Progressive Rep. Conglist. Has illustrated some 200 scientific publs. of Dr. David Starr Jordan and others, also of Carnegie Mus. and Calif. Acad. Science, and 3 vol. work entitled "Illustrated Flora of the Pacific States." Home: Stanford University, Calif. Deceased.

ATLEE, JOHN LIGHT, surgeon; b. Lancaster, Pa., Nov. 2, 1799; s. Col. William Pitt and Sarah (Light) A.; M.D., U. Pa., 1820; m. Sarah Franklin, Mar. 12, 1822, 3 children. First doctor to remove successfully both ovaries in 1 operation, 1843; a founder, pres. Lancaster County Med. Soc., 1844; a founder Pa. Med. Soc., 1848, pres., 1857; an organizer A.M.A., Phila., v.p., 1865, pres., 1882; a promoter of Franklin and Marshall Coll., Lancaster, prof. anatomy until 1869; mem. Pa. Pub. Sch. Bd.; trustee Pa. State Lunatic Asylum; hon. fellow Am. Gynecol. Soc. Died Lancaster, Oct. 1, 1885.

ATTWOOD, FREDERIC, business exec.; b. East Haddam, Conn., Apr. 23, 1883; s. Frederic J. H. and Margaret (MacConnell) A.; grad. Bklyn. Latin Sch., 1900; M.E., E.E., Columbia, 1904; m. Gladys Hollingsworth, Oct. 27, 1917; 1 son, William Hollingsworth. Traffic engr. N.Y. Telephone Co., 1904-07; European rep. Air. Reduction Co., 1915-17; gen. European rep. Ohio Brass Co., elec. mfrs., 1919; v.p., dir. Canadian Ohio Brass Co., Ohio Brass Co. from 1927; dir. Melville Shoe Corp. Commd. maj. C.E., A.E.F., Nov. 1917; attached to Gen. Hdqrs. A.E.F., C.W.S., Gen. Tech. Bd. War Damages Bd. Am. Commn. to Negotiate Peace, U.S. Liquidation Commn.; hon. disch. Oct. 1919; col. O.R.C. Decorated Officer Legion of Honor (France). Pres. U.S. nat. com. Internat. Conferences Large Elec. Systems; World Power Conf., Internat. Electrotech. Commn. Mem. Inst. Elec. and Electronic Engineers, Phi Gamma Delta. Republican. Episcopalian. Clubs: Bankers, Engineers, Columbia University (New York City); St. Cloud Country; University; Interallied (Paris, France). Home: New Canaan CT Died Aug. 26, 1969; buried Lake-View Cemetery, New Canaan CT

ATWATER, REGINALD MYERS, physician, pub. health official; b. Canon City, Colo., Aug. 6, 1892; s. Samuel Henry and Selina (Myers) A.; A.B., Colo. Coll., 1914, LL.D., 1949; M.D., Harvard, 1918; M.P.H., Johns HopkiHopkins, 1920, Dr. P.H., 1921; m. Charlotte Martin Penfield, July 10, 1919; children—Caroline Penfield (Mrs. Edwin Slater Leonard), Martha Martin (Mrs. John Bodine Duncan), Constance Avery (Mrs. Edward J. Bowser, Jr.), John Bancroft, David Sterline. Med. house officer Peter Bent Brigham Hosp., Boston, 1918-19; fellow in pub. health Rockefeller Foundation, 1919-21; cons. epidemiologist N.C. State Bd. of Health, 1920; asso. prof., hygiene, Hunan-Yale Coll. of Medicine, Changsha, Hunan, China, 1921-25; med. officer of health, Kuling Estate, Kiang-si, China, 1922-25; instr. preventive medicine and hygiene, Harvard Med. Sch., 1925-27; instr. epidemiology, Harvard Sch. Pub. Health, 1925-27; commr. of health, Cattaraugus County Dept. of Health, Olean, N.Y., 1927-35; exec. sec. Am. Pub. Health Assn., N.Y. City, since 1935; mng. editor Am. Jour. Pub. Health; spl. cons. U.S.P.H.S.; bd. dirs. Nat. Health Council; adv. com. Cleveland Health Museum. Served in Med. R.C., U.S. Army, 1918-19. Decorated Order of Carlos J. Finlay, Republic of Cuba, 1939; received Sedgwick Memorial Medal, 1947; received the Lasker award in public health, 1957. Fellow American Public Health Assn., American Med. Assn. (honorary) Royal Sanitary Inst. (Eng.); member New York State Med. Soc., Phi Beta Kappa, Alpha Omega Alpha, Delta Omega. Democrat. Mem. The Riverside Ch., N.Y. City. Contbr. to jours. Home: 2 Crows Nest Rd., Bronxville, N.Y. Office: 1790 Broadway, New York 19, N.Y. Died Oct. 18, 1957; buried Brookside Cemetery, Englewood, N.J.

ATWATER, RICHARD MEAD, chemist; b. Providence, R.I., Aug. 10, 1844; s. Stephen and Mary W. (Weaver) A.; A.B., Brown U., 1865, A.M., 1868; spl. studies in chemistry; m. Abby Sophia Greene, Sept. 29, 1867. Supt. schs., Millville, N.J., 1874-75; identified with chem. and mfg. interests, especially with coke and glass; in mercantile business, Paris, 1900-06; farmer, Chadds Ford, Pa., 1907—. Trustee, Brown U., 1878—; judge glass exhibits Chicago Expn. 1893. Hon. v.p. Internat. Chemists' Assn., Berlin, 1903. Contbr. to tech. jours. on glass and coke mfg. Commr. and mayor of Sea Isle City, N.J., 1913-17. Home: Chadds Ford, Pa. Died Oct. 30, 1922.

ATWATER, WILBUR OLIN, prof. chemistry Wesleyan Univ., 1873—; b. Johnsbrugh, N.Y., May 3, 1844; grad. Wesleyan U., 1865; Ph.D., Sheffield Scientific Sch., Yale, 2869; student univs. of Leipzig and Berlin; m. Marcia Woodard, Aug. 26, 1874. Prof. chemistry East Tenn. Univ., 1871-72, Me. State Coll., 1873; dir. Conn. Agrl. Expt. Sta., 1875-77; dir. Storrs (Conn.) Expt. Sta., 1887-1902; founded, 1888, and until 1891 dir., Office Expt. Stas., U.S. Dept. Agr., 1891—; spl. agt. Dept. Agr., and, 1908—, chief of nutrition investigations. Author over 150 papers on chem. and allied subjects, notably (with F. G. Benedict) An Experimental Inquiry Regarding the Nutritive Value of Alcohol, Vol. VIII, Nat. Acad. Sciences. Home: Middletown, Conn. Died 1907.

ATWOOD, WALLACE WALTER, geographer, geologist; b. Chicago, Ill., Oct. 1, 1872; s. Thomas Green and Adalaide Adelia (Richards) A.; B.S., U. of Chicago 1897, Ph.D., 1903 D.Sc., Worcester Polytechnic Institute, 1943; LL.D., Clark University, Worcester, Mass., 1946; married Harriet Towle Bradley, Sept. 22, 1900; children—Rollin Salisbury, Wallace Walter, Jr., Mrs. Harriet Olmsted, Mrs. Mary Hedge; Asst. geologist, N.J. Geol. Survey, 1897, Wis. Natural History Survey, 1898-99; instr. Lewis Inst., Chicago, 1897-99, Chicago Inst., 1900-01; fellow asst. and asso., 1899-1903, instr. and asst. prof. physiography and gen. geology, 1903-10, asso. prof., 1910-13, U. of Chicago; prof. physiography, Harvard, 1913-20; president Clark Univ., Sept. 1920-1946, president emeritus since 1946; dir. Clark School of Geography, 1920-46. Asst. geologist, U.S. Geological Survey, 1901-09, geologist since 1909; geologist, Ill. Geol. Survey since 1906. Recipient, distinguished service award, U. of Chgo. 1945, distinguished service medal, Chgo. Geog. Soc., 1948. Pres. Nat. Parks Assn., 1929-33. Fellow Geol. Soc. Am., Am. Acad. Arts and Sciences, Am. Antiquarian Soc.; mem. Assn. Am. Geographers (ex-pres.), Chicago Geog. Soc., Ill. Acad. Sciences, Chicago Museum and Library Extension Council, Nat. Council Geography Teachers, Delta Kappa Epsilon; pres. Pan-Am. Inst. of Geography and History, 1932-35, now hon. pres.; mem. Commn. Internationale de l'Atlas des Formes du Relief Terrestre; hon. member national Academy of Science of Mexico, Mexican Society of Geography and Statistics. Capt., Harvard R.O.T.C., 1917. Author: Physical Geography of the Drvils Lake Region (with R.D. Salisbury), 1899; Physical Geography of the Evanston-Waukegan Region of Ill. (with J. W. Goldthwait), 1908; Interpretation of Topographic Maps, 1908; Glaciation of the Uinta and Wasatch Mountains, 1909; Mineral Resources of Southwestern Alaska, 1910; Geology and Mineral Resources of the Alaska Peninsula, 1911; New Geography, Book 11, 1920; Home Life in Far Away Lands, 1928; The Americas, 1929; National Beyond the Seas, 1930; The United States Among the Nations, 1930; The World at Work, 1931; Physiography and Geology of the San Juan Mountains, Colorado, 1932; The Growth of Nations, 1936; Physiographic Provinces of North America, 1940; The Protection of Nature in the Americas (publ. No. 50, Pan-Am Institute of Geog. and History), 1941; The United States in the Western World, 1944; The Rocky Mountains, 1945; co-author (with Ruth E. Pitt) Our Economic World, 1948; also numerous sci., and ednl. papers. Founder and editor of Economic Geography, 1925. Clubs: Worcester, Worcester Economic; Tatnuck Country; Cosmos (Washington, D.C.); University (Boston and New York). Home: 21 Otsego Road, Worcester 5, Mass. Died July 24, 1949.

AUCHINCLOSS, WILLIAM STUART, author, inventor; b. New York, N.Y., Mar. 19, 1842; s. John A.; C.E., Rensselaer Poly. Inst., 1862. In construction dept. A.&G.W. Ry., and Jersey City Locomotive Wks., 1863-69; mfr. rolling stock and shipbuilder, 1871-79; commission merchant, 1879-95. Invented averaging instrument for rapid calculation of accounts. U.S. commr. Paris Expn., 1867. Author: Link and Valve Motions; Ninety Days in the Tropics; The Book of Daniel Unlocked; Chronology of the Holy Bible. Home: Atlantic Highlands, N.J. Died 1928.

AUCHTER, EUGENE CURTIS, horticulturist; b. Elmgrove, N.Y., Sept. 14, 1889; s. William David and Florence Monroa (Curtis) A.; B.S., Cornell U., 1912, M.D., 1918, Ph.D., 1923; m. Catherine Elizabeth Beaumont, Aug. 25, 1914. Asst. in pomology, Cornell U., 1911-12; asst. and asso. prof. of horticulture, U. W.Va., 1912-17— head dept. of horticulture, U. of Md., 1918-28; prin. horticulturist in charge div. of fruit and vegetable crops and diseases, U.S. Dept. of Agr., 1928-38, chief of Bureau of Plant Industry, 1938-42, administrator of Agricultural Research, 1942-45; pres. and dir. Pineapple Research Inst. of Hawaii, also v.p. Pineapple Growers Assn. since 1945. Mem. bd. of mgrs. New York Botanical Gardens. Hon. fellow Royal Hort. Soc. of London; fellow A.A.A.S.; mem. Am. Soc. Plant Physiologists, Wash. Acad. Sci., Am. Soc. Naturalists, Bot. Soc. of Washington, American Phytopathology Society, Am. Soc. Hort. Science, Am. Genetics Assn., Sigma Xi, Phi Kappa Phi, Alpha Zeta. Clubs: Cosmos (Washington, D.C.); Rotary, Pacific, Oahu Country, (Honolulu, Hawaii). Author: (with H.B. Knapp) Orchard and Small Fruit Culture, 1929; Growing Tree and Small Fruit, 1929. Home: 4471 Kahala Av., Honolulu, Hawaii. Office: Pineapple Research Institute, 2500 Dole St., Honolulu, T.H. Died July 8, 1952; buried Oahu Cemetery, Honolulu.

AUD, GUY, surgeon; b. Cecilia, Ky., Aug. 29, 1887; s. Charles Zachary and Lura (Bayne) A.; A.B., St. Xavier Coll., Louisville, 1904; M.D., U. Louisville, 1909; Fellow in surgery Mayo Clinic, Rochester, Minn., 1911-15. Surg. interne Lying-in Hosp., N.Y.C., 1909, N.Y. Hosp. for Relief of Ruptured and Crippled, 1910, Bellevue Hosp., 1911; pvt. practice surgery, Louisville, since 1919; faculty Sch. of Medicine, U. Louisville, since 1915, prof. surgery since 1946; attending surgeon Louisville Gen. Hosp., St. Joseph Infirmary and Kosair Crippled Children's Hosp. Served to maj. M.C., U.S. Army, 1917-19; comdg. officer Base Hosp. 210, Toul, France, 1918; lt. col. Med. Res. Corp., 1919-35; ret. 1935; surg. cons. to Med. Examining Bd., Selective Service Bd., 1942-46. Received Congl. Selective Service medal, 1947; Citation U. Louisville for 34 yrs. outstanding service, 1915; 1949 medal Am. Cancer Soc., Ky. div., for work in cancer control. Diplomate Am. Bd. Surgery, 1937. Fellow A.C.S., So. Surg. Assn. (v.p. 1950); mem. Am. Cancer Soc. (pres. 1951, regional dir. since 1944, chmn. exec. com. Ky. div., 1942-50), So. Med. Assn., Ky. State Med. Assn. (pres. 1948), Ky. Surg. Assn., Med. Research Commn. State of Ky., Phi Chi Democrat. Catholic. Contbr. chpts. in Ency. Medicine, Book of Health. Contbr. articles on surgery in med. jours. Editor Jour. Ky. State Med. Assn. Died Feb. 27, 1959; buried Calvary Cemetery, Louisville.

AUDRIETH, LUDWIG FREDERICK, chemist, educator; b. Vienna, Austria, Feb. 23, 1901; s. Ludwig Anton and Fredericka (Herrmann) A.; brought to U.S., 1902, naturalized, 1912; B.S., Colgate U., 1922; Ph.D., Cornell, 1926; m. Maryon Laurice Trevett, Mar. 27, 1937; children—Kaaren Laurice (Mrs. J. R. Tague, Jr.), Elsa Craven, Anthony Ludwig. Research asst. Cornell, 1926-28; faculty mem. dept. chemistry U. Ill., 1928-67, prof. emeritus, 1961-67; NRC fellow U. Rostock, Germany, 1931-32; chmn. cons., 1937-67 sci. attache Am. embassy, Bonn, West Germany, 1959-63; faculty Sch. Fgn. Affairs, Fgn. Service Inst., Washington, 1964-67. Mem. Chem. Corps Adv. Council, 1952-57. Served res. officer, Chem. Corps, 1930-42; active duty, capt., maj. Ordnance Dept., Picatinny Arsenal, as chief research div., 1942-46. Mem. Am. Chem. Soc., Ges. Deutscher Chemiker, A.A.A.S., Ill. Acad. Scis, Phi Beta Kappa, Sigma Xi, Sigma Nu, Alpha Chi Sigma, Phi Lambda Upsilon (nat. pres. 1950-54, editor Register 1938-42), Phi Mu Alpha, Sigma Gamma Epsilon, Phi Kappa Phi. Clubs: Cosmos (Washington). Author: The Chemistry of Hydrazine (with B.A. Ogg), 1950; Non-Aqueous Solvents (with J. Kleinberg), 1953. Bd. editors Inorganic Syntheses, 1934-67. Editor-in-chief, 1945-50. Contbr. profl. jours. Patentee in field. Home: 1515 Waverly Dr., Champaign, Ill. Died Jan. 28, 1967; buried Mt. Hope Cemetery, Champaign.

AUDUBON, JOHN JAMES, artist, ornithologist; b. Les Cayes, Santo Domingo (now Haiti), Apr. 26, 1785; illegitimate son of Jean Audubon and a Creole woman known as Mademoiselle Rabin, legalized by adoption (1794) as son of Jean and Anne (Moynet) A.; m. Lucy Bakewell, June 1808; children—Victor, John W. Went with father to live in France, 1789, baptized Jean Jacques Fougère Audubon, 1800; came to U.S., 1803, settled on father's estate "Mill Grove," nr. Phila., 1804; began studies of Am. birds, made 1st bird-banding expt., 1804; engaged in various bus. activities, N.Y.C. and Louisville, Ky.; jailed for debt, 1819; taxidermist Western Museum, Cincinnati, 1819-20; began trip down Mississippi and Ohio rivers to observe birds, 1820, paid expenses by painting portraits; tutor, drawing tchr., street sign painter, New Orleans; made unsuccessful trip to Phila. to find a publisher for his bird drawings, 1824; taught music and drawing (to wife's pupils), St. Francisville, La., 1825; took drawings to Europe, 1826, met with favorable reception; elected to Royal Soc. Edinburgh (Scotland), 1827; paid expenses by painting birds; engaged in preparing drawings and texts for his 1st book, Edinburgh, returned several times to continue work; returned to Am. with reputation as foremost American naturalist, 1831; elected fellow Am. Acad., 1830; settled on estate "Minnie's Land" (now Audubon Park), N.Y.C., 1841; subject of much controversy during his life; responsible for drawings and literature for his books (most of scientific identification and nomenclature supplied by others). Author: Birds of America, 4 vols., 1827-38; Ornithological Biography, 5 vols., 1831-38; Synopsis of the Birds of North America, 1839; Viviparous Quadrupeds of North America (completed by his sons), colored plates pub. in 2 vols., 1842-45, text in 3 vols., 1846-54. Died N.Y.C., Jan. 27, 1851.

AUER, JOHN, pharmacologist, physiologist; b. Rochester, N.Y., Mar. 30, 1875; s. Henry and Luise (Hummel) A.; S.B., U. of Mich., 1898; M.D., John Hopkins Med. Sch., 1902; m. Clara Meltzer, Oct. 1, 1903; children—James, Helen, John. Med. house officer, Johns Hospkins Hosp., 1902-03; fellow, asst., asso. and asso. mem. Rockefeller Inst. for Med. Research, 1903-06 and 1907-21; instructor in physiology, Harvard Medical Sch., 1906-07; prof. pharmacology and dir. Dept., St. Louis U. Sch. of Medicine, since 1921; pharmacologist, St. Mary's group of hosps., since 1924. Mem. Am. Assn. for Advancement of Science, Am. Physiological Society, Am. Society for Pharmacology and Exptl. Therapeutics (sec. 1912-16; pres., 1924-27), Soc. for Exptl. Biology and Medicine (v.p. 1917-19), Assn. Am. Physicians, Harvey Soc., St. Louis Acad. Sciences, St. Louis Med. Soc. Maj. Med. Officers' Reserve Corps, 1917-22. Contbr. researches: Investigations on Digestion; Respiration; Heart; Physiological Action of Various Drugs; Functional Disturbances Caused by Anaphylaxis; Studies on War Gas, Tetanus, Reflexes, Connective Tissue, Liver, Gall-bladder. Home: 1936 McCausland Av., St. Louis 17. Office: 1402 S. Grand Av., St. Louis 4, Mo. Died Aug. 30, 1948.

AUGENSTEIN, LEROY GEORGE, educator, biophysicist; b. Decatur, Ill., Mar. 6, 1928; s. Roy Henry and Minnie (Reifsteck) A.; student James Millikin U., 1944-46; B.S., U. Chgo., 1949; M.S., U. Ill., 1954, Ph.D., 1956; m. Elizabeth Schmalfuss, Sept. 23, 1950; children—David Leroy, Kimberly Beth. Began career as scientist at Brookhaven Nat. Lab., 1956-58, 60-62; research adminstr. AEC, 1958-60; sci. coordinator Seattle Worlds Fair, 1960-61; chmn. biophysics dept. Mich. State U., 1962-69, prof. biophysics, 1962-69. Mem. Mich. Bd. Edn., 1967-69; cons. NIH; lectr. for NATO, Internat. Atomic Energy Agy., Am. Inst. Biol. Scis. Mem. Ingham County Cancer Com., 1966-69. Precinct chmn., del. state Republican convs.; candidate for U.S. Senate, 1966. Bd. dirs. Univ. Internat. Served with AUS, 1946-48. Mem. Radiation Research Soc., Biophys. Soc., Sigma Xi, Sigma Alpha Epsilon. Author: Come Let Us Play God, 1969; also articles in field. Editor: Proceedings of Two International Symposia, 1960, 63; (rev. series) Advances in Radiation Biology, 1964-69. Home: Holt MI Died Nov. 9, 1969.

AULT, JAMES PERCY, magnetician; b. Olathe, Kan., Oct. 20, 1881; s. Addison and Mary Aleja (McElwain) A.; A.B., Baker U., Baldwin, Kan., 1904; A.M., Columbia, 1909; m. Mamie Alice Totten, Mar. 27, 1907; children—Evelyn Geraldine, Ruth Miriam (dec.), Marjorie Pearl. With Dept. Terrestrial Magnetism, Carnegie Instn. of Washington, 1904—, chief observer, 1918. Comd. yacht Carnegie, cruises in Arctic and Subantarctic regions, 1914-17; chief of section ocean work and comdr. of yacht Carnegie, Jan. 1919—. Lt. comdr. U.S.N. Res., 1927. Methodist. Author: (with others) Researches Dept. Terrestrial Magnetism (Carnegie Instn., Washington), 1917, 26. Home: Washington, D.C. Died 1929.

AUSTEN, PETER TOWNSEND, chemist; b. Clifton, S.I., N.Y., Sept. 10, 1852; s. John H. and Elizabeth (Townsend) A.; Ph.B., Columbia Sch. of Mines, 1872; studied chemistry, U. of Berlin, 3 yrs.; (Ph.D., U. of Zurich). Instr. chemistry, Dartmouth, 1876; prof. chemistry, Rutgers Coll. and N.J. Scientific Sch., 1877-87; continued with the coll. as univ. extension lecturer; prof. chemistry, Brooklyn Poly. Inst., 1893-98; has been chemist to Richmond Co. (N.Y.), New Brunswick (N.J.), Newark (N.J.) bds. of health, N.J. State Bd. Agr., etc.; also State chemist, N.J. Author: Kurtze Einleitung zu den Nitro-Verbindungen, 1876; Notes for Chemical Students, 1897. Transl. and revised Pinner's Organic Chemistry, 1893. Home: New York, N.Y. Died 1907.

AUSTIN, JAMES HAROLD, prof. research medicine; b. Phila., Pa., Sept. 22, 1883; s. James Smith and Louisa McKee (Sloan) A.; B.S., University of Pennsylvania, 1905; M.D., 1908; married Thelma Frances Wood, June 21, 1924; children—Thelma Frances Wood (Mrs. W. Warrin Fry), James Harold, John Brander, 3d. Interne Univ. Hosp., Phila., 1908-10; asst. demonstrator in pathology, U. of Pa., 1910-11, asso. in research medicine and medicine, 1911-17; asst. Rockefeller Inst., New York, 1919-20, asso., 1920-21; prof. of research medicine, University of Pennsylvania, 1922-50, emeritus prof. since 1950. Dir. William Pepper Lab. of Clin. Medicine, 1942-50; exec. sec. Coll. of Physicians of Philadelphia since 1949. Successively 1st lt., captain, major Medical Corps, U.S. Army, 1917-19. Mem. A.A.A.S., A.M.A., Assn. Am. Physicans, Assn. of Pathol. Bacteriology, Soc. Exptl. Biology, Soc. Clin. Investigation, Soc. Biol. Chemistry, Harvey Soc., Coll. of Physicans of Phila., Phi Beta Kappa, Sigma Xi, Alpha Omega Alpha, Delta Upsilon. Episcopalian. Club: University (Phila.). Editor Jour. Clin. Investigation, 1926-35; asso. editor Medicine since 1929. Home: 138 Chamounix Rd., St. Davids, Pa. Office: 19 S. 22d St., Phila. 3 Died Mar. 29, 1952; buried West Laurel Hill Cemetery, Bala Cynwyd, Pa.

AUSTIN, JOHN CORNEBY WILSON, architect; b. Bodicote, Oxfordshire, Eng., Feb. 13, 1870; s. Richard Wilson and Jane Elizabeth A.; ed. pvt. schs.; apprentice course in architecture; m. Hilda Violet Myton, Aug. 16, 1902 (died Nov. 25, 1931); 8 children. m. 2d, Dorothy Kathleen Bell. Feb. 5, 1935. Practiced architecture since 1894 in Los Angeles, Calif.; asso. with Frederic M. Ashley, 1912-37; designed and supervised constrn. Shrine Auditorium, Los Angeles Chamber of Commerce, Calif. State Bldg., St. Vincent's Hosp., Griffith Observatory, Saint Pauls Church (all in Los Angeles); one of three firms to design and supervise building of Los Angeles City Hall; past chmn. for Southern Calif. of President Hoover's orgn. for unemployment relief; past pres. State Bd. of Archtl. Examiners and past mem. Southern Dist.; mem. Com. of Seven apptd. to adjust claims resulting from failure of San Francisquito Dam in 1928; chmn. Citzens Com. of Metropolitan Water Dist.; mem. President Roosevelt's Labor Mediation Bd. (Los Angeles Dist.); chmn. Legislative Advisory Com. on Defense and Employment (State of Calif. 1940). Past pres. Los Angeles Chamber of Commerce. Fellow Am. Inst. Architects (past pres. Southern Calif. Chapter), Royal Soc. Arts; mem. Am. Soc. C.E. Mason (32 deg.); mem. Al Malaikah Shrine. Clubs: Jonathan (past pres.), Lincoln. Home: 1275 Kenilworth Av., San Marion CA

AUSTIN, LEONARD S., mining engr.; b. Stratford, Conn., Feb. 26, 1846; s. Thomas and Elvira (Reed) A.; Sheffield Scientific Sch. (Yale), Ph.B., 1868; post-grad work, Yale, Columbia, and Colo. State Sch. of Mines; m. Mary E. Watson, June 7, 1881. Mech. engring. work until 1877; chemist. Exploration Co., E. coast of Patagonia, S.A., 1877-79; chemist and foreman, Germania Lead Works, 1880-86; supt. various smelting works in U.S. to 1902; prof. metallurgy and ore dressing, Mich. Coll. of Mines, 1903-09; pvt. practice, 1909—. Episcopalian. Author: Metallurgy of the Common Metals, 1906, 5th edit., 1920; The Fire Assay, 1907. Annual contbr. to Industry, on "Metallurgy of Copper," 1903—; contbr. to Appleton's Yearbook, 1911-20. Home: Los Angeles, Calif. Died 1929.

AUSTIN, LOUIS WINSLOW, physicist; b. Orwell, Vt., Oct. 30, 1867; s. Prof. Lewis Augustine and Mary Louise (Taft) A.; A.B., Middlebury Coll., 1889, hon. D.Sc., 1920; student U. of Strassburg, 1889-90 and 1891-93, Ph.D., 1893; fellow Clark U., 1890-91; m. Laura A. Osborne, Aug. 16, 1898. Instr. and asst. prof. physics, U. of Wis., 1893-1901; in German govt. service (Phys. Tech. Reichsanstalt), 1902-04; with Bur. of Standards, Washington, 1904—; head of U.S. Naval Radiotelegraph Lab., 1908-23; chief Lab. for Special Radio Transmission Research, Bur. of Standards, 1923—. Fellow Inst. of Radio Engineers (pres. 1914); v.p. Internat. Union for Scientific Radiotelegraphy and chmn. Am. Sect.; mem. tech. advisory com. Conf. on the Limitation of Armament, Washington, 1921. Medal of Inst. of Radio Engrs., 1927. Author: Physical Measurement (with Prof. C. B. Thwing), 1896. Home: Washington, D.C. Died June 27m 1932.

AVERELL, WILLIAMS WOODS, army officer, inventor; b. Cameron, N.Y., Nov. 5, 1832; s. Hiram and Huldah (Hemenway) A.; grad. U.S. Mil. Acad., 1855; attended Cavalry Sch. of Practice, Carlisle, Pa., 1857; m. Kezia Hayward, Sept. 24, 1885. Drug clk., Bath, N.Y., until circa 1851; commd. brevet 2d lt. of mounted rifles U.S. Army, circa 1855; stationed Jefferson Barracks, Mo., 1855-56, ordered to frontier in N.M., 1857; received leave of absence due to wounds, 1859; became asst. adj. gen. on Gen. Andrew Porter's staff, 1861, served in 1st Battle of Bull Run; apptd. col. 3d Pa. Cavalry, U.S. Volunteers, Aug. 1861; lead charge with his brigade in Battle of 2d Manassas, Mar. 1862; served at Yorktown, Williamsburg, Fair Oaks, Malvern Hill, White Oak Swamp (all Va.), 1862; commd. capt. U.S. Army, apptd. brig. gen. U.S. Volunteers, 1862; made raids in Va., Dec. 1862; in command of 2d Calvalry Div. at Battle of Kelly's Ford (Va.), 1863, brevetted maj. U.S. Army for this action; served in Stoneman's Raid, Richmond, Va., May 1863, then transferred to W.Va.; brevetted lt. col. after Battle of Droop Mountain, 1863; took part in raids in Tenn., brevetted col. U.S. Army; commanded 2 Cavalry Div. in several battles under Gen. Philip Henry Sheridan, 1864; brevetted brig. gen. and maj. gen. U.S. Army, 1865, resigned 1865; apptd. U.S. consul gen. for Brit. N.Am. at Montreal, 1865-68; had interests in mfg. and engring.; invented and patented asphalt paving, 1879, insulating conduits and wires and conductors, 1884-85; insp. gen. Soldiers' Home, Bath, N.Y., 1880-98; awarded $700,000 in patent infringement suit against Barbour Asphalt Paving Co., 1898. Died Bath, Feb. 3, 1900.

AVERY, ELROY ACKENDREE, author; b. Erie Monroe Co., Mich., July 14, 1844; s. Caspar Hugh and Dorothy (Putnam) Ph.B. , U. of Mich., 1871, Ph.M., 1874; Ph.D., Hillsdale Coll., 1881, LL.D, 1894; D.C.L., 1911; served in Civil War; mustered out as sergt.-maj., 11th Mich. Cav.; m. Catherine Hitchcock Tilden, July 2, 1870 (died 1911); m. 2d, Ella Alice Wilson, June 15, 1916. Prin. high sch., Battle Creek, Mich., 1869, high and normal schs., Cleveland, O., 1871-79. Mem. Cleveland City Council, 1891-92, Ohio Senate, 1893-97. Author: Elementary Physics, 1876; Elements of Natural Philosophy, 1878; Physical Technics, 1879; Teacher's Hand Book of Natural Philosophy, 1879; Elements of Chemistry, 1881; Teachers' Hand Book of Chemistry, 1882; Complete Chemistry, 1883; First Principles of Natural Philosophy, 1884; Words Correctly Spoken, 1887; Columbus and the Columbia Brigade, 1892; School Physics, 1895; Elementary Physics, 1897; First Lessons in Physical Science, 1897; School Chemistry, 1904; The Town Meeting, 1904; The Groton Avery Clan, 2 vols., 1912; History of the United States and Its People, 12 vols.; John Humfrey, Massachusetts Magistrate, 1913; Cleveland and Its Environs, 3 vols., 1918; Genesis of New Port Richey, 1923. After living at Cleveland for 48 yrs., moved to Fla., 1919. Hon. pres. and chmn. bd. First State Bank of New Port Richey; first mayor of New Port Richey, 1924-25; founder and for 10 yrs. pres. Avery Pub. Library of New Port Richey (hon. life dir.). Home: New Port Richey, Fla. Died Dec. 1, 1935. 84/

AVERY, SAMUEL, chemist; b. Lamoille, Ill., April 19, 1865; s. Stephen B. and Mary T. Avery; A.B., Doane Coll., i887; B.Sc., U. of Neb., 1892, A.M., 1894; Ph.D, Heidelberg, 1896; LL.D, Doane and U. of Idaho, 1909; m. May B. Bennett, Aug. 4, 1897. Adj. prof. chemistry, U. of Neb., 1896-99; prof. chemistry and chemist, Agrl. Expt. Sta., U. of Ida., 1899-1901; prof. analytical and organic chemistry, U. of Neb., 1901; prof. agrl. chemistry and chemist, U. of Neb. Expt. Sta., 1902-05; head prof. chemistry, 1905-08, acting chancellor, 1908-09, chancellor, 1909, chancellor emeritus and prof. of research in chemistry, 1927—, U. of Neb. Leave of absence Jan.-Nov. 1918, as mem. and vice chmn. chemistry com. Nat. Research Council, and maj. chem. warfare service U.S.A., chief of univ. relations unit. U.S. mem. Internat. Councilation Commn. with Sweden, 1914-15. Mason. Recieved Kiwanis Medal. Home: Lincoln, Neb. Died Jan. 25, 1936.

AXELROD, HAIM IZCHAK, physician; b. Jerusalem, Palestine, Nov. 3, 1925; s. Louis and Sara Ethel Axelrod; B.A. in Physiology and Biochemistry, U. Toronto, 1947, M.D., 1951; m. Esther Gold, Dec. 20, 1952; children—Howard, David, Marsha, Caron. Jr. rotating intern Toronto (Ont., Can.) Western Hosp., 1951-52; postgrad. in anesthesiology U. Toronto, 1952-54; sr. anesthesiologist St. Michael's Hosp., Toronto, 1952, Toronto East Gen. Hosp., 1953, Toronto Gen. Hosp., 1954; asst. resident in anesthesiology Hosp. for Sick Children, Toronto, 1953; practice medicine specializing in anesthesiology, Toronto, 1954-71; attending physician dept. anesthesiology New Mt. Sinai Hosp., Toronto, until 1971. Diplomate Am. Bd. Anesthesiology, Nat. Bd. Med. Examiners. Fellow Am. Coll. Anesthesiology; mem. Canadian Med. Assn., Am. Soc. Anesthesists, Internat. Soc. Analgesia, Canadian Anesthesiologists Soc., Assn. Adminstrv. Assts. Home: Toronto Ontario Canada Died Jan. 4, 1971; buried Toronto Ontario Canada

AYER, JAMES BOURNE, neurologist; b. Boston, Dec. 28, 1882; s. James Bourne and Mary (Farwell) A.; grad. Roxbury Latin Sch., 1899; A.B., Harvard, 1903, M.D., 1907; m. Hannah Gilbert Palfrey, Dec. 15, 1909; children-James Bourne, Hannah Gilbert (Mrs. Robert Saltonstall), John Palfrey, Suzannah Cazneau (Mrs. John Harleston Parker), Mary Farwell (Mrs. James Saxton Haetzell), Elizabeth. Began practice medicine, 1909; prof. neurology Harvard Med. Sch., 1926-46. Served as capt. M.C., U.S. Army, 1918-19. Mem. Am. Neurol. Assn. (pres. 1931), Am. Acad. Arts and Scis., Royal Soc. Medicine. Home: 1350 Canton Av., Milton, Mass. Office: 319 Longwood Av., Boston. Died Oct. 25, 1963.

AYER, JOHN, consulting engr.; b. Oakland, Me., Apr. 29, 1883; s. John and Mary Annabel (Holt) A.; S.B., Mass. Inst. Tech., 1905; grad. student Tech. High Sch., Charlottenburg, Berlin, Germany, 1906-07; m. Josephine Flint Stevens, June 24, 1909; children—John, Jr., Mary Burnham (Mrs. John Hall). Asst. engr. Charles River Basin Commn., 1907-13; engineer and designer concrete dams and power houses, 1910-13; asst. engr. and dir. of Port of Boston, 1913-17; asst. engr. Fay, Spofford & Thorndike, 1917-18, exec. engr., 1918-19, div. engr., 1920-22, v.p., until 1961; dir., cons. Fay, Spofford & Thorndike, Inc., specializing in design and construction of waterfront projects; employed on large projects such as shipbuilding and graving docks for Bureau of Yards and Docks (U.S. Navy Dept.), Commonwealth Dry Dock and Pier, Hampden Co. Memorial Bridge (Springfield, Mass.), Victory Plant of Bethlehem Ship Bldg. Corp. (Quincy, Mass.); associated with three other engring. firms in design of dry docks and navy yard improvements for U.S. Navy, also work for U.S. Army in No. Can., Newfoundland, Greenland and Alaska. Served as chmn. Water and Sewer Commn., Medford, Mass., 1926-29; mem. Sch. House Bldg. Commn., 1929-33; dir. Lawrence Memorial Hospital of Medford Mem. Am. Society C.E., Newcomen Society, American Assn. Port Authorities, Am. Wood Preservers Assn. Republican. Conglist. Home: 22 Vernon St., West Medford, Mass. Office: 11 Beacon St., Boston. Died Aug. 31, 1961; buried Lindenwood Cemetery, Stoneham, Mass.

AYRES, MILAN VALENTINE, electric ry. engr.; b. Hamlin, Brown Co., Kan., Feb. 14, 1875; s. Milan Church (q.v.) and Georgiana (Gall) A.; S.B., Mass. Inst. Tech., 1898; course in elec. engring., Gen. Electric Co., Schenectady, N.Y., 1899-1900; studied law with C. H. Innis, Boston, and admitted to Mass. bar, 1909; m. Emma Gertrude Stevens, of Newton Highlands, Mass., Sept. 14, 1910. With Gen. Electric Co., 1899-1902; elec. and mech. engr., Boston & Worcester St. Ry., S. Framingham, Mass., 1902-11; asst. gen. mgr., Rockland Light & Power Co., Nyack, N.Y. (instituting methods of scientific management), July-Nov., 1911; chief engr. Mobile Light & R.R. Co., Nov., 1911-May, 1912; statistician with Ford, Bacon & Davis, consulting engrs., May, 1912-Apr., 1914; sr. elect. engr., Div. of Valuation, Interstate Commerce Commn., Washington, Apr. 1914-May 1918; maj. U.S.A. statistics branch, Gen. Staff, May 1918-Aug. 1920; chief statistical officer, Sept. 1919-Aug. 1920; chief statis. sect., adj. gens. office, Aug.-Dec. 1920; graphic statistician in private practice, Dec. 1920-Sept. 1921; editor of Index (weekly statis. pubn. Associated Gen. Contractors of America), 1921-2; statistician with Julian Armstrong, Inc., Chicago, since 1923. Conglist. Mem. Am. Statis. Assn., Progressive Ed. Assn. Maj. Signal Corps Reserve, U.S.A.; on gen. staff eligible list, U.S.A. Author of numerous technical papers and reports. Home: 5217 Dorchester Av. Office: 400 N. Michigan Av., Chicago IL

BAADE, WALTER, astronomer; b. Schroettinghausen, Germany, Mar. 24, 1893; student Gymnasium, Herford, 1903-12, U. Muenster, 1912-13, U. Göttingen, 1913-18, Ph.D., 1919; Dr. Naturwiss, Hamburg U. Asst. Hamburger Sternwarte, 1919-27, observator, 1927-31; privatdozent U. Hamburg, 1920-31; astronomer Mt. Wilson Observatory, Pasadena, Cal., 1931-47, Mt. Wilson, Palomar Observatories, 1948-58, ret.; Hitchcock prof. U. Cal., 1954. Recipient Gold Medal, Royal Astron. Soc., Bruce Gold Medal, Astron. Soc. Pacific. Corr. mem. Goettingen Acad., Royal Physiographical Soc. (Lund), Bayerische Akademie d. Wiss., Akademie d. Wiss. u. Lit. (Mainz). Asso. mem. Royal Astron. Soc. (London); hon. mem. Royal Canadian Astron. Soc.; fgn. mem. Royal Netherlands Acad.; mem. Am. Philos. Soc. Address: Mt. Wilson and Palomar Observatories, Pasadena 4, Cal. Died June 25, 1960; buried Germany.

BABASINIAN, V(AHAN) S(IMON), chemistry; b. Marsovan, Asia Minor, Nov. 28, 1876; s. Simon and Hripsimeh (Mallian) B.; A.B., Anatolia Coll., Asia Minor, 1895; A.M., Brown U., 1903, Ph.D., 1906; unmarried. Came to U.S., 1897, naturalized citizen, 1910. Instr. in chemistry, Brown U., 1903-06; Instr. in chemistry, Lehigh, untly 1909, asst. prof., 1909-11, asso. prof. 1911-22, prof. organic chemistry, 1922—. With Chem. Warfare Service (research), Washington, 1918, du Pont Co., Wilmington, Del., 1919. Republican. Conglist. Mason. Editor: Gattermann's Practical Methods of Organic Chemistry, 1914. Home: Bethlehem, Pa. Died May. 24, 1939.

BABB, CYRUS CATES, civil engr.; b. Portland, Me., June 18, 1867; s. Cyrus K. and Mary Lucretia (Judkins) B.: B.S., Mass. Inst. Tech., 1890; m. Grace Crowther, Mar. 7, 1906; children—Dudley cyrus, Kathryn. Hydrographer U.S. Geol. Survey 1890-1902. engr. same, 1902-06; project engr., U.S. Reclamation Service, 1906-09; dist. engr. U.S. Geol. Survey, 1910; chief engr. Me. State Water Storage Commn., July 1, 1911-Dec. 1914; cons. hydraulic engr., 1914-17; supervisor of lands, water, power, etc. The Rhodhiss (N.C.) Mfg. Co., and E. A. Smith Mfg. Co., 1917-18; cons. engr., 1919. Home: Granite Falls, N.C. Died 1937.

BABBITT, BENJAMIN TALBOT, inventor, mfr.; b. Westmoreland, N.Y., 1809; s. Nathaniel and Betsey (Holman) B.; m. Rebecca McDuffie, 2 daus. Established machine shop, Little Falls, N.Y., 1831, manufactured pumps, engines, farm machinery; developed new, cheaper way to make baking soda, 1843; manufactured various brands of soap; obtained 1st patent for pump and fire engine, 1842; patented brush trimming machine, 1846; patented over 100 devices, including car ventilator, automatic boiler feeder, steam generator cleaning apparatus, rotary engine, balance valve, air pump, air compressor, wind motors, pneumatic propulsion, air blasts for forges; 1st to use samples free for advt. Died Oct. 20, 1889.

BABBITT, ISAAC, inventor; b. Taunton, Mass., July 26, 1799; s. Zeba and Bathsheba (Luscombe) B.; m. Sally Leonard; m. 2d, Eliza Barney; 9 children. Made 1st Brittania-ware manufactured in U.S., 1831, 1st brass cannon cast in U.S., 1834; patented journal-box lined with alloy known as "Babbitt metal," (an anti-friction bearing metal used in all railroad car axle-boxes), 1839; awarded Gold medal by Mass. Mechanics Assn., 1841, also granted $20,000 by U.S. Congress for this invention. Died Somerville, Mass., May 26, 1862.

BABCOCK, ERNEST BROWN, prof. genetics; b. Edgerton, Wis., July 10, 1877; s. Emilus Welcome and Mary Eliza (Brown) B.; student Lawrence Coll., Appleton, Wis., 1895-96; grad. State Normal Sch., Los Angeles, 1898; B.S., U. of Calif., 1906, M.S., 1911, LL.D., 1950; m. Georgia Bowen, June 24, 1908. First instr. in agrl. nature study State Normal Sch., Los Angeles, 1906-07; instr., asst. prof. plant pathology, 1907-10, asst. prof. agrl. edn., 1910-13, prof. genetics 1913-47, professor emeritus 1947—, University of California; faculty research lecturer for the University of Calif., 1944; exec. v.p. Forest Genetics Research Found., 1952-54, pres., 1954. Y.M.C.A. ednl. dir., with A.E.F., Jan.-Apr. 1919; mem. Army Ednl. Corps, A.E.F., Apr.-June 1919. Research Asso., Carnegie Inst., 1925-37. President section of experimental taxonomy, VII International Botany Congress, Stockholm, 1950. Mem. A.A.A.S., American Soc. Naturalists (vice pres. 1934), Genetics Soc. Am., Western Soc. Naturalists, Am. Genetics Assn., Bot. Soc. Am., California Academy Sciences (1st vice president 1947-54, pres. 1954), California Botany Society (president 1940), Washington (D.C.) Academy Sciences, Nat. Acad. Sciences, Phi Beta Kappa, Sigma Xi, Alpha Zeta, Phi Sigma; hon. mem. Royal Bot. Soc. (Belgium), Japanese Bot. Soc. Congregationalist. Clubs: Faculty, City Commons (Berkeley, Calif.). Author: Genetics in Relation to Agriculture, (with Dr. Roy E. Clausen), 1918, 27; Genetics Laboratory Manual (with Dr. J. L. Collins), 1918; The Genus Crepins (in Bibliog. Genetica), (with Dr. M. Navashin), 1930; The Genus Youngia (with Dr. G. Ledyard Stebbins, Jr.), 1937; The Am. Species of Crepis, 1938; The Genus Crepis, Univ. Calif. Publ. Botany, vols. 21 and 22, 1947. Home: 1828 Hopkins St., Berkeley 7. Office: University of California, Berkeley 4, Cal. Died Dec. 8, 1954; buried Edgerton Fassett Cemetery, Edgerton, Wis.

BABCOCK, GEORGE HERMAN, inventor, mfr.; b. Unadilla Forks, N.Y., June 17, 1832; s. Asher M. and Mary (Stillman) B.; married 4 times. Chief draftsman Hope Iron Works, Providence, R.I.; inventor Babcock & Wilcox high pressure boiler; co-inventor 1st polychromatic printing press; pres. Babcock, Wilcox & Co., boiler mfrs., 1881-93; pres. bd. trustees Alfred U.; pres. Plainfield (N.J.) Bd. Ed. Plainfield Pub. Library; pres. Am. Soc. M.E., 1887. Died Plainfield, Dec. 16, 1893.

BABCOCK, HAROLD DELOS, astronomer; b. Edgerton, Wis., Jan. 24, 1882; s. Emilus Welcome and Mary Eliza (Brown) B.; B.S., U. Cal., 1907; m. Mary G. Henderson, Mar. 9, 1907; 1 son, Horace Welcome. With scientific staff, Bur. of Standards, Washington, 1906-08; staff of Mount Wilson Observatory, 1909-48. Mem. Nat. Acad. Scis. (mem. commn. on Standards of Wave-Length, past pres.), Internat. Astron. Union, Am. Astron. Soc. (member council 1943), Astron Soc. of Pacific (president 1937; Bruce Gold Medal, 1953); Sigma Xi; asso. Royal Astron. Soc. (England). Has specialized in spectroscopy. Shared award of 1929 prize, Pacific Div., A.A.A.S. Author of more than 100 sci. papers. Address: Altadena CA Died Apr. 8, 1968; buried Mountain View Cemetery, Altadena CA

BABCOCK, HARRIET (MRS. H. HOBART BABCOCK), psychologist; b. Westerly, R.I.; B.S., Columbia, 1922, A.M., 1923, Ph.D., 1930, Psychologist, Manhattan State Hosp., 1924-25; chief psychologist Bellevue Hosp., 1926-28; began research in measurement of mental deterioration, 1924; engaged in clinical work in efficiency phase of mental functioning since 1931. Fellow Am. Assn. Applied Psychology. N.Y. Acad. Science, Am. Psychol. Assn., A.A.A.S.; mem. eastern and local psychol. assns., Fgn. Policy Assn., Nat. Arts Club, N.Y. Pen and Brush. Author: An Experiment in the Measurement of Mental Deterioration, 1930; Dementia Praecox; A Psychological Study, 1933; Revised Examination for the Measurement of Efficiency of Mental Functioning, 1941; Time and the Mind, 1941. Contbr. to tech. and sci. jours. Orginator method of measuring and evaluating efficiency of mental functioning in normal and abnormal mental conditions by controlling abstract-verbal development; determined place of psychogenic psychoses between the normal and definitely abnormal; stated the level-efficiency theory of intelligence; and showed the relation of personality to basic mental functioning. Home: 15 Gramercy Park, New York 3. Office: 119 E. 19th St., New York, N.Y. Died Dec. 12, 1952.

BABCOCK, JAMES FRANCIS, chemist; b. Boston, Feb. 23, 1844; s. Archibald D. and Fannie F. (Richards) B.; attended Lawrence Scientific Sch. of Harvard U., 1862; m. Mary Crosby, Mar. 28, 1869; m. 2d, Marion Alden, Aug. 24, 1892; 5 children. Prof. chemistry Mass. Coll. Pharmacy, 1869-74, Boston U., 1874-80; state assayer Mass., 1875-85, introduced 3 percent limit as defining intoxicating liquor; insp. milk Boston, 1885; inventor Babcock fire extinguisher; pres. Druggists' Assn. Boston, 1894. Died Dorchester, Mass., July 19, 1897.

BABCOCK, JAMES WOODS, alienist; b. Chester, S.C., Aug. 11, 1856; s. Sidney E. (M.D.) and Margaret (Woods) B.; A.B., Harvard, 1882, M.D., 1886; (LL.D., S.C. Coll., 1905); m. Katharine Guion, Aug. 17, 1892. Asst. phys. McLean Hosp., Sommerville, Mass., 1885-91; phys. and supt. State Hosp. for Insane, Columbia, S.C., 1891-1914. One of 1st physicians in the South to recognize pellagra (Dec. 1907); pres. Nat. Assn. for the Study of Pellagra, 1909-12 and sec., 1912—; chmn. S.C. State Hosp. Commns., 1910-13; mem. Columbia Bd. Health, 1898-1901; chmn. Columbia Sewerage Commn., 1901-03, Columbia commn. on water and water works, 1903-07; prof. psychiatry. Med. Coll. of S.C., 1915—. Died Mar. 3, 1922.

BABCOCK, STEPHEN MOULTON, agrl. chemist; b. Bridgewater, N.Y., Oct. 22, 1843; s. Peleg B. and Cornella B.; A.B., Tufts, 1866; student chemistry, Cornell, 1872-75; Ph.D, U. of Göttingen, 1879; LL.D, Tufts, 1901; m. May Crandall, Oct. 27, 1896. Instr. chemistry, Cornell U., 1875-76; chemist, N.Y. Agrl. Expt. Sta., Geneva, N.Y., 1882-87; prof. agrl. chemistry. U. of Wis., 1887-1913 (emeritus); chief chemist Wis. Agrl. Expt. Sta., 1887-1913, asst. dir., 1901-13. Awarded bronze medal by Wis. legislature, 1899; grand prize, Paris Expn., 1900; mem. Jury of Awards, Buffalo Expn., 1901; grand prize St. Louis Expn., 1904. Inventor of Babcock test for butter. Home: Madison, Wis. Died July 2, 1931.

BABCOCK, WILLIAM WAYNE, surgeon; b. E. Worcester, Otsego County, N.Y., June 10, 1872; s. William Wayne and Sarah Jane (Butler) B.; grad. Binghamton (N.Y.) High Sch.; M.D., Coll. Physicians and Surgeons, Baltimore, 1893; studied summer sch., Harvard, 1893; M.D., Sch. of Medicine, U. of Pa., 1895; M.D., Medico-Chirurg. Coll., Phila., 1900; hon. A.M., Pa. Coll., Gettysburg, 1904; LL.D., Temple U., 1932; D.Sc., Ursinus Coll. 1944; L.H.D. Villenova, 1947; Med. Alumni Award, D.Sc., U. of Md., 1948; m. Marion C. Watters, May 14, 1918; children—Jane Butler, Catherine, Bonnie, William Wayne 3d (deceased). Resident physician St. Mark's Hosp., Salt Lake City, 1893-94, tng., Phila., 1895-1903; prof. gynecology Temple Coll., 1903, prof. surgery, clin. surgery, 1903-44, now emeritus; prof. oral surgery Phila. Dental Coll., 1907-08; surgeon to Temple U., cons. Phila. Gen. hosps., Phila. Has conducted researches leading to improved methods in surgery and invented a number of surg. instruments. Commd. capt., Med. Res. Corps, May 9, 1917; entered service Camp Greenleaf, Ga.; regtl. surgeon 318th F.A., Camp Jackson, August 1917; surg. chief, General Hospital No. 6, Fort McPherson, Georgia, September 1917-September 1919; commd. major, November 1917; lt. colonel, June 1918. Fellow Am. Coll. Surgeons, A.A.A.S; asso. mem. Academie de Chirurgie of France; hon. mem. Royal Soc. of Medicine (proctology), England; mem. A.M.A., Am. Therapeutic Soc. (pres. 1917-18), Pathol. Soc. Phila., Am. Assn. Obstetricians, Gynecologists and Abdominal Surgeons (pres. 1933-34), Internat. Coll. Surgeons, Am. Bd. Surgery, Societe des chirurgiens de Paris, Nat. Soc. Surgeons of Cuba, Phi Chi. Mason. Episcopalian. Clubs: Union League, Rotary. Home: 11 St. Asaph's Rd., Bala-Cynwyd, Pa. Office: 3401 N. Broad St., Philadelphia

BABOCK, HOWARD EDWARD, agricultural organizer, exec., teacher; b. Gilbertsville, N.Y., Feb. 23, 1889; s. Howard Worden and Mary Emma (Donahue) B.; B.A., Syracuse U., 1911 (hon. LL.D., 1941); m. Hilda Wall Butler, Oct. 23, 1913; children—Howard E., Barbara Elizabeth, John Butler. Teacher Elmira (N.Y.) Free Acad., 1912-13; county agt. Cattaraugus and Tompkins counties, 1913-14; asst. state dir. Farm Bureaus, sec. Agrl. Conf. Bd., N.Y. State, 1917-21; sec. N.Y. State Farm Bur. Federation, 1919-21; state dir. Farm Bureaus, 1915-19; leave of absence, 1917-18, to serve on N.Y. State Food Conservation Commn.; prof. of marketing, Cornell U., 1920-22; gen. mgr. Coop. Grange League Federation Exchange, 1922-32, 1935-36; pres. Coop, G.L.F. Holding Corp., 1932-35; pres. Coop. G.L.F. Products, Inc., 1937-40; dir. The G.L.F. School of Coop. Adminstrn., 1940-43; dir. research (G.L.F.) 1943-45; mem. bus. advisory council for U.S. Dept. Commerce, 1944-45; mem. Nat. Research Adv. Com. since 1946; asst. chmn. Federal Farm Bd., 1933; dir. Central Bank for Coop., 1933-39. Special consultant Farm Credit Adminstrn.; president Nat. Council Farmer Cooperatives, 1943. Chmn. N.Y. State Emergency Food Commn., 1943. Trustee Cornell U. (chmn. bd. 1940-47). Mem. Gov. Roosevelt's Agrl. Advisory Com., N.Y. State Council Farms and Markets, Guernsey and Aberdeen-Angus Breeders Assn., Delta Chi. Owns and operates poultry and stock farms totalling 1000 acres. Contbr. to agrl. jours. Conglist. H. Edward Babcock Fund for promotion of studies in nutrition established in his honor at Cornell U. Home: Ithaca, N.Y. Died July 12, 1950.

BACH, OSCAR BRUNO, indsl. designer, craftsman for metals; b. Germany, Dec. 13, 1884; s. Adolpho and Ernestine (Marco) B.; student Cath. Higher Gymnasium, 1890-98, Royal Art Acad., Berlin, Germany, 1898-1902; m. Pauline Marie Di Rufolo. Apr. 12, 1916. Came to U.S., 1913, naturalized, 1926. Began as designer of metallic architecture and sculpture in Berlin, Germany, mostly for German, British and Italian govts., at age of 20; came to U.S. before the World War, retained as indsl. designer for such cos. as Remington-Rand, Manning-Bowman, Edw. Budd Mfg. Co., Oneida Ltd., Galdwin Locomotive Works, Am. Radiator Co., Tappan Stove Co., etc.; maintained research labs. for metall. and engring. work; pres. Oscar B. Bach Studios, Inc.; pres. Bachite Development Corp. Recipient gold medal for native indsl. design and craftsmanship Archt. League of N.Y. Works include metall. design and execution for S.S.'s Washington and Manhattan, Empire State Bldg., Bank of Manhattan, Bank of N.Y. and Trust Co., Riverside Ch., Airlines Terminal Bldg., Rockefeller Center, Dept. of Health Bldg. (all in N.Y.), Williamsburgh Savings Bank, Bklyn., Toledo Mus. Art, other museums, Yale U., Telephone Bldg., Cin., Christ Ch., Sch. Indsl. Art, Cranbrook, Mich. Developed Bachite process, a treatment giving color, corrosion and abrasion resistance to all ferrous metals; designs for automobile bodies, trains, airplanes, building material, etc. Lecturer. Contbr. to tech. jours. Office: La Maison Francaise, 610 Fifth Av., N.Y.C. Deceased.

BACHARACH, ERIC WILLIAM, civil and sanitary engr., contractor; b. Cincinnati, O., June 14, 1883; s. Hugo and Hattie Louise (Karrmann) B.; student U. of Cincinnati, Engring. Coll., 1902-03 inclusive; U. of Mich., 1904-05, B.Sc. in Engineering (as of class of 1906), 1943; m. Lora Mary Hersey, July 15, 1911. With Pittsburgh Filter & Engring. Co., 1905-22, advancing to western mgr. and 1st v.p., in charge co.'s business west of Mississippi River; sole proprietor of E. W. Bacharach & Co., Kansas City, Mo., since 1922, pres. E. W. Bacharach, Inc. of Kansas City, Mo., 1948, chmn. bd., ret. 1960, now consultant, member board of directors; pioneer in introduction of modern methods of water purification; designed and installed plants for more than 800 towns, cities and indsl. concerns, and with others, for over 500 towns and cities, also has built many such plants for U.S. Govt. in connection with war projects. Inventor of chemical feeding machines and other devices used in connection with water purification plants used throughout the world. Received Modern Pioneer Award for achievements in sci., 1940; named hon. citizen Bacharach, Germany, 1956. Mem. bd. dirs., Juvenile Improvement Club; adv. bd. Salvation Army, Nat., Mo. socs. profl. engrs., Am. Soc. C.E., Am. Soc. Mil. Engrs., Starlight Theatre Assn. (dir.), Am. Water Works Assn., Kansas City Art Inst. Episcopalian. Clubs: Carriage, By-Line, Engineers (chmn. bd. dirs., 1925-26, 1928-29 and 1933-34), Kansas City, Rotary, Univ. of Mich. Home: Kansas City MO Died 1965.

BACHE, ALEXANDER DALLS, physicst, coll. pres.; b., Phila., July 19, 1806; s. Richard and Sophia (Dallas) B.; grad. U.S. Mil. Acad., 1825; LL.D., N.Y.U., 1836; U. Pa., 1837; Harvard U., 1851; m. Nancy Fowler, 1829, Commd Engrs. Corps, U.S Army, in constrn. Ft. Adams, Newport, R.I., 1825-29; prof. natural philosophy and chemistry U. Pa., 1828-41; 1st pres. Girard Coll., Phila., 1836-circa 1848; supt. U.S. Coast

Survey, 1843-67; a founder A.A.A.S.; an incorporator, regent Smithsonian Instn., 1846; a founder, 1st pres. Nat. Acad. Scis.; pres. Am. Philos. Soc., 1855; adviser to the Pres. U.S., also v.p. Sanitary Commn. during Civil War; Imperial Geog. Soc. London, Royal Acad. Turin, Imperial Geog. Soc. Vienna, Inst. of France. Author: Observations at the Observatory of Girard 3 vols, 1840-45. Died Providence, R.I., Feb. 17, 1867.

BACHE, FRANKLIN, physician, educator; b. Phila., Oct. 25, 1797; s. Benjamin Franklin and Margaret (Markoe) B.; grad. U. Pa., 1810, M.D., 1814; m. Aglae Dabadie, 1818. Entered U.S. Army as asst. surgeon, 1813, promoted to full surgeon, 1814, served until 1816; practiced medicine, Phila., 1816-24; physician to Walnut Street Prison, Phila., 1824-36; prof. chemistry Franklin Inst., Phila., 1826-32; an editor N.Am. Med. and Surg. Jour., 1826-31; fellow Coll. Physicians and Surgeons, Phila., 1829; prof. chemistry Phila. Coll. Pharmacy, 1831-41, Jefferson Med. Coll., Phila., 1841-64; pres. Am. Philos. Soc., 1853-55. Author: System of Chemistry for the Use of Students in Medicine, 1819; Dispensatory of the United States of America, 1833. Died Phila., Mar. 19, 1864.

BACHEM, ALBERT, prof. biophysics; b. Bonn, Germany, Feb. 26, 1888; s. Dr. Joseph and Gertrude (Tonger) B.; Ph.D., U. of Bonn, 1910; m. Erica Pietsch; children—Erica, Wolfgang Albert. Came to U.S., 1921, naturalized 1931. Served as asst. prof. physics, Univ. of Bonn and Univ. of Frankfurt; prof. biophysics, U. of Ill. Coll. of Medicine, since 1924. Mem. Am. Physiol. Soc., Soc. Experimental Biology and Medicine, Am. Congress Physical Therapy. Sigma Xi. Author: Principles of X-Ray and Radium Dosage; also 6 physical therapy charts. Home: 1337 Winona St. Office: 1853 Polk St., Chicago, Ill. Died April 3, 1957.

BACKFRAN, KENNETH D., prof. pediatrics; b. Cambridge, N.Y., Sept. 9, 1883; s. Harry Smith and Estella (Chase) Blackfan; M.D., Albany (N.Y.) Medical College (Union U.), 1905; m. Lulie Anderson Bridges, Aug. 15, 1920; 1 son, Turner Anderson Bridges. Pathologist Albany Hosp., and bacteriologist Bender Lab., 1905-06; instr. in pediatrics, Poly-clinic Hosp., Phila., 1910-11; asst. Washington U., St. Louis, 1911-12; instr. in pediatrics, Johns Hopkins, 1912-17, asso., 1917-19, asso. prof., 1919-20; prof. pediatrics, Coll. of Medicine, U. of Cincinnati, 1920-23; prof. pediatrics, Harvard Med. Sch., Boston, 1923—. Del. White House Conf. on Child Heatlh and Nature, 1899; A Nature Wooing, 1902; Orthoptera of Indiana, 1903; Boulder Reveries, 1906; Coleoptera of Indiana, 1910; Woodland Idyls, 1912; The Indiana Weed Book, 1912; Rhynchophora or Weevils of Northeastern America (with Charles W. Leng), 1916: Orthoptera of Northeastern America, 1920; Heteropters of Eastern North America, 1926; My Nature Nook, 1931; In Days Agone-Notes on the Fauna and Flora of Subtropical Florida When most of Its Area Was a Primeval Wilderness, 1932; South America as I Saw It, 1934; The Fishes of Indiana, 1938. Editor and part author Vols. XXXXXV, Annual Repts. Dept. Geology and Natural Resources of Ind. Home: Indianapolis, Ind. Died May 28, 1940.

BACON, CLARA LATIMER, mathematician; b. Hills Grove, Ill., Aug. 13, 1866; d. Larkin Crouch and Louisa (Latimer) Bacon; Ph.B., Hedding Coll., Ill.; A.B., Wellesley Coll., 1890; A.M., U. of Chicago, 1904; Ph.D., Johns Hopkins, 1911. Prin. pvt. schs., Dover, Kans., and Litchfield, Ky., until 1891; prof. mathematics, Hedding Coll., 1891-93; prin. high sch., Abingdon, 1893-95; prof. mathematics, Grand Prairie Sem., Onarga, Ill., 1895-97; instr. mathematics, 1897-1904, asso. prof., 1904-14, prof. since 1914, Goucher Coll. Mem. Am. Math. Soc., Math. Assn. Am., Am. Assn. Univ. Profs., Equal Suffrage League of Baltimore. Methodist. Club: College. Home: 2316 N. Calvert St., Baltimore. Died Apr. 14, 1948.

BACON, GEORGE WOOD, mech. engr.; b. Greenwich, N.J., May 6, 1869; s. Josiah and Caroline (Wood) B.; grad. Westtown (Pa.) Boarding Sch., 1888; M.E., Cornell U., 1892; m. Caroline Tilden Mitchell, June 1, 1904; 1 dau., Elizabeth Mitchell (Mrs. Ferdinand K. Rodewald); m. 2d, Elizabeth Ann Mitchel, June 11, 1943. A founder, mem. Ford, Bacon & Davis, Inc., pub. utility and indsl. engrs., 1894-1946, offices also in Phila., Chgo., Los Angeles, Monroe, La., Mexico City; identified with electrification of New Orleans street rys.; v.p. United Rys. Investment Co. (owners pub. utilities, Pittsburgh and San Francisco) for 8 yrs.; former pres. Sierra & San Francisco Power Co. hydro-electric power and transmission system; served as head of export dept. of J.P. Morgan & Co., 1915, making extensive purchases in U.S. of munitions for British and French govts.; pres., dir. East Long Beach (L.I.) Corp.; former chmn. bd. Ford, Bacon & Davis, Inc., ret. 1946. Fellow Nat. Geog. Soc.; mem. Am. Soc. M.E., Army Ordnance Assn., C. of C. State N.Y., Met. Mus. Art, Am. Museum Natural History, Cornell Soc. Engrs., Acad. Polit. Sci., Nat. Aero. Assn., N.J. Hist. Soc. Republican. Mem. Soc. of Friends. Clubs: University, Cornell, Economic (N.Y.C.); Recess, Piping Rock, St. George's Golf and Country. Home: 435 E. 52nd St., N.Y.C. 22. Deceased.

BACON, JOHN WATSON, engr., banker; b. Hartford, Conn., June 9, 1827; grad. Trinity, 1846; m. Caroline E. Botsford, Dec. 20, 1852; studied law 2 yrs., then became civil engr.; made first survey New York and New England R.R., and later was its gen. supt. until 1859; gen. supt. Danbury & Norwalk R.R., 1859-77; gen. R.R. commr. of Conn., 1877-87; pres. Savings Bank of Danbury, 1893—; State commr. of topog. survey of Conn. Home: Danbury, Conn. Died 1907.

BACON, RAYMOND FOSS, chem. engr.; b. Muncie, Ind., June 29, 1880; s. Rev. Charles and N.V. (Wiggs) B.; direct desc. of Bacons who settled in Mass., 1640, B.S., DePauw U., M.A., 1900, Ph.D., U. of Chicago; D.Sc., U. of Pittsburgh, 1918, DePauw, 1919; m. Edna Hine, Aug. 4, 1905. Chemist in U.S. Bur. of Science, Manila, P.I., 1905-10; asst. chemist Bur. of Chemistry, Washington, D.C., 1910-11; sr. fellow Petroleum Fellowship, Dept. Indsl. Research, U. of Pittsburgh, 1911-12; asso. dir., 1912-14, dir., 1914-21, Mellon Inst. Indsl. Research, U. of Pittsburgh; cons. chem. engr., New York, since Oct., 1921; scientific adviser to Philippine Govt., 1939. Col. Chem. Warfare Service, U.S. Army, Dec. 1, 1917-Dec. 16, 1918, spending 9 months in France as chief Tech. Div. C.W.S., A.E.F. Awarded SD.S.M., 1922. Mem. Am. Inst. Chem. Engrs., A.A.A.S., Societe de Chimie Industrielle, Chem. Soc. of London, D.K.E., Alpha Chi Sigma, Phi Lambda Upsilon. Clubs: Chemists', Siwanoy Country, Union League, Hudson River Country. Author: (with W.A. Hamor) American Petroleum Industry (2 vols.), 1916; (with same) American Fuels (2 vols.), 1922; also numerous papers on chemistry, technology of essential oils, reports, etc. Inventor of processes for mfr. of gasoline, recovery of cuprous sulphide from ores, for hydrogenating vegetable oils and for mfr. of sulphur from sulphide ores. Home: 98 Rockledge Rd., Bronxville, N.Y. Office: 500 Fifth Av., New York, N.Y. Died Oct. 14, 1954.

BADGER, WALTER LUCIUS, chem. engr.; b. Mpls., Feb. 18, 1886; s. Minor Campbell and Mary Helen (Albro) B.; B.A., U. Minn., 1907, B.S. in Chemistry, 1908, M.S., 1909; m. Helen Elizabeth Franklin, Apr. 8, 1913; 1 dau., Elizabeth Helen. Instr. chemistry U. Minn., 1908-09, spring 1910; chemist Gt. Western Sugar Co., fall 1909; asst. in chem. div. U.S. Bureau Standards, 1910-12; with U. Mich., 1912-37, prof. chem. engring., 1917-37; in charge research on water purification Detroit Edison Co., 1914-16; dir. research and cons. engr. Swenson Evaporator Co., 1917—; mgr. cons. engring. div. Dow Chem. Co., 1936-44; cons. chem. engr., 1944—; pres. W.L. Badger and Assos., Inc., 1957—. Recipient Wm. H. Walker award, 1940. Mem. Am. Chem. Soc., Am. Inst. Chem. Engrs., Sigma Xi, Tau Beta Pi, Alpha Chi Sigma, Phi Lambda Upsilon, Phi Delta Chi, Gamma Alpha. Conglist. Club: Chemists N.Y.C.). Author: Heat Transfer and Evaporation, 1925; Inorganic Chemical Technology (with E.M. Baker), 1928; Elements of Chemical Engineering (with W.I. McCabe), 1931; Introduction to Chemical Engineering (with J.T. Bancherd), 1955. Home: 1055 Cedar Bend Dr. Office: 309 S. State St., Ann Arbor, Mich. Died Nov. 19, 1958.

BAEKELAND, LEO HENDRIK, chemist; b. Ghent Belgium, Nov. 14, 1863; s. Karel L. and Rosalia (Merchie) B.; B.S., U. of Ghent, 1882, D. Nat. Sc., maxima cum laude, 1884; laureate of the 4 Belgian universities, 1887; hon. D.Ch., U. of Pittsburgh, 1916; hon. D.Sc., Columbia, 1929; hon.D.A.Sc., U. of Brussels, Belgium, 1934; hon. LL.D., U. of Edinburgh, 1937; m. Celine Swarts, Aug. 8, 1889; children—Jenny (dec.), George W., Mrs. Nina Baekeland Wyman. Asst., later asso. prof. chem., U. of Ghent, 1882-89; prof. chem. and physics, Govt. Higher Normal Sch. Science, Bruges, Belgium, 1885-87; came to America in 1889; founded 1893, and conducted until 1899, Nepera Chem. Co., mfg. photographic papers (Velox paper, etc.) of his invention; sold to Eastman Kodak Co., 1899, and since in research chem. work. Consulting chemist and helped develop Townsend electrolytic cell for Hooker Electrochem. Co., Niagara Falls, 1905; pres. Bakelite Corp., 1910-39, mfg. Bakelite (a Chem. synthesis from phenol and formaldehyde, replacing hard rubber and amber for uses in electricity and industrial arts where former plastics are unsuited). Mem. U.S. Naval Consulting Board since 1915; mem. U.Sn. Nitrate Supply Com., 1917, and chmn. com. on patents of Nat. Research Council, 1917; trustee of Inst. of Internat. Education since 1919; mem. advisory bd. Chem. Div. U.S. Dept. of Commerce since 1925. Awarded Nichols Medal, American Chemical Society, 1909; John Scott Medal, Franklin Institute, 1910; Willard Gibbs Medal, Am. Chem. Soc., Chicago sect. 1913; Chandler Medal (first award), Columbia U., 1914; Perkin Medal for industrial chemical research, 1916; grand prize, Panama-Pacific Exposition, 1915; Pioneer trophy, Chemical Foundation, 1936; scroll of hon. Nat. Inst., of Immigrant Welfare, 1937; Messel medal, Soc. of Chem. Industry, London, 1938; Franklin medal, Franklin Inst., 1940. Decorated Officer Legion of Honor (France); Order of Crown of Belgium; Comdr. Order of Leopold (Belgium), First Chandler lecturer, Columbia U., on occaison of 50th anniversary of Sch. of Mines, 1914; hon. prof. chem. engring., Columbia U., since 1917. U.S. del Internat. Congress Chemistry, 1909. Pres. Inventors' Guild, 1914; pres. sect. plastics, Internat. Congress Chemistry, 1912. Hon. mem. Electro-chem. Soc. (pres. 1909); mem. Am. Chem. Soc. (pres. 1924), Am. Inst. Chem. Engrs. (pres. 1912), Belgian-Am. Ednl. Foundation, Deutsche Chem. Ges., Soc. Chem. Industry of London (v.p. 1905), Nat. Acad. Sciences, Am. Inst. City N.Y., Phi Lambda Epsilon (hon.), Tau Beta Pi, Sigma Xi; life mem. Am. Philos. Soc., A.A.A.S., Franklin Inst., Royal Soc. of Arts (London), Société de Chimie Industrielle of Paris (hon.); hon. mem. Royal Soc. of Edinburgh, Soc. Belge des Electriciens, Am. Inst. Chemists. Clubs: Chemists' (honorary member; pres. 1904), University, Columbia Faculty (N.Y.); Cosmos (Washington); Engineers of Dayton (hon.); Cruising Club of America (N.Y.); Biscayne Bay Yacht (Fla.). Many patents U.S. and abroad, on the subjects of organic chemistry, elec. insulation synthetic resins, to-chemistry, electro-chemistry, organic chemistry, chem. industries, patent reform, social and philos. subjects, etc. Home: Coconut Grove, Fla.; and Yonkers, N.Y. Office: 30 E. 42nd St., New York, N.Y. Died Feb. 23, 1944.

BAENSCH, WILLY E., physician; b. Magdeburg, Germany, 1893; M.D., Halle (Germany) U., 1910. Intern surg., med. and univ. clinics Halle U., 1914-19; clin. tng. Curie Inst., Paris, France, Radiumhemmed, Stockholm, Sweden, 1926, also Central Roentgen Inst., Vienna Austria, 1926; dir. radiology and cancer research, prof. radiology Leipzig U., 1926-45; dir. dept. roentgenology Georgetown U., Washington, also prof., 1947-72, chmn. dept. radiology; sr. cons. VA, Washington. Recipient Gold medal Georgetown U., 1967. Diplomate Am. Bd. Radiology. Hon. mem. German Roentgen Soc. (Rieder medal 1969). Address: Bethesda MD Died Nov. 1, 1972; buried Woodstock NY

BAETJER, FREDERICK HENRY, roentgenologist; b. Baltimore, Md., Aug. 7, 1874; s. Henry and Fredricka B.; A.B., Johns Hopkins, 1897, M.D., 1901; m. Mary Yarnall Carey, Oct. 14, 1903. Prof. roentgenology and roentgenologist, Johns Hopkins U. and Hosp.; cons. roentgenologist, Union Memorial Hosp., Church Home and Infirmary, Hosp. for the Women of Md., Children's Hosp. Sch. Maj. Med. Corps U.S. Army, May 1917-Feb. 1919. Pres. Am. Roentgen Ray Soc., 1911-12. Home: Catonsville, Md. Died July 17, 1933.

BAGG, RUFUS MATHER, college prof.; b. at W. Springfield, Mass., Apr. 19, 1869; s. Rufus Mather and Mary E. (Bartholomew) B.; A.B., Amherst, 1891; Ph.D., Johns Hopkins, 1895; m. Grace Raybold, of W. Springfield, Mass., Apr. 8, 1896. Prin. high sch., Lubec, Me., 1891-2; instr. geology and mineralogy, Worcester Summer Sch. for Boys, 1891-2; asst. in geology, Johns Hopkins, 1895-7; asst. N.Y. State Mus., winter of 1897; prof. geology, Colo. Coll., 1898-9; instr. in science, Colo. Springs High Sch., 1899-1900; sub-master Brockton High Sch., 1901-3; prof. mineralogy and petrography, N.M. Sch. of Mines, 1903-4; instr. geology, U. of Ill., 1907-11; prof. geology and mineralogy, Lawrence Coll., 1911—. Hon. mineralogist to Paris Expn., 1900; lecturer on geology, Chautauqua of Mt. Lake Park, Md., Aug., 1900. Fellow A.A.A.S., Geol. Soc. of America; mem. Am. Inst. Mining Engrs., Geol. Soc. Washington, Nat. Geog. Soc., Ill. State Acad. Sciences, Paleontol. Soc. America, Sigma Xi (Ill. Chapter), Washington Acad. Sciences. Author of tech. articles and papers. Address: Appleton WI

BAILEY, BENJAMIN FRANKLIN, elec. engr.; b. Sheridan, Mich., Aug. 7, 1875; s. William Martin and Lucy (Stead) B.; B.S. in Elec. Engring., U. of Mich., 1898, A.M., 1900, Ph.D. , 1907; m. Elsie Marion Eggeman, Dec. 30, 1902; 1 son, Benjamin Franklin, Jr. Designer Edison Illuminating Co., Detroit, 1898; in testing dept., Gen. Electric Co., Schenectady, N.Y., 1898-99; instr. in electrotherapeutics, 1900-01, instr. in elec. engring., 1901-06, asst. porf., 1906-10, jr. prof., 1910-13, prof. since 1913, U. of Mich., also head Dept. of Elec. Engring. since 1925. Chief engr. Fairbanks-Morse Elec. Mfg. Co. and of Howell Elec. Motors Co.; inventor Bailey elec. lighting, starting and ignition system, also inventor of single-phase condenser motor; dir. Bailey Elec. Co., Howell Electric Motor Co.; v.p., dir. Fremont Motor Corp. Republican. Episcopalian. Fellow Am. Inst. E.E. (life); mem. Soc. Automotive Engrs., Sigma Xi, Tau Beta Pi, Eta Kappa Nu. Honored by Nat. Assn. Mfrs. as a modern pioneer. Clubs: Faculty, Michigan Union, Barton Hills Country, Ann Arbor Golf. Author: Induction Coils, 1903; Induction Motors, 1911; Elementary Electrical Engineering, 1913; Principles of Dynamo Electirc Machinery, 1915; Alternating Current Machinery, 1934. Home: Ann Arbor, Mich. Died Oct. 31, 1944.

BAILEY, EDGAR HENRY SUMMERFIELD, chemist; b. Middlefield, Conn., Sept. 17, 1848; s. Russell B. and Hannah (Miller) B.; Ph.B., Yale, 1873; Ph.D, Ill. Wesleyan, 1883; student Strassburg, 1881, Leipzig, 1895; m. Aravesta Trumbauer, July 13, 1876; children—Kenneth Russell (dec.), Herbert Stevens, William Hotchkiss, Edgar Lawrence, Austin. Instr. in chemistry, Yale, 1873-74. Lehigh U., 1874-83; prof. chemistry and metallurgy, 1883, dir. chem. lab., 1900, U. of Kan., emeritus. Chemist, Kan. State Bd. Agr., 1885—, State Bd. Health, 1899. Presbyn. Author: (with H. P. Cady) Laboratory Guide to Study of Qualitative Analysis, 1901; (with W. R. Crane) Gypsum (Vol. V); Mineral Waters (Vol. VII, Geol. Survey, Kan.); Sanitary and Applied Chemistry, 1906; The Source, Chemistry and Use of Food Products, 1914; Laboratory Experiments on Food Products, 1915; Report in the Dietaries of some State Institutions under the care of the Board of Administration, 1921; (with H. S. Bailey) Foods from Afar, 1922. Home: Lawrence, Kan. Died June 1, 1933.

BAILEY, EDWARD MONROE, chemist; b. New London, Conn., Aug. 27, 1879; s. Edward Monroe and Louise Maria (Hagan) B.; Ph.B., Yale, 1902, M.S., 1905, Ph.D., 1910; m. Myrtle Mix Studley, June 11, 1906; 1 son, Irvin Monroe. Asst. chemist Conn. Agrl. Expt. Sta., 1902-17, chemist in charge since 1917; state chemists, Conn., since 1919. Mem. Joint Com. on Definitions and Standards for Food Products, U.S. Dept. Agr., 1922-38; consultant Council Pharmacy and Chemistry, 1920-30; mem. Council Pharmacy and Chemistry, 1920-30; mem. Council Pharmacy and Chemistry and Council on Foods, A.M.A., 1930-38. Mem. Am. Chem. Soc., Assn., Official Agrl. Chemists, Assn. Feed Control Officials, Assn. Diary, Food and Drug Control Officials, Sigma Xi, Club: Graduate. Contbr. numerous articles on chemistry and biochemistry of foods, drugs and agrl. products in scientific jours. and station repts. Home: 854 Edgewood Av., New Haven, Conn. Died Apr. 13, 1948.

BAILEY, FRANCIS, printer, journalist; b. Lancaster County, Pa., circa 1735; s. Robert and Margaret (McDill) B.; married, at least 1 son, Robert. Publisher Lancaster Almanac, 1771-96; owner printing shop, Lancaster, after 1772, published many fgn. (chiefly German) materials, also 4th edit. of Common Sense (Thomas Paine), 1776; coroner Lancaster County, 1777; served as brigade maj. Pa. Militia at Valley Forge, 1778; published U.S. Mag., Phila., 1778-79; became ofcl. printer Continental Congress, also State of Pa., Phila., 1781; became editor Freeman's Journal of the N. Am. Intelligencer, weekly which opened columns to all polit. factions, 1781 (contbrs. included philip Freneau, James Wilson, George Osborne); established printing office, Sadsbury, Pa., 1797, continued as state printer; gradually turned business over to son, after 1800. Died Octoraro, nr. Phila., 1815.

BAILEY, GILBERT ELLIS, geologist; b. Pekin, Ill., Apr. 27, 1852; s. Rev. Gilbert Stephen (D.D.) and Sarah Eloise (Bunnell) B.; student U. of Chicago, 1868-72, U. of Mich., 1872-73; Ph.D., Franklin (Ind.) Coll., 1881; m. Martha Cobb, 1876 (died 1879); m. 2d, Reba Boston, 1902. Prof. chemistry, U. of Neb., 1874-79; geologist Wyo. Ty., 1883-87; prof. metallurgy, State School of Mines, S.D., 1888-89; asst., Calif. Mining Bur., 1900, 01; Death Valley explorations, 1901, 02, 03; prof. geology, U. of Southern Calif., 1909—. Republican. Episcopalian. Mason. Author: Saline Deposits of California, 1902; Mines and Minerals of San Bernardino County, California, 1902; California Soils, 1913; the Use of Explosives in Agriculture, 1914; Nitrating by Legumes, 1914; Vertical Farming, 1915; California, A Geologic Wonderland, 1924. Home: Los Angeles, Calif. Died Dec. 6, 1924.

BAILEY, IRVING WIDMER, prof. plant anatomy; b. Tilton, N.H., Aug. 15, 1884; s. Solon Irving and Ruth Elaine (Poulter) B.; A.B., Harvard, 1907, M.F., 1909, D.Sc. (hon.), 1955; hon. D.Sc., U. Wis., 1931; m. Helen Diman Harwood, June 15, 1911; children—Harwood, Solon Irving, II. Asst. in botany, 1909-10, instr., 1910, asst. prof., 1912, asso. prof., 1920, prof. plant anatomy, 1927-60, now prof. plant anatomy emeritus, Harvard; chmn. Inst. Research in Gen. Plant Morphol., since 1946; research asso. Carnegie Instn. Mem. advisory bd. U.S. Forest Products Lab., 1914-16; mem. Nat. Research Council, 1917-22 (exec. com. div. biology and agr. 1919-22, forestry com. 1917-20, biol. fellowship bd. 1928-32); mem. editorial bd. Am. Jour. Botany, 1915-18, Proc. Soc. Am. Foresters, 1914-16, Recipient Mary Soper Pope Award, 1954. Fellow A.A.A.S., Am. Acad. Arts Sci. (v.p. 1947-49); mem. emeritus Nat. Acad. Sci.; mem. Union of Am. Biol. Socs. (council 1924-26), Soc. Am. Foresters, Bot. Soc. America (pres. 1945), Am. Soc. Naturalists, Am. Phila. Soc. (Phila.), Bot. Soc. India (hon.), Royal Swedish Acad. Sciences, Linnaeau Soc. London, International Soc. of Plant Microphologists (pres. 1960), Phi Beta Kappa. Club: Faculty (Cambridge). Contbr. articles in field. Home: 985 Memorial Dr., Cambridge 38, Mass. Died May 16, 1967.

BAILEY, JACOB WHITMAN, educator; b. Auburn, Mass., Apr. 29, 1811; s. Isaac and Jane (Whitman) B.; grad. U.S. Mil. Acad., 1832; m. Maria Slaughter, Jan. 23, 1835, 1 son, 1 dau. Commd. 2d lt., arty. U.S. Army, 1832; became asst. prof. chemistry U.S. Mil. Acad., 1834, prof. chemistry and geology, 1838-57; did valuable research in botany (his field of greatest interest, specializing in minor algae, crystals of plant tissue); wrote many scientific papers on botany, chemistry and geology. Died West Point, N.Y., Feb. 27, 1857.

BAILEY, JOHN HAYS, bacteriologist; b. Chicago, Ill., May 3, 1900; s. George Troy and Clara (Koch) B.; B.S., U. of Chicago, 1924; Ph.D., 1928; D.P.H., U. of Michigan, 1938; m. Gertrude Boyer, Apr. 20, 1939; children—Martha Deborah, John Hoyne. Research fellow, bacteriology, Nelson Morris Inst., Chicago, Ill., 1928-29; fellow, James Whitcomb Riley Hosp., Indianapolis, Ind., 1929-32; resident bacteriologist, Municipal Contagious Disease Hosp., Chicago, 1932-35; senior bacteriologist, Ill. Dept. Pub. Health, 1935-38, on leave Sept. 1937-June 1938; asst. prof. bacteriology, Sch. of Medicine, Loyola U., Chicago, 1938-41; research bacteriologist, Winthrop Chem Co., Rensselaer, N.Y., 1942-43, Chief, div. of bacteriology, 1943-45; chief division of bacteriology, Sterling-Winthrop Research Inst., from 1946. Mem. Am. Acad. Microbiology (gov. 1956-59, sec.-treas. 1956-58), Soc. Gen. Micro-biology (Eng.), N. Am. Lily Soc., Soc. Am. Bacteriologists (sec.-treas., 1953-57, treas., 1957-59), Chgo. Inst. Medicine, A.A.A.S., Am. Hort. Soc., Sigma Xi, Chi Psi. Club: Ferndale Rod and Gun (Chgo. and New Auburn, Wis.). Adv. editor: Jour. Bacteriology. Home: Castleton-on-Hudson NY Died May 1, 1968.

BAILEY, JOHN WENDELL, cons. biologist; b. Winona, Miss., Jan. 9, 1895; s. Rev. Thomas Jefferson and Emma (Moseley) B.; B.S. Miss. State Coll., 1915, M.S., 1917; A.B., Cornell U., 1916, A.M., 1925; M.A., Harvard, 1927, Ph.D., 1928; m. Loui Lloyd, Dec. 27, 1917; children—Grances Bell, Loui Lloyd, John Wendell, Jr. Instr. in zoology and entomology, Miss. State Coll., 1916-17, asst. prof. and statistician, 1919-24; prof. biology, Miss. Coll., 1925-29; prof. biology, U. of Richmond, 1929-43; dir. of Biol. research, The Chesapeake Corp., 1937-41. Enlisted in U.S. Navy, 1918; trans. to U.S. Army; lt. Sanitary Corps, 1918-19; commd. maj., U.S. Army 1943, lt. col., 1945; overseas, 1943-46; educational advisor, Ft. Lee, Va., 1946-50; weapons effect directorate, historian Hdqrs., Field Command, Armed Forces Spl. Weapons Project, Sandia Base, Albuquerque, 1950-55; ret. as lt. col., 1955; cons. U.S. Army Transportation Research and Engring. Command, Ft. Eustis, Va., 1956-61; educational adviser U.S. Army logistical Mgmt. Center, Ft. Lee, Va., 1962-65, retired. Decorated with Croix de Guerre with gold star, Officer de l'Instruction Publique, Order of Palmes Academique (France); Croix Militaire de lere Classe (Belgium); Officer of Order Van Orange-Nassau (Netherlands). Winner Bowdoin prize, Harvard University, 1927. Fellow A.A.A.S.; mem. American Ornithologists, Biol. Soc. Washington, Mississippi Hist. Soc., Southern Hist. Assn., Miss. Educational Assn., Va. Acad. of Sci., George Rifles, Sigma Chi, Sigma Xi. Democrat. Clubs: Harvard of Va. (pres. 1942-43), Kiwanis. Author books and articles. Home: 27 Willway Rd., Richmond 26, Va. Died Dec. 1967.

BAILEY, LIBERTY HYDE, author, botanist, horticulturist; b. South Haven, Mich., Mar. 15, 1858; s. Liberty Hyde and Sarah (Harrison) Bailey; reared on farm; B.S., Mich. Agril. Coll., 1882, M.S., 1886; LL.D., U. of Wis., 1907, Alfred U., 1908; Litt.D., U. of Vt., 1919; D.Sc., U. of Puerto Rico, 1932; m. Annette Smith, June 6, 1883 (deceased); children—Sara May (deceased), Ethel Zoe. Has given particular attention to botany, horticulture and other biological subjects and to rural problems and education; asst. to Asa Gray, Harvard, 1882-83; prof. horticulture and landscape gardening, Mich. Agril. Coll., 1885-88; prof. horticulture, Cornell U., 1888-1903, dir. and dean Coll. of Agr., 1903-13. Awarded Veitchian silver medal, 1898, gold medal, 1927; George Robert White medal, 1927; gold medal Nat. Inst. Social Sciences, 1928; grande medaille Societe Nationale d'Acclimatation de France, 1928; gold medal of honor, Garden Club of America, 1931; Arthur Hoyt Scott medal and award, Swarthmore Coll. and Hort. Socs., 1931; Distinguished Service Award, Am. Assn. of Nurserymen, 1931; Centennial Medal, Am. Pomol. Soc.; Green Thumb Medal, Nat. Victory Garden Inst.; Johnny Appleseed Medal, Men's Garden Club of Am.; Medal Award, Nat. Garden Inst. 1948. Chmn. Roosevelt Commn. on Country Life, 1898. Fellow Am. Acad. Arts and Scis., A.A.A.S. (pres. 1926); mem. Nat. Acad. Scis., Am. Philos. Soc., Bot. Soc. Am. (pres. 1926), Am. Soc. Naturalists; hon. mem. Royal Hort. Soc. (London), Hort. Soc. Norway, Japan Agrl. Soc., Hort. Soc. Japan, Chinese Soc. Hort. Science, hort. societies Mass., R.I., and Ind., New Zealand Inst. Horticulture, Am. Soc. Hort. Science (1st pres.); corr. mem. Phila. Acad. Natural Science, Royal Acad. Agr. (Turin), Societe Lyonaise d'Horticulture; honorary member Botanical Society of Edinburgh. Author numerous publications relating to field. Editor: Cyclopedia of American Horticulture, 4 vols.; Cyclopedia of American Agriculture, 4 vols.; Standard Cyclopedia of Horticulture, 6 vols. (reprinted in 3 vols.); Rural Science series; Rural Textbook series; Rural Manual series; Rural State and Province series. Home: Ithaca, N.Y. Died Dec. 25, 1954; buried Lake View Cemetery, Ithaca.

BAILEY, LORING WOART, geologist; b. West Point, N.Y., Sept. 28, 1939; s. Prof. Jacob Whitman and Maria (Slaughter) B.; brother of William Whitman B.; A.B., Harvard, 1859, A.M., 1861; (hon. Ph.D., U. of N.B., Can., 1873; LL.D, Dalhousie, N.S., 1896; m. Laurestine M. d'Avray, Aug. 19, 1863. Prof. chemistry and natural science, 1861-1901, biology and geology, 1901-06, U. of N.B.; retired under Carnegie Foundation, Dir. Marine Biol. Sta. of Can., 1909. Author: Mines and Minerals of New Brunswick, 1864; Geology of Southern New Brunswick, 1870; Elementary Natural History, 1887. Home: Fredercton, N.B. Died 1925.

BAILEY, LYDIA R., printer; b. Phila., Feb. 1, 1779; no formal edn.; m. Robert Bailey, 1798, 4 children including Robert William. Took over printing bus. following death of husband, Phila., 1808; did much printing for govt. of Pa., circa 1800-20; printed 3d edition of Poems (Philip Freneau), 1809; city printer of Phila., 1830-50; trained many famous printers of Phila.; ret., 1861; contbd. 1st gift to endowment fund of 3d Presbyn. Ch., Phila. Died Phila., Feb. 21, 1869; buried 3d Presbyn. Ch. Cemetery.

BAILEY, MILUS KENDRICK, physician and surgeon; b. Euharlee, Ga., Sept. 4, 1891; s. Edward and Martha Jane (Kendrick) B.; student Daniel Baker Coll., 1908-12, U. Tex., 1915; M.D., Emory U., 1919; m. Martha Williams, Dec. 24, 1920 (dec.); m. 2d, Frances Riley, Dec. 10, 1950; 2 children. Interne, Emory U. Hosp., 1919-21; practice medicine and surgery, Hamilton, Ga., 1921-25, specializing in genito-urinary surgery since 1925; prof. urology and chmn. dept. urology Emory U. Sch. Medicine Atlanta, since 1934. Served as maj. M.C., AUS, 1942-45. Diplomate Am. Bd. Urology. Mem. A.M.A., Am. Urol. Assn., Phi Chi. Democrat. Presbyn. Clubs: Kiwanis, Druid Hills Golf. Author arricles on genito-urinary surgery. Home: 578 Ridgecrest Rd. N.E., Atlanta. Died June 21, 1964.

BAILEY, SOLON IRVING, astronomer; b. Lisbon, N.H., Dec. 29, 1854; s. Israel C. and Jane (Sutherland) B.; A.B., Boston U., 1881, A.M., 1884; A.M., Harvard, 1888; (Sc.D and hon. prof. astronomy, U. of San Agustin, Peru, 1923); m. Ruth Poulter, 1883; 1 son, Irving Widmer. Sent to Peru, S.A., to investigate conditions there in order to determine best location for a southern sta. for Harvard Coll. Obs., 1889; examined west coast from equator to Southern Chili, resulting in selection of Arequipa, Peru; in charge of work there, 1892—; established meteorol. sta. on summit of El Misti, at 19,000 feet, elevation, where observations were carried on for 10 yrs., by far the highest scientific sta. in world, 1893; various other meteorol. stas. jave been placed in Peru; asst. prof. astronomy, 1893-98, asso. prof., 1898-1913, Phillips prof., 1913-25, acting dir. observatory, 1919-22, Harvard, emeritus. In 1908 visited S. Africa and carried on astron. observations on elevated plateau in northern part of Cape Colony. Home: Cambridge, Mass. Died June 5, 1931.

BAILEY, VERNON, biologist; b. Manchester, Mich., June 21, 1864; s. Hiram and Emily B.; student U. of Mich., 1893, Columbian (now George Washington) U., 1894-95; m. Florence Augusta Merriam, Dec. 16, 1899. Served as chief field naturalist, U. S. Biol. Survey; retired July 31, 1933. Fellow A.A.A.S.; mem. Am. Ornithologists' Union, Cooper Ornithol. Club, Am. Forestry Assn., Washington Acad. Sciences, Biol. Soc. Washington. Author: Spermophiles of the Mississippi Valley, 1893; Pocket Gophers of Mississipi Valley, 1895; Reviison of Voles of the Genera Evotomys and Microtus, 1897; Mamals of District of Coumbia, 1900, 1923; Biological Survey of Texas, 1905; Life Zones and Crop Zones of New Mexico, 1913; Revision of the Pocket Gophers of the Genus Thomomys, 1915; Wild Animals of Glacier National Park (mammals); Beaver Habits and Beaver Farming, 1923; Biological Survey of North Dakota, 1927; Animal Life of Carlsbad Cavern, 1928; Animal Life of Yellowstone National Park, 1930; Mammals of New Mexico, 1931; Mammals of Oregon, 1936; Cave Life of Kentucky. Home: 1834 Kalorama Road, Washington. Died Feb. 14, 1942.

BAILEY, WILLIAM WHITMAN, botanist; b. West Point, N.Y., Feb. 22, 1843; s. Prof. Jacob Whitman and Maria (Slaughter) B.; brother of Loring Woart B.; entered Brown U., 1860; pvt. 10th R.I. Vols., 1862; returned to Brown and grad. 1864. Ph.B., 1873 (A.M., 1893; LL.D, U. of N.B., 1900); studied botany, Columbia, 1872, Harvatd Summer Sch., 1875, 1876, 1879; m. Eliza R. Simmons, Mar. 14, 1881. Asst. in chemistry, Mass. Inst. Tech., 1866; asst. chemist, Manchester (N.H.) Print Works, 1866; botanist U.S. Geol. Survey of 40th parallel, 1867-68; deputy sec. of State, R.I., 1868; asst. librarian Providence Athenaeum, 1869-71; taught botany pvt. schs., Providence; instr. botany, 1877-81, prof., 1881-1906, prof. emeritus, 1906—, Brown U.; spl. beneficiary of Carnegie Foundation, 1906. Sec. bd. visitors, U.S. Mil. Acad. 1896; del. centennial, U. of N.B., 1900, U.S. Mil. Acad. centennial, 1902; dir. Providence Athenaeum, 1900-03. Author: Botanical Collector's Handbook, 1881; Among Rhode Island Wild Flowers, 1885; Botanical Note-Book, 1894; New England Wild Flowers, 1897; Botanizing, 1899; Poems, 1910. Home: Providence, R.I. Died Feb. 20, 1914.

BAILOR, EDWIN MAURICE, psychologist; b. Culbertson, Neb., May 13, 1890; s. John Martin and Harriet (Shellhammer) B.; student Simpson Coll. (Ia.), 1907-09; A.B., Washington State Coll., 1914, A.M., 1916; Ph.D., Teachers Coll. (Columbia), 1924; hon. A.M., Dartmouth, 1928; m. Jane Galt, Apr. 21, 1920. Teacher, prin. and supt. schs., Lewis County, Wash., 1909-13 and 1914-15; instr. Wash. State Coll., 1915-18; psychol. expert, civilian service, U.S. Army, 1919-21; training officer U.S. Vets Bur., 1921-23; asst. Teachers Coll. (Columbia), 1923-24, instr., 1924-25; asst. prof. psychology, Dartmouth, 1925-28, prof. 1928-58. Served as 2d lt. Psychol. Corps, U.S. Army, 1918-19. Mem. A.A.A.S., Am. Psychol. Assn., Dartmouth Scientific

Assn., Am. Assn. Univ. Profs., Howe Library Corp., Phi Delta Kappa, Kappa Delta Pi, Kappa Phi Kappa, Lambda Chi Alpha. Mason. Author: Developed Lessons in Psychology, 1929; also Content and Form in Tests of Intelligence, 1925, Contbr. to mags. Home: Hanover NH Died Feb. 16, 1970; buried Southview Cemetery, Canton GA

BAIN, EDGAR COLLINS, metallurgist; b. Marion County, O., Sept. 14, 1891; s. Milton H. and Alice Anne (Collins) B.; B.Sc., Ohio State U., 1912, M.Sc., 1916, Sc.D. (hon.), 1947; honorary Dr. Engring., Lehigh University 1936; married Helen Louise Cram, February 18, 1927; children—Alice Anne, David. Began as chemist United States Bureau Standards, 1914, instructor Univ. of Wis., 1916-17; chem. engr. B. F. Goodrich Co., 1917; physicist Nat. Lamp Co. (Gen. Electric Co.), 1918-23; research metallurgist Atlas Steel Co., 1923-24, Union Carbide & Carbon Research Lab., 1924-28; dir. phys. metall. research U.S. Steel Corp., 1928-35, asst. to v.p. research and tech., 1935-43, v.p., 1950-57, assistant exec. vice pres. of operations, 1956-57; vice-pres. in charge of research and technology, Carnegie Ill. Steel Corp., 1943-56; retired; consulting metallurgist, from 1957; Howe memorial lecturer, 1932; E. DeM. Campbell memorial lecturer, 1932. Schwab Meml. lectr., 1952, Andrew Carnegie lecturer, 1958. Served to first lieutenant U.S. Army, 1918. Awarded Robert W. Hunt medal for work on nonrusting steels, 1929; Henry Marion Howe medal, for work on hardening of steel, 1931; Am. Iron and Steel Inst. medal, 1934, for work on alloy steel; Benjamin Lamme medal, Ohio State U., for eminence in engring., 1937 Albert Sauveur Achievement Award, 1946; John Price Wetherill medal, Franklin Inst., 1949; Gold medal Am. Soc. Metals, 1949; Grande Medaille de la Societe Francaise de Metallurgie, 1952; Ambrose Monell medal, 1958; gold medal Japan Inst. Metals, 1964; Meiji Centennial award Order Sacred Treasure, Govt. of Japan, 1968. Fellow American Physics Society; member Iron and Steel Institute of Japan (hon.), Iron and Steel Institute Great Britain (honorary), National Academy Sci. (chmn. div. engring., industrial research), Am. Phys. Soc., Am. Inst. Mining and Metall. Engrs., Am. Soc. Metals (past nat. pres., dir., chmn. N.Y. sect.), Am. Soc. Testing Materials, Japan Inst. Metals (hon.). Clubs: Duquesne (Pitts.); Cosmos (Washington). Author: (with M. A. Grossmann) High Speed Steel, 1931; Functions of the Alloying Elements in Steel, 1939, rev. edit. (with H. W. Paxton), 1961; also numerous papers on steel metallurgy. Discovered steel constituent later named Bainite. Home: Sewickley PA Died Nov. 27, 1971; interred Marion OH

BAIN, GEORGE GRANTHAM, writer, inventor b. Chicago, Jan. 7, 1865; s. George and Clara (Mather) B.; A.B., St. Louis Univ., 1883, A.M., 1890, Unmarried. News mgr. United Press at Washington; special corr. with headquarters in Washington and then New York; founded Bain News Service, New York, 1907; organized 1st news photograph service in America; inventor automatic photo-printer. Clubs: The Players, Aero ofinventor automatic photo-printer. Clubs: The Players, Aero of inventor automatic photo-printer. Clubs: The Players, Aero of America (a founder), Dutch Treat (gov.), Authors, Automobile of America. Contbr. short stories to leading mags. Home: 144 E. 22d St. Office: 255 Canal St., New York, N.Y.

BAIN, H(ARRY) FOSTER, mining engr.; b. Seymour, Ind., Nov. 2, 1872; s. William M. and Radie (Foster) B.; B.S., Moores Hill College, 1890; post-grad. study Johns Hopkins Univ., 1891-93; Ph.D. from Univ. of Chicago, 1897; m. Mary Wright, Dec. 1, 1902; 1 dau., Margaret. Asst. Ia. Geol. Survey, , 1893-95; asst. state geologist, Iowa, 1895-1900; mgr. mines, Ida. Springs and Cripple Creek, Colo., 1901-03; geologist, U. S. Geol. Survey, 1903-06; dir. Ill. Geol. Survey, 1905-09; editor Mining and Scientific Press, San Francisco, Apr., 1909-15; editor Mining Mag., London, 1915-16; explorations in Far East, 1916-17, 1920; asst. dir., U. S. Bur. of Mines, Apr. 1918-19, dir., 1921-24; cons. engr. Argentine, 1924-25, Columbia, 1929. Mem. Commn. for Relief in Belgium, 1915-16. Lecturer on econ. geology, Univ. of Ia., 1897, U. of Chicago, 1903-04. Fellow Geol. Soc., Am.; mem. Am. Inst. Mining and Metall. Engrs. (sec. since 1925), Mining and Metall. Soc. America. Canadian Mining Inst., Ins. of Mining and Metallurgy. Clubs: University (Urbana, Ill.); Engineers' (San Francisco and New York); Cosmos (Washington, D.C.). Home: 38 E. 53d St. Office: 29 W. 39th St., New York. Died March 9, 1948.

BAINBRIDGE, WILLIAM SEAMAN, surgeon; b. Providence, R.I.; s. Rev. William Folwell and Lucy Elizabeth (Seaman) B.; grad. Mohegan Lake School, Peekskill, N.Y., 1888; student Columbia; M.D., Coll. of Physicians and Surgeons (Columbia), 1893; grad. Presbyn. Hosp., 1895, Sloane Maternity Hosp., 1896; post-grad. Coll. Phys. and Surg., 1896; abroad 2 yrs.; hon. A.M., Shurtleff Coll., Ill., 1899; M.S., Washington and Jefferson Coll., 1902; Sc.D., Western U. of Pa., 1907; LL.D., Lincoln Memorial U., and Coe College; Litt.D., Lincoln Memorial U., and Coe College; Litt.D., Lincoln Memorial U., 1923; Dr. Honoris Causa, U. of San Marcos, Peru, 1941; m. June Ellen Wheeler, Sept. 9, 1911; children—Elizabeth (dec.). William Wheeler, John Seaman, Barbara (Mrs. Angus McIntosh). Professor operative gynecology, New York Post-graduate Medical School, 1900-06; professor surgery, New York. Poly. Med. Sch. and Hosp., 1906-18; surgeon, N.Y. Skin and Cancer Hosp., 1903-18; surg. dir. N.Y. City Children's Hosps. and Schs., Manhattan State Hosp., Wards's Island; cons. surg. or gynecologist to 16 metropolitan and suburban hosps.; hon. prof. med. faculty, Univ. Santo Domingo, Dominican Republic. Dir. Equitable Life Assur. Soc. of U.S., The Americas Foundation. Member Reserve Corps United States Navy, 1913-17; since Apr. 6, 1917 served as lieut. comdr., comdr. and capt. (med. dir.), M.C., U.S. N.R.; during World War operating surgeon on U.S.S. George Washington; med. observer for U.S. with allied armies in the field, later attached to surgeon general's office to write report; cons. surgeon and chief, Physiotherapeutic Division, U.S. Naval Hosptial, Brooklyn, New York; made consulting surgeon 3rd Naval Dist.; now cons. surgeon 3d Naval Dist. and attending specialist in surgery, U.S. Pub. Health Service, N.Y. City and vicinity. Official rep. of U.S. Govt. since 1921 at internat. congresses mil. medicine, surgery and sanitation; pres. 8th session Internat. office Medico-Military Documentation, Luxburg, 1938, chmn. 9th session, Washington and New York, 1939. On official mission to all republics of Central and South America for Navy Dept. and State Dept. 1941. Decorated U.S. Naval Reserve Medal; conspicuous Service Cross (N.Y. State); Officer, later Comdr. Legion of Honor (French); Officer Order of Leopold and Military Cross, 1st Class (Belgian); Commander, later Grand Officer Order of Crown of Italy, Vittorio-Veneto Commemorative Cross (Italian); Médaille Reconnaissance (French); Silver Medal of Merit (Italian R.C.); Officer, later Comdr. Order Polonia Restituta; Comdr. Order of White Lion (Czechoslovakia); Grand Officer Order of Crown (Rumania); Officer Orden del Libertador (Venezuela); Order of Gediminas (Lithuania); Cross of Merit (Hungary); Gold Cross of Merit (Poland); Comdr. Order of the Crown (Belgium); Comdr. Order of the Crown, Medal of Red Cross (Jugoslavia); Cruz de la Orden del Merito Naval (Spain); Comdr. Order of Saints Mauritius and Lazarus (Italy); Comdr. Order of the Sun (Peru); Comdr. of The Oak Leaved Crown (Luxemburg); Order of Merit, first class, Knigh, Order of White Rose (Finland); Gold Medal Order of Distinguished Auxiliary Service, Salvation Army. Hon. mem.Royal Acad. Medicine of Belgium, Royal Acad. Medicine Rome, Soc. of Surgeon of Poland, Soc. of Surgeons of Paris, Assn. Mil. Surgeons of Mexico, Union Medicale Latine, Assn. Mil. Surgeons of Hungary, Acad. of Surgery of Peru, Nat. Acad. Medicine Mexico, Acad. Sciences and Arts, Mexico, Nat. Acad. Med. Venezuela, French Gynecol. Soc., Nat. Acad. of Medicine of Spain; fellow Am. Assn. Obstet., Gynecol. and Abdominal Surgeons, Internat. Coll. Surgeons (internat. treas., 1935-46; surg. regent, New York State; chairman board trustees of U.S. chapter), American Geriatrics Society (hon.), International College Anesthetists, Royal Institute Pub. Health (life), fellow Royal Soc. Medicine (Eng.), A.M.A., N.Y. Acad. Medicine; mem. N.Y. State Med. Soc., Greater N.Y. Med. Assn., Assn. Mil. Surgeons of U.S. (pres. 1935), Internat. Med. Club of New York (pres. 3 terms, 1934-38). Am. Acad. Physical Medicine (pres. since 1941), St. Andrews Soc., Soc. Colonial Wars, S.R., S.A.R., Huguenot Soc., Soc. of Cincinnati (hon.), Mil. Order Foreign Wars (comdr. gen. Nat. Comdry., 1926-32), Military Order World War, Society Legion of Honor, Am. Soc. French Legion of Honor, Am. Soc. French Legion of Honor, St. Nicholas Society, Soc. of Am. Wars, Am. Legion (Comdr. Tiger Post 1932-35), Delta Upsilon, The Newcomen Soc., various foreign societies. Clubs: Authors, Columbia University, Pilgrims of United States, Quill (pres. 1938-39), Foreign Students Cosmopolitan, Union League, Nat. Arts, Rotary (pres. N.Y., Rotary 1933), Army and Navy of American (New York); Inter-allied Officer (London and Paris); Union Interalliée (Paris). Author: A Compend of Operative Gynecology, 1906; Life's Day Guide-Posts and Danger Signals in Health, 1909; The Cancer Problem 1914 (French, Italian, Spanish, Polish, Arabic edits.); also brochures, med. papers and repts. Address: 34 Gramercy Park, New York, N.Y. Died Spet. 22, 1947.

BAIRD, JULIAN WILLIAM, chemist; b. Battle Creek, Mich., Feb. 14, 1859; s. Abram Henry and Sarah Elizabeth (Wagoner) B.; A.B., U. of Mich., 1882, A.M., Ph.C., 1883; M.D. Harvard, 1890; m. Hattie Bell Ellinwood, Oct. 25, 1897. Asst. chem. analysis, U. of Mich., 1882-83; instr. qualitative chem. analysis and assaying, Lehigh U., 1883-86; prof. analytical and organic chemistry, 1886—, and dean, 1895—, Mass. Coll. of Pharmacy. Home: Boston, Mass. Died 1911.

BAIRD, MATTHEW, locomotive mfr.; b. Londonderry, Ireland, 1817; attended common schs., Phila. Came with family to Am., 1821, settled in Phila.; apprentice New Castle Mfg. Co. (Del.), 1834-37; supt. New Castle Railroad shops, 1837-38; supt. boiler div. Baldwin Locomotive Co., Phila., 1838-50, became partner, 1854, sole propr., 1866, reorganized co. as Baldwin Locomotive Works, M. Baird & Co., Proprs., ret., 1873; in marble bus., Phila., 1850-54; known for inventiveness in mfg. processes; a founder Am. S.S. Co.; active in many philanthropies, Phila. Died Phila., May 19, 1877; buried Phila.

BAIRD, SEPNCER FULLERTON, naturalist; b. Reading, Pa., Feb. 3, 1823; s. Samuel and Lydia (Biddle) B.; A.B., Dickinson Coll., 1841, M.A., 1843, Ph.D. (hon.), 1856; M.D. (hon.), Phila. Med. Coll., 1848; LL.D. (hon.), Columbia, 1875; m. Mary Helen Churchill, 1846; 1 dau., Lucy Hunter. Prin. founder Marine Lab., Wood's Hole, Mass.; prof. natural history Dickinson Coll., 1845; inaugurated the method of field study of botany and zoology in Am.; made explorations for U.S. Govt. in Wyo. Territory, 1850-60; sec. A.A.A.S., 1850-51; mem. Nat. Acad. Sci., 1864; 1st U.S. commr. Fish and Fisheries, 1871; elected asst. sec. Smithsonian Instn., 1850, sec., 1878. Author: Catalogue of North American Mammals, 1857; Catalogue of North American Birds, 1858; Review of American birds, 1864-66; editor Iconographic Ency., 1849; The Annual Record of Science and Industry, 1871-77; The Annual Reports of Smithsonian Instn., 1878-87; prepared Smithsonian Instn.'s Instructions to Collectors. Died Wood's Hole, Aug. 19, 1887; buried Oak Hill Cemetery, Washington, D.C.

BAKENHUS, REUBEN EDWIN, cons. engr.; b. Chgo., Sept. 10, 1873; s. Dietrich and Wilhelmnia (Kemper) B.; B. S., Mass. Inst. Tech., 1896; grad. Naval War Coll., 1924; m. Edith Steacy Rogers, 1901 (dec. 1946), 1 dau., Mrs. Dorinda Bakenhus Beck; m. 2d, Ethel Berg von Linde, July 22, 1953. Instructor civil engring., Mass. Inst. of Tech., 1896-97; with Metropolitan Water Bd., Boston, 1897-98; with U.S. Civil Service Commn., 1898-99; with U.S. Engineer Office, 1899-1901; commd. jr. lt. U.S. Navy, Feb. 27, 1901; advanced through grades to rear adm. C.E. Corps, Nov. 11, 1932, ret. Oct. 1937; sec. Am. Inst. Cons. Engrs., 1948-52, now secretary emeritus. Awarded Navy Cross, World War. Fellow A.A.A.S.; mem. Am. Soc. C.E. (ex-pres. Met. Sect.; former mem. bd. dirs.; sec., 1947-51), Society Engring. Edn., Soc. Am. Military Engrs. (ex.-pres. nat. soc., ex.-pres. N.Y.C. post); Am. sect. Permanent Internat. Assn. of Navigation Congresses; ex-pres. Am. Inst. Cons. Engrs. (mem. council), N.Y. Soc. Military and Naval Officers, World War, Military Order World War (ex-comdr. N.Y. Chapter), Amateur Fencers League of Am. Clubs: Army and Navy (Washington); N.Y. Yacht, Military Naval, Explorers. Author: The Panama Canal (with Capt. H.S. Knapp, and Emory R. Johnson), 1914. Editor of Activities of Bureau of Yards and Docks, Navy Dept. Contbr. to tech. mags. Home: 51 5th Av., New York 3. Office: care Am. Inst. of Consulting Engineers 33 W 39th St., N.Y.C. Died Oct. 7, 1967.

BAKER, ARTHUR LATHAM, mathematician; b. Cincinnati, May 7, 1853; s. John G. and Mary A. (Latham) B.; C.E., Rensselaer Poly. Inst., 1873; studied U. of Göttingen, 1896; hon. Ph.D., Lafayette Coll., 1889; m. Elizabeth Coit, d. Rev. Aaron H. Hand, Sept. 26, 1878; 1 dau., Dorothy (Mrs. J. Roy Allen). Adjunct prof. civ. engring., Lafayette Coll., 1873-80; atty. at law, Scranton, 1882; editor Commom Pleas Reporter and Weekly Digest, Scranton, 1885-87; prof. of mathematics, Stevens High Sch., Hoboken, N.J., 1889-91, U. of Rochester, 1891-1901; head of dept. of mathematics, Manual Training High Sch., Brooklyn, 1901-17. Author: Annual Digest Pennsylvania Supreme Court Decisions, 1886-87; Graphic Algebra, 1892; Elliptic Functions, 1890; Solid Geometry, 1893; Conic Sections, 1893; The Art of Geometry, 1905; Quaternions as the Result of Algebraic Operations, 1910; Elementary Thick-lens Optics, 1911; Mocrometry for the Amateur Microscopist, etc. Died 1934.

BAKER, CHARLES FULLER, zoölogist; b. Lansing, Mich., Mar. 22, 1872; s. Maj. Joseph Stannard and Alice (Potter) B.; B.S., Mich. Agrl. Coll., 1892; A.M., Stanford U., 1903; m. Ninette Evans, Aug. 29, 1894. Asst. in zoölogy, Mich. Agrl. Coll., 1891-92; asst. to zoölogist and entomologist, Colo. Agrl. Coll., 1892-97; zoölogist, Ala. Poly., and entomologist, Expt. Sta., 1897-99; teacher biology, Central High Sch., St. Louis, 1899-1901; asst. prof. biology, Pomona Coll., Calif., 1903-04; chief dept. botany, Estacion Agron. de Cuba, 1904-07; curator Bot. Garden and Herbarium, Museu Goeldi, Para, Brazil, 1907-08; dir.-elect Campo de Cultura Experimental Paraense, 1908; asso. prof. biology, 1908-09, prof., Sept. 1908-June 1912, Pomona Coll., Calif.; prof. agronomy, U. of the Philippines, July 1912—. In charge Colo. zööl. and forestry exhibit, Chicago Expn., 1893; zoölogist and asso. botanist, Ala. Biol. Survey, 1897-98; botanist, H. H. Smith exploring expdn. in Santa Marta Mountains, Columbia, S.A., 1898-99; also conducted field explorations in Southern Ill., Wis., Colo., N.M., Nev., Calif., Nicaragua, Cuba and Brazil. Pub. Invertebrata Pacifica. Home: Los Banos, P.I. Died 1927.

BAKER, CHARLES HINCKLEY, civil engr.; b. Chicago, Nov. 30, 1864; s. William T. and Eliza A. (Dunster) B.; C.E., Cornell, 1886; m. Gladys France, June 13, 1888. Resident engr. C.,B.&Q. Ry., C.,R.I.&P. Ry., and C.&N.-W. Ry., 1884-87; resident engr. Seattle, Lake Shore & Eastern Ry., 1887-90; civil engr. and contractor, 1890-95; reciever Merchants' Nat. Bank, Seattle, 1895-98. Built 3d St. and Suburban Ry., Seattle; organized and completed Snoqualmie Falls Power Co. (now Seattle-Tacoma Power Co.), transmitting, electrically, 19,000 h.-p. 30 miles to Seattle and 44 miles to Tacoma, 1898, also White River Power Co.; promoter reclamation Fla. Everglades; pres. Westchester-Putnam Co. Life Soc. Del. Dem. Nat. Conv., 1896; bolted and started Gold Dem. movement in State of Wash. Owner Mohegan Holstein and Knickerbocker farms, Moore Haven, Fla. Home: Mohegan Lake, N.Y. Deceased.

BAKER, DAVID, engr., metallurgist; b. Boston, Mass., May 31, 1861; grad. Mass. Inst. Technology (S.B.), 1885; also grad. mining engr.; m. Nov. 25, 1886, Kate M. Baker, Auburndale, Mass. In charge blast furnaces Pa. Steel Co.; then in charge erection and operation blast furnaces Md. Steel Co., 1887-97; metall. supt. same, 1897-98; supt. blast furnaces, South Works Ill. Steel Co., 1902-04. Address: Real Estate Trust Bldg., Philadelphia.

BAKER, DAVID FLOYD, engring. educator; b. Blue Springs, Mo., Sept. 19, 1919; s. Floyd Allen and Eula (Ketteman) B.; B.Indsl. Engring., M.Sc., Ohio State U., 1952, ph.D., 1957; m. Martha Estella Heacock, Feb. 6, 1944; children—Janet Estella, Jeffrey David. With Unitcast Steel Corp., Toledo, 1949, Buckeye Steel Castings Co., 1950, 51, 52; mem. faculty Ohio State U., 1953-70, prof. indsl. engring., 1961-70, chmn. dept., 1964-70, mem. adminstrv. com. Engring. Expt. Sta., 1963-65, dir. systems research group, 1964-70; cons. in field, ad hoc arbitrator labor-mgmt. disputes. Mem. engring. edn. and accreditation com. Engineers Council for Profl. Devel., 1968-70. Served with U.S. Navy, 1940-47. Decorated Bronze Star with gold star. Mem. Am. Inst. Indsl. Engrs., Am. Soc. Engineering Education, Institute Management Science, Nat. Soc. Profl. Engrs., A.A.A.S., Nature Conservancy, Aircraft Owners and Pilots Assn., Sigma Xi, Alpha Pi Mu (nat. pres. 1966-68), Tau Beta Pi, Pi Mu Epsilon, Phi Eta Sigma. Clubs: Wheaton (Columbus); Brooks Bird (past pres.) (Wheeling, W.Va.). Home: Columbus OH Died Feb. 10, 1970.

BAKER, ELLIS CRAIN, engineer; b. Brandon, Miss., Feb. 1, 1889; B.S., Miss. State Coll., 1911; M.S. in M.E., Ia. State Coll., 1930; m. Emma Pearson Davis, June 29, 1915; children—James Oliver, Ellis Crain. Efficiency Engr., Meridian (Miss.) Lt. & Ry. Co., 1911-12; instr. mech. engring., Miss State Coll., 1912-13, asst. prof., 1913-14; prof. Okla. Sch. Mines and Metallurgy, Wilburton, Okla., 1914-17; asst. prof. mech. engrg., Texas A. and M. Coll., Coll. Station, Tex., 1917-19; chief engr., asst. supt. boiler plant, Internat. Shipbldg. Co., Houston, Tex., 1919-21; asst. prof. mech. engrg., Okla. A. and M. Coll., 1921-23, asso. prof. 1923-30, prof. and head mech. engring. dept. since 1930. Mem. Am. Soc. Mech. Engrs., Am. Assn. Univ. Profs., Am. Soc. for Engring. Edn., Okla. Soc. Prof. Engrs., Pi Tau Sigma, Sigma Tau. Registered professional engr., Okla. Home: 801 Monroe St. Office: Okla. A. and M. Coll., Stillwater, Okla. Died Feb. 22, 1949.

BAKER, FRANK, anatomist; b. Pulaski, N.Y., Aug. 22, 1841; s. Thomas C. and Sybil S. (Weed) B.; sergt. 37th N.Y. Vols., 1861-63; M.D., Columbian (now George Washington) U., 1880; A.M., georgetown U., 1888, Ph.D., 1890 (LL.D, 1914); m. May E. Cole, Sept. 13, 1873. Prof. anatomy, Georgetown, 1883—; supt. Nat. Zoöl. Park, 1890-1916. Asst. supt. U.S. Life Saving Service, 1889-90; editor Am. Anthropologist, 1891-98. Has contributed anat. articles to Wood's Reference Handbook of the Medical Sciences, Standard Dictionary, Internat. Cyclopedia. Home: Washington, D.C. Died Sept. 30, 1918.

BAKER, FRANK COLLINS, zoöologist; b. Warren, R.I., Dec. 14, 1867; s. Francis Edwin and Anna Collins (Thurber) B.; ed. Brown U., 1888; Jessup scholar. Acad. Natural Sciences, Phila., 1889-90; B.S., Chicago Sch. of Science, 1896; m. Lillian May Hall, June 16, 1892 Idied Aug. 9, 1934). Was a member of Mexician exploring expdn. sent out by Acad. of Natural Sciences, 1890; invertebrate zoölogist, Ward's Natural Sciences Establishment and sec. Rochester Acad. Sciences, 1891-92; curator zoölogy, Field Columbian Mus., Chicago, 1894; curator Chicago Acad. of Sciences, 1894-1915 (life mem.); zoöl. investigator N.Y. State Coll. of Forestry, Syracuse U., 1915-17; curator Natural History Mus., U. of Ill., 1917-39; curator emeritus since 1939; consultant on Invertebrate Pleistocene Paleontology, Ill. Geol. Survey. V.-pres. Audubon Soc., 1900-15. Fellow A.A.A.S., Geol. Soc. America, Paleontol. Soc. America; mem. Am. Assn. Museums, Ill. Acad. Science (vice-pres. 1931), Museums Assn. (British), Ecol. Soc. America, Am. Malacological Union (pres. 1942), Limnological Soc. America, Sigma Xi; corr. mem. Zoöl. Soc., London. Clubs: University, Kiwanis, Author: A Naturalist in Mexico, 1895; Mollusca of the Chicago Area, 1898-1902; Shells of Land and Water, 1903; The Lynmoeidae of North and Middle America, 1911; Relation of Molusks to Fish in Oneida Lake, 1916; Life of the Pleistocene, 1920; Mollusca of Big Vermilion River (in relation to sewage pollution), 1922; Fresh Water Mollusca of Wisconsin, 1928; The Mollusca of the Shell Heaps or Escargotieres of Northern Algeria, 1939; Fieldbook of Illinois Land Mollusca, 1939; Use of Animal Life by the Mound-Builders of Illinois. Contbr. to zoöl. and geol. jours., principally on mollusca. Field zoölogist Wis. Geol. and Natural History Survey, 1920-22, Ill. Natural Hist. Survey 1920-22, Ill. Natural Hist. Survey, 1931-32. Home: Urbana, Ill. Died May 7, 1942.

BAKER, IRA OSBORN, civil engr.; b. Linton, Ind., Sept. 23, 1853; s. Hiram Walker and Amanda (Osborn) B.; B.S., U. of Ill., 1874, C.E., 1877 (D.Eng., 1903); m. Emma Burr, Aug. 5, 1877 (died 1911); m. 2d, Angie Ewing Ritter, Aug. 7, 1913. Assistant in civil engineering and physics, 1874-78, instr. civil engineering, 1878-80, asst. prof., 1880-82, prof., 1882—, U. of Illinois. Author: Leveling, 1886; Treatise on Masonary Constructionm 1889, 1899, 1909; engineer's Surveying Instruments, 1891; Treatise on Roads and Pavements, 1903, 13, 18, Home: Urbana, Ill. Died Nov. 8, 1925.

BAKER, MARCUS, cartographer; b. Kalamazoo, Mich., Sept. 23, 1849; s. John and Chastina (Fobes) B.; grad. U. of Mich., 1870; LL.B, Columbian Univ., 1896; m. Marian Strong, May 1899. Connected with U.S. Coast and Geodetic Survey, 1873-86; and with U.S. Geol. Survey, 1886—; spent several yrs. in explorations and surveys in Alaska and on Pacific coast; with William H. Dall, prepared the "Alaska Coast Pilot." Sec. U.S. Bd. on Geographic Names; was cartographer Venezuelan Boundary Commn. Asst. sec. Carnegie Instn. of Washington. Author: Dictionary of Alaskan Geographic Names; Northwest Boundary of Texas; Survey of Northwestern Boundary of United States; and other bulletins and geog. and math. papers. Died 1903.

BAKER, MARY FRANCIS, botanist; b. Plainfield, Conn., Nov. 29, 1876; d. Rev. John Manning and Sarah Joanna (Kinne) Francis; ed. Plainfield and Norwich acads. and under pvt. tutelage; m. Thomas R. Baker, of Winter Park, Fla., Oct. 12, 1918 (died 1930). Congregationalist. Author: The Book of Grasses, 1912; Florida Wild Flowers, 1926, rev. edit., 1938. Contbr. to mags. Home: 225 Holt Av., Winter Park FL

BAKER, WILLIAM JESSE, urologist; b. Dallas City, Ill., May 1, 1894; s. Eugene Hamilton and Elizabeth Edith (Prescott) B.; B.S., Knox Coll., 1917; M.D., Rush Med. Coll., 1923; m. Eloise Parsons, Aug. 30, 1923; children—William, Robert. Intern, resident intern urology Cook County Hosp., Chgo., 1924-26, asso. urologist, 1932-46, chief urol. dept., 1946—; urologist St. Luke's Hosp., 1926—; prof. urology Northwestern U. Med. Sch., 1955—; cons. urologist Municipal Contagious Hosp. Served with med. dept. U.S. Army, 1917-19, as lt. col., M.C., AUS, World War II. Fellow A.C.S.; mem. A.M.A., Am. Urol. Assn., Am. Assn. Genito-Urinary Surgeons, Clin. Soc. Genito-Urinary Surgeons, Internat. Soc. Urologists, Chgo. Urol. Sco., Am. Neissereian Soc., Tau Kappa Epsilon, Delta Sigma Rho, Nu Sigma Nu, Alpha Omega Alpha, Pi Kappa Epsilon. Conglist. Mason. Clubs: University, South Shore Country (Chgo.). Home: 5830 Stony Island Av., Chgo. Office: 7 W. Madison Street, Chgo. 2. Died Dec. 3, 1958.

BAKHMATEFF, BORIS ALEXANDER, civil engr.; b. Tiflis, Caucasus, Russia, May 14, 1880; s. Alexander Paul and Julia (Novitsky) B.; grad. Classical Gymnasium Tiflis, 1898; C.E., Inst. of Engrs. of Ways of Communication, St. Petersburg, 1903; studied at Poly. Inst., Zurich, 1903-04; D.Eng., Poly. Inst., St. Petersburg, 1911; m. Helen Speransky, July 15, 1905 (died 1921); m. 2d, Marie Helander Cole, June 7, 1938. Came to U.S., 1917, naturalized, 1935. Asst. dozent and prof. of gen. and advanced hydraulics, hydraulic structures, water power engring., theoretical mechanics and applied mechanics Polytech. Inst. Emperor Peter the Great, St. Petersburg, 1905-17; cons. engr. specializing on water power, St. Petersburg, 1907-15; enlisted with Red Cross, beginning of World War; chief plenipotentiary Central War Indsl. Com. to U.S., 1915-16; mem. Anglo-Russian Purchasing Commn., 1915-16; apptd. under-sec. of state (vice minister) Ministry for Commerce and Industry of Provisional govt. of Russia under premiership of Prince Lvov, 1917; apptd. head Extraordinary Russian Commn. to U.S. and Russian ambassador representing Provisional (Kerensky) Govt., 1917; continued as ambassador of the State of Russia until 1922; cons. engr. N.Y.C., 1923—; chmn. bd. Lion Match Co.; pres., dir. No. Mercury Felt Corp.; dir. Potash Co. Am., Research Corp.; prof. civil engring., Columbia, 1931, hon. prof., 1951; mem. bd. cons. engrs. Panama Canal, 1946-47. Dir. Humanities Fund, Russian Student Fund. Recipient Grand Medal, Soc. Drs. Engring., 1946, Order of Officer of Pub. Instrn., 1947 (France). Fellow Am. Geog. Soc., Fgn. Policy Council, N.Y. Acad. Scis., Inst. Aero. Scis. (asso.); mem. A.A.A.S., Am. Soc. C.E. (hon. 1946; chmn. com. research; mem. bd. engring. found.), Am. Soc. M.E., Engring. Inst. (Can.), Conn. Acad. Arts and Scis., Sigma Xi, Tau Beta Pi. Mem. Russian Orthodox Ch. Clubs: Century, University (N.Y.C.); Metropolitan (Washington). Author: Lectures on Hydraulics (Russian), 1912; Varied Flow of Liquid in Open Channels (Russian), 1912; Variable Flow of Liquids (Russian), 1914; Hydraulics of Open Channels, 1932; Mechanics of Turbulence, 1936. Contbr. to Foreign Affairs, Slavonic Review and jours. of Am. Soc. C.E., Am. Soc. M.E., others. Home: 876 Park Av., N.Y.C. Died July 21, 1951.

BAKST, HENRY JACOB, physician; b. Providence, May 19, 1906; s. Adolph and Sophie (Himowitz) B.; Ph.B., Brown U., 1927; M.D., Harvard, 1931; m. Ruth Elene Miller, June 23, 1933; 1 son, David Allan. Intern, resident physician Boston City Hosp., 1931-34, asst. vis. physician, 1935-72, teaching fellow histology and embryology Harvard, 1928-31; instr. medicine Boston U., 1935-45, asst. prof. medicine, 1946-48, asso. prof., preventive medicine, 1948-51, prof. preventive medicine, 1952-71, prof. emeritus, 1971-72, chmn. dept., 1952-66, asso. dean Sch. Medicine, 1965-69, dean, 1969-71, dir. med. scis. Boston U. Sch. Grad. Dentistry, 1971-72. dir. rehab. tng. Boston U., 1955-63; vis. physician Univ. Hosp., 1956-71, dir. ambulatory services, 1959-65, dir. div. health conservation, 1961-71, chief rehab. and phys. medicine. Chmn. health council United Community Services, Boston, 1953-57; mem. nat. adv. com. on pub. health tng. USPHS, 1965-69. Former trustee Univ. Hosp. Served as comdr. MC., USNR, World War II. Fellow A.C.P., Am. Pub. Health Assn.; mem. A.M.A., Mass. Assn. Mental Health (pres. 1956-57), Mass. Med. Soc., Assn. Tchrs. Preventive Medicine (sec.-treas. 1960-63, pres. 1963-64), Sigma Xi, Alpha Omega Alpha. Democrat. Jewish religion. Contbr. articles to med. jours. Home: Brookline MA Died Aug. 25, 1972.

BALBACH, EDWARD, metallurgist; b. Carlsruhe, Baden, Germany, July 4, 1839 (son of metallurgist of same name, 1804-90); came to U.S., 1850; ed. public schools; studied metallurgy and chemistry; m., Jan. 21, 1869, Julia Anna Nenninger. Invented de-silverizing process for argentiferous lead, known as the "Balbach process;" pres. Balbach Smelting and Refining Co. Address: Newark, N.J.

BALBOUR, DONALD CHURCH, surgeon; b. Toronto, Ont., Can., Aug. 22, 1882; s. Walter and Alice B.; M.B., U. Toronto, 1906, M.D., 1914, LL.D., Carleton College, 1934, Univ. of Toronto, 1941, St. Olaf Coll., 1943; D.Sc., McMaster U., 1941, Northwestern U., 1942, U. Western Ont., 1955; C.E., Nat. Acad. Medicine of France, 1952; m. Carrie L. Mayo, May 28, 1910; children—Mary Damon, William Mayo, Donald Church, Walter Mayo. Pvt. practice medicine, Rochester, Minn., 1907—; head sect. in div. surgery Mayo Clinic; dir. emeritus Mayo Found. for Med. Edn. and Research; prof. surgery emeritus U. Minn.; hon. cons. Med. Dept. USN, 1941, Army Med. Library, 1943; vis. lectr. U. Edinburgh, 1950; established Donald Church Balfour vis. professorship Mayo Found., 1960. Mem. com. on surgery NRC. Trustee Carleton Coll., also National Fund for Medical Education; elector Hall of Fame, N.Y.U. Decorated Cross of Knight Comdr. Royal Order of Crown of Italy; recipient citations Sec. of War, Sec. of Navy; President's Certificate of Merit, 1948; Builder of the Name medal U. Minn., 1950; Centennial award Northwestern U., 1951; D.S.M., A.M.A., 1955; Friednewald medal Am. Gastroenterological Assn., 1956. Diplomate Am. Bd. Surgery (a founder). Fellow A.C.S.; mem. Pan Am., Am. (adv. bd. med. specialties; chmn. surg. sect. 1928-29), Minn., So. Minn. med. assns., Am. (v.p. 1922), Western So., Central (charter), Interurban surg. assns., Soc. of Clin. Surgery, A.A.A.S., Interstate Postgrad. Med. Assembly of N.A. (pres. 1945), Assn, Am. Med. Colls., Assn. Am. Univs., Minn. Acad. Medicine, Minn. Acad. Sci. Societe des Chirurgiens de Paris, Societe Internationale de Chirurgie, Alumni Assn. Mayo Found. for Med. Edn. and Research, Alumni Association University of Toronto (hon. life), Academie de Chirurgie, Los Angeles Surg. Soc. (hon.), Southeastern Surg. Congress. Association Surgeons of Gt. Britain and Ireland, Assn. Mil. Surgeons; Sigma Xi, Nu Sigma Nu. also hon. fellow several fgn. profl. assns., including Royal Coll. Surgeons (England, Edinburgh, Australia and Canada), Royal Society Medicine, and others; hon. mem. several fgn. profl. assns. Republican. Conglist. Clubs: University (Chgo., Rochester); Minneapolis, Campus. Author: The Stomach and Duodenum (with graphs. Mem. editorial bd. Surgery, also Surgery, Gynecology and Obstetrics. Home: 322 8th Ave. S.W. Office: 200 1st St. S.W. Rochester, Minn. Died July 25, 1963.

BALDINGER, LAWRENCE H., educator; b. Galion, O., Jan. 12, 1907; s. Edward Nelson and Margaret (McCartney) B.; Ph.C., Western Reserve U., 1928, B.S., 1929; M.S., U. of Notre Dame, 1931, Ph.D., 1933; m. Helen Dwyer, Aug. 10, 1929; children—Lawrence H., Margaret Ann, James Edward, Charles Dwyer. Instr. dept. of pharmacy, U. of Notre Dame, 1929-33, instr. and head dept., 1933-39, asst. prof. chemistry, 1939-41, asst. prof. chemistry and asst. dean Coll. of Science, 1941-42, asst. prof. chemistry and acting dean, 1942-43, prof. of chemistry and dean, 1943-60, asso. dean, head dept. pre-profl. studies, 1960-70. Recipient of 1950 Notre Dame Lay Faculty award. Fellow A.A.A.S.; mem. Am. and Ind. chem. socs., Am. Pharm. Assn., Ind. Acad. Science (pres. 1961), Phi Delta Chi, Rho Chi, Sigma Xi. Contbr. to Jour. Am. Chem. Soc., Jour. Am. Pharm. Assn. Home: South Bend IN Died Nov. 28, 1970; buried South Bend IN

BALDWIN, A(RCHIBALD) STUART, civil engr.; b. Winchester, Va., Sept. 28, 1861; s. Robert Frederick and Caroline (Barton) B.; ed. Shenandoah Valley Acad., Winchester, Va., and Staunton (Va.) Mil. Acad.; m. Martha Frazier, Dec. 19, 1883. Rodman on Richmond & Allegheny R.R. (now C.&O. Ry.), 1879; asst. engr. and engr., Iron and Steel Works Assn. of Va., 1880-83; draftsman and asst. engr., Phila. extension B&O. R.R., 1883-85; pron. asst. engr., Mo. River Bridge, Kansas City, for C.M.&St.P. Ry., 1885-86; resident engr.

Louisville, St. Louis & Tex. R.R., 1886-87; asst. engr. and roadmaster, L.&N. R.R., 1887-1901; prin. asst. engr., 1901-03, engr. of constrn., 1903-05, chie- engr., Mar. 20, 1905-Aug. 1, 1918, then v.p. I.C. R.R. Co. Home: Chicago, Ill. Died June 26, 1922.

BALDWIN, ASA COLUMBUS, civil engr.; b. Austinburg, O., June 21, 1887; s. Adelbert Mortimer and Florilla (Williams) B.; B.A., Western Reserve U., Cleveland, O., 1908; student evenings law dept. George Washington Univ., 1910-13; m. Louis Smith, Dec. 8, 1917 (died May 6, 1933); children—Mortimer Wells, Frances Louise, Sylvia; m. 2d, Mrs. Marguerite Holliday, Dec. 12, 1935. Joined U.S. Coast and Geodetic Survey, 1909; was field officer Internat. Boundary Commn., establishing Alaska-Can. boundary, Mt. St. Elias to Arctic Ocean, 1909-13; leader in ascent of Mt. St. Elias, 1913. Pvt. engring. practice in Alaska, 1914-17, and in Seattle and Alaska since 1920; West Coast rep. Schlumberger Electrical Prospecting Methods of Paris since 1928; pres. Yellow Band Gold Mines, Inc., since 1938; mng. engr. Indianola Land Company, 1928-33. Geodetic engineer for International Boundary Commn. under NRA, 1933-34. Enlisted in Alaska for World War; entered O.T.C., Presidio, San Francisco, Aug. 27, 1917; 1st lt. Inf., Nov. 27, 1917; trans. to Engr. Corps and assigned to 29th Engrs., U.S. Army; sent overseas, June 1918; attached to G.H.Q., A.E.F., orientation officer for arty., Argonne-Meuse battle; hon. disch. Apr. 26, 1919. Mem. bar D.C. and Alaska; mem. Am. Soc. C.E., Beta Theta Pi. Lecturer on Alaska, seasons of 1926-27, making 2 transcontinental tours. Home: 3514 Wallingford Av. Office: Alaska Bldg., Seattle, Wash. Died Sept. 18, 1942.

BALDWIN, BIRD THOMAS, college prof.; b. Marshalltown, Pa., 1875; s. Bird L. and Sarah R. B.; B.S., Swarthmore (Pa.) Coll., 1900; studied U. of Pa., 1901-02, Harvard, 1902-03, 1904-05, U. of Leipzig, summer, 1906; A.M., 1903. Ph.D., 1905, Harvard; m. Claudia W. Wilbur, Sept. 1904 (died 1925); children—Bird Wilbur, Alan Wilbur and Jervas Wilbur (twins), Patricia. Supervising prin. Friends' schs., Morrestown, Pa., 1900-02; asst. in edn., Harvard Summer Sch., 1903; asst. in psychology and logic, Harvard, 1903-04; prof. psychology, West Chester (pa.) State Normal Sch., 1905-09; lecturer on psychology and edn., Swarthmore, 1906-10, U. of Chicago, 1909-10; asso. prof. edn. and head Sch. of Art of Teaching, U. of Tex., 1910-12; prof. edn., U. of Tenn., summers, 1912, 1913; prof. psychology and edn., Swarthmore, 1912-16; prof. ednl. psychology , Johns Hopkins, summers, 1915, 16, 17; lecturer in ednl. psychology, Johns Hopkins, 1916-17; research prof. in ednl. psychology and dir. Ia. Child Welfare Research Sta., State U. of Ia., 1917—. Chmn. Child Development Com. of Nat. Research Council. Washington, D.C. Mem. Friends Ch. Writer of numerous published articles, bulls, and reviews on ednl. and psychol. topics; collaborating editor psychol. and ednl. jours. Maj. Sanitary Corps U.S.A., Mar. 1, 1918-Aug. 1, 1919; in office of Surgeon Gen. of the Army, and chief psychologist and dir. rehabilitation of disables soldiers. Walter Reed General Hosp., Washington, D.C. Author: Physical Growth and School Progress; Physical Growth of Children from Birth to Maturity; The Mental Growth Curve of Normal and Superior Children; The Psychology of the Preschool Child. Home: Iowa City, Ia. Died May 12, 1928.

BALDWIN, EDWARD ROBINSON, physician; b. Bethel, Conn., Set. 8, 1864; s. Rev. Elijah C. and Frances Marsh (Hutchinson) B.; brother of Albertus Hutchinson B.; M.D., Yale Med. Sch., 1890; hon. M.A., Yale, 1914; Sc.D., Dartmouth, 1937; m. Mary Caroline Ives, June 1, 1895; 1 son, Henry Ives. Began practice at Cromwell, Conn., 1891; at Saranac Lake, N.Y., since 1893. Specializes in lung and throat diseases; researches in lab. since 1892; trustee Reception and Gen. hosps., Trudeau Sanatorium. Mem. Saranac Lake Sch. Bd., 1895; pres. Saranac Lake Bd. of Health, 1899-1901. Mem. Assn. Am. Physicians, A.M.A., Nat. Tuberculosis Assn. (pres. 1916-17), Am. Climatol. Assn., Assn. Am. Pathologists and Bacteriologists. Republican. Presbyterian. Home: Saranac Lake, N.Y. Died May 6, 1947.

BALDWIN, FRANCIS MARSH, prof. zoology; b. West Upton, Mass., Jan. 16, 1885; s. Ellory Albee and Rosa Arbella (Wood) B.; A.B., Clark U., 1906, A.M., 1907; Ph.D., U. of Ill., 1917; m. Bessie Mae Seay, July 15, 1912 (died Nov. 11, 1949); children—Gwendolyn, Francis Marsh; m. 2d Esther Pardee Harper, Aug. 5, 1950. Instr. nature and science, Ky. Normal Sch., 1908-11; independent investigator, U.S. Bureau Fisheries, Woods Hole, summers 1911-14; prof. biology, Western Maryland Coll., 1911-15; asst. zoology, U. of Ill., 1915-17; research, Marine Biol. Lab., Woods Hole, summer 1915; asst. prof. zoology, Ia. State Coll., 1917-19, asso. prof. 1919-20, prof. physiology, 1920-27, chmn. dept., 1929-36; dir. Marine Biological Station, 1928-36; chmn. Biological Div., 1936; spl. investigator, Marine Biol. Lab., summer, 1919; U.S. Biol. Survey, Barbary Erad, U.S.D.A., summer 1920; research, Freshwater Biol., Lakeside Lab. (Ia.) summers 1924-25. Fellow Ia. Acad. Science; mem. A.A.A.S., Am. Assn. Univ. Profs. (pres. local chapter 1931), Am. Physiological Soc., Soc. Exptl. Biol. and Medicine; mem. corp., Marine Biol. Lab., Woods Hole, Mass.; mem. So. Calif. Acad. Science, Sigma Xi (pres. local chapter 1943-44), Phi Kappa Phi (charter mem. local chapter). Author and contbg. editor: Elementary Manual for Physiology, 1927; Practical Exercises in Human Anatomy, 1932; Manual for Advanced Physiology (metabllism), 1933; Manual for Neurology, 1935. Contbr. articles on marine biology to Ency. Britannica, Book of the Year, collaborator for biol. abstracts. Frequent contbr. scientific articles to jours. Home: 5015 Angeles Vista Blvd., Los Angeles, 43. Office: 3551 University Av., Los Angeles 7, Cal. Died Feb. 2, 1951; buried Forest Lawn Cemetery, Glendale, Cal.

BALDWIN, HADLEY, civil engr.; b. Marshallton, Pa., Feb. 24, 1867; s. Barkley Cloud and Emily Kelly (Dowell) B.; B.S. in Civil Engring., U. Mich., 1893; m. Emily Wilson, Nov. 7, 1903; children—Wilson Barkley, Betty. With C.,C.,C.&St.L. Ry. Co., 1893—, successively masonry insp. and asst. engr., until 1896, supr. track, 1896, resident engr., at E. St. Louis, 1896-97, supr. track, 1897-98, engr. maintenance of way, Indpls., 1898-1902, engr. constrn., Cin., 1902, supt. St. Louis div., 1902-15, asst. chief engr., 1915-24, chief engr., 1924-31; chief engr. N.Y.C. R.R. Co. (C.C.C.&ST.L. Region), 1932-32; chief engr. Cin. No. R.R. Co. and Evansville, Indpls. & Terre Haute Ry. Co.; spl. engr. N.Y.C. R.R. Co., 1932—. Mem. Am. Ry. Engring. Assn. Republican. Unitarian. Clubs: Literary, Torch, Cincinnati Country. Home: 2565 Villa Lane. Address: Big Four Bldg., Cin. Died Nov. 22, 1949; buried Marshallton, Pa.

BALDWIN, JAMES MARK, psychologist; b. Columbia, S.C., Jan. 12, 1861; s. Hon. Cyrus II. and Lydia Eunice (Ford) B.; A.B., Princeton, 1884, A.M., 1887, Ph.D., 1889; hon. D.Sc., Oxford U., Eng., 1900 (first hon. degree in science ever given by Oxford), and U. of Geneva, 1909; LL.D, Glasgow U., 1901, S.C., Coll., 1905; studied Leipzig, Berlin and Tübingen; m. Helen Hayes, d. Prin. W. Henry Green, D.D., LL.D., Nov. 22, 1888; children—Helen Green (Mrs. John A. Sterrett), Elizabeth Ford (wife of Dr. Philip M. Stimson). Instr. French and German, Princeton, 1886; prof. philosophy, Lake Forest (Ill.) U., 1887-89, U. of Toronto, 1889-93; prof. psychology, Princeton, 1893-1903; prof. philosophy and psychology, Johns Hopkins, 1903-09; Nat. U. of ,exico, 1909-13. Hon. pres. Internat. Congress of Criminal Anthropology, Geneva, 1896; pres.-elect Internat. Congress of Psychology, 190913; awarded gold medal, Royal Acad. of Denmark, 1897. Author: Handbook of Psychology (2 vols.), 1889-91; Elements of Psychology, 1893; Mental Development in the Child and the Race, 1896; Social and Ethical Interpretations in Mental Development, 1898; Story of the Mind, 1898; Fragments in Philosophy and Science, 1902; Development and Evolution, 1902; Thought and Things, or Genetic Logic (vols. 1-3), 1906-11; Darwin and the Humanities, 1909; The Individual and Society, 1910; History of Psychology (2 vols.), 1913; Genetic Theory of Reality, 1915; France and the War, 1915; American Neutrality, 1916; The Super-State, 1916; Paroles de Guerre, 1919; Between Two Wars-Memories and Opinions (2 vols.), 1926. Joint Author: History of Psychology in Autobiography (volume 1), 1931. Editor of Psychological Review, 1894-1909, Dictionary of Philosophy and Psychology, 1901-06. His various books have been translated into French, German, Italian and Spanish. Decorated by Pres. of France, in person, with Cross Legion of Honor, 1917; Comdr. St. Saba (Serbian), 1918. Died Nov. 8, 1934.

BALDWIN, LOAMMI, JR., civil engr., lawyer; b. North Woburn, Mass., May 16, 1780; s. Loammi and Mary (Fowle) B.; grad. Harvard, 1800; m. Ann Williams; m. 2d, Catherine Beckford. Admitted to Mass. bar, 1804; helped construct Ft. Strong, Boston Harbor, 1814; engr. of improvements City of Boston, 1819; engr. Union Canal, 1821; mem. com. for erection Bunker Hill Monument, 1825. Designed and built dry docks at Charlestown (Mass.), Norfolk (Va.) navy yards, 1833; mem. Mass State Exec. Com., 1835; presdl. elector, 1836. Author: Thoughts on the Study of Political Economy as Connected with the Population, Industry and Paper Currency of the United States (pamphlet), 1809; Report on the Subject of Introducing Pure Water into the City of Boston, 1834. Died Charlestown, June 30, 1838.

BALDWIN, MAITLAND, neurosurgeon; b. N.Y.C., Sept. 29, 1918; s. Alvi Twing and Esther (McKean) B.; student Harvard, 1935-38; M.D., C.M., Queen's U., Kingston, Can., 1943; diploma neurol. surgery, M.Sc., McGill U., 1952. Asst. neurosurgeon Montreal Neurol Inst., 1950-52; lectr. in neurosurgery McGill U., 1950-52; asst. prof. neurosurgery U. Colorado, Denver, 1952-53; chief neurosurgeon, clin. dir. Nat. Inst. Neurol. Diseases and Blindness, Nat. Insts. Health, Bethesda, Md., from 1953, prof. clin. surgery Georgetown U. Hosps., from 1953; cons. NASA, Bethesda Naval Hosp. Served with USN, 1944-46. Diplomate Am. Bd. Neurol Surgery. Fellow A.C.S.; mem. Harvey Cushing Soc., Neurosurg. Soc. Am., Am. Acad. Neurology, A.A.A.S., N.Y. Acad. Scis., Soc. Neurol. Surgeons. Club: Cosmos (Washington). Home: Potomac MD Died Feb. 9, 1970; buried Gettysburg Nat. Cemetery.

BALDWIN, MATTHIAS WILLIAM, mfr., philanthropist; b. Elizabethtown, N.J., Dec. 10, 1795; s. William Baldwin; m. Sarah Baldwin (cousin), 1827, 3 children. Devised and patented process for gold plating; constructed Old Ironsides (one of 1st Am. locomotives used in transp.); a founder Franklin Inst. for Betterment of Labor, 1824; manufactured stationary engines, 1827, locomotives, 1831; mem. Pa. Constl. Conv., 1837; founded sch. for Negro children, 1835; founder M.W. Baldwin (now Baldwin Locomotive Works); donated money for 7 chs. and chapels in Phila.; mem. Pa. Legislature, 1854; mem. Am. Philos. Soc., Am. Hort. Soc., Pa. Acad. Fine Arts, Music Fund Soc. Died Phila., Sept. 7, 1866.

BALDWIN, SAMUEL PRENTISS, naturalist; b. Cleveland, O., Oct. 26, 1868; s. Charles Candee and Caroline Sophia (Prentiss) B.; A.B., Dartmouth, 1892, A.M., 1894, D.Sc., 1932; LL.B., Western Reserve U., 1895; m. Lillian Converse Hanna, Feb. 15, 1898. Admitted to Ohio bar, 1894, and began practice at Cleveland; discontinued practice because of ill health, 1902, has since devoted attention to science, principally ornithology; dir. Baldwin Bird Research Lab. for the study of live wild birds; originator of birdbanding method used in U.S. Biol. Survey; chmn. bd. The Williamson Co.; pres. The New Amsterdam Co. Research asso. in biology, Western Reserve U. Trustee Cleveland Mus. Natural History. Republican. Presbyn. Wrote: Bird Banding by Means of Systematic Trapping (Linnean Soc. of N.Y.), 1920; (with F. C. Lincoln) Manual for Bird Banding; Measurements of Birds; Physiology of the Temperature of Birds. Home: Cleveland, O. Died Dec. 31, 1938.

BALDWIN, THOMAS SCOTT, aeronaut; b. Quincy, Ill., June 30, 1860. Began with a circus at 10 as a gymnast, later becoming a tight rope walker; as a balloonist, 1887; invented and flew dirigible balloon at St. Louis Expn., 1904, also at Portland, Ore., and Buffalo expns. Apptd. by govt. to superintend bldg. of all spherical, dirigible and kite balloons; built first govt airship, 1908; commd. maj. Avaition Corps, 1917. Died May 17, 1923.

BALDWIN, WILLIAM, physician, botanist; b. Newlin, Pa., Mar. 29, 1779; s. Thomas and Elizabeth (Garretson) B.; M.D., U. Pa., 1807; m. Hannah M. Webster, 1808. Practiced medicine, Wilmington, Del., 1808-12; naval surgeon, St. Mary's, Ga., 1812-16; made bot. surveys of Del. and Ga., lived, collected specimens among Creek Indians in Ga. for several months; travelled to S.Am., 1816-17; apptd. botanist on expdn. to Rocky Mountains under command of Maj. Stephen H. Long, 1819. Died Franklin, Mo., Aug. 31, 1819.

BALDWIN, WILLIAM JAMES (ST. JOHN), mech. engr.; b. June 14, 1844, on shipboard; birth recorded at Waterford, Ireland; s. Capt. John and Giovanna Caterina (San Giovanni) B.; ed. Boston, and Charlottetown (St. Dunstan's), P.E.I., 2 yrs. spl. training in naval architecture; studied navigation drawing, engring. and physics; married. Began in mech. engring. and naval architecture, 1863; spl. work in naval constrn. during Civil War; was with Donald McKay, "prince of ship builders," at East Boston, in the construction of 3 monitors and the conversion of several blockade runners into U.S. cruisers; in the Brazilian service, as asst. naval constr., 1866-67. Was the first domestic engr. in the high buildings of New York; cons. engr. and designer for the U.S. War Coll., Washington, D.C., U.S. Immigrant Station, N.Y. Harbor, U.S. Soldiers' Home, Tennessee, etc., and cons engr. for Dept. Health, City of New York, hosps. and power-plants; over 24 yrs. cons. engr. N.Y. Telephone Co. and Empire City Subway Co. Asso. editor Engring. Record, 1880-89; lecturer and prof. thermal engring., Poly. Inst., Brooklyn. Mem. Commn. of Am. Soc. Mech. Engrs. that formulated the standard pipe threads (known as "the Briggs formula") for U.S.A. and Can., 1886; mem. internat. standard for pipes and fittings; mem. spl. com. Am. Soc. M.E. for electric screw thread standards. Life mem. A.I.A. Author: Steam Heating and Ventilation, 1897; An Outline of Ventilating and Warming, 1899; The Ventilation of the School-Room, 1901. Home: Brooklyn, N.Y. Died May 7, 1924.

BALK, ROBERT, geologist; b. Reval, Estonia, May 31, 1899; s. Hugo and Mary (Koch) B.; ed. Gymnasium, Dusseldorf, Germany; Ph.D., U. Griefswald, Gottingen, Breslau, Ger., 1924. Came to U.S., 1924, naturalized citizen. Independent field work since 1923 in Italy, Germany, Norway, U.S.A.; geologist, N.Y. State Mus., 1925-26, Minn. Geol. Survey, 1930, U.S. Geol. Survey, 1938-45; instr. Hunter Coll., 1925-28. asso. prof., 1928-35; vis. prof., Stanford U., 1934; asso. prof. Mt. Holyoke Coll., 1935-37, head dept. geol. and geography since 1935, prof. 1937-47, prof. geology U. Chgo., 1947-52; Prin. geologist N.M. Bur. Mines and Mineral Resources, 1952—. Fellow Geological Society America, Society Rheology, Am. Geophys. Union, Norsk Geol. Forening; mem. Phi Beta Kappa, Sigma Xi. Author: Structural Behavior of Igneous Rocks, i937. Editor, Geology of North America, 1936-39. Office: N.M. Died Feb. 19, 1955.

BALKE, CLARENCE WILLIAM, chemist; b. Auburn, O., Mar. 29, 1880; s. William Frederick and Clara Jacobena (Class) B.; A.B., Oberlin (O.) Coll., 1902;

Ph.D., U. of Pa., 1905; m. Minnie Maude Coddington, Apr. 21, 1905; children—Claire Coddington, Roger Redfield, Barbara, Hildegarde, Abigail Strader. Acting prof. physics and chemistry, Kenyon Coll., Gambier, O., 1903-04; instr. in chemistry, Oberlin Coll., summer 1903; instr. in chemistry, U. of Pa., 1906-07; asso. inchemistry, U. of Ill., 1907-10; asst. prof. inorganic chemistry, i910-13, prof., 1913-16; chem. dir. Franstell Products Co., North Chicago, Ill., since 1916. Mem. Am. Chem. Soc., Sigma Xi. Phi Eta, Phi Lambda. Club: Bonnie Brook Gol (Waukegan, Ill.). Contbr. papers on rare metals to Jour. Am. Chem. Soc., Chem. Bull., Chem. Age, etc. Discoverer of new methods of dehydrating, amalgamating, welding and processing; also methods for the mfr. of tantalum and columbius. Home: 40 Deere Park Drive, S., Highland Park. Office: Fansteel Products Co., North Chicago, Ill. Died July 8, 1948.

BALL, ELMER DARWIN, entomologist; b. Athens, Vt., Sept. 21, 1870; s. Leroy A. and Mary A. (Mansfield) B.; B.S., Ia. State Coll., 1895, M.Sc., 1898; Ph.D., Ohio State U., 1907; m. Mildred R. Norvell, June 14, 1899. Asst. in zoölogy and entomology, Ia. State Coll., 1895-97; asso. prof. same, Colo. Agrl. Coll., 1898-1902; prof. zoölogy and entomology, Utah Agrl. Coll., 1902-07; dir. Expt. Sta. and Sch. of Agr., Utah Agri. Coll., 1907-16; state entomologist of Wis., 1916-18; prof. zoölogy and entomology, Ia. State Coll., and state entomologist of Ia., i918-21, on leave as asst. sec. agr., June 12, 1920-Oct. 1, 1921; dir. scientific work, U.S. Dept. Agr., 1921-25; in charge of celery insect investigations, Fla. State Plant Bd., Sanford, Fla., 1925-28; dean of Coll. Agr. and dir. Agrl. Expt. Sta., Univ. of Ariz., 1928-31, now prof. zoölogy and entomology (on leave). Fellow A.A.A.S., Entomol. Soc. America, Utah Acad. Science (pres., 1910), Ia Acad. Science; mem. Washington Acad. Science, Biol. and Entomol. socs. Washington, Am. Assn. Econ. Entomolgists (pres. 1918), Pacific Slope Assn. Econ. Entomologists (pres., 1915-16), Ecol. Soc. America, Sigma Xi, Phi Kappa Phi, Gamma Sigma Delta (nat. pres. 1921-22). Author of systematic and life-history studies of Membracidae, Cercopidae, Jassidae and Fulgoridae, economic studies of codling moth, grasshoppers and leaf hoppers, causing "curly leaf" of sugar beets and "hopper burn" of potatoes, biol. studies of celery tyer, also studies of poultry breeding. Addres: University of Arizona, Tucson, Ariz. Died Oct. 5, 1943.

BALL, EPHRAIM, inventor; b. Lake Twp., O., Aug. 12, 1812; m. Lavina Babbs, circa 1835. Carpenter, Start County, O., circa 1832; built threashing machine (with brother), circa 1838, built factory for mfg. parts, Greentown, O., 1840, manufactured Blue Plough and Hussey Reaper during 1840's, reorganized firm with new partners, 1851; developed Ohio Mower (1st of 2-wheeled flexible mowers), patented, 1857, produced mower in his factory from 1859. Died Jan. 1, 1872.

BALL, FRANK HARVEY, mechanical engr.; b. Oberlin, O., May 21, 1847; s. Archibald McCullum and Sarah (Curtis) B.; ed. pub. and high schs., Buffalo, N.Y.; m. Katherine Deborah Bedell, of Grand Island, Erie Co., N.Y., Feb. 24, 1868. Organizer and mgr., Ball Engine Co., Erie, Pa., 1883-90, The Ball & Wood Co., Elizabeth, N.J., 1890-96; became v.p. and mgr. Am. Engine Co., Bound Brook, 1896; now mgr. carburetor dept. Penberthy Injector Co., Detroit. Mem. Am. Soc. Mech. Engrs. Address: 109 Willis Av., West Detroit, Mich.

BALL, HENRY PRICE, engineers; b. Phila., Pa., Jan. 8, 1868; s. Joseph and Sarah (Price) B.; B.S., U. of Pa., 1887, M.E., 1888; m. Anna Crosby Daily, May 30, 1891 (died April 23, 1934); 1 dau., Mabel; m. 2d, Miss Margaret A. Capeliss, April 3, 1937. With United Edison Mfg. Co., 1888-93, and designed and patented many devices for distribution of electricity for lighting, ry. and marine work; with Ward-Leonard Electric Co., 1893-1900, designed and patented complete line of rheostat theater dimmers and circuit breakers for control of electric current; chief engr. Gen. Incandescent and Arch Light Co., designed and patented apparatus for distbn. of high tension currents and automatic safety devices for control of same, large central sta. equipment, remote control switches and switchboard apparatus used by Commonwealth Edison Co., Chicago and Brooklyn, N.Y. Edison Co., etc.; cons. engr. Gen. Electric Co., 1903-08, designed and patented automatic machinery for reproduction of music played on piano and for mfr. of music rolls for use in piano players; engr. heating dept. Gen. Electric Co., Pittsfield, Mass., 1908-14, designed and patented complete line of electric heating devices for domestic and indsl. use; mem. firm, chief engr. and factory mgr. S. Sternan & Co., Brooklyn, 1914-17; supt. enamel factory of Lalande & Grosjean Co., Woodhaven, L.L., 1917-20; cons. engr. since 1920. Has taken out over 100 patents in U.S. and fgn. countries. Mem. Am. Inst. Elec. Engrs., Edison Pioneers, Beta Theta Pi. Republican. Home: 295 Parkside Av., Brooklyn, N.Y. Office: 141 5th Av., New York, N.Y. Died May 1, 1941.

BALL, JOHN RICE, geology and paleontology; b. Fremont, O., June 26, 1881; s. Oscar and Mary Ellen (Amsden) B.; prep. edn., Coll. of Puget Sound, Tacoma, Wash.; B.A., Northwestern U., 1913, M.A., 1917; B.D., Garrett Bibl. Inst., 1913; Ph.D., U. of Chicago, 1927; m. Cora Lena Goodman, Dec. 21, 1905; children—Clayton Garrett, Dorothy Margaret. With Northwestern University since 1916, asso. prof. geology and paleontology, 1928-45, prof. since 1945; with Univ. of Kansas City, 1946-51, U. of N.C. since 1951. Served on Illinois State Geological Survey, 1927, 1944; named several new fossils in the Silurian formations of Southeastern Missouri; served on North Dakota Geological Survey, summer, 1946; visiting and regular prof. geology and geography, U. of Kansas City, since June 1946. Fellow Geological Soc. America, A.A.A.S., Am. Paleontol. Soc.; mem. Am. Assn. Petroleum Geologists, Soc. of Economic Paleontologists and Mineralogists, Ill. Acad. Science, Chicago Acad. Science, Am. Assn. Museums, Sigma Xi. Methodist. Mason. Contbr. articles and brochures on researches. Address: University of Kansas City, Kansas City 4, Mo. Died Mar. 1, 1953.

BALL, MAX W(AITE), geologist; b. Henry Co., Ill., Sept. 9, 1885; s. Lewis Henry and Jennie Ann (Hoffstatter) B.; E.M., Colo. Sch. of Mines, 1906; LL.M., Nat. U., Washington, 1914; m. Amalia Maeder, Aug. 18, 1915; children—Douglas Schelling, Jean Katherine (Mrs. I.R. Kosloff). With U.S. Geol. Survey, 1906-16, chmn. oil bd., 1910-16; mining engr., law officer, U.S. Bur. of Mines, 1916-17; chief geologist, Royal Dutch Shell oil interests, Rocky Mountain region, 1917-18, gen. mgr., 1918-21; pres. Western Pipe Line Co., 1921-27, Marine Oil Co. and asso. cos., 1922-28; Argo Oil Co., 1925-28; consulting practice 1928-46; pres. Abasand Oils Ltd., 1930-43, Royal Royalties Ltd., Denver, 1931-44; spec. asst. to dep. petroleum adminstr., Petroleum Adminstrn. for War, 1944-46; dir. oil and gas div., Dept. Interior, 1946-48, oil and gas cons., 1948—, cons. to govt. Israel, drafting petroleum laws, 1950-53, govt. Turkey, 1953-54. Trustee Colo. Sch. of Mines, 1923-31. Recipient Medal of Merit for distinguished achievement Colo. Sch. of Mines, 1947; Gold Medal for distinguished service Dept. of Interior, 1948; Gold Medal for contbns. to Am. way of life, Freedom Founds. Inc., 1950. Fellow Am. Geog. Soc., Geol. Soc. of Am.; mem. Acad. of Polit. Sci., Am. Inst. Mining and Metall. Engrs. (vice chmn. Colo. chpt. 1923, 1926), Am. Assn. Petroleum Geologists (v.p. 1922-23; pres. 1923-24), Am. Petroleum Inst., Canadian Inst. Mining and Metallurgy (chmn. No. Alberta sect. 1942-43), Sigma Gamma Epsilon, Tau Beta Pi. Conglist. Club: Cosmos. Author: This Fascinating Oil Business; also bulls., articles on geology, econs., internat. relationships, etc. Home: 4705 Berkleley Terrace, Washington 7. Office: 1025 Vermont Av., Washington 5. Died Aug. 28, 1954.

BALL, OSCAR MELVILLE, biologist; b. Miami, Mo., Aug. 25, 1868; s. William Henry and Eliza Anne (Braden) B.; B.A., U. of Va., 1897; fellow in botany, U. of Va., 1898; student U. of Bonn, 1900, Leipzig, 1900-03; M.A., Ph.D., Leipzig, 1903; m. Mary B. Moon, June 16, 1900; 1 dau. Julia B. (wife of Lt. Robert M. Lee). Instr. in biology, U. of Va., 1896-97; prof. chemistry, Miller Sch., Va., 1897-1900; prof. botany and mycology, 1903-09, botany and zoology, 1909-11, biology, since June 1, 1911, Agrl. and Mech. Coll. of Texas. Mem. Deutsche Botanische Gesellschaft; fellow Tex. Acad. Science (v.p.); mem. A.A.A.S., Am. Econ. Soc., Nat. Inst. Soc. Sciences, Paleontol. Soc. Am., ect. Democrat. Mason (K.T., Shriner). Author of various papers on plant physiology, soil bacteriology and palaeobotany. Research in fossil flora of the Eocene. Address: College Station, Texas. Died Nov. 11, 1942.

BALL, SYDNEY HOBART, mining engr.; b. Chicago, Ill., Dec. 11, 1877; s. Farlin Q- and Elizabeth (Hall) B.; A.B., U. of Wis., 1901, Ph.D., 1910; m. Mary Ainslie, Dec. 8, 1913; 1 dau., Mary Virginia, Geologist, Mo. Bur. Mines and Geology, 1901-02; instr. geology, U. of Wis., 1902-03; asst. geologist, U.S. Geol. Survey, 1903-07; in charge expdn. exploring for minerals in Belgian Congo for Ryan-Guggenheim group, 1907-09; gen. practice in Europe, Asia, Africa, American and Greenland since 1909; cons. mineralogist U.S. Bur. of Mines; mining consultant War Production Rd., 1942-44. Mem. American Inst. Mining and Metall. Engrs. (dir. 1924-27), Geol. Soc. Am., Soc. of Econ. Geologists (pres. 1930), Mining and Metall. Soc. America (v.p. 1925-27; pres. 1933-34), Geol. Soc. of Belgium, Gemol. Inst. Am. (adv. bd., hon. mem.) C.R.B. Ednl. Fund (dir.), Psi Upsilon; hon. mem. Chem. Metall. and Mining Co. of South Africa. Officer Ordre Royal du Lion (Belgian). Republican. Clubs: Engineers' Explorers' (ex-gov.), Mining (pres. 1944-46). Author: Geology of Miller Co. (Mo. Bur. Mines), 1903; Geologic Reconnaissance in Southwestern Nevada and Eastern Calif., 1907; Geology of Clear Creek Quadrangle (U.S. Geol. Survey), 1906; annual chapter "Gemstones" in Minerals Yearbook; also pamphlets and tech. and geol. articles particularly on precious stones. Home: 829 Park Av. Office: 26 Beaver St., New York, N.Y. Died Apr. 8, 1949; buried Nantucket Island, Mass.

BALLANTINE, STUART, radio engr.; b. Germantown, Pa., Sept. 22, 1897; s. Charles Mansfield and Mary Stuart (Beverland) B.; ed. Grad. Sch. Harvard U., 1920-21, 1923-24; m. Virginia Gregory Orbision, June 18, 1927. With Marconi Co., 1914-15; bacteriol. lab., H. K. Mulford Co., 1916; research engr., Radio Frequency Labs., 1922-23; engaged in private research, 1924-27; dir. research Radio Frequency Labs., 1927-29; pres. Boonton Research Corp., 1929-34; pres. Ballantine Labs., Inc., elec. communication apparatus, Boonton, N.J., since 1935. Served as expert radio aide, U.S. Navy, 1917-20. Fellow Am. Phys. Soc., Acoustical Soc. Am., Inst. Radio Engrs. (pres. 1935); mem. Radio Club of Am., Franklin Inst. (mem. com. on science and the arts since 1935). Award for development of Navy radio compass, U.S. Navy, 1921; Morris Liebmann Memorial award by Inst. Radio Engrs., 1931; Elliott Cresson medal by Franklin Inst., 1934; John Tyndall fellow at Harvard, 1923-24. Mem. Ref. Episcopal Ch. Clubs: Harvard (Phila.); Rockaway River (Denville); Knoll (Boonton). Author: Radio Telephony for Amateurs, 1922. Contbr. about 40 articles on elec. communication. Home: 200 Overlook Av., Boonton, N.J. Died May 4, 1944.

BALLENGER, EDGAR GARRISON, physician; b. Tryon, N.C., Nov. 20, 1877; s. Thomas Theodore and Anna (Garrison) B.; student, Furman U., 2 yrs., Harvard U. part of 1896 and U. of N.C.; M.D., U. of Md., 1901; m. Nora Gorman, of Baltimore, Apr. 20, 1904. Interne, U. of Md. Hosp., 1901-2; surgeon Md. Granite Co., 1902-4; removed to Atlanta, Ga., 1904, and since made splty. of genito-urinary diseases. Lecturer genito-urinary diseases, Atlanta Sch. of Medicine, since 1905; editor Atlanta Journal Record of Medicine since 1905; mem. staff Presbyn. Hosp. Mem. A.M.A., Southern Med. Assn., Ga. Med. Soc., Fulton County Med. Soc. (pres.), Sigma Alpha Epsilon, Chi Zeta Chi. Clubs: Atlanta Athletic, Piedmont Driving, University. Author: Genito-Urinary Diseases and Syphilis, 1908. Home: 128 Myrtle St. Office: Century Bldg., Atlanta GA

BALLENGER, HOWARD C., physician, educator; b. Economy, Ind., Aug. 17, 1886; s. Jacob Oscar and Rachael Jane (Osborn) B.; student Indpls. Bus. Coll., 1906; Earlham Coll., 1906-07, U. Mich. Sch. Medicine, 1907-10, M.D., U. Ind. Sch. Medicine, 1911; m. Bessie Taylor, Aug. 15, 1912; children—Barbara Taylor (Mrs. Henry Churchill Williams), John Jacob, Howard Charles. Interne, Meth. Hosp., Indpls., 1911-12; asst. to Dr. W. L. Ballenger, 1912-15; instr. in otolaryngology U. Ill. Sch. Medicine, 1912-14, 1915-17; cons., surgeon, sect. otolaryngology USPHS (U.S. Marine Hosp.), Chgo., 1918-22; asst. surgeon otolaryngology Ill. Charitable Eye and Ear Infirmary, Chgo., 1917-20; asso. surgeon Evanston Hosp., 1918-36, surgeon since 1936; part time research Otho S. A. Sprague Inst. of Children's Meml. Hosp., 1928-31; asso. Northwestern U. Med. Sch., 1930-36, asst. prof., 1936-40, asso. prof. 1940-47, prof., chmn. dept. otolaryngology, since 1947. Fellow Am. Laryngol. Assn., Am. Otol. Soc., Am. Laryngol., Rhinol, and Otol. Soc., Am. Acad. of Ophthalmology and Otolaryngology, A.C.S., A.M.A.; mem. Chgo. Larnygol. and Otol. Soc. (past pres.). Co-author: Ballenger's Diseases of the Nose, Throat and Ear, (5th edition, 1925, 10th edition, 1957). Author: Eye, Ear, Nose and Throat (with A. G. Wippern), 1917; Otology, Rhinology and Larngology, 1st edit. 1940, 3d edit., 1947. Contbr. numerous articles to med. books, profl. jours. Home: 1570 Asbury Av., Winnetka. Office: 723 Elm St., Winnetka, Ill; Northwestern U. Med. Sch., 303 East Chicago Av., Chgo. Died Mar. 9, 1965.

BALLOU, WILLIAM HOSEA, mycologist, ichthyologist; b. Hannibal, Oswego County, N.Y., Setp. 30, 1857; s. Rev. Ransome R. and Mary Abigail (Green) B.; student Northwestern, 1877-81, U. of Pa., 1896; spl. studies in natural science; hon. Sc. D., Ft. Worth (Tex.) U., 1911; Litt.D., Chicago Law Sch., 1920; LL.D., Coll. of Oskaloosa, Ia., 1921; unmarried. Recorder U.S. Lake Survey, 1875-77; U.S. scientific survey of Niagara Falls, 1876; asst. engr. U.S. Yellowstone River Survey, 1878; govt. naturalist and representative of Harper's Weekly, Greely Relief Expdn., 1884; conducted crusade making animals safe in transport at sea (thanked by Queen Victoria and made perm. hon. commr. of U.S. by Sec. of Agr. Wilson), and other like crusades, 1892-95; editor New York Despatch (weekly), 1895-98; sec. Greater New York Despatch (weekly), 1895-98; sec. Greater New York Pub. Co., 1895-96; founder, sec. Westchester Free Hosp., 1892-95; Pres. Pocantico Water Works 1893-96; v.p. New York & Westchester Water 1891-98, etc.; owner and editor Science New Service. Hon. commr. U.S. Dept. Agr., del. of Davenport (Ia.) Acad. Natural Sciences, rep. of Am. Mus. Natural History and Popular Science Monthly at 7th Internat. Geol. Congress, St. Petersburg, 1897; conducted govt war propaganda to catch and eat more fish, under Herbert Hoover, 1917-18. Advocate of Louis Agassiz's theory of multiple origin of man, and species of animal and plant life. Discoverer of many species of fungi new to sicence, a number of which have been named in his honor; has listed over 1,000 species growing in Greater N.Y. City; founder nat. movement to conserve wild mushrooms, 1908. Mem. Nat. Inst. Social Sciences, Am. Soc. Ichthyologists and Herpetologists, American Soc. Mammalogists, Alumni Assn. of Northwestern Univ., Soc. Am. Military Engineers, Civic Forum, Alumni and Economic clus (New York); fellow Société Académique d'Histoire Internationale, France, which decorated him with the Sovereign's Grand Cross and Grand gold medal "for services to humanity"; also awarded hon chair of French Royal U., and of Paevia Sch. of Langs., Italy, for advocacy of Agassiz' theory of multiple origin of man and associated animals. Fellow Geopractic Soc.

of Am. (adv. editor for same). Life founder mem. Civil Legion of War Workers; awarded Divil Legion of Honor, 1931. Republican. Author: (novels) A Rider on a Cyclone, 1889; The Bachelor Girl, 1890; The Upper Ten, 1891; An Automatic Wife, 1891; Spectacular Romances, 1892; and over 300 poems. Donor of large collections of natural history to Northwestern U., and of fungi to State Museum, at Albany, N.Y., New York Bot. Garden, and Lloyd Inst., Cincinnati. Made geol. survey of Central Kans., discovering fossils of pre-fish, preamphibia, pre-reptiles with associated bivalves, and first plants in Devonian and Carboniferous Rock strata, and Upper Cretaceous marsupial, 1923; discovered fossil brachipods in Silurian rocks, West Virginia, by which Prof. Edward Drinker Cope and Dr. James Hall fixed geological age of the Appalachian System of mountains as Silurian, 1889; discovered cancer on tail of a boa constrictor in Honduras, 1890; first to define cancer as a fungus, originating in reptiles and fish and breeding by infinitely small spores, later investing entire reptile or fish and communicated to man by the drinking of infected water; scheduled 300 snakes and iguanas killed by cancer. Wrote poem, "The Unknown Soldier," for memorial service at Arlington, Nov. 11, 1921. Adv. editor Northwestern U. Alumni News and Living Age. Contbr. on popular science to Hearst syndicates; etc. Home: Closter, Bergen County, N.J. Died Nov. 30, 1937.

BALMER, FRANK EVERETT, agrl. educator and investment counselor; b. Woodston, Kan., Oct. 29, 1883; s. Elmer Denizen and Mary (Jencks) B.; B.S. in agr., Kansas State College 1905, also post grad. work, 1909; post grad. work Kansas University, June-August, 1909, U. Minn., 1924-26; m. Bertha Mabel Eastman, August 25, 1910 (she died July 18, 1942). Rural school teacher Rooks County, Kansas, 1900-01 and 1907-08; form mgr., 1906-08; dir. agrl. dept., Lewiston, Minn., 1909-11; prin. La Crosse County Sch. of Agr. and Domestic Sci., 1911-13; dist. supervisor county agrl. agts., West Central Minn., U. Minn., June 1913-Sept. 1914; asst. state leader county agt. work, U. Minn. Farm (St. Paul), Sept. 1914-July 1915; state county agt. leader, 1915-30; dir. agrl. extension, State Coll. of Wash. (Pullman), 1930-42; field representative Investors Syndicate and Investors Mutual Inc., Investors Stock Fund, Inc., conducted research in Minnesota relative cost of agricultural extension work also alfalfa prodn. possibilities. Awarded certificate of recognition for outstanding extension work, October, 1942. Member Agr. Hist. Soc. Am. Country Life Assn., Abraham Lincoln Assn., Acacia, Alpha Zeta, Epsilon Sigma Phi, Mu Beta Beta. Presbyn. Mason. Clubs: Nat. Travel, Kiwanis, Pullman Toastmasters (Pullman). Collector of Licolnana and Jeffersonia. Writer numerous articles on agr. and investment analysis. Home: Elmhurst Apts. C. Pullman, Wash. Died July 23, 1954; buried Riverside Park Cemetery, Spokane, Wash.

BANAY, RALPH STEVEN, psychiatrist; b. Hungary, July 26, 1896; s. George and Helen (Vadas) B.; M.D., Royal Hungarian U., 1920; post grad. studies, Vienna, Munich, Amsterdam; m. Mary C. Allen; two daughters, Suzanne Eve and Mary Clare. Came to the United States of America, 1927; naturalized, 1937. Asst. prof. psychiatry and neurology, Royal Hungarian U., 1921-23; clinical practice Budapest, 1923-27; sr. asst. physician Manhattan State Hosp., N.Y., 1927-29; pvt. practice N.Y. City, 1929-39; dir. clin. psychiatry Boston State Hosp., 1939-40; chief dept. psychiatry Sing Sing Prison, Ossining, N.Y., 1940-43; lecturer on criminal psychopathology, N.Y. Univ. Sch. of Edn., 1942-43; research psychiatrist, Columbia U., 1943-49. Dir. research on social deviations, dept. neurology, Columbia, 1943-49; attending psychiatrist, New York Sch. for Edn. of Blind, N.Y., 1942-47; med. dir., Yale Plan Clinic, Yale, 1944, Greenmont-on-Hudson Sanatorium, Ossining, N.Y. Civic Center Clinic, Bklyn., from 1954; project dir. Cyclazacine Plus program N.Y. State Narcotic Control Commn., psychiatrist charge Youth Institute, Incorporated, Ossining; adj. prof. forensic psychiatry Manhattan Coll. Chairman Committee on Prisons, Am. Psychiatric Assn., 1942 (chmn. sect. on Legal Aspects of Psychiatry, 1951-52); member sci. bd. of Research Council on Problems of Alcohol, since 1942; chmn. com. on research and edn. Nat. Pvt. Psychiat. Hosps.; cons. psychiatrist Armed Forces Induction Center, N.Y. Diplomate Am. Bd. Psychiatry and Neurology. Fellow Am. Med. Assn., Am. Psychiatric Assn., N.Y. Acad. Scis; mem. N.Y. State and County med. assns., A.A.A.S., Soc. Med. History, Soc. Med. Jurisprudence, Med. Correctional Association, Academy Forensic Scis. (chairman section psychiatry, 1957), Am. Correctional Assn. (v.p. 1957), Internat. Assn. Correctional Medicine in Tokyo (sec.), Contbr. N.Y. Times, and mags. Author: Youth in Despair, 1948; We Call Them Criminals, 1957. Editor: Corrective Psychiatry and Jour. Social Therapy. Home: New York City and Ossining NY Died May 15, 1970; Buried Ferncliff, Hartsdale NY

BANCROFT, EDWARD, inventor, Brit. agt.; b. Westfield, Mass., Jan. 9, 1744; no formal edn. Went to England, circa 1770, became contbr. articles on Am. to Monthly Review; acquainted with Benjamin Franklin, London; served as agt. for Franklin in London, at outbreak of Am. Revolution; agt. for Silas Deane (Am. commr.) in France while under pay Brit. govt., until 1783; gave to Brit. govt. information regarding treaties and movements of troops and ships from France to Am. during Revolution; lived in Eng. after 1873; invented dyes for use in textile mfg.; mem. Royal Soc. Author: Essay on the Natural History of Guiana, 1769; Experimental Researches Concerning the Philosophy of Permanent Colors, 1794. Died Margate, Eng., Sept. 8, 1821; buried Margate.

BANCROFT, HOWLAND, mining cons.; b. Denver, Sept. 19, 1886; s. Benjamin C. and Mary H. (Howland) B.; A.B., U. Mich., 1907; m. Alice R. Hannon, July 15, 1914; children—Howland, Lindgren (dec.), Jane. Mem. U.S. Geol. Survey, 1907-12; cons. engr., U.S. Bur. Mines, 1918-20; v.p. and mng. dir. Sinclair Panama Oil Corp., 1920-23; v.p. Lago Petroleum Corp., Lago Oil & Transport Co., Ltd., 1926-29; foreign rep. Pan-Am. Petroleum & Transport Co. (Standard Oil Indiana), 1929-31; European rep. Pan-Am. Petroleum & Transport Co., Pan-Am. Foreign Corp. (Standard Oil N.J.), 1932; cons. Latin-Am. enterprises; adviser, Metals Res. Co., Washington, 1941-44; cons. 1944-47; cons. Tsumeb Corp. Ltd., Tsumeb Exploration Co. Ltd. of Tsumeb, S.W. Africa; cons. exploration dept., O'okiep Copper Co. Ltd., Nababeep, C.P., 1947-50; cons. Sylvania Electric Products, Inc., 1951—, other mining, indsl. groups. Mem. S. Africa, Can. insts. mining and metallurgy, Am. Inst. Mining, Metall. and Petroleum Engrs., Mining and Metall. Soc. Am., Beta Theta Pl. Clubs: University (N.Y.); Cosmos (Washington); Union (Panama), Venezuela (Caracas). Author reports on mining dists. pub. by govt. and by tech. jours. Home: 22 E. 36th St., N.Y.C. 16. Died Sept. 12, 1964.

BANCROFT, J(OHN) SELLERS, mech. engr. b. Providence, R.I., Sept. 12, 1843; s. Edward and Mary (Sellers) B.; grad. Central High Sch., Phila., 1861; m. Beaulah Morris Hacker, Oct. 17, 1907. Began as apprentice Williams Sellers & Co., Phila., 1861; admitted to firm, 1873; gen. mgr., 1886-1902; gen. mgr., v.p. and treas. and mech. engr., Lanston Monotype Machine Co., 1902—. Mem. Soc. of Friends. Has taken out about 100 patents for mech. and elec. inventions. Home: Philadelphia, Pa. Died Jan. 29, 1919.

BANCROFT, WILDER DWIGHT, chemist; b. Middletown, R.I., Oct. 1, 1867; s. John Chandler and Louisa Mills (Denny) B.; A.B., Harvard, 1888; Ph.D., U. Leipzig, 1892; post-grad. Harvard, 1888-89, Strassburg, 1889-90, Berlin and Amsterdam, 1892-93; D.Sc. (hon.), Lafayette, 1919, Cambridge, 1923; LL.D., U. So. Cal. 1930; m. Katharine Meech Bott, June 19, 1895; children—Mary Warner, Hester, John Chandler, George, Jean Gordon. Asst. prof. phys. chemistry Cornell U., 1895-1903, prof., 1903-37, emeritus. Editor Jour. Phys. Chemistry, 1896-1932; asso. editor Jour. Franklin Inst., 1913—; chmn. div. chemistry NRC, 1919-20; adv. com. C.W.S. Tallman prof. Bowdoin Coll., 1937. Lt. col. C.W.S., 1918-19. Bd. visitors, Bur. Standards, 1922-25; v.p. Internat. Union Chemistry, 1922-25. Fellow Am. Acad. Arts and Scis. hon. mem. Am. Electro-chem. Soc. (pres. 1905, 1919), Am. Electroplaters Soc., English French, Polish chem. socs.; mem. Am. Chem. Soc. (pres. 1910), Am. Phys. Soc., Nat. Acad. Sci., Am. Philos. Soc. Author: The Phase Rule, 1897 Applied Colloid Chemistry, 1932; also numerous articles sci. jours. Address: 7 East Av., Ithaca N.Y. Died Feb. 7, 1953.

BANDELIER, ADOLPH FRANCIS ALPHONSE, archaelogist; b. at Berne, Switzerland, Aug. 6, 1840; m. Fanny Ritter, Dec. 30, 1893. Came to U.S. in youth; traveled under auspices of Archaeol. Inst. of America among native races of N.M., Ariz., Mexico and Central America, 1880-85; went to Peru and Bolivia, 1892, on scientific expdn. for Henry Villard, and has ever since pursued exhaustive archaeol., ethnol. and hist. researches in those countries (for six years for Am. Mus. Natural History, for which he has gathered its extensive collection of Peruvian and Bolivain antiquities). Resided in Santa Fe, N.M., 1885-92; in charge documentary studies for Hemenway Archaeol. Expdn., 1886-89. Lecturer Columbia U. on Spanish-Am. Literature in its connection with Ethnology and Archaeology, July 1904-11. Author: The Art of War and Mode of Warfare, 1877; Tenure of Land and Inheritances of the Ancient Mexicans, 1878; On the Social Organization and Mode of Government of the Ancient Mexicans; Historical Introduction to Studies Among the Sedentary Indians of New Mexico; An Archaeological Reconnoissance into Mexico, 1884; A Report on the Ruins of the Pueblo of Pecos, 1881; Final Report of Investigations Among the Indians of the Southwestern U.S., 1880-85, part 1, 1890, part 2, 1892; The Delight Makers (novel of Pueblo Indian Life); The Gilded Man; An Outline of the Documentary History of the Zuñi Tribe, 1892; The Indians and Aboriginal Ruins of Chachapoyas, Peru, 1907; The Islands of Titicaca and Koati (pub. by Hispania Soc. of America), 1910; The Ruins of Tiahuanaco in Bolivia, 1912. Home: New York, N.Y. Died Mar. 19, 1914.

BANDLER, CLARENCE G., surgeon, b. Owego, N.Y., Nov. 6, 1880; s. William and Eva (Fox) B.; A.B., Columbia, 1901, M.D., 1904; m. Miriam R. Zack, Aug. 17, 1951. Intern Bellevue Hosp., N.Y.C., 1904, adjunct attending urologist, chief of clinic, dept. urology, 1906-12; inst. asso. in urology. med. dept. Columbia, 1906-25; prof. urology N.Y. Post-Grad. Med. Sch. and Hosp. of Columbia U., 1909—; attending urologist Post-Grad. Hosp., 1934—, dir. dept. urology; cons. surgeon Home for Aged and Infirm, Yonkers, N.Y., 1908—; cons. urologist St. Francis Hosp., Port Jervis, N.Y., St. Vincent's Hosp., S.I., N.Y. U. Hosp., N.Y. U. Bellevue Med. Center, Bd. dirs. Asso. Hosp. Service. Served as capt., Med. Officers Res. Corps, World War I; sec. med. adv. bd. for draft registrants; with procurement and assignment com. Med. Adv. for Selective Service, World War II; with emergency med. service Office Civilian Def. Recipient Certificate, Medal of Merit, World War II. Diplomate Am. Bd. Urology (v.p.). Fellow A.C.S.; mem. Associete 'Internationale d'Urologie,' N.Y. State, N.Y. County med. socs. Clubs: Columbia University (N.Y.C.); Fairview Country, (Elmsford, N.Y.). Author numerous med. articles, including Tumors of the Urogenital Tract in the Young, Nephroptosis and Nephropexy, Urinary Obstruction. Home: 440 Park Av., N.Y.C. 22. Office: 77 Park Av., N.Y.C. 16. Died Nov. 15, 1957.

BANGHAM, RALPH VANDERVORT, biologist; b. Wilmington, O., Feb. 26, 1895; s. John Charles and Mary (Vandervort) B.; A.B., Wilmington Coll., 1915; B.S., Haverford Coll., 1916, A.M., 1917; Ph.D., Ohio State U., 1923; m. Margaret Williams, Sept. 5, 1925; children—John Williams (dec.), Jean. Instr. biology, Haverford Coll., 1917-18; prof. biology Agrl. and Mech. Coll., Arlington, Tex., 1918-19; asst. prof. anatomy Baylor U. Med. Coll., 1919-20, asst. prof. biology, 1920-22; asst. prof. biology Coll. of Wooster, 1923-24, prof. biology, 1924—, head dept., 1926—, on leave, 1947-48, 53-54; mem. staff Stone Lab., Ohio State U., summer, 1939, 40; research on fish parasitology U. of Toronto, summer 1941, 42, Jackson Hole Biol. Sta. of N.Y. Zool. Soc., 1949, 50; Inst. Biology U. Wyo., summer 1955; staff Rocky Mt. Biol. Lab., summer 1956; research asso. U. Wis., 1943-48; research U. B.C., 1953-54; parasitologist Ohio Div. Conservation on lake and stream survey; mem. Ohio Biol. Survey Board. Fellow A.A.A.S., Ohio Acad. Sci. (v.p. zoöl. sect. 1925); mem. Am. Zoologists Soc., Am. Soc. Parasitologists, Am. Fisheries Soc., Ecol. Soc. Am., Am. Micros. Soc., Limnological Soc., Am. Assn. U. Profs., Am. Soc. Naturalists, Soc. Systematic Zoölogy, Phi Chi, Gamma Alpha, Sigma Xi. Mem. Soc. of Friends. Club: Century. Author numerous sci. papers. Home: 1004 N. Bever St., Wooster O. Died Aug. 27, 1966; buried Wooster Cemetery.

BANGS, OUTRAM, zoölogist; b. Watertown, Mass., Jan. 12, 1863; s. Edward and Annie Outram (Hodgkinson) B.; ed. Noble's Sch., Boston, and Lawrence Scientific Sch., Harvard. Curator of mammals, Mus. of Comparative Zoölogy, Harvard, 1900—. Home: Cambridge, Mass. Died 1932.

BANISTER, JOHN, botanist; b. Twigworth, Eng., 1650; s. John Bannister; grad. Magdalen Coll., Oxford (Eng.) U., 1671, M.A., 1674; m. 1688. Came to Charles City County, Va., 1678, owned land on Appomattox River and acted as minister to Bristol Parish; engaged in studies local flora and fauna from his arrival, corresponded about his studies with other scientists including Compton, Sloane and Ray; trustee Coll. William and Mary, from circa 1690; part of his herbarium now in collection Brit. Museum; many of his scientific articles published posthumously in Philosophical Transactions of Royal Acad. Died nr. Roanoke River, Va., May 1692.

BANKER, HOWARD JAMES, biologist; b. Schaghticoke, N.Y., Apr. 19, 1866; s. Amos Bryan and Frances Alcena (Welling) B.; A.B., Syracuse U., 1892; A.M., Columbia, 1900, Ph.D., 1906; m. Mary Eugenia Wright, Aug. 23, 1894. Teacher, Troy Conf. Acad., Poultney, Vt., 1892-95 (vice prin., 1895); ordained deacon, 1894, elder, 1896, M.E. Ch.; pastor Union Ch., Proctor, Vt., 1895-98; teacher mathematics, Dickinson Sem., Williamsport, Pa., 1900-01; teacher biology, Southwestern State Normal Sch., Calif., Pa., 1901-14; investigator, Eugenics Record Office, Cold Spring Harbor, L.I., 1914-33 (acting supt. 1915-16; acting asst.-dir., 1920-21, 23); exec. com. and sec. sect. 2, 2d Internat. Congress of Eugenics. Fellow A.A.A.S.; mem. Phi Beta Kappa, Sigma Xi, Delta Upsilon. Author: The Hydnacae of North America, 1906; The Bancker or Banker Families of America, 1909. Editor The Underwood Families of America, 1913. Contbr. to scientific jours. of papers on mycology and eugenics. Address: 14 Myrtle Ave., Huntington, L.I. Died Sept. 23, 1943.

BANKS, EDGAR JAMES, archaeologist; b. Sunderland, Mass., May 23, 1866; s. John Randolph and Julia Maria (Dunklee) B.; student Amherst, 1886-87; A.B., Harvard, 1893, A.M., 1895; Ph.D., U. Breslau, 1897; m. Emma L. Lyford, July 16, 1893; m. 2d, Minja Miksich de Also Lukavecz; children—Edgar de Miksich, Daphne. Am. consul. Bagdad, Turkey, 1897-98; organized, 1899, expedition to excavate Babylonian city of Ur, but Sultan refused permission after 2 years waiting; acting prof. ancient history Robert College, Constantinople, 1902-03; pvt. sec. to Am. minister to Turkey, 1903; excavated Babylonian ruin, Bismya, 1903, for U. Chgo., discovering several thousand inscribed objects from 4500 B.C. to 2800 B.C. and the white statue of King David, a pre-Babylonian king of 4500 B.C. (oldest statue in the world); also much earlier ruins; field dir. of Babylonian expdn. and instr. Turkish and Semitic langs., U. Chgo., 1903-06; profl Oriental langs. and archaeology Toledo U., 1909; lectr. on Babylonia, Arabia, Turkey, etc., 1906—. Dir. Sacred Films, Inc., 1921-22; pres. Seminole Films Co., Inc. Climbed to summit of Mt. Ararat, 17,212 ft., Aut. 20, 1912 (1st Am.); crossed the Arabian desert by camel, 1912, on an exploring expdn. Author: Babylonische Hymnen der Berliner Sammlung, 1897; Jonah in Fact and Fancy, 1899; Bismya, or The Lost City of Adab, 1912; Bible and the Spade, 1913; Armenian Princess, 1914; Seven Wonders of the Ancient World, 1917. Also several hundred articles on archaeol. and other subjects. Address: P.O. Box 519, Eustis, Fla. Died May 5, 1945.

BANKS, JOHN HENRY, mining engr.; b. New York, N.Y., Nov. 28, 1861; s. Joseph and Ellen (Marsh) B.; E.,. Sch. of Mines, Columbian 1883; Ph.D., Columbia, 1894; m. Emilie S. Hultsch, June 9, 1886; children—Harold Purdy, Reginald Marsh. Mem. John H. Banks & Son. Republican. Episcopalian. Home: New York, N.Y. Died 1934.

BANKS, NATHAN, entomologist; b. Roslyn, N.Y., Apr. 13, 1868; s. Daniel Gerow and Maria (Hawxhurst) B.; B.S., Cornell, 1889, M.S., 1890; m. Mary A. Lu Gar, June 2, 1897 (dec. Feb. 24, 1956); children—Ruth, Bessie, Harold Bryant, Nellie May, Gilbert Shelley, Waldo Hawthorne, Dorothy Alice, Elsie Lucile, Douglas Hartley (dec.). Asst. entomologist U.S. Dept. Agr., 1900-16; curator insects Mus. Comp. Zoology, Harvard, 1916-36; also associate professor of zoology, Harvard University 1928-36, emeritus since 1936. Has largest collection of Arachinda and Neuroptera in United States. Member various entomological socs., Sigma Xi; fellow Am. Acad. Arts and Sciences. Prohibitionist. Wrote: Treatise on the Acarina, 1940; Catalogue of the Arcarina, 1907; Catalogue Nearctic Neuroptera, 1909; How to Collect and Preserve Insects, 1909; Catalogue Nearactic Spiders, 1910; Catalogue Nearctic Heteroptera, 1911; Index Economic Entomology, 1917. Contbr. many scientific and tech. papers to leading scientific jours. Home: Holliston, Mass. Died Jan. 24, 1953; buried Lake Grove Cemetery, Holliston.

BANNEKER, BENJAMIN, mathematician, abolitionist; b. Ellicott's Mills, Md., Nov. 9, 1731; s. Robert and Mary B.; ed. at home; attended integrated neighborhood sch. for a time. Inherited his father's farm; showed unusual mechanical ability, constructed a wooden clock with no previous training; took part in gentlemen's game of exchanging difficult math. problems; began making astron. calculations for almanacs, circa 1773; accurately calculated an eclipse, 1789, soon after sold his farm, concentrated on study of mathematics and astronomy; named to Capitol Commn. (1st presdl. appointment granted a Negro); assited L'Enfant in survey of D.C., 1790; published in almanac, 1792, wrote dissertation on bees; did study of locust plague cycles; wrote famous letter to Jefferson on segregationist trends in Am. Died Balt. Oct. 1806.

BANNISTER, HENRY MARTYN, physician; b. Cazenovia, N.Y., July 25, 1844; s. Rev. Henry and Lucy (Kimball) B.; Ph.B., Northwestern U., 1863, A.M., 1869; M.D., Nat. Med. Coll., Columbian (now George Washington) U:, 1871; m. Delia C. Ladd, of Chicago, June 14, 1887. On geol. survey of Ill., 1867-68, U.S. Geol. Survey of Territories, 1872; in med. practice since 1874; founded with Dr. J. S. Jewell and jointly edited Journal of Nervous and Mental Diseases, 1874-1881; has been connected with several other med. jours. Mem. A.M.A., Am. Med. Psychol. Assn. (hon.); asso. mem. Am. Neurol. Assn. Contbr. to med. publs. Home: 828 Judson Av., Evanston, Ill.

BANTA, ARTHUR MANGUN, zoölogist; b. near Greenwood Ind., Dec. 31, 1877; s. James Henry and Mary (Mangun) B.; B.S., Central Normal Coll., Ind., 1898; A.B., Ind. U., 1903, A.M., 1904; Edward-Austin fellow, Harvard, 1905-06, Ph.D., 1907; m. Mary Charlotte Slack, July 26, 1906; children—James Jerry, Ruth, Leah Margaret. Instr. in pub. schs., Ind., 1895-97; prin. high sch., 1899-1901, Johnson County Normal Sch., summer, 1901; asst. in zoology, Ind. U., 1903-05; instr. Ind. U. Biol. Sta., summers, 1903, 1904; asst. in zoölogy, Harvard, 1905-06, teaching fellow, 1906-07; with the U.S. Fish Commn., Woods Hole, lMass., summers, 1906, 09; prof. biology, Marietta Coll., Ohio, 1907-09; resident inv-estigator, Sta. for Exptl. Evolution of the Carnegie Instn., Cold Spring Harbor, N.Y., 1909-30; professorial lecturer in genetics, U. of Minn., 2d semester, 1927; visiting professor experimental zoölogy, Brown U., 1929-30, research prof. biology, 1930-45, prof. emeritus since June, 1945; associate Carnegie Instn. of Washington, 1930-32 and 1936-37. Mem. Nat. Research Council Board of Fellowships in the Biol. Sciences, 1933-37. Fellow A.A.A.S.; mem. Am. Soc. Zoölogists, Am. Soc. Naturalists (sec. 1935-37), Genetics Sco. of America, Limnological Soc. of America, Soc. Exptl. Biology and Medicine, Ecol. Soc. America, Sigma Xi. Investigator of effects of changed environment on cave animals; heredity, development longevity and sex determination in lower organisms, sex intergrades, etc. Author: The Fauna of Mayfield's Cave, 1907; Selection in Cladocera on the Basis of a Physiological Character, 1921; Studies on the Physiology, Genetics, and Evolution of some Cladocera, 1939. Contbr. to biol. jours. Home: 168 lMedway St., Providence, R.I. Died Jan. 2, 1946.

BARACH, JOSEPH H., physician, research medicine; b. Calvary, Poland-Russia, 1883; s. Zorach and Deborah (Oppenheim) B.; came to U.S., 1888, citizenship derived from father; student Park Inst., 1895-99; M.D., Univ. of Pittsburgh, 1903; post grad. student, Columbia, 1903; m. Edna S. Levy, Sept. 21, 1915; children—Joseph L., Richard L. Resident pathologist and interne West Pa. Hosp., Pittsburgh, 1904; asso. prof. medicine U. Pitts., also med. dir. U. Clins. Sch. Medicine, 1930—; sr. staff med. center hosps. 1910—; cons. dept. health Carnegie Inst. Tech., Pitts., 1910; cons. in medicine, Sewickley (Pa.) Valley Hosp., 1925—. Chmn. metabolism and endocrinology sect., research grants div. U.S.P.H.S., 1946-51, nat. council arthritis and metabolism sect., research grants div. since 1952. Served as capt. med. corps., World War I; chief selective service Dist. 1, Western Pa., World War II. Name inscribed on the Wall of Fame of the American Common—World's Fair of 1940, New York, for having made notable contribution to our living, ever-growing democracy devoted to peace and freedom. Fellow A.A.A.S., A.C.P., Am. Diabetes Assn. mem. council 1941, pres., 1944-46, chmn. sect. on metabolic and endocrine diseases, etc. member A.M.A., Sigma Xi, Republican-Liberal. Mem. Congregation Rodef Shalom, Pitts. Clubs: Cosmos (Washington); Concordia, Deep Creek Yacht. Author: Self Help for the Diabetic, 1934; Diabetes and Its Treatment, 1946; Diabetes, The Patients Book, 1948; Diabetes and its Treatment, 1949; Diabetes, The Foods and Facts on Diabetes, 1949. Contributor many articles to med. lit. in U.S. and abroad. Home: 5745 Beacon St., Pittsburgh 17, (summer) Manteo, N.C., Roanoke Island. Office: Fifth Av., Univ. Clinic Med. Center, Pitts. 13. Died Mar. 7, 1954.

BARAGWANATH, JOHN GORDON, mining engr.; b. Canaan, Conn., Oct. 4, 1888; s. Thomas Henry and Mary (Oakley) B.; student Newburgh Acad., 1902-05; A.B., Columbia U., 1910; m. Lelia Morris, 1914; 1 son, Albert Kingsmill; m. 2d, Neysa McMein (illustrator), May 18, 1923; 1 dau., Joan; married Dorothy Countess Beatty, June 26, 1950. Mining engr. in S. America, 1910-19; mem. firm Kingsmill & Baragwanath, N.Y., 1919-22; resident engr. Am. Smelting & Refining Co., 1922-28; pres. Pardners Mines, 1928-42; v.p. pres. Pardners Mines, 1928-42; gen. mgr. Nicaro Nickel Co. 1942-46; dir. explorations Freeport Sulphur Co., 1946-50; vice president Shelter Rock Development Corporation, 1950—. Member American Institute of Mining and Metall. Engrs., Mining and Metall. Soc. Am., Canadian Inst. of Mining and Metallurgy. Republican. Clubs: Explorers, Mining. Author: Pay Streak, 1936; A Good Time Was Had, published 1962. Co-author: All That Glitters (play), 1938; Farewell in Panama (novel), 1938. Contributor of scientific articles to engring. and mining mags.; also fiction. Home: 135 E. 54 St. Office: 485 Madison Av., N.Y.C. Died June 27, 1965; buried Rhinebeck, N.Y.

BARBA, CHARLES ELMER, mechanical engr.; b. Freemansburg, Pa., May 12, 1877; s. William Henry and Christiana (Smith) B.; student Bethlehem Prep. Sch., 1896-97; M.E., Lehigh U., 1901; m. Margarita E. Dunn, of Washington, D.C., June 22, 1904; children—Charles Elmer, Margarita Christiana, Dorothy Ann (Mrs. Dr. Bernard Wefers), Preston Albert, Francis William, William Henry, Elizabeth Dunn, Robert Eugene, John Edward. Draughtsman, Ordnance Dept., Washington, D.C., 1901-02; draughtsman, asst. chief draughtsman, asst. engr., Pa. R.R., Altoona, Pa., 1902-15; asst. engr., supt., Midvale Steel Co., Phila., 1915-17; supt. Mobile Carriage Shop, Watertown, Mass., 1917-19; supt. sea coast department, Watertown Arsenal, 1919-20, special duty, 1920-21; superintendent Osgood Bradley Car Co., Worcester, Mass., 1922-25; mechanical engineer, B.&M. R.R., N. Billerica, Mass., 1925-33; cons. practice, 1933-35; became chief engr., Junior Motors Corpn., Phila., and railroad consulting engr., 1936; now cons. engr. Ferrous Metals Corpn. Lecturer on railroads, State Coll. of Pa., 3 yrs.; on shop orgn. and management, foremanship and business administrations, Northeastern Univ., Boston, and mem. Mass. State Univ. Extension staff 3 yrs. Mem. Am. Soc. M.E. (chmn. r.r. div., 1935), Soc. for Promotion Engring. Edn., New England R.R. Club. Author of articles and tech. papers. Home: 11 Willard St., Newton, Mass. Office: 17 John St., New York NY

BARBORKA, CLIFFORD JOSEPH, diagnostician; b. Clinton, Ia., July 19, 1894; s. Joseph V. and Emma Marie (Schooley) B.; B.S., U. of Chicago, 1918; M.D., Rush Med. Coll., 1920; M.S., U. of Minn., 1923; D.Sc., Simpson Coll., 1932; m. Bessie Mae Long, July 28, 1919; children—Clifford Joseph, William Vincent. Interne, Presbyterian Hosp., Chicago, 1920-21; cons. physician Mayo Clinic, 1921-32; cons. gastroenterology, VA Research Hosp., Chgo.; professor medicine, chief gastrointestinal clinic, Northwestern U. Med. Sch. Attending phys., chief gastrointestinal service Passavant Memorial Hosp. Chairman international research committee World Orgn. Gastroenterology; member board directors of MEDICO, Incorporated; adv. panel gastroenterology U.S. Pharmacopea. Diplomate Am. Bd. Internal Medicine in gastroenterology. Fellow A.C.P.; mem. A.M.A., Ill. State Med. Soc., Inst. of Med. of Chicago, Soc. of Internal Medicine, Am. Gastroenterol. Assn. (pres. 1959), Central Soc. of Clinical Research, Assn. of Resident and Ex-Resident Physicians of Mayo Clinic, Am. Gastroscopic Soc. (pres. 1958), Beta Theta Pi, Nu Sigma Nu, Kappa Theta Psi, Sigma Xi, Alpha Omega Alpha. Author: Treatment by Diet, 1934, 5th Edition, 1948; also chpts. and sects. in books, articles, monographs. Co-author: Peptic Ulcer—Diagnosis and Treatment, 1955. Home: Chicago IL Died May 1971.

BARBOUR, ERWIN HINCKLY, geologist; b. Springfield, Ind.; s. Samuel Williamson and Adeline (Hinckly) B.; A.B., Yale, 1882, Ph.D., 1887; m. Margaret Roxanna Lamson, of New Haven, Conn., Dec. 7, 1887. Asst. palaeontologist U.S. Geol. Survey, 1882-88; Stone prof. natural history and geology, Ia. Coll., 1889-91; prof. geology, U. of Neb., state geologist, and curator Neb. State Mus., since 1891. Geologist Neb. State Bd. of Agr. since Feb., 1893. Supt. edn. for Neb., St. Louis Expn., 1904. Fellow Geol. Soc. America, A.A.A.S.; mem. Neb. Ornithologists' Union, Neb. Acad. Science, Palaeontol. Soc., Assn. of State Geologists, Seismol. Soc., Assn. Am. Museums. Contbr. on geol. and palaeontol. topics. Address: University of Neb., Lincoln NE

BARBOUR, HENRY GRAY, pharmacologist; b. Hartford, Conn., Mar. 28, 1886; s. John Humphrey and Annie (Gray) B.; A.B., Trinity Coll., Hartford, 1906; M.D., Johns Hopkins, 1910, fellow, 1910-11; research, Freiburg, 1911, Vienna, 1912, London, 1913; m. Lilla Millard Chittendent, Sept. 15, 1909; children—Henry Chittenden, Dorothy Gray (Mrs. John D. Hersey), Russel Chittendent. Asst. prof. pharmacology, Yale, 1912-21; prof. pharmacology, McGill U., 1921-23; prof. physiology and pharmacology, U. of Louisville, 1923-31; asso. prof. pharmacology and toxicology since 1937. U.S. gas investigations, 1917-18. Fellow Internat. Coll. Anesthetists; mem. A.M.A., Am. Physiol. Soc., Soc. Pharmacology and Exptl. Therapeutics, Am. Soc. Biol. Chemists, Soc. Exptl. Biology and Medicine, Cnetral Soc. for Clin. Research, Am. Soc. Anesthetists (hon.), Phi Beta Kappa, Sigma Xi, Alpha Omega Alpha, Nu Sigma Nu, Delta Phi. Republican. Episcopalian. Clubs: Pithotomists, Innominate (hon.), Graduate, New Haven County, Yale (New York). Author: Experimental Pharmacology and Toxicology. Contbr. to Am. Jour. Physicology. Jour. Pharmacology and Exptl. Therapeutics, Jour. Biol. Chemistry, and article Heat Regulation and Fever, in Blumer's Practitioner's Library. Asso. editor Archives Internat. de Pharmacodynamie et de Therapie. Home: 656 Prospect St., New Haven, Conn. Died Sept. 23, 1943.

BARBOUR, PERCY E., cons. mining engr.; b. Portland, Me., Aug. 1, 1875; s. Clifford S. and Clara A. (Ford) B.; Mayflower desc. on paternal side; B.S., Worcester Poly. Inst., 1896, C.E., 1908; m. Viola Grace Hackward, Mar. 21, 1909. Mgr. Mass. Fan Co., ventilating engrs., Boston, 1897-1900; engr. with Bingham Consol. Copper Co., Utah and Boston, 1900-03; engr. at smelter, Tenn. Copper Co., 1904; gen. mgr. Navaho Gold Mining Co., Bland, N.M., 1905-06; cons. mining engr., Goldfield, Nev., 1907-08; dep. sheriff Esmerelda County, Nev., 1907; engineer with Am. Smelting & Refining Co. and U.S. Smelting Co., Salt Lake City, Utah, 1909-10; gen. supt. Salt Lake Copper Co. (Ore. and Ida.), and lessee copper mine at Tecoma, Nev., 1910-11; gen. mgr. Uwarra Mining Co., Candor, N.C., 1911-14; editorial staff and mng. editor Engineering and Mining Journal, New York, 1915-17; asst sec. Am. Inst. Mining and Metall. Engrs., New York, counder and editor Minning and Metallurgy, 1919-25; asst. to mgr. exploration dept., St. Joseph Lead Co., 1915-27; cons. mining engineer since 1927. Mem. N.Y. State Bd. for Licensing Professional Engr. and Land Suveyors, 1920-29, chmn. bd., 1922-23 and 1927-28; sec. and treas. Mining and Metall. Soc. of America, 1925-29, asst. sec. and treas., 1929-30, sec. and treas. since 1931. Mem. Mass. Naval Brigade, 1898-1900; lt. Me. Coast Arty., 1914-16; service on Mexican border with 22d Regt., N.Y. Engrs., as lt. 1916-17; first dept. supt. and asst. organizer N.Y. State Troopers, Dept. State Police, 1917-18; capt. engrs., U.S. Army, 1918-19; hon. disch., 1919; maj. Engr. Res., 1919-22, lt. col. Engr. Res., 342d Engrs., exec. officer, 1922-33; comdg. 363d Engrs., 1933-39; promoted col., 1934, col. (inactive), 1939. Mem. N.Y. County Grand Jury, 1928-38. Mem. Am. Inst. Mining and Metall. Engrs., Mining and Metall. Soc. America; charter mem., sec., treas. and ex-dir. Soc. Am. Mil. Engrs. (gold medalist). Republican. Conglist. Mason, K.T. Club: Mining (New York). Author "Secondary Copper" and tech. articles and papers; internationally regarded as an authority on economics of copper, god and silver. Speaker on Gold at Norman Waite Harris Memorial Foundation, U. of Chicago, 1932, and People's Inst. of Pub. Affairs, U. of Va., 1932, and various associations and societies. Home: 540 Prospect Ave., Mamaroneck, N.Y. Office: 90 Broad St., New York, N.Y. Died May 4, 1943.

BARBOUR, THOMAS, naturalist; b. Martha's Vineyard, Mass., Aug. 19, 1884; s. William and Julia Adelaide (Sprague) B.; A.B., Harvard University, 1906, A.M., 1908, Ph.D., 1910, hon. Sc.D., 1940; Sc.D., Havana Univeristy, 1930, Dartmouth, 1935; Sc.D., University of Florida, 1944; m. Rosamond Pierce, Oct.

1, 1906; children—Martha Higginson (dec.), Mary Bigelow, William (dec.), Julia Adelaide, Louisa Bowditch, Rosamond (dec.). Made zoöl. explorations in East and West Indies, India, Burma, China, Japan, South and Central America, for Museum Comparative Zoölogy, Cambridge; student especially of Geog. distribution of reptiles and amphibians; now dir. of Harvard Univ. Museum and Museum Comparative Zoölogy; prof. of zoölogy; mem. facutlty, Peabody Museum, Harvard; custodian Harvard Biol. Station and Bot. Garden, Soledad, Cuba, since 1927; exec. officier in charge of Arro Colorado Island Lab., Gatun Lake, Panama, 1923-45. Del. Harvard U. to 1st Pan-Am. Scientific Congress, Santiago, Chile, Dec. 1907-Jan. 1908; del. at founding Nat. U. of Mexico, City of Mexico, 1910. Fellow Royal Geog. Soc. (London), Royal Asiatic Soc. (Straits br.), A.A.A.S., Am. Acad. of Arts and Sciences, Nat. Acad. Science, N.Y. Zoöl. Soc.; hon. fellow Acad. Sciences, Havana, Cuba; corr. mem. Hispanic Soc. America; mem. Am. Soc. Zoölogists, Am. Philos. Soc., lMass. Hist. Soc., Am. Antiquarian Soc., Washington Acad. Science (v.p.), Acad. Natural Sciences of Phila., Phi Beta Kappa and Sigma Xi fraternities; foreign mem. Zoö. Soc., London; Linnaean Soc., London; corr. mem. Nederlandesche Dierkundige Verlinigung, Amsterdam; hon. mem. Zoöl. Soc. Phila.; pres. Boston Soc. Natural History, 1924-27 and since 1940. Clubs: Somerset, Harvard, Tavern (Boston); Century, Harvard, Boone and Crockett (New York); Cosmos (Washington, D.C.). Author scientific papers in relation to reptiles and fishes, their systematic classifcation and geog. distribution. Home: 278 Clarendon St., Boston, Mass. Died Jan. 8, 1946.

BARCLAY, BERTRAM DONALD, botanist; b. Champaign, Ill., Nov. 9, 1898; Bachiller en Humanidades, Deutsche Schule, Santiago Chile, 1916; S.B., Coll. of Wooster 1923; S.M., W.Va. U., 1926; Ph.D., U. of Chicago, 1928; m. Harriet George, Sept. 4, 1928; children—Bertram Donald, Arthur Stewart. Instr. botany, W.Va. U., 1924-26, prof. botany, head dept., U. of Tulsa (Okla.) since 1929; staff, Rocky Mountain Biol. Lab., Crested Butte, Colo., since 1929, v.p., since 1940, acting dir., 1948. Fellow A.A.A.S., 1930; mem. Bot. Soc. of Am., Okla. Acad. of Sciences (pres. 1937), Ecol. Soc. of Am. Phi Beta Kappa, Sigma Xi, Phi Sigma, Pi Gamma Mu, Gamma Alpha. Republican. Presbyterian. Author: Origin and Development of Adventitious Roots in Hedera Helix L (unpub.), 1926; Organography of Elephantella Groenlandica at Varying Altitudes (unpub.), 1936; Origin and Development of Tissues in Stem of Selaginella Wildenovi, Botan. Gazette, 1931; contbd. articles. Home: R.D. 10, Box 56, Tulsa. Died June 6, 1953.

BARCLAY, ROBERT, M.D., aural surgeon; b. St. Louis, May 8, 1857; s. late David Robert Barclay, lawyer, author of Barclay's Digest; grad. Trinity Coll., Hartford, Conn., 1880 (A.M., 1883), Coll. Phys. and Surgeons, New York, 1883; asst. aural surgeon New York Eye and Ear Infirmary, 1883-85; removed to St. Louis, 1885; m. 1886, Minnie G. Hamilton, Hartford, Conn. Gives exclusive attention to otology, aural surgery and diseases of the ear; has devised improved instrumental devices for aural surgery and has written many monographs on otol. subjects; mem. many med. socs. and A.A.A.S.; aural surgeon to numerous instns. Address: 3894 Washington Blvd., St. Louis.

BARD, JOHN, physician; b. Burlington, N.J., Feb. 1, 1716; s. Peter Bard; m. Miss Valleau, 1 son, Samuel. One of 1st to conduct dissections for ednl. purposes; 1st to record extra-uterine pregnancy, 1759; apptd. health officer N.Y.C., 1759; 1st pres. Med. Soc. State N.Y., 1795. Died Hyde Park, N.Y., Mar. 30, 1799.

BARDEEN, CHARLES RUSSELL, anatomist;b. Kalamazoo, Mich., Feb. 8, 1871; s. Charles William and Ellen Palmer (Dickerman) B.; ed. Teichmann Sch., Leipzig, 1888-89; A.B., Harvard, 1893; M.D., Johns Hopkins, 1897; m. Althea Harmer, 1905; children—William, John, Helen, Thomas; m.2d, Ruth Hames, 1920; one dau., Ann. Asst. in anatomy, 1897-99, asso., 1899-1901, asso. prof., 1901-04, Johns Hopkins U.; prof. anatomy, 1904—, dean Med. Sch., 1907—, U. of Wis. Home: Madison Wis. Died June 12,1935.

BARKAN, OTTO, ophthalmologist; b. San Francisco, Apr. 5, 1887; s. Adolph and Louise (Besept) B.; B.A., Oxford, 1909, M.D., Munich, 1914; mem. Royal Coll. Surgeons, London, 1915; m. Margit Park, 1921; children—Park Otto, Thomas Adolph. House physician St. Mary's Hosp., London, 1915-16; with eye clinics, univs. of Munich and Vienna, 1916-17; asst. U. Munich, 1917-19, U. Zurich, 1919-20; practice of medicine, San Francisco Hosp., 1921—; mem. surg. staff San Francisco Hosp., 1921; asso. clin. prof. Stanford U. Med. Sch., 1921—; cons. ophthalmologist Veterans' Hosp. Recipient Howe medal for development surgery to relieve glaucoma in infants A.M.A., 1954. Mem. Am. Acad. Ophthalmology, Western Ophthal. Soc., A.M.A., Cal. Med. Assn., Assn. for Research in Ophthalmology, Pacific Coast Oto-Ophthal. Soc., Brit. Ophthalm. Soc., Alpha Kappa Kappa. Episcopalian. Clubs: Burlingame Country, Olympic. Contbr. articles on ocular surgery to med. jours. Home: 3435 Pacific Av. Office: 490 Post St., San Francisco. Died Apr. 26, 1958.

BARKER, BENJAMIN FORDYCE, physician; b. Wilton, Me., May 2, 1818; s. Dr. John and Phoebe (Abbott) B.; grad. Bowdoin Coll., 1837, M.D., 1841; m. Elizabeth Dwight, Sept. 14, 1843. Prof. obstetrics Bowdoin Med. Coll., 1844; pres. Conn. Med. Soc., 1848; an incorporator, prof. obstetrics N.Y. Med. Coll., 1849; pres. N.Y. State Med. Soc., 1856; prof. obstetrics and diseases of women Bellvue Hosp. Med. Sch., N.Y.C., 1861; founded, 1st pres. Am. Gynecol. Soc.; pres. N.Y. Acad. Medicine, 1882; 1st Am. physician to use hypodermic syringe. Author: Puerperal Diseases (translated into 6 langs.), 1874. Died N.Y.C., May 30, 1891.

BARKER, ERNEST FRANKLIN, coll. prof.; b. Listowel, Ontario, Can., Mar. 16, 1886; s. Charles Hewlett and Minnie (Feetham) B.; B.S., U. of Rochester, 1908; M.A., U. of Mich., 1913, Ph.D., 1915; m. Emma Swigart, Dec. 27, 1916; children—Paul Raymond, Stephen Francis; came to U.S., 1888, naturalized citizen, 1898. Physics teacher, East High Sch., Rochester, N.Y., 1908-11; instr. mathematics, U. of Rochester, 1911-13; asst. in mathematics, U. of Mich., 1913-14; prof. physics, U. of Western Ontario, 1915-19; nat. research fellow, U. of Mich., 1919-22; asst. prof. physics, 1922-27, asso. prof., 1927-31, prof., 1931-56, chmn. dept. of physics, 1941-55; prof. physics Alma Coll., 1956-58; Consultant to Argonne National Lab., 1950-55. Fellow A.A.A.S., Am. Phys. Soc. Mem. Am. Assn. Univ. Profs., Am. Assn. Physics Teachers, Phi Beta Kappa, Phi Kappa Phi, Sigma Xi, Sigma Pi Sigma, Theta Delta Chi. Congregationalist. Club: University (Mich.). Home: Ann Arbor MI Died Jan. 24, 1970.

BARKER, FRANKLIN DAVIS, prof. zoölogy; b. Ottawa, Kan., Sept. 16, 1877; s. Albert Wentworth and Martha Ella (Luther) B.; A.B., Ottawa U., 1898, A.M., 1900; grad. study U. of Chicago, 1898-1900; Ph.D, U. of Neb., 1910; fellow Harvard, 1912; m. Lena Lovett, 1905; 1 son, John Franklin. Prof. biology, Ottawa U., 1898-1903; prof. med. zoölogy, U. of Neb., 1903-26; also editor Jour. Paristology, 1915—; prof. zoölogy, Summer Schs. U. of Ill., 1917, Northwestern U., 1923; head prof. zoölogy, Northwestern, 1926—; investigator, Harpswell Biol. Sta., 1907, 12, 14, Bermuda Biol. Sta., 1912, 15. Research grant, Nat. Acad. Science. Republican. Baptist. Author: Synopsis of the Parasites of Man, 1926; Unit System Laboratory Outlines in General Zoölogy, 1926; Unit System Laboratory Outlines in Parisitology, 1926. Home: Evanston, Ill. Died July 10, 1936.

BARKER, GEORGE FREDERICK, physicist; b. Charlestown, Mass., July 14, 1835; s. George and Lydia Prince (Pollard) B.; Ph.B., Yale, 1858; M.D., Albany Med. Coll., 1863; (Sc.D, U. of Pa., 1898; LL.D, Allegheny, 1898, McGill, 1900); m. Mary M. Treadway, Aug. 15, 1861. Prof. natural sciences, Wheaton Coll., 1861; acting prof. chemistry, Albany Med. Coll., 1863; prof. natural sciences, Western U. of Pa., 1864; asst. chemistry, 1865-67; prof. physiol. chemistry and toxicology, 1867-73, Yale; professor physics, 1873-1900; prof. emeritus, 1900—, U. of Pa. Asst. editor Am. Jour. Science, 1868-1909; editor Jour. of the Franklin Inst., 1874-75. U.S. commr. Paris Elec. Exhbn., 1881; del. elec. congress and v.p. jury of award; recieved decoration comdr. Legion of Honor of France; U.S. commr. Elec. Exhbn. Phila., in poisons, criminal cases and in Edison, Berliner and other patent suits. Author: The Forces of Nature, 1863; Textbook of Elementary Chemistry, 1870; chemical Discoveries of the spectoscope, 1873; Conversion of Mechanical Energy into Heat by Dynamo-Electric Machine, 1880; Physics, 1892. Home: Philadelphia. Died 1910.

BARKER, NELSON W(AITE), physician; b. Evanston, Ill., Apr. 25, 1899; s. Earle Sherman and Ollive (Waite) B.; A.B., Dartmouth, 1921; M.D., U. Chgo., 1925; M.S., U. Minn., 1929; m. Florence Buswell, Apr. 6, 1926; children—Sylvia, David, Robert. Interne, Cook County Hosp., Chgo., 1924-26; fellow Mayo Found., 1926-29, 1st asst., path. anat. Mayo Clinic, 1927-28, 1st asst. medicine, 1928-30, asso. in med., staff, 1930-48, head sect. med. 1948-57; instr. med. Mayo Found. Grad. Sch., U. Minn., 1930-33, asst. prof. med., 1933-38, asso. prof., 1938-48, prof., 1948-64, emeritus prof., 1964-68; med. cons. Rochester State Hosp., 1957-68. Fellow Am. College Phys., circulation sect. Am. Heart Assn. Diplomate Am. Bd. Internal Medicine, 1937. Mem. A.M.A., Minn. State Med. Assn., Southern Minn. Med. Assn., Minn. Soc. Internal Medicine, Central Soc. for Clin. Research, Am. Soc. for Study of Arteriosclerosis (pres. 1953), Kappa Sigma, Alpha Kappa Kappa, Phi Beta Kapp, Sigma Xi (pres. Mayo Found. chpt. 1955-56). Independent. Author: Peripheral Vascular Diseases (with E. V. Allen and E. A. Hines), 1946, 2d edit. 1955, 3d edit., 1962; (with Florence B. Barker) Bird Songs of Southeastern Minnesota with birdsong recs.; many contbns. to med. lit. on diseases of the blood vessels and circulation, blood coagulation and anticoagulants. Home: Rochester MN Died Aug. 21, 1968.

BARLOW, CLAUDE HEMAN, physician; b. Lyons, Mich., Oct. 13, 1876; s. Nathan Pratt and Eliza Jane (Humphrey) B.; M.D., Northwestern U., 1906; certificate London Sch. of Tropical Medicine, 1914; D.Sc., Johns Hopkins U., 1929; m. Grace Eugenia Hawley, Dec. 31, 1907; (dec. 1967); children—Mary Ruth (Mrs. N. W. Abrahams), Harriet Hawley (Mrs. J. W. McConnell), Hester Hunt (Mrs. Donald Richon), Elizabeth Jean (Mrs. Steven Davids). Health officer, Engadine, Mich., 1906-07; med. missionary Am. Baptist Fgn. Missions Soc., Huchow, China, 1908-10; Shaohsing, 1911-25 (supt. of hosp., 1911, 1919), Ningpo, 1925-28 (supt. hosp. 1926); port physician, Ningpo, Chinese Maritime Customs, 1925-28; head Schistosom Studies, Rockefeller Foundation, Eqypt, from 1929; staff mem. Internat. Health Div., The Rockefeller Foundation; official examiner for British Red Cross. Discovered life cycle of Fasciolopsis buski; worked on Clonorchis sinesis; researches on Schistosomes in Eqypt. Director of Bilharzia Snail Destruction Section in the Ministry of Public Health, Cairo, Eqypt, resigned to contract with the South African Council for Scientific and Industrial Research for work on the control of Bilharzia Snail hosts. Awarded Cert. of Merit for medical research, February 8, 1948. Member of Soc. Tropical Medicine, Helminthological Soc., Soc. of Parasitologists (China branch), Ornithological Soc. of Mich., Royal Soc. of Tropical Medicine, China Med. Soc. Surgery, Delta Omega, Sigma Xi, Theta Kappa Psi. Author: Monograph on Fasciolopsis buski, 1925. Author articles on researches on control of Schistosomiasis in Eqypt. Amateur lapidist. Home: Trumansburg NY Died Oct. 9, 1969.

BARLOW, DE WITT DUKES, civil engr.; b. Phila., Pa., Oct. 4, 1880; s. Thomas Arnold and Elizabeth (Dukes) B.; B.S., Phila. High Sch., 1898; B.S. in C.E., U. of Pa., 1901; m. Elizabeth Hail Moody, May 16, 1905; children—Anne May, Esther Moody, Elizabeth Hall, De Witt D., Carlton Moutague, Jean Lewis. Began practice at Phila., 1901; pres. Atlantic Gulf & Pacific Co. since 1921; also pres. North Atlantic Dredging Co. Asso. chief of Dredging Setct., War Industries Bd., 1918-19; chmn. Dredge Owners' Proetcitvie Orgn. since 1920; chmn. Nat. Assn. River & Harbor Contractors. Mem. Alien Enemy Hearing Bd., Dist. of N.J. Mem. Common Council, Plainfield, N.J., 1922-23; mem. Bd. of Health, 1923-24; pres. Bd. of Edn., 1924-37; pres. Plainfield Symphony Soc.; mayor of City of Plainfield, 1937-38. Mem. bd. dirs., Metropolitan Popular Season, Inc. Chmn. N.J. Citizens Com. for the Princeton Local Govt. Survey. Chairman Plainfield and North Plainfield Chapter of the American Red Cross. Mem. Am. Soc. C.E., Sigma Xi. Republican. Presbyterian. Clubs: Engineers, U. of Pa. (New York); Plainfield Engrs., Plainfield Country. Home: 930 Woodland Av., Plainfield, N.J. Office: 15 Park Row, New York 7 N.Y. Died Sept. 23, 1945.

BARLOW, JOHN QUINCY, civil engr.; b. Bridgeport, Conn., Nov. 11, 1861; s. Daniel Sanford and Charity Whittemore (Johnson) B.; B.S., Worcester Poly Inst., 1882; m. Kate Ethel Newitt, of Salt Lake City, Utah, Feb. 10, 1900; Children—William Newitt, John Joseph. Asst. engr. N.P. R.R., 1882-87; div. engr. U.P.R.R., 1887-92; chief engr. r.r. and irrigation developments, 1892-98; div. engr. Ida. div. Ore. S.L. Ry., 1898-1903; chief engr. Western Md. R.R., 1903-08; chief of dept. of maintenance, S.P.R.R., 1908-19; regional engr. U.S. R.R. Adminstration 1919-23; cons. engr., San Francisco, since 1923; chief engr. Utah Constrn. Co. Republican. Home: 2803 Woolsey St., Berkeley, Calif. Office: 528 Phelan Bldg., San Francisco, Calif.

BARLOW, WILLIAM HARVEY, oil co. exec.; b. Neosho, Mo., Oct. 11, 1910; s. John T. and Diva E. (Rudy) B.; B.S. in Petroleum Engring., U. Okla., 1931; grad. Advanced Mgmt. Program, Harvard, 1957; m. Edna M. Lough, Dec. 20, 1937; 1 son, Michael Harvey. With Phillips Petroleum Co., 1932-36; petroleum engr. U.S. Bur. Mines, 1942-52; with Ohio Oil Co. (name changed to Marathon Oil Co. 1962), 1942-69, mgr. research dept., 1954-59, mgr. research and planning, 1959-61, dir. 1959-69, v.p. chems., planning and research, 1961-66, v.p. research and chems., 1967-69, also mem. research, computer policy, finance coms. Mem. exec. bd. Put-Han-Sen Area council Boy Scouts Am. Mem. Am. Petroleum Inst., Am. Inst. Mining, Metall. and Petroleum Engrs., Findlay Area (trustee), Ohio (dir.) chambers of commerce, N.A.M., Phi Gamma Delta, Tau Beta Pi, Sigma Tau. Presbyn. (deacon, bd. session). Clubs: Findlay Country, Rotary. Home: Findlay OH Died Feb. 9, 1969; buried Bartlesville OK

BARNARD, EDWARD CHESTER, U.S. boundary commr.; b. N.Y. City, Nov. 13, 1863; s. Owen Howard and Anne E. B.; E.M., Columbia, 1884; m. Mrs. Juliet Gill Rogers, Dec. 16, 1908. Topographer U.S. Geol. Survey, 1884-1907, geographer, 1907-15; mapped sections of Ky., Tenn., Va.and N.Y., in the East, and Calif., Ida., Mont., Ore. and Wash. in the West; had charge of party sent to Alaska by U.S. Geol. Survey to map Forty-Mile Dist., 1898, and Nome Dist., 1900; chief topographer U.S. and Can Boundary Survey, 1903-15, surveying and relocating U.S. and Can. boundary line, along 49th parallel from Pacific Coast to the Lake of the Woods and through Lake of the Woods, Rainy River and Rainy Lake; apptd. commr. on the part of the U.S. for defining and marking the boundary between U.S. and Can., except on Great Lakes and St. Lawrence River, and for marking and surveying boundary between Alaska and Can., 1915. Home: Washington, D.C. Died Feb. 6, 1921.

BARNARD, EDWARD EMERSON, astronomer; b. Nashville, Tenn., Dec. 16, 1857; learned photography in a studio as a boy; began astron. studies alone, in boyhood grad. Vanderbilt U., 1887 (Sc.D., 1893; A.M., U. of the Pacific, San José, 1889; LL.D., Queen's U., of 1909); m. Rhoda Calvert , Jan. 27, 1881. In charge Vanderbilt U. Obs., 1883-87; astronomer U. of Chicago and astronomer of the Yerkes Obs., 1895—. Mem. U.S. Naval Obs. Eclipse Expdn. to Sumatra, 1901. Discovered 5th satellite of Jupiter, 1892; also 16 comets and many other discoveries; has done much in celestial photography, making photographs of the Milky Way, comets, nebulae, etc. Recieved Lalande gold medal, French Acad. Sciences, 1892; Arago gold medal, same, 1893; gold medal, Royal Astron. Soc. of Great Britain, 1897; Janssen gold medal, French Acad. Sciences, 1900; Janssen prize, French Astron. Soc., 1906; Bruce gold medal, Astron. Soc. of the Pacific, 1917. Mem. Nat. Acad. Sciences; asso. fellow Am. Acad. Arts and Sciences. Died Feb. 6, 1923.

BARNARD, FREDERICK AUGUSTUS PORTER, coll. pres.; b. Sheffield, Mass., May 5, 1809; s. Robert and Augusta (Porter) B.; grad. Yale, 1828, LL.D. (hon.), 1859; LL.D. (hon.), Jefferson Coll., 1855; D.D. (hon.) U. Miss., 1861; m. Margaret McMurray, Dec. 27, 1847. Prof. mathematics and natural history U. Ala.; prof. mathematics and natural philosophy U. Miss., 1854-56, pres., 1856-58; published Letter to the President of the United States by a Refugee, 1863; pres. Columbia, 1864-89, founder Law Sch., Sch. Polit. Scis., Sch. Mines, Barnard Coll.; U.S. commr. Universal Exposition, Paris, France, 1867; asst. U.S. commr. gen. Paris Expostion, 1878; mem. U.S. Coast Survey; originator system of teaching deaf and dumb; mem. bd. Am. Bur. Mines; pres. Am. Meteorol. Soc., 1874-80; a founder, pres. A.A.A.S.; a founder Nat. Acad. Scis. Author: (principal works) Treatise on Arithmetic, 1830; Analytical Grammar, 1836; A History of the United States Coast Survey; Recent Progress of Science, 1859; The Metric System, 1871. Editor: Johnston's Cyclopedia. Died N.Y.C., Apr. 27, 1889; buried Sheffield.

BARNARD, HARRY EVERETT, chemist; b. Dunbarton, N.H., Nov. 14, 1874; s. Nelson H. and Celestia A. (Rider) B.; B.S., N.H. College of Agrl. and Mechanic Arts, 1899; Ph.D., Hanover (Ind.) College, 1913; D.Sc. from Univ. of N.H., 1928; m. Marion Harvie, June 20, 1910. Asst. chemist. N.H. Expt. Sta., 1899, U.S. Smokeless Powder Factory, Indian Head, Md., 1900-01; chemist, N.H. State Bd. of Health, 1901-05; Ind. State Bd. of Health, 1905-19; state food and drug commn. of Ind., 1907-19; state commr. of weights and measures of Ind., 1911-19; food and drug inspn. chemist, U.S. Dept. Agr., 1907-19; pres. H. E. Barnard, Inc. Pres. Ind. Sanitary and Water Supoly Assn.; dir. Am. Chem. Soc. (founder and 1st pres. Ind. Sec.); mem. Am. Inst. Chem. Engrs., Soc. Official Agrl. Chemists, Nat. Assn. State Food Commrs., Federal Food Standards Com., Indianapolis Technical Soc.; president Lake Michigan Water Commission; secretary Indiana Branch National Conservation Assn.; mem. exec. com. Nat. Conservation Congress, 1912. Federal Food Administrator for Ind., 1917-19. Pres. Am. Inst. of Baking, 1919, 27; sec. Am. Bakers' Health and Protection, 1929-31, Corn Industries Research Foundation, 1931-34; dir. research Nat. Farm Chemurgic Council, 1935-40, professional specialist in chemistry, War Manpower Commn., since 1941; with Fed. Economics Assn., 1945. Trustee New Hamphire Coll., 1903-06. Mem. Sigma Alpha Epsilon, Alpha Chi Sigma, Phi Kappa Phi. Clubs: Irvington Athenaeum, Indianapolis Literary; City. Chemists (Chicago); University (Evanston, Ill.); Cosmos (Washington, D.C.); Chemists' (New York). Author of N.H. and Ind. bd. of health reports and papers and adresses on subjects of food, drugs, water, sanitation, nutrition, child welfare, chemurgy, etc. Home: 5050 Pleasant RunParkway, Indianapolis, Ind. Office: Cosmos Club, Washington. Died Dec. 31, 1946; buried in Washington Park Mausoleum, Indianapolis.

BARNARD, WILLIAM NICHOLS, educator; b. Canton, Ill., Apr. 24, 1875; s. William Stebbins and Mary (Nichols) B.; M.E., Cornell U., 1897; m. Edith Nourse Robinson, Apr. 17, 1919. Instr. in machine design, Cornell U., 1897-99; engine designing, with Russel Engine Co., 1899-1903; asst. prof. of machine design and steam engring., Cornell U., 1903-07, prof. of steam engring., 1907-15, prof. of heat power engring., 1915-38; dir. of Sibley Sch. of Mech. Engring., 1910-15, prof. of heat power engring., 1915-38; dir. of Sibley Sch. of Mech. Engring. since 1938; coordinator of civilian pilot training, Cornell U. Served as pres. of academic bd. of U.S. Army Sch. of Mil. Aeronatuics, Cornell U., 1917-19. Registered Professional Engr., N.Y. Mem. Am. Soc. Mech. Engrs., Soc. for Promotion Engring. Edn., Cornell Soc. Engrs., Sigma Xi, Tau Beta Pi, Phi Kappa Phi, Atmos. Republican. Author: Valve Gears, 1907; Elements of Heat-Power Engineering (with C. F. Hirschfield), 1912; Heat-Power Engineering (with F. O. Ellenwood and C. F. Hirshfeld), Part 1, 1926, Parts 2 and 3, 1933. Home: 201 Bryant Ave., Ithaca, N.Y. Died Apr. 3, 1947.

BARNES, ALFRED EDWARD, architect; b. Kansas City, Mo., Mar. 5, 1892; s. Alfred Edward and Catherine (Cross) B.; ed. high sch., extension work under Soc. Beaux Arts Architects, 1912-14; m. Clara Frieda Knotter, Aug. 29, 1931; children—Gerardine Claire, Catharine Anne. Draftsman, Howe & Hoit, architects, Kansas City, 1909; chief draftsman, supt. Henry F. Hoit, 1910-18; mem. Hoit, Price & Barnes, 1919-41. Co-ordinating engr. Lake City Ordnance Plant, 1941; mech. engrs. Long-Turner, 1942-45. Prin. works: Kansas City Athletic Club (Archtl. League medal 1923), Southwestern Bell Telephone Bldg. (archtl. League medal 1929), Dierks Bldg., Kansas City Power & Light Bldg., Fideltiy Bank Bldg. (A.I.A. medal 1931), Municipal Auditorium (A.I.A. medal 1936), all in Kansas City; Cosden Bldg., Tulsa; others. Mem. A.I.A. (pres. Kansas City chpt. 1936), Soc. Am. Mil. Engrs., Archtl. League Kansas City (pres. 1925-26), Kansas City Art Inst., Am. Soc. C.E. Clubs: Engineers', Kansas City Club. Home: 439 E. 55th St., Kansas City 10, Mo. Died May 11, 1960.

BARNES, CHARLES REID, prof. of plant physiology, U. of Chicago, July, 1898—; b. Madison, Ind., Sept. 7, 1858; grad. Hanover (Ind.) Coll., 1877. (A.M., 1880; Ph.D, 1886), grad. study at Harvard, 1877, 1878, 1885-86), grad study at Harvard, 1877, 1878, 1885-86, 1892); m. Mary King Ward, Dec. 25, 1882. Prof. natural history, Purdue Univ., 1880-86; prof. botany, U. of Wis., 1886-98; co-editor Botanical Gazette, 1883—. Author: (with J. C. Arthur and J. M. Coulter) Plant Dissection, 1886; Keys to the Genera and Species of North American Mosses, 1896 (Univ. of Wis.); Plant Life, 1898; Outlines of Plant Life, 1900; and mumerous bot. papers Sec. Bot. Soc. of Am., 1893-98 (pres. 1903); gen. sec. A.A.A.S., 1893 (v.p. (v.p. 1899). Died 1910.

BARNES, FRANK HASLEHURST, neurologist, psychiatrist; b. Mohawk, Herkimer County, N.Y., June 1872; s. Charles Tappan and Flora Ann B.; grad. Utica (N.Y.) Free Acad., 1891; studied under pvt. tutor M.D., New York Med. Coll., 1896; m. Ella Betts Jerman, Sept. 22, 1897. Propr. Dr. Barnes Sanitarium, Stamford, since 1898. Formerly assistant prof. neurology, N.Y. Post-Grad. Hosp.; cons. neurologist Stamford Hospital; consultant psychiatrist Greenwich Hospital, St. Joseph's Hospital, Stamford, Conn. Ex-pres. Peoples Nat. Bank of Stamford. Ex-pres. Stamford Chamber of Commerce; ex-vice pres. Stamford Y.M.C.A.; ex-mem. Sch. Com. of Stamford. Mem. Med. Advisory Bd. during World War I. Diplomate Am. Bd. Psychiatry and Neurology. Mem. A.M.A., Am. Psychiatric Assn., Conn. State Med. Soc., Fairfield County Med. Assn. (ex-pres.). Republican. Presbyterian. Club: Woodway Country. Home: High Ridge Rd Stamford CT

BARNES, GLADEON MARCUS, army officer, engr.; b. Vermontville, Mich., June 15, 1887; s. Frank E. and Selinda (Cross) B.; B.C.E., U. Mihc., 1910, M.E., 1941; Eng. D., Ill. Inst. Tech., 1942; grad. Ordnance Sch. Tech., 1914; student Ordnance Sch. Application, 1916-17, Army Indsl. College, 1935-36, Army War Coll., 1937-38; m. Evelyn Mary Kopf, Apr. 3, 1912; 1 dau., Barbara Tufts (Mrs. Roderick Hamilton Sears). Commd. 2d lt., Coast Artillery, U.S. Army, 1910, and advanced through grades to major gen., 1943; charge design and prodn. of ry. and seacoast artillery, 1917-21, inspector fgn. munitions plants and materials, European countries, 1922, charge development anti-aircraft artillery, 1922-27, inspector Govt. Ordnance and Mfg. plants, Europe, 1928; chief engr. charge development and engrring., Watertown Arsenal, 1928-32; chief proof officer, automotive div., Aberdeen (Md.) Proving Ground, 1932-35; charge procurement planning officer, asst. sec.-war, 1936-37; chief tech. staff, 1939-40, asst. chief indsl. service in charge research and engring. ordnance dept., 1940-42; asst. chief ordnance, 1942-46, ret. 1946; cons. Porter International, Washington; v.p. charge engring. Budd Co., Phila., 1946-53. Decorated D.S.M.; Comdr. of Order Brit. Empire; Chevalier French Legion of Honor; recipient Elliott Cresson gold medal Franklin Inst., 1946. Mem. Am. Ordnance Assn., Newcomen Soc. Eng., Tau Beta Pi. Episcopalian. Clubs: Racquet (Phila.); Chevy-Chase, Army-Navy (Washington). Author: Weapons of World War II, 1947. Home: Osterville, Cape Cod, Mass.; also 4000 Cathedral Av., Washington 16. Died Nov. 15, 1961; buried Arlington Nat. Cemetery, Arlington, Va.

BARNES, HENRY A., traffic engr.; b. Newark, Dec. 16, 1906; s. Herman Myron and Maudie Louise (Henion) B.; student U. Mich., Mich. State Coll. Extension Sch., Gen. Motors Inst. Tech.; Sloan fellow, Yale, 1945; Ph.D. (honorary), Susquehanna Univ., 1965; married Hazel Mae Stone, Sept. 1, 1928; children—William Henry, Virginia Nancy. Elec. maintenance engr. Chevrolet Motor Co., 1933-37; traffic engr., capt. police, City of Flint, Mich., 1937-47; traffic dir., City and County of Denver, 1947-53; dir. traffic City of Balt., 1953-57, commr. of transit and traffic, 1957-62; commissioner of traffic for N.Y.C., 1962-68; cons. U.S. Congressonial sub-com. on traffic safety for Interstate and Fgn. Commerce Com., 1957-58; research and devel. traffic control devices; cons. devices; cons. traffic Am., European, S.- and Central Am. cities; developed traffic signal improvements and automatic electronic correlation of signal timing to traffic vols. Mem. Nat. Hyw. Research Bd. Bd. dirs. Eno Found. Hwy. Traffic Control, Inc., Saugatuck, Conn. Recipient Presdl. award for activities war transp.; Theodore M. Matson Meml. award, 1968 Mem. Am. Inst. E.E., Inst. Traffic Engrs., Am. Pub. Works Assn., Bklyn. Engrs. Club (life), Balt. Advt. Club, Chi Epsilon. Methodist. Mason (32 deg.), Elk. Author; The Man with the Red and Green Eyes, 1966. Author articles on traffic control, transp. Home: Bayside NY Died Sept. 16, 1968.

BARNES, MORTIMER GRANT, engr.; b. Reedsburg, Sauk Co., Wis., Jan. 17, 1867; s. James Brewster and Alice Jane (Randall) B.; B.S. in C.E., U. of Mich., 1896, C.E., 1900, M.E., 1922; m. Mary Wilhelmina Wood, Aug. 17, 1898; children—Alice Elizabeth, Florence Lillian, James Mathew. Worked on waterway constrs. and hydraulic power projects; in charge parties surveying and estimating of proposed Birmingham-Warrior River (Ala.) Canal, 1897, U.S. Deep Waterway, Gt. Lakes to Sea via N.Y. City, 1898; on design and constrn. Hennepin Canal, connecting Ill. and Miss. rivers, 1899, 1905; U.S. asst. engr. in charge design Moline Locks, Rock Island, Ill., 1905-06; design of locks for Panama Canal, 2907-07; mem. bd. cons. engrs., N.Y. State Barge Canal, 1907-15; also pvt. practice, Albany; apptd. by Gov. Lowden to devise means for utilizing waters of Ill. River for power and navigation, 1917; apptd. chief engr. Ill. Waterway, 1917; cons. engr. Ill. Waterway, June 1, 1928—. Mem. Christian (Disciples) Ch. Home: Oak Park, Ill. Died Oct. 7, 1930.

BARNES, OLIVER WELDON, civil engr.; b. Berlin, Hartford, Co., Conn., May 15, 1823; s. Henry and Marilla (Weldon) B.; grad. high sch., Burlington, N.J., and priv. sch. in engring., Phila.; also studied in Europe, 1846; apptd. asst. engr. in first corps assembled at Pittsburgh on Pa. R.R., May 1, 1847; prin. asst. engr., 1848; made final location of line of the Pa. R.R. form the Allegheny Mountains to Pittsburgh, and constructed Western div. between same points, 1848-53; chief engr. of Pittsburgh & Connellsville R.R. Co., 1853-57; built Western Div. Pittsburgh, Ft. Wayne & Chicago R.R., Plymouth to Chicago, 1858; commenced construction St. Paul & Pacific R.R. at St. Paul, 1861; built branch lines Pa. R.R., 1862; chief engr. Dutchess & Columbia R.R., 1866-70; chief engr. various lines, 1871-81; chief engr. South Pa. R.R., 1881; chief engr. N.Y. & Long Island R.R., 1887; 1892, chief engr. and pres. of the N.Y. Connecting R.R. Co., building from the N.Y. & Harlem R.R. across East River to Brooklyn; m. Elizabeth Denny, d. Maj. Ed Harding, U.S.A. Republican. Home: New York, N.Y. Died 1908.

BARNES, WILLIAM, surgeon, entomologist; b. Decatur, Ill., Sept. 3, 1860; s. William A. and Eleanor (Sawyer) B.; student State Normal Sch., Normal Ill., 1878, Ill. U., 1879; B.S., Harvard, 1883, M.D., 1886; post-grad. work, Boston City Hosp. and Heidelberg, Munich and Vienna; D.Sc., James Millikin U., Decatur, Ill., 1929; m. Charlotte L. Gillett, June 20, 1890; children—Joan Dean Gillett, William. Practiced at Decatur, 1890—; mem. Drs. Barnes & Tearnan; one of builders of Decatur and Macon County Hosp., of which was pres. Chmn., Med. Advisory Bd., Dist. No. 14, World War; chmn., also inspector AM. Protective League, Decatur Div., World War. Fellow Am. Coll. Surgeons; mem. various entomol. socs. Owner of largest collection of N.Am. Leipidoptera in existence; collection housed in fire-proof mus. and consists of several hundred thousand specimens-over 10,000 species and varieties and over 6,000 types of various kinds. Author: Contributions to the Natural History of Lepidoptera of North America, 23 parts, 1911-24; Check List of the Lepidoptera of Boreal North America, 1917; Illustrated Species of the Genus Catocala, 22 plates, 17 colored, 1918; also 95 articles in entomol. mags. Home: Decatur, Ill. Died May 1, 1930.

BARNETT, SAMUEL JACKSON, physicist; b. Woodson County, Kan., Dec. 14, 1873; s. Rev. James (D.D.) and Margaret Lees (Duff) B.; brother of James D. Barnett; A.B., U. of Denver, 1894; grad. Sch. of Astronomy, U. of Virginia, 1896; Ph.D., Cornell U., 1898; m. Lelia Jefferson Harvie, July 30, 1904. Instr. physics and biology, U. of Denver, 1894-95; asst. in Obs., U. of Va., 1895-96; univ. scholar, later Pres. White fellow Cornell U., 1896-98; instr., asst. prof., and prof. physics, Colo. Coll., 1898-1900, Stanford, 1900-05, Tulane, 1905-11, Ohio State U., 1911-18; physicist, Carnegie Inst. of Washington, 1918-26 (dept. of terrestrial magnetism, 1918-24; research associate, 1924-26); prof. of physics, U. of Calif. at Los Angeles since 1926, emeritus since 1944; research asso. Calif. Inst. of Technology since 1924. Magnetic observer U.S. Coast and Geod. Survey, 1902-04. Awarded Comstock prize for electricity, magnetism and radiation, Nat. Acad. Sciences, for discovery of magnetization by rotation, 1918. Faculty research lecturer, U. of Calif., Los Angeles, 1928. Mem. internat. Reunion d' Etudes sur le Magnetisme, Strasbourg, 1939. Mem. Nat. Research Council, 1922-24, (also mem. coms. on theories of magnetism and electromagnetic induction). Fellow Am. Assn. for Advancement of Science (mem. exec. com. Pacific Div., 1927-34), Am. Physical Soc., Am. Acad. Arts and Sciences; mem. Am. Geophys. Union, Philos. Soc. Washington, Sigma Xi (Cornell) (pres. Calif.-Los Angeles Chapter, 1933-34), Phi Beta Kappa (U. of Va.). Club: Athenaeum of Calif. Inst. Tech.

Author: Elements of Electro-magnetic Theory, 1903; co-author: Theories of Magnetism, 1922; Le Magnetisme, 1940. Contbr. articles, especially on theoretical and exptl. electricity and magnetism. Home: 315 S. Hill Av., Pasadena CA

BARNICKEL, WILLIAM SIDNEY, mfg. chemist; b. Lagrange, Ky., May 18, 1878; s. John and Mary (Dawkins) B.; Ph.G., St. Louis Coll. Pharmacy, 1902, Ph.C., 1903; m. Olive Edgeworth, June 4, 1904. Began as analyt. chemist with Allen Pfeifer Chem Co., St. Louis, 1903; chief chemist, Judge & Dolph Drug Co., 1904-10; prof. chemistry, Am. Med. Coll. St. Louis, 1905-10; pres. W. S. Barnickel & Co., 1910—. Served with 1st Inf. Tex. N.G., 3 yrs., 1st Inf., Mo. N.G., 3 yrs., Field Battery A, Mo. N.G., 9 yrs. Republican. Mason. (32 degree). Specialized in chemistry of petroleum; inventor of gasoline process; of chem. process for treating waste oil and petroleum emulsions. Home: St. Louis. Died May 19, 1923.

BARR, JOHN HENRY, mech. engr.; b. Terre Haute, Ind., June 19, 1861; s. John Henry and Eliza T. B.; B.M.E., U. of Minn., 1883, M.S., 1888; M.M.E., Cornell, 1889; m. Katherine L. Kennedy, June 4, 1884; 1 son, John H. Engaged in mech. dept. Calumet & Hecla Copper Mining Co. and Lake Superior Iron Works, 1883-85; instr. asst. prof. and prof. mech. engring., U. of Minn., 1885-91; asst. prof. and asso. prof., 1891-98, prof. machine design, 1898-1903, Sibley Coll., Cornell; factory mgr. Smith-Premier Works, Syracuse, N.Y., Feb. 1903; cons. engr. Union Typewriter Co., New York, Sept. 1909-13, and same, Remington Typewriter Co., May 1913-23; v.p. Barr-Morse Corp., 1923—; trustee of Ithaca (N.Y.) Savings Bank, Chairman N.Y. State Voting Machine Commn., 1903-14, Syracuse Lighting Commn., 1907; mem. Syracuse Intercepting Sewer Commn., 1908-12. Maj. ordnance, U.S.R.C., 1917-19, in office of chief of ordnance, U.S.A. and A.E.F., Aircraft Armament Sect., Paris, France. Trustee Cornell U., 1905-15. Author: Kinematics of Machinery, 1899; Notes on Machine Design; Elements of Machine Design (with D. S. Kimball), 1909. Home: Ithaca, N.Y. Died Mar. 29, 1937.

BARRALET, JOHN JAMES, artist, engraver; b. Dublin, Ireland, circa 1747. Successful painter of portraits and landscapes, book illustrator, drawing master, Dublin and London, Eng.; came to U.S., 1795, settled in Phila.; employed as book illustrator, worked in assn. with engraver Alexander Lawson; invented ruling machine for use of engravers, made improvements in ink used in copperplate printing; exhibited numerous paintings at Soc. Artists, Pa. Acad. Died Phila., Jan. 16, 1815.

BARRELL, JOSEPH, geologist; b. New Providence, N.J., Dec. 15, 1869; s. Henry Ferdinand and Elizabeth (Wisner) B.; B.S., Lehigh U., Pa., 1892, E.M., 1893, M.S., 1897 (Sc.D, 1916); Ph.D., Yale, 1900; m. Lena Hopper Bailey, Dec. 27, 1902. Pub. Sch. teacher, 1886-87; instr. in mining and metallurgy, Lehigh U., 1893-97; asst. mining engr., Lehigh Valley Coal Co., 1894, Butte & Boston, and Boston & Montana mining cos., Butte, Mont., 1897-98; field asst., U.S. Geol. Survey, 1899-1901; asst. prof. geology, Lehigh U., and in charge of dept. of natural sciences, 1900-03; asst. prof. geology, 1903-08, prof. structural geology, 1908—, Yale U. Home: New Haven, Conn. Died May 4, 1919.

BARRETT, ALBERT MOORE, psychiatrist; b. Austin, Ill., July 15, 1871; s. Edward Newton and Anna Sarah (Moore) B.; A.B., State U. of Ia., 1893, M.D., 1895; Heidelberg U., Germany, 1901-02; m. Eliza Jane Bowman, July 8, 1905; 1 son, Edward Bowman. Pathologist Independence (Ia.) State Hosp. for Insane, 1895-97, 1898-1901; asst. phys. Worcester (Mass.) Insane Hosp., 1897-98; pathologist Danvers (Mass.) State Hosp. for Insane, 1901-05, also asst. in neurol. pathology, Harvard, 1905-06. Called to U. of Mich., 1906, to organize the first univ. hosp. and clinic in America for mental diseases; apptd. asso. prof. of neuropathology, Med. Faculty, U. of Mich., 1906, also med. dir. State Psychopathic Hosp. of U. of Mich.; prof. psychiatry and nervous diseases, Dept. of Medicine and Surgery, U. of Mich., 1907-20; prof. psychiatry U. of Mich., Med. Sch., 1920—. Mem. Medical Council of U.S. Veterans Bureau. Republican. Episcopalian. Home: Ann Harbor, Mich. Died Apr. 2, 1936.

BARRETT, JOHN PATRICK, electrician; b. Auburn, N.Y., 1837; s. James and Bedelia (Gallagher) B.; went to Chicago, 1845; pub. sch. edn.; sailor 11 yrs.; m. Margaret Darcy, of Chicago, 1867. Asst., 1862-76, supt., 1876-97, fire alarm telegraph, Chicago; retired as consulting electrician for city. Invented fire alarm signals; orginated police patrol system; was first to conceive the idea of laying electric wires underground; chief electricity dept. Chicago Epn., 1893; installed 1st municipal electric light for streets, wires underground. Home: 4400 Michigan Av., Chicago.

BARRETT, MICHAEL THOMAS, dentist; b. Huntingdon, Que., Can., July 27, 1881; s. Dennis and Catherine (Timlin) B.; ed. acads., Can., and N.Y.; D.D.S., U. of Pa. Dental Dept., 1903; hon. M.S., Villanova, 1915; m. Della MacDonald, June 29, 1921. Came to U.S., 1900; demonstrator in prosthetic dentistry, U. of Pa., 1904-10; instr. in normal histology, same, 1910-14; instr. in oral pathology, Grad. Sch. of Medicine, U. of Pa. Discoverer pf amoebae in pyorrhea, 1914. Roman Catholic. Wrote: The Protozoa of the Mouth in Relation to Pyorrhea Alevolaris (pub. in Dental Cosmos, Aug. 1914); Clinical Report on Amoebic Pyorrhea (same, Dec. 1914); The Internal Anatomy of the Teeth with Special Reference to the Pulp with its Branches; The Effects of Thymus Extract on the Early Eruption and Growth of the Teeth of White Rats; A Study of the Etiological Factors Governing Dental Caries; etc. Home: Philadelphia. Died Aug. 22, 1940.

BARRETT, OTIS WARREN, agriculturist; b. Clarendon, Vt. Apr. 18, 1872; s. James and Alice W. (Kelley) B.; B.Sc., U. of Vermont, 1896; also certificate of proficiency in modern langs. (hon.D.Sc., 1934); m. Bessie Lou Stearns, Ph.B., Apr. 27, 1898. In Jamaica, 1894, in employ of West India Improvement Co.; apptd., 1898, traveling agt. of the commn. for the Mexican exhibit of Paris Expn. of 1900; hon. curator entom. collections of Museo de la Comision Geografico-Exploradora at Tacubaya, Fed. Dist., Mexico, 1898-1900; entomologist and botanist to P.R. Agrl. Expt. Sta., 1901-05; plant introducer, Office Seed and Plant Introduction and Distribution, U.S. Dept. Agr., 1905-08; Specially commd. by Agrl. Soc. of Trinidad and Tobago, B.W.I., to report upon cacao diseases in Trinidad, 1907; dir. of agr. for Mozambique, Portuguese E. Africa, 1908-10; chief of divisions expt. stas. and horticulture, Bur. of Agr., Manila, P.I., 1910-14; horticulturist of Canal Zone, 1914-17; mgr. coconut plantations in Nicaragua, Mar.-Sept., 1917; with U.S. Dept. Agr., 1917; carbon expert, U.S. War Dept., 1918-19; agrl. adviser to Liberia, 1920-21; agrl. survey of Haiti, 1922; with Dept. of Agr., San Juan, P.R., 1923-29; horticulturist of U. of Hawaii, 1929-30. Mem. Vermont Bot. Club, Bot. Soc. of Washington, Entomol. Soc. Washington, Soc. of Am. Mammalogists, Philippine Acad., Porto Rico Ateneo, S.A.R., fellow A.A.A.S. Club: Philippine. Author: The Changa, or Mole Cricket, in Porto Rico, 1902; The Yautias, or Taniers, of Porto Rico, 1905; Promising Root Crops for the South, 1910; Coconut Culture, 1911; The Philippine Coconut Industry, 1913; The Food Plants of Porto Rico, 1925; The Tropical Crops, 1928; The Animals on Postage Stamps, 1936. Address: N. Clarendon, Vt. Died Oct. 6, 1950; buried Clarendon Flats Cemetery.

BARRETT, SAMUEL ALFRED, anthropologist; b. Little Rock, Nov. 12, 1879; s. Samuel Eliphlet and Lillian Mary (Stryker) B.; B.S., U. Cal., 1905, M.S., 1906, Ph.D., 1908; grad. study Columbia, 1907-08; Sc.D., Lawrence U., 1929; m. Eileen C. Bray, Aug. 15, 1912. Levi Straus scholar, later Le Conte fellow and mus. asst. U. Cal., 1902-08; ethnologist George G. Heye S. Am. Expdn., 1908-09; curator anthropology Milw. Pub. Mus., 1909-20, dir., 1920-40, dir. emeritus since 1940; asso. dir. Army Specialized Tng. Program, Far Eastern, U. Cal. at Berkeley, 1943-44. Dir. Indian exhibits Golden Gate Internat. Expn. Commn., San Francisco, 1940. Mem. Am. Anthrop. Assn., Am. Ethnol. Soc., Am. Folk Lore Soc., Am. Assn. Museums, Mid-West Museums Conf., Wis. Acad. Sci., Arts and Letters, Wis. Hist. Soc., Wis. Archeol. Soc., Izaak Walton League Am., Phi Beta Kappa, Sigma Xi, Pi Gamma Mu; fellow Royal Geog. Soc., Royal Astron. Soc. Mason (K.T., Shriner). Clubs: Rotary, Milwaukee City; Explorers (New York); Adventurers' (Chgo.); Royal Socs. Club (London). Contbr. to Milw. Pub. Mus. Bull., and Yearbook; Indian, publs. U. Cal., others. Research in ethnology of Pomo and Miwok tribes of Cal., Cayapa Indians of Ecuador, and Wis. ethnology and archeology. Dist civic service citation Marquette U. Home: 9 Wolfe Av., San Rafael, Cal. Died Mar. 9, 1965; buried Sonoma, Cal.

BARRINGER, DANIEL MOREAU, mining engr., geologist; b. Raleigh, N.C., May 25, 1860; s. Hon. Daniel Moreau and Elizabeth (Wethered)B.; A.B., Princeton, 1879, A.M., 1882; LL.B, U. of Pa., 1882; spl. course in geology, Harvard, 1889, in chemistry and mineralogy, U. of Va., 1890; m. Matgaret Bennett, Oct. 20, 1897; children—Brandon, Daniel Moreau Sarah Drew, John Paul, Elizabeth Wethered, Lewin Bennitt, Richard Wethered, Philip Ellicott. Practiced law with brother, 1882-89; cons. mining engr. and geologist, 1890—; pres. and dir. of several mining cos. Trustee Jefferson Med. Coll. and Hosp. Republican. Author: The Law of Mines of Commercial Value, 1907. Discovered origin of Meteor Crater, 4,200 feet in diameter and 570 feet deep (to visible floor) in Northern Central Ariz., 1905, and "proved that it is due to impact of a meteoric mass, probably a compact cluster of iron meteorites." Home: Haverford, Pa. Died 1929.

BARRON, E. S. GUZMAN, biochemist; b. Huari, Peru, Sept. 18, 1898; s. Sebastian and Agripina (Barron) G.; M.D., U. San Marcos, Lima, 1924; D.Sc., U. Trujillo, Peru, 1947, U. Brazil, 1956; m. Cora Durkee, Aug. 8, 1930; 1 son, Richard. Came to U.S., 1926, naturalized, 1939. Fellow The Rockefeller Found., 1927-28; professor biochemistry U. Chicago; honorary professor of medicine, Faculty of Medicine, Lima, 1949; hon. prof. medicine and chemistry University Uruguay, 1956; hon. prof. science U. Arequipa, 1956. Recipient prize for study abroad, Faculty of Medicine, Lima, 1925-26. Mem. Am. Soc. Biol. Chemists, Am. Assn. Physicians, Am. Chem. Soc., Soc. Exptl. Biology and Medicine. Home: 5642 Kimbark Av., Chgo. 37. Died June 25, 1957; buried Woods Hole, Mass.

BARRON, ERNEST R., inventor; b. Meadville, Pa., May 23, 1844; m. March 18, 1869, Rachel R. Wyman, Cochranton, Pa. Improved typewriter, 1874, with James Densmore, his stepfather (now deceased); had charge assembling and aligning dept. Remington, 1874-79 (personally preparing first Remington typewriter used); same dept., Caligraph, 1880-85 (personally preparing first machine used); assisting James Densmore, 1885-90; mech. expert, with Densmore, Amos & Emmett Typewriter Co., 1890-93; supt. aligning and assembling dept. and expert on inventions, Franklin Typewriter Mfg. Co., 1893-95; since then has income from royalties on Remington typewriter. His inventions are used on Remington, Caligraph, Densmore and Franklin machines. Addresss: 519 Bedford Av., Brooklyn.

BARRON, GEORGE DAVIS, mining engr.; b. St. Louis, Mo., Jan. 20, 1860; s. of Samuel and Mary Ann (Williamson) B.; ed. Washington U., St. Louis, Mo.; m. Mrs. Josephine L. (Macy) Chamberlin, Oct. 29, 1918. Mining engr. since 1886; operated and owned important mines and metall. plants in Mexico, principally between 1898 and 1910; now retired. Trustee Village of Rye, 1903-04, United Hosp. Foundation of N.Y. Fellow A.A.A.S.; member Am. Inst. Mining and Metallurgical Engineers (trea. 1918-22). Republican. Protestant. Clubs: Union League, Engineers', Apawamis Golf, Blind Brook, American Yacht, Clve Valley Rod and Gun, Onteora, Lake Placid. Home and Office: Rye, N.Y. Died Apr. 1, 1947. *

BARRON, LEONARD, bioculturalist; b. Chiswick, Eng., Sept. 29, 1868; s. Archibald Farquharson and Eleanor (Ayres) B.; ed. Belmont House, Chiswick, Eng., Gunnersbury Coll., 1880-84, Birkbeck Inst., spl. courses in botany, vegetable physiology and morphology, chemistry and biology, 1884-92; came to U.S., 1894; m. Effie Maud, g.d. Adm. June 3, 1896; children—Eric Stuart, Dorothy Enid. Asst. editor Garderners' Chronicle, London, 1885-93; editor Am. Gardening, New York, 1894-1904; mng. editor Garden Mag., 1905-11, editor, 1911-24; editor Garden and Home Builder, 1924-28; hort. editor Am. Home and Country Life, 1928-36; editor The Flower Grower, 1936—; advisory editor Doubleday Doran & Co., pubs. Author: Lawns and How To Make Them, 1906; American Home Book of Gardening, 1931; (chief author) Roses and How To Grow Them, 1905. Editor: The Water Garden; The Garden Library; Flower Growing, 1924; The Pocket Garden Library. Home: Rockville Centre, N.Y. Died Apr. 9, 1938.

BARROW, WILLIAM MORTON, zoölogy; b. Rochester, N.Y., Apr. 7, 1883; s. Walter Bradford and Lizzie Mand (Withall) B.; B.S., Mich. State Coll., 1903; B.S. Harvard 1905, M.S., 1906, Sc.D., 1920; m. Eleanor S. Burton, June 25, 1908; children—William Morton, Arthur Burton. Prof. science, Manchester Coll., North Manchester, Ind., 1906-07; instr. in zoölogy, N.H. State Coll., Durham, 1907-09; with Ohio State U., since 1909, prof. zoölogy and entomology since 1923. Mem. A.A.A.S., Am. Soc. Zoölogists. Author: Science of Animal Life, 1927; Laboratory Exercises in Zoölogy, 1930. Contbr. many articles to scientific publs. Home: 123 Clinton St., Columbus, O. Died Feb. 24, 1946.

BARROWS, DAVID PRESCOTT, univ. prof.; b. Chicago, Ill., June 27, 1873; s. Thomas and Ella Amelia (Cole) B.; B.A., Pomona Coll., 1894; M.A., U. of Calif., 1895, Columbia, 1896; Ph.D., in anthropology, U. of Chicago, 1897; LL.D., Pomona, 1914, U. of Calif., 1919, Mills Coll., 1925; Dr. honoris causa, U. of Bolivia, 1928; Litt.D., Columbia U., 1933; m. Anna Spenser (Nichols), July 18, 1895; children—Anna Frances (wife of Brig. Gen. Floyd W. Stewart, Army of United States), Ella Cole (Mrs. Gerald Hagar), Thomas Nichols, Elizabeth Penfield (wife of Lieut. Col. F. G. Adams, United States Army); m. 2d, Mrs. Eva S. White, 1937. City supt. of schools, Manila, P.I., 1900; chief, Bureau Non-Christian Tribes of P.I., 1901; gen. supt. (afterwards styled director) of education for P.I., 1903-09; prof. edn. 1910, dean Grad. Sch., 1910, prof. polit. science, July 1, 1911, dean of faculties, 1913, and pres., 1919-23, prof. polit. science, emeritus, since 1943, Univ. of California. Pres. trustees Mills Coll., Calif., 1910-17; mem. bd. dirs. Calif. State Sch. for Deaf and Blind, 1912-17; mem. Calif. State Commmn. on Rural Credit and Colonization, 1915-17; dir. East Bay Pub. Utility Dist., 1924-27, 1932-34; trustee Carnegie Endowment for Internat. Peace. Mem. Belgian Relief Com., in charge food supply of Brussels, 1916, Commd. maj. of cav., N.A., 1917; lt. col. cav. U.S. Army, 1918; active duty in P.I. and Siberia, 1917-19; on original gen. staff list, U.S. Army 1919; col. 159th Inf., N.G., Calif., 1921; brig. gen. 79th Inf. Brigade, Calif. N.G., 1925; maj. gen. Army U.S., comdg. gen. 40th Div., Calif. N.G., 1926-37. First state comdr. for California, American Legion, 1920. Carnegie visiting prof. of Internat. Relations (Latin-America), 1928; Theodore Roosevelt prof., U. of Berlin, 1933-34; expert consultant to Secretary of War, 1941; representative Office Strategic Services, 1942; radio commentator, 1943-44; columnist International News Service, 1943-49. Decorated Chevalier Legion of Honor (French), promoted to officer, 1932; Order of the Crown (Belgian), Croix de Guerre (Czecho-Slovak); Order of the Sacred Treasure (Japanese); Order of the Crown (Italian); Comdr. Order of Polonia Restituta (Polish). Corr. mem. Royal Acad. of Polit. and Moral Science (Madrid), 1923. Republican. Conglist. Mem. Phi Beta Kappa. Clubs: Faculty (Berkeley); Bohemian (hon.), University (hon.), Commonwealth (San Francisco); Army and Navy (Los Angeles). Author: The Ethno-Botany of the Coahuilla Indians, 1900; A History of the Philippines, 1903, rev. 1924; A Decade of American Government in the Philippines, 1915; British Politics in Transition (with E. M. Sait), 1925; (with Thomas Barrows) Government in California, 1926; Berbers and Blacks (also transl. into French), 1927. Traveled in Asia, Malaysia, Central and South America and in Africa (Timbuktu, the French Sudan and British Nigeria). Home: 85 Parkside Dr., Berkeley 5 CA

BARROWS, HARLAN H., geographer; b. Armada, Mich., Apr. 15, 1877; s. David H. and Lucy Elizabeth (Tenney) B.; grad. Mich. State Normal Coll., Ypsilanti, 1896, Pd.M., 1912; S.B., U. Chgo., 1903, postgrad. 1903-06; m. Janie E. Gleason, Aug. 16, 1898 (dec. July 23, 1913); 1 son, Robert Harlan (dec.); m. 2d, Adda B. Weber, Sept. 4, 1915; children—Dorothy Elizabeth, Jean. Asst. in geology, 1904-07, instr. geology and geography, 1907-08, asst. prof., 1908-10, asso. prof. geography, 1910-14, prof. since 1914, chmn. dept., 1919-42, prof. emeritus sin-e 1942, U. Chgo. Head country sect. Bur. Research, U.S. War Trade Bd., 1918. Mem. Miss. Valley Com., Fed. Emergency Adminstrn. Pub. Works, 1933-34; mem. Water Planning Com. Nat. Resources Bd., 1934-35, Water Resources Com. 1935-41; chmn. cons. bd. Rio Grande Joint Investigation, 1935-38; mem. President's Gt. Plains Com., 1936; chmn. No. Gt. Plains Com., 1938-40; chmn. cons. bd. Pecos River Joint Investigation, 1939-41; planning cons. U.S. Bur. Reclamation since 1939; dir. Central Valley Project Studies, U.S. Bur. Reclamation 1942-44. Mem. Assn. Am. Geographers (pres. 1922), Swedish Soc. for Anthropology and Geography, Phi Beta Kappa, Sigma Xi. Co-Author: Elements of Geology (with Eliot Blackwelder); Elements of Geography (with R. D. Salisbury and W. S. Tower); Modern Geography (with same); Journeys in Distant Lands (with Edith P. Parker); United States and Canada (with same); Europe and Asia (with Edith P. and Margaret T. Parker); Southern Lands (with same); Our Big World; The American Continents, Old World Lands. Co-author numerous govt. reports. Home: 2740 Oak St., Highland Park, Ill. Died May 1960.

BARRUS, GEORGE HALE, steam engr.; b. Goshen, Mass., July 11, 1854; s. Hiram and Augusta (Stone) B.; B.S., Mass. Inst. Tech., 1874; m. Louise C. Williams, Oct. 2, 1897; 1 dau., Bella D. (Mrs. Edwin L. Bowman). Asst. in design and constrn., Steam Engring. Lab., Mass. Inst. Tech., 1874-75; cons. practice, Boston, 1875—. Judge of exhibits, Mass. Charitable Mech. Assn., Franklin Inst. Elec. Exhbn., Phila.; Mass. judge of power exhibits, World's Fair, Chicago, 1893. Mem. Govt. Advisory Bd. on tests of fuels and structural materials. Inventor of several forms of steam calorimeter, coal calorimeter, draft gauge, steam meter and drainage system. Home: Brookline, Mass. Died Apr. 1929.

BARRY, PATRICK, horticulturist; b. Belfast, Ireland, May 24, 1816; m. Harriet Huestis, 1847, 8 children including William C. Came to N.Y., 1837; a founder Mt. Hope Nurseries (became largest nursery in country, did much importing), Rochester, N.Y., 1840; hort. editor Genessee Farmer, 1845-53; editor The Horticulturist, until 1855; founder Fruit Growers' Soc. Western N.Y., 1855; chmn. exec. com.; mem. 1st bd. of control N.Y. Agrl. Expt. Sta., Geneva; organizer, pres: Flour City Nat. Bank, 1956; organizer, pres. Mechanics Savs. Bank, Rochester City R.R. Co., Powers Hotel Co.; pres. N.Y. State Agrl. Soc., 1877; pres. Western N.Y. Hort. Soc., 30 years. Author: The Fruit Garden, 1851; Catalogue of the American Pomological Society (guide for Am. fruit growers). Died June 23, 1890.

BARSTOW, EDWIN ORMOND, chemist; b. Rockport, O., Nov. 13, 1879; s. Edwin F. and Emma J. (Blodgett) B.; grad. Case Sch. Applied Sci., 1900, D.E., 1941; m. Florence Katherine Schade, July 21, 1903; children—Ormond Edwin, John Carlton, Robert Osborn, Frederick, Ruth Gertrude, Richard. With Dow Chem. Co. from 1900. Dir. Chem. State Savs. Bank, Midland, Mich. Patentee of electrolytic cells and apparatus and methods for oil extraction; also processes for mfr. lead arsenate, magnesium chloride, and other salts, phenol. benzoic acid, etc. Trustee Midland Community Center. Mem. Am. Chem. Soc., Sigma Xi, Tau Beta Phi. Presbyn. Mason. Club: Rotary. Home: Midland MI Died Apr. 21, 1967; buried Midland (Mich.) Cemetery.

BARSTOW, WILLIAM SLOCUM, elec. engr.; b. Brooklyn, N.Y., Feb. 15, 1866; s. Frank D. and Mary (Slocum) B.; A.B., Columbia, 1887; hon. Dr. Engring., Stevens Inst. Tech.; hon. Dr.Sc., Columbia; m. Francoise M. Duclos, Oct. 4, 1894; 1 son, Frederic D. With Edison Machine Works, Schenectady, N.Y., Paterson, N.J., New York and Brooklyn. 1887-89; asst. supt., 1889-90, gen.supt. and chief engr., 1890-97, gen. mgr., 1897-1901, Edison Electric Illuminating Co., Brooklyn; cons. elec. engr., 1901-06; practiced as W. S. Barstow & Co., Inc., 1906-12; organizer, 1912, Gen. Gas & Elevtric Corp. and pres. until 1929; now senior partner Barstow, Campbell & Co.; pres. Thomas Alva Edison Foundation, Inc. Trustee Stevens Ins. Tech. Fellow Am. Inst. Elec. Engineers; mem. Elec. Soc. (ex-pres.), Illuminating Engring. Soc., Edison Pioneers (pres. 8 yrs., tehn hon. pres.), Am. Electro-chemists So., United Engring. Soc., Edison Pioneers (pres. 8 yrs., then hon. pres.), Am. Electro-chemists Soc., United Engring. Societies (library bd.; mem. exec. com.). Clubs: Columbia University, Lawyers, Engineers, University, Delta Upsilon, N. Hempstead Country, Manhasset Bay Yacht, New York Yacht; Everglades, Boca Raton, Seminole, Sailfish Club of Florida, Hobe Sound Yacht (commodore). Home: Great Neck, N.Y. Office: 70 Pine St., New York. Died Dec. 26, 1942.

BARTH, CARL G(EORGE), mech. engr.; b. Christiania, Norway, Feb. 28, 1860; s. Jacob Böckman and Adelaide Magdalene (Lange) B.; grad. High School, Lillehammer, Norway, 1975; grad. Tech. Sch., Horten, 1876; m. Hendrikke Jacobibe Fredericksen, of Lillehammer, Mar. 4, 1882 (died Feb. 25, 1816); children—J. Christian, Carl. G., I. Adelaide (dec.), Elizabeth F.; m. 2d, Sophia E. Roever, Jan. 25, 1919. In machine ships, Norwegian Navy Yards; instr. in mathematics and mech. drawing, Tech. Sch., Horten to 1880; came to America, 1881; mech. draftsman with Wm. Sellers & Co., Phila., 1881-90, and instr. in mech. drawing, evening schs. of Franklin Inst., 1882-88; engr. and chief draftsman with Arthur Falkenau, Phila., 1890-1901; designer, Wm. Sellers & Co., 1891-95; engr. and chief draftsman, Rankin & Fritch Foundry & Machine Co., St. Louis, 1895-97; designer St. Louis Water Dept., Feb.-June, 1897; with Internat. Corr. Schs., Scranton, Pa., 1897-98; instr. in manual work and mathematics, Ethical Culture Schs., New York, 1898-99; machine shop engr. Bethlehem Steel Co., 1899-1901; there met Frederick W. Taylor, the father of scientific management, and was his prin. associate until Taylor's death in 1915; introducing Taylor system of scientific management, in machine shops, 1901-23; rep. of Yinius Olsen Testing Machines Co. in Japan, 1932-24; retired. Expert in shop management, Ordinance Dept., U.S. Army, 1909-18, and again during World War; lecturer on scientific management Harvard U., 1911-16, and 1919-23. U. of Chicag, 1914-16. Home: Philadelphia, Pa. Died Oct. 28, 1939.

BARTH, THEODORE H., inventor; b. New York, N.Y., Nov. 13, 1891; s. Ignatius and Johanna (Wollner) B.; unmarried. Co-inventor U.S. Navy catapult and arresting gear for launching and landing aircraft on the U.S.S. Saratoga and U.S.S. Lexington, 1928. Address: Carl L. Norden Inc., 141 Broadway, N.Y.C. Died June 19, 1967.

BARTHOLOMEW, TRACY, research engr.; b. Austin, Tex., Nov. 14, 1884; s. George Wells and Hettie Julia (Cole) B.; student Ohio State U., 1902-03; E.M., Colo. Sch. of Mines, 1906; m. Sarah Jane Anderson, Oct. 6, 1921; children—George Anderson, Jane Anderson. Construction engr. Federal Lead Co., Flat River, Mo., 1906-07; designing and test engr. Nev. Consol. Copper Co., McGill, Nev., 1907-09; gen. mgr. Alkali-Proof Cement Div. of Colo. Portland (now Ideal) Cement Co., Denver, Colo., 1909-11; mgr. Rico Tropical Fruit Co., Garrochales, P.R., 1911-21, pres. since 1921; sr. fellow Mellon Inst. of Industrial Reserach, Pittsburgh, 1921-39; mgr. of research Duquesne Slag Products Co., 1929-40; cons. engr. since 1940. Served as captain 374th Inf., United States Army, 1918-19. Mem. A.A.A.S., American Institute Mining and Metallurgical Engineers, American Society Civil Engineers, Am. Chem. Soc., Am. Ceramic Soc., Am. Soc. Municipal Engrs., Am. Soc. Testing Materials, Am. Concrete Inst., Engrs. Soc. of Western Pa., Beta Theta Pi, Phi Lambda Upsilon. Republican. Presbyterian. Mason (K.T., Shriner). Clubs: Faculty (U. Pittsburgh); Longue Vue. Home: 1545 Beechwood Blvd., Pitts. 17. Died Dec. 7, 1951.

BARTLETT, ELISHA, physician, educator; b. Smithfield, R.I., Oct. 6, 1804; s. Otis and Waite (Buffum) B.; grad. in medicine Brown U., 1826; m. Elizabeth Slater, 1829. Settled in Lowell, Mass., 1827, practiced medicine; prof. anatomy Berkshire Med. Instn., Pittsfield, Mass., 1832-40; an editor Med. Mag., Boston, 1832-35; prof. medicine Transylvania U., Lexington, Ky., 1841, 46, U. Md., Balt., 1844-45, U. Louisville (Ky.), 1849-50, N.Y.U., 1850-52, Coll. Physicians and Surgeons, N.Y.C., 1852-55. Author treatises: The Fevers in the United States, 1842; History, Diagnosis, and Treatment of Edematous Laryngitis, 1850. Died Smithfield, July 19, 1855; buried Smithfield.

BARTLETT, FRANK LESLIE, chemist; b. at Hanover, Me., Mar. 2, 1852; s. Cyrus and Caroline (Smith) B.; ed. Gould's Acad., Me., 1866-70; spl. course U. of Mich., 1872-73; in medicine, Dartmouth, 1878; spl. studies Westbrook Coll., Me., and abroad, 1879; m. Harriet W. Baldwin, of Bangor, Me., 1878. State chemist and assayer, Me., 1874-86; prof. science, Westbrook Coll., 1874-78; mining, treating ores and inventing since 1879. Has received more than 40 patents for handling, smelting and treating ores. Pres. Good Roads Assn., Chamber of Commerce, Board of Trade, Denver, Club: Automobile of Colo. (pres.). Author: Minerals of New England, 1877; Mines of Maine, 1879. Contbr. to scientific mags. Address: 944 Sherman Av., Denver, Colo.

BARTLETT, HARLEY HARRIS, botanist; b. Anaconda, Mont., Mar. 9, 1886; s. Jonathan Hodgkin and Harriet Amanda (Potter) B.; A.B., Harvard, 1908; grad. study, 1908-09. Asst. in biology and chemistry, Shortridge High Sch., 1902-04; asst. Gray Herbarium, Harvard, 1905-08; chem. biologist, Bureau Plant Industry, U.S. Dept. Agr., 1909-15; with U. Mich., 1915—, prof. botany, dir. Bot. Garden, to 1956, prof., dir., emeritus, 1956—; botantist Gorgas Memorial Lab., Panama, summer 1940; agent Office of Rubber Investigations, U.S. Dept. Agr., Philippines and Haiti, 1940-41; S.A., Mex., 1942-44. Mem. Sci. expdns. to Formosa and Sumatra, 1926-27, Mexico, 1930, Guatemala and British Honduras, 1931; exchange prof., U. Philippines, 1935, vis. prof., 1947. Certificate of merit Golden Jubilee, Bot. Soc. Am., 1956, Am. Soc. Agronomy, 1957. Mem. Bot. Soc. Am. (pres. 1927), Am. Soc. Naturalists, Mich. Acad. Science (pres. 1925), Wash. Acad. Sciences, A.A.A.S., Am. Philos. Soc., New Eng. Bot. Club, Sigma Xi, Republican. Author: Fire in Relation to Primitive Agriculture and Grazing in the Tropics, Vol. I, 1955, Vol. II, 1957. Home: 1601 Brooklyn Av., Ann Arbor, Mich. Died Feb. 21, 1960; buried Forest Hill Cemetery, Ann Arbor, Mich.

BARTLETT, ROBERT ABRAM, explorer; b. Brigus, Newfoundland, Aug. 15, 1875; s. William James and Mary J. (Leamon) B.; ed. Brigus High Sch., and Meth. Coll., St. Johns, Newfoundland; passed exam. for Master of British Ships, Halifax, N.S., 1905; hon. A.M., Bowdoin Coll., 1920; unmarried. Began explorations wintering with R. E. Peary, at Cape D'Urville, Kane Basin, 1897-98; on a hunting expdn., Hudson Strait and Bay, 1901; capt. of a sealer off Newfoundland coast, 1901-05; comd. the Roosevelt, 1905-09, taking active part in Peary's expdn. to the pole, reaching 88th parallel; comd. ship on pvt. hunting expdn. to Kane Basin, 1910; with Can. Govt. Arctic Expedition, 1913-14, as captain of the C.G.S. Karluk, which was crushed by ice, Jan. 1914; with 17 persons reached Wrangel Island; leaving 15 persons on island, with one Eskimo crossed ice to Siberia and returned with rescuing party, reaching Wrangel Island in Sept. 1914, and Sept. 12, 1915, reached Nome, Alaska, with 13 survivors. Cmdr. 3d Crocker Land Relief Expdn. to N. Greenland, returning with party, since Oct. 1917. Was sent, 1925, by Nat. Geog. Soc. to locate bases for aircraft, N.W. Alaska, and shores Arctic Ocean, also recording times and currents and dredging for flora and fauna. Expdn. to North Greenland and Ellesmere Land, 1926, to Fox Basin and West Shore Baffin Land, 1927, to Siberia, 1928, to Labrador, summer 1929, head of expdn. to N.E. coast of Greenland for Mus. of Am. Indian and Mus. of Natural History of Phila., 1930, expdn. to Greenland for Am. Mus. Natural History, Bot. Gardens of N.Y. City and Smithsonian Instn. (Washington), 1931, to N.W. Greenland (erecting monument in moemory of Admiral R. E. Peary), 1932, to Baffin Land, 1933, to N.W. Greenland, Ellesmere and Baffin Lands, under auspices of Acad. of Natural Sciences of Phila., 1934, to N.W. Greenland under auspices of Field Scientific research in Eastern Arctic, 1936-41; in government service, Hudson Bay, Baffin Land and Greeland (on own schooner Morrissey), 1942-44. Awarded Hubbard gold medal, National Geographic Society, 1909; Hudson-Fulton silver medal, 1909; silver medal, English Geog. Soc., 1910; Kane medal, Phila. Geog. Soc., 1910; silver medal, Italian Geog. Soc., 1910; gold medal, Harvard Travelers Club, 1915; awarded the Black Grant, Royal Geog. Soc., 1918, "in recognition of splendid leadership after the 'Karluk' was lost" gold medal Am. Geog. Soc. Hon. mem. "Society of Dorset Men in Lond" England, Boy Scouts of America; life mem. Am. Mus. Natural History; mem. Marine Soc. (New York), Am. Geophys. Union, Am. Legion Vets. Fgn. Wars, New York Garrison 194, Army and Navy Union of U.S.A.; corr. mem. Am. Geog. Soc. Confirmed rank of lt. comdr. U.S. N.R.F., 1920. Mason. Clubs: City Travelers' (Boston); Ends of the Earth, Explorers' Travel, Aero of America, Crusing of America , Coffee House (New York); Wilderness, Boone and Crockett. Author: Last Voyage of the Karluk, 1916; The Log of Bob Bartlett, 1928; Sails over Ice, 1934. Home: Brigus, Newfoundland. Address: Explorers' Club. 10 W. 72d St., New York, N.Y. Died Apr. 28, 1946.

BARTLEY, ELIAS HUDSON, M.D.; b. Bartley, N.J., Dec. 6, 1849; s. Samuel Potter and Anna (Ewalt) B.; B.S., Cornell, 1873; M.D., L.I. Coll. Hosp., 1879; m. Mary Frances Harloe, Nov. 5, 1888; Samuel Potter, Mrs. Mildred Simrel. Taught sciences, Princeton High Sch., 1873-741 instr. chemistry, Cornell, 1874-75; prof. chemistry, Swarthmore Coll., 1875-78; instr. chemistry, 1880-86, prof. chemistry and toxicology, 1886-1901, prof. of chemistry, toxicology and pediatrics, 1915-17, emeritus prof., 1917—, L.I. Coll. Hosp.; chief chemist, Health Dept., Brooklyn, 1882-88; mem. Kings Co, Bd. of Pharmacy, 1892-98; dean and prof. of organic chemistry, Brooklyn Coll. Pharmacy 1892-1902; consulting pediatrist, L.I. Coll. Hosp., Methodist, Kingston Av. Contagious Diseases, and S. Side hosps.; chief of the dept. of pediatrics Brownsville and East New York Hospital. Author: Textbook of Medical and Pharmaceutical Chemistry (7th edit.), 1909. Manual of Clinical Chemistry (3d edit.), 1907. Died Jan. 12, 1937.

BARTON, BENJAMIN SMITH, physician, botanist; b. Lancaster, Pa., Feb. 10, 1766; s. Thomas and Esther (Rittenhouse) B.; attended York Acad., Lancaster; M.D., U. Göttingen (Germany); studied medicine in England, 1786; m. Mary Pennington, 1792, 2 children including Thomas P. Became mem. Royal Med. Soc.; practiced medicine, Phila., 1789; prof. botany U. Pa., 1790-1813, prof. medicine, 1813-15; editor Phila. Med. and Phys. Jour., 1805-08. Author: Elements of Botany (1st elementary botany text by an American), 1803; Collections for an Essay Towards a Materia Medica of the United States (description of medicinal plants), 1804. Died Phila., Dec. 19, 1815; buried Phila.

BARTON, DONALD CLINTON, geologist; b. Stow, Mass., June 29, 1889; s. George Hunt and Eva May (Beede) B.; grad. Cambridge Latin Sch., 1907; Harvard, class of 1911, A.B., 1910, A.M., 1912, Ph.D, 1914; m. Margaret Dunbar Foules, June 26, 1923; 1 dau., Ann Foules. Instr. engring. geology, Washington U., 1914-16; field geologist Empire Gas and Fuel Co., 1916-17; geologist Gulf Coast div. Amerada Petroleum Corp., 1919-23; chief geologist Rycade Oil Corp., 1923-27; chief Torsion Balance and Magnetometer Div., Geophysica; Research Corp., 1925-27; cons. geologist and geophysicist, 1927-34; research and consulting geologist and geophysicist Humble Oil and Refining Comapny, 1935—. Private to Master Signal Electrician (weather forecaster), Meterological Section Signal Corps, A.E.F., 1917-29. Unitarian. Contbr. many papers on geology and geophysics. Home: Houston, Tex. Died July 8, 1939.

BARTON, GEORGE HUNT, geologist; b. Sudbury, Mass., July 8, 1852; s. George Washington and Mary S. (Hunt) B.; lived on a farm there until 21 yrs. old; S.B., Mass. Inst. Tech., 1880; m. Eva May Beede, Sept. 18, 1884; children—Harold Beede (dec.), Donald Clinton, Helen Mary. Asst. in drawing, Mass. Inst. Tech., 1880-81; asst. on Hawaiian govt. survey, Honolulu, 1881-83; asst. on geology, 1883-84, asst. prof. l till 1904, Mass. Inst. Tech.; same, Boston U., till 1904; now dir. Teachers' Sch. of Science. Lecturer on geology, Boston U., 1915, Welesley Coll., 1921-22. Was asst. geologist U.S. Geol. Survey; mem. 6th Peary expdn. to Greenland, 1896. Fellow Am. Acad. Arts amd Sciences. Author: Outline of Elementary Lithology, 1900; Outline of Dynamical and Sturctural Geology; also many geol. papers. Traveled extensively in U.S., British America, Hawaii, and Europe. Home: Cambridge, Mass. Died Nov. 25, 1933.

BARTON, JOHN RHEA, surgeon; b. Lancaster, Pa., Apr. 1794; s. William and Elizabeth (Rhea) B.; M.D., U. Pa., 1818; m. Susan Ridgeway. Practiced medicine, Phila., 1818-40; surgeon Phila. Hosp., 1920-22, Pa. Hosp., Phila., 1823; performed pioneer operation in case of anchylosis of hip joint, 1826; known for knowledge and treatment of bone fractures; author paper "A New Treatment in a Case of Anchylosis," 1837; chair in his honor established by his widow at U. Pa. Med. Sch. Died Phila., Jan. 1, 1871; buried Phila.

BARTON, LELA VIOLA, plant physiologist; b. Farmington, Ark., Nov. 14, 1901; d. Henry and Mary Frances (Miller) Barton; B.A., U. Ark., 1922; M.A., Columbia, 1927, Ph.D., 1939. Sci. tchr. Sr. High Sch., Van Buren, Ark., 1922-24; biology tchr. Sr. High Sch., Little Rock, Ark., 1924-26; plant-physiologist Boyce Thompson Inst. Plant Research, Yonkers, N.Y., 1928-66. Mem. Torrey Bot. Club (pres. 1956-57), A.A.A.S., Botanical Soc. Am., Sigma Xi, Sigma Delta Epsilon (nat. pres. 1947, nat. hon. mem.). Author: (with William Crocker) Twenty Years of Seed Research, 1948, Physiology of seeds, 1953; Seed Preservation and Longevity, 1961; Bibliography of Seeds, 1966. Home: Tucson AZ Died July 31, 1967; buried Fayetteville AR

BARTON, PHILIP PRICE, electrical engr.; b. Lock Haven, Pa., May 5, 1865; s. John Hervey and Hannah Davis (Price) B.; Ph.B., Cornell U., 1886, M.S., 1888; m. Georgia H. Thurston, of Pittsburgh, Dec. 28, 1899; 1 dau., Mary Elizabeth. Elec. engr. with Westinghouse Electric Co., Pittsburgh, 1888-91; with Brush Electric Co. and Gen. Electric Co., Pittsburgh, 1891-98; with the Niagara Falls Power Co., 1898-1920. Mem. Nat. Com. on Gas and Electric Service, 1917-20; maj. engrs. O.R.C., 1917. Republican. Fellow Am. Inst. E.E.; mem. Am. Geog. Soc., Psi Upsilon. Clubs: Niagara (Niagara Falls); Engineers (New York); Hartford, Hartford Golf (Hartford, Conn.). Home: 57 Forest St., Hartford, Conn.

BARTON, WILLIAM HENRY, JR., engr., curator; b. Baltimore, Md., July 7, 1893; s. William Henry and Helen E. (Pritchett) B.; B.S. in C.E., U. of Pa., 1917, C.E., 1921, M.S., 1923; M. Celia Mason. Aug. 19, 1920. Engring. work U.S. Bur. Public Roads. 1917-Jan. 1918 and Jan. 1919-Aug. 1920; teacher civil engring., U. of Pa., Set. 1920-June 1930, Pa. Military College, September 1935; lecturer curator of astronomy Hayden Planetarium since Sept. 1935. Corpl. then sergt. San Corps, U.S. Army, 1918-19; reserve, 5 yrs.; mem. Brit. Astron. Assn., Am. Assn. of Museums, N.Y. Acad. Sciences, Am. Astron. Soc., Royal Astron. Soc. of Canada, Tau Beta Pi. Sigma XI. Author: (with L. H. Doane) Sampling and Testing Highway Materials, 1925; (with S. G. Barton) Guide to the Constellations 1928; (with J. M. Joseph) Starcraft, 1935; An Introduction to Celestial Navigation, 1942; Stereopix, 1943. Contbr. articles to Sky mag. Home: 875 W 181st St. Address: American Museum of Natural History, New York. Died July 7, 1944.

BARTON, WILLIAM PAUL CRILLION, naval surgeon, botanist; b. Phila., Nov. 17, 1786; s. William and Elizabeth (Rhea) B.; grad. Princeton, 1805; studied medicine under uncle B.S. Barton, 1805-08; m. Esther Sergeant, Sept. 1814. Apptd. surgeon USN, 1809, served in hosps. in Phila., Norfolk, Pensacola; prof. botany U. Pa. (though still on Navy active list), 1815-18; charges brought by fellow Navy surgeons that he had criticized marine hosps. unjustifiably were dismissed, 1818; prof. medicine Jefferson Med. sch., circa 1825; 1st chief Bur. Medicine and Surgery, USN, 1842-44; as mem. inactive Navy list served as pres. Bd. Med. Examiners, 1852. Author: Vegetable Materia Medica of United States, 1817-19 (description medicinal plants). Died Phila., Feb. 29, 1865; buried Phila.

BARTOW, EDWARD, chemist; b. Glenham, New York, Jan. 12, 1870; s. Charles Edward and Sarah Jane (Scofield) B.; B.A., Williams Coll., 1892; Ph.D., U. Gottingen, 1895, Golden diploma, 1956; D.Sc., Williams Coll., 1923; m. Alice Abbott, Sept. 3, 1895 (dec. May 15, 1951); 1 dau., Virginia. Asst. in chemistry, 1892-94, instructor, 1895-97, Williams Coll., instr. in chemistry, 1897-99, asso. prof., 1899-1905, U. of Kan.; asso. prof., 1905-06, prof. sanitary chemistry, 1906-20, U. of Ill. Dir. State Water Survey, 1905-17; chief Water Survey Div., Dept. Registration and Education, Illinois, 1917-20; prof. and head dept. of chemistry and chem. engring., State Univ. of Ia., 1920-40, prof. emeritus, since 1940; research consultant Johns-Manville Corp. 1940-41. Del. 9th Internat. Congress Chemistry, Madrid, 1934, 10th Rome, 1938; mem. council Internat. chem. Union, 1922-25, 27-30, 33-38, v.p. for U.S.A., 1934-38. Sec. Lake Mich. Water Commn., 1908; Commn. on Standards of Water for Interstate Carriers, 1913, 22; sec.-treas. Ill. Water Supply Association, 1909-17. Served from maj. to lt. col., san. corps, U.S. Army, A.E.F., 1917-19. Awarded Medaille d'Honneur, des Epidemies, d'Argent (France). Mem. of American Chemical Society (dir. 1933, pres. 1936), A.A.A.S., Societe Chim. Industrielle (France), Soc. Chem. Industry (Great Britain), Am. Water Works Assn. (trustee, 1913, v.p., 1921; pres., 1922), Am. Inst. Chem. Engrs. (dir. 1923-25, 1936-39), Am. Soc. Civil Engrs. (life mem. 1946), Am. Assn. U. Profs., Franklin Inst., Am. Pub. Health Assn., Kan. Acad. Sci. (pres. 1904), Am. Soc. Testing Materials, American Society for Engineering Education, Am. Public Works Assn., Nat. Security League, Mil. Order World War, Nat. Inst. Social Science, Acad. Polit. Science, Am. Veterans Assn., Am. Legion Illinois Acad. Science, Iowa Engring. Society, Ia. Acad. Science, (vice president, 1933, president 1934), Am. Inst. Chemists, American Philatelic Society, Society Philatelic Americans, Spanish Academy Science (corr. mem.), Trans-Miss. Stamp Soc., Phi Beta Kappa Assos., Sigma Xi, Alpha Chi Sigma, Tau Beta Pi, Theta Delta Chi, Phi Lambda Upsilon. Conglist. Clubs: University, Chaos (Chgo.); Chemists (N.Y.C., Chgo.). Author 14 vol. report on Ill. waters; also papers relating to field. Asst. editor Chem. Abstracts, 1911—. Home: 304 Brown St. Office: Chemical Bldg., Iowa City, Ia. Died Apr. 12, 1958; buried Fishkill, N.Y.

BARTRAM, JOHN, botanist; b. nr. Darby, Pa., Mar. 23, 1699; s. John and Elizabeth (Hunt) B.; m. Mary Morris, Jan. 1723; m. 2d, Ann Mendenhall, Sept. 1729; 11 children including John, William. First native Am. botanist; founded 1st bot. garden in U.S., Kingsessing, Pa., 1728; apptd. Am. botanist to King George III, 1765; made bot. and sci. journeys adding new descriptions of plants and zool. specimens; conducted 1st experiments in hybridization in N. Am., 1728; name commemorated in Bartramia genus of mosses; designated by Linnaeus as greatest contemporary "natural botanist". Author: Observations on the Inhabitants, Climate, Soil, etc. made by John Bartram in His Travels from Pennsylvania to Lake Ontario, 1751; Descriptions of East Florida, 1769. Died Kingsessing, Sept. 22, 1777.

BARTRAM, WILLIAM, naturalist; b. Phila., Feb. 9, 1739; s. John and Ann (Mendenhall) B.; Apprenticed to mcht., 1757-61; in business as trader, Cape Fear, N.C., 1761; explored St. John's River with father, 1765-66; engaged in extensive travels through Southern part of nation gathering specimens and seeds along with drawings for Dr. John Fothergill of London, 1773-78; partner with brother John in operating botanic garden founded by father on bank of Schuylkill River, nr. Phila., 1777-1812; elected mem. Am. Philos. Soc., 1786; name commemorated in genus Bartramia of upland plovers, alos in Bartram's sandpiper; compiled list of 215 native birds (mcst complete in existence until Wilson's American Ornithology). Author: Travels (description of natural life in South of high literary quality), 1791; article "Account of the Species, Hybrids, and Other Varieties of the Vine in North America," 1804. Died Kingsessing, Pa., July 2, 1823; buried Phila.

BARTSCH, PAUL, biologist; b. 1871; B.S., State U. Ia., 1896; M.S., 1899, Ph.D., 1905; D.Sc., George Washington U., 1937. Smithsonian rep. Philippine Expdn., 1907-08; director breeding experiments with Cerions on Fla. Keys under Carnegie Inst. and Smithsonian Inst., 1912-33; science exploration Gulf Cal., Bahamas, W. Mex., Fla., Cuba, Haiti, Santo Domingo, Pureto Rico, all W. Indian Islands between Puerto Rico and Trinidad, Gulf St.Lawrence; Smithsonian del. 2d Pan Am. Sci. Congress, Washington, 1916; del. 1st Pan-Pacific Sci. Congress, Honolulu, 1920; dir. Johnson Smithsonian Deep Sea Expdn. to Puerto Rico Deep, 1932, Smithsonian Roebling Exploring Expdn., 1937; furnished poison gas detector to Chem. Warfare Service, 1918; asso. div. mollusks U. S. Natural Mus. since 1946; prof. emeritus George Washington U. since 1939. Fellow A.A.A.S.; mem. Washington Acad. Sci., Washington Biol. Soc., Am. Ornithol. Union, Am. Assn. Anatomists, Am. Soc. Zoologists, Am. Genetic Assn., Malacol. Soc. Gt. Brit. and Ireland, Am. Malacol. Soc., Sigma Xi. Author articles field. Home: Lebanon, Lorton, Va. Office: care The Smithsonian Instn., Washington. Died Apr. 24, 1960; buried Washington.

BARUCH, SIMON, physician; b. Schwersen, Germany, July 29, 1840; s. Bernard and Teresa (Green) B.; ed. Royal Gymnasium, Posen, Germany; M.D., Med. Coll. of Va., 1862; m. Isabel Wolfe, Nov. 27, 1867. Surgeon in the field in Gen. R. E. Lee's army, C.S.A., 1862-65; captured in charge of wounded on battlefields of South Mountain, Md/. and Gettysburg, Pa.; practiced medicine Camden, S.C., 1865-81; since then in New York; specialist as cons. physician in chronic diseases. Diagnosed first recorded case of perforating appendicitis successfully operated on, reported by Dr. Sands, in N.Y. Medical Journal, 1889; introduced free municipal bathhouses, prof. hydrotherapy, College Phys. and Surg. (Columbia) Chmn. S.C. State Bd. Health, 1880. Author: Uses of Water in Modern Medicine, 1892; The Principles and Practice of Hydrotherapy, 3 edits.; both books also translated and published in Germany and latter in France. Hosp. erected in his honor at Camden, S.C., 1913; free municipal baths named in his honor, Chicago, 1910, New York, 1917. Home: New York, N.Y. Died June 3, 1921.

BARUCH, SYDNEY NORTON, research engr.; b. Mamaroneck, N.Y., Mar 14, 1895; s. Joseph and Sophia (Van Kitzinger) B.; E.E., Cooper Union, 1911; D.Sc., Royal (Eng.), 1921; student special courses in engring. Cooper Union; spl. study elec. phenomenon, U. Cal.; unmarried. Chief engr. Fed. Telephone Co., radio div. Postal Telegraph Co., 1919-20, Gen. Petroleum Co. of Am., 1921; pres. Pub. Service Corp. of Cal., 1916-20; condr. pvt. research labs., N.Y.C., 1930—; dir., controller United Broadcasting chain of radio stations; chief research engr. Gen. Arc Lighting Co. Builder high power radio broadcast chain, 1925; designer broadcasting stations, CHCR, WBNY, WKBK, WKBQ, KIY (Bordeaux, France); cons. engr. (U.S. Signal Corp, 1948). Awarded gold medal Internat. Jury of Scientists, 1915. Cons. engr., special weapons div. U.S. Air Force, 1943—. Fellow Royal Soc. of London; mem. Am. Inst. Radio Engrs., Soc. Motion Picture Engrs. Mason (Shriner). Inventor thermo relay and other devices, also thyraton and norton type mercury rectifier tubes and sound recording on film, 1934; inventor depth bomb successfully used in destruction of submarines in World War I and World War II. Designer 300,000 volt direct current transmission system for Bonneville Project, U.S. Dept. Interior, 1941. Invented guides missile using jet propulson. Home: 145 E 54th St. Office: 1476 Broadway, N.Y.C. Died Sept. 22, 1959.

BARUS, CARL, physicist; b. Cincinnati, Feb. 19, 1856; s. Prof. Carl and Sophia (Mollman) B.; attended Columbia, 1874-76; U. of Wurzburg, Germany, 1876-80, Ph.D., 1879; LL.D., Brown, 1907, Clark U., 1909) m. Annie G. Howes, Jan. 20, 1887; children—Maxwell, Deborah Howes. Physicist, U.S. Geol. Survey, 1880-92; prof. Meteorology, U.S. Weather Bur., 1892-93; physicist, Smithsonian Instn., 1893-95; prof. physics, 1895-1926, prof. emeritus, 1926—, dean grad. dept., 1903-26, Brown Univ. Awarded the Rumford Medal of Am. Acad. Arts and Sciences for various researches in heat. Mem. advisory com. Carnegie Instn., 1902; mem. hon. com. of Internat. Congress on Radiology, Brussels, 1905, 1910. Fellow Am. Acad. Arts and Sciences; mem. numerous socs. Speaker for Am. Physics, World's Congress, St. Louis, 1904. Original contributions to science number about 400 titles. Author: The Electrical and Magnetic Properties of the Iron Carburets, 1885; Subsidence of Fine Solid Particles in Liquids, 1886; Physical Properties of Iron Carburets, 1886; The Measurement of High Temperatures, 1889; Viscosity of Solids, 1891; Die Physikalische Behandlung Hoher Temperaturen, 1892; Compressibility of Liquids, 1892; Mechanism of Solid Viscosity, 1892; Volume Thermodynamics of Liquids, 1892; High Temperature Work in Igneous Fusion, 1893; Condensation of Atmospheric Moisture, 1895; Experiments with Ionized Air, 1901; The Structure of the Nucleus, 1902; Nucleation of the Atmosphere, 1905; Nucleation of the Uncontaminated Air, 19O6; Condensation Induced by Nuclei and by Ions, 1907, part II, 1908, part III, 1909, part IV, 1910; Elliptic Interferences, 1911, 2d vol., 1913; 3d col., 1915; Diffusion of Gases through Liquids, 1913; Interferences of Reversed and Non-reversed Spectra, vol. I, 1916, vol. II, 1917, vols. III and IV, 1919; Interferometer Experiments in Acoustics, vol. I 1921, vol. II, 1923, vol. III, 1925; Acoustics Experiments with Pin-Hole Probe and the Interferometer, 1927. Edited The Laws of Gases, 1899. Home: Providence, R.I. Died Sept. 20, 1935.

BASCOM, FLORENCE, geologist; b. Williamstown, Mass.; d. John and Emma (Curtiss) Bascom; A.B., B.L., U. of Wis., 1882, B.S., 1884, A.M., 1887; Ph.D.., Johns Hopkins, 1893. Instr. geology and petrography, Ohio State U., 1893-95; lecturer and asso. prof., Bryn Mawr Coll., 1895-1906, prof. geology, 1906-28, prof. emeritus since 1928; geol. asst., U.S. Geol. Survey, 1896-1901, asst. geologist, 1901-09, geologist, 1909-36. Asso. editor Am. Geologist, 1896-1905. Fellow Geol. Soc. America (councilor 1924-26; 2d v.p. 1930). A.A.A.S.; mem. Phila. Acad. Natural Sicences, Geog. Soc. Phila., Washington Acad. Sciences, Seismological Soc. Am. Soc. of Women Geographers, Div. Geology and Geography of Nat. Research Council, Mineral. Soc. Am., Inst. Mineralogy and Meteorology, England, Geol. Soc. Washington, Pick and Hammer Club, Am. Geog. Soc., Petrologist Club, Phi Beta Kappa, Sigma Xi. Joint author and author geologic folios; also bulletins and numerous papers in tech. jours. Address Williamstown, Mass. Died June 18, 1945.

BASE, DANIEL, chemist; b. Baltimore, Md., Sept. 6, 1869; grad. Baltimore City Coll., 1888; A.B., Johns Hopkins, 1891, Ph.D, 1895. Prof. chemistry and plant histology, Md. Coll. Pharmacy, 1895-1920; prof. inorganic chemistry, Coll. Phys. and Surg., Baltimore, 1899-1904; prof. inorganic chemistry, Med. Dept., U. of Md., 1904-12; chief chemist Hynson, Westcott & Dunning, Baltimore, 1920—. Author: Elements of Vegetable Histology, 1898; (with Dr. William Simon) Simon-Base Manual of Chemistry, 1923. Home: Baltimore, Md. Died June 17, 1926.

BASKERVILLE, CHARLES, chemist; b. Noxubee Co., Miss., June 18, 1870; s. Charles and Augusta Louisa (Johnston) B.; studied U. of Miss., 1886-87; grad. U. of Va., 1890; studied Vanderbilt U., 1891; U. of Berlin, 1893; (Ph.D., U. of N.C., 1894); m. Mary Boylan Snow. Instr., 1891-94, asst. prof. chemistry, 1894-1900, prof. chemistry and dir. chem. lab., 1900-04, U. of N.C.; prof. chemistry and dir., Coll. City of New York, 1904—. Discovered the chem. elements, carolinium and berzelium; investigations on chemistry of anaesthetics. Mason. Author: School Chemistry, 1898; Key to School Chemistry, 1898; Radium and Its Applications in Medicine; General Inorganic Chemistry, 1909; Laboratory Exercises (with R. W. Curtis), 1909; Progressive Problems in Chemistry (with W. L. Estabrooke); Qualitative Analysis (with L. J. Curtman); Municipal Chemistry (and editor with other experts); Anesthesia (with J. T. Gwathmey); also numerous scientific, ednl. and technol. articles. Inventor processes for refining oils, hydrogenation of oils, plastic compositions, reinforced lead, etc. Died Jan. 28, 1922.

BASKETT, JAMES NEWTON, author; b. in Nicholas Co., Ky., Nov. 1, 1849; s. William B. and Nancy E. (Maffitt) B.; Ph.B., U. of Mo., 1872, A.M., 1893; m. Jeannie Gordon Morrison, Feb. 17, 1874. Student of comparative vertebrate anatomy, with ornithology as a specialty; presented paper at World's Congress of Ornithologists (Chicago, 1893) on Some Hints at the Kinship of Birds as Shown by Their Eggs. Author: The Story of the Birds, 1896; The Story of the Fishes, 1899; The Story of the Amphibians and Reptiles, 1902; also novels-At You-All's House, 1898; As the Light Led, 1900; Sweet Brier and Thistledown, 1902; also papers on the early Spanish Expdn. in the South and Southwest, etc. Home: Mexico, Mo. Died June 14, 1925.

BASQUIN, OLIN HANSON, physicist; b. Dows, Ia., Jan. 30, 1869; s. Oliver William and Hannah (Valentine) B.; A.B., Ohio Wesleyan U., 1892; A.B., Harvard, 1894; A.M., Northwestern Univ., 1895, Ph.D., 1901, D.Sc., 1930; m. Jessie C. Guthrie (died 1907); m. 2d, Anna Stuart, Sept. 12, 1908; children—Harold G., Maurice H. Chief engr., Lexfer Prism companies, at Chicago, 1897, at London, 1898, at Berlin, 1899; asst. prof. physics, 1901-09, prof. applied mechanics, 1909-26, Northwestern U.; with Haskelite Mfg. Corp. since 1926, now v.p. in charge of engineering. Editor: Luxfer Prism Pocket Book, 1898; Luxfer Prism Hand Book (tranlation into German and French), 1899; also papers on experimental work in physics and in strenghth of materials. Chanute Medal, 1915, by Western Soc. Engrs., for best paper in civ. engring. Republican Methodist. Mem. Western Soc. Engrs., Sigma Xi, Delta Tau Delta. Asso. engr.-physicist as specialist on study of tests of steel columns, U.S. Bur. Standards, summer, 1916; in charge exptl. investigations on steel for Navy Dept., summer 1917; investigations of engring. properties of plywood for use in mil. airplanes, 1918. Author: Tangent Modulus and the Strength of Steel Columns in Tests (Bur. of Standards), 1924. Home: 225 Kedzie St., Evanston, Ill. Office: 135 S. La Salle St., Chicago, Ill. Died Mar. 30, 1946.

BASS, CHARLES CASSEDY, M.D.; b. Carley, Miss., Jan. 28, 1875; s. Isaac Esau and Mary Eliza (Wilks) B.; M.D., Med. Dept., Tulane U., 1899; hon. D.Sc., U. of Cincinnati, 1921; LL.D., Duke U., 1937; m. Coraline Howell, Oct. 17, 1897; children—Cassie Juanita, Rachel Ernestine, Helen Corinne, Charles Cassedy. Practiced, Columbia, Miss., 1899-1904; began researches in hookworm disease, 1903; continued same in lab. of Dr. Charles E. Simon, Baltimore, and at Johns Hopkins Med. Sch., 1904; located in New Orleans, 1904, and conducted researches in intestinal parasites of man; pub. first successful cultivation of malaria plasmodia in vitro, 1911; made further research in cultivation of malaria plasmodia with Dr. F. M. Johns, in U.S. Govt. Hosp., Ancon, C.Z., 1912; successfully cultivated all 3 species of the malaria parasite; was scientific dir. malaria control demonstration of Internat. Health Bd., in Bolivar County, Miss.; prof. experimental medicine and director laboratories of clinical medicine, 1912-40, Sch. of Medicine, Tulane Univ., also dean Sch. of Medicine, same univ., 1922-40 (retired 1940). Mem. American Society Tropical Medicine (pres.), Southern Medical Association (pres.), Louisiana State Medical Society, Orleans Parish Medical Society, Soc. Am. Bacteriologists, Assn. Am. Physicians, American Coll. Physicians, Am. Soc. for Clin. Investigation (pres.), Am. Therapeutic Soc., Soc. for Exptl. Biology and Medicine, Stars and Bars Soc., Sigma Xi, Alpha Omega Alpha, Phi Chi. Awarded gold medal, Southern Med. Assn., 1912, for achievement in med. research; gold medal, A.M.A., 1913, for research exhibit in malaria; gold medal, Miss. State Med. Assn., 1913, for extraordinary scientific achievement; medal, Nat. Inst. Social Sciences, 1913, for contributions to welfare of mankind; spl. gold medal, Orleans Parish Med. Soc., 1914, for achievements in researches in malaria; given key to Stars and Bars Soc. of Tulane Med. Coll., 1915, for scholarship. Author: (with George Dock, M.D.) Hookworm Disease, 1909; (with F. M. Johns, M.D.) Alveolodental Pyorrhoea and Practical Clinical Laboratory Diagnosis, 1915; also more than 100 brochures and articles on hookworm disease, malaria, pellagra, test for typhoid fever, diphtheria, medical edn. prevention of the loss of teeth, etc. Home: 1445 Philip St., New Orleans 13. Office: 1430 Tulane Av., New Orleans 13 LA

BASS, FREDERIC HERBERT, civil engr.; b. Hyde Park, Mass., June 19, 1875; s. George Walter and Elizabeth (Bellamy) B.; S.B., Mass. Inst. Tech., 1901; m. Lillian Leggett, June 27, 1903; children—Jason Parker, Elizabeth Bellamy. With engring. dept., Met. Water Works, of Mass., dam, aqueduct and filter constrn., 1896-99, 1901-02; with U.S. engr. corps. Boston Harbor Improvement, 1900; instr. in civ. engring., 1901-04, asst. prof., 1904-10, prof. municipal and sanitary engring., Dec. 1910-19, head of civil engring. dept., 1919-43, U. of Minn.; exec. dir. American Public Works Assn., 1943-45; vice pres., Minn. State Bd. of Health, 1932-44, pres., 1936-39; mem. bd. engrs. Minneapolis-St. Paul San. Dist. Designed numerous water works, sewerage systems and other pub. works; retired 1947. Unitarian. Mem. Am. Soc. C.E., 1911. Am. Soc. Promotion Engring. Edn., Sigma Xi, etc. Mason. Clubs: Engineers, St. Paul Athletic. Address: 515 6th St. S.E., Mpls. Died May 13, 1954; buried Forest Hills Cemetery, Boston.

BASS, IVAN ERNEST, naval officer; b. Carley, Miss., July 29, 1877; s. Isaac E. and Mary Eliza (Wilkes) B.; grad. U.S. Naval Acad., 1901; m. Florence Victoria Bouché, Nov. 26, 1915. Commd. ensign, 1930, advanced through grades to rear adm., 1934; engr. officer Navy Yard, Boston, 1917-20, Navy Yard, N.Y., 1920-23; asst. to chief Bur. Engring., 1929-31; fleet engr. U.S. Asiatic Fleet, 1931-34; naval insp. machinery Newport News Ship Building & Dry Dock Co. (Va.), 1934-39; gen. insp. machinery Bur. Engring., sr. mem. Compensation Bd., U.S. Navy Dept., 1939-41; ret., 1941; mem. Contract Settlement Rev. Bd., Bur. Ships, Navy Dept., 1944-47; returned to inactive duty 1947. Mem. U.S. Naval Inst. Awarded medals Spanish-Am. War, Philippine Campaign, World War I, Yangtze Patrol, Am. Def., World War II; spl. commendation from Navy Dept. for service during World War I. Mem. Nat., Miss. geneal. socs., Inst. Am. Geneaology. Clubs: Army and Navy Country (Washington); New York Yacht. Author: History of Esau Bass (Rev. Soldier), His Brother Jonathan, and Their Descendants, 1955; Thomas Wilkes (circa 1735-1809) and His Descendants, 1965. Address: 3601 Connecticut Av., Washington 2008. Died 1967.

BASSET, WILLIAM RUPERT, industrial engineer; b. Boston, Nov. 12, 1883; s. William and Mary (Simpson) B.; ed. under pvt. tutors; m. Frances Warner, Mar. 2, 1907 (dec.); 1 dau., Beatrix; m. 2d, Mary McClane, 1914 (divorced); m. 3d, Amy Strand, Feb. 19, 1929; children—Amy Jane, William Rupert (dec.). Pres. Miller, Franklin, Basset & Co., indsl. engrs., 1909-28; partner Spencer Trask & Co., bankers, New York, 1928-39; partner Jas. B. Colgate & Co., brokers; pres. Basset, Colgate & Co. (indsl. engrs.), 1939-41; now practicing as indsl. and financial advisor; dir. and mem. exec. committee Colgate-Palmolive-Peet Co., Container Corp. Am., Vick Chem. Co.; dir. and chmn. of exec. com. Reinsurance Corp. of New York, National Reins Company; director Budd Company, Interstate Bakeries Corp. Clubs: Union League, Greenwich Country, Round Hill, Field, Special Car (Greenwich). Author: Accounting as an Aid to Business, 1918; When the Workmen Help You Manage, 1919; The Organization of Modern Business, 1921; Production Engineering and Cost Keeping for Machine Shops (with Johnson Heywood), 1922; Taking the Guesswork Out of Business, 1924; How to Solve Typical Business Problems, 1928; Operating Aspects of Industrial Mergers, 1930. Contbr. to Nation's Business, Saturday Evening Post, Colliers. Home: Old Church Rd., Greenwich, Conn. Died Jan. 9, 1953.

BASSETT, CARROLL PHILLIPS, cons. engr.; b. Bklyn. Feb. 27, 1863; s. Allen Lee and Caroline (Phillips) B.; C.E., Lafayette Coll., 1883, E.M., 1884, Ph.D., 1888, Sc.D., 1942; m. Margaret Condit Kinney, Apr. 14, 1904; children—Carroll Kinney, Estelle Condit (Mrs. R. Watson Pomery), Wm. B. K. Designed and erected water works, electric light, drainage sewerage disposal plants, in N.Y., N.J., Pa., Conn., W.Va. and S.C., 1886-1910; established and operated water and electric utility companies, 1900-22; cons. engr.; pres. Bassett Estates, Inc., Commonwealth Land Company, Commonwealth Water & Light Co., Lakewood Water & Coast Electric Company and subsidiaries; vice president Summit Home Land Company; chairman of the board of First Nat. Bank and Trust Co. (Summit); dir. State Title & Mortgage Guaranty Co., Firemen's Ins. Co., Commercial Casualty Co. (Newark). Trustee N.J. Hist. Soc. Lafayette Coll., YMCA (Summit); mem. exec. com. Sentinels of the Republic. Fellow Am. Geog. Soc.; mem. Am. Soc. C.E., Am., New Eng. water works assns., N.J. Public Utilities Assn., N.J. Soc. Colonial Wars, N.J. Hist. Soc., N.J. Washington Assn., Phi Beta Kappa, Tau Beta Pi, Phi Delta Theta (ex-pres.). Republican. Presbyn. Mason. Clubs: University (N.Y.C.); Baltusrol Golf, Canoe Brook Country. Home: Beacon Hill Summit. Office: 382 Springfield Av., Summit, N.J. Died Jan. 9, 1952; buried Mt. Pleasant Cemetery, Newark.

BASSETT, CHARLES A. II, astronaut; b. Dayton O., Dec. 30, 1931; s. Charles A. and Belle (James) B.; student Ohio State U., 1950-52; B.S. in Elec. Engring. with high honors, Tex. Tech. Coll., 1960; postgrad. U. So. Cal.; m. Jean Marion Martin; children—Karen Elizabeth, Peter Martin. Commd. 2d lt. USAF, 1952, advanced through grades to capt.; formerly exptl. test pilot, engring. test pilot Fighter Projects Office, Edwards AFB, Cal.; now astronaut with Manned Spacecraft Center, NASA. Mem. Am. Inst. Aeros. and Astronautics, Phi Kappa Tau. Home: 6848 Lindbergh St., Edwards, Cal. Died Feb. 1966.

BASSETT, WILLIAM AUSTIN, civil engr.; b. Boston, Mass., Sept. 29, 1876; s. Isaac Austin and Annie Mary (Tuson) B.; B.S., in C.E., Harvard, 1901; m. Grace Loring, Mar. 30, 1905. With engr. corps, Pa. R.R., 1901-04; engring. dept., Pittsburgh, Pa., 1905-07; mem. faculty, Carnegie Tech. Sch., Pittsburgh, 1908-10, also cons. practice; asst. chief editor Engineering Record, 1911-12; cons. engr. N.Y. Bur. Municipal Research, 1912—; expert on roads. Mem. Nat. Municipal League, Harvard Assn. Engrs. Unitarian. Author: Problems of Road Administration, 1917. Contbr. to tech. press on municipal and state problems relating to engring. Home: Mt. Vernon, N.Y. Died May 16, 1929.

BASSLER, ANTHONY, physician, author; b. N.Y.C., May 24, 1874; s. Louis and Louisa (Black) B.; M.D., Bellevue Hosp. Med. Coll., 1898; m. Harriette Matilda Seeley, July 1917; (died Dec. 14, 1951); children—Joan Mary, Anthony Seeley. Professor gastroenterology, N.Y. Polyclinic Medical School and Hospital, 1911-25, Fordham U., 1915-20; consultant in gastroenterology and internal medicine to 14 New York hosps.; sub chief advisory med. bds. of State of N.Y. Fellow Am. Coll. of Physicians; mem. A.M.A., Acad. of Medicine, Nat. Gastroenterologic Assn., N.Y.C., Internat. gastroenterol. assns., Am. Roentgen Ray Soc., Assn. for Study of Internal Secrettions, Am. Therapeutic Soc. Clubs: Pilgrims Soc., Canadian (N.Y.C.); Westchester Country. Author: Diseases of Stomach and Upper Alimentary Tract, 1907; Diseases of Intestines and Lower Alimentary Tract, 1920; Intestinal Toxemia, Biologically Considered, 1930; also author of over 200 monographs and papers on med. subjects. Home: 121 E. 71st St., N.Y.C.; (summer) Rye, N.Y. Died Aug. 20, 1959; buried Gate of Heaven Cemetery, Valhalla, N.Y.

BASTIN, EDSON SUNDERLAND, mining geologist; b. Chicago, Ill., Dec. 10, 1878; s. Edson Sewell and Christina (Boyd) B.; A.B., U. of Mich., 1902; M.S., Univ. of Chicago, 1903; Ph.D., 1909; Sc.D., hon., U. of Mich., 1941; m. Elinor Norton, June 30, 1910 (dec. Aug. 12, 1949). With U.S. Geol. Survey, in Me. and in western mining dists., 1904-16; examination of copper properties in Chile, 1916-17; mineral statis, and informational work, U.S. Govt., 1917-19; apptd. chief Div. of Mineral Resources, U.S. Geol. Survey, Jan. 1, 1919 (resigned); prof. economic geology, Univ. of Chicago, 1920-44 (retired); also chmn. Dept. of Geology, 1922-44; chmn. Div. of Geology and Geography of Nat. Research Council, 1935-37; mem. Ill. Bd. of Natural Resources and Conservation, 1922-44; cons. geologist. Fellow Geol. Soc. America (v.p. 1935), American Assn. for Advancement of Science (v.p. 1930), Am. Inst. Mining and Metall. Engrs., Soc. Econ. Geologists (pres. 1933); mem. Sigma Nu, Phi Beta Kappa, Sigma Xi. Unitarian. Author of numerous repts. pub. by U.S. Geol. Survey, also articles in geol. and mining jours. Home: 205 Bryant Av., Ithaca, N.Y. Died Oct. 9, 1953.

BATCHELDER, CHARLES FOSTER, naturalist; b. Cambridge, Mass., July 20 1856; s. Francis Lowell and Susan Cabot (Foster) B.; A.B., Harvard, 1878, C.E.,

1882; m. Laura Poor Stone, Feb. 19, 1895. Asso. editor The Auk, 1887-93; editor Proc. N.E. Zoological Club, 1899-1947. Associate Museum of Comparative Zoology; fellow Am. Ornithologists' Union (pres. 1905-08), A.A.A.S., Am. Acad. Arts and Sciences; mem. Boston Soc. Natural History (v.p. 1917-19), Nuttall Ornithol. Club, N.E. Not. Club, Biol. Soc. Washington. Home: Peterborough, N.H. Died Nov. 7, 1954; buried Cambridge, Mass.

BATCHELDER, JOHN PUTNAM, physician; b. Wilton, N.H., Aug. 6, 1784; s. Archelaus and Betty (Putnam) Batchelor; grad. Harvard. Licensed to practice medicine by N.H. Med. Soc.; settled in N.Y.C., lectr. anatomy and surgery, Castleton, Vt., also Berkshire (Mass.) Inst.; considered 1st Am. physician to perform operation to remove head of thigh bone; invented one-handed craniotome (instrument used in opening skull). Died N.Y.C., Apr. 8, 1868.

BATCHELDER, LOREN HARRISON, chemist; b. Montpelier, Vt., May 15, 1846; s. Isaac and Mary (Chase) B.; A.B., Middlebury Coll., Vt., 1874, A.M., 1877; grad. student in chemistry, Harvard, and elsewhere; LL.D., Hamline U., 1906; m. Fanny Gulick, of Elmira, N.Y., Dec. 20, 1882. Teacher chemistry and mathematics, and sr. prof., Centenary Collegiate Inst., Hackettstown, N.J., 1874-81; studied law, admitted to N.J., bar, 1882, Minn. bar, 1883; prof. chemistry, since 1883; acting president, 1888, dean, 1883-1918, and dean emeritus since 1918, Hamline University; professor chemistry Chautauqua (N.Y.) Summer Sch., 1890-01. Traveled in Europe summers, 1901, 03, 09. Methodist. Mem. Am. Chem. Soc., Minn. Ednl. Assn., Delta Upsilon. Author mag. articles on chemistry, published addresses, etc. Address: 877 Snelling Ave., St. Paul, Minn.

BATCHELDER, SAMUEL, mfr., inventor; b. Jaffrey, N.H., June 8, 1784; s. Samuel and Elizabeth (Woodberry) B.; m. Mary Montgomery, 1810, 6 children. Mgr., Hamilton Mfg. Co., Lowell, Mass., 1824-31, pres., 1859-70, treas., 1869-71; mem. 1st Bd. Selectmen, East Chelmsford, Mass., 1825; inventor stop-motion for drawing frame, 1832; perfected dynamometer (force-measurer), 1837; mem. Mass. Legislature, 1847; treas. Everett Mills, 1859-70; pres. Essex Co., 1867-70. Author: Responsibilities of the North in Relation to Slavery, 1856; Early Progress of Cotton Manufacture in United States, 1863, also newspaper articles. Died Cambridge, Mass., Feb. 5, 1879.

BATEMAN, ALAN MARA, geologist; born Kingston, Ontario, Canada, January 6, 1889; son of George Arthur and Elizabeth J. (Mara) Bateman; graduated Kingston Collegiate Institute, 1905; B.S., Queens University, Canada, 1910, D.Sc., 1970; Ph.D., Yale, 1913; m. Grace Hotchkiss Street, June 3, 1916. Asst. geologist German Development Co. Can., 1906-09; asso. geologist Can. Geol. Survey, 1910-12; instr. Yale, 1913; field geologist, Secondary Enrichment Investigation, Harvard U., 1913-15; asst. prof. geology, 1916-21, asso. prof., 1922-25, prof. geology Yale, 1925-41, Silliman prof., 1941, former chmn. department of geology; cons. geologist to Kennecott Copper Corp. from 1916; head of special U.S. mission to Mexico, 1942, dir. Metals and Minerals, Foreign Econ. Adminstrn., Washington, 1942-46; expert cons. S.C.A.P., Tokyo, 1949; cons. Department Interior E.C.A., NSRD, ODM, National Science Foundation; editor in chief Jour. of Econ. Geology; former editor Am. Jour. Science. Trustee Sheffield Scientific Sch. Yale U. Penrose Gold medallist, Soc. Econ. Geologists, 1962. Member American Inst. M.E., Inst. Mining and Metallurgy (pres. 1954), Geol. Soc. America, Soc. Econ. Geologists (pres. 1941-42), Am. Assn. Petroleum Geologists, Washington Acad. Sciences, Am. Academy Arts and Sciences; hon. mem. Chile Soc. Mineralogy and Geology; hon. member Soc. Geologique de Belgique; mem. Sigma Xi, Theta Xi. Republican. Conglist. Clubs: Graduate, New Haven Country, Yale, Lawn (New Haven, Connecticut); Cosmos Club (Washington); Mining, Yale Club (New York City). Author: Economic Mineral Deposits; Formation of Mineral Deposits; also papers on origin of mineral deposits. Home: New Haven CT also Pleasant Valley CT Died May 11, 1971; buried East Lawn Cemetery, East Haven CT

BATEMAN, GEORGE MONROE, retired educator; b. Bloomington, Ida., Sept. 12, 1897; s. Alfred John and Clara (Hess) B.; B.S., Utah State U., 1921; M.S. in Chemistry, Cornell U., 1926, Ph.D., 1927; m. Florence Harris, May 24, 1922; children—Cornella (dec.), Flora Mae, Georgia Rose, Harold Harris. Instr. sci. and math. Grace (Ida.) High Sch., 1921-22; prin. sch., Arimo, Ida., 1922-24; instr. dairy chemistry Cornell U., 1925-27, prof. chemistry, head sci. dept., 1927-51; prof. chemistry Ariz. State Univ., Tempe, 1936-69, emeritus prof., 1969-72, head phys. sci. div., 1951-64. Bishop, Tempe Ward, Church of Jesus Christ of Latter-day Saints, 1944-48. Served as pvt. U.S. Army, 1918; O.R.C., 1932-42; capt., C.W.S., 1941-42. Recipient Silver Beaver award Boy Scouts Am. Fellow A.A.A.S., Am. Inst. Chemists, Ariz. Acad. Sci., Phi Kappa Phi, Sigma Xi. Author scientific articles. Home: Tempe AZ Died Jan. 28, 1972; buried Double Butte Cemetery, Tempe AZ

BATES, CLINTON OWEN, coll. prof.; b. Washington Cl., Ark., June 4, 1858; s. James Francis and Margarette (Crawford) B.; A.B., U. of Ark., 1883; studied U. of Mich., 1885-86; U. of Chicago, summers, 1894, 1895; hon. Ph.D., Coe Coll., 1894; m. Mary Randall, of Cedar Rapids, Ia., June 27, 1893; children—Eleanor Avery, Ruth Crawford. Taught in Male Sem., Tahlequah, Okla., 1883-85; prin. high sch., Owosso, Mich., 1886-89; prof. chemistry, Coe Coll., 1889-1924; city chemist, Cedar Rapids, since 1924. Chemist for water supply of B.,C.R.&N.Ry., 1900-04; chemist for city water supply, Cedar Rapids, 1906-08. Fellow A.A.A.S.; mem. Am. Chem. Soc. (pres. Ia. sect. 1908), Ia. Acad. Science (pres. 1906), Am. Water Works Assn., S.A.R. Republican. Presbyn. Club: Rotary. Home: Cedar Rapids, Ia.

BATES, DAVID STANHOPE, civil engr.; b. Morristown, N.J., June 10, 1777; s. David and Sarah (Tappan) B.; m. Sarah Johnson, 1799; children—John, Timothy, David. Land surveyor, Oneida County, N.Y., 1810-11; mgr. iron factory, Rotterdam, N.Y., 1811-17; asst. engr. on mid-section Erie Canal, 1817-18, division engr., 1818-24; designed and built aqueduct over Genesee River at Rochester, N.Y., 1823; built system of locks at Lockport; cons. engr. for Ohio Canal Commrs., 1824-29, surveyed 800 miles of canal sites; chief engr. Louisville & Portland Canal Co., 1825-28; chief engr. Niagara River Hydraulic Co., 1828-34. Died Rochester, Nov. 28, 1839; buried Rochester.

BATES, FREDERICK (JOHN), phys. chemistry; b. Marysville, Kan., Jan. 2, 1877; s. Charles A. and Harriett (Roberts) B.; B.S., U. Kan., 1900; A.M., U. Neb., 1902; m. Gertrude C. Coyle, Jan. 5, 1905. Chief magneto-optical and carbohydrate sect. Nat. Bureau of Standards, 1903—; chief, optics div., 1941-47; cons. carbohydrate chemistry and optics, 1948; devised methods and prepared Treasury Dept. regulations for weighing, gauging, sampling, calssifying and testing imported sugars; supr. govt. sugar labs. of the Customs Service, Treasury Dept.; pres. Internat. Commn. for Uniform Methods of Sugar Analysis. Developed sensitive strip spectral polarizing system; Bates quartz compensating polariscope with adjustable sensibility; bates cadmium-vapor arc lamp, Bates polariscope tubes, Bates sugar balance, etc.; has pursued investigation of inversion of quartz and of rotary polarization of magnetic elements at high temperatures. Mem. Am. Chem. Soc., Am. Phys. Soc., Washington Philos. Soc., Am. Optical Soc., Internat. Soc. Sugar Cane Technologists, Internat. Union of Pure and Applied Chemistry, Sigma Xi. Republican. Methodist. Clubs: Cosmos, Columbia Country. Contbr. extensive researches in natural and magnetic rotary polarizations of light, and in the transformations in silica, especially anomalous rotary dispersion; co-author of Bur. of Standards of Baume scale. Co-author (circular) Polarimetry, Saccarimetry, and the Sugars. Home: 1649 Harvard St., Washington. Office: Nat. Bur. Standards, Washington 25. Died Nov. 1, 1958; buried Rock Creek Cemetery, Washington.

BATES, JAMES, physician, congressman; b. Greene, Me., Sept. 24, 1789; s. Solomon and Mary (Macomber) B.; ed. Harvard Med. Sch.; m. Mary Jones, July 27, 1815. Served with med. dept. U.S. Army, 1813; mem. U.S. Ho. of Reps. from Me., 22d Congress, 1831-33; supt. Insane Asylum, Augusta, Me., 1845. Died Yarmouth, Me., Feb. 25, 1882; buried Old Oak Cemetery, Norridgewock, Me.

BATES, LINDON, JR., engr.; b. Portland, Ore., July 17, 1883; s. Lindon Wallace (q.v.) and Josephine (White) B.; prep. edn., Harrow Sch., Eng.; Ph.B., Yale, 1902; unmarried. V.p. Bates Engring. Co.; has done engring work on Galveston grade raising and N.Y. Barge Canal; cons. engr. Western Engring. Corp., Denver Mining Investment Co. Am. mgr. Laguintos Oil Co., Maikop Areas, and Trinidad Cedrus Oil Co. Traveled to Russia, 1896; on exploring and hunting expdn. to islands N. of Hudson Bay, 1900; visited Panama, 1904; made midwinter sledge journey in Siberia and Mongolia, 1908; to Venezuela and up the Orinoco in 1911. Mem. N.Y. Assembly 1908, 1909; author of condemnation and civil service reform measures, direct nomination and employers' liability bills; mem. N.Y. County Com., 1908-11; apptd. by Gov. Hughes mem. of Nat. Conservation Congress. Author: The Political Horoscope (with Charles A. Moore, Jr.), 1904; The Loss of Water in New York's Distribution System, 1909; The Russian Road to China, 1910; Path of the Conquistadores, 1912. Home: New York, N.Y. Died May 7, 1915.

BATES, LINDON WALLACE, civil engr.; b. Marshfield, Vt., Nov. 19, 1858; s. William W. and Mary C. B.; ed. Yale; studied engring.; m. Josephine White; father of Lindon B., Jr. Asst. engr. N.P. and Oregon Pacific rys.; contractor engr. or mgr. various ry., dock and terminal contracts in Ore., Wash., Mont., Kan., Mo., Ill., La., Calif., etc., for transcontinental railways of their subsidiary cos., on Chicago Drainage Canal, etc.; built mammoth dredge "Beta," for U.S. Govt., earning bonus of $86,200 on test of capacity; retained 1896-1902 by Belgian Govt. to prepare reports and projects for improvement of port of Antwerp; on Suez Canal on the enlargement, etc., of the canal; by Russian Govt. on the rivers Volga, Dnieper and Bug, Azov Sea ports and channels, Black Sea ports, etc.; by the Queensland Govt. designed 8 harbors and regulation of Brisbane, Mary, Fitzroy, Norman and Albert rivers; built large hydraulic dredge for Russian Govt., earning bonus of $75,000 on capacity test. In collaboration with leading engrs. designated by govts. of Russia, Germany, Austria and Belgium prepared scheme for improvement of port of Shanghai, etc.; contracting engr. Galveston grade raising works; designed the "Three Lake" Panama Canal. Has been dir. various works in Korea, Trinidad and Peru. Grand prix and decoration from French Govt., 1900, for "distinguished services to science." Author: Retrieval at Panama; Colloidal Fuel, etc. Chmn. engring. com. Submarine Defense Assn., 1917. Inventor of colloidal fuel. Home: Mt. Labanin, N.Y. Died Apr. 22, 1924.

BATES, WILLIAM WALLACE, shipbuilder; b. Nova Scotia, Feb. 15, 1827; s. Stephen and Elizabeth (Wallace) B.; ed. common schs., Calais Me., beyond that self-educated; also self-educated in naval architecture; m. Marie Cole, Sept. 11, 1856. Began in shipwright trade, 1839; built 1st clipper shcooner, "Challenge," at Manitowoc, on the Great Lakes, 1851; editor Nautical Magazine and Naval Journal, New York, 1854-58; capt. in Union Army, 1861-63; in shipbuilding and drydock business, Chicago, 1866-81; dry-dock building, Portland, Ore., 1881-83; mgr. Inland Lloyds,Buffalo, 1885-88; U.S. commr. navigation, Washington, 1889-92; retired. Republican. Author: Rules for Shipbuilding, 1876, 1894; American Marine, 1892; American Navigation, 1902. Home: Denver, Colo. Died Nov. 1912.

BATJER, LAWRENCE PAUL, research horticulturist; b. Abilene, Tex., June 6, 1907; s. W.F.D. and Lois (Minter) b.; B.S., Tex. A. and M. Coll., 1928; M.S., Mich. State U., 1930; Ph.D., Cornell U., 1933; m. Irene Danner, July 2, 1936; children—William Dunbar, John Danner. Extension specialist pomology Cornell U., 1933-34; research and extension horticulturist W.Va. U., 1935-36; research plant physiologist Dept. Arg., Beltsville, Md., 1937-44, prin. physiologist regional lab., Wenatchee, Wash., 1945-67. Pres. Western region Am. Soc. Hort. Sci., 1950, nat. pres. elect, 1964; pres. N.W. Assn. Horticulturists, Entomologists and Plant Pathologists, 1961. Mem. Wenatchee Sch. Bd., 1954-67, pres., 1957, 61; chmn. jr. coll. com. Wash. State Sch. Dirs. Assn., 1964-65. Bd. dirs. N. Central Wash. Regional Library, 1948-51, Wenatchee YMCA, 1947-49. Recipient Norman J. Coleman award American Nurserymen's Association, 1966; Superior Service award U.S. Dept. of Agr., 1967. Fellow Am. Assn. Horticulture Scientists; mem. Am. Inst. Biol. Scis., Sigma Xi, Alpha Zeta. Lion (pres. Wenatchee 1949). Home: Wenatchee WA Died May 28, 1967.

BATTEY, ROBERT, surgeon; b. Augusta, Ga., Nov. 26, 1828; s. Cephas and Mary (Magruder) B.; attended Phila. Coll. Pharmacy, 1856; M.D., Jefferson Med. Coll., 1857; m. Martha Smith, Dec. 20, 1849, 14 children including Dr. Henry H. Performed successful operation for vesico-vaginal fistual, 1858; served as surgeon 19th Ga. Volunteers, Confederate Army, Civil War, established hosp., Macon, Ga., 1864; editor Atlanta Med. and Surg. Jour., 1872-76; founder Martha Battey Hosp., Rome Ga.; performed Battey's Operation (removal of normal human ovaries to establish menopause), 1872; prof. obstetrics Atlanta (Ga.) Med. Coll., 1873-75; pres. Ga. Med. Assn., 1876; introduced iodized phenol in gynecol. work, 1877; mem. Atlanta Acad. Medicine, Am. Gynecol. Soc., A.M.A. Died Rome, Ga., Nov. 8, 1895.

BATTLE, HERBERT BEMERTON, chemist; b. Chapel Hill. N.C., May 29, 1862; s. Kemp Plummer and Martha Ann (Battle) B.; brother of Thomas Hall and William James B.; B.Sc., U. of N.C., 1881, Ph.D., 1887; m. Alice M. Wilson, Nov. 25, 1885; children—Nell Lewis, James Wilson. Asst. chemist, N.C. Agrl. Expt. Sta., 1881-87; state chemist and dir. in charge of N.C. Agrl. Expt. Sta., 1887-98; pres. Southern Chem. Co., Winston, N.C., 1897-1901; with Southern Cotton Oil Col, Savannah, Ga., and Montgomery, Ala., 1902-06; pres. The Battle Lab. Corp., 1906—. Chemist N.C. State Bd. Health, 1887-97, N.C. Geol. Survey, 1887-92; prof. chemistry, Leonard Med. Sch., 1886-97. Author: (with F. B. Dancy) Chemical Conversion Tables, 1885; Chemical Conversion Tables (with W. J. Gascoyne), 1909. Home: Montgomery, Ala. Died July 3, 1929.

BAUER, GEORGE NEANDER, educator; b. Jordan, Minn. Jan. 8, 1872; B.S., U. of Minn. 1894; M.S., U. of Ia., 1898; Ph.D. Columbia, 1900; m. Bertha M. Blum, June 18, 1907 (died 1919); 1 dau. Elisabeth B.; m. 2d, Hildred Craig, Dec. 30, 1944. Instructor mathematics, University of Iowa, 1895-98; instr., 1900-02, asst. prof., 1902-07, prof. mathematics, 1907-18. U. of Minn. State chmn. War Savings Soc. for Minn. under the U.S. Treasury Dept. during 1918; asso. dir. War Savings Orgn. of 9th Fed. Reserve Dist., 1919; pres. East Hennepin State Bank, 1920-24; served as v.p. Exchange State Bank, Minneapolis; prof. of mathematics, University of New Hampshire, 1924-42, professor emeritus since 1942. Research worker in agrl. econ., during World War II. Member A.A.A.S., American Assn. Univeristy Profs., Am. Statistical Assn., Society for Quality Control. Author: The Parallax of Mu Cass, and the Positions of Fifty-six Neighboring Stars, 1900;

Plane and Spherical Trigonometry (with William E. Brooke), 1907; Transcendental Curves and Numbers and Algebraic and Transcendental Numbers (with Dr. H. L. Slobin); Mathematics Preparatory to Statistics and Finance, 1929. Home: 574 Circuit Rd., Portsmouth NH

BAUER, JOHANNES HENRIK, research physician; b. Upsala, Sweden, January 26, 1890; s. Gustav Hjalmar and Maria (Taën-Hedenstjerna) B.; student U. Upsala, 1909-10, U. Berlin, 1910-14; M.D., U. Upsala, 1915; m. Maria Louisa Gonzalez Garcia de Zuniga; children—Vivienne, John. Came to U.S., 1931, naturalized, 1937. Worked with A.R.C., Siberia, 1918-20; asso. in bacteriology, Pekin, Union Med. Co., China, 1920-25; mem. West African Yellow Fever Commn., Rockefeller Found., 1926-31; mem. staff div. medicine and pub. health Rockefeller Found. since 1926. Mem. Harvey Soc., Am. Soc. Exptl. Pathology, Am. N.Y. socs. of trop. medicine, Royal Soc. Trop. Medicine and Hygiene, Soc. Exptl. Biology and medicine. Home: Mount Airy, Md. Died Mar. 4, 1961; buried Mount Olive Cemetery.

BAUER, L(OUIS) A(GRICOLA), magnetician; b. Cincinnati, Jan. 26, 1865; s. Ludwig and Wilhemiina (Buehler) B.; brother of William Charles B.; C.E., U. of Cincinnati, 1888, M.S., 1894; Ph.D., A.M., U. of Berlin, 1895; (D.Sc., U. of Cincinnati, 1913, Brown, 1914); m. Adelia Francis Doolittle, Apr. 15, 1891; 1 dau., Mrs. Dorthea Weeks. Astron. amd magnetic computer, U.S. Coast and Geod. Survey, 1887-92; decent in math. physics, U. of Chicago, 1895-96; instr. in geophysics, 1896-97, asst. prof. mathematics and math, physics, 1897-99, U. of Cincinnati; insp. magnetic work and chief Terrestrial Magnetism Div., U.S. Coast and Geod. Survey, 1899-1906; dir. dept. Terrestrial Magnetism. Carnegie Instn., 1904-29, dir. emeritus and research asso., 1930—. Chief Div. of Terrestrial Magnetism, Md. Geological Survey, 1896-99; astronomer and magnetician, western boundary survey of Md.; lecturer in terrestrial magnetism, Johns Hopkins, 1899—; founder, 1896, editor until 1928, co-editor, 1928—, Terrestrial Magnetism and Atmospheric Electricity (mag.). Mem. permanent com. on terrestrial magnetism and atmospheric electricity of Internat. Meteorol. Conf. and of the Internat. Assn. of Academies; fellow A.A.A.S. (v.p. and chmn. Sect. B, 1909), Am. Acad. Arts and Sciences, Am. Geog. Soc. Recieved the Charles Lagrange prize (physique du globe) of Académie Royale des Sciences, des Lettres et des Beaux-Arts de Belgique, 1905, and Georg Neumayer Gold Medal, Berlin, May 1913; Halley lecturer on Terrestrial Magnetism at U. of Oxford, May 1913. Mem. Nat. Research Council, 1917—; chmn. com. navigation and nautical instruments, Council Nat. Defense, 1917-18; U.S. del. Brussels meetings, 1919. Internat. Research Council and Internat. Geodetic and Geophys. Union; U.S. del Rome meetings of latter, 1922, Madrid, 24, Prague, 27; sec. and dir. central bur. sect. terrestrial magnetism and electricity of Internat. Geodetic and Geophys. Union, 1919-27, pres., 1927-30; v. chmn. Am. Geophysical Union, 1920-22 (chmn. sect. terrestrial magnetism and electricity, 1920-22 and 1924-26); chmn. Am. Geophys. Union, 1922-24. Decorated comdr. 2d class Order of St. Olav (Norway). Frequent contbr. to scientific press on terrestrial magnetism, electricity, physics, etc. Died Apr. 12, 1932.

BAUER, LOUIS HOPEWELL, physician; b. Boston, Mass., July 18, 1888; s. Charles Theodore and Ada Marian (Shute) B.; A.B., Harvard, 1909, M.D., cum laude, 1912; honor grad. U.S. Army Med. School, 1914, U.S. Army School of Aviation Medicine, 1920; grad. Army War Coll., 1926; D.Sc., University of Sydney (Australia), 1955; m. Helena Meredith, Dec. 27, 1913; 1 son, Charles Theodore; m. 2d, Margaret Louise Macon, Aug. 9, 1930; 1 step-daughter, Joan Macon (Mrs. William B. Lawrence, Jr.). Intern, Mercy Hosp., Springfield, Mass., 1912-13; entered Med. Corps, U.S. Army, 1913, successively ranked as lt., capt., major, lt. col. (emergency); resigned, 1926; med. dir. aeronautics branch U.S. Dept. of Commerce (now Fed. Aviation Agy.), 1926-30; engaged in pvt. practice, confined to cardiology, Hempstead, N.Y., 1930-53; chmn. bd. dirs. United Med. Service, Inc., 1954-59, now cons. Past mem. N.Y. State Public Health Council. Mem. bd. of visitors Air University, 1957-59. Served as lt. col. and col., Med. Res. Corps, 1927-39; col., U.S. Army, retired. Recipient John Jeffries Award from Inst. Aeronautical Sciences, 1940; Theodore C. Lyster Award, Aero. Mem. Assn. 1947; hon. flight surgeon French Army, 1947; Carlos Finlay award Cuba, 1954: Bancroft medal, Queensland br. Brit. Med. Assn., in Australia, 1955; hon. gold key, Medical Faculty Univ. of Vienna, 1955; Paracelsus medal, German Medical Association, 1960. Diplomate Am. Bd. Internal Medicine, Am. Bd. Preventive Medicine, Am. Bd. Preventive Medicine (Aviation Medicine). Fellow A.C.P., Aero. Med. Assn. (pres. 1929-31); member World (sec. general 1948-61, now consultant), American (trustee 1944-51, chairman 1949-51, president 1952-53) med. assns., Med. Soc. State N.Y. (pres. 1947-48, pres. 2d dist. br. 1939-41), Nassau County Med. Soc. (pres. 1938-39), Am. Heart Assn., Alpha Omega Alpha, Kappa Gamma Chi, Phi Beta Kappa (hon. Harvard); hon. mem. Cuban, Burma med. assns. Mason. Club: Harvard (N.Y.C., Boston). Editor in chief Journal of Aviation Medicine (bi-monthly), 1930 1930-54, now editor-in-chief emeritus. Author: Aviation Medicine (textbook), 1926; Private Enterprise or Government in Medicine, 1947. Contributor chapter Medicine and Aeronautics in Tice's Practice of Medicine, 1942, Aviation Medicine chpt. in Cyclopedia of Medicine, Surgery and the Specialties, 1942, Aviation Medicine chpt. in Oxford Loose Leaf Medicine, 1943 (also pub. as monograph). Contbr. numerous articles on aviation medicine and cardiology to med. jours; The First Decade Report on the World Medical Association, 1958. Home: 341 Harvard Av., Rockville Centre, N.Y. Office: 10 Columbus Circle, N.Y.C., 10019. Died Feb. 3, 1964; buried Arlington, Va.

BAUER, WALTER, physician; b. Crystal Falls, Mich., June 7, 1898; s. John and Caroline (Schmid) B.; B.S., U. of Mich., 1920, M.D., 1922; M.A., honoris causa, Harvard, 1942; m. margaret Zeller, Sept. 12, 1931; childre—Walter Dale, Gretchen, Nancy Wallace. Interne, L.I. Coll. Hosp., Brooklyn, N.Y., 1922-23, asst. resident in medicine, 1923-24; resident physician, 1932-37, physician, 1937-51, chief med. service since 1951; instr. medicine Harvard Med. Sch., 1928-29, faculty instr. and tutor in medicine, 1929-32, asst. prof., 1932-36, asso. prof., 1936-51, Jackson prof. clin. medicine since 1951. Cons. physician Mass. Eye and Ear Infirmary cons. in med. research, Robert B. Brigham Hosp.; cons. Beth Israel, Lemuel Shattuck hosps. Director Robert W. Lovett Memorial Foundation for Study of Crippling Diseases, 1929-58. Chmn. sci. adv. com., v.p. bd. trustees Helen Hay Whitney Foundation. NRC fellowship in England (with Sir Henry H. Dale), 1927-28. Certified by Am. Bd. of Internal Medicine, 1937. Col., U.S. Army Med. Corps, med. consultant and dir. med. activities, 8th Service Comd., 1942-45. Fellow N.Y. Acad. Med. Royal Society of Medicine. (London, honorary); mem. A.M.A., Assn. of American Physicians (president 1959), Association Profs. Medicine, Royal Society of Medicine, American Coll. Physicians, Am. Soc. Clin. Investigation, Am. Rheumatism Assn., Am. Physiol. Soc., Assn. for Study of Internal Secretions, Mass. Med. Soc., Boston Soc. of Biologists, Am. Acad. Arts and Sics., A.A.A.S., Soc. of U.S. Med. Consultants in World War II; bd. dirs. Arthritis and Rheumatism Found.; hon. mem. Swedish Med. Soc., Pan Am. Med. Assn., Danish Soc. Medicine; Liga Argentina contra el reumatismo. Clubs: Harvard of Boston, Interurban, Peripatetic, Boston Orthopedic. Home: 10 Emerson Pl., Boston 02114. Office: Mass. General Hospital. Boston 02114. Died Dec. 2, 1963; buried Still River, Mass.

BAUER, WILLIAM CHARLES, elec. engr.; b. Cincinnati, Dec. 26, 1873; s. Ludwig and Wilhelmina (Buehler) B.; B.S. (in elec. engring.), U. of Cincinnati, 1896, post-grad. course and instr. civ. engring., 1896-97, student U. of Chicago, 1905; Sc.D., Baker U., Baldwin, Kan., 1908; m. Alice Jeannette Strahley, Aug. 24, 1896;children—Mary Virginia, William Malcolm. Prof. physics and chemistry, Baker U., 1897-1908; prof. physics and elec. engring., U. of Denver, 1908-09; prof. elec. engring., Northwestern U., 1909-39, acting dir. Coll. of Engring. many years, dean School of Engineering, 1927-38, retired, 1939; cons. engr., Northwestern U. in connection with a large group of buildings, 1925-33. Magnetic observer and dir. Baldwin Magnetic Obs., U.S. Coast and Geod. Survey, 1900-02; magnetic observer in Can. of eclipse for same, 1905; consulting elec. engr. since 1903; designed and built also supt. Baldwin (Kan.) Municipal Light Plant, 1906-08. Mem. Sigma Xi (pres. Northwestern Chapter, 1918-19); life mem. Tau Beta Pi. Home: 725 Milburn St., Evanston, Ill.; also 917 Alberca St., Coral Gables 34 FL

BAUER, WILLIAM HANS, pathologist; b. Prague, Austria, s. Aloysius Bauer; M.D., St. Charles U. Prague, 1912; Research fellow histology, med. sch., U. Insbruck, Austria, 1912-14; m. Mary Elizabeth Bauer, Nov. 4, 1913; children—John D. (M.D.), Inge Hynes, Annliese Lamb. Asst. Med. Sch. U. Insbruck, 1912-14, 1918-24, private dozent, 1925-38, associate prof., 1931-34, prof. and dir., 1934-38; prof. and dir. pathology, sch. dentistry, St. Louis U., 1938—, affiliated with dept. pathology, med. schs., St. Louis U., also Marquette U.; coordinator Cancer Control Program (sch. dentistry). Served in M.C., Austrian Army, 1914-18. Asso. A.M.A.; mem. Am. Assn. Pathologist and Bacteriologist, Internat. Dental Research Assn., A.A.A.S., St. Louis Soc. Pathology, Sigma Xi. Collaborator of Pathology by W.A. D. Anderson, 1948. Home: 3117 Russell St Office: 3556 Caroline St. St. Louis 4. Died June 14, 1956; buried Calvary Cemetery, St. Louis.

BAUM, FRANK GEORGE, electrical engr; b. Ste. Genevieve, Mo., July 18, 1870; s. Christian and Caroline (Kline) B.; A.B., Stanford U., Calif., 1898, E.E., 1899; m. Mary Dawson, July 18, 1900; children—Esther F., Helen E., Adah C. Elec. engr. Calif. Gas & Elec. Corp., 1902-07; consulting constrn. engr., 1907—; chief engr. hydro-electric work, Pacific Gas & Electric Co., 1912—. Author: Alternating Currents, 1902; Alternating Current Transformer, 1903; Atlas of U.S.A. Electric Power Industry, 1923. Inventor of constant potential electric transmission system. Home: Cassel via Redding, Calif. Died 1932.

BAUMGARDT, B.R., scientist; b. Liverpool, England, May 19, 1862; s. Theodore and Mary (Lathangue) B.; ed. Strengnäs, Sweden; grad. Strengnäs Coll., Sweden, spl. studies in astronomy and mathematics; m. Mary Louise Steinhauer, July 20, 1885; children—Mars Frederick, Howard Oscar. Sec. Ore. Acad. Sciences, 1892; pres. and for 10 yrs. chmn. astron. and math. sect. Southern Calif. Acad. Sciences; staff lecturer The Brooklyn Inst. Arts and Sciences, The Am. Inst. (New York), League for Polit. Edn. (New York), Am. Univ. Extension (Phila.), Nat. Geog. Society (Washington, D.C.) Goodwyn Inst. (Memphis), Acad. Science and Art (Pittsburgh), Phila. Forum; hon. mem. Am. Inst. (New York). Has pvt. astron. obs. with 4 1/2-inch refracting telescope. Mason. Author: Tidal Evolution; The Symbolism of the Universe. Contbr. to scientific publs. and daily press. Died June 19, 1935.

BAUSCH, WILLIAM, vice-pres. Bausch & Lomb Optical Co.; b. Rochester, N.Y., Mar. 25, 1861; s. John Jacob and Barbara (Zimmerman) B.; student Rochester pub. schs., Collegiate Inst., Rochester, and Hale's Prep. Sch.; m. Kate Zimmer, Oct. 1, 1891. Began in Father's Factory, 1875, and became interested in mfr. of eye-glasses; sec. Bausch & Lomb Optical Co., 1909-35, vi.p. since 1935; trustee East Side Savings Bank, Rochester. Pres. and trustee Rochester Dental Dispensary. Republican. Clubs: Rochester, Genesee Valley, Oak Hill Country, Country (Rochester). Home: 1063 St. Paul St. Office: 635 St. Paul St., Rochester, N.Y. Died Oct. 19, 1944. *

BAXLEY, HENRY WILLIS, surgeon; b. Balt., June 1803; s. George and Mary (Merryman) B.; attended St. Mary's Coll.; grad. U. Md., 1824. Attending physician Balt. Gen. Dispensary, 1826-29; physician Md. Penitentiary, 1831-32; co-founder Coll. Dental Surgery, Balt. (1st instn. of kind in U.S.), 1839, prof. anatomy, 1839-46; prof. surgery Washington Med. Coll., Balt., 1846-47; physician Balt. Alms House, 1849-50; prof. anatomy and surgery Med. Coll. of Ohio, Cincinnati, 1805-54; insp. hosps. U.S. Govt., 1865; Baxley Med. Professorship of Johns Hopkins Med. Sch. named after him. Author: Spain, Art Remains and Art Realities, Painters, Priests and Princes, 1875. Died Mar. 13, 1876.

BAXTER, DOW VAWTER, educator, forest pathologist; b. Hillsboro, Ill., Jan. 16, 1898; s. Charles C. and Emma C. (Vawter) B.; B.S.F., U. of Mich., 1921, M.S., 1922; Ph.D. (Univ. fellow, 1923-24), 1924; unmarried. Asst. in botany, U. of Mich., 1919-21; instr. botany, U. of Wis., 1924-26; asst. prof. forest pathology and silvics, sch. of forestry and conservation, U. of Mich., 1926-31, asso. prof., 1931-46, prof. since 1946; dir. U. Mich., forest pathology expdn., Alaska, 1952-60; mem. exec. bd. Horace H. Rackham Sch. of Grad. Studies, 1937-41; prof. botany since 1948; Charles Darwin lectr., Mich. State Coll., 1934; research associate University Cal., 1958. National Research Council fellow, Alaska, 1933. Sweden, 1934, Coll. U.S. Div. Forest Pathology since 1926; summer positions; mem. office blister rust control, U.S.D.A., 1919, 21, 23; field asst. office pathology, 1918, 19, asst. 1924-25; mem. of the expedition, Alaska, 1932, 33, 35-42, 45, 48-49, 51-53, 55-56; director expedition, Quebec and New Brunswick, Can., 1942, Alaska and the Yukon territory, 1958, 60, 61, 62, 63, 64; expdn. Newfoundland, 1946, Labrador, 1947, Icelan,d 1950, 54; spl. investigations Puerto Rico, 1944. Pres. forestry sect. VII, Internat. Bot. Congress, Stockholm, 1950, honorary president, VIII Congress, Paris, 1954; vice chairman of Forest Bot. IX International Botany Congress, Montreal, 1959. Member of the Society American Foresters Am. Forestry Assn., Mycol. Soc. Am., Am. Phytopathol. Soc., Soc. Foresters of Gr. Brit., Mich. Acad. Sci., Arts and Letters, Wash. Acad. of Sciences, New York Academy of Science, Xi Sigma Pi, Sigma Xi, Phi Sigma, Alpha Kappa Lambda, Gamma Alpha. Clubs: Senior Research (U. of Mich.); Explorers (New York). Author: On and Off Alaskan Trails; Pathology in Forest Practice; Fungus Development from Field to Forest in Spruce Plantings, 1904-64; The Chilkoot Pass, Then and Now. Contbr. to Ency. Brit.; also sect. Handbook Nat. Acad. Scis. Office: School of Natural Resources, U. Mich., Ann Arbor, Mich. Died Dec. 1966.

BAXTER, GEORGE EDWIN, physician; b. Griggsville, Ill., Oct. 27, 1874; s. Edwin Walter and Helen Maria (Harvey) B.; Ph.B., Ill. Coll., Jacksonville, 1896, A.M., 1924; M.D., Northwestern U., 1899; postgrad., Vienna, 1909; m. Maude Hitchcock, June 7, 1905. Interne, St. Luke's Hosp., Chgo., 1899-1901; practice in Chgo., 1901-36; instr. haemotology and pathology Northwestern U., 1903-05, instr. medicine, 1905-09; instr. grad. pediatrics, U. Chgo., at Children's Meml. Hosp. and asso. attending physician, 1910-36; cons. pediatrician Grant Hosp., 1930-35; attending pediatrician Ravenswood Hosp., 1907-36. Trustee Ill. Coll., Jacksonville, since 1924 (chmn. bd. 1932-36); trustee Chgo., Med. Soc., 1926-36; 1st sec., pres. North Shore br. Chgo. Med. Soc.; sec. and pres. former Physicians' Club, Chgo. Fellow A.C.P. (life mem.); mem. A.M.A., Ill. Med. Soc., Chgo. Pediatric Soc., Am. Acad. Pediatrics, Chgo. Inst. Medicine (bd. govs. 1927-30), Soc. Colonial Wars, S.R., Nu Sigma Nu, Phi Beta Kappa. Clubs: University (Chgo.); University (Claremont, Cal.). Address: Baxter Ranch, Glendora. Died July 22, 1966; buried Oakdale Meml. Cemetery, Glendora.

BAXTER, GREGORY PAUL, chemist; b. Somerville, Mass., Mar. 3, 1876; s. George Lewis and Ida Florence (Paul) B.; A.B., Harvard, 1896, A.M., 1897, Ph.D., 1899; hon. Sc.D. from U. of Mich., 1929; m. Amy Bailey Sylvester, June 2, 1906; 1 dau., Elizabeth Paul Boardman. Asst. chemistry, 1895-97, instr. 1897-99, Harvard; instr. chem., Haverford College, Pa., 1899-1900; asst. prof. chemistry, Swarthmore, 1900-02; instr. in chemistry, Harvard, 1902-05, asst. prof. 1905-15, prof. 1915-25, Theodore William Richards prof., 1925-44, Theodore William Richards prof. emeritus, 1944. Chmn. Internat. Com. on Atomic Weights, 1930-47. Rep. Unitarian. Theodore W. Richards medalist, 1934. Fellow Am. Acad. Arts and Scis.; mem. Nat. Acad. Sciences, Am. Chem. Soc., Phi Beta Kappa, Sigma Xi. Club: Harvard (Boston). Author: Researches upon the Atomic Weights, 1910, also papers in chemical periodicals. Home: 59 Francis Av., Cambridge MA

BAYLES, JAMES COPPER, engineer; b. New York, July 3, 1845; s. James and Julia Halsey (Day) B.; tech. edn. (M.E., Ph.D.) Lt. U.S. Arty., 1862-64; editor New York Citizen, 1865-67, Commercial Bulletin, 1868-69, Iron Age, 1870-89, Metal Worker, 1874. Has made a close study and much original research in electro-metallurgy, microscopic analysis of metals, sanitation and mech. hygiene, and has written much. Pres. health dept., N.Y., 1888. Address: Nat. Arts Club, 15 Gramercy Park, New York.

BAYLEY, RICHARD, physician; b. Fairfield, Conn., 1745; studied medicine under John Charlton, N.Y.C.; studied anatomy under William Hunter, London, Eng., 1769-71; m. Miss Charlton. Went to London, 1769-71; during croup epidemic made study of disease's causes and treatment which cut mortality rate in half, 1774; in England, 1775-76; surgeon Brit. Army under Gen. Howe, Newport, R.I., 1776-77; practiced medicine, N.Y.C., 1777; prof. anatomy and surgery Columbia, 1792; 1st physician in Am. to amputate arm at shoulder-joint; health physician Port of N.Y., 1795. Author: An Account of the Epidemic Fever which Prevailed in the City of New York during Part of the Summer and Fall of 1795, published 1796; Letters from the Health Office. Submitted to the New York Common Council. Died Aug. 17, 1801.

BAYLEY, WILLIAM SHIRLEY, geologist; b. Balt., Nov. 10, 1861; s. Robert P. and Emma (Downing) B.; A.B., Johns Hopkins, 1883, fellow, 1885-86, Ph.D., 1886; m. Lucie Jacobs, Mar. 11, 1894; 1 dau., Emily Elizabeth (Mrs. J. Howard Gillen). Prof. geology Colby Coll., 1888-1904; asst. prof. geology U. Ill., 1907-09, asso. prof. mineralogy and economic geology, 1909-13, prof. geology, 1913-31, head dept., 1928-31, retired, 1932. Asst. geologist U.S. Geol. Survey, 1887-1908, geologist, 1909-1931; asso. editor Am. Naturalist, 1886-1902; reviewer Neues Jahrbuch fur Mineralogie, Berlin, 1890-1908; bus. editor Economic Geology, 1905-43. Fellow A.A.A.S., Geol. Soc. Am. (1st v.p., 1929), Geol. Soc. Washington, Chemische Gesellschaft; mem. Soc. Econ. Geologists, Mineral Soc. America (pres. 1936). Ill. Acad. Sciences (pres. 1922-23), S.A.R., Phi Beta Kappa, Sigma Xi, Beta Theta Pi. Author: Elementary Crystallography, 1910; Minerals and Rocks, 1915; Descriptive Mineralogy, 1916; Guide to Non-Metallic Mineral Products, 1930; others. Home: Glen Rock, N.J. Died Feb. 13, 1943; buried Urbana, Ill.

BAYLIS, ROBERT NELSON, engineer; b. Englewood. N.J., Mar. 16, 1867; s. Robert and Martha N. (Smith) B.; M.E., Stevens Inst. Tech., 1887; m. Lilian Burt, Aug. 4, 1913. Draftsman, engr., chief engr. and factory mgr. C. & C. Electric Motor Co., New York, 1890-93; chief elec. engr. Walker Co., at Cleveland, O., 1893-97; pres. Baylis Co., engrs. and mfrs., Bloomfield, N.J., 1897. Pres. common council, Englewood, N.J., 1906-09. Mem. Am. Soc. Mech. Engrs., Am. Inst. Elec. Engrs., Nat. Geographic Soc., Delta Tau Delta. Home: Caldwell, N.J. Office: Bloomfield, N.J. Died Sept. 5, 1942.

BAYLISS, MAJOR WILLIAM, architect; b. Pictou, N.S., Nov. 8, 1848; s. John and Lillia (McKenzie) B.; pub. sch. edn., Pictou; studied architectural drawing at night schs.; m. Marion Francis, d. William A. Ray, Dec. 18, 1872. Became supt. hosp. constrn., office of surg. gen. U.S. Army, 1882. Invented combination steam and hot water heating system, 1893. Sovereign Grand Comdr., Supreme Council of Sovereign Grand Inspectors-Gen. Mason. Home: Washington, D.C. Died 1919.

BAYLOR, JAMES BOWEN, geodesist; b. Mirador, Albemarle Co., Va., ,ay 30, 1849; s. Dr. John Roy and Anne (Bowen) B.; hon. grad. Va. Mil. Inst., 1865; B.S., C.E., U. of Va., 1872; (LL.D., Baylor U., 1903); m. Ellen C. Bruce, Jan. 5, 1881 (dec.). Apptd. aid in U.S. Coast and Geod. Survey, 1874, after competitive exam; made magnetic survey of N.C.; field officer U.S. Coast and Geod. Survey, 1874—. Has determined the elements of earth's magnetism from Can. to Mex. in almost every state, and has done geod., astron. and hydrographic work for survey in various sections of U.S.; oyster surveys in La.; "Baylor survey" of oyster grounds of Va., 1899-94; commr. Supreme Ct. of U.S. for boundary of Va. and Tenn., 1900-02. Served with corps of cadets, Va. Mil. Inst., in Civil War, 1864-65. Boundary engr. for Va. (Va. and Md.); engr. on Pa.-N.Y. boundary and on U.S. and Can. Boundary Survey. Contbr. various reports of U.S. Coast and Geod. Survey. Home: Newmarket, Milford P.O., Va. Died May 1924.

BAYMA, JOSEPH, clergyman, mathematician; b. Cirie, France, Nov. 9, 1816; attended Royal Acad., Turin, France. Entered Jesuit novitiate, Chieti, France, 1832, ordained Jesuit priest, 1847; missionary to Algiers, 1847; asst. to astronomer Angelo Secchi and later dir. Osservatorio del Collegio Romano, Rome, Italy; rector Episcopal Sem., Bertinoro, Italy, 1852-58; prof. philosophy Stonyhurst Coll., Eng., 1858-69; pres. St. Ignatius Coll., San Francisco, 1869-72, prof. higher mathematics, 1872-80; retired to Santa Clara (Cal.) Coll. because of ill health, 1880. Author: (with Enrico Vasco) Il Ratio Studiorum adattato ai tempi presnti; De studio religiosae perfectionis excitando, 1852; Philosophia Realis, 1861; Elements of Molecular Mechanics, 1866. Died Santa Clara Coll., Feb. 7, 1892.

BAYNE-JONES, STANHOPE, bacteriologist; b. New Orleans, La., Nov. 6, 1888; s. Stanhope and Minna (Bayne) B.; A.B., Yale, 1910; M.D., Johns Hopkins, 1914, M.A., 1917, Sc.D., U. Rochester, 1943, Emory University, 1954; LL.D., Tulane University, 1956; married Nannie Moore Smith, June 25, 1921. Interne, Johns Hopkins Hosp., 1914-15; Rockefeller fellow in pathology, 1915-16, asso. prof. bacteriology, same, 1922-23; prof. bacteriology Sch. of Medicine, U. of Rochester, 1923-32; dir. Rochester Health Bur. Labs., 1926-32; prof. bacteriology, Yale Sch. of Medicine, 1932-47, and dean of the School of Medicine, 1935-40; also master of Trumbull Coll. (Yale), 1932-38. Served as capt. and maj., M.C., with British and Am. armies in France, Italy and Germany, 1917-19; sanitary insp. 3d Army, in Germany, 1919; brigadier gen. medical corps, U.S. Army, dept. chief preventive med. service, Office of the Surgeon Gen., 1942-46; adminstr. Army Epidermiological Board. Director, United States of America Typhus Commn., 1944-46; chmn. div. med. scis. National Research Council, 1932-33. Director Board of Scientific Advisers, Jane Coffin Childs Memorial Fund for Med. Research, 1937-47; scientific dir. Internat. Health Div., Rockefeller Foundation, 1939-41; director Josiah Macy, Jr. Foundation, 1939-41 and from 1948; president Joint Administration Board of New York Hospital-Cornell Medical Center, 1947-53; tech. dir. research Army Med. Research and Development Program, 1952-56; mem. Army Sci. Adv. Com., from 1954; chmn. sec.'s cons. on med. research and edn. U.S. Dept. Health, Edn. and Welfare, 1957-58; mem. Surgeon gen.'s com. on smoking and health USPHS from 1962. Mem. N.Y.C. Bd. Hosps., 1950-52, Nat. Manpower Council, 1951, Commn. on Financing Hosp. Care, 1951, Hosp. Council of Greater N.Y., 1948-51; mem. Yale Corp., 1956-57. Mem. A.A.A.S., A.M.A. (council on pharmacy and chemistry, 1930-34), Society Am. Bacteriologists (president 1929-30), Am. Assn. Immunologists (pres. 1930-31), Soc. Exptl. Biology and Medicine, Assn. Am. Physicians, Am. Assn. Pathologists and Bacteriologists (pres. 1940-41), Am. Pub. Health Assn., Am. Soc. Tropical Medicine, Assn. of Am. Med. Coll. (exec. council 1938-40), Am. Soc. for Control of Cancer (exec. com. 1938-1940), Am. Assn. for Cancer Research, Leonard Wood Memorial (med. advisory board 1937-41), Nat. Bd. Med. Examiner (1936-41), Zeta Psi, Nu Sigma Nu (hon. council), Phi Beta Kappa, Alpha Omega Alpha. Decorated Mil. Cross, Croix de Guerre, Distinguished Service Medal, U.S. of America Typhus Commn. Medal, Army Commendation Ribbon, Silver Star (with 2 oak leaf clusters), Order of British Empire (hon. comdr.). Episcopalian. Clubs: University, Metropolitan, Army and Navy, Cosmos. Contbr. on pathology and bacteriology. Home: Washington DC Died Feb. 20, 1970; buried Arlington Nat. Cemetery, Arlington VA

BAYNES, JOHN, inventor; b. Westmoreland, England, Aug. 24, 1842; s. Oswald and Agnes B.; took 5 yrs.' course at Ackworth (Soc. of Friends' Coll., England); m. Helen A. Norwill, Apr. 24, 1867; mem. Bengal Chamber of Commerce, 1864; engaged in gen. foreign shipping business until 1875. Came to U.S., 1875; invented celluloid photographic films, 1884; gold etching photo process, 1885, and numerous inventions in arts, including photographic modeling; photographically modeled records of sound vibrations. Invented process for producing musical and other sounds from graphic designs; mem. Asiatic Soc. Wrote Chronicles of Westchester Creek, Universal Review, London 1891. Home: Stamford, Conn. Died 1903.

BAYNHAM, WILLIAM, surgeon; b. probably S.C., Dec. 7, 1749; s. John Baynham; studied surgery under Dr. Walker, probably S.C., 1764-69, St. Thomas Hosp., London, Eng., 1769-72. Prepared anatomical demonstrations and instructed in dissection for med. students at Cambridge (Eng.) U., 1772-81; practiced surgery, London, 1781-85; returned to U.S., 1785; practiced medicine specializing in surgery, Essex, Va.; 1785-1814; gained reputation as surgeon in operations for stone, cataracts and extra-uterine pregnancy; descriptions of some of his operations in Vol. I of New York Med. and Surg. Jour. Died Essex, Dec. 8, 1814.

BEACH, ALFRED ELY, publisher, inventor; b. Springfield, Mass., Sept. 1, 1826; s. Moses Yale and Nancy (Day) B.; m. Harriet Eliza Holbrook, June 30, 1847. Founder (with Orson D. Munn) firm Munn & Co., publishers, 1846; editor Scientific Ameria; patentee typewriter, 1847, typewriter for blind, 1857, cable railways and tunneling shield, 1864; inventor pneumatic carrier system now used in mail tubes; recipient Gold medal for work on typewriter from Am. Inst., 1856. Died N.Y.C., Jan. 1, 1896.

BEACH, MOSES SPERRY, publisher, inventor; b. Springfield, Mass., Oct. 5, 1822; s. Moses Yale and Nancy (Day) B.; m. Chloe Buckingham, 1845. Apprentice printer on N.Y. Sun, 1834, circa 1840; co-owner Boston Daily Times, 1845; operated N.Y. Sun (with brother and father), 1845-52, sole owner, 1852-60, 62-68 (newspaper controlled by syndicate interested in religious affairs, 1860-62), designed Sun around tastes of working men, reprinting popular fiction liberally in its columns, expounded Democratic editorial policy, supported Buchanan and Douglas during 1850's; devised new method for feeding paper to presses and pioneered printing both sides of sheet at once; retired to estate in Peekskill, N.Y., following sale of Sun to group represented by Charles A. Dana, 1868; travelled widely abroad. Died Peekskill, July 25, 1892; buried Peekskill.

BEACH, MOSES YALE, publisher, inventor; b. Wallingford, Conn., Jan. 15, 1800; s. Moses Sperry and Lucretia (Stanley) B.; m. Nancy Day, Nov. 19, 1819; children—Moses Sperry, Alfred Ely; Apprentice cabinet maker, Hartford, Conn., 1814-18; developed engine using power of gunpowder explosions, 1819; partner in cabinet mfg. bus., 1819-circa 1828; invented rag cutting machine, circa 1826; part owner N.Y. Sun (a leading "penny paper" in N.Y.C.), 1834-38, owner, publisher, 1838-48, increased circulation to 38,000 in 1843 by such devices as "Balloon Hoax" (1844), quick reporting of news through such methods as ship news service, spl. trains and horse expresses; established N.Y. Asso. Press (with other N.Y.C. newspaper publishers) to gather news in all major cities in nation during Mexican War; apptd. by Pres. Polk as spl. emissary to Mexico, 1846; 1st publisher to use syndicated newspaper articles (1841), to publish fgn. edition (1848); publisher Weekly Sun (for farmers), Illustrated Sun and Monthly Literary Journal; lived in retirement, Wallingford, 1848-68. Died Wallingford, July 19, 1868; buried Wallingford.

BEACH, SPENCER AMBROSE, horticulturist; b. Sumner Hill, Cayuga Co., N.Y., 1860; s. Isaac Ambrose (M.D.) and Maria North (Wood) B.; B.S., Agr., Ia. State Coll., 1887, M.S., 1892; m. Norma Hainer, July 2, 1890. Prof. horticulture and botany, Tex. A. and M. Coll., 1890-91; horticulturist State Expt. Sta., Geneva, N.Y., 1891-1905; prof. horticulture, Sept. 1905—, vice-dean Coll. of Agr., 1906—, Ia. State Coll. Republican. Author: The Apples of New York (2 vols.), 1905. Home: Ames, Ia. Died Nov. 2, 1923.

BEACH, S(YLVESTER) JUDD, ophthalmologist; b. Dedham, Mass., Apr. 7, 1879; s. Seth Curtis and Frances Hall (Judd) B.; grad. Phillips Exeter Acad., 1897; A.B., Harvard Coll. 1901, M.D., Harvard U., 1905; m. Louise Harris, Oct. 7, 1909; children—Margaret Judd, Howell Williams (dec.), Edmund Beach. Surgical house officer, Boston City Hosp., 1904-06; house physician, Boston Lying-In Hosp., 1906, (acting) Mass. Eye and Ear Infirmary, 1907; practiced in Augusta, Me., Special practice, 1909; mem. staff Augusta Gen. Hosp., Gardner Gen. Hosp.; special practice, Portland, since 1920; consulting ophthalmic surgeon Me. Eye and Ear Infirmary (pres. staff 1946-48); mem. staff local hosps.; guest lecturer graduate courses George Washington, Florida, Virginia and Rochester univs.; mem. council State Dept. of Health, 1916-24. Oculist Medical Advisory Board, World War, 1916-18. Ex-pres. Wayneflete Sch.; sec. Am. Bd. Ophthalmology, vice president Foundation for Vision; member of executive committee, Ophthalmological Study Council. Fellow Am. Coll. Surgeons, Am. Med. Assn. (past chmn. Ophthalmology sect.); mem. Am. Ophthalmol. Soc. (member council, pres. 1944), Am. Acad. Ophthalmology and Otolaryngology (mem. council 1930-35), Soc. for Research in Ophthalmology (mem. commn.), Sigma Alpha Epsilon. Unitarian. Mason. Clubs: Cumberland, Aesculapian (Boston); Portland Rotary (pres. 1932), Fraternity (Portland); Torch of Western Maine (past pres.). Mem. editorial bd., Quarterly Review of Ophthalmology. Lecturer on Refraction. Author: Textbook of Refraction; The Eye and its Diseases (co-author). Home: Cragmoor, Cape Elizabeth, South Portland 7. Office: 704 Congress St., Portland, Me. Died Feb. 10, 1953; buried Augusta, Me.

BEACH, WILLIAM MULHOLLAND, surgeon; b. Stoneboro, Pa., Sept. 15, 1859; s. Oliver and Ann Elizabeth (Mulholland) B,; A.B., Waynesburg (Pa.) Coll., 1882, A.M., 1885; M.D., Jefferson Med. Coll., 1889; m. Lucy Lazear Miller, 1882. Prof. Latin and Greek, Ozark (Mo.) Coll., 1882-85; pres. Odessa (Mo.) Coll., 1885-87; an organizer and surgeon Presbyn. Hosp., Pittsburgh, 1895-1914; proctologist South Side Hosp., 1906-11. Examining surgeon for pensions, 1893-97; 1st lt. Med. Corps, N.G. Pa., 1894-97. Mem. bd. trustees Waynesburg College. Dem. Presbyn. Mason. Contbr. 2 chapters in Cook's Diseases of the Rectum and Colon. Inventor of proctoscope and colostomy supporter. Home: Pittsburgh, Pa. Died 1930.

BEACHLEY, RALPH GREGORY, educator; b. Hagerstown, Md., Aug. 12, 1895; s. Harry K. and Alice (Taylor) B.; grad. Mercersburg Acad., 1914; student Johns Hopkins, 1914-16; M.D., George Washington U., 1920; Dr. P.H. U. Ga., 1926; m. Carolyn Bates, Apr. 2, 1921; 1 dau., Eleanor Louise (Mrs. Roy Collins). Resident intern Children's and Emergency hosps., 1918-20; acting asst. surgeon USPHS, 1921; asst. dir., health officer Washington Co. Health Demonstration, 1922-23; dir. health dept. Dillon Co., 1923-25, Spartanburg Co., 1925-26; dep. state health officer Md. Health Dept., 1926-36; dir. student health service, instr. pub. health, hygiene Washington Coll., 1928-36; instr. pub. health nurses tng. sch. Southwest Hosp., Abingdon, Va., 1936-38; dir. dept. rural health Va. Health Dept., 1936-38; dir. pub. health and welfare Arlington Co., Va., from 1938; adj. prof. pub. health practice George Washington U., from 1938; asst. prof. pub. health and preventive medicine Med. Coll. Va., from 1938; guest lect., sch. pub. health Yale, 1953. Vice chmn. Council Social Agencies, Arlington Co., from 1939; chief med. officer Civil Def., No. Va. Orgn., 1950; dep. chief med. officer Civil Def., D.C., 1950. Served with U.S. Army, 1918. Diplomate Am. Bd. Preventive Medicine and Pub. Health, American Academy of Pediatrics. Fellow of the American Public Health Assn., Royal Soc. Health Eng.; mem. Am. Assn. Pub. Health Physicians, A.M.A., So. Med. Assn., Med. Soc. Va., Royal Soc. Med. Officers of Health Eng., Md. Hist. Assn. S.A.R., Am. Legion, (past comdr. 1924-25), Nat. Geog. Soc., Am. Sch. Health Assn., Arlington County Med. Soc., Met. Health Officers Assn. Washington (sec. treas. 1939, 1939-57, pres, 1957,), Washington Acad. Medicine (dir.), Alpha Omega Alpha, Phi Chi, Phi Sigma Kappa, Lambda Chi Alpha. Episcopalian. Clubs: Rotary, Cosmos (Washington). Editor of various publications on public health. Assistant editor Journal S.C. Medical Society, 1923-26. Home: Arlington VA Died Jan. 25, 1969; buried Columbia Gardens Cemetery, Arlington VA

BEADLE, CHAUNCEY DELOS, botanist; b. St. Catharines, Ont., Can., Aug. 5, 1866; s. Delos White and Harriet Converse (Steele) B.; student Ont. Agrl. Coll., 1884, Cornell U., 1885-86, 1889; m. Margaretta A. Wetzel, Nov. 11, 1891 (died May 11, 1924); m. 2d, Annie Louise (Paget) Rudolph, Mar. 3, 1928 (died June 1, 1941). Dir. Biltmore Herbarium, 1890-1916; supt. landscape dept. Biltmore Estate; sec.-treas. The Biltmore Co.; horticulturist, landscape architect. Democrat. Episcopalian. Contbr. numerous articles pertaining to botany of Southern States. Home: Biltmore, N.C. Died July 4, 1950.

BEAL, CARL H., petroleum geologist and engineer; b. in Kansas, July 16, 1889; s. William Harvey and Anna (Erwin) B.; A.B., Stanford U., 1913, M.A., 1915, E.M., 1919; m. Cynthia Hardy Anderson. Jan. 30, 1929; children—Carlton H., Thomas E. Engaged in oil production in Coalings, Calif., 1913; geologist in Calif. and Canada, 1914; oil and gas inspector, Okla., 1915; petroleum technologist U.S. Bur. of Mines and valuation expert U.S. Bur. of Internal Revenue, 1916-19; cons. petroluem geologist and engr., Calif. and Mexico, 191-25; v.p. Marland Oil Co., 1922-28; cons. petroleum geologist and engr. since 1928; pres. Northern Resources, Ltd., West Coast Royalty Co., Ltd.; dir. Tide Water Asso. Oil Co. Mem. Am. Assn. of Petroleum Geologists, Am. Geologists. Sigma Xi. Clubs: California, Bel-Air Country, Burlingame Country, Midwick Country, Uplifters' Polo, San Mateo-Burlingame Polo, Riviera Country, Bel-Air Bay Club. Contbr. tech. articles and bulls. on oil production, seismology, etc., for official governmental and institutional pubs. Died Sept. 7, 1946.

BEAL, FOSTER ELLENBOROUGH LASCELLES, naturalist; b. S. Groton (now Ayer), Mass., Jan. 9, 1840; s. Jacob Foster and Sarah Jane (Day) B.; B.S., Mass. Inst. Tech., 1871; m. Mary Louise Barnes, Jan. 9, 1877. Instr. mathematics, M.I.T., 1870-74; asst. prof. mathematics, U.S. Naval Acad., 1874-75; prof. civil engring., 1876-82, acting prof. zoölogy, 1879-82, prof. geology, 1883, Ia. Agrl. Coll.; asst. biologist, 1891-1901, economic ornithologist, 1902—, Biol. survey, U.S. Dpet. Agr. Writer on econ. ornithology. Home: Berwyn, Md. Died Oct. 1, 1916.

BEAL, GEORGE DENTON, chemist; b. Scio, O., Aug. 12, 1887; s. James Hartley and Fannie Snyder (Young) B.; Ph.C., Scio Coll. Pharmacy, 1906, Pharm. D., 1907; Ph.B., Scio Coll., 1908; A.M., Columbia, 1910, Richard Butler scholar in chemistry, 1910-11, Ph.D., 1911; Pharm.M., Phila. Coll. Pharmacy, 1933; Sc.D., Mount Union College, 1933; Sc.D., Rutgers University, 1943; m. Edith Downs, July 3, 1912; children—George Denton, Marjorie Downs. Assistant in chemistry, Scio Coll. Pharmacy, 1906-08; instructor in chemistry, University of Illinois, 1911-14, asso., 1914-18, asst. prof., 1918-20, asso. prof. analytical and food chemistry, 1920-24, prof., 1924-26; asst. dir. of the Mellon Inst., Pitts., 1926-51, dir. research since 1951; professorial lectr. pharmacy U. Pitts., 1946-72; dir. Am. Druggists' Insurance Company. Collaborator with com. on revision U.S. Pharmacopoeia, 1920; mem. com. of revision U.S. Pharmacopoeia, 11th to 15th revisions (chmn. subcom. on organic chemicals); member U.S. Pharmacopoeial Conv., 1930, 40, 50; 1st vice chmn. Commn. Rev., 1940, trustee 1955-72; adv. bd. Q.M. research and development problems, N.R.C., 1946. Trustee Mt. Union Coll. (Alliance, O.), Phila. Coll. of Pharmacy and Sci.; com. on pharm. survey, Am. Council on Education 1946-51. Fellow A.A.A.S. (vice president, chemistry 1951), American Public Health Association; member American Chemical Soc. (chmn. medicinal division 1938; councilor-at-large 1939-44; Pittsburgh award 1955), Am. Leather Chemists Assn., American Pharm. Assn. (1st vice-pres. 1934-35; pres. 1936-37; member of council 1942-52, 54-72, chmn. council 1945-52), Pa. Pharm. Assn., American Council on Pharm. Education (pres. 1948-72, Pa. Chem. Soc. (pres., 1946-48), Am. Soc. Testing Materials, Industrial Hygiene Found., Pa. Chamber of Commerce (com. on pollution abatement), Lambda Chi Alpha, Sigma Xi, Alpha Chi Sigma, Phi Lambda Upsilon (national president 1917-19), Gamma Alpha, Psi Kappa Omega. Winner Ebert prize, American Pharmaceutical Association, 1920, Remington medal, 1941. Republican. Methodist. Clubs: University, Univ. of Pittsburgh Faculty (Pittsburgh); Chemists' (New York); Contbr. to Jour. Am. Pharm. Assn., Jour. Am. Chem. Soc. Home: Pittsburgh PA Died 1972.

BEAL, JAMES HARTLEY, pharm. chemist; b. New Phila., O., Sept. 23, 1861; s. Jesse and Mary B.; student Buchtel Coll. (now Akron), and U. of Mich.; B.Sc., Scio (Ohio) Coll., 1884; A.B., 1888; LL.B., Cincinnati Law Sch., 1886; Ph.G. Ohio Med. Univ., 1894; Sc.D., Mt. Union Coll., 1895; Pharm.D., U. of Pittsburgh, 1902; Pharm.M., Phila. Coll. Pharamacy, 1913; m. Fannie Snyder Young. Sept. 29, 1886; children—George Denton. Nannie Esther. Dean dept. pharmacy and prof. chemistry and pharmacy, 1887-1907, acting pres. 1902-04, Scio (O.) Coll.; dir. era course in pharmacy, New York, 1889-1909; professor chemistry, metallurgy and microscopy, Pittsburgh Dental College, 1896-1904; prof. theory and practice of pharmacy, U. of Pittsburgh, 1903-11; gen. sec. and editor Jour. of the Am. Pharmaceutical Assn., 1911-14; dir. pharmacy research, U. of Ill., 1914-17. Mem. Ohio Ho. of Rep., 1901. Editor Midland Drugist and Pharmaceutical Review, 1908; chmn. com. on uniformity of legislation, methods of analysis and marking of food products, Nat. Pure Food and Drug Congress, 1898. Trustee U.S. Pharmacopoeial Conv., 1900 (pres. bd. trustees, 1910, 1940); pres. Am. Pharm. Assn., 1904-05. Ohio State Pharm. Assn., 1898. Am. Conf. Pharm. Faculties, 1907-08. Am. Druggists Fire Ins. Co., 1939-45; nat. councilor U.S. Chamber of Commerce, 1917-18; pharm. expert, War Industries Bd., 1918; pres. Nat. Drug Trade Conf., 1918-20. Remington medalist, 1919. Author: Notes on Equation Writing and Chemical and Pharmaceutical Arithmetic, 3d edition, 1903; Pharmaceutical Interrogations, 1896; Interrogations in Dental Metallurgy, 1900; Practical Pharmacy, 1907; Prescription Practice and General Dispensing, 1908; Principles of Theory and Practice of Pharmacy (5 Vols.). 1910 Contbr. to pharm. jours. Now retired. Home: Fort Walton, Fla. Died Sept. 20, 1945.

BEAL, WALTER HENRY, Agril. research; b. nr. Old Church, Va., Dec. 9, 1867; s. John and Charlotte Columbia (Ellett) B.; A.B., Va. Poly. Inst., 1886, M.E., 1886; m. Eleanor Gilliss Ashby, Apr. 27, 1910; children-Major Walter Henry, Jr., Mrs. Elizabeth B. Devlin, Ann Ashby, Ensign William Ashby. Assistant chemist, Massachusetts Agrl. Experimental Sta., 1887-91; specialist in agrl. meterology, soils and fertilizers, editor, and asso. in expt. sta. adminstration. Office of Experiment Stations, U.S. Dept. Agriculture, 1891-1938. Democrat. Episcopalian. Author various papers on scientfic agriculture; contbr. to Experiment Station Record, International Ency., Internat. Year Book, Webster's Internat. Dictionary, Ency. Americana. Fellow A.A.A.S.; mem. Agrl. Hist. Soc., Va. Hist. Soc. Club: Cosmos. Home: 1852 Park Road N.W., Washington, D.C. Died Jan. 1, 1946.

BEAL, WILLIAM JAMES, botanist; b. Adrian, Mich., Mar. 11, 1833; s. William and Rachael S. (Comstock) B.; A.B., U. of Mich., 1859, A.M., 1862; S.B., Harvard, 1865; M.S., U. of Chicago, 1875; (hon. Ph.D, U. of Mich., 1880; D.Sc., Mich. State Agrl. Coll., 1905; D. Agr., Syracuse U., 1916); m. Hannah A. Proud, Sept. 2, 1863. Teacher natural science, Frineds' Acad. and Howland Inst., Union Springs, N.Y., 1859-68; prof. botany, U. of Chicago, 1868-70; lecturer on botany, 1871, prof. botany and horticulture, 1871-81, prof. botany and forestry and curator of Bot. Mus., 1882-1903, prof. botany, 1903-10, emeritus prof., Mich. State Agrl. Coll. Dir. State Forestry Commn., 1888-92. Home: Amherst, Mass. Died May 12, 1924.

BEALS, EDWARD ALDEN, meteorologist; b. Troy, N.Y., Apr. 23, 1855; s. Alden Porter and Emma Z. (Waite) B.; ed. grade and high schs., Stamford, Conn., and Harvard, 1 yr.; m. Frances E. Middaugh, June 26, 1888; children—Nancy Augusta, Clyde Alden. Practiced dentistry until 1880, then entered U.S. Signal Corps; later transferred to U.S. Weather Bur.; in charge offices at New York, 1883, Atlanta, 1883, Mt. Washington, N.II., 1884-85, Chattanooga, 1886-87, La Crosse, Wis., 1887-90. Minneapolis, 1891-95, Cleveland, 1896-99, Portland, Ore., 1900-17, San Francisco, 1917-24; meteorologist on charge Hawaiian weather service, Honolulu, 1924-26, retired. Unitarian. Contbr. on meteorol. subjects to scientific publs. Home: Alameda, Calif. Died Dec. 26, 1931.

BEAMNA, WILLIAM MAJOR, topographic engr.; b. Annapolis, Md., Feb. 20, 1867; s. George William (q.v.) and Rebecca Swift (Goldsmith) B.; grad. Mass. Inst. Tech.; spl. studies in civ. and topographic engring.; m. Mary S. Parker, of Salem, N.J., Apr. 15, 1895. Engaged in engring. work in 1889 as topographer in U.S. Geol. Survey; has had change of topographic field work at various times in Me., Conn., N.C., Ga., N.Y., Tenn., Ala., Colo., Tex., Del., Nev., Utah, Ariz. and Md.; insp. topography U.S. Geol. Survey, 1907—. Inventor of Beaman stadia arc. Mem. Nat. Geog. Soc., Geol. Soc. Washington, Am. Forestry Assn., Washington Soc. Engrs. Club: Cosmos. Author of numerous published topographic maps of U.S. Geol. Survey. Home: The Burlington, Washington.

BEAN, BARTON A., ichthyologist; b. Bainbridge, Pa., May 21, 1860; s. George B.; ed. in acad., Smyrna, Del., and Normal Sch., Millersville, Pa.; spl. studies in ichthyology; m. Lida Berry Skeen, of Columbia, Pa. (died Nov. 19, 1925); children—George Tinny, Bertha O. (Mrs. M. Rea Shafer), Barton Adrian, Tarleton Smith, Lida Elizabeth (Mrs. W. H. Pilcher), John Berry, Edwin Temple. Asst. curator of fishes, U.S. Nat. Mus., Jan. 4, 1881-95; acting curator, Div. of Fishes, since Apr. 1, 1895. Writer on fishes of Indian River, Fla., fishes of D.C., andBahama Islands; History of the Whale Shark; papers on fishes in Proc. U.S. Nat. Mus. and bulls, of Fish Commn., also in Shooting and Fishing, and Forest and Stream. Wrote: (with Alfred C. Weed) Notes on the Genus Lepomis; Review of the Venomous Toadfishes; Coloration of Fishes; Descriptions of New Rays from Deepwater Off the South Carolina Coast (with H. W. Fowler), Chinese, Formosan, and Philippine Island Fishes; also report upon the fishes of the Wilkes Exploring Expdn. and The Fishes of Maryland. Address: U.S. National Museum, Washington. D.C.

BEAN, TARELTON HOFFMAN, zoölogist; b. Bainbridge, Pa., Oct. 8, 1846; s. George and Mary (Smith) B.; M.E., State Normal Sch., Millersville, Pa., 1866; M.D., Columbian (now George Washington) U., 1876; M.S., Ind. U., 1883; m. Laurette H. Van Hook, Jan. 1, 1878. Curator dept. of fishes, U.S. Nat. Mus., 1880-95; dir. N.Y. Aquarium, 1895-98; state fish culturist of N.Y., 1906—. Editor Proc. and Bulls, U.S. Nat. Mus., 1878-86, Report and Bull., U.S. Fish Commn. 1889-92; asst. in charge div. of fish culture, U.S. Commn., 1892-95; acting curator of fishes, Am. Mus. Natural History, New York, 1897. Rep. U.S. Fish Commn. at Chicago Expn., 1893, Atlanta Expn., 1895; dir. Forestry and Fisheries, U.S., Paris Expn., 1900; chief Depts. Fish and Game, adn Forestry, St. Louis Expn., 1902-05. Chevalier Legion of Honor and Officer of Mérite Agricole, France; Knight Imperial Royal Order of Red Eagle (Germany); Order of the Rising Sun (Japan). Author: The Fishes of Pennsylvania, 1893; The Salmon and Salmon Fisheries; Oceanic Icthyology (with late George Brown Goode), 1896; The Fishes of Long Island, 1902; The White World (part author), 1902; The Food and Game Fishes of New York, 1903; The Basses, Fresh-Water and Marine (part author), 1905; The Fishes of Bermuda, 1906. Died Dec. 28, 1916.

BEARCE, HENRY WALTER, physicist; b. Hebron, Me., Oct. 5, 1881; s. Herrick Mellen and Mary (Murch) B.; student Hebron Acad., 1897-1901; B.S., U. of Me., 1906; m. Kate Merrill, Dec. 1, 1907; children—Louis Merrill (dec.), Roger Mellen. Instr. physics, U. of Me., 1906-08; lab. asst. Nat. Bur. of Standards, 1908-09, asst. physicist, 1911-16, asso. physicist, 1917-19, senior and prin. physicist 1936-45, chief Div. Weights and Measures, 1940-45; owner and operator of apple orchards, Hebron, Maine, since 1945; Nat. Bur. Standards Rep. at Internat. confs. on standardization of screw threads, Paris, London, 1919, London, 1944, Ottawa, 1945; sec. Nat. Screw Thread Committee, 1918-32; member of Annual Assay Commission, 1926, 38, 41, 43, chmn., 1938. Elected Rep. rep. Me. Legislature, 1950, 1952. Member Adv. com. World Calendar Assn.; mem. Philol. Soc. of Washington, Washington Acad. of Science, Phi Beta Kappa, Sigma Alpha Epsilon. Club: Cosmos (Washington). Contbr. to Ency. Brit., 14th edit.; revised sect. on weights and measures, Marks Mech. Engrs. Handbook, 1941 and earlier edits.; cooperating expert Internat. Critical Tables, Vol. III, 1928. Author of Nat. Standard Petroleum Oil Tables; also of numerous tech. papers and bulletins. Home: Hebron ME Died June 24, 1968; buried Hebron Community Baptist Ch., Hebron ME

BEARD, CHARLES HEADY, physician; b. Spencer Co., Ky., Jan. 27, 1855; s. James P. and Emerin (Heady) B.; ed. Transylvania U., Lexington, Ky.; M.D., U. of Louisville, 1877; m. Laura Clark, Sept. 24, 1888. In med practice at Cannelton, Ind., 1877-83; studied at Post-Grad. Med. School, Polyclinic, Knapp's Inst., New York, and then became house surgeon Manhattan Eye and Ear Hosp.; studied in London, Paris, Zürich and Vienna about 2 yrs. In Chicago, 1887—, making speciality of eye and ear practice; asst. surgeon, 1887-90, surgeon, 1890—, Ill. Charitable Eye and Ear Infirmary; oculist to Cook Co. Hosp., 1 yr.; attending phys., Central Free Dispensary 1 yr.; oculist to Passavant Memorial Hosp. Author: Opthalmic Surgery, 1910-14; Opthalmic Diagnosis, 1911-13; Collection of

Pictures of the Fundus Oculi. Home: Chicago, Ill. Died June 3, 1916.

BEARD, GEORGE MILLER, physician; b. Montville, Conn., May 8, 1839; s. Spencer and Lucy (Leonard) B.; attended Phillips Acad., Andover, Mass., 1854-58; grad. Yale, 1862, Coll. Physicians and Surgeons, N.Y.C., 1866; m. Elizabeth Alden, Dec. 25, 1866. Began research in med. use of electricity, 1866, published 1st works in this field; lectr. diseases of nerves N.Y.U., 1868; mem. staff Demilt Dispensary, N.Y.C., from circa 1870; founded mag. Archives of Electrology and Neurology, 1874; del. Internat. Med. Congress, London, Eng., 1881; one of 1st neurologists in U.S.; 1st to formulate causes and treatment of seasickness, also pioneer in reforms for care of insane. Author: Medical and Surgical Uses of Electricity, 1871; Hay Fever, 1876; The Scientific Basis of Delusions, 1877; Nervous Exhaustion, 1880; numerous other publs. Died N.Y.C., Jan. 23, 1883; buried N.Y.C.

BEARD, JAMES THOMAS mining engr.; b. Brooklyn, Oct. 19, 1855; s. Ira and Isabella O. B.; grad. Adelphia Acad., Brooklyn, 1874; C.E., E.M., Columbia Sch. of Mines, 1877; m. Amelia E. Lawson, May 9, 1887; children—James Thom, Howard Iranaeus, Amelia Elizabeth. Asst. engr. Brooklyn Bridge, 1877-79; resident div. engr. C., B. & Q.R.R., 1880-83; U.S. dept. mineral surveyor, Colo., 1883-85; mining engr. Ottumwa Fuel Co., 1885-91; propr. Iowa Coal Exchange, 1891-96; asso. editor Mines and Mineral and prin. Sch. of Mines, Internat. Corr. Sch., Scranton, Pa., 1896-1911; sr. asso. editor Coal Age, New York, 1911. Sec. Ia. State Mine Examining Bd., 1888-94. Inventor: Beard-Mackie Sight Indicator for testing gas; Beard deputy safety lamp; Beard-Stine centrifugal mine fan. Republican. Mem. North Engring. Inst. Mining and Mech. Engrs., Am. Inst. Mining and Metall. Engrs.; founder, editor in chief Mine Inspectors' Inst. U.S.A.; fellow A.A.A.S.; etc. Author: The Ventilation of Mines, 1894; Design of Centrifugal Ventilators, 1899, Mines Gases and Explosions, 1908; Coal Age pocket Book, 1916; Mine Gases and Ventilation, 1919. Compiler: Mine Examination Questions and Answers (3 vols.). 1923. Contbr. to mining jours. Home: 58 Washington Av., Danburg, Conn. Died Dec. 26, 1941.

BEARD, WOLCOTT LE CLÉAR, engr., author; b. New York, Nov. 10, 1867; s. W.H. (artist, painter) and Carrie (Le Cléar) B.; grad. Hobart Coll., B.S., 1889, C.E., 1891; m. New York, June, 1902, Gabriella Smyth. Was engaged in irrigation works in Ariz.; 1st lt. 1st U.S. vol. engrs. in 1898. Contbr. of numerous stories to mags. Held govt. position in Lingayen, province of Pangasinan, as civ. engr., supervisor and head of adminstrative bds.; comd. exploring expdn., Bolivian headwaters of Amazon. Author: Sand and Cactus, 1898 S3. Address: Care Mrs. W. H. Beard, Lyndhurst, N.J.

BEARDSLEY, JAMES WALLACE, engineer; b. Coventry, Chenango County, N.Y., Sept. 11, 1860; s. William Hurd and Catherine Tremper (Phillips) B.; grad. State Normal Sch., Cortland, N.Y., 1884; C.E., Cornell, 1891; m. Ellen J. Pearne, Sept. 7, 1893; 1 son, Wllace Pearne. Asst. engr. with Santary Dist. of Chicago, in charge constrn., 1892-98; with U.S. Bd. Engrs., on deep waterways, in charge St. Lawrence River surveys, 1898-1900; with U.S. Corps of Engrs., in charge harbor work, 1900-02; in P.I., as cons. engr. to Philippine Commn., 1902-03; chief Bur. of Engring., 1903-05, dir. Pub. Works, P.I., 1905-08; cons. engr. investigating irrigation in Java, India and Egypt, 1908-09; irrigation engr. with J. G. White & Co., New York, 1909-10; chief engr. Puerto Rico Irrigation Service, 1910-16; private cons. practice, 1916-18; cons. engr. in ordnance, 1918; asst. chief engr. grand canal surveys of China, 1918-19; chief engr. and mem. Junta Central de Caminos, Panama, 1920-21; cons. engr., 1922-25; with Obras Publicas, Santo Domingo, R.D., 1926-29; private cons. practice since 1930. Mem. Am. Soc. C.E., Western Soc. Engrs., Delta Phi, Sphinx Head (Cornell). Republican. Methodist. Club: Technology (Syracuse). Home: 141 Franklin St., Auburn, N.Y. Died May 15, 1944.

BEARDWOOD, MATTHEW, M.D., chemist; b. Cape May City, N.J., June 22, 1872; s. Matthew and Jane (Mitchell) B.; A.B., Central High Sch., Phila., 1890, A.M., 1895; M.D., Medico-Chirug, Coll., Phila., 1894; spl. student, U. of Pa., 1906-08, U. of Edinburgh, 1909; (Sc.D, Ursinus, 1916); unmarried. In gen. med. practice, Phila., 1895—. Instr. chemistry, 1896-99, lecturer on clin. chemistry, 1899-1900, adj. prof. chemistry, 1900-14, prof. gen. chemistry and toxicology, 1914-16, Medico-Chirug. Coll.; prof. chemistry, Ursinus Coll., 1903—. Republican. Presbyn. Author: Students' Notes on Toxicology, 1904. Home: Philadelphia, Pa. Deceased.

BEATON, LINDSAY EUGENE, physician; b. Chgo., Jan. 25, 1911; s. David and Vera (de Lipkau) B.; A.B. summa cum laude, Dartmouth, 1932; M.D., Northwestern U., 1938, M.S., 1939, student Inst. Neurology, 1940-42; m. Eileen Barrows, Juen 28, 1962; children—Kathleen Fraser, Jeremy de Lipkau. Intern, Passavant Meml. Hosp., 1939-40; mem. fellow NRC, 1939-41; instr. anatomy and neurology Northwestern U. Med. Sch., 1936-38; lectr. dept. physiology U. Ariz.; attending physician St. Mary's Hosp., Tucson Med. Center, St. Joseph's Hosp.; cons. VA Hosp., Tucson, U.S. Army Hosp., Ft. Huachuca, Ariz. Mem. Ariz. Hosp. Bd, 1952. Pres., Family Service Agy., 1956-57, Tucson Child Guidance Clinic, 1958-59; chmn. social planning and priorities com. Tucson Community Council. Served from capt. to lt. col. M.C., AUS, 1941-46. Diplomate, asst. examiner Am. Bd. Psychiatry and Neurology. Fellow Am. Psychiat. Assn., Acad. Neurology, Am. Acad. Forensic. Scis.; mem. A.M.A. (del. Ho. Dels.; vice council mental health), Ariz. Med. Assn. (past pres.), Pima County Med. Soc., Am. Assn. Med. Colls. (editorial com. 1962), Phi Beta Kappa, Sigma Xi, Alpha Omega Alpha, Beta Theta Pi, Phi Kappa Epsilon. Contbr. chpt.; The Crisis in American Medicine, 1962; Today's Health Guide, A.M.A., 1964. Asso. editor U.S. Army Med. History of World War II, Neuropsychiatry in the War Against Japan, 1964. Contbr. numerous articles sci. jours. Home: 1615 N. Norton St. Office: 123 S. Stone Av., Tucson. Died Feb. 1967.

BEATTY, ALFRED CHESTER, mining engr.; N.Y.C., Feb. 7, 1875; s. John Cuming and Hetty (Bull) B.; M.E., Columbia, 1898; D.Sc., Birmingham, Eng., 1938, LL.D., 1939; m. Grace Madeline Rickard, Apr. 18, 1900 (dec.); children—Ninette, Alfred Chester; m. 2d, Edith Dunn, June 21, 1913 (dec. 1952). Went to Eng., 1913, naturalized, 1933. Dir. Am. Metal Co., Ltd. Awarded Columbia U. Medal, 1933; Egleston medal by Engring Alumni, 1948; Gold Medal of Instn. Mining and Metallurgy, 1935. Decorated Grand Cordon of Order of St. Sava (Yugoslavia); Comdr. Order of Leopold II (Belgium). Fellow Soc. Antiquaries; mem. Am., London C.'s of C., Am. Inst. Mining and Metall. Engrs., Am. Soc. in London, Automobile Assn., Bibliog. Soc., Egype Exploration Soc., Inst. Metals, Instn. Mining and Metallurgy, Royal Philatelic Soc., Pilgrims, L'Union Interllie (Paris). Clubs: Roxburghe; Travellers (Paris, France). Collector Oriental and Western manuscripts. Addresses: 10 Aliesbury Rd., Dublin, Eire; also Baitel-Azark, Mena, Cairo, Egypte. Died Jan. 19, 1968.

BEATTY, HENRY RUSSELL, coll. pres., machine mfg. exec., cons. mgmt. engr.; b. Eastport, Me., May 14, 1906; s. Harry Hamilton and Susan (Ferguson) B.; B.S., U. Me., 1927; M. Adminstrv. Engring., N.Y.U., 1945; D. Engring., Stevens Tech., Northeastern U., 1962; Doctor Engring. University of Maine, 1963; m. Alice C. Van Schagen, Feb. 14, 1934; 1 son, Robert C. Supr. indsl. engring. Gen. Electric Co., 1927-33; salesman Remington Rand, 1933-34; prodn. supt. Holtzer Cabot Electric Co., 1934-37; prof., asst. to pres., dean engring. Pratt Inst., 1937-53; pres., trustee Wentworth Inst., Boston, 1953-71; pres., trustee Wentworth Coll. Tech., 1970-72; cons. mgmt. engr., 1944-72; cons. Coll. Petroleum Minerals, Saudi Arabia, 1968-72. Dir. Reed & Barton Co., N.J. Machine Corp. of N.H., N.J. Packaging Corp. Mem. Mass. Health and Ednl. Facilities Authority; mem. adv. bd. Greater Boston Salvation Army. Mem. sci. edn. adv. com. NSF. Trustee Endicott Jr. Coll., Gordon Coll. Chmn. Corp. Open Ch. Found. Registered profl. engr., N.Y., N.J., Mass., Me. Fellow Am. Soc. M.E., Assn. Ind. Colls. and Univs. Mass. (sec.-treas. 1967-71); mem. Nat. Soc. Profl. Engrs., Engring. Soc. New Eng. (past pres.), Mass. Schoolmasters Club (past pres.), Am. Soc. Engring. Edn., Project Bd., A.A.A.S., Am. Nuclear Soc., Boston C. of C. Conglist. (trustee). Mason, Rotarian. Clubs: Congregational (pres.), Executives (Boston). Revised: Principles of Industrial Management (L.P. Alford), 1951. Home: Quincy MA Died Sept. 26, 1972.

BEAUMONT, WILLIAM, surgeon; b. Conn., Nov. 21, 1785; s. Samuel and Luctetia (Abel) B.; m. Mrs. Deborah Platt, 1821, 1 son, 2 daus. Apprenticed to physician, St. Albans, Vt., 1810-13; licensed to practice medicine by 3d Med. Soc. of Vt., 1812; surgeon 6th Inf., Plattsburg, N.Y., 1812-15; practiced medicine, Plattsburg, 1815-20; post surgeon Ft. Mackinac, Mich., 1820-25; treated patient with stomach wound and made important discoveries regarding digestive processes, 1822, conducted expts. with patient (Alexis St. Martin) until 1834 while stationed as post surgeon at Ft. Niagara, 1825-26, Ft. Howard, 1826-28, Ft. Crawford, 1828-34, corresponded with leading scientists about gastric fluids in digestion; served in St. Louis, 1834-39; resigned from Army Med. Corps, 1839; practiced medicine, St. Louis, until 1853. Author: Experiments and Observations on the Gastric Juice and the Physiology of Digestion (pioneer studies on digestion including over 200 expts.), 1833, 2d edit., 1847. Died St. Louis, Apr. 25, 1853; buried Bellefontaine Cemetery, St. Louis.

BECK, CARL, surgeon; b. at Neckargemuend, Germany, Apr. 4, 1856; s. Wilhelm and Sophia (Hoehler) B.; ed. Gymnasium of Heidelberg, 1869-74; studied at univs. of Heidelberg and Berlin; M.D., U. of Jena, 1879; m. Hedwig, d Chief Justice Heinrich F. von Loeser, of Saxony, Feb. 16, 1889. Came to U.S., 1882; pres. St. Mark's Hosp., New York; surgeon to St. Mark's, 1886— and German Poliklinik, 1883—; prof. surgery, N.Y. Post-Grad. Med. Sch., 1890—. Officer Med. Reserve Corp U.S.A. Author: Manual on Surgical Asepsis, 1895; Text Book on Fractures, 1900; Die Rötgendtrahlen im Dienstr der Chirurgie, 1902; Röntgen-Ray Diagnosis and Therapy, 1904; Röntgenshirurgie, Berlin, 1905; Amerikanishe, Streiflichter, 1905; Feuchtfroehliches and Feuchtunfroehliches, 1906; Der Schwedenkonrad (novel), 1906; Surgical Diseases of the Chest, 1907 (translated into German, 1909); Glimpses from Latin America, 1908; Röntgenuntersuchung der Lerber und Gallenblase, 1909. Died 1911.

BECK, CARL, surgeon; b. Milin, Austria, Mar. 26, 1864; s. Ignatz and Elizabeth (Pollak) B.; ed. Gymnasium, Prague, Bohemia; M.D., Royal and Imperial U. Prague, 1889; served as asst. in surg. and gynecol. clinics in Prague, assisting first Prof. Gussenbauer and later Dr. Schauta, gynegologist of Vienna; m. Eda Steln, Apr. 10, 1899; children—Helen Babette, Frances Eda, William. Made several trips to Am. as steamer surgeon, 1889-90; and in 1890 settled in Chgo. in gen. practice of medicine; prof. surgery, Chgo. Coll. Phys. and Surgeons (U. Ill.), Post-Grad. Med. Sch. and Chgo. Coll. of Dentistry; attending surgeon to Cook County, St. Joseph with N. Chgo. hosps. Founded St.Anthony Hosp., with the Sisters of Joliet. A founder German Med. Soc. and Bohemian Med. Soc. Chgo.; mem. A.M.A., German Soc. Surgeons of Berlin, Soc. Physicians of Prague, Royal Acad., Rome. Served as vol. in 11th Inf. Regt., Austrian Army, and later 1st lt. of 75th Inf. Regt. Author: Principles of Surgery, 1905; Crippled Hand and Arm, 1925; also many articles in med. jours.; collaborator of Internat. Jour. Gynecology and Obstetrics (internat. sec.). Home: 5121 Edgemoore Lane, Bethesda, Md.

BECK, CLAUDE SCHAEFFER, surgeon; b. Shamokin, Pa., Nov. 8, 1894; s. Simon and Martha (Schaeffer) B.; A.B., Franklin and Marshall Coll., 1916, D.Sc. (hon.), 1937; M.D., Johns Hopkins Univ., 1921; m. Ellen Manning, May 26, 1928; children—Mary Ellen, Kathryn Schaeffer, Martha Ann. House officer, Johns Hopkins Hosp., 1921-22; Meml. Cemetery, Chicago ILCabot fellow in research surgery, Harvard, and asso. surgeon Peter Bent Brigham Hosp., Boston, 1923-24; Crile fellow in surgery, Western Reserve Univ., Cleveland, 1924-25, various positions dept. of surgery since 1925, prof. neurosurgery, 1940-51, professor of cardiovascular surgery since 1951; with University Hospitals since 1924, asso. surgeon specializing in surgery of the heart since 1933; chief consultant neurosurgery, Crile Veterans Hosp., Cleveland, since 1945; visiting neurosurgeon, Cleveland City Hosp.; cardiac consultant Mt. Sinai Hospital, Cleve. Colonel, M.C., U.S. Army as surgeon consultant Fifth and Sixth Service Commands, 1942-45; awarded Legion of Merit, 1945. Spl. consultant Surgery Study Group, Nat. Institutes of Health since 1949. Fellow A.C.S. Mem. Am. Surgical Assn., Assn. for Thoracic Surgeons, Soc. Clinical Surgery, Am. Soc. for Exptl. Pathology, A.M.A., Am. Heart Assn., Am. Bd. of Surgeons, Am. Bd. Thoracic Surgeons (founders group), Eastern and Central surgical socs.; Cleveland Surgical Soc. (pres.), Cleveland Heart Soc. (pres.). Club: Halsted Contbr. about 125 chpts. and articles in med. books and jours. Home: East Cleveland OH Died Nov. 1971.

BECK, LEWIS CALEB, chemist, educator; b. Schenectady, N.Y., Oct. 4, 1798; s. Caleb and Catherine (Romeyn) B.; grad. Union Coll., Schenectady, 1817; attended Coll. Physicians and Surgeons, N.Y.C., 1816; m. Hannah Smith, Oct. 17, 1825. Licensed to practice medicine in N.Y., 1818; lived in various parts of U.S., 1818-24, began bot. collection; prof. botany Berkshire Med. Inst., 1824; prof. chemistry and botany Vt. Med. Acad., 1826; prof. chemistry Rutgers U., 1830, N.Y.U., 1836; prof. chemistry and pharmacy Albany (N.Y.) Med. Coll., 1840-53. Author: Botany of the Northern and Middle States, 1833; Minerology of New York, 1842. Died Albany, Apr. 20, 1853.

BECK, THEODRIC ROMEYN, physician, educator; b. Schenectady, N.Y., Aug. 11, 1791; s. Caleb and Catherine (Romeyn) B.; grad. Union Coll., Schenectady, N.Y., 1807; grad. Coll. Physicians and Surgeons, N.Y.C., 1811; m. Harriet Caldwell, 1814, 2 daus. Practiced medicine, Albany, N.Y., 1811-17; prin. Albany Acad., 1817-53; prof. medicine Western Coll. Physicians and Surgeons, Fairfield, N.Y., 1815-40, Albany Med. Coll., 1840-43; sec. N.Y. Bd. Regents, 1841-54; pres. N.Y. State Med. Soc., 3 terms; founder N.Y. State Library, N.Y. State Insane Asylum. Author: Elements of Medical Jurisprudence, 1823. Died Albany, Nov. 19, 1855.

BECKER, ELERY RONALD, zoölogy, Parasitology; b. near Sterling, Ill., Dec. 5, 1896; s. William Edgar and Emma Catherine (Gerdes) B.; A.B., U. of Colo., 1921, D.Sc., Johns Hopkins, 1923; m. Helen Pauline Grill, June 24, 1925; children—Helen Catherine, Ronald Ernest, William Elery. Instr. zoölogy, Ia. State Coll., 1925-35, prof., 1935-58; prof. zoology Arizona State Univ., 1958-61. Served as private, Medical Dept., World War I; maj., Sanitary Corps, A.U.S., World War II. Sec.-treas. Ia. Acad. Sci., 1941-43. Member American Society Zoölogists, Am. Society of Parasitologists (pres. 1954), Beta Beta Beta, American Soc. Naturalists, Soc. Protozoologists (sec.-treas. 1949-52, pres. 1959), Am. Soc. Tropical Medicine and Hygiene, Sigma Xi, Phi Beta Kappa, Phi Kappa Phi, Gamma Sigma Delta. Conglist. Author of Coccidia and Coccidiosis, 1934; Brief Directions in Histological Technique. Contbr. on sci. subjects. Editor Jour. of Parasitology, 1959-61. Home: 724 E. Granada Dr.,

Tempe, Ariz. Died Nov. 20, 1962; buried Green Acres Meml. Park, Scottsdale, Ariz.

BECKER, GEORGE FERDINAND, geologist; b. New York, Jan. 5, 1847; s. Alexander Christian Becker (member of a Danish family) and Sarah Cary (Tuckerman) Becker; B.A., Harvard, 1868; Ph.D., Heidelberg, 1869; passed final exam. Royal Sch. of Mines, Berlin, 1871; m. Florence Serpell Deakins, Feb. 11, 1902. Instr. mining and metallurgy, U. of Calif., 1875-79; U.S. geologist-in-charge, 1879-92 and 1894—; spl. agt. 10th Census, 1879-83. Examined gold and diamond mines of S. Africa, 1896. Detailed to serve as geologist with army in P.I., 2898-00; now charge div. chem. and physica; research, U.S. Geol. Survey; geophysicist, Carnegie Instn. Mem. com. Nat. Acad. apptd. Jan. 1903, to prepare report at Pres. Roosevelt's request, on desirability of instituting scientific explorations of the P.I. and on the scope proper to such an undertaking. Author: Atomic Weight Determinations, 1880; Geology of the Comstock Lode, 1882; Statistics and Technology of the Precious Metals (with S. F. Emmons), 1885; Geology of Quicksilver Deposits of the Pacific Slope, 1888; Gold Fields of Southern Appalachians, 1895; Gold Fields of Alaska, 1898; Gold Fields of South Africa, 1897; Geology of the Phillippine Islands, 1901; Experiments on Slaty Cleavage, 1904; Tables of the Hyperbolic Functions (with C. E. Van Orstrand), 1908. Home: Washington, D.C. Died Apr. 20, 1919.

BECKER, WILLIAM GERARD, mfg. chemist; b. Kempen, Rhein, Germany., Feb. 12, 1874; s. Gerard and Maria Magdalena (Frantzen) B.; student Poly Inst., Aix la Cnapelle; Ph.D., U. of Freiburg, 1897; m. Marie Antoinette Pothen; children—William Kurt, Elsa M. Served as 1st lt. German Army; asst. prof. chemistry Royal Dye Sch., Crefeld, 1898-1900; became connected with Bayer Co., mfrs. dyestuffs and chemicals, Elberfeld, 1900, and came to U.S., 1902, in charge tech. depts. of Am. br., same co.; founder, 1911, Beckers' Aniline & Chem. Works, of which was pres. and chmn. bd.; company consolidated with other cos., 1917, as Nat. Aniline & Chem. Co., Inc., of which is dir. and vice pres.; also dir. of Allied Chemical & Dye Corporation, Murray Hill Trust Co. (New York), Bolton Nat. Bank, Aviation Corp. (Del.), Canadian Colonial Airways, Inc. Naturalized citizen of U.S., 1911. Trustee Polytechnic Inst., Brooklyn. Mem. Am. Chem. Soc., Soc. Chem. Industries (Eng.). Republican. Clubs: Chemists, Lawyers' (New York); Montauk, Riding and Driving (Brooklyn, N.Y.); Country, Sagamore Golf (Lake George, N.Y.); Aviation Country Club, L.I. Home: 1067 5th Av., New York; (summer) Beckersville, N.Y. Office: 61 Broadway, New York. Died Nov. 3, 1948.

BECKET, FREDERICK MARK, chemist, metallurgist; b. Montreal, Can., Jan. 11, 1875; s. Robert Anderson and Anne (Wilson) B.; B.A.Sc., McGill U., 1895; LL.D., McGill U., 1934; A.M., Columbia U., 1899, grad. study, 1900-02, Sc.D., 1929; m. Geraldine McBride, Oct. 8, 1908; children—Ethelwynne (Mrs. Paul H. Folwell), Ruth Alene (Mrs. Ruth Becket Trauter). Came to U.S., 1895, naturalized citizen, 1918. With Westinghouse Electric & Mfg. Co., East Pittsburgh, Pa., 1895-96, Acker Process Co., at Jersey City, N.J., 1896-98, at Niagara Falls, N.Y., 1899-1900, Ampere Electrochem. Co., 1902-03, Niagara Research Labs., 1903-06; with Electro Metall. Co. and Union Carbide Co. since 1906; consultant Union Carbide & Carbon Corp. Fellow A.A.A.S.; mem. Am. Inst. of City of New York; N.Y. Acad. of Science, Am. Inst. Mining and Metall. Engrs. (pres. 1933), Electrochem. Soc. (pres. 1925-26, hon. mem. 1936), Mining and Metall. Soc. America, Am. Soc. for Metals, Iron and Steel Inst. of London. Awarded Perkin medal, 1924, Acheson medal, 1937; Elliott Cresson medal, 1940; Howe Memorial lecturer, 1938. Clubs: Chemsits' (pres. 1939), Engineers', Mining, Niagara (Niagara Falls). Contbr. to tech. publs. Home: 625 Park Av. Office: 30 E. 42d St., New York, N.Y. Died Dec. 1, 1942.

BECKETT, RICHARD CREIGHTON, engr.; b. Millville, N.J., Oct. 6, 1893; s. Bertrand Orris and Luphemia Creighton (McAvoy) B.; B.Sc. in San. Engring., Pa. State Coll., 1916; Certificate of Attendance in Chemistry and Govt., U. Nancy, France. Jan.-July, 1919; m. Sarah Sheppard, Oct. 7, 1922; 1 son, Richard Creighton. Asst. engr. Pa. Dept. of Health, Harrisburg, 1920-21; asst. san. engr., W.Va. Dept. of Health, Charleston, 1921-24; state san. engr. Del. Bd. of Health, Dover, 1924—. Mem. and sec. State Milk Commn., 1933-35, State Mosquito Control Commn., 1935-39; vice chmn. Commn. Interstate Cooperation, 1936—; mem. exec. com. Interstate Commn. Del. River Basin, 1936—; mem. post-war com. on reconstrn., Council of State Govts., gov's. com. post-war reconstruction, State Del. Registered profl. engr., Del. Mem. Am. Water Works Assn., Am. Pub. Health Assn., Am. Fedn. Sewerage Works Assn., New Castle County Regional Planning Commn., Conf. State San. Engrs. Independent. Author: various articles on sanitation and pub. health engring. in profl. mags. and publs. Home: Hazel Rd. Office: Delaware State Board of Health, Dover, Del. Died Dec. 16, 1948; buried Silver Lake Cemetery, Dover.

BECKMAN, P(HILIP) E(NOCH), engr.; b. San Francisco, May 7, 1899; s. Carl Erik and Selma Gustave (Carlson) B.; M.E., Stanford, 1921; m. Loretta Ann Hogan, July 13, 1923; children—Bethany Ann, Loretta Mae. With Pacific Gas & Electric Co., San Francisco, 1921—, beginning as draftsman, successively asst. engr., gen. supt. tech. services, v.p. in charge gas operations, 1953—; v.p., dir. Natural Gas Corp.; dir. Gas Lines, Inc., Standard Pacific Gas Lines, Inc. Mem. Am. Pacific Coast (dir.) gas assns., Cal. Natural Gasoline Assn. (dir.), Soc. Cal. Profl. Engrs. Mason. Home: 1101 Green St., San Francisco 9. Office: 245 Market St., San Francisco 6. Died Nov. 21, 1959.

BECKNER, LUCIEN, geologist; b. Winchester, Ky., Dec. 29, 1872; s. William Morgan and Elizabeth (Taliaferro) B.; ed. Centre Coll., Danville, Ky., U. of Ky., Transylvania Coll., Lexington, Ky.; studied law Centre Coll.; m. Marie Daveiss Warren, of Danville, Aug. 14, 1894; children—Jean Warren, Elizabeth Taliaferro, Marie Warren. Editor Sun-Sentinel and Winchester (Ky.) Sun, 1904-12; asso. editor Filson Club Quar., 1927-36; editor Tobacco News, 1908, and Clark Co. Republican, 1915-16; admitted to Ky. bar, 1895; geologist for oil and gas cos.; civil engr.; commr. for Ecuador to Pan-Am. Expn., Buffalo, N.Y., 1901. Capt. Inf. Ky. Militia. Fellow A.A.A.S.; mem. Ky. Acad. of Science (past pres.), Appalachian Geol. Soc., Am. Inst. Mining Engrs., Ky. State Park Commn., Ky. Ednl. Assn., Ky. Ornithol. Soc., Ky. State Hist. Soc. (life), Ky. State Bar Assn., Kappa Alpha; councillor Boy Scouts of America. Dir. Louisville Free Pub. Museum. Republican. Mason (K.T., Shriner). Clubs: Filson, Astronomy, Beckham Bird. Home: 411 Belgravia Court, Louisville KY

BECKWITH, THEODORE DAY, bacteriologist; b. Utica, N.Y., Dec. 8, 1879; s. Theodore George and Jane (Day) B.; B.S., Hamilton Coll., 1904, M.S., 1907; Ph.D., U. of Calif., 1920; m. Cornelia Lyon, June 14, 1910; children—Josephine Day, Jane Crosby, Stephen Lyon, Theodore Day. Algologist, U.S. Dept. Agr., 1904-05, scientific asst., 1905-07; asst. prof. bacteriology and plant pathology, N.D. Coll., 1907-10, prof., 1910-11, asst. botanist, N.D. Expt. Sta., 1907-11; head dept. bacteriology, Ore. State Coll., and bacteriologist Expt. Sta., 1911-20; asso. prof. of bacteriology, U. of Calif., and mem. Calif. Stomatological Research group, 1920-32; asso. prof. bacteriology, U. of Calif. at Los Angeles, 1932-33, prof. since 1933, head dept. since 1934; research asso. Calif. Expt. Sta., 1934-35; cooperated with Huntington Library in research dealing with foxing of paper 1933-39; consultant for pulp and paper industry. Capt. Sanitary Corps, U.S. Army, 1918-19. Fellow A.A.A.S., Calif. Acad. Sciences; mem. Soc. Exptl. Biology and Medicine (sec. Pacific Coast sect., 1925-32; chmn. Southern Calif. sec., 1935-36; council mem., 1935-36), Soc. Am. Bacteriologists (chmn. Southern Calif. sec.; council mem., 1936-37), Am. Pub. Health Assn., Southern Calif. Pub. Health Assn. (exec. com. 1938-1942); pres., 1941-42 Western Sco. Naturalists, Inst. Food Technology, Southern Calif. Dentral Assn. (hon.), Phi Beta Kappa, Sigma Xi, Alpha Zeta, Gamma Alpha, Kappa Psi, Delta Upsilon, Delta Omega. Presbyterian. Mason. Author: Causes and Prevention of Foxing in Books (with T. M. Iiams), 1937. Contbr. many articles on water supply, sewage germicides, metabolism, paper faults, medical and dental bacteriology. Home: 333 19th St., Santa Monica, Calif. Died July 18, 1946.

BEDELL, FREDERICK, physicist; b. Brooklyn, Apr. 12, 1868; s. Edwin Forrest and Caroline Louise (Cunningham) B.; A.B., Yale, 1890; M.S., Cornell, 1891, Ph.D., 1892; m. Mary L. Crehore, July 1, 1896 (died Mar. 17, 1936); children—Eleanor (Mrs. Robert Cady Burt), Caroline Cunningham (Mrs. Henry M. Thomas, Jr.); m. 2d, Grace Evelyn Wilson, July 19, 1938. Asst. prof. of physics, 1893-1904, prof. applied electricity, 1904-37, prof. emeritus since 1937, Cornell University; now consulting physicist, privately, Pasadena, Calif. Especially well known for investigations in alternating currents of electricity; author of several works in electricity and on areodynamics. Member of the jury of awards (electricity), Louisiana Purchase Exposition, St. Louis, 1904; asso. editor, 1894-1913, mng. editor, 1913-22, The Physical Review. Mem. Internat. Electrotech. Commn., 1913. Fellow A.A.A.S (sec. of council, 1898, gen. sec., 1899), American Physical Soc., American Inst. Elec. Engrs. (mgr. 1914-16, v.p. 1917-18), Phi Beta Kappa, Sigma Xi. Inventor systems of power transmission and communication and of scientific instruments, including aids for the deaf. Award (1940) as Modern Pioneer on Frontier of Industry for invention of Cathode ray oscilloscope and bone conduction hearing aids. Contbr. definitions in electricity to Webster's Internat. Dictionary. Home: 1147 Lura St., Pasadena 5, Calif. Died May 2, 1958.

BEEBE, WILLIAM, scientist, author; b. Brooklyn, July 29, 1877; s. Charles and Henrietta Marie (Younglove) B.; post-grad. course, 1898-99; Sc.D., Tufts, Colgate Univ., 1928; m. Mary Blair; m. 2d, Elswyth Thane, 1927. Curator ornithology, N.Y. Zoöl. Soc., since 1899, also dir. of Dept. Tropical Research. Fellow N.Y. Acad. of Sciences, A.A.A.S., N.Y. Zoöl. Soc., Am. Ornithologists' Union; mem. Linnaean Soc., Soc. Mammalogists, Ecol. Soc., Audubon Soc., corr. mem. Zoöl. Soc., London, Société d'Acclimatation de France; holder of the Elliot and John Burroughs medals. Author numerous books including: Book of Bays, 1942; Book of Naturalists, 1944; High Jungle, 1949; Unseen Life of New York, 1953; Adventuring with Beebe; also many sci. papers and monographs relating to birds, fish and evolution. Home: 33 W. 67th St., Wilmington, Vt. Office: Zoological Park, Bronx, N.Y.C. 60. Died June 6, 1962; buried Trinidad.

BEECHER, CHARLES EMERSON, prof. paleontology and curator of geol. collections, Yale; b. Dunkirk, N.Y., Oct. 9, 1856; grad. Univ. of Mich., 1878 (Ph.D., Yale, 1889); m. Mary Salome Galligan, Sept. 12, 1894. Author: Studies in Evolution, 1901; and over seventy papers in scientific jours. and proceedings of scientific societies, principally on modern evolution and the classification of Brachiopods and Trilobites, and on the development and detailed structure of Trilobites, etc. Home: New Haven, Conn. Died 1904.

BEEDE, JOSHUA WILLIAM, geologist; b. Raymond, N.H., Sept. 14, 1871; s. Hiram Pratt and Lydia Maria (Brown) B.; B.S., Washburn Coll., Kan., 1896, A.M., 1897; Ph.D, U. of Kan., 1899; m. Clara Frances McKee, Dec. 25, 1899; children—Genevieve (Mrs. G. G. Henderson), Lydia May (Mrs. T. O. Todd), Lucile Prosser, Clara Frances. Student asst. in paleontology, U. of Kan., 1897-99; teacher of science, Atchison Co. High Sch., Effingham, Kan., 1899-1901; instr. geology, 1901-06, asst. prof., 1906-09, asso. prof., 1909-17, Indiana U. geologist, bur. econ. geology and technology, U. of Texas, 1917-22; with Empire Gas & Fuel Co., 1922; with Dixie Oil Co., 1924-28; prof. geology and paleontology, Indiana U., 1928—. Mem. Kan. Geological Survey, 1896, 1898-99, 1903-10. Okla. Geol. Survey, 1911-17; aid U.S. Geol. Survey, 1901-02. Has made extensive researches in the carboniferous and permian formations and fossils from Neb. to Tex. and W.Va., and author of many papers on these topics and on Origin of Sediments and Coloring Matter of Red Beds, Kan.-Okla. Home: Bloomington, Ind. Died Feb. 26, 1940.

BEEKMAN, FENWICK, surgeon; b. N.Y.C., June 1, 1882; s. William Bedlow and Katherine Morris (Parker) B.; student in St.Mark's Sch., Southboro, Mass., 1896-1901, Columbia, 1901-03; M.D., U. of Pa., 1907; m. Sabina Wood Struthers, Oct. 12, 1912; children—Fenwick, Geradus, Robert Struthers; m. 2d, Vera Byerley Lindo, Dec. 8, 1933. Cons. surgeon Hospital for Special Surgery; cons. surgeon Lincoln and Beelevue Hosps., North County Community Hospital, Glen Cove, N.Y.; consulting pediatric surgeon Fitkin Memorial Hosp. (Neptune, N.J.). Trustee N.Y. Soc. Library, Greenwood Cemetery, Bklyn. Served A.E.F., World War, discharged as maj. Med. Corps. Cited for "meritorious service in Battle of Cambrai." Fellow Am. Coll. Surgeons; mem. A.M.A., N.Y. Co. Med. Soc., N.Y. State Med. Soc., N.Y. Acad. of Medicine, N.Y. Surgical Soc., N.Y. and New Eng. Assn. Ry. Surgeons, N.Y. Hist. Soc. (trustee, past pres.), Am. Assn. for Surgery of Trauma, Am. Assn. Oral and Plastic Surgery, N.Y. Gen. and Biog. Soc. (trustee); founder mem. Am. Bd. Surgery, Am. Bd. Plastic Surgery. Republican. Episcopalian. Mason. Clubs: Union, St. Anthony, St.Nicholas, Grolier, Pilgrims (exec. com.). Author: Office Surgery, 1932; also surg. papers. Home: 136 E. 64th St., N.Y.C. 10021. Died Nov. 21, 1962; buried Greenwood Cemetery.

BEELER, JOHN A(LLEN), cons. engr.; b. Towanda, Ill., June 28, 1867; s. John and Emma Walker (Mead) B.; ed. pub. schs.; m. Fannie Mary Gillette, Feb. 14, 1895 (died Nov. 19, 1908); children—Horace Gillette (dec.), Mrs. Dorothy Long; m. 2d, Amanda Rosini Gall, July 17, 1913; children—Betty Malvina, Esther Lois, Rosemary Virginia. Asst. engr. constrn. cable rys., Cincinnati and Denver, Colo., 1885-90; chief engr. Denver Contractors' Assn., 1889-90, Met. St. Ry. Co., Denver, 1891-92, Denver Tramway Co., 1890-1902; v.p. and gen. mgr. same, 1902-15; v.p. and gen. supt. D. & N.W. Ry. Co. (electric), 1903-15; dir. in charge operations, Denver & Intermountain R.R. Co. (electrified steam line), 1913-15; cons. practice since 1915. Cons. engr. on transit and other pub. utility problems for cities of New York, Boston, Washington, D.C., Kansas City, New Orleans, Richmond (Va.), Dallas, Houston, Atlanta, Louisville, Cincinnati, St. Louis, Toronto, Cleveland, Seattle; consulting traffic expert, New York Transit Commn., 1921-26; councillor and member advisory comm. of Eno Foundation for Highway Traffic Control; director The Beeler Organization, Transit Planners. Mem. American Soc. C.E. Baptist. Club: Scarsdale Golf (New York). Home: Scarsdale, N.Y. Office: 155 E. 44th St., New York, N.Y. Died July 11, 1945.

BEGG, ALEZANDER SWANSON, M.D., educator; b. Council Bluffs, Ia., May 23, 1861; s. Alexander Swanson and Lauretta (Slotterbeck) B.; grad. Collegiate Inst., Sarnia, Ont., Can., 1899; B.S., Drake U., 1906; M.D., 1907; m. Grace Waers, 1908; children—John, Charles, Barbara. Instr. in pathology, Drake U., 1907-09, asst. prof. pathology, histology and embryology, 1909-10, prof. histology and embryology, 1910-13; teaching fellow, Harvard Med. Sch., 1911-12, instr. in comparative anatomy, 1913-18, dean Grad. Sch. Medicine, 1917-18, demonstrator in anatomy and instr. of histology, 1919-21; research asso., Carnegie Inst., 1915-16; prof. anatomy, Boston U. Sch. of Medicine, 1921—, dean, 1923—. Served as 1st lt. and capt., Med. Res. Corps, 1917, major, 1918, lt. col., 1918, col., 1919—; active duty, office of surgeon gen., A.E.F., 1917-19. Republican. Unitarian. Home: West Roxbury, Mass. Died Sept. 26, 1940.

BEHAN, WILLARD, civil engr.; b. Watkins, N.Y., Jan. 15, 1854; s. James and Harriet (Griswold) B.; grad. Starkey Sem., Eddytown, N.Y., 1873; B.C.S., Cornell U., 1878; m. Bessie Bell De Witt, 1892; 1 son, James De Witt. Began under Jay Gould on his Southwest system of rys., 1880; chief of constrn., Chilean Ry., S.A., 1891; with Anderson & Barr, contractors, 1892-96; supt. constrn. for James J. Hill, at Cascade Tunnel, 1897-98; prin. engr. Lehigh Valley R.R., 1899-1901; div. engr., North Western R.R., 1901-05; 1st asst. engr., N.Y.C. R.R., at Cleveland, O., 1905-24; spl. engr. Nickel Plate R.R., 1924-26. Trustee Cornell U. Mem. Bur. Municipal Research, Cleveland. Democrat. Conglist. Home: Cleveland, O. Died Feb. 5, 1928.

BEHRENS, CHARLES AUGUST, bacteriologist; b. Grand Rapids, Mich., Jan. 5, 1885; s. August Charles and Anna D. (Bornemann) B.; B.S., U. Mich., 1909, M.S., 1910, Ph.D., 1913. Began teaching U. Mich., 1910; prof. bacteriology and san. sci. Purdue U., 1914—. Commd. 1st lt. San. Corps, U.S. Army, 1918. Fellow Ind. Acad. Sci. (pres. 1923), A.A.A.S., Am. Pub. Health Assn.; hon. mem. Tippecanoe Med. Soc.; mem. Soc. Am. Bacteriologists, Mich. Acad. Sci., Am. Assn. U. Profs., Sigma Xi. Presbyn. Mason (32 deg.). Died June 22, 1950.

BELCHER, JAMES ELMER, educator; b. Millville, Mo., Oct. 30, 1885; s. James Henry and Lydia (Dotson) B.; A.B., Okla. U., 1922, A.M., 1924; grad. work, U. of Chicago, 1929; m. Blanche Martin, Aug. 7, 1917; children—Myra Lael (Mrs. Homer B. Brown, Jr.), James Elmer. Public sch. teacher in Okla., 1907-20; mem. faculty, chemistry dept., Okla. Univ., from 1922, prof. of chemistry from 1948. Mem. Am. Chem. Soc., Okla. Acad. of Sci., Phi Beta Kappa, Alpha Chi Sigma. Mem. Church of Christ (elder). Author: A Course in Qualitative Analysis (with Guy Y Williams), 1938; Experiments and Problems for College Chemistry (with Dr. J.C. Colbert), 1928; Properties and Numerical Relationships of the Common Elements and Compounds (with Dr. J.C. Colbert), 1928, Scripture and Science Harmonized by the Scientific Method, 1970. Home: Norman OK Died May 5, 1972; buried IOOF Cemetery, Norman OK

BELDEN, CHARLES DWIGHT, physician; b. Boonton, N.J., Feb. 16, 1845; s. Rev. Henry and Caroline (Wilcox) B.; ed. Williams Coll., 1861-62; served in Civil War, 1862-65; Coll. Phys. and Surg. (Columbia), 1865-66; M.D., New York Homoe Med. Coll., 1868; m. Mary E. Noble, Feb. 21, 1866; m. 2d, Katinka, Countess de Rudzinski, of Poland, Apr. 26, 1907. In New York banking firms, 1875-82. Discoverer of therapeutic use of venom of Gila monster for paralysis, locomoter ataxia and kindred disorders. Mem. Mass. Ho. of Rep., 1882, 1883. Republican. Dept. comdr. G.A.R., Ariz., 1894. Author: Orations and Addresses, 1902. Home: Eureka Springs, Ark. Died July 27, 1919.

BELDING, DAVID LAWRENCE, teacher; b. Dover Plains, N.Y., July 24, 1884; s. Charles Walter and Ellinor (Frost) B.; A.B., Williams Coll., 1905; A.M., Harvard, 1915, M.D., 1914; M.D., Boston U., 1913; m. Isabel Wheeler, Aug. 18, 1915; children—Helen Wheeler (Mrs. Manson Meads), Ellinor Frost, Elizabeth Suzanne (Mrs. Leroy L. Eldredge, Jr.). Biologist, Mass. Fish and Game Commn., Mass. Dept. Conservation, Div. Fisheries and Game, 1905-33; cons. biol., Div. Fisheries and Game since 1923; asso. Biological Bd. of Can., 1931-33; pathologist Mass. Memorial Hosps., Boston, Mass., 1915-17, bacteriologist, 1923-26, dir. of laboratories, 1926-40; research asso. Evans Memorial Hosp., 1919-45; asst. prof. bacteriology, Sch. of Medicine, Boston U., 1921-23, asso. prof., 1923-26, prof. bacteriology and pathology, 1926-36, prof. bacteriology and exptl. pathology, 1936-49, emeritus, 1950; asso. Woods Hole Oceanographic Instn., 1950-70; lectr. Bowman Gray Sch. Medicine, 1953. Cons., Cape Cod Hosp., Norfolk County Hosp. Adv. bd. Cape Cod Nat. Seashore. Served with Med. Corps, U.S. Army, 1917-19, disch. with rank of capt. Mem. sch. com., Hingham, Mass., 1924-36, mem. bd. of health, 1934-35. Mem. salmon commn., Province of Quebec, Can. Mem. Soc. Am. Bacteriologists, Soc. Exptl. Pathologists, Am. Assn. Pathologists and Bacteriologists, Am. Bd. Pathology, A.M.A., Mass. Med. Assn. (mem. legislative com. 1944-51); Soc. Exptl. Biology and Medicine, Am. Fisheries Soc. (pres. 1929-30), Am. Acad. Arts and Scis., Phi Beta Kappa, Phi Sigma Kappa. Mason. Author: Textbook of Medical Bacteriology, 1938; Textbook of Clinical Parasitology, 1942; Basic Clinical Parasitology, 1958. Home: Hingham MA Died Dec. 5, 1970; buried Hingham Cemetery.

BELL, AGRIPPA NELSON, sanitarian; b. in Northampton Co., Va., Aug. 3, 1820; s. George and Elizabeth (Scott) B.; acad. edn.; studied Tremont Med. Sch., Boston, Harvard Med. Sch.; M.D., Jefferson Med. Coll., Phila., 1842; (hon. A.M., Trinity Coll., Hartford, 1860); m. Julia Ann Hamlin, Nov. 22, 1842. Asst. and passes asst. surgeon U.S.N., 1847-55; resigned. Deiscovered, 1848, and was first to use steam as disinfectant in yellow fever, nr. Vera Cruz. Located in Brooklyn, 1855, active in quarantine reform movement; mem. Quarantine Convs., 1857, 1858, 1859, 1860; chmn. Com. on External Hygiene of latter, which reported system of quarantine regulations upon which all subsequent regulations have been founded; supt. floating hosp. for yellow fever, New York lower bay, 1861-62; drew substance N.Y. Quarantine Law, passed 1863; supervising commr. quarantine, N.Y., 1870-73; insp. quarantine Nat. Bd. Health, 1879; had charge of yellow fever extermination, New Orleans and Memphis, 1879. Founder, editor and pub. The Sanitarian, 1873-1904, 52 vols. A founder Am. Pub. Health Assn. Author: Konwledge of Living Things, 1860; Records of Daily Practice-Scientific Visiting List, 1860; The Climatology and Mineral Waters of the United States, 1885. Home: Brooklyn, N.Y. Died 1911.

BELL, ALEXANDER GRAHAM, scientist, inventor; b. Edinburgh, Scotland, Mar. 3, 1847; s. Alexander Melville and Eliza Grace (Symonds) B.; ed. at Edinburgh and London U. (hon. Ph.D., Wurzburg, 1882; M.D., Heidelberg, 1886; LL.D., Harvard, 1896, Ill., Coll., 1896, Amherst, 1901, St. Andrews, 1902; Edinburgh, 1902; George Washington, 1913; Sc.D., Oxford, 1907); m. Mabel Gardiner, d. G. G. Hubbard, 1877. Went to Canada, 1870, and to Boston, 1871, becoming prof. of vocal physiology, Boston U. Invented telephone, for which patent was granted Mar. 17, 1876; also invented photophone, induction balance and telephone probe for painless detection of bullets in the human body, for which he was awarded hon. M.D. by U. of Heidelberg, at its 500th anniversary; with C.A. Bell and Summer Taintor invented the graphaphone, 1883. Awarded, 1880, by the French Govt., the Volta Prix; medal, London Soc. of Fine Arts, 1902; Royal Albert medal; Elliot Cresson medal; John Fritz medal, 1907; Hughes medal, 1914. Officer French Legion of Honor. Founded and endowed, 1887, Volta Bureau for increase of knowledge relating to deaf; founder, ex-pres. Am. Assn. to Promote Teaching of Speech to Deaf; regent Smithsonian Instn. Fellow Am. Acad. Arts and Sciences, A.A.A.S., etc. Author of many scientific and ednl. monographs, including Memoir on the Formation of a Deaf Variety of the Human Race. Died Aug. 2, 1922.

BELL, ALEXANDER MELVILLE, educator; b. Edinburgh, Scotland, March 1, 1819; studied under his father. Alexander Bell, inventor of a method for removing impediments of speech; m. Eliza Grace Symonds, 1844; m. 2d, Harriet Guess Shibley, 1898. Lectured at univs. of Edinburgh and London; went to Canada, 1870, and Washington, 1881; invented Visible Speech, a method of instruction in orthoepy. which has also been used in teaching deaf-mutes to speak; has written many works on orthoepy, phonetics, stenography and elocution: all V4. Father of Alexander Graham Bell. Died 1905.

BELL, E(RIC) T(EMPLE), author, mathematics; b. Aberdeen, Scotland, Feb. 7, 1883; s. James and Helen Jane (Lindsay-Lyall) B.; student U. of London, 1902; A.B., Stanford, 1904; A.M., U. of Wash., 1908; Ph.D., Columbia, 1912; Bôcher prize, for math. research, 1920-24; m. Jessie Lillian Brown, 1910 (she died 1940); 1 child—Taine Temple. Professor mathematics, University of Washington, Seattle, since 1921; same, University of Chicago, summers 1924, 1925; visiting professor mathematics, Harvard, 1st half 1925, Calif. Inst. of Technology since 1926. Mem. A.A.A.S. (v.p. sect. A, 1930), Am. Math. Soc. (council, 1924-27; v.p. 1926), Math. Assn. America (pres., 1931-33), Circolo Matematico di Palermo, Calcutta Math. Soc., Nat. Acad. of Sciences, Phi Beta Kappa, Sigma Xi. Gold medalist, Calif. Commonwealth Club, 1938. Author: (books) Sixes and Sevens, 1945; The Magic of Numbers, 1947; Mathematics, Queen and Servant of Science, 1950; several novels under pseudonym John Taine; also numerous math articles. Died Dec. 21, 1960.

BELL, JOSEPH CLARK, radiologist; b. Punxsutawney, Pa., Aug. 10, 1892; s. Franklin Welch and Mary (Smitten) B.; A.B., U. of Ore., 1917; M.D., Harvard, 1923; m. Lorraine Seeley, May 20, 1925; children—Nathaniel S., Edith M., Joseph Clark. Interne med. service, Presbyn. Hosp., N.Y. City, 1923-24, asst. resident in medicine, fall 1924, resident in radiology,1924-25; pvt. practiced medicine specializing in radiology, Louisville, since 1925; head dept. radiology, Norton Meml. Infirmary since 1931; cons. in radiology Kosair Crippled Children's Hosp. 1933—, Ky. State Tuberculosis Sanatorium since 1936; sr. consultant in radiology U.S. V.A. Hosp., Nichols, since 1945; asso. prof. radiology, U. of Louisville Med. Sch., 1949-52, clin. prof. roentgenology, 1952-53, professor of roentgenology, 1953-57, prof. radiology, 1957—; consultant Armed Forces Institute of Pathology 1952-57; bd. dirs. Ky. Physicians Mt. Ins. Co. (Blue Shield). Served with MC Army, 1917-19; staff sergeant, 91st Division, A.E.F., 1918-19; lt. comdr., U.S.N.R., 1934-37; served with U.S. Army, 1942-45; chief sect. radiology, Percy Jones Gen. Hosp., Battle Creek, Mich., 1942-45; disch. to inactive service as lt. col. Awarded Army Commendation ribbon; Silver medal by Am. Roentgen Ray Soc. for exhibit, abdominal arteriography (with associates), 1950. Certified Am. Bd. Radiology, 1934. Fellow Am. Coll. Radiology (chmn. commn. on pub. relations, 1947-51, member bd. chancellors, 1953-57); member Am. Roentgen Ray Soc. (mem. pub. com. 1950-54), Radiol. Soc. North America (bd. dirs. 1945-50, chmn. bd. dirs. 1950; pres. 1951-52), A.M.A., Southern (chairman sect. on radiology 1950-51), Ky. State and Jefferson Co. (pres. 1947-48, chmn. exec. com., 1950-51) med. assns., Ky. Radiol. Soc. (pres. 1945-46), member local med. socs. Episcopalian. Club: Louisville Country (bd. dirs., 1947-49). Editor: Case discussion sect. Kentucky State Med. Jour., 1954-57. Home: Glenview, Ky. Office: Heyburn Bldg., Louisville 2. Died Apr. 25, 1960.

BELL, LAWRENCE DALE, airplane mfr.; b. Mentone, Ind., Apr. 5, 1894; s. Isaac Evans and Harriet (Sarber) B.; student Poly. High Sch., Santa Monica, Cal.; m. Lucille Mainwaring, July 17, 1915. Became shop foreman Glenn L. Martin Co., airplane mfrs., Los Angeles, 1912, later v.p. and gen. mgr.; became gen. sales mgr. Consol. Aircraft Corp., Buffalo, 1928, later v.p. and gen. mgr.; with associates organized Bell Aircraft Corp., 1935; completed airplane, the Airacuda, twin-engine fighting plane mounting 2 cannons, 1937; began making the Airacobra, pursuit plane with 1 cannon, 1939, in mass production for U.S. Army. Pres. Aircraft War Prodn. Council. Received (with John Stack and Charles E. Yeager) Collier trophy for aid in supersonic flight; chariman board W.J. Schoenberger Co., Cleve., Erie Ins. Co.; Soc. Aeronaut. Sciences, Aero Club of Buffalo (pres. 1932-34), Aircraft Industries Assn. (board govs.) Mason. Clubs: Buffalo, Buffalo Country, Saturn. Home: 925 Delaware Av. Office: Bell Aircraft Corp., P.O. Box 1, Buffalo 5. Died Oct. 20, 1956.

BELL, LOUIS, elec. engr.; b. at Chester, N.H., Dec. 5, 1861; s. Gen. Louis (U.S.A.) and Mary Anne Persis (Bouton) B.; A.B., Dartmouth Coll., 1884; grad. student, 1884, fellow in physics, 1885-88, Ph.D., 1888, Johns Hopkins; m. Sarah G. Hemenway, Dec. 3, 1893. Prof. applied electricity, Purdue U., 1888 1888-89, and organized elec. course there; editor Electrical World, New York, 1890-92; chief engr. newly organized elec. power transmission dept. of the Gen. Electric Co.; designed and installed first polyphase plants used in this country, both for power and lighting and for ry. service; consulting engr. engaged mainly on work in connection with elec. power transmission, 1895—. Has taken out 40 patents relating to power transmission and optical apparatus. Lecturer on power transmission, Mass. Inst. Tech., 1895-1905; lecturer on public lighting, Harvard U., also on illumination, Harvard Med. Sch., 1914—. Tech. officer Vol. Elec. Corps, 1898. Fellow Am. Acad. Arts and Sciences; mem. Am. Inst. Elec. Engr., Illuminating Engring. Soc. (past pres.), etc. Mem. advisory com. Council of Nat. Defense. Unitarian. Republican. Author: The Electric Railway (with Oscar T. Crosby), 1892; Power Distribution for Electric Railroads, 1896; Electric Power Transmission, 1897; The Art of Illumination, 1902; Boston Electrical Handbook (as chmn. Publn. Com.), 1904; The Telescope, 1922. Home: West Newton, Mass. Died June 14, 1923.

BELL, WILLIAM BONAR, biologist; b. Milton, Ia., June 2, 1877; s. Robert Pollock and Isabell (Bonar) B.; M. Didactics, Ia. State Teachers Coll., Cedar Falls, 1899; A.B., State U. of Ia., 1902, M.S., 1903, Ph.D., 1905; m. Clara Carlton Preston, Sept. 5, 1906; children—Julia Carlton, David Bonar. Asst. prof. biology, later prof. zoölogy and physiology, N.D. Agrl. Coll., 1905-16; biol. Fish and Wildlife Service, U.S. Department Interior, Wasington, D.C., since 1916, title chief div. of wild life research. Retired Aug. 1, 1944. Fellow A.A.A.S.; mem. Am. Soc. Mammalogists, Soc. of Am. Foresters, Am. Forestry Assn., Am. Ornithologists Union, Washington Biol. Soc., Wash. Acad. Sci., Sigma Alpha Epsilon, Sigma Xi, Alpha Zeta. Episcopalian. Mason, Author of govt. reports and bulls. Home: 803 Rittenhouse St. N.W., Washington 11, D.C. Died March 30, 1949.

BELLAMY, LESLIE BURGESS, engr.; b. Wales, 1909; s. Henry and Sarah Alice (Adams) B.; student Beaufort Boys Sch., EBBW Vale Sch.; student U. Mich. (extension div.), 1933-35; m. Gwyneth Elizabeth Jones, June 13, 1935; children—Lloyd Burgess, John Stanley. Came to U.S., 1928, naturalized, 1934. Supt. materials specifications Packard Motor Car Co., 1937-44; chief tool research engr. Sterling Grinding Wheel div., Cleveland Quarries Co., 1944, mgr. Michigan, Ohio Territory, 1946-53, general manager, 1953—. v.p. Abrasive & Metal Products Company, 1956—. Member American Standards Assn. (certificate of appreciation 1950), Am. Soc. Tool Engrs. (pres. 1952-53, past nat. dir., chmn. nat. standards com.; certificate Det. chpt. 1950), Engring. Soc. Det., Nat., Mich. socs. profl. engrs. Methodist (trustee, mem. finance com.). Mason, Soujourner. Author tech. articles. Home: 14190 Rosemont, Detroit. Office: 729 Meldrum, Detroit. Died Jan. 20, 1962; buried Roseland Park Cemetery, Berkeley, Mich.

BELLANCA, GUISEPPE MARIO, airplane engr.; b. Sciacca, Italy, Mar. 19, 1886; s. Andrea and Concetta (Merlo) B.; tchrs.' certificate in math., Instituto Tecnico;

Milan, Italy; degree in engring. math., Politecnico, Milan; m. Dorothy Brown, Nov. 18, 1922; 1 son, August Thomas. Came to U.S., 1911, naturalized, 1929. Established lab. for spl. research in aviation, 1909; head of Bellanca Airplane Sch., Mineola, N.Y. 1912-16; cons. engr., Md. Pressed Steel Co., Hagerstown, 1917-20; cons. engr. for airplane constrn., Wright Aero. Corp., Paterson, N.J., 1923-26; organizer, 1927, former pres. Bellanca Aircraft Corp., Bellanca Aircraft Corp. Am.; also chmn. bd., dir. engring. Designer and builder 1st cabin monoplane in U.S., transatlantic monoplane, "Columbia," and 1st transpacific monoplane, "Miss Veedol." Mem. Am. Soc. M.E., Soc. Automotive Engrs., Aero. C. of C., Early Birds, Quiet Birdmen. Democrat. Catholic. Contbr. tech. papers on aviation. Home: Shorewood Farm, Galena, Md. Office: Bellanca Aircraft Corp., New Castle, Del. Died Dec. 26, 1960.

BELLOWS, HOWARD PERRY, M.D. (aurist); b. Fall River, Mass., Apr. 30, 1852; s. Albert F. (N.A., New York) and Candace (Brown) B.; B.S., Cornell U., 1875, M.S., 1879; M.D., Boston Univ. Medical Sch., 1877; hon. Sc.D., Boston Univ., 1931; also medical courses at Leipzig, Vienna, and Halle, etc.; m. Mary A. Clarke, June 20, 1880. Gen. Practitioner until 1890, since exclusively aural practice; for 7 yrs. actively engaged, by experimentation and writing, in promoting a more scientific investigating of drug action, with particular reference to needs of specialists; prof. , physiology, 1877-85, prof. otology, 1886-1929, now prof. emeritus, Boston U. Med. Sch.; consl. aural surgeon, Mass. Homeo. Hosp.; mem. consl. bd. Westborough State Hosp. Republican. Swedenborgian. Home: Cambridge, Mass. Died Oct. 16, 1934.

BELT, BENJAMIN CARLETON, geologist; b. Marshall, Mo., Apr. 9, 1889; s. Bailey Carleton and Jane (Barr) B.; B.S., U. Okla., 1910; m. Ruth Albertine Watson, Dec. 13, 1921; 1 dau., Ruth Althea. Field geologist Mexican Eagle Oil Co., Mexico, 1910-14; ind. geologist, Tulsa, 1914-16; chief geologist Mexican Gulf Oil Co., Mexico, also Cuba, 1916-17; chief geologist Gulf Oil Corp., Ft. Worth, 1917-21, 25-29, Houston, 1929-33, asst. to v.p., 1933-50, v.p., 1950. mng. exec. Houston Prodn. div. Gulf Oil Corp., Gulf Refining Co., 1950-55; mgr. Pantepec Oil Co., Tampico, Mexico, 1921-24; investigation petroleum resources Vacuum Oil Co., Australia, New Zealand, 1924-25, Houston, 1925; cons., 1955—; chairman of board Modular Bldgs., Inc.; director Sea Minerals, Incorporated, Western Natural Gas Corporation, Texas Gulf Sulphur Co.; chmn. proxy com. Sinclair Oil & Refinning Co. Chmn. trustees, mem. exec. com. United Fund, 1954-56, chmn. United Fund Nat. Agy. Com.; mem. adv. com. United Funds of United Community Funds and Councils Am., Inc., 1955; mem. nat. citizens com. United Community Campaigns Am., 1955; co-chmn. spl. gifts division United Fund campaign, 1956-61; hon. mem. bd. trustees United Fund, vice chmn. 1960 campaign; mem. bd. Cath. Charities; building and development com. Salvation Army, 1959; gen. chmn. building fund campaign St. Joseph's Hosp., 1959; mem. Tex. exec. com. Crusade for Freedom campaign, 1959. Exec. com., dir. Community Council, 1954-55; pres. Tex. County Home Rule Assn., 1958-59; mem. water adv. com. City of Houston; bd. dirs. Greater Houston Bowl Assn. Chmn. trustees U. St. Thomas, Houston, 1959-60; mem. bd. trustees Mus. Natural History, Houston, Hodgkin's Disease Meml. Research Center, Houston; mem. bd. dirs. Houston Council on Alcoholism; mem. adv. bd. Spindletop Fund for Advancement of Med. Research; mem. bd. govs. U. Houston, 1957—. Recipient award for leadership United Fund of Houston and Harrison County, 1956; distinguished service award Mid-Continent Oil and Gas Assn., 1956; award for leadership in orgn. better Tex. govt., Texas Research League, 1957; brotherhood citation Nat. Conf. Christians and Jews, Houston, 1958; award for distinguished service Houston C. of C., 1958. Mem. Am. Petroleum Inst. Mid. Continent Oil and Gas Assn., Am. Assn. Petroleum Geologists. Houston Geol. Soc., Texas Research League (dir. 1952-55, chmn. 1956-57, vice chmn. 1958, exec. com. 1959, 60), Houston C. of C. (pres. 1955-58, exec. com., dir. 1959, 60), Am., TEx., E. Tex., Houston hereford assns. Clubs: Serra; Interfaith-in-Action; River Oaks Country, Houston, Petroleum (mem. adv. com. 1959-60, past dir.) (Houston). Home: 2414 Rosamond, Apt. 120, Houston 6. Office: Houston Club Bldg., Houston 2. Died 1962.

BEMAN, WOOSTER WOODRUFF, univ. prof.; b. Southington, Conn., May 28, 1850; s. Woodruff and Lois Jane (Neal) B.; A.B., U. of Mich., 1870, A.M., 1873; (LL.D., Kalamazoo, 1908); m. Ellen Elizabeth Burton, Sept. 4, 1877. Instr. Greek and mathematics, Kalamazoo Coll., 1870-71; instr., mathematics, 1871-74, asst. prof., 1874-82, asso. prof., 1882-87, prof., 1887—, U. of Michigan. Treas. Mich. Bapt. Conv., 15 years; mem. exec. com. Northern Bapt. Conv., 1910-16; of Fed. Council Chs. of Christ in America, 1916-20. Democrat. Joint author (with David Eugene Smith): Plane and Solid Geometry, 1895; Higher Arithmetic, 1897; Famous Problems of Elementary Geometry (from the German of Klein), 1897; New Plane and Solid Geometry, 1899; Elements of Algebra, 1900; A Brief History of Mathematics (from the German of Fink), 1900; Sundara Row's Geometric Exercises in Paper Folding (revision), 1901; Academic Algebra, 1902. Author: Continuity and Irrational Numbers; Nature and Meaning of Numbers (from the German of Dedekind), 1901. Home: Ann Arbor, Mich. Died Jan. 18, 1922.

BEMENT, ALBURTO, engineer; b. at Appleton, Wis., Mar. 18, 1862; s. Cyrenius Elihu and Martha Ann (Gibson) B.; m. Eva, d. Daniel Delos Henderson, of Berkeley, Cal., 1910. Mem. advisory com. for Fuel Testing Expt. Sta., U. of Ill.; mem. bd. consulting engrs. smoke abatement commn., Chicago. Has conducted many spl. expts. and researches for improvement of efficiency of steam boilers and the prevention of smoke form Furnaces using bituminous coal, chem. composition of coal, etc.; thrice recipient of Chanute medal of Western Soc. of Engrs.; mem. com. Chicago Assn. Commerce to report on feasibility of electricication of Chicago ry. terminals, 1910; was chmn. com. apptd. by Western Soc. Engrs. to report on Chicago harbor problem; chmn. com. organized for purpose of securing establishment of Sch. of Mines at U. of Ill.; etc. Charter mem. Am. Inst. Chem. Engrs. Author of first comprehensive report on Ill. coal fields; etc. Home: Hubbard Woods, Ill. Office: 28 N. Market St., Chicago, Ill.

BEMENT, CALEB, N., agrl. writer, inventor; b. N.Y. State, 1790. Engaged as printer in N.Y., circa 1820; bought "Three Hills Farm" nr. Albany, N.Y., 1834, began agrl. experimentation; developed Bement's corn cultivator, Bement's turnip drill; breeder imported live stock; an editor monthly agrl. jour. Central N.Y. Farmer, 1844; mgr. Am. Hotel, Albany, 1844-circa 1850; propr., editor Am. Quarterly Jour. of Agr. and Science, 1848 (failed after 1 year); owner Albany Steam Mills producing substitute for yeast, 1853-55; farmer, Dutchess County, N.Y., 1855-67. Author: American Poulterer's Companion, 1844; The Rabbit Fancier, 1855; contbr. numerous articles to agrl. jours. Died Poughkeepsie, N.Y., Dec. 22, 1868; buried Poughkeepsie.

BENDIX, VINCENT, engr., inventor, industrialist; b. Moline, Illinois, 1882; son of Rev. John Bendix; mechanical, engineering and general education; m. Elizabeth Channon, Apr. 6, 1922 (divorced). Early pioneer in design and building of automobiles; inventor Bendix drive which made automobile self starting practicable, has been used on more than 65 million cars; introduced in U.S. first volume production 4-wheel brakes for automobiles; organized and chmn. bd. Bendix Aviation Corp., comprising allied group mfgs. here and abroad of automotive, aviation, marine and industrial apparatus until retired in 1942; instrumental in development and formation corp. for manufacture Bendix Home Laundry; dir. Pioneer Instrument Co., Bendix Eclipse of Can., Bendix Home Appliances, Jaeger Watch Co. Founder and sponsor Bendix Transcontinental Air Race and donor Bendix Trophy; sponsor Internat. Gilder Meet, Elmira, N.Y., and donor of Bendix Glider Trophy. Past pres. Soc. Automotive Engrs.; dir. Swedish Chamber of Commerce (New York). Clubs: Engineers (N.Y.); Metropolitan, Cloud, Economic, Lotos (New York); Bath and Tennis, Seminole (Palm Beach); Woodmount Rod and Gun Club (Berkley Springs, W.Va.); Havana Country (Cubs). Office: 401 Bendix Drive, South Bend, Ind.; also 30 Rockefeller Plaza, New York, N.Y. Died Mar. 27, 1945.

BENECKE, ADELBERT OSWALD, electrical engineer; b. Elbing, Prussia, Germany, July 31, 1855; s. of Adolph C. and Adelheid (Abs) B.; grad. Gymnasium, Elbing, 1876; U. of Koenigsberg, 1876-79 (studied mathematics, physics, chemistry and astronomy, 1877-79); asst. Royal Obs., Koenigsberg, 1880-82, continued studies at U. of Berlin; traveled through Europe to study phys. and elec. laboratory methods and equipments; m. Auguste Dreher, of Koenigsberg, Jan. 1884. Identified with the mfr. scientific instruments in Berlin, 1882-89; chief elec. engr. Weston Elec. Instrument Co., Newark, N.Y., 1891-05; chief engr. and factory mgr. Am. Instrument Co., Newark, 1906-09; chief engr. Industrial Instrument Co., Foxboro, Mass., 1909-12; consulting engr., Swampscott, Mass., 1913—. Fellow Am. Inst. E.E., A.A.A.S.; mem. Electrochem. Soc. Home: 374 Humphrey St., Swampscott, Massachusetts.

BENEDICT, C. HARRY, metallurgist; b. Pittsburgh, Pa., Sept. 24, 1876; s. Joseph and Hannah (Goldsmith) B.; B.S., Cornell U., 1897; D.Sc., Mich. Coll. of Mines, 1932; m. Lena Manson, Feb. 4, 1902; children—Manson, William S. Metallurgist for Calumet & Hecla Consol. Copper Co., 1898-1949; lecturer on hydro-metallurgy, Mich. Coll. of Mines, since 1919; mem. bd. control Mich. Coll. Mines and Metall. since 1952. Mem. Am. Inst. Mining and Metall. Engrs. (v.p. 1948-51, director, 1952—; recipient of Robert H. Richards Award, 1954), Mining and Metall. Soc. Am. (dir. 1947), Am. Chem. Soc., Am. Inst. Chem. Engring. Democrat. Jewish religion. Mason. Author: Red Metal. Inventor of ammonia bleaching process for copper. Home: Lake Linden MI

BENEDICT, HARRIS MILLER, botanist; b. Buda, Ill., Dec. 8, 1873; s. Miller Samuel and Anna Maria (Harris) B.; B.A., Doane Coll., Crete, Neb., 1894; B.S., U. of Neb., 1896, A.M., 1897; Ph.D., Cornell, 1914; m. Florence Stevens McCrea, 1906; children—Harris, Jean, Ann, Martha, McCrea. Head of biol. dept. Lincoln (Neb.) High Sch., 1897-99, Omaha High Sch., 1899-1902; instr. biology, 1902-03, asst. prof. 1904-08, asso. prof., 1908-11, prof. 1911-14, prof. botany, 1914—U. of Cincinnati; organized dept. of botany, U. of Cincinnati, 1914. Originator, 1908, and dir. Emery Bird Reserve (the first city bird reserve), Cincinnati and organized the first sch. garden courses, for teachers of Cincinnati shcs., and a pre-agrl. course for univ. students. Democrat. Presbyterian. Contbr. articles concerning researches on senility in perennial woody plants, as well as many minor papers of popular nature on botany, nature study and bird protection. Home: Cuncinnati. O. Died Oct. 17, 1928.

BENEDICT, RALPH C., prof. biology; Syracuse, N.Y., June 14, 1883; s. Abel Carter and Lizzie Miranda (Parmelee) B.; Ph.B., Syracuse Univ., 1906; Ph.D., Columbia U., 1911; m. Edna Diack Austin, Sept. 2, 1911; children—Ruth Austin (Mrs. Bertram H. Davis), Kathryn Parmelee (Mrs. Robert M. Eastman), Richard Austin, Albert Carter. Botanist, N.Y. Bot. Garden, 1906-11; resident investigator Bklyn. Bot. Garden, 1914-31. Fordham Univ., 1908-09; N.Y. U., 1908-10, high schs., N.Y.C., 1912-31; prof. biology, Bklyn Coll., 1931-53; dir. farm labor project, 1942-44. Founder, editor Am. Fern Jour., 1910—. Fellow A.A.A.S.; mem. Am. Assn. U. Profs., Am. Fern Soc., History of Science Soc., Am. Biology Tchrs. Assn., Torrey Bot. Club. Home: 1819 Dorchester Rd., Bklyn. 26. Died Aug. 1965.

BENEDICT, RUTH FULTON, anthropologist; b. New York, N.Y., June 5, 1887; d. Frederick S. and Beatrice J. (Shattuck) Fulton; A.B., Vassar Coll., 1909; Ph.D., Columbia U., 1923; m. Stanley R. Benedict, June 18, 1914 (died DEc. 21, 1936). Lecturer in anthropology. Columbia U., 1923-30, asst. prof., 1930-36, asso. prof., 1936-48, prof., 1948; field trips to Am. Indian tribes, 1922-39; on leave with Bureau of Overseas Intelligence, O.W. I., 1943-46. Author: Patterns of Culture, 1934; Zuni Mythology (2 Vols.), 1935; Race: Science and Policies, 1940; The Chrysanthemum and the Sword: Patterns of Japanese Culture, 1946. Home: 448 Central Park West, New York 25. Office: Dept. of Anthropology, Columbia University, New York, N.Y. Died Sept. 17, 1948.

BENET, LAURENCE VINCENT; mech. engr.; b. West Point, N.Y., Jane. 12, 1863; s. Brig. Gen. Stephen V. and Laura (Walker) B.; prep. edn., Emerson Inst., Washington; Ph.B., Yale, 1884; m. Margaret Cox, Dec. 20, 1899 (died July 20, 1941). With La Société Hotchkiss & Cie., Paris, since 1885; now hon. pres. Ensign U.S. Navy, Spanish-Am. War, 1898; with Am. Ambulance and Hosp. Service, Aug. 1914-1917, rank of comdt.; mem. adivsory com. Purchasing Bd., A.E.F., Sept. 1917-Jan. 1918. Past pres. and gold medalist Am. Chamber Commerce in France, Am. Aid Soc. Decorated Grand Officer Leigon of Honor, Medal of Honro, 1st Class (France); Comdr. Mil. Order of Christ (Portugal); Comdr. Order of Crown of Rumania; Officer of Osmania (Turkey); Am. Field Service, First Class, etc. Mem. Am. Soc. Mech. Engrs., Yale Engring. Assn., Nat. councillor Chamber Commerce of the U.S., Ingénieurs Civiles de France, U.S. Naval Inst., S.R., S.A.R., Loyal Legion, Mil. Order of Foreing Wars of the U.S., U.S. Army Ordnance Assn., United Vets. of Spanish-Am. War; fellow Am. Geog. Soc., St. Augustine's Hist. Soc. Republican. Episcopalian. Clubs: Metropolitan, Army and Navy (Washington); University (New York); Cercle Interallié. American (Paris) Home: 2101 Connecticut Av., Washington, D.C. Died May 21, 1948; buried in Arlington Nat. Cemetery.

BENIOFF, HUGO, scientist; b. Los Angeles, Sept. 14, 1899; s. Simon and Alfrieda (Wilderquist) Hamilton b.; B.A., Pomona Coll., 1921; Ph.D., Cal. Inst. Tech., 1935; m. Alice Silverman, Feb. 27, 1928; children—Paul, Dagmar (Mrs. E. Friedman), Elena (Mrs. E.G. Jackson, Jr.); m. 2d, Mildred Lent, Oct. 31, 1953; 1 dau., Martha Gwen. Asst. Mt. Wilson Obs., 1917-21, seismol. research Carnegie Inst. Washington 1923-24; staff seismol. lab. Cal. Inst. Tech., 1934—, prof., 1950-64, seismology prof. emeritus, 1964—; research engr. Submarine Signal Co., 1939-45, cons., Baldwin Piano Co., 1946-62; mem. Ad Hoc Group on Detection Nuclear Explosions; mem. panel on seismic improvement Dept. State; mem. adv. com. for geophysics Air Force Office Sci. Research; chmn. cons. bd. for earthquake analysis Cal. Dept. Water Resources; cons. Nat. Sci. Found., 1953; research on stress strain characteristics and structure of earth's crust. Recipient Arthur L. Day award Geol. Soc. America; William Bowie medal Am. Geophysical Union, 1965. Fellow Am. Acad. of Arts Sci., A.A.A.S., Geological Soc. Am.; mem. Nat. Acad. Sci., Am. Phys. Soc., Acoustical Soc. Am., Am. Geophys. Union, Seismol. Soc. Am., Royal Astron. Soc., Phi Beta Kappa. Patentee seismographs. Home: Camptche-Ukiah Rd., Mendocino, Cal. 95460 Died Feb. 29, 1968.

BENMOSCHE, M(OSES), surgeon; b. London, England, Dec. 5, 1883; s. Herman and Jane B.; student St. Mary's Male Acad., Norfolk, Va.; M.D. Med. Coll. of Va., 1904; student Middlesex Hosp. and Coll., London, Eng., 1908-11; m. Simma Guttwoch, 1908; children—Elkanah, Jacob; m. 2d, Gwladys Goodman, August 5, 1943. Instr. in histology, pathology, bacteriology, Medical Coll. of Va., 1904-06; asst. in cancer research, Middlesex Hosp., London, 1908-09;

dir. Pathol. Lab., Mobray Hsop., Capetown, S. Africa, 1911-12; dir. Pathol. Lab., Nashua, N.H., 1913-14; practice of surgery, Detroit, Mich., 1915-19; gen. surgery practice and research in cancer, N.Y. City, since 1920; senior in clin. surgery Mt. Sinai Hosp., N.Y. City; certified teacher of anatomy, dept. of anatomy, Middlesex Hosp. Med. Coll., London, Eng. First, with Dr. Frances I. Seymour, to describe the magnification of a fertile human spermatzoon under the electron microscope. Manhattan chmn. City Fusion party, N.Y. City, 1937. Apptd. by gov. of Va. as del. to International Congress on Tuberculosis, Washington, D.C., 1908; chairman, Am. Com. Nat. Sick Fund of Palestine. Hebrew religion. Mason, K.P. (chairman emeritus Grand Lodge com. ritual and instrn.; past supreme regent, Princess of Syracuse). Author: Waifs and Orphans, A Book of Selected Selected Poems; A Surgeon Explains to the Layman, 1940; also monographs on cancer research; also surgical papers on method of reconstructing the internal ring in indirect inguinal hernia. Address: 600 W. 111th St., N.Y.C. Died Sept. 5, 1952.

BENNER, RAYMOND CALVIN, chemist; b. Minneapolis, Minn., May 13, 1877; s. Webster and Clara Ellen (Hoak) B.; B.S. in chemistry, U. of Minn., 1902; M.A., U. of Wis., 1906, Ph.D., 1909; m. Lillian Brownell Stebbins, of Minneapolis, June 8, 1908; children—Eleanore, Priscilla, Mary. Instr. Mich. Agrl. Coll., 1902-03; U. of Wis., 1903-06; asst. prof. chemistry, U. of Ariz., 1906-11; prof. electrometallurgy, U. of Pittsburgh, 1911-13; dir. Fremont (O.) Labs. of the Nat. Carbon Co., 1913-25; research engr. Gen. Chemical Co., N.Y. City, 1925-26; dir. research, Carborundum Co., Niagara Falls, N.Y., since 1926. Chemist Wis. Geol. Survey, 1903-06; in charge of smoke investigation, Pittsburgh, 1911-13; mem. U.S. Assay Commn., 1912-13. Mem. Am. Chem. Soc., A.A.A.S., Am. Inst. Mining and Metall. Engrs., Am. Ceramic Soc., British Ceramic Soc., Am. Refractories Inst., Alpha Chi Sigma, Acacia, Chemists' Club (New York); Niagara Falls Chamber of Commerce. Mason. Democrat. Conglist. Contbr. many articles on metall. and tech. subjects. Granted over 200 patents in field of chemistry. Home: 640 College Av., Niagara Falls NY

BENNETT, ALBERT ARNOLD, mathematician, b. Yokohama, Japan, June 2, 1888; s. Albert Arnold and Mela Isabelle (Barrows) B.; came to U.S. in 1902; A.B., A.M., Brown Univ., 1910, Sc.M., 1911; Ph.D., Princeton, 1915; studied univs. of Paris, Gottingen, Bologna and Chicago; m. Velma McAfee Ely, June 17, 1922; one daughter, Betsy Bennett Miller. Instructor Princeton Univ., 1914-16; adj. professor U. of Tex., 1916-21, asso. prof., 1921-25; prof. and head of dept., Lehigh U., 1925-27; prof. mathematics, Brown U., from 1927. Editor in chief, Math. Monthly, 1923; mathematics editor Prentice-Hall, Inc. Student 1st O.T.C., Leon Springs, Tex., and Ft. Monroe, Va.; commd. capt. C.A.R.C., Aug. 15, 1917; trans. to ordnance, June 1918; hon. discharged Jan. 15, 1919; mathematics and dynamics expert, Ordnance Corps, June 1919-Sept. 1921; maj. Ordnance Corps, A.U.S., 1942-46, lt. col., 1946. Member Am. Math. Soc., Math. Assn. America (trustee 1922, v.p. 1925, 33), Am. Academy Arts and Sciences, Progressive Edn. Assn. (adv. council, 1933), A.A.A.S., Am. Assn. Univ. Profs., Am. Soc. Engring. Education, Assn. Computing Machines, Assn. Symbolic Logic (council), 1935, Assn. Teachers Math. New England (president 1941), Nat. Council Teachers of Math., Institute Math. Statistics, Rhode Island Sch. Design (Corp. mem.), Phi Beta Kappa, Sigma Xi, Delta Upsilon. Author: Introduction to Ballistic (Ordnance Dept. U.S.A.), 1921; Tables for Interior Ballistics (same), 1922; (with C.A. Baylis) Formal Logic, 1939. Address: Providence RI Died Feb. 17, 1971.

BENNETT, DONALD MENZIES, educator, b. Milw., Nov. 24, 1897; s. William Chase and Jean Louise (Menzies) B.; B.A., U. Wis., 1921, M.A., 1922, Ph.D., 1926; m. Irene Marie Schubring, Aug. 7, 1922; 1 son Robert Menzies. Asst. physics U. Wis., 1920-22, 24-26; instr. U. Colo., 1922-24; asst. prof. physics U. Louisville, 1926-29, asso. prof., 1929-44, professor heading engineering physics, 1944-56, acting head department of physics, College of Arts and Sciences, 1953-56; head, 1956; technical aide to dir. radiation lab. Mass. Inst. Tech., 1944; research participant Oak Ridge Nat. Labs., 1950. Regional counseler in physics for Kentucky. Member Louisville Engring. and Sci. Socs. Council (v.p. 1953-55), Ky. Assn. Physics Tchrs. (past pres.), Am. Phys. Soc., Am. Acoustical Soc., A.A.A.S., American Association University Professors, Kentucky Academy of Science, American Assn. Physics Teachers, Phi Beta Kappa, Sigma Xi, Sigma Tau, Phi Mu Alpha, Kappa Delta Pi, Sigma Pi Sigma, Phi Kappa Phi, Alpha Epsilon Delta. Club: Torch (pres. 1956-57) (Louisville, Ky.). Author: Fundamentals of Physics, 1936; Physical Basis of Music, 1956. Home: Louisville KY Died Nov. 7, 1971; inurned Columbarium, Resthaven Meml. Park and Cemetery, Louisville KY

BENNETT, EDWARD, cons. elec. engr.; b. Pitts., Oct. 26, 1876; s. Benjamin and Mary J. (Davis) B.; E.E., Western U. Pa., 1897; m. Ethel Moore, Aug. 16, 1911. Apprentice, Westinghouse Electric & Mfg. Co., 1897-98, research work, 1899; research engr. for George Westinghouse in development of Nernst lamp, later chief engr. Nernst Lamp Co., 1899-1904; mem. firm Beebe & Bennett, 1904-05; head electrician Nat. Electric Signaling Co., Washington, 1905-06; with Telluride Power Co., of Utah, 1906-09; with U. Wis., 1909-43, successively successively, asso. prof. elec. engring. until 1913, prof. 1913-43, chmn. dept., 1918-40, prof. emeritus 1943; cons. engr., 1943-50. Del. Internat. Dlectrotech. Commn. as rep. Am. Inst. E.E., Paris, France, 1950. Fellow Am. Inst. E.E. (v.p. 1924-26), Inst. Radio Engrs., Am. Phys. Soc.; mem. A.A.A.S., Am. Assn. U. Profs., Soc. for Promotion Engring. Edn. (v.p. 1929-30), Wis. Acad. Sci., History of Philosophy Assn., Acad. Polit. Sci., Sigma Xi, Tau Beta Pi, Eta Kappa Nu, Phi Kappa Phi. Club: University. Author: Introductory Electrodynamics for Engineers, 1926; also numerous bulls. and papers on edn. and engring. Home: 1919 Jefferson St., Madison, Wis. Died Jan. 10, 1951; buried Forest Hill Cemetery, Madison.

BENNETT, EDWARD HERBERT, architect; b. Cheltenham, Eng., May 12, 1874; s. Capt. Edwin C. and Margaret (Callas) B.; grad. Bristol Tech. Coll.; diploma in architecture Ecole des Beaux Arts, Paris, 1900; m. Catherine Jones, Oct. 18, 1913; 1 son, Edward II.; m. 2d, Olive Mary Holden, Jan. 5, 1930. Came to U.S., 1890; began in architect's office, San Francisco, 1892; with George B. Post, N.Y.C., 1-1/2 yrs.; with D.H. Burnham & Co., Chgo., 1904-09; specialized in city planning, 1909—; architect for Chgo. Plan Commn.; planner of Camp Grant, Rockford, Ill., and Camp Henry Knox, Stithton, Ky., cons. archtl. specialist to the sec. of the treasury, chmn. Bd. Architects of U.S. Treasury on Govt. Bldgs., 1927-33; organizer, mem. Bennett, Parson] sn, Frost & Thomas, changing in 1924 to Bennett, Parsons & Frost, city planners, designers archtl. development of Grant Park, Clarence Buckingham Meml. Fountain, Chgo., deptl. bldgs., Capitol Approach, Washington, D.C. Mem. Archtl. Commn. of Chgo. World's Fair Centennial Celebration, 1933. Decorated Chevalier Legion of Honor (France), 1928. Fellow A.I.A.; mem. City Planning Inst., Soc. Beaux Arts Architects. Episcopalian. Clubs: Century, Chicago, Casino, Onwentsia. Author many city planning reports, including Plan of San Francisco, 1905; Plan of Chicago, 1909; Plan of Ottawa and Hull, Can., 1915; Plan of Minneapolis, 1917; chapter on Public Buildings and Quasi-Public Buildings in City Planning by John Nolen, 1916; also chapters to City Planning, 1923, and City Planning for Detroit, 1925. As an artist has exhibited oil and water color paintings at Art Inst. of Chicago, Arts Club, New Orleans Mus. of Art, Artists League of Midwest, Lake Forest Acad., 1946, Tryon, N.C., 1947. Held one-man show, Quest Art Galleries, 1940, Mandel Bros. Art Galleries, Chgo., 1949-51. Recipient 1st Premium in oil, 2d in watercolores Piedmont Interstate Fair (amateur sect.), 1952. Home: 89 E. Deerpath, Lake Forest, Ill.; also Long Lane, Tryon, N.C. Office: 80 E. Jackson Blvd., Chgo. Died Oct. 14, 1954; buried Lake Forest, Ill.

BENNETT, HUGH HAMMOND, soil conservation; b. nr. Wadesboro, N.C., Apr. 15, 1881; s. William Osborne and Rosa May (Hammond) B.; grad. D. A. McGregor Sch., Wadesboro, 1896; B.S., University of N.C., 1903, LL.D., 1936; D.Sc., Clemson College, 1937; D.Sc., Columbia University, 1952; married Sarah Edna McCue, 1907 (died 1909); 1 dau., Sarah Edna (Mrs. Eugene Akers); m. 2d, Betty Virginia Brown, 1921; 1 son, Hugh Hammond. Soil scientist Soil Survey Div., Bur. of Soils, Dept. Agr., 1903-09, insp. in soil survey, 1909, 28; mem. agrl. expdn. Canal Zone, 1909; in charge explorative expdn., Alaska, 1914; mem. Chugach Nat. Forest Commn., 1916, Guatemala-Honduras Boundary Commn., 1919, Rubber Commn. to Central and S. America and W.I., 1923-24; in charge agrl. survey of Cuba, winters 1925-32; in charge, soil erosion and moisture conservation investigation, Bur. of Chemistry and Soils, U.S. Dept. of Agr., 1928-33; dir. Soil ErosErosion Service, U.S. Dept. Interior, 1933-35; chief Soil Conservation, Dept. Agr., 1935-52, ret. in 1952. Served as 1st lt., corps engrs., U.S. Army, 1918. Recipient Cullum Medal from American Geog. Soc. Fellow Soil Conservation Soc. of Am. (founder), Am. Soc. of Agronomy, Am. Geog. Soc., A.A.A.S.; mem. Canadian Conservation Assn. (hon.), Internat. Union for Protection of Nature (honorary president), Assn. Am. Geographers (pres. 1943), Washington Acad. Sci., Am. Soc. Agronomy, Friends of Land, Am. Forestry Assn., Phi Delta Theta. Democrat. Episcopalian. Clubs: Cosmos, Explorers. Author several boosk relating to field, 1913—. Contbr. to periodicals. Home: Eight Oaks, 5411 Kirby Rd., Falls Church, Va. Died July 7, 1960; buried Arlington Nat. Cemetery, Va.

BENNETT, WENDELL C(LARK), anthropologist; b. Marion, Ind., Aug. 17, 1905; s. William Rainey and Ethel (Clark) B.; Ph.B., U. of Chicago, 1927, Ph.D., 1930; m. Hope Ranslow, Oct. 30, 1935; children—Lucy, Martha. Asst. in anthropology, Am. Museum Natural History, 1931-38; asso. prof. anthropology, U. of Wis., 1938-40; asso. prof. of anthropology, Yale, 1940-45, prof. since 1945; specializes in Andean archeology. Exec. secretary Joint Com. Latin Am. Studies, 1942-44. Fellow Royal Anthrop. Inst. Gt. Britain and Ireland (hon.); mem. Am. Anthrop. Assn. (pres. 1952), Soc. Am. Archeology, Beta Theta Pi, Sigma Xi. Club: Cosmos. Author: The Tarahumara (with R.M. Zingg), 1935; (monographs) Excavations at Tiahuanaco; Excavations in Bolivia; Excavations on the North Coast of Peru; the North Highlands of Peru; Archeological Regions of Colombia; Excavations in the Cuenca region, Ecuador; Northwest Argentine Aracheology; Aneadn Culture History. Home: 176 Linden St., New Haven, Conn. Died Sept. 8, 1953.

BENNETT, WILLIAM ZEBINA, chemist; b. Montpelier, Vt., Feb. 25, 1856; s. George Hackett and Emiline (Young) B.; A.B., Harvard, 1878, A.M., 1881; Ph.D., U. of Wooster, 1883; studied twice abroad, first time, 1888, in Lab. of Imperial Bd. of Health, Berline, last time, 1901-10, in lab. of Emil Fischer, Berlin, last time, 1901-10, in lab. of Emil Fischer, Berlin, and in Sorbonne, Paris; m. Minnie Sinclair Proctor, Aug. 14, 1884. Asst. in chemistry, Harvard, 1878-80; asst. prof. chemistry, 1880-83. Kauke prof., natural sicences, 1883-86, Brown prof. chemistry and physics, 1886-1902, Brown prof. chemistry and dir. chem. lab., U. of Wooster, 1902-24; retired. Presbyn. Has done important research work in organic and physical chemistry and water analysis. Home: Pasadena, Calif. Died. 1938.

BENNITT, RUDOLF, educator; b. Springfield, Mass., Dec. 22, 1898; s. Francis Marion and Elizabeth Chandler (Allton) B.; B.S., Boston U., 1920, A.M., 1921; A.M., Ph.D., Harvard, 1923; m. Ruth Eunice Eynon, June 25, 1923; children—Elizabeth Allton, Eleanor Jackson. With Marine Biol. Lab., Woods Hole, Mass., summers 1918-20, 22, instr. in invertebrate zoology, 1925-29; with Bermuda Biol. Sta., summer 1921; with Winona Lake Biol. Sta., Ind. U., summer 1924; instr. in Biology Tufts Coll., 1924-27; asso. prof. zoology U. Mo., 1927-37, prof. zoology, 1937-44, William Rucker prof. zoology, 1944—; with Stone Lab., Ohio State U., summer 1930; survey of resident game and furbearers of Mo., under auspices Nat. Park Service, 1934-35. Fellow A.A.A.S.; mem. Am. Soc. Zoologists, Am. Soc. Mammalogists, Ornith. Union (asso), Wilson Ornith Club. Ecol. Soc. Am., Wildlife Soc. (pres. 1937-38), Phi Beta Kappa, Sigma Xi. Episcopalian. Author: (with Werner O. Nagel) A Survey of the Resident Game and Furbearers of Missouri, 1937; also sci. and miscellaneous papers. Home: 129 Edgewood Av., Columbia, Mo. Died Feb. 2, 1950.

BENOLIEL, SOLOMON D., electrochemist; b. New York, June 1, 1874; s. David J. and Pauline (Wasserman) B.; B.S., Coll. City of New York, 1893; E.E. and A.M., Columbia, 1896; m. Therese Lindeman, June 1, 1897; children—D. Jacques L. Osmond, Jean S. Teacher Adelphi Coll., 1897-1901; electrochemist, and gen. mgr. Roberts Chem. Co. (now Niagra Alkali Co.), 1901-06; gen. mgr. Internat. Chem. Co., Camden, from 1906, now of phila., Pa. Lecturer Bds. of Edn. New York and Brooklyn, and Brooklyn Inst. Arts and Science, 1899-1901. Has perfected new process for production of caustic potash and chemically pure hydrochloric acid by means of electric current; perfected a number of scientific cleaners, lubricants and burnishing compounds for industrial uses, particulary the metal mfg. trades. Writer on liquid air, photo therapy and electrochemistry. Home: Merion, Pa. Died Nov. 23, 1932.

BENSLEY, ROBERT RUSSELL, anatomist; b. Hamilton, Can., Nov. 13, 1867; s. Robert Daniel and Caroline (Vandeleur) B.; A.B., U. Toronto, 1889, M.B., 1892, D.Sc., 1919; m. Cariella May, Sept. 12, 1892; children—Caroline May, Alma Gladys (dec.), Robert Daniel. Asst. demonstrator biology U. Toronto, 1891-98, demostrator, 1898-1901; asst. prof. anatomy U. Chgo., 1901-05, asso. prof., 1905-07, prof., 1907-33, prof. emeritus, 1933—, research in functions of cellular organs. Editor Internationale Monatschrift fur Anatomie und Physiologie, 1912. Mem. Assn. Am. Anatomists (pres. 1918), Alpha Kappa Kappa. Club: Quadrangle. Home: 5447 Ellis Av., Chgo. 15. Died June 11, 1956.

BENSON, HENRY KREITZER, indsl. chemist; b. Lebanon, Pa., Jan. 3, 1877; s. William Frank and Catherine (Kreitzer) B.; A.B., Franklin and Marshall Coll., Lancaster, Pa., 1899, A.M., 1902, D. Sci., same coll., 1926; studied Johns Hopkins Univ., 1903-04; Ph.D., Columbia Univ., 1907; m. Eva A. Ronald, June 15, 1905; children—William Ronald, Margaret Elizabeth, Henry K., Betty. Prof. indsl. chemistry and chemical engineering, U. of Washington, 1905-47, professor emeritus since 1947; dir. research, I. L. Loucks' Laboratories, Inc., Seattle, 1949; former administrative head chem. dept. With U.S. Bureau of Soils, 3 summers; with U.S. Bur. Foreign and Domestic Commerce, as comml. agent, 1914, studying lumber by-products; state dir. with U.S. Naval Advisory Bd., 1916. Served as capt. research sect. of nitrogen div. of Army Ordnance, July 6, 1918-Feb. 20, 1919. Chmn. div. chemistry and chem. technology, Nat. Research Council, Washington, D.C., 1931-32. Del. Internat. Chem. Conf., Rome, Italy, 1938; chmn. Washington State Chemurgic Com. since 1942; Mem. Tech. Assn. of the Pulp Paper Industry, Am. Chem. Soc., Am. Inst. Chem. Engrs., Am. Legion (dist. comdr. 1923), Sigma Xi, Tau Kappa Epsilon, Phi Lambda Upsilon. Republican. Mem. Congl. Ch. Mason. Author: Industrial Chemistry, 1913; By-Products of the Lumber Industry, 1915; Chemical Utilization of Wood, 1932;

Potential Chemical Industries of Washington, 2 vols., 1936. Contbr. of some 90 articles to tech. jours. Home: 6027 Princeton Av., Seattle 5 WA

BENTLEY, GORDON MANSIR, zoologist, entomologist; b. Great Barrington, Mass., Sept. 23, 1875; s. Charles Harrison and Elvira E. (Mansir) B.; B.S.A., Cornell U., 1900, A.M., 1901; M.S., U. Tenn., 1928; m. Mary Catherine Elmore, June 12, 1912; children—Juanita Louise, Edna Elvira. Prof. botany and zoology Union Acad., Belleville, N.Y., 1901-04; instr. entomology N.C. State Coll., Raleigh, 1905; also asst. state entomologist N.C., 1905; instr. in zoology and entomology U. Tenn., 1905-08, asso. prof. entomology, 1908-23, prof., 1923-50, ret. Sept. 1950; state entomologist and plant pathologist 1909-50, ret.; now cons. entomologist and zoologist. Pres. So. Plant Quarantine Bd., 1929-30, 37-38, 39-44. Fellow A.A.A.S.; mem. N.E.A. Am. Assn. Econ. Entomologists (v.p. 1918-29, 36; pres. plant quarantine and inspection sect. 1925; pres. apiculture sect. 1929), Entomol. Soc. Am. (charter), Tenn. Acad. Sci., Am. Assn. U. Profs., Cotton States Entomologists (sec. 1923-27; pres. 1927), Tenn. State Hort. Society (sec.-treas. 1905-47, life hon. 1948), Tenn. Nurserymen's Assn. (organizer 1905, sec.-treas. 1905-48, hon. sec.-treas. for life), Tenn. Beekeepers Assn. (sec.-treas. 1906-45), Tenn. State Florists Assn. (organizer, 1909; sec. 1909-34), Tenn. Ornithol. Soc., Tenn and East Tenn. Tchrs. Assn., Am. Rose Soc., Izaak Walton League Am., So. Nurserymens Assn. (hon. life), Sigma Xi, Gamma Alpha, Alpha Zeta, Sigma Nu, Phi Kappa Phi. Presbyn (elder). Mason (32 deg., K.T., past comdr.; Shriner, past potentate; Royal Order of Jesters, Red Cross of Constantine, past Sovereign; past Viceroy). Clubs: National Travel, The Cabiri, Square & Compasses, Cornell, University of Tenn. Entomological (founder 1908), Shrine Luncheon (past pres.), Rotary, Knoxville Camera, Biologia, East Tennessee Automobile (dir.). Author: Lectures and Laboratory Guide for Economic Entomology, 1929; Insect Taxonomy, 1929; 120 bulls. on econ. entomology. Contbr. Jour. Econ. Entomology. Editor of Proceedings Tenn. State Hort. Soc., Tenn. Market Bulletin, State Dept. Agr. Reports. Home: Island Home Park, 141 W. Peachtree St. Office: 144 W. Peachtree St., Knoxville 15, Tenn. Died Oct. 8, 1954; buried Highlamb Meml. Cemetery.

BENTLEY, MADISON, psychologist; b. Clinton, Ia., June 18, 1870; s. Charles Eugene and Persis Orilla (Freeman) B.; B.S., U. of Neb., 1895 (LL.D., 1935); Ph.D., Cornell U., 1898. Assistant in psychology, instr., asst. prof., Cornell, until 1912; prof. psychology and dir. psychol. labs., U. of Ill., 1912-28; Sage prof. psychology, Cornell, 1928-38; consultant for psychology, Library of Congress, 1938-40, lecturer in psychology, Cornell Univ., 1942-44; chmn. division anthropology and psychology, Nat. Research Council, 1930-31. Capt. Air Service, 1917-18; major, J.S. Army, 1924-34. Fellow A.A.A.S.; mem. Am. Psychol. Assn. (pres. 1925), Phi Beta Kappa, Sigma Xi and Phi Kappa Psi. Wrote section on History in A Manual of American Literature, 1909; also articles on psychol. subjects in New Internat. Ency., Internat. Year Book, Ency. Americana, United Editors' Ency.; mag. articles. Editor of American Journal Psychology, 1903-51. Author: Studies in Social and General Psychology, 1916; Critical and Experimental Studies in Psychology, 1921; The Field of Psychology, 1924; Studies in Psychology from the University of Illinois, 1925; The New Field of Psychology, Pt. 1, The Psychological Functions and Their Government, 1934; The Problems of Mental Disability in England, 1938; Cornell Studies in Dynasomatic Psychology, 1938; The Theater of Living in Animal Psychology, 1943; Tools and Terms in Recent Researches since 1943; Sanity in the Life Course, 1946; Towards a Psychological History of the Hominids, 1947; Primary Factors in the Government of certain Biomechanical Systems, 1952. Address: 733 Oregon Av., Palo Alto, Cal. Died May 29, 1955.

BENTLEY, PERCY JARDINE, engineer; b. Brookfield, N.S., Can., Nov. 1, 1898; s. Robie Dugwell and Susan (West) B.; came ot U.S., 1925, naturalized, 1938; student Acadia Univ. Univ., N.S., 1919-21; B.S. in Mech. Engring., N.S. Tech. Coll., 1924; M.S., Mass. Inst. Tech., 1925; m. Virginia Deland Williams, Oct. 31, 1930; 1 son, David West. With Ingersoll-Rand Co., Phillipsburg, 1925—, gen. mgr., 1936-56, vice president, 1945—, member bd. dirs., 1943—. Served overseas with Canadian Expeditionary Force, World War I. Mem. Kappa Sigma. Presbyterian. Clubs: Northampton Country; Canadian (New York). Home: 660 Barrymore St., Phillipsburg, N.J. Office: 11 Broadway, N.Y.C. Died May 8, 1962; buried Old Greenwich Church Cemetery, Bloomsbury, N.J.

BENTLEY, WILLIAM BURDELLE, chemist; b. Maple Valley, N.Y., Aug. 8, 1860; s. William Henry and Elizabeth (Cummings) B.; A.B., Harvard, 1889, A.M., 1890, Ph.D., 1898; m. Susan E. Prescott, Dec. 15, 1891 (died 1923); children—William Prescott, Harold Jackson; m. 2d, Henrietta J. Prescott, July 1925 (died May 19, 1956). Asst. in chem. lab. Harvard, 1889-91, U.S. Torpedo Sta., Newport, R.I., summer 1890; adj. and asso. prof. chemistry and physics U. Ark., 1891-1900; prof. chemistry Ohio U., 1900-36, now emeritus. Served as capt. Ordnance Dept., U.S. Army, 1918-19, stationed Watertown (Mass.) Arsenal. Mem. Am. Chem. Soc., A.A.A.S. Mason (K.T.). Home: Athens, O. Died July 14, 1945; buried Athens.

BENTLEY, WILSON ALWYN, meterologist; b. Jericho, Vt., Feb. 9, 1865; s. Thomas Edwin and Fanny Eliza (Colton) B.; ed. pub. sch. Jericho; unmarried. Taught music, 1885-86; 1882—, a student of snow crystals and other meteorol. studies; has made 5,150 photomicrographs of snow crystals, hail, etc., and many hundreds of dew, clouds, raindrops, etc. Has written various monographs relating to these studies, published by U.S. Weather Bur., 1902, 1904, 1905, 1908, and articles "Snow" and "Frost" in Ency. Americana, contbns. to mags. and lectures on similar themes. Home: Jericho, Vt. Died Dec. 23, 1931.

BENTON, FRANK, apiculturist; b. Coldwater, Mich., July 5, 1852; s. Corydon Philemon and Phoebe Ann (Baldwin) B.; B.S., Mich. Agrl. Coll., 1879, M.S., 1886; attended lectures univs. of Munich and Athens, 1882-85; m. Harriet M. Wheeler, of Angelica, N.Y., Dec. 17, 1879. Spl. agt. and asst. entomologist, 1891-1901, apicul. investigator in charge of apiculture, Aug. 1, 1901-07, U.S. Dept. Agr.; naturalization examiner, U.S. Dept. of Justice, 1907-08; editor and translator, Dept. of Commerce and labor, since Dec. 17, 1908. Spent 11 yrs. (1180-91) investigating honey-bees of Europe, Africa and Asia; commd. by U.S. Dept. Agr. to make similar investigations in the Caucasus, Persia, India and P.I., 1905-06; 1st Am. importer of Oriental races of bees; inventor of transport cage for sending queen-bees long distances by mail, artificial queen-cells for use in breeding queen-bees, also numerous other apiarian appliances; lecturer on apiarian topics. Corr. sec. Entom. Soc. Washington, 1894-1905; mem. A.A.A.S., Nat. Geog. Soc., Allgemeiner Deutscher Sprachverein, Assn. Econ. Entomologists, Am. Entom. Soc., Bot. Soc. Washington, Am. Breeders' Assn., Nat. Bee-Keepers' Assn. (sec. 1892-93); hon. mem. many Am. and foreign apiarian socs. Author: The Honey-Bee, 1896; Bee-Keeping, 1897; also articles and translations on apiarian subjects, sketches of travel, etc. Home: Dominion Heights, Va. Office: Dept. of Commerce and Labor, Washington, D.C.

BERENS, CONRAD, ophthalmologist; b. Phila., Dec. 2, 1889; s. Conrad and Mary E. (Brockett) B.; prep. edn. Protestant Episcopal Acad., Phila.; M.D., U. Pa., 1911; m. Katherine Simpson Storrs, June 15, 1916 (dec. 1917); 1 son son, Richard; m. 2d, Katherine Andrea Parker, July 12, 1923; m. 3d, Frances Penington Cookman; children—Lawrence Penington, Rodney Bristal. Adv. attending surgeon-cons. pathologist, cons.-dir. research N.Y. Eye and Ear Infirmary; lectr. ophthalmology N.Y. U. Post-grad. Med. Sch.; prof. clin. ophthalmology Columbia, 1943-46; cons. ophthalmology St. Clare's Hosp., French Hosp., Midtown Hosp., Glen Cove Community Hosp., Nassau Hosp.; mem. med. bd. Doctor's Hosp.; vis. staff Hempstead Gen. Hosp.; cons. Riverview Hosp.; chmn. Council for Research in Glaucoma and Allied Diseases; staff Southside Hosp.; mng. dir. Ophthal. Found., Inc.; former cons. ophthalmology air surgeon, U.S. Army. Pres. Snyder Ophthalmic Found.; trustee Seeing Eye; dir. N.Y. Assn, for Blind, Nat. Soc. Prevention Blindness; chmn. Am. Com. on Optics and Visual Physiology; v.p. Internat. Assn. Prevention Blindness; v.p. Internat. Council on Ophthalmology chmn. Am. Bd. Ophthalmology, 1938-43, cons., 1948-59, emeritus. Commd. lt., Med. Res. Corps, 1917; France, World War I; lt. col., 1924—. Fellow A.C.S.; mem. A.M.A. (chmn. sect. ophthalmology 1943), Med. Soc. State N.Y. (chmn. eye sect. 1931), Am. Acad. Ophthalmology and Otolaryngology (pres. 1949), N.Y. Acad. Medicine (chmn. eye sect. 1923), Am., N.Y. (pres. 1939) ophthal. socs., Assn. Research Ophthalmology (chmn. 1945), Assn. Research Nervous and Mental Diseases, A.A.A.S., Illuminating Engring. Soc., Assn. Mil. Surgeons U.S., Optical Soc. Am. Pan-Am. Med. Assn. (exec. sec. 1929-32, treas. and sec. N.Am. sect. on ophthalmology 1934) Pan-Am. Assn. Ophthalmology (pres. 1948), Air Service Med. Assn. (pres. 1922), Med. Soc. County N.Y. (pres. 1944), Societe Francaise D'Ophtalmologie (Am. rep.). Clubs: Racquet and Tennis, Piping Rock, Seawanhaka Yacht, University, Author: The Eye and Its Diseases, 1936, 49; Diagnostic Examination of the Eye (with Zuckerman), 1946; Ency. of the Eye (with Siegel), 1950; Abstracts on Aviation and Military Ophthalmology, 5 vols. (with Sheppard and Bickerton, 1953-59; Ocular Surgery Manual (with Loutfallah); 1950, rev. (with King), 1956; also articles and sci. papers. Home: Centre Island, Oyster Bay, L.I. Office: 708 Park Av., N.Y.C.; also 13 Walnut Rd., Glen Cove, N.Y. Died Mar. 1963.

BERG, LOUIS, psychiatrist, author; b. London, Eng., June 19, 1901; s. Samuel and Ida B., brought to U.S. 1904, naturalized, 1919; A.B., Columbia 1920; M.D., Jefferson Med. Coll., Phila., 1923; grad. study U. Vienna, 1926; m. Lisa Conlin; adopted children—Leslie Lanham Berg, Wendy Lee Berg, Michael, David Berg. Intern. Beth David Hosp., N.Y.C., 1923-24; resident Montefiore Hosp., 1924-25; asst. physician Manhattan State Hosp. for Insane, 1924-25; Dist. med. Supr. Dept. of Health, N.Y.C., 1929-72; physician to N.Y. Dept. of Correction, Welfare Island, 1928-35; part-time instr. of edn., New York U., 1929-34; med. dir. Henry Meinhard Meml. Health Center 1931-72. Medico-legal expert, lectr., 1934-72; asso. in neuro-psychiatry Beth David Hosp.; neuro-psychiatrist to the army induction station, Grand Central Palace, N.Y.C., 1943—; mem. impartial specialist panel in neurology Workmens Compensation Bd. Bd. visitors Highland State Tng. Sch. Boys. Served in inf., U.S. Army, 1918. Diplomate Am. Bd. Psychiatry and Neurology. Fellow Royal Soc. Health; mem. A.M.A., N.Y. State, N.Y. County med. socs., Am. Psychiat. Assn. Mason. Author: (Novels) Prison Doctor; 1931; Prison Nurse, 1934; Devils Circus, 1934; Twilight Comes Early, 1939; other and later books include: The Human Personality; Sex, Methods and Manners (with Robert Treat), 1953; Psychiatry for the Layman, 1963; The Velvet Underground (with Michael Leigh) 1964. Contbr. articles in field to mags. Address: New York City NY Died Oct. 1, 1972.

BERGEY, DAVID HENDRICKS, bacteriologist; b. Montgomery Co., Pa., Dec. 27, 1860; s. G. R. and Susan (Hendricks) B.; M.D., B.S., U. of Pa., 1884; A.M., Ill. Wesleyan, 1894; Dr. of Pub. Hygiene, U. of Pa., 1916; m. Annie S. Hallman, June 5, 1884. First asst. Lab. of Hygiene, U. of Pa., 1896—, asst. prof. bacteriology, 1903-16, and asst. prof. of hygiene and bacteriology, 1916-26, prof. of hygiene and bacteriology, 1926-31, acting prof. hygiene, 1931-32; also dir. Laboratory of Hygiene, 1928-31. Dir. research in biology, Nat. Drug Co., 1931—. Commd. capt. Med. R.C., U.S.A., Apr. 1917; maj. May 1918. At training camp, Ft. oglethope, Ga., Aug. 4, 1917; placed in charge of clin. lab. Gen. Hosp. No. 14, Ft. Oglethorpe, Ga., Aug. 19, 1917; transferred to Gen. Hosp. No. 22, Richmond Coll., Va., Nov. 1918; discharge from service, Jan. 1919. Author: Handbook of Practical Hygiene, 1899; The Principles of Hygiene, 1901, 7th edit., 1921; also chapter on domestic hygiene in Pyle's Personal Hygiene, 1904. Home: Philadelphia, Pa. Died Sept. 5, 1937.

BERKELEY, JOHN, ironmaster; b. Eng.; m. Mary Snell, 10 children including Maurice. Came to Am. to establish ironworks for Va. Council, 1621; 1st ironmaster in Am.; set up machinery on Fall Creek, nr. what is now Richmond, Va.; 1st in Am. to smelt iron; Indians destroyed his machinery, 1622, ironmaking not reestablished in Am. until 1710. Killed by Indians led by Opechancanough, Mar. 22, 1622.

BERKEY, CHARLES PETER, geologist; b. Goshen, Ind., Mar. 25, 1867; s. Peter and Lydia (Stutsman) B.; B.S., U. of Minn., 1892, M.S., 1893, Ph.D., 1897, hon. D.Sc., 1940; hon. Sc.D., Columbia U., 1929; m. Minnie M. Best, Sept. 4, 1894; children—Paul Ainsworth, Virginia Dale. Instr. in geology, U. of Minn., to 1903; tutor, instr. and asst. prof., asso. prof. and prof. geology, Columbia U., 1903-41. A Specialist on geology applied to engineering. Employed on state surveys (geol.) of Minn., Wis. and New York; consulting geologist N.Y. Bd. Water Supply, 1906—; also consulting geologist of the Met. Dist. Water Supply Commn. of Mass., Dept. of Water and Power of Los Angeles; cons. engineer U.S. Reclamation Bureau, Tenn. Valley Authority; petrographer and geologist on many engring. and mining problems; chief geologist Central Asiatic Expdns., Am. Museum Natural History, 1922—; geologist Port of New York Authority; mem. U.S. Colo. River Bd. Ex-sec. and past pres. Geol. Soc. Am. Fellow A.A.A.S.; mem. N.Y. Acad. Scis. (past pres.). Rochester Acad. Science, Geol. Soc. China. Am. Inst. Mining and Metall. Engrs., Municipal Engrs. City of New York, Am. Soc. Civil Engrs. (hon.), Am. Philos. Soc., Nat. Acad. Sciences, Phi Beta Kappa, Sigma Xi, Tau Beta Pi, Phi Gamma Delta; corr. mem. Geol. Soc. of London. Home: 1076 Cumbermede Rd., Palisade, N.J. Died Aug. 22, 1955.

BERKNER, LLOYD VIEL, sci. research adminstr.; b. Milw., Feb. 1, 1906; s. Henry Frank and Alma Julia (Viel) B.; B.S., in Elec. Engring., U. Minn., 1927; student physics George Washington U., 1933-35; D.Sc. (hon.), Bklyn. Poly. Inst., 1955, U. Calcutta, 1957, Dartmouth, and U. Notre Dame, 1958, Columbia, 1959; D.Sc. (hon.), U. Rochester, 1960, Tulane U., 1961; D.Eng., Wayne State U., 1962; Ph.D. (hon.), U. Uppsala (Sweden), 1956; LL.D., U. Edinburgh, 1959; m. Lillian Frances Fulks, May 19, 1928; children—Patricia Ann Booth (Mrs. Charles Harrington), Phyllis Jean Ashley (Mrs. James Clay). Began as engr. in charge radio sta. WLB-WGMS, Mpls., 1925-27; elec. engr. airways div. U.S. Bur. Lighthouses, 1927-28; engr. 1st Byrd Antarctic Expdn., 1928-30, Nat. Bur. Standards, 1930-33; physicist, dept. terrestrial magnetism Carnegie Instn. Washington, 1933-41 (Australia 1938-93, Alaska 1941), head sect. of exploratory geophysics of atmosphere, 1947-51; exec. sec. Research and Devel. Bd., Dept. Def., 1946-47; spl. asst. sec. state on fgn. mil. assistance, 1950; pres., bd. trustees, chmn. exec. com. Asso. Universities Inc. 1951-60; pres. Grad. Research Center of Southwest, 1960-65, chmn. exec. com., 1965—, dir. Southwest Center for Advanced Studies, 1965—, Cons. several univs., govtl. agys. 1940—. Mem. com. on Rockefeller pub. service awards, 1954—. Chmn. 1957-59, 1962—. Mem. or officer of numerous U.S. delegations internat. sci. confs., 1936—. Naval aviator USNR, 1926—, rank of rear adm., 1955—; on active duty, head radar sect. Bur. Aero., USN, 1941-45. Decorated Legion of Merit (U.S.), Hon. Officer Order Brit. Empire; recipient spl. Congl. gold medal, silver medal Aero. Inst., sci award Washington Acad. Scis., 1941, Cleve. Abbe award Am. Metrol. Soc., 1962.

Fellow Am. Acad. Arts and Scis., I.E.E.E., Am. Phys. Soc., Arctic Inst. N.A., N.Y. Acad. Scis.; mem. Internat. Acad. Astronautics (corr.), Royal Swedish Acad. Sci., Am. Soc. Astronautics, Aerospace Med. Assn. (hon. mem.), Nat. Acad. Scis. 1960—, chmn. space sci. bd., 1958-62), NRC, A.A.A.S., Am. Geophys. Union (pres. 1959-62), Am. Philos. Soc., Philos. Soc. Washington, Washington Acad. Scis., Am. Geophysical Union (John A. Fleming award), Acacia (Founders award), Eta Kappa Nu (Eminent Members award), Theta Tau, Scabbard and Blade also several fgn. socs. Democrat. Conglist. Clubs: Cosmos (Washington); Explorers, Century Assn. (N.Y.C.); Bohemian (San Francisco). Contbr. to scientific and prof. jour. Home: 3632 N.E. 24th Av., Fort Lauderdale, Fla. Office: Grad. Research Center, Box 8478, Dallas 5. Died June 4, 1967.

BERL, ERNEST, research prof.; b. Freudenthal (formerly Austria), July 7, 1877; s. Max and Agnes B.; student chem. engring., Tech. U. of Vienna, 1894-98; Ph.D., U. of Zurich, 1901; m. Margaret Karplus, Mar. 28, 1912; children—Herbert, Walter George. Came to U.S., 1933, naturalized, 1938. Asst. U. and Tech. U. of Zurich, 1901, asst. prof., 1904-10; chief chemist rayon factory, Tubize, Belgium, 1910-14; chief chemist Austrian War Ministry, 1914-19; prof. chem. technology and electro-chemistry, Tech. U. of Darmstadt, 1919-33; research prof. Carnegie Inst. Tech. since 1933. Mem. Am. Chem. Soc., Am. Inst. Chem. Engrs., Faraday Soc., Soc. Am. Mil. Engrs., Army Ordnance Assn., N.Y. and Pa., Acad. of Sciences, Am. Inst. of Chemsits, Sigma Xi. Mem. U. S. Explosives Adv. Com. Home: Schenley Atps., Pittsburgh. Died Feb. 16, 1946; buried at Washington.

BERLIN, THEODORE H., physicist; b. N.Y.C., May 8, 1917; s. Abraham J. and Tillie (Rittoff) B.; B.S. in Chem. Engring., Cooper Union Inst. Tech., 1939; M.S., U. Mich., 1940, Ph.D. (Horace H. Rackham fellow), 1944; m. Patricia May Cleary, July 8, 1944; children—Geoffrey N., Dennis A., Michael K., Alexander L. Research physicist U. Mich., 1944-46; instr. Johns Hopkins U., 1946-47, asst. prof., 1947-48, asso. prof., 1949-54, prof., 1955-61; prof. Rockefeller Univ., 1961—; Guggenheim fellow, mem. Inst. Advanced Study, 1952-53; asso. prof. Northwestern U., 1948-49. Fellow Am. Phys. Soc.; mem. Sigma Xi, Phi Beta Kappa. Asso. editor Jour. Chem. Physics, Phys. Rev. Office: Rockefeller Inst., N.Y.C. 21. Died Nov. 16, 1962. Buried Prospect Hill Cemetery, Balt.

BERLINER, EMILE, inventor; b. Hanover, Germany, May 20, 1851; s. Samuel and Sarah (Friedman) B.; grad. Samson Sch., Wolfenbuttel, 1865; came to the U.S. in 1870; m. Cora Adler, 1881. Invented loose contact telephone transmitter or microphone, 1877; discovered that a loose contact will act as a telephone receiver (Apr. 1877), and was first to use an induction coil in connection with transmitters (pat. Jan. 1878); patentee of other valuable inventions in telephony; invented, 1887, the Gramophone, the first the first talking machine which utilizes a groove of even depth and varying direction, and in which the record groove not only vibrates but also propels the stylus across the record (known also as the Victor Talking Machine), for which he was awarded John Scott medal and Elliot Cresson Gold Medal by Franklin Inst., Phila.; also invented and perfected the present method of duplicating disc records; invented, 1925, the acoustic tile and acoustic cells for insuring good acoustics in halls, etc. Ednl. campaign against dangers of raw milk and other dairy products, 1901—. Author and co-author of pamphlets dealing with the prevention of sickness. Planned and was mem. Washington Milk Conf., 1907. First to have made and used in aeronautical experiments light weight revolving cylinder internal combustion motor, now extensively used on aeroplanes (1908). Under his general directions his son, Henry A., designed first successful helicopter, rising and sustaining himself in it, Nov. 1919. Pres. D.C. Tuberculosis Assn., 1915-21. Author: Health Rhymes. Home: Washington, D.C. Died Aug. 3, 1929.

BERMAN, PHILIP GROSSMAN, ophthalmologist, otolaryngologist; b. Lawrence, Mass., Feb. 12, 1900; s. Harris and Mary (Grossman) B.; M.D. cum laude, Tufts University, Medford, Mass., 1925; m. Anna Fidler, 1921; 1 son, Charles Samuel. Interne Roxbury Hosp., Boston, Mass., 1925; St. John's Hosp., Lowell, Mass., 1926; instr. Tufts Med. Sch., 1929-33; resident surgeon Boston City Hosp. for diseases of eye, ear, nose and throat, 1926-27; senior visiting surgeon St. Joseph's Hosp., Lowell, Mass., 1933; cons. surgeon Isolation Hosp., Lowell, Mass., 1934; vis. surgeon Boston City Hosp., Beth Israel Hosp., Boston, Mass., 1927-33; ex-pres. staff St. Joseph's Hosp., Lowell, Mass., mem. exec. com. and chief dept. eye, ear, nose and throat; dir. Concord Hardware Co., Canada Dry Bottling Co., Springfield, Mass. Trustee George A. Berman Trust. Diplomate Am. Bd. Ophthalmology. Fellow A.C.S., Am. Acad. Ophthalmology and Otolaryngology, N.E. Ophthal. Soc., N.E. Otol. Soc., Oxford Ophthal. Congress (Eng.); mem. Middlesex N. Dist. Med. Soc. (past pres.), chmn. com. on pub. relations, chmn. com. on mediation, A.M.A., Mass. Med. Benevolent Soc. (trustee), Societe Francaise D'Ophthalmologie (France). Mason (32 deg.). Clubs: Vesper, Country, Yorick (Lowell). Editor Middlesex North Bull. Home: Lowell MA Died Sept. 18, 1968; buried Temple Emanuel Cemetery, Lawrence MA

BERNARD, MERRILL, hydrologist; b. Burlington, Ia., July 25, 1892; ed. N.C. Mil. Acad., 1907; Mil. Coll. of S.C., 1908-10; A. and M. Coll. of Okla., 1911; m. Claudia Turner, Aug. 1, 1914. Engaged in municipal, irrigation and railroad engring. to 1916; civil engring., 1918-20; cons. engr. designing and supervising municipal, drainage and irrigation projects, La., Tex., Central Am., 1929-36; hydrologic specialist for Miss. Valley Com., 1934-36; hydraulic engr. Soil Conservation Service, 1936-37; with U.S. Weather Bureau since 1937, chief River and Flood Div., 1937-39, hydrologic director, 1939-46; chief, climatological and hydrological services since 1946. Served as 1st lt., U.S. Army, World War I. Mem. American Society Civil Engineers (Norman medalist, 1945), Am. Geophys. Union, Nat. Research Council (v.p. hydrology sect.), Wash. Acad. Sciences; mem. Internat. Union Geodesy and Geophysics (pres. internat. assn. hydrol. 1948), Internat. Meteorol. Orgn. (v.p. hydrol commn.), Research and Development Bd. (mem. com. on geophys. geog.), Am. Meteorol. Soc. Mem. Am. delegation 220th Anniversary Soviet Acad. Scis., Moscow; mem. Am. Meteorologic Mission to U.S.S.R., 1945. Club: Cosmos (Wash.). Contbr. papers to govt. bulls. and engring. jours. Home: 2205 42nd St., N.W., Washington, D.C. Died April 13, 1951.

BERNAYS, AUGUSTUS CHARLES, M.D.; b. Highland, Ill., Oct. 13, 1854; grad. McKendree Coll., 1872; M.D., Heidelberg, Germany, 1876; mem. Royal Coll. of Surgeons, London, Nov. 27, 1877; settle in practice at St. Louis, 1878; inventor of improved methods in operative surgery; noted as a teacher of anatomy in operative surgery; noted as a teacher of anatomy and surg. pathology and did much in introducing antispeptic method of surgery in the U.S. Unmarried. Author: Chips from a Surgeon's Workshop, 1880; Development of Valves of Heart, 1876 F5; Development of Joints in General and of the Human Knee Joint, 1877 F5. Home: St. Louis, Died 1907.

BERNE, ERIC LENNARD, psychiatrist, author; b. Montreal, Can., May 10, 1910; s. David Hillel and Sara (Gordon) B.; B.A., McGill U., 1931, M.D., C.M., 1935; student N.Y.C. Psychoanalytic Inst., 1941-43, San Francisco Psychoanalytic Inst., 1947-56; children—Ellen, Peter, Ricky, Terry, Robin Way, Janice Way (Mrs. Michael Farlinger). Intern Yale Psychiat. Clinic, 1936-38; clin. asst. psychiatry Mt. Sinai Hosp., N.Y.C., 1941-43; attending psychiatrist, mental hygiene clinic VA Hosp., San Francisco, 1950-56; pvt. practice, N.Y.C. and Norwalk, Conn., 1940-43, San Francisco, Carmel, Cal., 1946-70; cons. to surgeon gen. U.S. Army, 1951-56; adj. psychiatrist Mt. Zion Hosp., San Francisco, 1952-70; lectr. psychiatry U. Cal. Med. Sch., 1960-70; cons. group therapy McAuley Clinic, San Francisco, 1962-70. Served to maj., M.C., AUS, 1943-46. Diplomate Am. Bd. Psychiatry and Neurology. Fellow American Psychiatric Association (life member); member of the International Transactional Analysis Association (chairman board of trustees); corr. member Indian Psychiat. Society. Author: The Mind in Action, 1947; Layman's Guide to Psychiatry and Psychoanalysis, 1957; Transactional Analysis in Psychotherapy, 1961; The Structure and Dynamics of Organizations and Groups, 1963; Games People Play, 1964; Principles of Group Treatment, 1966; The Happy Valley, 1968. Home: Carmel CA Died July 1970.

BERNE-ALLEN, ALLAN, chem. engr., educator; b. S.I., N.Y., Aug. 13, 1902; s. Allan and Harriet Anna (Mallory) Berne-A.; B.S.E., U. Mich., 1924; Chem.E., Columbia, 1933. Ph.D., 1936; m. Helen Louise Kelsey, June 24, 1926. Research development tech. service Standard Oil Co. N.J., 1924-31. Vacuum Oil Co. (now Mobile Oil Co.), 1931-32; research, development, tech. asst. operation E.I. du Pont de Nemours & Co., Inc., 1934-47; prof. mech. engring. U. Cal. at Berkeley, 1947; prof. head dept. chemical engineering Clemson Agricultural College, 1948-55, profl. engr., 1955-69. Charter mem. bd. dirs. Fats and Protein Research Found., 1962-66. Served as maj. C.W.S., AUS, 1942-46; ret. lt. col. Reserves. Registered profl. engr., N.Y., S.C. Fellow Am. Inst. Chemists, A.A.A.S.; member Am. Oil Chemists' Soc., Am. Chem. Soc. (chmn. Va. sect 1941), Am. Inst. Chem.E., Am. Soc. Engring. Edn., Am. Assn. U. Profs., Va. Acad. Sci. Fla. Academy of Sciences, Res. Officers Assn. (pres. Staunton Va. 1936-37, pres. Gulf Coast chpt. 1958-59), Mil. Order World Wars, N.Y. Acad. Scis., Sarasota Power Squadron, Sigma Xi, Phi Lambda Upsilon, Phi Kappa. Phi, Phi Gamma Delta. Mason (past master). Clubs: Chemists (N.Y.C.); Army and Navy (Washington); Sarasota (Florida) Yacht; Michigan Union (Ann Arbor); Fla. N.; Highlands (N.C.) Country. Contbr. tech. mags. Patentee in field. Home: Sarasota FL Died Apr. 15, 1969; Meml. Army Marker in New Drop Moravian Cemetery.

BERNHEIM, BERTRAM MOSES, surgeon; b. Paducah, Ky., b. Feb. 15, 1880; s. Isaac Wolf and Amanda (Uri) B.; A.B., Johns Hopkins, 1901, M.D., 1905; p.-grad. work in Europe, 1906; in U.S., 1907; m. Hilda Marcus, July 26, 1905; children—Minda, Isaac Wolfe, Bertram. Practiced surgery, Baltimore, since 1908, specializing in blood-transfusion, and surg. of the blood vessels; asso. prof. emeritus surg., Johns Hopkins Med. Sch.; visiting surgeon Union Memorial Hosp., Hosp. for Women of Md., Church Home and Infirmary; visiting surgeon Johns Hopkins Hosp. Major, Medical Reserve Corps; member Johns Hopkins Hosp. Base Unit, A.E.F. in France, June 1917-Feb. 1919; received citation in France. Fellow and founder Am. Coll. Surgeons, Am. Bd. Surgery; fellow Am. Med. Assn.; mem. Medico-Chirurg. Faculty of Md. Jewish religion. Author: Surgery of the Vascular System, 1913; Blood Transfusion, Hemorrhage and the Anemias, 1917; Passed as Censored, 1918; Medicine at the Crossroads, 1939; Adventure in Blood Transfusion, 1942; A Surgeon's Domain, 1947 (Norton Award); The Story of The Johns Hopkins, 1948; also numerous articles dealing with surgery. Home: Pikesville 8, Md. Office: 2424 Eutaw Pl., Baltimore 17, Md. Died Nov. 28, 1958; buried Druid Ridge Cemetery, Pikesville, Md.

BERNSTROM, VICTOR, wood engraver; b. Stockholm Sweden. Pupil Royal Acad., Sweden. Awarded medal (1st class) World's Columbia Expn.; exhibited at Paris Expn., 1900; silver medal Pan-Am. Expn., 1901, St. Louis Expn., 1904. For a number of yrs. on staff London Graphic and Harper & Bros., New York. Home: Grand View-on-Hudson, N.Y. Died 1907.

BERQUIST, STANARD GUSTAF, prof. geology; b. Ironwood, Mich., Aug. 13, 1892; s. Charles John and Ellen Elizabeth (Walquist) B.; A.B., Univ. of Mich., 1915, M.Sc., 1927, Ph.D., 1933; m. Ada Evelyon Whitman, Aug. 6, 1924; 1 dau., Donna Jeanne. Instr. geology, Mich. State Coll., 1916, asst. prof. 1924, asso. prof., 1930, head dept. geology and geography, 1930, prof. geol., 1933, acting head dept. phys. sci., Basic College, 1945-48; head dept. phys. science, 1948-52; member of soil survey, Michigan, summers, 1921, 24, marl survey, Mich. Geol. Survey, summers, 1925-26; geol. Land Econ. Survey, Mich., summers, 1928-33; mem. gov.'s natural gas fact finding com., Mich., 1937; apptd. by gov. to investigate iron mines in Gogebic Co. for State Tax Commn., summer, 1942; field studies in glacial geology for Mich. Geol. Survey, summers, 1935-46; cons. geol. Engrs., Research Assn., 1936-37. Mem. East Lansing Council, 1930-31, East Lansing Bd. of Edn., 1938-44 (pres. 1939-41), East Lansing Charter Revision Commn., 1943; chmn. non-metallic sect. Mich. Minerals Industries Conf., 1942-43. Fellow A.A.A.S., Geol. Soc. of Am.; mem. Mich. Geol. Soc. (bus. mgr., 1936-37, 1940-41), Mich. Acad. of Sciences (pres. 1940), Am. Assn. Univ. Profs., Am. Legion, Sigma Xi, Phi Sigma, Sigma Gamma Epsilon, Phi Kappa Phi. Mem. People's Ch. Mason. Clubs: Inter City Wranglers (pres. 1941-42), Mich. Engineers. Author miscellaneous papers on geology, for sci. jours. Home: 164 Maplewood Dr., East Lansing, Mich. Died Mar. 31, 1956; buried Evergreen Cemetery, Lansing.

BERRY, CHARLES HAROLD, mech. engring. educator; b. Brooklyn, N.Y., June 8, 1889; s. Silas Hurd and Elsie (Brown) B.; Pratt Inst., Brooklyn, N.Y., 1907-09, M.E., Cornell Univ., 1912, M.M.E., 1916. A.M. (hon.) Harvard Univ., 1942; m. Natalie Daboll. Apr. 17, 1915; children—Carolyn (Mrs. G.R. Jacobs). Roberta (Mrs. P. R. Humez), Ruth Allyn (Mrs. B. D. Hilton). Instr. and asst. prof. heat power engring., Cornell U., 1913-18; U.S.A. Ordance Ordnance Dept., insp. div., 1918-19; research engr. Detroit Edison Co., Detroit, Mich., Summers, 1913-18, tech. engr. of power plants asst. to chief engr., 1918-25; asso. editor of Power, McGraw-Hill Pub. Co., New York, 1925-28; prof. mech. engring. Harvard U., 1928—, Gordon McKay prof. mech. engring. emeritus, 1955—; prof. mech. engring. Northeastern U., 1955-64. Fellow Am. Acad. Arts and Scis., Am. Soc. M.E.; mem. Sigma Xi, Tau Beta Pi, Pi Tau Sigma. Club: Harvard (Boston). Home: 162 Washington St., Belmont 78, Mass. Died Mar. 15, 1965.

BERRY, EDWARD WILBER, paleontologist; b. Newark, N.J., Feb. 10, 1875; s. Abijah Conger and Anna (Wilber) B.; educated privately; m. Mary Willard, Apr. 12, 1898; children—Edward Willard, Charles Thompson. Pres., treas. and mgr. Daily News, Passaic, N.J., 1897-1905; asst. in paleobotany Johns Hopkins U., 1907-08, instr., 1908-11, asso, 1911-13, asso. prof. of paleontology, 1913-17, prof. since, 1917, dean, 1929-42, provost, 1935-42; sr. geologist U.S. Geological Survey since 1910; asst. state geologist of Md., 1917-42. Fellow Paleontol. Soc. America (pres. 1924). Geol. Soc. America (pres. 1945); Am. Acad. Arts and Sciences, A.A.A.S., Am. Soc. Naturalists; mem. Am. Philos. Soc., Nat. Acad. Sciences, Washington Acad. Sciences, Torrey Bot. Club, Société Géologique de Frances, Academia Nacional de Ciencias en Cordoba, Argentina, Sociedad Geologica del Peru. Awarded Walker prize, Boston Society of Natural History, 1901. Conglist. Club: Hopkins. Wrote: Lower Cretaceous of Maryland (Md. Geol. Survey), 1911; Upper Cretaceous of Maryland (same), 1916; Eocene Floras of Southeastern North America (U.S. Geol. Survey), 1916; Tree Ancestors, 1923; Paleontology, 1929; also over 500 articles on paleontol., geol. and biol. subjects in Am. and foreign scientific periodicals. Has specialized on classification and evolution of plants, particularly in Southeastern N. America, equatorial America and South America. Home: 19 Elmwood Road, Baltimore, Md. Died Sept. 20, 1945.

BERRY, EDWARD WILLARD, geologist; b. Passaic, N. J., Nov. 24, 1900; s. Edward Wilber and Mary (Willard) B.; A.B., Johns Hopkins, 1924, Ph.D., 1929; m. Dorothy Everett Pidgeon, Oct. 12, 1925; children—Mary-Susan (Mrs. E.P. Robare), Edward Lewis, Samuel Stedman. Micropaleontologist Internat. Petroleum Co., Negritos, Peru, 1925-28; instr. geology Ohio State U., 1929-36; faculty dept. geology Duke 1936-68; prof. emeritus, 1967-68; cons. geologist coal and oil. Mem. council 21st Internat. Geol. Congress, 1960; prof. geology U. Malaya, Kuala Lampur, 1961-62. Fellow Geol. Soc. Am., Geol. Soc. London, A.A.A.S.; mem. Geol. Soc. South Africa, Geog. Soc. New Zealand, Assn. Geology Tchrs., Pan Am. Inst. Mining Engring. and Geology, Am. Geophys. Union, Am. Assn. Petroleum Geologists, geol. socs., France, Switzerland, Peru, Mexico, Am. Inst. Mining Metallurigal Engineers, N.C. Academy Science (pres. 1957-58), Yorkshire Geol. Soc., Carolina Geol. Soc. (sec.-treas. 1937-67), Paleontological Inst., Paleontological Assn. (London). Sigma Xi, Kappa Sigma. Mem. Soc. Friends, Contbr. tchr. jours. Editor: Southeastern Geologist. Home: Corpus Christi TX Died May 10, 1968; buried Clearbrook VA

BERRY, JOHN CUTTING, ophthalmologist; b. Sagadahoe Co., Me., Jan. 16, 1847; s. Stephen Decatur and Jane Mary (Morse) B.; ed. Monmouth (Me.) Acad.; M.D., Jefferson Med. Coll., Phila., 1871; studied New York, 1885, Vienna, 1894; m. Maria Elizabeth Gove, of Bath, Me., Apr. 10, 1872. Med. missionary A.B.C.F.M., in Japan, 1872-93; established hosps. and training sch. for nurses, and was intimately identified with med., religious, humanitarian and ednl. movements in Japan for 21 years; resident of Worcester, Mass., since 1896; consulting ophthalmic and aural surgeon, Worcester City Hosp.; visiting ophthalmologist, Baldwinsville Hosp. Cottages. Corporate mem. A.B.C.F.M.; pres. Memorial Home for Blind. Decorated by Emperor of Japan with Order of the Sacred Treasure. Mem. A.M.A., Mass. Med. Soc., N.E. Ophthalmol. Soc. S.A.R. (ex-pres. Worcester Chapter), etc. Clubs: Worcester Economic (ex-pres.), Congregational (ex-pres.). Home: 28 Trowbridge Rd. Office: 36 Pleasant St., Worcester, Mass.; (summer) "Wynburg," Phippsburg, Me.

BESSEY, CHARLES EDWIN, botanist; b. on farm, Milton, Wayne Co., O., May 21, 1845; s. Aduah and Margaret (Ellenberger) B.; B.Sc., Mich., Agrl. Coll., 1869. M.Sc., 1872; studied with Dr. Asa Gray at Harvard, 1872-73 and 1875-76; Ph.D., State U. of Ia., 1879; (LL.D., Ia. Coll., 1898); m. Lucy Athearn, Dec. 25, 1873; father of Ernest Athearn B. Prof. botany, 1870-84, acting pres., 1882, Ia. Agrl. Coll.; prof. botany, 1884—, acting chancellor, 1888-91, 1899-1900, and 1907, head dean, 1909—, U. of Neb. Bot. editor Am. Naturalist, 1880-97, of Science, 1897—, Johnson's Cyclo., 1893—. Mem. Neb. Rural Life Commn., 1911-13. Pres. A.A.A.S., 1910-11, Bot. Soc. America, 1895-96, Soc. Promotion Agrl. Science, 1889-91, dept. natural science N.E.A., 1895-96, Am. Micros. Soc., 1902. Progressive Republican. Conglist. Author: Geography of Iowa, 1876; Botany for High Schools and Colleges, 1880; The Essentials of Botany , 1884; Elementary Botanical Exercises, 1892; The Phylogeny and Taxonomy of Angiosperms, 1897; Elementary Botany, 1904; Plant Migration Studies, 1905; Synopsis of Plant Phyla, 1907; The Phyletic Idea in Taxonomy, 1908; Outlines of Plant Phyla, 1909, 11, 12, 13. Home: Lincoln, Neb. Died Feb. 25, 1915.

BESSEY, ERNST ANTHEARN, botanist; b. Ames, Ia., Feb. 20, 1877; s. late Charles Edwin and Lucy (Athearn) B.; B.A., U. Neb., 1896, B.Sc., 1897, A.M., 1898; U. Halle, Germany, 1902-04, Ph.D., 1904; Munich, 1904; m. Edith Carleton Higgins, July 25, 1906; children—Bertha Agnes, William Higgins, Robert John. Bot. collector for N.Y. Bot. Garden in Mont. and Yellowstone Park, 1897, for U.S. Dept. of Agr. in Colo., 1898; asst. in botany Colo. Summer Sch., Colorado Springs, 1894, 95, 96, asst. pathologist, Div. Vegatable Physiology and Pathology, 1899-1901, asst. in chrage of seed an plant introduction, 1901-02, agrl. explorer in Russia, the Caucasus, Turkestan and Algeria, 1902-04, in charge Subtropical Lab. and Garden of U.S. Dept. Agr. at Miami, Fla., 1906-08; prof. botany and bacteriology, La. State U., 1908-10; prof. botany Mich. State Coll., 1910-45, distinguished prof. botany, 1945-46, retired 1946, acting dean applied science div., 1927-30, dean grad. sch., 1930-44; vis. prof. botany U. Hawaii, 1939-40. Fellow A.A.A.S.; mem. Bot. Soc. Am., Torrey Bot. Club, Am. Phytopath. Soc., Mycol. Soc. Am. (pres. 1941), Mich. Acad. Scis. (pres. 1915-16), Deutsche Botan Gesell, Phi Beta Kappa, Sigma Xi, Alpha Zeta, Phi Kappa Phi, Phi Sigma. Author: Textbook of Mycology, 1935, rev. edit. 1947; with others working on Mich. State U. agrl. dictionary, 1956-57. Home: 213 University Dr., East Lansing, Mich. Died July 17, 1957; buried Deepdale Cemetery, Lansing.

BEST, GEORGE NEWTON, M.D., botanist; b. Round Valley, N.J., Oct. 16, 1846; s. Cornelius and Elsie (Alpaugh) B.; attended Lafayette Coll. (class '73); M.D., U. of Pa., 1875; m. Hannah W. Wilson, 1877. Pres. Lehigh Valley Med. Assn.; permanent del. Med. Soc. N.J.; mem. Torrey Bot. Club; fellow A.A.A.S.; hon. mem. Phila. Bot. Club. Author of numerous papers and addresses; specialty mosses; bryological contbns. including: Revision of the North American Thuidiums, 1896; Revision of the Claopodiums, 1897; Revision of the North American Pseudoleskeas, 1900; Revision of the North American Heterocladiums, 1901; Revision of the North American Leskeas, 1903. Asso. editor The Bryologist. Home: Rosemont, N.J. Died 1926.

BETTEN, CORNELIUS, prof. emeritus; born Orange City, Ia., Nov. 13, 1877; s. Antonie J. and Mary (Rhynsburger) B.; A.B., Lake Forest Coll., 1900, M.A., 1901, D.Sc., 1923; Ph.D., Cornell U., 1906; m. Myrtle Alice Sherer, Sept. 8, 1906; (died December 16, 1948); children—Robert S., Cornelius, Jr.; m. Mrs. Beatrice Hobson Argetsinger, Aug. 17, 1951. Prof. of biology at the Lake Forest College, 1907-15; sec., registrar, 1915-20, vice dean res., instrn., 1920-22, dir. res. instrn., 1922-40, acting dean, 1924-26, 1931-32, N.Y. State Coll. agr. at Cornell U.; dean faculty, 1932-45, prof. entomol., emeritus since 1945. Fellow A.A.A.S., Entomol. Society America, mem. Gamma Alpha, Sigma Xi, Phi Kappa Phi, Alpha Zeta. Author: The Trichoptera of New York State, 1934; (with M. E. Mosely) The Walker Types of Trichoptera in the British Museum, 1941. Home: 177 Woodland Rd., Asheville NC

BETTENDORF, WILLIAM PETER, inventor, mfr.; b. Mendota, Ill., July 1, 1857; s. Michael and Catherine (Reck) B.; m. Mary Wortman, 1879; m. 2d, Mrs. Elizabeth Staby, 1908. Worked for Peru Plow Co. (Ill.), 1872-75, supt. shops, 1882-86; worked for Moline Plow Co. (Ill.), 1875-82; invented power lift sulky plow, 1878, Bettendorf metal wheel, 1880; manufactured wheels, Davenport, Ia., 1886-1910; concentrated on substituting steel for wood in mfg. r.r. cars; other inventions include cast steel side frame truck, Bettendorf integral journal-box. Died June 3, 1910.

BETTS, PHILANDER, III, engineer; b. Nyack, N.Y., May 28, 1868; s. Philander, Jr., and Sarah Taulman (Demarest) B.; B.S., Rutgers Coll., N.J., 1891, M.S., 1895; E.E., Columbian (now George Washington) U., 1903, Ph.D., 1914, hon. Dr. Engring., 1932; m. Nancy Bell Hammer, Nov. 19, 1896 (deceased Nov. 22, 1938); 1 son, Philander Hammer; m. 2d, Mr.s Nelle Campbell Allen (widow of Lyman W. Allen), June 18, 1940. Constructing engr. Field Engring. Co., New York, directing constrn. of some of the earliest electric lines in Newark, N.J., and Phila., 1890-93; with Westinghouse Elec. & Mfg. Co., 1893-95; elec. engr., Washington Navy Yard, 1895-1901; instr. in mech. and elec. engring., Corcoran scientific Sch., Washington, 1901-05; asst. prof., George Washington U., head of elec. engring. dept. and in charge of all mech. and elec. engring. labs., 1905-10; chief engr. Pub. Utilities Commn., N.J., 1910-34. Has served as consulting engr. in many important elect. light and power projects. Fellow Am. Inst. Elect. Engrs.; mem. Am. Soc. Mech. Engrs., Illuminating Engring. Soc., Am. Electric Ry. Assn., S.A.R. (past pres. N.J. Soc.), Beta Theta Pi. Mason (33 deg.). Republican. Mem. Dutch Reformed Church. Maj. Engr. Res. Cops. July 14, 1917; lt. col. Q.M. Corps. Mar. 18, 1918; active city, War Dept., Washington; hon. discharged, May 31, 1919; citation of sec. of war "for efficient service in the Construction Division of the Army"; col. Engr. Res. Corps, comdr. 373d Engrs. Sr. past comdr., North Jersey Chapter Mil. Order of World Ward, also past comdr. N.Y. Chapter; v.p. and mem. gen. staff N.J. State Reserve Officers Assn. (hon. v.p. for life); mem. Am. Legion, Sojourners (ex-pres. Manhattan Chapter). Compiler and editor of the hist. records in connection with all War Dept. construction in this country. Prominent in field of pub. service regulation, valuation and rate-making. Home: 100 Tenth Av., Belmar, N.J. Died Feb. 5, 1945.

BEUTENMULLER, WILLIAM, entomolgist; b. Hobenk, N.J., Mar. 31, 1864; s. William and Mathilda (Hauser) B.; ed. pub. and pvt. schs. and business coll., New York; m. Edna L. Hyatt, Apr. 15, 1903. Curator dept. entomology, Am. Mus. Natural History, 1889-1910. Author: Butterfield, Moths, Gall-insects; Forestry Insects. Also numerous articles on entomology in scientific mags. Editor Journal of N.Y. Entomol. Soc., Vols. I-XI. Home: Tenafly, N.J. Died Feb. 24, 1934.

BEYER, GEORGE EUGENE, prof. biology, Tulane Univ.; b. Dresden, Saxony, Germany, Sept. 9, 1861; s. Otto and Henrietta von Reitzenstein B.; ed. in Dresden, 1867-70; then Realschule I. Ordnung, Plauen (Vogtland), Saxony and Dresden, until April, 1879; spl. studies in biology, bionomics, etc., in Dresden and Berlin under Dr. Alfred Brehm (author of Brehm's Thierleben), Dr. Otto Staudinger (entomologist), Dr. Engelhart, botanist, etc.; left Germany in 1880; traveled as naturalist in Central and South America, 1881-83; settled in New Orleans at the end of 1883; curator vertebrata Tulane Museum, 1893; instr. natural history, 1895; asst. prof., 1896; prof., 1899; m. Mildred, d. Maj. William M. Robinson, New Orleans. Fellow A.A.A.S.; asso. Am. Micros. Soc., Am. Ornithologists' Union; pres. La. Naturalists Soc., La. Hist. Soc.; v.p. La. Audubon Soc.; hon. mem. La. State Med. Soc., Orleans Parish Med. Soc., Am. Pub. Health Assn.; mem. U.S. Yellow Fever Inst.; mem. U.S. Yellow Fever Commn. to Vera Cruz; spl. insp. Biol. Survey U.S. Dept. Agr. Has written various monographs on biology and other subjects; also part author of Bionomics Experimental Investigation of B. Sanarelli in Connection with the Mosquitoes of New Orleans, 1902; etc. Residence: 4422 Coliseum St., New Orleans.

BEYER, OTTO STERNOFF, cons. engineer; b. Woodridge, N.J., Sept. 18, 1886; s. Otto Sternoff and Marie (Clobus) B.; M.E., Stevens Inst. Tech., 1907; grad. study U. of N.Y. and U. of Pa., 1907-10; m. Clara Mortenson, July 30, 1920; children—Morten, Donald, Richard. Engr. apprentice E. W. Bliss Co. and Midvale Steel Co., 1907-08; motive power engr. Erie R.R., 1908-12; gen. foreman C., R.I.&P. Ry. Shops. Horton, Kan., 1912-16; cons. engr. in development labor-management coöperative programs with several ry. systems and industrial cos., 1920-33; dir. sect. labor relations, Federal Coördinator of Transporation, 1933-35; mem. Nat. Mediation Board, Jan. 1936-Jan. 1942, chmn. 1937, resigned Feb. 1943; dir. div. transport personnel Office of Defense Tansportation, Jan. 1942-June 1944, representing transportation on War Manpower Commission. Consultant, T.V.A. Bonneville Power Administration, U.S. Marime Commission, The Alaska Railroad, U.S. Department of Interior. Special lecturer, George Washington University. Served in organization U.S. Army Sch. Aeronautics, Urbana, Ill., 1917; capt. U.S. Army, 1918-19, organizing and training tech. personnel for ry. and heavy arty. maintenance, later directing all training of ordnance personnel; after the war dir. arsenal orders sect. Army Ordnance Dept. Club: Cosmos. Pres. Baltic-American Soc. of Washington, D.C. Democrat. Author reports and bulls.; contbr. numerous professional articles. Home: Spring Hill, McLean, Va. Office: Albee Bldg., Washington. Died Dec. 8, 1948; buried in Arlington National Cemetery.

BEYER, SAMUEL WALKER, geologist; b. Clearfield, Pa., May 15, 1865; s. Abraham and Barbara Ann (Keagy) B.; B.S. Ia. State Coll., 1889; Ph.D., Johns Hopkins, 1895; m. Jennie Morrison, June 22, 1893; children—Jeanette, Mary Morrison. Instr., 1891-95, asst. prof., 1895-98, prof. geology and mining engring., 1898—, v.-dean engring. div., 1908-17, dean, 1917-18, dean Industrial Science Division, 1919—, Iowa State Coll. Geologist Iowa Geol. Quartzite and Certain Associated Rocks, 1895; Geology of Boone, Marshall, Story and Hardin Counties, Iowa, 1895-99; Clays and clay Industries of Iowa, 1903; Iowa Quarries and Quarry Products, 1906; Iowa Peat Deposits, 1908; Road and Concrete Materials in Iowa, 1914. Home: Ames, Ia. Died June 2, 1931.

BICKELHAUPT, CARROLL OWEN, elec. engineer; b. Roscoe, Dakota Territory, December 15, 1888; s. William George and Ida Emma (Owen) B.; B.S., U. of Wisconsin, 1911, E.E., 1914; D.Eng. South Dakota Sch. of Mines and Tech., 1947; m. Marie Helen Jewett, April 30, 1919; children—Nancy Jewett (Mrs. Joseph Harris), Alice Mary (Mrs. Charles B. Wilson). With Dakota Central Telephone Co., 1904-11; with Am. Telephone & Telegraph Co., 1911-25, toll traffic engr., 1922, comml. engr., 1922-25; v.p. Southern Bell Telephone & Telegraph Co., 1925-30, also dir. and mem. exec. com.; v.p., dir. and mem. exec. com., Cumberland Telep. & Teleg. Co., 1925-26; asst. v.p. Am. Telep. & Teleg. Co., 1930-41, v.p. 1941-45, v.p. and sec. since 1945; dir. Bell Telephone Securities Co., 1935-37. Maj. Signal Corps, AUS World War I; brig. gen. AUS (dir. communications office chief signal officer, ETO, U.S.A., U.S. Mil. Govt., Germany), World War II; recommd. brig. gen., 1947, ret. 1949. Decorated, Distinguished Service Medal, Legion of Merit, Bronze Star Medal, Army Commendation Ribbon, Armed Forces Res. Medal; (U.S.); Officer, Legion of Honor, Officier d'Academie et de l'instruction Publique, Croix de Guerre with Palm (France); hon. mem. Signal Corps French Army; Commander of Order of Leopold II (Belgium). Diploma of the Medal, Assn. Engr.-Drs. of France, 1947. Fellow Am. Institute Electrical Engrs. (v.p., dir., 1927-29); mem. Am. Engring. Council (v.p. 1933-41, mem. assembly and administrative board); N.Y. Elec. Soc.; del. to meetings of Internat. Cons. Com. on Telephony, Lucerne, Switzerland, 1935, Cairo, Egypt, 1938; tech. observer at meeting of Internat. Cons. Com. on Radio, Bucharest, 1937, and at meeting of Internat. Telecommunications Confs., Cairo, 1938; Am. Soc. Corporate Secs. (dir., past pres.), Armed Forces Communications Assn. (dir., past v.p.), Army Signal Assn., Grant Monument Association of New York (trustee), v.p. N.Y. chapt., Mil. Order of World Wars. Repub. Clubs: University, Downtown Assn.(N.Y.); Army and Navy (Wash., D.C.); Washington (Conn.). Home: 1075 Park Av. Office: 195 Broadway, N.Y.C. Died May 16, 1954; buried Washington, Conn.

BIDWELL, CHARLES CLARENCE, prof. phyics; b. Rochester, N.Y., Oct. 23, 1881; s. Charles Henry and May Isabelle (Millham) B.; A.B., U. of Rochester, 1904; Ph.D., Cornell U., 1914; m. Mary Delphina Moody, Sept. 12, 1912. High Sch. sci. tchr., 1907-10; grad. student, asst. and instr. physics, Cornell U., 1910-16, asst. prof. physics, 1917-25, prof., 1925-27; prof. physics and head of dept., Lehigh U., since 1927, also director curriculum in engring. physics. Employed at U.S. Naval Exptl. Lab. on submarine detection problems, World War. Fellow Am. Physical Soc.; mem. Optical Soc. Am. (sec. 1925-29), A.A.A.S., Soc. for Promotion Engring. Edn., Sigma Xi, Delta Kappa Epsilon. Am. Newcomen Soc. Episcopalian. Author: Principles of Physics, 1922;

Advanced Course in General College Physics (with P. L. Bayley), 1937. Home: Bethlehem, Pa. Died Apr. 1967.

BIDWELL, EDWIN CURTIS, physician; b. Tyringham (now Monterey), Mass., Feb. 20, 1821; s. Barnabas and Betsey (Curtis) B.; grad. Williams Coll., 1841, M.D., Yale, 1844; m. Isabella Calder Gibson, Nov. 24, 1856 (died 1888). Surgeon 31st Mass. vols., 1862-65; examining surgeon for pensions, 1869-81. Trustee Iowa State Univ., 1856-8; mem. Am. Inst. Civics, G.A.R.; corr. mem. N.Y. Hist. Soc.; pres. Vineland Hist. and Antiq. Soc. In 1849 wrote article on the Portability of Cholera Infections, which was at that time an important contribution to med. knowledge; discovered, 1880, fungus of the black rot of the grape, since named for him Laestadia Bidwellii (bulls. Dept. Agr., 1886-87-88); pres. Vineland New England Soc. Home: Vineland, N.J. Died 1905.

BIEBER, CHARLES L(EONARD), geologist; b. Reinbeck, Ia., Aug. 22, 1901; s. Andrew and Caroline Letitia (Franck) B.; A.B., Cornell Coll., 1924; A.M., U. ofIa., 1932; Ph.D., Northwestern U., 1942; m. Minerva Elizabeth Wagaman, Aug. 1, 1929; children—Carolyn (Mrs. Lynnwood Thompson), Dorothy Ann Bieber (Mrs. Richard Murphy) and Charles Richard Bieber. Teacher of mathematics and geography, athletic coach Reinbeck, Ia., 1924-27; assistant professor physical education. North Central College, Naperville, Illinois, 1927-37, professor geology, 1937-47, instructor in meterology Navy preflight and teacher geography Army Specialized Training Program, 1941-45; chmn. dept. geology and geography and prof. geology DePauw U. since 1947; with Mo. Geol. Survey, summers, 1944, 45, 55, 56, Ind. Geol. Survey, summers, 1949-52. National Science Foundation teacher geology, 1959, 61, 62; geol. research, Queensland, Australia, 1963. Mem. A.A.A.S., Geol. Soc. of Am. Am. Geophys. Union, Ill. and Ind. acads. sci., Assn. College Geology Teachers (pres. 1949-50), Am. Assn. Univ. Profs., Sigma Xi. Member Methodist Church. Contributor of papers on structure and stratigraphy Ill. and Ind. acads. sci.; also contbr. Tectonics in Mo. Home: 311 Greenwood Av., Greencastle, Ind. Died Dec. 21, 1965; buried Forest Hill Cemetery, Greencastle.

BIEFELD, PAUL ALFRED, prof. astronomy; b. Joehstadt, Saxony, Geramy, Mar. 22, 1867; s. Henry and Wilhelmina (Glaeser) B.; came to U.S., 1881; B.S. in Elec. Engring., U. of Wis., 1894; Ph.D., U. of Zurich, Switzerland, 1900; m. Emma Bausch, for Frankfort on the Main, Apr. 11, 1900; children—Carl H., Louise M., Lawrence P. Asst. prin. high sch., Appleton, Wis., 1894-97; lab. asst. in physics and elec. engring., Polytechnikum, Zurich, 1899-1900, prof. physics and elec. engring., Technikum Hildburghausen, Germany, 1900-06; prof. physics and astronomy, Buchtel Coll., Akron, O., 1906-11; became prof. astronomy and director Swasey Observatory, Denison University, 1911, now prof. emeritus. With Yerkes eclipse expdn., Denver, Colo., 1918; research asst. Yerkes Obs., summer quarter, 1919; eclipse expdn. (Yerkes), to Catalina Islands, Sept. 1923. Mem. Am. Astron. Soc., Astron. Soc. Pacific, A.A.A.S.; hon. mem. Am. Soc. Stationary Engrs. Republican. Baptist. Lecturer on astronomy. Home: Granville, O.

BIEGLOW, HENRY BRYANT, zoologist; b. Boston, Oct. 3, 1879; s. Joseph S. and Mary C. (Bryant) B.; A.B., Harvard U., 1901, A.M., 1904, Ph.D., 1906, Sc.D. (hon.), Yale, 1941, Harvard U., 1946; Ph.D. (hon.), Oslo, 1946; m. Elizabeth P. Shattuck, Aug. 14, 1906; children—Elizabeth P. (dec.), Mary C., Henry B. (dec.), Frederick S. With Harvard Univ. since 1905; curator of Coelenterates in the Museum of Comparative Zoology, Harvard U., 1914-26, research curator in Zoology, 1925-27, curator of oceanography, 1927-50, prof. emeritus Harvard U., 1950; also prof. zoology; dir. Woods Hole (Mass.) Oceanographic Instn., 1930-39. Fellow Am. Acad. Arts and Scis., Am. Assn. for Advancement Sci., Royal Geog. Soc., London; mem. Am. Philos. Soc., Am. Geophys. Union, Nat. Acad. Sci., Boston Soc. Nat. Hist. Am. Geog. Soc., Norwegian Acad. (Oslo); corr. mem. Acad. Nat. Sci., Zool. Soc. (London). Clubs: Faculty (Cambridge, Mass.), Harvard (Boston); Cosmos (Washington, D.C.). Author of numerous treatises on zoology and oceanography. Home: Concord, Mass. Address: Museum of Comparative Zoology, Cambridge. Died Dec. 1967.

BIEN, JULIUS, artist, lithographer; b. Hesse-Cassel, Germany, Sept., 1826; m. Miss A. M. Brown. Came to U.S., 1849; began business on small scale (1850) with one lithographic hand-press; filled in spare time painting portraits and banners; became specialist in scientific and artistic lithography; illus., 1852, American Locomotives and Railroads (by Colburn & Holly); later illus. Coast Survey Reports, Pacific Ry. surveys; Hayden's andowell's expdns.; Atlas of the Records of Rebellion; Statistical Atlas of U.S. Censuses, and many other Govt. and State reports. Then head of Julius Bien & Co., lithographers; pres., 1889-95. Nat. Lithographers' Assn.; mem. many sicentific socs. Received medals and diplomas Centennial Expn., Phila., 1876; Paris, 1878; Chicago, 1893; Paris, gold and silver medal, 1898. Home: New York, N.Y. Died 1909.

BIERBAUM, CHRISTOPHER HENRY, cons. engr.; b. Garnavillo, Ia. Feb. 14, 1864; B.S., Northern Illinois Normal School, 1886; M.E., Cornell U., 1891; unmarried. Instr. in exptl. engring., Cornell U., 1892-96; cons. engr. Am. Stoker Co., Dayton, O., 1896-98; mem. Bierbaum & Merrick, engrs., Cincinnati, 1898. Buffalo, N.Y., 1901; founder, v.p. and consulting engineer in charge of research Lumen Bearing Co. since 1901; private consulting office, Buffalo, 1903-28; Am. Soc. of Mechanical Engrs. Rep. on the Adv. Com. for Metall. Research in the U.S. Bur. of Standards. Fellow A.A.A.S., Am. Soc. Mech. Engrs. (formerly chairman bearings metals research committee); member American Institute Mining and Metall. Engring., Am. Soc. for Metals, Am. Microscopical Soc., Sigma Xi. Contbr. many articles to tech. jours. and to engring. handbooks. Inventor of microcharacter, a device for studying physical properties of the microspcopic constituents of metals, also determining the relative hardness of rolled metal sheets of less than two thousandths of an inch in thickness. Originator and patentee of phosphor nickel bearing bronzes. Pioneer in studies of corrosive effect of oxidized mineral lubricating oils. Home: 113 Florence Av., Buffalo 14. Office: 197 Lathrop St., Buffalo 12, N.Y. Died June 15, 1947.

BIERRING, WALTER LAWRENCE, physician; b. Davenport, Ia., July 15, 1868; s. Jeppe and Catherine Elizabeth (Jessen) B.; M.D., State U. Ia., 1892; grad. work U. Heidelberg, 1892. U. Vienna, Austria, 1892-93, 96, 1901, Ecole de Médecine, Pasteur Inst., Paris, 1894; m. Sadie Byrnes. Apr. 14, 1896; children—Florence Viola (Mrs. P. M. Hutchinson), Elza Elizabeth (Mrs. Rains-Radoff). Prof. pathology and bacteriology State U. Ia., 1893-1903, prof. theory and practice of med., 1903-10, prof. emeritus; prof. theory of medicine Drake U., 1910-14; pres. Ia. State Bd. of Health and Ia. State Bd. Med. Examiners, 1914-22; sec.-editor Am. Fedn. State Exam. Bds., 1915—; state commr. pub. health disease Ia. Dept. Health; cons. internal med. Mem. Nat. Bd. Med. Examiners (past pres.), Commn. Med. Edn. Diplomate Am. Bd. Preventive Medicine, Inc. (chmn. bd. emeritus), Am. Bd. Internal Medicine (chmn. 1936-39). Master A.C.P.; fellow Am. Heart Assn., Royal Sanitary Inst. (hon.); member A.M.A. (pres. 1934-35), A.A.A.S., Am. Assn. Pathologists and Bacteriologists, Am. Pub. Health Assn., Health Authorities of N.A. (pres. 1945-47), Royal Coll. Physicians of Edinburgh, Sigma Nu, Alpha Omega Alpha (pres.) Phi Beta Kappa. Republican. Presbyn. (Mason). Clubs: Des Moines, Prairie, University (Des Moines). Home: 3007 W. Grand Av. Office: State Office Bldg., Des Moines. Died June 24, 1961; buried Des Moines.

BIERS, HOWARD (WILLIAM RICHARD), cons. engr.; b. N.Y.C., Dec. 3, 1904; s. Arthur and Anne Eleanor (Zoll) B.; B.S., U. Va., 1925; S.M., Mass. Inst. Tech., 1927; Dr. mont., Montanistische Hochschule Leoben, Austria, 1954; m. Constance Lucie Mary Herzog, Nov. 10, 1937; 1 son, William Richard. Research metallurgist Union Carbide & Carbon Research Labs., Inc., N.Y.C., 1927-30; cons. engr., Paris, Brussels, London, 1930-40; tech. adviser to metals controller, tech. adv. com. mem. Dept. Munitions and Supply, Canadian Govt., 1940-48; also Canadian chmn. ferro alloy com. WPB; mem. (for Can.) Joint U.S.-U.K. Canadian Metall. Mission; spl. adviser Dept. Trade and Commerce; cons. engr. Union Carbide & Carbon Corp., N.Y.C., 1948-55, dir. sales devel. ore div., 1955-59; sr. cons. Union Carbide Internat. Co., 1959—. Recipient citation, Internat. Conf. World Metall. Congress, 1951. Fellow Inst. Metallurgists (Eng.); mem. Internat. Inst. Welding (pres.), Iron and Steel Inst. (hon. v.p.), Commission Permanente Internat. de l'Acetylene (Paris) (U.S. del), Am. Inst. Mining and Metall. Engrs. (hon. life), Iron and Steel Inst. (Eng.) (hon.), Am. Welding Soc. (hon chmn. com. Internat. Inst. Welding), Am. Soc. for Metals (hon.), Verein Deutscher Eisenhuettenleute (Germany) (hon.), Instituto del Hierro y del Acero (Spain), Société Francaise de Métallurgie (France) (hon.), Association des Ingénieurs Sortis de l'Ecole de Liége (Belgium) (hon.), Instituto de la Soldadura (Spain) (hon.), Eisenhuette Oesterreich (Austria), Association des Ingenieurs de la Faculté de Mons (hon. Belgium) Chevalier de Tastevin. Clubs: University (N.Y.C.); The Travellers (Paris, France); The Pilgrims (London, Eng. and N.Y.C.); Brooks's, The Athenaeum (London); Knickerbocker (N.Y.C.). Contbr. to tech. publs. Home: French Farm, Silvermine, Norwalk, Conn. Office: 270 Park Av., N.Y.C. 10017. Died Mar. 15, 1967.

BIGELOW, EDWARD FULLER, lecturer and writer; b. Colchester, Conn., Jan. 14, 1860; s. William S. and Mary J. B.; prep. edn. Bacon Acad., Colchester; spl. student Biol. Lab., Yale University, 1896-97; student Biol. Lab., Cold Spring Harbor, L.I., 1899; Nature Study School, Coll. of Agr., Kingston, R.I., 1899; Nature Study Class, Marine Biol. Lab., Woods Hole, Mass., 1900-01; also studied at Nature Study School. Cornell U.; A.M., Ph.D., Taylor U., 1899; m. Mary Augusta Pelton, July 2, 1882; children—Nellie Pelton, Woodbridge Fuller, Pearl Agnes (dec.). Editor Nature and Science dept., St. Nicholas Magazine, 1900-14; for 25 years, took about 4,500 boys and girls yearly on natural history excursions; editor of Poplar Science, New York, 3 yrs.; editor the Observer, 8 years; principal public school, 10 years; editor dailies, 18 years; nature lecturer for N.Y. Bd. of Edn., Marthas Vineyard Inst. for Teachers, Cornell U., Cold Spring Harbor Lab., etc.; dir. Conn. Summer Sch. of Nature Study and Natural Sciences, Conn. Coll. Agr., 1902, and Conn. Chautauqua Assembly Assn., 1903-04; lecturer nature study and astonomy, Castle Boarding Sch. for Young Ladies, Tarrytown, N.Y., 1900-31; lecturer and teacher in Miss Spence's School, N.Y. City, 1900-32; with Camp Kineowatha, Maine, and other camps for girls, 1916; gen. dir. Cornucopia Home-Camp, Sound Beach (now Old Greenwich), Conn., 1925-30. Instr. in nature pedagogy at co. teachers' insts., throughout U.S.; instr. nature pedagogy at co. teachers' insts., throughout U.S.; instr. nature study in univ. summer schs., Calif., Ohio, Mich., N.C., Ala., Ind., Iowa, Etc.; inventor chem. tablets for artificial nutriment of plants, 1901, an ednl. beehive, 1905. Author: (and designer) Bigelow's Descriptive Plant Analysis; How Nature Study Should Be Taught; The Spriit of Nature Study, 1907. Compiler: Walking, a Fine Art, 1907. Editor of The Guide to Nature, 1908-35. Scout naturalist of Boy Scouts of America, and editor "On Nature's Trail," in Boys' Life 1916-19. Curator The Bruce Museum, Greenwich, Conn., 1915-37, now curator emeritus. Home: Old Greenwich, Conn. Died July 13, 1938.

BIGELOW, ERASTUS BRIGHAM, inventor, economist; b. West Boylston, Mass., Apr. 2, 1814; s. Ephraim and Mary (Brigham) B.; m. Susan King; m. 2d, Eliza Means; 1 child. Inventor power loom for prodn. of coach lace, 1837, power loom for prodn. Brussels, Wilton tapestry and velvet carpetings, 1839; chartered Clinton Co., nr. Lancaster, Mass., to build and operate looms, 1841, built plants, Lowell, Mass., and Derby, Conn.; mem. com. founding Mass. Inst. Tech., 1861; an organizer Nat. Assn. Wool Mfrs. Author: The Tariff Question Considered in Regard to the Policy of England and the Interests of the United States, 1862; The Tariff Policy of England and the United States Contrasted, 1872. Died Boston, Dec. 6, 1879.

BIGELOW, FRANK HAGAN, meterologist; b. Concord, Mass., Aug. 28, 1851; s. Francis Edwin and Ann (Ilager) B.; A.B., Harvard, 1873, A.M., 1880; (hon. L.H.D., Columbia (now George Washington) U., 1899; m. Mary E. Spalding, Oct. 6, 1881. Astronomer at Cordoba Obs., Argentine Republic, 1873-76 and 1881-83; took part in Dr. B. A. Gould's exploration of the Southern heavens; prof. mathematics, Racine Coll., 188-89; asst. Nautical Almanac Office, 1889-91, and mem. U.S. Eclipse Expdn. to W. Africa, 1889. Newberry, S.C., 1900, Spain, 1905; prof. meterology, U.S. Weather Bur., 1891-1910; prof. solar physics, George Washington U., 1894-1910; prof. meteorology, Oficina Meterologica, Cordobs, Argentina, 1910-21; dir. Pilar Solar and Magnetic Obs., 1915-21. Rector, Natick, Mass., 1880-81; chaplain, Racine, Wis., 1885-89; asst. minister St. John's Ch., Washington, 1891-1910; was chief climatol. div. U.S. Weather Bur.; also in charge of researchers into the law of evaporation at the Salton Sea and in U.S. generally; then retired. Author of articles and monographs on meterology, solar physics, meterol. treatise on Circultation and Radiation of the Atmospheres of the Earth and Sun; Treatise on the Sun's Radiation and other solar phenomena. Deceased.

BIGELOW, HARRIET WILLIAMS, astronomer; b. Fayetteville, N.Y., June 7, 1870; d. Rev. Dana W. (D.D.) and Katherine (Huntington) B.; A.B., Smith Coll., 1893; Ph.D., U. of Mich., 1904. Asst. in astronomy, 1896-1901, instr., 1904-06, asso. prof., 1906-11, prof., 1911—, Smith Coll. Presbyn. Home: Northampton, Mass. Died June 27, 1934.

BIGELOW, HENRY JACOB, surgeon, educator; b. Boston, Mar. 11, 1818; s. Jacob and Mary (Scollay) B.; grad. Harvard, 1837, M.D., 1841; m. Susan Sturgis, May 8, 1847, 1 son, William Sturgis. Tchr. surgery Tremont Street Med. Sch., Boston, 1845-49; surgeon Mass. Gen. Hosp., 1846-86; published 1st account of use of ether in surg. operation; asso. with discovery of surg. anaethesia, 1846; prof. surgery Harvard Med. Sch., 1849-84; did research and experiments on anatomy of hip-joint and removal of bladder stones, circa 1852; 1st Am. surgeon to excise hip-joint, 1852; inventor operating chair. Author: Manual of Orthopedic Surgery (Boylston prize essay), 1844; Medical Education in America, 1871; writings collected in Works of Henry Jacob Bigelow (edited by William Sturgis Bigelow), 3 vols., 1900. Died Newton Creek, Mass., Oct. 30, 1890.

BIGELOW, JACOB, physician, botanist; b. Sudbury, Mass., Feb. 27, 1787; s. Jacob and Elizabeth (Wells) B.; grad. Harvard, 1806; M.D., U. Pa., 1810. Began practice medicine, Boston, 1811; gave 1st lectures on botany at Harvard, 1812, active next decade collecting bot. specimens in New Eng.; prof. medicine Harvard Med. Sch., 1815-35; Rumford prof. applied science Harvard, 1816-27; founded Mt. Auburn Cemetery, Cambridge, Mass., as public health project, 1831; pres. Am. Med. Arts and Scis., 1847-63. Author: Florula Bostoniensis, 1814; American Medical Botany, 3 vols., 1817, 18, 20; Treatise on Materia Medica, 1822; Discourse on Self Limited Diseases, 1835; Elements of Technology, 1829; Brief Expositions of Rational Medicine, 1858. Died Boston, Jan. 10, 1879; buried Mt. Auburn Cemetery.

BIGELOW, MAURICE ALPHEUS, biologist; b. Milford Center, O., Dec. 8, 1872; s. Alpheus Russell and Hattie (Parthemore) B.; B.S., Ohio Wesleyan U., 1894, LL.D., 1930; M.S., Northwestern U., 1896; Ph.D., Harvard, 1901; Sc.D., Columbia, 1929; m. Anna Neiglick, 1900. Instr. in biology, Ohio Wesleyan U., 1894-95; instr. in zoology, Northwestern U., 1896-98; instr. in biology, Teachers Coll., Columbia U., 1899-1903, adj. prof., 1903-07, prof., 1907-39, dir. practical arts, 1914-35, dir. Inst. Practical Science Research, 1934-39, prof. emeritus, 1939—. Founder and editor Nature-Study Review, 1905-10. Fellow A.A.A.S. (sec. zool. sect., 1908-13), Am. Soc. Naturalists; founder and sec. Am. Nature Study Soc., 1908-10; chmn. exec. com. Am. Social Hygiene Assn., 1925-39; pres. American Eugenics Soc., 1940-45. Educational consultant American Social Hygiene Association and U.S. Pub. Health Service, 1939-45. Author: Early Development of Lepas, 1902; Teaching of Zoology in the Secondary School, 1904; Applied Biology (with Anna N. Bigelow), 1911; Introduction to Biology (with wife), 1913; Sex-Education, 1916; Health for Every Day and Health in Home and Neighborhood (with Prof. Jean Broadhurst), 1925; Adolescence, Educational and Hygienic Problems, 1924; also papers in ednl. health and scientific jours. Co-editor Eugenical News, 1942—. Address: R.F.D. 1, Croton-on-Hudson, N.Y. Died Jan. 6, 1955; Rose Hill Cemetery, Chgo.

BIGELOW, ROBERT PAYNE, zoologist; b. Baldwinsville, N.Y., July 10, 1863; s. Otis and Margaret (Payne) B.; S.B., Harvard U., 1887; Ph.D., Johns Hopkins U., 1892; m. Caroline Evans Chase, Nov. 9, 1911; 1 son, Robert Otis. Inst. biology Mass. Inst. Tech., 1893-1912, asst. and asso. prof. zoology and parasitology, 1912-22, prof. same, 1922-33, prof. emeritus since 1933, librarian, 1895-1925; librarian Marine Biol. Lab., 1919-23. Editor Am. Naturalist, 1897-98, Technology Quarterly, 1895-1908. Fellow Am. Acad. Anatomists, History of Sci. Soc. Author of papers on zool. subjects; contbr. series of biol. articles to Reference Handbook of the Medical Sciences, 1900-04 and 1913-17; also author Directions for the Dissection of the Cat, 1925, revised edit., 1935. Contbr. chapters in Sedgwick and Tyler's Short History of Science, revised edit., 1939. Home: 72 Blake Road, Brookline 46, Mass. Died Sept. 6, 1955.

BIGELOW, S(AMUEL) LAWRENCE, chemist; b. Boston, Feb. 23, 1870; s. Samuel Augustus and Ella Harriet (Brown) B.; A.B., Harvard, 1891; B.S., Mass. Inst. of Tehc., 1895; Ph.D., U. of Leipzig, 1898; m. Mary Crawford Barry, May 10, 1892; children—John Lawrence, Robert Barry, Anne Harrison. Instr. gen. chemistry, 1898-1901, asst. prof. and acting dir. lab. of gen. chemistry, 1901-04, jr. prof. 1904-05, jr. prof. gen. and phys. chemistry, 1905-07, prof. from 1907, U. of Mich.; now emeritus. Episcopalian. Fellow A.A.A.S.; mem. Am. Chem. Soc., Am. Electrochem. Soc., Mich. Acad. Sciences, Franklin Inst., Phila., Sigma Xi. Author: Theoretical and Physical Chemistry, 1912. Home: 39 Highland St., West Hartford 7, Conn. Died Dec. 3, 1947; buried at Ann Arbor, Mich.

BIGELOW, WILLARD DELL, chemist; b. Gardner, Kan., May 31, 1866; s. William I. and Jennie (Lytle) B.; A.B., Amherst 1889; m. Nancy M. Nesbit, Apr. 9, 1896. Asst. prof. chemistry, Ore. State Coll., 1889-90; instr. chemistry, Washington High Sch., 1891-92; chemist, July 1, 1892-June 1, 1913, asst. chief, Bur. of Chemistry, 1903-13, chief Div. of Foods, 1901-13, U.S. Dept. Agr.; mem. bd. of food and drug inspection, U.S. Dept. Agr., Jan. 1-June 1, 1913; chief chemist, 1913-18, dir. research laboratories, 1918, Nat. Canners' Assn. Porf. chemistry, Nat. U., Washington, 1893-98. Author of bulls, on the composition and adulteration of food and on technology of canning. Home: Washington, D.C. Died Mar. 6, 1939.

BILGRAM, HUGO, machinist; b. Memmingen, Bavaria, Germany, Jan. 13, 1847; s. G. David and Rosina (Wiedemann) B.; grad. Poly. Sch., Augsburg, Bavaria, 1865; came to U.S., 1869; m. Mary Fischer, Dec. 8, 1872. Worked as machinist, instrument maker, draughtsman, until 1879; entered machinery business, 1879, producing spl. machinery. Author: Slide Valve Gears, 1877; Involuntary Idleness, 1889; The Cause of Business Depression, 1914; The Remedy for Overproduction and Unemployment, 1928. Home: Molylan, Pa. Deceased.

BILLINGS, FRANK SEAVER, pathologist; b. Boston, Jan. 15, 1845; s. George and Lucy E. B.; ed. in boarding schs. in Mass.; studied (and grad.) veterinary sch. and med. dept. Univ. of Berlin, 1875-80 (Doctor Veterinary Medicine); hon. M.D. Medico-Chirurg. Coll., Phila., 1888; m. Boston, Nov. 6, 1873, Harriet M. Roulstone. Brought up in Am. mcht. service, then went to stock farming; studied medicine in Europe, 1875-85. Did not practice medicine but became known as pathologist and bacteriologist. Pathologist to N.Y. Poly-clinic Sch. of Medicine; founded Pathol. Inst., Univ. of Neb., 1886; took Newark, N.J., boys over to Pasteur to be inoculated for rabies, 1885. Independent in politics. Retired as invalid, 1893. Author: Relation of Animal Diseases to Public Health, 1884 A2; many reports on infectious diseases for Univ. of Neb., 1886-92; How Shall the Rich Escape? (socialistic study), 1894 A3. Contbr. on pathol. and bacteriol. subjects in med. jours. Address: Sharon, Mass.

BILLINGS, FREDERICK HORATIO, educator; b. Chicago, Ill., May 26, 1869; s. Horatio Gilbert and Emily Amelia (Bowers) B.; grad. Calif. State Normal Sch., 1890; A.B., Stanford U., 1896; A.M., Harvard, 1897; Ph.D., U. of Munich, 1901; post grad. work, University of Wisconsin, Massachusetts Institute of Technology and Harvard Medical School; m. Louise Massey, Aug. 15, 1893; children—Frances Augusta, Bertha Mae. Prof. botany and bacteriology, La. State U., 1901-1907; asso. prof. botany and bacteriology, U. of Kan., 1907-13; prof. bacteriology, 1913-17; prof. botany and bacteriology, U. of Redlands, Calif., 1921-40. Fellow A.A.A.S.; mem. Sigma Xi, Alpha Epsilon Delta. Republican. Presbyterian. Mason (past comdr. K.T.; past high priest, R.A.M.). Author: Laboratory Exercises in Bacteriology, 1914. Contbr. numerous papers on researches in botany and bacteriology. Home: 260 High Drive, Laguna Beach CA

BILLINGS, GEORGE HERRICK, metallurgist; b. Taunton, Mass., Feb. 8, 1845; s. Warren and Mary Frances (Caswell) B.; ed. Pittsburgh and Mass. Inst. Tech.; m. Harriet Ann Goodwin, Apr. 24, 1879. Was employed in steel mills as roll turner, heater, roller, and later as chemist, mech. engr. and gen. mgr.; mfr. cold drawn steel, 1889—. Inventor of machines for drawing iron and steel bars for shafting and finishing rods. Contributor to current periodicals. Home: Boston, Mass. Died Dec. 8, 1913.

BILLINGS, J(OHN) HARLAND, educator; b. Orono, Can., Apr. 4, 1888; s. Samuel Martin and Evaline Elizabeth (Swanston) B.; B.A.Sc., U. of Toronto, 1912; S.M., Mass. Inst. Tech., 1915, Harvard, 1915; Eng.D., Drexel Institute of Technology, 1959; m. Anna Sibylla Stonehouse, Sept. 29, 1915; children—Julia Evelyn, Jean Harland (Mrs. Curtis A. Grundberg), John Kimball. Asst. engr., Can. Machinery Corp., 1912-13; instr. mech. engring., U. of Missouri, 1913-14, Johns Hopkins, 1915-16; lecturer in machine design, U. of Toronto, 1916-19; prof. and head dept. of mech. engring., Drexel Inst. Tech., Phila., from 1919, acting dean Engring. Sch., 1944-45; engring. cons. U.S. Army Ordnance, Bur. Ships, USN. Gage prodn. rep. Imperial Munitions Bd. Ottawa, Can., Apr.-Oct. 1917. Fellow A.A.A.S.; mem. Am. Soc. M.E. (chmn. Phila. sect. 1928-29), Soc. Promotion Engring. Edn. (chmn. Mid-Atlantic sect. 1944), Tau Beta Pi, Pi Tau Sigma, Phi Kappa Phi. Club: Llanerch Country. Author: Applied Kinematics, 1943; Mechanics and Design of Machines, 1951. Home: Broomall PA Died Sept. 29, 1971; buried Valley Forge Gardens, King of Prussia PA

BILLINGS, JOHN SHAW, surgeon, librarian; b. Switzerland Co., Ind., Apr. 12, 1839; s. James and Abbie (Shaw) B.; A.B., Miami U., 1857, A.M., 1860; M.D., Med. Coll. of Ohio, 1860; (LL.D., U. of Edinburgh, 1884, Harvard, 1886, Buda-Pesth, 1896, Yale, 1901, Johns Hopkins, 1902; M.D., Munich, 1889, Dublin, 1892; D.C.L., Oxford, 1889); m. Kate M. Stevens, Sept. 3, 1862. Demonstrator anatomy, Med. Coll. of Ohio, 1860-61; served in U.S.A., as asst. surgeon, Apr. 16, 1862; maj. surgeon, Dec. 2, 1876; lt. col. deputy surgeon gen., June 6, 1894; bvtd. capt., maj. and lt. col., Mar. 13, 1865, "for faithful and meritorious services during the war"; in hosp. service during Civil War; later med. insp. Army of the Potomac, in charge of library of surgeon-general's office until his appmt., Dec. 28, 1883, as curator Med. Mus. and Library; retired Oct. 1, 1895. In charge vital statistics 10th Census, vital and social statistics, 11th Census. Prof. hygiene, U. of Pa., 1891, and dir., 1893-96; dir. N.Y. Pub. Library, Astor, Lenox and Tilden foundations, 1896—; chmn. bd. Carnegie Instn., 1905—. Fellow Am. Acad. Arts and Sciences; pres. A.L.A., 1901-02. Author: principles of Centilation and Heating, 1886; Index Catalogue of the Library of the Surgeon-General's Office U.S.A. (16 vols.), 1880-1894; National Medical Dictionary (2vols.), 1889. Home: New York. Died March 11, 1913.

BILLINGSLEY, PAUL, mining geologist; b. N.Y. City, Nov. 30, 1887; s. John Alver and Lucy Ann (Smith) B.; A.B., Columbia, 1908, A.M., 1909; m. Harriet Bigelow, May 18, 1912; children—Lucy Ann, Harriet Joy (Compton), Paul. Geologist, explorer, mine examiner U.S. and S.A., 1910-24; consultant South American Development Company, 1925—; cons. various copper mining and smelting cos. 1925—; research tectonic controls of origin and placement of ore deposits, 1933—; consulting geologist Bunker Hill Co., Bear Creek Mining Co., 1956—. Commissioner, Vashon Island, Wash., 1949-50; president Puget Sound Ferry Users Association, 1949-50. Served as 1st lt. U.S. Army, 1918. Active civil def., World War II. Awarded Leonard medal, Engring. Institute of Can., 1942. Fellow A.A.A.S., Geol. Soc. of Am., Am. Geog. Soc.; mem. Soc. Econ. Geologists, Am. Inst. Mining and Metall. Engrs., Canadian Inst. Mining and Metall. Engrs. (Barlow medal, 1941), Acad. of Polit. Science, Nat. Council of Nat. Econ. League, Foreign Policy Assn., Am. Legion, Am. Acad. Polit. & Social Scis., Seismol. Soc. Am., Am. Polar Soc., Colo., N.W. sci. socs., S.A.R., Sigma Xi, Theta Delta Chi. Author reports, papers and articles. Home: Burton, Wash. 98013. Died May 18, 1962; buried Seattle.

BILLNER, KARL PAUL, civil engr., inventor; b. Billesholm, Sweden, Mar. 5, 1887; s. Oskar Frederik and Maria (Johansson) B.; C.E., Chalmers Tech. U., Gothenburg, Sweden, 1906; m. Gurli Soderman, Oct. 24, 1914; 1 son, Borje Frederik; m. 2d, Margareta Kohalnder, Sept. 24, 1931. Came to U.S., 1906. Irrigation engr. Moses Coulee Fruit Co., Wash., locating engr. Northern Pacific R.R., Mont., locating and resident engr. Wash. Hwy. Dept., 1907-12; bridge engr. Columbia River Hwy. Ore. (designed and supervised constrn. 1st concrete bridges in Ore.), 1913-14; engring. and bldg. constrn., Stockholm, 1916-24; formed Aerocrete Britain Ltd., London, 1925; organized Aerocrete Corp. Can., Montreal, Aerocrete Corp. Am. N.Y., interested in asso. cos. in 29 countries; pres. Vacuum Concrete Corp., Phila., Billner Vacuum Concrete, S.A. Phila.; dir. Societe du Vacuum Concrete, Paris, France, Sociéta Italiana del Vacuum Concrete, Rome, Italy. Bd. govs. Am. Swedish Hist. Found., Phila. Recipient Frank P.Brown medal Franklin Inst., 1946. Mem. Am. Concrete Inst. (Turner Gold medal 1962), Am. Soc. Swedish Engrs. (pres. 1933-34). Developed light weight concrete "aerocrete," 1st used in Imperial Brit. Expn., 1925, since by Bethlehem Steel Co., U.S. govt., others; inventor vacuum concrete (moisture removed by vacuum making possible rapid hardfreezing, elec. pretressing of reinforcing steel, method for eliminating centrifugal sway from trains, micro-filter. Contbr. to tech. jours. Home: Garden Court Plaza, Phila. 19143. Office: Girard Trust Bldg., Phila. 19102. Died June 6, 1965.

BINGHAM, EUGENE COOK, chemist; b. Cornwall, Vt., Dec. 8, 1878; s. W. Harrison and Mary Lucina (Cook) B.; B.A., Middlebury (Vt.) Coll., 1899, D.Sc., 1936; Ph.D., John Hopkins Univ., 1905; student univs. of Leipzig, Berlin and Cambridge, 1905-06; m. Edith Irene Snell, June 18, 1907. Prof. chemistry, Richmond (Va.) Coll., 1906-15; asst. physicist, U.S. Bureau of Standards, 1915-16; prof. chemistry, Lafayette Coll., since Aug. 1916. Chemist. U.S. Bureau of Standards, 1918-19, on lubrication investigation. Was awarded certificate of merit by Franklin Inst. for improved form of variable pressure viscometer, 1921. Chem. com. on plasticity Am. Soc. Testing Materials. Mem. Am. Chem. Soc., Soc. of Rheology, A.A.A.S., Am. Assn. Univ. Profs., Am. Inst. Chem. Engrs., Delta Kappa Epsilon, Phi Beta Kappa, Tau Beta Pi, Alpha Chi Sigma; hon. mem. Va. Chemists Club; sec. the Bingham Assn. Republican. Conglist. Club: Blue Mountain Club of Pa. (pres.). Author: Laboratory Manual of Inorganic Chemistry, 1911; Fluidity and Plasticity, 1921; also numerous papers pub. in Am., English and German scientific periodicals. Editor: Rheological Memoirs, 1940. Inventor: Improved laboratory hood, machine for ruling with waterproof inks, encased cement columns, self-lighting and non-glare surface for highways, instruments for the precise measurement of viscosity and plasticity. Home: 602 Clinton Terrace, Easton, Pa. Died Nov. 6, 1945.

BINGHAM, HIRAM, explorer, ex-senator; b. Honolulu, H.I., Nov. 19, 1875; s. Rev. Hiram and Minerva Clarissa (Brewster) B.; A.B., Yale, 1898; M.A., U. of Calif., 1900; M.A., Harvard, 1901, Ph.D., 1905; Litt.D., U. of Cuzeo, 1912; m. Alfreda Mitchell, Nov. 20, 1900; children—Woodbridge, Hiram, Alfred Mitchell, Charles Tiffany, Brewster, Mitchell, Jonathan Brewster; m. 2d, Suzanne Carroll Hill, June 28, 1937. Austin teaching fellow in history, Harvard, 1901-02 and 1904-05; preceptor in history and politics, Princeton U., 1905-06; explored Bolivar's route across Venezuela and Colombia, 1906-07; lecturer on South Am. geography and history, Yale, 1907-09; asst. prof. Latin Am. history, 1901-15, prof., 1915-24; Albert Shal lecturer on diplomatic history, Johns Hopkins, 1910. Del. U.S. Govt. to 1st Pan-Am. Scientific Congress. Santiago de Chile, 1908; explored Spanish trade route, Buenos Aires to Lima, 1908-09; dir. Yale Peruvian Expdn., 1911, discovered ruins of Machu Picchu, located Vitcos, last Inca capital, and made the first ascent of Mt. Coropuna, 21,703 ft.; dir. Peruvian expdns., 1912, 14-15, auspices of Yale U. and Nat. Geog. Soc.; adviser on the South Am. Collections in the Yale U. Library; lecturer on South Sea Islands, Naval Training Schools, 1942-43. Alternate, Rep. Conv., Chicago, 1916; del. at large, Cleveland, 1924, Kansas City, 1928, Chicago, 1932, Cleveland, 1936; presdl. elector, 1916; lt. gov. of Conn., 1923-24, elected gov., 1924, resigning Jan. 8, 1925; elected U.S. Senator, Dec. 16, 1924, re-elected for term, 1927-33; mem. President Coolidge's Aircraft Bd. (Morrow Bd.), 1925; chairman American Samoan Commission, 1930; chairman Loyalty Review Board, Director Washington Loan & Trust Co. Capt. 10th Field Arty., Conn. Nat. Guard, 1916; organized U.S. schools of military aeronautics; commd. lt. col., Air Service, Mil. Aeronautics, U.S. Army, Oct. 23, 1917; chief Air Personnel Div., Washington, Nov. 1917-Mar. 1918, and A.E.F., Tours, 1918; comdg. officer Aviation Instrn. Center, Issodoun, France (Allies' largest flying school), Aug.-Dec. 1918. Officer de l'Ordre de l'Etoile Noire (French); Gran Oficial de la Orden del Libertador (Venezuela); Gran Oficial de la Orden "El Sol del Peru" (Peru); awarded Mitre medal of Hispanic Soc.; H.G. Bryant Gold Medal. Fellow Royal Geog. Society; honorary life member National Geog. Society; member Geographic Soc. of Phila., Hispanic Soc. America (hon. president), American Antiquarian Society; honorary member Nat. Acad. Hist. (Bogota); corr. member Lima

Geog. Soc., Nat. Acad. Hist. (Caracas, Venezuela). Mem. Sigma Psi. Clubs: Elizabethan, Grad. (New Haven), Century (N.Y.), Metropolitan, Chevy Chase, Alfalfa (Wash.). Author: Journal of an Expedition across Venezuela and Colombia, 1909; Across South America, 1911; Vitcos, the Last Inca Capital, 1912; In the Wonderland of Peru, 1913; The Monroe Doctrine, An Obsolete Shibboleth, 1913; The Future of the Monroe Doctrine, 1920; An Explorer in the Air Service, 1920; Inca Land, 1922; Freedom under the Constitution, 1924; Machu Picchu, 1930; Elihu Tale—The American Nabob of Queen Square, 1939; Lost City of the Incas, 1948. Home: 1818 R St., Washington 9. Died June 6, 1956; buried Arlington Nat. Cemetery.

BINKLEY, ALMOND M(ADISON), educator, horticulturist; b. Franktown, Colo., May 23, 1900; s. Henry M. and Elizabeth (Davies) B.; B.S., Colo. State Univ., 1922; M.S., Ia. State Coll. (research fellow), 1923; grad. study Cornell, 1934-35; m. Alma Irene Harrington, July 22, 1932. Insp. fruit and vegetables Colo. Bur. Markets, 1923-24; research agriculturist Am. Beet Sugar Co., Rocky Ford, Colo., 1924-28; asso. prof. Colo. State Univ., Fort Collins, 1928-35, head horticulture and chief horticulturist Colo. Agri. Exptl. Sta. from 1939; Colo. state horticulturist, 1935-42; collaborator Bur. Plant Industry, U.S. Dept. Agr. from 1939. Attended Internat. Horticulture Congress, London, Eng., 1930. Served as pvt., inf. S.A.T.C., 1918. Mem. Am. Soc. Hort. Sci., A.A.A.S., Am. Potato Assn. Am. Carnation Soc. (hon.), Phi Kappa Phi (hon.), Tri-Beta (hon.), Sigma Phi Epsilon. Mason, Elk. Author tech. research, and popular articles. Home: Ft Collins CO Died Nov. 20, 1970; interred Fairmount Mausoleum, Denver CO

BINNEY, AMOS, naturalist; b. Boston, Oct. 18, 1803; s. Col. Amos and Hannah (Dolliver) B.; grad. Brown U., 1821; M.D., Harvard, 1826; m. Mary Ann Binney, Dec. 20, 1827, 5 children including William Greene. A founder Boston Soc. Natural History, 1830, curator, 1830-32, treas, 1832-34, corr. sec., 1834-37, v.p., 1837-43, pres. 1843-47; a founder Am. Assn. Geologists and Naturalists; mem. Mass. Legislature, 1836-37. Author: Terrestial Air-Breathing Moilusks of the United States and Adjacent Territories of North America. Died Rome, Italy, Feb. 18, 1847.

BINNS, CHARLES FERGUS, ceramic educator; b. Worcester, Eng., Oct. 4, 1857; s. Richard William B. (F.S.A.), dir. Royal Porcelain Works, Eng.; D.Sc., Alfred (N.Y.) Univ., 1925; m. Mary Howard Ferrar, June 7, 1882 (died 1925); children—Mary Elizabeth, William Hugh Ferrar (dec.), Annie Howard (Mrs. F. Bonnet, Jr.), Dorothy Neville (Mrs. A. H. Remsen), Norah Winifred (Mrs. A. D. Fraser). Was connected with the Royal Porcelain Works, Worcester, Eng., 1872-96; prin. Tech. School of Science and Art, Trenton, N.J., 1897-1900; dir. N.Y. State Coll. of Ceramics, 1900-31. Pres. Am. Ceramic Soc., 1901, sec., 1918-22. Ordained priest P.E. Ch., 1923. Author: Ceramic Technology, 1896; The Story of the Potter, 1897; The Potter's Craft, 1909, 2d edit., 1922. Home: Alfred, N.Y. Died Dec. 4, 1934.

BIRD, PAUL PERCY, mechanical engr.; b. Kalamazoo, Mich., Mar. 24, 1877; s. Charles H. and Mary A. (Warrant) B.; M.E., Cornell U., 1900; m. Elizabeth Hyatt, of Toledo, O., June 20, 1908. With Newport News (Va.) Shipbuilding Co., 1900-3; instr. in marine engring. Cornell U., 1904; steam engr., Ill. Steel Co., S. Chicago, 1904-7; smoke insp., City of Chicago, 1907-11; mech. engr. with Commonwealth Edison Co., Chicago, May, 1911-1913. Mem. Assn. of Commerce Com. on Smoke Prevention with Electrification of Ry. Terminals, Chicago. Pres. Internat. Assn. for Prevention of Smoke, 1910; mem. Am. Society Mech. Engrs., 1907, Nat. Electric Light Assn., Western Soc. of Engrs., Delta Tau Delta. Presbyn. Clubs: University, Exmoor Country. Office: 111 W. Monroe St., Chicago IL

BIRDSEYE, CLARENCE, processed foods exec.; b. Brooklyn, N.Y., Dec. 9, 1886; s. Clarence Frank and Ada (Underwood) B.; student Amherst, 1910, M.A., 1941; m. Eleanor Gannett, Aug. 21, 1915; children—Kellogg G., Ruth, Eleanor, Henry S. Field naturalist, biol. survey, U.S. Dept. Agr., 1910-12; fur trader, Labrador, 1912-17; U.S. purchasing agent U.S. Housing Corp., 1917-19; asst. to pres. U.S. Fisheries Assn., 1920-22; vice pres. and pres. of companies pioneering in quick freezing dressed seafoods, 1923-29; with Birdseye-Frosted Foods, Inc., and Birdseye Lamps, 1930-34; pres. Birdseye Electric Co., 1935-38; engaged in development of specialized food freezing and dehydrating processes and equipment, 1939—; pres. Process Evaluation & Development Corp., 1955-56. director Cape Ann Nat. Bank, Gloucester, Mass., consultant to Gen. Foods Corp. Mem. Am. Chem. Soc., Boston Hort. Club, Gloucester Chamber of Commerce, Am. Fisheries Assn., Am. Soc. Refrigerating Engrs., Inst. Food Technologists (chmn. northeast sect. 1945-46), Internat. Assn. Milk Sanitarians, Camp Fire Club. Author numerous papers and talks on food preservation. Granted approximately 250 U.S. and fgn. patents in fields of food preservation and incandescent light. Spent two months on hospital ship with Dr. Wilfred T. Grenfell, assisting in medical care given sick along coast of Labrador. Developed process for making paper pulp from sugar cane "bagasse", straw and other farm residues. Address: Eastern Point Blvd., Gloucester, Mass. Died Oct. 7, 1956.

BIRDSEYE; CLAUDE HALE, topographic engr.; b. Syracuse, N.Y., Feb. 13, 1878; s. George Frederick Hurd and Katharine Lamb (Hale) B.; A.B., Oberlin, 1901, Sc.D., 1931; post-grad. work, U. of Cincinnati and Ohio State U.; m. Grace Gardner Whitney, Nov. 23, 1904; children—Charles W., Frederick H., Florence W. Instr. in Physics, U. of Cincinnati, 1901; field asst., later topographer U.S. Geol. Survey, 1901-06; survey or Gen. Land Office, 1907-08; with U.S. Geol. Survey, 1909-29 (except when in war service), as topographer, geographer, and from Oct. 1919 to Sept. 1929, as chief topographic engr.; pres. Aerotopograph Corp. of America, 1929-32; asst. to dir. U.S. Geol. Survey, 1932; chief, division of engraving and printing, U.S. Geol. Survey, 1932—. Captain Corps of Engineers, U.S.A., Mar.-July 1917; maj. July 1917-Aug. 1918; lt. col. C.A.C., Aug. 1918-June 1919; served in France, on staff of chief of army arty., Aug. 1917-Jan. 1919. The col. engr., O.R.C. Decorated Officer de l'Instruction Publique (French), 1919; Daly medal (American Geol. Soc.), 1924. Author of engring. and tech. repts. Home: Chevy Chase, Md. Died May 30, 1941.

BIRKHOFF, GEORGE DAVID mathematician; b. Overisel, Mich., Mar. 21, 1884; s. David and Jane Gertrude (Droppers) B.; student Lewis Inst., Chicago, 1896-1902, U. of Chicago, 1902-03; A.B., Harvard, 1905, A.M., 1906; Ph.D., U. of Chicago, 1907; hon. Sc.D., Brown, 1923, U. of Wis., 1927, Harvard, 1933, U. of Pa., 1938, Sofia, 1939; LL.D., St. Andrews, 1938; hon. Dr., Poitiers, 1933, Paris, 1936, Athens, 1937, University of Buenos Aires, 1942; hon. mem. faculty, San Marcos, Lima, 1942; University of Chile, 1942; m. Margaret Elizabeth Grafius, Sept. 2, 1908; children—Barbara (Mrs. Robert Treat Paine, Jr.), Garrett, Rodney. Instr. in mathematics, U. of Wis., 1907-09; asst. prof. mathematics, 1909-11, Princeton U., prof., 1911-12; asst. prof. mathematics, Harvard, 1912-19, prof., 1919-33, Perkins prof. since 1933, dean faculty of arts and sicences, 1935-39; lecturer College de Frances, 1930. Decorated Officier French Legion of Honor. Editor of Annals of Mathematics, 1911-13; editor Trans. of Am. Math. Soc., 1920-25; editor Am. Journal of Mathematics since 1943. Mem. Nat. Acad. (pres. 1936-37), Nat. Acad. Sciences of Argentina, Circolo Mathematico di Palermo, Royal Danish Acad. Sciences and Letters, Göttingen Acad. Sciences, Inst. of France, Lima Acad. of Sciences, Royal Acad. of the Lincei, Royal Inst. of Bologana, Pontifical Acad. of Sciences; Royal Irish Acad., Royal Soc., Edinburgh; honorary member Edinburgh Mathematical Society, London Mathematical Soc., Peruvian Philosophic Society, Scientific Society of Argentina; member Sigma Alpha Epsilon, Phi Beta Kappa, Sigma Xi. Awarded Querini-Stampalia prize, 1918, Royal Inst. Science, Letters and Arts, of Venice, Bocher prize of Am. Math. Soc., 1923, for researches in dynamics, and prize awarded by A.A.A.S., 1926; biennial prize of Pontifical Acad. of Sciences, Vatican City, 1933, for research on systems of differential equations. Club: Century (N.Y. City). Author: Relativity and Modern Physcis, 1923; The Origin, Nature and Influence of Elativity, 1925; Dynamical Systems, 1928; Aesthetic Measure, 1933; Basic Geometry (with Ralph Beatley), 1941. Contbr. to mat. jours. Home: 987 Memorial Dr., Cambridge. Mass. Died Nov. 12, 1944.

BIRKINBINE, JOHN, cons. engr.; b. nr. Reading, Pa., Nov. 16, 1844; attended Poly. College of Pa. Served in U.S.A. in Civil War; became asst. to his father as engr. of Phila. water supply; has designed and constructed important water supplies, water power and blast furnace plants; examined and reported upon many mines and industries, in U.S., Can. and Mexico; spl. agt. 11th and 12th censuses; expert on iron and manganese ores for U.S. Geol. Survey for 17 yrs.; chmn. Water Supply Commn., Pa., 1905—. Pres. Am. Inst. Mining Engrs., 1891-93, Engrs.' Club, Phila., 1893, Franklin Inst., 1897-1907, Pa. Forestry Assn., 1897—. Editor for 9 yrs. Journal of Charcoal Iron Workers; now editor Forest Leaves. Home: Cynwyd, Pa. Died May 14, 1915.

BIRKMIRE, WILLIAM HARVEY, engr.; b. Falls of Schuylkill, Phila., June 25, 1860; s. John Harvey and Mary A. B.; ed. pub. and pvt. schs.; grad. Phila. Acad. of Music, 1883; studied architecture 4 yrs. with Samuel Sloan; m. Louisa A. Meny, July 12, 1888. Removed to New York, 1885, to take charge construction dept. Jackson Architectural Iron Works, and, 1892, of J. B. & J. M. Cornell Iron Works; made practical steel details for large bldgs. and the Astor hotels; etc. Author: Construction of High Office Buildings, 1898; Skeleton Construction in Buildings, 1893; Architectural Iron and Steel, 1891; The Planning and Construction of American Theatres, 1896; Compound Riveted Girders, 1893. Home: New York, N.Y. Died Feb. 9, 1924.

BISCH, LOUIS EDWARD, neuropsychiatrist; b. Bklyn., Mar. 10, 1885; s. Otto George and Dorothea Louise B.; A.B., Columbia, 1907, Ph.D., 1912, M.D., 1911; m. Henriette B. Bousquet; children—Barbara, Betty. Interne Manhattan State Hosp., N.Y. City, 1911-13; physician Clearing House for Mental Defectives, 1912-15, N.Y. Neurol. Inst., 1912-16; instr. neuropathology, N.Y. Post-Grad. Med. Sch., 1914-15; consulting neurologist, N.Y. City Children's hosps. and schs., 1913-15; lecturer and asso. in ednl. psychology, Teachers Coll., and lecturer psychology, Columbia, 1913-16; prof. of neuropsychiatry, N.Y. Polyclinic Med. Sch. and Hosp. 1926-63; organizer and dir. Psychopathic Lab. N.Y.C., 1916, Mental Hygiene Clinic, Norfolk, Va., 1918-19; cons. specialist in neuropsychiatry USPHS Hosp. 45, Biltmore, N.C., 1921-22; med. dir. Hillcrest Manor. Organizer, 1917, and dir. psychopathic div. 5th Naval Dist., U.S.N.R.F. until 1919. Fellow A.M.A.; mem. Eugenics Research Assn., Am. Psychiatric Assn., N.Y. State, N.C. med. socs., A.A.A.S., Authors' League of America, Am. Anthropol. Assn., N.Y. Acad. Clubs: Lotos (New York); Authors' (London, Eng.). Author several books, including: Your Nerves, 1945; Cure Your Nerves Yourself, 1953, also sci. paper and contbr. to mag. Home: New York City NY Died 1963.

BISHOP, ERNEST SIMONS, M.D., b. Patwtucket, R.I., Nov. 29, 1876; s. Phanuel Euclid (M.D.) and Louise (Simons) B.; A.B., Brown, 1899; M.D., Cornell Med. Sch., New York, 1908; m. Helen Earle, Jan. 20, 1912; children—Helen Kingsley, Amy. Interne and res. phys. Bellevue Hosp., 1908-12; clin. prof. medicine New York Polyclinic Med. Sch. Was mem. Med. Advisory Bd. of U.S. Army Draft. Frequently called upon as expert witness in courts, and in advisory capacity has modified and interpreted med. legislation, especially narcotic laws; originator and elaborator of modern conception of narcotic drug addiction as a definite and curable phys. disease. Fellow Am. Coll. Physicians, also of Acad. Medicine (New York). Episcopalian. Mason. Author: The Narcotic Drgu Problem; also the Chronic Drug Intoxications and Addictions in George Blumer edit. of Billings-Frochheimer's Therapeusis of Internal Diseases, 1925. Home: New York, N.Y. Died Nov. 16, 1927.

BISHOP, EVERETT L(ASSITER), pathologist; b. Savannah, Ga., Oct. 28, 1892; s. William Alfred and Iola (Getchell) B.; student Davidson Coll., 1912; M.D., U. Md., 1916; postgrad. Cornell Med. Sch. and Meml. Hosp., N.Y. (with Dr. James Ewing), 1922-25; m. Gladys Rose Young, Apr. 5, 1915; children—Everett L., William F., Amy Lou (Mrs. C.B. Henderson). Intern Oglethorpe Hosp., Savannah, 1916; pvt. practice medicine, Savannah, 1916-21; pathologist Steiner Cancer Clinic, Atlanta, 1925-46, Winship Clinic, Emory Univ., 1938—, asso. prof. pathology (neoplastic diseases) Emory Univ., 1935-47, prof. pathology (neoplastic diseases) 1947—; cons. pathologist Emory U. Hosp., Piedmont Hosp., Grady Meml. Hosp., Atlanta, 1948—, Lawson VA Hosp., Chamblee, Ga., 1947-53, Atlanta VA Hosp., 1953—; pvt. practice surg. pathology and cancer diagnosis, 1932—; chief cons. in pathology Area 3 VA, 1946-54; cons. to various hosps. in Atlanta and S.E. Served as 1st lt. M.C., U.S. Army, 1918; lt. comdr. M.C., USNR, 1934, 1941; served to capt., 1941-45, resigned 1947. Diplomate Am. Bd. Pathology, 1936; member com. Am. Registry of Pathology 1951-55. Founding fellow Coll. Am. Pathologists (gov. 1947); mem. Internat. Acad. Pathology (mem. council), 1939-47, pres. 1948-49), Ga. Assn. Pathologists (founder, pres. 1936-46, 57-58), James Ewing Soc., A.M.A., Am. Assn. Pathologists and Bacteriologists, Am. Soc. Clin. Pathologists and Bacteriologists, Am. Soc. Clin. Pathologists, Am. Assn. Cancer Research, Assn. Am. Med. Colls., Am. Cancer Soc. (dir. Ga. div. 1948—), So. Med. Assn. (chmn. sect. pathology 1938), Med. Assn. Ga. (mem. exec. com. cancer commn., 1945—, chmn. 1950, 58-59, mem. editorial bd. Jour. 1952), Am. Philatelic Society, American Topical Assn., N.Y. Path. Soc., Fulton County Med. Soc., A.A.A.S., Phi Rho Sigma. Presbyn. Mason (32 degree) Club: Rotary (dir. 1946-49). Contbr. numerous articles on splty., surg. pathology particularly tumor diagnosis and pathology of cancer to med. jours. Home: 48 Clarendon Av., Avondale Estates, Ga. Office: Medical Arts Bldg., Atlanta 8. Died Aug. 12, 1963; buried W. View Abbey, Atlanta.

BISHOP, FREDERIC LENDALL, physicist; b. St. Johnsbury, Vt.; s. Lendall and Ellen (Bishop) B,; B.S., Mass. Inst. Tech., 1898; Ph.D., University of Pittsburgh, 1938; m. Lelia Prio, Aug. 9, 1899 (died Feb. 26, 1925); 1 son, Frederic Lendall; m. 2d, Marie Thorne, Aug. 14, 1928; children—Ann Thorne, Ellen Marie. Prof. physics, U. of Pittsburgh since 1909, dean Sch. of Engring., 1909-27, Sch. of Mines, 1920-27; cons. engr., Am. Window Glass Co., Window Glass Machine Co. Editor Engineering Education. Fellow A.A.A.S.; mem. Am. Phys. Soc., Am. Inst. E.E., Soc. Promotion Engring. Edn. (sec.). Clubs: University, Field (Pittsburgh); Cosmos (Washington). Contbr. papers on engring. education, thermal conductivity, heat of dilution, electric furnaces, viscosity, mechanical mfr. of glass, etc. Home: Fox Chapel Manor, Fox Chapel Borough, Pittsburgh, Pa. Died 1948.

BISHOPP, FRED CORRY, entomologist; b. Virginia Dale, Colo., Jan. 14, 1884; s. Thomas Barton and Harriet Caroline (McKay) B.; B.S., Colo. State Coll., 1902, M.S., 1926; grad. student Southern Meth. U., 1923-24; Ph.D., Ohio State U., 1932; m. Eulalie Virginia Spencer, Dec. 9, 1908; children—Harriett Eloise, Fred Thomas, Howard Spencer (dec.), Hazel Eulalie.

Teaching fellow zoology and entomology, Colo. Agri. Coll., 1902-03; asst. prof. entomology and zoology, Md. Agrl. Coll., 1903-04; special field agt. Bureau Entomology, U.S. Dept. Agr., 1904-08, asst. entomologist, 1908-11, entomologist, 1911-26, chief Div. of Insects Affecting Man and Animals, 1926-41, asst. chief of bureau in charge research 1941-53; dir., coordinator fed., state and industry sponsored research on bollworm Oscar Johnston Cotton Found., 1953; Dept. State adviser to agr. minister Egypt, 1956; mem. Dept Agr. delegation to World Agr. Fair, New Delhi, India, 1959. Decorated His British Majesty's Medal for service in the cause of freedom. Fellow of American Public Health Associations A.A.A.S., Entomol. Soc. America (v.p. 1932); mem. Am. Assn. of Economic Enthomologists (pres. 1937), Am. Soc. of Parisitologists (pres. 1938), Washington Acad. Sciences, Enthomol. Society of Washington (pres. 1932), American Society Tropical Medicine and Hygiene, Acad. Trop. Medicine, Am. Mosquito Control Assn. (v.p. 1952), Biol. Soc. Washington, Am. Found. for Tropical Medicine. Phi Kappa Phi, Sigma Xi. Presbyn. Editor section on Insects Affecting Animals and Sanitary Entomology of Biol. Abstracts. Author of numerous bulletins and articles on Entomology. Home: Silver Spring MD Died May 8, 1970; buried Inglewood Cemetery, Inglewood CA

BISSELL, GEORGE HENRY, petroleum exec.; b. Hanover, N.H., Nov. 8, 1821; s. Isaac and Nina (Wempe) B.; grad. Dartmouth, 1845; LL.B., Jefferson Coll., 1846; m. Ophie Griffin, 1855. Admitted to N.Y. bar, 1853, organizer Pa. Rock Oil Co. (1st U.S. oil co. to develop Pa. oil lands), 1854; pioneer in technique of obtaining petroleum through drilled wells. Died Nov. 19, 1884.

BISSONNETTE, T. HUME, prof. biology; b. Dundas, Ont., Can., June 27, 1885; s. Julien Donald and Annie Isabel (Hume) B.; M.A., Queen's U., Kingston, Can., 1913; Ph.D., U. of Chicago, 1923; m. Julia Irene Powers, Mar. 1, 1924; children—Julien Hume, Donald King. Came to U.S., 1920, naturalized, 1931. Junior master, Galt Coll. Inst., 1906-09; prin. Victoria Pub. Sch., Saskatoon, Can., 1913; science master, biology and chemistry, Regina Coll. Inst., 1914-16; lecturer in biology, Queen's Univ., Can., 1919-20; asst. in zoology, U. of Chicago, 1921-23; instr. in zoology, Y.M.C.A. Coll. of Liberal Arts, Chicago, Ill., 1922-23; prof. biology, Coe Coll., Cedar Rapids, Ia., 1923-25; J. Pierpont Morgan prof. biology and head of dept., Trinity Coll., Hartford, Conn., since 1925; instr. in marine invertebrate zoology, Marine Biol. Lab., Woods Hole, Mass., 1926-36, in charge of course, 1936-41; research visiting prof., Cambridge U., Eng., 1931-32. Served with C.E.F., 1916-17; 2d lt., Lancashire Fusiliers, B.E.F., 1918-19; wounded and gassed, Harbonnieres, France, 1918; lecturer in botany, Canadian Khaki Coll., Ripon, Yorks, England, 1919. British Board of Education Scholar at U. of Chicago, 1920-21, for war service; head of biology branch, Biarritz Am. Univ. (Army), 1945-46, France; U.S.A.F.L. examiner Hockst, Germany, 1946. Walker Grand prize winner, 1945 for investigations in Photo periodism; for 5 yrs. Fellow A.A.A.S., Ia. Acad. Science; mem. Assn. for Research in Internal Secretions, Am. Soc. Zoologists, Genetic Assn., Genetics Soc., Am. Assn. Univ. Profs. (pres. Trinity chapter 1941), Northeastern Birdbanding Assn., Am. Naturalists, Corp. of Marine Biol. Lab., Nat. Geog. Soc., Gamma Alpha, Sigma Xi. Ind. Republican. Presbyterian. Mason. Lecturer to Conn. Air Raid Wardens' Sch. on prevention and control of panic, 1940-41. Contbr. of over 75 sci. articles in learned publs. Home: 622 Pard Rd., West Hartford, Conn. Office: Trinity Coll., Hartford 6, Conn. Died Nov. 30, 1951; buried Stirling, Ont., Can.

BITTNER, JOHN JOSEPH, cancer research; b. Meadville, Pa., Feb. 25, 1904; s. Martin and Minnie (Shults) B.; A.B., St. Stephen's Coll., Annandale-on-Hudson, N.Y., 1-25; M.S., U. of Mich., 1929. Ph.D., 1930; Doctor of Science, (hon.), Bard College 1950; Dr. Medicine and Surgery, U. Perugia, Italy, 1957; m. Mary Esther Mahaffy, June 23, 1930; children—Mary Margaret, Elizabeth Ann. Asst. in biology, St. Stephen's Coll., 1923-25; master, Donaldson Sch., Ilchester, Md., 1925-26; with N.Y. Telephone Co., 1926-27; asst. in cancer research, U. of Mich., 1927-30, incorporator Jackson Memorial Lab., Bar Harbor, Me., 1930, dir., 1935-42, treas., 1936-38, vice pres., 1940-42, research asso., 1930-40; George Chase Christian prof. cancer research and dir. cancer biology, med. sch. U. Minn., 1942—, prof. exptl. pathology, 1957—; cons. associate scientist Sloan-Kettering Institute, 1956—. Mem. 3rd Internat. Cancer Congress, Atlantic City. 1939. Fourth Congress, St. Louis (chmn. symposium on milk agent; official U.S. del.; program com.; proceeding publication com.). 1947; mem. of Unitarian Service Committee (World Health Organization Sponsored a medical teaching mission to Austria), 1947; Round Table on relation sex hormones to cancer (Am. Assn. Cancer Research), Richmond, Va., 1942. Endocrine-Cancer Conf., Atlantic City, 1942. Gibson Island Cancer Conference (A.A.A.S.), 1944. Recipient Alvaranga prize award Coll. of Phys. of Phila., 1941; Comfort Crookshank award and lecture, London, 1951; Bertner award and lecture U. Tex. M.D. Anderson Hosp. and Tumor Inst., Tex. Med. Center, 1957. Mem. Am. Assn. Cancer Research, Inc. (dir.; v.p., 1946-47; pres. 1947-48), NRC (chmn. milk factor panel, com. on growth, 1945-46, mem. exptl. genetics panel 1947-48), A.A.A.S., Am. Assn. U. Profs., Minn. Pathology Soc., Soc. Exptl. Biology and Medicine. Am. Cancer Soc. (dir. Minn. div. 1945-55, 2d v.p. 1947-48, reginal del. 1948-49). Harvey Soc., Soc. Physicians Vienna (corr. mem.), Royal Soc. Medicine London, N.Y. Acadmey Scis., Sigma Xi, Mason; Eulexian. Club: Dragon. Mem. editorial bd. Cancer Research, 1941-56; mem. editorial com. A.A.A.S. Gibson Island Symposium. 1945. Author and contbr. publs. in field. Home: 112 Seymour Av. S.E., Mpls. 55414. Died Dec. 14, 1961; buried Lakewood Cemetery, Mpls.

BIZZELL, JAMES ADRIAN, soil technologist; b. Glenwood, N.C., Apr. 13, 1876; s. Hannibal Newton and Mary Catherine (Underwood) B.; B.Sc., State Coll. Agr. and Engring., Raleigh, N.C., 1895, M.Sc., 1900; Ph.D., Cornell U., 1903; m. Elizabeth Tillotison Peters, April 15, 1924; children—Mary Catherine, James Royal. Asst. chemist N.C. Expt. Sta., 1895-1901; fellow in chemistry, Cornell U., 1901-02; asst. chemist Cornell U. Expt. Sta., 1903-08; asst. prof. soil technology, N.Y. State Coll. Agr., 1908-12, prof. since 1912. Mem. Am. Soc. Agronomy, Sigma Xi, Alpha Chi Sigma, Gamma Alpha, Acacia. Presbyterian. Mason (K.T., Shriner). Home: Forest Home, Ithaca, N.Y. Died Nov. 1, 1944.

BLACK, ERNEST BATEMAN, cons. eng.; b. Mt. Sterling, Ill., Jan. 13, 1882; s. Moses and Mary Ella (Winslow) B.; B.S., U. of Kans., 1906, C.E., 1924; m. Faye Irene Bunyan, Juen 16, 1914; children—Robert Winslow, Mary Helen, Patricia Ann, John Bunyan. Masonry insp., A.;T.&S.F. Ry., 1906-07; asst. engr. Riggs & Sherman Co., Toledo, O., 1907-09; jr. partner J.S. Worley Co. and Worley & Black, 1909-14; sr. partner Black & Veatch, cons. engrs., since 1915. Served as capt. and maj. Air Service, Air Craft Prodn. U.S. Army, 1917-18, Also chief engr. Craft Prodn. U.S. Army, 1917-18, also chief engr. War Credits Bd. and engr. Sect. B., Constrn. Div. of Army; consultant-chief Water Supply Unit, Civil Engr. Branch, Constrn. Div. Q.M.C., U.S. Army, 1941. Pres. Kansas City Area Boy Scouts of Am., 1940, 41, 42, 43. Mem. Nat. exec. bd. Boy Scouts of America, 1944-46, chmn. region VIII, 1946. Pres. U. of Kansas Gen. Alumni Assn., 1928-29. Mem. American Institute Consulting Engineers, American Society Civil Engrs. (president 1942), Society of Am. Mil. Engrs. Director, 1943, 44, 45, Am. and New England water works assns., Kansas Engineering Soc., Sigma Xi, Tau Beta Pi. Republican. Presbyterian. Mason (Shriner). Clubs: University, Mission Hills Country, Kansas City Engrs. (Kansas City, Mo.). Contbr. articles on engring. to tech. jours. Home: 824 W. 62d St. Office: 4706 Broadway, Kansas City, Mo. Died July 4, 1949.

BLACK, GREEN VARDIMAN, dentist; b. Scott Co., Ill., Aug. 3, 1836; D.D.S., Mo. Dental Coll., St. Louis, 1877; M.D., Chicago Medical Coll., 1884; (Sc.D., Ill. Coll., 1892; LL.D., Northwestern, 1898). Prof. operative dentistry, pathology and bacteriology and dean Northwestern U. Dental Sch. Author: Formation of Poisons oy Micro- organisms; Periosteum and Peridental Membrane; Anatomy of the Human Teeth; Operative Dentistry (2 vols.); also many soc. papers and journal articles. Home: Chicago, Ill. Died Aug. 31, 1915.

BLACK, NEWTON HENRY, educator; b. Putney, Vt., May 3, 1874; s. Newton Horace and Frances (Blanchard) B.; Phillips Exeter Acad., Exeter, N.H., 1892-93; A.B., Harvard, 1896, A.M., 1906; student U. of Berlin, 1912-13, Cambridge U., England, 1930-31; m. Elizabeth A. Herrmann, Aug. 3, 1918; children—Elizabeth Spalding (Mrs. W. J. Emlen), Margaret Persis (Mrs. Stephen A. Richardson). Teacher of science, St. George's Sch., Newport, R.I., 1896-98; High Sch., Concord, N.H., 1898-1900; Roxbury Latin Sch., Boston, 1900-24; asst. prof. edn., Harvard, 1924-32, asst. prof. of physics, 1932-40, asst. prof. emeritus since 1940, also dir. Harvard Univ. Summer Sch., 1932-34. Lecturer, U.S.N. Communication School, 1942-43, navy V-12, 1943-44. Fellow A.A.A.S., Am. Phys. Soc.; mem. Am. Inst. E.E., Coll. Entrance Exam. Bd., 1906-22. Rep. Conglist. Author: Lab. Manual in Physics, 1913; Revised Edition Jackson's Elementary Electricity and Magnetism, 1919; Laboratory Experiments in Chemistry, 1920, 27, 36; Laboratory Experiments in Practical Physics, 1923; Introductory Course in College Physics, 3d edit., 1948. Co-author: Black and Davis' Practical Physics, 1913-22, 29, 38; Black and Conant's Practical Chemistry, 1920, 27; Black and Davis' New Practical Physics, 1929; Black and Conant's New Practical Chemistry, 1936; Black and Weaver's Laboratory Experiments and Workbook in Physics, 1938; Black and Davis' Elementary Practical Physics, revised, 1949. Home: 21 Follen St., Cambridge 38, Mass.; also South Tamworth NH

BLACKBURN, WILLIS CLIFFORD, petroleum geologist; b. nr. Union Grove, Wis., Apr. 5, 1903; s. Roy Lindsey and Nellie (Moyle) B.; B.A., U. Tex., 1926; m. Annie Lenora Whitmire, June 19, 1930; 1 dau., Susie Ann (Mrs. William Martin Boyce). Exploration geologist to sr. exploration geologist Humble Oil & Refining Co., Houston, 1926-55, div. geologist, Ala., Ga., Fla., 1955-59; cons. geology, from 1959. Mem. Am. Assn. Petroleum Geologists, Soc. Econ. Paleontologists, Permian Basin Pioneers (charter), Southeastern Geol. Soc. (past pres.), Sigma Gamma Epsilon. Club: Skyline Country (Mobile, Ala.). Author: The Hilbig Oil Field. Address: Mobile AL Died Sept. 15, 1967; buried Houston TX

BLACKFORD, EUGENE GILBERT, fish mcht., icthyologist; b. Morristown, N.J., Aug. 8, 1839; common school edn.; m. Frances L. Green, May 16, 1860. Became fish dealer in Fulton Market, New York; was leader in introducing there red snapper, whitebait, pompano and other fine fish; commr. of fish and fisheries, N.Y., 1879; caused establishing of hatching sta. for fish at Cold Spring Harbor; has published many papers on fish. Pres. Bedford Bank, Brooklyn; Am. Writing Machine Co., N.Y.; Biol. School, Cold Spring, N.Y.; v.p. Union Typewriter Co., and v.p. Brooklyn Inst. of Arts and Sciences. Home: Brooklyn, N.Y. Died 1904.

BLACKFORD, KATHERINE M(ELVINA) H(UNTSINGER), character analyst; b. West Mineral, Kan., Mar. 18, 1875; d. Henry and Catherine (Schock) Huntsinger; ed. high sch., Columbus, Kan.; M.D., Coll. Phys. and Surg. (now Keokuk Med. Coll.), Keokuk, Ia., 1898; post-grad. work, Dearborn St. Med. Sch. and Hosp., Chicago, 1899; m. Everett F. Blackford, of Rochester, N.Y., June 1, 1899 (dec.); m. 2d, Arthur Newcomb, of New York, Nov. 28, 1912. Began practice of medicine at Rochester, N.Y.; research travel and lecturing, 1903-11; joined Emerson Engineers as employment and personnel specialist, 1912; individual practice, 1913, now retired; pres. Blackford Pubs., Inc. Mem. Authors' League America, League of Am. Pen Women. Club: Woman's Nat. Republican. Author: Employer's Manual, 1912; The Job, the Man, the Boss (with Arthur Newcomb), 1914; The Science of Character Analysis by the Observational Method, 1914; Analyzing Character (with Arthur Newcomb), 1916; Reading Character at Sight, 1918; The Right Job (2 vols.), 1924. Office: 50 E. 42d St., New York NY

BLACKMARR, FRANK HAMLIN, M.D.; b. Rouseville, Pa., Feb. 16, 1871; s. Hamlin L. and Mary C. (Gray) B.; Allegheny Coll., Meadville, Pa.; B.S., U. of Chicago, 1893; M.D., Hahnemann Med. Coll., Chicago, 1897; m. Catherine Strong, of Oil City, Pa., June 22, 1899. Practiced in Chicago, since 1897; specializes in X-Ray therapy, radium therapy, electro therapy. Dir. New York Radium Inst.; fellow A.M.A.; mem. Mo. Med. Soc., Radiological Soc. of N. America, Am. Chem. Soc., Ill. State and Chicago med. socs., Ill. and Chicago Homoe. med. socs., Western Electro-Therapeutic Assn., Western Soc. Engrs., Am. Med. Assn. of Vienna, Sigma Alpha Epsilon. Mason (32 deg. Shriner). Clubs: Unanimous (New York); Illinois Athletic (life), Press (life), Chicago Athletic, Medinah Athletic (life), Chicago Motor, South Shore Country (life). Home: 7350 Phillips Av. Office: 25 E. Washington St., Chicago IL

BLACKMORE, HENRY SPENCER, chemist, patent atty.; b. Yonkers, N.Y., Mar. 10, 1868; s. Isaac and Hannah M. (Dean) B.; grad. grammar sch., Mt. Vernon, N.Y., 1884, New York Coll. of Pharmacy, 1888 (Ph.G., F.C.S.); m. Isabelle Rostosky, of New York, June 2, 1904, V.p. Black-Ford Utility Oil Co.; consulting chemist Am. Automatic Disinfectant Co. and Mexican Nat. Leather Co.; inventor of processes for reducing aluminum and other metals, electric smelting, making alkali from feldspar, making caustic soda from common salt, making sulphuric acid, purifying water gas from poisonous carbonic oxide, making gas purifying agents, making formic aldehyde, disinfecting apparatus and disinfectants, a system of electric lighting, generating electricity from fuel, recording wireless telegrams, making cyanides, ammonia, alcohol, ketones, lithium salts, etc., having taken out more than 150 patents; discoverer, inventor and patentee of a process of making substances which are unstable at elevated temperatures, but which evolve heat upon their formation, such as sulphuric anhydride and sulphuric acid, and this process has economized and revolutionized the manufacture of these products; has also discovered what is believed to be two new chemical elements of non-metallic nature, found associated with sulphur, for which the names "Azureon" and "Vernon" have been suggested. Fellow Chem. Soc. of Great Britain, Am. Geog. Soc., Nat. Geog. Soc.; mem. Soc. Chem. Industry of Great Britain, Am. Chem. Soc., A.A.A.S., Am. Pharm. Assn., Internat. Chem. Congress, Inernat. Elec. Congress, Franklin Inst. of Phila.; mem. U.S. Navy League; chemist to 71st Regt. N.G.S.N.Y., and mem. Vet. Assn. same; Mason, Past Comdr. Bethlehem Commandery No. S3 K.T., life mem. Consistory of New York, 32 deg. Scottish Rite Masons and Mecca Temple A.A.O.N.M.S.; a gov. in state of N.Y. and D.C. for Am. Civic Alliance, 1911; mem. Alumni Assn. Coll. of Pharmacy, Columbia U. Mem. Dutch Reformed Ch., Mt. Vernon, N.Y. Home: Mt. Vernon, N.Y. Offices: 612 F St., N.W., Washington, D.C., and Niagara Falls, N.Y.

BLACKSTONE, RICHARD, engineers; b. Connellsville, Pa., Oct. 16, 1843; s. James and Nancy Campbell (Johnson) B.; studied Pa. Mil. Acad., Rensselaer Poly. Inst., Troy, N.Y.; m. Mabel R. Nobel, Dec. 28, 1871. Enlisted as pvt. in Co. C, 32d Ohio Vols., July 30, 1861; served in W. Va.; taken prisoner at Harper's Ferry Sept. 12, 1862; exchanged, and assigned to Army of Tenn., under Gen. Grant; participaed in many battles, siege of Vicksburg, March to the Sea, Grand Review at Washington; mustered out as capt., July 27, 1865. Placer miner, 2 seasons, Breckenridge, Colo., 1868 and 1869; draftsman in office U.S. surveyor gen., Denver, 1869-70, Cheyenne Wyo., 1870-78; went to Back Hills, 1878, and engaged in mining and mine surveying; asst. supt., chief engr., 1883-1914, gen. mgr. and supt., Sept. 1914-18. Homestake Mining Co., Lead, S.D. Built Black Hills & Ft. Pierre R.R.; water system for Homestake; hydro-electric sta. at Englewood; electric light and power plant, and hydro-electric power plant, Spearfish, including 5-mile concrete-lined, diverting dam tunnel; complete elec. equipment of Homestead Mine; etc. Mem. Am. Inst. Mining Engr., Ohio Commandery Loyal Legion. Republican. Home: Lead, S.D. Died Dec. 21, 1922.

BLACKWELDER, CHARLES DAVIS, engr.; b. Greenville, S.C., Apr. 15, 1895; s. Charles Burwell and May (Stradley) B.; student Furman U. Fitting Sch., 1910-13; Internat. Corr. Sch. extension courses, 1913-27, 41-45; m. Helen McLarin, Sept. 1, 1928 (dec. Mar. 1966); 1 dau., Helen McLarin (Mrs. Russell Cecil Scott). Began as draftsman and lab. asst. Am. Mach. & Mfg. Co., Greenville, 1913-14, chief draftsman, 1915-17, asst. chief engr., in charge of designing machinery, equipment, factories for U.S., also Mexico, India, China, S. Am., 1917-19, resident engr. in India and Ceylon, 1919-22; structural and mech. engr. J.E. Sirrine & Co., engrs., Greenville, 1922-25, chem. and mech. engr., head chm. engring. dept., 1925-37, partner, 1937-44; v.p. in charge engring. Reynolds Metals Co., Richmond, Va., 1944-45, v.p., cons. engr., 1955-59; v.p. Reynolds Reduction Co., 1953—, Reynolds International de Mexico, S.A., 1954—. Registered profl. engr. in 36 states. Mem. Am. Soc. M.E., Am. Inst. Chem. Engrs., Am. Chem. Soc., Am. Water Works Assn., Nat. Va. socs. profl. engineers, S.C. Soc. Engrs., Assn. Iron and Steel Engrs., Chi Beta Phi, Gamma Sigma Epsilon, Tau Beta Pi. Epsicopalian. Elk. Clubs: Central Va. Engrineers, Commonwealth, Country of Va., Va. Power Boat, Va. Writers. Home: Larinwel, Highland Rd., R.F.D. 13, Richmond 23226. Office: Reynolds Metals Bldg., Richmond, Va. 23219. Died Apr. 15, 1965; buried Hollywood Cemetery, Richmond.

BLACKWELL, ELIZABETH, M.D.; B. Bristol, England, Feb. 3, 1821; emigrated to U.S., 1832; ed. in private schools in bristol and New York; taught school in Ky., and the Carolinas; sought admission to several med. colls., but was refused until she entered the med. school at Geneva, N.Y., 1847; later studied in La Maternité and Hotel Dieu, Paris, and St. Bartholomew's, London. Established practice in New York, 1851; founded a hosp., and, in 1867, in conjunction with her sister, Dr. Emily Blackwell, organized Woman's Med. Coll. of New York Infirmary; lectured in England, 1858-59; registered as a physician in England, 1859, and, 1869— has practiced in London and Hastings; founded Nat. Health. Soc. of London; aided in founding London School of Medicine for Women. Author: Physical Education of Girls; Religion of Health; Counsel to Parents on Moral Education; Pioneer Work in Opening the Medical Profession to Women; The Human Element in Sex; Decay of Municipal Representative Institutions. Died 1910.

BLACKWELL, EMILY, formerly Dean Woman's Med. Coll., New York Infirmary; b. Bristol, Eng., 1926; M.D., Western Reserve U., Cleveland, O., 1854. One of the founders (1853), with Elizabeth Blackwell, M.D., and then connected with New York Infirmary for Women and Children, 1st woman's hosp. in the country. Home: Montclair, N.J. Died 1910.

BLAIN, ALEXANDER WILLIAM, surgeon; b. Detroit, Mich., Mar. 4, 1885; s. Alexander William and Mary (Gray) B.; M.D., Detroit Coll. of Medicine and Surgery, 1906; hon. M.S., Wayne U., 1930; m. Ruby Johnson, June 14, 1918; children—Alexander Wm. III, M.D., Shirley Ruth (Mrs. Robert L. Berry), Donald Gray M.D. Asst. H.O. Walker, 1903-06; interne Harper Hospital, 1906-17; sr. surgeon Detroit Meml. Hospital, 1917-22, now consulting surgeon. Receiving, Eloise Hospitals; prof. physiology, School of Dentistry, Wayne U., 1909-11, surgical pathology, Sch. of Medicine, 1911-29, prof. since 1929; chief of staff, Blain Clinic; senior surgeon Alexander Blain Hospital, Detroit, Mich., 1924—. President Detroit Museum of Science Society. Director Gorgas Memorial Institute; mem. Pub. Welfare Commn., Detroit, 1926-33, pres., 1931-32; mem. Supts. of Poor Of Wayne County, 1926-33; mem. Commn. of Conservation, State of Mich., 1939-45. Fellow Royal Soc. Arts, N.Y. Academy Sciences, A.C.S. (gov.), A.A.A.S., Detroit Acad. Surgery, mem. Mich. Horticultural Soc. (pres. 1944-45; mem. bd.), Detroit Zoological Society (trustee), Detroit Acad. Natural Sciences, Detroit Bd. of Commerce; hon. mem. Flint Acad.; mem. Am. Soc. Mammalogists, Am. Ornithologists Union, Wilson Ornithol. Club, Cooper Ornithol. Club, Wayne Co. Med. Soc. (ex-pres.), New York Acad. Sciences, Cranbrook Inst. of Sci. (mem. bd. trustees), Am. Acad. of Political and Social Sciences, Am. Forestry Assn., Nat. Audubon Society, Zoological Societies of New York and Philadelphia, Alumni Association of Wayne U. (pres. 1939-40), Nu Sigma Nu, Sigma Xi, Alpha Omega Alpha. Mason (K.T., Shriner). Clubs: Royal Socs. (London); Detroit, Detroit Athletic, Detroit Boat. Contbr. to mags.; mem. editorial staff Washington Inst. of Medicine (Washington, District of Columbia). Member editorial bd., Revista Argentino-Northeamericana de Ciencias Medicos. Home: 1028 Berkshire Rd., Gross Point; (country) Blain Island, Waterford, Michigan. Office: 2201 Jefferson Av., East, Detroit 48207. Died Dec. 14, 1958.

BLAIR, ANDREW ALEXANDER, chemist; b. Woodford Co., Ky., Sept. 20, 1848; s. Gen. Francis Preston and Apolline (Alexander) B.; grad. U.S. Naval Acad., 1866; midshipman, 1862-68, ensign, 1868-69, U.S.N.; m. Anna S. Biddle, Oct. 24, 1872. Chief chemist to U.S. Commn. to test iron, steel and other metals, Watertown Arsenal, N.Y., 1875-78; chief chemist U.S. Geol. Survey and 10th Census, Newport, R.I., 1879-81; in gen. practice, 1882—. Author: The Chemical Analysis of Iron, 1888, 7th edit., 1909. Contbr. article on assaying in Ency. Britannica, 1900. Home: Chestnut Hill, Pa. Died 1932.

BLAIR, HENRY ALEXANDER, physiologist; b. Winnipeg, Manitoba, Can., Jan. 6, 1900; s. Edward and Isabella (MacFarlane) B.; B.S., U. of Manitoba, 1925; M.S., 1927; Ph.D., Princeton U., 1930; m. Eva Andrews, Aug. 4, 1926; children—Shirley Isabelle, Barbara Elizabeth, Henry Alexander Blair. Came to U.S., 1927, naturalized, 1942. Demonstrator, physics, U. of Manitoba, 1924-27; lecturer, mathematics, Manitoba Agrl. Coll., 1926-27; research asst. physics, Princeton U., 1927-29; instr. biophysics, Western Reserve Med. School, 1930-32; instr. physiology, U. of Rochester, 1932-34, asst. prof., 1934-40, asso. prof., 1940-48, prof. since 1948, dir. dept. radiation biology, and U. of Rochester Atomic Energy Project. Mem. tech. information panel A.E.C. Served with C.E.F., 1918-19. Mem. Radiation Research Soc., Am. Phys. Society, Am. Physiol. Society, Society for Experimental Biology and Medicine, A.A.A.S., Am. Inst. of Physics, Sigma Xi. Editor: Biological Effects of External Radiation, 1954. Mem. editorial bd. Jour. Neurophysiology, 1945-55, Am. Jour. Physiology, 1953-56, Jour. Applied Physiology, 1953-56. Sec. AEC com. on fellowships in indsl. medicine. Home: Rochester NY Died Nov. 4, 1971.

BLAIR, JOSEPH CULLEN, horticulturist; b. Truro, N.S., Apr. 26, 1871; s. Col. William M. and Harriet (Blair) B.; grad. Provincial Coll. of Agr., Truro, 1892; Cornell, 1892-96; hon. M.S.A., Ia. Agrl. Coll., 1906; D.Sc. Coll. of Wooster, 1920; m. Sada Van Horne, June 16, 1898; children—Josephine Van Horne, Robert Collyer, Richard Gordon, Joseph Cullen. Instr. in chemistry, agr. and botany, Provincial Coll. of Agr., 1890-91; instructor in horticulture and horticulturist, Agrl. Expt. Sta., 1896-1901; prof. pomology and chief in horticulture, Coll. of Agr. and Expt. Sta., U. of Ill., 1901-12, prof. and chief in horticulture, 1912—; dean of Coll. of Agr., dir. Agrl. Expt. Sta. and dir. of extension service in agr. and home economics, 1938-39. Republican. Methodist. Prepared plans and directed work for restoration of Ft. Massac State Park, Urbana City Parks, University Heights Addition, Urbana Home: Urbana, Ill. Died April 2, 1940.

BLAIR, W(ILLIAM) REID, zoölogist; b. Phila., Pa., Jan. 27, 1875; s. William Reid and Jeannette (Houston) B.; D.V.S., McGill U., Montreal, Can., 1902, LL.D. from same univ. in 1928; m. Mildred Myrtle L.L.D. from same univ. in 1928; m. Mildred Myrtle Kelly, Oct. 29, 1896. Veterinarian and pathologist, N.Y. Zoöl. Park, 1902-22; prof. comparative pathology, Vet. Dept. New York U., 1905-17; cons. veterianrian, N.Y. State Dept. Agr. Asst. dir. N.Y. Zoöl. Park, 1922-26, dir., 1926-40; exec. sec. Am. Com. Internat. Wild Life Protection since 1938. Pres. Com. Internat. Wild Life Protection since 1938. Pres. Vet. Med. Soc., 1922-23; v.p. and trustee Bronx Soc. of Arts and Sciences; life mem., fellow N.Y. Zoöl. Soc.; fellow A.A.A.S., Am. Geog. Soc.; life mem. Quebec Zoöl. Soc.; mem. council N.Y. Acad. Sciences; corr. mem. Royal Zoöl. Soc. of Ireland, Zoöl. Soc. of London, Internat. Soc. for Preservation of European Bison; life mem. Soc. for Preservation of Fauna of the Empire; trustee Am. Soc. of Mammalogists; sr. fellow Am. Inst. of Park Execs.; mem. Nat. Inst. of Social Sciences, Am. Vet. Med. Assn., N.Y. Graduates Soc. of McGill U., Phi Beta Zeta. Commd. maj., Veterinary Corps, U.S. Army, 1917; served in France and Germany as chief vet. 4th Army Corps, 1918-19; hon. discharged, June 1919; col. Res. Corps. U. S. Army, 1923. Received Citation of Merit, Park Assn. of N.Y. City, 1940. Active in wild life conservation of birds and mammals. Clubs: Century, Authors, Boone and Crockett. Author: Disease of Wild Animals in Confinement (pub. N.Y. Zoöl. Soc.), 1911; In the Zoo, 1929. Also contbr. scientific publs. on comparative medicine. Home: 271 College Road, Riverdale, New York, N.Y. Died Mar. 1, 1949.

BLAKE, ELI WHITNEY, inventor, mgr.; b. Westborough, Mass., Jan. 27, 1795; s. Elihu and Elizabeth (Whitney) B.; grad. Yale, 1816; m. Eliza O'Brien, July 8, 1822, 6 sons, 6 daus. Partner firearms business with uncle Eli Whitney, New Haven, 1817-25, continued bus. with brother after uncle's death, 1825-36; propr. hardware factory, Westville, Conn., 1836-71; received patents for door lock, bedstead castors, stone crusher; a founder Conn. Acad. Scis.; contbr. to Am. Jour. of Science. Author: Original Solution of Several Problems in Aerodynamics, 1882. Died New Haven, Conn., Aug. 18, 1886; buried New Haven.

BLAKE, FRANCIS, inventor; b. Needham, Mass., Dec. 25, 1850; s. Francis and Caroline (Trumbull) B.; high sch. edn., Brookline, Mass.; (hon. A.M., Harvard, 1902); m. Elizabeth L., d. Charles T. Hubbard of Weston, June 24, 1873. Served on U.S. Coast Survey 13 yrs., resigned; during last 2 or 3 yrs. was engaged in field work and its reduction ot determine differences of longitude between observatories at Greenwich, Paris, Cambridge and Washington; devoted leisure to experimental physics, and in 1878 invented "Blake Transmitter," which has played important part in development of telephony throughout the world; has patented many other elec. devices. Fellow A.A.A.S., Am. Acad. Arts and Sciences. Home: Keewaydin, Weston (Auburndale P.P.), Mass. Died Jan. 1913.

BLAKE, FREDERIC COLUMBUS, prof. physics; b. Decatur, Ill., Oct. 30, 1877; s. Christopher Columbus and Rachel Ellen (Beam) B.; Ph.B., U. of Colo., 1901; univ. fellow, Columbia, 1903-04, John Tyndall fellow, 1904-07, Ph.D., 1905; studied Cambridge U., Eng., 1905-06, Berlin, 1906-07; m. Edith Sherwin Adams, Aug. 20, 1907 (died 1931); m. 2d, Jane Snow Hinkley, Apr. 23, 1933. Asst. prof. physics, Ohio State University, 1907-12, prof. since 1912; prof. of physics, emeritus since 1946. Pres. Academic Bd., U.S. Army Sch. of Mil. Aeronautics, Ohio State U., Nov. 1917-Sept. 1918. Fellow, Am. Physical Soc.; mem. Am. Assn. Physics Teachers, Sigma Xi, Phi Beta Kappa. Author: papers on X-ray diffraction and curved crystal spectrographs. Home: 1581 N Grand Oaks Av., Pasadena 7 CA

BLAKE, JOHN CHARLES, educator; b. Ottumwa, Ia., May 31, 1873; s. Christopher Columbus and Rachel (Beam) B.; B.S., U. of Colo., 1901; Ph.D., Yale, 1903; m. Jennie Archibald, of Trinidad, Colo., July 21, 1904; children—Charles Archibald, Mabel Myrtle, Frances, Ruth, Helen. Research asso. in physical chemistry, Mass. Inst. Tech., 1903-05; asst. physicist, Nat. Bur. Standards, 1905-06; head dept. of chemistry, Agrl. and Mech. Coll. of Tex., 1906-13, also chem. engr.; head dept. of chemistry, Hahnemann Med. Coll., Chicago, since 1913, dean 1921-22; dean Gen. Med. Coll. (successor to Hahnemann Med. Coll.), 1922-24. Mem. Am. Chem. Soc., Am. Inst. of Chemists, Sigma Xi, Pi Upsilon Rho. Author: General Chemistry, Theoretical and Applied, 1913; General Chemistry Laboratory Manual, 1913. Contbr. numerous articles to Jour. Am. Chem. Soc. Home: 6615 Kimbark Av., Chicago IL

BLAKE, LYMAN REED, inventor, shoe mfr.; b. South Abington, Mass., Aug. 24, 1835; s. Samuel and Susannah (Bates) B.; m. Susie Hollis, Nov. 27, 1855. Joined shoemaking firm Gurney & Mears (became Gurney, Mears & Blake), 1856, ret. before 1861; inventor form of shoe that could be sewed, 1857, also machine for sewing soles to uppers (essentially the modern process). Died Oct. 5, 1883.

BLAKE, SIDNEY FAY, botanist; b. Stoughton, Mass., Aug. 31, 1892; s. Walter Raymond and Harriot Elsie (Southworth) B.; A.B., Harvard, 1913, A.M., 1913, Ph.D., 1917; m. Doris Mildred Holmes, May 4, 1918; 1 dau., Doris Sidney. Asst., Gray Herbarium, Harvard, 1916-17; prof. botany, Stanford, 1927; with U.S. Dept. Agr., since 1917, sr. botanist, Bur. Plant Industry, Beltsville, Md., since 1928. Del. to Seventh Internat. Bot. Congress, Stockholm, 1950. Fellow Linnean Soc., London; mem. Am. Bot. Soc., American Society Plant Taxonomists (pres. 1943), Cal. Bot. Soc., Washington Acad. Sci., Biol. Soc. Washington (recording sec. since 1923), Bot. Soc. Washington, Washington Biologists' Field Club (pres., 1931-34), New England Bot. Club. Author: Geographical Guide to Floras of the World (with Alice C. Atwood), 1942, Vol. 2, 1961; Flora of Stoughton, Mass., 1963. Contbr. tech. papers on classification of flowering plants. Home: 3416 N. Glebe Rd., Arlington, Va. Office: Plant Industry Station, Beltsville, Md. Died Dec. 31, 1959; buried Stoughton, Mass.

BLAKE, WILLIAM PHIPPS, mineralogist; b. New York, June 1, 1826; s. Elihu and Adeline N. (Mix) B.; Ph.B., Yale, 1852; (hon. A.M., Darmouth, 1863; Sc.D., U. of Pa., 1906); m. Charlotte Haven Lord Hayes, of S. Berwick, Me., Dec. 25, 1885; father of Joseph Augustus B. Officially identified with great expositions, 1853—; geologist and mineralogist for U.S. Pacific R.R. expdn., 1853; edited Mining Magazine, 1858-60; mining engr. in service of Japanese Govt., 1862; explored the Stickeen River, Alaska, 1863 and made report to Sec. of State Seward; prof. mineralogy and geology Coll. of Calif., 1864; geologist and mineralogist U.S. Commn. to Santo Domingo, 1871; exec. commr. Centennial Expn., 1876; prof. geology and dir. Sch. of Mines, U. of Ariz., 1894-1905, emeritus, 1905—; territorial geologist, 1898—. Chevalier Legion of Honor, France, 1878. Author: Geological Reconnaissance, California, 1855; Sivler Ores and Silver Mines; Tombstone and Its Mines; Ceramic Art and Glass; Life of Capt. Jonathan Mix. Home: Tucson, Ariz. Deceased.

BLAKESLEE, ALBERT FRANCIS, botanist; b. Geneseo, N.Y., Nov. 9, 1874; s. Francis Durbin and Augusta Mirenda (Hubbard) B.; A.B., Wesleyan U., Conn., 1896, D.Sc., 1931; A.M., Harvard, 1900, Ph.D., 1904 (Bowdoin medal, 1905); D.Sc., U. of San Marcos (Peru), 1925; D.Sc., U. of Delhi (India), 1947; LL.D., University of Arkansas, 1947; D.Sc., Yale University, 1947; Wesleyan U., 1931. Paris, Sorbonne, France, 1951, Smith Coll., 1952; married to Margaret Dickson Bridges, June 26, 1919 (dec.). Asst. botany Harvard, 1899-1900; instr. Botany, Radcliffe Coll., 1900-02; teaching fellow, Harvard, 1901-03; asst. in botany, Summer Sch. of Cold Spring Harbor, L.I., 1901-02; collector in Venezuela for the Cryptogamic Herbarium of Harvard, summer of 1903; investigator in Europe for Carnegie Instn., 1904-06; instr. botany, Harvard, 1906-07; dir. Summer Sch. and prof. botany, Conn. Agrl. Coll., Sept., 1907-14, prof. botany and genetics, 1914-15; resident investigator, Carnegie Sta. for Exptl. Evolution, Cold Spring Harbor, 1912-13, in plant genetics 1915-41, asst. dir. dept., 1923-34, acting dir., 1934-35, dir., 1936-41, asso. in Genetics, Columbia U., 1940-42; William Allan Nellson research professor of botany, Smith College, 1942-43, visiting prof. and dir. Smith College Genetics Experiment Station, 1943—; visiting lecturer at Harvard University, 1948-49. Del. Carnegie Instn. to 3d Pan-Am. Scientific Congress, Lima, 1924-25; del. of A.A.A.S. to Indian Sci. Congress, 1946-48; mem. div. biology and agr., Nat. Research Council, 1931-33; mem. bd. mgrs. N.Y. Bot. Garden, 1933-34, director National Science Fund; trustee Biological Abstracts, 1931-46, president, 1942-46. Awarded A. Cressy Morrison prize, New York Academy Sciences, 1926, 36, also the Henry deJouvenal prize, Palais de la Decouverte, 1938. Honorary fellow, Nat. Institute Scis. of India; fellow A.A.A.S. (sec. Sect. G., 1916-17, v.p. 1918, pres. 1940), Am. Acad. of Arts and Sciences; mem. Am. Philos. Soc., Bot. Soc. Naturalists (v.p. 1916; pres. 1930), N.E. Bot. Club, Torrey Bot. Coub (asso. editor, 1924—, pres. 1933), The American Genetics Association, Genetic Soc. of America, Am. Eugenics Soc., Assn. for Research in Human Heredity, Human Genetics Society, Society for Study of Development and Growth (Pres. 1945-46), Phi Beta Kappa, Phi Sigma, Sigma Xi; asso. mem. Societe Royale de Botanique de Belgique, Soc. de Biologie de Paris, Royal Academy of Belgium; corresponding member of Nederlandsche Botanische Vereeniging, Acad. of Natural Sciences of Phila.; foreign mem. Acad. Sciences of Inst. of France, Linnean Soc. (London), Royal Danish Acad. of Science, Royal Physiographical Society of Lund (Sweden); Royal Swedish Acad. Scis., Botan. Soc. India; hon. mem. Soc. Naturalists (Moscow), Mycological Society of Leningrad, Genetics Soc. of Japan. Author: Sexual Reproduction in the Mucorineae, 1904; New England Trees in Winter (with C.D. Jarvis), 1911, and Trees in Winter (with C.D. Jarvis), 1913. Contbr. to scientific jours. Home: 32 Paradise Rd., Northampton, Mass. Office: Smith College Genetics Experiment Station, Northampton, Mass. Died Nov. 16, 1954.

BLAKESLEE, RAYMOND IVES, patent law; b. Bridgeport, Conn., Sept. 17, 1875; s. Cornelius and Mary (Sanford) B.; grad. high sch., Brooklyn, N.Y., 1893; acad. equivalent certificate, U. of State of N.Y., 1897; studied in law offices, N.Y. City, and N.Y. Law Sch., 1897-1903; m. Helene M. Beers, Dec. 22, 1906; children—Loren Ray, Anita Dawn. Admitted to N.Y. bar, 1907; patent solicitor, 1899-1907; in practice, specializing in patent law, at Los Angeles, Calif., 1907—. Was of counsel in famous Wright Bros. vs. Glenn Curtiss flying machine patent case, Carson smelting patent litigation and others of note. Republican. Home: Pasadena, Calif. Died Jan. 8, 1941.

BLALOCK, ALFRED, surgeon; b. Culloden, Ga., Apr. 5, 1899; s. George Zadock and Martha (Davis) B.; A.B., U. of Ga., 1918; M.D., Johns Hopkins, 1922; M.D. honoris causa, U. Turin, 1951; Sc.M., Yale, 1946; Sc.D. (hon.), Univ. Rochester, and U. Chgo., 1951, Lehigh U., 1953, Emory U., 1954, Georgetown U., 1959; LL.D., Hampden-Sydney Coll., 1954; m. Mary Chambers O'Bryan, Oct. 27, 1930 (deceased); children—William Rice, Mary Elizabeth, Alfred Dandy; m. 2d, Alice Seney Waters, Nov. 12, 1959. Intern Johns Hopkins Hosp., 1922-23, asst. res. surgeon, 1923-25; resident surg. Vanderbilt Univ. Hosp., 1925-26; instr. surgery Vanderbilt Med. Sch., 1925-27, assistant professor, 1928-30, asso. prof., 1930-38, prof. 1938-41; prof. of surgery and dir. dept. of surgery Johns Hopkins U. 1941-64; surgeon-in-chief Johns Hopkins Hosp. 1941-64; visiting prof. surgery U. Rochester, March 1959, also various other colls. and univs., 1961—. Delivered Agnew lecture, 1959. Mem. med. fellowship board National Research Council, 1939-51. Mem. com. John J. Carty Fund, Nat. Acad. Scis. Served with U.S. Army, 1918. Decorated Chevalier Legion of Honor (France); recipient Research medal Southern Medical Assn., 1940, Gordon Wilson medal, 1941, Charles Mickle Fellowship, 1947; Passano Award, 1948; Rene Leriche award, 1949, Matas award, 1950, Distinguished Service award, A.M.A., 1953, Internat. Feltrinelli prize for medicine, 1954, Lasker award, 1954, Roswell Park medal, 1955, Holland Soc. Potomac Branch award, Gairdner award, 1959; Modern Medicine award for distinguished achievement, 1960. Diplomate Am. Bd. Surg. (founder). Fellow A.C.S. (pres. 1954-55); mem. Nat. Acad. Sci., Nat. Soc. Med. Research (v.p.0, Am. (pres. 19-5-56), So. (pres. 1949) surg. assns., Am. Assn. Thoracic Surgery (pres. 1950). Internat. Soc. Surgery, American Philosophical Society, also member of A.M.A., Soc. Clin. Surgery (pres. 1950-52). Soc. Vascular Surgery (pres. 1951-52), Academie des Sciences, Institut de Fance, Royal College Surgeons of Eng. and Edinburgh, Phi Beta Kappa, Alpha Omega Alpha, Sigma Chi, Nu Sigma Nu, Am. Coll. Cardiology (hon.), also various fgn. societies. Methodist. Clubs: Gibson Island (Md.); Elkridge. Asso. editor, Surgery, 1936—; mem. editorial bd. Archives of Surgery, 1939—; mem. adv. editorial bd. Jour. of Thoracic Surgery, 1946—. Contbr. profl. jours. Home: 117 Churchwardens Rd., Balt. 12, Office: Johns Hopkins Hosp., Balt. Died Sept. 15, 1964; buried Balt.

BLANCHARD, ARTHUR HORACE, cons. engr.; b. Providence, R.I., Feb. 10, 1877; s. Horace Kennedy and Caroline Potter (Hill) B.; Providence High Sch.; C.E., Brown U., 1899; A.M., Columbia, 1902; m. Mary Temple Burt, of Providence, June 17, 1902; 1 son, Gerald Geoffrey. With highway dept., Providence, Am. Bridge Co., and in gen. consulting work, 1896-1903; dep. engr. State Bd. Pub. Rds. R.I., 1903-10; instr., asst. prof. and asso. prof. civ. engring., Brown U., 1899-1911; prof. highway engring., Columbia U., 1911-17, prof. highway engring. and highway transport, U. of Mich., Aug. 1919-27. Cons. highway engr., Oct. 1910—; mem. Advisory Commn. on State Highways, N.Y., 1912; consulting highway engr., Board Water Supply, to commr. public works of Borough of Manhattan, Mich., N.Y., and Pa. State Highway depts., Dominion of Can. and Nat. Highways Assn.; mem. Advisory Bd. on Highways, N.Y. State Dept. of Efficiency and Economy; chief Bur. of Pub. Works, Army Overseas Ednl. Commn., Feb.-June 1919. Consulting transport engineer and highway traffic control consultant, 1926—. United States reporter to Internat. Road Congresses, 2d at Brussels, 1910, 3d at London, 1913, 4th at Seville, 1923, 5th at Milan, 1926; U.S. rep. Internat. Com. on Standard Tests for Highway Materials, 1914. Episcopalian. Fellow A.A.A.S. (sec. sect. engring., 1913); mem. Am. Soc. C.E., Society Automotive Engineers, Institute of Transport of Great Britain, Societe des Ingenieurs Civils de France, Engring. Inst. of Can., Inst. of Traffic Engrs., Internat. Assn. for Testing Materials, Internat. Assn. Road Congresses, Am. Soc. Municipal Engineers, Nat. Highways Assn.; pres. Am. Road Builders' Assn., Nat. Highway Traffic Assn., Internat. Traffic and Transport Assn., Internat. Inst. of Transport; ex-dir. Nat. Pedestrians' Assn.; mem. highway research bd. Nat. Research Counsel; mem. Delta Tau Delta, Sigma Xi, Phi Kappa Phi, etc. Clubs: Michigan Union, University (Providence); Union Interalliee of Paris. Co-Author (with H. B. Drowne): Highway, 1910-12; Highway Engineering, 1913. Asso. editor on highways, American Civil Engineers Pocket-Book, 1913; Elements of Highway Engineering, 1915. Editor-in-Chief, American Highway Engineers' Handbook, 1919; Internat. Highway Transport Handbook; Internat. Highway Traffic Control Handbook; Internat. Highway Engineers' Handbook. Contbr. on engring. topics. Address: Box C, Edgewood Station, Providence RI

BLANCHARD, MURRAY, engineer; b. Peru, Ill., July 25, 1874; s. Murray and Helen A. (Dolliver) B.; B.S. in C.E., Univ. of Mich., 1898, C.E., 1903; m. Alice H. Fish, Feb. 6, 1902; 1 dau., Helen (dec.). Has operated extensively in the U.S. and Can. as engr. water power development, also as hydraulic engr.; with engring. dept. Pa. R.R. as asst. engr. on tunnel in N.Y. City, 1905-09; hydraulic engr. State of Ill., Div. of Waterways, 1920-30; prin. engr. U.S. Engring. Dept., 1930-31; cons. engr., Chicago, 1930-33; engr. U.S. Pub. Works Adminstrn., 1933-37; engr. U.S. Engring. Dept. since Feb. 1, 1938. Served in World War as major engrs. U.S. Army, 1917-19. Mem. Am. Soc. C.E. (life), Western Soc. Engrs., Soc., Am. Mil. Engrs., Am. Legion. Republican. Conglist. Clubs: Univ. of Mich., Chicago Engineers'. Home: 132 Peck St. Office: U.S. Engineer Office, Sault Ste Marie MI

BLANCHARD, THOMAS, inventor; b. Sutton, Mass., June 24, 1788; s. Samuel and Susanna (Tenney) B. Invented machine that could produce 500 tacks per minute, 1806; devised a lathe which performed 2 different operations (turned rifle barrels externally and when breech was reached, cut both flat and oval portions); with Springfield (Mass.) Arsenal, 5 years; patented machine which could produce various irregular forms from a single pattern, 1820; invented steam-wagon, 1825; unsuccessfully promoted co. to build railroads, 1826; patented steamboat which was able to ascend rivers against strong currents and rapids, 1831; developed heavy timber-bending process, 1851. Died Boston, Apr. 16, 1864.

BLANCHARD, WILLIAM MARTIN, prof. chemistry; b. Perguimans County, N.C., Aug. 25, 1874; s. William Stewart and Artemecia (Towe) B.; A.B., Randolph-Macon Coll., Ashland, Va., 1894, A.M., 1897; Ph.D., Ia., 1937; traveled and studied in Europe, 1912-13; m. Hattie Godwin, Sept. 10, 1901; 1 son, Wm. Godwin; m. 2d, Vera Worth, Aug. 9, 1933. Fellow in chemistry, Johns Hopkins U., 1899-1900; instr. chemistry Rose Poly. Inst., Terre Haute, Ind., 1900-01; prof. chemistry, De Pauw U., 1901-39, dean College of Liberal Arts, 1927-41; retired 1941; prof. chemistry, U. of Southern Calif., Los Angeles, summer 1936. Sec.-treas. Ind. Intercollegiate Conf., 1926-39. Fellow A.A.A.S., Chem. Soc. (London), Ind. Acad. Science; mem. Am. Chem. Soc., Deutsche Chemische Gesellschaft, Phi Beta Kappa. Del. Gen. Conf. M.E. Ch., 1920, 24, 32. Author: Laboratory Exercises in General Chemistry, 1909, 2d edit., 1918; An Introduction to General Chemistry, 1928; Laboratory Manual in General Chemistry, 1928. Contbr. to scientific periodicals. Home: Greencastle, Ind. Died Dec. 21, 1942.

BLANKENHORN, MARION ARTHUR, physician; b. Orrville, O., Nov. 13, 1885; s. Henry and Emma C. (Amstutz) B.; Ph.B., Wooster Coll., 1909; M.D., Western Reserve U., 1914, M.A. in medicine, Grad. Sch., 1920; hon. D.Sc., Wooster Coll., 1939; m. Martha Finley Taggart; children—Martha, Mary Margaret, David Henry. Prof. biology, Buena Vista (Ia.) Coll., 1909-10; resident physician in Lakeside Hosp., Cleveland, Ohio, 1914-17; instr. in medicine, 1919; voluntary asst. Rockefeller Inst. for Med. Research, 1925-26; professor medicine, Western Reserve U., 1929-35; prof. medicine U. Cin., 1935-56, prof. emeritus, 1956—; responsible investigator aviation medicine NRC; dir. edn. dept. internal medicine Jewish Hosp., Cin., 1957—. Served as capt. M.C., 1917-19; med. cons. 5th Corps Area; med. cons. Surgeon Gen., 1948, Far East Command, 1951, ETO. Fellow A.C.P. (regent v.p.; dir. survey of hsop. standards in internal medicine 1956-57); mem. A.M.A., Assn. Am. Physicans, Am. Soc. Clin. Investigation, Central Soc. Clin. Research, Am. Soc. Exptl. Pathology, Alpha Tau Omega, Nu Sigma Nu, Phi Beta Kappa, Alpha Omega Alpha, Sigma Xi. Home: 6 Rural Lane. Office: Jewish Hosp., Cin. Died Sept. 3, 1957; buried Wooster, O.

BLANKS, ROBERT FRANKLIN, civil engr.; b. Maplehill, Kan., Sept. 4, 1900; s. Thomas Franklin and Vida Florence (Fairbanks) B.; B.S. in Civil Engring., Kan. State Coll., Manhattan, Kan., 1924, C.E., 1936; D.Sc., Kansas State College, May 1949; married Laura Viola Denman, May 26, 1922; 1 son, Robert Franklin. Municipal engr., Burley, Ida., Jan.-May, 1921; field engring. on location and constrn. Carey (Ida.) Irrigation Project, May-Sept., 1921; sci. and math. instr., Burley (Ida.) High Sch., 1921-22; asst. supt. Burley (Ida.) public schs., 1922-23; inst. in physics, chemistry and math., also athletic coach, Hollister (Ida.) High Sch., 1924-25; asst. supt. and engr. irrigation project, Salmon River Canal Co., Hollister, Ida., 1925-27; instr. in physics, chemistry and math. Hollister High Sch., 1927-28; made hydraulic investigations Am. Falls Reservior and Basin Water Dist. No. 36, State of Ida., Idaho Falls, May-Oct. 1928; with Office Engring., Fort Hall Irrigation project, U.S. Indian Irrigation Service, Blackfoot, Ida., 1928-29; office and field engring., Columbia Basin Investigations, Washington U.S. Engr. Office, Seattle, Wash., 1929-30; chief, research and geology division U.S. Bur. of Reclamation, Denver, 1930-51. Vice pres., gen. mgr. Great Western Aggregates, Inc.; research cons. Ideal Cement Company. Chairman Reinforced Concrete Research Council Engineering Foundation Winner Thomas Fitch Rowland prize for paper Deterioration of Concrete Dams Due to Alkali-Aggregate Reaction. Mem. Am. Soc. C.E. (chmn., 1945, 46, 47; dir. at large, 1944-45; dir. 6th dist., 1941-42; adv. com., 1945; v.p., 1945, 46, 47, pres. 1948), Highway Research Board, Colorado Society Engrs. (dir. 1951-53, pres. 1955), Sigma Tau, Sigma Xi. Contbr. engring. publs. Patentee materials testing equipment for controlling rate of load application in testing materials. Home: 1062 S. Clayton Way, Denver 9. Office: Boston Bldg., Denver 2. Died July 14, 1958.

BLATCHLEY, WILLIS STANLEY, naturalist; b. N. Madison, Conn., Oct. 6, 1859; s. Hiram S. and Sarah J. B.; A.B., Indiana Univ., 1887, A.M., 1891, LL.D., 1921; m. Clara A. Fordice, May 2, 1882; children—Raymond S., Ralph F. Assistant Arkansas Geological Survey, 1889-90; mem. Scoville's scientific expdn. to Old Mexico, 1891; asst. on U.S. Fish Commission, 1893; was state geolgoist of Ind., 1894-1911. Author: Gleanings from physics, 1894-95, asst., 1895-98, asso., 1898-1901, collegiate prof. physics, 1901-28, Johns Hopkins, now emeritus. Fellow Am. Phys. Sco. Episcopalian. Author: Manual of Experiments in Physics (with J. S. Ames), 1897, Home: Baltimore, Md. Died Dec. 27, 1940.

BLATTEIS, SIMON RISEFELD, physician; b. Silesia, Austria, Mar. 27, 1876; s. Max and Sarah (Risefeld) B.; brought to U.S., 1882, naturalized 1897; student Coll. of Physicians and Surgeons, Columbia U., 1893-94; M.D., Bellevue Hosp. Med. Coll., 1898; m. Minnie Levison, Nov. 4, 1900 (dec. 1957); children—Victor Louis, Eleanor Miriam (Mrs. Edward A. Werner). Began practice in 1898; med. insp., New York Dept. of Health, and acting chief Div. of Epidemiology. 1915-17; pathologist in chief, Brooklyn Jewish Hosp., 1906-18, visiting physician, 1920-35; clinical prof. medicine, 1924-32, L.I. Coll.; prof. clinical med., 1932-41; emeritus prof. clinical med. 1941, L.I. Coll. of Medicine; physician-in-chief, Jewish Hosp., 1935-41, also consulting physician and cons. pathologist; cons. physician Adelphi Hosp., 1930; cons. physician Beth-El Hosp.; lecturer in medicine, clinical prof. med., N.Y. Univ. Med. Coll., 1900-40. Diplomate American Bd. of Internal Medicine. Fellow Am. Coll. of

Physicians; mem. Am. Medical Soc., N.Y. Academy of Medicine, Harvey Society, Phi Delta Epsilon. Mason. Home: Miami Beach FL Died June 11, 1968.

BLECKWENN, WILLIAM JEFFERSON, neuropsychiatrist; b. Astoria, L.I., N.Y., July 23, 1895; s. Alfred Paul and Julia A. (Lorenz) B.; student N.Y. U., 1913-15; B.S., U. Wis., 1917; M.D., Columbia, 1920; m. Marion J. Dougan, Jan. 28, 1919; children—Marion J. (Mrs. Birkenmeier), William Jefferson (dec.), Alfred T. Intern Bellevue Hosp., N.Y.C., 1920-22; grad. tng. Wis. Psychiat. Inst., 1922-24, asst. dir., 1926; instr. neuropsychiatry U. Wis., 1922-26, asst. prof., 1926-30, asso. prof., 1930-35, prof., 1935—, chmn. dept., 1948—; practice medicine, 1920—, specializing neuropsychiatry, 1922—; cons. neuropsychiatry Surg. Gen. U.S. Army, 1944—; chmn. med. adv. bd. Dept. Vets. Affairs, 1952. Chmn. boxing rules com. Nat. Collegiate Athletic Assn., 1948—. Served with U.S. Army, World War I, Col. M.C., World War II. Decorated Legion Merit with oak leaf cluster, Presdl. Citation. Mem. A.M.A., Am. Psychiatry Assn., Central, Milw. neuropsychiat. assns., Wis. Mental Health Soc., Sigma Xi, Sigma Sigma, Phi Gamma Delta, Phi Rho Sigma. Presbyn. Clubs: Madison, University. Contbr. articles on neurosyphilis, narcoanalysis, picrotoxin, epilepsy, shock therapy. Discoverer sodium amytal (truth serum). Home: 3441 Crestwood Dr., Madison 5, Wis. Died Jan. 4, 1965; buried Forrest Hills Cemetery, Madison.

BLEGEN, CARL WILLIAM, archeologist; b. Minneapolis, Minn., Jan. 27, 1887; s. John H. and Anna B. (Olsen) B.; B.A., Augsburg Sem., Minneapolis, 1904, U. of Minn., 1907; B.A., Yale, 1908, Ph.D., 1920, hon. M.A., 1927; student Am. Sch. of Classical Studies, Athens, Greece, 1910-13; honorary doctorate, University of Oslo (Norway), 1951, Thessalonike (Greece), 1951, U. Athens, 1963; D. Litt., Oxford, 1957; LL.D., U. Cin., 1958; L.H.D., Hebrew Union College, Jewish Inst. Religion, 1963; Litt.D., Cambridge U., 1963; m. Elizabeth Denny Pierce, July 11, 1924 (dec. 1966). Sec. Am. Sch. Classical Studies, 1913-20, asst. dir., 1920-26, actg. dir., 1926-27; professor classical archeology Grad. Sch. Arts and Sciences, University of Cincinnati 1927-57, prof. emeritus, 1957-71, Distinguished Service prof. emeritus, 1969-71, became fellow, 1927; head department of classics, 1950-57; field dir. University of Cincinnati Archaeol. Expdn., Turkey and Greece; on leave of absence, with Office of Strategic Services, Washington, 1942-45; cultural relations attache, American Embassy, Athens, Greece, 1945-46; dir. Am. Sch. Classical Studies, Athens, 1948-49. With the Am. Red Cross in Greece, 1918-19. Recipient gold medal Archaeological Inst. Am., 1965, gold medal Soc. Antiquaries of London, 1966, Gold medal from University of Cincinnati, 1969. Corresponding fellow of British Academy. Fellow American Academy of Arts and Sciences; mem. Am. Philos. Soc., Am. Philol. Assn., Archeol. Inst. Am., Am. Assn. Univ. Profs., German Archeol. Inst., Archaeol. Soc. Athens (hon. v.p.), Soc. Promotion of Hellenic Studies, London, England (honorary), Royal Soc. Letters of Lund (Sweden), Swedish Royal Acad. Letters, History and Antiquities, Norwegian Academy of Science and Letters, also Phi Beta Kappa (honorary), Sigma Xi. Lutheran. Clubs: Literary, University (Cinn.); Yale (New York); Cosmos (Washington). Author: Korakou, AA Prehistoric Settlement near Corinth, 1921; Zygouries, A Prehistoric Settlement in the Valley of Cleonae, 1928; Acrocorinth (with R. Stillwell, O. Broneer and A. Bellinger), 1930; Prosymna, the Helladic Settlement Preceding the Argive Heraeum (with Elizabeth Blegen), 1937; Troy, Vol. I (with J.L. Caskey, M. Rawson, J. Sperling), 1950, Troy, Vol. II (with J.L. Caskey and M. Rawson), 1951, Vol. III, 1953, Vol. IV (with C. Boulter, J. L. Caskey, M. Rawson), 1958; Troy and the Trojans, 1963; (with M. Rawson) The Palace of Nestor at Pylos, Vol. I, 1966, Vol. III, 1973. Contbr. archaeal. publs. Home: Athens Greece Died Aug. 24, 1971; buried Athens Greece

BLESSING, GEORGE FREDERICK, mech. engr.; b. Carrollton, Ky., July 2, 1875; s. John Jacob and Anna Elizabeth (Leesé) B.; B.M.E., State U. of Ky., 1897, M.E., 1905; Ph.D., Hanover Coll., Ind., 1906; studied and Taught at Cornell U., 1906-08; m. Martha Ripperdan White, Dec. 26, 1908. Draftsman various cos. to 1899; asso. prof., mech. engring., 1899-1900, prof., 1900-05, Nev. State U.; asst. engr. of tests, S.P. Co., Sacramento, Calif., summer, 1902; in charge design and research work, Eureka Oil Burning Co., San Francisco summer, 1903; designer Pacific Foundry, San Francisco, summer, 1903; designer Pacific Foundry, San Francisco, summer, 1904; design and research work in turbine pumps, Platt Iron Works, Dayton, O., 1905-06; designer in steam turbine dept., Gen. Electric Co., Lynn, Mass., 1906; asst. prof. machine design, Sibley Coll. Engring., Cornell U., 1906-08; lecturer Cornell U. Summer Sch., 1907-08; prof. mech. engring. and in charge engring. dept., Swarthmore coll., 1908—. Plant facilities engr., U.S. Ordnance Dept., Phila. Dist., 1918. Author: Elements of Drawing, 1912; Elements of Descriptive Geometry, 1913; The Small College and Technical Education, 1917. Home: Swarthmore, Pa. Died June 25, 1921.

BLEYER, J(ULIUS) MOUNT, physician; b. at Pilsen, Austria, Mar. 16, 1859; s. Samuel and Sophia B.; came to America with parents, 1868; student U. of Prague, 2 yrs.; M.D., Bellevue Hosp. Med. Coll. (New York U.), 1883; (LL.D., Central U. of Ind., 1896); m. Rose Floersheim, of New York, 1884. Has practiced in New York since 1883; specializes in diseases of nose, throat and lungs; consulting specialist on the throat, Met. Opera House, since 1888. Orginator of electrocution in the State of N.Y., 1884. V.p. Am. Congress on Tuberculosis, 1901-04; fellow Royal Acad. Medicine and Surgery, Naples, Italy, 1894; mem. A.M.A., Medico-Legal Soc. of N.Y. (v.p. since 1903), Anthropol. Soc. of Italy; corr. mem. Nat. Acad. Medicine (Mexico), Laryngol. Soc. and Elec. Soc. (Paris); mem. Am. Acad. Polit. and Social Science, A.A.A.S. Address: 725 Riverside Drive, New York.

BLISS, A(ANDREW) RICHARD, JR., pharmacologist; b. New York, N.Y., Nov. 10, 1889; s. Andrew Richard and Frances Revue (Sutton) B.; Ph.Ch., Columbia, 1908, Ph.D., 1909; B.S., Howard College, Ala., 1910, A.M., 1912, LL.D., 1932; M.D., U. of Ala., 1913; m. Loretta Ann Deering, Aug. 20, 1918. Adjunct prof. chemistry and pharmacology, Sch. of Medicine, U. of Ala., later dean of college of pharmacy and prof. biochemistry and pharmacology, 1910-15; prof. pharmacology, Emory U. Med. Sch., Atlanta, Ga., 1915-23; chief of division of physiology and pharmacology, U. of Tenn. Coll. of Medicine, 1923-33, and dean of Sch. of Pharmacy, 1925-33; director Reelfoot Lake Biological Station, 1931-36; head of dept. of pharmacology, and dean of pharmacy of Howard College, 1934—. Served Served as lt. M.C. und Adj. Gen. U.S. Army, World War; then passed asst. surgeon, U.S. Pub. Health Service Res. Awarded Conspicuous Service Medal Clumbia U., 1932. Mem. Com. of Revision of U.S. Pharmacopoeia, 1930-40; dir. pharmacol. and physiol. studies for Edn. Research Com. of Commonwealth Fund of Pa., 1923-26; dir. health programs, Station WSGN, Birmingham. Fellow Am. Inst. Chemists, A.A.A.S., Am. Acad. Polit. and Social Science, Am. Geolg. Soc. Episcopalian (mem. Bishop and Council, Diocese of Tenn.). Mason. Author: Essentials of Physiology (with G. Bachmann), 1939; Physics and Chemistry for Nurses (with A. H. Olive), 1926; Qualitative Analysis (with H. H. Schaefer), 1929; Properties and Uses of Drugs (with H. H. Rusby and C. W. Ballard), 1930; Experimental Pharmacodynamics, 1939. Mem. board editors Chemical Formulary; contbg. editor The Chemist; mem. editorial bd. Am. Professional Pharmacist; contbr. over 200 to scientific educational lit. Home: Birmingham, Ala. Died Aug. 12, 1941.

BLISS, COLLINS PECHIN, educator; b. Carlisle, Pa., Apr. 28, 1866; s. John Collins and Mary Newton (Pechin) B.; B.A., Princeton, 1888, M.A., 1891; Ph.B. in Arch., Columbia, 1891; spl. work, Cornell U., 1896; hon. Dr. Engring., Stevvens Ins. of Tech., 1936; m. Jessamine Coon, of Cleveland, Ohio, 1898. With Works (shipbuilding), Cleveland, O., 1893-96; instr. and asst. prof. mech. engring., 1896-1902, rpof., 1902-30, dean of Coll. of Engring., 1930-36, dean emeritus since 1936, New York U.; pres. Engring. Indes, Inc., cons. engr. in constrn., 1902-12. Trustee Robert Coll., Istambul. Mem. Am. Soc. M.E. (com. on standardization), Soc. Promotion Engring. Edn., Princeton Engring. Soc., Iota Alpha, Tau Beta Pi, Sigma Xi. Republican. Presbyterian. Clubs: Princeton, Faculty. Home: Eton Hall, Scarsdale, N.Y. Died Dec. 27, 1946.

BLISS, GILBERT AMES, mathematician; b. Chicago, May 9, 1876; s. George Harrison and Mary Maria (Gilbert) B.; B.S., Univ. of Chicago, 1897, M.S., 1898, fellow, 1899-1900, Ph.D., 1900; hon. Sc.D., Univ. of Wis., 1935; student Univ. of Gottingen, 1902-03; m. Helen Hurd, June 15, 1912 (died Dec. 22, 1918); children—Elizabeth, Ames; m. 2d, Olive Hunter, Oct. 12, 1920. Instr. mathematics, Univ. of Minn., 1900-02; associate in mathematics, Univ. of Chicago, 1903-04; asst. prof. mathematics, Univ. of Mo., 1904-05, Princeton, 1905-08; asso. prof. mathematics, 1908-13, prof., 1913-41, chmn. dept. of mathematics since 1927, Martin A. Ryerson distinguished service prof. of mathematics, 1933-41, prof. emeritus 1941, U. of Chicago. Asso. editor Annals of Mathematics, 1906-08. Trans. Am. Math. Soc., 1908-16. Mem. Am. Math. Soc. (pres. 1921-22), Nat. Acad. Sciences, Am. Philos. Soc., Am. Acad. of Arts and Sciences, Sigma Xi, Phi Beta Kappa, Delta Kappa Epsilon. Clubs: Quadrangle, University, Flossmoor Country. Home: Flossmoor, Ill. Died May 8, 1951.

BLISS, WILLIAM JULIAN ALBERT, physicist; b. Washington, Jan. 22, 1867; s. Alexander and Ellen Taylor (Albert) B.; A.B., Harvard, 1888; certificate in elec. engring., John Hopkins, 1890, Ph.D., 1894; m. Edith Grantham West, Nov. 19, 1896; children—Eleanor Albert, Frances McDowell. Asst. in elec. engring., 1890-91, lecturer in Protection, 1930 (chmn. com. on growth and development); chmn. gen. advisory com. on maternal and child welfare under Social Security Act, 1935-37; consultant Children's Bureau, 1935—; mem. Commn. on Grad. Medical Education, 1937—. General sec. 5th Internat. Congress on Pediatrics; del. Internat. Commn. on Nutrition, sponsored by Health sect. League of Nations, Berlin, 1932. Mem. bd. dirs. Infants' Hosp., Boston. Republican. Presbyn. Editor: Report of White House Conference on Child Health and Protection, 1932. Home: Brookline, Mass. Died Nov. 29, 1941.

BLODGET, LORIN, statistician-physicist; b. nr. Jamestown, Chautanqua Co., N.Y., May 25, 1823; ed. Jamestown Acad. and Geneva (now Hobart Coll.); asst. Smithsonian Instn., in charge of researches on climatology, 1851-52; on Pacific R.R. survey, 1852-56, for War Dept.; with Treas. Dept., 1863-77. Author: The Climatology of the United States; Commercial and Financial Resources of the United States, and about 150 volumes of financial and industrial reports and statistics. Died 1901.

BLODGETT, HUGH CARLTON, psychologist, educator; b. Zamora, Cal., Nov. 21, 1896; s. Carlton Salmon and Esther Cornelia (Heard) B.; A.B., U. Cal. at Berkley, 1921, Ph.D., 1925; m. Georgia Colombat, Sept. 20, 1926 (dec. July 1932); children—Joan, Carlton Colombat; m. 2d, Yvonne Bledsoe, Sept. 9, 1933; 1 dau., Carol Yvonne. Teaching fellow U. Cal. at Berkeley, 1922-23, research asst., 1923-25; research asst. Stanford, 1925; teaching asst. Harvard, 1926-27; instr. Lehigh U., 1927-28; faculty U. Tex., Austin, 1928, prof. psychology, 1944-69, prof. emeritus, 1969-72, chmn. dept., 1948-50, 60-62, research scientist def. research lab., 1951-64, radiobiol. research lab., 1957-64; vis. scientist Bekhterev Inst. of Brain, Leningrad, USSR, 1932; vis. prof. U. Cal. at Los Angeles, 1950; participant Mercury space project S.A.M., NASA, 1959-60. Served to ensign U.S. Navy, 1917-19. Fellow Am. Psychol. Assn. (council reps. 1949-51); mem. Tex. (pres. 1954), S.W. psychol. assns., Psychonomic Soc., A.A.A.S., Sigma Xi. Contbr. to profl. jours. Home: Austin TX Died Oct. 15, 1972.

BLOMQUIST, HUGO LEANDER, educator; botany; b. Sorsele, Sweden, June 5, 1888; s. Nils Edward and Eva (Dahlberg) B.; B.S., U. Chgo., 1916, Ph.D., 1921; m. Margaret Lane Mordecia, Dec. 26, 1928; 1 dau., Betty. Came to U.S., 1892, naturalized, 1900. Engaged in farming Kulm, N.D., until 1909; prin. high sch., Deering, N.D., 1912-14; asst. prof. biology, Trinity Coll. (now Duke U.), 1920-23, prof. botany, 1923-57, emeritus, 1957—, chmn. dept., 1935-53. Served as musician, 1st class, U.S. Army, 1917-19. Recipient Meritorious Teaching award Assn. Southeastern Biologists, 1956. Fellow A.A.A.S.; member Bot. Soc. Am., Bryological Soc., N.C. Acad. Sci., Sigma Xi, Phi Sigma. Author: Ferns of North Carolina, 1934; Grasses of North Carolina, 1948; (with Wilhelmina Greene) Flowers of the South, 1953. Home: 922 Demerius St., Durham, N.C. 27701. Died Nov. 28, 1964; buried Oakwood Cemetery, Raleigh, N.C.

BLOOD, WILLIAM HENRY, JR., elec. engr.; b. Charlestown, Mass., Mar. 29, 1866; s. of William Henry and Marianna (Williamson) B.; E.E., Mass. Inst. Tech., 1888; m. Grace Marie Nathan, Nov. 6, 1890. With Thomson-Houston Elec. Co., Lynn, Mass., in charge of mfg. elec. motors, etc., 1888-89; with the N. W. Thomson-Houston Co., St. Paul, Minn., 1889-90; partner Franklin Elec. Co., Kansas City, Mo., constructing elec. light and st. ry. plants and waterworks, 1890-96; superintendent Chase-Shawmut Company, mfg. electricians, Boston, 1896-97; vice-pres. Stone & Webster Engineering Corp., Boston, examination and report, construction, expert court work, 1897—. Asst. to pres. Am. Internat. Shipbuilding Corp., Phila., 1917-18. Lecturer on pub. utilities, Harvard U. Grad. Sch. of Business Admin. Republican. Conglist. Fellow Am. Inst. E.E. Home: Wellesley, Mass. Died Feb. 13, 1933.

BLOODGOOD, JOSEPH COLT, surgeon, cancer research; b. Milwaukee, Wis., Nov. 1, 1867; s. Francis and Josephine (Colt) B.; B.S., U. of Wis., 1888; M.D., U. of Pa., 1891; m. Edith d. Henry Holt, Sept. 1, 1908. Resident phys. Children's Hosp., Phila., 1891-92; asst. resident surgeon, Johns Hopkins Hosp., Baltimore, June-Nov., 1892; attended foreign clincis and hospitals, 1892-93; resident surgeon Johns Hopkins Hospital, 1893-97; associate in surgery, Johns Hopkins U. and Hosptial, 1897-1903; then adjunct prof. surgery, Johns Hopkins University; surgeon, St. Agnes' Hosp. Major Medical R.C., 1917. Mem. gen. med. com. Am. Nat. Red Cross; mem. editorial bd., in charge surgical pathology, Am. Jour. of Cancer; mem. adivsory bd. Radiol. Research Inst. Fellow Am. College Surgeons, A.A.A.S. Episcopalian. Died Oct. 22, 1935.

BLOOR, WALTER RAY, educator; b. Ingersoll, Ont., Can., July 2, 1877; s. George and Elizabeth B.; A.M., Queen's U., Kingston, 1902; grad. Ont. Normal Coll., 1903; A.M., Harvard, 1908, Ph.D., 1911; LL.D., Queen's, 1945; m. Cleo Holt, July 27, 1904; children—John Holt (dec.) and Norma (twins), Robert John. Instr., asst. prof. chemistry Wash. State Coll., 1903-07; asst. in biochemistry, Harvard Med. Sch., 1908-10; asso. in biochemistry, Washington U. Sch. of Medicine, St. Louis, 1910-14; asst. prof. biochemistry, Harvard, 1914-18; prof. biochemistry, U. of Cal., 1918-22; prof. same, Rochester U. Med. Sch. since 1922, emeritus, 1947. Mem. Am. Chem. Soc., Am. Physiol. Soc., Am. Soc. Biol. Chemists (pres. 1929-31), Soc. Exptl. Biology and Medicine, Sigma Xi. Baptist. Contbr. Jour. Biol. Chemistry. Home: 881 Ballantyne Rd., Scottsville, N.Y. Died Feb. 1966.

BLOSSOM, FRANCIS, engr.; b. N.Y. City, Oct. 17, 1870; s. Josiah B. and Grace Parish (Ludlam) B.; ed. Poly. Inst., New York, 1880-87; C.E., Sch. of Mines (Columbia), 1891; m. Madeline Buck, Feb. 27, 1900; children—Dudley Buck, June (Mrs. H. P. Moon). Design and construction industrial railway equipment, and assistant engineer gas plant construction, 1891-93; engineer and department mgr. Westinghouse, Church, Kerr & Co., 1892-99; mem. Sanderson & Porter, engrs., offices in New York, Chicago and San Francisco, since 1899. Chmn. bd. apptd. by sec. of war to review and report on constrn. work War Dept., 1918; mem. Constrn. Adv. Com. apptd. by sec. of war, 1940, to recommend firms qualified for handling Army constrn. projects World War II. Alumni trustee Columbia Univ., 1935-41; trustee N.Y. Med. Coll., Flower and Fifth Av. hospitals, N.Y. City. Mem. Am. Soc. C.E., Am. Inst. E.E., (honorary) Am. Soc. M.E., Alpha Delta Phi. Clubs: University, Columbia Univ., City Midday, Alpha Delta Phi, (New York). Home: 784 Park Av., N.Y. City 21. Office: 52 William Street, New York City 5

BLOSSOM, HAROLD HILL, landscape architect; b. Brooklyn, N.Y., Oct. 6, 1879; s. Frederick Augustus and Sarah Carson (Hill) B.; prep. edn., Poly. Inst., Brooklyn, and Pratt Inst. High Sch.; B.S. Amherst, Brooklyn, and Pratt Inst. High Sch.; B.S. Amherst, 1902; M.A., Harvard, 1906, Master in Landscape Architecture, 1907; m. Minnie Motley Dawson, Sept. 23, 1908 (died Oct. 19, 1922); children—Elizabeth Thornton, Thomas, Eleanor, Margaret Blackwell; m. 2d, Louise Barnes Thompson, Feb. 16, 1926; 1 dau., Deborah. With Olmstead Bros., landscape architects, Brooklyn, 1907-19, working on Atlantic Coast from Maine to Cuba, and from Seattle to San Diego, on Pacific Coast; practiced on own account in Boston, 1919—, specilizing in gardens and country estates, also real estate developments; mem. faculty Lowthorpe Sch. of Landscape Architecture, 1926-27; lecturer to Cambridge Sch. Domestic Architecture and Landscape Architecture; instr. landscape architecutre, Harvard, summer 1932. Landscape engr. Conn. Valley Park Commn., 1923; apptd. by gov. mem. Conn. Valley Regional Planning Bd., 1924. Awarded Medal of Honor in Landscape architecture by Architectural League of New York, 1923. Fellow Am. Soc. Landscape Architects, Boston Soc. Landscape Architects (pres. 1930-31), Archtl. League of N.Y. Republican. Unitarian. Home: West Roxbury, Mass. Died Dec. 3, 1935.

BLUM, WILLIAM, chemist; b. Phila., Pa., Dec. 28, 1881; s. Jacob and Catherine (Hoffman) B.; B.S., U. of Pa., 1903; Ph.D., 1908; m. Willetta Carr Baylis, Sept. 20, 1910; 1 son, William. Instr. in chemistry, U. of Utah, 1903-08, asst. prof., 1908-09; with U.S. Bureau of Standards, Washington, 1909-52, chemist 1918-52; cons. to numerous cos., Dept. Def., CIA. Member American Chemical Society, A.A.A.S., Washington Acad. Sciences, Electrochem Society (awarded Acheson medal, 1944); hon. mem. Am. Electroplaters' Society, Sigma Xi. Awarded medal Institute of Chemists, "for distinguished governmental service," 1926. Awarded Edward Goodrich Acheson gold medal and prize for achievement in electrochemistry, Oct. 1944. Chairman Citizens Committee, Section 4, Chevy Chase, Maryland, 1916-26. Presbyn. Clubs: Chemists (New York); Cosmos (Washington). Author: (with G. B. Hogaboom) Principles of Electroplating and Electroforming, 1924, 2d edit., 1930; also articles on analytical and electro chemistry. Home: Chevy Chase MD Died Dec. 7, 1972.

BLY, ELEANOR SCHOOLEY, bacteriologist; b. Montgomery, Pa., May 30, 1907; d. Joseph G. and Mabel (Fowler) Schooley; B.A., Bucknell U., 1928, M.S., 1937; Ph.D. in Bacteriology, Pa. State U., 1954; m. Earl W. Bly, Jan. 30, 1942 (dec. July, 1944). With Phila. Zool. Soc., Phila., 1928-29; mem. bacteriology dept. Bucknell U., Lewisburg, Pa., 1929-49; bacteriologist Williamsport (Pa.) Hosp., 1949-69. Mem. social services Watsontown (Pa.) Guild, 1930-54; active YWCA. Mem. Soc. Am. Bacteriologists, Am. Soc. Microbiology, D.A.R., Delta Delta Delta. Club: Soroptomist (Williamsport). Home: Williamsport PA Died July 4, 1969.

BOARDMAN, HAROLD SHERBURNE, educator; b. Bangor, Me., Mar. 31, 1874; s. James A. and Marilla M. (Leighton) B.; B.C.E., Me. State Coll., 1895; grad. student, Mass. Inst. Tech., 1896, Civil Engr., Univ. of Me., 1898, Dr. Engring., 1922; LL.D., Colby, 1927; Dr. Engring. R.I. Coll., 1928; LL.D., Bates Coll., 1929; m. Caroline A. Hilton, July 24, 1897 (died 1910); m. 2d, Nellie Frances Mann, July 2, 1912; children—James Alden, Rosemary (dec.). Tutor in drawing, U. of Me., 1896-99; draftsman Union Bridge Co., Pa., 1899-1900, Am. Bridge Co., Pa., 1900-01; instr. in civ. engring., 1901-03, asso. prof., 1903-04, prof. and head of dept., 1904-26, dean Coll. of Tech., 1910-26, acting pres., 1925-26, pres. 1926-34, U. of Me. (retired). While mem. of engring. faculty was actively engaged in many important hydrographic, structural, hydraulic and highway projects and active in professional and ednl. socs. Chmn. engring. sect. Assn. Land Grant Colleges, 1922-23. Served as chairman Me. Liquor Commn., 1937-41. Cadet maj. Coburn Cadets, Me. State Coll., 1894-95; Capt. Co. G, N.G.S.M., Edn. (vice pres. 1923-24; pres. 1930-31), Maine Assn. 1898-99. Mem. Am. Soc. C.E., Am. Soc. for Engring. Engineers, Beta Theta Pi, Tau Beta Pi, Phi Kappa Phi, Phi Beta Kappa, Scabbard and Blade. Republican. Mason (32 deg.). Home: 172 Main St., Orono ME

BOARTS, ROBERT MARSH, chem. engr.; b. Kittanning, Pa., Feb. 2, 1904; s. Robert Marsh and Annie (Fleming) B.; graduate Phillips Acad., Andover, Mass., 1922; B.S. in Ch.E., Lafayette Coll., 1922-26; M.S.E., U. Mich., 1932, Ph.D., 1937; m. Margaret Kapp, June 14, 1933. Sr. inspector of construction, Detroit Water Bd., 1927-29; chem. engr., chief draftsman Comstock & Westcott, Inc., Niagara Falls, 1929-31; successivley asst. prof., head dept. chem. engring., U. Tenn., since 1934; head Cooperative Chem. Engring. Research Lab., Tenn. Valley Authority, 1934-48; on leave as prin. physicist to Nuclear Reactor Sch., Atomic Energy Commn., Oak Ridge, Tenn., 1946-47; cons. Bur. Mines, 1939-41, Monsanto Chem. Co., 1947-48, Carbide & Carbon Chem. Corp. (name changed to Union Carbide Nuclear Company), 1948—. U.S. Air Force Arnold Engineering Development Center, 1951;

BOAS, FRAZ, anthropologist; b. Minden, Westphalia, July 9, 1858; s. M. and Sophie (Meyer) B.; univs. of Heidelberg, Bonn and Kiel, 1877-81; Ph.D., Univ. of Kiel, Germany, 1881, M.D., Honoris causa; LL.D., Sc.D., Oxford U., Clark U., Howard U. and Columbia Univ.; hon. citizen, honoris causa, Univ. of Bonn Graz; m. Marie A. E. Krackowizer, 1887; children—Mrs. Helene Marie Yampolski, Ernest P., Mrs. Marie Franziska Michelson. Explored Baffin Land, 1883-84; asst. Royal Ethnog. Museum, Berlin, and docent of geography, Univ. of Berlin, 1885-86; investigations in N.A., Mexico, Puerto Rico, 1886-193; docent anthropology, Clark U., 1888-92; chief asst. dept. of anthropology, Chicago Expn., 1892-95; lecturer physical anthropology, Columbia U., 1896-99, prof. anthropology, 1899-1937, prof. emeritus since 1937; asst. curator, 1896; curator, 1901-05, dept. anthropology Am. Mus. Natural History; hon. philologist, Bureau Am. Ethnology, 1901-19. In Mexico, 1910-12; hon. prof. Nat. Mus. of Archeology, Mexico; corr. sec. Germanistic Soc. America, 1914; pres. Emergency Soc. German and Austrian Science, 1927; nat. chmn. Com. for Democracy and Intellectual Freedom, 1939-40, hon. chmn. since 1940; mem. Nat. Acad. Sciences, Am. Philos. Soc., Am. Antil. Soc., Am. Folklore Soc. (editor 1908-25, pres. 1931); fellow A.A.A.S., (v.p. 1895, 1907; pres. 1931), N.Y. Acad. Sciences (pres. 1910), Am. Anthrop. Soc. (pres. 1907, 1908), Am. Acad. Arts and Sciences; honorary mem. Anthropology Soc. Vienna, Société des Americanistes, Paris, Senckenbergische Gesellschaft, Frankfort, Geog. Soc. Göteborg, Geographical Soc. Hamburg, Geographical Society of Würzburg; honorary fellow Anthropol. Inst. of Great Britain and Ireland, Folk Lore Soc. of London; cor. mem. Inst. for History of Civilization (Oslo), Anthrop. socs. of Berlin (until 1939), Brussels, Florence, Moscow, Paris, Rome, Stockholm, Washington, and of Am. Numis. Soc., German Anthropol. Soc., Prussian, Munich, Danish, Vienna Acad. Sciences, Leopoldina Acad. Halle, Soc. for Oriental Lang., Frankfort; senator Deutsche Akademie, Munich. Author: The Growth of Children, 1896, 1904; Changes in Form of Body of Descendants of Immigrants, 1911; The Mind of Primitve Man, 1911, 1938; Kultur und Rasse, 1913; Primitive Art, 1927; Anthrop. and Modern Life, 1928-38; General Anthropology (with others), 1938; Race, Language and Culture, 1940; Dakota Grammar (with Ella Deloria), 1941; also publs. on anthropometry, linguistics and anthropology of North America. Editor Jesup N. Pacific Expdn., Internat. Jour. Am. Linguistics, etc. Home: Grantwood, Bergen County, N.J. Address: Columbia Univ., New York, N.Y. Died Dec. 21, 1942.

BOATRIGHT, BYRON B(LACKBURN), cons. petroleum engr.; b. Colorado Springs, Feb. 10, 1900; s. William Louis and Minnie Ellen (Stump) B.; E.M., Colo. Sch. of Mines, 1922; Ph.D., U. of Colo., 1936; m. Sylva Dora Kerr, Mar. 10, 1922; children—Barbara Jeanne (Mrs. H.P. Oliver), William Gary (dec.). Flagman survey party, U.S. Gen. Land Office, 1919; rouster, fireman, and tool-dresser Midwest Refining Co., Big Muddy and Salt Creek Fields, Wyo., 1922-25; jr. engr., asst. engr. and later asso. engr. in charge oil and gas leasing div. U.S. Geol. Survey, state of Colo., 1925-26; dist. engr. Panhandle Dist., Marland Oil Co., 1926-28; head petroleum engring. dept. and prof. prodn. engring., Colo. Sch. Mines, 1928-37; cons. petroleum and natural gas engr., Golden, Colo., 1928-37; partner partner Parker Foran, Knode & Boatright (cons. engrs.), Houston, Tex., 1937-40, Foran, Knode, Boatright & Dixon, 1940-41, Foran, Boatright & Dixon, 1941-45, Boartright & Mitchell (cons. engrs. and geologists), 1945-46; vice pres. and chief engr. Republic Natural Gas Co., Dallas, Tex., 1946-48; 1st vice pres. Conroe Drilling Co., Austin, Tex., 1948-49, dir. 1949; gen. supt. Heep Oil Corp., Austin, Tex. 1948-49; consulting petroleum and natural gas engineer, 1949-53; v.p., gen. mgr., dir. Houston Natural Gas Producing Co., 1953—. Served with reserve force, U.S. Navy, 1918-19; 2d lt. 9th engr. reserve U.S. Army, 1930-35. Registered engr., Tex. Mem. Am. Inst. Mining and Mech. Engrs., Am. Petroleum Inst., Sigma Xi, Theta Tau, Sigma Phi Epsilon, Blue Key, Kappa Kappa Psi. Republican. Episcopalian. Mason (Shriner). Clubs: Petroleum Engineers (Dallas, Tex.), Houston, Ramada (Houston). Contbr. articles to tech. jours. Home: 11315 Smithdale Rd. Office: Capitol Petroleum Bldg., Houston. Died May 9, 1957; buried Crown Hill, Denver.

BODANSKY, MEYER, biochemist, pathologist; b. Elizabetgrad. Russia, Aug. 30, 1896; s. Phineas and Eva (Geiro) B.; brought to U.S., 1907; A.B., Cornell U., 1918, Ph.D., 1923; M.A., U. of Tex., 1922; M.D., U. of Chicago, 1935; m. Eleanore Abbott, June 15, 1925; children—Samona, Eleanore Ruth. In Ordnance Dept., U.S., later in lab. div. of Med. Corps., 1918-19; instr. in biol. chemistry, U. of Tex. Med. Sch., 1919-23, adj. prof., 1923-25; acting asst. prof., Stanford, 1925-26; asso. prof., U. of Tex., 1926-30, prof. pathol. chemistry, 1930—; dir. labs. John Sealy Hosp., John Sealy Memorial Research Lab.; visiting prof. of physiol. chemistry, Am. Univ. of Beirut, Syria, 1932-33. Certificate Am. Bd. of Pathology. Author: Introduction to Physiological Chemistry, 1927, 30, 34, 38; Laboratory Manual of Physiological Chemistry (with M. Fay), 1928, 31, 35, 38; Biochemistry of Disease (with O. Bodansky), 1940. Contbr. to Jour. Biol. Chemistry, Am. Jour. Clin. Pathology (mem. ediotrial bd.), etc. Home: Galveston, Tex. Died June 14, 1941.

BODER, DAVID PABLO, psychology; b. Libau, Latvia, Nov. 9, 1886; s. Bernard and Betty (Frank) B.; ed. Teachers Coll., Vilna, and Psycho-Neurol. Inst., St. Petersburg, until 1912; A.M., U. of Chicago, 1927; Ph.D., Northwestern U., 1934; m. Pauline Yvensky, July 20, 1907 (div. 1909); 1 dau., Elena, M.D.; m. 2d, Dora Neveloff (D.D.S.), October 14, 1925. Began as asst. in German at Psycho-Neurol. Inst.; served as officer in Russian Army, 1917; in charge adult edn., western div. Trans-Siberian R.R., 1917-18; went to Mexico, 1919; asst., later prof. psychology, Nat. Univ., Mexico, 1922-25; in charge psychol. research, penal instns., Federal Dist. of Mexico, later dir. psychol. investigations Mil. College and Nat. Agrl. schs.; came to U.S., 1926, naturalized, 1932; psychologist Michael Reese Hosp., Chicago, 1927-33; with Lewis Inst. (now Ill. Inst. Tech.), 1930-52 head department of psychology and philos., 1935-40, prof. emeritus since 1952; research associate Univ. California at Los Angeles since 1952. Study of the displaced people of Europe, in France, Switzerland, Italy and Germany, summer 1946; collection verbatim recordings of stories of the displaced people, by means of magnetic wire recorder; research on displaced people material under grants of Nat. Inst. Mental Health, USPHS, 1949-57. Trustee and executive dir. Psychol. Museum 1937-57. Mem. Am. Psychol. Assn.; mem. Chicago Psychol. Club (pres. 1935-36), Sigma Xi (Distinguished Faculty Lecture, 1950). Club: Chicago Literary, Author: La Education, el Maestro, y el Estado Mexico, 1921; Stanford-Binet Tests for Mexico, 1924; I.I.T. Morse Code Training Forms, 1943; I Did Not Interview the Dead, 1949; Topical Autobiographies of Displaced People, five series on 100 microcards (material also in sixteen mimeographed volumes), 1952-57. author of articles. Inventor of the Boder voice keys and with Joseph H. Stonekin of the metascope and disloscope; design of a traumatic index for assessment and evaluation of catastrophic events, 1954. Translator and analyst Russian neurophysiol. classics. Home: 911 S. Sierra Bonita Av., Los Angeles 90036. Died Dec. 18, 1961; buried Mt. Sinai Meml. Park, Los Angeles.

BODINE, JOSEPH HALL, prof. zoology; b. Lake Hopatcong, N.J., Sept. 19, 1895; s. Gilbert and Sarah Annie (Hall) B.; A.B., U. of Pa., 1915, Ph.D., 1920; m. Sarah Olivia Heimach, Nov. 19, 1919 (dec. June 1950); 1 son, Joseph Hall; m. 2d, Eunice Willis Beardsley, June, 1951. Inst. zoology, U. of Pa., 1915-16 and 1920-25, asst. prof., 1925-28, prof., 1928-29; prof. and head dept. zoology, U. of Ia., 1929—. Served in Med. Corps, A.E.F., World War. Chmn. scientific advisory com., Biol. Lab., Cold Spring Harbor, N.Y.; mem. exec. com. div. of agr. and biology, 1933-34, vice-chmn. of div., 1934-35, Nat. Research Council; mem. Ia. Basic Sci. Bd., 1935-50; mem. Nat. Research Council Fellowship Bd., 1941. Mem. Atomic Energy Commn. Fellowship Bd., 1948—. Director, Iwa Lakeside Laboratory, 1932—. Fellow A.A.A.S. (sec. sect. F., 1948-51, rep. Am. Physiol. Soc. 1948-49); mem. Am. Assn. Zoologists (v.p. 1933-34, pres. 1947, mem. exec. com. 1948-52), Nat. Acad. Scis., Am. Physiol. Soc., Soc. Exptl. Biol. and Med., Am. Soc. Naturalists (v.p. 1938, pres. 1940), Am. Micro. Soc., Am. Assn. Univ. Prof, Sigma Xi, Gamma Alpha. Mason. Club: Triangle. Mem. Editorial bd. Physiol. Zoology; asso. editor, Jour. Morphology, Am. Naturalists. Home: Pinehurst, R.R.2, Iowa City, Ia. Died July 23, 1954; buried Oakland Cemetery, Iowa City.

BOEING, WILLIAM EDWARD, b. Detroit, Mich., Oct. 1, 1881; s. Wilhelm and Marie (Ortman) B.; student Sheffield Scientific Sch. (Yale), 1899-1902; LL.D., State College of Washington, 1947; married Bertha Potter Paschall, Sept. 27, 1921; 1 son, William Edward, Jr. Instructed in flying by Glen L. Martin; founded Boeing Airplane Co., 1916. Awarded Daniel Guggenheim medal for the year 1934, "for successful pioneering and achievement in aircraft manufacturing and air transport." In U.S. Navy, World War; lieutenant (Jr. grade) U.S.N.R.F. Retired. King County Airport, Seattle, named Boeing Field, 1928; recipient award for econ. statesmanship Seattle U., 1955. Clubs: Seattle

Yacht; Royal Vancouver Yacht; Pacific Union (San Francisco); Chicago (Chicago); California (Los Angeles); Links (N.Y.); Rainier (Seattle). Home: Aldarra Frams, Fall City, Wash. Office: 1411 Fourth Av., Seattle 1. Died Sept. 28, 1956.

BOGARDUS, JAMES, inventor; b. Catskill, N.Y., Mar. 14, 1800; s. James and Martha (Spencer) B.; m. Margaret Maclay, Feb. 12, 1831. Awarded gold medals Am. Inst. N.Y. for 8-day, 3-wheeled chronometer clock, 1828, for invention of dry gas meter, 1835; won award for engraving machine and new method of making postage stamps, 1839; introduced cast-iron usage for frames, floors and all bldg. supports; built Bogardus Bldg. (1st all cast iron bldg. in world), 1850; designer Balt. Sun Bldg., Birch Bldg. Chgo., Pub. Ledger Bldg., Phila.; made numerous improvement in manufacture of tools and machinery. Died N.Y.C., Apr. 13, 1874.

BOGART, JOHN, engr.; b. Albany, N.Y., Feb. 8, 1836; s. John Henry and Eliza (Hermans) B.; B.A., Rutgers, 1853, M.A., 1856; (Sc.D. 1912)); m. Emma Cherington Jefferis, Nov. 2, 1870. In engr. corps N.Y.C. R.R., state canals of N.Y.; U.S. engr. Ft. Monroe, Va., and other points during the war, 1861-66; chief engr. park commn., Brooklyn; engaged on many important works for govt. and pvt. coprs., including pub. and municipal works at Albany, New Orleans, Chicago, Nashville, Baltimore, Buffalo, Norfolk, Kansas City, Toronto, Keene, Rochester, etc., 1877—; 6 yrs. chief engr. State Bd. of Health, N.Y.; constructing engr. of Washington Bridge, New York; Harbors of Venezuela; engr. hydraulic and electric development of power at Niagara Falls, Sault Ste. Marie, Massena, St. Lawrence River, Cascade, Brit. Columbia, Knoxville, Atlanta, Chattanooga, Verde, Ariz., and Southern Va., Neb., and Youghiogheny Power companies; cons. engr. several railways, Rapid Transit Commn., New York, Essex Commn. (N.J.), Southern Colo. Power & Rys.; advisory and expert engr. in many cases; chief engr. Chattanooga & Tenn. River Power Co.; mem. various bds. Lt. col. and chief engr. N.G.S.N.Y. Del. for U.S. Govt. at Internat. Congress of Navigation, Düsseldorf, Germany, 1902, Milan, Italy, 1905, St. Petersburg, Russia, 1908, pres. inland navigation sect., Phila., 1912; mem. Permanent Bd. of Internat. Navigation Congresses; only civilian mem. U.S. Govt. Bd. on the Lakes to the Gulf Waterway; mem. Municipal Art Commn. of New York. Hon. mem. A.I.A. Author: Engineering Feats; Papers and Discussions. Home: New York, N.Y. Died Apr. 25, 1920.

BOGEN, EMIL, physician; b. N.Y.C., Sept. 8, 1896; s. Boris David and Elizabeth (Scholtz) B.; A.B., U. Cin., 1920, M.D., 1923, M.S., 1927; m. Jane Skillen, Apr. 15, 1933; children—Elizabeth, Ellen, David. Intern Los Angeles Gen. Hosp., 1923-24, resident, 1924-26; grad. student, fellow U. Cin., 1926-27, Harvard, 1928; asst. prof. preventive medicine U. Cin., 1928-29; head pathologist, dir. labs. and research Olive View Sanatorium, Los Angeles County, 1929-59; chief pathologist VA Hosp., Alexandria, La., 1959-60; exchange prof. Vallabhbhai Patel Chest Inst., Univ. of Delhi (India), 1959-60; associate clinical prof., clinical professor infectious diseases U. Cal. at Los Angeles Co. Hosp., City of Hope Sanatorium; vis. dir. labs and research Leahi Hosp., Honolulu. Served from pvt. to cop. U.S. Army, AEF, 1917-19; comdr. USNR, 1942-46. Recipient prize awards Cal. Med. Assn., 1926, 27, 30; Alvarenga prize Coll. of Physicians Phila., 1927. Diplomate Nat. Bd. Med. Examiners, Am. Bd. Pathology. Fellow Am. Coll. Chest Physicians; mem. Am. Pub. Health Assn., A.M.A., A.A.A.S., Am. Soc. Clin. Pathologists, Nat. Tb. Assn., Internat. Union Against Tb., Cal. Trudeau Soc. (pres. 1941), Soc. for Experimental Biology and Medicine (pres. So. Cal. br., 1938). Author: (with Lehmann Hisey) What About Alcohol, 1934; Surgeon Errant, 1935; numerous contbns. to med. and sci. publs. Address: 445 W. Longden Av., Arcadia, Cal. Died Sept. 19, 1962.

BOGERT, MARSTON TAYLOR, chemist; b. Flushing, N.Y., Apr. 18, 1868; s. Henry A. and Mary B. (Lawrence) B.; A.B., Columbia, 1890, Ph.B., 1894, Sc.D., 1929; LL.D., Clark U., 1909; R.N.D., Charles U. (Prague); m. Charlotte E. Hoogland, Sept. 12, 1893; children—Annette B. (Mrs. Frank B. Tallman), Elise B. (Mrs. F. K. Huber). Asst. organic chemistry, 1894-97, tutor, 1897, instr., 1897-1901, adj. prof., 1901-04, prof., 1904-39, emeritus prof. in residence since 1939; mem. Univ. Council, 1909-11, 1916-17, and 1922-29, Columbia; also rep. Columbia U. on bd. trustees N.Y. Coll. of Pharmacy, 1930-36. Lecturer organic chemistry, New York U., 1919020. Mem. Am. Advisory Com. of Honor 7th Internat. Congress of Applied Chemistry, London, 1909; pres. Organic Sect., 8th Internat. Congress Applied Chemistry, Washington, D.C., and New York, 1912, chmn. com. of presidents of sections of same and v. chmn. com. of same; by invitation of President Roosevelt, mem. of White House Conf. on Conservation of Natural Resources, May 1908; also of the following Conf. with Governors of States and Tys., Washington, D.C., Dec. 1908; mem. Internat. Com. in Honor of Amedeo Avogadro, under patronage of King Victor Emmanual III of Italy; del. of U.S. Govt. and Nat. Research Council and pres. sect. on chemistry and nat. defense, X. Internat. Congress Chemistry, Rome, 1938; pres. Internat. Union Chemistry, 1938-47. Fellow A.A.A.S., London Chemical Soc., Royal Soc. of Edinburgh (hon.). Member Assn. chimica Italiana, Societe Chimique de Paris, Nederland Chem. Ver., Swiss Chemists' Society American Institute Chemists (medalist for 1935-36), Am. Chem. Society (ex-pres.; Nichols medal, 1905; Priestley medal, 1938); hon. mem. Soc. Chem. Industry Eng. (ex-pres.), Chemists Club (ex-pres.), Nat. Acad. Sciences (chmn. chem. sect., 1926-29), Washington Acad. Scis., N.Y. Acad. Scis., Am. Philos. Sco., Am. Acad. Arts and Sciences, Am. Assn. Univ. Profs. (pres. Columbia U. chapter 1932-37), Phi Beta Kappa, Delta Phi, Sigma Xi (councilor 1904; pres. Columbia Chapter, 1906, 1933-37; recipient of its Large Scroll 1936); hon. mem. Chemists' Soc. of Poland, Royal Soc. Sciences and Letters (Bohemia), Societe de Chimie Industrielle de France (pres. Am. sect. 1920-21); corr. mem. Am. Inst. in Prague. Medalist of Charles U. (Prague) and of the Comensky U. (Bratislava); Comdr. Order of White Lion of Czechoslovakia. Awarded Egleston Medal of Columbia Engineering School Alumni Assn., 1939. First Recipient Medal Award, Society of Cosmetic Chemists; Charles Frederick Chandler medalist and lecturer (selection by Columbia U.), 1948. An incorporator of Museums of Peaceful Arts, now New York Museum of Science and Industry, New York, 1915, member board directors since its organization; member national advisory board, Masaryk Institute. In World War I—member executive bd. Nat. Research Council (organizer and 1st chmn. div. of chemistry and chem. technology, with 32 subcoms.); mem. raw materials div. War Industries Bd.; mem. bd. on Gas Warfare; cons. chemist, Bur. Mines; mem. scientific staff, Bur. Standards; advisory bd. materials prodn. div., Signal Corps, War Dept.; consultant Fed. Trade Commn., mil. intelligence div. of Gen. Staff, War Dept., bur. investigation Dept. Justice, postal censorship Post Office Dept., etc. Commd. lt. col. and apptd. chief, Chem. Service Sect., U.S. Army, and asst. dir. Gas Service, Mar. 9, 1918; promoted col., July 13, 1918; served as chief of relations sect., intelligence sect., mem. bd. of review, claims bd. and exec. com. hdqrs. staff of Chem. Warfare Service; mem. standardization sect., purchase branch, Gen. Staff U.S. Army, etc.; hon. disch. May 1, 1919. Apptd. U.S. tariff commr. by President Wilson but declined; consultant in research and development work, Chem. Warfare Service; councillor of Internat. Union Pure and Applied Chemistry, 1926-33; and since 1937; 1st visiting Carnegie prof. of internat. relations to Czechoslovakia, 1927-28; v.p. Nat. Inst. Social Science, 1923-25; collaborator U.S. Dept. Agr., 1926-32 (chmn. advisory bd. to Color Lab. 1926-31); mem. board mgrs. N.Y. Bot. Gardens since 1927; mem. council of advisors, Fed Union, Inc; pres. supervisory bd., Am. Year Book Corp. Mem. Refereee Bd., Chem. Industries Br., Office of Production, Research and Development, War Production Bd., 1942-45. Mem. Mil. Order Foreign Wars, Mil. Order World War. Asso. editor Jour. Am. Chem. Soc., 1924-30; mem. bd. of editors and editor trustee, Jour. Organic Chemistry since 1937; contbr. Jour. Indsl. Engring. Chemistry, Science, Jour. Am. Chem. Soc., Jour. Organic Chemistry, etc. Clubs: Megantic Fish and Game, Columbia Men's faculty, Chemists' (hon.), Century Assn., Holland Soc. of N.Y., St. Nicholas Soc. of N.Y. Home: 1158 5th Av., N.Y.C. 29. Died Mar. 21, 1954; buried Flushing Cemetery, Flushing, L.I., N.Y.

BOGGS, ROBERT, cons. med. edn.; b. Portland, Ore., Sept. 22, 1903; s. Robert William and Martha (Horton) B.; A.B., U. Ore., 1928; M.D., C.M., McGill U., 1933; m. Barbara Field, Feb. 14, 1942 (div. Feb. 1961); children—Robert, Sarah Lenox, Evelyn Marshall; m. 2d, Jane Will, Teagle. Research fellow in surgery Harvard also fellow surgery Peter Bent Brigham Hosp., Boston, 1933-34; intern, asst. resideent surgery N.Y. Hosp., 1934-36; pvt. practice surgery N.Y.C., 1936-39; instr. N.Y. Med. Coll., 1939-40; asst. prof. anatomy N.Y. U. Coll. Med., 1945-47, asst. dean, 1947-48; acting dean N.Y. Post-Grad. Med. Sch., 1948-49; acting dean N.Y. U. Post-Grad. Med. Sch. (formed by consolidation of N.Y. Post-Grad. Med. Sch. and postgrad. div. N.Y. U. Coll. Medicine), 1948, Nat. Com. Resettlement of Fgn. Physicians; chmn. deans com. N.Y. Vets. Hosps., 1953-55; mem. adv. com. Unitarian Service Com. Bd. dirs. Field Found. Commd. lt. (j.g.), M.C., U.S. Navy, 1936; on active duty, 1940-45; promoted comdr., 1942; served in U.S.S. Wichita, P.T.O., 1942-44; capt., 1945. Mem. N.Y. Acad. Medicine, Harvey Soc., Royal Soc. Health, Chi Psi, Alpha Kappa Kappa. Clubs: University, Piping Rock, Links, Golf, Racquet and Tennis, River, Creek, Turf and Field, Seawanhako-Corinthian Yacht; Bath and Tennis, Everglades (Palm Beach, Fla.). Home: Cleft Rd., Millneck, N.Y. Office: 203 E. 62d St., N.Y.C. Died Oct. 1967.

BOGGS, S(AMUEL) WHITTEMORE, geographer; born Coolidge, Kan., Mar. 3, 1889; s. Charles F(airman) and Lillian Louise (Whittemore) B.; B.L., Berea (Ky.) Coll., 1909; student Yale U., 1912-13; M.A. Columbia U., 1924; D.Sc. (honorary), Berea College, 1949; married Amy Burt Bridgman, August 16, 1916; children—Mary Lillian, Barbara Bridgman. Private sec. to President Frost, Berea Coll., 1909-12; secretarial work U.P.R.R., Omaha, Neb., 1913-14; secretarial and exec. work Internat. Com. of Y.M.C.A. and other orgns., New York, 1914-19; geog. research, map compilation, editor Am. Book Co., etc., 1916-24, including editing maps for World Missionary Atlas, 1921-24; geographer U.S. Dept. of State, 1924—; lecturer on internat. boundaries, Columbia U., summers 1939, 40, 41, and 42; lecturer, Am. Univ., 1945-46. Tech. adviser, U.S. delegation, Conf. for Codification of Internat. Law, The Hague, 1930; ofcl. del. International Geog. Congresses, Cambridge, 1928, Paris, 1931, Warsaw, 1934, Lisbon, 1949, Pan Am. Inst. Geography and History, 3d gen. assembly, Lima, 1931, 4th gen. assembly Caracas, 1946, 1st consultation on geography Rio de Janeiro, 1949, 5th general assembly, Santiago, Chile, 1950, 3d consultation, Washington, 1952, 6th consultation on cartography, Ciudad Trujillo, 1952; member U.S. Geographic Bd., 1924-34, chmn. exec. com., 1927-34, U.S. Bd. on Geog. Names, 1947—, chairman, 1949-51. Fellow A.A.A.S., Royal Geog. Soc.; mem. Assn. Am. Geographers (councillor 1941-42), Am. Soc. Professional Geographers, Am. Council Learned Socs. (sec.-treas. 1942-48, treas., 1948-50), Acad. Polit. Sci., Am. Geophys. Union, Wash. Acad. Sci.; hon. mem. Mexican Soc. Geography and Statistics; corr. mem. Lima Geog. Soc. Presbyn. Clubs: Cosmos (Wash.); Exploers (N.Y.). Author: International Boundaries—a Study of Boundary Functions and Problems, 1940; Classification and Cataloging of Maps and Atlases (with Dorothy C. Lewis) 1945. Contbr. to Dist. Am. History and various mags. Home: 4119 Stanford St., Chevy Chase 15, Md. Office: U.S. Dept. of State, Washington 25. Died Sept. 14, 1954.

BOGUE, VIRGIL GAY, engr.; b. at Norfolk, N.Y., July 20, 1846; s. George Chase and Mary (Perry) B.; C.E., Rensselaer Poly. Inst., Troy, N.Y., 1868; m. Sybil Russell Bogue, Mar. 2, 1872. Asst. engr., Prospect Park, Brooklyn, 1868-69; asst. engr. Oroya Ry. and mgr. Trajille Ry., Peru, S.A., 1869-79; asst. engr. N.P. R.R. (discovered Stampede Pass), supervised constrn. across Ida., and Wash., 1880-86; chief engr. U.P. R.R., 1886-91; consulting engr., New York, 1891—. Mem. commn. apptd. by President Harrison to investigate methods for improving navigation of Columbia River; consulting engr. for Govt. of New Zealand on ry. across South Island; cons. engr. Dept. Pub. Works, New York, Western Md. R.R., 1903-06; chief engr. and v.p. Western Pacific Ry., 1905-09. Prepared the plan and report for Greater Seattle, Wash.; for harbor of Tacoma and for Grays Harbor, Wash., etc. Fellow Am. Geog. Soc. Office: 15 Williams St., New York. Died Oct. 14, 1916.

BOHR, NIELS HENRIK DAVID, Danish physicist; b. Copenhagen, Denmark, Oct. 7, 1885; s. Christian and Ellen (Adler) B.; Master's degree U. Copenhagen, 1909, Doctorate, 1911; hon. doctorates from more than 30 univs., worldwide; m. Margrethe Norlund, Aug. 1, 1912; 6 children, including Hans Henrik, Erik, Aage, Ernest. Carlsberg Found. grantee for study abroad, in Eng.; worked under J. J. Thomson at Cavendish Lab., Cambridge, Eng., 1911-12, under Rutherford at Manchester, Eng., 1912-13; lectr. physics U. Copenhagen, 1913-14, Victoria U., Manchester, 1914-16; prof. theoretical physics U. Copenhagen, 1916-62; a founder Inst. for Theoretical Physics, 1920, dir., 1920-62; visited U.S., 1938, 39; fled from German occupation in World War II, went 1st to Sweden, then Eng., finally to U.S., 1943, and served in adv. capacity Los Alamos Atomic Labs.; redeveloping peaceful uses of atomic energy; chmn. Danish Atomic Energy Commn.; organized 1st Atoms for Peace Conf., Geneva, 1955. Recipient Gold medal Acad. Scis. Copenhagen, 1908; Nobel prize in physics, 1922; 1st Atoms for Peace award, 1957. Pres.; Royal 1926; mem. French Acad. Scis., 1937, fgn. asso., 1945; mem. nearly all learned socs. of Europe. Author Atomic Constitution, 1922; Atomic Theory and the Description of Nature, 1934; The Unity of Knowledge, 1955; also many articles. Adapted Planck's quantum theory to Rutherford's model of atomic structure, thus devising Bohr's theory of the atom, 1913, which represents the atom as a dynamic system of electrons rotating around a nucleus (atom emits or absorbs electromagnetic radiation only when an electron passes from 1 orbit to another of different surgery level); his was 1st reasonably successful attempt to use spectroscopic data to describe the internal structure of atom; was among those who pointed out that electrons exist in sheels and that the electron content of the outer-most shell determines the chem. properties of the atoms of a particular element; developed principle phenomena may be examined in each of 2 mutually exclusive ways, with each being valid in its own terms; developed the correspondence principle, 1916. Died Copenhagen, Nov. 18, 1962.

BOLDHUAN, CHARLES FREDERICK, health educator; b. Bielefeld, Germany, May 7, 1873; s. William and Juliane (Dreibholz) B.; Ph.G., Coll. of Pharmacy, N.Y.C., 1893; M.D., Coll. Phys. and Surg., Columbia, 1901; student U. Berlin, 1903; m. Adele Jonsson, Sept. 15, 1906; 1 son, Nils W. (M.C. U.S. Army); m. 2d, Herma Engelsdorff, Mar. 1, 1928. Prof. bacteriology and hygiene Fordham U., 1905-08; bacteriologist Dept. of Health, City N.Y., 1904-07; asst. to gen. med. officer Dept. of Health, 1907-13; dir. Bur. Pub. Health Edn., 1913-18; chief, sec. Public Health Edn., USPHS, 1918-21; surgeon USPHS, detailed U.S. consular service, Europe, 1921028; dir. Bur. of Health Edn., Dept. of Health, N.Y.C., 1928-43; lectr. preventive medicine and hygiene Columbia, 1918-22, Sch. Sociology and Social Service, Fordham, 1928-42. Sec. N.Y. Tb Preventorium for Children. Founder, hon. pres. N.Y., Diabetes Assn. Fellow Am. Pub. Health

Assn., N.Y. Acad. Medicine; mem. N.Y. Soc. Med. History; hon. mem. Am. Diabetes Assn. Author: Immune Sera, 5th Edit. 1918; Applied Bacteriology for Nurses 8th edit. 1941; Public Health and Hygiene, 3d edit. 1941; Spanish edit. 1943. Translator of Suppression of Tuberculosis, etc., 1905; Serum Diagnosis, 1905; Collected Studies on Immunity, 1906; also scientific papers in medical jours.; numerous statistical studies on cancer, heart disease, infant mortality, typhoid fever, etc., hist. studies on health conditions in N.Y. City during 19th Century. Editor Bull., N.Y.C. Dept. Health. Address: Northport, L.I., N.Y. Died Apr. 4 1950.

BOLDT, HERMANN JOHANNES, gynecologist; b. nr. Berlin, Germany, June 24, 1856; s. Hermann and Amalie (Krüger) B.; came to U.S., 1865; ed. public grammar and high schs.; studied and practiced pharmacy; M.D., Univ. Med. Coll. (New York U.), 1879; m. Hedwig Krüger, 1891. In practice since 1879; since 1891 has confined practice to gynecology; prof. gynecology, N.Y. Post-Grad. Med. Sch. and Hosp. (now post-grad. dept. of Columbia U.), 1890-1923; now prof. emeritus; was cons. gynecologist, Stuyvesant Polyclinic, Post Graduate, Beth Israel, St. Vincent's and Union hosps.; retired, 1929. Extensive investigator into physiol. action of cocaine and gynecol. pathology. Inventor of various gynecol. instruments and an operating table for abdominal surgery which received medal at Paris Expn., 1900, and also a modern examining table for office work. Fellow Am. Coll. Surgeons (founder mem. and former mem. bd. govs.); hon. mem. Am. Gynecol. Soc., Am. Gynecol. Club, Westchester Surg. Soc.; mem. Nat. Soc. of Sciences, N.Y. Acad. Sciences, Internat. Gynecol. Soc. and Obstet. Soc. (ex-pres.), N.Y. Acad. Medicine (ex-chmn. gynecol. sec.), Southern Surg. Soc., Mil. Surgeons U.S.A., Royal Soc. of Medicine (London), Gynecol. Soc. of Germany; hon. mem., ex-pres. German Med. Soc. (New York); hon. mem. Gynecol. Soc. of Great Britain, Gynecol. Soc. of Germany. His only child, Hermann J., Jr., 1st. 102d Inf., was killed in France, July 20, 1918, while on vol. duty on hazardous mission as aerial observer attached to st Am. Escadrille; was awarded citation and Croix de Guerre with palm by order of General Petain. Home: (winter) Hotel Albemarle, St. Petsburg, Fla. Address: 29 Greenridge Av., White Plains, N.Y. Died Jan. 12, 1943.

BOLGER, HENRY JOSEPH, physicist; b. portland, Wis., Sept. 29, 1901; s. Michael Henry and Mary Rebecca (Roche) B.; A.B., Notre Dame, 1924; A.M., Catholic U. Am., 1929; postgrad. Cal. Inst. Tech., 1932-36. Ordained priest Roman Catholic Ch.; prof. physics, Notre Dame, 1936-, head de dept. physics, 1937-63. Dir. project under auspicies of Manhattan Dist., 1943-45. Mem. Council Argonne Nat. Labs. Mem. Am. Physics Soc., Am. Assn. Physics Tchrs., A.A.A.S. Address: Notre Dame, Ind. Died May 4, 1964.

BOLL, JACOB, geologist, naturalist; b. Bremgarten, Canton Aargau, Switzerland, May 29, 1828; s. Henry and Magdalena (Peier) B.; attended U. Jena; m. Henriette Humbel, 1854. Owned pharmacy, Bremgarten, 1854-74; studied natural history of Canton Aargau; visited Tex., 1869-70, collected specimens for Louis Agassiz; studied geology and natural history of Tex., 1874-80; collected fossils and reptiles in North and N.W. Tex.; employed by U.S. Entomol. Commn. for study of Rocky Mountain locust, 1877-80; commd. by Canton Aargau to collect specimens of Colo. potato beetle, seeds of woody plants, fresh water and marine mollusks of Tex. Died Wilbarger County, Tex., Sept. 29, 1880.

BOLLER, ALFRED PANCOAST, engr.; b. Phila., Feb. 23, 1840; s. Henry J. and Anna M. (Pancoast) B.; A.M. U. of Pa., 1858; C.E., Rensselaer Poly. Inst., 1861; m. Katherine Newbold, Apr., 1864. Was engr. with ry. and other corps., 1862-85; has for yrs. been cons. engr. or contractor for bridge constrn.; was engr. Albany and Greenbush bridge over Hudson at Albany; the Thames River Shore Line Bridge, New London, Conn.; the Central Bridge and viaducts over Harlem River, N.Y.; the 4-track, Duluth and Superior Interstate Bridge; etc.; cons. engr. Park Dept. and Public Works Dept., New York, under old charter; extension of Wabash lines into Pittsburgh, 1901-04, Brooklyn Rapid Transit Elevated R.R., etc., senior mem. Bolier & Hodges. Author: Treatise on the Construction of Iron Highway Bridges, etc. Home: E. Orange, N.J. Died Dec. 9, 1912.

BOLT, RICHARD ARTHUR, physician; b. St. Louis, Mar. 12, 1880; s. Richard Orchard and Mary Virginia (Belt) B.; student Washington U., 1899-1900; A.B., U. Mich., 1904, M.D., 1906; postgrad. Boston Children's Hosp., also Boston Lying-In Hosp., N.Y. Lying-In Hosp.; grad. Pub. Health, U. Cal., 1917, Dr. P.H., 1924; Dr.P.H. (fellow), Johns Hopkins, 1925; m. Rebecca Beatrice French, July 21, 1908; children—Elizabeth Rebecca (Mrs. E. C. Pendleton), Richard Henry, Marrion Jane (Mrs. Jack W. Field), Robert Bashford. Intern St. Vincent's Charity Hosp., Cleve., 1907-08, pathologist, vis. physician, 1907-09; actg. med. dir. Babies' Dispensary and Hosp., Cleve., 1909-10; med. dir. U.S. Indemnity Coll., Pekin, China, 1911-16; chief bur. child hygiene Cleve. Dept. Health, 1917-18; instr. and asso. in pediatrics Western Reserve Med. Sch., 1917-20, asso. in hygiene, pub. health and pediatric depts., 1929-45; lectr. Johns Hopkins U., 1920-25, Johns Hopkins Sch. Hygiene and Pub. Health, 1923-25, Nat. Catholic Welfare Sch.; asst. prof. child hygiene U. Cal., 1925-29, lectr. sch. pub. health, 1945-48, emeritus, 1948—, spl. summer lectr. 1920—, lectr. extension div., 1925-29. Dir. Cleve. Child Health Assn., 1929-45; specialist in maternal and infant hygiene U.S. Children's Bur., 1924—; adviser in child hygiene City Health Dept. and Pub. Schs. Berkeley, 1925-29, spl. lectr. Stanford, 1923; dir. child welfare div. Tb Commn., A.R.C. in Italy, 1918-19; dir. Alameda County (Cal.) Pub. Health Center, 1919-20; gen. dir. Am. Child Hygiene Assn., also sec sec.-treas. Nat. Child Health Council, 1920-22; med. dir. Am. Child Health Assn., 1923-24; mem. White House Conf. on Child Health and Protection; chmn. com. on prevention and research Internat. Soc. for Crippled Children; ofcl. del. from U.S. to 6th English-Speaking Conf. on Maternity and Child Welfare, London, 1933, also Congrés Internat. pour la Protection de l'Enfance, Paris; asso. in 44th congress Royal Sanitary Inst. of Eng. and Wales, Blackpool, Eng., 1933; mem. hygiene reference bd. Life Extension Inst.; mem. Conf. on Coll. Hygiene, Surgeon-Gen.'s Conf. on Control of Venereal Disease, Washington, 1936; mem. White House Conf. on Children in a Democracy, 1939; mem. exec. com. of gov.'s com. on follow-up of White House Conf. in Ohio, 1941; adv. bd. Living Age; mem. Carl Schurz Meml. Found., Cleve. Health Council, Civilian Def., Emergency Child Care and Nutrition Com.; mem. adminstrv. com. Sch. Pub. Health; rep. Spokesmen for Children, Inc.; mem. Emergency Com. to Save U.S. Children's Bureau. Recipient 2 decorations Chinese Red Cross for work during Chinese Revolution; Oberlaender Trust award for study maternal and child welfare in Germany and Austria, 1933. Fellow Am. Pub. Health Assn.; mem. Cleve. Dental Soc. (hon.), Sigma Xi, Alpha Kappa Kappa, Delta Omega, Phi Sigma. Methodist. Author: Tsing Hua College, Peking, 19i4; Japanese Justice on Trial in Korea, 1915; Sandflies in China in Relation to Disease, 1915; The Baby's Health, 1924; (with Chenoweth and Selkirk) School Health Problems, 1937; Maternal, Infant and Preschool Hygiene in Nelson's Loose Leaf Medicine and in Emerson's Adminstrative Medicine, 1941; Publications and Addresses, Including Editorials and Radio Scripts, 1900-1955. Home: 2954 Linden Av., Berkeley 5, Cal. Died Aug. 3, 1959; buried El Carmelo Cemetery, Pacific Grove, Cal.

BOLTON, BENJAMIN MEADE, bacteriologist; b. Richmond, Va., Apr. 7, 1857; s. James (M.D.) and Anna Maria (Harrison) B.; student Charlottesville (Va.) Inst., 1871-75; M.D., U. of Va., 1879; studied S.C. Coll., 1882-83, U. of Heidelberg, 1883-84, U. of Göttingen, 1884-86, U. of Berlin, 1886; m. Johanna Heriette Louise Liebau, Brunswick, Germany, 1886; children—Meade, Theodore; m. 2d, Laetitia Todd, 1898; 1 dau., Laetitia Todd. Asst., 1886-88, asso., 1892-95, Johns Hopkins; prof. hygiene and bacteriology, S.C. Coll., 1888-89; dir. bacteriol. dept., Hoagland Lab., 1889-92; dir. of lab., Bd. of Health, Phila., 1895-96; prof. pathology and bacteriology, U. of Mo., 1896-97; prof. pathology and bacteriology, U. of St. Louis, 1901-04; dir. of Lab., State Bd. of Health, N.J., 1907-08; expert in exptl. theapeutics Bur. of Animal Industry, Washington, D.C.; biologist, Md. Agrl. Expt. Sta., 1912-14; expert in diseases of animals, Cuban Agrl. Expt. Sta., 1914-15; dir. Virchow Lab., St. Louis, 1917-19; pathologist New Samaritan Hosp., Sioux City, Ia., 1920-21; pathologist New Samaritan Hosp., Sioux City, Ia., 1920-21; pathologist St. Joseph's Hosp., Paterson, N.J., 1921—; bacteriologist Rhode Island State Bd. of Health. Home: New York, N.Y. Died Aug. 12, 1929.

BOLTON, ELMER KEISER, chemist; b. Phila., June 23, 1886; s. George and Jane (Holt) B.; A.B., Bucknell U., 1908, hon. D.Sc., 1932; A.M., Harvard, 1910, Ph.D., 1913; student Kaiser Wilhelm Inst. fur Chemie, Berlin, 1913-1915; D.Sci. (honorary), U. Del.; m. Marguerite L. Duncan, December 6, 1916; children—Duncan G., Marjorie L., Elmer K. With E. I. du Pont de Nemours and Co. 1915-51, successively asst. mgr. Lodi Works, mgr. organic div. of chem. dept., dir. chem. sect. of dyestuffs dept., asst. chem. dir. of chem. dept., 1929-30, chem. dir., 1930-51; retired, 1951; mem. tech. advisory panel on materials Dept. of Def. Trustee Bucknell U.; bd. mgrs., The Wilmington Institute Free Library. Mem. Nat. Acad. of Sciences, Am. Chemical Soc. (dir., 1940-43), Am. Inst. Chem. Engrs., Sigma Xi, Phi Kappa Psi, Alpha Chi Sigma. Recipient Chemical Industry Medal, 1941, Perkin Medal, 1944; Willard Gibbs gold medal, Am. Chem. Soc., 1954. Clubs: Wilmington, Wilmington Country, du Pont Country, Harvard. Home: Wilmington DE Died July 30, 1968.

BOLTON, HENRY CARRINGTON, chemist; b. N.Y., Jan. 28, 1843; s. Jackson (M.D.) and Anna H. (North) B.; grad. Columbia, 1862; studied chemistry in Europe (Ph.D., Göttingen); m. Henrietta Irving, Oct. 10, 1893. Asst. in quantitative analysis, Columbia Sch. of Mines, 1872-77; prof. chemistry, Woman's Med. Coll. of N.Y. Infirmary; prof. chemistry and natural science, Trinity Coll., 1877-87. Fellow A.A.A.S. (gen. sec., 1878-79, and v.p., 1882); mem. (pres. 1898-99) Library Assn. of D.C.; mem. (pres. 1893) N.Y. Acad. Sciences; one of incorporators, 188, Am. Folk Lore Soc.; mem. (pres. 1900) Washington Chem. Soc. Author: The Student's Guide in Quanitiative Analysis, 1885; The Counting Out Rhymes of Children, 1888; Scientific Correspondence of Joseph Priestly, 1892; A Select Bibliography of Chemistry 1492-1892, 1893, supplements, 1899, 1900; The Family of Bolton in England and America 1100-1894, 1895; A Catalogue of Scientific and Technical Periodicals, 1897; Evolution of the Thermometer 1592-1743, 1900; The Follies of Science at the Court of Rudolph II, 1903. Died 1903.

BOLTON, REGINALD PELHAM, engring. expert; b. London, Eng., Oct. 5, 1856; s. Rev. James and Lydia Louisa (Pym) B.; ed. pvt. schs.; m. Kate Alice Behenna, May 4, 1878; children—Ivy, Guy; m. 2d, Ethelind Huyck, Sept. 3, 1892. Came to America, 1879. In cons. practice and traveling in Europe, designing and erecting machinery for mines, shipywards, marine engines, to 1894, since in New York; cons. engr. to Dept. of Water Supply, N.Y., Plant System, R. H. Macy Co., N.Y. Central Terminal, etc., also in connection with erection of numerous tall bldgs.; pres. Electric Meter Corp. Mem. Am. Scenic and Historic Preservation Soc.; trustee Dyckman Inst., City Hist. Club; sec. Washington Heights Taxpayers Assn., 1904-27; mem. Am. Soc. C.E., Am. Inst. Cons. Engrs., Am. Soc. M.E., Am. Soc. Heating and Ventilating Engrs. (pres. 1911); hon. life mem. N.Y. Hist. Soc.; asso. mem. Instn. Civil Engineers, England (Telford gold medal, 1902). Club: National Arts, Author: MOtive Powers, 1895; The Assault of Mt. Washington, 1776, 1901; Elevator Service, 1908; The Indians of Washington Heights, 1909; Building for Profit, 1911, 15, 22; Power for Profit, 1915; An Expensive Experiment, 1913, 17; A Municipal Experimetn, 1917; New York City in Indian Possession, 1920; Indian Paths in the Great Metropolis, 1922; Washington Heights-Its Eventful Past, 1924; Indian Life of Long Ago in the City of New York, 1934. Home: 638 W. 158th St. Office: Bolton Bldg., 116 E. 19th St., New York, N.Y. Died Feb. 18, 1942.

BONAPARTE, CHARLES LUCIEN, ornithologist; b. Paris, France, May 24, 1803; son of Lucien Bonaparte; nephew of Napoleon Bonaparte; ed. in Italy; married Zenaide (his cousin). Came to U.S. (Phila.), 1822; completed Wilson's Ornithology, (listing at least 100 species of birds he discovered), 1825-33; contbr. articles on ornithology to sci. journals; returned to Italy to continue studies, 1828; became prince of Canino and Musignano (upon death of his father), 1840; entered Italian politics, joined anti-papal faction, served as v.p. of republican assembly; fled Italy, 1848, settled in France, 1850; became dir. Jardin des Plantes, 1854. Author: Geographical and Comparative List of Birds of Europe and North America, 1838; several other studies, published 1827-58. Died Paris, July 29, 1857.

BOND, A(LEXADER) BUSSELL, editor and patent solicitor; b. of Am. parents, Stara Zagora, Bulgaria, June 12, 1876; s. Lewis and Fannie Grier (Russell) B.; came to U.S., 1890; A.B., Princeton, 1898; m. Edith Louise Pruden, Oct. 22, 1901; 1 son, Gordon Van Der Veer. Asso. editor Scientific American, 1902-15; mng. editor same, 1915-19; editor Scientific American Monthly, 1919-21; mgr. patent dept. Federated Engrs. Development Corp., 1921-26, also sec. and dir.; registered patent atty., 1908. Presbyn. Author: Scientific American Boy, 1905; Scientific American Boy at School, 1909; With Men Who Do Things, 1913; Pick, Shovel and Pluck, 1914; On the Battlefront of Engineering, 1915; American Boys' Engineering Book, 1918; Inventions of the Great War, 1919; Mechanics, 1922. Compiler and Editor: Handy Man's Workshop and Laboatory, 1909. Collaborator with A. A. Hopkins on Scientific American Reference Book, 1904 and 1912; editor Century Books of Useful Science. Home: Plainfield, N.J. Died June 3, 1937.

BOND, EDWARD AUSTIN, civil engr.; b. Dexter, Mich., Apr. 22, 1849; s. Hollis and Emily (Faxon) B.; ed. pub. schs. of Mich., and bus. coll., Utica, N.Y.; m. Gertrude Hollenbeck, Nov. 11, 1873; m. 2d, Clara E. Ellis, Nov. 10, 1904; mem. corps 15engrs. on construction of D.,L.&W. R.R., between Utica and Binghamton, N.Y., 1868-70; resident engr. Utica & Black River R.R., assisting in constrn. of road, 1870-71; chief engr. Clayton & Theresa R.R., 1872-75. Utica & Black River R.R., 1875-89; chf. engr., gen. supt., location, constrn., operations, Carthage & Adirondack R.R.; mem. Hines & Bond, cons. and advisory engrs. in promotion and constrn. of water works throughout U.S. and Can. State Engr. and suveyor of N.Y., 1898-1904; apptd. by Gov., chmn. advisory bd. engrs., and during 1900 as state engr. had full charge surveys, plans and estimates for a barge canal acorss state, for which appropriated $101,00,000, and which was ratified by people at polls; chmn. advisory bd. of cons. engrs. for constrn. of Barge Canal, 1904-July 21, 1911. Pres. Barrie (Ont.) Water Works Co., Chatham (Ont.) Water Works Co., Napenee (Ont.) Water Works Co. Mason. Home: New York, N.Y. Died Dec. 10, 1929.

BOND, GEORGE PHILLIPS, astronomer; b. Dorchester, Mass., May 20, 1825; s. William C. and Selina (Cranch) B.; grad. Harvard, 1845; m. Harriet Harris, Jan. 27, 1853, at least 3 children. Asst. observer Harvard Observatory, 1845-59, dir., 1859-65, Phillips prof. astronomy, 1859-65; credited with discovery of Hyperion (8th satellite of Saturn) and of crape ring, 1850; founder photographic astronomy; received gold medal from Royal Astron. Soc. of London; papers include "Cometary Calculations," "The Method of Mechanical Quadratures." Died Cambridge, Mass., Feb. 17, 1865.

BOND, WILLIAM CRANCH, astronomer; b. Portland, Me., Sept. 9, 1789; s. William and Hannah (Cranch) B.; A.M. (hon.), Harvard, 1842; m. Selina Cranch, July 18, 1819; m. 2d, Mary Roope Cranch, 1831; 6 children including William Cranch, George P. Independent discoverer Comet of 1811; did pioneer work on rates of chronometers, meteorology and magnetism, 1831-39; dir. Harvard Observatory, 1839-59, did intensive studies of planets, also Orion and Andromeda nebulae; constructed 1st sea-going chronometer made in Am.; discovered 8th satellite of Saturn, 1848; mem. Am. Acad. Arts and Scis., Am. Philos. Soc., Royal Astron. Soc. (Eng.). Died Cambridge, Mass., Jan. 29, 1859.

BONILLAS, YGNACIO, mining engr., diplomat; b. San Ygnaodo, Sonora, Mex., Feb. 1, 1858; s. Gervasio and Dolores (Fraijo) B.; S.B., Mass. Inst. Tech., 1884; m. Mary Borton, June 29, 1885. Mining insp., State of Sonora, 1911-13; sec. in first Carranza Cabinet, 1884-88, of Nogales, Mex., 1896-98; prefect of Magdalena Dist., 1890-92; mem. 23d Congress, State of Sonora, 1911-13; sec. in first Carranza Cabinet, 1913-17; A.E. and P. from Mexico to U.S. since Mar. 1917. Mem. commn. to settle difficulties arising from Villa's attack on Columbus, N.M., and Pershing Expdn., 1916-17. em. Am. Inst. Mining Engrs., Am. Acad. Polit. and Social Science, Alumni Assn. Mass. Inst. Tech. Mason. Address: Mexican Embassy, Washington. Died Jan. 31,1944.

BONNER, DAVID MAHLON, biologist, educator; b. Salt Lake City, May 15, 1916; s. Walter Daniel and Grace Amber (Gaylord) B.; B.A., U. Utah, 1936; Ph.D., Cal. Inst. Tech., 1940; m. Miriam Thatcher, Aug. 23, 1941; children—Matthew, Nicholas. Research asst. biology Cal. Inst. Tech., 1940-42; research asso. biology Stanford, 1942-46; research asso. microbiology Yale, 1946-56, prof. microbiology, 1956-60; professor biology U. Cal., LaJolla, 1960-. Recipient medal for achievement in biochemistry Eli Lilly, 1952. Fellow A.A.A.S., American Academy Arts and Sciences, Nat. Acad. Scis.; member Am. Chem. Soc., Genetics Soc. Am., Sigma Xi. Author: Heredity. Home: Arroyo Sorrento Rd., Del. Mar. Cal. Office: U. Cal., La Jolla, Cal. Died May 2, 1964.

BONNER, TOM WILKERSON, physicist; b. Greenville, Tex., Oct. 19, 1910; s. Medona and Bessie (Spears) B.; B.S., So. Meth. U., 1931; M.A., Rice Inst., 1932, Ph.D., 1934; NRC fellow Cal. Inst. Tech., 1934-36; Guggenheim fellow Cambridge U., Eng., 1938-39; m. Jarmila Prasilova, Sept. 7, 1937; children—Tom I., Susan P., Robert F. Asst. prof. Rice Inst., 1936-41, prof. physics, 1945—. chmn. dept., 1947—; asso. head airborne div. Radiation Lab., Mass. Inst. Tech., 1941-45; cons. Los Alamos Lab., 1946—. Vice chmn. council Oak Ridge Inst. Nuclear Studies, 1955-56, 58-59, dir., 1959—; mem. commn. on nuclear physics Internat. Union Pure and Applied Physics, 1960—; phys. adv. panel Nat. Sci. Found., 1959—; vis. com. Brookhaven Nat. Lab., 1959—; fellowship bd. NRC, 1947-54; mem. nuclear cross sects. adv. group to AEC, 1951—. Recipient Presdl. Certificate of Merit, 1946. Fellow Am. Phys. Soc., London, Dutch. Japanese phys. socs.; mem. Nat. Acad. Sci. Author publs. in field. Home: 1 Spring Hollow, Houston 77024. Died Dec. 6, 1961.

BONSER, THOMAS A., Spokane Museum curator; b. Dayton, O., Sept. 21, 1860; s. Thomas and Louisa (Guthbrod) B.; Ph.D., Otterbein Coll., Westerville, O., 1899; M.Sc., U. of Chicago, 1903; m. Edna Flory, 1886 (died 1904); m. 2d, Ethel F. Wilcox, June 15, 1906; children—Mildred Elizabeth, Donald Charles. Head of biol. dept., Spokane High Sch., 1903-07; head of scientific dept. Spokane Coll., 1907-12; head of biol. dept. N. Central High Sch., Spokane, 1912-33; curator Spokane Mus., 1918—; curator Mus. Eastern Washington State Hist. Soc.; cons. botanist Spokane Clin. Labo Mem. health and sanitation com. Spokane Chamber Commerce. Mem. Spokane Council Boy Scouts. republician. Conglist. Mason, Discoverer of cause of irregular tides on The Great Lakes, 1895. Author: Ecological Study of Big Spring Prairie, Ohio, 1903. Contbr. papers, repts. and articles on hay fever plants in the Northwest. Home: Spokane, Wash. Died Aug. 4, 1935.

BONWILL, WILLIAM GIBSON ARLINGTON, surgeon and dentist; b. Camden, Del., Oct. 4, 1833; ed. country school; worked, 1847-53, as carpenter, cabinet-maker and school teacher; studied dentistry (hon. degree Dental Coll., 1865, Jefferson Med. Coll., 1865); practiced dentistry, Dover, Del., 1854-71, then in Philadelphia; m. Abagail Elizabeth Warren, June 13, 1891. Invented first dental and surgical engine, 1869; first electrical mallet, 1869; merchanical mallet, 1878; the all-porcelain tooth- crown, 1879; first removable bridge, 1889; also numerous other dental appliances. Invented also first injector for boilers, 1856; first binder to a wheat reaper, 1856; the safety-pointed pin, 1863; the first machine to carve marble and rock by power, 1869, and many others. Author: Geometry and Mechanics Deny Evolution; also, 1888—, of 140 poems; many papers on dental and aural surgery in journals, etc. Home: Philadelphia, Pa. Died 1899.

BOOKWALTER, ALFRED GUITNER; b. Cedar Rapids, Iowa, Oct. 26, 1873; s. Lewis (LL.D.; retired clergyman) and Emma (Guitner) B.; A.B., Yale, 1897, A.M., 1901; m. Amy Mitchell Shuey, April 21, 1908; children—Alfred Shuey (dec.), Emily Guitner, Effie Mitchell (dec.), Edwina, Lewis. Master St. Paul's Sch., Concord, N.H., 1898-1903; in local, state and overseas service and on Nat. Council of Y.M.C.A.; instr. Yale Univ., 2 years; then pres. Willadena Nurseries, Inc., Sparta, Ky., and Berry Hill Nursery Co., Springfield, O. Rural rehabilitation work for U.S. Govt. at Washington, 1934-35; with cooperation of Ohio State U. and Antioch Coll. has conducted successful experiments on his Guernsey dairy farms in Ohio, in preserving green alfalfa as winter feed for dairy cattle, through packing with dry ice, in metal silos. Trustee Antioch Coll. Epsicopalian. Died Apr. 2, 1939.

BOORAEM, JOHN VAN VORST, engr.; b. Jersey City, lI.J., Oct. 30, 1838; s. Henry Augustus and Cornelia (Van Vorst) B.; studied mathematics and languages, Hamburg, Germany, 1854-56; M.E., Poly. Sch., Carlsrühe, Baden, 1859; m. Elizabeth Wreaks, Nov. 7, 1867. Followed general machinery and marine engring., 1860-72; designing building and running sugar refineries from 1872—; consulting engr. Am. Sugar Refining Co., 1882-98; retired; v.p. Am. Enamel Brick and Tile Co. Author of monograph, "Internal Energy," 1906. Home: Brooklyn, N.Y. Died 1923.

BOORAEM, ROBERT ELMER, mining engr.; b. Jersey City, N.J., Mar. 28, 1856; early edn., Germany and New York; E.M., Columbia School of Mines, 1878; unmarried. Mining engr. in practical field work in Colo. and Mont., 1879-91; cons. engr. for western mining cos., New York, 1891-1911; resumed mining work in Colo. and oil business in Calif., 1911. Gold mining in Arizona and Nev., 1915; working oil wells in Wyo., precious metal mining, Nev., 1917. Home: Denver, Colo. Died Sept. 21, 1918.

BOORD, CECIL ERNEST, research dir.; b. Veedersburg, Ind., June 29, 1884; s. Rev. John Summerbell and Rose Ann (Campbell) B.; grad. high sch., Veedersburg, 1904; B.A., Wabash Coll., 1907; M.A., Ohio State U., 1909, Ph.D., 1912; m. Augusta Corinne Brown, Aug. 20, 1913; 1dau., Mary Elizabeth (Mrs. Kenneth W. Greenlee). With Ohio State U. since 1907; successively fellow in chemistry till 1909, asst. in chemistry, 1909-12, instr., 1912-13, asst. prof., 1914-24, prof., 1924-51, research prof. of chemistry, 1951-54, emeritus, 1954, still in active service as dir. Air Research and Development Command project on oxidation of hydrocarbons. Mem. Nat. Research Council, 1924-26; mem., contbr. 3d World Petroleum Congress, The Hague, 1951. Dir. program of pure hydrocarbon research under the sponsorship Am. Petroleum Inst. and Ohio State U. Research Found. since 1938. Served as civilian dir. Ohio State U. Field Station, research div., Gas War Service, 1917-19. Recipient Joseph Sullivant Medal, Ohio State U., 1950-56. Dir. Ohio State U. Research Found., 1955-58. Fellow A.A.A.S., O. Acad. Sci.; mem. Am. Chem. Soc., Am. Petroleum Inst. (awarded Scroll 1954), N.Y. Acad. Sci., Am. Assn. Univ. Profs., Sigma Xi, Phi Lambda Epsilon, Gamma Alpha, Alpha Chi Sigma, Phi Beta Kappa. Republican. Presbyterian. Clubs: Faculty, Torch. Author: (with Wallace R. Brode and Roy G. Bossert) of Lab. Outlines for Organic Chemistry. Coinventor (with others) Chemistry of Petroleum Hydrocarbons, 1954; Knocking Characteristics of Pure Hydrocarbons, Mechanism of the Oxidation of Hydrocarbons, 1958. Coinventor (with Wallace R. Brode and Charles D. Hurd) of Molecular Models. Contbr. to chem. jours. and of chapters in Annual Survey of American Chemistry, Vols. VII, 1932; VIII, 1933, and in The Science of Petroleum, 1938. Home: Columbus OH Died Nov. 3, 1969; buried Union Cemetery, Columbus OH

BOOTH, HAROLD SIMMONS, chemist; b. Cleve., Jan. 30, 1891; s. Edwin and Lydia Ackley (Simmons) B.; A.B., Adelbert Coll., Western Res. U., 1915, A.M., 1916, Ph.D., Cornell U., 1919; m. Hazel Lavinia Anthnoy, Dec. 31, 1917; children—Robert (dec.), Marilyn Jane, Elizabeth Lydia. Comml. photographer, 1911-16; instr. chemistry Western Res. U., 1919-24, asst. prof., 1924-30, asso. prof., 1930-37, prof. 1937—; head of div. of sciences, 1926—, head of div. science and math., 1939—, chmn. summer session div. of chemistry, 1921-42. chmn. dept. chemistry, 1942—. Hurlbut prof. chemistry in univ., 1947. Civilian chemist Cornell Gas Def. Sta., 1917. Dir. Western Reserve sta. USN Research Lab., 1941-44. Fellow Am. Acad. Arts and Sciences; mem. Am. Chem. Soc. (council mem.; hon. chmn. conv. 1943), A.A.A.S., Electrochem. Soc., Phi Beta Kappa. Sigma Xi, Pi Kappa Alpha, Alpha Chi Sigma. Club: Cleveland. Author: (with V.R. Damerell) Text on Quantitative Analysis, 1940; (with Donald Ray Marin) Boron Triflourida and its Derivitives, 1949. Editor-in-chief, Inorganic Syntheses, Vol. 1; asso. editor, Vol. II, Vol. III. Contbr. profl. jours. Home: R.F.D. 3, Chagrin Falls, O. Office: 10940 Euclid Av., Cleve. Died June 23, 1950; buried Knollwood Cemetery, Mayfield Heights, O.

BOOTH, JAMES CURTIS, chemist; b. Phila., July 28, 1810; s George and Ann (Bolton) B.; A.B., U. Pa., 1829; LL.D. (hon.), Lewisburg U. (now Bucknell U.), 1867; Ph.D. (hon.), Rensselaer Poly. Inst., 1884; m. Margaret Cardoza, Nov. 17, 1853. Prof. chemistry Franklin Inst., 1836-45; melter and refiner Phila. Mint, 1849-88; prof. chemistry U. Pa., 1851-55; mem. 1st Geol. Survey of Pa.; state geologist Del. mem. Am. Philos. Soc., Acad. Natural Scis., Md. Inst. for Promotion Mechanic Arts, Phila. Soc. for Promotion of Agr., Hist. Soc. Pa.; pres. Am. Chem. Soc., 1883-85. Died Haverford, Pa., Mar. 21, 1888.

BOOTH, MARY ANN ALLARD, microscopist; b. Longmeadow, Mass., Sept. 8, 1843; d. Samuel Colton and Rhoda (Colton) B.; ed. Wilbraham (Mass.) Acad., and under pvt. teachers. Devoted many yrs. to research with the microscope; traveled widely in U.S., Can. and Alaska and lectured before many scientific socs.; made photomicrographs of germ-bearing fleas of rats, for stereopticon slides, during campaign against bubonic plague in San Francisco, 1907-09; has large pvt. collection of parasites and photomicrographs of same. Editor of Practical Microscopy, 1900-07. Medals and diplomas, New Orleans Expn., 1885, St. Louis Expn., 1904, San Francisco Expn., 1915. Conglist. Home: Springfield, Mass. Died Sept. 15, 1922.

BOOTH, RALPH DOUGLAS, cons. engr.; b. Methuen, Mass., Feb. 4, 1899; s. Harry Hodgson and Lucy (Bairstow) B.; S.B., Mass. Inst. Tech., 1920; m. Mary H. Armstrong, Oct. 18, 1930; 1 son, Ralph Douglas. With Jackson and Moreland, Boston, 1920—, gen. partner, 1930—; exec. v.p. Jackson & Moreland, Inc., 1956-59, president, 1959—. Fellow American Institute E.E.; mem. Am. Petroleum Inst., Am. Soc. M.E., Engring. Soc. N.E. Clubs: Engineers (Boston and N.Y.); Algonquin (Boston). Home: Salem Depot, N.H. Office: 31 St. James Av., Boston 02116. Died Nov. 21, 1960.

BOOTHBY, WALTER MEREDITH, medical research; b. Boston, Mass., July 28, 1880; s. Alonzo and Marie Adelaide (Stodder) B.; student Boston U. Sch. of Medicine, 1901-05; A.B., Harvard Coll., 1902; M.D., Harvard U. Med. Sch., 1906; M.A., Harvard Grad. Sch., 1907; m. Catharine Burns, Nov. 15, 1930; children (by previous marriage)—Gertrude (Mrs. Louis Schulze), Nancy (Mrs. Robert Reinhardt). Interne and house surgeon Boston City Hosp., 1908-09; practiced surgery in Boston, 1909-16; in charge metabolism and respiration labs., Peter Bent Brigham Hosp., 1913-16; instr. in anatomy, Harvard Med. Sch., 1910-16, also lecturer on anesthesia, 1914-16; head of sect. of metabolic research, Mayo Clinic, 1916—; asst. in medicine, Mayo Foundation, 1917-23, asso. prof. in medicine, 1923-26; prof. exptl. metabolism, 1936-48, emeritus professor, 1948—; chmn. Mayo Aero Med. Unit for Research in Aviation Med., 1942-48; guest prof. aviation medicine, Institute of Physiology, University of Lund, Sweden, 1948-50; advisor on research Sch. of Aviation Medicine, prof. physiology, Air U., Randolph Field, U.S. Air Force, Texas, 1950-51; Lovelace Found. for Med. research, 1951—, head of dept. of respiratory physiology. Served with A.R.C. Ambulance Hospital, Paris, summer 1915; capt., later major, Med. Corps, U.S. Army, with A.E.F. in France, 22 months; assigned as dir. 1st Corps Gas Sch., Chem. Warfare Service; later instr. Army Med. Sch., Lange, France; at front as chief of surgical team in battles of St. Mihiel and Argonne. President Roosevelt made personal award of Collier Trophy for 1938 to Dr. Walter M. Boothby, and Dr. William Randolph Lovelace II (both of Mayo Foundation), for med. edn. and research, and to Capt. Harry L. Armstrong, M.C., U.S. Army, for mutual contribution to aviation medicine in general and pilot fatigue in particular; certificate of merit, U. Minn., 1949; awarded order Comdr. of North Star by King of Sweden, 1952. Fellow A.C.S., A.C.P.; mem. A.M.A., Am. Physiol. Soc., Am. Soc. Biol. Chemists, American Soc. for Clin. Investigation, Soc. for Exptl. Biology and Medicine, Assn. Am. Physicians, Am. Inst. Nutrition, Am. Soc. for Exptl. Pathology, Am. Soc. for Pharmacology and Exptl. Therapy, Am. Soc. Anesthetists, Aero Med. Assn. of U.S., Inst. Aeronautical Sciences, Nat. Aeronautic Assn., Mass. Med. Soc., Alumni Assn. of Mayo Foundation, Minn. State Med. Assn., U.S. Inf. Assn., Sigma Xi. Democrat (liberal). Protestant. Author of 300 sci. papers on respiration, metabolism, thyroid diseases, aviation medicine. Home: 2819 Ridgecrest Dr. Office: Lovelace Found., Albuquerque, N.M. Died July 4, 1953.

BOOTHROYD, SAMUEL LATIMER, astronomer; b. Loveland, Colo., Aug. 10, 1874; s. Philip Henry and Edith Margaret (Latimer) B.; B.S., Colo. A.&M. Coll., 1893, M.Sc., 1904; U. of Colo., 1 semester, 1893-94, U. of Chicago, 1894-95, Cornell U., 1904-08; m. Alice Bell, Jan. 12, 1898; children—Philip Douglass, Robert Samuel, Lucy Elizabeth, Mary Alice. Prof. mathematics and astronomy, Mt. Morris (Ill.) Coll., 1895-97; asst. astronomer, Lowell Obs., Flagstaff, Ariz., 1897-99; asso. prof. physics, engring., Colo. A.&M. Coll., Ft. Collins, 1902-04; instr. civil engring., Cornell U., 1904-08, asst. prof. topographic and geodetic engring., 1908-12; asso. prof. mathematics and astronomy, U. of Wash., 1912-17, asso. prof. astronomy, 1917-21; prof. astronomy and geodesy, Cornell U., 1921-42, prof. emeritus, June 30, 1942; teacher navigation, Naval

Training Sta., Cornell U., Nov. 1942-Sept. 1945. In charge field work, Ariz. Meteor. Expdn., Harvard, Cornell, Lowell Obs., Flagstaff, 1931-32. Asst. surveyor Alaskan Boundary Commn., summers 1905-09; teacher of navigation, Naval Training Sta., U. of Wash., during World War I. Fellow A.A.A.S.; The Meteoritical Society; life member of Astronomical Soc. Pacific, Am. Astronomical Soc., Am. Assn. Variable Star Observers, Sigma Xi, Phi Kappa Phi. Conglist. Co-author: Manual of Astronomy. Contributor to publications of Dominion Astrophys. Obs., Victoria, B.C. Head of expdn. to secure ultra-violet spectra of stars at Mountain Station of Lowell Obs., 1933, using aluminum coated mirrors first made at Cornell U. Selected by Alumni of Colo. A. and M. Coll. as honor alumnus for 1946. Home: Warley Place RD 1, Ithaca NY

BOOTT, KIRK, mfr.; b. Boston, Oct. 20, 1790; s. Kirk and Mary (Love) B.; attended Harvard; m. Ann Haden, circa 1813. Went to Eng., served under Duke of Wellington in Peninsular War, commanded a force at siege of San Sebastian; returned to Boston, 1817; agt. Merrimack Mfg. Co., 1821; Pawtucket Canal enlarged under his direction; began machine-shop, manufactured 1st locomotives in Am.; built a village where his employees lived (became Lowell, Mass., 1826). Died Lowell, Apr. 11, 1837.

BORDEN, GAIL, surveyor, inventor; b. Norwich, N.Y., Nov. 9, 1801; s. Gail and Philadelphia (Wheeler) B.; m. Penelope Mercer, 1828; m. 2d, Mrs. A. F. Stearns; m. 3d, Mrs. Emeline Eunice (Eno) Church, 1860; several children. Moved with family to Covington, Ky., 1815, to Ind. Territory, 1816; sch. tchr. Ind. Ty., 1820-22; moved to Amite County, Miss., 1822; county surveyor, U.S. dep. surveyor Amite County, 1822-circa 1829; moved to Tex., circa 1829; supt. ofcl. surveys of Tex. colonies; del. San Felipe (Tex.) Conv., 1833; made 1st topog. map and planned layout of Galveston, Tex.; land agt. Galveston City Corp., 1839-51; became interested in concentrated foods, invented "meat biscuit" exhibited at London Fair, 1851; developed a form of condensed milk, Lebanon, N.Y., patented 1861; moved to Borden, Tex., after Civil War; continued research into concentration of foods, patented process of concentrated juices and fruit, 1862. Died Tex., Jan. 11, 1874.

BORGLUM, GUTZON (JOHN BUTZON DE LA MOTHE BORGLUM), sculptor, painter, author; b. Idaho, Mar. 25, 1871; s. Dr. James de La Mothe and Ida (Micheison) de la Mothe B.; ed. in pub. schs. of Fremont and Omaha, Neb.; studied art in San Francisco; went to Paris in 1890, studying in Julian Acad. and Ecole des Beaux Arts; awarded hon. M.A. by Princeton University, and LL.D. by Oglethorpe U.; Dr. of Letters, Dakota Wesleyan U., 1939; aerodynamic engr.; m. Mary Montgomery, 1909; children—James Lincoln, Mary-Ellis. Exhibited as painter and sculptor in Paris Salon and made associate Salon, 1891. Spent year in Spain; in Calif., 1893-94; returned to Europe and located in London and Paris until 1901, then settled in New York; held successful exhibitions abroad. Gold Medallist La. Purchase Expn. Sculptor St. John's Cathedral; produced Sheridan Equestrian, Washington, D.C.; Sheridan Equestrian, Sheridan Road, Chicago; colossal marble head of Lincoln in rotunda. Capitol Bldg., Washington; large bronze group. Mares of Diomedes, Metropolitan Museum; Ruskin (bronze); statue of Lincoln, Newark, N.J.; Trudeau memorial. Saranac Lake; Trail Drivers memorial, Tex.; statues-Mackay, Beecher, Altgeld, Vance, Huntington, Aycock, Alexander H. Stephens,John C. Greenway; O'Connell memorial, University of Virginia; Hoard memorial, Madison, Wis.; Wheeler memorial fountain, Bridgeport, Conn.; Bryan (Wm. Jennings) memorial, Washington, D.C.; Floulke memorial, Rock Creek Cemetery, Washington, D.C.; marbles-Wonderment of Motherhood, Modern Atlas (a woman), Conception, Martyr, The Centaurs; colossal monument 42 figures in bronze, Wars of America, Newark, N.J.; North Carolina memorial, battlefield of Gettysburg; memorial to Woodrow Wilson, Posnan, Poland; Northwest Territory memorial at Marietta, Ohio; Thomas Paine memorial. Paris, France; designed and began carving Confederate memorial on face of Stone Mountain, Ga., but a controversy arose with the Stone Mountain Memorial Assn., and all plans and models and work were destroyed; author and designer Confederate half dollar, struck in honor of the Confederate soldiers by nat. govt.; designer and sculptor of first nat. memorial federally authorized, on Mount Rushmore in Black Hills, S.D., dedicated and officially begun by President Coolidge, Aug. 10, 1927-money appropriated by Congress and commn. apptd. by President in 1929; head of Washington unveiled, 1930. Jefferson unveiled by President Roosevelt in 1936, Lincoln in 1937, Theodore Roosevelt in 1939, work still in progress. Non-Partisan leader in politics, identified with the agrarian revolt in the Northwest; investigated for President Wilson and exposed the colossal aircraft failure. Progressive Republican. Mason. Decorated Order of Knights of Dannebrog (Denmark), 1931; Order of "Reconstructed Poland," 1931. Home: Stamford, Conn. Died Mar. 6, 1941.

BORHEGYI, STEPHAN FRANCIS DE, educator, museum dir.; b. Budapest, Hungary, Oct. 17, 1921; s. Francis E. and Hildegard (Geiger) de Borhegyi; Doctor of Philosophy summa cum laude from the Royal Peter Pazmany U., Budapest, 1946; postdoctoral fellow U. Ariz., 1948-49, Yale, 1951-52; m. Suzanne Catherine Sims, July 5, 1949; children—Ilona-Maria, Stephan E., Carl, Christopher. Came to U.S., 1948, naturalized, 1955. Instr. class. archaeology Peter Pazmany U., 1946-47, asst. prof., asst. curator mus., 1947-48; asso. prof. anthropology San Carlos U., Guatemala, 1949-51; asst. prof. anthropology U. Mo., 1952; asst. prof. anthropology, mus. dir. U. Okla., 1954-59; dir. Milwaukee Pub. Mus., 1959-69; prof. dept. anthropology U. Wis. at Milw., 1959-69. Served as 1st lt. Mounted Arty., Royal Hungarian Army, 1941-44. Recipient diploma of merit for reorgn. Guatemalan Mus. (Rep. of Guatemala), 1951. Fellow Royal Anthrop. Assn. Gt. Britain and Ireland, Am. Anthrop. Assn., Soc. Am. Archaeology, Sociedad de Geographia de Guatemala; mem. Mountain Plains Museums Assn. (past pres.), Am. Assn. Museums (councilor), Central States Anthrop. Soc. (pres.), Midwest Museums Assn. (v.p.), Internat. Council Museums (U.S. del. to com. on ethnography museums, sec. U.S. nat. com. on ethnographical research and museums). Home: Milwaukee WI Died Sept. 27, 1969; cremated.

BORING, EDWIN GARRIGUES, psychologist; b. Phila., Pa., Oct. 23, 1886; s. Edwin McCurdy and Elizabeth Garrigues (Truman) B.; M.E., Cornell, 1908, A.M., 1912, Ph.D., 1914; hon. A.M., Harvard, 1942; Sc.D., University of Pa., 1946; D.Sc., Clark University, 1956; married Lucy May Day, June 18, 1914; children—Edwin Garrigues, Frank Henry, Mollie Day, Barbara (dec. 1950). Asst. psychol., 1911-13, instructor, 1913-18, Cornell; psychological examiner, rank of capt., Camp Upton, N.Y., 1918; in Surgeon General's Office, Washington, 1918-19; prof. exptl. psychology and dir. Psychol. Lab., Clark U., 1919-22; asso. prof. psychology Harvard, 1922-28 prof., 1928-56, Lowell TV lectr., 1956-57, Edgar Pierce professor 1956-57, emeritus, 1957-68. Phi Beta Kappa visiting scholar, 1958-59, director of the psychology laboratory, 1924-49. Hon. pres. XVII Internat. Congress of Psychology, 1963. Fellow A.A.A.S., Soc. Exptl. Psychologists, Am. Acad. Arts and Scis.; mem. Nat. Acad. Scis., Am. Psychol. Assn. (sec. 1920-22; council 1920-25; pres. 1928), Am. Philos. Soc., Brit. Psychol. Soc. (hon.), Soc. Franc de Psychol. (hon.), Society Espanol. de Psichol. (hon.), Soc. Ital. di Psicol. Scient. (hon.). Author: A History of Experimental Psychology, 1929, 2d edit., 1950; The Physical Dimensions of Consciousness, 1933; Sensation and Perception in the History of Experimental Psychology, 1942; Psychologist at large, 1961; History, Psychology and Science, 1963; (with R.J. Herrnstein) Source Book in the History of Psychology, 1965. Coeditor: Psychology: A Factual Textbook, 1935; Introduction to Psychology, 1939; Psychology for the Fighting Man, 1943; Psychology for the Armed Services, 1945; Foundations of Psychology, 1948. Editor: Contemporary Psychology, 1956-61; asso. editor Basic Books, 1961-68. Contbr. numerous articles to psychol. jours. Home: Cambridge MA Died July 1, 1968.

BORN, MAX, physicist; b. Breslau, Germany (now Poland), Dec. 11, 1882; s. Gustav and Margaret (Kauffmann) B.; student Breslau, Heidelberg, Zurich univs.; Ph.D., Goettingen U., 1907; D.Sc. (hon.), Bristol U., Eng., 1928; M.A., Cambridge U., Eng., 1933; D.Sc. (hon.), Bordeaux U., 1948, Oxford U., 1954; Dr. rer. nat., Freiburg U., 1957, Berlin U., Frankfurt U.; LL.D., Edinburgh U., 1957: Dr. Ing. (hon.), Stuttgart Tech. U., 1960; D.Sc. (hon.), Oslo U., 1961, Brussels University, 1961; Dr. rer. nat. (honorary), Frankfurt University, 1964; m. Hedwig Ehrenberg, August 2, 1913; children—Irene (Mrs. NewtonJohn), Margaret (Mrs. Pryce), Gustav V.R. Privat-docent, Goettingen U., 1909, prof., 1921; guest lectr. U. Chgo., 1912; prof. U. Berlin, 1915, Frankfurt University, 1919, Goettingen, 1921; guest lecturer at Massachusetts Inst. Tech., 1925; Stokes lectr. Cambridge U., Eng., 1933; guest prof. Indian Inst. Science, Bangalore, 1935-36; prof. natural philosophy, Edinburgh, Scotland, 1936-53, emeritus, 1953-70. Decorated Stokes medal, Cambridge, 1934; Macdougall-Brisbane and Gunning-Victoria Jubilee prize, Royal Soc. Edinburgh, 1945, 1950; Max Planck medaille, Germany, 1948; Hughes medal Royal Soc. London, 1950; Freedom City of Goettingen, 1953; Nobel prize, 1954; Grotius Medal, Munich, 1956. Fellow Royal Society of Edinburgh, Royal Society of London: mem. acads. Berlin, Goettingen, Copenhagen, Stockholm, Moscow, Dublin, Am. Acad. Arts and Scis., Nat. Acad. Sci. Author many books and articles, mostly on theoretical physics. Home: Bad Pyrmont Germany Died Jan. 5, 1970; buried Gottingen Germany

BOSCH, HERBERT MICHAEL, engineer; b. Jefferson City, Mo., Mar. 31, 1907; s. Herman and Katherine (Buehrle) B.; B.S. U. Mo., 1929; Master Pub. Health Sch. Pub. Health Johns Hopkins U., 1940; m. Jeanette E. Heinrich, Aug. 17, 1931. Tech. and administrative staff Mo. State Bd. Health, 1929-35, Minn. Dept. Health, 1935-41, 46-50; chief environmental sanitation sect. WHO, U.N., Geneva, Switzerland, 1950-52. mem. panel experts on environmental sanitation, 1952—; prof. environmental health School of Public Health, U. Minn. Mem. Minnesota Bd. Health, 1952—, v.p., 1954—. Mem. Mo. State Planning Bd., 1933-35; mem. com. on san. engring. and environment Nat. Research Council. Cons. san. engring. Surgeon Gen. Dept. Army, 1947—, WHO (govts. Jugoslavia, Finland) 1952, ECA (Brizil), 1954, ICA (Brazil), 1955-56, WHO (Eastern Mediterranean Region), 1956; cons. USPHS, ICA, WHO (Japan) 1957, Pan Am. Health Orgn., 1959; mem. Commn. Environmental San., Armed Forces Epidemiological Bd.; mem. com. on civil def. NRC, 1954-62; mem. Nat. Adv. Health Council, 1961—; mem. USPHS Environmental Health Study Team to USSR, 1962. Served as 1st lt. to col. San. and Gen. Staff Corps, U.S. Army, 1941-46. Decorated Bronze Star Medal with oak leaf cluster, Legion of Merit (U.S.); Legion of Honor, Croix de Guerre with Palm (France); Commander Order Orange-Nassau (Holland); Croix de Guerre with Palm (Belgium); recipeint medal for distinguished service in engring. U. Mo. Fellow Royal Sanitary Institute, London (hon.), Am. Pub. Health Association (governing council 1949, 57—); mem. Am. Soc. C.E., National, Minn. socs. profl. engrs., A.A.A.S., Am. Water Works Assn., Am. Assn. U. Profs., Central States Sewage and Indsl. Waste Assn., Minn. Acad. Sci., Nat. Research Council (exec. com. Div. Med. Scis. 1960-61), New York Academy of Sciences, also Sigma Xi, Tau Beta Pi, Delta Omega. Club: Campus (Mpls.). Home: 315 11th Av. S.E., Mpls. 55414. Office: care Sch. Pub. Health, U. Minn., Mpls. 55414. Died Sept. 16, 1962; buried Nat. Cemetery, Jefferson City, Mo.

BOSS, BENJAMIN, astronomer; b. Albany, N.Y., Jan. 9, 1880; s. Lewis and Helen M. (Hutchinson) B.; A.B., Harvard, 1901; m. Marguerite M. Guy, Aug. 30, 1906 (died 1919); children—Marguerite, Elizabeth; m. 2d, Helga S. Nordstrom, Aug. 7, 1923; 1 dau., (Helga) Lucinda. Asst. Dudley Obs. Albany, N.Y., 1901-05, U.S. Naval Obs., Washington, 1905-06; dir. U.S. Naval Obs., Tutuila, Samoa, 1906-08; mem. expdn. to observe solar eclipse at Flint Island, 1908; sect. Dept. Meridian Astrometry, Carnegie Instn., Washington, 1908-12, acting dir., 1912-15; acting dir., Dudley Obs., 1912-15; dir. Dept. Meridian Astronomy, Carnegie Instn., Washington, 1915-39; dir. Dudley Obs., 1915-56. Editor Astron. Jour. 1912-41. Mem. Am. Astron. Soc., A.A.A.S. Club: University. Specialized in determination of star positions and motions. Pub. General Catolog of 33342 Stars, 1937. Address: Albany NY Died Oct. 18, 1970.

BOSS, LEWIS, astronomer; b. Providence, R.I., Oct. 26, 1846; s. Samuel P. and Lucinda (Joslin) B.; A.B., Darmouth Coll., 1870; (LL.D., Union Univ., 1902); m. Helen M. Hutchinson, Dec. 30, 1871. Civilian asst. U.S. Northern Boundary Commn., 1872-76; dir. Dudley Obs., 1876—, and prof. astronomy, Union U. Mem. govt. expdn. to observe total eclipse in Colo., 1878; chief govt. expdn. to observe transit of Cenus, Santiago, Chili, 1882; state supt. weights and measurers, N.Y., 1883-1906; editor and mgr. Albany Express, 1885; dir. Dept. of Meridian Astronomy, Carnegie Instn., Washington, 1906; editor of Astron. Journal, 1909. Gold medal, Royal Astron. Soc., London, 1905; Lalande prize, Acad. Sciences, Paris, 1911. Mem. Nat. Acad. Sciences. Author: Declinations of Fixed Stars, 1878; Catalogue of 8,241 Stars, Leipzig, 1890 (Astronomische Gesellschaft). Monographs: The Solar Motion, and related papers, 1888; Prize Essay on the Physical Nature of Comets, 1881; Division Correction of the Olcott Meridian Circle, 1896; 179 Southern Stars, 1898; Solar Motion and Related Researches, 1901; Positions and Motions of 627 Standard Stars, 1903; Preliminary General Catalogue of 6,1888 Stars, 1910; Catalogue of 1,059 Standard Stars, 1910, etc. Home: Albany, N.Y. Died Oct. 5, 1912.

BOSS, WILLIAM, agrl. engr.; b. Zumbro Falls, Minn., Oct. 7, 1869, s. Andrew and Janet (Nisbet) B.; student U. Minn., 1890-92; D.Sc., Macalester Coll., 1956; Jamestown Coll., 1956; m. Edna Florence Rider, Oct. 2, 1895; children—Ronald William, Harlan David. Worked as carpenter and builder, 1887-90; instr. Sch. Agr., U. Minn., 1982-1906, prof. farm structures and farm mechanics, 1906-10, prof. agrl. engring. and chief of dept., 1919-38, emeritus, 1938—; founder, pres. Speciality Mfg. Co., St. Paul, chief counselor Boss Engring. Co., cons. devel. engrs., 1929—; pres. Boss Foundry, Bayport, Minn., established, 1944. Recipient outstanding achievement award U. Minn., 1958. Registered profl. engr., Minn. Fellow A.A.A.S.; charter mem., fellow Am. Soc. Agrl. Engrs. (John Deere medal 1943, past pres.); mem. Soc. Promotion Engring. Edn., Am. Assn. Univ. Profs., Engrs. Soc. St. Paul, Nat. Minn. socs. profl. engrs., Alpha Zeta Gamma Sigma Delta. Republican. Presbyterian. Clubs: Association, St. Paul, Midway. Author: Instructions for Traction and Stationary Engineers, 1906; The Heath Book for Threshermen, 1907; (with J. G. Dent and H. B. White) Mechanical Training, 1932. Home: 1439 Raymond Av., St. Paul 8. Office: 2356 University Av., St. Paul 4. Deceased.

BOST, RALPH WALTON, chemist; b. Rockwell, N.C., Jan. 5, 1901; s. James Walton and Mary Lee (Miller) B.; A.B., Newberry (S.C.) Coll., 1923; A.M., U. of N.C., 1924, Ph.D., 1928; m. Beulah Christine Cauble, July 12, 1927. Asst. in chemistry, U. of N.C., 1923-24; instr. chemistry, Tulane U. (La.), 1924-26; with U. of N.C. since 1926, instr. chemistry, 1926-28, asst. prof., 1928-34, asso. prof., 1934-37, prof. since 1937, head of chemistry dept. since 1939, also acting dean Sch. of Applied Science, 1933-35. Member American

Chemical Society, Chemical Society of London, Elisha Mitchell Scientific Soc., Am. Physical Society, North Carolina Academy of Science, Pi Kappa Delta, Sigma Xi, Kappa Psi, Alpha Chi Sigma. Pres. Chapel Hill (N.C.) Rotary Club, 1935-36. Author: Bibliography of Organic Sulfur Compounds, 1930. Home: 500 E. Rosemary St. Office: Venable Hall, Chapel Hill, N.C. Died Sept. 22, 1951; buried Chapel Hill Cemetery.

BOUTON, CHARLES LEONARD, mathematician; b. St. Louis, Apr. 25, 1869; s. William and Mary R. (Conklin) B.; M.Sc., Washington, U., 1891; A.M., Harvard, 1896; Ph.D., Leipzig, 1898; m. Mary G. Spencer, June 15, 1907. Instr. Smith Acad., St. Louis, 1891-94, Washington U., 1893-94; instr. mathematics, 1898-1904, asst. and asso. prof. 1904—, Harvard. An editor Bulletin of Am. Math. Soc., 1900-02; asso. editor Transactions Am. Math. Soc., 1902-11. Mem. Am. Math. Soc., Deutsche Mathematiker Vereinigung, Berliner Math. Gesellschaft, Circolo Matematico di Palermo; fellow Am. Acad. Arts and Sciences, A.A.A.S. Home: Cambridge, Mass. Died Feb. 20, 1922.

BOUTWELL, JOHN M(ASON), engr.; b. St. Louis, May 1, 1874; s. Henry Thatcher and Helen Grace (Willis) B.; A.B., Harvard, 1897, B.S., 1898, M.S., 1899; m. Esther G. Miner, Jan. 22, 1910; m. 2d Ruth Crellin, Sept. 28, 1922; 1 dau., Jean Miner (Mrs. Joseph B. Paul). Tchr. dept. ecology Harvard, 1896-1900; geologist U.S. Geol. Survey, 1898-1908; cons. mining geologist, examiner econ. possibilities of mines in U.S., Mexico and S.A., since 1908; cons. Metals Res. Co. (R.F.C.), 1942-44. Mem. nat. council Boy Scouts Am. Emeritus fellow Geol. Soc. Am., A.A.A.S.; mem. Soc. Econ. Geologists (pres. 1944, counsellor, mem. com. on Penrose medal), Am. Inst. Mining and Metall. Engrs. (dir. 1937-43), Mining and Metall. Soc. Am. (counsellor), Wash. Geol. Soc., Wash. Acad. Sci., S.A.R., Soc. Mayflower Descendants (founder Utah soc., gov. 1948-53). Clubs: Harvard (N.Y.C. and Boston); Alta (Salt Lake City). Author reports. Address: 105 E.S. Temple St., Salt Lake City 1

BOUTWELL, PAUL WINSLOW, educator; b. Lyndeborough, N.H., Feb. 6, 1888; s. Benjamin Jones and Louise Elizabeth (Knight) B.; B.S., Beloit Coll., 1910; A.M., U. Wis., 1912, Ph.D., 1916; m. Clara Gertrude Brinkhoff, June 12, 1915; children—Roswell Knight, Clara Barnes (Mrs. Leslie Paul Bunker, Jr.) Paul Winslow. Tchr. high sch., Mankato, Minn. 1910-11; instr. State Tchrs. Coll., summers 1911-15 instr. U. Del., 1916-17; asst. chemistry U. Wis. 1912-16, instr. agrl. chemistry, 1917-18, asst. prof. 1918-20; asso. prof. Beloit (Wis.) Coll., 1920-21, prof., head dept. chemistry from 1921, faculty athletic rep., 1923-52; research, prodn. div. synthetic chemistry Eastman Kodak Co., 1928. Fellow A.A.A.S.; mem. Am. Chem. Soc., Wis. Acad. Scis., Arts and Letters (v.p. 1936-39, pres. 1939-42), Am. Assn. U. Profs., Phi Beta Kappa, Sigma Xi, Gamma Alpha, Delta Sigma Rho, Omicron Delta Kappa, Sigma Chi. Republican. Conglist. Contbr. chem. jours. Home: Beloit WI Died Feb. 22, 1971.

BOUTWELL, WILLIAM ROWE, b. Surry Co., Va., Nov. 25, 1860; s. William Rowe and Sarah (Crittenden) B.; pub. sch. edn.; m. Mary Elizabeth Cocke, of Surry Co., June 26, 1889. Began as pilot, 1882; inventor of Boutwell gyro propeller. Chmn. Harbor Improvement Com. of Norfolk and Portsmouth, Va., 1907—, Harbor Improvement Com., Norfolk and Newport News, 1909—. Pres. Va. Pilot Assn. since 1904; mem. Bd. Pilot Commrs. of Va.; mem. exec. com. Am. Pilot Assn. Democrat. 32 deg. Mason. Clubs: Virginia (Norfolk), Westmoreland, Business Men's (Richmond), New York Press, Nat. Press (Washington). Home: Albemarle Ct. Office: Board of Trade Bldg. Norfolk, Va.

BOVIE, WILLIAM T., teacher, inventor; b. Augusta, Mich., Sept. 11, 1882; s. William and Henrietta (Barnes) B.; A.B., Mich., 1908; A.M., U. of Mo., 1910; Ph.D., Harvard, 1914; Sc.D. (hon.) Albion Coll., 1929; m. Martha Adams, Sept. 15, 1909; 1 son, William Adams. Prof. geology and biology, Antioch Coll., 1906-07; research fellow, Cancer Comm., Harvard U., 1914-20; instr. bacteriol., Harvard U., 1920-21, asst. prof. biophysics, 1920-27; prof. biophysics, Northwestern U., 1927-29; lecturer, social technology, Colby Coll., 1939-48. Awarded John Scott Medal, Franklin Inst., 1928. Mem. Botanical Soc., Physiol. Soc., Physical Soc., Soc. for Cancer Research, Soc. Tropical Medicine, Am. Acad. Arts and Sciences, Am. Chem. Soc. (chmn. biol. sect. 1919-23). Developed pioneer methods for therapeutic use of radio active substances; perfected electric apparatus for bloodless surgery and for prevention of metastasis of cancer cells; inventor various biophysical instruments. Address: 22 Summit St., Fairfield, Me. Died Jan. 1, 1958; buried Maplewood Cemetery, Fairfield, Me.

BOVING, ADAM GIEDE, entomologist; b. Saby, Denmark, July 31, 1869; s. Niels Orten Mathias and Otilia Louise Augusta (Giede) B.; A.B., U. of Copenhagen, 1889, M.S., 1894, Ph.D., 1906; m. Anna Kirstine Christensen, of Copenhagen, Jan. 31, 1916; 1 son, Bent Giede. Came to U.S., 1913, naturalized citizen, 1918. Asst. curator entomol. div. Zool. Mus., Copenhagen, 1902-13; zoologist, govt. expdn. to Iceland, 1908; entomologist, U.S. Bur. Entomology, Washington, D.C., 1913-39; sr. entomologist; retired July 31, 1939. Fellow Entomol. Soc. Am.; mem. A.A.A.S., Entomol. Soc. Washington (pres. 1923-24), Biol. Soc. Washington, Washington Acad. Science (v.p. 1924-30); honorary member Copenhagen Entomol. Society; corr. member "Vanamo," Finnish Zool.-Bot. Soc. Decorated Golden Cross Knights of Dannebrog. Author: Donaciinlarvernes Naturhistorie, 1906; Larvae of Coleoptera (with F. C. Craighead), 1931. Contbr. on entomol. subjects. Home: 221 Rock Creek Church Rd., Washington DC

BOWDEN, ABERDEEN ORLANDO, educator, anthropologist; b. Fulton, Ky., Dec. 13, 1881; s. Isaiah and Malenda Agnes (Emerson) B.; A.B., State U. of Ky., 1908, A.M., 1910; A.M., Harvard, 1912; studied U. of Chicago, 1 yr.; Ph.D., Columbia U., 1929; m. Katharine Kennan Marsh, Aug. 21, 1913; children—Gordon Townely, Anne Emerson. Prin. high sch., Maysville, 1908-09, Henry County High Sch., Paris, Tenn., 1909-11, high sch., Laurel, Mont., 1913-14, Hurson, S.D., 1914-18, Huron Jr.-Sr. High Sch., 1918-20; supt. city schs., Huron, 1920; head of dept. and prof. edn. and philosophy, Baylor Coll., Belton, Tex., 1920-22; pres. N.M. State Teachers' Coll., 1922-34; head of dept. of anthropology, U. of Southern Calif., and dir. Calif. branch of Sch. of Am. Research, since Sept. 1934; adviser Veterans Rehabilitation, Sawtelle, Calif.; dir. Jemez Field Sch. of Archeology, summer 1935; field work in anthropology in S.A., 1 semester. Was pres. N.M. Ednl. Council; mem. board of control, Sch. of Am. Research; mem. Nat. Illiteracy Commn., Geographical Board of N.M. Fellow A.A.A.S., American Geographical Board of N.M. Fellow A.A.A.S., American Geographic Society; mem. American Men of Science, N.E.A. (com. on tenure), Save Our Schools Com. (nat.), Am. Acad. of Polit. and Social Science, Am. Sociol. Soc., Am. Anthropol. Assn., Nat. Economic Council, Nat. Soc. for Study of Ednl. Sociology, N.M. Endl. Assn. (pres. 1928-29), School Master's Club of N.M. (pres. 1932-33), Phi Beta Kappa, Phi Delta Kappa, Kappa Delta Pi, Phi Sigma Pi, Pi Gamma Mu, Mu Alpha Nu, Sigma Xi; del. of N.E.A. to World Federation of Edn. Assns., Geneva, Switzerland, 1929; pres. N.M. Science Commn., 1931-32; pres. N.M. Assn. for Science, 1930-31; pres. N.M. Coll., Presidents' Assn.; pres. Southwestern Archeol. Soc., 1937-38. Baptist. Mason. Rotarian (Gov. 42d dist. 1932-33). Author: Consumers' Uses of Arithmetic, 1929; Tomorrow's Americans (with Ida Clyde Clarke), 1930; Social Psychology of Education, 1937; Man and Civilization, 1938; The American Scene, 1942; Preface to Human Nature; The Day Before Yesterday in America. Compiler of Bibliographies in Education Sociology (with others), 1928. Chmn. N.M. Elementary Course of Study, 1930. Contbr. to sicentific and ednl. press. Winner various awards for scholarship. Home: 4815 Angeles Vista Blvd., Los Angeles 43, Calif. Died Feb. 10, 1946.

BOWDEN, GARFIELD ARTHUR, chem. research; b. Dec. 19, 1880; s. John and Agnes (Lukey) B.; grad. Normal Sch., Platteville, Wis., 1901; B.S., U. of Chicago, 1913; grad. work, U. of Chicago and University of Cincinnati; m. Lucy E. Bell, September 10, 1902 (deceased June 9, 1942); children—Paul Webster, Isabel Agnes. Principal of the State Graded Sch., Revere, Minn., 1901-02, high sch., Pepin, Wis., 1902-06; in charge sicence and math. depts., high sch., Winona, Minn., 1906-08; head of science dept. Twp. High Sch., Waukegan, Ill., 1908-11, asst. prin., 1915-17; asst. prof. methods of science teaching, Teachers Coll., Normal (Ill.) U., 1917-18; head of science dept. University Sch., Cincinnati, 1918-37; head of chem. research and ednl. depts. A. S. Boyle & Co., Inc., Cincinnati, O., and Jersey City, N.J., and for Am. Home Products, Jersey City, N.J.; asst. prof. methods of science teaching, N.C. State Teachers Coll., Raleigh summers 1924-27. Fellow of Royal Soc. of Arts (London); mem. Acad. Polit. Science, A.A.A.S., Central Assn. Science Teachers, Am. Chem. Soc., Schoolmasters Club (Cincinnati), Cincinnati Astron. Soc., Cincinnati City Beautiful Assn., Torch Club, Phi Delta Kappa. Presbyterian. Author: Gen. Science, 1923; Foundations of Science, 1931. Home: 139 N. Arlington Av., East Orange, N.J. Office: 1934 Dana Av., Cincinnati, O.; and 257 Cornelison Av., Jersey City, N.J. Deceased.

BOWDITCH, HENRY INGERSOLL, physician; b. Salem, Mass., Aug. 9, 1808; s. Nathaniel and Mary (Ingersoll) B.; attended Boston Latin Sch., 1823-25; grad. Harvard, 1828, M.D., 1832; studied medicine, Paris, France, 1832-34; m. Olivia Yardley, 1838. Mem. Staff Mass. Gen. Hosp., Boston, 1831-32, 38-92; practiced medicine, Boston, from 1834; abolitionist leader from 1830's, friend of William L. Garrison; active in case of runaway slave George Latimer, 1842-43; became expert on diseases of chest, especially tuberculosis; pioneer in performing operations for pleural effusions with suction pump; prof. Harvard Med. Sch., 1859-67; an original mem. Mass. Bd. Health, 1869-79; noted for work in fields preventive medicine and public sanitation; fellow Am. Acad. Arts and Scis. Author: The Young Stethoscope, 1846; Public Hygiene in America, 1877. Died Boston, Jan. 14, 1892.

BOWDITCH, HENRY PICKERING, physiologist; b. Boston, Apr. 4, 1840; s. Jonathan Ingersoll and Lucy Orne (Nichols) B.; brother of Charles Pickering B.; A.B., Harvard, 1861, A.M., 1866, M.D., 1868; (D.Sc., Cambridge, Eng., 1898; LL.D., Edinburgh, 1898, Toronto, 1903, U. of Pa., 1904); lt., capt. and maj. U.S. Vol. Cav., 1861-65; studied physiology in France and Germany, 1868-71; m. Selma Knauth, of Leipzig, Sept. 9, 1871. Asst. prof., 1871-75, prof. physiology, 1876-1903, George Higginson prof. physiology, 1903-06, dean Med. Sch., 1883-93, Harvard. Trustee Boston Pub. Library, 1895-1902. Fellow Am. Acad. Arts and Sciences, A.A.A.S. (v.p., 1886, 1900); mem. Nat. Acad. Sciences. Author: Growth of Children, 1877; Hints for Teachers of Physiology, 1889; Is Havard a University?, 1894; Advancement of Medicine by Research, 1896. Home: Jamaica Pain, Mass. Died 1911.

BOWDITCH, NATHANIEL, astronomer, mathematician, ins. exec.; b. Salem, Mass., Mar. 26, 1773; s. Habbakkuk and Mary (Ingersoll) B.; A.M. (hon.), Harvard, 1802; m. Mary Boardman, Mar. 25, 1798; m. 2d, Mary Ingersoll (cousin), Oct. 28, 1800; 8 children including Jonathan Ingersoll, Henry Ingersoll. Prepared 1st Am. edit. The Practical Navigator (J.H. Moore), 1799, revised and enlarged under title The New American Practical Navigator, 1802, 9 edit. published during his lifetime, 56 reprints or edits. published since his death; portions of the work reprinted under title Bowditch's Useful Tables, 1844; his skill in mathematics led to positions Mass. Hosp. Life Ins. Co., 1823-38; made survey of Salem harbors, 1804-06; published 23 papers on nautical and astron. subjects in Memoirs of Am. Acad. of Arts and Scis., 1804-20; published translation with commentary of 1st 4 vols. of Mechanique Celeste (LaPlace) (most important sci. work); best known papers include one concerning meteor which exploded over Weston, Conn., 1807, another discussing the motion of a pendulum; mem. Am. Acad. Arts and Scis., 1799, pres., 1829-38. Died Boston Mar. 17, 1838; buried Mt. Auburn Cemetery, Cambridge, Mass.

BOWEN, ABEL, engraver; b. Greenbush, N.Y., Dec. 3, 1790; s. Abel and Delia (Mason) B.; m. Eliza Healy, 10 children. Moved to Boston, 1811, became printer and wood engraver; published many volumes illustrated with copperplates and woodcuts during 1820's and 1830's; an organizer Boston Bewick Co., (profl. group Boston wood engravers), circa 1833, instrumental in planning engravings in Am. Mag. of Useful and Entertaining Arts, published in Boston, 1834-circa 1838; influenced work of engravers including George Loring Brown, Hammat Billins; executed engravings and woodcuts for History of Boston (by Caleb Snow), 1825; Picture of Boston, 1828; The Young Ladies Book, 1830. Died Boston, Mar. 11, 1850; buried Boston.

BOWEN, EARL, biologist; b. Attica, Ark., Feb. 23, 1899; s. Thomas A. and Alice (Neal) B.; A.B., Hendrix Coll., 1919; student U. N.C., 1925; A.M., Harvard, 1929, Ph.D., 1931; m. Kathleen D. Lilliston, Apr. 15, 1921. Tchr., prin. high schs., Ark. and Fla., 1919-27; Jeffries Wymann scholar Harvard, 1927-28; Austin teaching fellow Harvard and Radcliffe Coll., 1928-30, asst. zoology, 1930-31; asst. prof. biology L.I. U., 1931-39; research asso. Am. Museum Natural History, 1936-40; Charles H. Graff professor biology, head department Gettysburg Coll., 1939—, on leave of absence 1958-60; sci. specialist ICA, U.S. OVerseas Mission. Afghanistan, 1958-60; biological research various laboratories; visiting professor. Member corp. Bermuda Biol. Station for Research.fServed as pvt. U.S. Army, 1918. Fellow, life mem. N.Y. Acad. Scis.; mem. A.A.A.S., Am. Soc. Ichthyologists and Herpetolagists, Am. Assn. U. Profs., Pa. Acad. Sci., Am. Soc. Zoologists, Sigma Xi. Contbr. articles profl. jours. Home: 34 E. Lincoln Av., Gettysburg, Pa. 17325. Died Feb. 3, 1965; buried Evergreen Cemetery, Gettysburg, Pa.

BOWEN, HAROLD GARDINER, naval officer, ring traveler mfg. exec.; b. Providence, Nov. 6, 1883; B.S., U.S. Naval Acad., 1905; M.A., Columbia, 1914; Sc.D., Brown U. 1947; m. Margaret Edith Brownlie, Sept. 27, 1911; 1 son, Harold Gardiner. Commd. ensign USN, 1907, advanced through grades to capt., 1927, rear adm., 1935, vice adm., 1946; apptd. asst. chief Bur. Engring., 1931, engr. in chief of navy, 1935, dir. Naval Research Lab., also tech. aide to sec. navy, 1939-42, spl. asst. to under-sec. navy and sec. navy, 1942-47, dir. Office Patents and Inventions, 1945, chief Office Research and Inventions, May 1947; exec. dir. Thomas Alva Edison Found., Inc., 1948-55; pres. U.S. Ring Traveler Co., 1955—. Mem. research adv. bd. Franklin Inst., 1946. Decorated D.S.M., nine letters of commendation from sec. navy; recipient Newcomen medal Franklin Inst., 1944. Hon. mem. Am. Soc. M.E. Author: The Edison Effect; (with Charles F. Kettering) Short History of Technology. Home: 65 Arlington Av., Providence 6. Office: U. S. Ring Traveler Co., 159 Aborn St., Providence 3. Died Aug. 1, 1965; buried Arlington Nat. Cemetery.

BOWEN, IRA SPRAGUE, astronomer; b. Senece Falls, N.Y., Dec. 21, 1898; s. James Henry and Philinda May (Sprague) B.; A.B., Oberlin Coll., 1919, D.Sc., 1948; postgrad. U. Chgo., 1919-21; Ph.D., Cal. Inst. Tech., 1926; Ph.D., U. Lund, 1950; Sc.D., Princeton, 1953; m. Mary Jane Howard, July 12, 1929. Asst. in physics U. Chgo., 1919-21; instr. physics Cal. Inst. Tech., 1921-26, asst. prof., 1926-28, asso. prof.,

1928-31, prof. 1931-45; dir. Mount Wilson Obs., 1946-64, Palomar Obs., 1948-64, Distinguished Service staff mem., 1964-69. Morrison research asso. Lick Obs., 1938-39. S.A.T.C., 1918. Recipient Potts medal Franklin Inst., 1946; Ives medal Optical Soc. Am., 1952. Mem. Nat. Acad. Sci. (Draper medal 1942), Am. Philos. Soc., Am. Acad. Arts and Scis. (Rumford Premium 1949), Am. Astron. Soc. Astron. Soc. Pacific (asso., Bruce medal 1957), Royal Astron. Soc. (Gold medal 1966). Contbr. articles to sci. jours. Home: Altadena CA Died Feb. 6, 1973.

BOWEN, NORMAN LEVI, geologist; b. Kingston, Ont., Can., June 21, 1887; s. William Alfred and Elizabeth (McCormick) B.; A.M., Queen's U., 1907, B.S., 1909, LL.D., 1941; Ph.D., Mass. Inst. Tech., 1912; hon. Sc.D., Harvard Tercent; m. Mary Lamont (M.D.), Oct. 3, 1911; 1 dau., Mrs. Jerold Orne. Came to U.S. 1909. Field investigator, Ont. Bur. Mines, 1907-09, Geol. Survey of Can., 1910-11; petrologist, Carnegie Instn., Washington, D.C., 1912-18, and 1920-37; Charles L. Hutchinson distinguished service prof. of petrology U. of Chicago, 1937-47, chmn. dept. geology, 1945-47; prof. mineralogy Queen's U., 1919-20; petrologist Carnegie Instn., Wash., 1947—. Supervisor optical glass production, War Industries Board, World War I. Member Geological Society American (v.p. 1938-45, pres. 1946), Mineral Society Am. (pres. 1937), Mineral Soc. London, Am. Geophysical Union, Am. Acad. Arts and Sciences, Washington Acad. Sciences, Am. Philos. Soc., Nat. Acad. Sciences, Indian Acad. Sciences (hon.), Kaiserlich deutsch Akademie der Naturforscher (Halle), Soc. Geol. Belgique, Finnish Acad. Sciences, All-Russian Mineral Soc. Bigsby medalist Geol. Soc. of London, Eng., 1941, Penrose medalist Geol. Soc. of America, 1941. Miller medalist Royal Soc. of Canada, 1943. Clubs: Cosmos (Washington, D.C.); Kingston Yacht. Author: The Evolution of the Igneous Rocks, 1928. Contbr. to Jour. of Geology, Am. Jour. Science, Jour. Physical Chemistry, Bull. Geol. Soc. America, Am. Mineralogist. Jour. Am. Ceramic Soc., Zeitschrift fur anoganische Chemie, etc. Joint discover of Mullite, the fundamental constituent of fire clay refractories. Prin. petrologist (consultant) U.S. Bur. of Mines, 1942; coordinator research and official investigator for N.D.R.C. contract, Geophysical Lab., 1943. Mem. bd. Natural Resources and Conservation, State of Illinois, 1944-47. Address: 3801 Connecticut Av., Washington 8. Died Sept. 11, 1956.

BOWEN, REUBEN DEAN, planter; b. Montgomery Co., Tex., Dec. 18, 1859; s. William Abraham and Clementine Dalmatia (Richards) B.; ed. St. Mary's Coll., Galveston, Tex.; Agrl. and Mech. Coll. of Tex., 1877-78; m. Bonnybel, d. Capt. Sam J. Wright, of Paris, Tex., May 15, 1890. Bookkeeper, Galveston and New Orleans; traveling salesman for G. R. Finlay, wholesale drugist, New Orleans, 1879-84; became connected with E. J. Hart & Co., New Orleans, 1884, advancing to partnership and gen. mgr., closed out shoesale bus., returned to Texas, 1895; active in promoting investments in Southwest and owner and mgr. of large farming interests in Tex.; pres. Kiomatia Planters' Co., Red River Co., Tex. Originator of movement to popularize use of cotton in U.S. and for many mfg. purposes; chmn. of com. of Farmers' Union on Greater Consumption of Cotton; largely instrumental in securing competition form other states in bidding for cotton-seed in Tex.; also in application of business methods to the farm; engaged largely in stock raising. Apptd. by gov. of Tex. as chmn. com. to receive delegation from Chicago on its visit to Tex., 1902, out of which originated Miss. Valley Assn., of which he was an organizer, and elected as dir. representing agriculture; del. from Tex. in orng. Am. Farm Bur. Fedn. in Chicago, 1919; one of organizers Farmers-Mfrs. Assn. Movement launched 1924; mem. permanent exec. com. Nat. Flood Control of Miss. River, mem. Farmers Union, Tex. Farm Bur., Tex. Hist. Soc., Southern Sociol. Assn., Improved Order of Red Men. Home: Paris, Texas. Died 1939.

BOWERS, ALPHONZO BENJAMIN, inventor and civ., mech., hydraulic engr.; b. W. Baldwin, Me., Sept. 25, 1830; s. Wilder and Sarah Hay (Thompson) B.; desc. from George B., Scituate, Mass., 1637, and through mother from James T., Charleston, Mass., 1630, and Dr. William Hay, Reading, Mass., about 1717; ed. Bridgton Acad., Maine Wesleyan Sem., Bridgewater State Normal Sch., Phillips Acad., Andover, Mass., and by pvt. study. Built 1st dam at 16; went to Calif., 1853; engaged in mining, teaching, writing and lecturing; invented, 1853, method of cheap transportation of earth by stream of water on down grade in open flume for building of dams and embankments; flexibly connected floating pipes, and method of building levees from old style dredges; hydraulic dredging, transportation, filling, and hydraulic dredge, with rotary excavator. Studied law, became his own atty. and obtained over 400 claims, engaging in more than 60 suits against infringers of his patents, costing over $250,000. Del. Rep. State convs., 1861, 1863; offered nomination surveyor gen. (declined); chief clerk office surveyor gen., 1863, deputy surveyor gen., 1864; in charge of sales of state lands, 1863-67. Mem. Internat. Congress of Commerce and Navigation, Brussels, 1898, and entertained by Leopold II; mem. Permanent Internat. Assn. of Navigation Congresses; del. from Calif. to Am. Civic Alliance, New York, 1909. Died Jan. 24, 1926.

BOWERS, WILLIAM GRAY, coll. prof.; b. nr. Franklin, W.Va., June 16, 1879; s. Josephus and Emily (Bond) B.; B.Sc., Ohio Wesleyan U., 1905; A.M., Ind. U., 1911; spl. student U. of Calif., 1915; Ph.D., Ohio State U., 1919; m. Ollie Quitera Smith, 1901; children—Emily Margaret, John Edward. Began teaching at 16; taught in pub. sch. of W.Va., 5 yrs.; asst. in Zoölogy, Ohio Wesleyan U., 1904; prin. ward sch., Urbana, O., 1905; prin. high sch., Aspen, Colo., 1906; supt. schs., Leesburg, O., 1907; science teacher summer, Ind. Normal Sch., Muncie, Ind., 1907; phys. science teacher, State Normal and Indsl. Sch., Ellendale, N.D., 1908-18; v.p. same, 1914, 16; prof. food chemistry, and head of lab. of State Food Commn., Agrl. Coll., N.D., 1918-20; head of chem. dept. Colo. State Teachers Coll. 1920. Mem. Am. Chem. Soc., Colo. Ednl. Assn., N.E.A., Colo. Science Club. Republican. Methodist. Wrote: The Nutrition Value of the Soy Bean; Laboratory Instruction in Elementary Chemistry; also articles on food adulteration, on methods in teaching of chemistry, etc. Commencement speaker and institute instr. Home: 1117 19th St., Greeley, Colo. Died May 29, 1945.

BOWIE, EDWARD HALL, meteorologist; b. Annapolis Junction, Md., Mar. 29, 1874; s. Thomas John and Susanna Hall (Anderson) B.; M.S., St. John's Coll., Annapolis, Md., 1920; m. Florence C. Hatch, Dec. 12, 1895; children—Mrs. Helen McKinstry Prentiss, Mrs. Margaret Lowndes Wallace, Mrs. Susanna Anderson Lindquist. Entered service U.S. Weather Bur., Dec. 1891; asst. observer at Memphis, 1891-95, Montgomery , Ala., 1896-98; observer, Dubuque, Ia., 1898-1901; section dir., Galveston, Tex., 1901-03; local Weather Bur., 1910-12, nat. forecaster, 1909-24, prin. meterologist and dist. forecaster, Pacific States, since 1924. Commd. maj. Signal Corps, July 9, 1917, and ordered to France for meterol. forecasts for A.E.F.; resigned and returned to Weather Bur., Dec. 1918. Geophys. Union. Fellow Am. Meterol. Soc., Calif. Acad. Sciences; mem. Philos. Soc. Washington, Washington Acad. Sciences. Mason. Clubs: Faculty (Berkeley, Calif.); Family (San Francisco, Calif.). Home: 844 Contra Costa Av., Berkeley, Calif. Office: U.S. Weather Bur., San Francisco, Calif. Died July 29, 1943.

BOWIE, WILLIAM, engr., geodesist; b. Annapolis Junction, Md., May 6, 1872; s. Thomas John and Susanna A(nderson) B.; St. John's Coll., Annapolis, Md.; B.Sc., Trinity Coll., Conn., 1893; C.E., Lehigh U., Pa., 1895, Sc.D., 1922; M.A., Trinity, 1907, Sc.D., 1919; LL.D., Univ. of Edinburgh (Scotland), 1936; Sc.D., George Washington Univ. 1937; m. Elizabeth Taylor Wattles, June 28, 1899; children—William Bladen (dec.), Clagett. Mem. field force, U.S. Coast and Geod. Surveys, 1895-1937, retired; engaged in field on coast or geod. surveys in many states of U.S. in P.R., P.I., and Alaska, 1895-1909; in charge Div. of Geodesy, 1909-36; commd. hydrographic and geodetic engr., 1917. Maj. engrs. U.S.A. Aug. 1918-Feb. 1919. In charge summer course in practicial astronomy and geodesy, Columbia U., 1912-17. Del. from U.S. to number internat. scientific confs. Pres. Internat. Geod. Assn., 1919-33; pres. Internat. Geod. and Geophys. Union, 1933-36; chmn. bd. Surveys and Maps of Federal Govt.; 1922-24. Special lecturer at Lehigh, 1922-36. Author of a number of publs. of the Coast and Geodetic Survey on the various branches of geodesy, including measurement of base lines, triangulation, gravity, isostasy, etc.; also geodetic and engrings. articles in scientific and engring. mags. Author of book "Isostasy,"1927. Awarded Cresson medal, Franklin Inst., 1937, Officer Order of Orange-Nassau, Holland; comdr. Order St. Sava, Yugoslavia. Home: Washington, D.C. Deceased.

BOWLER, EDMOND WESLEY, educator; b. Dedham, Mass., Jan. 15, 1892; s. Edmond Henry and Catherine Ellen (McAvoy) B.; S.B. in San. Engring., Mass. Inst. Tech., 1914. Asst., Mass. Inst. Tech., 1914-15, research asst., 1916-17, instr. hydrographic survey Civil Engring. Camp, summers 1926, 29; topographer U.S. Geol. Survey, 1915-16; research engr. for def. Boston Molasses Tank Collapse Lawsuits, 1919-20; asst. prof. math. U. N.H., 1920-27, asst. prof. civil engring., 1927-28, asso. prof., acting dept. head, 1928-31, prof. civil engring., 1931-61, emeritus, 1961—, head dept., 1931-58. Served from 2d to 1st lt. C.E., U.S. Army, 1917-19. Commnr. N.H. Fish and Game Commn., 1935-43; N.H. rep. U.S. Coast and Geodetic Survey, 1933-36. Mem. Am. Soc. C.E., Am. Acad. San Engrs., Nat., N.H. socs. profl. engrs., Am. Soc. Engring. Edn., Am. Pub. Health Assn., Soc. Am. Mil. Engrs., N.E. Sewage Works Assn., Phi Kappa Phi. Roman Catholic. Home: 12 Woodman Av., Durham, N.H. 03824. Died Oct. 28, 1963; buried Brookdale Cemetery, Dedham.

BOWLES, OLIVER, mining engr., geologist; b. nr. Lindsay, Ont., Can., Jan. 10, 1877; s. William Henry and Sarah A. (Glaspell) B.; prep. edn. Lindsay Collegiate Inst., Can., 1901-03; B.A., U. Toronto, Can., 1907, M.A., 1908; grad. work U. Mich., U. Minn.; Ph.D., George Washington U., 1922; m. Eva H. Workman, 1908; children—William George, Edgar Oliver. Came to U.S., 1908, naturalized, 1914. Field work, Bureau of Mines, Ont., summers, 1908-10; tchr. geology and mineralogy U. Mich., 1908-09, U. Minn., 1909-14; with State Geol. Survey, Minn., summers, 1911-13; temporary geologist U.S. Geol. Survey, parts of 1912-14; quarry technologist, U.S. Bureau of Mines, 1914-17, mineral technologist, 1917-23; supervising engr. nonmetallic minerals expt. sta., New Brunswick, N.J., 1923-28, supervising engr. building materials sect., 1928-37, asst. chief nonmetal economics div., 1937-42, chief, 1942-47, retired, 1947; parttime research prof. U. Md., 1948—. Received gold medal from Dept. of Interior for distinguished service in Bureau of Mines; Hardinge award, Am. Inst. Mining and Metall. Engrs. Mem. Am. Inst. Mining and Metall. Engrs., Mineral Soc. Am., Soc. Econ. Geologists, N.Y. Acad. Science, Sigma Xi; hon. mem. Inst. Quarrying of Great Britain. Republican. Christian Scientist. Club: Cosmos (Washington). Author: The Stone Industries; also numerous bulletins, reports and articles in tech. press on stone, slate, lime, cement, asbestos, etc. Address: 500 Masssachusetts Av., Washington 16. Died Aug. 1, 1958.

BOWMAN, HARRY LAKE, cons.; b. Philadelphia, Pa., May 17, 1889; s. Harry and Emma Louise (Lake) B.; B.S. in Civil Engring., Pennsylvania State Univ., 1911; S.M., Mass. Inst. Tech., 1914; Eng.D., Drexel Institute of Technology, 1957; m. Florence Foster, Sept. 18, 1915; children—Claire Elvira (Mrs. Hamilton W. Wells), Margaret Emma (Mrs. Bruce S. Hawley), Edward Harry. Began career as draftsman with American Bridge Co., Pencoyd, Pa., 1911-15; prin. asst. to C.E. Smith, cons. engr., St. Louis, Mo., 1915-18; asst. engr., Philadelphia & Reading R.R., Philadelphia, Pa., 1918-19; cons. engr. since 1920; instr. structural engring., Mass. Inst. Tech., Cambridge, Mass., later asst. prof., asso. prof., 1919-26; prof. civil engring. and head dept., Drexel Inst. Tech., Phila., 1926-53, dean engrineering, 1953-58, dean faculty, 1953-58, dean faculty, 1953-51, academic consultant, 1961—; cons. AEC, 1948—. Dir. physicial damage div. U.S. Strategic Bombing Survey. Member Am. Soc. C.E., Am. Concrete Inst., Am. Soc. for Engineering Edn., Alpha Tau Omega, Theta Tau, Phi Kappa Phi, Sigma Xi. Author: (with H. Sutherland) Structural Design, 1938; (with H. Sutherland) Structural Theory, 4th edit., 1950. Home: 7117 Wolftree Lane, Rockville, Md. 20852. Office: Drexel Inst. Tech., Phila. 19104. Died May 24, 1965.

BOWMAN, HOWARD H(IESTAND) M(INNICH), ednl. admn.; b. Lancaster, Pa., Nov. 3, 1886; s. Andrew Minnich and Kate Howard (Hiestand) B.; desc. of John Bowman, pioneer Swiss settler in Lancaster County, Pa., 1712, B.Ph., Franklin and Marshall Coll., Lancaster, 1913, M.Sc., 1914; Ph.D., U. of Pa., 1917; m. Edna Katherine Lockwood, July 28, 1928 (deceased 1960). Began career as instructor Franklin and Marshall College, 1913-14, Pa. Sch. of Horticulture, Ambler, 1915; asst. U. of Pa., 1916-17; prof. Heidelberg Coll., Tiffin, O., 1917-18; at U.S. Army Md. Sch., Washington, D.C., 1918-1919; prof. biology Toledo U., 1919-57, head dept. biology and pre-medical div. emeritus, 1957; dir. med. edn. Toledo Hosp., 1957-63. Insp. Ohio Bureau of Plant Industry, 1945-48. Mem. executive committee Toledo Pub. Health Council. Vice chmn. Mich. Acad. Science, 1935, mem. council, 1935-36. Fellow Assn. Am. Genealogists, Am. Geneal. Soc., Am. Assn. for Advancement Science, Ohio Acad. Sci. (v.p. 1924; chmn. finance com. 1940, pres. 1946-47); mem. Am. Assn. Univ. Prop. (pres. Toledo Chapter, 1947), Am. Genetic Assn., Am. Bot. Soc., Am. Physiol. Soc., Field Nature Soc., Mich. Acad. Science, American Heart Association (sec. bd. dirs. N.W. Ohio chpt.), Ohio Heart Assn. (pres. 1953-54), Sons of the American Revolution, Sigma Xi, Kappa Psi, Pi Kappa Alpha, Phi Kappa Phi; hon. mem. Toledo Acad. Medicine. Republican. Episcopalian. Mason. Club: Torch. Wrote: Botanical Ecology of the Dry Tortugas, 1918; A Manual of Botany, 1930; Work Book for General Biology, 1939; Ecology and Physiology of the Red Mangrove for Proc. American Philos. Soc., 1917; Brochure on Internship at Toledo Hospital. Contbr. to tech. journs.; author of papers on Eastern Pa. history and genealogy. Collaborator editorial bd. Biol. Abstracts, 1925-45. Home: Toledo OH Deceased.

BOWMAN, ISAIAH, univ. pres.; b. Waterloo, Ont., Can., Dec. 26, 1878; s. Samuel Cressman and Emily (Shantz) B.; grad. State Normal Coll., Ypsilanti, Mich., 1902; B.Sc., Harvard, 1905; Ph.D., Yale, 1909; hon. M.A., 1921; hon. M.Ed., Mich. State Coll., 1972; hon. Sc.D., Bowdoin Coll., 1931, Universities of Cuzco and Arequipa, Peru, 1941; Oxford Univ., 1918; LL.D., Dartmouth, Charleston, Dickinson and U. of Pa., 1935, U. of Wis. and Harvard, 1936, Queen's U. and U. of Western Ontario 1937, Washington Coll., 1940, Johns Hopkins, 1949; hon. Litt.D., Marietta College, 1947; m. Cora Olive Goldthwait, June 28, 1909; children—Walter Parker, Robert Goldthwait, Olive. Asst. physiography Harvard 1904-05; instr. geography State Normal Coll., Ypsilanti, 1903-04; instr. geography Yale, 1905-09, asst. prof., 1909-15; dir. Am. Geography Soc., 1915-35; pres. Johns Hopkins, 1935-48, pres. emeritus, 1949. Leader first Yale South Am. Expdn., 1907; geographer and geologist Yale Peruvian Expdn., 1911; leader expdn. to Central Andes under auspices Am. Geography Soc., 1913. Chmn. Nat. Research Council, 1933-35, vice chmn. Sci. Adv. Bd., 1933-35.

Chief territorial specialist Am. Commn. to Negotiate Peace, 1918-19; mem. various territorial commns. of the Peace Conf., Paris, 1919; physiographer U.S. Dept. Justice in Red River boundary dispute; Am. mem. Permanent Internat. Commn., China and U.S., since 1940; mem. London Mission of Dept. of State, 1944; chmn. territorial com. Dept. of State, 1942-43; vice-chmn. post-war adv. council Dept. of State, 1943-44; special adviser to Sec. of State, 1943-45; mem. American del. Dumbarton Oaks Conf., 1944; adviser to U.S. del. U.N. Conf., San Francisco, 1945; mem. Comm. on the Organization of the Exec. Branch of the Govt., 1948 (Hoover Commn.); mem. Pub. Adv. Com. on the China Program since 1948; cons. colonial development div. E.C.A., since 1949. Mem. bd. dirs. Am. Telephone & Telegraph Co., Council on Fgn. Relations, Woods Hole Oceanographic Inst., Am. Geog. Soc. of N.Y. (councilor, 1935); pres. Internat. Geog. Union, 1931-34. Fellow Am. Acad. Arts and Sciences; mem. Am. Philos. Soc. (council 1935), Assn. American Geographers (pres. 1931), Nat. Acad. Sciences (v.p., 1941-45), A.A.A.S. (pres. 1943), Phi Beta Kappa; mem. bd. overseers Harvard Coll. since 1948; asso. mem. Nat. Acad. Sciences, Peru, hon. corr. mem. Geog. Society La Paz, Bolivia, Hispanic Soc. Am., Royal Geog. Soc., London, Swedish Soc. Anthropology and Geography (former mem., 1939), geog. socs. of Phila., Berlin, Finland, Jugoslavia, Rome, Columbia, etc., corr. mem. Soc. Chilena de Hist. y Geog.; recipient Livingstone gold medal Royal Scottish Geog. Soc., 1928; Bonaparte-Wyse Gold Medal of Geog. Soc. of Paris, 1917, for explorations in the publs. on S. America; Gold Medal Geog. Soc., Chicago, 1927; Cvijic Medal Geog. Soc. of Belgrade, 1935; Henry Grier Bryant Gold Medal Geog. Soc. of Phila., 1937; Patron's Medal Royal Geog. Soc. (London), 1941; Delgado Medal of the Geogr. Soc. of Lima, 1949; Explorers Club Medal award postumously, 1950. Clubs: Explorers (ex-sec. and ex-v.p.), Century (New York); Cosmos (Washington). Author: Fores Physiography, 1911; South America, 1915; The Andes of Southern Peru, 1916; The New World—Problems in Political Geography, 1921; Desert Trails of Atacama, 1928; An American Boundary Dispute, 1923; The Mohammedan World, 1924; International Relations, 1930; The Pioneer Fringe, 1931; Geography in Relation to the Social Sciences, 1934; Design for Scholarship, 1936; Graduate School in American Democracy, 1939. Co-editor and part author of Human Geography; editor and collaborator for Limits of Land Settlement, 1937. Home: The Warrington Apts., Baltimore 18. Office: The Johns Hopkins University, Baltimore 18, Md. Died Jan. 6, 1950.

BOWMAN, KARL MURDOCK, physician; b. Topeka, Nov. 4, 1888; s. Homer Caleb and Isabelle Susanna (Murdock) B.; A.B., Washburn Coll., 1909, D.Sc., 1953; M.D., U. Cal. at Berkeley, 1913, LL.D., also Dr. J. Elliott Royer award, 1964; m. Eliza Abbott Stearns, Aug. 18, 1916 (dec. 1957); children—Richard Stearns, Thomas Elliot, Murdock Stearns, Walter Murdock; m. 2d, Anna Lowrey, July 18, 1959. Intern Children's Hosp., Los Angeles, 1913, Seton Hosp., N.Y.C., 1914, Roosevelt Hosp., N.Y.C., 1915, Bloomingdale Hosp., White Plains, N.Y., 1915-17, 19-21; chief med. officer Boston Psychopathic Hosp., 1921-36; asst. prof. psychiatry Harvard Med. Sch., 1921-36; dir. div. psychiatry Bellevue Hosp., N.Y.C., 1936-41; prof. psychiatry N.Y.U. Coll. Medicine, 1936-41; prof. psychiatry U. Cal. Sch. Medicine, San Francisco, 1941-56, prof. emeritus, 1956-73, med. supt. Langley Porter Clinic, San Francisco, 1941-56; vis. prof. U. Philippines Coll. Medicine, 1954-55; dir. div. mental health for Alaska, also supt. Alaska Psychiat. Inst., Anchorage, 1964-67. Sent to China by WHO to assist govt. China in setting up Nat. Psychiat. Inst., Nanking, 1947; cons. USPHS, Office Surgeon Gen., U.S. Army, U.S. Navy, USAF, VA; mem. com. neuropsychiatry NRC, 1944-47; dir. Cal. Sexual Deviation Research, 1950-54; mem. nat. health adv. com. USPHS, 1948-50; mem. profl. adv. com. Office Vocational Rehab., 1944-50; trustee Nat. Com. Mental Hygiene, 1944-47; mem. adv. bd. psychiatry A.R.C., 1938-50. Served as capt., M.C., U.S. Army, World War I; lt. comdr. USNR, 1935-52; ret., 1952. Diplomate in psychiatry Am. Bd. Psychiatry and Neurology (dir. 1943-46, 50-51). Fellow Am. Psychiat. Assn. (life fellow, pres. 1944-46), Physician Philippines (hon.), Am. Coll. Psychiatrists; hon. life mem. Philippine Mental Health Assn.; mem. Cal., San Francisco med. socs., N.Y., Mass. psychiat. socs., A.A.A.S., Boston Soc. Psychiatry and Neurology (sec.-treas. 1933-36), New Eng. Soc. Psychiatry, Assn. Research Nervous and Mental Disease (1st v.p. 1938, 41), Sigma Xi, Phi Delta Theta, Alpha Omega Alpha. Author: Personal Problems for Men and Women, 1931; also numerous articles. Asso. editor Geriatrics, Quar. Jour. Studies on Alcohol, 1942-73. Address: San Francisco CA Died Mar. 2, 1973.

BOWN, RALPH, physicist, cons. engineer; b. Fairport, N.Y., Feb. 22, 1891; s. Gardner W. and Bertha (Bruner) B.; Cornell U., M.E., 1913, M.M.E., 1915, Ph.D., 1917; m. Alma Crawford, June 28, 1919; children—Ralph, Crawford. Instr. in physics, Cornell U., 1913-17; with Am. Telephone & Telegraph Co., dept. of development and research, engaged in development of radio broadcasting and transoceanic comml. radiotelephony, 1919-34; dir. radio research, Bell Telephone Labs., N.Y.C. 1934-45, dir. TV research, 1938-46, dir. research 1946-51, v.p. research, 1951-54, v.p., 1954-56, ret.; cons. N.W. Ayer & Son, Inc., from 1956. Served at lt. later capt., Signal Corps, U.S. Army, 1917-19. Mem. Radar Division, Nat. Defense Research Com.; member Nat. Television Systems Com., 1940-41; expert consultant to secretary of war, 1941. Awarded Morris Liebmann Memorial prize by Institute of Radio Engineers, 1926, Medal of Honor, 1949, Founder's award, 1961. Fellow Am. Phys. Soc., Inst. Radio Engrs. (v.p. 1925; pres. 1926; dir.), Acoustical Soc. Am., Am. Inst. Elec. Engrs., A.A.A.S.; mem. Sigma Xi, Eta Kappa Nu, Gamma Alpha. Author of several technical papers; patentee. Address: Millburn NJ Died July 29, 1971; buried Old Brick Church, Bradevelt NJ

BOWNOCKER, JOHN ADAMS, geologist; b. nr. St. Paul, O., Mar. 11, 1865; s. Michael and Eliza (Adams) B.; B.Sc., Ohio State U., 1889, D.Sc., 1897; fellow U. of Chicago, 1892-94; grad. scholar, Yale, 1894-95; m. Anna K. Flint, June 12, 1911. Prin. high sch., Martins Ferry, O., 1898-99, asso. prof. inorganic geology, 1899-1901, prof., 1901-17, prof. geology, 1917—, curator of mus., 1899-1917, Ohio State U. Asst. geologist, 1900-06, State geologist of Ohio, 1906—. Fellow Geological Soc. America. Republican. Author of various reports of Geol. Survey of Ohio and numerous papers on geol. subjects. Home: Columbus, O. Died Oct. 20, 1928.

BOYAJIAN, SETRAK KRIKOR, chemist; b. Harpute, Armenia, Turkey, Nov. 9, 1889; s. Krikor Heroian and Kohar (Samueian) B.; student Euphrates Coll. (Harpute), 1904-06; U. Wis., 1910-13; M.A., Clark U., 1914; research student Boston U., 1923-26, Harvard, 1924-33. Came to U.S., 1906, naturalized, 1915. Proprietor, research dir. Precision Testing Labs., Worcester, Mass., 1920-70. Cons. chemist, 1920-70. Served as 1st lt. Ordnance Res. Corp., 1917. Mem. Am. Chem. Soc., A.A.A.S. Club: Harvard (Worcester, Mass.). Patentee in field. Home: Hudson MA Died Jan. 19, 1970; buried Woodlawn Cemetery, Wellesley MA

BOYD, D. KNICKERBACKER, architect, structural standardist; b. Phila., Jan. 5, 1872; s. David, Jr., and Alida Visscher (Knickerbacker) B.; ed. Friends' Central Sch., Rugby Acad., Phila., Pa. Acad. Fine Arts, Spring Garden Inst., Phila., and U. of Pa.; m. Elizabeth Hörnli Mifflin, Sept. 10, 1896; children—Barbara Mifflin (Mrs. Lawrence C. C. Murdoch), Lysbeth Knickerbacker (Mrs. Henry P. Borie). Practiced Phila. since 1892; designer Carnegie Library Bldg., Phila., chs., factories, apartment bldgs., schs. and suburban homes. Lecturer and writer on constrn. economics, archtl. adviser Structural Service Bur.; consultant on bldg. codes, zoning, production and applciation of bldg. materials and on informational publications. During World War, chief material infomration sec., U.S. Housing Corp., U.S. Dept. of Labor and rep. on War Industries Board. Editor Structural Service Book, Jour. A.I.A. Mem. correlating com. on legislation and adminstration of President's Conf. on Home Building and Home Ownership. Fellow Am. Inst. Architects (ex-sec., ex-v.p.); mem. coms. on buklding regulations and on pub. information and civilian defense of Phila. chapter A.I.A.; ex-pres. Pa. State Assn. A.I.A., Phila. chapter A.I.A.; ex-pres. Phila. Building Congress; v.p. Am. Constrn. Council (coms. on apprenticeship and better building); mem. Phila. com. Better Home in America; mem. exec. com. Zoning Fed. of Phila.; mem. Archtl. League of New York, Am. Federation of Arts (ex-dir.), N.E.A., Phila. Housing Assn., Regional Plan of Phila. (advisory com.), Com. to Revise Building Code of Philadelphia, Civil Legion, War Industries Bd. Assn., S.R. (chmn. com. on protection of historic bldgs.), Independence Hall Association (exec. sec.), Netherlands Society, Society of Cincinnati of Pennsylvania; honorary member N. Texas Chapter, A.I.A. Pa.; state archtl. advisor Home Owners Loan Cor.; adminstrative asst. Pa., Works Progress Administrn.; co-ordinator of exhibits, N.Y. State Worlds Fair Commn.; advisor on building industry relations. Russell Sage Foundation; consultant on housing and labor relations, U.S. Housing Adminstration; consultant Federal Committee on Apprenticeship. Contributing editor Pencil Points, N.Y. City. Episcopalian. Club: T Square (Phila.). Home: 320 W. Springfield Av., Phila., and 53 W. 33d St., New York, N.Y. Office: 4 S. 15th St., Philadelphia, Pa. Died Feb. 21, 1944.

BOYD, LOUISE ARNER, explorer, author; b. San Rafael, Cal., Sept. 16, 1887; d. John Franklin and Louise Cook (Arner) Boyd; ed. Miss Stewart's Sch., San Rafael, Miss Murison's Sch., San Francisco; hon. LL.D., U. Cal., 1939, Mills Coll., 1939. Explorer of East Greenland; explorer polar region, N.E. and West Greenland (Spitzbergen and Franz Josef Land); flew pvt. chartered plane over North Pole, 1955. Decorated Chevalier Legion of Honor (France), St. Olaf of Norway (1st fgn. woman to receive award); awarded Andree plaque by Swedish Anthropol. and Geog. Soc., Cullum gold medal Am. Geog. Soc., medal of King Christian Xth of Denmark; certificate of Appreciation, U.S. Army; made hon. citizen City of San Rafael. Mem. Royal Hort. Soc. (London), Am. Polar Soc. (hon., dir.), Cal. Acad. Sci. (hon.), Am. Soc. Photogrammetry, Am. Geog. Soc. (council), Assn. Pacific Coast Geographers, Brit. Glaciological Soc., Am. Hort. Soc., Soc. Woman Geographers, Cal. Bot. Soc., Nat. League Am. Pen Women, Geog. Soc. Phila. (hon.), Colonial Dames Am., Sigma Delta Epsilon. Republican. Episcopalian. Clubs: San Francisco Garden (hon.); Burlingame (Cal.) Country, Marin Garden (hon.); Colony (N.Y.); Garden of Am. (mem.-at-large). Author: Fiord Region of East Greenland, 1935; Polish Countrysides, 1937; Coast of Northeast Greenland. Contbr. to Geog. Rev. Office: San Francisco CA Died Sept. 1972.

BOYD, PAUL PRENTICE, univ. dean; b. Cameron, W.Va., Feb. 26, 1877; s. Milton Robin (M.D.) and Florence Virginia (Talbott) B.; A.B., Oberlin, 1898; M.A., Cornell U., 1905, Ph.D., 1911, LL.D., Park College, Parkville, Missouri, 1942; m. Cleona Belle Matthews, Aug. 2, 1906; children—Virginia Drue, Martha Elizabeth. Teacher pub. schs., Isle St. George, O., 1898-99, teacher mathematics, Park Coll. Acad., Parkville, Mo., 1899-1903; prof. mathematics and astronomy, Park Coll., 1903-04; fellow in mathematics, Cornell U., 1905-06; prof. mathematics, Hanover (Ind.) Coll., 1906-12; prof. mathematics, U. of Ky., 1912-1947, head of dept. 1913-1947, dean coll. arts & sciences, 1917-47, acting pres., 1917. Pres. Interstate Oratorical Association, 1911-12; chmn. bd. of trustees Lees Junior College; chmn. Kentucky com. Postwar Higher Edn., 1943-45. Fellow A.A.A.S.; mem. Am. Math. Soc., Math. Assn. America, Ky. Ednl. Assn., Ky. Acad. of Science (pres., 1919-20), Ky. Assn. Colls. and Secondary Schs. (sec. 1929-47), Southern Assn. Colls. and Secondary Schs. (sec. com. on postwar edn. 1943-45), N.E.A., Phi Beta Kappa, Sigma Xi, (pres. Ky. chapter, 1921-22), Phi Delta Kappa, Pi Mu Epsilon, Pi Gamma Mu, Sigma Delta Chi, Omicron Delta Kappa, Phi Sigma Kappa. Democrat. Presbyterian. Mason. Club: Lexington Executive (pres. 1944-45). Co-author: Boyd, Davis & Rees' Analytic Geometry, 1922; Boyd and Downing's Brief Course in Analytical Geometry, 1946. Contbr. to mags. on ednl. subjects. Home: 119 Waller Av., Lexington KY

BOYDEN, SETH, inventor, mfr.; b. Foxborough, Mass., Nov. 17, 1788; s. Seth and Susanna (Atherton) B.; m. Abigail Sherman; children—Susan, for making patent leather, 1819, malleable iron, Obadiah, Matilda, George, Seth. Inventor process for making patent leather, 1819, malleable iron, 1826; manufactured stationery steam engines; developed forerunner of "Am. Process' furnace grate bar, 1847, an inexpensive process for manufacturing Sheet-iron, a hat-forming machine; made 1st Am. daguerreo-tupe; originated machines for manufacturing nails and cutting files; described by Thomas Edison as one of America's greatest inventors. Died Hilton, N.J., Mar. 31, 1870.

BOYDEN, URIAH ATHERTON, engr., inventor; b. Foxborough, Mass., Feb. 17, 1804; s. Seth and Susanna (Atherton) children. Moved to Boston, 1811, became printer and wood engraver; published many volumes illustrated with copperplates and woodcuts during 1820's and 1830's; an organizer Boston Bewick Co., (profl. group Boston wood engravers), circa 1833, instrumental in planning engravings in Am. Mag. of Useful and Entertaining Arts, published in Boston, 1834-circa 1838; influenced work of engravers including George Loring Brown, Hammat Billins; executed engravings and woodcuts for History of Boston (by Caleb Snow), 1825; Picture of Boston, 1828; The Young Ladies Book, 1830. Died Boston, Mar. 11, 1850; buried Boston.

BOYÈ, MARTIN H. (BAPTIZED HANS MARTIN BOYÈ), chemist and geologist; b. Copenhagen, Denmark, Dec. 6, 1812; ed. Borgerdyskolen, Copenhagen; grad. U. of Copenhagen, 1832; Polytehcnic School, Copenhagen, 1835; Univ. of Pa., med. dept., 1844; spl. studies in analytical chemistry and physics (hon. A.M., Univ. of Pa., 1844). Came to U.S., 1836; assisted Dr. Robert Hare in chem. investigations, 1837-38; asst. geologist and chemist first geol. survey of Pa., 1838-43; jointly discovered new compound, chloride of platinum with binoxide of nitrogen, 1839; jointly discovered perchloric ether, the most explosive of all substances, 1841; conducted laboratory for analysis and instruction in analytical and practical chemistry, 1842-45; discovered, and with others applied the first process of refining cotton seed oil, 1845; specimens exhibited at Centennial Expn., Phila., 1876, received 1st premium; prof. chemistry and natural philosophy, Central High Sch., Phila., 1845-59; delivered many lectures; retired, 1859. Author: Pneumatics, or the Physics of Gases, 1856; Chemistry, or the Physics of Atoms, 1857. Wrote also, Explosive Power Perchloric Ether Proc. Am. Philos. Soc., vol. ii, p. 203; Perchloric Ether, Transactions, Am. Philos. Soc., vol. viii, art vi.; "Analysis" in Booth's Chemical Ency.; Analysis of the Bittern of a Saline on the Kiskeminetas; of Magnetic Iron Pyrites Containing Nickel; of Schuylkill, Croton and Rock Creek Waters, etc., in Silliman's and Franklin Inst., Journals, 1842-45. Home: Coopersburg, Pa. Eid 1909.

BOYER, FRANCIS, pharm. mfg. exec.; b. Penllyn, Pa., June 21, 1893; s. Henry Conover and Nathalie C. (Robinson) B.; student Groton Sch., 1912, Harvard, 1912-15, Cambridge (Eng.) U., 1919; LL.D., Hahnemann Medical College, 1956, Univ. of Pa., 1961; D.Sc., Trinity Coll., 1961; L.H.D., Jefferson Med. Coll., 1965, Pa. Mil. Colls., 1966; m. Marian Angell Godfrey, July 6, 1950;children—(by previous marriage) Markley

Holmes, Mary Robinson. Began in circulation dept. Curtis Pub. Co., 1915; advt. dept. Phila. Public Ledger, 1916; with Smith Kline & French Labs., pharm. mfrs., Phila., 1919-72, became asst. to pres., 1926, exec. v.p., 1936, pres., 1951, chmn. bd., 1958-66, dir.; mem. of the board of directors of The Philadelphia Contributionship. Mem. bd. advisers Nat. Fund for Medical Education. Mem. bd. mgrs. Wistar Institute Anatomy and Biology; formerly mem. nat. adv. com. Arthritis and Metabolic Diseases Council; dir. Project Hope, 1958-61; mem. Harvard Bd. Overseers, 1958-64; mem. Harvard overseers com. to visit Peabody Mus. and dept. anthropology, 1966-72; associate trustee, member board med. education and research University Pennsylvania 1960-72. Served as 1st lieutenant F.A., U.S. Army, 1917-19. Fellow Royal Soc. Medicine London (hon.); mem. Pharmaceutical Manufacturers Association (director, 1958-65), Phi Beta Kappa. Clubs: Philadelphia, Harvard (Phila.). Author articles profl. jours. Home: Ardmore PA Died May 21, 1972.

BOYER, JOSEPH, mfr.; b. Can., 1848; m. Clara A. Libby; children—George W. (dec.), Frank H., C. Pearl (Mrs. H. E. Candler), Myrion L., Ruby C. (Mrs. W. A. C. Miller), Lotta E. (Mrs. Standish Backus), Gertrude (Mrs. Harold S. Chase), Joseph. Inventor of the first successful pneumatic hammer; associated with William S. Burroughs in construction of the first Burroughs adding machine; formerly pres., now chmn. bd. Burroughs Adding Machine Co.; plant moved from st. Louis to Detroit, 1904. Died Oct. 24, 1930.

BOYLSTON, ZABDIEL, physician; b. Brookline, Mass., Mar. 9, 1679; s. Dr. Thomas and Mary (Gardner) B.; m. Jerusha Minot, Jan. 18, 1705, 8 children. First physician to introduce small pox inoculation into Am. during Boston epidemic, 1721, for which he was persecuted and his life frequently threatened; wrote books in defense of inoculation, including The Little Treaties on the Small pox, 1791; An Historical Account of the Small pox Inocculated in New England, 1726; fellow Royal Soc. Died Brookline, Mar. 1, 1766; buried Old Cemetery, Brookline.

BOYSEN JENSEN, PETER, plant physiologist; b. Hjerting, Denmark, Jan. 18, 1883; s. Nis Povlsen and Maren Knudsen Jensen; Ph.D., U. Copenhagen, 1910; Dr. honoris causa, U. Oslo, Aarhus U.; m. Olga Vogt, Nov. 18, 1911 (dec. July 7, 1931); 1 dau., Margrette (Mrs. Louis Ehlers). Lectr. plant physiology U. Copenhagen, 1922-27, profl. plant physiology, 1927-48. Decorated Comdr. Order of Dannebrog. Mem. acads., sci. socs. Denmark, Sweden, Norway, Germany, Austria; hon. fgn. mem. Am. Acad. Arts and Scis. Author: Die Stoffproduktion der Pflanzen, 1932; Growth Hormones in Plants, 1936. Home: Raadmandsgade 49, Copenhagen, Denmark. Died Nov. 21, 1959.

BOZELL, HAROLD VEATCH, elec. engineer; b. Beloit, Kan., May 31, 1886; s. Charles Fremont and Olive Arletta (Veatch) B.; B.S. in E.E., U. of Kan., 1908, E.E., 1915; m. Isadel Read Heath, Nov. 22, 1910; children—Mrs. Elizabeth Louise Forrest, Joan Virginia (dec.). Head of elec. engring. dept., U. of Okla., 1908-16, also cons. engr.; asst. prof. elec. engring., Yale, 1916-21, also editor Electric Ry. Jour., New York, 1920-21; First editor Bus. Transportation, 1922; editor Electrical World, 1922-25; connected with Bonbright & Co. investments, 1925-32; dir. and pres. General Telephone Corp.; dir. Gen. Pub. Utilities Corp. (N.Y.), The North Electric Company, Galion, O., Roanwell Corp., N.Y.C., N.E. Electronics Corp., Concord, N.H. Capt. Signal Corps., Oklahoma National Guard, 1913-16; in charge signal training Com. on Edn. and Spl. Training, World War, also with Com. on Spl. Problems of Naval Cons. Bd., World War, and dir. Okla. industrial survey 1916; mem. telephone operations industry adv. bd. W.P.B., World War II. Named to Hall of Fame, Ind. Telephone Pioneer Assn., 1970. Fellow Am. Inst. E.E.; mem. Sigma Xi, Tau Beta Pi, Beta Theta Pi. Republican. Methodist. Rotarian. Clubs: Bankers, Down Town Athletic, Univ., Yale (N.Y.); Larchmont Shore, University, Bonnie Briar Country (Larchmont). Home: Larchmont NY Died Nov. 27, 1972.

BRACKENRIDGE, WILLIAM ALGERNON, engineer. Engr. on constrn. New York elevated rys., 1876-80, D.L.&W.Ry., 1880-82, Brooklyn Elevated Ry. 1883-85, L.I. R.R., 1885-89; railroad commr. of Conn., 1890-91; cons. engr., Niagara Falls, N.Y., 1891-1904; became mem. advisory bd. of cons. engrs. of N.Y. State Canals, 1904; v.p. and gen. mgr. Southern Calif. Edison Co., Los Angeles, until 1928. Home: S. Pasadena, Calif. Died Nov. 29, 1929.

BRACKENRIDGE, WILLIAM D., botanist; b. Ayr, Scotland, June 10, 1810; studied under Friedrick Otto, Berlin, Germany. Head gardener of Dr. Patrick Neill's Grounds, Edinburgh, Scotland; came to Phila. in service of Robert Buist, 1837; mem. U.S. Govt. expdn. to explore Pacific, 1838-42 (collected 10,000 species of plants representing 40,000 specimens; findings formed core of Nat. Herbarium); in charge of greenhouse, Washington, D.C., entrusted with care of living plants and preparation of report on ferns of expdn., 1842-55; ret. to Balt., 1855, some years. Author: Filices, Including Lycopodiaceae and Hydropterides, Vol. XVI, 1854. Died Balt., Feb. 3, 1893.

BRACKETT, BYRON BRIGGS, dir. radio engring.; b. Ira, N.Y., Aug. 13, 1865; s. James Henry and Helen Maria (Pierce) B.; A.B., Syracuse U., 1890, A.M., 1893; B.C., Johns Hopkins, Ph.D., 1897; m. Tilla Wilson, 1900; 1 son, Richard Thomas. Inst. in charge elec. engring., Union Coll., Schenectady, N.Y., 1897-98; teacher of physics, Washington, D.C., 1898-1900; engr. for Rowland Telegraph Co., Baltimore, Md., 1900-01; with Inst. Elec. Engring. and Mathematics, Rutgers Coll., 1901-03; prof. elec. engrin, Clarkson Coll., Potsdam N.Y., 1903-09, S. Dak. State Coll., Brookings, 1909-23, U. of S.Dak., 1923-1931; dir. radio. U. of S.D., 1931—. Insp. torpedo cable for U.S. Army Engr. Corps. Spanish-Am. War; mem. S.Dak. Bd Industrial Preparedness and dir. training of radio operators and electricans in S.A.T.C. work, S.Dak. State College, World War. Republican Epsicopalian. Home: Vermillion, S.D. Died Dec. 12, 1937.

BRACKETT, CYRUS FOGG, physicist; b. Parsonfield, Me., June 25, 1833; s. John and Jemine (Lord) B.; A.B., Bowdoin Coll., 1859, M.D., 1863; LL.D., Lafayette Coll., 1883, Bowdoin, 1892, Princeton, 1909; A.M., Princeton, 1896; m. Alice A. Briggs, Dec. 29, 1864. Instr., Bowdoin Coll., 1863, prof. chemistry, 1864-73; prof. physics, Princeton U., 1873-1908, prof. emeritus, 1908. Home: Princeton, N.J. Died Jan. 29. 1915.

BRACKETT, DEXTER, civil engr.; b. Newton, Mass., Nov. 30, 1851; s. Cephas Henry and Louisa Thwing (Pierce) B.; grad. High Sch., Brighton Mass., 1868; Bryant & Stratton Bus. C oll., fall and winter, 1868-69; m. Josephine Dame, Sept. 21, 1875. Asst. engr. in charge of work in connection with Boston Water Works, 1872-88; supt. of distribution, Boston Water Works, 1888-91, and asst. engr., in charge of spl. investigations, 1891-95; dept. engr. Met. Water Works during constrn. of works, 1895-1907, chief engr., 1907—. Has served as consulting engr. or given advice as expert for many municipalities. Home: Binghton, Mass. Died Aug. 26, 1915.

BRACKETT, E(LMER) E(UGENE), engr.; b. Jamesburg, N.J., Nov. 22, 1876; s. Benjamin Franklin and Annie Eliza (Lary) B.; B.Sc. in Elec. Engring., U. of Neb., 1901; m. Minnie Burt Guile, Sept. 17, 1903; children—Mary (Mrs. Leo Barnell), Ruth (dec.), Annie L. (Mrs. Charles B. Heal), Elmer Eugene, Jane J. (wife of Dr. Elbert T. Phelps). Installation, operation and management of small pub. utilities in midwest, 1901-06 and 1911-12; instr. elec. engring. U. of Pa., 1907-10; instr. agrl. engring., advancing to prof., U. of Neb., 1913-47, chmn. dept. 1928-47, retired as emeritus prof., 1947; prin. U. of Neb. Trades Sch. (Vets. Rehabilitation), 1922-24. Mem. Neb. Bd. Tractor Test Engrs., 1919-47, chmn., 1928-47; former asso. Am. Inst. Elec. Engrs. Registered professional engr., Neb. Served as 1st lt., U.S. Army Air Service, 1918-19; overseas, France and Italy. Mem. Soc. Agrl. Engrs. (pres. 1940), Neb. Engring. Soc., Am. Soc. Engring. Edn., Neb. Reclamation Assn., Lincoln C. of C., Y.M.C.A., Farm House, Am. Legion, Sigma Xi, Gamma Sigma Delta. Republican. Presbyterian. Mason. Clubs: Engineers (past pres.), Rotary (Lincoln). Home: 6053 25th Rd. N., Arlington, Va. Office: University of Nebraska, Arlington VA

BRACKETT, FRANK PARKHURST, astronomer; b. Provincetown, Mass., June 16, 1865; s. S. H. and Mary (Thomas) B.; A.B., Dartmouth Coll., 1887, A.M., 1890, Sc.D., 1927; hon. fellow, Clark U., 1902-03; m. Lucretia Burdick, Aug. 15, 1889 (died 1937); children—Mary Amanda (dec.), Frederick Sumner, Frank Parkhurst. Instr. mathematics and astronomy, 1888-90, prof. mathematics, 1890-1924, prof. astronomy, 1924-33, dir. observatory, 1908-33, prof. emeritus since 1933, chmn. of faculty, 1927-30, Pomona Coll., Calif.; also chmn. faculty Claremont Colls., 1930-32. Prof. mathematics, U. of Calif., summer 1910, mem. Smithsonian Astron. Expdn. to Africa, 1911, to Mt. Whitney, 1913; sec. Local Exemption Bd., 1917-18; dir. Solar Eclipse Expdn. to the Isthmus, Santa Catalina Island, 1923, to Ramm's Ranch and Honey Lake, Calif., 1930. Trustee C.R.B. Ednl. Foundation, Belgian Am. Ednl. Foundation. Fellow A.A.A.S.; mem. Am. Math. Soc., Math. Assn. of America, Astron, Soc. America, Royal Astron. Soc. Can., Sigma Xi, Phi Beta Kappa. Lecturer and writer on astron. subjects. Am. del. of Commn. for Relief in Belgium, Province of Brabant, 1916. Author: History of San Jose Rancho, 1919; The Challenge of the Ages; Granite and Sage Brush. Home: Box 433, Balboa Island, Calif. Office: 11044 Kling St., N Hollywood CA

BRACKETT, GUSTAVUS BENSON, pomologist; b. Unity, Me., Mar. 24, 1827; s. Reuben and Elizabeth S. B.; ed. pub. schs., Cincinnati, 1838-41; acad. at Denmark, Ia., 1841-47; m. Anna Houston, Nov. 14, 1849. Served 3 yrs. in Civil War as Capt. engrs.; after war lt. col. Ia. Militia; commr. in charge Iowa exhibits, Centennial Expn., Phila., 1876; U.S. commr. to Paris Expn., 1878; del.-at-large from Ia., Nat. Cotton Expn., New Orleans 1885; represented pomol. div. Dept. of Agr. at Chicago Expn., 1893; was on jury of awards, Hort. Dept.; practical nurseryman and horticulturist; was 2 yrs. sec. and 4 yrs. pres. Ia. State Hort. Soc.; hort. expert of U.S. Commn. to Paris Expn., 1900; 2 yrs. sec. Am. Pomol. Soc. Was chief of div. of pomology, U.S. Dept. of agr. Home: Denmark, Ia. Died Aug. 2, 1915.

BRACKETT, RICHARD NEWMAN, asso. prof. chemistry Clemson Coll., since 1891; b. Richland Co., S.C., Sept. 14, 1863; s. Rev. Gilbert Robbins B.; early edn. private schools, Charleston, S.C.; grad. Davidson Coll., 1883; Ph.D., Johns Hopkins, 1887; spl. in chemistry, mineralogy and geology; chemist of geol. survey of Ark., 1887-91. Fellow A.A.A.S.; mem. Am. Chem. Soc. Contbr. papers on geol. chemistry to scientific jours. Address: Clemson College, P.O., S.C.

BRADBURY, ROBERT HART, chemist; b. Phila., Pa., Sept. 25, 1870; s. Robert and Margaret C. (Hart) B.; A.B., Central High Sch., Phila., 1887; Ph.D., U. of Pa., 1893; m. Mabel Bradner, June 27, 1901; children—Robert Hart, Mabel Campbell. Asst. chemist, Cambria Iron Co., 1889; chemist S. P. Wetherill Paint Co., 1891-92; prof. chemistry, Central Manual Training Sch., Phila., 1893-1907; head dept. of science, Southern High Sch., Phila., 1907-30; retired. Consulting chemist, Am. Chem. Paint Co. Lecturer on phys. chemistry, dept. of philosophy, U. of Pa., 1894-95. Mem. Am. Chem. Soc., Franlin Inst. Author: An Elementary Chemistry, 1903; A. Laboratory Manual of Chemistry, 1903; An Inductive Chemistry, 1912; Laboratory Studies in Chemistry, 1912; A First Book in Chemistry, 1922, 3d edit. revised, 1938; New Laboratory Studies in Chemistry, 1923; Looseleaf Work-book for the Chemistry, Laboratory, 1934. Home: 2114 Chestnut Av., Ardmore, Pa. Died March 27, 1949.

BRADEN, WILLIAM, mining engr.; b. Indianapolis, Mar. 24, 1871; s. William and Martha (Burford) B.; ed. pvt. schs. and Mass. Inst. Tech.; m. Mary Kimball, June 6, 1893; 1 child, Spruille. Asst. to chief engr., Montana Co., Marysville, Mont., 1889; surveyor Elkhorn Mining Co. and Anaconda Co.; chemist and assayer, later asst. supt., Ark. Valley Smelter, Leadville, Colo., to 1893; engr. and rep. in British Columbia, for Omaha and Grant Smelting & Refining Co., also examination of mines in North and South America, 1893-98; expert engr. for Boston and Mont. and Butte and Boston interests in litigation with F. Aug. Heinze, at Butte, 1898-1901; gen. manager Velardefia Mines, Mexico, Bruce Mines, Ontario, Can., and mine examinations in the U.S. and Mexico, 1901-03; organizer and gen. mgr. Braden Copper Co., Child; with Anaconda Copper Mining Co. and directing operations of Andes Exploration Co. in S.A., 1913-18; cons. and mining examinations, 1919-30; mining explorations in N. and S. America, 1931-39. Mem. Am. Inst. Mining and Metall. Engrs., Club de la Union, Santiago, Chile. Home: Monarch Hotel. Office: 730 Van Nuys Bldg., Los Angeles, Calif. Died July 18, 1942.

BRADFORD, WILLIAM, printer; b. Leicestershire, Eng., May 20, 1663; s. William Bradford; m. Elizabeth Sowle, Apr. 28, 1685; asso. founder 1st colonial paper mill, 1690; printer to King William and Queen Mary, N.Y., 1693-1742; printed Votes (proceedings of N.Y. Assembly, 1st Am. printed legislative proceedings); printed 1st N.Y. paper currency, 1709, 1st Am. Book of Common Prayer, 1710, 1st colonial written drama, 1714, 1st history of N.Y., 1727, 1st copperplate plan of N.Y., 1730; ofcl. printer N.J., 1703-33; founder, publisher N.Y. Gazette (1st newspaper in N.Y.C.), Nov. 8, 1725. Died N.Y.C., May 23, 1752.

BRADLEE, HENRY G., engineer; b. Boston, Mass., Jan. 25, 1871; s. John Tisdale and Sarah E. (Goddard) B.; S.B., Mass. Inst. Tech., 1891; m. Marion Chamberlin, Nov. 9, 1898; children—Mrs. Elizabeth Perry, Henry G. With Stone & Webster, enginers and mgrs. pub. service corps. since June 1, 1891, and mem. firm 1907-20; now vice president, chmn. executive committee and director, Stone & Webster, Inc.; dir. numerous traction, light, power and other cos. Clubs: Union, Country, Downtown. Home: Brookline, Mass. Office: 49 Federal St., Boston, Mass. Died Sept. 3, 1947.

BRADLEY, CHARLES SCHENCK, inventor; b. Victor, N.Y., Apr. 12, 1853; s. Alonzo and Sarah (Schenck) B.; prep. edn. De Graff Mil. Inst., Rochester, N.Y., 1868-71; student u. of Rochester, 1872; m. Emmaretta Orcutt Brackett, Feb. 16, 1876. Began with Edison Illuminating Co., New York, 1881; succesively in employ various elec. cos., 1883-1914; with U.S. Reduction Co., 1916—. Has taken out many patents, including patent for process for production of aluminum, patent for three phase transmision of power, rotary convertor, fixation of atmospheric nitrogen, etc. Home: New York, N.Y. Died 1929.

BRADLEY, FRANK HOWE, geologist; b. New Haven, Conn., Sept. 20, 1838; grad. Yale, 1863; m. Sarah M. Bolles, 1867, 2 children. Discovered new species of trilobite in Potsdam sandstone of N.Y., 1857; after graduation spent over year in Panama collecting coral and other zool. materials; asst. geologist in survey of Ill., 1867, of Ind., 1869; prof. geology and mineralogy U. Tenn., 1869-75; mem. Nat. Survey, 1872, assigned to Snake River area of Ida.; contbr. article On the Silurian Age of the Southern Appalachians to Am. Jour. Sci., 1876. Killed (while engaged in pvt. mining venture) in cave-in nr. Nacooche, Ga., Mar. 27, 1879.

BRADLEY, JOHN DAVIS, mining engr.; b. San Francisco, Oct. 26, 1910; s. Frederick Worthen and Mary (Parks) B.; B.S., U. Cal., 1933; m. Jane Easton, Jan. 12, 1935; children—John Easton, Lynn Bradley.

Dir. Bunker Hill Co. (formerly Bunker Hill & Sullivan Mfg. Co.), San francisco, 1938—, exec. v.p., 1954-55, pres., 1955—; dir. Bradley Mining Co., San Francisco, 1934—, v.p., 1936-46, exec. v.p., 1946—; pres., dir. Aircraft Service Co., Boise, Ida., 1947—; v.p., dir. Sullivan Mining Co., Kellogg, Ida., 1954-55, now subsidiary Bunker Hill Co.; v.p., dir. Pend Oreille Mines & Metals Co., Reeves MacDonald Mines, Ltd. Mem. Am. Inst. Mining, Metall. and Petroleum Engrs., Mining and Metall. Soc. Am., Lead Industries Assn. (pres., dir.), American Zinc Institute (vice president, director), also Newcomen Soc. Republican. Presbyn. Clubs: Pacific Union (San Francisco); Burlingame (Cal.) Country: Cypress Point (Pebble Beach, Cal.). Home: 2945 Ralston Av., Hillsborough, Ca. Office: 660 Market St., San Francisco 94104. Died Nov. 1959.

BRADLEY, JOHN HODGDON, geologist, author; b. Dubuque, Ia., Sept. 17, 1898; s. John Hodgdon and Margaret (Ferring) B.; grad. Phillips Exeter Acad., Exeter, N.H., 1917; A.B. magna cum laude, Harvard, 1921; Ph.D. magna cum laude, U. Chgo., 1924; m. Katharine Leighton Hilton, June 24, 1922 (dec. 1950); 1 dau., Margaret Ruth; m. 2d, Elinor M. Starke, 1952. Asst. in geology Harvard, 1920-21; instr. in geology U. N.C., 1921-22; again asst. in geology Harvard, 1922-23; asst. prof. geology U. Mont., 19325-26, asso. prof., 1926-28; prof. geology U. So. Cal., 1929-35. Served with USMC, 1918019. Fellow A.A.A.S., Geol. Soc. Am., Paleontol. Soc. Am.; mem. Alpha Sigma Phi, Phi Beta Kappa, Sigma Xi. Author: The Earth and Its Hist., 1928; Parade of the Living, 1930; Fauna of the Kimmswick Limestone, 1930; Autobiography of Earth, 1935; Farewell Thou Busy World, 1935; Patterns of Survival, 1938; The World at War, 1943; World Geography, 1945. Co-author, Exploring Our World, 1940; Our World Changes, 1940; Using Our World, 1941; Our World and Science, 1941. Contbr. to Jour. Geology, Biol. Abstracts, Sci. Monthly, New Republic, Forum, Yale Rev., Atlantic Monthly, others. Address: P.O. Box 966, Escondido, Cal. Died Aug. 18, 1962; buried Dubuque.

BRADLEY, MILTON, mfr.; b. Vienna, Me., Nov. 8, 1836; s. Lewis B.; ed. grammar and high schs., Lowell, Mass., and Lawrence Scientific Sch. (Harvard), 1854-55; spl. studies in engring. Began active life as civil and mech. engr. Became interested in lithography and through that in the publishing of home amusements. Organized the Milton Bradley Co. at Springfield, Mass., for the manufacture and publication of kindergarten and school material, 1863; developed the Bradley system of color instruction, based on spectrum standard colors with a complete and definite color nomenclature; publisher The Kindergarten Review. Author and publisher: Color in the School Room 1890; Color in the Kindergarten, 1893; Elementary Color, 1895; Water Colors in the Schoolroom, 1900. Home: Springfield, Mass. Died 1911.

BRADLEY, PHILIP READ, mining engr.; b. Georgetown, Calif., Oct. 12, 1875; s.Henry Sewell and Virginia (Shearer) B.; B.S. in Mining, U. of Calif., 1896; m. Mabel Harland, Feb. 13, 1903; children—Philip Read, Henry Harland, Ruth, Frances. Former mining supt. and mgr.; cons. engr. since 1897; pres. Alaska Juneau Gold Mining Co., Treadwell Yukon Co.; v.p. Pacific Mining Co., Atolia Mining Co., Bunker Hill and Sullvian Mining and Conc. Co. Mem. Am. Inst. Mining Engrs., Mining and Metall. Soc. Protestant. Clubs: Engineers, Bohemian, Press. Home: 506 Linden Av., Grass Valley, Calif. Office: Crocker Bldg., San Francisco, Calif. Died Dec. 31, 1948.

BRADLEY, SAMUEL STEWART, aeronautics; b. Medina, O., June 27, 1869; s. John Albro and Eleanor (Stewart) B.; grad. high sch., Ann Arbor, Mich.; student civ. engring., U. of Mich., 1887-89; hon. M.S., U. of Mich., 1937; m. Genevieve Cornwell, Dec. 17, 1901. Engaged in civ. engring., 1889-91; sec. and gen. mgr. New Duluth Co., 1891-97; treas. Atlas Iron & Brass Works, 1893-97; originated and perfected practical improvements in business systems, including perpetual stock inventory and constant balanced ledgers, 1898-1904; pres. patterson, Gottfied & Hunter, Ltd., 1901-11, Young Machine & Tool Co., 1905-11. Frasse Co., 1906-09, supt. Brooklyn (N.Y.) Park Dept., 1914-17, gen. mgr. Mfrs. Aircraft Assn., 1917-36, chmn. bd. since 1937; v.p. and gen. mgr. Aeronautical Expns. Corp., 1927-29; dir. Wilcox & Gibbs Sewing Machine Co. Mem. council Aeronautical Chamber of Commerce of America (v.p. and gen. mgr. 1921-29). Mem. and sec. Am. Aviation Mission to Europe, 1919; mem. various sub. coms. of Nat. Advisory Com. for Aeonautics, 1918-20; mem. Inst. of Aeronautical Sciences. Republican. Epsicopalian. Clubs: Univeristy of Michigan, Psi Upsilon, Union League (New York); "M" (Ann Arbor); Union Interallies (Paris). Ed. annual edits. of Aircraft Year Book, 1920-29; pub. Airplane Patent Digest (bi-monthly), 1929-36. Home: 45 Park Av. Office: 30 Rockefeller Plaza, New York, N.Y. Died April 10, 1947.

BRADLEY, WALTER PARKE, chemist; b. Lee, Mass., July 7, 1862; s. George Franklin and Mary Alverson (Freeman) B.; A.B., Williams Coll., 1884; U. of Gottingen, Germany, 1884-86, 1888-89, A.M., Ph.D., 1889; Sc.D., Wesleyan U., 1914; m. Adelaide Bartlett Huntting, June 26, 1888; 1 child, Marian Huntting. Prof. chemistry, Wesleyan U., Conn., 1893-1914; dir. General Lab., U.S. Rubber Co., 1912-13, research chemist same, 1914-19; pres. Bradstone Rubber Co., 1919-38. Dir. 1st laboratory in U.S. for research at extreme low temperatures. Mem. Phi Beta Kappa, Zeta Psi, Sigma Xi. Author: They Made Him Christ, 1942. Contbr. to scientific mags. on liquefaction of permanent gases, critical temperature, etc. Home: 196 College St., Middletown CT

BRADY, LIONEL FRANCIS, geologist; b. Dovercourt, Eng., Jan. 24, 1880; s. Henry and Anna Maria (Kinder) B.; B.A., St. Catharine's Coll., Cambridge U., 1903, M.A., 1905; m. Linden Van Every, Apr. 30, 1914 (dec.); married Gertrude E. Passey, February 5, 1956. Tchr. lower sch., Rubgy, Eng., 1905-1905-07, Racine (Wis.) Coll., 1908-10, Evans Sch., Mesa, Ariz. 1910-20; head-master Mesa Ranch Sch., 1920-42, Ariz. State Coll. 1942-47; curator geology, trustee Mus. Northern Ariz., Flagstaff, 1927—; asso. in geochronology U. of Arizona, Tucson. Trustee Verde Valley Sch. Fellow A.A.A.S., Meteoritical Soc. (pres. 1950-54), Geol. Soc. Am. Paleontol. Soc.; mem. Soc. Vertebrate Paleontol. Episcopalian. Address: Museum of Northern Ariz., P.O. Box 1389, Flagstaff, Ariz.; also 2603 E. Prince Rd., Tucson. Died Feb. 24, 1963; buried Mesa, Ariz.

BRAGG, EDWARD MILTON, prof. naval architecture and marine engring.; b. Chicopee, Mass., Feb. 22, 1874; s. Warren Sylvester and Mary Charlotte (Shores) B.; B.S., Mass. Inst. Tech., 1896; m. Helen Elizabeth Brooks (M.D.), July 2, 1907; children—Martha Shores (Mrs. John Clarke Moore), Edward Brooks; m. 2d, Marion Olive Wood, June 21, 1932. Assistant Instructor Mass. Inst. Tech., 1896-1900; draftsman at William Cramp & Sons, Philadelphia, Pa., William R. Trigg Company, Richmond Virginia, New York S. B. Co., Camden, N.J., 1900-03; with Newport News Shipbuilding & Drydock Co., 1907-08; instr. naval architecture and marine engring., U. of Mich., 1903-45, now prof. emeritus. Mem. Soc. Naval Architects and Marine Engrs., Inst. of Naval Architects, Royal Soc. of Arts, Sigma Xi, Phi Kappa Phi. Home: 1056 Ferdon Rd., Ann Arbor MI

BRAIN, WALTER RUSSELL, neurologist; b. Oct. 23, 1895; s. Walter John and Edith Alice (Smith) B.; D.M. (Theodore Williams scholar physiology), Oxford U., D.Sc. (hon.); Price Engrance scholar anatomy and physiology Dondon Hos.; LL.D. (hon.), Wales, Belfast, D.C.L. (hon.), Durham U.; m. Stella Langdon-Down; children—Christopher Langdon, Micahel Cotteril, 1 dau. Con. physician London Hosp., also Maida Vale Hosp. Nervous Disease. Recipient Osler medal U. Oxford, 1961. Mem. Royal Commns. on Marriage and Divorce, and Law Relating to Mental Illness. Mem. Assn. Physicians (pres. 1956), Assn. Brit. Neurologists (pres. 1960), Internat. Soc. Internal Medicine (pres. 1958), Am., French, German, Spanish neur. socs., Swiss Acad. Medicine, Royal Coll. Physicans (pres. 1950-57), British Assn. (pres. 1963), Family Planning Assn. (pres.) Clubs: Atheneum, Savile. Author: Man, Society and Religion, 1944; Mind, Perception and Science, 1951; Tea with Walter de la Mare, 1957; The Nature of Experience, 1959; Some Reflections on Genius, 1960; Speech Disorders, 1961; Recent Advances in Neurology, rev. edit., 1962; Diseases of the Nervous System, rev. edit., 1962; Clinical Neurology, rev. edit., 1964; Doctors Past and Present, 1964; Medicine and Government, 1967. Home: Hillmorton, Coombe Hill Rd., Kingston-upon-Thames, Eng. Died Dec. 29, 1966.

BRAINARD, OWEN, civil engr.; b. Haddam, Conn., Mar. 10, 1865; s. Hubert and Cynthia V. (Brainerd) B.; ed. pub. and pvt. schs.; m. Jean Sawyer, Mar. 10, 1901. Began as chief engr. Carrere & Hastings, architects, New York, 1893, admitted to partnership 1901. Architect of builder: New York Pub. Library; Yale bi-centennial bldgs.; Goldwin Smith Hall, Cornell U.; Senate and House office bldg., Washington; alterations to U.S. Captol; etc. 11Fellow A.I.A. Republican. Conglist. Home: New York, N.Y. Died Apr. 2, 1919.

BRAINERD, ARTHUR ALANSON, illuminating engr.; b. Durham, Conn., Apr. 6, 1891; s. Alanson Virgil and Alice Luella (Kelsey) B.; B.S., Ohio U., Athens, O., 1915, Dr. Engring. (honorary), 1954; student University of Michigan Graduate School, 1922-23; m. Zella Elizabeth Knoll, May 23, 1916; children—Elizabeth B. Kintz, Henry Alanson. Tester and insp. Hartford (Conn.) Electric Light Co., 1915-16; in commercial dept. Manchester (Conn.) Electric Co., 1916-18; head elec. dept., State Trade Sch., Danbury, Conn., 1918-20; inst. elec. engring., U. of N.H., 1920-24; asst. illuminating engr. Phila. Electric Co., 1924-28, illuminating engr., 1928-34, engr. and dir. lighting service division, 1934-56; cons. engr., Erwinna, Pa., now Fla. Created floodlighting effects for Edison Bldg., Phila., 1927, Art Museum, Phila., 1929, etc. Won James H. McGraw award, 1927, for best paper of year on an engring. subject. U.S. rep. on coms. Internat. Commn. on Illumination; mem. bd. of judges for price award in illumination, Beaux Arts Inst.; del. Internat. Commn. of Illumination, Holland, 1939, Paris, 1948, Stockholm, 1951; mem. Elec. Industry Com. on Handbook of Interior Wiring Design, representing Edison Electric Inst.; president U.S. Nat. Com. of International Com. on Illumination, Fellow Illuminating Engring. Society (regional v.p., chmn. lighting service com., papers com.; rep. on Nat. Elec. Code); mem. Nat. Electric Light Assn., Inst. Electric Science (chairman committee on Lighting of Central Station Properties), Commission Internationale De L'Eclairage (v.p., member coms. on pleasantness in lighting and lighting legislation, chairman attendance com., del. U.S. national com. Vienna 1963); member of executive committee 1967 sessions Washington, Am. Standards Assn. (lamp standards com.), Soc. for Elec. Development. Republican. Methodist. Mason. Author: (pamphlets) Three-Dimensional Seeing, Salvaging Waste Light for Victory. Contbr. to mags. Address: P.O. Box 8, Keystone Heights, Fla. Died Dec. 7, 1966; buried Keystone Heights.

BRAISLIN, WILLIAM C., otologist; b. Burlington, N.J., July 1, 1865; s. John and Elizabeth (Webber) B.; grad. Peddie Inst., 1885; student Princeton, 1885-87; M.D., Coll. Phys. and Surg. (Columbia), 1890; spl. courses in anatomy of the ear, human and comparative, under Drs. Huntington and Blake, 1901-02; m. Alice Cameron, Oct. 19, 1892 (died Sept. 30, 1927); children—William Donald (dec.), John Cameron, Gordon Stuart, Alice Cameron (Mrs. Robert Hadley Bennet). Began practice, Brooklyn, 1890; with Brooklyn Eye and Ear Hosp. since 1892, attending otologist and oto-laryngol. surgeon since 1903; sec. exec. com. bd. of dirs., same 1904-21, now lecturer to graduate in medicine and mem. bd. trustees; lecturer to undergraduates, L.I. Coll. Hosp., 1919-24, clin. prof. otology since 1920. Mem. advisory bd. (Norwegian Hosp. group) Federal Draft Com., World War. Mem. Am., N.Y. State and Kings County med. socs., Am. Otol. Soc., Am. Oto-Laryngol. Soc. Episcopalian. Author: Relief of Deafness by Medication of Custachian Tubes; (brochure) Study of Some Casts of the Infantile Pharynx, 1909; also abt. 90 papers, mostly on treatment of deafness. Home-Office: 425 Clinton Av., Brooklyn, N.Y. Died Dec. 3, 1948. *

BRAND, LOUIS, mathematician, educator; b. Cin., Sept. 27, 1885 s. Louis William and Josephine (Zingsheim) B.; Ch.E., U. Cin., 1907, E.E., 1908, A.M., 1909, Doctor of Science (honorary), 1956; Ph.D., Harvard University, 1917; m. Lulu Edith Shinkle, Aug. 14, 1915; children—Sara Josephine (Mrs. Oliver Marcy), Martha Louise (Mrs. Bruce Raymond). Head dept. mathematics and mechanics, coll. engring. U. Cin., 1919-56, head dept. mathematics, 1935-56, prof. emeritus, 1956-71; Whitney vis. prof. Trinity Coll., 1956-57; M.D. Anderson professor of mathematics University of Houston, Tex., 1957-71; vis. prof. University of Brazil, 1963. Fellow A.A.A.S., Ohio, Tex. acads. scis.; mem. Am. Math. Soc., Am. Math. Assn., Sigma Xi, Tau Beta Pi, Phi Kappa Phi. Author math. textbooks, latest being Differential and Difference Equations, 1967; also articles math. jours. Home: Houston TX Died Jan. 27, 1971.

BRANDENBURG, FREDERICK HARMON, meteorologist; b. Washington, D.C., Aug. 23, 1854; s. Frederick William and Martha Bolling (Sims) B.; ed. pvt. schs. and under pvt. tutors; m. Virginia Pauline Zeh, Nov. 29, 1881. Mem. Signal Corps, U.S.A., 1877-1901, when the dept. was transferred to Weather Bur.; with U.S. Weather Bur., 1901—; served various 1878-94; in charge at Denver, 1894—, apptd. local forecaster, 1895, dist. forecaster, 1901; section dir. Climatol. Service of Colo., 1894—; dist. editor Monthly Weather Review, Colo. River Valley, 1909-13; collected data regarding snowfall and published bulls, giving estimates of water available for irrigation, 1895; organized river and flood service of Colo. River, 1907. Republican. Mason. Home: Denver, Colo. Deceased.

BRANDES, ELMER WALKER, cons. sugar technologist; b. Washington, July 15, 1891; s. Frederick and Emma (Pangburn) B.; B.S., Mich. State Coll., 1913, M.S., 1915; student Cornell U., 1916-17; Ph.D., U. of Mich., 1919; m. Grace Newbold, 1915; children—Elizabeth Pangburn, William Frederick. Engaged as research asst. Mich. State Coll., 1914; plant pathologist Puerto Rico Agrl. Expt. Sta., 1915-16; 2d lt. A.E.F., France, 1918; pathologist U.S. Dept. Agr., 1919-22, sr. pathologist-in-charge Office of Sugar Plants, 1923-27, agrl. explorer, 1928; principal pathologist-in-charge div. of sugar plant investigations, Bureau of Plant Industry, U.S. Dept. Agr., 1928, head pathologist-in-charge, divs. of sugar plant investigations and rubber plant investigations, 1940-48, sugar plant investigations only, 1948-51; cons. sugar technologist, 1951-59. Sugar expert for the Pan-Pacific Food Conservation Congress, Honolulu, 1924. Organizer and officer Internat. Soc. Sugar Cane Technologists, gen. chmn., 1935-38; has been dir. of various scientific expeditions in Central and South America, Asia, Africa and Pacific Islands; leader U.S. Dept. Agr. airplane explorations, New Guinea, 1928; apptd. to organize research and stimulate plantation rubber production in 15 countries of Latin America for national preparedness, 1940. Received The Alumni Award, Mich. State Coll., 1948; Gold Medal for distinguished service U.S. Dep. Agrl., 1949. Hon. mem. Proefstation Voor de Java-Suikerindustrie, Pasoeroean, Java; honorary life member American Sugarcane League; fellow A.A.A.S., Am. Phytopath. Soc.; mem. Bot. Soc. Washington, Washington Acad. Science, Sigma Xi. Republican. Lectr. on geography and ethnology.

Author: numerous scientific papers on sugar and rubber technology, tropical crops, diseases of plants, bot., ethnol. and geog. subjects. Clubs: Cosmos, Chevy Chase. Home: 335 Seabreeze Avenue, Palm Beach, Fla. Office: Box 361 Canal Point, Fla. Died Feb. 4, 1964; buried Arlington Cemetery.

BRANDT, ALLEN DEMMY, engr.; b. Mountville, Pa., Nov. 8, 1908; s. Charles G. and Mary Bella (Demmy) B.; B.S. in Civil Engring. (White, Carnegie scholar), Pa. State Coll., 1931, M.S. in San. Engring., Harvard, 1932, D.Sc. (Rockefeller Found. fellow), 1933; B.S. in Law, LaSalle Extension U., 1954; m. Ella Nora Snavely, June 23, 1933; children—Patricia Ella, Barry Allen, Frederick Thomas. Dir. indsl. hygiene research Wilison Products, Inc., Reading, Pa., 1933-40; chief, engring. sect., indsl. hygiene div. USPHS, Washington, 1940-42; asst. chief indsl. hygiene br. safety and security div. Office Chief of Ordnance, War Dept., Chgo., 1942-45; research fellow, assigned by USPHS to research lab. Am. Soc. Heating and Ventilating Engrs., Cleve., 1945-46; chief indsl. hygiene dept. Bethlehem Steel Co. (Pa.), 1946-60, mgr., indsl. health engring., 1960-67, mgr. environmental quality control, 1967-71. Cons. environmental engring. problems; vis. lectr. indsl. hygiene engring. Harvard; chmn. Pa. Air Pollution Commn.; mem. council tech. advisers N.Y. Air Pollution Control Bd.; past chmn. Environmental Engring. Engring. Intersoc. Bd. Past pres. Bethlehem Area council Boy Scouts Am. Recipient certificate of commendation U.S. Army; Richard Beatty Mellon award Air Pollution Control Assn., 1971. Named adm. Navy Great State of Neb. Registered engr., Pa., Ohio. Fellow A.A.A.S.; mem. Am. Soc. Heating, Refrigerating and Air Conditioning Engrs., Am. Indsl. Hygiene Assn. (past pres., Cummings Meml. award), Am. Standards Assn. (mem. 3 coms. dealing with air sanitation and ventilation), Phi Kappa Phi, Tau Beta Pi, Delta Omega, Chi Epsilon. Republican. Club: Saucon Valley Country. Author: Industrial Health Engineering, 1947; also papers on phases of air sanitation, indsl. hygiene, ventilation chpts. in tech. handbooks. Home: Bethlehem PA Died Oct. 2, 1971; buried Meml. Park, Bethlehem PA

BRANHAM, SARA ELIZABETH, bacteriologist; b. Oxford, Ga., July 25, 1888; d. Junius Wingfield and Sarah Amanda (Stone) Branham; A.B., Wesleyan Coll., Ga., 1907; A.B., U. Colo., 1919, hon. Sc.D., 1937; Ph.D., U. Chgo., 1923, M.D., 1934; m. Philip S. Matthews, Dec. 22, 1945. Tchr. biology, Girl's High School, Atlanta, 1914-17; asst. bacteriology U. Colo., 1917-19, U. Chgo., 1919-23, instr. bacteriology, 1923-27; instr. bacteriology U. Colo., summer 1923; asso. bacteriology U. Rochester Sch. of Medicine and Destistry, 1927-28; asso. bacteriologist, USPHS, 1928-29, bacteriologist, 1929-30, sr. bacteriologist 1930-51, prin. bacteriologist, 1951-57, chief sect. Bacterial Toxins, 1957-58; vis. lectr. Am. Inst. Biol. Scis., 1959—; professorial lectr. preventive medicine George Washington U., 1939-53. Recipient Ricketts prize for research in pathology U. Chgo., 1924; outstanding Achievement award Wesleyan Coll. Alumnae Assn., 1950: Distinguished Service award U. Chgo. Med. Alumni Assn., 1952. Diplomate Nat. Bd. Med. Examiners, 1935, Am. Bd. Pathology, 1955. Del. from U.S. to 1st Internat. Congress for Microbiology, Paris, 1930, 2d London, 1936. Fellow Am. Pub. Health Assn. (chmn. lab. sect. 1946-47), A.A.A.S., mem. Soc. Am. Bacteriologists (councillor-at-large 1952-54), Am. Assn. Immunologists, Soc. Exptl. Biology and Medicine, Wash. Acad. Scis., Med. Soc. D.C., Am. Med. Women's Assn., Phi Beta Kappa, Sigma Xi, Alpha Omega Alpha, Sigma Delta Epsilon, Iota Sigma Pi, Alpha Epsilon Iota, Alpha Delta Pi. Methodist. Clubs: Am. Assn. Univ. Women. Co-author Practical Bacteriology, Hematology, Parsitology, 1948. Contbr. numerous articles on results of research to profl. jours. Deceased.

BRANNER, JOHN CASPER, geologist; b. New Market, Tenn., July 4, 1850; s. Michael T. and Elsie (Baker) B.; B.S., Cornell, 1874; Ph.D., Ind. U., 1885; LL.D., U. of Ark., 1897, Maryville Coll., 1909, U. of Calif., 1915; Sc.D., U. of Chicago, 1916; m. Susan D. Kennedy, June 22, 1883. Geologist Imperial Geol. Commn., Brazil, 1875-77; asst. engr. and interpreter S. Cyriaco Mining Co., Minas Geraes, Brazil, 1878-79; spl. botanist in S. America, 1880-81; agt. U.S. Dept. Agr. in Brazil, 1882-83; topog. geologist, Geol. Survey of Pa., 1883-85; prof. geology, Ind. U., 1885-92; state geologist of Ark., 1887-93; prof. geology, Leland Stanford Jr. U., 1892-1915, acting pres., i898-99, v.p., 1899-1913, pres., 1913-15, emeritus. Dir. Branner-Agassiz expdn. to Brazil, 1899; mem. Calif. Earthquake Commn., 1906-07; spl. asst. Geol. Survey of Brazil, 1907-08; dir. scientific expdns. to Brazil, 1899, 1911. Mem. Nat. Acad. Sciences. Asso. editor Journal of Geology. Address: Stanford University, Calif. Died Mar. 1, 1922.

BRANSON, EDWIN BAYER, geologist; b. Belleville, Kan., May 11, 1877; s. John McDowell and Harriet Melviney (Bullen) B.; A.B., A.M., U. Kan., 1903; Ph.D., U. Chgo., 1905; m. Grace Muriel Colton, Aug. 24, 1905; children—Carl Colton, Edwin Robert. Instr. in geology Oberlin Coll., 1905-07, asso. prof., 1907-09, prof., 1909-10; prof. geology U. Mo., 1910—. Served as geologist Mo. Bur. Geology and Mines intermittently, 1914-28; geologist Gypsy Oil Co., parts of 1920-28. Fellow Geol. Soc. Am., Paleontol. Soc. Am., A.A.A.S., Am. Assn. Petroleum Geologists; mem. Mo., St. Louis acads. sci., Phi Beta Kappa, Sigma Xi. Conglist. Author: Geology of Missouri, 1918; Geology and Geography of Middle Eastern Costa Rica; Devonian of Missouri, 1923; Conodonts, 1933; Introduction to Geology, 1935, 2d edit., 1941; The Lower Mississippian of Missouri, 1938; Geology of Missouri, 1945. Contbr. sci. jours. Home: 301 S. Glenwood Av., Columbia, Mo. Died Mar. 12, 1950. *

BRASHEAR, JOHN ALFRED, lense mfg. co. exec.; b. Brownsville, Pa., Nov. 24, 1840, s. Basil Brown Brashear; attended Duff's Merc. Coll., Pitts., 1955; m. Phoebe Stewart, Sept. 24, 1862. Pattern maker, Brownville, 1956-61, Pitts., 1961-81; founded lense making firm, Pitts., 1881; produced astron. lenses and precision instruments of internat. renown, from 1880's; perfected technique of making plane surfaces; produced plates from which Rowland Diffraction Gratings were made; invented method for silvering mirrors; trustee Western U. Pa. (now U. Pitts.), 25 years acting chancellor, 3 years; chmn. Allegheny Observatory Com.; helped plan Carnegie Inst. Tech., Frick Ednl. Commn. Died Pitts., Apr. 8, 1920; buried Pitts.

BRASHER, REX, ornithologist; b. Brooklyn, N.Y., July 31, 1869; s. Philip Marston and Laura Alida (Bull) B.; grad. St. Francis Coll., Brooklyn, 1884; unmarried. Studied birds, paintings all species in U.S. Mem. Rex Brasher Associates, pubs. Author: Secrets of Friendly Woods, 1926; Birds and Trees of North America (12 vols), 1934. Contbr. to Compton's Ency., Nature Lovers Library, Outdoor America, Yachting, American Mag., Mentor, Boys' Life, etc. Home: Kent, Conn. Died Feb. 29, 1960. *

BRASSERT, HERMAN ALEXANDER, consulting engr.; b. London, Eng., Jan. 24, 1875; s. Charles Alexander and Marie (Stein) B.; student Latin and Greek Sch., Freiburg, Baden, Germany, 4 yrs., Sch. of Mines, Leoben, Austria, 1 yr.; grad. Metallurgical engr., Coll. Mining and Metallurgy, Berlin, 1896; m. Sarah Maury Childs, May 1902 (died Nov. 1907); 1 son, Charles Alexander; m. 2d, Ethel Mohr, Oct. 6, 1909; children—William Ewing, James Elton. Came to the U.S. Oct. 1897. Worked six months at Warrick Furnaces, Pottstown, Pa.; asst. supt. and supt. Edgar Thomson Blast Furnaces, Carnegie Steel Co., Pittsburgh, 1898-1905; in charge of blast furnaces for Ill. Steel Company, Chicago Dist., 1905-16; charter mem. U.S. Steel Corp. Coke Committee; asst. gen. supt. South Works, Ill. Steel Company, 1916-18; organized and became chmn. bd., 1918-22, Freyn-Brassert Co., engineers; also vice pres. Miami Metals Co. of Chicago. Established cons. engineering business as H.A. Brassert, Inc. in 1922, and organized H.A. Brassert & Co., Chicago, cons. engineers, 1925; now chairman board and president with offices New York, Pittsburgh; organized British Company, H.A. Brassert & Co., Ltd.; also president and director various other companies. Internationally known for contribution to development of the modern blast furnace and for many improvements to iron and steel plants and processes; contributed ten technical papers these subjects. Designed and constructed plants in this country and abroad; modernized plants and methods; created new industries in many parts of the world. Mem. Am. Iron & Steel Institute, Mining and Metall. Engineers, Blast Furnace and Coke Assn.; British Iron & Steel Inst.; iron and steel institutes and engineering societies of other countries. Clubs: University (Chicago), Duquesne (Pittsburgh); Uptown (New York). Home: Nettleton Farm, Washington, Conn.; also 1165 Fifth Av., N.Y.C. Office: 69 E. 42d St. N.Y.C.; also 210 Blvd. of the Allies, Pitts

BRAUER, ALFRED, zoologist; b. Cherokee County, Ia., Jan. 13, 1895; s. Charles E. and Emma (Kionka) B.; A.B., U. Kan., 1918; M.A., U. Okla., 1924; Ph.D., U. Chgo., 1932; m. Ruth Conron, Aug. 21, 1919; children—Alfred Charles, Elizabeth Ann (Mrs. Sterling L. Bugg). Inst. zoology U. Ky., 1923-26, asst. prof., 1926-31, asso. prof., 1931-37, prof. since 1937; vis. investigator Oak Ridge Nat. Lab., 1948-49, cons. biol. div. Mem. Ky. Acad. Sci. (sec. 1937-46; pres. 1947-48), Am. Soc. Zoologists, Soc. for Study Growth, Am. Assn. U. Profs., Am. Soc. Human Genetics, Sigma Xi, Delta Chi. Democrat. Author articles on insect embryology, physiology of devel., histology, histol. technique. Home: 1020 Cooper Dr., Lexington, Ky. 40502. Died Jan. 26, 1965.

BRAUN, WERNER, microbiologist; b. Berlin, Germany, Nov. 16, 1914; s. Simon and Edith (Brach) B.; Ph.D., U. Gottingen, 1936; m. Barbara Melnikow, June 7, 1942; children—Renee, Stephanie, Robin. Came to U.S., 1936, naturalized, 1941. Guest investigator U. Mich., 1936-37; research asso. dept. zoology U. Cal. at Berkeley, 1937-42, asso. dept. vet. sci. Expt. Sta. Coll. Agr., 1942-48; med. bacteriologist, chief variation br. Chem. Corps Biol. Labs., Camp Detrick, Frederick, Md., 1948-55; prof. microbiology Inst. Microbiology, Rutgers U., New Brunswick, N.J., 1955-72; cons. U.S. Army Chem. Corps, 1955-68; USPHS, 1956-72, U.S. Dept. of Def., 1960-68, NSF, 1967-70; bd. sci. counselors Nat. Inst. Allergy and Infectious Diseases, NIH, 1966-69, chmn. bd. sci. counselors, 1968-69, vis. scientist, 1970-72; I.M. Lewis lectr. U. Tex., 1951; vis. prof. U. P.R. Med. Sch., 1957, 59, 60, 61, 63, 65, 67, 68; NIH research fellow, Israel, Paris, also vis. prof. Hebrew U., Hadassah Med. Sch., Jerusalem, 1962-63; vis. scientist Weizmann Inst., Israel, Pasteur Inst., Paris, Karolinska Inst., Stockholm, 1969-70; O. Stark lectr. Miami U., Oxford, O., 1971. Recipient Barnett Cohen award. Soc. Am. Bacteriologists, 1954; superior accomplishment award Chem. Corps, U.S. Army, 1954. Fellow Am. Acad. of Microbiology (pres. 1968-69), A.A.A.S.; mem. Theobald Smith Soc. (pres. 1957-58), Sci. Research Soc. Am., Am. Soc. Microbiology, Am. Assn. Immunologists, Genetics Soc. Am., Soc. Exptl. Biology and Medicine, Soc. Gen. Microbiology, Sigma Xi, Phi Sigma. Author: Bacterial Genetics, 1953, 2d edit., 1965. Editor several sci. books. Contbr. articles to sci. jours. Home: Princeton NJ Died Nov. 19, 1972.

BRAWLEY, FRANK, ophthalmologist; b. Orion, Ill., Nov. 23, 1875; s. Ellis T. and Eliza S. (Higgins) B.; Ph.G., Northwestern U., 1897; M.D., U. Ill., 1902; m. Mary Vernon Wilson, Apr. 24, 1907. Practiced in Chgo. since 1902; sr. ophthalmologist St. Luke's Hosp. Awarded Key of Honor Soc., Am. Acad. Ophthalmology and Otolaryngology. Fellow A.C.S.; mem. A.M.A., Ill. State Med. Soc., Chgo. Ophthal. Soc. (ex.-pres.), Phi Rho Sigma Fraternity. Clubs: Chicago Athletic Association, Flossmoor Country, Ill. Seniors Golf Assn. Author numerous monographs on eye and accessory sinuses of nose; contbr. to Am. Ency. Ophthalmology and Ophthalmic Therapeutics, Ophthalmic Operations. Home: 201 E. Walton St., Office: 30 N. Michigan Av., Chgo. Died Jan. 19, 1962; buried Oak Woods Cemetery, Chgo.

BRAY, JOHN LEIGHTON, metallurgist; b. Millbridge, Me., Aug. 11, 1890; s. Charles Ambergh and Vinetta (Cook) B.; B.S. Mass. Inst. of Tech., 1912, Ph.D., 1930; m. Jean Shaw, Aug. 23, 1925; children—Barbara Vilora, John Leighton. Metallurgist, Braden Copper Co., Rancagua, Chile, 1912-15, Consolidated Mining & Smelting Co., Trail, B.C., 1915-16, Blackbutte (Ore.) Quicksilver Co., 1916-17, N.Y. & Honduras Mining Co., Honduras, C.A., 1918-20; prof. metallurgy, N.S. Tech. Coll., 1920-21; metallurgist for U.S. Tariff Commn., 1921-23; prof. metallurgy, Purdue U., W. Lafayette, Ind., since 1947, head Sch. Chem. and Metallurgical Engring., 1935-47, prof. metall. engring. since 1947. Served as maj., Ordnance Dept., U.S. Army, World War I. Mem. Am. Inst. Mining and Metall. Engrs., Soc. of Metals, Am. Chem. Soc., Am. Inst. Chem. Engrs., Electrochem. Soc., Inst. of Metals (Eng.), Soc. for Promotion Engring. Edn., Scabbard and Blade, Sigma Psi, Tau Beta Pi, Phi Lambda Upsilon, Lambda Chi Alpha, Omega Chi Epsilon. Republican. Presbyn. Author: Textbook of Ore Dressing (with R.H. Richards and C.E. Locke), 1925; Principles of Metallurgy, 1930; German Grammar for Chemists, 1937; Introductory Readings in Technical German, 1940; Non Ferrous Production Metallurgy, 1941; Ferrous Production Metallurgy, 1942; Patent Law and Procedure, 1948. Home: 701 N. Chauncey Av., W. Lafayette, Ind. Died Dec. 6, 1952.

BRAY, WILLIAM CROWELL, chemist; b. Wingham, Ont., Can., Sept. 2, 1879; s. William Thomas and Sarah Jane (Willson) B.; B.A., U. of Toronto, 1902; Ph.D., U. of Leipzig, Germany, 1905; m. Nora Thomas, June 30, 1914. Research asso., 1905-10, asst. prof. physico-chem. research, 1910-12, Mass. Inst. Tech.; asst. prof. chemistry, 1912-16, asso. professor, 1916-18, prof. since 1918, University of Calif. Chmn. dept. chemistry, 1943-June 1945. Am. U. Experiment Sta., Washington , D.C., 1918; asso dir. Fixed Nitrogen Research Lab., Washington, 1919. Fellow Am. Acad. Arts and Sciences; mem. Nat. Acad. Sciences, Am. Chem. Soc., Am. Electrochem. Soc. Contbr. papers on inorganic and phys. chem. in Jour. Am. Chem. Soc. Home: 2708 Virgina St., Berkeley 4, Calif. Died Feb. 24, 1946.

BRAY, WILLIAM L., botanist; b. Burnside, Ill., Sept. 19, 1865; s. William and Martha Ann (Foster) B.; student State Normal Sch., Kirksville, Mo., 1883-85; Cornell U., 1889-91; A.B., Ind. U., 1893; A.M., Lake Forest U., 1894; U. Berlin, 1896-97; Ph.D., U. Chgo., 1898; D.S.C., Syracuse U., 1936; m. Alice Weston, Dec. 28, 1899; children—William Weston, Alice Roberta, Florence. Instr. botany Lake Forest U., 1894-95, adj. prof. biology, 1895; instr. botany U. Tex., 1897-98, adj. prof. 1898-1901, asso. prof., 1902-05, prof., 1905-07; prof. botany Syracuse U., 1907—, dean grad. sch. 1918-43, retired 1943. Collaborator U.S. Forest Service, 1899-1909; act. dean, N.Y. State Coll. of Forestry, 1911; chief Div. of Forestry, Tex. World's Fair Commn., 1903-04. Fellow A.A.A.S.; mem. Bot. Soc. Am., Ecol. Soc. Am., N.Y. Acad. Sciences, Phi Beta Kappa, Sigma Xi, Phi Kappa Phi. Methodist. Author: Development of Vegetation of N.Y. State, 1915; also several govt. bulls. on Texas forests and various articles on plant distribution and adaptation, in bot. jours. Bray Hall. N.Y. State Coll. Forestry named in his honor, 1933. Address: 863 Ostrom Av., Syracuse, N.Y. Died May 25, 1953.

BRAYMER, DANIEL HARVEY, electrical engr., editor; b. Hebron, N.Y., Nov. 29, 1883; s. George W. and Jennie Cordelia (Smith) B.; A.B., Cornell U., 1906, E.E., 1908; m. Ruth McGuire, 1925. Began practice as elec. engr., New York, 1908; editor Electrical Engineering (formerly Southern Electrician), Atlanta,

Ga., 1910-15; engring. editor Electrical World, New York, 1915-17; editor Electrical Record, 1917-19; returned to Electrical World as mng. editor, 1919, editor, 1921-22; editorial dir. Industrial Engr., 1922-25; consulting engr., Omaha, Neb., 1925—. Author: American Hydreolectric Practice, 1917; Armature Winding and Motor Repair, 1920; Rewinding Small Motors, 1925; Repair Shop Diagrams and and Connecting Tables, 1927; Rewinding and Connecting A.C. Motors, 1931. Died Oct. 29, 1932.

BRECHT, ROBERT PAUL, educator; b. Lancaster, Pa., Apr. 25, 1899; s. Milton Josiah and Mary Mehaffey (Wolfe) B.; B.S., U. Pa., 1922, A.M., 1925, Ph.D., 1931; m. June Dalbey Heller, Sept. 5, 1925; children—Robert Paul, Barbara June (Mrs. Benjamin Dawson, Junior), Mary Suzanne (now Mrs. Richard Mowry). Began as instructor industry Wharton Sch. Finance and Commerce, U. Pa., 1922-34, asst. prof., 1934-41, asso. prof., 1941-42, prof. industry, 1942-66, emeritus, 1967-70, chmn. geography and industry dept., 1941-58, mem. labor relations council, 1947-56; research asso. indsl. research dept, U. Pa., 1931; research cons. Work Project Adminstrn.-Nat. Research Project, 1936; lectr. management Pub. Service Inst., Department of Pub. Instrn., Commonwealth Pa., 1941-44; chmn. arbitrators Millville Mfg. Co., Textile Workers of America, from 1938; director several companies, 1956-62. Impartial chmn. adjustment bd. N.Y. Shipbldg. Corp., 1936-47, Phila. Knitted Outerwear Industry, from 1947; chmn., mem. various industry coms. Dept. of Labor, 1941, 43; pub. panel mem. 3d Regional War Labor Bd., 1943-45; spl. mediation rep. Nat. War Labor Bd., 1942-43; mem. panel of arbitrators Fed. Mediation and Conciliation Service; panel mem. N.J. Bd. Mediation, from 1959, Supervising Referees Election Inst., from 1959; research asso. Financial Execs. Research Inst., from 1960. Recipient Leffingwell medal Nat. Office Mgmt. Assn., 1948. Mem. Acad. Mgmt. (pres. 1941), A.I.M., Am. Assn. of University Profs., Nat. Academy of Arbitrators, The National Office Management Association (president 1951-52), Kappa Sigma. Author: Philadelphia Upholstery Wearing Industry (with Balderston, Hussey, Palmer and Wright), 1932; Management of an Enterprise (with Balderston, Karabasz and Riddle), 1937, rev., 1949; Practical Office Management (with Wylie and Gamber), 1937. Mem. cons. and adv. bd. Funk & Wagnalls New Standard Ency., 1947-50; mem. editorial cons. and advisers Harper & Bros. New Ency., 1955-60. Contbr. profl. jours. Home: Media PA Died May 21, 1970; buried Greenwood Cemetery, Lancaster PA

BRECK, JOHN H., mfg. chemist; b. Holyoke, Mass., June 5, 1877; s. Edward and Elizabeth (Devine) B.; D.Sc., American International College, 1958; m. Elizabeth R. Pratt, Oct. 11, 1905; children—Edward, M. Constance, Marion (Mrs. John F. Sullivan), John H. With J.H. Breck, Inc., Springfield, Mass., 1929—, beginning as chief chemist, successively pres. and treas., 1929-54, chmn. bd., 1954—. Mem. Am. Chem. Soc. Home: 26 Orlando St., Springfield 01108. Office: 115 Dwight St., Springfield, Mass. 01103. Died Feb. 16, 1965.

BRECKENRIDGE, JAMES MILLER, indsl. chemist; b. Jamestown, Ont., Can., Oct. 13, 1880; s. David and Jane (Lee) B.; A.B., Albion Coll., 1903; M.S., U. Wis., 1908, Ph.D., 1910; studied U. Chgo.; m. Alice Thurston, May 30, 1911; 1 dau., Margaret Jean. Prin. high schs., S.D., 1903-07; research chemist, Welsbach County, Gloucester, N.J., 1910-12; prof. chemistry Carroll Coll., 1912-13, Wabash Coll., 1914-46; asst. dir. Expt. Sta., Hercules Powder Co., Kenvil, N.J., 1917-19; dir. Sch. of Chemistry, Vanderbilt U., 1919-49, ret. Mem. Am. Chem. Soc., Soc. Chem. Industry, Am. Electrochem. Soc., Chem. Soc. (London), Am. Ceramic Soc., Deutsche Chemische Gesellschaft, Inst. Chem. Engrs., Gamma Alpha, Phi Lambda Upsilon, Sigma Xi. Meth. Research in alloys and electro-deposition of metals, industrial chem. problems, electrochem. potentials, conductivity of aluminum calcium alloys, and electro chem. potentials of copper in cyanide solutions, beryllium separation, preparation of beryllium chloride, preparation of beryllium-organo compounds. Home: 2001 Capers Av., Nashville 37212. Died Apr. 13, 1961; buried Woodlawn Meml. Park, Nashville.

BRECKENRIDGE, LESTER PAIGE, mech. engr.; b. Meriden, Conn., May 17, 1858; s. Moses Paige and Lucretia L. (Wetherell) B.; Ph.B., Sheffield Sci. Sch. (Yale), 1881; M.A., Yale, 1909; Eng.D., U. Illinois, 1910; m. May Brown, Dec. 19, 1883; children—Blanch F. (Mrs. Henry B. Dirks), Gladys S. (Mrs. Earl D. Finch), May H. (Mrs. D.B. Luckenbill); m. 2d, Susan W. Ford, July 26, 1911. Instr. mech. engring. Lehigh U., 1882-91, except 2 yrs. engaged in engring. work; prof. mech. engring. Mich. Agrl. Coll., 1891-93; prof. mech. engring. U. Ill., 1893-1909, dir. engring. expt. sta., 1905-09; prof. mech. engring. Sheffield Sci. Sch. (Yale) 1909-23, emeritus. Engr. in charge boilder div. U.S. Geol. Survey Fuel Testing Plant, St. Louis, 1904—. Contrived and equipped dynamometer cars, 1897-99; invented automatic recording machine, 1901. Mem. Am. Soc. M.E. (v.p. 1907-09), Soc. Promotion Engring. Edn., Western Soc. Engrs. (v.p. 1905-06), Am. Soc. Heating and Ventilating Engrs. (hon.). Chmn. adv. bd. Super-power Survey, 1920-21; mem. World Power Conf. Author articles in tech. jours., reports, bulls. Home: North Ferrisburg, Vt. Died Aug. 22, 1940; buried Westfield, Mass.

BREED, CHARLES BLANEY, engineer; b. Lynn, Mass., Nov. 28, 1875; s. Charles Otis and Sarah (Guilford) B.; S.B., Mass. Inst. Tech., 1897; married; children—Charles Alfred (by 1st marriage), David Edson and Nancy Eleanor (by 2d marriage). Began with city engring. dept., Lynn, 1894; resident engr., Walden Pond Dam, Lynn; consulting engr. for state commns. on pub. utility projects, also cities and railroads on eliminattion of grade crossings and transportation econ. problems; prof. r.r. and hwy. transportation, Mass. Inst. Tech., 1906-45, prof. emeritus, 1945—, head dept. civil engring., 1935-45; pres. acad. bd. U.S. Army School of Mil. Aeronautics, Mass. Inst. Tech., 1917-18; trustee Lynn Five Cents Savings Bank. Mem. Am. Soc. C.E. (ex-dir.); Am. Railway Engring. Assn., Am. Road Builders' Assn., Boston Soc. C.E. (ex-pres.), Chi Epsilon, Sigma Xi, Tau Beta Pi, Rep. Meth. Mason. Clubs: Boston City (ex-pres.), Algonquin, Brae Burn Country (Newton). Author: (with Prof. George L. Hosmer) Principles and Practice of Surveying (vols. I and II), 1906, 1908; also Surveying, 1942; also several brochures on highway transportation economics. Asso. editor American Civil Engineers' Pocketbook, 1911, American Mining Engineers' Handbook, 1913. Home: Harbor Rd., Camden, Me. Died Aug. 9, 1958; buried Mountain View Cemetery, Camden, Me.

BREED, ROBERT STANLEY, bacteriologist; b. Brooklyn, Pa., Oct. 17, 1877; s. Robert Fitch and Emma Marie (Beers) B.; B.S., Harvard, 1902; student U. Gottingen, 1910, U. Kiel, 1911; m. Louise Miller Helm, Aug. 23, 1899 (died Dec. 13, 1905); 1 dau., Alice Fitch; m. 2d, Emma Margaret Edson, July 2, 1913. Inst. biology U. Colo., 1898-99; asst. in zoology Harvard, 1900-02; prof. biology Allegheny Coll., 1902-13, sec. faculty, 1907-10; bacteriologist N.Y. State Agril Expt. Sta., Cornell U., 1913-47, emeritus prof. bacteriology, 1947—. Vice pres. World Dairy Congress, Washington, 1923, London 1928; del. Berne, 1914, Rome, 1934; permanent sec. Internat. Com. on Bect. Nomenclature, Internat. Assn. Microbiology and Internat. Bot. Congress, 1930—; del. 2d Inter-Am. Conf. Agr., Mexico City, 1942. Fellow A.A.A.S. (council 1932-34), Am. Pub. Health Assn. (vice chmn. lab. sect. 1932-33, chmn. 1933-34); mem. Soc. Am. Bacteriologists (pres. 1927), Am. Dairy Sci. Assn., Am. Biol. Soc., Internat. Assn. Milk Sanitarians, Brit. Soc. Applied Bacteriology (corr.), Cuban Soc. Microbiologists, Geneva Hist. Soc. (pres. 1935-42), Phi Beta Kappa, Sigma Xi, Phi Gamma Delta. Presbyn. Clubs: Rotary, University (pres. 1928-30). Author bulls. and articles on biol. subjects, especially milk hygiene and systematic bacteriology. Editor in chief Bergey's Manual Determinative Bacteriology, 1937—; asso. editor Jour. of Bacteriology and of Biol. Abstracts. Address: 6 Sunset Dr., Geneva, N.Y. Died Feb. 10, 1956.

BREIDENBAUGH, EDWARD SWOYER, chemist; b. Newville, Pa., Jan. 13, 1849; s. Rev. E. and Catherine Elizabeth (Swoyer) B.; grad. Pa. Coll., Gettysburg, 1868; studied chemistry, Sheffield Scientific Sch. (Yale), 1871-73; hon. Sc.D., Pa. Coll., 1883; m. Ida Kitzmiller, Nov. 20, 1873; children—Edna, Ida May. Instr. analytical chemistry, Sheffield Sch., 1872-73; prof. chemistry and mineralogy, Pa. Coll., 1874-1924; emeritus prof., 1925. Was mineralogist to State Bd. of Agr.; practiced as chemist. Author: Pennsylvania College Book; Lecture Notes on Inorganic Chemistry; Mineralogy on the Farm; Directory in Elementary Chemistry; Course in Qualitative Analysis; Syllabus of Lectures on Geology. Home: Gettysburg, Pa. Died Sept. 5, 1926.

BREMER, JOHN LEWIS, embryologist; b. N.Y.C., Nov. 3, 1874; s. John Lewis and Mary (Fransworth) B.; A.B., Harvard, 1896, M.D., 1901; post-grad. work, Oxford, 1896-97; m. Mary C. Bigelow, Sept. 29, 1906. Asst. in histology and embryology, 1902, instr., 1903-06, demonstrator in histology, 1906-12, asst. prof., 1912-15, asso. prof., 1915-31, Hersey prof. of anatomy, 1931-41, emeritus 1941—, Harvard University. Fellow American Acad. Arts and Sciences; Mem. Am. Assn. Anatomists, Boston Soc. Natural History. Clubs: Somerset, Harvard. Home: 113 Marlborough St., Boston, Mass. Died Dec. 25, 1959.

BREMNER, GEORGE HAMPTON, civil engr.; b. Marshalltown, Ia., Dec. 17, 1861; s. William and Catherine C. (Hampton) B.; C.E., State U. of Ia., 1883; m. Louie A. Stephenson, Sept. 5, 1888. Began in engring. work with C.G.W. Ry., 1883, and C.&N.W. Ry., 1884; with the C.,B.&Q. Ry. in various positions, 1884—, engr. of the Ill. dist., 1902—. Home: LaGrange, Ill. Died Apr. 2, 1927.

BRENEMAN, ABRAM ADAM, chemist; b. Lancaster, Pa., Apr. 28, s. Dr. Abraham and Anna B.; B.S., Pa. State Coll., 1866, M.Sc., 1871; unmarried. Instr. chemistry, Pa. State Coll., 1867-68, prof. 1869-72; asst. prof. industrial chemistry, Cornell U., 1875-79, prof. 1879-82; analyst, chem. expert, writer and lecturer, 1882—; also in consulting practice. Inventor Breneman process of rendering iron non-corrodible. Editor Journal, Am. Chem. Soc., 1884-93. Chmn. internat. jury on mineral waters, Chicago Expn., 1893, St. Louis Expn., 1904; expert mem. municipal explosives commn., New York, 1906-09. Author: (with Prof. G. C. Caldwell) A. Manual of Introductory Laboratory Practice, 1875; Report on the Fixation of Atmospheric Nitrogen, 1889; Report on Sewer and Conduit Explosions in New York, 1909, 1910. Address: New York, N.Y. Died May 10, 1928.

BRENKE, WILLIAM CHARLES, prof. mathematics; b. Berlin, Germany, Apr. 12, 1874; s. Frederick Martin and Wilhelmina (Kloepper) B.; brought to U.S., 1882; A.B., U. of Ill. 1896, M.S., 1898; Ph.D., Harvard, 1907; m. Kate Read, Aug. 16, 1898; children—Katherine (Mrs. R.T. Dunstan), Bernice. Instr. mathematics and astronomy, U. of Ill., 1896-1904; instr. in mathematics and astronomy, Harvard, 1905-07; successively asst. prof., asso. prof. and prof. math., U. of Neb., 1907-44, emeritus since 1944; chmn. dept. math. and astronomy, 1934-43. Member American Math. Soc., Math. Assn. of America, Nat. Council of Math. Teachers Am. Soc. for Engring. Edn., Am. Assn. Univ. Profs., A.A.A.S., Deutshe Mathematiker Vereinigung, Sigma Xi. Presbyterian. Author: Advanced Algebra and Trigonometry, 1910; Algebra, First Course (with Edith Long), 1913; Plane Geometry (with same), 1916; Elements of Plane Trigonometry, 1917; Advanced Algebra, 1917; Calculus (with E.W. Davis), 1918. Contbr. articles on mathematics and astronomy. Home: 1250 S. 21st St., Lincoln NB

BRES, EDWARD SEDLEY, cons. civil engr.; b. New Orleans, Sept. 15, 1888; s. Joseph Ray and Sara Ella (Hughes) B.; B.E. in Civil Engring., Tulane U., 1910, C.E., 1931; m. Ann Elizabeth Todd, Sept. 7, 1917; children—Edward Sedley (officer U.S. Army), Elizabeth (Mrs. Samuel D. G. Robbins). In engring. work, harbors, flood control, dredging, docks, highway constrn., New Orleans and State of La.; mem. Eustis & Bres, 1910-17; cons. engr. and contractor, 1919-26; mem. Scott & Bres, cons. and contracting engr., 1926-41. Served from lt. to maj. C.E., AEF, U.S. Army, 1917-19; col. C.E. Res., 1927, reentered Army, 1941, brig. gen., 1945, maj. gen., 1946; ret., 1950; cons. and regional engr. U.S. Army constrn. projects, 1941; dep. chief engr. U.S. Army Forces in Australia, 1942-43; regulating officer Office of G.H.Q., S.W. Pacific Forces, 1942-44; duty Gen. Staff Corps, Washington, 1945-50; mem. N.G. Res. policies com., 1945; exec. for Res. and R.O.T.C. affairs, 1945-47; mem. sec. of army personnel bd., 1947-50. Chmn. La. Com. for Trade Recovery, 1933; La. del. Nat. Rivers and Harbors Conf., 1935; mem. adv. bd. Soil and Foundation Survey, New Orleans and vicinity, 1935; mem. La. State Bd. Engring. Examiners, 1941; mem. housing code rev. com. D.C., 1954-55. Mem., chmn. Battle of New Orleans Sesquicentennial Celebration Commn., 1963 (apptd. by pres.). Mem. Tulane Athletic Council, 1937-40. Decorated Legion of Merit with oak leaf cluster, World War I Victory medal with 3 stars, World War II Victory medal, Asiatic-Pacific medal with 4 stars, and other medals. Recipient Freedom Found. award, 1965. Nat. dir. Soc. Am. Mil. Engrs. 1941; nat. pres. Res. Officers Assn. of U.S., 1939-40, pres. New Orleans chpt., 1930, La. dept. 1932, IV Corps area council, 1934-35; dir. Navy League of U.S., 1953. Mem. Am. Soc. C.E. (life mem., past pres. La. sect., past nat. dir.), La. Engring. Soc. (hon. mem., past pres.), Am. Legion, Tulane Alumni Assn. (sec. 1915, pres. 1941), Soc. War of 1812, Mil. Order World Wars, Delta Kappa Epsilon (nat. hon. pres. 1951), Theta Nu Epsilon, Kappa Delta Phi, Delta Tau Omega, Omicron Delta Kappa, Scabbard and Blade. Clubs: Boston (New Orleans); Army and Navy, Cosmos, Post Mortem (Washington). Home: New Orleans LA Died Sept. 24, 1967; buried Arlington Nat. Cemetery, Arlington VA

BRETHERTON, SIDNEY ELLIOTT, mining engr.; b. Gloucester, England, Apr. 16, 1854; s. George and Elvira (Legg) B.; brought to U.S., 1859; ed. pub. schs., Flinton, Ont., Can., and night sch., Oswego, N.Y.; m. Belle Wright, Sept. 1, 1886. Began as asst. assayer Morgan Smelter, Salt Lake City, Utah, 1877; assayer, Stockton Smelter, Utah, 1878; assayer and chemist, La Plata Smelter, Leadville, Colo., 1879-81; supt. and metallurgist, Bonanza Smelter, Colo., 1882, Ark. Valley Smelter, Leadville, 1882-83; gen. supt. and metallurgist, Am. Smelting Works, Leadville, 1883-93; in consulting practive, 1893-1905; consulting engr., Afterthourght Cooper Co., 1905-16; consulting practice, 1916; retired, 1926. Mason (K.T.). Home: Berkeley, Calif. Died Oct. 4, 1929.

BREWSTER, JAMES, wagon mfr.; b. Preston, New London County, Conn. Aug. 6, 1788; s. Joseph and Hannah (Tucker) B.; m. Mary Hequembourg, 1810. Apprenticed to wagon-maker, Northampton, Mass., 1804-09; moved to N.Y.C., 1809; opened wagon shop, New Haven, Conn., 1810; became known for quality in all types of horse drawn tranps.; opened warehouse and repair shop, N.Y.C., 1827; helped finance New Haven & Hartford R.R. (1st Conn. railroad), pres., 1834-48; contbr. to an orphan asylum, almshouse, street improvement, temperance movements, other philanthropic interests. Died Nov. 22, 1866.

BREWSTER, WILLIAM, ornithologist; b. Wakefield, Mass., July 5, 1851; grad. Cambridge High School, 1869; hon. A.M., Amherst, 1880, Harvard, 1899; m. Caroline F. Kettell, Feb. 9, 1878. Asst. in charge of collection birds and mammals, Boston Soc. Natural

History, 1880-87; in charge dept. of mammals and birds, Cambridge Museum Comparative Zoölogy, 1885-1900, curator, dept. of birds, 1900—; most of his time devoted to managing private museum of ornithology at his place in Cambridge. Trustee Brewster Free Acad. Address: Cambridge, Mass. Died July 11, 1919.

BRIDGES, CALVIN BLACKMAN, geneticist; b. Schuyler Falls, N.Y., Jan. 11, 1889; s. Leonard Victor and Amelia C. (Blackman) B.; B.S., Columbia, 1912, Ph.D., 1916; m. Gertrude Frances Ives, Sept. 7, 1912; children—Philip Newell, Norman Ives (dec.), Betsy Blackman, Nathan Ives. Research work in heredity under grants from Carnegie Inst., 1915-19; mem. staff, Carnegie Instn., 1919—. Mem. Nat. Acad. Sciences. Atheist. Author: The Mechanism of Mendelian Heredity, 1915; Sex-linked Inheritance in Drosophila (with T. H. Morgan), 1916; Contributions to the Genetics of Drosophila Melanogaster (with same), 1919, 23; Genetics of Drosophila, 1925. Home: Leonia, N.J. Died Dec. 27, 1938.

BRIDGES, ROBERT, physician; b. Phila., Mar. 5, 1806; s. Culpepper and Sarah (Clifton) B.; grad. Dickinson Coll., Carlisle, Pa., 1824; M.A., U. Pa., 1828. Became tchr. chemistry Phila. Coll. Pharmacy, 1831, turstee, 1839, prof. gen. and pharm. chemistry, 1842, prof. emeritus, 1879; vaccine physician, several years; apptd. dist. physician during cholera epidemic, 1832; prof. chemistry Franklin Med. Coll., 1846-48; became mem. Acad. Natural Scis., 1835, presented index of genera in its Herbarium (with Dr. Paul B. Goddard), 1835, revised index, 1843, pres. acad., 1864; became fellow Coll. Physicians of Phila., 1842, librarian, 1867-69, catalogued Urinary Calculi in Mutter Mus.; became mem. Franklin Inst. of Phila., 1836, Am. Philos. Soc., 1844; asso. editor Am. Jour. Pharmacy, 1839-46, mem. com. for revision of pharmacopoeia, 1840, 70; editor Am. editions of Elementary Chemistry (George Fownes), Elements of Chemistry (Thomas Graham). Died Feb. 20, 1882.

BRIDGMAN, PERCY WILLIAMS, Am. physicist; b. Cambridge, Mass., Apr. 21, 1882; s. Raymond Landon and Mary Ann Marie (Williams) B.; A.B., Harvard, 1904, A.M., 1905, Ph.D., 1908; Sc.D., 1934, 39, 41, Princeton, 1950; Yale, 1951; Dr. honoris causa, Paris, 1950; m. Olive Ware, July 16, 1912; children—Jane, Robert Ware. Fellow Harvard, 1908-10, instr. physics, 1910-13, asst. prof. 1913-19, prof. 1919, Hollis prof. math. and natural philosophy, 1926-50, Higgins U. prof. Harvard, 1950-54, emeritus. Fellow Am. Acad. Arts and Scis.; mem. Am. Philos. Soc., Washington, Nat. acads. scis., Am. Phys. Soc.; corr. mem. Academia Nacional de Ciencias (Mexico); hon. fellow, Phys. Soc. (London). Foreign mem. Royal Soc. (London), Indian Acad. of Scis. Recipient Rumford medal Am. Acad. Arts and Scis., 1917; Cresson medal, Franklin Inst., 1932; Rozeboom medal, Royal Acad. Scis. Amsterdam, 1933; Comstock prize Nat. Acad. Scis., 1933; Research Corporation award, 1937; Nobel prize in physics for researches in high pressure, 1946. Mem. Phi Beta Kappa, Sigma Xi. Author: The Logic of Modern Physics, 1927; The Physics of High Pressure, 1931; Thermodynamics of Electrical Phenomena in Metals, 1934; The Nature of Physical Theory, 1936; The Intelligent Individual and Society, 1938; The Nature of Thermodynamics, 1941; Reflections of a Physicist, 1950; The Nature of Some of Our Physical Concepts, 1952; Studies in Large Plastic Flow and Fracture, 1952; The Way Things Are, 1959. Showed that viscosity increases tremendously with pressure (except for water); obtained new form of phosphorus by heating under pressure, 1921; his work led to prodn. of synthetic diamonds in 1955; also studied electrical conduction in metals and properties of crystals; vigorous exponent of operationalism as a philosophy of science. Died, a suicide, Randolph, N.H., Aug. 20, 1961.

BRIGGS, LYMAN JAMES, physicist, dir. emeritus Nat. Bur. Standards; b. Assyria, Mich., May 7, 1874; s. Chauncey L. and Isabella (McKelvey) B.; B.S., Mich. State Coll., 1893, Sc.D., 1932; M.S., U. Mich., 1895, LL.D., 1936; Ph.D., Johns Hopkins 1901; D.Eng., S.D., Sch. Mines, 1935; Sc.D., George Washington U., 1937; Georgetown U., 1939; Columbia, 1944; m. Katharine E. Cook, Dec. 23, 1896; children—Mrs. Isabel Myers, Albert Cook (dec.). In charge Phys. Lab. Div. (now Bur. Soils), U.S. Dept. Agr., 1896-1906; physicist in charge Biophys. Lab., Bur. Plant Industry, 1906-12, in charge biophys. investigations, 1912-20; detailed to Bur. Standards by exec. order, 1917-19, chief div. mechanics and sound, 1920-33, asst. dir. research and testing, 1926-33, dir. Nat. Bureau, 1933-45; ret., 1945; Mem. Nat. Advisory Com. for Aeros., 1933-45; vice chmn., 1942-45, mem. aerodynamics sub-com., 1922-30; chmn. Fed. Specifications Bd., 1932-40; Fed. Fire Council, 1933-39; bd. dirs. Am. Standards Assn., 1933-45. Life Trustee Nat. Geog. Soc. 1933— (chmn. research com., 1934-60, chmn. emeritus, 1960-63); dir. sci. program stratosphere balloon flights, others. Trustee George Washington U., 1945—; mem. exec. com. engring. div. Nat. Research Council 1945-50. Awarded Medal for Merit, 1948, Gold medal U.S. Dept. Commerce for exceptional service. Fellow A.A.A.S., Am. Physics Soc. (pres. 1938); mem. Nat., Washington (pres. 1917) acads. sci.; Philos. Soc. Washington (pres. 1916), Am. Philos. Soc., Am. Acad. Arts and Scis., Inst. Aero. Scis., Phys. Soc. Eng. (hon.), Newcomen Soc. (Eng.), Washington Acad. Medicine (pres., 1945-46), Tau Beta Pi, Sigma Xi, Sigma Pi Sigma; hon. fellow Am. Coll. Dentists; mem. Am. Soc. M.E. Mem. U.S. nat. com. for internat. geophys. year. Awarded Magellan medal (with Paul R. Heyl), 1922. Clubs: Cosmos (pres. 1922), Federal (pres. 1928). Contbr. to govt. and tech. publs. Home: 3208 Newark St., Cleveland Park, Washington, D.C. Died Mar. 26, 1963.

BRIGHAM, ALBERT PERRY, geologist; b. Perry, N.Y., June 12, 1855; s. Horace A. and Julia (Perry) B.; A.B., Colgate, 1879, A.M., 1882, LL.D., 1925; student Hamilton Theol. Sem., 1879-82; A.M., Harvard, 1892; Sc.D., Syracuse, 1918; L.H.D., Franklin, 1921; m. Flora Winegar, June 27, 1882; children—Charles Winegar (dec.), Elizabeth (Mrs. Lawrence V. Roth). Ordained Bapt. ministry, 1882; pastor Stillwater, N.Y., 1882-85, Utica, 1885-91; pastor Stillwater, N.Y., 1882-85, Utica, 1885-91; became prof. geology, Colgate, 1892, emeritus prof. Instr. Harvard Summer Sch. of Geology, 4 summers; prof. Cornell Summer Sch., 1901-04, U. of Wis., 1906; lecturer, Oxford U. Sch. of Geogrophy, 4 summers and Hilary term, 1924, also at U. of London, 1924. Chief examiner geography, Coll. Entrance Exam. Bd., 1902-13; examiner in geography, N.Y. State Edn. Dept., 1911-13, 1917-19; vice chmn. div. geol. geography Nat. Research Council; mem. gen. geog. com. U.S. Commn. Washington Bicentenary. Author: A Text-Book of Geology, 1900; Introduction to Physical Geography (with G. K. Gilbert), 1902; From Trail to Railway Through the Appalachians, 1907; Commercial Geography, i911; Essentials of Geography (with C. T. McFarlane), 1916; Cape Cod and the Old Colony 1920; Manual for Teachers of Geography (with C. T. McFarlane), 1921; The United States of America (U. of London Press), 1927; Glacial Geology and Geographic Conditions of Lower Mohawk Valley, 1929. Collaborator, N.Y. State Museum; consultant in geography, Library of Congress. Contbg. editor Geog. Rev. Died Mar. 31, 1932.

BRILL, GEORGE MACKENZIE, cons. engr.; b. Poughquag, N.Y., Mar. 24, 1866; s. Thomas and Mary J. (Hurd) B.; M.E. from Cornell U. in 1891, M.M.E., same 1905; m. Achsah A. Quick, June 1, 1892; children—Elliot M., G. Meredith, Roland C.; m. 2d, Edith Seaman Brill, June 4, 1932. Research engr., Solvay Process Co., Syracuse, 1891-96; chief engr. Solvay Process Co., Detroit, 1896-97; cons. engr. Solvay Process Co., 1904-14; gen. engr., Swift & Co., Chicago, 1897-1900; cons. practice, Chicago, 1900-13, engring. investigations abroad, 1910, 12, 13; chmn. bd. engrs., smoke suppression, Chicago, 1907-12; mem. Jury of Awards and chmn. of jury covering gen. machinery, San Francisco Expn., 1915; joined staff of Guggenheim Bros. as cons. mech. engr. early in 1917, but resigned to enter mil. service; commd. maj. O.R.C., July 1917, and in charge of plant facilities in office of acting chief of ordnance to Apr. 1918; in charge requirements sect. of Emergency Fleet Corp., representing it on War Industries Bd., later cons. engr. for the corp.; determined condition and value of ships requisitioned by President Wilson, Aug. 3, 1917, upon which claims had not been settled, Jan. 1, 1919; cons. practice, N.Y. City, since 1919. Fellow A.A.A.S., Am. Geog. Soc., Am. Soc. M.E. (past v.p.), Sigma Xi. Republican. Home: 19 Kingston Av., Poughkeepsie NY

BRILL, HARVEY CLAYTON, chemist; b. Preble County, O., Dec. 29, 1881; s. John and Matilda (Velte) B.; A.B., Miami U., 1908; Ph.D., U. of Mich., 1911; m. Gertrude Davidson, June 17, 1913; 1 dau., Elizabeth. Asst. prof. chemistry, Miami U., 1911-13; organic chemist Bur. of Science, Manila, P.I., 1913-16; chief Div. of Organic Chemistry, same, 1916-18; member Food and Drugs Board, P.I., 1914-17; prof., head dept. chemistry, Miami U., from 1918. Chem. engr. Fellow A.A.A.S., Ohio Acad. Sci., Am. Institute Chemists; mem. American Chemical Society, Deutsche Chemische-Gesellschaft, Phi Sigma Kappa, Sigma Xi, Phi Lambda Upsilon, Phi Beta Kappa, Pi Gamma Mu. Democrat. Presbyterian. Author many papers dealing with original investigations in organic chemistry. Home: Oxford OH Died Jan. 11, 1972; buried Oxford Cemetery.

BRILL, NATHAN EDWIN, physician; b. New York, Jan. 13, 1860; s. Simon and Adelheit (Frankenthal) B.; A.B., Coll. City of New York, 1877, A.M., 1883; M.D., Univ. Med. Coll. (New York, 1877, A.M., 1883; M.D., Univ. Med. Coll. (New York U.), 1880; m. Elsa M. Josephthal, June 8, 1899; children—Elisabeth Joyce, John Lewis. Interne Bellevue Hosp., 1879-81, attending phys. 1st med. div., Mt. Sinai Hosp., 1893—; prof. clin. medicine, Coll. phys. and Surg. (Columbia), 1910—; consulting phys. Mt. Sinai Hosp. Discoverer, 1910, of previously unrecognized form of typhus fever known as Brill's disease. Major Med. O.R.C., 1917, and dir. Base Hospital N. 3. Trustee N.Y. Acad. Medicine; mem. Pub. Health Com.; fellow New York Acad. Medicine. Translator: Klemperer Clinical Diagnosis, 1898. Home: New York, N.Y. Died Dec. 13, 1925.

BRINCKE, WILLIAM DRAPER, physician, pomologist; b. Kent County, Del., Feb. 9, 1798; s. John and Elizabeth (Gordon) B.; grad. Princeton, 1816; M.D., U. Pa., 1819; m. Sarah T. Physick, 1821; m. 2d, Elizabeth Bishpam Reeves, 1832. Began practice of medicine, Wilmington, 1819, Phila., 1825; physician concerned with contagious diseases City Hosp., 1827-39; active in control of Asiatic cholera epidemic, 1832; a pomologist, developed numerous fruit varieties, worked primarily with small fruits and pears; published findings of strawberry expt. in Farmer's Cabinet, 1846; frequent contbr. to Horticulturist; a founder Am. Pomol. Soc.; retired from med. practice due to ill health, 1859. Died Dec. 16, 1862.

BRINCKERHOFF, HENRY MORTON, elec. engr.; b. Fishkill-on-Hudson, N.Y., Apr. 20, 1868; s. Peter Remsen and Helen (Morton) B.; grad. Stevens Inst. of Tech., 1890; m. Florence L. Fay, Jan. 20, 1903. Constrn. work Thomson-Huston Co. on West End Street Ry., Boston; asst. engr. in power house Utica Belt Line Street Ry., 1891-92; foreman in charge car equipment Gen. Elec. Co., Boston, Coney Island and Brooklyn Ry.; asst. elec. engr. Intramural Ry., World's Columbia Expn., Chicago, 1893, first 3d rail elevated road of U.S.; elec. engr. Met. West Side Elevated Ry., Chicago, first large elevated road for city Transportation equipped with electricity, Aug. 1, 1894, asst. gne. mgr. and gen. mgr. 1898-1906; elec. asso. of William Barclay Parsons since 1906. Mem. Am. Soc. Elec. Engrs., Western Soc. Engrs. Residence: 3 W. 8th St. Office: 60 Wall St., New York. Died Oct. 13, 1949.

BRINLEY, CHARLES A., chemist, metallurgist; b. Hartford, Conn., Aug. 23, 1847; s. George B.; attached to geol. survey in Calif., 1864-65; grad. Sheffield Scientific School, Yale, 1869; m. 1877, Mary Goodrich Frothingham. Took 3 yrs. post-graduate course in chemistry and metallurgy; supt. of steel works nr. Phila., and of a sugar refinery there, 1872-92; mng. dir. Am. Pulley Co. since 1899; since 1894 pres. Am. Soc. for Extension of Univ. Teaching. Address: 247 S. 16th St., Philadepia. Deceased.

BRINSMADE, ROBERT BRUCE, mining engr.; b. Elmira, N.Y., Aug. 27, 1873; s. Hobar and Ella Mary (Lyon) B.; B.S. in Mining, Washington U., 1894; E.M., Lehigh U., 1895; m. Helen Christine Steenbrock, July 24, 1909; children—Virginia Skidmore, Robert Trugot, Harold Steenbock, Akbar Farichild, Lyon Ruus, Alan Bruce, Christine. Mining eng., various mining cos. of Mont., 1896-99, War Eagle Mine, Rossland, B. C., 1899-1900; metallurgist, Columbia and other mining cos., Mo., 1900-0l; mine and smelter supt. at Cordoba, Argentina, S.A., 1901-02; designing engr., Ordnance Bur. U.S.A., Rock Island, Ill., 1902-03, Solvay Coke Co., Syracuse, N.Y., 1903-04; supt. Rossie Iron Mines, St. Lawrence Co., N.Y., 1904-05; prof. mining engring., State Mining Coll., Socorro, N.M., 1905-06; consulting engr., St. Louis, 1906-07; organizer and dir. State Mining Sch., Platteville, Wis., 1907-08; mining exploration, San Domingo, W.I., 1908-09; prof. mining engring., U. of W.Va., 1909-11; consulting practice, 1911—; economist Mexican Ministry of Finance, 1920-24. Unitarian. Author: Mining Without Timer, 1911; Latifundismo Mexicano, 1916; Catastro Democratico, 1926; Exploring Spanish America, 1927; Mexican Religious Crisis, 1928; What's the Use of Working?, 1931; Silver Cure for Uncle Sam, 1933; Engineer's Cure for Plutocracy, 1936. Address: Luis Potosi City, Mexico Died Sept. 28, 1936.

BRINTON, PAUL HENRY MALLET-PREVOST, chemist; b. Richmond, Va., May 8, 1882; s. Col. Joseph P. and Kate (Mallet-Prevost) B.; student, Trinity Coll., Hartford, Conn., and Stevens Inst. Tech., Hoboken, N.J., 1900-02; Chemisches Laboratorium Fresenius, Wiesbaden, Germany, 1907-09; B.S., U. Minn., 1912, M.S., 1913, Ph.D., 1916; m. Mary Adams Rice, 1906. With various elec. mfg. and mining cos. until 1907; instr. chemistry U. Minn., 1909-12; asst. prof. and prof., U. Ariz., 1912-20; prof. and head of div. of analytical chemistry, U. Minn., 1921-27; resigned to devote time to private research; cons. chemist; vis. prof. chemistry, U. So. Cal., 1932-42. Capt. Chem. Warfare Service, U.S. Army; chief of analyt. research unit, chem. research sect., 1918. Fellow A.A.A.S., Am. Inst. Chemists, mem. Am. Chem. Soc., Am. Assn. Univ. Profs., Phi Kappa Phi, Sigma Xi, Phi Lambda Upsilon, Phi Gamma Chi, Psi Upsilon. Christian Scientist. Contbr. numerous papers on analyt. chemistry and chemistry of rare elements. Address: Madre del Oro Mine, Oracle, Ariz. Died Nov. 16, 1966.

BRISBIN, CLARENCE FRANKLIN, pioneer telephone executive; b. Greenville, Pa., Oct. 12, 1871; s. James Montgomery and Martha (Showers) B.; ed. pub. and select schs., and Pricketts Sch. of Commerce, Phila.; m. Marion Perry, of Brooklyn, Pa., Jan. 9, 1902. Began active career with James Humphrey & Son, lumber mchts., Greenville; with W. T. Craig & Son, lumber, Greenville, 1885-94; mgr. flour mill of A. D. Mead & Son, Du Bois, Pa., 1894-95; installer and inspector Central Dist. and Printing Telegraph Co., Du Bois, 1895-97; first solicitor Central Pa. Telephone & Supply Co., Scranton, 1897-1900, local mgr., 1900-02; after merger with Pa. Telephone Co. served as div. supt., Wilkes-Barre, 1902-07; after merger with Phila. Bell Telephone Co. forming the Bell Telephone Co. of Pa. was dist. plant supvr. at Wilkes-Barre, 1907-10, dist. mgr. 1910-19, div. mgr., at Harrisburg, 1919-21; genl. connecting co. supervisor at Phila. in charge relations with state and federal govts., railroads, connecting and independent telephone cos., 1921-27; from formation of N.J. Bell Telephone, 1927, served as v.p. in charge personnel and pub. relations, retired, 1932. One of best known telephone pioneers; active in early telephone socs. which were forerunners of employees training courses now conducted throughtout Bell System. Director Bur. of Civilian Relief Am. Red Cross, of Wyoming Valley, World War; dir. and nat. councillor Mfrs. Council (N.J.); dir. and v.p. N.J. State Chamber of Commerce. Mem. H. G. McCully Chapter Telephone Pioneers of America. Mason. Clubs: Essex, Downtown, Newark Athletic (Newark); Braidburn Country (Madison). Home: 305 West End Av., New York NY

BRISTOL, CHARLES LAWRENCE, biologist; b. Ballston Spa, N.Y., Sept. 29, 1859; s. Lawrence W. and Carolina (Hawkins) B.; B.S., New York U., 1883. M.S., 1888; teacher sciences, Riverview Acad., Poughkeepsie, N.Y., 1884-87; m. Ellen Gallup, Jan. 28, 1890; children—Lawrence, Elisabeth (Mrs. W. E. Greenleaf). Prof. zoölogy, U. of S.D., 1887-91; fellow Clark U., 1891-92, U. of Chicago, 1892-93, Ph.D., 1895; prof. biology, New York U., 1894-1925 (emeritus); prof. biology on University World Cruise, 1926-27. Directed zoöl. expdns. to Bermuda and made successful expts. in transporting tropical marine animals alvie to New York Aquarium. Address: New York, N.Y. Died Aug. 27, 1931.

BRISTOL, WILLIAM HENRY, mathematician; b. Waterbury, Conn., July 5, 1859; s. Benjamin Hiel and Pauline (Phelps) B.; M.E., Stevens Inst. Tech., 1884; m. J. Louise Wright, Sept. 8, 1885 (died 1888); m. 2d, Elise H. Myers, June 28, 1899. Organized, 1882, manual training dept. of Workingman's Sch., New York, and teacher same, 1882-86; instr. mathematics, Stevens Inst. Tech., 1886-88, asst. prof., 1888-99, prof., 1899-1906. Organized, 1889, and pres. The Bristol Co. (mfg. his inventions). Inventor of numerous recording instruments for pressure, temperature and electricity, steel belt-lacing, sound ampilfying and talking motion picture apparatus, etc.; awarded John Scott Legacy medal, Franklin Inst., Phila., 1890; medal and diploma, Chicago Expn., 1893; silver medal, Paris Expn., 1900; gold medal, St. Louis Expn., 1904; grand prize, Panama P.I. Expn., 1915. Home: Waterbury, Conn. Died June 18, 1930.

BRISTOW, ALGERNON THOMAS, physician; b. Richmond, Eng., Nov. 29, 1851; s. Isaac and Charlotte (Andrews(B.; grad. Brooklyn Poly. Inst., 1869; A.B., Y-ale, 1873; M.D., Coll. Phys. and Surg. (Columbia), 1876; m. Emeline Ashmead, June 17, 1891. Surgeon L.I. Coll., Kings County, and St. John's hosps.; consulting surgeon to Bushwick Central and L.I. State hosps.; clin. prof. surgery, L.I. Coll. Hosp. Wrote chapter on post-mortem examinations in Hamilton's Legal Medicine; chapter on bacteriology Fowler's Surgery. Home: Brooklyn, N.Y. Died Mar. 26, 1913.

BRITTIN, LEWIS HOTCHKISS, engineer; b. Derby, Conn., Feb. 8, 1877; s. Edwin and Mary (Hotchkiss) B.; prep. edn., Gunnery and Ridge schs., Washington, Conn.; student Harvard, 1897-99; m. Arna Torkelson, 1919 (died July 25, 1935). Engineer Newhall Engineering Co., Sierra Madre Land & Lumber Co.; mgr, Nat. Lamp Div. of Gen. Electric Co.; v.p. and gen. mgr. Northwestern Terminal, Minneapolis; founder, vice pres. and gen. mgr. Northwest Airways, Inc.; consultant, Bureau Foreign and Domestic Commerce, U.S. Dept. of Commerce; cons. and collaborator, U.S. Dept. Agr.; cons. Bur. Fgn. and Domestic Commerce, N.Y. Bd. Trade, dir. Edward S. Evans Transportation Research, Washington, D.C. Pres. Chicago Air Traffic Assn.; v.p. St. Paul Assn.; mem. bd. govs. and cons. Aeronautical Chamber Commerce; pres. Nat. Assn. of State Aviation Officials; chmn. Minn. Aeronautics Commn.; dir. Airport Program, Dept. Commerce, State of Minn.; dir. Independent Air-Freight Assn. Cons. aeronautical engr. Cpl. Batt. A, 1st Mass. Vols., Spanish-Am, War; lt. col., assigned duty Gen. Staff, U.S. Army, World War; chmn. Minn. State Defense Com. Mem. Sons of Am. Revolution, Soc. of War of 1812, Sigma Alpha Epsilon, Pi Eta Soc. (Harvard). Clubs: Harvard (New York); Minnesota (St. Paul); Minneapolis (Minn.). Home: 1445 Ogden St., N.W. 813 Arlington Bldg., 1025 Vermont Av., N.W., Washington 5

BRITTON, EDGAR C., chem. co. exec.; b. Rockville, Ind., Oct. 25, 1891; s. Joseph A. and Bertha E. (Hirsbrunner) B.; student Indiana State Normal, 1909; student Wabash College, 1911-14, Doctor of Science, 1955; A.B., University of Michigan, 1915, Ph.D., 1918, D.Sc., 1952; m. Grace Van Huss, June 29, 1916; children—Harold E., Joseph H., Lennis G.; m. 2d, Mildred A. Proud, Dec. 25, 1937; children—Linda Ann, Daniel E. Instr. organic chemistry U. Mich., 1918-20; with Dow Chemical Co., Midland, Mich., 1920—, beginning as research chemist, dir. organic research lab., 2932—; dir. Dow Corning Corp. Recipient Perkin medal, Soc. Chem. Industry, 1956. Mem. Am. Chem. Soc. (pres. 1952), A.A.A.S., Chem. Soc. (London), Soc. Chem. Industry, Am. Inst. Chemists, Sigma Xi, Alpha Chi Sigma, Pi Lambda Upsilon. Clubs: Chemists (N.Y.C.); Torch, Country, Kiwanis, Benmark (Midland). Home: 438 Bldg., Midland, Mich. Died July 31, 1962; buried Midland Cemetery, Midland, Mich.

BRITTON, ELIZABETH GERTRUDE, bryologist; b. New York, Jan. 9, 1858; d. James and Sophie A. (Compton) Knight; girlhood spent in Cuba; grad. Normal Coll., 1875, taught in training dept., 1875-82, asst. botany, 1882-85; m. Nathaniel Lord Britton, Aug. 27, 1885. Edited Bulletin of Torrey Bot. Club, 1885-88; studied mosses, 1880—; devoted prin. part of time gratuitously to the collections of Columbia U. and New York Bot. Garden (hon. curator of mosses). Home: New York, N.Y. Died Jan. 1934.

BRITTON, NATHANIEL LORD, botanist; b. New Dorp, S.I., N.Y., Jan. 15, 1859; E.M., Columbia, 1879, hon. Sc.D., 1904; LL.D., U. of Pittsburgh, 1912; m. Elizabeth Gertrude Knight, Aug. 27, 1885. Asst. in geology, Columbia U., 1879-86, instr. in geology and botany, 1886-90, also instr. in zoölogy, 1887-88, adj. prof. botany, 1891-96, prof. emeritus, 1896—; dir.-in-chief New York Bot. Garden, 1896-1929; dir. emeritus, 1929—. On N.J. Geol. Survey, 5 yrs.; field asst. U.S. Geol. Survey, 1882; editor Bulletin Torrey Bot. Club, 1888-98. Pres. Bot. Soc. America, 1896-98 and 1921, N.Y. Acad. Science, 1905-07, N.Y. State Forestry Assn., 1913. Author: The Flora of New Jersey; Illustrated Flora of Northern United States and Canada, 3 vols., 1896-98, 2d edit., 1913 (with Addison Brown); Manual of the Flora of the Northern States and Canada; C.F. Millspaugh), 1920; monograph of the Cactus Family (with J. N. Rose), 1919-20. Home: Bronx, New York, N.Y. Died June 25, 1934.

BRITTON, WILTON EVERETT, entomologist; b. Marlboro, Mass., Sept. 18, 1868; s. Benjamin Howard and Emily Eliza (Wright) B.; B.S., U. of N.H., 1893, D.Sc., 1930; grad. study Cornell U., 1893-94; Ph.D., Yale, 1903; m. Bertha Madeline Perkins, Apr. 30, 1895. Horticulturist, Conn. Agrl. Expt. Sta., 1894-1901, entomologist, 1901—, also Conn. state entomologist, 1901—; lecturer, Yale Sch. Forestry, 1901-05; supt. Conn. Geol. and Natural History Survey, 1925—; asso. editor Jour. Econ. Entomology, 1909-28. Pvt., Governors Foot Guard, 1917-20. Chmn. Conn. Tree Protection Examining Bd.; pres. Donald G. Mitchell Library; dir. New Haven Pub. Library, 1926-32, Young Men's Inst., Westville Cemetery. Republican. Conglist. Author: Check-List of the Insects of Conn., 1920. Home: New Haven, Conn. Died Feb. 15, 1939.

BROADHEAD, GARLAND CARR, geologist; b. Albemarle County, Va., Oct. 30, 1827; s. Achilles and Mary Winston (Carr) B.; attended U. of Mo., 1850-51; M.S., 1873; Western Mil. Inst., Ky., 1851-52; m. Marion Wallace Wright, Dec., 1864 (died 1883); 2d, Victoria Regina Royall, June 1890. Civ. engr. Pacific R.R. of Mo., 1852-57; asst. geologist of Mo., 1857-61; U.S. deputy collector internal revenue, Mo., 1862-64; asst. engr. Mo. Pacific R.R., 1864-66; U.S. assessor 5th Dist., Mo., 1866; asst. geologist of Ill., 1868, of Mo., 1871-73; state geologist of Mo., 1873-75; on surveys and constrn. of rys. in Kan., 1879-80; prof. geology. U. of Mo., 1887-97. Mem. bd. of jurors, Centennial Expn., Phila., 1876; spl. agt. 10th Census, on quarry, industry, for Mo. and Kan.; mem. Mo. River Commn., 1884-1902. Author of several geol. reports of Mo. and Ill. and other geol. publs. Address: Columbia, Mo. Died Dec. 1912.

BROCKWAY, ZEBULON REED, penologist; b. Lyme, Conn., Apr. 28, 1827; ed. E. Haddam, Conn.; m. Jane Woodhouse, Apr. 13, 1853. Clerk Conn. State Prison, 1848; deputy supt. Albany Penitentiary, 1851; supt. Monroe Co. Penitentiary, 1854, Detroit House of Corrections, 1861, N.Y. State Reformatory, Elmira, 1876-1900; retired. Mayor Elmira, 1906-07. Spl. U.S. commr. to establish a U.S. Mil. Prison, 1873. Non-resident spl. lecturer on penology, Cornell U., 1901. Charter mem. Nat. Prison Assn. U.S.A. (pres. 1898). Author: Fifty Years of Prison Service (auto-biography). Address: Elmira, N.Y. Died Oct. 21, 1920.

BRODE, HOWARD STIDHAM, biologist; b. Stark Co., Ill., Aug. 28, 1866; s. Andres Jackson and Sarah Rodman (Stidham) B.; fellow, 1894-96, S.B. and Ph.D., 1896, U. of Chicago; m. Martha Catharine Bigham, of Chatsworth, Ill., Aug. 30, 1893; children—James Stanley, Harold Ross (dec.), Malcolm Donaldson, Wallace Reed, Robert Bigham. Instr., Marine Biol. Lab., Woods Hole, Mass., 1895; instr. in charge of ecology, Puget Sound Biol. Sta., Friday Harbor, Wash., various summers, prof. biology Whitman Coll., 1890-1935, prof. emeritus since 1935, curator of Mus. since 1899. Fellow A.A.A.S.; mem. Archaeol. Inst. America, Am. Assn. Museums, Washington State Tuberculosis Assn. (dir. since 1924, pres., 1924-29). Has made investigations on morphology of invertebrates, ecology, anthropology and social and industrial applications of biology. Home: 433 E. Alder St., Walla Walla, Wash.

BRODERICK, WILLIAM STEPHEN, engring. and constrn.; b. Fredericton, N.B., Can., Dec. 26, 1878; s. William Guy and and Margaret (Kirlin) B.; student pub. schs. of Butte, Mont.; m. Isabel Ingles Izett, June 22, 1912; children—Jean Elinor, William Rossiter. With Internat. Corr. Sch., 1900-20, rep., 1900-03, field supt., Western Can., 1903-06, mgr. Rocky Mountain States, Denver, 1906-19, v.p. in charge sales force in Western U.S. and Can., 1920; organized Western U.S. Jan., 1920; organized Western Paving Constrn. Co., Denver, 1923, and since prop.; pres. Ogden Quick Freezing & Storage Col, Ogden, Utah, Broderick Wood Products Co., Denver, Western Paving Constrn. Co., Denver, A. & W. Finance Co., Ogden, Utah. Named to Hall of Am.'s Builders, George Pepperdine Coll. Mem. Hudson Game Assn. Roman Catholic. Clubs: Denver, Athletic, Country, Wigwam (Denver). Home: 1228 E. 3d Av. Office: 5105 Washington St., Denver. Died Mar. 1, 1962.

BRODERS, ALBERT COMPTON, surg. pathologist; b. Fairfax County, Va., Aug. 8, 1885; s. John and Virginia (Woodyard) B.; grad. Potomac Acad., Alexandria, Va., 1905; M.D., Med. Coll. Va., 1910, hon. D.Sc., 1929; M.S. in pathology, Mayo Found. U. Minn., 1920; D.Sc. (hon.), Washington and Lee U., 1949; m. Webber Adlene Zimmerman, Sept. 8, 1915; children—Albert Compton, Charles William, Elizabeth Fairfax (Mrs. Armour T. Beckstrand). Served as interne Meml. Hosp., Richmond, Va., 1910-12; asst. in surg. pathology, Mayo Clinic, Rochester, Minn., 1912-19, asso., 1919-22, head a sect. on surg. pathology, 1922-35, 1936-45; dir. and cons., div. surg. pathol., 1945, emeritus dir., cons. since 1950; inst. pathol. Mayo Found., 1920-21, asst. prof., 1921-23, asso. prof., 1923-35, prof., 1936, emeritus prof. since 1951; sr. cons., dept. surg. pathology and pathologic anatomy Scott and White Clinic, Temple, Tex.; sr. cons. pathology, M.D. Anderson Hosp. for Cancer Research, U. Tex., Houston; emeritus prof. pathology U. Tex. Post-grad. Sch. Medicine, Temple Div., 1955—, lectr., prof. surg. pathology, dir. cancer research. Med. Coll. Va., 1935-36. Hon. mem. faculty biol. and med. scis. U. Chile. Fellow A.C.P., Coll. Am. Pathol.; mem. A.M.A., Am. Assn. Pathologists and Bacteriologists, Am. Soc. Clin. Pathologists, A.A.A.S., Alumni Assn. Mayo Found.; corr. gfn. mem. Asociacion Med. Argentina, Asoc. Med. Argentina Soc.; hon. mem. Acad. Nacional de Med. de Buenos Aires, Sociedad de Anatomia Normal y Pathol. de Chile, Argentina de Anat. Normal y Pathol., Sigma Xi, Alpha Omega Alpha. Democrat. Mason. Contbr. to med. jour. Originator numerical microscopic grading of cancer. Home: 1105 N. 6th St. Office: Scott and White Clinic, Temple, Tex. Died Mar. 27, 1964.

BROGLIE, DUC DE (MAURICE), physicist; b. Paris, Apr. 27, 1875; s. Victor Duc de Broglie and Pauline d'Armaille; student College Stanislaus, Ecole Navale; D.Sc. (hon.), Oxford U., Leeds U.; m. Camille de Rochetaille, 1904. Physicist x-rays, radiation, atomic physics. Decorated Grand Officer Legion of Honor; recipient Hughes gold medal Royal Soc. Mem. French acad., Academie des Sciences; fgn. mem. Royal Soc. Club: Union of Paris (pres.). Author sci. articles. Address: Rue de Chateaubriand 29, Paris 8, France. Died July 14, 1960.

BROMER, RALPH SHEPHERD, physician; b. Schwenksville, Pa., Mar. 21, 1886; s. Albert and Catherine (Schappert) B.; A.B., Yale, 1908; M.D., U. Pa., 1912; m. Alice Rupp, July 6, 1921; children—Ralph Shepherd, Catherine Brandes (Mrs. John Haughton Wrenn). Intern Pa. Hosp., Phila., 1912-14; house officer in orthopedic surgery Children's Hosp., Boston, 1915, roentgenologist, 1921-51; pvt. practice, specialist in radiology, 1915—; prof. clin. radiology grad. sch. medicine U. Pa., 1935—. Served with M.C., U.S. Army, World War I; roentgenologist and adj. Base Hosp. 34, comdg. officer Evacuation Hosp. 36, Nantes, France, 1918-19; disch. as lt. col. Fellow Am. Coll. Radiology; mem. Am. Roentgen Ray Soc. (past pres.), Radiol. Soc. N.A., A.M.A. Home: 318 Millbank Rd. Office: Bryn Mawr Hosp., Bryn Mawr, Pa. Died Sept. 25, 1957.

BROOKE, JOHN MERCER, prof. physics; b. Tampa, Fla., Dec. 18, 1826; s. Maj. Gen. George Mercer, and Lucy (Thomas) B.; ed. prep. school, Burlington, N.J., and Kenyon Coll., O.; entered U.S.N. as midshipman, Mar. 3, 1841; grad. Nval acad., 1847, with 1st class grad. from Annapolis; on duty Naval Observatory, Washington, 1851-53; while there invented deep-sea sounding apparatus; was in N. Pacific surveying and exploring expdn. in sloop-of-war Vincennes, under Commodore John Rogers, having charge of astron. dept.; comd. "Fennimore Cooper" in survey of route between San Francisco, Sandwich Islands, Japan and China; resigned from U.S.N. on secession of Va., 1861; entered C.S. service; made chief of bureau of ordnance and hydrography under Sec. Stephen Mallory; prof. physics, Va. Mil. Inst., 1866-99, emeritus, 1899. Invented Brooke gun; discovered the utility of the air-space in cannon; designed plans for iron-clad vessel with submerged ends-this plan being used in reconstruction of the Merrimac; drew directions for cruise of Shenanadoah for destruction of whaling fleet; received from King William of Prussia (Emperior William I.) gold medal of sicence awarded by Acad. of Berlin. Home: Lexington, Va. Died 1906.

BROOKE, WILLIAM ELLSWORTH, university prof.; b. Minier, Ill., Oct. 7, 1870; s. John P. and Rebecca A. (Reynolds) B.; B.C.E., U. of Neb., 1892, A.M., 1896; m. Helen Frances Langer, of West Point, Neb., Aug. 22, 1898. Fellow and asst. in mathematics, U. of Neb., 1894-97; prof. mathematics, Omaha High Sch., 1897-1901; instr. mathematics, 1901-05, asst. prof., 1905-07, prof. mathematics and mechanics since 1907, U. of Minn., also head of dept. of mathematics and mechanics and head dept. drawing and descriptive geometry. Emeritus prof. mathematics and mechanics, June, 1939. Mem. Am. Math. Soc., Circolo Matematico di Palermo, Deutschen Mathematiker Vereinigung, Soc. Promotion of Engring. Edn.; fellow A.A.A.S.; mem. Am. Soc. Mech. Engrs. Author: Plane and Spherical Trigonometry (with George N. Bauer), 1907; Engineering Mechanics (with H. B. Wilcox), 1929; Intermediate Algebra (with H. B. Wilcox), 1938. Home: 416 Walnut St., S.E., Minneapolis MN

BROOKS, ALFRED HULSE, geologist; b. Ann Arbor, Mich., July 18, 1871; s. Maj. Thomas Benton and Hannah (Hulse) B.; studied in Germany, 1890-91; B.S., Harvard, 1894; post-grad. study at Paris; hon. D.Sc., Colgate U., 1920; m. Mabel W. Baker, Feb. 23, 1903. Asst. geologist U.S. Geol. Survey, working in various states, and 1898-1923 engaged in geol. and exploratory work in Alaska; chief Alaskan geologist. Vice-chmn. Alaska R.R. Commn., 1911-12. Received gold medals, Am. Geog. Soc. and Geog. Soc. of Paris, 1913. Wrote The Geography and Geology of Alaska, and other papers on Alaska, and on military subjects. Commd. capt. of engrs., Apr. 1917, maj., July 1917, lt. col., Oct. 1918; was chief geologist, A.E.F.; served in France, Aug. 1917-Apr. 1919. With Am. Peace Commn., Feb.-Apr. 1919. Home: Washington, D.C. Died Nov. 22, 1924.

BROOKS, BENJAMIN TALBOTT, chemist; b. Columbus, O., Dec. 29, 1885; s. Nathaniel Wilson and Rae (Saunders) B.; A.B., Ohio State U., 1906; Ph.D., Gottingen U., 1912; m. Sarah Osgood, 1909; children—William Barker, Margaret, Benjamin Talbott, Robert Osgood. Asst. chemist Bur. of Standards, 1906-07; research chemist Bur. of Sci., P.I., 1907-11; fellow Mellon Inst., Pitts., 1912-17; prof. chem. engring. U. Pitts., 1913-17; chief chemist Comml Research Co., of N.Y., 1917-18; cons. practice, 1918-19; chem. engr. Mathieson Alkali Works, 1919-24; cons. chemist since 1924; petroleum cons. to Venezuela, 1940-41, cons. on U.S. Mexican Oil. Commn. 1942. Maj. Chem. Warfare Res., U.S. Army. Mem. bd. visitors Ohio State U., 1933. Mem. Am. Chem. Soc. (chmn. N.Y. sect.), Am. Inst. Chem. Engrs., Inst. Petrol. Tech. (London), Delta Upsilon, Phi Beta Kappa, Sigma Xi; fellow A.A.A.S., Mem. bd. editors Chem. Industries. Club: Chemists' (trustee N.Y.). Author: Non-Benzenoid Hydrocarbons, 1922; Peace, Plenty and Petroleum, 1944. Am. editor Science of Petroleum. Home: Old Greenwich, Conn. Died Aug. 1962.

BROOKS, CHARLES F., meteorologist; b. St. Paul, Minn., May 2, 1891; s. Morgan and Frona Marie (Brooks) B.; student U. of Ill., 1908-08; A.B., Harvard, 1911, as of 1912, A.M., 1912, Ph.D., 1914; m. Eleanor Merritt Stabler, June 4, 1914; children—Edward Morgan, Margaret, Sylvia, Barbara, Edith, Herrick, Norman Herrick, Frona. Research assistant, Blue Hill Observatory, 1912-13; assistant in meteorology and physiography, Harvard, 1913-14; assistant physiography, Radcliffe College, 1914; assistant and collaborator in farm management U.S. Dept. Agr., 1914-18; instr. geography, Yale, 1915-18; instr. meteorology, U.S. Signal Corps Sch. of Meteorology, College St., Tex., World War, May-Nov. 1918; meteorologist U.S. Weather Bur., editing Mo. Weather Review, 1918-21; asso. prof. meteorology and climatology, 1921-26, prof., 1923-32, Clark U., also instr. summers; prof. meteorology and dir., Blue Hill Obs., Harvard, 1931-57, professor of meteorology and climatology, 1921-26, prof., 1926-32, Clark U., also instr. summers; prof. meteorology and dir., Blue Hill Obs., Harvard, 1931-57, professor of meteorology emeritus, 1957—; visiting prof. University of Chicago, summer, 1939; visiting lecturer, Clark U., summer 1941, U.S. Weather Bur., 1943-44. Meteorologist Cons. for U.S. Weather Bureau, 1948. Expert Climatic Research Div., Q.M. Corps, War Dept.; cons. Nat. Defense Research Com. Pres. Mt. Washington Obs. Mem. internat. commns., Climatol., 1931-45, Snow and Glaciers, 1936-48, Instruments and Methods of Observation 1947-51 (pres. sub-committee on station instruments and methods 1947-53), Clouds and Hydrometeors 1947-53. Fellow A.A.A.S., Royal Meteorol. Society, Am. Geog. Soc.; asso. fellow Inst. Aeronaut. Sciences; mem. Am. Acad. Arts and Sciences, Am. Meteorol. Soc. (organizer, editor 1919-25, 27-36, 39; sec. 1919-54, hon. sec. 1954—), Assn. Am. Geographers (pres. 1947), Am. Geophys. Union (chairman meteorological section 1935-38), Phi Beta Kappa, Sigma Xi. Author: "Why the Weather?" Joint author: Climatology of N. Am. and West Indies (part of a 5 vol. series); Climatic Maps of North America; Eclipse Meteorology; Science from Shipboard; International Cloud Atlas. Home: 1793 Canton Av., Milton 86, Mass. Died Jan. 8, 1958.

BROOKS, FREDERICK A., agrl. engr.; b. Mpls., May 1, 1895; s. Morgan and Frona (Brooks) B.; B.Elec. Engring., U. Ill., 1917, M.E., 1927; Sc.D., Mass. Inst. Tech., 1920; m. Margaret H. Ward, Sept. 7, 1922; children—Audrey M. (Mrs. Preble Stolz), Emily F. (Mrs. Robert E. Lynde), Deborah A. (Mrs. Arthur Corra), Brenda D. (Mrs. Vinson Jester). Airplane designer Curtiss Aeroplane & Motor Corp., Buffalo, 1917-18; asst. engr. Dunlop Tire & Rubber Corp., Buffalo, 1920-21; sales engr. Hall-Scott Motor Car Co., Berkeley, Cal., 1923-25; chief engr. Johnson Gear Co., Berkeley, 1925-28; asst. to chief engr. Byron Jackson Co., Los Angeles and Berkeley, 1930-31; mem. faculty U. Cal. at Davis, 1931-67, research agrl. engr., prof. emeritus, 1962-67. U.S. del. UNESCO-Australia symposium on arid zone climatology, 1956; collaborator U.S. Forest Service div. forest fire research, 1953-67. Guggenheim fellow, 1959; recipient Cyrus Hall McCormick medal, 1960. Life fellow Am. Soc. M.E.; fellow Am. Soc. Agrl. Engrs.; mem. Am. Meteorol. Soc. (award bioclimatology 1966), Am. Geophys. Union, Sigma Xi. Contbr. numerous articles profl. jours. Spl. research parallel-beam measurement atmospheric radiation over short paths with hohlraum chilled with liquid nitrogen and through whole atmosphere simultaneously with spl. radiosonde flights; project leader extensive field research frost protection; coop. field expts. eddy transfers of momentum, heat, moisture over 12-acre irrigated turf surfaces. Author: An Introduction to Physical Microclimatology, 1960. Home: Davis CA Died Mar. 10, 1967.

BROOKS, HENRY TURNER, physician; b. at Baltimore, Sept. 18, 1861; s. James Henry and Rebecca (Turner) B.; ed. Friends' elementary and high sch., Baltimore, and pub. schs., N.Y.; M.D., Albany (N.Y.) Coll. Medicine, 1887; studied med. dept. Johns Hopkins, 1887-88, Wesleyan U., 1888-89, univs. of Berlin and Munich, 1890-92; m. at Baltimore, Agnes Davies, of Lancashire, Eng., Dec. 25, 1895. Asst. U.S. Agrl. Expt. Sta., Wesleyan U., Conn., 1888-89; instr. pathol. anatomy, 1893-97, adj. prof., 1897-1900, prof. since 1901, New York Post-Grad. Med. Sch.; formerly pathologist New York Post-Grad. Hosp., Beth Israel Hosp.; bacteriologist St. Mark's Hosp.; consulting pathologist Liberty (N.Y.) Sanitarium. Mem. N.Y. Acad. Medicine, etc. Republican. Author of English translation Lenhartz's "Mikroskopie und Chemie am Krankenbett] ," under title, Manual of Clinical Microscopy and Chemistry, 1904; Use of the Microscope, 1900; General and Special Pathology, 1911. Home: New Rochelle, N.Y. Office: 40 E. 41st St., New York.

BROOKS, JOHN PASCAL, civil engr.; b. Kittery, Me., Sept. 24, 1861; s. James W. and Anna A. (Wilson) B.; prep. edn. Phillips Acad., Exeter, N.H.; B.S. Dartmouth, 1885, M.S., 1893, Sc.D., 1915; Sc.D., Clarkson Coll. Tech., Potsdam, N.Y., 1931; m. Maude P. Perkins, of Red Bank, N.J., June 25, 1888; m. 2d, Belle C. Pearson, of Lexington, Ky., June 4, 1903. Prof. civ. engring., State U. of Ky., 1897-1906; asso. prof. civ. engring., U. of Ill., 1906-11; pres., Clarkson Coll. of Tech., Potsdam, N.Y., 1911-28, pres. emeritus since 1928. Republican. Mem. Am. Soc. C.E., Soc. Promottion Engring. Edn. Author: Handbook for Surveyors (with Mansfield Merriman), 1895; Handbook of Street Railroad Location, 1897; Reinforced Concrete, 1911. Home: Potsdam, N.Y.

BROOKS, MORGAN, electrical engr.; b. Boston, Mar. 12, 1861; s. Francis A. and Frances (Butler) B.; Ph.B., Brown U., 1881; M.E., Stevens Inst. of Tech., Hoboken, N.J., 1883; m. Frona Marie Brooks, Apr. 24, 1888; children—Henry M., Cahrles F., Frances (Mrs. Lincoln Colcord), Frederick A., Roger, Edith, Mrs. Frona B. Hughes, Dorothy Prescott (Mrs. Joseph M. Thomas). With Am. Bell Telephone Co., Boston, 1884-86; sec.-treas. St. Paul Gas Light Co., 1887-90; organizer Elec. Engring. Co. of Minneapolis; prof. elec. engring., U. of Neb., 1898-1901, U. of Ill., 1901-29, emeritus. Patented automatic telephone system, 1896. Fellow Am. Inst. Elec. Engrs. (dir. 1907-10, v.p. 1910-12); mem. Am. Soc. Mech. Engrs. (life), Illuminating Engring. Soc., Western Soc. Engrs., Delta Kappa Epsilon, Sigma Xi, Tau Beta Pi. Pres. Western Unitarian Conf., Chicago, 1917-22. Contbr. to engring. mags. Home: 907 W. Oregon St., Urbana, Ill. Died Apr. 25, 1947.

BROOKS, PHILLIPS MOORE, astronautics co., exec.; b. Independence, Cal., Feb. 18, 1908; s. Willis Moore and Wilhelmina (Singlaub) B.; student U. Cal., Los Angeles, 1931-34; A.B., U. Cal., Berkeley, 1935; Ph.D., Leland Stanford U., 1943; m. Jean Woodworth Smith, Aug. 21, 1941; 1 son, Phillips Robertson. Scientist Bikini Sci. Resurvey Group, USAF, 1947; head dept. bacteriology, botany, physiology, Riverside (Cal.) Coll., 1947-49; asst. prof. aviation physiology U. So. Cal., Los Angeles, 1949-51; chief nuclear safety analysis group Nuclear Div., Martin Co., Balt., 1960-62; staff physiologist McDonnell Douglas Corp., St. Louis, 1962—. Lectr. physiology dept. Ohio State U., Columbus, 1958-59; lectr. Washington U., St. Louis, 1963-65, cons. dept. radiation physics, 1965—; vice chmn. space simulator safety operations subcom. Aerospace Industries Assn. Am., St. Louis, 1962. Served to lt. col., USAF, 1943-47, 52-60. Recipient Huntington Meml. Library scholarship U. Cal., 1933-34; Am. Smelting and Refining Corp., fellowship, Stanford U., 1935-38. Mem. A.A.A.S., Am. Inst. Aeronautics and Astronautics, Health Physics Assn., Aerospace Indsl. Life Scis. Assn., Aerospace Physiologist Assn., Aerospace Bioenvironmental Engring. and Scis. Assn., Aerospace Med. Assn., Air Force Assn., Nat. Sojourners, Inc., Am. Inst. Biol. Scis., Sigma Xi, Chi Phi. Contbr. articles to profl. jours. Home: Creve Coeur MO Died Dec. 17, 1967.

BROOKS, ROBERT BLEMKER, cons. engr.; b. Jackson, Tenn., Mar. 17, 1889; s. Louis J. and Laura (Blemker) B.; B.S., Washington U., 1910, C.E., 1922; m. Estelle Goodfellow, Oct. 10, 1910 (died 1946); children—Robert B., Ernest A., Joseph B.; m. 2d, Anny Kneifel, Nov. 24, 1948; stepson, Ralph C. Chief engr. Moreno-Burkham Constrn. Co., St. Louis 1919-25; dir. streets and sewers, City of St. Louis, 1925-33; cons. engr., St. Louis 1933—; bd. of Freeholders Met. Transit Authority. Served as lt., later capt., AUS, 1918-19. Ofcl. rep. U.S. Dept. of State in dedication Pan-Am. Highway in Mexico, 1936, 8th Internat. Road Congress, The Hague, Holland, 1938, Pan Am. Conf., Mexico City, 1941, 5th ordinary Pan-Am. Highway Congress, Mexico City, 1952. Mem. City Plan Commn. of St. Louis, 1925-33 and 1945-47; mem. Mo. State Highway Commn., 1937-42. Mem. Mississippie River Parkway Planning Commission (Distinguished Service Award, 1956). Rep. of American Pub. Worls Officials at European confs., 1931, 35, 38, 47, 53. Mem. Am. Soc. C.E., Am. Rd. Builders Assn., Am. Legion, Safety Council of Greater St. Louis (pres. 1949-50), Municipal Theatre Assn., Republican. Methodist. Mason. Clubs: Missouri Athletic, St. Louis Engineers. Home: 6048 Cabanne Pl., St. Louis 12. Office: Ambassador Bldg., St. Louis 63101. Died Apr. 30, 1960; buried Bellefontaine Cemetery, St. Louis.

BROOKS, SUMMER CUSHING, biologist; b. Sapporo, Japan, Aug. 17, 1888; s. William Penn and Eva Bancroft (Hall) B., came to U.S., 1999, citizen by birth; B.S., Univ. of Mass., 1910; Ph.D., Harvard, 1916; m. Matilda Neuffer Moldenhauer, July 14, 1917. Asst. in botany, Mass. Agrl. Expt. Sta., Amherst, Mass., 1910-11; bio-chemist, Research Inst. Nat. Dental Assn., Cleveland, 1916-17; Hanna research fellow, pathology, Western Reserve U., 1917; research fellow tropical medicine, Harvard, 1917-19; asso. prof. physiology and biochemistry, Bryn Mawr Coll., 1919-20; biologist, hygienic lab., U.S. Pub. Health Service, Washington, 1920-26; prof. of physiology Rutgers Univ., 1926-27; prof. of zoology Univ. of Calif. at Berkeley, since 1927. Trustee Marine Biol. Lab., Woods Hole, Mass. Mem. A.A.A.S., Am. Bot. Soc., Am. Physiol. Soc., Am. Chem. Soc., Soc. Exptl. Biol. Medicine, Western Soc. Naturalists (pres. 1933), Phi Beta Kappa, Sigma Xi, Phi Kappa Phi, Phi Sigma Kappa. Club: Cooper Ornithol. (pres. Northern sect., 1946-48). Author: Permeability of Living Cells (with Matilda M. Brooks), 1941. Contbr. numerous articles to sci. periodicals. Home: 630 Woodmont Av., Berkeley 8, Cal. Died Apr. 23, 1948; buried Woods Hole, Mass.

BROOKS, THOMAS BENTON, engr.; b. Monroe, N.Y., June 15, 1836; grad. Union Coll., C.E., 1857 (A.M.); m. Hannah Hulse, 1868 (died 1883); m. 2d, Martha Giesler, 1887. Practiced as civil and mining engr.; in Civil war, lt. 1st N.Y. col. engrs., serving as engr. officer on staff Gen. Gilmore; bvtd. lt. col. and col.; later State geologist, Mich. and Wis.; published reports on Lake Superior iron regions, 1872-76; later farming; owned live-stock and tobacco plantations in S.W. Ga., spending winters at Bainbridge, Decatur County, Ga. Home: Newburg, N.Y. Died 1900.

BROOKS, WILLIAM KEITH, naturalist; b. Cleveland, O., Mar. 25, 1848; grad. Williams, 1870, Harvard, Ph.D., 1875; LL.D., Williams, 1893, also Hobart and U. of Pa.; m. Amelia Schultz, June 1878 (died 1901). Asst. Boston Soc. Natural History, 1875-76; asso. prof. and prof. zoölogy, Johns Hopkins, 1876. Mem. Nat. Acad. Sciences. Awarded medal, Soc. d'Acclamitation, Paris; challenger medal, Edinburgh; medal, St. Louis Expn., 1904. Author: Handbook of Invertebrate Zoölogy; The Stomatopoda of H. M. S. Challenger, A. Monograph of the Genus Salpa; The Foundations of Zoölogy; The Oyster; Rep. Md. Oyster Commn., etc. Address: Baltimore, Md. Died 1908.

BROOKS, WILLIAM PENN, agriculturist; b. S. Scituate, Mass., Nov. 19, 1851; s. Nathaniel and Rebecca Partridge (Cushing) B.; B.S. (valedictorian), Mass. Agrl. Coll., 1875, grad. student chemistry and botany, 1876; Ph.D., Halle, 1897; hon. degree Nogaku Hakushi, Japanese Dept. Edn., 1919; m. Eva Bancroft Hall, Mar. 29, 1882; children—Rachel Bancroft, Sumner Cushing. Prof. agr., Imperial Coll. of Agr., Japan, 1877-88, prof. botany, 1880-88, pres. ad interim, 1880-83 and 1886-87; prof. agr., Mass. Agrl. Coll., 1889-1908, lecturer on agr., 1908-18, pres. ad interim, Jan.-Apr., 1903, and 1905-06; agriculturist, Mass. Agrl. Exptl. Station, 1889-1921, dir., 1906-18; consulting agricultures, 1918-21, dir., 1906-18; consulting agriculturist, 1918-21. Decorated 4th Order of the Rising Sun, Japan, 1888. Contbr. to 2d, 3d and 4th and editor 5th and 6th ann. reports, Imperial Coll. Agr. of Japan. Author: Agriculture (3 vols.), 1901; General Agriculture, Dairying and Poultry Farming. Home: Amherst, Mass. Died 1938.

BROOKS, WILLIAM ROBERT, astronomer; b. Maidstone, Kent, Eng., June 11, 1844; s. Rev. William and Caroline (Wickings) B.; came to U.S., 1857; acad. end., Marion, N.Y.; hon. A.M., Hobart, 1891; D.Sc., Hamilton, 1898; m. Mary E. Smith, Oct. 15, 1868. Founded Red House Observation, Phelps, N.Y., 1874, where he discovered 11 comets; in charge Smith Observation, Geneva, N.Y., 1888—; prof. astronomy, Hobart Coll.; lecturer. Has discovered 16 additional comets, making 27 in all (many of these discoveries made with telescope of his own construction); early worker in photography and later in its application to astronomy. Winner of over $1,000 in Warner gold prizes for astron. discoveries; 10 medals from Astron. Soc. Pacific; Lalande medal, Paris Acad. Sciences; spl. gold medal for list and photographs of cometary discoveries, St. Louis Expn., 1904; spl. gold medal and diploma, Astron. Soc. of Mexico for discoveries of 25 comets. Address: Geneva, N.Y. Died May 3, 1921.

BROUWER, DIRK, educator; b. Rotterdam, Netherlands, Sept. 1, 1902; came to U.S., 1927, naturalized 1937; s. Martinus and Louisa (van Wamelen) B.; Ph.D., U. Leiden, Netherlands, 1927; Sc.C. (hon.), U. La Plata, 1959; m. Johanna Antonia Mathilda de Graaf, Nov. 1, 1928; 1 son, James Martin. Asst. in theoretical astronomy, Leiden U., 1923-27; fellow Internat. Edn. Bd. at Yale and U. Cal., 1927-28; instr. astronomy Yale 1928-33, asst. prof., 1933-39, asso. prof., 1939-41, prof. astronomy, dir. Obs., since 1941; editor Astron. Jour., 1941—. Recipient gold medal Royal Astron. Soc., 1955. Mem. A.A.A.S., Am. Astron. Soc., Am. Assn. Variable Star Observers (pres. 1941-43), Astron. Soc. of Pacific, Internat. Astron. Union, Nat. Acad. Scis., Am. Acad. Arts and Scis., Royal Astron. Soc. (fgn. asso.), Royal Netherlands Acad. Scis. (corr.), Am. Geophys. Union, Buenos Aries Acad. Scis. (corr. 1961), Sigma Xi. Contbr. papers on theoretical astronomy (motion of planets and satellites) to sci. jours. and obs. publs. Home: 363 Willow St. Office: Yale Univ. Observatory, New Haven 11. Died Mar. 31, 1966.

BROUWER, LUITZEN EGBERTUS JAN, sci. investigator; b. Overschie nr. Rotterdam, Netherlands, Feb. 27, 1881; s. Egbert and Henderika (Poutsma) B.; D.Sc., U. Amsterdam, 1907; Ph.D. (hon.), U. Oslo, 1929; D.Sc. (hon.), Cambridge U., 1955; m. Elisabeth Deholl, Aug. 31, 1904. External lectr. U. Amsterdam, 1909-12, prof., 1912-51, prof. emeritus, 1951-66. Decorated Knight Order Netherland Lion. Mem. Koninklijke Nederlandse Akademie van Wetenschappen, Am. Philos. Soc., Royal Soc. London, Royla Soc. Edinburgh, Real Academia de Ciencias Exactas, Fisicasy Naturates Madrid, Consejo Superior de Investigaciones Cientificas Madrid, Akademie der Wissenschaften in Gottingen, Leopoldinisch-Carolinische Akademie der Naturforscher Halle, Deutsche Akademie der Wissenschaften Berlin, Societas Scientiarum Fennica Helsinki, Societe des Sciences et des lettres de Varsovie, Societe Mathematique de Moscou, Edinburgh Math. Soc., Calcutta Math. Soc. Author: Life, Art and Mysticism, 1905; On the Foundations of Mathematics, 1907; Mathematics, Truth, Reality, 1919; also articles learned jours. Died Dec. 2, 1966.

BROWER, JACOB VRADENBERG, archaeologist, explorer, author; b. on farm at York, Mich., Jan. 21, 1844; s. Abraham Duryea and Mary R. B.; ed. pub. schs.; enlisted in vol. cav., 1862; in U.S. vol. navy, 1864; auditor Todd Co., Minn., 1867-73; mem. Minn. legistature, 1873; register U.S. land office, St. Cloud, Minn., 1874-79; Itasca State Park Commr., Minn., 1891-95; charted source of Miss. river, 1889, and source of Mo. river, 1896; discovered mounds and ancient village site at Itasca Lake, 1894-95; rediscovered site of Quivira, 1897-98; discovered 1,125 ancient mounds at Mille Lac, Minn., 1900. Pres. Quivira Hist. Soc. (assn. of explorers, authors and ethnol. students); well known as explorer and archaeologist. Author: The Mississippi River and Its Source, 1893; Prehistoric Man at the Head Waters of the Mississippi, 1895 O1; The Missouri River and Its Utmost Source, 1896 A7; Quivira, 1898 A7; Harahey, 1899 A7; Mille Lac, 1900 A7; Kathio, 1901 A7; Kakabikansing, 1902 S30; Minnesota-Discovery of Its Area, 1541-1665, 1903 S30; Kansas-Monumental Perpetuation of Its Earliest History, 1541-1896, 1903 S30. Home: St. Paul, Minn. Died 1905.

BROWN, A. PAGE, architect; b. 1859; grad. Cornell U. With office of McKim, Mead & White; toured Europe; returned to N.Y.C., 1885, opened office; practiced architecture, N.Y.C., several years; designed Clio and Whig halls, Mus. of Historic Art, Princeton; moved to San Francisco, 1889, began practice as architect; recognized as one of most progressive architects in San Francisco; architect numerous pub. and bus. structures, including Crocker Office Bldg., Sharon Office Bldg., 1892, Ferry Bldg., So. Pacific Depot (begun 1893, finished by Willis Polk, 1903), Donajue Office Bldg., Trinity Ch.; architect Cal. Bldg. erected at World's Columbian Expn., Chgo., 1893. Died Jan. 20, 1896.

BROWN, ARTHUR ERWIN, naturalist; b. Bucks County, Pa., Aug. 14, 1850; s. Samuel Corbin and Achsah Erwin (Kennedy) B.; ed. chiefly in Europe; hon. Sc.D., U. of Pa., 1907. Mem. bd. mgrs. Wistar Inst. of Anatomy; sec. Zoöl. Soc. of Phila.; v.p. and curator Acad. Natural Sciences of Phila. Home: Philadelphia, Pa. Died 1910.

BROWN, BARNUM, palaeontologist, geologist; b. Carbondale, Kan., Feb. 12, 1873; s. William and Clara (Silver) B.; A.B., U. Kan., 1897; postgrad. Columbia, 1897-98; D.Sc., Lehigh U., 1934; m. Marion R. Brown, Feb. 13, 1904 (dec. 1910); 1 dau., Frances Raymond; m. 2d, Lilian MacLaughlin, May 20, 1922. With Am. Mus. Natural History, N.Y.C., since 1897, asst. curator dept. palaeontology, 1897-1909, asso. curator, 1909-11, curator, 1927-42, now curator emeritus. Fellow A.A.A.S., Geol. Soc. Am., N.Y. Acad. Sci., Royal Geog. Soc. Contbr. to mags. on popular, sci. subjects. Home: 522 West End Av. Died Feb. 1963.

BROWN, CHARLES CARROLL, cons. civil engr.; b. Austinburg, Ohio, Oct. 4, 1856; s. George Pliny and Mary Louise (Seymour) B.; studied engring. Cornell University, 1874-75; C.E., U. of Mich., 1879, hon. A.M., 1913; m. Cora Stanton, Sept. 10, 1878 (dec.); children—Edith Stanton (dec.), Edwin Stanton (dec.); m. 2d, Eileen Finkle, Jan. 2, 1930. Prof. of civil engring., Rose Poly. Institute, 1883-86, Union College, 1886-93; consulting engr. N.Y. State Bd. Health, 1888-93; city engr., Indianapolis, 1894-95. Editor Municipal Engring., 1896-1917; in Ill. Div. of Highways, 1918-19; prof. engring., Valparaiso U., 1919-21; engr., Dept. Pub. Works, St. Petersburg, Fla., 1921-23; city engr., Lakeland, Fla., 1923-27; prof. civil engring., U. of Fla., 1927-33; also cons. engr.; ex-chmn. Gainesville City Plan Board; cons. engr. Fla. Mapping Project. Fellow Fla. Engrs. Soc. (ex-pres.); mem. Am. Soc. C.E. (life), Am. Pub. Works Assn. (ex-pres., sec.), Am. Assn. Engrs. (ex-pres. Fla. Chapter), Sigma Xi. (2d nat. pres.), Sigma Tau, Phi Delta Theta. Author: Report on Croton Water Shed of the City of New York, 1889; Directory of American Cement Industries (5 edits.), 1901-09; Handbook for Cement Users (3 edits.), 1901-05. Home: 848 Orange Park Av., Lakeland, Fla. Died Nov. 26, 1949.

BROWN, CHARLES WILSON, geologist; b. Overton, Neb., Aug. 11, 1874; s. Rev. Henry Wheaton and Abbie E. (Wilson) B.; student Boston U., 1896-97; Ph.B., Brown U., 1900, A.M., 1901; student Grad. Sch., Harvard, 1903-04; m. Anne Taft Peirce, June 10, 1908. With U.S. Geol. Survey, 1902-08; prin. high sch., Warren, R.I., 1901-03; instr. geology, Lehigh U., S. Bethelehem, Pa., 1904-05; instr., asst., asso. prof., prof. geology, and head dept., Brown U., 1905-40; emeritus prof. since 1940; supt. Natural Resources Survey of R.I., 1909-13; v.p. R.I. Ice Co. Fellow Geol. Soc. America, Am. Geog. Soc., Seismol. Soc. America, A.A.A.S., Am. Inst. Mining and Metall. Engineers; mem. Providence Engineer Soc., Am. Geophys. Union, Sigma Xi. Clubs: University, Art, Agawam Hunt (Providence); Joint author of Penobscot Bay (Me.) Folio (U.S. Geol. Survey), 1907. Writer of geol. and geog. bulls., articles and reviews. Home: 37 Barnes St., Providence RI

BROWN, C(HRISTIAN) HENRY, oculist; b. Lancaster, Pa., May 8, 1857; s. Edwin H. and Susan A. (Widmyer) B.; student Franklin and Marhsall Coll., Pa.; M.D., U. of Pa., 1878. Phys. Phila. Hosp., 1878-80, Lancaster County Hosp., 1881-83; located in Phila., 1887; specializes in diseases of the eye; founder, 1889, and pres. Phila. Optical Coll. Established Bd. of Health, Lancaster, and sec. same until left Lancaster. Mason (32 deg.). Author: Optometric Record Book, 1891; The Optician's Manual, Vol. 1, 1895, Vol. 2, 1901; Clincis in Optometry, 1905; State Board Questions, 1909. Home: Philadelphia, Pa. Deceased.

BROWN, D(ENTON) J(ACOBS), prof. of chemistry; b. Hampton, Pa., Apr. 13, 1882; s. A. David and Anna Mary (Jacobs) B.; A.B., U. of Tex., 1910; Ph.D. Chicago University, 1918; married Sallie Sloan (deceased); 1 son, Denton Sloan (deceased). Instructor chem. Univ. Texas 1914-15, 1917-18; asst. prof. chemistry Agrl. and Mech. Coll. of Tex., 1915-17; asso. prof. chemistry U. of Neb., 1918-27, prof. 1927-50, professor of chemistry emeritus since 1950. Mem. Am. Chemical Society, Am. Assn. Univ. Profs., Phi Beta Kappa, Sigma Xi, Phi Lambda Upsilon, Alpha Chi Sigma, Acacia. Mason (32 deg.). Conductor research in electrochemistry and rates of reaction. Home: 1935 S. 47, Lincoln 6, Neb. Died Oct. 4, 1955; buried Wyuka Cemetery, Lincoln, Neb.

BROWN, EARL THEODORE, physicist; b. Centralia, Wash., Nov. 20, 1890; s. William Chandler and Sarah Ellen (Axtell) B.; B.S., U. Wash., 1918, M.S., 1924; student Stanford, 1928-29, U. Cal., 1929-30; m. Lida Fake, Dec. 25, 1922; children—Nancy Jean, John Theodore. High sch. tchr. and prin., Wash., 1918-19; asso. in physics U. Wash., 1920-21; prof. physics Willamette U., 1921-55. Mem. Am. Assn. Physics Tchrs., Am. Inst. Physics. Republican. Presbyn. Mason. Mem. Men's Garden Club of America. Home: 293 S. 14th St. S.E., Salem, Ore. Died Mar. 3, 1959; buried Belcrest Cemetery, Salem.

BROWN, EDGAR, botanist; b. Ontario County, N.Y., Sept. 25, 1871; s. Amos C. and Emma L. (Smith) B.; Ph.B., Union Coll., N.Y., 1895; m. Harriet V. Tefft, Aug. 14, 1902; m. 2d, Elizabeth D. Gould, June 6, 1934. Botanist in charge seed testing labs. U.S. Dept. Agr., 1902-38, principal botanist. Mem. Washington Acad. Science, Phi Gamma Delta, Sigma Xi. Mem. Soc. of Friends. Club: Cosmos. Author of bulls. Dept. of Agr. Home: Mount Airy MD

BROWN, ERNEST WILLIAM, mathematician; b. Hull, Eng., Nov. 29, 1866; s. William and Emma (Martin) B.; B.A., Christ's Coll., Cambridge, Eng., 1887, fellow, 1889-95, hon. fellow, 1911, M.A., 1891, Sc.D., 1897, Adams prize, 1907; hon. A.M., Yale U., 1907; D.Sc., Adelaide U., 1914, Yale, 1933, Columbia, 1934; LL.D., McGill U., 1935; unmarried. Prof. mathematics, Haverford (Pa.) Coll., 1891-1907, Yale, 1907-32. Awarded Bruce Medal, 1920. Mem. Am. Acad. Arts and Sciences, Nat. Acad. Science (Watson medal 1937), Am. Astron. Soc. (v.p. 1923-25; pres. 1928-31). Author: Treatise on the Lunar Theory, 1896; A New Theory of the Moon's Motion, 1897-1905; Tables of the Motion of the Moon's Motion, 1897-1905; Tables of the Motion of the Moon, 1920; Planetary Theory (with C. A. Shook), 1933. Address: New Haven, Conn. Died July 1938.

BROWN, F(RANK) E(MERSON), chemist, coll. prof.; b. near Cuba, Kan., Feb. 9, 1882; s. Prairie Frank and Marie Elizabeth (Barnhill) B.; A.B. in edn.Kan. State Teachers Coll., Emporia, 1911, student 1902-10; B.S. in chemistry, Univ. of Chicago, 1912-17, Ph.D. (phys. chemistry), 1918; m. May Maria Holmes, Dec. 25, 1910; children—Frank Emerson, Holmes M.; m. 2d, Louise Jaggard, July 23, 1920; 1 dau., Louise Jaggard. Teacher country schs., Republic County, Kan., 1899-1902, supt. of schs., prin. of high sch., Portis, Kan., 1905-07, Hill City, Kan., 1907-09; supt. of schs., Collinsville, Okla., Jan., 1911-June, 1912; chemistry teacher, night classes, Chicago schs., Y.M.C.A. schs., 1912-18; chemistry teacher Fresno (Calif.) high sch. and jr. coll., spring, 1914; asst. prof. of chemistry, Ia. State Coll., Ames, Feb. 1917, asso. prof., 1918, prof., 1923-52, emeritus, 1952—. Dir. Ia. Acad. Sci., 1956—. Dir. Ia. Sci. Talent Search, 1947—. Recipient Ia. State Coll. Faculty citation for outstanding service, 1956; Sci. Apparatus Makers award in Chem. Edn., Am. Chem. Soc., 1958; Silver Beaver, Boy Scouts Am., 1943. Mem. Am. Chem. Soc. (local section sec., treas., 1918, chmn., 1921, councilor, 1931, 33, 39 and 45); chmn. local section officers group, 1940, chmn. Div. of Chem. Edn. 1942; Senate of Chemical Education (chmn. com. on membership affairs 1950-51); Ia. Acad. Sci. (chmn. com. high sch. relations, 1942-50, chmn. com. sci. talent search 1950—; v.p. 1950-51, pres. 1951-52), A.A.A.S., Sigma Xi, Phi Kappa Phi, Alpha Chi Sigma, Phi Lambda Upsilon, Phi Kappa Tau. Presbyterian. Mason. Contbg. ed. Jour. Chem. Edn., 1928-40; editorial bd. Ia. State Coll. Jour. Sci. 1945—. Author: A Short Course in Qualitative Analysis, 1932; articles on research and teaching of chemistry to chem. jours; abstractor Chemical Abstracts, 1922—. Home: 138 Hyland Av., Ames, Ia. Died Sept. 10, 1959.

BROWN, FRANKLIN STEWART, civil engr.; b. Chgo., Oct. 22, 1909; s. Charles Dickerson and Martha May (Swaney) B.; B.S. in Civil Engring., U. Ill., 1931; m. Aura Frances Clark, June 9, 1934; children—Charles Clark, Gail Frances, Richard Alan. With C.E., U.S. Army, 1931-46, 48-62, chief engring. div. No. Pacific, Portland, Ore., 1952-62; chief gen. engring. div. Panama Canal, 1946-48; chief bur. power FPC, from 1962, also chief engr.; staff dir. Nat. Power Survey. Registered profl. engr., Ore. Fellow Am. Soc. C.E. (pres. Ore. 1962); mem. U.S. Com. Large Dams (chmn. 1964-65), Nat. Soc. Profl. Engrs., Soc. Am. Mil. Engrs., P.I.A.N.C., Internat. Commn. Large Dams (chmn. com. dam failures). Home: McLean VA Died May 3, 1970.

BROWN, FREDERICK HARVEY, inventor; b. at Indiantown (now Tiskaiwah), Ill., May 11, 1843; s. Joseph Mortimer and Louisa M. B.; ed. St. Louis High Sch., Washington U. and by pvt. study of natural sciences; m. Ida Moore, 1861 (dec.); 2d, Catherine F. Norwood, Apr. 29, 1877. Asst. auditor and clerk, for Gen. T. J. Haines, purchasing q.-m. commissary U.S. Army St. Louis, 1862; v.p. Magneto Telegraph Co., New York, 1885-86, Brown Telegraph Co., Chicago, 1890; pres. Electra Geodetic Co., Los Angeles, 1900, Nat. Electric & Magnetic Co., Chicago. Holder many patents on electric inventions in U.S. and foreign countries. Awarded medal for telephone, Paris Expn. Agnostic, Author: One Dollar's Work, 1893; A Few Wise Things It Were Well for You to Read, 1893. Home: Los Angeles, Calif. Died 1911.

BROWN, GEORGE VAN INGEN, surgeon; b. St. Pau., Jan. 15, 1862; s. Matthew Wilson and Emily (Lynch) B.; ed. at home, high sch., St. Paul, and under pvt. tutor; D.D.S., Pa. Coll. Dental Surgery, Phila., 1881; M.D., Milwaukee Med. Coll., 1895; A.B., Northern Ill. Coll., Easton, 1898; M.D., Marquette U., Milwaukee, 1909; m. Elizabeth Kathleen Selby Jones, Sept. 22, 1884; 1 son, Selby Van Ingen. Practiced oral surgery and dentistry; St. Paul and Duluth, Minn., 1881-98; splst plastic surgery, Milwaukee, since 1898. Prof. operative dentistry and oral surgery, dental dept., Milwaukee Med. Coll., 1898-1902; spl. lecturer on oral surgery, dental dept., U. of Ill., 1902-03, State U. of Ia., 1903-04, U. of Tenn., 1904, Vanderbilt U., 1905, Southern Dental Coll., Atlanta, Ga., 1909-15; prof. oral surgery and oral pathology, State Univ. of Iowa, 1904-10; apptd. by U.S. Senate del. to Internat. Med. Congress, Madrdi, Spain, 1903; apptd. to make report on harelip and cleft palate before the Internat. Med. Congress, Budapest, 1911; chief of staff St. Mary's Hosp., 1936; on surg. staff Columbia Hos. and St. Mary's Hosp., of Milwaukee; plastic surgeon State of Wis. Gen. Hosp., at U. of Wis., and also at Wis. Orthopedic Hosptial, Madison; cous. staff Milwaukee Children's Hosp., Wis. Meth. Hosp. and Madison Gen. Hosp., Madison, Wis.; attending mem. on surg. staff, Milwaukee County Hosp., Wauwatosa, Wis. Served at 1st lt., cpat., maj., lt. col., Med. R.C., 1915-19; col., Officers Reserve Corps. U.S. Army, 1923; pres. bd.

examiners for applicants for apptmt. to Med. R.C., at Milwaukee; later at Office Surgeon Gen., Washington, D.C., in charge sect. of plastic and oral surgery of head surg. div.; organized shc. of plastic and oral surgery, at Ft. Oglethorpe, Ga., 1918; in charge plastic and oral surg. operative reconstruction work for returned soldier with disfigured faces and jaws, at U.S. Army Gen. Hosp. No. 11, Cape May, N.J-, and later chief of maxill-faciale service, Walter Reed Hosp., Takoma Park, D.C.; apptd. surgeon U.S.P.H.S., 1919; with Bur. War Risk Ins. as consultant in plastic surgery, at Milwaukee, 1919; consultant plastic surgery Vets. Adminstrn.; medical consultant, Veterans Service Exchange; professor of oral and plastic surgery, U. of Wis., 1920-37, now emeritus. Fellow Am. Coll. Surgeons, Tri-State Med. Soc. (pres. 1920-21); member A.M.A. and affiliated assns., Wis. State, and Milwaukee County med. socs., Milwaukee Acad. Medicine (honorary mem.), Companion Mil. Order World War, State Hist. Soc. of Wis., Sociëtë Scientifique Francaise de Chirurgie Rëparatrice, Plastique et Esthëtique (Paris, France), Pan-American Med. Assn., The American Society of Plastic and reconstructive Surgery, Am. Board of Platic and Reconstructive Surgeery, Am. Board of Plastic Surgery, Pi Gamma Mu, Delta Sigma Delta, Alpha Kappa Kappa and many other professional orgns., U.S. and Europe; hon. fellow Internat. Coll. of Surgeons (Geneva, Switzerland). Speaker Interstate Post-Grad. Med. Assn. of North America, 1920-35, trustee since 1920. Awarded Jarvie medal by N.Y. State Dental Society. Episcopalian senior warden of St. Paul's Church). Mason. Clubs: University, Rotary, Army and Navy (Washington, D.C.); Authors' (London). Author: The Surgey of Oral and Facial Diseases and Malformations, 4th edit., 1938; chapter in Ochsner's Surgical Diagnosis and Treatment, chapter in Sajous' Cyclopedia of Practical Medicine, also monographs, papers and occasional poems. Mem. advisory council Living Age (mag.). Home: 7152 North Beach Dr., Fox Point, Milwaukee, Wis. Office: 759 N. Milwaukee St., Milwaukee, Wis. Died Apr. 2, 1948.

BROWN, HARRY B(ATES), plant breeder, agronomist; b. Delphi, Ind., June 9, 1876; s. John Holton and Sue (Bates) B.; grad. Ind. State Tchrs. Coll., 1902; A.B., Ind. U., 1906, A.M., 1907; Ph.D., Cornell, 1910; m. Ina Isole Barker, Sept. 8, 1911; children—Harry B., Sue Eleanor (Mrs. T.S. Dietrich), Mary Etta (Mrs. Wm. H. Neal). Tchr. common and high schs., in Ind., 1894-1905; instr. botany Ind. U., 1907, Cornell U., 1908-11; prof. botany and forestry Miss. State Coll., 1911-15; cotton breeder and agronomist Miss. Agr. Expt. Sta., 1911-1911-21, vice dir. 1919-22; cotton breeder Stoneville Pedigreed Seed Co., 1922-26; cotton breeder and head crops and soils dept. La. Agr. Expt. Sta., 1926-46, ret. June 1946. Chosen Man of Year, in La. Agr., Progressive Farmer, 1946; originated Stoneville, and Delfos Cotton varieties. Mem. Sigma Xi, Phi Kappa Phi. Baptist. Mason. Clubs: Rotary, Science (La. State U., pres. 1935). Author: Cotton (gen. ref. work), 1926 and later edits. Home: 4601 Vanderbilt Dr., Baton Rouge 14. Died July 8, 1962; buried Greenoaks Meml. Park, Baton Rouge.

BROWN, HARRY FLETCHER, chemist; b. Natick, Mass., July 10, 1867; s. William H. and Maria F. (Osgood) B.; A.B., Harvard Univ., 1890, A.M., 1892; hon. D.Sc., U. of Delaware, 1930; m. Florence M. Hammett, Oct. 26, 1897. Chief chemist at U.S. Naval Torpedo Sta., lNewport, R.I., 1893-1900; engaged in the investigation and development of smokeless powder in the Navy Dept.; gen. supt. Internat. Smokeless Powder & Chem. Co., 1900-04; dir. of mfr. smokeless powder, E. I. du Pont de Nemours & Co., 1904-15, v.p. in charge smokeless powder dept., 1915-19, now v.p. and dir. E. I. du Pont de Nemours & Co.; also v.p. and dir. Christiana Securities Co. Trustee U. of Del. Mem. Am. Chem. Soc., Nat. Edn. Assn. Home: 1010 Broome St. Office: Du Pont Bldg., Wilmington, Del. Died Feb. 28, 1944.

BROWN, HUGH S(TEWART), engr.; b. Somerville, N.J., Nov. 1, 1896; s. James and Ellen (Lane) B.; grad. Pratt Inst., Brooklyn, 1920; m. Sara Daniels, Sept. 20, 1927. Chief engr. Buda Co., Harvey, Ill., 1924-41; dir. of engring Briggs & Stratton Corp., Milwaukee, 1941-43, vice pres. since 1943, dir. since 1948. Trustee Parsons Coll., Fairfield, Ia. Mem. Soc. Automotive Engrs., Engring. Soc. of Milwaukee, Am. Soc. M.E. Club: Professional Men's (Milwaukee). Home: 2020 Two Tree Lane, Wauwatosa, Wis. 53213. Office: 2711 N. 13th St., Milw. 53201. Died Dec. 15, 1961; buried Wis. Meml. Park, Milw.

BROWN, JAMES BARRETT, plastic surgeon; b. Hannibal, Mo., Sept. 20, 1899; s. Albert Sydney and Evelyn (Segsworth) B.; M.D., Washington U., 1923, D.Sc., 1970; m. Bertha Phillips Phillips, Sept. 30, 1946; children—Jane Hamilton, Frances Reith; (by previous marriage)—James Barrett, Charles Sydney. Interne and assistant resident surgical service, Barnes and Childrens' Hospital, 1923-25; engaged in private practice of plastic surgery, Saint Louis, Missouri, since 1925; professor clin. surgery, School of Medicine, Washington U., 1948-68, prof. emeritus plastic surgery, 1968-71; prof. maxillo-facial surgery, Sch. of Dentistry from 1936; mem. surg. staff, Barnes, St. Louis Children's, St. Luke's, Jewish, Deaconess and DePaul hosps., St. Louis Mo. consultant surgeon, Shriners. Barnard Free Skin & Cancer, Ellis Fischel State Cancer Hosps., and others; cons. surgeon M.P. & Frisco R.R.; cons. plastic surg. USAF; consultant Los Alamos Medical Center. Served as colonel, M.C., U.S. Army, 1942-1946; chief consultant plastic surgery, E.T.O., 1942-43; chief plastic surgeon, Valley Forge Gen. Hosp., 1943-45; senior consultant plastic surgery U.S. Army, 1945-46; sr. civilian cons. plastic surg., U.S. Army, Office Surgeon Gen.; chief cons. plastic surg., U.S. Vets. Adminstrn. Decorated Legion of Merit; Am. Design Award, Lord & Taylor, 1944; Alumni Citation, Washington U., 1955; award Am. Assn. Plastic Surgeons, 1967, Modern Medicine, 1968; Certificate Merit, St. Louis Med. Soc., 1969; James Barrett Brown vis. professorship established in his honor Washington U., 1969. Diplomate Am. Bd. Surgery (founders group), Am. Bd. Plastic Surgery (founders group), Fellow A.C.S. (v.p. 1959-60), Am. Assn. Plastic Surgeons (hon.; pres. 1954); mem. Am., Southern, Western (vice president 1955, president 1958), Central surg. assns., Am. Assn. Surg. Trauma. Assn. Mil. Surgs., Am. Society of Plastic and Reconstructive Surgery, International Society of Surgeons (Brussels), Assn. of Medical Consultants, World War II, Surgeons' and Halsted clubs, Am. Soc. Surgery Hands, Society Head and Neck Surgeons, Phi Delta Theta, Nu Sigma Nu, Alpha Omega Alpha. Presbyterian. Clubs: Grolier (New York City); University (St. Louis). Co-author: Skin Grafting, 1958; Plastic Surgery of the Nose, 1951; Neck Dissections, 1957; Surgery of Face, Mouth and Jaws, 1954; Post-Mortem Homografts, 1960; (with Dr. Thomas Zaydon) Early Treatment Facial Injuries, 1964; other books on plastic surgery. Editorial bd. Excerpta Medica, Amsterdam; and others. Contbr. chpts. textbooks and articles in surg. jours. and other sci. publs. Home: St. Louis MO Died Mar. 18, 1971; interred Oak Grove Mausoleum, St. Louis MO

BROWN, JAMES GREENLIEF, plant pathologist; b. St. Clair, Mich., Nov. 21, 1880; s. George Simeon and Ida Evelyn (Graham) B.; prep. edn. high sch., Marlette, and Ferris Inst., Big Rapids, Mich.; B.S., U. Chgo., 1916, M.S., 1917, Ph.D., 1925; m. Clara May McNeil, June 5, 1912; 1 dau., Imogene (dec.). Tchr. dist. and village schs., Mich., 1897-1903; tchr. sci. Cebu (P.I.) Normal Sch., 1904-06, acting prin., 1906; lab. asst. in botany U. Chgo., 1907-08; research asst. Carnegie Desert Lab., Tucson 1909-11; instr. in biology U. Ariz., 1909-15, asst. prof. biology, 1916-19, prof. plant pathology Agrl. Coll., and plant pathologist Agrl. Expt. Sta., 1920-52, also head dept. agr., 1922-26. Fellow A.A.A.S. (mem. council 1941); mem. Am. Soc. Plant Physiologists, Am. Phytopathol. Soc. Bot. Soc. Am., Mycol. Soc. Am., Soc. Am. Bacteriologists, Sigma Xi, Phi Beta Kappa, Phi Kappa Phi. Mason, Kiwanian. Author: Crown Gall on Coniefers; effect of penicillin on corwn gall; also various papers on cotton, cactus, and other plant diseases. Built machine used for delinting and surface sterilizing cotton seed with sulphuric acid. Home: 1733 E. 6th St., Tucson. Died Apr. 1, 1954.

BROWN, JAMES SALISBURY, mfr., inventor; b. Pawtucket, R.I., Dec. 23, 1802; s. Sylvanus and Ruth (Salisbury) B.; m. Sarah Phillips Gridley, 1829, 2 daus., 1 son James. Pattern maker for David Wilkinson, Pawtucket, 1817-19; joined Pitcher & Gay, cotton machinery mfrs., 1819, became partner, 1823, gained control of firm, 1842, changed name to Brown Machine Works, continually expanded firm; patented improvement for lathe slide-rest (1st invented by his father), 1820; designed cutter for cutting bevel gears, 1830; patented spl. drilling machine, 1838; produced guns and gun making machines during Civil War, returned to mfg. cotton machinery after war. Died Dec. 29, 1879.

BROWN, JOHN BERNIS, educator, biochemist; b. Rock Falls, Ill., Dec. 25, 1893; s. Frank T. and Kathryn (Robb) B.; B.S., U. Ill., 1915, M.S., 1917, Ph.D., 1921; m. Bertha G. States, Oct. 9, 1918; children—Phyllis Margery (Mrs. John Buchanan), Franklin S. Asst. chemistry U. Ill., 1915-21; asso. chemistry and pharmacology U. Pa., 1921-23; research chemist Swift & Co., Chgo., 1923-24; successively asst. prof., asso. prof., prof. and chmn. dept. physiol. chemistry and pharmacology Ohio State U., 1924-64, prof. emeritus, 1964-69, dir. Inst. Nutrition and Food Tech., 1950-64. Mem. Ohio Nutrition Com., from 1950; fat com. agrl. bd. NRC, from 1955, fat com. food and nutrition bd., 1956-58; oilseeds adv. com. Dept. Agr., from 1957; mem. biochemistry test com. Nat. Bd. Med. Exam., 1953-57. Mem. Grandview Heights Library Bd., from 1950; governor's adv. com. on atomic power, Ohio, 1956-57. Served as 2d lt., U.S. Army, 1918-19. Mem. Am. Inst. Nutrition (treas. 1956-59), Am. Soc. Biol. Chemistry, Am. Chem. Soc., Inst. Food Technologists, Sigma Xi (pres. Ohio 1946), Phi Lambda Upsilon. Methodist (chmn. bd. trustees). Mason. Clubs: Mercator, Ohio State U. Faculty (past pres.) (Columbus). Editor physiology sect. Chem. Abstracts, 1940; editorial bd. Jour. Am. Oil Chemists Soc., 1952-56. Home: Columbus OH Died Nqv. 21, 1969; buried Union Cemetery, Columbus OH

BROWN, JOHN HAMILTON, gun inventor; b. Liberty, Me., July 28, 1837; at 18 apprenticed to gunsmith's trade. Located in Haverhill, Mass., 1957; perfected steel die for heeling ladies' shoes; removed to New York, 1863. Became associated with Kursheedt Mfg. Co., 1873; devised combination pleating machine, rotary ruching press, ruffling machine. Engaged in business for himself quilting linings of overcoats and ladies' cloaks on machine of his own invention. Dir. Nat. Rifle Assn., Capt. New York Rifel Club; mem. Am. team which shot return internat. match at Wimbledon, Eng., July 1883 (rifle designed and perfected by him with wwhich Am. team on that occasion beat British team at 4 to 6 ranges). In 1886 invented segmental tube wire-wound gun. Address: 602 St. Nicholas Av., New York.

BROWN, J(OHN) HAMMOND, author, conservationist; b. Balt., Jan. 18, 1877; s. John Hammond and Georgia Childs (Shipley) B.; student Oakland Acad., Louisa Co., Va., Peddie Sch., Highstown, N.J., 1897, Richmond Coll., 1898; grad. U. Ky., 1902; m. Margaret Scott Bell, Jan. 18, 1903; children—Druscilla Bell (Mrs. Charles C. Rettberg), Virginia Hammond (Mrs. H.G. Emery), Georgia Shipley (Mrs. R.L. Carmichael). Explorer jungles S.A., Yucatan sector Mexico, W.I., 1898-1903; newspaperman Herald, also Democrat, Lexington, Ky., 1899-1905; columnist Balt. News-Post, Sunday Am., since 1905; writer outdoor subjects since 1907; editor monthly mag. Outdoors Unlimited since 1940. Mem. adv. com. on wild waterfowl U.S. Dept. Interior. Mem. Am. Waterfowl Com. (sec. since 1947), Guardians of the River (founder, exec. dir. 1939), Outdoor Writers Assn. (pres.), Brotherhood Jungle Cock (founder, hon. pres.). Club: Flying Fishermen's (originator, v.p. 1938). Editor (book): Outdoors Unlimited, 1947. Home: 3800 Egerton Rd. Office: 7 St. Paul St., Balt. Died Aug. 13, 1955; buried Woodlawn Cemetery, Balt.

BROWN, JOHN PINKNEY, arboriculturist; b. Rising Sun, Ind., Jan. 19, 1842; s. Capt. Elbridge G. and Adaline (Style) B.; ed. Hanover Coll., Ind.; studied div. engring.; m. Mary E. Stephens, 1868. Served 16th Ind. Regt., 1861-63; later Miss. River service in U.S. steamers. Organized and later sec. and treas. Internat. Soc. Arboriculture. Originated system of tree planting by rys. for future timber and tie supply; has established model forest farm of 200 acres on which were planted 200,000 young forest trees. Republican. Editor Arboriculture. Author: Practical Arboriculture, 1906. Home: Connersville, Ind. Died 1915.

BROWN, JOSEPH ROGERS, inventor, mfr.; b. Warren, R.I., Jan. 26, 1810; s. David and Patience (Rogers) B.; m. Caroline B. Niles, Sept. 18, 1837, 1 child. Perfected and built linear dividing engine, 1850; perfected vernier caliper reading to thousandths of an inch, 1851, applied vernier to protractors, 1852; became partner (with Lucian Sharpe) in firm J. R. Brown & Sharpe, 1853, incorporated as Brown & Sharpe Mfg. Co., 1868; micrometer caliper, 1867; invented precision gear cutter to make clock gears and to supply his jobbing customers with gears, 1855; greatest achievement was invention of universal grinding machine, patent issued, 1877 (after his death). Died Isle of Shoals, N.H., July 23, 1876.

BROWN, KENNETH RENT, chemist; b. Pendleton, Ind., July 30, 1896; s. Calvin Fletcher and Mary (Rent) B.; A.B., Swarthmore Coll., 1918; m. Rae A. Horrobin, Aug. 21, 1920; children—Kenneth Horrobin, Richard Calvin, Robert Winfield. Chemist Atlas Power Co., Wilmington, Del., 1918-26, asst. dir. Reynolds exptl. lab., 1926-28, acting dir., 1928-30, dir. research lab., 1930-40, dir. research dept., 1940-51, mem. bd., 1947, v.p., Atlas Powder Co., 1951—. Mem. Am. Chem. Soc. (councilor, 1935), Am. Inst. Chem. Engrs., Am. Inst. Chemists, Soc. Chem. Industry, Electro Chem. Soc., Am. Soc. Testing Materials, Am. Assn. Econ. Entomologists, Phi Beta Kappa, Sigma Xi, Phi Kappa Psi. Republican. Methodist. Clubs: New York Chemists; Philadelphia Engineers, Union League (Phila.). Home: 620 S. High St., West Chester, Pa. Office: Atlas Powder Co., Wilmington 99, Del. Died Mar. 18, 1958; buried Tamaqua, Pa.

BROWN, LUCIUS POLK, chemist; b. Maury County, Tenn., Aug. 1, 1867; s. Campbell and Susan R. (Polk) B.; grad. U. of Va., 1889; post-grad. work in chemistry; m. Susan Catherine Massie, Dec. 12, 1903. Engaged in farming, 1890-93; in Pvt. practice as mem. firms of Memminger & Brown and Lucius P. Brown & Co., analyt. chemists, 1894-1908; pres. Brown Labs., Inc., 1908-15. Acting chemist, Tenn. Agrl. Expt. Sta., Knoxville, Tenn., 1889-90; food and drugs commr. of Tenn., 1908-15; dir. Bur. of Food and Drugs, Dept. of Health, City of New York, 1915-20. Capt. Nutrition Div., Sanitary Corps U.S. Army, 1918-19. Episcopalian. Home: Franklin, Tenn. Died 1935.

BROWN, PAUL GOODWIN, engineer; b. Red Oak, Ia., 1871; s. Isaac W. and Helen (Goodwin) B.; prep. edn., Wyoming Sem., Kingston, Pa.; student Cornell U., 1892-93; m. Antoinette Knapp, 1924. Formerly pres. Keystone State Corp. Mem. Am. Soc. C.E., Western Soc. Engrs., Delta Kappa Epsilon. Director and member executive committee Universal Pictures. Director St. Mary's Hospital, Civic Association, Four Arts, Community Chest (Palm Beach). Clubs: Racquet, Philadelphia, Engineers, Phila. Country (Phila.); Engineers, Links, Turf and Field, United Hunts, Cornell, Metropolitan (New York); Boca Raton (Fla.); Gulf Stream Golf (Delray Beach, Fla.); Old Guard Soc.,

Bath and Tennis, Everglades (Palm Beach). Home: 151 Hammon Av., Palm Beach, Fla. Office: 1321 Arch St., Philadelphia, Pa. Died Mar. 24, 1950.

BROWN, PERCY, röntegenologist; b. Cambridge, Mass., Nov. 24, 1875; s. Isaac Henry and Mary Elizabeth (Kennedy) B.; grad. Browne and Nichols Sch., Cambridge, 1893; Lawrence Sci. Sch. (Harvard), 1893-96; M.D., Harvard, 1900; m. Bernice Mayhew, Dec. 7, 1904. Röntgenologist Carney Hosp., 1903-10, St. Elizabeth's Hosp., 1905-11, L.I. Hosp., Boston, 1906-10; cons. röntgenologist Carney Hosp., 1911-13; instr. röntgenology Harvard Med. Sch., 1911-22; röntgenologist to Boston Children's Hosp., Boston Infants' Hosp., 1903-06, 10-22, St. Luke's Hosp., N.Y.C., 1924-29; röntgenologist in chief Western Pa. Hosp., Pitts., 1923. Maj., M.C., U.S. Army, Base Hosp. 5, France, 1917-18. Gold medalist Radiol. Soc. N.A., 1922; Caldwell lectr. Am. Röntgen Ray Soc., 1923. Fellow A.C.P., Am. Coll. Radiology; mem. A.M.A., Mass. Med. Soc., Boston Soc. Med. Sciences, Am. Urol. Soc., Am. Röntgen Ray Soc. (pres. 1911), Röntgen Soc. of London, Deutsche Röntgen Gesellschaft (until 1917), N.Y. Röntgen Soc., Phila. Röntgen Ray Soc. (hon.), Röntgen Ray Soc. New Eng., Boston Sci. Soc., Boston Soc. Natural Hist., Bostonian Soc. Conglist. Clubs: University, Harvard, St. Botolph (Boston); Harvard (N.Y.C.); Aesculapian of Boston (hon.). Author: American Martyrs to Science through the Roentgen Rays, 1935. Co-author of Science of Radiology for Fist Am. Congress of Radiology, Chicago, 1933. Contbr. sci. jours. and author of sundry monographs on subjects dealing with the X-Ray. Home: Egypt (Scituate), Plymouth County, Mass. Died Oct. 8, 1950; buried Martha's Vineyard, Mass.

BROWN, PHILIP KING, physician; b. Napa, Cal., June 24, 1869; s. Henry Adams and Charlotte Amanda (Blake) B.; A.B., Harvard, 1890, M.D., 1893; U. of Berlin, 1895-96, Göttingen, 1896; m. Helen Adelaide Hillyar, Mar. 7, 1900; children—Hillywar Blake, Harrison Cabot, Phoebe Hearst, Bruce Worcester. In practice of medicine, San Francisco since 1893; asst. in nervous diseases, U. of Calif., 1894, asso. prof. clin. medicine, 1896-98, instr. animal pathology, 1896-99; vis. physician, 1896-97, later cons. physician. Mt. Zion Hosp., San Francisco; cons. pathologist French Hosp., 1896-1901; asso in medicine and instr. clin. pathology, Cooper Med. Coll., 1899-1902, instr. clin. pathology and exptl. medicine, U. of Calif.; med. dir. So. Pacific Hosp.; attending physician, City and County Hosp., 1905-17; founder. med. dir. Arequipa Sanatorium (for tuberculous wage-earning women), Manor, Calif. Mem. Assn. Am. Physicians, Am. Climatol. and Clin. Assn., A.M.A., Boylston Med. Soc., Calif. Acad. Medicine, Calif. State Med. Soc., Soc. Colonial Wars, Soc. Am. Wars, S.A.R., Royal Legion. One of organizers San Francisco Settlement Assn. and San Francisco Boys' Club. Democrat. Mem. Gov. Olsen's Com. on Health Ins., 1939. Clubs: Burlingame, Commonwealth. Contbr. on animal pathology, heart and lung diseases, leporsy, soical problems in medicine, etc. Home: 1 25th Av., N. Office: 909 Hyde St., San Francisco. Died Oct. 1940.

BROWN, SAMUEL, surgeon; b. Augusta County, Va., Jan. 30, 1769; s. Rev. John and Margaret (Preston) B.; B.A., Dickinson Coll., 1789; med. degree U. Aberdeen (Scotland); m. Catherine Perry, 1809, 2 children. Introduced smallpox vaccination at Lexington, Ky., 1802; prof. theory and practice of medicine Transylvania U., 1819-25; started North Am. Med. and Surg. Jour., 1825; founder Kappa Lambda Soc. of Hippocrates (soc. of men pledged to profl. ideals). Died Huntsville, Ala., Jan. 12, 1830.

BROWN, STIMSON JOSEPH, astronomer; b. Penn. Yan, N.Y., Sept. 17, 1854; s. John Randolph B.; ed. Cornell, 1871-72; grad. U.S. Nval Acad., 1876, at head of class; m. Alice Graham, Nov. 18, 1878; m. 2d, Elizabeth Sharp Pettit, Nov. 12, 1913. Served in U.S. Coast and Geod. Survey, 1879-81; prof. mathematics U.S. Navy, 1883—; astron. dir. U.S. Naval Obs., 1898-1901; dir. Nautical Almanac, 1900-01; on duty at U.S. Naval Acad., April 4, 1901, and head dept. mathematics and mechanics June 1907, retired. Observed Catalogue of Stars for the "Berliner Jahrbuch," at Annapolis, Md., 1885-87, and at the obs. of U. of Wis., 1887-90. Author of text book on algebra, analytical geometry, trigonometry and The Calculus, for use of midshipmen. Mem. Spl. Bd. on Naval Ordnance, 1912—. Address: Washington, D.C. Deceased.

BROWN, SYLVANUS, millwright, inventor; b. Valley Falls, R.I., June 4, 1747; s. Philip and Priscilla (Carpenter) B.; m. Ruth Salisbury, 1 son, James Salisbury. Learned millwright trade; served aboard Continental Navy vessel Alfred, at beginning of Am. Revolution; worked for State of R.I. arsenal; supervised constr. several grist and saw mills, New Brunswick; made short trip to Europe, returned to Pawtucket, R.I., reestablished machine shop; assisted Samuel Slater in construction Am.'s 1st practical power spinning wheel, 1790, credited with crucial part in turning Slater's memories of English spinning machines into working model; developed many machines essential to profitable constn. of textile machinery; possibly 1st to use slide-crest lathe; superintended furnaces in cannon factory, Scituate, R.I., 1796-1801. Died Pawtucket, July 30, 1824.

BROWN, WADE HAMPTON, medical research; b. Sparta, Ga., Oct. 18, 1878; s. Geroge Rives and Laura Virginia (Brown) B.; B.S., U. of Nashville, 1899; grad. student U. of Chicago, 1902-03; M.D., Johns Hopkins, 1907; m. Beth Gillies, Oct. 29, 1908; children—Wade Gillies, Elspeth, Wade Hampton. Instr. pathology, U. of Va., 1907-08; instr. same, U. of Wis., 1908-10, asst. prof., 1910-11; prof. pathology, U. of N.C., 1911-13; with Rockefeller Inst. since 1913, asso. mem., 1914-22, mem. scientific staff for medical research since 1922. Mem. Assn. Am. Physicians, Am. Soc. Pathologists and Bacteriologists, Am. Soc. for Exptl. Pathology, Am. Soc. for Pharm. and Exptl. Therapeutics, Soc. for Exptl. Biology and Medicine, A.A.A.S., Sigma Xi, Nu Sigma Nu. Democrat. Presbyterian. Contbr. of more than 75 papers in med. procs. and jours.; has specialized in study of biology of syphilitic infections, constitutional factors and physical environment in relation to heredity and disease. Home: 34 Westcott Rd., Princeton, N.J. Died Aug. 4, 1942.

BROWN, WILLIAM GEORGE, chemist; b. Newcastle-on-Tyne, Eng., Nov. 5, 1853; s. William Robert and Jane Gillie (Sanderson) B.; Miller scholar, U. of Va., 1875, B.S., 1877; Morgan fellow, Harvard, 1884, U. of Heidelberg, Germany, 1880-81; hon. Ph.D., U. of N.C., 1889; m. Isabelle White, Nov. 14, 1895. Prof.chemsitry and instrn. in geology and mineralogy, E. Tenn. U., 1877-79: prof. gen. and agrl. chemistry, 1879-80, chemistry and mineralogy, 1880-83, U. of Tenn.; instr. chemistry, U. of Va., 1883-85; prof. chemistry and physics, S.C. Mil. Acad., 1885-86; prof. chemistry, Washington and Lee U., 1886-94; asst. chemist U.S. Dept. of Agr., 1894-96; prof. chemistry, 1896—, and dir. of labs., 1905-10, prof. industrial chemistry, 1910-19, U. of Mo.; editor U. of Mo. Studies, 1904-11. Elected dir. Tech. Sch., Newark, N.J., 1884 (declined); elected adj. prof. agr., U. of S.C., 1885 (declined). Mem. U.S. Assay Commn., 1913. Home: Columbia, Mo. Died Aug. 8, 1920.

BROWN, WILLIAM HENRY, botanist; b. Richmond, Va., Oct. 6, 1884; s. John Henry and Julia (Wright) B.; B.S., Richmond Coll., 1906; Ph.D., Johns Hopkins, 1910; m. Mary Agus Blythe, June 3, 1927. Scientific asst., U.S. Fisheries Lab., Beaufort, N.C., 1908; grad. asst., Johns Hopkins, 1908, fellow, 1909-10, Bruce fellow, 1910; bot. investigation in Jamaica, 1910; asst. Desert Lab. of Carnegie Instn., 1910; scientific asst., Mich. Agrl. Expt. Sta., and instr. plant physiology, Mich. Agrl. Coll., 1910-11; plant physiologist, Bur. of Science, Manila, 1911-23; asso. prof. botany, 1915-18; prof. and head of dept., 1919-24, U. of Philippines; chief division of investigation, Bur. of Forestry, Manila, 1918-20; dir. Bur. of Science, Manila, 1924-33. Mason. Author: Vegetation of Philippine Mountains, 1919; A Textbook of General Botany, 1925; Laboratory Botany, 1925; The Plant Kingdom, 1935. Editor: Minor Products of Philippine Forests, vol. 1, 1920, vols. 2 and 3, 1921. Editor in chief Philippine Journal of Science, Manila, 1924-33. Address: Manila, P.I. Died Nov. 9, 1939.

BROWN, WILLIAM HENRY, civil engr.; b. Little Britain Tp., Lancaster County, Pa., Feb. 29, 1836; s. Levi K. and Hannah C. (Moore) B.; ed. Central High Sch., Phila.; m. Sallie A. Rimmel, Oct. 15, 1863. Asst. engr. survey dept., Phila., 1858; engr. constrn. U.S. mil. rys., 1861-63; asst. engr., 1863-64, prin. asst. engr., Jan.-Oct. 1864, Pan Handle R.R.; asst. engr. Pittsburgh div., 1864-65, engr. Oil Creek R.R., Mar. 17-July 1, 1865, prin. asst. engr. Phila. & Erie div., 1865-67; engr. same, 1867-69, engr. in charge constrn. Altoona shops, 1869-70, resident engr. middle div., 1870-71, chief engr. and supt. Lewiston div., 1871-72, supt. Bedford div., 1872-74, engr. maintenance of way, 1874-81, chief engr. July 1, 1881-Feb. 28, 1906, Pa. R.R.; during service made 133 changes and revisions of line, built 14 elevated rys. through cities, 41 tunnels, 163 stone bridges, including Rockville stone bridge (largest in world of stone), Broad St. Sta., Phila., etc. Retired Feb. 29, 1906. Republican. Presbyn. Address: Philadelphia, Pa. Died 1910.

BROWNE, ARTHUR WESLEY, educator; b. Brooklyn, N.Y., Nov. 24, 1877; s. Henry Bewley and Kate Matilda (Day) B.; B.S., summa cum laude, Wesleyaff U., 1900, M.S., 1901; Ph.D., Cornell U., 1903; Sc.D. from Wesleyan U., 1933; m. Helen Elizabeth Westgate, Feb. 20, 1904; children—Arthur Westgate, Robert Lewis, Ruth Westgate (dec.), Helen Westgate, Catherine Day. Asst. chemist, S.S. White Dental Mfg. Co., Prine Bay, N.Y., 1895-97; grad. scholar in chemistry, 1901-02, instr., 1903-06, asst. prof. inorganic and analytic chemistry, 1906-10, prof. same, 1910-22, prof. inorganic chemistry since 1922, actg. head dept. chemistry (2d semester), 1924-25, Cornell; visiting prof. chemistry, U. of Chicago, summer 1931. Served as consultant during World War, chem. expert Ordnance Dept. at large. Mem. Alpha Delta Phi, Omega Upsilon Phi, Gamma Alpha, Alpha Chi Sigma, Phi Beta Kappa, Sigma Xi, Aldjebar, Phi Kappa Phi, Tau Beta Pi. Independent Republican. Conglist. Contbr. articles to Am. Year Book, 1910-19; also numerous professional articles on original researches in Am. and European chem. jours. Home: 216 Dearborn Place, Itahac, N.Y., Died Dec. 15, 1945.

BROWNE, CHARLES ALBERT, chemist; b. North Adams, Mass., Aug. 12, 1870; s. Charles Albert and Susan (MacCallum) B.; B.A., Williams, 1892; M.A., 1896; M.A. and Ph.D., U. of Göttingen, Germany, 1902; hon. D.Sc., Williams, 1924, Stevens Inst. Tech., 1925; m. Louise McDanell (A.B., Stanford, A.M., Columbia, Ph.D., Yale), Feb. 9, 1918; 1 dau., Caroline Louise. Engaged as chemist, New York, 1892-94; instr. in chemistry, Pa. State Coll., 1895-96; asst. chemist, Pa. Expt. Sta., 1896-1902; studied sugar chemistry in Germany, 1900-02; research chemist, La. Sugar in Germany, 1900-02; research chemist, La. Sugar Expt. Sta., New Orleans, 1902-06; chief sugar lab., U.S. Bur. Chemistry, Washington, D.C., 1906-07; chemist in charge of N.Y. Sugar Trade Lab., Inc., 1907-23; chief, Bur. of Chemistry, U.S. Dept. Agr., 1923-27; acting chief Bur. of Chemistry and Soils, 1927, chief of chem. and technol. research, 1927-35, supervisor chem. research, 1935-40, retired as colaborator, Bur. Agrl. and Indsl. Chemistry, 1940. U.S. del 6th Internat. Soc. of Sugar Cane Technologists, Brisbane, 1935. Fellow A.A.A.S. (v.p. chemistry sec., 1931, sec. history sec. 1941); mem. Am. Chem. Soc. (bd. of editors, 1911-22; chmn. N.Y. sect., 1923; chmn. sugar sec., 1919-21; chmn. history of chemistry sect., 1922-23; editor, Golden Jubilee number, "A Half-Century of Chemistry in America" 1926), Assn. Official Agrl. Chemists (pres. 1924-25), Washington Acad. Sciences, History of Science Soc. (recording sec. 1926-28; president 1935-36), Agrl. History Soc., S.A.R., Nat. Geog. Soc. Phi Beta Kappa, Sigma Xi, Phi Lambda Upsilon; hon. mem. Am. Oil Chem. Soc.; hon. fellow Sugar Technol. Assn. of India. Historian, American Chemical Society since 1945. Gold and silver medals for sugar exhibits, St. Louis Expn., 1904; award of distinction, Associate Grocery Manufacturers of America for applications of science to food manufacturing, 1935. Nicholas Appert Medal for outstanding achievement in food tech., 1944. Unitarian. Mason (32 deg.). Club: Cosmos (Washington, D.C.). Author: Handbook of Sugar Analysis, 1912; Sugar Tables for Laboratory Use, 1912; (with F. W. Zerban) Physical and Chemical Methods of Sugar Analysis, 1941; Source Book of Agricultural Chemistry, 1943; Thomas Jefferson and the Scientific Trends of His Time, 1943; also numerous bulletins and papers. Contbr. to Ency. Britannica, 13th and 14th edits., to Ency. Americana, 1941 edit., and to Dictionary of Am. Biography. Advisory editor Chemistry in Agriculture, 1926; co-editor, Wiley's Principles and Practices of Agricultural Analysis, 3d edit. Home: 3408 Lowell St. N.W. Office: U.S. Bureau of Agrl. and Industrial Chemistry, Washington 25, D.C. Died Feb. 3, 1947.

BROWNE, RALPH COWAN, roentgenologist, inventor; b. Salem, Mass., Nov. 15, 1880; s. Josiah Hill and Katherine (Cowan) B.; grad. high sch., Salem, 1898; m. Mary Belle Moody, Jan. 15, 1908 (died Apr. 1952); m. 2d, Florence May Hart Cox, Nov. 21, 1952. Principally interested in research and invention; now pres. Brown Apparatus Co.; tech. expert L.E. Knott Apparatus Co.; Roentgenologist Salem Hosp. Inventor of elec. system and mechanism adopted by U.S. Govt. in North Sea mine barrage, World War I; inventor Brown portable X-ray apparatus. Brown air-lift mine pump, zincit chalcoprite detector (Used in wireless telegraphy), high resistance transmitters (used in telephony). Republican. Conglist. Home: Salem, Mass. Died Jan. 1, 1960; buried Green Lawn Cemetery.

BROWNING, JOHN M., inventor; b. Ogden, Utah, Jan. 21, 1855; s. Jonathan and Elizabeth (Caroline) B. Made first gun at 13, of scrap iron in father's gunshop; patented breech-loading rifle, 1879, repeating rifle, 1884, box magazine, 1895; also numerous other patents on rapid fire guns. Automatic guns adopted by European govts.; automatic pistol adopted by U.S. Govt., 1908, machine guns and machine rifle by U.S. Govt., 1918. Decorated Order of Leopold, of Belgium. Home: Ogden, Utah. Died Nov. 26, 1926.

BROWNING, PHILIP EMBURY, chemist; b. Rhinebeck, N.Y., Sept. 9, 1866; s. William Garretson and Susanna Rebecca (Webb) B.; A.B., Yale U., 1889, Ph.D., 1892; U. of Munich, 1893-94, also the Sorbonne (Paris), 1913-14; m. Elizabeth Sophia Bradley, Dec. 12, 1899. Asst. in chemistry, 1889-93, instr., 1894-98, asst. prof., 1898-1929, asso. prof. and curator of chemical exhibit, 1929-32, later curator of chem. exhibit, Yale U. Mem. New Haven City Council, 1900-02, board of park commrs., 1901-02. Treas. First Eccles. Soc. in New Haven (founded 1638), 1916-30 and 1931—. Conglist. Author: Notes on Qualitative Analysis (with prof. F. A. Gooch), 1898; An Introduction to the Rarer Elements, 1903, 08, 12; Outlines of Qualitative Chemical Analysis (with same), i906. Home: New Haven, Conn. Died Jan. 2, 1937.

BROWNLEE, JAMES LEAMAN, U.S. asst. engr.; b. Washington Co., Pa., July 4, 1863; ed. public schools, Knoxville, Tenn., and Univ. of Tenn. to end of junior year; m. Oct. 6, 1892, Nettie M. Betsworth. In office East Tenn., Va. and Ga. R.R., 1884-86; entered govt. service, engr. dept., Jan., 1887; U.S.A. asst. engr., located at New Orleans since Oct. 1, 1890; member La. Engring. Soc. and Am. Soc. Civil Engrs. Residence: 1304 Leontine St. Office: Custom House, New Orleans, La.

BROWNSON, MARY WILSON, educator; born Washington, Pa.; d. James Irwin (D.D., LL.D.) and Eleanor McCullough (Acheson) B.; A.B., Pa. Coll. for Women, 1904, Litt.D., 1920; A.M., Washington and Jefferson Coll., 1905; summer courses in U. of Chicago, U. of Wis., Oxford U., England, and at Harvard and Columbia; library research in British Mus., Bibliotheque Nationale, Paris, and Harvard U. Prof. mathematics, 1885-89, English Bible, 1898-1919, modern European hist., 1904-20 (resigned), Pa. Coll. for Women. Lecturer. Mem. Nat. Inst. of Social Sciences. Presbyn. Author: Old Testament Story (4 vols.), 1904; His Sister, 1904; Syllabus Old Testament History, 1917; Victory Through Conflict (with Vanda E. Kerst), a pageant produced at Pa. Coll. for Women, during the fiftieth anniversary of the instn., June 1920. Home: 4301 Spruce St., Philadelphia PA

BRUCE, GEORGE, type-founder; b. Edinburgh, Scotland, June 26, 1781; m. Margaret Watson, Jan. 1, 1803; m. 2d, Catherine Wolfe, 1811. Came to Phila., 1795; apprenticed to bookbinder, then to printer; with brother David traveled to Albany, N.Y., 1798; then began work in N.Y.C.; foreman N.Y. Daily Advertiser, 1803, also printer, publisher of paper for owner, 1803-06; opened book-printing office with David, N.Y.C., 1806-16, improved English stereotyping process; co-owner type foundry, 1816-22, concentrated on type-founding after partnership ended, developed successful type-casting machine with nephew; pres. Mechanics and Tradesmen; patron N.Y. Typog. Soc., Printers' Library; mem. N.Y. Hist. Soc. Died N.Y.C., July 5, 1866.

BRUES, CHARLES THOMAS, zoologist; b. Wheeling, W.Va., June 20, 1879; s. Charles Thomas and Ada (Mossie) B.; B.S., University of Texas, 1901, M.S., 1902; studied Columbia University, 1903-04; A.M., Harvard Univ., 1942; m. Beirne Barrett, June 16, 1904; children—Austin Moore, Alice Mossie. Fellow in zoology, Columbia, 1903-04; spl. field agt., U.S. Dept. Agr., 1904-05; curator invertebrate zoology, Milwaukee (Wis.) Pub. Mus., 1905-09; instr. in econ. entomology, 1909-12, asst. prof., 1912-26, associate professor, 1926-35, professor entomology 1935-45, professor emeritus, 1946—. Harvard; associate curator insects, Museum Comparative Zoology, Biological research West Indies, 1910, 12, 1926-27; Dutch East Indies, 1937; Philippines, 1949. Member National Research Council, 1917-19. Fellow Am. Acad. Arts and Sciences, A.A.A.S., Entomol. Soc. America (pres. 1929); mem. Am. Assn. Econ. Entomologists, Cambridge Entomol. Club, Am. Soc. of Naturalists Boston Soc. of Natural Hist., Chicago Acad. Sci. (hon.), Florida Academy Science, Florida Entomological Soc. (honorary), Sigma Xi. Club: Harvard Faculty. Author: (with A.L. Melander) A Key to the Families of North Amer. Insects, 1915, Insects and Human Welfare, 1920 (2d ed., 1947); Classification of Insects (with A.L. Melander), 1931. Insect Dietary; An Account of the Food Habits of Insects, 1945. Editor of Psyche (jour. of entomology) 1909—. Author several hundred articles in scientific jours., mainly on insects. Address: Biological Laboratories. Harvard Univ., Cambridge 38, Mass. Died July 22, 1955; buried Mount Auburn Cemetery, Cambridge.

BRUMLEY, DANIEL JOSEPH, engineer; b. Putnam Co., O., Mar. 19, 1865; s. Joseph and Phillippina (Leffler) B.; student Ohio Northern U., Ada. O., C.E., Ohio State U., 1895, hon. Dr. of Engineering, same university, 1934; m. Susanna Pinkerton Lytle, of Deshler, O., Sept. 1, 1908; 1 son, David Joseph. Entered ry. engring. service, June 18, 1895, as asst. section foreman, L. & N. R.R., Evansville, Ind., asst. engr. Columbus and Hocking Coal & Iron Co., New Straitsville, O., Aug.-Dec. 1896; with L. & N. R.R. successively as asst. supervisor, Belleville, Ill., section foreman, Evansville, Ind., rodman, Louisville, Ky., asst. engr., Clarksville, Tenn. and Louisville, Ky., until 1901; engr. maintenance of way, Nat. Ry. of Mexico, Sept. and Oct. 1901; roadmaster L. & N. R.R., Elizabethtown, Ky., 1901-04; div. engr. Ind. Southern R.R., 1904-05p prin. asst. engr., I.C.R.R. and Yazoo & Miss. Valley R.R., 1905-10, engr. of constrn., 1910-13; engr. maintenance of way, I.C. and Y. & M.V. rys., Apr.-Nov. 1913, and continued with same rds. as asst. chief engr., 1913-14, valuation engr., 1914-18 and chief engr. in charge of electrifying Chicago Terminal, I.C.R.R., 1920-35, retired and pensioned by rr. co.; consulting engineer, Itabira R.R. Co., Brazil. Ex-president Flossmoor (Ill.) State Bank. Pvt. Co. A, 14th Inf. Ohio N.G., 1893-95. Ex.-pres. bd. Sch. Dist. No. 161, Cook County, Ill., 1921-29; ex-pres. bd. Village of Flossmoor, Ill., 1924-27; served as justice of peace, Town of Rich, Cook Co., Ill., since 1925; chmn. Cook County Work Relief Com., 1933-34; chmn. state Advisory Com. I.E.R.C., 1934-35. Mem. Am. Soc. C.E., Am. Inst. Elec. Engrs., Am. Ry. Engring. Assn. (ex-pres.; editor and consultant Apr. 1, 1935-Mar. 1, 1937), Western Soc. Engrs. (ex-pres.), Ohio Soc. of Chicago, Ohio State U. Association (ex-pres.). Republican. Methodist. Club: Chicago Engineers'. Author: Preparation and Care of a Vegetable Garden (with Thomas G. Grier and Fred Menge), 1918. Home: Flossmoor, Ill.

BRUNDAGE, ALBERT HARRISON, M.D., toxiciologist; b. Candor, N.Y., Mar. 3, 1862; s. Amos H. (M.D.) and Sarah M. (Dimmick) B.; M.D., Univ. Med. Coll. (New York U.), 1885; Ph.G., Brooklyn Coll. Pharmacy, 1892, Pharm.D., 1897; hon. A.M., U. Nashville, 1898; M.S., R.I. Coll. Pharmacy and Allied Sciences, 1905; m. S. A. Holt, Sept, 26, 1888. Prof. emeritus toxicology and physiology, depts. medicine, dentistry and pharmacy, Marquette Univ., 2908—; prof. toxicology and physiology, Brooklyn Coll. Pharmacy, 1898-1903 (pres. 1893-94), and R.I. Coll. Pharmacy and Allied Sciences, 1903-07. Toxicologist to Bushwick Hosp., 1904-21; lecturer on tuberculosis, Brooklyn Com. for Prevention of Tuberculosis, from 1908; lecturer for Am. Red Coross from 1918; pres. New York State Bd. of Pharmacy, 1903, and Board examiner in toxicology and posology, 1901-04, chmn. state com. on poisions. Mem. Vol. Med. Service Corps, 1918-19; maj. med. staff, Police reserve, City of New York; cons. toxicologist Bushwick Hosp.; insp. Bd. of Health; asso. immuno-therapy Polhemus Clinic, L.I. Coll. Hosp. Founder of first open-air classes in Brooklyn public schools. Grand lecturer Order of Eastern Star, State of New York, 1912, and reviser of its ritual. Commr. of Brooklyn to Tennessee Centennial, 1897. Founder and hon. mem. Brooklyn Med. Soc. (pres. 1895-96). Mason (32 deg.). Author: A Manual of Toxicology, 13th editon, 1921; Practical Points in Physiology, 2 edits., 1904. Address: Woodhaven, N.Y. Died Mar. 12, 1936.

BRUNER, HENRY LANE, zoölogist; b. Knox County, Ill., Jan. 10, 1861; s. Frances Marion and Esther (Lane) B.; A.B., Abingdon (Ill.) Coll. (united with Eureka Coll., 1884), 1880; Yale, 1880-81; Ph.D., U. of Frieburg, Baden, 1896; D.Sc., Butler U., 1932; m. Carolyn Aumock, Sept. 10, 1890 (died 1894); 1 son, Harold Aumock; m. 2d, Emma Pfeiffer, June 15, 1897; children—Margaret Emilie (Mrs. H. W. Hudson), Henry Pfeiffer. Taught natural sciences various colleges, 1881-86; prof. biology and geology. Drake Univeristy, 1891-92, Butler University, 1892-1919, professor zoölogy, 1919-38, head of dept., 1892-38, dir. grad. studies 1932-38, prof. emeritus since 1938. Fellow A.A.A.S., Ind. Acad. of Science (pres. 1919), Ia. Acad. of Science (emeritus); mem. Am. Soc. Zoölogists, Eugeneics Soc., Am. Assn. Univ. Profs. (emeritus), New York Acad. Sciences (asso.), S.A.R., Phi Kappa Phi. Republican. Mem. Disciples Church. Club: Professional Men's Forum. Author: Laboratory Directions in College Zoölogy, 3d edit., 1942; contbr. to Anatomy and Physiology of Vertebrates. Home: 324 S. Ritter Av., Indianapolis. Died March 17, 1945; buried in Crown Hill Cemetery, Indianapolis.

BRUNER, LAWRENCE, entomologist; b. Catasauqua, Pa., Mar. 2, 1856; s. Uriah and Amelia (Brobst) B.; ed. U. of Neb., hon. B.Sc., 1897; m. Marcia Dewell, Dec. 25, 1881; children—Psyche E., Helen M., Alice (dec.). Asst. U.S. Entom. Commn., 1880; field agt. U.S. Dept. Agr., U. of Neb., 1888; in Argentina, S.A., 1897-98; entomologist, Neb. Agrl. Expt. Sta., 1888-90; instr. entomology, 1890-95, and prof., 1895—, U. of Neb. Author: Introduction to Study of Entomology; Destructive Locust of Argentina, 1st rept., 1898, 2d rept., 1900; Locusts of Paraguay, 1906; Vol. II Orthopt. Biol. Cent. Americana; Salt Orthopt. of Brazil, Locusts of Peru; Preliminary Catalog of Philippine Orthoptera. Also numerous monographs, reports and papers on insects and birds. Joint Author: New Elementary Argriculture. Named as most distinguisned Nebraskan by governor's com. to represent the State at the Panama P.I. Expn., 1915. Address: Lincoln Neb. Died Jan. 30, 1937.

BRUNS, THOMAS NELSON CARTER, bridge builder; v. Richmond, Va., June 4, 1902; s. Henry Dickson and Kate Virginia (Logan) B.; grad. Prep. Sch., Woodberry Forest, Orange, Va.; student U. Va., 1920-23; B.S. in Civil Engring., Tulane U., 1927, C.E. 1932; m. Bernard Peyton Llewllyn Early, Oct. 27, 1928; children—Thomas Nelson Carter, Peyton Llewellyn Early. Foreman, then supt. Doullut & Ewin, Inc., New Orleans, 1924-37; project mgr. Raymond Concrete Pile Co., N.Y.C., 1937-41; owner, mgr. Bruns Bridge Co., New Orleans, 1946-57; chief engr. Keller Constrn. Corp., 1957—; pres. Brunspile Corp., New Orleans, 1957—. Served as comdr. Civil Engr. Corps, USNR, 1942-46. Fellow Am. Soc. C.E.; mem. La. Engring Soc., Chi Phi, Tau Beta Pi. Patentee prestressed concrete piling. Contbr. articles to engring. lit. Home: 526 St. Peter St., New Orleans, 70116. Office: 7900 Palm St., New Orleans 70125. Died Oct. 1, 1966; buried Christ Ch., Glendower, Va.

BRUNSCHWIG, ALEXANDER, surgeon, gynecologist; b. El Paso, Tex., Sept. 11, 1901; s. Felix and Pauline (Harris) B.; B.S., U. of Chicago, 1923, M.S., 1924; M.D., Rush Med. Coll., 1927; post grad. work, Strasbourg and Paris, France; M.D. (honorary), Laval U., P.Q., Can.; Doctoris Honoris Causa. U. Strasbourg (France), 1959, University of Montpellier, University Bordeaux; married Lea Naye, June 16, 1926; children—Louise (Mrs. Paul Sivak), Roxane (Mrs. Bruno Pavia). Practice Chgo., from 1928; Nat. Research fellow, Strasbourg, 1930-31; surg. staff U. Chgo. Clinics, became prof. surgery U. Chgo., 1940; attending surgeon, chief gynecol., dept. Meml. Hosp. for Treatment Cancer and Allied Diseases; became prof. clin. surgery Cornell U. Coll. Med., 1947; cons. gynecologist, surgeon New York Infirmary; consulting surgeon at New York Polyclinic Hosp. Paris civilian cons. U.S. Govt., 1942-46; mem. Unitarian Service Com. Medical Teaching Missions to Czechoslovakia, 1946, Austria, 1947. Served as lt. (j.g.) USN, 1926-27. Awarded Medal of Charles U. of Prague, 1946; Order of White Lion of Czechoslovakia; Medal, U. Brussels (Belgium); Officer Legion of Honor (France); Gold Medal, Societie des Journees Medicales de Bruxelles; medal U. Bologna (Italy), Lucy Wortham James award, James Ewing medal; Ann Langer Cancer Research Found. Award, 1968. Fellow American College Surgeons, International College Surgeons (hon.), Am. Surgical Association; hon. or corr. member medical and professional socs. various foreign countries; member Society Clinical Surgery, Soc. U. Surgeons, A.M.A., Soc. Pelvic Surgeons, N.Y. Cynecol. Soc., Academie de Chirurgie Paris. Author: The Surgery of Pancreatic Tumors; Radical Surgery in Advanced Cancer of the Abdomen; L'exenteration pelvienne, 1964; also articles med. jours. Home: Pelham NY Died Aug. 7, 1969; buried Ferncliff, Hartsdale NY

BRUSH, CHARLES FRANCIS, scientist; b. Euclid O., Mar. 17, 1849; s. Col. Isaac Elbert and Delia Williams (Phillips) B.; M.E., U. of Mich., 1869; Ph.D., Western Reserve, 1880; hon. M.S., U., 1900, Kenyon Coll., 1903; Sc.D., U. of Mich., 1912; m. Mary E. Morris, Oct. 6, 1875; children—Charles Francis, Mrs. Edna Perkins, Helene. Chem. expert, Cleveland, 1870-73; iron and ore commn. mcht., 1873-77; pioneer investigator of electric lighting, and invented the Brush electric arc light, 1878, now in gen. use; also the storage battery (fundameal invention) and other devices essential to modern elec. engring.; founder the Brush Electric Co.; credited with "The Practical Development of Electric Are Lighting" (Rumford medal). Pres. Cleveland Arcade Co., 1887—; founder The Linde Air Products Co. (1st pres.). Trustee Western Reserve U., Adelbert Coll., Univ. Sch., Cleveland Sch. of Art, Lake View Cemetery; corporator Case Sch. Applied Science; Chevalier of Legion of Honor, France, 1881; Rumford medal, Am. Acad. Arts and Sciences, 1899; Edison medal, 1913. Fellow Am. Acad. Arts and Sciences. Warden Trinity Cathedral. Home: Cleveland, O. Died June 15, 1929.

BRUSH, GEORGE JARVIS, mineralogist; b. Brooklyn, Dec. 15, 1831; s. Jarvis and Sarah (Keeler) B.; pvt. sch. edn.; studied chemistry and mineralogy at New Haven; in Oct. 1850, went to Louisville as asst. to Prof. Silliman in univ. there; Ph.B., Yale, 1852; hon. A.M., 1857; LL.D., Harvard, 1886; m. Harriet Silliman Trumbull, Dec. 23, 1864. Asst. in chemistry, U. of Va., 1852-53; studied in Europe, 1853-56; prof. metallurgy, 1855-71, prof. mineralogy, 1864-98, prof. emeritus, 1898—, dir. 1872-98, Sheffield Scientific Sch. (Yale). Address: New Haven, Conn. Died Feb. 6, 1912.

BRUSH, WILLIAM WHITLOCK, civil engr.; b. Orange, N.J., July 28, 1874; s. Clinton Ethelbert and Eliza Thomson (Whitlock) B.; B.S., New York, U., 1893, C.E., 1894, M.S., 1895; m. Jean Evelyn Mitchell, Apr. 28, 1897; 1 son, John Mitchell. Engr. on water supply for Brooklyn, N.Y., 1894-1907; engr. with Bd. of Water Supply, on Catskill system, 1907-09; dept. engr. Bd. of Water Supply, on design of city aqueduct system, 1909-10; dep. chief engr. Bur. Water Supply Dept. of Water Supply, Gas and Electricity, N.Y. City, 1910-17; apptd. acting chief engr. same, July 1917, dep. chief engr., 1919, chief engr., 1927; retired, 1934; editor Water Works Engring., 1934. Designed system of delivery of Catskill water to the five boroughs of N.Y. City. Mem. of Council of New York Univ. Hon. mem. Am. Water Works Assn. (ex-pres. and treas.); mem. Am. Soc. C.E., Munic. Engrs. of N.Y. (ex-pres.), Am. Pub. Health Assn., Alumni Assn. Arts and Engineering of New York U. (ex-pres.) Gamma Chapter Delta Phi; hon. mem. N.E. Water Works Assn. Republican. Mem. Dutch Ref. Ch. Club: Engineers, Town Hall. Contbr. tech. papers on engring. subjects. Home: Hotel Drake, 440 Park Av., New York 22. Office: 24 W. 40th St., New York 18 NY

BRYAN, KIRK, geologist; b. Albuquerque, N.M., July 22, 1888; s. Richard W.D. and Susie Hunter (Patten) B.; A.B., U. of N.M., 1909; A.B., Yale U., 1910, Ph.D., in absentia, 1920; A.M.(honorary), Harvard, 1942, D.Sc. (honorary), U. of N.M., 1947; m. Mary Catherine MacArthur, July 11, 1923; children—Richard Conger, Mary Catherine, Kirk, Margaret Stuart. Entered service U.S. Geol. Survey, 1912, as geologic aid and advanced successively through grades to senior geologist, 1927; instr. geology, Yale U., 1914-17; lecturer physiography, Harvard, 1926-27, asst. prof., 1927-30, asso. prof., 1930-43, prof. since 1943. Served as pvt., then 2d lieut., engrs., geol. sec. in chief engrs. office, U.S. Army, 1918-19, with A.E.F. in France. Fellow Am. Assn. for Advancement of Science (v.p. and chmn. Sect. E., 1939), Geol. Soc. of America (vice pres. 1948), mem. Am. Acad. (council 1935-38), Assn. Am. Geographers (council 1935-38), Soc. Am. Military Engrs., Am. Geographical Soc., Am. Geophys. Union, Boston Geol. Soc. (pres. 1936), Geol. Soc. Wash., Northwest Scientific Assn., Sigma Xi, Pi Kappa Alpha. Spl. assignments—geologist Columbia Basin Project, 1923; Nat. Geo. Soc., Chaco Canyon Expdn., 1923-25; geologist Middle Rio Grande Conservancy Dist., 1927, 34, 35; geologist for Mexican Govt., San Juan Project.

Democrat. Clubs: Economy (pres. 1942-43), Faculty (Cambridge). Address: 5 Scott St., Cambridge, Mass. Died Aug. 22, 1950; buried Albuquerque, N.M.

BRYAN, WILLIAM ALANSON, ornithologist, zoölogist; b. nr. New Sharon, Ia., Dec. 23, 1875; s. William A. and Catherine M. (Pearson) B.; B.S., Ia. State Coll., 1896; m. Ruth M. Goss, June 20, 1900; m. 2d, Elizabeth Jane Letson, Mar. 16, 1909; (died 1919); m. 3d, Maud M. Robinson, June 21, 1921. Asst. dept. zoölogiy in charge Ia. State Coll. Museum, 1893; on expdn. to Big Stone Lake, 1894; spl. lecturer on museum methods, U. of Minn., Ind. U., U. of Chicago, Purdue U., Ia. Coll. and Drake U., 1895-97; asst. curator in charge dpt. ornithology, Field Columbian Museum, 1898-99; apptd. rep. U.S. Dept. Agr. to investigate fauna of H.I., 1899; traveled extensively in Europe, and America, studying museum adminstrn., 1900; curator, Bishop Museum of Ethnology and Natural History, Honolulu, 1900-07; organized, and was made pres. Pacific Scientific Instrn., 1907; prof. zoölogy and geology, U. of Hawaii, 1909-19; scientific expdn., Latin America, 1919-20; dir. Los Angeles Museum History, Science and Art, 1921-40 (retired). Presented pvt. collection, 10,000 natural history specimens, to New Sharon (Ia.) High Sch., 1903; hon. curator Pacific ornithology, Minn. Acad. Natural Sciences, 1904. Fellow A.A.A.S.; mem. Am. Orinthologists' Union, Cooper Ornith. Club, Am. Fisheries Soc., Am. Mus. Assn., Southern Calif. Acad. Natural Science (pres. 1925), Hawaiian Hist. Soc. (v.p.); mem. 4th Internat. Ornith. Congress. Author: Key to Birds of Hawaiian Group, 1901; Natural History of Hawaii, 1915; also monographs of Marcus Island, and various scientific papers. Home: 142 S. Hayworth Av., Los Angeles, Calif. Died June 18, 1942.

BRYANS, HENRY BUSSELL, cons. engr.; b. Phila., Mar. 26, 1886; s. Henry M. and Ella (Lonergan) B.; A.B., Central High School, Phila., 1903; B.S. in mech. engring., U. of Pa., 1907; m. Ada Matilda Trinkle, May 1, 1911; children—Henry Trinkle, Robert Trinkle. Began as engr. United Gas Improvement Co., 1907; gen. supt. Phila. Suburban-Counties Gas & Electric Co., 1927-28, asst. gen. mgr. Phila. Electric Co., 1928-29, v.p. in charge operations, 1929-38, exec. v.p., 1938-47, dir., 1940-52, pres., 1947-52; v.p., dir. United Engrs. & Constructors, Inc., 1952-55; dir. mem. exec. com. Bellevue-Stratford Hotel; dir. Baldwin Securities Corp.; mem. bd. mgrs. emeritus Western Sav. Fund Soc. of Phila. Mem. electrical utility Def. Adv. Council, 1950-51. Life trustee past chmn., mem. finance, investment and devel. coms., exec. bd. U. Pa. Fellow Royal Soc. Arts, Manufacturers and Commerce; mem. Am. Standards Assn. (past pres.), Am. Soc. M.E., I.E.E.E., Franklin Inst. (bd. mgrs., past chmn., mem. finance com., past mem. exec. com.), Pa. Elec. Assn. (past pres.), Elec. Assn. Phila. (past pres.), Hist. Soc. Pa., Newcomen Soc., Pa. Soc. N.Y. Republican. Presbyterian. Mason. Clubs: Engineers, Union League (past pres.), Midday (Phila.); Penn., Sunday Breakfast. Home: Bryn Mawr PA Died May 1973.

BRYANT, ARTHUR PEYTON, chemist; b. South New Market, N.H., May 7, 1868; s. George Nelson and Anna Maria (George) B.; B.S., Wesleyan U., Middletown, Conn., 1892, M.S., 1895; m. Fannie Wright Burr, Apr. 4, 1893; 1 son, Harold Burr (dec.). Teacher, English and Classical Sch., Providence, R.I., 1893, Swarthmore Coll., 1894; food and nutrition work with Prof. W. O. Atwater, Middletown, Conn., 1895-1901; chemist with Agrl. Expt. Sta., Storrs, Conn., 1901; research chemist Corn Products Co., Chicago, 1902-06; with Bryant-Miner Labs., 1906; directing chemist Clinton Corn Syrup Refining Co. (now Clinton Co.), 1907—, also v.p. and dir.; v.p. and dir. Clinton Corn Syrup Sales Co., Internat. Wheat Malt Syrup Co.; dir. City Nat. Bank of Clinton; cons. chemist Nat. Candy Co. Mem. and ex-pres. Clinton Bd. of Edn., Y.M.C.A., Clinton br. Boy Scouts of America. Republican. Methodist. York and Scottish Rite Mason. Home: Clinton, Ia. Died Feb. 3, 1935.

BRYANT, GRIDLEY, civil engr., inventor; b. Scituate, Mass., Aug. 26, 1789; s. Zina and Eunice (Wade) B.; m. Maria Fox, Dec. 3, 1815, 10 children. Contractor for U.S. Govt.; built Boston br. U.S. Bank, 1823; inventor portable derrick, 1823; supervising engr. Quincy (Mass.) R.R., 1826; inventor 8-wheeled railroad car; one of earliest railroad builders. Died Scituate, June 13, 1867.

BUCHANAN, GEORGE SIDNEY, geologist; b. Starling, Colo., Sept. 1, 1902; s. Julian Eugene and Alice (Propst) B.; A.B., U. Mich., 1922, M.S. 1924; grad. Advanced Mgmt. Program, Harvard, 1950; m. Dorothy E. Dodds, Apr. 21, 1928; children—Daphne Alice, Dodds Ireton, George Sidney. Geologist Carter Oil Co., 1924-28; chief geologist Tulsa Oil Co., 1928-32, Barnsdall Oil Co., 1932-34; pres. Adams Oil & Gas Co., 1934-39, Yequa Corp., 1938-44, v.p. Sohio Petroleum Co., 1949-52; sr. v.p., dir. Husky Oil Co., & Refining Co. Ltd., Rimrock Tidelands, Inc. Fellow Geol. Soc. Am.; mem. Societe Oili Minerali (pres.), Am. Assn. Petroleum Geologists (pres. 1958-59), Am. Geog. Soc., Sigma Xi, Home: Box 380, Cody, Wyo. Died July 21, 1967.

BUCHANAN, JAMES WILLIAM, prof. zoology; b. Basil, O., Jan. 30, 1888; s. James Wilson and Almeda (Jenkins) B.; B.S., Ohio U., Athens, O., 1913; student U. of London, Eng., 1919; Ph.D., U. of Chicago, 1921; m. Pearle Oliver, July 20, 1918; children—James O., William Ervine. Began as teacher, 1906; asso. prof. of biology, U. of Miss., 1913-15; fellow in zoology, U. of Chicago, 1915-16; instr. in zoology, N.Y. Univ., 1916-17; senior instructor 3d Army Post Schools, Coblenz, Germany, 1919; instr. and asst. prof. biology, Yale, 1921-30; asso. prof. zoology, Northwestern U., 1930-33, prof., 1933-49, chmn. dept., 1940-49; Morrison prof. zoology, 1945-49; acting dean, Coll. Liberal Arts, 1945-46. Hancock prof. zool., dir. research Hancock Found., U. So. Calif., since 1949. Served as 1st lt. inf., U.S. Army, with A.E.F., W.W.; maj. U.S. Inf. Reserve Fellow A.A.A.S. (sec., Sect. F., 1940-48), mem. American Soc. Zoologists, Am. Physiol. Soc., Am. Nature Assn., Chicago Acad. of Science (hon. life mem.), Phi Beta Kappa, Sigma Xi, Sigma Pi, Gamma Alpha. Mason. Address: Hancock Found., U. of So. Calif., L.A. 7. Died June 27, 1952; buried Inglewood Cemetery, Inglewood, Los Angeles County, Cal.

BUCHANAN, JOSEPH, educator, journalist, inventor; b. Washington County, Va., Aug. 24, 1785; s. Andrew and Joanna B.; attended Transylvania U., Lexington, Ky.; m. Nancy Rodes Garth; 1 son, Joseph Rodes. Apptd. prof. insts. of medicine Transylvania U., 1809; went to Phila. to study Pestalozzian ednl. methods, returned to Lexington, tested methods in his classes; studied law, then lectured in pvt. law sch.; with Lexington Reporter, Frankfort (Ky.) Palladium, Western Spy and Literary Gazette; editor Louisville (Ky.) Focus, 1826-29; developed spiral boiler, applied boiler to wagon, 1825. Author: Philosophy of Human Nature, 1812; A Practical Grammar of the English Language, 1826. Died Sept. 29, 1829.

BUCHANAN, ROBERDEAU, atronomier; b. Phila., Nov. 22, 1839; s. McKean (pay dir. U.S.N.) and F. Selina (Roberdeau) B.; B.S., Lawrence Scientific Sch. (Harvard) 1861; m. Lyla M. Peters, 1888, Nautical Almanac Office, U.S. Naval Obs.; has made calculations for Nautical Almanac. 1879—. Author: Genealogy of the Roberdeau Family 1876; Genealogy of the Descendants of Dr. William Shippen, The Elder, 1877; Genealogy of the McKean Family, 1890; Life of Gov. Thomas McKean of Pennsylvania 1890; Observations on the Declaration of Independence, 1890; Treatise on the Projection of the Sphere, 1890; The Mathematical of Eclipses. Died Dec. 18, 1916.

BUCHER, JOHN EMERY, chemist; b. Hanover, Pa., Aug. 17, 1872; s. Jacob F. and Elizabeth (Emery) B.; A.C., Lehigh U., 1891; Ph.D., Johns Hopkins, 1894; Sc.D., Brown U., 1917; m. Alcista Howard, of Milford, Mass., 1896. Instr. organic chemistry, Tufts Coll., 1894-97; asso. prof. chemistry, R.I. Coll., 1897-1901; same, Brown U., 1901-15, prof. and head of dept., 1915-17; with Penman-Littlehales Chem. Co., 1917-20. Mem. Naval Consulting Bd., World War. Mem. Civil Legion. Republican. Contbr. numerous articles in professional jours. Inventor of process for nitrogen fixation, and processes for mfr. of magnesium, beryllium and aluminium. Consulting chemist, New York. Home: 57 Davenport St., North Adams, Mass. Address: P.O. Box 401, Norwalk CT

BUCHER, WALTER H(ERMAN), geologist; b. Akron, O., Mar. 12, 1888; s. August J. and Maria (Gebhardt) B.; Ph.D. U. of Heidelberg, Germany, 1911; Sc.D. (hon.), Princeton, 1947, Columbia, 1957, U. Cincinnati, 1962, U. Durham (Eng.), 1963; m. Hannah E. Schmid; children—John Eric, Mary Dorothy, Margaret Louise, Robert Walter. With U. of Cincinnati, 1913-40 (prof. geology, 1925-37, head dept., 1937-40); prof. structural geology, Columbia, 1940-56, prof. emeritus, 1956, head dept., 1950-53; cons. Humble Oil & Refining Co., Houston. Recipient Bowie medal Am. Geophys Union, 1954; L. V. Buch medal Deutsche Geologische Gesellschaft, 1955; Penrose medal Geol. Soc. Am., 1960. Fellow Am. Acad. Arts and Scis.; mem. Nat. Acad. Sci., Nat. Research Council (div. chmn. 1940-43), Geological Soc. America (president 1954-55), Geophys. Union (pre. 1948-53), Paleontol. Soc. Am., Am. Assn. Advancement Sci., N.Y. Acad. Sci. (pres. 1944), Ohio Acad. Sci. (pres. 1935); hon. mem. Geol. de France, Deutsche Geol. Ges., Soc. Geol. Belgique, Methodist. Author: The Deformation of the Earth's Crust, 1933; also articles sci. jours. Home: 100 Paulin Blvd., Leonia, N.J. Died Feb. 17, 1965; buried Spring Grove Cemetery, Cin.

BUCHHOLZ, JOHN THEODORE, botanist; b. Polk County, Neb., July 14, 1888; s. Conrad C. and Christine (Weber) B.; B.S., Ia. Wesleyan Coll., 1909; A.B., State U. of Ia., 1909; M.S., U. of Chicago, 1914, fellow, 1916-17, Ph.D., 1917; studied Ia. Lakeside Lab. and Cold Spring Harbor, N.Y.; m. Olive Peterson, Aug. 15, 1912; children—Olive Miriam, Christine, Ruth Elizabeth. Instr. biology, 1909-11, head science dept., 1911-18, Ark. State Normal Sch., Conway; prof. biology, West Tex. State Normall Coll., Canyon City, 1918-19; prof. botany and head of dept., U. of Ark., 1919-26; prof. botany, U. of Tex., 1926-29; prof. botany U. of Ill., since 1929, head dept., 1938-42. Visiting investigator Carnegie Instn. dept. of genetics, Cold Spring Harbor, summers, 1921-41. Fellow A.A.A.S. (sec. sect. G, 1937-40, v.p., chmn. 1942); mem. Bot. Soc. America (pres. 1941), Am. Soc. Naturalists, Genetics Soc. of America, Am. Assn. Univ. Profs., Torrey Bot. Club, Calif. Bot. Soc., Sigma Xi. Contbr. on botanical subjects—morphology and embryology of conifers; on the genetics of Datura, especially the role of pollen-tube growth in the heredity of polyploids, on plants with extra chromosomes and gene affecting pollen-tube growth. Clubs: University and Dial (Urbana); Chaos (Chicago). Address: 706 S. Coler Av., Urbana, Ill. Died July 1, 1951; buried Mt. Hope Cemetery, Urbana.

BUCK, GURDON, surgeon; b. N.Y.C., May 4, 1807; s. Gurdon and Susannah (Manwaring) B.; M.D., Coll. Physicians and Surgeons, N.Y.C., 1830; studied in Paris (France), Berlin (Germany), Vienna (Austria), 1832-34; m. Henriette Wolff, July 27, 1836, 1 son, Albert H. Vis. surgeon N.Y. Hosp., 1837, St. Luke's Hosp., 1846; asso. with N.Y. Eye and Ear Infirmary, 1852-62; vis. surgeon Presbyn. Hosp., 1872; among chief contbns. was buck's extension (a treatment of thigh fractures by weights and pulleys); pioneer in plastic face surgery. Author: Description of an Improved Extension Apparatus for the Treatment of Fracture of the Thigh, 1867; Contributions to Reparative Surgery, 1876. Died N.Y.C., Mar. 6, 1877.

BUCK, HAROLD WINTHROP, elec. engr.; b. N.Y.C., May 7, 1873; s. Albert Henry and Laura S. (Abbott) B.; Ph.B., Yale, 1894; E. E., Columbia Sch. Mines, 1895; m. Charlotte R. Porter, 1902; children—Winthrop Porter, Gurdon; m. 2d, Mary Perry, 1941. Entered Schenectady works General Electric Co., 1895, student, later asst. engr.; elec. engr. Niagara Falls Power Co. from 1900; now retired. Took out several patents for mech. and elec. devices, a process for making corundum in an elec. furnace. Fellow Am. Inst. E.E. (pres. 1916-17); mem. Franklin Inst., Engring. Inst. Can. Home: 3 E. 71st St., N.Y.C. Died Aug. 5, 1958; buried Putnam Cemetery, Greenwich, Conn.

BUCK, SAMUEL JAY, mathematician; b. Russia, Herkimer Co., N.Y., July 4, 1835; s. Samuel and Amity (Millington) B.; A.B., Oberlin Coll., 1858, A.M., 1862; grad. Tehol. Sch., Oberlin, 1862; (D.D., Tabor Coll., Ia., 1903); m. Jane Cory (coll. classmate), Nov. 17, 1859. Ordained Congl. ministry, 1863; pastor Orwell, O., 1861-63, and prin. Orwell Acad., 1860-63; prin. prep. dept., 1864-69, prof. mathematics and natural philosophy, 1869-93, acting pres., 1884-87, prof. mathematics and astronomy, 1893-1905, prof. emeritus, July 4, 1905, Grinnell Coll. Preached at various place while teaching; co. supt. schs., 1866-69; pres. Ia. State Teachers' Assn., 1871; co. surveyor Poweshiek Co., Ia., 1890-1913. Republican. Was the guest of Gov. George W. Goethals on trip of U.S.S. Ancon through the Panama Canal, signalizing opening of the canal, Aug. 15, 1914. Home: Grinnell, Ia. Died May 10, 1918.

BUCKINGHAM, DAVID EASTBURN, veterinarian; b. Wilmington, Del., Mar. 21, 1870; s. David Eastburn and Sara (Van Trump) B.; grad. high sch., Wilmington, Del., 1888; V.M.D., U. of Pa., 1893; m. Roberta Randall, of N.Y. City, Dec. 8, 1897. Practiced at Washington, D.C., since 1893; insp. and veterinarian Q.-M. General's Office, U.S.A., 1898-1900, and 1916; organizer and dean George Washington U. Coll. of Vet. Medicine, 1908-18; organizer, and pres. Bd. Vet. Med. Examiners, D.C., 1909-12; made disease investigation of foxes, Alaska, for U.S. Biol. Survey, 1924; spl. distemper investigation, Paris, London, Belgium, Switzerland and Holland; consulting toxicologist, Insecticide Div. of U.S. Bur. Chemistry and Soils; propr. Hosp. for Animals; veterinarian to D.C. Republican. Baptist. Mason. Club: Rotary. Home: 3108 Hawthorne St. N.W. Office: 2115 14th St. N.W., Washington DC

BUCKINGHAM, EDGAR, physicist; b. Phila., Pa., July 8, 1867; s. Lucius Henry and Angelina Bradley (Hyde) B.; A.B., Harvard, 1887; post-grad. work same, 1887-89, U. of Strassbury, 1889-90, Ph.D., Leipsic, 1893; m. Elizabeth Branton Holstein, July 15, 1901; children—Katharine, Stephen Alvord. Asst. in physics, Harvard, 1888-89, 1891-92, Strassburg, 1889-90; mem. faculty, Bryn Mawr Coll., 1893-99; instr. physics, U. of Wis., 1901-02; asst. physicist Bur. of Soils, U.S. Dept. Agr., 1902-05; with Bur. of Standards, 1905-37, was physicist same. Lecturer on thermodynamics, Grad. Sch. U.S. Naval Acad., 1910-12; asso. scientific attachè, U.S. Embassy, Rome, Italy, 1918. Author: An Outline of the Theory of Thermodynamics, 1900. Home: Chevy Chase, Md. Died Apr. 29, 1940.

BUCKLAND, CYRUS, inventor; b. Manchester, Conn., Aug. 10, 1799; s. George and Elizabeth B.; m. Mary Locke, May 18, 1824, 3 children. Instrumental in manufacture of eccentric bit and auger used in cutting lock, guard plate, side plate, breech plate, rod spring and barrels to gunstocks; designed and patented rifling machine to cut groove of regularly decreasing depth from breech to muzzle (sec. of war paid $10,000 for U.S. Govt. Rights to invention). Died Springfield, Mass., Feb. 26, 1891.

BUCKLER, WILLIAM HEPBURN, archeologist; b. of Am. pareents, Paris, France, Feb. 1, 1867; s. Thomas Hepburn (M.D.) and Eliza (Ridgely) B.; M.A., Trinity Coll. (Cambridge U., Eng.), 1890; LL.B., Cambridge U.

1891; studied Law Dept., U. of Md., 1893-94 (prizeman, 1894 for thesis on Instalment Sales); M.A., Oxford, 1925, D.Litt., 1937; LL.D., Aberdeen, 1935, Johns Hopkins, 1940; m. Georgina Grenfell Walrond, May 25, 1892; children—Lucy Ridgely (Mrs. Vivian Seymer), Barbara Isabel (Mrs. Charles Wrinch). Practiced law, Baltimore, M.d, 1894-1902; sec. emergency com. after Baltimore fire, Feb. 1904; sec. U.S. special embassy to King's wedding, Spain, 1906; sec. U.S. Legation Madrid, Spain, 1907-09; mem. staff Am. Expdn. to Sardis, Asia Minor, 1910-14; special agent Dept. of State, Embassy, London, 1914-18; attached Am. Comm. to Negotiate Peace, Paris, June-Dec. 1919; made journeys in Asia Minor, 1924, 26, 30, 33; asso. All Souls Coll., Oxford, Eng., 1924-25. Mem. bd. trustees Johns Hopkins U., 1904-12. Member council American Society for Archeological Research in Asia Minor; v.p. Society for Hellenic Studies, Society for Roman STudies; fellow British Academy. Wrote: History of Contract in Roman Law (Yorke Prize, Cambridge), 1894; Relation of Roman Law to Other Historical Sciences (Vol.II, Proc. Internat. Congress Arts and Sciences, St. Louis), 1904; Chapter VI, in Hollander and Barnett's Studies in American Trade Unionism, 1906; Chapter XXII in Ripley's Railway Problems, 1907; Lydian Inscriptions, 1924; Sardis-Greek and Latin Inscriptions (with David M. Robinson), 1932; Monuments of Western Phygia, etc. (with W.M. Calder, C.M. Cox and K. Guthrie), 1933, 1939. Residence: 1 Bardwell Rd., Oxford, Eng. Died Mar. 2, 1952.

BUCKLEY, ERNEST ROBERTSON, mining geologist; b. Milbury, Mass., Sept. 3, 1872; s. Thomas M. and Grace R. B.; B.S., U. of Wis., 1895; Ph.D., 1898; married. Dir. Bur. of Geology and mines of Mo. and state geologist, 1901-08; mining geologist, Federal Lead Co., 1908—. Author: Building and Ornamental Stones of Wisconsin, 1898; Clays and Clay Industries in Wisconsin, 1900; Highway Construction in Wiscons, 1902; Quarrying Industry of Missouri, 1904; Public Roads in Missouri; The Geology of the Granby Area; The Geology of the Disseminated Lead Deposits of St. Francois and Madison Counties, Missouri. Home: Rolla, Mo. Died Jan. 19, 1912.

BUCKLEY, OLIVER ELLSWORTH, research engr.; b. Sloan, Ia., Aug. 8, 1887; s. William Doubleday and Sarah Elizabeth (Jeffrey) B.; B.S., Grinnell Coll., 1909, D.Sc., 1936; Ph.D., Cornell, 1914; D.Sc., Columbia, 1948; D.Eng., Case Inst. Tech., 1948; m. Clara Lane, Oct. 14, 1914; Children—Katherine Lane (Mrs. R.G. Nuckolls), William Douglas, Barbara (Mrs. Frederick B. Wolf), Juliet Georgiana (Mrs. Patrick Alsup). Instr., Grinnell (Ia.) Coll., 1909, Cornell, 1910-14; with the research department Western Electric Co., 1914-25; with Bell Telephone Labs., 1925-52, asst. dir. research, 1927-33, dir. of research, 1933-36, exec. v.p., 1936-40; pres. 1940-51, chmn. bd., 1951-52, dir., 1940-55; dir. Summit Trust Company. Mem. bd. of Edn. of South Orange-Maplewood, N.J., 1938-50, pres., 1948-50. Trustee Jackson Memorial Lab., Thomas A. Edison Foundation. Served as major, Signal Corps, A.E.F., World War I, in charge research section Div. Research and Inspection, Signal Corps, Paris; mem. communications and guided missiles divisions Nat. Defense Research Com., World War II. Medal for Merit. Chmn. sci. adv. com. O.D.M. 1951-52, Bd. Multiple Sclerosis Soc. Member gen. adv. com. AEC, 1948-54; mem. Army Ordnance sci. adv. com. 1951-55. Fellow Am. Phys. Society, Am. Acad. Arts and Scis., Am. Inst. E.E. (Edison medal 1954), Acoustical Soc. Am.; mem. Nat. Acad. Scis., Am. Philosophical Society (v.p. 1954-57), Franklin Institute, Engineering Foundation Board (chmn. 1939-42), National Inventors Council, Sigma Xi, Phi Beta Kappa, Phi Kappa Phi. Clubs: Century (N.Y.C.); Cosmos (Washington). Home: 13 Fairview Terrace, Maplewood, N.J. Died Dec. 1959.

BUCKMAN, HARRY OLIVER, soil technologist; b. West Liberty, Ia., July 4, 1883; s. Charles E. and Louisa M. (Walter) B.; B.S. in Agr., Ia. State Coll., 1906, M.S., 1908; Ph.D., Cornell U., 1912; post-grad. Harvard, 1914; m. Rita M. Shannon, Dec. 1912. With Cornell U. since 1910, prof. soil tech., 1917-49, emeritus. Mem. A.A.A.S., Am. Soc. Agronomy, Internat. Soc. Soil Sci., Sigma Xi, Phi Kappa Phi, Alpha Zeta, Gamma Alpha, Delta Upsilon. Republican. Presbyterian. Joint author: Soils, Their Properties and Management, 1914; The Nature and Properties of Soils, 1922, 29, 37, 43. Home: 118 Wait Av., Ithaca, N.Y. 14850. Died Dec. 7, 1964.

BUCKMAN, HENRY HOLLAND II, cons. civil engr.; b. Jacksonville, Fla., Oct. 25, 1886; s. Henry Holland and Sarah Caruthers (Allison) B.; B.S., Harvard, 1908; postgrad. student univs. Berlin, Leipzig, also Royal Tech. Coll., Charlottenburg; m. Mildred Regester, Apr. 26, 1911; children—Allison Caruthers (Mrs. B. Bassett), Henry Holland III, Yardley Drake. Mineral exploration, 1908, in Mongolia, 1909-15; designed, constructed 1st comml. electric furnaces in U.S., 1915-22; discovered rare earth, radioactive mineral deposits of Fla., developing for comml. uses 1915-22; dir. exploration for tin ores in fgn. countries, developed uses for titanium, made surveys for stream salinity and meteorological research and for nonmetallic minerals of Ala., Ga., Fla., 1922-68; cons. engr., specializing in river and harbors, stream pollution, inland navigation and transportation, canalization, 1934-68; engring. counsel Ship Canal Authority Fla., 1948-68; engring. counsel Fla. Inland Navigation Dist.; dir., vice chmn. project com. Nat. Rivers and Harbors Congress, 1939-68, pres., 1961. Tech. counsel com. fgn. affairs on strategic materials, U.S. Ho. of Reps., 1935-36; cons. Chem. Warfare Service, World War II, to Dept. of State at London Internat. Tin Conf., 1946. Mem. Am. Soc. C.E. (corp.). Jacksonville Hist. Soc. (past pres.), Sigma Alpha Epsilon. Protestant Episcopalian. Clubs: Harvard (past pres. Fla.; past v.p. asso. clubs). Author reports and documents. Home: Orange Park FL Died Mar. 5, 1968; buried Evergreen Cemetery, Jacksonville FL

BUCKWALTER, TRACY V., consultant Timken Roller Bearing Co.; b. Jersey Shore, Pa., Apr. 28, 1880; s. David B. and Ellen Virginia (Harmen) B.; grad. Woodward Township High Sch., Houtzdale, Pa., 1895; m. Hattie Mae Emmons, Oct. 22, 1902 (died May 21, 1941); children—Lawrence E., Emory T., Theodore J., Eugene P., Norman R., Tracy V.; m. 2d, Sara Porter Gregory, Nov. 18, 1941. Began as apprentice with elec. contractor, Phila., 1896; with Pa. R.R., Altoona, Pa., as machinist, 1900, asst. foreman, 1901, draftsman, 1906, foreman movitve power engring. dept., 1911; with Timken Roller Bearing Co., Canton, O., as chief engr., 1916-22, vice president, 1922-46; dir. Spun Steel Corp., developed electric trucks, gas-electric locomotives, while at Altoona roller bearing steel mills, roller bearing machine tools Timken locomotive, inexpensive bearing for automotive vehicles, etc.; has superviswd tests of locomotive and railroad car axles under auspices Assn. Am. Railroads since 1933, steam locomotive balancing since 1936. Mem. Soc. Automotive Engrs., Am. Soc. Mech. Engrs., Am. Welding Soc., A.A.A.S., Am. Geog. Soc., Ohio Forestry, Am. Museum Natural History, Ohio Chamber of Commerce, Princeton Engring. Assn. (Bracket mem), Awarded Modern Pioneer by Nat. Assn. Mfrs., 1939; Henderson Medal by Franklin Inst. for transportation of roller bearings, 1946. Presbyterian. Clubs: Canton, Brookside Country (Canton); Catawba Cliffs Beach, Catawba Cliffs Yacht (Lakeside, O.); Coral Rdige Yacht (Ft. Lauderdale); and railway clubs in N.Y. City, Pittsburgh, Buffalo, Toronto, Montreal, Chicago, Atlanta. Author of several technical booklets on axle testing, roller bearings, locomotives, automotive equipment, etc. Author: The Railroad. Home: 2310 Del Mar Place, Ft. Lauderdale, Fla. Died March 14, 1948; buried in Lauderdale Memorial Park, Ft. Lauderdale.

BUCKY, GUSTAV, physician, radiologist; b. Leipzig, Germany, Sept. 3, 1880; s. Theodor and Henriette (Pawel) B.; grad. Gymnasium, Leipzig, 1901; M.D., U. of Leipzig, 1907; m. Frida Sarsen, June 9, 1911; children—Peter Arthur, Thomas Lee. Came to U.S. 1923, naturalized, 1929. Practicing physician in Berlin, 1910-23, in N.Y. City since 1923, confining practice to radiology; was chief of X-ray dept. Municipal Children's Hosp.; of deep therapy dept. Third Univ. Clinic, and of X-ray dept. Virchow Hosp., all in Berlin; attending physician New York Univ.; director of physiotherapy department, Sea View Hospital; clin. prof. emeritus, New York University; visiting prof. Elbert Einstein Coll. for Medicine; consultant radiologist Bronx Municipal Hospital Center; inventor of diaphram in general use in roentgenography. Fellow A.M.A.; mem. N.Y. County Med. Soc., German Roentgen Society (corresponding member). Author: Grenz Ray Therapy (with F. Combes), 1955; also several works pub. in Germany. Contbr. to mags. Address: 16 E. 79th St., N.Y.C. 10021. Died Feb. 19, 1963.

BUDINGTON, ROBERT ALLY, zoologist; b. Leyden, Mass., Oct. 22, 1872; s. Stephen Buckland and Ereda (Baker) B.; B.A., Williams Coll., 1896, M.A., 1899, Sc.D., 1929; studied Columbia, 1899-1903; m. Mabel Frances Stone, Dec. 27, 1906; children—Robert Allyn, William Stone. Instr. science and mathematics Dow Acad., Franconia, N.H., 1896-99; asst. in biology Williams Coll., 1898-99; asst. demonstrator physiology Coll. Phys. and Surg. Columbia, 1900-02; instr. physiology and zoology Mt. Hermon (Mass.) Sch., 1903-05; inst. biology Wesleyan U., Conn., 1905-08; asso. prof. zoology, Oberlin Coll., 1908-13, prof. zoology, 1913-40, prof. emeritus, 1940—, head. dept., 1913-36, instr. invertebrate morphology, instr. Marine Biological Lab., Woods Hole, Mass., 1902-10, instr. embryology, 1912-19. Fellow A.A.A.S.; mem. Am. Soc. Zoologists, Am. Naturalists, Ohio Acad. Science. Conglist. Author: (with H. W. Conn) Advanced Physiology and Hygiene, 1909; Physiology and Human Life, 1927. Contbr. to Am. Jour. Physiology, Biol. Bulletin, School and Society, etc. Home: Winter Park, Fla. Died Oct. 23, 1954.

BUDROW, LESTER RUSK, mining engr.; b. Ogden, Ia., Mar. 17, 1877; s. William C. and Rebecca (Beauchamp) B.; Ph.B., State U. of Ia., 1897; spl. course, Sch. of Mines of Mo., Rollo, Mo., 1898-9; m. Ruth Niles, of San Diego, Cal., Nov. 20, 1906. With M. Guggenheim Sons or affiliated cos., 1899-05; general supt. Tiro General Mine, Charcas, S.L.P., Mexico, 1905-7; gen. supt. Cia Metalurgica de Michoacan, Angangneo, Mex., 1907-8; mgr. Michoacan & Pacific Ry. & Mining Co., 1908-9; gen. mgr. Tigre Mining Co., Yzabal, Sonora, Mexico, Nov., 1909—; v.-p. Hunter Av. Realty Co., Kansas City, Mo.; gen. mgr. The Tigre Mining Co., S.A., Esqueda, Sonora, Mex. Mem. Am. Inst. Mining Engineers, 1902, Beta Theta Pi. Club: American (Mexico City). Home: 2346 3d St., San Diego, Cal. Office: Douglas AZ

BUEHLER, HENRY ANDREW, geologist; b. Monroe, Wis., May 27, 1876; s. Andrew and Katherine (Bleiler) B.; A.B., U. of Wis., 1901; hon. D.Sc., U. of Mo., 1925; unmarried. Asst. state geologist, Mo., 1901-07; mining geologist, 1907-08; state geologist, Mo., since 1908, also dir. Mo. Bur. Geology and Mines. Mem. Am. Geol. Soc., Am. Inst. Mining and Metall. Engrs. (pres. 1935), Soc. Econ. Geologists, Am. Assn. Petroleum Geologists, A.A.A.S., St. Louis Acad. Science, Wis. Acad. Sciences, Arts and Letters Tau Beta Pi. Clubs: Noonday (St. Louis); Cosmos (Washington, D.C.). Home: Rolla, Mo. Died Mar. 14, 1944.

BUEK, GUSTAVE HERMAN, lithographer; b. Boston, Aug. 25, 1850; s. Herman and Augusta (Siemers) B.; ed. pub. sch., Brooklyn, and 2 yrs. in pvt. sch., Schmieder & Deghuée, Brooklyn; m. Louisa Valentine, Apr. 30, 1873. Apprenticed to Hatch & Co., lithographers, N.Y., 1866; later took charge of art dept. of newly established firm of Donaldson Bros.; started firm of Buek & Lindner, 1881, which soon after became G. H. Buek & Co.; joined in formation of Am. Lithographic Co., New York, 1891, of which is a v.p.; pres. Alco-Gravure, Inc.; dir. Crowell Pub. Co. Was first to introduce facsimile water-color work into commercial lithography. Republican. Home: Brooklyn, N.Y. Died Feb. 8, 1927.

BUELL, ABEL, inventor, engraver, silversmith; b. Killingworth, Conn., Feb. 1742; son of John Buell; m. Mary Parker, 1762; m. 2d, Aletta Devoe, 1771; m. 2d, Mrs. Rebecca Parkman, 1779; m. 4th, Sarah. Apprenticed to silversmith Ebenezer Cittenden, Killingworth; opened own shop, 1762; 1st signs of his ability were some Conn. 5 shilling bank notes which he artfully improved to 5 pound notes (this indiscretion cost him some months in jail plus branding and confiscation of property); upon release from prison, constructed lapidary machine for cutting and finishing precious stones; learned craft of typefounding, produced 1st known example of Am. typefounding, 1769; granted 100 pounds by Conn. Assembly to aid in establishing type-foundry at New Haven, 1769; began copperplate engraving, 1770; produced map of territories of U.S. according to Peace of 1783 (his chief engraving work), 1784; remained in New Haven where his business operations extended to operating packet boats; developed marble quarry; owned 2 privateersmen; fashioned silver; cast type; practiced engraving; a diffuse and rarely profitable businessman; constructed money coining machine, 1785; traveled to England, 1789; worked at N.Y. cotton mfg. plant, 1793; returned to Hartford (Conn.) and continued silversmithing and engraving, 1799; silversmith in Stockbridge, Mass., 1805; a believer in Thomas Paine's doctrines until 1813 when he embraced Christianity. Died in New Haven Alms House, Mar. 10, 1822.

BUELL, CHARLES EDWARD, electro. mech. engr.; b. Torrington, Conn., May 4, 1841; s. Joseph Case and Mary (Kellogg) B.; ed. Wesleyan Acad., Wibraham, Mass.,; m. Annie F. Cooper. Entered army, Co. E. 10th Mass. Vols., April 27, 1861; hon. disch. April 23, 2863 (wounds). Registered patent atty., solicitor of patents. Entered telegraph service, 1864, worked for Am. Tel. Co., Western Union Tel. Co., The Franklin Tel. Co., Bankers and Brokers' Tel. Co., as supt. Bankers and Merchants' Tel. Co., building lines; 3 yrs., 1865-68, ticket agent 4 railroads at Albany, N.Y.; 8 yrs., 1872-80, accountant N.Y.,N.H.& R.R., New Haven, Conn.; pres. U.S. Telephone Co.; pres. The Buell Elec. and Hydraulic Mfg. Co., (fire protection); spl. agt. class Telegraph and Telephones, U.S. 10th census, 1880; chief of div., class chs., 11th U.S. census, 1890; chief of div., class chs., 11th U.S. census, 1890; sec. U.S. spl. commn. to Puerto Rico, 1898-99. Republican. Seventh-day Sabbath-keeper. Home: Camden, N.J. Died 1903.

BUFFUM, BURT C., plant breeder; b. South Bend, Ind., Apr. 7, 1868; s. George W. and Harriet (Butts) B.; B.S., Colo. Agrl. Coll., 1890, M.S., 1893; m. Luda Maude Southworth, of Denver, June 24, 1890; children—Eugene Roy (dec.), Cecil Southworth (dec.), Harriet Eduma, Martha Maude, Burbank Brooks. Asst. in meteorology and irrigation engring., Colo. Agrl. Coll., 1890; prof. agriculture and horticulture, U. of Wyo., 1891-1900; v.-dir. Wyo. Expt. Sta., 1896-1900; prof. agr. Colo. Agrl. Coll., 1900-02; dir. Wyo. Expt. Sta. and prof. agr., U. of Wyo., 1902-07; gen. mgr. Wyo. Plant & Seed Breeding Co., 1907-13; plant breeder Buffum Pure Seed Co., 1913-14; pres. Emmer Products Co., 1914-18; in charge plant breeding, Wyo. State Industrial Inst., 1915-16. Commr. Lewis and Clark Expn., Portland Ore., 1905. Christian Scientist. Fellow A.A.A.S. Clubs: Consistory (Cheyenne, Wyo.), Alfalfa (Worland, Wyo.). Author: Arid Agriculture, 1909; Plant Breeding, 1912; Sixty Lessons in Agriculture (Buffum and Deaver), 1913. Home: 2837 W. 35th Av., Denver, Colo.

BULFINCH, CHARLES, architect; b. Boston, Aug. 8, 1763; s. Thomas and Susan (Apthorp) B.; grad. Harvard, 1781; m. Hannah Apthorp, Nov. 20, 1788, 11 children including author Thomas Bulfinch. Designed Old Hollis Sch. Ch., Boston, 1788; a designer Boston Theatre; designed Beacon Monument, 1789; selectman City of Boston, 1791-1817, chmn. bd., 1799-1817; designed

Boston State House, 1800; architect India Wharf, Cathedral of Holy Cross, New South Ch., Conn. State House, Me. State Capitol; successor to Benjamin Latrobe as architect Capitol bldg., Washington, D.C., 1817-30; considered one of best early Am. architects. Died Boston, Apr. 15, 1844.

BULL, CARROLL GIDEON, prof. immunology; b. Knoxville, Tenn., June 22, 1884; s. William G. and Emma (White) B.; B.S., Peabody Peabody Coll. (U. of Nashville), 1907; M.D., U. of Nashville, 1910; studied U. of Chicago, U. of Mich., Harvard; m. Zelma Smith, 1914; children—Nancy, Carrollyn. Teacher of bacteriology and pathology, Lincoln Memorial U., 1910-12; fellow Nelson Morris Inst., Chicago, 1912-13; asst. and asso. in pathology, Rockefeller Inst., N.Y. City, 1913-17; maj. Med. Corps, U.S.A., 1917-18; asso. prof. immunology, Sch. of Hygiene and Pub. Health, Johns Hopkins, 1918, prof. same, 1921—. Had specialized in researches in agglutination of bacteria in vivo and toxin and anti-toxin for B. Welchi. Home: Baltimore, Md. Died May 31, 1931.

BULL, GEORGE MAIRS, cons. civil engr.; b. Troy, N.Y., Mar. 15, 1873; s. Rice C. and Catharine (Johnson) B.; C.E., Rensselaer Poly. Inst., 1897; Dr. Engring., Colo. Sch. of Mines, 1938, U. of Colo., 1940; m. Sara E. Baker, June 1, 1910. Asst. engr. on contract work reconstructing original Erie Canal, 1897-98; employed by C.&W. Ry. Co. and located the foundation of Boone Viaduct across Des Moines River, 1899-1900; returned to Troy, N.Y., 1900; deputy city engr., Troy, N.Y., 1900-03, in charge of constrn. and maintaining municipal structures; resident engr. in office N.Y. State Barge Canal, 1903-06; with J. G. White Engring. Corp., 1906-09; engr. Arnold Co. of Chicago, 1909; private practice as cons. engr., Denver, 1910-18; developing Pub. Works Program for Denver, Colo., 1920-33; apptd. state engr. P.W.A., Colo., 1933, state dir. P.W.A., 1935-37, regional dir. for 7 southwestern states, 1937-40; in private practice as cons. engr., 1940; returned to service with the Office of Prodn. Management, 1941, as field rep. in the southwestern states; later apptd. regional dir. P.W.A. Defense Construction Program in the Rocky Mountain States; in 1943 appointed Colo. state dir. Office of Price Administration; returned to private practice as cons. engr., 1945. Served as 1st class private, 1st Vol. Engrs., 1898-99; lt. comdr. Civil Engr. Corps, U.S. Naval Res., 1918-22. Mem. Am. Soc. Civil Engrs., Colo. Soc. Engrs., Rensselaer Soc. of Engrs. Presbyterian. Club: Denver Athletic. Home: 3910 Perry St., Denver CO

BULL, LUDLOW (SEGUINE), Egyptologist; b. N.Y. City, Jan. 10, 1886; s. Dr. Charles Stedman and Mary Eunice (Kingsbury) B.; grad. Pomfret (Conn.) Sch., 1903; A.B., Yale, 1907; LL.B., Harvard, 1910; Ph.D., U. of Chicago, 1922; m. Katharine Davis Exton, Nov. 25, 1924; children—Frederick Kingsburg, 2d, Roger Ludlow, Agnes Davis. Admitted to N.Y. bar, 1911, and practiced in N.Y. City, 1910-15; fellow in Semitics, U. of Chicago, 1920-22; mem. Oriental Inst., U. of Chicago, expeditions to Egypt, Mesopotamia, Syria, 1919-20, Egypt, 1923; asst. curator Egyptian Dept., Met. Museum, N.Y. City, 1922-28, asso. curator, 1928—; lecturer in Egyptology, Yale, 1925-36, research asso. with rank of prof., 1936—; curator Yale Egyptian Collection, 1925—. Asso. fellow Davenport Coll. Served as pvt. Med. Corps, U.S. Army with Yale Mobile Hosp., A.E.F., 1917-18, 1st lt. San. Corps, A.E.F., 1918-19. Trustee Pomfret Sch. (pres. Alumni Assn., 1942-45), Kingsley Trust Assn. (New Haven), 1936-38 (adv. com., 1941—); trustee, Am. Schs. Oriental Research (Jerusalem and Baghdad). Mem. Com. Mediterranean Antiquities, Am. Council Learned Soc., 1930-36. Fellow Am. Geog. Soc.; mem. Am. Oriental Soc. (del. to centenary Royal Asiatic Soc. 1923; rec. sec. 1925-36; v.p. 1938-39; pres. 1939-40), Archeol. Inst. Am. (executive com. N.Y. soc.), Society Bibl. Lit., Egypt Exploration Soc. (London), trustee Cathedral St. John the Divine, N.Y., 1943—, Youth Consultation Service (N.Y.), Am. Research Center in Egypt, Antiquarian and Landmarks Society of Connecticut, Palestine Exploration Soc. (Jerusalem) Soc. Egyptol. Reine Elisabeth (Brussells), Scroll and Key (Yale), Psi Upsilon, Ind. Republican. Episcopalian. Clubs: Century, Church (past pres.), University (N.Y.C.); Lawn (New Haven); Litchfield (Conn.) Country (former pres.) Author: The Rhind Mathematical Papyrus, Vol. II (with A.B. Chace, and H.P. Manning), 1929; Inscriptions at Deir el Hagar, in H.E. Winlock, Ed Dakhleh Oasis, 1936. Editor of 6 vols. Publications of the Egyptian Expedition and 6 vols. Publications of the Egyptian Dept., Metropolitan Museum, N.Y. City. Mem. editorial board Metropolitan Museum Studies, 1928-34. Contbr. articles to professional jours. Home: Litchfield, Conn. Office: care Metropolitan Museum, N.Y.C. 28. Died July 1, 1954; buried Litchfield, Conn.

BULL, STORM, prof. steam engring., U. of Wisconsin, 1884—; b. Bergen, Norway, Oct. 20, 1856; grad. Federal Swiss Polytechnic Inst., Zurich, deg. M.E., 1877; in professional work, 1877-79; then became instr. Univ. of Wis. V.-p. of jury of class 21 (gen. machinery), Paris Expn., 1900; pres. jury steam engines, etc., St. Louis Expn., 1904. Author many scientific papers. Died 1907.

BULLARD, RALPH HADLEY, prof. chemistry; b. Worcester, Mass., Dec. 6, 1895; s. Charles Merrick and Mary Henrietta (Blake) B.; A.B., Clark U., 1917, M.S., 1918; student U. of Chicago, 1923; Ph.D., Brown, 1925; m. Adele Lillian Lipphard, Aug. 27, 1925; 1 dau., Barbara Jean. Instr. chemistry Hobart Coll., Geneva, N.Y., 1918-19; research chemist, Roessler & Hasslacher Chem. Co., 1919-20; instr. chemistry, Hobart Coll., 1920-21, asst. prof., 1921-25, prof. since 1925, on mil. leave, 1941-45; lt. comdr. 1942, capt., 1951. U.S.N.R.; on duty at Naval Research Lab., Washington, D.C.; chemist Eastman Kodak Co., summers, 1931, 34, 35. Dir. research, Norwich Pharmacal Comapny, 1948-50. Chemist fuel oil testing plant U.S. Navy Yard, Phila., during World War, U.S.N.R.F., 1917-21. Awarded Legion of Merit. Fellow A.A.A.S.; mem. Am. Chem. Soc., Phi Beta Kappa, Sigma Xi, Kappa Sigma. Republican. Episcopalian. Research on metallo-organic chemistry, organic synthesis, etc. (results pub.); also contbr. to scientific publs. Home: 101 St. Clair St., Geneva, N.Y. 14456. Died Nov. 2, 1961; buried Arlington Nat. Cemetery, Arlington, Va.

BULLARD, W(ASHINGTON) IRVING, banker, textile manufacturer and inventor; born in Waltham, Mass.; son of George E. and Mary E. (Green) Bullard; student Boston University, 1905; m. Annie E. Jacobs, Oct. 28, 1903; children—Barbara Anita, Charlotte Frances, Edward Jacobs (major Air Corps); m. 2d, Eleanor Gaither Clark, May 16, 1931; children—Mary Ann, Sarah Clar. Was newspaper reporter, editor bond market dept. Wall St. Jour.; now pres. and owner E. H. Jacobs Mfg. Co., Danielson, Conn.; pres. E. H. Jacobs Mfg. Corp., Charlotte, N.C.; Danielson, Conn.; v.p. McClain Distributing Co., Charlotte, N.C.; dir. and v.p. Wauregan Cotton Mills; treas. Williamsville Buff Mfg. Co.; organizer and 1st pres. Colonial Air Trnasport; pres. Vineyard Theatres, Inc.; formerly v.p. Merchants Nat. Bank (Boston) and Central Trust Co. (Chicago); was dir. Federal Mutual Fire Ins. Co., Danielson Building & Loan Assn., Federal Mutual Liability Ins. Co. Served in U.S. Navy, World War I; naval intelligence, U.S. Navy, 1939-42, Work War II. Mayor of Danielson 3 terms; mem. city council of Charlotte, 1943-45. Formerly treas. and dir. Nat. Assn. of Cotton Mfrs., 10 yrs., vice pres. and treas. Asso. Industries of Mass., 4 yres., vice pres. Boston C. of C., 4 yrs., treasurer Boston Music School, Settlement. American treasurer World Cotton Conference; dir. Am. Internat. Chamber of Commerce; chmn. com. on aeronautics, Chamber of Commerce of U.S.; chmn. com. on aviation, Chicago Assn. Commerce; mem. Chicago Aero Commn. Mem. Beta Theta Pi. Republican. Episcopalian. Clubs: Union League (N.Y. City); University (Boston); Charlotte (N.C.) Country; Union Interalliée (Paris). Author: Textile Mill Stocks as Investments, 1910; Women's Work in War Time, 1917; Whirl of the World, 1921. Lecturer and writer on economic, financial and industrial subjects. Home: 2208 Sherwood Av., Charlotte, N.C. Died June 28, 1948.

BULLOCK, WILLIAM A., inventor; b. Greenville, N.Y., 1813; 1 dau. Apprentice to iron founder and machinist, Catskill, N.Y., 1821-34; owner machien shop (developed shingle-cutting machine), Plattsville, N.Y., 1836-38; established unsuccessful shingle mfg. firm, Savannah, Ga.; then opened shop making hay and cotton presses of his own design, also artificial legs, N.Y.C.; opened patent agy., machine shop (3 original designs came from this shop, grain drill, seed planter, lath cutting machine), Phila., 1849; printed daily newspaper The Banner of The Union, 1849-53, became interested in printing machinery, devoted rest of life to devel. and eventual patenting of Bullock press which revolutionized printing by printing on both sides of the paper, printing from continuous roll of paper and cutting newsprint either before or after printing, 1863. Died Apr. 12, 1867.

BUMP, MILAN RAYNARD, elec. engr.; b. Rock Falls, Wis., Mar. 18, 1881; B.S. in E.E., U. of Wis., 1902; m. Mary Morrison, 1909. Asst. engr. Washington Water Power Co., Spokane, Wash., 1902-03; engr. Denver Gas & Electric Light Co., 1904-06; examining engr., Henry L. Dougherty & Co., 1907-09; gen. mgr. Empire Dist. Electric Co., Joplin, 1909-10; chief engr. Henry L. Dougherty & Co., 1910—; dir. of about 30 corps. controlled by the parent co. Home: Montclair, N.J. Died May 5, 1925.

BUMSTEAD, HENRY ANDREWS, physicist b. Pekin, Ill., Mar. 12, 1870; s. Samuel Josiah (M.D.) and Sarah Ellen (Seiwell) B.; A.B., Johns Hopkins, 1891; Ph.D., Yale, 1897; m. Luetta Ullrich, Aug. 18, 1896. Asst. in physics, Johns Hopkins, 1891-93; instr. in physics, Sheffield Scientific Sch., Yale., 1893-1900; asst. prof., 1900-06, prof., Yale Coll., and dir. Sloane Physicial Lab., 106—, Yale U. Scientific attaché, Am. Embassy, London, 1918. Fellow Am. Acad. Arts and Sciences. Home: New Haven, Conn. Died Dec. 31, 1920.

BUNCE, ALLEN HAMILTON, physician; b. Bulloch County, Ga., Sept. 5, 1889; s. James Allen and Georgia Anne (McElveen) B.; A.B., U. Ga., 1908; Emory U. Sch. Medicine, 1908-09, M.D., 1911; postgrad. U. Chgo., 1909-10; m. Angelina La Riviere, Aug. 28, 1916 (dec. 1939); m. 2d, Isabella Arnold, June 12, 1940. Formerly asso. in medicine Emory U. Sch. Medicine; physician Ga. Bapt. Hosp. (pres. 1928-29), Crawford W. Long Meml. Hosp. (pres. 1924-25, now cons.), Wesley Meml. Hosp., Grady Hosp. (pres. 1927-28), Piedmont Hosp.; cons. St. Joseph's Infirmary. Served as 1st lt. and capt. M.C., U.S. Army, in World War, Nov. 1, 1917-Apr. 7, 1919; with A.E.F. as chief of lab. service Base Hosp. 43. Officer Acad. Francaise for service in France. Pres. Atlanta Tb Assn., 1917-19. Phi Beta Kappa Assn. fellow, 1953. Recipient Lamartine Griffin Hardman award, 1947; 1st D.S.M. Med. Assn. Ga., 1958; Diplomate Am. Bd. Internal Medicine; fellow A.C.P., A.M.A. (vice speaker Ho. of Del.; trustee 1929-39; del. 1916, 1924-39, 1942-50); mem. Med. Assn. Ga. (sec.-treas. 1920-35, pres. 1941-42), Fulton County Med. Soc. (hon. pres. 1951), World Med. Assn. (charter mem), Internat. Soc. Internal Medicine, Phi Chi, Phi Beta Kappa, Omicron Delta Kappa, Pi Mu Gamma. Democrat. Mason (32 deg., Shriner). Club: Lotos (N.Y.). Author: Campus Verse, 1908; Outlines of Physiology (with E.G. Jones), 1912; also numerous articles on internal medicine and allied subjects. Editor Jour. Med. Assn. Ga., 1920-35, Elected chmn. com. on revision of Constrn. and By-laws, U.S. Pharmacopeal Conv., 1940-50; revision adopted, 1942, pres. conv., trustee, 1950-60. Club: Capital City (Atlanta). Home: 368 Ponce de Leon Av., N.E. Atlanta. 30308. Office: 98 Currier St., N.E., Atlanta 3. Died July 30, 1965; buried Oakland Cemetery, Atlanta.

BUNDESEN, HERMAN NIELS, pres. bd. health; b. Berlin, Germany, Apr. 27, 1882; s. Herman Niels and Ida Mae (Klein) B.; brought to U.S. in infancy; M.D., Northwestern U., 1909; M.D., U.S. Army Med. School, Washington, D.C., 1911; hon. Sc.D. from Northwestern U., 1927; m. Rega Russell, Mar. 6, 1909; children—Rega Jane, Herman N., Jr., Russell, Laurabelle, Betty, William Evans. Began practice at Chicago, 1909; epidemiologist Chicago Dept. Health, 1914-22; cons. surgeon Ill. Central Railroad since 1915; regional consultant contagious diseases, U.S. Vets. Bur.; health commr. of Chicago 1922-27; dir. of health Sanitary District of Chicago, 1927-28; coroner of Cook County, Ill., 1928-31; pres. Chicago Board of Health since 1931; trustee Municipal Tuberculosis Sanitarium Chicago, 1922, v.p. bd. dirs., 1947, v.p. 1947-53; med. pub. council Nat. Blood Research Found., 1954; professorial lectr. pub. health adminstrn. U. Chgo., 1926—. Served as 1st lt. U.S. Army, 1909-11. Hon. v.p. Child Conservation League of Am. Award for Distinguished Service, Am. Cancer Soc., Ill. div., 1956; Al Dibitetto award for outstanding achievement and devotion to humanity, 1958. Fellow A.C.P., Am. Pub. Health Assn. (bd. govs.; pres. 1927); mem. Am. Coll. Preventive Medicine, Ill. Pub. Health Assn. (pres. 1959—), Honorary Order of Ky. Colonels, A.M.A., Am. Assn. Public Health Physicans, Am. Med. Writers Assn., Assn. Mil. Surgeons U.S., Ill. State, Chgo. med. socs., Inst. Medicine, corr. mem. Danish Dermatol. Soc., Copenhagen, Denmark. Episcopalian. Club: South Shore Country. Candidate for the Democratic nomination for governor of Illinois, 1936. Awarded Chicago Daily News prize of $1,000 "for the most beneficial action for humanity by a resident of Greater Chicago" during the year ending Sept. 9, 1926. Apptd. sr. surgeon U.S.P.H.S., 1933, rank of lt. col. Author numerous publs. in field. Health editor Chgo. Am. and syndicated newspapers. Home: 7410 Oglesby Av. Office: 54 W. Hubbard St., Chgo. Died Aug. 25, 1960; buried Oakwood Cemetery, Chgo.

BUNDY, EDWIN S., business exec.; b. Cooperstown, N.Y., Oct. 12, 1889; s. Melvin C. and Ada (Marcy) B.; M.E., Cornell, 1911; m. Ethel May Manwaring, Oct. 18, 1916; children—Emily A., Edwin S. (dec.). Entire bus. career with Niagara Mohawk Power Corp. and predecessor cos., Buffalo, 1911—, chief engr., 1944-50, chief engr., mem. exec. com., 1950-56, v.p., dir., 1956—. Fellow (life mem) Am. Inst. E.E.; mem. N.Y. State Soc. Profl. Engrs., Tau Beta Pi. Presbyn. Clubs: Torch, Athletic, Wanakah Country (Buffalo); Rotary (Hamburg); Century (Syracuse, N.Y.). Home: 10 Woodview Ct., Hamburg, N.Y. 14075. Office: Elec. Bldg., Buffalo 3. Died Sept. 23, 1963.

BUNIM, JOSEPH J(AY), physician, educator; b. Volozin, Russia, Nov. 5, 1906; s. Moses and Minnie (Joselowsky) B.; brought to U.S., 1910, naturalized, 1914; B.Sc., Coll. City N.Y., 1926; M.D., N.Y.U., 1930, Sc.D. in Medicine, 1938; m. Miriam Schild, Dec. 30, 1934; children—Lesley, Elizabeth, Michael. Intern Medicine N.Y.U. div., Bellevue Hosp., 1930-32, resident medicine, 1933-35, successively adjunct vis. physician, asst. vis. physician, asso. vis. and vis. physician, 1936-52, founder, chief prenatal cardiac clinic, 1939-49, chief arthritis clinic, 1949-52; asst. physiology N.Y.U. Coll. Medicine, 1935-36, asst., 1939-49, instr., 1939-42, asst. prof. clin. medicine, 1942-49, asso. prof. medicine, 1949-52; fellow infectious diseases Yale Coll. Medicine, 1932, intern pediatric service New Haven Hosp., 1932-33; cons. Surg. Gen., U.S. Army, 1949-52, VA Hosp., 1951-52; asso. prof. medicine Johns Hopkins, 1953—; clin. prof. medicine Georgetown U., 1959—; clin. dir., chief arthritis and rheumatism br. Nat. Inst. Arthritis and Metabolic Diseases, Nat. Insts. Health, USPHS, 1953—; attending physician Walter Reed Army Hosp., 1955—; Sci. adv. com., bd. dirs. Arthritis and Rheumatism Found.; mem. expert adv. panel on chronic degenerative diseases WHO, 1963—. Recipient

Herberden medal for research rheumatic diseases, 1960, Presidential citation N.Y.U., 1965. Diplomate Am. Bd. Internal Medicine. Fellow A.C.P.; mem. Assn. Am. Physicians, N.Y. Acad. Medicine, N.Y., Washington acads. sci., Harvey Soc., A.M.A., Am. Rheumatism Assn. (pres. 1959), Nat. Rheumatism Soc. Argentina, Can., Mexico, NRC, Sigma Xi, Alpha Omega Alpha. Founder, editor Bull. on Rheumatic Diseases. Editorial bd. Jour. Chronic Diseases, Jour. Arthritis and Rheumatism. Contbr. sci. articles med. publs. Home: 7506 Maple Av., Chevy Chase, Md. Office: Nat. Inst. of Health, Bethesda, Md. Died July 8, 1964; buried Montefiore Cemetery, St. Albins, N.Y.

BUNN, PAUL AXTELL, physician, educator; b. Lorain, O., Dec. 9, 1914; s. Paul C. and Lois (Axtell) B.; A.B., DePauw U., 1936; M.B., U. Cin., 1940, M.D., 1941; m. Elizabeth Maxwell, June 14, 1941;children—Barbara (Mrs. Philip H. Howard), Paul Axtell, Mary Elizabeth. Intern, Univ. Hosps. of Cleve., 1940-41; resident in Tb, U. Mich. Hosp., Ann Arbor, 1941-42, resident in internal medicine, 1942-43; instr. medicine Cornell U. Coll. Medicine, N.Y.C., 1943-46, asst. in pharmacology, 1944-46, asst. prof. medicine, 1946-47; asst. physician out-patient dept. N.Y. Hosp., 1943-46, physician, 1946; asst. to chief Tb div. Central Office, VA, Washington, 1946-47; asso. prof. medicine State U. N.Y. Coll. Medicine at Syracuse, 1947-56, prof., 1956-70, acting chmn., 1967-70; asso. attending physician Syracuse Meml. Hosp., 1948-56, attending physician, 1956-70; attending physician Syracuse Univ. Hosp., 1947-70; cons. in internal medicine VA Hosp., Syracuse, 1953-70, St. Joseph's Hosp., Syracuse, 1957-70, Chenango Meml. Hosp., Norwich, N.Y., 1957-70; asso. dir. medicine Syracuse City Hosp., 1948-56; med. dir. Gen. Electric Co., Syracuse, 1970. Mem. panel on infectious diseases Com. on Revision U.S. Pharmacopeia, 1956-70. Mem. DeWitt (N.Y.) Central Sch. Dist. No. 11 Bd. Edn., 1950-56; v.p. DeWitt Community Assn., 1957-58; mem. DeWitt Planning Commn., 1957-60. Bd. dirs. Onondaga Health Assn., 1954-60; bd. visitors Roswell Park Meml. Inst., Buffalo, 1959-70. Diplomate Am. Bd. Internal Medicine. Fellow A.C.P. (gov. 1967-70), N.Y. Acad. Medicine; mem. Am., N.Y. (pres. 1954-55) Trudeau socs., N.Y. State, Onondaga County med. socs., Syracuse Acad. Medicine (pres. 1960), A.A.A.S., Am. Fedn. Clin. Research, Am. Soc. for Clin. Investigation, Am. Clin. and Climatol. Assn., Alpha Omega Alpha, Alpha Tau Omega, Nu Sigma Nu. Clubs: Onondaga Golf and Country, Thursday Night, Interurban. Assoc. editor: Cornell Conferences on Therapy, Vol. II, 1947, N.Y. State Jour. Medicine, 1956-70; abstractor Infectious Diseases, Excerpta Medica Found., 1952-70. Contbr. numerous articles to med. jours. Home: De Witt NY Died May 26, 1970; buried Oakwood Cemetery Syracuse NY

BUNN, WILLIAM HALL, physician; b. Salineville, O., Dec. 24, 1889; s. William Eliphalet and Alice Ophelia (Hall) B.; student U. Wooster, 1911-12; M.D., Jefferson Med. Coll., 1915; m. Helen L. Rownd, Jan. 17, 1925; children—Nancy, William Hall, Robert. Postgrad. study Sir James MacKenzie, St. Andrews, Scotland, 1921; intern Presbyn. Hosp., Phila., 1915-16; student Nat. Heart Hosp., London, 1924; instr. cardiology Youngstown Hosp. Nurses Tng. Sch., 1924-47; chief cardiac clinic Youngstown Hosps., 1924-56; chief med. services Youngstown Hosp. Assn., 1935-55; lectr. biology Youngstown U. Cons. in cardiology area VA, 1946; cons. FSA Pub. Health Service, 1951, Surgeon Gen. U.S. Army. Bd. govs., exec. com. Youngstown U.; trustee Youngstown YMCA. Chmn. Ohio Nat. Found. Scholarship Com., 1959-60. Served as capt. U.S. Army, 1917-19. Decorated Medaille D'Honneur des Epidemie (France). Diplomate Am. Bd. Internal Medicine, Cardiovascular Disease. Fellow A.C.P. mem. hosp. standards survey group 1956-57); mem. A.M.A., Am. Heart Assn. (dir. 1947-56, v.p. 1954-56), Central Soc. Clin. Research (pres. 1937), Youngstown Area Heart Assn. (past pres.), Mahoning Med. Assn. (pres. 1945), Alpha Omega Alpha. Clubs: Youngstown Country, Youngstown; Union (Cleve.). Contbr. articles med. jours. Home: 410 Tod Lane. Office: 275 W. Federal St., Youngstown, O. Died Aug. 15, 1961; buried Youngstown, O.

BUNNELL, STERLING HAIGHT, mech. engr.; b. Stratford, Conn., Jan. 30, 1871; s. Rufus William and Catharine Mary (Sterling) B.; Ph.B., Yale, 1891; M.E., 1893; m. Rebecca Lapham Peterson, Oct. 17, 1900;children—Charles Sterling, Elizabeth Lapham (Mrs. Edwin Marshall Deery). Began as with various manufacturing companies, 1893-99; engineer mgr., 1899-1916; chief engr., R. Martens & Co., N.Y. City, 1916-22; cons. engr., N.Y. City, 1922-27; with indsl. department Nat. City Co., N.Y. City, 1928-32; vice president George S. Armstrong & Co., Inc., financial consultants and indsl. engrs., 1932-51; staff mem. Stanford Research Inst., since 1951. Fellow American Soc. M.E.; mem. Franklin Inst., Nat. Geog. Soc., Yale Eng. Assn. Trustee Sterling Park and Community House. Republican. Episcopalian. Clubs: Yale (New York); Housatonic Boat and Cupheag (Stratford, Conn.), Technical writer, author. Address: 2225 Main St., Stratford CT

BUNTING, CHARLES HENRY, pathologist; b. La Crosse, Wis., May 22, 1875; s. Charles Hood and Florence Josephine (Smith) B.; B.S., U. of Wis., 1896, fellow in biology, 1896-97; M.D., Johns Hopkins U., 1901; m. Carlotta Mary Swett, June 19, 1907; children—Elizabeth (Mrs. John V. A. Fine), Henry. Served as medical house officer, Johns Hopkins Hosp., 1901-02; asst. demonstrator in pathology, U. of Pa., 1902-03; instr. and asso. in pathology, Johns Hopkins, 1903-06; pathologist, Bay View Hosp., Baltimore, 1903-06; professor pathology, University of Virginia, 1906-08; prof. pathology, U. of Wis., 1908-45, professor emeritus, since 1945; lecturer in pathology, Yale Medical Sch., since 1945. Fellow A.A.A.S., Am. Assn. Pathologists and Bacteriologists; mem. Assn. Am. Physicians; mem. Soc. Exptl. Biology and Medicine, Chicago Pathol. Soc., Am. Assn. of Anatomists, Am. Assn. for Cancer Research, Am. Soc. Exptl. Pathology, Beta Theta Pi, Nu Sigma Nu, Alpha Omega Alpha, Sigma Xi, Phi Beta Kappa; hon. mem. Milwaukee Surg. Soc. Wis. Acad. of Arts and Science, State Hist. Soc. of Wis., Soc. of Mayflower Descendants. Contbr. articles on gen. pathol. subjects, especially in hermatology, on anemias, pernicious anemia, Hodgkin's disease. Home: 139 Armory St., Hamden, 11, Conn. Office: 310 Cedar St., New Haven CT

BUNTING, RUSSELL WELFORD, educator; b. Ann Arbor, Mich., June 2, 1881; s. William Alfred and Emma (Welford) B.; D.D.S., U. Mich., 1902, D.D.Sc., 1908; m. Mattie Janes, August 10, 1904 (dec.); children—John Welford, Cyrenus Garritt; m. 2d, Dorothy G. Hard, June 26, 1948. Practiced dentistry, Ann Arbor, 1903; instr. in oral pathology, U. Mich. Sch. Dentistry, Ann Arbor, 1904-14, prof. Oral pathology since 1914, sec. dental faculty, 1912-23, dean 1937-50, ret.; dental cons. Fed. Civil Def. Adminstrn. since 1951. Recipient Callahan Meml. award, 1929, Fauchard medal, 1930. Dir. research on dental caries under grant from Children's fund of Mich. Former pres. Internat. Assn. for Dental Research. Fellow Am. Coll. Dentists; mem. Am. Dental Assn., Mich. State Dental Soc. (ex.-pres.), Sigma Xi, Phi Kappa Phi, Omicron Kappa Upsilon, Delta Sigma Delta, Acacia. Rep. Bapt. Mason (K.T.). Club: Ann Arbor Golf. Author: Oral Pathology, 1929, 2d edit., 1940; Oral Hygiene and Treatment of Parodontal Diseases, 1936; Oral Hygiene and Preventive Dentistry, 1950; The Story of Dental Caries, 1953. Contbr. to textbooks and profl. jours. Home: 2224 Vinewood Pl., Ann Arbor, Mich. Died Nov. 22, 1962; buried Forest Hill Cemetery, Ann Arbor.

BUNZELL, HERBERT HORACE, educator; b. Prague, Austria-Hungary, Jan. 13, 1887; s. Frederick B. and Mathilde (Brandeis) B.; came to U.S., 1903; B.S., U. Chgo., 1906, Ph.D., 1909; student U. Berlin, summer 1908, Marine Biol. Lab. Woods Hole, Mass., summers 1906, 07, 09. Asst. biochemistry U. Chgo., 1906-10; expert U.S. Dept. Agr., 1910-11, chem. biologist, 1911-16; prof. chemistry George Washington U., 1914-16; spl. lectr. biochemistry Georgetown U. Med. Sch., 1916; asst. prof. biochemistry U. Cin., 1916-17, prof., head dept., 1917-18; chief chemist Isko Corp., Hudson Motor Corp., and cons. chemist, Detroit, 1918-19; dir. Bunzell Labs., 1920—; prof. chemistry Woman's Med. Coll. of Pa., 1920-36; cons. practice, N.Y.C.; prof., head dept. biochemistry Essex Coll. Medicine and Surgery, 1944-45. Reviewer Am. biochem. lit. for Zentralblatt der Biochemie, and Physiol. Zentralblatt, 1906-13; dir. Am. Bd. Clin. Chemists, 1950-54. Developed methods for accurate measurement oxydases in tissues; studied enzymatic disturbances in various plant diseases; discovered method of controlling condition bakery products, 1930; study elec. impulses as related to crime detection. Fellow A.A.A.S.; mem. Am. Chem. Soc., Soc. Biol. Chemists, Sigma Xi, Phi Chi. Republican. Lutheran. Author: Everday with Chemistry, 1937. Contbr. articles to profl. jours. Died Sept. 23, 1964.

BURBANK, LUTHER, naturalist; b. Lancaster, Mass., Mar. 7, 1849; s. Samuel Walton and Olive (Ross) B.; boyhood on farm; ed. Lancaster Acad.; Sc.D., Tufts, 1905; m. Elizabeth J. Waters, Dec. 21, 1916. Always devoted to study of nature, especially plant life. Moved to Santa Rosa, Calif., 1985; conducted Burbank's Expt. Farms. Originator Burbank potato, rapid-growing edible thornless opuntias (cactus), Gold, Wickson, Apple, October, Chalco, America, San Fros, Formosa, Beaty, Eldorado, and and Climax plums; Giant Splendor, Sugar, Standard and Stoneless prunes; a new fruit, the Plumcot; Burbank and Abundance cherries; Peachblow, Burbank and Santa Rosa roses, gigantic forms of amaryllis, tigridias, the Shasta Daisy, Giant and Fragrance callas; and various new apples, peaches, nuts, berries and other valuable trees, fruits, flowers, grasses, grains and vegetables. Special lecturer on evolution, Leland Stanford Jr. University. Life mem. Red Cross; hon. pres. Chamber of Commerce, Santa Rosa; hon. pres. Sonoma Co. (Calif.) Boy Scouts; hon. mem. Am. Playground Soc. Author: Training of the Human Plant; Methods and Discoveries (12 vols.); How Plants Are Trained to Work for Man (8 vols.), 1921; also numerous mag. articles. Died Apr. 11, 1926.

BURBIDGE, FREDERICK, mining engr.; b. Stratford, Eng., Apr. 16, 1864; s. Enoch and Caroline (Green) B.; ed. Mechanics' Inst., Stratford; m. Rebecca Florence Williams, of Seneca Falls, N.Y., May 18, 1892 (died Dec. 24, 1915); children—Norman Elwell, Beatrice Frederick (Mrs. William Lambert Berry). Came to U.S., 1882; mgr. Butte (Mont.) Reduction Works, 1886-88; mining on own account, 1888-93; assayer, asst. mgr., mgr. Bunker Hill & Sullivan Mining & Concentrating Co., 1893-1901; gen. mgr. Frisco Mining Co., 1901-09; mining on own account, 1909-16; gen. mgr. Federal Mining & Smelting Co. since 1916; pres. Federal Mining & Smelting Co. since 1916; pres. Blackhawk Mining Co. Mem. Am. Inst. Mining and Metall. Engrs., Mining and Metall. Soc. America, A.A.A.S. Republican. Episcopalian. Club: Spokan City. Home: Wallace, Ida.

BURCH, EDWARD PARRIS, cons. engr.; b. Menomonie, Wis., Aug. 1870; s. Newell and Susan (Parris) B.; E.E., U. of Minn., 1892; m. Harriet Jackson; 1 dau., Mrs. Imogene Wolcott. Elec. engr. Twin City Rapid Transit Co., 1892-99, in charge of installing 10,000 horsepower plant for utilizing the water power of St. Anthony's Falls for operating the electric rys. of Minneapolis and St. Paul; consulting engr., specilaizing in water power and elec. power work since 1900; dir. Minneapolis, Northfield & Southern Ry. Lecturer on electric railroading, 1902-10, prof. ry. elec. engring., 1913-14, U. of Minn. Consulting engr. Detroit Electric Ry. Commn., 1914-15; mem. research com. Minn. Com. Pub. Safety, 1917; ry. and power valuations, 1921-26; receiver Minneapolis, Anoka & McWethy, 1930-36; mem. Mayor's Survey Commn., Minneapolis, 1930. Mem. Am. Inst. E.E., Geol. Soc. of Minn. (pres. 1938), Phi Gamma Delta. Presbyterian. Author: Electric Traction for Railway Trains, 1911, Telephone Rates in Detroit, 1916-20. Home: 1729 James Av. S., Minneapolis, Minn. Died May 4, 1945.

BURCH, LUCIUS EDWARD, gynecologist, obstetrician; b. Nashville, Dec. 10, 1874; s. John Christopher and Lucy (Newell) B.; prep. edn. Webb Sch. at Bellbuckle, Tenn., M.D., Vanderbilt U., 1896; studied surgery in Europe 1 yr.; m. Sadie Polk Cooper, Nov. 8, 1898; children—John C., Lucius E. Practiced in Nashville since 1896; prof. gynecology, Vanderbilt U. since 1904, also dean Sch. of Medicine, 1914-25; prof. obstetrics and gynecology; gynecologist and obstetrician in chief, Vanderbilt U. Hosp., 1924-46; prof. emeritus, obstetrics and gynecology Sch. Medicine, Vanderbilt U., sr. obstetrician and gynecologist, Vanderbilt U. Hosp., 1956—, also life mem. bd. trustees; gynecologist Nashville Gen., St. Thomas hosps. Served as capt. asst surgeon 1st Tenn Inf.; surgeon gen. N.G. Tenn.; commd. maj. Med. R.C., 1917; lt. col. M.C., A.E.F.; chief of surg. service, Base Hosp. 63. Ex-pres. Vanderbilt Athletic Assn.; former comdr. Nashville Post Vets. of World War I. Licentiate Am. Bd. Obstetrics and Gynecology. Fellow A.C.S. (bd. govs.); mem. A.M.A. (mem. ho. of dels. 1923; vice chmn. sect. on obstetrics and gynecology and abdominal surgery 1921), Central Assn. Gynecologists and Obstetricians, Tenn. State Med. Assn., So. Med. Soc., Vanderbilt Med. Alumni Assn. (pres.), So. Surg. Soc. (pres. 1929), Middle Tenn. Med. Soc. (pres. 1905), Nashville Acad. Medicine (pres. 1906, chmn. com. nat. fedn. obstetric and gynecologic soc.), Kappa Alpha, Phi Chi, Alpha Omega Alpha. Democrat. Episcopalian. Mason, K.P., Elk. Clubs: Army and Navy (Washington); Hermitage (ex-pres.), Belle Meade Golf and Country. Collaborator Pack-Livingston book The Treatment of Cancer. Former mem. adv. editorial bd., Am. Jour. Obstetrics and Gynecology. Home: Porter Rd. Office: 2112 West End Av., Nashville. Died Oct. 15, 1959; buried Mt. Olivet Cemetery, Nashville.

BURCHARD, ERNEST FRANCIS, mining geologist; b. Independence, Kan., May 20, 1875; s. George W. and Alice (Boyd) B.; student Lehigh U., 1897; B.S., Northwestern U., 1900, M.S., 1903; Sc.D., U. of Ala., 1935; m. Frances Elizabeth Baker, June 18, 1910 (died Jan. 1931). Instr. chemistry and geology, Sioux City (Ia.) High Sch., 1900-03; asst. geologist Wis. Geol. and Nat. Hist. Survey, 1903; on geologic staff of U.S. Geological survey, 1904-05; geologist in charge sect. non-metal resources, 1915-17, sect. iron and steel metals, 1917-44, prin. geologist, 1942-45, ret. 1945; sr. geologist, Geol. Survey of Ala., since 1945; cons. geologist, Bur. Bus. Research, Univ. of Ala., Tenn. Valley Authority, Ky. Geol. Survey, 1947; field work on iron ores, structural materials in all parts of the U.S. Organized World War I studies of U.S. Geol. Survey of reserves of ferro-alloy metals, 1917; mem. commn. to study chrome and manganese ores of Cuba, 1918; in petroleum fields of P.I., 1920, Argentina and Bolivia, 1922; made studies of iron ore reserves for Argentine Govt. and reconnaissance of iron and manganese ore fields of Brazil, 1925, Venezuela, 1929. Fellow Geol. Soc. America; mem. Am. Inst. Mining and Metall. Engrs. (chmn. com. on mining geology, 1924-27), Soc. Economic Geologists, Geol. Soc. Washington, Phi Beta Kappa, Sigma Xi, Phi Kappa Psi. Episcopalian. Author: Geology of Dakota County, Nebraska; Geology of Lancester-Mineral Point, Wis. (with U.S. Grant); Iron Ores of the Birmingham District, Ala., Red Iron Ores of East Tennessee, Northeast Alabama and Northwest Georgia, Marble Resources of Southeast Alaska, Chrome and Manganese Ores of Cuba, Bauxite in Mississippi; Iron Ore in Misiones Territory, Argentina, The Iron Ore Situation in the South, The Pao Deposits of Iron Ore, Venezuela, Geological Exploration for Iron Ore Deposits, Fluorspar Deposits in Western States,

The Sources of Ores of Iron and Ferro-alloy Metals, The Iron Ore Situation in the Western States and in California; National reserves and production of iron ore; Conservation of Iron Ore.; Red Iron Ore Outcrops in Northeast Alabama (with Thos. G. Andrews)—in bulletins of Federal and state geological surveys and tech. mags. Contbr. many other papers on geol. and economic subjects. Address: 3403 Lowell St., Washington 16

BURCKHALTER, CHARLES, astronomer; b. Taylorsville, O., Jan. 5, 1849; s. Adam and Elisabeth B.; grad. Ottumwa High Sch., 1866; m. Mary Catherine Nash, Sept. 23, 1878. Astronomer in charge Chabot Obs., Oakland, Calif., 1885—. Mem. eclipse expdn. from Lick Obs. to Japan, 1896; in charge from Chabot Obs. to India, 1898; Calif., 1889, and Ga., 1900. Mem. State Earthquake Investigation Commn., 1906. Fellow Royal Astron. Society. Died Sept. 20, 1923.

BURDEN, HENRY, ironmaster, inventor; b. Dunblane, Scotland, Apr. 20, 1791; s. Peter and Elizabeth (Abercrombie) B.; m. Helen McQuat, Jan. 17, 1821. Came to Am., 1819; patented machine for making wrought iron spikes, 1825; 1st patented horseshoe machine (his most widely known invention), 1835. Died Troy, N.Y., Jan., 19, 1871; buried family vault, Albany (N.Y.) Rural Cemetery.

BURDEN, JAMES ABERCROMBIE, mfr., inventor; b. Troy, N.Y., Jan. 6, 1833; s. Henry B. inventor; b. Troy, N.Y., Jan. 6, 1833; s. Henry B. (inventor); ed. by tutor at New Haven, Conn., supplemented by lectures at Sheffield Scientific Sch., Yale, and Rensselaer Poly. Inst.; m. Miss Irvin. Pres. Burden Iron Co.; dir. (pres.) Hudson River Ore & Iron Co. Has made many inventions. Presdl. elector, 1880, 1888. Home: Troy, N.Y. Died 1906.

BURGER, KATHRYN REYNOLDS (MRS. JOHN D. BURGER), pharm. and cosmetics mfr.; b. Chicago, Ill.; daughter of Richard J. and Catherine (Kurtz) Reynolds; ed. high school, also business course and beauty course; m. John D. Burger, June 12, 1918 (dec.). Participated (with husband) in development Kaywoodie Co (pipes) and Civic Briar Pipe Co. (Eng.), also designer leather items for latter company; sold cos. to Consol. Grocers Corp., Dec. 28, 1950; engaged in advertising and designing DuraGloss lines, Lorr Labs., Inc., Paterson, N.J., 1939; pres. of Lorr Laboratores, Inc., 1943-54; created, developed and packaged cosmetic lines, Milkmaid Cosmetics, 1941, originating concept of utilizing farm products (pasteurized milk and cream) in cosmetics. Mgr. of small village, Burgerville, Bouchette, Que., Can., 1943-52. Mem. Compagnons de Rabelais. Clubs: River Regency; Madistone (East Hampton, L.I., N.Y.); Everglades, Bath and Tennis. Home: Waldorf Astoria Towers, Park Av. and 50th St., N.Y.C. Died Feb. 6, 1958.

BURGER, OWEN FRANCIS, plant pathologist; b. Freeland, Pa., June 8, 1885; s. Amandus Kresge and Eliza Ann (Barthold) B.; A.B., Ind. U., 1909; M.S., U. of Fla., 1911; M.S., Harvard, 1915, D.Sc., Harvard, 1916; m. Helen Sanborn Lothrop, July 22, 1916. Asst. plant pathologist, Fla. Agrl. Expt. Sta., 1911-13; univ. scholar, Harvard, 1913-14, and Priscilla Clark Hodges scholarship, same univ., 1914-16; instr. plant pathology, Citrous Expt. Sta., U. of Calif., 1916-18; pathologist U.S. Dept. Agr., 1918-20; plant pathologist Agrl. Expt. Sta., U. of Fla., Dec. 1920—. Fellow A.A.A.S. Democrat. Episcopalian. Mason. Home: Gainesville, Fla. Died 1928.

BURGER, WILLIAM HENRY, civil engr.; b. Caribou, Colo., May 2, 1874; s. Henry and Caroline (Mohr) B.; B.S., U. Colo., 1896, post-grad., 1896-97; m. Elizabeth L. Shotwell, Aug. 7, 1912; children—William H(enry), Elizabeth Marie. Instr., U. Colo., 1896-97; with engring. corps. Colo. & N.W. Ry., 1897-99; aide and asst. U.S. Coast and Geod. Survey 1899-1910; asst. prof. civ. engring., 1910-15, prof., 1915-39; professor of civil engring. emeritus since 1939, Northwestern U. Cons. precision and geod. surveys. Author: Measurement of Flexure of Pendulum Supports with the Interferometer; Biographical Memoir of John F. Hayford. Fellow A.A.A.S., Am. Geophys. Union; mem. Sigma Xi, Delta Tau Delta. Home: 1220 Noyes St., Evanston, Ill. Died June 19, 1962; buried Meml. Park Cemetery, Evanston.

BURGESS, ALBERT FRANKLIN, entomologist; b. Rockland, Mass., Oct. 2, 1873; s. Emory and Mary (Lewis) B.; B.S., Mass. Agrl. Coll., 1895, M.S., 1897; m. Mary E. Dwight, June 20, 1904; children—Emory D., Albert F. Asst. entomologist, Mass. State Bd. Agr., 1895-99; asst. in entomology, U. of Ill., 1899-1900; asst. insp. 1900-02, chief insp. of nurseries and orchards, 1902-07, Ohio Dept. Agr.; expert in charge of breeding experiments, Bur. of Entomology, U.S. Dept. of Agr., 1907-43, in charge of preventing spread of the gypsy moth for same bureau, 1913-28; principal entomologist of U.S. Plant Quarantine and Control Adminstrn., 1928-34; principal entomologist U.S. Bur. of Entomology and Plant Qqarantine, 1933-43, ret. Asso. editor Journal of Economic Entomology, 1908-10, business mgr., 1910-24, 1931-32. Published 5 annual reports and 9 bulls. on nursery and orchard inspection, numerous bulls. issued by U.S. Bur. of Entomology and many scientific articles on entomol. subjects. Fellow A.A.A.S., Entomol. Soc. America; mem. Am. Assn. Econ. Entomologists (sec., 1903, 1906-23 and 1930-31; 1st v.p., 1904; pres., 1924), Washington Entomol. Soc., Entomol. Soc. of France, Am. Assn. Hort. Inspectors (past pres.), Cambridge Entomol. Club (past pres.), Nat. Shade Conf. (chmn. 1931), Phi Sigma Kappa, Sigma Xi. Republican. Mason. Club: Cosmos (Washington). Home: 24 Franklin St., Greenfield, Mass. Died Feb. 23, 1953.

BURGESS, CHARLES FREDERICK, chemical engr.; b. Oshkosh, Wis., Jan. 5, 1873; s. Frederick and Anna A. (Heckman) B.; B.S., U. of Wis., 1895, E.E., 1897, Ph.D., 1926; Dr. Engrg., Ill. Inst. Technology, 1944; m. Ida M. Jackson, June 25, 1903; children—Betty, Jackson. Instr. and asst. prof. elec. engring., 1895-1900, prof. applied electro-chemistry and chem. engineering, 1900-13, U. of Wis. Engr. for Wis. R.R. Commn., 1908-13. Pres., chmn. of bd., C.F. Burgess Lav.; dir. Burgess-Parr Co. and Burgess-Manning Co. Inventor process for electrolytic purification of iron; also inventor of various iron alloys, improvement in dry cells, etc.; has taken out over 400 patents covering various products and processes. Awarded Octave Chanute medal by Western Society Engrs., 1911; Perkin medal of Chemical Societies, 1932; Edward Goodrich Acheson award, 1942. Member District Draft Bd. for Southern Wisconsin, 1917-18. Mem. Internat. Jury of Awards, St. Louis Expn., 1904. Mem. Am. Electrochem. Soc. (ex-pres.), Soc. Chem. Industry, Am. Chem. Soc. Am. Gas Inst., Western Soc. Engrs., Am. Electroplaters' Soc., Royal Institution of Gt. Britain, Beta Theta Pi, Tau Beta Pi, Alpha Chi Sigma. Clubs: University, Union League, Lake Shore (Chicago); Chemists' (New York); Niagara (N.Y.). Author sci. and tech. papers dealing with chem. engrg. subjects. Home: Bokeelia, Fla. Address: 180 North Wabash Av., Chicago, Ill. Died Feb. 13, 1945.

BURGESS, EDWARD, entomologist, yacht designer; b. West Sandwich, Mass., June 30, 1848; s. Benjamin and Cordelia (Ellis) B.; A.B., Harvard, 1871; m. Caroline Sullivant, 2 children. Sec. Nat. History Soc. Boston, 1872; instr. entomology Harvard, 1879-82; mem. U.S. Naval Bd., 1887; permanent chmn. U.S. Life Saving Service, 1888; designed yachts Puritan, Mayflower and Volunteer (winners of Internat. Yacht Race). Died Boston, July 12, 1891.

BURGESS, EDWARD SANDFORD, botanist; b. Little Valley, N.Y., Jan. 19, 1855; s. Rev. Chalon and Emma (Johnston) B.; A.B., Hamilton Coll., 1879, A.M., 1882, Sc.D., 1904; fellow Johns Hopkins, 1880-81; Ph.D., Columbia, 1899; m. Irene S. Hamilton, Dec. 30, 1884. Taught botany in Washington, 1881-95, Marthas Vineyard Summer Inst., 1880-95, Johns Hopkins U., 1885; prof. natural science, Hunter Coll., 1895—, acting pres., Jan.-May 1908. Pres. Torrey Bot. Club, 1912-13. Author: History of Pre-Clusian Botany, 1902; Species and Variations of Biotian Asters, 1906. Died Feb. 23, 1928.

BURGESS, GEORGE KIMBALL, physicist; b. Newton, Mass., Jan. 4, 1874; s. Charles A. and Addie L. (Kimball) B.; S.B., M.I.T., 1896; D.Sc., Paris, 1901; hon. D. Engr., Case Sch. Applied Science, 1923. Lehigh U., 1925; m. Suzanne Babut, of Paris, Jan. 5, 1901. Taugh physics at Mass. Inst. Tech., U. of Mich., 1900-01, and U. of Calif.; asso. physicist, Nat. Bur. of Standards, Washington, D.C., 1903-13; physicist and chief of div. of metallurgy, same, 1913-23; dir. Bureau of Standards and member various coms. connected with it; engaged in pyrometric and metall. researches. U.S. del 7th Internat. Conf. on Weights and Measurers, Paris, 1927; U.S. del World Engring. Congress, Tokyo, 1929; pres. Annual Conf. on Weights and Measures Paris, 1927; U.S. del. World Engring. Congress, Tokyo, 1929; pres. Annual Conf. on Weights and Measures. Mem. foreign service and engring. coms., Nat. Research Council. Author: Recherces sur la constante de Gravitation, 1901; Experimental Physics-Freshman course, 1902; The Measurement of High Temperatures (with H. Le Chatelier), 1912. Died July 2, 1932.

BURGESS, JOHN ALBERT, mining engr.; b. St. John, N.B., Can., May 30, 1876; s. Rev. Joshua Chase and Mary Helen (Noble) B.; brought to U.S., 1883; B.S., U. of Calif. Coll. of Mining, 1906; m. Florence Helen DuBois, Sept. 25, 1907; children—Eleanor, John DuBois, Peter DuBois. Chief engr. and geologist, Tonopah Mining Co. of Nev., 1906-11; supt. Nevada Wonder Mining Co., Wonder, Nev., 1911-16; gen. mgr. United Eastern Mining Co., Oatman, Ariz., 1916-20; cons. engr. and geologist San Francisco, 1920-33; gen. mgr. Carson Hill Gold Mining Corp., 1933-43; agent Metals Res. Co., Yosemite Tungsten Project, 1943; gen. supt. U.S. Smelting Exploration, S.A., a subsidiary co. of U.S. Smelting & Refining Co. and cons. geologist Cia de Real del Monte y Pachuca, 1926-27; cons. engr. Mayflower Associates, New York, 1929; pres. Mother Lode Mining Assn. 1940-41. Brought into successful operation Nevada Wonder Mine (silver), United Eastern Mine (gold) and Carson Hill Mine (gold). Mem. Am. Inst. Mining and Metall. Engrs., Mining and Metall. Soc. of America; Sigma Xi. Republican. Presbyterian. Contbr. to Economic Geology, Mining and Scientific Press, etc. Home: P.O. Box 321, Sonora CA

BURKE, ARTHUR DEVRIES, author, dairy technologist; b. Wheeling, W.Va., Jan. 1893; s. Thomas Carrol and Anna (Little) B.; B.S., U. Wis., 1916; M.S., Ohio State U., 1920, grad. student, 1927-28; m. Marguerite Outcalt, Feb. 1, 1921. Dairy inspr. Huntington, W.Va., 1916-17; instr. dairy dept. Ohio State U., 1919-20; asst. prof. of dairying Okla. A. and M. Coll., 1920-22, asso. prof., 1922-29; prof. and head dairy dept. Ala. Poly. Inst., 1929-46. Mem. adv. council Sealtest, Inc., 1935-48. Served as 2d and 1st lt., C.A.C., U.S. Army, 1917-19. County chmn. A.R.C., 1940-47; apptd. welfare chmn. Lee County Defense Council, 1941; chmn. Campus Defense Council, Ala. Poly. Inst., 1942. Mem. Am. Dairy Science Assn. (former sec., v.p. and pres. so. sect.), Internat. Assn. Ice Cream Mfrs. (mem. statis, research com., 1939-47), Ala. Dairy Products Assn. (former pres., v.p., sec.; now exec. sec.) Am. Legion (comdr. Stillwater, Okla., 1925, Auburn, Ala., 1935), Alpha Gamma Rho, Gamma Sigma Delta. Democrat. Presbyn. Club: Auburn Kiwanis (pres. 1939; lt. gov. Ala. 1940). Author: Practical Ice Cream Making, 1933 revised 1945; Practical Dairy Tests, 1935; Practical Manufacture of Cultured Milks and Kindred Products, 2938. Tech. editor for Milk Dealer, 1920; Ice Cream Review, 1929—. Contbr. tech. jours. Home: Annalue Farm, Auburn, Ala. Died Aug. 16, 1950.

BURKE, MILO DARWIN, civil engr.; b. Ashland Co., O., Aug. 23, 1841; s. Sirenoe and Tirza B.; ed. common sch. and Oberlin Coll.; did not graduate; m. Ellen S. Bachtell, Dec. 25, 1866. Lfet coll., 1863, and served asst. topog. engr. at Gen. George H. Thomas' headquarters, Sept., 1864-Dec., 1965; has gen. practice in engring. work; constructed 4 inclined planes for passenger traffic (3 at Cincinnati and 1 at Hamilton, Ont.), and numerous steam, st. and electric roads, as well as municipal work, and developed mineral properties. Mem. Am. Inst. Mining Engrs., Am. Soc. C.E., Franklin Inst., A.A.A.S., Author: Brick for Street Pavements, 1893; also numerous tech. papers in current publications. Home: Kennedy, O. Office: Second Nat. Bank Bldg., Cincinnati, O.

BURKE, STEPHEN PATRICK, cons. engr.; b. N.Y. City, Mar. 18, 1897; s. Patrick Joseph and Ada May (Finney) B.; B.S., Columbia U., 1917, Chem. Engr., School of Mines, Engring. and Chemistry (Columbia), 1920, Ph.D., Columbia, 1922; m. Catharine Regis Moran, Oct. 1, 1924; children—Stephen Patrick, Joan, William Dennis. Research chemist Combustion Utilities Corp., N.Y. City, 1922-23, research dir., 1923-30; chmn. grad. council and dir. indsl. science div., W.Va. U., 1930-36; tech., consultant Federal Emergency Relief Adminstrn. also of W.Va. State Planning Bd.; econ. and financial adviser to Governor and W.Va. legislature, 1932-36; research dir., Consolidation Coal Company, 1936-39; cons. engr. since 1936, visiting prof. chem. engring., Columbia, 1939-41, prof. chem. engring. since 1941. Mem. Tech. Bd. of Arbitration on the Value Correlation of Coals, 1934; tech. adviser Northern W.Va. Subdivisional Code Authority, 1934; same Northern W.Va. Coal Ass., 1935; tech. adviser Joint Legislative Com. on Social Security, 1935-36; chmn. advisory bd., W. Va. Dept. of Public Assistance, 1936-37, member same, 1937-38; president, Fairmont Coal, Incorporated, 1939-42; mem. A.A.A.S., Am. Inst. Chem. Engrs., Am. Inst. Mining Engrs., Am. Gas Assn., Am. Chem. Soc., Tau Beta Pi, Sigma Gamma Epsilon, Phi Lambda Upsilon, Sigma Xi, Phi Beta Kappa. Catholic. Clubs: Columbia Univ., Chemists, Catholic (New York); Torch (Washington, D.C.). Home: 435 Riverside Dr. (25). Office: 301 Havemeyer Hall, Broadway and 118th St., New York, N.Y. Died Mar. 10, 1945.

BURKHOLDER, PAUL RUFUS, educator, microbiologist; b. Orrstown, Pa., Feb. 1, 1903; s. William Rankin William Rankin and Mary Ellen (Schubert) B.; A.B., Dickinson Coll., 1924; Ph.D., Cornell U., 1929; NRC fellow in botany, Harvard, 1932-33, Columbia, 1933-34; M.A. (hon.), Yale, 1944; Sc.D. (hon.), Dickinson Coll., 1949; m. Lillian Miller, Feb. 4, 1930; children—Franz M., Peter M., Karl M. Instr. botany Cornell U., 1924-28; biol. curator Buffalo Mus. Sci., 1929-32; asst. prof. Conn. Coll., 1934-37, asso. prof., 1937-38; asso. prof. U. Mo., 1938-40; asso. prof. Yale, 1940-43, Eaton prof. botany, 1944-53; chmn. dept. plant sci., 1950-53; head dept. bacteriology U. Ga., 1953-56; dir. research Bklyn. Botanic Garden, 1956-61; chmn. marine biology programs Lamont Geol. Obs. Columbia, 1961-69; vis. prof. microbiology U.P.R., Mayaguez, 1969-72. Mem. A.A.A.S., Nat. Acad. Sci., Bot. Soc. Am. (sec. 1940-45), Am. Soc. Naturalists (pres. 1948), Am. Soc. Microbiologists, Soc. Protozool., Soc. Gen. Microbiol., Torrey Bot. Club, Sigma Xi. Contbr. papers in field. Home: Madison WI Died Aug. 1972.

BURKS, JESSE DESMAUX, engr.; b. Adairville, Ky., Sept. 11, 1868; s. Jesse Herring and Sabine (Desmaux) B.; Ph.B., U. Chicago, 1893; M.L., U. of Calif., 1894; fellow Columbia, 1901-02, Ph.D., 1902, lecturer in adminstration, 1908; m. Frances Stoddard Williston, of Northampton, Mass., Aug. 9, 1900; children—Jesse Williston (dec.), Barbara Stoddard, Frances Williston. Survey and report or edl. system of Philippines for Bur. of Insular Affairs, 1907; later with Bur. Municipal Research, New York, and dir. Phila. Bur. Municipal Research, and municipal efficiency dept., Los Angeles.

Served in Washington, D.C., as adviser President's Nat. Industrial Conf., Income Tax Bur., Federal Tax Simplification Bd., also as Washington mgr. Nat. Industrial Conf. Bd.; spl. investigator Inst. for Pub. Service, New York, 1929. Dir. dept. of service Bd. of Edn., San Francisco, 1924-29; spl. adviser Oil Producers Sales Agency of Calif., 1931. Capt. Gen Staff, World War; maj. O.R.C., 1919-29; duty in Office Asst. Sec. of War, 1923-24. Unitarian. Clubs: X Club (Los Angeles); X Club (Palo Alto); Black Cat (New York). Writer on tech. subjects. Home: 1151 Guinda St., Palo Alto, Calif.

BURLINGAME, LEONAS LANCELOT, prof. biology; b. Guernsey County, O., Aug. 25, 1876; s. Gorton and Nancy Jane (Hamilton) B.; Ph.B., Ohio Northern U., 1901; A.B., U. of Chicago, 1906, Ph.D., 1908; m. Anna Irene Lesh, Jan. 1, 1902; children—Edith Mildred, Anna Lucile (Mrs. Howard Day). Prof. biology and geology, Ohio Northern U., 1902-04; asst. in botany, U. of Chicago, 1906-08; instr. in botany, Stanford, 1908-09, asst. prof., 1909-16; asso. prof., 1916-24, professor biology, 1924-41; professor emeritus since 1941; acting professor zoology, University of Oregon, summers 1924, 25. Field asst. U.S. Department Agr., 1918. Mem. A.A.A.S., Bot. Soc. America, Genetics Soc. of America, Am. Genetics Soc., Am. Eugenics Soc., Assn. for Research in Human Heredity, Am. Naturalists, Western Naturalist, Am. Assn. Univ. Profs., Sigma Xi, Phi Beta Kappa; fellow Calif. Acad. Sciences. Author: General Biology, 1921; Heredity and Social Problems, 1940. Also numerous scientific papers. Address: 426 Jordan Hall, Stanford University, Palo Alto CA

BURLINGAME, LUTHER D., mech. engr.; b. Whitesboro, N.Y., Jan. 12, 1865; s. Luther R. and Emeline S. (Aldrich) B.; ed. pub. schs.; m. Christine Ward; children—Mrs. Grace C. Lockwood, Harold L., Mrs. Ethel R. Spooner, Stanley W. With Brown & Sharpe Mfg. Co. since beginning of active career, industrial supt., 1914—, also patent expert. Mem. Nat. Screw Thread Commn.; mem. Joint Com. Am. Soc. Mech. Engrs. and Soc. Am. Engrs. as sponsors of Engring. Standards Com. Republican. Baptist. Home: Providence, R.I. Died June 2, 1932.

BURNETT, CHARLES HENRY, otologist; b. Phila., May 28, 1842; s. Eli Seal and Hannah (Mustin) B.; grad. Yale, 1864; M.D., U. Pa., 1867; studied otology in Europe, 1870-72; m. Anna Davis, June 18, 1874. Practiced medicine specializing in otology, Phila., 1872-1902; prof. otology Phila. Polyclinic; mem. Coll. Physicians of Phila.; pres. Am. Otol. Soc.; developed operation for relief of progressive deafness and vertigo by performing tympanotomy and removing incus. Author: The Ear; Its Anatomy, Physiology, and Diseases, 1877; Hearing and How To Keep It, 1879. Editor: System of Diseases of the Ear, Nose, and Throat, 1893; Textbook of Diseases of the Ear, Nose and Throat, 1901. Died Bryn Mawr, Pa., Jan. 30, 1902.

BURNETT, CHARLES HOYT, physician, educator; b. Boulder, Colo., Mar. 7, 1913; s. Clough Turrill and Lucille (Hoyt) B.; A.B., U. Colo., 1934, M.D., 1937; M. Eda Waugh, Apr. 27, 1940; children—Grosvenor Turrill, Mark Hoyt, Margaret Jamie. Asst. resident pathology, asst. pathology Presbyn. hosp., N.Y.C., Columbia U. Coll. Phys. and Surg., 1937-38; intern Harvard med. service Boston City Hosp., 1939-40; asst. resident medicine Mass. Gen. Hosp., Boston, 1940-42, chief resident medicine, 1945-46; asst. medicine, med. sch. Harvard, 1940-42, 45-46; asst. prof. medicine Boston U. Sch. Medicine, 1947-50, asso. prof., 1950; asst. mem. Robert Dawson Evans Meml. Hosp., 1947-50, asso. mem., 1950; prof. medicine, chmn. dept. Southwestern Med. Sch., U. Tex., Dallas, 1950-51; prof. medicine University N.C., Chapel Hill, 1951-67, head dept. medicine, 1951-65; consultant Surgeon Gen.'s Office, 1946-56, 63-67; chief med. service N.C. Memorial Hospital, 1952-65; chief cons. for research Richardson Merrell, Inc., 1965-67. Mem. Nat. Board Medical Examiners medicine test committee, 1955-56, chmn. 1956. Member of sub-com. on shock Nat. Research Council, 1951-54; sci. adv. bd. Armed Forces Inst. Pathology, 1952-56; mem. adv. com. for biology and medicine AEC, 1953-58; council Nat. Inst. for Arthritis and Metabolic Diseases, 1958-62. Served as maj. M.C., AUS, 1942-46. Decorated Bronze Star Medal Fellow A.C.P.: mem. Soc. for Clin. Investigation (emeritus), Assn. Am. Physicians. A.A.A.S., Endocrine Soc., A.M.A., Am. Acad. Arts and Scis., So. Soc. Clin. Research, Assn. Am. Profs. Medicine (v.p. 1963), Alpha Omega Alpha. Author sci. articles. Home: Chapel Hill NC Died Oct. 23, 1967.

BURNETT, JOHN TORREY, mfg. chemist; b. Southboro, Mass., Apr. 23, 1868; s. Joseph and Josephine (Cutter) B.; student Harvard, 1891; m. Phyllis Abbot, Nov. 13, 1909; children—Frances, Joseph. Pres. Joseph Burnett Co., Boston, Mass., 1906—; v.p. North End Savings Bank; sec. and treas. Mass. Bonding and Ins. Co.; treas. Big Sandy Co., City Central Corp. of America. Democrat. Episcopalian. Home: Southboro, Mass. Deceased.

BURNHAM, HUBERT, architect; b. Chicago, Ill., Sept. 7, 1882; s. Daniel Hudson and Margaret (Sherman) B.; grad. Chicago Manual Training Sch. and Phillips Acad. Andover, Mass; grad. U.S. Naval Acad., 1905; grad. Ecole des Beaux Arts, Paris, 1912; m. Vivian Cameron, June 24, 1908; children—Cherie (Mrs. Lawrence Kendall Morris), Margaret (mrs LeGrow). Mem. D.H. Burnham & Co. (founded by father), Chicago, 1910-12, Graham, Burnham & Co., 1912-17, re-established firm of D. H. Burnham & Co., 1917, Burnham Bros., Inc., 1928. Burnham Bros. & Hammond, Inc., 1933, now Burnham & Hammond; firm designed the Burnham, Bankers, Carbide and Carbon, Engring. and Medical and Dental Arts Bldg., Chicago, So. wing and boiler house Evanston (Ill.) Hosp., Presbyn.-St. Lukes Nurses Home, Chgo., Argo Elementary Sch., Meml. Hosp., Springfield, Ill. Past chmn. Evanston City Plan Commn. Ret., 1955. Lt. U.S. Navy, World War; aviation constrn. work in France 14 mos. Fellow Am. Institute of Architects; member Society Beaux Arts Architects, Chicago Archtl. Club. Republican. Club: Glen View. Mem. Archtl. Commn. Chicago World's Fair Centennial Celebration, 1933. Home: Chicago IL Died Dec. 31, 1968; buried Graceland Cemetery, Chicago IL

BURNHAM, SHERBURNE WESLEY, astronomer; b. Thetford, Vt., Dec. 12, 1838; (hon. A.M., Yale, 1878). Took up study of astronomy as an amateur, and made many discoveries, especially of double stars, with 6-inch refractor; observer in pvt. obs., Chicago, 1870-77, Dearborn Obs., Chicago, 1877-81 and 1882-84, Washburn Obs., Madison, Wis., 1881-82; astronomer Lick Obs., 1888-92; prof. practical astronomy and astronomer Yerkes Obs., U. of Chicago, 1893—. Has discovered 1,274 new double stars; expert commr. to test the seeing on Mt. Hamilton Cal., resulting in locating the Lick Obs. there, 1879. Gold medal, Royal Astron. Soc. (for discovery and measurement of double stars), 1894; Lalande prize in astronomy, Paris Acad. Sciences, 1904. Fellow, 1874, asso. 1898, Royal Astron. Soc.; asso. fellow Am. Acad. Arts and Sciences, etc. Author of Vol. I, publs. of Yerkes Obs. (gen. catalogue of stars discovered by him), 1900; also a gen. catalogue of all known double stars visible in Northern Hemisphere, for Carnegie Instr., Washington, 1907; Measurers of Proper-Motion Stars, 1912. (hon. Sc.D., Northwestern U., 1915) Died Mar. 11, 1921.

BURNS, BOB, actor; b. Greenwood, Ark., Aug. 2, 1890; s. William Robert and Emma (Needham) B.; student U. of Ark.; m. Elizabeth Fisher, Sept. 1921 (now dec.); 1 son, Robert; m. 2d, Harriet Foster, May 31, 1937; children—Barbara Ann, William, Stephen. Began professional career on vaudeville stage, 1911; now identified with motion pictures and radio programs. Served as sergt. U.S. Marine Corps. Episcopalian. Mason. Inventor of Bazooka (musical instrument). Home: Canoga Park, Cal. Died Feb. 2, 1956; buried Forest Lawn Meml. Park, Glendale, Cal.

BURNS, GEORGE PLUMER, botanist; b. Maroa, Ill., Oct. 30, 1871; s. George William and Emily Harriet (Mouser) B.; grad. Ill. State Normal U., 1891; B.S., Ohio Wesleyan U., 1898; A.M.; Ph.D., U. Munich, 1900; m. Annette May Hollington, June 20, 1898. Instr. in botany Ohio Wesleyan U., 1897; instr. botany, later asst. prof. and jr. prof., and dir. Bot. Gardens, U. Mich., 1900-10; prof. botany U. Vt., 1910—, head dept., 1910-44, prof. emeritus, 1944—. Mem. Vt. (pres.), N.E. bot. clubs, Bot. Soc. Am., Ecol. Soc. Am. Phi Delta Theta, Sigma Xi, Phi Beta Kappa. Republican. Methodist. Contbr. articles to bot. jours. on forest ecology. Address: 453 S. Willard, Burlington, Vt. Died 1953.

BURNS, KEVIN, physicist; b. Pleasant Ridge, N.B., Can., Mar. 1, 1881; s. John and Gertrude (Campbell) B.; brought to U.S., 1885; A.B., U. of Minn., 1903, Ph.D., 1910; studied in Europe, 1911, 12; hon. D.Sc., St. Bonaventure College, 1947; married Hazel Bunney, 1911 (died 1917); 1 son, Kevin; m. 2d, Ruth Buchanan, 1926 (dec. 1957); children—John Buchanan, George Campbell. Asst. at Lick Obs., Cal., 1904-07, U. of Minn., 1907-10; Martin Kellogg fellow, Lick Obs., residence in Europe, 1911-12; asst. physicist, Bur. of Standards, Washington, 1913-17, asso., 1917, physicist, 1917-19; astronomer, Allegheny Obs., Pitts., 1920-51, asst. dir., 1930-51. Mem. Sigma Xi, Philos. Soc. Washington, A.A.A.S., A.A.S. (tres. 1941-47), Internat. Astron. Union, Unitarian. Has specialized in spectroscopy, pioneer in spectrochemical analysis; measured standard wavelenghts; determined stellar velocities and distances. Home: 3444 Delaware Av. Address: Allegheny Observatory, Pitts. 14. Died Apr. 30, 1958.

BURNS, MATTHEW D., indsl. engr.; b. Emporium, Pa., July 29, 1897; s. Matthew G. and Margaret A. (Murry) B.; student indsl. engring., Pa. State U., 1919-21; m. Claire Johnston, Sept. 27, 1924; children—Margaret (Mrs. Martel Berge), M. David (U.S.A.F.). With Sylvania Electric Products, 1921—, beginning as mem. staff charge lamp quality, factory supt. Emporium receiving tube plant, mgr., gen. mfg. mgr. radio tube div., gen. mgr., gen. mgr. charge electronic tube operations, 1921-55, v.p. electronic tube operations Sylvania Electric Products, Incorporated, now senior vice president; director Emporium Trust Company, Director Emporium Foundation. Member Inst. Radio Engrs., Emporium-Cameron County C. of C. (dir.). Episcopalian (vestryman). Mason. Club: Emporium Country (dir.). Home: 321 W. 5th St. Office: Sylvania Electric Products, Inc., Emporium, Pa. Died Feb. 15, 1965.

BURPEE, GEORGE WILLIAM, civil engr.; b. Sheffield, New Brunswick, Can., Nov. 9, 1883; s. Moses and Caroline (Alexander) B.; A.B., Bowdoin Coll., 1904; hon. D.Sc., 1939; B.S., Mass. Inst. Tech., 1906; m. Katherine Jameson Kellam, June 2, 1915; children—George Alexander, Louise Kellam (Mrs. James B. Landreth), and also Elizabeth Holliday. Began as draftsman with L.&N. R.R.; with Westinghouse, Church, Kerr & Co., N.Y., 1907-20, mng. engr., 1919, mng. engr. Dwight P. Robinson & Co., N.Y., 1920-21; with Coverdale & Colpitts, N.Y., 1921—, mem. of the firm, 1924-63, cons., 1964—; pres. Gen. Aniline & Film Corp., 1943-47; dir. Kaiser Steel Corp., Lukens Steel Co., Coatesville, Pa., Bklyn. Union Gas Co., N.Y., Nat. Vulcanized Fibre Co., Wilmington Del. Emeritus trustee Fowdoin Coll. Mem. Nat. Indsl. Conf. Bd. (sr. mem.), Am. Inst. Cons. Engrs. (past pres.), Am. Soc. C.E. (hon.), Am. Ry. Engring. Assn., Engring. Inst. of Can., Phi Beta Kappa, Delta Kappa Epsilon. Republican. Episcopalian. Clubs: University, Engrs., Recess (N.Y.C.); Siwanoy Country (Bronxville). Home: 39 Woodland Ave., Bronxville, N.Y. Office: 120 Wall St., N.Y.C. Died Nov. 7, 1967.

BURPEE, W(ASHINGTON) ATLEE, seedsman; b. Sheffield, N.B., Can., Apr. 5, 1858; s. David (M.D.) and Ann Catherine (Atlee) B.; ed. Friends' Central Sch., Phila.; studied 2 yrs., U. of Pa., class of 1878; m. Blanche Simons, Apr. 30, 1892. Started in seed business with two partners, 1876; 2 yrs. later began alone, adopting name of W. Atlee Burpee & Co., now the largest exclusive mail order seed house in the world; owns 3 large seed farms in Bucks Co., Pa., Gloucester Co., N.J., and Santa Barbara Co., Calif. Mem. exec. bd. Nat. Farm Sch. Republican. Home: Doylestown, Pa. Died Nov. 26, 1915.

BURR, CHARLES WALTS, neurologist; b. Phila., Nov. 16, 1861; s. D. Ridgway and Hannah (Walts) B.; B.S., U. Pa., 1883, M.D., 1886, D.Sc., 1933. Neurologist Phila. Gen. Hosp., 1896-1931, psychiatrist, 1931-40; prof. mental diseases U. Pa., 1901-31, prof. emeritus, 1931—; physician to Orthopaedic Hosp. and Infirmary for Nervous Diseases, 1911-40. Pres. Am. Neurol. Assn., 1908, Phila. Psychiatric Soc., 1909, 10, Phila. Neurol. Soc., Pathol. Soc. Phila. Fellow Coll. Physicians of Phila.; mem. A.M.A. Phi Beta Kappa. Address: 1527 Pine St., Phila. Died Feb. 19, 1944; buried Soc. of Friends Cemetery, Phila.

BURR, FREEMAN F., geologist; b. Medford, Mass., Mar. 7, 1877; s. Horace Freeman and Susan Lydia (Sawyer) B.; B.S., Harvard, 1900; student Yale, 1908; A.M., Columbia, 1913; m. Lois Southwick Ives, June 30, 1904; children—Richard Southwick, Barbara (Mrs. Horton Flynt), Foster Ives (dec.), Jean (Mrs. Alexander F. Smith), Horace Freeman. Science teacher high and prep. schs., 1900-04; instr. State Normal Sch., New Haven, 1904-12; lecturer, instr. Barnard Coll. (Columbia U.), 1912-15; geol. to Me. State Commns., 1914-22; head dept. geol., St. Lawrence U., 1922-31; Me. State geol., 1935-46; retired; part time biology, Allendale Sch., Rochester, N.Y. Mem. Augusta City Council, 1921-22. Past pres. Knox Acad. of Arts and Sciences; mem. Me. Mineral, Soc. Republican. Unitarian. Author: Maine State Reports; also science and nature articles. Home: Sunrise Farm, Wayne ME

BURR, WILLIAM HUBERT, civil engr.; b. Watertown, Conn., July 14, 1851; s. George William and Marion Foote (Scovill) B.; C.E., Rensselaer Poly. Inst., 1872; m. Caroline Kent Seeyle, 1876 (died 1894); children—Mrs. Marion Elisabeth Mars. William Fairfield, George Lindsley; m. 2d, Gertrude Gold Shipman, 1900; 1 dau., Mrs. Anne Louisa Colgate. Began practice as civ. engr., 1872; prof. rational and tech. mechanics, Rensselaer Poly. Inst., 1876-84; asst. to chief engr., and later gen. mgr., Phoenix Bridge Co., 1884-91; prof. engring. Harvard, 1892-93; prof. civil engrine., 1893-1916, prof. emeritus, Columbia U.; civil engr. and consulting engr., N.Y. City, 1916—. Consulting engr. to dept. pub. works, 1893-95, parks, 1895-97, of docks, 1895-97, and then dept. of bridges and bd. of water supply, New York. Mem. bd. of engrs. to to investigate feasibility of proposed bridge across North River, 1894; mem. bd. to leocate deep water harbor on coast of Southern Calif., 1896; mem. Isthmian Canal Commn. to examine and report uptón most feasible and practicable route for an interoceanic canal across the Central American Isthmus, 1902; mem. and chmn. Commn. on Additional Water Supply of City of New York; mem. Isthmian Canal Commn. and mem. bd. consulting engrs., 1905—; cons. engr. to bd. of water supply, New York; mem. advisory bd. of engrs. for constrn. of Barge Canal by State of N.Y., 1911; mem. bd. cons. engrs. by commns. states of N.Y. and N.J. for constructing vehicular tunnel under Hudson river at N.Y. City, 1919; cons. engr. N.Y. State Transit Commn., 1923-14, for Port of New York. Authority, 1925—, for constrn. of Ft. Washington Suspension Bridge across Hudson River, and for other bridges being built for the Port. Awarded 1st place in national competition, 1900, for proposed memorial bridge across Potomac at Washington. Decorated Order of Sacred Treasure, 2d degree (Japan). Fellow Am. Acad. Arts and Sciences. Trustee Cathedral of St. John the Divine. Author: The Stresses in Bridge and Roof Trusses, 1881; Elasticity and Resistance of the Materials of Engineering, 1883; Ancient and Modern Engineering and the Isthmian Canal, 1902; The Graphic Method by influence Lines for Bridge and Roof Computation (with M. S. Falk), 1905; The Design and Construction of Metallic Bridges (with M. S. Falk), 1912; Suspension Bridges, Arch Ribs and Cantilevers, 1913. Home: New Canaan, Conn. Died Dec. 13, 1934.

BURRAGE, CHAMPLIN, author, archaeologist; b. Portland, Me., Apr. 14, 1874; s. Henry Sweetser and Caroline (Champlin) B.; A.B., Brown U., 1896, hon. A.M., in absentia, 1905; studied univs. of Berlin and Marburg, and traveled widely in Europe, 1899-1901, Oxford U., 1906-15; B.Litt., Oxford, 1909; hist. research in English libraries, 1901-15; m. at Oxford, Florence Dwight Dale, of Montclair, N.J., Sept. 3, 1907. Librarian Manchester Coll., Oxford, 1912-15; librarian John Carter Brown Library (Brown U.), and mem. faculty of Brown U., 1915-17; hist., archaeol. and philol. research in Am. libraries and museums, 1915-20; temporarily on staff Mus. of Fine Arts, Boston, summer 1923 and winter 1923-24. Corr. mem. N.E. Hist.-Geneal. Soc.; mem. Archaeol. Inst. America, Bibliog. Soc. America, Delta Kappa Epsilon, Phi Beta Kappa. Author: A New Year's Guift by Robert Browne, 1588, 1904; The Church Covenant Idea, 1904; The True Story of Robert Browne (Oxford Univ. Press), 1906; The Retraction of Robert Browne, 1907; New Facts Concerning John Robinson, 1910; The Early English Dissenters in the Light of Recent Research (Cambridge Univ. Press), 1912; John Penry, the So-Called Martyr of Congregationalism, 1913; Nazareth and the Beginnings of Christianity, 1914; John Pory's Lost Description of Plymouth Colony, 1918; An Answer to John Robinson, of Leyden, 1920; The Minoan Hieroglyphic Inscriptions, I; The Phaestos Whorl, 1921 (reprinted from Harvard Studies in Classical Philology, Vol. 32, 1921; this brochure is believed to contain a considerable number of first readings from the prehistoric Cretan inscriptions); Studies in the Hieroglyphic Inscriptions and Pictographs of Minoan Crete and Neighboring Countries and Islands; also contbr. hist. articles in English Historical Review, American Jour. of Theology, Harvard Theol. Review, etc. Collector Henry S. Burrage collection, Colgate U. library, relics of mound builders of Ohio (Muskingum valley and Blennerhassett island regions) and the Burrage collection of Cretan Antiquities, 1927—. Compiler and editor Seaman's Handbook for Shore Leave, 1st edit., 1919 (for U.S. Shipping Bd.). Made Minoan and Hittite investigations in the Ashmolean Mus., British Mus. and museums of Athens and Candia; also made first archaeol. visit to Crete, 1926-27, 2d visit 1927. Home: 5 Park Vale, Brookline MA

BURRELL, EDWARD PARKER, mech. engr.; b. Hall, N.Y., Feb. 11, 1871; s. Edward and Elizabeth (Parker) B.; M.E., Cornell U., 1898, M.M.E., 1899; m. Katharine Ward, Dec. 8, 1904. Successively designing engr., works engr., works mgr., Warner and Swasey Co., 1900-24, dir. of engring., 1924—; directed design of all large telescopes built by this co. in past 20 years, including 72-inch relecting telescope for Dominion Astrophys. Obs., Victoria, B.C.; 69-inch reflecting telescope for Ohio Wesleyan U.; 20-inch refractor for Chabot Obs., Oakland, Calif. Designed and constructed model of proposed 200-inch telescope for Mt. Wilson Obs. Inventor and is holder of many patents in his field. Home: Shaker Heights, O. Died Mar. 21, 1937.

BURRELL, GEORGE ARTHUR, chem. engr.; b. Cleve., Jan. 23, 1882; s. Alexander A. and Jane (Penny) B.; student Ohio State U., 1902-04, Chem. E., 1918; Sc.D., Wesleyan U., 1919; m. Mary L. Schafer, 1906; 1 dau., Dorothy May; m. 2d, Naomi L. Schafer, June 16, 1914. Chemist U.S. Geol. Survey, 1904-08; in charge research work, gas mine gas, and natural gas and gasoline investigations, U.S. Bureau mines, Pitts., 1908-16; cons. engr. petroleum and natural gas work, 1916-43; asst. to dir. Bureau of Mines, 1917; col. U.S. Army, in charge all research work, C.W.S., 1917-18; located supply of helium gas in Tex. and initiated the govt. helium program. Decorated D.S.M. (U.S. Army). During 1919-20 had charge constrn. of refineries for the Island and Raritan Refining Cos. (N.Y.C.), was pres. Island Refining Co. and v.p., gen. mgr. Raritan Refining Co.; pres. Burrell Corp., 1923-52, became chmn. bd.; pres. Atlantic States Gas Co., 1936-54; retained by Russian govt. to modernize natural gas industry, 1930-31. Inventor Burrell gas detector, Burrell gas analysis apparatus; coinventor Burrell-Oberfell process of extracting gasoline from natural gas by charcoal methods; designed and built many natural gasoline refineries. Recipient Lamme medal for achievements in engring. Ohio State U., 1935; Hanlon award, Nat. Gasoline Assn. Am., 1948. Mem. Am. Petroleum Inst., Am. Chem. Soc., Am. Inst. Chem. Engrs., Am. Inst. Chemists, Tau Beta Pi, Sigma Xi. Clubs: Uptown, Westchester Country (N.Y.C.). Author: Handbook of Gasoline, 1917; Recovery of Gasoline from Natural Gas, 1925; An American Engineer Looks at Russia, 1932; and also many papers and govt. publs. on gas, gasoline, petroleum and allied subjects. Home: 101 W. 57th St., N.Y.C. Died Aug. 16, 1957.

BURRELL H(ERBERT) CAYFORD, geologist; b. Boston, Dec. 16, 1903; s. Herbert Leslie and Caroline White (Cayford) B.; student Middlesex Sch., Concord, Mass., 1915-21; S.B., Harvard, 1928, A.M., geologist, Zinc Corp., Ltd., Broken Hill, N.S.E., 1929, Ph.D., 1946; student U. of Wis., 1932-33; m. Mary Josephine Runkel, July 25, 1929; children—Frederick R., Patricia R. Geologist Cerro de Pasco Copper Corp., Morococha, Peru, 1929-32; 1st resident Australia, 1934-37; with Central Geog. Survey, 1937-39; lab. research on Broken Hill ores Harvard, 1939-42; with coordinator Interam. Affairs Bd. Econ. Warfare, and Fgn. Econ. Adminstrn. in connection with development of operations and purchase manganese ores for U.S. Govt., 1942-45; staff geologist Oliver Iron Mining Co. (U.S. Steel Corp. subsidiary) in cos. exploration for iron ore in Venezuela, 1946-49; trans. to raw materials dept. U.S. Steel Corp. of Del., Pittsburgh, 1949, since served as geologist; mgr. raw materials development, Columbia-Geneva Steel Div., U.S. Steel. Mem. Am. Inst. Mining and Metall. Engrs., Mining and Metall. Soc. Am. Author: Geology of the Broken Hill Ore Deposit, Broken Hill, N.W.S., Austraila (with J.K. Gustafson, M.D. Garretty), 1950. Home: 424 Golden Gate Av., Belevedere, Calif., Office: 235 Montgomery St., San Francisco. Died Nov. 9, 1953; buried Harmony Grove, Salem, Mass.

BURRILL, THOMAS JONATHAN, botanist; b. Pittsfield, Mass., Apr. 25, 1839; s. John and Mary (Francis) B.; grad. Ill. State Normal U., 1865; (hon. A.M., Northwestern, 1876, LL.D., 1893; Ph.D., U. of Chicago, 1881, LL.D., U. of Illinois 1912); m. Sarah H. Alexander, July 22, 1868. Superintendent Urbana (Ill.) public schools, 1865-68; asst. prof. natural history, U. of Ill., 1868-70; prof. botany and horticulture, 1870-1903, prof. botany, 1903-12 (emeritus), v.p., 1879-1912, dean Coll. Science, 1878-84, dean gen. faculty, 1894-1901, dean Grad. Sch., 1894-1905, acting pres., 1891-94 and 1904, U. of Ill.; botanist, U.S. Agrl. Expt. Sta., 1888-1912. Fellow Am. Micros. Soc. (pres. 1885-86, sec. 1886-89); mem. Am. Acad. Arts and Sciences. Home: Ubrana, Ill. Died Apr. 14, 1916.

BURROUGHS, JOHN, naturalist; b. Roxbury, N.Y., Apr. 3, 1837; s. Chauncey A. and Amy (Kelly) B.; acad. edn.; (Litt.D., Yale, 1910; Doctor Humane Letters, Colgate, 1911); m. Ursula North, Sept. 13, 1857. Taught school about 8 yrs.; treasury clerk, 1864-73; nat. bank examiner, 1873-84; has lived on a farm, devoting his time to literature and fruit culture, 1874—. Mem. Am. Acad. Arts and Letters. Author: Notes on Walt Whitman as Poet and Person, 1867; Wake Robin, 1871; Winter Sunshine, 1875; Birds and Poets, 1877; Locusts and Wild Honey, 1879; Pepacton, 1881; Fresh Fields, 1884; Signs and Seasons, 1886; Indoor Studies, 1889; Riverby, 1894; Whitman, a Study, 1896; The Light of Day, 1900; Squirrels and Other Fur Bearers, 1900; Literary Values, 1904; Far and Near, 104; Ways of Nature, 1905; Bird and Bough (poems), 1906; Campbing and Tramping With Roosevelt, 1907; Leaf and Tendril, 1908; Time and Change, 1912; The Summit of the Years, 1913; The Breath of Life, 1915; Under the Apple Trees, 1916; Field and Study, 1919. Home: West Park, N.Y. Died Mar. 29, 1921.

BURROUGHS, WILLIAM SEWARD, inventor; b. Auburn, N.Y., Jan. 28, 1855; s. Edmund and Ellen Burroughs; m. Ida Selover, 1879, 4 children, Jennie, Horace, Mortimer, Helen. Worker in father's shop making models for castings and new inventions, St. Louis, 1881; employed by Future Great Mfg. Co., St. Louis, 1881-84; invented machine to solve arithmetical problems, 1844-85, (not commercially practical); organized Am. Arithmometer Co. to produce machines for solving arithmetical problems, St. Louis, 1885; granted patent for 1st practical machine, 1892; awarded John Scott medal of Franklin Inst. for his invention, 1897. Died Citronelle, Ala., Sept. 5, 1898.

BURROW, TRIGANT, phylobiologist, psychiatrist; b. Norfolk, Va., Sept. 7, 1875; s. John W. and Anastasia (Devereux) B.; pres. edn., St. Francis Xavier's Acad., N.Y.C., pvt. schs.; A.B., Fordham, 1895; M.D., U. Va., 1899, Ph.D., Johns Hopkins, 1909; grad. studies U. Va., Munich, Vienna, Johns Hopkins and Zurich, 1900-10; m. Emily Sherwood Bryan, Aug. 9, 1904; children—John D. (dec.), Emily Sherwood, (Mrs. Hans Syz). Demonstrator in biology, U. Va., 1899-1900; asst. physician U. Frauenklinik, Munich, i900; asst. in exptl. psychology Johns Hopkins, 1906-09, in clin. psychiatry Johns Hopkins Hosp., 1911-27; practice and research in psychiatry and psychoanalysis, 1911-23, social psychiatry and the group method of analysis, 1923-28; research in phylopathology, or in the modifications of behavior induced through adjusting the organism's internal tensional patterns; also to instrumental recording of these physiological changes, 1928—; sci. dir. the Lifwynn Foundation for Lab. Research in Analytic and Social Psychiatry, Westport, Conn., 1927—. Participant in 2d Internat. Symposium on Feelings and Emotions. Moosehart, Ill., 1948. Mem. A.M.A., A.A.A.S., Med. and Chirurg. Faculty of Md., Am. Psychopath. Assn., Am. Psychiatric Assn., Am. Psychol. Assn., Am. Anthropol. Soc., Human Genetics Soc. Am., N.Y. Acad. Scis., So. Soc. for Philosophy and Psychology, Phi Beta Kappa, Phi Delta Theta. Author: The Social Basis of Consciousness, 1927; The Structure of Insanity, 1932; The Biology of Human Conflict, 1937; The Neurosis of Man—An Introduction to a Science of Human Bahavior, 1949; (pub. posthumously) Science and Man's Behaviour, The Contribution of Phylobiology, 1953, A Search for Man's Sanity, The Selected Letters of Trigant Burrow, 1958; also articles in field of medicine, exptl. psychology, psychoanalysis, individual and social psychiatry and phylopathology. Home: S. Morningside Dr., Greens Farms, Conn. Office: 77 Park Av., N.Y.C. 16; also Lifwynn Foundation, 52 S. Morningside Dr., Westport, Conn. Died May 24, 1950.

BURROWS, MONTROSE THOMAS, surgeon; b. Halstead, Kan., Oct. 31, 1884; s. Thomas Forbes and Carolina Melvin (Richards) B.; grad. high sch., Halstead, 1901; A.B., University of Kansas, 1905; M.D., Johns Hopkins University, 1909; m. Flora Barbara Hege, Sept. 4, 1918; children—Bette Burrows Tanner, Helen Eugenia Ferrey, Zelta Reynolds, Loy Montrose. Fellow and asst. Rockefeller Inst. Medical Research, 1901-11; instructor in anatomy, Cornell U. Med. Sch., 1911-15; asso. in pathology and resident pathologist Johns Hopkins Med. Sch. and Hosp., 1915-17; acting prof. pathology, Washington U., 1917-20; asso. prof. surgery, same, and dir. research labs. Barnard Free Skin and Cancer Hosp., St. Louis, Mo., 1920-28; now specializing in cancer treatment and research, Pasadena, Calif. Served as 1st lt. Med. Corps, U.S. Army, 1916-19. Mem. A.M.A., A.A.A.S., Am. Assn. Antomists, Am. Soc. Exptl. Pathology, Soc. Experimental Biology and Medicine, Sigma Nu, Nu Sigma Nu, Sigma Xi. Republican. Methodist. Contributor to biological reviews. Research in tissue culture, vitamin theory of cancer, heart muscle contraction, poliomyelitis, cancer, focal infections, etc. Home: 5202 Maywood Av., Los Angeles, Calif. Office: 201 N. El Molino Av., Pasadena, Calif. Died Aug. 21, 1947.

BURROWS, WILLIAM RUSSELL, pub. utilities exec.; b. Lynn, Mass., May 20, 1872; s. William Albert and Sarah (Russell) B.; student Mass. Inst. Tech.; m. Helen Liese, 1899; children—William Russell, Alan Liese, Helen Frances (Mrs. Philip H. Reagan). Began as unskilled worker; inventor of labor saving machinery for lamp mfr. for 10 yrs.; later in various exec. positions and mgr., Edison Lamp Works; v.p. in charge mfg. Gen. Electric Co., Schenectady, N.Y., 1927-44, ret., in charge labor relations and cost reductions. Clubs: Essex Country Golf, Mohawk Golf (Schenectady). Home: 378 Oakwood Av., Orange, N.J. Office: 1 River Rd., Schenectady, N.Y., Died Mar. 2, 1955.

BURT, EDWARD ANGUS, botanist; b. Athens, Pa., Apr. 9, 1859; s. Howard Fuller and Miranda (Forsyth) B.; grad. N.Y. State Normal Sch., Albany, 1881; A.B., Harvard, 1893, A.M., 1894, Ph.D., 1895; m. Clara M. Briggs, Aug. 21, 1884; children—Angus Edward (dec.), Albert Forsyth, Farlow, Howard. Teacher, Albany Boys' Acad., 1880-85; prof. natural sci., State Normal Sch., Albany, 1885-91; prof. botany, Middlebury (Vt.) Coll., 1895-1913; asso. prof. botany, 1913-18, prof., 1918-25. Washington U., and librarian and mycologist, Mo. Bot. Garden, 1913-25. Home: Middle Grove, N.Y. Died Apr. 27, 1939.

BURT, HORACE GREELEY, engr.; b. Jan. 1849; C.E., Univ. of Mich., 1872. Began ry. service, 1868; resident engr., Mar., 1873-81, div. supt., 1881-87, chief engr., Aug., 1887-Nov., 1888, C.&N.W. Ry. Co.; gen. mgr. Fremont, Elkhorn & Mo. Valley and Sioux R.R. cos., 1888-96; gen. mgr. C.,St.P.,M.&O. Ry., July-Oct., 1896; 3d v.p. C.&N.W. Ry. Co., 1896-97; pres. U.P. R.R., 1898-1904; traveled around world, 1904-o5; cons. engr., 1905-09; receiver C.G.W. Ry., Jan.-Sept., 1909; cons. engr., Sept., 1909-11; chief engr. of com. of investigation smoke abatement and electrificaition of ry. terminals, Chicago, 1911—. Home: Oak Park, Ill. Died May 19, 1913.

BURT, JOHN, inventor, mfr.; b. Wales, N.Y., Apr. 18, 1814; s. William and Phoebe (Coles) B.; m. Julia Calkins, Dec. 3, 1835, 3 children. Dep. surveyor Mich., 1841; began constrn. railroad from Marquette to Lake Superior, completed in 1857; 1st supt. Saulte St. Marie Canal; devised number of improvements for manufacture of pig and wrought iron, involving methods of carbonization (patented 1869); Patented type of canal lock 1867, put into use, 1881; Republican elector-at-large, 1868; pres. Lake Superior & Peninsula Iron Co., Burt Freestone Co. Died Detroit Aug. 16, 1886.

BURT, WILLIAM AUSTIN, inventor, surveyor; b. Worcester, Mass., June 13, 1792; s. Alvin and Wealthy (Austin) B.; m. Phoebe Cole 1813; 5 children, including John. Served as justice of peace, postmaster, county surveyor Detroit; invented the typographer (predecessor of typewriter), patented, 1829; elected surveyor Macomb County, 1841; apptd. dist. surveyor in Mich; asso. judge Mich. Circuit Ct., 1833; postmaster Mt. Vernon (Mich.); apptd. U.S. dep. surveyor Washington D.C. by Gen. Land Office, constructed solar compass, patented, 1836, equatorial sextant, patented, 1856; mem. Mich., Territorial Legislative Council 1826-27; mem. Mich. Legislature, 1853, chmn. com. internal improvements. Recipient Scott medal Franklin Inst., 1840. Died Detroit, Aug. 18, 1858.

BURTON, EDWARD FRANCIS, aero. engring. exec.; b. Rock Island, Ill., Nov. 6, 1899; s. John R. and Mary A. (Hulsbrink) B.; student U. Ill., 1918, Cal. Inst. Tech., 1925; m. Mary A. Lewis, May 28, 1923; children—John L., James T. With Douglas Aircraft Co., Santa Monica, Cal., 1924—, successively draftsman, armament engr., project engr., designer, chief designer and asst. chief engr., chief engr., 1924-58, v.p. and dir.-engring., transport aircraft systems, 1958-60, vice president for engineering, 1960—. Fellow Institute of Aero. Scis.; member Nat. Def. Transportation Assn., Am. Rocket Soc. Club: Los Angeles Country. Home: 515 Homewood Rd., Los Angeles 49. Office: 3000 Ocean Park Blvd., Santa Monica, Cal. Died Apr. 1962.

BURTON, GEORGE DEXTER, inventor; b. Temple, N.H., Oct. 26, 1855; s. Dexter L. and Emily F. B.; ed. Appleton Acad. and Comer's Commercial Coll., Boston; m. Frances C. Jones, Jan. 1894. Editor and pub. New England Star, New Ipswich, N.H., 1873-77. Inventor of the Burton stock car, especially well known for his inventions of a liquid process of heating and welding metals by an electric current; pres. Am. Electric Forge Co.; invented process of unhairing and tanning animal skins and hides by electricity; also process of degumming and separating vegetable fibres by electricity, etc. Pres. Electro-chem. Pulp and Paper Co., Reno (Nev.) Reduction Works; pres. The Burton Co., Mills at Clinton and Holliston, Mass. Lecturer on heating and working metals by electricity before Harvard Lecture Club of Jefferson Physical Lab., Harvard Coll., before Soc. of Arts of M.I.T., Franklin Inst., etc. Had received over 500 U.S. and foreign patents; awarded more than a dozen gold and silver medals from scientific and corporate instns. for various discoveries and inventions. Home: New Ipswich, N.H. Died Jan. 7, 1918.

BURTON, HARRY EDWARD, astronomer; b. Onawa, Ia., June 11, 1878; s. William and Sarah Martha (Van Dorn) B.; A.B., U. of Ia., 1901, M.S., 1903; fellow in mathematics, State U. of Ia., 1902-03; m. Ina Burroughs Robinson, Aug. 22, 1911. Apptd. computer, U.S. Naval Obs., Feb. 1, 1909; advanced through the grades to prin. astronomer; head of equatorial div. since July 1, 1929. Mem. Am. Astron. Soc., Iinternat. Astron. Union. Sigma Xi. Discovered, May 8, 1915, the separation of Comet Mellish (1915a) into 2 components; derived new elements of orbits of satellites of Mars and redetermined position of equator of Mars in 1929 (A.J. 929). Wrote introduction to Observations of Double Stars, 1928-44. Received letter of commendation from Sec. of Navy, 1935. Co-author of Publications, U.S. Naval Observator, Second Series, Vol. XII. Editor Manual of Field Astronomy, for Naval Officers detailed to Hydrographic Surveys. Contbr. to Astronomical Joural. Address: U.S. Naval Observator, Washington 25, D.C. Died July 19, 1948.

BURTON, LAURENCE V(REELAND), consultant; b. Aurora, Ill., Apr. 15, 1889; s. Charles Pierce and Cora Lena (Vreeland) B.; B.S., U. Ill., 1911, M.S., 1914; Ph.D., Yale University, 1917; m. Isabel Clegg, Aug. 17, 1921 (deceased on August 12, 1965). With Libby, McNeil & Libby, 1915-17, 22-24, Nat. Canners Assn., 1919-21, Ill. Canners Assn., 1921-22, Foulds Milling Co., 1924-28, McGraw-Hill Pub. Co., 1928-47; exec. dir. Packaging Inst., N.Y.C., 1947-55, cons. food processing and packaging, from 1955; contbg. editor Package Engring. Leader 2-man Reverse Flow team under ECA invited by Anglo-Am. Council on Prodn. to visit Eng., 1951. Served as pvt. to 1st lt. San Corps, World War I; corr. SWPA, 1944, Combined Intelligence Objectives Survey, 1945. Recipient Internat. award Inst. Food Technologists, 1957. Mem. Am. Soc. Testing Materials, Tech. Assn. Pulp and Paper Industry, Inst. Food Technologists (pres. 1941-42), Am. Chem. Soc., Soc. Am. Microbiologists, Am. Assn. Cereal Chemists, Packing Inst., Met. Bakery Prodn. Men's Assn., N.Y. Acad. Scis., Soc. for Investigation of Recurring Events, Phi Kappa Sigma, Phi Tau Sigma. Club: Yale (N.Y.C.). Author: Week-End Painter, 1948. Contbr. profl. jours. Home: Scarsdale NY Died July 9, 1970.

BURTON-OPITZ, RUSSELL, physician, physiologist; b. Ft. Wayne, Ind., Oct. 25, 1875; s. Charles and Anna B.; M.D., Rush Med. Coll., 1895; S.B., U. Chgo., 1897; post-grad. work, 1897-98, S.M., 1902, Ph.D., 1905; post-grad. U. Vienna, 1898; m. Jeanette Jonassen, 1909 (dec. 1930); 1 dau., Arlyn; m. 2d, Elizabeth Elliot Phillips Cordts, 1932. Asst. in physiology U. Breslau, 1898-1901; investigator Marine Biol. Sta., Naples, 1901; asst. in physiology Harvard, 1901-02; asst. Columbia, 1902-03, instr., 1903-04, adj. prof., 1904-10, asso. prof. physiology, 1909-23, head dept. of physiology, 1909-11. lectr. in physiology, 1923—; cons. physician Cumberland Hosp.; cons. diseases of heart Lenox Hill, Englewood, North Hudson, Holy Name, Christ, Hackensack hosps. (all N.Y.C.). Fellow A.A.A.S.; mem. A.M.A., Am. Physiol. Soc., Soc. Exptl. Medicine and Biology, Am. Soc. Naturalists, Deutsche Physiol. Gesellschaft, Am. Soc. Biol. Chemists, Medical Soc. State N.Y., New York County Med. Soc., Am. Soc. Pharm. and Exptl. Therapy, N.Y. Cardiol. Soc. (pres.), Sigma Xi, Alpha Omega Alpha (pres.). Contbr. to Am. and fgn. physiol. and med. jours. Author: Text Book of Physiology, 1920; Advanced Lessons in Practical Physiology, 1920; Elementary Manual of Physiology. Home: 218 Bridle Way, Palisade, N.J. Died Nov. 18, 1954.

BURWELL, ARTHUR WARNER, chemist; b. Rock Island, Ill., Aug. 26, 1867; s. Charles A. and Cornellia P. (Bonnell) B.; student Kaiser Wilhelm Univ., Strassburg, Germany (Ph.D.); m. Bertha Schade, Dec. 22, 1898; children—Richard Bonnell, Oliver Peckham, Cornelia. Chemist Standard Oil Co., 1893-98; consulting chemist to 1922; research in oxidation of petroleum hydrocarbons, 1922-26; practical oxidation of petroleum hydrocarbons since 1926; v.p. and tech. dir. Alox Corp., Niagara Falls, N.Y. Awarded gold medal by Western N.Y. Sec. of Am. Chem. Soc. for "work in producing and utilizing fatty acids and other chemicals from petroleum" 1941. Mem. Am. Chem. Soc., German Chem. Soc., Automotive Engrs., Am. Soc. Testing Materials, Electrochem. Soc., Am. Petroleum Ins., Am. Inst. Chemistry. Republican. Mason (32 deg., Shriner). Clubs: Rotary, Torch. Author: Oiliness, 1935; also many articles to tech. jours. on decomposition of petroleum hydrocarbons, lubricants, etc. Holds many patents in mfr. of lubricants, etc. Home: Crescent Drive, Tuscorora Park, Wilson, N.Y. Office: Alox Corp., 3943 Buffalo Av., Niagra Falls, N.Y. Died May 24, 1946.

BURWELL, CHARLES SIDNEY, physician, educator; b. Denver, Colo., Apr. 10, 1893; s. Charles Sidney and Elizabeth (Clark) B.; A.B., Allegheny Coll., Meadville, Pa., 1914, LL.D., 1936; M.D., Harvard Med. Sch., 1919; S.D. (hon.) Syracuse U., 1944; m. Edith Mary Churchill, Oct. 10, 1922; children—Sidney Moseley, Eleanor Churchill. Med. house pupil Mass. Gen. Hosp., Boston, Mass., 1919-20; with Am. Red. Cross Commn. to West Russia, 1920; asso. prof. med., Vanderbilt Med. Sch. Nashville, Tenn., 1925-28, prof., 1928-35; vis. chief, 1928-35; dean faculty of med. Harvard Med. Sch., 1935-49, research prof. clin. med., 1935-55, Levine prof. med. emeritus, 1959—; physician Peter Bent Brigham Hosp., 1935-59; vis. physician 1959—. Recipient John Phillips Meml. award Med. Assn., Am. Coll. of Physicians, Am. Acad. Arts and Scis.; mem. Am. Soc. for Clin. Investigation (pres. 1933-34), Assn. Am. Phys., Am. Clin. and Climatol. Assn. (pres. 1942-43), Am. Heart Assn. Author: (with James Metcalfe) Heart Disease and Pregnancy, 1958. Home: 416 Marlborough St. Office: 25 Shattuck St., Boston 15. Died Sept. 1967.

BUSEY, SAMUEL CLAGETT, M.D.; b. on farm in Montgomery Co., Md., July 23, 1828; attended Rockville Acad.; M.D., Univ. of Pa., 1848 (LL.D., St. Mary's Univ., Baltimore). In practice, Washington. Pres. Med. Soc. of D.C., 1877, 1894-98; prof. materia medica, diseases of infancy and childhood, and theory and practice of medicine at different periods, and became emeritus prof. theory and practice of medicine, med. dept., Georgetown Univ., Washington, D.C. Author: Occlusion and Dilatation of Lymph Channels, acquired Forms; Lymph Channels. Died 1901.

BUSH, KATHARINE JEANNETTE, zoölogist; b. Scranton, Pa., Dec. 30, 1855; d. William Henry and Eliza Ann (Clark) B.; ed. New Haven pvt. and pub. schs. and New Haven High Sch.; studied many yrs. under Prof. A.E. Verrill; Ph.D., Yale, 1901; unmarried. Asst. Zoöl. dept. Yale U. Mus., 1879—; on U.S. Fish Commn. several yrs.; assisted in revision of Webster's Dictionary, resulting in Webster's Internat. Dictionary, edit. of 1890. Author: The Tubicolous Annelids of the Tribes Sabellides and Serpulides-Harriman Alaska Expedition, Vol. XII, 1905. Home: New Haven, Conn. Died 1937.

BUSH, LINCOLN, civil engr.; b. Cook Co., Ill., Dec. 14, 1860; s. Lewis and Mary (Ritchie) B.; M.S., Cook County Normal School, 1880; B.S., U. of Ill., 1888, hon. D.Engring., 1904; m. Alma R. Green, 1890; children—Cedric Lincoln, Denzil Sidney. Asst. engr. U/P. R.R. and Pacific Short Line, 1888-90; asst. engr. with E. L. Corthell, 1890-92; chief draftsman, West Office Pittsburgh Bridge Co., 1892-96; asst. bridge engr. and acting div. engr. C.&N.W.R.R., 1896-99; bridge engr., 1899-1900, prin. asst. engr., 1900-03, chief engr., D.,L.&W. Railroad, 1903-08; then retired. Inventor of a new method of constructing concrete and pile footings; also the Bush train shed, Bush track constrn. Col. Q.M.C., U.S.A., World War. Home: Kansas City, Mo. Died Dec. 10, 1940.

BUSHNELL, DAVID; inventor; b. Saybrook, Conn., 1742; grad. Yale, 1775. Completed man-propelled submarine boat, 1775; orginator modern submarine warfare; capt.-lt. Continental Army, 1779, capt., 1781. Died Warrenton, Ga. 1824.

BUSHNELL, DAVID I., JR., anthropologist; b. St. Louis, Mo., Apr. 28, 1875; s. David I. and Belle (Johnston) B.; ed. in St. Louis and abroad. Asst. in archaeology, Peabody Mus., Harvard, 1901-04; in Europe, 1904-07, studying collections in various museums and associated in field exploration in Italy and Switzerland. Fellow A.A.A.S., Royal Anthropol. Inst. of London; mem. Anthropol. Soc. of Washington, Washington Acad. Sciences, Va. Hist. Soc., Minn. Hist. Soc., Phi Beta Kappa; hon. mem. La. Hist. Soc. Episcopalian. Author: The Sloane Collection in the British Museum, 1906; Ethnological Material from North America in Swiss Collections, 1908; Archaeological Investigations in Ste. Genevieve County, Missouri, 1914; The Five Monacan Towns in Virginia, 1607, 1930; also bulls. of Bureau of Ethnology, The Choctaw of Bayou Lacomb, Louisiana, 1909; Villages of the Algonquian, Siouan, and Caddoan Tribes West of the Mississippi, 1922; Burials of the Algonquian, Siouan, and Caddoan Tribes West of the Mississippi, 1927. Club: Cosmos. Address: Care Smithsonian Institution, Washington DC

BUSHNELL, WINTHROP GRANT, elec. engr.; b. New Haven, Conn., Mar. 20, 1864; s. Cornelius S. and Emilie Fowler (Clark) B.; B.A., Yale, 1888; m. Harriet Elizabeth Scofield, June 7, 1911. Night editor New Haven Journal and Courier, 1889; commercial elec. engr. with Edison Electric Co. and Gen. Electric Co., 1890-1906; owner and mgr. various pub. utilities, water powers, etc.; v.p. Conn. Power Co. State chmn. Y.M.C.A. and chmn. exec. com. New Haven Chapter Am. Red Cross, 1917; Conn. state chmn. United War Work Campaign, 1918. Republican. Conglist. Home: New Haven, Conn. Died Oct. 23, 1921.

BUSWELL, ARTHUR MOSES, chemist; b. Madison, Wis., Mar. 20, 1888; s. James Oliver and Emeline (Porter) B.; grad. Carroll Acad., Waukesha, Wis., 1906; A.B., U. Minn., 1910; A.M., U. Me., 1912; Ph.D., Columbia, 1917; m. Helen Stobie, July 8, 1912 (div.); children—Robert James, Arthur Alexander (dec.); m. 2d, Marian Winifred Marshall, Apr. 13, 1941; 1 dau., Mary Ann. Instr. chemistry U. Me., 1910-12, Columbia, 1913-20; asso. prof. san. chemistry, U. Ill., 1920-22, prof., 1922-31, prof. chemistry, 1931-44; research prof., 1945-55, emeritus, 1955; research prof. chemistry U. Fla., 1955—. Chief Ill. State Water Survey, 1920-55, Ofcl. investigator Nat. Def. Research Com. 1941-43, 1st lt. San. Corps, U.S. Army, with 1st Div., A.E.F., 1917-18, capt., 1918-19; maj. San. Corps, Med. Research, Edgewood Arsenal June 29, 1943-Jan. 7, 1945. Civilian cons. Chem. Warfare Service 1945-46. Received Army Commendation Ribbon with citation, 1946. Fellow N.Y. Acad. Scis., A.A.A.S., Am. Pub. Health Assn., Am. Inst. Chemists; mem. Am. Chem. Soc., Royal Soc. Health U.K., Am. Water Works Assn. (Fuller award 1953), Am. Microscopic Soc., Soc. Chem. Industry, Sigma Xi, Phi Lambda Upsilon, Alpha Chi Sigma. Democrat. Presbyn. Clubs: University (Urbana); University, Chaos (Chicago). Author: The Chemistry of Water and Sewage Treatment, 1928. Editor 6th edit. Mason's Water Examination, 1931. Chem. referee of Water Analysis, Contbr. to Jour. Am. Chem. Soc., Bulls. Ill. State Water Survey, others, Outdoor Am. Author numerous patents on fermentation. Home: 2713 S.W. 5th Pl., Gainesville, Fla. Died June 6, 1966; buried Mount Hope Cemetery, Urbana, Ill.

BUTLER, AMOS WILLIAM, zoölogist; b. Brookville, Ind., Oct. 1, 1860; s. William Wallace and Hannah (Wright) B.; A.B., Indiana U., 1894, A.M., 1900, LL.D., 1922; LL.D., Hanover Coll., 1915; m. Mary I. Reynolds, June 2, 1880; children—Mrs. Carrie Hannah Watts, Mrs. Alice Kaylor (dec.), Wm. Reynolds, Gwyn Foster, Mrs. Anne Harrison, Hadley Butler (Dec.). Ornithologist, dept. of geology and resources of Ind., 1896-97; sec. Ind. Bd. State Charities, 1897-1923. Mem. White House Children's Conf., 1909. Lecturer on economics, Purdue U., 1905. Pres. Nat. Conf. Charities and Corrections, 1906-07; chmn. Am. com. on Internat. Prison Congress, Washington, 1910; mem. Am. Prison Assn.; v.p. Internat. Prison Congress; del from U.S. to Internat. Prison Congress, London (v.p. sec. 2), 1925, Prague, 1930; pres. Ind. Conf. Charities and Correction, 1915; fellow A.A.A.S.; chmn. exec. com. Ind. Soc. for Mental Hygiene, 1918-25, pres., 1925-30, emeritus; sec. Ind. Com. on Mental Defectives, 1915; senior sociologist U.S. Bureau of Efficiency, 1928-29; founder Internat. Com. on Mental Hygiene, Washington, 1930; mem. advisory com. to Nat. Commn. on Law Observance and Enforcement, 1928-31; sec. Ind. Com. on Observance and Enforcement of Law, 1929-31; mem. exec. bd. Am. Inst. of Criminal Law and Criminology, 1935—. Author: Birds of Indiana; Also Indiana—A Century of Progress, The Development of Public Charities and Corrections. Home: Indianapolis, Ind. Died Aug. 5, 1937.

BUTLER, BERT S. geologist; b. Grainesville, N.Y., Mar. 30, 1877; s. Dexter W. and Desire (Hawley) B.; grad. Geneseo State Normal Sch., 1899; A.B., Cornell, 1905, A.M., 1907; D.Sc., Colo. Coll. Mines, 1929; m. Elizabeth Martin (dec.), Feb. 17, 1908; children—Lawrence Proctor (dec.), Waldo Dexter; m. 2d, Mrs. Loretta Bergen Caine, Dec. 24, 1928. Instr. geology, Cornell U., 1905-07; mem. U.S. Geol. Survey, 1907-20; geologist Calumet & Hecla Mining Co., 1920-24; geologist U.S. Geol. Survey 1924-47; prof. geology, U. of Arizona since 1928. Penrose medalist, Soc. of Econ. Geologist, 1947. Mem. Geol. Soc. America, Am. Inst. Mining and Metall. Engrs., Soc. Economic Geologists (president 1933), Am. Assn. Advancement of Science. Author numerous reports, papers, articles on ore deposits. Home: 1838 Drachman St., Tucson. Died Nov. 20, 1960; buried South Lawn Meml. Park, Tucson.

BUTLER, ELMER GRIMSHAW, biologist; b. Parish, N.Y., Feb. 13, 1900; s. Frank Alexander and Elizabeth Jane (Grimshaw) B.; A.B., Syracuse U., 1921; A.M., Princeton U., 1925, Ph.D., 1926; hon. Sc.D., Syracuse

U., 1941; m. Eleanor Brill, June 30, 1927. Instr. zoology, U. of Vt., 1921-23; fellow in biology, Princeton U., 1923-26, instr. biology, 1926-28, asst. prof., 1928-31, asso. prof., 1931-37, Class of 1877 prof. of zoology, Princeton U., 1937-60, Henry Fairfield Osborn prof. biology, from 1960, chmn. dept. biology, 1933-48. Asso. editor, Journal of Morphology, 1941-43; mng. editor, 1946-54. Mem. editorial board Journal of Experimental Zoology, American Zoologist, also Biological Bulletin, 1955-58; cons. editor Developmental Biology. Mem. vis. com. for the biological sciences Johns Hopkins. Trustee Asso. Univs., Inc. (Brookhaven National Laboratory). Chmn. Am. Inst. Biol. Scis., 1949-50; chmn. cell biology study sect. Nat. Insts. Health, 1959-72. John Simon Guggenhiem Fellow, 1950. Fellow International Institute Embryology, A.A.A.S., New York Acad. Sci.; mem. Am. Soc. Zoologists (pres. 1956-57); Am. Soc. Naturalists, Am. Assn. Anatomists, Soc. for Exptl. Biol. and Medicine, Soc. for Growth and Development (pres. 1951-52), American Society for Cell Biology, Marine Biological Laboratory, Woods Hole (trustee), Bermuda Biol. Station, Am. Philos. Society, Mt. Desert Island Biol. Lab., Internat. Soc. Cell Biology, Phi Beta Kappa, Sigma Xi, Phi Kappa Psi. Presbyn. Club: Nassau (Princeton). Author sci. articles on normal and experimental embryology, including development of blood-vascular system in man and other mammals, effects of X-radiation on embryonic development, studies on regeneration. Home: Princeton NJ Died Feb. 23, 1972; buried Parish NY

BUTLER, ETHAN FLAGG, surgeon; b. Yonkers, N.Y., Jan. 4, 1884; s. Charles Henry and Marcia (Flagg) B.; grad. Hotchkiss Sch., Lakeville, Conn., 1902; A.B., Princeton, 1906; M.D., Johns Hopkins, 1910; m. Margaret M. Renshaw, Dec. 18, 1915; 1 dau., Agnes Reeves; m. 2d, Mrs. Edith Halliday; stepchildren—Gordon Halliday, Florence Halliday. Vol. asst. Labrador Med. Mission, summers 1908-10; asst., Mayo Clinic, Rochester, Minn., 1911-14; dir. A.R.C. (Serbia), 1914-15; mem. M.C. U.S. Army, 1917-20; chief surg. service Polyclinic Hosp., N.Y.C., 1920; adj. asst. attending surgeon 2d surg. div., Bellevue Hosp., 1920-21; asst. attending surgeon N.Y. Skin and Cancer Hosp., 1921-22; asso. surgeon Robert Packer Hosp., Sayre, Pa., 1922-29; dir. chest service Arntho-Ogden Meml. Hosp., Elmira, 1929-36; prin. thoracic surgeon N.Y. State Dist. Tb hosps., 1936-43; cons. surg. Onondaga Sanatorium, 1943-44; mem. med., surg. dept. VA 1947, 54, ret., 1954. Lt. col. ret. Diplomate Am. Bd. Surgery, Bd. Thoracic Surgery. Fellow A.C.S.; mem. A.M.A., Am. Assn. Thoracic Surgery (sec. 1924-28, v.p. 1930, pres. 1931), Mayo Alumni, Am. Broncho-Esophagol. Assn., N.Y. Soc. Thoracic Surgery (pres. 1936); Upstate Soc. Thoracic Surgeons (pres. 1946), N.Y. State Med. Soc., Assn. Mil. Surgeons U.S., Am. Legion. Decorated Comdr. Order of St. Sava and Serbian Red Cross medal. Republican. Presbyn. Club: Princeton (N.Y.); Country (Elmira). Contbr. articles on gen. and thoracic surgery. Home: 956 W. Water St., Elmira, N.Y. Died Jan. 27, 1964.

BUTLER, GEORGE FRANK, physician, author; b. Moravia, N.Y., Mar. 15, 1857; s. Isaac and Asenath (Chase) B.; grad. Baldwin's Acad., Groton, N.Y., 1874; pharmacist, Pittsfield, Mass., 1874-78; in sheep and drug business, southwestern Kan., 1878-86; M.D., Rush Med. Coll., Chicago, 1889; (hon. A.M., Valparaiso U., 1908); m. Nannie Blanche Porter, Mar. 21, 1882. Lecturer med. pharmacy and materia medica, Rush Med. Coll., 1889-92; prof. materia medica, and clin. medicine, Northwestern U. Women's Med. Sch., 1890-96, Coll. Phys. and Surg., Chicago, 1892-1906; prof. medicine, Dearborn Med. Coll., 1905-06; prof. internal medicine, Chicago Post-Grad. Med. Sch., 1905-07; med. supt. Alma Springs Sanitarium, Alma., Mich., 1900-05; prof. and head dept. therapeutics, and prof. clin. and preventive medicine, Chicago Coll. Medicine and Surgery, 1906-15, emeritus, 1915—; pres. faculty and prof. diseases of kidneys and nervous system, Practitioners' Coll., Chicago, 1910-12; co. phys. of Cook Co., Ill., Nov. 1911-13; med. dir. North Shore Health Resort, Winnetka. Author: Textbook of Materia Medica, Therapeutics and Pharmacology, 1896. Home: Wilmett, Ill. Died June 22, 1921.

BUTLER, RALPH otolaryngologist; b. Loag, Pa.; s. James and Rachel M. (James) B.; B.E., West Chester State Normal Sch. (now West Chester Tchrs. Coll.), 1893; M.D., U. Pa., 1900; studied diseases of ear, nose and throat, Vienna, 1901-02, Berlin, 2 mos., 1906; m. Ida Shaw, Dec. 18, 1905. Resident St. Joseph's Hosp., Phila., 1900-01; asst. aural surgeon U. Pa., 1902-06, instr. in otology, 1907-16, asst. prof. otology, 1916-24, prof. laryngology and vice dean of otolaryngology, grad. school of medicine, 1918-46, emeritus prof. laryngology, 1946—; prof. diseases of nose and throat Phila. Polyclinic and Coll. for Graduates in Medicine, 1912-18; cons. otolaryngology Lankenau Hosp., Drexel Home and Women's Hosp. of Phila. Fellow A.C.S.; mem. A.M.A., Am. Otol. Soc., Am. Laryngol. Assn., Am. Laryngol., Rhinol. and Otol. Soc., Med. Soc. State Pa., Phila. County Med. Soc., Phila. Med. Club, Alpha Kappa Kappa. Republican. Presybn. Mason. Address: 1930 Chestnut St., Phila., 3. Died Apr. 1954.

BUTTERICK, EBENEZER, inventor; b. Sterling, Mass., May 29, 1826; s. Francis and Ruhamah (Buss) B.; m. Ellen. Became tailor and shirt-maker, Sterling; idea conceived (by him or his wife) for method of unlimited reproduction of shirts with set of garded shirt patterns, circa 1859; placed 1st patterns on market, 1863, moved to larger town of Fitchburg, Mass., because of success, 1863; upon wife's suggestion made patterns for boys' suits ("Garibaldi" suits modeled from uniform of internat. hero Guiseppe Garibaldi); opened office on Broadway, N.Y.C., 1864, extended patterns to women's garments; formed (with J. W. Wilder and A.W. Pollard) E. Butterick & Co., 1867, opened branches in London, Paris, Berlin and Vienna, by 1876; reorganized firm as Butterick Publishing Co., Ltd., 1881, served as sec., 1881-94. Died Mar. 31, 1903.

BUTTRAM, FRANK, oil co. exec.; b. Chickasaw Nation, I.T., Apr. 2, 1886; s. Abe and Almira (Starritt) B.; A.B., U. Okla., 1910, A.M., 1912; m. Merle E. Newby, Feb. 18, 1914; children—Myron Franklin and Merle Frances (twins), Dorsey Randall, Donald A., Harold Eugene. Chemist and geologist, Okla. Geol. Survey, 1911-14; an organizer, later chief geologist and gen. mgr., Fortuna Oil Co., 1914-20; organizer, 1920, and owner Buttram Petroleum Corp., Oklahoma City; chmn. bd. Fed. Res. Bank, Okla. Div., 1926; dir. First Nat. Bank & Trust Co. Chmn. bd. of regents U. Okla., 1923-30; nat. chmn. Stadium-Union Meml. Dr., U. Okla.; chmn. State Recovery Bd. for Okla. under NRA, also state recovery council, NRA; chmn. Com. of 100 to establish city mgr. form of govt. for Oklahoma City Provident Assn.; mem. exec. com. Internat. Conv. Disciples of Christ. Mem. Petroleum Industry War Council, 1941-43. Mem. Am. Inst. Mining and Metall. Engrs., Am. Assn. Petroleum Geologists, Mid-Continent Oil and Gas Assn. (pres. 1939-43). Clubs: Beacon, Golf and Country, Twin Hills Golf and Country, Home: 7316 Nichols Rd., Oklahoma City 6. Office: First Nat. Bank Bldg., Oklahoma City, 2. Died Dec. 1966.

BUTTS, CHARLES, geologist; b. Portville, N.Y., Sept. 18, 1863; s. William Othello and Eliza Jane (Southworth) B.; B.S., Alfred (N.Y.) U., 1899; M.S., 1900; D.Sc., U. Ala., 1927; m. Mellye Arledge, Nov. 1903; m. 2d, Ella Virginia Rickles Pearson, Nov. 30, 1909. Field asst., U.S. Geol. Survey, 1900; asst. to N.Y. state palcontologist, 1900-01; asst. geologist, U.S. Geol. Survey, 1901-09, paleontoloeist, 1909-12, geologist, 1912-33, retired; geologist Va. Geol. Survey, 1933, 37. Mem. Geol. Soc. Am., Geol. Soc. Washington, Washington Acad. Sciences. Republican. Presbyn. Contbr. to geol. periodicals. Home: 1808 Kenyon St. N.W. Washington. Died Oct. 4, 1946.

BUTTS, EDWARD, civil engr.; b. Rensselaer Co., N.Y., Aug. 16, 1853; s. Anson and Anna (Stadler) B.; self ed.; learned surveying in boyhood, his father being civil engr., m. Hannah Knight, of Kansas City, Mo., Oct. 28, 1883. Asst. engr. 2 terms, city engr. 2 terms, Kansas City; chief engr. Met. St. Ry. Co. 15 yrs. Sec. Civil Service Bd., Kansas City, 1912. Curator Pub. Library Museum (devoted to science and art) since 1917; Pres. Kansas City Science Club, 1924-25. Author: Civil Engineers' Field Book, 1885; The Swastica, 1908; The Triskelion, 1926; Polaris, 1927; Along Old Trails, 1936. Contbr. on engring. subjects. Home: 3402 Prospect Av., Kansas City, Mo.

BUWALDA, JOHN PETER, prof. geology; b. Zeeland, Mich. Dec. 16, 1886; s. Peter John and Eva (Takoma) B.; B.S., U. of Calif., 1912, Ph.D., 1915; m. Irma Wann, Aug. 17, 1917; children—Peter John, May, William John, Robert John. Instr. in geology, U. of Calif., 1915-17; asst. prof. geology, Yale U., 1917-21; asso. prof. U. of Calif., 1921-25, prof., 1925-26, dean of summer sessions, 1923-26; prof. geology and head of div. geol. sciences, Calif. Inst. Tech., 1926-47, prof. geology, 1954—. Research asso., Carnegie Instn.; Professor of Geol. Cal. Inst. Tech. 1947-54, mem. federal bd. expert advisers on Yosemite Nat. Park, Mem. A.A.A.S., Geol. Soc. America, Seismological Soc. America (dir.), Am. Assn. Petroleum Geologists, Am. Assn. Univ. Profs., Sigma Alpha Epsilon, Sigma Xi, Theta Tau, Gamma Alpha. Republican. Club: Faculty (Calif. Inst. Tech.). Home: 2103 San Pasqual St., Pasadena 10, Cal. Died Aug. 19, 1954.

BUXTON, CHARLES LEE, obstetrician and gynecologist; b. Superior, Wis., Oct. 14, 1904; s. Edward Timothy and Lucinda (Lee) B.; B.S., Princeton, 1927; M.D., Columbia, 1932, Med. Sc.D., 1940; M.A. (honorary), Yale, 1954; m. Helen Morgan Rotch, Sept. 3, 1938 (div.); children—Timothy, Anthony, Edward, Lucinda; m. 2d, Margaret P. Mithoefer. Intern Bassett Hosp., Cooperstown, N.Y., 1932-33; fellow endocrinology, med. sch. Harvard, 1933-34; resident Sloane Hosp. for Women, 1934-38, dir. endocrine clinic, 1938-54, asso. attending obstetrician, 1947-54; instr. obstetrics and gynecology Coll. Phys. and Surg. Columbia, 1938-46, asso. prof., 1947; prof. obstetrics and gynecology, 1954-69, chmn. dept., sch. med. Yale, 1954-66; member consulting staff William W. Backus Hosp., Norwich, Conn., Charlotte Hungerford Hosp., Torrington, Conn., Meriden (Conn.) Hosp., New Britain (Conn.) Gen. Hosp., Stamford (Conn.) Hosp. Hartford Hosp., Sharon Hosp. Served as comdr. USNR, 1942-45. Recipient of Albert Lasker award, 1965. Diplomate Am. Bd. of Obstetrics and Gynecology (dir.). Fellow Am. College of Obstetrics and Gynecology; (first vice president 1963-1964, chairman district I, 1961-64); mem. A.M.A., Am. Endocrine Soc., Am. Soc. Study Sterility (pres. 1959-60, dir.), Am. Assn. Obstetricians and Gynecologists, New England, New Haven obstet. socs., Am. Gynec. Soc., Conn. Obstetrics Soc. (pres. 1955-56), Soc. Obstetricians and Gynecologists of Can., Assn. Profs. Gynecology Soc. Gynecol. Investigation, Sociedad Esterilidad Brasileria, Sociede de Obstetricia e Gynecologia de Brasil Soc. Royal Belge de Gynecologei etd' Obstetrique, Brit. Society for Study Fertility, Sigma Xi. Presbyterian. Author, co-author books on gynecology, endocrinology and sterility; contbr. med. jours. Asso. editor Jour. Fertility and Sterility. Home: New Haven CT Died July 7, 1969.

BYERLY, WILLIAM ELWOOD, mathematician; b. Phila., Dec. 13, 1849; s. Elwood B.; A.B., Harvard, 1871, Ph.D., 1873; m. Alice Worcester Parsons, May 28, 1885; children—Robert Wayne, Francis Parkman; m. 2d, Anne Carter Wickham Renshaw, July 23, 1921. Asst. prof. mathematics, Cornell, 1873-76; asso. prof. mathematics, 1876-81, prof., 1881-1913, prof. emeritus, Harvard. Fellow Am. Acad. Arts and Sciences, etc. Author: Elements of Differential Calculus, 1879; Elements of Integral Calculus, 1881; An Elementary Treatise on Fourier's Series and Spherical, Cylindrical and Ellipsoidal Harmonics, 1893; Problems in Differential Calculus, 1895; Generalized Coördinates, 1916; Introduction to the Calculus of Variations, 1917. Died 1935.

BYFORD, HENRY TRUMAN, gynecologist; b. Evansville, Ind., Nov. 12, 1853; s. Dr. William H. and Anne (Holland) B.; grad. Williston Sem., 1870; M.D., Chicago Med. Coll. (Northwestern U.), 1873; m. Lucy Larned, Nov. 8, 1882. Engaged in practice in Chicago; prof. gynecology, Coll. of Medicine of U. of Illinois, Chicago, 1892-1913, emeritus; cons. gynecologist, St. Luke's and Chicago Lying-In hosps. Fellow American Coll. Surgeons. Author: Manual of Gynecology; To Panama and Back, 1908; Diseases of Women (with late Dr. William Heath Byford). Joint author: American Text Book of Gynecology; Kelly and Noble's Operative Gynecology. Home: Chicago, Ill. Died June 5, 1938.

BYFORD, WILLIAM HEATH, gynecologist, educator; b. Eaton, O., Mar. 20, 1817; s. Henry T. and Hannah B.; M.D., Ohio Med. Coll., 1845; m. Mary Ann Holland, Oct. 3, 1840; m. 2d, Lina Flersheim, 1873. Apptd. prof. anatomy Evansville Med. Coll., 1850; prof. obstetrics and diseases of women and children Rush Med. Coll., Chgo. Med. Coll., 1859. Author med. works including Treaties on the Theory and Practice of Obstetrics, 1870. Died Chgo., May 21, 1890.

BYRD, RICHARD EVELYN, explorer, naval officer (ret.); b. Winchester, Va., Oct. 25, 1888; s. Richard Evelyn and Eleanor Bolling (Flood) B.; ed. Shenandoah Valley Mil. Acad., Va. Mil. Inst. and U. of Va.; grad. U.S. Naval Acad., 1912; m. Marie D. Ames, of Boston, Mass., Jan. 20, 1915. Ensign U.S. Navy, 1912; advanced through grades to lt. comdr.; ret. Mar. 15, 1916; promoted to grade to comdr. after north polar flight, 1926; promoted to rank of rear adm., 1930. Entered Aviation Service Aug. 1917; comdr. U.S. Air Forces of Can., July 1918, until Armistice; comdr. aviation unit of Navy-MacMillan Polar Expdn., June-Oct. 1925; made flight in aeroplane with Floyd Bennett over North Pole and back to base at Kings Bay, Spitzbergen, May 9, 1926, covering distance of 1,360 miles in 15-1/2 hours; made trans-Atlantic flight with 3 companions, from New York to France, distance of 4,200 miles, flight lasting 42 hours, June 29-July 1, 1927; flew over South Pole, Nov. 29, 1929; made 1st expdn. to Antarctic, 1928-30, 2d expdn., 1933-May 10, 1935; on both expdns. made important discoveries, among them being Edsel Ford Mountains and Marie Byrd Land; spent 5 mos. of winter night alone at scientific work in shadow of South Pole, In 1939 was made commander of United States Antarctic Service, an expedition sent to the Antarctic by Government; made four noteworthy flights resulting in discovery of five new mountain ranges, five islands, more than 100,000 square miles of area, a large peninsula, and 700 miles of hitherto unknown stretches of antarctic coast. During World War II served with Fleet Admiral King in Washington and Fleet Admiral Nimitz in Pacific; overseas 4 times (3 times in Pacific, once, Western front in Europe); cited 4 times; apptd. commanding officer U.S. Navy Antarctic Expdn., 1946. Advisor Dept. Defense, Polar defense and strategy. Holds 18 honorary degrees from colleges and universities. Presented by President Collidge with Hubbard gold medal, June 23, 1926, for valor in exploration, awarded Congressional Medal of Honor, 1926, Special Congressional Medals (1930, 37, and 46), Congressional Life Saving Medal of Honor, Navy D.S.M., Navy Cross, Navy Flying Cross. Patron's medal of Royal Geog. Soc. (British, 1931), and gold medal Reale Societa Geografica (Italy, 1931); Elisha Kent Kane medal of Phila. Geog. Soc.; Langley medal of aerodromics of Smithsonian Inst., David Livingstone Centenary medal by Am. Geog. Soc., D.S.M. of State of N.Y. presented by Gov. Franklin D. Roosevelt; also 65 other medals; received from President Roosevelt (Sept. 1940) gold star in recognition of services as commander of U.S. Antarctic Service Expedition, 1939-41; 22 citations from Navy Dept.; twice awarded Legion of Merit medal and special citation for service in Pacific, World War II; decorations by Portuguese and

Rumanian govts.; also Officer Legion of Honor and Comdr. Legion of Honor (France) Medal, Order of Christopher Columbus, Santo Domingo; Grand Lodge Medal for Distinguished Achievement; Loczy Medal, Hungarian Geog. Society; Vega Medal, Swedish Geog. Society Mem. Phi Beta Kappa, Kappa Alpha, and about 100 other orgns. Episcopalian. Clubs: Century, Explorers (New York); Chevy Chase (Washington); Tavern, University, Somerset, Union Boat, Engineers', Country (Boston); Dedham Polo and Country. Author: Skyward, 1928; Little America, 1930; Discovery, 1935; Exploring with Byrd; Alone, 1938. Address: 9 Brimmer St., Boston. Died Mar. 11, 1957.

BYRNE, JOHN, physician; b. Kilkeel, Ireland, Oct. 13, 1825; s. Stephen and Elizabeth (Sloane) B.; M.D., U. Edinburgh (Scotland), 1846; grad. N.Y. Med. Coll., 1853. Came to Am., 1848; practiced medicine, Bklyn., 1848-1902; mem. exec. bd., also clin. prof. uterine surgery L.I. Coll. Hosp.; surgeon-in-chief St. Mary's Hosp., N.Y.C., 1858-1902; devised means of using electric cautery-knife in surgery of malignant disease of uterus. Author: Clinical Notes on the Electric Cautery in Uterine Surgery, 1872. Died Montreux, Switzerland, Oct. 1, 1902.

BYRNES, EUGENE ALEXANDER, principal examiner electrochemistry and metallurgy, U.S. Patent Office; b. Belfast, N.Y., March 3, 1862; grad. Univ. of Mich., 1884 (LL.B., LL.M., Ph.D., 1900, Columbian Univ.); m. Nov. 17, 1892, Alice Stier. Address: 2539 13th St., Washington.

CABLE, FRANK T. torpedo boat expert; b. New Milford, Conn., June 19, 1863; s. Abijah and Olive L. (Taylor) C.; ed. Claverack (N.Y.) Coll.; m. Nettie A. Hungerford, May 29, 1892. Eneaged in elec. and engring. work in minor capacities, 1890-97; supt. Holland Submarine Boat Co., 1897-1901, and as elec. engr. developed the original Holland boat, commanding her on every trip until she was sold to the U.S. Govt., 1900; conducted trials of the first submarine built by the English Govt., and trained crew to operate same, 1902; also conducted trials of Adder class of submarines for U.S. Govt., 1903; of first Holland submarine bought by the Russian Govt., and trained the crew, 1904; of 5 submarines for the Japanese Govt. and trained crews for same, 1905; consulting engineer, Electric Boat Co.; organizer, 1910, New London Ship & Engine Co., Groton, Conn. Pres. New London Building & Loan Assn.; trustee New London Savings Bank. Member Soc. Naval Architects. Republican. Conglist. Clubs: Thames, Harbour (New London); Transportation (New York) Home: New London, Conn. Office: Groton, Conn. Died May 21, 1945.

CABOT, WILLIAM BROOKS, engr.; b. Brattleboro, Vt., Feb. 2, 1858; s. Norman F. and Lucy T. (Brooks) C.; student Sheffield Scientific Sch. (Yale); C.E., Rensselaer Poly. Inst., 1881; m. Elisabeth Lyman Parker, May 29, 1886. Began in civ. engring. dept. U.P. Ry., in the West, later in iron mfg., Everett, Pa.; v.p. Holbrook; Cabot & Rollins Corp., Boston and New York, 1895-1907. Mem. Am. Antiquarian Soc., Am. Acad. Arts and Sciences, Royal Geog. Soc. (London). Episcopalian. Clubs: Explorers' Boone and Crokett (New York); Harvard Travelers; St. Botolph (Boston). Author: Labrador, 1920. Home: 447 Marlboro St., Boston, Mass. Died Jan. 30, 1949.

CADDELL, ALBERT D(AVID), engr.; b. Toronto, Can., May 20, 1888; s. Walter William and Christine Margaret (Jack) C.; ed. Pub. and Collegiate Schs. and Toronto Tech. Coll.; m. Helen Margaret Remy, Dec. 28, 1916; children—Jack Remy, William David, Helen Margaret Ligman. Came to U.S., 1912, naturalized. 1923. Works mgr. North American Watch Co., Mansfield, O., 1916-26; exec. sec. Mfrs. Club, also sec.-mgr. Chamber of Commerce and sec., treas. Mfrs. Assn. Central Ohio. 1927-34; exec. sec. and spl. rep., Div. Safety and Hygiene, Indsl. Commn. of Ohio, 1934-41; dir. safety Curtis Wright Airplane Div., Columbus, O., 1941-44; exec. sec. AM. Soc. Safety Engrs. Since 1944; former mem. Ohio Indsl. Council; former dir. Mansfield Ohio Y.M.C.A. Mem. President's Conf. on Indsl. Safety. Professional engr., Ill. Evangelical Lutheran. Mason Club: Rotary (past pres.). Editor: Engineering for Safety. Home: 2440 W. Estes Av., Chicago, 45. Office: Amer can Society of Safety Engineers, 20 N. Wacker Dr., Chgo. 6 Died Jan. 3, 1952.

CADWALADER, THOMAS, surgeon; b. Phila., 1708; s. John and Martha (Jones) C.; m. Hannah Lambert, 1738. A founder (with Benjamin Franklin) Phila. Library, 1731; performed earliest recorded autopsies in Am. 1742; subscribed to founding Pa. Hosp., 1751; trustee U. Pa., 1751; mem. Common Council of Phila., 1751-74, Provincial Council of Pa., 1755-76; signer Non-Importation Agreement of 1765; mem. Am. Philos. Soc.; on most noted 18th century Am. physicians. Died Trenton, N.J., Nov. 14, 1799.

CADY, HAMILTON PERKINS, chemist; b. Camden, Kan., May 2, 1874; s. Perkins E. and Ella M. (Falkenbury) C.; Carleton Coll., Northfield, Minn.; A.B., U. of Kan., 1897, Ph.D., 1903; grad. work Cornell, 1897-99; m. Stella C. Gallup, June 5, 1900; children—Ruth Caroline, George Hamilton, Helen Frances. Asst. prof. chemistry, 1899-1905, asso. prof., 1905-11, prof. chemistry since 1911, U. of Kan., also chmn. chem. dept. until 1040. Fellow A.A.A.S.; mem. Am. Chem. Soc., Kan. Acad. Science, Sigma Xi, Alpha Chi Sigma. Conglist. Author: (with Edgar Henry Summerfield Bailey) A Laobratory Guide to the Study of Qualitative Analysis, 1901; The Principles of Inorganic Chemistry, 1912; General Chemistry, 1916. Home: Lawrence, Kan. Died May 26, 1943.

CAGLE, FRED RAY, scientist; b. Marion, Ill., Oct. 9, 1915; s. Fred and Agnes (Guiney) C.; B.E., So. Ill. Normal U., 1937; M.S., U. Mich., 1938, Ph.D. (univ. fellow, 1941-42, Rackham fellow, 1942-43), 1943; m. Josephine Alexander, June 18, 1938; children—Fred Ray, Mary Jo. Instr. zoology, critic teacher, Univ. High Sch., So. Ill. Normal U., Carbondale, 1938-39, dir. museum, asst. prof. zoology, 1939-46, instr. gen. biology course for teachers, 1939-40; vis. lecturer zoology, Tulane U., 1946, asso. prof. zoology, 1946-49, prof. zoology, chmn. dept., 1955-59, research coordinator, 1959-63, v.p. planning, 1963-65, v.p. instnl. devel., 1965-68; dir. Audubon Conservation Camp, summers 1948, 49. Mem. U.S. Commn. for UNESCO; cons. NASA, USPHS, Biol. Sci. Commn. Project, 1963-68, Sci. in Policy Devel. Countries, 1963-68. mem. sci. and tech. com. Library of Congress, 1962-68. Bd. dirs. Gulf U. Research Corp., Nat. Acad. Sci.-NRC Council Biol. Information. Served as aviation physiologist, capt., USAAF, 1943-45; India, PTO. Recipient Alumni Achievement award So. Ill. U., 1965. Fellow Herpetologists League, A.A.A.S.; mem. S.W. Assn. Naturalists, Am Soc. Naturalists, Nat. Council U. Research Adminstrs., Am. Assn. Icthyologists and Herpetologists (v.p. 1953-55), Am. Soc. Mammalogists, Wildlife Soc., Soc. Study Evolution, Soc. Systematic Zoology, Ecol. Soc. Am., Netherlande Assn. Herpetologists, Brit. Herpetology Soc., Am. Inst. Biol. Scis. (bd. govs. 1957-62, exec. com. information 1960-63, chmn. internat. com. 1961-68, chmn. com. transl. 1959-61), Conf. Biol. Editors (exec. sec. 1957-63), Am. Assn. U. Profs., Nat. Conf. Adminstrv. Research (program com. 1967), Fedn. Internationale de Documentation, Am. Council Edn. (chmn. com. sponsored projects 1966-68), U. Research Assn. (dir.), Gulf South Research Inst. (dir.), Sigma Xi (pres. Tulane chpt. 1963-64), Phi Sigma. Club: Cosmos. Author reptile sect. Vertebrates of N. Am.; also articles. Home: New Orleans LA Died Aug. 8, 1968.

CAHILL, GEORGE FRANCIS, Urologist; b. New Haven, Jan. 1, 1890; s. Thomas J. and Margaret A. (McMahon) C.; M.D., Yale 1911; Sc.D., Columbia, 1956; m. Eva Marian Wagner, Oct. 16, 1916; children—Margaret Frances (Mrs. H. Thomas McGrath), Marian Elizabeth (Mrs. Gordon Page Guthrie), George Francis Pathol. med. surgical interne Bellevue Hosp., N.Y.C., 1911-14; surg. resident N.Y. Post-Grad. Hosp., 1914; instr. surgery N.Y.U., 1915-22; instr., asst. prof., asso. prof. Urology N.Y., Post-Grad. Hosp., 1915-28, Columbia 1919-39, prof. Urology, dir. Squier Urol. Clinic, 1939-55, emeritus prof., 1955—. head dept. Urology Coll., Phys. and surg. Columbia, also exec. officer Columbia-Presbyn. Med. Center until 1955. cons. Urologist Presbyn. Hosp. and Vanderbilt Clinic; cons. Surgeon Willard Parker Hosp.; cons. Urologist at Babies and Yonkers Gen., Francis Delafield hosps.; pres. med. bd. Presbyn. Hosp. 1946-49. Commd. 1st lt. 1917. capt. Army, 1918, comdg. officer Base Hosp. 119, AEF, France, 1918-19. Mem. Spl. adv. com. U.S. VA, Medal, 1948. Fellow A.C.S. (gov.) N.Y. Acad. Sciences, A.A.A.S., Mem. Am. Bd. Urology (Pres. 1953-54, trustee), A.M.A., Am. Urol. Assn. (pres. 1952-53), Am. Assn. Genito-Urinary Surgeons, Internat. Soc. of Urology (pres. 9th Congress, N.Y.C., 1952) Harvey Society, Acad. Medicine (N.Y.), N.Y. Urol. and Surg. Soc., Soc. of Clin. Urology (pres. 1947-48), Phi Rho Sigma. Clubs.: Yale (N.Y.C.), Metropolitan, Camp Fire of America Contbr. med. Publs. on Urol. Surgery, adernals, Cancer. Home: Campbell Rd., Suffern., Rockland County, N.Y. Office: 121 E. 60th St. N.Y.C. 22. Died July 25, 1959.

CAHILL, THADDEUS, inventor; b. I., 1867; s. Timothy and Ellen (Harrington) C.; grad. Oberline (O.) High Sch., 1884; studied Oberlin Acad., 1994-85, and in laboratories; LL.M., 1893, D.C.L., 1900; unmarried. Admitted to bar, 1894, practiced several yrs. Invented the elec. typewriter; invented process of producing music electrically, known as telharmony; pioneer in U.S. of art of distributing music electrically from a central sta. to receiving telephones on premises of subscribers; also invention in composing machines, heat engines, wireless telphony and wired-wireless; removed laboratory from Washington to Holyoke, Mass., 1902, and to New York, 1911. Jeffersonian Democrat. Episcopalian. Home: New York, N.Y. Died Apr. 12, 1934.

CAIN, WILLIAM, univ. prof.; b. Hillsboro, N.C., May 14, 1847; s. William and Sarah Jane (Bailey) C.; A.M., N.C. Mil. and Poly. Inst., 1965; (LL.D.); unmarried. Engring, practice, 1868-74, 1880-82; prof. mathematics and civ. engring., Carolina Mil. Inst. 1874-79, S.C. Mil. Acad., Charleston, 1882-89; prof. mathematics, U. of N.C., 1889—. Author: Theory of Voussoir Arches, solid and Braced Elastic Arches, Steel-concrete Arches and Vaulted Structures, Bridges, Retaining Walls, Symbolic Algebra (all in Van Norstrand's Science Series), 1874-1909; A. Brief Course in the Calculus, 1905; Earth Pressure, Retaining Walls and Bins, 1916. Died 1930.

CAIRNS, FREDERICK IRVAN, mining engr.; b. Susquehanna, Pa., Mar. 6, 1865; s. Reb. John and Magdelena (Hardie) C.; A.B., Hamilton Coll., N.Y., 1887, A.M., 1891; Met. E., Columbia, 1890; m. Marie Budd, Apr. 16, 1895; 1 son, Samuel Budd. Supt. Mich. Smelting Co. Mem. Am. Inst. Mining Engrs., 1897. Republican. Presbyterian. Home: Houghton, Mich. Died Apr. 14, 1944.

CAIRNS, W(ILLIAM) D(EWEESE), educator; b. Troy, O., Nov. 2, 1871; s. Samuel Alexander and Mary Brook (Gunn) C.; prep. edn., high Sch., Troy, 1885-89; A.B., Ohio Wesleyan U., 1892; A.B., Harvard, 1897; A.M., 1898; Ph.D., U. Göttingen, Germany, 1907; m. Iva Crofoot, Aug. 25, 1898 (dec. Nov. 2, 1926); children—Mary Catherine, Robert William; m. 2d, Bertha Noble Pope June 17, 1930. Instr. Mathematics. high sch., Troy, O., 1894-96, Calumet, Mich. 1898-99; instr. mathematics, Oberlin Coll., 1899-1904; asso. prof., 1904-20, prof. 1920-39, emeritus, 1939—. Mem. Math. Assn. Am. (sec.-treas. 1915—.) A.A.A.S., Am. Math. Soc., Nat. Council Tchrs. of Mathematics, N.E.A., Phi Beta Kappa, Alpha Tau Omega. Republican, Conglist. Original investigations in integral equations in binomial theorem as applied to probability, Math. analysis investigation of preparation for Univ. Mathematics. Home: Oberlin, O. Died July 15, 1955.

CAJORI, FLORIAN, college prof.; b. St. Aignan, near Thursis, Switzerland, Feb. 28, 1859; s. George and Catherina (Camenisch) C.; came to U.S., 1875; B.S., U. of Wis., 1883, M.S., 1886; student Johns Hopkins; Ph.D., Tulane, 1894; LL.D., U. of Colo., 1912, Colo. Coll., 1913; Sc.D., U. Wis., 1913; m. Elizabeth G. Edwards, Sept. 3, 1890; 1 son, Florian Anton. Asst. prof. mathematics, 1885-87; prof. applied mathematics, 1887-88, Tulane U.; prof. physics, 1889-98, mathematics, 1898-1918, dean dept. of engring., 1903-18, Colo. Coll.; prof. history of mathematics, U. of Calif., 1918—. Fellow Am. Acad. Arts and Scienes: Author: A History of Mathematics, 2 ed., 1919; A History of Elementary Mathematics, 2 ed., 1917; A History of Physics, 1899; Early Mathematical Sciences in North and South America, 11928; Mathematics in Liberal Education, 1928; Career of F. R. Hassler, 1929; History of Mathematical Notations (2 vols.), 1928-29. Deceased.

CALABRESE, GIUSEPPE, educator; b. Oliveri, Italy, July 13, 1897; s. Vincent and Maria (Orlando) C.; B.Eng., Poly Inst. Turin, 1921; m. Florence Verderese, Oct. 12, 1929; children—Marianita, Vincent Paul. Came to U.S., 1923, naturaliced, 1930. Tester, Westinghouse Elec. Co., East Pittsburgh, 1923-24, transmission engr., 1926-28; elec.-insp. designer, predeccessors of the Consol. Edison Co. of N.Y. (Bklyn.), Edison and N.Y. Edison, respectively, 1924-26; asst. engr., div. engr. Colsol. Edison Co., 1928-48; prof. elec. engring. N.Y. U., 1948—. Registered profl. engr., N.Y. State Fellow Am. Inst. E.E. (chmn. sub-com. on application probability methods; mem. com. on power generation); mem. Soc. Sigma Xi, Eta Kappa Nu Assn. Home: 188-01 Dormans Rd. St. Albans 12, N.Y. Office: N.Y. U., University Heights, N.Y.C. Died Nov. 15, 1966.

CALDWELL, BENJAMIN PALMER, chemist; b. New Orleans, Apr. 2, 1875; s. Dr. John Williamson and Mary Howe (Palmer) C.; A.B., Tulane U., 1893, B.E., 1895, Ch.E., 1896; Ph.D., Johns Hopkins, 1901; m. Helen Mercer Wright, Dec. 23, 1902; children—Benjamin Palmer, Hamilton Mercer Wright(dec.) Fellow Tulane U., 1893-95; successively instr. in chemistry, 1895-1916; absent on leave as fellow in Chemistry, Johns Hopkins, 1899-1901; visited France, Germany, and Eng., 1901, examining chem. ednl. facilities; prof. chemistry Oglethorpe U., Atlanta, 1916-19; prof. analytical chemistry Bklyn. Poly. Inst., 1991-27, prof. physical chemistry, 1927-45, emeritus prof. physical chemistry 1945—. Fellow A.A.A.S., New Orleans Acad. Sciences; mem. Am. Chem. Soc. (charter mem. and ex-pres. La. sect.). Phi Beta Kappa (charter mem. and ex-pres. Alpha of La.). Phi Lambda Upsilon, Sigma Xi. Democrat. Presbyn. Home: 1725 Gen. Pershing St., New Orleans, 15. Died Sept. 21, 1950.

CALDWELL, BERT WILMER, hosp. cons.; b. Effingham, Ill., Feb. 20, 1875; s. Henry D. and Ann Mary C.; A.B. Austin Coll., Effingham, Ill., 1894; M.D., Barnes Med. Coll., St. Louis, 1898— m. Georgia Hanson, Jan. 26, 1894; 1 son Henry Hanson. Began practice of medicine at St. Louis, 1898; with Isthmian Canal Commn., in charge Santo-Tomas and other hosp. Republic of Panama, during building of Panama Canal, 1905-15; mem. Rockefeller Red Cross Commn. to the Balkans, 1915; attached to the Am. Embassy in Berlin, as Commr. to insp. Allied prison camps, Germany, 1916; supt. Allegheny Gen. Hosp., Pitts., 1916-17; in charge 8th dist. USPHS Chgo., 1919; mem. Yellow Fever Commn., Rockefeller Found. in Mexico, in charge Gulf Coast from Tampico to Yucatan, 1920-22; supt. University Hosp., State U. Ia., 1922-25; supt. Tampa (Fla.) Municipal Hosp., 1925-27; exec. sec. Am. Hosp. Assn., 1927-43; Served in Spanish-Am War; col. Med. Dept., U.S. Army, World War 1. Republican.

Presbyn. Mason. Editor: Hospitals, 1936-42. Home: Rockton, Ill. Died July 1951.

CALDWELL, EUGENE WILSON, physician; b. Savannah, Mo., Dec. 3, 1870; s. W. W. and Camilla (Kellogg) C.; B.S., U. of Kan., 1892; M.D., Univ. and Bellevue Hosp. Med. Coll. (New York U.), 1905; special student of the College of Physicians and Surgeons (Columbia), 1898-99; m. Elizabeth Perkins, 1913. Engaged in experiments in wireless telephony (with L.I. Blake) for United State Lighthouse Establishment, 1893-95; asst. engring. dept. New York Telephone Co., 1895-97; from 1897 has devoted nearly all time to experimental work with Rötgen rays and to their practical application in diagnosis. Inventor Caldwell Liquid Interrupter, spl. froms of Röntgen ray tubes for therapeutic uses and many other appliances used with Röntgen rays. Prof. Röntgenology, Coll. Phys. and Surg. (Columbia), Mar. 1917—. Commd. capt. Med. O.R.C., 1917, maj., 1918, in acitve service. Author: The Röntgen Rays in Therapeutics and Diagnosis (with William A. Pusey), 1903. Home: New York, N.Y. Died June 23, 1918.

CALDWELL, FRANCIS CARY, educator; b. Ithaca, N.Y., Dec. 25, 1868; s. George Chapman and Rebecca Stanly (Wilmarth) C.; A.B., Cornell U., 1890, M.E. in Elec. Engring., 1891; Nat. Polytechnicum, Zürich, Switzerland, 1892-93; m. Louise Taft, Orton, July 12, 1900; children—Anne Davenport (wife of Dr. W.A. Kramer, dec.), Edward Orton (dec.) With Thomson-Houston Electric Electric Co., 1891-92; asst. prof. elec. engring. Ohio State U., 1893-97, asso. prof., 1897-1901, prof., 1901-39, prof. emertius, 1939—. dir. Ranco, Inc.; engr. Div. of Vehicle Lighting of Bur. of Motor Vehicles, Ohio; lectr. on illumination Inst. of Technology, Prague, Czechoslovakia, 1924-25; hon. curator Collection of Applied Electricity,Ohio State Museum, 1931—. Trustee Antioch Coll., Yellow Springs, O., 1923-34;. U.S. rep. on pub. lighting, Internat. Commn. on Illumination, 1935—. Registered profl. engr., Ohio. Fellow Am. Inst. E.E.; Mem. Ohio Traffic Safety Council, Illuminating Engring. Soc. (dir. 1921-24), Soc. for Promotion Engring. Edn., Tau Beta Pi, Sigma Xi, Phi Beta Kappa, Theta Xi, Eta Kappa Nu. Republican. Unitarian. Clubs: Faculty (Ohio State University), Engineers. Author Notes and Questions for the Dynamo Laboratory, 1900; Electrical Engineering Problems, 1904-13; Electrical Engineering Test Sheets, 1911; Modern Lighting, 1930 Editor: Technical Letters on Industrial Lighting, 1919. Contributing editor E.M.F. Electrical Year Book, 1922-26; General Engineering Handbook, 1931-40; Pender's Handbook, for Electrical Engineers, 1935. Home: 206 16th Av., Columbus, O. Died July 21, 1953.

CALDWELL, FRANK CONGLETON, b. Indianapolis, June 22, 1866; s. Henry Wallace and Hannah Ann (North) C.; ed. Chicago pub. schs.; LL.B., Union Coll. of Law (Northwestern U.), 1887; m. Grace Bevis, of St. Louis, Jan. 4, 1888. Admitted to Ill. bar, and practiced, Chicago, 1887-92; v.p. H.W. Caldwell & Son Co., engrs. and machinists, 1892-1908, pres., 1908—; dir. Oak Park Trust & Savings Bank. Republican. Presbyn. Mem. Oak Park Sch. Bd.; mem. S.A.R. Mason. Clubs: Chicago Athletic, Union League, Engineers' (New York). Home: 445 N. Kenilworth Av., Oak Park, Ill. Office: 17th St. and Western Av., Chicago. Deceased.

CALDWELL, GEORGE CHAPMAN, prof. chemistry, Cornell, 1968-1903; b. Framingham, Mass., Aug. 14, 1834; grad., B.S., Lawrence Scientific School, Harvard, 1885; (Ph.D., Göttingen, Germany, 1857); m. Rebecca Stanley Wilmarth, 1961. Prof. chemistry and physics Antioch Coll., Ohio, 1959-62; prof. chemistry, 1864-67, v.p., 1867-68. Agrl. Coll. of Pa.; prof. emeritus, Cornell, 1903. Home: Ithaca, N.Y. Died 1907.

CALDWELL, JOHN WILLIAMSON, univ. prof.; b. Charleston, S.C., Jan. 31, 1842; s. John W. and Martha Catherine (Coates) C.; A.B., Coll. of Charleston, 1861, A.M., 1868; M.C., Va. State Med. Coll., 1864; pvt. and asst. surgeon C.S.A., 1861-65; m. Mary Palmer, Sept. 20 1865. Practiced medicine, New Orleans, 1965-74; Stewart prof. of natural sciences, Stewart Coll. (afterward Southwestern Presbyn. U.), Clarksville, Tenn., 1974-84; curator Tulane U. Mus., 1995; prof. chemistry and geology, 1886-1907, emeritus, Tulane U. Died 1923.

CALDWELL, MARY LETITIA, educator; b. Bogota, Columbia, Dec. 18, 1890; dau. Milton Etsil and Susanna (Adams) Caldwell; A.B., Western Coll., 1913; A.M., Columbia, 1919, Ph.D., 1921; unmarried. Instr. in chemistry, Western Coll., 1914-15, asst. prof., 1915-17, asso. prof., 1917-18; univ. fellow in chemistry Columbia, 1920-21, instr. in chemistry, 1922-29, asst. prof., 1929-43, asso. prof. 1943-1948; prof. from 1948. Recipient Gavvan medal, 1959. Fellow A.A.A.S., N.Y. Acad. Sci.; mem. Am. Chem. Soc., Am. Inst. Nutrition, Am. Soc. Biol. Chemists, Am. Assn. U. Profs., Am. Geog. Soc., Sigma Xi. Presbyn. Republican. Author sci. papers in sci. profl. jours. Home: New York City NY Died July 1, 1972; buried South Salem OR

CALDWELL, ORESTES HAMPTON, editor, elec. engineer; b. Lexington, Kentucky, Mar. 8, 1888; s. William Hampton, M.D., and Flora V. (Weed) C.; prep. edn., Dr. Duhrings Sch., Charlottenburg, Germany, and Shortridge High Sch., Indpls., B.S. in E.E., Purdue, 1908, E.E., 1931, D.Eng., 1933; m. Mildred Hope Bedard, Sept. 9, 1914; children—Joan Hope (Mrs. Edward Schempp), Mary Jane (Mrs. Robert E. Nickerson). Asso. editor Electrical World, 1910-17; editor Electrical Merchandising, 1916-29, Radio Retailing, 1925-35, Electronics, 1930-35, Radio Today, 1935-48, Radio and Television Retailing, 1941-52; federal radio commr., 1927-29; v.p., treas. Caldwell-Clements, Inc.; chmn. bd., treas. Caldwell-Elements Manuals Corpl; partner Electronic Devel. Assos.; Nat. Broadcasting Co. commentator on weekly programs, "Radio Magic," Chmn. Indsl. Relations Com. Armed Forces Communication Assn., N.Y. sect.; mem. Nat. Color-Television Standards Com.; mem. com. on ednl.-television station awards. Fellow Inst. Radio Engrs., Fellow Am. Inst. E.E. (chmn. N.Y. sect. 1931-32); mem. Am. Standards Assn. (chmn. civilian-radio com.), N.Y. Elec. Soc. (1st vp. 1931-32; pres. 1932-34), Radio Pioneers (treas., 1st vp), Am. Mus. Natural History (vice chmn. com. on planetarium), Epsilon Chi, Tau Beta Pi, Amateur Astronomers Assn. (pres. 1936-38). Trustee N.Y. Museum of Science and Industry. Club: Indian Harbor Yacht. Address: Walden Woods, Catrock Rd., at Bible Corners, Cos Cob, Conn. Died Aug. 27, 1967.

CALDWELL, OTIS WILLIAM, scientist; b. Lebanon, Ind. Dec. 18, 1869; s. Theodore Robert and Belle C.; B.S., Franclin (Ind.) Coll., 1894, Ph.D. from University of Chicago, 1898; LL.D., Franklin Coll., 1917; m. Cora Burke, Aug. 25, 1897. Prof. biology, Eastern Ill. State Normal Sch., 1899-1907; asso. prof. botany, 1907-13, prof. botany and dean Univ. Coll., 1913-17, U. of Chicago; prof. edn. in Teachers' Coll. (Columbia) and dir. Lincoln Exptl. Sch., 1917-27; dir. Div. of School Experimentation of Inst. of Ednl. Research, 1920-27; dir. Inst. of Sch. Experimentation, 1927-35; retired as emeritus prof. Gen. sec. A.A.A.S. 1933-47; prof. botany U. of Ind. Summer School of Biology, 1904; visiting prof., U. of Calif., 1931, Atlanta U., 1937-38. Fellow A.A.A.S. (chmn. com. on the place of science in education, 1924-40). Author: Laboratory and Field Manual of Botany, 1901; Plant Morphology, 1903; Practical Botany (with J.Y. Bergen), 1911; Introduction to Botany, 1914; Elements of General Science, 1914; Laboratory Manual of General Science (with others), 1915; Then and Now in Education, 1923; Biology in the Public Press, 1923; Open Doors to Science, 1925; Introduction to Science (with F.D. Curtis), 1929; Biological Foundations of Education (with C.C. Skinner and J.W. Tietz), 1931; Biology for Today (with F.D. Curtis and N.H. Sherman), 1933; Do You Believe It (with G.E. Dundeen), 1934; Everday Biology (with F.D. Curtis and N.H. Sherman), 1940; Everday Science (with F.D. Curtis), 1943. Editor: Science Remaking the World (with E.E. Slosson), 1923. Contbr. to science and ednl. jours. Home: New Milford, Conn. Office: Boyce Thompson Inst., Yonkers, New York Died July 5, 1947.

CALDWELL, SAMUEL HAWKS, educator; b. Phila., Jan. 15, 1904; s. Thomas B. and Margaret L. (Hogg) C.; B.S., Mass. Inst. Tech., 1925, S.M., 1926, Sc.D., 1933; m. Elva A. Powell, Dec. 24, 1923 (divorced); children—Samuel H., Richard L., Jane P.; m. 2d, Elizabeth M. Ward, Mar. 8, 1951. Apptd. to staff Mass. Inst. Tech., 1926, asst. prof. elec., engineering, 1934-40, associate professor, 1940-47, professor, 1947— (in charge of research division, 1929-35, and development and construction of new differential analyser, 1935-39). Section chief, Nat. Defense Research Com., 1940-46; past advisory asst. on staff of Mass. Memorial Hosps.; dir. research Graphic Arts Research Found. Recipient Medal for Merit, King's Medal for Service in Cause of Freedom; John Scott Medalist, 1943; Fellow American Association Advancement Science; mem. Am. Inst. E.E., A.A.A.S., Sigma Xi, Eta Kappa Nu. Republican. Episcopalian. Clubs: St. Botolph (Boston); Faculty (M.I.T.). Author: Switching Circuits and Logical Design. Author sci. papers on mech. analysis and electrocardiography. Inventor Linotype machine for composing Chinese. Home: 100 Memorial Dr., Cambridge, Mass. 02142. Died Oct. 12, 1960.

CALDWELL, WILLIAM E(DGAR), obstetrician, univ. prof.; b. Northfield, O., Feb. 23, 1880; s. Milton Etsil and Susanna Adams C.; M.D., N.Y. Univ. and Bellevue Hosp. Med. Sch., 1904; unmarried. Interne N.Y. Lying-In Hosp., 1904-05, 3d surg. div. Bellevue Hosp., 1905-08; resident obstetrician Manhattan Maternity Hosp., 1908-09; adjunct asst. attending physician, Bellevue Hosp., and instr. in obstetrics, N.Y. Univ. Med. Sch., 1909-14, asst. prof. and asst. attending physician Bellevue Hosp. Obstet. Service, 1914-20; asso. prof. and asso. dir. Sloane Hosp., Columbia U., 1920-27, prof. clin. obstetrics and gynecology and asso. dir. Sloane Hosp., Columbia U., since 1927. Served as capt. of Med. Corps, U.S. Army, 1918. Fellow Am. Coll. Surgeons; mem. A.M.A., Med. Soc. of State of N.Y., Med. Soc. of County N.Y., N.Y. Obstet. Soc., N.Y. Acad. Medicine, Am. Gynecol. Soc., Am. Gynecol. Club, Sigma Xi, Nu Sigma Nu. Republican. Presbyterian. Clubs: Century Assn., N.Y. Athletic, Ohio Soc. of N.Y.; Silver Springs Country (Ridgefield, Conn.). Contbr. many professional articles to Am. Jour. Obstetrics and Gynecology and other jours. Home: 875 Park Av., New York, N.Y. Died Apr. 1, 1943.

CALHANE, DANIEL FRANCIS, educator cons.; b. Bradford Mass., Aug. 19, 1869; A.B., Harvard, 1894, A.M., 1896. Ph.D., 1904; m. Luette E. Richmond, Sept. 8, 1906. With Worcester Poly. Inst., 1903-36, as instr., asst. prof. and prof. indsl. and applied eletro-chemistry, prof. emeritus, 1936—. now engaged in pvt. research and cons. work Fellow A.A.A.S.; mem. Electrochem. Soc. Inventor of small type electric furnace for high temperatures. Author: of papers on pure and applied chemistry. Address: 32 Berkmans St., Worcester, Mass. Died Sept. 20, 1951.

CALHOUN, FRED HARVEY HALL, geologist; b. Auburn, N.Y., June 27, 1873; s. John Hamilton and Ellen (Hall) C.; B.S., U. Chgo., 1898, Ph.D., 1902; m. Grace B.Ward, June 9, 1904; children—John Ward, Fred. Asst. in geol. dept. U. Chgo., 1899-1902; asst. prof. geology and physics Ill. Coll. 1902-04; prof. geology and mineralogy Clemson (S.C.) Coll., 1904—, also dir. agrl. dept., 1915-33, dean sch. chemistry and geology, 1933-50; cons. geologist S.A.L. R.R.: asst. geologist U.S. Geol. Survey, 1903-15; geologist U. Colo., Summer, 1903, 05, 09, U. Chgo., summer, 1907, U. Mich. summer 1911, U. Ia., summers 1914, 15. Fellow Geol. Soc. Am., A.A.A.S., mem. S.C. Acad. Science (pres.) Phi Delta Theta Alpha Nu, Alpha Chi Sigma, Phi Kappa Phi. Episcopalian. Rotarian. Author of geol. monographs. Home: Clemson, S.C., Died May 2, 1959; buried Churchyard St. Paul's Pendleton, S.C.

CALHOUN, RALPH EMERSON, mining engr.; b. Rockmart, Ga., Jan. 8, 1906; s.William A. and Mildred E. (Davitte) C.; student N. Ga. Agrl. Coll., Dohlonegg, 1923-26; m. Mary J. Pickett, Nov. 10, 1931;children—William Mitchell, Robert Lewis, Ann. Rodman, engring. dept. Am. Zinc Co. of Tenn., 1925-28; resident engr. Jarnigon Property, Jefferson City, Tenn., 1928-29; supt., Joplin, Mo., 1929-31; engring. dept., Tenn., 1932, supt. of mines, Joplin, 1933-36; gen. supt. Am. Zinc Lead & Smelting Co., Metaline Falls, Wash., 1936-42, Joplin, 1942, asst. dist. mgr. charge mining, exploration engr., 1946, mgr. Colo. operations, 1946-49, Southwestern rep., 1949-54, Western mgr., 1954-59, mgr. mines, 1959-65, v.p., St. Louis, 1965-68. Mem.Am. Inst. Mining Engrs., Mo. Soc. Profl. Engrs., Pi Kappa Alpha. Home: Mascot, Tenn and St. Louis MO Died Oct. 6, 1968; buried Mount Hope Cemetery, Joplin MO

CALKINS, GARY NATHAN, zoologist; b. Valparaiso, Ind., Jan. 18, 1869; s. John W. and Emma F. (Smith) C.; S.B., Mass. Inst. Tech., 1890; Ph.D., Columbia U., 1897, Sc.D., 1929; m. Anne Marshall Smith, June 28, 1894; m. 2d, Helen Richards Colton, 1909; children—Gary Nathan, Samuel Williston. Asst. biologist, Mass. State Bd. Health, and lecturer in biology, Mass. Inst. Tech., 1890-93; tutor biology, 1894-96, zoology, 1896-99, instr., 1899-1903, adj. prof., 1903-04, adj. prof. invertebrate zoology, 1904, prof., 1904-06, professor of protozoology, 1906-39, prof. emeritus since 1939, Columbia Univ. Biologist New York State Cancer Lab., 1904-08; clk of corp., Marine Biol. Lab. Fellow A.A.A.S., New York Zool. Soc.; mem. Am. Soc. Naturalists, Am. Morphol. Soc., Soc. Exptl. Biology and Medicine, Nat. Acad. Sciences. Pres. Am. Soc. Cancer Research, 1913-14, Soc. Exptl. Biology and Medicine, 1919-21. Dir. Am. Univ. Union, Paris, France, 1926-27. Author: The Protozoa (Vol. VI, Columbia U. Biol. Series), 1901; Protozoology, 1908; Biology, 1914; Biology of the Protozoa; 1926. Also numerous scientific papers. Home: Scarsdale, N.Y. Died Jan. 4, 1943.

CALLAHAN, WILLIAM PAUL, JR., pathologist; b. Sept. 20, 1917; s. William Paul and Catherine C.; B.S., Notre Dame U., 1939; M.D., Washington U., St. Louis, 1943; m. Jo Anne Aylward, June 19, 1941; children—Patricia (Mrs. Berry), Catherine (Mrs. Mandigo), William Paul, Michael. Intern, Washington Univ., St. Louis, 1943-44, asst. pathologist, 1943, instr. pathology, 1943-45, asso. pathologist, 1944-45; mem. staff St. Francis Hosp., Wichita Kans., 1947-48, dir. labs., 1948-66; founder, dir. Callahan Labs., Wichita, 1966-71. Chmn. Midwest Div., Field Survey Project for Lab. Assts.; med. dir. Kans. Certified Lab. Assts. Program; dir. cerivcal cytology screening program for the indigent of Kans.; cons. in field. Dir. fund raising Univ. Notre Dame Found., Kansas. Served M.C. AUS from lt. to capt., 1945-47. Diplomate Am. Bd. Pathology. Mem. A.M.A., Am. Soc. Clin. Pathologists (bd. Schs. of Med. Tech.), Am. Assn. Pathologists and Bacteriologists, Internat. Acad. Pathology, Coll. Am. Pathologists (rep. Kans.), Kans. Soc. Pathologists (sec.-treas.). Home: Wichita KS Died Aug. 16, 1971. Buried Old Mission Mausoleum Wichita KS

CALLAN, JOHN GURNEY, univ. prof.; b. Northfield, Conn., Apr. 7, 1875; s. Michael John and Olive Rebecca (Gurney) C.; B.S. in E.E., Mass. Ins. Tech., 1896; m. Martha Towns Litchfield, July 25, 2900 (now dec.); children—Malcolm Frederic (dec.), Rosalie Dorothea (Mrs. Sven A. Baeckström), Priscilla Elsa Gurney (Mrs. Georges Lucienne Houle), Hildegarde Muriel (Mrs. Donald T. Whittemore), John Gurney, Paul Litchfield. Began active career with the Edison Electric Illuminating Co., Boston, 1897, General Electric Company, experimental and engring. depts. and commercial engring., 1897-1909; mech. and elec. engr. of Arthur D. Little Co., Boston, 1909-15; prof. steam and gas engring., U. of Wis., 1915-20; prof. industrial management, Grad. Sch. of Business Administration, Harvard, 1920—, also consulting work. War work on investigation of marine Diesel engines in Great Britain, 1917-18. Chmn. Cotton Textile State Industrial Relations Bd. from Mass. Republican. Mem. Ch. of New Jerusalem (Swedenborgian). Has taken out about 70 patents, principally in connection with steam turbines. Home: Cambridge, Mass. Died Dec. 30, 1940.

CALLEN, ALFRED COPELAND (kal'len), mining engr.; b. Pen Argyl, Pa., July 17, 1888; s. Benjamin Tucker and Jennie (Fear) C.; E.M., Lehigh U., 1909, M.S., 1911; m. Ida C. Saylor, Apr. 9, 1912; children—Katharine Edna, Martha Saylor, Alfred Copeland. Instr. physics, Lehigh Univ., 1909-10, mining engring, 1910-11; mgr. Pottstown (Pa.) Machine Co., 1911-14; instr. mining engring., U. of Ill., 1914-16, asso., 1916-17; prof. mining engring. and dir. mining extension, W.Va. U., 1917-24; prof. mining engring. and head of dept., U. of Ill., 1924-39; prof. mining engring., Lehigh U., since 1939, dean Coll. of Engring., 1939-45. Editor: Coal Mine Management, Chicago, 1922-29. Gov. Ill.-E. Iowa Kiwanis Dist., 1930; trustee Kiwanis Internat., 1932-36, pres., 1936-37. Mem. Am. Inst. Mining and Metall. Engrs. (chmn. mineral industry education division 1944), Mining and Metallurgical Society of America, Illinois Mining Inst. (pres. 1930), American Soc. Engring. Edn. (member of council 1941-44), Theta Delta Chi, Tau Beta Pi, Sigma Xi, Omicron Delta Kappa, Pi Tau Sigma. Republican. Methodist. Mason (K.T., 33 deg.). Author: various engring. and ednl. bulletins and articles. Home: 820 Beverly Av., Bethlehem, Pa. Died July 30, 1951; buried Nisky Hill Cemetery, Bethlehem.

CALLENDER, (WILLIAM) ROMAINE, musician; B. South Shields, Eng., Aug. 16, 1857; s. Edwin and Jane (Carr) C.; ed. Wright pvt. sch. and Dr. Addison's coll. prep. sch.; studied science at Mechanics Inst., and Marine Sch., South Shields, and at Lit. and Philos. Inst., Newcastle-on-Tyne; studied piano, organ, harmony and compostion under pvt. tutors; m. Ella Cordelia Andrews, Aug. 2, 1878. Came to Can., 1876, to U.S., 1889; editorial and publicity work for several yrs. with J. B. Lippincott Co., Phila.; also publicity work with Canadian rys. and Canadian Govt.; prin. Metropolitan Coll. of Music, Phila., 1900—. Formerly dir. Haydn Orchestral Soc. and conductor Brantford (Can.) Philharmonic Soc.; organist Grace Episcopal and Zion Presbyn. chs., Brantford. Episcopalian. Author: Teachers' Manual and Elementary Method (piano), 1911; Prison-Flower, Kermadec Romance (novels), 1912, etc.; composer pieces for organ, compiler and editor. Inventor of pneumatic and electric organ actions, automatic telephone exchange system, autographic piano recording and reproducing apparatus, etc. Home: Philadelphia, Pa. Died July 1, 1930.

CALLOW, JOHN MICHAEL, mining engr., metallurgist; b. Northrepps, Norwich, Norfolk, Eng., July 7, 1867; s. Michael John and Emily (Neave) C.; ed. in England; came to U.S., 1890; m. Roberta More, 1893; children—Bessie Roberta, Margaret Roper More, Francis Marie, Michael John. Engr. and draftsman with Stearns, Roger Mfg. Co., 1892-93; engr. Metallic Extraction Co., 1894; operating mines and mills in San Juan Co., Colo., 1895-96; on engring. staff Samuel Newhouse, 1898-1901; pvt. practice, 1901-06, inventing Callow settling tank and Callow traveling belt screen; pres. and mgr. Gen. Engineering Co., New York, 1906—; designed and built 500-ton plant for Nat. Cooper Co., Mullan, Ida., installing pneumatic flotation cells, 1912; designing and constrn. engr., Mt. Isa Mines, Australia, 1928-31. Originator of pneumatic flotation in treatment of ores; awarded 18 patents. Awarded Douglas medal by Am. Inst. Mining and Metall. Engrs., 1925, for achievements in non-ferrous metallurgy. Mason. Episcopalian. Died July 27, 1940.

CALVERT, JOHN F., prof. elec. engring.; b. Columbia, Mo., Oct. 14, 1898; s. Sidney Calvert and Elizabeth (Fyfer) C.; B.S. in E.E., U. of Mo., 1922, E.E., 1924; M.S., U. of Pittsburgh, 1930, Ph.D., 1936; m. Harriet D. Johnston, June 28, 1927; 1 dau., Elizabeth C. Shick. Design and devel. engr. Westinghouse Electric & Mfg. Co., East Pittsburgh, 1924-36; asso. prof. of elec. engring., Iowa State Coll., 1936-38k prof. and chmn. dept. Northwestern U., 1938-54; prof., chmn. dept. elec. engring. U. Pitts., 1954—; design and constructor, USN, 1941-42; dir. U.S. Naval Radio Tng. Sch., 1942-43; dir. numerous nat. def. armed service contracts, Northwestern U., exec. dir. adv. bd. hardened electric power systems Nat. Academy of Sciences—NRC, 1963—. Served Mex. border, 4th Mo. Inf., 1916; 139th Inf., U.S. Army, with AEF, 1917-19. Recipient elect. engring. award Am. Inst. E.E., 1958; U. Mo. engineering award, 1959. Profl. engr. Ia., Ill., Minn. and Pa. Fellow Western Soc. Engrs., Eta Kappa Nu, Tau Beta Pi, Sigma Xi. Presbyn. Contbr. tech. papers in field. Home: 3603 Ridgewood Dr., Pitts. 35. Died Dec. 26, 1966.

CALVERT, PHILIP POWELL, entomologist; b. Phila., Jan. 29, 1871; s. Graham and Mary S. (Powell) C.; grad. Central High Sch., Phila., 1888; studied U. of Pa., 1888-89, 1891-95, Ph.D., 1895; Berlin, 1895-96, Jena, 1896; m. Amelia C. Smith, 1901. Instr. zoology, 1897-1907, asst. prof., 1907-12, prof., 1912-39, emeritus since 1939, U. of Pa. (studying natural history in Costa Rica on leave of absence, 1909-10). Asso. editor Entomological News, 1893-1910, editor 1911-43. Fellow A.A.A.S., mem. council Academy Natural Sciences of Phila., since 1897; pres. Am. Entomol. Society (Phila.), 1899-1915; pres. Entomol. Soc. America, 1914; mem. Limnological Soc. of Am., Am. Soc. Zoologists, Am. Soc. Naturalists, Ecol. Soc. America, Am. Philos. Soc., Am. Soc. Trop. Medicine, Sigma Xi. Known as student of the Odonata (Dragonflies). Contbr. to the sect. Odonata in Biologia Centrali-Americana (edited by F. D. Godman, F.R.S.), 1901-08; also catalogues and numerous articles on the Odonata of various regions. Author: (with Amelia S. Calvert) A Year of Costa Rican Natural History, 1917. Home: Box 14, Chevnev PA

CALVERT, ROBERT, patent atty., chemist; b. Milford, Mo., Mar. 15, 1889; s. William Samuel and Martha Ann (Newkirk) C.; A.B., U. Okla., 1909, A.M., 1910; S.M., U. Chgo, 1912; Ph.D., Columbia, 1914; m. Mary Power Siggers, Mar. 6, 1922; children—Robert, Carol (dec.), George Edward. Instr. chem. U. Okla., 1909-11, Columbia, 1913-15; chemist and research lab. dir. E. I. du Pont de Nemours & Co., 1915-20; asst. prof. chemistry U. So. Cal., 1921-22; research lab. dir. Celite Products Co., 1922-24; prof. indsl. chemistry U. Md., 1925-26; chief chemist Van Schaack Bros. Chem. Works, Chgo., 1926-31; patent atty. Johns-Manville Corp., 1931-38, cons., 1938-41, patent atty., 1941-58; patent atty. Borden Company, 1958-64; professor industrial chemistry American University Beirut, 1951-52. Distinguished Service citation University Oklahoma, 1965; American Institute Chemists' Freedman Patent Found. award, 1966. Mem. Del. Chemists Soc. (chmn. 1917), N.J. Chem. Soc. (vice chmn. 1920), Am. Chem. Soc. (vice chmn. Chgo. sect. 1931; chmn. N.Y. sect. 1940), Tech. Soc. Council of New York (pres. 1950-51), N.Y. Patent Law Assn., Japan Patent Attorneys Assn. (hon.), Ret. Chemists Assn. N.Y. (pres. 1965-66), Phi Beta Kappa, Beta Theta Pi, Phi Lambda Upsilon, Sigma Xi. Republican. Conglist. Clubs: Chemists (N.Y.); Scarsdale (N.Y.) Golf. Author: Diatomaceous Earth, 1930; Patent Practice and Management, 1950; Winds of Opportunity (autobiography), 1969. Editor; Ency. Patent Practice and Invention Mgmt., 1964. Home: Scarsdale NY Died June 26, 1969.

CALVERY, HERBERT ORION, pharmacologist; b. Eddy, Tex., Dec. 9, 1897; s. Luther and Theresa Irene (Marriele) C.; ed. Peniel Coll.; B.S., Greenville Coll., Ill., 1919; m. Gertrude V. Lane, June 2, 1925; children—Catherine Ann, George Herbert. Teacher, 1919; asst. chemistry, U. of Ill., 1920-21, fellowship, 1922-24; asst. prof. U. of Louisville, 1924-25; instr. Johns Hopkins Med. Sch., 1925-27; asst. prof. physiol. chemistry, University of Michigan Medical School, 1927-35; senior pharmacologist Food and Drug Adminstrn. 1935-36, chief div. pharmacology since 1936. Fellow A.A.A.S., John Simon Guggenheim Memorial Foundation Fellow in Europe in 1932-33. Mem. Am. Chem. Soc. (chmn. biol. div. 1939-40), Am. Soc. Biol. Chemists, Am. Soc. Pharmacology and Exptl. Therapeutics, Soc. Exptl. Biology and Medicine, Am. Pub. Health Assn., Sigma Xi, Alpha Chi Sigma, Phi Lambda Upsilon, Phi Sigma. Dem. Contbr. to jours., texts, encys. on biochemistry and toxicology. Home: 47 W. Baltimore St., Kensington, Md. Died Sept. 23, 1945.

CALVIN, SAMUEL, geologist; b. Wigtonshire, Scotland, Feb. 2, 1840; s. Thomas and Elizabeth C.; came to U.S. at 11; attended Lenox Coll., Hopkinton, Ia., but did not graduate on account of enlistment in Union Army, 1864; (hon. A.M., 1875, LL.D., 1904, Cornell Coll., Ia.; Ph.D., Lenox, 1888); m. M. Louise Jackson, Sept. 5, 1865. Prof. geology, State U. of Ia., 1874—, State geologist of Ia., 1892-1904, and 1906—; one of editors Am. Geologist, 1888-1905; mem. Nat. Advisory Bd. on Fuels and Structural Materials. Home: Iowa City, Ia. Died 1911.

CAMAC, CHARLES NICOLL BANCKER, M.D.; b. Phila., Pa., Aug. 6, 1868; s. William and Ellen (McIlvaine) C.; A.B., U. of Pa., 1892, M.D., 1895; student, Guy's Hosp. Med. Sch., London, 1893; Johns Hopkins U. Med. Sch., grad. studies, 1895-97; m. Julia Augusta Metcalfe, Nov. 17, 1897; m. 2d, Chritie M. Fraser, May 25, 1935. Instr. physiology, U. of Pa., 1895; asst. resident phys., Johns Hopkins Hosp., 1896-97; organizer and dir. lab. of clin. pathology, 1899-1905, instr. physical diagnosis, chief of med. clinic, lecturer in medicine, 1905-09, prof. clin. medicine, 1909-10, Cornell U. Med. Coll., New York; asst. prof. clin. medicine, College Physicans and Surgeons (Columbia), 1910-38; visiting phys., 1899-1916, cons. physicians, 1916-35, N.Y. City Hosptial; cons. physician, N.Y. Polyclinic Hosp. and Med. Sch., 1934-36 (emeritus prof. medicine). During World War served as physician in American War Hospital, England, and Ocean Ambulance Hospital, Belgium; chmn. Physicians, Surgeons and Dentists Fund for purchase of hosp. instruments and equipment for French mil, hosp., 1916; med. dir. Gouverneu Hosp. of the Bellevue and Allied hosp., N.Y. City, 1916-23; cons. phys., 1923—. Commissioned 1st lt. Med. R.C., Apr. 1917; student officer, Camp Greenleaf, Ft. Oglethorpe, Ga., Sch. of Gas Defense, Ft. Sill, Okla.; apptd. instr. in gas defense, Inf. Sch. of Arms, U.S. Army, Ft. Sill, Oka., Sept. 1917; promoted maj. Med. R.C., Oct. 1917; apptd. med. chief U.S. Army Gen. Hosp. No. 6, Ft. McPherson, Ga., Oct. 1917; apptd. dir. Officers' Training Sch., Ft. McPherson, Apr. 1918; promoted lt. col. M.C., Nov. 1918; apptd. med. chief Gen. Hosp. No. 38, Eastview, N.Y. Jan. 1919; hon. disch., July 1919. Author: Imhotep to Harvey—The Blackgrounds of the History of Medicine, 1931. Home: Altadena, Calif. Died Sept. 27, 1940.

CAMERON, EDWIN J(OHN), dir. research lab.; b. Cambridge, Mass., Sept. 17, 1895; s. John J. and Annie (Ellis) C.; B.S., Mass. Inst. Tech., 1920; Ph.D., George Washington U., 1927; m. Dorothy Ellouise Pray, Sept. 21, 1921; 1 son, John Pray. Bacteriologist Comml. Solvents Corp., Terre Haute, , Ind., 1920 1920-23; Nat. Canners Assn., Washington, 1923-36; asst. dir. research lab., 1936-39, dir. research lab., 1939-55, dir. all research labs., 1955—. Served with M.C., U.S. Army, A.E.F., World War 1, Mem. Soc., Am. Bacteriol., The American Chemical Society Institute of Food Technologists. Club: Cosmos Contbr. articles on thermophilic bacteria, sources of thermophilic bacteria and relations to canned food spoilage; thermophilic contamination of beet and cane Sugar. Home: 2651 16th St., N.W., Washington 9. Office: 1133 20th St., Washington 6. Died Mar. 21, 1955; buried Arlington Nat. Cemetery.

CAMERON, FRANK KENNETH, chemistry; b. Baltimore, Md., Feb. 2, 1869; s. Maj. John Malcolm and Elizabeth (Fitz-Patrick) C.; A.B., Johns Hopkins, 1891; Ph.D., 1894; m. Katherine Boyle, Sept. 14, 1899; (died Nov. 25, 1903); children—Francis, Katherine. Research fellow and instr. chemistry, Cornell U., 1894-95; asso. prof. chemistry, Catholic U. of America, 1895-97; research asst. and instr. in physical chemistry, Cornell U., 1897-98; expert U.S. Dept. Agr., 1898 chemist to Div. of Soils, U.S. Dept. Agr., 1899; in charge Lab. of Soil Chemistry U.S. Dept. Agr., 1899-1915; prof. chemistry, U. of North Carolina, 1926-46, emertius professor 1946—: cons. practice. Awarded Herty Medal, 1939. Roman Catholic. Mem. various Sci. socs., including A.A.A.S., Am. Chem., Soc., Soc. Electrochemistry, Elisha Mitchell Sci. Soc.; mem. S.A.R. K.C. Clubs: Cosmos (Washington); University, Alta. (Salt Lake City). Author: Les Constituants Mineraux des Solutions des Sols (with James M Bell), 1907; the Soil Solution, 1911; also over 200 research papers. Asst. editor Zeitschrift Kollide Chemistry, 1910-14, Jour. Phys. Chemistry, 1910-23, 31-33, Jour. Indsl. and Engring. Chemistry 1912-21. Home: 47 Maxwell Rd., Glen Lennox, Chapel Hill, N.C. Died Aug. 18, 1958 buried Old Chapel Hill Cemetery.

CAMP, THOMAS RINGGOLD, engineer; b. San Antonio, Nov. 5, 1895; s. Harmon Clark and Mildred Stella (Dashiell) C.; B.S., Tex. A. and M. Coll., 1916; M.S., Mass. Inst. Tech., 1925; Sc.D. (hon.), Clarkson Inst. Tech., 1970; m. Margaret Alice Evans, June 15, 1925; children—Frances, John, Emilie (Mrs. R. F. Stouffer). Practicing engineer, Tex., N.C., N.Y., N.J., 1916-29, hydraulic, san. engr. since 1921; asso. prof. san. engring., Mass Inst. Tech., 1929-44; consulting engr., 1944-1971; founded Camp Dresser & McKee, Boston, 1947. Served with U.S. Army, 1917-19. Received Boston Soc. C.E. san. sect. prize, 1941, hydraulic, 1944, Desmond FitzGerald medal, 1949; Karl Emil Hilgard prize, Am. Soc. C.E., 1941. J.C. Stevens hydraulic prize, 1945, J. James R. Croes medal, 1947; N.E. Water Works Assn. Dexter Brackett meml. medal, 1943, 56, Fuller award, Am. Water Works Assn., 1955; Rudolph Hering medal, Am. Soc. C.E., 1956, Friedman award 1964, C.E. Clemens Herschel award, 1970. Samuel A. Greeley award, 1969, posthumously awarded J.C. Stevens award, 1972; New Eng. award Engring. Socs. of New Eng., 1963, Distinguished Service award Nat. Clay Pipe Inst., 1966. Registered profl. engr., Mass., Me., Conn., Vt., R.I., N.H., Pa., N.Y., N.C. Diplomate Am. Acad. Sanitary Engrs., 1955. Fellow Am. Pub. Health Assn.; mem. Am. Soc. C.E. (hon.), Boston Soc. C.E. (pres. 1950; hon.), N.E. (pres. 1950; hon.), Am. water works assns., N.E. Sewage Works Assn. (pres. 1947), Am. San. Engring. Intersoc. Bd. (founder, chmn. 1956-62), Am. Inst. Cons. Engrs., Water Pollution Control Fedn. (hon. mem.; fedn. established Thomas R. Camp medal 1964), Sigma Xi, Tau Beta Pi. Author profl., tech. articles. Mem. adv. com. 1962. Revision USPHS Drinking Water Standards. Patentee in field. Author: Water and Its Impurities, 1963. Address: Boston MA Died Nov. 15, 1971.

CAMP, WALTER JOHN RICHARD, toxicologist; b. Chgo., Mar. 6, 1897; s. Robert Conrad and Mary Josephine (Laub) Heinekamp; B.S., U. Ill., 1919, M.S., 1920, M.D., 1923, Ph.D., 1927. Asst. pharmacology U. Ill. Coll. Medicine, 1918-22, asst. obstetrics, 1923, asso. pharmacology, 1923-27, asst. prof. pharmacology, 1927-31, asso. prof., 1931-35, prof., 1935-48, prof. pharmacology and toxicology, 1948—; intern Cook County Hosp., 1922-23; state toxicologist, 1948—. Mem. Am. Acad. Forensic Scis. (sec.-treas. 1954—), Inst. Medicine of Chgo., A.M.A., Am. Soc. Pharmacology and Exptl. Therapeutics, Soc. Exptl. Biology and Medicine, A.A.A.S., Sigma Xi, Phi Beta Pi, Alpha Omega Alpha, Pi Kappa Epsilon. Republican. Mason. Address: 1853 W. Polk St., Chgo. 60612. Died June 16, 1964.

CAMP, WENDELL H(OLMES), botanist; b. Dayton, O., Feb. 22, 1904; s. Rev. Peter Monroe and Martha Elnora (Flexer) C.; B.Sc., Otterbein College, 1925, D.Sc. (hon.), 1951; M.Sc., Ohio State U., 1926, Ph.D., 1932. Inst. botany Ohio State U., 1926-36; asso. curator N.Y. Bot. Garden, 1936-49; curator dept. exptl. botany and horticulture Acad. Natural Sci. Phila., 1949-54; lectr. botany U. Pa., 1950-54; dir. Taylor Meml. Arboretum, Garden City, Chester, Pa., 1951-54; prof. botany, head dept. University of Conn., 1954—; chairman editorial board International Rules Bot. Nomenclature, 1947; member of the editorial board International Horticulture Congress, Internat. Code Nomenclature for Cultivated Plants, pub. London, 1953. Prodn. research latex, fiber producing plants, Caribbean, also C.A., 1942-43, exploration quinine yielding Chinchona, Ecuador, 1944-45. Recipient Distinguished Service award N.Y. Bot. Garden. Fellow The Botanical Soc. of British Isles; mem. A.A.A.S., American Society Plant Taxonomists (pres. 1949, editor Taxonomic Index 1938-58), Bot. Soc. Am., Internat. Association Plant Taxonomists, Soc. Study Evolution, Am. Hort. Council (Pres. 1949-52, chmn. commn. nomenclature and registration 1952-54). Author tech. articles. Research taxonomy of woods plants, especially blueberries, beeches and oaks. Home: Clover Mill Rd., Mansfield, Conn. Office: University of Conn., Storrs, Conn. Died Feb. 4, 1963; buried South Lawn Cemetery, Beach City, O.

CAMPBELL, ALBERT H., civil engr., artist; b. Charlestown, Va. (now W.Va.), Oct. 23, 1836; grad-Brown U., 1847. Served as engr. and surveyor with several railroad surveys in S.W., circa 1850-60; chief Topographic Bur., Confederate States Army, during Civil War, made maps which were important to Confederate mil. tactics; chief engr. for several railroads in W.Va., after Civil War. Died Ravenswood, W.Va., Feb. 23, 1899.

CAMPBELL, ALLAN B(ERRY), elec. engr.; b. Morgan County, Ill., July 20, 1884; s. Clinton Samuel and Mary Ann (Eyre) C.; A.B., U. Ill., 1909, engring. degree, 1921; m. Mary Alma Butler, Oct. 15, 1909; children—Allan Bonham, Kenneth Butler. Student apprentice, 1909-11; telephone-operation, maintenance and engineering, 1911-15; tchr. Ia. State Coll. Agr. and Mech. Arts, 1915-20; elec. engr. Bd. R.R. Commrs., State of Ia., 1920-23; engr., Nat. Electric Light Assn. and Edison Electric Inst., 1923-43; eastern sales rep. Hughes Bros., 1943-46; exec. sec., Nat. Assn. Corrosion Engrs. since 1946. Fellow Am. Inst. E.E.; mem. Am. Soc. Testing Materials, Houston Engrs. Club, Vets. of Safety, Nat. Assn. Corrosion Engrs., Tau Beta Pi. Licensed prof. engr., Ia., N.Y., Mich. Republican. Home: 6518 Mercer St., Houston 77005. Office: M and M. Bldg., 1 Main St., Houston 2, Died Sept. 17, 1962.

CAMPBELL, ANDREW, inventor, mfr.; b. Trenton, N.J., June 14, 1821; married, 1848, 4 children. Brushmaker, S. Louis, 1842-50; built 1st St. Louis omnibus; patented printing machine, 1858, began The Campbell Country Press; erected plant, Bklyn., 1866; developed 2 revolution picture press, 1867, large press for fine illustrations, 1868; made 1st press which printed, inserted, pasted, folded and cut in 1 continuous operation. Died Bklyn., Apr. 13, 1890.

CAMPBELL, CHARLES MACFIE, M.D.; b. Edinburgh, Scotland, Sept. 8, 1876; s. Daniel and Eliza (McLaren) C.; student George Watson's Coll., Edinburgh; M.A., Edinburgh U., 1897, B.Sc., 1900, M.B., Ch.B., 1902, M.D., 1911; also student Paris, Heidelberg; m. Jessie Deans Rankin, June 3, 1908; children—Annie McNicol, Edith Storer, Charles Macfie, Katherine Rankin. Came to U.S., 1904, naturalized citizen, 1918. Asst. phys., Psychiatric Inst., Ward's Island, N.Y., later asst. phys. at Bloomingdale Hosp., White Plains, N.Y., until 1913; asso. prof. psychiatry, Johns Hopkins, 1913-20; prof. psychiatry, Harvard Med. Sch., since 1920. Dir. Boston Psychopathic Hosp. Mem. Am. Psychiatric Assn., Am. Neurol. Assn., Am. Sch. Hygiene Assn., etc. Home: 58 Lake View Av., Cambridge, Mass. Office: 74 Fenwood Rd., Boston, Mass. Died Aug. Aug. 7, 1943.

CAMPBELL, DONALD FRANCIS, actuary; b. East River, St. Mary's, N.S., Can., Apr. 26, 1867; s. George and Ellen Esther (Gunn) C.; B.A., Dalhousie Coll., Halifax, N.S., 1890; B.A., Harvard, 1894, M.A., 1895, Ph.D., 1898; m. Lou Rena Bates, Mar. 28, 1906 (died July 4, 1939); children—Donald Francis, Elizabeth Bates (Mrs. L. T. Arthur). Instructor mathematics, Harvard, 1897-1900; prof. and head dept. mathematics, Armour Inst. Tech., Chicago, 1900-27. Lecturer on ins., Northwestern U., 1909-11; sec. and actuary Illinois Pension Laws Commissions of 1916 and 1918; actuary, Pension Laws Commission of Milwaukee, 1921; deputy examiner of Pension Funds to which public moneys are contributed, 1929-30; president of Bates Laboratories, Inc., of Chicago. Member Am. Math. Soc.; fellow Am. Institute Actuaries, Am. Assn. Advancement of Science. Author: The Elements of the Differential and Integral Calculus, 1904; A Short Course in Differential Equations, 1907; A Short Course in Life Insurance, 1909. Actuary in charge of the preparation of bills for the following annuity and benefit funds for public employees which are now laws: Policemen of Milwaukee; Firemen of Milwaukee; Sheriffs of Milwaukee; Policemen of Chicago; Firemen of Chicago; Municipal Employees of Chicago; County Employees of Cook County; Sanitary District Employees; Peoria Police; Park Employees of Chicago; Park Policemen of Chicago; Laborers' and Retirement Board Employees of Chicago; Municipal Court and Law Department Employees of Chicago; Election Commissioners' Employees of Chicago. Home: 1209 Hinman Av., Evanston, Ill. Office: 3542 N. Clark St., Chicago 13

CAMPBELL, DOUGLAS HOUGHTON botanist; b. Detroit, Dec. 16, 1859; s. James Valetine and Cornelia (Hotchkiss) C.; Ph.M., U. of Mich., 1882; Ph.D., 1886, LL.D., 1932; stuided in Bonn, Tübingen and Berlin, 1886-88; unmarried. Instr. in biology, Detroit High Sch., 1882-86; prof. botany, Ind. U., 1888-91, Leland Stanford U., 1891-1925, prof. emeritus since 1925. Mem. Nat. Acad. Sciences, Am. Philos. Soc.; fellow Am. Acad. Arts and Sciences, Royal Soc. Edinburgh foreign mem. Linnaean Soc.; mem. various other Socs., Am. and European Clubs: University (San Francisco); Authors' (London). Author: Elements of Structural and Systematic Botany, 1890; Structure and Development of Mosses and Ferns, 1895; 3d edit., 1918. Lectures on Evolution of Plants, 1899, A University Text Book of Botany, 1902, 2d edit., 1907; Plant Life and Evolution, 1911; Outline of Plant Geography, 1926; Evolution of the Land Plants, 1940. Also many monographs and other scientific papers. Address: Box 943, Stanford University, Cal. Died Feb. 23, 1953

CAMPBELL, EDWARD DE MILLE, chemist; b. Detroit, Mich., Sept. 9, 1863; s. James Valentine and Cornelia (Hotchkiss) C.; B.S. in Chemistry, U. of Mich., 1886; m. Jennie M. Ives, 1888. Chemist Ohio Iron Co., Zanesville, 1886-87, Sharon (Pa.) Iron Co., 1887-88, Dayton (Tenn.) Coal & Iron Co., 1888-90; asst. prof. metallurgy, 1890, jr. prof. metallurgy and metall. chemistry, 1893, jr. prof. analytical chemistry, 1896, prof. chem. engring. and analytical chemistry, 1902, dir. chem. lab. and prof. chem. engring. and analytical chemistry, 1905, prof. chemistry and dir. chem. lab., 1914, prof. chemistry and metallurgy and dir. chem. lab., 1920—, all U. of Mich. Cons. chemist, Ordnance Dept. at large, Oct. 1917 to close of War. Home: Ann Arbor, Mich. Died Sept. 18, 1925.

CAMPBELL, ELMER GRANT, biology; b. Fairburn, Ga., Feb. 11, 1876; s. William Jackson and Sarah Elizabeth (Smith) C.; A.B., Hiram (O.) Coll., 1905; M.S., Purdue U., 1914; Ph.D., U. of Chicago, 1923; m. Elizabeth Fisher, Oct. 24, 1904; 1 son, Elbert Grant. Teacher, prin. and dir. biology, high schs., Ind. and Mich., 1907-12; instr. in biology, Purdue, 1912-15; asst. prof. botany, Tex. State Coll., 1915-18; head of dept. agrl. botany, Purdue U., 1919-27; became dean of men and head of biology dept., Transylvania Coll. and Coll. of the Bible, Lexington, Ky., 1927, head of institution, 1928-32; became dean of men and head of botany, Oglethorpe U., 1932; head of human biology and dean of students, U. of Ga., Atlanta Div., 1933, now research associate. Mem. Am. Assn. Advancement of Science, Sigma Xi, Phi Kappa Tau, Alpha Kappa Psi. Democrat. Mem. Christian (Disciples) Ch. Mason. Author: General Elementary Botany, 1929, rev. edit., 1941; Phantoms (nature sketches), 1940; Life's Temples (biology text), 1942; Man and Others. Contbr. research and academic papers. Home: 810 Virginia Circle N.E. Office: 24 Ivy St. S.E., Atlanta GA

CAMPBELL, GEORGE ASHLEY, telephone research engr.; b. Hasting, Minn., Nov. 27, 1870; s. Cassius Samuel and Lydia Lorraine (Ashley) C.; B.S., Mass. Inst. Tech., 1891; A.B., Havard, 1892; A.M., 1893, Ph.D., 1901; stuided Göttingen, Vennia and Paris; m. Caroline Gillis Sawyer, 1913; children—Alexander Hovey (dec.), Ashley Sawyer, With Am. Tel. and Tel. Co., 1897-1934; with Bell Telephone Labs., 1934-35. Mem. Am. Acad. Arts and Sciences Math. Soc., Math. Assn. America, Physical Soc., A.A.A.S. Distinguished Service medal, Inst. Radio Engrs., 1936; Elliott Cresson medal, Franklin Inst., 1939. Edison medal, Am. Inst. of Elec. Engrs., 1940. Pioneering research in connection with loading, crosstalk, 4-wire repeater circuits, sidetone reduction, electric wave filters, inductive interference, antenna arrays, maximum output networks, Fourier intergrals and electrical units. Author: Collected Papers, 1937. Republican. Conglist. Home: Upper Montclair, N.J. Died Nov. 10, 1954; buried Easthampton, Mass.

CAMPBELL, HARDY WEBSTER, soil culturist; b. Montgomery Centre, Vt., July 21, 1850; s. John and Mary M. (Hopkins) C., both of Scotch parentage; commn sch. edn.; m. 3d, Elizabeth M. Turney, of Seward, Neb., Dec. 20, 1902. Reared on farm until until 18; began as mfr. butter tubs and boxes in Vt., 1868; twice burned out; went to Norwood, N.Y., 1878, and built largest factory of the kind then in the U.S.; again burned out, 1879 (total loss). Took up homestead in Brown Co., Dak. Ty., in 1879; began studying soil production scientifically, owing to failure of wheat crop in that section, 1883; in 1894 raised 142 bushels of potatoes to the acre on 32 acres, while neighbors raised practically nothing; developed system of dry farming known as the "Campbell System," now adopted in many countries of the world. Has directed extensive experiments in soil culture in many states of the West; traveling agriculturist for C., B. & Q. Ry. several yrs. to Oct. 1916; agrl. agt. Southern Pacific Ry. Co., 1916—. Republican. Conglist. Author: Campbell's 1901 Soil Culture Manual, 1901; Campbell's 1905 Manual, 1905; Campbell's 1907 Manual, 1907; Campbell's Soil Culture Almanac, 1907; Campbell's Farming for Profit, 1914; Campbell's Farming for Profit, 1914; Campbell's Progressive Farming for Profit, 1914; Campbell's Progressive Agriculture, 1916. Inventor of several new implements for soil tillage. Home: 1350 Pine St. Office: S.P. Bldg., San Francisco, Calif.

CAMPBELL, HARRY HUSE, steel expert; b. W. Roxbury, Mass., Mar. 10, 1859; s. John H. C. and Caroline E. (Huse) C.; B.S., in mining engring., Mass. Inst. Tech., 1879; unmarried. Began in a minor capacity, 1879, with Pa. Steel Co., and advanced through various positons, including gen. supt. and gen. mgr.; metall. engr. same, Sept., 1905—, and also of Md. Steel Co., Spanish-Am. Iron Co. Investigated the scientific principles of open hearth process of making steel. Republican. Unitarian. Author: The Manufacture and Properties of Iron and Steel, 1895, 4th edit., 1906. Home: Steelton, Pa. Deceased.

CAMPBELL, JAMES LEROY, physician; b. Fulton County, Georgia, July 15, 1870; s. Thomas Jefferson II, and Mary Jane (Brown) C.; M.D., Atlanta Med. Coll.; m. Mary Jones, Sept. 20, 1899; children—Lula Grove (Mrs. George M. Ivey), James LeRoy, Jr. Prof. surg. anatomy, clinical surgery, 1920-40; chief, surg. service, Emory U. Div. of Grady Hosp., 1921-30; emeritus prof. clinical surgery, Emory U. Sch. of Medicien, since 1940. Author of present Ga. state law for control of cancer; established state aid cancer clinics for treatment of indigent cancer victims in Ga.; secured amendment to constitution of Ga., exempting ednl. institutions from taxation, 1918. Ga. state chmn. Am. Soc. for Control of Cancer, 1920-29; chmn. cancer commn. of Med. Assn. of Ga., since 1918; chmn. exec. com. Ga. Div. of Women's Field Army of Am. Soc. for Control of Cancer, 1937-47; member board of dirs. Am. Soc. for Control of Cancer, 1939-46. Fellow A.M.A., Am. Coll. of Surgeons; mem. Southern Med. Assn., Fulton Co. Med. Soc., Med. Assn. of Ga., Omicron Delta Kappa, Phi Beta Kappa, Alpha Omega Alpha. Democrat. Methodist. Author of numerous articles in professional journals. Home: 1315 Fairview Rd. N.E. Office: 478 Peachtree St., Atlanta 3, Ga. Died June 11, 1948.

CAMPBELL, JOHN LOGAN, civil engr.; b. Perry Co., Ill., Nov. 30, 1863; s. Hugh and Jane C.; ed. Ewing (Ill.) Coll. and Nat. Normal U., Lebanon, O.; M.C.E., Pa. Mil. Coll., 1916; m. Elizabeth Loretta Rule, of Perry Co., Ill., May 10, 1888; children—Marian Elizabeth, Logan, Doyle. Began as dep. co. surveyor, El Paso Co., Tex., 1888; city engr., El Paso, 1890-94; resident engr. constrn., Rio Grande Northern Ry., 1894; chief engr. Rio Grande Dam & Irrigation Co., 1894-98; locating engr. Rio Grande, Sierra Madre & Pacific Ry., of Mexico, 1895; chief engr. location and constrn., El Paso & Northeastern Ry., 1897, 98; locating engr. Santa Fe Ry., 1899-1900; engr. in charge location and construction Ariz. & N.M. Ry., 1900-01; chief engr. location and constrn. St. L., K.C. & Colo. Ry., now St. Louis line of R.I. Ry., 1901-05; apptd. engr. maintenance of way El Paso & S.W. System, 1905; chief engr., 1920-24; asst. to chief engr. S.P. Co., 1924-28; chief engr. Northwestern Pacific R.R. Co., 1928-31 (retired). Mem. Am. Soc. C.E., Am. Ry. Engring. Assn. (1st v.p. 1921-22, pres. 1922-23). Republican. Presbyn. Home: 2917 E. 29th St., Oakland, Calif.

CAMPBELL, JOHN LYLE, prof. physics and astronomy, Wabash Coll., 1850—; b. Salem, Ind., Oct. 13, 1827; s. David G. C.; grad. Wabash Coll., 1849 (A.M., 1852; LL.D., Ind. State Univ., 1876); m. Mary E. Johnston, July 27, 1854. Civ. engr., 1849-50; in 1866 made 1st suggestion to Mayor McMichael of Phila. concerning Centennial Expn., 1976; Centennial Commr. for Ind., 1874-78; sec. U.S. Centennial Commn., 1875-78; pres. Ind. Bd. of Commrs. for Columbia Expn., Chicago, 1893; asst. U.S. Coast and Geodetic Survey, 1881-89. Home: Crawfordsville, Ind. Died 1904.

CAMPBELL, JOHN PENDLETON, biologist; b. Cumberland, Md., Nov. 20, 1863; s. John B. H. and Ellen W. (Magruder) C.; A.B., Johns Hopkins, 1885, Ph.D., 1888; m. Martha F. Hunter, of Winchester, Va., Feb. 9, 1892. Prof. biology, U. of Ga., since June, 1888. Mem. Am. Soc. Naturalists, Am. Physiol. Soc., A.A.A.S., Phi Beta Kappa. Address: Athens, Ga.

CAMPBELL, JOHN TENBROOK, surveyor; b. nr. Montezuma, Ind., May 21, 1833; s. Joseph and Rachel (TenBrook) C.; ed. dist. schs.; one term Western Manual Labor Acad.; m. Annie Butterfield, Dec. 15, 1864. Capt. Co. H, 21st Ind. Vols., 1861; right leg permanently crippled in battle, Baton Rouge, La., Aug. 5, 1862; resigned, Oct. 29, 1862; asst. provost-marshal, 7th Congl. Dist. of Ind., June 24-Nov. 4, 1863; treas. Parke Co., Ind., 2 terms; asst. assessor internal revenue, 1870; Republican; later Greenbacker; returned to Rep. party, 1890; defeated for state senate as Greenbacker, 1870; journal clerk, Ind. Senate, 1878; 1st asst., Ind. Bur. of Statistics, 1878-83; co. surveyor 10 yrs. Devised 5 new problems in trigonometry as applied to surveying; also 2 new problems in curve work, with formula for application in practice. Home: Rockville, Ind. Deceased.

CAMPBELL, LEON astronomer; b. Cambridge, Mass., Jan. 20, 1881; s. William J. and Leonora(Rawding) C.; student pub. schs., Cambridge and spl. instrn., Harvard Obs.; m. Fredrica J. Thompson, June 15, 1905; children—Leon, Florence May, Malcolm Fredric, Ruth Evelyn, Eleanor Beatrice. Asst. at Harvard Obs., 1899-1911; in charge of Arequipa (Peru) sta., 1911-15, variable star investigator, and astronomer, 1915—; instr. in astronomy, Harvard, 1928, Pickering Meml. Astronomer, 1931—. Assists in extension of research among amateur astronomers. Mem. Am. Astron. Soc., Am. Assn. Variable Star Observers (pres. 1919-22), Internat. Astron. Union, Lima Geog. Soc. (hon.). Contbr. to annals of Harvard Obs., and astron. mags.; Co-author: the Story of Variable Stars. 1941. Died May 10, 1951.

CAMPBELL, MARIUS ROBISON, geologist; b. Garden Grove, Ia., Sept. 30, 1858; s. Alvah W. and Eliza (Davis) C.; ed. in common schs.; taught country schs.; attended Ohio-State U., 1885-86; m. Margaret Stevenson, Nov. 5, 1890. Civ. engr. on ry. constructions, 1886-88; geologist in U.S. Geol. Survey, 1889—. Fellow Geol. Soc. America. Home: Washington, D.C. Died Dec. 7, 1940.

CAMPBELL, SAM(UEL) (ARTHUR), naturalist, lecturer, author; b. Watseka, Ill., Augl 1, 1895; s. Arthur James and Katherine (Lyman) C.; ed. public school and high school, Chicago, Ill.; m. Virginia M. Adams, June 10, 1941. Began as musician, also in indsl. real estate, motion picture photographer; produced 150,000 feet of nature films to illustrate lectures; 9,000 lectures in 30 yrs.; plus radio and TV programs. Christian Scientist. Rotarian. Club: Lake Shore (Chicago). Author: How's Inky?, 1943; Too Much Salt and Pepper, 1944; Eeny, Meeny, Miney and Still Mo, 1945; A Tippy Canoe and Canado Too, 1946; On Wings of Cheer, 1948; Moose Country, 1950; The Seven Secrets of Somewhere Lake, 1952; Nature's Messages, 1952; Loony Coon, 1954; Fiddlesticks and Freckles, 1955; Beloved Rascals, 1957; Sweet Sue's Adventures, 1959; Calamity Jane, published in the year 1962. Known as Sam Campbell, the philosopher of the forest. Organizer, conductor of the Sam Campbell Nature Lover Tours; established Sam Campbell Conservation Scholarship, 1965. Home: Three Lakes, Wis. (winter); 220 Oak Knoll Rd., Barrington, Ill. Died Apr. 13, 1962.

CAMPBELL, THOMAS DONALD, mech. and agrl. engr.; b. Grand Forks, N.D., Feb. 19, 1882; s. Thomas and Almira Cathrine (Richards) C.; A.B., U. N.D., 1903, M.E., 1904, LL.D., 1929; post-grad. Cornell U., 1904-05; D.Eng., U. So. Cal., 1929; m. Bess McBride Bull, Oct. 3, 1906; children—Thomas D. (dec.), Elizabeth Ann, Jean, Cathrine. Engaged in farming since 1898; operated 95,000 acres of land in Mont. and raised wheat and flax; spl. investigator available farm lands on Indian reservations for U.S. Dept. Interior, World War I; pres. and chief engr. Campbell Farming Corp. since 1922; spl. adviser, cons. engr. for Russian Govt. to assist in forming plans covering operation 10 million acres in Russia, 1929; spl. adviser to Brit. Govt. on increased wheat prodn. and agrl. mechanization, 1941; made report for French Govt. on increased wheat prodn. in N. Africa, 1948. Serving as col. AC, U.S. Army, since 1942, overseas, 1943, 45; brig. gen., Apr. 1946; now gen. Army Res. Awarded Commandeur Degree, French Legion of Honor. Mem. Am. Soc. M.E., Am. Soc. Agrl. Engrs., Am. Assn. Engrs., Soc. Am. Mil. Engrs., Am. Inst. Cons. Engrs. Delta Tau Delta. Republican. Presbyn. Mason (Shriner). Clubs: University (Los Angeles); Twilight, Valley Hunt (Pasadena); Union League (Chgo.); University (Washington); Cornell (N.Y.C.). Author: Russia, Market or Menace. Inventor, Campbell Grain Dryer; developer Campbell windrow method of harvesting and threshing grain and furrow dammers on grain drills for conserving moisture. Home: Harden, Mont.; and Albuquerque. Office: Korber Bldg., Albuquerque. Died Mar. 1966.

CAMPBELL, WILLIAM, metallurgist; b. Gateshead-on- Tyne, England, June 24, 1876; s. Thomas and Francieska (Albrecht) C.; grad. Civil Service Dept., King's Coll., London, 1892; St. Kenelms Coll., Oxford, 1892-94; Durham U. Coll. Science, 1894-97, A.Sc., 1896, B.Sc., 1897, M.Sc., 1903, Sc.D., 1905; Royal Sch. of Mines, London, 1899-1901; Ph.D., Columbia, 1903, A.M., 1905, Sc.D., 1928; m. Estelle M. Campbell. Demonstrator in metallurgy and lecturer in geology, Durham Coll. of Science, 1898-99; "Royal Exhbn. of 1851" research scholar, Royal Sch. of Mines, London, 1899-1901; univ. fellow, Columbia, 1902, Barnard fellow, 1903; univ. fellow, Columbia, 1902, Barnard fellow, 1903; lecturer on European geology, 1903-06, instr. in metallurgy, 1904-07, adj. prof., 1907-12, asso. prof., 1912-14, prof., 1914-24, Howe prof., 1924—, Sch. of Mines, Columbia. Metallographer Technologic Branch U.S. Geol. Survey, 1907-11; metallographer Bur. of Mines, same, 1911-21; lecturer on metallurgy, U.S. Naval Acad. Post-Grad. Sch., 1913. Editor Sch. of Mines Quarterly, 1910; asst. editor Internat. Jour. of Metallography, Jour. Indsl. and Engineering Chemistry. Fellow Geol. Soc. London, New York Acad. Sciences (v.p. 1911). Awarded Saville Shaw Medal, Soc. Chem. Industry (British), 1903; Carnegie Scholarship, Iron and Steel Inst., 1903; Research Grant, Carnegie Instrn., 1905, Mem. com. on alloy steel, Nat. Research Council; metallurgist, Navy Yard, New York, 1917; mem. advisory com. U.S. Bur. of Standards; lt. comdr. U.S. N.R.F., 1918, comdr., 1919-29; advisory metallurgist, Navy Yard, New York, 1921-26; advisory metallurgist, Bd. of Transportation N.Y. City. Epsicopalian. Mason. Home: New York, N.Y. Died Dec. 16, 1936.

CAMPBELL, WILLIAM WALLACE, pres. emeritus U. of Calif., atronomer; b. on farm, Hancock Co., O., Apr. 11, 1862; s. Robert Wilson and Harriet (Welch) Wester U. of Pa., 1900, U. of Mich., 1905, U. of Western Australia, 1922, Cambridge U., 1925, Columbia U., 1928, U. of Chicago, 1931; LL.D., U. of Wis., 1902, U. of Calif., 1932; m. Elizabeth Ballard Thompson, Dec. 28, 1892; children—Wallace, Douglas, Kenneth. Prof. mathematics, U. of Colo., 1886-88; instr. astronomy, U. of Mich., 1888-91; astronomer, 1891-1930 (emeritus), acting dir., 1900, dir., 1901-20, emeritus, Lick Observatory; pres. U. of Calif., 1923-30, emeritus. In charge Lick Obs. eclipse expdn. to India, Jan. 1898, Ga., May 1900, Spain, Aug. 1905, Flint Island, Jan. 1908, Kiev, Russia, Aug. 1914, Goldendale, Wash., June 1918, Wallal, Western Australia, Sept. 1922; mem. expdn. to Lower Calif., Mexico, Sept. 1923. Silliman lecturer, Yale, 1909-10; William Ellery Hale lecturer, Nat. Acad. Sciences, 1914; Halley lecturer, Oxford, 1925. Lalande prize (gold medal), Paris Acad. Sciences, 1903; gold medal, Royal Astron. Soc., 1906; Draper gold medal, Nat. Acad. Sciences, 1910; Bruce gold medal, 1915. Comdr. Order of Leopold II, 1919; Officer Legion of Honor (France), 1927; comdr. Order Crown of Italy, 1928. Trustee Carnegie Instrn. (Washington), Internat. House (Berkeley, Calif.). Mem. Am. Acad. Arts and Sciences, Science. Author: The Elements of Practical Astronomy, 1899; Stellar Motions, 1913; Stellar Radial Velocities (with collaboration of J. H. Moore), 1928. Home: San Francisco, Calif. Died June 14, 1938.

CAMPBELL, WILLIS COHOON, orthopedic surgeon; b. Jackson, Miss., Dec. 18, 1880; s. Charles C. and Lula (Cohoon) C.; M.D., U. of Va., 1904; m. Elizabeth Yerger, June 30, 1908; children—Louise, Willis, Elizabeth, George. Practiced at Memphis, Tenn., 1906—; prof. of orthopedic surgery, U. of Tenn. Coll. of Medicine, 1910—; consultant in orthopedic surgery, Bapt. Memorial and St. Joseph's hosp., U.S. Marine Hops. No. 12; chief of staff Dr. Willis C. Campbell Clinic, Crippled Children's Hosp., Hosp. for Crippled Adults; attending orthopedic surgeon Methodist Hosp. Fellow Am. Coll. Surgeons. Democrat. Episcopalian. Author: Orthopedic Surgery, 1930; Orthopedics of Childhood (monograph), 1927; Operative Orthopaedics, 1939. Home: Memphis, Tenn. Died May 4, 1941.

CANFIELD, ROY BISHOP, M.D.; b. Lake Forest, Ill., July 22, 1874; s. Eli Lake and Sarah Maria (Bishop) C.; A.B., U. of Mich., 1897, M.D., 1899; studied U. of Friedrich Wilhelm, Berlin, Germany; m. Leila Marchant Harlow, Aug. 6, 1907. Interne, Mass. Charitable Eye and Ear Infirmary, 1900-01; chief of clinic, Jansensche Klinik und Poliklinik, Berlin, 1903; asst. surgeon, Manhattan Eye, Ear and Throat Hosp., New York, 1904; attending laryngologist, N.Y. City Clinic for Laryngeal Tuberculosis, 1904; clin. prof. diseases of ear, nose and throat, Med. Sch., U. of Mich., 1904-05; prof. oto-laryngology, same, 1905—; oto-laryngologist in chief to Univ. Hosp., 1904. Commd. maj. Med. C. U.S.A., Sept. 1917; chief of ear, nose and throat sect., Base Hosp., Camp Custer, till ordered to Neuro-Surg. Sch. and Rockefeller Inst., New York; chief of surg. service Base Hosp. 76, A.E.F.; later surg. consultant Base Sec. III; hon. disch., Jan. 11, 1918. Fellow Am. Coll. Surgeons. Protestant. Home: Ann Arbor, Mich. Died May 12, 1932.

CANNON, A. BENSON, physician; b. Wilcox County, Ala., Nov. 10, 1888; s. Edmund Rashe and Pencye (Bigger) C.; LL.D., Erskine Coll., S.C., 1909; M.D., Tulane U., 1913; student U. of Vienna, 1924-25; m. Eleanor Moore Reid, Nov. 9, 1916; 1 Presbyn. dau., Cynthia. Interne Hosp. New York City, 1913-16; asst. dermatologist in office Dr. John A. Fordyce, 1916; prof. dermatology, Coll. of Phys. and Surgs., Columbia Univ.; dir. dept. dermatology, City Hosp., consulant Woman's New York Neurological, St. Mary's Nassau County and Sharon hosps., Vassar Hosp. (Poughkeepsie, N.Y.). Trustee Erskine Coll. Mem. A.M.A., Am. Acad. of Dermatology and Syphiloloyy, Soc., New York Acad. of Medicine, Vienna Dermatol. Soc. (hon. mem.), Clin Research Soc., Sigma Alpha Epsilon, Alpha Kappa Kappa. Clubs: Millbrook Hunt; Rapahanock Hunt (Va.); New Canaan Golf. Contbr. articles to med. jours. Home: 1160 Park Av. Address: 371 Park Av., N.Y.C. Died Nov. 27, 1950; buried Millbrook, N.Y.

CANNON, ANNIE JUMP, atronomer; b. Dover, Del., Dec. 11, 1863; d. Wilson Lee and Mary Elizabeth (Jump) C.; B.S., Wellesley, 1884, M.A., 1907; spl. work in astronomy, Radcliffe Coll.; D.Sc., U. of Del., 1918; Dr. Astronomy, U. of Groningen, Holland, 1921; LL.D., Wellesley Coll., 1925; D.Sc., Oxford U., 1925, Oglethorpe, 1935; Mt. Holyoke, 1937. Asst. Harvard Coll. Obs., 1897-1911, curator astron. photographs, 1911-38, William Cranch Bond astronomer and curator, 1938—. In course of photographic work has discovered 300 variable stars, 5 new stars, 1 spectroscopic binary and numerous stars having bright liens or variabel spectra; has completed a catalogue of 272-150 stellar spectra which fills ten quarto volumes of the annals, all of which are published; made an extension to the catalogue, giving the spectra of fainter stars. Author of various Harvard Coll. Obs. Annals. Awarded Henry Draper medal, for investigations in astro. physics, 2931; Ellen Richards Research prize, 1932. Home: Cambridge, Mass. Died Apr. 1941.

CANNON, GEORGE LYMAN, JR., geologist; b. New York, Mar. 10, 1860; s. George Lyman and Frances Amelia (Downs) C.; ed. U. of Colo. and Colo. State Sch. of Mines; A.M., Denver U., 1900; unmarried. Mgr. Colo. Chem. Works, 1882-87; instr. geology and biology, East Side High Sch., Denver, since 1887. Asst. geologist, U.S. Geol. Survey, 1888-89. Discoverer of many species of extinct vertebrates, Colo. lepidoptera and phanerogams. Fellow A.A.A.S., Colo. Scientific Soc.; mem. N.E.A., Colo. Hist. Soc., Colo. Acad. Sciences, S.A.R. Club: University. Author: Geology of Perry Park, 1890; Geology of Palmer Lake, 1892; Colorado Science Literature, 1902; Geology of Denver and Vicinity, 1894; Outlines of Zoology, 1895; Nature Study for Denver Schools, 1895. Also various papers, etc., on geology and zoology. Home: 1918 Pennsylvania St., Denver, Colo.

CANNON, SYLVESTER QUAYLE, ch. official, cons. engr.; b. Salt Lake City, June 10, 1877; s. George Quayle and Elizabeth (Hoagland) C.; student Latter Day Saints Coll., Salt Lake City, 1889-93, U. of Utah, 1894-95; B.S. in Mining Engring., Mass. Inst. Tech., 1899; m. Winnifred Saville, June 15, 1904; children—Julian Saville, Elinor, Winfield Quayle, Sylvia, Lawrence Saville, Lucile, Donald James. Began as mining and civil engr., 1902-07 and since 1909; in charge Weber River Hydrog. Survey for state engr. of Utah, 1905-07; water supply engr., Salt Lake City, 1912-13, city engr. in charge of improvements costing $411,000,000, 1913-25; cons. engr., 1925-26; cons. engr. U.S. Reclamation Service, American Falls Project, Ida., 1923; mem., State Advisory Bd., Pub. Works Adminstrn., 1933-34. Presiding Bishop, Latter Day Saints Ch., 1925-38, financial affairs supervision 1,000 bishops, 9,000 Aaronic Priesthood mems. Asso. Council of Twelve Apostles, Ch. of Jesus Christ of Latter Day Saints (Mormon), 1938-39 (mem. to date). Pres. Deseret News Pub. Co., Cannon Investment Co.; dir. Amalgamated Sugar Co., Hotel Utah Co., U.S. Fuel Co., Zion's Coop. Merc. Instn., Zion's Savings Bank. Pres. McCune Sch. of Music and Art; chmn. bd. Deseret Symnasium. Mem. Am. Soc. C.E. Republican. Clubs: Commercial, Timpanogos. Home: 1334 Second Av. Office: 47 E.S. Temple, Salt Lake City, Utah. Died May 29, 1943.

CANNON, WALTER BRADFORD, physiologist; b. Prairie du Chien, Wis., Oct. 19, 1871; s. Colberg Hanchett and Wilma (Denio) C.; A.B., Harvard U., 1896, A.M., 1897, M.D., 1900, Sc.D., Yake Univ., 1923; LL.D., Wittenberg Coll., 1927, Boston Univ., 1929; Washington Univ.; Doctor, honoris causa, Univs., of Liege and Strasbourg, 1930, Paris, 1931, Madrid, 1938, Barcelona, 1939, Catholic Univ. of Chile, 1944. Baly medalist, Royal College Physicians, London, 1931. National Institute Social Science, 1934; m. Cornelia James, June 25, 1901; children—Bradford, Wilma Denio, Linda, Marian, Helen. Instructor zoology, 1899-1900, instr. physiology, 1900-02, asst. prof., 1902-06, George Higginson prof., Sept. 1, 1906-Aug. 31, 1942, emeritus prof. since Sept. 1, 1942. Harvard. Croonian lecturer, Royal Soc., London, 1918; Harvard exchange prof. to France, 1929-30; Linacre lecturer, Cambridge U., 1930; Herter lecturer, New York, 1932; Beaumont lecturer, Detroit, 1933; Kober lecturer, Assn. Am. Physicians, 1934; Caldwell lecturer, Am. Rontgen Ray Soc., 1934; Newbold lecturer, Phila. College of Physicans, 1934; Hughlings Jackson lecturer, McGill Univeristy, 1939; visiting prof. Peiping Union Med. Sch., 1935; hon. fellow Stanford U., 1941. Fellow A.A.A.S. (pres. 1939), Am. Acad. Arts and Sciences; mem. Nat. Acad. Sciences (fgn. sec.), Acad. of Sciences of U.S.S.R. (hon.), Am. Philos. Soc., Am. Physiol. Soc., Assn. Am. Physicians, Soc. Exptl. Biology and Medicine, A.M.A., Mass. Med. Soc., Phi Beta Kappa, Alpha Omega Alpha; corr. mem. Societe de Biologie (Paris), R. Academia delle Scienze, Bologna, Sociedad de Biologia, Buenos Aires, Societe Belge de Biologie (Brussels), Royal Soc. Medicine (Budapest); fgn. mem. Royal Soc. London, Royal Swedish Acad. of Science; hon. mem. Academic Nacionale de Medicina (Spain), Royal Soc. Edinburgh, British Physiol. Soc., Academia de Medicina (Barcelona), Academic Royale de Medicina de Belgique (Belgium), Nat. Acad. of Medicine (Mexico). Pres. Med. Research Soc. of Am. Red Cross, France, 1917-18. Awarded Friedenwald medal by the Am. Gastroenterological Assn., 1941. Lieut. colonel, Med. Corps, U.S. Army, 1918. Decorated Companion of the Bath (British), 1919; D.S.M. (U.S.). Author: A Laboratory Course in Physiology, 1910; The Mechanical Factors of Digestion, 1911; Bodily Changes in Pain, Hunger, Fear and Rage, 1915, revised edit., 1929; Traumatic Shock, 1923; The Wisdom of the Body, 1932, revised edition was published in 1939; Digestion and Health, 1936;

Autonomic Neuro-effector Systems (with A. Rosenblueth), 1937; The Way of an Investigator, 1945. Contributor of articles describing movements of stomach and intestines, effects of emotional excitement, organic stabilization, chem. mediation of nerve impulses, etc., and papers on med. edn. and in the defense of med. research. Club: Faculty (Cambridge). Died Oct. 1, 1945.

CAPPS, STEPHEN REID, geologist; b. Jacksonville, Ill., Oct. 15, 1881; s. Stephen Reid and Rhoda (Tomlin) C.; student Ill. Coll., Jacksonville, 1899-1901; A.B., U. of Chicago, 1903, fellow in Geology, 1906-07, Ph.D., 1907; m. Julia Isabelle Webster, Nov. 21, 1911; children—Louise C. Scranton, Stephen Reid, Mary Capps Stelle, Webster. Began as instructor Univ. High School, Chicago, 1904; geologist with U.S. Geological Survey since 1907, assistant chief geologist, 1942-44; geologist Military Geology Unit, 1944-45; engaged in areal study and economic studies in Alaska, 1908-36, of gold placers in Idaho and Colo. and of Manganese deposits in Brazil since 1936. Grant memorial lecturer Northwestern U., 1936. Mem. Geological Society of America, American Geophysical Union, Geological Soc. of Washington, Washington Acad. Sciences, Alpha Delta Phi, Sigma Xi. Club: Cosmos. Spent 2 yrs. in Near East in petroleum exploration for Standard Oil Co. of N.Y. Author of The Southern Alaska Range, Geology of the Alaska Railroad Belt, and many bulletins and articles on geol. subjects. Home: 3308 35th St N.W. Washington, D.C. Died Jan. 19, 1949.

CAPRO, JOSE ANGEL ANGEL univ. prof.; b. Cuzco, Peru, Nov. 2, 1888; s. Mariano Palcido and Cecilia Perez) C.; came to U.S., 1904; C.E., U. of Norte Dame, 1908, M.S. in E.E., 1909, M.E., Ph.D., 1913; Sc.D., U. of St. Anthony, Peru, 1910; M.A., U. of Chicago, 1919; m. Elizabeth Ella Kocsis, June 9, 1921; children—Edward Paul, Joseph Francis. Instr. mathematics, U. of Norte Dame 1908-10; prof. chemistry and anthropology, U.of St. Anthony, 1910-11; instr. physics and mathematics, U. of Notre Dame, 1912-13, acting head dept. elec. engring., 1913-18, head of dept., 1919-39, professor of electrical engineering, 1939-43, professor emeritus, 1946—; engineer Ind. and Mich. Elec. Co., 1923-25; with U. of St. Anthony, Cuzco, Peru, S.A., to 8th Internat. congress of Applied Chemistry, 1912, to the 2d Pan-Am. Scientific Congress, 1915. Served as war instr. E.E.: charter Mem. Math. Assn. Am. Democrat. Catholic Author: Desire for Gold and Conquest, 1953. Writer of elec. articles Home: 1024 Leeper Blvd., South Bend 17, Ind., Died July 12, 1954; buried Cedar Grove Cemetery, Notre Dame, Ind.

CAPRON, HORACE, agriculturist; b. Attleboro, Mass., Aug. 31, 1804; s. Dr. Seth and Eunice (Mann) C.; m. Louisa V. Snowden, June 5, 1834; m. 2d, Margaret Baker, 1854. Owner, supt. cotton factory, Laurel, Md., 1836-51; nationally known for his progressive farming techniques; commd. lt. col. 14th Ill. Cavalry during Civil War, 1863, commd. brig. gen. U.S. Volunteers, 1865, U.S. Army, 1866; U.S. commr. of agriculture, 1867-71; agrl. commr., chief adviser Japanese Govt., 1871-75; his farming methods revolutionized Japanese system of agriculture. Died Washington, D.C., Feb. 22, 1885.

CAPSTAFF, JOHN GEORGE, color photography authority; b. Gateshead-on-Tyne, Eng., Feb. 24, 1879; s. John Squier Squire and Elizabeth (Hogg) C.; ed. Heaton Sch. of Science and Art and Armstrong Coll., Durham; m. Alice Grace Wallace, of Newcastle-on-Tyne, Sept. 23, 1912; children—Phyllis Mary, Elizabeth. Came to U.S., 1913; engaged in research in photography with Eastman Kodak Co., Rochester, N.Y., 1913; pioneered in 16 millimeter motion pictures; responsible for application of the reversal process to motion pictures; holds many photographic patents; authority on color photography. Recipient Modern Pioneer award, 1940; Progress medal of Soc. Motion Picture Engrs., 1944; hon. fellowship Royal Photographic Soc., 1944; recipient progress Medal of Royal Photog. Great Britain, 1947; hon. fellowship Photographic Soc. of Am., 1950. Home: 5151 Roxbury Rd., San Diego 16, Cal. Died Jan. 31, 1960.

CARDIFF, IRA D., botanist; b. Stark Co., Ill., June 20, 1873; s. Edward Austin and Latrobe R. (Sellon) C.; B.S., Knox Coll., 1897; U. of Chicago, 1902-4; Ph.D., Columbia, 1906; m. Myrtle Sherman, of Galesburg, Ill., Aug. 14, 1902. Teacher and prin. pub. schs., Ill., 1897-1901; asst. in botany, Columbia, 1904-6; asst. prof. botany, 1906-7, prof., 1907-8, U. of Utah; prof. botany, Washburn Coll., Topeka, Kan., Sept., 1908-12; prof. plant physiology and bacteriology, 1912, head of dept. of botany and dir. State Expt. Sta., Washington State Coll., 1913—. Dir. Washburn Summer Sch., 1909-12; prof. botany, U. of Kan. Summer Sch., 1911-12. Mem. 6th Ill. Inf., Spanish-Am. War, 1898, in P.R. Fellow A.A.A.S.; mem. Utah Acad. Science (pres., 1908), Kan. Acad. Science. Contbr. Bot. Gazette, Bull. Torrey Bot. Club, Plant World, etc. Home: 302 Oak St., Pullman WA

CARDWELL, JAMES R., inventor, industrialist; b. Concord, Va., Oct. 27, 1873; s. Charles W. and Dolly Ming (Franklyn) C.; m. Zouella Durbin, Mar. 14, 1904; children—Dorothy (Mrs. Kenneth Kinckerbocker), Virginia Ann (Mrs. Reinhardt), Began as office boy Am. Cotton Oil Co., 1893, became master car builder, 1898; organized Cardwell Mfg. Co., 1905, Union Draft Gear Co., 1909 (reorginized as Cardwell-Westinghouse Co., 1930, of which is now chmn.); organizer Acme Visible Records Co., v.p. and dir. Diamond T. Motor Car Co.; dir. Allied Mills Co., Domestic Credit Co. Developed improved r.r. brake shoe draft gear. Home: 365 Oak Knoll Rd., Barrington Ill. Office: 332 S. Michigan Av., Chgo. Died Dec. 8, 1957.

CAREY, EBEN JAMES, physician, educator; b. Chicago, Ill., July 31, 1889; s. Frank White and Mary Anne (Curran) C.; pre-med. studies, U. of Calif., 1909-11; 1st and 2d yrs. in medicine, 1911-13; B.S., Creighton U., Omaha, Neb., 1916, M.S., 1918, D.Sc., 1920; M.D., Rush Med. Coll., Chicago, 1925; m. Helene Lichnovsky, Sept. 3, 1919; 1 dau., Mary Anne. Instr. and asst. prof. anatomy, Creighton U., 1914-20; prof. and dir. dept. of anatomy, Marquette U. Sch. of Medicine, Milwaukee, 1920-26, also dean med. student, 1921-26, acting dean, 1926, dean and prof. of anatomy since Aug., 1933; med. dir. Marquette Free Dispensary, 1924; chief of staff Marquette U. Hosp., 1926. Commd. 1st lt. R.O.T.C.; now lt col. State Staff, Wis. Nat. Guard. Chmn. Scientific Exhbn., Inter-State Postgrad. Med. Assembly, Wilwaukee, 1931; in charge med. sect., dept. exhibits, Chicago World's Fair, 1933-34; dir. med. science exhibits, Museum of Science and Industry, Chicago, since 1934. Mem. advisory com. med. exhibits Tex. Centennial, Dallas, 1935-36, Golden Gate Internat. Expdn., 1939; mem. scientific com. A.M.A., 1935-41. Chmn. program com. Council on Scientific Work, Med. Soc. of Wis. Silver medal for exhibit illustrating original investigation on intrinsic wave mechanics of the nervous and muscular systems, convention of A.M.A., Atlantic City, June, 1937. Hon. fellowship Am. Coll. of Dentistry, 1939. Fellow A.A.A.S., A.M.A., N.Y. Acad. Sciences; mem. Wis. State and Milwaukee County (pres. 1942) med. socs., Milwaukee Acad. Medicine (pres. 1939-40), Chicago Inst. Medicine, Newcomen Soc. Eng., Alpha Omega Alpha, Pi Kappa Epsilon, Phi Chi (chmn. exec. trustees, editor Quarterly since 1932). Democrat. Catholic. Fourth degree, K.C. Author: Studies in Anatomy, 1924; also many tech. articles. Silvgr medal for scientific exhibit on exptl. bone origin and pathology, at A.M.A. Conv., Minneapolis, Minn., 1928; citation of merit for scientific exhibit of continued exptl. studies on bone origin at A.M.A. Conv., Portland, Ore., July, 1929; citation of merit, A.M.A. Conv., Detroit, 1930, Philadelphia, 1931; gold medal for studies on origin of muscle and bone, Radiol. Soc. of N.A., 1933; gold medal for exhibit on motor nerve endings, A.M.A. meeting, Atlantic City, June 1942. Clubs: Rotary, University (Milwaukee); Rotary (Chicago). Home: 6119 W. Wisconsin Ave., Wauwatosa, Wis. Office: 561 N. 15th St., Milwaukee, Wis. Died June 5, 1947.

CAREY, JAMES WILLIAM, consulting civil and elec. engr.; b. Duluth, Minn., Aug. 28, 1892; s. Peter and Marie (Nichols) C.; ed. various schs. of Minn., Ohio, N.Y.; m. Sally B. Lofthus, Dec. 5, 1942. Transitman on railroad constrn. work, State of Washington, 1908-09; constrn. engr. building railroads, docks, power and sewer systems for Pacific Coast Steamship Co., Pacific Coast Coal Co., Pacific Coast R.R. Co., 1909-15; charge valuation work of Pacific Coast R.R. Co. of Wash. and Pacific Coast Ry. Co. of Calif. for Interstate Commerce Commn., 1915-17; constrn. engr., various positions, 1919-21; constrn. engr. transmission lines, Stone & Webster Engring. Corp., 1921-22; chief engr., State of Wash. Dept. Pub. Works and Tax Commn., Wash., 1922-28; cons. engr., Portland, Ore., and Tacoma, Wash., engaged in valuation, reports on water power sites, etc., including present Bonneville power site; outlined present public service laws Oregon, 1928-33; chief engr. Department Public Service, Wash., 1933-36; state engr. in charge construction. Fed. P.W.A., State of Wash., 1936-38; cons. civil and elec. engr., Seattle and Tacoma., Wash., 1938-43; member of firm of James W. Carey & Associates, Carey & Kramer, consulting engineers; member U.S.-Alaskan Internat. Highway Commn., 1938-54; member National Rivers and Harbors Congress. Served as officer U.S. Naval Reserve Force, World War, 1917-19; engaged as consulting engr. rebuilding City of Renton, Wash., as defense matter; new streets, water and sewer system, sewage disposal plant, 1944; designed Des Chutes Basin Project, dam, spillway; Tolt River Dam for Seattle Water Supply; design for USN, largest drydock in world, Bremerton, Wash. with N.Y. firm); co-designer met. sewage project City of Seattle; engaged in work with Hydro-Electric Project, Sitka, Alaska; widely known in electric light, power, water, sewerage and sewage disposal appraisals. Mem. Soc. Am. Military Engrs., Washington Soc. Profl. Engrs. (pres. 1942; nat. vice pres., 1944), Am. Legion, Forty and Eight, Seattle Exec. Assn., Seattle C. of C., Am. Water Works Assn., Northwest Sewage Assn., Am. Concrete Inst., Am. Arbitration Assn., Cons. Engrs. Assn., Nat. Rivers and Harbor Congress; past pres. Alaska-Yukon Pioneers. Mason (K.T.). Clubs: Rainier, Blue Ridge (past pres.), Washington Athletic, Arctic, Engineers (Seattle). Author numerous engring. papers. Home: Seattle WA Died Aug. 2, 1969.

CAREY, WILLIAM FRANCIS, contractor, engr.; b. Hoosick Falls, N.Y., Sept. 14, 1878; s. William and Catherine (Ryan) C.; ed. schools, Hoosick Falls; m. Ocean K. Daily, Oct. 28, 1904; children—Francesca, William Francis. Partner various contracting concerns engaged in building railways for Chinese Govt., financed by Am. Internat. Corp. of New York; gen. supt. of excavation during bldg. of Panama Canal; built railroad in Bolivia from Cochabamba to Santa Cruz; sanitary commr., N.Y.C., 1936-45; engaged in cement rock mining in Brazil and Argentina; pres. Carey, Baxter & Kennedy, Inc., Siems Carey Ry. & Canal Co.; v.p., The China Corp.; dir. Curtis-Wright Corp., Lone Star Cement Corp.; mem. Commn., Washington, as special advisor on construction of army, marine and aviation cantonments, World War II. Catholic. Clubs: Bankers, Engineers, Grand Street Boys Assn.; Hoosick Falls (N.Y.) Country; Bay Shore Yacht; Scranton (Pa.) Club: Split Rock (White Haven, Pa.) Home: 100 S. Montgomery Av., Bay Shore, L.I., N.Y. Office: Hotel Biltmore; also 342 Madison Av., N.Y.C. Died Feb., 1951.

CARHART, DANIEL, civil engr.; b. Clinton, N.J., Jan. 28, 1839; s. Charles and Christianna (Bird) C.; C.E., Poly. Coll. of Pa., 1859, M.C.E., 1869; Sc.D., Western U. of Pa., 1897; m. Josephine R. Stoy, Apr. 17, 1867. Practicing civ. engring., 1859-68; asst. prof. and prof. civ. engring. Poly. Coll. of Pa., 1868-78; prof. mathematics and civ. engring., 1882-92, dean collegiate and engring. depts., 1892-1908, emeritus prof. civ. engring., 1908—, Western U. of Pa. (now U. of Pittsburgh). Author: Plane Surveying (text-book), 1888. Apptd., Aug. 1913, by the pres. of Civ. Service Commn., leading advisory on the bd. to pass upon the eligibility of applicants to fill postions as sr. civ. engr. in the Interstate Commerce Commission under the act providing for the valuation of properties of common carriers. Home: Pittsburgh, Pa. Died Dec. 7, 1926.

CARHART, FRANK MILTON, cons. engr.; b. Ogden, Utah, Dec. 18, 1882; s. Sanford M. and Frank (Schramm) C.; B.S., Mass. Inst. Tech., 1905; m. Elizabeth Bush, 1911. Asst. state engr., Ida., 1908-13; engr. So. Ida. Water Power Co., American Falls, 1914-16; engr. Ida. Power Co., Boise, 1916-19, valuation engr., 1919-22; cons. engr. Thomas Conway, Jr., Phila., 1911-23; dept. mgr. Jackson & Moreland, cons. engrs., Boston, 1923-27, mem. firm, 1927-30, gen. partner, 1930-51, sr. partner, 1951-55, pres. Jackson & Moreland, Inc., 1956-58, chmn., 1958-63; pres. Wood-Regan Instrument Co.; dir. United Engrs. & Constructors, Inc. Fellow I.E.E.E.; mem. Am. Soc. C.E., A.S.M.E. Engring Soc. N.E., Am. Inst. Cons. Engrs., Boston Soc. C.E., Am. Gas Inst., A.A.A.S. Republican. Clubs: India House, Engrs., Algonquin, Brae Burn Country (Boston); Halifax (N.S.). Home: 21 Rockridge Rd., Wellesley Hills, Mass. Office: Park Square Bldg., Boston. Died June 25, 1965; buried Wellesley (Mass.) Cemetery.

CARHART, HENRY SMITH, physicist; b. Coeymans, N.Y., Mar. 27, 1844; s. Daniel S. and Margaret (Martin) C.; A.B., Wesleyan, Conn., 1869, A.M., 1872; student Yale, 1871-72, Harvard, 1876, U. of Berlin, 1881-82; (LL.D., Wesleyan, 1893, U. of Mich., 1912; Sc.D., Northwestern, 1912); m. Ellen M. Soule, Aug. 30, 1876. Prof. physics and chemistry, Northwestern U., 1872-86; prof. physics, 1886-1909, emeritus prof., 1909—, U. of Mich. Mem. Internat. Jury of Awards, Paris Expn., of Electricity, 1881; pres. Bd. Judges, Dept. Electricity, Chicago Expn., 1893; mem. Jury of Awards, Buffalo Expn., 1901; U.S. del. Internat. Elec. Congress, Chicago, 1893, St. Louis, 1904; guest of Brit. Assn. Adv. Science to S. Africa, 1905; mem. preliminary conf. on elec. units and standards, Berlin, 1905; U.S. del to conf., same, London, 1908; del. U. of Mich. to Darwin Centennial Celebration, Cambridge, Eng., 1909. Author: University Physics, 1894-96; Electrical Measurements (with G. W. Patterson), 1895; High School Physics (with H.N. Chute), 1901; College Physics, 1910; First Principles of Physics (with H. N. Chute), 1912; Physics with Applications (with H.N. Chute), 1917. Home: Pasadena, Calif. Died Feb. 13, 1920.

CARHART, WINFIELD SCOTT, mining engr.; b. Brooklyn, June 29, 1861; common school edn.; left school before 15 yrs. old because of failing health; went to Colo.; 1880; learned mining engring. by private study and practical experience; mem. Am. Inst. Mining Engrs.; a U.S. deputy mineral surveyor; fellow Nat. Geog. Soc.; unmarried. Address: Telluride, Colo.

CARLE, NATHANIEL ALLEN, engr.; b. Portland, Ore., May 28, 1875; s. Thomas Jackson and Mildred (Allen) C.; B.A., in M.E., Stanford, 1898; m. Heartie Wood, Aug. 2, 1902. Engr. Canadian Rand Drill Co., Sherbrooke, Can., 1899-1900, Westinghouse, Church, Kerr & Co., N.Y.C., 1900-09; v.p. and gen. mgr. No. Colo. Power Co., 1906-08; engr. Puget Sound Bridge & Dredging Co., Seattle, 1910-12; chief engr. Pub. Service Electric Co., Newark, 1912-22; designed and built Essex Power Sta. for this co.; v.p. and gen. mgr., Pub. Service Prodn. Co., 1922-25, design and installation of new Kearny Power Sta. for Pub. Service Electric Co.; became v.p. in charge of operation Pub. Service Prodn. Co., 1925; design and installation Harrison Gas Plant for Pub. Service Electric and Gas Co.; v.p. and gen. mgr. Seattle Toll Bridge Co.; cons. engr. of the Puget Sound Bridge & Dredging Co., Hallidie Machinery Co. (all Seattle). City engr. and chmn. Bd. Pub. Works, Seattle,

1936-38; with inspection dept. Wash. Hwys., 1939-40; cost engr., Puget Sound Bridge & Dredging Co., 1947-48; engr. Birch-Johnson-Little, constructing air bases at Anchorage and Fairbanks, Alaska; with Drake-Puget Sound at Adak and Attu, Alaska, 1948-50. Licensed prof. civil, elect., mech., hydraulic, mining engr., Wash. Life mem. Am. Soc. C.E., Am. Inst. E.E. (v.p.); mem. A.S.M-E., Am. Inst. M.E. Nat. Electric Light Assn. (ex-chmn. tech. sect. 1944-45), 1st chmn. Puget Sound Council Engring. and Tech. Socs. Mem. S.A.R., Sigma Xi, Beta Theta Pi. Republican. Episcopalian. Mason (K.T., Shriner). Address: 1656 E. Garfield St., Seattle. Died July 27, 1960.

CARLETON, BUKK, G., surgeon; b. Whitefield, H.H., Nov. 11, 1856; s. Ebenezer and Lucia M. (Dester) C.; ed. Littleton (N.H.) High Sch., 1870-73; M.D., N.Y. Homoe. Med. Coll., 1876; med. dept. U. City of New York, 1876-77; (hon. A.M., Rutgers, 1907); m. Sarah E. Robinson, Nov. 19, 1879 (died 1901); 2d, Clarice E. Griffith, Mar. 23, 1903. Mem. house staff, 1876-77, pathologist, 1877-81, visting phys., 1881-95, genito-urinary surgeon, 1895—, Homoe. and Metropolitan hosps., Dept. Pub. Charities, New York; demonstrator anatomy, 1879-80, adj. prof. of anatomy, 1880-82, N.Y. Homoe. Medical Coll.; cons. genito-urinary surgeon Hahnemann Hosp., 1897—; prof. genito-urinary surgery, 1902-10, med. ethics and clin. urology, 1910—, New York Homoe. Med. Coll. and Hosp. Author: Urological and Venereal Diseases, 1905. Died Oct. 20, 1914.

CARLETON, MARK ALFRED, plant pathologist; b. Jerusalem, O., Mar. 7, 1886; s. Lewis D. and Lydia Jane (Mann) C.; B.Sc., Kans. Agrl. Coll., 1887, M.Sc., 1893; m. Amanda Elizabeth Faught, Dec. 29, 1897. Cerealist, U.S. Dept. Agr., 1894—. Agrl. explorer for U.S. Govt. in Russia and Siberia, 11898-99; cereal expert, then plant pathologist Cuyamel (Honduras) Fruit Co. Has introduced several new grain crops from foreign countries, including especially the durum wheat industry; in charge U.S. grain exhibit and mem. jury of awards, Paris Expn., 1900; chmn. group 84, jury of awards, St. Louis Expn., 1904. Given leave of absence 15 mos., 1912-13, to conduct work of the Pa. Chestnut Tree Blight Commn. Decorated with order Mérite Agricole by French Govt. Died 1925.

CARLISLE, G(EORGE) LISTER, JR., engr., B. N.Y.C., Sept. 15, 1877; s. George Lister and Mary Swift (Coffin) C.; Harvard Sch., New York City; B.S. in Mech. Engring., Yale, 1900; m. Leila Laughlin, Feb. 28, 1915. Entered mining work on design of Experimental breaker, Auchincloss mine, Pa., 1900-02, in charge of erection of breaker; in goldmining, partner Pres. H.S. Zalaya, Nicaragua 1905-10; mining U.S., 1910-16; mem. Carlisle-Clark African expdn., Am. Museum of Natural History, N.Y.City, 1928; contbr. completed lion group to museum for Roosevelt African Hall, Trustee, Berry Coll., Rome, Ga.; mem. bd. Am. Geog. Soc., Nat. Audubon Soc., N.Y. City. Mem. Yale Engring. Assn., Am. Inst. Mining and Metall. Engrs. Rep. Conglist. Clubs: Century, Yale, Explorers (New York); Captains, Wharf Rats (Nantucket, Mass.). Home: Norfolk, Conn. Died Dec. 22, 1954.

CARLL, JOHN FRANKLIN, geologist; b. Long Island, N.Y., May 7, 1828; ed. Union Hall Acad., Jamaica, L.I.; m. Hannah A. Burtis, Nov. 15, 1853 (died 1859); 2d, Martha Tappan, Oct. 28, 1868. Published Daily Eagel, Newark, N.J., 1849-53; civil engr. and surveyor at Flushing, L.I., 1953-61; settled in Pleasantville, Pa., 1864, becoming identified with oil development; invented static pressure sand-pump, removable pump chamber and other devices now used in oil operations; in 1874 received an appmt. on the geol. survey of Pa. and as asst. in charge of the oil regions; compiled 7 vols. of the State reports; then in practice as cons. geologist. Died 1904.

CARLOCK, JOHN BRUCE, mining and mech. engr.; b. Carlock, Ill., Dec. 26, 1882; s. George Madison and Chloe (Canterbury) C.; State Normal Sch., Normal, Ill., 1895-97; State Normal Sch., Kirksville, Mo., 1897-99; Elgin (Ill.) Acad., 1899-1900; U.Chgo., 1900-01; E.M., Lehigh, 1907; m. Sidney Jane Whiteside, Feb. 4, 1919; children—Eleanor Jane (Mrs. H.H. Donaldson, Jr.), Sidney Frances (Mrs. Roger E. Beal), John Bruce. Constrn. engr. Bethlehem Steel Corp., 1907-09; field engr., supt. refineries, Gen. Petroleum Corp., Cal., 1909-14; supt. refineries, Richfield (Cal.) Oil Co., 1914-17; constr. engr. Dravo Contracting Co., Pitts., 1919-21; with Jones & Laughlin Steel Corp. 1921, chief engr. Pittsburgh South Side Works, 1926, chief engr. of plants, 1938-48, ret.; now chief cons. engr., Loftus Engring. Corp. Served as maj. Chemical Warfare Service, with 1st Gas Regt., in France, Dec. 1917-Jan. 1919; comdr. regt., Dec. 1918-Mar. 1919 Awarded Croix de Guerre (France); citation certificate and Victory Medal with six bars. Mem. Am. Iron and Steel Inst., Am. Soc. Mining and Metall. Engrs., Engrs., Soc. of Western Pa. (past pres.), Am. Soc. Mil. Engrs., Am. Ordnance Assn., S.A.R., Am. Legion, Mil. Order World War, Beta Theta Pi, Phi Beta Kappa, Tau Beta Pi. Republican. Mem. East End Christian Ch. Club: Pittsburgh Automobile (gov.). Home: D'Arlington Apts. Office: 610 Smithfield St., Pittsburgh, Pa. Died Oct. 20, 1965.

CARLSON, ANDERS JOHAN, educator, engr.; b. St. Peter, Minn., Aug. 3, 1894; s. John Sven and Mary Mathilda (Anderson) C.; B.S., U. Minn., 1916, C.E., 1917, M.S., 1925; Ph.D., U. Cal., 1929; m. Louise Josephine Thorson, Sept. 26, 1925; children—Anders Johnston, John Stanley, Mary Louise (Mrs. Gerald L. Hanes). Instr. sch. mines U. Minn., 1917-19, asst. prof., 1919-26; cons. engr., mine expert Minn. Tax Commn., 1918-26; research asst., jr. research fellow Am. Petroleum Inst., 1927-31; lectr. coll. mining U. Cal., 1926-30, asso. prof., 1930-42, prof. petroleum engring., 1942-43, prof. petroleum engring. div. mineral tech., from 1943, chmn. div., 1949-53. Ednl. supr. ESMWT, 1941-45; operations analyst USAAF, 1945. Profl. petroleum engr., Cal. Mem. Am. Petroleum Inst., A.A.A.S., Am. Chem. Soc., Sigma Xi, Tau Beta Pi, Alpha Sigma Phi, Sigma Rho, Pi Epsilon Tau, Scabbard and Blade. Clubs: Engrs. (Mpls.); Faculty (Berkeley); Univ. (Oakland, Cal.). Author research paper Inorganic Environment in Kerogen Transformation, 1937. Home: Berkeley CA Deceased.

CARLSON, ANTON JULIUS, physiologist; b. Bohuslan, Sweden, Jan. 29, 1875; s. Carl and Hedwig (Anderson) Jacobson; A.B., Augustana Coll., 1889, A.M., 1899; Ph.D. Stanford U., 1903; honorary degrees of M.D., LL.D., Sc.D. from 8 univs. and colls.; m. Esther Shegren, Sept. 26, 1905; children—Robert Bernard, Alice Esther, Alvin Julius. Came to U.S., 1891. Research asso. Carnegie Instn., 1903-04; asso., asst. prof., prof. and chmn. dept. of physiology, U. of Chicago, 1904-40, now Frank P. Hixon Distinguished Service prof. USPHS; lecturer in China under auspices of Rockefeller Found., 1935; with Am. relief expedition in Europe, 1918-19; mem. Internat. Congresses of Physiology in Vienna, 1909, Groningen, 1913, Stockholm, 1927, Boston, 1930, Leningrad and Moscow, 1935, Copenhagen, 1950, Montreal, 1953, member medical and research committees of the National Foundation of Infantile Paralysis. Served O.S.R.D. Lt. Colonel, Med. Corps. U.S. Army, 1917-19; Awarded Distinguished Service Gold Medal (A.M.A.), Distinguished Service Citation (Minn. Med. Assn.); Voted Humanist of Year, 1953. Fellow A.A.A.S. (past pres.); pres. Nat. Soc. for Med. Research, Research Council on Problems of Alcohol, Chicago Com. on Alcholism; past pres. Am. Biol. Soc., Am. Physiol. Soc., Fedn. of Am. Socs. for Exptl. Biology, Inst. of Medicine, Am. Assn. Univ. Profs.; mem. American Gerontological Society (president), Nat. Acad. Sci., National Reserach Council, A.M.A., Am. Inst. Nutrition, Am. Inst. Chemists, etc; mem. biological 1 and med. socs. of France, Germany, Sweden, China and Argentina. Author (books): Control of Hunger in Health and Disease; The Machinery of the Body; also some 200 research reports. Contbr. to Am. and German jours. on physiological subjects. Home: 5228 Greenwood Av., Chicago. 15. Died Sept. 2, 1956.

CARLSON, CHESTER, b. 1906. Inventor. Xerox copier, also leading stockholder Battelle Corp. Address: NYC NY Died Sept. 1968.

CARLSON, LOREN DANIEL, physiologist, educator; b. Davenport, Ia., May 5, 1915; s. Frank Daniel and Esther (Lind) C.; B.S., St. Ambrose Coll., 1937; Ph.D., U. Ia., 1941; Ph.D. honoris causa, U. Osio (Norway), 1969; m. Marion Dudley Gross, June 7, 1941; children—Eric Daniel, Christopher Dean, Allen David, Katherine Dudley. Research asso. cellular physiology dept. zoology U. Ia., 1941-42; instr. zoology U. Wash., 1945, asst. prof. to prof. physiology and biophysics, 1946-60; prof., chmn. dept. physiology and biophysics U. Ky. Coll. Medicine, 1960-66; chief of scis. basic to medicine U. Cal. at Davis, 1966-72, asso. dean curriculum and research devel., 1971-72. Mem. sci. adv. bd. to USAF, 1957-62. Served to maj. USAAF, 1942-46. Decorated Legion of Merit; recipient USAF Exceptional Civilian Service medal, 1962; John Jeffries award Am. Inst. Aeros. and Astronautics, 1968, Outstanding Achievement award Office Aerospace Research, Dept. Air Force, 1970. Asso. fellow Inst. Aeros. and Astronautics; fellow Aerospace Med. Assn., Am. Acad. Arts and Scis.,; mem. Am. Physiol. Soc. (pres. 1968-69), Fedn. Am. Socs. Exptl. Biology (pres. 1969-70), Soc. Exptl. Biology and Medicine, Am. Soc. Zoologists, A.A.A.S., Internationalis Astronautica Academia, Sigma Xi. Contbr. articles to sci. jours. Home: Davis CA Died Dec. 12, 1972.

CARLTON, A(RTHUR) C(LIFFORD), engr., museum dir.; b. Balt., Aug. 24, 1895; s. William Arthur and Dovie (Hutton)C.; S.B., Mass. Inst. Tech., 1917; m. Mabel Caldwell Jones, May 28, 1919. Engr. Chile Exploration Co., Chupuicamata, Chile, 1920-22; dept. supt., Gen. supt. Balt. Copper Smelting and Rolling Co., 1923-31; curator fuels, metals and chemistry Mus. Sci. and Industry, Chgo,, 1932-41; civilian engr. Ordnance Dist., 1942-46; exec. dir. mus. Franklin Inst., Phila., since 1946. Served as 2d lt. to capt. Inf., U.S. Army, 1917-19. Mem. Ordnance Assn., Radnor-Ithan-St. Davids Civic Assn., Phi Kappa Sigma. Home: Randor, Pa. Office: Franklin Institute, Parkway and 20th St., Phila. 3. Died Nov. 12, 1958. buried Chapel Cemetery, Valley Forge, Pa.

CARLTON, ERNEST W(ILSON), civil engr.; b. Fort Collins, Colo., May 6, 1897; s. Luther N. and Maude Alice (Mefford) C.; B.S., Colo. A. and M. Coll., 1920, M.S., 1926; B.S., Mo. Sch. Mines (now The University of Missouri at Rolla, Mo.), 1925, C.E., 1935; m. Myrtle Marie Fleming, Sept. 9, 1920; children—Paul F., Elaine Dorothy, Patricia Ann. Inst., dept. applied mechanics, Univ. Neb., 1920-23; asst. prof. engring. drawing, U. Mo. at Rolla, 1923-27, professor structural engineering, 1927-55, professor of civil engring. and chairman department, 1955-65, coordinator engring., sci. managment war training program, 1941-46; cons. civil engr., 1930—. Mem. American Society Civil Engineers (past nat. director district 14; past pres., Mid-Mo. sect., faculty advisor Mo. Sch. Mines student chpt.), Am. Soc. Engring. Edn., Nat. Congress on Surveying and Mapping (past v.p.), Mo. Soc. Professional Engrs. (past pres.; past pres. Rolla chpt.), Mod. Acad. Sci., Nat. Soc. of Profl. Engrs., Sigma Xi, Chi Epsilon, Phi Kappa Phi (hon.), Triangle, Sigma Chi. Republican. Presbyterian. Mason (past master, past high priest). Clubs: Engineers (member board of directors) Lions (past president). Reigstered profl. engr. Author publs. concerning hwy. constrn., concrete, also articles to tech. jours. and mags. Splty.; applied research in fields of highway constrn., steel and concrete. Home: 30 Sydney Ct., Rolla, Mo. 65401. Died Nov. 7, 1966; buried Rolla.

CARLYLE, WILLIAM LEVI, agricultural scientist; b. Chesterville, Ont., Can., Sept. 22, 1870; s. Thomas and Nancy (Thom) C.; Ont. Agrl. Coll., 1889-92; B.S., in agr. U. of Toronto, 1892; M.S., Colo. Agrl. Coll., 1905; m. Inez M. Fairbanks, of Herman, St. Lawrence Co., N.Y., July 7, 1896. Instr. dairying, Ont. Agrl. Coll., 1893; lecturer, live stock and dairy husbandry extension dept., U. of Minn., 1893-7; prof. animal husbandry, U. of Wis., 1897-1903; prof. agr., 1903-5, dean of agr., 1905-9, Colo. Agrl. Coll.; expert in animal husbandry, U.S. Dept. Agr., 1905-9; supt. in charge live stock div., Alaska-Yukon-Pacific Expn., 1909; dean Coll. of Agr. and dir. Expt. Sta., 1910-15, acting pres., Feb., 1913-May, 1915, U. of Ida.; dean of agr. and dir. Expt. Sta., Okla. Agrl. and Mech. Coll., since 1915. Dir. Western Live Stock Show, Portland, Ore.; mem. Internat. Live Stock Show, Chicago, Nat. Live Stock Show, Denver. Has judged live stock at leading state and nat. shows since 1900. Presbyn. Clubs: Saddle and Sirloin (Chicago). Author bulls. and ann. reports Wis. Expt. Sta., 1898-1904, Colo. Expt. Sta., 1904-7; contbr. to various agrl. periodicals and jours. Address: Stillwater OK

CARMAN, ALBERT PRUDEN, physicist; b. Woodbury, N.J., July 1861; s. Rev. Thomas C. and Phebe C. (Pruden) C.; A.B., Princeton, 1883. A.M., 1885, D.Sc., 1886; m. Maude W. Straight June 21, 1900. Fellow and tutor physics and mathematics Princeton, 1883-87; student Berlin, 1987-89; prof. physics and elec. engring. Purdue, 1889-92; Leland Stanford Jr. U., 1892-96; prof. physics and head of dept. U. Ill., 1896-1929. ret. Mem. Am. Physical Soc. Contbr. to tech. jours. Home: 910 W. California Av., Urbana, Ill. Died Feb. 10, 1946; buired Forest Home Cemetery, Oak Park, Ill.

CARMICHAEL, HENRY, chemist; b. Brooklyn, Mar. 5, 1846; s. Daniel and Eliza C.; A.B., Amherst, 1867, A.M., 1870; Ph.D., Göttingen, 1871; m. Annie Darling Cole (writer, composer). Prof. chemistry, Iowa Coll., 1871, Bowdoin Coll., 1872-86; lecturer Me. Med. Sch., 1872-86; state assayer of Me., 1872-86; lecturer M.I.T., 1899-1901. Moved to Boston, 1886; inventor or processes for manufacturer of fibreware, of soda and bleach by electrolysis, and many others; expert in patent causes; assayer, metallurgist and inventor metall. processes. Home: Malden, Mass. Died 1924.

CARMICHAEL, ROBERT DANIEL, mathematician; b. Goodwater, Ala., Mar. 1, 1879; s. Daniel Monroe and Amanda (Lessley) C.; A.B., Lineville (Ala.) Coll. 1898; Ph.D., Princeton, 1911; m. Eula Narramore, Nov. 24, 1901; children—Eunice Annie (Mrs. Keith H. Roberts), Erdys Lucile (Mrs. Ernest C. Hartmann), Gersham Narramore, Robert Lessley. Prof. Ala. Presbyn. Coll., 1906-09; fellow Princeton, 1909-10, Jacobus fellow, 1910-11; asst. prof. mathematics, Ind. U., 1911-12, asso. prof., 1912-15; asso. prof. U. Chgo. Summer Sch., 1915; asst. prof. mathematics, 1915-18, asso. prof., 1918-20, prof. since 1920, head of dept., 1929-34, acting dean Grad. Sch., U. of Ill., 1933-34, editor, Annals of Mathematics, 1916-18, Am. Math. Monthly, 1916-17, editor in chief, 1918; editor Transactions Am. Math. Soc., 1931-36. Fellow A.A.A.S. (v.p., Sect. A, 1934); mem. Am. Math. Soc. (councillor 1916-18, v.p. 1922, chmn. Chgo. sect. 1920-21), Math. Assn. Am. (councillor 1916-18, 20, 24, 25-27; v.p. 1921-22, pres. 1938), Am. Philos. Assn., Kappa Delta Rho, Pi Mu Epsilon, Sigma Xi, Phi Beta Kappa, Phi Kappa Phi. Mem. div. phys. science, Nat. Research Council, 1929-32. Clubs: Chaos, University, Philosophical. Author: Theory of Relativity, 1913, 20; Theory of Numbers, 1914, French edit., 1929; A Debate on Relativity (with others), 1927; The Logic of Discovery, 1930; Plane and Spherical Trigonometry (with E.R. Smith), 1930; Mathematical Tables and Formulas (with E.R. Smith), 1931; Theory of Groups of Finite Order, 1937; What Is Man, 1950. Contributor numerous articles on the philosophy of science; also articles in tech., math., and physical jours. Home: 6315 Robinhood Lane, Merriam, Kan. 66203. Died May 2, 1967.

CARMICHAEL, THOMAS HARRISON, prof. pharmaceutics; b. Phila., Jan. 27, 1959; s. William and Julia Baker (Hunter) C; A.B., Central High Sch., Phila.; M.D., Hahnemann Med. Coll., Phila., 1887; m. Emily H. Leonard, Nov. 23, 1897; 1 son, Leonard. Interne Ward's Island Hosp., New York, 1886-87; lecturer on pharmaceutics, 1897-1908, prof. of pharmacodynamics, 1908-13, asso. prof. materia medica, 1913-19, Hahnemann Med. Coll. Mem. Am. Inst. Homeopathy (1st v.p., 1908, pres., 1911-12, trustee, 1912-13), Homeo. Med. Soc. Co. of Phila. (pres. 1908, 1917, trustee since 1912); ex-pres. Allen Lane Sch. Assn.; chmn. Com. on Homeo. Pharmacopoeia, 1907, 08, 09, 10, 12, and since 1933; chmn. Com. on Revision Homeo. Pharmacopoeia of U.S., 1935; censor Sr. Mil. Med. Assn., 1917. Vice-pres. Pan.-Am. Homeopathic Congress, 1941. Dir. and chmn. Auxiliary Com. Germantown Hist. Soc., Pi Gamma Mu. Episcopalian; vestryman Christ Ch., and St. Michael's Ch., Germantown for 18 yrs. Club: Oxford Medical. Address: President's House, Tufts College, Mass. Died Oct. 9, 1942.

CARMICHAEL, WILLIAM PERRIN, civil engineer; b. Warren County, Ind., Apr. 14, 1858; s. Ralph Erskine and Rebecca (Dill-Kent) C.; A.B., Wabash Coll., Ind., 1879, A.M., 1886; m. Alice Norris, Mar. 2, 1887; 1 dau., Katherine Norris. Exec. sec. Ind. Engring. Soc., 1891-93; mgr. Williamsport (Ind.) Stone Co., 1893-98; pres. Wm. P. Carmichael Co., Williamsport, Ind., St. Louis, Mo., Mexico City, Mex., engring. contractors, 1898-1910; v.p. and gen. mgr. Unit Constrn. Co., St. Louis 1910-14; pres. Carmichael Cryder Co., Inc., St. Louis, 1914-29; pres. The Carmichael Gravel Co., Williamsport, Ind., and St. Louis, 1914-25; v.p. and treas. Midwest Constrn. Utilities, 1931-36; retired. Pres. of Winona Lake Instns., 1918-39; now pres. Nowata County Gas Co. Republican. Presbyterian. Mem. Am. Soc. Engring. Contractors. S.A.R. Clubs: City, Mo. Athletic. Home: 7749 Delmar Blvd., St. Louis, Mo.; (summer) Winona Lake, Ind. Died Dec. 17, 1944.

CARMODY, THOMAS EDWARD, surgeon; b. Shiawasee County, Mich., May 22, 1875; s. Thomas and Mary Ann (Gorman) C.; D.D.S. Dental Sch., U. of Mich., 1897, D.D.Sc., 1898; grad. Sch. of Medicine, U. of Colo., 1903; m. Mary Jane McBride, Nov. 7, 1899; children—David, Ruth R. (Mrs. William G. Summers), Mary Alice (Mrs. Howard D. Cobb). In practice as physician and surgeon since 1903, specializing in otohinolaryngology, bronchoesophagology, oral and plastic surgery; prof. bacteriology and histology, Dental Coll., U. of Denver, 1898-1905, prof. oral surgery and rhinology, 1905-32; asst. in laryngology and otology, Med. Sch., U. of Colo., 1905-33; chief of otolaryngology, child research council, research dept., U. of Colo., 1928-36. Surgeon general of Colo., 1909-11. Served as 1st lt., Med. Res. Corps, U.S. Army, 1917; major, Med. Corps, U.S. Army, 1918-19. Fellow Am. Coll. Surgeons, Am. Coll. Dentists, Internat. Coll. Surgeons. Mem. Denver County Med. Soc. (sec., 1904, pres., 1923), Denver Dental Soc. (pres. 1907), Colorado Otolaryngol. Soc. (1st pres.), Col. Soc. for Crippled Children (1st pres.), Am. Acad. of Opthal. and Otolaryn. (pres., 1923), Am. Bronchoesophagological Soc., Am. Laryn., Rhenol. and Otol. Soc. (pres., 1936), Am. Laryn. Assn. (pres., 1941), Am. Otol. Assn., Am. Soc. of Oral and Plastic Surgs., Am. Soc. of Plastic and Reconstructive Surgery, Am. Med. Assn. (chmn. otolaryn. sec., 1931); mem. 1st Internt. Otolaryn. Congress, Copenhagen, Denmark, 1929; mem. bd. dirs. Nat. Soc. for Crippled Children. Home: 1901 Hudson St. Office: 227 16th St., Denver, Colo. Died Aug. 30, 1946.

CARNAP, RUDOLF, educator; b. Wuppertal, Germany, May 18, 1891; s. Johannes S. and Anna (Dorpfeld) C.; student U. Freiburg Baden, Jena; Ph.D., U. Jena, 1921; Sc.D. (hon.), Harvard, 1936; LL.D. (hon.) U. of Cal. at Los Angeles, 1963; H.L.D. (hon.), U. of Mich., 1965; Ph.D. (honorary), Univ. of Oslo (Norway), 1969; m. Elizabeth Ina von Stoger, 1933 (dec. 1964). Came to U.S., 1935, naturalized, 1941. Instr. philosophy U. Vienna (Austria), 1926-31; prof. natural philosophy German U., Prague, Czechoslovakia, 1931-35; prof. philosophy U. Chicago, 1936-52; prof. philosophy University of California at Los Angeles, 1954-62, research philosopher, 1962-70; vis. prof. Harvard, 1940-41. Fellow Am. Academy of Arts and Sciences, British Academy (corresponding); mem. Am. Philosophical Assn., Assn. Symbolic Logic, Philos. Sci. Assn. Author: Der Raum, 1922; Physikal. Begriffsbildung, 1926; Der Logische Aufbau der Welt, 1928; Scheinprobleme der Philosophie, 1928; Abriss der Logistik, 1929; The Unity of Science, 1934; Logische Syntax der Sprache, 1934; Die Aufgabe der Wissenschaftslogik, 1934; Philosophy and Logical Syntax, 1935; Logical Syntax of Language, English translation, 1937; Foundations of Logic and Mathematics, 1939; Introduction to Semantics, 1942; Formalization of Logic, 1943; Meaning and Necessity, 1947; Logical Foundations of Probability, 1950; The Continuum of Inductive Methods, 1951; Einfuhrung in die symbolische Logik, 1954; Introduction to Symbolic Logic and its Applications, 1958; Induktive Logik und Wahr-Scheinlishkeit, 1958; Philosophical Foundations of Physics, 1966; The Logical Structure of the World, 1967; A Basic System of Inductive Logic, 1971; also book chpts., articles. Writings collected in The Philosophy of Rudolf Carnap (editor Paul A. Schilpp), 1963. Home: Los Angeles CA Died Sept. 14, 1970.

CARNEGIE, ANDREW, philanthropist; b. Dunfermline, Fifeshire, Scotland, Nov. 25, 1835; came with family to U.S., 1848, settling in Pittsburgh; (lord rector, St. Andrew's U., 1903-07, LL.D., 1905; lord rector, Aberdeen U., 1912-14, and LL.D.; also LL.D., univs. of Glasgow, Edinburgh, Birmingham, Manchester, McGill U. (Montreal), Queen's Coll. (Toronto), Erskine Coll., Allegheny Coll., U. of Pa., Brown U., Cornell U., Hamilton Coll.; Dr. Polit. Science, U. of Groningen); m. Louise Whitfield, 1887. First work was as weaver's asst. in cotton factory, Allegheny, Pa.; telegraph messenger boy in Pittsburgh office of Ohio Telegraph Co., 1851; learned telegraphy, entered employ Pa. R.R. and became telegraph operator, advancing by promotions until he became supt. Pittsburgh div. Pa. system; joined Mr. Woodruff, inventor of the sleeping car, in organizing Woodruff Sleeping Car Co., gaining through it nucleus of his fortune; careful investments in oil lands mincreased his means; during Civil War served as supt. mil. rys. and govt. telegraph lines in the East. After war developed iron works of various kinds and established, at Pittsburgh, Keystone Bridge Works and Union Iron Works. Introduced into this country Bessemer process of making steel, 1868; was principal owner a few years later of Homestead and Edgar Thomson Steel Works, and other large plants as head of firms of Carnegie, Phipps & Co. and Carnegie Bros. & Co.; interest were consolidate, 1899, in the Carnegie Steel Co., which in 1901 was merged in the United States Steel Corp., when he retired from business. Has given libraries to to many towns and cities in the U.S. and Great Britain, and large sums in other benefactions, including $24,00,000 to Carnegie Inst., Pittsburgh; $5,200,00 to New York for the establishment of branch libraries; $22,00,000 to Carnegie Instn. of Washington; $10,000,00 to Scotch universities; $5,000,000 to fund for benefit of employes of Carnegie Steel Co.; $1,000,000 to St. Louis Pub. Library; $5,000,000 to the Carnegie Hero Fund Commn., Pittsburgh; $1,150,000 to the Carnegie Hero Fund Trust, Dunfermline, Scotland (for Great Britain); $1,000,000 to the Hero Fund for Frances; $1,500,000 to the Hero Fund for Germany, $230,000 to the Hero Fund for Belgium; $125,000 to the Hero Fund for Denmark; $200,000 for the Hero Fund for Holland; $230,000 to the Hero Fund for Sweden; $130,000 to the Hero Fund for Switzerland; $750,000 to the Hero Fund for Italy; $125,000 to the Hero Fund for Norway; $3,500,000 to the Carnegie Dunfermline Trust; $1,500,000 for the Peace Temple at The Hague; $1,500,000 to United Engring. Soc. Total benefactions exceed $300,000,000, including over $60,000,000 for over 3,000 municipal library bldgs; also building and grounds for Pan-Am. Union, Washington, 1906; $16,250.000 for Foundation for Advancement of Teaching in U.S., Can. and Newfoundland. Life trustee Carnegie Corp. of New York ($125,000,000 foundation to carry on various works in which he has been engaged). Hon. mem. Am. Inst. Architects, Am. Soc. M.E., Am. Inst. Mining Engr.; trustee Cornell U., 1890—. Comdr. Legion of Honor, France, 1907; Grand Cross, Order of Orange Nassau; Grand Cross, Order of Danebrog. Has received freedom of 54 cities of Great Britain and Ireland. Author: An American Four-in-Hand in Briain, 1883; Round the World, 1884; Triumphant Democracy, 1886; The Gospel of Wealth, 1900; The Empire of Business, 1902 (translated into 8 langs.); The Life of James Watt, 1906; Problems of Today, 1909. Died Aug. 11, 1919.

CARNEY, FRANK, geologist; b. Watkins, N.Y., Mar. 15, 1868; s. Hugh and Esther R. (Breahan) C.; Starkey Sem., Eddytown, N.Y.; A.B., Cornell U., 1895. Ph.D., 1909; m. Mary E. Keegan, June 26, 1890; children—Esther L. (Mrs. H. H. Martin), Ewart Gladstone, Harry Beahan, Mary F. (Mrs. J. W. Cunnick), Frances E. (Mrs. P. A. Knoedler). Instr., 1887-90, prin., 1894-95, Starkey Sem.; instr. Keuka Inst., 1895-1900; asst. in geology, Cornell U., 1901, and instr., Cornell Summer Sch. of Geography, 1901-04; v.prin. Ithaca High Sch., 1901-04; prof. geology, 1904-14, prof. geology and geography, 1915-17, Denison Univ.; chief geologist, Nat. Refining Co., 1917—, in charge of Land Department, 1923-29; prof. geology and geography, Baylor Univ., 1929—. Lecturer on geography, Summer Sch., U. of Va., 1909-11; prof. geology, Summer Quarter U. of Chicago, 1912; acting prof. geology, U. of Mich., 1912-13; prof. geography, Cornell Summer Sch., 1914-16. Asst. geologist Ohio Geol. Survey, 1907-17. Baptist. Mason. Died Dec. 13, 1934.

CARNOCHRAN, JOHN MURRAY, surgeon; b. Savannah, Ga., July 4, 1817; s. John and Harriet (Putnam) A.; grad. U. Edinburgh (Scotland), 1834; M.D., Coll. Physicians and Surgeons, N.Y.C., 1836; studied medicine, Paris, France, 1836-42, London, Eng., 1842-47; m. Estelle Morris. Practiced medicine, N.Y.C., 1847-87; surgeon-in-chief N.Y. State Emigrant Hosp. Ward's Island, 1851; prof. surgery N.Y. Med. Coll., 1851-62; health officer port of N.Y., 1870-71; mem. N.Y. Medico-Legal Soc., 1871-87. Author: Etiology, Pathology, and Treatment of Congenital Dislocation of the Head of the Femur, 1850; Contributions to Operative Surgery and Surgical Pathology, 1858; Cerebral Localization in Relation to Insanity, 1884. Died Oct. 28, 1887.

CAROTHERS, WALLACE H(UME), chemist; b. Burlington, Ia., Arp. 27, 1896; s. Ira Hume and Mary Elizabeth (McMullen) C.; B.S., Tarkio (Mo.) Coll., 1920; M.S., U. of Ill., 1921, Ph.D., 1924; grad. study U. of Chicago; m. Helen E. Sweetman, Feb. 21, 1936. Instr. chemistry, Tarkio Coll., 1918-20, U. of S.D., 1921-22, U. of Ill., 1924-26, Harvard, 1926-28; research chemist du Pont Co., Wilmington, Del., 1928—; co-inventor of importatnt new synthetic rubbers. Editor: Organic Syntheses, 1933; asso. editor Jour. Am. Chem. Soc., 1930—. Home: Wilmington, Del. Died Apr. 29, 1937.

CARPENTER, ALLEN FULLER, prof. mathematics; b. Marengo, Ia., June 12, 1880; s. Henry Merritt and Sophronia Allen (Fuller) C.; A.B., Hastings Coll., Hastings, Neb., 1901, D.Sc. 1937; A.M., U. of Nebraska, 1909; Ph.D., U. of Chicago, 1915; m. Margaret Anna Daily, Aug. 30, 1905; children—Richard Henry (dec.), Eleanor Jane (Mrs. Robert William MacKay). Instr. in mathematics, Hastings Coll., 1901-08, U. of Nebraska, 1908-09; instr. in mathematics, U. of Washington, Seattle, Wash., 1909-15, asst. prof. 1915-19, asso. prof., 1919-26, prof. since 1926, exec. officer dept. of mathematics since 1936; asso. prof. mathematics, U. of Chicago, summer 1923. Served as pvt., Presidio Regt., S.A.T.C., July-Sept. 1918. Chmn. Seattle Civil Service Pension Commn., 1928. Fellow A.A.A.S.; mem. Am. Math. Soc., Am. Assn. Univ. Profs., Sigma Xi, Theta Chi. Club: Faculty Men's (U. of Wash.). Home: 6202 51st St. N.E., Seattle 5, Wash. Died Oct. 16, 1949.

CARPENTER, ARTHUR HOWE, metallurgist; b. Georgetown, Clear Creek County, Colo., Oct. 19, 1877; s. Franklin Reuben and Annette Fuller (Howe) C.; freshman class, U., 1894; A.M., 1914. student Northwestern U., 2 yrs.; m. Ohio U., Margaret Lucile, D. Dafydd J. Evans, June 5, 1901; children—Franklin Dafydd, Margaret Annette (Mrs. D.M. Dutton), Mary Elizabeth (Mrs. S.L. McCarthy,). Assayer and research chemist, 1894-96, assistant supt. Deadwood and Delaware Smelting and Refining Co., Deadwood, S.D., 1898-99; jr. partner firm of Carpenter and Carpenter, Denver, 1900; supt. Clear Creek Mining and Reduction Co., Golden, Colo., 1901-03; research work, Calumet, Mich., 1904; gen. mgr. Takilma (Ore.) Mining and smelting Co., 1905; chief chemist, Am. Smelting and Refining Co., Leadville and Denver, Colo., 1906-08; research work ect., 1909; prospecting Nev., 1910-11; research metallurgist, Am. Vanadium Co., 1912-18; gen. mgr. Colo. Vanadium Corp., 1918-20; asst. prof. metallurgy, Armour Inst. Tech. (Ill. Inst. Technology), Chicago, 1920-28; became Associate Prof., 1929, head metallurgy division; lecturer geology, astronomy, meterology; emeritus professor since November1,1944. Staff consultant, metallurgy, Armour Research Foundation; cons. practice. Fellow A.A.A.S.: Mem. Am. Inst. Mining and Metall. Engrs., Ill. Acad. Science, Am. Soc. Testing Materials, Soc. Promotion Engring. Edn., Astron. Soc. Amateur Telescope Makers of Chicago (pres.), Phi Lambda Upsilon Alpha Chi Sigma, Pi Gamma Mu, Delta Tau Delta, S.A.R. Repbulican. Espicopalian. Mason. Contbr. mining and metall. publs. Inventor methods of covering pipe with lead. Made 20 1/2 telescope used by Elgin Obs. for daily Arcturus ceremony at Century of Progress Expn., Chicago, 1933 and 1934. This telescope was made as a memorial to Dr. Franklin R. Carpenter and D.J. Evans, and presented to Ohio Univ., Athens, O. Club: Faculty. Home: 365 S. 5th Av., Middleport, O. Died Mar. 20, 1956; buired West Union St. Cemetery, Athens, O.

CARPENTER, CHARLES LINCOLN, civil engr.; b. Amherst, Mass., June 17, 1867; s. Charles Carroll and Feronia N. (Rice) C.; B.S., Darmouth, 1887; C.E., Thayer Sch. Civ. Engring. (Dartmouth), 1889; m. Charlotte Florence Sullivan, Dec. 15, 1892; children—James Sullivan, Thomas Rice, Charles Carrol. On surveys and constrn. Nicaragua Canal, Nicaragua Canal Co., 1889-91; asst. engr. with Boston Bd. of Survey, 1891-98; mining in Alaska, 1898-1900; locating Boston & Worcester R.R., 1900-01; asst. engr., location and constrn., Cuba R.R., Cuba, 1901-02; with U.S. engr. corps. dredging in Boston Harbor, 1902-04; with Isthmian Canal Commn. in Panama as asst. engr. on surveys, 1904-06, resident engr. in direct charge of Gatun Locks, 1906-08, in charge Gatun Dam and Porto Bello Quarry, 1906-07; supt. constrn. for J. G. White & Co., on reconstruction of Cuba Eastern R.R., 1908-09; gen. mgr. and chief engr. Guantanamo & Western R.R., which is the Cuba Eastern R.R. reorganized, 1909-11; supt. Ponce & Guayama R.R., Dec. 1911-12; v.p. and gen. mgr. Central Aguirre Sugar Co., Puerto Rico, 1912—; v.p. and gen. mgr. Central Machete Co., 1920—; v.p. Santa Gabei Sugar Co. Died Sept. 28, 1929.

CARPENTER, DELPH E., lawyer, agriculturist; b. near Greeley, Colo., May 13, 1877; s. Leroy S. and Martha Allen (Bennett) C.; student lit. dept. of Denver, 1896-97, law dept., 1897-99, LL.B., 1899; LL.D., from U. of Colorado, 1927; m. Michaelea, d. Capt. M.J. Hogarty, U.S. Army, June 5, 1901; children—Michaela Hogarty, Donald Alfred, Sarah Hogarty, Martha Patricia. Engaged in gen. practice until 1908, since in irrigation and interstate river practice; counsel in original proceeding in case of Wyo. vs. Colo., 1910-19, involing appropriation of waters of the Laramie River; managing and dir. counsel for Colo. in South Platte litigation between Neb. and Colo., spl. counsel for Colo. in Republican River litigation between Neb. and Colo.; counsel for Colo. in interstate Boundary, New Mexico vs. Colo., 1919-25; mem. Colo. Senate, 1908-12 (chmn. com. interstate water investigations, 1909-11); spl. asst. atty. gen. of Colo., in charge interstate water litigation, 1918; spl. envoy gob. gov. of Colo. to gov. of New Mexico to arrange submission La Plata River interstate water controversy to interstate compact commn.; originator program exercise treaty powers of states in interstate river controversies; drew legislation 1920-21, enacted by Calif., Colo., Nev. N.M., Ariz., Utah and Wyo., providing for formulation by interstate treaty commn. of compact between the seven states respecting the future use and disposition of waters of the Colorado River and tributaries, and prepared congressional legislation providing for a nat. representative on same commn.; apptd. interstate compact commr. for Colo., 1921, to serve on interstate treaty comms. respecting settlement of future use and disposition of Colo., La Plata, Ark., S. Platte and Laramie rivers; spl. counsel for Colo. for reargument Laramie River and Republican River Cases before U.S. Supreme Court, 1921-22; concluded Colorado River Compact, 1922, also La Plata River compact (Colo. and N.M.); apptd., 1923, treaty commr. colo., use and disposition waters of Rio Grande, Arkansas, S. Platte and N. Platte rivers; concluded compact bet. Colo. and Neb. in waters S. Platte; reappointed, 1925, Counsel for Colo., Rio Grande controversy with N.M., Tex. and U.S.; in charge of all interstate river controversies for Colo., 1923-27; commr. for Colo. at conf. of governors and commrs. of Colorado River States at Denver, Aug. and Sept. 1927; concluded compact between Colo., N.M., and Tex., respecting waters of the Rio Grande River, 1929—engaged in negotiations respecting North Platte and Colorado rivers, ano in miscellaneous interstate river work, 1928-31; counsel for Colo. in suit of Ariz. vs. Calif., et al., before U.S. Supreme Court, 1930-31; commr. for Colo., North Platte River compact negotiations (Colo. and Wyo.) Awarded University Recognition medal, U. of Colo., 1923, "for distinguished public service." Reclaimed by irrigation about 400 acres of arid land in Weld County, Colo.; breeder of registered shorthorn cattle. Mem. Am., Colo. and Weld County bar assns., Beta Theta Pi; hon. mem. Colo. Soc. C.E. Republican. Methodist. Mason. Home: 1112 Tenth St. Greeley, Colo., Died Feb. 27, 1951; buried Linn Grove Cemetery, Greeley, Colo.

CARPENTER, EUGENE R., brain surgeon; b. Knobnoster, Mo., Oct. 5, 1873; s. William D. and Emma (Shanks) C.; student U. of Mich., 2894-97; M.D., Jefferson Med. Coll., Phila., Pa., 1898 (winner de Schweinitz medal on ophthalmology, Dercums neurol. prize, and the otol. prize); interne Kings Co. Hosp., 1898-99; post-grad. work, Manhattan Eye and Ear Hosp., New York Cye and Infirmary, also Vienna and London, 1907-08; m. Lucile Snyder, July 20, 1916. Practiced at Dallas, Tex., 1921—. Maj. Med. R.C.; retired capt. U.S.A. Fellow Am. Coll. Surgeons. Democrat. Baptist. Mason. Designer of numerous surg. instruments. Home: Dallas, Tex. Died Oct. 11, 1934.

CARPENTER, FORD ASHMAN, meteorologist, aeronaut; b. Chicago, Ill., Mar. 25, 1868; s. Lebbaeus Ross and Charlotte (Eaton) C.; ed. Dilworth Acad.; Carson Astronomical Obs.; U.S. Balloon and Airship Schs., etc.; LL.D., Whittier (Calif) Coll., 1913; Sc.D., Occidental Coll., Los Angeles, Calif., 1921. With U.S. Weather Service various stations, 1888-1919; special observer, 1940-41; mgr. dept. meteorology and aeronautics, Los Angeles Chamber of Commerce, 1919-41. Hon. lecturer, summer sessions U. of Calif. 1914-16, 1939-41; lecturer, U.S. Army Aviation School, San Diego, 1915, Monterey Mil. Encampment, 1916-17; mem. faculty (lecturer meteorology) Southern br. U. of Calif., 1919-30; lecturer on meteorology, Air Service, War Dept., 1915-44, Babson Inst., 1921-35, Columbia, Cornell, and Northwestern, 1923-38, New York U., West Point Mil. Acad., Annapolis Naval Acad., Poly. Inst. Brooklyn, Carnegie Inst. Pittsburgh, Field Mus., 1925-38, Goodyear-Zeppelin Co., 1926-29, War Coll. (Washington), etc., Meteorological adviser Palos Verdes Estates, 1914-20, Pauba Rancho, 1921-31, TWA, 1927-30, Santa Fe Ry. Co., 1922-35; American Airways, TWA, United Arilines, 1927-38, Los Angeles Municipal Airport, 1927, Hollywood Bowl, 1928, Amer. Hawaiian Steamship Co., 1934-40. Climatol. adviser to Frank A. Vanderlip, 1927-37. Selected and surveyed L.A. Municipal Airport, 1927. Served as pvt., Signal Corps, U.S. Army, 1888; lt. U.S.N.R., class 5, 1920-21; lt. col. Inactive Res., U.S. Army aide, 9th Civilian Defense Area. Meteorol. in defense, World War I; in Intelligence, World War II, lecturing to pre-aviation cadets, 1943-44. Meteorol. observer of aerial bombing of former German battleships, 1921. Radio broadcaster over stations KFI, KFAC, and KMTR, 1923-41. International balloon pilot No. 913, Federation Aeronautique Internationale since 1921. Meteorological and aeronautic adviser to naval affairs com. of 72nd Congress, 1930; nat. councilor U.S. Chamber of Commerce, Washington, 1933-38. Mem. 8th Internat. Geog. Congress, Washington, D.C., 1904, Internat. Congress Tuberculosis, Washington, D.C., 1908; mem. photographic com. standards, U.S. Dept. Agr., 1908. Climatol. commr. Seattle Expn. (gold medal for meteorol. exhibit), 1909; first photographed red snow in natural colors, 1911; asst. in U.S. Weather Bur. meteorograph ascents into stratosphere, alt. 108,000 ft., 1913; mem. Pan Am. Med. Congress, 1915, 1st International Aero Congress (v.p.), Omaha, 1921. Past fellow A.A.A.S., Royal Meteorol. and Geog. Soc. (London), Am. Seismol. Soc., Am. Assn. Univ. Profs., S.A.R.; fellow San Diego Soc. Nat. History, Southern Calif. Acad. Science (pres. 1929-31, v.p. 1932-39), Nat. Assn. Balloon Corps Vets., Los Angeles Mus. (gov. 1920-40), Am. Climatol. and Clin. Assn., Nat. Aero. Assn., Assn. Mil. Engrs., Sigma Xi, Phi Beta Kappa. Republican. Episcopalian. Mason (32 deg., Shriner). Clubs: University, Sunset, Scribes (Los Angeles); Sojourners, Army and Navy (Washington, D.C.). Author of monographs, pamphlets, articles, etc., including the following: Climate and Weather of San Diego; Influence of the College Spirit; Aviator and Weather Bureau; Meteorological Methods; Aerial Pathways; Roadbeds of the Air; Weather and Flight; Aids to Air Pilots; Climatic Comparisions; Old Probabilities; Commercial Climatology; Gen. Billy Mitchell as I Knew Him; Sailing Around America's Shores of Two Oceans; Climatology of a Block of Ice, 1945. Contbr. Atlantic Monthly, Scientific Am., Nation's Business, etc. Editor, Meteorology and Aeronautics, 1919-41. Inventor of anemometric scale, hythergraph, televentscope and ventograph. Home: University Club. Office: 108 W 6th St., Los Angeles 14. Died Nov. 1947.

CARPENTER, FRANKLIN REUBEN, mining specialist; b. Parkersburg, W.Va., Nov. 5, 1848; s. John Woodward C.; academic edn. (A.M., Ph.D., Ohio); m. Dec. 23, 1874, Annette Howe, Athens, O. Was dean of faculty and prof. geology, State School of Mines, S. Dak.; inventor of the process of smelting now in use in the Black Hills; now gen. mgr. smelting works and mines; author of works on geology, and papers upon mining and smelting; fellow Geoll Soc. of America; mem. Am. Inst. Mining Inst. Engrs.; Colo. Scientific Soc.; etc. Writer of scientific papers. Residence: 1420 Josephine St. Office: Equitable Bldg., Denver.

CARPENTER, FREDERIC WALTON zoölogist; b. Millbrook, N.Y., May 12, 1876; s. Franklin T. and Jane (Willets C.; B.S., New York U., 1899; A.M., Harvard, 1902, Ph.D., 1904; studied Neurol. Inst., Frankfort-on-Main, Germany, 1908, univs. Berlin and Munich, 1910-11; m. Dorothy E. Dresler, June 26, 1906. Asst. in zoölogy, Harvard, 1901-02; lecturer in biology, summer sch. New York U., 1904, 05; instr. in zoölogy, 1904-08, asso., 1908-10, asst. prof., 1911-13, Univ. Ill.; dir. Bermuda Biol. Sta., summer, 1909; J. P. Morgan prof. biology, Trinity Coll., Conn., July 1, 1913—. Mem. editorial bd. of Folia Neuro-Biologica. Q.m., Am. Red Cross Sanitary Training Detachment No. 2, 1917; asso. field dir., later field dir., hosp. service of Am. Red Cross, at U.S.A. Base Hosp., Camp Devens, Mass., June 21, 1918-July 1, 1919. Died Mar. 1, 1925.

CARPENTER, HORACE FRANCIS; b. Pawtucket, Oct. 19, 1842; s. Horace and Charlotte C.; grad. high sch., Pawtucket; spl. course in analyt. chemistry, Brown U., 1860-61; m. Jennie Hastings, Feb. 23, 1895. Began in gold and silver refining business, 1860; retired from firm of H. F. Carpenter & Son, 1912; discoverer of process of extracting gold and silver from phoographic waste; also discovered process of obtaining chemically pure gold for commercial purposes. Treas. N.E. Mgr. Jewelers and Silversmiths' Assn. 18 yrs. Trustee and mem. library com. of William H. Hall Free Library Corp. Republican. Episcopalian. Mineralogist and conchologist; regarded as the leading authority in R.I. on mollusks; presented City of Providence his library on natural history (237 vols.) and his collection of 1,200 species and varieties of minerals and 4,000 species of shells, consisting of 75,000 specimens; discovered 3 new shell-bearing mollusks. Home: Edgewood, R.I. Died Feb. 28, 1937.

CARPENTER, HUBERT VINTON, electrical engr.; b. near Thomson, Ill., Jan. 29, 1875; s. Charles Higley and Mary Elizabeth (Burge) C.; B.S. in E.E., U. of Ill., 1897; M.S. in mathematics and physics, 1899; LL.D., State Coll. of Washington, 1938; m. Maggie Edith Staley, June 19, 1899; children—Charles R., Florence Edith, William Harold, Arthur C. Instr. physics, U. of Ill., 1897-1901; asst. prof. physics and elec. engring., State Coll. of Wash., 1901-03, head dept. of mech. and elec. engring. since 1903, dean coll. Mech. arts and engring. since June 1917; consultant Nat. Resources Planning Bd. Fellow Am. Inst. E.E.; mem. Am. Soc. M.E., Soc. Promotion Engring. Edn., Tau Beta Pi, Sigma Tau, Phi Kappa Phi, Sigma Xi, Theta Xi. Methodist. Home: Pullman, Wash. Died Nov. 15, 1941.

CARPENTER, LOUIS GEORGE, consulting engr.; b. Orion, Mich., Mar. 28, 1861; s. Charles K. and Jennette (Coryell) C.; B.S., Mich. Agrl. Coll., 1879. M.S., 1883; D.Eng. from same college, 1927; U. of Mich., winters, 1881-82, 1883-84; Johns Hopkins, 1885-86, 1887-88; m. Mary J. C. Merrell, Feb. 17, 1887 (died 1921); children—Charles L. (capt. U.S. Army), Jeannette (Mrs. Roe Emery); m. 2d, Katherine M. Warren, Sept. 30, 1922. Asst. and asst. prof. mathematics, Mich. Agrl. Coll., 1881-88; prof. engring. and physics, Colo. Agrl. Coll., 1888-1911. Irrigation engr., Colo. Expt. Station, later dir. of station, 1899-1910; irrigation expert U.S. Dept. of Agr.; organized 1st systematic instrn. in irrigation engring. and investigation in that line, 1888; spl. agt. and field geologist U.S. artesian wells investigation, 1890; expert in irrigation litigation, U.S. vs. Rio Grande dam, Elephant Butte Internat. Case; state engr., Colo., 1903-05; consulting engr. and irrigation expert for state in suit of state of Kans. against Colo., of Wyo. against Colo., etc.; cons. engr. many important dams, irrigation and hydraulic enterprises, etc.; mem. bd. arbitration selected by both parties as referee and chmn. to settle electric lighting controversy at Colo. Springs, 1907; mem. Irrigation Commn. of British Columbia, 1907-08, to determine foundations for new water code (adopted by B.C. Parliament, 1908); arbitrator chosen by both sides in dispute over waters of North Platte, U.S. vs. Wyo., 1920; expert for Pueblo, Canon City and Salida in stopping pollution of Arkansas River by mining debris; cons. engr. preparing case for Colo. in Wyo. vs. Colo., etc. Served in World War as dir. Dept. of Information, vice-chmn. Explosives Bd., Dept. of Information, vice-chmn. Explosives Bd., Edn. of Drafted Soldiers, etc. Chevalier du Mérite Agricole, France, 1895; gold medals, Paris and Portland expns. Mem. Colo. State Council Defense, 1917-19. Home: Denver, Colo. Died Sept. 12, 1935.

CARPENTER, RAY WILFORD, educator; b. Fontanelle, Neb., June 27, 1894; s. Ernest Harlow and Paulina Marie (Meier) C.; A.B., U. Neb. 1920; LL.B., Georgetown U., 1925; m. Kathrine Kreycik, Nov. 24, 1923; children—Barbara R., David H. Head, dept. agrl. engring. U. Md. since 1920; state drainage engr. Md. since 1937. Mem. Am. Soc. Agrl. Engrs., Farm House, Alpha Zeta, Sigma Tau, Omicron Delta Kappa. Home: 4804 College Av., College Park, Md. 20740. Died May 16, 1962; buried Arlington Cemetery.

CARPENTER, ROLLA CLINTON, engr.; b. Orion, Mich., June 26, 1852; s. Charles K. and Jennette (Coryell) C.; brother of Louis George and William Leland C.; B.S., Mich. Agrl. Coll., 1873, M.S.; C.E., U. of Mich., 1875; M.M.E., Cornell, 1888; (LL.D., Mich. Agrl. Coll., 1906); m. Marion Dewey, 1876. Instr. and prof. of mathematics and civ. engring., Mich. Agrl. Coll., 1875-90; asso. prof. engring., 1890-95, prof. exptl. engring., 1895-1917, Cornell U. (emeritus). Consulting engr. for Helderburg, Cayuga Lake, Quaker Portland, Great Northern, Belleville Portland, Cal. and Atlas Portland cement companies. Constructed numerous power stas. for elec. rys.; patent expert in several important cases; engr. for City of New York for high pressure pumping engines, 1911-12; engr. for Kopper's Co.; Brooklyn pumping engines, 1914; lighting and heating of city buildings, 1913-16; high pressure fire system, City of Baltimore, 1911. Judge of machinery and transportation, Chicago Expn., 1893, Buffalo Expn., 1901, Jamestown Expn., 1907. Author: Experimental Engineering (8 edits.), 1890, 1902; Heating and Ventilating (6 edits.), 1898, 1910; The Gas Engine (with Prof. Diedrichs); Heating and Ventilation (New Internat. Ency. and Kidder's Architectural Pocket Book). Home: Ithaca, N.Y. Died Jan. 19, 1919.

CARR, ARTHUR R.; dean engring.; b. Whitehall, Mich., Apr. 9, 1893; s. Harrison Burdette and Susie E. (Stearns) C.; B.Pd., Mich. State Normal Coll., Ypsilanti, 1914, A.B., 1915; B.S. in Engring., U. of Mich., 1920, M.S. in Engring., 1921, Ph.D., 1934; LL.D., Eastern Mich. Coll., 1956; m. Edith Ilone Smith, July 14, 1917. Supt. of schs. Stockbridge, Mich., 1915-18; instr. chem. engring., U. of Mich., 1920-24; asst. prof. chemistry. Coll. of City of Detroit, 1924-29, prof. of chem. engring. and head of dept. of engring., 1929-33; dean coll. engring., Wayne U., Detroit, 1933—; pres. Wayne Engineering Research Institute; assistant in Survey of Clays and Shales of Mich., Mich. Geol. Suvery 1923—; engr. in charge of inflation of Dirigible ZMC-2, Grosse Isle, Mich., 1929; chem. engr. in charge research, Shakespeare Co., Kalamazoo, 1929-30. Served with Engineer Reserve Corps as Instr. S.A.T.C., U. of Mich., 1918. Mem. Municipal Utilities com., Detroit. 1937; dir. engring. defense training, Wayne U. Mem. Am. Chem. Soc., Mich. Engring. Soc., Am. Soc. Testing Materials, Engring. Soc. of Detroit Sigma Rho Tau, Tau Beta Pi, Alpha Chi Sigma, Phi Lambda Upsilon, Mu Sigma Pi. Mason. Author: Fuels and Their Utilization (with C.W. Selheimer) 1940. Home: 25320 Waycross, R.D. 3, Birmingham, Mich. Office: Wayne U., Bd. of Edn., Detroit 1. Died June 12, 1956; buried Marshall, Mich.

CARR, HARVEY, psychologist; b. Morris, Ill., 1873; s. Hamilton and Bell (Garden) C.; student DePauw U., 1893-95; B.Sc., U. Colo., 1901, M.Sc., 1902; Ph.D., U. Chgo., 1905; m. Antoinette Cox, Dec. 30, 1908; children—Frances Garden, Laurence Hamilton, Virgina Virginia Thurston. Instr. psychology Pratt Inst., Bklyn., 1906-08; asst. prof. psychology U. Chgo., 1908-16, asso. prof., 1916-23, prof., 1923-38, chmn. of dept., 1926-38, prof. emeritus, 1938—. Adv. editor Journal of Gen. Psychology; coö preating editor comp. Psychology Monographs. Mem. Am. Psychol. Assn. (pres. 1926), Sigma Xi, Sigma Nu. Club: Quadrangle. Author: Textbook of Psychology, 1925; An Introduction to Space Preception, 1935. Contributor on Comparative Psycoholgy visual space perception ednl. theory, etc. Ind. Died June 27, 1954.

CARR, WILLIAM KEARNY, researcher; b. in Warren Co., N.C., Aug. 17, 1860; s. the late Gov. Elias and Eleanor (Kearny) C.; Hillsboro (N.C.) Mil. Acad., 1873-76; U. of Va., 1877-78; m. Martina Van Riswick, June 5, 1885. Engaged in sale and mfr. of cotton at Norfolk, Va., and N.C., 1878-90; dir. Rocky Mt. (N.C.) Cotton Mills; study and research in phys. sciences at Washington, 1890—. Home: Washington, D.C. Died Oct. 7, 1915.

CARREL, ALEXIS, surgeon; b. Sainte Foy les Lyon, France, June 28, 1873; s. Alexis and Anne (Ricard) C.; L.B., U. of Lyon, France, 1890, M.D., 1900; Sc.B., U. of Dijon, France, 1891; M.D., Belfast, 1919; Sc.D., Columbia U., 1913 Brown and Princeton Univs., 1920, U. of the State of N.Y., 1937 Manhattan Coll., 1938; LL.D., U. of Calif., 1936; m. Anne de la Motte, 1913. Interne hopitaux de Lyon, 1896-1900; prosector, U. of Lyon, 1900-01, came to America, 1904; U. of Chicago Physiol. Labs., 1905-06; staff Rockefeller Inst. for Med. Research, 1906-12, mem. 1912-39, mem. emeritus since 1939. Winner of Nobel prize, 1912, for success in suturing blood vessels and transplantation of organs; winner of Nordhoff-Jung Cancer prize, 1931; Newman Foundation award, U. of Ill., 1937; Phi Beta Kappa, Dartmouth, 1937; Rotary Club of New York Service medal, 1939. Served as maj. French Army Med. Corps, 1914-19. Special mission for French Minstry of Pub. Health, 1939-40. Decorated Comdr. Legion of Honour; France; Comdr. Order of Leopold; D.S.M.; C.M.G.; Orders of Northern Star of Sweden, Isabella of Spain. Sr. fellow Am. Surg. Assn.; mem. Am. Philos. Soc., Am. Coll. Surgeons, Am. Soc. Physiology; asso. mem. A.M.A.; Soc. Clin. Surgery (sr. mem.), Accademico Pontificio, Pontifica Accademia delle Scienze; hon. fellow Royal Soc. of Med.; foreign asso. Societa Italiana delle Scienze, corr. mem. various foreign academies. Club: Century (N.Y.C.). Catholic. Author: Treatment of Infected Wounds (with Georges Dehelly), 1917; Man, the Unknown, 1935; The Culture of Organs (with Charles A. Lindbergh), 1938. Contbr. on biol. and surg. subjects. Address: Rockefeller Institute, 66th St. and York Av., N.Y.C. Died Nov. 5, 1944; buried Ile St. Gildas, Penvenan, Cotes-du-Nord, France.

CARRELL, WILLIAM BEALL, orthopedic surgeon; b. Lawrenceburg, Tenn., 1883; s. Charles A. and Virginia L.C.; B.S., Southwestern U., 1905, M.D., 1908; m. Beulah Stewart, Sept. 20, 1905; children—W. Brandon, Mary Stewart, John Robert. House surgeon, St. Paul's Sanitarium, Dallas, 1901-10; prof. orthopedic surgery, Baylor Med. School; chief surgeon to Tex. Scottish Rite Hosp. for Crippled Children; orthopedic surgeon, Baylor Hosp., Parkland Hosp., Methodist Hosp. Served as capt., later maj. Med. Corps, U.S. Army. Fellow Am. Coll. Surgeons; mem. American and Southern med. assns., State Med. Assn. of Tex., Am. Orthopedic Assn., Dallas County Med. Soc., Tex. State Surg. Soc., Central States Orthopedic Soc., Internat. Orthopedic Society. Democrat. Methodist. Mason (33 deg., I.G.H.). Clubs: University, Dallas Athletic, Dallas Country. Given Dallas Service Award, 1926. Home: 3612 Overbrook Drive. Office: 3701 Maple Av., Dallas, Tex. Died Feb. 23, 1944.

CARRICK, MANTON MARBLE, sanitarian; b. near Keatchie, La., Aug. 17, 1879; s. White L. and Cammie Rozina (Thompson) C.; grad. Dallas Acad., 1897; M.D., Tex. Christian U., 1901; also post-grad. work in clinics of Chicago, New York, Boston and Philadelphia; m. Mai Connor Gordon, July 15, 1926. Asst. house surgeon, T.&P. Ry. Hosp., Marshall, Tex., 1899; resident phys., Parkland Hosp., 1900; quarantine officer State of Tex., 1906; asst. supt. State Epileptic Colony, Abilene, Tex., 1910-11; supt. Tex. State Lepers' Colony, 1912; pres. Tex. State Bd. of Health, and State health officer; chmn. pub. health com. United Charities, Dallas; prof. preventive medicine, Baylor U. Coll. of Medicine, 1914; dir. pub. health, City of Dallas, Aug. 20, 1927; has made sanitary surveys of many cities and towns of U.S. Surgeon (R.) U.S. Public Health Service. Retired as maj., Med. Corps., U.S. Army. Awarded scholarship in gen. medicine, New York Post-Grad. Med. Sch. and Hosp., 1925, also scholarship in diseases of children by same, 1926. Democrat. Epsicopalian. Mason. Home: Dallas, Tex. Died Sept. 17, 1932.

CARRIER, WILLIS HAVILAND, mech. engr.; born Angloa, N.Y. Nov. 26, 1876l s. Duane Williams and Elizabeth (Haviland) C.; grad. high schs. Angola and Buffalo; M.E., Cornell U., 1901; Dr. Engring., Lehigh U., 1935; D.Sc., Alfred University, Alfred, N.Y., 1942; m. Edith Claire Seymour, 1902 (died)1912) m. 2d, Jennie Tifft Martin, 1913 (died 1939); m. 3d, Elizabeth Marsh Wise, 1941. Engr. Buffalo Forge Co., 1901-06, chief engr. 1906-15; cons. engr., 1915—; pres. Carrier Engring. Corp., 1915-31, chairman bd. Carrier Corp., 1931-43, chmn. emeritus, 1948—. Member American Society Mechanical Engineers, American Soc. Refrigerating Engrs. (pres. 1927), Am.Soc. Heating and Ventilating Engrs. (pres. 1931), Sigma Xi. Republican. Presbyterian. Clubs: Engineers, Cornell (New York); Century, Bellevue Country, Onondaga Country (Syracuse). Author: Fan Engineering, 1914; Modern Heating, Ventilating and Air Conditioning (with others); also various Scientific Papers papers before American Society M.E. and Am. Soc. Refrigerating Engrs., among them, in 1911. a paper entitled "Rational Syychometric Formulae," presenting the theory and practical data on which the art of air conditioning has been founded. Home: 2570 Valley Drive Office: care Carrier Corp., Syracuse, N.Y. Died Oct. 7, 1950; buried Forest Lawn Cemetery, Buffalo.

CARROLL, CAROLINE MONCURE BENEDICT (MRS. MITCHELL CARROLL), archaeologist; b. Belair Plantation, La.; d. Judge E. D. and Caroline (Moncure) Benedict; A.B., Wells Coll., 1891; studied in Europe, 1893-94, later studied archaeology at Athens, Rome, Sch. Am. Research (Santa Fe, N.M.), Am. Sch. Prehistoric Research, Western Europe 1925; Central European Research, 1926; m. Dr. Mitchell Carroll, Sept. 6, 1897 (died Mar. 3, 1925); children—Mitchell Benedict, Randolph, Fitzhugh, Charles Doyal. Lecturer in current history, Nat. Cathedral Sch. for Girls, 1909-10; lecturer in archaeology, Chautaqua Summer Sch., 1914-16; lecturer in archaeology, George Washington U., 1925-1932 (succeeding husband); mem. editorial staff and bd. dirs. Art and Archaeology (monthly mag.). Active worker in Liberty Loan Campaign. Non-resident. mem. Woman's Bd. of Santa Fe; recorder bd. of mgrs. Sch. of Am. Research and State Mus., Santa Fe. Hon. life mem. Archaeol. Soc. Washington (sec. dir. and trustee), Art and Archaeol. League (pres.), Internat. Soc. Woman Geographers (member exec. council, chmn. Washington group), Fondation Egyptologique, Brussels, Anthropol. Soc. Washington, Am. Assn. Univ. Women, Lit. Soc. Washington, English-Speaking Union, Italy America Soc., Am. Classical League, Columbian Women (ex-pres.), Phil Beta Kappa (mem. Washington assn.). Del. Internat. Congress Univ. Women, Paris, 1922, Congress French A.A.S., Liege, 1924; U.S. del. 21st Internat. Congress Americanists, The Hague and Goteborg, 1924, Congress of Fed. Archaeology and History, Bruges, 1925; del. Pan American Inst. Geography and History, 1935, Internat. Fedn. Univ. Women Conf., Cracow, Poland, 1936; U.S. del. Am. Scientific Congress, Washington, 1940. Episcopalian. Clubs: Washington (bd. govs.), Arts, Nat. Club Am. Assn. Univ. Women. Author: Story of Flora MacDonald, 1914; Historical Sketches of Kashmir, 1915. Contbr. to mags. Research work in Southern Europe, 1928-29, Eastern Europe, 1930, 31, Baltic lands, 1936, Mexico, 1937. Home: 2320 Twentieth St., N.W. Office: 315 Southern Bldg., Washington DC*

CARROLL, JAMES, physician, army surgeon; b. in Eng., June 5, 1854; s. James and Harriet (Chiverton) C.; ed. Albion House Acad., Woolwich, Eng., to 1869; grad. med. dept., Univ. of Md., 1891; postgrad. course pathology, Johns Hopkins Hosp., 1891; in bacteriology, 1892; m. Jennie M. George Lucas, May 1888. Associated with late Maj. Walter Reed, surgeon U.S.A., in study of Sanarelli's supposed yellow fever bacillus, 1897-1902, U.S. and Cuba. To justify experimentation on other persons, voluntarily submitted to bite of a contaminated mosquito that had previously been caused to bite 3 well-marked cases of yellow fever. Within 4 days was taken ill and suffered a severe attack of the disease. First lt. and assistant surgeon U.S.A. Prof. bacteriology and clinical microscopy, Army Med. Sch.; prof. bacteriology, Washington Post-Grad. Sch.; prof. bacteriology and pathology, med. dept. George Washington Univ.; curator Army Med. Museum. Home: Washington, D.C. Died 1907.

CARROLL, PHIL, cons. indsl. engr.; b. Bucyrus, O., June 20, 1895; s. Phil and Martha Ada (Couts) C.; B.S. in Elec. Engring., U. Mich., 1918, M.E., 1940; m. Margaret Birdsell, Mar. 20, 1920; children—Margaret Birdsell (Mrs. L. Terry Finch), Jeane Durrell (Mrs. Thomas G. Custin), Phil III, Patricia Anne (Mrs. Martin H. Buchler, III). Engaged in r.r. work, track constrn., automatic signals, summers 1911-17; with Westinghouse, East Pittsburgh, 1919, timestudy Krantz Mfg. Co. (Westinghouse), Bklyn., 1921-22, Westinghouse, Mansfield, O., 1922-23; with Hydraulic Pressed Steel Co., Cleve., 1923-24; a founder Dyer Engrs., Inc., Cleve., 1924, engr., chief engr., v.p. in charge operations, 1924-40; own bus. specializing in timestudy, wage incentive, cost control, 1940-71. Lectr., Newark Coll. Engring., Stevens Inst. Tech., univs. Pa., Mich., Wis., Conn., N.Y. Chmn., Maplewood (N.J.) Planning Bd., 1965-69; mem. indsl. engring. adv. com. U. Mich. Served with Signal Corps, adv. com. U. Mich. Served with Signal Corps, U.S. Army, 1918. Awarded Gilbreth medal in 1950, Indsl. Incentive award, 1953, Distinguished Alumnus, U. Mich., 1953. Fellow Am. Soc. M.E. (Gantt medal bd. 1949-53, chmn. mgmt. div. 1954, chmn. gen. engring. dept., mem. bd. tech. 1962-63), Internat. Acad. Mgmt. (Frank and Lillian Gilbreth award 1970), Am. Inst. Indsl. Engrs. (regional v.p. 1956), Gilbreth award 1970), Am. Inst. Indsl. Engrs. (regional v.p. 1956), Soc. for Advancement Mgmt. (Distinguished Service award N.J. chpt. 1958, nat. sec. 1947, nat. treas. 1948-49, nat. sec. 1947, nat. treas. 1948-49, v.p. membership 1955-57, 1st v.p. 1957, pres. 1958, chmn. bd. 1959; mem. Wallace Clark Bd. Award 1960-66, chmn. 1962); mem. N.J. Tech. Socs. Council (pres. 1951), U.S. Adv. Group on European Productivity, Am. Mgmt. Assn., Nat. Soc. Profl. Engrs., Acad. Mgmt. Republican. Methodist (ofcl. bd.). Mason. Author: Timestudy for Cost Control, 1938; Timestudy Fundamentals for Foremen, 1944; Discussion Leaders Manual, 1948; How to Chart Data, 1950; rev., 1960; How to Control Production Costs, 1952; How Foremen Can Control Costs, 1955; Better Wage Incentives, 1957; Cost Control Through Electronic Data Processing, 1958; Profit Control, 1962; Overhead Cost Control, 1964; Practical Production and Inventory Control, 1966. Contbr.: Foremen's Handbook, 1943, 66; Industrial Engineering Handbook, 1956; profl. jours., encys. in field. Editorial bd. Advanced Mgmt. and Supervision. Home: Maplewood NJ Died Oct. 23, 1971.

CARROLL, ROBERT SPROUL, psychiatrist; b. Cooperstown, Pa. Feb. 18, 1869; s. Jonathan Edward and Margaret Jane (Sproul) C.; student Denison U., Granville, O., 1885-86; M.D., Marion Sims Coll. of Medicine(St. Louis YU.), 1893; M.D., Rush Med. Coll. (U. of Chicago), 1897; m. 2d Grace Stewart Potter (pianist), Feb. 28, 1918; children (1st marriage)—Mrs. Heloise Handcock, Donald Frederic (Major in U.S. Army). Practiced medicine at Calvert, Tex., 1893-1902; associate superintendent Marysville (Ohio) Sanatorium, 1902-04; established Dr. Carroll's Sanitarium, Inc., Ashville N.C., 1904, title changed 1912 to Highland Hosp., Inc., (hosp. donated to psychiatric dept. Duke U., 1939; retired as pres. and med. dir. 1946). Lecturer in psychiarty, Sch. Med., Duke U. Fellow Am. Psychiat. Assn. Assn. for Research in Nervous and Mental Disease. Assn. for Study of Internal Secretions, Southern Soc., Philosophy, A.A.A.S., Am. Eugenics Soc., Am. Ethnol. Soc., Eugenical Research Assn., Nat. Econ. League, Am. Museum Natural History, Assn. for Research in Human Heredity, N.Y. Acad. Sciences. Republican. Presbyn. Author: The Mastery of Nervousness, 1917; The Soul in Suffering, 1919; Our Nervous Friends, 1919; Old at 40 or Young at 60, 1920; The Grille Gate, 1922; Aseptic Meningitis in Combating the Parecox Problem. 1923; What Price Alchohol, 1941. Home: 400 Midland Drive, Asheville, N.C. Died June 26, 1949; buried Lakeview Cemetery Cleveland.

CARSON, HOWARD ADAMS, civil engr.; b. Westfield, Mass., Nov. 28, 1842; s. Daniel B. and Mary (Pope) C.; B.S., Mass. Inst. Tech., 1869; (hon. A.M., Harvard, 1906); m. Nancy Wilmarth, 1870. Asst. engr. Providence Water Works, 1871; in charge sewer constrn., Providence, 1873; prin. supt. constrn., Boston main drainage, 1878; designed, 1887, and later was chief engr., N.Met. and Charles River Valley sewerage systems for Mass.; chief engr. Boston Transit Commn., 1894-1909, bldg. the Boston subway, the E. Boston tunnel and the Washington St. tunnel; has been cons. engr. in various parts of the country, including double-track ry. tunnel under Detroit River. Author of annual reports as chief engr. Met. Sewerage, 1890-94, and as chief engr. Boston Transit Commn., 1894-1909, and other engring. reports. Trustee Mass. Inst. Tech. Home: Malden, Mass. Died Oct. 26, 1931.

CARSON, JOHN RENSHAW, research engr.; b. Pittsburgh, Pa., June 28, 1887; s. John D. and Ada R. (Johnstone) C.; B.S., Princeton, 1907, E.E., 1909, M.S., 1912; grad. study Mass. Inst. Tech., 1907-08; D.Sc., Brooklyn Poly. Inst., 1936; m. Frances Atwell, July 22, 1913; 1 son, John R. Instr. in physicis, Princeton, 1912-14; engr. transmission theory development, Am. Telephone & Telegraph Co., 1914-34; research mathematician, Bell Telephone Labs., N.Y.City, 1934—. Awarded Liebmann Memorial prize, Inst. Radio Engr., for invention in radio and contbns. to math. theory of electric circuits, 1924; Elliott Cresson medal, Franklin Inst., for contributions to the art of electrical communication, 1939. Author: Electric Circuit Theory and the Operational Calculus, 1927; Elektrische Ausgleichvorgänge und Operatorenrechnung, 1929. Home: New Hope, Pa. Died Oct. 31, 1940.

CARSON, JOSEPH, physician; b. Phila., Apr. 19, 1808; s. Joseph and Elizabeth (Lawrence) C.; grad. U. Pa., 1826, M.D., 1830; m. Mary Goodard, 1841; m. 2d, Sarah Hollingsworth, 1848; 4 children. Practiced medicine, Phila., 1832-76; mem. Acad. Natural Sciences of Phila., 1835-76; prof. materia medica Phila. Coll. Pharmacy, 1836; prof. materia medica and pharmacy U. Pa., 1850-76; physician lying-in dept. Pa. Hosp., 1849-54; editor Am. Journal of Pharmacy; mem. Coll. Physicians of Phila., Am. Philos. Soc. Author: Illustrations of Medical Botany, 1847; History of the Medical Department of the University of Pennsylvania, 1869. Died Dec. 30, 1876.

CARSON, RACHEL L(OUISE), scientist, author; b. Springdale, Pa., May 27, 1907; d. Robert Warden and Maria Frazier (McLean) Carson; A.B., Pa. Coll. for Women, 1929, D.Litt. (hon.), 1952; A.M., Johns Hopkins, 1932; D.Sc. (hon.), Oberlin Coll., 1952; Doctor of Letters (honorary) Drexel Institute Tech., 1952; D.Litt. (honorary) Smith College, 1953; spl. studies Marine Biol. Lab., various summers since 1929. Mem. zoology staff U. Md., 1931-36, Johns Hopkins, summer schs., 1930-36; joined staff Bur. Fisheries (now Fish and Wildlife Service) as biologist, 1936, editor-in-chief Fish and Wildlife Service 1949-52. Eugene Saxton Meml. fellowship, 1951-52. Recipient George Westinghouse A.A.A.S. Sci. Writing award, 1950; John Burroughs medal, 1952; Frances K. Hutchinson medal, 1952; Gold Medal, N.Y. Zoological Soc.; Silver Jubilee Medal, Ltd. Editions Club, 1954; Book award Nat. Council Women U.S., 1956; Schweitzer medal Animal Welfare Inst., 1962;

Constance Lindsay Skinner award Women's Nat. Book Assn., 1963; New Eng. Outdoor Writers Assn. award, 1963; Conservationist of the Year award Nat. Wildlife Fedn., 1963; Achievement award Einstein College Medicine (women's division), 1963; special citations Garden Club of America, Pa. Federation Women's Clubs, Izaak Walton League America, 1963. Fellow Royal Society Limited; member National Institute of Arts and Letters, Audubon Soc., Soc. Women Geographers. Presbyn. Author: Under the Sea Wind, 1941; The Sea Around Us, 1951; The Edge of the Sea, 1956; Silent Spring, 1962. Contbr. periodicals. Office: care Marie F. Rodell, 141 E. 55th St., N.Y.C. 10022. Died Apr. 14, 1964.

CARSON, WILLIAM WALLER, civil engr.; b. Adams Co., Miss., June 2, 1845; s. Dr. James Green and Catherine (Waller) C.; pvt. and sergt. maj. 4th La. Cav., C.S.A., 1863-65; C.E., Washington Coll. (now Washington and Lee U.), 1868; M.E., 1869; m. Rachel Finnie, Dec. 23, 1880; children—Katherine Waller, James Finnie (dec.) Emma Finnie, William Waller, Instr. engring., Washington Coll., 1868-69; prof. mathematics, Davidson Coll., 1877-83; prof. civ. engring., U. of Tenn., 1885-1916 (emeritus). Engr. on various rys. and on city, river and other public works. Comdr. Fred Ault Camp No. 5, U.C.V., 1912—. Home: Knoxville, Tenn. Died Feb. 7, 1930.

CARSTARPHEN, FREDERICK CHARLES, cons. engr.; b. Denver, Apr. 1, 1881; E.M., Colo. Sch. Mines, 1905, D.Eng., 1932; m. Kate Fullerton, June 23, 1908 (dec.); children—Catherine, Elizabeth (dec.), Charles Frederick, Florence, Marion. Began as newsboy Denver Post, 1897; Post " Kite expert," flying kites in western cities and from top of Pike's Peak, 1900-01; field engr. constrn. of water systems, Golden, Colo., 1904; U.S. dep. surveyor, 1905; engr. Colo. Portland Cement Co. 1906-07; mem. Hewitt-Carstarphen Co., cons. engrs., 1906-08; mem. Western Engring. Constrn. Co., 1908-09; mgr. Vulcan Sulphur Co., 1909, Gilsonite Co., of America, 1910-12; U.S. mineral surveyor, 1910-14; mining engr. Spring Canon Coal Co., 1913; chief aerial tramway engr. Am. Steel and Wire Co., Trenton, N.J., 1913-23; v.p. and chief engr. Mfrs. Selling Co., Trenton, 1923-26; has served as cons. for U.S. Smelting, Mining and Refining Co., Pittsburgh Coal Co., U.S. Bur.of Reclamation, Westinghouse Electric and Mfg. Co., Hardie Tynes Co., Consol. Steel Co., Nacional Comision de Irrigacion, Mex., Reconstruction Finance Corp., Moffat Tunnel Commn., Mosquito Mines Corp., V. Z., Reed Mines, Babcock and Wilcox Co. for city of Denver on Cherry Creek Flood control, Tenderfoot Mining Co., Mollie Kathleen Project (Cripple Creek, Colo.), Strong Leasing and Mining Co., (Victor, Colo.), Squaw Gulch Gold Mining Co., Golden Star Mining Co. (Cripple Creek) Pacific Gas and Electric Co. (San Francisco), Morrison-Utah-Winston-Lawler Co., Contractors Seminole Dam (Wyoming), Aguilar Mines (South America), etc.; designed ski tow at Denver's Winter Park, Colorado. Built telpher systems at the powder Plants, during World War; now mem. Commn. on Aerial Tramsways, and cons. engr. for Engr. Bd. U.S. Army, Ft. Belvoir, Va. Fellow A.A.A.S.; mem. Am. Soc. C.E. (Wellington award, 1929; ex pres. Colo. sect.), Am. Inst. Mining Engrs., Colo. Soc. Engrs. (past pres.), Engrs. Club of Trenton (past pres.), Tau Beta Pi, Kappa Sigma. Mason (Shriner). Author of brochures and articles on tech. engring. subjects. Special lecturer at Denver University on Mechanics and Strength of Materials, 1943. Home: 721 Marion St., Denver. Died 1942.

CARTER, EDWARD CARLOS, civil engr.; b. Waverly, Ill., Jan. 11, 1854; s. George and Louisa J. (Smith) C.; C.E., Rensselaer Poly. Inst., 1876; m. Fannie G. Fairbank, Dec. 16, 1880; children—Edward Fairbank, Paul Epler, Gertrude. Rodman, draftsman and mech. engr., 1870-77, asst. engr. on Kansas City extension, C.&A. R.R., 1877-78; prin. asst. engr. on Mississippi River observations, 1878; asst. engr. contrn., Indianapolis, Decatur & Springfield Ry., 1879-80; resident engr. Wabash, St. Louis & Pacific Ry., 1880-84, asst. to chief engr., 1884-85; asst. and contracting engr., Detroit Bridge & Iron Works, 1885-87; prin. asst. engr. C&N.W. Ry., 1887-99, chief engr., 1899-1914; later cons. engr. Home: Evanston, Ill. Died Dec. 23, 1930.

CARTER, HAROLD SAMUEL, civil engr.; b. Eden, N.Y.; Oct. 17, 1896; s. Harry J. and Elizabeth (Yager) C.; B.S., Ore. State Coll., 1921; M.S., Ia. State Coll., 1923, C.E., 1929; m. Doris Greenwood, Aug. 25, 1938; children—Elaine, Harold Nick. With Ore. Hwy. Commn., summers 1917-21; grad. asst. and instr. civil engring. Ia. State Coll., 1921-24; asst. prof. civil engring. S.D. State Coll., 1924-25; asso., 1925-26, prof. civil engring., 1926-36; prof. civil engring. Utah State Agrl. Coll., 1936-45, U. Utah, Salt Lake City, 1945-53; sec.-treas. Met. Engrs., since 1953; cons. engr., S.D., Utah since 1924. Chmn. engring. commn. Utah Traffic Safety. Profl. engr., Utah, S.D., Iowa. Mem. Am. Soc. C.E., Am. Soc. Engring. Edn. Presbyn. Mason, Kiwanian. Utah Hwy. Needs Study, 1950 (study and report for Utah Legislative Council). Home: 4121 S. Carter Circle, Salt Lake City 7. Office: 140 W. 2nd S., Salt Lake City. Died July 1965.

CARTER, HENRY ROSE, sanitarian; b. Clifton Plantation, Caroline Co., Va., Aug. 25, 1852; s. Henry Rose and Emma Caroline (Coleman) C.; C.E., U. of Va., 1873; post-grad. work in mathematics and applied chemistry, same, 1874, 1875; M.D., U. of Md. Sch. of Medicine, 1879; m. Laura Hook, Sept. 29, 1880. Entered Marine Hosp. Service (now U.S. Pub. Health Service), as asst. surgeon, May 5, 1979; passed asst. surgeon, July 1, 1882; surgeon Feb. 1, 1892; sr. surgeon, Oct. 15, 1912; asst. surgeon gen. by spl. act of Congress, Mar. 4, 1915—. Has devoted attention mainly to sanitation in connection with yellow fever and malaria, beginning at the Ship Island Quarantine Sta. on Gulf of Mexico, 1888; had charge in control of several yellow fever epidemics in Southern states; discoverer, 1900-01, of extrinsic incubation of yellow fever, this announcement leading to later discovery of Dr. Walter Reed, that mosquitoes are carriers of yellow fever; inaugurated quarantine system in Cuba, 1899, 1900. Democrat. Episcopalian. Mem. Rockefeller Yellow Fever Commn., sent to Central and S. America, 1916; in charge malarial work for U.S.P.H.S., 1917 and 1918, with special reference to anti-malarial measurer for cantonments; yellow fever work, Peru, S.A., and sanitary advisor Peruvian Govt., 1920-21. Mem. Yellow Fever Council, Internat. Health Bd., Rockefeller Foundation; hon. chmn. Nat. Malaria Com., also vice permanenet sec. Names was presented for Nobel prize, 1904, by Maj. Sir Ronald Ross. Home: Washington, D.C. Died Sept. 14, 1925.

CARTER, JAMES MADISON GORE, physician; b. Johnson Co., Ill., Apr. 15, 1843; s. Rev. William B. and Mary A. (Deans) C.; A.B., St. John's Coll., 1874; M.D., Northwestern U., 1880; A.M., McKendree Coll., 1881, Ph.D., 1887; Sc.D., Lake Forest U., 1887; m. Eunice R. Northrop, 1873 (died 1887); m. 2d, Mrs. Emogenen P. Earle, June 18, 1890. Served in Co. K. 60th Ill. Vols., 1861-6S; was at Island No. 10, Corinth, Nashville, Murfreesboro, Chattanooga to Atlanta, with Sherman to the sea, through Carolinas to Rockingham, N.C., where was captured and taken to Libby Prison. Prof. pathology and hygiene, 1891-95, clin. and preventive medicine, 1895-99, prof. emeritus, Coll. of Phys. and Surg., Chicago. Author: Outlines of Medicial Botany of the United States, 1888; Catarrhal Diseases of the Respiratory Organs, 1895; Diseases of the Stomach, 1902. Home: Los Angeles, Calif. Died Mar. 3, 1919.

CARTER, OBERLIN MONTGOMERY, capt. corps in engrs., U.S.A.; b. in Ohio, 1856; entered Mil. Acad. from Ohio, apptd. by Pres. Grant, June 14, 1876; 2d lt. engrs., 1880; 1st lt., June 15, 1882; capt., Dec. 14, 1891. Mem. Am. Soc. C.E.'s. Address: War Dept., Washington. Died July 1944.

CARTER, WILLIAM SPENCER, educator; b. Warren Co., N.J., Apr. 11, 1869; s. William and Ann (Stewart) C.; M.D., U. of Pa., 1890; m. Lillian V. McCleavy, Oct. 1894; children—Margaret Stewart (Mrs. R. M. Wilkinson), Mary Taylor (Mrs. H. C. Emery). Asst. demonstrator of pathology, U. of Pa., 1891-94, asst. prof. comp. physiology, 1894-97, demonstrator of physiology, 1896-97; prof. physiology, U. of Tex., 1897-1922, dean of med. faculty, 1903-22; asso. dir. med. science div. Rockefeller Foundation, 1922-1934; dean of med. faculty, U. of Tex., 1935-38. Former mem. Nat. Bd. of Med. Examiners. Mem. Am. Med. Assn., Am. Physiological Soc. Awarded Boylston prize, 1892; Alvarenga prize, 1903. Author: Notes on Pathology and Bacteriology (with David Riesman), 1895; Laboratory Exercises in Physiology, 1916. Address: 151 Day St., Auburndale, Mass. Died May 12, 1944.

CARTWRIGHT, C(HARLES) HAWLEY, indsl. cons.; b. Huntington, Ind., Aug. 27, 1904; s. Forest and Mable (Hawley) C.; B.S., Cal. Inst. Tech., 1926, Ph.D., 1930; m. Valentia C. Meng, Aug. 31, 1940; children—Edgar, Valentia. Research fellow in astro-physics Cal. Inst. Tech., 1930-31; nat. research fellow physics U. Wis. and Physikalisches Institut, Berlin, 1931-32; research with Prof. M. Czerny, Berlin, 1932-33; fellow in physics U. Brussels, Belgium, 1933-35; instr. physics, U. Mich., 1935-36; physicist R.C.A., Hollywood, Cal., 1936-37; instr. physics Mass. Inst. Tech., 1937-40; mem. research staff Corning Glass Works, 1940-44, 45-54; cons. physicist Paramount Pictures, Inc., 1944-45; prin. engr. Farnsworth Electronics, 1954-59; indsl. cons., Indpls., 1959—. Research in devel. radiometric instruments, thermocouples, galvanometers, infra-red spectroscopy, molecular structure, evaporation metals in high vacuum; developed non-reflecting glass especially valuable for high-speed lenses. Fellow Am. Picture Engrs., Sigma Xi. Republican. Contbr. numerous articles to sci. jours. Address: 539 E. 53rd St., Indpls. Died Dec. 19, 1964.

CARTY, JOHN J., elec. engr.; b. Cambridge, Mass., Apr. 14, 1861; ed. Cambridge Latin Sch.; D.Engring., Stevens Inst. Tech., 1915, New York U., 1922; D.Sc., U. of Chicago, Bowdoin, 1916, Tufts, 1919, Yale, 1922, Princeton, 1923; LL.D., McGill, 1917, U. of Pa., 1924; m. Marion Mount Russell, Aug. 8, 1891; 1 son, John Russell. Began with Bell System in Boston, 1879, served in various positions, including chief engr. New York Telephone Co., 1889-1907, chief engr. Am. Telephone & Telegraph Co., 1907-19, v.p. same, 1919-30. A pioneer in development of telephone, for which invented many improvements. Trustee of Carnegie Instrn., Washington, Carnegie Corp. (New York). Fellow Am. Academy of Arts and Sciences, American Institute E.E. (pres. 1915-16); hon. mem. Franklin Inst., etc. Longstreth medal, 1903, and Franklin medal, 1916. Franklin Inst.; Edison medal, 1918, Am. Inst. E.E.; John Fritz medal, 1928, engring. societies. Commd. maj. Signal Officers' R.C., Jan. 1917; col. (temp.) U.S. Army, 1917; served on staff chief signal officer U.S. Army, and in France on staff chief signal officer A.E.F.; signal officer during armistice, in charge of communications, Am. Commn. to Negotiate Peace; brig. gen. U.S. Army Res. Decorated D.S.M. (U.S.); Officer Legion of Honor (French), Order Rising Sun and Order Sacred Treasure (Japanese). Home: Winter Park, Fla. Died Dec. 27, 1932.

CARVER, GEORGE WASHINGTON, agrl. chemist, botanist; b. of slave parents, nr. Diamond Grove, Mo., circa 1864; in infancy lost father, and was stolen and carried into Ark. with mother, who was never heard of again; was bought from captors for a race horse valued at $300, and returned to former home in Mo.; worked way through high sch., Mpls., Kan., and later through coll.; B.S. Agr., Ia. State Coll. A. and M. Arts, 1894, M.S. Agr. 1896; D.Sc., Simpson Coll., 1928. Elected mem. faculty, Ia. State Coll. A. and M. Arts, placed in charge greenhouse, devoting spl. attention to bacterial lab. work in systematic botany; tchr. Tuskegee Inst. from 1896, also dir. Dept. Agrl. Research. Apptd. collaborator Bur. Plant Industry, U.S. Dept. Agr., div. mycology and disease survey, 1935. Recipient Spingarn medal, 1923, Roosevelt medal, 1939; plantation on which he was born made a nat. monument, 1953. Mem. Royal Soc. Arts, London. Developed 300 types of synthetic material from peanuts, including dyes, soap, cheese, milk substitutes; developed 118 by-products from sweet potatoes; made dyes from local clays; taught soil improvement; urged diversification of crops. Died Jan. 5, 1943.

CARVER, WALTER LEXOR, engr.; b. Cleve., Oct. 16, 1889; s. Loren D. and Margaret (Jacob.) C.; ed. pub. schs. spl. lab. and research work; m. Marie MacDonald, Dec. 10, 1914. Apprentice Nat. Screw and Tack Co., Cleve., 1908-10; with engring. dept. Peerless Motor Car Co., 1910-13; chief engr. and supt. production Wallis Tractor Co., Cleve. and Racine, Wis., 1913-16; fgn. countries, 1916-17; supt. production Moline (Ill.) Plow Co., 1917-20; chief engr. tractor dept. Midwest Engine Co., Indpls., 1920; V.P., treas. T.B. Funk Co., Indpls., 1922—. Traveled widely throughtout the world; tech. work with Russian Army, at Riga front, 1917; made first tech. test of tractor haulage of arty. for U.S. Govt. Mem. Soc. Automotive Engrs. Unitarian. Address: 39 Fifth Av., N.Y.C. Died Apr. 12, 1958.

CARVETH, HECTOR RUSSELL, electrochemist; b. Port Hope, Ont., Can., Jan. 23, 1873; s. Joseph and Martha Ann (Butterfield) C.; student Victoria U., 1892-96; A.B., U. of Toronto, 1896; fellow in chemistry, Cornell U., 1896-98, Ph.D., 1898; m. Josephine McCollum, Dec. 22, 1915; children—Florence Camille, Nancy Page, Marie Josephine, Hector Russell, Stephen Melhuish, Daniel Butterfield, Rodney Penrhyn. Came to U.S., 1896, naturalized, 1907. Lecturer in phys. chemistry, Cornell U., 1898-1905; chemist, Internat. Acheson Graphite, 1905-06; works mgr., Niagara Electro Chem. Co., 1906-17, pres., 1932; vice pres. The Roessler & Hasslacher Chem. Co., 1917-28, pres. 1928-32; dir. E. I. du Pont de Nemours, 1930-32; retired, 1932. Mem. Am. Chem. Soc., Am. Electrochem. Soc., D.U. Mason. Clubs: Republican. Chemists. Drug and Chemical, New York Athletic (New York); Empire State, Niagara, Rotary, Niagara Falls Country, Annisquam Yacht. Research in metallic chromium and production, properties, reactions and uses of sodium and other alkali metals. Home:352 Buffalo Av., Niagara Falls, N.Y. Died Sept. 17, 1942.

CARY, AUSTIN, forester; b. East Machias, Me., July 31, 1865; s. Charles and Mary C.; A.B., Bowdoin, 1887, A.M., 1890; studied biology, Johns Hopkins and Princeton univs., 1888-91; D.Sc. Bowdoin Coll., 1922; instr. Dept. Geology and Biology, Bowdoin, 1887-88; m. Lelia J. Chisholm, Oct. 8, 1916 (died 1917). In employ of forest commr., Me., and Forestry Div., U.S. Dept. Agr., 1893-96; forester for Berlin Mills Co., Portland, Me., 1898-1904; taught, spring terms, Yale Forest Sch., 1904-05; asst. prof. forestry, Harvard, 1905-09; supt. state forest, N.Y., 1909-10; U.S. forest service, 1910-35. Democrat. Conglist. Author: Woodsman's Manuel, 1909. Home: Brunswick, Me. Died Apr. 28, 1936.

CARY, EDWARD HENRY surgeon; b. Union Springs, Ala., Feb. 28, 1872; s. Joseph Milton and Lucy Janette (Powell) C.; pre. edn., Union Springs Acad. and high sch., N.Y. City; M.D. Bellevue Hosp. Med. Coll. (New York U.), 1898; LL.D., Baylor U., 1916; m. Georgie Fonda Schneider, Apr. 19, 1911; children—Georgie, Edward Henry, Florence, Jenette(dec.), Catherine. Intern, Bellevue Hosp., 1898-99, N.Y. Eye and Ear Infirmary, 1899-1901; prof. ophtalmology and Otolayngology and head of dept., Baylor University, 1902-43, dean of Medical School, 1902-22, chairman department surgery, 1921-29; chairman faculty, Med. Sch., 1909-29; chmn. staff, Baylor Hosp., 1909-29; prof. emeritus of ophthalmology, Southwestern Med. Sch., U. of Tex., chmn. adv. bd., sch. and hosp., 1909-29; now pres. Group Hosp. Service, Inc., Group Med. and Surg. Service; pres. Cary-Schneider Investment Co.; dir. Republic Nat. Bank. Recipient Linz Award for 1945. Pres. and chmn. exec. bd. National Physicians Com.; pres. Kesller Plan Assn. Chmn. dist. bd. med. examiners, Dallas, World War; organized Baylor Med. Appeal Board of Selective Service Dist. No. 7. Pres. Southwestern Med Foundation, Philos. Soc. of Tex. (past pres.), President Dallas Historical Society. Fellow Am. College Surgeons; mem. Am. Med. Assn. (trustee 1925-29; pres. 1932-33), Amer. Laryngol., Rhinol. and Otol. Soc., Southern Med. Assn. (ex-pres.), Tex. Texas State Med. Soc. (ex-pres.), Dallas County Med. Soc. (ex-pres.), Am. Acad. of Ophthalmology and Otolaryngology, mem. council, Phi Alpha Sigma , Alpha Omega Alpha, Soc. Colonial Wars. Mason (32 deg., Shriner). Clubs: Critic, Dallas Athletic, Dallas Brookhollow and Country. Home: 4712 Lakeside Drive, Dallas 5. Office: Medical Arts Bldg., Dallas. Died Dec. 11, 1953; buried Hillcrest Mausoleum, Dallas.

CARY, EDWARD RICHARD, engineer; b. Troy, N.Y., Dec. 19, 1865; s. Tallman, Jr., and Elizabeth (Lounsbury) C.; C.E., Rensselaer Poly. Inst., 1888; m. Mary Lyman, of Troy, June 21, 1892; 1 dau., Helen Elizabeth (Mrs. F. William Cappelmann). With Rensselaer Polytechnic Institute since 1888, professor surveying and railroad engring., 1904-36, emeritus prof. since 1936. Practiced as mem. Cary & Roemer, 1896-1906; city engr., Troy, 1900-02 and 1906-08. Mem. Am. Soc. C.E. (v.p. S.C. Sect. 1939), Rensselaer Soc. Engrs., S.C. Soc. Engrs., Sigma Xi, Tau Beta Pi. Republican. Episcopalian. Mason. Author: Solution of Railroad Problems by Use of the Slide Rule (text book), 1911; Geodetic Surveying, 1915; Elements of Diagrams, 1923. Home: 10 Wit-Mary Apts., Columbia, S.C.

CASE, ALBERT HERMON, mining engr.; b. Cambridge, Lenawee County, Mich., June 1, 1875; s. Marion and Mary Stirling (Ladd) C.; B.S. in Mech. Engring., Michigan State College, 1902, D.Eng., 1945; Co-University, 1905; D.Sc. (honorary), Tampa University, 1950; married Sarah B. S. Avery, August 14, 1906. Superintendent of Cliff Mine, Ophir, Utah, 1906-07, with various Lewisohn interests since 1907, as superintendent Santa Fe Gold & Copper Mining Co., general manager Tennessee Copper Co., S. A. Gold & Platinum Co.; v.p., dir. Tampa Southern Ry. Co., numerous mine examinations in U.S., Can., Alaska, Colombia and Panama. Trustee Tampa Univ. Dir. Lyons Fertilizer Co., Medal for Achievement, Col. University, 1947. Mem. Am. Inst. Mining and Metall. Engrs., S.A.R., Alpha Tau Omega, Tau Beta Pi, Sigma Xi. Democrat. Episcopalian. Mason (32 deg.). Club: Rotary (Tampa). Home: 1314 Rugby Rd., Charlottesville VA

CASE, ERMINE COWLES, paleontologist; b. Kansas City, Mo., Sept. 11, 1871; s. Theodore Spencer and Julia (Lykins) C.; A.B., A.M., U. of Kan., 1893; M.S., Cornell U., 1894; Ph.D., U. of Chicago, 1895, m. Mary Margaret Snow, of Lawrence, Kan., June 24, 1899; children—Francis Huntington, Theodore Johnston. Instr. chemistry, U. of Kan., 1893-94; instr. paleontology, U. of Chicago, 1895; prof. geology and phys. geography, State Normal Sch., Milwaukee, Wis., 1897-1906; asst. prof. hist. geology and paleontology, 1906-08; jr. prof., Sept. 25, 1908-12, prof., 1912—, U. of Mich. Research asso. Carnegie Instn. of Washington. Fellow A.A.A.S., Geol. Soc. America, Paleontol. Soc.; mem. Washington Acad. Science, Am. Soc. Mammalogists, Am. Soc. Naturalists, Paleontolog. Gesellsch., Mich. Acad. Science, Sigma Xi, Phi Delta Theta. Author: Geology and Physical Geography of Wisconsin. Contbr. numerous papers and 9 monographs, mostly on vertebrate paleontology. Home: Ann Arbor MI

CASE, GEORGE SESSIONS, mech. engr., mfr.; b. Interlaken N.Y., Oct. 16, 1882; s. Frank Castle and Fannie (Sessions) C.; B.S., Case Sch. Applied Science, 1904, M.E., 1927; m. Amey Ellen Hall, Dec. 4, 1906; children—Geo. S., Barbara Jane. With Lamson and Sessions Co., since 1904, became factury mgr., 1912, treas., 1921, v.p., 1926, pres., 1929, chmn. of bd. 1938; dir. Peck, Stow and Wilcox Co., Baker-Raulang Co., Johnston and Jennings Co., The Lamson and Sessions Co., J. Hungerford Smith Co. Maj. Chem. Warfare Service, 1918; station at Edgwood Arsenal and Washington. Mem. Am. Soc. M.E., Cleveland Engring. Soc., Soc. Automovtive Engrs., Phi Delta Thea, Tau Beta Pi. Republican. Presbyn. Clubs: Union, Mayfield Country. Home: 17414 S. Woodland Rd., Shaker Heights 20, O. Office: 1971 W. 85th St., Cleveland 2. Died Oct. 11, 1950; buried Lakeview Cemetery, Cleveland.

CASE, JAMES THOMAS, surgeon, roentgenologist; b. San Antonio, Tex., Jan. 5, 1882; s. James Henry and Fannie Elizabeth (Robertson) C.; M.D., Am. Med. Missionary Coll., U. of Ill. Med. Sch., 1905; D.M.R.E., U. of Cambridge, 1920; m. Helena Margaret Kallogg, Sept. 1, 1908; children—Herbert Roland, Margaret Frances. House surgeon, Battle Creek Sanitarium, 1908-10, asst. surgeon, 1910-19, chief surgeon, 1919-29, consultant, 1929-51, dir. of sanitarium's Roentgen department; also president of board of trustees, 1944-51; formerly director of X-ray dept. St. Luke's Hosp., Chicago and Evanston (Ill.) Hospital; professor roentgenology, Northwestern University Medical School, 1912-47, professor emeritus since 1947; mem. exec. com. Chicago Tumor Inst., 1947-52, pres., 1949-52; radiologist, U.S. Marine and Highland Park hosps., 1929-52; dir. Meml. Cancer Found., Santa Barbara, 1951—. Pres. Race Betterment Found., 1942-51. Served as lt. col. Med. R.C., 1917; in general charge of X-ray work, A.E.F., in France, 1917-18; col., 1920-32; exec. officer 108th Med. Regt., 33d Div., 1932-37. Decorated with Order of the Purple Heart (U.S.); with Order of Merito Militar (Mexico), 1948, Cuban Order of Merit, Carlos Finlay, 1955; Colombian Orden de Boyaca, 1955; recipient gold medal, Interamerican Congress of Radiology, 1955; honorary professor radiol. U. of San Marcos, Lima (Peru), 1949. Editor Annals of Roentgenology, 1920-38. Pres. Am. Roentgen. Ray. Soc., 1919-20, Caldwell lectr., gold medalist, 1939; pres. Am. Radium Society, 1923-24 (Janeway lecturer and medalist 1959), American Co-l. Radiology, 1929-30; treas. Internat. Coll. Surgeons, 1949-56; fellow A.C.S., Royal Soc. Medicine (Eng.), Radiol. Soc. of N.A. (Carman lectr., 1937; gold medalist, 1950); mem. Interam. Congress Radiology (pres. 1955); mem. roentgen and radiology profl. socs. Am. France, Spain, Brazil, Peru and other countries; mem. fgn. and domestic scientific socs. Del. to and sometimes officer of several internat. profl. congresses. Republican. Author X-ray Examination of the Alimentary Tract (4 vols.), 1914, Spanish Edition, 1918; also chapters in various med. books. Translator German books in field. Home: 416 Samarkand Dr. Office: 2315 Bath St., Santa Barbara, Cal. Died May 25, 1960.

CASE, JEROME INCREASE, mfr.; b. Williamstown, N.Y., Dec. 11, 1818; s. Caleb and Deborah (Jackson) C.; m. Lydia Bull, 1848, 4 children. Designed built, used combined thresher and separator, signed built, used combined thresher and separator, (eliminated the fanning mill), 1844; incorporated J.I. Case Threshing Machine Co., 1880; established Mfrs.' Nat. Bank of Racine (Wis.) and First Nat. Bank of Burlington (Wis.), 1871, pres. both banks; mem. bd. trustees Northwestern Mut. Life Ins. Co.; Republican mayor Racine, 1856, 59; mem. Wis. Senate; one of Wis. commrs. at Centennial Exposition, 1876; a founder Wis. Acad. Science, Art and Letters. Died Dec. 22, 1891.

CASE, RALPH E., indsl. engr.; b. Rowayton, Conn., Apr. 25, 1887; s. Elmer E. and Katie E. (Petty) C.; E.E., Rensselaer Poly. Inst., 1912; m. Mildred Fleming, June 30, 1917; children—Carolyn F. (Mrs. Renwick Tweedy), Renwick E. Engr. Crooker Wheeler & Co., Ampere, N.J., 1912-14; engr. R.U.V. Co., Norwalk, Conn., 1914-17; engr. Spicer Mfg. Co., South Plainfield, N.J., 1919-23; partner Stevenson, Jordan & Harrison, 1923-62; chmn. bd. Case & Co., N.Y.C., 1962-69; dir. Glen Alden Corp., Ivan Sorvell, Inc., Flexible Tubing Corp.; corporator of South Norwalk Savs. Bank; adv. bd. City Trust Co. Served as ensign USNRF, 1918-19. Mem. National Assn. Cost Accountants. Clubs: N.Y. Yacht, Cruising of America (N.Y.C.); Norwalk Yacht, Off Soundings, Essex Yacht. Home: Durham CT Died Feb. 1969.

CASON, HULSEY, psychologist; b. Lexington, Ga., Feb. 21, 1893; s. Emory Hugh and Jesse (Jones) C.; A.B., Mercer U., 1913; A.M., Columbia, 1920. Ph.D., 1922; m. Elosie May Boeker, Sept. 6, 1923; children—Roger Lee, Jean; m. 2d, Marion Conrad, Aug. 30, 1939; 1 son Emory Conrad. Asst. prof. psychology, Syracuse U., 1923-26, U. of Rochester, 1926-27, prof. psychology, 1927-30; prof. psychology, U. of Wis., 1930-40, U. of Miami since 1948; summers lecturer in psychology U. of N.C., 1923, Columbia, 1927, 29, U. of Wis. 1930; research psychologist, U.S.P.H.S., 1940-48. Served as 1st lt., Inf., 7th Div. Regular Army, 1917-19, Mexican Border and A.E.F. in France. Diplomate in Clin. psychology, Am. Bd. of Examiners in Professional Psychology, 1948. Fellow Am. Psychol. Assn., A.A.A.S., Mem. Am. Assn. U. Profs., Southern Soc. for Philosophy and Psychology, Midwestern Psychol. Assn. Fla. Psychol. Assn., Fla. Acad. Scis., Sigma Xi., Phi Delta Kappa, Psi Chi. Unitarian. Club: Country (Coral Gables). Author: Conditioned Pupillary and Eyelid Reactions, 1922; Laws of Exercise and Effect, 1924; Common Annoyances, 1930; Pleasant and Unpleasant Activities, 1932; Nightmare Dream, 1935; Psychopathic Personality, 1942; Concept and Symptoms of the Psychopath, 1948 (also in Spanish, 1950, 51). Mem. editorial bd. Jour. of Psychology since 1935. Genealogist. Home: 619 Anastasia Av., Coral Gables, Fla. Died May 1, 1950; buried Warren, Ca.

CASPARI, CHARLES EDWARD, cons. chemist; b. Baltimore, Md., Apr. 9, 1875; s. Charles and Leslie Virginia (Heinichen) C.; A.B., Johns Hopkins U., 1896, Ph.D., 1900; m. Emilie Ganz (b. in Paris, France), Mar. 4, 1903; children—Florence L. (Mrs. Oliver Abel, Jr.), Charles Edward, Emilie C. (Mrs. M.E. Gilderbloom, Jr.). Instr. organic chemistry, Columbia U., 1900-01; research chemist Mallinckrodt Chem. Works, St. Louis, 1901-03; prof. chemistry, St. Louis Coll. Pharmacy, 1903-30, prof. emeritus since 1930, dean since 1926; mem. Revision Com. U.S. Pharmacopoeia, 1910-40. Fellow A.A.A.S.; mem. Am. Chem. Soc., Am. Pharm. Soc., Franklin Inst., Phi Beta Kappa. Democrat. Unitarian. Clubs: Noonday, University, Missouri Athletic, Bellerive Country (St. Louis); Chemists (N.Y.C.). Contbr. to Proceedings Am. Pharm. Assn. Home: 6951 Kingsbury Blvd. Office: 4588 Parkview Place, St. Louis, Mo. Died June 9, 1942.

CASS, GEORGE WASHINGTON, engr., railroad exec.; b. Muskingham County, O., Mar. 12, 1810; s. George W. and Sophia (Lord) C.; grad. U.S. Mil. Acad., 1832. Detailed for duty with Corps. Engr., U.S. Army, as asst. to supt. in charge constrn. Cumberland Rd., 1832-36; erected 1st cast-iron tubulararch bridge built in U.S., 1837; established Adams Express Co., 1849, effected consolidation of company lines between Boston and St. Louis and South to Richmond Va., 1854, pres. co., 1855; became pres., dir. Ohio & Pa. R.R. Co. (later consol. and name Pitts., Ft. Wayne & Chgo. R.R.), 1856. Died Mar. 21, 1888.

CASSELL, WALLACE LEWIS, educator; b. Abilene, Kan., June 19, 1899; s. Levin Lewis and Mabel (Dooley) C.; B.S., U. of Colo., 1922, E.E., 1928; M.S., Purdue U., 1946; m. Louise L'Engle, Aug. 26, 1942; 1 dau., Hope (Mrs. Richard G. Ligon). Elec. engr. Gen. Electric Co., Schenectady, 1922-25; instr. elec. engring. U. Colo., 1925-28, asst. prof., 1928-32, asso. prof., 1932-39; asso. prof. elec. engring. Ia. State U., 1939-41, prof., 1941—, Anson Marston prof. engring., 1957—. Fellow Am. Inst. E.E. (v.p. 1952-54); mem. I.R.E. (sr.), Am. Soc. Engring. Edn., Tau Beta Pi, Phi Kappa Psi, Sigma Tau, Eta Kappa Nu, Phi Kappa Phi. Presbyn Mason, Kiwanian (past dist. gov.). Home: 415 Westwood Dr., Ames, Ia. Died Mar. 11, 1966; buried University Cemetery, Ames.

CASSIDY, M(ICHAEL) JOSEPH, govt. ofcl.; b. Macon, Ga., Mar. 29, 1893; s. Patrick John and Mary Ann (Campbell) C.; A.B., Spring Hill Coll., 1914; C.E., Cath. U., 1917. Cons. engr. Elroy G. Smith Co., Augusta, Ga., 1921-37; constrn. supervision Zone V, commr. Fed. Housing Adminstrn., L.A., 1938-42, asst. Zone commr. Zone V, Washington, 1943-46, zone commr., 1947-55, executive officer regional liaison, 1955—. Served as lt., 20th C.E., France, World War 1; supervision rehabilitaiton engr. troops after Armistice. 1918-20. Club: Columbia Country (Chevy Chase, Md.). Home: 6640 Hillandale Rd., Bethesda, Md. Office: 811 Vermont Av., Washington 11. Died Dec. 17, 1957.

CASSIN, JOHN, ornithologist; b. Delaware County, Pa., Sept. 6, 1813. Became mcht., Phila., 1834, later established engraving and lithographing bus.; mem. Acad. Natural Scis.; identified and arranged ornithol. specimens in collection of Dr. Thomas B. Wilson. (largest collection then in existence); studied taxonomy, synonomy and nomenclature of ornithology; contrbr. papers to govt. and scientific publs. Author: Illustrations of the Birds of California, Texas, Oregon, British, and Russian America, 1856. Died Jan. 10, 1869.

CASSIRER, ERNST, philosopher; b. Breslau, Prussia, July 28, 1874; s. Eduard and Jerry Cassirer; ed. univs. Berlin, Leipzig, Munich, Heidelberg; Ph.D., U. Marburg, 1899; LL.D., Glasgow (Scotland) U.; m. Toni Bondy, 1902, 3 children. Lectr., U. Berlin, before World War I; drafted for civil service in World War I; prof. U. Hamberg, 1919-33, rector, 1930-33, resigned when Hitler came to power; lectr. All Souls Coll., Oxford (Eng.) U., 1935-41; became Swedish citizen; vis. prof. philosophy Yale, 1941-44, Columbia, 1944-45. Hon. mem. Bedford Coll., London; mem. Svenska Vitesk Acad., Swedish Royal Acad. Sci., Historic Acad. (Stockholm). Regarded as leading rep. of Neo-Kantian Marburg sch.; worked chiefly in epistemology, logic, philosophy of sci., politics. Author: Substanzbegriff und Funktionsbegriff, 1910, Zur Einsteinschen Relativitatsheorie, 1921 (combined into English transl. as Substance and Function and Einstein's Theory of Relativity 1923); Language and Myth, 1925, transl., 1946; Philosophy of Symbolic Forms, 3 vols., 1923-29, transl., 1953-57; Essay on Man, transl., 1944; Myth of the State, transl., 1946; Problem of Knowledge, transl., 1950; Philosophy of the Enlightenment, transl., 1955; Determinism and Indeterminism in Modern Physics, transl., 1956; Logic of the Humanities, transl., 1961; Individual and the Cosmos in Renaissance Philosophy, transl., 1964; Question of Jean-Jacques Rousseau, transl., 1963; Rousseau, Kant and Goethe. Editor: (with others) Renaissance Philosophy of Man, 1948. Contbr. articles to Jour. de Psychologie, other jours. Died N.Y.C., Apr. 13, 1945.

CASTELLANI, ALDO (COUNT OF CHISIMAIO), physician; b. Florence, Italy, Sept. 8, 1877; s. Ettore and Violante (Giuliani) C.; M.D., U. of Florence, 1899; studied U. of Bonn, London Sch. of Tropical Medicine; m. Josephine Ambler Stead, of Yorkshire, Eng., Jan. 2, 1906; 1 dau., Jacqueline (wife of Sir Miles Lampson). Hon. physician to the King of Greece and Crown Prince and Princess of Italy. Mem. Foreign Office Royal Soc's. First Sleeping Sickness Commn., Uganda, Africa, 1902-03; prof. pathology, later prof. tropical medicine, Ceylon Med. Coll., 1903-15, also dir. Bacterial Inst., lecturer on dermatology, etc.; prof. tropical medicine, Royal U. of Naples, 1915-19, also lt. col. Italian Med. Service and mem. Internat. Sanitary Commn.; lecturer London Sch. Tropical Medicine and dir. tropical medicine, Ross Inst., 1919-33; prof. tropical medicine, Tulane U., 1926-30; prof. tropical medicine, Royal U. of Rome, 1930-71; prof. tropical medicine La. State U.

Med. Sch., 1932-71; surgeon gen. and inspr. gen. for Italian Army, Ethiopian War, 1935-36. Made the fundamental discovery in elucidation of etiology of sleeping sickness, 1902; discoverey in Ceylon, the micro-organism which causes yaws; described the organisms causing certain new diseases; etc. Fellow Royal Coll. Physicians, London, Royal Soc. Tropical Medicine, London, Am. Coll. Phys., Royal Soc. Medicine. Decorated Knight Comdr. of St. Michael and St. George (British); Grand Cross Crown of Italy; Officier Legion of Honor (French); Grand Cross Order of Civil Merit (Spain); Grand Cross Order of St. Sava and Officer White Eagle (Jugo Slavia); created Hereditary Count by King of Italy for services in Ethiopian War. Catholic. Clubs: Atheneum (London); Travellers (Paris); Caccia (Rome). Author: (with Dr. Albert Chalmers), Manual of Tropical Medicine, 4th edit. by Castellani, 1940; Fungi of Fungal Diseases (lectures), 1927; Climate and Acclimatization, 1930, 2d edit., 1938; also about 400 contributions on medical subjects. Editor of Journal of Tropical Medicine and Hygiene (London). Address: New Orleans LA DiedOct. 1971.*

CASTLE, WILLIAM ERNEST, zoologist; b. Alexandria, O., Oct. 25, 1867; s. William Augustus and Sarah (Fassett) C.; A.B., Denison U., 1889; A.B., Harvard, 1893, A.M., 1894, Ph.D. 1895; LL.D., Denison, 1921; Sc.D., Wisconsin, 1921; m. Clara Sears Bosworth, Aug. 18, 1896 (died May 22, 1940); children—William Bosworth, Henry Fassett (dec.), Edward Sears. Taught Latin, Ottawa (Kan.) University, 1889-92; instructor vertebrate anatomy, University of Wisconsin, 1895-96; instructor biology, Knox Coll., 1896-97; inst. zoology, Harvard, 1897-1903; asst. prof., 1903-08, prof., 1908-36, now emeritus; research asso. in genetics, U. of Calif. since 1936; also research asso. in genetics, Carnegie Instn., Washington. Kimber award genetics, Nat. Acad. Scis., 1955. Fellow Am. Acad. Arts and Scis.; mem. Nat. Acad. Sciences, Am. Philos. Soc., Boston Soc. Natural History, A.A.A.S., Am. Soc. Naturalists (pres. 1918), Am. Soc. Zoologists (pres. Eastern Branch 1905-06), Phi Beta Kappa, Sigma Xi. Author: Heredity in Relation to Evolution and Animal Breeding, 1911; Genetics and Eugenics, 1916, 4th rev. edit., 1930; Genetics of Domestic Rabbits, 1930; Mammaliam Genetics, 1940; also several publs. on subjects of heredity and evolution. Home: 421 Spruce St., Berkeley, Cal. 94708. Died June 3, 1962.

CASWELL, ALBERT EDWARD, physicist; b. Winnipeg, Manitoba Can., May 24, 1884; .s. John J. and Patience Ethel (Smith) C.; student U. of Manitoba, 1903-05; A.B., Stanford U., 1908; Ph.D., 1911; m. Mary Constance Edwards July 3, 1912; children—John Edwards, Miriam Esther (Mrs. Ford L. Danner), also Dwight Allan, Randall Smith. Came to U.S., 1905. naturalized 1916. Instr. in Physics Purdue U., Lafayette, Ind 1911-13; instr. in physics, U., of Ore., Eugene, Ore., 1913-15; asst. prof., 1915-17, prof., 1917-32, prof. physics and head of physicis department, 1934-49, professor emeritus, 1949—; on leave of absence to act as staff mem. Radiation Lab., Mass. Inst. Tech., 1942-45; nat. research fellow in physics, Princeton Univ., 1919-20; prof. physics , Ore. State Coll., Corvallis, Ore., 1932-34 . Westminster Foundation of Ore., 1921—; 1st v.p. Ore. Council of Churches 1938-42, 1945-46. Mem. Am. Assn. Physics Teachers, Am. Phys. Soc., Am. Astron. Soc., A.A.A.S., Am. Assn. Univ. Profs., Sigma Xi. Sigma Pi Sigma, Pi Mu Epsilon. Club: Kiwanis (Eugene, Ore.). Author: Experimental Physics, 1928; Outline of Physics, 1928, rev. edit., 1938; International Critical Tables (wrote section on thermoelectricity), 1929; Contbr. Physical Review and other scientific jours. Home: 1960 University St., Eugene, Ore. Died June 18, 1954.

CASWELL, ALEXIS, scientist, univ. pres.; b. Taunton, Mass., Jan. 29, 1799; s. Samuel and Polly (Seaver) C.; grad. Brown U., 1822, D.D. (hon.), 1841, LL.D. (hon.), 1865; m. Esther Thompson, 1830; m. 2d, Elizabeth Edmands, 1855; 6 children. Prof. ancient langs. Columbia U., Washington, D.C., 1825-27; entered ministry as pastor of a Baptist Ch., Halifax, N.S., Can., 1827; prof. mathemtatics and natural philosophy Brown U., 1828-63, pres., 1868-72, trustee, 1873-75; became asso. fellow Am. Acad. Arts and Scis., 1850; v.p. A.A.A.S., 1855; chosen by U.S. Govt. as one of 50 incorporators Nat. Acad. Scis., 1863; became pres. Nat. Exchange Bank, also Am. Screw Co. (both Providence, R.I.), 1863; pres. R.I. Hosp., 1875-77; dir., v.p. Providence Athenaeum. Author: Smithsonian Contributions to Knowledge, 1860; other works include: Lecutres on Astronomy, 1858, Memoirs of John Barstow, 1864. Died Providence, Jan. 8, 1877.

CATES, LOUIS SHATTUCK, mining engr.; b. Boston, Dec. 20, 1881; s. Edwin Wallace and Emily Allen (Johnson), C.; S.B., Mass. Inst. Tech., 1902; Dr. Engring. (hon.), Mich. Coll. Mining and Technology, 1936; D.Sc., U. Ariz., 1946; D.Sc. (hon.) Columbia, 1947; m. 3d. Ethel Chesbrough (hon.) Columbia, 1947; m. 3d. Lewis. May 12, 1951. Mine operator in Mexico, 1902; asst. to pres. Nat. Steel and Wire Co., N.Y., 1903-04; in charge of construction and developement at Bingham Canyon, Utah, for Boston Consolidated Mining Co., 1904-08; gen. mgr. 1909; with Ray (Ariz.) Consol. Copper Co., 1910-22; gen. mgr. 1922-30 also 1923-30; asst. gen. mgr. Bingham and Garfield Ry. Co., 1919-22, gen. mgr., 1922-30, also vice pres., 1923-30; pres. Phelps Dodge Corp., Copper, 1930-47, chmn. bd., 1947—; dir. of Phelps Dodge Copper Products Corp., Long Island R.R. Co., Dodge Refining Corp., Niagara Fire Ins. Co., So. Peru Copper Corp. Mem. Div. of engring. and indsl. research, Nat. Research Council, 1939-41 Developed system making it economically possible by underground methods, to mine low grade prophyrv ores. Decorated Comdr. Order of the Crown (Belgium); Knight Order of the Condor of the Andes (Bolivia); Chevalier of the Legion of Honor (France). Awarded Saunders Gold Medal by Am. Inst. Mining and Metall. Soc. Am., 1956; Knight Comdr. Agrl. & Indsl. Order Merit, Cuba, 1957. Mem. Corp. Mass. Inst. Tech. (life). Engr., 1939. Mem. Corp. Mass. Inst. Tech., 1933-38.V.p., dir. Copper and Brass Research Assn., 1931-32; mem. Am. Mining Congress (pres. 1925), Mining and Metall. Soc. of Am. (pres. 1931), Am. Inst. Mining and Metall. Engrs. (v.p. 1934-37, dir. 1919-21, 1931-34, 1936-39, pres. 1946), Nat. Inst. Social Scis. (life). Soc. Mayflower Descs.; Gen. Soc. Colonial Wars, The Pilgrims of the U.S., S.A.R., Chi Phi. Republican. Episcopalian. Mason (32 deg. Shriner). Clubs: India House, The Linds, The Brook, Pinnacle, University (N.Y.C.); Piping Rock (Loucst Valley, N.Y.). Home: 950 Fifth Av. N.Y.C. 21. Office: 300 Park Av., N.Y.C. 22. Died Oct. 29, 1959.

CATHCART, CHARLES SANDERSON, chemist; b. New Brunswick, N.J., Jan. 2, 1865; B.Sc., Rutgers, 1886, M.Sc., 1889. Asst. chemist to Austin & Wilber, chemists, 1886-89; asst. chemist N.J. Agrl. Coll. Expt. Sta., 1889-93; chief chemist Lister's Agrl. Chem. Works, Newark, N.J., 1893-1907; chief chemist N.J. Agrl. Expt. Sta. since 1907; state chemist since 1912. Fellow A.A.A.S.; mem. Am. Chem. Soc. Home: New Brunswick, N.J. Died Dec. 9, 1945.

CATHCART, STANLEY H(OLMAN), geologist; b. Millerstown, Pa., Aug. 20, 1889; s. Thomas Preston and Linda (Holman) C.; B.S., Pa. State Coll., 1912, M.S., 1916; grad. study Yale, 1917-18, 19-20; m. Iva Louise Waterbury, Oct. 20, 1921. Asst. geologist, geologist U.S. Geol. Survey, 1918-25; geologist Standard Oil Co., N.J., 1925-30, Socony Vacuum Oil Co., 1937-41, Tex. Oil. Co., 1943-47, Pa. Geol. Survey, 1930-37, advanced geologist, 1941-43, state geologist since 1947. Mem. Geol. Soc. Am., Am. Assn. Petroleum Geologist, Engring. Soc. Pa., Appalachian, Pittsburgh geol. Socs., Sigma Xi. Mason. Clubs: Torch, Rotary (Harrisburg, Pa.). Home: 3113 N. Front St. Office: Pa. Geological Survey, Harrisburg, Pa. Died Mar. 19, 1953; buried Liverpool, Pa.

CATHCART, WILLIAM LEDYARD, engr.; b. Mystic, Conn., Aug. 12, 1855; s. William and Eliza (Caldwell) C.; ed. U. of Pa., 1871-73; grad. U.S. Naval Acad., 1875. Served in Engr. Corps. U.S. Navy on Acad., 1875. Served in Engr. Corps U.S. Navy on N. and S. Atlantic, S. Pacific and Asiatic squadrons; resigned from Navy, 1891, to enter pvt. business; treas. mfg. co., 1891-97; prof. marine engring., Webb Acad. of Naval Architecture, New York, 1897-99; adj. prof. maech. engring., Columbia, 1899-1903; prof. engring., Webb Inst. Naval Architecture, N.Y. City, 1918—. Apptd. chief engr. U.S. Navy, and ordered to spl. duty as asst. to engr.-in-chief, Navy Dept., during Spanish-Am. War; apptd. lt. comdr. U.S.N.R.F., and on spl. duty office of engr.-in-chief, U.S. Navy, World War; later promoted to comdr. U.S.N.R.F. Author: Machine Design, 1903; Elements of Graphic Statics, with Prof. J. Irvin Chaffee, 1910; A Short Course in Graphic Statics (with same), 1911. Mem. Griffin & Cathcart, consulting engrs. Home: Germantown, Philadelphia, Pa. Died Mar. 192S.

CATHELL, WILLIAM T., M.D.; b. Baltimore, Dec. 4, 1864; grad. Coll. Phys. & Surg., Baltimore, March, 1886. Practice limited to diseases of nose and throat. Discoverer of Kissingen and Vichy treatment of obesity. Contributor of various articles to med. press. Residence: 1308 N. Charles St. Office: 1636 E. Baltimore St., Baltimore.

CATLIN, CHARLES ALBERT, chemist; b. Burlington, Vt., May 10, 1849; s. Henry Wadhams and Mary Cobb (Mayo) C.; bro. of Henry Guy and Robert Mayo C.; B.S., U. of Vt., 1872, Ph.B., 1873 (Sc.D., 1913); special course Mass. Inst. Tech., 1894, 95; m. Frances L. Herrick, June 20, 1877. Chemist, Rumford Chem. Works, Providence, 1873-75 and 1878—. Inventor and patentee of chem. processes and applications, many of which relate to mfr. of phosphates for dietetic purposes. Trustee U. of Vt. and R.I. Hosp. Author: Baking Powders, 1899. Home: Providence, R.I. Died Apr. 2, 1916.

CATLIN, HENRY GUY, mining engr.; b. Burlington, Vt., July 21, 1843; s. Henry Wadhams and Mary Cobb (Mayo) Catlin; University of Vermont, left in senior year to enter army and served in 12th Vt. Vols.; spl. studies engring. m. Mary C. Clarke, of Browneville, Pa., July 17, 1866; 2d, Josephine Robbins, of New York, Jan. 7, 1895. Engaged in mining since 1870; Republican. Author: Yellow Pine Basin, 1897. Has written sketches and stories of Western life to Youth's Companion, Saturday Evening Post, Ainslie's Magazine, etc. Address: 27 William St., New York, N.Y.

CATLIN, ROBERT MAYO, mining engr.; b. Burlington, Vt., June 8, 1853; s. Henry Wadhams and Mary Cobb (Mayo) C.; B.S., U. of Vt., 1872, C.E., 1873, hon. E.M., 1902; Sc.D., Rutgers, 1918; m. Ann E. Robertson, June 15, 1882; children—Bessie Margery, Mary Helen, Robert Mayo. Engaged as mining engineer, 1875; co. surveyor, Elko Co., Nev., 1876; supt. Navajo Mining Co., Tuscarora, Nov. 1880; supt. Victorine Gold Mining Co., 1882; supt. Navajo, Belle Isle, N. Belle Isle, N. Commonwealth and Nevada Queen mines (Tuscarora); gen. mgr. (under John Hays Hammond), of 8 deep level mines, Johannesburg, Transvaal, 1895-1906; gen. supt. N.J. Zinc Co., 1906-30; v.p. Sussex County Trust Co., Franklin, N.J. Acting cons. engr. of the Consolidated Gold Fields of South Africa, Ltd. Home: Oakland, Calif. Died Nov. 22, 1934.

CATTELL, WILLIAM ASHBURNER, civil engr.; b. Princeton, N.J., June 16, 1863; s. Rev. Thomas W. (Ph.D.) and Anna C. (Ashburner) C.; C.E., Lafayette Coll., 1884; m. Jennie W. Woodhull, Sept. 17, 1889. Asst. engr., State Bd. of R.R. Assessors, N.J., and later on preliminary location surveys for A.T.&S.F. R.R. in Kans. and Ind. Ty., 1884-89; asst. chief engr., constrn. L.I. R.R., 1889-97; consulting practice, New York, 1897-1905; cons. engr. for E. H. Rollins & Sons, San Francisco on various projects, 1905-08, including Western Pacific R.R.; report for Hirsch Syndicate, Ltd., London, on Valdez-Yukon R.R. project in Alaska; chief engr. Clear Lake Power and Irrigation project, also the Trona Ry.; cons. engr. San Francisco-] Oakland Terminal Rys., Peoples Water Co., Los Angeles Ry. Corp. Gen. consulting practice, San Francisco, 1908-17; mem. Cattell, Howard & Ashton, 1917. Commd. maj., Engr. R.C., Mar. 1, 1917; ordered to active duty, Dec. 28, 1917; at Camp Lee, Va., Jan. 5-Feb. 22, 1918; staff duty Office Chief of Engrs., Washington, in charge of hist. unit, Feb. 23, 1918-Sept. 30, 1919. Mason. Home: Washington, D.C. Died Oct. 10, 1920.

CAULLERY, MAURICE JULES GASTON CORNEILLE, biologist; b. Bergues, Nord, France, Sept. 5, 1868; s. Jules and Uranie (Godbille) C.; ed. Lycée de Douai, Ecole Normale Superieure; m. Sabine Hubert, Nov. 3, 1900; children—Solange (Mrs. L. Godard), Michel. Denise (Mrs. D.Van Den Berghe), Francine (Mrs. V. Elisséef). Lectr., Faculté des Sciences, Université de Lyon, 1896-1900; prof. Falculté des Sciences de Marseille 1900-03; prof. Faculté des Sciences de Paris. 1909-40; chair of evolution of present organisms. Decorated Commandeur De La Legion d'Honneur. Mem. Academie des Sciences; fgn. mem. Royal Soc. London, Royal Soc. Edinburgh Royal Acad. Belgium, Am. Acad. Scis. (Boston), N.Y. Acad. of Scis., Philos. Soc. Phila., Linnaeus Soc. London, and other sci. orgns. Author numerous publs. in field. Home: 6 rue Mizon, Paris XV. Office: Laboritorie d'Evolution des Etres Organisés, 106 Blvd. Raspail, Paris VI. France. Died July, 13, 1958.

CAUSEY, WILLIAM BOWDOIN, civil engr.; b. Suffolk, Va., June 24, 1865; s. Charles Henry and Martha Josephine (Prentis) C.; ed. pvt. schs.; unmarried. Began as chairman Atlantic & Danville R.R., Va., 1883; with engring. depts. various rys., including U.P. Ry., N.Y., N.H.&H. R.R., C.&N.W.,C&A. R.R., C.G.W. R.R., also was chief engr. E.J.&E. Ry., supt. Ill. lines C.&A. R.R., supt. C.G.W. Ry.; v.p. and gen. mgr. Norwood-White Coal Co., Des Moines, Ia., 1914-17; city mgr. Norfolk, Va., 1923-25; then v.p. White Construction Co. and M. E. White Co., gen. contractors, Chicago. Commd. capt. engrs., June 13, 1917, and assigned to 17th Engrs., U.S.A.; landed in France Aug. 1917; maj., Mar. 1918; lt. col., Sept. 1918; mem. Am. sect. Inter-Allied Mission sent to Vienna from Paris by Supreme War Council to investigate financial, economic and fuel transportation conditions in former Austro-Hungarian Empire, Dec. 1918-July 1919; was coal and transp. expert of the Mission, pres. Allied Ry. Mission, Austro-Hungary, Jan.-Oct. 1919; tech. adviser to Austrian Govt., Sept. 1919-July 1923; then lt. col. O.R.C., U.S.A. Asst. U.S. commr. to Century of Progress Expn., Chicago, July 1932-Apr. 15, 1935. Decorated Officer Legion of Honor (France); Order of Saint Sava 2d class (Kingdom of the Serbs, Croats and Slovenes-Jugo-Slavia); The Great Silver Cross of Honor (Republic of Austria); citation from Gen. Pershing "for distinguished services" in Frances. Republican. Episcopalian. Mason. Home: Chicago, Ill. Died Aug. 10, 1936.

CAVANA, MARTIN, physician, surgeon; b. Marcy, Oneida Co., N.Y., Feb. 24, 1849; s. M.P. and Mary (Hughes) C.; ed. dist. schs., Whitestown (N.Y.) Acad., Univ. of Mich., Bellevue Hosp. Med. Coll., M.D., 1872, Post-grad. Med. Sch., New York; m. Holland Patent, N.Y., June 5, 1872, Sarah J. Robinson. Engaged in practice of medicine since 1872; now mgr. Oneida Pvt. Hosp., Sanitarium and Training Sch. for Nurses, Sylvan Beach, N.Y. Inventor Cavana operating vaginal speculum, Mem. Am. Med. Assn., N.Y., State Med. Sco.; permanent mem. Am. Assn. Ry. Surgeons; ex-pres. N.Y. and New Eng. Assn. of Ry. Surgeons, Medico-Legal Soc. of N.Y. Pres. corporation council of Sylvan Beach, N.Y.; 1st lt. 35th Separate Co. of Inf., N.G.S.N.Y.; capt. Oneida Battery, Light Arty.; pres. Civ. Service Commn., City of Oneida. Baptist. Republican; mem. and ex-chmn. Madison Co. Rep.

Com. Residence: Oneida, N.Y. Office: Sylvan Beach, N.Y.

CEDERBERG, WILLIAM EMANUEL, prof. mathematics; b. Upsala, Seden, Jan. 26, 1876; s. Rudolph and Charlotte (Fleur) C.; brought to U.S., 1895; B.A., Augustana Coll., Rock Island, Ill., 1900; Ph.B., Yale, 1902; student Brown U., Providence, R.I., 1902-03; student Goettingen, Germany, 1905-07; Ph.D., U. of Wis., 1922; m. Martha M. Sievers, June 9, 1923; children—Rita Charlotte, Enid Augusta. Instr. Brown U., Providence, R.I., 1902-03; prof. mathematics, Augustana Coll. since 1908. Mem. Am. Math. Soc., Math. Assn. Am., A.A.A.S. (fellow), Sigma Xi. Lutheran. Author: On the Solution of Differential Equations of a Double Pendulum, 1923. Home: 2542 22 1/2 Av. Office: Augustana Coll., Rock Island IL

CELL, JOHN W(ESLEY), coll. prof.; b. Kansas City, Mo., Mar. 29, 1907; s. John Franklin and Mary Florence (Musson) C.; A.B., U. of Ill., 1928, A.M., 1929, Ph.D., 1935; m. Mary Louise Keith, Apr. 3, 1931; children—John Whitson, Howard Robert, Mary Linn. Part time instr. in mathematics U. of Ill., 1928-29, 1933-35; asst. prof. mathematics School of Engring., Southern Methodist U., 1929-32; instr. mathematics N.C. State Univ., 1935-36, asst. prof., 1936-38; asso. prof., 1938-46, prof., 1946-67, chmn. dept. mathematics, 1957-67, dir. research project, 1952-59, director of applied math. research group, 1959-67; prof. mathematics, rocket research, Aberdeen Proving Grounds, 1944-45. Fellow A.A.A.S.; mem. Society of Indsl. and Applied Mathematics, Am. Math. Soc., Math. Assn. Am., Am. Soc. Engring. Edn., Am. Inst. Aeros. & Astronautics, Am. Ordn. Assn., Engineering Science Society, Phi Kappa Phi, Sigma Xi, Pi Mu Epsilon. Democrat. Baptist. Author: Engineering Problems Illustrating Mathematics, 1943; Analytic Geometry, 1951. Researcher in applications of mathematics in engring., in ballistics, operational mathematics, and in visual aids in teaching mathematics. Home: Raleigh NC Died Nov. 9, 1967.

CHADBOURN, WILLIAM HOBBS, JR., civil engr.; b. Nashville, Tenn., Oct. 17, 1865; s. William H. and Adelaide S. (Peters) C.; B.S., Mass. Inst. Tech., 1886; m. Jane E. Cheney, of Boston, June 19, 1888. Chief engr. branch Atlantic Coast Line R.R., 1886-88, Wilmington Seacoast R.R., 1888-89; served in engr. corps, U.S.A. (lt. 3d Regt. engrs., 1898), 1890-1906; chief engr. C.G.W. Ry., since 1906. Mem. Am. Soc. C.E. Address: Grand Central Sta., Chicago.

CHADBOURNE, PAUL ANSEL, coll. pres.; b. North Berwick, Me., Oct. 21, 1823: S. Isaiah and Pandora (Dennett) C.; grad. Williams Coll., 1848, LL.D., 1868; D.D., Amherst Coll., 1872. m. Elizabeth Page, Oct. 9, 1850. First prof. botan and chemistry Williams Coll., 1853; dean Me. Med. Sch., 1852-58; mem. Mass. Senate, 1865; 1st pres. Mass. Agrl. Coll. Amherst, 1866-67, 1882-83; pres. U., Wis., 1867-70, Williams Coll., 1872-81; mem. Mass. bd. Agr., 1874-83. Mem. Royal Soc. Northern Antiquaries of Copenhagen. Author: Lectures on Natural History, Its Relations to Intellect, Taste, Wealth and Religion (presented at Smithsonian Instrn. 1859), 1860; Lectures on Natural Theology (Lowell Inst. lectures), 1867; Instinct in Animals and Men, 1872; Hope of the Righteous, 1877. Conducted exploring and scientific expdns. to Newfoundland, 1855, Fla., 1857, Greenland, 1861. Died N.Y.C., Feb. 23, 1883.

CHADWICK, CHARLES WESLEY, engraver; b. Red-Hook- on-the-Hudson, N.Y., Feb. 8, 1861; s. Rev. T. W. and Mary F. C.; A.B., Wesleyan U., Conn., 1884, A.M.; studied wood engraving under Frederick Juengling, William Miller and Frank French; m. Agnes F. Hardy, Oct. 30, 1902; children—John Vincent, Sumner Stone (dec.), Donald Hardy, Charles W. Work has appeared mostly in Century Magazine and Scribner's Magazine; later engaged in finishing and engraving halftone plates. Exhibited at Paris Expn., 1900; bronze medal, Buffalo Expn., 1901, St. Louis Expn., 1904; silver medal, Panama Expn., San Francisco, 1915. Home: Milford, Conn. Died Aug. 25, 1940.

CHADWICK, GEORGE HALCOTT, geologist;b. Catskill, N.Y., May 27, 1876; s. Nathaniel Kimball and Celia Serena (Halcott) C.; Ph.B., U. Rochester, 1904, M.S., 1907; hon. Sc.D. St. Lawrence U., 1940; m. Bertha Elisabeth Ellwanger, Feb. 22, 1908 (died Mar. 22, 1937); children—Elizabeth Ellwanger, George Halcott; m. 2d Irene Brugger, Sept. 30, 1944. With Ward's Natural Sci. Establishment, 1896-1906, N.Y. State Museum, 1906-07, St. LawrenceU., 1907-14, U. Rochester, 1914-23, Empire Gas and Fuel Co., Okla., 1923-25, Williams Coll., 1925-26, Vassar, 1929, U. Newark, 1943-44, The Natural Sci. Assn. of the Catskills, Inc., 1944—; surveys: N.Y. State Pa. Topographic and Geologic, 1926-31, Cities Service Group, 1930-31, Nat. Park Service, 1935-37. Fellow Geol. Soc. Am.; mem. Alpha Delta Phi, Phi Beta Kappa, Sigma Xi. Republican. Episcopalian. Contbr. on Devonian Stratigraphy, geology of Mount Desert Island Me. Address: The Natural Science Assn. of the Catskills, Inc., Box 165 Catskill, N.Y. Died Aug. 1953.

CHADWICK, HENRY DEXTER, physician; b. Boscawen, N.H., Jan. 2, 1872; s. Jeremiah Clough and Eliza (Austin) C.; M.D., Harvard, 1895; m. Edith Nichols Clark, May 24, 1898; children—Maurice Place (U.S. Army), Barbara. House officer, surg. service, Boston City Hosp., 1895-96; began practice at Waltham, Mass., 1896; mem. staff Waltham Hosp.; bacteriologist, Waltham Bd. of Health, 1898-1905; supt. Vt. Sanatorium for Tuberculosis, Pittsford, 1907-09; supt. Westfield (Mass.) State Sanatorium, for tuberculous children, 1909-29; tuberculosis controller, Detroit Health Dept., 1929-33; Mass. Commn. Pub. Health, 1933-38; med. dir. Middlesex County Sanatorium, 1938-41; med. dir. Cambridge (Mass.) Sanatorium, 1942-47; retired. Acting asst. surg., U.S. Mil. Hosp., Ponce, Porto Rico, 1898; capt. Mass. Vol. Militia, 1899; mem. bd. tuberculosis examiners, Camp Bartlett, Westfield, 1917, U.S. Vol. Med. Service Corps, 1918. Acting dir. Div. of Tuberculosis, Mass. State Dept. Pub. Health, 1927; lecutrer post grad. medicine, U. of Mich., 1931-33; lecturer in medicine Harvard, lecturer Harvard Sch. Pub. Health; retired, 1946. Mem. White House Conf. Child Health and Protection. Member National Tuberculosis Assn. (pres. 1939), American Sanatorium Association (president eastern sect. 1928; v.p. 1929; pres. 1930), Mich. Tuberculosis Assn. (pres. 1932, 33), Am. Climatol. and Clin. Assn., Mass. Med. Soc., Mass. Tuberculosis League (pres. 1942-45), Hampden County Tuberculosis and Public Health Association (pres. 1928), American Public Health Association, Massachusetts Public Health Assn. (president 1940, 41), Boston Trudeau Soc., S.A.R., Westfield C. of C. (1st pres. 1920). Conglist. A Pioneer in tuberculosis investigation among children; orginator of "Ten Yr. Program" (now known as the Chadwick Clinics) in Mass., providing for examination of sch. children. Author: The Modern Attack on Tuberculosis (with Dr. A. S. Pope), 1942. Contbr. of articles on tuberculosis and pub. health to med. periodicals. Home: Worcester Lane, Waltham MA

CHAFFEE, ROGER B., astronaut; b. Grand Rapids, Mich., Feb. 15, 1935; s. Donald L. Chaffee; B.S. in Aero. Engring., Purdue U., 1957; postgrad. Air Force Inst. Tech., Wright-Patterson AFB, O.; m. Martha Louise Horn; children—Sherly Lyn, Stephen Bruce. Joined USN, 1957, advanced through grades to lt. comdr.; former safety officer, quality control officer Navy Photog. Squadron 62, Jacksonville (Fla.) Naval Air Sta.; now astronaut with Manned Spacecraft Center, NASA. Mem. Tau Beta Pi, Sigma Gamma Tau, Phi Kappa Sigma. Office: care Manned Spacecraft Center, NASA, Houston 1. Died Jan. 27, 1967.

CHAFFEY, GEORGE, engineer; b. Kingston, Ont., Can., Jan. 28, 1848; s. George and Ann (Leggo) C.; ed. pub. schs., Brockville and Kingston, Ont.; m. Annette Augusta McCord, of Toronto, Ont., 1870 (dec.); children—Andrew McCord, Benjamin, Col. John Burton. Apprenticed in mech. engring. and ship-building, Brockville, 1866-69; designer, also builder and comdr. fast lake steamers, 1869-80; moved to Calif., 1881, and founder (with bro. William B.) Etiwanda and Ontario colonies; initiated device of mutual water co., with 1 share of stock for each acre of land; built first hydroelectric power plant in western America, and wired first house electrically lighted west of Miss. River; builder and owner of system which made Los Angeles first municipality in U.S. to be electrically lighted; established colonies at Mildura, Victoria, and Renmark, South Australia, canal system of Imperial Valley, Calif., 1900-02; founder since 1902 of various banks, water companies and irrigation projects; dir. Calif. Bank, Founder Chaffey Union High Sch., Ontario, Calif.; trustee Chaffey Coll. Trust. Mem. Instn. of Mech. Engrs. (London). Republican. Episcopalian. Club: San Diego Yacht. Home: 1004 Rosecrans Av., Point Loma, Calif.

CHAMBERLAIN, CHARLES JOSEPH, botanist; b. Sullivan, O., Feb. 23, 1863; s. Esdell W. and Mary (Spencer) C.; A.B., Oberlin Coll., 1888, A.M., 1894, D.Sc., 1923; Ph.D., U. of Chicago, 1897; research at Bonn, 1900-01; m. Mary E. Life, July 30, 1888 (died Feb. 27, 1931); 1 dau., Mas. Mabel Allsopp; m. 2d, Martha Stanley Lathrop, Oct. 30, 1938. Prin. Crookston (Minn.) High School, 1889-93; student U. of Chicago, 1893-96; asst. and asso. in botany, 1897-1901, instr. 1901-07, asst. prof. morphology and cytology 1908-11, asso. prof., 1911-15, prof., 1915-29, now emeritus, U. of Chicago. Am. editor cytology in Botanisches Centrallblatt since 1902. Mem. Bot. Soc. Am. (pres. 1931-32), Assn. Internationale des Botanistes, Kaiserlich Deutsche Akademic der Natufforscher, Deutsche Botanische Gesellschaft; fellow A.A.A.S., Naturforscher Gesellschaft an der K. Universitat zu Kiew (hon.), Correspondant Societe de Geneve; Botanical Soc. of India (corr. mem.). Author: Methods in Plant Histology, 1901, 5 edits. to 1932; The Morphology of Gymnosperms (with Prof. John M. Coulter), 1901, 17; The Morphology of Angiosperms (with same), 1903; The Living Cycads, 1919; Elements of Plant Science, 1930; Gymnosperms, Structure and Evolution, 1935. Contbr. to Bot. Gazette since 1895. Has collected Cycadaceae in Mexico, Cuba, Australia and Africa, and has pub. numerous researches upon this family. Clubs: Quadrangle, Chaos. Home: 6127 Greenwood Av., Chicago. Died Jan. 5, 1943.

CHAMBERLAIN, MONTAGUE, ornithologist; b. St. John, N.B., Apr. 5, 1844; s. Samuel M. and Catherine W. (Stevens) C.; ed. pvt. schs., St. John, until 1958; m. Anna Sartoris Prout, June 15, 1907. Bookkeeper 18 yrs., and partner, 1885-87, firm of J. & W. F. Harrison, wholesale grocers, St. John; recorder Harvard U., 1889-93, sec., 1893-1900, Lawrence Scientific Sch. For 10 yrs. was active mem. of Canadian army; retired with rank of capt. Editor: Popular Handbook of the Birds of the United States and Canada, by Thomas Nuttall, 1903. Home: Groton, Mass. Died 1924.

CHAMBERLAIN, OSCAR PEARL, civil engr.; b. Pittstown, N.Y., Nov. 26, 1870; s. Alonzo Bradner and Laura Arceville (Munson) C.; A.B., Central High Sch., Phila., 1885; A.B., U. of Pa., 1889; unmarried. Rodman and asst. engr., Pa. R.R., 1889-1902; asst. engr., C.G.W. Ry., 1902-04; div. engr., N.P. Ry., 1904-05; chief engr. C.&I.W. R.R., 1905; chief operating engr. Dolese & Shepard Co., 1910—; gen. mgr. Union Paving Co.; v.p. and gen. mgr. Dolese & Shepard Co., 1913. Republican. Home: LaGrange, Ill. Died Dec. 10, 1932.

CHAMBERLAIN, PAUL MELLEN, cons. mech. engr.; b. Three Oaks, Mich., Feb. 28, 1865; s. Henry and Rebecca (Van Devanter) C.; B.S., Mich. Agrl. Coll., 1888; M.E., Cornell, 1890; m. Olivia Langdon Woodward, Apr. 23, 1891 (died 1920); children—Rebecca Van Devanter (Mrs. Elmer J. Baker, Jr.), Wheelock Paul, Olivia Langdon (Mrs. Clinton G. Johnson), Julia Ada (Mrs. Frank Alexander Farnham III); m. 2d, Margaret Phelps Graham, Feb. 21, 1935. Assistant engr. Frick Co., 1890-92; mech. engr. Hercules Iron Works, Aurora, Ill., 1892-93; asst. prof. mech. engring., Mich. Agrl. Coll., 1893-96; asst. prof. drawing and design, 1896-99, prof. mech. engring., 1899-1906, Lewis Inst., Chicago; cons. practice, Los Angeles, 1906-07; chief engr. The Underfeed Stoker Co. of America, Chicago, 1907-10; cons. practice, 1910-17; inventor various machines. Commd. maj., Ordnance R.C., Oct. 3, 1917; called into active service, Nov. 1, 1917; insp. ordnance, Toledo, O., Dec. 1917-Feb. 1919, Cleveland Dist. Claims Bd., Feb.-July 1919; apptd. chmn. Chicago Dist. Salvage Bd., Oct. 1919; comdg. officer Chicago and St. Louis Ordnance dists., Apr.-Dec. 1920; disch. Dec. 28, 1920. Home: Keene, N.Y. Died May 27, 1940.

CHAMBERLAIN, ROBERT F., educator, engr.; b. Newark Valley, N.Y., May 19, 1884, S. Theodore F. and M. Eloise (Slosson) C.; student Phillips-Exeter Acad., 1902-04, M.E., Cornell, 1908; m. Mabelle Sandwick, Aug. 19, 1914; children—J. Theodore, Robert Sandwick, Phyllis Jane (Mrs. P. A. Kilbourne). Student tng. course Westinghouse Elec. & Mfg. Co.; instr. Purdue U., 1908-10; mem. faculty Cornell, 1910—, prof. elec. engring., 1921-52, asst. dean, personnel officer, 1946-52, prof. emeritus elec. engring., 1952—; switchboard engr. Gen. Elec. Co., 1920; cons. engr., 1930—; chmn. elec. examining bd. City of Ithaca, 1935-50. Mem. Am. Soc. Engring. Edn., Am. Inst. E. E. (mem. com. on indsl. power 1924-40, chmn. summer conv. com., 1935), Eta Kappa Nu, Tau Beta Pi. Republican. Clubs: Masonic, Statler, Ithaca Country (Ithaca); Tompkins County Fish and Game. Revised Gray's Principles and Practice of Electrical Engineering, 1924. Home: 125 Merlin Av., North Tarrytown, N.Y. Died July 15, 1967; buried Hope Cemetery Newark Valley.

CHAMBERLIN, ROLLIN THOMAS, geologist; b. Beloit, Wis., Oct. 20, 1881; s. Thomas Chrowder and Alma Isabel (Wilson) C.; student univs. of Geneva and Zurich, Switzerland, 1899-1900; S.B., Univ. of Chicago, 1903, Ph.D. from same, 1907; Sc.D., Beloit Coll., 1929; m. Dorothy Ingalis Smith, Nov. 11, 1922; children—Frances Dresser, Isabel Chrowder, Louise Ingalls. Mem. U.S. Geol. Survey, 1907-08; with U. of Chicago Oriental Ednl. Investigation Commn. to China, 1909; research asso., U. of Chicago, 1909-11; investigation of Brazilian iron ore resources, 1911-12; inst. in geology, 1912-14, asst. prof., 1914-18, asso. professor, 1918-23, prof. since 1923, U. of Chicago, Carnegie Institution Expedition to Samoa, 1920. Mng. editor Jour. of Geology, 1922-28, editor since 1928. Fellow Geol. Soc. America; (v.p. 1922), A.A.A.S. (v.p. 1933), British A.A.S., Am. Geophys. Union, Seismological Soc. of America; mem. Nat. Acad. Sciences, Am. Philosophical Soc., Phi Gamma Delta, Phi Beta Kappa, Sigma Xi, Gamma Alpha; v-chmn. div. geology and geography, Nat. Research Council, 1922-23. Republican. Episcopalian. Clubs: University, Quadrangle, South Shore Country, Am. Alpine. Contbr. numerous scientific articles. Home: 9300 Pleasant Av., Chicago. Died Mar. 6, 1948.

CHAMBERLIN, THOMAS CHROWDER, geologist; b. Mattoon, Ill., Sept. 25, 1843; A.B., Beloit Coll., 1866, A.M., 1869; grad. science, U. of Mich., 1868-69 (Ph.D., univs. of Mich. and Wis., 1882; LL.D., U. of Mich., Beloit Coll., Columbian U., 1887, U. of Wis., 1904, Toronto U., 1913; Sc.D., U. of Ill., 1905, U. of Wis., 1920); m. Alma Isabel Wilson, 1867. Prof. natural science, State Normal Sch., Whitewater, Wis., 1869-72; prof. geology, Beloit, 1873-82, Columbian, 1885-87; pres. U. of Wis., 1887-92; prof. and head dept. of geology and dir. Walker Mus., U. of Chicago, 1892-1919 (prof. emeritus). Asst. state geologist, Wis., 1873-76, chief geologist, 1876-82; studied glaciers of

Switzerland, 1878; U.S. geologist in charge of glacial div., 1882-1907; geologist Peary Relief Expdn., 1894; cons. geologist, Wis. Geol. Survey; commr. Ill. Geol. Survey; cons. geolgists U.S. Geol. Survey; investigator fundamental problems of geology, Carnegie Instrn., 1902-09; research asso., same instrn., 1909—; mem. commn. for Oriental Edn. Investigation, 1909. Fellow Am. Acad. Arts and Sciences. Author: Geology of Wisconsin; General Treatise on Geology (with R. D. Salisbury), 1906; The Origin of the Earth, 1916. Home: Chicago, Ill. Died Nov. 15, 1928.

CHAMBERS, CHARLES AUGUSTUS, horticulturist; b. Portland, Me., Feb. 22, 1873; s. Joseph Augustus and Maria (Charles) C.; ed. pub. schs., Ark. and La.; m. Alice Roland, of Oakland, Cal., Oct. 6, 1913. Trained in horticulture under George C. Roeding, of Cal.; connected with nursery business in Fresno, 1891—; with Fancher Creek Nurseries 10 yrs.; sec.-treas. Fresno Nursery Co., 12 yrs.; later mgr. nursery dept. of Luther Burbank Co., of San Francisco; now industrial agt. Memphis, Dallas & Gulf Ry. Co. Regarded as an authority on hort. and agrl. topics on Pacific Coast. Democrat. Unitarian. Mem.'Pacific Coast Assn. of Nurserymen, Nat. Geog. Soc. Contbr. hort. articles and widely known as writer of humorous stories and feature writer for agrl. press. Address: 1630 3d St., San Diego CA

CHAMBERS, FRANK WHITE, exec. engr.; b. Beaver, Pa., Sept. 14, 1908; s. Frank and Lena (Gourley) C.; student U. Pitts., 1929; m. Helen Stoddard, July 12, 1934. With Koppers Co., 1936—, project mgr. Butadiene-Styrene plant, 1942-43, mgr. control dept., engring. and constrn. Div., Pitts. 1949-51; dir. engring. Kennecott Copper Corp., N.Y.C., 1951-59; pres., dir. Strategic Materials Corp. 1959—; dir. Nochols Wire & Aluminum Co., Internat. African-Am. Corp. Cons., W.P.B., 1941-42. Served lt., U.S.N.R., 1943-46. Mem. Nat. Soc. Prof. Engrs., Am. Inst. Mech. Engrs., A.I.M., Am. Mgmt. Assn. Mason (Shriner), Elk. Presbyn. Clubs: Union League (N.Y.C.); Weeburn Golf (Darien). Home: 74 Pembroke Rd., Darien, Conn. Office: 235 E. 42d St., N.Y.C. 10017. Died Apr. 8, 1962.

CHAMBERS, ROBERT, biologist; b. Erzerum, Turkey, Oct. 23, 1881; s. Rev. Robert and Elizabeth (Lawson) C. (both Canadians) B.A., Robert College, Constantinople, Turkey, 1900; M.A., Queens University, Kingston, Canada, 1902, hon. LL.D., 1944; Ph.D., University of Munich, Germany, 1908; research student, Columbia, 1911-12; m. Bertha Inez Smith June 15, 1910; children—Robert, killed in action, Pacific, December, 1941, William Nesbit, Edward Lucas, Bradford; married 2d Elosie Parkhurst, December 3, 1954. With A.B.C.F.M. in Turkey until 1909; lecturer in Biology, Toronto University, 1909-11; assistant professor histology, Univ. of Cincinnati, 1912-15; instructor anatomy, Cornell Univ. Med. Coll., N.Y. City, 1915-19, asst. prof., 1919-23, prof. microscopic anatomy, 1923-28; research prof. biology, Washington Sq. Coll. (N.Y. U.), 1928-48, prof. emeritus continuing research through Nat. Inst. Health grant. Trustee Marine Biol. Corp., Woods Hole, Biological Lab., Cold Spring Harbor. Naturalized citizen of US. Fellow A.A.A.S.: mem. Marine Biol. Lab., Am. Soc. Zoölogists (pres. 1948-49), Am. Soc. Naturalists, Am. Assn. Anatomists (v.p. 1939), Am. Assn. Cancer Research, Soc. (pres. 1944-45, 1945-46), Union Am. Biol. Soc. (pres. since 1946), British Biol. Corp., Am. Physiol. Soc., Am. Soc., Am. Soc. Bot., Soc. Gen. Physiology; asso. fellow N.Y. Acad. Med. N.Y. Acad. Scis., fgn. corr. mem. Nat. Acad. Med., France Investigations, Summers, Marine Biol. Lab., Woods Hole; has made investigations in cytology and on phys. nature of protoplasm and the constituents of the living cells by means of an instrument divised for dissecting and injecting living cells under highest magnification of compound microscope, cellular cancer in tissue culture, and of blood capillary circulation in traumatic shock. Awarded Traill medal Linnean Society. Londoninvention of devices for microdissection of living cells, 1925. Contributor to Encyclopedia Britannica also numerous research articles to American and European journals. Co-editor of "Protoplasma" (journal). Home: Woods Hole, Mass. Office: New York University, N.Y. City 3. Died July 22, 1957.

CHAMBERS, ROBERT FOSTER, prof. chemistry; b. Providence, R.I., Oct. 8, 1887; s. William Spicer and Annie Andrews (Foster) Chambers; Ph.D., Brown Univ., 1909, M.S., 1910, Ph.D., 1912; m. Helen Newman Peirson, 1915 (deceased); 1 daughter, Frances C. Wesson; m. 2d, Nettie Mildred Sumner of Attleboro, Mass., 1930. Instr. in chemistry, Brown Univ., 1915, asst. prof., 1916-22, asso. prof., 1922-32, prof. since 1932. Mem. Am. Chem. Soc., Providence Engring. Soc., Rhode Island Hist. Soc., Delta Phi, Phi Beta Kappa, Sigma Xi. Mason. Clubs: University Art (Providence). Home: 254 Irving Av., Providence 6, R.I. Died Nov. 17, 1947.

CHAMBLISS, CHARLES EDWARD, agronomist; b. Petersburg, Va., Aug. 20, 1871; s. David Lewis and Lucy Jane (Mann) C.; B.S., U. of Tenn., 1892, M.S., 1894; m. Lucy Page Smith, June 11, 1896; children—Charles Edward, Bathhurst Lee. Instructor zoology and entomology, U. of Tenn., and entomologist, Tenn. Agrl. Expt. Sta., 1894-1900; state entomologist, Tenn., 1900-01; asso. prof. zoology and entomology, Clemson Coll., and entomologist S.C. Agrl. Expt. Sta., 1901-07; state entomologist of S.C., 1907-08; agronomist in charge of rice investigations, U.S. Dept. of Agr., 1908-30, in Puerto Rico, 1917-19, in Dominican Republic, 1918-19, in Cuba for Tropical Plant Research Foundation, 1927, in charge rice technology and botany, 1930-41, collaborator since 1941. Fellow A.A.A.S.; mem. Am. Soc. Agronomy, Bot. Soc. Washington (sec. 1913-20; pres. 1920), Biol. Soc. Washington (pres. 1933-36), Washington Acad. Sciences (v.p. 1934-36; pres. 1939), Sigma Alpha Epsilon, Phi Kappa Phi. Club: Cosmos. Home: 1833 Kilbourne Pl., Washington DC

CHAMBLISS, HARDEE, educator; b. Selma, Ala., Dec. 4, 1872; s. Nathaniel Rives and Anna Dummett (Hardee) C.; grad. Va. Mil. Inst., 1894; M.S. Vanderbilt U., 1899; Ph.D., Johns Hopkins, 1900; m. Julita McLane Sturdy, 1903 (died 1916); children—Joseph Hardee, John Lockwood, Hardee C., Allan McLane Francis; m. 2d, Emma Marie Henne, June 27, 1918. Inst. Columbia U., 1900-01; research chemist Moore Electric Co., Newark, N.J., 1901-03; Gen. Chem. Co., New York, 1903-09; prof. in charge chemistry, Oklahoma Coll., Stillwater, 1909-15; asst. commr. of health, Okla., 1915-16; chem. dir. Commercial Acid Co., St. Louis, Mo., 1916-17. Commd. maj. O.R.C., Aug. 1917; called to active duty, Dec. 7, 1917, and assigned to Gun Div., Ordnance Dept.; trans. to Nitrate Div. of Ordnance, Feb. 3, 1918, and directed researches, N.Y.C., conducted by War Dept. in cooperation with Gen. Chem. Co.; later put in charge all research work of Ordnance Dept., Nitrate Div., in New York, and vicinity; detailed as comdg. officer U.S. Nitrate Plant No. 1, Sheffield, Ala., Feb. 1919; promoted lt. col., July 1919; hon. discharged, Nov. 29, 1920, and apptd. plant mgr., U.S. Nitrate Plant 1, resigned Sept. 1, 1921, prof. chemistry, Catholic U. of Am., 1921, dean Sch. of Science, 1925-30, dean Sch. of Engring., 1930-34; retired; now cons. chemist. Promoted col. O.R.C., 1929. Fellow A.A.A.S.; mem. Am. Chem. Soc., Sigma Alpha Epsilon. K.C. (4 deg.). Democrat. Home: 1715 Varnum St. N.W. Washington. Died June 1, 1947.

CHAMOT, EMILE MONNIN sanitary chemist, microscopist; b. Buffalo, Mar. 4, 1868; s. Christopher Peter and Eugenie (Monnin) Chamot; B.S. in Chemistry, Cornell U., 1891, Ph.D., 1897; studied U. Nancy (France), 1897, Tech. Hochschule, Branunschweig (Germany) and Polytechicum (Delft, Holland), 1898; m. Cora Ellen Genung, June 1897; Began as asst. in chemistry Cornell U., 1890, became prof. chem. microscopy and sanitary chemistry, 1910, now retired; Am. exchange prof. to France, 1924-25. Expert on questions dealing with purity and purification of water and industrial Microscopy. Mem. Am. Chem. Society, Am. Acad. Arts and Sciences, Sigma Xi, Alpha Chi Sigma. Author: Analysis of Water for Household and Municipal Purposes (wity H.W. Redfield), 1911; Elementary Chemical Microscopy, 1915; Handbook of Chemical Microscopy (with C.W. Mason), 1930; also many papers on sanitary chemistry, microscpy, etc. Home: 927 E. State St., Ithaca, N.Y. Deceased.

CHAMPION, CHARLES SUMNER, patent lawyer; b. Washington, D.C., Jan. 22, 1871; s. Charles and Catherine Elizabeth (Hyde) C.; ed. grammar and high schs., Washington, D.C.; studied law N.Y. Univ. Law Sch.; m. Charlotte Amelia Flentjé, June 26, 1895. Practiced in Washington, D.C., Phila., Hartford and N.Y. City, 1888-1901, for or against leading inventors of U.S. and Europe, including Thomas A. Edison, Francis H. Richards and Dr. Werner von Siemens; practiced in N.Y. City, 1901—; a pioneer in movement in N.Y. State, 1905, for direct primary nominations. Home: Montclair, N.J. Died July 31, 1916.

CHANCA, DIEGO ALVAREZ, physicians, 15th century. Court physician to Ferdinand and Isabella of Spain; acompanied 2d expdn. of Columbus to Am., 1493, saved life of Columbus and others suffering malaria; selected site for 1st permanent settlement of Isabella, Haita. Author of detailed and accurate account of New World as he saw it during 3-month stay; also wrote study of treatment of pleurisy, published 1506, after his return to Spain.

CHANCE, EDWIN MICKLEY, pres. United Engineers and Constructors, Inc.; b. Phila., Pa., Jan. 13, 1885; s. Henry Martyn and Lillie E. (Mickley) C.; grad. DeLancey Sch., 1903; B.S. in Chemistry, U. of Pa., 1907; m. Eleanor Kent, Jan. 11, 1909 (died Nov. 21, 1940); children—Henry Martyn II, Britton. Assaying and mining in Nev., 1907-09; chemist and engr. Phila. and Reading Coal and Iron Co., Pottsville, Pa., 1909-13; cons. practice Wilkes-Barre, 1913-17; engring. mgr. Day and Zimmerman Inc., Phila., 1919-25; v.p. Day and Zimmerman, Inc., 1925-28; pres. Day and Zimmerman Engring. and Constrn. Co., Inc., 1928; v.p. United Engrs. and Constructors, Inc., 1928-31, pres., 1931—; Pres. Dwight P. Robinson andCo., ,Inc., U.G.I. Contracting Co. Served as capt. to lt. col. Ordnance Dept., Chem. Warfare Service, U.S. Army, in Charge design, construction and operation of poison gas, shell filling plant, Edgewood Arsenal, 1917-18; with A.E.F., 1918. Trustee and mem. ex. bd. U. of Pa., chmn. bd. grad. edn. and research member bd. (U. Pa.). trustee Henry Phipps Inst. (U. of Pa.). Mem. Acad. Natural Science (Phila.), Franklin Inst. , Army Ordnance Assn. Awarded Edward Longstreth Medal of merit, Franklin Institute. Clubs: Midday, Racquet (Philadelphia); New York Yacht, Mantoloking Yacht, Crusing Club of America, Sportsmen's Club of America. Contbr. tech. publs.; chem. and metall. inventions. Home: Ocean Av., Mantoloking N.J. Office: 1401 Arch St., Phila. 5. Died Nov. 26 1954.

CHANCE, HENRY MARTYN, cons. engr.; b. Phila., Pa., Jan. 18, 1856; s. Jeremiah Chambers and Augusta (Mitchell) C.; C.E., U. of Pa., 1874; M.D., Jefferson Med. Coll., 1881; m. Lillie E. Mickley, Apr. 20, 1882; children—Edwin Mickley, Thomas Mitchell (died 1933). In gen. consulting practice, 1884—; developed, 1921—, sand flotation process for cleaning coal, an invention of Thomas M. Chance, largely used in cleaning Pa. anthracite coal, and also bituminous coal. Home: Philadelphia, Pa. Died Feb. 19, 1937.

CHANDLER, ASA CRAWFORD, biologist; b. Newark, Feb. 19, 1891; s. Frank Thomas and Augusta (Jappá) C.; A.B., Cornell 1911; M.S., U. Cal., 1912, Ph.D., 1914; m. Belle Clarke, June 1, 1914 (dec.); 1 dau., Dorothy Belle; m. 2d Ina Henrietta Sands, July 9, 1921 (dec.) children—Frank Sands, Emily Alice; m.3d, Mrs. Lillie More Laughlin, Dec. 23, 1944, Grad. asst. Zoöl. dept. U. Cal., 1911-14; instr. Zoölogy, later asst. prof., Oregon State Agrl. Coll., 1914-18; instr. biology Rice Inst., Houston, 1919-24; charge bookworm research lab. Sch. Tropical Medicine, Calcutta, India, 1924-27; prof. biology Rice Inst., 1927—, also spl. cons. USPHS, 1942-47. Served as 2d lt. San. Corps, U.S. Army, 1918-19. Fellow A.A.] A.S., Mem. Am. Soc., Parasitologist,Am. Soc. Tropical Medicine and Hygiene, Am. Micros. Soc., Am. Soc. Naturalist, Sigma Xi. Repubilcan Author: Animal Parasites and Human Disease, 1918; Anthelmintics and Their Uses (with R. N. Chopra)., 1928; Hookworm Disease, 1929; Introduction to Parasitology, 9th edit. 1955; The Eater's Digest. 1941. Made helminthological survey of India. 1924-27. Home: 6315 Vanderbilt Av., Houston 5. Office: Rice Inst., Houston 1, Died Aug. 23, 1958.

CHANDLER, CHARLES DEFOREST, aeronautics; b. Cleveland, O., Dec. 24, 1878; s. Francis Marion and Effie May (Barney) C.; student Case Sch. of Applied Science, 1899-1901; grad. Army Signal Sch., Fort Leavenworth, Kan., 1911; unmarried. Served as 1st lt. U.S. Vol. Signal Corps, June 1898-May 1899; apptd. 1st lt. U.S.A., Feb. 2, 1901, and advanced through grades to col., Aug. 5, 1917; trans. to Air Service, July 1, 1920; retired, Oct. 18, 1920; aeronautic editor Ronald Press Co., 1925—. Served in Spanish-Am. War, Philippine Insurrections, Punitive Expdn. in Mexico; chief of balloon sect., Air service, U.S.A., in Frances, World War. Comdr. U.S. Cableship Burnside, laying of 1st submarine cable to Alaska, 1903-04; 1st winner of Lahm trophy for balloon racing 1907; comdr. 1st Army aviation sch., College Park, Md., 1911-13. Awarded D.S.M. (U.S.); Officer Legion of Honor (France). Republican. Author: Free and Captive Balloons (with R. H. Upson), 1926; Balloon and Airship Gases (with W. S. Diehl), 1926. Home: Washington, D.C. Died May 18, 1939.

CHANDLER, CHARLES FREDERICK, chemist; b. Lancaster, Mass., Dec. 6, 1836; student Lawrence Scientific Sch. (Harvard), univs. of Berlin and Göttingen; A.M., Ph.D., Göttingen, 1856; (hon. M.D., New York U., 1873; LL.D., Union, 1873; Sc.D., Oxford, 1900; Ph.D., Göttingen, 1906; LL.D., Columbia Univ., 1911). Prof. chemistry, Union College, 1857-64; one of organizers, and prof. analytical and applied chemistry, Columbia Sch. of Mines, 1864-77; adj. prof. chemistry and med. jurisprudence Coll. Phys. and Surg., 1872-76; prof. chemistry, 1877—, dean Faculty of Mines, 1864-97, dean Faculty of Science, 1897, Columbia; then prof. organic chemistry, and pres. New York Coll. of Pharmacy. Chemist and later pres. Met. Bd. of Health, 1867-84. Asso. editor (with his brother, Prof. W. H. C.) American Chemist, 1870-77; chem. editor Johnson's Encyclopedia. Address: New York, N.Y. Died Aug. 25, 1925.

CHANDLER, SETH CARLO, astronomer; b. Boston, Sept. 17, 1846; s. Seth and May (Cheever) C.; ed. Boston English High Sch.; (LL.D., DePauw Univ., Ind., 1891); m. Carrie M. Herman, Oct. 20, 1870. Aid, U.S. Coast and Geod. Survey, 1864-70; life ins. actuary, 1870-85; editor Astronomical Journal, 1896—. Received the Watson gold medal and the gold medal of the Royal Astron. Soc. of Eng. Fellow Am. Acad. Arts and Sciences. Home: Wellesley Hills, Mass. Died Dec. 31, 1913.

CHANEY, LUCIAN WEST, statistician; b. Heuvelton, N.Y., June 26, 1857; s. Lucian West and Happy T. (Kinney) C.; A.B., Carleton Coll., 1878, B.S., 1879, M.S., 1882, D.Sc., 1916; Woods Hole, Mass., 1890-95; m. Mary E. Hill, June 20, 1882. High sch. prin. and supt. schs., Faribault and Glencoe, Minn., 1879-82; instr. biology, 1882-83, prof., 1883-1908, Carleton Coll.; spl. agt. U.S. Bur. of Labor on dangerous occupations of women and children, 1907-09; expert in accident prevention, U.S. Bur. Labor Statistics, 1901—. Explored in Rocky Mountains, Mont., 1895, 1903, 1905; visited several glaciers for first time; one bears name of Chaney

Glacier. Author numerous bulls. of the U.S. Bur. of Labor. Died May 6, 1935.

CHANEY, NEWCOMB KINNEY, research chemist, chem. engr.; b. Northfield, Minn., Apr. 27, 1883; s. Lucian West and Mary (Hill) C.; B.S., Carleton Coll., 1904 (honors in philosophy and biology), M.S. in chemistry and physics, 1905; Rhodes scholar, Ballion Coll., Oxford U., 1907-10, B.A. in chemistry, 1910; Harrison fellow in chemistry U. Pa., 1910-11, Ph.D., 1912; m. Elsie Elizabeth Webb, July 19, 1911; children—Elizabeth Webb (Mrs. Bassett Ferguson, Jr.), David Webb. Research chemist Nat. Carbon Co., 1914-20; in charge carbon and battery divs. Union Carbide & Carbon Research Labs. Inc., Long Island City, N.Y., June 1912-May 1925; asst. dir. Research Labs., Nat. Carbon Co., Inc. 1925-35; asst. dir. research United Gas Improvement Co., 1935-36, dir. reserach, 1936-54, research cons., 1955—; research cons. Am. Gas Assn., 1947—. Research fgn. and U.S. patentee in carbon products, synthetic resins, processes for ultra-violent irradiation of foods, petroleum cracking. Recipient Potts medal Franklin Inst., May 1939. Recipient Modern Pioneer N.A.M., 1940; Alumni Achievement award Carleton Coll., 1956; award of merit Am. Gas Assn., 1957. Fellow A.A.A.S., Am. Inst. Chemists, Chem. Soc. (London); mem. Am. Inst. Chem. Engrs. (dir. 1925-28), Am. Chem. Soc. (past chmn. Cleve. sect., chmn. Phila. sect. 1939-40), Am. Gas Assn., Inst. Petroleum Engrs. (London), Soc. Chem. Industry, Alembic Club (Oxford, Eng.), Phi Beta Kappa Assos. Conglist. Mason. Clubs: Chemists (v.p. N.Y.C.); Oxford Union (Eng.). Contbr. prof. articles. Home: Possum Hollow Rd., Rose Valley, Wallingford. Address: 1401 Arch St., Phila. Died July 1966.

CHANNING, J(OHN) PARKE, mining engr.; b. New York, Mar. 24, 1863; s. Roscoe H. and Susan (Thompson) Channing; E.M., Columbia, 1883, M.S., 1914; unmarried. Engr. and supt. iron and copper mines, Lake Superior Mining Dist., 1885-94; deputy commr. mineral statistics, Mich., 1884; insp. mines, Gogebic Co., Micn., 1897-1900; made several trips to Mexico and C.A. to examine and report on properties; asst. mgr. Calumet & Hecla Mining Co., 1893-94; with old Boston & Mont. Consolidated Mining Co. (now part of Anaconda Copper Co.), 1895-96; consulting engr., New York, . 1896; developed and equipped mines and reduction works of Tenn. Copper Co., also pres., 1903-08; made original report on Nev. Consolidated Mine; organized Gen. Development Co., 1905, which found and developed properties of Miami Copper Co., one of porphyry coppers; dir. Tenn. Corp., Kerr Lake Mines, Ltd., San Cayetano Mines, Ltd., Miami Copper Co.; retired 1926. Democrat. Unitarian. Mem. Mining and Metall. Soc. Am. (pres. 1910-12), Am. Inst. Mining and Metall. Engrs., Lake Superior Mining Inst., Am. Geog. Soc., Instn. of Mining and Metallurgy (England). Author numerous tech. articles for mining socs., engring. and scientific mags., etc.; delivered course of lectures on mine plants at Columbia and various addresses elsewhere. Address: 61 Broadway, New York, Died Oct. 11, 1942.

CHANNING, WALTER, physician, coll. dean; b. Newport, R.I., Apr. 15, 1786; s. William and Lucy (Ellery) C.; B.A., Harvard, 1808, M.D., 1812; M.D., U. Pa., 1809; m. Barbara Higginson Perkins, 1815; m. 2d, Elizabeth Wainwright, 1831. First prof. obstetrics and med. jurisprudence Harvard Med. Sch., 1815-circa 1844, dean, 1819-47; co-editor Boston Med. and Surg. Jour., 1828; librarian Mass. Med. Soc., 1822-25, treas., 1828-40; a founder Boston Lying-In Hosp., 1832; mem. Am. Acad. Arts and Scis.; 1st to use ether in childbirth cases. Died Boston, July 27, 1876.

CHANNING, WILLIAM FRANCIS; inventor; b. Boston, Feb. 22, 1820; s. William Ellery and Ruth (Gibbs) C.; M.D., U. Pa., 1844; m. Mary Jane Tarr. Asst., 1st geol. survey of N.H., 1841-42; asst. editor Latimer Jour., Boston, 1842; asst. on geol. survey of Lake Superior copper region, 1847; worked with Moses Farmer on devel. of fire-alarm telegraph, 1845-51, 1st used in Boston, 1851, patented and sold to Gamewell & Co., 1857; patented ship ry. for inter-oceanic transport of ships, 1865; invented portable electromagnetic telegraph, 1877. Died Mar. 19, 1901.

CHANUTE, OCTAVE, engineer; b. Paris, France, Feb. 18, 1832; s. Joseph and Eliza (De Bonnaire) C.; came to U.S., 1838; ed. pvt. schs., New York; (Dr. Engring., U. of Ill., 1905); m. Annie James, Mar. 12, 1857. Civ. engr. on various rys., 1849-63; chief engr. C.&A. R.R., 1863-67, Sundry Kan. R.R., 1867-73, Erie R.R., 1873-83; pres. Chicago Tie Preserving Co., 1893—. Author: The Kansas City Bridge (with George Morison), 1870; Progress in Flying Machine, 1894. Home: Chicago, Ill. Died 1910.

CHAPIN, CHARLES VALUE, health officer; b. Providence, R.I., Jan. 17, 1856; s. Joshua B. and Louise (Value) C.; A.B., Brown U., 1876; M.D., Bellevue Hosp. Med. Coll. (New York U.), 1879; Sc.D., Brown 1909. R.I. State Coll., 1932; LL.D., Yale 1927; m. Anna Augusta Balch, May 6, 1886; 1 son, Howard M. House physician Bellevue Hosp., 1879-80; supt. of health, Providence, 1884-1932, then 80; supt. of health, Providence, 1884-1932, then emeritus; prof. physiology, Brown U., 1886-96; city registrar of Providence, 1889-1932. Lecturer, Harvard Med. Sch., 1909, Harvard-Mass. Inst. of Tech. School for Health Officer, 1913-22, Harvard School of Hygiene, 1923-35; spl. agenct of A.M.A. for study of State sanitation, 1913. Providence City Hosp. named Charles V. Chapin Hosp., 1931. Author: Sources and Modes of Infection, 1910; State Public Health Work, 1916; How to Avoid Infection, 1917; Changes in Type of Contagious Disease, 1926. Mem. med. advisory bd. Am. Red Cross, World War. Fellow Am. Acad. Arts and Sciences, Royal Soc. Medicine (Eng.). Awarded Marcellus Hartley gold medal by Nat. Acad. of Sciences, 1928; Sedgwick memorial medal for distinguished service in pub. health, 1929; Susan Colver Rosenberg special honor medal, Brown U., 1935. Home: Providence, R.I. Died Jan. 31, 1941.

CHAPIN, HENRY DWIGHT, physician, author; b. Steubenville, O., Feb. 4, 1857; s. Henry Barton and Harriet Ann (Smith) Chapin; A.B., Princeton, 1877, A.M., 1885; M.D., Coll. Phys. and Surg. (Columbia), 1881; m. Alice Delafield, June 1, 1907. Prof. emeritus, diseases of children, N.Y. Post-Grad. Med. Sch. and Hosp. Former pres. Hosp. Social Service Assn. of New York; dir. Havens Relief Fund Soc., Life Saving Benevolent Assn., N.Y. Post-Grad. Med. Sch. and Hosp., Working Women's Protective Union, Children's Welfare Fedn. Mem. Am. Pediatric Soc. (pres. 1910-11), N.Y. Acad. Medicine, N.Y. County Med. Soc., Soc. of Mayflower Descendants Soc. Colonial Wars, S.R. Club: Century. Author: Theory and Practice of Infant Feeding, 1902 (3 edits.); Vital Questions, 1905; A General Treatise on Diseases of Children, 1909 (6 edits.); Health First—The Fine Art of Living, 1917; Heredity and Child Culture, 1922. Also sociol. and med. articles in various mags. Chmn. pub. health div. of N.Y. State Reconstruction Commn. Awarded Columbia U. medal for outstanding contributions to problems relating to the care of children and as a pioneer in hospital social service, 1933. Home: Lawrence Park W., Bronxville, N.Y. Died June 27, 1942.

CHAPIN, HENRY EDGERTON, biologist; b. Wilbraham, Mass., May 9, 1859; s. Samuel W. and Maria (Damon) C.; B.Sc., Mass. Agrl. Coll., Amherst, Mass., and Boston U., 1881; post-grad. student chemistry and biology, Johns Hopkins, 1886-87; M.Sc., Mich. Agrl. Coll., 1893; (Sc.D., McKendree Coll., 1908); m. Eudora M. Hoffman, June 29, 1893. Taught in secondary schs. and engaged in agrl. journalism, 1881-86; teacher Pa. State Normal Sch., 1888-90; prof. biology, Ohio U., 1891-1900; instr. in biology and physciography, high sch., New York, 1900—. Lecturer and mem. Council Brooklyn Inst. Arts and Sciences and pres. dept. of botany, 1904-14; editor "Tomahawk," mag. of Alpha Sigma Phi, 1916-21. Capt. Ohio N.G., 1892-93; capt. New York reserve list for commd. officers, 1917—. Joint author: Chapin's and Rettger's Elementary Zoölogy and Guide, 1896. Died Mar. 1922.

CHAPIN, JAMES PAUL, ornithologist; b. N.Y.C., July 9, 1889; s. Gilbert Granger and Nano (Eagle) C.; A.B., Columbia, 1916, A.M., 1917, Ph.D., 1932; m. Suzanne Drouel, Oct. 3, 1921 (div. 1939); children—Mary Louise, Suzanne Caroline (dec.), James Drouel, Pauline Thomas; m. 2d, Ruth Trimble, Sept. 5, 1940. With Am. Mus. Natural History, 1905, asst. on Congo Expdn., 1909-15, asst. dept. ornithology, 1914-19, asst. curator same dept., 1919, asso. curator, 1923-48, curator emeritus, research asso. African ornithology, 1949—; expdns. to Canadian Rockies, 1915, Panama, 1923, East Africa and Belgian Congo, 1926-27, Galapagos Islands, 1930, Belgian Congo, 1930-31, Polynesia, Juan Fernandez, Galpagos Islands, 1934-35, Belgian Congo, 1937, for IRSAC, Belgian found 1953-58, Ascension Island, 1942. Served as 1st lt. U.S.R.C.; 1917-19. Decorated Ordre de la Couronne, Officer Ordre de l'Etiole Africaine (Belguim); recipient Elliott medal Nat. Acad. Scis.; medal Explorers Club. Mem. S.I. Inst. Arts and Scis. (pres. 1934-50), S.I. Zool. Soc. (pres. 1937-46), Am. Ornithologists Union (pres. 1939-42), Brit. Ornithologists Union, Cercle Zoologique Congolais, Deutsche Ornithologische Gesellschraft, Societe Orinthologique de France (hon. mem.), Linnean Soc. N.Y. (pres. 1928-29), Newcomen Soc., S. African Ornigh. Soc., Delta Upsilon, Phi Beta Kappa, Sigma Xi. Club: Explorers (pres. 1949-50 N.Y.C.). Author: Birds of the Belgian Congo, 4 vols. 1932-54. Contbr. articles to jours. Home: 419 W. 119th St., N.Y.C. 10027. Office: American Museum Natural History, N.Y.C. 24. Died Apr. 5, 1964; buried Moravian Cemetery, S.I., N.Y.

CHAPIN, JOHN BASSETT, physician; b. New York, Dec. 4, 1829; s. William and Elizabeth H. (Bassett) C.; A.B., Williams Coll., 1850; M.D., Jefferson Med. Coll., Phila., 1853; (LL.D., Jefferson, and Williams); m. Harriet E. Preston, Mar. 18, 1858. Resident phys. N.Y. Hosp. State Lunatic Asylum, 1854, Brigham Hall, Canandaigua, 1860-69; med. supt. State Hosp., Willard, N.Y., 1869-84; phys.-in-chief, Pa. Hosp. for Insane, Phila., 1884-1911. In a public communication communication, 1862, recommended changes in asylum construction which would provide for segregation and conditions; views were adopted in Willard Hosp. Author: Compendium of Insanity for Physicians and Students, 1899. Retired, June 1911. Died Jan. 18, 1918.

CHAPLIN, WINFIELD SCOTT, engr.; b. Glenburn, Me., Aug. 22, 1847; s. Col. Daniel and Susan D. (Gibbs) C.; grad. U.S. Mil. Acad., 1870; (hon. A.M., Union Coll., 1885; LL.D., Harvard, 1893; Doc. of Tech., Imperial Univ. of Japan, 1915); m. Harriet B. Caldwell, 1873. Second lt. 5th U.S. Arty., 187072; civil engr., on ry., 1872-73; prof. mech. engring., Me. State Coll., 1873-76; prof. engring., Imperial U. of Japan, 1877-82; prof. mathematics and adj. prof. physics, Union Coll., 1883-86; prof. engring. and dean, Lawrence Scientific Sch. (Harvard), 1886-91; chancellor Washington U., 1891-1907. Decorated Order of the Rising Sun (Japan). Fellow Am. Acad. Arts and Sciences. Home: San Antonio, Tex. Died Mar. 12, 1918.

CHAPMAN, ALVAN WENTWORTH, botanist, physician b. Southampton, Mass., Dept. 28, 1809; s. Paul and Ruth (Pomeroy) C.; A.B., Amherst Coll., 1830; m. Mary Ann (Simmons) Hancock, Nov. 1839. Practiced medicine, Quincy, Marianna and Apalachicola, Fa.; became leading botanist in South; friend and correspondent of Asa Gray; genus Chapmania named in his honor; helped Union soldiers escape from prison nr. his home at Apalachicola during Civil War. Author: Flora of the Southern States (only manual for Southern botany until after turn of century), 1860. Died Apalachicola, Apr. 6, 1899.

CHAPMAN, FRANK MICHLER, ornithologist; b. Englewood, N.J., June 12, 1864; s. Lebbeus and Mary A. (Parkhurst) C.; acad. edn. (Sc.D., Brown, 1913); m. Fannie Bates Embury, 1898; 1 son, Frank Michler. Asso. curator ornithology and mammalogy, Am. Museum Natural History, 1888-1908, curator ornithology since 1908; originator there of the habitat of bird groups and seasonal bird exhibits. Zoological explorations in temperate and tropical America since 1887. Dir. Bureau of Publications Am. Red Cross, 1917-18; commr. Am. Red Cross to Latin America, 1918-19. Pres. Linnaean Soc., New York, elected 1897; pres. Burroughs Memorial Assn., 1921-25; fellow Am. Ornithologists' Union (pres. 1911); v.p. Explorers Club, 1910-18; hon. mem. N.Y. Zool. Soc., British Ornithologists' Union, Sociedad Ornithologica del Plata, Deutschen Ornithologischen Gesellschaft; mem. Nat. Academy of Sciences, Am. Phil. Soc., Soc. Colonial Wars. Awarded first Linnaean medal by Linnaean Soc. of New York, 1912; first Elliot medal by Nat. Acad. of Sciences, 1918; medal Roosevelt Memorial Assn., 1928; awarded medal Burroughs Memorial Assn., 1929. Clubs: Explorers, Century (New York). Author: Handbook of Birds of Eastern North America, 1895; Bird—Life, a Guide to the Study of Our Common Birds, 1897; Bird Studies with a Camera, 1900; A Color Key to North American Birds, 1903; The Economic Value of Birds to the State, 1903; The Warblers of North America, 1907; Camps and Cruises of an Ornithologist, 1908; The Travels of Birds, 1916; The Distribution of Bird—Life in Colombia, 1917; Our Winter Bids, 1918; What Bird Is That?, 1920; Birds of Urubamba Valley, Jeru, 1921; The Distribution of Bird—Life in Ecuador, 1926; My Tropical Air Castle, 1929; Autobiography of a Bird—Lover, 1933; Life in an Air Castle, 1938; The Post—Glacial History of Zonotrichia capensis; Birds and Man; also numerous papers on birds and mammals. Editor and founder Bird—Lore. Office: American Museum Natural History, New York, New York. Died Nov. 15, 1945.

CHAPMAN, GEORGE HERBERT, civil engr.; b. Chgo., Dec. 9, 1898; s. George Orlando and Nellie (Cross) C.; diploma Chgo. Tech. Coll., 1922-26; m. Mary Lucille McNamara, Oct. 20, 1921; 1 son, Gerald McNamara. Project engr. Allen & Garcia Co., Chgo., 1946-48; chief engr., v.p. Mines Engring. Co., Chgo., 1949-54; sr. civil engr. Paul Weir Co., Chgo., 1954-61; pvt. practice cons. engring., Chgo., 1961-67. Served as maj. AUS, 1943-46. Named officer Order of Leopold II (Belgium). Registered profl. engr., Ill., Mich., W. Va.. Mem. Nat., W.VA. socs. profl. engrs., Am. Soc. C.E., Am. Inst. Mining Engrs., Ill. Mining Inst. Presbyn. Mason. Home: Arlington Heights IL Died Dec. 29, 1967.

CHAPMAN, GERALD HOWARD, chemist, educator; b. Kent, O., June 3, 1902; s. Howard I. and Maude (Shilliday) C.; B.S., Kent State U., 1925; M.A., Ohio State U., 1929; Ph.D., Western Res. U., 1938; m. Vera Morris, June 16, 1928; 1 dau., Linda. Sci. tchr. Niles (O.) High Sch., 1925-29; critic supr. sci. Kent State High Sch., 1929-36; mem. chemistry dept. Kent State U., 1938—, prof., 1947—, chmn. phys. sci. course, 1960—; prof. chemistry Western Res. U., nights 1940-45. Mem. Am. Chem. Soc., Sigma Xi. Home: 122 University Dr., Kent, O. 44240. Died Mar. 31, 1965; buried Homeland Cemetery, Rootstown, O.

CHAPMAN, HENRY CADWALADER, physician; b. Phila., Aug. 17, 1845; s. George William and Emily (Markoe) C.; grad. Univ. of Pa., 1864 (A.M.), med. dept. same, M.D., 1867; M.D., Jefferson Med. Coll., 1878; studied 3 yrs. in Europe; m. Hannah Neylee Megargee, Dec. 2, 1876. Resident physician Pa. Hosp. and lecturer on anatomy and physiology, Univ. of Pa., 1870; prof. institutes of medicine and med. jurisprudence, Jefferson Med. Coll., 1880; coroner's physician. Phila., 1876-81. Mem. Phila. Acad. Natural Sciences, 1868—, curator same, 1875—; fellow Coll. Physicians, Phila., 1880; prosector Zoöl. Soc., Phila.

Author: Evolution of Life: History of the Discovery of the Circulation of the Blood; Treatise upon Human Physciology; Medical Jurisprudence and Toxicology, 1903. Home: Philadelphia. Died 1909.

CHAPMAN, JAMES RUSSELL, civil engr.; b. Boston, Oct. 31, 1851; s. Ozias Goodwin and Elizabeth (Russell) C.; A.B., U. of Vt., 1873; m. Antoinette Hagar, of Salem, Mass., Nov. 19, 1879. Engr. various ry. cos., 1873-1901; chief engr. Underground Electric Rys. Co. of London, 1901-10; retired, 1910. Mem. Am. Soc. C.E. Address: 1712 Anacopa St., Santa Barbara, Cal.

CHAPMAN, NATHANIEL, physician; b. Fairfax County, Va., May 28, 1780; s. George and Amelia (Macrae) C.; grad. U. Pa. Med. Sch., 1800; M. D., U. Edinburgh (Scotland), 1804; m. Rebecca Biddle, 1808. Founder Med. Inst. Phila., 1817; editor Jour. Med. and Phys. Scis.; pres. Phila. Med. Soc.; 1st pres. A.M.A.; pres. Am. Philos. Soc. Author: Elements of Theraputics and Materia Media, 1817; Lectures on the More Important Diseases of the Thoracic and Abdominal Viscera, 1844; Lectures on the More Important Eruptive Fevers, Hemorrhages and Dropsies and on Gout and Rheumatism, 1844; A Compendium of Lectures on the Theory and Practice of Medicine, 1846. Died Phila., July 1, 1853.

CHAPMAN, ROBERT HOLLISTER, topographic engr.; b. New Haven, Conn., July 29, 1868; s. Charles Welsey and Etta (Sperry) C.; ed. Corcoran Scientific School, Washington, D.C.; m. Frances Beardsley Andrews, June 1, 1907. With U.S. Geol. Survey, 1880—; has made topographic surveys and explorations in prin. Western and Southern states, maps of portion of Death Valley and adjacent deserts and high Sierras, Cal.; sent to Ottawa, May 1909, to introduce U.S. topographic methods in Geol. Survey of Can.; in charge of field work, on Vancouver Island, 1909, 1910, 1911; acting supt. Glacier Nat. Park, Mont., 1912; returned to U.S. Geol. Survey, 1913. Maj., Engrs. R.C. and on active duty, June 1917. Author many bulletins published by governments of United States and Canada. Personal explorations in Northern Selkirks, B.C., 1915, and Northern Canadiann Rockies, 1919. Home: Washington, D.C. Died Jan. 11, 1920.

CHAPMAN, THOMAS GARFIELD, metall. engr.; b. Can., Sept. 21, 1886; s. Alexander and Elizabeth (MacDonald) C.; came to U.S., 1887; S.B., Mass. Inst. Tech., 1909, Sc.D., 1925; m. Dorothy Spears, Aug. 1925; 1 son, Thomas G. Inst. Mass. Inst. Tech., 1909-12; asst. prof. metallurgy Mich. Coll. of Mines, 1912-16; prof. metallurgy, U. Ariz., since 1916, dean grad. coll. 1937-40, dean coll. mines since 1940; dir. Ariz. Bur. Mines. Mem. Am. Inst. Mining and Metall. Engrs., Sigma Xi, Phi Kappa Phi, Tau Beta Pi. Mason (32 deg.). Home: 2724 E. 8th St., Tucson. Died Nov. 6, 1965; buried Forest Hills Cemetery, Boston.

CHAPMAN, W(ILBERT) M(CLEOD), ichthyologist, writer; b. Kalama, Washington, Mar. 31, 1910; s. Albert Bradford and Ivy Myrtle (McLeod) C.; B.S., U. of Wash., 1932, M.S., 1933, Ph.D., 1927; m. Mary Elizabeth Swaney, Mar. 22, 1935; children—Lewis McLeod, Alan Bruce, Jane Elizabeth, Thomas Malcolm, Jonathan Emery, Kathryn Ann. Scientific assistant with the International Fisheries Commn., 1933-35; biologist, Wash. State Dept. of Fisheries, 1935-41; aquatic biologist, U.S. Fish and Wildlife Service, 1941-42; oyster biologist, Wash. State Planning Council, 1942; curator of fishes, Calif. Acad. of Sciences, 1943-47; sr. fisheries specialist in charge Fisheries Project, Bd. of Econ. Warfare, South Pacific, 1943-44; dir., Sch. of Fisheries, U. of Wash., 1947; spl. asst. to under sec. of state, U.S. Dept. of State, 1948-51; dir. of research American Tunaboat Assn., 1951-70. Fellow, Calif. Academy of Sciences, John S. Guggenheim Memorial Foundation; mem. Inst. of Food Technologists, Am. Soc. of Ichthyologists and Herpetologists (bd. of govs., pres., West. Div., 1940), Oceanographic Soc. of Pacific, A.A.A.S., Pacific Fishery Biologists, Western Soc. of Naturalists. Methodist. Author: Fishing in Troubled Waters, 1948. Contbr. numerous articles on fish and fisheries to Scientific and popular periodicals, since 1932. Home: San Diego CA Died July 1970.

CHASE, FRANK DAVID, industrial engr.; b. Riverside, Ill.; S. David Fletcher and Emily Frances (Tabor) C.; B.S. in C.E., Mass. Inst. Tech., 1901. Pres., 1913—, Frank D. Chase, Inc., engineers and architects, specialists in design of industrial and mercantile bldg., operating throughout U.S. Home: Evanston, Ill. Died July 23, 1937.

CHASE, FREDERICK LINCOLN, astronomer; b. Boulder, Colo., June 28, 1865; s. George Franklin and Augusta Ann (Staples) C.; A.B., U. of Colorado, 1886; Ph.D. Yale, 1891; unmarried. Asst. in Yale Obs., 1890; asst. astronomer, 1891-1911, acting dir. same, 1910-13. Wrote: Heliometer Triangulation of the Victoria Comparison Stars (Annals of the Cape Observatory, 1897); Triangulation of the Prinicipal Stars of the Cluster in Coma Berenices (trans. Yale Univ. Obs., Vol. I, Part V, 1896); Parallax Investigations on 163 Stars, mainly of Large Proper Motion (trans. Yale Univ. Obs., Vol. II, Part I, 1906); Parallax Investigations on 35 Selected Stars, Vol. II, Part II, 1910; Parallax of 41 Southern Stars, Vol. II, Part III, 1912; Catalogue of Yale Parallax Results, Vol. II, Part IV, 1912. Home: Boulder, Colo. Died Nov. 8, 1933.

CHASE, ISAAC MCKIM; mech. engr.; b. Baltimore, May 27, 1837; s. Alexander and Mary Ann (Cruser) C.; grad. Md. Inst.; m. Emeline Hall, Apr. 1, 1878. Entered Washington Navy Yard, 1868, becoming master mechanic; expert in marine Propellers and propulsion. Author: Screw Propellers and Marine Propulsion, 1895; Art of Pattern Making, 1903. Died 1903.

CHASE, JOHN CARROLL, civil engr.; b. Chester, N.H., July 26, 1849; s. Charles and Caroline (Chase) C.; grad. Pinkerton Acad. (Derry, N.H.), 1869; student Mass. Inst. of Tech., 1870-71; m. Mary Lizzie Durgin, Oct. 21, 1871 (died 1927); children—Caroline Louise (wife of Raffaele Lorini, M.D.), Benjamin (dec.), Alice Durgin (wife of Samuel C. Prescott, S.B., Sc.D.); m. 2d, Florence Anne Buchanan, July 14, 1928. Began as civil engr., 1871; asst. engr. on water works constrn., N.H. and Mass., 1871-77; asst. engr. on Elevated R.R. constrn., New York, 1877-79; asst. cashier, N.Y. Custom House, 1880-81; supt. Clarendon Water Works, Wilmington, N.C., 1881-97; city surveyor and engr., Wilmington, 1886-94; gen. practice as civil engr., 1871-1907; pres. and treas. The Benjamin Chase Co., Derry, N.H., 1907—. Mem. N.C. State Bd. of Health, 1893-97. Trustee and sec. Pinkerton Acad.; trustee and treas. Taylor Library, Derry, N.H. Republican. Mason. Author: History of Chester, N.H., 1926; Descendants of Aquila and Thomas Chase, 1928; Descendants of William Chase. Home: Derry, N.H. Died Apr. 1936.

CHASE, MRS. (MARY) AGNES, botanist; b. Iroquois Co., Ill., Apr. 20, 1869; d. Martin John and Mary (Cassidy) Merrille; ed. Lewis Inst. U. Chgo. (u. extension courses); m. William Ingraham Chase, Jan. 21, 1888 (dec. Jan. 2, 1889). Asst. in botany Field Mus., Chgo., 1901-03; bot. illustrator U.S. Dept. Agr., 1903-07, sci. asst. in systematic agrostology, 1907-23, asst. botanist, 1923-25, asso. botanist, 1925-36, sr. botanist, 1936-39; ret.; custodian grasses U.S. Nat. Mus., Smithsonian Instn., since 1939. Recipient numerous awards. Mem. A.A.A.S., Bot. Soc. Am., Chgo. Acad. Scis., Bot. Soc. Washington, Biol. Soc. Washington; corr. mem. Natural History Mus. (Vienna, Austria). Author: First Book of Grasses, 1922. Contbr. to bot. jours. Home: 5403 41st St., Washington 20015. Office: Smithsonian Institution, Washington, D.C. Died Sept. 24, 1963.

CHASE, PLINY EARLE, educator, scientist; b. Worcester, Mass., Aug. 18, 1820; s. Anthony and Lydia (Earle) C.; grad. Harvard, 1839, M.A. (hon.), 1844; LL.D. (hon.), Haverford Coll., 1844; m. Elizabeth Brown Oliver, 1843, 6 children. Prof. natural sciences Haverford Coll., 1871, prof. philosophy and logic, 1875, acting pres., 1886; lectr. psychology and logic Bryn-Mawr Coll.; mem. Am. Philos. Soc. (v.p., sec., recipient Magellanic medal for paper "Numerical Relations between Gravity and Magnetism"); linguist; mgr. Franklin Inst.; fellow A.A.A.S., 1874. Author textbooks including: Elements of Arithmetic, 1844; The Common School Arithmetic, 1848; Elements of Meterology for Schools and Households, 1884. Died Haverford, Pa., Dec. 17, 1886.

CHATARD, THOMAS MAREAN, mining engr.; b. Baltimore, Dec. 15, 1848; s. Ferdinand E. and Eliza M.C.; A.B., Mt. St. Mary's Coll., 1867; S.B., Harvard, 1871; Ph.D., Heidelberg, 1876; m. Eleanor A. Williams, of Baltimore, Feb. 12, 1889. Mem. Am. Inst. Mining Engrs. and other socs. Contbr. scientific articles to various jours. Address: 1716 R. I. Av., Washington.

CHATBURN, GEORGE RICHARD, civil engr.; b. near Magnolia, Ia., Dec. 24, 1863; s. Jonas Wellington and Mary (Burton) C.; B.C.E., Ia. State Coll., 1884, C.E., 1910; A.M., U. of Neb., 1897; Dr. Engring. from Iowa State Coll., 1928; m. Anna Murphy, July 21, 1889; children—Mary Frances, Alice (dec.), George Richard. Teacher dist. schs., Shelby County, Ia., 1884-85; prin. sch., Plattsmouth, Neb., 1885-89; supt. pub. schs., Humboldt, Neb., 1889-91. Wymore, 1891-94; instr. and adj. prof. civ. engring., 1894-1905, asso. prof. and prof. applied mechanics and machine design, 1905—, U. of Neb., also head dept. applied mechanics and machine design; ry. and highway consulting engr. During World War has charge of publicity and instructional work of S.A.T.C., U. of Neb. Republican. Mason. Author: Highway Engineering, 1921; Highways and Highway Transportation, 1923. Home: Lincoln, Neb. Died Jan. 30, 1940.

CHAUVENET, REGIS, mining engr.; b. Phila., Pa., Oct. 7, 1842; s. William and Catharine (Hemple) C.; bro. of William Marc C.; A.B., Washington U., 1862, A.M., 1864 (LL.D., 1900); B.S., Harvard, 1867; m. Virginia Mellon, Dec. 20, 1887. Analytical chemist. St. Louis, 1871-83; chemist to Mo. Geol. Survey and city gas insp., St. Louis, 1872-75; pres. and prof. chemistry and metallurgy, Colo. Sch. of Mines, 1883-1902; resigned to devote attention to practice as mining engr. Author: Chemical and Metallurgical Calculations, 1911. Home: Denver, Colo. Died Dec. 6, 1920.

CHAUVENET, WILLIAM, astronomer, mathematician, univ. chancellor; b. Milford, Pa., May 24, 1820; s. William Marc and Mary B. (Kerr) C.; grad. with high honors Yale, 1840; m. Catherine Hemple, 1842. Prof. mathematics in Naval Asylum, Phila., 1841, serving on U.S.S. Mississippi; influenced orgn. of U.S. Naval Acad., 1845, chmn. dept. mathematics and astronomy, 1853-55; prof. Washington U., St. Louis, 1855-69, chancellor, 1862-69; elected mem. Am. Philos. Soc., Am. Acad. Arts and Scis.; an incorporator Nat. Acad. Scis.; pres. A.A.A.S. Author: A Treatise on Plane and Spherical Trigonometry, 1850; A Manual of Spherical and Practical Astronomy, 1863; A Treatise on Elementary Geometry with Appendices Containing a Collection of Exercises for Students and an Introduction to Modern Geometry, 1870. Died St. Paul, Minn., Dec. 13, 1870; buried Bellefontaine Cemetery, St. Louis.

CHAUVENET, WILLIAM MARC, chemist; b. in Naval Acad., Annapolis, Md., Mar. 4, 1855; s. William and Catharine (Hemple) C.; brother of Regis C. (q.v.); grad. Washington U., 1879; unmarried. Expert spl. agt. U.S. Geol. Survey, div. mining geology, 10th census, 1879-83; chemist U.S. Geol. Survey, 1881-82, making reports on iron ores of Ala., Tenn., Ky., and Mo., 10th Census; asst. U.S. Geol. Survey, Lake Superior div., 1882-85. Fellow A.A.A.S., mem. Am. Inst. Mining Engrs. Juror for Bulgaria, St. Louis Expn., 1904. Author: Notes on Minnesota Geology on Northern Boundary, 1885. Also reports on Mexico, Venezuela, California, Missouri. Home: The Pendennis. Office: 620 Chestnut St., St. Louis.

CHEEK, F(RANK) J(ACOBS), JR., coll. prof.; born Paris, Ky., Aug. 25, 1893; s. Rev. F. J. and Elizabeth Ann (Ingels) C.; A.B., Centre Coll. of Ky., 1914; C.E., Rensselaer Poly Inst., 1919; S. M., Mass. Inst. Tech., 1933; m. Martha A. Butt, Aug. 26, 1924; 1 dau., Martha R. High Sch. teacher mathematics, 1914-15; office mgr. state agency Northwestern Mutual Life Ins. Co., 1915-16; constrn. engr. and field supt. Turner Constrn. Co., N.Y. City, 1919-22; operated own office. 1922-23; asso. prof. Kan. State Coll.,1923-37; prof. hydraulic and sanitary engring. U. of Ky., 1937-59. Consultant in Engring. Curricula Central U. of Venezuela; mem. State Bd. of Examiners for Waterworks Operators; mem. State Bd. of Examiners for Sanitary Engrs.; nat. vice chmn. Engring. College Magazines, Associated, 1948-49, national chairman, 1949-51. Member American Soc. C.E., Am. Soc. Engring. edn., Ky. Soc. Professional Engrs., Sigma Chi, Alpha Rho Chi, Sigma Xi, Tau Beta Pi. Registered profl. engr., Ky. Democrat. Presbyn. Home: 1492 Tates Creek Rd., Lexington 5, Ky. Died Apr. 23, 1959.

CHELDELIN, VERNON H(ENDRUM), biochemist, educator; b. Clatskanie, Ore., Mar. 15, 1916; s. John Frederick and Marie Cecelie (Thurgersen) C.; B.A., Reed Coll., 1937; M.S., Ore. State U., 1939; Ph.D., U. Tex., 1941; m. Irene Hinnells, Sept. 7, 1938; children—Verene B. (Mrs. Billy R. Finley), Ronald H., Lawrence V., Sandra I. Instr. chemistry R.R. Williams Labs., Summit, N.J., 41-42; research asso. biochem. inst. U. Tex., 1942; faculty Ore. State U., 1942—, prof. chemistry, 1948—, dir. sci. research inst., 1952—, dean Sch. Sci., 1962—. Mem. study panel biochemistry and nutrition USPHS, 1951-55, 61-65; adv. council Army Chem. Corps., 1957—; study panel bldg. facilities NSF, 1961-63; mem. for Ore., Sci. and New Technologies Com., 1961—. Rockefeller fellow Enzyme Inst., U. Wis., 1949-50; Guggenheim fellow Oxford (Eng.) U., 1957; recipient Carter award outstanding teaching Ore. State U., 1954, Sigma Xi research award, 1956; citation Ore. Acad. Sci., 1958; Squibb lectr. microbiology Rutgers U., 1960. Mem. Am. Chem. Soc. (exec. council bio chemistry div. 1948-50, chmn. Ore. sect. 1949, nat. councilor 1944, 53-55, chmn. nat. conv. Portland 1948; Harrison Howe lectr. 1956) Am. Soc. Biol. Chemists (editorial policy com. 1953-59), Pacific Slope Biochem Assn. (pres. 1961), Am. Inst. Nutrition, Biochem. Soc. (Britain), Soc. Exptl. Biology and Medicine, Soc. Am. Microbiologists, Sigma Xi, Phi Kappa Phi, Phi Lambda Upsilon. Home: 3453 Hayes St., Corvahlis, Ore. Died Aug. 23, 1966.

CHELSLEY, ALBERT JUSTUS, health ofcl.; b. Mpls., Sept. 12, 1877; s. Clarence Percival and Aline Kilbourne (Goodale) C.; M.D., U. Minn., 1907; m. Placida Garner (M.D.). Feb. 13, 1920; 1 dau., Emma Louise. With Minn. Bd. Health 1902—. Successively in lab. service epidemologist, dir. dv. epidemiology, dr. dv. preventable diseases, 1902-21, sec., exec. officer state bd., 1921—. became prof. pub. health dept. preventive medicine U. Minn., 1925, ret.as clin. prof. emeritus. pres. conf. of State and Provinical Health Authorities of N.A., 1924, sec., 1927-45. Arthur T. McCormack award, 1950. Mem. bd. sci. dir., internat. health expert to A.R.C. Commn. to France, also chief of staff to Poland, later commr. to Poland, 1918-20. Decorated War with Spain, Philippine campaign medals. 8th Army corps. Congl. Medal for Philippine Service (U.S.); Medaille de la Reconnaissance Francaise 3d classe (France) three decorations from Polish govt.; recipient distinguished service medal Minn. Med. Assn., 1948; Outstanding Achievement award U. Minn., 1951; Sedgwick Meml. medal Am. Pub. Health Assn., 1955. Diplomate Am. Bd. Preventive Medicine and Pub. Health Fellow Am. Coll. Preventive Medicine, Royal

San. Inst. Gt. Britian (hon.); life mem. Am. (Pres. 1930;). Canadian (hon.) pub. health assns., Am. Social Hygiene Assn. (hon.) mem. Am., Minn., Hennepin County med. assns., Assn. Mil. Surgeons U.S., Am.-Epidemiology Soc., Am. Assn. Pathologists and Bacteriologists. Vets. Fgn. Wars, Nu Sigma Nu. Mason. Home: 11 River Terrace St., Mpls. Died Oct. 17, 1955; Buried Fort Snelling Nat. Cemetery, Mpls.

CHENERY, WILLIAM ELISHA, laryngologist; b. Wiscasset, Me., June 14, 1864; s. Elisha (M.D.) and Harriet Ann (Grose) C.; prep. edn., Boston Latin Sch.; A.B., Boston U., 1887; M.D., Harvard U., 1890; D.S., Boston University, 1938; Dr. Humane Letters, Tufts College, 1945; studied in Europe, Freiburg, Vienna, and Berlin; m. Marion M. Luse, Oct. 14, 1896. Prof. laryngology, Tufts College Med., now emeritus prof.; consultant in nose, throat and ear dept. Boston Dispensary, also of Roxbury and Booth hosps., Walter E. Fernold State Sch. and Forsyth Dental Infirmary for Children; consultant in laryngology, New England Deaconess Hosp.; mem. staff N.E. Bapt. Hosp.; chief surgeon med. staff, Aleppo Temple; lecturer dental hygiene Forsyth Dental Infirmary. Volunteered for service with U.S. Med. Corps, Sept. 24, 1918. Fellow Am. Laryngol., Rhinol. and Otol. Soc., N.E. Otolaryngol. Soc., Am. Acad. Ophthalmology and Oto-Laryngology, Am. Coll. Surgeons; mem. A.M.A., Mass. Med. Soc., Mass. Soc. Examining Physicians, A.A.A.S., S.A.R. (Boston chapter), Ancient and Honorable Arty. Co. of Mass., Nat. Geog. Soc., Harvard Brotherhood of Brookline, Theta Delta Chi, Phi Chi, Phi Beta Kappa. Mem. exec. com. and trustee Boston Univ.; ex-pres. Boston Methodist Social Union, Interchurch Fellowship; co-founder and ex-pres. Friends of China, Inc. (Sino-Am. Soc.), Boston; v.p., Boston Industrial Home; treas. New England Com. for Relief in China. Republican. Methodist; trustee and chmn. finance com. St. Marks Ch., Brookline. Mason (32 deg., K.T.). Clubs: Boston City, University, Harvard, Algonquin, Appalachian Mountain, Tufts College Masonic, Kiwanis of Brookline, Cosmopolitan. Address: 377 Commonwealth Av., Boston MA

CHENEY, CLARENCE ORION, psychiatrist; b. Poughkeepsie, N.Y., 1887; s. Albert Orion and Caroline (Adriance) C.; A.B., Columbia, 1908; M.D., Coll. Physicians and Surgeons, Columbia, 1911; m. Josephine Scott, June 7, 1915; 1 son, Robert Scott. Intern Manhattan State Hosp., 1911; asst. physician and pathologist, same, 1912-17; asst. dir. N.Y. State Psychiatric Inst., 1917-22; asst. supt. Utica State Hosp., 1922-26; supt. Hudson River State Hosp., Poughkeepsie, 1926-31; dir. N.Y. State Psychiatric Institute and Hosps., 1931-36; dir. New York Hospital, Westchester Div., 1936-46, emeritus since 1946; instructor in psychiatry, Cornell Med. Sch., 1917-22; lecturer in psychiatry, Syracuse Med. Sch., 1922-26; prof. clin. psychiatry, Columbia U., 1931-33, prof. psychiatry, 1933-36; prof. clin. psychiatry, Cornell Med. Sch., since 1936. Fellow Am. Psychiatric Assn. (sec.-treas. 1928-33; chmn. bd. examiners 1933-38; pres. 1935-36); mem. New York Psychiatric Soc. (pres. 1943-44), N.Y. Soc. for Clinical Psychiatry (pres. 1934-35), N.Y. Neurological Society, A.M.A., New York State Med. Soc. (ex-chmn. sect. on neurology and psychiatry), Westchester County Med. Soc., Assn. for Research in Nervous and Mental Diseases, Royal Medico-Psychol. Assn. England (corr. mem), U. Council of Columbia U. (mem. 1935-36) Alpha Chi Rho, Alpha Omega Alpha, Sigma Xi; fellow N.Y. Acad. Medicine, American College of Physicians. Clubs: Kiwanis of Utica (pres. 1925-26); Rotary, University (White Plains). Editor: Outlines of Psychiatric Examinations, 1934. Asso. editor of Psychiatric Quarterly and Am. Jour. of Psychiatry. Address: 11 Burling Av., White Plains, New York. Died Nov. 4, 1947.

CHENEY, MONROE GEORGE petroleum geologist; b. Franklinville, N.Y., Sept. 1893; s. Monroe George and Annie Naomi (Button) C.; B.S., Cornell U., 1916; student Royal Sch. of Mines, London, Eng., 1919; m. Margaret Booth, June 8, 1918; children—Monroe George, Harris Graham. Geologist, various business interests, 1916-17; cons. geologist and prgs. Anzac, Oil Corp., Coleman, Tex., since 1919. Served with U.S. Army, 1917-19; 111th Engrs., 36th Div., 1918-19. Fellow Geol. Soc., Am., A.A.A.S., mem. Am. Assn. Petroleum Geologists, (Sec.-treas., 1934; pres. 1945), Soc. Econ. Explor. Geophysicists, Am. Geog. Soc., Am. Geophysical Union, Am. Petroleum Inst., Sigma Phi Epsilon. Contributor numerous articles on geology and oil developements to tech. jours. Home: 1015 W. Walnut St. Office: State Bank Bldg., Coleman, Tex. Died Sept. 28, 1952; buried Overall Lease, near Coleman, Tex.,

CHENEY, SHERWOOD ALFRED, army officer (ret.) b. S. Manchester, Conn., Aug. 24, 1873; s. John S. Cheney; grad. U.S. Mil. Acad., 1897, Army War Coll., 1907, Gen. Staff Coll., 1921; m. Louise Delano, Sept. 10, 1921 (died 1923); m. 2d, Charlotte S. Hopkins, Nov. 23, 1925. Comd. additional 2d lieut. engrs., June 11, 1897; 2d lieut., July 5, 1898; advanced through the grades to brig. gen., (temp.), Oct. 1, 1918; brig. gen. U.S. Army, Apr. 1, 1933. In field in Cuba, May-Sept., 1988; in Philippines, 1899-1901; participated in operations about San Fabian, later in Cavite Province and in expdn. to Nueva Caceres, and chief engr. officer Dept. of Southern Luzon; a.-d.-c. to Maj. Gen. J. C. Bates, at Chicago and St. Louis, 1903-05; duty with Gen. Staff, 1907-11; dir. Army Field Engr. Sch., 1914-15; on Mexican border, 1915-17; went to France on special commn., June 1917; comdr. 110th Regt. Engrs., 1918; rep. of chief of engrs. at Gen. Hdqrs., A.E.F., 1918; dir. Army Transport Service, later dir. gen. transportation, 1919; Am. mem. Inter-Allied Mil. Mission to Baltic Provinces, Nov. 1919-Jan. 1920, in Baltic States and Germany; mem. Gen. Staff Corps, 1921-24; military attaché to China, 1921-24 retired Aug. 24, 1937. Awarded D.S.M. "for services in organization of engineer units and repatriation of A.E.F. from France." Clubs: Hartford (Hartford, Conn.); Army and Navy (Washington). Home: 34 Park St., Manchester, Conn. Died March 13, 1949.

CHENOWETH, ALEXANDER CRAWFORD, cons. engr.; b. Baltimore, June 5, 1849; s. Rev. George Davenport and Frances Ann (Crawford) C.; A.B., Dickinson Coll., 1868, A.M., 1869 (LL.D., 1908); course in engring. Rensselaer Poly. Inst.; m. Catherine Richardson Wood, Apr. 19, 1876. Engaged on engring. force of Prospect Park, Brooklyn, 1870; asst. engr. Middletown-New Haven R.R., 1871, Brunswick & Western R.R., Ga., 1872; asst. under Gen. George Green, pub. works, Washington; contractor for dock and ry. work, West Shore R.R., 1882; cons. engr. to Gen. M. Prado, President of Peru; prepared foundation for Bartholdi Statue of Liberty, Bedloe's Island, N.Y., 1884; apptd. asst. engr. Croton Aqueduct Commn., New York Feb. 16, 1885, resident engr. in charge Croton Aqueduct, July 26, 1889; resigned, 1895, to enter into constrn. work for U.S. Govt. at Sandy Hook; contractor for drainage work, D.C., 1896, built Nagle Av., New York 1898; specialist in foundation work; pres. Chenoweth Concrete Revetment Co. Served in 7th Regt. N.G.N.Y.; was 1st lt. Vet. A.C. and Washington Continental Guard. Episcopalian. Democrat. Home: New York, N.Y. Died Apr. 13, 1922.

CHERONIS, NICHOLAS DIMITRIUS, educator, research chemist; b. Sparta, Greece, June 29, 1896; s. Dimitrius George and Panghiota (Machinis) C.; came to U.S., 1911, naturalized by Act of Congress; student Third Gymnasium of Athens, Greece, 1911; B.S. with honors, U. of Chicago, 1919, Ph.D., 1929; m. Irene Hamlin, June 29, 1923; children—Thaleia Eleni Selz (Mrs. Peter Howard), Dion Dimitrius Lorenzo. Spl. work in carbon monoxide under Julius Stieglitz (war project), 1917; spl. work on organic compounds, Chem. Warfare Service, U.S. Army, Cath. Univ. Lab., 1918-19; asst., U. of Chicago, 1919-20; instr., Crane City Coll., Chicago, 1930-33; chmn. div. of physical sci., Wright City Coll., 1934-50; chmn. dept. of chemistry, Brooklyn (N.Y.) Coll. 1950-62; dir. Synthetical Labs., 1921-29, consultant since 1930. Mem. A.A.A.S., Am. Chem. Soc., Ill. Acad. of Sci., N.Y. Acad. Sci., Sigma Xi. Author books including: Semimicro Qualitative Organic Analysis (with J. Entrikin), 1948, 2d edit., 1957; Micro and Semimicro Methods; Technique of Organic Chemistry, Volume VI, 1954; Semimicro Experimental Organic Chemistry, 1958; (with T.S. Ma) Functional Group Analysis; also articles in chem. publs. Home: Halycon Hill, R.D. 2, Oregon, Ill. 61061. Office: Bklyn. Coll., Bklyn. 11210. Died July 2, 1962; buried Deerfield, Ill.

CHERRIE, GEORGE KRUCK, field naturalist; b. Knoxville, Ia., Aug. 22, 1865; s. Martin and Agnes (Breckenridge) C.; ed. Knoxville, Ia., and State Agrl. Coll., 1880; m. Stella M. Bruere, Dec. 1, 1895; m. 2d, Esther Atwell, Jan. 12, 1934. Asst. taxidermist, U.S. Nat. Museum, 1888; accepting position in Am. Museum, New York later; appointed taxidermist and curator of birds, mammals and reptiles, Nat. Museum, Costa Rica, 1889; asst. curator ornithology, in charge of dept., Field Museum of Natrual History, Chicago, 1894-97; conducted explorations in Valley of the Orinoco for Lord Rothschild, 1897-99; ornithol. explorations for Tring Museum, in French Guiana, 1902-03; explorations in Trinidad and Valley of Ornioco, for Brooklyn Inst. Museum, 1905 and 1907; curator ornithology and mammalogy, Brooklyn Inst. Arts and Sciences, 1899-1911; mem. Am. Museum expdn. to Columbia, S.A., valley of the Magdalena River and the high interior, 1913; rep. Am. Museum Natural History on Roosevelt expdn. through So. America, 1913-14; naturalist Collins-Day S. Am. expdn., 1914-15; dir. Cherrie-Roosevelt South American expdn. for Am. Museum Natural History, 1916-17; South Am. service for U.S. Bur. Naval Intelligence, 1918-19; a leader Anthony-Cherrie expdn. to Ecuador for Am. Museum Natural History, 1920-21; Cherrie expdn. to Ecuador for same, 1921; Mazaroni River diamond fields, British Guiana, 1922; expdn. to Central Brazil, 1924; naturalist Roosevelt-Simpson Asiatic expdn. for Field Museum, Chinese Turkestan, 1925-26; leader Marshall Field Brazilian expdn., 1926. Mem. Am. Ornithologists' Union; hon. fellow Am. Museum Natural History, 1921; Boone and Crocket Club, New York; Explorers Club, New York; Ends of the Earth Club, New York; Camp Fire Club of Chicago; hon. Boy Scout Field Museum, 1926. Wrote on Central American Birds with descriptions of new species, etc., in The Auk and Proc. U.S. Nat. Museum, 1890-96; also The Ornithology of Santo Domingo (Publs. Field Museum of Natural History, Chicago), 1896; New Birds of the Orinoco Region and of Trinidad, 1909; Dark Trails, Adventures of a Naturalist, 1930. Home: Newfane, Vt. Died Jan. 20, 1948.

CHERRY, WILLIAM STAMPS, African explorer; b. Clark Co., Mo., Feb. 14, 1868; s. L.S. and Elizabeth (Allen) C.; ed. pub. schs., Warsaw, Mo., 1974-81; Brooklings, (S.Dak.) Coll., 1882-86; took thorough course as mech engr., 1886-89; m. Morgan Park, Ill., Feb. 14, 1902, Olive Isabel Harvey. Went to Africa, 1889; traveled over Congo basin, 1890-93; returned to U.S.; took spl. course Armour Inst., Chicago; returned to Africa; engaged in original exploration and scientific research on the Upper Mobangui, 1896-1901; explored Kotto river and water shed of Bahr el Gazahl and Chari rivers; made maps of the region and gathered much information on African arts, customs and religions; lived among natives while making researches; supported himself and expdn. by elephant hunting; now editing his notes for publ. Wrote: Elephant Hunting in Central Africa, McClure's Mag., Oct. 1901. Address: Santa Ana, Cal.

CHESNEY, ALAN MASON, physician, internist; b. Baltimore, Md., Jan. 17, 1888; s. Jesse Mason and Annie (Atkinson) C.; student Balt. City College, 1905; A.B., Johns Hopkins, 1908, M.D., 1912, LL.D., 1957; m. Cora Chambers, May 17, 1917; children—Joan, Alan Dukehart, Peter. Began practice at Baltimore, 1912; asst. in medicine, Johns Hopkins, 1913; asst. resident physician, Rockefeller Inst. Hosp., 1914-17; asso. in medicine, Washington U., 1919-21; asso. prof. medicine, Johns Hopkins since 1921, asst. dean of medical school, 1927-29, dean, 1929-53, dean emeritus, 1953—; managing editor Medicine, 1923-47. President Med. and Chirurgical Faculty, State of Md., 1952. Served as lt., advancing to majl, Med. Corps, U.S. Army, 1917-19. Pres. Assn. of Am. Med. Colls., 1937-38. Member Johns Hopkins Med. and Surg. (pres. 1959-61), Assn. Am. Physicians, Soc. for Clin. Investigation, Soc. Exptl. Pathology, Baltimore City Medical Society (vice pres. 1951), Phi Beta Kappa, Alpha Omega Alpha, Phi Gamma Delta. Clubs: 14 W. Hamilton St., Deer Isle Yacht, Author: Immunity in Syphilis, 1926; The Flowering of an Idea, 1939; The Johns Hopkins Hospital and The Johns Hopkins Hospital and the Johns Hopkins University School of Medicine—A Chronicle, 1943. Home: 700 N. Charles St., Balt. 21201. Died Sept. 22, 1964.

CHESNEY, CUMMINGS C., elec. engr.; b. Selinsgrove, Pa., Oct. 28, 1863; s. John C. and Jane (McFall) C.; B.S., Pa. State Coll., 1885; taught mathematics and chemistry, Doylestown Sem. and Pa. State Coll., 1885-88; m. Elizabeth Cutler, 1891; children—Malcolm M., Elizabeth, Margaret, Katherine, Barbara. Joined William Stanley's laboratory force, Great Barrington, Mass., 1888; with U.S. Elec. Lighting Co., Newark, 1889-90; one of incorporators, 1890, Stanley Elec. Mfg. Co., mgr. Pittsfield works of Gen. Electric Co., 1906-27; v.p. and chmn. mfg. com., Gen. Electric Co.; pres. Berkshire Morris Plan Bank, 1931-35, Berkshire Trust Co., 1934-39; pres. Pittsfield Coal Gas Co.; hon. v.p. Gen. Electric Co.; dir. G.E. Employees Securities Corp., Mass. Mut. Life Ins. Co., Agrl. Nat. Bank, Pittsfield, Springfield Fire and Marine Insurance Co., N.E. Fire Ins. Co., Sentinel Fire Ins. Co., Boston & Albany R.R. Co. Pioneer in many elec. improvements; laid out first polyphase power transmission plant to be put into successful operation in America; also pioneer in designing alternating current generators for high voltages, and many other developments. Pres. Am. Inst. E.E., 1926-27; mem. Soc. of Arts, London. Awarded Edison medal by Am. Inst. E.E., 1922. Home: 74 Dawes Av., Pittsfield, Mass. Died Nov. 27, 1947.

CHESNUT, VICTOR KING, chemist, botanist; b. Nevada City, Calif., June 28, 1867; s. John A. and Henrietta S. (King) C.; B.S., U. of Calif. 1890; grad. student U. of Chicago and Columbian (now George Washington) U.; m. Olive Branch Spohr, July 18, 1899; children—George S., Alma E. , Frank T., Gertrude V. Asst. in chemistry, U. of Calif., 1890-93; asst. botanist in charge of poisonous plant investigations, Bur. of Plant Industry, U.S. Dept. Agr., 1894-1904; prof. chemistry and geology, Mont. Agrl. Coll.; chemist Mont. Expt. Sta., 1904-07; collaborator, poisonous plant investigations, U.S. Dept. of Agr. 1904-06; asst. chemist. div. of drugs, 1907-16, asst. chemist, Phytochemical Lab., 1916-24, asso. chemist, 1924-33, Bur. Chemistry, U.S. Dept. Agr., Food and Drug Adminstration; retired on pension, July 1, 1933. Elder in Presbyterian Ch. Author: Principal Poisonous Plants of the United States, 1898; Determination of Pepsin in Liquids, 1913 and 1916; Determination of the Proteoclastic Activity of Papaya latex and the Detection of Enzyme Adulterants, 1916; (with F. B. Power) An Improved Method for the Quantitative Determination of Caffeine in Vegetable Material, 1919; Ilex Vomitoria as a Native Source of Caffeine; The Odorous Constituents of Apples, 1920, 22; Odorous Constituents of Peaches, 1921; Methyl Anthranilate in Grape Juice, 1921; The Odorous Constituents of the Cotton Plant, 1925; The Nonvolatile Constituents of the Cotton Plant, 1926. Home: Hyattsville, Md. Died Aug. 1938.

CHESSIN, ALEXANDER, mathematician, patent atty.; b. St. Petersburg (Leningrad), Russia, Dec. 14, 1866; A.M., Imperial Inst. History and Philosophy, St. Petersburg, 1889; C.E., Poly. Sch., Zurich, Switzerland, 1892; unmarried. Came to U.S., 1893. Lecturer on advanced mathematics, Harvard, 1894; lecturer on celestial mechanics, 1894-95, asso. prof. pure and applied mathematics, 1895-99. Johns Hopkins; prof. mathematics, Washington U., St. Louis, Mo., 1901-09; patent atty., YN.Y.C., since 1915. Fellow A.A.A.S. Mem. Greek Orthodox Ch. Writer of 36 papers on mathematics, astronomy and mechanics. Home: 87 Gramatan Drive, Bryn Mawr, Park, Yonkers, N.Y. Office: 7 E. 42nd St., New York, N.Y.

CHESTER, ALBERT HUNTINGTON, prof. chemistry and mineralogy, Rutgers Coll., 1892—; b. Saratoga Springs, N.Y., Nov. 22, 1843; s. Albert Tracy and Elizabeth (Stanley) C.; grad. (M.E.) Columbia Sch. of Mines, 1868; Ph.D. in course, 1878 (Sc.D., Hamilton, 1892); m. Alethea Sandford Rudd, 1869 (died 1891); m. 2d, Georgiana Waldron Jenks, 1898. Had large practice as mining engr.; was, 1870-92, prof. chemistry, Hamilton Coll., N.Y. Author: Dictionary of the Names of Minerals, 1886-97; Catalogue of Minerals with Their Chemical Compositions and Synonyms, 1896. Home: New Brunswick, N.J. Died 1903.

CHESTER, FREDERICK DIXON, bacteriologist; b. San Domingo, Hayti, Oct. 8, 1861; s. Edwin Smith and Elizabeth (Walthall) C.; B.S., Cornell, 1882, M.S., 1885; m. Emma L. Sherwood, June 1883. Prof. geology and botany Del. Coll., 1992-89; mycologist and bacteriologist, Del. Agrl. Expt. Sta., and bacteriologist, in charge of the State bacteriol. and pathol. lab., 1899-1906; in business since 1906. Fellow A.A.A.S.; mem. Am. Geol. Soc., Soc. for the Promotion of Agrl. Science, Am. Bacteriol. Soc. Author: Manual of Determinative Bacteriology, 1901. Also monographs on the geology of Del. and Eastern Md., and papers and reports on mycology and bacteriology. Address: Chester Springs, Pa. Died Jan. 1, 1943.

CHESTER, JOHN NEEDELS, civil and mech. engr.; b. Columbus, O., Sept. 24, 1864; s. Hubert and Melvina S. (Needels) C.; B.S., U. of Ill., 1891, M.S. and C.E., 1909, M.E., 1911. Began as field supt. Nat. Water Supply Co., 1891; constrn. engr. Am. Debenture Co., Chicago and New York, 1892-94; sales engr. Henry R. Worthington Co., New York, 1894-99; chief engr. Am. Water Works Electric Co., Pittsburgh, Pa., 1899-1906; gen. mgr. Epping-Carpenter Pump Co., Pittsburgh, 1906-11; founder, 1911, J. N. Chester, Engrs., head 1911-41, retired; pres. Edgeworth and Fayette City water cos., Jamestown Water Co. Mem. bd. dirs. U. of Ill. Foundation. Mem. Am. Soc. C.E. (former v.p. and dir.), Am. Soc. Mech. Engrs., Engrs. Soc. Western Pa. (pres. 1929), Am. Water Works Assn., American Pub. Health Assn. Methodist. Club: Duquesne. Inventor of apparatus for water filtration. Contbr. to tech. publs. Collector of rare books and manuscripts. Visited every continent, every state of the U.S., every province of Canada, and practically every European country many times. Home: 4200 Center Av., Pittsburgh PA*

CHESTER, K(ENNETH) STARR, scientist, biologist; b. Turner's Falls, Mass., July 21, 1906; s. John Daboll Webster and Alice Josephine (Starr) C.; S.B., Boston Univ., 1928, S.M., 1929; S.M., Harvard, 1930, Ph.D., 1931; Harvard Sheldon fellow Switzerland, 1931-32; children—Desire Packer (now Mrs. Greenidge), Lois Faxon (now Mrs. Sousa). Research fellow Rockefeller Inst. Med. Research. Princeton, 1932-37; prof. and head dept. botany and plant pathology, Okla. A. and M. Coll., 1937-48, dir. coll. research found., 1944-48; supervisor Battelle Meml. Inst., Columbus, O., 1948-54, cons., 1954-55; tech. adviser Alton Box Board Co. (Ill.), 1955-63; prof. biology Ohio Northern Univ., Ada, 1964-69; v.p. and chmn. research com., council for Agrl. and Chemurgic Research; chmn. Internat. Commn. on Plant Diseases Losses, in coop, with UNESCO. Fellow A.A.A.S.; mem. Am. Phytopath. Soc., Ohio Forestry Assn. (pres. 1955; hon. v.p.); adviser Pres. Bipartisan Commn. and Indsl. Use Agrl. Products, 1956. Mem. American Pulpwood Association, Phi Beta Kappa, Sigma Xi, Pi Gamma Mu. Author: Nature and Prevention of Plant Diseases, 1942; The Cereal Rusts, 1946; Selected Writings of N.J. Vavilov (Russian trans.), 1951; Plant Disease Losses: Their Appraisal and Interpretation, 1950; Papermaking Raw Materials. Contbr. numerous scientific articles in professional and popular pub's. Home: Ada OH Died Feb. 26, 1969.

CHESTER, WAYLAND MORGAN, zoologist; b. Noank, Conn., Mar. 10, 1870; s. Charles I. and Harriet (Morgan) C.; A.B., Colgate, 1894, A.M., 1896; student Harvard U., 1909-10; Sc.D., Hillsdale (Mich.) Coll., 1926; m. Laura Davis, Aug. 30, 1897; children—Morgan Elliott, Harry Wilbur, Margaret Ashbey, Albert Brigham. Asst. in geology and natural history, 1894-96, instr. biology, Colgate U., 1896-1900, prof., since 1900. Republican. Baptist. Fellow A.A.A.S.; mem. Am. Soc. Zoologists, Am. Micros. Soc., Am. Assn. Univ. Profs., Phi Beta Kappa, Beta Theta Pi. Contbr. papers on Coelenterata. Home: Hamilton, N.Y. Died Feb. 7, 1945.

CHICKERING, JONAS, piano mfr.; b. Mason Village, N.H., Apr. 5, 1797; s. Abner and Eunice (Dakin) C.; m. Elizabeth Sumner Harraden, Nov. 30, 1823; 4 children. Mem. Handel and Haydn Soc., 1818, trustee, pres., 1843-50; with partner (James Stewart) began piano mfg. bus. Stewart & Chickering, 1823; founded, developed one of earliest and largest Am. piano mfg. houses, 1830; introduced many improvements; casted iron frame able to sustain great tension needed in good quality piano, 1837; pres. Mass. Charitable Mechanics Assn.; know as father of Am. piano-making. Died Boston, Dec. 8, 1853.

CHILCOTT, ELLERY CHANNING, agriculturist; b. E. Hamburgh, N.Y., Apr. 8, 1859; s. Benjamin Franklin and Philenda (Freeman) C.; ed. common schs. and Friends' Inst. there; (M.S., S.C. Agrl. Coll., 1898); M. Alice Bushley, Jan. 2, 1884; children—Ellery Franklin, Ralph Waldo, Amos Huerd, Minnie (Mrs. Edwin A. Reeves). U.S. deputy surveyor, 1882-92; owned and managed stock ranch, Campbell County, S.D., 1883-92; mem. S.D. Senate, 1892; prof. agr., 1892-97, prof. geology and agronomy and vice dir., 1897-1905, S.D. Agrl. Coll.; agriculturist U.S. Expt. Sta., S.D., 1893-1905; in charge of dry land agrl. investigations, Bur. of Plant Industry, Dept. Agr., 1905—; organizer of Central Great Plains Field Station, near Cheyenne, Wyo., for U.S. Dept. Agr., 1928-29. Mem. S.D. State Bd. Agr., 1928-29. Mem. S.D. State Bd. Agr., 1901-02; collaborator U.S. Dept. Agr. Cereal Investigations, 1902. During summer and fall of 1918 was head of an agrl. mission sent to France and Algeria by the U.S. Dept. of Agr. at the request of the French High Commn. Author of numerous bulls. and reports, U.S. Dept. Agr. Home: Vienna, Va. Died Nov. 14, 1930.

CHILD, CHARLES MANNING, biologist; b. Ypsilanti, Mich., Feb. 2, 1869; s. Charles Chauncey and Mary Eilzabeth (Manning) C.; Ph.B., Wesleyan U., Conn., 1890; M.S., 1892; hon. D.Sc., 1928; Ph.D., U. Leipzig, Germany 1894; m. Lydia Van Meter Aug. 15, 899; 1 daug. Jeannette Manning. Grad. asst. Wesleyan U., 1890-92; Naples Zoöl. Sta., 1894 and 1902; asst in Zoölogy U. Chgo., 1895-96, successively asso. instr., asst. prof., asso. and prof., 1916-34 prof. emeritus, 1934—; vis. prof. Duke U., Sendi, Japan, 1930-31; now lecture in biology Stanford. Fellow A.A.A.S., mem. Acad. Scis., Am. Zoölogists, Am. Naturalists, Am. Physiol. Soc. , Am. Assn. Anatomists, Linneau Soc. London (fgn. mem.), Société Royale Zoologique de Belgique (hon.), Phi Beta Kappa. Author: Die Physiologische Isolation Von Teilen des Organismus (Leipzig), 1911; Senescence and Rejuvenescence, 1915; Individuality in Organisms, 1915; The Origin and Developement of the Nervous System from a Physiological Viewpoint,1921; Physiological Foundations of Behavior, 1924; Patterns and Problems of Development, 1941; also numerous articles giving results of researches in Am. and European mags. Home: 571 Kingsley Av., Palo Alto, Cal. Died Dec. 19, 1954 buried Greenmount Cemetery, Balt.

CHILD, CLEMENT DEXTER, physicist; b. Madison, O., May 15, 1868; s. Increase and Artemisia (Lincoln) C.; grad. Normal Sch., Fredonia, N.Y., 1886; A.B., U. of Rochester, 1890; Ph.D., Cornell U., 1897; studied Berlin and Cambridge, Eng., 1897-98; m. H. Aerion Stiles, June 26, 1902; children—Aileen Mary (adopted), James Alfred. Instr. in physics, Cornell U., 1893-97; prof. physics, Colgate U., 1898—. Republican. Baptist. Author: Electric Arcs, 1913. Home: Hamilton, N.Y. Died July 15, 1933.

CHILDE, JOHN, civil engr.; b. West Boylston, Mass., Aug. 30, 1802; s. Zachraiah and Lydia (Bigelow) C.; grad. U.S. Mil. Acad., 1827; m. Laura Dwight, 1832, at least 1 dau.; m. 2d, Ellen Healy, 1856. Served with Corps Engr., U.S. Army 1827-35, resigned, 1835; cons. civil engr. to railroads in survey and location work, from 1835; became well-known in profession after locating route for Albany and W. Stockbridge R.R. through Green Mountains, 1844; became chief engr. Mobile R.R. Co., 1848, supervised constrn. of 500 miles of track through 4 states, obtained land grant from Congress, 1849, active in promotion of stock of co. until 1856; head of engring. corps which made survey regarding contrn. of new harbor facilities for Bd. Harbor Commrs., Montreal, Can., 1857. Died Springfield, Mass., Feb. 2, 1858; buried Springfield.

CHILDS, ARTHUR EDWARD, elec. engr., ins. pres.; b. Montreal, Can., Sept. 16, 1869; s. George and Christian C.; B.Sc., McGill U., 1888, M.S., 1892; asso., 1891, and fellow Central Tech. Coll., London, Eng., 1893; m. Alice Grant Moen, Feb. 1, 1894; children—Philip Moen, Alice Muriel. Began as wireman, with Canadian Gen. Electric Co. and became asst. to Dr. Coleman Sellers in development of Niagara Falls power plant; dist. engr. Westinghouse Elec. & Mfg. Co., Phila., 1893-95, and later N.E. mgr. Electric Storage Battery Co., Boston; organized, 1896, the Light, Heat & Power Corp. to acquire lighting, heating and power plants in the Eastern states, and became actively connected with a large number of gas, electric light and power cos.; one of organizers, 1902, and pres. Columbian Nat. Life Ins. Co.; pres. Am. Investment Securities Co., Hotel Somerset Co., Mass. Lighting Cos., Mass. Utilities Investment Co. (chmn. bd.). Republican. Conglist. Home: Boston, Mass. Died Nov. 9, 1933.

CHILDS, FRANK AIKEN, architect, engr.; b. Evanston, Ill., Jan. 12, 1875; s. Shubael Davis and Mary Anne (Wright) D.; student Armour Inst. Tech., 1894-96, Atelier Umbdenstock, Paris, 1905-07. Designer L.D. Dutton, San Francisco, 1910, Holabird & Roche, Chgo., 1910-12; with Childs & Smith, Inc. Chgo., specializing ednl. and comml. work, univs., coll., elementary and high schs., office bldgs., 1912—, now chmn. works include pub. schs. Oak Park, Evanston, Jackson, Mich., LaSalle, Ill., Wisconsin Rapids, Wis., Davenport, Ia., Park Ridge, Ill., Crystal Lake, Ill., Arlington Heights, Ill. Regional adviser on sch. bldgs. U.S. Office Edn., 1928. Fellow A.I.A.; mem. Ill. Soc. Architects, Art Inst. Chgo. (life). Republican. Home: 1745 Orrington Av., Evanston, Ill. Office: 20 N. Wacker Dr., Chgo. 6. Died Jan. 25, 1965.

CHILDS, ROSS RENFROE, agronomist; b. Wayside, Ga., Jan. 22, 1888; s. William Simpson and Nancy Antonette (Walker) C.; B.S.A., U. of Ga., 1912, M.S.A., 1913; m. Claudia Lamb, Nov. 29, 1923. Instr. agronomy, Ga. State Coll. Agr., 1913-14; scientific asst., Office of Creal Investigations, U.S. Dept. Agr., 1914-18; prof. agronomy, in charge cotton industry, U. og Ga. State Coll. Agr., May 1919-July 1934, exec. sec. cotton adjustment, under Agrl. Adjustment Adminstrn., 1934-39; extension agronomist, Ga. Agr. Extension Service, since 1939. Served as 2d lt. Air Service, U.A. Army, 1918-19. Fellow A.A.A.S.; mem. Am. Soc. Agronomy, Am. Genetic Assn., Ga. Acad. Science, Phi Kappa Phi. Democrat. Baptist. Mason (32 deg., shriner). Home: 175 University Drive, Athens, Ga. Died Feb. 20, 1942.

CHILDS, SAMUEL BERESFORD, roentgenologist; b. East Hartford, Conn., Nov. 5, 1861; s. Seth Lee and Juliet (Wood) C.; grad. high sch., Hartford, Conn., 1879; A.B., Yale, 1883; M.D., Univ. City New York, 1887; m. Henrietta Willett, of West Hebron, N.Y., 1890 (died 1906); 1 son, John Wood; m. 2d, Anne Starling, of Henderson, Ky., Sept. 2, 1908 (died Apr. 19, 1935); 1 son, Samuel Beresford; m. 3d, Nan Bullions Palmer, of Pittsburgh, Sept. 5, 1936. Asst. in out-patient dept., Chambers St. Hosp., N.Y. City, 1887; interne Hartford Hosp., 1887-88; in general practice at Hartford, 1888-95; practiced at Denver, since 1898, specialist in Roentgenology since 1902; prof. anatomy, Denver and Gross Med. Coll., 1900-11; asso. prof. Roentgenology, Med. Sch. U. of Colo., 1911-36, emeritus since 1936; president staff, St. Luke's Hospital, 1923-24; Roentgenologist, St. Joseph's Hospital; cons. Roentgenologist, Colo. Gen. Hosp., Denver Gen. Hosp., St. Luke's Hosp., Nat. Jewish Hosp. Fellow Am. Coll. Radiology, Pres. 1925; mem. A.M.A., Radiological Soc. N.A., Am. Roentgen. Ray Soc., Colo. State Med. Soc. (pres. 1928-29), Denver Co. Med. Soc. (pres. 1917), Colo. Yale Assn. (pres. 1911), Am. Med. Golf Assn., (Pres. 1927). Episcopalian. Club: Denver Country. Home: 930 Pearl St. Office Metropolitan Bldg., Denver, Colo.

CHILTON, CECIL HAMILTON, engineer, economist; b. N.Y.C., Sept. 25, 1918; s. Claudius Lysias and Clara Caroline (Weidmann) C.; B.S., Auburn U., 1939; M.S., Carnegie-Mellon U., 1940; m. Florence Edna Zitzman, Oct. 1, 1941; children—Edward Morgan, Margaret Arnold (Mrs. W. Owen BeMent). Chem. engr. Mobil Oil Corp., 1940-41, E.I. duPont de Nemours & Company, 1941-50; editor McGraw-Hill, Inc., 1950-66, editor-in-chief Chem. Engring., 1959-66; tech. economist Battelle Meml. Inst., Columbus, 1966-72. Recipient Am. Bus. Press editorial achievement award, 1966. Mem. Am. Inst. Chem. Engrs. (dir. 1971-72), Am. Assn. Cost Engrs. (award of merit, pres. 1962-63), Am. Society for Engring. Edn. Mem. Ch. of Nazarene. Editor: Cost Engineering in the Process Industries, 1960; co-editor: Chemical Engineers' Handbook, 1963, 5th edit., 1972. Home: Columbus OH Died Nov. 13, 1972; buried Union Cemetery, Columbus OH

CHILTON, THOMAS HAMILTON, chem. engr.; b. Greensboro, Ala., Aug. 14, 1899; s. Claudius Lysias and Mabel Cecilia (Pierce) C.; student Starke's U. Sch., Montgomery, Ala., 1910-13, Lanier High Sch., Montgomery, Ala., 1914-15, U. Ala., 1915-16, Columbia U., 1917-22. Chem. Engr., 1922; D.Sc. (hon.) U. Del., 1943; m. Cherridah McLemore, June 29, 1926 (dec. Mar. 1969); children—Thomas McLemore, Daniel Tanner; m. 2d, Elizabeth Crafs Rinehart, Jan. 2, 1971. Research chemist F.J. Carman, N.Y.C., 1922-25; chemist; chem. dept. Exptl. Sta., E.I. du Pont de Nemours & Co., Wilmington, Del., 1925-30, group leader, chem. engring. research, 1930-35, asst. div. head, tech. div., engring. dept., 1935-38, dir. tech. div., 1938-45, mgr. devel. engring. div., 1945-46, tech. dir. devel. engring. div., 1946-58, tech. adviser, 1958-59; Regent's prof. U. Cal. at Berkeley, 1959-60; Fulbright lectr. Japan, 1960-61; vis. prof. U. New S. Wales, Australia, 1961, U. Del., 1963-64, Cal. Inst. Tech., 1965, U. Va., 1965-66, Biria Inst. Tech., Pilani, Rajasthan, India, 1967, U. Wash. at Seattle, 1968, U. Ala., spring 1969, U. Mass., Amherst, fall 1969, U. P.R., spring 1970, U. Natal, Durban, South Africa, fall 1970; Fulbright lectr. France, 1961-62; Neely vis. prof. Ga. Inst. Tech., 1962-63. Recipient Presdl. Certificate of Merit, 1948; Chandler medal Columbia, 1939, Univ. medal, 1950; Egleston medal Columbia Engring. Sch. Alumni Assn., 1943; Founders award Am. Inst. C.E.,

1958. Mem. adv. bd. for books in chem. engring. John Wiley & Sons, 1939-59. Mem. Am. Inst. Chem. Engrs. (pres. 1951), Am. Chem. Soc. (bd. editors Monographs 1938-57), Am. Soc. Engring. Edn., A.A.A.S., Sons of Am. Revolution, Automobile License Plate Collectors Assn., Nat. Acad. Engring., Sigma Xi, Tau Beta Pi, Phi Lambda Upsilon, Omega Chi Epsilon. Presbyn. (elder 1944-50). Clubs: University and Whist (Wilmington, Delaware); Chemists (N.Y.C.). Author: Strong Water, 1968. Section editor for Indsl. Chemistry, Chem. Abstracts, 1945-51. Contbr. profl. publs. Address: Wilmington DE Died Sept. 15, 1972.

CHINN, ARMSTRONG, railroad official; b. Dallas, Tex., Sept. 26, 1894; s. William Yates and Kate (Armstrong) C.; B.S. and C.E., Va. Poly. Inst., 1916; m. Edith E. Shumadine, Apr. 6, 1920; children—Armstrong, Edith Elizabeth wife of Dr. Scott Sears. Instrumentman, C., B. and Q. R.R., 1916-17 and 1919-22, asst. engr., 1923, div. engr. and roadmaster, 1923-25, asst. roadmaster, 1925-26, asst. dist. engr., maintenance of way, 1926-27, dist. engr., maintenance of way, and supervisor work equipment, 1927-29; chief engr., The Alton Railroad, 1929-43, gen. mgr., 1943-45, chief exec. officer 1945-46; pres. Terminal R.R. Assn. of St. Louis since 1946. Served as 2d lieutenant F.A., A.E.F., France, 1918-19. Mem. Am. Ry. Engring. Assn., (past pres.), Roadmasters and Maintenance of Way Assn. of Am., Am. Ry. Bridge and Bldg. Assn. Clubs: Western Railway; Maintenance of Way, Union League (Chgo.); Missouri Athletic, Bellerive Country, Noonday (St. Louis). Home: 4399 McPherson Av., St. Louis 8. Office: Union Sta., St. Louis 3. Died Aug. 27, 1958; buried Norfolk, Va.

CHISHOLM, WILLIAM, SR., inventor, mfr.; b. Scotland, Aug. 12, 1825; was a sailor, then, 1847-52, builder at Montreal; removed, 1852, to Cleveland, O.; became mgr. Cleveland Rolling Mills, then mfr. of spikes, bolts, etc.; discovered practical method for manufacture of screws from Bessemer steel; organized Union Steel Co.; invented new method for mfg. steel shovels and and spades; also invented new method of steam hoisting and pumping engines, conveyors for coal and ore, etc. Home: Cleveland, O. Died 1908.

CHISOLM, JOHN JULIAN, surgeon, oculist; b. Charleston, S.C., Apr. 16, 1830; s. Robert Trail and Harriet Chisolm; M.D., Med. Coll. S.C., 1850; m. Mary Edings Chisolm, Feb. 3, 1852; m. 2d, Elizabeth Steel, Jan. 14, 1854. Practiced medicine, Charleston, 1852-61; conducted free hosp. for slaves, also 1 of 1st Am. summer schs. of medicine, 1853-58; prof. surgery Med. Coll. of S.S., 1858-61, dean, 1865-69; 1st commd. med. officer in Confederated Army, 1861; served as chief surgeon mil. hosp., Richmond, Va., later dir. plant for manufacture of medicines, Charleston; prof. eye and ear surgery U. Md., 1869, dean, 1869-95, prof. emeritus, 1895-1903; founder Balt. Eye and Ear Inst., 1870; founder Presbyn. Eye and Ear Chaity Hosp., Balt., 1877, chief surgeon, 1877-98; limited his practice to opthamology, after 1873; 1 of 1st to use cocain in eye surgery and to used chloroform anesthesia. Died Petersburg, Va., Nov. 2, 1903; buried Greenmount Cemetery, Balt.

CHITTENDEN, FRANK HURLBUT, entomologist; b. Cleveland, O., Nov. 3, 1858; s. S. King and Harriet M. C.; ed. Cleveland, O., and Cornell U., licentiate, 1881 (hon. Sc.D., Western U. of Pa., 1904); unmarried. Asst. entomologist, U.S. Dept. Agr., Apr. 25, 1891—; entomologist, truck crop insect investigations, 1917—. Author: Insects Injurious to Vegetables; also bulls. and other papers on econ. and tech. entomology published by the U.S. Dept. Agr. Home: Washington, D.C. Died Sept. 15, 1929.

CHITTENDEN, RUSSELL HENRY, univ. prof. and dir.; b. New Haven, Conn., Feb. 18, 1856; s. Horace Horatio and Emily Eliza (Doane) C.; Ph.B., Sheffield Scientific Sch. (Yale) 1875, Ph.D., 1880; student Heidelberg U., 1878-79; LL.D., U. of Toronto, 1903, U. of Birmingham, 1911, Wash. U., 1915, Yale, 1922; Sc.D., U. of Pa., 1904; m. Gertrude Louise Baldwin, June 20, 1877; children—Edith Russell, Alfred Knight (dec.) Lilla Millard (Mrs. Harry Gray Barbour). Asst. 1974-77, inst., 1877-78, 1879-82, prof. physiol. chemistry, 1882-1922 (emeritus), dir., Sheffield Scientific Sch., 1898-1922, all of Yale; lecturer physiol. chemistry, Columbia, 1898-1903. Mem. referee bd. of consulting scientific experts to Sec. of Agr. Hon. M.D., Conn. State Med. Society, 1934. Mem. Nat. Acad. Sciences, Am. Philos. Soc., Societe des Sciences Medicales et Naturelles de Bruxelles; corr. mem. Societe de Biologie, Paris; pres. Am. Soc. of Naturalists, 1893, Am. Physiol. Soc., 1895-1904, Am. Soc. Biol. Chemists, 1907. Fellow Am. Acad. Arts and Sciences; hon. fellow N.Y. Acad. of Medicine, 1930. Mem. advisory com. on food utilization; mem. exec. com. Nat. Research Council, 1917; U.S. rep. on Inter-Allied Scientific Food Commn. at London, Paris, and Rome, 1918. Clubs: Graduate (New Haven); Yale (New York). Editor: Studies in Physiological Chemistry, 4 vols., 1884, 1901. Author: Digestive Proteolysis, 1895; Physiological Economy in Nutrition, 1905; Nutrition of Man, 1907; History of the Sheffield Scientific School (2 vols.), 1928; Development of Physiological Chemistry in the United States, 1930; also many papers on physiol. subjects in Am. and foreign jours. Home: 83 Trumbull St., New Haven, Conn. Died Dec. 26, 1943.

CHOATE, JOSEPH KITTREDGE, managing engr.; b. Salem, Mass., Aug. 22, 1853; s. George C. S. (M.D.) and Susan (Kittredge) C.; B.S. in C.E., U. of Colo., 1899. With engr. corps, Central Park, N.Y. City, 1873-74; asst. engr. Dept. Pub. Works, N.Y. City, 1874-77; and chief engr. constrn., 1877-79; supervisor and asst. engr. Pa. Railway, 1879; prin. asst. engr. construction, Erie R.R., 1879-84; supt. U.P. Ry., 1884-96; consulting practice, 1896-1913; v.p. J. G. White Management Corp., 1913—; pres. Morris County Traction Co.; v.p. Manila Electric Corp., Augusta-Aiken Ry. & Electric Co., Staten Island Edison Corp., Helena Light & Ry. Co., Richmond Light & R.R. Co. Home: New York, N.Y. Died June 19, 1928.

CHOUTEAU, PIERRE, engr.; b. St. Louis, July 30, 1849; s. Charles P. and Julia Augusta (Gratiot) C.; ed. tech. schs., St. Louis and Royal School of Arts, Mines and Manufacturers, Liege, Belgium; m. Lucille M. Chauvin, Nov. 27, 1882. Has devoted leisure to invention of various devices and appliances now in gen. use; has also done much in collection and preservation of ancient documents, papers and books illustrating early conditions and history of St. Louis; originated project for commemoration of centennial anniversary of purchase of La. Ty., being chmn. of several preliminary coms., which originated the La. Purchase Expn., of which he served as 8th v.p. Home: St. Louis, Mo. Died 1910.

CHRISMAN, OSCAR, paidologist; b. Gosport, Ind., Nov. 16, 1855; s. Benjamin and Eliza (Bastian) C.; grad. Ind. State Normal Sch., 1887; A.B., Ind. U., 1888, A.M., 1893; fellow in Clark U., 1892-94; student in Jena and Berlin, 1894-96; Ph.D., U. of Jena, 1896; m. Drusilla Likenbill, Oct. 6, 1883; children—Chrisman, Oscie Drusilla (Mrs. R. D. Gladding, dec.). Teacher pub. schs., 1876-83, prin., 1883-85; prin. Longfellow Sch., Houston, Tex., 1888-89; supt. schs., Gonzales, Tex., 1889-92; prof. Kan. State Normal Sch., 1896-1901; prof. of paidology, 1902-26, also prof. psychology, 1904-22, Ohio Univ. Republican. Methodist. Formulated idea of the science of the child, 1893, originated the term paidology, and has since made this his life's work. Author: The Historical Child, 1920. Home: Athens, Ohio. Died Feb. 2, 1929.

CHRISTENSEN, J(ONAS) J(ERGEN), plant pathologist; b. Hutchinson, Minn., Aug. 22, 1892; s. Chris C. and Christina (Borg) C.; B.S., U. of Minn., 1921, M.S., 1922, Ph.D., 1925; Guggenheim Memorial fellowship for study in Germany and other countries, 1929-30; m. Hildur Minerva Lundeen, Aug. 16, 1922; children—Philip, Donn, Robert. Rural sch. teacher, Mercer, N.D.,1915-16; instr. plant pathology University of Minnesota, 1920-25, asst. prof., 1925-31, asso. prof., 1931-38, prof., 1938-61, acting chief 1948-53, head dept., 1953-61, now professor emeritus; also fed. collaborator in charge Cooperative Rust Lab.; agent U.S. Dept. Agr., 1922-29 and 1930-37; vis. expert N.R.S., G.H.Q., S.C.A.P., Jan., 1950; cons. Chem. Corps, A.U.S., since 1947. Served as sergt., M.C., U.S. Army, 1917-19; Received Caleb Dorr Prize, 1920; named hon. Premier Seed Grower, 1948; Elvin Charles Stakman award, 1959. Fellow A.A.A.S.; mem. Am. (pres. 1944, pres. N. Central div. 1957), Japanese phytopath. socs., Am. Assn. U. Profs., Mycol. Society of America, Botanical Society of Am. Indian Phytopath. Soc. Flax Institute of U.S., Minn. Agricultural Coll. Alumni Assn. (sec.-treas. 1940-41), Minn. Acad. Sci., Biol. Club, Sigma Xi (vice president Minnesota chapter, 1944, president 1949), Alpha Zeta, Gamma Sigma Delta (v.p. Minn. 1944), Gamma Alpha. Author numerous chpts. and articles on pathology. Home: 2116 Como Av., St. Paul 55108. Died June 20, 1964.

CHRISTENSEN, NIELS ANTON, engr.; b. Toerring, Denmark, Aug. 16, 1865; s. Christian and Anne Marie (Nielsen) Jensen; apprentice in shipbuilding and marine engring.; grad. Tech. Inst. Copenhagen; m. Mathielde Thomesen, Aug. 19, 1894; 1 dau., Esther Marie (Mrs. Charles Jacob Young). Came to U.S. 1891, naturalized citizen. Successively in charge machinery for waterworks of Calcutta, India, then charge refining nitrate soda, Chile; asso. with Fraser-Chalmers, machinery mfrs., 1892-93; asst. to supt., chief engr. Edward P. Allis Co., Milw., 1894-96; founded Chirstensen Engring. Co., for mfr. air brakes on cable cars, 1896, with company until 1903. Active during World War 1, World War 2 developing special hydraulic and compressed air equipment for aircraft. Royal Danish vice-consul, Ohio, 1928—. Decorated Denmark Victory Medal, King Christian X. Republican. Episcopalian. . Mason (32 deg.). Club: Mayfield Country (Cleve.). Owns over 200 patents. Address: 1719 Sheridan Rd., S. Eucild, O. Died Oct. 1952; buried Van Hornesville, N.Y.

CHRISTIAN, EUGENE, author, dietitian; b. nr. McMinnville, Tenn., May 30, 1860; s. William Thornton and Harriet (Freeman) C.; Irving Coll., Warren Co., 1 yr.; m. Mollie Griswold, Apr. 30, 1889; children—Eugenia, Lorita. Traveled for mercantile house until 1894; in mercantile bus., Atlanta, Ga., 1894-97; mgr. Binghamton, N.Y., 1897-1900; settled in N.Y. City, 1900; began teaching and practicing as dietitian; was prosecuted by Med. Soc. of N.Y. City, and by decision of Supreme Court of New York established right of food scientist to diagnose and prescribe diet as a remedy for disease; founded Am. Vitamin Food Co., Westifeld, Mass. Pres. Chrisitan Realty Co., New York, Christian-Boice Corp. and Hotel Co., St. Petersburg Fla.) Christian Foundation; chmn. bd. Canada Health Foods, Ltd., Toronto, Can. Author: Ency. of Diet (5 vols.), 1913; How to Live 100 Years, 1914; 24 Lessons in Scientific Eating, 1915; Eat and Be Well, Encyclopedia of Cookery (4 vols.), 1919. Home: Forest Hills, L.I., N.Y. Died Mar 10, 1930.

CHRISTIAN, HENRY ASBURY, physician (ret.); b. Lynchburg Va., Feb. 17, 1876; lineal descendant of Thomas Chrisitan, who patented land in Virginia, Jan. 15, 1657; s. Camillus and Mary Elizabeth (Davis) C.; A.B., A. M., Randolph-Macon Coll., 1895, LL.D., 1923; M.D., Johns Hopkins, 1900; A.M., Harvard 1903; hon. Sc.D., Jefferson Med. Coll., 1928, U. of Mich., 1938; LL.D., Western Reserve U., 1931, U. of Western Ontario, 1938; m. Eilzabeth Sears Seabury (Mayflower desc.), June 30. 1921. Asst. pathologist, 1900-02; Asst. visting pathologist, 1902-05, Boston City Hosp. asst. pathologist children's Hosp.,1903-07; instr. pathology, Harvard, 1903-05, theory and practice of Physic, 1905-07; asst. prof., 1907-08, dean Faculty of Medicine and Med. Sch., 1907-12, Hersey prof., 1908-39, emeritus since 1939, recalled to active teaching, 1942-46; clin. prof. medicine, Tufts Coll. Med. Sch., 1943-46; dean Faculty of Medicine and Medical School Boston, Mass., 1908-12; asst. visting physician Long Island Hosp., 1905; phys.-in-chief Carney Hosp., 1907-12, and to Peter Bent Brigham Hops., 1910-39, emeritus s since 1939; visting physician, Beth Israel Hospital, Boston, 1942-46. Major Med. Reserve Corps, U.S. Army, 1918-21; commd. but not called to service in World War 1. Resident chmn. division medical scis., Nat. Research Council, Oct. 1, 1919-Oct. 1, 1920. Awarded D.S.M. by A.M.A., 1947. Fellow Am. Acad. Arts and Scis., Am. Coll. Phys.; hon. fellow Royal Coll. Phys.; (Can.); mem. Assn. Am. Phys. (pres. 1935), Am. Assn. Pathologists and Bacteriologists, A. M.A., Am. Soc. for Clin. Investigation (pres. 1919),.A.A.A.S., Boston Med. Library Assn., Mass. Med. Soc., Am. Soc. Exptl. Pathology, Am. Assn. Univ. Profs., Interstate Post Grad. Med. Assn. of North America (pres. 1931), Sigma Chi, Phi Beta Kappa (asso.), Alpha Omega Alpha, Sigma Xi fraternities; corresponding mem. Medico-Chirugical Society (Edinburgh), Wien Gesellsch. f. inner. Med. und Kinderheilkunde, Sociedad de Medecina Interna de Buenos Aries. Clubs: Thursday Evening, Examiner, Somerset, Harvard St. Botolph (Boston); Century (N.Y. City): Country (Brookline). Author: Diagnosis and Treatment of Heart Disease; Principles and Practice of Medicine (4 editions); Bright's Disease; Purpuras; Non-Vascular Heart Disease; also papers on Pathological and Clinical med. subject. Editor (for Oxford University Press) Oxford Medicine and Oxford Monographs. Home: Longwood Towers, 20 Chapel St., Brookline 46, Mass. Died Aug. 24, 1951; buried Mt. Auburn Cemetery, Cambridge, Mass.

CHRISTIE, ALEXANDER GRAHAM, educator; b. Manchester, Ont., Can., Nov. 19, 1880; s. Peter and Mary Honor (Graham) C.; M.E., Sch. Practical Sci., U. Toronto, 1913; hon. D.E., Stevens Inst., 1939, Lehigh, 1940; LL.D., Johns Hopkins; m. Flora Brown, June 28, 1919; children—Peter Graham, Catherine Graham. Came to U.S., 1901, naturalized, 1918. With Westinghouse Machine Co., East Pittsburgh, Pa., 1901-04; instr. mech. engring. Cornell U., 1904-05; with steam turbine dept. Allis-Chalmers Co., 1905-07; mech. engr. Western Can. Cement & Coal Co., 1907-09; asst. and asso. prof. steam and gas engring. U. Wis., 1909-14; asso. prof. Johns Hopkins, 1914-20, prof. mech. engring., 1920-48, prof. emeritus, 1948; dir. div. engring. McCoy Coll., Johns Hopkins since 1917; cons. practice in Am., Gt. Britain, chmn. Md. State Bd. Registration for Profl. Engrs. and Land Surveyors, 1939-49. Lomme award for Achievement in Engring. Edn., 1928. Mem. Internat. Electrotech. Commn.; chmn. Power Test Codes Com. Am. Soc. M.E.; hon. mem. Am. Soc. M.E. (pres. 1938-39); mem. (life) Inst. Mech. Engrs. (Gt. Britain), Engring. Inst. Can., Soc. for Promotion Engring. Edn., Newcomen Soc. (Eng.), Sigma Xi, Tau Beta Pi, Omicron Delta Kappa, Pi Tau Sigma. Clubs: Engineers (N.Y.); Engineers, Johns Hopkins (Balt.). Author of Steam Turbine Sec. Sterling's Marine Engineers Handbook, and Steam Turbine Sec. Kent's Mechanical Engineer's Handbook, also numerous sci. papers, articles. Home: 211 Tunbridge Road, Balt. 12, Md. Died Oct. 24, 1964; buried Pine Grove Cemetery, Port Perry, Ont.

CHRISTIE, ARTHUR CARLISLE, physician, radiologist; b. W. Sunbury, Butler County, Pa., Dec. 29, 1879; s. Milton Hughes and Harriet Josephine (Rhodes) C.; grad. high sch., Corry, Pa., 1898; M.D., Cleveland Coll. Physicians and Surgeons (medical department Ohio Wesleyan University), 1904; M.S., Ohio Wesleyan 1919; D.Sc., The American University, 1942; grad. Army Med. Sch., Washington. D.C., 1907; m. Maude Irene Hopkins, June 1, 1904; children—Mrs. Geneva Irene Morris Carlisle Van Dyke, Milton Arthur, Harriet Inez Beck. Practiced Clymer, N.Y., 1904-06; joined Med. Corps., U.S. Army, 1906; served in Philippines, 1907-10, Columbus (O.) Barracks, 1910-12; prof.

Operative surgery and Roentgenology, Army Med. Sch., Washington, D.C., 1912-16; resigned as capt.; in World War as maj., lt. col. and col. M.C.; gen. charge X-ray work for Army, 1917-Aug. 1918; apptd. sr. consultant in Roentgenology, A.E.F. in France, Sept. 1918; hon. discharged, Feb. 1919; col. M.R.C. Formerly Prof. of radiology George Washingtoh U. Med. Coll . Mem. firm Drs. Groover, Christie and Merritt, specializing in Roentgenology; formely prof. clinical radiology, Georgetown Univ. Med. School; counsulant U.S. Public Health Service. Mem. special advisory group Veterans Adminstration; cousulants in radiology Walter Reed General Hosp. pres. Fifth Internat. Congress of Radiology, Chicago, 1937; chmn. com. on Radiology, Natl. Research Council; hon. consulant U.S. Army Medical Library. Hon. fellow British Faculty of Radiologists, 1950. Mem. editorial bd. Am. Jour. Roentology and Radium Therapy. Fellow Am. Med. Assn., Am. Coll. of Physicians, International College Surgeons member Am. Coll. Radiology (pres.), Med. Society of D.C. (President). Republican. Methodist. Mason (32 deg.). Club: Army and Navy, Rotary. Author: Manual of X-ray Technique, 1913, 17; Roentgen Diagnosis and Therapy, 1924; Economic Problems of Medicine, 1935. Home: Crescent City Fla. Office: 1835 I St. N.W., Washington 6. Died June 22, 1956.

CHRISTIE, JAMES, mech. engr.; b. nr. Ottawa, Can., Aug. 28, 1840; s. Thomas A. and Elizabeth (Holmes) C.; ed. pub. schs., Ottawa; m. Miss M. J. Maxwell, 1866. Served U.S.A., 1863. Machinist's apprentice, Detroit and Phila.; bridge builder, 1872-76; mem. town council and mayor, Phillipsburg, N.J., 1874; chief mech. engr. Pencoyd Iron Works, 1876—, and Am. Bridge Co., 1899-1905. Awarded Norman medal, Am. Soc. C.E., 1884. Home: Philadelphia, Pa. Died 1912.

CHRISTIE, WILLIAM WALLACE, mech. engr.; b. Paterson, N.J., July 12, 1866; s. James C. and Louisa (Jones) C.; grad. high sch., Paterson, N.J., 1882, spl. student, Cornell, 1889-91; spl. musical edn. (organ); m. Carrie E. Ker, Mar. 14, 1895. In practice as mech. engr. from 1882. Republican. Author: Chimney Formulae and Tables, 1897; Chimney Design and Theory, 1899; Furnace Draft, 1901; Boiler Waters; Scale, Corrosion, Foaming, 1906; Furance Draft, Its Production and Mechanical Methods, 1905. Editor Mech. Section Foster's Electrical Pocket Book, 1909; Water: Its Purification and Use in the Industries, 1912. Home: Ridgewood, N.J. Died Apr. 13, 1925.

CHRISTY, SAMUEL BENEDICT, metallurgist; b. San Francisco, Calif., Aug. 8, 1853; s. James C.; Ph.B., U. of Calif., 1874; studied mining and metallurgy U. of Calif., 1874-79; (Sc.D., Columbia, 1902); m. Sarah Adele Field, Feb. 22, 1881. Grad. student and instr. analytical chemistry, 1874-79, instr. mining and metallurgy, 1879-85, prof., 1885—, U. of Calif. Life mem. Calif. Acad. Sciences (corr. sec., 1881-86). Patented, 1900, improved process for recovering gold and silver from dulute cyanide solutions. Home: Berkeley, Calif. Died Nov. 30, 1914.

CHRYSLER, MINTIN ASBURY, botanist; b. Berlin, Ont., Can., Aug. 25, 1871; s. Edgar and Sarah (Green) C.; B.A., U. of Toronto, 1894; certificate, Ont. Normal Coll., 1894-95, grad. student, 1902-03, fellow in botany, 1903-04; Ph.D., U. of Chicago, 1904; m. Clara Belle Van Duzen, of Grimsby, Ont., Sept. 15, 1910; 1 son, Sidney Van Duzen, Science master, Toronto Junction Collegiate Inst., 1895-1902; asst. in botany, Marine Biol. Lab., summer 1904; on bot. survey of Md., summers 1904-05; asst. in botany, 1904-05, instr., 1905-07, Harvard; asso. prof. botany, 1907-10, prof., 1910-11, prof. biology, 1911-23, U. of Me.; asso. prof. botany, Rutgers U., 1923—. Fellow A.A.A.S. mem. Bot. Soc. America, Torrey Bot. Club. Conglist. Mason. Joint Author: Plant Life of Maryland, 1910. Home: 208 Lawrence Av., New Brunswick NJ

CHRYSLER, WALTER PERCY, mfr. motor cars; b. Wamego, Kan., Apr. 2, 1875; s. Henry and Anna Maria (Breyman) C.; desc. of Tuenis Van Dolsen, who was first male child born in New Amsterdam (now Manhattan), New York; grad. of high sch., Ellis, Kansas; m. Della V. Forker, June 5, 1901 (died 1938); children—Thelma (Mrs. Byron C. Foy), Bernice (Mrs. E. W. Garbisch), Walter, Jack. From machinist's apprentice with r.r. to supt. motive power and machinery of C.G.W. Ry. at age of 33; apptd. asst. mgr. Pittsburgh works of Am. Locomotive Co., 1910, mgr. 1911; works mgr. Buick Motor Co., 1912-16, pres. and gen. mgr., 1916-19; v.p. in charge operations Gen. Motors Corp., 1919-20; exec. v.p. Willys-Overland Co., 1920-22; served as chmn. reorganization com. Maxwell Motor Corp.; became chmn. bd. Chrysler Corp. Republican. Episcopalian. Mason. Home: New York, N.Y., and Great Neck, L.I., N.Y. Died Aug 18, 1940.

CHUBB, LEWIS WARRINGTON, research dir.; b. Fort Yates, N.D., Oct. 22, 1882; s. Col. Charles St. John and Sarah L. (Eaton) C.; high school, Columbus, O.; M.E. in Elec. Engring., Ohio State U., 1905; Sc.D., Allegheny Coll., 1933; m. Mary Porter Everson, Mar. 28, 1910; (died 1919); children—Lewis Warrington, John Everson, Morris Wistar; m. 2d, Ora Lee (Dias) McGregor, May 10, 1926; 1 dau., Vivian McGregor. Vivian McGregor. With Westinghouse Elec. and Mfg. Co., 1905-30; engring. apprentice, 1905-06; in research and development magnetic materials 1906-18, in charge research sect.; with elec. development sect., materials and process engring. dept., 1916-20; mgr. radio engring. department 1920-30; asst. v.p. in charge engring. RCA Victor Co., Camden, N.,J., Jan.-June 1930; dir. Westinghouse Research Labs., East Pittsburgh, 1930-48. Mem. spl. uranium com. Nat. Acad. Scis., 1941-42; mem. spl. planning bd. on atomic energy Office Sci. Research and Development 1941-42, consulant to dir. (O.S.R.D.), 1941-43. Awarded John Fitz medal for 1947. Fellow Am. Inst. E.E., Inst. Radio Engrs.; mem. O. State U. Research Found. (bd. dirs.), Phys. Soc., Sigma Xi, Tau Beta Pi. Republican. Episcopalian. Clubs: University, Edgewood Country. Awarded between 100 and 200 patents as result of elec., and chem. researches; Lamme medal, Ohio State U., 1934. Contbr. many articles and papers. Home: "Sunnytop" Churchill Churchill Road, Pitts. 35. Died Apr. 2, 1952; buried Allegheny Cemetery, Pitts.

CHUPP, CHARLES DAVID, plant pathologist; b. Millersburg, Elkhart County, Ind., June 2, 1886; s. Levi N. and Margaret Rebecca (Weaver) C.; A.B., Wabash Coll., Crawfordsville, Ind., 1912; Ph.D., Cornell U., 1916; m. Nora Mae Scrugham, Aug. 23, 1913; children—Karl Richard, William Howard, Frank Marsh, John Paul. Asst. in plant pathology, Cornell, 1912-14, instr. 1914-16; acting prof. botany, Wabash Coll., 1916-17; instr. plant pathology, Cornell, 1917-19, asst. prof., 1919-27, prof., 1927-54; prof. emeritus, 1954-67; on leave at Rutgers U., 1926-27; visiting prof., Puerto Rico, 1946-47. Recipient Superior Service award U.S. Dept. Agr., 1954. Member A.A.A.S., American Mycological Soc., Am. Phytopathol. Soc. (councilor 1937-38; v.p. 1939; pres. 1940, recipient Award of Merit 1964), Sigma Xi, Sigma Phi. Methodist. Mason. Author: Manual of Vegetable-Garden Diseases, 1925; (with other) Vegetable Diseases and Their Control, 1960. Contbr. numerous articles to scientific jours. Has been working on monograph of fungus genus, cercospora, 30 yrs.; studied European herbaria, especially at London and Berlin, summer 1938. Home: Ithaca NY Died Nov. 9, 1967; buried East Lawn Cemetery, Ithaca NY

CHURCH, ARTHUR LATHAM, mech. engr.; b. Phila., Pa., Oct. 11, 1858; s. William A. and Elizabeth I. (Barker) C.; B.S., U. of Pa., 1878; m. Louise Brant, Dec. 5, 1888; 1 son, Herbert, In machine shop and Draughting room of The William Cramp & Sons Ship & Engine Bldg. Co., Phila., 1878-82; with engine depts. of steamships Queen of the Pacific, City of Peking and Granada, and draughtsman Union Iron Works, San Francsico, 1882-84; chief engr. Franklin Inst. Elec. and Novelties Exhbns., Phila., 1884-85; supt. Spring Garden Inst., 1885-86; with Baldwin Locomotive Works, Phila., 1886—, now sec. and asst. treas. Trustee U. of Pa.; mgr. Preston Retreat, Spring Garden Inst., Univ. Hosp. Republican. Home: Philadelphia, Pa. Died June 25, 1931.

CHURCH, IRVING PORTER, univ. prof.; b. Ansonia, Conn., July 22, 1851; s. Dr. Samuel P. and Elizabeth (Sterling) C.; C.E., Cornell, 1873, M.C.E., 1878; m. Elizabeth P. Holley, June 15, 1881. Asst. and asso. prof. civil engring., 1876-92, prof. applied mechanics and hydraulics, 1892-1916 (emeritus), Cornell Univ. Author: Statics and Dynamics for Engineering Students, 1886; Mechanics of Materials, 1887; Hydraulics and Pneumatics, 1889 (these three afterward published as Mechanics of Engineering, 1890); Notes and Examples in Mechanics, 1892; Diagrams of Mean Velocity of Water in Open Channels, 1902; Hydraulic Motors, 1905; Mechanics of Internal Work, 1910. Home: Ithaca, N.Y. Died May 8, 1931.

CHURCH, JAMES EDWARD, educator; b. Holly, Mich., Feb. 15, 1869; s. James Edward and Mary Alice (Eisenbrey) C.; A.B., U. Mich., 1892, post-grad. work, 1898-99; Ph.D., U. Munich, 1901; LL.D., U. Nev. 1937; studied archeology, Italy and Greece, 1901; m. Florence Humphrey, July 2, 1894 (dec. Feb. 1922); children—Willis Humphrey, Donald Eisenbrey. Tchr., prin. pub. schs., Mich., 1885-88; instr. Latin and German, U. Nev., 1892-94, asst. prof. Latin, 1894-95, asso. prof., 1895-96, prof., 1896-1939; founder, 1905, meteorologist and dir. Mt. Rose Meteorol. Obs.; adviser to cooperative snow surveys for State Nev.; meteorologist Mich-Greenland Expdn., 1926-27-28, Nev. Agrl. Expt. Sta., 1906-19, 31-48; snow specialist U.S. Weather Bur., 1942-48, ret.; now engaged in research and writing. Sec. Rhodes Scholarship Com. for Nev., 1904-29, pres., 1933, 1935—; co-founder Nev. Art Gallery Incorporated, pres. 1943—. Recipient award of merit D.A.R.; Distinguished Nevadan award University of Nevada, 1958. Fellow A.A.A.S., Am. Meteorol. Soc. (councilor 1933-35); mem. Aeroarctic, British Glaciological Society (honorary), American Geophysical Union (Chmn. com. on hydrology of snow 1931-47; v.p. sect. hydrology 1936-39, pres. 1942-47), Internat. Assn. Sci. Hydrology (pres. commn. on snow 1933-39, snow and glaciers 1939-48), Internat. Commn. on Snow and Ice (hon. life mem.), Am. Philol. Assn., Phi Beta Kappa, Phi Kappa Phi, Sigma Xi. Baptist. Clubs: Sierra, Explorers. Author of Snow Surveying: Its Problems and Their Present Phases (proc. 2d Pan-Am. Sci. Congress); Climate and Evaporation in Alpine and Arctic Zones; Temperatures of Arctic Soil and Water; Chapter on Snow and Ice in Volume on Hydrology (Physics of the Earth Series; The Human Side of Snow; Saga of Mount Rose Observatory, Snow Sport and Transport, Perennial Snow and Glaciers, Snow Perils and Avalanches; Snow Surveying in Southern Andes (with Dagoberto A. Sardina); Snow and Life; Physics of Snow Melt; also monographs and articles pertaining to philol., meteorol., winter mountaineering, snow conservation, and stream-flow forecasting; chpts. in Snow Surveys in the Himalayas (Govt. India), 1956. Guest CCXX anniversary Soviet Acad. Scis., 1945; organized snow surveys in Himalayas for India Govt., 1946-47, in Andes for Artentina, 1947-48. Home: 358 Washington St., Reno. Died Aug. 5, 1959; buried James Edward Church Fine Arts Bldg., U. Nev., Reno.

CHURCH, JOHN ADAMS, mining engr.; b. Rochester, N.Y., Apr. 5, 1843; s. Rev. Pharcellus and Chara E. (Conant) C.; bro. of William Conant C.; E.M., Columbia, 1867, Ph.D., 1879; studied in Europe, 1868-70; m. Jessie A. Peel, July 30, 1884. Acting prof. mineralogy and metallurgy, Columbia School of Mines, 1872-73; editor Engineering and Mining Journal, 1872-74; on U.S. Geog. and Geol. Survey, and examined Comstock Lode; prof. mining and metallurgy, State U. of Ohio, 1878-81; became supt. Tombstone (Ariz.) Mill & Mining Co.; in service of Viceroy Li Hung Chang, opening silver mines in Mongolia and introducing Am. methods and machinery, 4 yrs., 1886-90; now practicing as mining engr. Author: Notes on a Metallurgical Journey in Europe, 1875; The Comstock Lode, 1880; Report on Artesian Wells in Arizona, 1882; etc. Home: New York, N.Y. Died Feb. 12, 1917.

CHURCHILL, CHARLES SAMUEL, civil engr., ry. official; b. New Britain, Conn., Sept. 22, 1856; s. Samuel W. and Ellen (Hubbard) C.; C.E., Sheffied Sci. Sch. (Yale), 1878; m. Anna D. Green, Nov. 11, 1885, Ry. surveys and constrn., Conn. and Pa., 1879-81; div. engr. constrn. Pittsburgh & Lake Erie R.R., 1881-84; prin. asst. engr. constrn., Schuylkill Valley div. Pa. R.R., 1884-87; engr. maintenance of way, Shenandoah Valley R.R., 1887-88; engr. in charge Ohio extension of N.&W. Ry., May-Oct. 1888, engr. maintenance of way, 1888-1903, chief engr., 1903-14, chmn. valuation com., 1913-14, asst. to pres. and chief of valuation, 1914-18, Norfolk & Western Ry. System; v.p. N.&W. Ry. Co., 1918-26, in charge purchases, real estate and valuation, 1920-26, also chmn. coms. representing Southern group of rys. on federal valuation, 1913-26, and engaged in ventilation of ry. tunnels; retired from ry. service, Oct. 1, 1926; cons. engring. practice. Elected hon. mem., 1931, Am. Ry Engring. Assn., "in recognition of outstanding contributions to the science of railway engineering." Home: Roanoke, Va. Died Jan. 25, 1934.

CHURCHILL, EDWARD DELOS, surgeon; b. Chenoa, Ill., Dec. 25, 1895; s. Ebenezer Delos and Maria A. (Farnsworth) C.; B.S., Northwestern U., 1916, A.M., 1917; M.D. cum laude, Harvard, 1920; Dr. Honoris Causa, of Algiers, 1944; D.Sc., Princeton, 1947, U. Ala., 1959, Harvard, 1961; LL.D., Queen's U., 1954; m. Mary Lowell Barton, July 7, 1927; children—Mary Lowell, Frederick Barton, Edward Delos, A. Coolidge. Student intern Faulkner Hosp., Boston, 1919-20; surg. intern Mass. Gen. Hosp., 1920-22, resident, 1922-23, chief West Surg. Service, 1931-48, chief Gen. Surg. Services, 1948-72; asso. surgeon and dir. Surg. Research Lab., Boston City Hosp., 1928-30; asst. in surgery Harvard, 1922-23, Alumni asst. in surgery, 1923-24, instr. surgery, 1924-28, Moseley traveling fellow, 1926-27, asso. prof. surgery, 1928-31, John Homans prof. surgery, 1931-62, emeritus, 1962-72. Adv. med. bd. Am. Hosp., Paris, 1957-72; mem. adv. council Shiraz Med. Center, Nemazee Hosp., Iran, 1957-72; charter mem. sci. adv. bd. Walter Reed Inst. Research, Washington, 1958. Served in Med. Res., U.S. Army, 1918, 1st lt., 1924-29; col. M.C., cons. surgeon N. African and Mediterranean theatres, 1943-46. Decorated Legion of Merit, 1944; European Theater Service medal with 4 bronze battle stars; Cross of Knight Legion of Honor, 1953; War medal of Brazil; comdr. Order Crown of Italy; hon. officer Mil. Div. Order Brit. Empire, 1945; D.S.M., 1946; officer de l'Ordre National du Cedre (Lebanon). Chmn. med. adv. com. to sec. of war, 1946-48; vice chmn. task force, Fed. Med. Services, Commn. on Orgn. Exec. Br. Govt., 1948-49, 1953-55; mem. Armed Forces Med. Adv. Com. to Sec. Def., 1948-51; chmn. com. on surgery NRC, 1946-49; sr. civilian cons. in thoracic surgery to Surgeon Gen., 1953-72; cons. to Surgeon Gen., 1954-55; mem. edit. bd. Annals of Surgery. Fellow Royal Coll. Surgeons Eng. (hon.), Royal Coll. Univ. Surgeons Denmark (hon.), Am. Acad. Arts and Sci.; lectr. Royal Coll. Physicians and Surgeons (Can.); mem. Am. Assn. for Thoracic Surgery (pres. 1948-49), Am. Bd. Surgery Founders' Group (mem. bd. 1937-49), A.C.S., A.M.A., Am. Soc. for Clin. Investigation (emeritus 1941-72), Am. Surg. Assn. (pres. 1946-47), Assn. Mil. Surgeons U.S., Internat., New Eng. Boston, Excelsior (hon.) surg. socs., Halsted Club, Mass. Med. Soc., No. Pacific Surg. Assn. (hon.), Soc. Clin. Surgery (pres. 1949-50), Soc. U.S. Med. Cons. in World War II, Trudeau Soc., Korean Communications Zone Med. and Dental (hon.), 38th Parallel Med. Soc. of Korea (hon.), So. Honshu Med. Soc., Alpha Omega Alpha, Sigma Xi, Delta Tau Delta; hon. mem. U.S. and fgn. surg. socs. Presbyn. Clubs: Tavern, Century Assn., Harvard

(Boston and N.Y.C.), Aesculapian. Home: Belmont MA Died Aug. 28, 1973.

CHURCHMAN, JOHN WOOLMAN, bacteriologist; b. Burlington, N.J., Jan. 8, 1877; s. Horace and Edith Anna (Woolman) C.; A.B., Princeton, 1898, A.M., 1901; M.D., Johns Hopkins, 1902; A.M., Yale University, 1915; m. Martha Bertrand Jaramillo, Oct. 27, 1923. Resident house officer and clin. asst. in surgery, Johns Hopkins Hosp., 1902-05; vol. asst. Surg. Clinic, Breslau, Germany, 1905-06; asst. resident surgeon and resident surgeon, Johns Hopkins Hosp., 1906-11; instr. in surgery, Johns Hopkins, 1909-11; asst. prof. surgery, 1912-14, prof. 1914—, Yale, also acting head of dept.; médecin chef Hôp. Militaire, 32 bis, Château de Passy, France, 1916; attending surgeon and acting surgeon in chief, New Haven Hosp. and Dispensary; prof. of exptl. therapeutics and dir. Lab. of Exptl. Therapeutics, Cornell U. Med. Sch. Maj., Med. R.C.; pres. Bd. Examiners of Med. R.C., State of Conn. Fellow Am. College of Surgeons and of the N.Y. Acad. of Science. Officier de l'Instruction publique, and Officier d'Académie, France. Awarded Alvarenga prize, College Physicians of Philadelphia, 1921. Republican. Home: New York, N.Y. Died July 12, 1937.

CHUTE, HORATIO NELSON, physicist; b. Grovesend, Ont., Can., Dec. 26, 1847; s. Walter and Catherine C.; ed. Woodstock Coll., Ont., 1860-63; B.S., U. of Mich., 1872, M.S., 1875; m. M. Lucretia Clappison, Aug. 21, 1872. Prin. Aylmer pub. schs., Ont., 1866-69; asst. prof. Latin. Woodstock Coll., Ont., 1869-70; engaged in astron. work under Dr. J.C. Watson, 1872-73; instr. physics, Ann Arbor High Sch., 1873-1922. Author: Practical Physics, 1889; Physical Laboratory Manual, 1894; Elements of Physics (with Henry S. Carhart), 1892-97; Laboratory Note-Book, 1898; A Laboratory Guide, 1913. Home: Ann Arbor, Mich. Died 1928.

CIOCCO, ANTONIO, biostatistician; b. Columbus, O., May 1, 1908; s. Michael and Gelsomina (Ferraro) C.; Sc.D. (economics), U. Naples (Italy), 1930; Sc.D. (hygiene), Johns Hopkins, 1936; m. Augusta Kershaw, Feb. 16, 1942; 1 dau., Angela. Research asso. otology Johns Hopkins Sch. Medicine, 1930-35, asso. biology Sch. Hygiene and Public Health, 1936-39; biometrician, pub. health adminstr. U.S.P.H.S., Washington, 1939-49; prof., head dept. biostatistics U. Pittsburgh Grad. Sch. Pub. Health, 1949-69, professor of biostatistics, 1969-72; sometimes cons. U.S.P.H.S., United States Children's Bur., Rockefeller Found., War Manpower Commn., Nat. Security Resources Bd. Mem. Am. Pub. Health Assn., Biometrics Soc., Soc. Research in Child Development, Am. Soc. Human Genetics, A.A.A.S. Roman Catholic. Author monographs, contbr. articles various jours. dealing with investigations fields deafness, physical growth and development, human genetics, etc. Home: Pittsburgh PA Died Jan. 5, 1972; buried Gate of Heaven Cemetery, Silver Spring MD

CIST, JACOB, naturalist, inventor; b. Phila., Mar. 13, 1782; s. Charles and Mary (Weiss) C.; m. Sarah Hollenback, Aug. 25, 1807, at least 2 daus. Postmaster, Wilkes-Barre, Pa.; mined anthracite coal, Mauch Chunk, Pa., 1815-21; collected fossil plants and flora, described coal formations, 1815-21; founder, corresponding sec. Luzerne County Agrl. Soc.; invented artist's paint mixing mill, 1803, printer's ink from anthracite coal, 1808, anthractie coal burning stove, 1817. Died Dec. 30, 1825.

CLAASSEN, PETER WALTER, biologist; b. Hillsboro, Kan., Mar. 17, 1886; s. Deitrich and Elizabeth (Wall) C.; grad. normal course, McPherson (Kan) Coll., 1909; A.B., U. of Kans., 1913, A.M., 1915; Ph.D., Cornell U., 1918; m. Evelyn Strong, Dec. 22, 1917; children—Sarah Evelyn, Richard Strong. Prin. pub. sch., Hillsboro, Kan., 1909-11; asst. state entomolgist of Kan., 1913-15; instr. biology, Cornell U., 1915-16; asst prof. entomology, U. of Kan., 1916-17; asst. prof. biology, Cornell U., 1918-26, prof., 1926—; prof. biology (leave of absence), Tsing Hua Coll., Peking, China, 1924-25. Republican. Presbyn. Specialized in study of plecoptera. Author: Laboratory Text in General Biolgoy; Plecoptera Nymphs of North America. Home: Ithaca, N.Y. Died Aug. 16, 1937.

CLABAUGH, HINTON GRAVES, industrial engineer; b. Talladega, Alabama; s. John Henry and Martha Hinton (Graves) Clabaugh; m. Mary Louise Farson, Aug. 16, 1909 (died 1937); children—Louise Farson, Hinton Graves, George Francis; m. 2d, Mary Elizabeth Law, Mar. 22, 1939 (div.). Confidential investigator United States Government service as special agent Department of Justice, May 1910, asst. supt. at Chicago, 1911, 12, in charge in Cincinnati, 1913; asst. supt. N.Y. City, 1913, div. supt. at Chicago, Sept. 1914-Dec.1918; asst. to pres. Peabody Coal Co. and pvt. practice as industrial engr., Dec. 1918-22; represented U.S. Govt. and Chicago and Ill. bar assns. in special cases; identified with Commonwealth Edison Co., Public Service Co. of Northern Illinois, Peoples Gas Light & Coke Co. and other utilities since 1922. Lieut. United States Naval Reserve, 1917-21, lt. commander, 1926-30, comdr. since July 1939. Chmn. Ill. Pardon and Parole Bds., 1926-29. Mem. Ry. Spl. Agts. Assn., Am. Gas Assn., Am. Electric Ry. Assn., Am. Legion, Mil. Order World War. Reserve Officers Assn. of U.S., Sojourners. Republican. Mason. Clubs: Lake Shore, Electric, Army and Navy. Home: 153 Bertling Lane, Winnetka, Ill. Office: 79 W. Monroe St., Chicago, Ill. Died May 31, 1946.

CLAPP, CHARLES HORACE, geologist; b. Boston, Mass., June 5, 1883; s. Peleg Ford and Mary Lincoln (Manson) C.; B.S., Mass. Inst. Tech., 1905, Ph.D., 1910; studied Harvard, 1911; m. Mary R. Brennan, Apr. 19, 1911; children—Daniel Brennan, Michael Manson, Mary Lincoln, Francis Coyle, Lucy Ford, Prudence, Paul, Margaret. Instructor geology and mining, Univ. of N.D., 1905-07, also asst. state geolgoist; instr. geology, Mass. Inst. Tech., 1907-10; with Geol. Survey of Can., 1908-13; prof. geology, U. of Ariz., 1913-16; prof. geology, Mont. State Sch. of Mines, 1916-21, pres., 1918-21; pres. State U. of Mont., 1921—. Dir. and geologist Mont. Bur. Mines and Metallurgy, 1919-22; asst. geologist U.S. Geol. and Metallurgy, 1919-22; asst. geologist U.S. Geol. Survey, 1914-25. Democrat. Unitarian. Home: Missoula, Mont. Died May 9, 1935.

CLAPP, CORNELIA MARIA, zoölogist; b. Montague, Mass., Mar. 17, 1849; d. Richard and Eunice Amelia (Slate) C.; grad. Mt. Holyoke Coll., 1871; Ph.B., Syracuse U., 1888, Ph.B. and Ph.D., 1889; Ph.D. U. of Chicago, 1896; studied at Penikese, 1874, and at Marine Biol. Lab., Woods Hole, 1888-1902, during summer sessions carried on investigations; unmarried. Prof. zoölogy, Mt. Holyoke Coll., 1896-1916. Home: Montague, Mass. Died Jan. 1, 1935.

CLAPP, EARLE HART, forester; b. North Rush, N.Y., Oct. 15, 1877; s. Edwin Perry and Ermina Jane (Hart) C.; student Geneseo (N.Y.) Normal Sch., Cornell U., 1902-03; A.B., U. of Mich., 1905, D.Sc., 1928; m. Helen Adele Roberts, Oct. 15, 1908; children—Stewart, Helen Ermina. Asst. in forest service, U.S. Dept. Agr., 1905, chief of office forest management, 1908, asso. dist. forester, 1909-12, forest insp., 1912-15, asst. forester in charge research, 1915-35, asso. chief of forest service, 1935-44; except when acting chief forest service, 1940-42; organized research bureau; planned and helped obtain legislation to insure planwise development of research commensurate with nat. needs, resulting in 12 regional forest expt. stas. and further development of a nat. forest products lab.; as acting chief formulated Fed. legislation leading towards nation-wide forestry, with primary emphasis on pub. regulation of forest practices on privately owned land and greatly increased pub. ownership. Fellow Soc. Am. Foresters (twice v.p.); mem. Soc. Forestry Finland (corr.), Sigma Xi. Clubs: Cosmos (Washington); U. of Mich. Union (Ann Arbor, Mich.). Author: National Program of Forest Research, 1926, Supervised report "A National Plan for American Forestry," 1933; "The Western Range, A Great but Neglected National Resource," 1936; also various other govt. reports. Contbr. to forestry jours. Home: 6802 Meadow Lane Chevy Chase 15 MD

CLAPP, FREDERICK GARDNER, cons. geologist; b. Boston, July 20, 1879; s. Edward Blake and Mary Frances (Jones) C.; S.B. in Geology, Mass. Inst. Tech., 1901; m. Helen Drew Ripley, Dec. 28, 1908; children—Clara Frances, Edward Gardner, Priscilla. Instr. in U.S. Geol. Survey, 1902-08; consulting geologist and petroleum engr., specializing in reports on oil and gas properties since 1908; mng. geologist, The Associated Geol. Engrs., 1912-18; chief geologist, The Associated Petroleum Engrs. since 1919; also petroleum and natural gas expert, Canadian Dept. of Mines, 1911-15; in charge geol. explorations in China, 1913-15; in charge investigations in Australia and New Zealand, 1923-25; petroleum adviser Imperial Govt. of Iran, 1927, 28, 33; explorations in Iran and Afghanistan, 1934-38; Oklahoma oil operations, 1939-43; special lecturer on oil geology, Harvard, 1921; reported to committee of United States Senate in Teapot Dome Case, 1923. Christian Scientist. Fellow Geol. Society America, A.A.A.S., Am. Geog. Societyk Royal Engrs., Geol. Soc. Washington, Am. Asiatic Assn., Royal Geog. Soc.; mem. Am. Inst. Mining and Metall. Engrs., Am. Geophys. Union, Am. Petroleum Inst., Am. Assn. Petroleum Geologists, Inst. of Petroleum (London), Am. Inst. for Iranian Art and Archeology, Societe Geologique de France; hon. mem. Sociedad des Ingemieros del Peru. Clubs: Explorers (New York); Teheran (Iran). Author of books and papers on travel, geology, petroleum, natural gas, geography and water supply. Home: 91 Warwick Rd., Bronxville, N.Y. Office: 50 Church St., New York, N.Y. Died Feb. 18, 1944.

CLAPP, PAUL SPENCER, elec. engr; b. Toledo, Ia., July 20, 1890; s. Samuel E. and Nellie (Morse) C.; B.S. in E.E., Ia., State Coll., 1913; E.E., From same coll., 1923; m. Rosalind Wainwright, June 24, 1932; children—Paul, Rosalind, Julia Ann. With the Western Electric Co. at Chicago and New York, engring. research, engr. on first transcontinental telephone line, also on early transoceanic telephone experiments, 1913-17; assistant purchasing agent Allied Machinery Corporation, Feb.- Sept. 1917; with International Western Electric Co., 1918-19; managing director Nat. Electric Corp., 1932-42; v.p. Ohio Fuel Gas and elec. Co., 1942—; Cincinnati Gas and Elec. Co., 1942—; mem. bd. Columbia Engring. Corp., v.p. since 1945. Sec. St. Lawrence Commn. of U.S., 1924-26, Second Nat. Radio Conf., 1925. Commissioned 1st lieut. Signal Corp. U.S. Army, 1917, later captain; served in U.S. and France; with Peace Commission, Paris, and Am. Relief Adminst., in Central Europe and Russia, to U.S., 1923; spl. asst. to Herbert Hoover Secretary of Commerce, 1923-26; retired Colonel Engineers Corps. 1949. Decorated by Roumanian Govt., 1919. Awarded Anson Marstin medal for achievement in engineering, Iowa State Coll., 1945. Received Alumni Merit Award, Iowa State Coll., 1948. Member Am. Inst. E.E., Edison Electric Inst. Nat. Assn. Mfrs., Tau Beta Pi Delta Upsilon. Republican. Prostestant. Clubs: University Recess (New York); Manhasset Bay Yacht (Washington). Address: 123 E. 78th St., N.Y.C. Died Dec. 5, 1953; buried Arlington Nat. Cemetery.

CLARK, ALLAN JAY, metallurgical engr.; b. Jersey City N.J., Apr. 12, 1874; s. Bernard Stearns and Adele (Shiffer) C.; grad. Berkeley Sch., New York. 1891; E.M., Sch. of mines (Columbia). 1896— hon. Dr. Engring., S.D. Sch. of Mines. 1940; m. Jane Parfrey. Oct. 2, 1901; children—Elizabeth Adele, Bernard Stearns, Marian Louise. Engr. with Tenn. Coal, Iron and R.R. Co., 1896; metallurgist with Homestake Mining Co., 1897-1927, chief metallurgist since 1907; cons. practice; retired. 1943. State chmn. for S.D., Naval Cons. Bd., 1915. Mem. Am. Inst. Mining and Metall. Engrs., Alpha Delta Phi. Repbulican. Episcopalian. Contbr. paper "Metallurgy of the Homestake Ores." of which was co-author. Home: Spearfish. S.D. Died March 23, 1950; buried Rosehill Cemetery, Spearfish, S.D.

CLARK, ALVA BENSON, elec. engr.; b. Clay Center O., Feb. 15, 1890; s. George Frederick and Nellie Judith (McIntyre) C.; B.E.E., U. of Mich., m. Anna C. Harper. Nov. 25, 1920 (now dec.); children—Judith H., Patricia H. (dec.) m. 2d, Helen Kerstetter. Aug. 13, 1938. Elec. engr. Am. Telephone and Telegraph Company, 1911-34; with Bell Telephone Laboratories since 1934. as director of transmission development 1935-40, director of systems development 1940-44. vice pres. since 1944. Delegate to Comite. Consulatif International Telephonique and Internat. Electro-Tech. Commn. meetings, Belgium and Scandinavia, 1930. Consultant or member of various division. Office Scientific Research and Development, 1941-45 became expert cons. to sec. War, 1944; dir. research and development. Nat. Security Agency, 1954—. Cited as Distinguished Alumnus by U. of Mich., 1941. Fellow Am. Inst. Elec. Engrs., Acoustical Soc. America; senior member of the Institute of Radio Engineers; mem. Tau Beta Pi. Sigma Xi. Clubs: Downtown Athletic, Michigan Alumni (N.Y. City). Author: of several pub. papers; holds 44 patents on elec. communication devices. Home: 4301 Massachusetts Av., N.W., Washington. Office: Washington. Died Nov. 14, 1955.

CLARK, ALVAN, astronomer, lens maker; b. Ashfield, Mass., Mar. 8, 1804; s. Alvan and Mary (Bassett) C.; A.M. (hon.), Amherst Coll., Chgo. U., Princeton, Harvard; m. Maria Pease, Mar. 25, 1826, children include Alvan Graham, George Bassett. Started firm Alvan Clark & Sons, 1852, produced world's largest telescopes; produced lenses for Vienna Obervatory, Wesleyan U., Middletown, Conn., Lick Obs., Cal., 18 inch lens for Dearborn Obs., Evanston, Ill., 23, inch for Princeton, 26 inch telescopes for Naval Observatory and U. Va., 30 inch telescope for Pulkova Observatory, Russia, 1879; made 36 inch lens for Lick telescope. Recipient Rumford medal Am. Acad. Arts and Scis. Died Cambrdige, Mass., Aug. 19, 1887.

CLARK, ALVAN GRAHAM, astronomer, lens maker; b. Fall River, Mass., July 10, 1832; s. Alvan and Maria (Pease) C.; m. Mary Willard, Jan. 2, 1865. Discovered star Sirius for which he was awarded Lalande gold medal French Acad.; discovered 16 double stars; made 40 inch lenses of Yerkes telescope (then world's largest), at U. Chgo.; made 30 inch refractor for Imperial Observatory, St. Petersburg, Russia; mem. total Eclipse expdn. to Spain, 1870, Wyo. Mission, 1878. Fellow Am. Acad. Arts and Scis., A.A.A.S. Died Cambridge, Mass., June 9, 1897.

CLARK, AUSTIN HOBART, biologist;b. Wellesley, Mass., Dec. 17, 1880; s. Theodore Minot and Jeanette (French C.; grad. high sch., Newton. Mass., 1899; A.B. Harvard, 1903. grad study 1904; m. Mary Wendell Upham. Mar. 6, 1906 (died Dec. 28, 1931); children—Austin Bryant Jackson, Sarah Wendell Hugh Upham, Anne Bradstreet, Mary Holmes. m.2d, Leala Gay Forbes. Sept. 23, 1933. Organizer of expedition to Margarita Island, Venezuela. 1901; in zoöl. research Lesser Antilles. 1903-05; acting chief of scienitfic staff of U.S. Fisheries S.S. Albatross, 1906-07; mem. staff Smithsonian Inst., 1908-50. ret. dir. press service, A.A.A.S., press. relation ofcr. 8th Pan-Am. Sci. Congress. 1940; pub. relations ofcr. Centennial Celebration. A.A.A.S.; 1948; vice-chmn. Am. Geophys. Union; pres. Washington Acad. of Sciences; pres. Entomological Society of Washington; member long range planning com. Va. Acad. of Science; mem. exec. com. and long range planning com. Southern Association of Science and Industry; member advisory board Virginia Fisheries Laboratory; research work in Oceanography, marine biology. ornithology and entomology. served as aide-de-camp to the Prince of Monaco 1921. Exec. com., bd. trustees Nat. Parks Assn. exec. com., bd. govs. Nature Conservancy. Fellow Royal Geog. Soc. Decorated Knight of Order of

Danneborg (Denmark). Club: Cosmos. Author: Animals of Land and Sea. 1925; Nature Narratives, Vol. 1 1929, Vol. 2 1931; The New Evolution. 1930; Animals Alive. 1948; also monographs and bulletins and about 600 scientific articles in English. French, Italian, German and Russian. Home: 1818 Wyoming Av., N.W., Washington 9, D.C. Died Oct. 28, 1954. buried Mt. Auburn Cemetery, Cambridge, Mass.

CLARK, CHARLES CLEVELAND, statistician, meteorologist; b. Washington, D.C., Mar. 6, 1875; s. Ezra Wescote and Sylvia (Nodine) C.; student Columbia U.; LL.B., Phila. Law Sch. (Temple Coll.), 1899; LL.M., Columbia, 1900, D.C.L., 1901; m. Mary Duncan Swingle, July 12, 1905; children—Charles Cleveland, Robert Duncan, Mary Elizabeth, Anita. Asso. statistician in charge Bur. of Statistics, Dept. of Agr., Washington, D.C., 1906-08, also chmn. crop-reporting bd.; statistician Internat. Inst. Agr., Rome, Italy, 1909, 1910; chief clk. U.S. Dept. Agr., 1911-13; exec. asst. U.S. Weather Bur., 1913-14; asst. chief same since 1915. Represented U.S. in organizing Internat. Inst. Agr., at Rome, Italy, 1908. Mem. bar States of Pa. and Wash. and of Washington, D.C. Mem. Am. Statis. Assn., Am. Meteorol. Soc., Loyal Legion, Columbia Hist. Soc., Am. Forestry Assn., Inst. of Aeronautical Sciences. Clubs: University, Torch, Federal, Congressional Country (Washington, D.C.). Author various bulls., and monographs on statis. and crop reporting subjects. Home: 21 W. Irving St., Chevy Chase MD

CLARK, CLAUDE LESTER, metall. engr.; b. Saginaw, Mich., Mar. 6, 1903; s. Jason and Addie (Leaman) C.; B.S., U. Mich., 1925, M.S., 1926, Ph.D., 1928; m. Irene Marie Hansen, Aug. 8, 1930 (dec. 1960); children—Joanne (Mrs. Victor Long), Claude Leaman. Profl. research engr., lectr. metallurgy U. Mich., 1928-40; metall. engr. in charge spl. steel products Timken Roller Bearing Co., 1940-58, staff Alumnus citation U. Mich., Albert Sauveur Achievement award Am. Soc. Metals 1961; 25 year Appreciation certificate Am. Soc. M.E. Mem. Am. Soc. Testing Materials (dir., chmn. com. on tubular products), Am. Soc. M.E., Am. Inst. Mining and Metall. Engrs., Nat. Assn. Corrosion Engrs., Am. Soc. Metals, T.A.P.P.I., Sigma Xi, Phi Lambda Upsilon, Iota Alpha, Tau Beta Pi. Episcopalian. Clubs: Engineers (N.Y.C.); Michigan Union (U. Mich.). Author: 15 Lesson Course on High Temperature Metals; tech. papers. Patentee in field. Home: 3510 Croyden Rd., Canton 8. Office: 1835 Bueber Av. S.W., Canton 6, O. Died Jan. 6, 1966; buried Forest Lawn Cemetery, Saginaw.

CLARK, EDWARD, architect U.S. Captiol, 1865—; b. Phila., 1822; common school and academic edn.; m. Evaline F. Freeman, Dec. 13, 1860. Studied architecture under Thomas U. Walter; became asst. to latter on his apptmt. as architect of the U.S. Capitol extension and succeeded him when he resigned, 1865; apptd. by Congress on commn. for completion of Washington monument; has served on various other commns. for Govt. work, including that for construction of Congressional Library. Is trustee for construction of Congressional Library. Is trustee for construction of Congressional Library. Is trustee Corcoran Gallery of Art; mem. various scientific socs. Mem. A.I.A. Home: Washington, D.C. Died 1902.

CLARK, EDWARD LEE, geologist; b. Springfield, Mo., Jan. 23, 1908; s. Edward William and Nell (Brassfield) C.; B.S., Drury Coll., 1929; M.S., State U. Ia., 1931; Ph.D., U. Mo., 1941; m. Catherine Call, July 6, 1930; children—Edward Lee, Catherine Jean. Prof. geology Drury Coll., 1932-42; mining geologist, Potosi, Bolivia, 1935-36; geologist Mo. Geol. Survey, summers 1937-41; regional tech adv. mining div. WPB, 1942-44; state geologist of Mo., 1944-55; ex-officio mem. Mo. Highway Commn., 1944-55; v.p. Four Corners Uranium Corp., Grand Junction, Colo., 1955-59; dir. dept. Natural Resources, State Colo., 1959—; mining geologist charge exploration and development. Mem. Engring. Joint Council Water Panel; mem. adv. bds. other state agencies. Trustee Midwest Research Inst., Kansas City, Mo. Fellow Geol. Soc. Am.; mem. Am. Inst. Mining and Metall. Engrs., Soc. Econ. Geologists, Colo. Mining Inst. (past dir.), Sigma Xi. Mason. Author adminstrv. reports, tctech articles profl. jours. Home: 6835 S. Adams Way, Littleton, Colo. Office: State Services Bldg., Denver. Died Mar. 7, 1962; buried Springfield, Mo.

CLARK, ELIOT ROUND, educator; b. Shelburne, Mass., Nov. 13, 1881; s. George Larkin and Emma Frances (Kimball) C.; A.B., Yale, 1903; M.D., Johns Hopkins, 1907; D.Sc., Washington and Jefferson Coll., 1940; studied U. Munich, U. Cracow; m. Eleanor Acheson Linton, Mar. 21, 1911; 1 dau., Margaret Brownson; adopted son, Douglas. Inst. anatomy Johns Hopkins Med. Sch., 1907-10, asso., 1910-14; prof. anatomy U. Mo., 1914-22; prof. anatomy U. Ga., 1922-26 also asst. dean, med. dept., 1923-25; prof. anatomy and dir. dept. anatomy U. Pa., 1926-47; prof. anatomy emeritus U. Pa. Contract surgeon U.S. Army, Sept. - Nov. 1918. Fellow A.A.A.S.; mem. Am. Assn. Anatomists (sec.-treas. 1938-42, 43046), Am. Assn. Physiologists, Coll. Physicians Phil., Physiol. Soc. Phila., Sigma Xi, Phi Beta Kappa, Alpha Omega Alpha, Phi Kappa Epsilon, Phi Beta Pi. Corp. mem. of Marine Biol. Lab. (trustee 1930-46). Club: Woods Hole Yacht (vice commodore, 1942-48, commodore 1948-52). Contbr. results original researches to profl. jours., chiefly growth and reactions of lymphatics, blood vessels, connective tissue cells, blood cells, microscopic study of cells and tissues in the living mammal. Home: 315 S. 41st St., Phila. 4. Office: Wistar Inst. Anatomy and Biology, Woodland Av. and 36th St., Phila. 4. Died Nov. 1, 1963.

CLARK, EUGENE BRADLEY, engineer, mfr.; b. Washington, D.C., July 27, 1873; s. Ezra W. and Sylvai Anne (Nodine) C.; M.E., Cornell U., 1894; m. Laura Wolfe, Oct. 28, 1899 (died 1917); children—Helen Cecil (Mrs. Leo Wolman), Eugene B., John M.; m. 2d, Mrs. Luella M. Coon, 1919. Began as elec. engr. for Westinghouse Electric & Mfg. Co., Pittsburgh, 1894; elec. engr., later asst. mgr. Ill. Steel Co., South Chicago, 1896-1906; pres. Am. Sintering Co. since 1906; pres. Clark Equipment Co., Am. Ore Reclamation Co., Buffalo Sintering Corp. Mem. Soc. Automotive Engrs., Art Inst. Chicago, Field Museum of Natural History, Oriental Inst. Clubs: Chicago, University, Bob O'Link Golf, Tavern (Chicago); South Bend (Ind.) Country; Detroit Athletic; India House (New York); Surf, Indian Creek (Miami, Fla.). Home: Buchanan, Mich.; and Chicago, Ill. Offices: Buchanan, Mich.; and 310 S. Michigan Av., Chicago, Ill. Died July 29, 1942.

CLARK, FREDERICK HUNTINGTON, mining engr.; b. Minneapolis, Minn., Apr. 13, 1877; s. John Bates and Myra Almeda (Smith) C.; student Amherst, 1895-96, Worcester Poly. Inst., 1896-97, law dept. U. of Minn., 1897-98; M.E., Sch. of Mines (Columbia), 1907; m. Eleanor Phelps, Dec. 30, 1908; children—Eunice, Eleanor. Engr. El Oro Mining & Ry. Co., 1907; mgr. San Cayetano Mines, Ltd., and consulting engr. various companies, 1908-10; field engr. Gen. Development Co., 1910-13; gen. practice since 1913; v.p. Peninsula Development Corp. (Bradentown, Fla.); now gen. mgr. and dir. The Trans-Lux Movie Ticker Corp., New York. Engr. U.S. Shipping Bd. and Emergency Fleet Corp. until June 1917. Originated plan for construction of emergency fleet of wooden vessels to meet war crises in shipping. Mem. Minn. N.G., 1897-98. Mem. Delta Kappa Epsilon, Tau Beta Pi, Sigma Psi. Club: University. Home: 35 Fifth Av. Address: 24 State St., New York 4 NY

CLARK, GEORGE LINDENBERG, chemist; b. Anderson, Ind., Sept. 6, 1892; s. Ralph Bliven and Olive (Burnett) C.; B.A., DePauw U., 1914; M.S., U. of Chicago, 1914, Ph.D., 1918; Sc.D., DePauw U., 1937; m. Mary Mason Johnson, June 19, 1919; children—Mary Ann (dec.), Ralph Burnett, George Mason, Jean Louise, Carolyn Johnson. Instr. in chemistry, DePauw U., 1914-16, 19; asso. prof. chemistry, Vanderbilt, 1919-21; nat. research fellow, Harvard, 1921-24; asst. prof. applied chm. research, Mass. Inst. Tech., 1924-27 (installed and directed first industrial X-ray research lab.); prof. chemistry U. Ill., 1927-53; research prof. analytical chemistry, 1953-60, emeritus 1960, vis. prof. DePauw U., 1961; chmn. Merchants Property Ins. Co. of Ind.; dir. Clark-Mchts., Inc. Mem., past chmn. Concert and Entertainment Bd., U. Ill., 1934-36, 38-51; mem. Nashville Symphony Orch., 1920-21, U. Ill. Symphony Orch., 1938-44. Served as lt. C.W.S., Am. U. Expt. Sta., 1918. Fellow A.A.A.S.; mem. Am. Chem. Soc., (Mobile-Pensacola sect. award, 1952), Am. Crystallographic Assn., Am. Inst. Chemists, Radiol Soc. Am., Am. Soc. Testing Materials (Marburg Meml. lectr. 1927), Phi Beta Kappa, Phi Beta Kappa Associates, Sigma Xi, Phi Lambda Upsilon, Beta Theta Pi, Alpha Chi Sigma; founder, Electron Microscope Soc. Am., 1943. Methodist. Mason (32 deg., K.T.). Clubs: Nat. Exchange, Torch, University. Author: Applied X-Rays, 1926, 4th edit., 1955; also many papers in chem. and physical jours. Awarded Grasselli medal, 1932; Mehl. medal, 1944; Orton Lectureship award, 1946. Editor-in-chief Ency. of Chemistry, 1957, co-editor 2d edit., 1965; editor: Supplement, 1958. Editor Ency. Spectroscopy, 1960, Microscopy, 1961; Ency. X-Rays and Gamma Rays, 1963. Home: Urbana IL Died Jan. 8, 1969; buried Eastlawn Cemetery, Urbana IL

CLARK, HARRY WILLARD, chemist, sanitary engr.; b. Melrose, Mass., Sept. 15, 1863; s. John Hobart and Emily (Peters) C.; ed. Cornell U. and M.I.T.; m. Gertrude Fuller, of N. Andover, Mass., July 21, 1891 (died 1927). Assistant chemist, 1887-93, chemist, 1893-95, dir., 1895-1933, Lawrence (Mass.) Experimental Sta.; chief chemist Mass. State Bd. Health, 1897-1933. Chemist Metropolitan Sewerage Commn., 1898, Charles River Dam Commn., 1901, Mass. Highway Commn., 1908-21; lecturer on sanitary engring., Harvard, 1925; engaged in sanitary engring. practice since 1933. Consulting expert in regard to purification of water and disposal and purification of sewage and industrial wastes of many cities, bds. and corps. Mem. Boston Soc. C.E., N.E. Water Works Assn., Am. Water Works Assn., New England Sewage Works Assn., etc. Author of numerous papers on sanitary, chem. and bacterial subjects, reports upon methods for the purification of sewage and water, etc. Home: N. Andover, Mass. Office: 89 Broad St., Boston, Mass.

CLARK, HENRY JAMES, educator; b. Easton, Mass., June 22, 1826; s. Rev. Henry Porter and Abilgail (Orton) C.; grad. U. City N.Y., 1848, Lawrence Scientific Sch., 1854; m. Mary Young Holbrook 1854, 8 children. Pvt. asst. to Louis Agassiz, 1854-65; asst. prof. zoology Scientific Sch. at. Harvard, 1860-65; prof. botany, zoology and geology Pa. State Coll., 1866-69, U. Ky., 1869-72; prof. Mass. Agrl. Coll., 1872-73. Author: Mind in Nature; or the Origin of Life, and the Mode of Development of Animals, 1965. Died July 1, 1873.

CLARK, HUBERT LYMAN, zoologist; b. Amherst, Mass., Jan. 9, 1870; s. William Smith (pres. Mass. Agrl. Coll.) and Harriet Kapuolani Richards (Williston) C.; A.B., Amherst Coll., 1892; Ph.D., Johns Hopkins U., 1897; hon. Sc.D., Olivet (Mich.) Coll., 1927; m. Fannie Lee Snell, Apr. 4, 1899; children—William Smith, Stirrat (dec.), Janet Stirrat, Edith. Prof. biology, Olivet Coll., 1899-1905; asst. Museum Comparative Zoology, Harvard, 1905-12, curator of echinoderms, 1912-27, became curator of marine invertebrates, and asso. prof. zoology, 1927, emeritus prof., also curator; acting prof. Williams Coll., 1920-21; acting asso. prof., Stanford U., 1936; research associate Hancock Foundation, University of So. Calif., 1946-47. Received Clarke Memorial Medal, Royal Soc. of New South Wales, Australia, for research in Australian sci., 1947. Sci. investigations in Jamaica (5 visits), Tobago, Bermuda, Galapagos Islands and Australia (3 visits). Chmn. bd. visitors Andover-Newton Theol. Sem. 1930-40. Republican. Conglist. Author of numerous sci. papers, including 3 monographs on Austrian Echinoderms, 1921, 38, 46. Home: 97 Lakeview Av., Cambridge 38, Mass. Died July 31, 1947; buried in West Cemetery, Amherst, Mass.

CLARK, JANET HOWELL, scientist; b. Balt., Jan. 1, 1889; d. William Henry and Anne Janet (Tucker) Howell; A.B., Bryn Mawr Coll., 1910; Ph.D., Johns Hopkins, 1913; m. Admont Halsey Clark, July 9, 1917 (dec. Oct. 1918); 1 dau., Anne Janet (Mrs. Peter Picard Rodman). Lectr. physics Bryn Mawr Coll., 1914-15; instr. physics Smith Coll., 1916-17; instr. Johns Hopkins, 1918-20, asst. prof. physiology, 1920-22, asso. prof., 1922-35, lectr. physiology, 1935-38; prof. biophysics, dean Coll. for Women U. Rochester, 1938-52; lectr., researcher Johns Hopkins, 1952-69. Mem. bd. trustees Bryn Mawr Sch., 1952-58, St. Paul's Sch. for Girls, 1958-69. Huff fellow Bryn Mawr Coll., 1913-14; Am. Assn. U. Women Sarah Berliner fellow, 1915-16. Mem. Am. Assn. U. Women (chmn. internat. grants com., 1953-59), Internat. Fedn. U. Women (chmn. fellowships com. 1960-69), Am. Physical Soc., Am. Optical Soc., Am. Physiological Soc., Radiations Research Soc., A.A.A.S., Phi Beta Kappa, Sigma Xi. Author: Lighting in Relation to Public Health, 1924; also articles in profl. jours. Home: Baltimore MD Died Feb. 12, 1969.

CLARK, JOHN ARVINE, engring. exec.; b. Syracuse, N.Y., May 22, 1889; s. George Arvine and Margaret (Flanigan) C.; M.E., Cornell U., 1910; m. Ivel L. Martin, June 7, 1934. Student engr. Westinghouse Machine, Pitts., 1910-12; engr. Hope Natural Gas Co., Clarksburg, W.Va., 1912-50, pres., 1950-52. chmn. bd. 1953, dir., 1946—; dir. River Gas Co., Mariteta, O., 1947—; Nat. Gas Co., N.Y.C., 1952—. Served as 2d lt. U.S. Army, Engrs. Corp., 1918-19. Mem. Am. Gas Assn., Newcomen Soc. Home: 600 E. Main St. Office: 445 W. Main St., Clarksburg, W.Va., Died Aug. 8, 1954.

CLARK, JOHN EDWARD, M.D.; b. England, Jan. 13, 1850; s. Fred J. and Ellen (Petley) C.; came to America, 1856; ed. Victoria Coll., Toronto; M.D., U. of Mich., 1877; m. Frances Hutchins, June, 1887; children—Harold E., Frances. In practice at Detroit, 1877—; prof. gen chemistry and physics, Mich. Coll. of Medicine, 1879-85, Detroit Coll. of Medicine, 1885—; dean dept. pharmacy and prof. chemistry and toxicology, Detroit Coll. of Medicine, 1892—. Surgeon-gen. Mich. N.G., 1892; pres. U.S. Pension Examining Bd., 1899—; then chemist and analyst Wayne Co., Mich. Mem. Detroit Bd. of Edn., 1893-97 (pres., 1895); pres. Detroit Pub. Library Commn., 1902. Author Clark's Physical Diagnosis and Urine Analysis, 1890; Laboratory Technique for Medical Students, 1900. Home: Detroit, Mich. Died Sept. 19, 1934.

CLARK, JOHN EMORY, mathematician; b. Northampton, N.Y., Aug. 8, 1832; s. Rev. John and Sarah Miller (Foote) C.; A.B. U. of Mich., 1856, A.M., 1859; (hon. A.M., Yale, 1873); m. Caroline C. Doty, Aug. 20, 1856 (dec.). Professor of mathematics, Mich. State Normal Sch., 1856-57; asst. prof. mathematics, U. of Mich., 2857-59; studied at univs. of Heidelberg, Munich and Berlin, 1859-60; U.S. deputy surveyor in Dak., 1861-62, in Colo., 1869; capt. and maj. 5th Mich. Cav., 1862-65; bvtd. lt. col. U.S. Vols., Mar., 1865; prof. mathematics and astronomy, Antioch Coll., 1866-72; asst. astronomer, Northern Boundary Commn., 1872; prof. mathematics, 1873-1901, emeritus, Sheffield Scientific Sch. (Yale). Home: Springfield, Mass. Died Jan. 3, 1921.

CLARK, LEE HINCHMAN, chem. cons.; b. Bklyn., Dec. 27, 1895; s. Cornelius Jones and Arabella (Hinchman) C.; B.Chemistry, Cornell U., 1919; m. Margaret Bellows, Mar. 7, 1923; children—Lee

Hinchman, Everett Reynolds, Mary Lee (Mrs. Gray E. Mather, Jr.). Engr., Nat. Sugar Refining Co., Long Island City, 1919-20; chemist Gen. Chem. Co., Marcus Hook, Pa., 1920-21; chemist Sharples Corp., Phila., 1921-23, chief chemist, 1923-29; v.p. Sharples Chems. Corp., Wyandotte, Mich., 1929-50, exec. v.p., 1950-54, pres., 1954-55; v.p. Pennsalt Chems. Corp., Phila., 1955-61; chem. cons., 1961—. Mem. township bd., Grosse Ile, Mich., 1940-50. Trustee Oakwood Hosp., Dearborn, Mich., Pennsalt Chem. Found. Mem. Am. Inst. Chem. Engrs., Am. Chem. Soc., Sigma Xi, Tau Beta Pi, Psi Upsilon. Club: Marion Gold (Ardmore, Pa.). Patentee in field. Author articles chem. processing, use of centrifugals in process industries. Home: 923 Waverly Rd., Bryn Mawr, Pa. Office: 3 Penn Center, Phila. 19102. Died Dec. 25, 1962.

CLARK, MELVILLE, piano mfr.; b. Oneida Co., N.Y.; s. Thomas W. and Susan M. (Medole) C.; ed. pub. schs. and commercial coll.; m. Elizabeth Baughman, Oct. 1, 1873. Began mfg. organs, Oakland, Calif., 1875; removed to Quincy, Ill., 1876, Chicago, 1880; became mem. Story & Clark, mfrs. of organs, 1884; firm began mfr. of piano, 1894; dissolved partnership 1899; organizer, 1900, and pres. Melville Clark Piano Co. Extensive experimenter in field of pneumatics. Invented and put on market first 88-note piano player, revolutionizing the player piano industry of the world; built first player, 1901. Invented, 1911, the recording machine which reproduces the temperament and tech. peculiarities of the pianist playing a grand piano to which recorder is attached; used for cutting music rolls. Progressive. Home: Chicago, Ill. Died Nov. 5, 1918.

CLARK, VIRGINIUS E., aeronautical engr.; b. in Pa., Feb. 27, 1886; grad. U.S. Naval Acad., 1907; mil. aviator, 1913; postgrad. course in aeronautical engring., Mass. Inst. Tech., 1914; chief aero engr. U.S. Army, 1915-20; mem. Nat. Advisory Com. for Aeronautics, 1917-18; mem. Joint Army and Navy Bd. for Aeronautics, 1917-20; mem. Biling Aero Mission to Europe, 1917; comdg. Army Exptl. Sta., McCook Field, Dayton, O., 1917; chief engr. Dayton-Wright Co., 1920-23; v.p. and chief engr. Consolidated Aircraft Corp., 1923-27; gen. mgr. and chief engr. Am. Airplane & Engring. Corp., 1931-32. Fellow Inst. of Aeronautical Sciences. Mem. Nat. Aeronautical Safety Code Com., 1920-24; v.p. Soc. Automotive Engrs., 1922-23. Address: 1067 Corsica Drive, Pacific Palisades, Calif. Died Jan. 30, 1948.

CLARK, WALLACE, consulting engr.; b. Wyoming, Cincinnati, O., July 27, 1880; s. William Allen and Mary (Rankin) C.; A.B., U. of Cincinnati, 1902; hon. deg. D.Eng., Stevens Inst. Technology, 1943; m. Pearl Franklin, May 11, 1922. With Remington Typewriter Co., 1907-17; staff engr. H.L. Gantt, 1917-20; head of scheduling div., U.S. Shipping Bd., 1918; cons. cons. management engr.; head Wallace Clark & Co. since 1920; engineer member Kemmerer Finance Commission to Poland, 1926; Am. representative, committee on scientific management, International Labor Office, Geneva, Switzerland. Fellow American Society M.E.; mem. Am. Management Assn., Soc. for the Advancement of Management, Association Consulting Management Engineers, Civil Engineers of France, Masaryk Acad., also other foreign management insts. Decorated Comdr. Cross Poland Restored; Gantt medalist, 1934. Clubs: Engineers, University (N.Y.C.); Cosmos (Washington); Interalliee (Paris, France). Author: The Gantt Chart, 1922; Shop and Office Forms, 1925; The Foreman and His Job, 1926. Address: 521 Fifth Av., New York 17, N.Y. Died July 4, 1948.

CLARK, WALTON, engr.; b. Utica, N.Y., 1856; s. Erastus and Frances A. (Beardsley) C.; ed. High Sch., Utica; M.E., Sc.D.; m. Alice M. Shaw (died); 1 son, Frank Shaw; m. 2d, Louise Beauvais, 1885; children—Walton, Theobald Forstall, Beauvais, Darthela. Began in New Orleans, 1873, and has been identified with pub. service corps.; cons. engr. United Gas Improvement Co., Phila. Republican. Home: Chestnut Hill, Pa. Died 1934.

CLARK, WILLIAM BULLOCK, geologist; b. Brattleboro, Vt., Dec. 15, 1860; s. Barna A. and Helen C. (Bullock) C.; A.B., Amherst, 1884; Ph.D., U. of Munich, 1887; continued studies in Berlin and London; (LL.D., Amherst, 1908); m. Ellen C. Strong, Oct. 12, 1892. Instr. and asso., 1887-92, asso. prof., 1892-94, prof. geology, and dir. Geol. Lab., from 1894, Johns Hopkins. Asst. geololgist, 1888-94, geologist, 1894-1907, coöperating geologist, 1907—, U.S. Geol. Survey; dir. Md. Weather Service, 1891—; state geologist, 1896—; commr. for state of Md. on re-survey of Mason and Dixon line, 1900-06; mem. and exec. officer Md. State Forestry Commn., 1906—; mem. White House Conf. on conservation, 1908; mem. Md. State Conservation Commn., 1908-12. Asso. editor Jour. of Geology., 1896—; pres. Children's Aid Soc., Baltimore, 1901—. Author: The Eocene Deposits of the United States, 1891; The Physical Features of Maryland, 1906; The Mesozoic and Cenozoic Echinadermata of the United States, 1915. Home: Baltimore, Md. Died July 27, 1917.

CLARK, WILLIAM MANSFIELD, physiol. chemistry; b. Tivoli, N.Y., Aug. 17, 1884; s. James Starr and Caroline S. (Hopson) C.; grad. Hotchkiss Sch., Lakeville, Conn., 1903; B.A., Williams Coll., 1907, M.A., 1908; hon. Sc.D. from same coll. 1935; Ph.D., Johns Hopkins, 1910; Sc.D., U. Pa., 1940; m. Rose Willard Goodard, Sept. 14, 1910 (dec. June 1958); children—Harriet Allen (Mrs. Everett B. Gladding), Miarian Goddard. Research chemist, dairy division United States Dept. Agriculture, 1910-20; prof. chemistry, and chief division of chemistry Hygenic Lab., U.S. Public Health Service, 1920-27; De Lamar prof. physiol. chemistry, Johns Hopkins, 1927-52, DeLamar professor emeritus since 1952, research professor chemistry, 1952-64; First Hon. Lectr. Albany Med. Coll., 1957. Chmn. division chemistry and chem. technology of Nat. Research Council, 1941-46. Cons. O.S.R.D., 1941-46. Awarded William H. Nichols medal, 1936; Hotchkiss Alumni award, 1938; Borden award, chemistry of milk, 1944; Remsen Memorial lecturer, 1952; Passano award, 1957. Fellow A.A.A.S.; mem. American Chemical Society, Soc. Am. Bacteriologists (pres. 1933), Am. Soc. Biological Chemists (pres. 1933, 34, edit. bd. Jour. Biol. Chem., 1933-51), Nat. Acad. of Scis., (mem. council, 1940-46), Gargoyle, Alpha Zeta Alpha, Phi Beta Kappal Sigma Xi. Club: 14 W. Hamilton St. Author: The Determination of Hydrogen Ions, 1920, 22, 28; Studies on Oxidation Reduction, 1928; Topics in Pnysical Chemistry, 1948, 52; Oxidation-Reduction Potentials of Organic Systems, 1960. Home: 1533 Stonewood Rd., Balt. 21212; also Lakeville, Conn. Died Jan. 19, 1964; buried Salisbury, Conn.

CLARK, WILLIAM TIMOTHY, b. Delphos, O., July 21, 1860; s. Henry Dutton and Mary A. (Garbutt) C.; ed. high sch.; m. Adelaide M. Wear, of Topeka, Kan., Oct. 31, 1882; children—William Wear (dec.), Madeline (dec.), Henry Dutton, Mary Adelaide, Joseph Forrest (dec.). A founder of Lamar, Colo., 1886, later mgr. Union Pacific Town & Land Co., Topeka, Kan.; moved to Wash., 1889, and has been prominently identified with irrigation and development enterprises, including the Wenatchee Canal, the Selah and Moxie Canal, the Billings (Mont.) Land and Irrigation Co., the Columbus (Mont.) Dist. and Canal etc.; now pres. Monitor Orchard Co., Clark Co., Republic Farms; owner East Side Land Co.; mem. firm Clark-Oliver Apple Co.; instrumental in bldg. the first bridge over Columbia River, at Wenatchee. Republican. Club: Rainier (Seattle, Wash.). Home: Santa Monica, Calif.

CLARK, WINFRED NEWCOMB, pub. utility exec.; b. Paxton Ill., Oct. 13, 1876; s. Abram L. and Sarah E. (Foster) C.; student of U. of Ill., 1894-96; B.Sc., in E.E., Colo. Sch. of Mines, 1898; m. Mary Ward, Apr. 15, 1903; children—Muriel (Mrs. James Gittinger), Helen Louise (Mrs. Geo. Ashby), Winfred Ward. Asst. engr. Colo. Telephone Co., 1898; elec. engr. Silver Lake Mines Co., 1898-99; operating engr. La Bella Mill Water and Power Co., 1899-1900; constr. and operation of Pikes Peak Power Co. and successor companies, 1900-12; pres. Southern Colo. Power Co., (successor to Pike Peak Power Co.), 1931-51, ret.; registered C.E., State of Colo. Rocky Mt. Elec. Assn. award, 1935. Chmn. Pueblo Co. Relief Assn., 1932-33. Mem. Am. Inst. E.E., Pueblo Engrs. Soc., Colo. Engring. Soc., Am. Mining Congress. Republican. Epsicopalian, Mason, Shriner, K. of P., Elk. Clubs: Rotary, Pueblo Golf and Country. Home: 2201 Greenwood. Office:. Southern Colorado Power Co., Pueblo, , Colo. Died July, 19, 1952.

CLARKE, ALFRED, mech. engr.; b. Leicester, Eng., June 4, 1849; s. Thomas Alfred William and Susanna (Cott) C.; ed. pub. schs., Leicester, and dept. of science and art, S. Kensington, London; m. Lucia Evelyn Whiting, Nov. 3, 1880. Came to America, 1874; chief engr., Bradley Fertilizer Co., N. Weymouth, Mass., 1876-77; supt. Kitson Machine Co., Lowell, Mass., 1877-85, and while there invented and patented improvements in cotton machinery then in general use; gen. mgr. Prospect Machine & Engine Co., Cleveland, O., 1885-87; asso. with Arthur E. Childs in founding The Light, Heat & Power Corp., Boston, which led to formation of the Mass. Lighting Cos., owning a number of gas, electric light and power cos. in Mass. Republican. Mem. Ch. of England, Mason. Home: Walpole, N.H. Died Apr. 27, 1922.

CLARKE, CHARLES LORENZO, elec. engr.; b. Portland, Me., Arp. 16, 1853; s. Daniel and Mary Lewis (Bragg) C.; B.S. with honors, Bowdoin, 1875, M.S., 1879, C.E., 1880; m. Helen Elizabeth Sparrow 1881; 1 son, John Curtis; m. 2d, Henriette Mary Augusta Willatowski, 1894; children—Mary Willatowski (dec.), Daniel William; m. 3d, Edna Florence Thurston, Aug. 30, 1916; 1 son, Charles Lorenzo. Became asst. Edison lab., Menlo Park, N.J., 1880; chief engr. parent Edison Electric Light Co., 65 Fifth Av., New York, 1881-84; engr. Telemeter Co., New York, 1884-87, Gibson Electric Co. (storage batteries), 1887-89; cons. practice, 1889-1901; cons. engr. Bd. of Patent Control. Gen. Electric Co. and Westinghouse Electric & Mfg. Co., 1901-11; cons. engr. General Electric Co., 1911-31, retired Nov. 1, 1931. Intalled first (now historically noted) Edison electric lighting central station system, 1882, with central station at 257 Pearl St., New York. Republican. Protestant. Diagonal Patentee of several inventions. Home: Newton, Mass. Died Oct. 9, 1941.

CLARKE, CHARLES W(ARRINGTON) E(ARLE), cons. engr.; b. Chicago, Ill., Jan. 23, 1882; s. John Robert and Izelia (Smith) C.; ed. Lewis Inst., Chicago; m. Lucy Sima, Dec. 27, 1900; 1 dau., Lucille V. Successively draftsman Hawley Downdraft Furnace Co. (Chicago); draftsman and engr. Armour & Co. then Sargent & Lundy, Chgo.; steam engr. electric zone, N.Y.C.&H.R. Ry. (New York); mech. engr. Stone & Webster (Boston); (power and cons. engr. Dwight P. Robinson & Co., Inc. (New York); cons. engr. United Engineers & Constructors, Inc. (Phila), 1928-35, private practice as cons. engr., 1935-37; cons. engr. United Engrs. & Constructors, Inc., 1937-56, v.p., cons. engr., 1945-56, dir., 1955-56, ret.; pvt. cons. practice Narbeth, Pa., 1956-60. Served at civilian engr. on constrn. project, World War, France. Fellow and hon. mem. Am. Soc. M.E.; mem. Am. Iron and Steel Inst., Edison Electric Inst., Assn. Iron and Steel Engrs., Instn. Mech. Engrs. (Gt. Britain; life), Newcomen Soc. N. Am. Republican. Mason (32 deg., Shriner), Clubs: Engineers (past pres.) (N.Y.C.); Clinkers (Phila.); Merion Golf. Home: 728 Clarendon Rd., Narberth, Pa. Died Jan. 20, 1965; buried All Saints Ch., Wynnewood, Pa.

CLARKE, ELIOT CHANNING, engr.; b. Boston, May 6, 1845; s. Rev. Dr. James Freeman and Anna (Huidekoper) C.; A.B., Harvard, 1867; studied civ. engring. 1 yr. Mass. Inst. Tech.; m. Alice de Vermandois Sohier, Apr. 4, 1878 (died 1901). Practiced as civ. engr. in different parts of U.S., in connection with building rys., bridges, tunnels, water works and sewerage systems, 1868-86; treas. of cotton mill, 1886-1904. Fellow Am. Acad. Arts and Sciences (treas. 13 yrs.). Author: Report of a Commission Appointed to Consider a General System of Drainage for the Valleys of Mystic, Blackstone and Charles Rivers, 1886 (state publ.); Astronomy from a Dipper, 1909. Home: Boston, Mass. Died May 4, 1921.

CLARKE, FRANK WIGGLESWORTH, chemist; b. Boston, Mar. 19, 1847; s. Henry Ware and Abby Mason (Fisher) C.; S.B., Lawrence Scientific Sch. (Harvard), 1867; D.Sc., Columbian, 1891, Victoria, Manchester, 1903; LL.D., Aberdeen U., 1906, U. of Cincinnati, 1914; m. Mary P. Olmsted, Sept. 9, 1874. Instr. Cornell, 1869; prof. chemistry, Howard U., Washington, D.C., 1873-74; prof. chemistry and physics, U. of Cincinnati, 1874-83; chief chemist U.S. Geol. Survey and hon. curator minerals, U.S. Nat. Museum, 1883—. Hon. pres. Internat. Com. on Chem. Elements. Chevalier de la Légion d'Honneur; Wilde medallist. Manchester (Eng.) Literary and Philos. Soc., 1903. Mem. Internat. Jury Awards, Paris Expn., 1900. Author: Weights, Measurers and Money of All Nations; Elements of Chemistry; Constants of Nature; Report on the Teaching of Chemistry and Physics in the United States, 1881; Elementary Chemistry (with Louis M. Dennis), 1902; Laboratory Manual of Elementary Chemistry (with same), 1902. Home: Washington, D.C. Died May 23, 1931.

CLARKE, HANS THACHER, educator, biol. chemist; b. of Am. parents, Harrow, Eng., Dec. 27, 1887; s. Joseph Thacher and Agnes (Helferich) C.; B.Sc., Univ. Coll., London, 1908, D.Sc., 1914; grad. study U. of Berlin, 1911-13; Sc.D., U. Rochester, 1953, Columbia, 1957; m. Frieda Planck, October 8, 1914 (dec. Aug. 1960); children—Eric, John, Rebecca, Heidi; m. 2d, to Flora de Peyer, July 1963. Demonstrator in chemistry, Univ. Coll., 1908-09, lecturer in stereochemistry, 1910-11, asst. in chemistry, 1913-14; research organic chemist, Eastman Kodak Co., Rochester, N.Y., 1914-28; prof. biol. chemistry, Coll. Physicians and Surgeons, Columbia U., 1928-56, prof. emeritus, 1956; lecturer Yale, 1956-64; research guest Boston Children's Hosp., 1964-72; science attache American Embassy, London, 1951-52. Fellow Inst. Chemistry of Great Britain, Chem. Soc. London, Univ. Coll. (London); mem. Nat. Acad. Science, Am. Philos. Soc., Am. Chem. Soc., Am. Soc. Biol. Chem. (pres. 1947-49), Harvey Soc. (pres. 1942-44). Club: Century. Author: Organic · Analysis, 1911; Introduction to Study of Organic Chemistry, 1914. Editor: Organic Syntheses, 1921-32; The Chemistry of Penicillin, 1949, asso. editor Jour. of Am. Chem. Soc., 1928-38; mem. editorial com. Jour. of Biol. Chemistry, 1930-37, mem. editorial board, 1937-51, 53-58. Home: Cambridge MA Died Oct. 21, 1972; buried Scotland CT

CLARKE, HOPEWELL, mining; b. Williamsport, Pa., Mar. 10, 1854; s. Hopewell and Mary A. (Strebeigh) C.; ed. pub. schs. Dickinson Sem., Williamsport, and spl. study in civ. and mining engring.; m. Rosetta Cline, Nov. 18, 1884. Entered engring. dept. Pa. R.R., 1871; engr. for various rys. in Minn., 1880-83; surveyor, land examiner and chief clerk N.P. R.R., 1883-88; land commr. St. Paul & Duluth R.R., 1888-99; then engaged in the development of mines, especially on the Mesabi Iron Range, with which and the settlement of Northern Minn. he was early identified. During controversy over the source of Miss. River made survey of its headwaters; report pub. in Science, 1886. Mason. Home: St. Paul, Minn. Died Feb. 3, 1931.

CLARKE, JOHN MASON, geologist; b. Canandaigua, N.Y., Apr. 15, 1857; s. Dr. Noah T. and Laura Mason (Merrill) C.; brother of Lorenzo Mason C.; A.B., Amherst, 1877, A.M., 1882; U. of Göttingen, 1882-84; (Ph.D., Marburg, 1898; LL.D., Amherst, 1902, Johns

Hopkins, 1915; Sc.D., Colgate, 1909, U. of Chicago, 1916, and Princeton U., 1919), m. Fannie V. Bosler, 1895. Professor of geology and mineralogy, Smith Coll., 1881-84; lecturer geology Mass. State Agrl. Coll., 1885-86; asst. N.Y. State paleontologist, 1886; prof. geology and mineralogy, Rensselaer Poly. Inst., 1894—; asst. state geologist, 1894, state paleontologist, 1898-1904, state geologist and paleontologist and dir. State Mus. and Science Dept., U. State of N.Y., 1904—. Hayden gold medal, 1908; gold medal. Permanent Wild Life Protection Fund, 1920; Wampum keeper of Iroquois Nation; Spindiaroff prize, Internat. Congress of Geologists, Stockholm, 1910. Chmn. geol. com. Nat. Research Council, 1917. Pres. Albany Inst., and Hist. and Art Soc.; trustee Dudley Obs., Schuyler Mansion. Fellow Am. Acad. Arts and Sciences, Geol. Soc. America (pres. 1916-17), Paleontol. Soc. (1st pres.). Mem. Nat. Research Council (chmn. geology); v.p. Nat. Parks Assn.; mem. Nat. Council Boy Scouts America. Author: Sketches of Gaspé; The Magdalen Islands; Heart of Gaspeé; The Life of JeJames Hall; Organic Dependence and Disease; L'Ile Percée. Home: Albany, N.Y. Died May 29, 1925.

CLARKSON, COKER FIFIELD, manager and editor; b. Des Moines, Ia., May 11, 1879; s. James S. and Anna (Howell) C.; A.B., Harvard, 1894; Harvard Law Sch., 1894-96; m. Lucy Miller Corkhill, 1898. Admitted to Phila. bar, 1896; practiced with Alexander & Magill, Phila., 1896-98; removed to New York, 1898, and practiced with Tracy, Boardman & Platt, later in own office as tech., corp. and patent atty.; became head of engring. dept. Assn. of Licensed Automboile Mfrs., operating under Selden patent; edit. 2 volumes mech. branch bulls. and reports of tests; inaugurated and edited A.L.A.M. Digest of Current Technical Literature; mgr. and head of publicity department A.L.A.M., 1909; sec. and gen. mgr. Soc. Automotive Engrs., which took over engring. work of A.L.A.M., 1910—. Mem. automotive products sect. of War Industries Bd., Council of Nat. Defense; Internat. Aircraft Standards Bd.; sec. war truck com. Q.M. Dept., U.S. Army, 1917; sec. Soc. Automotive Engrs., ordnance com. Home: Scarborough, N.Y. Died June 4, 1930.

CLARKSON, JAMES A(NDREW), educator; b. Newburyport, Mass., Feb. 7, 1906; s. Edward Hale and Alice Channing (Batchelder) C.; A.B., Dartmouth, 1929; A.M., Brown U., 1933, Ph.D., 1934; member Inst. Advanced Study, 1934-36; Nat. Research Council fellow Inst. Advanced Study, also Princeton, 1935-36; m. Jessie Murdoch McIntosh, June 14, 1930. Instr. Phillips Andover Acad., 1929-30; instr. U. Pa., 1936-40, asst. prof., 1940-47, asso. prof., 1947-48; prof., chmn. mathematics dept. Tufts U., 1948-69, Robinson prof., 1949-70. Exec. sec. div. mathematics Nat. Research Council, 1951-55. Chmn. board trustees Medford Public Library. Served as operations analyst hdqrs. 8th A.F.. U.S.A.A.F., 1943-45. Medal of Freedom, USAAF, 1948. Mem. Dansk Matematisk Forening, Am. Math. Soc., Math. Assn. Am., Am. Assn. U. Profs., Phi Beta Kappa, Sigma Xi, Sigma Pi Sigma. Republican. Unitarian. Contbr. articles profl. math. jours. Home: West Medford MA Died June 6, 1970; buried Dover NH

CLAS, ANGELO ROBERT, architect; b. Milw., Feb. 13, 1887; s. Alfred Charles and Louise (Wick) C.; grad. E. Div. High Sch., Milw., 1905; B.S. in Architecture, Harvard, 1909; m. Norma Huette, Oct. 12, 1910 (dec. 1963); 1 dau., Mary Louise (Mrs. Delmar W. Holloman); m. 2d, Alice Beier Nicholson, 1965. Began as architect in Milw., 1908; engaged in mfg. business, Sheboygan, Wis., also Toledo, 1909-23; manufactured truck and tractor motors and shells during World War; traveled abroad, 1924; partner D.H. Burnham & Co., architects, Chgo., 1924-26, W.W. Ahischlager, 1927-29, Holabird & Root, 1929-34; apptd. mem. housing div. Fed. Emergency Adminstrn. of Pub. Works, Washington, 1934, dir. of housing, 1935-36; asst. adminstr. pub. works, 1936-37; now cons. Clas, Riggs, Owens & Ramos. Recent work: Fed. Loan Agy., Internat. Bank for Reconstrn. and Devel., YMCA Addition, Washington Statler Hotel, Wyatt Bldg. (winner 1952 Archtl. award of Merit); large scale housing devels. in Md., Va., Pa. and Tenn.; office bldg. Govt. of India, also Nat. Rifle Assn., Phillip Murray, IMF bldgs. of Washington (winner 1959 Archtl. award of Merit). Recipient Bronze award for outstanding contbns. to architecture of Nat. Capitol, Bldg. Stone Inst.; bronze medal Am. Heart Assn., 1965. Fellow A.I.A.; mem. Washington Bldg. Congress, Honolulu Acad. Arts, Delta Upsilon. Mason. Methodist. Club: Harvard, Outrigger Canoe. Home: Honolulu HI Died Dec. 4, 1970; interred Wildwood Cemetery, Sheboygan WI

CLAUSEN, JENS (CHRISTIAN), research botanist; b. North Eskilstrup, Denmark, Mar. 11, 1891; s. Christen Augustinus and Christine (Christensen) C.; M.A., U. Copenhagen, 1921, Ph.D., 1926; Doctor of Agr. (hon.), University of Uppsala, 1957; m. Anna Hansen, October 28, 1921 (deceased August 24, 1956). Came to the United States, 1931, naturalized, 1943. Farmer, 1905-15; tchr. secondary schools, 1910-16, 18-20; research asst., dept. genetics Royal Agrl. and Vet. Coll., Copenhagen, Denmark, 1921-31; research fellow Internat. Edn. Bd., U. Cal., 1927-28; staff dept. plant biology Carnegie Inst. of Washington, Stanford, Cal., 1931-69; lectr. U. Copenhagen, 1936, universities of Brazil, 1953, Messenger lecturer Cornell, 1950, U. Chgo., Wash. State U., 1961, Vanderbilt U., 1962; prof. biology Stanford U., 1951-69; vis. professor genetics, University Cal. at Davis, 1963-64. Trustee Berkeley Bapt. Div. Sch., 1950-61. Served with Arty. Corps, Denmark Army, 1916-18. Recipient Mary Sope Pope medal of botany. Cranbrook Inst. Sci., 1949; certificate of merit Botanical Soc. Am., 1956; decorated Knight of Dannebrog (Denmark), 1961. Fellow Bot. Soc. Edinburgh (hon.), California Academy of Sciences, American Academy of Arts and Sci., A.A.A.S.; mem. Soc. Study Evolution (pres. 1956), Royal Swedish Acad. Sci., Nat. Acad. Genetics Soc. Am., Am. Soc. Agronomy, Royal Danish Acad. Sci. and Letters. Republican. Baptist. Author: Experimental Studies on the Nature of Species I-III (with D. D. Keck and William M. Hiesey) 1940-48, IV (with William M. Hiesey), pub. 1958 Stages in the Evolution of Plant Species, 1951. Author sci. articles on hybridization, race ecology, plant evolution, world forest compositions. Home: Palo Alto CA Died Nov. 22, 1969.

CLAUSEN, ROY ELWOOD, Univ. prof.; b. Randall Ia., Aug. 21, 1891; s. Jens and Mathilda (Chrisitanson) C.; B.S., Okla., Agrl. and Mech. Coll., 1910; B.S., U. of Calif., 1912, Ph.D., 1914; m. Mae Winifred Falls, July 19, 1916; 1 son, Roy Elwood. Instr. genetics, U. of Calif., 1914-16, asst. prof., 1916-24, associate prof., 1924-28, prof., 1928—; special dutied at the Los Alamos Sci. Lab., Manhattan Dist., 1944-45. Served in U.S. Army, 1917-19. Fellow for special study in cytogenetics. International Education Bd., Stockholm Högskolan, 1926-27; travel fellow for inspection of genetics instns. in Northwestern Europe, May- Sept. 1927; spl. consulant in genetics Hawaiian Agrl. Expt. Station and expt. stations of Hawaiian Sugar Planters Assn. and Pineapple Producer Cooperative Assn., May-June 1941; faculty research lectuer U. Cal. At Berkeley, 1954. Mem. Nat. Acad. Science, A.A.A.S., (v.p. chmn. exec. com. 1940-44), Bot Soc. America, Am. Genetic Assn., Genetics Society of America (vice president 1952; president 1953), American Soc. Naturalists, Am. Assn. Univ. Profs., Western Soc. Naturalists, Alpha Zeta, Phi Sigma, Sigma Xi, Phi Kappa Phi. Sec.-gen. 6th Pacific Science Congress, 1939. Democrat. Clubs: Faculty (Berkeley). Author: Genetics in Relation to Agriculture (with E. B. Babcock), 1918, 2d edit., 1927. Contbr. articles to Scientific jours. Home: 1885 San Juan Av., Berkeley 7, Cal. Died Aug. 21, 1956; buried Golden Gate Nat. Cemetery, San Bruno, Cal.

CLAYBOURN, JOHN GERONOLD, civil engineer, consultant on marine development and dredging; b. Albert Lea, Minn., May 23, 1886; s. John Bethel and Ellen (Clink) C.; grad. high sch., Albert Lea; student College of Engineering, University of Minnesota, 3 yrs., B.S. (hon.), 1964; m. Elsie Kathryn Grieser, Sept. 1, 1928. Served as rodman, levelman and transitman Isthmian Canal Commn., 1910-14; with dredging div. of Panama Canal since 1914, jr. engr., 1917-18, asst. engr. 1919-20, supt. of div., 1921-48, mem. Gov.'s staff, 1924-48, salary bd., 1926-48; retired; cons. engr. on marine developments, nav., rivers, harbors, canals; cons. on harbor developments, Colombia and Venezuela, 1949; collaborator on design of Diesel electric and turbo-driven suction dredges, Diesel electric tugs, floating electric compressor, floating electric grader, floating electric relay booster plant; original design and lay-out of new dredging div. hdqrs. and townsite Gamboa, Canal Zone, 1924-36; cons. engr. Dique Canal, Colombia, 1917, harbor development at Puntarenas, Costa Rica, 1925-46, 48; Aguadulce, Panama, 1926; Trans-Fla. Ship Canal, 1933, Panama Harbor, 1940-44, 46-48; study and layout docks and warehouses, Colon, 1948; reconnaisance covering Inland Waterway of Guatemala for I.B.E.C Tech. Service Corp., New York City, 1949; consultant for Inland Water Transport, Government of Union of Burma, 1951-53. Mem. commission for revision Colombian Code covering vessel construction and navigation, 1955-56. Mem. Pres.'s Club, U. Mich. Decorated Commendador, 1945, Gran Official, 1946, La Orden Vasco Nunea de Balboa (Panama). Mem. American Soc. Civil Engrs., Society of American Military Engineers, Tau Beta Pi. President of Gamboa Civic Council, 1937-48; pres. gen. com. Canal Zone Civic Councils, 1939-41; pres. The Panama Canal Employees' Mutual Benefit Assn., 1943-48, Minn. Club of Canal Zone, 1942-47. Mason (K.T. and Red Cross of Constantine, Shriner). Clubs: Union, Panama City, Panama Golf, Gamboa Golf and Country (pres. 1937-47). Author: Dredging on the Panama Canal, 1931; The Dredging Division of The Panama Canal, Its Function, Organization and Equipment, 1937; Evolution of the Panama Canal, 1944; Streamlining the Panama Canal for Maximum Safety and Unlimited Capacity, 1946; Suggested Methods and Equipment, Dredging and Mining for Convering the Present Locktype Canal to Sea Level, 1947. Contbr. to Mil. Engr., The Dock and Harbor Authority, London. Home: Ann Arbor MI Died June 26, 1967; buried Graceland Cemetery, Albert Lea MN

CLAYPOLE, EDWARD WALLER, geologist; b. England, June 1, 1835; grad. U. of London, B.A., 1862; B.Sc., 1864; D.Sc., 1888. Has been engaged in teaching of 40 yrs., now prof. geology and biology, Poly. Inst., Pasadena, Calif.; was for a time on geol. survey of Pa. Author of many papers and essays on geol. and biol. subjects. Mem. geol. socs. of London, Edinburgh and America. Home: Pasadena, Calif. Died 1901.

CLAYPOOL, J(OHN) GORDON, physician; b. Kansas City, Kan., Oct. 8, 1916; s. Charles William and Ruby (Larey) C.; A.B., U. Kan., 1939, M.D., 1941; m. Martha Roena Tillman, June 30, 1938; children—John Mark, Martha Ann. Asst. instr. anatomy U. Kan. Med. Sch., 1938; mem. teaching staff student health service Kan. State Coll., 1946-47; preceptor gen. practice U. Kan. Med. Sch., 1949-55, research fellow in medicine, 1955-56; practice medicine, specializing in internal medicine, Howard, Kan. Dir. Howard Nat. Bank (Kan.). Breeder Hereford cattle, buffalo. Trustee Kan. Blue Shield, 1963-67, v.p., 1967; trustee 4 County Mental Health Assn. Served as capt. M.C., AUS, 1944-46. Diplomate Am. Bd. Internal Medicine. Fellow A.C.P.; mem. A.M.A., Kan. (mem. council 1960-63, v.p. 1967), Greenwood County (pres. 1965), Elk County (sec.-treas., 1948-67) med. socs. Methodist. Contbr. papers in hemodynamics, other tech. studies to profl. jours. Home: Howard KS Died Sept. 22, 1967.

CLAYTON, HENRY HELM, meteorologist; b. Murfreesboro, Tenn., Mar. 12, 1861; s. Dr. Henry Holmes and Maris L. (Helm) C.; ed. pvt. schs., 1869-77; m. Frances Fawn Coman, Sept. 21, 1892; children—Henry Comyn (deceased), Lawrence Locke, Frances Lindley. Asst., Astron. Obs., Ann Arbor, Mich., 1884-85; asst. Harvard Astronomical Obs., 1885-86; observer, Blue Hill Meteorol. Obs., 1886-91; local forecast official U.S. Weather Bur., 1891-93; meteorologist, Blue Hill Meteorol. Obs., 1894-1909; dean Sch. of Aeronautics Assn. Inst., Boston, 1909-10. Employed by Oficina Meteorologica Argentina to study methods of weather forecasting in the Argentine Republic and also to inaugurate near Cordoba a sta. for exploring the upper air by means of kites, Mar.-Oct. 1910; engaged in business, 1911-12; forecast official, Oficina Argentina, Buenos Aires, 1913-22; researches, in cooperation with the Smithsonian Instn., in regard to the relation of world weather changes to observe conditions on the sun, 1923-25; pvt. weather service and cons. meteorologist for business orgns., 1925-42; research associate, Harvard University, 1943-44. In charge, 1905, of Tiesseren de Bort-Rotch expdn. for exploring the atmosphere over the Atlantic ocean with kites and sounding balloons; accompanied Oscar Erbsloh in the German balloon Pommern, Oct. 1907, when record-making balloon voyage was made from St. Louis to Asbury Park, N.J. Inaugurated a new system of weather forecasting, based on solar head changes in Argentina, 1918. Cons. expert in Cloud Atlas prepared for Hydrographic Office, under Capt. Sigsbee, U.S. Navy; invented attachment for anemometers, Blue Hill box kite, etc. Del. Pan.-Am. Scientific Congress, Washington, D.C., 1915; del. Argentine Weather Service to 6th Internat. Meteorol. Conf., Holland, 1923. Fellow Am. Acad. Arts and Sciences. Author: World Weather, 1923; World Weather Records (pub. by Smithsonian Instn.), 1927 and 1934; Solar Relations to Weather, 1943; also numerous papers on meteorol. subjects (1939-41); studies of periodic changes in solar activity pub. by Smithsonian Institution and in JOur. of Atmosphere, Electricity and Terrestrial Magnetism of Carnegie Institution. Home: Canton, Mass. Died Oct. 27, 1946.

CLAYTON, JOHN botanist; b. Fulham, Eng., 1685; Came to Am., 1705. Asst. clk. Gloucester County, Va., 1905-22, 1st clk., 1722-73; collected bot. specimens in Middle Tidewater dist. of Va.; his specimens identified and categ] orized in John Frederick Gronovius' book Flora Virginia, 1739, 43; part of his collection now in Nat. Herbarium in England, Died Dec. 15, 1773.

CLAYTON, POWELL; . b. Bethel, Pa., Aug. 7, 1833; s. John and Ann (Clark) C.; ed. pub. schs. and Partridge Mil. Acad., Bristol, Pa.; studied civ. engring., Wilmington, Del.; went to Kans., 1855. Inc. civ. engring. practric to 1861; city engr. Leavenworth, Kan., 1859-61; capt. 1st Kan. Inf., May 29, 1861; lt. col. 5th Kans. Cav., Dec. 18, 1861; col., Mar. 7, 1862; brig. gen. vols., Aug. 24, 1864; hon. discharged, Aug. 24, 1865; m. Adaline McGraw, Dec. 14, 1865. Purchased and settled upon a plantation near Pine Bluff, Ark., after close of war; removed to Eureka Springs, Ark., 1882, where same yr. built the Eureka Springs Ry.; later built the st. ry. and as chmn. water and sewer boards constructed sewer system and water works there; pres. Crescent Hotel Co.; Eureka Springs, and dir. Mo.&N.Ar. Ry. Co. Active in politics from orgn. of Rep. party; mem. State Central Com., Ark., 1867—; mem. Rep. Nat. Com., 1872-1913 (except about 3 yrs.). Gov. of Ark., 1868-71; U.S. senator, 1871-77; attended every Rep. Nat. Conv., 1872-1912; mem. com. or arrangements Rep. Nat. Conv., St. Louis, 1896, and mem. exec. com. Rep. Nat. Com. and chmn. of speaker's bur., at New York, during following campaign; Am. ambassador to Mexico, 1897-1905. Address: Washington, D.C. Died Aug. 25, 1914.

CLEARY, ALFRED JOHN, engr.; b. San Francisco, Calif., June 24, 1884; s. Patrick and Julia Agnes (Tarpey) C.; B.A., U. of San Francisco, 1902; B.S., U. of

Calif., 1906; m. Marie Alouise Ryan, Mar. 2, 1918; children—Alfred John, Louis Xavier. Cons. engr. for State of Calif. on development of its water resources, 1921-30; chief engr. Construction Co. of N. America, in charge of Hetch Hetchy tunnel, Muscle Shoals analysis and bid, Kennet project, and San Francisco-Oakland Bridge via Rincon Hill; pioneer engring. on Mokelumne River water supply project and American River Reservoir development, in Sacramento-San Joaquin Delta; formerly chief asst. city engr. of San Francisco, and acting city engr.; apptd. city adminstr. of San Francisco, Jan. 8, 1932. Catholic. Author: The Engineering Works of San Francisco, 1915. Home: San Francisco, Calif. Died Feb. 16, 1941.

CLEGG, MOSES TRAN, bacteriologist; b. Red Bluff, Ark., Sept. 1, 1876; s. Joseph Thomas and Ida Neal (Daugherty) C.; Siloam Springs (Ark.) High Sch.; U. of Ark., 1892, 93, 96; m. Edna Wisner, July 26, 1911. Mem. U.S. Army Hospital Corps. Mar. 31, 1899-Apr. 1, 1902, serving through Philippine insurrection; asst. bacteriologist in Bureau of Science, Philippine Civ. Service, Apr. 2, 1902-Sept. 1910; in U.S. Pub. Health and Marine Hosp. Service as asst. dir. U.S. Leprosy Investigation Sta., Hawaii, 1910-15; bacteriologist, U.S. Public Health Service, San Francisco, 1916-17; supt. Queen's Hosp., Honolulu, H.T., 1918—. Mason. Died Aug. 9, 1918.

CLELAND, HERDMAN FITZGERALD, prof. geology; b. Milan, Ill., July 13, 1869; s. David James and Margaret (Betty) C.; Gates Coll., Neligh, Neb.; B.A., Oberlin, 1894; Ph.D., Yale, 1900; post-grad. work, U. of Neb., 1895, U. of Chicago, 1896, Cornell U., 1901; m. Helen Williams Davison, 1910; children—Margaret Jane, Elizabeth Davison; m. 2d, Emily Leonard Wadsworth, 1925. Asst. in geolgoy, Cornell U., 1900-01; instr. in geology and botany, 1901-04; asst. prof. geology and mineralogy, Williams, 1905-07, prof. geology from 1907; instr., Cornell Summer Sch., 1900-02, U. of Tenn. Summer Sch., 1904. Mem. Internat. Geol. Congress, Mexico, Belgium and Spain; Internat. Geog. Congress, Geneva, Switzerland. Author: Fossils and Stratigraphy of the Middle Devonic of Wisconsin, 1911; Physical and Historical Geology (2vols.), 1917; Practical Applications of Geology and PhPhysiography, 1920; Our Prehistoric Ancestors, 1928; Why Be an Evolutionist, 1930. Home: Williamstown, Mass. Died Jan. 24, 1935.

CLELAND, RALPH ERSKINE, botanist; b. Le Claire, Ia., Oct. 20, 1892; s. Charles Samuel and Edith Eleanor (Collins) C.; A.B., U. of Pa., 1915, M.S., 1916, Ph.D., 1919, Sc.D., 1958; LL.D., Hanover College, 1957; Sc.D., Ind. U., 1970; married Elizabeth Prentice Shoyer of East Orange, N.J., June 11, 1927; children—William Wallace, Robert Erskine, Charles Frederick. Asst. in botany, U. of Pa., 1915-16, Harrison fellow, 1916-18; instr. biology, Goucher Coll., 1919-20, asst. prof., 1920-23, asso. prof., 1923-30, prof., 1930-38, chmn. of dept., 1937-38; prof., chmn. botany dept. Ind. U., 1938-58, dean of Grad. School, 1950-58, Distinguished Service prof. botany, 1958-63, Distinguished Service prof. botany emeritus, co-dir. aerospace applications center, 1963-68; instructor botany Marine Biol. Lab., Woods Hole, 1925; editor plant cytology, Biol. Abstracts (trustee, 1943-48); cons. Nat. Sci. Found.; editor in chief Am. Jour. of Botany, 1940-46. Mem. U.S. Nat. Commn. for UNESCO, 1958-60; mem. of the program committee U.S. Nat. Com., 1958-60. Pvt., arty., U.S. Army, with A.E.F., 1918-19. Rec. John F. Lewis award, Am. Philos. Soc., 1937, J. S. Guggenheim traveling fellowship, 1927-28. Fellow A.A.A.S. (mem. council 1932-37, v.p. 1944), Ind. Acad. Sci. (pres. 1959), Am. Acad. Arts and Scis.; mem. Nat. Research Council (chmn. div. biol. and agr. 1948-51), Bot. Soc. Am. (pres. 1947), Genetics Society of Am. (v.p. 1955, pres. 1956), Nat. Acad. Scis. (chmn. Pacific sci. bd.), Nat. Assn. Biology Tchrs., Am. Soc. Naturalists (sec. 1938-40, pres. 1942), Am. Inst. Biol. Sci. (chmn. 1948-49), Soc. Study Evolution, Am. Philos. Soc. (v.p. 1965-68), Genetics Soc. Japan (hon. fgn. mem.), Bot. Soc. Korea (hon. life), Deutsche Botanische Gesellschaft (corresponding member), Phi Beta Kappa, Sigma Xi. Presbyterian. Author: OenotheraCytogenetics and Evolution, 1971. Contbr. numerous articles to scientific jours. Home: Bloomington IN Died June 11, 1971.

CLEMENTS, EDITH SCHWARTZ, ecologist, illustrator; b. Albany, N.Y., d. George and Emma G. (Young) Schwartz; B.A., U. of Neb., 1898, Ph.D., 1906; m. Frederic E. Clements, 1899. Fellow in German, U. of Neb., 1898-1901, asst. in botany, 1903-07; instr. botany, U. of Minn., 1909-13; investigator and illustrator, Carnegie Institution, Washington, D.C., 1918-41. Mem. Sigma Xi, Phi Beta Kappa, Kappa Alpha Theta fraternities. Author: Relation of Leaf Structure to Physical Factors, 1905; Rocky Mountain Flowers (with husband), 1913, 19; Flowers of Mountain and Plain, 1913, 19; (monograph) Herbaria Ecadium Californiae, 1914; (booklet) Wild Flowers of the West, 1927; Flower Families and Ancestors (with husband), 1928; Flowers of Coast and Sierra, 1929; Flower Pageant of the Midwest, 1939; Flowers of Prairie and Woodland, 1947. Editor: Dynamics of Vegetation, 1949. Illustrator: Experimental Pollination, 1923; Genera of Fungi, 1931. Home: La Jolla CA Died June 30, 1971.

CLEMENTS, FREDERIC EDWARD, ecologist; b. Lincoln, Neb., Sept. 16, 1874; s. Ephraim G. and Mary (Scoggin) C.; B.Sc., U. of Neb. 1894; M.A., 1896, Ph.D., 1898, LL.D., 1940; m. Edith Schwartz, May 30, 1899. Instr. and asso. prof. botany, 1894-1906, prof. plant physiology, 1906-07, U. of Neb.; prof. and head of dept. of botany, U. of Minn., 1907-17; State botanist, dir. bot. survey of Minn.; in charge ecol. research, Carnegie Instn., Washington, 1917-41; collaborator U.S. Soil Conservation Service since 1934; cons. National Highway Research Bd., 1935. Fellow A.A.A.S., (gen. sec., 1910), Am. Geographers Assn., Am. Nomenclature Commn., Internat. Nomenclature Commn., Internat. Cong. of Science, Am. Nature Study Soc. (dir. 1905), Am. Breeders Assn., St. Paul Inst., Minn. Mycol. Soc. (pres. 1908), Minn. Garden Club (pres. 1910), Ecol. Soc. of Am., Paleontol. Soc., Soc. Am. Foresters, Am. Meteorol. Soc., Am. Soc. Mammologists, Am. Soc. Naturalists, Am. Soc. Plant Physiologists, Brit. Ecol. Soc., Societas Phytogeographica Suecana of Sweden (hon.), Reale Academia Agricultura of Italy (hon.), Sigma Xi, Phi Beta Kappa. Author: The Phytogeography of Nebraska (with Dr. Pound), 1898; 2d edit., 1900; Histogenesis of Caryophyllales, 1899; Greek and Latin in Biological Nomenclature, 1902; Development and Structure of Vegetation, 1904; Research Methods in Ecology, 1905; Plant Physiology and Ecology, 1907; Cryptogamae Formationum Coloradensium, 1908; Genera of Fungi, 1909; Minnesota Mushrooms, 1910; Rocky Mountain Flowers, 1913 (with Dr. Edith Elements); Plant Succession, 1916; Plant Indicators, 1920; Aeration and Air-Content, 1921; The Phylogenetic Method in Taxonomy (with Dr. Hall), 1923; Experimental Pollination (with Dr. Long), 1923; Experimental Vegetation (with Dr. Weaver), 1924; Phytometer Method in Ecology (with Dr. Goldsmith), 1924; Plant Succession and Indicators, 1928; Flower Families and Ancestors (with Dr. Edith Clements), 1928; Home: Manitou, Colo. (Alpine Lab.). Died July 26, 1945.

CLEMENTS, GEORGE P., counselor agr., conservation; b. Dumfries, N.B., Can., Nov. 12, 1867; s. Frederick William William dePyster and Mary Anna (Jones) C.; came to U.S., 1881; M.D., U. of Nebraska, 1896; LL.D., University of California, 1944; m. Esther W. Hoag, May 25, 1898; 1 dau., Catherina Emily (Mrs. John Clifford Argue). in Passenger dept. C.B.&Q. R.R., 1886-89; with Armour & Co., Armour & Cudahy and Cudahy Packing Co., 1890-92; in gen. med. and surg. practice, Clarkson and Albion, Neb., 1896-1900; owner and operator of pureblood stock farm, 1897-99; engaged in gen. and exptl. agr., Riverside, Calif., 1900-18; organizer, 1918, and mgr. agrl. dept. Los Angeles (Calif.) Chamber of Commerce, 1918-39, counselor on agr. and conservation, 1939-47. Chmn. City Council, Clarkson. Neb., 1897-98; dep. state health cbmmr., Neb., 1897-99; coroner, Colfax County, Neb., 1898. Decorated Chevalier du Merite Agricole (France), 1933; selective service medal, U.S. Congress, World War II Dir. Los Angeles Co. Farm Bur., Calif. Jr. Republic; mem. Calif. State Land Use Planning Com., 1941—; mem. adv. com. on land utilization for state planning Bd., Mem. Soil Conservation Service Regional Bd., Mem. Appeal Bd. No. 10. Selective Service; mem. S.W. Museum, Museum Hill Com. Fellow (1940) Pacific Geog. Soc. (dir. v.p. and treas., 1921-31); mem. Los Angeles Tb and Health Assn. (dir. and sec. 1921-37, Fellow, 1940), State Assn. County Agrl. Commrs. (hon.), Southern California Conservation Assn. (dir.) Sigma Xi. Democrat. Episcopalian. Mason. Clubs: University, Andreas Canyon (pres. 1922-39, dir. since 1939). Contbr. articles and papers on agrl. economics. Home: 26 4805 Alta Canda Road, La Canda, Calif. Office: Chamber of Commerce, Los Angeles 15. Died Aug. 7, 1958; buried Lawn, Glendale, Cal.

CLEPHANE, JAMES OGILVIE, lawyer, financier; b. Washington, D.C., Feb. 21, 1842; s. James and Ann (Ogilvie) C.; m. Pauline M. Harrison, Oct. 9, 1867. In early life became interested in the typewriter and other inventions, and expended much captial in their development; under his direction the first Sholes of Remington Typewriter was built; brought C. T. Moore from W.Va. in 1871 and had him construct the Moore Typewriter and Linomatrix machine, of which companies he became officer and dir.; these cos. were subsequently merged with the Am. Planograph Co., of which he became v.p. and dir.; suggested to Mr. Ottmar Mergenthaler the idea of a typesetting machine and furnished the means whereby was evolved the present successful linotype machine. Later was assisted by Whitelaw Reid, William C. Whitney and Ogden Mills; organized Am. Graphophone Co. to develop invention of the graphophone of Profs. Graham Bell and Summer Tainter; also organizer and pres. Horton Basket Machine Co., the Locke Steel Belt Co., and the Aurora Mining Co.; pres. Oddur Mfg. Co. Home: Englewood, N.J. Died 1910.

CLERGUE, FRANCIS HECTOR, b. Bangor, Me., May 28, 1856; s. Joseph H. and Frances (Lombard) C.; ed. U. of Me.; unmarried. Admitted to Me. bar, 1877, and later to Supreme Court of U.S. Engaged in mfg. and hydraulic engring., 1880; in 1894 as pres. Lake Superior Power Co., Algoma Steel Co., and Algoma Central Ry., began development of the hydraulic power of the falls of St. Mary at Sault Ste. Marie, Mich., and Ont., and the constrn. and operation there of various factories and transportation lines, comprising blast furnaces, steel rolling mills, iron mines, pulp mills, stemship lines, the Algoma Central Ry., and Algoma Eastern Ry. Home: 692 Mountain St. Office: Place d'Yonville, Montreal, Can.

CLEVELAND, LEMUEL ROSCOE, zoologist; b. Newton County, Miss., Nov. 14, 1892; s. Daniel Frank and Donna (Taylor) C.; B.S., U. of Miss., 1917; U. of Chicago, 1919-20; Sc.D., Johns Hopkins U. Sch. of Public Health, 1923; m. Mabel Bush, Mar. 27, 1925; 1 dau., Margaret Elaine; m. 2d, Dorothy Eleanor Colby, June 17, 1936; 1 son, Bruce Taylor. Asst. prof. protozoology, Harvard Med. Sch., 1925-36, asso. prof. zool., 1936-46, prof. biol., 1946-59, prof. emeritus, 1959-69. Mem. Am. Acad. Arts and Sci., Am. Acad. Tropical Med., Am. Soc. Zool., Am. Soc. Parasitol., Am. Naturalists, Gamma Alpha, Sigma Xi. Contbr. to scientific jours. Home: Boston MA2Died Feb. 12, 1969.

CLEVELAND, PARKER, educator, scientist; b. Byfield, Mass., Jan. 15, 1780; s. Parker and Elizabeth (Jackman) C.; grad. Harvard, 1799. Taught sch., York, Me., 1799-1802; tutor mathematics and natural philosophy Harvard, 1803-05; prof. mathematics and natural philosophy Bowdoin Coll., Brunswick, Me., 1805-58; prof. materia medica Med. Sch. of Me., Brunswick, 1820-58; mineral Cleavelandite named for him. Author: Elementary Treatise on Mineralogy and Geology (1st Am. work on subject), 1816; Agricultural Queries, 1827. Died Oct. 15, 1858.

CLIFFORD, HARRY ELLSWORTH, elec., engr.; b. Lowell, Mass., Apr. 21, 1866; s. Raeburn Gilman and Helen Rebecca (Hodgdon) C.; S.B., Mass. Inst. Tech., 1886. S.D. (hon.), 1937; grad. student, Harvard. 3 yrs.; m. Harriet Briggs Rogers, June 24, 1896; 1 dau., Gretchen. Asst. prof. theoretical physics, 1895-1902, asso. prof. theoretical electricity, 1902-04, prof. theoretical and applied electricity, 1904-09, Mass. Inst. Tech.; became Gordon McKay Prof. elect. engring., Grad. Sch. Applied Sci. (Harvard), 1909, now emeritus became dean Harvard Engring. Sch., 1930, now emeritus; cons. practice prof. Post Grad. Sch., U.S. Naval Acad., 1913-15, mem. Bd. Visitors; mem. adv. bd., U.S. Coast Guard, 1933—; cons. editor, McGraw-Hill Book Co., 1910—. Fellow Am. Acad. Arts Scis., A.A.A.S., Am. Inst. E.E. (past chmn. Boston br. mem. Edison medal com.); Illuminating Engring. Soc.; mem. Nat. Electric Light Assn. (past chmn. N.E. br.), Am. Electric Ry. Assn., Circolo Matematico di Palermo, Tau Beta Pi, Sigma Xi, etc. Republican. Untarian. Clubs: University, Harvard (Boston); Brae Burn Country. Home: Newton Center, Mass. Died 1952.

CLIFFORD, LESLIE FORBES, heating and ventilating engr.; b. Reedsburg, Wis., July 18, 1913; s. Cecil Leslie and Margaret (Forbes) C.; student Intermountain Coll., 1932-33; A.B., Mont. State U., 1936; grad. study U. Minn., 1943-44, Ill. Inst. Tech., 1946-47, Northwestern U., 1949-50, 52-53; m. Almira Rita Santell, Dec. 26, 1953. Head music dept. Ronan (Mont.) High Sch., 1936-37; asst. prin. Inverness (Mont.) High Sch., 1937-38; Flathead Co. (Mont.) ednl. supervisor, W.P.A., 1938, zone supervisor edn., 1938-40, Mont. State librarian, edn. and recreation, 1940-41; sales engr. Holland Furnace Co., 1941-42; application engr. Cardox Corp., Chgo., 1942-43; prof. Chgo. Tech. Coll., 1943-45, head refrigeration and air conditioning dept., 1944-45; mech. engr. Skidmore-Owings & Merrill, 1945-46, asst. chief mech. engr., 1946-47; research engr. Assn. Am. R. Rs., 1947-49; organized, 1944, pres. Clifford-Johnson & Asso., 1944-66; cons. Vern E. Alden Co., U. Chgo.; chief cons. engr. Horozon Corp.; adminstrv. engr. William A. Pope Co.; cons. engr. U. Chgo., Ragnar Benson, Inc. Pres. Industry's Profl. Tng. Registered profl. engr.; licensed ins. broker. Mem. Nat. Assn. Practical Refrigerating Engrs., Am. Assn. Engrs., Am. Soc. Heating Refrigerating and Airconditioning Engrs., Chgo. Tech. Socs. Council, Nat. Assn. Power Engrs., Refrigeration Service Engrs. Soc., Mont. State Alumni Assn. (pres. Chgo. chpt.), Eagle, Associate editor Nat. Engr., 1951-52, editor-in-chief, 1952-55; pres. Forbes Pubs., Inc., 1955-66; editor, LISTEN, High Fidelity and FM Guide, 1955-65. Author several manuals and numerous tech. articles. Home: Riverside IL Died Oct. 5, 1966; buried Bronswood Cemetery, Oakbrook IL

CLINE, ISAAC MONROE, meteorologist; b. Madisonville, Tenn., Oct. 13, 1861; s. Jacob Leander and Mary Isabel (Wilson) C.; A.B., Hiwassee College, Tenn., 1882, A.M., 1885; M.D., U. of Ark., 1885; Ph.D., Texas Christian U., 1896; hon. Sc.D., Tulane U., 1934; m. Cora M. Ballew, Mar. 17, 1887 (died Sept. 8, 1900); children—Allie May (wife of Ernest E. B. Drake) Rosemary (Mrs. Vora Williams), Esther Ballew (Mrs. Albert Allen Jones), Entered U.S. Weather Service (then Signal Corps, U.S.A.), July 7, 1882; asst. Observer, Little Rock, Ark., 1883-85; in charge of observation sta., Abilene, Tex., 1885-89, Galveston, Tex., 1889-91; local forecaster and sect. dir. Tex. Sect. Climatol. Service, Weather Bur. of U.S. Dept. of Agr., 1891-1901; at New Orleans, 1901-35, in charge forecast center embracing Tex., Okla., Ark. and La.; also in charge coöperation between Mexican Weather Service and U.S. Weather Bur.; prin. meteorlogist U.S. Weather Bur. retired Dec. 31, 1935. Instr. Climatology, U. of

Tex., 1897-1901. Fellow Am. Meterol. Soc. (pres. 1934-35), New Orleans Acad. of Sciences(pres. 1934-35), Am. Geog. Soc., A.A.A.S., mem. Nat. Inst. Social Sciences, Pi Gamma Mu. Del. 2d Pan-Am. Scientific Congress, Washington, 1915; mem. Union Goedesique et Geophysique, Commission pour l'Etude des Raz de Maree. Hon. curator of paintings. Louisiana State Museum. Conglist. Club: Nat. Arts (New York). Author of many bulls. and published articles on climate of the Southwest, its effect on health and on agr., "Summer Hot Winds on the Great Plains," "Relation of Storm Tides to the Center and Movement of Tropical Hurricanes" (a contbn. to the knowledge and forecasting of hurricanes), "Tropical Cyclones " (Introducing the integration method for the first time in study of storms, and presenting new conclusions which define and descirbe cyclone characteristics), 1926; Storms, Floods and Sunshine (giving important and interesting happenings in the United States Weather Service during its first sixty years), 1945 revised third edition, part 1 Memoris; part 2 Characteristics of Tropical Cyclones. In Mississippi flood of 1927 issued flood warnings predicting area and depth two weeks in advance of arrival of flood and for this work was commended by President Hoover, and presented by Southern Pacific Co. with bronze tablet eugolizing work. Has made a spl study of art and has brought together a notable collection of American paintings and antique oriental bronzes. Bronze bust placed permanently in the Isaac Delgado Museum of Art by citizens on New Orleans Address: 29 Farnham Pl., New Orleans. 20. Died Aug. 3, 1955; buried Metairie Cemetery.

CLINE, LEWIS MANNING, educator; b. Duncan, Okla., Sept. 25, 1909; s. Edgar Betel and Leila (Sims) C.; B.S., U. Tulsa, 1931; M.S., U. Ia., 1934, Ph.D., 1935; m. Grace Ellen Shaw, Nov. 27, 1935; children—Ellen Sperling, Catherine Arlene, Charles Harry. Instr. geology U. Tulsa, 1931-32; research asst. U. Ia., 1932-35; instr. Tex. A. and M. Coll., 1935-36; instr. Ia. State Coll., 1936-37, asst. prof., 1938-42; mem. Ia. Geol. Survey, summers 1936-42; dist. geologist Standard Oil Co. Tex., 1943-45; faculty U. Wis., 1946-71, prof. geology, 1947-71, chmn. dept., 1960-65; cons. Natural Gas Pipeline Co. Am., 1940-42, Ia. Ins. Commn., 1939-41, Mobil Oil Research Lab., 1957-61, also other cos.; distinguished prof. Tex. Tech. Coll., 1952-53. Recipient Lew Wentz prize U. Tulsa, Lowden prize U. Ia. Fellow Geol. Soc. Am. (rep. Am. Stratigraphic Commn. 1957-60, chmn. publs. com. 1965, mem. council 1966-71, tech. program chmn. nat. meeting 1970); mem. Paleontol. Soc. Am. (chmn. nominating com. 1962), Am. Geol. Inst. (mem. geol. orientation study 1962-63, chmn. publs. com. 1966-71), Internat. Assn. of Sedimentalogy, Am. Assn. Petroleum Geologists (dist. rep. 1958-59, distinguished lectr. 1965), Soc. Econ. Paleontologists and Mineralogists (president 1965, chairman publications committee 1965), editor of Journal of Sedimentary Petrology 1961-64, Sigma Xi (sec.-treas. Iowa State College 1940-42), (president Univ. of Wisconsin chapter 1965-66), Gamma Alpha (v.p. U. Ia. 1934-35). Republican. Methodist. Rotarian (chmn. fellowship com. Madison 1951, Uthrotar com., Madison, 1959, vice president of Madison chpt. 1964-65). Author: Late Paleozoic Rocks of the Quachita Mountains, 1960. Editor, contbr.; Guidebook to Ouachita Mountains, 1956. Co-editor, contbr.; Geology of Ouachita Mountains, a symposium, 1959. Home: Madison WI Died Mar. 10, 1971; buried Forest Hill Cemetery, Madison WI

CLINTON, GEORGE PERKINS, botanist; b. Polo, Ill., May 7, 1867; s. John Waterbury and Carrie Adelia (Perkins) C.; B.S., U. of Ill., 1890, M.S., 1894; M.S., Harvard, 1901, Sc.D., 1902; m. Anna J. Lightbody Aug. 9, 1892; 1 son, Harry Lightbody (dec.). Asst. botanist Ill. Agrl. Expt. Sta., and asst. in botany, U. of Ill., 1890-1902; botanist Conn. Expt. Sta., 1902—; lecturer forest pathology, Yale Univ., 1915-26, research asso., 1926-1929. Fellow Am. Acad. Arts and Sciences. Author bot. monograph and expt. sta. bulls. dealing with parasitic fungi. Home: New Haven, Conn. Died 1937.

CLINTON, LOUIS ADELBERT, agriculturist; b. Grand Rapids, Mich., Feb. 13, 1868; s. Frederick Henry and Rhoby Ann (Allen) C.; B.S., Mich. Agrl. Coll., 1889, M.S., 1901; post-grad. Cornell Univ., 1901-02; dir. Mich. Expt. Sta., 1890-93; asst. prof. agr., Clemson Coll., S.C., 1893-95; asst. agriculturist, Cornell U. Expt. Sta., 1895-1902; dir. Storrs Agrl. Expt. Sta., and prof. agronomy, Conn. Agrl. Coll., 1902-12; agriculturist in charge of farm management N. Atlantic States of U.S. Dept. Agr., 1912-15; agrist. and asst. chief, Office of Extension North and West, for U.S. Dept. Agr., 1915-18; dir. agrl. extension, Rutgers Coll. and State U. of N.J., 1918—. Lecturer before farmers' insts. in Mich., N.Y., Pa., Del., Conn., Mass., N.H. and R.I. Home: New Brunswick, N.J. Died Jan. 21, 1923.

CLOKE, PAUL, educator; b. Trenton, N.J., Sept. 4, 1882; s. William and Hannah Virginia (Chatten) C.; grad. N.J. State Normal and Model Schs., 1901; E.E., Lehigh U., 1905, M.S., 1913; grad. work Columbia, 1921; Dr. Engring., U. Me., 1934; m. Ruth Gaines Thurber, June 28, 1916; children—Donald Thurber, Paul LeRoy. Engring. apprentice Westinghouse Electric Mfg. Co., 1905-06, 08; engr. Pub. Service Co. of N.J., 1906-07; physics instr. Pa. State Coll., 1909; with Westinghouse Lamp Co., 1909-10; asst. prof. physics and electric engring. R.I. State Coll., 1910-14; prof. physics Clarkson Coll. Tech., 1914-18; prof. elec. engring. U. Ariz. 1918-26; dean coll. tech. U. Maine, 1926-50, emeritus, 1950; dir. Me. Tech. Expt. Sta. since 1927. Pres. Me. chpt. Am. Planning; and Civic Assn.; vice chmn. Me. Bd. Registration for Profl. Engrs.; past v.p., Am. Soc. for Engring. Edn.; mem. Am. Inst. E.E., Am. Assn. Engrs., A.A.A.S., Phi Gamma Delta, Ind. Republican. Methodist. Mason. Rotarian, (past pres.), Home: 49 Forest Av., Orono, Me. Died Sept. 25, 1963.

CLOUD, MARSHALL MORGAN, surgeon; b. Carroll Co., Va., Oct. 9, 1868; s. Columbus Henry and Mary Emily (Parker) C.; M.D., honor medalist U. of Kan., 1892; grad. U.S.A. Med. Sch., 1897; B.S., U. of Southern Calif., 1904. A.M., 1906; grad. study Stanford, 1905, U. of Chicago, 1906; m. Mary Frances Moore, June 19, 1894; children—Dorothy (Mrs. Frederick B. Pinkus), Marguerite (Mrs. Allison J. Walllace, Jr.), Mary, Frances. Asst. supt. Kan. State Hosp., Topeka, 1893-95; commd. 1st lt., Med. Corps, U.S.A., 1896, and advanced through grades to maj., 1919; retired for disability in line of duty, 1921; clin. prof. ophthalmology, U. of Southern Calif., 1910-13, prof. mil. medicine, 1920-23; ophthalmologist, Nat. Soliders Home, Sawtelle, Calif., 1910-13; same, Santa Fe Ry., 1910-21; examining surgeon, U.S. Pension Bur.; on staff Hollywood Hosp. and Gen. Hosp., Los Angeles; partner Angeles Mesa Land Co.; owner Cloud Heights Subdivision, La Crescenta, Calif. Comdr. div. hosp., Mobile, Ala., Miami, Fla., and Anniston, Ala., Spanish-Am. War; served on operations div., commd. personnel br., Gen. Staff, World War. Fellow Am. Coll. Surgeons. Democrat. Episcopalian. Author: Sanitary Analysis of Water, 1905; Curing Our Nerves, 1934; Facts About Alcholic Drinks, 1934. Inventor, with M.F. Volkman, of horizontal-base range finder for artillery fire, 1904. Home: Los Angeles, Calif. Died 1937.

CLOWES, GEORGE HENRY ALEXANDER research dir.; b. Ipswich, Eng., Aug. 27, 1877; s. Josiah Pratt and Ellen (Seppings) C.; student Royal Coll. Sci., London, Göttingen U., Berlin U., Pasteur Inst. (Paris);Ph.D., Göttingen 1899; D.Sc. (hon.) Butler U., 1931; LL.D., Wabash Coll., 1938; m. Edith Whitehill Hinkel June 1910; children—Alexander Temple (dec.) George H.A. Allen Whitehill. came to U.S., 1900. naturalized citizen abt. 1921. With Eli Lilly & Co., mfg. chemists. Indpls., 1918—. dir. research lab., Indpls., Woods Hole, Mass., 1920-46. Pres., chmn. bd. Indpls. Symphony Orchestra, 1939—; v.p., dir. John Ilirron Art Mus., 1933—. Recipient Banting Medal, 1947. Served Chem. Warfare Service, World War 1. Mem. Am. Chem. Soc., Soc. for Exptl. Biology and Medicine . Bio-Chem. Soc., Cancer Assn., Immunologist and Pathologist, Chem. Soc. (Eng.), Republican. Episcopalin. Clubs: Indianapolis Athletic, Indianapolis University; Woodstock; Meridian Hills County; Cosmos (Washington) Woods Hole Golf. Research in Cancer; coöperated in development of insulin, liver extract. penicillin etc. Home: 3744 Spring Hollow Rd. Golden Hill Indpls. Office: Lilly Research Lab. Indpls. Died Aug. 25, 1958; buried Ch. Messiah, Woods Hole, Mass. (;

CLUETT, SANFORD LOCKWOOD, civil and mechanical engr.; b. Troy, N.Y., June 6, 1874; s. Edmund and Mary Alice (Stone) C.; student Albany (N.Y.) Acad., 1889; grad. Troy Acad., 1894; C.E., Rensselaer Poly. Inst., 1898, D.Eng., 1952; D.Sc., Russell Sage Coll., 1958; m. Camilla E. Rising, Feb. 1916; children—Gregory Stone, Sanford Lockwood, Camilla Trent, Marvin Vaughan. With Walter A. Wood Mowing & Reaping Machine Co., Hoosick Falls, N.Y., successively as chief engr., asst. supt., v.p., and v.p. and gen. supt., 1901-19; with Cluett, Peabody & Co., Inc., Troy, N.Y., 1919-68, in charge engring. and research until 1944; dir. from 1921, vice pres. from 1927; trustee Troy Savings Bank; director Albany & Vermont R.R. Co., Saratoga & Schenectady Railroad Company. Member board directors Troy Orphan Asylum. Enlisted as private, Nat. Guard N.Y., 1897, later N.Y. Vol. Inf., Spanish Am. War; trans. to 1st U.S. Vol. Engrs., June 1898; promoted lt. and capt.; served in Porto Rican campaign; again with N.G.N.Y., 1904-17, advancing to maj. Signal Corps.; Reserve list, May 11, 1917. Designed one-horse and two-horse vertical lift mowing machines; steel work for Govt. locks on Big Sandy River, Kentucky, 1900; valves for St. Andrews Rapids locks, Manitoba; etc. Trustee, v.p. Rensselaer Poly. Inst. Received Modern Pioneer award N.A.M.; Longstreth medal Franklin Inst., Holley medal Am. Soc. M.E., 1952. Fellow Am. Numis. Soc., Am. Soc. M.E.; hon. mem. Rensselaer Soc., Soc. Engrs.; mem. N.Y. State Hist. Assn., Franklin Institute, Mil. Order of Foreign Wars, Society Colonial Wars, Founders and Patriots America, Sons of the Revolution, Army Ordnance Association, U.S. Naval Institute, Soc. Am. Mil. Engrs., U.S. Inst. for Textile Research, Sigma Xi, Chi Epsilon. Republican. Episcopalian. Clubs: Troy, Troy Country; Univ., New York Yacht (N.Y.C.); Bath and Tennis, Everglades (Palm Beach, Fla.). Inventor of Sanforized process, Clupak (extensible paper). Home: Palm Beach FL Died May 17, 1968; buried Troy NY

CLUTE, WALKER STILLWELL, cons. geologist, petroleum engr.; b. Vancouver, B.C., Sept. 12, 1891; s. James M. and Mary Ella (Saunders) C.; student Occidental Coll., 2 yrs.; A.B. (Geology and Mining), Stanford, 1915; m. Helen Marie Day, Mar. 31, 1923; 1 son, Walker Van. Oil insp. City of Los Angeles; dep. oil assessor Los Angeles County; geologist for various Doheny interests; oil exploration in Colombia, S.A., in gulf coast and mid-continent, U.S.; oil and gas valuation engr. U.S. Treasury Dept.; field mgr. Wyo. and Mont. properties; U.S. Geol. survey, Washington, Tulsa; chief oil and gas sect. Cal. Tax Research Bur., State Bd. Equalization; cons. practice, Los Angeles, 1933-44; specializes in geology and econs. petroleum industry. Has written many tech., sci. articles on oil devel. Served with AS, U.S. Army as 2d lt., R.M.A., pursuit pilot, World War I. Mem. Am. Inst. Mining and Metall. Engrs., Am. Assn. Petroleum Geologists. Am. Legion, Los Angeles C. of C.; former mem. Am. Petroleum Inst., Cal. Oil and Gas Assn., Seismol. Soc. Am., Alpha Tau Omega. Clubs: Newport Harbor Yacht, Petroleum of Los Angeles. Republican. Conglist. Home: 811 W. 7th St., Los Angeles 17. Died Nov. 23, 1964.

CLUTE, WILLARD NELSON, author; b. Painted Post, N.Y., Feb. 26, 1869; s. George N. and Ruth (Wright) C.; student U. Chgo.; m. Ida Martin, Dec. 22, 1897; 1 dau.; Beulah Katharine. Asst. curator bot. dept. Columbia, 1897; curator N.Y. Bot. Garden, 1898-99; instr. biology Joliet (Ill.), High Sch., Chgo., 1903-10; instr. botany Curtis High Sch., 1910-11; tchr. biology, Flower Tech. High Sch. for Girls, Chgo., 1911-28; instr. botany and dir. Bot. Garden, 1938-41. Founder, pub. Plant World, Bryologist, Fern Bulletin, Am. Botanist, also editor last two. Founder Am. Fern Soc. (hon. mem.), Binghamton Acad. Sciences, Joliet Bot. Club (dir.). Fellow A.A.A.S.; Mem. Am. Genetic Assn., Soc. Midland Authors, Ill. State Acad. Science (pres. 1927). Author: A Flora of the Upper Susquehanna Valley, 1898; Our Ferns in Their Haunts, 1901; The Fern Collector's Guide, 1902; The Fern Allies of North America, 1905; Laboratory Botany for High School, 1909; Agronomy for High Schools, 1912; Laboratory Manual and Notebook in Botany, 1913; Experimental General Science, 1917; American Plant Names, 1923; Practical Botany, 1924; Useful Plants of the World, 1927— Botanical Essays, 1929; Common Names of Plants, 1931; Swamp and Dune, 1931; Off the Record, 1935; Our Ferns, Their Haunts, Habit and Folklore 1938; A Second Book of Plant Names, 1930. Home: 5257 Hinesley Av., Indpls. 8. Died Mar. 7, 1950.

CLYDE, NORMAN ASA, explorer western mountains; b. Phila., Apr. 8, 1885; s. Charles and Isabelle (Purvis) C.; A.B., Geneva Coll., Beaver Falls, Pa., 1909, Sc.D., 1939; postgrad. U. Wis., 1910, U. Cal., 1911-13; postgrad. in English, U. Cal. at Berkeley, 1923-24, in edn. U. So. Cal., 1926. Tchr. high schs. N.D., Utah, Ariz., Cal., 1898-10; engaged in solitary mountaineering, exploring (over 1000 ascents, 200 1st ascents including new routes), 1910-72, in various mountain ranges and peaks including Sierra Nevadas (Cal.), Cascades (Wash. and Ore.) Selkirks (B.C., Can.), Canadian Rockies (Alta., B.C. and Yukon, Can.), Tetons (Wyo.), Colo. Rockies, Wasatch Mountains (Utah), Sawtooth Range (Ida.), Sierra Madre (So. Cal.), Mt. Whitney, North Palisade (both in Sierra Nevadas), Beartooth Range (Mont.), Wind River Range (Wyo.), Salmon Alps (Cal.), Sierra San Pedro Martir (Baja, Cal.); much individual exploratory climbing in Glacier Park, Mont. (36 peaks in 36 days), 1926; cons. A.C., U.S. Army, on various occasions; collector zool. specimens U. Cal.; guide, climbing leader Sierra Club base camp, summers; ascents with Sierra Club (Glacier Park Canadian Rockies), Seattle Mountaineers (Canadian Rockies, No. Cascades of Wash. State), Alpine Club Can. (Selkirks). Recipient Distinguished Service award Geneva Coll., 1962. Mem. Nat. Rifle Assn., Cal. Acad. Scis. (wildlife observer 1943-72). Clubs: Sierra (San Francisco); American Alpine; Appalachian (corr.). Expert on high altitude flora and fauna (Hudsonian and Arctic Alpine zones of Sierra Nevada), geol. history and structure of mountain ranges of Western U.S., ski mountaineering. Classical scholar, linguist. Author: Close Ups of the Sierra, 1961; also over 300 articles on various phases of mountains, trout fishing, camping, wild life, other subjects, pub. in various mags., newspapers including Field and Stream, Touring Topics, Westward, Sierra Club Bull., Am. Alpine Jour., Nat. Motorist, Sports Afield. Made several rescues of lost mountain climbers, dead and alive, locating them by knowledge of the terrain, sometimes after other searchers had given up. Numerous mountain features in the Sierra named after him including Clyde's Minaret, Clyde's Spires, Clyde's Ledge, Clyde Meadow, Clyde Peak. Address: Inyo County CA Died Dec. 23, 1972.

COATES, CHARLES EDWARD, chemist; b. Baltimore, Aug. 13, 1866; s. Charles Edward and Anna Hunter (Roberts) C.; A.B., Johns Hopkins, 1887; Königliche Bergacademie, Freiberg in Sachsen, 1888; U. of Heidelberg, 1889; Ph.D., John Hopkins, 1891; LL.D. form Louisiana State University, 1934; m. Ollie Maurin, June 26, 1901; children—Charles Hunter, Victor Maurin, Jesse, Caroline Pennock, Prof. chemistry, St. John's Coll., 1891-93, La. State U., 1893—; dean Audubon Sugar Sch., 1907-37, then emeritus, also dean Coll. of Pure and Applied Sci., 1931. Dir. Institute for Industrial Research, 1931. Episcopalian. Herty medalist, 1938. Home: Baton Rouge, La. Died Dec. 27, 1939.

COBB, COLLIER, geologist; b. Mt. Auburn Plantation, Wayne Co., N.C., Mar. 21, 1862; s. Needham B. (D.D.) and Martha Louisa (Cobb) C.; student Wake Forest Coll., hon. Sc. D., 1917; student University of North Carolina; A.B., Harvard University, 1889, A.M., 1894; m. Mary L. Battle, Jan. 27, 1891 (died 1900); children—Wm. Battle, Collier, Mary Louisa; m. 2d, Lucy P. Battle, Apr. 6, 1904 (died1905); m. 3d, Mary Knox Gatlin, Oct. 27, 1910. Taught in pub. schs. of N.C.; lecturer in State normal schs.; asst. Harvard, 1888-90; instr. Mass. Inst. Tech., 1890-92; prof. geology, U. of N.C., 1892; Kenan research prof., 1920-21, studying shore lines N. Pacific, Gulf of Mexico, and Caribbean Sea. Taught geology, summer, Harvard, 1891, Knoxville, 1902, 09, Biltmore Forest Sch., 1905-12, Cornell, 1928, and U. of N.C.; student of moving sands, coast lines and soils. Mem. Baltimore Conf. on China-America Relations, 1925. Fellow Geol. Soc. America, A.A.A.S., Assn. Am. Geographers. Edited and published small illustrated paper, 1871-75; pub. map of North Carolina, 1879, 6 editions. Author: Where the Wind Does the Work; Human Habitations: Landes and Dunes of Gascony: Pocket Dictionary of Common Rock and Rock Minerals, edit., 1915. 1915; Geography of North Carolina, 1880, 5th edit., 1915. Discoverer of Enfield horse, in early Pleistocene deposits of N.C. Home: Chapel Hill, N.C. Died Nov. 28, 1934.

COBB, JOHN NATHAN, author, naturalist; b Oxford, N.J., Feb. 20, 1868; s. Samuel S. and Louise (Richards) C.; ed. pub. schs.; m. Harriet C. Bidwell, Oct. 18, 1898; 1 dau., Genevieve Catherine. Newspaper reporter and editor, 1886-90; field agt. U.S. Bur. Fisheries, 1895-1904; aast. Alaska salmon agt., with same bur., 1904-12; editor Pacific Fisherman, Seattle, Wash., 1913-17; dir. Coll. of Fisheries, U. of Wash., Seattle, 1919—. Mem. Advisory Scientific Bd., Internat. Fisheries Commn., 1915—. Mem. Am. Fisheries Soc., Pacific Fisheries Soc. (pres., 1921, 23). Conglist. Author: The Canning of Fishery Products, 1919; Fish Cookery (with Mrs. Evelene Spencer), 1921. Deceased.

COBB, LLOYD JOSEPH, lawyer; b. New Orleans, July 19, 1904; s. William Holmes and Katherine Mary (Salter) C.; LL.B., Tulane U., 1924; m. Mireille LeBretón, 1934; 1 dau., Mary. Admitted to La. bar, 1924; asso. Milling, Godchaux, Saal & Milling, 1924-26; practiced in New Orleans, 1928-72; partner firm Cobb & Wright, 1949-72; asst. to gen. counsel Pan Am. Petroleum Corp., 1926-28, gen. counsel, 1928, and to successor firm Pan Am. So. Corp., 1948-72; founder Marydale Products Co., Inc.; pres. New Orleans Internat. Trade Mart. Recipient Thomas A. Cunningham award, 1952; hon. consul Dominican Republic, 1956, 57. Club: Internat. House (pres. 1949-51). Pioneered dehydration sweet potatoes for cattle feed, for food for mil. use, World War II; developer model grassland farming operation Marydale Farm nr. St. Francisville, La., 1944. Home: New Orleans LA Died Nov. 27, 1972.

COBB, NATHAN AUGUSTUS, scientist, educator; b. Spencer, Mass., June 30, 1859; s. William H. and Jane A. (Bigelow) C.; both of English Puritan stock; B.Sc., Worcester Poly. Inst., 1881; Ph.D., U. of Jena, 1888, honors under Haeckel, Hertwig, Lang and Stahl; m. Alice Vara Proctor, Aug. 8, 1881; children—Russell Harding (dec.), Margaret Vara, Victor, Roger (dec.), Mrs. Frieda Blanchard, Mrs. Ruth Ross, Mrs. Dorothy Adams. Teacher pub. schs., Spencer, 1877-78; prof. chemistry and natural science, Williston Sem., Mass., 1881-87; appointee British Assn. Adv. Science, Naples Zoöl. Sta., 1888-89; locum tenens prof. biology, Sydney U., N.S.W., 189-91; pathologist Dept. of Agr., N.S.W., 1891-98; mgr. Wagga Expt. Farm, 1897-98; agrl. commr. N.S.W. to U.S. and Europe, 1898-1901; pathologist Dept. Agr., N.S.W., 1901-04; dir. div. Physiology and Pathology, Hawaiian Sugar Planters' Expt. Sta., Honolulu, 1904-07; agrl. technologist, Dept. of Agr., 1907—; acting asst. chief, Bur. Plant Industry, Dept. Agr., Jan. 1, 1911—. Awarded medal by Nat. Cotton Mfrs. Assn. "for work in establishing methods of determining the properties and value of cotton." Home: Falls Church, Va. Died 1932.

COBB, STANLEY, neuropsychiatrist; b. Brookline, Mass., Dec. 10, 1887; s. John Candler and Leonore (Smith) C.; A.B., Harvard, 1910, M.D., 1914; D.Sc., University of Maryland, 1952; m. Elizabeth M. Almy, July 10, 1915; children—Sidney, Helen Jackson, John Candler, 2d. Surgical house officer, Peter Bent Brigham Hosp., Boston, Mass., 1914-15; asst. prof. neuropathology, Harvard, 1920, asso. prof., 1923. Bullard prof. 1926-54, emeritus, 1954—; Rockefeller fellow in Europe, 1923-25; neurologist Boston City Hosp., 1934-54, ret. 1st lt., Med. Res. Corps, 1918-19. Mem. A.M.A., Am. Neurol. Assn. (pres. 1948). Assn. Am. Phys., Assn. Research Nervous and Mental Disease (pres. 1941), Am. Assn. Neuropathology (pres. 1943), Interurban Clinical Club, Am. Soc. Clin. Investigation, Am. Psychiatric Assn., Mass. Med. Soc., Am. Ornithologists Union, Boston Soc. Natural History, Boston Soc. Psychiatry and Neurology (pres. 1938), Am. Psychosomatic Soc. (pres. 1955), Royal Soc. Med. (hon.), Phi Beta Kappa. Unitarian. Clubs: Harvard, Tavern. Author books including: Emotions and Clinical Medicine 1950; Case Histories in Psychomatic Medicine, 1952. Editor American Journal of Psychiatry, Psychosomatic Medicine. Home: 34 Fernald Dr., Cambridge, Mass. Died Feb. 18, 1968.

COBLEIGH, WILLIAM MERRIAM, dean emeritus of engring., Montana State Coll.; b. Haverstraw, N.Y., Sept. 7, 1872; s. William and Julia Adelaide (Merriam) C.; E.M., School of Mines, College of Montana, 1894; A.M., Columbia University, 1899; m. Esther Rose Cooley, August 7, 1901; children—Winifred Merriam (wife of Dr. Robert K. Curry), Arthur Cooley (dec.), Lois Esther (Mrs. William H. McCall, Jr.), Norman Blake (dec.). Instr. chemistry, Mont. State Coll., 1894-99, asst. prof., 1899-1902, prof., 1902-15, prof. chemical engineering, 1915-42, dean of engineering, 1929-42, acting pres., 1942-43, dean emeritus of engineering since 1943. Director division of water and sewage, Montana State Board of Health, 1910-22, cons. engr. since 1923; state chemist Mont. Oil Commn., 1919-29. Fellow A.A.A.S.; mem. Am. Inst. of Chem. Engrs., Mont. Soc. of Engrs., Soc. for Promotion of Engring. Edn. (council 1933-35), Am. Chem. Soc., Am. Water Works Assn., Newcomen Soc., Tau Beta Pi, Alpha Chi Sigma, Phi Kappa Phi, Sigma Xi, Kappa Sigma. Republican. Presbyterian. Mason. Clubs: Chamber of Commerce, Kiwanis, Country. Contbr. to tech. jours. Home: 909 S. 3d, Bozeman MT

COBLENTZ, VIRGIL, chemist; b. Springfield, O., Mar. 12, 1862; s. John Philip and Susan (Zitzer) C.; grad. Wittenberg Coll.; Ph.G. and Pharm.M., Phila. Coll. Pharmacy, 1882; Ph.D., U. of Berlin, 1891; M.D., U. of Wuerzburg, 1895; m. Anna Bauer, of Strassburg, Mar. 7, 1889. Prof. materia medica and toxicology, Cincinnati Coll. Pharmacy, 1884-87; prof. chemistry, New York Coll. Pharmacy (Columbia), 1891-1911; chief chemist, E.R. Squibb & Sons, N.Y. City, 1911-17; pathologist to Hazard Hosp., Long Branch N.J. Chmn. N.Y. sect. Soc. Chem. Industry of Gt. Britain, 1902-04, N.Y. sect. Verein Deutscher Chemiker, 1909-14; mem. com. of revision of U.S. Pharmacopoeia, 1900-20. Mason. Author: Handbook of Pharmacy, 1895; The Newer Remedies, 1897; Sadtler and Coblentz Medical and Pharmaceutical Chemistry, 1899; Volumetric Analysis. Home: West End, N.J. Died 1932.

COBLENTZ, WILLIAM WEBER, physicist; b. North Lima, O., Nov. 20, 1873; s. David and Catherine (Good) C.; B.S., Case Inst. Tech., 1900, D.Sc., 1930; M.S., Cornell U., 1901, Ph.D., 1903; m. Catherine E. Cate, June 10, 1924 (dec.); children—Catherine Joan (dec.), David William (dec.). Research asso. Carnegie Instn., Washington, 1903-05; physicist Nat. Bur. Standards, 1905-45, ret. cons. physicist. Recipient numerous awards for researches and achievements in radiation and related fields, including: Howard N. Potts gold medal, Franklin Inst., 1910; Janssen medal L'Institut de France, 1920, John Scott medal and a premium of $1,000, 1924; gold key, Am. Congress Physical Therapy, 1934; Rumford medal, Am. Acad. Arts and Sciences, 1937; Frederick Ives medal, Opt. Soc. Am., 1945; silver medal, Soc. Applied Spectroscopy, 1953; Niels Finsen medal, Internat. Congress Photobiology 1954; Coblentz Society, organized in his honor, 1955. Member Am. Soc. Psych. Research A.A.A.S., Am. Phys. Soc., Optical Soc. Am., Am. Astron. Soc., Nat. Acad. Scis., Council on Physical Medicine, A.M.A., Internat. Union Geodesy and Geophysics (internat. com. solar radiation, internat. com. measurement and standardization ultraviolet for use in medicine), Soc. Francaise de Physique, Sigma Xi; corr. mem. Illuminating Engring. Soc. (London). Presbyn. Author: From the Life of a Researcher, 1951; Man's Place in a Superphysical World, 1954; also publs. of Carnegie Instn. and Nat. Bur. of Standards. With Harvard eclipse expdn., Middletown, Conn., 1925, Benkuelen, Sumatra, 1926. Home: 2737 Macomb St., Washington 20008. Died Sept. 15, 1962; buried Rock Creek Cemetery, Washington.

COCHRAN, CAROLOS BINGHAM, chemist; b. Albion, Mich., July 1, 1854; s. Isaac Cook and Julia A. (Bingham) C.; B.A., U. of Mich., 1877, M.A., 1888, Sc.D., 1907; m. Sarah B. Marshall, July 16, 1885. Microscopist and hygienist to Pa. State Bd. Agr., 1884—; chemist to Pa. dairy commr., 1885-95, to Phila. Milk Exchange, 1890-1905; chemist dairy and food division, Dept. Agr., 1895-1918; mem. West Chester Bd. Health, 1897—; prof. natural sciences, 1879, prof. physical sciences, 1895-1918; mem. West Chester Bd. Health, 1897—; prof. natural sciences, 1879, prof. physical sciences, 1895-1903, prof. chemistry, 1903-09, West Chester State Normal Sch.; chemist, Charles E. Hines Co., Phila., 1918—. Home: West Chester, Pa. Died 1929.

COCHRAN, JAMES HARVEY, educator; b. Abbeville, S.C., Sept. 14, 1913; s. Harvey Nickles and Leona (Greene) C.; B.S., Clemson A. and M. Coll., 1935; M.S., Ia. State Coll., 1936, Ph.D., 1946; m. Mildred Viola Batson, Aug. 28, 1940; children—Andrew, Sandra, Jennifer. Research entomologist E. I. DuPont De Nemours & Co., Wilmington, Del., 1938-42, 46-47; asso. entomologist S.C. Expt. Sta. in charge fruit and nut research, 1947-53; head entomology and zoology dept., prof., state entomologist Clemson Coll., 1953-69. Served from 2d lt. to maj., AUS, 1942-46. Mem. S.C. Entomol. Soc. (pres. 1955), S.C. Acad. Sci., Entomol. Soc. Am., S.C. Pest Control Assn., Sigma Xi, Alpha Zeta, Phi Kappa Phi, Gamma Sigma Delta (pres. chpt. 1961). Kiwanian. Home: Clemson SC Died May 9, 1969; buried Upper Long Cane Cemetery, Abbeville SC

COCHRANE, EDWARD LULL, ret. naval Officer; b. Mare Island, Cal., Mar. 18, 1892; s. Brig. Gen. Henry Clay (U.S. Marine Corps.) and Elizabeth (Lull) C.; student U. Pa., 1909-10; S.B., (with distinction), U.S. Naval Acad., 1914; post grad., 1916; M.S., Mass Inst. Tech., 1920; at U.S. Naval War Coll., 1939; LL.D., Hahnemann Med. Coll., 1943; E.D. (hon.), Tufts Coll., 1950; m. Charlotte Osgood Wilson, June 3, 1916; children—Richard Lull (comdr. United States Navy,), Edward Lull, Jr. (lt., U.SN.). Command ensign U.S. Navy, 1914, and advanced through grades to vice admiral, 1942; on U.S.S. Rhode Island, 1914-16; selected for post-grad. in naval constrn., 1915; assigned Phila., Navy Yards, 1917; in charge of constrn. of 2 battle cruisers, 1920-24; Bur. Constrn. and Repair, Navy Dept., 1924-29; submarine and general design; tech. adviser Internat. Conf. Safety of Life at Sea, London, 1929; in charge of design and constrn. submarines, Navy Yard, Portsmouth, N.H., 1929-33; Force constrn. staff, comdr. Scouting Force, U.S. Fleet, 1933-35; New Design Bur. Constrn. and Repair, Navy Dept., 1935-39; Bur. of Ships, Navy Dept. as hull asst. to head design div., 1939-40. also head preliminary design branch, 1941-42; asst. naval attaché Am. Embassy, London, 1940; chief of Bur. of Ships, Nov., 1942-Nov., 1946; chief Material Div., Navy Dept., 1946-47; ret.; professor of naval construction, head dept. of naval architecture and marine engring., Mass. Inst. Tech., 1947-50; chmn. Fed. Maritime Board and Maritime Adminstrn., Dept. of Commerce, 1950-52; dean engring. Mass. Inst. Tech., 1952-54, v.p. indsl. and governmental relations, 1954—. Awarded Mexican campaign medal, 1915; Victory medal World War I; Nat. Dev. medal, 1944; Am. Def. medal, Asiatic-Pacific campaign medal, Victory medal, World War II; David W. Taylor medal for notable achievement in naval architecture and marine engring., 1945; Knight Comdr. Mil. Div., Order British Empire. Navy Distinguished Service Medal. Mem. Soc. Naval Architects and Marine Engrs., Am. Soc. Naval Engrs., British Inst. Marine Engrs., British Inst. Naval Architects, U.S. Naval Inst., Nat. Acad. Sics., Am. Acad. Arts and Scis., United Seaman's Service Army and Navy, Chevy Chase (Washington); Country (Brookline, Mass.); Army and Navy Country (Arlington, Va.); University (N.Y.C.). Home: 2 Larchwood Dr., Cambridge 38, Mass. Died Nov. 14, 1959; buried Arlington Nat. Cemetery.

COCKERELL, THEODORE DRU ALLSON, naturalist; b. Norwood, Eng., Aug. 22, 1866; s. Sydney John and Elizabeth (Bennett) C.; ed. at pvt. schs. in Eng. and Middlesex Hosp. Med. Sch.; m. Annie S. Fenn, 1891 (died 1893); children—Austin (dec.), Martin (dec.); m. 2d, Wilmatte Porter, 1900. Resided in Colo., 1887-90, studying entomology, botany, etc.; curator pub. mus., Kingston, Jamaica, 1891-93; prof. entomology, N.M. Agrl. Coll., 1893-96, and 1898-1900; entomologist, N.M. Agrl. Expt. Sta., 1893-1901; cons. entomologist, Ariz. Agrl. Expt. Sta., 1900-09; teacher of biology, N.M. Normal U., 1900-03; curator Colo. Coll. Mus., 1903-04; lecturer on entomology, Univ. of Colo., 1904-06, professor systematic zoology, 1906-12; professor of zoology, 1912-34, professor emeritus since 1934. Author: Zoology; Zoology of Colorado; also of over 3,000 articles and notes in scientific publs., principally on mollusca, insects, fishes, palaeonotology and subjects connected with evolution. Fellow A.A.A.S., Am. Mus. Natural History (hon.); corr. mem. Phila. Acad. Natural Sciences, Am. Entomol. Soc.; mem. Am. Philos. Soc. Has made scientific explorations in Siberia, Japan, South America, Madeira Islands, Russia, Australia, Morocco, Central and South Africa, etc. Home: Boulder, Colo. Died Jan. 26, 1948.

CODE, CHARLES JOSEPH, civil engr., consultant; b. La Crosse, Wis., Mar. 9, 1900; s. James Grant and Frances Shepherd (Cleaver) C.; B.S. in Civil Engring., Carnegie Inst. Tech., 1921, C.E., 1925; m. Anne Fairfax Porter, Nov. 1, 1930; children—Charles Joseph, Anne Fairfax (Mrs. Arthur E. Barta), James Grant. With Monogahela So. Ry. Co., 1918; with Pa. R.R., 1920-65, asst. chief engr. tests maintenance of way, 1953-58, asst. chief engr. staff, 1958-65, asst. chief engr., 1965, retired; 1965; private consulting practice, 1965—. Mem. Am. Ry. Engring. Assn., 1942—, hon. mem., 1965—, dir., 1956-59, v.p. 1960-62, pres., 1962-63, chmn. joint com. relation between track and equipment with Assn. Am. Railroads, 1953-65. Dist. commnr. Blair Bedford council Boy Scouts Am., 1949-50, dist. commnr. Chester County Council, 1954-56, dist. com. mem., 1956—. Served to 2d lt., inf., U.S. Army, 1918. Recipient Distinguished Pistol Shot award Dept. of Army, 1953. Mem. Nat. Rifle Assn. (dir. 1948-53), Am. Soc. Testing Materials, Soc. Exptl. Stress Analysis, Tau Beta Pi. Republican. Episcopalian. Home: Box 283, Devon, Pa. Office: Pennsylvania R.R. Co., 6 Penn Center Plaza, Phila. 4. Died Dec. 20, 1966.

CODE, WILLIAM HENRY, civil engineer; b. Saginaw, Mich., Nov. 22, 1865; s. James and Elizabeth C.; ed. city schs. of Saginaw and Harrisville, Mich., U. of Mich., class of 1892; m. Martha E. Devlin, of Bay City, Mich., Sept. 14, 1893. On railroad work for U.P., Cheyenne, Wyo., 1890-91; asst. state engr., Wyo., 1891-92; chief engr. consolidated Canal System, Salt

River Valley, Ariz., 1892-1902; chief irrigation investigations, writing several dept. bulls. on irrigation subjects, 1901-02; mem. advisory bd. of engrs. City of Los Angeles, 1910, in matter of disposition of surplus waters from Owens River aqueduct; resigned from Govt. work, 1911; mem. Quinton, Code & Hill, consulting engrs., hydraulic work in U.S., Mex. and Can.; engr. consultant to Dept. of Interior. Mem. Am. Soc. C.E., Am. Assn. of Engrs. Home: 7231 Hillside Av., Hollywood, Calif. Office: Edison Bldg., Los Angeles, Cal.

CODY, CLAUDE CARR, university dean; b. Covington, Ga., Nov. 5, 1854; s. Madison Derrel and Fanny (Carr) C.; A.B. (with honor), Emory Coll., Oxford, Ga., 1875, A.M., 1878, Ph.D., 1881; student Cornell U., 1898; m. Mattie Hughes, of Georgetown, Tex., Dec. 20, 1883. Prof. mathematics, Jan. 20, 1879-1916, dean academic dept., 1906-16, and since emeritus. Southwestern U. (longest continuous record as coll. prof. of any man now living in Tex.); treas., and twice acting pres. of univ. Democrat. Mem. M.E. Ch., Author: Life of Dr. Mood, 1886; Elements of Plane and Solid Geometry, 1910. Formerly editor of Texas Methodist Historical Quarterly. Mem. Gen. Conf. M.E. Ch. S., 1894, 1918. Address: Georgetown, Texas.

COE, JOHN PARKS, chem. engr.; b. Rock Falls, Ill., Dec. 15, 1889; s. Decious Octavius and Emma Elizabeth (Parks) C.; student U. Kan.; A.B., Washburn Coll., 1911, D.Sc. (hon.), 1954; B.S., Mass. Inst. Tech., 1913; m. Mary Elizabeth Gleed, June 26, 1913; children—Willis Gleed, Mary Elizabeth. Began with US. Rubber Co., 1913 at Indpls. tire plant, 1913-14, Gen. Labs., N.Y.C., 1914-26, engaged in devel. gas masks for Army and Navy, Gen. Labs., Naugatuck and Providence plants, 1917-18, in charge tire devel., other product activities Gen. Labs., 1919-26, organized tire devel. dept., Detroit, 1927-30, asst. to pres. Naugatuck Chem. Co. (N.Y.), 1930, factory mgr., Naugatuck, Conn., 1931-36, gen. sales mgr. 1936-39, gen. mgr. Naugatuck Chem. Div. since 1939, also Synthetic Rubber div. since 1942; became v.p. U.S. Rubber Co., 1945, now v.p. and gen. mgr.; chmn. bd. Tex.-U.S. Chem. Co. Incorporator Naugatuck Savs. Bank; Rubber Reclaimers Assn., Inc. Named Chemist of Year, Comml: Chem. Devel. Assn. Mem. Am. Chem. Soc. (past pres. N.Y. Rubber Group), Am. Inst. Chem. Engrs., A.A.A.S., Naugatuck council Boy Scouts Am (chmn. 1936), Kappa Sigma. Club: Lotos (N.Y.). Lectr., Bklyn. Inst. Arts and Scis. Contbr. to profl. jours. Home: Amity Rd., Woodbridge, New Haven 15. Office: 1230 Av. of the Americas, N.Y.C. 20. Died June 24, 1961.

COE, ROBERT, civil engr.; b. Oakfield, N.Y., July 14, 1868; s. Rev. James Roger and Mary (Cleveland) C.; ed. pvt. tutor; Catskill (N.Y.) grammar sch., 1 yr.; short period U.S. Naval Academy; married. On engring. force Norfolk & Western R.R., 1886-94; resident engr. Choctaw, Okla. & Gulf R.R., 1894-95; field asst. and topographer, U.S. Geol. Survey, 1895-1907; asst. to sec. of Panama Canal Commn., 1907-09; with Carnegie Steel Co., Feb. 1, 1910-Apr. 1, 1915; asst. supt. transportation, Canadian Copper Co., since July 1, 1915. Address: Copper Cliff, Ontario, Can.

COE, WESLEY ROSWELL, biologist; b. Middlefield, Conn., Nov. 11, 1869; s. Henry Seth and Hannah (Bailey) C.; grad. Conn. Agrl. Coll., 1888, Meriden (Conn.) High Sch., 1889; Ph.B., Sheffield Scientific School (Yale), 1892, Ph.D., 1895; D.Sc. (hon.) Yale, 1947; investigator University of Wurzburg, 1895-96, Naples, 1896; married Charlotte Eliza Bush, July 25, 1905. Assistant in biology, Sheffield Scientific School, 1892-95; instructor biology, Yale University, 1895-1901, assistant prof. comparative anatomy, 1901-07, prof. biology, 1907-38, prof. emeritus since 1938; curator zool. collections, Peabody Mus., 1914-26. Research associate, Scripps Institute of Oceanography. Mem. sci. expedns. to Alaska. Fellow A.A.A.S. (v.p.; chmn. Sec. F, 1930); mem. Am. Soc. Naturalists, Am. Soc. Zoologists (pres. 1940), Am. Assn. Anatomists, Am. Genetic Society, N.Y. Zool. Soc., Conn. Acad. Arts and Scis. (fellow), San Diego Hist. Soc. (pres. 1946-47, pres., 1947-48). Has written over 100 monographs and papers on biol. and anat. subjects, chiefly on morphology and embryology of invertebrates, regeneration, and change of sex in animals. Asso. editor Am. Jour. of Science, 1917-44. Journal of Morphology, 1928-30. Address: Osborn Zoological Laboratory, Yale University, New Haven CT

COES, HAROLD VINTON engr., mfr.; b. Hyde Park, Mass., June 21, 1883; s. Zorester Bennett and Alice (Miller) C.; prep. edn., Northeast. Manual Tng. Sch., Phila.; B.S. Mech. Engring., Mass. Inst. Tech., 1906; m. Agnes Wickfield Day, June 5, 1909; children—Kent Day, Harold Vinton. Mech. engr. Liquid Carbonic Cho., Chgo., 1908-11; indsl. engr. Lockwood, Greene and Co., Chgo. and Boston, 1911-14; v.p., mgr. Sentinel Mfg. Co., New Haven, Conn., 1914-16; indsl. engr. Gunn, Richard & Co., engrs., N.Y., 1916-18, Ford Bacon & Davis, Inc., 1918-24, gen. mgr. Platt Iron Works, Dayton, O., for same; v.p., gen. mgr. Belden Mfg. Co., mfrs. elec. wire, cables, etc., Chgo., 1924-28; v.p. Ford, Bacon & Davis, Inc., N.Y., 1928-37, partner 1937-48, dir., 1943; ret. exec. v.p., dir. Vulcan Iorn Works, Wilkes-Barre, Pa., 1934; past pres. United Engring. Trustees, Inc., dir. Easy Washing Machine Corp., Syracuse, N.Y. Mem. Adv. council, Coll. Engring., Princeton, Indsl. Engring. Dept., Columbia; Civilian Asst. in operation and adminstrn. munition Plant in U.S., Can., World War. Cons. engr. Planning and Development Dept., Govt. of India for Ford, Bacon, & Davis, 1945-46. Chmn. finance com. Engrs. Nat. Hoovers Com. Fellow Am. Soc. M.E. (past pres); Inst. Mgmt. (past pres.) mem. Soc. Advancement of Mgmt., Am. mgmt. Assn. (chmn. exec. com.), Indsl. Marketing Execs. Assn., Assn. Cons. Mgmt. Engrs. (past pres.). Montclair Soc. Engrs. Army Ordanance Assn., Newcomen Soc. of England, St. Andrews Soc. (hon.), Pi Tau Sigma. Republican. Unitarian. Club: Engineers (N.Y.C.). Author: Production Control (Alex. Hamilton Inst.). Asso. editor Handbook of Business Adminstration, also of Cost and Production Handbook. Home: 18 Braemore Rd., Upper Montclair, N.J. Office: 39 Broadway, N.Y.C. Died Dec. 4, 1958; buried Mount Hebron Cemetery, Upper Montclair, N.J.

COFFEY, GEORGE NELSON, agriculturalist; b. Patterson, N.C., Jan. 17, 1875; s. Elijah and Mary Ann (Nelson) C.; Ph.B., U. of N.C., 1900; M.S., George Washington Univ., 1907, Ph.D., 1911; m. Clara Estella Kean, Apr. 22, 1914. Assistant in geological laboratory, Univ. of N.C., 1899-1900; scientist, soil survey, Bur. of Soils, U.S. Dept. Agr., as asst., 1900-4, in charge, 1904-05, in charge soil classification and correlation, 1905-9, in charge, Great Plains Div., July, 1909-July 1911; asst. in charge soil survey, Ohio Expt. Sta., July 1, 1911-Dec. 1912; asso. in charge Div. of Soil Tech., same, Dec., 1912-Feb., 1915; asst. state leader for county farm advisers, U. of Ill., 1915-17, state leader, 1917-22; sec. Wayne County Abstract Co., May 1922—. Lecturer on soils of Univ. of N.C., Feb. 1905; has made exhaustive study of classification and correlation of soils of U.S. and constructed soil maps and written reports upon numerous areas in N.C., Ohio, Ill., Pa., Ia., Kan., N.D., S.D., and Tex.; assisted Ontario Agrl. Coll. in beginning soil survey of Ont., May-June, 1915. Pres. Am. Soc. Agronomy, 1909 (chmn. com. of 15 mem. to secure a more uniform system of soil classification and nomenclature for soils of U.S. and Can.). Mem. Am. Title Assn., Ohio Title Assn. (v.p. 1923). Mason, Rotarian. Home: Wooster OH

COFFEY, ROBERT CALVIN, surgeon; b. Caldwell Co., N.C., Oct. 20, 1869; s. Patterson Vance and Nancy Martitia (Estes) C.; prep. edn., Globe (N.C.) Acad.; M.D., Ky. Sch. of Medicine, Louisville, Ky., 1892; m. Clarissa Ellen Coffey, Aug. 9, 1893; children—Jay Russell, Wilson Bryan, Robert Mayo. Began practice at Moscow, Ida., 1892; moved to Portland, Ore., 1900; owner and chief surgeon Dr. Robert C. Coffey Clinic and Hosp. Fellow Am. Coll. Surgeons. Democrat. Presbyterian. Devised method of treatment of gastro-enteroptosis, entitled the "hammock operations." Wrote monograph on Gastroptosis; chapter on Diseases of the Pancreas, in Binnie's Regional Surgery. Home: Portland, Ore. Died Nov. 9, 1933.

COFFIN, FREEMAN C., civ. engr.; b. Boston, Sept. 14, 1856; s. Alonzo King and Mary Morean C.; ed. pub. schs., and Patten (Me.) Acad.; studied engring. Pvtly. and by practice; m. Oct. 10, 1885, Janet Agnes Lighthall, Boston. Began practice 1884; opened office in Boston as civ. and hydraulic engr., Jan. 1, 1894. Mem. Am. Soc. Civ. Engrs., Canadian and Boston Soc. Civ. Engrs., Canadian and Boston Soc. Civ. Engrs., New England Water Works Assn. Club: Twentieth Century. Author: The Graphical Solution of Hydraulic Problems, 1897. Contbr. to tech. jours. Residence: W. Medford, Mass. Office: 53 State St., Boston.

COFFIN, HOWARD EARLE, cons. engr.; b. West Milton, O., Sept. 6, 1873; s. Julius V. and Sarah E. (Jones) C.; U. of Mich., 1893-96, 1900-02, B.S. in M.E., 1911, as of 1903, hon. Dr. Engring., 1917; LL.D., Mercer U., Macon, Ga., 1929; Sc.D., Ga. Sch. of Tech., 1931; m. Matilda V. Allen, Oct. 30, 1907 (died 1932). With the U.S. Civil Service, 1896-1900; chief of exptl. dept., Olds Motor Works, Detroit and Lansing, 1902-05, and chief engr., 1905-06; v.p. and chief engr., E. R. Thomas Detroit Co., 1906-08; v.p. and cons. engr., Chalmers Detroit Motor Co., 1908-10; v.p. and cons. engr. Hudson Motor Car Co., 1910-30; pres. Nat. Air Transport, Inc., 1925-28, chmn. bd., 1928-30; chmn. bd. Sea Island Co., Southeastern Cottons, Inc. Mem. Naval Consulting Board, 1915—; mem. Advisory Commn. of Council of Nat. Defense, 1916-18, and chmn. Aircraft Board of U.S., 1917-18; mem. Am. Aviation Mission, 1919; mem. Morrow Bd., 1925. Home: Sea Island Beach, Ga. Died Nov. 21, 1937.

COFFIN, JAMES HENRY mathematician, meteorologist; b. Williamsburg, Mass., Sept. 6, 1806; s. Matthew and Betsy (Allen) C.; grad. Amherst Coll., 1828, M.A. (hon.), 1831; LL.D., (hon.), Rutgers, 1859; m. Aurelia Jennings, 1833; m. 2d, Abby Young, 1851. Opened pvt. sch. for boys, Greenfield Mass., 1829, added manual labor dept, 1830 (1st sch. of its kind in U.S., was beginning of Fellenberg Manual Labor Instn.); tutor Williams Coll., 1840-43; prof. mathematics and natural philosophy Lafayette Coll., 1846-73; collaborated in work of Smithsonian Instn., published results of meterol. studies under auspices Smithsonian Instn. as: Winds of the Northern Hemisphere, 1853; Psychrometrical Tables, 1856; The Orbit and Phenomena of a Meteoric Fire Ball, 1869; The Winds of the Globe, or the Laws of the Atmospheric Circulation over the Surface of the Earth, published posthumously, 1876; author textbooks Solar and Lunar Eclipses, 1845; Analytical Geometry, 1849; Conic Sections, 1850. Died Easton, Pa., Feb. 6, 1873.

COFFIN, JOHN HUNTINGTON CRANE, mathematician; b. Wiscasset, Me., Sept. 14, 1815; grad. Bowdoin Coll., 1834, LL.D. (hon.), 1884; married, 5 children. Prof. mathematics on various vessels, U.S. Navy, 1836-43; with U.S. Naval Observatory, Washington, D.C., 1843-53; prof. mathematics, astronomy and navigation U.S. Naval Acad., 1853-66; chief editor Nautical Alamanac, 1866-77; mem. Am. Acad. Scis; wrote various math. papers. Bied Washington, Jan. 8, 1890.

COFFIN, SELDEN JENNINGS, astronomer; b. Ogdensburg, N.Y., Aug. 3, 1838; s. late Prof. James Henry and Aurelia M. (Jennings) C.; A.B., Lafayette Coll., 1858, A.M., 1861; grad. Princeton Theol. Sem., 1864; (Ph.D., Hanover Coll., 1876); m. Mary A. Angle, N.J., Dec. 22, 1875 (died 1889); 2d, Emma F. Angle, Dec. 23, 1891. Tutor and adj. prof. mathematics, 1864-76, prof., 1876-86, registrar, 1886-1904, prof. astronomy, 1873—, Lafayette Coll. Ordained Presbyn. ministry, 1874. Author: Conic Sections, 1878; Record of the Men of La Fayette, 1891. Compiled his father's The Winds of the Globe, 1876; revised Olmsted's Astronomy, 1882. Home: Easton, Pa. Died Mar. 15, 1915.

COFFIN, WILLIAM CAREY, engr., architect; b. Pittsburgh, Sept. 7, 1862; s. William Carey and Jane McCormick (Osborne) C.; C.E., Western U. of Pa. (now U. of Pittsburgh), 1883; D.Sc., U. of Pittsburgh, 1936; m. Vida Hurst, 1889. With Keystone Bridge Co., 1883; chief engr. Fort Pitt Boiler Works 1883-85; with Riter-Conley Mfg. Co., 1885-1908; v.p. from incorporation 1898; asst. gen. sales agent Jones & Laughlin Steel Co., 1909-15; v.p. Blaw-Knox Co., 1915-23; engr. and architect, 1923-27, is now retired. Designed and built some of the largest blast furnaces, steel plants and oil refineries in U.S. and Can. and secured many large contracts in U.S. and foreign countries, including electric power houses in Dublin, Ireland, Glasgow, Scotland, and Bristol, England; later designed and built several residences at Miami Beach, Fla. Mem. council Nat. Civil Service Reform Assn., 1908-18; mem. Fed. Trades Com. of Chamber of Commerce U.S.A., 1913-18; proponent codes of fair trade practice to Congress, 1913, 35; president of board of trustees University of Maimi. Mem. American Iron and Steel Inst., Pittsburgh Chamber of Commerce. Republican. Presbyterian. Mason (32 deg.). Author: Governmental Regulation of Cooperation in Trade, Seeds of Progress and Success, New Approach to Spiritual Revival, The Place of Big Business in a Democracy, Enduring Faith; also studies of social economic conditions in Europe, and S. America. Tech. consultant War Manpower Commn. Home: 238 E. San Marino Dr., Miami Beach, Fla.; also 5731 Bartlett St., Pittsburgh, Pa. Died Dec. 4, 1944.

COGGESHALL, ARTHUR STERRY paleontologist; b. Bridgeport, Conn., July 17, 1873; s. Sterry Israel and Harriet Ellen (Jeffries) C.; ed. pub. schs., New Haven, Conn.; D.Sc., hon.) Occidental Coll., 1950.; m. Jennie Louise Smith, Apr. 25, 1895; Children—Ethyl Adele (Mrs. Elmer P. Kuhn), Mildred Olive (Mrs. Benedict Kristoff), Hazel Eloise (Mrs. Rigby, Pogmore); m. 2d, Adelaide Arneson, Oct. 28, 1946. With Am. Mus. Natural History, N.Y.C., 1896-99, curator pub. edn. and preparator-in-chief f dept. of paleontology, Carnegie Mus., Pitts. 1899-1929; designed and perfected cast steel method of mounting large dinosaurus, 1904; dir. St. Paul Inst., St. Paul, Minn., 1929-31; chief Ill. State Mus., Springfield, 1931-37; dir. Santa Barbara (Cal.) Mus. Natural History, 1937—; Specialized work, Dinosaur, Brit. Mus. Natural History Br., 1905; Natural History Mus., Jardin des Plantes, Paris, France, 1901; Mus. Fur Nature Künde, Berlin, Ger., 1908; Royal Mus. Natural Hist., Vienna, Austria, 1909; Musco Geologico Bologna, Italy, 1909; Imperial Mus., St. Petersburg, Russia, 1911; Nat. Mus. of Argentina, La Plata, Argentina, 1912; National Mus. of Spain. Madrid, Spain, 1913. Prostestant. Officer de l'Instruction Publique de France, 1908; Francis Joseph Order of Merit with Golden Crown, Austria, 1909; Cavaliere della Corona d' Italian, 1909; Order of St. Anne, Russia, 1910; Caballero de la Orden civil de Alfonso XII, Spain, 1914; Caballero de la Real Orden de Isablea La Catolica, Spain, 1914. Mem. forest adv. com., sec., Western Mus. Conf. Fellow A.A.A.S., Mem. Council Am. Assn. Mus. Lectr. natural history subjects and travels; instr. U. Cal. Nature Sch. Home: 653 Mission Canyon Rd. Santa Barbara, CA. Died Aug. 13, 1958.

COGGESHALL, GEORGE WHITELEY, chemist; b. Des Moines, Ia., Dec. 21, 1867; s. John M. and Mary J. (Whiteley) C.; B.S., Grinnell (Ia.) Coll., 1890; grad. work, Harvard, 1891-92; Ph.D. Leipzig, 1895; grad. work, Harvard, 1891-92; m. Anna Torrey Sept. 6, 1900; children—Elizabeth (Mrs. John C. West), Mary (Mrs. John H. Hollands), Dorothy (Mrs. Walter P. Wilson). Inst. in physical chemistry, Harvard, 1895-97; developing new chem. products, 1898-1910; chief chem. engr., Inst. Industrial Research, Washington,

D.C., 1911-23; dir. Industrial Research Laboratories, 1923-29; dir. research, S.D. Warren Co., 1924-40. In charge surfacing concrete vessels, Emergency Fleet Corp., 1918. Fellow A.A.A.S., Am. Acad. Arts and Sciences; mem. Am. Chem. Soc., Am. Electrochem. Soc., Am. Inst. Mining and Metall. Engrs., Soc. Chem. Industry, Am. Inst. Chem. Engrs., Washington Acad. Sciences, American Genetic Association, American Geographical Soc. Clubs: Cosmos (Washington); St. Botolph (Boston); Cumberland (Portland); Faculty (Cambridge). Contbr. papers on standard calomel, electrodes, titanium mordants, potash from feldspathic rocks, etc. Developed various chem. processes, including Portland cement, rare metal compounds, gasoline from heavy oils, phosphates, paper pulp, paper specialities, etc. Home: Princes Point, Yarmouth, Me. Died Nov. 18, 1944.

COGHILL, GEORGE ELLETT, anatomist; b. Beaucoup, Ill., Mar. 17, 1872; s. John Waller and Elisabeth (Tucker) C.; student Shurtleff Coll., Alton, Ill., 1891-94; A.B. Brown, 1896, Ph.D., 1902, D.Sc., 1934; M.S., U. of N.M., 1899; Sc.D., Pittsburgh, 1931, Dension, 1933; M. Muriel Anderson, Sept. 13, 1900; children—Robert De Wolf, James Tucker, Louis Waller, Muriel, Benjamin Anderson. Asst. prof. biology, U. of N.M., 1899-1900; prof. biology, Pacific U., Forest Grove, Ore., 1902-06; prof. biology and embryology, Williamette U., Salem, Ore., 1906-07; prof. zoölogy, Dension U., Granville, O., 1907-13; asso. prof. anatomy, U. of 1913-15, prof., 1915-25, head of dept., 1918-25, sec. Sch. of Medicine, 1918-24; prof. comparative anatomy, Wistar Inst. Anatomy and Biology, 1925-27, mem. bd. advisers, Wistar Inst., 1926—, mem. inst., 1927-36; mng. editor Jour. Comparative Neurology, 1927-33; visiting lecturer on advanced anatomy, Univ. Coll., London, 1928. Awarded Daniel Giraud Elliot gold medal in 1934 by National Academy of Sciences. Baptist. Author: Anatomy and the Problem of Behavior, 1929. Home: Gainesville, Fla. Died July 23, 1941.

COGHILL, WILLIAM HAWES, metall. engr.; b. Roseville, Ill., Mar. 14, 1876; desc. James Coghill who came from Eng. to Va. 1664; s. John Waller and Elisabeth (Tucker) C.; student Shurtleff Coll., Alton, Ill., 1892-94, 1896-97; E.M., Colo. Sch. of Mines, 1903; m. Maria Robinson, May 16, 1906; children—Elizabeth, William Waller, Robert Gregory. Began as public sch. teacher, 1894; engr. Albuquerque (N.M.) Land & Irrigation Co., 1897-98; asst. mine surveyor, Bisbee, Ariz., 1901-02, 1903-04; asst. engr. Calumet & Ariz. Mining Co., Bisbee, 1904-05, Tamarack Mining Co., Calumet, Mich., 1905-06; gen. engring. work N.M., and Joplin, Mo., 1906-07; asst. prof. mining and metallurgy, Northwestern U., 1907-14; cons. engr. El Paso, Tex., 1914-15; prof. mining and metallurgy and head dept. chem. engring., Ore. State Agrl. Coll., Corvallis, Ore., 1915-17; metallurgist U.S. Bur. of Mines, Seattle, Wash., Golden, Colo., Platteville, Wis., Miami, Okla., 1917-25; supervising engr. in charge of ore dressing sect., U.S. Bur. Mines, Rolla, Mo., 1926-37; prin. engr. nonmetals div., U.S. Bur. Mines and supervising engr. Southern Expt. Sta., U. Ala., 1938-45; chief, Tuscaloosa div. Metall. branch, U.S. Bureau of Mines 1945, retired Dec., 1945. Milling research St. Joseph Lead Co., Bonne Terre, Mo., 1946-47; ret. Mem. American Inst. Mining and Metall. Soc. of Am., A.A.A.S., Sigma Xi, Tau Beta Pi. Club: Rotary. Author: many papers and govt. bulls. on cyaniding, flotation, concentration and grinding. Home: 145 W. Lincoln Av., Delaware OH

COGSHALL, WILBUR ADELMAN, prof. astronomy; b. Mendon, Mich., Feb. 8, 1874; s. Wilbur I. and Martha (Leavitt) C.; B.S., Albion (Mich.) Coll., 1895; studied U. Chgo., Yerkes Obs.; A.M., Ind. U., 1902; m. Harriet Bayliss, Jan. 21, 1899; children—Wilbur Bayliss, Sarah Louise, Frederick John. Prof. Astronomy Ind. U. Mem. Am. Astron. Soc., Ind. Acad. Science, Sigma Xi, Alpha Tau Omega. Methodist. Has specialized in astro- photography. Home: Rockford, Ill. Died Oct. 5, 1951; buried nr. Flagstaff, Ariz.

COGSWELL, WILLIAM BROWN, mfr.; b. Oswego, N.Y., Sept. 22, 1834; s. David and Mary (Barnes) C.; ed. Syracuse and Seneca Falls, N.Y.; attended Rensselaer Poly. Inst., 1850-52 (hon. C.E., 1884); twice married; m. 2d, Cora Louise Brown, Apr. 29, 1902. Apprentice Lawrence (Mass.) Machine Shop, 1852-55; asst. supt. Marietta & Cincinnati R.R., 1856-59; in U.S.N., 1861-65; erecting and operating blast furnaces at Franklin Iron Works, Oneida Co., N.Y., 1869-73; in charge mines La Motte Estate, Mo., 1874-79; established Solvay Process Co. (chem. works; soda products), 1881, of which was v.p. and mng. dir. Home: Syracuse, N.Y. Died June 7, 1921.

COHEN, ABRAHAM, university prof.; b. Baltimore, Sept. 11, 1870; B.A., Johns Hopkins, 1891, fellow in mathematics, 1893-94, Ph.D., 1894; student at Sorbonne, Paris, 1894-95; married; 1 dau., Inez Teress. Instr. mathematics, 1895-98, asso., 1898-1914, asso. prof., 1914-26, prof. since 1926, Johns Hopkins; lecturer summers, U. of Colo., 1916-25. Co-editor Am. Journal of Mathematics since 1899; asso. editor Am. Math. Monthly, 1916-17. Fellow A.A.A.S.; mem. Am. Math. Soc., Math. Assn. America (pres. Md.-Va.-D.C. Sect.), Phi Beta Kappa, Johns Hopkins Chapter Sigma Xi. Author: Elementary Treatise on Differential Equations, 1906; The Lie Theory of One-parameter Groups, 1911; Differential and Integral Calculus, 1925. Home: 233 E. University Pkwy., Baltimore MD

COHEN, BARNETT, biochemist, bacteriologist; born Rogachev, Russia, Feb. 16, 1891; s. Louis and Rose (Goedelberg) C.; brought to U.S., 1893, naturlized, 1900; student Townsend Haris Hall, N.Y. City, 1904-07; B.S., Coll. City of N.Y., 1911; Ph.D., Yale, 1921. Asst. Chem. bacteriologist, City of Savannah, Ga., 1915-16; chemist, hygienic lab. U.S. P.H.S., Washington, 1920-18; asso. prof. physiol. chemistry Johns Hopkins since 1928. Ofcl. investigatior Office Scientific Research and Development, 1941-45. Served as 2d lt., U.S. Army, 1918. Mem. A.A.A.S., Am. Chem. Soc., Am. Pub. Health Assn., Soc., Biol. Chemist, Soc. Am Bacterologists (pres. 1950, archvist since 1935). Club: Cosmos (Washington). 1937. Editor Bacteriological Reviews since foundation 1937. Home: 10 W. Read St., Balt. 1. Died Oct. 22, 1952; buried Linden Hill Cemetery of Central Synagogue, Queens, N.Y.

COHEN, LOUIS, cons. engr.; b. Kiev, Russia, Dec. 16, 1876; s. Abraham and Nattie (Resnik) C.; B.Sc., Armour Inst. Tech., 1901; student U. of Chicago, 1902; Ph.D., Columbia, 1905; m. Ethel Slavin, Jan. 3, 1904; 1 dau., Mrs. Louis P. Sissman. With scientific staff, Bur. of Standards, Washington, 1905-09; with Elec. Signaling Co., 1909-12; cons. practice since 1913; prof. elec. engring., George Washington U., 1916-29; cons. engr., War Dept., 1920-24; lecturer Bur. of Standards, Washington since 1928; U.S. del. Provisional Tech. Com. Internat. Conf. on Elec. Communication, Paris, France, 1921; mem. advisory tech. bd., Conf. on Limitation of Armament, Washington, 1921-22; technical expert German-Austrian claim commn., 1929-31. Fellow A.A.A.S., Am. Inst. E.E., Am. Inst. Radio Engrs., Am. Physical Soc. Author: Formulae and Tables for Calculation of Alternating Current Problems, 1913; Heaviside's Electrical Circuit Theory, 1928; also many papers in scientific and tech. jours. Inventor of many devices in radio and cable telegraphy. Home: 303 Roosevelt St., Bethesda, Md. Died Sept. 28, 1948.

COHEN, MENDES, civil engr., b. Baltimore, May 4, 1831; s. David I. C.; ed. pvt. schs.; studied engring., 1847-51, in locomotive works Ross Winans, Baltimore; m. 1865. In engr. corps and other service of B.&O. R.R., 1851-55; asst. supt. Hudson River R.R., 1855-61; pres. and supt. Ohio & Miss. R.R. (of Ill.), 1861-63; then in spl. service of Phila. & Reading; comptroller and asst. to pres. Lehigh Coal & Navigation Co., 1868-71; pres. Pittsburgh & Connellsville, 1872-75; afterward retired from active professional work; mem. bd. apptd. by Pres. Cleveland, 1894, to examine and report route from Chesapeake and Delaware Ship Canal; chmn. sewerage commn., Baltimore, 1893-1904. Died Aug. 13, 1915.

COHN, ALFRED EINSTEIN physician; b. N.Y. City, Apr. 16, 1879; s. Abraham and Maimie (Einstein) C.; A.B., Columbia, 1900; M.D., Coll. Physicians and Surgeons (Columbia), 1904, D.Sc. (hon.), 1940; studied U. of Freiburg, U. of Vienna and Univ. Coll., London; m. Ruth Walker Price, Apr. 24, 1911. In practice in N.Y. City, 1909-11; with Rockefeller Inst. for Med. Research since 1911, mem. since 1920, mem. emeritus since 1944. Lt. Col. M.C., U.S. Army, cons. in cardio vascular diseases, 1918; served in France. Mem. bd. of govs. N.Y. Tuberculosis and Health Assn., 1925-45; chmn. of com. on research N.Y. Heart Assn., 1921-48 (mem. advisory commn. on research 1946-48); councillor to VA, Washington, 1921-46; member executive committee group on adult edn. Carnegie Corp., 1924-26; member Laskers Found., 1928-40; mem. China Med. Board, 1934-45; mem .com. on Library, 1934-41; Member bd. of editors Bulletin of N.Y. Acad. of Medicine; mem. Am. Com. on Refugee Scholars, Writers and Artists (treas. from 1945); mem. med. bd. Irvington House, Irvington-on Hudson, 1930-45; chairman subcom. on heart diseases and rheumatic fever, N.Y. World's Fair, 1937-40. Mem. exec. committee Internat. Student Service, 1934-42; mem. bd. directros, sec.-treas. Student Service of America, Incorpoated, 1943-47; member Club. for Research on Ageing, from 1939; vice pres. com. for Nat. Morale, 1940-42, chmn. exec. com., 1942-49; chmn. science com. Research Council of Department of Hosps., New York, 1935-51, treas., 1943-51. Spl. adviser Board of Economic Warfare, 1942-44; bd. dirs. Iranian Inst. and Sch. Asiatic Studies, 1944-49, pres., 1947-49; bd. dirs. Sydenham Inst., 1947-48; member health committee American Jewish Joint Distribution Committee since 1944; Council on Foreign Relations since 1946. Visiting prof. medicine, Union Med. Coll., Peking, China Spring of 1925. Fellow N.Y. Academy of Medicine; mem. Am. Soc. Pharmacology and Expermental Therapeutics, Am. Assn. Hist. Medicine, Assn. Am. Phys., Am. Assn. Anatomists, Am. Physiol. Soc., Am. Assn. Pathol. and Bacteriol., Am. Soc. Clin. Investigation, Am. Med. Assn., Botanical Soc. of Am. (physiol. sec.t), Hist. of Science Soc., Harvey Soc. (pres. 1930,), Internat. Assn. Geographical l Pathology, New York Academy of Sciences, Soc. for Experimental Biology and Meicine (Councillor 1929-33), A.A.A.S., Am. Assn. on Adult Edn., Am. Soc. For Research in Psychomatic Medicine N.Y. Scientists Assn. since 1945, Am. Assn on Indian Affairs, 1945-47; Author: Medicine, Science and Art, 1931; Minerva's Progress, 1946; No Retreat from Reason, 1948; The Burden of Diseases in the United States (with Claire Lingg), 1950; also about 180 med. Investigations. Home: 200 E. 66th St., N.Y.C. 21. Died July 20, 1957.

COHN, ALFRED I., pharmacist, chemist; b. at New York, Nov. 1, 1860; s. Marx and Rose (Harris) C.; ed. Coll. City of New York; grad. Coll. Pharmacy City of New York, 1881; Pharm.D., Ph.G.; m. Laura Lambert, of New York, Sept. 8, 1887. Mem. Am. Chemical Soc., Soc. of Chemical Industry. Author: Indicators and Test Papers - Tests and Reagents. Translated and enlarged Quantitative Analysis: Lunge's Techno-Chemical Analysis. Contbr. on pharmacy and pharm. chemistry to jours. Home: 122 E. 74th St. Office: Care Merck & Co., 43-45 Park Pl., New York.

COHN, EDWIN JOSEPH, prof. biological chemistry; b. New York, N.Y., Dec. 17, 1892; s. Abraham and Maimie (Einstein), Cohn; student Amherst Coll., 1910-13; B.S., U. of Chic Chicago, 1914, Ph.D., 1917; grad. student Harvard 1915-17, M.A., (hon.) Harvard, 1945; M.D. (hon.), Geneva, 1946, Berne, 1947; m. Marianne Brettauer, July 30, 1917 (dec.); children—Edwin J., Alfred; m. 2d, Rebekah Higginson June 15, 1948. Nat. Research Council fellow in chemistry, 1919-22, studied at Carlsberg Laboratory, Copenhagen and Cambridge U., Eng.; Asst. prof. physical chemistry, Harvard, 1922-28. asso. prof., 1928-35; prof. biol. chemistry and head of dept. of physical chemistry, Harvard Med. Sch., 1935-49, Higgins University Professor Harvard, since 1949; chairman of division medical sciences, 1936-49; dir. U. Lab. of Physical Chemistry related to med. and pub. health, Harvard since 1949; chairman department biophys. chemistry since 1950. Served as first lieutenant Sanitary Corps, United States Army, 1918-19; honorary consultant to the Medical Dept. of the Navy since 1942. Received Alvarenga Prize Coll. of Phys. of Phila., 1942. Passano Award for distinguished service to American Clin. Medicine, 1945; John Scott Medal, Phila., 1946; John Phillips Memorial Medal, Am. College of Physicians, 1946; Theodore William Richards Medal from Am. Coll. Physicians, 1948; Medal of Science Free University of Belgium, 1947; Medal of Merit, U.S. Govt., 1948 French Legion Honor, 1952. Silliman Lectr. Yale, 1946; Am. Swiss Found. lectr., 1947; Belgian Am. Ednl. Found. lectr., 1947; Julius Streglitz meml. lectr., A.C.S. 1949. Fellow A.A.A.S., Am. Acad. Arts and Sci., N.Y. Acad. Sci.; mem. Nat. Acad Sci., Am. Philos. Soc., Am. Chem. Soc. Am. Soc. Biol. Chem., Am. Physiol. Soc., Sigma Xi. Contbr. articles on chem. of natural products and systems, liver fractions, plasma fractions, physical chem. of proteins, blood, and other tissues, to professional journals. Author: (with J. T. Edsall) Proteins, Amino Acids and Peptides, 1943; Research in Medical Sciences Sciences, March of Medicine, 1946. Clubs: Harvard, St. Botolph (Boston); Faculty (Cambridge). Home: 183 Brattle St., Cambridge, Mass. Died Oct. 1, 1953.

COKER, DAVID ROBERT, plant breeder, agrl. and cotton expert; b. Hartsville, S.C., Nov. 20, 1870; s. James Lide and Susan (Stout) C.; A.B., Univ. of S.C., 1891; hon. D.Sc. from Duke Univ., 1930; LL.D., U. of N.C., 1931; LL.D., Coll. of Charleston, 1935; D.Sc., Clemson Coll., 1937; m. Jessie Ruth Richardson, Sept. 10, 1894 (died 1913); Katherine, Hannah, Eleanor, Robert, Samuel; m. 2d, Margaret May Roper, 1915; children—Martha, Mary, Carolyn. Originator of varieties of staple cotton widely planted in the U.S. and elsewhere; pres. J.L. Coker & Co., merchants; mem. Coker Cotton Co.; pres. Coker's Pedigreed Seed Co. Mayor of Hartsville, S.C., 1902-04; chmn. S.C. Council of Defense, World War, also of Federal Food Adminstration for S.C.; mem. Nat. Agrl. Advisory Com.; mem. Nat. Agrl. Commn. to Europe, 1918, S.C. Land Settlement Commission; mem. Business Advisory Council of Dept. of Commerce, Trustee U. of S.C., Coker Coll. for Women. Awarded McMaster medal, U. of S.C. Democrat. Home: Hartsville, S.C. Died Nov. 28, 1938.

COKER, ROBERT E(RVIN), biologist; b. Society Hill, Darlington County, S.C., June 4, 1876; s. William Caleb and Mary Ervin (McIver) C.; S.C. Coll., 1892-93; B.S., U. of N.C., 1896, M.S., 1897; Ph.D., Johns Hopkins Univ., 1906; Doctor of Science, Univ. of South Carolina, 1948; m. Jennie Coit, Oct. 11, 1910; children—Robert Ervin, Coit McLean. Asst. in biology, 1895-97; prof. zoology, U. of N.C., 1922-39, Kenan prof. zoology, 1939-53, now emeritus, chmn. div. natural scis., 1935-44, chmn. bd. trustees Chapel Hill Schools, 1935-1947; mem. Council on Human Relations, A.A.A.S., 1939-41; collaborator U.S. Forest Service, 1939-41; consultant U.S. Public Health Service and mem. Nat. Advisory Com. on Gerontology, 1940-42; chairman Survey of Marine Fisheries of N.C., 1946; director U. of N.C. Inst. of Fisheries Research, 1947-48, chairman executive committee, 1948-50. O. Max Gardner award (for service in organization of Fisheries Survey and Institute), 1950. Delegate to Peruvian Government to 4th Internat. Fisheries Congress (v.p.), Washington, 1908. Fellow A.A.A.S., Chgo. Acad. Scis.; member Am. Fisheries Soc., Ecological Soc. Am. (president 1937), Am. Soc. Zoologists (pres. 1941), North Carolina Academy Science (president 1941), Elisha Mitchell Scientific

Society (president 1929-30), Limnological Society of America (vice-pres. 1935, pres. 1938), Assn. S.E. Biologists, Society Syst. Zoology, Sigma Xi, Phi Beta Kappa, Chi Psi; corr. member Davenport (Ia.) Acad. Science. Mason. Author: The Great and Wide Sea, 1947 (Mayflower award); various papers relating to oyster culture, fisheries and guano industry of Peru, mussels, copepods, etc. Home: Chapel Hill NC

COKER, WILLIAM CHAMBERS, botanist; b. Hartsville, S.C., Oct. 24, 1872; s. James Lide and Susan Armstrong (Stout) C.; B.S., S.C. Coll., Columbia, S.C., 1894; Ph.D., Johns Hopkins, 1901; studied at Bonn, Germany, 1901-02; LL.D., U. of S.C., 1925; D.Sc., U. of N.C., 1947; m. Louise Venable, Oct. 28,, 1934. With Atlantic Nat. Bank, Wilmington, North Carolina, 1894-97; teacher summer school, Brooklyn Inst. Arts and Sciences, Cold Spring Harbor, L.I., 1900; asso. prof. botany, U. of N.C., 1902-07; prof., 1907-20, Kenan professor botany, 1920-44; Kanan Research professor botany, 1944-45, emeritus since 1945; also director Coker Arborerum. Chief of botancial staff of Bahama expedition of the Geographical Society of Baltimore, 1903. Fellow A.A.A.S. mem. Bot. Soc. Am. (chmn. Southeastern sect), Am. Soc. Naturalistis, Am. Mycological Soc., Elisha Mitchell Scientific Soc., N.C. Acad. Sciences, American Forestery Assn. N.C. Forestry Assn., Chi Psi, Phi Beta Kappa, Sigma Xi. Democrat. Editor Journal. Elisha Mitchell Scientific Soc., 1904-45; chmn. bd. Univ. N.C. Press, 1936-43; pres. Highlands Biol. Laboratory 1933-44; honorary president since 1944; honorary curator of botany, Charleston Museum, 1943-53; trustee, Brookgreen Gardens, S.C., 1944-47. Author: Vegetation of the Bahama Islands, 1905; The Plant Life of Hartsville, S.C., 1912; The Trees of North Carolina (with H. R. Totten), 1916; The Saprolegniaceae, 1923; The Clavarias of the United States and Canada, 1923; The Gasteromycets of the Eastern United States and Canada (with J. N. Couch), 1928; Trees of the Southeastern States (with H. R. Totten), 1934; The Boletaceae of North Carolina (with A. H. Beers), 1943; The Stipiate Hydnums of the Eastern United States (with A. H. Beers), 1951. Contbr. numerous articles on morphological botany, particularly on the gymnosperms and fungi. Home: Chapel Hill, N.C. Died June 27, 1953; buried Chapel Hill Hill.

COLBERT, LEO OTIS, hydrographic and geodetic engr; b. Cambridge Mass., Dec. 31, 1883; s. P. John and Margaret (Byrnes) C.; B.S. in C.E., Tufts Coll., 1907, hon. Sc.D., 1939; m. Florentine Odou, Sept. 12, 1912; children—Mary Louise (Mrs. Raphael A. Neale), Jeanne (Mrs. William L. Doonan). With U.S. Coast and Geodetic Survey, 1907-50, on various survey parties; comdg. officer on survey ships, 1912-17; chief sect. vessels in Washington office, 1919-28; director of coast surveys in P.I., 1928-30; comdg. officer ship "Oceanographer," 1931, 32; chief div. of charts, 1933-38; dir. with rank of rear adm., 1938-50, ret. U.S. rep. Joint Colorado River Boundary Commns. Ariz.-Cal. Mem. adv. council Princeton University Department Civil Engring., Am. Con. on Surveying and Mapping. Hon. trustee Woods Hole Oceanograhic Instn. Awarded Dept. of Commerce Exceptional Service Citation; USC & GS Meritorious Service Ribbon, 1950; Gold medal by Society Am. Mil. Engrs., 1959. Fellow Arctic Inst. N.A.; mem. Am. Soc. C.E. (honorary member), Newcomen Soc. of North Am., Soc. Am. Mil. Engrs. (dir., past pres.), Am. Geophys. Union, Inst. Nav., Am. Shore and Beach Preservation Assn. (past pres.) Nat. Geog. Soc. (life trustee), Alpha Tau Omega, Tau Beta Pi. Clubs: Adventurers (Honolulu); Army and Navy. Home: Washington DC Died Dec. 23, 1968.

COLBURN, ALLAN PHILIP, educator b. Madison, Wis., June 8, 1904; s. Willis Paul and Jane (Grimm) C.; student Marquette U., Milwaukee, 1922-24; B.S., U. Wis., 1926, M.S., 1927, Ph.D., 1929; m. Evelyn Safford, Nov. 21, 1931; children—Judith, Willis, Carolyn. Research chem. engr., Dupont Co., Wilmington, Del., 1929-38; asso. prof. chem. engring., U. of Del., 1938-41, prof. since 1941, asst. to the pres., 1947-50, acting pres., Apr.-Nov. 1950, provost since 1950, chmn. engring. expt. sta. since 1947; cons. chem. engr. since 1941; sec. Haskell Research Found., Inc., since 1949. Cons. to Research and Development Bd., Dept. of Defense since 1948. Recipient Walker Award, Am. Inst. Chem. Engrs., 1936, Profl. Progress award, 1948. Dir. Del. chpt. Am. Red Cross since 1946. Mem. Am. Inst. Chem. Engrs. (dir., 1944-47, chmn. awards com., 1946, 47 1951), N.E.A., Am. Soc. Engring. Edn. (chmn. grad. studies div. 1952, chmn. ednl. methods div. 1953), Am. Soc. M.E. (chmn. heat transfer div., 1948), Am. Chem. Soc., A.A.A.S., Sigma Phi Epsilon, Tau Beta Pi Sigma Xi, Phi Lambda Upsilon, Phi Kappa Phi. Home: 49 Winslow Rd., Newark, Del. Died. Feb. 6, 1955.

COLBURN, WARREN, educator; b. Dedham, Mass., Mar. 1, 1793; s. Richard and Joanna (Eaton) C.; grad. Harvard, 1820; m. Temperance Horton, Aug. 28, 1823, 7 children. Conducted pvt. sch., Boston, 1820-23; supt. cotton mill of Merrimac Mfg. Co., Lowell, Mass., 1824-33; mem. 1st sch. bd. of Lowell, 1826-29; co-founder Am. Inst. of Instrn., Boston; mem. Am. Acad. Arts and Scis.; mem. examining com. for mathematics Harvard. Author: First Lessions in Arithmetic, on the Plan of Pestalozzi, with Some Improvements, 1821-26; An Introduction to Algebra upon the Inductive Method of Instruction, 1825; Lessions in Reading and Grammar, 1830-33. Died Sept. 13, 1833.

COLBY, ALBERT LADD, metallurgist; b. New York, N.Y., June 26, 1860; s. John Ladd (M.D.) and Mary Ann C.; student Coll. City of New York; Ph.B., Columbia Sch. of Mines, 1881; m. Agnes Wilson Lee, June 20, 1894. Engaged in steel metallurgy, 1886—; sec. of Assn. Am. Steel Mfrs., 1897-1905; U.S. Juror, Paris Expn., 1900; iron and steel comr., St. Louis Expn., 1904. Author: American Standard Specifications for Steel, 1902; Reinforced Concrete in Europe, 1909. Home: Bethlehem, Pa. Died May 2, 1924.

COLBY, BRANCH HARRIS, civil engr.; b. Cherry Valley, O., July 20, 1854; s. Lewis and Celestia (Rice) C.; C.E., U. of Mich., 1877, post-grad. course in mining engring., 1877-78; m. Minnie Bary, June 28, 1883; children—Vine (Mrs. Charles O. McCasland), Dorothy (Mrs. Victor H. Lawn). Asst. on survey of Great Lakes, 1875-78; U.S. asst. engr., Miss. River, 1878-84; in pvt. practice, 1885-89; U.S. asst. engr. in charge of survey of Portage Lake Ship Canal, 1888-89, for Straight Channel, Sandusky (O.) Harbor, 1889; U.S. asst. engr. Miss. River Commn., 1889-90; prin. asst. engr. sewer dept., St. Louis, 1890-95; sewer commn. and mem. Bd. of Pub. Improvements, 1895-99; civ. and consulting engr. Am. Car & Foundry Co., 1900; pvt. practice, 1901, until retired. Engineer on building steel ships at Hog Island Pa., 1917; supervised constrn. Govt. Island Shipyard, San Francisco, July-Dec. 1918; mem. bd. to investigate and report upon condition and operation of ship yards upon Atlantic Coast; resident engr. in charge of constrn. of a dry dock, marine ry. and repair plant at Jacksonville, Fla. Mem. Mich. Nat. Guard, 1873-76. Unitarian. Mason. Home: Normal, Ill. Died Jan. 3, 1933.

COLBY, CHARLES CARLYLE, educator; b. Romeo, Mich., Apr. 13, 1884; s. Frank and Anna Morton (Stephen) C.; B.Pd., Mich. State Normal Coll., 1908, hon. M.Ed., from same, 1922; B.S., U. Chgo., 1910, Ph.D., 1917; m. Mary McRae, Apr. 25, 1931; children—Stephen McRae, Bruce Redfearn. Asst. in geography Mich. State Normal Coll., 1906-08, U. Chgo., 1910; head. dept. geography State Normal Sch., Winona, Minn., 1910-13; fellow in geography U. Chgo., 1913-14; asso. prof. geography George Peabody Coll. for Tchrs., 1914-16; with U. Chgo. since 1916, as instr. geography, asst. professor, asso. prof. until 1925, prof. since 1925, chmn. dept., 1942-49, vis. prof. Grad. Coll. U. of Ill., 1949-50, vis. prof. geography U. Cal. at Los Angeles, 1950-51; lectr. So. Ill. U., 1951. Spl. expert div. planning and statistics U.S. Shipping Bd., 1918-19. Adviser to War Shipping Administration, 1942. Mem. div. geology and geography, NRC, 1924-27, 40-42, chmn. Sub.-Com. on Land Classification, 1939, and Sub.-Com. on Regional Approach to Employment Stblzn. 1940; cons. Hdqrs. Commn., Selection Site, UN, 1946. Fellow A.A.A.S.; mem. Assn. Am. Geographers (sec. 1923-29, pres. 1935), Ill. Acad. Sci., Geog. Soc. Chgo., (Gold medal) 1948; dir., pres. 1944, Phi Kappa Sigma, Sigma Xi; hon. corr. mem. Am. Geog. Soc. Dem. Clubs: Quadrangle, Chaos. Author: Source Book for the Economic Geography for Secondary Schools (with A. Forster), 1931; dir. Studies in Economic Geography (with same), 1932; Changing Currents of Geographic Thought in America, 1936; Economic Geography; Industries and Resources of the Commercial World, 1940; area analysis—A Method of Public Works Planning (with V. Roterus), 1942. Editor: Geographical Aspects of Internat. Relations, 1937; (with A. Foster) Economic Geography, 1953; Pilot Study of Southern Ill., 1956; Water Transport: Component of Civilization, 1965; The North Atlantic Arena, Water Transport in World Order, 1966. Editor and contbr. Land Classification in the United States, 1941. Contbr. to Annals of Assn. Am. Geographers and Econ. Geography. Home: 5737 Kimbark Av., Chgo. 60637. Died July 16, 1965; buried Oak Woods Cemetery, Chgo.

COLBY, IRVING HAROLD, govt. ofcl.; b. Booque, S.D., Mar. 6, 1908; s. Charles E. and Julia H. (Bly) C.; B.S., S.D. State U., 1931; m. Frances U. Ryland, Feb. 20, 1935; 1 dau., Carole. Served with U.S. Army, 1933-35; engr. S.D. State Hwy., Pierre, S.D., 1936-40, 46-68, emergency planning engr. Served to lt. col. AUS, 1941-46. Mem. Nat. Soc. Profl. Engrs., V.F.W., Am. Legion. Lutheran. Mason, Elk. Home: Pierre SD Died June 15, 1968.

COLBY, WALTER FRANCIS, physicist; born Rockford, Mich., July 28, 1880; s. Joshua and Sarah (Massie) C.; A.B., U. of Mich., 1901, Ph.D., 1909; grad. study U. Vienna, 1901-04; post doctoral study U. Munich, 1910-11, U. Copenhagen, 1922, U. Hamburg, 1921; m. Martha Guernsey, 1930. Mem. faculty U. Mich., 1909-44, prof. physics, 1919-44; staff Mt. Wilson Obs., 1914-15; dep. chief Office Sci. Research and Development, 1944-45; became dir. intelligence, U.S. AEC, 1948; asst. dir. Office Sci. Personnel, Nat. Acad. Scis., from 1953. Mem. Am. Phys. Soc. Club: Cosmos. Home: Washington DC Died July 1970.

COLCORD, FRANK FOREST, cons. engr.; b. Boston, Nov. 12, 1877; s. Benjamin F. and Ada I. (Reed) C.; S.B., Mass. Inst. Tech., 1898. Asst. to supt. Chgo. & Aurora Smelting Refining Co., 1898-1900; chief chemist Am. Smelting & Refining Co., Perth Amboy, N.J., 1900-08; chief clerk U.S. Metals Refining Co., Carteret, N.Y., 1908-10; asst. to v.p. U. S. Smelting Refining & Mining Co., N.Y.C., 1910-38, v.p., mgr. metal sales, 1938-47. now dir. Apptd. mem. primary lead producers industry adv. com. and mem. silver producers industry adv. com., W.P.A., 1942. Mem. Mining and Metall. Engrs., Electro-chem, Soc. Mason. Club: Lawyers (N.Y.C.). Contbr. tech. atricles profl. jours. Home: 2595 Devonport Rd., San Marino, Cal. Died Mar. 21, 1952.

COLE, AARON HODGMAN, biologist; b. Greenwich, N.Y., Oct. 21, 1856; s. Morgan C. (M.D.) and Lydia Ann (Hodgman) C.; A.B., Colgate U., 1884, A.M., 1887; grad. student Johns Hopkins, 1889, U. of Chicago, 1893, 1896, 1898; m. Emma Sarah Mason, Dec. 29, 1885. Instr. natural sciences, Peddie Inst., 1884-88; lecturer in zoölogy and geology, Colgate, 1888-92; instr. zoölogy, Cold Spring Harbor Biol. Laboratory, 1893; lecturer in biology, U. of Chicago, extension div., 1895-1906; instr. of biology, Chicago Teachers College, 1906—. Instr. technique of biol. projection and anesthesia of animals, U. of Chicago, 1901. Popular lecturer on bacteriology, 1895—; then delivering popular lectures on vital phenomena of lower animals and plants. Inventor of scientific apparatus, eye-shields, and of methods of highly magnifying on screen images of microscopic animals and plants; demonstrated method of "teaching biology from living plants and animals with a projection microscope," 1905; discovered a successful method of culture ofor amoeba, and a method of showing the movement of sap in the leaves of plants. Asso. editor United Editors Ency. and Dictionary and author of articles on "The Projection Microscope and Its Use" and "Anesthesia of Animals and Plants." Author and publisher: Manual of Biological Projection and Anesthesia of Animals, 1907. Home: Chicago, Ill. Died Dec. 31, 1913.

COLE, ALFRED DODGE, physicist; b. Rutland, Vt., Dec. 18, 1861; s. Israel D. and Alice (Ware) C.; A.B., Brown, 1884, A.M., 1887; studied Johns Hopkins, 1884-85, Summer Sch., Harvard, 1888, Berlin, 1894-95, Summer Sch., Cornell, 1897, U. of Chicago, summers, 1898, 1899, 1900, 1904; m. Emily Downer, June 18, 1889. Instr. chemistry and physics, 1885-87, acting prof., 1887-88, prof., 1888-1901, Denison U.; prof. physics, Ohio State U., 1901-07, Vassar Coll., 1907-08; prof. of physics and head of dept., Ohio State U., 1908-26; prof. physcis, 1926—. Trustee Denison U., Ohio., 1901-07, 1911—. Research guest, Nat. Bur. of Standards, Washington, and U. of Berlin, 1912-13. War work on electron radio receivers U.S. Navy Lab., Washington, summer 1917, and U.S. Bur. Standards, summer 1918. Deceased.

COLE, EDWARD SMITH, hydraulic engr.; b. Washington, D.C., Dec. 29, 1871; s. John Adams and Julia Mead (Alvord) C; student U. of Ill., 1890-92; M.E., Cornell U., 1894; m. Mary Watkinson Rockwell, June 26, 1901; children—John Rockewell, Edward Shaw, Mary Watkinson (Mrs. William E. Jordan). Prin. asst. John A. Cole, cons. engr., Chicago, Ill., 1894-1903; active in development of pitometer and method for measurement of flow of water in pipes under pressure, 1896-98; in charge of studies with the pitometer for dept. of water supply, gas and electricity, City of N.Y., 1903-04; founder The Pitometer Company, New York City; formed British Pitometer Co. with Glenfield Kennedy, Limited, of Kilmarnock, Scotland and London, England, 1920. Fellow American Soc. Mech. Engineers (awarded Worcester Reed Warner Medal, Dec. 1948); mem. Montclair, N.J. Engrs. Soc., Am. Water Works Assn. (hon. mem.), Am. Soc. Civil Engrs. Republican. Conglist. Home: 133 Bellevue Av., Upper Montclair, N.J. Office: 50 Church St., New York 7; and 237 Lafayette St., New York, N.Y. Died Mar. 18, 1950.

COLE, HARRY OUTEN, constrn. engr.; b. Morgantown, W.Va., Apr. 3, 1874; s. Minrod and Sarah Jane (Lough) C.; B.Sc., in Civil Engring., W.Va. U., 1898; m. Mable Wilson, June 12, 1901 (died 1921); 1 dau., Catherine; m. 2d, Margaret Buchanan, Feb. 14, 1929. Draftsman, estimator and designer of steel work until 1903; with V. G. Bogue, N.Y.C., as asst. engr. bridges, also cons. engineer rys. and bridge engr. Mexican projects; apptd. asst. engr. in charge designs Pacific Div. Isthmian Canal, 1908, later resident engr. and div. engr. until completion of canal; mem. . Cole Bros., Balt. until 1916; asst.,later constrn. engr. Braden Copper Co. and Chile Exploration Co., hdqrs. . N.Y.C.; pres. Cole Bros. Constrn. Co., Morgantown, 1921—; sec., dir. Morgantown Hotel Co. Mem. Am. Soc. C.E., Phi Kappa Sigma. Republican. Presbyn. Mason (K.T., Shriner), Elk. Kiwanian. Home: Morgantown, W.Va. Died Feb. 13, 1950.

COLE, HOWARD I(RVING), chemist; b. New Rochelle, N.Y., Apr. 12, 1892; s. Abram Henry and Anna Marie (Kammermeyer) C.; B.Chem., Cornell U., 1914; Ph.D., 1917; m. Nancy Ruth Fields, May 27, 1927. Expert chem. microscopist A.D. Little & Co., Cambridge, Mass., 1919-20; prof. chem. U. Ore., 1920-22; organic research chemist Bur. Sci., Manila, P.I., 1922-24; head dept. chemistry Robert Coll., Istanbul, Turkey, 1924-26; chief chemist Philippine Health Service, Culion Leper Colony, 1926-34; expert

League of Nations, stationed Rio de Janeiro, 1935-39; exec. dir. com. on biol. Warfare Research and Devel. Bd., Sec. def., Washington, 1947-54; mem. staff Nat. Acad. Scis., Washington, 1955-57. Served as lt. Gas Def., Service, U.S. Army, 1917-18; capt. 42d and 1st Inf. divs. Chem. Warfare Service, 1918-19; maj., lt. col. chem. Warfare Service, 1942-47. Awarded Legion of Merit. Fellow A.A.A.S., Mem. Am. Chem. Soc., Internat. Leprosy Assn., Washington Acad. Scis., Sigma Xi. Clubs: Army and Navy (Manila); Army-Navy (Washington), Pan-Am. Doctors (Huasca, Mexico); Cosmopolitan (Santa Barbara). Home: 2279 Alston Rd., Santa Barbara, Cal. Died Nov. 28, 1966; buried Santa Barbara (Cal.) Cemetery.

COLE, JOHN ADAMS, civil engr.; b. Westmoreland, N.H., Dec. 16, 1838; s. John and Elizabeth (Shaw) C.; Kimball Union Acad., and spl. math. studies; m. Julia Mead Alvord, of Boston, Dec. 15, 1870. In Office of Thomas Doane, civil engr., Boston, 1856-59; gen. field agent, Christian Commn., 1862 to close of Civil War, in charge of work in armies of Potomac and the James delivered addresses in principal cities of N.E. and directed expenditure of over $3,000,000; with army in Tex., 1865-66. Civ. engr., Washington, D.C., 1867-69, Chicago, 1873-1904; specialized in municipal engring.; was engr. Lake View and Hyde park, Ill., and consulting engr. many cities of U.S. and Can.; designed and built many water works and sewerage systems, etc.; pres. and treas. Pitometer Co. Hon. trustee Howard U. (sec. and treas., 1867-71); pres. Chicago Tract Soc., 1911-13, Training Sch., 1912-13. Mem. Am. Soc. C.E. Republican. Presbyn. Club: Literary Home: 1346 E. 53d St., Chicago, Ill.

COLE, LEON J(ACOB); b. Allegany, N.Y., June 1, 1877; s. Elisha Kelley and Helen Marion (Newton) C.; student Mich. Agrl. Coll., 1894-95, 1897-98; A.B., Univ. of Mich., 1901; Ph.D., Harvard, 1906; Sc.D., Michigan State College, 1945; married Margaret Belcher Goodenow, August 28, 1906; children—Margaret Valeria, Edward Goodenow. Asst. in zoology U. of Mich., 1898-1902, teaching fellow, Harvard U., 1902-06, chief of Div. of Animal Breeding and Pathology, Agrl. Expt. Sta., R.I., 1906-07; instr. in zoology, Sheffield Scientific Sch. (Yale), 1907-10; asso. prof. exptl. breeding, U. of Wis., Apr. 1910-14, prof., 1914-18, prof. genetics, 1918-47; on leave as chief Animal Husbandry Div., Bur. Animal Industry, U.S. Dept. Agr., 1923-24; chmn. Div. Biology and Agr., Nat. Research Council, 1926-27. Mem. Harriman Alaska Expdn., 1899; zool. expdn. to Yucatan, 1904. Investigator, U.S. Bur. of Fisheries, summers, 1901-06. Fellow A.A.A.S. (v.p. Sect. F., 1940); Poultry Science Assn.; mem. Am. Soc. Zoologists, Am. Genetic Assn., Genetic Soc of America (vice president 1937, president 1940), Eugenics Soc., Am. Soc. Naturalists (v.p. 1917; sec. 1927-31), Am. Ornithologists' Union, Am. Soc. Mammalogists, Soc. Animal Production, Board Biol. Fellowships of Nat. Research Council (1928-36), Wis. Acad. Science (pres. 1924-27), Sigma Xi (pres. Wis. Chapter 1917-18; nat. exec. com. 1932-34), Phi Kappa Phi, Gamma Sigma Delta, Phi Sigma (hon. nat. pres., 1940-46); corr. mem. Czechoslovak Acad. Agr. Contbr. on zoology, animal behavior, genetics and animal breeding. Organizer Am. Bird Banding Assn., 1909. Home: 312 N. Prospect Av., Madison 5, Wis. Died Feb. 17, 1948.

COLE, WILLIAM H(ARDER), educator; b. Cayuga N.Y., June 23, 1892; s. Wesley Walter and Floretta Elmina (Groves) C.; student Ballston Spa, 1910; A.B., Hamilton Coll., Clinton, N.Y., 1914, Sc.D. (hon.), 1954; A.M., Harvard, (Root fellow of Hamilton Coll., 1914-15; Thayer scholar. 1915-16), 1916, Ph.D., 1921; D.Dc. (hon.), Rutgers U., 1957; m. Florence Augusta Hanagan, July 7, 1918. Austin teaching fellow Harvard, 1920-21; instr. Pa. State Coll., 1916-20;prof. biology Lake Forest (Ill.), Coll., 1921-24, Clark U., 1924-28; prof. physiology and biochemistry, Rutgers U., 1928—, asst. dean coll. arts and scis., 1943-44, dir. research council, 1944—. Trustee Mt. Desert Island Biol. Lab., 1931-54, dir. labs., 1931-40, v.p., 1946-50, pres., 1950; investigator Bermuda Biol. Lab., 1915, Woods Hole, 1925, Mt. Desert Island Biol. Lab., 1931-44, Pacific Grove Lab., 1929, Cold Spring Harbor Lab., 1930, Cal. Inst. Tech., 1937; OSRD, Columbia, 1942-44; cons. A.S.T.P. 2d Corps area, 1942-44; med. dispatcher Middlesex Country (N.J.) Civilian Def., 1942-45, 50-53. Served with San. Corps, U.S. Army, 1927-29 Fellow A.A.A.S.,N.Y. Acad. Sci. (v.p. 1955); mem. Am. Assn. U. Profs. (pres. Rutgers chpt. 1931-32), Am. Soc. Zoologists (sec. 1930-33), Am. Soc. Naturalists, New Brunswick Sci. Soc. (pres. 1932-33), Phi Beta Kappa (pres. Rutgers chpt. 1948-49), Sigma Xi (pres. Rutgers chpt. 1933-34), Delta Upsilon. Independent Republican. Clubs: Outing (pres. 1933-35) Union of New Brunswick. Contbr. articles to profl. jou jours. Home: New Brunswick, N.J. Died Feb. 6, 1967.

COLEMAN, CLAUDE C., neurol. surgeon; b. Caroline County Va., July 21, 1879; s. Henry Frank and Jane (Patrick) C.; student William and Mary Coll., 1894-97, D.Sc. (honorary), 1948; M.D., Med. Coll. of Va., 1903, D.Sc., 1950; student at the New York Polyclinic Postgraduate Med. Sch., 1906; m. Julia Langhorne Cone, Apr. 28, 1917; children—Anne Putney, Julia Langhorne, Claude C., Jane Patrick; m. 2d, Ruth Threadcraft Putney, June 16, 1931; married 3d, Constance Cardoza, Dec. 30, 1948. Began practice at Richmond, 1910; prof. principles of surgery, Med. Coll. of Va., 1912-13, prof. Surgery-, 1924-51, consultant in neurol. surgery, 1951—; clinical prof. neurol. surgery, University of Va., 1937-1941. Served as maj. Med. Corps, U.S. Army, during World War; dir. Sch. of Brain Surgery. U.S. Army, Ft. Oglethrope, 1918; civilian consultant in neurol. surgery, to surgeon general, World War II; neruosurgical consultant Special Medical Advisory Board Veterans' Adminstration. Member Board of of Visitors Coll. of William and Mary. Fellow Am. Coll. Surgeons; mem. Soc. Neurol. Surgeons (pres. 1926). Southern Surgical Assn., A.M.A., Kappa Alpha, Phi Beta Kappa. Democrat. Clubs: Country Club of Va., Gloucester Country. Author: Medical Department U.S. Army in the World War, Vol. 2 (with others), 1924; section on the nervous system in Horsley and Bigger's Operative Surgery, 4th edit., 1937; sect. on Peripheral Nerves in Bancroft's Surgery, 1945. Contbr. surgical articles to jours. Home: 5115 Cary St. Rd. Office: 1200 E. Broad St., Richmond, Va. Died Jan, 9, 1953; buried Hollywood Cemetery, Richmond, Va.

COLEMAN, GEORGE PRESTON, civil engr., banker; b. Williamsburg, Va., May 4, 1870; s. Charles Washington and Cynthia Beverley (Tucker) C.; m. Mary Haldane Begg, Feb. 21, 1900; children—Janet Haldane (Mrs. Raymond de Witt Kimbrough), Cynthia Beverley Tucker (Mrs. Singleton P. Morehead). City engr., Winona, Minn., 1901-06; asst. Va. state highway commr. 1906-11, commr., 1911-23; pres. Peninsula Bank & Trust Co., Williamsburg, Va., since 1927; also pres. Williamsburg Finance Corp., Jamestown Corp., Williamsburg Inn., Inc., Williamsburg Gazette, Noting First Mortgage, South Atlantic Corp., Richmond; dir. Am. Gas Accumulator Co. and Signal Service (Elizabeth, N.J.), Argaloy Tubing Co. (Springfield, O.). Mayor of Williamsburg, 1929-34. Organizer Va. Good Road Association (president three terms); member committee to formulate Va. State Highway System. Member American Assn. of State Highway Officials, (organizer, past pres. and past chmn.; as chmn. of legislative com. wrote 1st Federal aid road bill, Bankhead Bill, which made possible the participation of the Nat. Gov. in constrn. of comprehensive road system); Am. Road Builders Assn. (v.p.), Va. Hist. Soc., Southern Soc. of New York, S.R., Sons of Confederacy, Soc. of the Cincinnati of Va., Colonial Wars, Jamestown Soc., Kappa Sigma, Phi Beta Kappa. Democrat. Episcopalian. Clubs: Commonwealth (Richmond), Flat Hat. Awarded medal by French Govt. for services connected with Sesquicentennial celebration. Home: Williamsburg, Va. Died June 17, 1948.

COLEMAN, JOHN DAWSON, engr.; b. Clarksburg, W.Va., Feb. 17, 1903; s. Thomas Jr., and Lida P. (Power) C.; B.S., W.Va. U., 1925; m. Elizabeth Gilmour Dunham, July 18, 1934; children—Constance II, Robin P., Thomas II, John D. Fuel research engr. Gen. Motors Corp., 1925-27; prodn. engr. Gen. Motors Export Co., 1927-28; chief chemist Fisher Body div. Gen. Motors Corp., 1928-33, mfg. methods engr. Frigidaire div., 1933-39, asst. supt. mfg. research, 1939-43, asst. supt. propeller plant, 1943-45, supr. mfg. process plan , 1945-46, supt. methods and material utilization, 1947-58, supr. field tests, product engring., 1958—. Chmn. Profl. Engrs. Conf. Bd. for Industry, 1953-55. Mem. exec. council Miami Valley council Boy Scouts Am., chmn. orgn. and extension com., 1952, v.p., 1953-56, chmn. N.W. Dist., 1955-56. Mem. Am. Chem. Soc. (chmn. Dayton sect. 1943), Dayton Tech. Socs. Council (chmn. 1947-48), Nat. (v.p. Central zone 1949-50, 50-51, pres. 1952-53), Ohio (pres. 1947-48), 1947-48), Dayton (Pres. 1945) socs. Profl. engrs., Am. Inst. Indsl. Engrs. (pres. 1951-52), Izaak Walton League (dir. Dayton chpt. 1948-50, v.p. 1951-53, pres. 1954-55), Phi Lambda Upsilon. Presbyn. (trustee 1945-49, 57-60, pres. bd. trustee 1959, elder 1952-54). Club: Engrs. (Dayton). Home: 5715 Free Pike, Dayton, 5. Office: 300 Talyor St., Dayton, O. Died Dec. 23, 1963; buried Meml. Gardens, Dayton.

COLEMAN, JOHN FRANCIS, cons. engr.; b. Jefferson County, Miss., Nov. 23, 1866; s. James Wood and Elizabeth Treeby (Chaffe) C.; hon. Dr. of Engring., Tulane U., 1935; m. Annie Hunter, Nov. 12, 1890; 1 son, Eugene Hunter (dec.). Rodman, Guatemala Northern R.R., 1884-85; levelman, later resident engr., Kansas City, Memphis & Birmingham R.R., 1885-88; asst. engr. Phila. Smelting & Refining Co., Pueblo, Colo., 1888-89; asst. U.S. engr., Miss. River, 1889-90; asst. engr. Tex. & Pacific Ry., 1890-93; contractor, New Orleans, 1893-94; div. engr., New Orleans & Western R.R., 1894-96; prin. asst. city engr., New Orleans, 1896-99; cons. civ. engr. since 1900; chief engr. New Orleans Great Northern R.R., 1905-07. Cons. engr. Bd. Commrs. Port of New Orleans, 1901-30; also formerly cons. engr. for ports of Corpus Christi, Freeport, Houston, Beaumont (all in Tex.), Lake Charles, La., Mobile, Ala., Jacksonville, Fla., Charleston, S.C., Richmond, Va.; builder of ship yard at Mobile for U.S. Steel Corp., Nov. 1917-Nov. 1919; now sr. partner J.F. Coleman Engring Co., cons. engrs. Mem. Engrs. Advisory Bd., Reconstruction Finance Corporation, 1932-33, adv. engr. since 1938. Trustee Eye, Ear, Nose and Throat Hosp., New Orleans, Hon. mem. Am. Soc. C.E. (ex-pres.), Am. Ry. Engring. Assn., Am. Shore and Beach Preservation Association, Am. Assn. Port Authorities, La. Engring. Soc. (ex-pres.; hon. mem.), Am. Engring. Council (pres. 1934-35). Democrat. Episcopalian. Home: 3116 Prytania St. Office: Carondelet Bldg., New Orleans, La. Died June 3, 1944.

COLEMAN, WARREN, M.D.; b. Augusta, Ga., Jan. 19, 1869; s. John Scott and Hetty Kennedy (McEwen) C.; A.B., Transylvania, Transylvania U., Lexington, Ky., 1888; grad. work Johns Hopkins, 1888-89; M.D., Univ. Med. Coll., New York, 1891; hon. M.A., Transylvania, 1899; m. Mrs. Bertie A. Twiggs, March 18, 1946. Practiced New York, 1891-1938; physician City (Charity) Hospital, 1896-99; instructor pathology, University Med. Coll., 1891-98; asst. curator, Bellevue Hosp., 1892-98, asst. visiting phys., 1899 visiting physician, 1908-27, cons. physician since 1927; prof. clin. medicine and applied pharmacology, Cornell U. Med. Coll., New York, 1909-17; asst. prof. medicine, U. of Ga. Sch. of Medicine, since 1938; cons. physician Lenox Hill Hosp. (N.Y. City); formerly cons. physician Monmouth (N.J.) Memorial Hosp., Med. Center of Jersey City (N.J.). Fellow Am. Coll. Physicians, A.M.A.; mem. Assn. American Physicians, American Board of Internal Medicine, New York Academy of Sciences, Georgia Academy of Science, Am. Nat. Red Cross, N.Y. Pathol. Soc., N.Y. Med. and Surg. Soc. (hon.), Society American Bacteriologists, American Gastroenterological Assn., A.A.A.S., Richmond County (Ga.) Med. Society (hon.), Assn. Military Surgeons, Sons of Revolution in State of Ga., Soc. of the Cincinnati in the State of Ga., Phi Alpha Sigma, etc.; non-resident fellow New York Acad. Medicine, retired member New York State Med. Med. Soc., New York County Med. Soc., formerly member Am. Genetic Assn., Soc. Exptl. Biology and Medicine, Assn. for Study of Internal Secretions, Am. Bible Soc., Harvey Soc. Democrat. Mem. Christian (Disciples) Ch. Clubs: Century Assn., Pilgrims, Camp-Fire of America. Writer on med. subjects. Home: 2749 Hillcrest Av., Augusta, Ga. Died Feb. 13, 1948.

COLEMAN, WILLIAM WHEELER, mfr., engr.; b. Balt., Nov. 21, 1873; s. William Wheeler and Eleanor Gibbons (Hiss) C.; B.S., in Metallurgy, Lehigh U., 1895; m. Alice Frazier, June 20, 1899; 1 dau., Isabel. With Bethlehem (Pa.) Steel Co., 1895-1902, Crucible Steel Co. and Latrobe Steel & Coupler Co., 1902-05; with Bucyrus-Erie Co., mfrs. machinery, 1905—, v.p., 1909-11, pres., 1911-43, chmn., 1943-57, hon. chmn., 1957—; chmn. Rushton-Bucyrus Ltd., 1929-57, hon. life chmn. 1957—, dir., 1929—; pres. Bucyrus-Erie Found., Inc., 1952-57, dir., 1952—. Dir. Columbia Hospital, 1928-55; trustee Milw. Downer Coll., 1923-47; bd. dirs. Nat. Fgn. Trade Council, 1932-54, Nat. Indsl. Conf. Bd., 1927-57. Apptd. spl. asst. to chief of ordnance, Washington, Oct. 1918; col. Ord. Res., ret. Mem. Am. Soc. M.E., Am. Inst. Mining and Metall. Engrs., Iron and Steel Inst. (Gt. Britain), Am. Acad. Polit. and Social Sci., Newcomen Soc., Soc. Colonial Wars, Sigma Phi. Clubs: Milwaukee, University (N.Y.); Century (N.Y.C.). Home: Harrison, N.Y. Died Jan. 1966.

COLES, DAVID SMALLEY, physician; b. nr. Plainsfield, N.J., Mar. 17, 1844; s. William and Catherine (Smalley) C.; grad. Princeton, 1871, A.M., 1874; divinity student Boston Sch. of Medicine, 1887. Homeo. Physician, practicing since 1887; discoverer of a new treatment for cancer and other blood diseases. Mem. Am. Peace Soc. Methodist. Address: Wakefield, Mass.

COLEY, WILLIAM BRADLEY, surgeon; b. Westport, Conn., Jan. 12, 1862; s. Horace Bradley and Clarine Bradley (Wakeman) C.; B.A., Yale, 1884; M.D., Harvard, 1888; New York Hosp., 1890; hon. A.M., Yale, 1910, Harvard, 1911; m. Alice Lancaster, June 4, 1891; children—Bradley Lancaster, Malcolm (deceased), Helen Lancaster (Mrs. William Boone Nauts). In practice as physician, 1888—; cons. surgeon Memorial Hospital; surgeon in chief emeritus Hospital for Ruptured and Crippled; surgeon in chief Mary McClellan Hosp. (Cambridge, N.Y.); cons. surgeon Fifth Avenue Hosp. and Sharon (Conn.) Hosp. Fellow Am. Surgical Assn.; Am. Coll. Surgeons; hon. mem. Assn. of Surgeons of Great Britain and Ireland. Author: Twentieth Century Practice of Medicine—part on Cancer (Vol. XVII), 1897; Hernia (in Dennis' System of Surgey), 1896; Hernia (in Warren and Gould's International Text Book of Surgery), 1898; Chapter of Hernia, in Progressive Medicine, 1898—; Hernia (in Keen's Surgery), 1907. Home: New York, N.Y. Died Apr. 16, 1936.

COLLES, CHRISTOPHER, engr.; b. Ireland, May 3, 1739; s. Richard and Henrietta (Taylor) C.; m. Anne Keugh, Jan. 14, 1764. Came to Am., 1765; lectr. pneumatics, Phila., 1772, on indland navigation, N.Y.C., 1773; devised plan (not used) for replacing N.Y.C.'s well and spring water system with system of reservoirs and pipes; instr. arty. of Continental Army, 1775-77; designed one of 1st Am. steam engines; suggested system of canals and river improvements to connect Great Lakes with Hudson River planned and surveyed roads between N.Y.C. and Phila.; mfr. small household utensils, N.Y.C., 1796, also traded in Indian goods and furs; built, operated semaphoric telegraph at Castle Clinton (N.Y.) during War of 1812; later employed in customs service, N.Y.C.; supt. Am. Acad. Fine Arts. Author: Syllabus of Lectures on Natural

Philosophy, 1773; A Survey of the Roads of the United States of America, 1789; Proposals of a Design for Inland Communication of a New Construction, 1808; Description of the Universal Telegraph, 1813. Died N.Y.C., Oct. 4, 1816.

COLLETT, JOHN, geologist and farmer; b. Eugene, Ind., Jan. 6, 1828; grad. Wabash Coll., 1847 (A.M., 1850; Ph.D., 1879); M.D., Central Med. Coll. State senator (Ind.), 1870-73; asst. State geologist, 1870-78; member New State House Commn., 1878-79; chief bureau of statistics and geology, 1879-80; State geologist, 1881-85. Has published numerous geol. reports, 6 vols., 110 papers, 22 maps and gen. sections, nearly 2,000 figures, most of which were since copied by Mo. and Pa. Unmarried. Home: Indianapolis, Ind. Died 1899.

COLLIDGE, JULIAN LOWELL, educator; b. Brookline, Mass., Sept. 28, 1873; s. Joseph Randolph and Julia (Gardner) C.; A.B., Harvard, 1895, LL.D., 1940; B.Sc., Oxford, 1897; Ph.D. U. Bonn, Prussia, 1904; D.Sc., Lehigh U., 1938; m. Theresa Reynolds, Jan. 17, 1901; children—Jane Revere, Julian Gardner, Archibald Cary, Margaret Wendell, Elizabeth Peabody, Rachel Revere, John Phillips, Theresa Reynolds. Teacher mathematics Groton (Mass.) School, 1897-99; instr. mathematics Harvard, 1900, assistant prof., 1908; prof., 1918-40, prof. emeritus, 1940—. Served as major, U.S. Aumy, 1917-19; liaison officer attached to French Gen. Staff, Paris, 1918-19. Decorated Cross Legion of Honor, Officer and Officer de l'Instruction Publique, Frnace, 1919. Fellow American Acad. Arts and Sciences; mem. Am. Math. Sco. (past v.p.), Math. Assn. Am. (pres. 1925), Assn. Math. Teachers in N.E. (past Pres.), Phi Beta Kappa. Club: Harvard (Boston). Author: Elements of Non-Euclidean Geometry 1909; Treaties on the Circle and the Sphere, 1916; Geometry of the Complex Domain, 1924; Introduction to Mathematical Probability, 1925; Algebraic Plane Curves 1931; History of Geometrical Methods, 1940; History of the Conic Sections 1943. Home: 27 Fayerweather St., Cambridge 38, Mass. Died Mar. 5, 1954.

COLLIE, GEORGE LUCIUS, geologist; b. Delavan , Wis., Aug. 11, 1857; s. Joseph and Ann Elizabeth (Foote) C.; B.S., Beloit Coll., 1881; A.M., Harvard, 1891; Ph.D., 1893; m. Katharine E. Burrows of Chicago. Mar. 26, 1896; (dec.); Helen Tannisse (dec.), Kenneth Gordon. Asst. prin. and prin. Delavan High Sch., 1885-90; Morgan fellow, Harvard, 1891-92; prof. geology, 1892-1923, prof. of anthropology, 1923-31, curator of Logan Museum of Archaeology 1893-1931, acting pres., 1902-03 and 1905-08, Beloit Coll., also dir. Logan Mus. Sch. for Prehistoric Research, Les Eyzies, France, and Tebersa, Algeria; Asst. Wis. Geol. Survey, 1898. Fellow Geol. Soc. of America, A.A.A.S., mem. Am. Anthrop . Assn., Phi Beta Kappa. Traveled around the World, 1910-11, on geol. trip covering 40,000 miles. Writer on geol. and ednl. topics. Y.M.C.A. sec., overseas service with A.E.F. in France and Eng., 1918-19. Engaged in research for early man in France and Algeria, 1926-28. Home: Beloit, Wis., Died Dec. 28, 1954; buried Spring Grove Cemetery, Delavan, Wis.

COLLIER, PETER, educator, chemist; b. Chittenango, N.Y., Aug. 17; 1835; s. Jacob and Elizabeth Mary Collier; grad. Yale, 1861, Ph.D. in Chemistry, 1866; M.D. (hon.), U. Vt., 1870; m. Caroline Angell, Oct. 18, 1871; at least 1 child. Prof. chemistry, mineralogy and metallurgy U. Vt., 1867-77, prof. toxicology and chemistry, med. sch., dean med. faculty, 1871-74; sec. Vt. Vd. Agr., Mining and Manufacture, 1872-76; chief chemist U.S. Dept. Agr., 1877-83; dir. N.Y. Agrl. Expt. Sta., Geneva, 1887. Author: Sorghum: Its Culture and Manufacture Economically Considered, and as a Source of Sugar Syrup and Fodder, 1884. Died Ann Arbor, Mich., June 29, 1896.

COLLIN, (HENRY) ALONZO, physicist; b. Hillsdale, N.Y., Aug. 14, 1837; s. Henry Augustus and Sarah Ann (White) C.; A.B., Wesleyan U., Conn., 1858, A.M., 1862; (Sc.D., Upper Ia. U., 1888); m. Chloe Matson, June 30, 1868. Prof. mathematics and natural science, 1860-68, natural sciences, 1868-81, Cornell Coll.; prof. chemistry and exptl. physics, U. of Neb., 1881-82; prof. physics and chemistry, 1882-99, physics, 1899-1906, emeritus, 1906. Cornell Coll. Home: Mt. Vernon, Ia. Died Apr. 17, 1918.

COLLINGS, CLYDE WILSON urological surgeon; b. Vancouver, Wash., Feb. 28, 1892; s. Dellbert A. and Emma May (McCafferty) C.; student U. Wash., 1913-15; M.D., Ore. U., 1919; m. Martha Monigle, 1944; 1 son, Anthony; children by previous marriage—Clyde Wilson, Amzell Iona. Urological interne and resident urologist Bellevue Hosp., N.Y.C., 1919-21, asst. attending urologist, 1921-36; asst. vis. clinic N.Y.U. Med. Coll., 1921-36; asst. vis. urologist St. Vincent Hosp., 1921-26; cons. urologist St. Joseph's Hosp., Far Rockaway, L.I., 1921—; founder mem. med. staff doctors Hosp., 1929—; sr. surgeon attending staff Los Angeles County Gen. Hosp.; Asso. prof. surgery (urology) Sch. Medicine, Coll. Med. Evangelists; chief urologic staff White Meml. Hosp. Served with USN Med. Dept. World War I, lt. comdr., World War II. Fellow Royal Society Medicine Eng., A.C.S.; mem. A.M.A., N.Y. State and County med. socs., N.Y. Acad. Medicine, Cal., Los Angeles County med. socs., Am. French urol. assns., Delta Tau Delta. Republican. Episcopalian. Clubs: Midwick Polo, Santa Barbara Polo, U.S. Polo Assn. Contbr. to med. jours. of U.S., England and France. Inventor of radio electric knife for transurethral surgery, 1923; devised the first operation with the cutting high frequency current and knife electrode through the urethrocope, 1923. Home: Collingswood, Encino, Cal. Office: 1930 Wilshire Blvd., Los Angeles. Died July 4, 1952; buried Inglewood Park Cemetery, Inglewood, Cal.

COLLINGS, GILBERT HOOPER, agronomist; b. Crewe, Va.; Jan. 13, 1895; s. Thomas James and Helen Thomas (Luke) C.; B.S., Va. Poly. Inst., Blacksburg, Va., 1915; M.S., U. of Ill., 1917; Ph.D., Rutgers U., New Brunswick, N.J., 1925; m. Hazel Winifred Cover, Dec. 9, 1917; children—Gilbert Hooper, Hazel Cover, Thomas Albert. Fellow in agronomy, U. of Ill., 1916-18; instr. French to Am. soldiers, World War I, 1918; asst. agronomist S.C. Agrl. Expt. Sta., 1918-23; asst. prof. agronomy, Clemson (S.C.) Agrl. Coll., 1918-25, asso. prof., 1925-29, actg. head agronomy dept. 1929-30, asso. prof. agronomy 1930-38, acting prof. of agronomy, 1938-39, prof. soils, 1939-60, head dept. agronomy, 1955-58, head dept. agronomy and soils, soils 1958-60, emeritus, 1960—; instr. history Am. soldiers World War II, 1943-44; agronomist, South Carolina Agricultural Exptl. Sta., 1944, 55, 60, emeritus, 1960—; organizer Collings & Assos., fertilizer cons., 1945; rep. S.C. Agrl. Expt. Sta. charge state soil surveys, 1946-56; dir. Buffalo Coal Corp., 1923-34, Wilson-Berger Coal Corp., 1931-42; dir. Mary Helen Coal Corp., 1931—; v.p., 1951-53; director Va.-Jellico Coal Corporation, 1940-55, vice president 1941-55. Member South Carolina Agricultural Council, 1960—. Fellow A.A.A.S. (mem. council, 1948-49), Am. Soc. Agronomy; mem. S.C. Acad., Sci. (sec. treas., 1938-40; mem. council, 1940-46, pres. 1947). Internat. Soc. Soil Science, Soil Conservation Society of Am. (charter mem.), Soil Science Society of America, Pendleton Farmers' Soc. (life mem.; pres. 1941-47), Southern Agrl. Workers Assn., Kappa Alpha Sigma, Alpha Zeta, Chi Beta Phi, Gamma Sigma Delta. Democrat. Baptist. Mason, Kiwanian. Author and editor agrl. books. Contbr. to mags. Home: 220 N. Clemson Av., S.C. 29631. Died Jan. 10, 1964; buried Clemson University Cemetery, Clemson, S.C.

COLLINGWOOD, FRANCIS, civil engr.; b. Elmira, N.Y., Jan. 10, 1834; acad. edn., Elmira, N.Y.; C.E., Rensselaer Poly. Inst., 1855; m. Eliza W. Bonnett. City engr. Elmira, 1865-69; asst. engr. East River Bridge constrn., New York, 1869-83; expert examiner New York Civ. Service, 1895—; lecturer on foundations, New York U., 1895-1904. Awarded Thelford medal and Thelford premium by Brit. Inst. C.E., 1884. Home: Elizabeth, N.J. Died 1911.

COLLINGWOOD, G(EORGE) HARRIS, forester; born Fayetteville, Ark., May, 27, 1890; s. Charles Barnard and Harriet (Thomas) C.; B.S., Mich. State U., 1911; student U. of Munich, Germany, 1913-14; M.A., U. of Mich., 1917; m. Jean Cummings, Sept. 1, 1916; children—Charles Cummings, Thomas Peeke, Eloise (Mrs. Baxter C. Prescott). Jean (Mrs. John H. Spelman), Rebecca Cummings (Mrs. James P. McHale), George Harris. Engaged as forest ranger Apache National Forest , 1911-15; assistant extension prof. forestry, Cornell, 1916-23, extension forester, U.S. Dept. Agr., 1923-28; forester, Am. Forestry Assn., 1928-40; chief forester , Am. Nat. Lumber Mfrs. Assn. 1940-46; dir. office of forest products. Nat. Housing Agency (all at Washington), 1946, asst. dir. forest products, div., Office Housing Expediter, 1947; research dir. on agrl. activities, Hoover Commn., 1948; forestry cons., C. of C. of u.S., 1949; analyst in conservation and natural resources Legislative Reference Service, Library of Congress 1949—, head natural resources sect., 1958—. Consultant to secretary of agricultrue for evalution of insect and plant disease control programs, 1951-52. Recipient Mich. State College Alumni Award, 1954; Conservation and Distinguished Service awards, American Forestry Association, 1956. Fellow American Association for the Advancement Sci., mem. Society American Foresters, Am. Forestry Assn. (hon. v.p. 1955). Republican. Conglist. Clubs: Cosmos, Torch. Author: The Proudction of Maple Syrup and Sugar in New York State Cornell Extension Bull., 1928; Farm Forestry Extension, U.S.D.A., Bull., 1925; Knowing your Trees, 1937; Manual for Chambers of Commerce, 91949. Contbr. numerous articles to mags. and jours. Home: 2853 Ontario Rd., Washington 9. Office: Library of Congress, Washington 25. Died Apr. 2, 1958; buried Centerville, Mich.

COLLINS A(RCHIE) FREDERICK, elec. physicist; b. South Bend, Ind., Jan. 8, 1869; s. Capt. Thomas Jefferson and Margaret Ann (Roller) C.; ed. pub. schs. and old U. of Chicago; m. Evelyn Bandy, June 28, 1897; 1 son, Virgil Dewey. Invented the wireless telephone, 1899; gold medal, Alaska-Yukon-Pacific Expn., 1909; invented rotating oscillation arc, 1909; discovered effect of electric waves on brain cells, 1902; formulated neutron theory of the ether, 1937. Lecturer New York Bd. Edn., 1900-10; technician Collins Wireless Telephone Co., 1904-10; scientific corr. New York Herald, 1901-03; editor: Collins Wireless Bulletin, 1908-10. Fellow Royal Astron. Society (Great Britain). Member of the American Heart Association. Clubs: Royal Aero of United Kingdom, Authors (London). Author: Wireless Telegraphy, Its History, Theory and Practice, 1905; and over 97 other books on arithmetic, astronomy, aviation, business, chemistry, electricity, gardening, internal combustion engines, hobbies, magic, mechanics, metallurgy, microscopy, motor cars, motor boating, natural history, optics, philately, physics, photography, shooting, submarines, tops and gyroscopes, tractors, travel, wireless telegraphy and telephony, television, invention, etc., and over 500 articles in encys. and Am., English and French tech. papers and mags. Home: The Antlers, Congers, Rockland County, N.Y. and Jacksonville FL

COLLINS, BERTRAND ROBSON TORSEY, mech. engr.; b. York, Me., Nov. 10, 1866; s. John (D.D.) and Laura Smith (Horne) C.; B.S. in Mech. Engring., Mass. Inst. Tech., 1888; m. Katharine Greer, of Chicago, June 20, 1900; children—Dorothea, Katharine Sallie. Began as instr. in mech. engring., Mass. Inst. Tech., 1888; mech. engr., Spray Engring., Co., since 1912, also v.p. Served as ensign U.S.N., Spanish-Am. War. Gen. mgr. Technology steamer Cadet, 1893, to the World's Fair, Chicago; lt. comdg. U.S.S. Dorothea, cruise of 2,800 miles from League Island Navy Yard, Phila., to Chicago, 1901. Mem. Am. Soc., Mech. Engrs.; charter mem. Naval and Mil. Order Spanish-Am. War. Progressive. Methodist. Clubs: Chestnut Hill Golf (Brookline), Great Chebeague Golf of Me. (sec., treas. and dir.). Home: 18 Athelstane Rd., Newton Center, Ma Mass., Office: 114 Central St., Somerville, Mass.

COLLINS, CHARLES EDWIN, civil engr.; b. at Roxbury, Vt., Feb. 23, 1868; s. Michael and Mary (Cushing) C.; B.S. in C.E., Norwich U., 1890, C.E., 1892; m. Mabel May Tuggey, of Pittsfield, Mass., Oct. 8, 1902. Asst. engr. Locks & Canal Co., Lowell, Mass., 1890-92, Pittsfield, Mass., 1892-95, Cambridge, 1895-96; asst. engr. in charge plans, or constrn. various rys., etc., 1896-1901; mem. Collins Bros., consulting engrs., Phila., 1901-03; designed and supervised constrn. of sewerage systems and sewerage disposal plants for more than 20 municipalities, water 7 hydro-electric power plants, etc. Mem. Am. Soc. C.E. Baptist. Mason. Address: Drexel Bldg., Philadelphia, Pa.

COLLINS, FRANK SHIPLEY, botanist; b. Charlestown, Mass., Feb. 6, 1848; s. Joshua Cobb and Elizabeth Ann (Carter) C.; grad. high Sch., Malden (Mass.), Oct.1863; A. M., Tufts 1910; m. Anna Lendrum Holmes, Oct. 18, 1875. In commerical pursuits 1864-1912. Has been a student of botany many yrs. Asso. Univ. Mus. Harvard U. Fellow Am. Acad. Arts and Sciences; mem. Boston Soc. Natrual History, Mass. Hort. Soc., N.E. Bot. Club (ex- pres.), A.A.A.S., Bot. Soc. America; corr. mem. Torrey Bot. Club: Author: Flora of Middlesex County, 1888; The Green Algae of North America, in Tufts College Studies, 1908-18; Phyotheca Boreali-Americana, 1894-1919 (subscription) Contbr. to bot. jours. Home: North Esatham, Mass. Died May 25, 1920.

COLLINS, GUY N., botanist; b. Mertensia, N.Y., Aug. 9, 1872; s. George and Maria Anne (Hathaway) C.; prep. edn., high sch., Syracuse, N.Y.; student Syracuse U., 1890-91; m. Christine Hudson, Aug. 3, 1903; children—George Briggs, Perez Hathaway. Asst. botanist Bur. Plant Industry, U.S. Dept. Agr., 1901-10, botanist, 1910-20, botanist in charge bio-physical investigations, 1920—. Conducted explorations in Liberia for N.Y. Colonization Soc., 1891-97; visited Mexico, Guatemala, Costa Rica, Puerto Rico and Haiti for U.S. Dept. Agr. Author: Economic Plants of Puerto Rico (with O. F. Cook), 1903; also numerous articles on tropical agr. and genetics of maize. Home: Lanham, Md. Died Aug. 14, 1938.

COLLINS, HUBERT EDWIN, cons. engr.; writer; b. Boonesboro, Ia., Mar. 27, 1872; s. Mahlon Day and Keturah Ann (Williams) C.; ed. high sch., Clarinda, Ia.; m. Ethelyn Ella Cropsey, June 30, 1897. Machinist and erecting engr., Laek Erie Engring. Works, Buffalo, N.Y., 1891-96; operating engr., New York & Queens Co. Electric Light & Power, Long Island City, N.Y., 1896-98; supt. shops and gen. mgr. in charge engring., Ambrose Machinery Co., Brooklyn, N.Y., 1898-1902; cons. and advisory engr., 1902—. Teacher of power plant design, Sch. of Fine Arts, Columbia, 1911-12. Conducted coal survey of Oneida and Herkimer counties, World War; N.Y. States Res. officer, Wright-Martin Aircraft Corp.; mem. mil. police, Utica, Sec. Inst. Operating Engrs. (N.Y. City); mem. Coal Survey Commn. of Federated Engr. (Washington, D.C.), Mason. Methodist Author: Value Setting, Shaft Governors, Erecting Work, Boilers, Steam Turbines, Pumps, Knocks and Kinks, Pipes and Belting, Shafting, Pulleys and Belting (9 vols.), 1907-08; Warpath and Cattle Trail, 1928. Home: Utica, N.Y. Died Oct. 31, 1932.

COLLINS, J(AMES) FRANKLIN, botanist; b. N. Anson, Me., Dec. 29, 1863; s. James H. and Josephine (Witherell) C.; ed. pub. schs. N. Anson and Providence, R.I.; hon. Ph.B., Brown Univ., 1896; unmarried. Art metal worker, Providence, 1879-99; became interested in botany in 1883 (pvt. study); curator, Brown U. Herbarium, 1894-1911 and 1924-38; inst. in botany,

Brown U., 1899-1905, asst. prof., 1905-11, head. dept., 1906-11, demonstrator, 1913-25, lecturer, 1925-38, pathologist, U.S. Dept. Agr., 1911-33, retired. Mem. N.E. Bot. Club (ex-pres.), R.I. Bot. Club (ex-pres.), Sullivant Moss Soc., Sigma Xi. Author: Illustrated Key to the Trees of Northeastern North America (with H.W. Preston), 1912; also many bulls. on tree surgery and tree diseases. Contbr. Bull. Torrey Bot. Club, Rhodora, Bryologist, and U.S. Govt. publs., 1893—, Rhode Island Arbor Day Programs, 1910-11; also illustrations in Botanizing, 1899, and 200 illustrations in Gray's Manual (7th Edit.), 1908. Club: Faculty. Home: 37 Circuit Drive, Edgewood, R.I. Died Nov. 29, 1940.

COLLINS, WILLIAM HENRY, astronomer; b. Peekskill, N.Y., Oct. 22, 1859; s. William B. and Mary (Griffen) C.; B.S., Haverford Coll., Pa., 1881; A. M. 1892; m. Julia Cope, May 22, 1894. Dir. Haverford Coll. Astron. Observatory, 1892-1904; prefect Haverford Coll., 1897-1919. Author: Proceeding of Haverford College Observatroy, 1892-1904. Home: Haverford, Pa. Died 1939.

COLLISSON, NORMAN HARVEY, engr.; b. Phila., Mar. 3, 1902; s. William Henry and Gertrude Elizabeth (Dunlevy) C.; B.S. in C.E., Swarthmore Coll., 1924; m. Marjorie Shoemaker, Oct. 19, 1932 (dec. 1937); 1 dau., Joan; m. 2d, Rita Altmiller, Mar. 5, 1945; children—Peter, Kathleen, Anne. Partner, Wm. Collisson, Jr. & Bro., civil engrs., 1924-35. Commd. lt. USNR, 1942, advanced through grades to capt., 1946; served as chief enging. officer, Office Procurement and Material, 3d, Naval Dist., 1942-44, officer in charge Navy Dept., operating plant York Safe and Lock Co., York, Pa., Mar-Oct., 1944, Lord Mfg. Co., Erie, Pa., Oct. 1944-45; dep. adminstr. Naval Petroleum Plants Office, Washington, Oct. 1945-May 1946; dep. Coal Mines Adminstr., Washington, May-Oct. 1946, Coal Mines adminstr., 1946-47; spl. asst. to sec. interior, 1947-48; became chief spl. ECA mission to Western Zones Germany, 1948; v.p. operations Olin Mathieson Chem. Corp., 1954-55, exec. v.p., 1955-59, became v.p. and gen. mgr. Metals div., 1959, sr. v.p. chmn. staff com., 1960-63, pres., 1963-65, chmn. bd., 1964—; pres. chmn. bd., Olin Foil Packaging Corp., dir., Pres., Ormet Corp., Ormet Shipping Corp., Ormet Generating Corp., 1958—. Trustee Welfare and Retirement fund, United Mine Workers Am. (govt. rep.). Mem. Am. So. C.E., Am. Soc., M.E., Am. Soc. Mil. Engrs., Illuminating Engring. Soc., Newcomen Soc. Epsicopalian. Club: Metropolitan (N.Y.), Author: Handbook of Industrial Machine Tool Survey 1942. Home: 1219 Greenville Hwy., Hendersonville, N.C. Office: 400 Park Av., N.Y.C. Died Oct. 31, 1966; buried Arlington Nat. Cemetery.

COLPITTS, EDWIN HENRY, electrical engr.; b. Point de Bute, N.B., Can., Jan. 19, 1872; s. James Wallace and Celia Eliza (Trueman) C.; A.B., Mt. Allison U., Sackville, N.B., 1893, LL.D. (hon.), 1926; A.B., Harvard, 1896, A.M., 1897; m. Annie Dove Penney, Aug. 17, 1899; 1 son, Donald Bethune. Came to U.S., 1895, naturalized 1920. Asst. in physics, Harvard, 1897-99; telephone engr. Am. Telephone & Telegraph Co., Boston, 1899-1907; research engr. Western Electric Co., New York, 1907-17, asst. chief engr., 1917-24; asst. v.p. dept. of development and research, Am. Telephone & Telegraph Co., 1924-34; v.p. Bell Telephone Laboratories, 1933-37; retired. Iwadare lecturer, Japan, 1937. Served with U.S. Signal Corps on staff Gen. Edgar Russel, 1917-18. Fellow Am. Inst. E.E., Inst. Radio Engrs., Am. Phys. Soc., Acoustical Soc. of Am., A.A.A.S.; mem. Am. Chem. Soc., Harvard Engring. Soc. of New York, Telephone Pioneers of Am. Republican. Presbyterian. Club: Canoe Brook Country. Home: 309 Lawn Ridge Rd., Orange, N.J. Died March 6, 1949.

COLPITTS, WALTER WILLIAM consulting engr.; b. Moncton, N.B., Can., Sept. 17, 1874; s. Henry Herbert and Lucy Anne (Bissett) C.; B.Sc., McGill U., Montreal, 1899 (valdeictorian; winner Brit. Assn. Medal), M.Sc., 1901, LL.D., 1921; m. Florence Rossington, Oct. 15, 1907; children—Lucy Anne, Jeremy Rossington. Came to U.S., 1901, naturalized citizen. 1921. Began as office boy to chief engr. of Intercolonial Ry., 1891; served as draftsman engr. rodman and instrumentman on r.r. Surveys; chief clk. to Sir Thomas Shaughnessy, pres. Canadian Pacific Ry., 1889-1900; transferred to constrn. dept., 1900-01; engaged in r.r. constrn., irrigation and power projects in southwestern States and Mexico, 1901-13; mem. Coverdale & Colpitts, cons. engrs., New York, since 1913; dir. of the Bank of New York, Pepsi-Cola Co., The Budd Co., Carriers & General Corp., Celotex Corp.; trustee Bank of N.Y. Gov., McGill Univ. Mem. Am. Inst., Cons. Engrs., Am. Soc. C.E. Am. Ry. Engring. Assn., Engring. Inst. of Can., Alpha Delta Phi. Republican. Methodist. Clubs: Lawyers, Canadian (ex.- pres.). Recess, Economic (New York); Nassau, Tiger Inn (Princeton); Chicago; Faculty (Montreal). Home: 75 Cleveland Lane, Princeton N.J., (summer) Big Moose, N.Y. Office: 120 Wall St., N.Y.C. Died Dec. 23, 1951.

COLT, SAMUEL, inventor, firearms mfr.; b. Hartford, Conn., July 19, 1814; s. Christopher and Sarah (Caldwell) C.; m. Elizabeth H. Jarvis, June 5, 1856. Invented multi-shot firearm of revolving barrell type, constructed wooden model; constructed 2 postols, 1831, sent description to U.S. Patent Office, 1832, received 1st U.S. patent for 1st practical revolving firearm (widely used in opening of Am. West), 1836; introduced electricity as agt. for igniting gun powder; operated mfg. plant, Hartford. Died Hartford, Jan. 10, 1862.

COLTER, FRED(ERICK) TUTTLE, cattleman, irrigation reclamation; b. Neutrioso, Ariz., Feb. 2, 1879; s. James H. G. and Rose (Rudd) C.; parental grandmother was a Tuttle, a direct descendant of the family of Tuttles who came from Tuttlefield, England, on the Good Ship Planter in 1627, founded New Haven, Conn., and gave of their homestead for site of Yale College; grad. high sch. and business college; m. Dorothy Burton, Aug. 20, 1927. Began cattle business at 12 as hired hand; had charge of outfit at 19; was pres. Cross Bar Land &Cattle Co., Colter-Greer Sheep Co., Colter Construction Co.; pres. Colter Live Stock & Agricultural Co., pres. Northern Ariz. Land Co., 1921; dir. Lyman Reservoir Co.; vice-pres. Stockman's State Bank, St. Johns, Ariz. Formerly vice-president Arizona Cattlemens Assn., and a director of National Livestock Assn.; was mem. Constl. Convention, ARiz.; mem. Arizona Senate, 8 terms; State Fair commissioner, Ariz., 5 yrs.; mem. Bd. Supervisors, Apache County, 5 yrs.; chmn. Dem. Central Com., Apache County; mem. Dem. Nat. Com. 1916-20; del. Dem. Nat. Conv., New York, 1924 (platform com.); Dem. nominee for gov. of Ariz., 1918 (defeated in gen. election by 300 votes); road commr. Apache County; rep. of gov. and State of Ariz., with Los Angeles Chamber of Commerce, before the U.S. Senate Irrigation and Reclamation Com., Oct. 1925, and before Congress and President of U.S., 1926, 27, 28, 37, 38, in relation to Colorado River irrigation; pres. since 1923, Ariz. Highline Reclamation Assn. (non-profit orgn.), to defeat Colorado River compact and build dams and High Line Canal, irrigating 4 million acres of land, developing 5 million electric H.P. Now pres. Colter, Ariz. Water Filing and Reclamation Assn. Trustee for Ariz. of major future water resources, filing on them in behalf of State, since 1923. Candidate for gov. of Ariz., 1930; mem. Ariz. House of Reps., 1934 and 1940-41. First pres. of Ariz. White Mountain Game and Fish Assn. Mem. advisory board Am. Hist. Soc.; mem. Correspondence Com. of Guards of Washington. Filed Pub. Works Adminstrn. loan application as Ariz. water trustee for $350,000,000 for construction of the Grand Canyon-Glen-Bridge-Verde-Highline Project, Nov. 1933, and renewed application, May 1935, of which sec. of interior has approved $173,000,000. Pub. of Highline (book regarding Colo. River), 1934; Colter's Reclaimer (mag.); wrote book Diligence in Protection and Development of Arizona Water Resources. Mem. advisory bd. Nat. Rivers and Harbors Congress; governor's rep. bn. Colo. River matters before legislature and congress; expert and adviser to Colo. River Commn. of Ariz. Candidate for Congress, 1942. Elk. Home: Colter, Springerville, Ariz. Office: 210-212 S. Third Av., Phoenix, Ariz. Deceased.

COLTON, CHARLES ADAMS, educator; b. at New York, Mar. 29, 1852; s. John Adams and Ruth Ann (Ely) C.; M.E., Sch. of Mines (Columbia), 1873; m. Augusta H. M. Beyer, of Newark, N.J., June 29, 1901. Asst. in mineralogy and metallurgy, sch. of Mines (Columbia), 1873-82; prof. chemistry and mineralogy, Rose Poly. Inst., Terre Haute, Ind., 1882-84; organizer, and dir. Newark (N.J.), Tech. Sch., since 1884. Mem. Am. Inst. Mining Engrs., Republican. Presbyterian. Home: 26 Stratford Pl. Office: 367 High St., Newark, New Jersey.

COLTON, GARDNER QUINCY, dentist, inventor; b. Georgia, Vt., Feb. 7, 1814; s. Walter and Thankfur (Cobb) C.; studied medicine under Dr. Willard Parker, N.Y.C., 1842. Gave exhbn. of effects of nitrous oxide (laughing gas) when inhaled, N.Y.C., 1844, toured other cities with laughing gas; invented an electric motor, 1847; participated in Cal. gold rush, 1849; justice of the peace San Francisco; reporter Boston Transcript, 1860; laughing gas became popular in dental anesthesia. Died Rotterdam, Holland, Aug. 9, 1898.

COMEY, ARTHUR COLEMAN city planner, regional planner and Landscape architect; b. Somerville, Mass., Sept. 6, 1886; s. Arthur Messinger and Kate (Coleman) Comey; A.B., Cum laude, Harvard, 1907; Harvard Sch. of Landscape Architecture, 1904-07; m. Eugenia Louise Jackson, Oct. 2, 1915; children—Katherine, Richard Jackson; m. 2d, Janet I. Mowry, June 26, 1930; married third, Elizabeth Pattee, July 25, 1950; m. 4th Janet Mowry, Jan. 24, 1954. Supt. parks Dixon, Ill., 1908; Utica, N.Y., 1909-10 ; city planner Milwaukee County, Wis., 1910; St. Paul, 1911; cons., from 1912; zoning dir. Boston Boston City Planning Bd., 1922-24; lectr. Harvard Sch. of Landscape Architecture, 1928-29; asst. prof. Harvard Sch. City Planning, 1930-36; asso. prof. Harvard Dept. of Regional Planning, 1937-40. Cons., Houston , Tex.; Dover, N.J.: Detroit; Milw.; Birmingham, , Mich. Manchester, N.H.; Portland, Me. Meriden. Conn., also to Boston and other N.E. Cities; UN Hdqrs. Commn., T.V.A. Recipient 1st prize in Richmond (Cal.) competition. Member Mass. Homestead Com., 1913-19, Town Planner, U.S. Housing Corp., 1918-19, World War. Fellow Am. Soc. Landscape Architects; mem. Am. Inst. of Planners (ex-gov.), Am. Soc., C.E., Boston Soc. Landscape Architects (pres.), Am. Inst. Cons. Engrs., Mass. Fed. Planning Bds., Am. Planning and Civic Asso. Mass. Governor's Com. on Open Spaces, Trustees of Public Reservations, President's Conf. on Home Building and Home Ownership. Consultant, Nat. Resources Planning Board, 1934-43 (mem. urbanism committee, local planning com.), Maine State Planning Bd., Mass. State Planning Bd., New England Regional Planning Commission. Clubs: Harvard Faculty, Appalachian Mountain, Chocorua Mountain (ec-v.p.), Harvard Mountaineering, Ski Club of Great Britain, Harvard Ski Club. Author: Houston-Tentative Plans, 1913; Regional Planning Theory, 1923; Transition Zoning (Harvard City Planning Studies, V.), 1933; State and National Planning Classification (with K. McNamara), 1937; Planned Communities (with M. Wehrly), 1940; Integration of The New England Regional Plan, 1942; Sudbury Valley Regional Planning (with Howard M. Turner), 1950. Editor: City and Regional Planning Papers, by A. Bettman (Harvard City Planning Studies, XIII), 1946. Asso. editor: Nat. Municipal Rev., 1927-32. Home: Kittery Point, Me. Died Jan. 26, 1954.

COMEY, ARTHUR MESSINGER, chemist; b. Boston, Nov. 10, 1861; s. Elbridge C. and Josephine L. (Messinger) C.; A.B., Harvard, 1882; Ph.D., U. of Heidelberg, 1885; m. Kate Coleman, Sept. 9, 1885; 1 son—Arthur Coleman Comey, Instr. in chemistry, Harvard, 1885-89; prof. chemistry, Tufts Coll., 1889-93; analyt. and cons. chemist. Boston, 1893-1906; dir. Eastern (research) Lab. of E. I. du Pont de Nemours 1920-21. Fellow Am. Acad. Arts and Author: Dictionary of Chemical Sciences. 1896, 2d 1921. Chmn. sub-com. on explosives Nat. Research Council, 1917. Home: Cambridge, Mass. Died Apr. 6, 1933.

COMFORT, MANDRED WHITSET, physician; b. Hillsboro, Tex., June 10, 1895; s. Edgar Whitset and Eulah (Stoud) C.; A.B., Austin Coll., 1916, LL.D., 1954; M.D., Univ. of Tex., 1921; M.S. in Neurology, Univ. of Minn., 1926; m. Aurelia Jones, Mar. 14, 1931. Teacher Sterling City Tex., 1916-17; adj. prof. of anatomy, Univ.of Tex., 1921-23; fellow Mayo Foundation, Rochester, Minn., 1923; apptd. asso. in medicine The Mayo Clinic, July 1, 1928, prof. of medicine The Mayo Foundation Grad. Sch., 1946—; cons. physician St. Mary's Hosp., 1928—; cons. Nat. Cancer Inst., 1946-50, and 1952—. Member board of governors The Mayo Clinic. Diplomate American Bd. Internal. Medicine. Fellow A.M.A., A.C.P., mem. Assn. Am. Physicians, Am. GastroEnterological Assn. (pres. 1957), Southern Minn. Med. Assn. Central Soc. for Clin. Research, Minn. Soc. Internal Med., Alumni Assn. of Mayo Foundation, Sigma Xi, Alpha Kappa Kappa Alpha Omega Alpha. Presbyterian. Contbr. numerous articles on gastroenterology br. of internal. medicine to professional jours. Home: 701 Ninth Av., S.W. Office: 102 110 Second Av. S.W., Rochester, Minn. Died Aug. 7, 1957; buried Hillcrest Meml. Park, Dallas.

COMPTON, ALFRED GEORGE, educator; b. London, Eng., Feb. 1, 1835; s. William and Elizabeth G. C.; A.B., Coll. City of New York, 1853, A.M.; m. Frances E. Feeks, June 10, 1874. Teacher mathematics, 1853-1911; prof. physics, 1902, acting pres., 1902-Sept. 15, 1902, Coll. City of New York. Author: A Manual of Logarithmetic Computations, 1881; First Lessons in Wood-Working; First Lessons in Metal-Working, 1890; The Speed-Lathe (Compton and De Groodt), 1898; Some Common Errors of Speech, 1898. Died Dec. 12, 1913.

COMPTON, ARTHUR H(OLLY), physicist, univ. chancillor; b. Wooster, O., Sept. 10, 1892; s. Elias and Celia Catherine (Augspurger) C.; B.S., Coll. Wooster, 1913, Sc.D., 1927; M.A., Princeton, 1914, Ph.D. (Porter Ogden Jacobus fellow), 1916, Sc.D., 1934; postgrad. Cambridge (Eng.) U., 1919-20; Sc.D., Ohio State U., 1929, Yale, 1929, Brown U., 1935, Harvard, 1936, U. San Marcos, 1941, U. Arequipa, 1941, Lehigh U., 1946, LL.D., Washington U., 1928, U. Cal., 1930; M.A. Oxford U., 1934; L.H.D., U. Tampa, 1941, Jewish Theol. Sem. Am., 1942; m. Betty Charity McCloskey, June 28, 1916; children—Arthur Alan, John Joseph. Inst. physics U. Minn., 1916-17; research engr. Westinghouse Lamp Co., 1917-19, also civilian asso. U.S. Signal Corps, developing airplane instruments, 1917-18; nat. research fellow physics Cavendish Lab., Cambridge, 1919-20; prof. physics, head dept. Washington U., 1920-23; prof. physics U. Chgo., 1923-29, Charles H. Swift distinguished service prof., 1929-45, chmn. dept. physics, dean div. phys. scis., 1940-45, dir. Metall. Atomic Project, 1942-45; chancellor Washington U., St. Louis, 1945-53, prof. natural history, 1953-61. Chmn. com. on X-rays and radioactivity NRC, 1922-25; Guggenheim fellow, spl. lectr. Punjab U., Lahore, India, 1926-27; mem. Solvay Internat. Congress Physics, 1927; Eastman vis. prof. Oxford U., fellow Balliol Coll., 1934-35; research asso. Carnegie Instn., 1931-41; Walker-Ames vis. prof. U. Wash., 1940; mem. nat. Cancer Adv. Bd., 1937-44; v.p. Chgo. Tumor Inst., 1937-45; pres. Am. Assn. Sci. Workers, 1939-40; active Com. for Econ. Devel., 1946, UN AEC, 1946; mem. civilian adv. com. to sec. navy, 1946; U.S. del. UNESCO, Paris, 1946. Gen. chmn. Laymens Missionary Movement, 1937-41; co-chmn. Nat. Conf. Christians and Jews, from 1938. Chmn. bd. trustees Coll. Wooster from 1940; regent Smithsonian Instn., from 1938. Recipient Rumford Gold medal Am.

Acad. Arts and Scis., 1927; Nobel prize for physics, 1927; Gold medal Radiol. Soc. N.Am., 1928; Matteucci Gold medal Italian Acad. Scis., 1930; Hughes medal Royal Soc. London, 1940; Franklin medal Franklin Inst., 1940; St. Louis Distinguished Service award, 1946; Medal for Merit, U.S. Govt., 1946. Fellow Am. Phys. Soc. (v.p. 1933, pres. 1934), A.A.A.S. (v.p. sect. B., 1927, pres. 1942), Western Soc. Engrs. (hon., Washington award 1945); mem. Am. Philos. Soc. (Franklin medal 1946), Nat. Acad. Scis. (chmn. physics sect. 1938-41), Phi Beta Kappa, Sigma Xi, Alpha Tau Omega, Gamma Alpha; fgn. mem. Reale Accademia dei Licei, Rome, Prussian Acad. Scis., Berlin, Royal Akademie, Amsterdam, Royal Soc. Scis., Upsala, Brazilian Acad. Scis., Peruvian Acad. Scis.; hon. mem. Royal Soc. New Zealand, Deutsche Akad. der Naturforscher, Indian Acad. Scis., Akad. der Wissenchaften in Vienna, Chinese Phys. Soc. Presbyn. Clubs: University, Tavern, Noonday, St. Louis Country (St. Louis); Cosmos (Washington). Author: (monograph) Secondary Radiations Produced by X-rays, 1922; X-rays and Electrons, 1926; The Freedom of Man, 1935; with S.K. Allison, X-rays in Theory and Experiment, 1935; Human Meaning of Science, 1940, also numerous sci. articles; co-author: On Going to College, 1938. Discovered change in wave-length of X-rays when scattered; total reflection of X-rays; (with C.H. Hagenow) complete polarization of X-rays; (with R.L. Doan) X-ray spectra from ruled gratings; elec. character of cosmic ray; directed world cosmic ray survey, 1931-34; directed work resulting in 1st atomic chain reaction. Home: 6510 Ellenwood Av. Office: Washington Univ., St. Louis. Died Mar. 15, 1962. ((

COMPTON, KARL TAYLOR, physicist; b. Wooster, O., Sept. 14, 1887; s. Elias and Otelia (Aguspurger) C.; Ph.B., Coll. of Wooster 1908, m.S., 1909, D.Sc., 1923; Ph.D., Princeton, 1912, D.Sc., 1930; D.Sc., Lehigh U., 1927, Stevens Inst. Tech., 1931, Clarkson Coll., 1932, Boston U., 1932, Columbia, 1940, N.Y.U., 1946, W.Va. U., 1948, Cambridge U., 1952, Israel Inst. Tech., 1954; LL.D., Harvard, 1930, U. Wis., 1934, Middlebury Coll., 1936, Williams Coll., 1936, Johns Hopkins, 1937, Frnaklin and Marshall Coll., 1937, Northeastern U., 1938, St. Lawrence U., 1939, U. Cal., 1941, Northwestern U., 1942, Tufts Coll., 1943, Norwich U., 1944, Coll. of William and Mary 1947, Rollins Coll., 1949; D. Eng., Bklyn. Poly. Inst., 1930, Case Sch. Applied Sci., 1931, Rutgers U., 1941, Worcester Poly. Inst., 1946; Dr. Applied Sci., Ecole Polytechnique, Montreal, 1944; L.H.D., U. Hawaii, 1947; Dr. Tech., Finnish Inst. Tech., 1949; m. Rowena Rayman (dec.); 1 dau., Mary Evelyn (Mrs. Russell Alderman) m. 2d, Margaret Hutchinson; children—Jean Corrin (Mrs. C. W. Boyes), Charles Arthur. Instr. chemistry Coll. Wooster, 1909-10; instr. physics Reed Coll., Portland, Ore., 1913-15; asst. prof. physics Princeton, 1915-19, prof., 1919-30, chmn. dept. Physics 1929-30; pres. Mass. Inst. Tech., 1930-48, chmn. of cor., 1948-54. Trustee Am. Optical Co., 1952-54; dir. Fed. Res. Bank Boston, 1951-54. Gen. Foods Corp., 1952-54 Gen. Motors Corp., 1952-54, High Voltage Engring. Corp., 1950-54, John Handcock Mut. Life Ins. Co., 1948-54, McGraw-Hill Pub. Co., 1949-54, Research Corp. of N.Y., 1933-53, Tracerlab, 1948-54. Served as aero engr., Signal Corps, U.S. Army, 1917; asso. sci. attache Am. Embassy, Paris, 1918. Chmn. research and development bd. Nat. Mil. Establishment, , 1948-49; cons. physicist Dept. Agr. and Gen. Electric Co., 1924-30; mem. vis. com. U.S. Bur. Standards, 1931-41; mem. bus. adv. and planning council Dept. Commerce, 1933-36; mem. adv. com. U.S. Weather Bur., 1935-48; mem. Adv. Com. on Research for Railroads, 1935-36; mem. War Resources Bd., 1938-40; mem. nat. defense research com. Office Sci. Research and Development, 1940-47, chief Office of Field Service, 1943-45, dir. Pacific br., 1945; mem. Sci. Intelligence Mission to Japan, 1945; mem. Baruch Rubber Survey Com., 1942; chmn. U.S. Radar Mission to U. K., 1943; spl. rep. sec. war in S,W. Pacific Area, 1943-44; mem. Secs. War and Navy Com. on Postwar Research, 1944; mem. sec. war's spl. adv. com. on atomic bomb, 1945; chmn. Research Bd. Nat. Security, 1945-46, Joint Chiefs of Staff Evaluation Bd. on Atomic Bomb Tests, 1946, Research and Development Bd., 1948-49, New Eng. Com. on Atomic Energy, 1954, President's Adv. Commn. on Universal Tng., 1946—47; mem. Naval Research Adv. Com., 1946-48, War Dept. Research Adv. Panel, 1946-48, Nat. Security Tng. Commn., 1951-54, Trustee Edison Found., 1946-53, Ford Found., 1946-51, Meml. Found. Neuro-Endocrine Research 1932-47, New Eng. Indsl. Research Found., 1941-48, Nutrition Found., Ind. (chmn. bd. trustees1941-54), Rockfeller Found. and gen. Edn. Bd., 1940-53 (exec. com. 1941-42, nominating com. 1941-44), Sloan Found., 1942-54, Sloan-Kettering Inst., 1947-54, Brookings Inst., 1940-50, Norwich U., 1935-50, Princeton (charter 1952-54), Western Coll., Oxford, O., 1947-49, Population Council, 1953-54; mem. adv. bd. Bartol Research Found., 1927-36, Watumull Found., 1944-54; chmn. governing bd. Am. Inst. Physics, 1931-36; chmn. com. on engring. schs. E.C. P.D., 1932-39; chmn. Sci. Adv. Bd., 1933-35. Chmn. adv. com. sci. research Nat. Assn. Mfrs., 1937-41; mem. Mass. Commn. on Stabiliaztion of Employment, 1931-33; dir. Boston C.of C. 1932-33; chmn. instns. div. Boston Community Fund, 1938-39; chmn. new products com. New Eng. Council, 1939-41. Cons. Brit. Parliamentary and Sci. Com., 1954. Pilgrim Trust lectr. Royal Soc. London, 1943. Fellow Am. Phys. Soc., (councillor; v.p. 1925-27; pres. 1927-29), Optical Soc. of Am.; Mem. A.A.A.S., (pres. 1935-36; exec. com. 1931-40), Am. Philos. Soc., Am. Chem. Soc., Franklin Inst., Am. Inst. E.E., Am. Soc. M.E., Inst. Aero. Scis., Am. Acad. Arts and Scis., Am. Inst. N.Y., Am. Soc. Engring Edn. (v.p. 1937; pres. 1938-39), Phi Beta Kappa, Sigma Xi, Alpha Tau Omega, Tau Beta Pi. Recipient Rumford medal Am. Acad. Arts and Scis., 1931, Medal for Merit, 1946, Washington Award, 1947, Marcellus Hartley medal Nat. Acad. Sci., 1947, Lamme medal Am. Soc. Engring. Edn., 1949, Col. Thacher E. Nelson award Advt. Club Boston, 1949, William Procter prize for Sci. achievement Sci. Research Soc., of Am. 1950, Hoover medal Founder Engring. Socs., 1951, Joseph Priestley award Dickinson Coll., 1954; Hon. Comdr. Order Brit. Empire, 1948; Comdr. Royal Norwegian Order St. Olav, 1948; French Legion of Honor, 1951. Presbyn. Clubs: Tavern, Algonquin, Union, University (Boston); University (N.Y.C.,); Cosmos (Washington). Home: 100 Memorial Dr., Cambridge Mass. Died June 22, 1954.

COMSTOCK, GEORGE CARY, astronomer; b. Madison, Wis., Feb. 12, 1855; s. Charles Henry and Mercy (Bronson) C.; Ph.B., U. of Mich., 1877; LL.B., U. of Wis., 1883 (LL.D., U. of Ill., 1907; Sc.D., U. of Mich., 1907); admitted to bar, but never practied; m. Esther Cecile Everett, June 12, 1894; 1 dau., Mary (Mrs. George Carey). Recorder and asst. engr. U.S. Lake Survey, 1874-78; asst. engr. on improvement Miss. River; asst. astronomer Washburn Obs.; computer Nautical Almanac Office; prof. mathematics and astronomy, Ohio State U., 1885-87; prof. astronomy, 1887-1922, dir. Washburn Obs., 1889-1922, dir. and dean Grad. Sch., 1906-20, U. of Wis., retired, 1922. Fellow Am. Acad. Arts and Sciences. Author: Method of Least Squares, 1890; Text-Book of Astronomy, 1900; Field Astronomy for Engineers, 1902; The Sumner Line as an Aid to Navigation, 1919. Home: Beloit, Wis. Died May 21, 1934.

COMSTOCK, JOHN HENRY, entomologist; b. Janesville, Wis., Feb. 24, 1849; s. Ebenezer and Susan (Allen) C.; B.S., Cornell, 1874; grad. student Yale, 1874-75, U. of Leipzig, 1888-89; m. Anna Botsford, Oct. 7, 1878. Instr. entomology, 1875-77, asst. prof., 1877-78, Cornell; U.S. entomologist, Washington, 1879-81; prof. entomololgy, invertebrate zoölogy, Cornell U., 1882-1914 (emeritus). Lecutrer on zoölogy, Vassar College, 1877; non-resident prof. entomology, Leland Stanford Jr. U., 1891-1900. Author: Insect Life; Notes on Entomology; Introduction to Entomology; How to Know the Butterflies (with his wife); The Spider Book; The Wings of Insects. Home: Ithaca, N.Y. Died Mar. 20, 1931.

COMSTOCK, LOUIS KOSSUTH, elec. engr.; b. Kenosha, Wis.; s. Charles Henry and Mercy (Bronson) C.; Ph.B., U. Mich., 1888; m. Anne Wilson, Sept. 12, 1902; 1 son, Thomas B. With North Am. Constrn. Co., Pitts., 1888-91; in practice as cons. engr., Chgo., 1891-97; supt. constrn. for Western Electric Co., 1897-1900; elec. engr. George A. Fuller Co., N.Y., 1900-04; organizer, 1904, L.K. Comstock & Co., pres., 1904-26, chmn. bd., 1926-43; chmn. Bd. Rev., WPB, 1941-46, to carry out stblzn. agreement with AFL and govt. agys. Has installed elec., mech. equipments in many of largest bldg. and indsl. plants in N.Y., Chgo., Can., and other localities; cons. engr., N.Y. C., since 1946. Vice pres., former mem. bd. mgrs. Montclair (N.J.) Savs. Bank, 1934-43; commr., dir. Pub. works, Montclair, N.J., 1936-43; chmn. Council on Indsl. Relations for Elec. Constrn. Industry, 1920-43. Mem. War Industries Bd., 1918; del. 4th congress, Internat. C. of C., Stockholm, 5th Congress, Amsterdam, 6th Congress, Washington, 5th Internat. Congress, Bldg. and Pub. Works, London. Fellow Am. Inst. E.E., Am. Soc. M.E.; mem. Commerce and Industry Assn. N.Y. (past pres., dir.), Am. Arbitration Assn. (past dir.), China Soc. Am. (dir.), Pilgrims U.S., Soc. Medalists. Clubs: Bankers, University (N.Y.). Home: 195 Fernwood Av., Montclair, N.J. Office: 101 Park Av., N.Y.C. 17. Died Jan. 1, 1964.

COMSTOCK, THEODORE BRYANT, mining engr., geologist; b. Cuyahoga Falls, O., July 27, 1849; s. Calvin J. and Amelia (Hanford) C.; B. Agr., Pa. State Coll., 1868; B.S., Cornell, 1870 (Sc.D., 1886); m. Blanche Huggins, Dec. 9, 1880. First asst. and photographer, Morgan expdn. to Brazil, 1870; prof. natural sciences, Pellham Priory, N.Y., 1871-72, pvt. sch., Cincinnati, 1873; geologist, Capt. W. W. A. Jones' N.W. Wyo. and Yellowstone Park expdn., 1873; founder, and dir. Kirtland Summer Sch. of Natural History, Cleveland, 1875; acting prof. geology and paleontology (founded dept. of econ. geology), Cornell, 1875-79; prof. mining engring. and physics, U. of Ill., 1885-89; asst. state geologist of Tex., 1889-91; founder and dir. Ariz. Sch. of Mines, 1891-95; pres. U. of Ariz., 1893-95. Asst., Harvard Summer Sch. of Geology, 1876; led expdn. to N.W. Ty., Can., 1877; asst. state geologist of Ark., 1887-88; dir. Ariz. Agrl. Expt. Sta., 1894. Pres. Calif. Farm & Home Builders; cons. engr. some of the largest mining cos. in the world; sec. and chief engr. Bd. of Pub. Utilities, Los Angeles, 1910-12. V.p. (presiding) Nat. Irrigation Congress, Los Angeles, 1893; mem. exec. com. Trans-Mississippi Congress, 1892-94. Author: Outline of Geology, 18978. Editor, Bulletin Southern California Academy Sciences, 1901. Home: Los Angeles, Calif. Died July 26, 1915.

COMSTOCK, DANIEL FROST, physicist, engineer; b. Newport, R.I., Aug. 14, 1883; s. Ezra Young and Nellie Preston (Barr) C.; S.B., Mass. Inst. Tech., 1904; studied U. of Berlin, 1905, U. of Zurich, 1905-06, U. of Basel, 1906, Ph.D., studied U. of Cambridge, Eng., 1906-07, under J.J. Thomson; m. Joan Barton, June 30, 1925; children—Daniel Frost, Charles Barton. Apptd. to teaching staff, Mass. Inst. Tech., 1904, instr. in theoretical physics, 1905-10, asst. prof., 1910-15, asso. prof., 1915-17; directed scientific work on development of means for detection of hostile submarines, World War I, president Comstock & Wescott, Inc., Engrs. 1912-14; v.p. Kalmus, Comstock & Wescott, Inc., engrs., 1914-25; dir. of scientific work on, and principal inventor of the process for producing Motion Pictures in natural color known as the Technicolor process, developed by Kalmus, Comstock & Wescott, Inc., for the Technicolor Motion Picture Corp., during 1914-25; v.p. Technicolor Motion Picture Corp., 1918-25; pres. Comstock & Westcott, Inc., 1925-67, chmn. bd., 1967-70; engaged almost exclusively with research and development on war projects during World War II; now engage in industrial research. Pres., treas., dir. Stator Co., co-inventor of new refrigeration process owned by same. Member National Advisory Council to Committee on Patents, Ho. of Reps., 1939. Fellow Am. Academy Arts and Sci., Am. Physical Society; mem. Am. Chemical Society. Club: St. Botolph (Boston). Author: Nature of Matter and Electricity (with L.T. Troland), 1917. Contbr. original research articles on modern theory of electricity and optics to Am. and English tech. jours. Home: Cambridge MA Died Mar. 2, 1970; buried Mt. Auburn Cemetery, Cambridge MA

CONANT, HENRY DUNNING, mining engr.; b. Rochester, N.Y., 1863; E.M., Sch. of Mines (Columbia), 1886. Asst. mining engr., Tamarack and Osceola mines, Mich., 1886-88; locating and constructing engr., Norfolk & Western R.R., Va., 1888-92; construction engr., N.Y., N.H. & H. R.R., 1892-93; engr., 1893-95, gen. mgr., 1895-98, Playa de Oro Mining Co., Ecuador; asst. supt., 1898-1904, supt., 1904, The Lake Superior Smelting Co.; later supt. Calumet & Hecia Smelting Wroks; cons. mining engr. and metallurgist since 1934. Mem. Am. Inst. Mining Engrs., 1888. Republican. Baptist. Home: 826 N. 70th St., Wauwatosa, Wis.

CONANT, HEZEKIAH, mfr., inventor; b. Dudley, Mass., July 28, 1827; s. Hervey and Dolly (Healy) C.; m. Sarah Williams Learned, Oct. 4, 1853; m. 2d, Harriet Knight Learned, Nov. 1859; m. 3d, Mary Eaton Knight, Dec. 6, 1865; 2 children. Patented pair of lasting pinchers for use in shoe mft., 1852; journeyman machinist, Boston, Worcester, Mass., 1852-55; employed at Colt Firearm Co., Hartford, Conn., 1885-circa 1859; invented gas check for breech loading firearms, 1856; invented machines for dressing sewing thread and winding thread on spools automatically, 1859, sold patent to Willimantic Linen Co. (Conn.), 1860, mech. expert, 1860-68; organized Conant Thread Co., Pawtucket, R.R., 1868, merged with J. & P. Coates Co. of Paisley, Scotland (largest thread mfrs. in Europe), 1869, name changed from Conant Thread Co. to J. & P. Coates Co., Ltd., 1893. Died Jan. 22, 1902; buried Dudley.

CONANT, LEVI LEONARD, mathematician; b. Littleton, Mass., Mar. 3, 1857; s. Levi and Annie W. (Mead) C.; A.B., Darmouth, 1879, A.M., 1887; A.M., Ph.D., Syracuse, 1893; m. Laura M. Chamberlain, July 24, 1884 (died 1911); m. 2d, Emma B. Fisher, June 19, 1912. In public school work, 1879-87; prof. mathematics, Dak. Sch. of Mines, 1887-90; post-grad. student mathematics, Clark U., 1890-91; prof. mathematics, Worcester Poly. Inst., 1891—, and acting pres., 1911-13. Mem. Worcester Bd. Edn. (chmn., 1909), Mass. State Bd. Edn., 1901-14. Republican. Author: The Number Concept—Its Origin and Development, 1894; Original Exercises in Plane and Solid Geometry, 1905; Plane and Spherical Trigonometry, 1909; Logarithmic and Trigonometric Tables, 1909. Editor Jour. of Worcester Poly. Inst., 1897-1905. Home: Worcester, Mass. Died Oct. 11, 1916.

CONARD, HENRY SHOEMAKER, botanist; b. Phila., Pa., Sept. 12, 1874; s. Thomas Pennington and Rebecca Savery (Baldwin) C.; B.S., Haverford, Coll., Pa., 1894, M.A., 1895; Ph.D., U. of Pa., 1901; Johnston scholar, Johns Hopkins, 1905-06; Sc.D., Grinnell, 1944, Haverford, 1945; m. (E) Laetitia Moon, Apr. 13, 1900; children—Elizabeth M., Rebecca S., Alfred F. Teacher of science, Westtown Sch., 1895-99; instr. botany, U. of Pa., 1901-05; prof. botany, Grinnell Coll., 1906-44, retired since June 1944; research professor State Univ. of Iowa since 1944. Instr. in plant ecology, Summer Sch., L.I. Biol. Assn., Cold Spring Harbor, L.I. Fellow A.A.A.S., Ia. Acad. Science. Mem. Bot. Soc. America, Sullivant Moss Soc., Am. Mycological Soc., Ecological Soc. of America, American Assn. Univ. Profs., Phi Beta Kappa (Haverford); Sigma Xi (U. of Pa.). Mem. Soc. of Friends (orthodox). Author: Waterlilies, 1905; Waterlilies and How to Grow Them (with Henry Hus), 1907. Translator and Editor: (with G. D. Fuller) Plant Sociology (by J. Braun-Blanquet), 1932.

Ranger-naturalist, Yellowstone Park, summers, 1924-26. Home: 1310 Elm St., Grinnel IA

CONCANNON, CHARLES CUTHBERT chemist; b. Boston, Mar. 13, 1889; s. John Stephen and Gertrude (Kavanagh) C.; grad. Boston Latin Sch., A.B., Harvard, 1911. Asso. with Dr. Jokichi Takamine, Japanese sci. and philanthropist, to 1922; chief of chem. Div., Bur. Foreign and Domestic Commerce, U.S. Depart. of Commerce, 1922—, in charge of export licensing chemicals, 1948—. chmn. Am. delegation 10th Internat. Congress of Chemistry, Rome, 1938; on leave from U.S. govt., 1945. Mem. Am. Inst. Chemists, Am. Chem. Soc., Am. Marketing Soc. Soc. for the Advancement of Mgmt. Clubs: University, Harvard (pres. 1951-52). (Washington), Harvard, Chemists (N.Y.C.), Harvard (Boston), Widely Known as lectr., writer on econs., comml. development of chem. industry. Contbr. many articles on chem. topics, Home: 1200 16th St. N.W. Office: Dept. of Commerce, Washington. Died 1957.

CONDICT, GEORGE HERBERT, electrical engr.; b. Newark, N.J., Mar. 7, 1862; s. J. Elliot and Sarah (Johnson) C.; ed. schs. New York and Phila., and U. of Pa.; m. Anna Neill, Jan. 10, 1888; children—Elizabeth Richards, Margaret, Harold Vail. Entered employ Central Gas Light Co., San Francisco, 1882; built gas works in Calif. and Ore.; connected with Pacific Coast Electric Constrn. Co., 1884; Pacific Coast agt. Van Depoele Electric Co., 1885; visited Chicago and was asst. to Mr. Van Depoele in electric ry. and lighting experiments; installed Van Depoele's exhbn. trolley line, New Orleans Expn., 1885; afterward in electric constrn. in Calif. Calif.; invented improved controller, which has been important factor in electric ry. development; was gen. mgr. Electric Car Co. of America; developed improved storage batteries and in 1894 built, at Merrill, Wis., 1st storage battery plant to be used as auxiliary to provide for fluctuations of ry. load; became chief engr. Electric Vehicle Co., 1897, and cons. engr. other automobile companies; v.p. and gen. mgr. Electro-Dynamic Co., 1903-06; now cons. electric and mech. engr. Mem. Common Council, Plainfield, N.J., 1917-20. Mem. com. of examiners Naval Cons. Bd., 1917-19; mem. tech. advisory com. War Claim Bd., War Dept., Washington, 1919-20. Home: Plainfield, N.J. Died Apr. 9, 1934.

CONDRON, THEODORE LINCOLN, cons. engr.; b. Washington, D.C., Apr. 16, 1866; s. Rev. George M. and Abbie (Smith) C.; B.S., Rose Poly. Inst., 1890, M.S., 1892, C.E., 1918, D.Engr. (hon.), 1947; m. Grace E. Layman, June 9, 1896; children—George Tolman, Helen (Mrs. Charles E. McGuire), Arnold Layman. Retired; formerly mem. Condron & Post, designers of railroad and highway bridges, factories and warehouse buildings of reinforced concrete and steel. Advisory engr. Reconstruction Finance Corp. on Tacoma Narrows Suspension Bridge, 1938-39. Awarded Chanute medal by Western Soc. Engrs., 1905. Mem. Structural Engrs.' Commn., State of Ill. Mem. Am. Soc. C.E. (dir. 1923-25), Am. Ry. Engrs. Assn., Am. Soc. for Testing Materials, Western Soc. Engrs. (v.p. 1899; hon. mem. 1945). Republican. Conglist. Clubs: Union League, Engineers; (hon. mem. 1938). Home: 212 S. Scoville Av., Oak Park IL

CONE, RUSSELL G., civil engr.; b. Ottumwa, Ia., Mar. 22, 1896; s. Frank and Alice (Haddon) C.; B.S. in Civil Engring., U. of Ill., 1922; m. Izetta Lucas, June 10, 1922 (div.); 1 son Russell Glenn; m. 2d, Jeanne Fozard Hamilton, Jan. 6, 1939 (div.); m. 3d, Pearl Janet Bloomquist, Feb. 3, 1957. Jr. engr., asst. engr., resident engr. charge constrn. main span Del. River Bridge, Phila., 1922-27; resident engr. charge constrn. Ambassador Bridge, Detroit, 1927-30; gen. mgr. Tacony-Palmyra Bridge, Phila., 1930-33; resident engineer in charge construction of Golden Gate Bridge, San Francisco, California, 1933-37; engr. in charge maintenance of thew the structure, Golden Gate Bridge and Highway Dist., 1937 to May 1, 1941; mem. board of investigation Tacoma-Narrows Bridge collapse, State of Washington, cons. engineer; engineering study of passenger tramway, Palm Springs, California, 1939-41; v.p., gen. mgr. Silas Mason Co.; gen. mgr. Ia. Ordnance Plant Cornhusker Ordnance Plant; engr. Pantex Ordnance Plant; cons. design and constrn. of Green River Ordnance Plant, Dixon, Ill.; constrn. and operation antitank rocket loading and Explosive loading; archtl. engr. New Test Site, AEC; mgr. Carquinez Bridge foundations contract, 1956. Served with 149th F.A., U.S. Army, 1917. Mem. Am. Soc. C.E., Am. Soc. Testing Materials, Am. Ordnance Assn., Am. Soc. Mil. Engrs., Tau Beta Pi, Sigma Tau, Chi Epsilon. Episcopalian Clubs: Engineers (N.Y.C.); Press and Union League (SAN San Francisco); Commonwealth of California. Author articles in tech. jours. and papers before tech. schs. socs. Home: 1083 Hargus Av., Vallejo, Cal. Office: Box 518, Corckett, Cal. Died Jan. 21, 1961; buried Golden Gate Nat. Cemetery, San Bruno, Cal.

CONEY, JABEZ, millwright, engr.; b. Dedham, Mass., Oct. 21, 1804; s. Jabez and Irene (Gay) C.; m. Mary Whiting, Oct. 25, 1827, 3 children. Believed to have built 1st iron vessel constructed in New Eng.; build 1st large marine engine, 1st gravel excavator; represented Ward 10 (South Boston) in Boston City Council, 1847, 50. Died Jan. 23, 1872.

CONEY, JOHN, silversmith; b. Boston, Jan. 5, 1655; s. John and Elizabeth (Nash) Conney; m. Sarah Coney; m. 2d, Mary Atwater; at least 2 children. Apprenticed to silversmith Jeremiah Dummer, Boston; owned large silver-work business, Boston; engraved plates for 1st paper money issued by Mass. Bay Colony; signed petition acknowledging King Charles II's authority; served with Mass. Militia. Died Aug. 20, 1722.

CONGDON, ERNEST ARNOLD, chemist; b. New York, Aug. 9, 1866; s. Henry Martyn and Charlotte (Greenleaf) C.; Ph.B., Columbia, 1887; specialized in chemistry, U. of Berlin, 1889. Instr., Lehigh U., 1889-92; prof. and dir. chemistry, Drexel Inst., of Art, Science and Industry, 1892-1906; chemist, New York Bd. of Health, 1906-08; chemist, H. M. Congdon & Son, New York, since 1908. Fellow London Chem. Soc.; mem. Am. Chem. Soc., MS. Soc. Clubs: Faculty of U. of Pa., University, Contemporary, Orpheus. Author: Brief Course in Qualitative Analysis, 1898; Laboratory Instruction in General Chemistry, 1901. Home: 194 Clinton St., Brooklyn. Office: 18 Broadway, New York.

CONKLIN, CLIFFORD TREMAINE, agrl. editor; b. Struthers, O., July 18, 1890; s. William and Isabelle (Bidwell) C.; B.S., Ohio State U., 1916; m. Ora B. Kistler, June 3, 1913; children—Clifford Tremaine, Richard Kistler, Martha Jeanne. Engaged in county extension work, 1916-17; asst. prof. animal husbandry Ohio State U., 1917-25; exec. sec. Nat. Ayrshire Breeders' Assn., also editor Nat. Ayrshire Digest, 1925-52, ret. 1952. Mem. bd. Rutland (Vt.) Hosp.; bd. dirs. Brandin Free Pub. Library. Named to Hall of Fame, Dept. Animal Husbandry Ohio State U.; recipient Distinguished Service award Ayrshire Breeders Assn., 1951; honored by Dairy Shrine Club. Mem. Am. Soc. Animal Prodn., Am. Dairy Sci. Assn., Agrl. Soc. Methodist. Mason. Clubs: Saddle and Sirloin (pres.), La Boheme. Created head test plan; instituted approved sire and dam program, type classification plan. Home: 14 High St., Brandon, Vt. Died Apr. 6, 1956; buried Pinehill Cemetery, Brandon, Vt.

CONKLIN, EDWIN GRANT, biologist; b. Waldo, O., Nov. 24, 1863; s. Dr. Abram V. and Maria (Hull) C.; S.G., Ohio Wesleyan U., 1885; A.B., 1886; A.M., 1889; Ph.D., Johns Hopkins, 1891; hon. Sc.D., U. Pa., 1908, Ohio Weselyan U., 1910, Yale, 1930; LL.D., Western Reserve U., 1925, Johns Hopkins, 1940, U. Pa., 1943, Princeton 1945; m. Belle Adkinson, June 13, 1889 (died Mar. 7, 1940); children—Paul, Mary (Mrs. Samuel Masland, dec.), Isabel. Prof. biology Ohio Wesleyan, 1891-94; prof. zoölogy Northwestern, 1894-96, U. Pa., 1896-1908; prof. biology Princeton, 1908-33, emeritus, 1933—; spl. lecturer in biology Trustee Woods Hole Lab., 1897—; also Woods Hole Oceanographic Instn., Pres. Bermuda Biol. Station 1926-36. Fellow A.A.A.S. (pres. 1936), Am. Acad. Arts and Sciences; mem. Nat. Acad. Scis., Am. Soc. Zoölogist (pres. 1899), Assn. Am. Anatomists, Am. Soc. Naturalists (pres. 1912), Am. Philos. Soc. (sec. 1900-08, v.p. 1932-42, , exec. officer, 1936-42, pres. 1942-45, 48—.), Phila. Acad. Natural Sciences (v.p. 1901—.), Phi Beta Kappa, Sigma Xi; mem. adv. bd. Wistar Institute; pres. Science Service, 1936-45; foreign mem. Royal Soc. of Edinburgh, Zoölogy Societé of London, Scieté Belge de Biologie, Academie Rouale de Belgique (1948), Societé Royale de Sci. Md. et Naturelle de Bruxelles, Königlich, Böhmische Gesellschaft der Wissenschaften. Lecturer; Harvey Soc., 1913; Hariss Foundation, Northwestern, 1914; Hale Lectures, Nat. Acad. Sci., 1917; NcNair Lectures, U. N.C., 1920; Lowell Inst., 1922; Rice Inst. 1923; Sedgwick Meml., 1929; Potter Meml., Jefferson Med. Coll., 1930; Penrose Meml., Am. Philos. Soc., 1934; Milton Acad. War Meml., 1935; Barnwell Address, 1938; Sharp Lectures, Rice Inst., 1941. Co-editor Biological Bulletin, Journal of Experimental Zoölogy, Genetics. Author: Heredity and Environment; Mechanism of Evolution; Direction of Human Evolution; Synopsis of General Morphilogy; Future of Evolution; Revolt Against Darwinism; Science and the Faith of the Modern Embryology and Evolution; Problems of Development; Biology and Democracy; Freedom and Responsibility; What Is Man?; Man, Real and Ideal; and about 200 other works on heredity, development, education, etc. Recipient of John J. Carty gold medal and award, 1942-43; Nat. Inst. Social Science gold medal, 1943. Home: 139 Broadmead, Princeton, N.J. Died Nov. 21, 1952.

CONKLIN, WILLIAM AUGUSTUS, zoölogist; b. New York, Mar. 17, 1837; s. Benjamin and Netta (Adams) C.; ed. pub. schs.; D.V.S., Columbia Vet. College, 1884; Ph.D., Manhattan Coll., 1886. Connected with Central Park, New York, 1858-98, dir. zoöl. dept., 1865-98; engaged in importing wild animals, 1898—. Editor Journal of Comparative Medicine and Veterinary Archives, 1878-93. Home: New York, N.Y. Died June 17, 1913.

CONN, HERBERT WILLIAM, biologist; b. Fitchburg, Mass., Jan. 10, 1859; s. Reuben Rice and Harriet E. (Harding) C.; A.B., Boston U., 1881, A.M.; Ph.D., Johns Hopkins, 1884; m. Julia M. Joel, Aug. 5, 1885. Instr. biology, 1884-86, asst. prof., 1886-88, prof., 1889—, Wesleyan U. Dir. Cold Spring Harbor Biol. Lab., 1889-97; bacteriologist, Storrs Expt. Sta., 1890-1906; dir. lab. of Conn. State Bd. Health, 1905—; lecturer, Trinity Coll., 1887-89. Specialist on the bacteriology of dairy products. Author: The Story of the Living Machine, 1899; The Method of Evolution, 1900; An Elementary Physiology and Hygiene for Use in Schools, 1903; practical Dairy Bacteriology, 1907; Introductory Physiology and Hygiene (rev. edit.), 1908; Biology (an introd. study for use in colls.), 1912; Elementary Physiology and Hygiene (for upper grammar grades), 1913; Social Heredity and Social Evolution, 1914; Bacteria, Yeasts, and Molds in the Home, 1917; Physiology and Health (rev. edit.), 1924. Home: Middletown, Conn. Died Apr. 18, 1917.

CONNELL, WILLIAM HENRY, civil engr.; b. N.Y. City, Jan. 12, 1878; s. Edward J. and Emma Augusta (McGean) C.; ed. De La Salle Inst., New York; m. E. Nena Watters, Apr. 23, 1913. Civ. engring. work, various depts., N.Y. City, 1908-12, including topog. surveys, water supply, highway and bridge dept. service, dept. commr. pub. works assisting boro pres. in reorganization of engring. depts., also built service test roadway and installed modern methods of highway maintenance and constrn.; chief engr. Bur. Highways and Street Cleaning, Phila., modernizing highway and street cleaning work and built service test rd., 1912-17; engring. exec. with Day & Zimmerman, placing a number of large orgns. in the field for war work, 1917-19; spl. staff engr. Phila. Rapid Transit Co., 1919-23; chief exec., dept. sec. and engring.and maintenance of state highway system, comprising 11,500 miles of rd., 1923-27; in cons. practice, 1927-29; exec. dir. Regional Planning Federation of Phila. Tri-State Dist., 1929-40; civil works adminstr., Phila. County, 1933-34; dir. local work division Federal Emergency Relief Adminstrn., Phila. County, 1934-35; consulting engineer. Mem. Nat. Highway Research Council, Am. Roadbuilders Assn. (ex-pres.), Am. Assn. State Highway Officials, Am. Soc. C.E.; hon. mem. Street and Road Assn. of England. Clubs: Engineers, Racquet. Address: 112 S. Oxford Av., Ventnor, N.J. Died Aug. 3, 1943.

CONNER, ELI TAYLOR, mining engr.; b. Mauch Chunk, Pa., Mar. 1, 1864; s. William Isaac and Anna Elizabeth (Hawk) C.; ed. pub. schs. E. Mauch Chunk, 1870-79; m. Florence Isabel Towar, June 30, 1887 (died 1889); m. 2d, Caroline Yarnall Minshall, Sept. 21, 1893; children—Margaret Yarnall (Mrs. Henry H. Strater), Walter Leisenring, Caroline Minshall, Eli Taylor. Operator and asst. chief clk. C.R.R. of N.J., Mauch Chunk, 1879-82; rodman, chainman, transitman, engr. and asst. supt. Sandy Run, Pond Creek Harleigh Collieries of M. S. Kemmerer & Co., 1882-88; supt. Mt. Jessup (Pa.) Coal Co., Ltd., Florence Coal Co., Dupont, Pa., and Spring Brook Coal Co., Moosic, Pa., 1888-96; supt. Shamokin Div. Lehigh Valley Coal Co., 1896, Wyoming Div., 1897-1902; apptd. gen. supt. Webster Coal & Coke Co., 1902, merged with Pa. Coal & Coke Co. of which was gen. mgr. until 1907; gen. mgr. New River Collieries Co. of W.Va., 1907-09; cons. coal mining engr. in Phila., N.Y. City and Scranton, Pa., 1909—. Republican. Episcopalian. Home: Scranton, Pa. Died Jan. 3, 1938.

CONNER, JAMES KEYES, civil engr.; b. Wabash, Ind., Apr. 12, 1871; s. Ovid Washington and Annie (Keyes) C.; ed. pub. schs. and Rose Poly. Inst.; m. Winifred Lamport, June 24, 1896. Asst. engr. and supvr. of track, C.C.C. & St. L. Ry. Co., 1895-99; asst. engr., B. & O. R.R., 1899-1900; asst. engr., designer and engr. N.Y.C. Lines, 1900-06; 1st asst., engr., 1906-14, chief engr., Feb. 10, 1914—. L.E. & W. R.R. Co. Republican. Presbyn. Home: Indianapolis, Indiana. Died May 18, 1925.

CONNICK, HARRIS DE HAVEN, constrn. engr.; b. Eureka, Cal., May 22, 1873; s. John Warren and Sarah (De Haven) C.; student Stanford, 1893-97; m. Edith J. Russ, June 15, 1908. Asst. in county suverory's office Humboldt County, Cal., 1890-93; asst. in city engr.'s office Eureka, 1897-98; in engring. dept. S.P. Co., San Francisco, 1898-99; asst. engr. in charge design new sewer system for San Francisco, 1900-02; asst.engr. Bd. Pub. Works, San Francisco 1902-06; chief asst. city engr., 1906-11 dir. works Panama-Pacific Internat. Expn., 1911-17, charge design constrn. and operations. Vice Pres. Am. Internat. Corp., 1917-20; dir. Am. Internat. Steel Corp., Am. Internat. Ship Bldg. Corp., 1917-20. Constrn. engr. numerous sewer and water supply systems of West. Chmn. finance and exec. co coms., dir. Famous Players Lasky Corp., 1920-22; dir. Famous Players Cal., Famous Players of Can., Famous Players of Mo., Real Art Rictures, Inc., 1920-22; pres., dir. Asso. Music Pubs., Inc., Bretikopf Publs., Inc., v.p., dir. Muzak Corp. of Ohio, Wired Radio, Inc.; dir. Am. Cities Power & Light Corp., Consol. Holdings Corp., Electric Shareholdings Corp., Falkland Corp., until March 1937; dir. Z. Russ Properties, Inc., Russ Investment Co., Russ Market Co., 1937-40; Russ Connick Livestock Corp. Mem. Am. Soc. C.E. Club: Bohemian (San Francisco). Home: 1408 Hawthorne Terrace, Berkeley, Cal. Died Dec. 28, 1965; buried Ferndale (Cal.) Cemetery.

CONNOR, WILLIAM DURWARD, army officer; b. nr. Beloit, Wis., Feb. 22, 1874; s. Edward D. and Adeline (Powers) C.; grad. U.S. Mil. Acad., 1897. Army

Staff Coll., 1909; m. Elsa Van Vleet, Nov. 6, 1907. Commd. add. 2d, lt., engrs., June 11, 1897; promoted through grades to lt. col., May 15, 1917; col. N.A., Aug. 5, 1917; brig. gen. N.A., June 26, 1918; brig. gen. U.S. Army, Apr. 27, 1921; maj. gen., Sept. 1, 1925. Served in Philippine Campaign and during Filipino Insurrection, 1898; city engr., Manila, 1899-1900; fortification work, New London, Conn., 1903; in charge 1st and 2d dists., Miss. River improvement, 1905-08; dir. civ. engring., U.S. Engr. Sch., 1910-12; duty Gen. Staff, 1912-16; chief of Staff Southern Dept. July-Nov. 1916; dept. engr., Philippine Div., Dec. 1, 1916-May 1917; duty Gen. Staff, A.E.F., July 28, 1917, as asst. chief of staff, A.E.F., Nov. 4, to May 1, 1918; chief of staff, 32d Div., to June 26, 1918; comdr. 63d Inf. Brigade, 32d Div., to Aug. 5, 1918; comdr. Base Sect. No. 2, Bordeaux, to Nov. 12, 1918; chief staff, Services of Supply, to May 26, 1919; comdg. gen. same to Sept. 1, 1919, comdg. gen. Am. Froces in France, to Jan. 7, 1920; chief of transportation Service, Aug. 15, 1920-July 14, 1921; asst. chief of staff, U.S. Army, Aug. 4, 1921-Nov. 10, 1922; comdr. U.S. Army Forces in China, Apr. 12, 1923-May 13, 1926; comdg. 2d Div., June 15, 1926-Dec. 18, 1927; Comdt. Army War Coll., Dec. 22, 1927-Apr. 30, 1932; supt. and comdt. U.S. Mil. Acad., May 1932-Jan. 1938; retired, Feb. 28, 1938; recalled to active duty, May 7, 1941; chmn. Construction Advisory Committee, U.S. War Dept., 1941-42, returned to inactive status, Mar. 21, 1942. Awarded D.S.M. and Silver Star (with Oak Leaf Cluster) by U.S.; commander Legion of Honor, Black Star of Morocco, Croix de Guerre (French); Companion Order of the Bath (British). Clubs: Army and Navy Chevy Chase (Washington); Bass Rocks Beach, Eastern Point Yacht (Gloucester, Mass.). Address: 2412 Tracy Pl. N.W. Washington 20008. Died June 16, 1960; buried U.S. Mil. Acad. Cemetery, West Point, N.Y.

CONRAD, CHARLES WEARNE, consulting engr.; b. Fennimore, Wis., May 28, 1887; s. Anthony Lee and Anne (Wearne) C.; E.E., U. of Tex., 1909; m. Flora D. Tandy, June 3, 1913; children—Charles Tandy,Anthony Lee, II Mgr. Canadian Water, Light & Power Co., Canadian, Tex., 1909-13; asst. elec. engr., Chicago Assn. Commerce, 1913-15; elec. engr. Eddystone (Pa.) Rifle Plant, Midvale Steel & Ordnance Co., 1915-16, plant engr., 1916-19; supt. Eddystone Rifle Storage Arsenal, U.S. Ordnance Dept., 1919-20; plant engr., Bird & Son, Inc., paper and bldg. Products, , East Walpole, Mass., 1920-30, gen. supt., 1930-35, v.p., 1935-46; pres. Conrad & Young, Inc. since Feb. 1946, name now changed to Conrad & Son, Inc., Member Engring. Socs. of New Eng., Am. Soc. M.E., Plant Engrs. Club (hon.), Boston, Delta Tau Delta. Republican. Home: 808 Washington St., Walpole, Mass. Office: 33 Union St., East Walpole Mass. Died Oct. 24, 1954; buried Maple Grove Cemetery, Walpole, Mass.

CONRAD, CUTHBERT POWELL, utility exec.; b. Osceola, Mo., Jan. 28, 1893; S. Cuthbert Powell and Sara Eugenia (Harris) C.; B.S., U. of Wis., 1915; C.E., 1916; m. Beatrice Carroll Tabor, Apr. 17, 1920. Instr. hydraulic engring., U. of Wis., 1916-17; jr. partner, Mead & Seastone, Cons. hydraulic engrs., Madison, Wis., 1921-24; chief hydraulic engr., Brazilian Traction Co., Rio de Janeiro and Sâo Paluo, 1925-40; pres. Ia.-Ill. Gas and Electric Co., Davenport Ia., 1946-54, chmn., 1954—. Served in Civil Engring. Corps, USN, 1917-20 and 1940-46, retiring to inactive duty with the rank of Commodore, April, 1946. Awarded Legion of Merit, World War II. Member American Society of Civil Engineers, Tau Beta Pi. Clubs: Army and Navy, Army and Navy Country (Washington), Davenport, Davenport Country, Outing (Davenport, Iowa); Rock Island (Ill.), Arsenal Golf, Short Hills Country (Moline); Blackhawk Hiking (Davenport, Rock Island, Moline). Home: 11 Edgehill Terrace, Davenport, Iowa. Office: 206 E. 2d St., Davenport Ia. Died Jan. 24, 1956; buried Arlington Nat. Cemetery.

CONRAD, FRANK, elec. engr.; b. Pittsburgh, Pa., May 4, 1874; s. Herbert M. and Sadie (Cassidy) C.; ed. pub. schs., Pittsburgh; hon. D.Sc., U. of Pittsburgh, 1928; m. Flora Selheimer, June 18, 1902; children—Francis H., Crawford J., Jane L. Began as bench-hand, Westinghouse Elec. & Mfg. Co., Pittsburgh, 1890; became gen. engr., 1914, asst. chief engr., 1921—. Early experimenter in radio, using phonograph records and local talent for broadcasting, 1919; exptl. programs developed into Station KDKA, first on the air, Nov. 2, 1920. Has patented over 200 inventions including round watt-hour electric meter, pantagraph trolley for electric trains, electric clock and devices for Automobile starting, lighting and ignition. Served in U.S. Army during World War; then lt. comdr. U.S. Naval Reserve. Awarded Edison medal of Am. Inst. Elec. Engr., 1931; John Scott medal of City of Phila., 1933; Morris Liebman prize by Inst. Radio Engr., 1936; Lamme medal by Am. Inst. Elec. Engrs., 1936. Home: Wilkinsburg, Pa. Died Dec. 11, 1941.

CONRAD, G(EORGE) MILES, biologist, documentalist; b. Seattle, Mar. 19, 1911; s. George Ellsworth and Ethel Elizabeth (Miles) C.; A.B., Oberlin Coll., 1933; A.M., Columbia, 1938; m. Mary Elizabeth Gibson, July, 27, 1935; 1 son, Thomas Miles. Research asst. Am. Mus. Natural History, N.Y.C., 1934, asst. curator comparative and human anatomy, 1935-43; lectr. zoology Columbia 1937-39; research dir., tech. editor Hazard Advt. Co., 1943-48; editor Graphic Sci. Assos., 1948-50; documentation specialist, chief documentation research sect. Library of Congress, Washington, 1950-53; sec. Am. Documentation Inst. 1951-54; temporary mgr. for Trustees Biol. Abstracts, Inc., Phila., 1953; dir. Biol. Abstracts, Inc., 1953-64. Dir. Spl. Libraries Council, Phila., 1955-58; president National Federation of Science Abstracting and Indexing Services, 1958-61, study missions to U.S.S.R., 1959, Japan, 1961. Member committee on biological abstracting International Council Scientific Union, 1957-64, was observer Abstracting Bd., Zurich, 1955, Chamonix, France, 1956, Columbus, 1958, Monte Carlo, 1959, Paris 1960, 62, London, 1961; adv. bd. office Critical Tables, NRC, 1960-63. Served as staff sgt. AUS, 1944-46, Decorated Bronze Star Medal, Conspicuous Service Cross, N.Y. State. Fellow N.Y. Acad. Scis., A.A.A.S. (mem. council 1961-63); mem. Spl. Libraries Assn., Conf. Biol. Editros, Editors, Am. Documentation Inst., Sigma Xi, Phi Delta Kappa. Clubs: Cosmos (Washington); Explorers. Author articles on biol. and documentation subjects. Home: Red Fox Lane, Strafford, Pa. Office: Biological Abstracts, Care U. Pa., Phila. Died Sept. 9, 1964.

CONRAD, TIMOTHY ABBOT, conchologist; b. nr. Trenton, N.J., June 21, 1803; sons of Solomon White Conrad; studied natural history and science privately. Assisted his father in printing bus. until father's death, 1831; became especially interested in conchology; became mem. Phila. Acad. of Scis., 1831; state geologist and paleontologist of N.Y., 1837-42; mem. Am. Philos. Soc.; his work is not well known because of his opposition to Darwin's theory of evolution; contbr. articles to various journals; drew many of plates for his own works. Author: American Marine Conchology; or, Descriptions and Colored Figures of the Shells of the Atlantic Coast, 1831. Died Trenton, Aug. 9, 1877.

CONROY, PETER JOSEPH, educator; b. Watervliet, N.Y., Oct. 26, 1894; s. William Patrick and Mary Ellen (Birmingham) C.; Diploma. Fordham Prep. Sch., 1915; Ph.G., Fordham Coll. Phram., 1917; B.S., Fordham U., 1926; M.S., 1927, Ph. D., 1929 1929; A.M., Columbia, 1940; student, New York, U. and Bellevue Hosp. Med. Coll., 1921-23; m. Marguerite E. Schoenstadt, May 13, 1919; 1 dau., Marguerite Ellen. Mem. faculty Fordham U., 1924—; lecturer chemistry and gen. sci., Fordham Sch. Edn., 1924-44; prof. of chemistry and head dept. Fordham U. Coll. Pharmacy, 1927—; asst. prof. pharmacology N.Y. Med. Coll., 1929-30. Lecturer food and nutrition, A.R.C., Crestwood, N.Y., 1942-43. Awarded Alumni medal, 1917; Bene Merenti medal (20 yr. service and achievement), 1945. Fellow A.A.A.S., Am. Inst. Chemists, Am. Geog. Soc., Mem. Am. Chem. Soc., Am. Pharm. Assn. (also N.Y. br.), German Apothecary Sco., N.Y. Acad. Sci., N.Y. State Pharm. Assn., Westchester Pharm. Assn. (hon. life mem.). Cons. pharm. chem. editor, Pharm. editor, Chain Store Age, 1942-47. Home: 410 Scarsdale Rd., Crestwood, P.O. Tuckahoe 7, N.Y. Office: Frodham Univ., Fordham 58, N.Y.C. Died June 17, 1955; buried Holy Mount Cemetery, Eastchester N.Y.

CONSTANT, FRANK HENRY, civil engr.; b. Cincinnati, O., July 25, 1869; s. Henry and Catherine (Ange) Constant; grad. Woodward High Sch., Cincinnati, 1887; C.E., with highest distinction, Cincinnati U., 1891, Sc.D., 1915; Sc.D., Lafayette, 1915; m. Annette G. Woodbridge, June 19, 1901; 1 son, Frank Woodbridge. Asst. engr. King Bridge Co., Cleveland, 1891-93; prin. asst. engr. Osborn Engring. Co., Cleveland, 1893-97, prof. 1897-1914, U. of Minn. prof. civ. engring. and head of dept., Princeton, 1914-37, prof. emeritus since 1937. Mem. Am. Soc. C.E., Soc. Promotion Engring. Edn., Phi Beta Kappa, Sigma Xi, Beta Theta Pi. Club: Princeton (N.Y. City). Home: 57 Battle Rd., Princeton, N.J. Died March 16, 1950.

CONSTANTINOPLE, PANAGIOTES S., surgeon; b. Arcadia Greece, June 27, 1901 (parents U.S. citizens); s. James and Georgia (Chios) C.; brought to U.S., 1905; B.S., Gerogetown U., 1921, M.D., 1923; student of Dr. Heinrich Neumann, Allgemeiner Krankenhaus, Vienna, 1925-26, U. of Vienna, 1925-26, U. of Budapest, 1926; m. Patricia Dowling, Oct. 6, 1934; children—James Dowling, Elena Talcott, Anne Patricia and George Robert and Nicholas Lely (twins). Associate prof. in physiology, Gerogetown U. Med. Sch., 1923-26, prof., 1929-31, asso. prof. otolaryngology, 1931-39, clin. prof. since 1939; in private practice since 1926; attending otolaryngologist, Garfield Hosp., 1939, senior attending surgeon and chief of ENT service; chief otolaryngology clinic, Georgetown Hosp., 1935—, senior attending surgeon Epsicopal Eye Ear Nose and throat Hosptial; consulting oto-laryngologist to Columbia Hosp. for Women; vice chmn. dept. otolaryngology Washington Hosp. Center; associate otolryngology Children's Hosp., Prof. ciln. otolaryngology, Georgetown Univ. Recipient Vi-cennial Medal, Georgetown U., 1950; Order of St. Sepulcher from Greek Orthodox Church. Fellow A.C.S., American Acad. Otolaryngology; mem. A.M.A., Pan-Am. Med. Assn., Internat. Med. Club (pres.), Clinical Club (sec. treas), Washington Society for Hard of Hearing (1st vice pres.), Alpha Omega Alpha (faculty member). Member of Greek Orthodox Ch. Clubs: Cosmos, Torch, Chevy Chase. Contbr. to med. jours. Home: 4840 Glenbrook Rd. Office: 1801 I St. N.W., Washington. Died Feb. 18, 1967.

COOK, ALBERT JOHN, naturalist; b. Owosso, Mich., Aug. 30, 1842; s. Ezekiel and Barbara Ann (Hodge) C.; B.S., Mich. Agrl. Coll., 1862, M.S., 1865 (D.Sc., 1905); studied at Harvard, 1867-88; m. Mary H. Baldwin, June 30, 1870; m. 2d, Mrs. Sarah J. Eldredge, July 3, 1897. Instr. mathematics, 1867-69, prof. zoölogy and entomology, 1868-93, curator Gen. Mus., 1875-93, entomologist Expt. Sta., 1888-91, Mich. Agrl. Coll.; prof. biology, Pomona Coll., Cal., 1893-1911; state commr. of horticulture Cal., Oct. 1911—. Conductor Univ. Extension work in agr., U. of Cal., 1894-1905. Author: Manual of the Apiary; Injurious Insects of Michigan; Silo and Silage; Maple Sugar and the Sugar Bush; Birds of Michigan; California Citrus Culture, 1913. Died Sept. 29, 1916.

COOK, ALFRED NEWTON, chemist; b. Cornell, Ill., Feb. 22, 1866; s. Ira and Harriett Ann (DeVelbiss) C.; grad. Geneseo (Ill.) Normal Sch., 1886; B.S., Knox Coll., Galesburg, Ill., 1890; Ph.D., U. of Wis., 1900; m. Annie G. McClelland, July 10, 1894; children—Herbert Edward, Harold Lewis. Prof. natural sciences, Amity Coll., College Springs, Ia., 1892-94; prof. chemistry and physics, Upper Ia. U., 1894-98; asst. in chemistry, U. of Wis., 1898-1900; prof. chemistry, Morningside Coll., 1900-04; prof. chemistry, U. of S. Dak., 1904-20; prof. of chemistry, Occidental Coll., Los Angeles, 1924—. State food and drug commr., S. Dak., 1909-13. Republican. Conglist. Mason. Deceased.

COOK, CLINTON DANA, educator, chemist; b. St. Johnsbury, Vt., Feb. 20, 1921; s. Clinton Dana and Anna Francis (Kubavec) C.; S.B., Mass. Inst. Tech., 1942; M.S., U. Vt., 1948; Ph.D. in Chemistry, Ohio State U., 1951; m. Alice Maclaren Fisher, May 21, 1944; children—Dana, Allison, Polly, Timothy, Cynthia. Group leader chemistry Gen. Electric Co., W. Lynn (Mass.) works, 1942-46, supervising chemist liquid dielectrics sect., Pittsfield, Mass., 1951-52; instr. chemistry U. Vt., 1946-48; asst. instr., research fellow Ohio State U., 1948-51, vis. grad. prof. chemistry, summer 1959; faculty U. Vt., 1952-69, prof. chemistry, 1959-69, chairman dept. chemistry, 1960-63, became dean of faculties, 1963, v.p. acad. affairs, 1965-69, chmn. premed. adv. sect. 1956-60; cons. organic chemistry U.S. Rubber Co., 1956-59; cons. NSF Instnl. Programs, 1965—. Trustee St. Johnsbury (Vt.) Acad. Mem. Am. Chem. Soc., Sigma Xi (pres. Vt. chpt. 1956), Phi Lambda Upsilon. Contbr. articles profl. jours. Home: Burlington VT Died June 25, 1969.

COOK, EDWARD NOBLE, former physician; b. St. Paul, Aug. 21, 1905; s. Edward and Jessie Gertrude (Noble) C.; B.A., U. Minn., 1926, B.S., 1927, B. Medicine, 1928, M.D., 1929, M.S. in Urology, 1935; m. Jean Elizabeth Moore, June 14, 1934; children—Margaret (Mrs. C.M. Berndt, Jr.), Edward Noble, Nancy (Mrs. L. Bruce Nelson). Intern, Kings County Hosp., Bklyn., 1929-30; mem. staff Mayo Found., U. Minn., from 1930-72, prof. urology, from 1958-72; staff Mayo Clinic, 1935-70, cons. urology, 1935-70; cons. urology Meth., St. Mary's hosps.; spl. research infections urinary tract, transurethral surgery; ret., 1970. Served as lt. M.C., USN, 1939-47. Mem. Am. Urol. Assn., A.M.A. (sec. sect. urology 1946-49), chmn. sec. 1949-50), Societe Internationale de Chirugie, Minn. Med. Assn., Olmsted County Med. Soc., Sigma Xi, Delta Upsilon, Alpha Kappa Kappa. Clubs: Country, University. Contbr. profl. jours. Home: Rochester MN Died July 26, 1972; buried Oakwood Cemetery, Rochester MN

COOK, ERNEST FULLERTON, pharm. chemist; b. Lionville, Pa., Feb. 1, 1879; s. Herman Sidney and Celia (Failor) C.; Pharm.D., Phila. Coll. Pharmacy, 1900, Pharm.M. 1918; grad. study U. Berne, Switzerland, 1926-27; M.Sc., U. Mich., 1937; D.Sc. (hon.), Phila. Coll. Pharmacy and Sci., 1950; m. Marguerite Shaffer (dec.), June 17, 1909; children—Ruth Ernestine, Bruce Shaffer (killed in action Feb. 1945), Theodore Failor, John Samuel (dec.); m. 2d, Helen Marr, May 12, 1948. Tchr., Phila. Coll. Pharmacy and Sci. since 1900, prof. operative pharmacy, dir. pharm. labs., 1918-45. Dir. USN Tng. Sch. for Pharmacists, 1917-18. Mem. com. of revision Nat. Formulary, 1908; chmn. com. revision Pharmacopeia of U.S., 1920, 30 and 40, now ret.; mem. Internat. Commn. Pharmacopoeial Experts. Awarded Remington medal, 1931. Fellow (hon.) Academia de Ciencias Medicas, Fisicas y Natruales of Havana, Cuba; Real Academia de Farmacia, Madrid, Spain, 1946. Mem. Am., Pa., Me. and N.H. pharm. assns., Internat. Pharm. Fedn. Republican. Presbyn. Co-editor: Remington's Practice of Pharmacy since 1926. Home: 719 Beechwood Rd., Pine Ridge, Media, Pa. Died Mar. 2, 1961. 1961.

COOK, GEORGE HAMMELL, geologist, educator; b. Hanover, N.J., Jan. 5, 1818; s. John and Sarah (Munn) C.; grad. Rensselaer Poly. Inst., 1839, B. Natural Scis., 1840, M.S., 1841; Ph.D. (hon.), U. City N.Y., 1875, LL.D. (hon.), Union Coll., 1866; m. Mary Thomas, Mar. 6, 1846. Prof. geology and civil engring. Rensselaer Poly. Inst., 1842, prof. mathematics and natural philosophy, 1848; prof. mathematics and natural philosophy, Albany Acad., 1848-52, prin., 1851; prof. chemistry and natural scis. Rutgers Coll., 1853-89; state geologist N.J., 1864-89; organizer N.J. State Coll. (for promotion agr. and mech. arts), attached to Rutgers, 1864; helped form, mem. exec. bd. N.J. Bd. Agr.; dir. agrl. expt. stas. in N.J., 1880; influential in promotion Act of Congress 1887 creating agrl. expt. stas. in all states; pres. New Brunswick (N.J.) Bd. Water Commrs.; mem. N.J. Bd. Health; chief dir. N.J. Weather Service, 1886. Died New Brunswick, Sept. 22, 1889.

COOK, GEORGE WYTHE, M.D.; b. Front Royal, Va., Oct. 28, 1846; s. Giles and Elizabeth Van Meter Lane C.; descendant of Mordecai Cooke, who settled in Va., 1650; ed. Front Royal Acad.; M.D., U. of Md., 1869; LL.D., Nat. U., 1890; m. Rebecca, d. Richard Lloyd, of Alexandria Co., Va., Oct. 1877; 1 son, Richard Lloyd. Pvt. 7th Va. Cav., Rosser's brigade, C.S.A.; severly wounded at Hawe's Shop, Hanover Co., Va., May 28, 1864. Practiced medicine at Front Royal, 1869-71, Upperville, Va., 1871-78, Washington since 1878. Formerly prof. physiology, Nat. U., and prof. clin. medicine George Washington U.; ex-attending phys., now mem. consulting staff Garfield Memorial Hosp.; phys. to Louise Home; consulting phys. Govt. Hosp. for the Insane; pres. med. staff of the Episcopal Eye, Ear and Throat Hosp.; pres. Bd. Med. Examiners of D.C., 1898; was acting asst. surgeon U.S.A., stationed in Washington 1898; member exec. board Emergency Hosp. Med. Soc. D.C., 1893, 1917, Med. Assn. D.C., 1897, Washington Obstet. and Gynecol. Soc., 1901-03; mem. Washington Acad. Sciences (v.p. 1917). Med. History Club; ex-treas. U.S. Pharmacopoeial Conv.; fellow A.M.A., Assn. Mil. Surgeons of U.S.; hon. mem. Clinico-Pathol. Soc. and Med. and Surg. Soc. Club: Cosmos. Address: 3 Thomas Circle, Washington, D.C.

COOK, HAROLD JAMES, paleontologist, geologist; b. Cheyenne, Wyo., July 31, 1887; s. James Henry and Kate (Graham) C.; student U. Neb., 1907-08; Columbia, 1909-10; lab. research, Am. Mus. Natural History, N.Y., 1909-10; m. Eleanor Barbour, Oct. 13, 1910; children—Margaret, Dorothy, Winifred, Eleanor. Rancher, Neb. since boyhood; became mem. Neb. State Geol. Survey, 1906; field staff, Am. Mus. Natural History, 1909; curator of paleontology, Colo. Mus. History, Denver, 1925-30; spl. lectr. Chadron (Neb.) State Normal Coll., 1925-26, Western State Coll., Colo. 1929; part owner, dir. Cook Mus. Natural History; custodian Scotts Bluff Nat. Monument, 1934-35. Mem. Neb. State Park Bd. Charter mem. Neb. Reclamation Assn. Fellow A.A.A.S., Am. Nature Assn., Am. Soc. Mammalogist; mem. Southwestern Colo. Archaeol. Soc., Am. Mus. Natural History (hon. life), Paleontol. Soc. Am., Internat. Soc. Archaeology, Neb. State Hist. Soc., Nat. Inst. Social Scis., Am. Assn. Petroleum Geologists, Am. Inst. Mining and Metall. Engrs., Am. Forest Assn., Neb. Acad. Sci., Colo.-Wyo. Acad. Sci., Soc. Econ. Paleontologists, Archaeol. Inst. Am., Neb. Alumni Assn., Sigma Gamma Epsilon, Phi Sigma, Delta Sigma; hon. mem. Tex. Archaeol. and Paleontol. Soc. Co-Author: Fossil Vertebtates in Am. Mus. of Natural History, 1915; also articles giving results of discoveries made in fossil fields of Neb. and Colo., among them New Trails of Acient Man, New Geological and Paleontological Evidence Bearing on the Antiquity of Man in America; discovered, in Neb., Hesperopithecus haroldcookii, Osborn, "oldest known nr. relative of the human race." Practices as cons. geologist. Home: Agate, Sioux County, Neb. Died Sept. 29, 1962; buried Scottsbulff, Neb.

COOK, J(AMES) CLINTON, JR., engr., educator; b. Atlanta, Sept. 21, 1918; s. James Clinton and Alline (Wellborn) C.; B.M.E., Clemson Coll., 1939, M.M.E., 1951; M.S. (fellow Gen. Edn. Bd., Rockefeller Found.), U. Mich., 1953, Ph.D., 1955; m. Irene Schwarz, Feb. 26, 1946; children—James Clinton III, Frances Alline, Robert Wellborn. Engr., Westinghouse Electric Corp., 1939-41; chief movements br. transport div. Office Mil. Govt. for Germany, 1946-48; asst. and asso. prof. mech. engring. Clemson Coll., 1948-54, prof. head dept., 1954—; sr. mech. engr. Lockheed Aircraft Corp., summers 1955, 56, 57, 59. Served from 2d lt. to maj. AUS, 1941-46; lt. col. Res. Decorated Bronze Star medal (U.S.); Croix de Guerre avec palme Belgium). Registered Profl. engr., S.C. Mem. Am. Soc. M.E., Am. Soc. Engring. Edn., Tau Beta Pi, Phi Kappa Phi. Methodist. Home: 116 Riggs Dr., Clemson, S.C. 29631. Died Sept. 28, 1965; buried Cemetery Hill, Clemson, S.C.

COOK, JAMES HENRY, naturalist; b. Kalamazoo, Mich., Aug. 26, 1858; s. Henry and Elizabeth (Shaw) C.; ed. pub. schs.; m. Kate Graham Cook, Sept. 28, 1886; children—Harold James, John Graham (dec.). Mgr. WS Ranch, Socorro County, N.M., 1882-87; owner Agate Springs Ranch, Agate, Sioux County, Neb., since 1887. Discovered Agate Springs Fossil Quarries, from which many valuable prehistoric specimens have been secured; maintains with Harold J. Cook, a free mus. of natural history, at Agate. Guide and scout with Texas Rangers in early 70's; Scout for U.S. cav. in Geronimo Indian Campaign, 1885, 86. Mem. Am. Inst. Social Sci., Nebraska State Hist. Soc., Nat. Indian War Vets; hon. mem. Boy Scouts America; asso. mem. Order Indian Wars of U.S. Republican. Protestant. Author: Fifty Years on the Old Frontier, 1923; also stories of adventure. Lecturer on geology, evolution, etc. Home: Agate, Neb. Died Jan. 26, 1942.

COOK, MELVILLE THURSTON, botanist; b. Coffeen, Ill., Sept. 20, 1869; s. William Harvey (M.D.) and Elizabeth Frances (Robinson) C.; student, DePauw U., 1888-89, 91-93, A.M., 1902; A.B., Leland Stanford Jr. U., 1894; Marine Biol. Lab., Woods Hole, Mass., 1896, 1899, 1900; U. Chgo., summers, 1897, 1898; Ohio State Lab., Sandusky, summers, 1902, 1903; Ph.D., Ohio State U., 1904; hon. Sc.D., U. P. R., 1940, DePauw U., 1940; fellow New York Bot. Garden, 1906-07; m. Dora Reavill, Sept. 8, 1897; children—Harvey Reavill, Harold Thurston, Elizabeth (Mrs. Harry A. Ross). Prin. high sch. Vandalia, Ill. 1894-95; instr. in bioloby De Pauw U., 1895-97, prof. 18970 1897-1904; chief dept. plant pathology and econ. entomology Estacion Central Agronomica, Santiago de las Vegas, Cuba, 1904-06; plant pathologist Del. Agrl. Expt. Sta., Newark, 1907-11; State plant pathologist of N.J., and prof. plant pathology Rutgers Coll., 1911-23; plant pathologist N.J. Agrl. Expt. Sta., Insular Expt. Station, Rio Piedras, P.R., retired 1940; vis. prof. botany La. State U., 1944—; editor Journal of Dept. Agr. of P.R., 1928-40, research lectr. sch. tropical medicine, 1926. Lecturer on embryology, Central Coll. Phys. and Surg., Indlps. 1902-03; on comparative anatomy Med. Coll. Ind., 1903-04. Fellow A.A.A.S., (v.p. 1921, sec. bot. sect. 1918-20, chmn. of sect. 1921), Ind. Acad. Sci., Bot. Sco. Am.; mem. Am. Phytopathol. Soc. (v.p. 1916, pres. 1917), Ecol. Soc. Am., Am. Assn. Econ. Entomologists, Entomol. Soc. Am., Ind. Acad. Sciences, N.J. Science Teachers' Assn. (pres. 1920-22), S.A.R., Delta Upsilon, Sigma Xi, Phi Beta Kappa, Pi Gamma Mu, Gamma Sigma Delta. Mason (32 deg., K.T., Shriner, grand sr. warden P.R., 1929). Author: Disease of Tropical Plants, 1912; Applied Economic Botany, 1919; College Botany, 1920; Los Enfermedades de las Plantas Economica de las Antillas, Los Virosis delas Plantas, 1943; Viruses and Virus Diseases of Plant 1947. Contbr. to bot. jours. Home: care Mrs. Harry A. Ross, 1045 Via Tranquila, Santa Barbara, Cal. Died Aug. 11, 1952.

COOK, ORATOR FULLER, JR., botanist; b. Clyde, N.Y., May 28, 1867; s. Orator Fuller and Eliza (Hookway) C.; Ph.B., Syracuse U., 1890; hon. D. Sc., 1930; m. Alice Carter, Oct. 11, 1892. In charge dept. biology, Syracuse U., 1890-91; made (1891-97) extended visits to Liberia for exploration and investigation as agr. N.Y. State Colonization Soc., prof. natural sciences in Liberia Coll., 1891-97, pres. same, 1896-97; secured extensive collection of plants and animals now under investigation in U.S. Nat. Mus., custodian and asst. curator U.S. Nat. Mus., 1898—. Spl. agt. in charge plant importation, U.S. Dept. of Agr., 1898-1900, in charge of investigation in tropical agr., 1900—, visting P.R., Guatemala, Mexico, Costa Rica, etc., prof. botany, George Washington U., 1904. Author of various articles and reports on Liberia and Africa colonization, P.R., topical agr., botany, Zoölogy, evolution, history of cultivated plants, especially on breeding, acclimatization, and cultrual improvement of cotton and rubber plants, also on classification of palms and millipeds. As botanist representing U.S. Dept. Agr. With Bingham expdn. to Peru under auspices of Nat. Geog. Sco. and Yale U., Mar.-Sept. 1915. investigating plants used by the Incas; expdn. to Haiti summer of 1917 on agrl. exploration and study for improvement of agricultural conditions. Expdn. to China for study of agrl. conditions, summer of 1919; Carnegie Instn. expdn. to Central America to study ancient Maya civilization, 1922; expdns. to Haiti, Panama, Mexico, Columbia, and Ecuador, to investigate native cottons and sources of rubber, 1923-31; botantist in charge palm classification, Fairchild Tropical Garden, Cocoanut Grove, Fla., 1937. Home: Lanham, Md. Died Apr. 23, 1949.

COOK, SAMUEL RICHARD, physicist; b. Minden, Haliburton County, Can., Feb. 14, 1865; s. Richard and Jane (Craig) C.; brought to Kan., 1871; B.S., U. of Mich., 1895, M.S., 1897; A.M., U. of Neb. 1898; Ph.D., Cornell U., 1905; studied univs. Chicago and Berlin; m. Mary Elizabeth Crothers, of San Jose, Calif., Sept. 8, 1905 (died 1917); 1 son, Richard Crothers; m. 2d, Eva Belle McConnell, June 14, 1931. Fellow in physics, U. of Neb., 1897-99; prin. of high sch., Wahoo, Neb., 1899-1901; instr. physics and chemistry, Washburn Coll., Topeka, Kan., 1901-02, Case Sch. of Applied Science, 1902-04; fellow in physics, Cornell U., 1904-05; acting prof. physics and astronomy, Allegheny Coll., Meadville, Pa., 1905-06; prof. mathematics, physics and astronomy, Coll. of Pacific, 1907-22. Fellow A.A.A.S.; mem. Am. Assn. of Engrs. Physical Soc., Sigma Xi. Republican. Methodist. Patentee pneumatic shock absorber. Home: 167 Stadium Drive, Stockton, Calif.

COOKE, (ALEXANDER) BENNETT, surgeon; b. Bowling Green, Ky., 1867; s. William Alexander and Nancy (Burnam) C.; A.B., Ogden Coll., Bowling Green, Ky., grad. work New York, Chicago, London, Berne, Vienna; m. Dorothy Daisy Soden, Louisville, Ky., July 10, 1894; dau., Dorothy Soden C. (Mrs. Raymond Tremaine). Began practice, Nashville, Tenn., 1895; removed to Los Angeles, Calif., 1913; prof. of anatomy, med. dept., U. of Nashville, 1897-1900; prof. of anatomy and clinical surgery, med. dept., Vanderbilt U., 1900-03; sr. attending surgeon Los Angeles County Hosp. since 1914; prof. of surgery, Coll. of Medical Evangelists, Los Angeles. Fellow Am. Med. Assn. (judicial council, 1913-17); fellow Am. Coll. of Surgeons, since organization; mem. Sons of Revolution. Pres. Tenn. State Med. Assn., 1907. Author: Diseases of the Rectum and Anus, 1914; Life—What Is It? Contbr. to med. journals. Address: 402 S. Manhattan Pl., Los Angeles, Calif. Died Dec. 9, 1946.

COOKE, C(HARLES) MONTAGUE, JR., zoologist; b. Honolulu, T.H., Dec. 20, 1874; s. Charles Montague and Anna Charlotte (Rice) C.; A.B., Yale U., 1897, Ph.D., 1901; Sc.D., University of Hawaii, 1936; m. Eliza Lefferts, Apr. 25, 1901; children—Carolene Alexander, Charles Montague. Has studied nearly all the large collections of Hawaiian land shells in museums of Europe and America; malacologist with Bishop Museum, Honolulu, T.H. Trustee Honolulu Acad. Arts, Bishop Museum. Mem. Washington Acad. Sciences, Acad. Natural Sciences, Phila., Malacological Soc., London. Republican. Conglist. Club: Pacific (Honolulu). Home: 2859 Manoa Rd., Honolulu, T.H. Died Oct. 29, 1948.

COOKE, HEREWARD LESTER, physicist; b. Montreal, Can., Mar. 26, 1879; s. Miles Woodifield and Clara Maude (Eager) C.; B.A., McGill, 1900, M.A., 1903; studied Emmanual Coll., Cavendish Lab., Cambridge U., 1903-06; m. Olive Lois MacCallum, 1911; children—Margaret Priscilla, Hereward Lester. With Princeton U. since 1906, prof. physics since 1919. Researches in radioactivity, thermionics, 1903-13; surveying with aeroplane photographs since 1919; theatre acoustics since 1928. Served as capt. Royal Engrs., B.E.F., in France, 1916-19. Mem. Am. Physical Soc., Acoustical Soc. America, Am. Soc. Photogrammetry, Optical Soc. of America. Clubs: Princeton (New York); Nassau Club, Princeton, N.J. Died Sept. 30, 1946.

COOKE, JOSIAH PARSON, chemist, educator; b. Boston, Oct. 12, 1827; s. Josiah and Mary (Pratt) C.; grad. Harvard, 1848, LL.D. (hon.), 1889; LL.D. (hon.), Cambridge (Eng.) U., 1882; m. Mary Huntington, 1860. Erving prof. chemistry and mineralogy Harvard, 1850-94; 1st coll. instr. to use lab. in undergrad. course; noted for investigation of atomic weight of Antimony; Mem. Nat. Acad. Scis., Am. Acad. Arts and Scis. (corr. sec. 1873-92, pres. 1892-94). Author: Elements of Chemical Physics, 1860; First Principles of Chemical Philosophy, 1868; The New Chemistry, 1872, rev. edit., 1884; Chemical and Physical Researches, 1881. Died Cambridge, Mass., Sept. 3, 1894.

COOKE, MORRIS LLEWELLYN, consulting engr. in management; b. Carlisle, Pa., May 11, 1872; s. William Harvey (M.D.) and Elizabeth Richmond (Marsden) C.; M.E., Lehigh U., 1895, Sc.D., 1922; m. Eleanor Bushnell Davis, June 16, 1900. Reporter on Phila. Press, Denver News and Evening Telegram (New York), 1890-94; served apprenticeship in Cramp's Shipyard, Phila., later journeyman machinist at Southwark Foundry; engr. for Acetylene Co., Washington, D.C., 1896-97; asst. engr. U.S. Navy during Spanish-Am. War; engaged in commerical orgn. work, 1899-1905; consulting engr., 1905-11; dir. Dept. Pub. Works, Phila., 1911-15; chmn. storage sect. War Industries Bd. of Council Nat. Defense and Mem. Depot Bd. U.S. Army, 1917; exec. asst. to chmn. U.S. Shipping Bd., 1918. Made study of collegiate adminstrative methods in U.S. and Can. for Carnegie Foundation, 1910; dir. Giant Power Survey Pa., 1923; chmn. Miss. Valley Com. of Pub. Works Adminstrn., 1933; dir. Water Resources sect. of Nat. Resources Bd., 1934; adminstr. Rural Electrification Adminstrn., 1935-37; chmn. Great Plains Com., 1936-37; tech. cons. Labor Div., office of Production Management, 1940-41; U.S. expert adjudication Mexican Oil dispute, head Am. Tech. Mission to Brazil, 1942. Trustee of Power Authority, State of New York, 1928-33; member Com. to Survey Patent System, 1946-47; chmn. President's Water Resources Policy Commn., 1950-51. Co-chmn. Comm. for an Effective Fgn. Aid Program. Fellow A.A.A.S., fellow Am. Soc. (Pres. 1927), Franklin Inst., Delta Phi, Sigma Xi; hon. mem. Masaryk Acad. (Prague), Czechoslovak Order of the White Lion, Order Aztec Eagle (Mexico), Legion Honor (France). Democrat. Episcopalian. Clubs: Engineers (N.Y.C.); Engineers (Philadelphia, Pa); Cosmos (Washington, D.C.). Author: Academic and Industrial Efficiency, 1910; Snapping Cords, 1915; Our Cities Awake, 1918; (with Philip Murray) Orgnaized Labor and Production, 1940; Brazil on the March, 1944. Editor: Public Utility Regulation, 1922; What Electricity Costs, 1933. Homes: St. Georges Rd., Phila. 19; also New Hope, Pa. Died Mar. 5, 1960.

COOLBAUGH, MELVILLE FULLER, coll. pres. emeritus; b. Coolbaugh, Pa., Feb. 8, 1877; s. John and Abbie (Woodward) C.; B.S., Colorado Coll., 1902, LL.D., 1925; M.A., Columbia, 1905; LL.D.., U. Colo., 1927; spl. research work Mass. Inst. Technology, 1914-15; m. Osie Frances Smith, Nov. 17, 1905; children—John, Franklin, Lois May Hinkley, David Fogg. Instr. chemistry Colo. Coll., 1902-04; asst. in chemistry Columbia, 1904-05; prof. chemistry, S.D. State Sch. Applied Science, Cleve., 1915-17; prof. chemistry Colo. Sch. Mines, 1917-18; with C.W.S., U.S. Army, World War, June-Dec., 1918; private research, 1919; dir. metall. research for Metals Exploration Co., Denver, 1919-25; pres. Colo. Sch. of Mines, 1925-46, pres. emeritus, 1946—. investigations in ore roasting, hydro and electro metallurgy; sec. Colo. Geol. Survey; mem. Colo. Planning Commn., 1934-45; mem. State Mineral Resources Bd., regional rep., Region 11, Engring., Science and Management War Training; mem. Pres. Truman's Com. of 19 on Fgn. Aid, 1947. Mem. Am. Chem. Soc., Am. Electro-Chem. Soc., Am. Inst. Mining and Metall. Engrs., Colo. Mining Assn., Colo.-Wyo. Acad. Science, Mining and Metall. Soc. of America, Sigma Gamma Epsilon, Sigma Xi. Mason. Clubs: Teknik, Schoolmasters Mile High, University (Denver); Kiwanis (Golden). Home: Golden Colo. Died Sept. 9, 1950.

COOLEY, LEROY CLARK, physicist; b. Point Peninsula, N.Y., Oct. 7, 1833; s. James and Sally (Clark) C.; grad. N.Y. State Normal Coll., 1855; A.B., Union Coll., 1858, M.A., 1861, Ph.D., 1870; m. M. Rossabella Flack, May 30, 1859. Prof. mathematics, Fairfield Acad., 1858-59; prof. physical science, N.Y. State Normal Coll., 1860-74; prof. physics and chemistry, 1874-94, physics, 1894-1907 (emertius), Vassar Coll., Poughkeepsie, N.Y. Author: New Text-Book of Physics, 1880; New Text-Book of Chemistry, 1881; Beginner's Guide to Chemistry, 1886; Laboratory Studies in Chemistry, 1894; Student's Manual of Physics, 1897. Died Sept. 20, 1916.

COOLEY, LYMAN EDGAR, civil engr.; b. Canandaigua, N.Y., Dec. 5, 1850; s. Albert Blake and Achsah (Griswold) C.; bro. of Mortimer Elwyn C.; C.E., Rensselaer Poly. Inst., 1874; (hon. E.C., U. of Mich., 1915); m. Lucena McMillan, Dec. 31, 1874. Taught in Canandaigua Acad., 1871-72; prof. Northwestern U., 1874-77; asso. editor Engineering News, 1876-78; asst. engr. ry. bridge over Mo. River, Glasgow, Mo., 1878; asst. U.S. engr. on Miss. and Mo. River improvements, 1878-84; editor Am. Engineer, 1884; promotoer and consecutively asst. and chief engr. and trustee, cons. engr. Chicago Sanitary Dist.; mem. Internat. Deep Waterways Commn., 1895-96; consulting engr. on contractors' and engrs.' trip to Nicaragua, 1897-98; advisory engr. investigation of $9,000.000 expenditure Erie Canal, State of N.Y., 1898; made econ. investigation on deep waterway, lakes to Atlantic, 1899; cons. engr. Union Water Co., Denver, 1899-1904; mem. U.S. Postal Commn. on pneumatic tubes for mail in cities, 1901; advising engr. on water works appraisement, Omaha, 1904; engr. water power project by damming Miss. River at Keokuk, and other projects; cons. engr. Rochester, N.Y., on location of barge canal, 1905; and Grand Rapids, Mich., on flood problem, 1905-10, Saginaw, 1912; sec. and cons. engr. Internat. Improvement Commn. of Ill., 1906-09; cons. engineer Lakes-to-the-Gulf Deep Waterways Assn., 1909—, and Sanitary Dist. of Chicago, 1912-15. Lecturer Ill., Wis., and Mich. univs. Author: The Lakes and Gulf Waterway; The Diversion of the Waters of the Great Lakes; The Illinois Valley Problem. Home: Evanston, Ill. Died Feb. 3, 1917.

COOLEY, MORTIMER ELWYN, engr.; b. Canandaigua, N.Y., Mar. 28, 1855; s. Albert Blake and Achsah (Griswold) C.; ed. Canandaigua Acad.; grad. U.S. Naval Acad., 1878; hon. M.E., U. of Mich., 1885; LL.D., Mich. Agrl. Coll., 1907; Eng.D., U. of Neb., 1911; Sc.D., Armour Inst. Tech., 1923; Eng.D., University of Michigan, 1929; B.Sc. from U.S. Naval Academy, 1938; m. Carolyn Elizabeth Moseley, December 25, 1879; children—Lucy Alliance (Mrs. Wm. O. Houston), Hollis Moseley, Anne Elizabeth (Mrs. E.C. Howe), Margaret Achsah (Mrs. Harvey F. Cornwell). Professor mechanical engineering, 1881-1928, dean College Engineering, 1904-28, University of Michigan, now dean emeritus, Colleges Engineering and Architecture. In navy on cruise in Mediterranean, 1879, Atlantic Coast, 1880, Bureau Steam Engineering, 1881; chief engineer U.S. Navy, 1898-99, serving on U.S.S. Yosemite during Spanish-American War and at League Island Navy Yard; chief engr. office Mich. Naval Brigade, 1895-1911. Dist. ednl. dir. S.A.T.C., 7th dist. (Mich., Wis., Ill), 1918. Mem. Bd. of Public Works, Ann Arbor, 1888-90; pres. common council, two terms, 1890-91; Dem. candidate for U.S. senator, Mich., 1924. Appraised rolling stock and power plants Detroit st. rys., 1899; in charge appraisal of Mich. rys., telegraphs, telephones, etc., 1900-01; assisted in appraisal mech. equipment, Newfoundland rys., 1902; cons. engr., Wis. railroad appraisal, 1903; in charge reappraisal of Mich. rys., 1903-04-05; mem. traction valuation com. Chicago, 1906; appraised Mich. telephone properties, 1907; in charge appraisal of hydro and steam electric cos. and rys. for Mich. R.R. and Utilities Commn., 1910-21; spl. investigation public utility properties in Minneapolis, Milwaukee, Cleveland, St. Louis, Boston, New York, Sault Ste. Marie, Red Wing, Buffalo, Evansville, Washington, D.C., N.J., etc., since 1906. State engr. for Mich. under Federal Pub. Works Adminstrn., 1933-34, becoming director, 1935; chmn. Mich. State Highway Advisory Bd. since 1934. Mech. expert in patent causes, 1893-1925. Chmn. Block Signal and Train Control Board, Interstate Commerce Commn., 1907-12. Mem. Engring. Com., Chicago Expn., 1893; com. on awards, Pan-Am. Expn., Buffalo, 1901; mem. advisory council Joint Commn. on Postal Service, 1920-23; pres. Am. Engring. Council, 1921-23. Mem. Gilbert Wilkes Camp No. 17, Spanish Am. War. Awarded navy service medal, Sampson, Detroit Naval Res. medal; recipient Washington Award of Western Society of Engineers. Mem. Internat. Board of Judges, Fisher Body Craftsmen's Guild, Hon. citizen, Boys Town; hon. mem. Nat. Council, Boy Scouts of America. Mem. National Committee on Independent Courts, 1937; member council National Economics League. Past mem. Am. Inst. Cons. Engrs.; fellow Am. Geog. Soc., Inst. of Am. Genealogy, Royal Soc. of Arts (London); past fellow A.A.A.S. (v.p. sect. D, 1898); hon. mem. Am. Soc. M.E. (v.p. 1902-03, pres. 1919, chmn. Detroit sect. 1916-17), Am. Soc. C.E. (dir. 1913-16), Franklin Inst., Soc. Promotion Engring. Edn. (pres. 1920-21), Mich. Engring. Soc. (pres. 1903), Nat. Assn. Power Engrs.; mem. Detroit Engring. Soc., Cooley Family Association of America (founder; pres. 1936-38), Griswold Family Assn. of America, Soc. of Descendants of Henry Wolcott, Sigma Phi, Tau Beta Pi, Sigma Xi, Phi Kappa Phi, Iota Alpha, Acacia, Aero. Soc., Vulcans, Michigamua, Scabbard and Blade, Sigma Rho Tau. Clubs: Army and Navy (Washington); Sigma Phi (New York); Detroit, Yondotega, Prismatic, Witenagemote (Detroit); University, Scientific, Town and Gown (Ann Arbor); hon. life mem. Heart o'Nature Club. Author: Cooley Genealogy. The Mortimer E. Cooley Foundation at U. of Mich. named in his honor. Home: 1405 Hill St., Ann Arbor, Mich. Died Aug. 25, 1944.

COOLEY, ROBERT ALLEN, entomologist; b. Deerfield, Mass., June 27, 1873; s. Alfred A. and Charlotte Maria C.; B.S., Mass. Agrl. Coll., 1895; studied entomology under Prof. C. H. Fernald, of Mass. Agrl. Coll.; D.Sc., Mont. State Coll., 1936; m. Edith M. Cooley, June 7, 1899 (died Aug. 1920) children—Charlotte Packard (Mrs. Gray D. Dickason), Robert Allen (dec.), Genevieve (Mrs. Kenneth M. McIver); m. 2d, Elsie Eddy Jolliffe, Aug. 13, 1925. Prof. entomology, Mont. Coll., and entomologist, Mont. Experiment Sta., 1899-1931; state entomologist, Mont., 1903-31; leader of African tick parasite expdn., 1928; entomologist U.S.P.H.S., 1931-41, sr. entomologist from 1941. Fellow A.A.A.S.; mem. Assn. Econ. Entomologists. Republican. Presbyn. Home: Hamilton MT Died Nov. 16, 1968.

COOLIDGE, EMELYN LINCOLN, pediatrist; b. Boston, Mass., Aug. 9, 1873; d. George A. and Harriet Abbot (Lincoln) Collidge; ed. pub. and pvt. schs., Boston, New York and Washington, Woman's Med. Coll., New York, and Cornell U. Med. Coll., M.D., 1900; unmarried. Engaged in practice as children's specialist since June 1900, asst. supt. Babies' Hosp., New York, 1892-1900, acting supt., 1900-01, res. phys., 1902, visiting phys. out-patient dept. same, 1903-05; pediatrist to Soc. of the Lying-In Hosp., New York, 1903-32. Conducted The Baby's Page, Ladies Home Journal, 1902-21; became editor Babies' Dept., Pictorial Review, 1921, resigned 1937; also occasional contbr. to other papers. Mem. Cornell Alumnae, Am. Child Health Assn., Authors' League, Com. of One Hundred, etc. Unitarian. Author: How to Feed the Baby from Birth to Three, 1902; The Mother's Manual, 1904; First Aid in Nursery Ailments, 1910; The Home Care of Sick Children, 1916 The Young Mother's Guide, 1916. Home: 220 W. 98th St., N.Y.C. Died Apr. 14, 1949.

COON, JOHN SAYLER, prof. mech. engring. and drawing, and supt. of shop, Ga. School of Technology, since 1889; b. Burdett, N.Y., Nov. 22, 1854; s. William Clarke and Susan (Sayler) C.; ed. Claverack Coll., and Hudson River Inst., Calverack, N.Y., grad. Cornell, 1877; spl. studies mech. engring.; m. Alice Spencer, Houston, Tex., May 23, 1888. Mem. Am. Soc. Mech. Engrs. Address: Atlanta, Ga.

COONAN, FREDERICK LEO, educator; b. Worcester, Mass., Aug. 3, 1899; s. George Henry and Margaret Agnes (Campbell) C.; A.B., Holy Cross Coll., Worcester, Mass., 1922, M.S., 1924; Sc.D., Mass. Inst. Tech., 1931; m. Anna Rita Hussey, June 12, 1933; children—Thomas George, Frederick Leo, Patricia Began as Asst. metallurigist Compton & Knowles Loom Works, Worcester; asst. prof. chemistry Holy Cross Coll. 1926-28, asso. prof., 1929-31; consultant metallurgist Arcade Malleable Iron Works, Worcester, 1929-30; became asst. prof. metallurgy and chemistry U.S. Naval Postgrad. Sch., 1931, chmn. dept. metallurgy and chemistry since 1947. Served with U.S. Army, World War I; comdr., U.S. Navy, 1941-45. AWarded silver certificate Am. Soc. for Metals. Licensed Profl. engr., Md. and Calif. Mem. Am. Soc. for Metals (chmn. ednl. com. Washington chapter), Am. Soc. Engring. Edn., Am. Soc. Profl. Engrs., Mil. Order World Wars, Sigma Xi. Clubs: Officers (Bethesda and Annapolis).Author: Principles of Physical Metallurgy, 1958. Contbr. tech. publs. Home: 1131 Sylvan Pl., Monterey, Cal. Died Nov. 30, 1961; buried St. John's Cemetery, Worcester Mass.

COONRADT, ARTHUR C., prof. mech. engring.; b. Rockford, Ill., Aug. 12, 1887; s. Arthur R. and Carrie B. (Chapin) C.; A.B. in Mech. Engring., Stanford, 1909; Aero. Engr., N.Y.U., 1928; m. Ann Rock, Apr. 17, 1911; 1 son, Frederic C. Power plant desinger Portland Electric Power Co., 1911-19; sales mgr. Grays Harbor Ry. and Light Co., 1919; dist. rep. Lidgerwood Mfg. Co., Seattle, 1920-24; power plant designer Stone & Webster Co., Seattle, 1924; instr. in mech. engring., Ore. State Coll., 1925-27; asst. prof. mech. engring., N.Y.U., later prof. Mem. Tau Beta Phi, Iota Alpha. Club: Gnome (Cal. Inst. Tech.). Home: 2120 W. 93d St., Los Angeles 47. Died Aug. 8, 1949.

COOPER, ELLWOOD, horticulturist; b. Lancaster Co., Pa., May 24, 1829; s. Morris and Phebe C.; ed. at Harmony, Pa.; m. Sarah P. Moore, Aug., 1853. Engaged in business for 10 yrs. at Port Au Prince, Hayti; for 5 yrs. in New York; went to Cal., 1870; since then in fruit culture at Santa Barbara; 1st to manufacture olive oil in U.S.; invented machines for that industry; also machines for hulling and pitting almonds and hulling and washing English Walnuts; 3 yrs. prin. Santa Barbara Coll.; pres. Cal. State Bd. of Horticulture, 1885-1903; horticultural Commr., Cal., 1903-1907. Author: Treatise on Olive Culture; Forest Culture and Eucalyptus Trees; also Statistics of trade with Hayti; Bug vs. Bug; Do Plants Think? Life History of the Author; etc. Address: Santa Barbara, Cal.

COOPER, HERMAN CHARLES, chemist; b. Glen Ellyn, Ill., Nov. 22, 1875; s. Lawrence Charles and Emma Parthenia (Yalding) C.; Ph.B., Beloit Coll., 1896; U. of Gottingen, 1896-97, Heidelberg, 1897-1900, various colls. of Paris, 1899; independent research worker, U. of Chicago, 1899-1900; m. Agnes Kent Packard, of Stratford, Conn., June 20, 1905; children—Elizabeth Packard, Lawrence Carleton, Cynthia Pamelia. Teacher chemistry, Lincoln (Neb.) High Sch., 1900-01; instr. chemistry, Syracuse U., 1901-03; research asso. phys. chemistry, Mass. Inst. Tech., 1903-04; asst. prof. chemistry, 1904-06, asso. prof., 1906-12, prof. 1912-18, Syracuse U.; asst. prof., Coll. City of New York, 1918-20; factory mgr. Acids Mfg. Corpn., 1920-22; research dir. Bauer & Black, Chicago, 1923-24; v.p. Glen Ellyn State Bank, since 1925. Mem. Am. Chem. Soc. (pres. Syracuse sect., 1909-10), Am. Electro-chem. Soc. (chmn. N.Y. sect., 1922-23, Chicago sect., 1925); Am. editor Holleman-Cooper Textbook of Inorganic Chemistry, 1902, 05, 08, 11, 16, 20, 26. Author: Laboratory Manual of Elementary Chemistry, 1917. Contbr. research monographs on physical and inorganic chemistry. Home: Glen Ellyn IL

COOPER, HUGH LINCOLN, hydraulic engr.; b. Sheldon, Minn., Apr. 28, 1865; s. George Washington and Nancy (Marion) C.; grad. High Sch., Rushford, Minn., 1883; hon. LL.D., Univ. of Mo.; Eng.D., Syracuse U. and Rensselaer Poly. Inst.; m. Frances Bliss Graves, Oct. 12, 1892; children—Agnes (Mrs. Ralph M. Sheldon), Elizabeth (Mrs. John R. Hardin, Jr.). Began bridge engring., 1883; chief engr. and supt. Chicago Bridge & Iron Co., 1890, 1891; engaged in hydraulic engring. as applied to power development for electric uses, 1891—; designed and largely built works totaling over 2,000,000 h.p. and costing over $200,000,000, in U.S. Canada, Brazil, Chile, Mexico, Russia and Egypt, the prin. begin the hydro-electric plant of the Miss. River Power Co. at Keokuk, Ia., Toronto Power Co.'s plants at Niagara Falls, Penn. Water & Power Co., at Holtwood, Pa., 620,000 h.p. water power project at Muscle Shoals. Ala., and 750,000 h.p. water power and navigation project in Ukraine, Russia. Hon. prof. civil engineering Republic of Brazil Govt. Sch. of Engineering. Republican. Conglist. Home: Stamford, Conn. Died June 24, 1937.

COOPER, JAMES GRAHAM, naturalist; b. N.Y.C., June 19, 1830; s. William and Frances (Graham) C.; grad. Coll. Physicians and Surgeons, N.Y.C., 1851; m. Rosa Wells, Jan. 9, 1866. Physician Pacific R.R. Survey Expdn., 1853-55; contract surgeon to U.S. Army; zoologist Geol. Survey of Cal.; became expert on geog. and biologic aspects of Pacific coast regions; one of 1st to collect materials and write about natural history of Cal. and Ore.; wrote chapter on Zoology for Natural Wealth of California (T. F. Cronise), 1868; practiced medicine, Santa Cruz, Cal., 1866-71; lived in Ventura Couty, Cal., 1871-75, Oakland, Cal., 1871-1902. Cooper Ornithol. Soc. named in his honor. Died July 19, 1902.

COOPER, PETER, mfr., inventor, philanthropist; b. N.Y.C., Feb. 12, 1791; s. John and Margaret (Campbell) C.; m. Sarah Beedell, Dec. 18, 1813, 6 children. Mfr. glue, N.Y.c., 1828; built Canton Iron Works, Balt., 1828; built 1st Am. steam locomotibve, 1830; promoter, financial backer laying of Atlantic Cable; rolled 1st structural iron for fireproof bldgs. in his Tenton (N.J.) factory, for which he received Bessemer gold medal award Iron and Steel Inst. of Gt. Britain, 1870; pres. N.Y., Newfoundland & London Telegraph Co., N. Am. Telegraph Co.; founder Cooper Union Coll., N.Y.C., 1857-59; Greenback Party candidate for Pres. U.S., 1876; owner foundries at Ringwood, N.J., wire factory, Trenton, rolling mill, N.Y.C.; inventor washing machine, machine for using tides as source of power. Died N.Y.C., Apr. 4, 1883.

COOPER, THEODORE, cons. engr.; b. Cooper's Plains, N.Y., Jan. 12, 1838; s. John and Elizabeth (Evans) C.; C.E., Rensselaer Poly. Inst., 1858; unmarried. Engr. officer U.S.N., 1861-72; asst. prof. Naval Acad., 1865-68; with Capt. James B. Eads, 1872, in charge mfg. and constrn. St. Louis bridge; later resident engr. in charge of its erection; engr. and supt. after its completion; later supt. Delaware Bridge Co.'s shops and asst. gen. mgr. and supt. Keystone Bridge Co.; asst. engr. in charge constrn. of the 1st elevated railroads in New York; from 1879 cons. engr. in charge of many important bridges, aqueducts, buildings, railroads shops, etc.; was one of the 5 expert engrs. selected by the President to determine the Hudson River bridge span; cons. engr. for N.Y. Pub. Library and for the Quebec bridge; mem. bd. of experts on Manhattan Bridge plan, 1903; retired. Authority on iron and steel constrn. Home: New York, N.Y. Died Aug. 24, 1919.

COOPER, THOMAS, scientist, coll. pres.; b. London, Eng., Oct. 22, 1759; s. Thomas Cooper; entered Oxford (Eng.) U., 1779; studied medicine London and Manchester; LL.D. (hon.), U.S.C., 1834, m. Alice Greenwood; m. 2d, Elizabeth Hemming, 1811; 8 children. Came to Am. in reaction to English conservative policies, 1794; convicted, sentenced and fined under Sedition Act, 1800; commr. in Luzerne County, Pa., 1801-04; state judge Pa., 1804-11; prof. chemistry Dickinson Coll., 1811-15; prof. applied chemistry and mineralogy U. Pa., 1816-19; prof. chemistry U. S.C., 1820, pres., 1821-34; influential in establishing 1st sch. medicine and 1st insane asylum in S.C., mem. Am. Philos. Soc. Author: On the Constitution, 1826; Lectures on Political Economy, 1826. Editor: Statutes at Large of South Carolina, 5 vols, 1836-39; Thomson System of Chemistry, 4 vols., 1818. Died Columbia, S.C., May 11, 1839; buried Trinity Churchyard, Columbia.

COOPER, WILLIAM ALBERT, photographer; b. London, Can., Aug. 27, 1843; ed. Union Sch., London, Ont.; studied photography under his brother, John C.; practice in St. Thomas, Ont. Studied the carbon process, London, Eng., and assisted Lambert to introduce it into America, 1876; studied photo-mech. printing with Obernetter at Munich, and in 1878 introduced the Artotype process into U.S.; studied with Guillaume, Paris, and in 1889 brought the half-tone process to America and established it in Chicago. In 1892 took up the study of reproducing paintings with "color values" and has since reproduced many private galleries. Address: 106 E. 23rd St., New York.

COPE, EDWARD DRINKER, zoologist, paleontologist; b. Phila., July 28, 1840; s. Alfred and Hanna (Edge) C.; ed. U. Pa., Phila. Acad. Scis., Smithsonian Instn.; A.M. (hon.), Haverford Coll., 1870; Ph.D. (hon.), Heidelberg (Germany) U., 1885; m. Annie Pim, Aug. 14, 1865, 1 child. Prof. comparative zoology and botany Haverford Coll., 1864-67; mem. Phila. Acad. Natural Scis., 1861, curator, 1865, mem. council, 1879; paleontologist U.S. Geol. Survey, 1870, discovered about 1000 new species extinct vertebrata; prof. geology and mineralogy U. Pa., 1889-95, prof. zoology and comparative anatomy, 1895-97, mem. Nat. Acad. Scis., A.A.A.S. (pres. 1896). Author: Synopsis of the Extinct Cetacea of the United States, 1867-68; Systematic Arrangement of the Extinct Batrachia, Reptilia and Aves of North America, 1869-70; Relation of Man to Tertiary Mammalia, 1875. Died Phila., Apr. 12, 1897.

COPE, THOMAS PYM, mcht.; b. Lancaster, Pa., Aug. 26, 1768; s. Caleb and Mary (Mendenhall) C.; m. Mary Drinker. Established 1st regular line of pact ships between Phila. and Liverpool, Eng., 1821; mem. Pa. Legislature, 1807; mem. Pa. Constl. Conv., 1837; a founder, pres. for many years Merc. Library Co., an original mem. Phila. Bd. Trade, pres., 1832-54; instrumental in completion Chesapeake & Delaware Canal; active in pioneering constrn. Pa. Central R.R.; bd. dirs. Girard Coll. Died Phila., Nov. 22, 1854.

COPELAND, ARTHUR H(ERBERT), SR., mathematician, educator; b. Rochester, N.Y., June 22, 1898; s. Albert E. and Jenny M. (Morris) C.; A.B., Amherst Coll., 1921; M.A., Ph.D., Harvard, 1926; m. Dorothy Eleanor West, June 16, 1925; 1 son, Arthur Herbert. Instr. math. Harvard, 1922-23, Rice Inst., 1924-28; asst. prof. math. U. Buffalo, 1928-29, U. Mich., 1929-37, asso. prof., 1937-42, prof. math., 1942-68, prof. emeritus, 1968-70; research worker Office Naval Research project, 1947-49, project dir., 1949-54; Guggenheim Memorial Found. fellow, 1935-36. Fellow Institute Math. Statistics; mem. Am. Math. Soc., Math. Assn. Am., Sigma Xi, Phi Beta Kappa, Phi Delta Theta. Home: Ann Arbor MI Died July 6, 1970; cremated.

COPELAND, EDWIN BINGHAM, botanist; b. Monroe, Wis., Sept. 30, 1873; s. Herbert Edson and Alice (Bingham) C.; A.B., Leland Stanford Jr. U., 1895; student Leipzig, 1895-96; Ph.D., U. of Halle, 1896; studied U. of Wis., 1896-97, 1898, U. of Chicago, 1901-02; m. Ethel Faulkner, of Chico, Calif., Dec. 19, 1900; children—Herbert Faulkner, Mary Faulkner, Alice Bingham, Charles Faulkner, John Bingham. Asst. prof. botany, Ind. U., 1897-98, State Normal Sch., Chico, Calif., 1899; asst. prof., 1899-1900, prof. botany, 1900-01, W.Va. U.; instr. botany, Stanford U., 1901-03; botanist, Philippine Govt., 1903-08; supt. Philippine Agrl. Sch., 1908-09; dean Coll. of Agr., and prof. plant physiology, U. of the Philippines, 1909-17; in charge herbarium, U. of Calif., 1928-32; established Los Banos Economic Garden, 1932; retired as dir. of same and as tech. adviser in agr., Philippine Govt., 1935. Mem. Phi Gamma Delta. Mason. Author: Philippine Agriculture, 1908; The Coco-nut, 1914; The Ferns of Borneo, 1917; Rice, 1924; Natural Conduct, 1928; Fiji Ferns, 1929; also some 140 pieces of bot. research. Home: Chico, Calif.; also Butte Meadows, Calif., and 1322 Euclid Av., Berkeley CA

COPELAND, FREDERICK KENT, engineer; b. Lexington, Mass., Aug. 22, 1855; s. Robert Morris and Josephine G. (Kent) C.; B.S. in C.E., Mass. Inst. Tech., 1876; m. Anna L. Boyd, Dec. 7, 1884; children—Margaret Boyd (Mrs. N. H. Blatchford, Jr.), Frederick W. With operating dept. C., C.,B.&Q. R.R., 1876-78; coal mining engr. in Ia., 1878-80; mining engr. in Colo., 1882-84; organized, 1884, Diamond Prospecting Co., merged, 1892, with Sullivan Machinery Co., mine and quarrying machinery (pres.). Democrat. Home: Winnetka, Ill. Died Nov. 10, 1928.

COPELAND, LENNIE PHOEBE, mathematician; b. Brewer, Me., Mar. 30, 1881; d. Lemuel and Emma (Stinchfield) Copeland; B.S., U. Me., 1904, Sc.D., 1948; M.A., Wellesley Coll., 1911; Ph.D., U. Pa., 1913. Instr. math. Wellesley Coll., 1913-20, prof., 1920-36, emeritus prof., 1946—. Pres. New Eng. Assn. Tchrs. Mathematics, 1925-27. Counselor in natural history Appalachian Mountain Club. Mem. A.A.A.S., Am. Math. Soc., Math Assn. Am., Phi Beta Kappa, Sigma Xi. Contbr. profl. jours. Home: 1190 8th St. N., St. Petersburg, Fla., Died Jan. 11, 1951; buried Bangor, Me.

COPELAND, PAUL L(AVERN), . coll. prof.; b. Holdredge, Neb., Apr. 13, 1905; s. Charles Finney and Nettie (Knowlton) C.; A.B. with honors, Neb. Wesleyan U., 1927; M.S., State Univ. of Ia., 1930, Ph.D., 1931; m. Gertrude Phelps, Jan. 1, 1929; children—John Stuart, William Charles. Instr. in physics, Mass. Inst. Tech., 1931-34; asst. prof. physics, Mont. State Coll., 1934-37; asso. prof., Armour Inst., 1937-42; prof., Ill. Inst. Tech., since 1942, chairman of department of physics since 1951. Fellow Am. Phys. Soc.; mem. Am. Assn. Physics Teachers, Electron Microscope Soc. of Am., Sigma Xi, Phi Kappa Phi. Methodist. Contbr. tech. papers to professional jours. Research in electron physics. Home: 17 W. 80 Oak Lane Dr., Bensenville, Ill. 60106. Died Dec. 21, 1964; buried Chapel Hill Gardens, Elmhurst, Ill.

COPPEE, HENRY ST. LEGER, asst. U.S. engr. in charge of U.S. levees in Miss.; b. West Point, N.Y., 1853; C.E., Lehigh Univ., 1872; engr. on rys., 1872-76; with Bethlehem (Pa.) Iron Co., 1876-78; from 1878 in U.S. Engr. Corps in improvement of rivers and harbors in Southwest; mem. Am. Soc. Civ. Engrs., and received its Roland prize, 1896, for papers on Bank Revetment on the Mississippi; mem. and State sec. for Miss. Mil. Order of Foreign Wars of the U.S. Home: Greenville, Miss. Died 1901.

COQUILLETT, DANIEL WILLIAM, entomologist; b. McHenry Co., Ill., Jan. 23, 1856; s. Francis Marquis Lafayette and Sarah Ann (Cokelet) C.; ed. dist. sch.; studied entomology and kindred sciences at home at odd moments, principally at night; married. Taught dist. sch., 1876; prepared, 1880, for Tenth Annual Rept., state entomologist of Ill., a descriptive paper on the caterpillars of U.S., with analytical keys to groups and species. Contributor on applied entomology Germantown Telegraph, 2 yrs.; asst. state entomologist of Ill., 1881, and wrote major portion Eleventh Annual Rept.; removed to Southern Calif., 1882; assisted Matthew Cooke on two works on entomology, 1883; investigated, 1885, for U.S. Dept. Agr., outbreak of destructive grasshoppers in Central Calif. and perfected method for destroying them by use of poisoned mash; also investigated for same, 1886, cottony cushion scale insect, infesting citrus trees in Southern Calif.; investigation suspended Aug. 1, 1886, for want of funds; experimented on own account with poisonous gases for destroying these and other noxious insects on trees and plants, inaugurating the hydrocyanic gas treatment; from 1887 in employ U.S. Dept. Agr.; asst. entomologist, Sept. 1893—; removed to Washington 1893; apptd., 1896, hon. custodian diptera, U.S. Nat. Museum. Died 1911.

CORBETT, LAURENCE JAY, Cons. elec. engr.; b. Saratoga, Cal., May 19, 1877 s. John Jay and Margaret Anne (Johnstone) C.; U. Ida., 1896-1900; B.S. in Elec. Engring., U. Cal., 1902; post-grad., Union Coll., Schenectady, 1903; m. Laura Gertrude Arthur, June 12, 1906; children—Ethel Jane, Arthur, Laurence. Successively with Gen. Electric Co., Schenectady, 1902-03, Union Iron Works, San Francisco, 1904, Spokane & Inland Empire (elec.) Ry., Spokane, Wash., 1905. Washington Water Power Co., Spokane 1905-06; cons. practice, Spokane, 1906-11; head dept. elec. engring. U. Ida., 1911-18; asso. prof. Mech. engring. U. Cal., 1920; engr. Pacific Gas & Electric Co. (hydro-electric and transmission div.); 1920-35; and on Pacific Coast and nat. tech. coms.; cons. elec. engr. and writer, 1935-42; engring. plan approval sect. U.S. Maritime Commn., Oakland, Cal., 1942-47, in charge deck machinery. Mem. Bd. Examiners of Architects, State of Ida., 1917-18; with Fed. Bd. for Vocational Edn., 1919. Served as capt. C.E., U.S. Army; commd. col. Engr. Res., 1931-41. Fellow A.A.A.S., mem. Am. Inst. E.E., (life), Pacific Coast Elec. Assn., Astron. Soc., Am. Mil. Engrs. (past pres. San Francisco post), Reserve Officers Assn. (pres. East Bay chpt. Ca. Cal. Dept. 1941); pres. bd. trustees for the duration). Mason (32 deg.). Club: National Writers. Author: Inductive Coordination, 1936. Contbr. to tech. press and to soc. proceedings on insulation of long transmission spans, inductive coordination, etc. Home: 1010 Shattuck Av., Berkeley 7, Cal. Died May 3, 1951.

CORBETT, LEE CLEVELAND, horticulturist; b. Watkins, N.Y., Oct. 21, 1867; s. J. Wallace and Lucia M. C.; B.S., Cornell, 1890, M.S., 1896; D.Agr., U. of Md., 1921; m. Evelyn L. Northrup, Mar. 23, 1893 (died 1931); children—Ruth Eleanor, Frances Lee (Mrs. Colston E. Warne), Roger Bailey, Laurence Ward, Thurston Lee; m. 2d, C. Louise Phillips, Feb. 22, 1936. Asst. horticulturist, Cornell, 1891-93; prof. horticulture and forestry, S.D. Agrl. Coll., 1893-95, W.Va. U., 1895-1901; horticulturist, U.S. Dept. Agr., 1901-13; asst. chief, Bur. Plant Industry, U.S. Dept. Agr., 1913-15; in charge hort. and pomol. investigations, U.S. Dept. Agr., 1915-29, prin. horticulturist; retired. Del. Internat. Inst. Agr., Rome, 1920. Author: Garden Farming, Intensive Farming. Also Agrl. Expt. Sta. bulls. of Cornell U., S.D., W.Va., and U.S. Dept. Agr., and articles in yearbook of latter. Home: Washington, D.C. Died July 13, 1940.

CORBIN, HENRY PINKNEY, civil engr.; b. Franklin, N.C., Oct. 5, 1867; s. Harvey Leander and Lucinda Hasseltine (Brendle) C.; ed. pub. schs.; m. Lulu Hannah White, June 1, 1899. Served as surveyor and engr. various irrigation projects in Colo.; owner 2 live stock ranches in Colo.; mem. Dem. State Central Com., Colo., 1898-04; presdl. elector, 1912; cons. engr. Internat. Boundary Commn., U.S. and Mexico, Oct. 7, 1914—. Baptist. Mason. Home: Foxton, Colo. Died Feb. 1922.

CORBUS, BUDD CLARKE surgeon; b. La Salle, Ill., July 22, 1876; s. Dr. Josephus R. and Sarah Angle) C.; M.D., Coll. Phys. and Surg., Chicago, 1901; m. Gertrude Pitkin, Dec. 15, 1903; (died July 1915); 1 son, Budd Clarke; m. 2d, Ruth Bent Dec. 22, 1917; children—William Godfrey, Josephus R. Mem. house staff Alexian Brothers' Hosp., 1902-03; practiced Chgo. since 1903; now in research cancer with H. T. Davis, Northwestern U. Certified by American Board of Urology. Fellow American College Surgeons; mem. A.M.A., Am. Urol. Assn., Chicago Med. Soc., Chicago Urol. Soc. Republican Conglist. Author: Diathermy in Genito-Urinary Diseases with Special Reference to Cancer (with V. J. O'Conor), 1925. Collaborator Cabot's American Textbook on Urology, History of Urology. Contbr. to med. jours. Home: 1415 Grove St., Evanston, Ill. Died Nov. 6, 1954; buried Graceland Cemetery, Chgo.

CORCORAN, GEORGE FRANCIS educator, author; b. Redfield, S.D., Sept. 26, 1900; s. George Francis, Sr., and Louise (Haag) C.; B.S., S.D. State College, 1923, Doctor of Science (honorary), 1962; M.S., U. of Minn., 1926; student University of Mich., summer 1937; m. Mary L. Kerr, June 28, 1962. Teaching fellow, U. of Minn. 1925-26; instr., Kan. State Coll., 1927-28; asso. prof., State U. of Iowa, 1931-39, prof. of elec. engring., 1939-41; prof. of elec. engineering and chairman of the department, University of Maryland, 1941-63; consultant Am. Council on Edn.; cons. elec. engr. in Washington-Baltimore area. Registered Profl. engr. Fellow Am. Institute E.E. (recipient nat. educational award 1961), Inst. Radio Engrs.; member Am. Society Engring. Edn., Am. Assn. U. Profs., Sigma Xi, Phi Kappa Phi, Tau Beta Pi. Sigma Tau, Eta Kappa Nu, Sigma Alpha Epsilon. Author: Basic Electrical Engineering 1949; Alternating Current Circuits (with R. M. Kerchner), 1950; Electrical Communications Expts. (with H.R. Reed and T. C. G. Wagner), 1952; Electronics (with H. W. Price), 1954; Electrical Engineering (with H.R. Reed), 1957. Adv. editor for pub. houses. Research worker in the field of active network analysis and synthesis. Home: 604 Palm Av., Belleair, Clearwater, Fla. 33516. Died June 24, 1964; buried Hollywood Cemetery, Richmond, Va.

CORDES, FREDERICK CARL, educator, physician; b. San Francisco, June 12, 1892; s. Frederick and Marie (Schwilk) C.; A.B., U. Cal., 1914, M.D., 1918, LL.D., Sch. Medicine, 1962; m. Faun Hope Lancaster, Sept. 4, 1920 (div.); children—Virginia Virginia Dayle, Fauno Lancaster. Engaged in pvt. practice, specializing in ophthalmology, 1919—; chmn. div. ophthalmology, Med. Sch., U. Cal., 1934-59, clin. prof. ophthalmology 1934—. Civilan cons. in ophthalmology to surgeon gen. U.S. Army, 1943—. to surgeon gen. U.S. Navy, 1946—. cons. ophthalmology Cal. Bd. Pub. Health, 1949-53; cons. Nat. Soc. for Prevention Blindness, 1949, bd. dirs., 1955-57; mem. Nat. Interprofl. Com. on Eye Care, 1951-54; Asso. chief examiner Nat. Bd. Med. Exaniners, 1948-54; dir. ophthalmic Pub. Co. Trustee Heed Ophthalmic Found., Francis I. Proctor, Found. for Research in Ophthalmology, 1954. Recipient Howe medal, eye sect. A.M.A., 1960. Mem. Am. Bd. Ophthalmology (chmn. 1949); mem. sub.-com. ophthalmology NRC, 1953-58; mem. Eye Research Fund, 1954—; adv. com. Variety Club for Blind Babies (chmn. 1955); adv. bd. K.T. Eye Found., 1956. Pres., Pacific Coast Oto-Ophthalmol. Soc., 1939, Assn. for Research in Ophthalmology, 1944; adv. bd. Pan-Am. Congress of Ophthalmology, 1955; mem. exec. com Internat. Congress Ophthalmology, 1954. Recipient Leslie Dana Gold medal, 1961. Fellow A.C.S. (adv. council ophthalmology 1956, mem. bd. regents

1957-59, 60-62); mem. A.M.A. (chmn. sect. ophthal. 1945), Cal. Med. Soc. (chmn. sect. ophthal. 1930), Am. Ophthal. Soc. (pres. 1956), Am. Acad. Ophthalmology and Otology (pres. 1953), San Francisco Opthal. Round Table (pres. 1950), San Francisco Med. Soc. (press cons. panel 1955 Am. Com. on Optics and Visual Physiology, Nu Sigma Nu, Alpha Chi Rho. Asso. editor Am. Jour. Ophthalmology, 1929—; editorial bd. Archives Ophthalmology, 1944—, Cal. Medicine. Clubs: Bohemian Club, San Francisco. Office: 384 Post St., San Francisco 8. Died Apr. 4, 1965; buried Cyress Lawn Cemetery, Coloma, Cal.

COREY, ROBERT BRAINARD, chemist; b. Springfield, Mass., Aug. 19, 1897; s. Fred Brainard and Caroline Louise (Heberd) C.; Ch.B., University of Pittsburgh, 1919, Doctor of Science (honorary), 1964; Ph.D., Cornell, 1924; m. Dorothy Gertrude Paddon, July 7, 1930. Instr. analytical chemistry, Cornell, 1923-28; asst. in biophysics, Rockefeller Inst. Med. Research, 1928-30, asso., 1930-37; research fellow, Calif. Inst. Tech., 1937-38, sr. research fellow in structural chemistry, 1938-46, research asso., 1946-49, professor of structural chemistry, from 1949; civilian with the OSRD, 1942-45, Bureau of Ordnance, U.S. Navy, 1945-46. Fellow John Simon Guggenheim Found., 1951-53. Member Nat. Acad. Scis., Am. Chemical Soc., A.A.A.S., Am. Crystallog. Assn., Sigma Xi, Phi Kappa Phi, Phi Lambda Upsilon, Alpha Chi Sigma. Contbr. articles to scientific jours. Home: Pasadena CA Died Apr. 23, 1971; buried Glenwood Cemetery, Homer NY

CORI, GERTY THERESA RADNITZ, biochemist; b. Prague, Czechoslovakia, Aug. 15, 1896; d. Otto and Martha (Neustadt) Radnitz; grad. Realgymnasium of Tetschen, Czechoslovakia, 1914; M.D., German U. Prague Med. Sch., 1920, Sc.D., Boston U., 1948, Smith Coll., 1949, Yale, 1951, Columbia, 1954; m. Carl F. Cori, Aug. 5, 1920; 1 son, C. Thomas. Came to U.S., 1922, naturalized, 1928. Asst., Children's Hosp., Vienna, 1920-22; asst. biochemist State inst. for Study Malignant Diseases, Buffalo, 1922-31; research Asso. Washington U. Med. Sch., 1931-47, prof. biol. chemistry, 1947-57, Mem. adv. bd. NSF. Recipient Midwest award Am. Chem. Soc., 1946; Squibb award in endocrinology, 1947; Nobel prize in medicine, and Physiology (with C. F. Cori and B. A. Houssay), 1947; Garvan medal, 1948; Sugar research prize Nat. Acad. Scis., 1950; Borden award Assn. Med. Colls. Mem. Nat. Acad. Sci., Am. PHilos. Soc., Am. Soc. Biol. Chemists, Harvey Soc., Am. Chem. Soc., Sigma Xi. Research (with husband) in carbohydrate metabolism, especially discovery of glycolysis in live tumors, isolation (1936) of glucose-phosphate (Cori ester), which led to discovery of course of catalytic conversion of glycogen to glucose by means of phosphorylase (Nobel prize 1947); also immunological study of complement of human serum; research into mechanism of action of hormones (particularly pituitary). Died St. Louis, Oct. 26, 1957.

CORIAT, ISADOR HENRY, psychiatrist, neurologist; b. Phila., Pa., Dec. 10, 1875; s. Harry and Clara (Einstein) C.; prep. edn. high sch., Boston; M.D., Tufts Coll. Med. Sch., 1900; spl. student in philosophy, Harvard, 1909-10; m. Etta Dann, Feb. 1, 1904. Asst. and 1st asst. phys., Worcester Insane Hosp., 1900-05; neurol. staff Boston City Hosp., 1905-19; neurologist, Mt. Sinai Hosp., 1905-14; cons. neurologist Chelsea Memorial and Beth—Israel hosps., 1919-28; neuropsychiatrist Forsyth Dental Infirmary, 1913-29; instr. neurology, Tufts Coll. Med. Sch., 1914-16. Instructor; mem. training com. and training analyst, Boston Psychoanalytic Inst. Neruologist Med. Advisory Bd., World War; contract surgeon in neuropshchiatry, U.S. Army, 1917. Fellow A.M.A., Mass. Med. Sco., Boston Med. Library, Am. Psychiatric Assn.; mem. Am. Psycho-Pathol. Assn. (v.p. 1931-32), N.E. Soc. Psychiatry, Internat. Psycholoanalytic Assn. (v.p. 1936-37), Boston Med. History Club, Mass. Psychiatric Soc., Am. Psychoanalytic Assn. (pres. 1924-25 and 1936-37; v.p. 1935-36), Boston Soc. Neurology and Psychiatry, Boston Psychoanalytic Soc. (pres. 1930-32 and 1941-42), Jewish Acad. of Arts and Sciences, Am. Bd. Psychiatry and Neurology; hon. mem. Tau Epsilon Phi. Collaborating editor Journal of Abnormal Psychology, 1906-26; now same Psychoanalytic Review; collaborator for psychoanalytic terms for Dictionary of Psychology. Republican. Mason. Author: A Laboratory Manual of Clinical and Physiological Chemistry (with Dr. A.E. Austin), 1898; Religion and Medicine (with Drs. Worcester and McCoomb), 1908; Abnormal Psychology, 1910, 2d edit., 1914; The Hysteria of Lady Macbeth, 1912, 2d edit., 1919; The Meaning of Dreams, 1915; What Is Psychoanalysis?, 1917; Repressed Emotions, 1920; Stammering, 1928; also monographs and articles on nervous and mental diseases, psychopathology and psychoanalysis. Address: 416 Marlboro St., Boston, Mass. Died May 26, 1943.

CORK, JAMES M., physicist; b. Yale, Mich., July 9, 1894; s. George M. and Jennie (Lee) C.; B.S., University of Michigan 1916, M.S., 1917, Ph.D., 1921; m. Laurie Kaufmann, 1918; children—Janet Lee (wife of Dr. John C. Wahr), James A. Asst. physics, Penn. State College, 1919-20; instr. physics, U. of Mich., 1920-25; Asst. prof. 1926-31, asso. prof. 1932-37, prof. since 1937, exchange prof., Victoria U., Manchester Eng., 1926-27; consultant Argonne National Laboratory, 1950, Served as lieut. Signal Corps, U.S. Army, 1918. Mem. National Defense Research Com., 1942-45. Fellow Am. Physical Society, A.A.A.S.; member Washington Philos. Soc. Sigma Xi, Gamma Alpha. Author: Pyrometry (with W. P. Wood), 1927, 1941; Heat 1933, 1942; Radioactivity and Nuclear Physics, 1946, 1957. Contbr. articles to tech. jours. on heat, X-rays and radioactivity. Home: 2034 Day St., Ann Arbor, Mich. Died Nov. 27, 1957; buried Forest Hills Cemetery, Ann Arbor.

CORLETT, WILLIAM THOMAS, physician; b. Orange, O., Apr. 15, 1854; s. William and Ann (Avery) C.; ed. Oberlin Coll., 1870-73; M.D., Wooster Univ., 1877; student and intern London Hosp., 1879-81, Hopital St. Louis, Paris, France, 1881; diploma Royal Coll. Phys., London, 1881; later studied in Vienna, Berlin and Breslau; m. Amanda Marie Leisy, June 26, 1895; children—Christine L. (Mrs. Horace F. Henriques), Ann E. (Mrs. Daniel B. Ford), Helen A., Edward L. Prof. diseases of the skin and genito-urinary diseases, Wooster U., 1883-85; prof. dermatology and syphilology, Western Reserve U., 1885-1914, sr. prof., 1914-24, emeritus prof. since 1924. Fellow Royal Soc. of Medicine (Great Britain), A.A.A.S., A.M.A.; mem. Am. Dermatol. Assn. (hon. mem., pres. 1905), Am. Acad. Dermatology and Syphilology (hon.); corr. mem. British Assn. Dermatology and Syphilology. Clubs: Union, Kirtland. Author: Treatise on the Acute Infectious Exanthemata, 1901; The American Tropics, 1908; The People of Orrisdale and Others, 1918; Early Reminiscences, 1920. Wrote: The , Morrow's System of Dermatology, etc.), 1894; The Vegetable Parasitic Diseases of the Skin (in Bangs and Hardaway's American Text-Book of Genito-Urinary Diseases, etc.), 1898; Purpura, Pompholyx and Pellagra, in Reference Handbook of the Medical Sciences, 1903; also on Lichen, Lentigo, Granuloma, Annulare in 1915 edition; The Medicine-Man of the American Indian and His Cultural Background, 1935. Also articles on diseases of the skin in leading Am. and foreign jours. Home: 11015 East Blvd., Cleveland. Died June 11, 1948.

CORLISS, GEORGE HENRY, inventor, mfr.; b. Easton, N.Y., June 2, 1817; s. Dr. Hiram and Susan (Sheldon) C.; attended Castelton Acad., 1835-38; m. Phoebe F. Frost, Jan. 1839; m. 2d, Emily A. Shaw, 1866. Invented machine for sewing boots (as a result of customer's complaints), patented 1842; joined firm Fairbanks, Bancroft & Co., 1844; invented improvements for steam engines, patented 1849; merged John Barstow and E.J. Nightingale Co. into Corliss, Nightingale & Co., 1849; incorporated, became pres. Corliss Engine Co., 1856; mem. R.I. Legislature, 1868-70; built Corliss steam engine (1st to use rotary valves); patented gear cutting machine, an improved boiler with condensing machine, an improved boiler with condensing apparatus, pump engine for water-works. Died Providence, R.I., Feb. 21, 1888.

CORNELL, EZRA, telegraph magnate, philanthropist; b. Westchester, N.Y., Jan. 11, 1807; s. Elijah and Eunice (Barnard) C.; m. Mary Ann Wood, Mar. 19, 1831, 1 son, Alonzo B. Worked in flour and plaster mills of J. S. Beebe, Ithaca, N.Y., 1828-41, became gen. mgr.; with Samuel F. B. Morse devised means for insulating telegraph wires on poles and helped erect line from Balt. to Washington, D.C.; owned cos. bldg. lines between many major cities in East and Midwest, including Magnetic Telegraph Co., Erie & Mich. Telegraph Co., N.Y. & Erie Telegraph Co., merged with competing lines to form Western Union Telegraph Co., dir., 1855-74, largest stockholder until 1870; built free pub. library, Itahca, 1863, model farm, nr. Ithaca; pres. N.Y. State Agrl. Soc., 1862; mem. N.Y. State Assembly, 1861-63, N.Y. State Senate, 1863-67; founded, endowed Cornell U., 1868, provided for edn. of women and poor students in liberal and mech. arts. Died Dec. 9, 1874.

CORNING, FREDERICK GLEASON, mining engr.; b. Brooklyn, Mar. 27, 1857; s. Rev. James Leonard and Sarah Ellen (Deming) C.; ed. Realschule, Stuttgart, Germany, Stuttgart, Poly. Royal Sch. of Mines, Freiberg, 4 1/2 years, M.E., 1879; LL.D., U. of Pittsburgh, 1911; m. Marion Adeline Vernon, June 18, 1891. Practiced as mining engr. and metallurgist in U.S., Central and S. America and Can.; from 1897 has been at head of cos. operating gold and silver mines in Mexico, S.A. and Can. Pres. The Exploration Co. of New York. Hon. senator in Freiberg Mining Acad. Home: New York, N.Y. Died July 12, 1937.

CORNING, J(AMES) LEONARD, neurologist; b. Stamford, Conn., Aug. 26, 1855; s. Rev. James Leonard and Sarah Ellen (Deming) C.; bro. of Frederick Gleason C.; ed. Riverview Mil. Acad., Poughkeepsie, N.Y.; U. of Heidelberg; M.D., U. of Würzburg, 1878; (hon. A.M., Williams Col., 1888; LL.D.); m. Julia Crane, May 12, 1883. Discoverer spinal anaesthesia, 1885; demonstrated that the action of certain medicinal substances, notably stimulants and sedatives, may be increased and prolonged while subject remains in compressed air; also first to inject liquid paraffin into the tissues and solidify it in loco; consultant in nervous and mental diseases to various hosps., New York. Author: Carotid Compression, 1882; Brain Rest, 1883, Brain Exhaustion; Local Anaesthesia, 1886; Hysteria and Epilepsy, 1888; A Treatise on Headache and Neuralgia, 1888; Pain in Its Neuro-Pathological and Neuro-Therapeutic Relations, 1894. Died Aug. 24, 1923.

CORNISH, LORENZO DANA, civil engr.; b. Lee Centre, N.Y., Mar. 30, 1877; s. James Bennett and Frances Emeline (Ward) C.; C.E., Syracuse U., 1902; m. Mary Elizabeth Brodhead, Jan. 15, 1901 (died 1911); 1 son, Eugene Brodhead; m. 2d, Jeanette Welsh, May 18, 1916. Jr. U.S. civ. engr. and supt. constn., at Pittsburgh, 1902-06; asst. engr. Internat. Consulting Bd. Panama Canal, 1906; designing engr. Isthmian Canal Commn., 1907-13; prin. asst. engr. Am. Red Cross Bd. Engrs., China, 1914; prin. U.S. engr., U.S. Engr. Dept., Cincinnati, O., 1915-17; asst. chief engr., 1919, became chief engr., 1928, Div. of Waterways, State of Ill., building Waterways, Lockport to LaSalle. Served as pvt. Co. C, 3d N.Y. Vols., June-Oct. 1898; capt. 15th Engrs., U.S.A., June 11, 1917-Feb. 13, 1919; maj. Feb. 13-Oct. 30, 1919; hon. disch. Oct. 30, 1919. Republican. Baptist. Home: Chicago, Ill. Died May 12, 1934.

CORNWALL, BEDINGER, chemist; b. Southport, Conn., July 29, 1844; s. Rev. Nathaniel Ellsworth and Susan Peyton Ellsworth (Bedinger) C.; A.B., Columbia, 1864, A.M., 1867, E.M., 1867 Ph.D., 1888; student Royal Acad. Mining, Freiberg, 1866-68; (hon. A.M., Princeton U., 1896); m. Mary Hall Porter, June 3, 1875. Asst. gen. chemistry and metallurgy, 1864-66, asst. gen. chemistry, 1868-70, Columbia; supt. mining co. in Mexico, 1870-71; prof. applied chemistry and mineralogy, 1873-1910 (emeritus), Princeton U. Author: A Manual of Blow-Pipe Analysis, 1882; etc. Died Apr. 1, 1917.

CORRIGAN, SEVERINUS JOHN, astronomer, physicist; b. Troy, N.Y., Jan. 8, 1852; s. John and Ann C.; family removed to St. Paul, Minn., 1862; ed. Troy, N.Y., St. Paul, Minn., Cape Girardeau, Mo., and Collegeville, Minn.; St. Paul Minn., m. Helena C. Birmingham, Sept. 2, 1884. Studied law several yrs. in St. Paul; then studied natural sciences 6 yrs.; especially astronomy, physics, chemistry and geology; asst. in office of Am. Ephemeris and Nautical Almanac Bureau of Navigation, U.S. Navy Dept., 1879-87; made spl. studies in electrical science; advanced new Kinetic theory of gases. Author: The Constitution and Function of Gases, the Nature of Radiance and the Law of Radiation (3 parts), 1895-97; Pioneer Press Co., St. Paul. Has contributed numerous papers of original research in astronomy and physics to tech. jounals. Address: 475 Hopkins St., St. Paul, Minn.

CORSE, WILLIAM MALCOLM, metall. and chem. engr.; b. Malden, Mass., May 25, 1878; s. William Alexander and Genevieve Hancock (Alexander) C.; grad. high sch., Medford, Mass., 1895; S.B., Mass. Inst. Tech., 1899; m. Edith Wright Bell, June 4, 1902 (died 1923); 1 dau., Margaret Bell (Mrs. Richard Southwick Burr); m. 2d, Ruth Winifred Albert, Sept. 20, 1924. Began as chemist for William S. Merrell Chemical Co., Cincinnati, O., 1899; with Detroit (Mich.) White Lead Works, 1900-02; chemist, foundry supt. and asst. supt., Detroit Lubricator Co., 1902-06; asst. gen. mgr. Mich. Smelting & Refining Co., Detroit, 1907; works mgr. Lumen Bearing Co., Buffalo, N.Y., 1908-12; gen. mgr. Empire Smelting Co., Depew, N.Y., 1913, and for Titanium Bronze Co., Niagara Falls, 1914-18; mfg. supt. Ohio Brass Co., Mansfield, O., 1918; gen. mgr. Monel Products Co., Bayonne, N.J., 1919-22; with Nat. Research Council, Washington, D.C., 1922-24; cons. metallurgist, Washington, since 1925. Special duty and brass foundry practice, at Portsmouth (N.H.) Navy Yard, 1918. Sec. Am. Institute of Metals (A.I.M.E.) for 25 years, treas. 30 yrs., and ex-pres. sec. trustees Internat. Critical Tables; sec. Advisory Com. on Non-Ferrous Alloys to Bur. of Standards 21 yrs.; mem. Am. Inst. Mining and Metall. Engrs., Am. Inst. Chem. Engrs., Am. Chem. Soc., Am. Soc. for Metals, Am. Soc. for Naval Engrs., Electrochem. Soc., Soc. Am. Mil. Engrs., Army Ordnance Assn., U.S. Naval Inst., Washington Acad. Sciences, S.A.R., Soc. Colonial Wars; hon. corr. mem. on Council of Inst. of Metals of Gt. Britain. Republican. Conglist. Clubs: Cosmos, Arts, Burning Tree (Washington); Rotary (Keene, N.H.); Chemists (New York); Lake Placid (Lake Placid, N.Y.). Author: Bearing Metals and Bearings. Home: Westmoreland, N.H. Office: 810 18th St. N.W. Washington. Died June 3, 1944; buried in Woodlawn Cemetery, Everett, Mass.

CORTHELL, ARTHUR BATEMAN, civil engr.; b. Whitman, Mass., July 3, 1860; s. James Hosea and Charlotte (Almy) C.; ed. Providence High Sch., 1875-77; Brown U., 1877-81 (hon. A.M., 1898); m. Lena Cynthia Foster, Sept. 26, 1882. Draftsman with Hereshoff Mfg. Co., Bristol, R.I., 1878-81; rodman, city engineer's office, Providence, Mar.-June 1881; again with Hereshoff Mfg. Co., June-Sept. 1881; asst. engr., supervisor and div. engr., N.Y., West Shore & Buffalo R.R., 1881-84; civ. engr. Knickerbocker Ice Co., New York, 1884-86; prin. asst. engr., Fitzgerald & Mallory Construction Co., building railroads for M.P. Ry., in Kans. and Colo., 188687; 1st asst. engr. constrn. Sioux City Bridge over Missouri River, 1887-88; asst. engr. on Thames River bridge, 1888-89, N.Y., Providence & Boston R.R., 1889-92; 1st asst. engr. Providence passenger sta. and approaches, 1892-97; prin. asst. engr.

on constrn. South Sta. for Boston Terminal Co., Boston, 1897-99; with Westinghouse, Church, Kerr & Co., Boston, 1899-1900; resident engr. Boston Terminal Co., 1900-02; terminal engr. N.Y.C.&H.R. R.R., at New York, 1902-06; asst. exec. Grand Central Sta. architects, 1906-08; sec. and cons. engr. auxiliary facilities com., Grand Central Terminal, 1908-11; chief engr. B.&M. R.R., July, 1911—. Mason. Home: Winchester, Mass. Died May 1924.

CORTHELL, ELMER LAWRENCE, civil engr.; b. S. Abington (now Whitman), Mass., Sept. 30, 1840; s. James Lawrence C.; A.B., Brown U., 1867, A.M., 1868 (Sc.D., 1894); m. Emily T. Davis, 1867 (died 1884); m. 2d, Marie Küchler (b. Switzerland), 1900. Served pvt. to capt. of battery 1st R.I. Light Arty., 1861-65; began civil engring. Providence, 1867; served on ry. surveys and constrn., Ill. and Mo.; chief engr. bridges over Mississippi River, Hannibal and Louisiana, Mo.; also levees on Miss.; resident engr. in constrn. Mississippi jetties with James B. Eads; chief engr. Atlantic & Pacific Ship Ry., to build ship ry. over Isthmus of Tehuantepec, Mex., with Capt. Eads; chief engr. contrn. N.Y., West Shore & Buffalo Ry.; cons. engr. bldg. rys. into Chicago; asso. chief engr. several large bridges over Mo., Ohio and other rivers; chief engr. Merchants Bridge, St. Louis, Brazos River jetties, Tex., Tampico Harbor Works, Mex.; consulting engr. Nat. Pub. Works Argentine Govt., 1900-02; mem. advisory bd. of engrs., 1903-05, to build 1,000-ton barge canals, N.Y. State, to cost over $100,000,000; chief engr. Port of Para, Brazil, and Rio Grande do Sul. Contbr. articles Jetties, Levees, Ship Canals, Ship Railways, etc., in Johnson's Cyclopedia; Railway Passenger Stations of the World, in Ency. Americans, 1904, etc. Home: North Egremont, Mass. Died May 16, 1916.

CORY, CHARLES BARNEY, ornithologist; b. Boston, Jan. 31, 1857; s. Barney and Eliza A. B. C.; ed. Boston schs. and Lawrence Scientific Sch. (Harvard), 1879; m. Harriet W. Peterson, May 29, 1883. Hon. curator of ornithology, Boston Soc. Natural History until 1905; hon. curator of ornithology, 1895-1906, prof. and hon. curator dept. zoölogy, 1906—, Field Mus. Natural History, Chicago. Pres. Am. Ornithologists' Union, 1904-05; fellow Zoöl. and Linnean socs. London. Author: Catalogue of West Indian Birds; Hunting and Fishing in Florida; The Birds of Eastern North America; How to Know the Shore Birds of North America; How to Know the Ducks, Geese and Swans of North America; The Birds of the West Indies; Key to the Water Birds of Florida; Hunting and Fishing in Florida; Key to the Birds of Eastern North America; The Birds of Illinois and Wisconsin. Home: Chicago, Ill. Died July 29, 1921.

CORY, CLARENCE LINUS, electrical engr.; b. Lafayette, Ind., Sept. 4, 1872; s. Thomas and Carrie (Stoney) C.; B.M.E., Purdue U., 1889, E.D., 1914; M.E., Cornell, 1891; m. Mayme Pritchard, Dec. 25, 1905; 1 dau., Marion Elizabeth. Prof. elec. engring. Highland Park College, Des Moines, Ia., 1891-92; prof. elec. engring., 1892—, and dean Coll. Mechanics, 1901—, U. of Calif. In practice as cons. elec. and mech. engr., San Francisco, Jan. 1, 1899—. Asst. dir. U.S. explosive plants, in charge of elec. power supply, 1917-18. Home: Berkeley, Calif. Died Aug. 2, 1937.

CORY, HARRY THOMAS, engineer; b. Lafayette, Ind., May 27, 1870; s. Thomas and Carrie (Stoney) C.; B.M.E., Purdue U., 1887 (first to receive degree in electrical engineering), B.C.E., 1889, Dr. Engring., 1929; M.C.E., Cornell, 1893, M.M.E., 1896; m. Ida (Judd) Hiller, Oct. 4, 1911; children—Thomas Judd, Clarence Richard and John Harry (twins, both dec.). Asst. engr. A.&M. Ry., 1888; asst. city engr. Lafayette, Ind., 1889; dep. county engr. Tippecanoe County, Ind., 1890-92; prof. civ. engring., U. of Mo., 1893-98; in Europe, 1898; prof. civ. and sanitary engring., U. of Mo., 1898-1900; dean Coll. of Engring. and prof. civ. engring., U. of Cincinnati, 1900-03; on leave of absence, 1901-03, with Mex. Central, Tex. & Pacific and S.P. railroads; asst. to gen. mgr. S.P. Co., July 1904-May 1905; in personal charge of diverting Colo. River from running to Salton Sea, 1906-07; asst. to pres. associated Harriman lines in Ariz. and S.P.R.R. in Mex., May 1905-Apr. 1911; gen. mgr. and chief engr. of the Calif. Development Co. and La Sociedad de Riego y Terrenos de la Baja California, April 1906-Dec. 1910; consulting engr. at San Francisco, 1909-17; dir. gen. foreign relief, Am. Red Cross nat. hdqrs., 1917-18; cons. engr. of U.S. Reclamation Service on soldier's land settlement plan, 1918-20; Am. mem. Internat. Nile Projects Commn. for the Egyptian and Sudanese govts., Cairo, Egypt, and Khartum, Sudan, Jan.-Sept. 1920; cons. engr. San Francisco, Calif., 1920-21; cons. engr. Los Angeles, Calif., and also for the U.S. Reclamation service, 1921-23; chief of engring. Palos Verdes project, Redondo Beach, Calif., 1922-24; chief engr. Guadalquivir marismas desalting and irrigation project, Seville, Spain, 1925-27; cons. engr. Muluya Valley irrigation project. French and Spanish Morocco, 1926; cons. engr. Los Angeles, Calif., since 1928; advisory engr. Los Angeles Agency, R.F.C., 1932-34; advisory com. on R.F.C. earthquake rehabilitation loans, 1933-34; mem. Passamaquoddy Bay Tidal Power Project Commn., 1934-35; cons. engr. Soil Conservation Service, U.S. Dept. Agr., Albuquerque, N.M., and Washington, D.C., 1935-40, supervising engineer, Defense Plant Corp., U.S. Govt., 1941-42; manager Los Angeles Office Bureau of Economic Warfare, 1942-43; consulting engr., Los Angeles, Calif., since 1943. Member Laymen's Advisory Council of National Conference of Jews and Christians. Life member American Society C.E. (Thomas Fitch Rowland prize 1914), Phi Delta Theta, Theta Nu Epsilon, Sigma Xi, Tau Beta Pi, Chi Epsilon, Kappa Phi Sigma. Mason (K.T., 32 deg., Shriner). Clubs: Bohemian (San Francisco); University, Los Angeles Athletic (Los Angeles). edn., (with T. Cory) Manual of U.S. System of Land Surveying, 1888; Imperial Valley and Salton Sink, 1915; Democratization of Family Planning, 1940; also atlases of Boone (1888), Clay (1890) and Tippecanoe (1892) counties, Ind. Contbr. tech. reports, scientific papers and mag. articles. Home: Los Angeles Athletic Club. Office: 431 W. 7th St., Los Angeles CA

CORYELL, CHARLES DUBOIS, chemist; b. Los Angeles, Feb. 21, 1912; s. William Harlan and Florence Elizabeth (Cook) C.; B.S., Calif. Inst. Tech., 1932, Ph.D., 1935; m. Meta Patricia Seward, Dec. 6, 1930 (div. 1936); 1 daughter, Patricia Louise Huber; m. 2d, Grace Seeley, Dec. 2, 1937 (dec. May 1965); dau., Julie Esther; m. 3d, Barbara Buchman, Mar. 30, 1969. Research asst. Calif. Inst. Tech., 1935-38; instr. chemistry Deep Springs Jr. Coll., Deep Springs, Calif., 1937-39; mem. staff, chemistry dept. U. of Calif. at Los Angeles, instr., 1938-40, asst. prof., 1940-44, asso. prof., 1944-45 (on leave, 1942-45); chief fission products sect., Metall. Lab., U. of Chicago, 1942-43, Clinton Labs., Oak Ridge, Tenn., 1943-46; prof. chemistry Mass. Inst. Tech., 1946-71. Consultant to AEC Laboratories, 1946-71. Louis Lipsky fellow Weizmann Inst. Science, Rehovoth Israel, 1953-54. Mem. board inc. Midwest Bus. Inst., Utopia Coll., 1947-68; mem. adv. bd. Williams-Waterman Fund, 1947-68; trustee Windham Coll., 1963-71, Mark Hopkins Coll., 1966-71. Guggenheim fellow, Fulbright lectr., Paris, 1963. Fellow Am. Nuclear Soc., Council for A Livable World, Am. Acad. Arts and Scis., Am. Phys. Soc., Am. Association for Advancement of Science; mem. Am. Chem. Soc., United World Federalists, Internat. Sci. Found., Fedn. Am. Scientists, Sigma Xi, Tau Beta Pi. Author numerous articles for sci. publs. Editor: Radiochemical Studies: The Fission Products, 1951. Home: Lexington MA Died Jan. 7, 1971.

COSBY, SPENCER, army officer; b. Baltimore Oct. 2, 1867; s. Frank C. and Charlotte M. (Spencer) C.; prep. edn. high sch., Washington, and 3 yrs. in France; grad. U.S. Mil. Acad., 1st in class, 1891; grad. U.S. Engr. Sch. of Application, 1894; m. Yvonne Shepard of Washington, Sept. 15, 1909. Apptd. additional 2d lt. engrs., June 12, 1891; 2d lt., Apr. 12, 1894; 1st lt., Oct. 13, 1895; maj. engrs. U.S.V., June 13, -Dec. 31, 1898; capt., Feb. 2, 1901; maj., June 9, 1907; lt. col., Feb. 28, 1915; col., Aug. 5, 1917. In Charge of river and harbor and fortification works, Phila., Mobile and Washington; engr. officer on staff Maj.-Gen. Brooke in P.R. during Spanish-Am. War; in charge lighthouse constrn. in P.I., 1903-05; in charge watersupply system, Washington, 1905-09; in charge pub. bldgs. and grounds, Washington with rank of col., Mar. 15, 1909-13; mil. attaché, U.S. Embassy, Paris, 1913-17; comdg. 5th Regt. Engrs., 1917-18; chief engr. 9th Div., 1918; in charge Galveston engr. dist., 1919—. Officer of Legion of Honor, France, 1917. Mem. Am. Soc. C.E., Internat. Congress Navigation. Clubs: Rittenhouse, University (Phila.), Metropolitan, Chevy Chase, Army and Navy (Washington). Home: 2027 Massachusetts Av. N.W., Washington, D.C.

COTHERN, LELAND (IRVIN), mining engr., educator; b. Pana, Ill., May 12, 1900; s. Harvey Bertram and Elizabeth Anna (Hebel) C.; B.S., U. Ill., 1922; M.S., U. Ala., 1930; m. Dorothy Elizabeth Mack, June 23, 1926; children—Jean Elizabeth (Mrs. Basil L. Jackson), John Mack, Dorothy Lee (Mrs. Ralph Nugent). Mining engineer Bethlehem Mines Corp., Heilwood, Pa., 1922. Peale, Peacock & Kerr Coal Co., St. Benedict, Pa., 1923; grad. asst. Sch. Mines, Pa. State Coll., 1924; instr. math. Beloit (Wis.) Coll., 1925; mining engr. Am. Smelting & Refining Co., Charcas, San Luis Potosi, Mexico; instr. Sch. Mines, U. Ala., 1927; asst. prof., 1927-37, asso. prof., 1937-39; head dept. mining engring. Va. Poly. Inst., 1939-48; prof. mining engring. Ohio State U. since 1948; cons. engr. Dir. engring. Jewel Ridge Coal Corp., 1950-62. Mem. Am. Inst. Mining and Metall. Engrs. (chmn. central Appalachian sect. 1942), Am. Soc. Engring. Edn., Sigma Gamma Epsilon, Gamma Sigma Epsilon, Delta Mu Epsilon. Methodist. Home: 242 E. North Broadway, Columbus 2, O. Died July 6, 1962; buried Monte Vista Cemetery, Bluefield, W.Va.

COTHRAN, FRANK HARRISON, cons. engr.; b. Millway, S.C., Aug. 28, 1878; s. Wade Elephare and Sara Elizabeth (Chiles) C.; m. Blanche Clardy, June 15, 1910; children—Frank Harrison, James Clardy, Samuel Alexander. Surveying with ry. and land surveys, 1899-1900; primary levelman U.S. Geol. Survey, 1901; asst. mining engr. Cranes Nest Coal Co., Toms Creek, Va., 1902; res. engr. South & Western Ry. (now Carolina, Clinchfield & Ohio Ry.), in charge location and constrn. in Breaks of Sandy, 1902-03, locating engr., 1905-06, asst. engr. in plant and equipment, Va.-Pocahontas Coal Co., Coalwood, W.Va., 1903; asst. locating engr. Coal and Coke Ry., W.Va., 1903-04; resident engr. Clover Fork (W.Va.) Tunnel, 1904-05; locating engr. proposed Bristol & Kingsport Ry., 1907-08; mem. Cothran and Cothran, engrs. and contractors, Greenwood, S.C., 1908-10; locating engr. Coal & Coke Ry., 1910, also Atlanta N.E. Ry., 1910-11; reconnaissance engr. Va.-Carolina Ry., 1910; engr. Ga. Granite Co., Atlanta, Ga., 1911; locating engr. Piedmont & Northern Ry., 1911-12; div. engr., 1912-14; in charge field surveys Quebec (Canada). Development Company, 1914-15, Southern Power Co., Charlotte, N.C., 1915-16; resident engineer in charge Bridgewater Development, Western Carolina Power Co., 1916-20; resident engr. in charge additions, Lookout Shoals Dam, Southern Power Co., 1916; division engr. for Southern Power Co., Bridgewater, N.C., 1920-22; v.p. and gen. mgr. Alma & Jonquiere Ry., Duke-Price Power Co., Ltd., also v.p. Quebec (Can.) Development Co., 1923-27; chief engr. Piedmont & Northern Ry., 1927-29; v.p., gen. mgr. and chief engr. Beauharnois Constrn. Co., 1929-33; cons. engr. from 1933; pres. Durham & Southern Ry., and Piedmont & Northern Ry. since Mar. 1937, also cons. engr. Sergt. 1st South Carolina Volunteer Infantry, Spanish-Am. War. Mem. Am. Soc. C.E., Am. Ry. Engring. Assn., Inst. Engrs. of Canada, Corp. Professional Engrs. of Que. (Can.). Mason. Clubs: Charlotte Country (Charlotte, N.C.); Poinsett (Greenville, S.C.); Traffic (New York); Biltmore (N.C.) Forest Country. Home: 917 Queens Rd. Office: Power Bldg., Charlotte, N.C. Died Sept. 1, 1948.

COTTERILL, GEORGE FLETCHER, consulting civil engr.; b. Oxford, Eng., Nov. 18, 1865; s. Robert and Alice (Smith) C.; came to U.S., 1872; grad. (valedictorian) Montclair (N.J.) High Sch., 1881; m. Cora Rowena Gormley, Feb. 19, 1890 (died Feb. 26, 1936); children—Ruth Eileen (dec.), (adopted) Marjorie Alice (Mrs. Paul J. Avery). Studied engineering with James Owen, civ. engr., Essex County, N.J., 1881-83; landscape engring., Arlington Cemetery. Hudson County, N.J., 1883-84; moved to Seattle, Wash., 1884, and since engaged in various lines of engring.; asst. city engr., Seattle, 1892-1900, spl. duties development city water supply and harbor platting; gen. engring. practice Seattle and N.W. since 1900; mem. Wash. State Irrigation Commn., 1903-05; mem. Seattle City Planning Commn., 1926-28; specialty landscape platting, municipal plans, etc.; chief engr. Wash. State Highway Dept., 1916-19. Charter mem. and first sec., 1902-03, Pacific Northwest Soc. Engrs. Dem. nominee for mayor of Seattle, 1900; for rep. in Congress, 1902 and 1916; mem. Wash. Senate, 1907-11; Dem. direct primary nominee for U.S. Senate, 1908, 10, 20; mayor of Seattle, Wash., 1912-14; commr. Port of Seattle, 1922-34; federal cons. to Wash. State Planning Council, 1934-35; cons. engr. State Dept. of Conservation and Development and liaison supervisor for state sponsor of U.S. Works Progress Adminstrn. Flood Relief Projects, 1935-36; consultant engr. State Dept. Social Security and Federal Work Projects Administration on Water Resources Research, 1937-39; supervisor U.S. Works Projects Adminstrn., Island County, Washington, 1940-41; cartographer asst. King County assessor, 1943-47. Dir. Am. Assn. Port Authorities, 1927-34; also of Assn. of Pacific and Far East Ports, 1927-30. Active in temperance reform, especially through Good Templars; sec. G.L. of Washington, 1889-90; rep. Internat. Supreme Lodge, 1893, and all sessions to 1930; U.S. Nat. Chief Templar Internat. Order of Good Templars, 1905-13, and internat. counselor, 1899-1902, and 1908-30; U.S. national counselor, 1936-39; Grand Chief Templar, Wash. Grand Lodge since 1945; U.S. del. 12th, 14th and 16th Internat. congresses against alcoholism, London, 1909, Milan, 1913, Lausanne, 1921. Mem. Washington State Pioneers Assn. (historian 1940-41, pres. 1942-43). Public speaker, writer and extensive traveler in Europe and America. Congregationalist. Mason (K.T., Shriner). Club: Seattle Press (life). Wrote: Puget Sound—The Mediterranean of the Pacific, 1927; The Climax of a World Quest, 1928; also various papers relating to Pacific Ocean and world commerce. Designed New World Map, Pacific Planisphere Projection, 1929. Home: 2020 E. 65th St., Seattle WA

COTTING, JOHN RUGGLES, geolgoist; b. Acton, Mass., 1783; attended Harvard, Dartmouth Med. Sch. Ordained to minsitry Congregational Ch., circa 1810; devoted most of his life to scientific pursuits; state geologist of Ga., 1835-37, made 1st geol. survey of state; gathered valuable collection of plants, minerals and fossils (divided among various colls. at his death); a copy of his state geol. report (1836) was requested by Czar of Russia for Royal Library. Author: Introduction to Chemistry, 1822; Synopsis of Lectures on Geology, 1825. Died Milledgeville, Ga., Oct. 13, 1867.

COTTINGHAM, IRVEN A., civil engr.; b. St. Marys, Tex., Oct. 14, 1866; C.E., Agrl. and Mech. Coll. of Tex. Began as asst. engr. S.P. C., 1889; div. engr. Galveston, Harrisburg & San Antonio Ry., until 1904; successively engr. maintenance of way and asst. gen. mgr. Houston & Tex. Central R.R. at Houston, 1904-16; sp. engr. in charge of valuation work Sunset Central Lines, 1916-18; chief engr. Texas lines of S.P. Co., 1918-22; engaged in pvt. practice and cons. engr. on valuation, Southern Pacific lines, Tex. and La.; retired, 1932. Home: Houston, Tex. Died Nov. 8, 1934.

COTTON, WILLIAM EDWIN, supt. expt. station; b. Oskaloosa, Ia., Sept. 17, 1866; s. George E. and Mary M.(Binns) C.; D.V.M., George Washington U., 1911; M. Grace E. Caskey, Sept. 20, 1898 (died Sept. 11, 1928); children—Corneila Marie, Edwin Rowland, John Caskey. Asst. Bur. Animal Industry, U.S. Dept. Agr., 1893-94, expert asst., 1894-1910, asst. supt. expt. station (now Animal Disease Sta.), Beltsville, Md., 1910-28, supt. 1928-37; prof. of infectious disease, Vet. Coll., Ala. Poly. Inst., Auburn, Ala., retired, 1948. Mem. Am. Veterinary Med. Assn. (first v.p., 1933-34, mem. exec. com., 1939-44), Internat. Vet. Congress, U.S. Livestock Sanitary Assn., Research Workers in animal diseases in N. N. Am. (pres. 1931-32); fellow A.A.A.S. Presbyterian. Contbr. repts. and bulletins, U.S. Dept. Agr. Research in animal diseases, tuberculosis, infectious abortion, etc. 1946. Home: Brockwood, Wilson Lane, Bethesda, Md. Died Sept. 7, 1951; buried Rockville Union Cemetery, Rockville, Md.

COTTRELL, CALVERT BYRON, inventor, mfr.; b. Westerley, R.I., Aug. 10, 1821; s. Lebbeus and Lydia (Maxson) C.; m. Lydia W. Perkins, May 4, 1849, 5 children. Machinist and employing contractor for Levalley, Lanphear & Co., Phoenix, R.I., 1840-55; in partnership (with Nathan Babocck) firm Cottrell & Babcock, mfrs. printing presses, Westerley, 1855-80, name changed to C. B. Cottrell & Sons, 1880; invented air spring for reversing bed of press, tapeless sheet delivery to drum cylinder, rotary color printing press, shifting tympan for a web perfecting press. Died Westerley, June 12, 1893.

COTTRELL, FREDERICK GARDNER, Am. chemist; b. Oakland, Cal., Jan. 10, 1877; s. Henry and Cynthia L. (Durfee) C.; B.S. U. Cal., 1896, LL.D., 1927; postgrad. U. Berlin, 1901; Ph.D., U. Leipzig, 1902; m. Jessie M. Fulton, Jan. 1, 1904; 2 children. LeConte fellow U. Cal., 1896-97, instr. phys. chemistry, 1902-06, asst. prof., 1906-11; chem. tchr. U.S. Bur. Mines, 1911, chief phys. chemist (field duty), 1911-14, chief chemist, 1914-15, chief metallurgist, 1916-19, asst. dir., 1919, 20, dir., 1920; chmn. div. chemistry and chem. tech. NRC, 1921-22; dir. Fixed Nitrogen Research Lab., U.S. Dept. Agr., 1922-27, chief div. fertilizer and fixed nitrogen investigation Bur. Chemistry and Soils, 1927-30, cons. chemist Bur. Chemistry and Soils, 1930-40, Bur. Plant Industry, 1940-43; pres. Research Associates, Inc., 1935-38; tech. cons. Smithsonian Instn., 1928-29, Research Corp., N.Y.C., from 1930. Mem. Am. Chem. Soc., Am. Inst. Mining Engrs., Am. Electrochem. Soc., Nat. Acad. Scis., Am. Philos. Soc., Societe de Chimie Industrielle (hon.), Sigma Xi, Phi Beta Kappa. Research on nitrogen fixation, liquefaction of gases, recovery of helium; inventor Cottrell precipitator for precipitation of particles from gases, built device for prodn. of positive ion rays, 1930. Died Nov. 16, 1948.

COUES, ELLIOTT, naturalist; b. Portsmouth, N.H., Sept. 9, 1842; grad. Columbia Univ., 1861; (M.D., 1863; hon. A.M., 1862; Ph.D., 1869). Medical cadet to asst. surgeon U.S. army (filling all intermediate grades), 1862-81, resigned; was prof. anatomy and zoölogy in several colleges; was surgeon and naturalist U.S. Northern Boundary Commn., 1873-76; sec. and naturalist U.S. Geol. and Geog. Survey of the Territories, 1876-80; long connected with Smithsonian Instn. Member Nat. Acad. Sciences; one of the founders and v.p.'s Am. Ornithologists' Union; mem. and corr. mem. on nearly 50 Am. and fgn. scientific and psychical societies. Author: Key to Nroth American Birds; Field Ornithology; Birds of the Northwest; Fur-Bearing Animals; Montographs of North American Rodentia; Birds of the Colorado Valley; New England Bird Life; Biogen, a Speculation on the Origin and Nature of Life; The Daemon of Darwin; Kuthumi; Can Matter Think; Buddhist Catechism; A Woman in the Case; Signs of the Times; Citizen Bird; etc. Was chmn. gen. and joint coms. of Psychical Science Congress, World's Congress Auxlliary, 1893. Died 1899.

COULTER, JOHN LEE, economist and statistician; b. Mallory, Minn., Apr. 16, 1881; s. John and Catherine (McVeety) C.; A.B., U. of N.Dak., 1904, A.M., 1905; LL.D., 1922; studied law, 1904-05; Ph.D., U. of Wis., 1908, studied U. of Minn., Ia. State Coll.; Doctor of Sci. (hon.) N.Dakota A. and M., 1950; m. Phoebe Everett Forst, Sept. 23, 1911; children—John Lee, Kirkley Schley, David Creswell. Instr. Ia. State Coll., 1907. U. of Wis., 1907-08, U. of Minn., 1908-09; asst. prof. economics, U. of Minn., 1909-10; spl. agent Minn. Board of Health, 2909-20; expert spl. agent U.S. Census Bureau, 1910-12, in charge of Div. of Agr., 1912-14; prof. rural economics, Kapp Sch. of Country Life, Nashville, Tenn., 1914-15; dean W.Va. Coll. Agr. and dir. Expt. Sta., 1915-21; pres. N.D. A. and M. Coll. 1921-29; became chief economist and chmn. advisory bd. U.S. Tariff Commn., 1929. mem. commn., 1930-34; mem. U.S. Com. for Reciprocity Information, 1934-35; lecturer George Washington U., 1910-13, Summer School of the South, 1910, 11. Mem. and Sec. U.S. Com. and Am. Com. sent to Europe to investigation rural credit and cooperation. Formerly mem. editorial staff Quaterly Jour. of Am. Statis. Assn. and Am. Econ. Review. Mem. W.Va., State Council Defense, 1917-18; expert for Nat. Council, 1917, War Industries Bd., 1918; maj. A.S.A.P., 1918; with Army Overseas Ednl. Commn., 6 months, 1918-19. Prog. Republican. Presbyterian. Mason. Fellow Am. Statis. Assn.; mem. Am. Econ. Assn. Am. Polit. Science Assn., Am. Assn. Labor Legislation, Am. Assn. of Agrl. Colls. and Expt. Stas. (v.p. 1917 and 1927), Farm Economics Assn., Nat. Econ. League, Phi Beta Kappa, Phi Beta Kappa Associates (pres. Washington chpt.). Club: Cosmos (Washington, D.C.). Author: Economic History of Red River Valley of the North, 1910; Cooperation Among Farmers, 1911; Postwar Fiscal Problems and Policies, 1945; also author numerous bulletins. reports and articles. Lecturer and cons. economist. Home: 2100 S.St. N.W. Office: Investment Bldg., Washington 5. Died Apr. 16, 1959; buried Arlington (Va.) Cemetery.

COULTER, JOHN MERLE, botanist; b. Ningpo, China, Nov. 20, 1851; s. Moses Stanley and Caroline E. (Crowe) C.; A.B., Hanover Coll., 1870. A.M., 1873. Ph.D., 1882; Ph.D., Ind. U., 1884; m. Georgie M. Gaylord, Jan. 1, 1874. Botanist, U.S. Geol. Survey in Rocky Mountains, 1872-73; prof. natural sciences, Hanover Coll., 1874-79; prof. biology, Wabash Coll., 1879-91; pres. and prof. botany, Ind. U., 1891-93; pres. Lake Forest U., 1893-96; prof. and head dept. botany, U. of Chicago, 1896-1925; adviser of Boyce Thompson Inst. Plant Research, Yonkers, N.Y., 1925—. Prin. Bay View Summer Univ., 1893-96, Winona Summer Sch., 1895-98; founder and editor Botanical Gazette, 1875—. Fellow Am. Acad. Arts and Sciences, A.A.A.S. (gen. sec. 1901, pres. 1918); pres. Chicago Acad. of Sciences; mem. Nat. Research Council, 1923—. Author: Manual of Rocky Mountain Botany, 1885; Manual of Texan Botany, 1891; Plant Relations, 1899; Plant Structures, 1899; Plant Studies, 1902; Morphology of Gymnosperms (with Charles J. Chamberlain), 1901; Morphology of Angiosperms (with same), 1903; A Text-book of Botany, 1906; Elementary Studies in Botany, 1913; Foundamentals of Plant Breeding, 1914; Evolution of Sex in Plants, 1914; Plant Genetics, 1918. Died Dec. 23, 1928.

COULTER, STANLEY, biologist; b. Ningpo, China, June 2, 1853; s. Moses Stanley and Caroline E. (Crowe) C.; brother of John Merle C.; A.B., Hanover Coll., 1871, A.M., 1974; Ph.D. 1889, LL.D., in 1907; Sc.D., Purdue Univ., 1931; Sc.D. from Wabash Coll., 1933; m. Lucy E. Post, June 21, 1877. Prof. biology and dir. Biol. Lab., 1887-1926, dean Sch. of Science, 1907-26, and dean of men, 1919-26, acting chmn. of faculty, 1921, Purdue Univ., now emeritus. Mem. State Bd. of Forestry, 1902-16. Mem. Conservation Commn. of Ind., since 1916 (chmn., 1925-33). Fellow A.A.A.S., Ind. Acad. of Science, Western Soc. Naturalists, Bot. Soc. of Am., Am. Genetic Assn.; pres. Indiana Tuberculosis Assn., 1927. Author: Forest Trees of Indiana, pamphlet, 1892; Flora of Indiana, 1890; Pharmacology of Remedies in Common Use; also 11 pamphlets upon nature study; 45 pamphlets of scientific studies and reports, and 70 other titles, book reviews, biog. sketches, etc. Address: Eli Lilly & Co., Indianapolis. Died June 26, 1943.

COUNTS, GERALD ALFORD, army officer, educator; b. Ranger, Tex., Sept. 24, 1895; s. John Ellis and Willa Bailey (Shelton) C.; student U. Cal. at Berkeley, 1913-14; B.S., U.S. Mil. Acad., 1917; B.S. in Civil Engring., Mass. Inst. Tech., 1921; postgrad. Cal. Inst. Tech., 1930-31; m. Anne Earle Harris, Nov. 21, 1921; 1 dau., Anne Harris (Mrs. John M. Minor). Commd. 2d lt. C.E., U.S. Army, 1917, advanced through grades to brig. gen., 1957; assigned 109th Engrs., 604th Engrs., 6th Engrs., World War I; river and harbor engring. Los Angeles, Galveston engr. dists., also field charge constrn. Houston Ship Channel, 1921-25; faculty U.S. Mil. Acad., 1925-30, 31—, acting prof. physics, 1931-34, prof. physics, 1934-46, head dept. physics and chemistry, 1946-57, dean acad. bd., 1957—; dep. chief engr. MTO, 1943-44; dep. G-4, 12th Army Group, Normandy to Germany, German occupation, World War II; ret., 1959. Decorated Legion of Merit with cluster, Bronze Star; Legion of Honor, Croix de Guerre with palm (France); Order of Leopold, Croix de Guerre with palm (Belgium); Courone de Chene (Luxembourg); Order Brit. Empire. Mem. Am. Soc. Engring. Edn., Am. Soc. Mil. Engrs., Kappa Alpha. Episcopalian. Home: Quarters 107. Office: Office of the Dean, West Point, N.Y. Died July 30, 1964; buried West Point, N.Y.

COUPER, JAMES HAMILTON, planter; b. nr. Brunswick, Ga., Mar. 4, 1794; s. John and Rebecca Hamilton, John. Owned half of "Hopeton" (a Ga. rice plantation), also rice plantation on Cannon's Point, St. Simon's Island, Ga.; supervised over 1800 slaves; 1st American to operate rice plantation scientifically, using diking and drainage system; built 1st cotton-seed oil mill in U.S., Natchez, Miss., 1834; one of 1st to grow Bermuda grass and olives in U.S.; plantations and fortune destroyed in Civil War. Died June 3, 1866; buried Frederika St. Simon's Island.

COURANT, RICHARD, mathematician, educator; born Lublinitz, Poland, January 8, 1888; s. Siegmund and Martha (Freund) C.; student U. of Breslau (Germany), U. of Zurich (Switzerland); Ph.D., U. of Goettingen (Germany), 1910; E.D., Technische Hochschule (Darmstadt); Sc.D., Case Inst. Tech., 1958, N.Y.U., 1958; D.E., Technische Hochschule, Aachen, Germany, 1958; m. Nerina Runge, Jan. 1919; children—Ernest David, Gertrude A. Elizabeth, Hans Wolfgang Julius, Marianne Leonore. Came to U.S., 1934, naturalized, 1940. Asst. and instr. of mathematics, U. of Goettingen, 1910-14; prof. of mathematics, U. of Muenster, 1919-20; prof. of mathematics and dir. of Math. Inst., Goettingen, 1920-33; lecturer, U. of Cambridge, Eng., 1933-34; prof. of mathematics and head mathematics dept. N.Y.U., 1934-58, prof. emeritus, science adviser, from 1958; also dir. Inst. Mathematical Scis. Served in German Army, 1914-19. Decorated Knight Comdr. Order of Merit (Fed. Republic of Germany; recipient Navy Distinguished Pub. Service award, 1958. Mem. Am. Math. Soc., A.A.A.S., American Physical Society, National Academy Sciences, New York Academy Sciences, Math. Assn. Am., American Philos. Soc., Accademia Nazionale dei Lincei, Acad. Scis. USSR, Royal Netherlands, Acad. Sciences and Letters, Akademie der Wissenschaften (Goettingen), Royal Danish Acad. Sci. and Letters, Sigma Xi. Club: Cosmos. Author textbooks including: (with H. Robbins) What is Mathematics?, 1941; Supersonic Flow and Shock Waves (Interscience), (with K. O. Friedrichs), 1948; Methods of Mathematical Physics (Wiley) (Interscience) (with D. Hilbert), vol. I, 1953, vol. II, 1962. Home: New Rochelle NY Died Jan. 27, 1972.

COURTIS, WILLIAM MUNROE, mining engr.; b. Boston, Mass., Jan. 7, 1842; s. William and Mehitable (Appleton) C.; A.B., Harvard, 1864, A.M., 1867; studied civ. engring., Lawrence Scientific Sch. (Harvard), 1 yr.; 3 yrs. at Royal School of Mines, Freiberg; m. Lizzie Easton Folger, Apr. 2, 1873. Was supt. and gen. mgr. of many mines and smelting works in Mich., Colo., Cal., N.M., etc., and cons. engr. to extensive operators; was chief engr. on survey of Santo Domingo, etc.; patented improved mill apparatus for saving waste in tailings. Interested in the search for potash in the U.S. to which devoted 5 yrs. and traveled 100,000 miles. Home: Highland Park, Detroit. Died 1922.

COURVILLE, CYRIL BRIAN, physician; b. Traverse City, Mich., Feb. 19, 1900; s. Philip Albert and Emma Amelia (Kroupa) C.; student Cedar Lake (Mich.) Acad., 1915-16; A.B., Emmanuel Missionary Coll., Berrien Springs, Mich., 1921; M.D., Coll. of Med. Evangelists, Loma Linda and Los Angeles, Calif., 1925; M.Sc. in embryology U. of So. Calif., 1930; D.M.S., Teijo University, Tokyo, Japan; married Margaret Louise Farnsworth, June 10, 1939. Instr. in anatomy Loma Linda University, Loma Linda, 1926-29, prof. neurology since 1934, head sect. nervous diseases; vol. asst. neurosurg. clinic Dr. Harvey Cushing, 1927; resident neurology and nerosurgery Los Angeles Co. Gen. Hosp., 1929-33, dir. Cajal Lab. Neuropathology, 1934-68; consultant neuropathology, Los Angeles County coroner White Meml. Hosp., Los Angeles. Founder, organizer med. cadet corps, 1935, organized 47th Gen. Hosp., 1937. Diplomate Nat. Bd. Med. Examiners; fellow Am. Acad. Neurology; mem. Cal., Los Angeles County med. assns., Am. Neurol. Assn., Am. Acad. Forensic Scis., Am. Acad. Cerebral Palsy, Los Angeles Neurological Society, Am. Assn. Neuropathologists, British Anthropological Association. Republican. Adventist. Author sci. books, including Commotio Cerebri, 1953; Effects of Alcohol in the Nervous System of Man; contributor to the Study of Cerebral Anoxia, 1953, Forensic Neuropathology, 1964, others. Author and editor, Medical Cadet Corps Training Manual, 1942, 43. Author essays and articles profl. jours. Home: Pasadena CA Died Mar. 22, 1968; buried Forest Lawn, Glendale CA

COUSINS, RALPH P., ret. army officer, ins. exec.; b. Mexia, Tex., Dec. 1, 1891; s. Robert Bartow and Dora (Kelly) C.; B.S., U.S. Mil. Acad., 1915; M.S., Yale, 1922; grad. AC Flying Sch., San Diego, 1916, AC Tactical Sch., Langley Field, 1931; m. Diana Wilson Fitzmaurice, May 10, 1945; stepchildren—Shelia Fitzmaurice (Mrs. William Shay), Patricia Fitzmaurice (Mrs. Les Baxter). Command and Gen. Staff Sch., 1933, Army War Coll., 1937, Commd. 2d, lt., U.S. Army, 1915; advanced through grades to maj. gen., 1942; developed radio beam, built communication systems of model airways, 1926-28; comd. Clark Field, Fort Stotsenburg, P.I., 1928-30; charge aviation units N.G., Washington 1933-36; asst. chief staff (personnel), Air Force, Langley Field, Va., 1937-41, Air Staff, Washington, 1941-42; Comdg. gen. Army Air Forces Western Flying Tng. Command, Santa Ana, Cal., 1942-46; ret. as maj. gen., 1946. Co-founder Founders' Fire & Marine Ins. Co. Los Angeles, v.p., sec., mem. bd. since 1946, past pres. Los Angeles Airport Commn. Decorations: War Dept. Commendation medal; Air medal; D.S.M.; Cloud Banner of Chinese Govt. Clubs: Army and Navy (Washington); California, Los Angeles. Home: 1125 Angelo Drive, Beverly Hills, Cal. Office: 523 W. 6th St., Los Angeles 4. Died Mar. 15, 1964.

COVER, RALPH, lawyer and inventor; b. Carrol Co., Md., June 13, 1892; s. Harry Fisher and Dora May (Hiteshew) C.; A.B., Western Md. Coll., Westminster, Md., 1910; LL.B., Harvard, 1913; m. Anna Saulsbury Fisher, Dec. 11, 1919; 1 son, Paul Fisher; m. 2d, Edna Arnold, Apr. 10, 1943. Admitted to Md. bar, 1913; asso. with Bond, Robinson & Duffy, Balt., 1913-15; mem. firm Smith & Cover, 1915-17; pvt. practice, Westminster, Md., 1930-69; chmn. bd. United Company, engaged in development and mfr. of inventions, machines and methods employed in food processing industry, Westminster, Md., 1914-69; pres.

The United Products Co., licensor of canning methods and processes. Served as asst. sec. priorities com., War Industries Bd., World War I. Mem. Am., Md. bar assns., Old Guard Soc. of Canning Industry, Am. Inst. Food Technologists (charter mem.). Club: Illinois Athletic (Chicago). Inventor various machines and methods employed in food processing industry; dir. tech. experts in development of such machines and methods; writer tech. articles. Home: Westminster MD Died Sept. 6, 1969.

COVERDALE, WILLIAM HUGH, cons. engr.; b. Kingston, Ont., Can., Jan. 27, 1871; s. William Miles and Fannie (O'Neill) C.; prep. edn., Collegiate Inst., Kingston; B.A., Geneva Coll., Beaver Falls, Pa., 1891, Dr. Sci., 1914; LL.D., Queen's U., 1922; m. Harriet E. Hinchliff, June 30, 1911; children—William Hugh, Mary, Harriet Hinchliff, Miles. With Engring. dept. Pa. Lines West of Pittsburgh, 1891-1900; engring. practice N.Y. City, since 1900, except 1 yr. traveling in Europe; mem. firm Coverdale & Colpitts, cons. engrs. since 1913; chmn. bd. and pres. Am. Export Lines; pres., mng. dir. Canada Steamship Lines, Ltd., Century Coal Co., Davie Shipbuilding & Repairing Co., Canadian Shipbuilding & Engineering, Ltd., pres. and dir. 1020 Fifth Av. Corp.; dir. mem. exec. com., Gen. Airline and Film Corp., Republic Steel Corp., Seaboard Air Line R.R. Co.; Georgia & Florida Railroad, Angle-Newfoundland Development Co., Montreal Trust Co., Richmond, Fredericksburg & Potomac R.R. Co., Richmond-Washington Co., Tenn., Ala. & Ga. Ry. Co., Comml. Nat. Bank, Canadian Car and Foundry Co., Ltd., dir. Schenley Industries, Inc. trustee Atlantic Mutual Ins. Co., Atlantic Mut. Indemnity Co. Dir. American Arbitration Association. Member American Soc. Civil Engrs., Am. Inst. Cons. Engrs. Clubs: Metropolitan, University, Engineers, Recess, Mt. Royal, Mt. Bruno Country, St. James, Beaconsfield Golf (Montreal); Kingston Yacht, Cataraqui Golf and Country (Kingston Can.). Home: 1020 5th Av., New York, N.Y.; (summer) Le Moine's Point Farm, Portsmouth, Ont. Can. Office: 120 Wall St., New York, N.Y. Died Aug. 10, 1949.

COVILLE, FREDERICK V(ERNON), botanist; b. Preston, N.Y., Mar. 23, 1867; s. Joseph Addison and Lydia (More) C.; A.B., Cornell U., 1887; D.Sc., George Washington U., 1921; m. Elizabeth Harwood Boynton, Oct. 4, 1890; children—Arthur Boynton (dec.), Stanley, Katharine, Cabot, Frederick. Instr. botany, Cornell, 1887-88; asst. botanist, 1888-93, botanist, 1893—, U.S. Dept. Agr.; curator U.S. Nat. Herbarium, 1893—; acting dir. Nat. Arboretum, 1929—. Procured foundation of the Desert Botanical Lab. by Carnegie Instn. Fellow (v.p. botany, 1902) A.A.A.S. Author: Botany of the Death Valley Expdn.; Standardized Plant Names (joint author); and many bot. papers. Awarded George Robert White medal of honor, Mass. Hort. Society, 1931. Home: Washington, D.C. Died Jan. 9, 1937.

COWAN, FRANK AUGUSTUS, communications engr.; b. Escatawpa, Ala., Aug. 30, 1898; s. James T. and Annie Ellen (Adamson) C.; B.S. in Elec. Engring., Ga. Inst. Tech., 1919; m. Dorothy L. Rush, July 3, 1942. With Am. Tele. & Tel. Co., 1920—. successively spl. services engr., div. transmission engr., asst. dir. operations, asst. dir. operations long lines, 1950—. Served as lt. comdr. USNR, 1942-49. Recipient Lamme Gold Medal, Am. Inst. E.E., 1953. Fellow Am. Inst. E.E. (chmn. communications group N.Y. sect. 1944-45), Inst. Radio Engrs. Home: 44 E. 67th St., N.Y.C. 21. Office: 32 Av. of Americas, N.Y.C. 13. Died June 21, 1957.

COWEN, JOSHUA LIONEL, inventor; b. N.Y.C., Aug. 25, 1880; student Coll. City N.Y., Columbia; m. Cecilia Liberman, Feb. 25, 1904 (dec. 1946); children—Lawrence, Isabel (Mrs. Harold Brandaleone); m. 2d, Lillian Herman, Nov. 1949. Pioneer devel. dry-cell battery, flashlight; builder galvanic and faradic batteries, also cytoscopic lamps; inventor fuse to set off magnesium flash powder use in photography; awarded contract to equip mines with detonators USN, 1898; builder model r.r.s., 1900—, early engines equipped with battery, later engines electricified; founder Lionel Corp., N.Y.C., chmn. 1945—. Home: 945 Fifth Av., N.Y.C. 21. Office: 15 E. 26th St., N.Y.C. 10. Died Sept. 1965.

COWLES, ALFRED HUTCHINSON, engineer; b. Cleveland, Dec. 8, 1858; s. Edwin C. (founder and editor Cleveland Leader) and Elizabeth (Hutchinson) C.; Ohio State U., 1875-77; Cornell, 1877-82; m. Helen J. Wills, Nov. 1906. With bro. Eugene H., organized, 1885. The Electric Smelting & Aluminum Co., pres., 1895—; pres. Cowles Detergent Co., 1923—, Pecos Copper Co., 1902-21. V.p. Cleveland Leader Printing Co., 1898-1904. Awarded Elliott Cresson and John Scott Legacy medals, Franklin Inst., 1886; medal, Paris Expn., 1889. With bro., Eugene H. Cowles, was a pioneer in electric smelting, beginning in 1884. Fellow Am. Inst. Elec. Engrs., A.A.A.S. Home: Sewaren, N.J. Died Aug. 13, 1929.

COWLES, HENRY CHANDLER, botanist; b. Kensington, Conn., Feb. 27, 1869; s. Henry Martyn and Eliza (Whittlesey) C.; A.B., Oberlin Coll., 1893; fellow in geology and botany, 1895-97, lab. asst., 1897-98, Ph.D., 1898 , U. of Chicago; Sc.D., Oberlin, 1923; m. Elizabeth Waller, June 25, 1900; 1 dau., Harriet Elizabeth. Prof. natural sciences Gates Coll., Neb., 1894-95; spl. field asst. U.S. Geol. Survey, summer, 1895; instr. botany, 1902-07, asst. chmn. dept. of botany, 1925-34 (emeritus), U. of Chicago. Pres. ecology sect., Internat. Bot. Congress, 1930. Conglist. Author: Vegetation of Sand Dunes of Lake Michigan, 1899; Plant Societies of Chicago, 1901; Text-book of Plant Ecology, 1911; Plant Societies of Chicago and Vicinity, 1913. Editor Botanical Gazette, 1925-34. Home: Chicago, Ill. Died Sept. 12, 1939.

COX, ABRAHAM BEEKMAN, civil engr.; b. New York, N.Y., Apr. 16, 1844; s. Abraham Beekman and Levantia White (Livingston) C.; grad. Yale, 1864; C.E. Rensselaer Poly. Inst., 1867; m. April 30, 1873, Augusta McBlair, d. late U. S. Senator John C. Ten Eyck of N.J. (died 1876). Practiced civ. engring 1st in R.R. work afterward building iron bridges until 1876; retired. Home: Cherry Valley, N.Y. Died 1906.

COX, FRANK P., elec. engr.; b. Terre Haute, Ind., Dec. 31, 1866; s. Robert S. and Frances (Strain) C.; ed. pub. sch schs., grad. Rose Poly. Inst., B.S., 1887; postgrad. course elec. engring., Johns Hopkins; m. at Baltimore, June 7, 1888, May Vaughen. In employ Kester Elec. Co., Terre Haute, 1888-89; in testing dept. Thomson Elec. Welding Co., 1889-90; in charge meter-testing dept. Thomson-Houston Co., and successor, General Elec. Co., 1890-94; then became engr. meter and inst. dept. Has taken out numerous patents handwritten for tech. press on meters and a treatise on direct-current dynamos and motors, etc. Address: Care of General Eelctric Co., Lynn, Mass.

COX, GUY HENRY, geologist; b. Lehigh, Ia., May 4, 1882; s. Edward Henry and Ada (Wilson) C.; B.S., Northwestern U., 1905; studied Sch. of Mines, U. of Calif., 1906; M.A., U. of Wis., 1908, Ph.D., 1911; E.M., Mo. Sch. of Mines and Metallurgy (U. of Mo.), Rolla, 1914; m. Kittie May Gates, Dec. 27, 1909. Geol. work in Wis., Wyo., Ill., summers 1904-11; instr. geology, U. of Calif., 1909; asst. prof. mineralogy and petrology, 1910-11, prof. geology and mineralogy, 1911-20, Mo. Sch. of Mines and Metallurgy. Civilian supervision govt. training camp, sections A and B, Rolla, Mo., 1917-18. Mem. Cox & Radcliffe, cons. engr., 1917-19; chief geologist, Jersey Oil Co., 1920—. Methodist. Author: Field Methods in Petroleum geology, 1920. Home: Pine Bluff, Ark. Died 1922.

COX, HENRY JOSEPH, meteorologist; b. Newton, Mass., Apr. 5, 1863; s. Thomas and Hannah M. (Perkins) C.; A.B., Harvard, 1884; hon. A.M., Norwich U., 1887, and ScD., 1914; m. Mary Cavanagh, Sept. 8, 1887; children—Henry Perkins, Arthur Cavanagh, Paul Greenwood (killed in action nr. Soissons, France, 1918). Prof. Norwich U., 1886-88; in weather service from Aug. 1, 1884; sr. meteorologist, July 1, 1924—; became sr. in charge North Central Forecast Dist., Chicago; also in charge of corn and wheat region service of Weather Bur., and formerly in charge spl. researches in agrl. meteorology. Fellow Am. Meteorol. Soc. (councilor). Author: Weather Buueau Records in Court; Lantern Slides in Teaching of Meteorology (Bull. 3, Geog. Soc. Chicago); Recent Advances in Meteorology; Notes of a Meteorologist in Europe; The Weather Bureau and the Cranberry Industry; Weather and Climate of Chicago; Weather Forecasting in United States (joint author); Influence of Great Lakes upon Movement of Storms; Thermal Belts and Fruit Growing in North Carolina Mountain Region. Home: Chicago, Ill. Died Jan. 7, 1930.

COX, JOHN REDMAN, physician; b. Trenton, N.J., Sept. 16, 1773; s. Daniel and Sarah (Redman) C.; M.D., U. Pa., 1794; m. Sarah Cox, 6 children. Introduced Jalap plant into U.S.; editor Medical Museum, 1805-11; prof. chemistry U. Pa., 1809-19, prof. materia medica and pharmacy Med. Dept., 1819-35. Died Phila., Mar. 22, 1864.

COX, LEMUEL, engr.; b. Boston, 1736; s. William and Thankful (Mandsley) C.; m. Susannah Hickling, 1763. Supervised constrn. of 1st bridge over Charles River, between Charlestown (Mass.) and Boston, 1785-86; architect, builder Essex Bridge from Salem to Beverly (Mass.); built bridge at Waterford, Ireland, 1793; received grant of land from Mass. for inventing 1st machine to cut card wire, 1796. Died Charlestown, Feb. 18, 1806.

COX, W(ILLIAM) ROWLAND, mining engr.; b. Salt Lake City, Utah, May 29, 1872; s. William Judson and Johanna M. (O'Farrell) C.; U. of Denver Business Coll.; student Mo. Sch. of Mines, 1893-96, hon. E.M., 1911; m. Gertrude Potter, May 25, 1907; children—Harriet, Barbara, Potter. Mine and mill supt., Aspen, Colo., 1897-1902; gen. mgr. Silver Lake Mines, Silverton, Colo. 1903-05; asst. gen. supt. mining dept. Guggenheim Exploration Co. and Am. Smelters Securities Co., hdqrs. Aguascalientes, Mexico, 1905-07; mem. Spurr & Cox, Inc., 1908-10; consulting practice. Mem. Am. Inst. Mining and Metall. Engrs., Mining and Metall. Soc., Canadian Inst. Mining and Metall. Engrs., Tau Beta Pi. Catholic. Office: 120 Broadway, New York NY*

COXE, ECKLEY BRINTON, mining engr., inventor; b. Phila., June 4, 1839; s. Charles Sidney and Ann (Brinton) C.; grad. U. Pa., 1858; studied mining in Europe, 1860-63; m. Sophia G. Fisher, June 27, 1868. Organized Coxe Bros. Co., 1865; pres. Cross Creek Co.; pres. Del., Susquehanna & Schuylkill R.R., 1890; a founder Am. Inst. Mining Engrs.; pres., 1878-89; pres. Am. Soc. M.E., 1892-94; mem. Pa. Senate, 1880-84; an original trustee Lehigh U., invented automatic slate-picking machine, mech. stocker, gyrating screens, steel measuring tapes. Died May 13, 1895.

COXE, WILLIAM BRISCOM, marine engr.; b. Reading, Pa., Feb. 25, 1869; s. Charles Chauncey and Annie Ellen (Griscom) C.; grad. Royal Tech. Coll., Charlottenburg, Berlin, 1891; served apprenticeship as marine engr., with J. & G. Thompson, Clyde Bank, Scotland, also with North German Lloyd repair plant, Bremerhaven, Germany; m. Helen Baer, Apr. 30, 1904. Fgn. rep. and asst. gen. supt. William Cramp & Sons Shipbuilding Co., Phila., 1898-1904; delivered to Russia, from Cramps, the battleship Retvizan and the cruiser Variag; to Japan, the cruiser Kasagi; pres. Harland & Hollingsworth Corp., Wilmington, Del., 13 1/2 yrs.; pres. Reading Paper Mills Co.; gen. mgr. for Pusey & Jones Co. of the Wilmington and Gloucester, N.J., plants. Served as sr. lt. U.S.N., Spanish-Am. War, 1898; dist. mgr. Emergency Fleet Corp., Delaware River Dist., World War, 1917-19. Pres. Atlantic Coast Shipbuilders' Assn., 1917-20. Democrat. Episcopalian. Mason. Home: Bellevue, Del. Died July 4, 1927.

COYLE, DAVID CUSHMAN, cons. engr.; b. North Adams, Mass., May 24, 1887; s. John Patterson and Mary Allerton (Cushman) C.; A.B., Princeton, 1908; C.E., Rensselaer Poly. Inst., 1910; m. Isadore Douglas, Sept. 3, 1914 (died 1927); children—Anne Douglas, John Patterson, Lawrence Thompson; m. 2d Chalice Kelly, Dec. 8, 1934 (died 1940); m. 3d, Doris Porter, Dec. 17, 1949. Began with Gunvald Aus Co., cons. engrs., N.Y.C., 1910; practicing under own name, 1930-69. Mem. Tech. Bd. of Review, PWA, 1933-35; cons. various govt. agencies, Washington, 1935-42, 1945-53, London, 1942-45. Club: Cosmos (Washington). Author about 12 books 1932-69, including: The American Way (recipient Harpers prize), 1938; The U.S. Political System, 1954; The United Nations, 1955; Conservation, 1957; Ordeal of the Presidency, 1959. Address: Washington DC Died July 15, 1969.

CRABTREE, FREDERICK, engineer; b. Bramley, York, Eng., Feb. 1, 1867; s. Joseph and Isabella (Clegg) C.; grad. high sch., Lawrence, Mass.; B.S. in Chemistry, Mass. Inst. Tech., 1889; m. Mary Odessa Moore, Aug. 30, 1894. Chemist, Ill. Steel Co., 1889, Nat. Tube Co., 1890-1900; supt. Western Steel Co., 1900-01; supt. blast furnace, Colo. Fuel & Iron Co., 1901-04; prof. mining and metallurgy, Colo. Coll., 1904-06; prof. mining and metall. engring., Carnegie Inst. Tech., 1906—. Republican. Episcopalian. Home: Pittsburgh, Pa. Died Feb. 14, 1925.

CRABTREE, JAMES ANDERSON, physician; b. Greenfield, Tenn., Aug. 30, 1902; s. Charles H. and Rosa Lee (Mitchell) C.; B.S., U. of Tenn., 1923, M.D., 1925, Dr. P.H. Johns Hopkins U. Sch. of Hygiene and Pub. Helath, 1932; m. Elizabeth Patterson, June 12, 1928; children—Nancy Lee, Patricia. Asso. with Tenn. State Health Orgn., 1926-34, dir. div. of preventable diseases, 1930-34; dep. dir. health and safety, Tenn. Valley Authority, 1934-38; entered commd. corps, U.S.P.H.S., 1938, serving in Nat. Cancer Inst., subsequently as exec. asst. to surgeon gen., dep. surgeon gen., 1946-48; on loan from U.S.P. H.S., to serve as med. dir. Nat. Security Resources Bd., June, 1948-May 1949; prof. and head dept. pub. helath practice, Graduate School Public Health, U. Pitts., 1949-58, dean 1958—; organized health division of U.N.R.R.A., director of health, 1943. Mem. bd. of trustees Am. Hosp. Assn. Mem. A.A.A.S., Washington Acad. of Medicine, A.M.A., Am. Pub. Health Assn., Sigma Phi Epsilon, Alpha Kappa Kappa, Alpha Omega Alpha, Delta Omega. Clubs: Cosmos, Kenwood Golf and Country (Washington, D.C.). Home: 4609 Bayard St., Pitts. 15213. Died Nov. 10, 1966; buried Arlington (Va.) Nat. Cemetery.

CRAFT, CLARENCE CHRISTIAN, M.D., magnetician; b. Gaston, S.C., Sept. 28, 1880; s. of David Elmore and Mary Louisa (Richter) C.; B.S., S.C. Mil. Acad., 1902; M.D., George Washington U., 1909; m. Charlotte Maye Thomas, Dec. 6, 1911; children—Hume Richter, Warren Frederick. Aid, U.S. Coast and Geod. Survey, 1903-05, on U.S.S. Patterson, assisting in making soundings for Army and Navy cable, from Cape Flattery to Sitka, Alaska, summer of 1903; surveying harbor of Kiska, Aleutian Is., summer of 1904, and survey of H.I., Oct. 1904-Mar. 1905; magnetic observer in various states, 1905-07; computer Dept. Terrestrial Magnetism, Carnegie Instn. of Washington, to 1909; magnetic observer, Comdr. Peary's auxiliary ship Erik, July-Oct. 1908, going as far north as Etah, Greenland; surgeon and magnetic observer aboard yacht Carnegie from Aug. 3, 1909-June 1, 1911; in pub. health work, Florence, S.C., 1914-16, and from Sept. 1, 1921. Home: Hickory, N.C. Died May 25, 1935.

CRAFT, EDWARD BEECH, electrical engr.; b. Cortland, Trumbull Co., Oc., Sept. 12, 1881; s. Charles C. and Nora A. (Trowbridge) C.; prep. edn., high sch., Warren, O.; D. Engring., Worcester Poly. Inst., 1926; m. Mary Ann Richards, Oct. 21, 1902; 1 dau., Clara Virginia. With Warren (O.) Electric and Specialty Co., 1898-1902 (last 2 yrs. as supt. lamp dept.); with dept. design of communication equipment, Western Electric Co.; Chicago, 1902-07; development engr., in charge telephone apparatus design, Western Electric Co., New York, 1907-17; asst. chief engr. same, in charge development and design, 1917-22; chief engr. same and Internat. Western Electric Co., 1922-25; exec. v.p. Bell Telephone Labs., Inc., New York, 1925—. Capt. Signal Corps, U.S.A., Mar. 1917; maj., Dec. 1917; tech. adviser U. S. Navy, London, June-Oct. 1918. Vice chmn. div. of engring. and industrial research Nat. Research Council; chmn. bd. Engring. Socs. Library; mem. of council Am. Inst. Weights and Measures. Republican. Home: Hackensack, N.J. Died Aug. 20, 1929.

CRAFTS, JAMES MASON, chemist; b. at Boston, Mar. 8, 1839; s. R. A. and Marian (Mason) C.; S.B., Lawrence Scientific Sch. (Harvard), 1858; (LL.D., 1898); studied chemistry at Bergacademie, Freiberg, and univs. of Heidelberg and Paris, 1850-55; m. Clemence Haggerty, June 13, 1868. Examined mines in Mex., 1866-67; prof. chemistry and dean chem. faculty, Cornell, 1868-71; prof. chemistry, 1871-80, organic chemistry, 1892-97, pres., 1898-1900, Mass. Inst. Tech.; engaged in chem. research, Boston, 1900—. Jecker Prize, Paris Acad. Sciences, 188S; chevalier Legion of Honor, France, 1885. Fellow Am. Acad. Arts and Sciences; mem. Nat. Acad. Sciences; hon. mem. Royal Inst. Great Britain. Author: Qualitative Chemical Analysis, 1870. Also published Researches Upon Silicic Compounds, 1865; Arsenic Ethers, A Method of Synthesis by Means of Chloride of Aluminum, 1879; Studies in Thermometry, 1880; Catalysis in Concentrated Solutions, 1908; Thermometry, 1913-15. Home: Boston, Mass. Died June 20, 1917.

CRAFTS, LEO MELVILLE, M.D.; b. Minneapolis, Minn., Oct. 3, 1863; s. Maj. Amasa and Mary Jane (Henry) C.; B.L., U. of Minn., 1886; M.D., Harvard, 1890; m. Amelia I. Burgess, Sept. 4, 1901. House phys., Boston City Hosp., 1889-91; practiced in Minneapolis, 1892—; prof. nervous and mental diseases, 1893-1908, dean, 1897-1903, Hamline Med. Sch., also trustee Corp. Hamline Med. Sch.; visiting neurologist various hosp. Pres. Progressive Club, Hennepin Co., 1912; v.-chmn. Prog. State Central Comp., 1912. Mem. Com. Am. Physicians on Med. Preparedness, Med. Advisory Bd. of U.S. Selective Service, etc.; del. Internat. Congress of Medicine, London, 1913; del. to Internat. Neurol. Congress, Berne, Switzerland, 1931. Pres. Minn. State S.S. Assn., 1893-95. Congregationalist. Chief neurologist on special neuro-psychiatric bd., examining the command at Camp Funston, summer 1918; attending specialist in neuro-psychiatry for U.S. Vet. Bur. Author of text book on Epidemic Encephalitits and numerous monographs on med. topics. One of originators of movement for Minn. Nat. Park and Forest Reserve. Home: Minneapolis, Minn. Died Sept. 22, 1938.

CRAFTS, WALTER, metallurgist, assn. ofcl.; b. Oberlin, O., May 16, 1903; s. Walter Nathan and Annie (Francis) C.; A.B., Yale, 1924; M.S., Mass. Inst. Tech., 1926; m. Suzanne Clifton, Oct. 15, 1932; children—Walter, Suzanne. Metallurgist U.S. Steel Corp., Chgo., 1926-29; asso. dir. tech. Union Carbide Metals Co., Union Carbide Corp., 1929—. Recipient achievement award Tech. Socs. Council of Niagara Frontier, 1955. Mem. Am. Soc. Metals (past pres.), Am. Inst. Mining, Metall. and Petroleum Engrs. (Francis L. Toy award 1953), Soc. Automotive Engrs., Iron and Steel Inst., Inst. Metals. Author: (with A.B. Kinzel) Alloys of Iron and Chromium, 1937; (with J.L. Lamont) Hardenability and Steel Selection, 1949. Home: 844 College Av., Niagara Falls, N.Y. 14305. Died Oct. 31, 1963; buried Riverdale Cemetery, Niagara Falls.

CRAGIN, FRANCIS WHITTEMORE, prof. geology, Colorado Coll., since 1891, examiner of mineral lands; b. Greenfield, N.H., Sept. 4, 1858; s. Dr. Francis Whittemore and Mary Ann (Le Bosquet) C.; studied in Wis. and Kan.; Washburn Coll., Topeka, Kan., and Brooklyn Polytechnic Inst.; grad. Lawrence Scientific School, Harvard, B.S., 1882; (Ph.D., Johns Hopkins, 1899); m. Aug., 1884, Catherine Officer. Studied marine zoology at Dr. A. Agassiz' private laboratroy Newport, R.I., prof. natural history, Washburn Coll., 1882-91. Inaugurated, 1883, and continued until 1891, the 1st so-called "biological survey" -that of Kan., publishing on connection therewith Bull. of Washburn Coll. Laboratory of Natural History; asst. geologist Texas State Geol. Survey, 1892-93. An editor and propr. American Geologist, 1890-96; author of many scientific papers, the earlier chiefly on zoology and botany, the later principally on geology and palaeonthology; mem. since 1880, fellow since 1890, A.A.A.S., original fellow Geol. Soc. of America; mem. Nat. Geog. Soc., Internat. Congress of Geologists; etc. Address: 1715 Wood Av., Coloardo Springs, Colo.

CRAIG, CHARLES FRANKLIN army officer, author; b. Danbury, Conn., July 4, 1872; s. William Edward and Maria Hamlin (Payne) C.; M.D., Yale, 1894, hon. M.A., 1914; D.Sc., Tulane U., 1945; m. Lillian Osmun, July, 7, 1893; children— Marjorie Lilian, Edward Arthur. Acting asst. Surgeon U.S. Army, 1898-1903; advanced through grades from 1st lt. to col. M.C., 1918; pathologist and bacteriologist Sternberg U.S. Army Gen. Hosp., Chickamauga Park, Ga., 1898, Simpson Gen. Hosp., Fortress Monroe, Va., 1898-99, Camp Columbia Hosp., Havana, 1899, U.S. Army Gen. Hosp., Presidio, Cal., 1899-1905, Div. Hosp., Manila, 1906; mem. U.S. Army, Bd. for Study of Tropical Diseases, Manila, 1906-07; lab. Ft. Leavenworth, Kan., 1907-09; attending surgeon, N. Y.C., 1909; asst. curator Army Med. Museum, 1909-13, curator, 1919-20; asst. prof. bacteriology and clin. diagnosis Army Med. Sch., Washington, 1909-13, prof. bacteriology, parasitology and preventive medicine, also dir. labs., 1920-22, condt. and dir. clin. pathology and preventive medicine, 1926-30; asso. prof. bacteriology, med. Dept. George Washington U., 1910-11; comdg. officer Central Dept. Lab. U.S. Army, Ft. Leavenworth, 1913-16, Dept. Lab. No. 2, So. Dept., El Paso, Tex., 1916-17, Ft. Leavenworth 1917-18; organized and comd. Yale Army Lab. Sch., 1918-19; med. insp. Hawaiian Dept. 1922-26; asst. cmdt. Army Med. Center, Washington, 1930-31; prof. tropical medicine and dir.dept., sch. medicine Tulane U., 1931-38, emeritus prof. tropical medicine 1939—. Asso. editor Am. Jour. Parasitology; editor Am. Jour. Tropical Medicine, etc. Fellow A.C.S., A.C.P., Assn. Mil. Surgeons U.S. (life), A.M.A., Am. Pub. Health Assn., mem. Am. Soc. Tropical Medicine (pres. 1914-15), Royal Soc. Tropical Medicine and Hygiene, Conn. Med. Soc., Wash. Acad. Sciences, Internat. Leprosy Assn. Soc. Tropical Medicine and Hygiene of Egypt, Internat. Soc. Parasitiologists (pres. 1934-35), Am. Acad. Tropical Medicine (pres. 1935), Bexar County (Tex.) Med. Soc. (hon.), Am. Soc. Clin. Pathologists. Recipient gold medal Am. Acad. Tropical Med., 1943. Founder's medal Assn. Mil. Surg., 1948. Mem. Alpha Omega Alpha, Sigma Xi, Nu Sigma Nu; pres. Yale Med. Alumni Assn., 1910-11. Decorated D.S.M., 1922. Club: Army and Navy Country (Washington). Author: the AEstivo-Autumnal Malarial Fevers, 1901; The Malarial Fevers, Haemoglobinuric Fever and the Blood Protoza of Man, 1909; The Parasitic Amoebae of Man, 1911; The Wassermann Test, 1918, 21; A Manual of the Parasitic Protozoa of Man, 1925; Amebiasis and Amebic Dysentery, 1935; Clinical Parasitology (With Faust), 1937; The Laboratory Diagnosis of Protozoan Diseases, 1941; The Etiology, Diagnosis and Treatment of Amebiasis, 1944. Also wrote chapters in Osler's Modern Medicine, 1907, 14, in Hare's Mod. Treatment, 1911; Oxford medicine and Oxford Tropical Medicines, 1919; Musser's Internal Medicine, 1932; Brennemann's Pediatrics, 1935; Riemann's Treatment in General Medicine, 1939; Barr's Modern Medical Therapy in General Practice, 1940; Blumr's Therapeutics of Internal Diseases, 1941. Clinical Tropical Medicine, Bercovitz. Home: 225 Henderson St., San Antonio. Died Dec. 9, 1950; buried Ft. Sam Houston Cemetery.

CRAIG, JOHN, horticulturist; b. at Lakefield, P.Q., Can., Apr. 27, 1864; s. William and Mary (Hamilton) C.; Ia. State Coll., 1885-88; asst. Ia. Expt. Sta., 1888-89; horticulturist Dominion Expt. Sta., Ottawa, Can., 1890-97; B.S., Ia. State Coll., 1898; M.S. in agr., Cornell U., 1899; m. Florence Augusta Slater, Nov. 1895. Prof. horticulture and forestry, Ia. State Coll., 1899-1900; prof. extension teaching, 1900-03, horticulture, 1903—, Cornell U. Editor National Nurseryman, 1904—; pres. N. Fla. Pecan Co., S. Ga. Pecan Co., Empire-Ga. Pecan Co. Mem. Jury of Awards, Chicago Expn., 1893, St. Louis Expn., 1904, Nat. Apple Show, Spokane, Wash., 1908. Mason (32deg.). Author: Practical Agriculture, revised edit., 1901. Contbr. to Cyclopedia of American Horticulture. Home: Ithaca, N.Y. Died Aug. 12, 1912.

CRAIG, PALMER HUNT, electrical engineer and physicist; b. Cheviot, O., Jan. 10, 1901; s. Charles Harry and Florence Irene (Hunt) C.; A.B. with honors, U. Cin., 1923; M.A. (Hanna grad. fellow), 1924, Ph.D., 1926; m. Hedwig Feltner, Apr. 5, 1927; children—Palmer Hunt, Marian Jean. Prof. physics, head of dept., dean of coll. of pre-engring., Mercer U., 1926-27; chief physicist, Premier Lab. Co., Inc., New York, 1927-29; research physicist, consulting engr., Harris Hammond Interests, New York, 1929; v.p. and dir., lab. of the Crason Corp., New York, 1929-30; v.p. and dir., lab. of Invex, Inc. (patent holding company developing, marketing his inventions) 1930-50; head of dept. elec. engring., U. of Fla., 1941-46; supervisor, War Research Lab., U. of Fla., 1943-46; chief engineer of radio station WRUF, 1943-47; radio supervisor State of Fla., under Federal E.S.M.W.T. program, 1942-45; associate technical director Pan American Technological and Manufacturing Corp., Miami; pres., dir. research Invex, Inc. Miami; cons. engineer; dir. electronics research lab., prof. engring. U. Miami, 1947-51; cons. engr. and physicist; with ICA, U.S. Dept. State, Indian Inst. Sci., Bangalore, India, 1957-59, guest prof. electronics, 1957-59; prof. electronics on fgn. assignment, U. Wis., 1957-59; tech. dir. Electronic & Chem. Research, Inc., Newark; cons. Airpax Electronics, Inc., Ft. Lauderdale, Fla.; U.S. del. Indian Sci. Congress, Madras, 1958, del., leader, Delhi, India, 1959, lectr. throughout India, Orient, Asia, Middle-East, Europe; dean of scis. and mathematics, also dir. indsl., govt. relations Fla. Atlantic U., Boca Raton, Fla.; 1961-66, dean emeritus, 1966-67; cons. to electronics corps. Mem. exec. com. S. Fla. Edn. Center; member com. on Oceanographic research Fla. U. System; cons. Broward County Bd. Public Instrn. Registered profl. engr. Recipient Naval Ordnance Award for Civilian Service; bldg. named in his honor Fla. Atlantic U. Fellow I.E.E.E., Am. Phys. Society, A.A.A.S.; I.R.E. (post chmn. Miami sect.), Am. Inst. Elec. Engrs.; mem. Fla. Engring. Soc. (life sr.), Fla. Acad. Sci. (sr.); Fla. Soc. Profl. Engineers (senior mem., past president of Miami chapter); member of Phi Beta Kappa, Sigma Xi, Sigma Tau, Omicron Delta Kappa, Sigma Phi Epsilon. Clubs: Coral Gables Country; Rotary; Bangalore (India). Author of numerous technical articles; inventor many electronic devices, including the Craig System of Television. Holder of over 40 issued patents. Contbr. articles on physics, electronics and electricity, in World Book Ency. Home: Boca Raton FL Died Apr. 7, 1967; interred Forest Lawn Meml. Gardens Mausoleum, Pompano Beach FL

CRAIG, THOMAS, mathematician; b. Ayrshire, Scotland, Dec. 20, 1855; s. Alexander and Mary (Hall) C.; grad. Layfayette Coll., 1875; Ph.D., Johns Hopkins, 1878; m. Louise Alvord, May 4, 1880. Lect., John Hopkins, 1877-79, fellow, later asso. prof. mathematics, 1881-92, prof., 1892-1900; mathematician U.S. Coast and Geodetic Survey, 1879-81; editor Am. Jour. of Mathematics, 1894-99. Author: Elements of the Mathematical Theory of Fluid Motion, 1879; A Treatise on Projections, 1882; A Treatise on Linear Differential Equations, 1889. Died May 8, 1900.

CRAIG, WALLACE, zoologist, psychologist; b. Toronto, Can., July 20, 1876; s. Alexander and Marion (Brookes) C.; B.S., U. of Ill., 1898, M.S., 1901; Ph.D., U. of Chicago, 1908; m. Mrs. Mima Davis Jenness, Oct. 12, 1904. Prof. philosophy, U. of Me., 1908-22; lecturer, psychology, Harvard, 1922-23, librarian, bio-physics, 1923-27; engaged in research since 1929. Fellow A.A.A.S.; mem. Am. Philos Assn., Am. Psychol. Assn., Boston Soc. Nat. History, Sigma Xi, Phi Kappa Phi, Phi Sigma. Author: Song of the Wood Pewee, a study of bird music, 1943. Contbr. on animal behavior, psychology. Address: 18 Martin St., Cambridge MA

CRAIG, WINCHELL MCKENDREE, neurosurg; b. Washington Ct. House, O., Apr. 27, 1892; s. Thomas Henry and Eliza Orlena (Pine) C.; student Culver Mil. Acad., 1911; A.B., O. Wesleyan U., 1915; D.Sc., 1937; M.D., Johns Hopkins Med. Sch., 1919; M.S. in surgery, U. Minn., 1930; m. Jean Katherine Fitzgerald, Feb. 16, 1928; children—Winchell McKendree, James Stewart, Jean Mary Patricia, Graham Fitzgerald. Resident surg., St. Agnes Hosp., Baltimore, 1919-21. Fellow Mayo Foundation, Grad. Sch. Univ. of Minn., 1921-24, instr., 1925, professor neurosugery, 1937; senior cons. Surgery Mayo Clinic, St. Mary's Hosp., Methodist Hospital. Served as commander, capt. and rear adm., M.C., U.S.N.R., chief surgeon, U.S. Naval Hosp., Corona, Calif., 1941-42; chief surg. Nat. Naval Med. Center, Bethesda, Md., 1942-45; dir. Grad. Training Program, Bur. Med. and Surg., Washington, D.C., 1945-46; res. cons. to Surg. Gen. U.S. Navy; cons. VA. Trustee Ohio Wesleyan U. Awarded Legion of Merit, Naval Res. Medal, Bronze Star. Fellow A.M.A., Am. Coll. of Surgeons; mem. Italian Soc. Neurosugery (hon.), Surgical Assn., Am. Neurol. Assn., Western Surg. Assn., Southern Surg. Assn., Minn. Soc. of Neurology and Psychiatry, Internat. Surg. Soc., Central Society Clinical Research Harvey Cushing Society, Am. Acad. Neurol. Surgery (hon.), Johns Hopkins Alumnae Assn., Minn. Surg. Soc., Internat. Neurol. Assn., Am. Legion, Association of Military Surgeons of the United States (pres. 1953), Res. Officers Assn., Sigma Xi, Beta Thea Pi, Phi Beta Pi. Clubs: University (Rochester, Minn.); Golf and Country (Rochester, Minn.); Ohio Society of New York. Author 300 med. papers and chapter chapters in monographs or systems of medicine. Editorial bd. Journal of Neurosurgery. Home: 828 Eighth St. S.W. Address: Care Mayo Clinic, Rochester, Minn. Died Feb. 12, 1960.

CRAIGHILL, WILLIAM PRICE, .chief of engrs. U.S.A.; b. Charlestown, Va., July 1, 1833; grad. West Point, 1853; (LL.D., Washington and Lee, 1897); m. Mary A. Morsell, Oct. 14, 1856; m. 2d, Rebecca Churchill Jones, Sept. 22, 1874. Assigned to engr. corps and superintended work on Ft. Sumter, 1854-55, and Ft. Delaware, 1858; several yrs. instr. West Point; built defenses of Pittsburgh, 1863; bvtd. lt. col., Mar. 1865, for services at Cumberland Gap; afterward engaged on defenses of New York and Baltimore, and many public works. Mem. Light House Bd. several yrs., also of Bd. Consulting Engrs; to Dept. of Docks of City of New York; after centennial of Surrender of Cornwallis, 1881; built the monument at Yorktown, Va., which though ordered to be built by Continental Congress, did not have funds provided until over a century later; colonel engineers, Jan. 10, 1887; brig. gen., chief of engrs. U.S.A., May 10, 1895, until retired, Feb. 1, 1897. Dir., 1892-93, pres., 1894-95, hon. mem., Mar. 23, 1896—, Am. Soc. Civ. Engrs.; 7 times deputy from W.Va. to Gen. Conv. P.E. Ch. Author: Army Officers' Pocket Companion, 1862. Address: Charles Town, W.Va. Died 1909.

CRAMER, JOHN WESLEY, cons. engr.; b. North Platte, Neb., May 15, 1914; s. W. H. and Elizabeth (Bonner) C.; student Wentworth Mil. Acad.; B.S., U. Neb., 1940; m. Henrietta Irene Peterson, Jan. 23, 1937;

children—John Henry, James Peter. Designer, Lockheed Aircraft Corp., Burbank, Cal., 1940-44; chief engr. Chemold Co., Glendale, Cal., 1944-45; partner Fulton & Cramer, cons. engr., Lincoln, Neb., 1949-59, sr. partner, 1959—. Fellow Am. Soc. C.E. (pres. Neb. 1961-62); mem. Am. Water Works Assn. (dir. 1951-53; Fuller award 1954; chmn. water resources div. 1958-59; pres. 1961-62), Am. Soc. M.E., Neb. Engring. Soc. (pres. 1957-58), Am. Inst. Cons. Engrs., Brit. Instn. Water Engrs., Nat. Soc. Profl. Engrs., Sigma Xi, Sigma Tau. Republican. Episcopalian. Rotarian. Home: 3401 S. 31st St. Office: Terminal Bldg., Lincoln 8, Neb. Died Feb. 1, 1966.

CRAMER, STUART WARREN, mfr.; b. Thomasville, N.C., Mar. 31, 1868; s. John Thomas and Mary Jane (Thomas) C.; grad. U.S. Naval Acad., 1888; studied Sch. of Mines (Columbia), 1888-89; Sc.D., N.C. State Coll., 1929; m. Bertha Hobart Berry, June 24, 1889 (died 1895); children—Katherine (wife of James R. Angell, pres. Yale U.), Stuart Warren; m. 2d, Kate Stanwood Berry, Sept. 7, 1896 (died 1897); m. 3d, Rebecca Warren Tinkham, Jan. 28, 1902; 1 son, George Bennett. Resigned from U.S.N., 1888; assayer in charge U.S.N., Assay office, Charlotte, N.C., 1889-93; engr. and mgr. D. A. Tompkins Co., Charlotte, 1893-95; mill engr. and contractor, Charlotte, designing or equipping nearly one-third of cotton mills in South, 1895-1918; pres. and treas. Mays Mills, Mayflower Mills, Cramerton Mills, Inc. Owner of Mayfarm and Orchards; officer or director of various financial, manufacturing and railway corps. Granted about 60 U.S. and foreign patents as result of research in industry, trade chemistry and physics. Organizer and first comdr. N.C. Naval Reserve, 1890-93; mem. Bd. Visitors, U.S. Naval Acad., 1912-26; life mem. U.S. Naval Inst., 1889; state chmn. for N.C. of Navy League of U.S.; mem. production engineering com. Council Nat. Defense, World War; was also mem. war service com. and advisory tax board of Treasury Dept. Mem. Am. Cotton Mfrs. Assn. (pres. 1916-17), Nat. Council Am. Cotton Mfrs. (pres. 1917-18, 1920-27), Nat. Assn. Cotton Mfrs. (medalist 1913); Cotton Textile Inst. (1st v.p.). Mem. Nat. Industrial Conf. Board; mem. Am. com. of Internat. Chamber of Commerce, 1923, Nat. Com. on Inheritance Taxation, 1925; mem. executive com. Nat. Business Survey Conf., 1929. Mem. Tax. Com. U.S. Chamber of Commerce, Del. to Rep. Nat. Conv., 1928, 32; (mem. com. to notify Herbert Hoover of presdl. nomination); chmn. finance com. N.C. Rep. State Exec. Com. and campaign mgr. 1928; mem. nat. advisory com., President's Orgn. on Unemployment Relief, 1931; mem. President's Conf. on Home Building and Home Ownership (chmn. subcom. on industrial decentralization and housing), 1931. Dir. and treas. The Textile Foundation. Mem. Cotton Textile Code Authority under NRA. Episcopalian. Author: Useful Information for Cotton Manufacturers (4 vols.), 1904-09. Home: Cramerton, N.C. Died July 2, 1940.

CRAMER, WILLIAM, pathologist; b. Brandenburg, Germany, June 2, 1878; s. Siegmund and Olga (Harff) C.; student chemistry Munich U., 1896-97, Berlin U., 1897-1900; D.Sc., Edinburgh U., 1903; M.R.C.S. and L.R.C.P., Ohio Coll., London, 1915-17; m. Belle Klauber, of New York, 1906; children—Ian William David, Michael William Valentine. Naturalized British subject, 1914; came to U.S., 1939. Research chemist and asst. to prof. pharmacology, U. of Berlin, 1900; jr. mem. scientific staff Imperial Cancer Research Fund, London, 1903-05; lecturer chem. physiology, U. of Edinburgh, 1905-14; sr. mem. scientific staff, Imperial Cancer Research Fund, London, 1915-39; research asso., Barnard Free Skin and Cancer Hosp., St. Louis, Mo., since 1940; mem. med. faculty, Washington U., St. Louis, since 1940; Middleton Goldsmith lecturer Pathol. Soc. of New York, 1940; lecturer British Med. Assn. and German Soc. for Cancer Research. British del. Council. of Internat. Union against Cancer (mem. statis. com.), Internat. Cancer Congress, Madrid, 1933, Brussels, 1936, Atlantic City, 1939. Awarded Ellis prize in physiology, 1906. Mem. Pathol. Club (Edinburgh), Biochem. Soc., Physiol. Soc. and Pathol. Soc. (England), Royal Soc. Medicine (London), Leewenhoek Vereeniging (Amsterdam), Am. Assn. for Cancer Research; mem. British Med. Assn. Com. on Radium Beam Therapy. Author: Practical Course in Chemical Physiology, 3d edit., 1918; Fever, Heat Regulation, Climate and the Thyriod Adrenal Apparatus, 1928; also chapters in various text books. Editor Cancer Review; mem. editorial com. Acta of Internat. Union Against Cancer. Home: 5364 Cabanne Av. Office: Barnard Free Skin and Cancer Hosp., St. Louis, Mo. Died Aug. 10, 1945.

CRAMP, WILLIAM, shipbuilder b. Phila., Sept. 22, 1807; m. Sophia Miller, 1827, several children including Charles Henry. Established William Cramp Shipbldg. Co., Phila., 1830, pres., 1830-79, name changed to William Cramp & Sons' Ship and Engine Bldg. Co., 1872, one of 1st shipbuilders to make change from wood to iron and steel vessels; built ships for U.S., Russian and Venezuelan navies; built U.S.S. New Ironsides (largest ironclad used in Civil War), 1862. Died Atlantic City, N.J., July 6, 1879.

CRAMPTON, CHARLES ALBERT, chemist; b. Davenport, Ia., Feb. 18, 1858; s. Albert Aulich and Harriet Jones (Weaver) C.; B.L., Ph.C., U. of Mich., 1882; A.C., Purdue, 1882; M.D., Columbian (now George Washington) U.; 1884; m. Lillie Dunn, June 25, 1890. Asst. chemist, U.S. Dept. Agr., 1883-90; chemist, 1890-93, chief chemist, 1893-1910, Internal Revenue Bur., Treas. Dept.; chief div. food and drug products, Institute Industrial Research, Washington, 1910—. Home: Bethesda, Md. Address: Institute of Industrial Research, Washington. Died July 26, 1915.

CRAMPTON, C(HARLES) WARD, b. N.Y.C., May 26, 1877; s. Henry Edward and Dorcas (Miller) C.; student Coll. City N.Y.; spl. student N.Y. U.; M.D., Coll. Physicians and Surgeons, 1900; m. Grace Tully, June 4, 1900; m. 2d, Dora Horwitz, June 30, 1919; 1 son, Charles Ward. Began practice, N.Y.C., 1900; asst. in embryology, Woods Hole (Mass.) Biol. Labs., 1899; asst. in pathology Coll. of Phys. and Surg., 1900-03; dir. phys. tng. and hygiene N.Y.C. Dept. Edn. 1907-19; dir. and dean of Battle Creek (Mich.), Normal Sch. Phys. Edn., 1919-21; in med. practice, N.Y.C., 1921—. Chmn. adv. com. on geriatrics N.Y.C. Dept. Health, 1947-49; chmn. sub-com. on geriatrics and gierontology Med. Soc. County of N.Y., since 1947; mem. com. on longevity, N.Y. State Legislature on Problems of Ageing, since 1947; mem. sub.-com. on ageing Med. Soc. State of N.Y., since 1947. Maj., Sch. Men's Bn., and dir. mil. tng., N.Y.C., World War maj. Med. R.C., U.S. Army. Organizer Health Service Clinic, Post Grad. Med. Sch., 1925, also asso prof. medicine. Mem. 1st bd. dirs., 1911, and pres., 1914-15, N.Y.C. (Manhattan) council Boy Scouts Am.; mem. 1st bd. dirs. Pub. Sch. Athletic League, 1903, exec. sec., 1907-09; organized, 1915, 1st Interborough Com. Boy Scouts (subsequently Boy Scout Found.), N.Y.; mem. 1st Sch. Lunch Com., N.Y.C., 1911; 1st chmn. Com. on Health Examinations, Med. Soc., State of N.Y., 1929-33, also 1st chmn. com. on Preventive Medicine, N.Y. County Med. Soc., 1933-39; mem. Fed. Com., Nat. Phys. Fitness, Fed. Security Agy. Mem. Council West Side YMCA since 1938, City Council since 1940. Fellow Nat. Inst. Social Sci., N.Y. Acad. Medicine; mem. A.M.A., Soc. Exptl. Biology and Medicine A.A.A.S., Aristogenic Assn. founder and pres.); mem. Fed. Com. chmn. sub. com., nat. fitness agys., Phi Sigma Kappa. Mem Dutch Ref. Ch. Mason. Author: The Folk Dance Book, 1903; The Second Folk Dance Book, 1905; The Pedagogy of Physical Training, 1920; Physical Exercises for Daily Use, 1924; (monograph) Dyskinesia, 1926; The Daily Health Builder, 1929; The Boys' Book of Strength, 1936; The Basic Health Record, 1938; Science Looks Toward God, 1938; Training for Championship Athletics, 1939; Your Guide to Physical Fitness, 1942; Preliminary Fitness Training, 1943. Author of page "Physically Fit." for Boys Life, 1934-43; 1st nat. broadcast series on preventive medicine for N.Y.State Med. Assn., 1933-34; Columbia Womans Health radio series (anonymous), 1936. Awarded Silver Buffalo for Outstanding Services to the Boyhood fo Am., 1941. Pioneer research in physiol. age and blood pressure, since 1900; vitamin A in treatment of colds, since 1943. Awarded gold medal St. Louis Olympic Congress, 1903, Crampton test of circulatory efficiency. Author: What Geriatrics Mean to the Medical Profession, 1947; Live Long and Like It, 1948; Dietary Aids and Dangers for the Ageing, 1948; Essentials of the Geriatric Examination, 1949. Died Oct. 1964.

CRAMPTON, HENRY EDWARD, zoölogist; b. N.Y.C., Jan. 5, 1875; s. Henry Edward (M.D.) and Dorcas Matilda (Miller) C.; student Coll. City of N.Y., 1889-92; A.B., Columbia 1893; Ph.D., 1899; m. Marion M. Tully, Oct. 27, 1896; Asst. in biology Columbia, 1893-95; instr. Mass. Inst. Tech.; 1895-96; fellow, lecturer, tutor and and instr. in zoölogy Columbia, 1896-1901; adj. prof., 1901-04, prof., 1904-43, emeritus prof., 1943—; instr. embryology Marine Biol. Lab., Woods Hole, Mass., 1895-1902; in charge of embryology, Cold Spring Harbor, 1903-06; asso. Carnegie Inst.; curator invertebrate zoölogy Am. Mus. Natural Histroy, 1902-20; asso. Bishop Museum, Honolulu. Scientific expdns. Islands of South Pacific Ocean, 1906-07, 08, 09, British Guiana and interior of Brazil, 1911; expdns. to Bahamas, 1912, Porto Rico, 1913-14, 14-15, South Seas, 1919, Western Pacific, Asia, Malaysia, Australia, 1920-21, South Seas, 1923-24, South Seas and Asia, 1928-29, Hawiian Islands, 1929, 20, 31, 35; research asso., Am. Mus. Natrual History, 1943, Former Sec. treas. Eugenics Soc. U.S. Fellow N.Y. Acad. Sciences (ex-v.p., sec. res. pres. and corr. sec.), A.A.A.S., Washington Acad. Scis.; mem. Am. Soc. Naturalists (v.p., 1921), Am. Sco. Zoölosgist (v.P. 1911), Theta Delta Chi, Sigma Xi, Phi Beta Kappa. Clubs: Century. Explorers (v.p. 1926-30) (N.Y.C.). Author: The Doctrine of Evolution, 1911; also various monographs on evolution, embryology, exptl. zoölogy and travel. Home: 315 W. 106th St., Died Feb. 26, 1956.

CRANDALL,CHARLES LEE, civil engr.; b. Bridgewater, N.Y., July 20, 1850; s. Peter B. and Eunice C. (Priest) C.; family removed to Ithaca, 1868; C.E., Cornell, 1872; served in architect's office and asst. ry. engr., 1872-74; m. Myra G. Robbins, Aug. 20, 1878. City engr., Ithaca, N.Y., 1870-91; instr. civ. engring. 1874-75, asst. prof., 1875-91, asso. prof., 1891-95, prof. ry. engring. and geodesy, 1895-1908, prof. ry. engring., 1908—, in charge of Coll. of Civil Engring., 1903-06. Cornell. Author: Tables from Computation of Railway and Other Earthwork, 1886, 1893, 1902, 1907; Notes on Descriptive Geometry, 1888, 1893; Notes on Shades, Shadows and Perspective; The Transition Curve, 1893, 1899; Text-Book on Geodesy and Least Squares, 1907; (joint author) Field Book for Railroad Surveying, 1909. Home: Ithaca, N.Y. Died Aug. 25, 1917.

CRANDALL, CHARLES SPENCER, pomologist; b. Waverly, N.Y., Oct. 22, 1852; s. Richard Orson and Marie Louise (Cushman) C.; B.S., Mich. Agrl. Coll., 1873, M.S., 1889; m. Maud Bell, June 9, 1897. Asst., dept. of horticulture, Mich. Agrl. Coll., 1885-89; prof. botany and horticulture, Colo. Agrl. Coll., 1890-1900; instr. horticulture, 1902-03, asst. prof., 1903-06, asso. prof., 1907-10, prof. pomology, Sept. 1, 1911—, U. of Ill. Home: Urbana, Ill. Died July 12, 1929.

CRANDALL, LEE SAUNDERS, zoologist; b. Sherburne, N.Y., Jan. 26, 1887; s. Charles Spencer and Ada (Harwood) C.; grad. Utica (N.Y.) Prep. Sch., 1907; student Cornell U. Med. Coll., 1907-08; Columbia, 1908-09; m. Celia Mary Dowd, Jan. 15, 1910; 1 dau., Sylvia. Asst., dept. of birds, N.Y. Zool. Park, 1908-11, asst. curator, 1911-19, curator, 1920-43, gen. curator, 1943-52, emeritus. Mem. sci. expeditions of New York Zoological Society to British Guiana, 1909, Costa Rica, 1914, New Guinea, 1928-29. Fellow New York Zool. Soc., N.Y. Acad. Science, Am. Ornithologists Union; mem. Linnaean Soc., Soc. Mammalogists, Am. Soc. Icthyologists and Herpetologists; corr. mem. Zool. Soc., London. Author: Pets and How to Care for Them, 1917; Paradise Quest, 1931. Contbr. many articles and papers on natural history. Home: Bronxville NY Died June 25, 1969.

CRANE, ALBERT SEARS, hydraulic engr.; b. Addison, N.Y., May 30, 1868; s. Albert Gallatin and Julia Ayrault (Holden) C.; grad. Addison Union Sch., 1884; C.E., Cornell U., 1891; unmarried. Asst. engr., Newton, Mass., 1891-95; asst. engr. dept. of sewers, Brooklyn, N.Y., 1895-1900; chief asst. engr. Mich. Lake Superior Power Co., Saulte Ste. Marie, Mich., 1898-1900; chief engr. The Lake Superior Power Co., Saulte Ste. Marie, Ont., Can., 1900-02; prin. asst. engr. Chicago Drainage Canal, 1902-05; hydraulic engr. J. G. White & Co., New York, 1905-13, vice-pres., 1913-28; cons. hydraulic engr. since 1928. Mem. Am. Soc. C.E., Am. Inst. E.E., Western Soc. Engrs., Boston Soc. C.E., Chi Psi. Republican. Presbyterian. Clubs: Engineers, Cornell, Lawyers (New York). Has engaged in constrn. of 30 large earth dams, 60 masonry dams, 40 hydroelectric stations, 6 irrigation projects, etc. Home: 32 W. 40th St. Office: 80 Broad St., New York. Died Aug. 25, 1946; buried at Addison, N.Y.

CRANE, A(UGUSTUS) W(ARREN), M.D,; b. Adrian, Mich., Nov. 13, 1868; s. Nathan Seeley and Julia Etta (Chaffee) C.; student lit. dept. U. of Mich., 1889-90, M.D., 1894, M.A., 1932; m. Caroline Bartlett, Dec. 31, 1896; children—Juliana Bartlett, Warren Bartlett. Practiced at Kalamazoo, 1894-1907; specialized as diagnostician, 1915—; investigator of X-rays, 1897—. Chmn. Kalamazoo Co. sect. Mich. State Com. of Med. Preparedness, and mem. Mich. Med. Advisory Bd. No. 12, 1917-18; apptd. mem. Nat. Research Council, 1919. Pres. Am. Roentgen Ray Soc., 1916 (Caldwell lecturer for 1932); pres. Kalamazoo Acad. Medicine, 1908. Acting editor Am. Jour. Roentgenology, 1917-18, later mem. editorial bd. Award gold medal, 1921, by Radio. Soc. of N. America "in recognition of achievement in science of radiology," Mem. People's Ch. Home: Kalamazoo, Mich. Died Feb. 20, 1937.

CRANE, CHARLES KITTREDGE, narcotics research; b. Dalton, Mass., Aug. 28, 1881; s. Zenas and Ellen Judith (Kittredge) C.; Ph.B., Sheffield Scientific Sch. (Yale), 1903; m. Margaret Diana Wilson, 1914 (divorced 1926); 1 son, Peter. With Z. and W. M. Crane, paper mfrs., Dalton, Mass., 1903-11; asst. hon. sec. Lord Knutsford's Shell Shock Hosps., London, 1914-17; research on internat. narcotics problem, 1925—. Republican. Conglist. Home: Pasadena, Calif. Died Jan. 24, 1932.

CRANE, WALTER RICHARD, mining engr.; b. Grafton, Mass., Feb. 5, 1870; s. Richard Reed and Arethusa Thorndyke (Barret) C.; grad. Franklin (Neb.) Mil. Acad., 1891; A.B., U. of Kan., 1895, A.M., 1896; Ph.D., Columbia, 1901; m. Margaret M. Gray, Dec. 28, 1898; children—Dorothy G., Margaret E., Aldyth C. Asst. in chemistry, U. of Kan., 1896; asst. to prin., Beloit High Sch., 1896-98; dir. manual training, city schs., Janesville, Wis., 1898-99; asst. geologist, Univ. Geol. Survey of Kan., 1893-1905; asst. prof. mining, U. of Kan., 1900-05; gas expert, Univ. Geol. Survey of Kan. and U.S. Geol. Survey, 1902-05; mem. faculty, Sch. of Mines, Columbia, 1905-08; dean Sch. of Mines and prof. mining, Pa. State Coll., 1908-18; mining engr., U.S. Bur. of Mines, 1918-33. Mem. State Commn. for Establishment U.S. Mining Expt. Sta. at Pittsburgh, 1913-18; war minerals investigation, U.S. Bur. of Mines, 1918-19; chief engr. War Minerals Relief Commn., Dept. Interior, 1920; apptd. supt. Southern Mining Expt. Sta., U.S. Bur. Mines, Birmingham, Ala., 1921; then supervising research engr., U.S. Bur. Mines until 1933; now cons. mining engr. Mem. Am. Inst. Mining and Metall. Engrs., Coal Mining Inst. America, Sigma Xi, Tau Beta Pi, Arctic Brotherhood. Republican. Congregationalist. Author: A Treatise on Gold and

Silver, 1908; Index of Mining Engineering Literature, 1909; Ore Mining Methods, 1910; also French and Russian edits.; also writer of numerous pub. monographs, papers and reports on mining and kindred subjects. In Alaska, investigating the coal resources of that territory, 1912 and 1913. Address: P.O. Box 453 Oakland CA

CRANNELL, ELIZABETH KELLER SHAULE (MRS. WINSLOW CRANNELL), writer, anti-suffragist; b. Sharon Springs, N.Y.; d. Solomon and Elizabeth (Keller) Shaule; ed. pvt. schs.; m. Winslow Crannell, of Albany, N.Y., Oct. 3, 1870 (died 1908). First woman to appear against extension of suffrage to women; addressed Rep. Nat. Conv., St. Louis, 1896, in opposition to female suffrage plank in party platform, conv. refusing to endorse the plank, appeared before Dem. Nat. Conv., Chicago, 1896, against female suffrage, conv. also refusing to embody female suffrage in its platform; organized anti-suffrage assns. in S.D., Wash. and Ore. and toured the country several times in opposition to female suffrage; addressed N.Y. Legislature annually, 1896-1911, in opposition to female suffrage. An organizer, 1892, and pres. Albany Assn., mem. exec. com. Pittsburgh Assn., and mem. Nat. Assn. Opposed to Woman Suffrage. Mem. Nat. Indian Assn. (exec. bd.), Albany Indian Assn. (ex-pres.), Albany Hist. and Art Soc., Dana Natural History Soc. (ex-president), Consumer's League, Authors' League America, Mohawk Chapter D.A.R. (charter mem. and 1st historian), etc. Episcopalian. Founder and editor Indian Advocate, also of the Anti-Suffragist; founder and 1st editor Church Record. Home: 9 Hall Pl., Albany NY

CRATHORNE, ARTHUR ROBERT, mathematics; b. Scarborough, Eng., Oct. 26, 1873; s. Francis and Ann (Harrison) C.; B.S., Univ. of Ill., 1898; U. of Wis., 1900-02; Ph.D., Goettingen U., 1907; m. Charlotte Pengra, 1904 (died 1915); children—Mary Preston (Mrs. Laurence Coughlin), Anne Harrison (Mrs. Carter L. Loth), Arthur Robert (died in service 1943); married 2d, Katherine Layton, 1917. Tutor in mathematics, University of Maine, 1898-1900; instructor in mathematics, University of Wis., 1901-04, with U. of Ill. since 1907, successively as instructor, asso., asst. prof., asso. prof., and prof. since 1935. Mem. Nat. Com. on Math. Requirements, Nat. Research Council Com. on Statistics; fellow A.A.A.S., Royal Statis. Soc., Inst. of Math. Statistics, Am. Statis. Assn. (v.p.); mem. Am. Math. Soc., Math. Assn. America, Econometric Soc., Phi Kappa Sigma, Sigma Xi, Phi Kappa Phi and Pi Mu Epsilon. Episcopalian. Club: University. Author: College Algebra (with H.L. Rietz), 1909, 4th edit., 1939; School Algebra (with H.L. Reitz and E.H. Taylor), Vols. 1 and 2, 1915; Mathematics of Finance (with H. L. and J. C. Reitz), 1921; Introductory College Algebra (with H.L. Reitz), 1923, 3d edit., 1943; Handbook of Mathematical Statistics (with others), 1924; Trigonometry (with E.B. Lytle), 1930, 2d edit., 1938; Brief Trigonometry (with G.E. Moore), 1941; Intermediate Algebra (with H.L. Reitz and L.J. Adams), 1942. Math. editor Nelson's Loose Leaf Ency. Contributor to math. and statis. jours. Home: 802 Pennsylvania Av., Urbana, Ill. Died Mar. 7, 1946; buried in Mount Hope Cemetery, Urbana.

CRATTY, ROBERT IRVIN, botanist; b. Butler Co., Pa., Feb. 5, 1853; s. William and Martha (Hirsch) C.; ed. pub. schs. Schs. and private study; m. L.E. Canon, Apt. 19, 1878 (died Dec. 22, 1896); children—Mabel Estelle, Edna Roberta (Mrs. C. B. Murtagh), Alta Medora (Mrs. C.W. Moore), Ralph William; m. 2d, Mrs. Mollie E. Webster, Mar. 4, 1910; of Minneaoplis, Minn. Teacher in pub. schs., Ill. and Ia., 1875-95; farming, 1895-1918; curator bot. dept., Iowa State Coll., 1918—. Has made extensive collections of Iowa and Minn. plants Fellow Ia. Acad. Sciences (pres., 1925-26); mem. Ia. Conservation Assn., Sigma Xi. Osborn Research Club, A.A.A.S. Presbyn. Republican. Writer onnflora of Ia., Delegate to 5th Internat. Bot. Congress, Cambridge, England, 1930. Home: Ames, Ia.

CRAVEN, ALFRED, civil engr.; b. Bound Brook, N.J., Sept. 16, 1846; s. Thomas Tingey and Emily (Henderson) C.; grad. U.S. Naval Acad., 1967; m. (Henderson) C.; grad. U.S. Naval Acad., 1967; m. Nina Florence Browne; children—Lucy Egerton, Emily Henderson, Truxtrin Tingey (dec.), Nana Florence. Resigned as master, U.S.N., 1871; engaged in geol. survey and irrigation work, Calif., and in mining engring., Calif. and Nev., 1871-74; div. engr. new Croton Aqueduct, N.Y. City, 1884-95; in charge constrn. Jerome Park Reservoir, 1895-1900; apptd. div. engr. Rapid Transit Commn., N.Y. City, 1900, and was in charge constrn. of sect. of subway at 42d St. and Broadway to 104th St.; dep. chief under same commn., 1905-07; dep. engr., subway constrn. of Pub. Service Commn., 1st Dist. N.Y., 1907-10; acting chief engr., later chief engr. in charge constrn. dual system of subways for N.Y. City, 1910-16; was consulting engr. Pub. Service Commn. and its successor, the Transit Constrn. Commn. Apptd. by Sec. of Navy, as one of two representatives of Am. Soc. C.E. on Naval Consulting Bd., 1915. Awarded Civil War Medal by Act of Congress, 1908. Republican. Episcopalian. Home: Pleasantville, N.Y. Died Sept. 30, 1926.

CRAVEN, GEORGE WARREN, electrical engr.; b. Helena, Mont., Apr. 1, 1871; s. Robert Martin and Mary Eleanor (Frasier) C.; B.S. in E.E., Mass. Inst. Tech., 1898; m. Marthell Arnold of Butte, Mont., June 30, 1903. Engr. with Highland Boy's Smelter, Murray, Utah, 1899; engr. with Butte Water Co.'s steam pumping plant, 1901; engr. Boston & Mont. Consol. Cooper & Silver Mining Co., 1901-03; with Mont. Power Co., 1903—, also cons. practice; pres. Mont. State Sch. of Mines, 1921-27. Democrat. Methodist. Mason. Home: Butte, Mont. Deceased.

CRAVEN, JOHN JOSEPH, physician, inventor; b. Newark, N.J., Sept. 8, 1822; m. Catherine S. Tichenor. Devised gutta-percha insulation for cables which pointed way for later successful ocean cable; med. dir. Dept. of South, U.S. Army, 1862, 10th Corps, 1864; physician to Jefferson Davis while the latter was in prison at Ft. Monroe, Va. Author: The Prison Life of Jefferson Davis, 1866. Died Patchague, N. Y. Feb. 14, 1893.

CRAVEN, TUNIS AUGUSTUS MACDONOUGH, radio engineer; b. Phila., Pa., Jan. 31, 1893; s. T. A. and Harriet Baker (Austin) C.; prep. edn. St. Paul's Sch., Baltimore, Md., 1902-08; grad. U.S. Naval Acad., 1913; m. Josephine La Tourette, Sept. 25, 1915; children—Eugenie La Tourette, Tunis Augustus Macdonough, Jr.; m. 2d, Emma Stoner, Dec. 1931; 1 son, Thomas Tingey; m. 3d, Margaret Preston, Dec. 1963; m. 4th, Emma Stoner, Mar. 1971. Commd. ensign U.S.N., 1913, radio officer, 1913-23; chief radio research and design section Bureau of Engineering, 1923-26; tech. adviser Internat. Radio-telegram Conf., Washington, 1927; resigned from navy, 1930, to enter private practice as cons. engr.; chief engr. Fed. Communications Commn., 1935-37; commr., 1937-44; senior executive and technical adviser Cowles' broadcasting stations, 1944-49; partner, Craven, Lohnes and Culver, cons. radio engrs., 1949-57; mem. FCC, 1957-63; consulting radio engineer, 1963—. Fellow Inst. Radio Engineers; member of U.S. Naval Inst., Mil. Order Loyal Legion of the U.S. Episcopalian. Clubs: Nat. Press (Washington, D.C.); Army and Navy Country; Ends of the Earth Club, Kilocycle Wave Length Club. Home: McLean VA Died May 31, 1972.

CRAWFORD, CHARLES WALLACE, ret. govt. ofcl; b. Lorena Tex., July 21, 1888; s. John Tilly and Alice Lee (Clark) C.; B.S., Okla. A. and M. Coll., 1909, M.S., 1916; m. Relia Brewer, Jan. 3, 1915; children—Alice Florence (Mrs. J. Prescott Blount), John Justin. Asst. chemist Okla. Agrl. Expt. Sta., Instr. in chemistry Okla. A. and M. Coll., 1909-10; asst. Wash. State chemist and instr. in chemistry Wash. State Coll., Pullman, 1910-11; chemist Internat. Refining Co., Cushing, Okla., 1916-17; asst. chemist Bur. of Chemistry (later became Food and Durg Adminstrn.) U.S. Dept. Agr. Chgo., New Orleans, Washington, D.C. 1917-54, trans. with Food and Drug Adminstrn. to Federal Security Agency, 1940. asso. commr. Food and Drugs, 1945-48; dep. commr. Food and Drugs, 1948-51, commr., 1951-54 ret, Mem. Assn. of Food and Drug Officials of the U.S., A.A.AS., Home: 762 Summit Av., Mill Valley, Cal. Died Sept. 15, 1957; buried Angeles Garden, Mount Tamapaes Cemetery, San Rafael, Cal.

CRAWFORD, GEORGE GORDON, engineer, metallurgist; b. Madison, Ga., Aug. 24, 1869; s. George Gilmore and Margaret Reed (Howard) C.; B.S., in mech. more and Margaret Reed (Howard) C.; B.S., in mech. engring., Ga. Sch. of Tech., Atlanta, 1890, Sc.D., 1931; Karl-Eberhard U., Tübingen, Germany, 1891-92; m. Margaret Richardson, Feb. 1, 1911. Chemist, 1892-94, draughtsman , 1894-95. Edgar-Thomson Works; asst. supt. Edgar-Thompson Blast Furnaces, Carnegie Steel Co., 1895-97; supt. blast furnaces and steel works, Nat. Tube Co., McKeesport, Pa., 1897-99; supt. Edgar-Thomson Blast Furances, Carnegie Steel Co., 1899-1901; mgr. nat. dept. Nat. Tube Co., McKeesport, Pa., 1901-07; pres. Tenn. Coal, Iron & R.R. Co., Birmingham, Ala., 1907-30; pres. Jones & Laughlin Steel Corp., Pittsburgh, 1930—. Mem. metall. advisory bd. Carnegie Inst. Tech. Dir. Am. Iron and Steel Inst. Home: Pittsburgh, Pa. Died Mar. 20, 1936.

CRAWFORD, IVAN CHARLES, cons. engr., educator; b. Leadville, Colo., June 2, 1886; s. Harvey Burton and Elizabeth (Fountain) C.; B.S., in C.E., U. of Colo., 1912, C.E., 1915; D.Sc., (honorary) University of Colorado, 1944; grad., Army School of the Line, Langres, France, 1918; short course, War Coll., Washington, D.C., 1926; m. Helen May Lee, Aug. 27, 1913; children—Ivan Charles, Jean Anne (dec.). Miner in Colo., 1906; surveying and bridge constrn., various periods, Ore. Short Line, D. & R. G. and I.C. rys.; successively instr., asst. prof. and asso. prof. civ. engring., U. of Colo., 1912-23; prof. civ. engring. and dean Coll. of Engring., U. of Ida., 1923-37; also dir. Ida. Engring. Expt. Sta., 1928-37; on leave of absence, 1933-34, as state engr., dir. for Ida., Fed. Pub. Works Adminstrn.; prof. civil engring., dean Sch. Engring. and Architecture, U. of Kan., 1937-40; dean Coll. of Engring., prof. civil engring., U. of Mich., 1940-51. Director Colorado Water Conservation Bd., 1953-58. Rep. in Idaho, U.S. Coast and Geodetic Sruvey, 1934; asso. consultant Nat. Resources Com., 1936; consultant on training programs of Ordnance Dept., United States Army, 1942, Navy Department Bureau of Naval Personnel, 1943-45; mem. bd. visitors U.S. Mil. Acad., 1957-60. Licensed civil engineer in Kansas, Mich., Colorado. Capt. Colo. N.G., 1916; maj. Engineer Corps, U.S. Army, 1917-19; chief of gen. buildings sect., Belgian Mission, Am. Commn. to Negotiate Peace; with Army of Occupation, A.E.F.; col. Engrs. Res. since 1938; ret. officer A.U.S., 1949. Awarded Norlin Alumni Medal for distinguished achievement, U. of Colo., 1950. Mem. Am. Soc. C.E.(dir. 1935-38), Soc. Am. Mil. Engrs., Northwest Sci. Soc. (pres. 1933), Am. Soc. for Engring. Edn. (v.p. 1936-37), Engrs. council for Professional Development (com. on engring. schs 1936-42), Nat. Soc. Profl. Engrs., Sigma Xi, Tau Beta Pi, Phi Kappa Phi, Sigma Tau, Alpha Sigma Phi, Acacia. Episcopalian. Mason. Clubs: Cosmos (Washihgton); Denver; Univ. Author: Legal Phases of Engineering: Contracts and Specifications. Contbr. to engring. press. Home: 645 Fifteenth St., Boulder, Colo. 80302. Office: State Office Bldg., Denver. Died Nov. 19, 1960; buried Boulder, Colo.

CRAWFORD, JOHN JONES, mining and metall. engr.; b. Newcastle, Pa., Feb. 12, 1846; s. J. M. and Elizabeth J. C.; grad. Polytechnic Coll. of Pa., Phila., 1867; Freiberg, Saxony, Royal School of Mines, June, 1870; supt. Great Basin Mining Co., White Pine, Nev., 1871; afterward supt. of other mines in Nev. and Calif. up to 1890; mem. of Calif., 1890-91; since, owner of canal and mines in Eldorado, Placer, Amador and Calaveras cos., Calif.; State mineralogist Calif., 1893-97; sec. Gwin Mine Development Co.; edited 3 reports, 11 bulls. Mem. Am. Inst. Mining Engrs. Address: 1209 Spreckels Bldg., San Francisco.

CRAWFORD, JOSEPH E(MANUEL), ry. official; b. San Diego, Calif., Dec. 1, 1876; s. Joseph U. and Harriet (Henriques) C.; B.S. in civil engring., U. of Pa., 1895; m. Alice Marion Christeson, May 15, 1904. Draftsman and designer Pencoyd (Pa.) Iron Works, 1895-1903; with N.&W. Ry. since 1903, as bridge engr., 1903-14, chief engr., 1914-24, gen. mgr., 1924-36, vice-pres. in charge of operation 1936-39, vice-president, assistant to president, 1939-41, retired Jan. 1, 1942. Member Am. Soc. Civil Engrs., Am. Ry. Engrs. Assn., Psi Upsilon. Republican. Episcopalian. Clubs: University (Phila.); Shenandoah, Roanoke Country (Roanoke, Va.). Home: 645 Wellington Av., Roanoke VA*

CRAWFORD, MORRIS BARKER, physicist; b. Sing Sing (now Ossining), N.Y., Sept. 26, 1852; s. Morris D'Camp and Charlotte (Holmes) C.; A.B., Wesleyan U., Conn., 1874, A.M., 1877; univs. of Leipzig and Berlin, 1877-80; m. Caroline L. Rice, Dec. 25, 1883; children—Holmes (dec.), Frederick North (dec.), Margaret. Tutor mathematics, Wesleyan U., 1874-77, instr. physics, 1880-81, asso. prof., 1881-84, prof., 1884-1921, prof. emeritus since 1921. Fellow A.A.A.S.; mem. Am. Physical Soc. Home: Middletown, Conn. Died. Oct. 9, 1940.

CRAWFORD, RALPH DIXON, geologist; b. nr. Peotone, Ill., Mar. 7, 1873; s. Ralph and Nancy Elizabeth (Cotes) C.; prep. edn. No. Ind. Normal Sch., B.A., U. Colo., 1905; M.A., 1907; Ph.D., Yale, 1913; m. Theophania Huntington, Sept. 5, 1907. Tchr. pub. schs., Ill., Tex., Colo. Until 1902; with U. Colo., 1904—, successively as asst. in geology, 2904-07, instr., 1907-08, asst. prof., 1908-14, prof. mineralogy and petrology, 1914—. Field asst. U.S. Geol. Survey, Summer 1906; asst. Colo. Geol. Survey, 1907-09, geologist, 1909-25. Fellow A.A.A.S., Mineral Soc. Am., Geol. Soc. Am.; mem. Am. Assn. Univ. Profs., Sigma Xi. Republican. Conglsit. Wrote (bulls.); Geology and Ore Deposits of Monarch and Tomichi Districts, Colo., 1913; Geology and Ore Deposits of Gold Brick Dist., Colo. (with P. G. Worcester), 1916; Geology and Ore Deposits of Red Cliff District, Colo. (with Russell Gibson), 1925. Home: 1050 Tenth St., Boulder, COlo. Colo. Died Mar. 7, 1950.

CRAWFORD, RUSSELL TRACY, astronomer; b. Davis Calif., Mar. 26, 1876; s. Frederick Gustavus and Mary Lanette (Foster) C.; B.S., U. of Calif., 1897, Ph.D., 1901; studied U. of Berlin, Winter semester, 1911; m. Mary Crooke McCleave, Oct. 20, 1902 (died Apr. 21, 1903); m. 2d, Helen Alice Young, May 22, 1913. Mem. examining force U.S. Civ. Service Commn., 1902-03; with University of Calif. since 1903, instr., in astronomy until 1906, asst. prof., 1906-10, asso. prof., 1910-19, prof., 1919-46, emeritus since 1946; chairman of dept., 1938-41, since 1942. Dir. Students Observatroy, 1939-46; dir. emeritus since 1946. Mem. Bd. of Edn., Berkeley, 1906-09. Maj. Air Service, U.S. Army, 1918-19. Fellow A.A.A.S., mem. Astron. Soc. Am., Astron. Soc. (pres. 1914), Astronomische Gesellschaft, Phi Beta Kappa, Sigma Xi. Investigated the orbits of many comets and two stellites; computed general pertubations of several asteroids. Club: Faculty (Berkeley). Author: The Dertermination of Orbits of Comets and Asteroids. Editor: Cajori's Newton's Principia, A Revision of Motte's Translation. Home: 2740 Hillegass Av., Berkeley 5. Cal. Died Dec. 21, 1958.

CRAWFORD, STANTON CHAPMAN, zoölogist, univ. dean; b. Steubenville, O., Oct. 30, 1897; s. George Moore and Minnie (Chapman) C.; A. B., Bethany (W.Va.) Coll., 1918; A.M., U. Cin., 1921; Ph.D., U. Waynesburg Coll., 1948; m. Mary Belle Parks, Mar. 23,

1920; children—Nancy Elizabeth (Mrs. Nancy C. Scott), Mary Alice (Mrs. Alan Rush Brown). Ordained Christian (Disciples) ministry, 1918; pastor Oakley-Hyde Park Ch., Clin., 1918-21; prof. biology Lynchburg (Va.) Coll., 1921-24; instr. zoölogy U. Pitts., 1924-26; prof. biology and dean Lynchburg Coll., 1926-27; asst. prof. zoology U. Pitts., 1927-28, asso. prof., 1928-30, prof., 1930-35, prof. zoölogy, 1935—, also head Johnstown Campus, 1927-33, dir. high sch. relations, 1933-35, dean coll. arts and scis., 1935-56, sec. univ., dean faculties, 1956—, acting chancellor, 1965-66. Mem. Allegheny county Bd. Assistance, 1954-57. Fellow A.A.A.S.; mem. Middle States Assn. Colls. and Secondary Schs. (commn. instns. higher edn. 1956-62, sec. 1960-62), Pa. Assn. Colls. and Univs. (exec. com. 1963—.), Pa. Soc., Pa. Acad. Sci. Fgn. Policy Assn. (pres. Pitts. 1955-56), Newcomen Soc., Sigma Xi, Omicron Delta Kappa, Sigma Nu, Phi Beta Kappa (hon.), Beta Beta Beta (hon.), Scabbard and Blade (hon.), Alpha Epsilon Delta (hon.). Republican. Presbyn. Mason. Clubs: University, Skytop, Junta (Pitts.); Faculty (U. Pitts). Contbr. to zoö;., hist. and ednl. jours. Home: 4716 Ellsworth Av., Pitts. 13. Died Jan. 26, 1966; buried Homewood Cemetery, Pitts.

CRAWLEY, CLYDE B(ROOKS), physicist, educator; b. Hopkinsville, Ky., July 3, 1907; s. Thomas Bacon and Wilmoth (Pace) C.; student Rransylvania Coll., 1927-28; A.B., U. Ky., 1930, M.S., 1931; Ph.D., Cal. Inst. Tech. (fellow, 1931-34), 1934; m. Urah Betty Divine, Dec. 31, 1928; 1 dau., Judith Fay. Prof. and head dept. of physics and mathematics Blue Mountain (Miss.), Coll., 1934-35; asst. prof. physics U. Ala., 1934-41, asso. prof., 1941-43; asso. prof. physics U. Kay., 1943-46, prof., 1946—. Mem. Am. Phys. Soc. (also Southeastern sect.), Am. Assn. Physics Tchrs., Am. Assn. U. Prof., So. Assn. Sci. and Industry, Ky. Assn. Physics Tchrs., Sigma Xi, Phi Beta Kappa, Sigma Pi Sigma, Pi Mu Epsilon. Mem. Christian Ch. Home: 170 Cherokee Park, Lexington 10, Ky. Died Oct. 26, 1949.

CRAWLEY, EDWIN SCHOFIELD, univ. prof.; b. Phila., July 31, 1862; s. Joseph S. and Elmira (Hammell) C.; B.S., U. of Pa., 1882, Ph.D., 1892; m. M. Annie Reckefus, Apr. 3, 1888 (died 1908); children—Mildred, Marion; m. 2d, Marjorie Bond, Mar. 1, 1924. Instr. civ. engring., 1882-85, instr. mathematics, 1885-89, asst. prof., 1889-99, Thomas A. Scott prof. mathematics, 1899—, U. of Pa. Author: Elements of Plane and Spherical Trigonometry, 1889, 96, 1907, 14; Tables of Logarithms, 1899; Short Course in Plane and Spherical Trigonometry, 1902; One Thousand Exercises in Trigonometry, 1914; Analytic Geometry (with Prof. H. B. Evans), 1918; Trigonometry (with Prof. H.B. Evans), 1922. Home: Philadelphia, Pa. Died Oct. 18, 1933.

CREAGER, WILLIAM PITCHER, civil engr.; b. Balt., Sept. 21, 1878; s. Nobel Harwood and Mary (Neal) C.; C.E., Rensselaer Poly. Inst., 1901; m. Margaret Burns, Apr. 9, 1904; 1 dau., Elizabeth Mary. Provincial Supr. Philippine Govt., 1901-04; designer N.Y. State Barge Canal, 1904-06; draftsman to chief hydraulic engr. J.G. White Engring. Corp., 1906-22; v.p. and chief engr. Power Corp. of N.Y. and other Corps, 1922-31; cons. engr., 1931—. Lt. col. U.S. Aumy, retired. Mem. Buffalo War Council; dep. comdr. Buffalo Office Civilian Protection; former trustee Rensselaer Poly. Inst.; mem. adv. engring. council, Princeton U. Mem. Am. Soc. C.E., AM. Inst. Cons. Engrs., Theta Xi, Sigma Xi. Clubs: Wanakah Country. Saturn. Author: Engineering for Masonry Dams, 1917; La Construction des Grands Barroges en Amerique, 1923; Hydro Electric Handbook (with others), 1927; Engineering for Dams (with others), 1942; also chapter in Handbook for Electrical Engineers and Structural Engineers Handbook Library Handbook for Mechanical Engineers. Contbr. many articles to sci. mags. Home: Sheraton Hotel. Office: Electric Bldg., Buffalo. Deceased.

CREASER, CHARLES W(ILLIAM), biologist; b. nr. Britton, N.D., Oct. 31, 1897; s. Philip William and Lena Electa (Jacokes) C.; student Alma (Mich.) Coll., 1916-19; A.B., U. Mich., 1920, M.S., 1921, Ph.D., 1924; m. Hulda M. Ward, July 20, 1924. Asst. curator of fishes Mus. of Zoology, U. Mich., 1921-23, prof. vertebrate zoology U. Mich. Biol. Sta., Pellston, 1925-62; instr. zoology U. Kan., 1923-24; asst. prof. zoology Wayne State U. (coll. of Detroit) 1924-28, asso. prof., 1928-34, prof., zoology, 1934-64, prof. emeritus, 1964—, chmn. dept. biology, 1935-57; spl. field work Mich. Dept. Conservation, 1921-31. Served with U.S. Army, 1918. Mem. A.A.A.S., Am. Soc. Zoologists, Soc. Ichthyologists and Herpertologists, , Soc. Exptl. Biology and Medicine, Detroit Physiol Soc. (pres.), Sigma Xi (pres. Wayne chpt.), Mich. Acad. Sci. (pres. 1957). Author: The Skate, 1927; (with J. L. Metcalf) Guide to Zoological Experiences (pvtly pub.), 1946; Manual (with Jessie L. Metcalf) Dissectional Study of a Shark, 1960. Contbr. articles and reports to sci. publs. on biology fishes, radio-active iodine and the thyroid gland, and other biol. topics, especially conservation. Home: 15 E. Kirby St. E., Detroit 48202. Died June 26, 1965; buried Riverside Cemetery, Alma, Mich.

CREHORE, ALBERT CUSHING, physicist; b. Cleveland, O., June 8, 1868; A.B., Yale, 1890; student Johns Hopkins, 1891; Ph.D., Cornell U., 1893. Instr. physics Cornell U., 1893-94; asst. prof. physics, Dartmouth, 1874-78; now research physicist Nela Research Lab., Nela Par, Cleveland. Fellow A.A.A.S.; mem. Am. Physical Soc. Am. Soc. Elec. Engrs. Address: Nela Research Laboratory, Nela Park, Cleveland, O.

CREHORE, WILLIAM WILLIAMS, civil engr.; b. Cleveland, Feb. 3, 1864; s. John Davenport and Lucy (Williams) C.; A.B., Yale, 1886, Ph.B. (Sheffield Scientific Sch.), 1888; m. Anna Ballard, July 11, 1888. Prin. Hemenway High Sch., Norfolk, Va., 1888-90; practicing as civ. engr., 1890—; pres. Typewriting Telegraph Co., 1906—. Author: Tables and Diagrams for Use of Engineers and Architects, 1894; Protection's Brood, 1912. Contributor to engring. jours.; also chapter on Modern High Buildings in DuBois' Stresses in Framed Structures, 1896; chapter on Theoretical Considerations of Design in Foster's Wooden Trestle Bridges, 1894. Home: Westfield, N.J. Died Sept. 13, 1918.

CREIGHTON, WILLIAM HENRY, engineer; b. Cincinnati, June 29, 1859; s. Peter and Mary A. (Woods) C.; grad. U.S. Naval Acad., 1882; m. Mathilda Mathis, Dec. 26, 1904; 1 son, William Henry. Asst. engr. U.S. Steamships Lackawanna and Mohican, to 1887; prof. engring., Purdue U., 1887-91; chief engr. U.S.C.S. Blake, 1891; retired from naval service, 1892; prof. mech. and sugar engring, 1894-1930, dean Coll. of Tech., 1911-19, Tulane U.; ordered to active duty U.S.N., Apr. 6, 1917. Democrat. Catholic. Author: The Steam Engine and Other Heat Motors, 1907, 3d edit., 1911. Has taken out number of patents on sugar making machinery. Home: New Orleans, La. Died Jan. 24, 1933.

CREIGHTON, WILLIAM J. architect; b. Los Angeles, Calif., July 31, 1892; s. William St. Clair and Lilly (Vaccaro) C.; student Sch. of Aeronautical Engring., Mass. Inst. Tech., 1918; m. Alice Townley Smyth, June 12, 1920; children—William Smyth, Suzanne Meade, Edward Telfair, Alice Townley. Registered architect in New York, New Jersey, Connecticut, Pennsylvania, Virginia and Dist. of Columbia. Designer in office of McKim, Mead & White, New York, 1920-27; partner, La Farge, Clare & Creighton, N.Y., 1927-30; pvt. practice, William J. Creighton, N.Y., 1930-45; with Toombs & Creighton 1945-48; pvt. practice, 1949—; architects 6th Dist. Fed. Reserve Bank, Georgia Warm Springs Foundation, Fulton County Adminstrn. Bldg., Rich's Inc. Dept. Store; designed building for New York Geneal and Biological Society; designed residence for Garrard Winston, New York; estates for John Hay Whitney (Va.), Philip B. Cole (Harrytown, N.Y.), Henry Pratt (Bristol, Pa.), Theodore Montague (Greenwich Conn.); architect for Atlanta Pub. Library; architect for Fulton Co. Adminstrn. Building. Served as 1st lt., R.M.A. Pilot, U.S. Army, World War I. Awarded medals, archtl. projects, Beaux Arts Inst. Mem. Mayor's Com. of Architects of New York, Planning bd. Township of New Caltle, Westchester County, New York. Mem. Am. Arbitration Soc., Am. Inst. of Architects (pres. Ga. chapter), Beaux Arts Inst. of Design, Phi Gamma Delta. Club: Athletic (Atlanta), Home: R. 3, Windy Hill Rd., Marietta Ga., Office: 1205 Spring St. N.W., Atlanta. Died July 17, 1955.

CREIM, BEN WILTON elec. engr.; b. Chicago, Sept. 19, 1898; s. Nathan B. and Ida (Belovitch) C.; student Los Angeles Poly. Jr. Coll., 1916, George Washington U., 1917, 1918; m. Mardel Bernadine Brinkmann, Mar. 24, 1923; children—Donald Henry, Audrey Jane (Mrs. Arthur T. Sturgess). Elec. engr. Bur. Power & Light, Los Angeles, 1919-27; chief elec. engr. Modesto (Calf.) Irrigation Dist., 1927-35; regional engr. Rural Electrification Adminstrn., Washington, 1936-39; asst. chief engr. Bonneville Power Adminstrn., Portland, Ore., 1939-42; regional power mgr. Bur. Reclamation Sacramento, 1945-50; adminstr. Southeastern Power Adminstrn., Dept. Interior, Elberton, Ga. since 1950. Served as machinist mate 1st class, U.S.N.R., World War I, comdr. II. Fellow Am. Inst. E.E.; mem. Am. Legion, 40 et 8. Home: 130 Lake Forest Dr. Office: Southeastern Power Adminstration, Elberton, Ga. Died Feb. 4, 1952; buried Arlington Nat. Cemetery.

CRELLIN, EDWARD WEBSTER, civil engr.; b. Carroll County, O., May 15, 1863; s. Edward Mortimer and Sarah Jane (Simmons) C.; C.E., State U. of Ia., 1890; m. Amy Hutchison, June 10, 1896. Founder Des Moines Bridge and Iron Works (later named Pittsburgh, Des Moines Co.), being pres. of both cos. until retirement, 1921. Mem. Am. Soc. C.E., A.A.A.S., Calif. Inst. Assos., Sigma Xi, Tau Beta Pi. Republican. Methodist. Address: 1550 San Pasqual St., Pasadena 4, Calif. Died May 16, 1948.

CRENSHAW, BOLLING HALL, prof. mathematics; b. Greenville, Ala., May 18, 1867; s. Walter Henry and Sarah (Anderson) C.; B.S., Ala. Polytechnic Institute, 1889, M.E., 1890, LL.D., 1932; m. Willie Glenn, Apr. 29, 1896; children—Mary Glenn (Mrs. Carl E. Wideberg), Sarah Hall. Railroad construction work, 1890-91; instr. mech. engring. and mathematics, 1891-96, asso. prof., 1896-1905, prof. mathematics and head of dept., 1905—, Ala. Poly. Inst. Democrat. Presbyn. Co-Author: Crenshaw & Derr's Plane Trigonometry, 1923; Crenshaw & Killebrew's Analytic Geometry and Calculus, 1925; Crenshaw & Harkin's College Algebra, 1929; Crenshaw, Pirenian & Simpson's Mathematics of Finance, 1930. Home: Auburn, Ala. Died Nov. 25, 1935.

CRESSEY, GEORGE BABCOCK, geographer, geologist b. Tiffin, O., Dec. 15, 1896; s. Frank Graves and Minnie Frances (Babcock) C.; B.S., Denison U., 1919, L.H.D., 1948; M.S., U. Chgo., 1921; Ph.D., (geology), 1923; student Yale, 1921-22, Coll. Chinese Studies Peking, 1923-24, Harvard, 1929-30; Ph.D. (geography), Clark U., 1931; m. Marion Holbrook Chatfield, June 29, 1925; children—Marjorie Holbrook, Richard Chatfield, Frances Graves, Eleanor Earl. Prin. Walworth (N.Y) High Sch., 1919-20; asst. prof. U. Shanghai, 1923-29 prof. and chmn. dept. geology and geography Syracuse U., 1931-45, chmn. dept. geog., since 1945; vis. prof. summers Harvard, 1930-32, Western Res. U., 1937, U. Mich., 1939, Columbia, 1941-44, China Under Dept. State, 1943-44, Stanford, 1945-46; field work in Mongolia, Tibet and interior China, 1923-29, 1943-44; in Soviet Asia, 1923, 1937, 1944. Geog. cons. China, 1934, U.S.] U.S.S.R., 1937, U.S., 1941-44. Del. to Pacific Sci. Congress, Japan, 1926; Java, 1929; del. Internat. Geol. Congress, 1949. Soviet Union, 1937, Eng., 1948, Lisbon, Portugal, 1949. Mem. Internat. Geog. Union (v.p. 1947-48, pres. 1949-52). Geol. Soc. Am., Assn. Am. Geographers (councillor 1947-49), Am. Inst. Pacific Relations; Fgn. Policy Assn., Nat. Council Geog. Tchrs., Am. Geog. Soc., Nat. Council Social Studies, Am. Geophys. Union, N.R.C., A.A.A.S., Am. Assn. U. Profs., Geog., Geol. Socs. China, Royal Asiatic Soc., Far Eastern Assn., Sigma Xi, Phi Beta Kappa. Mem. Presbyn. Bd. Fgn. Missions. Club: Cosmos (Washington). Asso. editor Econ. Geog.; adv. editor Far Eastern Quar. Author: Indiana Sand Dunes and Shore Lines of Lake Michigan Basin, 1928; China's Geographic Foundations, 1934 (N.Y.), 1939 (Paris); Asia's Lands and Peoples, 1944 (Buenos Aries, 1946, Shanghai, 1946); Basis of Soviet Strength, 1945. Editorial com. Am. Slavic and East European Rev. Contbr. articles on geography of Asia to jours. Home: 101 Windsor Pl., Syracuse 10, N.Y. Died Oct. 21, 1963; buried Granby, Conn.

CRET, PAUL PHILIPPE, architect; b. Lyons, France, Oct. 23, 1876; s. Paul Adolphe and Anna Caroline (Durand) C.; ed. Lycee of Bourg, Ecole des Beaux Arts, Lyons, Ecole des Beaux Arts, Paris; architecte diplome du gouvernement francais, 1903; Sc.D., U. of Pa., 1913; M.A. Brown, 1929; Dr. Arts, Harvard University, 1940; m. Marguerite Lahalle, Aug. 1905. Prof. design, U. of Pa., 1903-37, prof. emeritus since 1937, now associate trustee. Paris prize, 1896, Rougevin prize, 1901, and grand medal of emulation, Ecole des Beaux Arts, Paris, 1901; gold medal, Salon des Champs Elysees, Paris, 1903; medal of honor, Architectural League of New York; Phila. award (Bok prize), 1931; distinguished award Washington Soc. Architects; gold medalist of A.I.A.; gold medal Pan.-Am. Expn.; grand prize, Paris, 1937; Prize of Honor, 5th Pan.-Am. Congress of Architects, Montevideo, 1940; Award of Merit, U. of Pa. Alumni Soc., 1940. Architect (with Albert Kelsey) of Pan-American Union (Washington, D.C.); Valley Forge memorial arch. Rittenhouse Square, Phila., Indianapolis Pub. Library (With Zantzinger, Borie, and Medary); Detroit Inst. of Arts (with Zantzinger, Borie and Medary): Hartford County Bldg. (with Smith & Bassette, Hartford, Conn.); Folger Shakespeare Library (Washington, D.C.); Hall of Science at Century of Progress Expn., Chicago, 1933; Federal Reserve Bank and Delaware River Bridge, Phila., war memorials at Varennes, Fismes (France); memorials at Chateau Thierry, Bony, Waereghem and Gibraltar for Am. Battle Monuments Commn.; Central Heating Plant, Washington; new bldgs. U. of Tex.; Federal Res. Bd. Bldg., Washington; Calvert St. Bridge; new buildings U.S. Military Academy; new buildings U.S. Naval Academy; designer for Budd Co. streamlined trains since 1933; Philadelphia Zoo, new bldgs.; concealment projects for J.S. Army; Naval Medical center, Bethesda, Md., Nat. Academician; mem. Philos. Soc. N.Y. Acad. Arts and Letters, pres. Art Jury, City of Phila.; mem. Pa. State Art Commn., Nat. Commn. of Fine Arts. Mem. Societe architects diplomes, Soc. Beaux Arts Architects, T-Square Club (hon. pres.); fellow A.I.A.; mem. Phi Beta Kappa, Sigma Xi; hon. corr. mem. Royal Inst. Brit. Architects; hon. mem. Acad.d'Architecture Lyon, Mich. Soc. Architects. Trustee Phila. Museum. Consultant bd. of design N.Y. Expn., 1939; consultant U.S. Navy Dept. since 1938. Consultant U.S. Engineers, and Pub. Roads Adminstrn. Served in French Army and with 1st Div. A.E.F., 1914-19. Decorated Officer Legion of Honor and Croix de Guerre (France). Mem. Archtl. Commn., Chicago World's Fair Centennial Celebration 1933; consulting architect Am. Battle Monuments Commn., also Brown Univ. and univs. of Texas, Pennsylvania and Wisconsin. Clubs: Racquet, Art Alliance (Phila.); Century (N.Y.); Cosmos (Washington, D.C.). Home: 516 Woodland Terrace. Office: 1518 Walnut St., Philadelphia 2, Pa. Died Sept. 8, 1945.

CREW, HENRY, physicist; b. Richmond, O., June 4, 1859; s. Wm. Henry and Deborah A. C.; A. B., Princeton, 1882; Ph.D., Johns Hopkins, 1887; m. Helen C. Coale, July 17. 1890; children—Alice H., Mildred, William H. Instr. physics, Haverford Coll., 1888-91; astronomer Lick Obs., 1891-92; prof. physics,

Northwestern U., 1892-1930; chief of div. of basic sciences, Century of Progress Expn., Chicago, since 1930. Collaborator Astrophysical Journal, 1892-1942. Del. Congress of Physicists, Paris, 1900; mem. Nat. Acad. Sciences, Am. Physical Soc. (pres. 1909), Ill. Acad. Sciences (Pres. 1929-30), History of Science Soc. (pres. 1930); fwllow Am.Acad. Arts and Sciences, Phi Beta Kappa. Recipient of Oersted Medal of Am. Assn. Physics Teacher, 1941. Author: Principles of Mechanics, 1908; General Physics, 1908; Rise of Modern Physics, 1928. Translator of Maurolcyus' Optics, 1940. contbr. to scientific jours. Clubs: University (Chicago and Evanston,); Westmoreland Golf. Home: 620 Liberty Pl., Evanston, Ill. Died Feb. 17, 1953; buried Wilmington, O.

CRILE, DENNIS RIDER WOOD, surgeon; b. Baltic, O., May 27, 1891; s. Austin D. and Winifred Augusta (Wood) C.; B.S., U. of Wis., 1914; M.D., Harvard, 1917; m. Mary Dorothea Webb, Jan. 1, 1919; children—Dennis Michael, Dorothea Mary. Asst. prof. surgery, U. of Ill. Coll. Medicine, Served in France and Belgium, with Harvard Unit under British May 1916-Aug. 1918; in Eng., Aug. 1918-July 1919; commd. hon. capt. Royal Army M.C. Contbr. to medical jours., and chapters dealing with compound fractures in Ochsner's Surgical Diagnosis and Treatment, Originator of method of resuscitation of dying persons by injection of adrenalin into the heart. Died Mar. 21, 1937.

CRILE, GEORGE (WASHINGTON), surgeon; b. Chili, O., Nov. 11, 1864; s. Michael and Margaret (Dietz) C.; B.S., Ohio Northern U., 1885, A.M., 1888, M.D., Wooster U. (now Western Reserve U.), 1887, A.M., 1894; student Vienna, 1893, London, 1895, Paris, 1897; hon. Ph.D., Hiram Coll., 1901; LL.D., Wooster U., 1916; M.Ch., U. of Budlin, 1925; LL.D., U. of Glasgow, 1928; Doctor honoris causa, U. of Guatemala, 1939; m. Grace McBride, Feb. 7, 1900; children—Margaret (Mrs. Hiram Garretson), Elisabeth (Mrs. J.A. Crisler, Jr.), George Jr., Robert. Lecturer and demonstrator histology, 1889-90, prof. physiology, 1890-93, prof. principles and practice of surgery, 1893-1900, Wooster U., prof. clin. surgery, 1900-11, surgery, 1911-24, Western Reserve U.; visiting surgeon Lakeside Hosp., 1911-24; one of founders Cleveland Clinic Foundation, now dir. research, Brigade surgeon vols., maj., Cuba and Porto Rico, 1898; maj. Med. O.R.C. and professional dir. of U.S. Army Base Hosp. No. 4, Lakeside Unit (B.E.F., No. 9), in service in France, May 1917-May 1918; sr. consultant in surg. research, May 1918-Jan. 1919; lt. col., June 1918, col., Nov. 1918, brig. gen. Med. O.R.C., 1921; brig. general Auxiliary R.C., since 1929. Awarded D.S.M. (U.S.), 1919; Chevalier Legion of Honor (French), 1922, Alvarenga prize, Coll. Phys., Phila., 1901; Cartwright prize, Columbia, 1897 and 1903; Senn prize, A.M.A., 1898; Am. med. medal for service to humanity, 1914; Nat. Inst. Soc. Sciences medal, 1917; Trimble Lecture medal, 1921; 3d laureate of Lannelongue Foundation (Lannelongue Internat. medal of surgery presented by Societe Internationale de Chirurgie de Paris), 1925; Cleveland medal for public service, 1931; Distinguished Serivce Gold Key, American Congress of Physical Therapy, 1940. Fellow American Assn. Anatomists, A.A.A.S., American Surgical Association (president 1923), Am. Coll. Surgeons (pres. 1916; mem. bd. regents since 1913; chmn. bd. regents 1917-39), A.M.A., Am. Physiol. Soc., Am. Assn. Obstetricians, Gynecologists and Abdominal Surgeons, Southern Surg. Assn., Southern Med. Assn., Am. Philos. Soc.; mem. Assn. Am. Pathologists and Bacteriologists, Am. Soc. Clin. Surgery, Soc. Exptl. Biology and Medicine, Nat. Inst. Social Sciences, National Research Council, Assn. Study Internal Secretaions, Am. Heart Assn., Am. Med. Editors' Assn., Ohio State Medical Assn., Cleveland Acad. Medicine, Cleveland Med. Library Assn.; Interstate Post Grad. Med. Assn. of N. America (chmn. program com.); hon. corr. fellow or mem. many Am. and European societies. Clubs: Union (Cleveland); 100,000 Mile Club. Author: Surgical Shock, 1897; Surgery of Respiratory System, 1899, Certain Problems Relating to Surgical Operations, 1901; On the Blood Pressure in Surgery, 1903; Hemorrhage and Transfusion, 1901; Anemia and Resuscitation, 1914; Anoci-Association (with Lower), 1914, 2d edit., title, Surgical Shock and the Shockless Operation through Anoci-Association, 1920; Origin and Nature of the Emotions, 1915; A Mechanistic View of War and Peace, 1915; Man, An Adaptive Mechanism, 1916; The Kinetic Drive, 1916; The Fallacy of the German State Philosophy, 1918; A Physical Interpretation of Shock Exhaustion and Restoration, 1921; The Thyroid Gland (with others), 1922; Notes on Military Surgery, 1924; A Bipolar Theory of Living Processes, 1926; Problems in Surgery, 1928; Diagnosis and Treatment of Diseases of the Thyroid Gland (with others), 1932; Diseases Peculiar to Civilized Man, 1934; The Phenomena of Life, 1936; The Surgical Treatment of Hypertension, 1938; Intelligence Power and Personality, 1941. Home: 2620 Derbyshire Rd. Office: Cleveland Clinic, Euclid Av. at E. 93d St. Cleveland. Died Jan. 7, 1943.

CRITTENDEN, EUGENE CASSON, physicist, b. Oswayo, Pa., Dec. 19, 81880; s. Shuble Edgar and Ida Viola (Rowlee)C.; grad. Mansfield (Pa.) State Normal Sch. Applied Sci., 1946; m. Norma Snyder, May 10, 1910; children—Marjorie, Eugene. Inst. Physics Cornell U., 1905-06; physicist, various grades Nat. Bur. Standards, Washington, 1909—. chief div. of electricity, 1921-46, asst. dir. bur., 1933-46, asso. dir., 1946-50; retired; specilaized in surveys of measurement and use of light, adminstrn. research, testing work in electricity. Official del. from U.S. to Internat. Commn. on Illumination, Geneva. 1924, Saranac Inn, 1928. Great Britain, 1931, Holland, 1939. V.p. Internat. Commn., 1939-48; pres. U.S. Nat. Com of Internat. Electrotech. Commn., 1939-46. Mem. Internat. Com. on Weights and Measures, 1946—. chmn. Standards council, dir. Am . Standards Assn., 1939-48. Recipient Illum. Engring. Soc. medal. 1946. Mem. Am. Inst. E.E., Am. Physical Soc., Optical Soc. Am. (pres. 1932-33), Illum engring. Soc. of U.S. (pres. 1925), Illuminating Engring. Soc., of Great Britain, A.A.A.S., Washington Acad. Scis. (pres. 1940), Philos. Soc. Washington (pres. 1922) Gamma Alpha, Sigma Xi, Phi Beta Kappa Unitarian. Club: Cosmos. Home: 1715 Lanier Pl. N.W., Washington 9. Died March 28, 1956.

CROASDALE, STUART, mining engr.; b. Delaware Water Gap, Pa., Nov. 21, 1866; s. Evan Thomas and Ellen (Andre) C.; of early Quaker ancestry in America; B.S. in chemistry, Lafayette Coll., Easton, Pa., 1888, M.S., Ph.D., 1891; m. Elma G. Shaw, 1891; children—Dorothy, Ernest Shaw, Evan Thomas. Was chief chemist, Holden Lixiviation Works, Aspen, Colo., 1891-93, Gillette (Colo.) Reduction Works, 1894-95, Globe Smelting & Refining Co., Denver, 1896-1900; cons. practice, 1900—; cons. engr. Anaconda Copper Co., Mont., 1903. Burro Mt. Copper Co., 1903-07, Calumet & Ariz. Copper Co., 1912-13, and many other cos., including Utah Copper Co., Nipissing Mines Co., etc.; pres. Alma Gold Corporation, Denver, Colo. Pioneer in smelter smoke investigation, and commercial leaching of copper ores; inventor, volatilization process for treatment of ores, improved process for concentration orof ores. hydometallurgical process for treatment of mercury ores., etc. Republican Home: Denver, Colo. Died Sept. 30, 1934.

CROCKER, FRANCIS BACON, electrical engr.; b. New York, N.Y., July 4, 1861; s. Henry H. and Mary (Eldridge) C.; E.M., Columbia, 1882, Ph.D., 1894 (hon. M.S., 1914); unmarried. Instr. elec. engring., 1889-92, adj. prof., 1892-93, prof., 1893-1914, Columbia. Founder and v.p. C. & C. (Curtis & Crocker) Electric Co., 1887, and Crocker-Wheeler Electric Co., 1889. Pres. Am. Inst. Elec. Engrs., 1897-98, N.Y. Elec. Soc., 1889-92. Author: Management of Electrical Machinery, 8th edit., 1908; Electric Lighting, 8th edit., 1908; Electric Motors, 2d edition, 1914. Home: Ampere, N.J. Died July 9, 1921.

CROCKER, TEMPLETON, scientific research; b. San Francisco, Calif., Sept. 2, 1884; s. Charles Frederick and Jennie (Easton) C.; grad. Westminster Sch., Simsbury, Conn., 1903; A.B., Yale, 1908; unmarried. Research in South Seas, Galapagos Islands, for Calif. Acad. Sciences, 1932; Solomon Islands for Bishop Museum, Honolulu, 1933, Eastern Polynesia, Pitcairn and Easter Islands for Am. Museum of Natural History, 1934-35, Lower Calif. and west coast of Gulf of Calif. for Dr. William Beebe, New York Zoological Society, 1936, Hawaii, Tongareva, Samoa for American Museum Natural History, 1936-37. Decorated Chevalier Legion of Honor (France). Fellow Royal Geographical Soc.; mem. Am. Museum Natural History, N.Y. Zool. Soc., Field Museum, Calif. Acad. Sciences, S.A.R., Native Sons of the Golden West, Soc. Mayflower Descendants. Republican. Episcopalian. Clubs: Pacific Union, Bohemian (San Francisco); The Brook (N.Y. City); St. James', Royal Automobile, Authors (London). Author: The Cruise of the Zaca, 1933. Author of libretto of opera Fay-Yen-Fah. Home: 945 Green St. Office: Shreve Bldg., San Francisco, Calif. Died Dec. 12, 1948.

CROCKER, WALTER JAMES, veterinarian; b. Ada, Minn., Nov. 20, 1885; s. Walter Joseph and Helen (Wiley) C.; B.S.A., Utah Agrl. Coll., 1909; V.M.D., U. of Pa., 1911; m. Rosa Binder, Feb. 6, 1915; 1 dau., Helen Marie. Lecturer and instr., Vet. Sch., U. of Pa., 1911-13, asst. prof. vet. pathology, 1913-14, asst. prof. vet. pathology and bacteriology, 1914-16, prof. vet. pathology since Apr. 1916; asst. dir. Wistar Inst. of Anatomy and Biology, U. of Pa., 1920-21; dist. mgr. J. Lee Nicholson Inst., 1921; gen. mgr. Glove Labs., 1922-24; dir. Glove Labs, Glove Livestock Co. and Cleo Ranch Co., 1923-25; clin. pathologist Phila. Gen. Hosp., since 1925. Mem. Am., Pa. State and Keystone vet. med. socs., Phila. Pathol. Soc., Internat. Assn. Vet. Med. Museums, Dallas and Fort Worth Vet. Med. Assn., Tex. Vet. Med. Assn., Pa. Fish and Game Protect. Assn., Sigma Xi, Sigma Alpha, Alpha Psi. Republican. Episcopalian. Mason (32 deg., Shriner). Clubs: University, Norristown Rifle. Author: Veterinary Post Mortem Technic, 1917. Translator: Mastitis of the Cow and Its Treatment (by Sven Wall), 1918. Contbr. numerous scientific articles on hematology; hemography in diagnosis, prognosis and treatment; hemography in the diagnosis of appendicitis; nonspecific immune-transfusion in treatment septicemia and typhoid fever. Home: 5909 Christian St., West Philadelphia, Pa. Deceased.

CROCKER, WILLIAM, botanist; b. Medina, O., Jan. 27, 1876; s. Charles David and Catherine C.; grad. Ill. State Normal U., Normal, Ill., 1898; A.B., U. of Illinois, 1902, A.M., 1903; Ph.D., University of Chicago, 1906; married Persis D. Smallwood, September 3, 1910 (she died July 2, 1948); children—Major John Smallwood, Lt. Colonel David Rockwell. Inst. biology, Northern Ill. State Normal Sch., 1903-04; asso. plant physiology, 1907-09, instr., 1909-11, asst. prof., later asso. prof., 1911-21, Univ. of Chicago; managing director Boyce Thompson Inst. for Plant Research, Yonkers, N.Y., since 1921; Walker-Ames visiting prof. U. of Wash., winter 1943; pres. Yonkers Board of Education, 1937-46. Fellow A.A.A.S. (vice chmn. Sect. G 1925-26), member Botanical Society America (pres. 1924-25), Am. Chem. Soc., Am. Phytopathol. Soc., Phi Kappa Phi, Sigma Xi, Gamma Alpha. Mem. Nat. Research Council (chmn. div. of biology and agr., 1927-28); trustee Tropical Plant Research Foundation; pres. Welfare Federation of Yonkers, N.Y., 1940. Research on delayed germination in seeds, effect of noxious gases on plants, plant hormones, etc. Mem. Am. Philos. Soc., Soc. of Arts and Sciences (medalist, 1931), Am. Inst. N.Y. (gold medal, 1938). Club: Hudson River Country. Author: Growth of Plants—Twenty Years' Research at Boyce Thompson Institute, 1948; (with Lela V. Barton) Seeds and Germination (in press). Home: 27 Arden Pl. Office: 1086 N. Broadway, Yonkers 3, N.Y. Died Feb. 11, 1950.

CROCKETT, EUGENE ANTHONY, otologist; b. Calais, Me., Oct. 22, 1867; s. Frederick and Susan (George) C.; M.D., Harvard, 1891; m. Elizabeth Le Bourgeois. July 28, 1900. Has served as prof. otology, Harvard Med. Sch., and chief of Staff Eye and Ear Infirmary of same. Commr. Red Cross Service, Italy, 1917-18; maj. Med. Corps. O.R.C. Home: Ipswick, Mass. Died June 13, 1932.

CROCKETT, WILLIAM GOGGIN, pharm. chemist; b. Tazewell, Va., Jan. 9, 1888; s. John Ward and Mary Grace (Hopkins) C.; student Hampden-Sydney Coll., 1906-08, D.Sc., 1939; Pharm.D., Columbia U., 1913; M.S., New York U., 1917; m. Ethel May Dulin, Dec. 27, 1919; 1 dau., Mary Leila. Chemist Dept. of Health, New York, 1914-16; asst. in chemistry, New York U., 1916-17; chemist E. R. Squibb & Sons, Brooklyn, N.Y., 1917; chemist E. I. du Pont de Nemours & Co., Wilmington, Del., 1919; prof. of pharmacy, Baylor U., Dallas, Tex., 1920; prof. of pharmacy, Med. Coll. of Va., 1920—. Served as sergt. 1st class Research Div., Chem. Warfare Service, Am. Univ. Expt. Sta., Washington, D.C., 1917-18. Mem. revision com. U.S. Pharmacopoeia, term 1930-40. Presbyn. Mason. Home: Richmond, Va. Died Oct. 29, 1940.

CROES, JOHN JAMES ROBERTSON, civ. engr.; b. Richmond, Va., Nov. 25, 1834; s. Rev. Robert Brown and Helen (Robertson) C.; grad. Coll. of St. James, Md., 1853; unmarried. In practice as civ. engr., 1856—; resident engr. first high masonry dam in U.S. at Boyd's Corners, N.Y., 1865-70; topog. engr., New York Park Dept., 1872-78; chief engr., Suburban Rapid Transit R.R., New York, 1885-91; made expert reports on Quaker Bridge Dam (New York Aqueduct Commn.), 1888, New Croton dam and reservoir, 1901, and on New York water supply to Comptroller, 1899, and Merchants' Assn., 1900; consulting engr., N.Y. State Health Dept., 1903-05. Has made numerous reports on water supply, sewage, etc., to various cities. Pres. Am. Soc. Civil Engr., 1901. Home: Yonkers, N.Y. Died 1906.

CROMPTON, GEORGE, inventor, mfr.; b. Lancashire, Eng., Mar. 23, 1829; s. William and Sarah (Low) C.; m. Mary Pratt, Jan. 9, 1853; 9 children. Sole owner Crompton Loom Works (at the time one of Am.'s largest and best-known machine shops), 1859; Crompton looms in world-wide competition received 1st award at Paris Exposition; commn. pronounced them the best looms for fancy weaving at Centennial Exposition, 1876; a founder, 1st policy holder Hartford Steam Boiler Inspection & Ins. Co. (Conn.); a founder, pres. Crompton Carpet Co. Died Worcester, Mass., Dec. 29, 1886.

CROMPTON, WILLIAM, inventor, mfr.; b. Preston, Eng., Sept. 10, 1806; s. Thomas and Mary (Dawson) C.; m. Sarah Low, May 26, 1828, 8 children including George. Came to Am., 1836; perfected a weaving loom, 1837; went to Eng. for patent, 1838; designed looms to produce patterned woolens at Middlesex Mills, Lowell, Mass., 1839; opened mill, Millbury, Mass. Died Windsor, Conn., May 1, 1891.

CRONEIS, CAREY, educator, geologist; b. Bucyrus, Ohio, Mar. 14, 1901; s. Frederick William and Nell (Garner) C.; B.S., Denison U., 1922, D.Sc., 1945; M.S., U. of Kan., 1923; Ph.D., Harvard, 1928; LL.D., Lawrence College, 1944, Beloit College, 1954; D.Sc. (honorary), Ripon College, 1945; D.Eng. (honorary), Colorado School of Mines, 1949; L.H.D. (honorary), Tampa University, 1964; D.Sc., Tex. Christian U., 1965, Tex. Tech., 1967; D.Sc., Beloit College, 1968; married to Grace Williams, on September 15th, 1923; children—Christine (Mrs. Wm. C. Sayres), Catherine (Mrs. Theodore Alfred). Instructor in geology at Kansas, U. of 1922-23, Ark. U., 1923-25, Harvard and Wellesley Coll., 1927-28; geol. surveys Ark., Kan., Ill.; asst. prof. geology, U. of Chicago, 1928-31, asso. prof., 1931-41, prof. 1941-44, also curator paleontology, Walker Mus., U. of Chicago, 1928-44; pres. Beloit

(Wis.) Coll. 1944-54; provost, Harry C. Wiess prof., Rice University Houston 1954-60, acting pres., 1960-61, chancellor, 1961-71; cons. Nat. Defense Research Com., 1943-44. Mem. Beloit Coll.-Logan Mus. Expdn. to Colombia, 1947. Designed geology sect., Mus. of Science and Industry, Chicago; in charge geology sect. (1933), and chief of basic sciences (1934), A Century of Progress Expn., Chicago. Mem. com. math., physics, engring. sciences, Nat. Scientific Found., 1954-56; mem. sci. information council NSF, from 1969. Mem. com. on edn. Internat. Geophysical Year. Mem. panel sci. and tech. manpower Pres.' Sci. Adv. Com., 1962-64; adv. com. grad. edn. U.S. Office of Edn., 1964-66. Pres. bd. dirs. Gulf Univs. Research Corp., 1964-66. Mem. academic bd. U.S. Naval Acad.; chmn. Houston City Charter Com. Bd. dirs. Grad. Research Center S.W.; chmn. bd. educators United Educators, Chicago, American Society Oceanography. Erasmus Haworth award University of Kansas, 1952, Distinguished Alumni award, 1962; citation, Govt. Guatemala, 1956; Sidney Powers award Am. Assn. Petroleum Geologists, 1967; also Founder's medal of Austin College, 1968. Trustee Kinkaid Sch.; dir., former chmn. bd. Houston Mus. Contemporary Art; dir. Nat. Hist. Mus. Houston; v.p. Nat. Space Hall Fame, Houston, 1968; chmn. edn. subcom. Tex. Constn. Revision Com. Fellow A.A.A.S., Geol. Soc. of America, Am. Geol. Inst. (pres. 1951-52), American Association Petroleum Geologists, The Academy of Texas (charter mem.), Paleontology Society Am. (v.p. 1937), Houston C. of C. (past dir.), Houston Symphony Soc. (dir.), Houston Council World Affairs (pres. 1962-63), National Association Geology Teachers (pres. 1959-60), Society Econ. Paleontologists and Mineralogists (pres. 1940-41), Chicago Literary Club, Phi Delta Theta, Phi Beta Kappa, Sigma Xi, Phi Eta Sigma, Omicron Delta Kappa. Mason. Clubs: River Oaks Country, The Houston Petroleum (honorary). Editor of the Harper &Brothers Geoscience Series since 1941; associate editor of the Journal of Geology, 1930-45. Author: Paleozoic Geology of Arkansas; Down to Earth (with W. C. Krumbein); also numerous scientific articles and reviews. Home: Houston TX Died Jan. 22, 1972.

CROOK, ALJA ROBINSON, chief State Museum Div.; b. Circleville, O., June 17, 1864; s. Rev. Isaac and Emma (Wilson) C.; A.B., Ohio Wesleyan U., 1887; studied in British Mus., Jardin des Plantes (Paris), univs. of Berlin, Zürich and Munich, 1889-92; Ph.D., U. of Munich, 1892; m. Florence Wayne Purdum, Dec. 28, 1904; children—Elinor Josselyn, William Henry, Robert Purdum, Frederick Sherwood, Richard Bradford. Supt. Mt. Carmel, O., pub. schs., 1887-89; prof. natural history, Wheaton (Ill.) Coll., 1892-93; prof. mineralogy and economic geology, Northwestern U., 1893-1906; curator Ill. State Mus. Natural History, 1906-17; chief State Museum Div. of Ill., dept. of registration and edn., 1917—. Pres. Ill. Acad. Science, 1914— 15 (sec. 1908-10, 1915-16). Pres. Springfield Christian Laymen's Federation; v.p. Ill. State S.S. Assn.; pres. Ill. Conf. M.E. Laymen's Assn. Author: Guide to Mineral Collection. Home: Springfield, Ill. Died May 30, 1930.

CROSBY, WALTER WILSON, cons. civil engr.; b. Brooklyn, N.Y., Sept. 2, 1872; s. Wilson and Hannah A. (Seaver) C.; B.C.E., Me. State Coll., 1893, C.E., 1896; D.Sc., Maryland State Coll., 1912; D. Engring. U. of Maine, 1926; m. Florance Lapham Fletcher, 1921. Ry. and gen. engring. work, 1893-97; res. engr. for Mass. Highway Commn., 1897-1901; roads engr., Baltimore County, Md., 1901-04; gen. supt. Bd. of Park Commrs., Baltimore, 1904-05; chief engr. Md. Geol. and Econ. Survey, 1905-17; chief engr. State Roads Commn. of Md., 1908-12; capt. and maj. N.G. Md., 1904-17; maj. and asst. chief of staff 15th Div., U.S. Army, 1916-17; maj. Engr. O.R.C., U.S. Army, Aug. 31, 1917, lt. col.. 104th Engrs., 29th Div., A.E.F., Sept. 8, 1917-June 30, 1919; lt. col. U.S. Army, retired, 1928. Awarded Order of Purple Heart (U.S.). With U.S. Nat. Park Service, 1921; supt. Grand Canyon Nat. Park, 1922-24; location engineer Highway Dept. of Pa., 1924-26. Chmn. Coronado City Planning Commn., 1928-45. Del. 1st Internat. Road Congress, London, 1913, 4th Congress, Seville, 1923, 5th Congress, Milan, Italy, 1926; fellow A.A.A.S., American Geog. Soc.; mem. American Society Civil Engineers (life), Internat. Assn. Road Congresses (life), American Fisheries Soc., Izaak Walton League, Maine Soc. S.A.R., Md. Soc. S.R., Mil. Order Foreign Wars, Mil. Order World War, Am. Legion, Beta Theta Pi, Phi Kappa Phi. Unitarian. Clubs: Coronado Riding, Engineers (Baltimore, Maryland; hon. life mem.). Author: Some Western Fishing Notes on Highway Location and Surveying (with G.E. Goodwin), 1929. Wrote 3 sects. of Am. Highway Engineers' Handbook; also many official reports and tech. articles. Home: 1040 Adelia Av., Coronado, Calif. Deceased.

CROSBY, WILLIAM OTIS, geologist; b. Decatur, O., Jan. 14, 1850; s. Francis William and Hannah Everett (Ballard) C.; B.S., Mass. Inst. Tech., 1876; m. Alice Ballard, Sept. 4, 1876. Was engaged in mining in N.C. and Colo.; mem. faculty of Mass. Inst. Tech., 1883-1907, retired. Consulting geologist, chiefly engaged in original research; spl. geologist, U.S. and N.Y. surveys, U.S. Reclamation Service, U.S. Army Engineers, Met. Water Bd. of Mass., Bd. of Water Supply, New York; geologic investigations in connection with engring. projects in U.S. Can., Mexico, Alaska and Spain, Author: Contributions to the Geology of Eastern Massachusetts, 1880; Common Minerals and Rocks, 1881; Guide to Mineraology, 1886; Tables for the Determination of Common Minerals, 1887; Guide to Dynamical Geology and Petrography, 1892; Geology of the Boston Basin, 1893-94; Geology of Long Island, Home: Jamaica Plain, Mass. Died Dec. 31, 1925.

CROSKEY, JOHN WELSH (krôs'ke), ophthalmologist; b. Phila., Pa., Jan. 26, 1858; s. Henry and Ann (Dunnohew) C.; student Swarthmore Coll., 1886-87; M.D., Medico-Chirurg. Coll., Phila., 1889 (gold medalist); certificate of proficiency, Phila. Sch. of Anatomy, 1889; m. Elisabeth Estes Browning. Dec. 15, 1880 (dec.); children—Henry B., Elisabeth B. (Mrs. L.E. Bailey, dec.), Marion L., John Welsh Croskey, Jr. (dec.), m. 2d, Marie Lanche Bretschneider, January 21, 1939; two stepsons, Gordon Bretschneider, Louis Lanche Bretschneider. Began as chief assistant to surgical clinic, Medico-Chirurgical Coll., 1889, later lecturer on minor and operative surgery; assistant surgeon to Wills Hopsital, 1891-97; surgeon same, 1897-1902; appointed consulting ophthalmic surgeon to George Nugent Home for Baptists, 1899; ophthalmic surgeon to Philadelphia Gen. Hosp., apptd. 1900, cons. surgeon, apptd. 1925; also lecturer to training Sch. for Nurses; ophthalmic surgeon to Samaritan Hosp., Annie M. Warner Hosp., 1902-05; prof. ophthalmology, laryngology and otology, Temple U., 1902-05, etc.; acting assistant surgeon, United State Public Health Service; now retired; ophthalmologist Home of the Merciful Saviour for Crippled Children. Formerly editor and owner International Medical Magazine, and editor Medico-Chirurg. Jour. Fellow Am. Acad. Ophthalmology and Oto-Laryngology, A.M.A.; mem. Med. Soc. State of Pa., Phila. County Med. Soc. (sec. bd. of censors), W. Phila. Med. Assn. (ex-pres.), Hist. Soc. Pa., Valley Forge Historical Society, Fort Washington Historical Society. Academy Natural Science of Phila., Am. Med. Authors Assn., Colonial Soc. America, S.R., Gen. Alumni U. of Pa., Medical Alumni U. of Pa., Alumni Assn. Medico-Chirurg. Coll. (ex-pres.), Navy League (life), St. George Soc., St. Andrews Soc., Dickens Fellowship. Republican. Mason. Clubs: Kiwanis, Paxon Hollow Golf, Overbrook Golf, Merion Cricket, Golfers Association of Medical Society State of Pa. (ex-pres.), Am. Med. Golfing (ex-pres.), Penn Club (dir.). Author: Dictionary of Ophthalmic Terms, 1907; History of Blockley; Anatomy and Physiology of the Eye and Its Appendages; Historical Catalogue of the St. Andrews Society. Home: Fort Washington, R.F.D. No. 1, Ambler, Pa. Died July 30, 1951.

CROSS, CHARLES ROBERT, physicist; b. Troy, N.Y., Mar. 29, 1848; s. George and Lucy Ann (Brown) C.; B.S., Mass. Inst. Tech., 2870; m. Mariana Pike, July 15, 1873 (died 1900). Instructor, 1870-71, asst. prof., 1871-75, prof., 1875-76, Thayer prof. physics, 1877-1917, emeritus prof., 1917, dir. Rogers Laboratory, 1885-1917, Mass. Inst. Tech. (the first course in elec. engring. in U.S. leading to a degree was established at the inst., at his instance, 1882). Home: Brookline, Mass. Died Nov. 16, 1921.

CROSS, C(HARLES) WHITMAN, geologist; b. Amherst, Mass., Sept. 1, 1854; s. Rev. Moses Kimball and Maria (Mason) C.; B.S., Amherst, 1875; Ph.D., U. of Leipzig, 1880; D.Sc., Amherst, 1925; m. Virginia Stevens. Asst. geologist U.S. Geol. Survey, 1880-88, geologist, 1888-1925; retired account of age limit; chief sect. petrology, 1903-06. Mem. Nat. Acad. Sciences (treas. 1911-19), Geol. Soc. America (pres. 1918), Washington Acad. Sciences, Am. Philos. Soc.; hon. corr. Acad. Nat. Sc. Phila., 1924; foreign mem. Geol. Soc. London. Mem. Nat. Research Council, 1918-22 (treas. 1918-19), vice chmn. division of geology and geography 1918). Author of geol. reports and maps published by U.S. Geol. Survey, and of many papers in periodicals, on geol., petrographical or mineral subjects. Part author: Quantitative Classification of Igneous Rocks, 1903. Engaged in rose cultivation and cross-breeding since retirement. Home: 3901 Connecticut Av., Washington 8, D.C. Died Apr. 20, 1949.

CROSS, HARDY, civil engr.; born in Nansemond Va., Feb. 10, 1885; s. Thomas Hardy and Eleanor Elizabeth (Wright) C.; B.A., Hampden-Sydney Coll., 1902, B.S., 1903, hon. Sc.D., 1934; B.S. in C.E. from Mass. Inst. of Tech. , 1908; M.C.E., Harvard, 1911; hon. M.A., Yale Univ., 1937; m. Edythe Hopwood Fenner, Sept. 5, 1921. Instr. in English, Hampden-Sydney Coll., 1902-03; instr. in English and mathematics, Norfolk Acad., 1903-06; engr. bridge dept. M.P. Ry., 1908-10; asst. prof. civ. engring., Brown U., 1911-18; gen. Practice structural engring., 1918-21; prof. structural engring., Univ. of Ill., 1921-37; became prof. civil engineering Yale, 1937, former head dept. now prof. emeritus Stathcoma. Mem. Am. Soc. C.E., (awarded Norman medal, 1933), Am. Ry. Engring. Assn., Am. Concrete Inst. (awarded Wason medal 1936), Western Soc. Engrs., Conn. Soc. Civil Engineers, Am. Soc. Engring. Edn., Royal Society Arts, American Institute Consulting Engineers (awarded Lamme medal, 1944), Am.Acad. Arts and Sciences, Kappa Alpha, Sigma Xi, Tau Beta Pi, Sigma Tau, Chi Epsilon, Omicron Delta Kappa. Democrat. Mason. Author: Continuous Frames of Reinforced Concrete (with N. D. Morgan), 1932; also bulls. a and tech. articles. Home: 107-78th St., Virginia Beach, Va. Died Feb. 11, 1959.

CROSS, LEWIS JOSEPHUS, chemist; b. Hoosick Falls, N.Y., Oct. 15, 1874; s. Waite J. and Hannah M. (Scriven) C.; A.B., Cornell, 1909, Ph.D., 1912; m. Jessie B. Kerr, of Adams, Mass., Dec. 23, 1915. Asst. prof. chemistry, 1912-14, prof. 1914-23, Cornell U.; research chemist N.Y. State Dept. Farms and Markets since 1923. Developed process of pectin mfr. Editor Cornell Chemist, 1912-14. Mem. Am. Chem. Soc., Sigma Xi, Gamma Alpha. Republican. Presbyn. Mason. Home: 933 E. State St., Ithaca NY

CROSS, ROY, chemist; b. Ellis, Kan., Jan. 13, 1884; s. George Washington and Ada (Pendleton) C.; A.B., U. of Kan., 1905; M.D., U. Med. Coll., Kansas City, 1908; m. Mary Forbes, Oct. 1, 1917. Teaching fellow chemistry, U. of Kan., 1905-06; teacher chemistry Univ. Med. Coll., Kansas City, 1906-12; mgr. or pres. Kansas City Testing Lab. since 1908; v.p. and consultant Gasoline Products Co., 1922-26; pres. Silica Products Co., 1924-35; v.p. Cross Development Co., 1924-35; pres. Cross Engring Co., Cross Development Corp., Cross Labs.; cons. chemist. Trustee, Midwest Research Inst., Kan. City Museum Assn. Kan. City Art Institute, Kansas Univ. Research Foundation, Kansas Univ. Endowment Assn. Fellow A.A.A.S.; mem. Am. Inst. Chem. Engring., Am. Chem. Soc., Am. Concrete Inst., Am. Petroleum Inst., Am. Soc. for Testing Materials, Kansas City Engrs., Am. Forestry Assn., Phi Beta Kappa, Sigma Xi. Co-inventor of Cross Cracking process and designer of approximately 200 refining plants for gasoline. Holder of about 100 U.S. patents. Republican. Clubs: University, Mission Hills Country. Kansas City Farmer's (Kansas City, Mo.). Author: Handbook of Petroleum, Asphalt and Natural Gas, 1931; Handbook of Bentonite, 1935; Random Recollections of a Chemist, 1941; From a Chemist's Diary, 1943; also bulletins on mineral waters, air conditioning, etc. Home: 4511 Holmes St. Office: 700 Baltimore Av., Kansas City, Mo. Died Mar. 21, 1947.

CROSSEN, GEORGE, EDWARD, coll. dean; b. St. Paul, Minn., July 21, 1905; s. William and Ellen Agnes (Burke) C.; B.S., Univ. of Minn., 1933, M.S., 1937, Ph.D., 1940; m. Eleanor Ruth Curry, Sept. 22, 1934; 1 son, George William. Instructor Pharmacy, College of Pharmacy, University of Minnesota, 1933-41, asst. prof., 1941-42; dean and prof. of pharmacy Drake Univ., 1942-45; dean and prof. of pharmacy Ore. State Coll., Corvallis, since 1945; tech. consultant since 1945. Mem. Am. Pharm. Assn. (chmn. pract. sect., 1944-46; pres. North Pacific br., 1947-49), Am. Assn. College Pharmacists (exec. com. 1948-49), Am. Chem. Soc., A.A.A.S., Minn. Ia. and Ore. pharm. assns., C. of C., Rho Chi (exec. com. 1947-52), Kappa Psi (1st grand vice regent 1947-49), Sigma Xi, Phi Lambda Upsilon. Republican. Roman Catholic. Elk, K.C., Kiwanian. Author: Laboratory Manual of Inorganic Pharmaceutical Chemistry (with Karl J. Goldner), 1942; The Art of Compounding (with Justin L. Powers), 1942. Mem. Revision Com., U.S. Pharmacopeia, 1950-60. Home: 1260 Spring Lane, Corvallis, Ore. Died June 28, 1958.

CROTTI, ANDRÉ, surgeon; b. 1873; grad. U. of Lausanne, Switzerland, 1902; M.D., Starling-Ohio Med. Coll., Columbus, O., 1908; former prof. clin. surgery, Ohio State U., Coll. of Medicine: mem. staff Grant Hosp., Children's Hosp., Mt. Carmel Hosp. Regarded as a leading authority on goiter. Fellow Am. Coll. Surgeons; past pres. Internat. Coll. Surgeons; mem. A.M.A., and others Med. Socs. Home: 1592 E. Broad St. Office: 1 S. 4th St., Columbus, O. Died Jan. 31, 1958.

CROUCH, CALVIN HENRY, mech. engr.; b. Oswego, N.Y., Apr. 25, 1870; s. Henry Theodore and Ruth Lydia (Kenyon) C.; M.E., Cornell U., 1892; m. Della U. Newman, Oct. 6, 1898. Coll. vacations spent in machine shops; spl. apprentice, Ames Iron Works, Oswego, N.Y., 1892-93; machinist with Rome, Watertown & Ogdensburg R.R., Oswego, 1893-94; erecting engr. Deane Steam Pump Co., Holyoke, Mass., 1894-97; instr. in machine shop practice, Williamson (Pa.) Free Sch. of Mech. Trades, 1897-1900; traveling engr., erecting locomotives in Europe for Baldwin Locomotive Works, 1900-01; dean U. of N.Dak. Coll. Mech. and Elec. Engring., 1901-16; prof. mech. engring. and dir. of ships Coll. of Engring., U. of N.D., 1916-19; actg. dean and prof. engring., New Hampshire Coll., 1919-20; dean Coll. of Technology and prof. mech. engring., U. of N.H., 1920-25; mech. engr. with E. L. Phillips & Co., New York, 1925-32. Republican. Baptist. Mason. Home: Grantwood, N.J. Died July 13, 1937.

CROWE, FRANCIS TRENHOLM, civil engr.; b. Trenholmville, Quebec, Can. (parents Am. citizens), Oct. 12, 1882; s. John and Emma Jane (Wilkinson) C.; grad. Dummer Acad., South Byfield, Mass., 1901; B.S., U. of Me., 1905, Dr. Engring., 1935; m. Linnie Korts, Dec. 9, 1913; children—Patricia, Betty. Began as civil engr., 1905; construction engr. Jackson Lake, McDonald Lake, Tieton dams; asst. gen. supt. Arrowrock Dam; gen. supt. Guernsey, Combie,

Deadwood, Parker, Gene Wash., Copper Basin dams, 1931-37; gen. supt. of constrn. in charge of constrn. Boulder Dam for Six Companies, Inc., since 1938; gen. supt. constrn. Shasta Dam, for Pacific Constructors, Ind. Mem. Am. Soc. Civil Engineers, Sigma Alpha Epsilon, Tau Beta Pi. Republican. Episcopalian. Masson (32 deg., Shriner). Elk, Rotarian. Home: 1658 Orange St., Redding, Calif. Died Feb. 26, 1946.

CROWE, THOMAS BENNETT, engring. consultant; b. Emporia, Kan., Sept. 6, 1876; s. Alexander Fulton and Sophia (Bennett) C.; E.M., Colo. Sch. of Mines, 1900; m. Blanche Stonehouse, Oct. 19, 1901. Mine foreman Ophelia Tunnel, Cripple Creek, Colo., 1900-03; assayer, chemist, metallurgist and supt. mills, Portland Gold Mining Co., Cripple Creek and Colorado Springs, Colo., 1903-22; cons. engr. The Merrill Co., San Francisco, Calif., 1922—; best known as consultant, designer, builder and operator ore reduction plants; inventor and co-inventor metall. processes and apparatus. Republican. Mason. Home: Palo Alto, Calif. Died Nov. 13, 1940.

CROWELL, BOWMAN CORNING, pathologist; b. Yarmouth, N.S., Can., Jan. 10, 1879; s. Samuel Atwood and Mary Edna (Corning) C.; A.B., McGill U., 1900; M.D. and C.M., 1904; D.Sc., Marietta Coll., 1949; m. Frances Everett Horton, Apr. 25, 1909 (died Mar. 9, 1935); m. 2d, Frances Beatrice Henry, June 24, 1937. Resident pathologist, later interne, N.Y. City Hosp., 1904-07; instr. in pathology New York U. and Bellevue Med. Coll., 1907-11; pathologist, Bur. Science, Manila, P.I., 1911-15; asso. prof. pathology and bacteriology, and chief of dept., U. of Philippines, 1912-14, prof. and chief of dept., 1914-18, dir. Grad. Sch. Tropical Medicine and Pub. Health, 1916-18; chief of service, pathol. dept., Oswaldo Cruz Inst., Rio de Janeiro, Brazil, 1918-22; prof. pathology, Med. Coll. State of S.C., 1922-23, Jefferson Med. Coll., Phila., 1923-26; also pathologist and dir. labs., Jefferson Hosp., 1923-26; asso. dir and dir. clin. research, Am.Coll. Surgeons, Chgo., 1926-49, as Asso. dir. emeritus, 1949; lectr. in pathology, Northwestern U. Med. Sch., 1927—. mem. Nat. Malaria Com. Dir. Gorgas Meml. Inst., Washington; mem. bd. Am. Cancer Society, Recipient 1st ann. award Am. Cancer Soc., 1949. Mem. Internat. Assn. Med. Museums, Ill., Chgo. med. socs., Chgo. Pathol. Soc., A.A.A.S., Am. Assn. for Cancer Research, Am. Soc. Clin. Pathol. (hon.), Inst. of Medicine Chgo., Brazilian Acad. of Medicine (hon.), Chgo. Acad. of Sciences, Phi Delta Thea, Nu Sigma Nu. Republican. Presbyn. Clubs: Chicago Literary, University. Office: 40 E. Erie St., Chgo. 11. Died Apr. 26, 1951; buried Vancouver, B.C.

CROWELL, JAMES FOSTER, civil engr.; b. Oct. 13, 1848; s. John and Catherine (Roney) C.; grad. Poly. Coll. of Pa., June 27, 1867; m. Anna McK. Whiting, Jan. 27, 1881. Home: Flushing, N.Y. Died Mar. 29, 1915.

CROWELL, LUTHER CHILDS, inventor; b. West Dennis, Cape Cod. Mass., Sept. 7, 1840; s. Francis B. Crowell (sea capt.); ed. West Dennis, Pine Grove Sem., Harwich, Mass., 1844-56, Pierce's Acad., Middlebury, Mass., 1856-57; m. Mrs. Margaret D. Howard, Aug. 18, 1863. In merchant marine service, 1857-61. Invented an aerial machine, 1860; invented and patented metallic tie paper bag, 1867; square bottomed grocers' paper bag, also machine for making same, 1872; also (placed in Boston Herald, 1873) first mechanism for associating webs of paper in printing, by which the multiple newspaper is produced; also the supplement newspaper press, and the double and quadruple presses, pamphlet printing and combined wire binding machines; has received 280 patents from U.S. for printing machinery alone; since 1879 engaged with R. Hoe & Co. Died 1903.

CROWLEY, HENRY J., engineer; b. Unionville, Conn., 1865; s. Robert and Ann (O'Reilly) C.; ed. high sch.; m. Serena Virginia Ford, Nov. 25, 1892. Served as apprentice in mech. and elec. engring., later in constrn. electric light plants and as chief of students' course in elec. engring., Thomason-Houston Elec. Co.; dist. mgr. Gen. Elec. Co., Philadelphia, 1893-99; gen. mgr., Am. Ry. Co., constrn. and operation of pub. utilities, 1899—; v.p. in charge construction of plants and operation of about 30 subsidiary corps. in 12 states. Republican. Catholic. Home: Philadelphia, Pa. Died Oct. 27, 1924.

CROZET, CLAUDE, mil. engr., educator; b. Villefrauche, France, Jan. 1, 1790; ed. Polytechnic Sch. in Paris, France, Jan. 1, 1790; ed. Polytechnic Sch. in Paris, France. Came to U.S., 1816; served as engr. U.S. Army; asst. prof. U.S. Mil. Acad., 1816, prof., head dept., 1817-23; state engr. Va., 1823; mem. original bd. vistors Va. Mil. Inst., pres. until 1845; prin. Richmond Acad., 1858-64; introduced study of descriptive geometry to Am. Author: A Treatise of Descriptive Geometry for the Use of the Cadets of the United States Military Academy (1st Am. texbook on the subject), 1821. Died Jan. 29, 1864.

CROZIER, HERBERT WILLIAM, cons. engineer; b. San Francisco, Calif., June 28, 1875; s. William J. and Elizabeth (Mackeon) C.; student Cogswell Poly. Engring. Sch., San Francisco, 1891-92, Mechanics Inst. Schs., San Francsico, 189295; B.S., U. of Calif., 1899; m. Elizabeth Hyde, June 9, 1904; children—Elizabeth (Mrs. Milton G. Mauer), Hallett; m. 2d, Mary E. Sevison, Feb. 22, 1925. Engaged in constrn. work, Pacific Electric Ry., Between Vallejo and Napa, Stockton and Sacramento; with Ore. Electric Ry., 1902-1905; hydro-electric installation on Stanislaus River, Calif.; 1905-09; hydro-electric exploration on Klamath River, Calif., 1912-15, same and development work, Hoh, Queets, Cowlitz, North and Columbia rivers, Wash., 1922; cons. engr., State of Nev. (mem. Ariz.-Nev. Engrs. Conf., Ariz., Nev. and Calif. Engrs. Conf., Boulder Canyon project), 1923-26; appraisal commr. Islais Creek Reclamation Dist., San Francisco, and cons. engr. Nev.-Colo. River Commn., 1927-28; v.p. Calif. Desert Products Co. Rep. Monterey Breakwater before Bd. Engrs. for Rivers and Harbors, Washington, D.C., 1929; West Coast Naval Airship Base, Sunnyvale, Calif., before House Naval Affairs Committee, 1930; Redwood Harbor project before U.S. dist. engr., 1931. Cons. engr., Central Valley project, 1935; project mgr. Boulder-Pioche project, 1936-37. Home: San Francisco, Calif. Died Apr. 14, 1939.

CROZIER, W(ILLIAM) J(OHN), univ. prof.; b. N.Y. City, Aug. 28, 1892; s. William George and Bessie (MacKay) C.; Townsend Harris Hall, 1905-08; B.S., Coll. City of New York 1912; A.M., Harvard, 1914, Ph.D., 1915; Frederick Sheldon, travelling fellow, 1915-18; m. Blanche Maude Benjamin, June 25, 1915; children—Priscilla, Ruth; m. 2d, Louise Baylis Hoagland. June 2, 1934: 1 dau., Mary Louise. Resident naturalist Bermuda Biol. Station for Resarch, 1915-18; asst. prof. physiology, Coll. of Medicine, U. of Illinois, 1918-19, of Zoölogy, U. of Chicago, 1919-20; prof. zoölogy, Rutgers, 1920-25; asso. prof. gen. physiology, Harvard U., 1925-27, prof. since 1927, research prof. since 1934, Lowell lecturer, 1934, also dir. Lab. of Gen. Physiology to 1934. Visiting lecturer Belgian Universityes, C.R.B. Foundation, 1934; Roscoff Banyuls, Naples, 1934-35. Rece Received Townsend Harris Alumni medal, Coll. of City of N.Y., 1942. Operations analyst, U.S. Army Air Forces, 1944-45. Co-editor Journal of Gen. Physiology; mem. editorial bd. journal of Gen. Psychology, and Monograph on exptl. biology Fellow Am.Acad. Arts and Sciences; mem. Am. Soc. Naturalists, Am. Physiol. Soc., Phi Beta Kappa. Sigma Xi. Home: 18 Woodbine Rd., Belmont, Mass. Died Nov. 2, 1955.

CRUM, ROY W(INCHESTER), civil engr.; b. Galesgurg, Ill., Apr. 9, 1885; s. George and Elizabeth (Martin) C.; B.C.E., Ia., State Coll., 1907, C.E., 1914; m. 1st Nina Bates (dec.), 1909; children—George Winchester, Joseph, Elizabeth; m. 2d, Bertha Gates Roberts, 1924. With engr. corps, Pa. R.R. , Parts of 1906, 07, 10; instr., asst. prof., asso. prof., Ia. State Coll., 1907-19; Engr. Materials and Tests, Ia. State Highway Commn., 1919-28; dir. Highway Research Bd., NRC, 1928—. S.A.T.C., 1918. Mem. Am. Soc. C.E. (pres., Ia. sect., 1926, pres. D.C. sect., 1944, chmn. Highway Div., 1932-1941; director, 1946-49), American Concrete Institute (chairman Standards committee, 1931-44; president 1944), American Society for Testing Materials (chmn. com. on Concrete and Concrete Aggregates, 1932-38, chmn. com on Road Materials, 1929-30), Ia. Engring. Soc. (pres. 1922), A.A.A.S. (fellow), Sigma Xi, Tau Beta Pi, Phi Kappa Phi, Alpha Tau Omega. Congregationalist Mason (K.T., Shriner). Clubs: Cosmos, Engineers (Washington). Editor: Annual Proceedings Highway Research Abstracts, 1931—. Received Ia. State Coll. Alumni Merit Award, 1947, Marston Medal, 1948. Home: Ashton Md. Office: 2101 Constitution Av., Washington. Died May 13, 1951; buried Ames, Ia.

CRUM, WILLIAM LEONARD, A.B., Williams Coll., 1914; M.A., Yale, 1916, Ph.D., 1917. Became instr. mathematics, Yale, 1917; then prof. of economics, Harvard. Author: Corporate Size and Earning Power, 1939; co-author: Economic Statistics, 1938; Fiscal Planning for Total War, 1942; Rudimentary Mathematics for Economists and Statisticians, 1946. Address: Harvard University, Cambridge 38, Mass. Died May 1967.

CRUMLEY, THOMAS RALSTON, elec. engr.; b. Wayne, Pa., Sept. 20, 1878; s. David and Mary (Coleman) C.; B.S., Pa. State Coll., 1901; m. Nancy Bartlett, 1908. Constrn. engr. Hudson River Water Power Co., 1901-14; asst. supt. Phila. and Westchester Traction Co., 1904-08; elec. engr. Evansville & Ind. Ry. Co., 1908-15; chief engr. Gen. Engring & Management Corp., 1915-21, pres., 1921-27; v.p. Nat. Pub. Service Corp., 1925-27; v.p. Jersey Central Power & Light Co., 1925-28, pres. and gen. mgr. since 1928. Mem. Am. Inst. E.E. Republican. Episcopalian. Mason. Club: Deal Golf. Home: Eatontown, N.J. Office: 501 Grand Av., Asbury Park, N.J. Died Oct. 5, 1944.

CUDAHY, MICHAEL, merchant; b. Callan, Co. Kilkenny, Ireland, Dec. 7, 1841; s. Patrick and Elizabeth (Shaw) C.; came to U.S., 1849, family settling in Milwaukee; married; became employe in packing house, 1855; became packing house mgr. and meat insp.; partner in Armour & Co., 1873-90; then pres. Cudahy Packing Co., packers, Omaha, Sioux City and Los Angeles. Home: Chicago, Ill. Died 1910.

CULBERTSON, EMMA VALERIA (PINTARD) BICKNELL, physician; b. New Albany, Ind., Dec. 2, 1854; d. John C. and Mary P. C.; ed. by governess and tutors at home and in Europe; A.B., Vassar, 1877, A.M., 1881; M.D., Woman's Med. Coll. of Pa., 1881; unmarried. Attending surgeon N.E. Hosp. for Women and Children, 1891—. Home: Boston, Mass. Deceased.

CULIN, (ROBERT) STEWART, museum dir., curator; b. Phila., July 13, 1858; s. John and Mira (Barrett) C.; ed. Nazareth Hall, Pa.; m. Alice (Mumford) Roberts, Apr. 11, 1917. Director U. of Pa. Mus., 1892-99; curator ethnology, Brooklyn Inst. Mus., 1903—. Made numerous scientific expdns. to Japan, Korea, China and India, and among Am. Indian tribes. Knight of Royal Order of Isabella the Catholic; Officer Order of the White Lion (Czechoslovakian). Author: Korean Games, 1896; Chess and Playing Cars, 1896; American Indian Games, 1905. Home: Brooklyn, N.Y. Died Apr. 8, 1929.

CULLEN, GLENN E(RNEST), university prof.; b. Isle Saint George, O., Apr. 1, 1890; s. Charles and Emma (Gould) C.; A.B., U. of Mich., 1912, B.Chem. Engring., 1913; Ph.D., Columbia, 1917; m. Marie Wherry, June 22, 1917; children—Mary Alice, Donna Jean, Glenn Wherry. Research chemist at Rockefeller Inst. for Med. Research, New York, 1913-22; asso. prof. research, medicine, U. of Pa., 1922-24, prof. biochemistry, Vanderbilt U., 1924-31; traveling fellow, Rockefeller Foundation, 1924-25; prof. biochemistry, Grad. Sch., and prof. research pediatrics, Coll. of Medicine, U. of Cincinnati, 1931—; dir. laboratories of Children's Hosp. Research Foundation, 1931—. Served as capt. Sanitary Corps. World War. Pres. Am. Soc. Biol. Chemists, 1937-39. Writer on enzymes, antiseptics, chemistry of blood in health and disease, diseases of children. Home: Cincinnati, O. Died Apr. 11, 1940.

CULLEN, THOMAS STEPHEN, surgeon; b. Bridgewater, Ontario, Nov. 20, 1868; s. Rev. Thomas and Mary (Greene) C.; ed. Collegiate Instiute, Toronto; M.B., U. of Toronto 1890, also LL.D., hon. D.Sc., Temple U. Specialist in abdominal surgery; formerly prof. gynecology, Johns Hopkins U., now prof. emeritus; visiting gynecologist, JohnsHopkins Hosp. Honorary member La Societa Italiana Ostericia Ginecologia, Rome; corr. mem. Gesellschaft für Genrutshülfe, Leipzig; corr. mem. Gynecol. Soc. of München; hon. Obstet. Socl; pres. Southern Surg. of and Gynecol. Assn., 1916; Med. and Chirurg. Faculty of Md., 1927. Trustee and pres. of Enoch Pratt Library, Baltimore; trustee American Medical Association, 1929-41; chairman Chesapeake Bay Authority, Public Works District 10, 1933-34. Member Phi Beta Kappa. Author: Cancer of the Uterus, 1900; Adenomyoma des Uterus, Verlag Von August Hirschwald, 1903; Adenomyoma of the Uterus, 1908; Myomata of the Uterus (with Howard A. Kelly), 1909; Embryology, Anatomy and Diseases of the Umbilicus Together with Diseases of the Urachus, 1916; Henry Mills Hurd, 1920; Early Medicine in Maryland, 1927; also wrote Accessory Lobes of the Liver for Archives of Surgery. Contbr. to med. jours. on gynecol., pathology and abdominal surgery. Editor of 2 vols. on gynecology, Lewis System of Surgery, 1928. Home: 20 E. Eager St., Balt. Died Mar. 4, 1953; buried Easton, Md.

CULLOM, MARVIN MCTYEIRE, physician; b. Woodford, Tenn., Nov. 9, 1868; s. of Rev. Jeremiah Walker and Mary Bowling (Isom) C.; prepared for college at Webb School; A.B., Vanderbilt U., 1894, M.D., 1896; grad. Manhattan Eye and Ear Hospital, 1898; post-grad. study in London, Paris, Berlin and Vienna; m. Eva Bellinger, Oct. 30, 1899; Children—Isabelle Payne, Hale Ellicott. Practice at Nashville, Tenn., since 1899; prof. clin. ophthalmology and otolaryngology, Vanderbilt U.; eye, ear, nose and throat surgeon to St. Thomas Hosp.; cons. oculist, Louisville & Nashville Ry.; head of dept. of ophthalmology and otolaryngology, Nashville Gen. Hosp. Trustee Vanderbilt U., Webb School; mem. bd. trustees Joint Library of Vanderbilt U., Peabody Coll. and Scarritt Coll.; pres. bd. trust Ladies' Hermitage Assn.; commr. of State of Tenn. to N.Y. World's Fair; colonel in the Tenn. State Nat. Guard on the staff of Gov. Prentice Cooper. Certified ophthalmologist by the Am. Board of ophthalmology; oto-laryngologist by the Am. Bd. of Oto-Laryngology. Citation in publ. Scope, also in Vanderbilt Alumnus, 1956. Fellow A.C.S. Acad.-Internat. of Medicine; mem. A.M.A. (mem. Ho. of Dels., 1923, 25, 27, 28), Am. Geriatric Soc., Pan-Am Assn. Ophthalmology, XVII Internat Congress Ophthalmology, Am. Laryngol., Rhinol. and Otol. Soc., So. Med. Assn. (chmn. sect. ophthalmology and Otolaryngology 1911), Tenn. State Med. Assn. International Society of Ophthalmology, American Acad. of Ophthalmology and Otolaryngology, Nashville Acad. Opthal. and Otolaryngology (ex-pres.), Delta Kappa Epsilon, Alpha Kappa Kappa, Alpha Omega Alpha; pres. Am. Med. Golfing Assn., 1935-36; ex-pres. Nashville Acad. Medicine, Davidson County Med. Soc. Mem. Med. Advisory Bd., World War. Democrat. Methodist. Mason (32 deg., Shriner). Clubs: University, Old Oak, Bellemeade Golf and Country, Chamber of Commerce, Exchange, Cumberland; Royal Knocke Golf (Knockesur-Mer, Belgium); U.S. Seniors Golfing Assn. (1st vice president, member board of directors). Author numerous monographs in field; contbr. Wall St. Jour. Inventor surg. instruments. Home: 103 24th Av. S. Office: Bennie-Dillon Bldg., Nashville. Died June 29, 1959; buried Mt. Olivet Cemetery, Nashville.

CULVER, JOHN YAPP, civil engr.; b. New York, May 18, 1839. After tech. study became asst. engr. Central Park, New York; asst. sec. U.S. Sanitary Commn., 1st yrs. of Civil War; entered U.S. engr. service and was engaged on defenses South of Potomac under Gen. J.G. Barnard; to Central Park; later asst. engr. in charge Brooklyn Parks; chief engr. and supt. same, 1872-86; has done much work as landscape architect and engr. Inventor road-making and tree planting implements and machinery. Active mem. Brooklyn Bd. Edn. for 25 yrs. Lt.-col. and engr. N.G.S.N.Y. Mem. commn. which established rapid transit in Brooklyn; engr. Atlantic Av. Elevated R.R., in charge constrn. of Concourse at Coney Island; associated with the projectors at Brighton Beach, and Prospect Park & Coney Island R.R. and coast protection work on the ocean front; also mem. of com. on pollution of the waters of the State of N.Y. Home: Brooklyn. Office: Morton Bldg., New York.

CUMINGS, EDGAR ROSCOE, geologist; b. North Madison, O., Feb. 20, 1874; s. Charles and Rebecca A. (Sullivan) C.; A.B., Union College (N.Y.), 1897; grad. study Cornell U., 1897; fellow Yale University, 1901-03, Ph.D., 1903; Sc.D., Union College, 1912; m. Frances Lois Crowther, June 28, 1905; children—Edith Katharine, Edgar Crowther. Instr. paleontology, 1898-1903, asst. and asso. prof. and head dept. geology, 1903-09, prof. and head dept. geology since 1909, professor emeritus since 1944, secretary faculty, 1913-20, acting dean Graduate School, 1914-19 and 1923, Ind. University. Author of numerous papers on geology and paleontology with spl. reference to the stratigraphy of the Ordovician formations of N.Y. and Ind., the development, morphology and phylogeny of Brachiopoda and Bryozoa, Silurian of the Michigan Basin region, and the structure of ancient coral reefs. Fellow A.A.A.S., Geol. Society of America (v.p. 1931), Paleontol. Soc. America (v.p. 1928; pres. 1931), Ind. Acad. Science (pres. 1925); mem. Am. Assn. Univ. Professors (council 1916-19 and 1923-26), Phi Beta Kappa, Sigma Xi. Home: Painesville OH

CUMMER, CLYDE LOTTRIDGE, dermatologist; b. Cadillac, Mich., Feb. 23, 1882; s. Robert James (M.D.) and Abbie A. (Stone) C.; Ph.B., Adelbert Coll. (Western Reserve U.). 1904; M.D., Western Reserve U., 1907; m. Marienne Dix North, Feb. 25, 1915; children—Robert North, Katharine Anne (Mrs. H. Lansing Vail, Jr.). With School of Medicine, Western Reserve University, 1909-46, successively as teacher and asso. prof. of clin. pathology. asst. clinical prof. in dermatology and syphilology; visting dermatologist Charity Hosp., grad., study. dermatology dept. Vanderbilt Clinic and College Physician and Surgeon, N.Y. City, 1924-25. Mem. Med. Advisory Bd. No. 7. Selective Service. U.S. Army. World War I and Bd. of Appeals No. 8. Selective Service 1942-47, appeal bd. N. Fed. Judicial Dist. Ohio, 1951-52; hon, consultant U.S. Army med. Library 1942-46. Received Distinguished Service Award, Acad. of Medicine of Cleveland, 1942. Mem. Am. Dermatol. Assn., Am. Med. Assn. (mem. Council on sci. assembly 1937-47; mem house of Dels., 1932-33, 1934-43; chmn. sect. on dermatology and syphilology, 1944-46; mem. War Participation Com., 1942-45), American Academy Dermatology and syphilology, (teeas. 1938-46, pres. 1947-48), Ohio State Med. Assn.(pres. 1933-34; chmn. com. on education, 1936-43; Cleveland Dermatological Society (pres. 1929), Acad. Medicine of Cleveland (pres. 1923), Cleveland Medical Library Assn. (chmn. bd. 1929-37; sec. com. for building Amm Allen Meml. Library Bldg. 1923-26; pres. 1940-41; chmn. Pub. Health Council State of Ohio, 1939-40; mem. S.A.R., Beta Theta Pi, Nu, Phi Beta Kappa, Sigma Xi, Alpha Omega Alpha. Republican. Episcopalian. Author: Cummer Memoranda (geneal. record), 1912; Manual of Clin. Lab. Methods, 1922, 26, 31. Contributor to Blakiston's New Gould Medical Dictionary, 1949. Contbr. to med. lit. and med. history. Home: 19201 Van Aken Blvd., Shaker Heights, Cleve. 22. (summer) Indian River, Mich. Office: Hanna Bldg., Cleve. 15. Died June 7, 1958; buried Lake View Cemetery, Cleve.

CUMMINGS, GEORGE DONALD, pub. health lab. dir.; b. Qunicy, Mass., Oct. 20, 1904; s. George and Jane (Fixter) C.; B.S., Mass. Inst. Tech., 1926; Ph.D., U. Mich., 1934; M.D., Wayne U., 1942; m. Kathleen Mathieson, Jan. 29, 1927; children—Cynthia Jane, Bruce Donald. Joined staff Mich. Dept. of Health Labs., 1926, successively Jr. bacteriologist, sr. bacteriol asst. dir., asso. dir., 1926-44; dir. 1944-57, asso. commnr., dir. lab. services, 1957—; spl. lectr. pub. health U. Mich.; lectr. preventive medicine Wayne U.; cons. infant gastroenteritis control; spl. cons. helath resources adv. com., Office Def. Moblzn., Washington; spl. cons. Pan Am. San Bur., W.H.O.; chmn. Assn. State & Provincial Pub. Helath Lab. Dirs. Com. Research Grants. Recipient Career award Mich. Soc. Pub. Adminstrs., 1959; Achievement award Mich. Health Council, 1961. Diplomate Bd. Preventive Medicine and Pub. Health, Am. Bd. Microbiology, Pan Am. Med. Assn. Mem. A.M.A., Conf. State and Provincial Pub. Health Lab. Dirs. (chmn. com. research activities, grants and tng.), Assn. State and Territorial Pub. Health Lab. Dirs. (ad hoc. com. on impact of National Vaccination Assistance Act), Michigan Med. Soc. (certificate commendation 1962), Ingham County Med. Soc., Am. Coll. Preventive Med., Am. Pub. Health Assn. (mem. lab. council); asso. mem. Mich. Pathol. Society, Delta Omega, Nu Sigma Nu, Sigma Xi, Alpha Omega Alpha. Episcopalian. Club: Lansing City. Author: chapter on Epidemic Diarrhea of the Newborn, Handbook of Communicabel Diseases, 1947, 54; contbr. articles on gastro-enteritis in infants and children to scientific jours. Home: 511 Westmoreland St. Office: Michigan Dept. of Health Laboratories, Lansing, Mich. Died July 27, 1967.

CUMMINGS, HAROLD NEFF, engineer; born.Oxford, Me., Dec. 30, 1884; s. Charles Summer and Carrie A. (Neff) C.; A.B., Bates Coll., Lewiston, Me., 1906; student Harvard Summer Sch., 1906 and 1908; S.B. in Civil Engring., Mass. Inst. Tech., 1910; M. Engring. Edn., Newark Coll. Engring., 1950; m. Katherine Austin Taaffe, June 11, 1912; 1 son, Charles Summner II. Instr. science, Worcester (Mass.)Acad., 1906-08; instrumentman, Buck & Sheldon, cons. engrs. Hartford, Conn., 1910-11; prin. asst.engr., Great Northern Paper Co., Millinocket, Me., 1911-13; head of civil engring. dept., Mechanics Inst., Rochester, N.Y., 1913-14; head of mathematics dept., English High Sch., Lynn, Mass., 1914-17; instr. mathematics and mechanics, Wentworth Inst., Boston, Mass., 1917-18; hydraulic computer H.K. Barrows, Boston, summer 1918; asso. prof. civil engring. and acting head of dept., U. of Delaware, 1918-20; prof. applied mathematics and head of dept., Newark (N.J.) Coll. of Engring., 1920-26, prof. civil engring. and head of dept., 1926-42, vice pres. of coll. 1942-50, emeritus since 1950; engr. structures sect. Curtiss Wright Corp., Propeller Div., Caldwell, N.J., 1952-55, cons. engr., 1955—. Mem. Essex County Mosquito Extermination Commn., 1939-52, treas., 1940, pres. 1948-52. Fellow A.A.A.S., Am. Society C.E.; mem. Am. Soc. for Engring. Edn., Phi Beta Kappa, Tau Beta Pi, Phi Beta Kappa Assos., Chi Epsilon. Home: 695 Grove St., Upper Montclair, N.J. Office: Curtiss Wright Corp., Propeller Division, Caldwell, N.J. Died Mar. 14, 1962; buried Upper Montclair, N.J.

CUMMINS, CLESSIE LYLE, engine co. exec.; b. Honey Creek, Ind., Dec. 27, 1888; s. Francis M. and Josephine E. (Ed) C.; ed. Columbus (Ind.) schs.; m. Ethel M. McCoy, May 18, 1910 (dec. 1925); children—Brainard L., Beatrice M., Mary E., Joseph W., George T., m. 2d, Estella M. Feldmann, Oct. 8, 1926; 1 son, Clessie Lyle. With Am. Motors Co., Indpls., 1904-08; final tester, insp. Marmon Motor Car Co., Indpls., 1908-12; organizer, pres. Cummins Machine Works, Columbus, 1912-18; organizer, pres. Cummins Engine Co., Columbus, 1918-48, chmn. bd., 1948-50, dir., 1948-54, hon. chmn. bd., 1950-54. Mem. WPB, 1942-44. Mem. Soc. Automotive Engrs. (v.p., 1935), Am. Soc. M.E. Inventor first automotive diesel. Home: Sausalito CA Died Aug. 18, 1968; buried Columbus IN

CUMMINS, WILLIAM FLETCHER, geologist; b. Webster Co., Mo., June 13, 1840; s. John C.; ed. in common schools at Hazelwood, Mo.; pursued spl. studies in geology, mineralogy and archaeology; m. Mrs. Minnie Darnell, Mar. 17, 1871. Has written numerous articles on geol. subjects; now asst. State geologist of Tex.; fellow Tex. Acad. Natural Science; mem. A.A.A.S. Residence: Gano Av. Office: 253 Main St., Dallas, Tex.

CUMMINS, WILLIAM YAYLOR, physician; b. Media, Pa., May 17, 1879; s. Joseph Grubb and Sarah Jane (Otley) C.; grad. Biol. Dept., U. of Pa., 1902, M.D., Med. Dept., 1902; m. Josephine Widdicombe, Sept. 9, 1908 (died 1932) m 2d, Laura E. Anderson Sept. 28, 1938. Asst. demonstrator of pathology, U. of Pa., 1902-11; demostrator of pathology Woman's Med. Sch., Phila., Pa., 1907-10; Physician Henry Phipps Inst., Phila., 1907-10; bacteriologist Dept. of Health, N.Y. City, 1911; dir. labs., Southern Pacific Gen. Hosp., San Francisco, Calif., since 1911; Mem. A.M.A. Am. Assn. Pathologists and Bacteriologist, Am. Soc. Clin. Pathologist, Alpha Kappa Kappa Republican. Presbyterian. Clubs: Commonwealth, Olymipc. Author: Syllabur of General Pathology, 1908; Syllabur of Speical Pathology, 1909. Home: 217 25th Av. Office: 1400 Fell St., San Francisco. Died May 5, 1953.

CUNHA, FELIX gastroenterologist; b. Somerville, Mass., Mar. 10, 1896; s. John Felix and Florence (King) C.; M.D., Tufts Coll. Med. Sch., 1917; student U. of Vienna (Austria), 1928-30; m. Cornelia Tarleton Skinner, Dec. 31, 1922. On Visiting staff, St. John's Hosp., also visiting staff Cheney-Allard Hosp., Lowell, Mass., 1920-28; at Lexer Clinic (Munich, Germany), Hartman Clinic (Paris, France), Von Haberer Clinic (Dusseldorf, Germany), Polya Clinic (Budapest, Hungary) Koch Clinic (Prague, Czechoslovakia), 1928; first asst. to Prof. Weibel, Prague, June-Sept. 1928; asst. to Prof. Denk, U. of Graz Stryia, Austria, 1928; first asst. with Prof. Hans Finsterer, Finsterer Clinic, Vienna, 1929-30; formerly mem. faculty U. of Calif. Med. Sch.; mem. staff U. of Calif. Hosp.; formerly mem. Gastroenterological Clinic, San Francisco. Post-grad. and Polyclinic Hosp. Served as 1st lt., Med. Corps, U.S. Army, 1917-19, capt. Med. Res., 1919-23. Honorary fellow International College of Proctology Fellow Internat. Coll. Surgeons (former regent, mem. electoral bd. Hall of Fame) A.M.A., Nat. Gasenterol. Assn. (pres.), Am. Gastroenterological Assn.; hon. fellow Pan-Am. and Mex. Gastroenterological associations, member Pacific Coast District Int. College of Surgeons (regent), member A.M.A. of Vienna, 1929-30 (president 1929), Austro-American Soc. (Vienna; v.p. 1929), San Francisco County and California state medical societies, Association for Study of Internal Secretions, Assn. for Study of History of Medicine. Am. Coll. Gastreonterology (p.p.), Am. Gastroscipic Club, Phi Chi. Republican. Clubs: Cercle de L'Union, Press and Union League Commonwealth. Author: Osler as a Gastroenterologist, 1945; Osler and His Books, 1950; numerous articles for medical and surgical journals; member editorial board internat. Abstracts Surgery, Review of Gastro-enterology. Formerly lecturer in med. bibliography and history, instr. in medicine and consultant in gastroenterology, U. of Calif. Med. Sch. and Hosp. Home: 1150 Union St. Office: 450 Sutter St., San Francisco. Died May 17, 1960; buried Golden Gate Cemetery, San Bruno, Cal.

CUNNINGHAM, ANDREW OSWALD, civil engr.; b. Rangoon, Burma, July 8, 1866; s. Gen. Percy S. (British Army) and Annie Sarah (Stroud) C.; ed. South Eastern Coll., Eng., 1879-83; came to U.S., 1883; B.C.E., U. of Minn., 1894; m. Georgia Townsend Quinn, July 11, 1903. Rodman and leveler on N.P. R.R., 1886-88; land surveyor in N.D., 1890-91; draftsman, 1894-95, and asst. engr., 1895-96, Gillette-Herzog Mfg. Co., Minneapolis; gen. contracting and engring., and southern agt. for Schultz Bridge & Iron Co., Pittsburgh, 1896-98; with Pittsburgh Reduction Co., Pittsburgh, 1896-98; with Pittsburgh Reduction Co., designing improvements in old bldgs. at Niagara Falls and making designs for new bldgs. and improvements at New Kensington Works, 1898-99; in gen. cons. and civ. engring. bus., 1899-1900; contracting mgr. in charge estimates, designs and blds. for Am. Bridge Co., Cleveland, 1900-02; bridge engr., 1902-05; chief engr. Wabash R.R., 1905-23; in pvt. practice as cons. engr. Mayor University City, 1924—. Deceased.

CUNNINGHAM, BERT, biology; b. McLean County, Ill., June 3, 1883; s. Parker Dresser and Susie (Hammond) C.; B.S., Ill. Wesleyan U., 1908, M.S., 1909; A.M., Trinity Coll. (now Duke U.), 1916; Ph.D., U. of Wis., 1920; m. Jean Knapton, Oct. 1, 1907. Prof. science, Mo. Wesleyan Coll., 1909-11; Durham (N.C.) High Sch., 1911-16; instr. biology, Trinity Coll., 1917-20; prof. biology, Duke U., since 1920. Fellow A.A.A.S.; mem. Am. Soc. Zoologists, Am. Mus. Natural History, N.C. Acad. Science (ex-pres., sec.), Sigma Xi, Phi Sigma, Kappa Delta Pi, Phi Gamma Delta. Methodist. Author: Axial Duplicity in Serpents (monograph), 1937. Home: 1200 Markham Av., Durham, N.C. Died Sept. 27, 1943.

CUNNINGHAM, DAVID WEST, engineer; b. Boston, Dec. 24, 1829; s. Andrew and Abby L. (west(C.; ed. Chauncy Hall Sch. and Lawrence Scientific Sch. (Harvard); m. Mary B. S. Fuller, 1859 (died 1869); 2d, Caroline S. Thomas, 1873. Commenced as civ. engr. asst. in Boston water works, 1848; later civ. engr. on railroads in U.S. and Can., and 6 yrs. in Chile, S.A. on r.r. and govt. work; was engaged in construction Charleston water works and Lowell water works; sewerage systems, Lowell, Mass., and Stillwater, Minn.; chief asst. engr. for Boston water works additonal supply, 6 yrs.; built Tarkio Valley R.R.; was consulting engr., Minneapolis water works and Lowell water works; sewerage systems, Lowell, Mass., and Stillwater, Minn.; chief asst. engr. for Boston water works additional supply, 6 yrs.; built Tarkio Valley R.R.; was consulting engr., Minneapolis water works; worked 4-section wheat farm in N.D. until 1894, when he removed to Calif. Died May 11, 1916.

CUNNINGHAM, HOLLY ESTIL, author, lecturer, educator; g. Jackson County, W.Va., Jan. 13, 1883; s. Nathan Decatur and Sarah Ann (Shafer) C.; A.B., Lebanon (O.) Coll., 1908, LL.B., 1910; student U. of Cincinnati; Ph.D., U. of Chicago, 1918; m. Lelia Jane Morris, 1905. Began teaching in pub. schs. of W.Va.; pres. and prof. philosophy Lebanon (O.) Coll., 1914-17; prof. and head dept. philosophy U. of Okla., 1917-23; prof. and head dept. W.Va., U., 1923-29; prof. and dir. summer session Atlantic U., 1930-32, also trustee and sec. of Univ.; pres. Alfred Holbrook Coll., 1932-40; pres. Edison Coll. 1941-50; prof. philosophy Asbury Coll., Wilmore, Ky., since 1950. Chairman Lee County Red Cross, 1945-46. Lecturer Asso. Clubs, Inc., 1949. Mem. A.A.A.S., Southern Soc. for Philosophy and Psychology, Am. Philos. Assn. (Westerm and Eastern branches), Am. Assn. Univ. Profs., W.Va. Acad. Sciences, Southwestern Polit. Sci. Assn., Acacia, Kappa Delta Phi, Phi Delta Kappa. Baptist. Mason (32 deg.), Odd Fellow, Rotarian. Author: Types of Logical Theory, 1918; An Introduction to Philosophy, 1920; Textbook of Logic, 1924; Fundamental Concepts in the Physical Sciences 1927; The New Deal in Education, 1932; New Concepts in Educatoin, 1935; A Program of Education, 1937; Education and the Concept of Utility, 1939; Modern Science and Ancient Morality, 1947; An Introduction to Philosophy, revised, 1949; Adventures in Philosophy, vol. 8, 1951. Home: 108 Bellevue St., Wilmore, Ky. Died Jan. 23, 1952; buried buried Asbury College Plot, Wilmore, Ky.

CUNNINGHAM, PAUL DAVIS; b. Monroe Co., Ga., Nov. 27, 1869; s. Sumner Archibald and Laura N. (Davis) C.; ed. public schools Monroe Co., Ga., 1878-85; undergraduate Emory Coll., Oxford, Ga.; unmarried. Engaged in ry. location and construction, from rodman to asst. resident engr., July 1887, to Feb. 1890; resident engr. ry. construction, June 1890, to March, 1891; hydrographic work engr. dept., U.S.A., Oct. 1891; topographical work Internat. Boundary Commn., U.S. and Mexico, 1892-94; U.S. asst. engr. Internat. Boundary Commn., U.S. and Mexico, 1894-96; engr. clerk, N.W. and S.W. divs., engr. dept., U.S.A., 1896-98; asst. to chief engr. on duty at headquarters of army, July 1898-Jan. 1899; prin. asst. engr., Engr. Dept., Dept. of Havana, Cuba, Jan.-Dec. 1899; acting chief engr. Dept. of Havana, Dec. 1899-April 1900; chief engr. City of Havana, April-Aug. 1900; cons. engr. U.S. Internat. Boundary Commn. (U.S. and Mexico), 1900—. Home: El Paso, Tex. Died 1901.

CUNNINGHAM, ROBERT SYDNEY, anatomist; b. Anderson, S.C., Nov. 14, 1891; s. Robert Campbell and Annie Hortense (Cooley) C.; B.S., A.M.A., Davidson (N.C.) Coll., 1911; M.D., Johns Hopkins, 1915; Sc.D., Union Coll., Schenectady, 1938. Asst. in anatomy, 1915-16, instr., 1916-17, asso., 1919-22, asso. prof., 1922-25, Johns Hopkins; prof. anatomy, Vanderbilt Med. Sch., 1925-37; prof. anatomy and dean Albany Med. Sch., 1937-46, prof. histology and dean, 1946-50, prof., 1950-52, prof. emeritus, 1952, adminstr. Albany Hosp., 1942-50; exec. dir. Albany Med. Center, 1950-52; ret., 1952; vis. prof. Med. Coll. Va. Served as 1st lt. M.R.C., 1917-19. Mem. Am. Assn. Anatomists, Am. Physiol. . Soc. Richmond Med. Acad., Phi Beta Kappa, Sigma Xi. Author sci. articles on anatomy and physiology of peritoneum, origin and function of cells of blood changes in blood and tissues in tb and syphilis, and structure and function of lymphatic system. Home: 2023 Hanover Av., Richmond, Va. 23220. Died May 24, 1963; buried Old Silverbrook Cemetery, Anderson, S.C.

CURLEY, JAMES, astronomer; b. Athleague, Roscommon, Ireland, Dec. 26, 1796. Came to U.S., 1817, became bookkeeper in Phila.; taught mathematics, Frederick, Md.; joined Soc. of Jesus, 1827; ordained priest Roman Catholic Ch., 1833; tchr. philosophy and mathematics at Georgetown, also chaplain Visitation Convent, Washington, D.C., nearly 50 years; planner, 1st dir. and historian Georgetown Observatory. Died Georgetown, July 24, 1889.

CURRIE, DONALD HERBERT, sanitarian; b. in Jefferson Co., Mo., Mar. 25, 1876; s. Daniel McNeil and Martha (Dent) C.; M.D., Washington U., 1899; m. Helen Hope Hanson, May 10, 1900. Apptd. asst. surgeon U.S.P.H. Service, July 25, 1899; passed asst. surgeon, 1904; surgeon, 1912. At Hygienic Lab., Washington, 1900-01; served in plague epidemic, San Francisco, 1901-05, yellow fever epidemic, New Orleans, 1905; boarding officer San Francisco Quarantine Sta., 1905-07; on duty in Honolulu, 1907-11, in Calif., 1911-13; state health officer, Calif. (leave of absence), 1914-15; dir. U.S. Leprosy Sta., Honolulu, 1909-11, 1915-17; was sanitary adviser to gov. of Hawaii; apptd. quarantine officer, Boston, Mass., Aug. 1917. Represented U.S. in Internat. Leprosy Conf., Bergen, Norway, 1909. Episcopalian. Elk. Died Dec. 23, 1918.

CURRY, JAMES ROWLAND, educator; b. Wooster, O., Dec. 29, 1903; s. William R. and Edna (Smith) C.; B.S., Dartmouth Coll., 1925; Ph.D., Johns Hopkins, 1930; m. Leota DeVore, July 24, 1939. Lumber business, 1925-26; research in chemistry and physics, Kaiser Wilhelm Inst. and Univ. of Berlin, 1930-32, at Technische Hochschule in Darmstadt, 1933; research asst., Columbia, 1934-35; instr., Williams Coll., 1935-39, asst. prof., 1939-43, asso. prof., 1943, prof. and chmn. chemistry dept., 1946-47, Ebenezer Fitch prof. and chmn. dept. since 1947; spl. research asso., Radio Research Lab., Harvard, 1943-45; with Office of Scientific Research and Development, 1943-45. DuPont Fellow, 1929-30; German American Exchange Fellow, 1930-31. Fellow A.A.A.S.; mem. Am. Chem. Soc., Am. Phys. Soc., Inst. Radio Engrs., Phi Beta Kappa, Sigma Xi, Gamma Alpha, Theta Chi. Clubs: Faculty, Williams (N.Y.C.). Contbr. scientific papers. Home: Williamstown MA Died Apr. 5, 1968; buried Westlawn Cemetery, Williamstown MA

CURTIS, AUGUSTUS DARWIN, illuminating engr.; b. Hawley, Pa., Oct. 14, 1865; s. George B., M.D., and Augusta (Cook) C.; ed. Honesdale (Pa.) High Sch. and Athanaeum, Chicago, Ill.; student Art Inst. Chicago; m. Marette Hotchkin, 1891; children—Kenneth, Darwin. Sec. M. & M. Box Co., Marinette, Wis., 1890-1900; was half owner and bus. mgr. Popular Mechanics; pres. Curtis Lighting, Inc., Chicago, New York and Antwerp, 1900—. Former mem. Ill. N.G. Republican Presbyn. Mason. A pioneer in development of indirect lighting. Died Apr. 29, 1931.

CURTIS, CARLTON CLARENCE, botanist; b. Syracuse, N.Y., Aug. 26, 1864; s. Harlow and Martha (Shumway) C.; A.B., Syracuse U., 1891, A.M., Ph.D., 1893; A.M., Columbia, 1892; student universities of Cambridge, 1899, Leipzig, 1900; married. Principal, Fayette Union Sch., N.Y., 1892-94; inst. natural science, Brooklyn Poly. Inst., 1894-96; instr. botany, Columbia, since 1899. Mem. Am. Soc. Naturalists, Bot. Soc. Am. and other bot. socs., Phi Beta Kappa. Contbr. to bot jours. Author: Text-Book of General Botany, 1897; Nature and Development of Plants, 1922; Guide to the Trees, 1927. Address: Columbia University, New York. Died Apr. 10, 1945.

CURTIS, CHARLES GORDON, inventor; b. Boston, Apr. 20, 1860; s. George Ticknor and Louise A., C.; C.E., Columbia, 1881, M.S., 1907; LL.B., N.Y. Law Sch., 1883. Patent lawyer, 8 yrs.; organized C.&C. Electric Motor Co., the first to make electric motors and electric fans; organized Curtis Electric Mfg. Co., of which was pres.; invented and developed the Curtis Steam turbine; sold steam turbine rights to Gen. Electric Co.; introduced turbine of own design into British, Japanese, German and U.S. Navies. Recipient Count Rumford Gold and Silver medals Am. Soc., of Arts and Sciences. Republican. Invented Curtis Scavenging Systems for 2-cycle engines. Home: University Club. 1 W. 54th St., N.Y.C. Died Mar. 10, 1953; buried Westchester, N.Y.

CURTIS, EDWARD, physician; b. Providence, R.I., June 4, 1838; s. George and Julia (Bridgham) C.; A.B., Harvard, 1859, A.M., 1862; M.D., U. of Pa., 1864; m. Augusta Lawler Stacey, Nov. 16, 1864; father of Constance and Natalie C. Entered army as med. cadet, Sept. 6, 1861; acting asst. surgeon, May 5, 1863; asst. surgeon, Mar. 30, 1864; bvtd. capt. and maj. U.S.A., Mar. 13, 1865, "for faithful and meritorious services during the war;" resigned, June 7, 1870. Lecturer, 1871-73, prof. materia medica and therapeutics, 1873-86, emeritus, 1886, Coll. Phys. and Surg. (Columbia); med. dir Equitable Life Assurance Co., 1876-1904; retired, 1904. Author: Manual of General Medicinal Technology, 1883; Months and Moods; A Fifteen-year Calendar, 1903; Nature and Health, 1906. Died Nov. 28, 1912.

CURTIS, FRANCIS JOSEPH, chemist, chem. exec.; b. Cambridge, Mass., Apr. 22, 1894; s. James Henry and Mary Ellen (McCarthy) C.; A.B., Harvard, 1915; unmarried. With Monsanto Chemical Co. and subsidiaries, St. Louis, since 1915 as mem. research dept., 1915-20, mem. prodn. dept., 1920-25, sales dept., Merrimac Chem. Co., subsidiary, Everett, Mass., 1925-30, development dir., 1930-35; asst. development dir., Monsanto Chem. Co., 1935-39, development dir., 1939-43, v.p., 1943—, dir., 1949—. Civilian cons. Chem. Warfare Ser., 1945; asst. adminstr. Nat. Prodn. Authority 1951-52. Fellow Am. Inst. of Chemists; mem. Am. Inst. of Chem. Engrs. (past pres., N.Y.; past chmn. div. of indsl. and engring. chemistry, Washington), Soc. of Chem. Industry (past chmn. Am. section, London and N.Y., pres. London, 1952-53). Home: 410 N. Newstead Av., St. Louis 8. Office: Monsanto Chemical Company, 1700 S. 2d St., St. Louis 63104. Died Apr. 21, 1960.

CURTIS, GEORGE CARROLL, geographic sculptor; b. Abington, Mass., July 15, 1872; s. George E. and Mary Adeline (Browne) C.; S.B., Harvard, 1896; grad. work in physiography and geographic modeling, 1895-98; m. Helen Louise Waters. Asst. in geol. dept., Harvard Univ.; asst. field geologist, U.S. Geol. Survey; model Met. Boston (for State of Mass.), gold medal, Paris, 1900 (aerial perspective first applied to topog. models); stiudied with Heim in Zurich; made, for U.S. Senate (Congressional Library), models (1) Washington City, 1902 (2) Washington City as proposed future development—1st Am. city to be modeled on a photographic survey; gold medal, Geog. Models, St. Louis, 1904; rep. Nat. Geog. Soc., Dixie Expdn. to W. Indian eruptions; first to reach crater of La Soufrière; discovered new summit of Mt. Pelee; Curtis Geography Models of land from types; year among Coral Islands, S. Pacifiv, for Agassiz Mus. Coral Id. Bora Bora, 1st naturalistic landscape model to be made in America; sailed single handed, in study of coast, from Me. to Newfoundland, 1910-11, made photographic survey of Kilauea crater, for Harvard U.; went around the World examining volcanoes, 1913; landscape paintings in relief of Josemite, Niagara, and Grand Canyon, 1923-25. Author: (and illustrator) Topography of the Region about Boston, 1900. Deceased.

CURTIS, GEORGE LENOX, M.D., author; b. Apr. 19, 1854; s. Chas. Thomas and Jane C.; grad. Univ. of Pa., M.D., 1887; m. Janie Elizabeth Richmond, Feb. 12, 1896. Studied abroad; successor to Prof. James E. Garrotson, of Phila.; ex-prof. and ex-clinical instr. surgery of mouth and face; confines practice to that branch of surgery and to electro-therapeutics. Has contributed many articles on these subjects in which he is recognized authority. Mem. Soc. Am. Authors, Am. Med. Assn., and N.Y. State and County Med. assns., Med. Assn. of the Greater City of New York, A.A.A.S., Am. Electro-Therapeutic Assn., Harlem Med. Assn., Nat. Geog. Soc. Club: N.Y. Athletic, North Lakes Fish and Game, Canadian Camp (pres.) Residence: 7 W. 58th St., New York.

CURTIS, GEORGE MORRIS, surgeon; b. Big Rapids, Mich., Apr. 2, 1890; s. Anson Bartie and Mary (Christie) C.; A.B., U. Mich., 1910; M.A., 1910, Ph.D., 1914, Sc.D., 1952; student Vanderbilt U., 1918; M.D., Rush Coll., 1920; postgrad. U. Berne, Switzerland, 1924-27; m. Lucille Atcherson, Jan. 16, 1928; children—Charlotte Murray, Mary Darling. Asst. in biology U. Mich., 1908-11, asst. in anatomy, 1911-13; prof. anatomy Vanderbilt U., 1913-20, chmn. dept., 1915-20; interne USPHS Hosp. No. 30, 1920; mem. resident staff Presbyn. Hosp., Chicago, 1921-23; fellow in surgery NRC, 1923-25, asst. in surgery Rush Med. Coll., 1923-24, Inselspital, Brene, 1924-27; asso. prof. surgery U. Chgo., 1927-32, prof. surgery, 1932; prof. surgery Ohio State U. since 1932, surg. research, 1932-36, chmn. dept. Research Surgery since 1936; cons. surgeon Franklin County Tb Hosp.; editorial bd. Internat. Surg. Digest, So. Surgeon, Jour. Ohio Acad. Sci. Served in M.E.R.C.., 1918. Iodine award Am. Pharm. Assn., 1950. Fellow Am. Surg. Assn., A.C.S., Internat. Coll. Surgeons (hon.); Am. Coll. Chest Physicians; mem. A.A.A.S., Am. Assn. Thoracic Surgery, Am. Assn. Surgery Trauma, A.M.A., Chgo. Surg. Soc., Columbus Surg. Soc. (pres. 1948), Detroit Acad. Surgeons (hon.), Midwest Clin. Soc. (hon.), St. Paul Surg. Soc. (hon.), Inst. of Medicine Chgo., Ohio Acad Sci. (v.p. 1939), So., Western, Central (a founder; pres. 1946), Surg. assns., Am. Bd. Surgery (a founder), Am. Bd. Thoracic Surgery (founders group), Am. Physiol. Soc., Am. Assn. Anatomists, Am. Soc. Exptl. Pathology, Am. Soc. Clin. Investigation, Am. Assn. History of Medicine, Am. Goiter Assn., Am. Assn. Human Genetics, Assn. Study Internal Secretions, Chgo. Pathol. Soc., Central Soc. Clin. Research, Columbus Acad. Medicine, Soc. Exptl. Biology and Medicine, Ill. Acad. Sci., Phi Beta Kappa, Alpha Kappa Kappa, Alpha Omega Alpha, Beta Epsilon, Gamma Alpha, Sigma Xi, Phi Sigma. Clubs: Coffee House (Nashville); Michigan Union (Ann Arbor); Chaos (Chgo.); Kit Kat (Columbus). Writer chapts. textbooks, monographs Cited for progress in research (iodine) by Am. Medicine, 1933, and Jour. Am. Med. Assn. in 1939. Home: 1178 E. Broad St., Columbus 5, O. Died Dec. 1965.

CURTIS, HARRY ALFRED, chemist; b. Sedalia, Colo., Feb. 16, 1884; s. Frederick A. and Lydia A. Cramer) C.; B.S., U. Colo., 1908, M.A., 1910; Sc.D., 1930; Ph.D., U. Wis., 1914, Sc.D., 1937; D.Eng. (hon.), U. Louisville, 1948; m. Irene Hall, May 14, 1911 (dec.); children—Jeanne Carol, Patricia. Instr. later prof. chemistry, U. Colo., 1908-17; prof. chemistry Northwestern U., 1919-20; chief chemist, later plant supt. Internat. Coal Products Corp., Irvington, N.J., 1920-21; gen. mgr. Clinchfield Carbocoal Corp., South Clinchfield, Va., 1921-23; chief nitrogen survey U.S. De Dept., Commerce, 1923-24; prof. chem. engring. Yale, 1923-30, chmn. dept. chem. engring., 1929-30; chmn. div. chemistry and chem. tech. NRC, 1930-34; dir. research Vacuum Oil Co., 1931-33; chief chem. engr. TVA, 1933-38; dean Coll. Engring., U. Mo., 1938-48, dir. TVA 1948-57. Mem. Pres. Collidge's Muscle Shoals Commn. Mem. Colo. N.G., 1915-17; Mexican border service 3 mos., 1916; capt. ordnance, U.S. Army, World War I; assinged to nitrate div. ordnance and engaged in chem. engring. Mem. Am. Chem. Soc., A.A.A.S., Sigma Nu, Alpha Chi Sigma. Club; Cosmos (Washington). Home: 3730 Dellwood Dr., Knoxville, Tenn. Died July 1, 1963.

CURTIS, HARVEY LINCOLN, physicist; b. Mason, Mich., Dec. 14, 1875; s. Wm. Howell and Sarah Bowen (Ormsby) C.; Ph.B., U. Mich., 1900; A.M., 1903, Ph.D., 1910; m. Anna Puffer, Aug. 26, 1903; children—Roger W., Howard J., Alvin G.(dec.), Norma L., Mildred A. Asst. in phys. lab. u. Mich., 1902-03; instr. physics Mich. State Agrl. Co Coll., 1903-07; with Bur. of Standards, Washington, successively asst. physicist, 1907-13, asso. physicist, 1913-18, physicist, 1918-24, sr. physicist, 1924-28, prin. physicist, 1928-46; retired 1947. Recipient Joint Army and Navy cert. of Appreciation, 1948. Fellow Am. Physical Soc., A.A.A.S., Am. Inst. E.E. (chmn. Washington, sect. 1935), mem. Washington Acad. Scis. (pres. 1942), Washington Philos. Soc. (pres. 1931), Am. Soc. for Testing Materials, Am. Optical Soc., Phi Beta Kappa; mem. Internat. Electrical Congress, Paris, France, 1933. Methodist. Club: Cosmos. Author: Electrical Measurements; also scientific papers of Bur. of Standards and articles in technical journals. Home: 6816 Delaware St., Chevy Chase 15, Md. Died Apr. 17, 1956; buried Rock Creek Cemetery, Washington.

CURTIS, HEBER DOUST, astronomer; b. Muskegon, Mich., June 27, 1872; s. Orson B. and Sarah E. (Doust) C.; A.B., U. of Mich., 1892, A.M., 1893 Ph.D., U. of Va., 1902; m. Mary D. Rapier, July 12, 1895; children—Margret Evelyn (Mrs. Alexander Walters), Rowen Doust, Alan Blair, Baldwin Rapier. Prof. Latin, Napa Coll., 1894-97; prof. mathematics and astronomy, U. of the Pacific, 1897-1900; fellow in astronomy, Leander McCormick Obs., U. of Va., 1900-02; asst. 1902-04, asst. astronomer, 1904-06, Lick Obs.; acting astronomer in charge of the D. O. Mills Expdn. to the Southern Hemisphere, 1906-09; astronomer, Lick Obs., 1909-20; dir. Allegheny Obs., 1920-30; dir. obs. of U. of Mich., 1930—. Observed 11 total solar 1900, Sumatra, 1901, Labrador, 1905, Russia, 1914. Washington, 1918, Mexico, 1923, New Haven, 1925, Sumatra, 1926, 29, Nevada, 1930, Maine, 1932; in charge Lick Observatory Eclipse Sta., Labrador, 1905. Mem. Nat. Acad. Sciences. Died Jan. 8, 1942.

CURTIS, HOWARD JAMES, physiologist; b. Lansing, Mich., Dec. 11, 1906; s. Harvey Lincoln and Anna (Puffer) C.; B.S., U. Mich., 1928; A.M., Swarthmore Coll., 1929; Ph.D., Yale, 1932; Rockefeller fellow Johns Hopkins Sch. Medicine, 1938-40; m. Dorothy Albert, Aug. 27, 1932; children—Brian Albert, Richard Harvey, Barbara Ann. Biophysicist, The Biol. Lab., Cold Springs Harbor, N.Y., 1932-35; asso. in physiology Coll. Physicians and Surgeons, Columbia, 1935-38, asst. prof. physiology, 1941-43, asso. prof., 1946-47; prof. of physiology and head physiology dept. Vanderbilt U. Med. Sch., 1947-50. Med. cons. to AEC, 1946-72; cons. in radiobiol. to USPHS, 1946-72, chmn. radiation study sect., 1955-72; mem. Nat. Com. on Radiation Protection; mem. sci. council of Am. Cancer Soc., 1956; cons. in radioisotopes to VA, 1948-72. Del. Atoms for Peace Conf., Geneva, 1958. Active in adv. capacity in formulating nat. legislation of atomic energy and on NSF; mem. Nat. Council Radiation Protection, 1962-72. Mem. NRC (mem. space sci. bd. 1959-72, mem. com. on growth; chmn. com. on radiobiology); v.p. Radiation Research Soc., 1956; chmn. biology dept. Brookhaven Nat. Lab., 1950-72. Mayor of Village of Shoreham, N.Y. Mem. bd. of sci. councilors Nat. Inst. Neurol: Diseases and Blindness, 1958-72. Mem. L.I. Biol. Assn. (dir.), Am. Phys. Soc., Am. Physiol. Soc., Harvey Soc., A.A.A.S., N.Y. Acad. Sci. Author: (with J.H. Lawrence) Advances in Medical Physics, Vol. II, 1949; (with F. M. Liver) Biophysical Research Methods, 1949; (with Philip Bard) Medical Physiology; Biological Mechanisms of Aging. Editor: Physiological Reviews, 1951. Contbr. research articles to sci. publs. Home: Shoreham LI NY Died Sept. 13, 1972.

CURTIS, JOHN GREEN, physiologist; b. New York, Oct. 29, 1844; s. George and Julia (Bridgham) C.; A.B., Harvard, 1866, A.M., 1869; M.D., Coll. Phys. and Surg. (Columbia), 1870; (LL.D., Columbia, 1904); m. Mrs. Martha (McCook) Davis, Oct. 20, 1871. Apptd. jr. asst. Bellevue Hosp., Apr. 1, 1869, sr. asst., Oct. 1, 1869, house surgeon, Apr. 1, 1870, attending surgeon, 1879-80; asst. and demonstrator of anatomy, 1870-75, adj. lecturer, 1875-76, adj. prof. physiology, 1876-83, prof. physiology, 1883, emeritus prof. physiology, 1909, Coll. Phys. and Surg. Joint Author: American Text-book of Physiology, 1896. Died Sept. 20, 1913.

CURTIS, MOSES ASHLEY, botanist, clergyman; b. Stockbridge, Mass., May 11, 1808; s. Jared and Thankful (Ashley) C.; grad. William Coll., 1827; m. Mary de Rosset, Dec. 3, 1834. Ordained to ministry Episcopal Ch., 1835; missionary, N.C., 1835-37; tchr. Episcopal Sch., Raleigh, N.C., 1837-39; pastor in Hillsboro, N.C., 1841-47, 56-72, Society Hill, S.C., 1847-56; studied vegetation of N.C. during his many missionary travels, specialized in study of fungi. Author: Natural History Survey of North America, Part III, Botany; Containing a Catalogue of the Plants of the State, with Descriptions of History of the Trees, Shrubs, and Woody Vines, 1860. Died Hillsboro, Apr. 10, 1872.

CURTIS, OTIS FREEMAN, plant physiology; b. of Am. parents, Sendai, Japan, Feb. 12, 1888; s. William Willis and Lydia Virginia (Cone) C.; A.B., Oberlin, 1911; Ph.D., Cornell U., 1916; m. Lucy Marguerite Weeks, Aug. 27, 1913; children—Otis Freeman, William Edgar, Margaret Ann. Tutor Oberlin Acad., 1911-12; with Cornell U. since 1913, instr., later asst. prof. botany until 1922, prof. botany, plant physiologist, Expt. Sta., since 1922; visiting prof., U. of Leeds, Eng., 1926-27, Ohio State U., 1930-31. Mem. A.A.A.S., Bot. Soc. America, American Assn. Naturalists, Am. Soc. for Hort. Science, Am. Society Plant Physiologists (v.p. 1936-37, pres. 1937-38), Phi Kappa Phi, Gamma Alpha, Sigma Xi. Unitarian. Author: Translocation of Solutes in Plants; Introduction to Plant Physiology, 1949. Contributed findings of research along lines of translocation of foods in green plants, vegetative propagation and water and temperature relations of plants. Home: Forest Home, Ithaca, N.Y. Died July 4, 1949.

CURTIS, WINTERTON CONWAY, zoologist; b. Richmond, Me., Nov. 4, 1875; s. William Conway and Fanny Mary (Norton) C.; A.B., Williams, 1897, A.M., 1898, Sc.D., 1934; Ph.D., Johns Hopkins, 1901; m. Marion Hitchcock Peck, Sept. 5, 1902; 1 son, William Dwight. Instr. on staff, Marine Biol. Lab., Woods Hole, Mass., 1899-1903; in charge of the Invertebrate course, 1908-11; instr. zoology, 1901-04, asst. prof. 1904-08, prof. since 1908, acting dean, College of Arts and Science, 1939, dean of same 1940-45, dean and professor emeritus since 1946; director of instruction Armed Forces, 1943-44, University of Mo.; scientific assistant U.S. Bur. Fisheries, 1907-10. Visiting prof. Keio U., Tokio, 1932-33. Expert witness, Scopes trial, Dayton, Tenn., 1925. Mem. Nat. Research Council (div. biology and agr., 1924-26; chmn. same, 1930-31, mem. exec. bd., 1935-38); pres. Union of Am. Biol. Socs., 1931-35; trustee Marine Biol. Lab., Woods Hole, Mass., 1923-35, and since 1937. Fellow A.A.A.S. (v.p. sect. F, zoology, 1926); member American Society Zoologists (sec. 1913, pres. 1932), American Society of Naturalists, Phi Beta Kappa, Sigma Xi, Phi Gamma Delta. Has made investigations in embryology, morphology, parasitism in platoda and mollusca and in effects of radiations upon animals, also in humanistic aspects of biol. science. Club: Faculty (Univ. of Mo.). Author: Science and Human Affairs, 1922; Laboratory Directions in General Zoology, 1938, 48. Textbook of General Zoology (both with Mary J. Guthrie), 1938-47. Asso. editor Jour. of Morphology and Physiology, 1927-29. Home: 210 Westmount Av., Columbia MO

CURTISS, CHARLES FRANKLIN, agriculturist; b. Nora, Ill., Dec. 12, 1863; s. Franklin and Margaret (Schmitz) C.; B.Agr., Ia. Agrl. Coll., 1887, M.Agr., 1894; D.Sc., Mich. Agrl. Coll., 1907; m. Olive Wilson, Feb. 15, 1893. Managed farm, 1887-90; asst. dir., 1890-97, dir., 1897-32. Ia. Expt. Sta. and sr. dean of agr., now dean emeritus. A founder, dir., mem. exec. com. Internat. Live Stock Expn. Assn; mem. Am. Soc. Promotion Agrl. Science. Club: Saddle and Sirloin (Chicago). Home: Ames, Ia. Died July 30, 1947.

CURTISS, DAVID RAYMOND, mathematician b. Derby, Conn., Jan. 12, 1878; s. Hamilton Burton and Emily Wheeler (Curtis) C.; A.B., U. Cal., 1899; A.M., 1901; Ph.D., Harvard 1903; traveling fellow , 1903-04; studied Ecole Normale Supérieure Paris France; m. Sigrid Eckman, June 25, 1907 (dec. Apr. 1941); children—John Hamilton, Margaret Eckman, Alice Judson; m.2d, Ruth C. Kneen, July 23, 1943. Instr. mathematics Yale, 1904-05; asst. prof. mathematics Northwestern L., 1905-07, asso. prof., 1907-09, prof., 1909-43, prof. emeritus, 1943—; lectr. mathematics Harvard, 1920-21. Fellow A.A.A.S. (vice-pres sect. A, 1921); mem. Am Math. Soc. (council, and vice-pres.), Math Assn. America (pres.), Société Mathématique de France, Circolo Mathematico di Palermo, Delta Tau Delta, Phi Beta Kappa, Sigma Xi. Author: Analytic Functions, (with E. J., Moulton) Trigonometry, 1927, High School Trigonometry, 1940, Essentials fof Trigonometry, 1942, Essentials of Analytic Geometry, 1947. Contbr. to Math. jours. Editor Trans. Am. Math. Soc., 1913-19, also Bulletin Am. Math. Soc. and Carus Monographs. Home: 1249 Montery A St., Redlands, Cal. Died Apr. 28, 1953.

CURTISS, GLENN HAMMOND, inventor, aviator; b. Hammondsport, N.Y., May 21, 1878; s. Frank R. and Lua (Andrews) C.; ed. pub. schs.; m. Lena P. Neff, 1898; 1 son, Glenn Hammond. Former pres. G. H. Curtiss Mfg. Co., Curtiss Aeroplane Co., Curtiss Motor Co., Curtiss Engring. Co., Curtiss Aeroplane & Motor Corp.; dir. Curtiss Aeroplane & Motor Corp., Curtiss Flying Service. Early began expts. with motor vehicles, establishing motorcycle factory at Hammondsport, 1902. Set speed records for motorcycle, riding his own machines, 1905; at Ormond Beach, Florida, 1907, made record for mile of 46 2/5 seconds with 110 pound motorcycle. Designed aeronatuical motors for dirigibles with Capt. T. S. Baldwin, 1907-09, building for U.S.A., Dirigible No. 1; director of experiments for Aerial Expt. Assn., 1907-09, and supervised construction of and piloted "June Bur," July 4, 1908, for first public flight of mile in U.S., winning Scientific American trophy; experimented with the "Loon," an aeroplane fitted with pontoons, 1908; won Gordon Bennett cup and prix de la Vitesse at Rheims, Frances, Internat. Aviation Meet as rep. Aero Club America, Aug. 1909, with aeroplane and motor of Curtiss design; won N.Y. World prize of $10,000 in flight from Albany to New York in 2 hours, 51 minutes, May 29, 1910; made public demonstration of hydroaeroplane, Jan, 1911, with which had been experimenting for number of years, following demonstration of this invention with that of flying boat (awarded prize by Aero Club America, 1912). Established flying schs. at Hammondsport, San Diego, Buffalo, Newport News, Miami, Atlantic City, 1909-19; introduced flying boat to Brazil, Russia, Austria, Italy and Germany, 1913-14; designed and built for Rodman Wanamaker, the "America," the first multi-motored flying boat, and first heavier-than-air flying craft designed for transatlantic flight, 1914. With J. N. Willys expanded Curtiss factories to meet war demands of Great Britain, Russia, and U.S., 1917. Developed "Wasp" (holder of world's records for speed, climb, and altitude) and other types of aeroplanes, flying boat types, and with U.S. Navy, the Navy-Curtiss flying boats 1, 2, 3 and 4, the latter of which made the first Altantic crossing, May 16-27, 1919. Hon. mem. Nat. Aeronautic Assn., 1924. Author: (with Augustus Post) Curtiss Aviation Book. Home: Hammondsport, N.Y. Died July 23, 1930.

CURTISS, RALPH HAMILTON, astronomer; b. Derby, Conn., Feb. 8, 1880; s. Hamilton Burton and Emily Wheeler (Curtiss) C.; B.S., U. of Calif., 1901, Ph.D., 1905; m. Mary Louis Welton, June 17, 1920. Asst. Astron, Obs., U. of Calif., 1900; mem. Lick Obs. Eclipse Expdn. to Sumatra, 1901; fellow at Lick Obs., 1901-04; Carnegie asst., same, 1904-05; astronomer, Allegheny Obs., 1905-07; asst. prof. astronomy, 19907-11, asso. prof., 1911-18, prof., 1918—, U. of Mich., and asst. dir. Detroit Obs., dir., 1927—. Principal line of investigation, the properties of stars having bright line spectra in Classes B to A of the Draper Classification, Died Dec. 25, 1929.

CURTISS, RICHARD SYDNEY, chemist; b. at Stratford, Conn., Nov. 8, 1864; s. Elbert O. and Emma (Reeve) C.; Ph.B., Sheffield Scientific Sch. (Yale), 1888; studied U. of Munich, 1890; Ph.D., U. of Würzburg, 1892; Sorbonne, Paris, 1892-93; m. Jessie Eleanor Loop, of New York City, June 14, 1899. Chemist, Conn. Agrl. Expt. Sta., 1888-90 and 1893; docent and instr. in organic chemistry, U. of Chicago, 1893-97; prof. chemistry, Hobart Coll., Geneva, N.Y., 1897-1901; prof. of chemistry, Union Coll., Schenectady, N.Y., 1901-04; asst. prof. organic chemistry, U. of Ill., 1904-12; prof. organic chemistry and dir. Lab. of Petroleum Research and Technology, Throop Coll. Technology, Pasadena, Cal., since Sept. 1, 1912. Fellow A.A.A.S.; mem. Am. Chem. Soc. (pres. Southern Cal sect., 1914), Deutsche Chemische Gesellschaft, Ill. Acad. of Science (charter mem.), Am. Health League, Sigma Xi, Alpha Chi Sigma. Address: Pasadena, Cal.

CUSHING, HARVEY, Am. neurologist; b. Apr. 8, 1869; s. Henry Kirke and Betsey M. (William) C.; A.B., Yale, 1891, hon. A.M., 1912, Sc.D., 1919; A.M. and M.D., Harvard, 1895, Sc.D., 1931; M.D., hon., causa, Belfast, 1918, Strasbourg and Brussels, 1930, Budapest and Bern, 1931, Paris, 1933; Sc.D., Washington U., 1915; LL.D., Western Res. U., 1919, Cambridge, 1920. Edinburgh and Glasgow univs., 1927; Litt.D., Darmouth, 1929; m. Katharine Stone Crowell, June 10, 1902; children—Mary Benedict, Betsey, Henry Kirke, Barbara. Engaged in practice surgery, 1895-1933; asso. prof. surgery Johns Hopkins, 1902-12; prof. surgery, Harvard, and surgeon-in-chief, Peter Bent Brigham Hosp., 1912-32; Sterling prof. neurology, Yale, from 1933. Decorated D.S.M. (U.S.); Companion of Bath (Eng.); Officer Légion d'Honneur (France); recipient Cameron prize U. Edinburgh, 1924; Lister medal (London), 1930. Fellow Royal Soc., 1933; hon. fellow Royal Coll. Surgeons (Eng., Ireland and Edinburgh); mem. Nat. Acad. Scis., Am. Neurol. Assn. (pres. 1923), A.C.A. Author: The Pituitary Body and Its Disorders, 1912; Tumors of the Nervus Acusticus, 1917; The Life of Sir William Osler, 1925 (Pulitzer prize); A Classification of the Gliomata (with P. Bailey), 1925; Consecration Medici and other Essays, 1928; Intracranial Tumours, 1932; Pituitary Body and Hypothalamus, 1932. Renowned for brain operations, particularly with local anesthesia; performed 1st successful operation for intracranial hemorrhage in the newborn, 1905; demonstrated (with S. J. Crowe, J. Homans) that excision of pituitary gland results in atrophy of genital organs, 1910; suggested term, third ciruclation, to designate cerebrospinal fluid system, 1926; demonstrated evolution of different histological types of intracranial and intrapinal neoplasms; formulated Cushing's law (increase of intercranial tension causes increase of blood pressure to a point above pressure exerted against medulla). Died Oct. 8, 1939.

CUSHING, HENRY PLATT, geologist; b. Cleveland, Oct. 10, 1860; s. Henry Kirke and Betsey M. (Williams) C.; Ph.B., Cornell U., 1882; post-grad. work, same, 1882-83, 84, 85, M.S., 1884, Ph.D., 1909; Columbia, 1883-84; U. of Munich, 1891-92; m. Florence E. Williams, June 1886. Prof. of geology, Western Reserve U., 1892—; geologist on the N.Y. state Geol. Survey, 1893—. Died Apr. 14, 1921.

CUSHING, HERBERT HOWARD, physician; b. Toungoo, Burma, June 5, 1872; s. Josiah N. and Ellen H. C.; spl. scientific course Brown U., 1891-3; M.D., U. of Munich, 1898; M.D., Jefferson Med. Coll., Phila., 1899; also studied at Heidelberg, Giessen and Glasgow; m. Claudia D. Thompson, of Phila., Apr. 8, 1901. Demonstrator histology and embryology, Jefferson Med. Coll., 1901-2; dir. histol. and embryol. laboratories Woman's Med. Coll. of Pa. since 1899. Author: Cushing's Compend of Histology, 1903. Translator: Boehm, Davidoff and Huber's Histology, 1900. Address: 5710 Market St., Philadelphia

CUSHMAN, ALLERTON SEWARD, chemist; b. (U.S. Consulate) Rome, June 2, 1867; s. Edwin and Emma (Crow) C.; B.S., Worcester Poly. Inst., 1888; Freiberg, and Heidelberg, 1889-90; A.M., Harvard, 1896, John Harvard fellow, Ph.D., 1897; pvt. to capt., 6th Mass. Vol. Inf., 1898; m. Sarah Dunn Hoppin, June 20, 1901 (died 1921); children—Charles Van Brunt, Agnes Hoppin (dec.). Asso. prof. chemistry, Bryn Mawr Coll., 1900-01; asst. dir. Office of Pub. Roads, U.S. Dept. Agr., and chemist in charge of investigations, 1902-10; founder and dir. Inst. of Industrial Research, Washington, 1910-24. Commd. maj. Ordnance R.C., June 4, 1917; stationed at Frankford Arsenal, Pa.; promoted lt. col. Ordnance, U.S.A., Jan. 1918; discharged Dec. 1918. Prin. researches; extraction of potash from feldspathic rocks; use of ground rock as fertilizer; properties of road materials; cause and prevention of the rusting of iron and steel. Franklin medal, 1906. Author: The Corrosion and Preservation of Iron and Steel, 1910; Chemistry and Civilization, 1920, 2d edit., 1925. Died May 1, 1930.

CUSHMAN, JOSEPH AUGUSTINE, biologist; b. Bridgewater, Mass., Jan. 31, 1881; s. Darius and Jane Frances (Fuller) C.; student Bridgewater (Mass.) Normal School 4 yrs.; S.B., Harvard U., 1903; Ph.D. from same, 1909, hon. Sc.D., 1937; m. Alice Edna Wilson, Oct. 7, 1903 (died Jan. 25, 1912); children—Robert Wilson, Alice Eleanor, Ruth Allerton; m. 2d, Frieda G. Billings, Dept. 3, 1913. Museum dir. Boston Soc. Natural History, 1913-23; dir. Cushman Laboratory for Foraminiferal Research since 1923. Lecturer in micropalaeontology Harvard, 1926-40; research asso. in micropaleontology, Harvard, since 1940. Consulting geologist U.S. Geol. Survey; mem. Carnegie Instn. Expdn. to Jamaica, 1912. Chairman com. on micropaleontology National Research Council; since 1930. Fellow Am. Acad. of Arts and Sciences; mem. Geol. Soc. America (v.p. 1938), Washington Acad. Sciences, Paleontol. Soc. (pres. 1937), Am. Geog. Soc., Boston Soc. Natural History (trustee), N.E. Bot. Club, Am. Assn. Petroleum Geologists, A.A.A.S., Soc. Econ. Paleontology and Mineralogy (pres. 1930-31), Calif. Acad. Sciences, Sigma Xi, hon. fellow Royal Microscopical Society of London. Recipient of Hayden Memorial gold medal, 1945. Unitarian. Mason. Author: Monograph of Foraminifera of North Pacific Ocean (Smithsonian Instn.), Parts I-VI, 1910-17; Foraminifera of Atlantic Ocean, Parts I-VIII, 1918-31; also various papers on fossil and living Foraminifera in publs. U.S. Geol. Survey, U.S. Nat. Museum, Carnegie Instn., Washington, and publs. of Cushman Lab. Editor Jour. of Paleontology, 1927-30. Home: Brook Rd., Sharon, Mass. Died Apr. 16, 1949.

CUTBUSH, JAMES, chemist; b. Pa., 1788; s. Edward and Anne (Marriot) C. Authored 15 article series "Application of Chemistry to the Arts and Manufactures," Phila. Aurora, beginning 1808; contbr. article about mercury fulminate to Med. Museum, 1808, article describing method of purifying ether and production of ethylene, 1809, article about value of hop to brewers, 1811; contbr. article "Subjects and Importance of Chemistry" to Freemason's Mag., 1811; founder, 1st pres. Columbian Chemistry Soc., 1811; v.p. Linnaen Soc.; mem. Soc. for Promotion Rational System of Edn.; prof. chemistry, mineralogy and natural philosophy St. John's Coll., Phila.; apptd. asst. apothecary gen. U.S. Army, 1814; chief med. officer U.S. Mil. Acad., 1820, acting prof. chemistry and mineralogy; article on improvement Voltaic electric lamp to Am. Jour. of Science, 1820. Author: A Useful Cabinet, 1808; An Oration on Education, 1812; Philosophy of Experimental Chemistry, 1813; A Synopsis of Chemistry, 1821; A System of Phyrotechny, 1825. Died West Point, N.Y., Dec. 15, 1823; Died West Point, N.Y., Dec. 15, 1823; buried West Point.

CUTLER, CONDICT WALKER, JR., surgeon; b. Morristown, N.J., Aug. 9, 1888; s. Condict Walker and Cora (Carpenter) C.; B.S., Columbia, 1910, M.D., 1912; unmarried. Interne Roosevelt Hosp. 1913-15, asst. surg., 1927-32, asso. surg., 1932-38, attending surgeon, 1948-53, cons. surgeon 1953—. sec. med. bd., 1948-53; resident gynecologist Sloane Hosp. for Women, 1915-16; attending surg. Lincoln Hosp., 1929-31, dir. surgery Goldwater Meml. Hosp., 1939-53; pres. med. bd. 1949-51, cons. surgeon, 1953—; consulting surgeon, 1954—; consulting surgeon and trustee N.Y. Dispensary, 1932-48; Rockland State Hosp., since 1943; instr. surgery, Volumbia, 1920-28, asso. prof. clin. surgery 1947, prof. clin. surgery, 1947-54; chief Emergency Med. Service, Manhattan Nat. Office of Civilian Defense, 1941-43; surg., mem. cons. bd. and chmn. procurement and assignment service, New York, War Manpower Commn., 1940-43; pvt. practice, N.Y.C. since 1916. Served as 1st Lt. M.C., U.S. Army, A.E.F., 1918-19; Lt. Col M.C., U.S. Army, 1943-44, Col., 1945-46; surg. consultant, 1st Service Command. Received Legion of Merit, 1946. Presidential citation, 1943. Congressional Medal for Meritorious Service, 1946, Columbia Medal for Excellence 1944, Alumni medal, 1946. Trustee Columbia , 1940-43, 1949-51, N.Y. Acad. Medicine, 1941—. (chairman committee on medical education, 1945-47, chairman section of surgery, 1935-36); member joint administrator board Columbia-Presbyn. Med. Center, 1949-51. Fellow A.C.S.; mem. Am. Surg. Assn., Internat. Surg. Assn., N.Y. Acad. Medicine, Society Consultants to Armed Forces, American Assn. Surg. of the Hand (president, 1950), A.M.A., Med. Soc. of County of New York (treas., 1947-52), Am Legion (past condr. Columbia U. post), Mil. Order Fgn. Wars, Asso. Alumni Columbia College (pres. 1938-40); asso. Alumni Coll. Physicians and Surgeons (pres. 1950). Republican. Methodist. Club: University of New York City. Author: The Hand: Its Diseases and Disabilities 1941. Co-author: Histroy of Roosevelt Hospital, 1956. Contbr. numerous monographs and articles to med. publs. Home: 225 Central Park West, N.Y.C. 24, Office: 630 Park Av., N.Y.C. 21. Died July 6, 1958.

CUTLER, ELLIOTT CARR, prof. surgery; b. Bangor, Me., July 30, 1888; s. George Chalmers and Mary Franklin (Wilson) C.; A.B., Harvard, 1909, M.D., 1913; hon. doctorate U. of Strasbourg, 1938; D.Sc., U. of Vermont, 1941, University of Rochester, 1946; m. Caroline Parker, May 24, 1919; children—Elliott Carr, Thomas Pollard, David, Marjorie Parker (dec.), Tarrant. Surgical house officer, Peter Bent Brigham Hosp., 1913-15; resident surgeon, Harvard Unit, Am. Ambulance Hosp., Paris, 1915; resident surgeon, Mass. Gen. Hosp., 1915-16; alumni asst. in surgery, Harvard, 1915-16; voluntary asst., Rockefeller Inst., N.Y. City, 1916-17; resident surgeon, Peter Bent Brigham Hospital, 1919-21, associate in surgery, 1921-24; instructor in surgery, Harvard, 1921-24; professor of surgery, Western Reserve Univ., School of Medicine, 1924-32; dir. of Surgical Service, Lakeside Hosp., Cleveland, 1924-32; consulting surgeon, New England Peabody Home for Crippled Children, since 1932, Children's Hosp., Boston, since 1945; Moseley Prof. of surgery, Harvard, since 1932; chief consultant to professional services division, Vet. Adminstrn., 1945; civilian consultant to Sec. of War since May, 1946; acting asst. med. dir. Vets. Adminstrn., since 1947. Trustee, Dexter Sch., 1938-43 (chmn. med. com., 1938-43), Nobel and Greenough School, Boston Sch. Occupational Therapy, Mass. State Infirmary; mem. exec. com., Hugh Cabot Memorial Fund; mem. Mass. Med. Benevolent Soc., trustee, 1934-37; sponsor Walter Cannon Memorial Fund, 1946. Served as lt. Med. Reserve Corps, 1916-17; capt., M.O.R.C., 1917-18, major, 1918-24, lt. col., 1924-42, col., 1942-45, brig. gen., A.U.S., 1945, retired April, 1946; chief surgical consultant, E.T.O., U.S. Army, 1942-45; chief, professional services div., E.T.O., U.S. Army, 1945. Awarded Distinguished Service Medal with Battle Clasps for Champagne-Marne, Aise-Marne, St. Mihiel, (Meuse-Argonne Defensive Sector), Victory Medal World War I; Campaign Medal, E.T.O., World War II, Legion of Merit, Croix de Guerre with Palm, Order of British Empire; Oak Leaf Clusters & D.S.M., World War II. Fellow, Am. Coll. Surgeons, Boston Med. Library, Internat. Society of Surgery (chmn. Am. Com., 1929-47, del., chmn., U.S. Exec. Com., 1932). Mem. A.A.A.S., Am. Assn. Advancement of Sci., Am. Geog. Soc., Mass. Foundation, Am. Acad. Surgery, Am. Assn. for Thoracic Surgery, Am. Bd. of Surgery, Founders Group, 1937, Am. Bur. for Med. Aid to China, Inc., Am. Soc. for Clinical Investigation (emeritus, 1932), Am. Heart Assn., Inc., A.M.A., Am. Soc. for Exptl. Pathology, Am. Surgical Assn. (pres. 1947), Am. Soviet Medical Soc. (regional v.p. 1945-47; American Committee for the Protection of Medical Research, chmn., 1926-42), Assn. Mil. Surgeons of the U.S., Boston Surgical Soc.; Boylston Med. Soc. of Harvard U., L'Europe Medicale (hon. scientific mem., patronage com.), Friends of Med. Progress; Federation of Am. Socs. for Exptl. Biology (chmn. of com. for defense of Biological Reserach), Gerontological Soc., Inc., Harvard Med. Alumni Assn., Mass. Med. Soc.; Med. Exchange Club; New England Heart Assn., New England Surgical Soc.; Norfolk Med. Soc.; Omaha Med. Soc., Soc. for Exptl. Biology and Medicine, Soc. of Clinical Surgery, (senior mem. 1943, pres., 1941-46); Soc. of Univ. Surgeons, (hon. mem. 1938); Suffolk Dist. Med. Soc., Soc. U.S. Med. Consultants of World War II (pres. 1946). Mem. Town of Brookline Unemployment Com., U.N. (official, Mass. Com.), Mass. Foundation, exec. com., Mass. com. on Public Safety, (dir. Med. Div.), Mass. Com. for Public Safety, (dir. Med. div.).,Mass. Com. for retaring wild life, Parker River Wild Life Refuge, Mem. Alpha Omega Alpha, Sigma Xi, American Legion Inc. (Also corresponding member of many foreign medical societies). Unitarian. Clubs: Harvard, Somerset, Thursday Evening, Friday Evening, (all Boston), Aesculapian, Asso. Harvard Clubs (pres. 1936), Porcellian, Hasty Pudding (all affiliated Harvard U.), Harvard (New York), Mayfield Country (Cleveland), Country (Brookline), N. American Yacht Racing Union, Vineyard Haven Yacht Club (Commodore, 1938-42; 1946), Bonaventure Assos., Rotary (distinguished service award, 1946); Henry Jacob Bigelow medal from Boston Surg. Soc., 1947. Editor: America Clinica (adv. bd.), American Heart Journal, (adv. bd.), Macmillan Co. Surgical Monograph Series, (editor), Journal of Clinical Investigation (editorial com.), Surgery (adv. council), Am. Jour. of Surgery, (asso. editor), Brit. Jour. Surgery, (editorial bd. and exec. com.), Washington Inst. of Medicine, (editorial and consulting bd. in surgery). Author: Atlas of Surgical Operations (with R. Zollinger), 1939. Home: 61 Heath St., Brookline, Mass. Office: Peter Bent Brigham Hospital, 721 Huntington Av., Boston 15, Mass. Died Aug. 16, 1947.

CUTLER, GARNET HOMER, agronomist; b. Arkona, Can., June 12, 1882; s. Albert Elgin and Annie Sarah (Belton) C.; student Ont. Agrl. Coll., 1905-09; B.S.A., Toronto U., 1909; M.S., U. Wis., 1926, Ph.D., 1928; m. Gertrude Margaret Campbell, June 6, 1911; children—Mabelle Gertrude (Mrs. John Chatfield O'Toole), Garnet Campbell, Robert Thompson. Came to U.S., 1924, naturalized, 1934. Lectr., MacDonald Coll., McGill U., 1909-13; prof. field husbandry Saskatchewan U., Saskatoon, 1913-17; head dept. field husbandry and prof. field husbandry Alta. U., Edmonton, 1917-25; asst. chief dept. of agronomy and prof. agronomy, since 1926. Fellow Royal Metereol. Soc.; co-founder Internat. Corp Improvement Assn., mem. Am. Breeders Assn., Am. Genetic Assn., A.A.A.S., Am. Assn. U. Profs., Am. Soc. Agronomy, Inda. Acad. Sci., Canadian Soc. Tech. Agriculturists Ceres, Sigma Xi. Methodist. contbr. articles to tech. and sci. jours.; attended 4th Internat. Grassland Congress, Aberystwyth, Wales, 1937; visited agrl. expts. in Eng., Scotland, Norway, Sweden, Denmark, Germany, France; developed Doughball Test of gluten quality, granulation test for flour fineness. Home: 901 N. Chauncey, West Lafayette, Ind. Died Sept. 4, 1962; buried Bethel Cemetery, Watford, Ont., Can.

CUTLER, IRA EUGENE, college prof.; b. Putnam, Conn., Oct. 8, 1863; s. Frederick and Georgia Ann Frances (Stead) C.; B.S., Albion (Mich.) Coll., 1893, LL.D., 1919; A.M., U. of Denver, 1906; studied at U. of Chicago; m. Amelia Perkins, Aug. 1, 1894; children—Alice Zilpha, Marian Frances, Owen Perkins, Marjorie Mitchell, Laura Ann. Teacher of science, Menominee, Mich., 1895-97; supt. schs. Crystal Falls, Mich., 1897-98; with U. of Denver, 1898—, becoming prof. zoölogy, U.S. Govt. expert work upon Indian corn, 1916-20, developing many promising hybrids; has the largest pharm. and botanic garden in the Middle West; extensive geol. researches in the Florissant Dist., Colo. Commd. staff capt. R.O.T.C., U. of Denver, 1918; chmn. Colo. State Com. on Sch. Gardening. Conglist. Died May 25, 1936.

CUTLER, JAMES GOULD, inventor, mayor; b. Albany, N.Y., Apr. 24, 1848; s. John Nathan and Mary E. (Gould) C.; m. Anna K. Abbey, Sept. 27, 1871. Draftsman, Rochester, N.Y., 1872; invented mail chutes for office bldgs. known as letter box connection, patented 1883; formed (with brother) Cutler Mfg. Co. to build and install letter chute, 1884; mem. White Charter Commn. of N.Y. State, 1895; cons. architect N.Y. State Capitol, 1897; commr. pub. safety Rochester, mayor, 1903-07. Died Apr. 21, 1927.

CUTRIGHT, HAROLD GLEN, consulting management engineer; born in the town of Ivanhoe, West Va., July 14, 1900; son Averill Curtright and Idella Dove (Neely) Cutright; A.B., W.Va., Wesleyan Coll., 1922, student Harvard Business Sch., 1923-24; M.B.A., New York U., 1930; m. Gayle Evans, Dec. 20, 1924; 1 son, Langdon Cooper. Asst. prof., accounting, Virginia Poly. Institute, 1924-26; senior accountant, Elkins & Durham, C.P.A.'s, 1926-29; v.p. John Van Range Co., Cincinnati, O., 1929-31; financial exec. Nat. Dairy Products Corp., N.Y. City, 1932-39; comptroller and asst. treas. Minn.-Honeywell Regulator Co., Minneapolis, 1939-42; v.p. in charge of finance, Standard Brands, Inc., also dir., mem. exec. com., officer and dir. of subsidiaries, 1942-44; pres. R. Hoe Co., N.Y., 1944-46; v.p. The Pittston Co., Hoboken, N.J., dir. The Cliffs Corp., Cleveland, O., pres. and dir. North Kansas Development Corp., North Kansas City Bridge and Railroad Corp., Guinotte Land Co., Parkside Land Co. and North Kansas City Power and Light Co., Kansas City, Mo. vice pres. Clinchfield Coal Corp., Dante, Va.; Davis Coal and Coke Co., Baltimore, Md., 1946-48; dir. Nat. Tea Co., Chicago; Ralston Steel Car Co., Gen. Electric Co., N.Y.C., dir. sales Am. Machine & Foundry Co.; gen. sales mgr. Omark Industries, Inc., Portland, Ore., 1957, v.p. marketing; now cons. mgmt. engr., N.Y.C.; owner Glengayl Farms, Ivanhoe, W.Va., pedigreed Hereford vis. prof. mgmt. So. Ill. U., Alton Center and Edwardsville; dean finance So. Ill. U., 1966. Mem. Am. Acad. Polit. Sci. Democrat. Methodist. Clubs: Harvard, Harvard Business (N.Y. C.), Home: Glengayle Farms, Ivanhoe, W.Va. Office: Glengayle Assos., 509 Fifth Av., N.Y.C. Died Mar. 21, 1967; buried Hampton Cemetery, Ivanhoe, W.Va.

CUTTER, EPHRAIM, physician, food expert; b. Woburn, Mass., Sept. 1, 1832; s. Benjamin and Mary (Whittemore) C.; B.A., Yale, 1852, M.A., 1855; M.D., Harvard, 1856; M.D., U. of Pa., 1857 (LL.D., Ia. Coll., 1887); spl. lab. work in Sheffield Scientific Sch. and at Harvard under Oliver Wendell Holmes and J.P. Cooke; m. Rebecca Smith Sullivan, 1856 (died 1899); m. 2d, Mrs. Anna L. Davidson, 1901. Practiced at Woburn, Boston and New York, 1875—. Inventor of many surg. and gynecol. instruments, and procedures in relation to same; successfully with George B. Harrimon, D.D.S., of Boston, in 1876 used in microphotography of blood and sputum the higer and highest power lenses extant then and now. Mem. 9th and 10th Internat. Med. Congresses. Mem. Com. of One Hundred, Mass. Soldiers' Fund, 1961; was spl. military agt. during Civil War. Author: Versions and Flexions and Food in Motherhood; Fatty Ills and Their Masquerades (with John A. Cutter); Food—Its Relation to Health and Disease (with same), 1907. A pioneer of Am. laryngology; has studied the morphology of raw beef, 1854—; proved that the galvanic currents penetrate the human body, 1871; discovered tuberculosis cattle test, 1894; etc. Died Apr. 24, 1917.

CUTTING, CHARLES SUYDAM, naturalist; b. New York, N.Y., Jan. 17, 1889; s. Robert Fulton and Helen (Suydam) C.; prep. edn. Groton Sch., 1903-09; A.B., Harvard, 1912; m. Helen McMahon, 1932 (dec. 1961); m. 2d, Mary Pyne Filley, Apr. 8, 1964. Trustee Robert F. Cutting Estate from 1913; field work on expdns. to Central Asia for Am. Museum Natural History, Field Museum of Natural History, Chicago, Pitt River Museum of Oxford, Eng. Trustee Am. Museum Natural History, New York Zool. Soc. Hon. fellow Field Museum of Natural History, Chicago. Served as 1st lt., U.S. Army during World War; with A.E.F. in France 15 months. Performed active duty abroad as lt. col., U.S. Army. Decorated Croix Noire (French), Croix de Guerre with Gold Star, Honorary Comdr. Most Excellent Order of British Empire. Member of Bombay Natural History Society, Royal Geog. Soc., Royal Central Asia Soc. (all Brit.); Himmalyan Club. Republican. Episcopalian. Clubs: Knickerbocker, Brook, Racquet (New York). Author: The Fire Ox and Other Years, 1940; also series of articles pub. by Am. Museum Natural History. Home: Bernardsville NJ Died Aug. 24, 1972.

CUTTING, HIRAM ADOLPHUS, scientist, physician; b. Concord, Vt., Dec. 23, 1832; s. Stephen Church and Eliza Reed (Darling) C.; A.M. (hon.), Norwich (Vt.) U., 1868, Ph.D. (hon.), 1870: M.D. (hon.), Dartmouth, 1870; m. Maranda E. Haskell, Feb. 3, 1856, no children. An extremely precocious child, headed a sch. in Guildhall, Vt., by age 16; mainly self-educated, attended formal sch. for only breif periods; surveyor for a time; partner (with and uncle) in dry goods store, Lunenburg, Vt., 1854-79, sole owner, 1879-92; examining surgeon U.S. War Dept., 1861-65; prof. gen. science Norwich U., various times before and after Civil War; lectr. in med. coll. Dartmouth, 1870; became state geologist Vt., 1870; also practiced medicine during this period, later (1885-92) specialized solely in practice of medicine; became mem. Vt. Bd. of Agr., 1880; chmn. Vt. Fish Commn., for a time; Vt. del. to Internat. Forestry Congress, 1885; credited with devising improved camera lens; did research on capability of various building stones; also interested in agrl. improvements; contbd. many articles to mags. and newspapers. Author works including: Mining in Vermont, 1872; Microscopic Revelations, 1878; Scientific Lectures, 1884. Died Lunenburg, Apr. 18, 1892.

CUTTING, JAMES AMBROSE, inventor; b. Hanover, N.H., 1814; s. Abijah Cutting. Invented a bee hive, patented 1844; patented photographic process "ambrotype," 1850, photolithographic process, 1858; committed to an asylum, Worcester, Mass., 1862. Died Worcester, Aug. 6, 1867.

DABOLL, NATHAN, mathematician, educator; b. Groton, Conn., Apr. 24, 1750; s. Nathan and Anna (Lynn) D.; m. Elizabeth Daboll; m. 2d, "Widow Elizabeth Brown," Discovered errors in almanac prepared by Clark Elliott and published by Timothy Green), 1773, 74, 75; prof. mathematics and astronomy Plainfield (Conn.) Acad., 1783-88; taught navigation aboard frigate President, 1811. Author: Daboll's Complete Schoolmaster's Assistant, 1799; Daboll's Practical Navigation, published posthumously, 1820. Died Mar. 9, 1818.

DADANT, CAMILLE PIERRE, apiarist; b. Langres, France, Apr. 6, 1851; s. Charles and Gabrielle (Parisot) D.; came to America, 1863; ed. in France and pub. shcs., Hamilton, Ill.; m. Mary Marinelli, Nov. 1, 1875; children—Louisa G. (Mrs. L. G. Saugier), Valentine, Louis C., Henry C., Maurice G., Clemence S., Harriette G. (Mrs. F. A. Bush). Associated with his father, as Dadant & Son, in bee culture, and publisher of books, The Hive and Honey Bee, 1874-1902; with 3 sons and 2 daughters as Dadant & Sons, 1902—; began mfr. of bee comb foundations, 1879; editor Am. Bee Journal 1912—. Mem. Nat. Bee Keepers' Assn. (ex-sec., v.p., pres., later treas.). Editor and reviser of various edits. of The Hive and Honey Bee (by L. L. Langstroth), 1888—. Decorated Order of the Crown for services rendered Belgian bee-keepers during World War. Author: First Lessons in Bee-Keeping, 1915; Bee Primer; The Dadant System of Bee-Keeping. Home: Hamilton, Ill. Died Feb. 25, 1938.

DAFT, LEO, elec. engr.; b. Birmingham, Eng., Nov. 13, 1843; s. Thomas B. and Emma Matilda (Sturges) D.; m. Katherine Anna Flansburgh, Mar. 11, 1871, at least 4 children. Came to U.S., 1866; owner, operator photographic studio, Troy, N.Y., 1871-79; with N.Y. Electric Light Co. (later Daft Electric Co.); experimented with electric railroad, built electric locomotive for Saratoga & Mt. McGregro R.R., 1883; installed Balt. Union Passenger Ry. (1st comml. electric railroad in U.S.), 1885; mem. Am. Inst. E.E., A.A.A.S., Electro-Chem. Soc. Died Mar. 28, 1922.

DAGGETT, ELLSWORTH, mining engr.; b. Canandaigua, N.Y., May 24, 1845; s. Rev. Oliver Ellsworth and Elizabeth (Watson) D.; Ph.B., Sheffield Scientific Sch. (Yale), 1864; post-grad. courses in chemistry there, 1864-65; 1 yr. upon mineralogy and blow-piping elsewhere, 1865-66; 1 yr. at Bergakademie, Berlin, 1874-75; m. June Spencer, June 24, 1874. In practice as mining engr., 1866—; connected with Geol. Survey of 40th parallel, 1970; U.S. surveyor-gen., Utah, 1888-92; U.S. del. to Am. Mining Congress, Portland, Ore., Aug. 20, 1904. Home: Salt Lake City, Utah. Died 1923.

DAGGETT, PARKER HAYWARD, educator; b. Boston, Apr. 5, 1885; s. Gilbert Alden and Elizabeth Jane (Hayward) D.; student Phillips Exeter Acad.; S.B., Harvard, 1910 as of 1907; m. Esther Jarvis, Jan. 17, 1910; children—Parker Hayward, Mary Elizabeth, Emma Jarvis, William Bosworth, Jane Alden, Jonathon Hayward (dec.), Thomas Randolph. Asst. in elec. engring. Harvard, 1908-09; engr. toll traffic dept. Am. Tel. & Tel. Co., 1909-10; asso. prof. elec. engring., 1910-13, prof. and head dept. 1913-29, U. N.C., also acting dean Sch. Applied Sci., 1915-16; dean Coll. Engring., Rutgers U., New Brunswick, N.J., since July 1, 1929. Acting dist. ednl. dir. 4th Dist., S.A.T.C., Oct. 1918-Jan. 1919; mem. N.C. State Bd. Registration Engrs., 1921-29, sec. 1925-29; sec. Council of State Bds. of Engring. Examiners, 1922-23, pres., 1925-26; mem. Engrs., Council for Profl. Devel., 1933; chmn. regional com. in charge of accrediting of engring. schs. in Ohio., Ill., Ia., Minn., Wis., Mich., 1933-39. Mem. Soc. for Promotion Engring. Edn. (council 1921-24, v.p. 1935-36), N.C. Soc. Engrs. (pres. 1929), Phi Beta Kappa, Tau Beta Pi, Sigma Xi, Kappa Gamma Chi; asso. Am. Inst. E.E. Home: New Brunswick, N.J. Died June 6, 1964; buried Chapel Hill, N.C.

DAGGETT, ROGERT FROST, architect; b. Indianapolis, Ind., Mar. 13, 1875; s. Robert Platt and Caroline (Rraot) D.; B.S., U. of Pa., 1896; grad. Ecole des Beaux Arts, Paris, 1901; m. Lizette Lothian, Oct. 30, 1901; children—James Lothian, Robert Frost. Began practice at Indpls., 1901; architect fo Indpls. Athletic Club, James Whitcomb Riley Hosp. for Children, LaRue D. Carter Meml. Hosp., Community Hosp. Indpls. bldg. of Ind. U. Med. Center, Eli Lilly & Co., Indpls. Chamber of Commerce Building, Buildings for Indiana, DePauw, Purdue, and Butler Universities, churches and public schools Served as capt. U.S. Engrs., World War 1; col. Coast Arty. Res. Fellow A.I. A.; mem. Alpha Tau Omega. Republican. Mason. Home: 4904 Washington Blvd. Office: 567 W. Westfield Blvd., Indpls. Died. Sept. 6, 1955.

DAHLGREN, JOHN ADOLPHUS BERNARD, naval officer; b. Phila., Nov. 13, 1809; s. Bernard Ulric and Martha (Rowan) D.; m. Mary C. Bunker, Jan. 8, 1839; m. 2d, Sarah Madeleine Vinton Goddard, Aug. 2, 1865; 10 children, including Capt. Charles Bunker, Lt. Paul, John Vinton, Ulric, Eric. Apptd. acting midshipman U.S. Navy, 1826, passed midshipman, 1832, lt., 1837; assigned to make observations of solar eclipse, 1836; on leave to undergo treament for oncoming blindness, 1837-43; patented percussion lock, 1847; chief Buf. of Ordnance, Washington, D.C., 1847-63, 68-69, established ordnance system used by U.S. Navy during Civil War; formulated and equipped Navy Ordnance Yard, Washington; inventor 11 inch Dahlgren gun; introduced boat howitzers to navy, 1850; commd. comdr., 1855, capt., 1862, rear adm., 1863; commanded S. Atlantic blockading squadron, 1868; prof. gunnery U.S. Naval Acad.; mem. A.A.A.S.; comdr. Washington Navy Yard, 1869-70. Author: 32 Pounder practice for Ranges, 1850; The System of Boat Armament in the United States Navy, 1852, Naval Percussion Locks and Primers, 1853; Shells and Shell Guns, 1856. Died Washington Navy Yard, July 12, 1870.

DAHLGREN, ULRIC, biologist; b. Brooklyn, N.Y., Dec. 17, 1870; s. Charles Bunder and Augusta (Smith) D.; student State Model Sch., Trenton, N.J., 1883-85; grad. Mt. Pleasant Mil. Acad., Ossining, N.Y., 1890; A.B., Princeton, 1894, M.S., 1896; m. Emilie Elizabeth Kuprion, Sept. 3, 1896. Instr., 1896, prof. biology, 1911-39, prof. emeritus since 1939, Princeton U. Asst. dir. Marine Biol. Lab., Woods Hole Mass., 1899; trustee Harpswell (Me.) Biol. Lab., 1912-16; dir. Mount Desert Island Biol. Lab., Bar Harbor, 1921, pres. of Corp. since 1937. Pres. Princeton (N.J.) Bd. of Health. Fellow A.A.A.S., Phila. Acad. Sciences; mem. Am. Soc. Zoologists, Am. Soc. Naturalists, Am. Philos. Soc., N.J. Soc. of the Cincinnati, N.J. Soc. S.R., Loyal Legion, Sons Colonial Wars. Clubs: Princeton (Phila.), Nassau (Primate Preisdent), 1942-45. Author: Principles of Animal Histology (with W.A. Kepner), 1908. Wrote series on Production of Light by Organisms (Jour. of Franklin Inst.), 1915; also zool. memoirs in German and Am. jours., mostly on production of light and electricity by animals. Home: 7 Evelyn Pl., Princeton, N.J. Died May 30, 1946.

DAINS, FRANK BURNETT, chemist; b. Gouverneur, N.Y., Jan. 15, 1869; s. Rev. George G. and Celestia Stone (Burnett) D.; Ph.B., Wesleyan U., Conn., 1890, M.S., 1891, D.Sc., Wesleyan U., 1940; Ph.D., U. of Chicago, 1898; Freiburg and Berlin, 1901-02; m. Alice, d. Rev. W.H. Haight, Sept. 24, 1898. Asst. in chemistry, Wesleyan U., 1891-93; asst. prof., U. of Kan., 1893-94; fellow U. of Chicago, 1894-95; asst. prof. chemistry, Northwestern U., Schs. of Medicine and Pharmacy, 1895-1901; prof. chemistry, Washburn Coll., 1902-11; prof. chemistry, U. of Kan., since 1911, emeritus professor since Feb. 1942, acting dean Graduate School, 1926-27. Original investigator in chemistry and contributor of numerous papers on chem. subjects in Am. and fgn. jours. Mem. Sigma Xi, Phi Beta Kappa, Kan. Acad. Science, Am. Chem. Soc., History of Science Soc., Psi Upsilon; fellow A.A.A.S. Club: University (Lawrence). Home: 1224 Louisiana St., Lawrence, Kan. Died Jan. 5, 1948.

DAKIN, HENRY DRYSDALE ret. research chemist; b. London. Eng., Mar. 12, 1880; s. Thomas Burns and Sophia (Stevens) D.; B.Sc., Victoria U., Manchester, Eng., 1901; D.Sc., U. Leeds, 1907, LL.D., 1936; Ph.D., (hon.). U. Heidelberg; Sc.D., Yale; m. Susan Dows Herter, July 1916 (died 1951). Demonstrator in chemistry U. Leeds, 1901-02; research worker Lister Inst. Preventive Medicine, successively at London and Heidleberg, 1901-05, and Herter Lab., N.Y.C., 1905-20; sci. adviser to Merck Inst. Therapeutic Research; dir. Merck & Co. Fellow Royal Soc. Eng.; mem. Soc. Exptl. Biology, Inst. Chemistry of Great Britain and Ireland, London Chem. Soc., others. Decorated Chevalier Legion of Honor; recipient Philip A. Conne medal by Chemists' Club, Davy medal by the Royal Soc. (Eng.). Author: Oxidation and Reductions in the Animal Body, 1912; Handbook of Chemical Antiseptics (with E. K. Dunham), 1917. Editor Jour. Biol. Chemistry, 1911-13. Home: Scarborough-on-Hudson, N.Y. Died Feb. 10, 1952.

DALE, SIR HENRY HALLETT, scientist; b. London, Eng., 1875; s. C. J. Dale; scholar, Leys Sch., Coutts-Trotter Student Trinity Coll., Cambridge; St. Bartholomew's Hosp.; George Henry Lewes student, Sharpey Scholar, U. Coll., M.A., M.D., D.Sc., LL.D.; m. 1904; one son (deceased), two daughters. Director of Wellcome Physiological Research Lab., 1904-14; mem. Gen. Med. Council, 1927-37; dir. Nat. Inst. for Med. Research, Hampstead, 1928-42; Crown nominee to Ct. of London U., 1939-50; Fullerian prof. Royal Instn., 1942-46; Croonian lectr. Royal Soc., 1919, Herter Lectures, Balt., 1919, Harvey lectures, N.Y.C., 1919, 37, Croonian lectr. Royal Coll. Physicians, 1929; Dohme lectures, Balt., 1933, Welch lectures, N.Y.C., 1937, Pilgrim Trust lecture, Philadelphia, 1946; chairman Wellcome Trust, 1938-60. Mem. sci. adv. commn. to War Cabinet, 1940-47, chairman, 1942-47 Knighted, 1932. Decorated Medal of Freedom with Silver Palm (U.S.A.); Orden Pour le merite (Fed. Republic Germany); Order of Merit, Grand Cross Order Brit. Empire; recipient Nobel prize (with O. Loewi), 1936. Fellow of the Royal Society (president 1940-45); fellow Royal College of Physicians; fgn. asso. Nat. Acad. Sci. U.S.A. Clubs: Athenaeum. Author articles profl. jours. Home: Cambridge England Died Aug. 1968.

DALE, THOMAS NELSON, cons. geologist; b. New York, N.Y., Nov. 25, 1845; s. Thomas Nelson and Sarah Patten (Monson) D.; gen. edn. Europe and Williston Sem., Mass.; geol. training under Zittel and Pumpelly; m. Margaret Brown, Dec. 22, 1874; children—Sarah, Norman Brown, Nelson Clark, Oswald, Margaret, Arthur. Connected with U.S. Geol. Survey, 1885-1920, geologist, 1892-1920. Instr. geology and botany, Williams Coll., 1893-1901. Author: The Marbles of Western Vermont, 1912; Slate in the United States, 1914; The Commerical Granites of New England, 1923; etc. Home: Pittsfield, Mass. Died Nov. 16, 1937.

DALL, WILLIAM HEALEY, naturalist; b. Boston, Aug. 21, 1845; s. Rev. Charles Henry Appleton and Caroline (Healey) D.; ed. pub. shcs.; pupil in natural sciences under Louis Agassiz; spl. courses anatomy and medicine; hon. A.M., Wesleyan, 1888; D.Sc. U. of Pa., 1904; LL.D., George Washington U., 1915; m. Annette Whitney, Mar. 3, 1880; children—Charles Whitney, Marcus Hele, Marion, William Austin (dec.). Lt. in Internat. Telegraph Expdn. to Aalska, 1865-68; in U.S. Coast Survey, Alaska, 1871-84; paleontologist, U.S. Geol. Survey, 1884-1925; also from 1880, hon. curator U.S. Nat. Mus.; also prof. invertebrate paleontology, Wagner Inst. of Science, Phila., Feb. 1893—. Mem. Nat. Acad. of Sciences; fellow Am. Acad. of Arts and Sciences. Author: Tribes of the Extreme Northwest; Scientific Results of the Exploration of Alaska; Reports on the Mollusca of the Blake Expedition; Alaska and Its Resources; Coast Pilot of Alaska; Biography of Spencer Fulleton Baird. Died Mar. 27, 1927.

DALLA VALLE, JOSEPH MARIA, educator; b. N.Y.C., Mar. 7, 1906; s. Henry J. and Maria C. (Campiotti) Dalla V.; B.S., Harvard, 1927, M.S., 1928, ScD., 1930. Cons. engr., Cleve., 1930-32; field and research engr. USPHS, Washington, 1933-41; cons. engr., N.Y.C., 1941-48; faculty Ga. Inst. Tech., 1948—. asso. prof., 1948-49, prof. chem. engring., 1950-54; regents prof., 1954—. Fulbright lecturer Med. Sch., U. Milan. 1953-54. Mem. bd. dir. Oak Ridge Inst. Nuclear Studies, 1955. Author: Micromeritics, 1943; The Industrial Environment, 1948; Fine particle Measurements (with Clyde Orr, Jr.), Contbr. articles Profl. Publs. Office: Georgia Institute of Technology, Atlanta. Died June 1, 1958; buried Dalton, Ga.

DALSTROM, OSCAR FREDERICK, engineer; b. Wyanet, Ill., Aug. 15, 1871; s. Anders John and Anna Christina (Jacobson) D.; grad. Fremont (Neb.) Normal Sch., 1895; student civ. engring. course, U. of Neb., 1897-98; C.E., Rensselaer Poly. Inst., 1901; unmarried. Teacher dist. and village schs., 1894-97; draftsman and shop inspector, bridge dept., Pa. Steel Co., 1901-03 and 1904-06; draftsman Scherzer Rolling Lift Bridge Co., 1903-04; draftsman Riverside Bridge Co., Martin's Ferry, O., Apr.-Dec. 1904; with C. & N.W. Ry. Co. since 1906, draftsman bridge dept. until 1909, chief draftsman same dept., 1909-17, engr. of bridges since 1917. Mem. Am. Soc. C.E., Am. Ry. Engring. Assn., A.A.A.S., Western Soc. Engrs. Republican. Club: Engineers. Home: 4109 N. Paulina St. Office: 400 W. Madison St., Chicago IL

DALTON, JOHN CALL, physiologist, coll. pres. b. Chelmsford, Mass., Feb. 2, 1825; s. Dr. John Call and Julia (Spalding) D.; grad. Harvard, 1844; M.D., Harvard, 1847; studied physiology under Claude Bernard, Paris, France; never married. Never practiced medicine; became 1st U.S. physician to devote life to exptl. physiology and related scis.; recipient annual prize from A.M.A. for essay on Corpus Luteum, 1851; prof. physiology U. Buffalo (N.Y.), 1851-54, U. Vt., 1854-56; prof. physiology Coll. Physicians and Surgeons, N.Y.C., 1855-83, pres., 1884-89; with L.I. Coll. Hosp., 1859-61; served as surgeon with rank of brig. gen. med. corps. 7th N.Y. Regt., in Civil War, 1861-64; became mem. Nat. Acad. Sciis., 1864. Author: Treastise on Human Physiology, 1859; A Treatise on Physiology and Hygiene, 1868; Doctrines of the Circulation, 1884; other med. works. Died N.Y.C., Feb. 12, 1889.

DALTON, WILLIAM, mech. engr.; b. Albany, N.Y., Sept. 12, 1869; s. Philip W. and Harriet A. D.; M.E., Cornell, 1890; m. Ida M. Hill, of Nashville, Sept. 3, 1895; m. 2d, Sylvia Loines, of Schenectady, N.Y., 1929. Began in machine shop, Buffalo, N.Y., 1890; chief engr. Am. Locomotive Co., 1902-16; gen. mgr. Washington (D.C.) Steel & Ordnance Co., 1916-18; with Gen. Electric Co., Schenectady, N.Y., since 1918. Mem. Am. Soc. Mech. Engrs. Home: R.D. No. 2, Schenectady NY

DALY, REGINALD ALDWORTH, educator; b. Napanee, Ont., May 19, 1871; s. Edward and Jane Maria (Jeffers) D.; A.B., Victoria U., Toronto, 1891; A.M., Harvard, 1893, Ph.D., 1896, Sc.D., (hon.), 1942; studied Heidleberg 1897-98. Paris, France, 1898; Sc.D. (hon.), U. Toronto, 1923, U. Chgo., 1941; m. Louise P. Haskell, June 3, 1903; 1 son, Reginald Aldworth (dec.). Geologist for Can., internat. boundary surveys, 1901-07; prof. phys. geology Mass. Inst. Tech., 1907-12; Sturgis-Hooper Prof. geology Harvard, 1912-42, emeritus Sturgis-Hopper prof. geology, 1942—. Fellow Am.Acad. Arts and Scis., Geol. Soc. Am. (pres. 1932), Royal Soc., Edinburgh (hon.), mem. Am. Philos. Soc., Phila., Acad. Natural Sci. Nat. Acad. Scis., Seismol. Soc. Am., Am. Geophys. Union, Geol. Soc. South Africa; hon. mem. Norwegian Acad., Russian Acad., Swedish Acad., Mineral Soc. of Leningrad, Glasgow, Edinburgh. Stockholm, Belgium geol. socs.; fgn. mem. Geol. Soc. London; fgn. corr. Acad., Sci. France. Author: Geology of the North American Cordillera at the 49th Parallel of Latitude (3 vols.); Ingeous Rocks and Their Origin, 1914; Our Mobile Earth, 1926; Igneous Rocks and the Depths of the Earth, 1933; The Changing World of the Ice Age, 1934; Architecture of the Earth, 1938; Strength and Structure of the Earth 1940; The Floor of the Ocean, 1942. Asso. editor Am. Jour. Science. Home: 23 Hawthorn St., Cambridge 38, Mass. Died Sept. 19, 1957; buried Elmwood Cemetery, Columbia, S.C.

DALY, WILLIAM BARRY, mining engr.; b. Smartsville, Yuba County, Calif., Jan. 4, 1873; s. Lawrence and Ann (Barry) D.; grad. high sch., Smartsville, 1889; m. Mary E. Nevin, June 28, 1905; 1 son, Eugene William. Teacher, pub. grade schs., Brady, Calif., 1890-91; admitted to Calif. bar, 1894, and practiced at San Francisco untill 1899; successively foreman, supt., efficiency engr., gen. supt. mines, asst. gen. mgr. mines, Anaconda Copper Mining Co., until 1924, gen. mgr. mines, 1924-40; cons. mining engr. since Jan. 1, 1940. Mem. Am. Inst. Mining and Metall. Engrs. Am. Mining Congress. Democrat. Mem. Knights of Columbus. Clubs: Silver Bow. Country. Home: 808 W. Galena St. Office: Hennessey Bldg., Butee, Mont. Deceased.

DALZELL, ROBERT M., millwright, inventor; b. Belfast, Ireland, 1793; s. John Dalzell; m. Lucy S., 2 children. Came to Vernon, N.Y., 1801; apprentice to a millwright in N.Y.; worked as a millwright until 1826; moved to Rochester, N.Y., 1826, millwright for flour mill, 1826-51; designed almost all flour mills in Rochester (became known as "Flour City"); perfected and introduced elevator storage system for grain and meal. Died Rochester, Jan. 19, 1873.

DAME, FRANK LIBBY, electrical engr.; b. Boston, Mar. 21, 1867; s. Seth T. and Josephine R. (Libby) D.; E.E., Mass. Inst. Tech., 1889; m. Mary Elizabeth Elvidge, 1906; children—Frank E., Edward L., Robert O. Engr. Portland (Ore.) office of Westinghouse Co., 1889-90; supt. Vancouver (B.C.) Ry. & Light Co., 1891-92; engr. local office Gen. Electric Co., 1901-09; v.p. Electric Bond & Share Co., 1909-12; official various Public Utilities cos., 1912-24; now pres., chmn. exec. com. North American Co.; chmn. bd. exec. com. Cleveland Electric Illuminating Co., North Am. Edison Co., Wired Radio, Inc.; pres. Edsion Securities Co., North Am. Utilities Securities Corp., Sixty Broadway Building Corp., Western Power Corp.; v.p., mem. exec. com. and dir. Union Electric Light & Power Co.; dir. numerous cos. Episcopalian. Home: Garden City, N.Y. Died Dec. 30, 1933.

DAMESHEK, WILLIAM, physician, hematologist, editor; b. Voronezh, Russia, May 22, 1900; s. Isadore and Bessie (Muskin) D.; brought to U.S., 1902, naturalized, 1921; M.D., Harvard, 1923; m. Rose Thurman, Oct. 14, 1923; 1 dau., Elinor Thurman (Wife of Dr. Seymour Reichlin). Intern, Boston City Hosp., 1923-25, asst. blood lab., 1925-28; chief blood lab. Beth Israel Hosp., Boston 1928-39; sr. physician, hematologist, dir. blood research lab. New Eng. Center Hosp., Boston, 1939-69; cons. hematologist Lynn. Waltham, Mt. Auburn, Malden, U.S. V.A. hosp.; consultant Surgeon-Gen., U.S. Army; successively asst., instr., asst. prof., prof. medicine Tufts University Sch. of Medicine, 1925-67, professor emeritus, 1967-69; extraordinary prof. medicine at National Univ., Mexico, 1945; prof. medicine, honoris causae, U. Santiago, Chile; grad. lectr. hematology in many countries in Europe, South Am. and the Orient. Awarded Certificate of Merit, A.M.A., 1945, Silver medal, 1951; Claude Bernard medal University of Montreal, 1950; Premia Ferrata, Rome, 1958; decorated Commander Order of Carlos Finlay (Cuba). Fellow A.M.A., A.C.P., A.A.A.S., Am. Soc. Clin. Investigation, Internat. Soc. Hematology (pres. 1954-56), Am. Soc. Immunology, Am. Soc. Exptl. Pathology; Am. Acad. Arts and Scis., N.Y. Acad. Scis.; mem. Greater Boston Med. Soc. (pres. 1933), Peruvian Soc. Pathology (hon.), Am. (pres. 1964), Italian, Swiss, Chilean, French, European societies hematology (hon.), Chilean Soc. Internal Medicine, Soc. Exptl. Biology and Medicine. Club: Harvard (Boston). Author: Leukopenia and Agranulocytosis, 1944; Hemolytic Syndromes, 1945; Spleen and Hypersplenism, 1947; Chemotherapy of Leukemia and Leukosarcoma, 1949; Leukemia, 1958; also numerous articles medical jours. Co-author: Hemorrhagic Disorders, 1955. Founder and editor-in-chief Blood, the Jour. of Hematology, 1945-69; Home: New York City NY Died Oct. 1969.

DAMON, GEORGE ALFRED, consulting engr.; b. Chesaning, Mich., Apr. 7, 1871; s. Brazil Monroe and Martha Angeline (Gould) D.; B.S. in elec. engring., U. of Mich., 1895; m. Harriett Diller, June 8, 1904; children—George Alfred, Harriet Antha. On staff Electrical Industries, World's Fair, Chicago, 1893; in shops of Fisher Electric Works, Detroit, 1894; draftsman and engr. with Bion J. Arnold, Chicago, 1895-1900; mng. engr. The Arnold Co., in design and constrn. railroad shops, elec. rys., hydro-electric plants and industrial work, 1900-09; asso. with Mr. Arnold in reports on subway operations and constrn., New York, transportation problems of Pittsburgh and Los Angeles, Calif., and surrounding dists., etc., 1911; dean engring., Throop Coll. of Tech. etc., 1911; dean engring., Throop Coll. of Tech. (Calif. Inst. Tech.), 1911-17. Cons. engr. Bd. Pub. Utilities, Los Angeles, 1912-13; tech. dir. City Planning Com. of Pasadena, 1915-17; cons. engr. City Plan, San José, 1917; consultant City Plan, Long Beach, Calif., 1918-19; mem. Zoning Commn., Pasadena, 1923. Republican. Presbyn. Fellow Am. Inst. E.E.; chmn. Joint Tech. Socs., Los Angeles, 1918-19, Am. City Planning Inst.; charter mem. City Planning Assn., Los Angeles (pres. 1918-19, sec. 1922, 25); mem. Los Angeles Co. Regional Planning Commn., 1922-26 (v. chmn. 1923-25); co-ordinator for "Damon-Jubb Plan" for Los Angeles Union Depot, started Dec. 1933; program chmn. Pasadena 60th Anniversary Celebration, 1934. Author: Inter and Intra Urban Transit and Traffic as a Regional Planning Problem (proc. Nat. Conf. City Planning), 1923; The Influence of the Automboile on Regional Transportation Problems (trans. Am. Soc. C.E.), 1925. Home: Pasadena, Calif. Died June 23, 1934.

DAMON, HOWARD FRANKLIN, physician; b. Scituate, Mass., 1833; grad. Harvard, 1858, M.D., 1861. Supt., Boston Dispensary, 1862-64; admitting physician Boston City Hosp., 1864-84; mem. Boston Microscopical Soc., Boston Soc. for Med. Improvement. Author: Leucothythaemia: A Boylston Prize Essay, 1864; Neurosis of the Skin, 1868; Structural Lesion of the Skin, 1869; Photographs of Skin Diseases, 1870. Died Boston, Sept. 1, 1884.

DANA, EDWARD SALISBURY, mineralogist; b. New Haven, Conn., Nov. 16, 1849; s. James Dwight and Henrietta F. (Silliman) D.; A.B., Yale, 1870, A.M., 1874, Ph.D., 1876; studied Heidelberg and Vienna; m. Caroline, d. William Brooks Bristol, of New Haven, Oct. 2, 1883; children—Mary Bristol (Mrs. Alexander C. Brown), James Dwight, William Bristol. Tutor 1874-79, curator mineral collection, 1874-1922, asst. prof. natural philosophy, 1879-90, prof. natural philosophy, 1879-90, prof. physics, 1890-1917, and prof. emeritus, 1917—, Yale U. Trustee of Peabody Mus., 1885-1929; editor Am. Jour. of Science, 1875—. Fellow Am. Acad. of Arts and Sciences; mem. Nat. Acad. Sciences. Author: Text-book of Mineralogy, 1877, new edit., 1898; Text-book of Elementary Mechanics, 1881; Dana's System of Mineraology, 6th edit., 1892; Minerals and How to Study Them, 1895. Home: New Haven, Conn. Died June 16, 1935.

DANA, JAMES DWIGHT, geologist, educator; b. Utica, N.Y., Feb. 12, 1813; s. James and Harriet (Dwight) D.; grad. Yale, 1833; Ph.D. (hon.), U. Munich (Germany), 1872; LL.D. (hon.), Harvard, 1886, U. Edinburgh (Scotland), 1890; m.Henrietta Silliman, June 5, 1844, 4 children. Geologist, mineralogist on capt. Weekes expdn. to South Seas, 1837-40; editor Am. Jour. Science, 1840; Silliman prof. natural history Yale, 1849, prof. geology and mineralogy, 1864-90; pres. A.A.A.S., 1854. Recipient Woolaston medal Geol. Soc. London (Eng.), 1872; Copley medal Royal Soc. London, 1877; $1,000 Walker prize Boston Soc. Natural History, 1892. Author: Manual of Geology, 1862; Textbook of Geology, 1864; Corals and Coral Islands, 1872; Characteristics of Volcanoes, 1890. Died New Haven, Conn., Apr. 14, 1895.

DANA, JAMES FREEMAN, chemist; b. Amherst, N.H., Sept. 23, 1793; s. Luther and Lucy (Giddings) D.; A.B., Harvard, 1813; M.D., 1817; studied under Fredrich Accum, London, Eng., 1815; m. Matilda Webber, 1818. Changed name from Jonathan to James by legilsative act, 1820; organizer Hermetic Soc. at Harvard for informal scientific study; received Boylston prize for paper Tests for Arsenic; selected by Corp. of Harvard to purchase new chem. equipment in London, 1815; received 2d Boylston prize for Compostion of Oxymuriatic Acid, 1817; lectr. in chemistry to med. students Dartmouth, 1817-20, prof. chemistry and mineralogy, 1820-26; prof. chemistry Coll. Physcians and Surgeons, N.Y.C., 1826. Author: (with brother Samuel) Outlines of Mineralogy and Geology of Boston and its Vicinity, 1818; Epitome of Chymical Philosophy, 1825. Died N.Y.C., Apr. 14, 1827.

DANA, RICHARD TURNER, civil engr.; b. Lenox, Mass., June 13, 1876; s. Richard Starr and Florine (Turner) D.; Ph.B. in C.E., Sheffield Scientific Sch. (Yale), 1896; m. Mary R. Meredith, 2d, Apr. 22, 1902. With maintenance of way dept., Erie R.R., 1896-1902; cons. practice in N.Y. City, 1902—, chief engr. Construction Service Co., pres. Codex Book Co.; v.p. and treas. Construction Service Co.; sec. and treas. R. T. & D. T. Dana Co. Served in 1st Div. Naval Battalion, Conn. N.G., 2 yrs., 130th Separate Co., 1 yr. Republican Episcopalian. Mason. Author: Cost Keeping and Management Engineering (with H. P. Gillette), 1909; Rock Drilling (with W. L. Saunders), 1911; Handbook of Construction Equipment, 1921, 26. Joint author: Mechanical and Electrical Cost, 1918; Construction Costkeeping and Management, 1922; Concrete Computation Charts, 1922; The Bridge at Windsor (Vt.) and Its Economic Implications, 1926; The Human Machine in Industry, 1927. Home: New York, N.Y. Died Aug. 26, 1928.

DANA, SAMUEL LUTHER, chemist; b. Amherst, N.H., July 11, 1795; s. Luther and Lucy (Giddings) D.; grad. Harvard, 1813, M.D., 1818; m. Ann Willard, June 5, 1820; m. 2d, August Willard; 4 children. Served in War of 1812; discovered system of bleaching cotton known as Am. system of bleaching; devised improvements in printing calicoes. Author: Outlines of Mineralogy and Geology of Boston and its Vicinity, 1818; A Muck Manual for Farmers (one of 1st sci. works on agr. written and published in U.S.), 1842. Died Lowell, Mass. Mar. 11, 1868.

DANCEL, CHRISTIAN, inventor; b. Cassel, Germany, Feb. 14, 1847; 2 children. Learned machinet trade in Germany; came to N.Y.C., circa 1865; machinist in various N.Y. shops, 1865-67; devised shoe-sewing machine (bought by Charles Goodyear, Jr. for his shoe-machine factory), became supt. Goodyear's factory; began making machinery for stitching out soles and sewing shoe-welts, circa 1870; invented machine to sew both welts and turns, 1874 (still used with minor improvements); opened own machine called by Goodyear Co. to perfect machine to sew upper and outer sole of shoe, finished it (machine with curved needle sewing a lock-stitch), 1885; patented straight-needle machine, 1891; organized Dancel Machine Co., Bklyn., circa 1895; invented many other shoe-making devices; co-patentee machines for making leather buttonholes, barbed-wire fence, rubbing type. Died Bklyn., Oct. 13, 1898.

DANDY, WALTER E(DWARD), surgeon; b. Sedalia, Mo., Apr. 6, 1886; s. John and Rachel D.; A.B., U. of Mo., 1907; Ll.D., 1928; M.D., Johns Hopkins, 1910, A.M., 1911; m. Sadie Martin, Oct. 1, 1924; children—Walter E., Mary Ellen, Kathleen Louise, Margaret Martin. Began practice, Baltimore; now prof. neurol. surgery in charge surgery of nervous system, Johns Hopkiins. Mem. Am. Surg. Assn., Am. Neurol. Assn., Southern Surgical Assn., Phi Beta Kappa, Sigma Xi. Author of a textbook on neurological surgery and several books on various lesions of the brain. Contbr. numerous articles to surgical and neurological journals. Introduced new operative procedures for tumors and aneurysms of the brain. for hydrocepholus, neuralgias and other disturbances of cranial nerves; introduced ventriculography, ventricular estimation and cerebral pneumography, for diagnosis and localizing of tumors of the brain and intracranial lesions; discovered ruptured intervertebral disks which cause low backaches and sciaticas, and introduced surgical procedure for their cure. Home: 3304 Juniper Rd., Baltimore 18. Office: Johns Hopkins Hosp., Baltimore 5, Md. Died Apr. 19, 1946.

DANFORTH, CHARLES, inventor, mfr.; b. Norton, Mass., Aug. 30, 1797; s. Thomas and Betsey (Haskins) D.; m. Mary Willett, Oct. 18, 1823, at least 2 children. Foreman cotton-mfg. factory, Matteawan, N.Y.; factory worker Sloatsburg, N.Y., 1825; patented cap-spinner (important spinning frame improvement), 1828; machinist for firm Godwin, Rogers & Clark, Paterson, N.J., took over Roger's place in firm, but continued to work in machine-shop, designed and patented 5 improvements on original capspinner; purchased machine-shop branch of firm, 1840, bought firm's cotton mill, 1842 (became locomotives; incorporated Danforth Locomotive and Machine Co. 1865, pres., 1865-71. Died Paterson, Mar. 22, 1876.

DANFORTH, GEORGE WASHINGTON, naval officer, retired; b. Charleston, Mo., Feb. 22, 1868; s. Lewis William and Mary Jane (Yates) D.; State Normal Sch., Cape Girardeau, Mo., 1883-84; Manual Training Sch., Washington Univ., St. Louis, 1884-85; grad. U.S. Naval Academy, 1889; postgrad. course and practical engring. and engine bldg., Navy Yard, New York, 1891-92; m. Aileen R. Hennicke, of Brooklyn, Dec. 15, 1896. Commd. in engr. corps, U.S.N., July, 1891; engineering duties of various kinds at sea and on shore, July 1, 1891-June 1, 1899, retired. Insp. machinery for Navy Dept., at Union Iron Wks., San Francisco, 1902-03 and 1906-07; Navy Dept. detail at St. Louis Expn., 1904; instr. engring. dept., Naval Acad.,

1908-11; in charge summer naval sch., Culver (Ind.) Mil. Acad., 1912; chief Machinery Exhibits Dept., Panama-Pacific Internat. Expn., 1912-15; insp. engring. material for U.S.N. in central dist. of Pa., 1917-19. Mem. Soc. Naval Engrs. Mason. Club: Army and Navy (Washington). Author: Mechanical Processes, 1917. Home: Charleston, Mo. Address: Navy Dept., Washington.

DANIEL, JOHN, physicist; b. Perry County, Ala., July 6, 1862; s. John and Susan Lee (Winfield) C.; A.B., U. of Ala., 1884, A.M., 1885, LL.D., 1914; Johns Hopkins, 1886-88; U. of Berlin, 1892; m. Grace Olive Knight, Sept. 2, 1896; children—Landon Garland, Ray Knight, John Harben Winfield, Robert Bradley (dec.), Grace Olive. Asst. prof. physics U. of Ala., 1884-86; fellow, 1888, instr. physics, 1889, adjunct prof., 1890-93, prof., 1894-1939, prof. emeritus of physics since 1939, Vanderbilt U. Designed and installed the first electric dynamo at Vanderbilt Univ. (before commercial lighting); discovered depilatory and buring effect of X-Ray; describing same in Science for May, 1896; mem. Jury of Awards, Tennessee Centennial Expn., 1897. Fellow A.A.A.S.; charter mem. Tenn. Acad. Science. Mem. Phi Delta Theta, Phi Beta Kappa, Sigma Xi. Clubs: The Old Oak, The IV, The Faculty. Contbr. papers to Annales de Physique et Chimie, Philosophical Mag., Science, Physical Rev., etc. Home: 2500 Woodlawn Dr., Nashville, Tenn. Died Mar. 2, 1950.

DANIEL, J(OHN) FRANK(LIN), zoologist; b. O'Fallon, Mo., July 31, 1873; s. Dr. John Franklin and Martha Short (Henry) D.; Southern Ill. Normal U., 1901; with dept. of edn., P.I., 1901-05; S.B., U. of Chicago, 1906; Adam T. Bruce fellow from Johns Hopkins, Pasteur Inst., Lille, France, 1908-09; Ph.D., Johns Hopkins, 1909; m. Menetta White Brooks, Feb. 16, 1909. Inst. zoology, U. of Mich., 1910-11; instr. zoology, 1911-12, asst. prof., 1912-17, asso. prof., 1917-19, prof. zoology since 1919, U. of Calif. U.S. del. to 12th Internat. Congress. of Zoology, Lisbon, 1935. Decorated Chevalier of Legion of Honor (France), 1936. Fellow A.A.A.S., Am. Acad. of Arts and Sciences; mem. Am. Zool. Soc., Western Soc. of Naturalists, Soc. Explt. Biology and Medicine, Calif. Acad. Sciences, Am. Genetic Assn., Societe Zoologique de France, Assn. des Anatomistes. Author: Animal Life of Malaysia, 1905; The Elasmobranch Fishes, 1922; also papers on breeding of mice for scientific purposes, experimental studies on alcohol, morphogenesis, etc. Chmn. U. of Calif. Publs. in Zoology; collaborator Internat. Jour. of Cytology (Japan). Home: 615 Woodmont Av., Berkeley, Calif. Died Nov. 2, 1942.

DANIELLS, WILLIAM WILLARD, chemist; b. Oakland Co., Mich., 1840; s. Nathaniel I. and Lucinda (Reed) D.; B.S. Mich. Agrl. Coll., 1864, M.S., 1867; Lawrence Scientific Sch. (Harvard), 1867; Halle and Berlin, 1881; (D.Sc., Mich. Agrl. Coll., 1897); m. Hontas Augusta Peabody, June 21, 1871. Asst. in chemistry, Mich. Agrl. Coll., 1864-68; prof. chemistry, 1868-68, prof. agrl. and analytical chemistry, 1869-70, prof. chemistry, 1879-1907 (emeritus), U. of Wis. Chemist Wis. State Geol. Survey, 1872-76; asst. U.S. Geol. Survey, 1882-83; mem. Wis. State Bd. Health, 1885-89. Home: Madison, Wis. Died Oct. 12, 1912.

DANIELS, FARRINGTON, prof. chemistry; b. Minneapolis, Minn., Mar. 8, 1889; s. Franc Burchard and Florence Louise (Farrington) D.; B.S., U. of Minn., 1910, M.S., 1911; Ph.D., Harvard, 1914; D.Sc., Univ. Rhode Island, University Minnesota, University Dakar, U. Louisville, University Wis.; m. Olive M. Bell, Sept. 15, 1917; children—Farrington, Florence Mary (Drury), Miriam (Ludwig), Dorin. Instr. in chemistry, Worcester (Mass.) Poly. Inst., 1914-17, asst. prof., 1917-18; electrochem. U.S. Nitrogen Research Lab., Washington, 1919-20; asst. prof. chemistry, U. of Wis., 1920-24, asso. prof., 1924-28, prof., 1928-59, emeritus, 1959-72, chmn. dept. chemistry 1952-59, research Solar Energy Laboratory, Engineering Expt. Sta.; prof. chemistry Stanford, summer 1930; George Fisher Baker non-res. lecturer chemistry, Cornell Univ., Feb.-June 1935; vis. scholar Cranbrook Institute Sci., 1968. Dir. metall. lab., U. of Chicago, 1945-46; chmn. bd. govs., Argonne Nat. Laboratory, 1946-48. Served as 1st lt., U.S. Chem. Warfare Service, 1918. Recipient Outstanding Achievement award U. Minn., 1950, Norris award for excellence in teaching, 1957, Distinguished Service Citation U. Wis., 1972. Guggenheim fellow, 1952. Fellow A.A.A.S. (chmn. chem. sect. 1937, 1947); mem. Am. Chem. Soc. (pres. 1953; Willard Gibbs Medal; Priestley medal), Nat. Acad. Scis. (vice president 1957-61), Am. Acad. Arts and Scis., Geochemical Society (president 1958), American Philosophical Society, Solar Energy Society (president 1964-66), Sigma Xi (president 1965-66), Phi Beta Kappa, Alpha Delta Phi, Alpha Chi Sigma. Conglist. Author: Mathematical Preparation for Physical Chemistry; Chemical Kinetics; Direct Use of the Suns Energy. Co-author: Physical Chemistry; Experimental Physical Chemistry; Challenge of Our Times: Solar Energy Research. Research chem. kinetics, nitrogen oxides, thermoluminescence of crystals, atomic energy and solar energy. Home: Madison WI Died June 24, 1972.

DANIELS, FRED HARRIS, mech. engr.; b. Hanover Centre, N.H., June 16, 1853; s. William Pomeroy and H. Ann (Stark) D.; borther of Charles Herbert D.; M.E., Worcester Poly. Inst., 1873; spl. study in chemistry, under Dr. Thomas M. Drown, of Lafayette Coll.; m. Sarah Lydia White, May 17, 1883. Entered employ Washburn & Moen Mfg. Co., Worcester, 1873, and became gen. supt. and chief engr.; visited Europe, and made spl. studies of advanced methods in mfr. of iron, steel, etc.; apptd. chief engr., Am. Steel & Wire Co. when latter acquired business of Washburn & Moen Co., 1899, and became dir. in co., 1902; apptd. chmn. bd. of engrs. U.S. Steel Corp. when latter acquired interests of Am. Steel & Wire Co., 1901; pres. Washburn & Moen Co., and Worcester Wire Co., 1900—; also mem. bd. engrs. Ind. Steel Co., Gary, and Minn. Steel Co., Duluth. Awarded grand prize and gold medal, Paris Expn., 1900, for achievements in development of wire industry. Republican Conglist. Home: Worcester, Mass. Died Aug. 30, 1913.

DARBY, JOHN, educator, coll pres.; b. North Adams, Mass., Sept. 27, 1804; s. Joseph and Farrand Darby; grad. Williams Coll., Williamstown, Mass., 1831; m. Julia P. Sheldon, Aug. 20, 1833, at least 2 children. Taught at Williamstown Acad., also Barhamville Sem., Columbia, S.C.; prof. natural science Wesleyan Female Coll., Macon, Ga., 1842; prof. mathematics Williams Coll.; dir. Sigoruney Inst., Culloden, Ga., 6 years; dir. Masonic Female Coll., Auburn, Ala., 1855-56; prof. natural science East Auburn Male Coll., Auburn 1856-61; prof. science, later pres. Ky. Wesleyan Coll., Millersburg, 1869-76. Author: A Botany of the Southern State, 1841. Died N.Y., Sept. 1, 1877.

DARBY, WILLIAM, geographer; b. Hanover Twp., Pa., Aug. 14, 1775; s. Patrick and Mary (Rice) D.; m. Mrs. Boardman; m. 2d, Elizabeth Tanner, Feb. 1816; at least 2 children. Became cotton-planter, Natchez, Miss., 1781; dep. surveyor for U.S., 1804-09; mem. Andrew Jackson's topog. staff, 1814-15; a surveyor designating boundary line between U.S. and Canada, 1818; lectured and wrote geog. volumes, during next 35 years. Author: A Geographical Description of the State of Louisiana. . . Being an Accompaniment to the Map of Louisiana, 1816; A Tour from the City of New York to Detroit, 1819; (with Theodore Dwight, Jr.) A New Gazetteer of the United State of America, 1833; The Northern Nations of Europe, Russia and Poland, 1841. Died Oct. 9, 1854.

DARGEON, HAROLD WILLIAM, physician; b. N.Y.C., May 7, 1897; s. William Joseph and Florence (Kinghorn) D.; M.D., Albany Med. Coll., 1922; m. Muriel Mosher, Sept. 21, 1926; 1 dau., Jill Elizabeth. Intern 4th div. Bellevue Hosp., N.Y.C., 1922-24; attending in pediatrics St. Luke's Hosp., N.Y.C., 1924-29, asst. attending pediatrician, chief clinic, 1929-33, chief Tb clinic, 1929-33, asso. attending pediatrician, 1933-48, attending pediatrician, 1949-60, cons. pediatrician, 1960-70; asst. attending physician Knickerbocker Hosp., N.Y.C., 1924-29, dir. pediatrics, 1941-45; asst. pediatrician N.Y. Nursery and Children's Hosp., 1926-29; asst. attending physician Willard Parker Hosp., 1926-29; asst. attending pediatrician N.Y. Foundling Hosp., 1933-36; pediatrician Meml. Hosp. for Cancer and Allied Diseases, N.Y.C., 1935-46, attending pediatrician, 1946-62, chmn. dept. pediatrics, 1960-62, attending pediatrician emeritus, 1962-70; attending pediatrician St. Vincent's Hosp., 1948-51; cons. pediatrician Monmouth Meml. Hosp., Long Branch, N.J., 1949-70, House of Calvary, 1948-70, Lawrence Hosp., Bronxville, N.Y., 1954-70, Strang Clinic, Meml. Center, 1954-63, Fitkin Hosp., Neptune, N.J., 1958-70, Misericordia Hosp., Bronx, N.Y., 1958-70, N.Y.C. Dept. Health, 1961-70, N.Y. Infirmary, 1964-70, Riverview Hosp., Red Bank, N.J., 1968-70, Point Pleasant (N.J.) Hosp., 1969-70; spl. cons. USPHS, 1965-70; instr. pediatrics Columbia Coll. Phys. and Surg., 1931-46; asst. prof. clin. pediatrics Cornell U. Med. Coll., N.Y.C., 1947-51, asso. prof., 1951-61, clin. prof., 1961-63, clin. prof. emeritus, 1963-70. Otto Faust lectr. Albany Med. Coll., 1961; lectr. in U.S. and fgn. countries. Served with U.S. Army, 1917-18; to comdr., M.C., USNR, 1942-44. Recipient Hon. Alumni award Albany Med. Coll., 1969. Diplomate Am. Bd. Pediatrics. Mem. A.M.A., N.Y. State, New York County, N.Y. Celtic (pres. 1949) med. socs., Am. Acad. Pediatrics (past chmn. com. on tumor registry), Am. Radium Soc. (v.p. 1960, Janeway medal 1963), James Ewing Soc. (medal 1963), N.Y. Acad. Medicine, N.Y. Otolaryng. Soc., Bellevue Hosp. Alumni Assn. (pres. 1952), Alpha Omega Alpha. Roman Catholic. Author: Tumors of Childhood, 1960; (monograph) Reticuloendothelioses in Childhood, 1966. Editor, contrbr. Cancer in Childhood, 1940. Contbr. articles to med. jours. Pioneer in pediatric oncology. Home: Sea Girt NJ Died Oct. 29, 1970; buried Gate of Heaven Cemetery, Hawthorne NY

DARLING, WILLIAM LAFAYETTE, civil engr.; b. Oxford, Mass., Mar. 24, 1856; s. William E. and Cynthia M. (Steere) D.; B.S., Worcester Poly. Inst., 1877, hon. Dr. Engring., 1927; m. Alice E. Bevans, 1877, hon. Dr. Engring., 1927; m. Alice E. Bevans, Apr. 15, 1901. Engaged in constrn. and maintenance of steam rys. in various capacities, mostly with the Northern Pacific, 1878-1901; chief engr. St. Andrew's Bay & Chipley R.R., in Fla., 1884; engr. terminals for Burlington R.R., St. Paul and Minneapolis, 1885; chief engr. location and constrn. of Duluth, Watertown & Pacific Ry. and chief engr. Yankton, Sioux Falls R.R., for City of Yankton, later built by G.N. Ry., 1887-88; construction branch lines for N.P. Ry., 1888-91; chief engr. N.P. System, 1901-03; chief engr. Rock Island System, 1903-05, also v.p. Gulf Constrn. Co., line for the Rock Island between St. Louis and Kansas City; later in 1905 made report on extension of Milwaukee Road from Butte, Mont., to Pacific Coast; chief engr. N.P. Ry., Jan. 1906-Oct. 1916, also v.p. and engr. in charge fo engring. and constrn. of Portland & Seattle Ry. from Spokane to Portland; also pres. Union Depot Co., 1906-09. Apptd. asso. mem. U.S. Naval Consulting Bd., 1916; mem. U.S. commn. of ry. experts to Russia, May 1917-Jan. 1918; in nat. and state to Russia, May . 1918; in nat. and state war work, 1918; cons. engr., St. Paul, 1919-21; mem. Bd. of Economics and Engring. of Nat. Assn. Owners of Ry. Securities, 1922-May 1923; then cons. practice, St. Paul, Minn. Died Oct. 27, 1938.

DARLINGTON, CHARLES GOODLIFFE, pathologist; b. Bklyn., Jan. 28, 1892; s. Gustavus Cornelius and Kate Annabel (Bearns) D.; student Haverford Coll., 1909-10; M.D., Medico Chirurgical Coll. of Phila., 1915; m. Mabel Heinz, June 16, 1915; 1 dau., Annabel (Mrs. Ricker). Intern Flusning (L.I.), Hosp., 1915, Met. Hosp., N.Y.C., 1916; pathologist, serologist Bellevue Hosp., N.Y.C., 1917-19; asst. pathology N.Y.U. Coll. Medicine, 1919, instr., 1920, asst. prof., 1923, asst. prof. pathology Coll. Dentistry, 1925, asso. prof., 1932, prof. pa pathology, 1934—, dir. Undergraduate Cancer Teaching, Coll. Dentistry; asst. pathologist, 1926, pathologist, 1935-39; pathologist St. Vincent's Hosp., N.Y.C., 1922-24; pathologist dir. Pathology Lab., Muhlenberg Hosp., Plainfield, N.J., 1924-53, now cons. tissue pathology; pathologist Beekman-Downtown Hosp., N.Y.C., 1926-47, Somerset Hosp., Somerville, N.J., 1928-48; cons. pathologist Steon Hosp., N.Y.C., 1940-43; cons. oral pathologist VA Hosp., N.Y.C., 1954—. Served from 1st lt. to capt., U.S. Army, 1917-19, as col. AUS, 1943-45. Diplomate Am. Bd. Pathology. Fellow Coll. Am. Pathologists; mem. A.M.A., N.Y. Acad. Medicine, Acad. Medicine No. N.J., Am., N.J. Socs. clin. pathologists, N.Y. State Soc., Pathologists, N.Y. Acad. Sci., N.Y. Path. Soc., Harvey Soc., Internat. Assn. Dental Research, Sci. Research Soc., Am., Am. Legion, Mil. Order World Wars, Res. Officers Assn., N.Y. Soc. Mil. and Naval Officers World Wars, S.R., Sigma Xi. Home: 802 Belvidere Av., Plainfield, N.J., Office: 421 First Av., N.Y.C. 10010. Died Nov. 5, 1960.

DARLINGTON, FREDERICK, cons. engr., mfg. exec.; b. Lincoln University, Pa., Apr. 23, 1856; s. Franklin and Mary (Jackson) C.; B.S., Pa. State Coll., 1886; m. Josephine Sanford, Sept. 16, 1890; children—Mrs. Josephine Stanley, Mrs. Helen McCandless. With Am. Bridge Co., 1888-89, Hunt & Clap chem. Lab., Pitts., 1890, Westinghouse Electric Co., Pitts., 1891; with United Electric Light & Power Co. and Bursh Illuminating Co., N.Y.C., 1892-98; engring. and scientific investigations with William Stanley, Great Barrington, Mass., 1898-1903; with Westinghouse Electric & Mfg. Co., 1905-12, cons. engr., 1914-17, 23—. also asst. to v.p., 1923—; v.p. and mgr. Ala. Power Co., 1913; chief of power sect. of War Industries Bd., Washington, 1918. Repubilcan. Fellow Am. Inst. E.E. Clubs: Union League, Lawyers (N.Y.C.). Home: Great Barrington, Mass.; and 38 E. 37th St., N.Y.C. Died Oct. 27, 1943.

DARLINGTON, WILLIAM, botanist, congressman; b. Dilworthtown, Chester County, Pa., Apr. 28, 1782; s. Edward and Hannah (Townsend) D.; studied medicine under Dr. John Vaughan, Wilmington, Del.; M.D., U. Pa., 1804; m. Catherine Lacey, June 1808. Surgeon aboard ship to Calcuta, 1806-08; maj. in "Am. Grays" (Pa. Volunteers), during War of 1812; me. U.S. Ho. of Reps. from Pa., 14th, 16th-17th congresses, 1815-17, 19-23; organized Chester County Cabinet of Natural Scis., 1826; dir., pres. Nat. Bank of Chester County, 1830-63. Author: Florula Cestrica, 1826; Flora Cestrica, 1837; Reliquiae Baldwinianae, 1843; Agricultural Botany, 1847; Memorials of John Bartram and Humphry Marshall, 1849; American Weeds and Useful Plants, 1859. Died West Chester, Pa., Aug. 23, 1863; buried Oakland Cemetery, West Chester.

DARROW, CHESTER WILLIAM, psychophysiologist; b. Ft. Plaine, N.Y., Nov. 7, 1893; s. William E. and Harriet (Mills) D.; A.B., Des Moines Coll., 1915; M.A., Oglethorpe U., 1922; Ph.D., U. Chgo., 1924; m. Ruth Rentor, 1926; children—Virginia (Mrs. Robin Oggins), Diane (Mrs. Roland Grybek), Gale (Mrs. Anthony Kaliss); m. 2d, Alice Hale Waterman, Dec. 22, 1961. With Behavior Research Fund, Inst. for Juvenile Research, Chgo., 1924-26, psychophysiologist, psychophysiol. lab., 1926-67; asso. prof. physiology U. Ill., 1950-66, asso. prof. emeritus, 1966-67. Diplomate, fellow Am. Psychol. Assn. Mem. Am., Central (pres. 1954-55) electro-encephalographic socs., Soc. for Psychophysiol. Research (pres. 1960-61), Am. Physiol. Soc., Am. Psychopath. Soc., Am. Acad. Neurology, A.A.A.S., Chgo. Neurol. Soc., Soc. Biol. Psychiatry, Psychonomic Soc., Chgo. Inst. Medicine, Sigma Xi. Home: Chicago IL Died Apr. 7, 1967.

DART, CARLTON ROLLIN, civil engr.; b. Lansing, Mich., Feb. 1, 1862; s. Rollin Charles and Sarah Elizabeth (Darrling) D.; B.S., Mich. Agrl. Coll., 1881; post grad. in engring., U. of Mich., 1882-83; m. Ella Weinland, Feb. 8, 1908 (died 1923). Asst. to city engr., Lansing Mich., 1881-82; draftsman Marquette & Western R.R., Marquette, Mich., 1883-84, G.R.&I. Ry., Grand Rapids, 1885-86; asst. engr. U.P. System, on constn. of terminals, 1886-91; in gen. engring. work, 1891-97; in bridge, structural and waterway engring., 1897—; bridge engr. Sanitary Dist. of Chicago, Feb., 1901-11, asst. chief engr., 1912, chief bridge engr., 1913-21, cons. engr. and bridge eng., Chicago, 1921—. Died June 23, 1929.

DARTON, NELSON HORATIO, geologist; b. Brooklyn, N.Y., Dec. 17, 1865; s. William and Caroline M. (Thayer) D.; hon. D.Sc., U. of Ariz., 1922; m. Alice Weldon Wasserbach, 1903; Chemist N.Y., 1880-86; geologist, U.S. Geol. Survey, 1886-1910 and 1913-36 (ret.) geologist, Bur. Mines, 1910-13. Inventor of a sugar process; researches in tannic acid and water analysis, etc. Lectured at various colleges. Fellow Geol Soc. America (ex. v-p), A.A.A.S.; mem. Washington Acad. Sciences (former v.-p.), Geol. Soc. Washington (former pres.), Soc. Econ. Geologists, Mining and Metall. Soc., Am. Inst. Mining and Metall. Egnrs., Soc. Linn de Lyons, Inst. Francais, Pi Gamma Mu, Soc. Geol. de France, Assn. Am. Geographers, Internat. Geol. Congress, Soc. Fine Arts, Wyo. Valley Geol. Soc., Am. Geophysical Union, Archaeol. Soc., Federal Bd. of Surveys and Maps, English Speaking Union, Italy-America Soc., Alliance Francaise (v.p.), Spanish Atheneum (ex. pres.), Instituto de las Espanas; hon. mem. Am. Assn. of Petroleum Geologists; mem. sub-com. Nat. Council. Awarded Daly gold medal by Am. Geog. Soc., 1930, and Penrose gold medal by Geol. Soc. of Am., 1940; Legion of Honor, Am. Inst. Mining and Metall. Engrs., 1944. Wrote: The Story of the Grand Canyon; Geologic Guide to Santa Fe R.R.; Geologic Guide to Southern Pacific R.R.; Geology of Great Plains, Black Hills, Bighorn Mts., Owl Creek Mts., Geology Dist. Columbia region; Geologic maps Great Plains, Grand Canyon, S.D., Neb., Ariz., N.M., Lower Calif. and Tex.; many folios U.S. Geol. Survey, etc. Contributor on geol. subjects; geol. maps and reports on many districts, topog. maps states of Ariz., N.M. N.M., Tex., Nebr., N.D., S.D.; many articles in Ency. Americana and other publications. Explored ruins of the temple of Cuicuilco, Mexico, for Nat. Geog. Soc. and oil geology of Lower Calif., Santo Domingo, Eastern Cuba and Central Venezuela. Clubs: Cosmos, Inquirendo. Home: 6969 Brookeville Rd., Chevy Chase, Md. Office: U.S. Geological Survey, Washington, D.C. Died Feb. 28, 1948.

DARWIN, CHARLES GALTON, physicist; b. Cambridge, Eng., Dec. 19, 1887; s. George H. and Maud (DuPuy) D.; B.A., Trinity Coll., Cambridge U., 1909, Sc.D., 1937; fellow Christ's Coll., Cambridge U. 1919-22; Sc.D., Bristol U., 1937; LL.D., St. Andrews U., 1939, Edinburgh U., 1946, Manchester U., 1947, Delhi U., 1948, U. Chgo., 1959, U. Cal., 1961; m. Katharine Pember, Sept., 24, 1925; children—Cecily (Mrs. John Littleton), George, Henry Francis, Edward. Staff physics lab. Manchester U., 1910-14; vis. prof. Cal. Inst. Tech., 1922-23; prof. natural philosophy Edinburgh U., 1923-37; master Christ's Coll., Cambridge U., 1937-39; dir. Nat. Phys. Lab., 1939-49; dir. Brit. Central Sci., Office, Washington, 1941; now ret. Served as capt. Royal Engrs., France, 1914-19. Decorated Mil. Cross, Knight Brit. Empire; recipient Royal medal, 1936. Fellow Royal Soc.; mem. Am. Philos. Soc. Author: The New Conceptions of Matter, 1931; The Next Million Years, 1951. Home: Newnham Grange, Cambridge, Eng. Died Dec. 31, 1962.

DASHER, BENJAMIN JOSEPH, educator; b. Macon, Ga., Dec. 27, 1912; s. Benjamin Joseph and Odille (King) D.; B.S., Ga. Inst. Tech., 1935, M.S., 1945; Sc.D., Mass. Inst. Tech., 1952; m. Anne Moore Brooks, June 7, 1941; children—Benjamin Joseph III, Anne B., Preston B., Elizabeth S., David, Carole. Instr., asst. prof. elec. engring. Ga. Inst. Tech., 1940-46, asso. prof., 1952, prof. elec. engring., 1953-71, dir. Sch. Elec. Engring., 1954-69, asso. dean engring., 1969-71. Fellow I.E.E.E.; mem. Am. Soc. Engring. Edn., Nat. Soc. Profl. Engrs., Sigma Xi, Eta Kappa Nu. Home: Atlanta GA Died Dec. 13, 1971.

DATES, HENRY BALDWIN, electrical engr; b. New Britain, Conn., July 15, 1869; s. Henry Masten and Sarah E. (Baldwin) D.; B.S. in E.E., Mass. Inst. Tech., 1894; E.E., Case Sch. Applied Science; m. Harriet Burt Haskell, Dec. 29, 1896. Engr. Westinghouse Electric & Mfg. Co., 1894-96; prof. physics and elec. engring. Clarkson Sch. of Technology, Potsdam, N.Y., 1896-1903; dean Coll. Engring. and prof. elec. engring, U. of Colo., 1903-05; prof. elec. engring., Case Sch. Applied Science, 1905-38, now prof. emeritus. Fellow Am. Inst. Elec. Engrs.; mem. Illuminating Engr. Soc. (U.S.), country mem. Illuminating Engr. Soc. (London, Eng.); mem. U.S. Com. of Internat. Commn. on Illumination. Registered professional elect. engr., Ohio. Home: 3071 Euclid Heights Blvd., Cleveland 18 OH

DATTNER, BERNHARD, neuropsychiatrist; b. Ustron, Silesia, Austria, July 7, 1887; s. Adolf and Anna (Hechter) D.; jur. D., U. of Vienna, 1911; M.D., 1919; m. Margeret Friedrich, Jan. 14, 1939. Came to U.S., 1938. naturalized, 1943. cons. U.N. World Health Orgn. since 1950; N.Y. State Dept. of Health, Albany, since 1949; cons. in neurology U.S.P.H.S., Marine Hosp., Staten Island and Ellis Island since 1948; special cons., U.S.P.H.S., Washington, since 1946; asso. clin. prof. of neurol., N.Y. Univ. Sch. of Med., 1943-47; asst. clin prof. of neurol., Coll. Phys. and Surg., Columbia, 1945-47; acting attending neurologist, Goldwater Meml. Hosp., N.Y. City, since 1946. Bronx Hosp. since 1942; attending neurologist, Montefiore Hosp., since 1945; asso. visiting neuropsychiatrist Bellevue Hosp. since 1943. Diplomate Am. Bd. Psychiatry and Neurology; fellow N.Y. Acad. Medicine, Am. Neurol. Soc., N.Y. Neurol. Soc., Mexican Soc. Neurology and Psychiatry (hon.); corr. mem. Vienna Med. Soc., Vienna Neuro-spychitric Soc. Aurhor: Moderne Therapie der Neuro-syphilis, (Vienna, Austria), 1933; Management of Neruosyphilis, 1944. Home: 235 22d St., N.Y. City 10. Office: 133 58th St., N.Y.C. 22. Died Aug. 11, 1952.

DAUGHERTY, LEWIS SYLVESTER, zoölogist; b. Belmont Co., Ohio, Aug. 10, 1857; s. Samuel and Rachel Ann (Mechem) D.; student, Ill. State Normal U., Normal, Ill., 1881-82; 1881-82; B.S., U. of Ill., 1889, M.S., 1893; grad. student, U. of Chicago, 1894-96; Ph.D., Ill. Wesleyan U., 1901; spol. study, various summer schs. and in univs. of Germany, 1907; m. Millie Crum, July 8, 1885. Prof. science, 1889-92, biology, 1892-94, Township High Sch., Ottawa, Ill.; prof. natural science, 1897-1900, zoölogy, 1900-13, State Normal Sch., Kirksville, Mo.; prof. zoölogy and chemistry, Mo. Wesleyan Coll., 1913—. Republican. Methodist. Mason. Author: (with wife) Principles of Economic Zoölogy, 1912; Field and Laboratory Guide, 1912. Home: Cameron, Mo. Died Feb. 28, 1919.

DAVENPORT, CHARLES BENEDICT, biologist; b. Stamford, Conn., June 1, 1866; s. Amzi B. and Jane Joralernon (Dimon) D.; B.S., Poly Inst., Brooklyn, 1886; A.B., Harvard, 1889, A.M., Ph.D., 1892; m. Gertrude Crotty, June 23, 1894; children—Mrs. Millia Davenport Harvey, Mrs. James A. deTomasi, Charles Benedict (dec.). Engr. survey of Duluth, S. Shore & Atlantic Ry., 1886-87; asst. zoology, 1888-90, instr., 1891-99, Harvard; asst. prof. zoology and embryology, 1899-1901, asso. prof. and curator Zool. Mus., 1901-04, U. of Chicago; dir. dept. of genetics, Carnegie Instn. Comprising Sta. for Experimental Evolution, 1904-34, and Eugentics Record Office, 1910-34, Cold Spring Harbor, N.Y.; dir. Biol. Lab., Brooklyn Inst. Arts and Sciences, 1898-1923. Maj. Sanitary Corps, U.S. Army, in charge of anthropology, 1918-19. Asso. editor Jour. Experimental Zoology since 1896. Jour. of Physical Anthropology since 1918, Genetics since 1919, and others. Fellow Am. Acad. Arts and Sciences, A.A.A.S. (vice-pres. 1900-01, 1925-26), New York Zool. Soc.; mem. Nat. Acad. Sciences, Am. Philos. Soc., Am. Soc. Zoologists (pres. 1902-08, 29-30), Am. Genetic Assn., Am. Soc. Naturalists (sec. 1899-1903, v.p. 1906), Soc. Exptl. Biology and Medicine, Eugenics Research Assn. (hon. pres., 1937), N.Y. Acad. Medicine (asso.), Galton Soc. (pres. 1918-30), Nat. Inst. of Social Sciences (gold medal, 1923), L.I. Biol. Assn. (sec.), Internat. Fedn. of Eugenic Organizations (pres. 1927-32), Anthropologische Gesellschaft in Wien, Kaiserleih Deutsche Akad. Naturforscher (Halle), Berliner Gesellschaft fur Anthropologie, Ethnologie und Urgeschichte (corr. mem.), Acad. Royale de Belegique; foreign corr. Zool. Soc., London; pres. Third Internat. Eugenics Congress, New York City, 1932. Author: Graduate Courses, 1893; Experimental Morphology Part 1, 1897, Part 2, 1899; Statistical Methods in Biological Variation (4th edit.), 1936; Introduction to Zoology (with G.C. Davenport), 1900; Elements of Zoology, 1911; Inheritance in Poultry, 1906; Inheritance of Characteristics of Fowl, 1909; Eugenics, 1910; Heredity in Relation to Eugenics, 1911; Heredity to Skin Color in Negro-White Crosses, 1913; The Feebly-inhibited-Nomadism and Temperament, 1915; Naval Officers-Their Development and Heredity (with M. Scudder), 1919; Physical Examination of First Million Draft Recruits, 1919; Defects Found in Drafted Men, 1920; Army Anthropology, 1921 (the last 3 with Major A. G. Love); Body Build and Its Inheritance, 1923; Race-Crossing in Jamaica (with M. Steggerda), 1929; Genetical Factor in Endemic Goiter, 1932; How We Came by Our Bodies, 1936. Contbr. to biol. jours. Home: Cold Spring Harbor, L.I., N.Y. Died Feb. 18, 1944.

DAVENPORT, EUGENE, agriculturist; b. Woodland, Mich., June 20, 1856; s. George Martin and Esther (Sutton) D.; B.S., Mich. Agrl. Coll., 1878, M.S., 1884, M.Agr., 1895, LL.D., 1907; D.Sc. from Iowa State College, 1920; also LL.D., Univ. of Ky., 1913, Univ. of Ill., 1931; m. Emma Jane Coats, Nov. 2, 1881 (now dec.); children—Dorothy (dec.), Margaret (Mrs. H. B. Tukey, dec.). Asst. botanist Expt. Sta., 1888-89, prof. practical agr. and supt. of farm, 1889-91, Mich. Agrl. Coll.; pres. Collegio Agronomica, Sao Paulo, Brazil, 1891-92; dean Coll. of Agr., Univ. of Ill., 1895-1922; dir. Agrl. Expt. Station, and prof. thremmatology, U. of Ill., Sept., 1896-1922 (emeritus). Author: Principles of Breeding, 1907; Education for Efficiency, 1909; Domesticated Animals and Plants, 1910; Vacation on the Trail, 1923; The Farm, 1927. Republican. Conglist. Home: Woodland, Mich. Died Mar. 31, 1941.

DAVENPORT, GEORGE EDWARD, botanist; b. Boston, Mass., August 3, 1833; educated Boston schs.; has resided in Medford from 1875; devoted much attention to botany research; best known for his work on the ferns. One of founders Middlesex Field Club, which became Middlesex Inst.; became mem., 1872, of Mass. Hort. Soc. to which he gave, 1875, his collection of ferns now known as the Davenport Herbarium; was made life mem. of soc. and given Appleton gold medal. Has written various monographs and papers on ferns. Home: Medford, Mass. Died 1907.

DAVENPORT, THOMAS, inventor; b. Williamstown, Vt., July 9, 1892; s. Daniel and Hannah (Rice) D.; m. Emily Goss, Feb. 14, 1827. Built small circular ry. (1st electric ry. on record), 1835; invented early model of electric train motor, 1836, patented, 1837, unable to improve and market because of financial difficulties; patented 2d model, 1837. Died Salisbury, Vt., July 6, 1851.

DAVEY, JOHN, tree surgeon; b. Somersetshire, Eng., June 6, 1846; Samuel and Ann (Shopland) D.; largely self-ed.; m. Bertha A. Reeves, Sept. 21, 1879. Learned floriculture and landscape architecture, Torquay, Eng., 1866-72; came to U.S. and settled at Warren, O., 1873; moved to Kent, O., 1881; introduced tree surgery, 1890; pres. Davey Tree Expert Co. and Davey Inst. Tree Surgery (school), 1908—. Mem. Christian (Disciples) Ch. Author: The Tree Doctor, 1901; A New Era in Tree Growing, 1905; Davey's Primer on Trees and Birds, 1905; Instruction Books on Tree Surgery and Fruit Growing, Nos. 1-23, 1914. Home: Kent, O. Died Nov. 8, 1923.

DAVEY, WHEELER P(EDLAR), physics and chemistry; b. Cleve., Mar. 19, 1886; s. Thomas George and Myra Eliza (Christian) D.; A.B., Western Reserve U., 1906; M.S., Pa. State Coll., 1911; grad. study U. Chgo., summers, 1909, 10, 11; Huntingdon fellow, Cornell U., 1912-13, Ph.D., 1914; m. Laura L. Gunn, Aug. 28, 1912; children—Myra Ellen, George Thomas, Ruth Barton, Mary Louise. Tchr. physics and chemistry, Central Inst., Cleve., 1906-08; high sch., Mansfield, O., 1908-09; instr. in physics, Pa.State Coll., 1909-11 asst. in physics, Cornell U., 1911-12, instr. in 1913-14; research physicist research lab. Gen. Electric Co., Schenectady, N.Y., 1914-25; prof. physical chemistry and prof. indsl research, Pa. State Coll., 1926-31; research prof. physics and chemistry, 1931-49. research prof. emeritus 1949—. Chmn. Schenectady (New York), Civil Service Commn. 1916-17. Lecturer on X-rays and crystal structure, Union U., 1920-26; lecturer in physics dept., Grad.Sch., Pa. State Coll., summers, 1922, 23, 24; lecturer on crystal structure U. Mich., summer, 1925; Thurston lectr., Am.Soc. M.E., 1928. Mem. elect. insulation com. N.R.C., 1828-41, chmn. physics sub-com., 1935-40. Mem. Optics sub-com., Chicago Century of Progress Expn; mem. Am. Inst. Physics Council of Applied Applied Physics, 1935-38. Mem. editroial bd. Jours. of Chemical Physics, 1933. Award of merit, Am. Soc. Testing Materials, 1952. Fellow Am. Phys. Soc. for Metals, Soc. Rheology (pres. 1930-33; asso. editor, 1933-36, editor, 1936-41), Sigma Xi., Phi Lambda Upsilon, Sigma Pi Sigma Chmn. placement bd., 1934-45, Alpha Pi Mu, Acacia. Mem. joint com. (A.S.T.M., I.P. and American Chrystallographic Society) on chemical analysis by X-ray diffraction methods, 1940—. chairman, 1940-56. Republican. Presbyn. Mason. Contributor to Fairbanks' Investigation of Ores, 1928. Author: A Study of Crystal Structure, 1934; also articles on X-rays, crystal structure, automatic X-ray diffraction apparatus, criterions for the rating of Physics departments, planning new physics buildings. Home: Glennland Bldg., State College, Pa. Died Oct. 12, 1959; buried Diamond Grove Cemetery, Jacksonville, Ill.

DAVID, HENRY GASSETT, surgeon; b. Trenton, Me., Nov. 4, 1807; s. Isaac and Polly (Rice) D.; M.D., Yale, 1839; m. Ellen W. Deering, 1856; 3 children. Practiced in Worcester, Mass., also Milbury, Mass., 1838-54; went to N.Y.C., 1855; founder traction sch. of orthopedic surgery; his theories concerning the nature and treatment of club foot, congenital dislocation of the hip, chronic diseases of the joints and polimyelitis form the basis for the modern approach to these problems; unique treatment of abscesses anticipated the Cassel-Dahin therapy; 1st to devise a splint for traction and the protection of the hip joint. Author: Conservative Surgery, as Exhibited in Remedying some of the Mechanical Causes that Operate Injuriously both in Health and Diseases, 1867 (1st significant textbook in history of Am. orthopedic surgery). Died Everett, Mass., Nov. 18, 1896.

DAVID, WILLIAM THORNWALL, ophthalmologist; b. Little Rock, Arkansas; son William Thornwall and Terese (Atkin) D.; student Ky. Military Institute, 1890-92; M.D., George Washington, 1901; grad. U.S. Army Med. Sch., 1902-03, Univ. of Vienna, 1906, 12, Royal Ophthalmic Hosp., London, 1906; m. Renee Tolson, 1912; children—William Joseph Graham, Roger Has Brouck, Rene Sheldon, Akin Thornwall. Interne Garfield Memorial Hosp., Washington, D.C., 1901-02; 1st lt., later capt. Med. Corps, U.S. Army, 1902-13 (under Gen. Leonard Wood, Moro campaigns, 1904-05); maj. Med. Corps, U.S. Army, World War; prof. ophthalmology, U.S. Army Med. Sch., 1917-18;

prof. same, George Washington, since 1920; sr. surgeon Episcopal Eye and Ear Hosp.; cons. ophthalmologist at Garfield, Columbia, Gallinger, Casualty hosps.; ophthalmologist in chief George Washington U. Hosp.; consultant in ophthalmology to the surg. gen. U.S. Army, Feb. 1943. Mem. advisory bd. Selective Service Draft, 1941. Mem. bd. dirs. Washington Loan & Trust Co. Official Orden Nacional de Merito Carlos J. Finley (Cuba). Fellow American College Surgeon; mem. A.M.A., Southern Med. Assn., Am. Acad. Ophthalmology and Otolaryngology, Med. Soc. of D.C., S.A.R., Mil. Order of Foreign Wars of U.S., Soc. of the Cincinnati of State of Va., The Filson Club of Ky., Pan-Am Med. Assn., Acad. of Medicine (Washington, D.C.), Mil. Order Carabao, Spanish Am. War Veterans, Am. Legion (A.P. Gardner Post), Phi Sigma Kappa, Sigma Xi. Episcopalian. Mason. Rotarian. Clubs: Army and Navy, Metropolitan (Washington); Chevy Chase (Maryland). Contributed papers read before Am. Acad. Ophthalmology, Ophthal. Sect. A.M.A., etc. Office: 927 Farragut Sq., Washington, D.C. Died June 16, 1944.

DAVIDGE, JOHN BEALE, anatomist, surgeon; b. Annapolis, Md., 1768; s. capt. and Honor (Haward) D.; M.D., St. John's Coll.; Annapolis, Md., 1793; m. Wilhelmina Stuart, 1793; m. 2d, Mrs. Rebecca Troup Polk. Asso. with many operations, among them shoulder joint amputations, 1792; wrote treatise on yellow fever, 1798; a founder Coll. Medicine of Md. (now U. Md.), 1813, prof. anatomy and surgery, 1813-29, uni. dean. Died Aug. 23, 1829.

DAVIDSON, DONALD MINER, geologist; b. Quincy, Ill., Feb. 20, 1902; s. Isham Gaylord and Frances (Stillman) D.; A.B., magna cum laude, U. Minn., 1925, M.Sc., 1926, Ph.D., 1928; m. Bernadine Marie Dunn, Oct. 28, 1937 (dec. 1956); 1 son, Donald Miner. Geol., sr. engr. Selection Trust, Ltd., London, Eng., 1928-39; lectr. mineral economics, mining, geology various univs.; became chief geologist, v.p., dir. E. J. Longyear Co., 1939, now pres., director; also pres., dir. Canadian Longyear Ltd., Longyear N.V. Holland; cons. mining, mineral econs.;dir. vis. lectr. U. Minn., 1933-40, Columbia, 1948-49; guest lectr. Nat. War Coll., 1951. Mem. Nat. Mineral Adv. Council, 1950-52; cons. President's Materials Policy Commn., 1951-52, A.E.C., U.S. Bur. Mines, U.S. Corps Engrs., Siamese Bur. Mines, Portuguese Govt. Cons. Bureau Econ. Warfare, W.P.B., World War II. Fellow Geol. Soc. Am., mem. .A.A.A.S., Am. Inst. Mining Engrs., Inst. Mining and Metallurgy London, Soc. Econ. Geologists (pres. 1953), Mining and Metall. Soc., Sigma Xi, Sigma Alpha Epsilon. Episcopalian. Clubs: Minneapolis; Cosmos (Washington); Mining Engineers (N.Y.C.); Engineers (Toronto). Author many atric articles on mining, geology, mineral econs. Home: 4513 Wooddale Av. S., Mpls. 24. Office: 76 S. 8th St., Mpls. 55402. Died Sept. 16, 1960.

DAVIDSON, GEORGE, geodesist, astronomer; b. Nottingham, Eng., May 9, 1825; s. omas and Janet (Drummond) D.; came to U.S., 1832; A.B., Central High Sch., Phila., 1845, A.M., 1850; (Ph.D., Santa Clara Coll., 1876; Sc.D., U. of Pa., 1889; LL.D., U. of Calif., 1910); m. Ellinor Fauntleroy, Oct. 5, 1858. Secretary to Prof. A. D. Bache, supt. Coast Survey, 1845-46; member U.S. Coast and Geod. Survey, 1845-95; in geod. field and astron. work in Eastern states, 1845-50; in coast survey work of Calif., Ore., Wash. and Alaska, 1850-95, in charge of Pacific Coast work, 1868-95; hon. prof. geodesy and astronomy, 1870—, regent, 1877-84, prof. geography, 1898—, U. of Calif. Expert U.S. mints, Phila. and San Francisco 1872, 85, 86; mem. U.S. Irrigation Commn. Cal., 1873-74, India, Egypt, etc., 1875; mem. U.S. Advisory Bd. of Harbor Improvement, San Francisco, 1873-76; in charge Transit of Venus Expdn. to Japan, 1874, to N.M., 1882; mem. Miss. River Commn., 1888-90; spl. agt. U.S. 9th Internat. Geod. Congress, Paris, 1889. Medal, Paris Expn., 1878; Daly gold medal, Am. Geog. Sco., 1908; decorated with Order of St. Olof, Norway, 1907. Fellow Am. Acad. Arts and Sciences, A.A.A.S. Died Dec. 1, 1911.

DAVIDSON, J. BROWNLEE, prof. agrl. engring.; b. Douglas, Neb., Feb. 15, 1880; s. James H. and Margaret Jane (Dickson) D.; B.S., M.E., U. of Neb., 1904; A.E., 1914, Dr. Engring., 1931; m. Jennie Baldridge, June 14, 1906; children—Margaret Elizabeth, Ethel Brownlee, James Vincent (dec.), Helen Mary (dec.). instr. farm mechanics, U. of Neb., 1904-05; asst. prof. and profl. agrl. engring., Ia. State Coll. Agr. and Mechanic Arts, 1905-15; prof. agrl. engring., U. of Calif., 1915-19, Ia. State Coll. Agr. and Mechanics Arts, 1919-56. Dir. Survey of Research in Mech. Farm Equipment for U.S. Dept. Agr. (on leave), 1926; mem. Am. Com. on Colonization, Russia (on leave), 1929; cons. farm equipment mfrs.; Hon. mem. Am. Soc. Agrl. (chmn. com. History); life mem. Am. Soc. Engring. Edn., Ia. Engring. Soc.; "Estranger" mem. Swedish Royal Agrl. Soc.; mem. Sigma Xi, Phi Kappa Phi, Gamma Sigma Delta, Sigma Tau (nat. pres.), Tau Beta Pi, Alpha Zeta; Assn. of College Honor Societies (mem. council). Congregationalist. Author: Farm Machinery and Farm Motors, 1908; Agricultural Machinery, 1931; (with others) A Study of Extension Service, 1933; farm equipment consultant, War Production Board, 1943; United Nations Relief and Rehabilitation Adminstrn., 1944. Chmn. com. on Agricultural Engineering, Ministry of Agricultural and Forestry, China (on leave, 1946-48). Recipient of Cyrus Hall McCormick medal for achievement in engring. of agr., 1933. Club: Rotary Address: 1610 E. 14th Av., Denver. Died May 8, 1957; buried College Cemetery, Ames, Ia.

DAVIDSON, ROBERT JAMES, chemist; b. Armagh, Ireland, Apr. 3, 1862; s. John and Hannah (Donaldson) D.; B.S., S.C. Coll., 1885, A.M., 1887; m. Anna Maria, d. of John McLaren McBryde (q.v.), May 2, 1892. Tutor in chemistry, S.C. Coll., 1885-88, asst. prof. and sec. of faculty, Univ. of S.C., 1888-91; asst. chemist, S.C. Expt. Sta., 1888-90; chemist, Va. Expt. Sta., 1891-1907; prof. chemistry, 1891—, dean scientific dept., 1903—, Va. Poly. Inst., Blacksburg, Va. Democrat. Episcopalian. Del. Internat. Congress Applied Chemistry, London, 1909. Died Dec. 19, 1915.

DAVIDSON, WARD FOLLETT, elec. and mech. engring.; b. Commonwealth, Wis., Oct. 21, 1890; s. Otto Conrad and Charlotte S. (Dickinson) D.; B.S., U. Mich., 1913; M.S., 1920; m. Elizabeth Thurber Bostwick, Aug. 17, 1917; children—Ward F., Elizabeth Sargent (Mrs. Ralph Smith-Johannesen). Student, jr. engr. Westinghouse Electric & Mfg. Co., 1914-16; instr. in elec. engring. U. Mich., 1916-17, 19-20, asst. prof., 1920-22; dir. research Bklyn. Edison Co. and Consol. Edison Co. of N.Y., since 1922. Cons to chmn. and dep. exec. officer Nat. Def. Research Com., cons. Smaller War Plants, 1943-46. Awarded Presdl. Cerificate of Merit. Served as lt., later capt. C.E., U.S. Army, 1917-19; with A.E.F. in Eng., France and Germany; maj., Engr. Res., 1919-42. Sec. conf. on elec. insulstion NRC, 1927-39, chmn. 1939-48; mem.-at-large Div. Engring. and Industrial Research, NRC, 1950-54; chmn. com. on electric power cables Am. Standards Assn., 1927-54; chmn. joint com. on plant coordination, Edison Elec. Inst., 1933-37; mem. U.S. Delegation Internat. Electro-tech. Commn., Torquay, 1938; chmn. engring. sub-com. U.S. Nat. Com., Conference internat., des Grande Reseaux Electriques á Haut Tension (Cigre). Fellow Am. Inst. E.E. (chmn. com. on basic scis. 1936-38; chmn. com. on research, 1938-40, chmn. com. on nucleonics 1950-52), Am. Soc. M.E.; asso. Fellow Inst. Aero. Scis.; mem. Instn. Elec. Engrs. (London), Am. Phys. Soc., Am. Chem. Soc., Am. Meteorol. Soc. Am. Geophys. Union, Sigma Xi, Tau Beta Pi. Clubs: Engrs. (N.Y) Cosmos (Washington); Manhasset Bay (N.Y.) Yacht. Author numerous tech. papers, including several on nuclear (atomic) Power. Home: 12 Summit Rd., Port Washington, L.I., N.Y. Office: 4 Irving Place, New York 3, N.Y. Died July 12, 1960.

DAVIES, CHARLES, educator; b. Washington, Litchfield County, Conn., Jan. 22, 1798; son of Thomas John Davies; grad. U.S. Mil. Acad., 1815; LL.D. (hon.), Geneva (N.Y.) Coll., 1849; m. Mary Ann Mansfield. Brevetted 2d lt. U.S. Army, 1815, assigned to Engr. Corps., 1816, resigned soon after; prof. mathematics, natural and exptl. philosophy U.S. Mil. Acad., 1816-37; toured Europe, 1836-37; prof. mathematics Trinity Coll., 1837-41; paymaster with rank of maj. West Point, 1841-46; prof. mathematics, philosophy U. City N.Y., 1848-49; prof. higher mathematics Columbia, 1857-65, emeritus prof. mathematics, 1865-76. Died Fishkill-on-Hudson, N.Y., Sept. 17, 1876.

DAVIES, HYWEL, mining engr.; b. Breconshire Co., Wales, Sept. 26, 1859; s. Howell and Tydfil (Watkins) D.; ed. pub. schs.; m. Sarah Williams, of Wales, 1883 (died 1886); m. 2d, Ella C. Brooks, 1888; children—Hywel Brooks, Alwilda Tydfil, Winnefred Jeannette (dec.), Arthur Wayne, Paul Drummond, Alleine Blodwen, Helen Gwendolen, John Franklyn. Teacher and bookkeeper, 1875-85; came to U.S., 1885, naturalized citizen, 1892. In charge mine officer of East Tenn. Coal Co., later supt. until 1890; gen. mgr. du Pent mining operations in 3 counties in Ky., 1890-1912; consulting and mining engr. coal cos. Southern States and Mexico. Govt. mediator Colo. coal strike, 1914, Eastern Ohio coal strike, 1915, Alaska Govt. railroad strike, 1916; commr. of conciliation U.S. Dept. Labor, 1914—; Govt. labor adminstr. copper industry, World War; sole referee Calif. oil industry, 1919-21; mem. Govt. commn. on labor conditions in Hawaiian Islands, 1922. Trustee Ky. State U., 1908-14. Republican. Baptist. Mason. Home: Los Angeles, Calif. Died Feb. 17, 1927.

DAVIES, JOHN VIPOND, civil engr.; b. Swansea, South Wales, Oct. 13, 1862; s. Andrew and Emily (Vipond) D.; Wesleyan Coll., Taunton, Eng.; U. of London; m. Ruth Ramsey, Apr. 16, 1895 (died 1931). Engaged in coal mining, steel mfr. and other engring, work to 1889, when came to New York and employed as engr. with late Austin Corbin; chief asst. engr. tunnel under East River for East River Gas Co.; pres. Jacobs & Davies, Inc., cons. engrs., New York; v.p., chief engr. Hudson & Manhattan R.R.; chief engr. in charge design and constrn., W.Va. Short Line R.R. and Kanwaha & Pocahontas R.R. in W.Va.; chief engr. Atlantic Av. improvement, L.I. R.R., Brooklyn; consulting engr. Brooklyn Rapid Transit Co.; cons. engr. City of Detroit for water supply tunnel under Detroit River; engr. in charge for contractors of terminal improvement of N.Y.C. R.R., New York City; designed and built 4 turnnels under Hudson River and under New York, Jersey City and Hoboken, for Hudson & Manhattan R.R.; constrn. engr. for 26 aqueduct tunnels, aggregating 18 miles, in Mexico; one of bd. of 3 engrs. on constrn. of Moffat Tunnel in Rocky Mountains nr. Denver; firm prepared original studies for Pa. R.R. tunnels under North and East Rivers, New York; engr. in charge Astoria Tunnel, Consol. Gas. Co. of N.Y.; engr. in charge constrn. Hales Bar Dam across Tenn. River at Chattanooga; engr. in charge constrn. intake and discharge tunnels of N.Y. Edison Co.; on constrn. bridge or tunnel of N.Y. Edison Co.; on constrn. bridge or tunnel crossing of Miss. River at New Orelans; mem. bd. cons. engrs. N.Y. State Bridge and Tunnel Commn. and N.J. interstate Bridge and Tunnel Comvehicular tunnel under Hudson River, 1912-22); one of two engrs. on tunnel and bridge crossing of San Francisco Bay. Awarded Telford gold medal by the Institute of Civil Engineers, 1914; Norman gold medal, 1913, and Thomas Fitch Rowland prize, 1917, by Am. Soc. C.E.; Fowler professorial award, 1930. Episcopalian. Home: Flushing, N.Y. Died Oct. 4, 1939.

DAVIES, PERCY ALBERT, prof. of biology, scientist; b. Fort Collins, Colo., Feb. 10, 1896; s. Harry and Elizabeth Martha (Thompson) D.; B.S., Colo. State Coll., 1922, M.S., 1923; Ph.D., Harvard, 1926; m. Celestia May Johnson, Dec. 25, 1925; 1 dau., Lois Elaine. Asst. prof. biology, Univ. of Louisville, Louisville, Ky., 1926-28, asso. prof., 1928-29, prof., 1929—, head dept. of biology, 1931-56, chmn. div. of natural sciences. Mem. A.A.A.S., Soc. Am. Bacteriologists, Am. Mus. Nat. Hist., Bot. Soc. Am., Soc. Plant Physiology, Acad. Sci., Ornith. Soc., Soc. Nat. Hist. of Ky., Alpha Gamma Rho, Gamma Alpha, Phi Kappa Phi. Clubs: Torrey Bot., Filson Hist. Contbr. numerous sci. articles in sci. and hist. pubs. Home: 3124 Meadow Lark Av., Louisville 40213. Died Jan. 4, 1961.

DAVIS, ACHILLES EDWARD, ophthalmologist; b. Harrodsburg, Ky., Feb. 18, 1866; s. H. C. and Josephine (Le Compte) D.; A.B., Centre Coll., Danville, Ky., 1886, A.M., 1889; M.D., U. of Louisville, 1889; studied abroad in 1891; m. Josephine K. Robinson, 1914; children—Achilles Edward, Clay Robinson, Le Compte Kirkwood. Engaged in practice in New York City since 1892; consultant on diseases of the eye, New York Post-Graduate Med. Sch. and Hosp.; consulting ophthalmic surgeon, Manhattan State Hosp., Central Islip, New York since 1889, United Port Chester Hosp. since 1911, Ossining Hosp. since 1913. Capt. O.R.C. Mem. N.Y. State Med. Soc., N.Y. Ophthal. Soc., N.Y. Acad. Medicine, A.M.A., Am. Acad. Ophthal. Soc., Pacific Coast Oto-Ophthal. Soc., S.A.R., The Kentuckians, Huguenot Soc. N.Y., Ass. Mil. Surgeons of the U.S. Army Med. Mus. Author: The Refraction of the Eye, 1900; Handbook of the Anatomy and the Diseases of the Eye and Ear (with D. B. St. John Roosa), 1904; Eye, Ear, Nose and Throat Nursing (with Beaman Douglass), 1905; Medical Treatment of the Cataract, 1937. Contbr. to med. press; wrote sect. on Refraction in Am. Encyclopedia Ophthalmology, 1919. Home: Scarsdale, N.Y. Office: 40 E. 61st St., New York, N.Y.

DAVIS, ALEXANDER JACKSON, architect; b. N.Y.C., July 24, 1803; s. Cornelius and Julia (Jackson) D.; m. Margaret Beale, July 14, 1853. With firm Town & Davis, 1829-43; self employed as architect, 1843-80; architect: New York Customs House, 1832; Ind. (1832-35), N.C. (1831), Ill. (1837), Ohio (1839) state capitols; U.S. Patent Office, Washington, D.C., 1832; Va. Mil. Inst., 1852, 59; Assembly Hall, U. N.C., Alumni Hall, Yale; Gilmer House in Balt. (1832) and U. Mich. (1838) are advanced Gothic designs for that period; a founder Llewellyn Park, West Orange, N.J.; exponent of classic and gothic styles; an early experimenter with structural iron. Died West Orange, Jan. 14, 1892.

DAVIS, ALVA RAYMOND, educator; b. Cascade, Ida., Feb. 15, 1887; s. John William and Elizabeth (Orr) A.B., Pomona Coll., 1912, D.Sc. (h.c.), 1948; Ph.D., Washington U., 1915; LL.D., U. Cal., 1957; m. Eugenie Scharle, Aug. 31, 1916; children—Alva R., Jr., Margaret Ellen (Mrs. Robert Imrie). Rufus J. Lackland research fellow Washington U., 1912-15; Yale fellow Bishop Mus., Honolulu, 1925-26; instr. Woods Hole Biol. Lab. summers, 1913-14; research asst. Mo. Bot. garden, 1915-16; instr. Pomona Coll., summer 1915, asst. prof. botany and plant pathology U. Neb., 1916-19; instr. soil chemistry and bacteriology U. Cal., 1919, asst. prof. plant nutrition, 1921, asso. prof. plant physiology, 1925-19, prof. since 1929; chmn. dept. botany, 1936-47, dean Coll. Letters and Sci., 1947-55, vice chancellor, 1955-56, ret., 1956; acting chancellor, July-Aug., 1953, Aug.-Sept. 1954. Mem. Dept. State-ICA Mission U. Concepcion, Chile, 1959; chmn. Nat. Acad. Scis. survey Chilean univs., 1960. Adv. com. Regional Park Bd., San Francisco Bay Area; mem. exec. com. Assn. Land Grant Colls. and Univs. Chmn. bd. trustees Willis Lynn Jepson Found. Served in USN, 1903-07; capt. U.S. Army (CAC), 1917-19; lt. col. (CAC, AA), 1942-45; comdt. enlisted specialists schs. Camp Callan; dir. centralized schs. Anti-aircraft Replacement Tng. Center, Fort Bliss, Tex., 1944-45. Mem. acad. adv. bd. (chmn.) U.S. Maritime Acad., Kings Point, L.I., N.Y. Knight first class Royal Norweigian Order St. Olaf. Fellow A.A.A.S. (mem. exec. com. Pacific Div., 1932-37); mem. Soc. Plant Physiologists (pres. Pacific div. 1946-47), Bot. Soc. Am., Cal. Bot. Soc., (pres. 194041), Western Soc. Naturalist (v.p. 1932), Phi Beta Kappa, Sigma Xi (pres. U. Cal. chpt. 1937). Clubs: Sierra, Sierra

Ski, Faculty (pres. U. Cal. 1946); Commonwealth, Bohemian (San Francisco). Author numerous tech. pubs. on various phases plant metabolism. Editor Univ. of Cal. Bot. series, 1938-40. Home: 1159 Keeler Av., Berkeley 8, Cal. Died July 15, 1965; buried Pacific View Meml. Park, Corona del Mar. Cal.

DAVIS, ARTHUR POWELL, civil engr.; b. Decatur, Ill., Feb. 9, 1861; s. John and Martha P. D.; grad. State Normal Sch., Emporia, Kan.; B.S., Columbian (now George Washington) U., 1888, Sc.D., 1917; D.Eng., Ia. State Coll., 1920; m. Elizabeth Brown, June 20, 1888 (died Apr. 13, 1917); children—Mrs. Rena Peck, Mrs. Florence Eslin, Mrs. Dorothy Smith, Mrs. Elizabeth Smith; m. 2d, Marie MacNaughton, June 19, 1920. Topographer U.S. Geol. Survey, 1884-94, conducting surveys and explorations in Ariz., N.M., and Calif.; hydrographer in charge of all govt. stream measurements, 1895-97; hydrographer in charge hydrographic exam. of Nicaragua and Panama canal routes, 1898-1901; chief eng., U. S. Reclamation Service, 1906-14, dir. same, 1914-23. Consulting engr., Panama Canal, 1909. Examined and reported on irrigation in Puerto Rico, 1909; in Turkestan, 1911; mem. bd. of engrs. reporting on flood control in China, 1914; cons. engr. on many high dams; mem. joint conf. on standard specifications for Portland cement, 5 yrs.; tech. adviser to U.S. on Pecuniary Claims Arbitration, London, 1923. Chief engr. and gen. mgr. East Bay Municipal Utility Dist., Oakland, Calif., 1923-29; built large reservoir on Mokelumne River, aqueduct and tunnels, 95 miles long, now delivering mountain water to Oakland, San Francisco and eight other cities around San Francisco Bay; chief cons. engr. for irrigation projects in Turkestan and Transcaucasia 2 yrs. Fellow Am. Acad. Arts and Sciences, Washington Soc. Engrs. (pres. 1907; hon. mem. 1923). Author: Irrigation Works Constructed by the U.S. Government, 1917. Home: Oakland, Calif. Died Aug. 7, 1933.

DAVIS, BERGER, physicist; b. White House, N.J., Mar. 31, 1869; s. John and Catherine Marie (Dilts) D.; B.S., Rutgers, 1896, Sc.D. (hon.), 1929; A.M., Columbia, 1900, Ph.D., 1901, Sc.D., (hon.), 1929; studied Gottingen 1901-02, Cambridge, 1902-03; m. Matie Pearl Clark, 1922. Instr. physics Columbia 1903-09, adjunct prof. 1909-13, asso. prof. 1913-18, prof. of physics, 1918-39, professor emeritus, 1939—. Awarded medal and prize of Research Corporation 1929. Fellow A.A.A.S. (v.p. sect. (v.p. sect. B 1932), Am. Phys. Soc., Am. Optical Soc.; mem. Nat. Acad. Scis., Sigma Xi, Delta Upsilon, Mem. Reformed Dutch Ch. Author of numerous articles and papers. Home: 44 Moringside Dr., N.Y.C. 25. Died June 30, 1958; buried Dutch Reformed Cemetery, Readington, N.J.

DAVIS, BRADLEY MOORE, botanist; b. Chgo., Nov. 19, 1871; s. Charles Wilder and Emma Frances (Moore) D.; A.B., Stanford, 1892; A.B., Harvard 1893, A. M., 1894, Ph.D., 1895; research at Boon, 1898, Naples, 1904; m. Annie Elizabeth Paret, Sept. 22, 1908; 1 dau., Margery French (Mrs. Allen M. Boyden). Asst. in botany, U. Chgo., 1895, asso. in botany, 1896-98, instr. botany, 1898-1902, asst. prof. plant morphology, 1902-06, head dept. botany Marine Biol. Lab., Woods Hole 1897-1906, in charge of bot. sec. biol. survey Woods Hole, Bur. of Fisheries, 1903-09; asst. prof. botany. U. Pa., 1911-14, prof., 1914-19; prof. botany U. Mich. 1919-42, prof. emeritus, 1942—. Editor statis. div. U.S. Food Adminstrn., 1918. Chmn. Ann Arbor Com. to Defend America, 1940-44. Asso. editor Genetics. Fellow Am. Acad. Arts and Scis.; mem. Am. Philso. Soc. (sec. 1918-19), Bot. Soc. America, Am. Soc. Naturalists (sec., 1913-19, pres 1921), Am. Genetic Assn., A.A.A.S., Mich. Acad. Science, N.E. Bot. Club, Am. Assn. U. Profs.; Loyal Legion, Club: Chicago Literary. Co-author: Principles of Botany, 1906; Laboratory and Field Manual of Botany (with Joseph Y. Bergen), 1907. Also writer of many papers on plant cytology and plant genetics. Home: 2814 S.W. Labbe Av., Portland 1, Ore. Died Mar. 13, 1957.

DAVIS, CARL BRADEN, surgeon; b. Chgo., Oct. 9, 1877; s. Dr. Charles Gilbert and Isabella (Braden) D.; A.B., U. Chgo., 1900; M.D., Rush Med. Coll., 1903; m. Elsie Florence Booth, Dec. 10, 1907 (died June 5, 1933); m. 2d, Virginia Winslow Smith, Feb. 1945. Practiced in Chgo., 1903—; clin. prof. surgery Rush Med. Coll.; attending surgeon Presbyn. Hosp. Fellow A.C.S., Am. Surg. Assn., Soc. Clin. Surgery; mem. A.M.A., Chgo. Med. Soc. Clubs: University, Glenview Country. Home: 156 Chestnut St., Winnetka, Ill. Office: Peoples Gas Bldg., Chgo. Died Dec. 11, 1950.

DAVIS, CHARLES ALBERT, geologist; b. Portsmouth, N.H., Sept. 29, 1861; s. Lewis Gilman and Cyrena Frances (Peirce) D.; A.B., Bowdoin, 1886, A.M., 1889; Cornell Sch. of Forestry, 1 semester, 1900-01; Ph.D., U. of Mich., 1905; m. Frances Margaret Humphreys, Aug. 26, 1886. Teacher natural science, Hyde Park (Ill.) High Sch., 1886-87; prof. natural science, 1887-96, prof. biology and geology, 1896-1900, Alma (Mich.) Coll.; instr. forestry, 1900-05, curator Herbarium, 1905-08, U. of Mich.; peat expert U.S. Geol. Survey, 1907-10, Bur. of Mines, Washington, July 1, 1910-12; fuel technologist, 1912-14, geolgoist, 1914—. Field agent, Mich. Geol. Survey 1896-1907; instr. geology, U. of Mich. Summer School, 1900, 1901; field asst., U.S., Geol. Survey, 1904. Editor Jour. of Am. Peat Soc., 1907—. Republican. Conglist. Fellow Geol. Soc. America, A.A.A.S. Died Apr. 9, 1916.

DAVIS, CHARLES MOLER, ret. geographer, educator; b. Denver, Dec. 11, 1900; s. Charles Moler and Margaret Bigger (Porter) D.; A.B., U. Mich., 1925, A.M., 1926, Ph.D., 1935; m. Margaret Beal, Oct. 31, 1931. Instr. in geography, U. Mich., 1931-38, asst. prof., 1938-42, asso. prof., 1945-49, prof., 1949-71, prof. emeritus, 1971-72, chmn. dept. geography, 1956-66. Vis. prof. U. Cal. at Los Angeles, summer 1947, U. Tex., summer 1951, also U. Wash., summer 1963; Fulbright research scholar, Australia, 1952; geographer, Inst. for Fisheries Research, 1931-32; asst. land negotiator, U.S. Biol. Survey, 1935; Carnegie vis. prof. U. Hawaii, 1962; sect. organizer 10th Pacific Science Congress, Honolulu, 1961; geographer U.S. Geol. Survey, 1966-67, mem. NRC Com. on Remote Sensing Adv., 1966-72; dir. Inst. on Remote Sensing for Geographers. Served from lt. comdr. to capt., USNR, 1942-60; plans officer, Spl. Air Task Force, U.S. Fleet, 1943-44; mem. acad. library adv. bd. USAF Acad., 1958. Chmn. com. on geog. field techniques NRC, 1949-53; mem. com. adv. to geog. br. Office of Naval Research, 1949-51. Recipient Carnegie Corp. grant-in-aid, 1939-40. Mem. Assn. of Am. Geographers (del. to Nat. Acad. Science-NRC 1959-62), Mich. Acad. Sci., Phi Kappa Phi, Phi Sigma, Chi Gamma Phi, Delta Tau Delta. Club: University (Ann Arbor). Contbr. articles on geog. subjects to profl. mags. Home: Ann Arbor MI Died Nov. 26, 1972.

DAVIS, DAVID JOHN, pathologist, coll. dean emeritus; b. Racine, Wis., Aug. 9, 1875; s. David W. and Catherine (Jones) D.; B.S., U. Wis., 1893; M.D., Rush Med. Coll., 1904; Ph.D., U. Chgo., 1905; studied univs. of Vienna and Freiburg; m. Myra H. Jones, July 17, 1908— children—Dorland Jones, Edward David. Practiced in Chgo., 1904—; prof. pathology U. Ill., 1914-43, 1943—. dean emeritus, 1943—. dirs. Chgo. Municipal Tb. 1946; Dir. Chgo. Inst. Medicine. Mem. A.M.A., Ill. Med. Soc. (permanent historian 1946). Soc. Am. Bacteriologist, Am. Assn. Pathologists and Bacteriologist, Am. Assn. Pathologists and Bacteriologist, Chgo. Pathol Soc., Sigma Xi, Phi Beta Kappa, Alpha Omega Alpha. Republican. Conglist. Clubs: Univeristy, Crystal Downs. Contbr. about 150 papers, chiefly in Jour. Infectious Disease and Jour. A.M.A., on infection with influenza bacilli, streptococci, sporotricha and med. edn. Home: 721 Elmwood Av., Wilmette, Ill. Died Dec. 20, 1954.

DAVIS, D(ELBERT) DWIGHT, zooloigst; b. Rockford, Ill., Dec. 30, 1908; s. James Walter and Ada Iron (Fager) D.; B.S., North Central Coll., 1930, D.Sc., 1963; postgrad. U. Chgo., 1941-42; m. Charlotte M. Fraley, Jan. 3, 1931. Curator div. vertebrate anatomy Chgo. Natural Hist. Museum since 1941; lecturer zoology University of Chicago since 1950; head of dept. zoology U. of Malaya, 1963-64; member Field Museum Texas Expedition, 1937, Field Museum-Mandel Caribbean Expedition, 1940, Bornean Zoological Expedition, North Borneo, 1950, Malaya Zoological Expedition, 1958-59; visiting professor paleontology Cal. Inst. Technology, 1954. Mem. Am. Soc. Mammalogists, Am. Society Ichthyologists and Herpetologists, Soc. Study Evolution, Soc. Vertebrate Paleontology, Am. Soc. Zoologists. Author: Field Book of Snakes of the United States and Canada, 1941 (with K. P. Schmidt); The Giant Panda, 1964; articles tech. jours. Mng. editor: Evolution, 1961. Home: 22102 Millard Av., Richton Park, Ill. 60471. Office: Chicago Natural History Museum, Chgo. 60605. Died Feb. 6, 1965.

DAVIS, EDWIN HAMILTON, physician, archeologist; b. Hillsboro, O., Jan. 22, 1811; s. Henry and Avis (Slocum) D.; grad. Kenyon Coll., 1833, Cincinnati Med. Coll., 1838; m. Lucy Woodbridge, 1841, 9 children including John Woodbrirdge. Prof. materia medica and therapeutics N.Y. Med. Coll., 1850-60; surveyed and escribed (in collaboration with E.G. Squire) 100 of the more important earthworks of the Mound Builders, So. Ohio; compiled findings in the Ancient Monuments of the Mississippi Valley (1st work published by Smithsonian Instn.; continues to be a standard on the subject); noted for his collections of cultural objects of the Mound Builders. Died N.Y.C., May 15, 1888.

DAVIS, GEORGE H., engineer; b. Oswego, N.Y., 1863; son Samuel A. and Esther T. (Parks) D.; grad. Oswego State Teachers College, 1885; M.E., Cornell U., 1892; m. Katherine McGrath, 1898; children—Philip McGranth, Putnam. Design, constrn. and management mills and pub. utilities, Baltimore and New York, 1892-95; partner and dir. Ford, Bacon & Davis, Inc., New Orleans, New York and San Francisco, 1895-1941; engaged with partners in design, constrn. and management various pub. utilities, railways and indsl. plants, New Orleans, San Francisco and other southern and Western cities, 1895-1907, including resurveys and reconstruction of San Francisco because of the earthquake and fire of 1906; vice-pres. and mgr. Am. Cities Railway & Light Co., 1907-11 pres. Am. Cities Co., 1911-13; design, constrn. and reconstruction various terminals, railways, warehoures, harbor structures, etc., New Orleans, Mobile and Galveston, 1914-18; preparation of a report to the secretary of war on the strategic seclusion and mil. strength of the New Orleans area for airplane, army and naval base and operating terminals, 1918; Supervision of production Platt Iron Works, Dayton O., of army tanks for A.E.F., 1918; supervision of construction New Orleans Army Supply Base, 1918-19; dir. Atlantic Aircraft Corp., 1925-27, Fokker Aircraft Corp., 1927-30; active in development and manufacture of airplane engines; general engineering practice and capital management since 1921. Member American Society Mech. Engrs., American Society Civil Engrs., Louisiana Engring. Soc. Clubs: University, Engineers', Cornell City Midday, Boston Club (New Orleans). Home: 6 Guion Lane Larchmont N.Y. Office: 20 Exchange Pl., N.Y.C. 5. Died May. 1957.

DAVIS, HARVEY NATHANIEL, mech. engr.; b. Providence, R.I., June 6, 1881; s. Nathaniel French and Lydia Martin (Bellows) D.; A. B., Brown U., 1901, M.A., 1902; A.M., Harvard, 1903, Ph.D., 1906; Sc.D., Brown U., 1928, Northeastern Univ., 1938, Columbia Univ., 1940; LL.D., Rutgers, 1928; E.D., Stevens Institute of Technology, 1948; D.Eng., New York University, 1936, Rose Polytechnic Institute, 1938, Rensselaer Polytechnic Institute, 1949; m.Suzanne C. Haskell June 28, 1911 (died Jan. 1, 1919); children—Suzanne, Louisa Frederika; m. 2d., Alice M. Rohde, Sept. 20, 1920 (died Aug. 22, 1933); children—Marian, Nathaniel,; m.3d, Helen Clarkson Miller Feb. 8, 1935. Instr. mathematics, Brown Univ., 1901-02; inst. physics, 1904-10, asst.prof., 1910-19; prof. mech. engring., 1919-28, Harvard; became pres. Stevens Inst. Tech., 1928, retired, 1951. Dir. Office Production Research and Development of War Production Bd. Nov. 1942-June 1944. Engr. in turbine dept., Gen Electric Co., 1917-18; aeronautical mech. engr. A.S., 1918-22; cons. engr. Franklin Ry. Supply Co., 1920-27, United States Bureau of Mines, 1921-25, also Air Reduction Company, 1922-25. Regent Smithsonian Inst. Since 1938; trustee Blair Acad. Stevens-Hoboken Acad. Fellow Am.Acad. Arts and Sciences, American Phys. Society, A.A.A.S., American Soc. M.E. (pres. 1937-38); mem. Am. Math. Soc. (life), Franklin Inst. (hon.), The Inst. of M.E.; (London), Am. Philos. Soc., Newcomen Soc., Washington Acad. Sciences, American Association for Adult Education also Phi Beta Kappa, Sigma Xi, Tau Beta Pi, Delta Phi. Conglist. Clubs: Cosmos (Washington), Brown University (President, 1935), Harvard, Century (New York). Author: (with L. S. Marks) Steam Tables and Diagrams, 1908; with N. Henry Black Practical Physics for High Schools, 1913; Elementary Practical Physics, 1938. Home: Hoxie House, Castle Point, Hoboken, N.J. Died Dec. 3, 1952.

DAVIS, HERBERT SPENCER, zoologist; b. Oneida, N.Y., Mar. 28, 1875; s. Edson Warburton and Anna Maria (Griswold) D.; Ph.B., Wesleyan U., Conn., 1899; Ph.D., Harvard, 1907; m. Raynor Nicolson Harris, Aug. 12, 1912; 1 dau., Muriel Griswold. Instr. zoology, 1901-04, asst. prof., 1904-06, Wash. State Coll.; prof. zoology, U. of Fla., 1907-22; pathologist U.S. Bur. Fisheries since 1922. in charge aquicultural investigations. Cons. Oregon Game Commn., 1945-47; retired Sept. 1947. Mem. A.A.A.S., Am. Soc. Zoologists, Ma. Micros. Soc., Alpha Delta Phi. Congregationalist. Home: Claiborne MD

DAVIS, HERMAN S(TEARNS), astronomer; b. Milford, Del., Aug. 6, 1868; s. Thomas Josiah and Mary Jane (Potter) D.; prep. edn., Wilmington Conf. Acad., Dover, Del., and Phillips Acad., Andover, Mass.; A.B., cum laude, Princeton, 1892, grad. study, 1892-93, A.M., 1912; Univ. fellow in astronomy, Columbia, 1893-95, A.M., 1894, Ph.D., 1895; m. Coreita Register Hoffecker, May 24, 1894; 1 son, Herman Stearns. Asst. astronomer, U.S. eclipse expdn. to W. Africa, 1889-90; teacher of astronomy and geodesy, Columbia, 1895-99; lecturer, Bd. of Edn., N.Y. City, 1896-99, 1905-07; asst. U.S. Coast and Geodetic Survey, 1900; dir. Internat. Latitude Observatory, Gaithersburg, Md., 1900-05; cons. engr. and auditor, N.Y. City and Pittsburgh, Pa., 1905-10; sec. to pres. Gulf Refining Co., Pittsburgh, 1910-20; sec.-treas. Indian River Fruit & Vegetable Co., Indian River Grove & Farming Co., Dupont Land Co., Indian River Corp., Matson Oil Co. Astronomer Carnegie Instn., Nat. Acad. Sciences. Am. editor Astronomischer Jahresbericht, 1900-14; dir. New Reduction of Piazzi's Star Catalog, 1895—. Republican. Methodist. Mason. Author: Glossary to Homer's Iliad, 1888; Parallax of Eta Cassiopeiae, 1895; Catalogue of 62 Stars about Eta Cassipelae, 1895; Computation Forms for the Use of Classes in Practical Astronomy, 1897; An Abbreviated Form for Least Square Solutions, 1898; Private Cipher-Book, 1911; Dictionary of Telegraphic Code-Words, 1912. Home: Pittsburgh, Pa. Died May 23, 1933.

DAVIS, JAMES SHERMAN, educator; b. Troy, Ala., Feb. 16, 1918; s. John Sherman and Sally (Simpson) D.; B.S., Birmingham-So. Coll., 1941; M.A., U. Wis. 1948, Ph.D., 1952; m. Mary Lou Overall Mar. 14, 1941; children—Beatrice Anne, James Sherman. Research asst. zoology U. Wis., 1946-51; mem. faculty U. Tenn. Med. Units, Memphis, 1952-69, prof. anatomy, 1963-69, asst. dean basic med. scis., 1965-68, asso. dean, 1968-69; head research career sect. Nat. Inst. Gen. Medicine (spl. cons. to dir. 1965-66), NIH, 1964-65. Served to 1st lt. USAAF, 1942-45. Decorated

Air medal. Mem. Am. Assn. Anatomists, Endocrine Soc., Am. Soc. Zoologists, Am. Assn. Med. Colls., So. Soc. Anatomists, Sigma Xi. Home: Memphis TN Died Apr. 29, 1969.

DAVIS, JESS HARRISON, coll. pres.; b. Columbus, O., July 29, 1906; s. Willard Ellsworth and Winifred (Jones) D.; B.S., Ohio State U., 1928. M.S., 1933, D.Sc., 1956, St. Lawrence U., 1949; D.Eng., Clarkson Coll. Tech., 1951, Newark Coll. Engring., 1963; LL.D., Rutgers, 1954; m. Dorothy Carrigan, 1928 (dec. 1969); 1 dau., Sarah Louise (Mrs. Edward S. Boslow, Jr.); m. 2d, Mary Grattan Roper, July 1970. Student engr., asst. to maintenance supt. Ohio Bell Telephone Co., Columbus, 1928-29; mech. engr. Atmospheric Nitrogen Corp., Hopewell, Va., 1929; instr. mech. engring. Clarkson Coll., Potsdam, N.Y., 1929-31, asst. prof., 1931-36, asso. prof., 1936-40, prof. heat power and exptl. engring., 1947, pres. 1948; pres. Stevens Inst. Tech., Hoboken, N.J., 1951-72; prof., chmn. dept. mech. engring Speed. Sci. Sch., U. Louisville, 1944-46; mech. engr. Ala. Power Co., 1936, Am. Locomotive Co., 1937, Central N.Y. Power Co., 1940, Foster Wheeler Corp., 1941; cons. engr. Hydraulic Controls, Inc., 1942, N.Y. Air Brake Co., 1943-45, D.M. McBean, 1945-47, DeWolfe Furnace Corp., 1945-47; dir. Philip Morris, Inc., Pub. Service Electric & Gas Co., Nat. Biscuit Co., Prudential Ins. Co. Am., 1st Jersey Nat. Bank, Carrier Corp., Bethlehem Steel Corp., Pennwalt Corp. Commr., Port of N.Y. Authority, 1952-59. Registered Profl. engr., N.J., N.Y., Ky. Mem. Engrs. Council Profl. Devel., Am. Soc. M.E.s (bd. tech. 1954, Richards award 1952), Am. Soc. for Engring Edn., Am. Soc. Testing and Materials, Ky. Soc. Profl. Engrs., Louisville Adv. Com. on Smoke Abatement (chmn. 1944-45), Sigma Xi, Tau Beta Pi, Pi Mu Epsilon. Clubs: University, Engineers (N.Y.C.); Saucon Valley Country (Bethlehem, Pa.). Home: Hoboken NJ Died Sept. 17, 1972; buried Charlottesville VA

DAVIS, JOHN ROSE WILSON, civil engr.; b. Phoenixville, Pa., Oct. 26, 1868; s. Thompson and Annie Supplee (Rose) D.; C.E., Lehigh U., 1891; unmarried. Began as rodman N.Y., L.E. & W. R. R., 1891; asst. supervisor same Apr.-Dec., 1892, asst. engr., 1892-98; div. engr. Chicago & Erie R.R., at Huntington, Ind., 1898-1900; engr. maintenance of way, Eire R.R., at Jersey City, N.J., 190001; same, C. & A. Ry., at Bloomington, Ill., Jan.-Nov., 1901; engr. maintenance of way, Erie R.R., at Jersey City, 1900-01; same, C. & A. Ry., at Bloomington, Ill., Jan.-Nov., 1901; engr. maintenance of way, Erie R.R., at Jersey City, 1901-03; with Gt. Northern Ry. since Sept. 1, 1903, chief engr. since 1925. Mem. Am. Soc. C.E., Am. Ry. Engring. Assn. Republican. Presbyn. Address: Great Northern Ry. St. Paul, Minn.

DAVIS, JOHN WILLIAMS, engr.; b. Petersburg, Va., Nov. 21, 1887; s. Richard Beale and Annie Warwick (Hall) D.; prep. edn., Petersburg Acad., 1897-1904; Randolph Macon Coll., Ashland, Va., 1904-06; M.E., Cornell U., 1910; M.S., U. of Ill., 1917; m. Elizabeth Grimes Walker, Oct. 22, 1921; children-John Williams, Elizabeth Walker, Timothy Pickering. Instructor in elec. engring., Harvard U., 1910-11, Vanderbilt, 1912-13, Stanford, 1913-14, Univ. of Ill., 1914-17; also with various engring. firms for short periods, 1910-17; research in helium gas, U.S. Bur. Mines (inventor process for separation of helium from natural gas), 1919-25; head of development div., later head of tech. dept. Atmospheric Nitrogen Corp., Syracuse, N.Y., and Hopewell, Va., 1925-29; has been cons. engr., Atmospheric Nitrogen Corp. and The Solvay Process Co., 1929— (inventor of improvements in processes for nitrogen fixation). Mem. commn. of Toronto, Can., on establishment of schs. of mil. aeronautics in U.S., 1917; asst. in establishment of sch. of mil. aeronatuics at U. of Ill., 1917; adj. Flying Dept., U.S.A., Kelly Field, San Antonio, Tex., later asst. to exec. officer U.S. Air Service, Washington, D.C., and later in charge helium work for Air Service, World War; reserve mil. aviator, capt. Air Service Reserve, Democrat. Home: Petersburg, Va. Died Oct. 4, 1938.

DAVIS, JOHN WOODBRIDGE, civil engr.; b. New York, Aug. 19, 1854; s. Dr. Edwin Hamilton and Lucy (Woodbridge) D.; C.E., Columbia School of Mines, 1878 (Ph.D., 1880); began practice as civ. engr., New York. Devised plan for securing life lines ashore from ships by means of kites; in April, 1893, with cooperation of U.S. Govt., sent out a stout life line, dragged by a large steerable kite, from Brenton Reef lightship to Brenton's Point, a tongue of land 3,141 miles distant. Author: Dynamics of the Sun, 1891. Died 1902.

DAVIS, JOSEPH BAKER, engr.; b. Westport, Mass., July 31, 1845; s. Ebenezer Hawthaway and Mehitabel C. (Gifford) D.; C.E., U. of Mich., 1868; m. Mary H. Baldwin, July 10, 1872. Asst. prof. civ. engring., 1872-91, prof. geodesy and surveying, 1891-1910, asso. dean dept. engring., 1904-07, U. of Mich.,; chief engr. St. Clair Flats Survey, Mich., 1899-1902. Retired, 1910. Home: Dexter, Mich. Died Mar. 9, 1920.

DAVIS, JOSEPH PHINEAS, engr.; b. Northboro, Mass., Apr. 15, 1837; s. William E. and Almira L. (Sherman) D.; C.E., Rensselaer Poly. Inst., 1856; unmarried. Asst. engr. on constrn. of Brooklyn water wks., 1856-61 and 1865; topog. engr., Govt. Peru, S.A., 1861-65; chief engr. Brooklyn park commrs., 1866; prin. asst. engr. on constrn. St. Louis water works, 1867-69; chief engr. on constrn. Lowell (Mass.) water works, 1870-71; chief engr. Boston Water Bd., 1872; city engr., Boston, 1873-80; chief engr. Am. Bell Telephone Co. and its successor, Am. Telephone & Telegraph Co., 1880-1905; cons. engr. Croton Aqueduct Commrs., 1884-86, Mass. State Bd. Health, 1886-1904, Met. Water Bd., Mass., 1895-1907, Met. Sewerage Commrs., Mass., 1898. V.p. and gen. mgr. Met. Telephone Co., New York, 1880-86; pres. Hudson River Telephone Co., 1889-95, Westchester Telephone Co., 1890-93. Home: Yonkers, N.Y. Died Mar. 31, 1917.

DAVIS, JOSEPH SMITH, electronics engr.; b. Balt., July 15, 1923; s. Joseph S. and Theresa (Mueller) D.; student U. Balt., 1941-42, Johns Hopkins, 1948-53, U. Cin., 1962-64, Miami U., 1964-65; m. Dorothy Gough Fiege, Feb. 28, 1942; children—Cheryl D., Kevin B. Asst. foreman Bethlehem Fairfield Shipyard, Balt., 1942-43; supr. Bendix Radio, Towson, Md., 1948-56; product supr. Whirlpool Corp., Marion and Hamilton, O., 1956-62; sr. engr. Aeronca Mfg. Corp., Middletown, O., 1962-65; project supr. Access Corp., Cin., 1965-67; project supr. Philco-Ford Corp., Connersville, Ind., 1967-68. Served with AUS, 1943-46. Registered profl. engr. Ohio. Mem. I.E.E.E., Instrument Soc. Am., Ohio Soc. Profl. Engrs. (chpt. dir. 1965). Presbyn. Home: Hamilton OH Died May 18, 1969; buried Parkwood Cemetery, Baltimore MD

DAVIS, NATHAN SMITH, M.D.; b. Greene, N.Y., Jan. 9, 1817; s. Dow and Eleanor Smith D.; ed. common school and Cazenovia Sem.; grad. Coll. Phys. & Surg., Fairfield, N.Y., 1837; (A.M., Northwestern; LL.D., Ill. Wesleyan); m. Anna Maria Parker, Mar. 1838. Practiced medicine at Vienna and Binghamton, N.Y., and 1847-49, at New York; from 1849 at Chicago. Lecturer, Coll. Phys. & Surg., New York, 1848; prof. Rush Med. Coll., Chicago, 1849-59; one of founders, 1859, of Chicago Med. Coll. (now med. dept. Northwestern U.); prof. there for 30 yrs. and dean of faculty until 1898, resigned. Was editor of The Annalist, New York; afterward of Chicago Med. Journal, and later of Chicago Med. Examiner; 6 yrs. editor of Journal of the A.M.A. One of founders of Mercy Hosp., and one of its physicians over 40 yrs.; a founder and trustee Northwestern Univ. Union Coll. of Law (prof. med. jurisprudence), and Washingtonian Home for Reformation of Inebriates. Author: Principles and Practice of Medicine; Medical Education and Reform. Home: Chicago, Ill. Died 1904.

DAVIS, NELSON FITHIAN, biologist; b. Seeley, N.J., Aug. 10, 1872; s. George D. and Frances (Moore) D.; Sc.B., Bucknell U., Lewisburg, Pa., 1895, Sc.M., 1896, Sc.D., 1903; student Marine Biol. Lab., Cold Spring Harbor, L.I., N.Y., summers, 1895, 96; m. Nellie Taylor, 1899 (died 1904); children—Nelson Fithian, Frances Moore; m. 2d, Ella Marion Briggs, 1905. With biol. dept. Bucknell U., 1898—, prof. biology and head of dept., 1910—; instr. biology, Marine Biol. Lab., Cold Spring Harbor, summers, 1898-1903; in charge zoölogy, U. of Vt. Summer Sch., 1914. Republican Presbyn. Mason. Home: Lewisburg, Pa. Died Nov. 11, 1939.

DAVIS, PAUL ARTHUR, physician; b. Chillicothe, O., Dec. 8, 1889; s. Robert W. and Minerva A. (Tomlinson) D.; A.B., Ohio State, 1911, A.M., 1915; A.M., Univ. of Chicago, 1915; M.D., Ohio State, 1916; m. Clarie T. Russell, Dec. 23, 1939. Instr. in chemistry, Med. Coll., Ohio State, 1911-16; interne Children's and Protestant Hosps., Columbus, O., 1916-17; asst. med. dir. Goodyear Hosp., Akron, O., 1917-40; mem. staff City Hosp., Akron, O., 1924-47, pvt. practice, 1920-47; med. dir. Akron Standard Mold Co. since 1942; med. cons. Gen. Tire & Rubber Co., 1939—; med. dir. Pitts. Plate Glass Co., Akron Div.; indsl. toxicologist and dir. Industrial Hygiene Labs., 1940—; regional cons. Occupational Health Inst.; dist. counselor Industrial Medical Assn. Mem. Ohio State Med. Board Reviews since 1942; mem. pres. com., Employment Physically Handicapped; mem. Gov.'s Com. on Rehabilitation, 1954; chmn. evaluation com. Mayor's Committee Handicapped. Served as post surgeon, flight surgeon, U.S. Army, 1917, World War I. Diplomate Bd. Preventive Medicine. Fellow Am. Public Health Assn., Am. Assn. Indsl. Phys. and Surgs.; mem. Am. Coll. Preventive Medicine Royal Health Soc. England, A.M.A. (chmn. sect. on practice gen. medicine, 1946-47; House Delegates), Assn. American Phys. and Surgs. of Summit Co. (past pres., mem. bd. dirs.), Am. Assn. Gen. Practitioners (pres. 1944-49 chmn. bd. dirs. 1949), Am. Acad. of Nutrition, Ohio State Med. Soc. (pres. elect, 1952; councilor 6th dist.), Summit Co. Med. Soc. (pres. 1946—), Am. Rheumatism Assn., Am. Acad. Gen. Practitioners (chmn. bd., 1949). Tuberculosis and Health Assn. (chmn. indsl. med. sect.), Phi Rho Sigma, Alpha Chi Sigma, Acacia, Phi Lambda Upsilon, Sigma Xi. Republican. Mason. (32 deg., Shriner). Club: Physicians of Akron (past pres.). Contbr. articles on industrial medicine and toxicology to various med. jours. and trade and safety pubs. Home: 1436 Delia Av., Akron 2. Office: 633 E. Market St., Akron 4, O. Died Aug. 1967.

DAVIS, REUBEN NELSON, museum dir.; b. Lemon, Pa., Apr. 13, 1858; s. Charles R. and Julia A. (Sheldon) D.; grad. Wyoming Sem., Kingston, Pa., 1880; Ph.B., Ill. Wesleyan U., 1902; m. Sarah M. Evans 1883; children—Harold E., Jennie E., Catherine. Formerly teacher high schs. and Y.M.C.A.; curator Everhart Mus., Scranton, Pa., 1912-24, dir., 1924—. Conducted nat. history expdn. to Panama, 1921. Republican. Presbyn. Mason. Author: Butterfies of Lackawanna County, Pa., 1914; The Nature of Gravitation, 1931. Home: Dunmore, Pa. Died Jan. 1934.

DAVIS, ROYALL OSCAR EUGENE, chemist; b. at Newberry, S.C., July 11, 1880; s. of William Alexander and Sarah Isabelle (Payne) D.; Ph.B., U. of N.C., 1901; Ph.D., 1903; student University of Leipzig, 1904; m. Birdie Pritchard, July 26, 1905. Inst. chemistry, U. of N.C., 1903-09, asso. prof. 1909; soil physicist, 1910-27, U.S. Department of Agr., Washington; in charge soil water investigations, same, 1912-13, in charge soil physics investigations, 1915-26, sr. chemist fertilizer and fixed nitrogen investigations, 1927-29, in charge nitrogenous fertilizer materials, fertilizer investigations, 1930-42; asst. head soil, fertilizer investigations, 1942-45; asst. Div. Soils, Fertilizer and Investigations since 1944. Mem. Am. Chem. Soc., A.A.A.S., Soc. Agronomy, Internat. Soc. Soil Science. Democrat. Methodist. Mason. Club: Cosmos. Contbr. numerous articles on soils, nitrogen, fertilizers and related subjects; asst. editor Chemical Abstracts. Home: 7130 Alaska Av. N.W., Washington. Died Oct. 30, 1949; buried at Chapel Hill, N.C.

DAVIS, TENNEY LOMBARD, chemist; b. Somerville, Mass., Jan. 7, 1890; s. Thomas Lombard and Martha W. (Tenney) D.; student, Dartmouth Coll., 1907-08; B.S., Mass. Inst. Tech., 1910; M.S., Harvard, 1914, Ph.D., 1917; U. Calif., 1916-17; m. Dorothy Theresa Munch, Aug. 28, 1923. Austin teaching fellow, Harvard, 1913-16; instr. organic chem., Mass. Inst. Tech., 1919-20, asst. prof., 1920-26, asso. prof., 1926-38, prof., 1938-42, prof. emeritus since 1942; summer lecturer Western Reserve Univ., 1931, 1938; sect. chairman National Defense Research Committee, June 1940-April 1941; director of scientific research and development, National Fireworks, Inc. since 1942; trustee South Scituate Savings Bank. First lt. Ordnance Dept., U.S. Army, 1917-19. Mem. Am. Chem. Soc. (chmn. history chem. div., 1932-29), History of Science Soc. (v.p. 1941), A.A.A.S., Am. Acad. Arts and Sciences (corr. sec. 1930-37, rec. sec. 1937-38), corr. mem. Royal Soc. Bohemia (Prague, Czechoslovakia), Newcomen Soc. Editor-in-chief Chymia. Associate editor, Journal of Chemical Education, Isis, Tech. Review. Author: The Chemistry of Powder and Explosives. Contbr. various articles on chemical subjects, history of chemistry, Chinese alchemy. Home: Central St., Norwell, Mass. Died Jan. 25, 1949.

DAVIS, WATSON, editor; b. Washington, Apr. 29, 1896; s. Allan and Maud (Watson) D.; B.S. in Civil Engring., George Washington U., 1918; C.E., 1920, D.Sc., 1959; m. Helen Augusta Miles, Dec. 6, 1919 (dec.); children—Charlotte, Miles; m. 2d, Marion Shaw Mooney, Nov. 21, 1958. Asst. engr., physicist U.S. Bureau Standards, 1917-21; sci. editor Washington Herald, 1920-22; mng. editor Sci. Service, 1921—, dir., 1933—; editor Sci. News Letter, 1922—, THINGS of sci., 1940—, Chemistry (mag.), 1944-62; CBS radio program, 1930-59; pres. Am. Documentation Inst., 1937-47. William L. Honnald lectr. Knox Coll., 1939. Chmn., U.S. delegation World Congress Documentation, 1937; mem. Nat. Inventors Council, 1940—; dir. Sci. Clubs Am., 1941—; dir. Westinghouse Sci. Talent Search, 1942—, Nat. Sci. Fair Internat., 1949—; emeritus mem. exec. bd. Nat. Child Research Center; chmn. Sci. Clubs Com., UNESCO, 1949, Popularization Sci. Conf., Madrid, 1955; mem. Sec. Navy's Adv. Bd. Ednl. Requirements, 1959-61; mem., chmn. Sec. Commerce's Patent Office Adv. Com., 1960-62; mem. Nat. Adv. Dental Research Council, 1949-53; trustee George Wash. U., 1949-61, Jackson Lab., 1949; mem. vis. com. Harvard Obs., 1941-54. Awarded Syracuse U. Journalism medal, 1944; Westinghouse Sci. Writing award, 1946; War-Navy certificate Appreciation, 1946; Phila. Sci. Council Award, 1951; Thomas Alva Edison Found. award, 1955, 56; Pioneer medal, Nat. Microfilm Assn., 1959; James T. Grady medal, Am. Chem. Soc., 1960. Registered profl. engr., D.C. Fellow Am. Inst., A.A.A.S.; mem. Overseas Writers, Congl. Press Gallery, White House Corr. Assn., Am. Soc. for Testing Materials, Am. Eugenics Soc., Am. Polar Soc., Am. Concrete Inst., Nat. Assn. Sci. Writers (founder mem.), Aviation Writer's Assn., Acad. Medicine Washington (pres. 1956-58), Population Soc. Am.; Brit. Assn. Advancement Sci., Assn. francaise pour l'avancement des scis., Hist. Soc., Newcomen Soc., Seismol. Soc. Am., Philos., Soc. Washington, Geol. Soc. Washington, Washington Soc. Engrs., Sigma Xi, Pi Delta Epsilon, Sigma Delta Chi. Clubs: Cosmos, Nat. Press, Torch, Harvard. Editor: Sci. Today, 1931; New World of Science Series, 1931; The Advance of Science, 1934; Atomic Bombing, 1950. Author: The Story of Copper, 1924; Science Picture Parade, 1940; From Now On, 1950; The Century of Science, 1963. Contbr. to mags. and engring. jours. Home: 3620 Garfield St. N.W., Washington 20007. Office: 1719 N St. N.W., Washington 20036. Died June 27, 1967.

DAVIS, WILLIAM MORRIS, geographer, geologist; b. Phila., Pa., Feb. 12, 1850; s. Edward M. and Maria (Mott) D.; S.B., Lawrence Scientific Sch. (Harvard), 1869, M.E., 1870; Sc.D., U. of Cape of Good Hope, 1905; Ph.D., U. of Greifswald, 1906; Ph.D., U. of Christiania, 1911; S.D., U. of Melbourne, 1914; m. Ellen B. Warner, Nov. 25, 1879 (died 1913); m. 2d, Mary M. Wyman, Dec. 12, 1914 (died 1923); m. 3d, Lucy L. Tennant, Aug. 13, 1928. Asst., Nat. Obs., Cordoba, Argentina, 1870-73; joined faculty Harvard U., 1876, prof. geology, 1899-1912 (emeritus). Fellow Am. Acad. Arts and Sciences A.A.A.S. Was decorated Chevalier Legion of Honor (France). Author: Elementary Meteorology, 1894; Physical Geography, 1898; Practical Exercises in Physical Geography, 1908. Gold medalist of Harvard Travellers Club, Am. Geol. Soc., Geog. Socs. of Phila. and Chicago, Acad. Natural Sciences, Phila., Royal Geol. Soc. London, Geog. Soc. Stockholm. Republican. Unitarian. Died Feb. 5, 1934.

DAVISON, ALBERT WATSON, cons. engr.; b. Alexandria, O., Apr. 24, 1888; s. Watson and Hester Ann (Beaumont) D.; student Doane Acad., Granville, O.; B.S., Denison U., 1910, D.Sc., 1950; M.S., Ohio State U., 1912; Ph.D., Cornell, 1914; D.Eng., Rensselaer Poly. Inst., 1942; m. Ida Corena MacDaniel, June 22, 1915; children—Frances Ann (Mrs. Stuart Sturges), Albert Watson, Fellow in chemistry Ohio State U., 1910-11, asst. in chemistry, 1911-12; same, Cornell U., 1913-14; asst. prof. phys. chemistry U. Cin., 1914-17; mgr. Virginia Haloid Co., N.Y.C., 1919-21; prof. phys. chemistry Rensselaer Poly. Inst., 1921-25, prof. chem. engring. and head dept., 1925-42; sci. dir. Owens-Corning "Fiberglas" Corp., Newark, Ohio, 1943-48, dir. research, 1949-53; cons. chem., engr. since 1953. Served as 1st lt. Ordnance Dept., U.S. Army, 1917-18, capt. Chem. Warfare Service, 1918-19. Trustee Denison U. Mem. Am. Chem. Soc., Am. Inst. Chem. Engrs., Am. Soc. for Engring. Edn., Rensselaer Soc. Engr., Am. Ceramic Soc., A.A.A.S., Am. Ordnance Assn., Sigma Xi, Phi Beta Kappa, Phi Lambda Upsilon, Sigma Chi. Alpha Chi Sigma. Republican. Presbyn. Mason Club: Chemists (N.Y.). Author: Laboratory Manual of Physical Chemistry (with Henry S. van Klooster, W. A. Bauer), 1941, Contbr. to chem. publs. Address: 1199 Moundview Av., Newark, O. Died Nov. 2, 1960; buried Alexandria, O.

DAVISON, GEORGE STEWART, civil engr.; b. Pittsburgh, Pa., Sept. 21, 1856; s. Edward and Isabel (Kennedy) D.; C.E., Rensselaer Poly. Inst., 1878; D.Sc., U. of Pittsburgh, 1926; Dr. Engring., Rensselaer, 1926; m. Clara Elizabeth Lape, May 19, 1881; 1 son, Allen Stewart. Began with engring. dept. Pa. Lines West, 1878; with U.S. Engring. Corps, 1879; with engring. dept. A.T.&S.F. Ry. and Pa. Lines West, 1880-82; chief engr. Pittsburgh Chartiers & Youghiogheny R.R., 1882, gen. supt., 1883-90; mem. Wilkins & Davison, 1890-1900; gen. mgr. Monoongahela and Pittsburgh and Birmingham Ry. Lones, Pittsburgh, 1900-02; president Pa. Water Co. since 1902; asst. to pres. subsidiary cons. of Gulf Oil Corp., 1905-11. In 1911 became pres. Gulf Refining Co. and other subsidiaries of Gulf Oil Corp., resigned, 1929; v.p. Green Bag Cement Company of West Va.; chairman of the board Pittsburgh Coke & Iron Company, Pittsburgh & Ohio Valley R.R., Green Bag Cement Company of Pa., Allegheny River Limestone Co.; dir. Bellefield Co., Schenley Hotel Co.; pres. bd. mgrs. Homewood Cemetery; trustee Rensselaer Poly. Inst.; pres. and dir. West Penn Hosp., Pittsburgh; mem. Bd. of Industrial Preparedness, 1916, Com. of Public Safety of Pa., oil sub-com. Nat. Council of Defense and Nat. Petroleum War Service Commn., World War. Mem. Am. Soc. C.E. (past-pres.), Am. Inst. Consulting Engrs. Soc. of Western Pa. (past-pres.), Delta Phi. Republican. Presbyterian. Clubs: Pittsburgh, Athletic, Duquesne (Pittsburgh). Home: Pittsburgh Athletic Assn. Office: Oliver Bldg., Pittsburgh, Pa. Died Oct. 3, 1942.

DAVISON, WILBURT CORNELL, pediatrician; b. Grand Rapids, Mich., Apr. 28, 1892; s. William L. (D.D.) and Mattie E. (Cornell) D.; A.B., Princeton, 1913; Sr. Demy (Rhodes scholar 1913-16), Magdalen Coll., Oxford, Eng., 1915-17; B.A., Oxford U., 1915, B.Sc., 1916, M.A., 1919; M.D., Johns Hopkins, 1917; D.Sc., Wake Forest Coll., 1932; LL.D., U. N.C., 1944, Duke, 1961; m. Atala Thayer Scudder, June 2, 1917; children—William Townsend, Atala Jane Scudder Levinthal, Alexander Thayer. Instr., asso. prof., acting head dept. pediatrics, asst. dean, Johns Hopkins Med. Sch., 1919-27; asso. pediatrician, acting pediatrician in charge, editor Bull. Johns Hopkins Hosp., 1919-27; dean, James D. Duke prof. pediatrics Duke Sch. Medicine, 1927-61; cons. Womack Army Hosp; mem. medico adv. bd. CARE; trustee Duke Endowment; v.p. bd. dirs. Doris Duke Found. Mem. div. med. scis. NRC, vice chmn. 1942-43; cons. office Surgeon Gen., U.S. Army; adv. group Armed Forces Med. Library; mem. com. on vets. med. problems; mem. com. atomic casualties NRC; mem. med. adv. com. N.C. Bd. Mental Health; mem. med. adv. panel Oak Ridge Inst. Nuclear Studies; mem. council chief cons. VA; mem. dean's com. Durham VA Hosp.; mem. N.C. gov.'s working com. Research Triangle Devel. Council, N.C. Nuclear Energy Adv. Com; dir. Playtex Park Research Inst.; med. adv. com. Research Found.; nat. adv. com. Chronic Disease and Health of Aged; trustee Ednl. Council Fgn. Med. Grad.; mem. Civilian Health and Med. Adv. Council; chmn. OSD Hosp. Planning Group. Served with AEC, 1914-15. France, Serbia; capt. M.C., U.S. Army AEF, 1917-19; served to col. AUS. Recipient Alvaranga prize, 1917. Master A.C.P.; mem. Am. Acad. Pediatrics, Am. Coll. Clin. Adminstrn. (hon.), Am. Pediatric Soc., Soc. for Pediatric Research, Am. Soc. Clin. Investigation, N.C. Pediatric Soc., Am. Acad. Gen. Practice (hon.), Assn. Pediatricians de Guatemala (hon.), Phi Beta Kappa, Sigma Xi, Omicron Delta Kappa, Alpha Omega Alpha (pres.). Democrat. Methodist. Clubs: Cosmos (Washington). Hope Valley Country, Roaring Gap Yacht. Author: Pediatric Notes, 1925; (with S.A. Waksman) Enzymes; 1926; The Compleat Pediatrician, 1934, 38, 40, 44, 46, 49, 57, 61. Contbr. articles to profl. jours. Home: Roaring Gap NC Died June 26, 1972; cremated.

DAVISSON, CLINTON JOSEPH, physicist; b. Bloomington, Ill., Oct. 22, 1881; s. Joseph and Mary Calvert) D.; B.S., U. of Chicago, 1908; Ph.D., Princeton Univ., 1911; D.Sc. (hon), Purdue Univ., 1937, Princeton, 1938; Dr. (hon.), Lyon, 1939, D.Sc., (hon.), Colby, 1940; m. Charlotte Sara Richardson Aug. 4, 1911; children—Clinton Owen Calvert, James Williams, , Elizabeth Mary Dixon, Richard Joseph. instr. in physics, Carnegie Inst. Tech., 1911-17; mem. tech. staff Bell Telephone labs. (formerly engineering dept. Western Electric Co.), 1917-46; visiting prof. of physics, U. of Va., 1947-49; member editorial board physical Review. Mem. Nat. Research Council. Became hon. life mem. N.Y. Acad. Sciences, 1942. Fellow A.A.A.S. (chmn. sect. B. 1933), Am. Phys. Soc., Optical Soc. America; mem. Nat. Acad. Scis., Am. Philos. Soc., Am. Acad. Arts and Scis., Franklin Inst., Am. Inst., Sigma Xi, Phi Beta Kappa. Awarded Comstock prize ($2,300), Nat. Acad. Sciences, 1928, for "most important research in electricity, magnetism and radiant energy made in N.A., during the past 5 years"; Elliot Cresson medal 1931; Hughes medal, Royal Soc. London, 1935; Nobel prize for physics, 1937; Alumni medal U. of Chicago, 1941. Discoverer (with Dr. L. H. Germer) of diffraction of electrons by crystals, 1927. Republican. Contbr. on scienfific subjects. Home: 2605 Jefferson Park Circle, Charlottesville, Va. Died Feb. 1, 1958.

DAWLEY, FRANK E., farm expert; b. Elbridge, N.Y., Sept. 10, 1863; s. William Walker and Charlotte A. (Lamson) D.; ed. Munro Collegiate Inst.; spl. work in chemistry and agr.; m. Carrie L. Barnes, June 16, 1891; children—Marian B., Laura A., Helen F., Katherine L., Lamson E., Dorothy J. Has devoted attention largely to scientific breeding of horses, cattle, sheep and poultry and the domestication of fur-bearing wild animals, in which is regarded as an authority; founder and owner of Dotshome Farms and Karakul Fur Sheep Farms. Awarded gold medal for alfalfa hay exhibit, San Francisco Expn., 1915. One of first to introduce pure Karakul sheep, producing Persian lamb fur, in America; organized Am. Karakul Fur Sheep Record Assn. Dir. N.Y. State Farmers' Insts., 1896-1908. Trustee Cornell U. Sec. Am. Cheviot Sheep Soc. 20 yrs. (awarded gold medal by world soc. for services to Cheviot breed); master of Onondaga Pomona Grange. N.Y. state master of Onondaga Pomona Grange. N.Y. state appraiser of animals, Dept. Agriculture and Markets, 1917-33. Republican. Home: Fayetteville, N.Y. Died June 13, 1936.

DAWSON, WILLIAM LEON, ornithologist; b. Lon, Ia., Feb. 20, 1873; s. William Edwy and Ada Eliza Sarah (Adams) D.; Washington U., 1887-90; A.B., Oberlin, 1897, A.M., 1903; B.D., Oberlin Theol. Sem., 1899; m. Frances Etta Ackerman, May 1, 1895; children—William Oberlin, Giles Edwin, Barbara Dorothy. Ordained Congl. ministry, 1899; pastor North Ch., Columbus, O., 1900-02; organizer Wheaton Pub. Co., Columbus, 1902. Occidental Pub. Co., Seattle, Wash., 1905. Birds of Calif. Pub. Co., 1911, Birds of Ohio Pub. Co., 1926, Birds of Fla. Pub. Co., 1927. Dir. Internat. Mus. Comparative Oölogy, Santa Barbara, Calif. Progressive. Author: The Birds of Ohio, 1903; The Birds of Washington (2 vols.), 1909; The Birds of California (4 vols.), 1923. Home: "Los Colibris," Mission Canyon, Santa Barbara, Calif. Died Apr. 30, 1928.

DAY, ARTHUR LOUIS, physicist; b. Brookfield, Mass., Oct. 30, 1869; s. Daniel P. and Fannie M. (Hobbs) D.; A.B., Yale, 1892, h.D., 1894; Sc.D., Groningen, 1914, Columbia, 1915, Princeton, 1918, U. Pa., 1938; m. 2d, Ruth Sarah Easling, Mar. 27, 1933. Instr. physics Yale, 1894-97; mem. sci. staff Physikalisch-Technische, Reichanstalt, Charlottenburg, Germany, 1897-1900; phys. geologist, U.S. Geol. Survey, 1900-06; dir. Geophys. Lab., Carnegie Instn. Washington, 1907-36, ret.; v.p. Corning Glass Works since 1919. Mem. Nat. Acad. Scis. (home sec. 1913-18, v.p. 1933-41); fellow Am. Acad. Arts and Scis.; mem. Washington Acad. Scis. (pres. 1924), Geol. Soc. Am. (pres. 1938), Am. Phys. Soc., Am. Chem. Soc., Geol. and Philos. socs. Washington, Am. Philos. Soc., Franklin Inst.; fgn. mem. Acad. dei Lincei (Rome), Turin Acad., Geol. Soc. London, Norwegian, U.S.S.R., Swedish acads. sci. In charge optical glass prodn. War Industries Bd., World War; mem. Commn. Inquiry on Pub. Service Personnel, 1934-35. Awarded John Scott medal, 1923; Roozeboom medal Royal Acad. Sci., Amsterdam, 1939; William Bowie medal Am. Geophys. Union, 1940; Wollaston medal Geol. Soc., London, 1941; Penrose medal Geol. Soc. Am. 1947. Clubs: University (N.Y.); Cosmos of Washington (pres. 1933). Home: 9113 Old Georgetown Rd., Bethesda 14, Md. Died Mar. 2, 1960; buried Rock Creek Cemetery, Washington.

DAY, BENJAMIN HENRY, printer, journalist; b. West Springfield, Mass., Apr. 10, 1810; s. Henry and Mary (Ely) D.; m. Eveline Shepherd, Sept. 13, 1831, 4 children. Started N.Y. Sun, 1st one-cent daily newspaper, 1833, the Sun surpassed the 17,000 circulation of the London Times, Aug. 28, 1835, sold the Sun in 1838 for $40,000; first to apply steam power to move printing machine in newspaper office, 1835; founder penny paper True Sun, 1840, monthly Brother Jonathan (reprinted British novels), 1842, publisher, 1842-62; ret. from business, 1862. Died N.Y.C., Dec. 21, 1889.

DAY, CHARLES, mech. engr.; b. at Phila., May 15, 1879; s. Richard H. Day; M.E., U. of Pa., 1899. Began engring. work in Phila., 1899; mem. Dodge & Day, specializing in engring. management and constrn. work, 1901-11; pres. Day & Zimmermann, 1911-26; chmn. bd. Day & Zimmermann, Inc., 1926—. Superintendent of installation of power plant machinery, Phila. Export Expn. 1899; asst. supt. and engr. works for Link Belt Engring. Co., 1900-01; dir. Pennsylvania R.R., Fidelity-Phila. Trust Co., United Gas Improvement Co. Has lectured before grad. Sch. of Business Adminstration, Harvard, and at Columbia; mem. civilan bd. apptd. by Sec. of Navy to investigate the efficiency of the navy yards; mem. Storage Com. of Gen. Munitions Bd. during World War; mem. Depot Bd. apptd. by Sec. of War; engring. advisor Col. House's Commn.; spl. mission to France for Sec. of War; trustee Emergency Fleet Corp. Mem. bd. mgrs. Franklin Inst.; trustee U. of Pa. Republican. Author: Industrial Plants, 1911. Home: Chestnut Hill, Pa. Died May 10, 1931.

DAY, CHARLES IVAN; b. Damariscotta, Me., Jan. 23, 1882; s. George Oliver and Charlotte M. (Hodgkins) D.; B.S., U. of Me., 1904; M.E. Cornell U., 1905; m. Isabelle Merry Chapman. Apr. 30, 1908; 1 son Laurence Chapman. Lieut. U.S. Revenue Cutter Service, 1905-07; chief engr. Fla. East Coast Hotel Co., 1907-13; v.p. and gen. mgr. Southern Utilities Corp., Jacksonville, Fla., 1913-19; with W. & L.E. Gruley Co., mfrs. of Engring. and surveying instruments, since 1919, gen. mgr., now pres.; pres. Am. Tool & Machine Co. since 1928; dir. Troy Prudential Assn. Mem. Troy C. of C. (pres. 1932). Trustee of Russell Sage College, Samaritan Hosp.; treas. of Kinckerbocker Playground Mem. Am. Soc. Mech. Engrs. Am. Soc. Civil Engrs., Alpha Tau Omega. Baptist. Mason. Clubs: Engineers (New York); Troy, Rotary, Country (Tory). Home: 7 Whitman Court. Office: 514 Fulton St., Troy, N.Y. Died June 22, 1950; buried Hillside Cemetery, Damariscotta, Me.

DAY, DAVID TALBOT, geologist; b. E. Rockport (Lakewood), O., Sept. 10, 1859; s. Willard Gibson and Caroline (Cathcart) D.; A.B., Johns Hopkins, 1881, Ph.D., 1884; m. Elizabeth Eliot Keeler, Mar. 17, 1886. Demonstrator chemistry, U. of Md., 1884-85; chief, mining and mineral resource div., 1886-1907, expert in charge petroleum investigations, U.S. Geol. Survey, 1907-14; cons. chemist U.S. Bureau Mines, Washington, 1914-20. Exhibitor Centennial Exhbn., 1876; spl. agt. U.S. Geol. Survey, 1883-85; in charge petroleum exhibits, Chicago Expn., 1893; dir. of mining, Cotton States and Internat. Expn., Atlanta, 1896; sec. Jury of Awards, Tenn. Centennial, 1897; dir. of mining, Trans-Miss. Expn., 1898; in charge mining, Buffalo Expn., 1901; hon. chief dept. of mines and metallurgy, St. Lewis Expn., 1904; hon. commr. of mining, Lewis and Clark Expn., Portland, Ore., 1905, Jamestown Expn., 1907; U.S. commr. Internat. Commn. for Petroleum Test, 1907-09; pres. fuel sect., Internat. Congress Applied Chemistry, 1912. Compiler of Mineral Resource of the United States, 1885-1904. Author: Day's Handbook of the Petroleum Industry. Home: Washington, D.C. Died Apr. 15, 1925.

DAY, JESSE ERWIN, chemistry; b. Yorkshire, O., Feb. 16, 1888; s. John and Mary Elizabeth (Smith) D.; grad. Miami U. Acad., 1907; A.B., Miami U., 1911; A.M., Ohio State U., 1913, Ph.D., 1917; m. Frances Elizabeth Leech, Aug. 26, 1913; children—Cora Elizabeth, Donald Erwin. Fellow in chemistry, Ohio State U., 1911-12, asst. in chemistry, 1912-15; instr. in chemistry, La. State U., 1915-17; instr. in same, O. State U., 1917-18, asst. prof., 1918-20; chemist Nat. Electric Light Assn., summer 1920; asst. prof. chemistry, U. of Wis., 1920-23; same, Ohio State U., Coloumbus, 1923, asso. prof., 1928; prof., 1932—. Active in Liberty Loan drives, World War, aslo for Community Chest and K.C. Methodist. Died Apr. 19, 1935.

DAY, MARY ANNA, botanist; b. Nelson, N.H., Oct. 12, 1852; d. Sewell and Hannah (Wilson) D.; ed. Lancaster Acad., 1869-70; unmarried, Teacher in public schools of Mass., 1871-80. Wrote: The Local Floras of New England, Rhodora, vols. 1, 2, 1899-1900; The Herbaria of New England, same, vol. 3, 1901. Home: 43 Langdon St., Cambridge, Mass.

DAY, WILLIAM CATHCART, prof. chemistry Swarthmore (Pa.) Coll.; b. Urbana, O., May 30, 1857; s. Willard G. and Caroline Cathcart Day; grad. Johns Hopkins Univ. (Ph.D.); spl. studies in chemistry and physics; m. Jane Leamy, Baltimore, Dec. 27, 1884. Articles in Am. Chemical Jour., Analysis of Chrome Iron Ore, Oxidation of Brom. Cymene; Action of Carbon Dioxide on Sodium Aluminate; Production of Asphalt from Organic Materials; also wrote a series of tech. reports for U.S. Geol. Survey. Deceased.

DAYTON, WILLIAM A(DAMS), forest ecologist; b. N.Y.C., Dec. 14, 1885; s. William Adams (M.D.) and Emma (Samson) D.; grad. Irving Inst. (now Irving sch. for Boys), Tarrytown, N.Y., 1901; B.A., Williams Coll., 1905, M.A., 1908; corr. courses, U. Chgo.; student U.S. Dept. Agr. Postgrad. Sch. m. Helen Rollins, Aug. 18, 1918; children—William Adams, 3d, Elva Samson (Mrs. Merrill F. Aukland), Orlo Hazen Variously employed as teacher, clerk, farmer, stenographer to 1906; Office of 2d Asst. Postmaster Gen., Washington, 1906-10; with U.S. Forest Service, 1910-55, beginning as plant ecologist, in charge range forest investigations, 1911-55, principal dendrologist, 1942-55, retired, now adviser. Rep. U.S. Dept. Agr. on Editorial Com. on Standardized Plant Names, 1939; chmn. tree name com. U.S. Forest Service; del. to Internat. Union Protection of Nature, Lake Success, N.Y., 1949; del. 7th International Bot. Congress, Stockholm, 1950; sec., chmn. 6th Internat. Grassland Congress, State Coll., Pa., 1952; mem. com. of Fullbright fellowships NRC, 1949-51. Recipient gold medal by. Mass. Hort. Soc., 1940; distinguished service gold medal, U.S. Dept. Agr., 1955. Fellow A.A.A.S. (mem. of council 1945); mem. Am. Forestry Assn., Am. Genetic Assn., Am. Fern Soc., Internat. Assn. Plant Taxonomy, Am. Nature Assn., Am. Soc. Plant Taxonomists, Biol. Soc. Washington, Bot. Soc. Am., Bot. Soc. Washington, Cal. Bot. Soc., Ecol. Soc. Am. (charter mem.; rep. on bd. govs. Am. Inst. Biol. Sci., 1948-58), Internat. Dendrology Union, Am. Soc. Range Mgt., N.E. Bot. Club, Soc. Am. Foresters (sec.-treas. Wash. sect. 1933-36; chmn. 1940-41) So. Appalachian Bot. Club, So. Cal. Acad. Sciences, Wildlife Soc. (charter Mem.), Torrey Botanical Blub, Washington Acad. Sci., (v.p. 1938-52). Baptist. Club: Cosmos (Washington). Author: Notes on National Forest Range Plants, Part 1, Grasses (with W. R. Chapline), 1914; Important Western Browse Plan plants, 1931; Range Plant Handbook (with others), 1937; Rev. Edition of Standardized Plant Names (with H. P. Kelsey and others), 1942. The Forest of Costa Rica (with others), 1943. Contbr. articles to jours. and bulletins. Home: 4818 24th St. N., Arlington, Va. Died Oct. 20, 1958; buried Nat. Meml. Park.

D'AZAMBUJA, LUCIEN HENRI, astronomer; b. Paris, France, Jan. 28, 1884; s. Antonio and Blanche (Gagniot) D'A.; D.Sc.; m. Marguerite Roumens, July 4, 1935. Joined Observatoire de Meudon, 1899, named titular astronomer, 1938; titular astronomer astrophysics sect. Observatoire de Paris. Laureat de l'Institut, 1915, 27, 35, 43, Societe Astronomique de France, 1932, 48. Mem. Societe Astronomique de France (pres. 1949-51), Conseil des Observatoires Astronomiques, Federation des Societes Francaises de Physique, Comite Francais de Radio-Electricite Scientifique, Bur. Longitudes (corr.), Research and publs. on structure of solar chromosphere and evolution of protuberances. Home: Salies-de-Bearn (P.-A.) France Died July 18, 1970.

DEAKYNE, HERBERT, army officer; b. Deakyneville, Del., Dec. 29, 1867; s. Napoleon B. and Mary A. (David); student Delaware Coll. (now U. of Del.), 1884-85; grad. U.S. Mil. Acad., 1890; Engr. Sch. of Application, 1893; Army War Coll., 1917; m. Sadie M. Nickerson, June 15, 1899; children—Ramona (Mrs. John B. Hughes), Rosaline (Mrs. George W. Waldron). Commd. additional 2d lt. col., Feb. 27, 1914; col. Nat. Army, July 6, 1917; brig. gen. (temp.), Oct. 1, 1918-May 31, 1919; col. engrs., Feb. 6, 1920; brig. gen., June 27, 1926; retired, Dec. 31, 1931. River and harbor improvements, California, 1893-96; fortification works, Calif., 1896-1900; mem. Calif. Debris Commn., 1897-1901; in charge fortification works and river and harbor improvements in Fla., 1901-03; at Fort Leavenworth, Kan., 1903-05; in Philippines, 1905-07; chief engr. officer Philippines Div., Aug.-Nov. 1907; mem. Bd. Engrs. for Rivers and Harbors, 1909-12; at Phila., Pa., in charge of fortification works and river and harbor improvements, 1908-12; at Kansas City, Mo., in charge of river and harbor improvements, 1912-16; duty officer of Chief of Engrs., Washington, D.C., 1916; at Army War Coll., 1916-17. Organized 19th Engrs. (Ry.) at Phila., May-Aug. 1917; sailed for France via Halifax and Eng., Aug. 9, 1917; arrived in France Aug. 30, 1917; comd. 19th Engrs. at St. Nazaire, Sept. 1917-Jan. 1918; comd. 11th Engrs. (Ry.) on British Front and with A.E.F., Jan.-May, 1918; at G.H.Q., A.E.F., as dir. of Light Rys. and Roads, May-July 1918; chief engr. Paris Group, Aug.-Sept. 1918; chief engr., 2d Army, Sept. 1918-Apr. 1919; at New Orleans, La., in charge of fortification works and river and harbor improvements, May 1919-Sept. 1920; mem. Miss. River Commn., Mar.-Sept. 1920; at San Francisco, Calif., as div. engr. Pacific Div., and in charge fortification works and river and harbor improvements, Sept. 1920-Jan. 1925; mem. California Debris Commn., 1920-25; as division engr. Northeast division and in charge river and harbor improvements, Feb. 1925-June 1926; asst. chief of engrs., Aug. 8-Sept. 30, 1929. Mem. Board of Engineers for Rivers and Harbors, Feb. 6, 1925-Dec. 31, 1931; mem. Permanent Internat. Commn. of Internat. Assn. of Navigation Congresses; pres. Soc. Am. Mil. Engineers, 1932; cons. engr. to Chamber of Commerce, Eureka, Calif., Mar.-May 1934, to Trinity River Canal Assn., Fort Worth, Tex., Jan.-May 1937. Clubs: Army and Navy, Army, Navy, and Marine Corps Country (Washington, D.C.). Home: San Francisco, Calif. Address: 2248 Washington St., San Francisco 15, Calif. Died May 28, 1945.

DEAN, ARTHUR LYMAN, ex-coll. pres., corp. exec.; b. Southwick, Mass., Oct. 1, 1878; s. William Kenderick and Nellie May (Rogers) D.; A.B., Harvard, 1900; Ph.D., Yale, 1902; m. Leora Elevena Parmlee, Aug. 11, 1904; children—Sylvia, Layman Arnold, Pierson Goddard. Asst. Instr., Sheffield Sci. Sch. (Yale), 1902-03; instr. plant physiolo Yale, 1903-07, instr. indsl. chemistry 1908-09, asst. prof., 1909-14; with A.D. Little, chemist and engr., Boston, 1907-08; prof. U. Hawaii, 1914-27; dir. experiment Sta. of Assn. of Hawaiian Pineapple Canners; pres. Alexander and Baldwon Co. Research asst. Carneige Inst., 1904-05; chief, science of wood chemsitry U.S. Forestry Service 1905-07. Mem. A.A.A.S., Am. Chem. Soc., Sigma Xi, Kappa Gamma Chi, Phi Sigma Kappa. Republican. Club: University (Honolulu) Developed process for refinement chaumoogra oil for use in treatment leprosy. Home: Honolulu, Hawaii. Died June 1952.

DEAN, BASHFORD, zoölogist, armor expert; b. New York, Oct. 28, 1867; A.B., Coll. City of New York, 1886; A.M., Columbia, 1889, Ph.D., 1890; m. Mary Alice, d. Isaac Michael Dyckman, of Kingsbridge, N.Y., 1893. Tutor natural history, Coll. City of New York, 1886-90; instr. biology, 1891-96, adj. prof. zoölogy, 1896-1904, prof. vertebrate zoölogy, 1904-27, hon. prof., 1927—, Columbia. Asst. N.Y. State Fish Commn., 1886-88; asst., 1889-92, biologist, 1900-01, spl. investigator U.S. Fish Commn.; dir. Biol. Lab., Cold Spring Harbor, N.Y., 1890; mem. Advisory Bd., New York Aquarium, 1902—; curator of herpetology and ichthyology, 1903-26, hon. curator of ichthyology, 1926—, Am. Mus. Natural History; curator arms and armor, Met. Mus. Art, 1903—; prof. Fine Arts, New York U., 1925; pres. Dyckman Inst., curator Dyckman House Mus. Trustee N.Y. Museum. Chevalier Legion of Honor. Adviser on armor U.S. War Dept.; maj. of Ordnance U.S.A.; mem. Mission to France, Belgium, England, 1917. Author of numerous works on paleichthyology and embryology of fishes (myxinoid, chimaeroid and ganoid), and of bibliography of fishes (50,000 titles). Many pubs. on armor and arms. Home: Riverdale, New York, N.Y. Died Dec. 6, 1928.

DEAN, FRANCIS WINTHROP, mill engr., architect; b. Taunton, Mass., May 24, 1852; s. Samuel Augustus and Charity Williams (Washburn) D.; S.B., Lawrence Scientific Sch. (Harvard), 1875; m. Lydia Clarkson Hale Cushing, Mar. 8, 1893 (died Sept. 15, 1926); children—Samuel Winthrop, Francis Hale. Instructor in civil engineering, Harvard Engineering Sch., 1874-82; entered office of E. D. Leavitt, Cambridge, Mass., as spl. asst., and afterwards draftsman and insp. of machinery; chief draftsman, 1886-89; opened an office in Boston, 1889; head of Dean & Main, engrs. and architects, 1893-1907. With Emergency Fleet Corp., Jan. 1, 1918-Octo. 1, 1920; now practicing as engr. and architect. Mem. Bd. of Sewer and Water Commrs., Lexington, Mass., 7 yrs. Fellow, Am. Soc. M.E. (v.p. 1895-97). Home: Lexington, Mass. Died May 25, 1940.

DEAN, GEORGE ADAM, entomologist; b. Topeka, Kan., Apr. 19, 1873; s. Thomas Jackson and Harriet (Reese) D.; state teachers' certificate, Kan. State Teachers Coll., 1898; B.S., Kan. State Coll., 1895, M.S., 1905; D.Sc. Southwestern College, Kansas, 1943; m. Minerva Blachly, August 30, 1903; children—Helen Elizabeth, George Thomas, Loua Marjorie, Paul McConnell, Dorothy. With Kan. State Agl. Coll. since 1902, prof. entomology, also Experiment Station entomologist, state entomologist of Kan. since 1912; sr. entomologist, U.S. Dept. Agriculture, 1923-25. Mem. Mediterranean Fruit Fly Com. Federal Fruit Fly Board. Developed heat method for control of injurious insects and the poison bait method for control of grasshoppers, cut worms and army worms. Fellow A.A.A.S., Entomol. Soc. America (pres. 1925); mem. Am. Assn. Econ. Entomologists (pres. 1921), Sigma Xi, Phi Kappa Phi, Gamma Sigma Delta. Republican. Conglist. Mason (32 deg.). Home: 1725 Poyntz Av., Manhattan KS*

DEAN, JOHN CANDEE, mfr. and astronomer; b. Deansboro, N.Y., Sept. 15, 1845; s. John and Harriet R. (Peck) D.; scientific course, Whitestown Sem., Utica, N.Y.; Sc.D. Lombard Coll., Galesburg, Ill., 1917. Entered iron foundry and machine business, 1867; now pres. and treas. Dean Bros. Co., mfrs. pumping and condensing machinery. Republican. Unitarian. Author: "Life of Count Rumford," "Astronomical Superstitions," "Mysteries of Matter." Home: Indianapolis, Ind. Died Dec. 31, 1928.

DEAN, LEE WALLACE, otolaryngologist; b. Muscatine, Ia., Mar. 28, 1873; s. Henry Munson and Emma (Johnson) D.; B.S., State U. of Ia., 1894, M.S., 1896, M.D., 1896; studied in Vienna, 1896-97; m. Ella May Bailey, Dec. 29, 1904; 1 son, Lee Wallace. Prof. and head of otolaryngology and oral surgery, State U. of Ia. until July 1, 1927; also dean Coll. of Medicine, same univ., 1912-27; prof. otolaryngology, Washington U. Sch. of Medicine, since 1927; mem. staff Barnes, St. Louis Children's and Jewish hosps.; otolaryngologist in chief McMillan Eye, Ear, Nose & Throat Hospital and Oscar Johnson Research Inst., St. Louis (emeritus 1943). Served as lieut. col. Med. O.R.C., comdg. offr. Gen. Hosp. No. 54, World War. Mem. Am. Bd. Otolaryngology; editor Annals of Otology, Rhinology and Laryngology. Fellow Am. Coll. Surg.; mem. Am. Laryngol. Assn. (past pres.), Am. Laryngol., Rhinol. and Otol. Soc. (past pres.), Am. Otol. Soc. (past pres.), Am. Peroral Endoscopists, Mo. State Med. Soc., Am. Acad. of Ophthalmology and Otolaryngology (pres.), La Societe de Laryngologie des Hopitaux de Paris. Home: Kirkwood, Mo. Recipient of de Roaldes prize award, 1937. Address: Washington University Medical School, St. Louis, Mo. Died Feb. 9, 1944.

DEAN, REGINALD SCOTT, metall. engr.; b. Rolla, Mo., Aug. 23, 1897; s. George Reinald and Luella C.(Scott) D.; B.S., U. of Mo., Sch. of Mines, 1915, M.S., 1916, Metall. Engr., 1920; grad. study Harvard U. and U. of Chgo., Ph.D., U. of Maryland, 1936; m. Mattie McGregor, 1930. Research chemist for the American Zinc, Lead & Smelting Co., St. Louis, Mo., 1917-18; metallurgist, research dept. Anaconda Copper Mining Co., 1918; instr. in metall. engring., Armour Inst. Tech., 1919-20; devel. engr., Western Electric Co., Chgo., Ill., 1920-29; chief engr., metall. div., U.S. Bur. Mines, Washington, D.C., 1929-42; asst. dir., 1942-46; cons. metall. since 1946. Pres. Chgo. Devel. Co. Mem. Am. Inst. Mining and Metall. Engrs. Am. Chem. Soc., Am. Soc. for Steel Treating. Mason. Author: Electrolytic Manganese and Its Alloys, 1951. Home: 6900 Oak Ridge Rd., University Park, Md. Office: 5810 47th Av., Riverdale, Md. Died May 26, 1961.

DEAN, RICHARD DOGGETT, educator, engr.; b. Nesbitt, Miss., Sept. 10, 1884; s. Thomas Jefferson and Eliza Francis (Doggett) D.; student Randall U. Sch., Hernando, Miss., 1900-04; B.S., Miss. State, 1908, post grad. in elec. engring. 1909; D.D.S., U. of Tenn., 1922, M.D., 1931; m. Marguerite Gladys Tayolr, Sept. 5, 1914. Inspector Municipal Elec. Taylor, ing Labs., Seattle, 1909-12; dir., 1912-18; active practice dentistry, Memphis, 1922-24, student instr. U. of Tenn. Coll. Dentistry, 1922, prof. applied dental physics, metall. and materials, 1922-24, prof. surgery and pathol., chief div. oral medicine and surgery since 1924. dean coll. of Dentistry since 1941. Served in S.A.T.C., U.S. Army, 1918. Expert cons. Univ. of Tenn. presented to U. of Tenn. the liknesses of Dr. Dean and of his wife, Dr. Marguerite Dean, done in oils, which are hanging on the walls of new dental bldg, 1948; colleagues founded the Richard Doggett Dean and Marguerite Taylor Dean hon. Odontol. Soc., Dec. 6, 1948. Mem. Am., Tenn. dental assns., Internat. Assn. Dental Research, Ninth Dist. Dental Soc., Omicron Kappa Epsilon, Alpha Omega Alpha, Delta Sigma Delta. Research and investigation (with wife) in physical properties of dental materials, bacteriol., serol. and immunogenic studies on Vincent's Infection, bacteriophage as a therapeutic measure in treatment of dental pulps, etc. Contbr. articles to prof., Sci. jours. Home: R. 1, Box 39, Lake Cormorant Miss. Office: 847 Monroe Av., Coll. of Dentistry, University of Tenn., Memphis 3, Died Aug. 29, 1950.

DEAN, WILLIS JOHNSON, cons. engr.; b. Owensboro, Ky.; s. John Allen and Mary (Hale) D.; B.C.E., Univ. of Kentucky, 1908; m. Margaret Elizabeth Gage. Engaged in design and supervision of constrn. of comml. bldgs. and indsl. plants. Representative buildings and plants; Spalding Bldg., Multnomah Hotel, Portland, Ore.; Bryson Apt. Hotel, Los Angeles,; Watts Office Bldg., San Diego; Robbins & Myers Co., Plant, Springfield, O.; Army Supply Base, Brooklyn, N.Y.; Goodyear Tire & Rubber Co. plants, Akron, O., and Los Angeles, Calif.; Hamilton Club, Edgewater Beach Hotel, Union League Club, Daily News Bldg., Cook County Nurses Home, Chicago, etc. Capt. constrn. div. U.S. Army, during the World War. Kappa Alpha (Southern). Baptist. Mason (32 deg., Shriner). Home: Hotel Sovereign. Office: 400 W. Madison St., Chicago, Ill. Died Oct. 5, 1944.

DEANE, RUTHVEN, ornithologist; b. Cambridge, Mass., Aug. 20, 1851; s. Charles and Helen Elizabeth (Waterston) D.; ed. at Cambridge; m. Martha R., d. Henry A. Towner, of Chicago, Dec. 16, 1885; children—Charles, Henry Towner. Fellow Am. Ornithologists' Union, 1883—; pres. Ill. Audubon Soc., 1898-1914; mem. Chicago Acad. Sciences. Home: Chicago, Ill. Died Mar. 20, 1934.

DEANE, WALTER, botanist; b. Boston, Apr. 23, 1848; s. Charles and Helen Elizabeth (Waterston) D.; A.B., Harvard, 1870; m. Margaret Chapman Coolidge, Dec. 31, 1878. Pvt. tutor, 1870-71; instr. St. Mark's Sch., Southborough, 1871-78; instr. John P. Hopkinson's pvt. sch., 1878-95; pvt. tutor, 1895-97; associated with William Brewster in his ornithol. mus., as asst. in charge, 1897-1907. Compiled and edited, Flora of the Blue Hills, Middlesex Fells, Stony Brook and Beaver Brook Reservations of the Met. Park Commn. Home: Cambridge, Mass. Died July 30, 1930.

DEARBORN, EARL HAMILTON, research adminstr.; b. Manhattan, Kan., June 10, 1915; s. Edgar Hamilton and Gladys (Nichols) D.; A.B., U. Kan., 1938, M.A., 1940; Ph.D., U. Chgo., 1942; M.D., Johns Hopkins, 1949; m. Margaret Ann Kuchta, Dec. 24, 1943; children—Margaret K., Barbara Ann, Earl, Hamilton II, Patricia. Asst. pharmacology U. Chgo., 1940-43, instr., 1943; instr. pharmacology, exptl. therapeutics Johns Hopkins, 1943-49, asst. prof., 1949-52; prof. pharmacology, chmn. dept. Boston U., 1952-56; head dept. pharmacological research, Lederle Labs. div. Am. Cyanamid Co., Pearl River, N.Y., 1956-60, assistant director experimental therapeutics research, 1960-63, director, 1963-65, assistant director research, 1965-69; pres. therapeutics research div. Dome Labs., 1969-71; pharmacologist pres. Miles Research div. Miles Labs., Inc., 1971-73. Fellow A.A.A.S.; mem. N.Y. Acad. of Sciences, Soc. Experimental Biology and Medicine, Society of Toxicology, American Society Pharmacology and Exptl. Therapeutics, American Chemical Soc., Phi Beta Kappa, Sigma Xi, Alpha Omega Alpha, Phi Sigma. Home: Montvale NJ Died Feb. 28, 1973.

DEARBORN, GEORGE VAN NESS, psychiatrist; b. Nashua, N.H., Aug. 15, 1869; s. Cornelius Van Ness and Louisa Frances (Eaton) D.; 7th generation from Godfreye D., Exter, New Hampshire, 1637, and John Eaton of Haverhill, 1638; Litt.B., Dartmouth, 1890; M.D., Coll. Phys. and Surg. (Columbia), 1893; A.M., Harvard, 1896; Ph.D., Columbia, 1899; m. Blanche V. S. Brown, June 18, 1893; 1 dau., Lucia Eaton (Mrs. Seabury B. Hough). Assistant in philosophy, Harvard, 1896; asst. in physiology, Harvard Med. Sch., 1899; prof. and dir. lab. of physiology, 1900-16, Tufts College; professor psychology and education, Sargent Normal School, Cambridge, 1906-21; instr. psychology, School of Engenics, Boston, 1912-15; cons. physchology, School of Eugenics, Boston, 1912-15; cons. physiologist and psychologist, Forsyth Dental Infirmary for Children, Boston, 1913—; Med. Corps, U.S.A., Apr. 29, 1918; 158th Depot Brig., Camp Sherman, Ohio, neuropsychiatric board; chief of neuropsychiatric service, Camp Devens, Mass., Base Hosp., May 1919, until discharge, July 2, 1919. Asst. phys. for nervous diseases, Boston City Hosp., 1919-21; phys. August (Me.) State Hosp., June-Nov. 1921; suregon (R) U.S.P.H.S., neuropsychiatric sect., Sept. 28, 1921—; med. officer expert, U.S. Vets.' Bureau, 1924. Med. O.R.C., U.S.A., 1922. Fellow Boston Soc. Natural History, Am. Psychiat. Assn. Republican. Mason. Author: The Emotion of Joy, 1899; A Textbook of Human Physiology, 1908; Moto-Sensory Development, 1910; Relations of Mind and Body, 1914; The Physiology of Exercise, 1918; The Influence of Joy, 1916; How to Learn Easily, 1916; The Psychology of Clothing, 1918; Physiology and Hygiene. Editor: Our Senses Series, 1916. Home: Maplewood, N.J. Died Dec. 12, 1938.

DEARBORN, NED, biologist; b. Alton, N.H., Nov. 24, 1865; s. Josiah and Sara Morrill (Haines) D.; B.S., Dartmouth, 1891; M.S., N.H. State Coll., 1898, D.Sc., 1901; m. H. Josephine Hill, of Northfield, N.H., June 13, 1894. Was pub. sch. teacher, 2 yrs.; supt. lens dept., Lord Bros. Optical Co., Tilton, N.H., 4 yrs.; inst. in N.H. State Coll., 4 yrs.; asst. curator birds, Field Mus. of Natural History, Chicago, 1901-09; asst. biologist, Bur. Biol. Survey, U.S. Dept. Agr., July 1, 1909-June 30, 1920; mgr. Dearborn Fur Farm, Sacket Harbor, N.Y., July 1, 1920—. Mem. Cooper Ornithol. Club, Am. Genetic Assn., Biol. Soc., Washington, Am. Soc. Mammalogists. Author: Birds of Belknap and Merrimac Counties, N.H., 1898; Birds of Durham and Vicinity, N.H., 1902; Birds in Their Relation to Man (joint author), 1903. Home: Sacket Harbor, N.Y.

DEARBORN, RICHARD HAROLD, dean engring.; b. Salem, Ore., Nov. 2, 1874; s. Richard H. and Helen Azubah (Flint) D.; A.B. Willamette U., 1895; E.E., Cornell U., 1900; m. Julia Isabelle Braun, June 23, 1903; children—Katherine (Mrs. Henry Frulan DeBoest), Isabelle (Mrs. L.B. Forbes). Electrical engineer Portland General Electric Company, 1900; inaugurated course in electrical engineering, U. of Ore., Sept. 1901, successively instr., asst. prof. and prof., 1901-14; part time appraisal engr. Ore. State Tax Commn., 1908-10; half-time elec. engr. Ore. Pub. Utilities Commn., 1912-14; prof. elec. engring. and head of department, Oregon State College, 1914-33 conolidation of all engineering instruction at Oregon State College); became dean of engring., 1933, now dean emeritus. Dir. Engineering, Science, and Management War Training for Oregon. Member administrative council Ore. State Coll. Fellow Am. Inst. Elec. Engrs.; mem. Soc. for Promotion Engring. Edn., Northwest Electric Light & Power Assn., Corvallis Chamber of Commerce, Delta Upsilon, Tau Beta Pi, Sigma Tau, Pi Tau Sigma, Eta Kappa Nu. Republican. Episcopalian. Club: Corvallis Country. Writer of tech. articles. Home: 6212 S.E. 28th Av., Portland 2, Ore. Died Mar. 21, 1946.

DE BARR, EDWIN, chemist; b. Ingham Co., Mich., Jan. 14, 1859; s. Matthew and Mary Ann (Bell) D.; grad. State Normal Coll., Ypsilanti, Mich., 1866, B.Pd., 1892; B.S., Mich. Agrl. and Mech. Coll., 1891, M.S., 1893; Ph.B., U. of Mich., 1892, Ph.D., 1899; (hon. M.Pd., State Normal Coll., 1913); m. Cora Belle Reid, of Port Huron, Mich., July 7, 1900. Head of dept. of chemistry, 1892-, and v.p. and dir. Sch. of Chem. Engring., Sept. 1, 1909—; commd. as pure food expert by Sec. of Agr. James Wilson, 1909; city chemist of Norman, Okla. Democrat. Presbyn. Fellow A.A.A.S.; mem. Am. Pharm. Assn., Am. Chem. Soc., Okla. Pharm. Assn., Okla. Acad. Science, 33 deg. Mason. Clubs: Commercial Science. In Europe making investigations in industrial chemistry, 1913-14. Mem. Hon. Naval Consulting Bd. for Okla.; mem. Nat. Research Comm. for Okla.; chmn. Food Conservation Comm. for Assn. Food Officals for Okla., Tenn., Miss., La., Tex., Mo., and Ark. Address: Norman, Oklahoma.

DEBERARD, WILFORD WILLIS, city engr.; b. Farifax, Ia., Oct. 31, 1874; s. Wilford Henry and Lovie (Whitney) DeB.; A.B., Deloit (Wis.) Coll., 1896; Mass. Inst. Tech., 1901; m. Blendena E. Emmons, Sept. 15, 1902 (dec. Apr. 1953); children—Elizabeth, Emmons Wilford (dec.). Chemist and bacteriologist Denver Union Water Co., 1896-99; in charge water testing station, Phila., 1902-03; bldg. filter plant, Harrisburg, Pa., 1903-05; asst. in designing filter plant, pumping sta., others, Columbus, O., 1905-07; in charge water-testing sta., Oakland, Cal., 1907-08; chemist and bacteriologist Denver Union Water Co., 1908-09; asst. engr. U.S. Reclamation Service, 3 mos., 1909; same, Met. Sewerage Commn., N.Y., 6 mos., 1909; western editor Engring. News Record, Chgo., 1910-26; chief engr. Chgo. Regional Planning Assn., 1926-27; asso. editor Engring. News Record, 1927-41; city engr., Chgo., since Feb. 1, 1941. Established W. W. DeBerard Fund, Beloit. Trustee Village of Wilmette. Treas. Fedn. Sewage Works Assns. Mem. Am. Soc. C.E. (dir.), Western Soc. Engrs., Am. Assn. Engrs., Am. Waterworks Assn., Am. Rd. Builders Assn., Am. Soc. San Engring., Hwy. Research Bd., Theta Delta Chi, Phi Kappa Psi. Conglist. Clubs: Chicago Engineers', Collegiate, Town. Home: 505 N. Michigan Av., Chgo. 60611. Office: City Hall, Chicago 2. Died Sept. 23, 1962; buried Crown Hill Cemetery, Denver.

DE BOOY, THEODOOR, archeologist, explorer; b. Hellevoetsluis, The Netherlands, Dec. 5, 1882; s. C. J. G. and May (Hobson) de B.; ed. Royal Inst.; m. Elizabeth Hamilton Smith, Mar. 29, 1909. Came to U.S., 1906; naturalized citizen, 1916, in charge West Indian archeol. work of Mus. of Am. Indian, New York, 1911—. Explored previously unknown regions of Santo Domingo and Venezuela; conducted archeol. investigations in Bahamas, Cuba, Jamaica, Hayti. Santo Domingo, Turks and Caicos Islands, Margarita, Trinidad, Martinique, Venezuela and Virgin Islands of U.S. Commander Order of Liberator of Venezuela. Democrat. Author: The Newly Acquired Virgin Islands of the U.S. and the British Virgin Islands, 1918. Home: Yonkers, N.Y. Died Feb. 18, 1919.

DE BRAHM, WILLIAM GIRARD, geographer; b. 1717; m. 2d, Mary (Drayton) Fenwick, Feb. 18, 1776; at least 1 child. Came to Am., 1751; founded Town of Bethany, Ga., 1751; surveyor of Ga., 1754-64, planned towns of Ebenezer, 1757. Ft. George, 1761; supervised constn. of fortifications at Charleston, S.C., 1755, Savannah, Ga., 1762; drew 1st map of Ga. and S.C., 1757; surveyor gen. for So. Dist., 1764-70; commr. to mark No. boundary line of N.J., 1765; drew map of Atlantic Ocean, 1772. Author: The Atlantic Pilot, 1772; The Levelling Balance and Counter-Balance, 1774; DeBrahm's Zonical Tables for the Twenty-Five Northern and Southern Climates, 1774; Time an Apparition of Eternity, 1791; Apocalyptic Gnomon Points Out Eternity's Divisibility, 1795. Died 1799.

DEBUYS, LAURENCE RICHARD pediatrician; b. New Orleans, Nov. 12, 1878; s. James and Stella (Rathbone) DeB.; B.S., Tulane U., 1899, M.D., 1904; post grad. work in pediatrics Harvard, 1907, 08; clincs in Germany, Austria, England, France; m. Miriam Duggan, June 14, 1904; children—Laurence Richard, William Eno, Herbert Fowler, John Forester, Henry Duggan. Intern Charity Hosp., 1902-04; practiced medicine, Houma, La., 1904-07, New Orleans , 1907—, practice limited to pediatrics 1910—; head chief of clinic, dept. of gynecology and obstetrics and clin. asst., dept. of pediatrics Tulane U., 1907-08, asso. prof. pediatrics, 1912-17, clin. prof., 1917-19, asst. prof. pediatrics post grad. sch. medicine, 1912-17, prof. of pediatrics 1919-29; chief pediatric staff New Orleans Presbyn. Hosp., 1910-11; vis. pediatrist Charity Hosp. of La., 1907-22, chief of staff in pediatrics, 1919-22; mem. staff Touro Infirmary 1910—, chief of pediatric dept., 1919-39, cons. pediatrician, 1939—, chmn exec. com. med. staff 1937-38, prof. pediatrics nurses Tng. Sch., 1924-34; chmn pediatric div. U.S. Marine Hosp., 1931-34; chmn. Pediatric div. Emergency Med. Service, OCD, 1942; sec. La. State Com. on Nat. Defense Med. Sect., and mem. Vol. Med. Service Corps, World War 1. mem. White House Conf. on Child Health, 1929; mem. follow-up com., 1929-31. Mem. Court of Honor, Boy Scouts Am.,1918-21. Diplomate Am. Bd. Pediatrics. Fellow A.C.P. (bd. govs. 1925-26), Am. Acad. Pediatrics (emeritus); mem. La. Pediatric Soc. (organizer and pres. 1924-28), So. Med. Assn. (hon.) (chmn. pediatrics sect. 1925), A.M.A. (hon., chmn. sect. disease of children 1917-18), Assn. Am. Med. Colls., Am. Child Health Assn. (charter mem.; mem. bd. dirs. 1923-29), Abraham Jacoby Mem. Fund of A.M.A. (an organizer, chmn. com. 1923-24), Archivos Americnaso editor), de Medicina (corr. Pan. Am. Med. Assn. (v.p. pediatrics sect. 1933), Orleans Parish Med. Soc. (hon.) (v.p. 1911-14), La. Med. Soc. (hon.) (sec. 1912-15; sec.-treas. 1915-19; chmn. many coms.), Assn. Am. Tchrs. of Disease of Children (pres. 1916-17), Milk commn. New Orleans Pure Milk Society, (pres. 1931-35). Child Welfare Association, Alumni Assn. Tulane U. (member executive committee 1913-15). American Assn. Med. Milk Commrs. (councillor 1918-23; pres. 1919-20). Assn. for Study of Internal Secretions (councillor 1916-31), Am. child Health Assn. (emertius), Am. Pediatric Soc., (v.p. 1930-31; now emeritus), Assn. Study Internal Secretions (life) hon. mem. Dallas So. Clin. Soc., Tri-State Dist. Med. Assn., Lafourche Valley Med. Soc.; Alpha Omega Alpha, Alpha Tau Omega, Theta Nu Epsilon, Phi Chi Med. Fraternity (charter mem.). Del. to Conf. on Maternity and Child Welfare, London, 1928; 2d Internat. Pediatric Congress, Stockholm, 1930, Rome, 1936; Internat. Hygiene Congress, Germany, 1930. Mem. bd. dirs. New Orleans Golf Assn., 1933—, v.p., 1939-40, pres., 1941-42, 42-43 (one of 3 hon. life members). Democrat. Roman Catholic. Clubs: New Orleans Country (chmn. tournament com. 1935) La Kennel (pres. 1943-1944). Contributor chpts. abt's Pediatrics. Member editorial board American Journal Diseases of children, 1926-39; mem. cons. staff Archives of Pediatrics, 1919-26; Collaborator American Jour. of Syphilis, 1916-23. Contbr. numerous articles to med. jours. Pioneer in use of motion pictures in medicine demonstratiog peristaltic waves by motion pictures in 1913. Address 1417 Delachaise St., New Orleans, Died June 20, 1957; buried Metarie Cemetery, New Orleans.

DEBYE, PETER JOSEPH WILLIAM, educator; b. Maastricht, Netherlands, Mar. 24, 1884; s. Wilhelmus and Maria (Reumkens) D.; E.E., Engring. Sch., Aachen; Ph.D., U. Munich; hon. degs.; Harvard, Bklyn. Poly., St. Lawrence U., Colgate U., Oxford, Brussels, Leige, Sofia Eidgenossiche Technische Hochschule, Boston Coll., U. Notre Dame, Providence Coll., Clarkson Coll. Tech., Technische Hochschule, many others; m. Mathilde Alberer Apr. 10, 1913; children—Peter Paul Ruprecht, Mathilde Maria Gabriele. Came to U.S. 1940. Prof. theoretical physics U. Zurich, 1911; prof. univs. Utrecht, Goettingen, Leipzig, Berlin; prof. chemistry and chmn. dept. Cornell U., 1940-50, emeritus, 1950—. Recipient Lorentz, Faraday, Rumford, Franklin medals; Nobel award in chemistry, 1936; Wilard Gibbs medal, 1949; Max Planck medal, 1950; Kommandeur des Ordens Leopold II; Kendall award, colloid chemistry Am. Chem. Soc., Miami, 1957; Nichols medal N.Y. sect. Am. Chem. Soc., 1961, Priestly medal, 1963; Am. Phys. Soc. High-Polymer Prize, Ford Motor Co., 1965, Madison Marshall award N.Ala. sect. Am. Chem. Soc., 1965, also National medal of science, 1965. Fgn. Mem. Royal Soc. Amsterdam, Pontifical, Royal Irish, Royal Danish, Berlin, Gottingen, Munich, Brussels, Liege, Indian, Nat. (U.S.A.), N.Y., Am. (Boston), Papal (Rome), Indian (Bungalore), Royal Irish (Dublin), Royal Danish (Denmark), Royal Dutch (Amsterdam) acads.; scis.; Nat. Instn. Sci. India, Real Sociedad Espanola de Fisica y Quimica Madrid, Am. Philos. Soc. Home: 104 Highgate Rd., Ithaca, N.Y. Died Nov. 2, 1966.

DECKER, CHARLES ELIJAH, prof. Palecontology; b. Dixon, Ill., Sept. 27, 1868; s. Henry and Emogene (Bunnell) D.; A.B., Northwestern U., 1906; A.M. U. of Chgo., 1908, Ph.D., 1917; hon. D.Sc., Oklahoma City U., 1935; m. Gertrude Monlux, May 31, 1900 (died Jan. 31, 1954) m. 2d, Mrs. Ethelyn Wolfard, Sept. 30, 1955. Tchr. Allegheny Coll., 1909-16; instr. in geology U. Okla., 1916-17, asst. prof., 1917-19, asso. prof., 1919-25, prof. paleontology, 1925-43, research prof. emeritus of paleontology, 1943—;a also taugh geology summers, U. Ill., Cornell U., Colo. State Tchrs. Coll., and 1 semester Northwestern U. Mem. Silurian Com. NRC. Fellow A.A.A.S., Geol. Soc. Am., Paleontol. Soc., Okla. Acad. Science (pres. 1 yr.); mem. soc. Economic Paleontology and Mineralogy, Sigma Gamma Epsilon (nat. sec. 6 yrs., nat. pres. 8 yrs.), Sigma Xi; hon. mem. Am. Assn. Petroleum Geologist (sec.-treas. 7 yrs.), Alpha of Omega chpt. Phi Beta Kappa, 1927. Author: Minor Folds, 1920; List of Characteristic Fossils, 1925; Physical Characteristics of the Arbuckle Limestone (with C. A. Merritt), 1928 1928; Statigraphy and Physical Characteristics of the Simpson Group (with C.A. Merritt and R.W. Harris), 1931; Two Lower Paleo-oic Groups, Okla., 1939; Timbered Hills and Arbuckle Groups, Arbuckle and Wichita Mountains, Okla., 1939; Stratigraphic, significance of graphtolites of the Athens Shale, 1952; Upper Cambrian Graptolties from Virginia and Tennessee (with I. B. Gold), 1958; What higher magnification is doing for the study of graphtolites (with N. R. Hassinger), 1958; numerous graptolite papers also various tech. brochures articles. Home: 508 Chautuqua Av., Norman, Okla., Died. Aug. 23, 1958; buried Dixon, Ill.

DECKER, FLOYD F(ISKE), mathematician; b. Ednison, Tex., Mar. 23, 1881; s. Alonzo Wertz and Hannah Lucretia Amos D.; A. B., Syracuse U,. 1901, A.M., 1905, Ph.D., 1910; m. Mary Makepace, Aug. 30, 1910; children—Elizabeth Carol (Mrs. Curton B. Corwin), Robert Makepeace. Instr. in mathematics Syracuse U., 1904-10, asst. prof., 1910-14, asso. prof., 1914-17, prof., 1917—, dir. extension sch., 1919-30,

Fellow A.A.A.S.: mem. Am. Math. Soc., Math. Assn. Am., Am. Assn. U. Profs., Sigma Xi, Phi Beta Kappa, Phi, Kappa Phi, Pi Mu Epsilon, Republican. Methodist. Author: Symmetric Functions, 1910; Second Year Algebra, 1922. Contbr. to Math. jours. Home: 312 Marshall St., Syracuse 10, N.Y. Died Nov. 28, 1949; buried Oakwood Cemetery, Syracuse.

DEERE, JOHN, Am. inventor; b. Rutland, Vt., Feb. 7, 1804; s. William Rinold and Sarah (Yates) D.; m. Damaris Lamb, Jan. 28, 1827; m. 2d, Lucinda Lamb, 1867. First mfr. plow steel in U. S., organizer various mfg. firms; incorporated, became pres. firm Deere & Co., 1868. Mayor, Moline, Ill.; pres. 1st Nat. Bank Moline. Originated, developed idea that successful self-scouring of a steel moldboard depended upon its shape; devised new plow with steel blade; manufactured 1st cast plow steel in U. S. and other farm implements. Died May 17, 1886.

DEESZ, LOUIS A(SPELL) dean of engring.; b. Denver, May 22, 1888; s. Louis Phillip and Lucy (Soper) D.; student Colo. Coll., 1907-11; B.S., Carnegie Inst. Tech., 1922, E.E., 1936; m. Henrietta Davis, Aug. 13, 1913; children—Lucy Ann (Mrs. Duncan Huebner); m. 2d. Myrtle May Robbins, May 28, 1939. Elec. engr. Colo. Light & Power Co., Cripple Creek, 1912; supt. of transmission Fed. Light & Power Co., Trinidad, Colo., 1913; constrn., engr. Federal Light & Power, Deming, N.M., 1914; asst. chief engr. Intermountain Ry. Light & Power Co., Colo. Springs, Colo., 1915-16; asst. elec. supt. Colo. Fuel & Iron Co., Pueblo, 1917-19; gen. engr. Westinghouse Elec. Corp., 1919-22; engr. of tests Colo. Fuel & Iron Co., 1922-30; cons. engr. Freyn Engring. Co., Chgo., assigned to "Energocenter" and "Stalproect" Moscow and Siberia, USSR, 1930-33; lecturer on engring. U. Moscow, Russia, 1931; chief dist. combustion engr. Republic Steel Corp., Youngstown dist., 1933-42;instr. instr. in physics and math . Deming (N.M.) High Sch., 1914-14; prof. elec. engring., Youngstown (Ohio) Coll., 1939—, dean of night sch., 1940, dean Wm. Raven Sch. of Engring., 1942—. Chmn. Rockefeller Com. on Edn., Pueblo, Colo., 1925-39; mem. Mahoning Valley Indsl. Council River Survey, Youngstown, 1936-42. Served as 1st lt., 120th Constrn. Corp., U.S. Army, 1918. Decorated Udarnick of the SUSSR, 1932. Registered engr., Colo., Mem. Nat. Soc. Profl. and Registered Engrs., Am. Soc. Engring. Edn., Am. Inst. E.E., Kappa Sigma, Mu Pi Epsilon. Republican. Methodist. Mason (32 deg. Shriner). Author articles on electrical precipitation, combustion engring., and rotating elec. machinery. Home: 21 East Avondale Av., Youngstown 5, O. Died Apr. 19, 1950 buried Forest Lawn Cemetery, Youngstown.

DEETZ, CHARLES HENRY, cartographic engr.; b. Sellersville, Pa., Apr. 10, 1864; s. Thomas Berber and Caroline (Nase) D.; Phillips Exeter Acad., 1885; student civil engring. (geodetic course). Mass. Inst Tech., 1885-88; m. Clarissa Hannah Wilson, Dec. 7, 1892. Field worker with U.S. Coast and Geod. Survey in Ala. and Fla., 1888, also served in Eastern States; assigned to cartographic work in preparation nautical charts; specializes in map projection; U.S. Coast and Geodetic Sruvey for Army War Service, revising publs. on map. projection and cartography, 1942-43, ret. Mem. Philos. Soc. Washington, Am. Numis. Assn. Author: Lambert Conformal Conic Projection, 1918; Lambert Projection Tables for France, With Conversion Tables for the use of the Army, 1918; (with Oscar S. Adams) Elements fo Map Projection, with applications to map and chart construction, 1921, revised edit., 1944; Cartography, a review and guide for the construction and use of maps and charts, 1936; revised edition, 1943. Contbr. cartographic articles to sci. and tech. publs. Home: 2504 Cliffbourne Pl. N.W., Washington 9. Died Mar. 1946.

DE FLOREZ, LUIS, consulting engineer; born in New York City, Mar. 4, 1889; s. Rafael and Marie Stephanie (Bernard) deFlorez; B.S., in M.E., Mass Inst. Tech., 1912; D.Sc., Rollins College, 1939; D.Eng., Stevens Institute of Technology, 1946, Northwestern University, 1948; Doctor of Science, Tufts Coll., 1946; married Marian Elizabeth King, July 2, 1912; 1 son, Peter Rafael. Began as research engr. Burgess Co., Marblehead, Mass., 1912, W. A. Hall, chem. engr., 1913; chief engr. Hall Motor Fuel Co., Ltd., Eng., 1914-16; cons. engr. N.E. and Invincible Oil corps., 1919-21; chief engr. N.E. Oil Refining Co., 1921-23; cons. engr. A. D. Little & Co., Gasoline Products Co. and Pierce Oil Company, 1923-25; cons. engr. Texas Co. and Gulf Refining Co. 1926-56, Standard Oil Co. of N.Y., Vacuum Oil Company and Gasoline Products Co., 1929-46; director The deFlorez Company, Incorporated; director American—Optical Co., Nat. Aviation Corporation, Douglas Aircraft Company, Incorporated; engaged in the design, construction and operation of cracking plants for various oil refineries in U.S. and foreign, 1913-40; now aviation and mechanical engrs. cons. inventions; deFlorez Cracking Process, deFlorez Temperature Control System, deFlorez Vertical Stills, Safety Drilling Systems, Remote Control Devices. Former pres. Flight Safety Found. Served inspector naval construction in charge of research, design and prodn. instruments and accessories, aviation, U.S. Navy Dept., Washington, 1918-19; served as naval aviator U.S. Navy, 1940; spl. asst. to chmn. Bur. of Aero., Navy Department, 1940-43; director special devices division Bureau Aeronautics, 1943-45; dep. chief of Office Research and Inventions, Navy Dept., 1945-46, dep. chief Naval Research, Nvay Dept., Aug. 1946-Oct. 1946, Rear Admiral inactive service since Oct. 1946. Awarded the Collier Trophy 1943, for development Naval Aviation synthetic tng.; decorated D.S.M., Legion Merit, D.F.C., Comdr. Mil. div. Order Brit. Empire. Mem. Am. Soc. M.E.; asso. fellow Royal Aero. Soc.; fellow Inst. Aeronautical Sciences. Professional engr. N.Y. State. Catholic. Clubs: Union, St. Anthony, Century Assn. (N.Y. City); Metropolitan (Washington). Contbr. of tech. articles to mags. Home: Pomfret, Conn. Office: 200 Sylvan Av., Englewood Cliffs, N.J. Died Dec. 6, 1962; buried Arlington Nat. Cemetery.

DEFOE, HARRY JOSEPH, shipbuilding; b. Bay City Mich., Sept. 2, 1875; s. Joseph and Lucy Ann (Covey) D.; grad. West Bay City (Mich.) High Sch., m. Verna Herric Lusk, Aug. 15, 1900 (dec.,1913); m. Maude Ethel Currey, July 15, 1916; children—Thomas Joseph, William Martin, Lucy Helen. Began as school teacher; engaged in shipbuilding since 1905; mng. partner Defoe Shipbuilding Co. (Defoe Boat & Motor Works) since 1905. Began boat building by construction of wooden boats to 80 ft. in lenght, shipped chiefly in knockdown form; during World War 1 established steel shipyard (now conducted as Defoe Shipbuilding Co.); in 1940, when tremendous expansion of U.S. govt. shipbuilding required conservation of both manpower and space, devised "bottom up and rollover" construction, by which method steel hulls of ships between 300 and 400 ft. long were built bottom up on building forms, then rolled over to upright position by means of two wheels, or hoops, which encircle the hull and rested on heavy steel tracks; this made possible vast savings, in manhours, and almost all downhand welding, which proved to average twice as fast as overhead welding and gave better results; firm has built large number of vessels for the U.S. Navy, and has been awarded Navy E Mem. Soc. Naval Architects and Marine Engrs., Engring. Soc. of Detroit, Propellor Club of U.S., Newcomen Soc. of Eng. Mason. Clubs: India House (New York); Yacht (Detriot); Saginaw (Mich.); Country, Boat, Rotary International (Bay City). Recipient President's Certificate of Merit, 1947. Home: 1412 Center Av., Bay City, Mich. Died Mar. 21, 1957; buried Elm Lawn Cemetery, Bay City, Mich.

DE FOREST, ERASTUS LYMAN, mathematician; b. Watertown, Conn., Jun 27, 1834; s. John and Lucy (Lyman De F.; B.A., Yale, 1854, Ph.B., Sheffield Scientific Sch., 1856, M.A., 1867; never married. Inherited fortune from grandfather; went to Cal. as gold miner, 1848; later travelled in Australia, Orient and Europe; devoted time to study of theory of probability and errors; made important contributions to devel. of formulas for graduation by linerar compounding; endowed mathematics chair at Yale, 1888. Died June 6, 1888.

DE FOREST, LEE, inventor; b. Council Bluffs, Ia., Aug. 26, 1873; s. Henry Swift and Anna Margaret (Robbins) D.; grad. Mt. Hermon (Mass.) Boys' Sch., 1893; B.S., Sheffield Scientific Sch. (Yale), 1896; Ph.D., Yale, 1899, D.Sc., 1926; D.Sc., Syracuse, 1919, Dr. Engring., 1937; LL.D., Talladega College, 1951, Beloit Coll., 1951; D.Sc., College Osteopathic Surgery, 1951; married Nora Stanton Blatch, 1908; m. 2d, Mary Mayo, 1912; m. 3d, Marie Mosquini, 1930; children—Harriet S., Eleanor Peck, Marilyn Swanke. Pioneer in development wireless telegraphy in America; started radio broadcasting cos., 1902; officer numerous pioneering broadcasting orgns. Patented in U.S. and foreign countries 300 inventions in wireless telegrpahy, radio, wire telephone, sound-on-film, high speed fascimile and picture tranmission and television, numerous smaller items in field. Broadcast voice of Caruso, by radio, 1910, and in 1916 first radio news broadcast; established broadcast station, 1916. Showed sound-onfilm program Rivoli Theatre, N.Y. City, Apr. 1923. Awarded Gold Medal, Worlds's Fair, St. Louis, 1904, Panama Pacific Expn., San Francisco, 1915; medal of honor Inst. of Radio Engineers; Elliot Cresson medal, Franklin Inst.; John Scott medal, City of Phila.; Prix La Tour. Inst. of France; Officer Legion of Honor (France); Edison medal, 1946; Legion of Honor, France. Asso. several profl. socs. Author: "Television Today and Tomorrow"; (autobiography) Father of Radio; Conqueror of Space; also various sci. papers. Home: 8190 Hollywood Blvd., Los Angeles 90069. Office: 1027 N. Highland Av., Los Angeles 90028. Died June 30, 1961; buried San Fernando Mission Cemetery.

DEGERING, EDWARD FRANKLIND, author, radiation chemist; b. Dodge City, Kan., May 17, 1898; s. Irving Harrison and Talitha (Cogill) D.; grad. Forest Home Acad., Mt. Vernon, Wash., 1916; student Walla Walla Coll., 1917-19; Canadian Jr. Coll., Alta, Can., 1919-20; B.A., Union Coll., Lincoln, Neb., 1924; M.S., U. Neb., 1929, Ph.D., 1930; student U. Wash., Cornell U. (summers); m. Clara Mae Ogden, Aug. 12, 1921; 1 son, John Edward (dec.). Professor mathematics, Canadian Jr. Coll., 1919-20; contracting bus. with father, Seattle, 1920-21; principal Oriens High Sch., Seattle, 1921-23; grad. asst. and fellow, U. of Neb., 1924-30; instr. Purdue U., 1930-31, asst. prof., 1931-38; asso. prof., 1938-42, prof., 1942-49; asst. chmn. chemistry and chem. engring. Armour Research Found., 1949-50; research cons. Miner Research Found., 1949-50; research cons. Miner Labs., 1950-51; research mgr. Buckman Labs., Inc., 1951-53; chief chems. and plastics OQMG, 1953-54; chief phys. chemistry sec. pioneering research div. Q.M. Research and Devel. Command, U.S. Army, 1954-59, head Radiation Chemical Lab., 1959—. Mem. Ind. Acad. Sci. (v.p. 1940-41, pres. 1945-46), Ind. Chem. Soc. (pres. 1940), Am. Chem. Soc. (chmn. med. div., 1945-46, past sec. chmn. and counsellor for Purdue sect.), A.A.A.S. (pres. Acad. Conf. 1945-46, sec. div. chemistry since 1946), Am. Inst. Chemists, Am. Sch. Tchrs. Assn., Alpha Chi Sigma, Phi Lambda Upsilon, (editor of The Register, 1936-38), Sigma Xi. Clubs: Catalyst, Lions (dep. gov. Ind. 25-B, 1944-46; gov. Ind. 25-C, 1946-48). Holder of numerous patents on organic syntheses. Author: An Outline of Organic Chemistry, 1937; The Quadri-Service Manual of Organic Chemistry, 1938; The Workbook of Fundamental Organic Chemistry, 1941; Fundamental Organic Chemistry, 1942; An Outline of the Chemistry of the Carbohydrates, 1943; An Outline of Organic Nitrogen Compounds, 1945. Contbr. over 150 articles on chem. subjects to sci. jours. Home: Lakeview Garden Apts., 15 Kansas St. Office: Radiation Chemistry Lab., Pioneering Research Div., U.S. Army Natick Labs., Kansas St., Natick, Mass. 01762. Died May 11, 1967; buried Washelli Cemetery, Seattle.

DEGOLYER, E(VERETTE) L(EE), geologist, oil producer; b. Greensburg, Kan., Oct. 9, 1886; s. John William and N. Kagy Huddle) De G.; A.B., U. of Okla., 1911; hon. D.Sc., Colo. Sch. of Mines, 1925, Souhtern Methodist University, 1945, Tulane University, 1954; LL.D., Trinity College, 1947, Princeton, 1949, U. Mexico, 1951, Washington U., 1952; m. Nell Virginia Goodrich, June 10, 1910; children—Nell Virginia, Dorothy Margaret, Cecelia Jeanne, Everette Lee. With U.S. Geol. Survey, 1906-091; geologist and chief geologist Mexican Egal Oil Co., 1909-14; cons. practice, 1914-19; v.p. and gen. mgr., 1919-26, pres. and gen. mgr. 1926-29, chmn. bd., 1929-32, Amerada Crop., Amerada Petroleum and Amerda Refining Corp.; v.p. and gen mgr. Geophys. Research Corp., Pres. Atlanta Royalty Corp., 1932—; pres. Felmont Corp., 1934-39; sr. mem. DeGolyer & McNaughton, 1936—. Asst. dep. petroleum adminstr. for war, Washington, 1941-43; head Petroleum Adminstrn. for War mission to Mexico, 1942; head Dept. Interior Petroleum Reserves Corp. mission to Middle East, 1943 1943-44; tech. N.R.A. oil code, 1933; mem. Nat. Petroleum co Council, 1946—; mem. U.S. Mil. Petroleum Adv. Bd., Energy Commn., 1947—; mem. U.S. adv. com. on raw materials U.S. Atomic Energy Commn., 1947—; mem. U.S. adv. com. Am. participation Internat. Sci. Conf. on Conservation and Utilization fo Resources, 1948—; mem. adv. bd. Nat. Security Resources Bd., 1948—; cons. War Dept. and Bur. Mines Survey of Coal, Oil Shale and Natural Gas Reserves, 1948—; Aldred lecturer Mass. Inst. Tech., 1929; Cyrus Fogg Brackett lecturer Princeton, 1929, Lewis Clark Vanuxem 1941. Anthony F. Lucas medalist, 1941, John Fritz medalist, 1942; Sidney Powers gold medal from the American Association fo Petroleum Geolgoists, 1950; received a distingusihed service citation University of Oklahoma, 1948. Fellow Geol. Soc. Am., A.A.A.S., N.Y. Acad. Scis., Brit. Inst. of Petrolrum, Am. Geog. Soc.; mem. Am. Assn. Petroleum Geologists (pres. 1925; hon. mem. 1945), Am. Inst. Mining and Metall. Engrs. (pres. 1927; became hon. mem. 1952), Nat. Academy of Sciences, Am. Petroleum Inst. (dir. 1935—.)Am. Geophys. Union, Instituto Sudamericano del Petroleo, Soc. Econ. Geologist, Soc. Exploration Geologists, Soc. Exploration Geophysicists (hon. 1930), Pan Am. Inst. Mining Engring. and Geology (U.S. sect.), Dallas Mus. Fine Arts (pres., 1948—.), Phi Brta Kappa, Sigma Xi, Tau Beta Pi, Kappa Alpha, Pi Epsilon, Sigma Gamma Epsilon, Pi Gamma Mu. Conglist. Mason. Clubs: Bankers, Engineers, University, Mining, Grolier (New York) Cosmos (Washington); Houston (Tex.); Brook Hollow Country, Dallas Country, Petroleum, Thirteen (Dallas); Zamorano (Los Angeles). Chmn. editorial bd. Sat. Rev. Lit., 1948—. Asso. editor New Colophon, Southwest Rev. Home: 8525 Garland Rd.Office: 5625 Daniels Av., Dallas. Died Dec. 14, 1956.

DEISS, CHARLES F(REDERICK) geologist; b. Covington, Ky., Mar. 18, 1903; s. Charles Fred and Anna Dorothea (Reinhart) D.; A.B., Miami Univ., 1925; Ph.D., Univ. of Mich., 1928; m. Minnette Blanch Davison Jan. 22, 1929. Asst. prof. geology Mont. State Univ., Missoula, Mont., 1928-30, asso. prof., 1930-36, prof. 1936-42, dir. of library 1937-40; consultant Mont. Power Co., 1940-41; asst. geologist U.S. Geol. Survey, hdqrs., Missoula, Mont., 1940-41, geologist since 1942, in charge exploration for dolomite in western U.S., 1942-45, and for phosphate in Ida., 1944-45; prof. and chmn. dept. geology Ind. Univ. and State Geologist of Ind. since Sept. 1945. Mem. Geol. Soc. Am., Paleontological Soc., A.A.A.S., Am. Inst. Mining, Metall. and Petroleum Engrs., Am. Association of Petroleum Geologists. Soc. Econ. Geologists, Ind. Acad. Sci., Assn. Am. State Geologists (pres. 1954), Sigma Xi, Sigma Gamma Epsilon, Delta Upsilon. Author Sci. bulls. Contbr. articles on geologic subjects to various jours. Address: Owen Hall, Indiana University, Bloomington, Ind. Died June 13, 1959; buried Bloomington, Ind.

DE KALB, COURTENAY, mining engr.; b. Loudoun Co., Va., Sept. 18, 1861; s. E. E. and Emma A. De K.; acad. education; m. Frances Douglas. Practiced as mining engr. in Western and Southern states; went on expdns. through Brazil up the Amazon River and through Peru, Ecuador, Central America and Mexico; prof. mining and metallurgy, U. of Mo., 1895-98, Queen's U., Can., 1898-1901; mgr. San Fernando mine, Durango, Mex., 1901-02, Exposed Treasure mine, Calif., 1902-05; asso. editor Mining and Scientific Press, San Francisco, 1908-10; pres. and gen. mgr. Pacific Smelting & Mining Co., Guaymas, Mexico, 1910-12; asso. editor Mining and Scientific Press, 1917-19; trade commr. U.S. Dept. of Commerce, for investigation of mineral resources of Spain, Portugal and Morocco, 1919-20; cons. engr., New Orleans; and Roadside Mine, Ariz., 1921-25; prof. mining engring., U. of Ala., 1925-26; investigations in Spain and other countries for St. Joseph Leade Company, 1926-27. Lectured De Pauw Univ., 1925. Author: Handbook of Explosives; Nicaragua Canal-Ours of Englands's; A Vist to King Solmon's Mines; Fixed Nitrogen for National Defense. Home: New York, N.Y. Died Sept. 2, 1931.

DE KLEINE, WILLIAM, physician; b. Jamestown, Mich., Nov. 27, 1877; s. Hilbert and Alice (Kremers) DeK.; A.B., Hope College, 1902; hon. D.Sc., 1937; M.D., Northwestern Univ., 1906; M.Sc., U. of Mich. Sch. of Pub. Health, 1915; grad. student Mass. Inst Tech., summer 1924; m. Lottie Maria Hoyt, June 28, 1906; 1 son, Edwin Hoyt (M.D.). Practiced medicine, Grand Haven, Mich., 1906-14; dir. Mich. Tuberculosis Survey Campaign (state-wide clinical survey), State Bd. of Health, 1915-17; health officer (full time), Flint, Mich., 1917-22, Saginaw, Mich., 1922-25; dir. child health demonstrations, Mansfield, O. (conducted by Am. Child Health Assn.), Fargo, N.D., and Salem, Ore. (conducted by Commonwealth Fund of New York), and organized full-time health dept. in each city, 1925-28; became asso. with Am. Red Cross during Miss. flood, 1927, med. director Am. Red Cross, 1928-42; participated in all major disasters as organizer med. relief activities; in pvt. practice of internal medicine (spl. interest in nutritional therapy). 1942-43; state commissioner of health, Mich., 1944-47; engaged in private practice of medicine, 1947-56; now retired Formerly president Mich. Tuberculosis Assn., Mich. Pub. Health Assn.; formerly mem. bd. dirs. Nat. Tuberculosis Assn. Fellow Am. Pub. Health Assn., A.M.A.: mem. Ingham County (Mich.) Med. Soc., Southern Med. Assn. Presbyn. Contbr. to med. and health jours. Pioneer in in field of pub. health and traveling tuberculosis clinics and nutrition in clinical medicine. Address: 90 Concord Dr., Buffalo 15. Died Sept. 20, 1957; buried Forest Grove Mich.) Cemetery.

DELABARRE, FRANK ALEXANDER, orthodontist; b. Conway, Mass., Apr. 8, 1868; s. Edward and Maria L. (Hassell) D.; A.B., Amherst, 1890, fellow, 1890-91; Boston Dental Coll., 1891-92; D.D.S., U. of Pa., Dental Dept., 1894; M.D., U. of Pa. Med. Dept., 1895; m. Anna E. Sweeney, 1893; children—Lawrence, Katharine, Dorothy. In practice in Boston, 1895—; asst. prof. orthodontia, 1907-10, porf., 1910-18, Tufts Coll. Dental Sch.; chief of staff orthodontia department and dean Postgrad. Sch. of Orthodontia. Forsyth Dental Infirmary for Children, 1914-19; consultant Mass. Dept. of Health; lecturer, Tufts Coll. Dental Sch., Harvard Univ. Dental Sch. Member dental advisory com., Mass. Dept. Pub. Health. Fellow Am. Coll. Dentists. Home: Greenbush, Mass. Died Apr. 15, 1938.

DE LACY, WALTER WASHINGTON, engr.; b. Petersburg, Va., Feb. 22, 1819; s. William and Eliza (Lee) De L.; grad. St. Mary's Catholic Coll., 1838; studied engring., informally under Prof. Manhan, U.S. Mil. Acad., 1838. Constn. engr. I.C., Iron Mountain railroads 1839; asst. prof. French, U.S. Mil. Acad., 1840-46; served in Mexican War and Nez Perce War in Wash., 1855; in charge of constn. of a portion of Mullan Rd. from Ft. Benton to Walla Walla, Wash., 1858-60; prospected for gold in Mont., 1861-64; made 1st map of Mont. on commn. from Mont. Legislature, 1864-65; participated in survey for location line of N.P. R.R.; employed in Mont. Surveyor Gen.'s Office, 1890-92; co-founder Mont. Hist. Soc., Mont. Soc. Engrs. Died Helena, Mont., May 13, 1892.

DELANY, PATRICK BERNARD, electrician; b. Kings Co., Ireland, Jan. 28, 1845; s. James and Margaret D.; ed. pvt. and parochial schs., Ireland and U.S.: m. Annie M. Ovenshine, Mar. 31, 1869. Learned telegraphy in Hartford, Conn., worked at same, office boy to supt. of lines; expert operator, newspaper corr., editor and writer. Inventor 150 patents, covering anti-induction cables, synchronous multiplex telegraphy. Awarded gold medal and diploma Internat. Inventions Exhibition, London, 1885; automatic systems for ocean cables; rapid machine telegraphy for land lines; vox Humana talking machines; etc. Claims to have perfected system of automatic telegraphy, transmitting and plainly recording 3,000 words per minute over single wire; also patented method for locating submerged metallic bodies. Awarded Elliott Cresson gold metal twice, and John Scott legacy medal, Franklin Inst.; gold medal, Buffalo Expn., 1901, St. Louis Expn., 1904. Home: South Orange, N.J. Died Oct. 19, 1924.

DE LAUBENFELS, MAX W., zoologist; b. Mt. Pleasant, Ia., May 9, 1894; s. Harry J. and Hattie M. (Walker) deL.; A.B., Oberlin Coll., 1916; A.M., Stanford U., 1926, Ph.D., 1929; also studies U. Cal., Art Inst. Chgo., several European Univs. m. Beth Jones, Aug. 10, 1921; children—Peter Max, Leroy Arthur, David John, Allan Neal, Marilyn Beth. Business in Chgo., 1916-21; instr. Oberlin Coll., 1927, Pasadena City Coll., 1928-47; prof. zoology U. Hawaii, 1947-50, Ore. State Coll., 1950—; research for 10 univs. (incl. fgn.); for govt. agencies incl. Bur. Fish, Office Naval Research, Nat. Research Council, State Fla., various biol. stas., museums and pvt. corps., others. Fellow A.A.A.S.; mem. many sci. socs. Conglist. Mason. Author 50 sci. articles incl. 7 monographs on Porifera; also textbooks. Home: 200 Allen Lane, Corvallis, Ore. Died Feb. 4, 1958; buried Corvallis.

DELEE, JOSEPH BOLIVAR, obstetrician; b. Cold Springs, N.Y., Oct. 28, 1869; s. Morris and Dora (Tobias) D.; ed. 1 yr. at Coll. City of New York; M.D., Chicago Med. Coll. (now Northwestern U. Med. Sch.), 1891; interne Cook County Hosp., 1891-92; studied in univs. of Vienna and Berlin, 1893-94, Paris, 1894; hon. A.M., Northwestern, 1906; unmarried. Demonstrator anatomy, Chicago Med. Coll., 1892-93; lecturer in physiology, Dental Sch., 1892-93; became demonstrator obstetrics, Northwestern U. Med. Sch., 1894; lecturer on obstetrics same, 1895; took chair of obstetrics, 1896, and given title prof. obstetrics, 1897; now prof. emeritus obstetrics and gynecology, U. of Chicago. Founded, 1895, Chicago Lying-in Hosp. and Dispensary, opened hosp. in connection with same, 1899, now consultant in obstetrics Chicago Lying-in Hosp. and Dispensary; founder, 1932, and cons. obstetrician Chicago Maternity Center. Hon. fellow Edinburgh Obstet. Soc.; fellow Am. Gynecol. Soc. (v.p. 1929), Am. Coll. Surgeons; mem. A.M.A., Chicago Med. Soc. (councillor 1902), Ill. State Med. Soc. (sec. 1899), Chicago Gynecol. Soc. (pres. 1908), Miss. Valley Med. Assn., Chicago Hist. Soc. Author: Obstetrics for Nurses, 1904; Yearbook of Obstetrics, 1904-41, The Principles and Practice of Obstetrics, 1913, 7th Edit., 1938. Home: 5028 Ellis Av. Office: 5841 Maryland Av., Chicago, Ill. Died Apr. 2, 1942.

DELEUW CHARLES EDMUND, cons. engr.; b. Jacksonville, Ill., July 3, 1891; s. Oscar Anthony and Bessie Mary (Tribbey) DeL.; B.S., U. of Ill., 1912, C.E., 1916; married Martha Guthrie, Aug. 21, 1917 (dec.); 1 dau., Martha Guthrie (Mrs. Donald E. Stende); m. 2d, Ethel Buckmaster, July 29, 1927 (divorced 1948); children—Charles E., Sally (Mrs. Jon Peak) m. 3d, Sylvia Ffennell, Feb. 25, 1948 (dec. Oct. 1960); m. 4th, Emilene Brown, November 11, 1961. Chmn. bd. De Leuw, Cather & Co., cons. engrs.; transit and highway reports and plans for Chgo., Det., Los Angeles, Montreal, Toronto, Balt., Washington, Cleveland, Cin., Louisville, Boston, St. Louis, Providence, Buffalo, NY., Portland, San Francisco, Caracas, El Paso, Milwaukee, Norfolk, Oakland, Richmond, Istanbul, Sydney, Australia, Perth, Australia, New Jersey Turnpike; New York Thruway, Ohio Turnpike, Okla. Turnpike; consulting engineer for Department of Subways, City of Chicago, 1936-40, chief engr. 1941-44. Served as capt., 4th U.S. Engrs., 1917-19. Awarded D.S.C. Mem. Engring. Inst. of Can., Am. Institute Cons. Engrs., Am. Soc. C.E., Soc. Am. Mil. Engrs., Western and Ill. socs. engrs., Am. Transit Assn., Inst. Civil Engrs., Inst. Traffic Engrs., Phi Delta Theta. Clubs: University, Tavern; Mid-America. Home: Chicago IL Died Oct. 1970.

DELLINGER, JOHN HOWARD, physicist; b. Cleveland, July 3, 1886; s. John Pfohle and Catherine (Clark) D.; student Western Reserve U., Cleveland, 1903-07; A.B., George Washington U., 1908; Ph.D., from Princeton, 1913; D.Sc., George Washington U., 1932; m. Carol Van Benschoten. Oct. 11, 1909. Instr. physics, Western Reserve U., 1907-08; physicist. Nat. Bureau of Standards, 1907-48, chief of Radio Sect., 1918-46; chief Central Radio Propagation Lab., 1946-48, chief engr. Federal Radio Commn., 1928-29; chief of radio sect. of research div., Aeronatuics br., Dept. of Commerce, 1926-34; chief Interservice Radio Propagation Lab. 1942-46; chmn. Radio Tech. Com. for Aero, 1941-57 (Collier award for 1948); chmn. Radio Tech. Commn. for Marine Services, 1947-56; chmn. study group of radio propagation International Radio Consultative Com., 1949-57. Chairman general arrangements com. for 1957 Gen. Assembly International Radio Consultative Com., 1949-57. Chairman general arrangements com. for 1957 Gen. Assembly International Scientific Radio Union. Delegate to Conference Inter-allied Technical Committee on Radio Union. Delegate to Conference Inter-allied Technical Committee on Radio Communication, Paris, 1921; member technical staff Conference on Limitation of Armament, Washington, D.C., 1921; tech. adviser Internat. Radio Conf., 1927; U.S. del Internat. Tech. Cons. Com. on Radio Communications, The Hague, 1929, Copenhagen, 1931, and chmn. U.S. delgation, Lisbon, 1934, Bucharest, 1937; U.S. rep. at Internat. Electrotechnical Commn., Italy, 1927, and Scandinavia, 1930; tech. adviser Internat. Telecommunication Conf. Madrid, 1932; chmn. U.S. com. on radio frequency allocations for scientific research National Academy Sci. United States rep., Com. on Radio Wave Propagation, London, 1937; chmn. radio propagation sec., Nat. Defense Research Committee, 1942-46; mem. U.S. delgation Five-Power Telecommunications Conf., Moscow, 1946; U. S. del. Internat. Radio Consultive Com., Stockholm, 1948, Geneva, Switzerland, 1951, London, 1953, Los Angeles, 1959; International Scientific Radio Union, Zurich, 1950, Sydney, Australia, 1952, The Hague, 1954, Boulder, Colo., 1957, London, Eng., 1960. Recipient Pioneer award, Inst. Radio Engrs., 1960. Fellow Inst. Radio Engrs. (vice pres., 1924; pres. 1925); chmn. U.S. Govt. Interdepartment Radio Adv. Com., 1941-43; mem. Inst. of Navigation (v.p. 1949-52), Am. Geophys. Union, Internat. Sci. Radio Union (hon. pres. 1952—), Associazone Italiana di Aerotecnica (hon.), Alpha Tau Omega, Phi Beta Kappa, Eta Kappa Nu (eminent member). Unitarian. Club: Cosmos (Washington). Radio editor: Webster's Dictionary. Author: (with others) The Principles Underlying Radio Communication (govt. publ.), 1918; Radio Instruments and Measurements (govt. publ.), 1918; Radio Handbook (with L. E. Whittemore), 1922; also many articles and treatises on radio and elec. topics. Discoverer simultaneous occurence of solar eruptions and radio effects (Dellinger effect). Address: 3900 Connecticut Av., Washington 8. Died Dec. 28, 1962.

DEL MAR, ALEXANDER, mining engr., author; b. New York, N.Y., Aug. 9, 1836; attended Rev. Dr. Barry's Poly., Maurice's Mil. Acad., Madrid Sch. of Mines and New York U. Edited Daily American Times, 1854, Hunt's Merchants' Magazine, 1860, Social Science Review, 1864. Financial Chronicle, 1865; organized and dir. 1865-69, U.S. Bur. of Commerce, Naviation, Emigration and Statistics (now Dept. Commerce and Labor); U.S. del Internat. Congress, Turin, Italy, 1866. The Hague, 1868. St. Petersburg, 1872; mining commr. to U.S. Monteary Commn., 1876. Pres. Latin-Am. Chamber of Commerce. Home: New York, N.Y. Died July 2, 1926.

DEL MAR, ALGERNON, mining engr.; b. New York, Mar. 3, 1870; s. Alexander (author and historian) and Emily D.; ed. public schs., San Francisco; degree A.R.S.M., Royal School of Mines, London, 1891; m. Belle Rogers, Aug. 20, 1903; children—Roger Alexander, Bruce Eugene, Walter Homer. Practiced in S. Africa, Europe, Can., U.S., Mexico; specialty stamp mill constrn. and metall. treatment of gold and base metal ores; cons. metall. engr. Mem. Am. Inst. Mining Engrs. Author: Stamp Milling, 1912; Tube Milling, 1917; and number metall. articles in tech. press. Home: 4524 Alpha St., Los Angeles CA

DELMATER, CORNELIUS HENRY, mech. engr.; b. Rhinebeck, N.Y., Aug. 30, 1821; s. William and Eliza (Douglass) D.; m. Ruth O. Caller, 6 children. Built iron boats; built 1st steam fire engines used in U.S.; built engines for Monitor; partner (with Peter Hogg, ret. 1856) in iron works, 18S0-56, pres. Delameter Iron Works, 1856-89, constructed 30 gunboats for Spanish govt., 1869; noted for propellors, air compressors, for consconstn. 1st successful submarine torpedo boat, 1881; an original mem. Am. Soc. Mech. Engrs. Died N.Y.C., Feb. 7, 1889; buried Woodlawn Cemetery, N.Y.C.

DELOACH, ROBERT JOHN HENDERSON, investigator; b. Statesboro, Ga., Dec. 21, 1873; s. Zachariah Taylor and Jane (Williams) D.; A.B., U. of Ga., 1898, A.M., 1906; m. Bessie Holland of Johnston, S.C., Apr. 2, 1900; children—Edward Lowell, Louise, Evelyn, Julia Helen. Supt. city schs., Swainsboro, Ga., 1900; prin. teacher, U.S. Indian Sch., Ft. Sill, Okla. Ty., 1900-02; prin. Statesboro High Sch., 1903-05; botanist, Ga. Expt. Sta., 1906-08; prof. cotton industry, State Coll. of Agr., Ga., Oct. 1908-13; dir. Ga. Expt. Sta., 1913-17; dir. Armour's Bur. of Agr. Research, Chicago, since 1917. Collaborator, Bur. of Plant Industry, Washington, summer 1911. Mem. Am. Ornithologists' Union, Sigma Chi (Delta Chapter), Phi Beta Kappa, 1922; fellow A.A.A.S. Democrat. Clubs: Chicago, Cliff Dwellers, Quadrangle, Saddle and Sirloin. Baptist. Author: Rambles with John Burroughs, 1912; Agriculture for the Common Schs. Writer bulls. on plant breeding and diseases, also contbr. to current mags. Some time editor agrl. dept. Atlanta Constitution. Address: Statesboro GA

DELONG, IRA MITCHELL, prof. mathematics; b. Monroe, Jasper County, Ia., Jan. 7, 1855; s. William and Susan Adeline (Tool) D.; B.A., first honors, Simpson Coll., Indianola, Ia., 1878, M.A., 1881; LL.D., U. of Denver, 1914; m. Elizabeth A. Wright, Aug. 28, 1879; children—Edith E., Ruth; m. 2d, E. Vivian Sloan, April 3, 1929. Prof. mathematics, Central Bapt. Coll., Pella, Ia., 1878-86; prof. Latin and principal Preparatory Sch., Ia. Wesleyan Coll., Mt. Pleasant, 1886-88; prof. mathematics, U. of Colo., 1888-1925, now prof. emeritus. Organizer, mgr. Boulder Bldg. & Loan Assn. since 1890; an organizer, and dir. Merc. Bank & Trust Co., 1904-11, dir., 1918-37, pres. 1924-37. Organizer and ex-pres. Colo. Chatutaqua Assn. Del. Prog. Nat. Conv., 1912, 16; mem. Prog. Nat. Com., 1914-16; del. and pres. Boulder City Charter Conv., Aug.-Sept. 1917. Del. Gen. Conf. M.E. Ch., 1909; Colo. M.E. del. London Ecumenical Conf., 1921. Life mem. Am. Math. Soc., A.A.A.S.; mem. Math. Assn. of America, Colo. Math Soc. (pres.), Colo. Ednl. Council (ex-pres.), Sigma Xi (charter mem.), Delta Tau Delta. Mason (32 deg.,

Scottish Rite). Home: 201 Faculty Club House, Boulder, Colo. Died Sept. 2, 1942.

DELSASSO, LEO PETER, physicist, educator; b. Central City, Colo., Oct. 9, 1895; s. Fortunato and Elizabeth (Bitzenhoffer) D.; A.B., U. Cal. at Los Angeles, 1925; Ph.D., Cal. Inst. Tech., 1941; m. Mary Mussen, Dec. 18, 1948. Jr. engr. Southern Cal. Edison Co., 1917-19; instr. to prof. U. Cal. at Los Angeles, 1925-51, asst. to asso. dean grad. div., 1953-59, prof. physics, 1941-63. asso. dean grad. sch., 1958-59, chmn. dept. physics, 1959-63. Served from ensign to comdr. USNR, 1941-46. Fellow Acoustical Soc. Am. (v.p. 1957), Am. Phys. Soc.; mem. Am. Assn. Physics Tchrs., Sigma Xi Research in archtl. acoustics in auditoria; designer, builder sonic depth sounder giving continuous graphical record of depth of ocean, 1927. Home: Los Angeles CA Died July 26, 1971.

DELWICHE, EDMOND JOSEPH, prof. agronomy; b. Orbais, Belgium, Mar. 25, 1874; s. Desire Joseph and Marie Joseph (Dethy) D.; brought to U.S., 1879; Dixon (Ill.) Coll.; Interstate Sch. of Correspondence (Northwestern U.); B.S.A., U. of Wis., 1906; M.S., 1909; m. Alice Josephine Collin, 1899; children—Mary A. (Mrs. W.E. Hansen), Anthony J., Edmond D., Joseph J., Francis R., Richard O., Eugene A., Constant C. Teacher country schs. until 1903; with U. of Wis. since 1904, successively as field asst. Expt. Sta., supt. branch stations, asst. prof. agronomy, 1920-45 (emeritus since 1945), also supt. branch experiment stations. Fellow of the A.A.A.S.; mem. Am. Society Agronomy, Am. Genetics Assn.; Wis. Acad. Art Letters and Sciences, Alpha Zeta Fraternity. K.C. Originator two varieties of corn, also varieties of wheat, disease resistant peas, oats, soybeans. Author numerous expt. sta. publications. Home: R.F.D. 2, Green Bay. Office: Green Bay, Wis. Died Jan. 19, 1950.

DEMEREC, MILISLAV, geneticist; b. Kostajnica, Yugoslaiva, Jan. 11, 1895; s. Ljudevit and Ljubica (Dumbovic) D.; B.Sc., Coll. of Agr., Krizevci, Yugoslavia, 1916; student Grignon, France, 1919; Ph.D., Cornell U,, 1923; LL.D., Hofstra Coll.; Dr. hon. causa, U. Zagreb, 1960; D.Sc., L.I. U., 1961; m. Mary Alexander Zeigler, Aug. 24, 1921; children—Zlata Elizabeth, Vera Radoslava. Came to U.S., 1919, naturalized, 1931. Adjunct Krizevci Exptl. Sta., Yugoslavia, 1916-19; asst. in plant breeding Cornell U., 1921-23; resident investigator dept. genetics Carnegie Instn. Washington, 1923-35, asst. dir., 1936-41, acting dir., 1942, dir., 1943-60; dir. Biol. Lab., 1941-60; sr. geneticist Brookhaven Nat. Lab., 1960-65; research prof. biology C. W. Post Coll., L.I. U., 1966—; vis. prof. Rockefeller snst. Med. Research, N.Y.C., 1958-60; chmn. sec. zoology and anatomy NRC, 1958-61; associate genetics Columbia, 1943-65; hon. faculty medicine U. Chile. Mem. permanent internat. com. Genetics Congress, 1939-53; council 6th Internat. Congress, Genetics, Ithaca, N. Y., 1932; v.p. 7th Congress, Edinburgh, 1939, mem. organizer Cold Spring Harbor Symposia on Quantitative Biology, 1941-60. Recipient Order of St. Sava by Yugoslav Govt.; Kimber Genetics award Nat. Acad. Scis., 1962. Fellow A.A.A.S., mem. Acad. Scis. Yugoslavia (hon.), Genetics Soc. Japan, Soc. Biol. Santiago, Royal Danish Acad. Scis. and Letters, Am. Philos. Soc., Am. Soc. Naturalists (treas., v.p., pres.), Radiation Research Soc. (mem. council), Nat. Acad. Sci., Soc. Am. Bacertiologists, Soc. for Study Evolution, Genetics Soc. Am. (sec.-treas., v.p., pres.), Radiation Research Soc. (mem. coun-Am. Soc. Zoologists, Sigma Xi, Phi Kappa Phi. Contbr. many articles sci. jours. Home: Stewart's Lane, R.D., Syosett, N.Y. 11791. Office: Dept. Biology, Brookhaven Nat. Lab., Upton, L.I., N.Y. 11973. Died Apr. 12, 1966; buried Meml. Cemetery St. John's Ch., Syosset.

DE MOTTE, HARVEY CLELLAND; prof. mathematics, Ill. Wesleyan U.; b. nr. Greenfield, Ill., July 17, 1838; s. John L. and Phoebe A. DeMotte; grad. Ill. Wesleyan U., 1861; Ph.D., Syracuse U. (in mathatmatics); admitted to bar; m. Sarah J. Kern, July 26, 1864. Prof. mathematics, Ill. Wesleyan U., 1961-84; 1st lst. Co. G, 68th Ill. vols., 1862; pres. Chaddock Coll., Quincy, Ill., 1884-87; supt. Ill. Soldiers' Orphans' Home, 1887-93; lay delegate to Gen. Conf. M.E. Ch. 1892; editor and pub. Alumni Journal 7 yrs.; editor Daily and weekly Leader, Bloomington, Ill., 1896-99. Home: Bloomington, Ill. Died 1904.

DEMPSTER, ARTHUR JEFFREY, prof. physics; b. Toronto, Ont., Can., Aug. 14, 1886; s. James and Emily (Cheney) D.; A.B., U. of Toronto, 1909, A.M., 1910; grad. study univs. of Gottingen, 1911-12, Munich, 1912, Wurzburg, 1912-14, Chicago, 1914-16; 1851 Exhibition Scholar, 1912; Ph.D., U. of Chicago, 1916; Sc.D., U. of Toronto, 1937; married. Came to U.S., 1914, naturalized, 1918. Asst. prof. physics, U. of Chicago, 1919-23, asso. prof., 1923-27; prof. since 1927. Served as pvt. inf., U.S. Army, Nov. 1917-Mar. 1918, master signal electrician, Signal Corps, Mar.-Aug. 1918, 2d lt., in France, Oct. 1918-May 1919. Mem. Nat. Acad. Science, Am. Philos. Soc. Club: Quadrangle. Research in positive ray analysis of chem. elements, excitation of light and elec. discharges in gases. Home: 5757 Kenwood Av., Chicago, Ill., Died Mar. 11, 1950.

DENISON, A(LBERT) RODGER, geologist; b. Oklahoma Co., Okla., June 7, 1897; s. Jesse Irvin and Ada Irene (Naylor) D.; B.S., U. Okla., 1921, M.S., 1925; D.Sc., S.D. Sch. Mines and Tech., 1952; m. Maud Espy, Oct. 8, 1929; children—Cordelia Ann, Rodger Espy. Tchr. grad and high schs., Okla., 1913-21; part-time with Okla. Geol. Survey, 1920-22; teaching fellowship geology U. Okla., 1921-22; geologist Amerada Petroleum Corp., Tulsa, 1922, dist. geologist, 1925, div. geologist, 1927, chief geologist, 1937, v.p. 1950—; lectr. geology colls. and univs., 1940—. Mem Mem. Mil. Petroleum Adv. Bd., 1957—, chmn. Prodn. Panel, 1958—; mem. delegation from U.S. Govt. to Internat. Geol. Congress, 1956. Dir. Community Chest, Tulsa, 1955-61, Tulsa Council Social Agys., 1958-61. Fellow Geol. Soc. Am. (councilor 1954-57), Am. Assn. Advancement Sci., Am. Geol. Soc.; mem. Am. Assn. Petroleum Geologists (sec.-treas. 1929-30, pres. 1943-44), Am. Geol. Inst. (dir., chmn. finance com., mem. exec. com. 1948-51), Am. Inst. Mining and Metall. Engrs. (rep. bd. dirs. Am. Geol. Inst. 1948-51, mem. Lucas Medal award com. 1948-52), Am. Geophys. Union, Am. Petroleum Inst. (chmn. adv. com. Research Project 51, 1950-51), Kappa Alpha, Sigma Gamma Epsilon. Mason. Club; Tulsa. Contbr. profl. jours. Home: 7400 S. Harvard, Tulsa. Office: P.O. Box 2040, Tulsa 2. Died July 22, 1962.

DENISON, CHARLES SIMEON, engr.; b. Gambier, O., July 12, 1849; s. Rev. George and Janett Balloch (Ralston) D.; Norwich U., Northfield, Vt., 1 yr.; C.E., U. of Vt., 1871 (Sc.D., 1907); unmarried. Asst. engr. in constrn. Milwaukee & Northern R. R., 1871-72; instr. engring. from 1872, prof. stereotomy, mechanism and drawing from 1885, U. of Mich. U.S. astronomer and surveyor, locating boundary line between Wash. and Ida., part of 1873 and 1874. Republican. Episcopalian; mem. standing com. Diocese of Mich. Home: Ann Arbor, Mich. Died July 30, 1913.

DENMAN, IRA O., M.D., surgeon; b. Lenna, Kan., June 9, 1872; s. Francis M. and Lydia (Harding) D.; Allen Co. Normal Sch., Iola, Kan.; M.D., Hahnemann Med. Coll.; Chicago, 1897; post-grad. work Chicago Post-Grad. Med. Coll.; N.Y. Eye and Ear Infirmary; Harvard Med. Coll.; univs. of Vienna and Freiburg; Morfields Hosp., London, Eng.; m. Sabra Blair, Sept. 14, 1893; chidlren—Loraine, Ira O., Patti. Practiced general medicine and surgery, and eye, ear, nose and throat, Charleston, Ill., until close of 1907; moved to Toledo, O., Jan. 1908; practice limited to eye, ear, nose and throat. Chief of staff, Toledo Hospital, 1913—; oculist Pa. R.R., Detroit & Toledo Shore Line Railroad, Nickel Plate Railway. Chairman Bd. of Health, Charleston, Ill., 1903-07. Memeber Am. Bd. of Oto-Laryngology and Am. College of Physical Therapy. Republican. Mem. Christian (Disciples) Ch. Fellow A.C.S. Originated technique and designed chair for tonsilectomy under nitrous oxide and oxygen gas anesthesia. On editorial staff of Archives of Physical Therapy, X-Ray and Radium. Co-inventor of Physical Therapy, X-Ray and Radium. Co-inventor of vocaphone and artificial larynx for use in talking after a laryngectomy; v.p. The Vocaphone Co. Home: Toledo, O. Died Sept. 28, 1933.

DENNEY, OSWALD EVANS, officer U.S. Pub. Health Service; b. Smyrna, Del., July 21, 1885; s. Robert and Henrietta (Holding) D.; M.D., U. of Pa., 1913; D.T.M., U. of Philippines, 1915; m. Bertha Oliva Harris, Oct. 27, 1920; children—Robert Harris, Philip Holding, Oswald Evans, Mary Elizabeth Anne. Resident physician at Philippine General Hospital, 1913-14, San Lazaro Hospital, Manila, 1914-15; resident physician and later chief, Culion Leper Colony, P.I., 1915-19; exec. officer 4th dist. U.S. Pub. Health Service, 1919-20; med. officer in charge Nat. Leprosarium, Carville, La., 1921-35; chief quarantine officer Panama Canal Zone, 1936-39; traveling rep. Pan-Am. Sanitary Bureau, 1940; med. officer in charge U.S. Marine Hosp. and chief quarantine officer, Galveston, Texas, since 1940. Fellow Am. Coll. Physicians; mem. A.M.A., Am. Soc. Tropical Medicine, assn. Mil. Surgeons of U.S., Internat. Leprosy Assn., Am. Legion, Phi Chi, Sigma Xi. Democrat. Presbyterian. Clubs: Marine Hospital Golf (Carville). Author numerous papers on tropical medicine, particularly on Asiatic cholera and leprosy. Home: Smyrna, Del. Address: U.S. Marine Hospital, Galveston, Texas. Died Feb. 19, 1944.

DENNIE, CHARLES CLAYTON, physician; b. Excelsior Springs, Mo., Oct. 20, 1883; s. Arthur Doggett and Catherine (Heffley) D.; B.S., Baker U., 1908; M.D., U. of Kan., 1912; m. Glynn Bowden, July 29, 1940. Interne, Kan. City Gen. Hosp., 1912-13, Mass. Gen. Hosp., 1913-15; house officer and instr. in syphilis, Harvard Med. Sch., 1914-15; prof. of dermatology, Med. Sch., U. of Kan., from 1938, becoming prof. emeritus; clin. prof. medicine U. Mo.; dermatologist to Kansas City Gen., Mercy, St. Luke's, hosps. Served A.U.S., 1918-19; major, Med. Corps. A.E.F. Mem. Am. Bd. Dermatology and Syphilology, Am. Med. Assn., Am. Dermotol. Assn. (pres., hon. mem.), Am. Acad. Dermatology and Syphilology, Pan-Am. Med. Assn., French Soc. Dermatology and Syphilology, Brazilian (asso.), N.Y. (hon.) dermatol. assns. Author: Congenital Syphilis, 1940; A History of Syphilis, 1962; also monograph, Syphilis, 1928. Translator of Francisco Lopez de Villalobos book relating to syphilis, written 1498 (pub. in Bull. of History of Medicine). Home: Kansas City MO Died Jan. 13, 1971.

DENNING, REYNOLDS MCCONNELL, educator, mineralogist; b. Fitchburg, Mass., Sept. 3, 1916; s. William Wallace and Emma (McConnell) D.; B.S., Mich. Tech. U., 1939, M.S., 1949; Ph.D. in Mineralogy, U. Mich., 1953; m. Helen Green, June 25, 1942; 1 son, William Charles. Geologist, C.E., U.S. Army, 1939-40, Ark. Geol. Survey, 1940-41; Austin F. Rogers teaching fellow, Stanford, 1941-42; geologist Patino Mines and Enterprises, Cons., Inc., Llallagua, Bolivia, 1942-45; inst., then asst. prof. Mich. Tech. U., 1945-52; mem. faculty U. Mich., 1952-67, asst. prof., 1952-56, asso. prof., 1956-61, prof. mineralogy, 1961-67; cons., lectr. in field, 1945-67. Mem., acting chmn. panel indsl. diamonds Nat. Acad. Scis.-NRC, 1956-58. Mineral denningite named for him, 1961. Fellow Mineral. Soc. Am., Geol. Soc. Am., Royal Microscopical Soc., A.A.A.S.; mem. Mineral. Assn. Can., Geochem. Soc., Am. Crystallographic Assn., Mineral. Soc. Great Britain, Mich. Acad. Sci., Research Club Mich., Sigma Xi. Presbyn. Author papers in field. Researcher, cons. in crystal optics, phys. crystallography, diamond technology and gemology. Home: Ann Arbor MI Died Nov. 1, 1967; cremated.

DENNIS, LOUIS MUNROE, chemist; b. Chicago, May 26, 1863; s. Joseph S. and Faustina (Munroe) D.; Ph.B., U. of Mich., 1885, B.S. (Chem.), 1886; D.Sc., Colgate, 1923; d.Sc., U. of Mich., 1926; advanced study at U. of Munich, Polytechnikum of Dresden and of Aix-la-Chapelle, and pvt. lab. of Fresenius, Wiesbaden; m. Minnie Clark, Aug. 25, 1887; children—Faustine, Clark M., Frank S. Instr. chemistry, 1887-89, asst. prof., 1891-93, asso. prof. inorganic and analyt. chemistry, 1893-1900, prof. inorganic chemistry from 1900, head dept. of chemistry, 1903-1933 (emeritus), Cornell. Mem. Com. of Nat. Research Council on design of laboratories of chemistry. Fellow A.A.A.S. Author: Elementary Chemistry (with Frank W. Clarke), 1902; Laboratory Manual of Elementary Chemistry (with same), 1902; manual of Qualitative Analysis (with Theodore Whittlesey), 1902; Gas Analysis, 1913; Gas Analysis (with M.L. Nichols), 1929; Laboratory Manual and Problems (with A.W. Laubengayer); The Baker Laboratory of Chemistry at Cornell. Home: Ithaca, N.Y. Died Dec. 9, 1936.

DENNIS, WILLIAM B.; mining engr.; b. Cincinnati, Dec. 8, 1865; s. Rev. Mendenhall John and Sophia D.; Central U. of Ky., 1884; m. Queen H., d. Capt. D. M. Littlefield, of Port Townsend, Wash., June 1900. Entered newspaper work at Dayton, O., as spl. corr. Dayton Daily Journal and other papers; pub. The Farmers' Home, 1885-90; editor and mgr. Port Townsend (Wash.) Leader (daily and weekly), 1890-92; was several yrs. pres. and gen. mgr. Eureka-Pacific Consol. Mining Co. of Idaho; pres. and gen. mgr. Black Butter Quicksilver Mine of Ore.; v.p., mgr. Carlton & Coast R.R. Co.; v.p., mgr. Carlton Consol. Lumber Co. Inventor of The Dennis Roasting Furnace, Chmn. Ore. State Bur Mines and Geology, 1917-25; mem. Ore. State Bd. of Engring. Examiners, 1919-31; from Yamhill Co. in Ore. Ho. of Rep., 1919-20. Home: Carlton, Ore. Died Jan. 7, 1937.

DENSMORE, HIRAM D., botanist; b. Richmond, Wis., Jan. 20, 1862; A.B., Beloit (Wis.) Coll., 1886, M.A., 1890, D.Sc. (hon.), 1932; studied Cornell U., 1887-88, U. of Calif., 1896, Harvard, 1916; m. Effie Morse, 1889; children—Margaret, Dorothy, Janet, Theodora. Prof. botany, Beloit Coll., 1889, emeritus. Conglist. Author: General Botany (text), 1920; Laboratory and Field Exercises in Botany, 1920. Home: Beloit, Wis. Died July 18, 1940.

DENTON, JAMES EDGAR, mech. engr.; b. Piermont, N.Y., 1855; ed. pub. schs. and bus. coll.; grad. Stevens Inst. Tech., 1875. Asst. instrn. and lecturer, 1875-98, prof. mech. engring. and shopwork many yrs. from 1898. Stevens Inst. Tech. (emeritus). Engaged in mgr. rock-drilling machinery, 1882-86; constructed about 3 miles of the new Croton Aqueduct tunnel. Mem. Jury Awards in engring., Chicago Expn., 1893. Home: Maplewood, N.J. Died July 1928.

DE POUTALES, LOUIS FRANCOIS, naturalist; b. Neuchatel, Switzerland, Mar. 4, 1823; m. Elise Bachmann, 1 child. Accompanied Jean Agassiz on expdns. to study glaciers of Alps, 1840; came to U.S., 1846; with U.S. Coast Survey, 1848-73, in charge of tidal div., 1864-73; keeper Museum of Comparative Zoology, Harvard, 1873-80; collected and studied animal life at great depths; engaged in explorations carried on by Coast Survey steamer Bibb in waters of So. Fla., No. Cubs, Western Bahamas, located Pourtales Plateau off Southeastern Fla.; accompanied Agassiz on voyage in Hassler around Cape Horn to San Francisco, in charge of dredging and other deep sea work, 1871; did his most important work Deep Sea corals, published 1871; collected sea-urchin off So. Fla., named Pourtalesia. Died Beverly Farms, Mass., July 18, 1880.

DERBY, ELIAS HASKET, mcht., shipowner; b. Salem, Mass., Aug. 16, 1739; s. Capt. Richard and Mary (Hodges) D.; m. Elizabeth Crowninshield, Apr. 23, 1761, 7 children. ONe of wealthiest mchts. in New Eng. at close of Revolutionary War; sent ship Ligh Horse from Salem to St. Petersburg, Russia with cargo of sugar (1st ship to display Stars and Stripes to the Baltic), 1784; sent ship Grant Turk to Canton, China (1st New Eng. ship to Orient), 1785 most of fleet built under his personal supervision; his advice led to adoption by govt. of bonded warehouse system; built mansion, Salem, 1797. Died Salem, Sept. 8, 1799.

DERBY, GEORGE MCCLELLAN, colonel U.S. Army; b. at sea, Nov. 1, 1856; s. Capt. George H. Derby, U.S.A. and Mary A. (Coons) D.; ed. pvt. schs. Paris, Dresden and Lausanne, Switzerland, 1865-71; Washington U., St. Louis, 1872-73; Symonds Acad., Sing Sing, N.Y., 1873-74; grad. U.S. Mil. Acad. 1878, U.S. Engrs. Sch. of Application, 1881; m. Clara Matteson McGinnis, Nov. 6, 1878; m. 2d, Bessie Kidder, Apr. 4, 1904; children—George Townsend (U.S.A.), 13 Roger Barton (U.S.A.), Hollis Hasket, Elizabeth Crowninshield. 2d lt. Engr. Corps, 1878; 1st lt., 1881; capt., 1888; maj., 1898; lt. col. chief engr. U.S.V., May 9, 1898; hon. discharged, May 12, 1899; lt. col. engrs., U.S.A., 1906. on duty with battalion of engrs. U.S.A., 1878-81; asst. to Gen. John Newton in local charge of works at Hell Gate, E. River, and other river and harbor work in N.Y. and N.J., 1881-89; instr. practical mil. engring., U.S. Mil. Acad., 1889-93; and was mem. Academic Bd., U.S. Mil. Acad.; asst. to commr., D.C., 1893-94; in charge 4th dist. Mi Miss. River improvemtnt, 1894-1902; chief engr. 5th Army Corps in Cuba during Santiago cmapaign, and chief engr. 2d, Army Corps, 1898; in charge Louisville and Portland canal and toher river and harbor work, Louisville, Ky., 1902-03; in charge reserviors at headwarters of Miss. River, etc., Minn., 1903-06; retired at own request after 33 yrs. service, June 7, 1907. On active duty in charge 4th dist. Miss. River improvement, 1917-19; promoted col. U.S.A., 1919. Cited for gallantry in action. Fellow A.A.A.S.; mem. Am. Soc. of Civil Engrs. Active in civic and social work in New Orleans, 1899-1921, serving on parking commn. and other commns.; was pres. of La.S.P.C.A.; dir. New Orleans Charity Orgn. Soc., La. Free Kindergarten Assn., Home for Homeless Men, etc. Club: Round Table (New Orleans). Home: 1015 S. Carrollton Av., New Orleans. Died Oct. 1948.

DERICKSON, DONALD, civil engr.; b. Meadville, Pa., July 14, 1878; s. Charles Albert and Annie (Moorhead) D.; C.E., Thayer Sch. Civil Engring., Dartmouth, 1902; post grad. structural engring. Cornell U., 1905-07; D.Sc., Allegheny Coll., 1948; m. Margaret Kirby-Smith Gayden, June 27, 1912; 1 son, Gayden. With U.S. Coast and Geodetic Survey, 1898-1900; asst. prof. structural engring. Cornell U., 1907-12; prof. civil engring., head sch. civil engring. Tulane U., 1912-46, ret. 1946; cons. practice, founds., bridges, bldgs., marine and harbor works. Former mem. tech. adv. bd. Am. Inst. Steel Constn.; mem. La. Bd. Engring. Examiners. Hon. mem. Am. Soc. C.E. (past pres. La. sec.), Gulf Inst. Cons. Engrs., La. Engring. Soc. (past pres.); mem. Soc. Colonial Wars, Sigma Xi, Tau Beta Pi, Sigma Alpha Epsilon. Presbyn. Home: 1311 Henry Clay Av., New Orleans 18. Died May 5, 1962.

DERICKSON, SAMUEL HOFFMAN, prof. biology; b. Perry County, Pa., Apr. 9, 1879; s. Henry Benner and Lizzie Nomi (Hoffman) D.; student Lebanon Valley Acad., 1897-98; B.S., Lebanon Valley Coll., 1902, M.S., also hon. D.Sc., 1925; student Johns Hopkins U., 1903 and 1910; also student biol. labs., Cold Springs Harbor, N.Y. and Bermuda Islands; m. Jennie Vallerchamp, June 28, 1905; children—George Vallerchamp. Mary Elizabeth (dec.) Actg. prof. of biology Lebanon Valley College, 1903, professor 1907-50, emeritus professor of biology since 1950, actg. pres., 1912, treas. and trustee since 1918. Fellow A.A.A.S.; mem. Bot. Soc. of America, Am. Fern Soc., Pa. Acad. Science (pres.), Am. Soc. Zoölogists (asso.), Torrey Botanical Club Am. Assn. Univ. Profs. Republican. Mem. United Brethern Ch. Mason (past master). Address: 473 E. Main St., Annville, Pa. Died Nov. 27, 1951; buried Mt. Annville Cemetery, Annville.

DERLETH, CHARLES, JR., coll. dean; b. New York, Oct. 2, 1874; s. Charles and Annie (Taubert) D.; B.S., Coll. City of New York, 1894; C.E., Columbia University, 1896; LL.D., University of Calif., 1930; m. Emily Bush, May 19, 1904; children—Charles Edward, Dorothy. Instr. and lecturer, dept. of civ. engring., Columbia, 1896-1901; prof. of civ. engring., U. of Colo., 1901-1903; asso. prof. structural engring., 1903-07, prof. civ. engring, since 1907, dean Coll. of Civ. Engring, 1907-30, dean Coll. of Engring., 1930-42, U. of Calif. Cons. engr. U. of Calif., Alameda County, San Francisco Civic Center; chief engr. Carquinez Strait Highway Bridge; cons. engr. Oakland Estuary Tunnel, Golden Gate Bridge, San Francisco-Oakland Bay Bridge, Broadway Tunnels, Oakland, California. Mem. Am. Soc. C.E., Am. Soc. Testing Materials, Soc. Promotion Engring. Edn., Seismol. Soc. America, Internat. Assn. Testing Materials, Pacific Assn. Cons. Engrs., Am. Philos. Soc., Phi Gamma Delta, Phi Beta Kappa, Sigma Xi, Tau Beta Pi. Clubs: Engineers' (San Francisco); Claremont Country (Oakland). Home: 2834 Webster St., Berkeley 5 CA

DERR, HOMER MUNRO, engineering geologist; b. Turbotville, Pa., Feb. 5, 1877; s. John Frederick and Sarah (Houseknecht) D.; student U. of Mich., U. of Minn., Mich. Coll. of Mines; A.B., Stanford 1898; scholar in geology, Columbia, 1899, A.M., 1901; Ph.D., U. of Pa., 1903; m. Anna Laurie Stacy, Apr. 1, 1903; children—Coralie, Stacy. Asst. in physics, Columbia, 1899-1901; instr. mining engring. and geology, U. of Wyo., 1901-02; Tyndale fellow in physics, U. of Pa., 1902-03; supt. mines, Santa Margarita Gold Mining Co., Colombia, S.A., 1903-04; prof. of mathematics and civil engring. Clarkson College of Technology, 1904-06; professor civil engineering, S. Dak. State Coll., 1906-13; state engr., S. Dak., 1913-21; prof. mathematics, Ala. Poly Inst., 1921-22; prof. mathematics and engring., Southwestern Presbyn. U., 1922-25; prof. mathematics and engring., State College, West Virginia, 1925-33. Mathematician, Douglas Aircraft Co. 1942-45. Engineer S.D. Bd. of Railroad Commrs., 1908-10; sec. S.D. Highway Commn., 1917-19; mem. Commn. to Investigate Feasibility of Power Project at Big Bend (Missouri River), 1917; mem. Commn. to Report on Drainage and Prevention of Overflow in Valley of Red River of the North, 1917. Conducted survey leading to Angostura Irrigation Project (100,000 acres), in South Dakota. Mem. Am. Soc. C.E., Mathematical Association of America, Chi Beta Chi, Beta Kappa Chi. Author: Siliceous Oolites of Sweetwater County, Wyo., 1902; A Method of Petrographic Analysis, 1903; Biennial Reports of the State Engineer of S.D., 1914, 16, 18; Plane Trigonometry (with B. H. Crenshaw), 1923; Key to Plane Trigonometry, 1928; also examinations and reports on various mines in Calif., Ariz., Nev., Ida., Wyo., Colo., and Mexico. "Expert rifleman," Nat. Rifle Assn. Home: 16113 S. Caress Av., Compton CA

DERR, LOUIS, physicist; b. Pottsville, Pa., Aug. 6, 1868; s. Simon and Sarah Ann (Sieger) D.; B.A., Amherst, 1889, M.A., 1892; S.B., Mass. Inst. Tech., 182; student Harvard Grad. Sch., 1892-93; m. Jane E. Coy, June 7, 1893. Asst. in physics, 1892-93, instr., 1893-1901, asst. prof., 1901-04, asso. prof., 1904-09, prof. from 1909, Mass. Inst. Tech. Inst. physics, Boston U., 1893-98; in charge of instruction in physics, Boston Normal Sch. of Gymanstics, 1895-1908. Fellow Am. Acad. Arts and Sciences, Royal Photo. Sco. Gt. Britain. Author: Notes on the Principles of Dynamo and Transformer Design, 1902; Photography for Students of Physics and Chemistry, 1906. Home: Brookline, Mass. Died May 11, 1923.

DESLOGE, JOSEPH, engineer; b. St. Louis, Jan. 26, 1889; s. Firmin and Lydia (Davis) D.; A.M., St. Louis U., 1909; B.S., Mass. Inst. Tech., 1912; m. Anne Farrar, Oct. 10, 1922 (dec.); children—Joseph, Anne (Mrs. Louis Werner, II), Bernard, Zoe (Mrs. Samuel Fordyce); m. 2d, Marie Saalfrank, October 26, 1953. Pres. Killark Electric Mfg. Co. since 1913; pres. Minerva Oil Co. from 1940; v.p. Chemalloy Foundry Co. from 1945; dir. St. Joseph Lead Co. Pres. United Charities, 1942-43. Served as lt. French Army, World War I. Decorated Croix de Guerre, Legion of Honor (France); named Papal Chamberlain. Mem. Mo. Hist. Soc. (past pres.), St. Louis Acad. Sci. (past pres.), A.A.A.S., Am. Inst. Mining and Metall. Engrs., Am. Geog. Soc. Home: Florissant MO Died Mar. 11, 1971.

DESMOND, THOMAS CHARLES, retired engr.; b. Middletown, N.Y., Sept. 15, 1887; s. Thomas Henry and Katherine (Safried) D.; A.B magna cum laude, Harvard, 1908; S.B. in C.E., Mass. Inst. Tech., 1909; L.H.D., Union Coll., 1939; m. Alice B. Curtis, Aug. 16, 1923. Engaged in constrn. work in various parts of U.S., 1909-14; pres. T. C. Desmond & Co., engrs. and contractors, N.Y. from 1914, pres. Colonial Terraces Corp. Mem. N.Y. State Senate, 1930-58. Nat. treas. Roosevelt Non-Partisan League, 1916; pres. N.Y. Young Republican Club, 1926-29; del. Rep. Nat. Conv., Kansas City, Mo., 1928, Phila., 1940; mem. N.Y. Rep. Co. Com., 1915-30. Trustee or office several profl., sci. or ednl. instns. Mem. bd. mgrs. N.Y. Bot. Garden, N.Y.C. Trustee Theodore Roosevelt Assn.; mem. nat. adv. com. White House Conf. Aging, 1959. Mem. vis. com. bd. overseers dept. of astronomy Harvard; mem. at large nat. council Boy Scouts Am.; mem. adv. bd. Inst. Nutrition Scis., Columbia, 1959; life mem. governing bd. Mass. Inst. Tech. Recipient Silver Antelope award Boy Scouts Am., 1947; Brotherhood Award, 1956, Distinguished Service award N.Y. chpt. N.Y. Soc. Profl. Engrs., 1958; 1957 annual award Gerontological Research Found.; N.Y. State YMCA youth and govt. award, 1958; 1959 Ann. War Meml. award N.Y. Young Rep. Clubs, Eloise Payne Luauer medal, Garden Club Am., 1961. Mem. Nat. Geriatrics Soc. (hon.), Am. Astron. Soc., Astron. Soc. of the Pacific, Nat. Municipal League, State Soc. Profl. Engineers, C. of C. State New York, Acad. Scis., Am. Acad. Polit. and Social Sci., Royal Astron. Soc. of Can., Harvard Engring. Soc., Am. Soc. C.E. (life), Nat. Inst. Social Scis., A.A.A.S., Phi Beta Kappa, Phi Beta Kappa Assos., Sigma Alpha Epsilon. Mason (K.T.), Elk. Clubs: Newburgh City, Powelton; University, Union League, Union, Engineers, Harvard, Technology, Tuxedo, City, Century, Explorers (N.Y.C.); Harvard (Boston). Fort Orange (Albany); Adirondack; Lake Placid. Contbr. articles to mags. Owner and developer pvt. arboretum containing nearly 800 species trees and shrubs. Recipient medal award Fed. Garden Clubs of N.Y. State, 1950; large gold medal award Mass. Hort. Soc., 1950; Mass. Inst. Tech. Silver Stein Award, 1952; N.Y. Hort. Soc. Amateur award, 1971. Address: Newburgh NY Died Oct. 7, 1972; buried Fairfield CT

DESMOND, THOMAS HENRY, land architect, engr.; b. Hyde Park, Boston, Dec. 19, 1884; s. John Jerome and Margaret (Conway) D.; student Roxbury (Mass.) Latin Sch., Roxbury, 1897-99; diploma in horticulture, Conn. Agrl. Coll., 1906; B.S.A., Cornell, 1908; student landscape architecture in Europe, 1913; m. Olive Antionette Eddy, June 1, 1910; childrJohn E., Thomas C., Robert C., Philip D., Elizabeth (Mrs. Dana A. Keil), MacChesney, James M., Sylvia E. (Mrs. Austin M. Sheldon). Draftsman, superintendent construction, designer, office chief, Townsend & Fleming, landscape architects, Buffalo, N.Y., 1908-13; independent practice landscape architect, Hartford, Conn., 1913-18; dist., town planner, U.S. Housing Corp., Washington, 1918; pvt. practice, Simsbury, Conn., 1919-28; pres., treas., Thomas H. Desmond, Inc., Simsbury, Conn., 1928—; inspector C.C.C. State Park Development in New England and asst. regional officer, regional 1, Nat. Park Service, 1934-37; supt. . landscape constrn. Pentagon Bldg., U.S. War Dept., Washington, 1942-43; planning cons. Conn. State Park and Forest Conn. 1943—; supt. Conn. State Parks 1948-49; president Town and City Planning, New Haven, Conn. Sec. Simsbury Development Co. Important works: Willow Brook Park, New Britian Conn., estates F. B. Rentschler, Geo. J. Mead, etc., U.S. Coast Guard Acad., New London, Conn., U. Conn. campus; developed plans for Westminster Sch., Taft Sch., Conn. Masonic Home, etc. Registered engr. and land surveyor, Conn. Mem. Pres. Hoover's conf. on small home bldg. and ownership (collaborator report on Home Grounds Planning), 1932. Fellow Am. Soc. Landscape Architects (vice pres. 1942-49; trustee) mem. American Arbitration Assn. (mem. nat. panel arbitrators 1941—;) bd. edn., Town of Simsbury, Conn., 1924-28, chmn. town plan commn., 1928-34, mem. zoning bd. appeals, 1940—, Am. Planning and Civic Assn., Conn. Soc. C.E., Conn. Hort. Soc., Conn. Forest and Park Assn., Wilderness Soc., Eta Lambda Sigma. Republican. Conglist. Mason (Grand master, grand lodge of Conn., 1939-40, bd. mgrs. Masonic Charity Found. Conn., 1939—), co-founder, Philosophic Lodge of Reserach, 1941. Office: One Drake Hill Rd., Simsbury, Conn. Died May 20, 1950; buried Simsbury (Conn.) Center Cemetery.

DE SOLLAR, TENNEY COOK, cons. mining engr., b. Denver, Mar. 15, 1881; s. Henry Cook and Ellen Josephine (Waggoner) D.; E.M., Colo. Sch. of Mines, 1904; m. Edythe Longnecker Hoffman, June 20, 1906. Engaged in mining projects, Rico, Idaho Springs, Eldora, Colo., Hancock, Mich., 1908-24; Bessemer, Ala., 1924-42. Capt., C.E., 1918, lt. col., 1942-43, Distinguished Achievement medal Colo. Sch. of Mines, 1954. Licensed cons. engr. (mining). Mem. Am. Inst. Mining and Metall. Engrs. (Legion of Honor 1954), Colo. Colorado Sci. Soc., Am. Soc. Mil. Engrs., Am. Legion, S. A.R., Beta Theta Pi. Episcopalian. Mason (Shriner). Address: 1160 Lafayette St., Denver 80128. Died Jan. 22, 1966.

D'ESPOSITO, JOSHUA cons. civil engr.; b. Sorrento, Italy, July 30, 1878; s. Antonio and Louisa Marie (di Pontecorvo) D'E.; student Royal Nautical Inst., Sorrento; hon.Eng.D., Ill. Inst. Tech., 1941; m. Katherine Von Olnhausen, Aug. 18, 1908; children—Louise, Joshua, Julian. Came to U.S., 1898, naturalized citizen, 1907. Began as draftsman Pa. R.R. Co., 1904, advanced to asst. to chief engr., 1913, in charge Chgo. terminal developments, 1913; asst. mgr. Emergency Fleet Corp., U.S. Shipping Bd., Washington, 1917-19; returned to Chgo., 1919, in charge Union Station project until completed, 1925; in pvt. practice, 1927—; apptd. state engr. Pub. Works Adminstrn., 1933; project engr. Sanitary Dist. Chgo., 1934. Mem. Commn. and federal project engr. Chgo. Subway, cons. engr. subway, also Chgo. Plan Commn. Mem. Am. Soc. C.E., Am. Ry. Engring Assn., Western Soc. Engrs. Independent Republican. Clubs: Union League, Engineers Exmoor Country. Home: 2744 Ridge Av., Evanston, Ill. Office: 20 N. Wacker Drive, Chgo. Died Nov. 16, 1954; buried All Saints Cemetery, Des Plaines, Ill.

DETMOLD, CHRISTIAN EDWARD, civil engr.; b. Hanover, Germany, Feb. 2, 1810; s. Johann Detmold; m. Phoebe Crary, 2 children. Came to U.S., 1826; became surveyor, Charleston, S.C.; completed survey for Charleston & Hamburg R.R. & Canal Co., 1830, won $500 prize for designing best locomotive used by this company; worked for U.S. War Dept., 1833-34, supervised constrn. Ft. Sumter, S.C.; surveyor on various Eastern railroads, 1834-44; iron mfr., Md., 1845-52; constrn. engr. of famous crystal palace, World's Fair "Exhibition of the Industry of All Nations" (opened 1853); lived for time in Europe. Author: The Historical, Political and Diplomatic Writings of Niccolo Machiavelli; Translation from the Italian, 1882. Died N.Y.C., July 2, 1887.

DETRICK, JACOB STOLL, mechanical engr.; b. Frederick Co.; Md., Aug. 1, 1839; s. Henry and Eliza (Cronise) D.; ed. dist. sch. 3 yrs.; m. Harriet Markell, of Frederick City, Md., Nov., 1869. Began as apprentice, machinists' trade, with A. & W. Denmead & Sons, Baltimore, 1857; draftsman, foreman and supt., Union Iron Wks., San Francisco, 1861-76; mfr. gen. machinery, gun sights, gun carriages, etc. (for the govt.), Baltimore, 1879-1915; pres. Detrick & Harvey Machine

Co., Inc., 1890. Has designed and built a great variety of machinery; invented the open side iron planer, etc. Trustee Md. Inst. Schs. Art and Design fro Promotion of Mech. Arts. Progressive. Protestant. Mem. Am. Soc. Mech. Engrs. Home: 205 E. Preston St., Baltimore.

DETWEILER, A(LBERT) HENRY, educator; b. Perkasie, Pa., Oct. 4, 1906; s. Wm. H. and Lillian M. (Myers) D.; B.Arch., U. of Pa., 1930; m. Catharine S. Bunnell, Feb. 7, 1939; children—John H., Katharine D., Alice M., Mary S. Architect and archaeologist Univ. Museum, Tell Billa, Iraq, 1930-31; student Am. Sch. Oriental Research, Jerusalem, 1932-35, archtl. fellow, 1933-35; architect and archaeologist Tell Beit Mirsim, Gerasa, Bostra, Samaria, 1933-35; Yale, Dura Europos, 1935-37; Mich., Seleucia-on-the Tigris, fall 1936; asst. on survey Mosque d'Juma, Isfahan, summer 1936; asst. in research, Yale, 1937-39; mem. faculty Cornell since 1939, prof. architecture, 1948-56; asso. dean Coll. Architecture, Cornell, 1956-70; Langley scholarship Am. Inst. Architects, Eng., 1947; acting dir. Am. Sch. Oriental Research, Jerusalem, summer 1949, dir. 1953-54, president, 1955-66, trustee, 1955-66, life trustee, 1966-70; mem. Jerusalem Sch. Com., 1951-54; vis. prof. Roman archaeology Am. Sch. in Jerusalem, Jan. 1951; Haskell lectr. Oberlin Grad. Sch. Theology, 1964; Guggenheim fellow in Italy, 1961-62; associate director of Cornell-Harvard Expdn. to Sardis, 1958-70; archaeol. adviser Cosa Expdn., Am. Acad. Rome, 1954; mem. nat. com. to decide how to salvage Abu Simbel tombs, Egypt, 1963; mem. com. to survey ancient and medieval monuments in Egypt for Am. Research Inst., Egypt, 1966; mem. U.S. nat. com. Internat. Council Monuments and Sites-Icomas, 1967-70. Fellow A.I.A.; mem. Am. Inst. Archaeology, Soc. Archtl. Historians (1st v.p.), DeWitt Hist. Soc., N.Y. State Assn. Architects. Democrat. Unitarian. Clubs: Statler (Ithaca); Cornell (N.Y.C.). Author: Manual Archaeological Surveying, 1948. Contbr. articles in profl. publs.; chpts. and drawings in books. Home: Ithaca NY Died Jan. 30, 1970; buried Perkasie PA

DETWILER, SAMUEL RANDALL, prof. anatomy; b. Ironridge, Pa., Feb. 17, 1890; s. Isaiah H. and Mary (Hallman) D.; student Ursinus Coll., Collegeville, Pa., 1910-12; Ph.B,, Yale U., 1914, A.M., 1916, Ph.D., 1918, hon. M.S., 1931; m. Gladys I. Hood, July, 1942; children (previous marriage)—Samuel Randall (dec.), Ross Harison. Asst. Instr. biology, Yale, 1914-17, instr. in anatomy, 1917-20; asso., Peking (China) Union Med. Coll., 1920-23; asst. prof. Zoölogy, Harvard, 1923-26, asso. prof., 1926-27; prof. anatomy and exec. officer of dept., Columbia, 1927—. Served as Physiologist (civilian basis), U.S. C.W.S., 1917-18. Mem. Am. Assn. Anatomists (mem. exec. com. 1930-34, v.p. 1952-54, pres. 1954-56), Am. Physicians Art Assn., N.Y. Acad. Scis., Am. Naturalists, Am. Neurol. Assn. Anatomists (mem. exec. com. Soc. Exptl. Biology and Medn., Am. Acad. Arts and Sciences, Harvey Soc., Am. Philos. Soc., Sigma Xi, Gamma Alpha, Nu Sigma Nu, Omicron Kappa Upsilon. Author: Neuroembryology, 1936; Vertebrate Photorecptor, 1943. Mem. editorial bds.: Exptl. Biology, monograph series; Jour. Exptl. Zoology; Columbia Biol. series. Mem. adv. board of Human Biology. Contbr. to Jour. Exptl. Zoology, Jour. Comparative Neurology, Proc. Soc. Exptl. Biology and Medicine, Am. Jour. Anatomy, Anat. Record and other journals. Home: 160 Cabrini Blvd., New York 33. Office: 630 W. 168th St., N.Y.C. 22. Died May 2, 1957.

DEUEL, HARRY JAMES, JR., college dean; b. St. Paul, Minn., Oct. 15, 1897; s. Harry James and Mrytle Lillian (Mouser) Deule; A.V., Carleton College, 1918; Ph.D., Yale Univerity, 1923; married Grace Antionette Cutting July, 16, 1924. Chemists aid, later junior chemist, office home econ., U.S. Dept. Agriculture, 1917-20; instr. dept. physiology med. sch., Cornell U., 1923-27, asst. prof., 1927-28; prof. physiology med. sch., U. of Md., 1928-29; prof. biochemistry med. sch., U. of S. Calif. since 1929, dean of graduate school, 1949—; Fulbright lecturer, Dunn Nutritional Laboratory, Cambridge, England, 1955-56, Member of food, and nutrition adv. com. Cal. State Disaster Council. Served in Students' Army Training Corps, 1918. Vice chmn., city and county food and nutrition com., Los Angeles. Mem. Am. Soc. Biol. Chemists, Am. Physiol. Soc., American Inst. Nutrition (received) Broden award, 1949). Soc. of Experimental Biology and Medicine (chmn. Southern Calif. sect. 1941-42), Biochem. Soc. (London), Am. Chem. Soc., Harvey Soc., A.A.A.S., Am. Oil Chemists Assn., Assn. Study Internal Secretions, Sigma Xi (chmn. of U. of S. Calif. chapter 1939-41), Phi Kappa Phi (pres. U. of S. Calif. chapter 1945-46), Phi Lambda Upsilon, Phi Beta Pi. Author: The Lipids, Vol. 1 Chemistry, Intersci., 1951; Vol. 2 Bio-Chemistry, Intersci., 1954. Mem. and dir. Annual Reviews, Inc., 1946—, pres. 1953—; asso. editor, Am. Jour. Physiol., Circulation Reserach; contbr. 250 articles to sci. publs. Home: 365 W. Bellevue Dr., Pasadena 2, Cal. Office: 3518 University Av., Los Angeles 7. Died Apr. 17, 1956; buried Olive Wood Cemetery, Riverside, Cal.

DEUSSEN, ALEXANDER cons. geologist; b. San Antonio, Jan. 19, 1882; s. Charles and Chlotilda (Nordhaus) D.; B.S., U. Tex., 1903, M.S., 1904; m. Sue Burnett Campbell, Aug. 23, 1905; 1 dau., Lucile (Mrs. John F. McRae). Instr. geology U. Tex., 1905-14; asst. geologist U.S. Geol. Survey, 1907-14; geologist Gulf Prodn. Co., 1915-16, cons. geologist, 1916-28; v.p. Marland Oil Co., Tex., 1928-30, cons. geologist, 1930—; dir. Perforating Guns-Atlas Corp., Awarded Sidney Powers medal for distinguished service petroleum geology. Am. Assn. Petroleum Geologists, 1947. Fellow Geol. Soc. Am.; mem. Am. Assn. Petroleum Geologists (past pres., hon. mem. for distinguished service 1953), Am. Inst. Mining and Metall. Engrs., A.A.A.S., Houston Geol. Soc. (hon.), Houston Philos. Soc. (past pres.), Soc. Econ. Geologists, Tex. Geog. Soc., Soc. Exploration Geophysicists, Soc. Econ. Paleontogists and Mineralogists, Am. Petroleum Inst., Tex. State, West Tex. hist. assns., Phi Beta Kappa, Sigma Xi. Contbr. articles profl. jours. Home: R.F.D. 1, Ponder, Tex. Office: San Jacinto Bldg., Houston 2. Died Sept. 3, 1959.

DEVLIN, THOMAS FRANCIS, physician; b. Phila., Jan. 20, 1869; s. Thomas and Helen (Sanford) D.; A.B., LaSalle Coll., Phila., 1887; student Georgetown U., 1887-88; M.D., U.Pa., 1891, post-grad., 1891-92; m. Stella Hill, May 29, 1905; children—Thomas Francis, John Joseph. Physician, Phila., 1892—; asso., with St. Mary's Hosp.; staff mem. Misericordia Hosp., Archbishop Ryan Meml. for Deaf-mutes; pediatrist; pioneer in endocrinology as applied to children. Dir. and partner with wife, Marydell Sch. for physically and mentally retarded children. Republican. Catholic. Home: Manor Av., Langehorne, Pa. Died June 30, 1952.

DEVOE, ALAN author, naturalist; b. Montclair, N.J., Oct. 13, 1909; s. William Beck and Edith Guy (Taylor) D.; student Montclair High Sch., 1923-27, Columbia U., 1927-30; m. Mary Sheridan Berry, June 14, 1932. Author monthly department "Down to Earth" American Mercury, 1937—; asso. editor The Writer; contributing editor Audubon Mag., Am. Mercury; spl. contbr., editorial cons. natural history Reader's Digest. Sponsor, Defenders of Furbearers, Washington. Author: Phudd Hill, 1937; Down to Earth, 1940; Lives Around Us, 1942; Mind in Nature (monograph), 1946; Speaking of Animals, 1947; This Fascination Animal World, 1951; Our Animal Neighbors (with Mary Berry Devoe), 1953. Contribution to Atlantic Monthly, Country Gentleman, The Land, Nature Magazine, etc. Lectr. radio and television. Home: Phudd Hill, Hillsdale N.Y., Died Aug. 17, 1955; buried Mt. Hebron Cemetery, Montclair, N.J.

DEWEY, FREDERIC PERKINS, chemist; b. Hartford, Conn., Oct. 4, 1855; s. Daniel S. and Elizabeth (Perkins) D.; Ph.B., Sheffield Scientific Sch. (Yale), 1876; m. Charlotte Esther Candee, Apr. 12, 1877. Asst. analytical chemistry, Lafayette Coll., 1876-77; chemist with iron and steel mfrs. until 1881; with Dr. George W. Hawes investigated the building stone of the U.S. for the 10th census, 1881; curator metallurgy, U.S. for the 10th census, 1881; curator metallurgy, U.S. Nat. Museum, 1882-89; propr. commercial lab., 1890-1903; assayer Mint Bur., U.S. Treasury, 1903—; acting dir. Mint Bureau, 1913. Author: Descriptive Catalogue Collections in Economic Geology and Metallurgy (bull. No. 42), 1891. Deceased.

DEWEY, LYSTER HOXIE, botanist; b. Cambridge, Mich., Mar. 14, 1865; s. Francis Asbury and Harriet (Smith) D.; B.S., Mich. Agrl. Coll., 1888; m. Etta Conkling, Aug. 22, 1889; children—Grace Marguerite, Mary Genevieve (dec.). Inst. botany, Mich. Agrl. Coll., 1888-90; asst. botanist, 1890-1902, botanist in charge of fiber investigations since 1902, U.S. Agrl. Dept. Conducted investigations on grasses and troublesome weeds; U.S. rep. to Internat. Fiber Congress, Soerabaia, Java, 1911. Fellow A.A.A.S.; mem. Washington Acad. of Sciences, Bot. Soc. Washington, Biol. Soc. Washington. Democrat. Presbyterian. Home: 4512 9th St., Washington. Died Nov. 1944.

DEWITT, SIMEON, univ. chancellor, state ofcl.; b. Wawarsing, N.Y., Dec. 25, 1756; s. Dr. Andries and Jannetje (Vernooy) DeW.; B.A., Queen's Coll. (now Rutgers), 1776, M.A., 1788; m. Elizabeth Lynott, Oct. 12, 1789; m. 2d, Jane Varick Hardenberg; m. 3d, Susan Linn, Oct. 29, 1810; 6 children. Left coll. to join N.Y. Militia; served as asst. geographer Continental Army, 1778-80, chief geographer, 1780-81; surveyor gen. State of N.Y., 1784-1834; a commr. to settle N.Y.-Pa. boundary dispute, 1786-87; surveyor of various canal routes for N.Y.; published map of N.Y. State, 1802; regent, then vice-chancellor Univ. State of N.Y., 1798-1829, chancellor, 1829-34; a founder N.Y. Soc. for Promotion of Agr., Arts and Manufactures (later became part of Albnay Inst.), v.p. Albany Inst., many years; mem. Am. Philos. Soc. Author: The Elements of Perspective (collection of writings), 1813; contbr. scientific papers to various journals. Died Ithaca, N.Y. Dec. 3, 1834.

DE WOLF, FRANK WALBRIDGE, geologist; b. Vail, Ia., Mar. 22, 1881; s. John Horton and Carrie M. (Tempest) D.; S.B., U. Chgo., 1903, post-grad., 1903-04; m. Fanny Davis, Dec. 26, 1904; children—John Walbridge, Eleanor, Robert William, Frank Tempest. Geologic aid and asst. geologist U.S. Geol. Survey, Washington, 1904-08; asst. state geologist, Ill., 1908-09; acting dir. Ill. Geol. Survey, 1909-11, dir. 1911-23. Asst. dir. U.S. Bur. of Mines and chmn. sub-com. on geology cantonments NRC, 1927, div. of states relations, 1919-23; chief geologist Humphreys Corp., 1923-27; v.p., and gen. mgr. La. Land and Exploration Co., oil producers, 1927-31; head of dept. geology U. Ill., 1931-46, emeritus, 1946—; cons. on petroleum geology. Fellow Geol. Soc. Am. Soc. Econ. Geologists; mem. Am. Inst. Mining Engrs., Am. Assn. Petroleum Geologist (ex-v.p.), Ill. State Acad. Science (ex-pres.), Phi Delta Theta, Sigma Xi. Conglist. Clubs: University, Urbana Golf and Country, Kiwanis, Home: 601 W. Delaware Av., Urbana, Ill. Died Sept. 16, 1957.

DEXTER, GREGORY MUMFORD, cons. indsl. engr.; b. East Providence, R.I., Oct. 3, 1887; s. Walter Mumford and Emily O. (Potter) D.; C.E., Mass. Inst. Tech., 1908; M.E., Bklyn. Poly. Inst., 1929; m. Katie W. Jaecker, Nov. 24, 1934; children—Gregory Warren, Nancy Lee, Susan Marcy. Draftsman Hazen & Whipple, 1908-10; chief draftsman constrn. Ore. Short Line R.R., 1910-14; jr. engr. U.S. Engrs., Wheeling, W.Va., 1914-16; exec. engr. Honolulu Iron Works Co., 1916-28; engr. Peabody, Smith & Co., 1928-29; v.p. and gen. mgr. Finn, Iffland & Co., 1930-31; engring. asso. Bitting, Inc., 1932-44; in pvt. practice as cons. indsl. engr. since 1944. Fellow Am. Soc. M.E.; mem. Am. Society for Engring. Edn. Clubs: New York Athletic; Scarsdale (N.Y.) Town; Chemists. Contbr. tech. articles on mech. and chem. engring. to jours. Home: Scarsdale NY Died July 20, 1969.

D'HERELLE, FELIX, prof. bacteriology; b. Montreal, Can., Apr. 25, 1873; s. Felix and Augustine (Meert) d'H.; prep. edn., Lycee Louis le Grand, Paris; B.A., Lille, France, 1888; M.D., U. of Leiden, Holland; hon. M.A., Yale, 1928; hon. M.D., Montreal (Can.) U., 1930, Laval U., Quebec, Can., 1930; m. Mary Kerr, of France, July 11, 1893; children—Marcelle, Huberte. Director bacteriol. lab., Guatemala, 1902-06, Merida, Mexico, 1907-08; asst., Inst. Pasteur, Paris, 1908-14, chief of lab., 1914-21; lecturer U. of Leiden, 1922-23; dir. Internat. Sanitary Council of Egypt, 1923-27; prof. protobiology, Yale, 1928-34; hon. prof. University of Tiflis (U.S.S.R.), 1934. Fellow Royal Soc. Canada; member Harvey Soc., Am. Assn. Univ. Profs., Leningrad Soc. Microbiology; foreign mem. Societe de Biologie of Paris. Awarded Leewenhoek medal, Dutch Acad. Sciences, 1925; William Wood Gerhard medal, Philadelphia Pathol. Society, 1928; Shaundim medal, Institute Tropical Medicine, Hamburg, 1930; medal of Royal Asiatic Society, 1930. Author: Le Bacteriophage, 1921; The Bacteriophage, 1922; Les Defenses de l'Organisme, 1923; Immunity in Natural Infectious Diseases, 1924; Le Bacteriophage et son cemportement, 1926; The Bacteriophage and Its Behavior, 1926; Etudes sur le Cholera, 1929; The Bacteriophage and Its Therapeutical Applications, 1929; Le phenomene de la Guerison dans les Maladies infectieuses, 1938. Discoverer of a parasite of microbes, the bacteriophage, 1917. Home: 40 Olivier de Terres, Paris France

DIBBLE, BARRY, cons. engr.; b. St. Paul, Minn., July 6, 1881; s. Charles Augustus and Julia Maynard (Barry) D.; student Washington State Coll., 1899; E.E., U. of Minn., 1903; studied St. Paul Law Sch., 1905-06; m. M. Belle Butler, June 18, 1907; children—Elizabeth Hoxsie (Mrs. Fitzhugh Smith Rollins, Jr.), Ada Plummer (Mrs. Philip Siebenbaum Buckingham), Barry, Evelyn (Mrs. Samuel Wallace Hartshorn), Mary Belle (Mrs. Victor Mario Margutti), Edward Fitzgerald, Charles Gordon, Richard Brudenell. Formerly with Union Light, Heat & Power Co. (Covington, Ky.), Great Northern Ry., La. Purchase Expn., Cincinnati & Columbus Traction Co., and Jackson & Battle Creek (Mich.) Traction Co.; operation Shawinigan Water & Power Co., P.Q., Can., 1904; asst. supt. St. Paul Gas Light Co., 1905-06; asst. elec. engr. Twin City (Minn.) Rapid Transit Co., 1906-08; with U.S. Reclamation Service, 1909-24; as asst. engr., Los Angeles, 1909-10; elec. engr. in charge constrn. and operation of power and pump system of Minidoka Project, Ida., 1910-15; and project mgr. same, 1916-23; chief elec. and mech. engr. Bur. of Reclamation, Denver, Colo., 1923-24; pvt. practice since 1924, as cons. engr. on works including Coolidge Dam, San Carlos Irrigation Project, Ariz., Wapato Project, Wash., Flathead Project, Mont., Pensacola Dam and hydroelectric development, Oklahoma, Bonneville Project, Wash.-Ore., Denison hydro electric development, Tex., Metropolitan Water Dist. of So. Calif.; studies for development of Columbia, Clark's Fork, Missouri and Osage River, Bear Valley Mut. Water Co., Nat. Irrigation Commn. of Mexico, Garrison hydroelectric development, N.D., Chief Joseph hydroelectric development, Washington. Fellow American Institute E.E. (life mem.); mem. Am. Soc. C.E. (life) Am. Soc. Agrl. Engr., Am. Assn. Engrs., C. of C. (Redlands). Republican. Mason (K.T.). Kiwanian. Home: 120 E. Palm Av., Redlands, Cal. Died Jan. 9, 1961; buried Redlands.

DICK, GEORGE FREDERICK, internist; b. at Fort Wayne. Ind., July 21, 1881; s. Daniel and Elizabeth H. (Binsley) D.; M.D., Rush Med. Coll., 1905; m. Gladys R. Henry, Jan. 28, 1914. In practice of medicine, Chgo., since 1905; interne Cook County Hosp., 1905-07; prof. and chmn. dept. of medicine, U. of Chgo., since 1933. Mem. staff McCormick Memorial Inst. for Infectious Diseases. Served as maj., M.C., U.S. Army, World War. Mem. A.M.A., Ill., State and Chgo. med. socs., Inst. of Medicine of Chgo., Chgo. Pathol Soc., Chgo. Soc.

Internal Medicine, Assn. Am. Physicians, Am. Assn. Pathology and Bacteriology. With wife isolated the germ of and originated serum for scarlet fever. Clubs: University, Glenview Country. Home: 1915 Greenwood Blvd., Evanston, Ill. Office: 950 E. 59th St., Chgo. Died Oct. 11, 1967.

DICK, GLADYS HENRY, bacteriologist; b. Pawnee City, Neb., Dec. 18, 1881; d. William Chester and Azelia H. (Edson) Henry; B.S., U. Neb., 1900, also LL.D.; M.D., Johns Hopkins, 1907; D.Sc., U. Cin., 1925, Northwestern U., 1927; m. George Frederick Dick, Jan. 28, 1914; children—Roger Henry, Rowena Henry. Pres., Scarlet Fever Com. With husband isolated germ of scarlet fever and originated method of prevention; engaged in med. research. Home: 1015 Greenwood Blvd., Evanston, Ill. Died Aug. 24, 1963.

DICKENS, ALBERT, horticulturist; b. Anoka, Minn., Oct. 24, 1867; s. of William and Sarah (Ridge) D.; B.S., Kan. State Agrl. Coll., 1893, M.S., 1901; state teachers' certificate, Kan., 1895, life, 1898; m. Bertha Kimball, Jan. 1, 1898. Foreman, Munger Orchards, Eureka, Kan., 1895; instr., Ellinwood High Sch., 1897-98; asst. in horticulture, 1899-1901, actg. prof., 1901-02, prof., 1902—, Kan. State Agrl. Coll., Manhattan. Republican. Mason. Died Nov. 28, 1930.

DICKERSON, MARY CYNTHIA, zoölogist; b. Hastings, Mich., Mar. 7, 1866; d. Wilbur F. and Melissa R. D.; student of U. of Mich., three years, and spent several summers at Woods Hole, Mass.; B.S., U. of Chicago, 1897; unmarried. Instr. biology, Central High Sch., Grand Rapids, Mich., 1891-94, High Sch., La Grange, Ill., 1894-95; head dept. of zoölogy and botany, R.I. Normal Sch., Providence, 1897-1905; zoölogist, Instr. zoölogy, Stanford U., 1907-08; on scientific staff, Am. Mus. Natural History, New York, 1908-09, curator of dept. of woods and forestry, 1909-21, asst. curator of herpetology, 1910-13, asso. curator and curator, 1913-21. Asso. editor Am. Mus. Jour. Natural History, 1908-10, editor, 1910-21; lecturer N.Y. City Bd. Edn., 1908-17. Fellow N.Y. Acad. Sciences, Am. Mus. Natural History. Author: Moths and Butterflies, 1901; The Frog Book, 1906. Home: New York, N.Y. Died Apr. 8, 1923.

DICKEY, DONALD RYDER, zoölogist; b. Dubuque, Ia., Mar. 31, 1887; s. Ernest M. and Anna (Ryder) D.; B.A., Yale, 1910; hon. M.A., Occidental Coll., Los Angeles, 1925; m. Florence Van Vechten Murphy, June 15, 1921; 1 son, Donald R. Writer, lecturer and field naturalist; specializes in mammals and birds of N. and Central America; research asso. in vertebrate zoölogy, Calif. Inst. Tech., 1926—. Has collected over 50,000 specimens of birds and animals, regarded as the largest pvt. collection of the kind in U.S. Formerly mem. bd. Pasadena Br. Pacific S.W. Trust & Savings Bank. Trustee Southwest Mus., 1920-28; pres. bd. Pasadena Hosp. Assn., 1924-25, dir., 1923-27. Home: Pasadena, Calif. Died Apr. 15, 1932.

DICKEY, HERBERT SPENCER, physician, explorer; b. Highland Falls, N.Y., Feb. 24, 1876; s. Charles Henry and Marie (Brosseau) D.; prep. edn., Phillips Exeter Acad., Exeter, N.H.; student New York U. Med. Sch., 1895-98; M.D., Boston, 1899; m. Elizabeth Steley, Oct. 6, 1925 (div. 1933). Served as surgeon for the Tolima Mining Company, Colombia, S.A., 1900-06; resident physician, Peruvian Amazon Co., 1907-08, Antunes Rubber Estates, Remate de Males, Brazil, 1908-10, again with Peruvian Amazon Co., 1911-12, La Romana Sugar Estates, Dominican Republic, 1914-16; chief surgeon, Guayaquil & Quito R.R., 1923-25. Served as officer, rank of capt., Mil. Intelligence Div., U.S. Army, Southern Dept., 1918-19; maj., Mil. Intelligence Div. Res. Associate in South American research, Southwest Museum, Los Angeles. Decorated Order Al Merito by Ecuador, for important services to the Country, 1937. Mem. American Ethnological Society. Presbyterian. Clubs: Explorers, Ends of the Earth (N.Y.); Adventurers (Los Angeles), Author: The Misadventures of a Tropical Medico (with Daniel Hawthorne), 1929; My Jungle Book, 1932. Contributor to the New York Times. Believed to be 1st white man to descend Caqueta River from Colombia to its mouth. Principal explorations: 5 times on foot over Ecuadorian Andes, exploring affluents of Amazon; explored River Tomo, affluent to Orinoco; located source of Orinoco, July 14, 1931; organized and led first Dude expdn. over the Andes and down the Amazon, 1932; accompanied Sir Roger Casement on his trip to Amazon, 1911; discovered and removed from Ecuador nearly 500 archaeol. specimens for Southwest Mus., 1936; originated process for extracting quinine from lowgrade cinchona bark in Ecuador, 1941. Address: Explorers Club, 10 West 72d St., New York, N.Y.; and Huigra, Ecuador. Died Oct. 28, 1948.

DICKEY, ROBERT W(ILLIAM), educator; b. Mountain Grove, Va., May 13, 1891; s. Robert James and Martha (Jones) D.; B.S., Washington and Lee Univ., 1910, A.B., 1911, A.M., 1912; A.M., Johns Hopkins, 1915, Ph.D. (fellow in physics, 1915-16), 1916; m. Eliabeth Drury, Sept. 10, 1918; 1 son, Robert W., Jr. Instr. in physics and mathematics, Washington and Lee Univ. (Howard Houston teaching fellow, 1911-13), 1910-13, asso. prof. physics, 1916-22, asso. prof. elec. engring., 1922-24, prof. elec. engring., 1924-28, prof. of physics and elec. engring., 1928-34, McCormick prof. of physics, 1934-61, distinguished lecturer in physics, 1961-72, engring. cons. bldg. program, 1921-40 (designed and installed elec. lab.), elected prof. on Ball Foundation, 1947. Served as aeronaut. mech. engr., A.A.F., 1917-19; 2d lt., A.A.F., 1918-19. Mem. Am. Assn. Physics Teachers, Va. Acad. Scis., Phi Beta Kappa, Omicron Delta Kappa, Gamma Alpha, Phi Kappa Psi, Alpha Epsilon Delta. Episcopalian. Club: Hopkins (1913-16). Home: Lexington VA Died Mar. 24, 1972; buried Stonewall Jackson Cemetery, Lexington VA

DICKIE, GEORGE WILLIAM, naval architect, marine eng.; b. Arbroath, Scotland, July 17, 1844; s. William and Jane (Watson) D.; ed. Tay Port, Fife, Scotland, until 1860; learned engring. business with N. British R.R. Co. and in father's shipyard; arrived in San Francisco from Scotland, 1869; m. Anna Jack, of Tay Port, Aug. 5, 1873. Engr. Risdon Iron Works, San Francisco, 1870-83; mgr. Union Iron Works, San Francisco, 1883-1905; now cons. marine and mech. engr. San Francisco. Took prominent part in steamship work on the Pacific Coast and in designing machinery for the Comstock mines, etc. Pres. and life mem. Tech. Soc. Pacific Coast. Author: Pumping and Hoisting Works, 1876. Home: San Mateo, Calif. Died Aug. 16, 1918.

DICKINSON, HOBART CUTLER, physicist; b. Bangor, Me., Oct. 11, 1875; s. George Lyman and Emma T. (Cutler) D.; A.B., Williams Coll., 1900, A.M., 1902; studied Clark U., 1902-03, Ph.D., 1910; m. Elizabeth Wells, 1903 (died 1921); children—David (dec.), Bradley Wells (adopted); m. 2d, Mabel V. Kitson, 1923; 1 dau., Anne Katherine. Became connected with Bur. of Standards, Washington, 1903, asst. physicist, 1906-10, asso., 1910-16; physicist, 1916-21; research mgr. Soc. Automotive Engrs., 1921-23; chief Div. of Heat and Power, Bur. of Standards, 1923-45. Fellow A.A.A.S., Am. Physical Soc.; mem. Am. Soc. Testing Materials, Am. Soc. Refrigerating Engrs., Washington Acad. Sciences, Washington Philos. Soc. Conglist. Clubs: Cosmos (Washington, D.C.); Williams (New York). Home: 4629 30th St. N.W., Washington, D.C. Died Nov. 27, 1949; buried Washington.

DICKINSON, ROBERT LATOU, gynecologist; b. Jersey City, N.J., Feb. 21, 1861; s. Horace and Jeannette (Latou) D.; ed. Poly. Inst. Brooklyn and in Switzerland and Germany; M.D., L.I. Coll. Hosp., 1882; m. Sarah Truslow, May 7, 1890 (dec.); children—Margaret (dec.), Dorothy (wife of Prof. George B. Barbour), Jean (wife of Truman Squire Potter, M.D.), Former gynecologist and obstetrician, Brooklyn Hospital former Prof., L.I. Coll. Hosp.; asst. chief, Med. sec. Nat. Council Defense, Washington, 1917; lt. col., med. adviser and mem. Gen. Staff, Washington, 1918-19; on mission to China for Public Health Service, 1919, Near East, 1926. Fellow of A.C.S. (dir.); member American Assn. Marriage Counsellors Am. Assn. for the study of Sterility, Am. Gynecol. Soc. (ex-pres.), N.Y. Academy Medicine, N.Y. Obstetrical 1 Society (ex-pres), Brooklyn, Chicago and British gynecol. Socs., Am. Gynecol. Club (ex-pres.), Am. Geog. Soc.; sec. Nat. Com. on Maternal Health, 1927-37 (hon. chmn. since 1937); senior vice pres. Planned Parenthood Federation since 1939; Pres. Euthanasia Soc. 1946; member National Sculpture Society. Awards received; Long Island Med. Coll. Alumni Assn., 1944; Am. Phys. Edn. Assn., 1945; A. and M. Lasker (for research), 1946. Democrat. Clubs: Century, Town Hall, Hamilton, Cosmos. Author: (boollet) Palisades Guide 1921; New York Walk Book (with Others),. 1923, 39, 50; A Thousand Marriages, 1931; Control of Conception, 1931-38- Atlas of Human Sex Anatomy, 1933; The Single Woman, Her Sex Education, 1933; Co-author Sex Variants, 1941; Birth Atlas, 1941; Techniques of Conception Control, 1941; Human Sterilization, 1950; also 200 researches and reports on obstetrics, diseases of women, hosp. orgn. and sex problems Co-editor of American Text Book of Obstetrics, 1895. Illustrator of own writings. Sculpture (with A. Belskie) of Birth Series for N.Y. World's Fair, 1939; Pelvic teaching models 1941-47. Home: 360 E. 50th St., Office: 2 E. 103d St., N.Y. City 29. Died Nov. 30, 1950.

DICKINSON, ROSCOE GILKEY, univ. prof., b. Brewer, Me., June 10, 1894; s. George Edward Mott and Georgie Estelle (Gilkel) D.; B.S., Mass. Inst. Tech., 1915; Ph.D., Calif. Inst. Tech., 1920; m. Madeline Grace Haak, Apr. 7, 1917; children—Robert Winchester, Dorothy. Asst. in theoretical chemistry, Mass. Inst. Tech., 1915-16, asst., 1916-17, research associate in chemistry, Calif. Inst. Tech., 1917-26, nat. research fellow, 1920-23, Internat. Edn. Bd. fellow (Europe), 1924-25, asst. prof. physical chemistry, 1926-28, asso. prof., 1928-38, prof. since 1938, acting dean of Grad. Sch., 1942-45. Engaged in war research, Office of Sci. Research and Development, since 1941. Mem. Am. Chem. Soc., Sigma Xi. Home: 530 Bonita Av., Pasadena 8. Office: California Inst. of Technology, E. California St., Pasadena 4, Calif. Died July 13, 1945.

DICKSON, LEONARD EUGENE, prof. mathematics; b. Independence, Iowa, Jan. 22, 1874; s. Campbella and Lucy (Tracy) D.; B.S., Univ. of Tex., 1893, M.A., 1894; Ph.D., U. of Chicago, 1896; student U. of Leipzig, Germany, 1896, U. of Paris, France, 1897; hon. D.Sc., Harvard, 1936, Princeton, 1941; m. Susan Davis, Dec. 30, 1902; children—Campbell, Eleanor (Mrs. Harlow Higinbotham). Instr., U. of Calif., 1897—; prof. . mathematics, U. of Chicago, 1900—; editor, Am. Math. Monthly, 1902-08, Trans. Am. Math. Soc., 1910-16. Corr. de l'Académie de l'Institute de France. Mem. Nat. Acad. of Science, Phi Beta Kappa, Sigma Chi. Home: Quadrangle Club. 57th and Univ. Av. Office: Univ. of Chicago, Chgo. Died Jan. 17, 1954; buried Cleburne, Tex.

DIDUSCH, JAMES FRANCIS medical artist; b. Baltimore, Md., June 17, 1890; s. Joseph Martin and Katherine (Rena) D.; student Md. Institute School Mechanical Arts, 1904-08, Maryland Institute School Fine Arts, 1908-11, Dept. of Art as Applied to Medicine, Johns Hopkins 1910-13; m. Theresa Merie Eder, July, 1, 1915; children—George James, Anne Therese (Mrs. Hans Schuler, Jr.), Joseph Martin. Artist on staff dept. embryology, Carnegie Instn. of Washington, 1913-40; asso. prof. art as applied to medicine, Johns Hopkins, Med. Sch. 1940-43; mem. staff dept. embryology Carnegie Instn. of Washington since 1943. Mem. Johhs Hopkins Med. Soc., Md. Inst. Sch. of Fine Arts Alumni Assn. Illustrator: Surgery of Blood Vascular System (Bertram Bernheim), 1913; Operative Gynecology, (Richard W. TeLinde), 1945; chapter on embryology, Encyclopedea Brittanica; Vol. 32, Contributions to Embryology, Carnegie Instn. of Washington. Yearly Publs. Dept. Embryology, Carnegie Instn. Washington, 1913-40. Translated and revised treaties on development of human mesonephres by Jujior Shikinami 1926. Home: 1001 E. Biddle St., Baltimore 2, Office: 1902 E. Madison St., Balt. Died Mar. 16, 1955.

DIEDERICHS, HERMAN, mech. engr.; b. Muenchen-Gladbach, Germany, Aug. 12, 1874; s. John Peter and Anna Marie (Kamps) D.; came to U.S., 1888, naturalized, 1893; M.E., Cornell U., 1897; unmarried. Began as instr. mech. engring., Cornell U., 1898, asst. prof., 1902, prof., 1907, dir. Sibley Sch. of Mech. Engring., 1921—, John E. Sweet prof. engring. from 1928—all of Cornell U. Author: (with R. C. Carpenter) Internal Combustion Engines, 1905; (with same) Experimental Engring, 1910; (with W. C. Andrae) Experimental Mechanical Engineering (Vol. I), 1931. Died Aug. 31, 1937.

DIEKE, GERHARD HEINRICH, physicist; b. Reheda, Germany, Aug. 20, 1901; s. Gerard and Bertha (Fischer) D.; student U. Leiden, Holland, 1920-25; Ph.D., U. Cal., 1926; m. Sally Fairfax Harrison, June 8, 1938. NRC fellow Cal. Inst. Tech., 1926-27; research asso. Inst. Phys. Chemistry Research, Tokyo, 1927-28; conservator and privaat docent, U. Groningen, Holland, 1928-30; asso., Johns Hopkins, 1930-31, asso. prof. physics, 1931-39. prof. physics 1939-65, chmn. dept., 1950-65; investigator for War Metallurgy Com. and Office Prodn. Research and Devel. Cons., Argonne, Oak Ridge, Los Alamos labs., also indsl. cos.; contractor OSRD, AEC, Bur. Naval Ordnance, NASA, Office Naval Research. Fellow Am. Phys. Co., Optical Soc. Am.; mem. Royal Dutch Acad. Sci. Author of publs. on atomic and molecular physics, spectroscopy, entomology (genus Epilachna). Home: 1101 Argonne Drive, Balt. 21218. Died Aug 25, 1965; buried Ivy Hill Cemetery, Alexandria, Va.

DIEMER, HUGO, industrial engr., author; b. Cincinnati, O., Nov. 18, 1870; s. Theodore and Bertha L. (Huene) C.; M.E. in Electrical Engring., Ohio State U., 1896; student U. of Chicago, 1900; B.A. in history and polit. science, Pa. State Coll., 1913; m. Mabel N. Hudson, June 26, 1901 (died 1934); children—Theodore Hudson, Natalie Elizabeth, Dorothy Arnold, Mary Louise. With Addyston Pipe & Steel Co., Cincinnati, 1888-92; Bullock Electric Mfg. Co. and Westinghouse Electric & Mfg. Co., 1896-1900; asst. prof. mech. engring., Mich. Agrl. Coll. 1900-01; asso. prof. mech. engring., U. of Kan., 1901-04; cons. engr., Indianapolis and Chicago, 1904-07; prof. mech. engring., in charge of dept., 1907-09, prof. industrial engring., 1909-19, Pa. State Coll. Commd. maj. ordnance dept., 1917, then lieut. col.; in charge at U.S. Cartridge Co., Lowell, Mass., 1917, Bethlehem Steel Co., 1918; personnel supt. Winchester Repeating Arms Co., 1919-20; dir. management courses and personnel, La Salle Extension U., 1920—. Summer lecturer on organization and managment, University of Chicago, 1915; lecturer on industrial orgn., dept. of univ. extension Mass. State Bd. of Edn., 1917. Fellow and dir. Inst. of Management (div. of Am. Management Assn.), 1927—. Episcopalian. Mason. Author: Factory Orgnaization and Adminstration, 1910, 5th edit., 1935; Modern Foremanship and Production Methods (with Meyer Bloomfield), 1921; Personnel Adminstration (with Daniel Bloomfield), 1921; Foremanship Training, 1927; Production Control, 1930. Home: Chicago, Ill. Died Mar. 3, 1939.

DIETZ, CARL F. corp. official; b. N.Y. City, Feb. 12, 1880; s. Frederick A. And Caroline (Bher) D.; M.E., Stevens Institute fo Technology, 1901, Doctor of Engring. (honoris Causa); P.G., Royal Tech. Coll., Berlin, 1902; m. Katherine Vane, Nov. 26, 1907; children—Kathernie Caroline, Caroline Vane, Alan Vane. Metall. and cons. engr., 1903-11; successively plant engr., asst. sales mgr., gen. sales mgr. and v.p.

Norton Co., Worcester, Mass., 1911-21; pres. and gen. mgr. Bridgeport Brass Co., 1921-27; industrial and banking consultant. 1928-29; exec. v.p. Commander Larabee Corp., Minneapolis, 1930-32; nat. code dir. wheat flour milling industry under NRA, 1933-35; now chmn. Lamson Corp., Del., pres. N.Y. Mail & Newspaper Transportation Co., Boston Pneumatic Transit Co., director Financial Cons., Tucson, Ariz. Profl. engr. State of N.Y., and Conn., 1932, and all states with engring. registration burs. Nat. Bur. of Engring. Registration; chmn. Lamson Moblift Crop., Portland, Ore. Mem. Munitions Board Packaging and Materials Handling Industry Avd. Coam Industry Panel mem. War Labor Board, Region 2. Mem. New York Com. on Displaced persons; tripartite mem. for industry, N.L.R.S., New York State. Civic award, Humanitarian, Polish Legion Am. Vets. Mem. Council of Defense, Syracuse and Onondaga Co.; dir. War Fund and Community Chest of Onondaga County. Ex-chmn. Conn. Mfrs. Indsl. Relations Committee; national councilor U.S. C. of C., mem. advisory bd. dept. of mfr. Mem. finance bd. Bridgeport Community chest, 1923-27; dir. Conn and Bridgeport Mfrs. Assn., 1923-27; also dir. Boy's Club; formerly pres. Rotary and Engineers Clubs of Bridgeport Fellow Am. Soc. M.E., mem. Am. Inst. Mining and Metall. Engrs., Nat. Assn. Mfrs. (pres., mem. com. on labor negotiations), Mfrs. Assn. of Syracuse (chmn., mem. exec. con., chmn. govt. affairs com.), Conveyer Equipment Mfrs. Assn. (pres.), Technl. Club. of Syracuse (bd. govs., chmn., civic affairs com.), Syracuse C. of C. (dir.), Am. Soc. Professional Engrs., Onondaga Health Assn. (dir.), Technology Club of Syracuse (hon.). Machinery and Allied Products Inst. (mem. Council for Technical Advancement), American Ordnance Association (dir. of Empire Post), Industrial College Armed Forces Against Discrimination. Mem. Phi Sigma Kappa, Theta Nu Epsilon, Pi Tau Sigma (hon.), Republician. Episcopalian (vestryman). Mason (32 deg. Shriner). Clubs: Engineers (New York); Union League (Chgo.), Syracuse Technology (Hon.), Century (Syracuse, N.Y.); Oswelewgois (Redfield, N.Y.). Contbr. engring and indsl. articles. Address: 515 Ponce de Leon Blvd., Belleair, Fla. Died Oct. 4, 1957; buried Mountain Grove Cemetery, Bridgeport, Conn.

DIETZ, SHERL MELVIN, botanist; b. Garner, Ia., Apr. 6, 1893; s. Fredrick Michael and Rosina Elizabeth (Lackore) D.; B.S., Ia. State Coll., 1917, M.S., 1918, Ph.D., 1924; postgrad. Cornell, 1920-21; m. Lorraine Best, Oct. 16, 1921; children—James, Phil, Sherl, Annetta. Asst. pathologist, U.S. Dept. Agr., Ames, Ia., 1918-26, asso. pathologist, 1926-27; asso. prof. botany Ia. State Coll., 1927-32, prof. botany, 1932-37, 1938-47; plant pathologist, Wash. State Coll., 1937-38; head botany and plant pathology dept. Ore. State Coll., Corvallis, 1947-58, prof. of botany and plant pathology, 1958-62. Mem. Am. Phytopath. Soc., Ia. Acad. Sci., Ore. Acad. Sci., Sigma Xi, Gamma Sigma Delta, Phi Kappa Phi, Alpha Sigma Phi. Author: Laboratory and Field Problems in Botany, 1940. Home: 3420 Willamette St., Corvallis, Ore. Died May 6, 1962; buried Corvallis.

DIKE, CHESTER THOMAS, civil engr.; b. Woodstock, Ill., Aug. 13, 1870; s. Chester B. and Rose (Mayne) D.; B.C.E., Cornell Coll., Mt. Vernon, Ia., 1893, C.E., 1903; m. Bonnie Elder, Feb. 19, 1900; children—Edwin Berck, Gardner Elder. Began as chainman N.P.Ry.; chief engr. Mason City & Clear Lake Ry., 1896-97, Ia., Minn. & N.W. Ry., 1898-99; with C. & N.-W. Ry. since 1899, successively resident engr., div. engr., supt. constrn. various branches, gen. supt. Minn. and Dak. divs., asst. gen. supt. of the rd., 1918-19, asst. gen. mgr. Lines West of Mo. River, 1919-20, engr. maintenance of way, 1920-30, chief engr., 1930-34, v.p. and chief engr.; also v.p. way and structures C.,St.P.,M&ORy., 1934-35; v.p. and chief engr. C. & N.-W. System since 1935. Mem. Western Soc. Engrs. Club: Union League. Home: 821 Ridge Av., Evanston Ill. Office: 400 W. Madison St., Chicago IL

DILLEHUNT, RICHARD BENJAMIN surgeon; b. Decatur, Ill., July 12, 1886;s s. Benjamin Webster and Augusta (Buchert) D.; student U. of Ill., 1904-06; M.D., Rush Med. Coll. (U. of Chicago), 1910; unmarried. Began Practice at Portland, (Ore.)1914; with U. of Ore. Med. Sch. as prof. anatomy and asst. dean, 1912-17, dean, 1920-43, also clinical professor orthopedic surgery and head of dept.; surgeon in chief Shriners' Hospital for Crippled Children, 1923-43; member surg. staff Emanuel Hosp., Multnomah County Hosp.; chief of orthopedic surg. staff, Dorenbecher Memorial Hosp. for Children, 1926-43. Commd. 1st lt. Med. Corps U.S. Army, June 1917; capt. Jan. 1918; major Jan. 1919; served as orthopedic surg. Base Hosp. No. 46. Am Expeditionary Forces. Chmn. com. on Survey Oregon State Mental Hosps. since 1951. Member American Medical Assn. State Med. Soc., Multnomah County Med. Soc., N. Pacific Surg. Assn. Pacific Northwest Med. Assn.,Pacific Coast Surg. Assn. (pres. 1939-40), Am. Acad. of Orthopedic Surgeons, Am. Orthopedic Assn., Western Orthopedic Association (honorary mem.), Orgeon Mental Health Association (dir. 1950), North Pacific Orthopedic Society (president 1934), Phi Rho Sigma, Alpha Omega Alpha; fellow of A.C.S.; hon. mem. Seattle Surg. Assn. Republican. Mason (32 deg., Shriner). Clubs: University, Arlington. Home: 2607 N.W. Roanoke St., Portland 10, Ore. Died Oct. 31, 1953.

DILLER, JOSEPH SILAS, geolgoist; b. Plainfield, Pa., Aug. 27, 1850; s. Samuel and Catharine (Bear) D.; S.B., Lawrence Scientific Sch. (Harvard), 1879; 4 yrs. in post-grad. studies, Harvard and Heidelberg; m. Laura I. Paul, June 5, 1883. Taught in State Normal Sch., Westfield, Mass., 1873-77; geologist Assos. expdn., 1881-83; geologist U.S. Geol. Survey, 1883. Published many geol. papers in jours. and reports of U.S. Geol. Survey. Home: Washington, D.C. Died Nov. 13, 1928.

DIMITROFF, GEORGE ZAKHARIEFF, educator, astronomer; b. Svistove, Bulgaria, Aug. 24, 1901; s. Zakharia and Elenka Hadji (Nikolova) D.; student Robert Coll., Constantinople, 1916-17, 19-20; B.S., Boston U., 1927; M.A., Harvard, 1929, Ph.D., 1937; M.A. (hon.), Dartmouth, 1947; m. Mary Alice Sweeney, June 14, 1928; John David Barbara Ann. Came to U.S., 1921, naturalized, 1930. Asst. prof. physics Colo. State Coll., 1929-34; instr. astronomy, tutor div. phys. sics. Harvard, also Radcliffe Coll., 1934-37; supt. Oak Ridge sta. Harvard Obs., also research asso. astronomy Harvard, 1937-42; prof. astronomy Dartmouth, 1946—. Mem. Combined Priorities Subcom. 1943-44, ALSOS Mission, 1944-45, Naval Tech. Missions to Europe and Japan, 1943-46; dir. tng. research res. program office Naval Research, 1951-52. Served as comdr. USNR, 1943-46, and 1951-52, captain reserve, 1960—. Fellow Royal Astronomical Society, A.A.A.S.; mem. International Astron. Union, Am. Astron. Soc., Physics for the Laboratroy, 1930; Telscopes and Accessories 1945; Astronomy in Brief, 1956. Home: R.F.D. 1, Hartland, Vt. Office: Shattuck Observatory, Dartmouth Coll., Hanover, N.H. Died Jan. 3, 1968.

DIMMOCK, GEORGE, zoöloigst; b. Springfield, Mass., May 17, 1852; s. George Monroe and Elizabeth (Learned) D.; A.B., Harvard, 1877, taking spl. studies there until 1879; A.M., Ph.D., U. of Leipzig, 1881; Sorbonne, U. of Paris, 1881-82; m. Anna Katherina Hofmann, Mar. 30, 1878; 1 dau., Mrs. Anna D. Nash. Editor of Psyche, 1877-90, a jour. of entomology; engaged in anat. study of the early stages of beetles, and in compiling a history of the Dimmock family in America, 1900—. Author: The Anatomy of the Mouth-parts and of the Sucking Apparatus of Some Diptera, 1881. Home: Springfield, Mass. Died May 17, 1930.

DIMOCK, WILLIAM WALLACE, prof. vet. sci.; b. Tolland, Conn., Feb. 20, 1880; s. Henry Eugene and Ellen M. (Clark) D.; B.Agr., Conn. Agrl. Coll., 1901; D.V.M., N.Y. State Veterinary College (Cornell U.), 1905; D.V.M. University of Habana, Cuba, 1908, Professor Honoris Causa, 1945; m. Ruth Attwill Mudge, Nov. 27, 1909; children—Phoebe, Betty Anne, Shubael Eugene, Gladys Eusebia, Ruth Mudge. began practice as veterinarian in Conn., 1905; asst.chief animal husbandry, Cuban Expt. Sta., Santiago de los Vegus, Cuba, 1980-09; chief veterinarian, Nat. Bd. of Health, Cuba, 1908-09; prof. pathology and bacteriology, State Coll. of Ia. 1909-19; prof. vet. science, U. of Ky., since 1919, ex-head dept. animal pathology, Ky. Agrl. Expt. Sta. Mem. Am. Vet. Med. Assn. (pres. 1942-43), A.A.A.S., Ky. Vet. Med. Assn., Ia. Vet. Med. Assn., Ky. Acad. Science, U.S. Live Stock Sanitary Assn., Gamma Alpha, Phi Kappa Phi, Sigma Xi (pres. U. of Ky. Chapter 1930-31). Democrat. Presbyn. Author or joint author of 100 publs. on animal diseases. Home: Swigert Av., Lexington, KY. Died Oct. 1953.

D'INVILLIERS, EDWARD VINCENT, geologist, mining engr.; b. Germantown, Pa., Aug. 2, 1857; s. Camille S. and Ann S. (Maitland) d'I.; B.S., U. of Pa., 1878; (D.Sc., 1913); spl. studies in geology and mining engring.; m. Ann Maitland, of Phila., June 6, 1894. Asst. geologist, 2d Geol. Survey of Pa., 1875-85; geologist and consulting engr., 1885-1919. Fellow Geol. Soc. America; mem. Am. Inst. Mining and Metall. Engrs., Am. Philos. Soc., Franklin Inst. Author numerous geol. reports, etc. Home: 6630 McCallum St., Germantwon, Pa. Office: 518 Walnut St., Philadelphia, Pa.

DISERENS, PAUL, consulting engineer; b. Cincinnati, O., Jan. 9, 1882; s. Albert Day and Alice (Jefferies) Ds.; B.S., Purdue U., 1904, M.E., 1906; student U. of Ill., 1906-08; unmarried. Research asst. with Dr. W.F.M. Goss, 1904-08; in charge locomotive test in study of superheated steam locomotive service, Carnegie Inst. of Washington, 1905-06; research asst., studing Ill. coal, U. of Ill., 1907-09; engr. of test in charge research, Laidlaw Dunn Gordon Co., Cincinnati, O., 1909-19; asst chief engr., Worthington Pump and Machine Corp., New York City, 1919-28. chief cons. engr., 1928—. dir. research, 1944-45. dir. research and development, Worthington Pump and Machine Corp. and Subsidiaries, (Worthington) Gamon Meter Co., Ransome Machinery Co., Electric Machinery Co.), 1945-54; tech. advisor Compressed Air and Gas Inst. 1954—. Cons. Nat. Defense Research Com., 1941-44. Fellow Am. Soc. Mech. Engrs. (mem. power test codes Com) Mem. Am. Soc. Refrigerting Engineers, U.S. Nat. Com. Internat. Electrotech. Com., director, sec. and also chairman of the Technical committee on internat. Electrotech. combustion engines). Republican. Clubs: Engineers (New York); Canoe Brook Country (Summit, N.J.); Baltusrol Golf (Springfield, N.J.); Cornell (N.Y.) Inventor of expander engines for refrigeration in gasoline industry; valves for compressors; hot oil pumps for oil refineries; holds U.S. and Fgn. patents. Contbr. of articles to professional jours. Home: 1 Euclid Av., Summit, N.J. Died Oct. 6, 1958; buried Spring Grove Cemetery, Cin.

DISQUE, ROBERT CONRAD, educator; b. Burlington, Ia., Mar. 14, 1883; s. Frederick Jacob and Marie Louisa (Holstein) D.; B.L., U. of Wis., 1903, B.S. in E.E., 1908; Sc.D., Northwestern, 1942; D.Eng., Stevens Inst., 1946; grad. study, U. of Pa., 1925-31; m. Laura Maud Crafts, June 14, 1921; children—Sarah Marie, Robert Otis, Helen Cushman. Teacher high sch., Burlington, Ia., 1903-05; engr., Milwaukee Electric & Ry. Co., 1908; instr. in elec. engring., U. of Wis., 1908-17; prof. elec. engring., Drexel Inst., Philadelphia, Pa., 1919-24; academic dean, 1924-32, dean of the faculty, 1932; acting president, 1943-44. Educational consultant Walter P. Murphy Foundation. Served as 1st lt. Air Service, United States Army, 1917, capt. 1918; maj. United States Res., 1918-24. Dir. School Dist. of Swarthmore. Fellow Am. Inst. E.E.; mem. Am. Society for Engring. Edn., The Newcomen Soc., Phi Beta Kappa, Sigma Xi, Tau Beta Pi, Alpha Sigma Phi, Eta Kappa Nu, Phi Kappa Phi. Democrat. Mason. Home: Swarthmore PA Died May 7, 1968.

DIX, JOHN HOMER, opthalmologist; b. Boston, Sept. 30, 1811; s. John and Sarah Taffrey (Eddy) D.; grad. Harvard, 1833; M.D., Jefferson Med. Coll., 1836, m. Helen Perhan Curtis Curtis, June 9, 1859. Became mem. Mass. Med. Soc., 1837; practiced medicine, specializing in eye and ear diseases, Boston; became interested in opthalmology, one of 1st to import opthalmoscope developed by Helmholtz; built one of 1st apt. houses in U.S., Boston, 1856-57; mem. Am. Opthal. Soc.; Author: Treatise on Strabismus, or Squinting, and the New Mode of Treatment, 1841; also wrote papers on rare diseases of eyes. Died Aug. 25, 1884.

DIXON, JOSEPH, inventor, mfr.; b. Marblehead, Mass., Jan. 18, 1799; s. Joseph and Elizabeth (Reed) D.; m. Hannah Martin, July 28, 1822. Inventor machine for cutting files, in his youth; took up printing, made wood type, became skilled in wood-engraving and lithography; later invented matrix for casting metal type; recognized that used this substance (such as pencils and stove polish); opened mfg. plant, Salem, Mass., 1827; invented photolithographic process and process for producing colored inks to prevent counterfeiting, 1832; granted patent for anti-friction bearing metal, 1845; relocated his mfg. plant, Jersey City, N.J., 1847; received patents on processing graphite crucible, 1850, also received other patents on mfg. improvements; organizer, head Joseph Dixon Crubible Co., 1867-69. Died June 15, 1868.

DIXON, ROBERT M., mech. engr.; b. East Orange, N.J., Sept. 19, 1860; M.E., Stevens Inst. Tech., 1881. Draftsman Del. Bridge Co. until 1883; with Pintsch Lighting Co., 1883-88; became engr. Safety Car Heating and Lighting Co., and mgr. Pintsch Compressing Co., 1888, later pres. both companies, also pres. Realty Security Co.; dir. Vapor Car Heating Co.; patentee of many inventions. Home: East Orange, N.J. Died Oct. 16, 1918.

DIXON, ROYAL, naturalist, author, lect.; b. Huntsville, Tex., Mar. 25, 1885; s. Elijah and Frances Elizabeth (Watlington) D.; student Sam Houston State Tchrs. Coll., Columbia U.; unmarried; 1 foster son, Chester Snowden. With dept. botany Field Mus., Chgo., 1905-10; became writer Houston Chronicle, 1919; spl contbr. N.Y. World, Tribune and Sun, 1911-15; newpaper feature, The Human Side of Life, Houston Chronicle; formerly lectr. N.Y.C. Bd. Edn.; lectr. for Renaissance Soc.; dir. publicity Com. for Immigrants in Am.; mng. editor Immigrants in Am. Rev. (quar.); founder 1st Ch. for Animal Rights, N.Y.C., 1930; founder Wildflower Day in Am., 1929, S. W. Writers Guild, 1935; organizer Dixon's Sch. of Creative Writing (now S.W. Writers Sch.), Houston, 1933; spl. lect. Estes Park (Colo.) Conf., also for YMCA, Camp Chief, Ouray, Colo., summer 1920, Chautauqua Inst., Chautauqua, N.Y., Boulder, Colo., Monteagle (Tenn.) Assembly; head writer group Art Colony of S.W., Ruidosa, N.Y.; under auspices YMCA, spl. lectr. War Dept., AEF, 1918-19, Mental Sci. Inst., Denver, 1939; lectr. U. Ark. extension, 1941; nature instr., lectr. Lost Valley Ranch for Boys, 1949—; v.p. League of Foreign-born Citizens; founder (with Rose Ralbe) and pres. N.Y. Salon. Became radio broadcaster, Children's Hour; sta. WRNY, 1928, later in series original stories, What I sez, I sez; series, Wonders of Nature, sta. KTRH, Houston, 1953. Mem. Poetry Soc. Am., Am. Renaissance Soc., Univ. Forum Am., Little Roc, (Ark.) Authors and Composers Club, Knickerbockers Storytelling Club, Writers Club; hon. mem. Dayton Beach (Fla.) Garden Club, Southmore Garden Club (Houston), Chautauqua (N.Y.) Bird and Tree Club, Jacksonville (Fal.) Humane Soc. Author of numerous books, 1914—, latest being: Young Man of Manhattan, 1957; The Lost Angel, 1957; Behold Elizabeth Ney, 1953. Contbr. nat. mags. Asso. editor The Southerner, 1949. Home: The Patio, 1310 Truxillo Av., Houston; 2115 Riley Fuzzle Rd., Spring, Tex. Died June 4, 1962; buired Glenwood Cemetery, Houston.

DIXON, SAMUEL GIBSON, bacteriologist; b. Phila., Pa., Mar. 23, 1851; s. Isaac and Ann (Gibson) D.; grad. Mercantile Coll.; studied law, admitted to bar, 1877; M.D., with honors, U. of Pa., 1886; grad. dept. of bacteriology, King's Coll., London; studied in State Coll. of Medicine, London, and Pettenkofer's Lab. of Hygiene, Munich; (LL.D., U. of Pa., 1909); m. Fannie Gilbert. Prof. hygiene in med. and scientific depts. and dean auxiliary dept. of medicine, U. of Pa., 1888-1910; prof. bacteriology and micros. technology, 1890—, curator, 1891-92, exec. curator, 1892—, pres., 1896—, Acad. Natural Sciences, Phila. Mem. Bd. Pub. Edn., Phila., 1898; Commr. of Health, Pa., 1905—. Trustee U. of P., Wistar Inst. of Anatomy; 1st v.p. Ludwick Inst.; mgr. Grandom Instn. Author: Physiological Notes, 1886. Home: Bryn Mawr, Pa. Died Feb. 26, 1918.

DOAN, GILBERT EVERETT, metall. engr.; b. Lansdale, Pa., Jan. 16, 1897; s. William E. and Agnes Sibbald (McKinlay) D.; Chem. E., Lehigh University, 1919; Ph.D., University of Berlin, Germany, 1927; m. Alice Curtis Olney, Nov. 23, 1929; children—Gilbert Everett, Julia Alice (Mrs. Ben M. Cart), Agnes Sibbald (Mrs. Ronald Gregson). Metallographist, U.S. Naval Experiment Station, Annapolis, 1919-20; dir. research Una Welding Co., Cleveland, 1920-24; company mission to Germany, 1922-23; prof. metallurgy, Lehigh U., 1926-52, head of the dept., 1939-52; mgr. metall. research, Koppers Co., Pitts., 1952-59, cons., 1959-70; cons. U.S. Naval Research Lab., 1929; Spl. cons. Gen. Electric Co., Westinghouse, Bethlehem Steel Co, Union Carbide. Guest lecturer Franklin Inst.; exec. sec. Vol. Com. to Make Poor TV Better, 1961-70. Guest lectr. Osaka University, Kyushu Institute of Technology, Japan, Benares Univ., India, Lafayette College. Dir. Nat. Assn. Better Radio and TV. Investigator Office of Scientific Research Development, 1942-46. Awarded Lincoln gold medal for advancement of science of welding, 1943; Navy Certificate, 1947; The Stoughton Award, 1949. Member Board of Awards American Welding Society, Howe Medal Committee American Society for Metals. Del. London Conf. English Speaking Union, 1952. Fellow Royal Soc. Arts (London); mem. Newcomen Soc., and many sci. and tech. socs., Sigma Xi, Tau Beta Pi, Omicron Delta Kappa, Delta Upsilon. Author: The Principles of Physical Metallurgy 1935; Our Sons Specialize; Summer Enchantment: The New Position of Science; Science Changes the Scientist; The New American. Co-author: The Principles of Metallurgy, 1933; The Post-Scientific Era Arrives, 1965; Bradley Stoughton—Mankind Was My Business, 1966; also tech. and sci. papers. Home: Nazareth PA Died Oct. 27, 1970; buried Montgomery Square Methodist Ch., Lansdale PA

DOANE, SAMUEL EVERETT, electrical engr.; b. Swampscott, Mass., Feb. 28, 1870; s. Capt. Edward E. and Helen M. (Nickerson) D.; grad. Swampscott High Sch., 1886; hon. E.E., Case Sch. of Applied Science, 1927; m. Marion M. Jackman, of Marlboro, Mass., Oct. 17, 1900; children—Dorothy Helen, Edward Everett. Entered employ of Thomson-Houston Electric Co., Lynn, Mass., 1886; asst. engr. Harrison (N.J.) Lamp Works of Gen. Electric Co., 1892-96, supt., 1893-94; acting engr. foreign dept. Gen. Electric Co., at Schenectady, 1896-97; supt. Bryan-Marsh Co., Marlboro, Mass., 1897-1901; chief engr. Nat. Electric Lamp Assn. (now Nat. Lamp Works of Gen. Electric Co.), 1901-30, consultant, 1930-35, retired. Fellow Am. Inst. E.E., A.A.A.S.; mem. Am. Soc. M.E.; ex-pres. Illuminating Engring. Soc. of U.S. Address: 651 State St., Bridgeport CT

DOANE, THOMAS, mech. engr.; b. Orelans, Mass., Sept. 20, 1821; s. John and Polly (Eldredge) D.; m. Sophia Dennison Clark, Nov. 5, 1850; m. 2d, Louisa Amelia Barber; 4 children. Served 3 year apprenticeship with Samuel Felton, civil engr., Charlestown, Mass.; worked for Vt. Central R.R.; resident engr. Cheshire R.R. in N.H., 1847-49; pvt. engring., surveying practice, Charlestown, 1849-97; apptd. chief engr. in charge of constrn. Hoosac Tunnel, 1863; introduced new methods of engring. including new uses of explosives and compressed-air machinery; chief engr. Burlington & Missouri River R.R., 1869-73; completed constrn. Hoosac Tunnel, 1873-77; mem. Am. Soc. C.E., 1882; pres. Boston Soc. Civil engrs.; founder, trustee Doane Coll., Crete, Neb., 1872. Died West Townsend, Vt., Oct. 22, 1897.

DOBBIN, CARROLL EDWARD, geologist; b. Jonesport, Me., Oct. 2, 1892; s. Edward Butler and Myrtie Grace (Rumery) D.; A.B., Colby Coll., 1916; hon. D.Sc., 1941; Ph.D., Johns Hopkins, 1924; D. Engineering (hon.), Colorado School of Mines, 1952; m. Catharine Dorcas Barncord, Nov. 13, 1921. Geologist U.S. Geol. Survey, 1918-59, ret. Recipient U.S. Dept. Interior Honor award, 1959. Mem. Geol. Soc. America, Am. Assn. Petroleum Geologists (v.p. 1936-37, pres., 1947-48, hon. mem. 1958-67), Rocky Mountain Geologists (pres. 1932), Am. Inst. Mining Metall. and Petroleum Engrs., A.A.A.S., Colo. Sci. Soc., Geol. Soc. Washington, Am. Geophys. Union, Colo. Engring. Council (pres., 1945-47), Colo. Soc. Engrs. (pres. 1951), Soc. Econ. Geologists, Wyo. Engring. Soc., Wyo. Geol. Assn., N.M. Geol Soc., Sigma Xi, Sigma Gamma Epsilon, Lambda Chi Alpha, Gamma Alpha, Tau Beta Pi. Mason (32 deg.). Club: Teknik. Author bulls. and profl. papers of U.S. Geol. Survey; articles to geol. jours. Home: Denver CO Died Mar. 15, 1967; cremated.

DOBBINS, JAMES T(ALMAGE), chemist, educator; b. Boonville, N.C., Feb. 11, 1888; s. Nathan C. and Sophronia C. (Reece) D.; A.B., U. of N.C., 1911, A.M., 1912, Ph.D., 1914; m. Lila Shore, June 20, 1917; children—Christine (Mrs. Robert W. Taylor), James Talmage. Instr., N.C. State U., 1914-18; asso. prof. chemistry U. of N.C., 1918-30, prof. chemistry, 1930-60, emeritus prof., 1960-72. Chmn., Chapel Hill City Bd. Adjustment, 1948-68. Recipient 1st Ann. Distinguished Prof. award U. N.C. Sch. Pharmacy, 1961. Mem. Am. Chem. Soc., Soc. Pub. Analysts, Sigma Xi, Alpha Chi Sigma. Democrat. Baptist (lifetime deacon). Author: Semi Micro Qualitative Analysis, 1943. Home: Chapel Hill NC Died May 13, 1972; buried Chapel Hill Cemetery, Chapel Hill NC

DOBRINER, KONRAD research physician; b. Elberfeld, Germany, Oct. 14, 1902; s. Paul and Laura (Drey) D.; Gymansium Lennep, 1909-21, U. of Freiburg, 1921-25, U. of Munich, 1925-27; m. Shirley Fitzgerald, June 28, 1945; children—Madeleine Joan, Mark George. Came to U.S., 1934, naturalized, 1940. Intern II Medizinische Abteilung Kankenhaus Munich-Schwabing, 1927-28, assistenzarzt, 1928-33; speicalist for internal med., Munich, 1932; research fellow U. of Rochester Med. Sch., 1934-36, Hosp. of Rockefeller Inst., 1936-39; head dept. research chemistry Memorial Hosp., N.Y. City, 1939-47; mem. Sloan-Kettering Inst., N.Y. City since 1947, Mem. Am. Soc. Biol. chemists, Assn. Study Internal Secretions, Am. Assn. Cancer Research, Am. Soc. Clin. Investigation, Soc. Exptl. Biol. and Med., Harvey Soc., N.Y. Acad. Scis Research in metabolism of steroid hormones; cancer research; prophyrin metabolism, metabolism of carcinogens, infra-red spectrometry Home: 345 E. 68th St., N.Y. City 21. Office: 444 E. 68th St., N.Y.C. 21. Died Mar. 10, 1952; buried Simsbury, Conn.

DOCHEZ, ALPHONSE RAYMOND physician, teacher; b. San Francisco, Calif., Apr. 21, 1882; s. Louis and Josephine (Dietrich) D.; A.B., Johns Hopkins, 1903, M.D., 1907; Sc.D., N.Y.U., 1925, Yale U., 1926, Western Reserve U., 1931, Columbia U., 1954; unmarried. Formerly member staff Rockefeller Inst. for Med. Research; asso. prof. medicine, Johns Hopkins Med. Sch., 1919-21; asso. prof. medicine, Coll. Phys. and Surg. (Columbia), 1921-25, prof., 1925-37, John E. Borne prof. of med. and surg. research, 1939-49, emeritus professor medical and surgical research since 1949; visiting physician Presbyn. Hospital. Former trustee Rockefeller Institute for Med. Research. Maj. Medical Corps, U.S. Army, World War. Mem. Assn. Am. Physicians, Am. Soc. for Clin. Investigation, Am. Soc. for Exptrl. Pathology, Soc. for Exptl. Biology and Medicine, Harvey Soc., Nat. Acad. Science, Alpha Delta Phi. Democrat. Catholic. Clubs: University, Century, Maryland. Developer antitoxin for scarlet fever, also serum for lobar pneumonia; identified viral origins of common cold. Home: 1 W. 54th St., N.Y.C. Office: 620 W. 168th St., N.Y.C., 10032. Died June 30, 1964; buried Balt.

DOCK, GEORGE, physician, educator; b. Hopewell, Pa., Apr. 1, 1860; s. Gilliard and Livinia Lloyd (Bombaugh) D.; M.D., U. of Pa., 1884; hon. A.M., Harvard, 1895; Sc.D., U. of Pa., 1904; LL.D., University of Southern Calif., 1936; m. Laura McLemore, July, 5, 1892; children—George, William William; m. 2d, Miriam Gould, Oct. 17, 1925. Asst. clin. pathology, U. of Pa., 1887-88; prof. pathology, Tex. Med. Coll. and Hosp., 1888-91; prof. theory and practice of medicine and clin. medicine, U. of Mich., 1891-1908; prof. theory and practice of medicine, Tulane U., 1908-10; prof. medicine, Washington U. Med. School, 1910-12; hon. prof. medicine, University of Southern Calif. Member Assn. American Physicians (pres. 1916-17), A.M.A., etc; fellow A.A.A.S. Club: University, Valley Hunt, Twilight (Pasadena); Athletic (Los Angeles). Author: Hookworm Disease (with C. C. Brass), 1940. Also numerous articles on med. subject in jours. and text-books Home: 397 E. Calaveras, Altadena, Calif. Died May 30, 1951.

DOD, DANIEL, inventor, steam engine builder; b. Va., Sept. 28, 1788; s. Lebbens and Mary (Baldwin) D.; ed. Rutgers; m. Nancy Squier, 1901, 8 children, including Albert Baldwin. Granted U.S. patents on steam engines, including boilers and condensers, for use in steamboats and mills, 1811, maufactured ferryboats, put 1st products into service, 1813; greatest contbn. was products into service, 1813; greates contbn. was machinery for Savannah (first steamboat to cross Atlantic Ocean, 1819). Died in boiler explosion in steamboat test on East River, N.Y.C., May 9, 1823.

DODGE, BARNETT FRED, educator; born Akron, Ohio, Nov. 29, 1895; s. Fred Bradley and Charlotte Ida (Barnett) D.; B.S., Mass. Inst. Tech., 1917; D.Sc., Harvard, 1925; D.Sc. (hon.), Worcester Polytechnic Institute, 1956; Honorary Diplome de Docteur, University of Toulouse (France), 1961; Huesped de Honor, U. Central de Venezuela, Caracas, 1961; m. Constance Woodbury, June 5, 1918; children—Richard Woodbury, Phyllis. Chem. engineer E. I. du Pont Nemours Company, 1917-20; with Lewis Recovery Corp., Boston, 1920-22;- lecturer on chem. engring., Harvard U., 1922-25; asst. prof., Yale U., 1925-30, asso. prof., 1930-35, prof. and head of department, 1935-60, dean sch. engring., 1960-61, professor of chemical engineering, 1961-64, professor emeritus, 1964-72; lecturer Worcester Polytechnic Inst., 1922-25; official investigator for Nat. Defense Research Com., 1941-45; asso. dir. Central Engring. Lab. U. of Pa., 1943-44; tech. dir., Fercleve Corp., Oak Ridge, Tenn. (on leave from Yale); former chmn. chem. engring. dept., Yale U.; cons. to various organizations; Fulbright lectr., Univ. Toulouse, Fr., 1951; mem. Engring. Mission to Japan, Am. Soc. Engring. Edn., 1951; lecturer Univ. of Barcelona, Spain, 1954, U. Central de Venezuela (Carcaras), 1957; Fulbright lectr. U. Lille, also Cath. U. Lille (France), 1958; Ford Found. grant tchr. U. Buenos Aires, 1965-61; Sigma Xi lectr. Central and South Am., 1966; taught U. Uruguay, 1966; lectr. U. New South Wales, Sydney, Australia, 1967; Am. Acad. Sci. rep. to Yugoslavia, 1968; taught Pahlavi U., Shiraz, Iran, 1970; lectr. U.S. Bahia Blanca (Argentina), 1969. Recipient Walker award American Institute of Chemical Engineers, Warren K. Lewis award, 1963. Fellow Am. Inst. Chem. Engrs. (dir. 1939-41, 43-45, v.p. 1954, pres. 1955, chmn. com. on chem. engring. edn., 1942-47, chmn. spl. task com. for new engring. center site; rep. on Bd. United Engring. Trustees 1956-57, recipient founders award, 1962), Am. Acad. Arts and Scis.; mem. Am. Chem. Soc., American Society for Engring. Edn., Engrs. Council Profl. Development (chmn. region IV 1947-51), A.A.A.S., Sigma Xi, Tau Beta Pi. Republican. Club: Appalachian Mountain (Boston), Harvard of New Haven. Author: Chemical Engineering Thermodynamics, 1944. Contbr. to tech. jours. Home: Hamden CT Died Mar. 16, 1972.

DODGE, BERNARD OGILVIE, plant pathologist; b. Mauston, Wis., Apr. 18, 1872; s. Elbridge Gerry and Mary Ann (Nourse) D.; grad. Milw. Normal Sch., 1901; Ph.B., U. Wis., 1909; Ph.D., Columbia, 1912; m. Jennie S. Perry, June 14, 1906. Prin. high sch., Greenwood, Wis., 1897-1900, 02, Algoma, Wis., 1903-08; asst. research fellow and instr. in botany Columbia, 1910-19, lectr. dermatology, 1929—; pathologist U.S. Dept. Agr., 1920-28, N.Y. Bot. Garden, 1928-47, plant pathologist emeritus, 1947—; cons. mycology Presbyn. Hosp., N.Y.C., 1929-39. Mem. com. on microbiology of the soil, Nat. Research Council. Convener 3d Internat. Microbiol. Congress, N.Y., 1939. Recipient Distinguished Service award N.Y. Bot. Garden, 1951; Golden Jubilee award of merit Bot. Soc. Am., 1956. Fellow A.A.A.S.; mem. Nat. Acad. Sciences, Am. Acad. Arts and Sciences, Am. Soc. Naturalists, Linnean Soc. London (fgn.), Bot. Soc. Am., Am. Phytopathol. Soc., Mycol. Soc. Am. (pres. 1935), Am. Genetic Assn., Torrey Bot. Club (pres. 1940), Wis. Acad. Sci., Genetic Soc. Am., British Mycological Soc. (hon.) Sigma Xi. Author: Diseases and Pests of Ornamental Plants (with H. W. Rickette); also many papers on morphology, pathology and genetics of fungi. Collaborator Cytologia. Contbr.: Winge Jubilee Vol., Copenhagen, 1955. Asso. editor Mycolgia, 1923-32. Home: 39 Claremont Av., N.Y.C. 190027. Office: N.Y. Botanical Gardens, N.Y.C. 10027. Office: N.Y. Botanical Gardens, N.Y.C. Died Aug. 9, 1960; buried Cedar Lawn Cemetery, Paterson, N.J.

DODGE, CHARLES RICHARDS, textile fibre expert; b. in Miss., July 17, 1847; s. Hon. Jacob Richards and Frances Gove (Buxton) D.; 2 yrs. spl. course Sheffield Scientific Sch. (Yale); m. Mira. d. Col. Josiah Reab, of New Haven, Conn., Jan. 23, 1868. Dept. Agr., 1867, asst. entomologist, and had charge Agrl. Mus. 10 yrs.; began study of fibres, 1870; spl. agt. in charge fibre investigation, Dept. Agriculture, 1890; has since published 20 spl. reports on fibres and fibre industries, including a Dictionary of the Fibre Plants of the World. Officially connected with 11 internat. mem. jury awards, Paris, 1889, Chicago, 1893, Atlanta, 1895, Nashville, 1897, Omaha, 1898, Paris, 1900, Buffalo, 1901, St. Louis, 1904, Jamestown Expn., 1907. Chevalier du Mérite Agricole Frances; Chevalier Légion d'Honneur. Home: East Haven, Conn. Deceased.

DODGE, CHARLES WRIGHT, biologist; b. Cape Vincent, N.Y., Jan. 15, 1863; s. Jasper Newton and Charlotte Augusta (Wright) D.; B.S., U. of Mich., 1886, M.S., 1889; m. Louise W. Hooker, July 18, 1894; children—Charlotte Wright, Eleanor Wolcott (dec.). Instr. biology, 1890-92, prof., 1892-1931, emeritus prof., 1931—, U. of Rochester. Biologist, Rochester Health Bur., 1895-1925. Author: Introduction to Elementary Practical Biology, 1894. Reviser: Orton-Dodge General Zoölogy, 1903. Home: Rochester, N.Y. Died 1934.

DODGE, GRENVILLE MELLEN, civil engr.; b. Danvers, Mass., Apr. 12, 1831; s. Sylvanus and Julia T. (Phillips) D.; grad. Capt. Patridge's Mil. Acad.; C.E., Norwich U., Vt., 1850 (A.M., M.M.S., LL.D., 1892; LL.D., Cornell Coll., Ia., 1904). Was engr. Ill. Central and Rock Island roads; later on U.P. R.R. survey and banker at Council Bluffs, Ia. Entered Civil War as col. 4th Inf., July 6, 1861; brig. gen. vols., Mar. 21, 1862; maj. gen. vols., June 7, 1864; resigned May 30, 1866. Chief engr. U.P. R.R. and supervised its building, 1866-70; chief engr. Tex. & Pacific Ry., 1871-81. Mem. 40th Congress (1867-69), 2d Ia. Dist. Republican. Succeeded Gen. Sherman as pres. Soc. Army of the

Tenn.; comdr.-in-chief Mil. Order Loyal Legion, 1907-08. Apptd. maj. gen. U.S.V., 1898, but declined; apptd., 1898, pres. of the President's commn. to inquire into the management of the war with Spain; chmn. bd. dirs. C.&S. Ry. to Feb. 1909; dir. Ft. Worth & Denver City Ry.; v.p. Abilene & Southern Ry. Died Jan. 3, 1916.

DODGE, JAMES MAPES, mech. engr.; b. Waverly, N.J., June 30, 1852; s. William and Mary (Mapes) D.; ed. Acad., Newark, N.J., Cornell U. to junior yr., and Rutgers Coll.; m. Josephine Kern, Sept. 10, 1879. Has given spl. attention to improvement and manufacture of conveying machinery and devices; now chmn. Link Belt Co. Pres. Am. Soc. M.E., 1903; v.p. Franklin Inst. Republican. Home: Germantown, Phila., Pa. Died Dec. 4, 1915.

DODGE, RAYNAL, machinist, botanist; b. at Newburyport, Mass., Sept. 9, 1844; s. Alvin Dodge (Puritan ancestry); grad. high sch.; lifelong student; spl. studies in cryptogramic botany; served through Banks' campaign in La., Civil War. Author: The Ferns and Fern Allies of New England, 1896. Contbr. to various scientific and mech. jours.; lecturer on subjects connected with natural history. Address: Newburyport, Mass.

DOHARTY, ROBERT ERNEST coll. pres.; b. Clay City, Ill, Jan. 22, 1885; s. Anthony and Clara (Sauther) D.; B.S., U. of Ill., 1909; MS. Union Coll., Schenectady, N.Y., 1921; hon. A.A., Yale, 1931; hon. LL.D., Tufts Coll. and U. of Pittsburgh, 1936; honorary D.Sc. from Waynesburg College, 1948; m. Pearl Edna Mills, June 20, 1911; children—Robert Ernest, Vera Maud, James Anthony. With Gen. Elec. Co., Schenectady, 1909-31, test engr., 1909-10, designing engr., 1910-18; asst. to Dr. C. P. Steinmetz, 1918-23, cons. engr., 1923-31; prof. elec. engring., Yale, 1931-33; dean of Sch. of Engring., Yale, 1933-36; pres. Carnegie Inst. Technology, Pittsburgh, 1936-50; chmn. Engrs. Council for Prof. Development, 1941-43; Production Planning Bd., O.P.M., 1941; Mem. Nat. Advisory Com. for Aeronautics, 1940-41; mem. Advisory Com. for Engineering Science and Management War Training, 1940-46; chmn. Allegheny Conf. on Community Development, Pittsburgh, 1943-46; adv. committee, Army Specialized Training Division. 1943-46; Civil Adv. Council office chief of Ordnance, 1942-45; mem. Bd. of Vistors to the United States Naval Acad., 1944. Dir. Forbes Nat. Bank, Montour Railorad; chmn. Bd. Fed. Reserve Br., Pittsburgh, 1942-45; Mayor of Scotia, N.Y., 1922; mem. Bd. of Education, 1925-29. Awarded Lamme medals: for engring., Am. Inst. E.E., 1937; for edn., Soc. for Promotion Engring. Edn., 1945, 1st prize, oil painting, Asso. Artist of Pittsburgh, 1944. Mem. Am. Inst. Elec. Engrs., Social Science Research Counicl, Am. Soc. for Engring. Edn. (pres. 1943044), Theta Tau, Sigma Xi, Tau Beta Pi, Eta Kappa Nu. Theta Delta Chi, Omicron Delta Kappa. Conglist. Clubs: Engineers, Duquesne, University. Author: Mathematics of Modern Engineering (with E. G. Keller), 1936; (paper) Edn. for Professional Responsibility, 1948. Contbr. tech. and ednl. articles. Home: 900 Park Av. N., Winter Park Fla. Died Oct. 19, 1950; buried Clay City, Ill.

DOHENY, EDWARD LAURENCE, petroleum producer; b. Fond du Lac, Wis., Aug. 10, 1856; s. Patrick and Eleanor Elizabeth (Quigley) D.; grad. high sch., Fond du Lac, 1872; m. Carrie Estelle Betzold. Prospected for gold and silver 20 yrs.; prospected for and produced petroleum, 1892—; discovered several oil dists. in Calif., also petroleum fields in Mexico; chmn. bd. Petroleum Securities Co.; pres. Doheny-Stone Drill Co., Los Nietos Producting & Refining Co., Ltd. Apptd. mem. sub-com. on oil of Council Nat. Defense, July 1917. Died Sept. 8, 1935.

DOHERTY, HENRY LATHAM, operator gas and elec. cos.; b. Columbus, O., May 15, 1870; s. Frank and Anna (McIlvaine) D.; pub. school edn.; hon. Dr. Engring., Lehigh U., 1931; m. Mrs. P. F. Eames, 1929. Office boy Columbus Gas Co. at 12, advancing through various positions until 1890; engr. or mgr. pub. utility cos., Madison, Wis., St. Paul, Minn., San Antonio, Tex., Denver, Colo., and 25 other cities until 1905; organized 1905, and since mgr. Henry L. Doherty & Co., bankers and operators of pub. utility coprs.; organized, 1910, and since pres. Cities Service Co., holding co. for more than 190 pub. utility and petroleum properties with assets of more than $1,000,000.000. Recognized as one of the leaders in America in gas and electric arts and industries; leader in movement for oil conservation by means of unit operation of pools under federal control; patentee of many combustion processes and apparatus and originator of many standard practices. Awarded 1st Beall gold medal, 1898, by Am. Gas Light Assn., for paper on "Gas for Fuel"; mem. orgn. bd. World's Congress of Electricity, St. Louis, 1904; awarded Walton Clark medal, 1930, by Franklin Inst., "in consideration of his outstanding and valuable work in development of the manufactured gas industry." Died Dec. 26, 1939.

DOHME, ALFRED ROBERT LOUIS, chemist; b. Baltimore, Md., Feb. 15, 1867; s. Charles E. and Ida (Schultz) D.; A.B., Johns Hopkins, 1886; Ph.D., 1889; post-grad. courses in chemistry, geology and mineralogy; U. of Berlin, lab. of Fresenius Wiesbaden, and U. of Strassburg, 1889-91, U. of Paris, 1905; m. Emma D. Blumner, Feb. 15, 1893 (dec.); m. 2d, Paula Carl, Nov. 22, 1909. In bus. as mfg. chemist, 1891-1929; pres. Sharp & Dohme, 1911-29. Instr. pharmacy, Johns Hopkins, 1901-12; sec. Nat. Com. of Revision of Pharmacopoeia of U.S. for 1900-10 at decennial conv., Washington, 1900, and mem. Committee of Revision, 1900-30; president The Lync Co., Baltimore, Md. President of the Maryland Pharmaceutical Assn., 1899-1900. Am. Pharmaceutical Assn., 1918, Baltimore Drug Exchange, 1916-18; trustee Walters Art Gallery, Gilman Country Sch. for Boys; mem. bd. dirs. Sharp &Dohme, Fidelity Trust Co.; pres. City Wide Congress, Baltimore, 1911-21; vice pres. Baltimore Museum of Art. Clubs: University, Maryland, Elkridge Country, Baltimore Country, Merchants. Home: 5204 Roland Av., Office: Baltimore Life Bldg., Baltimore 1 MD

DOLAND, JAMES JOSEPH, educator and consulting engr.; b. Denver, Colo., Aug. 1, 1890; s. William and Catherine (Morgan) D.; B.S. Univ. of Colo., 1914; C.E., 1928; M.S., U. of Ill., 1932; D.Sc., St. John's Univ., 1944; m. Mary Hoy, Apr. 19, 1917. Instr. engring. mathematics, U. of Colo., 1914-16; engr. and supt. Hoy Constrn. Co., St. Paul, Minn., 1916-18 and 1919-23; designer and engr. U.S. Bur. of Reclamation, Denver, 1923-26; prof. civil engring., U. of Ill., 1926-58; cons. engr. Nat. Resources Planning Bd., Urbana, Ill., 1936-1943; prin. engr. U.S.E.D., Trinidad, B.W.I. Dist on lend-lease airbases, Trinidad, St. Lucia, Antigua, and Br. Guiana, 1941; cons. engr., War Prodn. Bd., 1943-44; cons. airport engr., Univ. of Ill. and Springfield, Ill. Airports since 1943; cons. hydraulic engr. Union Electric Co., St. Louis, since 1944. Mem. econ. com. Engrs. Joint Council on Nat. Water Policy, 1950. Served as engr. and lt. Constrn. Div., War Dept., U.S. Army, 1918-19. Mem. Am. Inst. Cons. Engr., Joint Council on Nat. Water Policy, 1950. Served as engr. and lt. Constrn. Div., War Dept., U.S. Army, 1918-19. Mem. Am. Inst. Cons. Engr., Am. Soc. C.E., A.A.A.S., Am. Geophys. Union, Tau Beta Pi, Sigma XI. Roman Catholic. Author: books-latest: Hydro-Power Engineering, 1953. Home: 1119 W. Charles S., Champaign, Ill. Died Dec. 23, 1960; buried St. Paul.

DOLBEAR, AMOS EMERSON, educator, inventor; b. Norwich, Conn., Nov. 10, 1837; grad. Ohio Wesleyan U., 1866 (A.M., M.E., Ph.D., all U. of Mich.; LL.D., Tufts College, 1902); from 1874 prof. physics, Tufts Coll. Invented writing telegraph, 1864; magneto telephone, 1876; static telephone, 1879; spring ballance ammeter, 1889; air space telegraph cable, 1882; discovered convertibility of sound into electricity, 1873; telegraphing without wires, 1881; photographing with electric waves, 1893. Received bronze medal for acoustic appartus, Centennial Expn., Phila., 1876, and silver medal, Paris, 1881, and gold medal, London, 1882, for static telephone. Was twice mayor Bethany, W.Va. Author: Chemical Tables; Art of Projecting; The Speaking Telephone; Matter, Ether and Motion; Modes of Motion; Natural Philosophy. Died 1910.

DOLKART, LEO, cons. engr.; b. Caucasia, Sept. 14, 1881; s. Abraham and Julia (Brownstein) D.; came to U.S., 1893, naturalized, 1900; B.S. in Elec. Engring., U. Ill., 1903; student Northwestern U., 1936-37, U. Chgo., 1956; m. Clara Elson, Mar. 12, 1908; children—Elynore (Mrs. Meserow), Ralph. Chief engr. Tri-City Elec. Co., also propr. Moline Elec. Co. (Ill.), 1910-30; designer elec. devel. Stalingrad tractor plant and combine, Siberian projects, 1930-31; cons. elec. engr., Chgo., 1931-40; chief engr. design and constrn. U.S. Navy fuel oil storage projects, 1941-43; chief engr. fgn. projects Leonard Constrn. Co., N.Y.C., 1943-45, charge design and constrn. cement plant, therapy; dir. Mexico, 1945-47; cons. elec. engr., Chgo., 1931-40; chief engr. design Ill., Wis. and Ia., 1951-66; mem. air pollution com. Engring. Found., com. engring. techniques for univs. and hosps. USPHS. Chmn. Moline Elec. Commn., 1924-26. Commr. Moline council Boy Scouts Am., 1926-29. Mem. adv. bd. Moline Salvation Army, 1927-66; bd. mgrs. Rogers Park YMCA, 1926-29. Served as capt., C.E., U.S. Army, World War I. Recipient G. W. Flood Safety award Kiwanis Club, 1938. Registered profl. engr., Ill., Wis., R.I. Fellow Am. Inst. E.E., I.E.E.E.; mem. Illuminating Engring. Soc. (charter emeritus; award of merit 1956, 61, 50 yr. gold pin 1956), Soc. History Tech. (charter, adv. council), Soc. Am. Mil. Engrs. (charter), Chgo. Tech. group (award of merit 1961), Ill. Soc. Profl. Officers Assn. (bd. dirs. Cook County chpt.), Jewish War Vets. U.S., Future Engrs. Am. (sec.), Engrs. Council Profl. Devel. (adv. council Ill.). Kiwanian (v.p. Roger Park); mem. B'nai B'rith (Distinguished Service award 1964). Contbr. profl. jours. Editor Sci-En-Tech News, 1950-60, Vector mag., 1960-64, 65-66, Near North B'nari B'rith News, 1962-66, also sec. Address: 222 E. Chestnut St., Chgo. 60611. Died Oct. 1966.

DOLL, ALFRED W., educator; b. Phila., June 5, 1903; s. Valentine and Katherine (Stift) D.; B.S., Central High Sch., Phila., 1920; B.S. in M.E., U. of Pa., 1924, M.E., 1931; M.A., Columbia, 1928; Ph.D., N.Y. Univ., 1932; P.E., U. of State of New York, 1936; m. Helen A. Nicholson, June 4, 1932; children—Katharine Ruth, Susan Josephine, Mem. faculty Pratt Inst. Sch. of Engring., 1925—; beginning as instr. now prof. physics, head dept. physics, 1938-42, 1946-53. acting dean sch. engring., 1953-56, asst. dean, 1956—. head dept. mech. engring., 1942-46, curriculum chmn. mech. engring., 1940-46, supervisor of vasci instrn., 1946—; Defense Training Inst. of Brooklyn as chmn., dept. of physics, 1940-43. Mem. Am. Assn. Physics Teachers, Am. Inst. Physics, Am. Soc. M.E., Am. Soc. E.E., Tau Beta Pi, Sigma Xi (hon. asso.). Presbyn. Author: Mechanics, Fluids and Heat Texts published by Pratt Inst. Home: 115 Dogwood Av., Malverne, L.I., N.Y. Office: 215 Ryerson St., Bklyn. 5, Died Dec. 23, 1957 buried Hillside Cemetery, Roslyn, Pa.

DOLLENS, BURL AUSTIN, engr.; b. Elnora Ind., Dec. 10, 1901; s. James and Mary (Stalcup) D.; B.S., Purdue U., 1925. D.S. in engr. (hon.), 1951; m. Neva E. Johnson, Dec. 20, 1924; daughters—Marilyn, Marjorie. With Gen. Motors Corp. since 1925, student tng. course. Delco Remy div., 1925-26; successively, industrial engineer, foreman prodn. dept. asst. supt., motor plant, plant engr. for entire div., asst. chief inspector of div., supt. Grey Iron Foundry, Supt. motor plant, gen. supt. three aircraft aluminum foundries, mgr. foundries and world's largest automotive battery plants, Delco-Remy Div., Muncie, Ind., New Brunswick, N.J., 1926-45; gen. mgr. Saginaw (Mich.) Malleabel Iron Div. (now Central Foundry Div.), 1945-46; asst. gen.mgr. Electro-Motive Div., La Grange, Ill., 1946-50; vice pres. General Motors Corp. and gen. mgr. Electro-Motive Div. since 1950. Mem. Ill. State C. of C. (dir.), Newcomen Society of England. Republican. Conglist. Clubs: Chicago, Executives, Indiana, Western Railway, Economic (Chicago). Home: 340 Cottage Hill Avd., Elmhurst, Ill. Office: Electro-Motive Div., General Motors Corp., La Grange, Ill. Died Feb. 9, 1952.

DOLLEY, CHARLES SUMNER, biologist, b. Elyria, O., June 16, 1856; s. Dr. Lester C., and Sarah R.A.D.; mother was the 2d woman to grad. in medicine in the U.S.; ed. Syracuse U. to jr. yr., class 1878; M.D., U. of Pa., 1882; postgrad. work, Johns Hopkins U., 1883-84, U. of Leipzig, 1884, Zool. Sta., Naples, Italy, 1885; m. Elizabeth G. Gilman, of Groveland, N.Y., Nov. 28, 1876; children—Gilman Corson (dec.), Loilyn Carlota (Mrs. Homer St. Gaudens, dec.), Lester Adamson (dec.); m. 2d, Adelaide Clark O'Gorman, Leicester, Eng., 1908. Prof. biology, Swarthmore, 1885-89, U. of Pa., 1885-92, Central High Sch., Phila., 1891-1907; pub. sanitation and chem. engring. work in Mexico City, 1907-12; biol. research, Bahamas, 1912-18; pres. Bahamas Plantation Co., Ltd. In charge Research Laboratory for Marine Biology and Biochemical Investigation, Old Fort, Bahamas. Invented many improvements in the methods and machinery of industrial processes, particularly in food preservation, filtration, tanning. Mem. Am. Philos. Soc., Am. Soc. Naturalist, Acad. Natural Sciences of Phila., Franklin Inst., Am. Chem. Soc., Am. Ceramic Soc., Psi Upsilon. Editor biol. terms, Standard Dictionary; biol. editor Gould's Illustrated Dictionary of Medicine and Biology; contbr. to scientfic jours. Home: Nassau, · N.P., Bahamas, B.W.I.

DONHAM, C(HARLES) R(UMPEL), veterinarian; b. Rockport, Ind., Aug. 1, 1898; s. Lewis Singleton and Amelia Rebecca (Rumple) D.; D.V.M., Ia. State Coll., 1921; M.S., Ore. State Coll. 1927; student, sch. of med., Washington U., summer parttime student U. Minn., 1929-35; m. Margaret Hyde Lysinger, June 18, 1921; children—Marion Margaret (Mrs. Joseph F. Jamison), James Charles. Pvt. practice in vet. medicine, 1921-22; instr., asst. prof. vet. medicine Ore. State Agr. Coll., 1922-29; asst. prof., asso. prof. vet. Medicine U. Minn., 1929-35; prof. vet. medicine Ohio State U., 1935-40; prof. vet. sci. Purdue U., 1940—. Mem. Com. on brucellosis U.S. Live Stock Sanitary Assn.; adv. com. Bur. Animal Insdustry, U.S. Dept. of Agr.; mem. Nat Workers in Animal Disease in N. Am., Inda., Am. vet. med. assns., Sigma Xi, Phi Kappa Phi, Zeta Iota, Sigma Nu. Methodist. Mason. Rotarian. Home: 1519 Summit Dr., West Lafayette, Ind. Died Apr. 24, 1956 buried Ames (Ia.) Cemetery.

DONKIN, MCKAY, univ. adminstr.; b. Westport, Conn., Oct. 17, 1904; s. George W. McKay and Leah (Gaydenne) D.; Petroleum Engr., Colo. Sch. Mines, 1929; grad. student U. Tex., 1936, Harvard, 1937; m. Agnes Denison McLean, June 25, 1935; children—Carla Swan (Mrs. Donald C. Jenkins), Deborah (Mrs. William Wells the third). Engaged as geologist, corporation official, and oil producer in oil and petroleum engring, 1929-50; with Dept. Def., 1950-51; spl. asst. chmn. AEC, 1951-57; v.p., treas. Pa. State U., 1957-68. Served to lt. comdr. USNR, 1942-46. Clubs: Metropolitan (Washington); Rolling Rock (Ligonier, Pa.). Home: State College PA Died Mar. 17, 1968; buried Graysville Cemetery, Spruce Creek, Huntington County PA

DONOVAN, JOHN JOSEPH, civil engr., lumber; b. Rumney, N.H., Sept. 8, 1858; s. Patrick and Julia (O'Sullivan) D.; grad. Plymouth (N.H.) State Normal Sch., 1877; B.S. in C.E., Worcester Poly. Inst., 1882, later C.E., also D.Sc., 1932; m. Clara Isabel Nichols, Apr. 29, 1888; children—Helen Elizabeth (Mrs. Leslie Craven), John Nichols, Philip Laurence. Civ. engr. N.P. Ry., 1882-88, in charge Cascade div., 1886-87, in charge Mont. constrn., 1887-88; chief engr. and mgr. 3 rys. radiating from Bellingham and sold to G.N., N.P. and C.,M.&St.P. respectively; built and operated many miles of railroad, etc.; has been engaged in lumber business exclusively, 1906—; dir. Bloedel Donovan Lumber Mills. Mem. City Council, Fairhaven, Washington, 1890-92; developed Nooksack Falls, and sold to Stone & Webster, 1905. Trustee Bellingham State Normal Sch., 8 yrs., Bellingham Chamber Commerce (pres.), State Chamber Commerce (pres.) Republican. Catholic. Home: Bellingham, Wash. Died Jan. 9, 1937.

DOOLEY, M(ARION) S(YLVESTER), physician, author: b. Cedar Grove, Mo., Dec. 23, 1879; s. Thomas Jefferson and Elizabeth Caroline (Howell) D.; A. B., U. Mo., 1907; med. student U. Mo., Harvard 2 yrs.; M.D., Syracuse U., 1914; m. Mary Elizabeth Jadwin, Sept. 1, 1908; children—Elizabeth (Mrs. Frederick D. Becker), Alice Ann (Mrs. David Radford Serpell); m. 2d, Constance Howell, Mar. 1, 1943. Successively instr., asst. prof. asso. prof., prof. physiology and pharmacology, Syracuse U. Coll. of Medicine, 1907-17, prof. pharmacology, 1917-45, emeritus prof., 1945—; drugs cons. University Hosp. staff, 1922-47, Bureau Hosp. Standards and Supplies, Inc., 1935—, W.P. B., 1943-45. Mem. U.S. Pharmacopoeia Revision Com., 1920-50. Fellow Internat. Coll. Anesthesia, A.M.A., Syracuse Acad. Medicine; mem. Internat. Anesthesia Research Soc. (hon.pres.), Am. Soc. Pharmacology and Therapeutics, Soc. Exptl. Biol. and Medicine, Sigma Xi, Phi Kappa Phi, Alpha Omega Alpha. Unitarian. Author: Pharmacology and Therapeutics in Nursing, 1948; chmn. editorial com. Practitioners and Interns Handbook, 4 edits, 1928-49; co-chmn. editorial com. Drug Manual, 1949. Home: 417 Waverly Av., Syracuse 10, N.Y. Died Dec. 13, 1958; buried Fayetteville (N.Y.) Cemetery.

DOOLEY, THOMAS ANTHONY III, physician, author; b. St. Louis, Jan. 17, 1927; s. Thomas Anthony and Agnes (Wise) D.; student U. Notre Dame; M.D., St. Louis U., 1953; postgrad. U. Paris. Served with USNR, 1944-46, 53-56; served at Naval Hosp., Camp Pendleton, Cal., 1 year, trans. to Naval Hosp., Yokosuka, Japan; volunteered for duty in USS Montague, transporting no. Vietnamese refugees to Saigon, 1954; later French interpreter, med. officer Navy preventive medicine unit, Haiphong, 1954; duty at Naval Hosp., Yokosuka, 1955; made lecture tour of U.S. under auspices U.S. Navy, 1956; organized pvt. med. mobile unit to work in Laos, 1956; an organizer Med. Internat. Corp. (MEDICO). Named 1 of ten outstanding men of 1956, Look mag.; decorated Legion of Merit; officer Ordre National de Vietnam. Author: Deliver Us from Evil, 1955; The Edge of Tomorrow, 1958; The Night They Burned the Mountain, 1960. Died Mar. 1961.

DOOLITTE, CHARLES LEANDER, astronomer; b. Ontario, Ind., Nov. 12, 1843; s. Charles and Celia D.; C.E., U. of Mich., 1874 (hon. Sc.D., 1897; LL.D., Lehigh U., 1912); m. Martha Cloyes Farrand, Sept. 18, 1866, m. 2d, Helen Eugenia Wolle, May 11, 1882; father of Eric D. On U.S. Boundary Survey, 1873-75; prof. mathematics and astronomy, Lehigh U., 1875-95; prof. astronomy, U. of Pa., and dir. Flower Astron. Obs. 1895-1912 (emeritus). Author: Practical Astronomy as Applied to Geodesy and Navigation; Results of Observation with Zenith Telescope, Sayre Obs., 1876-95; Results of Observation with Zenith Telescope, Sayre Obs., 1876-95; Results of Observation with Zenith Telescope, Flower Obs., 1894-1911. Home: Philadelphia, Pa. Died Mar. 3, 1919.

DOOLITTE, ROSCOE EDWARD, chemist; b. Fowlerville, Mich., Jan. 16, 1874; s. Edward Jefferson and Caroline M. (Hoyt) D.; high schs., Howell and Morrice, Mich.; B.S., Mich. Agrl. Coll., 1896; m. Ivah May Stewart, Nov. 6, 1895; children—Stewart Edward, Kenneth Hoyt. Asst. chemist, Mich. State Dairy and Food Dept., 1896-98; state chemist, 1898-1904; asst. chemist. Bur. of Chemistry, U.S. Dept. Agr. and chief of New York Lab., 1904-11; transferred to Washington, as asso. chemist same bureau and mem. Bd. of Food and Drug Inspection, Oct. 1911; served as acting chief Buf. of Chemistry, Mar.-Dec. 1912, after resignation of Dr. H. W. Wiley; returned to former position as chief of New York Lab., 1912-17; chief eastern dist., Bur. Chemistry, Jan. 8-Oct. 1, 1917, chief central dist., Chicago, Oct. 1, 1917—. Home: Evanston, Ill. Deceased.

DOOLITTLE, ERIC, astronomer; b. Ontario, Ind., July 26, 1869; s. Charles Leander (q.v.) and Martha Cloyes (Farrand) D.; ed. prep. sch. Lehigh U., 1883-87; C.E., Lehigh U., 1891; post-grad. work astronomy, 1894-96; m. Sara Bitler Halliwell, Mar. 31, 1902. Instr. astronomy, Lehigh U., 1891-92, State U. of Ia., 1892-93, U. of Pa., 1896-1904; asst. prof. astronomy, U. of Pa., 1904-12; prof. astronomy and dir. Flower Astron. Obs., 1912—. Presbyn. Author: Measures of 900 Double and Multiple Stars, 1901; Measures of 1066 Double and Multiple Stars, 1905; Catalogue and Remeasurement of the 648 Hough Double Stars, 1907; Measures of 1954 Double Stars, 1914. Home: Upper Darby, Pa. Died Sept. 21, 1920.

DOOLITTLE, THOMAS BENJAMIN, engr., inventor; b. Woodbury, Conn., June 30, 1839; s. Benjamin and Betsey C. (More) D.; ed. Woodbury Acad.; (Sc.D., Darmouth, 1909); m. Mary Louise Bradley, Dec. 24, 1866. In early life was a mfr. of brass articles at Bridgeport, in which he made many inventions in connection with mfr. of barbed wire; was originator of buffer platform and coupler, of which modifield types are in general use on passenger cars; became connected with Bell Telephone Co. at early day; originated the first telephone switchboard, the hard drawn copper and the telephone call bell, etc.; originated and placed in use a fare registering device on street cars; retired from active service of Am. Telephone & Telegraph Co., June 1909. Received Edward Longstreth medal from Franklin Inst. of Phila., 1898, for origination of process of producing hard drawn copper wire. Home: Branford, Conn. Died Apr. 4, 1921.

DORAN, JAMES M., chemist; b. Frand Forks, N.D., Aug. 17, 1885; s. Frank and Edwinna (Brainerd) D.; B.S. in Chemistry, U. of Minn., 1907; post-grad. study, George Washington U., 1912-13; m. Roxana Brook, Aug. 22, 1908; children—James Edward, Frances. Chemist Internal Revenue Bur., U.S. Treasury, since 1907, head of chem. and tech. div. since 1920; commr. of prohibition, 1927-30; commr. of industrial alcohol 1930-33; supervisor Assn. of Distilled Spirits Industry (code authority), Dec. 1933-May 1935; tech. dir. Distilled Spirits Inst. since Dec. 1933. Mem. Am. Chem. Soc., Sigma Xi. Republican. Protestant. Club: Cosmos. Contbr. on industrial alcohol to scientific periodicals. Home: 1231 31st St., N.W., Washington. Died Sept. 8, 1941.

DOREMUS, CHARLES AVERY, chemist; b. New York, N.Y., Sept. 6, 1851; s. Robert Ogden and Estelle Emma (Skidmore) D.; A.B., Coll. City of New York, 1870; A.M., Ph.D., U. of Heidelberg, 1873; student U. of Leipzig, 1873; (hon. M.D., U. of Buffalo, 1879); m. Elizabeth Johnson Ward (playwright), Aug. 4, 1880. Reporter on photography for U.S. govt., Vienna Expn., 1873; chemist U.S. Dairy Co., 1873; in gen. practice of chemistry, 1873—. Asst. chemistry, toxicology and med. jurisprudence, Bellevue Hosp. Med. Coll., 1874-79, adj. prof., 1879-97; prof. chemistry and toxicology, med. dept., U. of Buffalo, 1879-82; prof. chemistry, 1882-92, emeritus prof., 1892-98, Am. Veterinary Coll., New York; asst., 1882-97, asst. prof. chemistry and physics, 1897-1901, asst. prof. chemistry, 1901-03, acting prof., 1903-04, Coll. City of New York. Wrote sect. on Gaseous Poisons, Text-Book of Legal Medicine and Toxicology, 1903. Home: New York, N.Y. Died Dec. 2, 1925.

DOREMUS, ROBERT OGDEN, chemist; b. New York, Jan. 11, 1824; grad. N.Y. Univ., 1842; med. dept., 1850 (LL.D., 1872); studied chemistry in Paris, 1847-48, establishing laboratory in New York latter yr. Has held several important chairs in collegiate instns., becoming, 1861, prof. chemistry and toxicology, Bellevue Hosp. Med. Coll.; also, 1864, prof. chemistry and physics, Coll. City of New York. In Paris, 1862-64, developing the use of compressed granulated gunpowder, which was adopted by the French govt.; has patented methods of extinguishing fires and other chem. processes. Died 1906.

DORN, HAROLD F(RED), statistician; b. Tompkins County, N.Y., July 30, 1906; s. Fred E. and Minnie Elizabeth (Miller) D.; B.S., Cornell U., 1929, M.S., 1930; Ph.D., U. of Wis., 1933; student, Miami U., 1931-32; U. of Chicago, summer, 1933; Univ. Coll., London, 1933-34; m. Celia Camine, June 25, 1932; children—Eleanor Louise, Patricia Elizabeth. Research analyst, Fed. Emergency Relief Adminstrn., W.P.A., 1934-35; staff mem., com. on population problems, Nat. Resources Com., 1936; statistician, USPHS, 1936—. Cutter lectr. preventive medicine Harvard U., 1959—. Del. to Internat. Union for the Scientific Investigation of Population Problems, Paris, 1937; mem., U.S. Com. on Joint Causes of Death, 1946-48; del.to the Internat. Conf. for the 6th Decennial Revision of the Internat. List of Causes of Death, Paris, 1948; Interagency Com. on Med. Records, U.S. Govt. (chmn. since 1946), Tech. Adv. Com. on Population for the 1950 Census; mem., U.S. Nat. Com. on Vital and Health Statistics. Served as lt. col., Med. Adminstrative Corps, dir., med. statistics div., Office of the Surgeon-Gen., U.S. Army, 1943-46. Awarded Legion of Merit. Fellow Am. Pub. Health Assn., A.A.A.S., Am. Statis. Assn.; member Am. Assn. Cancer Research, American Sociological Society, Population Assn. American (pres.), Internat. Union Against Cancer (gen. sec.), Am. Eugenics Soc., Washington Acad. Scis., Am. Cancer Society (science advisory council 1956-62), Washington Statis. Soc. (pres.), Social Sci. Research Council, Internat. Population Union, Public Health Cancer Assn., Am. Soc. Human Genetics, Am. Epidemiological Soc., Alpha Zeta, Phi Kappa Phi. Home: 15 Burning Tree Ct., Bethesda, Md. 20034. Died May 9, 1963; buried Arlington Nat. Cemetery.

DORR, GEORGE BUCKMAN, scientist, student; b. Jamaica Plain, Mass., Dec. 29, 1853; s. Charles Hazen and Mary Gray (Ward) D.; A.B., Harvard, 1874, post-grad. work, 1888-91, hon. M.A., 1923; hon. M.Sc., U. of Me., 1924; unmarried. Studied and traveled in Europe and Near East; has devoted much time to plant life, pub. reservations and landscape gardening; founder, and supt. under U.S. Govt., of Acadia National Park, on coast of Me. Fellow Harvard Travellers Club; mem. N.E. Bot. Soc.; treas. The Wild Gardens of Acadia. Home; (legal) Bar Harbor, Me. Died Aug. 5, 1944.

DORR, JOHN VAN NOSTRAND, metall. chem. engr.; b. Newark, N.J., Jan. 6, 1872; s. John Van Nostrand and Nancy H. (Higginson) D.; b.Sc., Rutgers Coll., New Brunswick, N.J., 1894, honorary Eng.M., 1914, D.Sc., 1927; hon. D. Engring., S.D. Sch. of Mines, 1940, Mich. Coll. Mining and Tech., 1940, Colo. Sch. Mines, 1956; D.Sc., Columbia, 1943; m. Sally Harman Doughty, Apr. 24, 1897; children—Antoinette Nott (Mrs. Malcolm Oakes), Rosalind Higginson (Mrs. R. D. McMillan, deceased); m. 2d, Ellen Faulkner Swift, June 20, 1924; m. 3d, Mrs. Virginia Nell Becker, Aug. 20, 1935. Lab. research under Thomas A. Edison 2 yrs.; pres. The Dorr Co., engrs., 1910-49, chmn., 1949-54; founder, chmn. Dorr-Oliver, Inc., 1955, hon. chmn., 1956; chmn. bd. Dorr-Oliver, Ltd., London; pres. Dorr Associates. Chairman board Dorr Found. Inventor Dorr Classifier, Dorr Thickener, Dorr Agitator, used metall., chemical and san. engring. fields. John Scott medal, Franklin Inst., 1916; James Douglas medal, Am. Inst. Mining and Metall. Engrs., 1930; Chem. Industry medal, 1938, Perkin medal, 1941, Soc. Chem. Industry medal, 1938, Perkin medal, 1941, Soc. Chem. Industry, 1938; Modern Pioneers award, Nat. Assn. Mfrs., 1940. Mem. Am. Inst. Mining and Metall. Engrs., Am. Electro-chem. Soc., Am. Inst. Chem. Engrs. (pres. 1932-33), Am. Chem. Soc., Soc. of Chem. Industry (London), Thomas Alva Edison Foundation, Council on Foreign Relations, Mining and Metall. Soc. America, Canadian Inst. Mining and Metallurgy, Chem. Metall. and Mining Soc. S. Africa (hon.), Institute Mining and Metallurgy (London), Zeta Psi (nat. pres. 1931); Tau Beta Pi, Phi Lambda Upsilon, Phi Beta Kappa. Trustee Rutgers U. Republican. Episcopalian. Clubs: Explorers, Mining, Chemists, Century, University (N.Y.C.); Cosmos (Washington); Union Interalliée (Paris); Mining and Metallurgical (London); Chem. Industries (London); Author: The Cyanidation and Concentration of Gold and Silver Ores, 1936, rev., 1950. Home: 30 E. 37th St., N.Y.C.; also Villa Serena, Washington, Conn. Office: 99 Park Av., N.Y.C. 10016. Died June 29, 1962.

DORRANCE, GEORGE MORRIS, surgeon; b. Bristol, Bucks County, Pa., Apr. 24, 1877; s. John and Eleanor Gillingham (Thompson) D.; prep. edn., Peekskill Mil. Acad., Ossining, N.Y.; M.D., U. of Pa., 1900; m. Emily Fox, Nov. 10, 1921; children—George Morris, Emily Fox. Practiced at Phila. since 1900; prof. surgery Women's Med. Coll. of Pa., 1923-24; prof. maxillo-facial surgery, Thomas Evans Inst., U. of Pa., surgeon to Doctors Hosp., Philadelphia; surgeon, Cooper Hosp., Camden, N.J.; consultant oral surgery State and Montgomery Hospitals, Norristown, Pa.; chmn. bd. Campbell Soup Co. Served overseas as maj. Med. Reserve Corps, U.S. Army. Fellow Am. Coll. Surgeons, Coll. Physicians of Phila.; mem. A.M.A., Pa. State Med. Soc., Phila. County Med. Soc., Pathol. Soc., Phila. Acad. Surgery, Republican. Episcopalian. Clubs: Racquet Medical, Physicians, Motor, Phila. Country. Home: 2218 Delancey St. Office: 2101 Spruce St., Philadelphia, Pa. Died Nov. 21, 1949.

DORSET, MARION, chemist; b. Columbia, Tenn., Dec. 14, 1872; s. Walter Clagett and Jane (Mayes) D.; B.S., U. of Tenn., 1893; M.D., Columbia (now George Washington Univ. U.), 1896; also studied at U. of Pa.; m. Emily K. Jackson, Oct. 10, 1900; children—Walter Clagett (dec.), Jane Mayes (dec.), Virgil Jackson. Has taught bacteriology and pathology; now engaged in research work on bacterial toxins, especially those of tuberculosis, etc.; asst. chemist biochemic lab., Dept. Agr., 1894-1903; chief biochemic div., 1904—. Home: Washington, D.C. Died July 15, 1935.

DORSETT, P(ALEMON) H(OWARD), foreign plant introduction to U.S.; b. Carlinville, Ill., Apr. 21, 1862; s. William (Newman) and Laura (Oceola) D.; B.A., U. of Mo., 1884; m. Mary Virginia Payne, of Columbia, Mo., Sept. 12, 1892 (died Aug. 13, 1905); 1 son James H. (dec.). With U.S. Dept. Agr. since 1891; field office worker, and has assisted in building up 6 plant introduction gardens under Dept. of Agr.; leader agrl. exploring expdn. to Brazil, 1913-14; to China, 1914-26; Dorsett and Morse Agrl. Expdn. to Japan, Chosen, Manchuria and Northern China, 1929-31. Member American Genetic Assn. (life), Am. Red Cross (life), Bot. Soc. Washington. Episcopalian. Mason. Home: Bell, Md. (P.O. Glendale, Md., R.F.D. 1). Address: U.S. Dept. Agr., Washington, D.C.

DORSEY, CLARENCE WILBUR, agrl. engineer; b. Kirkersville, O., July 6, 1872; s. Edwin Jackson and Mary Elma (Grove) D.; brother George Amos D. (q.v.); Litt.B., Denison U., 1894; A.B., Harvard, 1896; m. Florence May Juilliard, of Louisville, O., Dec. 28, 1898. Asst. physicist, Md. Agrl. Expt. Sta., 1896-8; in charge field work in Div. of Soils, U.S. Dept. Agr., 1898-1902; soil physicist, Bur. of Agr., P.I., 1902-3; in charge Soil Survey, Bur. of Soils, U.S. Dept. Agr., 1903-9; in pvt. practice as agrl. engr., in Cal., 1909—. Author of bulls. and papers relation to soil investigations in U.S., P.R. and P.I. Home: 520 S. St. Andrews Pl. Office: Central Bldg., Los Angeles CA

DORSEY, HERBERT GROVE, physicist; b. Kirkersville, O., Apr. 24, 1876; s. Edwin Jackson and Mary Elma (Grove) D.; B.S., Denison U., Granville,

Ohio, 1897, M.S., 1898, Sc.D., 1938; Ph.D., Cornell Univ., 1908; m. Virginia Rowlett, June 21, 1906; children—Herbert Grove, William Rowlett. Instr. physics, U. of Me., 1898-1900; asst. prof. U. of Fla., 1901-03; instr. physics and electricity, Mechanics Inst., Rochester, 1903-04; asst. instr. physics, Cornell U., 1904-05, instr., 1905-10; engr. research br., Western Electric Co., 1910-12; research engr. Nat. Cash Register Co., 1912-16, Hammond Radio Research Lab., 1916-22, Submarine Signal Co., 1922-26; senior elec. engr. U.S. Coast and Geodetic Survey, 1926-28, prin. elec. engr. and chief research sect., 1923-46; lecturer in physics, George Washington Univ., 1947; instr. physics Capitol Radio Engring. Inst. since 1948. Invented Dorsey Phonelescope, dynamic loudspeaker, Fathometer, Sono Radio Buoy. and improved acoustics contrivances in telephone and radio fields; Sonar, the fathometer used horizontally has been employed extensively to locate enemy craft and submarines. Recipient 1st annual award, Washington Soc. Engrs., 1941. Fellow A.A.A.S., Am. Phys. Soc., Acoustical Soc. of America, Inst. Radio Engrs. (chmn. Washington sect., 1933), American Institute Elec. Engrs. (chmn. Washington sect., 1934); member American Optical Society, American Assn. Physics Teachers, Internat. Com. on Radio, Am. Geophys. Union, Am. Radio Relay League, Washington Acad. Science, Philos. Soc. of Washington, Washington Soc. Engrs., Sigma Xi, Phi Kappa Phi, Beta Theta Pi. Baptist. Club: Cosmos. Home: 3708 33d Pl., Washington 8 DC

DORSEY, MAXWELL J., horticulturist; b. Dresden, O., May 3, 1880; s. Samuel and Martha Jane (Magruder) D.; B.S., Mich. State Coll., 1906; M.S. in Agr., Cornell U., 1910, Ph.D., 1913; m. Jean Muir, Dec. 9, 1914; 1 son, John Muir. Instr. in horticulture, U. Me., 1906-06; asst. horticulturist, N.Y. State Exptl. Sta., Geneva, 1907-10; asst. in plant breeding Cornell, 1910-11; asst. and asso. horticulturist, U. Minn., 1911-21; head, dept. horticulture, W.Va. U., 1921-25; chief in pomology, U. of Ill., 1925-66; head, dept. horticulture, U. of Ill., 1941, ret. Sec.-treas. Nat. Peach Council Mar. 1949-66. Fellow Am. Soc. Hort. Sci., Am. Naturalists, Am. Pomol. Soc., Am. Genetic Assn., Ill. Hort. Soc.; mem. A.A.A.S., Sigma Xi, Sigma Nu, Gamma Alpha, Gamma Sigma Delta, Alpha Zeta, Alpha Tau Alpha. Republican. Baptist, Mason, Rotarian. Assisted Dr. U. P. Hedrick in writing Grapes of New York, 1908; Plums of New York, 1910. Prepared the report on hort. Nomenclature for Internat. Hort. Congress held in Rome and Berlin. Contbr. articles to sci. and hort. jours. Home: 1502 S. Lincoln St., Urbana, Ill. Died July 22, 1966.

DOTEN, CARROLL WARREN, statistician; b. Panton, Vt., Jan. 27, 1871; s. Elisha Morton and Ida Lucretia (Hatch) D.; Ph.B, U. of Vt., 1895, A.M., 1899; A.M., Harvard U., 1902; m. Carrie Kingsland Mitchell, Sept. 6, 1899 (died July 9, 1933); children—Robert Kingsland, Dana Morton; m. 2d, Mary Helen Wyman, May 2, 1936. Instructor, 1895-1903, sec. and register, 1896-1903, U. of Vt.; instr., 1903-05, asst. prof. economics, 1905-14, asso. prof., 1914-18, prof. on economics, 1918-36, emeritus since Feb. 1, 1936, Mass. Inst. of Tech. Head of research work, Boston School for Social Workers, 1907-09; expert spl. agt. U.S. Bur. of Census, 1909; chief investigator, Mass. Commn. on Compensation for Industrial Accidents, 1910-12; pres. Cambridge (Mass.) Asso. Charities, 1914-17; pres. Cambridge Park Commission, 1921-1928 and 1934-1939; member Mass. Bureau Immigration, 1917-19. Head of industrial service section of U.S. Shipping Board Emergency Fleet Corp., 1918; in charge statis. audit, U.S. Central Bur. of Planning and Statistics, 1919; mem. advisory com. U.S. Census, 1919-24; cons. specialist Bur. Agrl. Economics, U.S. Dept. of Agr., 1922-27; cons. economist Nat. Retail Dry Goods Assn. since 1929; cons. specialist to secretary of interior, 1933-34; collaborator, consumers' counsel, Agricultural Adjustment Adminstrn. since 1934. Pres. Am. Statis. Assn., 1920-21; member American Economics Association, Massachusetts Reform Club (president), N.E.R.R. Club (pres. 1921-22), Phi Beta Kappa, Phi Delta Theta. Republican. Conglist. Clubs: Cosmos (Washington); City (Boston); Cambridge. Home: Basin Farm, Brandon, Vt. Office: 222 Charles River Rd., Cambridge, Mass. Died June 14, 1942.

DOTEN, SAMUEL BRADFORD entomologist; b. in Gold Hill, Storey County, Nevada, Dec. 14, 1875; s. Alfred and Mary Calista (Stoddard) Doten; B.A., Univ. of Nevada, 1898, M.A., 1912; D.Sc., 1950; m. Laura Katherine Schweis, June 16, 1915. Instr. history and mathematics, 1898-1900, instr. mathematics and entomology, 1900-02, asst. prof., 1902-03, asst. prof. entomology, meterology and mathematics, 1903-05, prof. entomology, since 1906, U. of Neb.; also entomologist and dir. Nev, Expt. Station, 1913-46. Fellow A.A.A.S.; member Phi Kappa Phi. Rebuplican. Episcopalian. Rotarian. Author numerous bulls. and articles on entomol. subjects. Home: 129 Elm St., Reno, Neb. Died May 9, 1955; buried Masonic Cemetery, Reno.

DOTY, PAUL, mech. engr.; b. Hoboken, N.J., May 30, 1869; s. William Henry Harrison and Anna (Langevin) D.; M.E., Stevens Inst. Tech., 1888; m. Mary Reddy, Apr. 8, 1913; 1 dau., Diana. Engr. with United Gas Improvement Co., Phila., 1888-95; engr. with Am. Light and Traction Co., New York, 1895-1917; chmn. Minn. Bd. Registration for Architects, Engrs., and Land Surveyors, 1921— v.p. St. Paul Trust & Savings Bank, 1921-24; regional reconditioning supervisor Home Owners' Loan Corp., Atlanta, Ga., 1934-35. Served as lt. col. Corps of Atlanta, Ga., 1934-35. Served as lt. col. Corps. of Engrs., U.S.A., 1917-18; gen. staff U.S.A., constrn. adviser to Sec. of War, Washington, 1918-19. Democrat. Catholic. Home: St. Paul, Minn. Died Dec. 3, 1938.

DOUGHERTY, PROCTOR LAMBERT;, b. Boston, Mass., 1873; s. M. Angelo and Mary Elizabeth (Proctor) D.; B.S., Mass. Inst. Tech., 1897; m. Grace C. Holmes, Oct. 12, 1910; children—Proctor L., Frances, Elizabeth, Faith. Mgr. Otis Elevator Co., Washington, D.C., 1919-26; pres. Bd. of Commissioners of D.C., 1926-30; now cons. engr. Mem. Washington Soc. of Engrs., Washington Soc. Mass. Inst. Tech. Mem. Massachusetts Soc. Republican. Conglist. Club: University (past pres.). Home: 3723 Jenifer St. Office: National Press Bldg., Washington DC

DOUGHERTY, RICHARD ERWIN, cons. engr., ry. ofcl. (ret.); b. N.Y. City, Feb. 13, 1880; s. Richard and Emma (Erwin) D.; student Coll. City of N.Y., 1894-97; C.E., Columbia, 1901; m. Jessie Evelyn Sprugeon, Mar. 2, 1905; children—Evelyn E. (Mrs. James C. Sharp), Blanche H. (Mrs. John G. Horsman). Instr. in engring. Columbia U., 1901-02; spl. lectr. Cooper Union, 1917-21. With N.Y. Central System, 1902-51, started as rodman, retired as v.p., 1951; cons. Seelye, Stevenson, Value and Knecht, 1951—; Transportation Cons., Washington, 1954—. Mem. adv. com. on safety of White House, 1948; chmn. adv. com. to N.Y. State Civil Def. Commn. Chmn. bldg. planning com. for new Columbia U. Engring. Sch.; mem. adv. council civil engring. Columbia, U. Notre Dame, Norwich University. Recipient Egleston medal Columbia Engineering Schools Alumni Assn., 1945, University medal Columbia, 1948, Townsend Harris medal Assn. Alumni Coll., City of N.Y., 1949, others. Licensed profl. engr. N.Y., Conn., D.C., Ohio, Mass., Cal., Va. Mem. sometime officer several profl. assns. Conglist. Clubs: N.Y. Railroad; University (pres. 1938, White Plains); Westchester Country. Home: 2 Murchison Pl., White Plains, N.Y. Office: 101 Park Av., N.Y.C. Died Sept. 29, 1961.

DOUGHTY, MRS. ALLA, vol. observer for weather bur., 1903—. Catholic. Suuplies at own expense reading matter to persons living in isolated places, garrisons, hosps., Indian police agencies, etc.; also spl. periodicals for scientific use in S. Africa and Japan. Mem. Geog. Soc. of Phila., Pa. Nat. Conservation Assn., etc. Home: Milford, Pa. Nat. Conservation Assn., etc. Home: Milford, Pa. Deceased.

DOUGHTY, HOWARD WATERS, prof. chemistry; b. Baltimore, Md., Aug. 13, 1871; s. Thomas Paramour and Margaret Mustard (Waters) D.; student Johns Hopkins, 1890-93, 1900-04, Ph.D., 1904; M.A., Amherst Coll., 1916; Bachelor of Engring. extra ordinem, Johns Hopkins, 1927; m. Anna Elizabeth Bates, Nov. 29, 1905 (died Jan. 22, 1913); children—Mary Elizabeth (dec.), Odbert Bates, Howard Waters; m. 2d, Rebecca Thompson Pue, Dec. 22, 1920; Research asst., Carnegie Foundn., 1904-05; instr. chemistry, U. of Mo., 1905-06, U. of Wis., 1906-07; mem. faculty, Amherst since 1907, prof. chemistry 1913 since. Fellow A.A.A.S.; mem. Am. Chem. Soc., Phi Gamma Delta, Phi Beta Kappa, Sigma Xi, Phi Lambda Upsilon. Presbyterian. Home: Amherst, Mass. Died Jan. 25, 1949.

DOUGLAS, FREDERIC HUNTINGTON, curator, anthropologist; b. Evergreen, Colo., Oct. 29, 1897; s. Charles Winfred and Mary Josepha (Williams) D.; A.B., U. of Colo., 1921; post-grad. U. of Mich., 1921-22; student Pa. Acad. Fine Arts, 1922-26; Doctor Sci., University of Colorado. 1948; m. Freda Bendix Gillespie, May 21, 1926; children—Ann Pauline and Eve (twins), David. Painter and wood-caver, 1926-29; pres. sch. bd. Evergreen, Colo., 1929-34; curator, dept. Indian Arts, Denver Art Museum 1929-47, curator, dept. Native Arts, since 1947; dir. Denver art. Mus., 1940-42; asst. prof. anthropology U. Denver, from 1934; lecturer in anthropology, U. Colo., from 1946; research fellow in ethnology, Harvard, 1952; director of edn. Fed. Indian Exhibit, San Francisco Fair, 1938-39; co-cir. North Am. Indian Art, Museum Modern Art, N.Y.C., 1940-41; mem. Anglo-Am. group inspecting Swedish and Finnish museums, 1946; commr. Fed. Indian Arts and Crafts Board, from 1946. Served as private, U.S. Inf., 1918; commd. capt. Med. Adm. Corps, Nov. 1942, major, 1944, lt. col., 1945; registrar 31st Gen. Hosp., 25 mos., on New Hebrides and Luzon; disch., Feb. 1946. Trustee Denver Art Museum, Museum of Northern Arizona, Museum of Man, San Diego; mem. of the editorial Board F. W. Hodge Anniversary Fund. Sec. Clearinghouse for Southwestern Museums, 1938-51. Research in design, styles and techniques appearing in work of Indian tribes north of Mexico, in last 150 yrs., with special emphasis on history of each design, style and technique. Fellow A.A.A.S. (v.p. Southwest Div., 1942-47, pres., 1947-48), Royal Anthrop. Soc. of Gt. Britain; mem. Am. Anthrop. Assn., Soc. for Am. Archeology, Am. Folklore Soc., Societe ded Americanistes de Paris; mem. Phi Gamma Delta, Sigma Delta Chi, Mu Alpha Nu. Republican. Episcopalian. Clubs: Denver Country, University, Mile-High, The Westerners (Denver, Colorado). Author and editor, Denver Art Mus. publs. in Indian art; Indian Leaflet Series, since 1930, Indian Design Series since 1938; etc.; author (with Rene d'Harnoncourt), Indian Art of the United States. 1941; The Inner Light (verses, 4 vols.), 1946-53. Contbr. articles to newspapers and jours. Home: 745 S. Jackson St. Office: 1300 Logan St., Denver. Died Apr. 23, 1956; buried Fairmount Cemetery, Denver.

DOUGLAS, HENRY TROVERT, JR., civil engr.; b. in Richmond Co., Va., June 16, 1863; s. William Walter and Betty Landon (Chinn) D.; ed. pub. schs. and under pvt. tutors; m. Ella Merryman Todd, of Baltimore Co., Md., Nov. 15, 1899. Began as civ. engr., Baltimore, Md., 1883; chief engr. Wheeling & Lake Erie and Wabash & Pittsburgh Terminal rys., 1902-12; chief engr. C.&A. R.R. since 1912; v.p. Joliet & Chicago R.R.; dir. Miss. River Bridge Co. Commd. maj., Engr. R.C., June 14, 1917. Mem. Am. Ry. Engring. Assn. Episcopalian. Home: 666 Irving Park Blvd., Chicago, Ill.

DOUGLAS, JAMES, mining engr.; b. Que., Cana., 1837; s. Dr. James and Elizabeth (Ferguson) D.; A.B., Queen's U., Kingston, Can., 1858; (LL.D., McGill U., 1899); m. Naomi, d. late Walter Douglas, of Glasgow, Scotland, Nov. 1860. Was prof. chemistry, Morrin Quebec; has resided in U.S. 1875—, coming to take charge of copper works at Phoenixville, Pa.; later identified with copper industry of Ariz., and Sonora and R.R. of the S. West & Northern Mexico; chmn. bd. Phelps Dodge Corp., Copper Queens Consol. Mining Co., El Paso & Southwestern Co., El Paso & Southwestern R.R. Co.; pres. Old Dominion Co. of Me., etc. With late Dr. T. Sterry Hunt did much original work in hydrometallurgy of coppers. Awarded Instn. of Mining and Metallurgy (Eng.) gold medal, 1908; John Fritz medal, 1915. Home: Spuyten Duyvil, N.Y. Died June 25, 1918.

DOUGLAS, SILAS HAMILTON, chemist; b. Fredonia, N.Y., Oct. 16, 1816; s. Benjamin and Lucy (Townsend) D.; M.D., Coll. Surgeons and Physicians, Balt. Practiced medicine, Dearborn, Mich., for a time; instr. chemistry U. Mich., 1844-45, lectr. in chemistry and geology, 1845-51; an organizer dept. of medicine, prof. chemistry and pharmacy, dept. of medicine, 1855-70, prof. chemistry, 1870-75, prof. mineralogy, 1875-77. Author: Tables for Qualitative Chemical Analysis, 1864; co-author: Qualitative Chemical Analysis: A Guide in the Practical Study of Chemistry, 3d edit., 1880. Died Ann Arbor, Mich., Aug. 26, 1890.

DOUGLAS, WALTER, mining engr.; b. Quebec, P.Q., Can., Dec. 19, 1870; s. James and Naomi (Douglas) D.; ed. Upper Can. Coll., Morrin Coll., Royal Mil. Coll., all of Can.; Sch. of Mines (Columbia); m. Edith Margaret Bell, Sept. 10, 1902; children—Elizabeth Margaret, Katherine Studart, Naomi Margaret, Walter,. Robert Bell. Engr. Commercial Mining Co. of Prescott, Ariz., 1890-92; metallurgist, Consol. Kansas City Smelting & Refining Co., 1892-94; chemist Copper Queen Consol. Mining Co., 1894-95; Detroit Copper Mining Co., 1896-99; supt. 1899-1902, gen. mgr. since 1902, Copper Queen Consol. Mining Co.; gen. mgr. Phelps Dodge & Co. since 1910; ex-pres. Phelps Dodge Crop., now dir. officer numerous addlied corps; formerly chmn. bd. in active charge of property Southern Pacific R.R. Co. of Mexico; div. Southern Pacific Co.; etc. Mem. Am. Mining Congress (ex-pres.) Am. Inst. Mining Engrs., Mining and Metall. Soc. of America, St. Andrew's Soc., etc. Clubs: Century, Grolier, Down Town, St. Andrew's Golf. Home: Glenalla, Chauncey, N.Y. Office: 233 Broadway, New York, N.Y. Died Oct. 3, 1946.

DOUGLASS, ANDREW ELLICOTT, astronomer; b. Windsor, Vt., July 5, 1867; s. Rev. Malcolm and Sarah E. (Hale) D.; A.B., Trinity Coll., Conn., 1889, hon. D.Sc., 1908; hon. D.Sc., U. Ariz., 1938; m. Ida E. Whittington, Aug. 3, 1905. Asst. Harvard Coll. Obs., 1889-94; 1st asst. atronomer, Lowell Obs., Flagstaff, Ariz., 1894-1901; probate judge Coconino County, Ariz., 1903-06; instr. No. Ariz. Normal, 1905-06; prof. physics and astronomy U. Ariz., 1906-18, acting pres. Dec. 1910-May 1911, dean Coll. of Letters, Arts and Scis., 1915-18, dir. Steward Observatory, 1918-38, emeritus 1938-62, prof. astronomy, 1918-62; prof. dendrochronology 1936-62; director Laboratory of Tree Ring Research 1937-58, emeritus, 1959-62. Research asso. Carnegie Instrn. Washington, 1925-38. Fellow Royal Astron. Soc., A.A.A.S. (pres. S.W. div., 1921); mem. Nat. Geog. Soc. (hon. life), Am. Philos. Soc., Am. Meteorol. Soc. (v.p., 1924-25), So. Cal. Acad. Sci., Ariz. Archeol. and Hist. Soc. (pres. 1929-30), Am. Astron. Soc., Astron. Soc. Pacific, Phi Beta Kappa (pres. Ariz. chpt. 1934-35), Phi Kappa Phi, Sigma Xi (pres. Ariz. chpt., 1930-31), Psi Upsilon. Author: Annals of Lowell Obs., Vol. I, pt. II, and Vol. II; Climatic Cycles and Tree Growth, Vols. I, II and III (Carnegie Instn.), 1919, 1928, 1936. Made photographs of shadow bands, zodiacal light, Mars; research in dating prehistoric ruins by tree rings; invented the cycloscope for climatol. and cycle studies of same. Received award Research Corp., New York, for studies in tree rings and chronology, 1931. Corr. Acad. Natural Sci., Phila., 1936. Home: Tucson, Ariz. Address: Lab. Tree-Ring Research, U. Ariz., Tucson. Died Mar., 1962.

DOUGLASS, DAVID BATES, civil engr., army officer, coll. pres.; b. Pompton, N.J., Mar. 21, 1790; s. Nathaniel and Sarah (Bates) D.; grad. Yale, 1813, LL.D. (hon.); m. Ann Eliza Ellicott, Dec. 1815. Commd. 2d lt. engrs., sent to U.S. Mil. Acad., 1813; commd. 1st lt., brevetted capt., 1814; asst. prof. natural philosophy U.S. Mil. Acad., Jan. 1, 1815; prof. natural philosophy Univ. City N.Y., 1832-33; became civil engr., architect; designed N.Y.U. bldg. in Washington Sq.; as engr. N.Y. comrs. selected Croton water shed, determined essential features of system including crossing Harlem River on a high bridge; system supplied N.Y.C. with water, 75 years; pres. Kenyon Coll., 1840-45; prof. mathematics and natural philosophy Hobart Coll., 1848. Died Geneva, N.Y., Oct. 21, 1849; buried Greenwood Cemetery, N.Y.C.

DOUGLASS, EARL, geologist, paleontologist; b. Medford, Minn., Octo. 28, 1862; s. Fernando and Abigail Louisa (Carpenter) D.; ed. U. of Dak., Vermillion, S.D., 1888; S.D. Agrl. Coll., 1889 and 1892; B.S., Ia. State Coll., 1893; M.S., U. of Mont., 1900; fellow, Princeton U., 1900-02; m. Pearl C. Geotschius, Oct. 20, 1905; 1 son, Gawin Earl. Taught sch. with interruptions, 1883-1900; prin. schs., Virginia City, Mont., 1897-98; taught geology, physical geography and physics, U. of Mont., 1899-1900; received life teacher's certificate in Mont.; asst. under Prof. William Trelease in Mo. Bot. Gardens, St. Louis, 1890-91; engaged in research work in dept. of vertebrate paleontology, Carnegie Mus., Pittsburgh, 1902-24. In charge obtaining U. of Utah collection of skeletons from the Dinosaur Nat. Monument, 1923, 24. Teaching in pub. schs., studying geol. and making collections especially of fossil vertebrates, 1894-1900; with Princeton scientific expdn. in Mont., summer 1901, collecting Cretaceous dinosaurs and marine reptiles, also made collections from Tertiary and other formations of Montana and N.D.; discovered, 1909, an immense deposit of Comanchean dinosaurs and marine reptiles, also made collections from Tertiary and other formations of Montana and N.D.; discovered, 1909, an immense deposit of Comanchean dinosaur skeletons near Jensen and Vernal, Utah; this region later set aside as the Dinosaur Nat. Monument. Investigating oil problems, including the origin of oilshales, asphalts, etc. Home: Salt Lake City, Utah. Died Jan. 13, 1931.

DOULL, JAMES ANGUS, medical director; born New Glasgow, Nova Soctia, Sept. 8, 1889; son James Forbes and Mary (Chisholm) D.; B.A., Dalhousie University (Can.), 1911, M.D., C.M., 1914; D.P.H., Cambridge University (England) 1919, Johns Hopkins, 1921; m. Ethel Mary MacQuarrie, Dec. 16, 1919; children—Ethel Dorothy (Mrs. Richard M. Miller), James Angus. Came to the United States 1920, naturalized, 1931. Interne N.S. Hosp., 1913-14; practiced medicine in Glace Bay, 1914-15; provincial insp. health, N.S., 1919-20; Rockefeller fellow Johns Hopkins, 1920-21, and asso. in epidemiology, 1921-24, asso. prof., 1924-30, dir. clin. lab. (John J. Abel Fund) for research on the common cold, 1928-30; prof. hygiene and pub. health, Western Reserve U. School of Medicine, Cleveland, 1930-45; lecturer in epidemiology, U. of Rio de Janeiro, 1926; visiting prof. of epidemiology, Sch. of Tropical Medicine, Columbia University, Puerto Rico, 1941; visiting professor of bacteriology, Ohio State University, 1941; special mission officer, Lend-Lease Adminstration, 1943; medical consultant for U.N.R.R.A., 1944; medical consultant, Foreign Economic Adminstration 1944-46; mem. U.S. delegation UNCIO, 1945, International Health Conference, 1946; Pan American Sanitary Conference, 1947, First World Health Assembly, 1948; U.S. representative, Intern. Office Public Health, Paris, 1946-49; medical director (R), United States Public Health Service, 1944-45; med. dir. since 1945; chief Office of Internat. Health Relations, 1945-49; detailed Leonard Wood Memorial as med. dir., 1949. Served in M.C., the British Army, 1915-19, retiring as major. Chairman of medical advisory board American Leprosy Foundation (Leonard Wood Memorial), 1940-43. Member A.M.A., American Public Health Association, Am. Epidemiol. Soc. (pres. 1937-38), A.A.A.S., Delta Omega, Sigma Xi, Alpha Omega Alpha; honorary fellow of the Royal Sanitary Institute (Gt. Britain). Awarded Military Cross (Great Britain and Croix de Guerre (France), 1918; Chevalier, Ordre de Sante Publique (France), 1945; Comdr. Order of St. Lazarus of Jerusalem, 1959. Presbyn. Club: Cosmos (Washington). Contbr. to professional journals. Home: 4202 N. 25th St., Arlington, Va. Address: 1832 M St. N.W., Washington. Died Apr. 6, 1963; buried Arlington (Va.) Nat. Cemetery.

DOVE, W(ILLIAM) FRANKLIN, biologist; b. Marion, Ia., Apr. 11, 1897; s. William Franklin and Edith (Gregory) D.; B.S., Ia. State Coll., 1922; M.S., U. of Wis., 1923, Ph.D. in Genetics, 1927; m. Ruth Rebecca Stone, Sept. 5, 1933; children—Edith Felicia, William Franklin, Ellen Rebecca, Christopher Stone, John Gregory. Asst. in genetics, U. Wis., 1923-26; asso. biol., Me. Argr. Expt. Sta., U. Me., 1926-31, head dept. biology, 1931-43. Cons., Subsistence Research Br., Mil. Planning Div. O.Q.M.G., Washington, 1944; biologist in charge Food Acceptance Research Br., Subsistence Research and Devel. Lab., C.Q.M.D. (later Quartermaster Food and Container Inst. for Armed Forces, C.Q.M.D.), Chgo., 1944-45; coordinator for Food Acceptance Com. on Food Research, 1945; chief, Food Acceptance Research Branch, Q.M. Food and Container Inst. for the Armed Forces, 1946-48; biologist USPHS, (nutrition br.), also dir. food acceptance Studies Dept. Pub. Health, Coll. of Medicine, U. Ill., 1950, research asso., 1950-66, research asso. emeritus, 1966-72; adv. bd. U.S. Soil, Plant Nutrition Lab., Cornell U., 1939-42. Served AS, USN, Pensacola, Fla., 1918. Mem. A.A.A.S., Am. Soc. Human Genetics, Soc. for Study of Growth and Devel., Genetics Soc. Am., Am. Statis. Assn. (Biometrics), Inst. Food Technologists, Sigma Xi. Contbr. to sci. jours. on physiol. genetics, transplantation of tissues, artifical production of the fabulous unicorn, individual vs. group-growth and need-getting, the theory of aggrid ascendance, bio-economics, appetite levels of food consumption, food acceptance research, water and the consumer. Home: Oak Park IL Died Mar. 24, 1972; buried Mt. Vernon IA

DOW, ALEX, chmn. exec. com. Detroit Edison Co.; b. Scotland, 1862; hon. Master Engring., U. of Mich., 1911; hon. D.Engring., U. of Mich., 1924; D.Sc., U. of Detroit, 1936; Dr. of Arts, Wayne U., 1938; m. Vivienne Kinnersley, 1889. Came to U.S., 1882; naturalized, 1895. Elec. engr. City of Detroit, 1893-96; water commr., Detroit, 1916-21, reapptd., 1925-32; pres. Detroit Edison Co., 1932-40, now chmn. exec. com. Mem. Am. Soc. C.E., Am. Soc. M.E., Am. Inst. E.E., Inst. Elec. Engrs., Inst. Mech. Engrs. (Great Britain), etc. Republican. Episcopalian. Clubs: Detroit, etc. Home: Barton Hills, Ann Arbor, Mich. Office: 2000 2d Av., Detroit, Mich. Died Mar. 22, 1942.

DOW, ALLAN WADE, chemical engr.; b. New York, N.Y., Aug. 24, 1866; s. Capt. John Melmoth and Elizabeth K. (Allan) D.; ed. pvt. sch.; Ph.B., Sch. of Mines, Columbia, 1888; m. Jessie Ceclia Frank, Nov. 10, 1892; childern—F. Miriam, Allan W., John A. Asst. chemist, Barber Asphalt Paving Co., 1889-94; chemist to engring. dept. and insp. asphalt and cement for D.C., 1894-1906; mem. firm Dow & Smith, cons. engrs., specialists on road paving and paving materials, 1906-32; cons. engr. under name of A. W. Dow, Inc., same specialities, 1932—; v.p. and chief Asphalt Paving Technologist; mem. Am. Chem. Soc., Internat. Soc. for Testing Materials, A.A.A.S., Am. Soc. for Testing Materials Home: Old Gulph Rd., Bridgewater, Conn. Office: 801 2d Av., N.Y.C. 17. Died Dec. 8, 1955; buried Bridgewater.

DOW, HERBERT HENRY, chemist, mfr.; b. Belleville, Ont., Feb. 26, 1866; s. Joseph H. and Sarah J. (Bunnell) D.; grad. Case Sch. Applied Science, 1888, hon. D. Eng., 1924; Doctor of Engring., U. of Mich., 1929; m. Grace A. Ball, Nov. 16, 1892. Prof. chemistry and toxicology, Huron Street Hosp. Coll., Cleveland, 1888-89; mfr. chemicals, 1889—, as partner, or officer Midland Chem. Co., Inc., Dow Process Co., and Dow Chem. Co., pres. and gen. mgr. latter. Awarded Perkin medal by Soc. of Chem. Industry, 1930. Has developed many new chem. processes on which over 100 patents have been grated. Formerly member Advisory Com. of Council of Nat. Defense, The Chem. Alliance, Inc.; mem. Board Public Works, and Bd. of Edn., Midland, Mich. Trustee Case Sch. Applied Science. Presbyn. Mason. Home: Midland, Mich. Died Oct. 15, 1930.

DOW, LORENZO, inventor, businessman; b. Sumner, Me., July 10, 1825; s. Huse and Zilpha (Drake) D.; grad. Wesleyan U., 1849; studied law, N.Y.C., 1853; Topeka, Kans., 1854-57; m. Elizabeth Penfield, Dec. 25, 1853; m. 2d, Mrs. Sabrina Smith, Oct. 2, 1862, 1 son, 1 dau. Went to Cal., 1850-53; judge Kan. Supreme Ct., 1858; mayor Topeka, 1859; editor Kan. Tribune, Topeka, 1859; patented waterproof cartridge, 1861; experimenter for Remington Arms Co., N.Y., 1861-62, 64-66; went to S.Am., 1866, established steamboat service in Colombia; engaged in mining, Venezuela, 1870-73; returned to U.S., 1873, became mining engr. in Colo., 1873-circa 1883; lived in N.Y.C., circa 1883-99; organized Dow Composing Machine Co. of W.Va., N.Y.C., 1896. Died N.Y.C., Oct. 12, 1899.

DOW, WILLARD HENRY, corp. official; b. Midland, Mich., Jan. 4, 1897; s. Herbert Henry and Grace Anna (Bell) D.; Bachelor of Science, University of Mich., 1919, D.E., from same university, 1941; D.Sc., Mich. Coll. of Mining and Tech., 1944; m. Martha L. Pratt, Sept. 3, 1921; children—Helen Dow Whiting, Herbert Henry II. Began as chem. engr. Dow Chem. Co., 1919, dir. since 1922, asst. gen. mgr., 1926-30, pres. and gen. mgr. since 1930, chmn. bd. since 1941; pres. Ethyl-Dow Chem. Co., 1933-46; Midland Ammonia Co., 1937-45, Dow of Can., Ltd., 1942-46, Io-Dow Chem. Co., 1936-39, Dowell, Inc., 1932-39, Cliffs Dow Chem. Co., 1935-39; dir. Dowell, Inc., Dow Magnesium Corp., Dow Corning Corp., Midland Ammonia Co., Dow Chem. of Can., Ltd., Saran Yarns Co., Ethyl-Dow Chem. Co. (1933-36), Cliffs Dow Chem. Co. (1035-42). Mem. Chem. Corps Adv. Bd., chmn. adv. com. Munitions Bd., 1940-49; adviser to Resources Div. Office Quartermaster Gen., 1942-49. Mem. bd. control Mich. Coll. of Mining and Tech., 1946-49; Corp. of Mass. Inst. Tech., 1942-46. Mem. Am. Chem. Soc. (dir. 1945-49), Am. Inst. Chem. Engrs., Am. Inst. of Chemists, Soc. Chem. Industry, A.A.A.S., N.E. Historic Geneaol. Soc., Engring. Soc. of Midland, Newcomen Soc., Tau Beta Pi, Pheta Delta Chi, Alpha Sigma. Chandler Medalist, Columbia, 1943; recipient; Gold Medal of Am. Inst. Chemists, 1944; Chem. Industry Medal of Am. sect. of Soc. of Chem. Industry, 1946; Medal for Advancement of Research by Am. Soc. for Metals, 1948. Chosen one of America's 50 foremost bus. leaders by Forbes Mag., 1948. Presbyterian. Mason (33 deg., Shriner). Clubs: Chemists, Rockefeller Center (New York); Detroit, Midland Bohemian (San Francisco); York (Toronto); Crystal Downs Country (Frankfort, Mich.). Home: 923 W. Park Drive. Office: Dow Chemical Co., Midland, Mich. Died Mar. 31, 1949.

DOWELL, FLOYD DEE, agriculturist; b. Lamont, Okla., May 3, 1910; s. Stephen Mathias and Cora Agnes (Lanning) D.; student Phillips U., 1926-27; B.S., Okla. State U., 1930; student La. State U., summer 1937, Colo. State U., summer 1939; m. Dorotha Mae Kirby, Mar. 23, 1929; children—Troy D., Steve Richard, Dorotha (Mrs. Fred H. Jester). County agrl. agt., Blaine County, Okla., 1934-44; supr., instr. vets. fgn. tng. program, Garfield and Grant counties, Okla., 1946-52; bd. suprs. Grant County (Okla.) Soil Conservation Dist., 1946-52; agrl. adviser FOA, Govt. of Nepal, 1952-56; dept. chief food and agrl. div. U.S. Operations Missions to Yugolslavia, 1956-61, Tehran, Iran, 1961—. Mem. P.T.A. (pres. Hunter, Okla. 1950). Mem. Christian Ch. Mason. Home: Hunter, Okla. Office: American Embassy, Tehran, Iran. Died Apr. 18, 1961; buried Lamont, Okla.

DOWNEY, HAL, educator emeritus; b. State Coll., Pa., Oct. 4, 1877; s. John F. and Stella (Osborn) D.; B.A., U. Minn., 1903, M.A., 1904, Ph.D., 1909; studied U. Berlin, 1910, U. Strassburg, 1911; m. Iva Mitchell, June 7, 1905; children—Phyllis Mitchell, Richard Thomas, Jean Annis. Asst. in dept. of zoölogy U. Minn., 1903, successively instr., asst. prof., asso. prof., prof., 1917-29, prof. anatomy, Med. Sch. 1929-46; lectr. hematology Mayo Found. for Medical Research; research in hematology Dept. Anatomy, U. Minn., Mayo Found., 1947—. Pvt. Co. A, 13th Minn. Vol. Infantry, in P.O., 1898-99. Recipient Outstanding Achievement award, 1951; Distinguished Service award, 1957. Fellow Internat. Sco. Hematology (hon.), European, Soc. Hematology (hon.), Mem. Assn. Am. Anatomists, Minn. Pathol. Soc., Sigma Xi. Contbr. Handbook of Hematology (4 vols.), 1938; Am. editor Folia Haematologia, 1928-41. Home: 2 Barton Av. S.E., Mpls. 14. Died Jan. 9, 1959; buried Ft. Snelling Nat. Cemetery.

DOWNING, ELLIOT ROWLAND, zoologist, educator; b. Boston, Mass., Nov. 21, 1868; s. Orrien Elliot and Mary Jane (Rowland) D.; B.S., Albion (Mich.) Coll., 1889; M.S., 1894; Ph.D., U. of Chicago, 1901; Columbia, 1907-08; U. of Wurzburg, Naples Aquarium, 1908; m. Grace Emma Manning, June 24, 1902; children—George Elliot, Mary Elizabeth, Lucia Grace. Instr. science, Ft. Payne (Ala.) Acad., 1890-91, Beloit (Wis.) Coll. Acad., 1891-98; supt Brooklyn Training Sch. for Boys, 1896-98; sec. Brooklyn Children's Aid Soc., 1898-99; fellow in zoology, U. of Chicago, 1899-1901; instr. embryology, summer sessions same, 1900, 1901; prof. biology Northern State Normal Sch., Marquette, Mich., 1901-11; asst. prof. natural science, 1911-13, asso. prof., 1913-34, emeritus since 1934; asst. dean School of Edn., 1913-16, Univ. of Chicago, Editor Nature Study Review, 1911-17. Pres. Mich. State Non-Game Bird Commn., 1907-11. Fellow A.A.A.S.; mem. Am. Eugenics Assn., Wis. Acad. Science, Am. Nature Study Soc., Nat. Assn. Research in Science Teaching (pres. 1930-32), Sigma Xi, Alpha Tau Omega. Republican. Conglist. Club: Quadrangle. Author: Elementary Eugenics; A Naturalist in the Great Lakes Region; Our Living World; Our Physical World; Teaching Science in the Schools; Science in the Service of Health; Introduction to the Teaching of Science; Living Things and You. Home: Williams Bay, Wis. Died Sept. 10, 1944.

DOWNING, LEWIS KING, coll. dean; b. Roanoke, Va., Jan. 2, 1896; A.B., Johnson C. Smith U., 1916, Sc.D., 1953; B.S. in Civil Engring., Howard U., 1921; B.S. Mass. Inst. Tech., 1923; M.S., U. of Michigan, 1932; D.Sc., Virginia State College, 1995; married Morease M. Chisholm, December 26, 1925; children—Charlotte C., Morease M. With Howard University, 1924-67, professor, 1938-67, became dean School of Engineering and Architecture, 1936, dean emeritus until 1967. Chairman engring. com. D.C. Commrs. Traffic Adv. Bd., 1958—; mem. D.C. Commrs. Urban Renewal Council, 1958, D.C. Commrs. Planning Adv. Council, 1959-62; vice chmn. Washington Met. Area Joint Bd. on Sci. Edn., 1959, sec., 1960, D.C. Bd. for Registration of Professional Engineers, 1962-67. Recipient Distinguished Alumni award, Howard University, 1953, cited by N.Y. chpt. Howard U. Alumni Assn., 1957, 58. Registered civil engr., Va., 1936, D.C., 1951. Fellow Am. Soc. C.E. (dir. nat. capital sect. 1962-64); mem. Washington Acad. Sci., Am. Soc. Engring. Edn. (sec., dir. 1957-58, chmn. civil engring. div. 1959-60), Nat. Tech. Assn., Pi Mu Epsilon, Alpha Phi Alpha, Beta Kappa Chi, Tau Beta Pi. Home: Washington DC Died Oct. 19, 1967; buried Lincoln Meml. Cemetery, Washington DC

DOWNING, PAUL M., elec. engr.; b. Newark, Mo., Nov. 17, 1873; s. Thomas B. and Margaret (Sanford) D.; A.B., July 20, 1897; With Tacoma (Wash.) Light & Power Co., 1895-96, Market St. Ry. Co., San Francisco, 1896-97, Blue Lakes Water Co., 1898-99; Standard Consol. Mining Co., 1899-1901; mgr. Colusa Gas & Electric Co., 1901-02; div. supt. Bay Counties Power Co., 1902-03; various positions with Calif. Gas and Electric Corp. and Pacific Gas and Electric Co.; 1st V.P. and general manager Pacific Gas and Electric Co., 1929-43, executive vice-president since August, 1943, vice-president Edison Electric Institute; mem. Am. Inst. Elec. Engrs., Pacific Coast Elec. Assn., Pacific Coast Gas Assn. Republican. Mason (K.T., Shriner). Clubs: Engineers', Olympic, Commonwealth, Sutter, Commercial, Pacific Union, Lakeside Country, Menlo Country, San Francisco Golf. Home: 1980 Washington St. Office: 245 Market St., San Francisco, Calif. Died Dec. 11, 1944.

DOWNS, WILLIAM SMITH, cons. engr., prof. ; b. Martinsburg, W.Va., Mar. 15, 1883; s. Joseph Allen and Caroline Janet (Evans) D.; B.S. in Civil Engring., W.Va. U., 1906, C.E., 1915; m. Nellie Jane Albright, June 22, 1910; children—William Richard, James Albright, Jane. Topographer, Bolivian R.R. Commn., Bolivia, S.A., 1905-06; chief draftsman, M. & K. R.R., 1906-09; resident engr., Hydro Elec. Co. of W.Va., 1909-15; County, W.Va., 1915-19; div. engr., W.Va., nonglaia county, W.Va., 1915-19; div. engr., W.Va., Satat Rd. Commn., 1919-29; cons. engr., Morgantown, W.Va., 1929—; Prof. Ry. and Highway Engring., W.Va., U.; consultant for Assn. Am. Railroads, W.Va. Pub. Service Commn., Pa. R.R., West Assn. R.R. Execs., Princeton U. State and Local Govt. Sect. Morgantown Municipal Planning Commission. Mem. Am. Soc. Civil engring. (past pres. W.Va. sect.), W.Va. Soc. Prof. Engring. (past pres.), Am. Rd. Builders Assn. (dir. edn. div.), Soc. Promotion Engring. Edn., Beta Theta Pi, Tau Beta Pi, Chi Epsilon. Republican. Presbyterian. Club: Rotary (Morgantown, W.Va.), Contbr. to professional jours. Home: 204 Euclid Av., Morgantown, W.Va. Died July 12, 1954; buried East Oak Grove Cemetery, Morgantown.

DOZIER, ORION T., physician; b. Marion Co., Ga., Aug. 18, 1848; s. of Dr. T. H. D.; ed. Atlanta, Ga., schs., grad. Atlanta Med. Coll., 1874; m. Elizabeth Powers, of Atlanta, Ga., Apr. 30, 1874. Began practice of medicine at Attalla, Ala., May, 1874; moved to New Madrid Co., Mo., 1878, to Rome, Ga., 1881; began practice of medicine in Birmingham, Ala., May, 1890, as specialist in genito-urinary, rectal and cutaneous diseases, Was the originator and organizer of The Regents of the White Shield, 1892; has held office of Supreme Regent Commander since 1896. Inventor and patentee of hame for harness, portable elevator, mailing machine. Author: Foibles of Fancy and Rhymes of the Times, 1894; Poems Patriotic, 1898; Galaxy of Southern Heroes, and Other Poems, 1905. Contbr. poems, essays, to various papers. Home: 2112 Humboldt Av., Birmingham, Ala.

DRAGER, WALTER LOUIS, civil engr.; b. Hamilton, Ill., Feb. 23, 1886; s. Charles and Lesa P. Winters) D.; student U. Cal., 1905-06, Cornell U., 1906-09; m. Alice E. Sickly, Feb. 29, 1908; children—Carl (dec.), Donald G., Susan Winters (Mrs. Kenneth K. Lawshe), Alice Anne (Mrs. M Macon J. Fussell). Asst. tCity engr., Auburn, N.Y., 1909-10; asst. to cons. engr. Johnstown, Pa., 1910-11; asst. City engr., Schenectady, N.Y., 1912-13; asst. to constrn. engr. Grand Valley Dam, U.S. Reclamation Service, Grand Junction, Colo., 1914-15; asst. engr. Pub. Utilities Commn. on Denver water supply investigation, 1915-16; asst. engr. in charge investigations for Castel Peak Project, Utah Reconnaissance, U.S. Reclamation Service, 1917-20; office engr. Reclamation Service, Denver, 1920-22; engr. Bear River div. Salt Lake Basin Investiations, Utah 1922-26; resident engr. J. G. White Co., Agusacalientes, Mexico, 1926-29; field engr. Stevens & Wood, Inc., 1929-31; asst. div. engr. N.J. State Water Policy Commn., Trenton, 1932-37, chief engr. same and Def. Plant Corp., 1937-47, ret. 1947. Mem. Am. Soc. C.E., Theta Xi. Democrat Mason. Home: 1919 Maine Av., Long Beach, Cal. Died Aug. 10, 1953; buried Forest Lawn Meml. Park.

DRAKE, NATHAN LINCOLN, univ. prof.; b. Watertown, Mass., Dec. 21, 1898; s. Frederick Lincoln and Ada (Hales) D.; A.B., Harvard, 1920, A.M., 1921, Ph.D., 1922; Sheldon Traveling fellow Harvard, Technische Hochschule, Zurich, Switzerland, 1922-23; m. Ruth Esther Johnson, Dec. 26, 1923; children—Ruth (Mrs. Wilbur Chamberlain Davis), Robert Lincoln, Dorothy Ann (Mrs. Orville Morton Weston, Jr.). Research chemist Mallinckrodt Chemical Works, St. Louis, 1923-25, Procter and Gamble, Ivorydale, O., 1925-26; prof. indsl. chem. U. of Md., 1926-28, prof. organic chemistry, 1928-41, prof. and head chemistry dept. since 1941. Panel mem., sythesis of anti-malarials, Nat. Research Council, 1942-45; vice chmn. com. on organic chemistry Chem. and Biological Coordination Center, 1947. Awarded Hillebrand prize for work on anti-malarial drugs by Chem. Soc. of Washington, 1948. Mem. Chem. Soc. of Washington, 1948. Mem. Chem. Soc. of Washington (pres. 1938), Am. Chem. Soc. (chmn. organic sect. 1940; chmn. com. on membership affairs 1948), Washington Acad. Sciences, Sigma Xi, Alpha Chi Sigma, Phi Beta Kappa. Republican Mason. Editor of vols. 21 and 24 of Organic Syntheses, 1941, 1944. Contbr. to vol. 1 of Organic Reactions, 1942. Home: 6820 Pineway, College Heights, Hyattsville, Md. Office: Department of Chemistry, University of Maryland, College Park, Md. Died Oct. 13, 1959.

DRAKE, NOAH FIELDS, geologist; b. Summers, Washington County, Ark., Jan. 30, 1864; s. Wesley and Martha (Kellam) D.; C.E., U. of Ark., 1888; A.B., 1894, A.M., 1895, Ph-D., 1897, Stanford U.; m. Mary Elenor Shockley, July 30, 1904 (died Dec. 25, 1926); m. 2d, Lota West Fairchild, Dec. 23, 1932. Geologic work, Ark. Geol. Survey, 1887, Texas Geol. Survey, 1889-93, U.S. Geol. Survey, 1897; prof. geology and mining, 1898-1900 and 1905-11, Pei Yang U., Tientsin, China; asso. prof. economic geology, Leland Stanford Jr. U., 1911-12; prof. geology and mining, U. of Ark., 1912-20; cons. geologist since 1920. Engr. Pub. Worls Dept., Tientsin, China, 1900-01; cons. geologist Am. China Development Co., 1902-04; chmn. bd. Tientsin Land & Investment Co., Ltd., 1904-11; v.p. Am. Machinery & Export Co., Tientsin, 1910. Fellow Geol. Soc. America; mem. Am. Inst. Mining Engrs., Seismol. Soc. America, Royal Asiatic Soc. (N. China branch), China Philos Soc. Home: Fayetteville, Ark. Died May 4, 1945.

DRAPER, DANIEL, meteorologist; b. New York, Apr. 2, 1841; s. late Dr. John William and Antonia U. Grammar School; (Ph.D., New York U., 1880); m. Ann Maury Ludlow, Apr. 28, 1887 (died 1911). Studied science under his father; was his asst. in chemistry and physiology for several yrs. and his amanuensis for his Intellectual Development of Europe and other works. Served mech. apprenticeship of 5 yrs. at Novelty Iron Works, New York; dir. New York Meteorol. Obs., 1868-July 1, 1911, retired. Designed and made the self-recording instruments there; also helped his brother, late Henry Draper, M.D., to construct the telescopes, grind the mirrors and build his oberservatory at Hastings-on-Hudson. Home: Hastings-on-Hudson, N.Y. Died Dec. 21, 1931.

DRAPER, GEORGE OTIS, mfr.; inventor; b. Hopedale, Mass., July 14, 1867; s. William Franklin and Lydia Warren (Joy) D.; ed. W. Newton English and Classical Sch. and Mass. Inst. Tech. (non-grad.); m. Lily Duncan, Apr. 28, 1892. Learned details of mfr. of cotton machinery in father's shops; partner, George Draper & Sons, Hopedale, from 1889 to its consolidation with Draper Co., 1897; an officer in some 25 corps. connected with textile mfr., quarrying, mining and the development of patented mech. devices and improved details of the Northrop loom; expert on patents, and in cotton mfr. Pres. Draper Realty Co., Draper-Hansen Co., Michener Stowage Co., Sapphire Record & Talking Machine Co., Draper-Latham Magneto Co., Scholz Fireproofing Co., Farrmington Co., Phillips Mfr. Co., Hilton Mfg. Co. Author: Searching for Truth, 1902; Still on the Search, 1904, More, 1908. Home: New York, N.Y. Died Feb. 7, 1923.

DRAPER, HENRY, astronomer; b. Prince Edward County, Va., Mar. 7, 1837; s. John William and Antonia Coetana de Paiva Pereira (Gardner) B.; M.D., U. City N.Y., 1858; m. Mary Anna Palmer, 1867. Mem. staff Bellevue Hosp.,N.Y.C., 1858-60; prof. natural science U. City N.Y., 1860-66, prof. physiology, 1866-73, dean of faculty, also prof. analytical chemistry, 1870-82, prof. chemistry, 1882; built observatory at Hastings-on-Hudson, N.Y., 1860; devoted career to study of stellar spectroscopy; directed photographic work in U.S. govt. expdn. to observe transit of Venus, 1874; led expdn. to Wyo. to observe total eclipse of sun, 1878; mem. Nat. Acad. Scis., Am. Philos. Soc. Died N.Y.C., Nov. 20, 1882.

DRAPER, JOHN WILLIAM, scientist, historian; b. St. Helen's, Eng., May 5, 1811; s. Rev. John Christopher Draper; attended London U.; M.D., U. Pa., 1836; m. Antonia Coetana de Paiva Pereira Gardner, circa 1830; children—Henry, John Christopher, Daniel, Virginia, Antonia. Came to Am., circa 1832; operated own scientific lab.; prof. chemistry and natural philosophy Hampden-Sydney (Va.) Coll., 1836-38; prof. chemistry Univ. of City N.Y. (now N.Y.U.), 1838; pioneer in photography, took 1st complete portrait of person by sunlight, circa 1839; founder sch. of medicine of Univ. Sicty of N.Y., 1838, prof. chemistry and physiology, 1839-50, pres. med. sch., 1850. Author: A Treatise on the Forces Which Produce the Organization of Plants, 1844; Human Physiology, Statical and Dynamical, 1856; History of the Intellectual Development of Europe, 1863; Thoughts on the Future Civil Policy of America, 1865; History of the American Civil War, 3 vols., 1867-70; History of the Conflict Between Religion and Science, 1874. Died Jan. 4, 1882.

DREIKURS, RUDOLPH, psychiatrist; b. Vienna; s. Sigmund and Fanny (Cohn) D.; M.D., U. of Vienna, 1923; m. Sadie Garland; children—Eric, Eva. Came to U.S., 1937, naturalized citizen. Began practice of medicine in Vienna, organizing mental hygiene and psychiat. social work; dir. clinics for child guidance, alcoholics and psychopathics, asst. and collaborator Alfred Adler from 1923; prof. psychiatry Chicago Med. Sch., 1942-66, emeritus, 1966-72; with Tex. Tech. Coll., from 1966; vis. prof. U. Vt., from 1968; dir. Alfred Adler Inst., Chgo.; cons. psychiatrist Hull House, 1940-43; vis. prof. U. of Rio de Janeiro, 1946, Northwestern U. Sch. Edn., 1947-51, U. Ore., 1957, Bar Ilan University, Ramat Gan, Israel; lecturer in edn. Ind. U. Gary extension, 1951-54, Loyola U., from 1959; lecturer in psychology Roosevelt U., 1954-56. Medical dir. Community Child Guidance Centers of Chgo. Fellow Am. Psychiat. Assn., Am. Soc. Group Therapy and Psychodrama (pres. 1954-55); mem. Am. Soc. Adlerian Psychology (pres. 1954-56), Internat. Assn. Individual Psychology (vice chmn. from 1954), American Humanist Association (vice president 1950-56), Ill. Soc. for Personality Study (pres. 1954-56), Sociedade de Psychologia Individual of Rio de Janeiro (hon. pres.) Author: Introduction to Individual Psychology (pub. in English, German, Dutch, Czech, French), Psychic Impotence (German), The Nervous Symptom (German), Education Without Coercion (Dutch); The Challenge of Marriage, 1946; The Challenge of Parenthood, 1947; Character Education and Spiritual Values in an Anxious Age, 1952; Fundamentals of Adlerian Psychology, 1950; Psychology in the Classroom, 1957; (with Dr. Donald Dinkmeyer) Encouraging Children to Learn, 1962; (with Vicki Solts) Children: The Challenge; (with Loren Grey) Logical Consequences, a New Approach to Discipline, 1968; (with Loren Grey) A Parent's Guide to Child Discipline, 1970; (with Berniece Grunwald and Floy Pepper) Maintaining Sanity in the Classroom, 1971; Social Equality: Training-A Parent's Guide, 1972; Coping with Children's Misbehaviour, 1972; (with Pearl Cassel) Discipline without Tears, 1972. Developed Alfred Adler's system of individual psychology into techniques for understanding purposes of disturbing behavior in children and for stimulating coop. behavior without punishment or reward; founded Alfred Adler Inst. of Chgo. and Tel Aviv; inspired internat. movement of family edn. centers, parent study groups. Home: Chicago IL Died May 25, 1972; buried Chicago IL

DRESBACH, MELVIN, physiologist; b. Hallsville O., July 8, 1874; s. Harvey and Amanda (Orr) D.; B.Sc., Ohio State U., 1897, M.Sc., 1900; M.D., Ohio Med. U., 1903; spl. work, Woods Hole, Mass., 1911; m. Sylvia Reedy, Dec. 28, 1899. Asst. in physiology Ohio State U., 1897-1902, instr., 1902-05; instr. physiology, Cornell Med. Coll., 1908-09, asst. prof. pharmacology, 1909-10, asst. prof. physiology Albany Med. Coll. (Union U.), 1918-36; now engaged in research. U. Pa., Mem. Am. Physiol. Soc., Soc. Exptl. Biology and Medicine, A.A.A.S., Sigma Xi, Nu Sigma Ny. Democrat. Contbr. to med. publs. Home: 817 Madison Av., Albany, N.Y. Died Oct. 15, 1946; buried Chillocothee, O.

DRESDEN, ARNOLD, mathematician; b. Amsterdam, Netherlands, Nov. 23, 1882; s. Mark and Anna (Meyerson) D.; student U. of Amsterdam, 1901-03; S M., U. of Chicago, 1906, Ph.D., 1909; m. Louise Schwendener, June 12, 1907; 1 son, Mark Kenyon. Came to U.S., 1903, naturalized citizen, 1912. Teacher of mathematics, University High Sch., Chicago, 1906-09; instr. mathematics, 1909-12, asst. prof., 1912-21, asso. prof., 1921-27, U. of Wis.; prof. mathematics, Swarthmore Coll., 1927—. Service with A.R.C. in France, Sept. 1918-June 1919. Fellow A.A.A.S.; mem. Math. Assn. America (pres. 1933-35), Am. Math. Soc., Académie of Macon, France, Société Mathématique de France. Author: Plane Trigonometry, 1921; Solid Analytical Geometry and Determinants, 1930; An Invitation to Mathematics, 1936; Introduction to the Calculus, 1940. Home: 606 Elm Av., Swarthmore, Pa. Died Apr. 10, 1954; buried Cumberland Cemetery, Media, Pa.

DREW, CHARLES RICHARD, surgeon; b. Washington, June 3, 1904; s. Richard Thomas and Nora R. (Burrell) D.; grad. Amherst Coll,. 1926; M.D., C.M., Faculty Med., McGill U., 1933; Med. D.Sc., Columbia Coll. Phys. and Surg., 1940; hon. D.Sc., Va. State, 1945, Amherst Coll., 1947; children—Bebe Roberta, Charlene Rosella, Rhea Sylvia, Charles Richard. Intern Royal Victroia Hosp., Montreal, Can., 1932-33; intern Gen. Hosp., Montreal, Can., 1933-34, resident in medicine, 1934-35; instr. in pathology Howard U., Washington, 1935-36, asst. in surgery, 1935-36, prof. surgery, head dept., 1941—; Rockefeller fellow in surgery Coll. Phys. and Surg. Columbia, also redident in surgery Presbyn. Hosp., N.Y.C., 1938-40; chief surgeon and chief of staff Freedman's Hosp., Washington, med. dir. 1946-47; surg. cons. ETO (Army), 1949. Dir. first plasma div. Blood Transfusion Assn., supplying plasma to British, 1940-41; first dir. A.R.C. Blood Bank, supplying plasma to U.S. forces, 1941. Recipient Springarn award, 1944, dir. D.C. chpt. Nat. Founds. Polyomyelitis, 1946, D.C. Soc. for Crippled Children. Mem. Am.-Soviet Science Com., 1944. Home: 328 College St. N.W. Office: Dept. of Surgery, Howard U., Washington Died Apr. 1, 1950.

DREW, GILMAN ARTHUR, biologist; b. Newton, Ia., Nov. 15, 1868; s. Orrin Gilman and Mary Emily (Drew) D.; B.S., State U. of Ia., 1890; Ph.D., John Hopkins, 1898; m. Lena E. Slawson, Nov. 24, 1892. Acad.

teacher, 1890-91; high sch. teacher, Oskaloosa, Ia., 1892-94; fellow, 1897-98, Bruce fellow, 1898, asst. in zoölogy, 1898-1900. Johns Hopkins prof. biology, U. of Maine, 1900-11. Asst. dir. Marine Biol. Lab., Woods Hole, Mass., 1909-26. Fellow Am. Acad. Arts and Sciences. Home: Eagle Lake, Fla. Died Oct. 26, 1934.

DREYER, GEORGE PETER, physiologist; b. Baltimore, Md., Sept. 22, 1866; Baltimore City Coll., 1879-84; A.B., Johns Hopkins, 1887, Ph.D., 1890; Harvard, summer 1888, Coll. Phys. and Surg., Baltimore, 1890-91; m. Aug. 1890. Teacher, acad. dept., Johns Hopkins, 1890-93, Med. Sch., same, 1893-1900; prof. physiology and head dept. of physicology and physiol. chemistry, Coll. of Med., U. of Ill., 1900—, jr. dean, 1913-15. Best known research was discovery of the secretory nerves of the suprarenal glands. Home: LaGrange, Ill. Died Feb. 27, 1931.

DREYER, WALTER, utility co. exec.; b. San Francisco, May 20, 1892; s. Claus and Frederike (Schuttler) D.; B.S., U. Cal., 1916; m. Letitia Ann Curtis, Oct. 30, 1920; children—Barbara Ann (Mrs. Donald K. McIntosh), Curtis. With Warren Bros. Co., 1910-11; surveyor Pacific Gas & Electric Co., 1912-13, successively civil engring. designer, in charge structural and hydraulic design, asst. chief civil engring. div., chief div., 1916-52, v.p., chief engr., 1952—. Cons., Nat. Security Resources Bd., 1948-51, Def. Electric Power Adminstrn. Served as 1st lt. U.S. Army, 1918-19. Mem. Am. Soc. C.E., Structural Engrs. Assn. No. Cal., Newcomen Soc. Mason. Club: Engineers (San Francisco). Home: 492 Staten Av., Oakland, Cal. 94610. Office: 245 Market St., San Francisco 6. Died Aug. 5, 1966.

DRINKER, CECIL KENT, physician; b. Philadelphai, Pa., Mar. 17, 1887; s. Henry Sturgis and Amiee Ernesta (Beaux) D.; B.S., Haverford College, 1908; D.Sc., (hon.), 1933; M.D., Univ. of Pa. med.School., 1913; A.M. (hon.), Harvard, 1942; m. Katherine Livingston Rotan, Sept. 7, 1910; cihldren—Anne, Cecil. Interneship and residence in hosps., 1913-17, became acting head dept. physiology Harvard Univ., Med. Sch., 1917-18, asst.prof. physiology, 1818-19, asso. 1919-23; sec. com. on Indsl. Hygiene, 1918-22; mng. editor jour. of Indsl. Hygiene, 1919-32; asst. to visiting physician Boston City Hosp., 1922-24; prof. physiology, Harvard Univ. Sch. Pub. Health, 1923-48, asst. dean, 1924-35, dean, 1935-42; asso. editor Jour. of Indsl. Hygiene and Toxicology, 1932-48; lecturer in physiology, Cornell Med. College, 1948-49; consulting physiologyst U.S. Navy since 1951. Emeritus mem. American Soc. for Clin. Investigation; mem. Assn. of Am. Physician, Am. Physiol. Soc., Royal Danish Acad. Sci. and Letters, Phi Beta Kappa, Alpha Omega Alpha, Sigma Xi. Republican Home: Sippewissett Rd. Address: Box 502 Falmouth, Mass. Died Apr. 14, 1956; buried Phila.

DROKE, GEORGE WESLEY, mathematician; b. Morgan Co., Ind., Sept. 26, 1854; s. George and Diana (Etter) D.; A.B., U. Ark., 1880; A.M., 1884, LL.D., 1929; U. Mich., Johns Hopkins, U. Chgo., brief periods; LL.D., Hendrix Coll., 1919; m. Josephine Campbell, Sept. 24, 1879 (died 1886); children—George Prentice, Lelia Rugh (dec.), Marvin Josesphine; m. 2d, Inez James, Aug. 18, 1887 (died Apr. 1931); children—Albert Hill (dec.), Mary Inez, Louise Blanche, James Walling (adopted); m. 3d, Mrs. Belle Clayton Fenner, Feb. 20, 1932. Asst., 1st asst. tchr., prep. dept. U. Ark., 1880-85; head dept. of English, Coronal Inst., San Marcos, Tex., 1885-86; prin. high sch., Bentonville, Ark., 1886-87; with U. Ark., 1887-1929, prof. mathematics, astronomy, 1897-1929, emeritus prof., 1929—; dean coll. Arts and Scis., 1915-25. Mem. Math. Assn. Am., Ark. State Tchrs' Assn. (pres. 1910), Phi Beta Kappa (1932). Methodist. Home: Fayetteville, Ark. Died Sept. 4, 1936.

DROUGHT, ARTHUR BERNARD, acad. dean.; b. Racine County, Wis., Oct. 24, 1914; s. Arthur Benjamin and Anna M. (Morley), D.; B.Ed., Milw. State Tchrs. Coll., 1935; M.A., Northwestern U., 1942; M.S., Harvard, 1949, S.D., 1950; m. Ruth H. Spink, Dec. 27, 1939; children—Richard M., Michael H., Arthur Bernard II. Engring. draftsman Harnischfeger Corp., Milw., 1935-37; tchr. Milw. pub. schs., 1937-42; teaching fellow elec. engring. Harvard, 1946-47, instr., 1947-48, Henry Weidemar Locke fellow 1948-49; faculty Marquette U., 1949-63, asso. prof. elec. engring., 1953-63, dean Coll. Engring., 1956-63; academic dean United States Naval Academy, 1963-70. Cons. electronics dept. investigative med. VA Hosp., Wood, Wis.; mem. Wis. Adv. Com. Sci., Engring. and Specialized Personnel; asst. to bd. registration for architects and engrs., Wis. Served to lt. (j.g.) USNR, 1942-46. Registered prof. engr., Wis. Mem. Am. Inst. E.E., Engrs. Council Profl. Development (chmn. guidance com. region VI), Nat. Soc. Profl. Engrs. (pres. Milw. chpt. 1960-61), Am. Soc. Engring. Edn. (gen. council 1956-60), engring. faculty devel. com. 1960-61, chmn. 1961-62), Engrs. Soc. Milw., Am. Interprofl. Inst., Sigma Xi, Eta Kappa Nu, Tau Beta Pi. Conglist. (moderator). Author articles profl. jours. Home: Annapolis MD Died Sept. 18, 1970.

DRUCKER, ARTHUR ELLERT, educator, metall. engr.; b. San Francisco, Calif., Aug. 25, 1877; s. Ellert and Emma Florence (Cootey) D.; grad. Calif. Sch. Mech. Arts, 1897; B.S., Univ. of California, 1902; LL.D., Washington State College, 1944; married Minnie Barstow, Feb. 14, 1912. Assayer and mill foreman, Roosevelt M. & M. Co., Calif., 1904-05; cyanide foreman and research metallurgist, Oriental Con. Mining Co., Korea, 1905-08; metall. exams in Japan, Philippines, Malay States, Australia, U.S., etc., 1908-10; chief metallurgist and constrn. engr. Oriental Con. Mining Co., Korea, 1910-13; technical mgr. Concession Miniere Francaise, North Korea, 1913-14; cons. metall. engr., London, 1914-15; engaged in metall. exams. and constrn. of plants for Pellew-Harvey & Co., in Columbia, S.A., 1915-16; cons. engr., New York, 1916-20; prof. metall. engring., Wis. State Sch. of Mines, 1920-21; asst. prof. mining engring., U. of Ill., 1921-26; dean Sch. of Mines and Geology, Washington State College, 1926-45; dir. Mining Expt. Sta., State Electrometall. Research Labs., 1937-45; dean emeritus since 1945. Tech. adviser Wash. State Planning Council. Mem. Northwest Mining Assn., Asso. Engrs. Spokane, Central Washington Mining Assn., Eastern Oregon Mining Assn. (hon. life), Newcomen Soc. of England (hon.), Northwest Sci. Assn., Pullman Chamber Commerce, S.A.R., Sigma Xi, Tau Beta Pi, Sigma Tau, Epsilon Chi, Sigma Gamma Epsilon, Delta Mu Epsilon, Phi Eta, Acacia. Mason (32 deg., Shriner). Clubs: Kiwanis, Wranglers. Cosmopolitan; Seoul (Korea). Contbr. of many articles to mining jours. Home: Hotel Washington, Pullman, Wash. Died Feb. 7, 1949.

DRUECK, CHARLES, surgeon; b. Chgo., Mar. 15, 1906; s. Charles John and Helen Mable (Martin) D.; A.A., Ill. Inst. Tech., 1924; M.D., Northwestern U., 1929; m. Alice Lucille Finch, Sept. 11, 1943; children—Charles III, Ethel Irene. Surg. residency St. Luke's Hosp., Chgo., 1929-30; practice of medicine, Chgo., since 1929, specializing proctology since 1948; mem. staff of Illinois Masonic Hospital; sec.-treas. Indsl. Med. Pub. Co., 1937-48; editor Proctology Journal Anal, Rectal and Colon Diseases, 1953. Received Borglum life saving medal. Mem. Chgo. Soc. Indsl. Medicine and Surgery (treas.), A.M.A., Internat. Coll. Surgeons, Am. Proctologic Soc., Am. Med. Writers Assn. Home: 1404 N. Astor St., Chgo. Office: 55 E. Washington St., Chgo. 2. Died June 11, 1964; buried Mt. Hope Cemetery, Chgo.

DRUM, A. L., cons. engr.; b. San Francisco, Calif., 1875; s. John Drum (maj. U.S.A.) and Margaret (Desmond) D.; B.S. in Elec. Engring., Mass. Ins. Tech., 1896; m. Jane Hunter, 1892; children—John, Charlotte, Hunter. Began engring. practic in Boston, 1896; moved to Chicago, 1904; head of A. L. Drum & Co., consulting and constructing engrs. Pres. Eastern Michigan Railways. Consulting engr. for U.S. Shipping Board and U.S. Housing Corp., World War. Fellow Am. Inst. E.E. Home: Detroit, Mich. Died Mar. 17, 1933.

DRUMHELLER, JOSEPH, chem. engr.; b. Spokane, Sept. 25, 1900; s. Daniel Montgomery and Eleanor (Powell) D.; B.S. in Chem. Engring., U. Wash., 1924; m. Helen Elizabeth Chamberlain, Dec. 14, 1956; children—Mrs. William J. McAllister, Frederick Corbin. Owner, Drumheller Labs., Spokane, 1924—; pres. Densow Drugs Inc., Richland, Wash., 1952—, Idaho Lakeview Mines, Inc., Fern Gold Mining Co., Drumheller Estates, Inc.; dir. West Coast Airlines, Pacific N.W. Bell Telephone Co., Sunshine Mining Co., First Nat. Bank Spokane, Union Iron Works, Spokane. Chmn. Gonzaga U. Great Tchrs. Program, 1955-58; incorporator, dir. Pacific Sci. Center, Seattle. Member Wash. State Senate from Spokane County, 1934-42; mem. city council, Spokane, 1960-64. Bd. regents U. Wash., 1945-50, 55-69, Gonzaga U., 1958-70. Mem. Am. Assn. Cereal Chemists, Spokane C. of C. (pres. 1948-49), Sigma Nu. Democrat. Elk. Home: Spokane WA Died Apr. 28, 1970.

DRUMMOND, I(SAAC) WYMAN, chemist; b. Roxbury, Mass., June 19, 1855; s. James F. and Sarah (Wyman) D.; E.M., Columbia Sch. of Mines, 1878, Ph.D., 1880; unmarried. Formerly chmn. bd. and chemist, Devoe & Raynolds Co., New York; trustee Bowery Savings Bank. Retired. Unitarian. Editor dept. of colors and dyes, Century Dictionary. Home: New York, N.Y. Died Apr. 15, 1933.

DRUMMOND, THOMAS RUSSELL, mining engr.; b. Colombo, Ceylon, Aug. 27, 1873; s. Russell and Charlotte Hawtrey (Thwaites) D.; ed. George Watson's Coll. and Herriott-Watt Tech. Coll., Edinburgh (Scotland), School of Mines (London); m. Harriet Blake, of Chariton, Lucas Co., Ia., May 1900; children—Charlotte Blake, George Russell, Thomas Arthur, Ronald Blake. Engr. and assayer for Clarkson-Stanfield Concentration Co., London, 1896-97; mill man and constrn. engr. Prussian Mine, Boulder, Colo., 1897; with Utah Consolidated Mine, Bingham, Utah, 1897-1905; mgr. Dominion Copper Co., B.C., 1905-07, Nipissing Mining Co., Cobalt, Ont., Can., 1907-08, Cactus Copper Co., Newhouse, Utah, 1908-09, Inspiration Copper Co., 1909-12; supt. mines Inspiration Consolidated Copper Co., 1913; pvt. practice, Philippines, China, etc., 1913-18; sec. and treas. Zenda Gold Mining Co.; mgr. Zenda Leadville Mfg. Co. Mem. Am. Inst. Mining and Metall. Engrs. (life). Naturalized citizen of U.S. Republican. Presbyn. Mason. Home: 1627 N. Genesee St., Hollywood, Calif. Office: I.W. Hellman Bldg., Los Angeles CA

DRURY, WALTER MAYNARD, mining engr.; b. Chicago, Ill., Feb. 8, 1880; s. Myron M. and Ida (Osborn) D.; B.S., Mass. Inst. Tech., 1903; m. Mary Kane, 1915; children—Maynard Kane, Innes. Gen. mgr. mining dept. Am. Smelting & Refining Co. of New York since 1912; dir. Cia Minera Asarco, Cia Minera Nacional, Cia Minera Loteria, Cia Minera Magistral, Cia Metalurgica Maxicana, Potosi & Rio Verde R.R., Montezuma Lead Co., Sombrerette Mining Co., Descubridora Mining Co., Cia Minera Tepic, Cia Minera La Ventura, Brandreth Mgf. Co., Intercontinental Rubber Co., Towne Securities Co. Mem. Am. Inst. Mining and Metall. Engrs. Clubs: Bankers, Tuxedo, Sleepy Hollow Country (New York). Address: care American Smelting & Refining Co., 120 Broadway, New York, N.Y. Died July 16, 1946.

DRYDEN, HUGH LATIMER, physicist; b. Pocomoke City, Md., July 2, 1898; s. Samuel Isaac and Nova Hill (Culver) D.; A.B. Johns Hopkins, 1916, A.M. 1918, Ph.D., 1919, LL.D., 1953; Sc.D., Poly. Inst. Bklyn., 1949, U. Pa., 1951, Western Md. Coll., 1951, Princeton, 1965; D.Eng., N.Y. U., 1950, Rensselaer Poly. Inst., 1951, U. Md., 1955; LL.D., Adelphi Coll., 1959; D.Sc., Case Inst. Tech., 1961, Northwestern U., 1963; D.Eng., S.D. Sch. Mines and Tech., 1961; L.H.D., Am. U., 1962; M.E., Politecnico Milan, 1964; Sc.D., Worcester Polytech. Inst., 1964, Swiss Federal Institute of Tehcnology, 1964; m. Mary Travers, Jan. 29, 1920; children—Hugh Latimer, Mary Ruth (Mrs. Andrew Van Tuyll), Nancy Travers. Lab asst. Nat. Bur. Standards, 1918-19, asso. physicist, chief of aerodynamics sec., 1920-34, chief mechanics and sound div., 1934-46, asso. dir., 1946-47; dir. NACA, 1947-58; dep. adminstr. NASA, 1958-65; U.S. del. adv. group aero. research and devel. NATO. Mem. Nat. Inventors Council, Dept. Commerce; Wilbur Wright lectr., Royal Aero. Soc., London, 1949. Hon. Officer, Civil Div., Order Brit. Empire. Recipient Wright Brothers Meml. Trophy, 1955; Nat. Civil Service League Career award, 1958; Rice medal, Am. Ordnance Assn., 1958; Langley medal Am. Philos. Society, 1962; Rockefeller Pub. Service award, 1962; John Fritz medal, 1963; gold medal Internat. Benjamin Franklin Soc., 1963; Dr. Theodore von Karman Meml. citation, 1963; Dr. Robert A. Godard Meml. Trophy, 1964; Hill space transp. award Am. Inst. Aeros. and Astronautics, 1964. Hon. fellow Inst. Aero. Scis. (pres. 1943), Royal Aero. Society (London); fellow Am. Acad. Arts and Scis.; mem. Nat. Acad. Scis. (home sec.), French Acad. Scis., Rocket Soc., Internat. Council Aero. Scis., Nat. Geog. Soc. (life mem., trustee), Am. Soc. M.E., Am. Phys. Soc., Washington Acad. Scis., Philos. Soc. (Washington), Phi Beta Kappa, Sigma Xi. Wright Bros. lecturer, Inst. of Aeronautical Scis., 1940; Medal of Freedom, 1946; Daniel Guggenheim medal, 1951; Nat. medal Sci., 1965, Space Flight award Am. Astron. Soc., 1966, Distinguished Service medal NASA, 1966. Methodist. Club: Cosmos. Author books; contbr. to tech. jours. Home: 5606 Overlea Rd., Washington 20016. Address: 4th and Maryland Av. S.W., Washington 20546. Died Dec. 2, 1966; buried Woodlawn Cemetery, Balt.

DRYDEN, JAMES, poultry breeder; b. Galt, Ont., Can., Feb. 27, 1863; s. James and Mary (Swan) D.; ed. Collegiate Ins., Galt; m. Alice Keim, June 15, 1892; children—Leone (dec.), Robert James, Winfield Joseph, Horace Walter. Came to U.S., 1889, naturalized, 1892. Sec. of com. of Canadian senate, on Resources of MacKenzie River Basin, 1886; sec. to Lt. Gov. Schultz, Manitoba, 1887-88; writer Salt Lake Daily Tribune, 1889-91; instr. poultry husbandry and investigator, Utah Agrl. Coll., Logan, 1892-1907. Ore. State Agrl. Coll., Corvallis, 1907-21; pres. mgr. and chief owner, James Dryden Poultry Breeding Farm, Ltd., 1922—. Developed method of estimating laying capacity of poultry. Republican. Methodist. Woodman. Author: Poultry Breeding and Management, 1916. Home: Modesto, Calif. Died Feb. 4, 1935.

DRYER, CHARLES REDWAY (WILMARTH), geographer; b. Victor, N.Y., Aug. 31, 1850; s. Daniel and Fidelia (Perry) D.; A.B., Hamilton Coll., 1871; M.D., U. of Buffalo, 1876; m. Alice Mary Peacock, 1874; children—Helen Eliza, Alice Judith, Reginald Peacock, Clare Mary. Teacher sciences, high sch., Ft. Wayne, Ind., 1877-90; prof. chemistry and toxicology, Ft. Wayne Coll. of Medicine, 1878-93; prof. geography and geology, Ind. State Normal Sch., 1893-1913. Chemist, Ft. Wayne Electric Co., 1890-93; asst. Ind. Geol. Survey, 1886-93. Author: Studies in Indian Geography, 1897; Lessons in Physical Geography, 1901; Geography, Physical, Economic and Regional, 1911; Elementary Economic Geography, 1916. Home: Fort Wayne, Ind. Died Mar. 21, 1927.

DUANE, WILLIAM, physicist; b. Phila., Pa., Feb. 17, 1872; s. Charles Williams and Emma Cushman (Lincoln) D.; A.B., U. of Pa., 1892; A.B., Harvard, 1893, A.M., 1895; univs. of Berlin and Göttingen, 1895-97, Ph.D., Berlin, 1897; hon. Sc.D., U. of Pennsylvania, 1922; hon. Sc.D., U. of Colo., 1923; m. Caroline Elise Ravenel, Dec. 28, 1899; children—William, Arthur Ravenel (dec.), John P., Margaretta C. Asst. in physics, 1893-95, Tyndall fellow, 1895-97, Harvard; prof. physics, U. of Colo., 1898-1907; research, Curie Radium Lab., U. of Paris, 1907-12; asst. prof. physics, 1913-17, prof. bio-physics, 1917—. Harvard. Mem. Am.

Acad. Arts and Sciences. Episcopalian. Awarded John Scott medal and premium, 1922; Comstock prize, Nat. Acad. of Science, 1922; first Leonard prize, Am. Roentgen Ray Soc., 1923; all three prizes for researches in radioactivity and X-rays. Died Mar. 7, 1935.

DUBILIER, WILLIAM, inventor, engr.; b. New York, July 25, 1888; s. Abe and Anna D.; Geo. DeWitt Clinton High Sch., Tech. Inst., Cooper Inst., New York; m. Florence Don. Inventor several systems of wireless telephony and telegraphy, also med. apparatus; has obtained over 300 patents; wireless telephone and telegraph apparatus used by U.S., French, English and Russian govts.; originated, developed and patented the mica condenser now universally used in all broadcasting stations and for high frequency equipment; invented means for locating, obtaining speed and direction of submarines, used by France and England. Supplied first aeroplane wireless communication installations for U.S. Govt., 1914-15, pioneer X-ray equipment for dental surgery, 1910, chief electrician, Continental Wireless Telegraph & Telephone Co., 1908; pres. and tech. dir. Commercial Wireless Telegraph & Telephone Co., Seattle, Wash., 1910; organized Dubilier Condenser Co., Ltd., London, 1910, Dubilier Electric Co., N.Y., 1913, Dubilier Condenser Corp., N.Y., 1916, Radio Patents Corp., N.Y., 1917, Deutsche Dubilier Kondensator Gesellschaft, Berlin, 1922, Cornell-Dubilier Electric Corp., 1933; at present officer or dir. in above orgns.; member board of directors Seagrave Corporation. Patents licensed to Radio Corporation of America, General Electric Company, Westinghouse Electric and Manufacturing Company, Canadian Gen. Electric Co., Gen. Electric Co., England, German Gen. Electric Co. (Hydra), Berlin, Siemens & Halske, A.G., Berlin, etc. Decorated Order Academic Palms, 1949, Chevalier Legion of Honor, 1950; Gano Dunn Medal, Cooper Union, 1955. Fellow Am. Inst. E.E., Inst. Radio Engrs.; mem. Franklin Inst., etc. Co-author articles, books on wireless telegraphy, etc. Home: New Rochelle NY Died July 1969.

DU BOIS, AUGUSTUS JAY, civil engr.; b. Newton Falls, O., Apr. 25, 1849; s. Henry Augustus and Catherine Helena (Jay) D.; Ph.B., Sheffield Scientific Sch. (Yale), 1869; C.E., 1870, Ph.D., 1873; studied mechanics 2 yrs. at Freiberg (Saxony) Mining Acad.; m. Adeline Blakesley, June 23, 1883. Prof. civ. and mech. engring., Lehigh U., 1875-77; prof. mech. engring., 1877-84, civ. engring., 1884—. Sheffield Scientific Sch. Author: Elements of Mechanics (3 vols), 1893-95. Home: New Haven, Conn. Died Oct. 19, 1915.

DUBOIS EUGENE FLOYD, physiologist; b. West New Brighton, N.Y., June 4, 1882; s. Eugene and Anna Greenleaf (Brooks) DuB.; A.B., Harvard 1903; M.D., Coll. Phys. and Surg. (Columbia), 1906; Sc.D., U. Rochester (N.Y.), 1948; m. Rebeckah Rutter, June 4, 1910. Interne Presbyn. Hosp. N.Y., 1907-08, asst. pathologist, 1909; instr. applied pharmacology, Cornell U. Med. Coll., N.Y., 1910-17; asso. prof. medicine, 1919-30, prof. medicine, 1930-41, prof. physiology, 1941-50, emeritus prof., 1950—; med. dir. Russell Sage Inst. Pathology, 1913-50 1913-50; dir., vis. physician Second Med. Div. of Bellevue Hosp., 1919-32; cons. physician, 1932—; physician-in-chief N.Y. Hosp., 1932-41. Chmn. com. on aviation medicine NRC, 1940-45. Lt., lt. comdr. Med. Corps, USNRF, 1917-18; capt. 1927; during war had charge of investigations dealing with aviation, gas warfare and submarine ventilation. Served as capt. M.C., USNR, 1942-45, Bur. Medicine and Surgery, U.S. Decorated Navy Cross. Mem. Assn. Am. Physicians, Am. Assn. Clin. Investigation. Am. Physiol. Soc., Nat. Acad. Scis. Democrat. Episcopalian. Club: Century Assn. Author: Basal Metabolism in Health and Disease, 1924, 27, 36; The Mechanism of Heat Loss and Temperature Regulation; Compiler of Harvard University Songs, 1902. Research in metabolism. Home: 1215 Park Av., N.Y.C. 28. Died Feb. 1959.

DUBOSE, FRANCIS GOODWIN, M.D., surgeon; b. Maplesville, Ala., Sept. 27, 1873; s. Franklin Davis and Anna M. (Goodwin) DuB.; prep. edn., Orrville (Ala.) Acad. and Marion (Ala.) Mil. Inst.; student U. of Va.; M.D., Tulane U., 1893; grad. study N.Y. City, Baltimore, Phila. and Chicago, 1893-99, London, Berlin, Vienna, 1900, London and Paris, 1902, Paris, 1924; m. Aimee Nelson, of Selma, Ala., June 11, 1902. Began practice at Selma, 1893; founder, 1911, later mgr. and chief of staff Vaughan Memorial Hosp.; retired, 1931. Mem. Ala. State Com. Nat. Defense, World War. Mem. State Bd. Examiners for Nurses, Ala. Fellow Am. Coll. Surgeons (a founder), Southern Surg. Assn.; mem. A.M.A., Med. Assn., State of Ala., Dallas Co. Med. Soc., Southern Med. Assn. (ex-chmn. sect. on surgery), Ala. State Hosp. Assn. (ex-pres.), Pi Gamma Mu. Presbyterian. Club: Town and Country. Wrote: Episodes in Black and White, 1932. Writer over 30 monographs on surg. subjects. Discoverer of muscle in female perineum; research in gall bladder and pelvic inflammatory disease; devised original technique in many surg. operations; originated and first used paravertebral alcohol block for treatment of asthma. Home: Maplesville AL

DUCE, JAMES TERRY, geologist; b. Worcester, Eng., Dec. 29, 1892; s. James and Annie Mabel (Terry) D.; came to U.S., 1902, naturalized, 1903; A.B. in Geol., U. Colo., 1916, LL.D., 1964; m. Ivy Oneita Judd, Aug. 22, 1923; 1 dau., Charmian (Mrs. John L. Corrinet). Geologist, Texas Co., 1918-38; v.p., dir. Tex. Petroleum Co., 1926-38; v.p. Colombia Petroleum Co., 1939; v.p. charge govt. relations Arabian-Am. Oil Co., 1940-58; cons. Middle East Colls. Survey Commn., 1959—, Carroll E. Bradberry & Assos., Los Altos, Cal., 1962—. Dir. fgn. div. Petroleum Adminstrn. War, 1941-43; mem. Mil. Petroleum Adv. Bd., 1947-60. Bd. dirs. Middle East Inst., 1955—, pres., 1960-64, emeritus, 1964—; bd. dirs. Am. Friends Middle East, 1958—; bd. visitors Harvard, 1954-64; adv. com. dept. Oriental studies Princeton, 1945—; trustee Am. U. Beirut, 1962—. Decorated comdr. Nat. Order Cedars Lebanon. Mem. A.A.A.S., Am. Assn. Petroleum Geologists, Am. Inst. Metall. and Mining Engrs. (bd. dirs. 1939-41), Soc. Econ. Geologists (bd. dirs. 1938-41), Am. Petroleum Inst., Fgn. Policy Assn., Acad. Polit. Sci., Pan Am. Soc., Council Pvt. Internat. Devel., Council World Affairs No. Cal., Council Fgn. Relations, Nat. Security Indsl. Assn., Am. Soc. Internat. Law, Am. Geog. Soc., U.S. Internat. C. of C., Inst. Internat. Edn., Syrian Lebanese Am. Fedn. Eastern States, Council Islamic Affairs. Club: Metropolitan (Washington). Author numerous articles in field. Address: 1100 Sacramento St., San Francisco 94108. Died Aug. 15, 1965; buried Golden Gate Nat. Cemetery, San Francisco.

DU CHAILLU, PAUL BELLONI, explorer, author; b. New Orleans, July 31, 1838; sailed from New York to the French settlement at the mouth of the Gaboon river, W. Africa; at his own expense traveled 8,000 miles, with only native companions; covered much miles, with only native companions; covered much previously unexplored country and added 60 species of birds and 20 species of mammals (including the gorilla) to the known zoölogy of Africa. His accounts of the gorillas and Obongo dwarfs were contradicted by scientists, but have since been confirmed. Made a second exploration, 1863-65; discovered many new species of animals and birds; also traveled in Sweden, Norway, Lapland and Finland and other countries. Author: Wild Life Under the Equator; My Apingi Kingdom; The Country of the Dwarfs; Lost in the Jungle; The Land of the Long Night, 1899; The World of the Great Forest, 1900; How Animals, Birds, Reptiles and Insects Talk, Think, Work and Live, 1900. Home: New York, N.Y. Died 1903.

DUCOMMUN, JESSE CLARENCE, engr.; b. Cleghorn, Ia., Sept. 16, 1904; s. Louis H. and Rose (Stahly) D.; B.A., Morningside Coll., 1926; B.S., U. Ia., 1927, M.S., 1928, C.E., 1932; postgrad. U. Ill., Chgo., Lewis Inst., Harvard; m. Elizabeth B. Rasmus, Oct. 3, 1927; children—Dale J., Donald P., Diane E. Research asst. U. Ia., 1927-28; instr. U. Ill., 1928; design engr. Standard Oil Co., 1929-32, chief inspection engr., 1932-34, various refinery operations, 1934-48, Whiting (Ind.) refinery mgr., 1948-52, dir., gen. mgr. mfg., 1956-60; dir. Calumet Nigrogen Products Co., 1955—, pres., 1961—; pres., dir. Waterview Seafood Corp., 1961—; v.p., dir. Am. Oil Co. (Md.), 1961—, (Tex.), 1961—. Chmn. Whiting unit Salvation Army, 1955—; past pres. Lake County Tb Assn., Lake County X-ray Survey Found.; adv. bd. St. Margaret Hosp.; trustee Whiting (Ind.) Community Center; dir. Jr. Achievement of Chgo. Registered profl. engr., Ind. Mem. Ill. State, Whiting East Chgo. C.'s of C., Chgo. Assn. Commerce and Industry, Am. Petroleum Inst. (creator operating practices com.), Nat. Petroleum Refiners Assn. (dir.), Chgo. Athletic Assn., Ia. Hist. Soc., Indiana Soc. Chgo. Clubs: South Shore Country (gov.), Executives (Chgo.). Author (with others) books on refinery process safety. Home: 1536 Amy Av., Whiting, Ind. Office: 910 S. Michigan Av. Chgo. 80. Died July 5, 1966; buried Marcus (Ia.) Amhurst Cemetery.

DUDLEY, BENJAMIN WINSLOW, surgeon; b. Spotsylvania County, Pa., Apr. 12, 1785; s. Ambrose Dudley; M.D., U. Pa., 1806; m. Anna Maria Short, 1821, 3 children. Studied medicine under Dr. Fred Ridgely; began practice of medicine, Lexington, Ky.; traveled, studied in Europe, 4 years; mem. Royal Coll. Surgeons; returned to Lexington, 1814; prof. anatomy and surgery Transylvania U., 1817-50; performed 1st successful cataract operation in West, 1836; ret., 1853. Died Lexington, Jan. 20, 1870.

DUDLEY, CHARLES BENJAMIN, chemist; b. Oxford, N.Y., July 14, 1842; s. Daniel and Maranda (Bemis) D.; A.B., Yale, 1871, Ph.D., 1874; m. Mary V. Crawford, Apr. 17, 1906. Asst. in physics, U. of Pa., 1875, then chemist to Pa. R.R. Co.; has made noteworthy chem. researches in to the quality of metals of railroad use. Home: Altoona, Pa. Died 1909.

DUDLEY, GUILFORD SWATHEL, physician; b. N.Y.C., Jan. 23, 1890; s. Frederick William and Ada Agnes (Hall) D.; A.B., Cornell, 1910, M.D., 1913; m. Marie Adele Irwin, Aug. 12, 1918; children—Guilford Allerton, Richard Irwin. Interne, St. Luke's Hosp., N.Y.C., 1913-15, resident in surgery, 1915-16; interne Sloan Hosp. for Women, 1916; pvt. practice surgery, N.Y.C., 1917—; mem. faculty Cornell U. Med. Coll., 1925—, prof. clin. surgery, 1949—; dir. Second Surg. Div., Bellevue Hosp., 1931-49, cons. surgeon surgeon, 1949—; cons. surgeon Lawrence Hosp., Bronxville, N.Y., 1938—, French Hosp. N.Y.C.; vis. surgeon William Booth Meml. Hosp., 1926—; asso. attending surgeon N.Y. Hosp., 1934-49, attending surgeon, 1949—; attending gen. surgeon Manhattan Eye, Ear and Throat Hosp., N.Y.C. 1st lt., Med. Officer's Res. Corps, U.S. Army, 1917. Hon. med. officer, N.Y.C. A.M.A., A.C.S.; mem. N.Y. Surg. Soc., Acad. Medicine, County Med. Soc. N.Y., Gen. Soc. Mayflower Descs., Hosp. Grads. Club, Medico-Surg. Soc., Med. Strollers, West Side Clin. Soc., Bellevue Alumni Soc., Cornell Med. Coll. Alumni Assn., Soc. Alumni Sloane Hosp. for Women, St. Luke's Hosp. Alumni Soc., Sigma Xi, Nu Sigma Nu. Home: 510 E. 23rd St., N.Y.C. 10. Office: 653 Park Av., N.Y.C. 21. Died May 1, 1962; buried Greenwood Cemetery, N.Y.C.

DUDLEY, PLIMMON HENRY, civil and metall. engr.; b. Freedom, O., May 21, 1843; s. Charles and Sarah (Leete) D.; ed. Hiram (O.) Coll., Ph.D.; m. Lucy May Bronson, Dec. 12, 1871. Chief engr. Valley Ry., 1872-74; chief engr. City of Akron, O., 1866-72; now cons. engr. N.Y.C. lines. Invented dynamometer, 1874; track indicator, 1880, designed, 1883, the first 5-inch steel rail used in U.S., and in 1892 introduced the first 6-inch 100-lb. rails; invented stremmatograph for obtaining and registering strains in rails under moving trains; made first announcement, 1884, that fungi was the cause of decay in wood. Reporter for U.S. on the "Nature of the Metal for Rails" to internat. Ry. Congress, 6th sessions, Paris, 1900, and on "Rails for Lines with Fast Trains," to 7th session, Washington, 1905. Died Feb. 25, 1924.

DUDLEY, SAMUEL WILLIAM, educator; b. New Haven, Oct. 18, 1879; s. Charles Samuel and Mary Elizabeth (Austin) D.; Ph.B., Sheffield Sci. Sch. (Yale), 1900; M.E., 1903; D. Engring., Clarkson Coll. Tech., 1943; m. Mabel Eva Allen, Sept. 21, 1907 (dec. June, 1940); children—John Russell, Mrs. Elizabeth Udella Waters, George Austin, Mrs. Martha Allen Gilbert. With Westinghouse Air Brake Co., 1905-21, asst. chief engr., 1910-14, chief engr., 1914-21; prof. mech. engring. Yale Sch. Engring., 1921-48, chmn. dept. 1923-46, dean, 1936-48, emeritus, 1948—. Fellow Am. Soc. M.E.,; mem. Am. Soc. Engring. Edn., Air Brake Assn., Yale Engring. Assn., N.Y. Ry. Club. Republican. Conglist. Clubs: Graduate, Country (New Haven); Yale (N.Y.). Home: Hamden, Conn. Died Dec. 24, 1963.

DUDLEY, WILLIAM LOFLAND, chemist; b. Covington, Ky., Apr. 16, 1859; s. George Reed and Emma (Lofland) D.; B.S., U. of Cincinnati, 1880; (hon. M.D., Miami Med. Coll., 1885); unmarried. Demonstrator of chemistry, 1879-80, prof. chemistry and toxicology, 1880-86, Miami Med. Coll.; prof. chemistry in Vanderbilt Univ., 1866—, dean Medical Dept., 1895-1913. Commr. Cincinnati Industrial Expn., 1881-85 (2d v.p. 1884); dir. of affairs Tenn. Centennial Expn., 1897; sec. sect. inorganic chemistry, Internat. Congress Arts and Sciences, St. Louis, 1904. Devised a process for working and electro-plating with iridium which has caused its enlarged use in the arts. U.S. commr. 7th Congress Applied Chemistry, London, 1909; v.p. sect. on law and legislations as affecting chem. industry, 8th Congress Applied Chemistry, 1912; spectrographic studies on tellurium and atomic weight determinations of tellurium. Home: Nashville, Tenn. Died Sept. 8, 1914.

DUDLEY, WILLIAM RUSSEL, botanist; b. Guilford, Conn., Mar. 1, 1849; s. Samuel William and Lucy (Chittenden) D.; B.S., Cornell, 1874, M.S., 1876; studied natural history in the Agassiz School, Penikese Island, 1874, Harvard Summer Sch., 1876; studied at univs. of Strassburg and Berlin, 1887-88. Instr. botany, 1873-76, asst. prof., 1876-83, asst. prof. in charge cryptogramic botany, 1883-92, Cornell; prof. botany, Leland Stanford Jr. U., 1892—. Asso. editor Sierra Club Bull., 1898—. Author: The Cayuga Flora, 1886; Lackawanna and Wyoming Flora, 1887; Manual of Histology (with Prof. M. B. Thomas), 1894; etc. Died 1911.

DUELL, PRENTICE, archaeologist; b. New Albany, Ind., Aug. 17, 1894; s. Martin H. and Mary Hannah (Gray) D.; A.B., U. of Calif., 1916; A.M., U. of Ariz., 1917; studied architecture, Paris, 1919; U. of Pa., 1919-20; M. Arch., Harvard U., 1924. Charles Eliot Norton fellowship, Am. Sch. Classical Studies at Athens, 1923-25; Guggenheim fellowship to study Etruscan tomb painting in Italy, 1929-30. Instr. history of architecture, U. of Ill., 1921-22; asst. prof., 1925-26, and prof., 1926-27, ancient architecture, U. of Cincinnati; lecturer, 1927-29, and asso. prof., 1929-30, classical archaeol., Bryn Mawr College; Archaeologist, Restoration of Williamsburg, Va., 1929-31; field dir. Sakkarah (Egypt) Expdn., Oriental Inst., U. of Chicago, 1930-36, and non-resident asso. prof. ancient Mediterranean art, same, 1931-36; research in London and Vienna, 1936-38; research fellow in Etruscan art Fogg Museum of Art, Harvard U., since 1939. Exhibitions of water colors and photographs of Etruscan wall paintings, Met. Mus., New York, and other museums and univs. Enlisted in U.S. Army, aviation sect., 1917, commd. 2d lt., 1918; balloon pilot-observer with A.E.F., San Mihiel and Argonne offensives, also Army of Occupation, 1918-19; apptd. 1st lt. aviation section, Reserve Corps, 1920-22, and Mil. Intelligence, Reserve Corps, 1922-35. Member N.Y. State Assn. of Architects, Archaeol. Inst. Am., A.I.A., Am. Academy in Rome, Instituto di Studi Etruschi ed Italici (Florence,

Italy), l'Assn. Internationale d 'Archéologie Classique (Rome). Sigma Xi. Theta Xi. Clubs: Century. Harvard, (New York); Army and Navy (Washington); Faculty of Harvard. Author: Mission Architecture, Exemplified in San Xavier del Bac, 1919; The Tomba del Triclinio, at Tarquinia, 1927; The Mastaba of Mereruka, at Sakkarah, (2 vols.), 1938. Contbr. articles to archaeol. jours. Address: Fogg Museum of Art, Harvard University, Cambridge 38, Mass. Died Apr. 16, 1960; buried Arlington (Va.) Nat. Cemetery.

DUFF, G(EORGE) LYMAN, educator, pathologist; b. Hamilton, Ont., Can., Jan. 16, 1904; s. Charles and Elizabeth Anne (Ostler) D.; B.A., U. Toronto, 1926, M.A., 1927, M.D., 1929, fellow pathology, 1929-31, Ph.D., 1932; Nat. Research Council fellow medicine Johns Hopkins, 1931-32; m. Isobel Farrell Griffiths, Oct. 23, 1935; children—Shelia Louise, Graham Lyman, Ian Griffiths, Catharine Isobel. Asst. pathology Johns Hopkins, 1931-33, instr. pathology, 1933-35; Pathologist Johns Hopkins Hosp., 1933-35; lectr. pathology U. Toronto, 1935-37, asst professor pathology, 1937-39; asst. pathologist Toronto General Hosp., 1935-39; asso. editor Am. Am. Jour. Med. Sci. since 1938; prof. pathology, dir. path inst. McGill U. since 1939, hon. curator Royal Canadian Army Med. Corps. Med. Mus., 1941-48, dean faculty medicine since 1949; cons. pathologist Montreal General Hosp., Childrens Meml. Hosp., Alexandria Hospital, Reddy Meml. Hosp., Jewish Hosp. of Hope, Montreal; asso. examiner pathology and bacteriology, Med. council. Can., 1942-45; mem. asso. com. med. research Nat. Research Council Can., Ottawa, 1943-48, executive com., 1944-48; examiner pathology Royal Coll. Phys. and Surg. Can. since 1944; hon. cons. pathology Royal Victoria Hosp., lectr. medicine Royal Coll. Physicians Can., 1947; editroial bd. Am. Heart Jour. Since 1950, Lab. Investigation since 1953. Certified specialist in pathology Royal Coll. Phys. and Surg. Can. Recipient Flavelle Medal, Royal Soc., Can., 1956. Fellow Royal Society Can., Royal Coll. Physicians Can.; mem. Nat. Cancer Inst., Can. (dir., v.p. 1953-54, pres. 1954-55), Path. Soc. Gt. Brit. and Ireland, Am.Assn. Pathologist and Bacteriologist (mem. council 1950-55, v.p. 1953-54 pres. 1954-55), Canadian Cancer Soc. (nat. dir.), Internat. Assn. Med. Mus. (mem. council 1942-47, mem. editroial bd. Bull. 1947-52, v.p. 1949-50, pres. 1950-51), Montreal Medico-Chirurgical Soc., Que. Association Pathologist (pres. 1946-47), Am. Soc. Study Arteriosclerosis (bd. dirs. 1947-50, v.p. 1950-51, pres. 1951-52), Soc. Exptl. Biology and Medicine, Canadian Med. Assn., Canadian Assn. Pathologists. Contbr. Contbr. articles med. jours. Home: 730 Upper Roslyn Av., Westmount 6. Office: 3775 University St., Montreal 2. P.Q., Can. Died Nov. 1, 1956.

DUFFIELD, WILLIAM WARD, civil engr.; b. Carlisle, Pa., Nov. 19, 1823; grad. Columbia, 1841 (A.M., 1844); m. A. Louise Ladue, June 27, 1854. Lt. on staff Gen. Gideon P. Pillow in Mexican war, 1847-48; lt. col. 4th Mich. inf., 1861, in Civil War; col. 9th Mich. inf., 1862; twic severely wounded at Murfreesboro; State senator Mich., 1878-79; chief engr. of railways in Mich., N.Y., Ill., Texas and other states; U.S. engr. of improvements on Wabash and White rivers in Ind. and Ill., 1892-93; supt. U.S. Coast and Geodetic Survey, 1894-98. Author: School of the Brigade and Evolutions of the Line; Treatise on Logarithms—with Tables of Logarithms to Ten Place. Home: Washington, D.C. Died 1907.

DUFOUR, FRANK OLIVER, civil engr.; b. at Washington, Jan. 1, 1873; s. John Francis Ruter and Florida E. (Everett) D.; C.E., Lehigh U., Pa., 1896; m. Sarah Breisch, of S. Bethlehem, Pa., Sept. 2, 1901; 1 son, Robert Seton. Asst. engr. Lehigh Valley R.R., 1896-98; instr. civil engring., Lehigh U., 1898-1902; prof. civ. engring., U. of Cincinnati, 1902-04; acting prof. bridge engring., U. of Wis., 1904-05; asst. prof. structural engring., U. of Ill., 1905-13; prin. asst. engr. with D.A. Keefe, 1913; consulting engr., Athens, Pa., 1913-14; sr. structural engr., central dist. Div. of Valuation, Interstate Commerce Commn., Chicago, 1914-15; structural engr. with Stone & Webster, Boston, 1915-21; prof. civ. engring. and dir. Materials Testing Labs., Lafayette Coll., Easton, Pa., 1921-28; now cons. engr., United Engrs. & Constructors, Inc., Philadelphia, Pa. Mem. Am. Soc. C.E., Am. Ry. Engring. Assn., Sigma Xi, Theta Delta Chi. Clubs: Explorers (New York); Penn Athletic, Phila. Cricket, Engineers', Midday, Business Men's Art, Tredyffrin Country (Philadelphia); Camp Fire Club of America (New York). Author: Bridge Engineering, 1908, revised edit., 1931; Roof Trusses, 1908; Structural Drafting, 1911. Contbr. to various tech. mags. Home: Narberth, Pa. Office: 1401 Arch St., Philadelphia PA

DUFOURCQ, EDWARD LEONCE, mining engr.; b. New York, Aug. 6, 1870; s. Leonce Felix and Hortense Louise (Geer) D.; Columbia, 1886-87; E.M., Sch. of Mines (Columbia), 1892; m.Ernestine King, June 29, 1896 (died 1911); m. 2d, Effie E. Mason, 1917. Assistant engr., mining, railroad and municipal work, Central America, Mexico and U.S., 1892-94; supt. Internat. Mining Co., San Miguel del Mezquital, Mexico, 1894-96; supt. Consol. Kansas City Smelting & Refining Co., Sierra Mojada, Mex., 1896-98; mem. Olcott, Fearn & Peele, cons. engr., New York, 1898-1901; mgr. Andes Mining Co., Chimbote, Peru, 1901; gen. supt. Montezuma Lead Co., Santa Barbara, Mex., 1901-04; cons. mining engr., N.Y. City 1904—; pres. Dufourcq & Co., Inc., export trade. Democrat. Epsicopalian. Died Apr. 15, 1919.

DUGGAR, BENJAMIN MINGE, univ. prof.; b. Gallion, Ala., Sept. 1, 1872; s. Dr. Reuben Henry and Margaret Louisa (Minge) D.; brother of John Frederick D.; student U. of Ala., 1887-89; B.S., Miss. A. and M. Coll. (1st honors), 1891; M.S., Ala. Poly. Inst. 1892; A.B., Harvard, 1894, A.M., 1895; Ph.D., Cornell, 1898; German Universities and at Naples, Paris, and Montpelier, 1899-1900, 1905-06; LL.D., U. of Mo., 1944; D.Sc., Washington U., 1953; m. Marie L. Robertson, Oct. 16, 1901 (died 1922)—children—Marie Louise, Benjamin Minge, Anna St. Julian Guerard, George Strowan, Emily Westwood; m. 2d, Elsie Rist, June 5, 1927; 1 daughter, Gene Lorraine. Asst. dir. Uniontown (Ala.) Agrl. Expt. Sta., 1892-93; asst. botanist of Ill. State Lab. Natrual History, 1895-96; cryptogamic botanist, Agrl. Expt. Sta. and instr. plant physiology, 1896-1900; 1896-1900; asst. prof., 1900-01, Cornell; physiologist, Bur. Plant Industry, U.S. Dept. Agr., 1901-02; prof. botany, U. of Mo., 1902-07; prof. plant physiology, Cornell U., Feb. 1, 1907-12; research prof. plant physiology Mo. Bot. Garden and Washington U., 1912-27; prof. physiology and economic botany, University of Wisconsin, 1927—; emeritus, June, 1943—; consultant, mycological research and production Lederle Laboratories Div. American Cyanamid Co., Pearl River, N.Y., 1944. Acting prof. biology chemistry Washington U. Med. Sch., 1917-19. Awarded Medal of Honor of Public Education, Venezuela, 1951. Trustee emeritus Marine Biol. Lab., Woods Hole Oceanographic Instn. Fellow A.A.A.S., (v.p. section G, 1925); mem. Nat Acad. Scis., Am. Philos. Soc., Phila. Acad. Science, Botanical Soc. of America (pres. 1923), Am. Soc. Plant Physiol. (pres. 1946-47), American Phytopathol. Soc., American Chem. Society, Soc. American Naturalists, American Pub. Health Assn., Torrey Botanical Club, Nat. Research Council (chmn. div. biology and agr., 1925-26), Sigma Xi, Phi Beta Kappa, Phi Sigma. Chairman Organizing Com. and general secretary Internat. Congress Plant Sciences, 1926. Speaker in sect. plant physiology, Internat. Congress of Arts and Sciences, St. Louis, 1904. Editor for Physiology, Botanical Abstracts, 1917-26, Biological Abstracts, 1926-33, and Biological Abstracts of Radiation, 1936. Author: Fungus Diseases of Plants, 1909; Plant Physiology, 1911; Mushroom Growing, 1915; A Textbook of General Botany with B. M. Smith, et al; also research articles. Home: 198 Braunsdorf Rd., Pearl River, N.Y. Died Sept. 10, 1956; buried Oak Hill Cemetery, Nyack, N.Y.

DUGGAR, JOHN FREDERICK, agriculturist; b. Faunsdale, Ala., Aug. 24, 1868; s. Dr. Reuben Henry and Margaret Louisa (Minge) D.; brother of Benjamin Minge D.; ed. Southern U., Greensboro, Ala.; B.S., Miss. Agrl. and Mech. Coll., 1887, M.S., 1888; student Columbian (now George Washington) U., Cornell U., and U. of Colo.; m. Frances Ambrose Camp, June 17, 1891; children—John Frederick, Frances Camp, Mrs. Margaret McCormick, Ambrose Camp, Llewellyn Goode, Dorothy. Asst. prof. agr., Tex. Agrl. and Mech. Coll., Bryan, Tex., 1887-89; editor Southern Live Stock Journal, Starkville, Miss., 1890; asst. dir. Expt. Sta., Clemson Coll., S.C., 1890-92; editor dept. field crops, Expt. Sta. Record, U.S. Dept. Agr., 1893-95; prof. agr., Alabama Poly. Inst., 1896-1921; also dir. Alabama Expt. Sta., 1903-21, and dir. Ala. Extension Service, 1914-20; research prof. farm management and special investigations, Ala. Poly. Inst., 1922-31, research prof. since 1931. Lecturer in agronomy, U. of Calif., 1922-24. Mem. Phi Kappa Phi. Recipient (1939) medal for distinguished service, from Assn. Southern Agrl. Workers. Author: Agriculture for Southern Schools; Southern Field Crops; Southern Forage Crops; also numerous articles and pamphlets. Home: Auburn, Ala. Died Dec. 25, 1945.

DUGMORE, ARTHUR RADCLYFFE, author, artist; b. England, Dec. 25, 1870; s. Capt. F.S. and Hon. Emily Evelyn (Brougham) D.; ed. Elizabeth Coll., Guernsey, and Turrell's Sch., Smyrna (Asia Minor); studied painting at Belle Arti, Naples; came to U.S., 1889, from Naples; studied ornithology and continued drawing, painting and illustrating by photography; m. Henrietta Louise Watkins, Jan. 17, 1901. Mem. Am. Ornithologists' Union, Linnaean Soc.; fellow Royal Geog. Soc. (Eng.), Royal Photographic Soc.; hon. life mem. Am. Mus. Natural History, New York Zool. Soc. Clubs: Royal Societies, Shikar (London), Players, Explorers, Camp Fire of America (New York). Author: Bird Homes, 1899; Nature and the Camera, 1902; Camera Adventures in the African Wilds (pub. in English, French and German); Wild Life and the Camera; The Romance of the Newfoundland Caribou. Also writer and lecturer on nature subjects in periodicals. Address: Royal Societies Club, St. James St., London SW England

DUKE, WILLIAM WADDELL, physician; b. Lexington, Mo., Oct. 18, 1882; s. Henry Buford and Susie (Waddell) D.; Ph.B., Yale, 1904; M.D., Johns Hopkins, 1908; grad. study, Mass. Gen. Hosp., Boston, 1909-10, U. of Vienna, 1910-12, U. of Berlin, m. Frances Thomas, May 18, 1920; Children—Henry Basil, Frances Suzanne. Practicing physician in Kansas City, Mo., since 1912, limiting practice to internal medicine; prof. exptl. medicine U. of Kan. Sch. of Medicine, Rosedale, 1914-18; visiting physician Christian Ch. Hosp., Kansas City, 1918-24. Mem. Council of Nat. Defense and capt. in Am. Red Cross, World War; lt. col. O.R.C. since World War. Fellow A.M.A.; mem. Am. Coll. Physicians. Awarded silver medal, 1924 by A.M.A. for research in allergy; annual gold medal, 1941, by the Midwest Forum of Allergy for distinguished and outstanding contributions in the field of allergy. Episcopalian. Mason (K.T., Shriner). Clubs: Kansas City, University, Kansas City Country. Author: Oralsepsis in Relationship to Systemic Disease, 1918; Allergy, Asthma, Hay Fever, Uricaria and Allied Manifestations of Reaction, 1925; also chapters in Practitioners' Library of Medicine and Surgery, Cyclo. of Medicine, Modern Home Med. Adviser. Contbr. tech. articles. Discovered in field of Allergy and physical allergy, oral sepsis, transfusion and anemia, palm color test, bleeding time, relation between platelets and hemorrhagic disease; co-discoverer physiology of heart beat in relationship to the potassium and calcium content of the blood; also made polien surveys. Home: 1220 W. 62nd St. Office: Professional Bldg., Kansas City, Mo. Died Apr. 10, 1946.

DUKES, RICHARD GUSTAVUS educator; b. Findlay, O., De Pauw U., Mass. Inst. Tech.; M.E. in Elec. Engring., Cornell 1896; m. Harriet Campbell, June 22, 1901 (died Dec. 1943); m. 2d, Mary Irene Hughes, Feb. 23, 1946; children—Elizabeth Mitchell (Mrs. C. D. Phillips), Martha Campbell (Mrs. F. H. Ryan). With Gen. Electric Co., Schenectady, 1898-1900; instr. in mech. engring. Worcester Poly. Inst., 1900-01; instr. dept. exptl. engring. Cornell U., 1901-03; prof. in charge applied mechanics Case Sch. Applied Science, 1903-09; prof. applied mechanics and head dept. Purdue U., 1909-42, prof. emeritus, 1942—, dean Grad. Sch., 1929-42, dean emeritus, 1942—. Mem. Soc. Promotion Engring. Edn., Am. Soc. for Testing Materials, Ind. Acad. Science, Scabbard and Blade, Sigma Xi, Delta Kappa Epsilon, Alpha Phi Omega, Tau Beta Pi. Presbyn. Club: Town and Gown. Home: 2 Stadium Rd., W. Lafayette, Ind. Died Aug. 12, 1950.

DUMBLE, EDWIN THEODORE, geologist; b. Madison, Ind., Mar. 28, 1852; s. James F. and Mary A.D.; B.S., Sc.D., Washington and Lee U., Va.; m. Fanny Doswell Gray, June 15, 1876; children—Mrs. Milly Gray Mitchell, Mrs. Rosalie McCoy Davis. State geologist of Tex., 1887-96; cons. geologist and mgr. oil properties Southern Pacifc Co. (Rio Bravo Oil Co., Tex., East Coast Oil Co., Mex.), 1897-1925; also cons. geologist Pacific Oil Co.; cons. practice, Houston, Tex. Fellow Geol. Soc. America, A.A.A.S., Tex. Acad. Science. Author: Brown Coal and Lignite; Geology of East Texas. Died Jan. 26, 1927.

DU MEZ, ANDREW GROVER, pharmaceutical chemist; b. Horicon, Wis., Apr. 26, 1885; s. Andrew Alexander and Anna (Meister) Du M.; Ph.G., U. of Wis., 1904, B.S., 1907, M.S., 1910, Ph.D., 1917; m. Mary Elizabeth Fields, June 9, 1912. Inst. in pharm. chemistry, U. of Wis., 1905-10; prof. chemistry, Pacific U., Forest Grove, Ore., 1910-11; asst. prof. chemistry, Okla. Agrl. and Mech. Coll., 1911-12; dir. Sch. of Pharmacy, U. of the Philippines, 1912-16; Hollister fellow, U. of Wis., 1916-17; asso. pharmacologist, Hygenic Lab., U.S. Public Health Service, Washington, D.C., 1917-26; dean of Sch. of Pharmacy, U. of Md., since 1926. Pharmacy consultant to the surgeon general, U.S. Army. Sec. spl. com. Treasury Dept. to investigate traffic in narcotics in United States, 1918-19; vice chairman Revision Com. of Pharmacopoeia of U.S. for term 1930-40; chairman sub.-com. on nomenclature since 1920; U.S. Govt. del. to Second Conf. on Unification of Standards for Potent Remedies, Brussels, 1925; sec. Am. Council on Pharmaceutical Edn. since 1932. Fellow A.A.A.S.; member American Association Colleges of Pharmacy (pres. 1929), Am. Chem. Soc., Am. Pharm. Assn. (pres. 1939-40, awarded Remington Medal, 1948), Am. Pub. Health Assn., Wis. Acad. Science, Arts and Letters, Sigma Xi, Phi Delta Chi. Congregationalist. Mason. Joint Author: Quantitative Pharmaceutical Chemistry (with Glenn L. Jenkins), 1931. Advisory editor, joint author, American Pharmacy. Editor: Digest of Comments on the Pharmacopoeia of the U.S. and the National Formulary, 1916-22; Yearbook of Am. Pharm. Assn., 1921-34, Pharm. Abstracts, 1935-41. Science editor Jour. Am. Pharm. Assn., 1938-41. Contbr. to Philippine Jour. Science, Jour. Am. Med. Assn., Jour. Am. Pharm. Assn., Am. Jour. Pharmacy, etc. Home: Stony Run Lane and 40th St., Baltimore 10. Office: 32 S. Greene St., Baltimore 1, Md. Died Sept. 26, 1948.

DU MONT, ALLEN BALCOM, tehc. cons.; b. Bklyn., Jan. 29, 1901; s. William Henry Beaman and Lillian Felton (Balcom) Du M.; E.E., Rensselaer Poly. Inst., 1924, Dr. Engring., 1944; Dr. Engring., Bklyn. Poly. Inst., 1949; LL.D.., Fairleigh Dickinson Coll., 1955; D.Sc., N.Y.U., 1955; Litt. D., Montclair State Coll., 1959; m. Ethel Martha Steadman, Oct. 19, 1926; children—Allen Balcom, Yvonne. Engr., Westinghouse Lamp Co., Bloomfield, N.J., 1924-28; chief engr. De Forest Radio Co., Passaic, N.J., 1928-31; pres. Allen B. Du Mont Labs., Inc., cathode ray and TV equipment, Clifton, N.J., 1931-56, chmn. bd., 1956-60; group gen.

mgr. Allen B. DuMont Labs. div. Fairchild Camera & Instrument Corp., 1960-61, sr. tech. consultant, 1961—. Mem. Nat. Television Systems Com., 1940-44. Pub. gov. Am. Stock Exchange. Vice pres. bd. trustees Rensselaer Poly. Inst. Decorated Chevalier Order French Legion of Honor, 1952. Fellow I.R.E., Soc. Motion Picture and Television Engineers, Television Soc., Eng.; mem. Am. Inst. E.E. (hon.), Television Pioneers, Radio and Television Execs. Soc., Vet. Wireless Operators Assn., Am. Rocket Soc., Radio Pioneers. Recipient Westinghouse award for most outstanding accomplishment, Am. Television Society award for advancement comml. TV, 1943, Television Award devel. of cathode ray tube, 1944, Marconi Meml. medal Achievement for pioneer work in field of communication, 1945, AAAA Gold medal award for work in television, 1947, Am. Schs. and Colls. award. Inventor of magic eye tube, cathautograph, photovision, electron turbine, duoscopic television and has received over 30 patents on cathode ray tubes and television. Mem. Champlain Soc., Hunguenot Soc., Eastern Cruiser Assn. (commodore 19155-56), S.A.R., Sigma Xi, Sigma Delta Chi. Baptist. Clubs: New York Athletic (N.Y.C.); Englewood Y.C.; Upper Montclair Country; Explorers. Became the National Champion, power crusier div. Am. Power Boat Assn., 1953-55, 58. Home: 275 Bradford Av., Cedar Grove, N.J. Office: 750 Bloomfield Av., Clifton, N.J. Died Nov. 16, 1965.

DUN, JAMES, civ. engr.; b. Chillicothe, O., Sept. 8, 1844; s. James and Virginia Walke D.; ed. Miami Univ., 1865-66; m. Mrs. Belle R. Otterson, Mar. 11, 1885; m. 2d, Mrs. Lucy J. Rucker, Oct. 31, 1899. Chainman with engring. corps Indianpolis & Cincinnati R.R., 1866; asst. engr. A.&P. Ry., 1867-71; asst. engr., Mo. Pacific Ry., 1871-74; engr. Union Depot Co., St. Louis, 1874-77; supt. bridges and bldgs., 1877-78, chief engr., 1878-90, S.L.&S.F. R.R.; chief engr. A.,T.&S.F. Ry. Co., 1890-1900; chief engr. entire A.,T.&S.F. Ry. System, Aug. 1, 1900—. Home: Chicago, Ill. Died 1908.

DUNBAR FLANDERS, psychiatrist; b. Chgo., Ill., daughter Francis William and Edith (Flanders) Dunbar; grad. Sch., N.Y. City, 1919; B.A., Bryn Mawr Coll., 1923; M.A., Columbia, 1924; Ph.D., 1929, Med. Sc.D., 1935; B.S., Union Theol. Em., 1927; M.D., Yale, 1930; m. George Henry Soule (retaining own name by law); 1 dau., Marcia Winslow Dunbar-Soule. Clinical research Worcester (Mass.) State Hosp., summer 1925, and various periods later; sub-internship New Haven Hosp., 1928; hospitant in Gen. and Psychiatric-Neurological Hops. and Clinic of U. of Vienna, and asst. at Burghölzli, Zurich, 1929-30; asst. in medicine Columbia U. Coll. of Phys. and Surg. and Presbyn. Hosp., 1930-34; clin. asst. vis. physician Bellevue Hosp., 1935-37; instr. in psychiatry Columbia Univ. Coll. of Phys. and Surg. and asst. attending psychiatrist Presbyn. Hosp. and Vanderbilt Clinic, 1931-36. asso. in psychiatry, asst. physician and asso. attending psychiatrist, 1936-49; in charge psychosomatic research, 1932-49; in charge asso. mem. staff Greenwich (Conn.) Hosp., 1944-49; practicing med. as specialist in psychiatry and psychosomatic problems; instructor N.Y. Psychoanalytic Institute, 1941-49. Diplomate Nat. Bd., Am. Bd. Psychiatry and Neurology. Qualified Psychiatrist, N.Y. State, Conn. Mem. exec. com. N.Y. City Com. on Mental Hygiene; sec. Welfare Council and chmn. sub-com. on psychiat. problems in somatic disorders, 1936-48. Fellow N.Y. Acad. Medicine (neurology and psychiatry; sec., asso. treas., com. emotions and health 1932-38), Am. Psychiat. Assn. (sec.-treas. 1939-40, vice chmn. 1940-41, sect. psychoanalysis), Am. Geriatrics Soc., Internat. Assn. Gerontology, N.Y. Acad. Sci.; mem. A.M.A., A.A.A.S., Academy of Psychoanalysis, Asso., for Psychiatric Treatment of Offenders, New York Society of Clinical Psychiatry, Am. Psychoanalytic Assn. (treas. 1942-45,), N.Y. Psychoanalytic Soc. (edn. com. 1942-44) Am. Psychopath. Assn. (v.p. 1942-45), Assn. for Research in Nervous and Mental Diseases, Internat. Psycholanalytic Assn., med. socs. County N.Y., State. N. Y. Nat. Com. on Alcoholism, Nat. Safety Council, N.Y. State Acas. Gen. Practice, World Med. Assn., UNICEF (U.S. Com., Inc.), American Orthopsychiat. Assn., Am. Psychomatic Soc. (Council 1947; formerly Am. Soc. Research Psychosomatic Problems), American Com. for World Fedn. for Mental Health, Greenwich Med. Soc. Clubs: Colonial Dames, Bryn Mawr, Cosmopolitan. Author: Symbolism in Medieval Thought, 1929; Emotions and Bodily Changes, 1935, rev. 1954; Psychosomatic Diagnosis. 1943, rev. 1956; Mind and Body; Psychosomatic Medicine, 1947, rev. 1955; Synopsis of Psychosomatic Diagnosis and Treatment, 1948; Your Child's Mind and Body, 1949; Psychiatry in the Medical Specialties, 1959. Translator: Eugene Kahn's Psychopathic Personalities, 1931. Inaugurator Jour. Psychosomatic Medicine, exptl. and clin. studies, monogrpah supplements, editor in chief, 1938-47. now emeritus. Contbr. numerous sci. articles. Collaborating editor Psychoanalytic Quarterly, 1938-40, editor, 1939-40. Editor Acta Psychotherapeutica, Psychosomatica et Orthopaedagogica. Home: South Kent, Conn. Office: South Kent, Conn., 1 E. 69th St., N.Y.C. 21. Died Aug. 1959.

DUNBAR, WILLIAM, planter, scientist; b. Elgin, Scotland, 1749; s. Sir Archibald Dunbar; married, 7 children. Came to Fort Pitt (now Pitts.), began trading with Indians, 1771-73; partner John Ross in plantation, West Fla., 1773; founded 2d plantation, nr. Natchez, Miss., 1792; surveyor gen. Dist. of Natchez, 1798; conducted 1st meteorol. observations in Miss. Valley, 1799; mem. Am. Philos. Soc.; apptd. explorer of Hot Springs, Ark. area, 1804, for Red River area, 1805; mem. Territorial Legislature, Miss.; chief justice Ct. of Quarter Sessions; contrbr. numerous articles on natural and phys. to various jours. including Jour. Am. Philos. Soc. Died "The Forest," nr. Natchez, Oct. 1810.

DUNCAN, CHARLES, state health commr., pathologist; b. Chelsea, Mass., Mar. 18, 1872; s. James and Margaret (Patterson) D.; B.L., Dartmouth, 1898; M.D., Harvard, 1903; m. Charlotte Ilsley (A.B., Radcliffe), June 28, 1905; children—Laurence Ilsley, Eleanor (wife of Rev. Walter Priest Brockway), Margaret (wife of Rev. Howard E. Short). Practiced at Concord, N.H., 1903—; pathologist and bacteriologist; State Bd. of Health, 1903-18, became sec., 1918, now state commr. of health; pathologist to Memorial Hosp. Republican. Congregationalist. Editor of "Health" (mag.). Home: Concord, N.H. Died Nov. 12, 1936.

DUNCAN, GREER ASSHETON, civil engr.; b. Alexandria, La., Mar. 31, 1887; s. Herman Cope and Maria Elizabeth (Cooke) D.; B.C.E., U. of South, 1911; B.S., U.S. Naval Acad., 1908; C.E., Rensselaer Poly. Inst., 1912; m. Marie Louise Chauvin, June 17, 1911; children—Marie Louise (wife of Capt. Robert F. Jones), Greer Assheton, Jr. (lt. comdr., U.S. Navy). Line officer on cruisers, torpedo boats and battleships, U.S. Navy, 1908-10; mem. Civil Engr. Corps, U.S. Navy, 1911—, advancing through the ranks from ensign to captain; pub. works officer Navy Yard, Mare Island, Cal., 1938-41; asst. naval attache, spl. naval observer, mem. staff Comdr. of Naval Forces in Europe, 1941-43; pub. works officer, 13th Naval Dist., Seattle, 1943-46. Owner's rep. Constrn., Seattle, 1948; cons. engr., 1947—. Hon. life trustee Rensselaer Poly. Inst. Recipient Sec. of Navy Commendation with bronze star, Comdr. Order of Honor and Merit Republic of Haiti, 1931, Marine Expeditionary Medal, 1908, Victory Medal, 1917, Def. Medal with Star, European Theatre medal, 1941-43, Am. Theatre medal, 1946; World War Victory medal, 1941-46. Mem. Rensselaer Soc. Engr., Soc. Am. Mil. Engrs., Soc. Naval Architects and Marine Engrs., Kappa Sigma. Episcopalian. Mason. (R.A.M., R.&S.M., K.T.). Home: Alexandria, La.; also 3218 Esplanade Dr., Seattle 7. Office: care Bureau of Yards and Docks, Navy Dept., Washington 25. Died June 26, 1962.

DUNCAN, LOUIS, elec. engr.; b. Washington, D.C., Mar. 25, 1862; s. Thomas and Maria (Morris) D.; grad. U.S. Naval Acad., 1880; Ph.D., Johns Hopkins U., 1885; m. Edith McKee, 1887. Resigned from navy, 1887; maj. 1st vol. engrs., Spanish War; asso. and asso. prof. applied electricity, Johns Hopkins U., 1887-98; head dept. elec. engring., Mass. Inst. Tech., 1902-04. Fellow Am. Philos. Soc.; hon. mem. Franklin Inst. Home: Pelham Manor, N.Y. Died Feb. 13, 1916.

DUNCAN, ROBERT KENNEDY, chemist; b. Brantford, Ont., Can., Nov. 1, 1868; s. Robert Augustus and Susan (Hawley) D.; bro. Norman D.; B.A., U. of Toronto (with 1st class honors in physics and chemistry), 1892; fellow in chemistry, Clark U., 1892-93; grad. student in chemistry, Columbia, 1897-98; m. Charlotte M., d. of George Foster, of Brantford, Ont., Dec. 27, 1899. Instr. physics and chemistry, Auburn (N.Y.) Acad. High Sch., 1893-95, Dr. Julius Sach's Collegiate Inst., New York, 1895-98, The Hill Sch., Pottstown, Pa., 1898-1901; studied abroad, 1900, 03, 04, 07; prof. chemistry, Washington and Jefferson College, 1901-06; prof. indsl. chemistry, U. of Kan., 1906-; dir. indsl. research, U. of Kan., 1910—; dir. indsl. research and prof. industrial chemistry, U. of Pittsburgh, 1910—; visiting lecturer, Clark U., 1911—. Discoverer and patentee of new process for mfg. phosphorus, of a new lowmelting glass, and of processes of decorating glass; consultant in chemistry. Initiated in 1907 at U. of Kans. a new scheme of industrial fellowships which has since grown to remarkable proportions at U. of Kan. and U. of Pittsburgh. Send abroad by McClure's Mag., summer of 1901, to study radio-activity; by A. S. Barnes & Co., summer of 1903, for material for The New Knowledge; by Harper's Mag., 1905-06, to study relations of modern chemistry to industry. Author: The New Knowledge, 1905; The Chemistry of Commerce, 1907; Some Chemical Problems of Today, 1911. Died Feb. 18, 1914.

DUNCKLEE, JOHN BUTLER, civil engr.; b. Boston, July 7 1848; s. John and Harriet (Gillmore) D.; S.B., Lawrence Scientific Sch (Harvard), 1866; course in mining engring. Mass. Inst. Tech., 1866-68; m. Libbie S. Adams, Jan. 1875. Civil engr., 1868-74; div. engr., 1870-74, in construction of Brooklyn parks; civ. engr. connected with U.S. Engr. Dept. at Washington, on river and harbor improvements, 1874-82, and on improving Potomac River and reclaiming its flats at Washington, 1882-99; had charge construction Aqueduct bridge and Pennsylvania Av. bridge, Washington, 1901-11; consulting and bridge engineer; designed new long bridge across Potomac River, Washington. Home: S. Orange, N.J. Deceased.

DUNHAM, FRANKLIN, educator; b. Brooklyn, N.Y., May 17, 1892; s. Frank and Gertrude (Quarles) D.; ed. Poly. Inst., Brooklyn, 1911-12 Columbia, 1912-15 (grad.); Columbia Law Sch., 1915-16, New York U. Sch. of Music, summers 1916-17; Mus.D., N.Y. Coll Music, 1935; Litt. D., St. Bonaventures Coll., 1937; L.H.D., St. Michael's Coll., 1949; LL.D., Marquette U., 1955; fellow Trinity Coll., London, 1938; m. Mary Elizabeth Burke, Oct. 15, 1921; children—Alvin, Franklin, Mary Gertrude. Ednl. dir. corps., broadcasting cos., 1916-41; spl. cons. U.S. Commr. of Education, joint Army and Navy Com. on Welfare and Recreation, chief radio, U.S. Office Edn., 1945—; tchr. music depts., several univs., 1919—; chief radio and television U.S. Office of Edn., Washington; mem. faculty Am. U., Washington, 1951. Decorated Officer de l'Intstruction Publique (France); Cross with palms of d'Academie (France). Served as pvt. and 2d lt., U.S. Army, 1917-19; 1st lt. O.R.C. Permanent exec. sec. Interparliamentary Union, 1945—. Recipient Nat. Assn. Ednl. Broadcasters award, 1958. Decorated Knight of Holy Sepulchre (Papal), 1950. Mem., sometime officer several profl. orgn., Pi Delta Epsilon (nat. pres. 1919-21), Sinfonia (hon.). Democrat. Roman Catholic, K.C. (4deg.). Clubs: Authors (London); Beethoven (Bonn, Germany); Conservatoire National (Paris); Cliff Dwellers (Chicago); Cosmos (Washington, D.C.); Columbia University (N.Y.C.); St. Nicholas (L.I., N.Y.). Author of radio programs; contbr. to musical jours.; inventor of musical appliances. Editor-in-chief Pictorial Encyclopedia. Associate editor N.A.E.B. Journal World Affairs Mag. Home: 1200 S. Cleveland, Arlington, Va.,; Thetford, Vt. Office: U.S. Office of Education, Washington 25. Died Oct. 27, 1962.

DUNKIN, DAMON DUFFIELD, mining engr.; b. Albia, Ia., May 10, 1875; s. John McFarland and Ida Ada (Haskell) D.; A.B., Woodland Coll., Mo., 1892; B.S., Sch. of Mines, U. of Mo., 1905; m. Dorothy Julian Perry, Aug. 10, 1910 (died 1925); m. 2d, Mertie Arnold, Mar. 4, 1928; 1 daughter, Ida Kate. Bookkeeper and credit man with wholesale house, to 1900; with bridge dept. I.C. R.R., 1902-04; supt. Midnight Mining Co., 1904-06; Moseley Lead & Zinc Co., 1906-07; supt. E. E. Dwight properties, 1907-08; prof. mining, Okla. Sch. of Mines, 1908-13; v.p. and gen. mgr., McAlester Coal & Coke Co., 1913-17; mgr. Coahuila Lead and Zinc Co., 1917-20, Standard Zinc Lead Co., 1920-21; pres. and gen. mgr. Silica Products Co., Inc., 1921—. Mem. Co. F, 3d Mo. Vols., Spanish-Am. War. Mason. Home: Harrison, Ark. Died Sept. 13, 1933.

DUNLAP, FREDERICK LEVY, consulting chemist; b. Chillicothe, O., May 16, 1870; s. Joseph Levy and Ann Marie (Clingman) Dunlap; student Ohio State University, 1888-89; B.Sc., University of Mich., 1892; D.Sc., Harvard, 1895; studied Yale, 1895-96; m. Eleanor Baldwin, of Worcester, Mass., Aug. 26, 1901; children—Rosalie (Mrs. Paul E. Boyle), Stanton Baldwin. Instr. industrial chemistry, Worcester Poly. Inst., 1896-1900; instr. chemistry, 1900-05, asst. prof. 1905-07, U. of Mich.; asso. chemist, Bur. Chemistry, Dept. Agr. 1907-12, and mem. Bd. of Food and Drug Inspection; consulting chemist, Victor Chem. Works, 1912-15. Mem. Am. Chem. Soc., A.A.A.S., Am. Inst. of Chem. Engineers, Am. Assn. Cereal Chemists, Sigma Xi, Chi Phi; foreign mem. Masaryk Acad. of Work, Czechoslovakia. Republican. Mem. Disciples of Christ Church. Club: Quadrangle (Chicago). Translator: Dr. Hugo Erdmann's Introduction to Chemical Preparations (from the German), 1900. Contbr. in organic chemistry, cereal chemistry, etc. Home: 5527 University Av., Chicago IL

DUNLAP, RENICK WILLIAM, agrl. scientist; b. Kingston, O. Oct. 21, 1872; s. Nelson J. and Elizabeth J. (Bell) D.; B.Sc., Ohio State U., 1895; Dr. Agriculture, Rhode Island State Coll. 1929; m. Maxine C. Cummins, June 9, 1897; children—Nelson Henderson (deceased in 1942), Mary Maxine. Farmer; president Columbus Wire Fence Company. Member Ohio Senate, 76th General Assembly; dairy and food commissioner of Ohio, 1907-11; secretary of agriculture, Ohio, 7 mos., 1915; asst. sec. of agr. by appointment of President Coolidge, April 1, 1925, reapptd. by President Hoover, Mar. 1929 (resigned Mar. 1933) apptd. mem. Com. on Recent Economic Changes by Sec. of Commerce Hoover, Mar. 1928; chmn. Am. delegation to World's Dairy Congress, London, 1928. Advocate of enforcement of pure food laws; author of the commercial feed stuff law of Ohio. Mem. Ohio Farm Bur., The Grange, Alpha Zeta, Kappa Sigma. Mem. Com. on Agr. Kiwanis Internat. Republican. Presbyn. Mason (Shriner). Clubs: Torch, Kiwanis. Named one of 48 leading alumni of O. State U., 1929; presented with testimonial by Am. Soc. Annual Production and other orgns., 1931, and portrait hung in Saddle and Sirloin Club, Chicago. Home: Kingston, Ohio. Died Mar. 2, 1945.

DUNN, BEVERLY CHARLES, army officer; b. Fort Monroe, Va., July 16, 1888; s. Beverly Wyly and Stella (Kilshaw) D.; B.A., U.S. Military Acad., 1910, Engr. Sch., U.S. Army, 1911-12, Army Indsl. Coll., 1927-28, Army War Coll., 1937-38; m. Helen Ward Fay, Nov. 22, 1916; children—Beverly Charles, William Wyly. Commd. 2d lt., engring. corps, 1910 and advanced through grades to brig. gen.; served with engr. installations doing flood control and river and harbor improvement work at Rock Island, Illinois, Memphis, Tenn., Pittsburgh, Pa., New Orleans, La., 1st N.Y. District, Seattle, Wash., Jacksonville, Fla. (intercoastal canal from Jacksonville to Miami); Isthmian Canal Commn. in Panama, supt. 13th Lighthouse District; military aide to the President; chief of finance div., Office Chief of Engrs.; dir., procurement branch, office of Asst. Sec. War, mem. Budget Adv. Bd.; troop duty with 1st battalion engrs., Washington Barracks, Washington, D.C., 3rd engrs., Philippines, 10th engrs. (forestry), Washington, D.C., 5th engrs. training regiment and 33d engrs., Ft. Hunphreys, Va., 209th engrs. Camp Sheridan, Ala., 28th engr. regiment (aviation), Marsh Field, Calif., commd. 6th engrs., Ft. Lawton, Wash.; chief engr. Supreme Hdqrs., Allied Expeditionary Force. Decorated D.S.M. with oak leaf cluster; comdr. Order Brit. Empire; Croix de Guerre, Legion d'Honneur (France and Belgium. Mem. Soc. Am. Military Engrs., Am. Soc. Civil Engrs. Clubs: Army and Navy, Chevy Chase (Washington, D.C.); University (N.Y.C.), N.Y. Athletic. Home: New York City NY Died Aug. 14, 1970; buried U.S. Mil. Academy, West Point NY

DUNN, CHARLES PUTNAM, engring. exec.; b. Marcus, Ia., Sept. 28, 1886; s. John Leander and Mary Ida (Putnam) D.; C.E., Wash. State Coll., 1909; m. Lillian Hilda Hulseman, Dec. 23, 1913; 1 son, Robert Charles. Chief engr. Portland (Ore.) Electric Power Co., 1919-29, Alcoa Power Co., Arvida, Que., Can., 1929-32; contractors chief engr. Transbay Constrn. Co., San Francisco, 1932-34; chief engr., Morrison-Knudsen Co., Inc. (took part in U.S. Navy Pacific Island projects), 1934-42, v.p., dir., 1942—; v.p., gen. mgr. Morrison-Knudsen Internat. Co., Inc., 1946—; pres., dir., Morrison-Knudsen Afghanistan, Inc., 1946—; pres., gen. mgr. Internat. Engring. Co., Inc., 1946—; pres. B.C. Internatn. Engring. Co., Ltd., 1947—, v.p., gen. mgr. Morrison-Knudsen, Ltd., San Francisco, 1933—. Cons. to govt. on spl. classified projects, World War II. Mem. Am. Soc. C.E. Home: 98 Selby Lane, Atherton, Cal. Office: 74 New Montgomery St., San Francisco. Died Jan. 1966.

DUNN, ELIAS BOUND, pres. Excellograph Co.; b. Brooklyn, March 23, 1855; ed. in public schools; entered U.S. Weather Bureau, 1874; steadily advancing to position of local forecast official at New York; had charge New York sta. 14 yrs. Predicted great rise in Ohio at Cincinnati in 1884 and floods in Mississippi, 1891. Sec. Vacuum Cleaner Co., 1905. Address: E. Orange, N.J.

DUNN, GANO, elec. engr.; b. New York, N.Y., Oct. 18, 1870; s. N. Gano and Amelia (Sillick) D.; B.S., Coll. City of New York, 1889; M.S., 1897; E.E., Columbia, 1891, hon. M.S., 1914; hon. D.Sc., Columbia 1938, Rutgers, 1938, N.Y. University, 1941; Doctor of Engineering, Lehigh University, 1942; D.Sc. (honorary), City College, New York, 1947; LL.D. (honorary), Bowdoin College, 1947; m. Julia Gardiner Gayley, Aug. 26, 1920 (died May 12, 1937). With the Western Union Telegraph Co., 1886-91, also Crocker-Wheeler Electric Mfg. Co., v.p. and chief engr., 1898-1911; v.p. in charge engring. and constrn., J. G. White & Co., v.p. and chief Inc., New York, 1911-13; pres. The J. G. White Engring. Corp. since 1913; trustee Greenwich Savings Bank; dir. Guaranty Trust Co.; trustee and dir. Panhandle Eastern Pipe Line Co., 1936-43; dir. Radio Corp. of Am., Nat. Broadcasting Co., R.C.A. Communications, Inc.; dir. Regional Plan Assn., Inc. President New York Elec. Soc., 1900-02, Am. Inst. Elec. Engrs., 1911-12, United Engring. Soc., 1913-16; chmn. The Engring. Foundation, 1915-16; chairman Nat. Research Council, 1923-28; v.p. Internat. Elec. Congress, 1911; U.S. delegate and mem. exec. com., World Power Co Conf., 1946-52; mem. N.Y. State Committee on Tech. Industrial Development since 1944. Member War Dept. Nitrate Commn., 1916-18; chmn. Visiting Com. Bur. of Standards since 1928; chmn. State Dept. special com. on submarine cables, 1918. Hon. mem. Assn. Iron and Steel Engrs., Am. Institute E.E. (pres. 1911-12). Fellow Inst. Radio Engrs., Royal Micros. Soc., A.A.A.S., N.Y. Acad. Sciences, N.Y. Micros. Soc.; member Pan-American Society (honorary president), Am. Society Mech. Engrs. (hon. mem. 1944), Am. Soc. C.E., British Instn. E.E. (hon. sec. for U.S.), Franklin Inst., Illuminating Engring. Soc., New York Hist. Soc., N.Y. Zoöl. Soc., Pilgrims (chmn. exec. committee, Optical Society of America, Horological Institute of America, Nat. Acad. Sciences, Am. Acad Arts and Sciences, Am. Philos. Soc. Mem. Sr., N.Y. Chamber Commerce. Mem. Visiting com. Harvard Engineering School. Trustee Barnard College; chmn. trustee Cooper Union for Advancement Sci. and Art; mem. President's Com. on Civil Service Improvement, 1939; mem. Patent Office Adv. Com., 1939-41; member mayors Bus. Advisory Com., City of New York; consultant on power and steel, Office of Production Management, member board trustees Catherdal of St. John the Divine, Grant Monument Association, member Business Advisory Council for Department of Commerce; member Science Advisory Board, 1932-36; president Society of Older Graduates of Columbia 1933-38; pres. Phi Beta Kappa Alumni in New York, 1940, Phi Beta Kappa Associates, 1944. War Dept. cons., 1947— mem. N.Y. State Univ. Commn., 1947. Awarded Townsend Harris medal, 1933, Edison medal, 1937; Hoover medal, 1939; Modern Pioneer Award, National Association of Manufactures, 1940; Pan-American Soc. Medal, 1947; Peter Cooper medal, 1950. Decorated Order Honor and Merit, Republic of Haiti, 1940. Clubs: Union Univ., Knickerbocker, Fencers, Columbia Univ., Engineers', Recess Century, Church, New York Yacht, Crusing Club of America, Tuxedo, Downtown (New York); Cosmos (Washington, D.C.). Contributor various papers on elec. and engring. subjects. Office: 80 Broad St., N.Y.C. 4. Died Apr. 10, 1953.

DUNNING, HENRY ARMITT BROWN, mfg. pharmacist; b. Denton, Md., Oct. 24, 1877; s. Charles Alexander and Ella M. (Redden) C.; Ph.G., Maryland Coll. of Pharmacy, 1897; hon. Pharm.M., Phila. Col. Pharmacy and Science, 1925; grad. work at Johns Hopkins U. and Johns Hopkins Hosp.; Pharm. D., Univ. of Maryland, 1908, D.Sc., 1941; hon. D.Sc., Washington., 1940; LL.D., Johns Hopkins U., 1942, College of Notre Dame of Maryland, 1958; married Beatrice Fitzgerald, Oct. 24, 1901 (died 1906); children—James H. Fitzgerald, Katherine Ellen (Mrs. H. Charles Kersten); m. 2d, Ethel Adams, 1908; children—Henry Armitt Brown, Charles Alexander. With Hynson, Westcott & Co., mgr. pharmacists, Baltimore, since 1894, purchased part ownership, 1901, chmn. of board, Hynson, Westcott & Dunning, Inc.; Formerly asso. prof. of chemistry, U. of Md. Trustee Maryland Acad. of Sciences, Home for Incurables; pres. American Found. for Pharmaceutical Education; v.p. Friends of Library, Johns Hopkins U. Served with 4th U.S. Vols. in Cuba, Spanish-Am. War. Donated organic chemistry lab. to U. of Md.; also contbr. to Johns Hopkins Hosp. and Y.M.C.A.; established 1st scholarships in pharmacy in the U.S.; established Science Bldg., Washington Coll., Chestertown, Md.; Kelly Meml. Bldg. completed, 1953, under his supervision; gift of $30,000.00 to Notre Dame Coll. Md. for scholarship meml. and $30,000.00 to Incarnation Parish House. Balt. to erect a chapel as memorial; subscriber to Nat. fellowship movement Johns Hopkins U., mem. alumni adv. com. and councillor to dept. of chemistry. Contributed to and supported nuclear research years before World War II resulting in the employment of the atomic bomb in war. Awarded Remington hon. medal, 1925; received First Alumni award as outstanding graduate, Department of Pharmacy, Univeristy of Maryland, 1950; recipient illuminated scroll, 1953, honoring all time services to all branches pharmacy; gold life membership card Am. Pharm. Assn. on retiremnt; new pharmacy bldg. U. Md. dedicated in his honor 1958. Apptd. 1st capt. of first United States Life Saving Corps by President Wilson. Pres. American Pharmacy Assn., Md. Pharm Assn.; chmn. bldg. plans. Am. Inst. of Pharmacy. Mem. Am. Chem. Soc. (chmn. of various coms.), Am. Inst. Chemists, Inc., Am. Drug. Mfrs. Assn. (chmn. scientific sect.), Rho Chi, St. George's Soc., U.S. Seniors Gold Assn. Quaker-Methodist. Clubs: Elkridge (Baltimore); Lake Placid; Batimore Country. Firm of Hunson, Westcott & Dunning, Inc., received Army-Navy "E" award, Apr. 12, 1943, Army and Navy production Star, 4 times. Home: 4215 Greenway, Baltimore 18, Office: Charles and Chase Sts., Balt. 1. Died July 26, 1962; buried Loudon Park Cemetery, Balt.

DUNNINGTON, FRANCIS PERRY, chemist; b. Baltimore, Mar. 3, 1851; s. William Augustus and Sarah Brice (Keener) D.; B.S., Univ. of Va., 1871, C.E., M.E., 1872; m. Marion S. Beale, of Fredericksburg, Va., Aug. 20, 1878; children—Sarah Brice (wife of Dr. Thomas H. Daniel), Margaret Bell (wife of Dr. Thomas Dwight Sloan), Francis Howison (dec.), Jean McDonald (wife of Dr. Rockwell Emerson Smith). Adj. prof. analyt. chemistry, 1872-1885, prof. analyt. and agrl. chemistry, 1885-1908, analyt. and industrial chemistry, 1908-19, U. of Va. Discovered and first pointed out universal distribution of titanic oxide in soils of the earth. Fellow A.A.A.S.; mem. British Assn. Adv. Sci., London Chemical Soc., Am. Chemical So., Am. Electrochem. Soc., Franklin Int., Phi Beta Kappa, Va. State Anti-Saloon League (exec. com.). Retired upon Carnegie Pension Fund. Contbr. to jours. Presbyn. Home: University, Va.

DUNTLEY, JOHN WHEELER, mfr.; b. Wyandotte, Mich., Aug. 16, 1863; ed. public schools; married. Began as foundryman, 1878; in ry. supply business, 1884-95; founded Chicago Pneumatic Tool Co., 1895, of which was pres. until 1909; organized ans was dir. Taite-Howard Pneumatic Tool Co., of London, Eng., 1898, to exploit products of the Chicago company, under its foreign patents; organized New York Air Compressor Co., 1899, at Arlington, N.J., and in 1900 merged it with Franklin (Pa.) Air Compressor Co., of which became v.p.; merged the Franklin Air Compressor Co., Chisholm & Moore Mfg. Co. (Cleveland), and the Boyer Machine Co. (Detroit) with the Chicago Pneumatic Tool Co., 1901; absorbed the Standard Pneumatic Tool Co., of Aurora, Ill., 1902, and consolidated the Taite-Howard Pneumatic Tool Co. with the Internat. Pneumatic Tool Co., of London, Eng., into the Consol. Pneumatic Tool Co., with offices at London and works at Fraserburgh, Scotland; absorbed the Phila. Pneumatic Tool Co., 1905, making it part of the Chicago Pneumatic Tool Col. From the first amalgamation of interest with the Chicago company was a mem. of the exec. bd. and a dir.; organized, 1909, and pres. Duntley Mfg. Co., mfrs. of Duntley Pneumatic Cleaners; pres. Libertad Mining and Smelting Co. (mines in Sonora, Mex.). Decorated with cross of Legion of Honor by President of Frances in 1900, in recognition of services in introducting pnuematic tools into gen. and practical use. Home: Chicago, Ill. Died 1921.

DUNWOODY, WILLIAM HOOD, flour mfr.; b. Westtown, Pa., Mar. 14, 1841; s. James and Hannah (Hood) D.; acad. edn. at Phila.; m. Katie L. Patten. Began business in Phila., 1864; moved to Minneapolis, Sept., 1869; was ifrst to introduce new process for milling wheat, and to export flour from Minneapolis direct to Europe; now v.p. Washburn-Crosby Co.; pres. Northwestern Nat. Bank, St. Anthony & Dakota Elevator Co., Barnum Grain Co.; v.p. Minneapolis Trust Co.; St. Anthony Elevator Co. Mem. Minneapolis and New York chambers of commerce. Home: Minneapolis, Minn. Died Feb. 8, 1914.

DU PUY, RAYMOND, civil engr.; b. Pittsburgh, Jan. 4, 1860; s. T. Haskins and Martha L. (Allen) D.; Georgetown U., D.C., 1876-77; m. Doretta Greve, Oct. 15, 1888. Began as water boy, M.K. & T. Ry., Tex., 1877; asst. engr. same rd. and M.P. Ry., 1881; chief engr. Tioga R.R. (br. N.Y., L.E. & W. Ry.), 1881-85; gen. supt. Minn. & Northwestern Ry., 1885-87; gen. mgr. C., St. P. & K.C. Ry., 1887-88; pres. Leavenworth & St. Joseph and DeKalb & Great Western rys., to 1896; gen. supt. C.G.W. ry., 1898-99; supt. D.L.&W. R.R., 1899-1900; v.p. and gen. mgr. St. Joseph & Grand Island Ry., 1900-05, Virginian Ry., Apr. 15, 1905—; pres. Virginian Ry. Co.; v.p. Industrial Finance Co., Norfolk (Va.) Terminal Ry. Co. Home: Norfolk, Va. Died May 14, 1933.

DURAN, WILLIAM FREDERICK, mech. engr.; b. Bethany, Conn., Mar. 5, 1859; s. William L. and Ruth (Coe) D.; U.S. Naval Acad., 1880; Ph.D., Lafayette Coll., 1888; LL.D., U. Cal., 1927; m. Charlotte Kneen, Nov. 23, 1883. Served in Engr. Corps, USN, 1880-87; prof. mech. engring. A. and M. Coll., Mich., 1887-91; prof. marine engring. Cornell U., 1891-1904; prof. mech. engring. Leland Stanford Jr. U., 1904-24; now prof. emeritus. Sci. Atachè A. Embassy, Paris and mem. Interallied Commn. on Inventions, 1918-19; mem. President's Aircraft Bd., 1925; adv. bd. engrs. Boulder Dam Project, 1929; chmn. Navy Depts. Spl. Com. in Airship Design and Constrn., 1935. Mem. NACA, 1915-33, 41-45, Nat. Research Council, 1915-45. Recipient Guggenheim medal award, 1935; John Fritz medal award, 1935;Franklin Inst. medal award, 1938; Presdl. Award of Merit, 1946; Wright Mem. Trophy, 1948. Fellow Am. Acad. Arts. and Scis., A.A.A.S., Royal Aero. Sco., Inst. Aero Schs. (hon.); mem. Nat. Acad. Scis. (J. J. Carty medalist 1944), Am. Philos. Soc., Soc. Naval Architects and Marine Engrs., Société Technique Maritime, Am. Soc. Naval Engrs. (life Mem., gold medalist), A.S.M.E. (hon. mem. medalist 1945; Assn. Italiana di Aerotecnica (hon.). Author Fundamental Principles of Mech., 1889; Resistance and Propulsion of Ships, 1898; Practical Marine Engineering, 1901; Motor Boats, 1907; Hydraulics of Pipe Lines, 1921; Biography of Robert Henry Thurston, 1929. Gen. editor Aerodynamic, Theory (6 vols.), 1934. Contbr. to engring. jours. Home: 379 Washington Av., Bklyn. 38. Died Aug. 9, 1958.

DURAND, CYRUS, engraver, inventor; b. Feb. 27, 1787; s. John and Rachel (Meyer) D.; m. Mrs. Phoebe Woodruff. Inherited his father's silversmithie, Newark, N.J., 1814; served with U.S. Army in War of 1812 for short time; made carding and weaving machines, 1815; patented "grammatical mirror," also machine to ornament columns, 1818; in engraving partnership with brother Asher, 1824-32; govt. engraver, Washington, D.C. Died Irvington, N.J., Sept. 18, 1868.

DURAND, E(DWARD) DANA, statistician; b. Romeo, Mich., Oct. 18, 1871; s. Cyrus Y. and Celia (Day) D.; A.B., Oberlin, 1893; Ph.D., Cornell, 1896; m. Mary Elizabeth Bennett, July 15, 1903; children—Dana Bennett, Bennett, Mary Cecelia, Eric. Legislative librarian N.Y. State Library, 1895-97; asst. prof. adminstrn. and finance, Leland Stanford Jr. U., 1898-99; sec. U.S. Industrial Commn., 1900-02; instr. economics, Harvard, 1902; spl. expert agt. U.S. Census Office on street rys. and elec. light plants, 1902; spl. examiner Bur. of Corps., 1903-07; deputy commr. of corps., 1907-09; dir. of the U.S. Census, 1909-13; prof. statistics agrl. economics Univ. of Minn., Sept. 1913-17; employed by U.S. Food Adminstrn., chiefly in Europe, 1917-19; adviser to food minister of Poland, 1919-21; chief Eastern European Div. U.S. Bur. Foreign and Domestic Commerce, 1921; chief of Div. of Statis. Research, Dept. of Commerce, 1924-29; statis. asst. to U.S. sec. commerce, 1929; chief economist U.S. Tariff Commn., 1930-35, mem. of commn. since Dec. 1935. Mem. Com. of Experts under Internat. Treaty on Econ. Statistics and United States Central Statistics Bd.; mem. joint U.S.-Canada econ. com. Member International Inst. Statistics, Inter-American Inst. Statistics, Am. Econ. Assn., Am. Statis. Assn. Author: Finances of New York City, 1898; The Trust Problem, 1915; Industry and Commerce of the United States, 1930. Contbr. on econ. and polit. subjects. Home: 3613 Norton Pl., Washington DC

DURAND, ELIAS JUDAH, botanist; b. Canandaigua, N.Y., Mar. 20, 1870; s. Rufus and Ann M. (Sisson) D.; A.B., Cornell U., 1893, D.Sc., 1895; m. Anna Louise Perry, Sept. 6, 1899 (died 1901); 2d, Sue G. Stone, July 24, 1917. Fellow, Cornell U., 1893-95; asst. in botany and asst. botanist in Expt. Sta., Cornell, 1895-96; instr. botany, Cornell, 1896-1910; asst. prof. botany, 1910-11, asso. prof., 1911-18, U. of Mo.; prof. botany, U. of Minn., 1918—. Home: St. Paul, Minn. Died Oct. 29, 1922.

DURAND, ELLE MAGIORIE, pharmacist, botanist; b. Mayenne, France, Jan. 25, 1794; s. André Durand; m. Polymnia Rose Ducatel, Nov. 20, 1820; m. 2d, Marie Antoinette Berauld, Oct. 25, 1825; at least 1 son. Apprenticed to pharmacist; pharmacist in French army, 1813-14; came to U.S., 1816; in pharmacy partnership with Edme Ducatel, Balt., 1817-24; made trip to France, 1824-25; began drugstore, Phila., 1825 (became profl. and social center of Phila.'s physicians and botanists); mem. Phila. Acad. Natural Scis., Am. Philos. Soc.; v.p. Coll. of Pharmacy, 1844; retired, 1851, devoted rest of life to bot. studies; transported his herbarium to Paris, France, 1868, gave it to Jardin des Plantes. Co-translator: Manual of Materia Medica and Pharmacy, 1829. Author: Memoirs of Francois André Michaux and Thomas Nuitall. Died Aug. 14, 1873.

DURAND, LOYAL, JR., former educator; b. Milw., July 12, 1902 s. Loyal and Lucia Relf (Kemper) D.; A.B., U. Wis., 1924, A.M., 1925, Ph.D., 1930; m. Dorothy Lillian Lee, Dec. 25, 1929; children—Loyal, Philip, Lee Mcv., Kemper B. Asst., Wis. Geol. Survey, summer 1926; instr. U. Wis., 1928-30, asst. prof., 1930-44; faculty U. Tenn., 1944, prof. geography, 1946-70. Vis. summer prof. Mankato (Minn.) Tchrs. Coll., 1929, Pa. State Coll., 1938, 40, 53, U. Utah, 1943, U. Wis., 1945, U. Colo., 1946, U. Cal. at Los Angeles, 1947, U. Neb., 1948,52, Central Coll. Edn., Ellensburg, Wash., 1950, 60, U. Wash., 1954, U. Ore., 1956, U. Mich., 1957, 61, 66, U. Hawaii, 1957-58, U. Mont., 1959, U. Minn., 1962; land planning cons. Nat. Resources Bd., 1934-35, spl. land planning cons., 1941; research and analysis div. O.S.S., Washington, 1944. Mem. Nat. Acad. Scis. (nat. research council com., adv. to Office Naval Research 1951-54), Am. Assn. U. Profs., Assn. Am. Geographers (v.p. 1951), Nat. Council Geography Tchrs. (exec. bd. 1947, v.p. 1949, pres. 1950), Wis. Acad. Scis., Arts and Letters (sec.-treas., editor 1935-44), Tenn. Acad. Sci., Phi Beta Kappa Assos., Phi Beta Kappa, Sigma Xi, Sigma Chi. Episcopalian. Author books including: World Economic Geography (with George T. Renner, C. Langdon White), 1951; World Geography, 1954; World Geography Today, 1960; Economic Geography, 1961. Geography editor: Macmillan social studies series; contbg. editor Economic Geography, 1947. Contbr. articles to geog. mags. Home: Knoxville TN Died Oct. 14, 1970.

DURANT, CHARLES PERSON, aeronaut; b. N.Y.C., Sept. 19, 1805; s. William and Elizabeth (Woodruff) D.; m. Elizabeth Hamilton Freeland, Nov. 14, 1837. First native Am. balloonist, made about 40 ascensions; printer, lithographer. Author: Algae and Corallines of the Bay and Harbor of New York; Exposition, or a New Theory of Animal Magnetism with a Key to the Mysteries, 1837. Died Mar. 2, 1873.

DURANT, WILLIAM CRAPO, mfr.; b. Boston, Mass., Dec. 8, 1861; s. William Clark and Rebecca Folger (Crapo) D.; g.s. Hon. H.H. Crapo, governor of Mich., 1864-68; ed. pub. schs., Flint, Mich.; m. Catherine Lederer, May 28, 1918. Founder Durant-Dort Carriage Co., Flint, 1886, and developed business reaching 150,000 carriages a yr.; organized the Buick Motor Car Co., 1905, The General Motors Co., 1908; purchased the Cadillac, Oakland, Oldsmobile and Northway motor cos., 1908-09; secured controlling interest in Gen. Motors Co., 1915, and in same yr. organized the Chevrolet Motor Co., an $80,000,000 corp., with plants in 11 prin. cities of U.S.; held controlling interest in Gen. Motors Co. and Chevrolet Motor Co. until 1920; organized Durant Motors, Inc., Jan. 1921; pres. Crown Point Products, Inc., Pomeroy-Day Land Co.; v.p. C.V.S. Mfg. Co.; dir. Huntman Stabilizer Corp. Republican. Presbyterian. Clubs: Detroit, Detroit Athletic, Flint Country; Calumet, Lotos (New York). Home: 45 Gramercy. Office: 230 Park Av., New York, N.Y. Died Mar. 18, 1947.

DURFEE, WILLIAM FRANKLIN, civil and mech. engr.; b. New Bedford, Mass., Nov. 15, 1833; ed. at home and Lawrence Scientific School, Harvard; established and engr. and architect, 1853; city surveyor, New Bedford, 5 years; mem. Mass. legislature, 1861; examined iron ores of Lake Superior, 1862, with reference to their suitability for steel manufacture, and erected exptl. works where ingots of steel were produced from which were rolled, May 25, 1865, the first steel rails ever made in U.S.; built at Wyandotte, Mich., first analytical laboratory built as adjunct to steel works in U.S.; built at Ansonia, Conn., first successful furnaces for refining copper by gaseous fuel ever erected in U.S.; was mgr. U.S. Mitis Co.; etc. Consulting engr. and expert in patent causes. Home: West New Brighton, N.Y. Died 1899.

DURHAM, CALEB WHEELER, inventor; b. Tunkhannock, Pa., Feb. 6, 1846; s. Alpha and Elizabeth (Riggs) D.; attended Williston Acad. (Mass.), 1866; studied civil engring. U. Mich. at Ann Arbor, 1867-69; m. Clarissa Safford Welles, May 28, 1873. Served with 42d Regt., Pa. Militia, 1861-62, with 195th Pa. Volunteers, 1862-64; with Phila. & Reading R.R., 1864-66; employed engring. dept. several railroads including N.Y.C. R.R., 1869-73; became civil engr. specializing in sanitation, Chgo., 1873; invented hot-air heater, 1875, manufactured heater for brief period; devised spl. fittings for drainage pipes, 1880; devised house drainage method later known as Durham System; established Durham House Drainage Co., Chgo., 1881; built drainage system for entire town of Pullman (Ill.); moved business to Peekskill, N.Y., 1883; designed installations for Carnegie Hall, N.Y.C., also Captiol Bldg., Washington, D.C.; mem. Engrs. Club N.Y. Died Peekskill, Mar. 28, 1910; buried Peekskill.

DURHAM, HENRY WELLES, civil engr.; b. Chicago, Sept. 15, 1874; s. Caleb Wheeler and Clarissa Safford (Welles) D.; father inventor of Durham system of house drainage now universally employed in large bldgs.; C.E., Sch. of Mines (Columbia), 1895; m. Josephine Belden Trowbridge, Oct. 1, 1903; 1 dau., Elisabeth Trowbridge. Asst. on surveys for N.Y. Rapid Transit Commn. and with U.S. Geol. Survey, 1895-98, Nicaragua Canal Surveys 1898-1900; asst. engr. in charge of constrn., New York Subway, 1900-04; resident engr. in charge of design and constrn. of all municipal improvements in City of Panama for U.S. Isthmian Canal Commn., 1904-07; resident engr. in charge of surveys and constrn. of Cape Cod Canal, 1907-12; chief engr. of highways Manhattan Borough, 1912-15; engineer, Bergeon Co., N.J., 1916. Mem. Co. I, 7th Inf., N.G.N.Y., 1900-17; Mexican border service, 1916; commd. capt., Engr. R.C., 1917; promoted maj., Engrs. U.S. Army, Dec. 10, 1917, assigned command 41st Engrs.; took battn. overseas, Feb. 25, 1918; in charge forestry operations near St. Dizier, France, advance section, A.E.F., till July, then on staff Brig. Gen. Jadwin, Tours, France, in chg. road maintenance in A.E.F. till July 1919; discharged Oct. 17, 1919; in Peru on studies and plans for sanitation of Lima, Cuzco and other cities, 1920-22; designs, etc., N.Y., Mass. and N.C., 1923-24; engaged in sanitation and paving for govt. of Nicaragua, 1925-30; highway studies in Guatemala, 1931-32; municipal improvements in Barranquilla, Colombia, 1933-34; mine valuation in El Salvador, 1935; paving engr., New York World's Fair 1939, 1936-39; building first highway in Paraguay, 1939-42; C.E., research, Mil. Intelligence, Office Chief of Engrs., U.S. Army, 1943-45. Del. to Third Internat. Road Congress, London, 1913; studied European street paving for President McAneny and Mayor Gaynor; mem. Am. Soc. C.E., Boston Soc. C.E., Permanent Internat. Assn. Road Congresses, A.A.A.S., Am. Road Builders Assn., Am. Public Works Assn., Municipal Engrs. of N.Y., Internat. Engring. Congress, San Francisco, 1915, Soc. Am. Mil. Engrs., Reserve Officers' Assn. of U.S. Mil. Order World Wars, New York Soc. Mil. and Naval Officers of World Wars, Sociedad de Ingenieros del Peru; fellow Am. Geog. Soc. Officier du Merite Agricole, Sept. 1919, for work on restoration of French highways; Conspicuous Service Cross, N.Y. State, also 7th Regt. Cross (15 yrs. service). Col., Army of the U.S. Hon. Res. (ret.). Clubs: Columbia University, Beta Theta Pi. Author: Street Paving and Maintenance in European Cities, 1915; various monographs and articles. Home: Halfway House Sandwich MA

DURY, CHARLES, entomologist; b. Cincinnati, Nov. 14, 1847; s. Francis W. and Louisa M. (Gibson) D.; pub. sch. edn.; m. Pearl A. Welch, of Cincinnati, Oct. 28, 1896. Mem. Ohio Acad. Science (pres. 1907), Cincinnati Soc. Natural History (pres. 1897-98 and 1914-22), Cuvier Press Club (trustee 1906—). Contbr. numerous papers on entomology and ornithology to proc. scientific socs. Address: 537 Ridgeway Av., Cincinnati, O.

DURYEA, CHARLES EDGAR, automobile inventor, mfr.; b. nr. Canton, Ill., Dec. 15, 1861; s. George Washington and Louisa Melvina (Turner) D.; m. Rachel Steer, 1884; children—Rhea Edna, Grace Louise Merle Junius. Owner bicycle bus., Peoria, Ill.; invented 1st Am. car, 1893, improved car (used 4 cycle water-cooled motor, clutch and gear transmission, pneumatic tires) by 1905; his car won over an imported fgn. model in Chgo. Times Herald race, 1895; pres. Am. Motor League; co-owner Duryea Motor Wagon Co., Springfield, Ill., until 1898; owner Duryea Power Co., Reading, Pa., circa 1900-14. Author: The Handbook of the Automobile, 1906. Died Phila., Sept. 28, 1938; buried Ivy Hill Cemetery, Phila.

DURYEA, EDWIN, civil engr.; b. Craigville, Orange Co., N.Y., July 12, 1862; s. Edwin and Hannah (Rumsey) D.; B.C.E., Cornell U., 1883, C.E., 1890; m. Roberta Vincent Taylor, of Ithaca, N.Y., Dec. 13, 1888. Began with engring. dept. N.P. Ry., 1883; engaged in constrn. of bridges over Miss., Mo. and Ohio rivers and in Kan. and Mich., until 1891; engr. or supt. for contracting firms, Chicago and New York, 1891-95; resident engr. Brooklyn end Williamsburg Suspension Bridge (N.Y. City), 1895-1900; in pvt. practice, New York, 1900-02; chief engr. Bay Cities Water Co., San Francisco, and its allied interests, 1902-10; engr. in charge South San Joaquin (Calif.) Irrigation Dist., 1909-13; mem. Duryea, Haehl & Gilman since 1907. Mem. Com. of 40 to advise on rehabilitation of San Francisco after the great fire, 1906. Mason (32deg.). Home: Palo Alto, Calif. Address: Humboldt Bank Bldg., San Francisco.

DUSCHAK, LIONEL HERMAN, univ. prof., cons. engineer; b. Buffalo, N.Y., Sept. 25, 1882; s. Adolf and Agnes Hannah (Day) D.; A.B., U. of Mich., 1904; M.A., Ph.D., Princeton, 1908; m. Frances Eschenburg, Oct. 13, 1909. Instr. in chemistry, Princeton, 1907-09; research engr. Corning (N.Y.) Glass Works, 1909-13; chem. engr. U.S. Bur. Mines, in charge Expt. Sta., Berkeley, Calif., 1915-21; cons. practice since 1921; prof. metallurgy, U. of Calif., since 1938. Mem. Am. Chem. Soc., Am. Am. Inst. Mining and Metall. Engrs., Pacific Assn. of Cons. Engrs., A.A.A.S., Phi Gamma Delta, Theta Tau, Sigma Xi, Tau Beta Pi. Republican. Unitarian. Clubs: Engineers (San Francisco); Commonwealth Club of Calif., Faculty. Home: 86 Tamalpais Rd., Berkeley 8, Calif. Office: Hobart Bldg., San Francisco, Calif. Died Nov. 27, 1948; buried at Santa Barbara, Calif.

DUSHANE, GRAHAM (PHILLIPS), univ. dean; b. South Bend, Ind., July 20, 1910; s. Donald and Harriette Graham (McLelland) D.; A.B., Wabash Coll., 1930; Dr. of Laws (honorary), 1958; Ph.D., Yale, 1934; m. Susan Elizabeth White, September 5, 1933; children—Linda (Mrs. Robert G. Knechtel), Harriette Graham, Susan (Mrs. Michael J. Tihila). Research associate State University of Iowa, 1934-35; NRC fellow Stanford, 1935-36; instr. zoology U. Chgo., 1936-41, asst. prof., 1941-45, asso. prof., 1945-46; prof. Stanford, 1946-56; editor Science, 1956-62; dean grad. scis., chmn. dept. biology Vanderbilt University, 1962—. Mem. sci. information council Nat. Science Foundation, 1958-60, 1962—. Mem. adv. council American Cancer Soc., 1958—. Fellow A.A.A.S.; member American Society Zoologists, Am. Assn. Anatomists, Sigma Xi, Phi Beta Kappa, Kappa Sigma, Gamma Alpha. Clubs: Cosmos (Washington, D.C.). Received Campbell award Wabash Coll., 1930, award for excellence in undergrad. tchg., U. Chgo., 1945; Alumni Merit award Wabash Coll., 1962. Trustee Biol. Abstracts, 1959—. Contbr. papers and reviews on development of pigmentation, nervous system and behavior to jours. and books. Home: 2248 Wellesley, Palo Alto, Cal. Died July 19, 1963; buried Los Angeles.

DUSHMAN, SAUL phys. chemist; b. Rostov, Russia, July 12, 1883; s. Samuel and Olga (Hurwitz) D.; came to America, 1891; B.A., U. of Toronto, Can., 1904, Ph.D., 1912; hon. D.Sc., Union Coll., Schenectady, N.Y., 1940; m. Amelia Gurofsky, May 1, 1907 (died May 6, 1912); m. 2d, Anna Leff June 28, 1914; 1 dau., Beulah. Demonstrator electro-chemistry, U. of Toronto, 1904-09; lecturer, 1909-12; with Research Lab., Gen. Electric Co., Schenectady, N.Y., since 1912, asst. dir., 1928-48; dir. research div. Edison Lamp Works, Harrison, N.J., 1922-25; research consultant since 1950. Mem. Am. Phys. Soc., Am. Chem. Soc. Naturalized citizen of U.S., 1917. Jewish religion. Author: High Vacuum, 1923; Elements of Quantum Mechanics, 1938; Scientific Foundations of Vacuum Technique, 1949; Fundamentals of Atomic Physics, 1951; also numerous tech. articles. Office: Gen. Electric Research Lab., P.O. Box 1088, Schenectady, N.Y. Died July 7, 1954; buried Temple Gates of Heaven Cemetery, Schenectady, N.Y.

DUTCHER, WILLIAM, ornithologist; b. Stelton, N.J., Jan. 20, 1846; pub. sch. edn. Pres. Nat. Assn. of Audubon Socs.; fellow A.A.A.S., Am. Ornithologists' Union, N.Y. Acad. Sciences, N.Y. Zoöl. Soc., Royal Soc. for Protection of Birds (London). Home: Plainfield, N.J. Died July 2, 1920.

DUTTON, WALTER C(URTIS), horticulturist; b. Hockingport, O., July 27, 1889; s. Edwin Augustus and Lethe Rebecca (Curtis) D.; student Ohio U., 1905-08; B.S. in Agr., Ohio State U., 1912; M.S., Mich. State U., 1925; m. Marie Graham England, Oct. 15, 1913; children—Charles Edwin, Nancy Bartlett (Mrs. William B. Rowe). Asst. horticulturist, research asso. horticulture Agrl. Expt. Sta., Mich. State U., 1913-36; horticulturist, dir. field research, asst. dir. agrl. chem. research Dow Chem. Co., Midland, Mich., 1936-57; mem. agrl. bd. NRC, 1956-59, chmn. com. agrl. pests, 1956—. Recipient award North Central Weed Control Conf. Mem. Agrl. Research Inst. (pres. 1956-57), Am. Soc., Delta Theta Sigma. Club: Michigan State University. Home: 523 Bailey St., East Lansing, Mich. Died Nov. 2, 1962.

DUVAL, CHARLES WARREN, pathologist; b. Annapolis, Md., Nov. 28, 1876; s. George W. and Madelaine J. (Stump) D.; A.B., St. John's Coll., Annapolis, 1897; M.D., U. of Pa., 1903; m. Hilda von Stuckradt, Mar. 19, 1906. Rockefeller fellow, U. of Pa., 1902; 1st asst. pathologist, Boston City Hosp., 1905; dir. pathology, Montreal Gen. Hosp., 1908; lecturer on pathology, McGill U., 1906; prof. pathology and bacteriology, Tulane U., since 1909; dir. pathol. labs. of Charity and Presbyn. hosps., New Orleans. Mem. Am. Coll. Physicians. Soc. Experimental Biology and Medicine, Am. Acad. Science, Soc. Am. Pathologists, Soc. Am. Bacteriologists, Am. Federation Allied Sciences, Soc. Experimental Pathology, A.M.A., Nu

Sigma Nu, Phi Delta Theta. Mason (32deg). Contbr. research articles on dysentery, tuberculosis, leprosy, scarlet fever. Home: 8 Richmond Pl. Office: 1430 Tulane Av., New Orleans LA*

DUVEL, JOSEPH WILLIAM TELL, crop technologist; b. Wapakoneta, O., Nov. 16, 1873; s. August and Amanda (Myers) B.; B.Sc., Ohio State U., 1897; D.S., U. of Mich., 1902; m. Elva Smith, May 11, 1904; children—Maxine, William August. Asst. botanist, Ohio Agrl. Expt. Sta., 1898-99; with Bur. Plant Industry, U.S. Dept. of Agr., Washington, 1902-18, crop technologist in charge of grain standardization investigations 1910-18; with U.S. Grain Corp., New York, 1918-20; grain mcht., Winnipeg, Can., 1920-21; U.S. grain exchange supervisor, Chicago, 1922-25; chief, Commodity Exchange Adminstrn., Washington, D.C., 1925-42; retired March 1, 1942. Fellow A.A.A.S., mem. Washington Botanical Soc., Potomac Grange, Washington Biologists' Field Club, Kappa Sigma, Pi Gamma Mu; hon. life mem. of Royal Agrl. Soc. of New South Wales, Australia. Club: Cosmos. Home: 1225 Decatur St., N.W. Office: U.S. Dept. Agr., Washington, D.C. Died Jan. 8, 1946.

DWIGHT, ARTHUR SMITH, mining and metall. engr.; b. Taunton, Mass., Mar. 18, 1864; s. Benjamin Pierce and Elizabeth Fiske (Dwight) S.; assumed maternal surname on coming of age—authorized by Kings' County (N.Y.) Court, Dec. 15, 1886; grad. Poly. Inst., Brooklyn, 1882; E.M., Sch. of Mines (Columbia), 1885, hon. M.Sc., 1914, hon. D.Sc., 1929; m. Jane Earl Reed, June 4, 1895 (died Feb. 1929); m. 2d, Mrs. Anne Howard Chapin. Mining and metallurgical work, 1885-1906, in charge smelting operations at Pueblo and Leadville (Colo.), El Paso (Tex.), Argentine (Kan.), San Luis Potosi and Cananea (Mexico); cons. practice and directing business of Dwight & Lloyd cos., New York, since 1906; pres. Dwight & Lloyd Sintering Co.; pres. Dwight & Lloyd Metall. Co. Commd. major engrs., U.S.R., Jan. 23, 1917; assisted organizing 1st Reserve Engrs., later 11th Engrs., the first A.E.F. unit in action in France (Cambrai); served in Somme sector, Cambrai offensive, Lys defensive, N. Picardy sector, Meuse-Argonne offensive; in France 22 mos., on British front 9 mos., comdg. 1st Batt., 11th Engrs.; later on spl. duty as metall. consultant French companies; engr. salvage officer A.E.F.; now colonel engrs., U.S.R. (inactive); vice chmn. mineral advisory com. Army and Navy Munitions Board. Alumni trustee Columbia U., 1915-21. Mem. American Institute Mining and Metallurgical Engineers (life, ex-pres.; Douglas medallist), Mining and Metallurgical Society America, Society American Mil. Engrs. (ex-pres. N.Y. Post), Mass. Society of Mayflower Descendants, Mil. Order of the World War, Am. Legion, Great Neck Post, American Vets Assn., Institution Mining and Metallurgy of London (hon.), Mass. Soc. of the Cincinnati, Sigma Xi, Tau Beta Pi; hon. mem. Soc. Engineers of Louvain Univ., Belgium. Citation by Gen. Pershing; Order of Purple Heart (U.S.); Companion D.S.O. (British); Chevalier Legion d'Honneur (French). Republican. Episcopalian (hon. Warden All Saints Church, Great Neck). Clubs: University, Engineers', Mining, Columbia Univ., North Hempstead Country, Hobe Sound Yacht (vice commodore), Jupiter Island; Army and Navy (Washington); Union Interalliee (Paris). Co-inventor with R.L. Lloyd of Dwight and Lloyd system of ore treatment. Home: West Shore, New Fairfield, Conn. and Beau Rivage, Hobe Sound, Fla. Office: 19 Rector St., New York, N.Y. Died Apr. 1, 1946.

DWIGHT, EDWIN WELLES, M.D.; b. Auburn, N.Y., Aug. 11, 1863; s. Henry Williams and Mary Jane (Winslow) D.; M.D., Harvard, 1891. Engaged in practice in Boston, 1891—; asst. commr. pub. instns., Boston, 1895-96; med. dir. N.E. Mut. Life Ins. Co.; formerly instr. legal medicine and surgery, Harvard Med. Sch., prof. legal medicine, Tufts Coll. Med. Sch., asst. visiting surgeon Boston City Hosp. Conglist. Democrat. Author: Medical Jurisprudence, 1903; Toxicology, 1904. Home: Marshfield, Mass. Died Jan. 14, 1931.

DWIGHT, THOMAS, anatomist; b. Boston, Oct. 13, 1843; s. Thomas and May Collins (Wareen) D.; A.B., Harvard, 1866, M.D., 1867, A.M., 1872; studied abroad 2 yrs.; (LL.D., Georgetown, 1889); m. Sarah C. Pasigi, Sept. 18, 1883. Instr. comparative anatomy, Harvard, 1872-73; lecturer and prof. anatomy, Bowdoin, 1872-76; instr. in histology, 1874-83, instr. topog. anatomy, 1880-83, Parkma prof. anatomy, 1883—, Harvard, succeeding Dr. Oliver Wendell Holmes. Editor Boston Med. Journal, 1873-78; gave course of lectures, Lowell Inst., on "Mechanism of the Bone and Muscle," 1884. Author: Anatomy of the Head, 1876; Variations of the Bones the Hand and Foot, 1907. Home: Nahant, Mass. Died 1911.

DWIGHT, WILLIAM BUCK, geologist, educator; b. Constantinople, Turkey, May 22, 1833; s. Harrison Gray Otis (Am. missionary) and Elizabeth (Barker) D.; came to U.S. permanently, 1849; grad. Yale, A.B. 1854, A.M. 1857, B.S. 1859, Union Theol. Sem., 1857; m. Nov. 17, 1859, Eliza Howe Schneider (died 1901). Founder and prin. 1859-65; Englewood (N.J.) Female Inst.; in mining explorations Va. and Mo., 1865-67; taught at West Point, N.Y., 1867-70; asso. prin. and prof. natural sciences, State Normal Sch., New Britian Conn., 1870-78; prof. natural history, dept. of geology and mineraology, and curator mus., Vassar Coll. Apptd. univ. examiner in geology, State of N.Y., 1894. Invented and patented, 1891, a rockslicing machine for scientific section of minerals; awarded bronze medal at Paris Exp'n, 1900. Fellow A.A.A.S.; original fellow Am. Soc. Naturalists and Geol. Soc. of America. Home: Poughkeepsie, N.Y. Died 1906.

DYAR, HARRISON GRAY, biologist; b. New York, Feb. 14, 1866; s. Harrison Gray and Eleonora Rosella (Hannum) D.; B.S., Mass. Inst. Tech., 1889; A.M. Columbia, 1894, Ph.D., 1895; m. Zella Peabody, Oct. 14, 1889; children—Dororthy, Otis Peabody; m. 2d, Wellesca Pollock Allen, Apr. 26, 1921; children—Roshan Allen, Harrison Golshan, Wallace Joshan. Asst. bacteriology, Columbia, 1895-97; custodian of lepidoptera, U.S. Nat. Mus., 1897—; entomol. asst., Bur. of Entomology, U.S. Dept. of Agriculture, 1915-17. Capt. Santiary Dept., Organized Reserves, U.S.A., 1924. Co-author: (with L. O. Howard and the late Frederick Knab) The Mosquitoes of North and Central America and the West Indies (Carnegie Inst., Washington), 1912-17. Editor Journal of the N.Y. Entomol. Soc., 1904-07. Procs. of Entomol. Soc., Washington, 1909-12. Home: Washington, D.C. Died Jan. 19, 1929.

DYCHE, HOWARD EDWARD prof. elec. engring.; b. Spring Valley, O., Jan. 19, 1884; s. Samuel Edward (M.D.) and Flora Alice (Carey) D.; grad. high sch., Spring Valley, 1901; M.E. in E.E., 1910; 1 son Howard Edward. Engr., ry. dept. Westinghouse Electric & Mfg. Co., 1906-11 prof. elec. engring., Westinghouse Tech. School, Pittsburgh, 1909-11; instr. in mathematics and physics, U. of Pittsburgh, 1911, instr. in elec. engring., 1912-14, asst. prof. and elec. engring., 1914-17, asso. prof., 1917-19, prof. and head of dept., 1919—; director of graduate work in industry, 1927-52, acting dean School of Engring. and Mining, 1950; cons. engr., registered profl. engr. Commonwealth of Pa., Asst. dir. war training, U. of Pittsburgh, 1918 and 1944. Member Am. Inst. E.E. (past chmn. Pittsburgh, sect.). Soc. Promotion Engring. Edn., Sigma Xi, Sigma Tau, Eta Kappa Nu. Lutheran. Mason (32 deg.). Clubs: University, Faculty. Home 317 South Av., Wilkinsburg, Pa., and Spring Valley, O., Address: University of Pittsburgh Died Apr. 11, 1954; buried Homewood Cemetery, Pitts.

DYCHE, LOUIS LINDSAY, zoölogist; b. Berkely Springs, W.Va., Mar. 20, 1857; s. Alexander and Mary (Reilly) D.; B.A., B.S., U. of Kan., 1884, A.M., 1886, M.S., 1888. Asst. prof. zoölogy, 1885-86, prof. comparative anatomy, 1886-90, prof. zoölogy and curator of birds and mammals, 1890-1900, prof. systematic zoölogy and taxidermy and curator of birds and mammals, 1900—, U. of Kan. Has made 23 scientific expdns. and hunted all over N. America, from Mexico to Alaska and including Greenland and the arctic regions, resulting in securing for U. of Kan. one of the largest and finest collections of large N. Am. mammals in the world. State game and fish warden of Kans., Dec. 1, 1909. Home: Pratt, Kan. Died Jan. 20, 1915.

DYER, FRANK LEWIS, mech. and elec. expert and inventor; b. Washington, D.C., Aug. 2, 1870; s. George Washington and Kate (Huntress) D.; ed. pub. schs., and Columbia (now George Washington) U. Law Sch.; m. Annie Augusta Wadsworth, 1892; children—John Wadsworth, Frank Wadsworth; m. 2d, Isabelle Dawson Archer, 1924; m. 3d, Eliza J. Martin, 1939. Practiced patent law, Washington, 1892-97, New York, 1897-1903; gen. counsel Edison interest, 1903-08; exec. officer T. A. Edison's indus. corps., 1908-1912; pres. Gen. Film Co., 1912-14; treas. Condensite Co. of America, 1910-20; officer and dir. numerous corps.; has secured over 100 patents in various arts, including talking books for the blind; practicing from 1914 as mech. and elec. expert. Democrat. Mason. Author: Edison—His Life and Inventions (with T. Commerford Martin), 1910-29. Home: Ventnor, N.J. Died June 4, 1941.

DYER, LEONARD HUNTRESS, inventor; b. Washington, D.C., May 13, 1873; s. George Washington and Kate (Huntress) D.; student Corcoran Scientific Sch., Columbian (now George Washington) U.,1893; Georgetown U. Law Sch., 1895. Nat. Law Sch., Washington, D.C., 1896— D.Sc., Rollins College, Winter Park Fla., 1949; m. Josephine Duncan, July 10, 1905; children—Duncan (dec.), Katherine Huntress (Mrs. Elmer Puddington); m. 2d, Jessica Hofstetter, Oct. 14, 1927. Was admitted to D.C. bar, 1894; practiced patent law with brother, Frank L. Dyer, until 1897; practiced alone, 1897-1903. in N.Y. City, unitl 1917. Commd. lt. U.S.N.R.F., Mar. 6, 1917, and apptd. comdr. 2d Sec., 3d Naval Dsit., hdqrs. Bridgeport, Conn.; also assigned as comdr. Squadron 6, 3d Naval Dist. Invented an automobile with a direct drive, sliding transmission, selective gear shift and unit power plant; more than 100,000,000 automobiles have been made embodying this invention; also a landscape painter. Fellow Am. Geog. Soc. Mem. Soc. Colonial Wars, Spanish Inst. of Florida. Clubs: New York Yacht, University of Winter Park (Fla.); Anglers' Yacht. Author: The Evolution of the Motor Vehicle as Shown by Patents, 1955. Home: Winter Park Fla. Died Nov. 16, 1955.

DYSTON, JAMES LINDSAY, educator, geologist; b. Lancaster, Pa., May 23, 1912; s. Herbert Pannebecker and Mary Emma (Lindsay) D.; B.S., Lafayette Coll., 1933; M.A., Cornell U., 1935, Ph.D., 1938; m. Lolita Gill Brown, Oct. 10, 1942; children—Dolores Gill, Deborah Ann. Instr. geology Cornell U., 1935-38; instr. geology, phys. scis. Colgate U., 1938-41; ranger-naturalist Nat. Park Service, summers 1935-40, 46, 48; asso. prof. geology Hofstra Coll., 1946-47; mem. faculty Lafayette Coll. 1947—, prof., 1948-64, Markle professor, 1964—, head dept. of goelogy and geography, 1948—; lectr., cons. geologist, 1947—; cooperating geologist Pa. Geol. Survey, 1952—. Chmn. geology selection com. Fulbright Awards, Nat. Acad. Scis.-NRC, 1961-62, Mission 66 com., 1957-65. Served to lt. col. AUS, 1941-46; col. Res. Decorated Legion of Merit; recipient Thomas L. Jones superior teaching award Lafayette Coll., 1956, 57, 64, Distinguished Alumnus citation, 1964. Fellow Geol. Soc. Am., Am. Geog. Soc., A.A.A.S. (council 1958-60); mem. Pa. Acad. Sci. (past pres.; dir.), Nat. Assn. Geology Tchrs., Am. Alpine Club, Am. Geol. Inst. (chmn. mission 66 com. 1957—), Glaciological Soc., Arctic Inst. N.A. (asso.), Sigma Xi, Phi Kappa Phi. Author: The World of Ice (Phi Beta Kappa Sci. award 1962), 1962; also articles. Home: 32 McCartney St., Easton, Pa. Died Mar. 1967.

DYKSTRA, JOHN, indsl. exec.; b. nr. Stiens, Netherlands, Apr. 16, 1898; s. Theodore and Nellie (DeVries) D.; came to U.S., 1902, naturalized, 1919; mech. engring. course, Cass Tech. Sch., nights, 1915-17; corr. course, LaSalle Extension U., 1921-26; m. Marion S. Hyde, Mar. 2, 1918; children—Betty H. (Mrs. John Steele), John O. Diemaker, later mgr. body plant, Hudson Motor Co., Detroit, 1919-34; with Oldsmobile Corp., Lansing, Mich., 1934-47, works mgr., 1942-47; asst. to v.p. charge mfg., Ford Motor Co., 1947, gen. mgr. plants in Detroit, Canton (O.). and Cincinnati, 1947-49, v.p. aircraft engine, tractor and machined products group 1950-53, vice pres. and group executive, Dearborn, 1953-56, group v.p., Dearborn, 1957-58; v.p. mfg., v.p. def. products group 1958-61, pres., 1961-63, dir., from 1958; dir. Philco Corp. Mem. Society Automotive Engrs. Clubs: Detroit Athletic, Recess, Detroit Golf. Home: Birmingham MI Died Mar. 2, 1972; buried Oakview Cemetery, Royal Oak MI

EADS, JAMES BUCHANAN, engr., inventor; b. Lawrenceburg, Ind., May 23, 1820; s. Thomas C. and Ann (Buchanan) E.; LL.D. (hon.), U. Mo., 1877; m. Martha Dillion; m. 2d, Eunice Eads, 1857; 5 children. Inventor diving bell; became partner in steamboat salvaging firm, 1842; called by Pres. Lincoln to Washington, D.C., 1861, recommended means of employing Western rivers for Union war operations, undertook constrn. of fleet of steam-powered armor-plated gunboats which he had proposed, built total of 14 armoured vessels (in record time), featuring his own patented ordnance inventions; constructed Eads Bridge (steel and masonry bridge across Mississippi at St. Louis, best known achievement), incorporated engring. features conquering difficulties considered insuperable by prominent authorities of day, 1867-74; reputation as hydraulic engr. established by river control work completed 1879 at South Pass in Mississippi River, controlled placement of river's sediment so as to keep channel clean; improved harbor facilities at Liverpool (Eng.), Toronto (Ont., Can.), Tampico and Veracruz (Mexico); mem. Am. Soc. C.E., v.p., 1882; fellow A.A.A.S.; mem. Brig. Instn. Civil Engrs., Brit. Assn.; recipient Albert medal from Brit. Soc. for Encouragement of Art, Manufacture and Commerce, 1884. Died Nassau, Bahama Islands, Mar. 16, 1887.

EARDLEY, ARMAND JOHN, educator; b. Salt Lake City, Oct. 25, 1901; s. John Alma and Elizabeth Emma (Brown) E.; A.B., U. Utah, 1927, D.Sc. (hon.), 1970; Ph.D., Princeton U., 1930; m. Norma Ashton, May 6, 1930; 1 son, Michael John. Mem. faculty U. Mich., 1930-51, prof., dir. geology field work, 1943-49; mem. faculty U. Utah, 1951-72, chmn. Div. of Earth Scis., Coll. Mines and Mineral Industries, 1951-54, prof. geology, prof. emeritus, 1965-72, dean coll. of mines and mineral industries, 1954-65. Distinguished lectr. Am. Assn. Petroleum Geologists, 1951; Reynolds lectr. U. Utah, 1955; nat. lectr. Sigma Xi, 1957. Recipient Distinguished award in sci. Utah Acad. Sci., Arts and Letters, 1956; Distinguished Achievement award Am. Fedn. Mineral Soc., 1968. Fellow Geol. Soc. Am.; mem. Am. Assn. Petroleum Geologists, Geophys. Union of Am., Nat. Assn. Geology Tchrs. (pres. 1962-63), Am. Geol. Inst. (pres. 1964-65). Author: Aerial Photographys; Their Use and Interpretation, 1942; Structural Geology of North America, 1951, 2d edit., 1962; General College Geology, 1965. Contbr. articles tech. lit. Specialist in continental tectonics; structural geology (Utah, Wyo., Mont.), sedimentation, petroleum geology. Home: Salt Lake City UT Died Nov. 7, 1972.

EARHART, ROBERT FRANCIS, physicist; b. Toledo, Ia., Feb. 2, 1873; s. Robert N. and Frances (Fidlar) E.; B.S., Northwestern U., 1893; Ph.D., U. of Chicago, 1900; m. Darline Scofield, of Columbus, O., Aug. 1906; children—Daniel S., Robt. N., Edwin W.,

Frances, Warren S. Formerly in engring. practice at Moline, Ill.; with Ohio State U. since 1903; prof. physics same, since 1912. Mem. Am. Physical Soc., Sigma Xi. Methodist. Original researches in discharge of electricity through gases. Home: 342 W. 9th Av., Columbus OH

EARL, GEORGE GOODELL, civil engr.; b. Monmouth Co., N.J., Oct. 9, 1863; s. Holmes and Annie (Taylor) E.; grad. Freehold (N.J.) Inst., 1880; C.E., Lafayette Coll., Easton, Pa., 1884, D.Sc., 1918; m. Anna L. Riddell, June 1890 (died 1911); children—Anna Taylor (dec.), Ralph; m. 2d, Frances H. Fowler, Jan. 1912; 1 son, Thomas Collins. With U.S. Geol. Survey in N.J., 1884-85; r.r. location and constrn. with A.T.&S.F. R.R., in Mo., 1886-87; sewer constrn., Montgomery, Ala., 1888; gen. engring. practice, 1888-92; city engr., Americus, Ga., 1890-91; chief engr. New Orleans Sewerage Co., 1892-99; gen. supt. and chief engr., Sewerage and Water Bd., New Orleans, 1900-30, cons. engr. of same, 1931—. Has specialized in development of new methods for regulation, measurement and recording of fluid flows and pressures, especially in proportional flows, and in improvement of liquid meters to record fully on low rates of draft heretofore not recordable. Home: New Orleans, La. Died Sept. 16, 1940.

EARLE, CLARENCE EDWARDS, engr.; b. Bengies, Md., Aug. 27, 1893; s. William George and Annie Rebecca (Edwards) E.; student Baltimore Polytech. Inst., 1913; B.S. in Chem. Engring., George Washington U., 1923; m. Dorothy B. Stone, April 16, 1919; children—Leslie Marie (Mrs. Richard O. Thomas), Richard Stone. Teacher manual arts, science, mathematics, Del Norte, Colo., Richmond, Va., 1913-18; head aeronautical gas sect., Bur. Aeronautics, U.S. Navy, 1920-25; rep. U.S. helium plant, Ft. Worth, Tex., 1925-30; head chem. research and development sec., Bur. Aeronautics, U.S. Navy, 1930-42, chief chem. consultant, 1942-43; dir. Earle Research Lab., since 1939; research dir. Baltimore Engring. and Chem. Co.; president Breco Mfg. Company, director Medical Chemicals, Inc., Insl-X Company, Ossining, N.Y.; chief tech. consultant R.R. Engring. Co. (all Baltimore). Entered U.S. Naval Aviation, Jan. 8, 1918 as machinist mate 2d class, disch. as ensign U.S. Naval Res., Apr. 1920. Mem. Am. Chem. Soc. Automotive Engrs., Washington Soc. Engrs. Protestant. Mason (Shriner). Clubs: University, Congressional Country (Washington, D.C.), Merchants' (Baltimore). Discovered and developed Lithium soap lubricating greases used in aircraft mfg., U.S. and fgn., World War II; originated, developed all-purpose hydraulic oil, chem. polar compounds for thin film preservation of metallic surfaces against corrosion, aircraft carbon monoxide detector, etc.; pioneered discovery and development of series of chem. compounds known as phenyl-amino salts used as mycotic drug in South Pacific. Home: 5025 Glenbrook Terrace, Washington 16. Office: Marsh Bldg., Washington 6. Died Nov. 25, 1953.

EARLE, FRANKLIN SUMNER, botanist and agriculturist; b. Dwight, Ill., Sept. 4, 1856; s. Parker and Melanie (Tracy) E.; ed. schs., Cobden, Ill., and U. of Ill.; special studies, chiefly botany and biology, but did not graduate; M.S., Ala. Poly. Inst., 1902; m. Susan B. Skeham, 1886; children—Melanie Tracy (Mrs. William L. Keiser), Ruth Esther (Mrs. David Sturrock); m. 2d, Esther J. Skehan, 1896. Connected with U. of Ill., 1886, doing spl. mycol. work, results of which were published with title "The Erysiphaceae of Illinois" (joint author with T. J. Burrill); connected with Miss. Agrl. Expt. Sta., 1894-95; joint author (with S. M. Tracy), "Mississippi Fungi," 1895; asst. pathologist in charge mycol. herbarium, U.S. Dept. Agr., 1895-96; horticulturist, Ala. (Coll.) Agrl. Expt. Sta., Jan. 1896; prof. biology, Ala. Poly. Inst., 1896-1901; issued "Preliminary List of Alabama Fungi" (with Dr. L. M. Underwood), 1897; asst. curator in charge mycol. collections, N.Y. Bot. Garden; sent by N.Y. Bot. Garden to Jamaica and Cuba, and by U.S. Dept. Agr. to make scientific investigations in Puerto Rico, 1903; dir. Estacion Central Agronómica of Cuba (on recommendation U.S. Dept. Agr.), 1904-06; consulting agriculturist to Cuban-Am. Sugar Co., 1908-11; pres. Cuba Fruit Exchange, 1911—. Sent to P.R. by U.S. Dept. of Agr., July 1918, to investigate serious sugar cane disease; expert in sugar cane disease Insular Govt. of P.R., July 1, 1919-Sept. 1, 1921; cons. agriculturist Aguirre Sugar Co.; dir. of agriculture Gen. Sugar Co., Havana, Cuba, 1923-24; sugar cane technologist Tropical Plant Research Foundation (in charge of work with sugar cane varieties in Cuba), 1924—. Author: "Southern Agriculture," 1907. Home: Herradura, Cuba. Died Jan. 31, 1929.

EARLE, RALPH, naval officer, educator; b. Worcester, Mass., May 3, 1874; s. Stephen Carpenter and Mary Eaton (Brown) E.; student Worcester Poly. Inst., 1892, hon. D.Sc., 1925; grad. U.S. Naval Acad., 1896; m. Janet Turner, d. of late Pay Dir. Caspar Schenck, U.S.N., Sept. 29, 1898; children—Ralph, Mary Janet. Ensign, U.S.N., May 6, 1898; lt. (jr. grade), May 6, 1901; promoted through grades to rear adm., Dec. 23, 1916, continuing during World War; capt. May 5, 1920; promoted to rank of rear adm., Sept. 1930. Served on U.S.S. Massachusetts, 1896-98; navigator and watch officer, Hornet, Apr.-Sept. 1898, participating in battles of Manzanillo, June 30 and July 18, 1898; on San Francisco, Sept. 19-25, 1898; on Essex, 1898-1901; at naval proving ground, Indian Head, 1901-02; on Lancaster, 1902-03, Yankee, May-Oct. 1903, Missouri, 1903-05; insp. of powder for East Coast, 1905-07; gunnery officer U.S.S. Maine, 1907-08, also navigator part of time; exec., navigator and gunnery officer U.S.S. Galveston, July-Oct. 1908; in charge magazine and chem. lab., P.I., 1908-10; in elec. dept., Naval Acad., 1910-11; exec. officer Iowa, May-Sept. 1911; discipline dept. Naval Acad., 1911-13; head of English dept., same, Aug.-Sept. 1912; mem. spl. bd. on naval ordnance, 1912-13; comd. Balch, Sept.-Oct. 1913, Dolphin, 1913-15, during which time (Apr. 9, 1914) occurred the "Tampico incident"; exec. officer Arkansas, June-Sept. 1915; head dept. of ordnance and gunnery, Naval Acad., 1915-16, dept. of English, June-Aug. 1916; comd. naval proving ground, Indian Head, Md., Sept.-Dec. 1916; apptd. chief Bur. of Ordnance, Navy Dept., Dec. 23, 1916; comd. U.S.S. Connecticut, May 5, 1919-Sept. 28, 1921; chief of staff of control force, U.S.S. Florida, Oct. 10, 1921-May 31, 1922; Naval War Coll., July 1, 1922-May 26, 1923; comdr. Naval Torpedo Sta., Newport, R.I., May 26, 1923-May 25, 1925; retired Aug. 25, 1925. Pres. Worcester Poly. Inst., 1925—. Mem. U.S. Naval Inst. Episcopalian. Author: Life at the U.S. Naval Academy, 1917; Makers of Naval Tradition; (brochure) Practical Interior Ballistics, 1917. Accomplished origination of and developed plans for and provided the material for the mine field across the North Sea, known as the Northern Barrage; directed making a type of mine entirely new to naval warfare; originator of the 14-inch Navelry. batteries in France. Originated plans for depth charges, and many other ordnance projects. Home: Worcester, Mass. Died Feb. 13, 1939.

EAST, EDWARD MURRAY, biologist; b. Du Quoin, Ill., Oct. 4, 1879; s. William Harvey and Sarah Granger (Woodruff) E.; Case Sch. Applied Science, 1897-98; B.S., U. of Ill., 1900; grad. study, 1900-05, M.S., 1904, Ph.D., 1907; LL.D., Kenyon Coll., 1926; m. Mary Lawrence Boggs, Sept. 2, 1903; children—Elizabeth Woodruff, Margaret Lawrence, Edward Murray (dec.). Asst. chemist, 1900-03, 1st asst. in plant breeding, 1903-05, U. of Ill. Agrl. Expt. Sta.; agronomist Conn. Agrl. Expt. Sta., 1905-09; asst. prof. exptl. plant morphology, 1909-14, prof. exptl. plant morphology, 1914-26, prof. genetics, 1926—, Harvard U. Collaborator tobacco investigations, U.S. Dept. Agr., 1908-18. Chmn. bot. raw products com., and mem. bot. and agr. com., Nat. Research Council, 1917-18; actg. chief statistics div. U.S. Food Administration, 1918. Editorial bd. Genetics, 1916—; contbg. bd. Bot. Abstracts, 1918-22; Harvard lectureship at Yale, 1924-25; lecturer U. of Chicago, 1911, Grad. Sch. Agr., 1914; De Lamar lecturer Johns Hopkins, 1920; lecturer Cornell U., 1922; Larwill lecturer Kenyon Coll., 1927; lecturer of U. of Mich., 1930; Harvey lecturer New York U., 1931. V.p. 2d International Congress on Eugenics, 1921; hon. v.p. 6th International Botanical Congress, 1935. Fellow Am. Acad. Arts and Sciences, A.A.A.S. Author: Heterozygosis in Evolution and Plant Breeding, 1912; Inbreeding and Outbreeding, 1919; Mankind at the Crossroads, 1923; Heredity and Human Affairs, 1927. Editor: Biology in Human Affairs, 1931. Home: Boston, Mass. Died Nov. 9, 1938.

EASTIN, BERTRAND P., oil co. exec.; b. Indpls., Apr. 27, 1911; s. Paul and Minnie (Elzea) E.; B.S., U. Cal. at Berkeley, 1937, M.S., 1939; m. Margaret I. Sandeman, Dec. 26, 1941; 1 son, Gary Brian. With Shell Oil Co., 1938-68, dir. prodn. research, exploration and prodn. research div. Shell Devel. Co., 1958-61, v.p. prodn. parent co., 1961-68. Mem. Am. Petroleum Inst., Am. Inst. Mining and Metall. Engrs., Sigma Xi. Home: Darien CT Died July 28, 1968.

EASTMAN, CHARLES ROCHESTER, geologist, palaeontologist; b. Cedar Rapids, Ia., June 5, 1868; s. Austin V. and Mary (Scoville) E.; A.B., Harvard, 1890, A.M., 1891; Ph.D., Munich, 1894; m. Caroline A., d. Alvan G. Clark (famous telescope-maker), 1892. Studied natural science at Harvard, Johns Hopkins, and abroad; served on U.S., Iowa, N.Y., N.J., and other state geol. surveys; taught geology and palaeontology in Harvard and Radcliffe colls.; curator at Carnegie Mus., Pittsburgh, and prof., U. of Pittsburgh, 1910-13; engaged in scientific research and editor at Am. Mus. Natural History, New York, 1913—. Editor Am. Palaeontol. Soc.; translator of Von Zittel's Palaeontology, 3 vols., 1900-2. Home: New York, N.Y. Died Sept. 27, 1918.

EASTMAN, GEORGE, mfr.; b. Waterville, N.Y., July 12, 1854; s. George W. and Maria (Kilbourn) E.; ed. Rochester, N.Y. Became an amateur photographer and experimenter and perfected a process for making dry plates; began to mfr. dry plates on small scale, 1880; originated the kodak and transparent film for use in same; chmn. bd. Eastman Kodak Co. of N.Y., and of Eastman Kodak Co. of N.J. A leader in business and philanthropic movements; donor of more than $75,000,000 to various philanthropic objects. Home: Rochester, N.Y. Died Mar. 14, 1932.

EASTMAN, JOHN ROBIE, astronomer; b. Andover, N.H., July 29, 1836; s. Royal Friend and Sophronia (Mayo) E.; M.S., Dartmouth Coll., 1962; Ph.D., 1877; m. Mary J. Ambrose, Dec. 25, 1866. Asst., U.S. Naval Obs., 1861-65; prof. mathematics U.S.N., 1865—. Retired for age, July 29, 1898, with rank of capt. U.S.N., but retained on active duty till Oct. 12, 1898; promoted to rank of read-adm. U.S.N., June 29, 1906. Engaged in astron. observations, computations and research, 1862—. Most of published work in the annual volumes of the govt. observatory. Was first pres. Washington Acad. Sciences. Was in charge of the Meridian Circle work at the observatory, 1874-91; observed total solar eclipses Aug. 7, 1869, at Des Moines, Iowa; Dec. 22, 1870, Syracuse, Sicily; July 29, 1878, at West Las Animas, Colo., and May 28, 1900, at Barnesville, Ga. Prepared and edited the Second Washington Star Catalogue, which contains the results of nearly 80,000 observations made at the U.S. Naval Obs., 1866-91. Author: Transit Circle Observations of the Sun, Moon, Planets and Comets, 1903. Home: Andover, N.H. Died Sept. 26, 1913.

EASTON, STANLY ALEXANDER, mining engr.; b. Santa Cruz, Calif., Apr. 7, 1873; s. Giles Alexander and Mary Esther (Gushee) E.; B.S., Univ. of California College of Mines, 1894; D.Sc., Whitman Coll., Walla Walla, Wash., 1934; LL.D., U. of Calif., 1939, U. Idaho, 1950; H.H.D., College Idaho, 1951; married Estelle Greenough, Nov. 15, 1906; children—Ruth (Mrs. John B. Rodgers), Jane (Mrs. John D. Bradley), Anne (Mrs. Everett A. Black). Chmn. Bunker Hill & Sullivan Mining and Concentrating Co. (one of largest lead and silver mines in the world); honorary chmn. of the board directors Bunker Hill Company, and Pend O'Reille Mines and Metals Co. Certificate of Merit, Washington State College, 1947. Recipient Wm. Lawrence Saunders Gold Medal, 1949. Mem. Board of overseers Whitman Coll.; mem. exec. com. Region No. 11, Boy Scouts of America. Mem. Am. Inst. Mining and Metall. Engrs., Mining and Metall. Soc. America, Am. Mining Congress, Idaho Mining Assn., Instn. of Mining and Metallurgy (London), S.A.R., Soc. Calif. Pioneers, Delta Kappa Epsilon. Episcopalian. Mason, Elk. Clubs: Spokane, Spokane Country (Spokane); Pacific Union, Engineers (San Francisco); Mining (N.Y.). Home: El Mirasol Hotel, Santa Barbara, Cal. Died Dec. 17, 1961; buried Cypress Lawn Cemetery, Colma, Cal.

EASTWOOD, ALICE, botanist; b. Toronto, Can., Jan. 19, 1859; d. Colin Skinner and Eliza Jane (Gowdey) E.; grad. E. Denver High Sch., 1879. Tchr. E. Denver High Sch., 1879-89; curator herbarium Cal. Acad. Scis., 1892-49, ret. Fellow A.A.A.S., Cal. Acad. Scis. Author: Popular Flora of Denver, Colo., 1893; Popular Flora and Pacific Coast Edition, Bergen's Botany, 1897; Popular Flora and Rocky Mountain Edition, Bergen's Botany, 1900; Hand-Book of Trees of California, 1905; also many papers on systematic botany and articles for scientific mags. Address: 1221 Lombard St., San Francisco. Died Oct. 29, 1953; buried Toronto, Can.

EASTWOOD, EVERETT OWEN, prof. emeritus mechanical engineering; born at Portsmouth, Virginia, on February 5, 1876; son of Matthew D. and Mary Anne (Thornton) E.; A.B., University of Virginia, 1899, B.S., 1897, A.M., 1899, C.E., 1896; B.S. in naval architecture, Mass. Institute of Tech., 1902; fellow in astronomy, U. of Va., 1897-1900; m. Nelle Dorothy Halliwall, Dec. 20, 1905; children—Emily Louise (Mrs. R. S. Bunker, Jr.), Mary Elizabeth (Mrs. Oliver Ashford). Draftsman Navy Dept., 1902-03, office of the chief constructor, 1903-04; with Fore River Shipbuilding Co., Quincy, Mass., 1904; instr. mech. engring. and naval architecture, Lehigh U., 1904-05; asst. prof. mech. engring, U. of Wash., Seattle, 1905, asso. prof., prof. and head of dept., 1905-29, dir. aeronautical engring., 1929-46, chmn. com. on Campus Planning, 1938-43, mem. U. Senate. Pres. board of trustees Univ. Congl. Ch., 1913-27; chmn. bd. dirs. Univ. Nat. Bank, Seattle, 1913, 1929. Charge of training course for engr. officers, U.S. Merchant Marine, U. of Wash., during World War I; in charge aviation training courses, Naval cadet classes, U. of Wash. Mem. Am. Soc. Heating and Ventilating Engrs. (v.p. 1941, pres. 1942), Am. Soc. Mech. Engrs. (mem. council, v.p. 1923-29), Am. Arbitration Assn., Am. Engring. Council (mem. council 1929-32), Sigma Alpha Epsilon, Tau Beta Pi, Sigma Xi. Conglist. Clubs: Faculty (U. of Wash.); Seattle Municipal League. Contbr. to tech. jours. Home: 4702 12th Av. N.E., Seattle WA

EATON, AMOS, scientist; b. Chatham, N.Y., May 17, 1776; s. Capt. Abel and Azuba (Hurd) E.; grad. Williams Coll., 1797; attended Yale, 1815-17; m. Polly Thomas, Oct. 16, 1799, 1 son; m. 2d, Sally Cady, Sept. 16, 1803, 5 sons; m. 3d, Ann Bradley, Oct. 20, 1816, 3 children; m. 4th, Alice Johnson, Aug. 5, 1827, 1 son. Admitted to N.Y. bar, 1802; became lawyer and land agt., Catskill, N.Y., also studied science; lectured on botany and geology throughout Northeast; prof. natural history Med. Sch., Castleton, Vt., 1820-24; prof. Rensselaer Sch. (now Poly. Inst.), 1824-42; wrote papers in all scientific fields. Author: A Manual of Botany for the Northern States, 1817. Died May 10, 1842.

EATON, DANIEL CADY, botanist; b. Ft. Gratiot, Mich., Sept. 12, 1834; s. Gen. Amos B. and Elizabeth (Seldon) E.; grad. Yale, 1857; attended Harvard, 1857-60; m. Caroline Ketcham, Feb. 13, 1866. Served with army commissary, N.Y.C., during Civil War, 1860-64; prof. botany Yale, 1864-95; specialized in study of ferns, did much field work; wrote bot.

definitions for Webster's Internat. Dictionary. Author: The Ferns of North America, 2 vols. Died New Haven, Conn., June 29, 1895.

EATON, GEORGE FRANCIS, zoölogist and archeologist; b. New Haven, Conn., May 30, 1872; s. Daniel Cady and Caroline (Ketcham) E.; B.A., Yale, 1894, Ph.D., 1898; m. Julia Henrietta Hammer, Oct. 24, 1899. Curator of osteology, 1899-1920, asso. curator vertebrate paleontology, 1904-10, asso. paleontologist, 1919-20, Yale. Sec. Conn. Acad. Arts and Sciences, 1905-46, editor publs., 1916-46; now retired. Mem. A.A.A.S., Am. Soc. Naturalists. Home: 85 Laurel Rd., New Haven, Conn. Died Nov. 6, 1949.

EATON, HUBERT, scientist, business exec., patron of arts and Christian education; b. Liberty, Mo., s. James Rodolphus and Martha (Lewright) E.; A.B., William Jewell Coll., 1902; hon. Sc.D., U. Redlands; also hon. doctorates in sci., letters, laws, fine arts; m. Anna Munger-Henderson, Dec. 10, 1918 (dec. Nov. 1960). Chief research chemist B.&M. Consol. Copper & Silver Mining Co. (now Anaconda Copper Co.), Great Falls, Mont.; chief chemist Teziutlan Copper Co., Mexico; gen. mgr. metallurgist Adaven Mining & Smelting Co. Nev.; chmn. adv. bd. Bank of Am. (Glendale); mem. adv. board St. Joseph's Hosp., Burbank, Cal.; founder all Forest Lawn Meml. Parks, Forest Lawn Co., Forest Lawn Life Ins. Co., Forest Lawn Found., Council of Regents of Meml. Court of Honor, American Security & Fidelity Corp. Originated Meml.-Park Plan, 1916, and as example built Forest Lawn Meml.-Park, where bronze tablets set level with lawn are substituted for tombstones; where also are collections of paintings and stained glass; large-size works of famous European and Am. Sculptors; Moretti re-creation of Leonardo da Vinci's The Last Supper; paintings, The Crucifixion, by Jan Styka, The Resurrection by Robat Clark, Bonguereau's famed Song of the Angels; outdoor mosaic of Signing of Declaration of Independence; The Ascension, The Birth Liberty; 7 chs., mus. Mem. nat. council, v.p. Boy Scouts Am. Knighted by King Victor Emanuel III; recipient D.S.M. vets. com. People to People Program; decorated Star of Solidarity (Italy). Recipient NSE 1955 Mgmt. award; Good Citizenship medal S.A.R., 1959; Diplome d'Honneur, Combattants de Belgique. Past trustee William Jewell Coll., established Found. Sci. and Art of Persuasion; bd. dirs., trustee Redlands, Temple Baptist Ch.; established writing awards programs, at four liberal arts Christian colls.; asso. Caltech, Occidental Coll., asso. also Pomona Coll. Fellow Royal Soc. Arts (Great Britain), (profl. mem.), Italian. Acad. Fine Arts (Carrara), Acad. Arts of Design (Florence); mem. C. of C. (past dir.), Western Cemetery Alliance (v.p.), Nat. Cemeteries Assn., Interment Assn. Cal., S.R., Soc. Colonial Wars, Sigma Nu, Alpha Phi Gamma. Baptist. Mason (K.T., Shriner). Clubs: Hidden Valley, California, Los Angeles Country, Aliso Gun. Chief Blackfoot Indians. Author: The Comemoral, also pamphlets on cemetery Devel. Home: 837 Greenway Dr., Beverly Hills, Cal. Died Sept. 20, 1966.

EATON, JAMES TUCKER, chem. co. exec.; b. Bonne Terre, Mo., Feb. 24, 1907; s. James A. and Nannie (Tucker) E.; A.B., Central Coll., Fayette, Mo., 1928; M.A., U. Ill., 1931, Ph.D., 1934; m. Margaret B. Alexander, Dec. 24, 1933; children—Shirley, Patricia (Mrs. Thomas M. Scott), and Barbra. Instructor of chemistry Central Coll., Fayette, Mo., 1928-29; asst. instr. U. Ill., Urbana, 1929-33; research chemist Ill. Geol. Survey, Urbana, 1934, Nat. Aniline div. Allied Chem. and Dye Corp., Buffalo, 1934-37; research chemist, E. F. Houghton & Co., Phila., 1938-41, asst. to v.p., 1941-46, mgr. research, 1946-50, dir. research, 1950-68, asst. dir. plants, 1951-54, v.p. prodn., 1955-68; dir., exec. v.p. E. F. Houghton and Co. of Can., Ltd., Toronto, 1955-68; dir. Houghton, S.A. in Buenos Aires. Mem. Hatboro-Horsham Joint Authority, Hatboro, Pa., 1950-53, chmn., 1950-52; mem. Hatboro School Board, 1952-61, president, 1952-55; mayor of Hatboro, 1962-68; Chairman Hatboro committee for Community Advance, 1957-60. Trustee Houghton-Carpenter Found. Dir. Mary Bailey Found.; trustee Presbyn. Hosp. of Phila., 1959-61. Pres. Elder's Assn. of Phila., 1947-49; mem. Presbyn. Social Union of Phila., 1943-68, (pres., 1957-58). Recipient Distinguished Alumnus citation Central College, Fayette, Missouri, in 1963. Mem. Am. Chem. Soc. (councilor 1951-54), A.A.A.S., Am. Leather Chemists Assn., Montgomery County Mayor's Assn. (pres. 1967-68), Alpha Chi Sigma, Sigma Xi. Presbyn. (elder). Home: Hatboro PA Died Mar. 21, 1968; cremated.

EATON, L(EALDES) MCKENDREE (LEE M.), physician; b. Owaneco, Ill., Feb. 3, 1905; s. Jordan Stewart, Sr., and Margaret (Barrett) E.; student James Millikan U., 1923-25; B.S., U. Chgo., 1927, M D., 1932; M.S., U. Minn., 1938; m. Mary Louise Long, Apr. 2, 1936; children—Elizabeth Barrett. Lynne St. Pierre, Emily Jordan, Charles McKendree, Thomas Lee. Intern Cook County Hosp., Chgo., 1931-33; fellow internal medicine Mayo Found., Rochester. 1933-34, fellow neurology, 1934-36, instr. neurology, 1938-41, asst. prof., 1941-46, asso. prof., 1946-50, prof., 1950—; cons. neurology Mayo Clinic, 1936-47, head neurologic sect., 1947-54, chmn. neurology sections, 1954—; research myasthenia gravis, polymyositis, other neuromuscular diseases. Med. adv. bd. Myasthenia Gravis Found., Inc., 1954—. Diplomate Am. Bd. Psychiatry and Neurology. Mem. Central Neuropsychiat. Assn. (pres. 1953), Am. Neurological Assn., Am. Acad. Neurology, Assn. Research Nervous and Mental Disease (president 1958), American Medical Association (chairman section on nervous and mental disease 1956), Sigma Xi, Alpha Omega Alpha. Universalist. Author articles on neurologic subjects. Home: 909 Eighth St. S.W. Office: 200 First St. S.W., Rochester, Minn. Died Nov. 17, 1958.

EATON, LUCIEN, mining engr.; b. St. Louis, Mo., July 6, 1879; s. Lucien and Hannah Orr (Noyes) E.; A.B., magna cum laude, Harvard, 1900, M.S., 1902; S.B. in mining and metallurgy, Lawrence Scientific Sch., 1901; m. Eleanor Archibald Stevens, June 15, 1907 (dec. May, 1949); children—Elizabeth Stevens, Eleanor, Lucien; m. 2d, Charlotte Vose, July 8, 1952. On engring. staff Cleveland Cliffs Iron Co., Ishpeming and Ironwood, Mich., 1902-06; supt. Iron Belt & Shores Mines, same co., Iron Belt, Wis., 1906-09; supt. Ishpeming Dist. (with exception of few months), 1909-29; cons. mining engr. Roan Antelope Copper Company and Rhodesian Selection Trust, Ltd., 1929-33; consulting mining engineer gold mines of Australia, Western Mining Corp., Bendigo Mines, North Broken Hill, Broken Hill S., Zinc Corp., and other Australian mining cos., 1934-35; consulting engr. Copper Range Co. and Isle Royale Copper Co., 1937-38; general manager Isle Royale Copper Co., 1938-39; cons. mining engineer with H. A. Brassert & Co., New York, 1940-46; cons. engr. with Pierce Management, Scranton, Pa., for Turkish Govt. in Turkey, 1947; Cons. engr. Copper Range Co., since 1947; Big Sandy and other mining cos. and with H. A. Brassert & Co. (Mex.), 1946; pres. dir., Inca Mining & Development Co., Santo Domingo, Peru, 1925. Capt. engrs. U.S. Army, June-Dec. 1918. Mem. Am. Inst. Mining and Metall. Engrs., Mining and Metall. Soc. America, Lake Superior Mining Inst. (v.p. 1929), Am. Mining Congress (chairman standardization committee 1929) Republican. Mason. Unitarian. Member of Milton Hoosick Club. Made various improvements in mining practice and in design of rock drills and mech. equipment for handling ore. Author: Practical Mine Development and Equipment, 1934. Contbr. to tech. jours. Address: 79 Vose's Lane, Milton 87, Mass. Died Dec. 9, 1952; buried Milton Cemetery, Milton, Mass.

EAVENSON, HOWARD NICHOLAS, (ev'en-sun), mining engr.; b. July 15, 1873; s. Alben Taylor and Susan (Bean) E.; student Public and Friends' Central School, Phila., Pa.; B.S., Swarthmore Coll., 1892, C.E., 1895; Dr. Engring., Univ. of Pittsburgh, 1928; m. Ada J. Daugherty, Sept. 20, 1898. Engring. work in Va., N.J. and with U.S. Lake Survey, 1892-97; with H. C. Frick Coke Co. and Allied cos. as div. engr., asst. chief engr., chief engr., Uniontown, Pa., 1897-1902; chief engr. U.S. Coal and Coke Co., Gary, W.Va., 1902-20; cons. engr., 1920—, now head of Eavenson & Auchmuty; dir. Boone Co Coal Corp., Appalachian Coals, Inc.; pres. Bituminous Coal Research Inc., 1939-48. Trustee, Carnegie Inst. Mem. Am. Soc. C.E., Am. Inst. Mining and Metall. Engrs. (pres. 1934), Am. Soc. Testing Materials, Delta Upsilon, Tau Beta Pi. Republican. Mem. Society of Friends. Clubs: University, Duquesne, Rolling Rock. Author: Coal Through the Ages; The Pittsburgh Coal Bed—Its Early History and Development; First Century and a Quarter of American Coal Industry. Home: 4411 Bayard St. Office: Koppers Bldg., Pitts. 19. Died Feb. 16, 1953.

EBAUGH, FRANKLIN GESSFORD, psychiatrist; b. Reistertown, Md., May 14, 1895; s. Zachariah Charles and Elizabeth Bell (Gessford) E.; A.B., Johns Hopkins, 1915, M.D., 1919; m. Dorothy Reese, Apr. 9, 1921; children—Franklin G., David C., Donald R., Nancy Haines. Res. med. officer, Henry Phipps Clinic, 1919-20; asst. physician, New Jersey State Hospital., 1920-21; director neuro-psychiatric dept., Philadelphia Gen. Hosp., 1920-24; instr. in psychiatry, U. of Pa., 1922-24; dir. Colo. Psychopathic Hosp., Denver, since 1924; clin. prof. psychiatry University of Colorado, Denver, 1924-53, prof. emeritus 1953-72; pvt. practice psychiatry, 1953. Served as col. M.C., AUS, neuropsychiat. consultant Eighth Service Command, Dallas, Texas, 1942-45, served in Pacific area. Office of Chief Surgeon, June 1945-46. Director Division of Psychiatric Edn., Nat. Com. for Mental Hygiene, 1933-42; mem. Am. Bd. of Psychiatric Examiners, 1933-41; chmn. sect. nervous and mental diseases, Am. Med. Assn., 1931-32; pres. Colo. Soc. for Mental Hygiene; chmn. Gov's. Com. Mental Health, Colo., 1960-61; mem. Ft. Logan Mental Health Center Adv. Com., 1964-65; mem. Am. Bd. of Psychiatry and Neurology, 1934-42; cons.-at-large U.S.P.H.S.; cons. office of Surgeon Gen.; mem. editorial bd. Am. Jour. of Psychiatry, Current Med. Digest, Post-Grad. Medicine, Am. Practitioner, Diseases of Nervous System; contbg. editor Am. Jour. of Med. Sciences; mem. advisory bd. Med. Specialties, 1934-42, Council on Mental Health, Colorado, from 1957. Recipient Distinguished Service award American Psychiatric Association, 1966. Fellow of the American Psychiatric Association (council 1931-34); mem. A.M.A., Colo. Med. Soc. (past chmn. com. mental health), Am. Neurol. Assn., Canadian Neuropsychiatric Assn. (hon.), Nat. Research Council (com. on neuropsychiatry), Am. Psychiatric Association (Colorado District branch president 1960-61, chmn. com. on psychiatry in med. edn.), Assn. Research Nervous and Mental Disease (pres. 1944). Central Psych. Assn. (pres. 1930), Grad. Med. Edn. (mem. commn. 1936-41), Alpha Kappa Kappa, Sigma Xi, Alpha Omega Alpha; corr. mem. Royal Medico-Psychol. Assn. since 1929. Rep. Episcopalian. Mason. Clubs: Mile High, Cactus, Denver Country. Co-author: Practical Clinical Psychiatry (with E. A. Strecher), 1925, 8th edit., 1946; Psychiatry in Medical Education (with Charles A. Rymer), 1942. Contbr. to Am. Jour. Psychiatry, Am. Jour. Med. Sciences, Archives Neurology and Psychiatry, Am. Practitioner, Jour. Nervous and Mental Diseases, Postgrad. Medicine. Home: Denver CO Died Jan. 4, 1972.

EBERBACH, CARL WALTER, (e'ber-bak), surgeon; b. Ann Arbor, Mich., Dec. 9, 1889; s. Ottmar and Katherine (Haller) E.; A.B., U. of Mich., 1912, M.D., 1916; m. Elisabeth Louise Falk, Nov. 10, 1930; 1 dau., Elisabeth Katherine. Intern and asst. resident in medicine, Barnes Hosp., Washington U., St. Louis, 1916-17; served as capt. Med. Reserve Corps, with Base Hosp. No. 21, A.E.F.; also Base Hosp. No. 12, B.E.F., during World War, 1917-19; instr. in surgery U. of Mich., 1920-23; asst. dean of Med. School, 1922-26; asst. prof. of surgery, 1924-27; asso. with Drs. Sifton and Evans, Milwaukee, in practice of surgery since 1928; asso. clin. prof. in surgery Marquette U., Milwaukee, 1932-50, clinical professor surgery, 1950—, chief dept., 1950-58; chief staff Milwaukee Hospital, 1946-51. Fellow Am. College of Surgeons; founder member Am. Board of Surgery; member Am. Med. Assn., Western Surg. Assn., Milwaukee Surg. Soc. (pres. 1940-42), Milwaukee Acad. Medicine (pres. 1944-45), Wis. State Board of Health, Milwaukee County Med. Society (president 1942), Sigma Xi, Alpha Omega Alpha, Sigma Chi, Nu Sigma Nu. Republican. Clubs: Milwaukee, Milwaukee Country, University, Rotary. Home: 4514 N. Lake Dr. Office: 324 E. Wisconsin Av., Milw. 2. Died July 31, 1962.

EBY, IVAN DAVID, marine engr.; b. Waterloo, Ont., Can., Mar. 24, 1887; s. Cyrus and Maria (Buehler) E.; ed. pub. schs., Waterloo; m. Ruth Mary Burroughs, Apr. 30, 1920; children—Barbara Kathleen (Mrs. Richard Hopkins Aime), Elsie Patricia, Adelaide (Mrs. Richard Edward Barkhorn). Came to U.S., 1909, naturalized, 1914. Practiced marine engring., principally Trans-Pacific and Trans-Atlantic, 1910-19. Charge engring. and repairs all Moore-McCormack Lines vessels, N.Y.C., 1920-49, v.p. 1949-52. Engr. officer on Naval troop transport, East Coast U.S. ports to France, World War I. Mem. Am. Soc. M.E., Am. Soc. Naval Architects and Marine Engrs. Mason. Holder patents. Home: 299 West 12th St., N.Y.C. 14. Office: Pier 32, North River, N.Y.C. 13. Died Sept. 24, 1967.

ECCLES, ROBERT G(IBSON), M.D.; b. Scotland, Jan. 1, 1848; s. David and Isabella E.; ed. in schools in Scotland, Ireland, Mo., Kan., etc.; M.D., L.I. Coll., 1881; Pharm.D., Scio Coll., 1903; m. Mary Hançe, Sept. 1876; 1 son, David Charles. Was chemist U.S. Dept. Indian Affairs, prof. and dean Brooklyn Coll. of Pharmacy, editor Merck's Archives, and mem. com. of revision of U.S. Pharmacopoeia. Discoverer of the alkaloids calycanthine, glaucosine, etc., and of calycanthic acid; devised the 1900 ofcl. method of assaying pepsin; investigator of effects of drugs on peptic digestion. Fellow A.A.A.S., New York Acad. Sciences. Author: Food Preservatives, 1905; Darwinism and Diabetes, 1908; Letters from Foreign Lands, 1908; Darwinism and Malaria, 1909; Parasitism and Natural Selection, 1909; Touring the Lands Where Medical Science Evolved, 1909; Darwinism and Anaphylaxis, 1911. Home: Brooklyn, N.Y. Died June 9, 1934.

ECKEL, CLARENCE LEWIS, univ. dean; b. Buffalo, Ill., Mar. 2, 1892; s. John Louis and Ida Francis (Jack) E.; B.S., U. of Colo., 1914, C.E., 1921; m. Florence Robinson, June 12, 1917; children—Patricia Fairchild (Mrs. Carroll Wilson Griffin), Robert Bruce. Concrete detailer and designer, H. S. Crocker, cons. engr., Denver, 1914, engr., 1926 and 1929; constrn. supt. M. S. Ketchum, Cons. Engr., Longmont, Colo., 1915; detailer, Am. Bridge Co., Pencoyd, Pa., 1922-23; chief constrn. engr., Crocker & Ryan, architect-engr., Air Support Command Base, Colorado Springs, Colo., 1942; instr. in civil engring., U. of Colo., 1914; asst. prof. U. of Pa., 1919-23; prof. U. of Colo., 1923-26, also engr., constrn. dept., 1925, head dept. of civil engring., 1926-43, cons. engr. constrn. dept. since 1936, dean coll. of engring. and prof. civil engring. from 1943; vis. lectr. Coll. Engring., San Diego State Coll., 1960-62. Served as 1st lt., Co. B, Engrs., Colo. Nat. Guard; capt., Co. A, 115th Engrs., AEF, 1917-19, part-time; commander 1st Bn., 115th Engrs. Technical editor civil engring. class, Lefax, Phila., 1920-25. Recipient Faculty Appreciation award Asso. Engring. Student Faculty, 1960; Distinguished Engring. Alumnus award U. Colo., 1966; All Conf. Center Football U. Colo. Hall Honor award, 1972. Mem. Colo. Bd. Examiners for Engrs. and Land Surveyors, from 1942; dir. Western Zone, Nat. Council State Bds. Engring. Examiners, 1946-48; v.p. Nat. Council State Bds. Engring. Examiners, 1948-49 (pres. 1949-50). Mem. Am. Soc. C.E. (pres. Colo. sect. 1932, nat. dist. dir. 1955-58; rep. Engrs. Council for Profl. Development subcom. from 1936), Colo. Engring. Council (pres. 1956), A.I.A. (hon. asso. Colo. chpt. 1956), Am. Society of Engineering Education (member council 1934-37, v.p. 1957), American Concrete Inst., Colo. Soc. Engrs. (Gold Medal award, hon. life), Am. Soc. Mech. Engrs., Colo. Sch. Masters Club, Nat., Colo. edn. assns., Acacia, Alpha Sigma Phi, Tau Beta Pi, Sigma Tau, Sigma Xi, Chi Epsilon (pres. 1950-52). Licensed profl. engr. Pa. and Colo. Mason (Shriner). Club: Rotary (Boulder). Home: Boulder CO Died July 31, 1972; cremated.

ECKEL, EDWIN CLARENCE, (ek'el), engr., geologist; b. New York, Mar. 6, 1875; s. August and Helena S. K. (Butt) E.; B.S., New York U., 1895, C.E., 1896; m. Julia Egerton Dibblee, July 9, 1902; children—Edwin Butt, Julia Dibblee, Richard Egerton. Asst. geologist of N.Y., 1900-02; asst. geologist, 1902-05, U.S. Geol. Survey, and geologist in charge sect. of iron ores and structural materials, 1906-07; spl. commr. in charge cement exhibits, Jamestown Expn., 1907; cons. engr. and geologist since 1907; pres. Dominion Cement Co., 1910-12. Expert on southern and eastern iron ores for U.S. Steel Corp. during the Stanley investigation and dissolution suit, 1911-13; iron ore investigations in Europe, 1928-30; cement mill valuations for U.S. Treasury Dept., 1931-32; chief geologist Tenn. Valley Authority since 1933. Commd. capt., Engr. R.C., Jan. 23, 1917; maj. engrs., U.S. Army, Apr. 1919; service in France, July 1917-July 1919. Fellow Geol. Soc. America; mem. Soc. of Econ. Geologists, Am. Inst. Mining Engrs., Delta Kappa Epsilon; life mem. Am. Soc. C.E. Author: Cements, Limes and Plasters, 1905; Portland Cement Industry from the Financial Standpoint, 1908; Building Stones and Clays, 1911; Iron Ores, 1914; Coal, Iron and War, 1920; Le Ciment Portland, 1927; Report on Economic Sanctions, 1931. Wrote Ency. Britannica article on Iron Ore Resources of World; Engineering Geology of Tennessee Valley, 1939. Home: 1503 Decatur St. N.W., Washington, D.C. Died Nov. 22, 1941.

ECKER, ENRIQUE E(DWARD), immunologist, bacteriologist, educator; B. Willemstad, Curacoa, Netherlands, W.I., Jan. 26, 1887; s. Johannus Petrus Gerardus and Marie Arsene (Fidanque) E.; student Wageningen, the Netherlands; Ph.D., U. Chgo., 1917; postgrad. Lausanne, 1924, Cambridge, 1927; m. Marie Josephine van Reeth, June 22, 1918; children—Paul Gerard (M.D.), Enrique Edward. Came to U.S., 1914, naturalized, 1927. Demonstrator hygiene and bacteriology Western Res. Univ., 1918, instr. immunology, 1919-22, sr. instr., 1922-24, asst. prof., 1924-27, asso. prof., 1927-42, prof. immunology, 1942—; vis. immunologist, bacteriologist Univ. Hosps., Cleve. City Hosp., St. Luke Hosp. Mem. Consejo Superior de Investigaciones Cientificas (hon.), Soc. Microbiologists, Soc. Clin. Pathologists; corr. mem. Real Academia de Medicina (all at Madrid). Recipient Silver medal from people of the Netherlands for postwar relief, 1947. Mem. Am. Assn. Immunol., Soc. Am. Bacteriologists, Am. Chem. Soc., Am. Soc. Expt. Pathology, A.A.A.S., Soc. Exptl. Biol. and Med., N.Y. Acad. Scis. Roman Catholic. Clubs: Professional, Print. Contbr. articles to sci. jours. Home: 3387 Superior Park Dr., Cleveland Heights 18. Office: Inst. of Pathology, 2085 Adelbert Rd., Cleve. 6. Died Mar. 5, 1966; buried Chgo.

ECKERT, WALLACE J., astronomer; b. Pittsburgh; June 19, 1902; s. John and Anna (Heil) E.; A.B., Oberlin Coll., 1925, D. Sc., 1968; M.A., Amherst Coll., 1926, U. of Chicago, 1925, Columbia U., 1928, Ph.D., Yale, 1931; m. Dorothy Applegate, May 14, 1932; children—Alice Applegate, John Wallace, Penelope D. Asst., dept. of astronomy, Columbia, 1926-27, instr., 1927-31, asst. prof. 1931-40 and prof., 1940; dir. U.S. Nautical Almanac, U.S. Naval Observatory, 1940-45, dir. dept. pure science, Internat. Business Machines Corp., 1945-52; dir. Watson Scientific Computing Lab., 1945-67; prof. celestial mechanics, Columbia U. Councillor Am. Astronomical Soc. Recipient James Craig Watson medal Nat. Acad. Sci., 1966; IBM award, 1969, IBM fellow, 1967, Fellow A.A.A.S. Mem. Internat. Astron. Union, Am. Astron. Soc., Washington Acad. Science, Am. Math. Society. Author: Punched Card Methods in Scientific Computation, 1940; Coordinates of the Five Outer Planets 1653-2060, 1951; Construction of the Improved Lunar Ephemeris, 1954; Faster, Faster, 1954. Home: Leonia NJ Died Aug. 24, 1971.

ECKFELDT, HOWARD, mining engr.; Conshohocken, Pa., Oct. 17, 1873; s. Jacob B. and Jeanette R. (Latch) E.; B.S., Lehigh U., 1895; E.M., 1896; m. Catalina Trousselle, Oct. 3, 1898; children—Jacob Trousselle, Emily Catherine, Jeannette Matilde. Mining engr. for Mazapil Copper Co., Concepcion del Oro, 1896-1900; instr. in mining engring., Lehigh U., 1900-02, prof. since 1902, now head of dept. In charge survey of F. C. de Zacatecas Oriente, June-Sept. 1907. Absent on leave from Lehigh U., Aug. 1910-Sept. 1911, on engring. work in Mexico. Mem. Am. Inst. Mining and Metall. Engrs., Soc. Promotion Engring. Edn., Sigma Xi. Presbyterian. Home: Bethlehem, Pa. Died March 4, 1948.

ECKFORD, HENRY, marine architect, shipbuilder; b. Irvine, Scotland, Mar. 12, 1775; s. John and Janet (Black) E.; m. Marion Bedell, Apr. 13, 1799, 2 daus. Settled in N.Y.C., 1786; supr. shipbldg. in Lake Ontario during War of 1812; reduced size of stern frame, altered details of rigging; naval constructor Bklyn. Navy Yard, 1817-20; built steamer Robert Fulton (made 1st successful steam voyage from N.Y.C. to New Orleans and Havana, Cuba, 1822). Died Turkey, Nov. 12, 1832.

ECKMAN, DONALD PRESTON, educator; b. Hillsdale, Mich., Dec. 30, 1915; s. Harold Raymond and Eva Mae (Crall) E.; B.S. in Engring., U. Mich., 1938, M.S., 1939; Ph.D., Cornell U., 1950; m. Jeannette Eliene Putnam, Sept. 29, 1940; children—Martha Lynn, Louise Karen, David Preston, Richard Raymond, Mark Andrew. Test engr. Brown Instrument Co., Phila., 1937-38; devel. engr. Cox Labs., Detroit, 1938-39; research engr. Mpls.-Honeywell Regulator Co., Phila., 1939-46; teaching fellow Cornell U., 1946-50; faculty Case Inst. Tech., 1950-62, prof. engring., 1953-62, dir. systems research center, 1959-62; research scientist Royal Dutch Shell Co., 1957-58; lectr. Tech U. Barcelona (Spain), 1960; research scientist Michelsen Inst., Bergen, Norway, 1960; engring. cons. corps. Mem. Am. Soc. Engring. Edn., Am. Assn. U. Profs., Instrument Soc. Am., Internat. Fedn. Automatic Control (chmn. adv. com.). Recipient Edn. award. Am. Soc. M.E-Indsl. Regulator Div., 1958. Author: Principles of Industrial Process Control, 1945; Industrial Instrumentation, 1950; Automatic Process Control, 1958, Polish edit., 1961, Japanese, 1962; Systems Research and Design, 1961. Patentee in field. Home: 2625 Exeter Rd., Cleveland Heights 18, O. Office: 10900 Euclid Av., Cleve. 6. Died May 26, 1962.

EDDY, BRAYTON, author, entomologist, lectr.; b. Providence, Jan. 13, 1901; s. Charles Zimri and Alace Edith (Kerr) E.; grad. Moses Brown Sch., Providence, 1917; Ph.B., Brown U., 1921; postgrad. Biol. Lab., Cold Spring Harbor, 1931, Cornell U. summers 1932-34; m. Emilia Robison, Feb. 13, 1928; 1 son, Charles Zimri II. Founder R.I. Insect Zoo, 1935, dir., 1936, 38; dir. Mich. Insect Zoo, 1937; extension lectr. Brown U., 1938; adminstr. R.I. Office of Entomology and Plant Industry, 1939-45; curator insects and reptiles N.Y. Zoöl. Soc., 1945—. Fellow N.Y. Zoöl. Soc., 1946; mem. Am. Assn. Econ. Entomology, A.A.A.S., Entomol. Society Am., Bronx Beekeepers Assn., Am. Nature Study Soc., Am. Soc. Ichthyol. and Herpetol., Brown Alumni Assn., Delta Upsilon. Author: Strangeways (play), 1922; Rock Bottom (novel), 1923; Personality of Insects (with Royal Dixon), 1924; Personality of Water-Animals (with same), 1925; The Pick-up (skit), 1925; also plays Shallow Wells (with Michael Kallesser), 1926; The Way Out (with Michael Kallesser), 1926; Plenty Palavar; Night Caps (children's stories), 1928; A Couple of Brokers (skit), 1929. Contbr. short stories and articles to mags., newspapers. Address: care N.Y. Zoölogical Soc., Bronx Zoo, N.Y.C. 60. Died July 17, 1950; buried Palmer Cemetery, Somerset, Mass.

EDDY, HARRISON PRESCOTT, civil engr.; b. Millbury, Mass., Apr. 29, 1870; s. William Justus and Martha Augusta (Prescott) E.; B.S. Worcester Poly. Inst., 1891, hon. D.Engring. 1930; m. Minnie Locke Jones, June 1, 1892; children—Willard Jones (dec.), Harrison Prescott, Randolph Locke, Charlotte Frances. Supt. sewage treatment works, Worcester, 1891-92; supt. sewer dept., 1892-1907; mem. Metcalf & Eddy, May 1907—; has been cons. engr. on sewage, drainage, etc., to cities of Boston, Louisville, Milwaukee, New York, Dayton (O), Cincinnati, Pittsburgh, Portland, Ore., San Francisco, Cleveland, Chicago. Mason. Author: (with Leonard Metcalf) American Sewerage Practice, Vol. I, Design of Sewers, 1914, Vol. II, Construction of Sewers, 1915, Vol. III, Disposal of Sewage, 1915; Sewerage and Sewage Disposal (with Leonard Metcalf), 1922. Home: Newton Centre, Mass. Died June 15, 1937.

EDDY, HENRY TURNER, univ. dean; b. Stoughton, Mass., June 9, 1844; s. Rev. Henry and Sarah Hayward (Torrey) E.; A.B., Yale, 1867, Ph.B., Sheffield Scientific Sch., 1868, A.M., 1870; C.E., Cornell, 1870, Ph.D., 1872; studied at U. of Berlin and Physikalische Inst., Berlin, 1879; Sorbonne and Collége de France, Paris, 1880; (LL.D., Center Coll., 1892; Sc.D., Yale, 1912); m. Sebella Elizabeth Taylor, Jan. 4, 1870. Instr. in field work, Sheffield Scientific Sch., 1867-68; instr. Latin and mathematics, U. of Tenn., 1868-69; asst. prof. mathematics and civ. engring., Cornell, 1869-73; adj. prof. mathematics, Princeton, 1873-74; prof. mathematics and astronomy and civ. engring., 1874-90, dean academic faculty, 1874-77, 1884-89, acting pres. and pres.-elect, 1890, U. of Cincinnati; pres. Rose Poly. Inst., 1891-94; prof. engring. and mechanics, 1894-1907, head prof. mathematics and mechanics Coll. Engring., 1907-12, dean Grad. Sch., 1906-12, prof. and dean emeritus, 1912—, U. of Minn. Author: Concrete Steel Construction (with C. A. P. Turner), 1914, new edit., 1919. Home: Minneapolis, Minn. Died 1921.

EDDY, NATHAN BROWNE, pharmacologist; b. Glens Falls, N.Y., Aug. 4, 1890; s. Charles Appleton and Aletta Amelia (Norcross) E.; M.D., Cornell U., 1911; D.Sc., U. Mich., 1963; m. Wilhelmina Marie Ahrens, Sept. 7, 1913; 1 son, Charles Ernest. Began practice of medicine, N.Y.C., 1911; instr. physiology McGill U., 1916-20; asst. prof. physiology and pharmacology U. Alta., 1920-28, asso. prof., 1928-30; research prof. pharmacology U. Mich., 1930-39; formerly cons. biologist in alkaloids, USPHS, prin. pharmacologist, 1939-48, med. officer, 1948-60, cons. on narcotics, 1960-73. Co-recipient 1st annual award Am. Pharm. Mfrs. Assn., 1939. Profl. asso. NRC, 1960-67, chmn. com. on drug dependence, 1970-71; exec. sec. com. on drug addiction and narcotics, 1947-67; mem. Expert Com. on Narcotic Drugs, WHO, chmn., 1949-51, 57, 63, 67, 68; chmn. adv. com. to Bur. Narcotics under Narcotics Mfg. Act. of 1960; cons. Bur. Narcotics and Dangerous Drugs, 1968-73. Recipient citation Dept. Health and Welfare; Sixth Lister Meml. Lect., Edinburg, 1960; William Freeman Snow award Am. Social Health Assn., 1967; Hillebrand prize Chem. Soc. Washington, 1968; Meml. award WHO, 1968; gold medal Eastern Psychiat. Research Assn., 1970. Fellow A.A.A.S.; mem. Soc. Pharmacol. and Exptl. Therapeutics (mem. council 1944). Soc. Exptl. Biology and Medicine, Coll. Clin. Pharmacology, Coll. Neuro-psychopharmacology, Internat. Narcotics Enforcement Officers Assn., Sigma Xi. Republican. Methodist. Club: Cosmos. Co-author: Pharmacology of Opium Alkaloids; Synthetic Drugs with Morphine-Like Effect; Codeine and Its Alternates for Pain and Cough Relief. Contbr. to med., sci. jours. Address: Bethesda MD Died 1973.

EDDY, WALTER HOLLIS, physiol. chemist; b. Brattleboro, Vt., Aug. 26, 1877; B.S., Amherst, 1898; A.M., Columbia, 1908; Ph.D., 1909, Instr. sci., high sch., Amherst, 1898-1900, Passaic, N.J., 1900-03; head dept. biology, N.Y.C. High Sch. Commerce, 1903-17; asso. in biochemistry Coll. Phys. and Surg. (Columbia), 1908-13; research chemist N.Y. Hosp., 1913—; with Tchrs. Coll. (Columbia), 1919-41, prof. physiol. chemistry, 1922-41, now emeritus; dir. Bur. Food, Sanitation and Health, Good Housekeeping Mag., 1927-41; cons. chemist and conductor, Food Forum program WOR, 1941-48; sci. dir. Am. Chlorophyll, Inc., Lake Worth, Fla., 1948-52, Am. Chlorophyll Div., Strong Cobb Co., 1952; research dir. Mangrove Products, Inc., West Palm Beach, Fla., cons. chem. engr., 1953—; research cons. U.S. Vitamin and Pharm. Corp. Served from capt. to maj. Nutrition Div., U.S. Army, 1917-19; an organizer Div. Food and Nutrition, A.E.F., and made chief div. Author: Experimental Physiology and Anatomy, 1906; Vitamin Manual, 1921; Nutrition, 1928; The Avitaminoses, 1937, rev. edit., 1941, 1945. What Are the Vitamins?, 1941; We Need Vitamins, 1941; Vitaminology 1949, also many articles on foods and vitamins. Home: 1227 N. Lakeside Dr., Lake Worth, Fla. Died Oct. 1959.

EDGAR, CHARLES LEAVITT, electrical engr.; b. Griggstown, N.J., Dec. 23, 1860; s. Thomas and Annie (Veghte) E.; A.B., Rutgers Coll., 1882, E.E., 1887, D.Sc., 1927; also LL.D., Tufts College, 1927; m. Annette M. Duclos, June 16, 1886. In employ of Edison Electric Light Co., New York, 1883-87; gen. supt., 1887-90, v.p. and gen. mgr., 1890-1900, pres. and gen. mgr., 1900—, Edison Electric Illuminating Co. of Boston; chmn. bd. N.E. Power Assn. Trustee Rutgers U., Employers Group Associates, Mass. Utilities Associates (exec. com.); dir. Life Extension Inst. Republican. Episcopalian. Home: Brookline, Mass. Died Apr. 14, 1932.

EDGAR, GRAHAM, chemist; b. Fayetteville, Ark., Sept. 19, 1887; s. George Mathews and Rebecca (Fry) E.; B.S., U. Ky., 1907; Ph.D., Yale, 1909; m. Luena N. Dunbar, Oct. 9, 1926; 1 dau., Nancy (Mrs. Warren Fales). Asst., later asso. prof. chemistry U. Va., 1909-17; prof. chemistry Cal. Inst. Tech., 1917-18; sec. research information service NRC, 1918-19; prof. chemistry U. Va., 1919-24; dir. research Ethyl Corp., 1924-52, v.p., 1932-52; v.p. Ethyl-Dow Chemical Co., 1933-52, retired; now cons. chem. engr. Cons. chemist Ordnance Dept., U.S. Army, 1918-19. Mem. Am. Chem. Soc., Am. Petroleum Inst., Soc. Automotive Engrs., Inst. Aero. Scis., Am. Soc. Testing Materials, Inst. Petroleum Technologists (London), Phi Beta Kappa, Sigma Xi, Tau Beta Pi. Democrat. Clubs: Chemists (N.Y.C.); Field (Bronxville). Contbr. Jour. Am. Chem. Soc., Am. Jour. Sci. Home: Riversville Rd., Greenwich, Conn. Died Sept. 8, 1955.

EDGECOMBE, SAMUEL (WHEELER), horticulturist; b. Decatur, Ill., July 7, 1907; s. Robert and Luella (Wheeler) E.; B.S.A., U. Manitoba (awarded U. Gold Medal for Scholarship), 1930; M.Sc., Ia. State Coll. (fellow in pomology), 1931, Ph.D., 1936; m. Winnie Davis Slusser, June 10, 1932; children—Virginia Elaine (Mrs. Richard K. Johnson), Roberta-Gay (Mrs. Stephen Shadle). With Ia. Emergency Garden Relief Program, Ia. State Coll. Extension Service, 1933, forest pathologist, 1933; dir. subsistence gardens, Ia. Emergency Relief Adminstrn., 1934, dir. Ia. Service Bur. Transients, 1934-35; extension asst. prof. horticulture and chmn. hort. extension service, Ia. State Coll., 1935-42, extension asso. prof. and asso. research prof., 1941-42; asso. prof. plant sci., U. Manitoba, 1942-44; research dir., v.p., dir. of bd. W. Atlee Burpee Co., Phila., 1944-47, vegetable prodn. head, 1945—; head, prof. horticulture, Winnipeg Victory Garden Program; chmn. Winnipeg Food Conservation Program Com., 1942-44; vegetable judge, All Am. Selections, 1946; 1st v.p. Am. Garden Found., 1947; pres. Winnipeg Hort. Soc. Assn., 1943-44; hon. pres. Ft. Garry Hort. Soc., 1943-44; dir. Manitoba Hort. Assn., 1942-44. Mem. Soc. Econ. Entomologists, Ia. Acad. Sci., Am. Soc. Hort Sci. (mem. com. edn., chmn. 1950-51), A.A.A.S., Am. Polmol. Soc., Ia. State Hort.

Soc. (dir. at large 1941-42), Utah, Wash., Colo. hort. socs., Western Canadian Soc. Hort. (1st pres., 1943-44), Agrl. Inst. Can., N.Y. Bot. Garden, Am. Acad. Polit. and Social Sci., Am. Hort. Soc., Pan Am. Assn. Phila., Am. Beekeepers Fedn. (chmn. honey and pollen plants com., 1948-52), Sigma Xi. Presbyn. Club: Utah Associate Garden. Contbr. articles hort. jours. Home: 493 W. 3d North, Logan, Utah. Died Feb. 5, 1959.

EDISON, OSKAR E(DWIN), educator; b. Gothenburg, Neb., Jan. 2, 1892; s. Erik Edward and Ingrid (Carlson) E.; B.S., U. Neb., 1914; M.S., 1915, E.E., 1924; m. Vella Wolcott, Oct. 23, 1915; children—Elizabeth (Mrs. H. C. Christian), Edward, Eleanor (Mrs. E. J. Busch, Jr.). Switchboard operator Commonwealth Edison Co., Chgo., 1915-17; instr., elec. engring., U. Neb., 1917-19, asst. prof., 1919-25, asso. prof., 1925-44, prof. elec. engring., 1944-60; spl. cons. Moon Lake Electric, Vernal, Utah, 1960-64. Cons. engr. elec. engring., 1939—. Fellow Am. Inst. Elec. Engrs.; mem. Am. Assn. U. Profs., Am. Soc. Engring. Edn., Sigma Xi, Sigma Tau. Author: Electrical Engineering Laboratory Practice (with Prof. F. W. Norris), 1928. Home: 3248 T St., Lincoln, Neb. 68503. Died July 6, 1964.

EDISON, THOMAS A(LVA), inventor; b. Milan, O., Feb. 11, 1847; s. Samuel and Nancy E.; received some instruction from his mother; (hon. Ph.D., Union Coll., 1878; D.Sc., Princeton U., 1915; LL.D., Univ. of the State of N.Y., 1916); m. Mary G. Stillwell, 1873; children—Marion Estelle, Thomas A., William L.; m. 2d, Mina Miller, 1886; children—Madeleine, Charles Theodore. At 12 years of age became newsboy on the Grand Trunk Ry.; later learned telegraphy; worked as operator at various places in U.S. and Canada; invented many telegraphic appliances, including automatic repeater, quadruplex telegraph, printing telegraph, etc. Established workshop at Newark, N.J., removing to Menlo Park, N.J., 1876, and later (1887) to West Orange, N.J. Invented machines for quadruplex and sextuplex telegraphic transmission; the electric pen and mimeograph; the carbon telephone transmitter; the microphone; the microtasimeter for detection of small changes in temperature; the megaphone; the phonograph; the incandescent lamp and light system; the electric valve, (at first called the "Edison effect"), now fundamentally essential in wireless telegraphy; a system of wireless telegraphy to and from moving railway trains; motion pictures; the telescribe; alkaline storage battery; since commencement of European War, 1914, designed, built and operated successfully several benzol plants; also 2 carbolic acid plants; also other chemical plants for making myrbane aniline oil, aniline salt, and paraphenylenediamine; has received patents for more than 1,000 inventions. Was made Chevalier, Officer, and afterwards Comdr. Legion of Honor, by French Govt.; apptd. 1903, hon. chief consulting engr., St. Louis Expn., 1904. Awarded John Fritz medal, 1908; Rathenau medal (German), Am. Mus. of Safety, 1914; congressional gold medal, 1928, "for development and application of inventions that have revolutionized civilization in the last century." Pres. Naval Consulting Bd., July 1915—. Made many war inventions for U.S. Govt. Home: West Orange, N.J. Died Oct. 18, 1931.

EDMANDS, SAMUEL SUMNER, engr., educator; b. Kalamazoo, Mich., Apr. 30, 1877; s. John and Maria Clara (Goodwin) E.; B.S. in E.E., 1899, D.Eng., 1930, Worcester Poly. Inst.; m. Althea Florence Miller, Nov. 28, 1916; 1 dau., Patricia. With Am. Tel. & Tel. Co., Providence, R.I., 1899-1900; instr. elec. engring., Ohio State U., 1900-01; teacher and head of dept. elec. engring., 1901-10, dir. Sch. of Science and Technology, 1910—, Pratt Inst., Brooklyn, N.Y. Died May 24, 1938.

EDMONDS, HARRY MARCUS WESTON, physicist; b. Oshkosh, June 25, 1862; s. Marcus A. and Mary E. (Weston) E.; A.B., U. of Calif., 1882; M.D., Hahnemann Med. Coll., Phila., 1893; postgrad work; univs. of Gottingen, Bonn and Leipzig; m. Mary D. Bigelow, June 8, 1889; children—Marc Weston, Dorothy, Katherine. With U.S. Coast and Geol. Survey, 1889-1909; magnetician, Dept. Terrestrial Magnetism, Carnegie Instn., 1909-30, retired. Comdr. yacht Carnegie, 1917-18; in charge Huancayo Magnetic Obs., Peru, 1919-21; co-operated with New Zealand in the operation of Apia Observatory, Samoa, 1921-22. Address: Carnegie Institution, Washington. Died Apr. 4, 1945.

EDSON, CYRUS, physician; b. Albany, N.Y., Sept. 8, 1857; s. Franklin E., ex-mayor of New York; ed. Columbia Coll.; grad. Coll. Phys. & Surg., 1881; became asst. sanitary insp., 1882, and promoted through grades to commr. of health of New York; 3 terms pres. Bd. of Pharmacy, city and Co. of New York; apptd. commr. of health of State of N.Y., 1893; was surgeon and lt. col. N.Y. Nat. Guard; has served in various other positions; inventor of many useful surg. instruments; m. Virginia Churchill Page (died 1889); m. 2d, Mary E. Quick. Home: New York, N.Y. Died 1903.

EDSON, HOWARD AUSTIN, plant pathologist; b. Randolph, Vt., Aug. 14, 1875; s. Franklin Howard and May Eunice (Bell) E.; grad. Vt. State Normal Sch., 1892; B.S. in Chemistry, U. of Vt., 1906; M.S. in Biology, 1910; Ph.D., U. of Wis., 1913; m. Lillian Sarah Buck, June 21, 1906; children—Thelma Cecilia (dec.), Ralph Howard, Margaret May. Asst. botanist and instr. bacteriology, U. of Vt. and Vt. Agr. Expt. Sta., 1906-09; bacteriologist and asst. prof. bacteriology, same, 1909-10; plant pathologist U.S. Dept. Agr., 1910-27, sr. pathologist in charge cotton, truck, and forage crop disease investigations, 1924-27; chief examiner of U.S. Civil Service Commn., 1927-33, and prin. examiner same, 1933-34; prin. pathologist in charge mycology and plant disease survey, U.S. Dept. of Agr., 1934-45; retired, 1945. Made plant disease survey of Philippines, 1916, and study of sugar beet and Irish potato diseases in Europe, 1914; service for Joint Congl. Commission on Reclassification of Salaries, 1919-20, on staff of Personnel Classification Bd., 1923-24. Fellow A.A.A.S.; mem. Am. Phytopathol. Soc. (treas. and business mgr. Phytopathology, 1935-43). Bot. Soc., America Bot. Soc., Washington, Washington Acad. Sciences, Sigma Xi, Phi Beta Kappa, Phi Delta Theta. Republican. Presbyn. Clubs: Cosmos, Federal (pres. 1932). Home: 3810 4th St. N.W., Washington 11 DC

EDWARDS, ALBA M., statistician; b. Savannah, Mo., Sept. 21, 1872; s. Phineas and Mary (Osborn) E.; A.B., U. of Okla., 1903; A.M., Yale, 1905, Ph.D., 1906; m. Edith Winifred Schurr, Aug. 2, 1910; children—Earl Lester, John Bruce, Lloyd Grant. Special agent Carnegie Instn., of Washington, 1906-07; acting professor Bowdoin Coll., 1907-09; statistician for occupations, Bureau of the Census, 1909-43. Member Am. Statis. Assn. Author: Labor Legislation of Connecticut, 1907; also census reports and articles on statis. subjects. Address: 2522 12th St. N.W., Washington DC

EDWARDS, IRA, geologist; b. Hulberton, N.Y., Apr. 22, 1893; s. Frank S. and Alice M. (Sherman) E.; B.S., U. of Rochester, 1913, M.S., 1914; Ph.D., George Washington U., 1930; m. Nora E. Dicke, July 17, 1917. Began as lab. asst., U. of Rochester, 1910; expert in paleontology, N.Y. State Museum, Albany, 1914-16; asst. Milwaukee Pub. Museum, 1916-19, asst. curator geology, 1919-20; adjunct prof. geology, U. of Tex., 1920-21; curator of geology, Milwaukee Pub. Museum, 1922-39, dir. since 1940; geologist Wis. Natural History and Geol. Survey, 1924-30, asst. editor Museum publs., 1925-39, editor since 1940; instr. U. of Wis. Extension Div., 1935-39. Fellow Paleontol. Soc., Geol. Soc. America; mem. A.A.A.S., Wis. Acad. Sciences, Arts and Letters, Am. Museums Assn., Wis. Archeol. Soc., British Museums Assn., Theta Chi, Sigma Gamma Epsilon, Sigma Xi. Conglist. Club: Rotary (Milwaukee). Contbr. to Milwaukee Pub. Museum Yearbook. Home: 2651 N. 60th St. Address: Milwaukee Public Museum, Milwaukee, Wis. Died Oct. 31, 1943.

EDWARDS, PHILIP R(ARICK), bacteriologist; b. Owensboro, Ky., Aug. 30, 1901; s. Elza and Celishia (Rarick) E.; B.S., U. Ky., 1922, D.Sc., 1959; Ph.D., Yale, 1925; m. Katherine Brewer, Sept. 20, 1927; children—Katherine E., Dorothy. Bacteriologist dept. animal pathology, Ky. Agrl. Exptl. Sta., 1925-48; distinguished prof. U. Ky., 1498; chief enteric bacteriology unit Communicable Disease Center, USPHS, Atlanta, 1948-62, chief bacteriology sect., 1962—. Recipient Distinguished Service award U.S. Dept. Health, Edn. and Welfare, 1955; Kimble Methodology Research award, 1956. Fellow Am. Acad. Microbiology (bd. govs.); mem. Soc. Am. Bacteriologists (v.p. 1958, pres. 1959), Soc. Exptl. Biology and Medicine, Am. Pub. Health Assn., Am. Vet. Med. Assn. (hon.), Sigma Xi, Gamma Alpha, Alpha Gamma Rho. Presbyn. Home: 207 Upland Rd., Decatur, Ga. 30030. Office: Communicable Disease Center, Atlanta 22. Died May 16, 1966.

EDWARDS, ROBERT WILKINSON, microbiologist; b. Portland, Ore., Apr. 6, 1914; s. William Dresser and Lucy (Wilkinson) E.; B.S., Memphis State Coll., 1948; M.S., U. Tenn., 1949; m. Ruth Mae Rawlins, Apr. 19, 1941; 1son, Robert Wilkinson. Civilian pilot, 1930-40; pres. Edwards Aircraft Corp., Memphis, 1938-40; asst. traffic mgr. Chgo. & So. Airlines, Houston, 1945-46; asst. prof. Tenn. Poly. Inst., Cookville, 1949-51; chief bacteriologist Cook County Hosp., Chgo., 1951-53; microbiologist U.S. Army, 1956-66; tech. staff scientist Airtronics, Inc., Washington, 1966-69; cons. applied microbiology. Served to maj. USAAF, 1940-45; USAF, 1953-56. Decorated Bronze Star medal, Air medal. Mem. N.Y. Acad. Scis., Am. Soc. Microbiologists, Soc. Indsl. Microbiologists, Nat. Assn. Corrosion Engrs., Marine Tech. Soc., Am. Assn. Contamination Control, Quiet Birdmen. Club: OX-5 of America (Md.). Home: Braddock Heights MD Died Sept. 24, 1969.

EGAN, LOUIS HENRY, elec. engr.; b. La Crosse, Wis., Nov. 21, 1881; s. John M. and Susanna (Gallagher) E.; Ph.B., Yale, 1904; m. Fanny James, Oct. 2, 1912. Asst. engr., div. mgr. Detroit Edison Co., 1905-09; gen. mgr. Kansas City Light & Power Co., 1910-16; with Union Electric Co. of Mo., 1916—, successively asst. gen. mgr., v.p., pres., 1920—; pres. Mississippi River Power Co. (Keokuk, Ia.), Ia. Union Electric Co., Union Electric Co. of Ill., Union Colliery Co., The St. Louis County Gas Co., Union Electric Land and Development Co., St. Louis & Belleville Electric Ry. Co.; dir. Mercantile-Commerce Bank & Trust Co., Mercantile-Commerce Nat. Bank. Trustee Edison Electric Inst. Mem. Am. Inst. Elec. Engrs. Home: 30 Brentmoor, Clayton, Mo. Office: 315 N. Twelfth Boul., St. Louis. Deceased.

EGGERS, HAROLD EVERETT, pathologist; b. Royalton, Wis., Mar. 1, 1882; s. Frederic and Louise (Matchinski) E.; B.S., U. Wis., 1903, M.A., 1905; M.D., Rush Med. Coll., 1909; m. Eunice Cartwright, Nov. 15, 1911; children—Olden Cartwright (adopted), Harold E., Leigh (Mrs. William F. Bryce), Eunice Cartwright. Fellow in pathology U. Chgo., 1906-07; research appointment Meml. Inst. for Infectious Diseases, 1907-08, 08-09, 10-11; resident physician Cook County Hosp., Chgo., 1909-10; prof. pathology and bacteriology Harvard Med. Sch. of China, 1911-16; prof. U. Neb. Coll. Med., 1916-47, prof. emeritus, 1947—. Ednl. dir. Neb. div. Am. Cancer Soc., 1946—; dir. Bur. Cancer Control, Neb. Health Dept., 1947—. Instr. medicine O.T.C., Ft. Riley, Kan., Camp Greenleaf, Ga., New Haven, Conn. Mem. Soc. Am. Bacteriologists, Phi Beta Kappa, Alpha Chi Sigma, Alpha Omega Alpha, Phi Beta Pi. Research in normal opsonins, racial immunity, tropical ulcer in China. Home: 303 S. 51st Av. Office: 809 Brandeis Theater Bldg., Omaha. Died Nov. 1966.

EGGLESTON, CARY, physician; b. Brooklyn, N.Y., Aug. 18, 1884; s. George Cary and Marion (Craggs) E.; grad. Berkeley School, New York, 1902; studied U. of Jena, Germany, 1903; M.D., Cornell U. Med. Coll., 1907; m. May Appleton Parker, June 3, 1916; children—Nancy May (Mrs. Edward Holcomb), Forrest Cary. Intern New York Hosp., Sloane Hosp. for Women, 1907-09; phys. Spence Sch. Soc. for Crippled Children, 1910-12; mem. Asso. Tuberculosis Clinics, N.Y., 1910-12; chief clinic Children's Dept., Demilt Dispensary, 1911-12; sr. asst. phys. N.Y. Hosp., out-patient dept., 1910-12; asst. phys. Bellevue Hosp. Dispensary, tuberculosis div., 1910-12; instr. pharmacology, 1911-18; asst. prof., 1918-23, Cornell U. Med. Sch., asst. prof. clin. medicine, July 1923-39; asso. prof. clin. medicine since 1939; asst. attending phys., City Hosp., 1915-18; adj. asst. visiting physician Bellevue Hospital, 1919-23; assistant visiting physician, 1923-33, visiting physician, 1933-50, consulting physician from 1950; associate attending physician New York Hospital, 1932-44, attending physician from 1944, cons. phys. from 1951; cons. phys. N.Y. Infirmary for Women and Children since 1934; cons. cardiologist Willard Parker Hosp. since 1932; cons. cardiologist, 1938, Hosp. Special Surgery, Manhattan Eye, Ear and Throat Hosp. from 1945. Fellow (founder) Am. Acad. Compensation Med., 1948. Fellow N.Y. Acad. Med., A.M.A., Assn. Am. Phys., Am. Soc. Clin. Investigation; mem. N.Y. State and N.Y. Co. med. socs., A.A.A.S., Alpha Omega Alpha, Phi Alpha Sigma Dem. Clubs: Quill, West Side Tennis, Univ. Author: Essentials of Prescription Writing, 1913. Contbr. to textbooks. Asso. editor New York Medical Journal, 1911-19; editor in charge dept. of therapeutics, Am. Jour. of. Med. Sciences. Second v.p. U.S. Pharmacopoeial Conv. (XII Revision), 1940, pres., 1941-50. Home: New York City NY Died Nov. 15, 1966; buried Eggleston Cemetery, Brooklyn NY

EGGLETON, FRANK E(GBERT), univ. prof.; b. Rutland Center, N.Y., Sept. 24, 1893; s. Lewis Edmund and Eleanor Rickett (Bennett) E.; A.B., Hillsdale Coll., 1922; M.A., U. of Mich., 1923, Ph.D., 1930; m. Gladys Jane Vary, Aug. 6, 1919; children—Reginald Charles, Phylis Roberta, Richard Elton. Asst. biology, Hillsdale Coll., 1919-22; asst. zoology, U. of Mich., 1922-23; instr. zoology, Syracuse Univ., 1923-26; instr. Zoology, U. of Mich., 1926-30, asst. prof., 1930-37, asso. prof., 1937-51, prof. from 1952. Asst. limnology, U. of Mich. biol. sta., 1927-30, mem. station staff since 1931. Served U.S. Army, 1917-19. Received Russel award, Mich., 1937; distinguished alumni award Hillsdale Coll., 1958. Fellow A.A.A.S. (council 1946-52); mem. Am. Micros. Society (v.p. 1938, sec. 1946-51, editor 1946-51, president 1952), Am. Soc. Zoology, Ecol. Soc. Am., Am. Soc. Limnol and Oceanog., American Fish Society, Wilderness Society, Michigan Academy Science, Wis. Academy Science, American Association University Professors, American Soc. Systematic Zoology, Sigma Xi, Phi Kappa Phi, Phi. Sigma. Epsilon Delta Alpha. Delta Sigma Phi. Baptist. Club: University. Co-author: Problems of Lake Biology; Plant and Animal Communities. Contbr. research articles to scientific jours. Editor of Transactions, Am. Micros. Soc., 1946-51, mem. editorial board, 1952-60, mem. exec. com., 1938, and from 1960. Home: Ann Arbor MI Died May 3, 1970; buried Washtenong Meml. Park, Ann Arbor MI

EGLOF, WARREN K., chemist; b. Troy, N.Y., Mar. 19, 1899; s. Frederick E. and Eliza (Baumbach) E.; Ch.E., Rensselaer Poly. Inst., 1921; M.S., Niagara (N.Y.) U., 1935, Ph.D., 1938; m. Marguerite A. Frentz, Dec. 31, 1927; 1 dau., Marcia A. Instr., Rensselaer Poly. Inst., 1921-24; chemist City of Newburgh, 1924-26; prof. chemistry, Niagara U., 1926—; became chief operator, chemist Niagara County Water Dist., 1960. Mem. Am. Chem. Soc., Am. Water Works Assn., N.Y. State Sewage Works Assn., Sigma Xi. Home: 3763 McKoon Av., Niagara Falls, N.Y. 14305. Office: Niagara U., Niagara, N.Y. Died July 3, 1965; buried Mt. View Cemetery, Pekin, N.Y.

EGLOFF, GUSTAV, research in petroleum; b. N.Y. City; s. August and Mary E.; A.B., Cornell U., 1912; A.M., Columbia, 1913, Ph.D., 1915; D.Sc., Polytechnic Inst. Bklyn., 1938, Armour Inst. Tech., 1940, Philadelphia Coll. of Pharmacy and Science, 1944; married. Asst. in Chandler Mus., Barnard research fellow, 1914-15; chemist U.S. Bur. Mines, 1915-16, Aetna Chem. Co., Pittsburgh, 1916-17; dir. research Universal Oil Products Co., Chicago, 1917—. Holder of 250 patents on processing petroleum oil, coal, shale oil and chemical derivatives of hydrocarbons; delegate World Power Conference, London, 1928, 36, Berlin, 1930, Washington, 1936, London, 1950; delegate Congress for Automobile Transportation, Rome, 1928, World Engring. Congress, Tokyo, 1929, Internat. Bituminous Coal Conv., Pittsburgh, 1926, 28, 31, World Petroleum Congress, London, 1933, 37 (v.p. Congress); Internat. Congress of Chem., Rome, 1938; lectured before chem. symposium of Royal Inst. Chem., St. Andrews, Scotland, July 1947, Internat. Congress of Pure and Applied Chem., 1947, 1951; dir. sci. and tech. com., International Petroleum Expn. and Congress, Tulsa, Okla., 1948. Has lectured at Columbia, Princeton, Chicago, Northwestern, California, Southern Calif., Stanford, Mo., Mich., N.Y., Johns Hopkins; mem. com. on petroleum exhibits, Century of Progress, Chicago, 1933; chmn. sci. exhibit Internat. Oil Expn., Tulsa, 1938-42; apptd. by Am. Inst. Mining and Metall. Engrs. advisor to Mus. of Science and Industry, Chicago; mem. adv. bd. Chem. Warfare Service, Washington, D.C. Awarded gold medal of Am. Inst. Chemists, 1940; Octave Chanute medal (1939-40), by Western Soc. Engrs.; named "Modern Pioneer," by National Assn. of Manufacturers, 1940; Columbia Univ. Medal for Excellence, June 1943. Head of mission sponsored by Nat. Resources Commn. of China and Acting in an advisory capacity in establishment and development of modern petroleum refining industry in Republic of China; mem. Scandinavian research and industry tour sponsored by Royal Swedish Acad. of Engring. Research, 1946. Fellow Am. Inst. Chemists (pres. 1942-46), A.A.A.S., Royal Society of Arts of Great Britain; member American Chemical Society (councillor at large, dir. Chicago sect.; chmn. petroleum div. 1946-47), Am. Inst. Chem. Engrs. (dir.), Am. Inst. Mining and Metall. Engrs. (chmn. Chicago Section, 1934), Wash. Academy Sciences, Chmn. Inst. of Can., Ill. Soc. Engrs., Franklin Inst., Soc. Chem. Industry, Am. Petroleum Inst. (dir.), Nat. Petroleum Assn., Inst. Petroleum Technologists (London), Soc. Am. Mil. Engrs., Western Soc. of Engrs., (v.p., mem. development and library committees), Soc. Automotive Engrs., Am. Soc. for Testing Materials, Adult Edn. Soc. of Chicago (dir.), Ill. Acad. Science, Am. Geog. Society (fellow), Washington Award Commn., Sigma Xi, Phi Lambda Upsilon. Clubs: Chemists of Chicago (pres. 1934); Chemists of New York (v.p. 1939-41); Cosmos (Washington, D.C.). Author: Earth Oil, 1933; The Reactions of Pure Hydrocarbons, 1937; The Physical Constants of Hydrocarbons, Vol. 1, 1939, Vol. 2, 1940; Catalysis, 1940; Emulsions and Foams, 1941; Isomerization of Pure Hydrocarbons, 1942; Physical Constants of Hydrocarbons, Vol. III, 1946. Contbr. over 425 articles to tech. and trade journals on petroleum industry, particularly cracking and refining of oil. Elected by U. Edinburgh to give Romanes lecture in chemistry, 1951. Home: 2100 Lincoln Park West, Chicago 14. Office: 30 E. Algonquin Rd., Des Plaines, Ill. Died Apr. 29, 1955; buried Yonkers, N.Y.

EHRLICH, HARRY, surgeon; b. West Farms, N.Y., Mar. 22, 1909; s. Louis and Anna (Spummburgh) E.; U. Va., 1929; M.D., L.I. Coll. Medicine, 1933; m. Estelle Monaghan, July 13, 1935; children—Margery, John. Intern Kings Count Hosp., Brooklyn, 1933-35; asst. surgeon Nathan Littauer Hosp., Gloversville, N.Y., 1935-40; resident pathologist Beth Israel Hosp., 1940-42; asst. surg. resident, Rockefeller fellow and chief surg. resident Meml. Hosp., 1942-46; asso. Dr. Hayes Martin, 1946-47; asso. surgeon in charge head and neck surgery Mt. Sinai Hosp. since 1947, cons. head and neck surgeon, tumor clinic since 1947; specialist in treatment cancer of head and neck. Diplomate Am. Bd. Surgery. Fellow A.C.S.; mem. Am. Radium Soc., N.Y. Co. Med. Soc., A.M.A., N.Y. Acad Medicine, Am. Cancer Soc., James Ewing Soc., N.Y. Cancer Soc. Author articles med. jours. Asst. editor of Cancer, 1949-51. Home: 860 Fifth Av. Office: 715 Park Av., N.Y.C. 21. Died July 31, 1952; buried Ferncliff Cemetery, Hartsdale, N.Y.

EICHELBERGER, WILLIAM SNYDER, astronomer; b. Baltimore, Sept. 18, 1865; s. Albert G. and Martha (Snyder) E.; A.B., Johns Hopkins, 1886, Ph.D., 1891; m. Vola McCrea, Mar. 21, 1894; children—Emily Louise (dec.), Donald McCrea (dec.), Adele Marie (Mrs. Bernard Tallman). Asst. Nautical Almanac Office, 1889-90, 1896-98; instr. mathematics and astonomy, Wesleyan U., Conn., 1890-96; computer in U.S. Naval Observatory, 1898-1900; prof. mathematics U.S. Navy since 1900; was head of div. meridian instruments, 1902-07; in charge dept. of astron. observations, U.S. Naval Obs., 1907-08; in charge cataloguing Washington Zone Observations of 1846-52, 1908-11; in charge reducing and cataloguing meridian circle observations of 1903-11, 1908-19, dir. Nautical Almanac, 1910-29, U.S. Naval Obs.; with Eastman Kodak Co., Rochester, N.Y., since 1929. Mem. U.S. eclipse expdn., Pinehurst, N.C., 1900; in charge U.S. eclipse stas. at Fort de Kock, Sumatra, 1901, Daroca, Spain, 1905. Asso. Royal Astron. Society; fgn. corr. Bureau des Longitudes; fellow A.A.A.S.; mem. Am. Astron. Soc. Astronomische Gesellschaft, Washington Acad. Sciences, Philos. Soc. Washington (pres. 1915), Phi Beta Kappa. Wrote: "Positions and Proper Motions of 1504 Standard Stars," in Astron. Papers of Am. Ephemeris, 1925; (with Arthur Newton) "The Orbit of Neptune's Satellite and the Pole of Neptune's Equator," in Astron. Papers of Am. Ephemeris, 1926; contbr. papers to Govt. pubs. and Astron. Jour.; etc. Address: 1447 St. Paul St., Rochester NY

EICKEMEYER, RUDOLF, inventor, mfr.; b. Altenbamberg, Bavaria, Germany, Oct. 31, 1831; s. Christian and Katherine (Brehm) E.; m. Mary True Tarbell, July 1856 6 children. Came to America, 1850; devised 1st "whip-stitch" for hatbands, 1st successful hat stretching machines; patented 1st hatblocking machine, 1865; designed machine to pounce hats, 1869; developed 1st direct-connected ry. motor for use on N.Y. Elevated R.R.; developed differential gear for mowing and reaping, 1870; secured about 150 patents in U.S. and abroad, including 1st symmetrical drum armature, iron clad dynamo; discovered and was 1st employer of Charles P. Steinmetz; bus. consol. with Gen. Electric Co., 1892; v.p. Yonkers Sch. Bd., trustee 23 years. Died Washington, D.C., Jan. 23, 1895.

EIDMANN, FRANK LEWIS, prof. mech engring.; b. Kingston, N.Y., Dec. 20, 1887; s. John Frederick and Susanna (Reinmuth) E.; prep. edn. Stevens Prep. Sch., 1902-05; M.E., Stevens Inst. of Tech., 1909; m. Ethel Irene Fischbeck, 1924; 1 son, John Frank. Began as instr., Stevens Inst. Tech., 1909; with engring. dept. Olds Gas Power Co. and Seager Engine Works, Lansing, Mich., 1909-13; instr. in gas engines, Y.M.C.A. Evening Sch., Lansing, 1910-13; instr. in mech. engring., Rensselaer Poly. Inst., 1913-15; instr. in gas engines, Albany (N.Y.) Evening Schs., 1914-15; engr. for developing mfg. processes, Am. LaFrance Fire Engine Co., Elmira, N.Y., 1915-16; plant engr. Heald Machine Co., Worcester, Mass., 1916-17; factory mgr. and chief engr. Cowan Truck Co., Holyoke, Mass., 1917-18, 1919-20; travel around the world, 1921-22; cons. engr. Barrett-Cravens Co., Chicago, and Revolvator Co., Jersey City, N.J., 1922-23; asso. prof. of machine design and industrial practice, Princeton U., 1923-30; prof. mech. engring., Columbia, 1930—; dir. research lab., Gen. Time Instruments Corp., New York, 1931—. Served as lt. j.g., U.S. Naval Aviation, 1918-19. Republican. Presbyterian. Author: Economic Control of Engineering and Manufacturing, 1931. Editor: Aircraft Engine Manual, 1919. Home: Princeton, N.J. Died Sept. 4, 1941.

EIESLAND, JOHN (ARNDT), mathematician; b. Ny Hellesund, nr. Christianssand, Norway, Jan. 27, 1867; s. Andreas and Angnete (Abrahamsen) E.; Normal Sch. and Gymnasium, Christianssand; Ph.B., U. of S.Dak., 1891; Ph.D., Johns Hopkins, 1898; Johns Hopkins Scholar, 1897-98; m. Clara June Snyder, Sept. 15, 1904. Came to U.S., 1888; teacher Lutheran Acad., Albert Lea, Minn., 1891-92; prof. mathematics, Thiel Coll., Greenville, Pa., 1895-1903; instr. mathematics, U.S. Naval Acad., 1903-07; prof. mathematics and head of dept., W.Va. U., 1907-38, prof. emeritus since 1938. Sec. W.Va. Acad. Science, 1905-06, pres., 1906-07. Fellow A.A.A.S.; mem. Am. Math. Soc., Math. Assn. America, Circolo Matematico di Palermo (Italy), Deutsche Mathematiker Vereinigung, Phi Beta Kappa. Democrat. Lutheran. Author: Advanced Algebra for Technical Schools and Colleges, 1910; also numerous memoirs in math. jours. Home: Morgantown WV

EIGENMANN, CARL H., zoölogist; b. Flehingen, Germany, 1863; s. Philip and Margaretha (Lieb) E.; A.B., Ind. U., 1886, A.M., 1887, Ph.D., 1889; m. Rosa Smith, Aug. 20, 1887; children—Lucretia Margaretha, Charlotte Elizabeth, Theodore Smith, Adele Rosa E. (Mrs. John O. Eiler), Thora Marie. Prof. zoölogy, 1891—, dean Grad. Sch., 1908—, Ind. U.; curator of fishes, Carnegie Mus., Pittsburgh, 1909-18. Founder and dir. biol. sta., Ind. U., 1895-1920. Explorations in Calif., Ore., Ida., Mont., Dak. and Western Can., 1890-92, Cuba, 1902-04, British Guiana, 1908, Colombia, 1911-12, Peru and Bolivia, 1918, Chile, 1919. Author: Cave Vertebrates of North America, The Archiplata-Archhelenis Theory, The American Characidae, The Fresh-water Fishes of British Guiana, The Fishes of Western South America, and The Doradidae. Home: Bloomington, Ind. Died Apr. 24, 1927.

EILERS (FREDERIC) ANTON, mining engr., metallurgist; b. Nassau, Germany, Jan. 14, 1839; s. E. J. A. Frederic and Elizabeth E.; ed. Mining School, Clausthal, and U. of Göttingen; m. Elizabeth Emrich, May 3, 1863. Came to U.S., 1859; asst. to Adelberg and Raymond, mining engrs., 1863-66; in charge mines and copper smelting works, W.Va., 1866-69; deputy U.S. commr. mining statistics, 1869-76; part owner and mgr. Germania Smelting & Refining Works, Salt Lake City, 1876-79; in smelting business (Billing & Eilers), Leadville, Colo., 1879-82; pres. The Colorado Smelting Co. of Pueblo, Colo., 1883-99; dir. and gen. mgr. United S. & R. Co. of Mont. and Chicago, 1890-99; dir. and tech. mem. of exec. com. of Am. Smelting & Refining Co., and of Am. Smelters' Securities Co., 1899-1910, when retired from active business. V.p. Last Dollar Gold Mining Co.; pres. Colo. Mines Exploring Co. Homes: Brooklyn, and Sea Cliff, L.I., N.Y. Died Apr. 22, 1917.

EILERS, KARL (EMRICH), metallurgist; b. near Marietta, O., Nov. 20, 1865; s. F. Anton and Elizabeth (Emrich) E.; grad. in arts, Poly. Inst. Brooklyn, 1884; E.M., Sch. of Mines (Columbia), 1889; postgrad. work, U. of Berlin, 1889, until spring of 1891; France and Spain 4 mos. each; m. Leonie Jeannette Wurlitzer, Oct. 19, 1896; children—Marguerite E., K. Fritz, F. Farny. Successively assayer Colo. Smelting Co., Pueblo, Colo., St. Louis Smelting & Refining Co., St. Louis, United Smelting & Refining Co., Chicago, until 1893; supt. Colo. Smelting Co., Pueblo, 1893-98; manager, 1899, dir. and mem. exec. com., 1906-20, v.p., 1916-20, Am. Smelting & Refining Co.; cons. practice, N.Y. City, Apr. 1920—; pres. Colo. Mines Exploring Co. Home: Sea Cliff, L.I., N.Y. Died Aug. 18, 1941.

EIMBECK, WILLIAM, geodesist, asst. U.S. Coast and Geod. Survey, since July 1, 1871; b. city of Brunswick, Germany, Jan. 29, 1841; s. Frederick and Henrietta E.; ed. public school and coll., and private instruction; largely self-ed. Draftsman in locomotive works, St. Louis, 1857; later asst. civil engr. in public offices, St. Louis; prof. mechanics and engring., Washington Univ., 2 yrs.; mem. Govt. solar eclipse expdns. to Ill., 1869, and to Italy, 1870. Has been chiefly occupied with the western div. of 39th parallel triangulation across the continent. Fellow A.A.A.S., since 1879; mem. other learned socs. of Washington. Inventor of the invariable reversible pendulum, and the duplex base apparatus of Coast and Geodetic Survey; unmarried. Address: U.S. Coast and Geodetic Survey, Washington.

EINSTEIN, ALBERT, theoretical physicist; b. Ulm an der Donau, Germany, Mar. 14, 1879; s. Hermann and Pauline (Koch) E.; ed. Luitpold Gymnasium, Munich, Aarauer Kantonsschule, Aarau, Switzerland, Technische Hochschule, Zurich, 1895-1900; Ph.D., U. Zurich, 1905; D. honoris causa univs. Oxford, Cambridge, Manchester, Princeton, Paris, Madrid, Harvard, London, numerous others; m. Mileva Marec, 1901; children—Albert, Eduard; m. 2d, Elsa Einstein, 1971 (dec. 1936). Tech. asst. Swiss Patent Office, Berne, 1902; privatdozent, Bern, 1908; prof. extraordinary, Zurich, 1909; prof. theoretical physics, Prague, 1911; returned to corr. post, Zurich, 1912; prof. physics U. Leyden, 1912-28; dir. Kaiser Wilhelm Inst. for Physics, prof. physics U. Berlin, 1914-33; lectr. in Europe, U.S., Far East, 1920's; vis. lectr., Eng., U.S., 1930-33; renounced German citizenship, came to U.S., 1933, naturalized, 1940; apptd. for life as mem. Inst. Advanced Studies, Princeton, N.J., 1933; leading figure in world govt. movement after war; offered presidency of Israel, declined; collaborated with Chaim Weizmann in establishing U. Jerusalem. Recipient Nobel prize for physics, 1921; Fellow Royal Soc., 1921 (Copley medal 1925), medal Franklin Inst., 1935. Mem. Prussian, French (fgn.) acads. scis. Author: Meaning of Relativity, 1923; Sidelights on Relativity, 1923; Investigation on the Theory of Browning Movement, 1926; Builders of the Universe, 1932; On the Method of Theoretical Physics, 1933; (with Sigmund Freud) Why War?, 1933; The World as I See It, 1934; (with Leopold Infeld) Evolution of Physics, 1938, also articles. Originator of spl. and gen. theories of relativity, 1905, 16, which deal with systems in uniform non-accelerated motion, gen. accelerated systems, respectively; assumed for his theory constancy of speed of light in vacuum, particle-like properties of light and relativity of motion and rest; developed law of simultaneity; worked out inter-relationship of mass and energy, showed these are different aspects of same phenomenon; developed in math. detail new theory of gravitation of which Newton's classic theory is but spl. case; developed law of photoelectric effect by applying quantum theory to light, did much to establish quantum mechanics, 1905; worked out math. equation to explain Brownian motion, showed it could be used to determine sizes of molecules; deduced influence of gravity on propagation of light; developed gas theory, derivation of Planck's radiation law, concept of duration of excited states, calculation of probability coefficients of emission and absorption, law of photochem. reactions, theory of specific heats; worked on unified field theory in later years. Died Princeton, N.J., Apr. 18, 1955.

EISEN, GUSTAVUS A(UGUSTUS), biologist, archeologist; b. Stockholm, Sweden, Aug. 2, 1847; s. Frans August and Amalia (Markander) E.; Ph.D., U. of Upsala, Sweden, 1873; came to U.S., Oct. 1873, naturalized, 1887; unmarried. Known specially for researches in Oligochaeta (earthworms) of America, researches in the elements of blood of batrachians and man, and the amoeba of carcinoma. Publns. on antique glass, antique beads and antique bronzes; author of "The Fig," and "The Raisin Industry," articles, the biol. nature of caprification, explorations in Lower Calif., Mexico, Central Am. republics (1880-1903); archeol. explorations, especially Christian archeology and antique glass (1903-15), in Spain, Italy, Algiers, Tunis, Morocco and Egypt; studies in the principal museums of Europe, 1910-15. One time docent in zoölogy, University Upsala, and collaborator, U.S. Dept. Agriculture; late curator Calif. Acad. Sciences. Pres.

San Francisco Micros. Soc. Comdr. Order of North Star (Sweden), 1935; Knight of the Gothic Golden Griffin, 1939. Originator of Sequoia Nat. Park in Calif., 1890. Described and classified the Gellatly and Freer Museum collections of antique glass, Smithsonian Inst. Wrote: (monograph) The Great Chalice of Antioch, 1924; Glass—Antique Glass—Its History and Classification (monograph), 2 vols., 1927. Died Oct. 29, 1940.

EISENHARDT, RAYMOND, research engr., cons., writer; b. Phila., June 29, 1901; s. William George and Mary Augusta (Klaus) E.; M.B.A., Temple U.; m. Mildred Bachman, Nov. 1, 1924; 1 son, Raymond. Cons., writer, editor on tech. matters Dando Co., Phila., 1921-25; asst. to pres. James F. Newcomb & Co., N.Y.C., 1925-30; chmn., dir. Edgar Steiner & Co., Inc., research engring., N.Y.C., 1931—, also chmn.; cons. on sci. research, new product devel., materials handling, packaging techniques. Trustee Parkinson Found. Mem. Sigma Kappa. Lutheran. Mason. Clubs: Pen and Pencil, Poor Richard. Author: Knowledge, 1925; Direct Relections, 2 vols. 1927-28; The Cubby Hole, 1930; The Third Ingredient, 1927; How to Develop Ideas, 1932; Perish the Thought, 1935; The Bull's Eye, 1939; The Mathematics of Physical Design, 1942; Imagination Unlimited, 1952; The Facts of Life, 1959; also articles on methods and econs. of research. Author light verse under pseudonym E. Henry Ray. Patentee in field. Home: 310 Manor Rd., Ridgewood, N.J. Office: 45 Rockefeller Plaza, N.Y.C. 20. Died Aug. 9, 1965.

EISENHART, LUTHER PFAHLER, mathematician; b. York, Pa., Jan. 13, 1876; s. Charles Augustus and Emma Catharine (Pfahler) E.; A.B., Gettysburg Coll., 1896, Sc.D. (hon.), 1921, LL.D., 1926; Ph.D., Johns Hopkins, 1900; hon. Sc.D., Columbia, 1931, U. Pa., 1933, Lehigh, 1935, LL.D., Duke, 1940, Johns Hopkins, 1953; Sc.D. (hon.) Princeton, 1952; m. Anna Maria Dandridge Mitchell, Aug. 17, 1908 (dec. Mar. 1913); 1 son, Churchill; m. 2d, Katharine Riely Schmidt, June 1, 1918; children—Anna Small, Katharine Riely. Instr. prep. dept., Gettysburg Coll., 1896-97; instr. math. Princeton, 1900-05, asst. prof., 1905-09, prof., 1909-45, prof. emeritus, 1945—, dean of the faculty, 1925-33, dean grad. school 1933-45. Trustee Pa. Coll., 1907-14; pres. Assn. Am. Colleges, 1930; chmn. Order Crown of Belgium, 1937; named Pa. Ambassador, York, 1952; archway on Graduate College Rd., Princeton, named in his honor, 1951. Episcopalian. Mem. Am. Math. Soc. (pres. 1931-32, editor Trans. 1917-23), Am. Philos. Soc. (exec. officer 1942-59), A.A.A.S. (v.p., chmn. Sect. A, 1916-17), Phi Kappa Psi, Phi Beta Kappa, Nat. Acad. Sci. (v.p. 1944-48). Clubs: Nassau (Princeton, N.J.); Princeton, Century (N.Y.C.). Author: Differential Geometry of Curves and Surfaces, 1909; Transformations of Surfaces, 1923; Reimannian Geometry, 1925; Non-Riemannian Geometry, 1927; Continuous Groups of Transformations, 1933; Coordinate Geometry, 1939; An Introduction to Differential Geometry, 1940; The Educational Process, 1945; also number of papers on math. Home: 25 Alexander St., Princeton, N.J. Died Oct. 28, 1965; buried Princeton Cemetery.

EISENSCHIML, OTTO, (i'zen-shim-'l), chemist, author; b. Vienna, Austria, June 16, 1880; s. Alexander and Eleanor (Koretz) E.; Chem. Engr., Polytech. Sch. of Vienna, 1901; hon. Litt.D., Lincoln Memorial U., Harrogate, Tenn., 1937; Diploma, Lincoln College, Lincoln, Ill., 1960; m. Bertha Eisenschimel, Jan. 14, 1912; children—Rosalie Ruth, Gerald Alexander, Ralph Eugene. Chemist with Carnegie Steel Co., Pittsburgh, Pa., 1901-04; chief chemist Am. Linseed Co., Chicago, 1904-07, mgr. South Chicago plant, 1907-12; cons. chemist, Chicago, 1912; pres., now chmn. of bd. Scientific Oil Compounding Co., Inc., distributors of materials for paints, varnishes, fungicides, since 1912. Chmn. State Commn. on Purity of Paint Materials (Ill.), 1927-42; chmn. com. cons. Chicago Civil Defense, 1951. Recipient Honor Scroll Award of American Institute Chemists. Mem. National Research Council, American Chemical Society (chmn. 1914), Paint, Oil and Varnish Assn. of U.S., Chicago Hist. Soc., West Side Hist. Soc. of Chicago (president 1936-37, chairman 1938-45), American Institute Chemists (hon.), N.Y. Academy Sciences. Founder, 1st pres. Nat. Soybean Oil Mfrs. Assn. Club: Chgo. Chemists (pres. 1922). Editor Chem. Bull., 1914-17. Author: Why Was Lincoln Murdered?, 1937; Reviewers Reviewed, 1940; In the Shadow of Lincoln's Death, 1940; Without Fame, 1942; The Case of A. L—, Aged 56, 1943; Chicago Murders (co-author), 1945; The Story of Shiloh, 1946. Co-author: The American Iliad, 1947; As Luck Would Have It, 1948; The Celebrated Case of Fitz John Porter, 1950; The Civil War, 1956; Why The Civil War?, 1958; The Hidden Face of the Civil War, 1961; The Civil War in Miniature, 1962. Author tech. and hist. treatises. Editor: Vt. Gen., 1960. Lectr. Home: 2300 Lincoln Park W. Office: 1637 S. Kilbourn Av., Chgo. Died Dec. 9, 1963; ashes scattered at Shiloh.

EKBLAW, WALTER ELMER, (ek'blaw), geographer; b. Rantoul, Ill., Mar. 10, 1882; s. Andrew and Ingrid (Johnson) E.; prep. edn., Austin Prep. Coll., Effingham, Ill., and Central Y.M.C.A. Night Sch., Chicago; A.B., U. of Ill., 1910, A.M., 1912; hon. fellow Clark Univ., 1924-26, Ph.D., 1926; Sc.D. (hon.) Upsala College, 1947; married Augusta May Krieger. February 28, 1918; children—Walter Elmer, Neil William, Elsa May; m. 2d, Ellen L. Lindblad, Jan. 23, 1933. Geologist and botanist, Crocker Land Arctic Expdn., 1913-17; research fellow, U. of Ill., 1917-20; also research asso. Am. Museum Natural History, 1917-22; consultant geologist, 1922-24; editor Economic Geography since 1924; prof. geography, Clark U., since 1926. Decoration: Order of the North Star (Sweden). Member Assn. American Geographers, Am. Assn. of Professional Geographers (vice pres.), Mass. Archeol. Soc. (pres.), A.A.A.S., Am. Anthrop. Soc., Soils Science Society of America, Am. Ornithol. Union, Swedish Colonial Society, Sigma Xi, Gamma Alpha, Theta Nu Epsilon, Acacia. Republican. Episcopalian. Mason. Clubs: Explorers (N.Y.); Cosmos (Washington); Kiwanis (Champaign, Ill.). Contbr. to Annals of Assn. Am. Geographers. Explored large areas of Grant Land and Ellesmere Land. Home: The Homelands, N. Grafton, Mass. Office: Clark University, Worcester, Mass. Died June 5, 1949.

EKELEY, JOHN BERNARD, (ek'le), chemist; b. Orebro, Sweden, Jan. 1, 1869; s. John and Ingeborg (Olson) E.; brought to U.S., 1872; A.B., Colgate U., Hamilton, N.Y., 1891, A.M., 1893 (Sc.D., 1911); Ph.D., U. of Freiburg, in Baden, Germany, 1902; studied Sorbonne, Paris, 1909-10, U. of Berlin, 1910; married Adelaide Evelyn Hobbs, July 18, 1894 (died August 5, 1943); married 2d, Viola Winifred Gaylord, Mar. 16, 1946. Assistant in chemistry at Colgate University, 1891-93; science master, St. Paul's School, Garden City, N.Y., 1893-1900; professor and head dept. of Chemistry, U. of Colo., 1902-37, emeritus, 1937, State chemist of Colo., 1911-33. Inventor, with W. B. Stoddard, of process for extraction of tungsten from tungsten ores; pres. Tungstic Acid Corp., 1922-28. Dir. Nat. State Bank, Boulder, Colo., mem. Colo. Coal Mine Commn., 1911. Fellow A.A.A.S.; mem. Am. Chem. Soc., Am. Electrochem. Soc., Am. Institute of Chemical Engineers, American Institute of Chemists, Colorado-Wyoming Academy of Science, Faraday Society, Royal Central Asian Society, Delta Kappa Epsilon, Phi Beta Kappa, Sigma Xi, Alpha Chi Sigma. Author: A Laboratory Manual of Inorganic Chemistry, 1912, revised, 1923, 28, 34; The Chief Laws and Theories of Chemistry Briefly Stated, 1924; also various research articles in Am. and European chem. jours. Home: 703 11th St., Boulder, Colo. Died Nov. 8, 1951.

EKSERGIAN, RUPEN, (ek-ser'jun), consulting engr.; b. Somerville, Mass., Mar. 30, 1889; s. Carnig and Zoe Elizabeth (Huntington) E.; S.B., Mass. Inst. Tech., 1914, S.M., 1915; S.M., Harvard, 1915; Fellow in physics, Clark U., 1916-17, Ph.D., 1928; m. Maydell Hagenbuch, Aug. 14, 1920; 1 dau., Gloria (Mrs. Gilbert Shaw). Asst. to vice pres. in charge engring. Baldwin Locomotive Works, 1920-29, developed methods of analysis on locomotive design; cons. engr., E. I. du Pont de Nemours & Co., 1929-34; chief cons. engr. E. G. Budd Mfg. Co., 1934-45; cons. engr. The Budd Co., 1945-51; responsible for tech. phase of stainless steel train developments, starting with Pioneer Zephyr) cons. engr. Bethlehem Steel Co.; sometime cons. Am. Car & Foundry, Lukens Steel Co., Day & Zimmermann, Inc., Atomic Power Development Assos., formerly research adviser Am. Locomotive Co. Mem. bd. mgrs. The Franklin Institute, co-founder, sr. staff adviser The Franklin Institute Laboratories for Research & Development, also serves as editor of Franklins Inst. Journal. Served as 1st lt., capt., major, Ordnance Dept., U.S. Army, during World War I; organized ordnance design office Franklin Inst., also served as tech. consultant to Chief of Ordnance Office, and specialist on arty. and heavy ordnance, World War II. Recipient George R. Henderson medal Franklin inst., 1937, Worcester Reed Warner medal Am. Soc. M.E., 1939. Fellow Am. Soc. M.E. Mem. Div. I, Nat. Defense Research Com. Recipient Louis E. Levy medal of Franklin Inst., 1945. Contbr. of articles for Am. Soc. M.E., including Stresses in Locomotive Frames, The Balancing and Dynamic Rail Pressure of Locomotives, The Design of Light Weight Trains and The Design of Axles and Locomotive Crank Pins; also papers for Franklin Inst., including The Dynamical Analysis of Machines, Some Applications of Normal Coordinates to Engring. Vibration System, The Fluid Torque Converter and Coupling, The Efficiency of Power Units and The Reaction of Fluids and Fluid Jets. Author of a book on ordnance engring. for U.S. Army, 1920. Analytical research in applied dynamics and dynamics of machinery. Home: Rose Tree Rd., Media, Pa. Died Dec. 1961.

ELDRED, BYRON E., mech. engr.; b. Jackson, Mich., Feb. 12, 1873; s. Zenas C. and Helen (Carter) E.; B.S., Dartmouth (class of 1896), hon. D.Sc., 1916; m. Mildred Carter, 1896 (div. 1911); m. 2d, Mary Victoria Lawson, Apr. 22, 1911 (died 1930); m. 3d, Mrs. G. Norden Hawthorne, 1931. Engaged in research and engineering work; inventor of many comml. processes and products, among which is a substitute for platinum used extensively in mfr. of electric lamps and electrical contacts, temperature and volume of flame control, the optical light slit used generally in sound recording for theatre pictures, the Talking Book micro-photographic record of sound, and waste coal recovery process utilizing property of absorption of carbonaceous materials. Discoverer of effect of sinusoidal air wave for correcting defective audition and method for continuous casting of metals known as draw-casting. War work during World War I. Recipient John Scott legacy and medal City of Phila., Elliott Cresson gold medal by Franklin Inst. Pres. Nat. Assn. Engrs. Hoover for President, 1928; mem. exec. com. NRC, 1931-32. Del. U.S. Govt. to World Engring. Congress, Tokyo, 1929. Club: Engineers New York (pres. 1938-39). Home: Lime Rock, Conn. Died May 27, 1956. *

ELIASBERG, WLADIMIR G., psychiatrist, neurologist, psychologist, author; b. Wiesbaden, Germany, Dec. 10, 1887; s. Samuel and Rachel E.; student med. colls., univs. Berlin and Heidelberg, M.D., 1912; Ph.D., U. Munich, 1924; m. Esther Talbot; four children. Intern Prof. Kraepelin Hosp., Munich, 1912; voyage as ship's Dr., Far East, 1913; physician Hosp. for Brain Diseases, Munich, 1919-23; founder, sec. gen. German Congress for Psychotherapy, 1926; editor Allg. Aerztl. Ztschrft. f. Psychother.; attending physician and supt. Hosp. for Nervous and Mental Diseases, Munich-Thalkirchen, 1928-30; mem. delegation 7th Internat. Congress for Psychotechnics, 1931; lectr. forensic psychiatry Munich Bar Assn., 1932; chmn. div. indsl. pathology 8th Internat. Congress for Psychotechnics, Prague, 1934; vis. prof. Academie des Sciences Politiques, Prague, 1937; chmn. sci com. for Advancement of Psychotherapy, 1940; Psychiatrist, O.P.D., Mt. Sinai Hosp., 1941-44; lectr. psychology Rutgers U., 1946; psychiat. cons. Bulova Watch Co., 1946; med. dir. Bklyn. treatment unit Citizens Com., N.Y., 1952, Convent Av. and Neighborhood guidance clinics, N.Y., 1953. Certified psychiatrist N.Y. State Bd. Mental Hygiene, 1940; certified examiner State N.Y., 1940. Served as capt. Ger. Army Med. Corps, 1915-18. Diplomate Am. Bds. Neurology and Psychiatry. Fellow Am. Psyhciat. Assn., N.Y. Acad. Medicine, Am. Sociol, Assn.; mem. A.M.A. (life), Rudolf Virchow Med. Soc., Am. Soc. Criminology, Assn. for Psychiat. Treatment Offenders (hon. mem.), Am. Soc. Psychoanalytic Physicians (pres. 1958), N.Y. Soc. Clin Psychiatry, Am. Psychol. Assn., Pirquet Society Clin. Medicine, N.Y. State Assn. Psychology, N.Y. Assn. for History of Medicine, Allg. Aerztl. Ges. f Psychotherapie Vienna (hon.), 1952, Prague Inst. of Psychotechnics (hon.), 1937, Am. Mental Health Found., (v.p.), Acad. Polit. and Social Sci. Phila. Author med. and other books, also numerous articles concerned with psychiatry, psychology, sociology, criminology, child psychology, propaganda, indsl. psychology, grapho-diagnostics, history of medicine. Contbr.: Handbook of Child Guidance, 1940; Handbook of Scientific Proof and Relations of Law and Medicine (Harvard Law Sch.), 1946; Handbook of Correctional Psychology, 1947; Encyclopedia of Criminology, 1948; Handboak of Therapeutic Abortion, 1954; Speaking and Thinking (symposium), 1954; Handbuch d. Neurosenlehre u. Psychotherapy, 1957. Present-Day Psychology, 1955; Psychotherapy and Soc., 1959. Address: NYC NY Died June 1969.

ELIOT, WALTER GRAEME, civil engr.; b. New York, Nov. 16, 1857; s. Augustus G. (M.D.) and Elizabeth (Proctor) E.; E.M., Ph.B., Columbia, 1878, C.E., 1879, Ph.D., 1882; LL.D., St. Francis Xavier Coll., 1892; admitted to senior class, Harvard; m. Maud Stoutenburgh, Feb. 4, 1892; children—Marion Elinor Viola (wife of Lt. Carlton James), Amory Vivion (U.S.A.), Van Cortlandt Stoutenburgh, Priscilla Alden. Insp. tenements, N.Y. Health Dept., 1877-78; judge, municipal, competitions, 1878-80; sanitary engr. of health dept., New York, 1880-81; engring. expert on water supply, 10th Census, 1881; gen. mgr. Am. Photo Litho. Co., 1881-82; sec., auditor Westcott Express Co., 1884-87; editor and a propr. University Magazine, 1890-94; asst. chemist, and insp. foods. health dept., 1896-98. Active for 4 yrs. in orgn. of milk interests of New York; on tech. staff. dept. taxes and assessments, New York, 1898-1902; asst. engr. topog. bur., Borough of Queens, New York, 1902-10, engr. in charge, 1910; commr. parks, Borough of Queens, New York, 1911-14. Author of 1st bill to license professional engrs.; apptd. mem. N.Y. State Board of Licensing for Professional Engrs., term 1921-30 (chmn. 1925). Member Co. K, 7th Regt., N.G. N.Y. and of its victorious rifle teams of 1904, 05, 06; 1st lt. Co. A, 71st Inf., N.G.N.Y., Oct. 1907-09; maj. Coast Arty. Corps., N.G.N.Y., 1911-13; lt. col. Inf., 1918. Trustee New York Coll. Dentistry, 1903-25. Pres. Technical League of Engrs., 1908-11; a founder and mem. Soc. Municipal Engrs., New York. Episcopalian. Author: Sketch of the Eliot Family, 1889; History of the Stoutenburgh Family, 1905. Home: Hyde Park-on-Hudson, N.Y. Deceased.

ELKIN, DANIEL COLLIER, surgeon; b. Louisville, Ky., Mar. 26, 1893; s. Robert and Roberta (Collier) E.; A.B., Yale, 1916; M.D., Emory University, Atlanta, Ga., 1920; Sc.D., Northwestern University, 1952; D.Sc. (honorary), Centre Coll., 1956; married Helen McCarty, November 3, 1923; 1 son, Daniel C. Intern and resident surgeon, Peter Bent Brigham Hosp., Boston, Mass., 1920-24; asst. in surgery, Harvard, 1924; Whitehead prof. of surgery, Emory U., 1929-55, now emeritus. Mem. bd. trustees Univ. Kentucky. Served as colonel Medical Corps, Army of U.S., unit dir. 43d Gen. Hosp., 1941, chief of surg. service Ashford (W.Va.) Gen. Hosp., 1942-46. Apptd. brigadier gen., O.R.C., A.U.S., 1949. Awarded Matas medal for vascular surgery Tulane U., 1940; Legion of Merit, 1945, Fellow A.C.S. (pres.); mem. Soc. Vascular Surgery (president

1948), Soc. Medical Consultants (president 1949), Southern Surgical Assn. (president 1946), American Surgical Assn. (past pres.), American Assn. Thoracic Surgery, Soc. Clinical Surgery (pres. 1947). Presbyn. Clubs: Piedmont Driving, Capital City, (Atlanta); Pendennis (Louisville); Graduates (New Haven). Author: Medical Reports of John Y. Bassett, 1941. Contributor numerous papers relating to surgery of heart and blood vessels to sci. publs. Home: Lancaster, Ky. Office: Emory University, Ga. Died Nov. 3, 1958; buried Lancaster, Ky.

ELKIN, WILLIAM LEWIS, astronomer; b. New Orleans, Apr. 29, 1855; s. Lewis and Jane (Fitch) E.; C.E., Royal Poly. Sch., Stuttgart, 1876; Ph.D., U. of Strassburg, 1880; (hon. M.A., Yale, 1893, Ph.D., Christiania, 1911). Associated with Sir David Gill, Royal Obs., Cape of Good Hope, investigating parallaxes of southern stars, 1881-83; astronomer, 1884-96, dir., 1896-1910 (emeritus), Yale Obs. Lalande prize, Paris Acad. Sciences, 1908. Home: New Haven, Conn. Died May 30, 1933.

ELLEFSON, BENNETT STANLEY, engring. adminstr.; b. Canby, Minn., Jan. 10, 1911; s. Halvor S. and Sarah (Lewison) E.; A.B., St. Olaf Coll., 1932; M.S., U. Minn., 1933; student N.Y.U. 1933-34; Ph.D., Pa. State U., 1937; m. Dorothea Kinter, Nov. 25, 1948; children—Dana, Kristi Gayle. Teaching fellow N.Y.U., 1933-34; research asst. Pa. State U., 1934-37; with Sylvania Electric Products, Inc., Bayside, N.Y., 1937-60, successively research chemist, asst. to v.p. engring., dir. central engring. labs., dir. research, 1937-56, v.p. engring and research, 1956-59, v.p. tech. planning, 1959-60; v.p. Gen. Telephone and Electronics Labs., Inc., 1960-73. Fellow I.E.E.E., A.A.A.S.; mem. Am. Chem. Soc., Am. Ceramic Soc. Home: Bayside NY Died 1973.

ELLENWOOD, FRANK OAKES, univ. prof.; b. Little Hocking, O., Nov. 10, 1878; s. Douglas Harlow and Cynthia Clough (Oakes) E.; A.B. in Mech. Engring., Stanford, 1904, M.E., 1922; m. Cecelia Freeman Atherton, June 30, 1909; children—Ruth Cecelia (Mrs. Prince McGuyre), Hazel Adaline (Mrs. Warner S. Hammond), Cecelia Atherton (dec.). Asst. to erection foreman, steam power plants, C. C. Moore & Co., San Francisco, Calif., 1904-05; asst. to master mechanic, Tonopah (Nev.) R.R. Co., 1905-06: asst. engr. Am. Smelting and Refining Co., South San Francisco, Calif., 1907-08; instr. mech. engring., Stanford, 1908-11; asst. prof. heat-power engring., Cornell U., 1911-15, prof., 1915-40, head of dept. heat-power engring. since 1940, John Edson Sweet prof. engring. since 1941. Served as head of engine dept. U.S. Army Sch. of Mil. Aeronautics, Cornell U., 1917-19. Mem. Am. Soc. M.E. (chmn. com. on thermodynamic terminology, 1936; mem. com. on symbols for heat and thermodynamics 1927-44), Am. Soc. Refrigerating Engrs., Soc. Promotion Engring. Edn., Sigma Xi, Tau Beta Pi, Phi Kappa Phi, Atmos, Triangle. Mem. First Unitarian Ch., Ithaca, N.Y. Clubs: Research Cornell U., Ithaca Country (Ithaca, N.Y.). Author: Steam Charts, 1914. Co-author: Heat-Power Engineering, Vol. I, 1926, Vol. II, 1932, Vol. III, 1933; Vapor Charts, 1939; Thermodynamic Charts, 1944. Home: 111 Harvard Place, Ithaca, N.Y. Died Sept. 7, 1947.

ELLERMAN, FERDINAND, astronomer; b. Centralia, Ill., May 13, 1869; s. Mathias and Rosa Augusta (Fleischbein) E.; ed. high sch., Belleville, Ill., and special studies U. of Chicago; hon. A.M., Occidental College, 1927; m. Hermine Louise Hoenny, May 16, 1895; children—Leola, Louise. In mercantile business, 1885-92; asst., Kenwood Obs., 1892-95, Yerkes Obs., 1895-1901; instr. in astrophysics, 1901-04. asst. astronomer, 1905-15, astronomer, 1915-37, Mt. Wilson Obs. of Carnegie Instn., Washington, D.C. Presbyn. Home: Pasadena, Calif. Died Mar. 20, 1940.

ELLERY, EDWARD, educator, chemist; b. Albany, N.Y., July 24, 1868; s. Edward and Abbie Maria (Bellows) E.; A.B., Colgate, 1890, A.M., 1893, Sc.D., 1912; S.C., U. of Pittsburgh, 1931; Univ. of Berlin, 1894, 1909; Ph.D., Univ. of Heidelberg, 1896; LL.D. from George Washington U., 1937; m. Adelaide F. True, Feb. 20, 1909. With Union Coll. since 1904, prof. chemistry, 1904-40, dean of faculty, 1918-40, acting pres., 1933-35, chmn. of faculty, 1935-40, emeritus prof. chemistry since 1940. Expert chemist for various industrial concerns; chemist for Schenectady Bureau of Health. Member Schenectady Board of Education. Made tour of American Universities, 1914-15, for Union College. Phi Beta Kappa lecturer, Univ. of N.D. and U. of Wash., 1923; lecturer Univs. of London and Belfast, 1925, St. Andrew's Aberdeen, Glasgow and Durham, 1926; Sigma Xi lecturer U. of Fla., 1938, W.Va U., 1939, U. of Ala. 1939; visiting lecturer Univ. of Hawaii, 1941. Mem. Nat. Research Council. Fellow A.A.A.S.; mem. Am. Chem. Soc., Sigma Xi, (exec. com., chmn. research fellowship com., nat. sec., nat. pres.), Phi Beta Kappa (pres. Upper Hudson Assn., also N.Y. State Assn.), Beta Theta Pi. Baptist. Clubs: Forthnightly, Mohawk (Schenectady). Author: The Half Century Record and History of Sigma Xi, 1937; also articles on training of chemists; corr. editor Scientific American, 1921. Address: Union College, Schenectady, N.Y.; and South Paris ME

ELLET, CHARLES, civil engr.; b. Penn's Manor, Pa., Jan. 1, 1810; s. Charles and Mary (Israel) E.; attended Ecole Polytechnique, Paris, France; m. Elvira Daniel, 1837, 1 son, Charles Rivers. Chief engr. James River and Kanawha Canal, 1836; designed, built wire suspension bridge across Schuy-lkill River nr. Phila., 1842; designed, built suspension bridge across Niagara River below the falls, 1847; completed Wheeling (W.Va.) Bridge for B. & O. R.R., 1849; engr. Hempfield R.R., 1851-55, Va. Central R.R., 1853-57; served as col. engrs. U.S. Army 1861-62; converted fleet of Mississippi steamers into rams, sank or disabled several Confederate vessels off Memphis, 1862; considered one of Am.'s great engrs. Author: Physical Geography of the Mississippi Valley with Suggestions as to the Improvement of Navigation of the Ohio and Other Rivers, 1853; Coast and Harbor Defenses, or the Substitution of Steam Battering-rams for Ships of War, 1855. Died Cairo, Ill., June 21, 1862.

ELLICOTT, EUGENE, engr.; b. Baltimore, Md., Dec. 8, 1846; s. Benjamin Ellicott of Ellicott's Mills, Md.; ed. private school, Baltimore; mem. of the bar; m. 1st, Baltimore, Jan., 1877, & Margaret Tyson; 2d, Phila., Jun 1895, Eleanor Cuyler Patterson. On duty engr. corps, U.S.A., 1964-65, defenses of Baltimore and Washington; on U.S. Coast Survey, 1864-90; connected with San Juan boundary line work, 1871; determined line between Me. and N.B. from Calais, Me., 25 miles inland, 1887-88; asst. to provost, Univ. of Pa., 1894-1901; capt. 1st regt., U.S.V. Engrs. on duty in Porto Rico and Cuba. Republican. Mem. Sons Revolution, Soc. Spanish-Am. War, Columbia Hist. Soc. Clubs: Metropolitan (Washington), University (Baltimore). Residence: 2205 De Lancey Pl., Philadelphia. *

ELLIOT, DANIEL GIRAUD, zoölogist; b. New York, Mar. 7, 1835; s. George Thompson and Rebecca Giraud (Foster) E.; acad. edn.; studied zoölogy; (Sc.D., Columbia, 1906); m. A. E. Henderson, 1858 (died 1905). Traveled in Europe, Africa, Palestine and Asia Minor, 1856-78; later in greater part of U.S., Can., Alaska, S. America; hon. and supervisory curator zoölogy, Field Mus. of Natural History, Chicago, 1895—. Led expdn. into interior of E. Africa, 1896, and into the recesses of the Olympic Mountains, 1898, being first naturalist to penetrate that little-known range. Fellow Royal Soc. Edinburgh; decorated 10 times by European govts. for labors in natural science. Author: Shore Birds of North America, 1895; Gallinaceous Game Birds; Wild Fowl of the United States and the British Possessions, 1898; Synopsis of the Mammals of North America and the Adjacent Seas, 1901; Land and Sea Mammals of Middle America and West Indies (2 vols.), 1894, and many others. Part author The Deer Family, 1902; Check List Mammals N. American Continent and W. Indies, 1905; Catalogue Mammals in Field Columbian Museum, 1906. Died Dec. 22, 1915.

ELLIOTT, DANIEL STANLEY, coll. prof., physicist; b. Baltimore, Md., Aug. 3, 1885; s. George llerbert and Minnie (Prinz) E.; A.B., Johns Hopkins U., 1911, A.M., 1913, Ph.D., 1914, fellow, 1913-14; m. Nora A. Nilson, June 11, 1917. Instr. physics, Ga. Inst. Tech., 1914-15, asst. prof., 1915-16, asso. prof., 1916-17, acting prof., 1918-19; W. R. Irby prof. of physics and head dept., Tulane U., New Orleans, La., since 1920. Served as v.p. acad. bd. and head depts, radio and airplanes, Ga. Tech. Sch. of Mil. Aeronautics, U.S. Army, 1917-18; at O.T.C., Plattsburg, N.Y., 1918. Fellow Am. Phys. Soc., A.A.A.S.; mem. Am. Assn. Physics Teachers (mem. exec. com. 1938-39), Soc. for Promotion of Engring. Edn. (council mem., 1937-39); Southeastern Sect. of Am. Phys. Soc. (chmn. 1936), New Orleans Acad. of Sciences (treas. 1933), La. Sect. of Am. Assn. Physics Teachers (chmn. 1940), La. Engring Soc., Gamma Alpha, Phi Kappa Phi, Omicron Delta Kappa, Kappa Delta Phi. Democrat. Methodist. Contributor articles to technical journals, etc. Home: 7922 Freret Street, New Orleans, La. Died Dec. 1, 1944.

ELLIOTT, HENRY WOOD, artist, naturalist; b. Cleveland, O., Nov. 13, 1846; s. Franklin Reuben and Sophia A. E.; ed. public and pvt. schs.; m. Alexandra Melovidov, of St. Paul's Is., Alaska, July 22, 1872. Pvt. sec. to Joseph Henry, sec. of Smithsonian Instn., 1862-78; artist U.S. Geol. Survey, 1869-71; spl. commr. for investigation of Seal Islands of Alaska under spl. act of Congress, 1872-74, and again, 1890. Under authority of act approved April 8, 1904, prepared the fur-seal treaty of "mutual concession and joint control," March 7, 1905, which was ratified by U.S. Senate, July 24, 1911, with Can., Japan, and Russia, for the protection and preservation of the fur seal herd of Alaska. Author: Condition of Affairs in Alaska, 1875 (Treasury Dept.); Monograph of the Seal Islands of Alaska (U.S. Fish Commn.), 1882; The Seal Islands of Alaska, 1884; Our Arctic Province, 1886. Also many papers on seal life, pomology, horticulture, and on scientific subjects. Address: Lakewood, nr. Cleveland, O. *

ELLIOTT, JOHN STUART, engr., insular official; b. Savannah, Ga., Mar. 20, 1859; s. Stuart and Lucy Ireland (Sorrel) E.; ed. in schs. in U.S. until 12 yrs. old, then for 5 yrs. in sch. in Europe; grad. Univ. of Pa., B.S., 1879, later C.E.; m. New York, Sept. 4, 1890; now widower. Engaged in practice as civ. and mining engr., 1879-1905; commr. of the Interior, Island of Porto Rico, 1905. Mem. Am. Soc. Civ. Engrs., Am. Inst. Mining Engrs. Club: Racquet and Tennis (New York). Address: San Juan, P.R. *

ELLIOTT, JOSEPH ALEXANDER, dermatologist; b. Moundville, Ala., Nov. 19, 1888; s. Joseph Alexander and Ludie (Whitfield) E.; A.B., Birmingham-Southern U., 1910; M.D., U. of Mich., 1914; m. Anne Cross, Aug. 24, 1918 (deceased); children—Joseph Alexander, Stuart Whitfield; married 2d, Emily Harrell Sebrell. Interne Barnard Skin and Cancer Hosp., St. Louis, 1914, Dept. Dermatology and Syphilology, U. of Mich. Hosp., 1915, resident, 1916, acting asst. prof., 1917-18; dermatologist Crowell Clinic, Charlotte, N.C., 1919-29; cons. dermatology, Presbyn. Hosp., Mercy Hosp.; pvt. practice, 1929—; pres. Elliott Realty Co., Doctors Bldg., Inc. Served as 1st lt., Med. Res. Corps.; assigned to U. Mich. Med. Dept. from beginning of war to 1918; active service, 1918-19, Camp Stuart. Diplomate Am. Bd. Dermatology and Syphilology. Fellow Am. Acad. Dermatology and Syphilology; mem. Macklenburg Medical Society (past president), N.C. State Med. Soc. (pres. 1953), A.M.A., Southern Med. Assn., Tri-State Med. Assn., Am. Dermatol. Assn., Southeastern Dermatol. Soc. (past pres.), Soc. for Investigative Dermatology, Alpha Tau Omega (past pres.), Alumni Assn. (Charlotte), Alpha Omega Alpha, Sigma Xi, Phi Chi. Democrat. Methodist. Clubs: Charlotte Country; past. pres. Myers Park Country and Kiwanis clubs. Contbr. over 40 articles to med. jours. Home: 2700 Sherwood Av. Office: 1012 Kings Dr., Charlotte, N.C. Died May 6, 1961; buried Forest Lawn, Charlotte, N.C.

ELLIS, CALVIN, physician, educator; b. Boston, Aug. 15, 1826; s. Luther and Betsey E.; grad. Harvard, 1846, M.D., 1849. Mem. 1st Harvard Boat Club; asst. in pathology Harvard Med. Sch., prof., 1867-83, dean, 1869; admitting physician, pathologist Mass. Gen. Hosp.; leading exponent of diagnosis by elimination of symptoms of disease; bequeathed $150,000 to Harvard Med. Sch. Mem. Am. Acad. Arts and Scis. 1859. Author: Obstruction of the Lungs, caused by Pressure on the Primary Bronchus; The Tendency of Disease in One Part to Excite it in Another; also 40 or more med. articles, including Boylston prize essay "Tubercle", 1860. Died Boston, Dec. 14, 1883.

ELLIS, CARLETON, research chemist, author; b. Keene, N.H., Sept. 20, 1876; s. Marcus and Catherine (Goodnow) E.; B.Sc., Massachusetts Institute of Technology, 1900; m. Birdella M. Wood, Nov. 28, 1901. Instr. M.I.T., 1900-02; has worked extensively in field of edible oils, fats, waxes, synthetic resins, paints, varnishes, petroleum products, and gasoline mfr.; has taken out about 750 patents; dir. Ellis-Foster Company. Gold medal for inventions at Jamestown Expn., 1907; Edward Longstreth medal, Franklin Institute, 1916. Selected as a "modern pioneer" by a committee of which Karl Compton is the chairman. Author: Hydrogenation of Organic Substances, 3d edit., 1930; Synthetic Resins and Their Plastics, 1923; 2d edit., 1935; Chemistry of Petroleum Derivatives, 1934; Vol. 2, 1937; Chemistry of Printing Ink, 1939. Co-author: The Vital Factors of Foods; Ultra Violet Light; Soilless Growth, etc. Home: Montclair, N.J. Died Jan. 13, 1941.

ELLIS, CHARLES ALTON, educator; born Parkman, Me., June 23, 1876; s. David B. and Eliza Wharff (Lombard) E.; A.B., Wesleyan U., 1900; C.E., U. of Ill., 1922; m. Elsie Louise Ney, Sept. 29, 1913. Draftsman, checker, squad foreman, Am. Bridge Co., 1902-08; asst. prof. civil engring., U. of Mich., 1908-12; designing engr., Dominion Bridge Co., 1912-14; asst. prof. civil engring., U. of Ill., 1914-15, prof. structural engring., 1915-21; v.p. Strauss Engring. Corp., 1921-32; cons. engr., private practice, 1932-34; prof. and head of div. (structural engring., Purdue U., 1934-46; prof. emeritus since 1946; lecturer in Civil engring., Northwestern Tech. Inst., since 1946; designer (with P. L. Pratley), Montreal Harbor Bridge; designing engineer, Golden Gate Suspension Span. Member Am. Soc. C.E. (life), Am. Ry. Engr. Assn., Am. Concrete Inst., Soc. Promotion Engring. Edn., Sigma Xi, Tau Beta Pi, Chi Epsilon, Delta Kappa Epsilon, Triangle. Contbr. articles on engring. to jours. Home: 638 Garrett Place, Evanston, Ill. Died Aug. 22, 1949.

ELLSWORTH, HENRY LEAVITT, agriculturist, U.S. commr. of patents; b. Windsor, Conn., Nov. 10, 1791; s. Chief Justice Oliver and Abigail (Wolcott) E.; grad. Yale, 1810; m. Nancy Goodrich, 1813, 3 children; m. 2d, Marietta Mariana Bartlett; m. 3d, Catherine Smith. Practiced law, Windsor, Conn., 1813; sec. Hartford County Agri. Soc., 1818; pres. Aetna Ins. Co., 1819-21; commr. to superintend the settlement of Indian tribes south and west of Ark., 1832; mayor Hartford (Conn.), 1835; 1st U.S. commr. patents, 1835-45; influential in gaining 1st Congl. appropriation for agri. research, 1839; land commr. U.S., 1845; called father of Dept. of Agri. Died Fair Haven, Conn. Dec. 27, 1858.

ELLSWORTH, LINCOLN, explorer, civil engr.; b. Chgo., May 12, 1880; s. James William and Eva (Butler) E.; prep. edn. Hill Sch., Pottstown, Pa.; student Columbia 2 years; M.S., Yale; LL.D., Kenyon Coll.; m. Mary Louise Ulmer, May 23, 1933. Axman on 1st survey Grand Pacific R.R. surveys of transcontinental route across Canada, 1902-07, then resident engr. Prince Rupert Terminal; later resident engr. on constrn.

work west of Montreal, C.P. Ry.; prospector for gold, Peace River, 1909; became asst. engr. Kougarock Mining Co., Alaska, 1910; organizer Ellsworth Expdn., sponsored by John Hopkins, making geol. cross section of Andes Mountains from Pacific Ocean to headwaters of the Amazon, 1924; condr. and navigator N 24 on Amundsen-Ellsworth Polar Flying Expdn., reaching 88 deg. N. Latitude; co-leader of Amundsen-Ellsworth-Nobile Transpolar flight from Kingsbay, Spitzbergen, to Teller, Alaska, May 11-13, 1926; dir. of scientific investigation Wilkins-Ellsworth Trans-Arctic Submarine Expdn., 1931; represented Am. Geog. Soc. on Graf Zeppelin Arctic flight, 1931; made airplane flight of 2,300 miles, crossing Antarctic, Nov. 1935; in recognition of this flight and for claiming 30,000 square miles of new land for U.S., awarded special gold medal by Congress; in 1939 made flight into interior of Antarctica on Indian Ocean side, south of Australia, claiming 81,000 square miles of ty. for U.S. Lt. comdr. USNR. Fellow Am. Museum Nat. History, Royal Geog. Soc.; asso. mem. Am. Soc. C.E.; hon. fellow and trustee Am. Mus., New York; trustee Western Reserve Acad., Hudson, O. Decorated Comdr. 1st Class Order St. Olav (Norway); awarded gold medal by Norwegian Parliament for saving 2 companions from drowning, 1925; awarded Great King Humbert medal of Italian Geog. Soc., 1920; Grand Cross Order of St. Olav, Norway, 1926; spl. gold medal, by President Hoover from Congress of U.S., 1931; David Livingston Centenary medal, Am. Geog. Soc.; Hubbard gold medal, Nat. Geog. Soc., also Explorer's gold medal; Elisha Kent Kane gold medal, Phila. Geog. Soc.; gold medal, Geog. Soc. of Chicago; Patron's gold medal, Royal Geog. Soc. Clubs: Union, Century Association, Explorers, Boone and Crockett (New York). Author: The Last Wild Buffalo Hunt, 1915; (with Capt. Roald Amundsen) Our Polar Flight, 1925; First Crossing of the Polar Sea, 1926; Search, 1932; Beyond Horizons, 1938. Address: care Morris & McVeigh, 60 Wall St., N.Y.C. Died May 26, 1951; buried Hudson, O.

ELMAN, ROBERT, surgeon; b. Boston, Mass., Nov. 9, 1897; s. Samuel and Bessie Marian (Schmidt) E.; B.S., Harvard, 1919; M.D., Johns Hopkins, 1922; m. Mima Kreykenbohn, June 15, 1928. Resident house officer Johns Hopkins, 1922-23; asst. in pathology Rockefeller Inst., 1923-25; mem. teaching staff Washington U. Med. Sch., St. Louis, since 1925, now prof. clin. surgery; asso. surgeon Barnes Hosp. and St. Louis Children's Hosp.; in pvt. practice surgery, St. Louis, since 1928. Dir. surg. service and chief of staff Homer Philips Hosp. Mem. committee on infected wounds and burns, committee on convalescence and rehabilitation, National Research Council, 1943-45. Member National Professional Advisory Council, Office of Vocational Rehabilitation. Federal Security Administration (chairman Missouri State Office of Vocational Rehabilitation Advisory Council). Diplomate American Bd. Surgery; fellow A.C.S., A.A.A.S., Internat. Soc. Surgery; mem. Harvey Society, Am. Surgical Assn., Am. Gastroenterological Assn. (president, 1955). Society Exptl. Biology and Med. (pres. Mo. sect. 1948), American Medical Association, Phi Beta Kappa, Alpha Omega Alpha, Sigma Xi. Author: (with Warren H. Cole) Textbook of General Surgery, 5 edits. since 1936; Parenteral Alimentation in Surgery, 1946 (awarded the quinquennial Samuel D. Gross award, Phila. Acad. of Surgery, 1945); numerous single chapters in surg. texts, many papers on surg. subjects including first report on use plasma transfusions in burns and on successful use of amino acid mixtures injected intravenously in the human for parenteral protein feeding; mem. editorial bd. of Gastroenterology, Archives of Surgery. Home: 4456 Maryland Av., St. Louis 8. Office: 600 S. Kingshighway, St. Louis 10. Died Dec. 23, 1956.

ELMEN, GUSTAF WALDEMAR, elec. engr.; b. Stockholm, Sweden, Dec. 22, 1876; s. Claes Julius and Josephine (Ericson) E.; B.S., U. of Neb., 1902, M.A., 1904, D.Eng., 1932; m. Ruth M. Halvorsen, 1907; children—James Frederick, Richard Spencer, Paul Halvorsen; came to U.S., 1893, naturalized, 1918. Fellow in physics, U. of Neb., 1902-04; elec. engr. for Gen. Electric Co., 1904-06, for Western Electric Co., 1906-25, for Bell Telephone labs., 1925-41; magnetic consultant for Naval Ordnance Lab., Washington Navy Yard, 1941—. Mem. Sigma Xi. Awarded John Scott medal by City of Philadelphia, 1927, Elliott Cresson medal by Franklin Inst., Phila., 1928. Modern Pioneer Award Nat. Assn. Mfrs., 1940. Republican. Inventor magnetic materials used in elec. communications. Author of papers on magnetic properties of alloys. Home: 104 High St., Leonia, N.J. Address: Naval Ordnance Laboratory, Navy Yard, Washington. Died Dec. 10, 1957.

ELMENDORF, JOHN E(DWARD), JR., physician; b. New Brunswick, N.J., May 28, 1893; s. John Edward and Helen Aline (Decker) E.; B.A., Rutgers U., 1914; D.Sc. (hon.), 1954; M.D., Johns Hopkins, 1918, spl. studies, sch. hygiene and pub. health, 1926-29; m. Virginia Knower, May 20, 1922 (div. 1934); children—Virginia DuBarry (Mrs. Francis A. Sokol), Joan Loomis (Mrs. Russell McCandless); m. 2d, Harriet Camac, Oct. 25, 1935. Intern Johns Hopkins Hosp., 1918-19; asst. resident medicine Barnes Hosp., St. Louis, 1919-20; dir. field studies dept. medicine and pub. health Rockefeller Found., 1920-52; engaged in yellow fever and malaria control work 1930-41; dir. civilian sch. to train army and navy officers in malaria control, 1942-43; dir. Carlos Finlay Yellow Fever Inst., Bogota, Columbia, 1947-51; promoted, planned and organized Superior Sch. of Hygiene, Colombia, and served as sci. dir., 1951-52; now engaged in writing. Served from lt. col. to col., AUS, 1943-47. Decorated Legion of Merit; Hon. Officer Most Excellent Order of British Empire; Distinguished Visitor and Citation (Mexico); Medal and Citation Crux de Boyaca (Colombia). Fellow A.A.A.S., Am. Pub. Health Assn., N.Y. Acad. Medicine; mem. Am. Soc. Tropical Hygiene and Medicine, Soc. Colonial Wars. Clubs: Strollers, Military Naval (N.Y.C.). Office: care Rockefeller Found., 49 W. 49th St., N.Y.C. 20. Died May 25, 1960; buried Elmwood Cemetery, New Brunswick, N.J.

ELMSLIE, GEORGE GRANT, architect; b. Aberdeenshire, Scotland, Feb. 20, 1871; s. John and Jane (Wans) E.; ed. Duke of Gordon Schs., Huntly, Aberdeenshire, Scotland; came to U.S., 1885; m. Bonnie Marie Hunter (A.B., Wellesley Coll.), Oct. 12, 1910 (died 1912). Pupil in architecture with Adler & Sullivan, Chicago, 1890-95; asso. with Louis H. Sullivan in planning and designing, 1895-1910; in partnership with W. G. Purcell and George Feick, Jr., 1910-12, and with Purcell, 1912-20; practiced alone in Chicago since 1920. Fellow A.I.A. Democrat. Presbyterian. Author papers on architecture, etc. Home: 5723 Blackstone Av., Chgo. Died Apr. 23, 1952.

ELROD, MORTON JOHN, biologist; b. Monongahela, Pa., Apr. 27, 1863; s. John Morton and Mary (Elliott) E.; A.B., Simpson Coll., 1887, A.M., 1890, M.S., 1898; Ph.D., Ill. Wesleyan, 1905; hon. LL.D., University of Montana, June 1938; m. Emma A. Hartshorn, of Corydon, Ia., 1888; 1 dau., Mary J. Prin. high sch., Corydon, Ia., 1887-88; adj.-prof. natural science, 1888-89, prof. biology and physics, 1891-97, Ill. Wesleyan U.; prof. biology, 1897-1935, dir. Biol. Sta., 1899-1935, prof. emeritus since 1935, U. of Mont. Editor 1st vol. Ill. Wesleyan Magazine; instr. Des Moines Summer Sch. of Methods, 8 sessions. Dir. Nature Guide Service, Glacier Nat. Park, since 1922. Editor of Elrod's Guide and Book of Information of Glacier National Park. Pres. Western Div. of Mont. Edn. Assn., 1924; pres. Inland Empire Edn. Assn., 1928. Fellow A.A.A.S.; member Ecol. Soc. America, Am. Entomol. Soc., Am. Bison Soc. (dir.), Am. Soc. Mammalogists, Am. Soc. Zoologists, Northwest Science Assn., Mont. Acad. (pres. 1901-04), Am. microscopical Soc. (pres. 1933), Phi Kappa Psi. Contbr. to scientific and other mags. and jours. Editor Inter-Mountain Educator, 1913-24. Home: 205 S. 5th E., Missoula Mont. *

ELROD, RALPH (PERRY), bacteriologist; b. Oakland, Cal., Jan. 17, 1913; s. Ralph Leroy and Rose (Gyson) E.; A.B., Brown U., 1936, M.S., 1938; Ph.D., Ohio State U., 1941; m. Elizabeth Virginia Keefe, Oct. 30, 1942; children—Perry Keefe, Ralph George. Instr. Brown U., Providence, 1940-41; asso. Rockefeller Inst., Princeton, N.J., 1941-47; prof., chmn. dept. microbiology U. S.D., 1947—. Served as maj. San. Corps, U.S. Army, 1942-45, bacteriologist, serologist, and parasitologist. Mem. Am. Assn. Immunologists, Soc. Am. Bacteriol., Sigma Xi, Alpha Tau Omega. Author numerous articles in field of microbiology. Home: 920 E. Clark St. Office: U.S.D., Vermillion, S.D. Deceased.

ELSBERG, LOUIS, laryngologist; b. Iserlohn, Prussia, Apr. 2, 1836; s. Nathan and Adelaide E.; M.D., Jefferson Med. Coll., 1857; m. Mary Van Hagen Scoville, 1876. Resident physician Mt. Sinai Hosp., N.Y.C.; one of editors North Am. Med. Reporter, 1859; mem. faculty med. dept. Univ. City N.Y.; held 1st course of lectures on diseases of throat in U.S., 1862; recipient gold medal A.M.A. for publ. Laryngoscopal Surgery Illustrated in the Treatment of Morbid Growths within the Larynx, 1865; published Regeneration, or the Preservation of the Organic Molecules (his most important contbn. to med. science), 1874; founder, 1st pres. Am. Laryngological Assn., 1878; founder quarterly Archives of Laryngology, 1880; other publs. include: Neuroses of Sensation, 1882; Structure of Hyaline Cartilage, 1881-82; On Angioma of the Larynx, 1884. Died N.Y.C. Feb. 19, 1885.

ELSER, WILLIAM JAMES, pathologist, bacteriologist; b. Milwaukee, Wis., Nov. 28, 1872; s. John and Frances (Auer) E.; M.D., Bellevue Hosp. Med. Coll., 1895; post-grad. study, univs. of Berlin, Vienna and Gratz; m. Saturnina Beatrice Rodriquez, Sept. 8, 1911; children—Frances (Mrs. John Pehle), John (dec.), Ramona. Interne Bellevue Hosp. Med. Coll., 1895-97; instr. pathology, Cornell U. Med. Coll., 1901-06, asst. prof. bacteriology and immunology, 1906-09, prof., 1909-32, prof. applied pathology and bacteriology, 1932-38, professor emeritus since 1938; asst. pathologist New York Hosp., 1902-05, director Div. of Labs., 1905-32, dir. Central Labs., 1932-38, retired; consulting bacteriologist Grasslands Hosp., Valhalla, N.Y., since 1920. Served as pathologist and bacteriologist Base Hosp. No. 9, A.E.F., 1917; asst. dir. Div. of Labs. and Infectious Diseases, A.E.F., 1917-18; col. O.R.C. since 1919. Fellow A.A.A.S.; mem. Am. Assn. Pathologists and Bacteriologists, Assn. Mil. Surgeons of U.S., New York Acad. Medicine, Soc. for Exptl. Biology and Medicine, N.Y. City br. of Soc. Am. Bacteriologists, Harvey Soc., New York Bacteriol. Club, Phi Alpha Sigma. Contbr. to publs. dealing with epidemic cerebral meningitis and methods of preserving immune sera. Home: Kent, Conn. Address: New York Hosp., 525 E. 68th St., New York NY

ELVEHJEM, CONRAD ARNOLD, (el-ve-yem), univ. pres.; b. McFarland, Wis., May 27, 1901; s. Ole Johnson and Christine (Lewis) E.; B.S., U. Wis., 1923, Ph.D., 1927; student Cambridge U., England, 1929-30; D.Sc., Ripon Coll., 1942, Beloit Coll., 1958, Northwestern U., 1959; LL.D., U. Cal., 1959; m. Constance Walts, June 30, 1926; children—Peggy Ann (Mrs. Calvin Henninger), Robert Stuart. Instructor biochemistry, University of Wisconsin, 1925-29, assistant professor, 1920-32, asso. prof., 1932-36, prof. 1936-58, chmn. dept., 1944-58, dean Grad. Sch., 1946-58, pres., 1958—; Harvey Soc. lectr., 1940, Herter lecturer, 1942; Sigma Xi lecturer, 1943. Vice president of Johnson Foundation, 1959—. Recipient the Mead Johnson award for research in Vitamin B Complex 1939, Grocery Mfrs. America Award, 1942, Willard Gibbs medal, 1943, Nicholas Appert Medal, 1948, Osborne-Mendel award, 1950; Lasker Award in Medical Research, 1952; Charles F. Spencer award, Am. Chem. Soc., 1956; American Inst. of Baking award, 1957. Chmn. Food Nutrition bd. National Research Council, 1955-58; mem. Nat. Adv. Heart Council, 1948-50, Nat. Sci. Found. Bd., 1960—, Research Corp. Bd., 1960—, Sugar Research Found., Inc. Bd., 1959; mem. edn. adv. com. Upper Midwest Research and Development Council, 1960—; mem. Council Foods and Nutrition, A.M.A., 1940-59; member Scientific Advisory Committee Nutrition Foundation, 1941-58, board trustees, 1958—; member National Adv. Dental Council, 1950-56, Fed. Security Agy. Mem. Am. Acad. Arts and Scis., Biochem. Soc. England, American Chemical Society, American Assn. for Advancement of Science, Am. Soc. Biol. Chemists, American Inst. Nutrition (vice pres. 1952-53, president 1953-54), Society of Experimental Biology and Medicine, Inst. Food Technologists, Nat. Acad. Sciences, Am. Pub. Health Assn., Am. Philos. Soc., Assn. Grad. Schs. (pres. 1948-49), Alpha Chi Sigma, Phi Beta Kappa (hon.), Gamma Alpha, Sigma Xi, Phi Sigma, Alpha Zeta, Delta Theta Sigma, Phi Kappa Phi (hon.), Phi Lambda Upsilon. Congregationalist. Clubs: Chaos (Chgo.); University, Rotary, Ygdrasil Literary Soc., West End (Madison). Editor: Respiratory Enzymes, 1939. Author: Vitamin Content of Meat (with H. A. Waisman). Contbr. papers on biochemistry and nutrition to Jour. Biol. Chemistry, Jour. of Nutrition and med. jours. Home: 130 N. Prospect Av., Madison, Wis. Died July 27, 1962; buried Forrest Hills Cemetery, Madison, Wis.

ELVEY, CHRISTIAN THOMAS, astronomer, physicist; b. Phoenix, Ariz., Apr. 1, 1899; s. John A. and Lizzie Christena (Miller) E.; A.B., U. of Kansas, 1921, A.M., 1923; Ph.D., University of Chicago, 1930; m. Marjorie Purdy, Sept. 1, 1934; children—Thomas Christian, Christena Vivian. Instructor in astronomy, University of Kansas, 1921-25, fellow in astronomy, U. of Chicago, 1925-26; instr. in astronomy, Northwestern U., 1926-28; instr. in astro-physics, Yerkes Observatory, U. of Chicago, 1928-32, asst. prof., 1932-35; astronomer and asst. to dir. McDonald Observatory, Fort Davis, Tex., 1935-42, on leave of absence to work with Office of Sci. Research and Development, 1942-45; head, interior ballistics sect. Naval Ordnance Test Station, Inyokern, Calif., Apr.-Nov. 1945, head, applied research div., 1945-47, head research dept., 1947-49, sr. research scientist, 1949-51, head of staff, 1951; head dept. geophysics, and dir. geophys. inst. U. Alaska, 1952-63, vice president research and advanced study, 1961-63, University research professor and spl. asst. to the pres., 1963-67, director emeritus geophysical institute, from 1967. Mem. sci. adv. bd. USAF, 1956-63. Fellow Arctic Inst. of North Am., A.A.A.S., Am. Physics Soc.; mem. Internat. Astron. Union, American Astron. Soc., Am. Geophys. Union (pres. sect. geomagnetism and aeronomy), Internat. Com. Geophysics, Internat. Assn. Geomagnetism and Aeronomy (chmn. com. number 2 aurora and airglow 1957-62), Sigma Xi. Rotarian (pres. 1954-55). Home: Tucson AZ Died Mar. 25, 1970.

ELWELL, CHARLES CLEMENT, civil engr.; b. Belfast, Me., July 16, 1855; s. Benjamin Tyler and Martha (Wilson) E.; B.C.E., U. of Me., 1878, C.E., 1890, D.Engring., 1927; m. Nancy Bolton, Mar. 25, 1885; children—Francis Bolton, Charles Clement, Supt. constrn. and repairs, Southern Coast, U.S. Light House Engring. Dept., 1878-82; asst. engr., constrn. and maintenance, N.Y.&N.E. Ry., 1882-85; asst. engr. and roadmaster, Wilmington & Northern R.R., 1885-91; engr. maintenance of way, B.&O. R.R. Co., 1891-93; roadmaster, in charge 4-track constrn., N.Y., N.H.&H. R.R., 1893-95, supt., 1895-1908, in charge Shore Line, Air Line, Northampton, Norwich and Worcester divs., and chief engr. trolley lines of same co., in N.Y. and Conn., 1908-11; chief engr. Pub. Utilities Commn. Com., 1911-15, mem. Commn., 1915—. Republican. Conglist. Mason. Home: New Haven, Conn. Died May 21, 1931.

ELY, STERLING, chemist; b. Nelsonville, N.J., Mar. 20, 1899; s. Charles Elmer and Laura Bell (Ely) E.; B.S., Univ. of Md., 1921; grad. law studies, Washington,

D.C., 1927-30; m. Helen Barker Tompkins, Feb. 14, 1925; children—Lloyd (dau.), Stephen. Research chemist, San-I-Sal Labs., Washington, D.C., 1924-29; admitted to Ind. bar, 1931; chemist and consultant for National Carbon Co., Haynes Stellite Co. and affiliated cos., Washington, D.C., 1929-44; Union Carbide Corporation, Washington, 1944—. Sec., trustee Woodlawn Pub. Found. Mem. Am. Chem. Soc., Am. Bar Assn., Am. Judicature Soc., Delta Sigma Phi. Mem. Unity Sch. of Christianity. Clubs: University, 1925 F St. (Washington); Beachcombers (Provincetown, Mass.). Home: 2025 Hillyer Pl., Washington 9. Office: Woodward Bldg., Washington 5. Died Sept. 16, 1961.

ELY, SUMNER BOYER, educator; b. Watertown, N.Y., Nov. 5, 1869; s. Frederick Gustavus and Matilda Caroline (Boyer) E.; S.B., Mass. Inst. Tech., 1892; m. Mary Rodman Updike, Jan. 25, 1899; children—Esther Stockton, Frederick Sumner. Asst. supt. Pressed Steel Car Co., McKees Rocks, Pa., 1900; chief engr. Am. Sheet Steel Co., Pittsburgh, 1901; chief engr. Am. Sheet & Tin Plate Co., Pittsburgh, 1903-06; v.p. Chester B. Albree Iron Works, Pittsburgh, 1906-16; prof. comml. engring., Carnegie Inst. of Tech., 1920-40, emeritus; now supt. Bureau of Smoke Prevention, Pittsburgh. Consulting engr. Pa. Giant Power Survey, 1923-24. Sec. Internat. Conf. on Bituminous Coal held under the auspices of Carnegie Inst. Tech., Pittsburgh, 1926, 28; consultant to director of World's Power Conf., Washington, D.C., 1936; technical mem. Pittsburgh Smoke Abatement Commn., 1941. Ex-pres. Univ. Extension Soc., Pittsburgh; mem. Am. Soc. Mech. Engrs., Engrs.' Soc. Western Pa., A.A.A.S. Presbyterian. Home: 520 Roslyn Pl., Pittsburgh PA

EMBURY, AYMAR, II, architect; b. New York, June 15, 1880; s. Aymar and Fannie Miller (Bates) E.; C.E., Princeton U., 1900, M.S., 1901; L.H.D., Hofstra College, Hempstead, N.Y., 1951; m. 1st, Dorothy Coe (now dec.); children—Aymar (dec.), Edward C., Carl Richard, Peter A. (dec.); m. 2d, Ruth Dean (deceased); one daughter, Judith Dean (Mrs. Hugh Hack); m. third, Jane Schabbehar. Engaged in architectural practice, N.Y.C. since 1901; instr. in architecture, Princeton, U., 1904-05; specializes in college buildings; architect of New York City Building, Argentine Building, New York Worlds Fair, 1939-40, Triborough, Whitestone, Henry Hudson, Jamaica Bay (N.Y.), Rainbow (Niagara), and 70 other bridges; chief engr. for contractors, N. African Mil. Mission; architect Park Department City of N.Y. Mem. President's Advisory Com. on Architecture, 1934-43. Capt. 40th Engrs., U.S. Army, 1917-19, with 14 months' foreign service; lt. col. O.R.C., 1923. Mem. Princeton Engring. Soc., Nat. Inst. Arts and Letters. Clubs: The Players; Maidstone (East Hampton, L.I., N.Y.). Author books including: The Aesthetics of Engineering Construction, 1943. Home: 430 E. 57th St., N.Y.C.; also 223 Main St., East Hampton, L.I., N.Y. Died Nov. 14, 1966.

EMCH, ARNOLD, mathematician; b. Hessigkofen, Switzerland, Mar. 24, 1871; s. Albrecht and Maria (Zurbuchen) E.; Cantonal Coll. of Solothurn, 1886-90; Eidgenossische Technische Hochschule, Zurich, 1890-93; came to U.S., 1893; Ph.D., U. of Kan., 1895; m. Hilda Walters, of Lawrence, Kan., Aug. 31, 1895; children—Walter, Arnold Frederick, Karl. Asst. prof. graphics, U. of Kan., 1895-97; prof. graphics and mathematics, Technikum Biel, Switzerland, 1897-98, Kan. State Agrl. Coll., 1898-1900, U. of Colo., 1900-05, Cantonal Colls. of Solothurn and Basel, 1905-11, U. of Ill., 1911-27; prof. mathematics, U. of Ill. since 1927. Mem. Am. Math. Soc., Sigma Xi, Swiss Math. Soc., Swiss Naturforschende Gesellschaft, Swiss Alpine Club. Author: An Introduction to Projective Geometry, 1905; also writer in various languages on math. subjects. Home: Urbana IL

EMERSON, CHERRY LOGAN, consulting engineer; born Atlanta; s. Dr. William Henry and Lily (Cherry) E.; B.S. in Mech. Engring., Ga. Sch. Tech., 1908, B.S. in Elec. Engring., 1909; student Phila. Textile Sch., 1911-12; m. Sina White, Nov. 11, 1914; children—Dorothy Elizabeth (wife of Dr. Richard W. Cross), Cherry Logan. Apprentice, Westinghouse Elec. and Mfg. Co., Pitts., 1909, asst. engr., Boston, 1910-11, engr., Phila., 1911-12, Charlotte, N.C., 1912-14; application engr. Duke Power Co., Charlotte, 1914-16, asst. to chief engr., 1916-19; v.p. and chief engr., Robert & Co., Inc., Atlanta, 1919-45; dean engring. Ga. Inst. Tech., Atlanta, 1945-55, v.p. Ga. Inst. 1948-55; mem. A. Thomas. Bradbury & Assos., 1955—; director of the Bank of Georgia. Life member national board directors Boy Scouts America; awarded Silver Antelope, also Silver Buffalo); mem. bd. Atlanta Boy Scout Found. Director Georgia Tech. Foundation. Fellow of the Am. Inst. E.E.; mem. Am. Soc. M.E., Am. Soc. C.E., Alpha Tau Omega, Phi Kappa Phi, Anak. Clubs: Capital City, Atlanta Athletic, Ansley Park (Atlanta). Home: Atlanta Athletic Club, Atlanta. Office: 60 Fifth St. N.E., Atlanta 8. Died Oct. 26, 1959.

EMERSON, GEORGE BARRELL, educator; b. Wells, Me., Sept. 12, 1797; s. Samuel and Olive (Barrell) E.; grad. Harvard, 1817, LL.D. (hon.), 1857; m. Olivia Buckminster, June 11, 1823, 3 children m. 2d, Mrs. Mary Rotch Fleming, Nov. 12, 1834. Became mathematics tutor Harvard, 1819; prin. English High Sch., Boston, 1821-23; opened pvt. sch. for young ladies, Boston, 1823; an organizer Boston Mechanics Inst.; a founder Am. Inst. Instrn., 1830; pres. Boston Soc. Natural History, 1837-43; mem. Am. Acad. Arts and Scis. Author: Report on the Trees and Shrubs Growing Naturally in the Forests of Massachusetts, 1846, 2d ed., 1875; Manual of Agriculture, 1861. Died Newton, Mass., Mar. 4, 1881.

EMERSON, JAMES EZEKIEL, retired machinist; b. Norridgewock, Me., Nov. 2, 1823; ed. at Bangor, Me., 1829-39; m. Mary Shepherd, 1849; 2d, Mary Belle Woods, 1878. Was farmer, carpenter, saw-mill worker; mfr. wood-work, machinery, Lewiston, Me., 1850-52; went to Calif., 1852; engaged in saw-mill enterprises; visited Europe, 1869. Invented inserted tooth circular and band saws and many other devices. Manufactured edge tools at Trenton, N.J., and during Civil war, cavalry sabres; later supt. Am. Saw Co.; and then pres. and supt. Emerson Smith & Co. Saw Works, Beaver Falls, Pa.; retired. Home: Columbus, O. Died 1900.

EMERSON, KENDALL, surgeon; b. Northampton, Mass., June 27, 1875; s. Benjamin Kendall and Mary Annette (Hopkins) E.; A.B., Amherst Coll., 1897, M.A. (honorary), 1922, Doctor of Science, 1950; M.D., Harvard University, 1901; married Josephine Devereux Sewall, Oct. 1, 1903; children—Sewall, Kendall. Intern, Mass. Gen. Hosp., Boston, 1901-02; began practice orthopedic and gen. surgery, Worcester, Mass., 1902; asst. surgeon, Memorial Hosp., Worcester, 1903-10, orthopedic surgeon, 1910-28, cons. surgeon since 1928; mng. dir. Nat. Tuberculosis Assn. 1928-48, retired, 1948, consultant since 1948; president of New York Tuberculosis and Health Association, 1948-49; exec. sec., Am. Pub. Health Assn., 1931-35. Maj., Royal Army Med. Corps (Brit.), 1916-18; maj., Med. Corps, U.S.A., 1918-19, instr., surgeon general's office, Washington, D.C., 1918-19, detailed as spl. Red Cross commr. to Siberia; dir. Am. Hosp. in Paris, 1920; consultant U.S. Pub. Health Serv.; counselor Med. Council of Vets. Adminstrn. Mem. permanent bd. hon. consultants to Army Med. Library. Trustee Smith Coll., Potts Memorial Hosp. Mem. exec. com. Internat. Union Against Tuberculosis; mem. U.S. Commn. to Meeting of Pan-Am. Sanitary Union, Buenos Aires, 1934. Awarded Trudeau Medal for tuberculosis work, 1947. Fellow Am. Coll. Surgs.; mem. A.M.A., N.Y. Acad. Medicine, New York County Med. Soc., Mass. Med. Soc., New England Surg. Soc., Phi Beta Kappa, Alpha Delta Phi. Decorated Order St. Sava, 1st Class (Rumania). Republican. Episcopalian. Clubs: Century (New York); Cosmos (Washington). Contbr. articles to med. jours. Home: 1070 Beacon St., Brookline, MA Office: 1790 Broadway NY 19

EMERSON, MERTON LESLIE, engineer; b. Brockton, Mass., Aug. 11, 1882; s. Edwin Leslie and Lora Gertrude (Kingman) E.; student Thayer Acad., Braintree, Mass., 1900; S.B., Mass. Inst. Technology, 1904; m. Frances Elizabeth Dike, Oct. 25, 1906; children—Elizabeth Kingman (dec.), Merton Leslie (dec.), Mary Leslie (wife of Major Thos. B. Mechling, U.S.A.). Engineer with U.S. Geological Survey, 1903-04; engr. Boston Pneumatic Transit Co., 1904-06; mng. dir. The Housing Corp., 1920-21; operating mgr. Am. Pneumatic Service Co., 1906-16, v.p., 1916-27, pres., 1927-29; treas. The Lamson Co., 1916-18, pres., 1927-29; pres. Boston Pneumatic Transit Co., New York Pneumatic Service Co., Chicago Pneumatic Service Co., St. Louis Pneumatic Tube Co.; cons. engr. with Scovell Wellington & Co. and United Engrs. & Constructors; dir. Arkwright Mut. Fire Ins. Co., Braintree Nat. Bank. Mem. Tech. Board of Rev., U.S. Fed. Adminstrn. Pub. Works; New England dir. NRA, 1935; consultant Nat. Resources Com., asst. dir. U.S. Drainage Basin Studies; tech. adviser Social Security Bd. Served as major, U.S. Army, chief of adminstrn., gas defense div., Chem. Warfare Service, 1918-19; Army Specialist Corps, 1942. Trustee Wentworth Inst., Boston, Thayer Acad., Thayerlands Sch.; term mem. Mass. Inst. Tech. Corp. Mem. Am. Soc. C.E., Am. Soc. Mil. Engrs., Am. Inst. Cons. Engrs., Soc. Advancement of Management, Am. Soc. Public Adminstrn., Am. Legion, Mil. Order World War, Tech. Alumni Council, Tau Beta Pi, Soc. Mayflower Descendants. Republican. Unitarian. Mason. Clubs: Engineers, Technology (New York); University (Boston); Cosmos, Army and Navy Country (Washington). Home: Braintree, Mass.; 218 S. Royal St., Alexandria, Va. Office: 75 Federal St., Boston, Mass. Died Feb. 1945.

EMERSON, ROBERT, educator, researcher; b. N.Y.C., Nov. 4, 1903; s. Haven and Grace (Parrish) E.; A.B. cum laude, Harvard, 1925; Ph.D., Friedrich Wilhelm U., Berlin, Germany, 1927; m. Claire Garrison, Feb. 9, 1929; children—Kenneth, Stephen, David, Ruth. Nat. Research fellow, Harvard. 1927-29; asst. prof. biophysics Cal. Inst. Tech., 1929-46; on leave as research asso. Carnegie Inst. Washington, Stanford, 1937-40; research prof. botany U. Ill., 1946—; research on photosynthesis, especially investigation of maximum efficiency; Fulbright fellow, 1954. Mem. Nat. Acad. Scis., Am. Bot. Soc., Am. Soc. Plant Physiologists. Author sci. papers. Home: 806 W. Main St., Urbana, Ill. Died Feb. 4, 1959.

EMERSON, ROBERT ALTON, engr., ry. exec.; b. Plum Coulee, Man., Can., Apr. 12, 1911; s. Bertram H. and Lillian (Hughes) E.; B.Sc. in Civil Engring.; U. Man., 1930, LL.D., 1962; postgrad. (Strathcona Meml. fellow in Transp.), Yale, 1933-34; m. Katherine West, Nov. 12, 1935. Rodman Manitoba dist. C.P. Ry. Co., 1928-29, rock ballast insp. Kenora div., 1929-30, transitman, Kenora, 1930-35, B.C. dist., 1935-36, Regina div., 1936-39 roadmaster Man. dist. 1939-41, div. engr. Brandon div., 1941-43, Moose Jaw div., 1943-44, asst. dist. engr. B.C. dist., 1944-46, dist. engr., 1946-48, engr. track system, Montreal, 1948-50, asst. chief engr., 1950-51, chief engr., 1951-55, v.p., operation and maintenance, 1955-58, v.p. exec. com., dir., 1958-64, pres., chief operating officer dir., mem. exec. com., 1964—, dir. affiliates, dir. Soo Line R.R. Co., Toronto. Consol. Mining & Smelting Co., Can. Ltd., Can. Marconi Co., Canadian Pacific Investments Ltd., Canadian Pacific Air Lines, Ltd., Canadian Pacific Oil & Gas Ltd., Toronto, Hamilton & Buffalo Ry. Co. Bd. govs. Royal Victoria Hosp. Decorated comdr. bro. Order of St. John. Mem. Am. Ry. Engring. Assn., C.E. Que., Canadian C. of C. (exec. council), Engring. Inst. Can., Phi Delta Theta. Anglican. Clubs: Mt. Royal, Mt. Stephen. Home: 945 Dunsmuir Rd., Montreal 16. Office: Windsor Station, Canadian Pacific Ry., Montreal 3, Que., Can. Died Mar. 13, 1966; buried Chapel Lawn Meml. Gardens, Winnipeg, Man., Can.

EMERSON, ROLLINS ADAMS, geneticist; b. Pillar Point, Jefferson County, N.Y., May 5, 1873; s. Charles D. and Mary C. (Adams) E.; moved to Neb., 1880; B.Sc., U. of Neb., 1897, LL.D., 1917; Sc.D., Harvard, 1913; m. Harriet Hardin, May 23, 1898; children—Mrs. Thera Kahler, Sterling Howard, Eugene Hardin, Mrs. Myra Ryan. Horticulturist, office of expt. stas., U.S. Dept. Agr., Washington, D.C., 1897-98; asst. prof. and prof. horticulture, U. of Neb., 1899-1914; prof. plant breeding, Cornell U., 1914-42, and dean grad. school, 1925-30. Mem. A.A.A.S., Am. Soc. Naturalists, Am. Assn. Univ. Profs., Nat. Acad. Sciences, Am. Genetic Assn. Home: 501 Dryden Rd., Ithaca, N.Y. Died Dec. 8, 1947.

EMERY, ALBERT HAMILTON, civil and mech. engr.; b. Mexico, N.Y., June 21, 1834; s. Samuel and Catherine S. E.; ed. Mexico Acad.; C.E., Rensselaer Poly. Inst., 1858; m. Mrs. F. B. Myers, Mar. 3, 1875; 1 son, Albert Hamilton. Invented and designed the well-known testing machine at Watertown Arsenal, as well as several others including two installed at Bur. of Standards, Washington, one of 230,000 lbs. capacity for tension and compression, and one of 1,150,000 lbs. capacity for tension, and 2,300,000 lbs. for compression on specimens of all lengths up to 33 ft. Invented and developed the method of constructing guns by hydraulic radial expansion. Home: Stamford, Conn. Died Dec. 2, 1926.

EMERY, CHARLES EDWARD, engr.; b. Aurora, N.Y., Mar. 29, 1838; s. Moses Little and Minera (Prentiss) E.; attended Canandaigua Acad., circa 1852-56; Ph.D. (hon.), U. City N.Y., 1876; m. Susan Livingston, 1863. Served as asst. engr. U.S. Navy, 1861-65; engr., Bklyn. Navy Yard, 1865-68, resigned from Navy, 1868, served as cons. engr. to Navy, from 1868; supt. Am. Inst. Fair, N.Y.C., 1869; cons. engr. to Coast Survey, designed over 20 revenue cutters, 1870's; chief engr., mgr. N.Y. Steam Co., N.Y.C., from 1879; cons. engr. to many communities and orgns.; expert on isochronism of timeplaces; constructed dynamos and motors which operated by direct current without commutator; recipient Watt medal Instn. Civil Engrs. of Britain, 1889; results of his experiments with steam engines published in Tables and Diagrams Relating to Non-Condensing Engines and Boilers (W. P. Trowbridge), 1872, also in Transactions of Am. Soc. C.E., Vol. III, 1875. Died N.Y.C., June 1, 1898.

EMERY, WILLIAM ORRIN, chemist; b. Vernon, Vt., Mar. 29, 1963; s. Ira and Emmeline (Stearns) E.; B.S., Worcester Poly. Inst., in civ. engring., 1885, in chemistry 1886; spl. work in chemistry, physics, geology, mineralogy, and bacteriology, Bonn and Berlin, 1886-93; pvt. asst. to Prof. Kekule and instr. chemistry, U. Bonn, 1887-92; Ph.D., U. Erlangen, 1888; m. Auguste Josephine Roetzel, Apr. 8, 1893; children—Alice, Gustav Harold. Pvt. docent in chemistry, U. Bonn, 1891-92, absent on leave, 1893-97; research chemist in Berlin and Chgo., 1893-94; prof. chemistry, Wabash Coll., 1895-1901; was research chemist, Crawfordsville, Bonn and Berlin, beginning 1902; organic chemist (1907; and chief Synthetic Products Lab., Bur. Chemistry, Dept. Agr., 1908—; also charge spl. collaborative investigations of Food and Drug Adminstrn., 1929—. Fellow A.A.A.S.; mem. Am. Chem. Soc., Washington Acad. Scis., Phi Beta Kappa, Sigma Xi. Club: Cosmos. Contbr. numerous papers Am. and fgn. periodicals. Home: 2232 Cathedral Av. N.W. Address: Bur. of Chemistry, Washington. Died May 3, 1946; buried Fort Lincoln Cemetery, Washington.

EMLAW, HARLAN STIGAND, mining engr.; b. Grand Haven, Mich., Aug. 8, 1873; s. Andrew Jackson and Louisa (Yates) E.; student Mich. State Coll., 1890-92; B.S. and M.E., Mich. Coll. of Mining and Tech., 1895, Dr. of Engring., 1942; m. Alice Lucy Bilz, June 26, 1901; 1 dau., Alice Louise (Mrs. Donald A. Lacoss). Engr. with Anaconda Copper Co., 1896-1903; acting and gen. superintendent of mines for Cerro de Pasco Mining Co., Peru, S.A., 1903-07; pvt. practice to 1919; gen. mgr., pres. and dir., Am. Potash and Chem.

Corp., 1919-45; retired 1945. Mem. Am. Inst. Mining and Metall. Engrs., Mining and Metall. Soc. Am. Republican. Club: Mining (New York). Home: 724 Charlotte Av., Rock Hill, S.C. Died Feb. 5, 1953; buried Grand Haven, Mich.

EMMET, WILLIAM LEROY, electrical engr.; b. New Rochelle, N.Y., July 10, 1859; s. William J. and Julia Colt (Pierson) E.; grad. U.S. Naval Acad., 1881; Sc.D., Union Coll., 1910, Trinity Coll., Hartford, Conn., 1925. D.Eng., Stevens Inst. of Technology, 1939; unmarried. Left navy, 1883; elec. engr., 1887—; in service Gen. Elec. Co., 1892—; reentered navy during Spanish-Am. War; most important work has been in steam turbine inventions and developments, and invention of mercury vapor power process. Awarded Edison medal, 1919, Elliott Cresson medal, 1920; gold medal from Am. Society M.E.; David W. Tayloe medal from Am. Soc. of Naval Architects and Marine Engrs., 1938. Author: Alternating Current Wiring and Distribution 1894; The Autobiography of an Engineer, 1931. Mem. Naval Consulting Bd., 1915, and chmn. com. on submarines, Home: Schenectady, N.Y. Died Sept. 26, 1941.

EMMONS, EBENEZER, physician, geologist, educator; b. Middlefield, Mass., May 16, 1799; s. Ebenezer and Mary (Mack) E.; grad. Williams Coll., 1818, Rensselaer Inst., 1826; attended Berkshire Med. Sch., 1826-28; m. Maria Cone, 1818. Apptd. lectr. chemistry Williams Coll., 1828; apptd. jr. prof. Rensselaer Inst., 1830; prof. chemistry Albany Med. Sch., 1838, later prof. obstetrics until 1852; apptd. state geologist N.C., 1851. Author: Manual of Mineralogy and Geology (5 papers dealing with investigation of agrl. resources of N.Y. State), 1846-54; Zoology of Mass., 1840; American Geology, 3 vols., 1855. Died Brunswick County, N.C., Oct. 1, 1863.

EMMONS, WILLIAM HARVEY, geologist; b. Mexico, Mo., Feb. 1, 1876; s. St. Clair Peyton and Elizabeth Harvey (Ford) E.; A.B., Central Coll., Fayette, Mo., 1897; Ph.D., U. of Chicago, 1904; m. Virginia Cloyd, Sept. 6, 1910; children—Elizabeth, William Cloyd. Geologic aid, 1904-06, asst. geologist, 1906-10, geologist, 1910-15, U.S. Geol. Survey; lecturer on ore deposits, 1907, on petrology, 1908, asst. prof. petrology and econ. geology, 1908-09, asso. prof. econ. geology, 1909-12. U. of Chicago; prof. and head of dept. geology and mineralogy, University of Minnesota since 1911, professor emeritus since 1944; also director Minnesota Geol. Survey. Asso. editor Jour. of Geology. Mem. Am. Commn. to China, 1920, to study coal and iron for S. Manchurian Ry. Mem. Geol. Soc. America (v.p. 1923), Geol. Soc. Washington. Am. Inst. Mining Engrs., Soc. Econ. Geology (pres. 1928); mem. (hon.) American Assn. Petroleum Engrs., Geological Societies of France and of Belgium, Sigma Xi, Sigma Nu, Gamma Alpha. Methodist. Author: Ore Deposits of Maine, 1910; Ore Deposits of Bull Frog, Nev., 1910; Ore Deposits of Elko, Lander and Eureka Counties, Nev., 1910; Ore Deposits of Phillipsburg, Mont. (with F. C. Calkins), 1913; Enrichment of Ore Deposits, 1917; Ore Deposits of Ducktown, Tenn., 1926—(all pub. by U.S. Geol. Survey); also several text books on ore deposits and on petroleum. Home: 1225 7th St. S.E., Minneapolis. Died Nov. 5, 1948.

EMSWELLER, SAMUEL LEONAR, biologist; b. Tarentum, Pa., Nov. 1, 1898; s. Samuel Peter and Catherine (Waltzinger) E.; B.Sc., W.Va. U., 1920; Ph.D., U. Cal., 1932; m. Frances P. Fitzgerald, June 30, 1920; children—Eugene S., Frances T. Research asst. U. Cal., 1928-32, asst. prof., 1932-35; prin. horticulturist, head floriculture research Dept. Agr., 1935-51, head horticulturist, ornamental plant crops sect., Beltsville, Md., from 1952. Mem. Internat. Hort. Congress, London, 1952, Netherlands, 1955, sectional chmn., 1955-58, Hort. Congress, France, 1958, Internat. Genetic Congress, Montreal, 1960. Recipient achievement award Am. Hort. Council, gold medal N.E. Gladiola Soc., gold medal Mass. Hort Soc., Jackson-Dawson Medal, 1950; citation for research, Mens Gardens Club of Am., 1958; Superior Service award by U.S. Dept. Agr., 1959; Lytel Cup, Royal Hort. Soc., London, 1959; Medal of Honor, Garden Club Am., 1959, George Robert White Medal of Honor, 1964, Norman J. Colman medal, 1964; named to Floriculture Hall of Fame, 1964. Fellow A.A.A.S.; mem. Am. Genetic Soc. (pres.), Am. Soc. Hort. Sci. (past pres.). American Bot. Soc., Genetics Soc. Am. (rep. div. biology and agr. Nat. Research Council, Bot. Soc. Washington (past pres.), Washington Acad. Sci., Sigma Phi Epsilon, Sigma Xi, Alpha Zeta. Clubs: Bohemian (asso.) (San Francisco); Cosmos (Washington). Office: Beltsville MD Died Aug. 22, 1966; buried Arlington National Cemetery, Arlington VA

ENDERS, HOWARD EDWIN, dean emeritus, professor zoology; b. Enders, Pa., June 18, 1877; s. Charles Washington and Phoebe A. (Buffington) E.; B.S., Lebanon Valley Coll., Anville, Pa., 1897, M.S., 1900; B.S., U. of Mich., 1898; post-grad. work 3 summers, U. of Mich. and Harvard Univ., and Johns Hopkins U., 1903-06; Ph.D., Johns Hopkins Univ., 1906, Sc.D. (hon.), Lebanon Valley College, 1946; m. Susie S. Moyer. Oct. 16, 1901; children—Mrs. Katherine Eleanora Flack, Charles M., Sue E (Winston). Science teacher, Hulst High Sch., Iron Mountain, Mich., 1898-1900; with field party Mich. Geol. Survey, summer, 1899; prof. biol. sciences, Lebanon Valley Coll., 1900-03; research in zoology, U.S. Fisheries Lab., Beaufort, N.C., summers, 1903-08; with Purdue U. since 1906, successively instr. in zoology, asst. prof., asso. prof., 1917, prof. zoology, head of gen. biology, head of dept. of biology since 1926, acting dean Sch. of Science, 1931, and dean, February, 1932-46, on leave, 1946-47; retired July 1, 1947; professor of zoology and biology, 10 summers, Ind. U. and Johns Hopkins; research in parasitology at Kartabo Jungle Lab. of Tropical Biology, British Guiana, S.A., summer, 1925, at research lab. of Inst. of Tropical Biology, Gatun Lake, Panama Canal Zone, summer, 1927; tropical research in Lancetilla Expt. Sta., Honduras, summer, 1933. Lecturer on physiology, St. Elizabeth Hosp., Lafayette, Ind., 1915-1940. Fellow A.A.A.S. (sec. 1928; chmn. acad. conf. 1929 and 1933), Ind. Acad. Science (sec. 1913-20; pres. 1921); state sponsor Indiana Junior Acad. of Science; member Am. Soc. Zoologists, Phi Beta Kappa (Johns Hopkins), Sigma Xi of Purdue (pres. 1931). Republican. Mem. U.B. Ch. Clubs: Rotary (pres. 1931-32), Town and Gown (pres. 1933-34). Author: Laboratory Directions in General Biology, 1912, 4th edit., 1936. Home: 249 Littleton St., West Layfayette, Ind.; Winter; Venice FL

ENGELHARDT, FRANCIS ERNEST, chemist; b. Gieboldehausen, Hanover, June 23, 1835; s. Ernest Philipp and Marie Antonette (Schwachheim) E.; studied U. of Göttingen, 1854-57; came to U.S., 1857; Ph.D., St. Francis Xavier Coll., New York, 1864; m. Anna M. Miller, of Syracuse, N.Y., Sept. 8, 1870. Asst. in chemistry, Amherst, 1857-58; chemist, Phila., 1858-60; asst. in chemistry, Francis Xavier Coll., 1862-67; prof. materia med-Columbia, Coll., 1861-62; prof. chemistry, St. ica, New York Coll. of Pharmacy, 1868-69; chemist to Onondaga Salt Co. since 1869; chemist to state salt supt. of Onondaga Salt Reservation, 1878-90; apptd. 1881, and again, 1885, by State Bd. of Health, chemist of liquors, wines beers, State of N.Y.; now in gen. practice; also chemist for City of Syracuse. Author of papers on petroleum, salt, liquors, beers, etc., in various journals. Home: 504 Catharine St. Office: 405 City Hall, Syracuse, N.Y. *

ENGELKEMEIR, DONALD WILLIAM, nuclear chemist; b. Nehawka, Neb., June 10, 1919; s. Julius G. and Mathilda (Ploeger) E.; B.A., U. Cal., Los Angeles, 1942; Ph.D., U. Chgo., 1952; m. Antoinette M. Greiner, July 19, 1947; children—Richard, Ann, Gregory, Jean. Asso. chemist Metall. lab., U. Chgo., 1942-45; asso. chemist Los Alamos (N.M.) Sci. Lab., 1945-46; nuclear chemist Argonne (Ill.) Nat. Lab., 1948-69. Mem. Am. Physical Soc., Am. Assn. Variable Star Observers, Sigma Xi. Democrat. Roman Catholic. Home: Hinsdale IL Died Apr. 29, 1969.

ENGELMANN, GEORGE, botanist, physician; b. Frankfurt-am-Main, Germany, Feb. 2, 1809; s. George and Julia (May) E.; M.D., U. Wurzburg, 1831; m. Dorothea Horstmann, June 11, 1840, 1 son, George J. Came to U.S., 1832; an early user of quinine for treatment of malaria; discoverer adaptation of Pronuba moth for accomplishing pollination of yuccas; discovered immunity of Am. grape to phylloxera; a pioneer meteoroligist; organizer St. Louis Acad. Science, 1856. Works collected in Botanical Works of the Late George Englemann Collected for Henry Shaw, 1887. Died St. Louis, Feb. 4, 1884.

ENGERRAND, GEORGE C., (an-zhe-ran'), anthropologist; b. at Libourne, France, Aug. 11, 1877; s. of Georges and Clara (Dormoy) E.; B.S., of Bordeaux, France, 1895; licencié in geology, same univ., 1897, in botany, 1898; Ph.D., U. of Texas, 1935; hon. prof. at New U., Brussels, 1907; M.A., U. Miss., 1920; m. Alice Delsaute, 1898; children—Elisee, Gabriel; m. 2d, Jeanne Richard, 1904; children—Jacques J., Mrs. W. F. Helwig, Mrs. F. H. Gafford. Prof. geology and prehistoric archaeology, New U., 1898-1907; geologist Belgian Geological Survey, 1901-07; chief geologist Mexican Geological Survey, 1907-15; professor prehistoric archaeology, Nat. Mus., Mexico City, 1908-14; dir. Internat. Sch. Am. Archaeology and Ethnology, Mexico City, 1912-13; asst. prof. Romance langs. and instr. geology, Univ. of Miss., 1919-20; adjunct prof. anthropology, 1920-23, asso. prof. anthropology, 1923-29, prof., 1929-38, grad. prof. since 1938, U. of Texas; prof. extraordinario, Nat. U. of Mexico, summers, 1943, 44, 45, 46. Member bd. of governors Latin-American Orgn. for Continental Solidarity. Decorated officer d' Acadénice by French Government. Member American Anthropological Assn., Davenport (Ia.) Acad., Berliner Gesellschaft für Anthropologie, Ethnologie und Urgeschichte, Academia Nacional de Ciencias Antonio Alzate (Mexico); hon. mem. Académie Malgache; corr. mem. Sch. of Anthropology, Anthropol. Soc., Soc. des Américanistes—all of Paris. Author: Six leçons de Préhistoire, 1905; Article on Mexico in 14th edit. Ency. Brit.; The So-called Wends of Germany and their Colonies in Texas and Australia, 1934. Contbr. numerous articles in geol. and archaeol. jours. on eoliths, petroglyphs in Lower Calif., geology of Yucatan, paleontology of Chiapas (Mexico), etc. Address: U. Texas, Austin 12. Died Sept. 2, 1961; buried Meml. Hill Park and Mausoleum.

ENGLE, EARL T., med. research, editor; b. Waterloo, Ia., Mar. 19, 1896; s. Levi H and Mary C. (Stephens) E.; A.B., Nebraska Wesleyan U., 1920; A.M., U. of Colorado, 1923; Ph.D., Stanford, 1925; m. Mirth Richardson, Jan. 1, 1917; children—Audrey Engle Hawthorn, Robert Gregg. Instr. zoölogy, U. of Colo., 1921-23, anatomy, Stanford, 1925-27; asst. prof., 1927-28; Coll. Physicians and Surgeons, Columbia, 1928-29; asso. prof., 1929-39, professor since 1939, assigned to obstetrics and gynecology, 1949; Sir William F. Shaw lecturer Royal College of Obstetrics and Gynecology, London, 1952. Director research, National Committee Maternal Health, 1937-47; chairman editorial com., Assn. Internal Secretions, 1942-48. Recipient award from Am. Urological Assn., 1946; award for research Am. Gynecol. Soc., 1950. Hon. mem. N.Y. Soc. Am. Urol. Assn., Western Urol. Association; mem. Am. Soc. Anat., Am. Soc. Physiol., Soc. Exp. Biol. Med., Soc. Gerontol. Assn., Study Internal Secretions, Nat. Research Council (mem. com. growth, 1945-50, committee human reprodn., 1947-50). Editor: (books) Diagnosis in Sterility, 1946; Problem of Fertility, 1946; Menstruation and Its Disorders, 1948; Studies on Ovary and Testis, 1952; Pregnancy Wastage, 1953; (with G. Pincus) Hormones and the Aging Process, 1956. Mem. Atomic Bomb Casualty Commn., Hiroshima, 1949. Address: La Orilla, Rancho Santa Fe, Cal. Died Dec. 17, 1957.

ENGLE, WILBUR DWIGHT, chemist; b. Portland, Mich., Aug. 31, 1870; s. David and Ann (Guernsey) E.; A.B., Albion (Mich.) Coll., 1893, A.M., 1894; Ph.D., Columbia, 1898; Sc.D. from the University of Denver in 1914; LL.D. from the University of Colorado, 1927; m. Emma G. Agard, of Litchfield, Mich., Aug. 22, 1895; children—Earl Agard, Dorothy Gail. Instr. in chemistry, Albion Coll., 1893-95; prof. chemistry, 1895-1937, dean Summer Sch., vice chancellor, 1917-37, acting chancellor, 1920-22 and 1927-28, dean Sch. of Science and Engineering, 1930-37, and dean of the Graduate School of the U. of Denver, 1933, retired, 1937. Prof. chemistry, Denver and Gross Colleges of Medicine, 1898-1910. Mem. American Chemical Society, The Teknik Club (Denver), also Phi Lambda Upsilon, Omega Upsilon Phi, Alpha Tau Omega. Methodist. Mem. exec. com. 8th Internat. Cong. Applied Chemistry, 1912-13; has done much expert work in chemistry, especially in toxicology, and recognized as an authority in that subject; especially interested in chemistry of uranium and vanadium, and has devised successful methods for the treatment of their ores. Home: 2233 S. Columbine St., Denver CO

ENGLISH, GEORGE LETCHWORTH, mineralogist; b. Phila., Pa., June 14, 1864; s. John A. and Amanda (Evans) E.; grad. Friends' Central Sch., Phila., 1881; m. Louise T. Baltz, June 17, 1890 (died Mar. 10, 1920); children—Mrs. Gwendolen Burleson, Henry Rowland, Kathrine Louise (dec.); m. 2d, Jane Parsons Hanna, Mar. 29, 1923. Collected minerals in Europe, North and South America, Africa and Australia; head firm George L. English & Co., Phila. and New York, dealers in scientific minerals, 1886-1904; monazite expert, and in charge of mining monazite in N. and S. Carolina for Nat. Light & Thorium Co., 1903-13; mgr. dept. of mineralogy and petrography, Ward's Natural Science Establishment, Rochester, N.Y., 1913-21; cons. mineralogist for the same (later The Frank A Ward Foundation of Natural Science of the University of Rochester), 1921-34. Has lectured on mineralogy for N.Y. City Board of Edn., also before various socs. Fellow and life mem. Rochester Acad. Science (pres. 1919-21); mem. Phila. Acad. Natural Sciences, Brooklyn Inst. Arts and Sciences (life), New York Mineral Club, Mineral. Soc. America (v.p. 1927), etc. Author: Getting Acquainted with Minerals; Descriptive List of the New Minerals, 1892-1938; A Catalogue of Minerals, and articles on mineralogy in Ency. Americana, etc. Home: 50 Brighton St., Rochester, N.Y. Died Jan. 2, 1944.

ENGSTROM, HOWARD THEODORE, scientist, corp. exec.; b. Boston, Apr. 23, 1902; s. Gustav W. and Anna K. (Ranvik) E.; B.Chem. Engring., Northeastern U., 1922; M.A. in Math., U. Me., 1925; Ph.D. in Math., Yale, 1929; NRC fellow, Cal. Inst. Tech., 1929-30; Internat. Research fellow, Gottingen, Germany, 1930-31; m. Karin Ekblom, Apr. 18, 1935; children—Karin S. (Mrs. William Agosta), Anna K., Morten H. Engr. Western Union Telegraph Co., 1922-23; instr. U. Me., 1923-25; instr. math. Trinity Coll., Hartford, Conn., 1925-26; instr. Yale, 1926-29, asst. prof. math., 1931-35, asso. prof., 1935-41; founder, v.p. Engring. Research Assos., St. Paul, 1945-52; company bought by Remington Rand Co., 1952; v.p. Remington Rand div. Sperry Rand Co., 1952-56, 58—; dep. dir. Nat. Security Agy., 1956-58; chmn. bd. Computer Export Corp., Atlanta, 1958—. Adviser Dept. of Def. Served with USNR, 1941-45; capt. Res. Decorated Distinguished Service medal, Naval Res. medal, Presdl. Unit citation; Officer British Empire; recipient medal of appreciation Dept. of Def., Nat. Security Agy. medal; fellow Davenport Coll., Yale. Fellow Inst. Radio Engrs. mem. Am. Math. Soc., Math. Assn. Am., Assn. Computing Machinery. Club: Cosmos (Washington). Editor: High Speed Printing Devices, 1950. Author numerous articles in field. Home: Ellisville, Buzzard's Bay, R.F.D., Mass. Office:

Remington Rand, 315 4th Av., N.Y.C. 10. Died Mar. 8, 1962; buried Arlington Cemetery.

ENNIS, WILLIAM DUANE, engineer; b. in Bergen County, N.J., Jan. 6, 1877; s. William C. and Kate E. (Burroughs) E.; M.E., Stevens Inst. Tech., 1897, Dr. Engring., 1934; married Margaret Schuyler, December 28, 1898. Mechanical engineer in various companies, including Am. Linseed Co., 1897-1905; engr. Am. Locomotive Co., 1905-07; served as prof. mech. engring., Poly. Inst. of Brooklyn, Columbia U., U.S. Naval Acad. Consultant in mech. engring. and industrial management. Commd. maj. U.S.R. and on active duty, Ordnance Dept., Washington, and Watervliet Arsenal, N.Y., 1917-18. Vice pres., Technical Advisory Corp., N.Y., 1920-29. Alexander Crombie Humphreys prof., economics of engring., Stevens Inst. Tech., 1929-44; now professor emeritus. Fellow A.A.A.S., Royal Econ. Soc.; Am. Soc. M.E. (treas. 1935-44); mem. American Economic Assn., Tau Beta Pi. Author: Linseed Oil, 1909; Applied Thermodynamics, 1910; Vapors for Heat Engines, 1912; Flying Machines Today, 1911; Works Management, 1911; Thermodynamics Abridged, 1920; Business Fundamentals for Engineering Students, 1941. Home: Wyckoff, N.J. Died Oct. 14, 1947.

ENO, WILLIAM PHELPS, highway traffic engr.; b. N.Y. City, June 3, 1858; s. Amos Richards and Lucy Jane (Phelps) E.; B.A., Yale, 1882, M.A., 1923; m. Alice Rathbone, Apr. 4, 1883 (died Dec. 21, 1911); m. 2d, Alberta Averill Paz, Apr. 18, 1934. Studied highway traffic regulation in Europe many yrs.; actively identified with the cause in U.S. since 1899; incorporated the Eno Found. for Highway Traffic Regulation, 1921; organized and directed Home Defense League of D.C. (an auxiliary police force); now mem. adv. bd. on Highway Research of Nat. Research Council. Served as chmn. div. of transportation of War Industries Bd. and as chmn. adv. bd. highway transport com of Council of Nat. Defense. Chevalier Legion of Honor (France), 1925, promoted to officer, 1935. Hon. mem. Inst. of Traffic Engrs., Traffic Squad Benevolent Assn. of Police Dept., N.Y. City; hon. pres. Nat. Pedestrian Assn., Nat. Highway Traffic Assn.; hon. mem. Chember Syndicale des Cochers et Chauffeurs de Voitures de Place de la Seine (Paris). Clubs: Yale, University, New York Yacht (New York); Cosmos, Metropolitan (Washington, D.C.); Union Interalliee, American (Paris). Author: Street Traffic Regulation, 1909; Le Probleme de la Circulation, 1912; The Science of Highway Traffic Regulation, 1920; Fundamentals of Highway Traffic Regulation, 1926; Simplification of Highway Traffic, 1929. Home: Washington, D.C.; and Saugatuck, Conn. Died Dec. 3, 1945.

ENSIGN, ORVILLE HIRAM, electrical mech. engr.; b. Ithaca, N.Y., July 8, 1863; s. Hoffman W. and Jennie (Chambers) E.; ed. pub. and high schs., Ithaca, N.Y., and 2 yrs.' course in mech. arts, Cornell U.; m. Jennie Kirtland, Aug. 15, 1888. Machinist, Ithaca, N.Y., 1882-83; with Schenectady Locomotive Works, 1883-87; with Edison United Co., New York, in charge power plant construction for N.Y., 1887-89; with Gen. Elec. Co., Schenectady, N.Y., in charge of tests, 1889-90, chief insp. factory, 1890-93; consulting engr. Redlands (Calif.) Electric Light & Power Co., and in other miscellaneous pvt. work on telephone patents; elec. and mech. engr. on construction and operation of power plants, Pasadena & Los Angeles Elec. Ry. and Los Angeles, Santa Monica Ry., 1894-95; supt. and chief engr. Redlands Electric Light & Power Co., 1896; supt. and chief engr., 1897, of Southern Calif. Power Co., planning and constructing 30,000-volt long distance transmission line, and when this, with other cos., was consolidated as Edison Electric Co. of Los Angeles, became supt. and chief elec. and mech. engr. until 1904; was chief elec. and mech. engr. U.S. Reclamation Service, in charge of hydroelectric power and pumping problems; now cons. engr. U.S. Reclamation Service and of Los Angeles Aqueduct Power; mfr. of carburetors. Republican. Methodist. Home: Pasadena, Calif. Died June 1, 1935.

ENTRIKIN, JOHN BENNETT, educator; b. Canton, Kan., Oct. 6, 1899; s. James Bennett and Addie Mae (Powers) E.; A.B., Southwestern U., 1922; A.M., 1923; Ph.D., State U. Ia., 1929; m. Minnie Sue Stewart, July 29, 1924; children—Jean Marie (Mrs. Dr. Wm. S. Harwell), Connie Mae (Mrs. E. L. Gibson). Instructor Southwestern University, 1924-26; professor Temple (Texas) Junior College, 1926-27; professor and head dept. chemistry. Centenary Coll. of La. since 1929; indsl. consultant, chemistry since 1929. Served with S.A.T.C., 1918; dep. dir. Shreveport Civilian Def. from World War II, 1955. Fellow Am. Inst. Chemists; mem. Am. Chem. Soc. (past chmn. Ark-La-Tex. sect.), Am. Legion, A.A.A.S., Am. Assn. U. Profs., La. Acad. Sci. (past pres.), Shreveport Soc. for Nature Study (past pres.), Shreveport C. of C. (chmn. com. on chemurgy), Sigma Xi, Alpha Chi Sigma, Phi Lambda Upsilon, Omicron Delta Kappa, Kappa Alpha Order. Methodist. Author (with N.D. Cheronis): Semimicro Qualitative Organic Analysis, 1947, 3d edit. (with E. M. Hodnett), 1965; Identification of Organic Compounds, 1962. Home: 3789 Greenway, Shreveport, La. Died June 17, 1966; buried Forest Park Cemetery, Shreveport, La.

EPSTEIN, PAUL SOPHUS, physicist; b. Warsaw, Poland, Mar. 20, 1883; s. Siegmund Simon and Sophia Sarah (Lourie) E.; grad. Humanistic High Sch., Minsk, Russia, 1901; B.S., U. Moscow, 1906, M.S., 1909; Ph.D., U. Munich, 1914; m. Alice E. Ryckman, June 17, 1930; 1 dau., Sari Sophia (Mrs. Frank Mittelbach). Came to United States, 1921, naturalized, 1927. Asst. Agricultural Inst. Moscow, 1906; asst., U. Moscow, 1907-09; privatdocent U. Moscow, 1909-13, U. Zurich, 1919-21; prof. Cal. Inst. Tech. since 1921; exchange prof. Inst. Tech., Aachen, Germany, 1927 and 1929. Fellow Am. Phys. Soc., A.A.A.S.; mem. Nat. Acad. Scis. Author: Textbook of Thermodynamics, 1937. Address: 1484 Oakdale St., Pasadena, Cal. 91106. Died Feb. 8, 1966.

EQUEN, MURDOCK, nose and throat surgeon; b. New Orleans, Apr. 9, 1892; s. Jonte and Willie (Sykes) E.; student Vanderbilt, 1912-13; M.D., Emory U., 1916; postgrad. U. Pa., 1920-21; m. Anne Hart, Oct. 25, 1922; children—Anne Hart (Mrs. W. Perry Balland), Carol Sykes (Mrs. Sebastian Miller). Intern Bklyn Eye and Ear Infirmary, 1916-17; practice of nose and throat surgery, Atlanta, 1921—; founder Ponce de Leon Infirmary, Atlanta, owner, operator, 1936—. Served as 1st lt. MC, Base Hosp. 43, World War I. Recipient Thomas A. Edison Found. Gold award for achievement and contbn. to arts and scis., 1944. Diplomate Am. Bd. Otolaryngology. Fellow A.C.S.; mem. A.M.A., Am. Laryngol. Assn., Am. Broncho-Esophagol. Assn., Am. Laryngol. Phinol. and Otol. Soc., Am. Acad. Ophthalmology and Otolaryngology, So. Med. Assn., Med. Assn. Ga., Fulton County Med. Soc., Atlanta Eye, Ear, Nose and Throat Soc., Kappa Sigma, Phi Rho Sigma. Clubs: Kiwanis, Piedmont Driving, Capitol City. Author: Magnetic Removal of Foreign Bodies, 1957. Originator various modifications of magnetic instruments used in air and food passages. Author articles profl. jours. Home: 2505 Habersham Rd. N.W., Atlanta 30305. Office: 144 Ponce de Leon Av. N.E., Atlanta. Died Nov. 11, 1964; buried West View Abbey, Atlanta.

ERB, CARL LEE, JR., civil engr.; b. Lincoln, Neb., Sept. 11, 1913; s. Carl Lee and Clarence Lillian (Larson) E.; B.Sc. in Civil Engring., U. Neb., 1935; m. Phyllis Lenore Richey, Dec. 6, 1936; children—Julann (Mrs. Lauren E. Meyers), Philip Michael. Constrn. engr. C., B. & O. R.R., 1935-37; office engr. Kingsley Dam Western Neb., designer hydropower and irrigation structures Central Neb. Power & Irrigation Dist., 1938-41; with Howard, Needles, Tammen & Bergendoff, cons. engrs., Kansas City, Mo., Cleve., N.Y., 1941-71, partner, 1957-71; dir. Grand Av. Bank, Kansas City, Mo. Recipient Thomas Arkle Clark award Alpha Tau Omega, 1935, Man of Year award, 1971. Registered profl. engr., Conn., Ida., Ind., Ky., La., Mo., Mont., Neb., N.Y., Ohio, Okla., Pa., W.Va., Wis. Mem. Am. Inst. Cons. Engrs. (nat. pres. 1971), Am. Soc. C.E., Nat. Soc. Profl. Engrs., Kansas City Engrs. Club, Engring. Inst. Can., Am. Rd. Builders Assn., Cons. Engrs. Council, Sigma Xi, Alpha Tau Omega, Sigma Tau, Pi Mu Epsilon. Methodist. Rotarian. Clubs: Mission Hills (Kan.) Country; Kansas City (Mo.); Mid-Ocean (Bermuda). Prin. designer, adminstr. maj. bridges and expressways including Del. Meml. Bridge, Pres. Truman Bridge, Kansas City, Mo. Turnpike, Denver-Boulder Turnpike, urban expressways systems in Cleve., Akron (O.), Toledo, other large cities. Home: Mission Hills KS Died Dec. 5, 1971.

ERDMAN, FREDERICK SEWARD, educator and cons. engr.; b. Sidon, Syria (Lebanon), Oct. 27, 1901 (parents U.S. citizens); s. Paul and Amanda C. (Jessup) E.; B.S., Princeton, 1924; B.S. in M.E., Mass. Inst. Tech., 1927; M.S., in M.E., Cornell, 1937, Ph.D., 1941; m. Mary Nicol, June 15, 1928; children—Barbara Gertrude (Mrs. David E. Blais), Carol Amanda (Mrs. Douglas H. Merkle), Frederick Seward Erdman, Elizabeth Anna (Mrs. Horace J. Mann), Constance Rebecca (Mrs. George F. Feissner). Tchr. Am. U., Beirut, Lebanon, 1924-25; jr. engineer Worthington Pump & Machinery Corp., Cincinnati, 1927-28; asst. prof. mech. engring. Robert Coll., Istanbul, Turkey, 1928-36; grad. student and instr. coll. of engring., Cornell, 1936-41, asst. prof. mech. engring., 1941-44, asso. prof., 1944-49, prof., 1949-67, emeritus prof., 1967-68, asso. dean, 1962-67; vis. engr. Brookhaven Nat. Lab., 1948, cons., 1949-52; cons. engr., 1942-68. Licensed profl. engr. Mem. Am. Assn. U. Profs., A.S.M.E., Am. Soc. Engring. Edn., Phi Kappa Phi, Sigma Xi. Presbyterian (elder). Author: Principles of Food Freezing (with Gortner and Masterman), 1948. Contbr. articles to tech. jours. and Encyclopaedia Britannica. Home: Ithaca NY Died Sept. 22, 1968.

ERDMAN, JOHN FREDERIC, surgeon; b. Cin., Mar. 27, 1864; s. Zacharia and Maria Elizabeth (Lippert) E.; M.D., Bellevue Hosp. Med. Coll. (N.Y.U.), 1887, D.Sc., 1948; m. Georgiana Wright, June 20, 1894; children—Olivia Sturtevant, Sturtevant, Jane. Practiced at N.Y.C., 1887—; clin. prof. surgery, Univ. and Bellevue Hosp. Med. Coll. (N.Y.U.), 1893-1908; prof. practical anatomy, N.Y.U., 1895-1900; dir., prof. surgery, N.Y. Post-Grad. Med. Sch. and Hosp. Columbia, 1908-34; attending surgeon Post-Grad. Hosp., 1934-39; cons. surgeon since July, 1939; cons. surgeon, Gouverneur, Nassau, Mt. Vernon, Greenwich Gen. and Nyack, Rockland States, St. Luke's (Newburgh) hosps., State Hosp. at Central Islip, Home for Incurables, Hosp. Joint Diseases, Jersey City Med. Center, Union Hosp. (Bronx), Southampton Hosp. Capt., asst. surg., N.Y. Nat. Guard, 6 yrs. asst. surgeon U.S.R.C., 1912-15; lt. col. M.O.R.C. until 1929. Pres. Interstate Post. Grad. Med. Assn. N.A., 1936-37. Fellow A.C.S.; mem. A.M.A., Am. Assn. Obstetricians, Gynecologists and Abdominal Surgeons, N.Y. Surg. Soc., Am., N.Y. urol. socs., N.Y. Acad. Medicine, N.Y. County Med. Assn., Ohio Soc. N.Y., Bellevue Alumni. Episcopalian. Clubs: Union League, Devon Yacht, Maidstone (L.I.), L.I. Country, Hospital Graduates. Address: 122 E. 70th St., N.Y.C. Died Mar. 1954.

ERICKSON, J(ULIUS) L(YMAN) E(DWARD), univ. prof.; b. Lake Charles, La., Oct. 8, 1901; s. Charles Edward and Ella Jessie (Finlayson); B.A., Rice Inst., 1923, M.S., 1926; A.M., Harvard, 1927, Ph.D., 1932; m. Olivia Bradshaw, Aug. 28, 1928; 1 dau., Jane Vincent. Instr. in chemistry La. State U., 1930-32, asst. prof., 1932-37, asso. prof., 1937-44, prof. organic chemistry from 1944. Fellow The Chem. Soc. (London), Am. Inst. of Chemists, A.A.A.S., La. Acad. Sci.; mem. Am. Chem. Soc., Sigma Xi, Phi Lambda Upsilon, Kappa Sigma. Democrat. Presbyterian. Clubs: Harvard of Louisiana (New Orleans); Faculty (La. State U.). Contbr. articles to professional jours. Holder patents on macrocyclic musk compounds, U.S., British and Canadian; research in organic chemistry dealing with synthesis, mechanism of reactions and natural products. Home: Baton Rouge LA Died Feb. 22, 1968; buried Graceland Cemetery, Lake Charles LA

ERICSSON, JOHN, engr., inventor; b. Province of Vermland, Sweden, July 31, 1803; s. Olof and Brita (Yngstrom) E.; m. Amelia Byam, Oct. 15, 1836. Came to U.S., 1839; built a caloric engine, 1833; developer transmission of power by compressed air, use of centrifugal blowers for boiler forced draft, new types of steam boilers; placed warship engines below water line for protection; constructed railroad steam locomotive, 1829; introduced screw propellers for boats, 1840, designed much of U.S.S. Princeton (1st screw-propelled vessel of war), 1844; designed and built the Monitor (with a friction recoil mechanism for its guns) for U.S. Navy, 1861; designer, builder 13 inch wrought iron gun for U.S. Govt., 1863. Died N.Y.C., Mar. 8, 1889; buried Sweden.

ERIKSON, HENRY ANTON, physicist; b. Mt. Morris, Wis., July 30, 1869; s. Hemming and Elizabeth (Tommeraas) E.; B.E.E., U. of Minn., 1896, Ph.D., 1908; student U. of Chicago, 1899, Cambridge U., Eng., 1908-09; m. Winifred Boynton, of New Lisbon, Wis., June 21, 1899; children—Hemming (dec.), Elizabeth W., Henry B. Instr. in science, high sch., Rochester, Minn., 1896-97; instr. physics, 1897-1906, asst. prof., 1906-14, asso. prof., 1914-15, prof. 1915-38, also chairman of dept., professor emeritus, 1938—, University of Minnesota. Fellow A.A.A.S.; mem. Am. Physical Soc., Sigma Xi, Tau Beta Pi, Theta Chi. Club: Cosmopolitan. Author: Elements of Mechanics; Manual of Physical Measurements, 1902. Contbr. on ionization in Physical Rev., Philos. Mag., others. Address: 1207 Genoa St., Coral Gables, Fla. Died June 22, 1957; buried Mount Morris, Wis.

ERLANGER, JOSEPH, physiologist; b. San Francisco, Jan. 5, 1874; s. Herman and Sarah (Galinger) E.; B.S., U. Cal., 1895, LL.D., 1932; M.D., Johns Hopkins, 1899, LL.D., 1947; Sc.D., U. Wis., 1936, U. Pa., 1936, Washington U., St. Louis, 1946; D. (hon) Free, U. Brussels, 1949; m. Aimée Hirstel, June 21, 1906 (dec. May 22, 1959); children—Margaret Ruth (Mrs. R. H. Swinney), Herman (dec. 1959). Asst. prof. dept. physiology Johns Hopkins, 1900-06; prof., head dept. physiology U. Wis., 1906-10; prof., head dept. physiology Washington U., St. Louis, 1910-48, prof. emeritus, 1948—; Hitchcock lectr. U. Cal., 1930; Johnson lectr. U. Pa., 1936. Recipient Nobel Prize in physiology and medicine (with Herbert S. Gasser), 1944. Mem. A.A.A.S., Am. Physiol. Soc., Am. Philos. Soc., Nat. Acad. Scis., Deutsche Academie Naturforscher, Société Philomathique (Paris), Soc. Exptl. Biology and Medicine, Sigma Xi, Alpha Omega Alpha. Author: (with others) Symposium on the Synapse, 1936; (with Herbert S. Gasser) Electrical Signs of Nervous Activity, 1937; also numerous articles. Research on action potential nerves, heart block, blood pressure; (with Herbert Gasser) devised means for use of cathode ray oscillograph for studying transmission of impulses through single nerve fibers; contbns. to circulatory physiology with devel. of device to record blood pressure; studied influence in field of electrophysiology. Died Dec. 5, 1965.

ERNSBERGER, MILLARD CLAYTON, mechanical engr.; b. Varick, N.Y., June 12, 1862; s. Daniel W. and Hannah (Warne) E.; A.B., U. of Rochester, 1888; M.E., Sibley Coll. (Cornell U.), 1908; unmarried. Admitted to N.Y. bar, 1891, and practiced at N.Y. City until 1897; mgr. illustrating depts. New York Tribune 2 yrs.; draftsman and designing engr. with MacIntosh, Seymour & Co., steam engines, Auburn, N.Y., 1899-1906; asst. and instr. in power engring., Sibley Coll. until 1909; prof. mech. engring., U. of Rochester, 1909-21; prof. heat-power engring., Sibley Sch. Mech. Engring., Apr. 30, 1921—. Home: Ithaca, N.Y. Died Jan. 25, 1940.

ERNST, EDWIN CHARLES, radiologist; b. St. Louis, Mo., June 26, 1885; s. Charles W. and Catherine (Koche) E.; grad. Moravian Coll., Bethlehem, Pa., 1905; student St. Louis U., 1906-09; M.D., Washington U., St. Louis, 1912; m. Mildred V. Vogt, Aug. 2, 1916; children—Edwin C., Roland, Richard. Began practice at St. Louis, 1912. Commd. maj. Med. R.C., Apr. 15, 1917; served in Base Hosp. 21, France, 1917-18; dir. x-ray dept. and radiologist of the De Paul Hosp., St. Louis; radiologist St. Joseph Hospital, Kirkwood, Mo. President board of dirs. of Beaumont Medical Building. Awarded gold medal of Radiol. Soc. of North America for researches in X-ray unit measurement; the highest IX Internat. Congress Radiology Scientific award, 1959; citation German Roentgen Society of Munic, 1959. Mem. A.M.A., A.C.P., Am. Roentgen Ray Soc., Chgo. Roentgen Soc., Radiol. Soc. of N. America (ex-pres.), Am. Coll. of Radiology, (past pres.), Am. Radium Soc. (past pres.), Radiological Research Inst., Inc. (past pres.), Am. College of Radiology (past pres.), Am. Cancer Soc. (past pres. Mo. div.), Southern Medical Association (2d vice president), Phi Beta Pi. Republican. Protestant. Clubs: University, Mo. Athletic (pres. 1956-57), Algonquin Country. Contbr. to Am. Roentgen Ray Jour. Research in cancer, radiology. Home: Kirkwood MO Died Mar. 1969; buried Sunset Burial Park.

ERNSTENE, ARTHUR CARLTON, physician; b. Parker, S.D., Aug. 4, 1901; s. Edwin Carl and Alice (Goddard) E.; A.B., State U. Ia., 1922, M.D., 1925; D.Sc. (hon.), John Carroll U., 1959, Baldwin-Wallace Coll., 1964; m. Beatrice McGarvey, June 25, 1925 (dec. 1925); 1 son, Marshall Paul; m. 2d, Audra N. Miller, Nov. 20, 1954. Intern Henry Ford Hosp., Detroit, 1925-26; asst. resident Thorndike Meml. Lab., Boston City Hosp., 1926-27, resident 1927-28; research asso. Beth Israel Hosp., Boston, 1928-32; asst. in medicine Harvard, 1927-30, instr., 1930-32; head dept. cardiovascular disease Cleve. Clinic, 1932-48, chmn. div. medicine, 1948-66. Served as lt. comdr. M.C., USNR, 1942-44; chief of medicine, hosps. at Auckland, New Zealand, Espiritu Santo, New Hebrides. Bd. lay trustees John Carroll U. Recipient Gold Heart award Am. Heart Assn., 1964. Diplomate Am. Bd. Internal Medicine (mem. sub-specialty bd. on cardiovascular disease 1956-61). Fellow A.C.P. (gov. Ohio 1957-63, regent 1963-69, pres. 1965-66), A.A.A.S.; mem. A.M.A. (sec. sect. internal medicine 1953-56, chmn. 1956-57), Am. Clin. and Climatol. Assn. (v.p. 1950), Am. Soc. for Clin. Investigation, Central Soc. Clin. Research, Assn. Am. Physicians, Am. (dir. 1953-63; chmn. sect. clin. cardiology 1952-54, pres. 1959-60), Ohio State (founders group, 1st pres. 1950-52) heart assns., Cleve. Area Heart Soc. (founders group, 1st pres. 1949-51), Acad. of Medicine of Cleve. (sec.-treas. 1940-42, dir. 1946-49), Ohio State Med. Assn. (chmn. com. on sci. work 1951-59), Interurban Clin. Club Cleve. Med. Library Assn. (trustee), Phi Beta Kappa, Sigma Xi, Alpha Omega Alpha, Phi Kappa Psi, Nu Sigma Nu. Author: Coronary Heart Disease, 1948; also articles and papers in field. Home: Cleveland OH Died Mar. 3, 1971.

ESKOLA, PENTTI EELIS, educator, geologist; b. Honkilahti, Finland, Jan. 8, 1883; s. Kustaa Eskola and Eeva Kristiina Ellaa; B.Sc., U. Helsinki, 1906, Dr. Philosophy, 1915; Dr. honoris causa, univs. Oslo, 1938, Padova, 1942, Bonn, 1943, Prague, 1948; m. Mandi Josefiina Wiiro, Jan. 9, 1915; children—Matti (killed in war 1941), Päivätra. Tchr. geology and mineralogy, agrl. and forestry faculty U. Helsinki, 1910, docent of petrology, 1916, geologist Geol. Survey of Finland, 1922, prof. geology and mineralogy since 1924. Field work in Transbaical as mem. Russian expdn. in search of radium, summer 1914; field work in East Carelia, with stipend from Russia Acad. Sci., summers, 1916, 17; research work with U. Oslo, 1919-20, Geophys. Lab., Washington, 1921-22 (with stipend from U. Helsinki); field work for Geol. Survey of Can., summer 1922. Mem. Academia Scientiarum Fennica, Societas Scientiarum Fennica, Duetsche Akademie der Naturforscher, Heidelberger Akad. Wiss., Det Norske Videnskapsakademiet i Oslo, Det Kongel. Norske Vid. Selskab (Trondheim), Geologische Vereiningung, Nat. Acad. Scis. (Washington); corr. mem. Geol. Soc. Am., Mineral. Soc. Am., Am. Natural History, Die Physik.-mediz. Sozietat su Erlangen, Am. Geophys. Union; hon. mem. Naturforscherverein zu Riga, Deutsche Mineralogische Gesellschaft; fgn. mem. Svenska Vetenskapsakademien, Osterreich Akad. der Wiss.; asso. mem. Académie Royale de Belgique; fgn. corr. Soc., Géologique de France. Awarded Gustav Steinman medal of Geol. Vereiningung, 1943, William Smith lectr. Geol. Soc. London, 1948, Penrose medal Geol. Soc. Am., 1951, Wollaston medal Geol. Soc. London, 1958, Friedrich Becke-Medaille Osterreich, Min. Gesellsch., 1962, Leopold von Buch-Plakette Deutsche Geol. Gesellsch., 1962, Eskola medal Geol. Soc. Finland, 1963, Vetlesen prize Columbia U., 1964. Home: Kauppiaankatu 10. Office: Geologian Laitos, Snellmaninkatu 5, Helsinki 17, Finland. Died Dec. 6, 1964.

ESPY, JAMES POLLARD, educator, meteorologist; b. Westmoreland County, Pa., May 9, 1785; s. Josiah and Elizabeth (Patterson) E.; grad. Transylvania U., Lexington, Ky., 1808; m. Margaret Pollard, 1812. Tchr. mathematics and classics Franklin Inst., Phila., 1817; recipient Magellanic prize Am. Philos. Soc., 1836; apptd. meteorologist U.S. War Dept., 1842; submitted 1st annual weather report, 1843; formulated convectional theory of precipitation (his chief contbn.), laid foundation of weather forecasting; 1st govt. ofcl. to use telegraph to get weather reports from across nation. Author: Philosophy of Storms, 1841. Died Cincinnati, Jan. 24, 1860.

ESSELEN, GUSTAVUS JOHN, research chemist; b. Roxbury, Mass., June 30, 1888; s. Gustavus John and Joanna (Blyleven) E.; A.B. magna cum laude, Harvard, 1909, A.M., 1911, Ph.D., 1912; m. Henrietta W. Locke, Sept. 18, 1912; children—Rosamond (Mrs. Bradford K. Bachrach), Josephine (Mrs. George Byron Hanson), Gustavus John, 3d. Mem. research lab. staff Gen. Electric Co., Lynn, 1912-14; asst. mgr., later mgr., Chem. Products Co., 1914-17; research staff Arthur D. Little, Inc., 1917-21; v.p. and dir. research Skinner, Sherman & Esselen, Inc., 1921-30; pres. and treas. Gustavus J. Esselen, Inc. (name changed to Esselen Research Corp. 1946), Boston, 1930-49; v.p. U.S. Testing Co., Inc., mgr. Esselen Research Div., 1950-52; President American Council of Commercial Laboratories, Incorporated, 1951-52. National Academy of Sciences delegate to Internat. Union of Chemistry, Liege, 1930, Lucerne, 1936. Chmn. bd. trustees Swampscott Pub. Library, 1928-38. Mem. Nat. Research Council, 1936-39 and 1940-43; mem. Mass. Bd. Registration Professional Engrs. and Land Surveyors, 1942-49, chmn. 1943, 48; mem. Referee Bd. Office Prodn. Research and Development, 1942-45 (chmn. joint Army-Navy-N.D.R.C. Committee on Tropical Deterioration, 1943-46). Served as a major and lt. colonel, Chemical Warfare Reserve, 1925-40. Received Pioneer Award of Nat. Assn. of Mfrs., 1940, Norris Award, 1948. Fellow A.A.A.S., Am. Inst. Chemists, Am. Acad. Arts and Scis. (council 1944-48); mem. Am. Chem. Soc. (dir. 1934-41; trustee permanent trust fund), Assn. Cons. Chemists and Chem. Engrs. (dir. 1936-39, 1946-49), Am. Inst. Chem. Engrs. (dir. 1931-33, 1934-36), Boston C. of C. (dir. 1943-46), Asso. Industries of Mass., Engineering Socs. N.E., N.E. Council, Tech. Assn. Pulp and Paper Industry, Soc. Chem. Industry of Great Britain (chmn. Am. sect. since 1949), Electrochem. Soc., Soc. Plastics Industry, Soc. Plastics Engrs., Alpha Chi Sigma, Sigma Xi. Conglist. Clubs: Harvard, Rotary, Union, Chemists (New York); Cosmos (Washington, D.C.). Author of numerous tech. papers and chapters on chem. products. Lecturer. Address: 99 Gale Rd., Swampscott, Mass. Died Oct. 22, 1952; buried Swampscott (Mass.) Cemetery.

ESSIG, EDWARD OLIVER, educator; b. Arcadia, Ind., Sept. 29, 1884; s. Monroe Franklin and Isabel (Todd) E.; B.S., Pomona Coll., 1909, M.S., 1912; m. Ethel Mildred Langford, May 13, 1910; 1 dau., Mary Isabel; m. 2d, Marie W. Mauerhan, Sept. 11, 1950. Hort. commr. Ventura County, Cal., 1910-11; sec. Cal. Commn. on Horticulture, 1911-14; instr. in entomology U. Cal., 1914-16, asst. prof. entomology, 1916-20; asso. prof., 1920-27, prof. 1927-54, emeritus, 1954-64; entomologist Cal. Agrl. Expt. Sta. since 1928; head div. entomology and parasitology 1943-50 Agt., Ventura County, World War, 1917-18; com. for relief Belgium, World War. Mem. sci. adv. bd. Palm Springs Desert Mus. Fellow A.A.A.S., Am. Assn. Econ. Entomology (pres.), Entomol. Soc. Am. (pres.), Cal. Acad. Scis. (mem. council), mem. Am. Iris Soc. (dir., Dykes Medal award for hybridizing), Am. Fuchsia Soc., Pacific Coast Entomol. Soc., Cal. Entomol. Club, Cal. Hort. Soc., Western Soc. Naturalists, Sigma Xi, Phi Sigma, Alpha Gamma Rho, Alpha Zeta. Was awarded rank of Chevalier du Merite Agricole, 1932. Dykes medal, 1935. Republican. Conglist. Author books and articles; editor publs. on entomology U. Cal. Mem. U.S. Dept. Agr. Dehydration Sch. staff, 1942; NRC, 1941-47. Home: 744 Creston Rd., Berkeley, Cal. 94708. Died Nov. 23, 1964; buried Sunset View Cemetery, El Cerrito, Cal.

ESTABROOK, JOHN D., civ. eng'r; mem. Am. Inst. Mining Eng'rs; grad. Rensselaer Polytechnic Inst., Troy, N. Y., 1856; employed on Western ry., in city eng'rs' office, Boston, and on sea coast defenses of Mass. Bay.; eng'r of public parks and comm'r of highways, Phila.; supt. of parks, St. Paul, Minn.; sec. and eng'r Union Depot Co., St. Paul, Minn., and sec. and eng'r of C. C. Washburn's Flouring Mills Co., Minneapolis. Address: Westboro MA

ESTERLY, GEORGE, inventor, mfr.; b. Plattekill N.Y., Oct. 17, 1809; s. Peter and Rachel (Griffith) E.; m. Jane Lewis, Mar. 4, 1832; m. 2d, Mrs. Amelia Shaff Hall, Mar. 1855; m. 3d, Caroline Esterly, May 1884; 7 children. One of earliest farm machinery mfrs.; patented horsepushed harvester (1st successful Am. harvester), 1844; invented 1st sulky cultivator, 1854, seeder, 1865, self-rake reaper, 1870. Author: A Consideration of the Currency and Finance Question, 1874; A Plan for Funding the Public Debt, and a Safe Return to Specie Payment, 1875. Died Hot Springs, S.D., June 7, 1893.

ESTY, WILLIAM, electrical engr.; b. Amherst, Mass., July 9, 1868; s. William Cole (q.v.) and Martha Ann (Cushing) E.; A.B., Amherst, 1889, A.M., 1893; B.S., Mass. Inst. Tech., 1893; m. Julia Louise Coy, June 14, 1894; children—William Cole, Lucien Coy, John Cushing. With Thomson-Houston Electric Co., Lynn, Mass., 1892-93; instr., asst. prof. and asso. prof. elec. engring., U. of Ill., 1893-1901; asst. prof., 1901-03, prof. elec. engring., 1903—, Lehigh U. Fellow Am. Inst. Elec. Engrs., A.A.A.S. Author: Alternating Current Machinery, 1911, new edit., 1920; Elements of Electrical Engineering, 2 vols. (with W. S. Franklin), 1906-07; Dynamo Laboratory Manual; Dynamos and Motors, 1909. Home: Bethlehem, Pa. Died July 6, 1928.

ETCHEVERRY, BERNARD ALFRED, irrigation engr.; b. San Diego, Calif., June 30, 1881; s. Bernard and Louise (Earle) E.; B.S. in C.E., Coll. Civ. Engring., U. of Calif., 1902; m. Helen Maude Hanson, of Berkeley, Calif., Aug. 6, 1903; children—Bernard Earle, Alfred Starr. Instr. in civ. engring., U. of Calif., 1902-03; asso. prof. civ. engring., U. of Nev., 1903-05; asso. prof. irrigation engring., 1905-17, prof. same, 1917—, U. of Calif. Consulting engr. for various projects and cos. in B.C., Wash. and Calif. Mem. Am. Soc. C.E., 1909; mem. Psi Upsilon, Phi Beta Kappa, Sigma Xi, Tau Beta Pi, Alpha Zeta, Chi Epsilon. Officer de l'ordre du Ouissam Alouite (Morocco), 1932. Dir. American Society Civil Engineers, 1934-36. Republican. Clubs: Commonwealth, University. Author: Irrigation Practice and Engineering, 3 vols.; Land Drainage and Flood Protection. Contbr. numerous articles on irrigation problems to tech. jours. Home: 2678 Buena Vista Way, Berkeley, Cal. Died Oct. 26, 1954; buried Sunet View Cemetery, Berkeley.

ETHEREDGE, M(AHION) P(ADGETT), chemist; born near Saluda, S.C., Sept. 27, 1897; s. Joseph Wolfe and Julia Ella (Padgett) E.; B.S., Clemson Coll., 1918; M.S., Miss. State Coll., 1940; Ph.D., Mass. Inst. Tech., 1945; m. Lucile Davis, Sept. 30, 1926; children—Sarah, Dot. Asst. chemist Miss. State Chem. Lab., 1918-23, asst. state chemist of Miss., 1923-45, state chemist from 1945; instr. Miss. State College, 1935-45, head, department of chemistry 1945-63, dean of school of arts and sciences, 1951-63, prof. chemistry and state chemist, 1963-67. Member Council of Oak Ridge Institute for Nuclear Studies, 1949-64. Member board dirs. Miss. Agrl. Indsl. Bd., 1945-67. Attended Officers Training Camp, World War I; War Dept. Civilian Gas Sch., World War II. Awarded 6 Cups for Miss. State Chem. Lab. from Am. Oil Chemists Soc., 1926-39, resulting in a grant-in-aid from Gen. Edn. Bd., 1943-45. Recipient Herty Medal, American Chem. Soc., 1956; Honor Scroll, La. chpt. Am. Inst. Chemists, 1962. Fellow A.A.A.S. (council 1952-54). mem. Am. Chem. Soc. (chairman Mississippi section), American Oil Chemists Society, Association Am. Feed Control Ofcls. (past pres.), Assn. Ofcls. Agr. Chemists (pres. 1957), Assn. Am. Fertilizer Control Ofcls. (pres. 1956), Food and Drug Ofcls. U.S.A., So. Assn. Sci., Industry (past pres.), Newcomen Soc., So. Feed and Fertilizer Control Ofcls. (pres. 1956), Food and Drug Ofcls. S. Central States (past pres.), N.E.A., Internat. Platform Assn., Alpha Chi Sigma, Alpha Epsilon Delta, Phi Kappa Phi, Omicron Delta Kappa. Baptist. Mason (32 deg., Shriner). Contbr. articles to profl. jours. Home: Starkville MS Died July 12, 1971; buried Memorial Gardens, Starkville MS

ETS-HOKIN, LOUIS, engring. co. exec.; b. Chgo., July 28, 1893; s. Samuel and Esther (Simon) Ets-H.; A.B., Cornell U., 1915, M.E., 1917; m. Rose Hartman, June 19, 1921; children—Jeremy M., Esther Naomi (Mrs. Robert S. Leuter). Pres. Ets-Hokin Corp., and prececessor, San Francisco, 1920-59, chmn. bd., 1959-71; chmn. bd. Murphy-Pacific Co., 1963-71, Tech. Constrn. Co., 1962-71; also Murphy Pacific Marine Salvage Company. Pres. Assn. Boat Industries, 1946-49, San Francisco Marine Exchange, 1954-56, Western Shipbldg. Assn., 1959-61; environmental engineer Civil Defense, 1968-71; chmn. Gov. Cal. Com. Shipbldg., 1953-58; mem. San Francisco Bay Conservation and Development Commn., 1965-71. Member board directors San Francisco Federation Jewish Charities, 1950-53; pres. San Francisco Maritime Mus. 1955-57; adv. bd. San Francisco Bay Transp. Study. Served with U.S. Navy, 1917-19. Registered profl. engr., Cal. Home: San Francisco CA Died Aug. 10, 1971.

EUSTIS, FREDERIC AUGUSTUS, metallurgical engr.; b. Milton, Mass., Oct. 7, 1877; s. William Ellery Channing and Edith (Hemenway) E.; A.B., Harvard, 1901, A.M., 1902, S.M., 1903, Sc.D., 1915; studied Mass. Inst. Tech.; m. Edith Tileston, Sept. 15, 1908 (died June 28, 1927); m. 2d, Muriel B. Churchill, Sept. 20, 1937. Secretary and treasurer Virginia Smelting Co.; director Penobscott Chemical Fibre Co., Spl. agt. U.S. Shipping Board, from Feb. 1917-Feb. 1919. Republican. Unitarian. Clubs: Union, Brookline Country, Milton-Hoosic-Whesick, Beverly Yacht (all of Mass.); Harvard, Century (New York). Home: 1452 Canton Av., Milton, Mass. Office: 131 State St., Boston, Mass.; and 270 Madison Av., New York NY

EUSTIS, HENRY LAWRENCE, engr., educator, army officer; b. Boston, Feb. 1, 1819; s. Gen. Abraham and Rebecca (Sprague) E.; grad. Harvard, 1838, A.M., 1850; grad. U.S. Mil. Acad., 1842; m. Sarah Eckley, May 2, 1844; m. 2d, Caroline Hall, July 10, 1856; 6 children. Asst. prof. engring. U.S. Mil. Acad., 1847-49; prof. engring. Harvard, 1849-85, organized dept. engring. Harvard's Lawrence Scientific Sch., dean sci. faculty, 1862-63, 71-85; commd. brig. gen. U.S. Volunteers, 1863, served in many important battles;

fellow Am. Acad. Arts and Scis. Died Cambridge, Mass., Jan. 11, 1885.

EVANS, ANTHONY WALTON WHYTE, civil engr.; b. New Brunswick, N.J., Oct. 31, 1817; s. Thomas M. and Eliza (Whyte) E.; grad. Rensselaer Poly. Inst., 1836; m. Anna Zimmerman, at least 1 dau. Worked on Erie Canal; asst. to Allan Campbell in constrn. N.Y. & Harlem R.R., also Copiapo R.R., Chile; built other S.Am. railroads; became cons. engr., N.Y.C., continued designing S.Am. railroads, served as agt. for fgn. railroad cos. Died Nov. 28, 1886.

EVANS, ARTHUR THOMPSON, botanist; b. Wellington, Ill., May 22, 1888; s. Robert M. and Anna Caldwell (Johnstone) E.; A.B., U. of Ill., 1912; studied U. of Mich., summers, 1913, 14; M.A., U. of Colo., 1915; Ph.D., U. of Chicago, 1918; m. Anna Mathilde Hansen, Aug. 22, 1914; children—Margaret Louise, Arthur T., Lewis Hansen, Dorothy Ann. Grad. asst. in botany, U. of Colo., 1914-15, instr., 1915-17; fellow in botany, U. of Chicago, 1917-18; in charge cereal disease investigations, U.S. Dept. of Agr., in Great Plains Region, World War, 1918, corn investigations, 1919; dean of coll. and prof. botany, Huron (S.D.) Col., 1919-20; asso. prof. agronomy, 1920-23, head of dept. and prof. botany and plant pathology, 1923-28, S.D. State Coll.; now prof. botany, Miami University. Fellow A.A.A.S., Ohio Academy of Science; member Botanical Society America, Phi Sigma (biological), Sigma Xi, Delta Pi. Republican. Presbyterian. Mason (K.T., Shriner). Author: (textbook) First Course in Botany (with R. J. Pool); Laboratory Manual for First Course in Botany. Contbr. on original research in morphology and cytology, also coll. bulls, etc. Home: Oxford, O. Died Oct. 5, 1943.

EVANS, CADWALLADER, JR., mining engr.; b. Pitts., Sept. 21, 1880; s. Cadwallader and Margaret Brown (Oliver) E.; M.E., Lehigh, 1901; m. Myra Thornburg, Jan. 21, 1911; children—Kathleen, Cadwallader III. Engaged in mining engring., Western Pa., Mexico, Dutch Guiana, N.S., 1901-16; gen. mgr. Hudson Coal Co., Scranton, Pa., since 1916; dir. Abington Nat. Bank, Clarks Summit, Pa., Scranton Air Port. Trustee Lehigh U. Mem. Am. Inst. Mining Engrs. (trustee). Mem. Disciples of Christ Ch. Home: Waverly, Pa. Office: Hudson Coal Co., Scranton, Pa. Died Apr. 1966.

EVANS, EDWARD STEPTOE, manufacturer; b. Thaxtons, Va., May 24, 1879; s. Thomas Davis and Mary Elizabeth (Murrell) E.; law student Columbian (now George Washington) Univ., Washington, D.C., 2 1/2 yrs.; spl. course in library science; m. Virginia Epes McCormick, Apr. 5, 1905; children—Edward Steptoe, Robert Beverly. In Library of Congress, 1900-04; asst. state librarian, Va., 1904-07; founder, 1915, pres. and treas. Evans Products Co., Inc., mfrs. loading material and devices for loading automobiles loading material and devices for loading freight cars, airplanes and trucks, road and rail locomotives and vehicles and other equipment for railroads, battery separators, heating and ventilating units for motor vehicles and airplanes, molded plywood, airplane engine mounts, etc.; president and treasurer Saven Corporation, investments; farmer, breeder of registered Guernseys. Served as captain in Q.M.C., U.S. Army, 1918-19 inclusive; lieutenant colonel specialist reserve attached to U.S. Air Corps. Fellow American Geographical Society; member Society Automotive Engrs. Episcopalian. Mason (32 deg., K.T., Shriner). Clubs: Explorers (New York); Detroit, Detroit Athletic, Detroit Boat, Country, Players, Adventurers (Chicago); Commonwealth (Richmond, Va.). Held record for circumnavigating the globe in 28 days, 14 hours and 36 minutes, 1926; mgr. Detroit Arctic Expdn., 1925, 26. Founder and 1st pres. Nat. Glider Assn. Donor annual silver trophy U.S. nat. glider champion and bronze trophy U.S. Army Air Corps grand glider champion presented to U.S. War Department, 1941. Author: Encyclopaedic Guide to Richmond, Va., 1907; History of Seals of Virginia (monograph), 1908. Compiler: Calendar of Virginia Transcripts, 1906. Contbr. to numerous mags. on freight transport. Pioneer in aircraft mfr. and air transportation. Home: 1005 Three Mile Drive, Grosse Pointe, Mich. Office: 15310 Fullerton St., Detroit, Mich. Died Sep. 6, 1945.

EVANS, EVERETT IDRIS, surgeon; b. Norfolk, Neb., Apr. 15, 1909; s. Rhys and Mary (Jones) E.; Ph.D., U. of Chicago, 1935, M.D., 1937; m. LaVerne Veatch, Sept. 14, 1936; children—Robert Rhys, Melissa Lee, Richard Idris. House surgeon, Pa. Hosp., Phila., 1937-39; asst. resident surgery, Med. Coll. of Va. Hosp., Richmond, 1939-40; Rockefeller Foundation Fellow in surgery, Mass. Gen. Hosp., Boston, 1940-41; resident in surg., Med. Coll. of Va. Hosp., 1941-42, asst. prof. surg., Med. Coll. of Va., 1942-43, asso. prof., 1943-48, prof. surg. and dir. surg. research lab. since 1948; responsible investigator, Office Sci. Research and Development, Med. Coll. of Va., 1940-46, prin. investigator Research and Development Bd., Office Surg. Gen., Dept. of Army since 1948; surg. cons., Atomic Bomb Casualties Commn., Far East Command (Japan) since 1948, Office of Surg. Gen., Dept. of Army since 1948; vis. prof. surgery pro tem, Ohio State Univ., 1950; MacArthur lecturer U. of Edinburgh, 1952-53. Member committee on surg., Nat. Research Council since 1946; mem. com. on blood and blood substitutes, Am. Red Cross since 1947, com. on atomic casualties, Nat. Research Council since 1947; mem. adv. bd. on Health Services, Am. Nat. Red Cross, since 1947. Mem. adv. com. on annual scientific award, Am. Pharm. Mfrs. Assn. since 1947. Awarded certificate of appreciation by Depts. of Army and Navy for work during World War II. Mem. Internat. Soc. Surgery, Soc. for Vascular Surg., Am. Surg. Assn., Southern Med. Assn., A.M.A., Am. Physiol. Soc., Am. Surg. Assn., Am. Coll. Surgs., Southern Surg. Assn., Richmond Acad. Med., Sigma Xi, Nu Sigma Nu, Alpha Omega Alpha. Democrat. Episcopalian. Club: Commonwealth. Mem. editorial bd. Annals of Surg. since 1947. Home: Llanfair, River Rd., Richmond. Office: 1200 E. Broad St., Richmond 19, Va. Died Jan. 14, 1954; buried St. Mary's Episcopal Church, Goochland County, Va.

EVANS, GEORGE WATKIN, mining engr.; b. Ystrad, Rhonnda Valley, Wales, Mar. 5, 1876; s. Watkin and Catherine (Hughes) E.; student Internat. Corr. Schs., Scranton, Pa., 1892-96; B.S. and E.M., State Coll. of Wash., Pullman, Wash.; m. Olivia Laird, Mar. 12, 1902; children—Watkin L., Blodwyn E., Lloyd George. Practical work in coal mines, 1888-96; later in the Klondyke and placer mines, Yukon; with Wash. Geol. Survey, 1899-1901; cyanide practice in gold mines, Colo., 1902; practiced as engr., 1903-08; geologist in charge coal surveys Wash. Geol. Survey, 1909-12; cons. mining engr. U.S. Bur. of Mines, 1911—, also cons. Mining Engr. U.S. Navy; dist. mining engr. U.S. Bur. of Mines during World War I; cons. engr. for large fuel cos., also Canadian Nat. Rys.; now in practice as cons. mining engr. Mem. Am. Inst. Mining and Metall. Engrs., West Coast Engineers. Unitarian. Rotarian. Home: 3134 37th Pl., Seattle 44. Died Jan. 11, 1951.

EVANS, HERBERT P(ULSE), mathematician; born Chattanooga, Tenn., Jan. 5, 1900; s. Oscar Ewel and Effie Gertrude (Pulse) E.; B.S., Univ. Wis., 1923, M.S., 1927, Ph.D., 1929; student Columbia, 1924-25; m. Rae Elbertine White, Dec. 27, 1929; children—Douglas Sherwood, Gail Kristine. Research engr. Bell Tel. Lab., N.Y. City, 1923-25; instr. elec. engring., Univ. Wis., 1925-28, research asst. in physics (and Columbia) 1928, mem. dept. of math. since 1928, instr., 1928-29, asst. prof., 1929-38, asso. prof., 1938-42, prof. since 1942, charge univ. extension math. dept. since 1945. Served in U.S.N.R.F. as elec. 3c, 2c, 1c, and chief p.o., 1917-19, in France, 1918-19. Fellow A.A.A.S. Mem. Am. Math. Soc., Math. Assn. of Am., Inst. Math. Statistics, Am. Statistical Assn., Am. Assn. Univ. Profs.; Sigma Xi, Pi Mu Epsilon. Club: Univ. Asso. ed. Am. Math. Monthly, 1944-49. Contbr. articles on electric circuit theory, boundary value problems, probability theory, and mathematical edn. in scientific jours. Home: 1101 Seminole Highway, Madison 5, Wis. Died June 2, 1959.

EVANS, NEWTON (GURDON), pathologist; b. Hamilton, Mo., June 1, 1874; s. William and Emma Beulah (Newton) E.; student Battle Creek (Mich.) Coll., Am. Med. Missionary Coll., Chicago; B.S. Union College, Lincoln, Neb., 1895; M.D., Cornell Univ. Med. Sch., New York, 1900; m. Cora Mildred Deming, Aug. 27, 1901 (died 1942); children—Emma Elizabeth (Mrs. Howard A. Ball), William Dustin. In general practice until 1914, prof. pathology, Med. Dept. U. of Tenn., 1908-11; prof. pathology, College Medical Evangelists, Loma Linda and Los Angeles, California, since 1914, president, 1914-27, dean, 1928-31, and since 1943; vice-pres., 1931-36; pathologist Los Angeles County Gen. Hosp. since 1928, Lt. col. Med. Res. (now retired), comdg. officer U.S. Gen. Hosp. 47, 1926-32 and 1935-37. Chmn. bd. Alumni Research Foundation, Coll. Med. Evangelists. Fellow A.M.A., Am. Cell. Physicians, A.A.A.S.; mem. Am. Soc. Clin. Pathologists, Los Angeles Acad. Medicine, Los Angeles Pathological Soc. (pres. 1929), Los Angeles Cancer Soc. (pres. 1936), Am. Assn. Pathologists and Bacteriologists, Med. Assn. State of Calif. Republican. Seventh Day Adventist. Contributor results of research to various med. jours. Home: 2000 Milan Av., South Pasadena. Address: 312 N. Boyle Av., Los Angeles, Calif. Died Dec. 19, 1945.

EVANS, OLIVER, inventor, steam-engine builder; b. New Castle County, Del., 1755; s. Charles Evans; m. Miss Tomlinson, 1780; 2 children. Perfected machine for wool manufacture that could produce 1500 cards a minute; completed series of improvements in flour-mill machinery operated by means of water-power in 1785, then petitioned legislatures Pa. and Md. for exclusive rights to use his "improvements in flour mills and steam carriages" in those states (partially granted in Pa., wholly granted in Md.); in engine building bus., 1803; established Mars Iron Works, 1807; designed and constructed water works in Phila., 1817; 1st steam engine builder in Am., 50 of his engines in use throughout Atlantic coast states by 1819. Author: The Young Mill-Wright and Miller's Guide, 1795; The Abortion of the Young Engineer's Guide, 1805. Died N.Y.C., Apr. 5, 1819.

EVANS, RICHARD JOSEPH, civil engr.; b. Washington, D.C., July 14, 1837; s. Dr. John and Sarah Zane (Mills) E.; ed. Rittenhouse Acad.; studied architecture and building under his grandfather, Robert Mills, govt. architect; m. Anais D. Lagarde, Feb. 4, 1861. Served several yrs. as aide in U.S. Coast Survey; removed to New Orleans during mil. occupation of that city; apptd. engr. New Orleans, Carrollton & Lake Pontchartrain Ry.; later chief engr. New Orleans, Opelousas & Great Western Ry.; afterward in employ of the Morgan Co. (steamship and ry. lines); devised adaptation of stern wheel steamboats for transferring loaded freight cars over Mississippi River; one of 3 engrs. apptd. to pass upon plans for the drainage of New Orleans and its protection from overflow; built and superintended Gulf, Western Tex. & Pacific Ry. to Cuero; in Bur. of Steam Engring., Navy Dept., 1875-77; took charge of engring. of terminals. New Orleans Pacific Ry., 1877; later chief engr. Memphis, Selma & Brunswick Ry.; supt. Brunswick & Western Ry. of Ga.; chief engr., 1885, v.p. and gen. mgr., 1888 to 1894, Tex., Sabine Valley & N.W. R.R.; in constrn. drainage, sewerage and water system of New Orleans, 1898—. Home: New Orleans, La. Died Dec. 30, 1916.

EVANS, WALTER HARRISON, botanist; b. Delphi, Ind., Jan. 3, 1863; s. Joseph and Catharine (Bricker) E.; A.B., Wabash Coll., 1887, A.M., 1889, Ph.D., 1896; m. Bessie Binford, Oct. 22, 1890; 1 dau., Margaret B. Instr. botany, Wabash Coll., 1888-90; botanist Eli Lilly Co., Indianapolis, 1890-91; spl. agt. Dept. Agr., 1891-92; chief Div. Insular Stas., Dept. Agr., 1902-33; acting chief, Office of Expt. Stas., 1929-32. Associate and bot. editor Experiment Station Record, 1892-1933. Made agrl. reconnaissance of Alaska, 1897-98; rep. U.S. Dept. of Agr. to congresses of Horticulture, Forestry and Expt. Stas., Paris, 1900; gold medal, Paris Expn., 1900; grand prize, St. Louis Expn., 1904. Fellow A.A.A.S.; mem. Biol. and Bot. socs., Washington, Am. Phytopathol. Soc. Wrote chapters on Economic Botany in New Internat. Ency., 1902-03 and 1914-15, Internat. Yearbook, 1902-24, Am. Yearbook, 1910-19. Contbr. to bot. jours. and publs. Dept. Agr. Special editor Webster's Internat. Dictionary, 2d edit. Home: R.F.D. 2, Florence SC

EVANS, WILLIAM AUGUSTUS, hygienist; b. Marion, Ala., Aug. 5, 1865; s. William Augustus and Julia Josephine (Wyatt) E.; B.S., Agrl. College of Miss., 1883, M.S., 1898; M.D., Tulane Univ. of La., 1885, med. dept. U. of Ill., 1899; LL.D., Tulane, 1910; D.P.H., Univ. of Mich., 1911; LL.D., Univ. of Miss., 1921; m. Ida May Wildberger, Nov. 20, 1907 (died Jan. 13, 1926). In practice of medicine since 1885; demonstrator pathology, 1891-95, prof., 1895-1908, Coll. of Medicine of U. of Ill.; commr. of health of Chicago, 1907-11; prof. san. science, Northwestern U. Med. Sch., 1908-28, now emeritus. Home: Aberdeen, Miss. Died Nov 8, 1948.

EVE, DUNCAN, surgeon; b. Augusta, Ga., May 1, 1853; B.S., U. of Nashville, 1870; A.M., Greenville and Tusculum Coll., 1885; M.D., Bellevue Hosp. Med. Coll. (New York U.), 1874. Prof. microscopy, Tenn. Coll. Pharmacy, 1975; dean and prof. surgery and clin. surgery, U. of Tenn., 1877-95; prof. surgery Vanderbilt U., since 1895. Address: 2112 West End Av., Nashville, Tenn. *

EVE, JOSEPH, inventor, scientist; b. Phila., May 24, 1760; s. Oswald and Anne (Moore) E.; m. Hannah Singletary, 1800, 1 son Joseph Adams. Inventor machine for separating seed from cotton (an early version of cotton gin); manufactured gunpowder and cotton gins, nr. Augusta, Ga., 1810, also experimented with steam; inventor cottonseed huller, 1803, metallic bands for power transmission, 1828, 2 steam engines, 1818, 26. Contbr. several short poems, also long poems "Better to Be" (pub. in book form 1823) and "The Projector" to Augusta newspapers. Died Augusta, Nov. 14, 1835; buried "The Cottage," nr. Augusta.

EVE, PAUL FITZSIMONS, surgeon; b. Augusta, Ga., June 27, 1806; s. Capt. Oswell and Aphra (Pritchard) E.; B.A., Franklin Coll. (now U. Ga.), 1826; M.D., U. Pa., 1828; m. Sarah Twiggs; m. 2d, Sarah Duncan, 1852; 3 children including 2 sons who became doctors. Practiced medicine in clinics, London, Eng., also Paris, France, 1828-30; participated as physician in Revolution of July 1831, Paris; offered services to Polish Govt., served in hosp., Warsaw; an organizer Med. Coll. Ga., 1832, prof. surgery, 1839-50; prof. surgery U. Louisville (Ky.), 1850, U. Nashville (Tenn.), 1851-61, 70-77, Nashville Med. Coll., 1877; served in Mexican War; served as surgeon gen. Tenn., then chief surgeon Gen. Joseph E. Johnston's Army, also surgeon Gate City Hosp., Atlanta, Ga., in Civil War; pres. A.M.A., 1857-58; leading surgeon and tchr. of surgery in South; perfected operation for vesical calculus; 1st Am. surgeon to perform hysterectomy; co-editor So. Med. and Surg. Jour.; asst. editor Nashville Jour. of Medicine and Surgery. Author (most noted med. works): A Collection of Remarkable Cases in Surgery, 1857; A Contribution to the History of the Hip-join Operations Performed During the Late Civil War, 1867. Died Nashville, Nov. 3, 1877.

EVERIT, EDWARD HOTCHKISS, telephone engr.; b. New Haven, Conn., Aug. 5, 1870; s. Richard Mansfield and Mary Talman (Lawrence) E.; grad. Hillhouse High Sch., New Haven, 1888; spl. studies, Columbia U., 1891-92; m. Cordelia S. Peck, of New Haven, Nov. 26, 1895 (died 1901); children—Elizabeth C. (Mrs. Robert P. Heald), Arthur M., Mary L. (Mrs. Joseph C. Bauer); m. 2d, Marie S. Withmar, nee Bigger, of Richmond, Va., June 1, 1911. Began in employ of

Southern N.E. Telephone Co., 1889, supt. of equipment, 1892, engr., 1903, chief engr., 1910, asst. to gen. mgr., 1927-30, now retired. Fellow Am. Inst. E.E.; mem. A.A.A.S., Soc. for Promotion Engring. Edn., Conn. Soc. C.E., New York Elec. Soc., Telephone Pioneers of America, Zeta Psi. Republican. Epsicopalian; vestryman Trinity Ch. Clubs: Quinnipiack, Rotary, New Haven Country, Applachian Mountain; Zeta Psi (New York). Home: 25 Edgehill Terrace, New Haven CT

EVERMANN, BARTON WARREN, naturalist; b. Monroe County, Ia., Oct. 24, 1853; s. Andrew and Nety (Gardner) E.; B.S., Indiana Univ., 1886, A.M., 1888, Ph.D., 1891; LL.D., Univ. of Utah, 1922, and of Indiana U., 1927; m. Meadie Hawkins, Oct. 24, 1875; children—Toxaway Bronté, Edith (Mrs. Wm. E. Humphrey). For 10 yrs. teacher and supt. of schs. in Ind. and Calif.; prof. biology, Ind. State Normal Sch., 1886-91; asst. ichthyologist, 1888-91, ichthyologist, 1891-1914, chief Div. Statistics and Methods of Fisheries, 1902-03, asst. in charge of scientific inquiry, 1903-10, chief Alaska Fisheries Service, July 1, 1910-14, U.S. Bur. of Fisheries. U.S. fur seal commr., 1892; spl. lecturer, Stanford U., 1893-94 and 1926—; lecturer on fish and game protection, Cornell, 1900-03, Yale, 1903-06; chmn. fur seal bd., 1908-14; v.p. Bd. of Edn., D.C., 1906-10; dir. Museum Calif. Acad. Sciences, 1914—, and of Steinhart Aquarium, 1922—. Editor Proc. Washington Acad. Sciences, 1904-11, Calif. Acad. Sciences, 1914—. Chmn. com. on zoöl. investigation of State Council of Defense, and mem. exec. com. Calif. Research Conf. of same, 1917-19; mem. com. Pacific investigation, Nat. Research Council, and chmn. Com. on Conservation of Marine Life of the Pacific. Author: The Fishes of North and Middle America, 4 vols. (with Dr. David Starr Jordan), 1896, 1900; American Food and Game Fishes, 1902; The Aquatic Resources of the Hawaiian Islands (with David Starr Jordan); The Alaska Salmon Fisheries; Fishes of the Phillippines, 1906; The Golden Trout of the Southern High Sierras, 1906; The Fishes of Alaska, 1907; The Fishes of Peru, 1915; A Review of the Giant Mackerel-like Fishes, Tunnies, Spearfishes, and Swordfishes (with David Starr Jordan); etc. Home: Berkeley, Calif. Died Sept. 27, 1932.

EVVARD, JOHN MARCUS, (ev-vard'), consultant animal nutrition and prodn., author: b. Saunemin, Ill., Nov. 6, 1884; s. John B. and Mary (Leitel) E.; B.S., U. of Ill., 1907; M.S. in Agr., U. of Mo., 1909; Ph.D., U. of Ariz., 1927; m. Mattie Casey Cooper, Aug. 10, 1911; children—Mary Margaret Batman, John Cooper, Martha Jane Shemer. Asst. city editor Pontiac Daily Sentinel, 1904; asst. to dean and dir. Mo. Agrl. Coll. and Mo. Agrl. Expt. Sta., 1907-10; asst. chief, animal husbandry, Ia. Agrl. Expt. Sta., 1910-14; charge animal husbandry sect. and chief in swine prodn., 1911-30, chief in beef cattle and sheep production, 1919-30, Ia. Agrl. Expt. Sta.; asso. prof. animal husbandry, 1916-18, prof., 1918-30, Ia. State Coll. Agr. and Mechanic Arts, chief in nutrition, 1914-19; special assistant in the Office of Secretary of Agriculture, 1922-23; staff of Am. Inst. of Agriculture, 1922-23; v.p. McMillen Co., Allied Mills, Ft. Wayne, Ind., 1930-33; research consultant Soya Products, Inc., Chicago, since 1932; advisory to exec. staff Allied Mills, Inc., since 1933; pres. Universal Supply, Inc., Phoenix, 1933-36; professor and head of dept. of agriculture, Ariz. State Coll., Tempe, (part time), 1935-37. Contbg. editor Chester White Journal, 1920-30, corr. editor Farm and Fireside, 1924-30. Chmn. swine commn. U.S. Food Administration, 1917-18; mem. U.S. Livestock Industrial Com., 1917; member Farmers' Livestock Marketing Com. of 15. Fellow A.A.A.S., Ia. Acad. Science; mem. Am. Soc. Animal Production (ex-pres.), Alpha Zeta, Sigma Xi, Phi Lambda Upsilon, Phi Kappa Phi, Gamma Sigma Delta, Sigma Delta Chi, Lambda Gamma Delta. Advanced Unitarian. Author over 700 bulls., papers, etc., covering investigations principally in field of animal feeding and nutrition. Home: "Casita Querida," 317 W. Cypress, Phoenix, Ariz. Died July 30, 1948.

EWBANK, THOMAS, inventor, govt. ofcl.; b. Durham, Eng., Mar. 11, 1792. Came to N.Y.C., 1819; developed improved methods of tinning lead, patented 1832, improved steam safety valves, patented 1831; U.S. commr. patents, 1849-52; founder, active mem. Am. Ethnol. Soc. Author: Descriptive and Historical Account of Hydraulic and Other Machines Ancient and Modern, 1842 (16th edit. 1870); The World a Workshop or the Physical Relation of Men to the Earth, 1855; Thoughts on Matter and Force, 1858. Died N.Y.C., Sept. 16, 1870.

EWELL, ARTHUR WOOLSEY, physicist; b. Bradford, Mass., Oct. 20, 1873; s. John Lewis and Emily Spofford (Hall) E.; A.B., Yale, 1897, Ph.D., 1899; studied Johns Hopkins, 1899-1900, U. of Berlin, 1904, Radium Inst., Paris, 1924; hon. D. Sc., Worcester Polytechnic Inst., 1946; m. Jane Dodge Estabrook, Sept. 6, 1905; children—Milicent, Jane Estabrook, John Woolsey. Asst. in physics, Yale, 1897-99; instr. physics, 1900-04, asst. prof., 1904-10, prof. since 1910, dir. of physics and gen. science depts., 1935 to retirement 1938, Worcester (Mass.) Poly. Inst.; trustee Bancroft School, Worcester, Mass., 1915-18, treasurer, 1918-28, president, 1928-30; lecturer Massachusetts Institute of Technology; member research staff Westinghouse Electric Mfg. Co., Bloomfield, N.J.; cold storage engr. Dir. Worcester Airport, Am. Soc. Refrigeration Engrs. Trustee Worcester County Instn. for Savings; v.p. board of Gov. Dummer Acad. Capt. U.S.R., Dec. 15, 1917; head of bomb unit, Air Service, A.E.F., after armistice, in charge expt. development and tests of bombs, until May 1, 1919; lt. col. O.R.C.; apptd. spl. aerial bomb expert War Dept., Nov. 1919. Fellow Am. Acad. Arts and Sciences, Am. Physical Soc. (hon. life mem.); mem. American Society Refrigeration Engineers (dir.; hon. member 1945), French Physical Soc., Newcomen Soc. of England, Am. Legion (past comdr. Devens Post), Phi Beta Kappa, Sigma Xi. Episcopalian. Democrat. Clubs: Century, Yale (New York); Myopia Hunt, Worcester, Worcester Fire Society, St. Wulstan. Author: Physical Chemistry, 1909; Physical Measurements, 1910, 1913; numerous papers upon artifical rotatory polarization, magnetic double refraction, aerial bombs and bombing, electrolytic electrode potentials, properties of gases and vapors, refrigeration, ozone, ultra-violet light, food preservation, etc. Mem. editorial staff Refrigeration Data Book, 1940, 1945. Home: Rowley, Mass. Address: 55 Jackson St., Worcester 8 MA

EWEN, JOHN MEIGGS, engr.; b. Newtown, N.Y., Sept. 3, 1859; s. Warren and Sarah (Faulkner) E.; grad. Stevens Inst. Tech., 1880; m. Grace Patterson, Mar. 29, 1889. Asst. engr. J. B. and J. M. Cornell, iron works, New York, 1884-86; archtl. engr. W. L. B. Jenny, Chicago, 1886-90; engr. and gen. mgr. Burnham & Root, architects, 4 yrs.; v.p. and gen. mgr. (4 yrs. in London, Eng.) and western contracting agent George A. Fuller & Co., Chicago, 1890-1902; v.p. and western rep. Thompson-Starrett Co., bldg. contractors, New York, 1902-04; now pres. John M. Ewen Co., engrs. and builders, Chicago. Republican. Presbyn. Home: Evanston, Ill. Died Dec. 19, 1933.

EWING, HENRY ELLSWORTH, entomologist; b. Arcola, Ill., Feb. 11, 1883; s. Joseph Henry and Ann Louisa (McDonald) E.; student Knox Coll., 1902-04; A.B., U. of Ill., 1906, A.M., 1908; Ph.D., Cornell U., 1911; m. Bertha May Wood Riley, Aug. 7, 1916; children—Paul McDonald, Lydia Frances. Science teacher Marshall (Ill.) High Sch., 1908-09; asst. in zoölogy, Ia. State Coll., 1909-10; Schuyler fellow Cornell U., 1910-11; asst. entomologist Ore. Agrl. Expt. Sta., 1911-14; asst. prof. of entomology, Ia. State Coll., 1914-16, asso. prof., 1916-19; specialist Bur. of Entomology, U.S. Department of Agriculture, 1919-23, associate entomologist, 1923-29, entomologist, 1929-45, collaborator since 1947. Fellow A.A.A.S., Iowa Academy of Science, Entomol. Soc. of America; mem. Am. Assn. Econ. Entomologists, Soc. of Mammalogists, Am. Soc. of Parasitologists (pres. 1944), Am. Soc. Ichthyologists and Herpetologists, Ecol. Soc. of Am., Ill. Acad. of Sci., Biol. Soc. Washington, Washington Acad. of Science, Helminthological Soc. of Washington (past pres.), Entomol. Society of Washington (pres. 1941), Phi Delta Theta, Sigma Xi. Author: A Manual of External Parasites, 1929, and scientific and tech. articles. Contbr. Encyclopaedia Britannica. Home: 7308 Willow Av., Takoma Park, Md. Office: U.S. National Museum, Washington. Died Jan. 5, 1951; buried Rock Creek Cemetery, Washington.

EWING, JAMES, pathologist; b. Pittsburgh, Dec. 25, 1866; s. Thomas and Julia R. (Hufnagel) E.; A.B., Amherst, 1888, A.M., 1891; Sc.D., 1923; M.D., Coll. Phys. and Surg. (Columbia), 1891; Sc.D., U. of Pittsburgh, 1911, Amherst, 1923, U. of Rochester, 1932, Union U., 1938; LL.D., Kenyon, 1931, Western Reserve, 1931; m. Catherine C. Halsted, June 19, 1900; 1 son, James Halsted. Tutor histology, 1893-97. Clark fellow, 1896-99, instr. clin. pathology, 1897-98, Coll. Physicians and Surgeons; prof. pathology, Cornell, 1899-1932, prof. of oncology since 1932. Charles Mickle fellow, Toronto, 1935; John Scott medalist, Phila., 1937; hon. mem. Phila. Pathol. Soc., Acad. Med., Brazil, Swedish Roentgen. Soc., Acad. Med. Budapest; mem. Nat. Acad. Sciences, Assn. Am. Physicians, Am. Roentgen Ray Soc., Am. Med. Museums Soc., Am. Assn. Pathologists and Bacteriologists, Soc. Exptl. Biology and Medicine, Harvey Soc., Am. Assn. for Cancer Research, N.Y. Acad. Med. N.Y. Pathol. Soc. Decorated Officer Order Southern Cross, Brazil; Officer Order of Leopold, Belgium. Republican. Presbyterian. Clubs: Century, University, Amherst. Author: Clinical Pathology of Blood, 1900-03; articles on Identity, The Signs of Death, and Sudden Death, in Text-Book of Legal Medicine and Toxicology, 1903; on Blood, etc., in Text-Book of Legal Medicine, 1910; Neoplastic Diseases, 1919-27, 40. Home: 415 Central Park W. Office: 444 E. 68th St., New York, N.Y. Died May 16, 1943.

EWOLDT, HAROLD BOADEN, mining engr.; b. Bennett, Ia., Dec. 12, 1908; s. Henry Hans and Leitha (Boaden) E.; B.S., S.D. Sch. Mines, 1930; m. Florence Thomas Lead, Aug. 14, 1930; children—Betty (Mrs. William F. McKissock, Jr.), Dorothy (Mrs. E. Dennis Posey), Harold Boaden; m. 2d, Millard Curlin, Apr. 4, 1947. Supt., Double Rainbow Mines, Inc., Deadwood, S.D., 1930-33; sr. foreman constrn., maintenance, U.S.F.S., Deadwood, 1933-36; supt. Gregory Bates Mining Co., Black Hawk, Colo., 1936-39; dist. engr. U.S. Bur. Mines, Norris, Tenn., 1939-44; mgr. Calumet & Hecla, Shullsburg, Wis., 1946-50; v.p., gen. mgr. Copper Range Co., Boston, 1950-56; dir. planning Cerro Corp., N.Y.C., 1956-60; chief mining engr. Le Tourneou Westinghouse, Peoria, Ill., 1960-69; sr. mining engr. WABCO, C.E. div., 1967-69. Served to lt. USNR, 1944-46. Registered profl. engr., Colorado, Wisconsin. Mem. Am. Inst. Mining Engrs., Mining and Metall. Soc., Am. Assn. Cost Engrs. Republican. Presbyn. Mason (Shriner), Elk. Home: Peoria IL Died Dec. 20, 1969; buried Ridgecrest Cemetery Jackson TN

EXTON, WILLIAM GUSTAV, pathologist, urologist; b. Savannah, Ga., Feb. 25, 1876; s. Gustav and Rosalie (Unger) E.; M.D., Coll. Physicians and Surgeons (Columbia), 1896; house physician, Mount Sinai Hosp., N.Y. City, 1896-99; post grad. and research work, Pathol. Inst., Vienna, also in London and Paris, 1906-07; m. Florence Phillips, Sept. 20, 1905; children—William, Manning Mason, John Marshall. Practiced, N.Y. City, 1901-06; spl. practice and research in urology-metabolism, 1907-16; dir. laboratories Prudential Ins. Co., Newark, N.J., since 1914, planned and directed longevity service since 1917. Mem. A.M.A., Med. Soc. State of N.Y., New York County Med. Soc., Am. Pub. Health Assn., Am. Urol. Assn., Am. Soc. Clinical Pathologists (pres.), Assn. Life Ins. Med Dirs., Optical Society of America, Am. Assn. Advancement of Science, Am. Chem. Soc. Inventor of gastroscope, 1906; urological table, 1907; immiscible balance, 1915; protein tests, 1918; turbidimeter, 1918; euscope, 1920; spectroscopic method of colorimetry, 1921; scopometer, 1924; junior scopometer, 1927; quantitative microscopy, 1928; photoelectric scopometer, 1929; a new test for sugar tolerance, 1930; new methods for identifying the various sugars that occur in urine, 1932; new method for measuring the number, diameters, volume and hemoglobin content of red blood cells, 1933; the one-hour-two-dose dextrose tolerance test, 1934; incidence of sugars and reducing substances other than glucose in 1000 consecutive cases, 1934; instrument and method for measuring size of sub-microscopic particles photoelectrically by transmitted light and Tyndall beam, 1934; fibrinogen as an index of disease and its clinical determination by photoelectric scopometry, 1935; partition of blood fats, 1936; one hour renal condition test, 1937; colorimetric determination of oxygen in blood, 1938; determination of blood water and its distribution between cells and plasma, 1940; inventor of Photo-panometer; a photoelectric photometer and spectrophotometer having scale readings linear with concentration, 1940; clinical significance and measurement of acidosis and alkalosis by colorimetry of carbon dioxide in blood. Author: The Prudential Urinalysis System, 1934. Contbr. on preclinical medicine, longevity, clinical pathology, etc. Awards Ward Burdick memorial medal, Am. Soc. Clin. Pathologist; N.Y. State and N.J. State Med. socs and others. Home: Flofields, Millbrook, N.Y.; also 240 Central Park S., New York, N.Y. Office: Prudential Ins. Bldg., Newark, N.J. Died Mar. 12, 1943.

EYCLESHYMER, ALBERT CHAUNCEY, anatomist; b. Cambridge, N.Y., June 16, 1867; s. David C. and Anna M. (Perry) E.; B.S., U. of Mich., 1891; fellow, Princeton, 1891, Clark U., 1892. U. of Chicago, 1893, Ph.D., latter, 1895; student, U. of Cambridge, Eng., 1895-96; Austin fellow, Harvard U., 1901; M.D., St. Louis U., 1909; m. Mary Elizabeth Donovan, Sept. 23, 1895. Asst. prof. human embryology, Rush Med. Coll., Chicago, 1897-99; asst. prof. human anatomy, U. of Chicago, 1903; dir. of anatom. dept., 1903-13, acting dean Coll. of Medicine, 1913, St. Louis U.; prof. and head of dept. anatomy, 1913—, and dean of faculty, 1917—, Coll. Medicine of U. of Ill., Chicago. Member Nat. Board of Medical Examiners. Received grand prize for embryol. work from La. Purchase Expn., 1904. Author: Manual of Surgical Anatomy for U.S. Army and Navy, 1919. Home: Oak Park, Ill. Died Dec. 30, 1925.

EYERLY, JAMES BRYAN, physician, educator; b. Neb., 1895; s. James Harlan and Laura Mae (Ford) E.; B.S., U. Neb., 1918; M.D., Rush Med. Coll., 1920; grad. student, Paris, Berlin, Vienna, 1927; m. Dorothy Catherine Dal, Sept. 12, 1923; m. 2d, Mary Virginia Boyd Ashby, Aug. 30, 1933. Intern, Presbyn. Hosp., Chgo., 1920-22, asst. attending physician, 1925-30, asso. attending physician, 1930-47, attending physician, 1947, service head gastroenterology, 1947; clin. asst. Rush Med. Coll., Chgo., 1924, clin. asso., 1925-27, clin. instr., 1927-38, asst. clin. prof., 1938-43; clin. asso. prof. U. Ill. Med. Sch., 1943-45, clin. prof., 1945—. Diplomate Am. Bd. Internal Medicine, specializing gastroenterology. Mem. A.M.A., A.C.P., Am. Gastroent. Assn., Sigma Xi, Phi Chi, Alpha Sigma Phi. Republican. Club: University (Chgo.). Co-author: A Method of Measuring Acidity and Protein Digestion within the Human Stomach, 1939. Contbr. articles to sci. jours. Home: 1200 Lake Shore Dr., Chgo. Office: 20 N. Michigan Av., Chgo. 2. Died Oct. 26, 1963.

EYERMAN, JOHN, mineralogist, mining geologist; b. Easton, Pa., Jan. 15, 1867; s. Edward H. and Alice S. (Heller) E.; direct desc. Capt. Sieur Jean Jacques and Jean Eyerman, 1531; ed. Lafayette, Harvard, Princeton; m. Lucy E. Maxwell, 1888; children—Marguerite (Pardee), John. Formerly lecturer on determinative mineralogy, Lafayette; asso. editor American Geologist, 1890-1900; asso. editor Jour. Analytical Chemistry; chief research chemist Kemet Laboratories; director

G.M.N.A. Laboratories; consulting geologist Calif. mining cos. Member scientific expeditions to Mont., Colo. and Calif. Fellow Mineral. Soc. America, Palaeontol. Soc. America, etc.; life mem. British Assn. Sec. 10 yrs. and dep. gov. gen. Soc. Colonial Wars N.J. Author: The Mineralogy of Pennsylvania (2 vols.), 1891, 1911; A Course in Determinative Mineralogy, 1892; Some Letters and Documents (2 vols.), 1900; Genealogical Studies, 1902. Contributions to Mineralogy (in 10 parts). Research work on the rarer metals. Over 100 scientific monographs, articles and reports; also writer on genealogy. Address: P.O. Box 567, Hollywood Calif. *

EYSTER, WILLIAM HENRY, botanist; b. Fishers Ferry, Pa., July 13, 1889; s. Henry and Alice (Star) E.; A.B., Bucknell U., 1914, A.M., 1915; Ph.D., Cornell U., 1920; grad. study Harvard, 1923, U. of Berlin, 1928, Botanisches Institut, Erlangen, Germany, 1928; m. Elmira Snyder, June 18, 1914; children—William Henry, Paul Morris, Helen Elizabeth. Asst. prof. botany, U. of Mo., 1920-24; prof. U. of Me., 1924-27; fellow John Simon Guggenheim Memorial Foundation for Study Abroad, 1927-28; prof. botany Bucknell U., 1928-45; president Eyster Hybrid Seed Co., 1945-46; professor of botany, Baldwin-Wallace College, 1945-46; prof. edn. Moravian Coll., Bethlehem, Pa., 1959; genetic adviser W. Atlee Burpee Co., Phila.; mng. editor Organic Gardening; asso. editor Organic Farmer; soil scientist for National Soil Conservation, Inc., N.Y. City; agrl. cons. Atlantic Organic Company, Williamsport, Md.; Scientific consultant to Wandel Machine Company, Inc., also Zook & Ranck, Inc., Gap, Pennsylvania; scientific adviser Bally Products, Bally, Pa.; v.p. and dir. research Eastern States Soilbuilders, Inc., Sharpsburg, Md.; v.p. Wandel Machine Co., Inc., Dowingtown, Pa.; agrl. dir. Roper Lumber Co., 1951-52; v.p., dir. prodn. Soil-Tone Corp., Plymouth, North Carolina, 1952-55; director of research for Fertilium, Inc., 1956-58; science director Fertilium Co., 1958-61; inventor organic soil conditioner and plant food; dir. Zeolite Chem. Company, N.Y.C. Trustee Soil and Health Foundation. Fellow A.A.A.S.; member Am. Bot. Soc., German Bot. Soc., Am. Genetic Soc., Am. Soc. of Plant Physiologists, Am. Soc. Naturalists, Torrey Botanical Club, Pennsylvania Acad. Sciences; fellow N.Y. Acad. of Sciences, Sigma Xi, Phi Kappa Phi, Phi Sigma, Phi Gamma Delta. Originator of hybrid corns and marigolds. Author: College Botany, 1931; Genetics of Zea Mays, 1934; Biological Science, 1941. Author many articles. Asst. editor Biological Abstracts. Investor Eysterlite soil conditioner 1963. Address: Emmaus PA Died Apr. 16, 1968.

EZEKIEL, WALTER NAPHTALI, plant pathologist; b. Richmond, Va., Apr. 26, 1901; s. Jacob Levy and Rachel (Brill) E.; B.S., U. of Md., 1920, M.S., 1921, Ph.D., 1924; m. Sarah Ritzen, of Minneapolis, Minn., Feb. 15, 1926; children—Herbert Mordecai, David Hirsch, Joseph Lewis, Raphael Safra, Miriam. Asst. plant pathologist, Md. Agrl. Expt. Sta., 1920-25; nat. research fellow in biol. sciences, U. of Minn., 1925-27; agt. Bur. Plant Industry, U.S. Dept. of Agr.; plant pathologist, Tex. Agrl. Expt. Sta., since 1928. Fellow A.A.A.S., Tex. Acad. Sciences; mem. Am. Phytopathol. Soc., Mycol. Soc. of America, Phi Alpha. Democrat. Jewish religion. Has made extensive investigations of fruit-rotting Sclerotinias, physiology of resistance to plant diseases, Phymatotrichum root rot. Author bulls. and articles on plant pathology. Home: Bryan, Tex. *

FABING, HOWARD DOUGLAS, physician; b. Cin., Feb. 21, 1907; s. Henry Charles and Jessie (Ammann) F.; A.B., U. Cin., 1927, M.D., 1931; m. Esther Clare Marting, Dec. 16, 1939; children—Suzannah Jane, Priscilla Ruth, Howard William. Rotating intern Cin. Gen. Hosp., 1931-32, resident neurology, 1932-33; pvt. practice psychiatry and neurology, 1936-70; faculty physiology and neurology dept. U. Cin., 1936-42. Served from maj. to lt. col. M.C., AUS, 1942-46; neurologist Walter Reed Hosp.; chief neuropsychiatry Finney Gen. Hosp.; dir. sch. and standardized treatment combat fatigue ETO; research cerebral blast concussion; chief neurology div. VA, Washington, 1945-46; cons. Surg. Gen. U.S. Army, Korea, 1950. Decorated Legion of Merit. Mem. Am. League Against Epilepsy (chmn. legislation com.), Nat. Multiple Sclerosis Soc. (med. adv. bd.), Am. Neurological Assn., Am. Psychiat. Assn., Assn. Research Nervous and Mental Disease (member Commission 1957) Electroshock Research Assn., Cin. soc. Neurology and Psychiatry (pres. 1941), Ohio Med. Assn. (chmn. sect. nervous and mental diseases 1942), Am. Acad. Neurology (pres. 1953-55), Soc. Biol. Psychiatry (pres. 1955-56), Cin. Acad. Medicine (pres. 1956-57). Author: Fischerisms (rev. edit.), 1956; Epilepsy and the Law (with Roscoe Barrow), 1956. Author sci. papers. Home: Cincinnati OH Died July 29, 1970.

FAGET, JEAN CHARLES, physician, author; b. New Orleans, June 26, 1818; s. Jean Baptiste and Mrs. (Le Mormand) F.; attended Collège Rolin, Paris, France, 1830-37; M.D., Faculté de Paris, 1844; m. Glady Ligeret de Chazet, many children. Practiced medicine, New Orleans, 1845; published articles in La Gazette Médicale, also New Orleans Med. Jour.; published discovery of difference in symptoms between yellow fever and malaria, 1859; apptd. to La. Bd. Health; mem. San. Commn. apptd. by Gen. Nathaniel Banks, 1864. Author: Memoires et Lettres sur la Fièvre Jaune et la Fièvre Pauludeénne, 1864 (named chevalier Legion of Honor by France for this work, 1864). Died New Orleans, Dec. 7, 1884.

FAILLA, GIOACCHINO, (fa-el'-la), physicist; b. Italy, July 19, 1891; s. Nicolo and Sara (Spoleti) F.; brought to U.S., 1906, naturalized, 1916; E.E., Columbia, 1915, M.A., 1917; D.Sc., U. Paris, 1923; D.Sc. (hon.), University of Rochester, 1949; m. Marie Muller, June 9, 1925 (dec. 1936); children—Marie Louise (Mrs. J. D. Campbell), Evelyn Sara (Mrs. Robert Kent Rockhill); married second Patricia McClement, Jan. 22, 1949. Physicist, establishing physics and biophysics lab. Memorial Hosp., N.Y. City, 1915-42; prof. Coll. Phys. and Surgeons, Columbia, 1943-60, emeritus prof., 1960—; sr. physicist (emeritus) Argonne Nat. Lab., Argonne, Ill., 1960—; asst. to sci. attache Am. Embassy, Rome, 1918-19; consultant, metall. lab. U. Chicago, 1943-46, Argonne Nat. Lab. 1946-60, Los Almos Sci. Lab., 1947-48, Brookhaven Nat. Lab., 1947-57, Nuclear Engine Propulsion Aircraft Project, 1948-50; member council physical therapy A.M.A., 1941-48, U.S.P.H.S., U.S. V.A. since 1942; chief biophysics br., div. biology and medicine A.E.C., 1948, mem. adv. com. biology and medicine, 1951-57, chmn., 1955-57; mem. Nat. Def. Research Com., 1942-45, radiobiology panel, com. growth. Nat. Research Council, 1945-47, subcom. human applications, chmn. Adv. com. isotope distbn., 1947-50; mem. exec. com., chmn. subcom. external radiation, Nat. Com. Radiation Protection, 1946-57; chmn. radiol. instrument panel Armed Forces Spl. Weapons Project, 1948—. Ofcl. rev. Am. Phys. Soc. to 1st Internat. Congress Radiology London, 1925; Am. Radium Soc. del. to 4th Internat. Congress Radiology, Zurich, Switzerland, 1934; chmn. radiophysics sect., hon. chmn. internat. com. radiol. units 5th Internat. Congress Radiology, Chicago, 1937; v.p. emeritus 6th Internat. Congresses Radiology, London, 1950, Copenhagen, 1953, Mexico City, 1956; chairman of biophysics sect. Internat. Cancer Congress, Atlantic City, 1939; chmn. subcom. external radiation Internat. Commn. Radiol. Protection; hon. mem. Brit. Inst. Radiology, Internat. Joint Com. Radiobiology 1950-56. Awarded Pulitzer Scholarship, 1911-15; Leonard prize Am. Roentgen Ray Soc., 1923, 25, Caldwell medal, 1945; Am. Radium Soc., 1939; Gold medal, Radiol. Soc. N.A., 1947; Ann. National award Am. Cancer Society, 1956; Ewing Soc. honorary lecture medal, 1961. Fellow A.A.A.S., Am. Phys. Soc.; mem. Optical Soc. Am., N.Y. Acad. Scis., Am. Radium Soc., Am. Roentgen Ray Soc., Radiol. Soc. N.A., Harvey Soc., Corp. Marine Biological Laboratory (trustee), Radiation Research Soc. (president 1954), Internat. Congress Radiation Research, Burlington, Vt., 1958 (organizing com.), Gerontological Soc., Sigma Xi. Author articles in sci. jours. Home: 575 Warren Terrace, Hinsdale, Ill. Office: Radiological Physics Division, Argonne Nat. Lab., Argonne, Ill. Died Dec. 15, 1961.

FAIR, GORDON MASKEW, prof. engring.; b. Burghersdorp, Union of South Africa, July 27, 1894; s. Charles and Maria (Maskew) F.; grad. Werner Siemens Gymnasium, Berlin, 1913; S.B., Mass. Inst. of Tech., 1916; S.B., Harvard, 1916; hon. M.S., Tufts Coll., 1934; Dr. Ing. Technische Hochschule, Stuttgart, 1951; hon. fellow Imperial Coll. Sci. and Tech., 1951; Dr. honoris causae, Universidad Nacional de Ingenieria, Lima, Peru, 1960; Doctor of Science, Rose Polytechnic Institute, 1963; Doctor of Science, Rutgers, The State Univ., 1965; m. Esther Lansing Mead, December 21, 1918; children—Gordon Maskew, Cornelius Lansing. Began as sanitary engr., 1917; instr. to prof. Harvard Univ., 1918-35, Gordon McKay prof. of sanitary engring. 1935-65, Abbott and James Lawrence prof. of engring. 1938-65, McKay and Lawrence prof. emeritus, from 1965, dean faculty of engring., 1946-49; master of Dunster House, 1948-61; cons. on san. engring. to govt. agencies, industries; and founds., including National Mil. Establishment 1946-53; internat. health div., Rockefeller Found. 1945-48, 1949-54, Commn. on Environmental Hygiene, Army Epidemiological Bd. 1946-54; chmn. environmental health study sect. NIH, 1952-55; mem. NRC committee on sanitary engineering 1942-64; mem. panel on environmental sanitation WHO. Registered profl. engr., Mass. Served C.E.F., World War I. Fellow Am. Soc. Civil Engrs., Am. Acad. Arts and Scis.; mem. Am. Water Works Assn., Am. Pub. Health Assn., A.A.A.S. (v.p, 1947), Sigma Xi, Nat. Acad. engring., other profl. and scientific socs. and assns. Clubs: Cosmos (Washington); Faculty (Harvard). Author books and chpts. on water supply, and waste water disposal. Contbr. scientific articles to jours. Home: Cambridge MADied Feb. 11, 1970.*

FAIRBANK, HERBERT SINCLAIR, highway engineer; b. Baltimore, Md., Sept. 16, 1888; s. Charles Alexander and Sarah Sherwood (Sinclair) F.; C.E., Cornell U., 1910; unmarried. Civil engr. student U.S. Bureau of Mines, Sept.-Nov. 1910; with U.S. Office Pub. Roads since 1910, as civil engr. student, 1910-11, asst., then speaker on Good Roads Trains operated over rys. of South and West, 1912-13, object lesson road building, highway research. etc., 1911-17, editor "Public Roads" mag., 1920-27, chief div. of information, 1927, dir. statewide highway planning surveys, U.S. Bur. Pub. Roads in cooperation with highway depts. of 48 states, 1935-43, dep. commr., 1943-55. Chmn. dept. of econs., finance and adminstrn., Hwy. Research Bd., Nat. Research Council, 1944-56, mem. com. econs. of size and weight motor vehicles, 1956—, exec. com., 1959-62. Aternate mem. Pres.'s. Sci. Research Bd., 1946. Aide to sec.-gen. Internat. Road Congress, Washington, 1930, del. U.S. Govt., Munich, 1934; v. chmn. U.S. delegation United Nations Conference on Road and Motor Transport, Geneva, 1949. Served as 1st lieut., later capt., Chem. Warfare Service, U.S. Army, 1918-19. Received George S. Bartlett Award for outstanding contribution to highway progress, 1947; Dept. of Commerce award for Exceptional Service, 1949; Roy W. Crum award in highway research, 1953; Thomas H. MacDonald award, 1957. Member Tau Beta Pi. Presbyn. Home: 2041 E. 32d St., Baltimore 21218. Died Dec. 14, 1962; buried Green Mount Cemetery, Balt.

FAIRBANKS, HAROLD WELLMAN, geologist; b. Conewango, N.Y., Aug. 29, 1860; s. Daniel and Harriet N. (Wellman) F.; B.S., U. of Mich., 1890; Ph.D., U. of Cal., 1896; m. Bertha Helena Kemp, June, 1888. Engaged since graduation upon the geology and geography of the Pacific Coast. Author: Stories of Our Mother Earth, 1899; Home Geography, 1902; Physiography of California, 1903; Stories of Rocks and Minerals, 1903; The Western United States; Physical Geography for High Schools; also about 40 articles on geology, mineralogy and physical geography of California and adjoining regions. Address: Berkeley, Cal. *

FAIRBANKS, HENRY, inventor, mfr.; b. St. Johnsbury, Vt., May 6, 1830; s. late Thaddeus (inventor of scales) and Lucy P. (Barker) F.; A.B., Dartmouth, 1853, A.M., 1856 (Ph.D., 1880); grad. Andover Theol. Sem., 1857; m. Annie S. Noyes, Apr. 30, 1862 (died 1872); m. 2d, Ruthy Page, May 5, 1874; father of Arthur F. Ordained Congl. ministry, 1857; in pastorates, 1857-60; prof. natural philosophy, 1859-65, natural history, 1865-68, Dartmouth. Identified with E. & T. Fairbanks & Co., mfrs. of scales, etc., 1868—; has received more than 30 patents on various devices. Trustee Dartmouth Coll., 1870-96; pres. St. Johnsbury Acad.; mem. Nat. and Internat. Congl. councils. Home: St. Johnsbury, Vt. Died June 7, 1918.

FAIRBANKS, THADDEUS, inventor, scale mfr.; b. Brimfield, Mass., Jan. 17, 1796; s. Joseph and Phebe (Paddock) F.; m. Lucy Barker, Jan. 17, 1820, 2 children including Henry. In partnership with brother Erastus Fairbanks, 1792-1864; established iron foundry E. & T. Fairbanks Co., 1823; patented a plow, 1826, flax and hemp dressing machine, 1830, platform scale, 1831; devised parlor stove, cook stove; invented draft mechanism for furnaces, 1843, hot water heater, 1881, also feedwater heater; established St. Johnsbury (Vt.) Acad., 1842. Recipient knightly cross Order St. Joseph from Emperor Austria, Golden medal from King of Siam, token of comdr. Order of Iftikar from Bey of Tunis. Died St. Johnsbury, Apr. 12, 1886.

FAIRCHILD, DAVID, agrl. explorer; b. Lansing, Mich., Apr. 7, 1869; s. George Thompson and Charlotte Pearl (Halsted) F.; student Kan. State Agrl. Coll.; hon. degrees from Oberlin Coll., Fla. State Coll., Kan. State; m. Marian H. Bell, Apr. 25, 1905; children—Graham Bell, Barbara (Mrs. Leonard Muller), Nancy Bell (Mrs. Marston Bates). Expdns. in search of plants for introduction to U.S., with Barbour Lathrop, to Dutch E. Indies, 1895, to S. Sea Islands, Siam, Australia, New Zealand, 1896-97, to W. Indies, S.A., Egypt, Ceylon and Persian Gulf, 1901-02, Africa, 1903; organizer, in charge office plant introduction Dept. of Agr., 1904-28; Allison V. Armour expdns. to Morocco, Dutch E. Indies, W. Africa, Carribbean, 1925-27, 32-33; in charge sci. work of Fairchild Garden expdn. to Philippines, Celebes, Java, Bali and Moluccas, on Mrs. Anne Archbold's Chinese junk, Cheng Ho, 1939-40; collected plants in Colombia, Panama and Guatemala and Yucatan, 1944. Mem. bd. trustees Nat. Geog. Soc. Medallist Societe d'Acclimatacion France, Harvard Traveller's Club, Mass. Hort. Soc. (George Robt. White), Nat. Acad. Scis., Garden Club of Am., Men's Garden Clubs (Johnny Appleseed), Nat. Council State Garden Clubs (Gold seal), Fairchild Tropical Garden (Meyer medal, plant introduction); Fairchild Tropical Garden, Coconut Grove Fla. named in his honor. Fellow Linnean Soc. London; pres. Am. Genetic Assn.; hon. mem. Committee of One Hundred, Miami Beach. Author: Book of Monsters, 1914; Exploring for Plants, 1930; The World Was My Garden, 1938; Garden Islands of the Great East, 1945; The World Grows Round My Door, 1947. Home: 4013 Douglas Rd., Coconut Grove, Fla.; (summer) Beinn Bhreagh, Nova Scotia, Can. Died Aug. 2, 1954.

FAIRCHILD, HERMAN LE ROY, geologist; b. Montrose, Pa., Apr. 29, 1850; s. Harmon C. and Mary A. (Bissell) F.; B.S., Cornell, 1874; D.Sc., U. of Pittsburgh, 1910; m. Alice Egbert, of Ithaca, N.Y., July 25, 1875; children—Katherine (Mrs. Charles T. Lewis), Lillian (dec.), Jessie Evelyn (Mrs. Guy Bogart), Le Roy Frink (dec.). Teacher Wyoming Sem., Kingston, Pa., 1875-76; lecturer N.Y. schs., 1876-88, and in Cooper Union, 1878-88; prof. geology and natural history, 1888-96, geology, 1896-1920, Univ. of Rochester, now emeritus. Fellow A.A.A.S. (gen. sec. 1894, v.p. 1898), Geol. Soc. Am. (sec. 1890-1906, pres. 1912); mem. N.Y. Acad. Sciences (sec. 1885-88), Rochester Acad.

Sciences (past president). President Commn. Govt. Assn. of N.Y. State, 1911-12; mem. N.Y. State Bd. of Geographic Names, 1913-23. Author: History of the New York Academy of Sciences, 1887; Revision of Le Conte's Elements of Geology, 1903; Geologic Story of the Genesee Valley and Western New York, 1928; The Geological Society of America (a chapter in Earth Science History), 1932; also over 270 monographs and contbns. on geol. and biol. subjects, especially on the glacial geology of N.Y. Home: 106 Winterroth St., Rochester, N.Y. *

FAIRCHILD, SHERMAN M., aviation exec.; b. Oneonta, N.Y., Apr. 7, 1896; ed. U. of Ariz., Harvard and Columbia. Inventor of Fairchild aerial camera; chmn. of the bd. Fairchild Camera and Instrument Co., 1925-71, head, Dynar Corporation; owner of Fairchild Recording Equipment Corp.; chmn. bd. Fairchild Industries; director Conrac. Corp., IBM Corp. Mem. bd. govs. Audio Engring. Soc. Fellow Inst. Aeronautical Scis., Royal Aero. Soc. Home: Huntington LI NY Died Mar. 28, 1971; buried Oneonta NY

FAIRCLOTH, JAMES M(ANNING), engr.; b. Clinton, N.C., Aug. 4, 1903; s. Cyrus Mills and Alice Lerina (Wade) F.; grad. Ga. Mil. Acad., 1922; B.S., N.C. State Coll., 1928; M.S., U. Ala. 1938; m. Annie Moore Parker, Aug. 22, 1928 (dec. 1957); children—Elise, Alice Wade, James M., Anne Moore; m. 2d, Louise Goodwyn, June 10, 1958. Instr. civil engring. U. Ala., 1928-31, asst. prof., 1931-39, asso. prof., 1939-45, prof., 1945—, asst. dean engring., 1939-45, head dept. civil engring., 1946—, acting dean coll. engring., 1952-53, various profl. jobs in hwy. engring., san. engring. and gen. civil engring., 1928—. Mem. Ala. State Water Improvement Commn., Tuscaloosa (Ala.) City Planning Bd.; mem. Tuscaloosa Housing Authority. Fellow Am. Soc. C.E. (dir. dist. 10 council, pres. Ala. sect., mem. nat. com. on student chpts. faculty adviser); mem. Am. Soc. for Engring. Edn., Am. Assn. U. Profs., Tau Beta Pi, Chi Epsilon, Theta Tau (faculty adviser), Sigma Phi Epsilon. Kiwanian. Home: 2 L Northwoods Lake, Northport, Ala. Office: P.O. Box Z, University, Ala. Died July 12, 1964; buried Memorial Park Cemetery, Tuscaloosa.

FAIRMAN, JAMES FERDINAND, engr.; b. Big Rapids, Mich., Apr. 8, 1896; s. George Ferdinand and May (Trowbridge) F.; B.S., U. Mich., 1918, M.S., 1921; Dr. Engring. (hon.), 1953; m. Bertha Esther Wright, Aug. 25, 1920; children—Julia (Mrs. W.W. Stifler, Jr.), Barbara Wright (Mrs. J. W. Jickling), James F., Jr. Instr. in elect. engring., U. Mich., 1919-22, asst. prof., 1922-25; outside plant engr., Bklyn. Edison Co., Inc., 1925-26, asst. electrical engr., 1927-32, electrical engr., 1932-36, Consol. Edison Co. of N.Y., Inc., 1937-40, asst. v.p. 1941-45, v.p., 1946-57, sr. v.p., 1957-61; pres. United Engring. Trustees, Inc. adminstr. Defense Electric Power Adminstrn., Dept. of Interior, 1951-52 (on leave); trustee Faltbush Savs. Bank. Mem. bd. examiners Profl. Engrs. and Land Surveyors, N.Y. State, 1953-62. Fellow Am. Inst. Elec. Engrs. (pres., 1949-50); mem. Bklyn. C. of C., Nat. Soc. Profl. Engrs. Republican. Episcopalian. Clubs: University, The Engineers' (N.Y.C.). Address: 170 Baldwin, Birmingham, Mich. Died Apr. 25, 1967.

FALCONER, ROBERT CLEMONS, civil engr.; b. St. Mary's, Pa., Mar. 21, 1874; s. Nathaniel Sill and Elizabeth (Clemons) F.; B.S., in C.E., U. of Wis., 1895; m. Clara Eliza McLain, Oct. 25, 1906; children—Clara Evans, Elizabeth, Robert McLain. With Purdy & Henderson, New York, 1895-97, Cambria Steel Co., Johnstown, Pa., 1897-98, Pa. Lines West of Pittsburgh, 1898-1901; sales engr. Am. Bridge Co., Pittsburgh, 1901-02; prospecting for Pittsburgh Zinc Co., 1902-03; designer, Walton Iron Co., Cincinnati, 1903-04; designer and estimator McClintock-Marshall Constrn. Co., Pittsburgh, 1904-05; with Erie R.R., 1905—, advancing through various positions in engineering dept. to asst. v.p. and chief engr., and asst. v.p. in charge of engring.; also dir. Paterson & Ramapo, Paterson, Newark and New York. Home: Cleveland, O. Died Feb. 20, 1941.

FALK, K. GEORGE, chemist; b. N.Y. City, Sept, 8, 1880; s. Arnold and Fannie (Wallach) F.; B.S., Columbia, 1901; Johns Hopkins, 1901-03; Ph.D., Strassburg U., 1905; Berlin U., 1905-06; m. Dora Lichten, May 31, 1909; m. 2d, Carolyn Rosenstein, Oct. 16, 1935. Asst. in phys. chemistry, Columbia, 1906-07, tutor in physics, 1907-09; research asso. in phys. chemistry, Mass. Inst. Tech., 1909-11; chemist Harriman Research Lab., Roosevelt Hosp., New York, 1911-28, Harriman Research Fund, New York U. Med. Coll., 1929-31; biol. chemist, Bureau of Labs., Health Dept., N.Y. City, 1931-39; prof. chemical bacteriology in preventive medicine, New York U. Med. Coll., 1933-36; dir. Lab. of Industrial Hygiene, Inc., since 1936; also consultant for various chem. companies. Capt. Sanitary Corps, U.S. Army, 1918-19. Pres. Hebrew Tech. Inst. Mem. Am. Chem. Soc., Am. Pub. Health Assn., Am. Soc. Biol. Chemists, A.A.A.S., Soc. Exptl. Biology and Medicine, Harvey Soc., N.Y. Acad. Sciences, London Chem. Soc., Am. Assn. for Cancer Research, Am. Inst., Am. Inst. of Chemists, Sigma Xi, Phi Lambda Upsilon. Clubs: Chemists, Columbia, Harmonie. Author: Chemical Reactions, Their Theory and Mechanism, 1920; Chemistry of Enzyme Action, 1921, 2d edit., 1924; Catalytic Action, 1922. Contbr. to scientific jours. Home: 40 E. 66th St., N.Y. City 21. Office: 254 W. 31st St., N.Y.C. 1. Died Nov. 22, 1953; buried Ferncliff Cemetery, Hartsdale, N.Y.

FALK, MYRON SAMUEL, cons. engr.; b. New York, N.Y., Sept. 13, 1878; s. Arnold and Fannie (Wallach) F.; C.E., Columbia, 1899, Ph.D., 1903; M.E., Stevens Inst. Tech., 1900; m. Milly Einstein, June 3, 1903 (died Nov. 9, 1915); children—Eleanor Arnold (Mrs. Joseph B. Lenzner), Myron Samuel, Mildred (Mrs. Edgar P. Loew). Successively tutor, instr., lecturer in civil engring., Columbia, 1900-10; mem. N.Y. Bay Pollution Commn., 1903-05; cons. engr. N.Y. State Water Supply Commn., 1905-08; chief engr. Godwin Constrn. Co., New York, 1905-30, H.H. Oddie, Inc., 1909-28; chmn. bd. dirs. Wonham, Bates & Goode Trading Corp., 1920-23; v.p. Am. Bemberg Corp., 1925-27. Served as major, later lt. col., Ordnance Dept., U.S. Army, 1918-19. Chmn. bd. trustees Lavanburg Found.; trustee Mount Sinai Hosp. Mem. Am. Soc. Civil Engrs., Am. Soc. Testing Materials. Clubs: Engineers. Columbia University, Harmonie (New York); Century Country (White Plains, N.Y.); Tamarack Country (Port Chester, N.Y.). Author: Cements, Mortars and Concretes, 1904; Graphic Method by Influence Lines for Bridge and Roof Computation (with Wm. H. Burr), 1908; Design and Construction of Metallic Bridges (with Wm. H. Burr), 1908. Address: King St., Greenwich, Conn. Died Nov. 26, 1945.

FANNING, JOHN THOMAS, civil engr.; b. Norwich, Conn., Dec. 31, 1837; s. John Howard and Elizabeth (Pridde) F.; acad. and normal sch. edn.; m. M. Louise Bensley, June 14, 1865. Studied architecture and civil engring. until 1861; served during Civil War, lt. to lt. col., 3d Conn. S.M. After war became prominent in engring., particularly in planning and constructing pub. water works and water powers in N.E., and later in the West, notably on the power of the Miss. River at Minneapolis, of the Spokane River in Washington, and Missouri River nr. Helena and at Great Falls, Mont., and on the Weenatahee River in Wash. for the electrification of the G.N. Ry.'s cascade tunnel; was cons. engr. St. Paul, Minneapolis & Manitoba R.R. and G.N. Ry., and v.p. Minneapolis Union Ry. Home: Minneapolis, Minn. Died 1911.

FARAGHER, DONALD QUALTROUGH, architect; b. Rochester, N.Y., Apr. 11, 1906; s. William Henry and Ella (Qualtrough) F.; B.Arch., Syracuse U., 1930; m. Harriet Miller Thistlethwaite, June 20, 1931; children—Anthony Thistlethwaite, Rachel Qualtrough. Draughtsman, F.R. Scherer, Architect, Rochester, 1926-33; architect engrs. office City of Rochester, 1933-34; pvt. practice, Rochester, 1934-42, 45-71; partner Faragher & Macomber, 1951-71; supervising architect Rochester-Monroe County Civic Center, 1954-71, master plan Rochester Civic Center 1954-71. Mem. Bd. Examiners Architects N.Y. State, 1950-59, pres., 1954-57; chmn. finance com. Nat. Council Architects Registration Bds., 1959-71; adv. com. facilities and planning N.Y. Dept. Edn.; adviser Rochester Bldg. Bd. on N.Y. State Code, 1951-71; mem. Bldg. Research Inst. representing A.I.A. on Nat. Acad. Sci., 1959; mem. sr. thesis juries Syracuse U. Sch. Architecture, 1949-59, coop. com., 1952-71; bd. appeals N.Y. State Bldg. Constrn., 1960-71. Recipient Lillian Fairchild award U. Rochester, 1952; Arents medal Syracuse U., 1960; citation for Ellison Park Apts., Central N.Y. chpt. A.I.A. and N.Y. State Assn. Architects, 1950; certificate of merit for outstanding design of Rochester E. High Sch., N.Y. State Assn. Architects, 1958. Fellow A.I.A. (mem. commn. on edn. and research, dir. N.Y., trustee Found.); member N.Y. State (pres. 1951-52, dir. 1959-61, chmn. edn. com. 1953-60), Assn. Architects, Rochester (pres. 1948-50, chmn. legislative com. 1959-63), Soc. Architects, Rochester Engring. Soc. (pres. 1957-58, dir. 1958-61), Am. Soc. Testing Materials, Rochester C. of C., Rochester Music Assn., Syracuse U. Archtl. Alumni Assn. (pres. 1958), Sigma Alpha Epsilon, Sigma Upsilon Alpha. Republican. Presbyn. Clubs: Lake Placid (N.Y.); Rochester Country, Torch (dir. 1957-59), University (Rochester). Home: Rochester NY Died Feb. 5, 1971.

FARAGHER, WARREN FRED, research chemist; b. Sabetha, Kan., Apr. 25, 1884; s. William Henry and Delphine A. (Davis) F.; A.B., U. Kan., 1905; Ph.D., 1910; m. Nina May Poole, June 23, 1909; children—Robert Vance, William Arthur. Instr. chemistry, 1905-07; Dir. research Houdry Process Corp. (holding co. of Catalytic Devel. Co.), 1931-44, tech. adv., 1944-51, tech. cons. to Houdry Process Div., World Commerce Corp., N.Y., Europe and Near East, 1952-54; chem. engring. cons., 1954—; v.p. Temple U. Research Inst., 1958—. Mem. Tech. Oil Mission to Germany, 1945; field chief liquid fuels and lubricants sect. Field Intelligence Agy. Tech. (Germany), 1946-47 (on loan to U.S. Govt.). Mem. Am. Chem. Soc., Am. Petroleum Inst., French Assn. Petroleum Technologists, German Soc. for Petroleum Technology and Coal Chemistry, Kan. Acad. Sci., France Forever (nat. v.p.; pres. Phila.), Phi Beta Kappa, Sigma Xi, Phi Lambda Upsilon, Sigma Gamma Epsilon, Alpha Chi Sigma. Republican. Methodist. Contbr. to manuals and handbooks. Home: Swarthmore Apts. Office: 101 S. Chester Rd., Swarthmore, Pa. Died Feb. 1, 1966.

FARBER, SIDNEY, physician; b. Buffalo, Sept. 30, 1903; s. Simon and Matilda (Goldstein) F.; B.S., U. Buffalo, 1923; M.D., Harvard, 1927; post-grad. research, Germany, 1928-29, Belgium, 1935-36; D.Sc., (hon.), Suffolk U., 1960, Boston U., 1961, Providence Coll., 1961, Albert Einstein Coll. Medicine, 1966, N.Y. Med. Coll., 1970; M.D. (hon.), U. Ghent (Belgium), 1962, Cath. U. Louvain (Belgium), 1965, Karolinska Institute, Stockholm, Sweden, 1969; L.H.D. (hon.), Brandeis U., 1963; m. Norma C. Holzman, July 3, 1928; children—Ellen, Stephen Burt, Thomas David, Miriam. Faculty, Harvard Med. Sch. 1927-70, S. Burt Wolbach prof. pathology, 1967-70, prof. emeritus, 1970-73; prof. pathology, Harvard Med. Sch. at Children's Hosp., 1948-67; pathologist-in-chief, chmn. div. labs. and research, Children's Med. Center 1946-70; chmn. staff Children's Hosp. Med. Center, 1964-70, cons. in pathology and oncology, 1970-73. Founder, sci. dir. Children's Cancer Research Found. 1948-73; cons. Armed Forces Inst. Pathology, U.S. Pub. Health Services, Nat. Cancer Inst. Trustee Worcester Found. Exptl. Biology, Southwest Found. Research and Edn., San Antonio; founding trustee United Cerebral Palsy Research and Ednl. Found.; mem. Nat. Adv. Cancer Council; chmn. panel on cancer. Pres.'s Commn. Heart Disease, Cancer and Stroke, 1964. Pres., Am. Assn. Pathologists and Bacteriologists, 1957-58, Soc. Pediatric Research, 1947-48; pres. New Eng. Pathol. Soc., Boston Pathol. Soc.; bd. dirs. Belgian Am. Ednl. Found.; trustee Brandeis U., sec. bd. trustees, 1967; mem. sci. adv. bds. Rosell Park Research Inst., New Eng. Deaconess Hosp. Recipient Gt. medal U. Ghent, 1959; Modern Medicine award, 1962; Albert Lasker award for clinical research, 1966; Boston medal for distinguished achievement, 1967; Jurzykowski award in med. sci., 1970; Papnicolou award, 1971. Diplomate Am. Bd. Pathology. Fellow N.Y. Acad. Scis., Am. Acad. Arts and Scis.; mem. A.M.A., Am. Pediatric Soc., Asso. Cancer Inst. Dirs. (pres. 1963-65), Am. Assn. Cancer Research (hon.), James Ewing Soc. (hon.), Sigma Xi, Phi Beta Kappa, Alpha Omega Alpha. Club: Harvard. Editorial bd. Cancer, Biochem. Pharmacology. Home: Cambridge MA Died Mar. 30, 1973.

FARIS, ROBERT LEE, civil engr.; b. Caruthersville, Mo., Jan. 13, 1868; s. James White and Willie Ann (Stovall) F.; C.E., U. of Mo., 1890; spl. course in mathematics, Columbian (now George Washington) U., 1893; m. Carrie Elizabeth Hellen, June 8, 1897; children—Robert Lee, Hellen Mills, Carolyn, Elizabeth R., Charles William. U.S. asst. engr., survey Mo. River, 1890-91; recorder, 1891, aid, 1893, asst., 1895—. Coast and Geod. Survey; assisted in survey Yukon delta and N. Coast Behring Sea, Alaska, etc.; comd. coast survey steamers at P.R. and on East Coast, U.S., 5 yrs.; insp. magnetic work and chief of div. of Terrestrial Magnetism, Sept. 1906-Nov. 1914; asst. insp. hydrography and topography, Nov. 1914-Mar. 1915; asst. dir. Coast and Geod. Survey, Mar. 1915—. Mem. com. on navigation and nautical instruments of Nat. Research Council, 1917; mem. Miss. River Commn.; mem. Federal Bd. on Surveys and Maps. Home: Washington, D.C. Died Oct. 5, 1932.

FARISH, FREDERICK GARESCHÉ, (far'ish), mining engr.; b. St. Louis, Sept. 14, 1866, s. Edward Tilghman and Elizabeth (Garesché) F.; ed. St. Mary's Coll., Montreal, Can., 1880-86; St. Louis (Mo.) U., 1887-88; m. Alice Harwood, Oct. 1, 1808; 1 son, Edw. T. Asst. supt. Old Dominion Mining Co., Ouray, Colo., 1892-93; supt. Silver Age Mining Co., Idaho Springs, Colo., 1893-95; assayer and chemist, Grand Central Mining Co., Ltd., Torres, Sonora, Mex., 1896-99; mgr. Japan-Flora Mining Co., Telluride, Colo., 1900-01; cons. and exam. engr., 1902-11; supt. Humboldt mine, Sneffels, Colo., 1912-13; mgr. Lluvia de Oro Gold Mining Co., Chihuahua, Mex., 1915-16; mgr. Mineral Hill Consol. Copper Co., Ariz., 1917-18; gen. mgr. Metals Exploration Co., 1919-23; gen. supt. Silvermane Mines Co., Lake City, Colo., 1924-25; gen. mgr. Rico Mining & Reduction Co. since 1926. Cons. practice N.Y. City since 1927; cons. engr. to Campbell Mining Co., Inc., N.Y. City, 1934-40; retired. Mem. Am. Inst. Mining and Metall. Engrs. Catholic. Home: "The Pines," R.F.D. 2, Bel Air, Md. Died Aug. 14, 1946; buried in Calvary Cemetery, St. Louis.

FARLOW, WILLIAM GILSON, botanist; b. Boston, Dec. 17, 1844; s. John Smith and Nancy White (Blanchard) F.; A.B., Harvard, 1866, A.M., 1869, M.D., 1870; studied botany in Europe several yrs.; (LL.D., Harvard, 1896, U. of Glasgow, 1901, U. of Wis., 1904; Ph.D., Upsala, 1907); m. Lillian, d. E. N. Horsford, of Cambridge, Jan. 10, 1900. Asst. prof. botany, 1874-79, prof. cryptogamic botany, 1879—, Harvard. Fellow A.A.A.S. (v.p. 1887, 1898, pres. 1905), Am. Acad. Arts and Sciences. Author: The Gymnosporangia, or Cedar; Apples of the United States, 1880; Marine Algae of New England, 1881; The Potato Rot; Index of Fungi; etc. Home: Cambridge, Mass. Died June 3, 1919.

FARMER, F. MALCOLM, ret. elec., engr.; born Ilion, N.Y., Mar. 28, 1877; s. William Chesterton and Agnes (MacCrum) F.; prep. edn., Ilion Acad.; M.E., Cornell U., 1899; m. Lucy Merriman, June 6, 1906 (died August 20, 1949); one dau.; Alison (Mrs. Paul Wescott). Served as student engr. of General Electric Co., Schenectady, N.Y., 1899-1900; insp. U.S. Navy Dept., Brooklyn,

N.Y., 1901-03; lecturer Cooper Union Inst., New York, 1902-06; tech. asst. Elec. Testing Labs., New York, 1903-06, engr., 1906-12, chief engr., 1912-42, cons. engr. since 1942, v.p. 1929-49, pres., 1949-53, dir., hon. chmn. bd., 1953-57. Tech. cons. insp. methods, N.Y. Ordnance Dist., U.S. Army, 1942-45. An authority on elec. measurements, elec. insulating materials, testing engring. materials and high voltage cables. Awarded War Dept. Certificate of Commendation, 1946. Past chmn. standards council Am. Standards Assn., Engring. Found., John Fritz Medal Com. and Hoover Medal Com.; past pres. United Engring. Trustees. Fellow Am. Inst. Elec. Engrs. (pres. 1939-40); mem. A.A.A.S., Am. Soc. Mech. Engrs., Instn. Electrical Engrs. (British), Am. Soc. Testing Materials (pres. 1924-25, hon. member, 1948), Am. Welding Society (pres. 1926-28). Republican. Club: Engineers. Author: Electrical Measurements in Practice, 1917; also numerous tech. papers before Am. Inst. Elec. Engrs., (paper on high tension cables received both first nat. first dist. prizes, 1926), etc. Contbr. to Standard Handbook of Electrical Engineers, 1933; asso. editor American Civil Engineers' Handbook, 1930; Underground Systems Reference Book, 1931. Made investigation and report on high tension cable practice in Europe, 1923. Home: 331 W. Miner St., West Chester PA

FARMER, JOHN, cartographer; b. Halfmoon, N.Y., Feb. 9, 1798; s. John and Catharine (Stoutenburgh) F.; m. Roxana Hamilton, Apr. 5, 1826, 3 children. Tchr., Lancasterian sch., Albany, N.Y.; in charge one of U. Mich. schs., Detroit, 1821; engaged in surveying, map-making, 1825; made map of Mich., accompanied by small gazetteer, 1830; influential in promoting extensive immigration into Mich., 1825-40; produced map of Detroit, 1831, published in Am. State Papers, Public Lands, Vol. VI; sold copyrights to a N.Y. map house; produced new map of Mich., 1844; noted for large map of Mich. and Wis., published 1859. Died Detroit, Mar. 24, 1859.

FARMER, MOSES GERRISH, inventor, electrician; b. Boscawen, N.H., Feb. 9, 1820; s. Col. John and Sally (Gerrish) F.; attended Dartmouth, 1840-43; m. Hannah Shapleigh, Dec. 25, 1844, 1 child. Civil engr., Portsmouth, N.H., 1842; asst. in pvt. sch., Portsmouth, 1843; accepted preceptorship Eliot (Me.) Acad., 1843; prin. Belknap Sch. for Girls, Dover, N.H., 1844; devised machine that printed paper shades for lamps; experimented with electric railroad, 1845, constructed miniature electric train of 2 cars; wire examiner of new electric telegraph between Boston and Worcester (Mass), 1847; telegraph operator between Boston and Newburyport (Mass.), 1848; invented electric-striking apparatus for fire alarm service, 1848; supt. 1st electric fire alarm system in Am., installed Boston, 1851; discovered means for duplex and quadruplex telegraph, 1855; became supt. of tobacco-extracting manufactory, Somerville, Mass., 1861; invented an incadescent electric lamp, 1858-59, "self-exciting" dynamo, 1866; electrician U.S. Torpedo Sta., Newport, R.I., 1872-81; cons. electrician for U.S. Electric Light Co. of N.Y.; established public library, Eliot, Me. Died Chgo., May 25, 1893; buried Eliot.

FARNAM, HENRY, railroad builder, philanthropist; b. Scipio, N.Y., Nov. 9, 1803; s. Jeffrey Amherst and Mercy (Tracy) F.; m. Ann Whitman, 1839. Surveyor on Erie Canal, 1821-24; asst. engr. in constrn. Farmington Canal, 1825, chief engr., 1827 until canal abandoned, 1846, then engr. and supt. railroad replacing canal; completed Mich. So. R.R. from Hillsdale connecting to East, 1852; built Chgo. & Rock Island R.R., 1852-54, pres. until 1863; designed and built 1st railroad bridge crossing Mississippi River, extended Miss. & Mo. R.R. to Grinnell (Ia.); contbr. to Yale, also civic causes. Died New Haven, Conn., Oct. 4, 1883.

FARNELL, FREDERIC JAMES, psychiatrist; b. Providence, R.I., Jan. 14, 1885; s. George and M. Elizabeth (Topham) F.; M.D., Cornell U. Med. Coll., 1908; hon. M.B.A., Bryant and Stratton Coll. Business Administration; m. Jessie Worrell, Dec. 23, 1909 (divorced); children—F. Richard, Marjorie E. (dec.); m. 2d, Eva May Edgett, Jan. 25, 1939. Licensed to practice medicine, R.I., 1909, N.Y. State, 1909; settled in Providence, 1911; clin. prof. psychiatry, New York Med. Coll; asst. psychiatrist, Psychiatry Dept., Flower-Fifth Av. Hosp.; asso. attending neuro-psychiatrist, Met. Hosp., N.Y., attending neurologist, historian, from 1944; attending neurologist Murray Hill Hosp., N.Y. City; visiting neuro-psychiatrist, St. Vincent's Hosp., New Brighten, S.I.; psychiatrist R.I. State Hosp. for Mental Diseases; has served as psychiatrist or neurologist to Providence City Hosp., St. Joseph's Hosp., Newport Hosp., French Hosp. (Pawtucket, R.I.), pub. schs. of Providence, etc.; asst. in research, neuro-pathology, Mt. Sinai Hosp., 1945-47; cons. neuro-psychiat., U.S. Vets. Bur., Dist. 4.; chief neurology and therapist in psychiatry, Jamaica Center for Psychotherapy, 1958; attending staff Gracie Sq. Hosp., N.Y.C.; courtsey staff neuro-psychiatry Medical Arts Center, N.Y.C., Past chmn., R.I. State Public Welfare Commn.; chmn. com. on spl. legislation on prision labor, Nat. Com. on Prisons and Prison Labor; formerly mem. bd. of dirs. Am. Prison Assn. mem. bd. of Nat. Com. on Prisons and Prison Labor. Qualified psychiatrist N.Y. State Bd. Psychol. Examiners, Mental Hygiene. Diplomate in neurology and psychiatry. Mem. Am. advisory council, Euthanasia Soc. of America. Mem. N.Y. Acad. of Medicine, Internat. Psychoanalytic Soc., N.Y. Psychoanalytic Soc. (ex-pres.), Am. Coll. Physicians (gov.), R.I. Soc. for Mental Hygiene (dir. and exec. com.), R.I. Med. Assn., Am. Neurol. Assn., Nat. Com. of Mental Hygiene, New York Acad. Sciences; asso. mem. Medico-Psychol. Soc. of Paris; hon. mem. Young Men's Council of U.S.; hon. mem. Eugene Field Lit. Soc. Patron Smithsonian Institute (science). Republican. Protestant. Co-author (with Dr. Harms) Handbook of Socio-Psychiatry. Contbr. to Sir William Osler's publs., and med. jours.; collaborating editor Am. Jour. Nervous and Mental Diseases; asso. editor The Nervous Child; mem. editorial bd. Jour. Child Psychiatry. Address: New York City NY Died Nov. 4, 1968.

FARNHAM, ROBERT, chief engr.; b. Washington, D.C., Dec. 19, 1877; s. Robert and Emma Jane (Lowry) F.; student Columbian (now George Washington) U., 1894-95; C.E., Lehigh U., 1899; m. Gertrude Hanley, of St. Paul, Minn., Nov. 22, 1911; 1 son, Robert. Asst., engr. corps, engring. dept., D.C., 1899-1902; with J. H. Gray & Co., N.Y. City, 1902-03; with Pa. R.R. Co. since 1903, transitman, engrs. corps, Mar.-Aug. 1903, asst. engr. constrn., in charge constrn. work, Washington, D.C., 1903-10, asst. engr. office of engr. bridges and bldgs., 1910-13, asst. to engr. bridges and bldgs., 1913-16, asst. engr. bridges and bldgs., 1916-23, engr. same, 1923-27, chief engr., Philadelphia improvements, 1927-37, asst. chief engr. Eastern Region of Pa. R.R. since Sept. 1937. Mem. Am. Soc. C.E. (dir. 1924-26), Am. Ry. Engring. Assn., Am. Soc. Testing Materials, Sigma Chi. Republican. Episcopalian. Clubs: Engineers, Pennsylvania Golf. Home: 7126 Cresheim Rd., Mount Airy. Office: Broad St. Station, Philadelphia PA

FARNSWORTH, PHILO TAYLOR, research engr.; b. Beaver, Utah, Aug. 19, 1906; s. Louis Edwin and Serena (Bastian) F.; student Rigby (Ida.) High Sch., 1922-23, Brigham Young U., 1923-25); Sc.D. (honorary), Indiana Inst. Tech., 1951; D.Sci. (honorary) Brigham Young Univ., 1968; m. Elma Gardner, May 27, 1926 children—Philo Taylor, Kenneth Gardner (dec.), Russell S., Kent. Associated with Farnsworth Television & Radio Corp., Fort Wayne, Ind., and predecessors, 1926-58; former pres., dir. Farnsworth Research Corporation division Internat. Tel. & Tel. Co.; former v.p., tech. dir. Farnsworth Electronics Co., lab. cons. International Tel. and Tel. Corp.; founder, pres., dir. Philo T. Farnsworth Assos., Inc. Fellow A.A.A.S., Institute of Electric and Electronic Engineers; mem. Franklin Institute, American Physical Society, Sigma Xi, also mem. Eta Kappa Nu. Recipient of the Brigham Young U. Alumnus award, 1937; hon. mention, 1937, Eta Kappa Nu; Morris Leibnan Memorial Prize, Inst. of Radio Engrs. 1941, named one of 10 outstanding young Am. Pioneers, 1940, 1st medal Television Broadcasters Assn., 1944, Distinguished Alumnus award Brigham Young U., 1953. Mem. Ch. of Latter Day Saints. Holder over 300 Am. and fgn. patents, television, radar, electronics; now directing nuclear research. Home: Salt Lake City UT Died Mar. 11, 1971; buried Provo UT

FARR, MARCUS STULTS, zoologist, paleontologist, geologist; b. Cranbury, N.J., Feb. 19, 1870; s. James and Mary A. (Stults) F.; grad. Princeton Univ., A. B., 1892, M. Sc., 1893; A. M., Univ. of Chicago, 1894; D. Sc., Princeton, 1896; m. Oct. 24, 1894, Luella C. Bergen, Cranbury, N.J. Fellow in biology, Princeton, 1892-3; fellow zoology, Univ. of Chicago, 1893-4; graduate student, Princeton Univ., 1894-6; laboratory asst. paleontology, Princeton, 1896-8; asst. zoologist, N.Y. State Museum, Univ. State N. Y., Albany, 1898-1900; since Oct., 1900, asst. geology and curator dept. vertebrate paleontology, Princeton. Mem. Nat. Geog. Soc. A. A. A. S.; asso. mem. Ornithologists Union; hon. mem. Delaware Valley Ornith. Club. Wrote: Notes on the Osteology of the White River Horses, Proc. Am. Philos. Soc., 1896; Check List of New York Birds, Bull. 33, N. Y. State Museum, 1900. Address: 12 Maple St., Princeton NJ

FARRAR, JOHN, educator; b. Lincoln, Mass., July 1, 1779; s. Deacon Samuel and Mary (Hoar) F.; B.A., Harvard, 1803, M.A., 1806; LL.D. (hon.), Brown U., 1833; m. Lucy Buckminster; m. 2d, Eliza Rotch. Tutor of Greek, Harvard, 1805, Hollis prof. mathematics and natural philosophy, 1807-36; fellow Am. Acad. Arts and Scis., 1808, recording sec., 1811-23, mem. com. on publs., 1828-29, v.p., 1829-31, contbr. articles to its Transactions; author various monographs on meteorology and astronomy; helped make European astron. and math. lit. known in America through translations. Died Cambridge, Mass., May 8, 1853.

FARRELL, THOMAS FRANCIS, cons. engr.; b. Brunswick, Rensselaer County, N.Y., Dec. 3, 1891; s. John J. and Margaret (Connelly) F.; grad. La Salle Inst., Troy, N.Y., 1907; C.E., Rennselaer Poly Inst., Troy, 1912; grad. Engr. Sch., U.S. Army, Ft. Humphreys, Va., 1923; Dr. Engring. (hon.) Renssalaer Poly Inst., 1945; LL.D., Siena Coll., 1947; m. Ynez White, July 23, 1917; children—Thomas F. (killed in action, Anzio, Italy, Feb. 25, 1944), Barbara, Peter B., Patricia Anne, Stephen Stuart. Engring. work, Panama Canal, 1913-17; chief engr. Dept. Pub. Works, Jan. 1930-June 1947; chmn. N.Y. Housing Authority, July 1947-Dec. 1951; dep. adminstr. D.P.A., 1951; asst. gen. mgr. AEC, 1951-52; mng. dir. ARO, Inc. Tullahoma, Tenn., 1952-57; cons. N.Y. Worlds Fair of 1964-65, Power Authority of N.Y. Commd. 2d lt. Corps of Engrs., U.S. Army, 1916, promoted through grades to maj., 1918; served 2 yrs. overseas. On active duty, with rank col., Engrs. Corps, Army of U.S., Feb. 1941-Jan. 1944, brig. gen., Jan., 1944, maj. gen. Nov. 1945; Served as chief engr. China-Burma-India Theatre, Nov. 1944-Jan. 1945; deputy comdr. Atomic Bomb Project, 1945-46; comdg. gen. 301st Logistical Command, and comdg. gen. Camp Rucker, Ala., 1950-51. In chg. of field operations in Mariannas in atomic bomb operns. against Japan. Headed mission to Japan to check damage and Japanese atomic bomb activities; mem. evaluation bd. for test of atomic bomb against naval vessels; advisor to the U.S. rep. on U.N. Atomic Energy Commn. Com. Mem. Am. Society of Military Engineers. Decorated D.S.C., D.S.M., Legion of Merit (with Oak Leaf Cluster). Silver Star Medal (two oak leaf clusters). Order of the Purple Heart (U.S.); N.Y. State Conspicuous Service Cross; 3 citations; Croix de Guerre with Palm (French); Order of British Empire (degree of comdr.). Democrat. Clubs: Army-Navy (Washington). Contbr. to The Military Engineer. Home: 30 W. 60th St. Office: care Power Authority, 10 Columbus Circle, N.Y.C. Died Apr. 11, 1967; buried Arlington Nat. Cemetery, Washington.

FARRIS, EDMOND J., research anatomist; b. Buffalo, N.Y., July 28, 1907; s. George and Sultana (Baddour) F.; B.A., U. of Buffalo, 1928; Ph.D., U. of Pa., 1938; m. L(ouise) Augusta Stroman, June 5, 1932; children—Louise Augusta, Edmond J., Suzanne Lartique. Research asso., dept. exptl. biology, Am. Museum Natural History, 1928-29; instr. anatomy, Med. Coll. of S.C., 1929-34; instr. anatomy, Georgetown U., 1934-35; instr. anatomy, U. of Buffalo, 1935-36; fellow in anatomy, in charge of operations, The Wistar Inst., 1936-38, exec. dir. and asso. mem. in anatomy, 1938-58, cons., mem., 1959—; prof. anatomy, Pa. Academy Fine Arts; visiting lecturer grad. school medicine Univ. Pa.; member film commn. Wistar Institute; director The Farris Institute for Parenthood. Citation Outstanding Medical Research, Buffalo U. 1956. Member Society Phys. Anthropology, Soc. Panamenade Obstetrics and Gynec., Brazilian Soc. Sterility (corr. mem.), Am. Assn. Anatomists, Am. Soc. for Study of Sterility, Internat. Association Medical Museums, Physiol. Society Philadelphia, Biological Photographical Association, (director, pres., 1947-49), N.Y. Acad. Scis. (fellow), American Soc. Zoologists, A.A.A.S., Phi Beta Kappa, Sigma Xi. Mason (K.T.). Special award from Nat. Research Found. for Alleviation of Human Sterility, 1945; Ann. award, Am. Urol. Assn., 1949. Author textbooks. Co-author (and co-editor with J. Q. Griffith): Care and Breeding of Lab. Animals, 1950; Human Fertility and Problems of the Male, 1950; Human Ovulation and Fertility, 1956. Contbr. to, also editor sci. jours. Home: 329 Bala Av., Bala-Cynwyd, Pa. Address: The Wistar Inst., 36th St. and Woodland Av.; Farris Inst., 133 S. 36th St., Phila. Died Apr. 13, 1961; buried McClellanville, S.C.

FARROW, EDWARD SAMUEL, cons. engr.; b. Snow Hill, Md., Apr. 20, 1855; s. William H. and Catherine A. F.; A.B., Baltimore City Coll., 1872; grad. U.S. Mil. Acad., 1876; m. Elizabeth E. Downing, 1897. Commd. 2d lt., 21st Inf., June 15, 1876; 1st lt., Sept. 17, 1883; instr. tactics, U.S. Mil. Acad., 1880-85; resigned from army, Feb. 24, 1892. Served against Indians in Ore., Mont., Dak. and Wash. Ty.; captured the hostile Sheep-Eater Indians, in Salomon Mountains, Ida., 1879, and was recommended for brevets "for conspicuous bravery, energy and soldierly conduct" in Nez Perce, Bannock, Piute and other Indian campaigns. Engring. operations include exploration of mining dists. in eastern Ore. and northwestern Ida.; ry. constn. and timber operations in Adirondacks; surveys and reports on Appalachian fields on Va.; exams. and reports on gold and copper deposits in Black Hills of S.D., mica deposits of Me., arsenical ore deposits in Putnam Co., N.Y., mineral deposits in Bland Co., Va., also reports on Panama Canal and Canal Zone, etc. Founder of Farrow Pub. Library, Pinewald, and Pinewald Mil. Camp of Instrn. Episcopalian. Author: American Small Arms, 1904; West Point and the Military Academy, 1900; Camping on the Trail, 1902; Dictionary of Military Terms, 1917; Farrow's Manual of Military Training, 1919; Riots and Riot Duty, 1919; Gas Warfare, 1919; American Guns in the War with Germany, 1919. Compiler: Farrow's Military Ency. (3 vols.), 1885; owner and editor Pinewald Bull. (newspaper advocating peace). Inventor of toxic gases and gas grenade; discoverer of gravity control by intensification of Hertsian waves. Home: Pinewald, N.J. Died Sept. 25, 1926.

FAST, GUSTAVE, cons. engr.; b. Sweden, May 18, 1884; s. Johan P. and Maria Charlotta (Swenson) F.; ed. Chalmers Tech. Coll., Goteborg, Sweden, 1900-04, City and Guild Tech. Coll., London, Eng., 1904-06; m. Ganna Kjaergaard-Nielsen, Aug. 23, 1929; 1 son, Jon Gustave Viking. Came to U.S., 1910, naturalized, 1924. Mech. engr. Gwynne's, Ltd., London, Eng., 1906-07, Atlas Iron Works, Birmingham, Eng., 1908-09, Swedish State Ry., 1909-10, Worthington Pump & Machinery Co., Harrison, N.J., 1910-12, Crown Cork & Seal Co., Baltimore, 1912-15, Poole Engine & Machine Co.,

Baltimore, 1915-25, Bartlett Hayward Co., Baltimore, since 1919, pres. Gustave Fast Engring. Co., Annapolis, since 1931; pres. The Fast Bearing Co., Annapolis, since 1936; cons. engr. Koppers Co., Baltimore, since 1919. Fellow Am. Soc. M.E. Awarded John Price Wetherill medal by Franklin Inst. for "discovery and invention in the physical sciences," 1929; "Modern Pioneer" plaque, by Am. Assn. Mfrs., 1939. Club: Cosmos (Washington, D.C.). Home: Salisbury, Md. Office: Gustave Fast Engineering Co., Annapolis, Md. Died May 9, 1946; buried at Goteborg, Sweden.

FASTEN, NATHAN, prof. zoölogy; b. Austria, Dec. 4, 1887; s. Schneier and Jane (Drillman) F.; brought to U.S., 1889, naturalized, 1896; B.S., Coll. City of New York, 1910; Ph.D., U. of Wis., 1914; m. Frieda Mayer, June 18, 1916; children—Janet Rebecca (Mrs. Leon Benson Levy), Marion (Mrs. Alexander Grinstein), Natalie (Mrs. Gilbert E. Rosenwald, Jr.), Head dept. of biology, Marshall College, Huntington, W.Va., 1910-11; asst. instr. zoölogy U. Wis., 1911-14; instr., asst. prof. zoölogy U. Wash., 1914-20; asso. prof. zoölogy and physiology Ore. State Coll., 1920-21, prof., head dept., 1921-45; chief biologist, chief tech. div. Wash. Pollution Control Commn., 1945-50, ret. chief biologist, cons. biologist, 1950—; summer work as asst. U.S. Bur. Fisheries, Woods Hole, Mass., 1911, investigator Wis. Fish Commn., 1912, 13, 14, Wash. Fish Commn., 1919, Ore. Fish and Game Commn., 1923, in charge invertebrate zoölogy Puget Sound Biol. Sta., 1915, 16, 20, charge animal biology B.C. Summer Session for Tchrs. 1922, 23; spl. investigator Oyster Culture and Pollution Problems, Pacific Spruce Corp., 1927-28; chmn. Ore. Basic Sci. Exam. Com., 1934-45. Fellow A.A.A.S.; mem. Am. Soc. Zoölogists, Am. Soc. Naturalists, Genetics Soc. Am., Western Soc. Naturalists (pres. 1924-25), Sigma Xi, Phi Kappa Phi, Gamma Sigma Delta, Phi Sigma. Jewish religion. Clubs: B'nai B'rith, Seattle Lodge, Mens, Temple de Hirsch. Author: Origin Through Evolution, 1929; Principles of Genetics and Eugenics, 1935; Principles of General Zoölogy, 1938; Introduction to General Zoölogy, 1941; General Zoölogy Laboratory Outlines, 1941; also articles profl. jours. Home: 2504 25th Av. N., Seattle 2. Died Sept. 19, 1953; buried Seattle.

FAUCETTE, WILLIAM DOLLISON, (faw-set), civil engr.; b. Halifax, N.C., June 27, 1881; s. Charles William and Florence Relinda (Dickens) F.; B.E., N.C. State Coll., Raleigh, N.C., 1901, C.E., 1910, D. Sc., 1929; m. Belle Edwards Nash, Nov. 11, 1908; children—Ellen Nash (Mrs. W. E. Black, Jr.), Florence Wilcox (Mrs. J. L. Weller, Jr.), Belle Dollison. Began with Seaboard Air Line Ry., 1901, and served as asst. engr., in Savannah office and adjacent region until 1906; in chief engineer's office, 1906-10, chief clk. to pres., 1910-12; chief engr., all Seaboard Air Line Railway System 1913-44; executive rep. of receivers, Seaboard Airline Railway System, 1944-46, executive, representative of receivers and chairman of committee, for Research and Planning, Seaboard Air Line Railroad Co. since 1946. Del. for Va., at Southern Forestry Congress, 1923-26; official del. for Ga., to Southern Appalachian Power Conf., Chattanooga, Tenn., 1927; on council American Inst. Weights and Measures; chmn. Joint Comm. on Metric System, Assn. Am. R.R. (mem. spl. com. on grade crossing elimination; railroad com. to study post-war transportation); chmn. zone 3, Assn. Am. R.A. com. on Waterway Projects. For many yrs. mem. exec. com. U. of N.C. (former trustee). Mem. Norfolk (Va.) City Council com. on higher edn. Mem. bd. dirs. Central Y.M.C.A., Travelers Aid Society, Norfolk. Mem. Am. Ry. Engring. Assn. (past pres.); mem. spl. com. on uniform gen. control forms and cooperative relations with univs., waterways and harbors, Am. Soc. C.E. (ex-pres. Va.), N.C. Soc. Engrs., Phi Kappa Phi, Tau Beta Pi. Democrat. Episcopalian (vestryman St. Andrews Church, Norfolk). Mason. Clubs: Engrs. of Hampton Roads; Norfolk German (past pres.), Norfolk Yacht and Country, Virginia (Norfolk, Va.). Home: 1024 Graydon Av. Office: 756 Seaboard Air Line Railroad, General Office Bldg., Norfolk, Va. Died May 19, 1947.

FAWCETT, HOWARD S(AMUEL) (faw'set), plant pathologist; b. Salem, O., Apr. 12, 1877; s. Thomas F. and Sidney Ann (Bonsall) F.; B.S., Ia. State Coll., 1905; M.S., U. of Fla., 1908; Ph.D., Johns Hopkins, 1918; m. T. Helen Tostenson, Sept. 15, 1909; 1 dau., Rosamond Annette. Asst. prof. botany and horticulture, U. of Fla., 1905-06; plant pathologist Fla. Agrl. Expt. Sta., 1906-11, Calif. Commn. of Horticulture, 1911-13; asso. prof. plant pathology, U. of Calif., 1913-18, prof. since 1918; collaborator for U.S. Dept. Agr. for study of citrus and date diseases, N. Africa and Mediterranean lands, 1929-30. Fellow A.A.A.S.; mem. Bot. Soc. America, Phytopathol. Soc. (pres. 1930), Am. Soc. Naturalists, Western Soc. Naturalists, Phi Beta Kappa, Sigma Xi. Mem. Soc. Friends—Quakers (went to Russia to aid their relief work 1922). Author: Citrus Diseases and Their Control (used by the citrus industry as authority), 1926; revised, 1936; also many scientific papers and bulletins. Home: 3594 Larchwood Pl. Address: Citrus Experiment Station, Riverside, Calif. Died Dec. 12, 1948.

FAXON, WILLIAM OTIS II, engineer; born Stoughton, Mass., Oct. 19, 1910; s. Nathaniel W. and Marie B. (Conant) F.; A.B., Harvard, 1932, M.S., 1933; m. Frances Parker, Sept. 27, 1941; children—David, Susan, Thomas, Roger. Instr. Harvard, 1933-35; comptroller Dorr Co., 1935-42; v.p. Harrison Abrasive Corp., 1946-52, also dir.; v.p. Metals Disintegrating Co., 1952-54; exec. v.p. Tracer Lab., Inc., Boston, 1954-56, dir., 1954-57, pres., 1956-57; pres. Keleket X-Ray Corp., 1956-57, dir., 1954-57, exec. v.p., dir. Comstock & Wescott, Inc., 1957-67, pres., dir., 1967-68. Selectman, Town of Concord. Dir. Manchester (N.H.) Community Chest, 1946-52, Boys Club. Served as lt. comdr. USNR, 1942-46. Registered profl. engr., N.H., Mass. Mem. Harvard Engring. Soc. (sec. 1940-42), Am. Soc. Metals, Am. Soc. Engring. Scis., Am. Metal Powder Inst. Conglist. Home: Concord MA Died Dec. 31, 1968.

FAY, ALBERT HILL, mining engr.; b. Appleton City, Mo., Mar. 12, 1871; s. L. Lankton and Adeline (Hill) F.; B.S., Mo. Sch. of Mines, 1902, E.M., 1905; A.M., Columbia, 1907; m. Clara Louise Constable, Nov. 4, 1908; 1 son, Albert Hill. Engr. with Greene Consolidated Copper Co., Cananea, Mex., 1903-05; prospecting and development, Bartel's Tin Mining Co., Alaska, 1906-07; mining engr. with John T. Williams & Son, Bristol, Tenn., 1907-08; editorial staff Engineering and Mining Journal, New York, 1908-11; editor Mineral Industry, 1911; with U.S. Bur. Mines, 1911-20; valuation engr. and head of natural resources div., Income Tax Unit, Internal Revenue Bur., Treas. Dept., specializing in petroleum, 1920-23; cons. mining engr., 1923-25; asst. editor Engineering Mining Journal-Press, New York, 1925-27; cons. engr. U.S.S.R., 1929-30; now cons. mining engr. and asst prof. mining engring., Lafayette Coll., Easton, Pa. Sec. mining sect. Pan-Am. Scientific Congress, Washington, 1915. Republican. Conglist. Author: Glossary of the Mining and Mineral Industry (20,000 terms and words), 1920. Home: Easton, Pa. Died Aug. 7, 1937.

FAY, FREDERIC HAROLD, civil engr.; b. Marlboro, Mass., July 5, 1872; s. John Sawyer and Elizabeth (Ingalls) F.; S.B., Mass. Inst. Tech., 1893; M.S., 1894; m. Clara May Potter, Apr. 21, 1897; children—Allen Potter (dec.), Beatrice, Mildred E., Dorothy C., Eleanor P., Elizabeth. Transitman, with city engr., Marlboro, Mass., summer, 1892; draftsman Boston Bridge Works, summer, 1894; city engr.'s office, Boston, as draftsman and asst. engr. in charge design and constrn. of city's bridges, 1895-1911; engr. in charge bridge and ferry div. Pub. Works Dept., Boston, 1911-14 (resigned), also commr. for Boston on Boston and Cambridge Bridge Commn.; mem. Fay, Spofford & Thorndike, cons. engrs., since June 1914. Served as cons. engr. for railroads, Federal, State and provincial authorities, municipalities, etc., in U.S. and abroad, and as engr. to War Dept. on design and supervision of Boston army base, 1918-19, and Newfoundland and other northern army bases since 1940, also jointly with other firms, engr. to Navy Dept. on design of dry docks and Navy Yard improvements since 1940; former chmn. Boston City Planning Bd. and vice chmn. Met. Planning Div. of Mass.; chmn. Boston Bd. Zoning Adjustment; mem. Mass. State Planning Board, N.E. Regional Planning Commn. and Nat. Conf. of City Planning (dir. 1931-34); alumni mem. Corp. Mass. Inst. Tech. 1914-19; trustee Northeastern Univ., Dorchester Savings Bank. Fellow Am. Acad. Arts and Sciences, A.A.A.S.; mem. Am. Inst. Cons. Engrs. (pres. 1927), Am. Soc. C.E., Engring. Inst. of Canada, Boston Soc. C.E. (pres. 1913-14), Engineers Soc. Western Mass., N.E. Water Works Assn., Am. Concrete Inst., Internat. Assn. Navigation Congresses, Mass. Highway Assn., Mass. Charitable Mechanics' Assn., Boston Chamber Commerce (ex-v.p. and chmn. com. on municipal and met. affairs), Alumni Assn. Mass. Inst. Tech. (pres. 1913). Life mem. and dir. Am. Unitarian Assn.; v.p. Unitarian Laymen's League. Clubs: Union, Engineers, Boston City, Wollaston Golf (Boston); Engineers, Technology (New York). Compiler of "The Population and Finances of Boston," 1901. Home: 227 Savin Hill Av., Dorchester. Office: 11 Beacon St., Boston, Mass. Died June 5, 1944.

FAY, HENRY, chemist; b. Williamsburg, Pa., Jan. 12, 1868; s. John (M.D.) and Sarah C. F.; A.B., Lafayette Coll., 1889, A.M., 1892, hon. D.Sc., 1915; Ph.D., Johns Hopkins, 1895; m. Marie F. Phelps, of Boston, Sept. 19, 1908; 1 dau., Margery. Instr. chemistry, Johns Hopkins, 1893-95; instr. analytical chemistry, 1895-1900, asst. prof., 1900-05, asso. prof., 1905-07, prof., 1907-20, prof. anal. chemistry and metallography, 1920, Mass. Inst. Tech., retired, 1926. Consulting chemist Gillette Safety Razor Company, 1905-12; consulting metallurgist Winchester Repeating Arms Co., 1916-20, and U.S. Arsenal, Watertown, Mass., 1906-19; lecturer at U.S. Mil. Acad. and U.S. Naval Acad., 1919. Republican. Unitarian. Fellow Am. Acad. Arts and Sciences; mem. Am. Chem. Soc., British Iron and Steel Inst., Inst. of Metals, Phi Kappa Psi. Author: Microscopic Examination of Steel; An Advanced Course in Quantitative Analysis, 1917. Contbr. articles on chemistry and metallography to various jours. Home: 11 Worthington Rd., Brookline, Mass. *

FAY, IRVING WETHERBEE, prof. chemistry; b. Natick, Mass., Nov. 3, 1861; s. Gilbert Park and Laura Sophia (Brigham) F.; A.B., magna cum laude, Harvard, 1886; Ph.D., U. of Berlin, 1897; m. Elizabeth Webster Schwefel, Aug. 18, 1897; 1 dau., Ernestine (Mrs. Herbert Thompson Scott). Instr. in sciences, Montpelier (Vt.) Sem., 1886-87; instr. in chemistry and physics, Belmont (Calif.) Sch., 1887-93; prof. chemistry, Ohio U., 1896-97; prof. chemistry, Poly. Inst. of Brooklyn, 1897—. Fellow Brooklyn Inst. Arts and Sciences (pres. dept. chemistry). Republican. Conglist. Author: Coal Tar Dyes, 1910. Home: Brooklyn, N.Y. Died 1936.

FAY, TEMPLE, neurol. surgeon; b. Seattle, Jan. 9, 1895; s. John Purinton and Alice Isabelle (Ober) F.; B.S., U. Wash., 1917; M.D., U. Pa., 1921; m. Marion Hutchinson Button, June 8, 1923; children—Jane Dundas (Mrs. Quinley R. Schulz), Alice Amelia (Mrs. Robert Hutton), Marion Biddle (Mrs. David C. Henry), Marie-Louise (Mrs. Samuel R. Hazlett). Resident physician, U. Pa. Hosp., 1920-23, neurologist, 1922-29; asst. instr. in neurology, Sch. Medicine, U. Pa., 1923-25, asso. in neurology, 1927-29; prof. neurosurgery, Sch. Medicine, Temple U., 1929-36, prof., head dept. neurology, neurosurgery, 1936-43; prof. neurosurgery Women's Med. Coll. Pa., 1949-54; chief neurosurgeon Temple U. Hosp., 1929-43; neurologist Phila. Gen. Hosp.; hon. neuro-surg. cons. Phila. Gen. Hosp.; neuro-surg. cons. Meml. Hosp., Sarasota, Fla.; med. cons. Pa. Bur. Vocational Rehab.; sr. neuro-surg. cons. U.S. Naval Hosp., Phila. Dir. D. J. McCarthy Found. for Investigation Nervous and Mental Diseases, 1928-42; dir. Temple U. Med. Sch. unit for investigation malignancy, Internat. Cancer Research Found. grant, 1935-37. Served with Med. Enlisted Res. Corps and S.A.T.C. during World War I, med. officer base No. 17, Coastal Patrol, 1942-43; mem. U.S.C.G. Aux., 1942—. Mem. Bd. Appeals Selective Service, Eastern Jud. Area, Pa.; mem. med. adv. com. Nat. Hdqrs. Civil Air Patrol, rank of lt. col.; wing med. officer, Pa. Civil Air Patrol; owner patrol plane lost in action off N.Y. Harbor, 1942. Recipient Gold Medal award, Class A, Sci. Exhibit, A.M.A., 1929, spl. award of merit, 1935. Dir. Neuro-Phys. Rehab. Clinic. Mem. med. adv. com. Nat. Soc. for Crippled Children and Adults (also Pa. Soc.). Co-founder Harvey Cushing Soc. (pres. 1937), Am. Acad. Cerebral Palsy, 1947; research council United Cerebral Palsy Assn., Inc.; bd. dirs., vice chmn. brs. S.E. chpt. A.R.C. Vice pres. Internat. League Against Epilepsy (pres. Am. chpt. 1937). Diplomate Nat. Bd. Med. Examiners. Fellow A.C.S., Soc. Neurol. Surgeons; mem. Internat. Coll. Surgeons, Am. Neurol. Assn., Am. Psychiat. Assn., A.M.A., Pan-Am., Phila. County med. assns., Phila. Neurol. Soc., Phila. Psychiat. Soc. Royal Soc. Medicine, Assn. Research in Nervous and Mental Diseases, Am. Bd. Neurol. Surgery, Pa. Soc. S.R., Phi Kappa Psi, Nu Sigma Nu, Alpha Omega Alpha, Sigma Xi. Clubs: Country, University, Art Alliance, Art, Pylon, Union League, Rotary, Phila. Cricket (Phila.); Gibson Island Yacht, Rock Hall Yacht, Sportsman Pilot Assn. Contbr. numerous med. papers and articles to sci. publs.; also author: My First Baby, 1933; serial (Sat. Eve. Post), Ambulance Anecdotes, 1932. Home: 7304 Elbow Lane, Philadelphia 19. Office: 8811 Germantown Av., Chestnut Hill, Pa. Died Mar. 7, 1963; buried Ivy Hill Cemetery, Mount Airy, Pa.

FEDERSPIEL, MATTHEW NICHOLAS, (fed'er-spel), plastic and maxillo-facial surgeon; b. Lincoln, Kewaunee Co., Wis., Sept. 15, 1879; s. Peter and Kathryn (Forster) F.; D.D.S., Milwaukee Medical Sch., 1900; M.D., Marquette U., 1910, B.S., 1912; m. Bertha Agatha Knocke, June 24, 1903. Practiced at Milwaukee since 1910; prof. oral and maxillo-facial surgery, Dental Sch. Marquette U.; prof. plastic and maxillo-facial surgery, Med. Sch. Marquette U.; plastic and facial surgery, Milwaukee Hosp., St. Joseph's and St. Michael's Hosps. Fellow Am. Coll. Surgeons, Am. Coll. Dentists; mem. Am. Board Surgery, A.M.A., Am. Bd. Plastic Surgery, Am. Dental Assn., Wis. Acad. Dentists, Am. Soc. Orthodontists, Am. Assn. Ry. Surgeons, Wis. State and Milwaukee County med. societies, Wis. State Dental Soc., Milwaukee Acad. Medicine (life mem.). Republican. Roman Catholic. Elk. Author: Harelip and Cleft Palate, 1927; numerous articles in med. and dental publs. Address: 1403 N. Astor St., Milwaukee. Died Sept. 6, 1951; buried Holy Cross Cemetery, Racine, Wis.

FEIKER, FREDERICK MORRIS, (fi'ker), engineer, univ. dean; b. Northampton, Mass., June 14, 1881; s. Frederick Christian and Fanny Barnes (Thayer) F.; B.S. in E.E., Worcester Poly. Institute, 1904, hon. E.D., Worcester Poly. Inst., 1938; M.S. in textile, tech. (hon.), Lowell Textile Inst., 1953—; married Elizabeth Baker Campbell, Oct. 3, 1906; children—Elizabeth Stuart (Mrs. Carl S. Weist), Capt. Frederick Christian (killed in action), Gretchen, Janet (Mrs. Robert J. Delaney), Barbara Jean (Mrs. H. Franklin Barrus, Jr.), George Campbell William Gordon. Technical journalist, General Electric Co., 1906-07; editor Factory Magazine, Chicago, 1907-09; chairman editorial board "System," and Factory Mag., 1912-15; editor of Electrical World New York, 1915-18; v.p. McGraw-Hill Co., Inc. (pubs. of tech. and industrial jours.), 1920-23; leave of absence as asst. to Sec. of Commerce, Herbert Hoover, 1921; spl. agt. Bur. Foreign and Domestic Commerce, 1922; expert consultant Dept. of Commerce; operating v.p. Society for Elec. Development, 1923-26; mng. dir. Associated Business Papers, Inc., 1927-31; dir. U.S. Bur. Foreign and Domestic Commerce, 1931-33; ednl. consultant for Textile Foundation since 1936; elected executive sec. Am. Engring. Council, 1934; dean Sch. Engring., George Washington U., 1939, dean emeritus, 1952;

cons. management, government and industry; dir. Northampton Cutlery Co., Mass.; dir., research cons. Ward Motor Vehicle Co., Mount Vernon, N.Y. Chairman adv. com., Census of Distribution, Dept. of Commerce of U.S. Lecturer and organizer course in industrial management, Grad. Sch. of Business, Harvard, 1909, 10. Chairman div. of industrial and engring. research of the Nat. Research Council, Washington, 1946-48. Mem. Nat. Inventors' Council, U.S. Dept. of Commerce, 1940. Fellow Am. Inst. Elec. Engrs.; mem. Am. Soc. Mech. Engrs., A.A.A.S., Soc. Advancement Management, Washington Society of Engineers, American Society for Engineering Education, Sigma Alpha Epsilon, Sigma Xi, Sigma Tau, Theta Tau, Phi Psi, Omicron Delta Kappa. Republican. Congregationalist. Clubs: Engineers (N.Y.C.); Rotary (hon.), Cosmos (Washington). Editor: The Sphere, Williamsburg, Mass. Home: Box 301, Williamsburg, Mass. Died Jan. 13, 1967; buried Northampton.

FEJOS, PAUL, (fay ush), anthropologist; b. Budapest, Hungary, Jan. 24, 1897; s. Desiré Emery and Aurora (Novelty) F.; M.D., Royal Hungarian Med. University, Budapest, 1921; m. Lita Sophia Binns, 1958. Came to the United States of Am., 1922, naturalized, 1930. Research technician Rockefeller Inst. Med. Research, 1923-26; motion picture dir. Universal, Metro-Goldwyn-Mayer Studios, Hollywood, Cal., 1926-30; producer, dir. films, including ethnographical films, Africa, East Indies, Far East; dir. Danish Ethnographic Expdn. to Madagascar, also Seychelles Archipelago, 1934-36; field collector ethnographic div. Nat. Museum, Copenhagen, 1935-37; dir. Swedish Film Industry Ethnographic Expdn. to East Indies, also Siam, 1936-38; dir. Wenner-Gren Sci. expdn. to Hispanic Am., 1939-41; hon. prof. U. Cuzco Peru 1941; dir. research Wenner-Gren Found. for Anthrop. Research (formerly The Viking Fund), 1955-63, pres., 1955-63; consulting professor anthropology Stanford University, 1943-63; professorial lectr. anthropology Yale, 1949-51, acting dir. S.E. Asia studies, 1951; asso. in anthropology Columbia, 1951-52. Mem. bd. dirs. Electrolux Corp., 1957-63. Decorated Knight Comdr. Order of Sun (Peru); awarded Orellana Medal, Geog. Soc. Lima, Peru, 1943; Golden Medal, Italy, 1958; Commander Cross, Austrian Medal of Honor, 1960. Honorary fellow Royal Anthrop. Inst.; fellow A.A.A.S., Am. Anthrop. Assn., New York Academy of Medicine, New York Academy Sciences (chmn. sect. anthropology 1950-51, pres. 1954); mem. Am. Acad. Polit. and Social Sci., Am. Assn. Phys. Anthropologists, Am. Ethnol. Soc. Am. Soc. Human Genetics, Society of American Archeology, Institute of Human Paleontology, Austrian Acad. Scis. (hon.). Author: Ethnography of the Yagua, 1944; Archeological Explorations in the Cordillera Vilcabamba, Peru, 1944. Office: 14 E. 71st St., N.Y.C. 10021. Died Apr. 23, 1963.

FELGAR, JAMES HUSTON, mechanical engr.; b. Stuart, Ia., July 27, 1874; s. David and Margaret (Huston) F.; A.B., U. of Kan., 1901; B.S., Armour Institute Technology (now Illinois Institute of Technology), Chicago, 1905, M.E., 1911, honorary Dr. Engring. 1929; m. Etta Judd, 1906. Instr. mech. engring., Okla. Agrl. and Mech. Coll., 6 mos., 1906; instr. mech. engring., coll. of engring., U. of Okla., 1906-08, prof., 1908-37, dean coll. of engring., 1909-37, dean emeritus and prof engring. since 1937. Mem. Am. Soc. M.B., Okla. Soc. Engrs. (ex-pres.), Okla. Society Professional Engrs., Soc. Promotion Engring. Edn., Phi Betta Kappa, Tau Beta Pi, Sigma Tau, Beta Theta Pi, Lions Internat. (ex-pres.). Presbyterian. Home: 743 De Barr Av., Norman, Okla. Died July 19, 1946.

FELLER, WILLIAM, educator; b. Zagreb, Yugoslavia, July 7, 1906; s. Eugene V. and Ida (Perc) F.; M.S., Zagreb Univ., 1925; Ph.D., Gottingen Univ., 1926; m. Clara Mary Nielsen, July 27, 1938. Came to U.S., 1939, naturalized, 1944. In charge of applied math. lab., Univ. of Kiel, 1929-33; research asso., Univ. of Stockholm, 1933-39; asso. prof. and exec. editor, Math. Reviews, Brown Univ., 1939-45; prof. Cornell Univ., 1945-50; Eugene Higgins prof. of math., Princeton Univ., from 1950; consulting and war work; visiting prof. at Rockefeller University. Recipient Nat. medal Science, 1970. Honorary fellow Royal Statistical Society; foreign associate of the Royal Danish Academy; member of National Acad. Scis., Internat. Inst. Statistics American Math. Soc., Am. Acad. Arts Scis., London Math. Soc. (hon.), Inst. Math. Statistics (pres. 1949), Yugoslav Acad. Sciences, Am. Philos. Soc. Former editor Math. Review. Contbr. articles on probability statistics, geometry, differential equations, real variables, etc. Address: Princeton NJ Died Jan. 14, 1970.

FELSING, WILLIAM AUGUST, chemist; b. Denton, Tex., May 19, 1891; s. William and Anna Judith (Kurner) F.; A.B., U. of Texas, A.M., 1916; Ph.D., Mass. Inst. Tech., 1918; m. Stella Elizabeth Scorgie, Sept. 8, 1920; children—Barbara Ann, William August. Asst. prof. chemistry, U. of Texas, asso. prof., now prof., part-time research scientist, defense research lab.; with Underwater Sound Lab., Harvard, Mar.-Nov. 1943. Served as 1st lt., later capt., Chem. Warfare Service, U.S. Army, Mar.-Dec. 1918; engaged in making poison gas Edgewood Arsenal. Mem. Tex. Acad. Sciences, Am. Chem. Soc., Sigma Xi, Phi Lambda Upsilon, Phi Beta Kappa, Acacia. Mason. Author: Notes on Descriptive Chemistry, 1928; General Chemistry (with E. P. Schoch and G. W. Watt) 1938; (revised edit. 1946). Contbr. more than 50 research articles to sci. jours. Home: 3007 Washington Square, Austin 21, Tex. Died Oct. 5, 1952; buried Austin Meml. Park, Austin, Tex.

FELT, CHARLES FREDERICK WILSON, civil engr.; b. Salem, Mass., Apr. 29, 1864; s. Charles Wilson and Martha Seeth (Ropes) F.; B.S., Mass. Agrl. Coll., 1886; m. Clara C. Root, Apr. 6, 1904. Axman, rodman and bridge engr., A.,T.&S.F. Ry., 1886-88; levelman, D.&R.G. Ry., Feb.-May 1888; instrument-man, Ariz. & Southeastern R.R., 1888-89; transitman, Topolobampo Ry., Mex., 1889-90; resident engr., Gulf, Colo. & Santa Fe Ry., at Cleburne, Tex., 1890-92; office engr. Rio Grande Southern Ry., 1892-93; div. engr. Gulf, Colo. & Santa Fe Ry., Feb.-May 1893; resident engr. same rd., Galveston, Tex., 1893-96, chief engr., 1896-1909; chief engr., A.,T.&S.F. Ry., 1909-13, and of entire system, 1913—. Home: Chicago, Ill. Died Feb. 4, 1928.

FELT, DORR EUGENE, inventor; b. Beloit, Wis., Mar. 18, 1862; s. Eugene Kincaid and Elizabeth (Morris) F.; ed. pub. schs., Beloit; m. Agnes McNulty, Jan. 15, 1891; children—Virginia, Elizabeth, Constance, Dorothea. Inventor first key operator calculating machines, also first practical adding and listing machines; organized firm Felt & Tarrant, 1886, to manufacture his inventions, and in 1887 inc. Felt & Tarrant Mfg. Co., of which is pres. Regional adviser War Industries Bd., for Ill., Ind. and Ia. (Region No. 9), 1918; mem. Employers' Commn., by appmt. of Sec. of Labor William B. Wilson, and sent to Eng. to study and report on labor conditions and governmental policies in Great Britain, 1919. Dir. Chicago Assn. of Commerce; mem. Chamber of Commerce U.S.A. Republican. Baptist. Home: Chicago, Ill. Died Aug. 7, 1930.

FELT, EPHRALM PORTER, entomologist; b. Salem, Mass., Jan. 7, 1868; s. Charles Wilson and Martha Seeth (Ropes) F.; grad. Mass. Agrl. Coll., 1891; appointed specialist in entomolgy by Gypsy Moth Commn., Mass., S.D., Cornell, 1894; m. Helen Maria Ottetson, June 24, 1896; children—Margaret, Ernest Porter, Helen, Elizabeth. Taught natural sciences, Clinton Liberal Inst., Ft. Plaib, 1893-95; asst. to state entomologist, 1895; acting state entomologist, 1898, state entomologist of N.Y., 1898-1928; dir. and chief entomologist Bartlett Tree Research Labs. since 1928. Published extended work on park and woodland insects, a manual of tree and shrub insects, key to American insect galls, our shade trees, plant galls and gall makers, pruning trees and shrubs, shelter trees in war and peace, 25 official reports, a number of bulletins and many articles in agricultural, horticultural and scientific jours. Hon. editor Jour. of Econ. Entomology. Collaborator U.S. Bur. of Entomology, New York State Museum. Emeritus life mem. A.A.A.S.; fellow Entomol. Soc. of America; mem. Am. Assn. Econ. Entomologists (pres. 1902), Conn. Tree Protective Assn. (pres.), Entomol. Soc. Washington, N.Y. Entomol. Soc., Sigma Xi; hon. mem. Entomol. Soc. Ontario. Chief Entomologist, Gypsy Moth Bur., N.Y. State Conservation Commn., 1923-24. Co-author: (with W. H. Rankin) Insects and Diseases of Ornamental Trees and Shrubs. Address: Stamford, Conn. Died Dec. 14, 1943.

FELTON, SAMUEL MORSE, civil engr., railroad exec.; b. Newbury, Mass., July 17, 1809; s. Cornelius and Anna (Morse) F.; grad. Harvard, 1834; m. Eleanor Stetson, 1836; m. 2d, Maria Lippitt, 1850. Engr. for Loammie Baldwin, Jr., 1836, took over business after Baldwin's death, 1838; built Fresh Pond R.R. to transport ice into Boston, 1841; began constrn. Fichtburg R.R., 1843, supt., 1845; pres. Phila., Wilmington & Balt. R.R., 1851-64 (important in Civil War Union troops movements); officially commended by War Dept. for his role in transporting Gen. Butler's troops to Annapolis and preparing plans for cooperation of all railroads centering in Phila.; commr. Hoosac Tunnel, 1862-65; pres. Pa. Steel Co., 1865; organizer, dir. N.P. R.R. Died Jan. 24, 1889.

FENN, GEORGE KARL, physician; b. Ashland, Wis., Oct. 30, 1890; s. Clarence Christian and Catherine Mary (Ryder) F.; M.D., Northwestern U., 1913; m. Vera Eleanor Wallace, June 4, 1918; children—Elizabeth Wallace, George Karl. Intern St. Luke's Hosp., Chgo., 1913-15, sr. attending physician, 1934-59, chief staff, 1943-45, dir. electrocardiograph lab., 1945-59; attending physician emeritus Passavant Meml. Hosp., 1959—; med. research, 1915-17; gen. practice medicine, 1917-25; asso. prof. medicine Northwestern U., 1940-51, prof., 1951-56, prof. medicine emeritus, 1956—. Served as lt., M.C., U.S. Army, 1918-19. Fellow A.C.P.; mem. Inst. Medicine Chgo., Chgo. Soc. Internal Medicine (pres. 1935), Central Soc. Clin. Research, Am. Heart Assn. (dir.), Chgo. Heart Soc. (pres. 1947), Sigma Xi. Republican. Club: University (Chgo.). Home: 5807 Dorchester Av., Chgo. 60637. Office: 122 S. Michigan Av., Chgo. Died Nov. 28, 1960.

FENN, WALLACE OSGOOD, physiologist; b. Lanesboro, Mass., Aug. 27, 1893; s. William Wallace and Faith Huntington (Fisher) F.; A.B., Harvard U., 1914, A.M., 1916, Ph.D., 1919; D.Sc. (hon.), U. Chgo., 1950; Cathedratico Honoraria, U. San Marcos, Peru, 1959; Doctor honoris causa, U. Paris, 1960; D.Sc. (hon.), U. Rochester, 1965; hon. doctorate, U. Libre de Brussels, Belgium, 1965; m. Clara Bryce Comstock, Sept. 9, 1919; children—William Wallace, Ruth, Priscilla, David Bryce. Instr. physiology, Harvard Med. Sch., 1919-22; traveling fellow Rockefeller Inst., 1922-24, prof., chmn. dept. physiology, School Medicine and Dentistry, U. Rochester, 1924-59, asst. dean, 1949-53, asso. dean grad. studies, 1957-58, distinguished univ. prof. physiology, 1961-71; dir. space science center, 1962-66. Pres., 24th Internat. Congress Physiol. Scis., D.C., 1968. Served as 2d lt. Food Division, U.S. Army, and camp nutrition officer, Camp Dodge, 1918-19. Mem.-at-large Div. Biology and Agr., Nat. Research Council 1932-35; mem. com. on med. sci., Research and Development Bd., 1949-52; mem. biol. adv. com., Nat. Sci. Found., chmn. 1953. Recipient; Gold medal award Rochester Med. Alumni, 1958; certificate merit Rochester Acad. Medicine, 1961. Daniel and Florence Guggenheim award Internat. Acad. Astronautics, 1964; Antonio Feltrinelli internat. prize exptl. medicine, Rome, 1964; Distinguished Achievement award Modern Medicine, 1965; Research Achievement award Am. Heart Assn., 1967; Johannes Muller medallion German Physiol. Soc., 1971; Ville de Monaco medal, 1971. Mem. Internat. Union Physiol. Scis. (pres. 1968-71), Can. Physiol. Soc. (hon.), Brit. Physiol. Soc. (hon.), Nat. Inst. of Health (chmn. Physiol. Study Sect. 1947-51), Am. Inst. Biol. Sci. (pres. 1957-58), Am. Philos. Soc. (John F. Lewis prize 1949), A.A.A.S., Nat. Acad. Sciences, Am. Physiol. Soc. (treas. 1936-40, sec. 1942-46, pres. 1946-47), Soc. Experimental Biology and Medicine (pres. 1957-59), British Physiol. Soc., Am. Assn. U. Profs., Internat. Acad. Astronautics, Undersea Med. Soc., Italian Soc. Exptl. Biology, Rochester Museum and Sci. Centers, Am. Acad. Arts and Scis., N.Y. Acad. Scis., Sigma Xi, Alpha Omega Alpha, Harvey Soc. (hon.). Corr. mem. Sociedad de Biologia, Argentina. Unitarian. Club: Cosmos (Washington). Author: Graphical Analysis of Respiratory Gas Exchange, 1955; Handbook of Respiration (2 vols.), 1964. Contbr. numerous articles to sci. jours. Home: Rochester NY Died Sept. 20, 1971; buried Walnut Hill Cemetery, Brookline MA

FENNEMAN, NEVIN M., geologist; b. Lima, O., Dec. 26, 1865; s. William Henry and Rebecca (Oldfather) F.; A.B., Heidelberg Coll., Tiffin, O., 1883; Ph.D., U. of Chicago, 1901; LL.D., Cincinnati, 1940; m. Sarah Alice Glisan, Dec. 26, 1893 (died 1920). Prof. physical sciences, Colo. State Normal Sch. (now Colo. State Coll. of Edn.), 1892-1900; prof. geology U. of Colo., 1902-03, U. of Wis., 1903-07, U. of Cincinnati, 1907-37, emeritus prof. since 1937; asst. geologist, 1901-19, asso. geologist, 1919, geologist, 1924, U.S. Geol. Survey; geologist, Wis. Geol. and Natural History Survey, 1900-02, Ill. State Geol. Survey, 1906-08, Ohio Geol. Survey, 1914-16. Awarded gold medal, Geog. Soc. Chicago, 1938. Fellow A.A.A.S. (v.p., chmn. sec. E., 1923), Geol. Soc. America (pres. 1935); mem. Assn. Am. Geographers (pres. 1918), Am. Soc. Naturalists, Sigma Xi, Phi Beta Kappa (hon.). Mem. Nat. Research Council, 1917-24, 1932-35, chmn. div. of geology and geography, 1922-23. In charge science work on Africa for inquiry preparatory to Paris Peace Conf. Presbyterian. Clubs: Literary of Cincinnati (pres. 1924-25); Cosmos (Washington, D.C.). Author: Physiographic Divisions of the United States; Physiography of Western United States; Physiography of Eastern United States; also numerous government bulls. and scientific papers. Home: 348 Shiloh St. Address: Univ. of Cincinnati, Cincinnati, O. Died July 4, 1945.

FENNER, CLARENCE NORMAN, geologist; b. nr. Paterson, N.J., July 19, 1870; s. William Griff and Elmina Jane (Carpenter) F.; E.M., Sch. of Mines (Columbia), 1892, A.M., Columbia, 1909, Ph.D., 1910. Mining and econ. geol. work in U.S., Can., Mexico, Central and S. A., 1892-1907; petrologist Geophys. Lab., Carnegie Instn., Washington, 1910-37, research asso., 1937-38, engaged on researches in application of physics and chemistry to geology, ret., 1938; expdn. of N.Y. Acad. Sci. on geolog. reconnaissance of P.R., 1914; researches on optical glass for mil. purposes under War Industries Bd. (in charge one of prin. plants), 1917-1918; geologist Nat. Geog. expdn. to Valley of 10,000 Smokes, Alaska, 1919; leader of 2d expdn. sent by Geophys. Lab. to same locality, 1923; geol. investigations in Peru, 1939; rep. of Geol. Soc. Am. on Nat. Research Council, 1925-28 (mem. exec. com. div. geology and geography, 1926-28). Fellow Geol. Soc. Am., Am. Phys. Soc., A.A.A.S.; mem. Am. Inst. Mining and Metall. Engrs., Washington Acad. Scis., N.Y. Acad. Scis., Am. Geophysical Union (chmn. sect. of volcanology, 1933-35), Geol. Soc. of Washington (pres. 1933); fgn. corr. Geol. Soc. of London. Writer of many sci. papers, especially on geol. and volcanological subjects. Club: Cosmos. Home: 64 Broad St., Clifton, N.J. Died 1949.

FENSKE, MERRELL ROBERT, chem. engr.; b. Michigan City, Ind., June 5, 1904; s. William A. and Minna (Glassman) F.; A.B., DePauw U., 1925, D.Sc., 1946; D.Sc., Mass. Inst. Tech., 1928. Research asso. Mass. Inst. Tech., 1928-29; asst. prof. chmn. engring. Pa. State U., 1929-34, asso. prof., 1934-36, prof., 1936-71, in charge Petroleum Refining Lab., 1932, dir. Div. Indsl. Research, 1936-47, head dept. chem. engring., 1959-69; ofcl. investigator and cons. Nat. Def. Research Com., 1941-45; chmn. rev. com. div. chem.

engring. Argonne Nat. Lab., 1962-63; cons. NACA, NASA, AEC, Argonne Nat. Lab.; mem. ad hoc com. chem. warfare and biol. warfare programs Dept. Def.; mem. U.S. nat. com. Seventh World Petroleum Congress; mem. air pollution subcom. Nat. Acad. Scis.-Nat. Acad. Engring. Environmental Studies Bd.; dir. Def. Research and Engring., USAF, Baruch Rubber Survey Com., 1942, Metallurgy Lab., U. Chgo., 1944-45. Recipient Naval Ordnance Devel. award, 1945, Certificate of Merit, OSRD, 1945; Nat. award Am. Soc. Lubrication Engrs., 1966; USAF Systems Command certificate of Merit; Mayo D. Hersey award, 1970. Fellow Am. Inst. Chemists, Inst. Petroleum (London) (Redwood medal 1964), Royal Soc. Arts; mem. Soc. Chem. Industry, Am. Soc. M.E., Am. Soc. Lubrication Engrs., A.A.A.S., Nat. Acad. Engring., Am. Assn. U. Profs., Am. Petroleum Inst., Am. Chem. Soc. (past chmn. div. indsl. and engring. chemistry), Am. Soc. Engring. Edn., Soc. Automotive Engrs., Am. Inst. Chem. Engrs., Am. Soc. Testing Materials, Phi Beta Kappa, Tau Beta Pi, Sigma Xi, Phi Lambda Upsilon, Sigma Pi Sigma, Alpha Chi Sigma, Alpha Tau Omega. Club: Chemists (N.Y.). Author chpts., tech. papers and various publs. Home: State College PA Died Sept. 28, 1971; interred Michigan City IN

FENTON, RALPH ALBERT, surgeon; b. Lafayette, Ore., Nov. 5, 1880; s. William David and Katherine (Lucas) Fenton; student University of California, 1899-1901; A.B., University of Oregon, 1903, Sc.D., 1943; M.D., Northwestern University, 1906; married Mabel Copley-Smith, June 24, 1908. Senior house surgeon Ill. Charitable Eye and Ear Infirmary, 1906-07; in practice as eye, ear, nose and throat surgeon, Portland, Ore., since 1907; mem. faculty, U. of Ore. Med. Sch., since 1911, prof. and head. dept. of otolaryngology since 1927; mem. staffs Multnomah County Hosp. since 1911, St. Vincents Hosp. since 1907, Portland Sanitarium, Doernbecher Children's Hosp.; senior partner Fenton, Lupton, Bolton & Titus. Served as 1st lieutenant, captain, maj. Med. Corps, U.S. Army, 1917-19; senior consultant in ophthalmology, 3d Army, A.E.F., 1918-19; now colonel Medical Reserve. Awarded The Casselberry prize by American Laryngological Association (with O. Larsell), 1928; De Roaldes Medal, 1943. Member American Board Otolaryngology since 1927. Fellow Am. Coll. Surgeons; mem. Am. Laryngol. Assn. (pres. 1950), Am. Otol. Soc., Am. Laryngol., Rhinol. and Otol. Soc., Am. Acad. Ophthalmology and Otolaryngology (vice pres. 1927), A.M.A. (trustee 1935-45), Pacific Coast Oto-ophthal. Soc. (pres. 1941), Portland Acad. Medicine (pres. 1931), Portland City and County Med. Soc., Ore. Acad. Ophthalmology and Otolaryngology (pres. 1930), Assn. Mil. Surgeons, Chi Psi, Nu Sigma Nu, Phi Beta Kappa, Sigma Xi, Alpha Omega Alpha. Republican. Protestant. Clubs: Arlington Club, University Club (Portland, Oregon). Contbr. many articles to professional jours.; mem. editorial bd. Archives of Otolaryngology. Home: 13100 S.W. Pacific Hwy., Oswego, Ore. Office: 1020 S.W. Taylor St., Portland 5, Ore. Died Mar. 1960.

FERGUSON, CHARLES EUGENE, obstetrician; b. Indianapolis, Ind., May 29, 1856; s. Norval Wilson and Julia (Rexford) F.; M.D., Med. Coll. of Ind., 1892; Berlin and Vienna, 1907; m. Isabel J. Lamb, of Indianapolis, Feb. 14, 1882. In wholesale dry goods business, 1873-84; teacher histology, Ind. Med. Coll., 1982-96; prof. bacteriology, same, 1896-1907; apptd. clin. prof. obstetrics, Ind. Univ. Sch. of Medicine, 1910, now emeritus prof. obstetrics; attending obstetrician City Hosp.; staff St. Vincent's and Methodist hosps.; formerly supt. City Dispensary, supt. City Hosp., sec. Bd. of Health, Indianapolis. Awarded Mear's medal in obstetrics, 1892. Demonstrated the pollution of the city water supply of Indianapolis, compelling the installation of a complete filter system. Mem. Vol. Med. Service Corps, 1918. Fellow Am. Coll. Surgeons; mem. A.M.A., Ind. State Med. Soc., Indianapolis Med. Soc. (ex-pres.), Phi Rho Sigma, Ind. Hist. Soc., etc. Club: Indianapolis Literary. Address: 3919 Washington Blvd., Indianapolis, Ind. *

FERGUSON, FARQUHAR, M.D.; prof. pathology and clinical medicine and phys., Post-Grad. School and Columbia Hosp., New York, since 1887; b. Sydney, Cape Breton Island, Canada, 1852; ed. Sydney Acad.; grad. L.I. Coll. Hosp., 1880; practices in New York; m. 1890, Juliana, e.d. H. O. Armour. Pathologist, L.I. Coll. Hosp., 1883-85; prof. histology and pathol. anatomy, same, 1883-89; has held various hosp. apptmts.; consulting pathologist, N.Y. bd. of health, 1892; mem. N.Y. Path. Soc.; N.Y. Acad. Med.; N.Y. Mutual Aid Assn.; Alumni Assn. Post-Grad. Med. School; N.Y. Neurolog. Soc. Address: 20 W. 38th St., New York. *

FERGUSON, GEORGE ALBERT, chemist; b. Brooklyn, Aug. 31, 1868; s. David W. and Ellen T. F.; Ph.B., Columbia Sch. Mines, 1890; m. Elsie Loeb, 1893. Examiner med. supplies, etc., U.S. Interior Dept., 1893—; asst. instr., demonstrator, chem. laboratory, prof. analytical chemistry and mathematics, New York Coll. of Pharmacy, 1896—; chemist N.Y. State Bd. of Pharmacy, 1898—; expert in clin. chemistry and toxicology, United Labs. Co., of New York; sr. mem. Ferguson-Hancock Labs., Blue Point, L.I., N.Y.; dir. Ferguson Labs., New York; official chemist Internal Revenue Service, Treas. Dept. Author: Elliott and Ferguson's Qualitative Chemical Analysis. Home: Brooklyn, N.Y. Deceased.

FERGUSON, HENRY GARDINER, geologist; b. San Rafael, Cal., June 21, 1882; s. Henry and Emma J. (Gardiner) F.; B.A., Harvard, 1904, M.A., 1906; Ph.D., Yale, 1923; m. Alice L. Lowe, Sept. 14, 1914. With Cleveland Cliffs Iron Co., Ishpeming, Mich., 1906-07. Phillippine Bur. Sci., 1907-10; geologist U.S. Geol. Survey, Washington, 1911—. Mem. Am. Inst. Mining Engrs., Geol. Soc. Am., Soc. Econ. Geologists (pres.), Geol. Soc. Washington, A.A.A.S. Home: 2330 California St., Washington 8. Office: U.S. Geol. Survey, Washington 25. Died 1966.

FERGUSON, LOUIS ALOYSIUS, electrical engr.; b. Dorchester, Mass., Aug. 19, 1867; s. Denis and Louisa (Doherty) F.; B.S., Mass. Inst. Tech., 1888; m. Martha Sargent Jenkins, June 21, 1892. Joined staff Chicago Edison Co., Aug. 1888, as engr. underground dept., promoted asst. elec. engr. constrn. dept., 1889, elec. engr. of co. 1890, gen. supt. Chicago Edison Co., 1897-1902, and of Commonwealth Elec. Co., 1898-1902; 2d v.p. Chicago Edison Co., and Commonwealth Elec. Co., 1902-07; 2d v.p. Commonwealth Edison Co., 1907-14, v.p., 1914-36. Has done much notable work in central station practice. Apptd. 1895 on staff of lecturers U. of Wis. Catholic. Home: Evanston, Ill. Died Aug. 25, 1940.

FERGUSON, MARGARET CLAY, botanist; b. Phelps, N.Y., Aug. 20, 1863; d. Robert Bell and Hannah Maria (Warner) F.; B.S., Cornell U., 1899, fellow, 1899-1900, Ph.D., 1901; Sc.D., Mount Holyoke College, 1937. Teacher and prin. pub. schs., 1877-86; in charge Dept. of Science, Harcourt Place Sem., Gambier, O., 1892-93; instr. in botany, 1894-96 and 1902-04, asso. prof. and head dept. of botany, 1904-06, prof. and head of dept., 1906-32, now research prof. botany, Wellesley Coll. Asst. in botany, summer, Cornell, 1901, 02, instr., 1903. Fellow A.A.A.S.; mem. Sigma Xi, Bot. Soc. America, California Acad. of Science, Am. Assn. Univ. Profs., Am. Genetic Assn., Am. Soc. Naturalists, Am. Assn. Univ. Women, Science League of America, Mass. Hort. Soc., Eugenics Soc. of U.S., Am. Micros. Soc. (v.p., 1914), Bot. Soc. America (v.p., 1922; pres. 1929). Author of scientific papers dealing with problems in plant physiology, genetics, cytology and comparative morphology. Home: Wellesley, Mass. Died 1951.

FERMI, ENRICO, physicist; b. Rome, Italy, Sept. 29, 1901; s. Alberto and Ida (de Gattis) F.; Doctorate, U. Pisa, 1922; D.S. univs. Heidelberg, 1936, Utrecht, 1936, Columbia, 1946, Washington, 1946, Yale, 1946, Harvard, 1948, Rochester, 1952; LL.D., Rockford Coll., 1947; m. Laura Capon, July 10, 1928; children—Nella, Giullo. Came to U.S., 1939, naturalized, 1945. Lectr. physics U. Florence, 1924-26; prof. theoretical physics U. Rome, 1927-38; prof. physics Columbia, 1939-42; research on atomic bomb U. Chgo., 1942-45, prof. physics Inst. for Nuclear Studies, 1946-54. Recipient Nobel prize, 1938, Hughes medal Royal Soc., 1942, Congl. medal for merit U.S.A., 1946, Barnard medal Columbia, 1950, award of merit Pres. of U.S., AEC, 1954, also numerous others. Fellow Am. Acad. Arts and Scis. (Rumford medal 1953), Royal Soc. Edinburgh; mem. Am. Philos. Soc. (Lewis prize 1946), Nat. Acad. Scis., Franklin Inst. (Franklin medal 1947), Italian Physics Soc., Royal Soc. London, Am. Phys. Soc. (pres. 1953), numerous others. Author: Thermodynamics, 1937; Elementary Particles, 1951, also several books in Italian and articles. Investigated formation of artificial radioactive substances; 1st to bring about nuclear transformations of heavy elements by neutron bombardment, 1934; discovered thermal (or slow) neutrons are more easily absorbed by nucleii than accelerated particles; developed statis. model of atom (Thomas-Fermi model), 1927-28; named neutrino which Pauli had postulated, maintained it has character of real particle, worked out some of math. involved in neutrino emission; responsible for constrn. 1st atomic pile (or nuclear reactor) and 1st self-sustaining chain reaction at U. Chgo., 1942 (marked the beginning of the atomic age); helped develop atom bomb, 1942-45; worked on high energy physics, including pion-nucleon interactions; developed theory of cosmic ray origin; worked on quantum electrodynamics; investigated theory of hyperfine structures of spectrum lines; artificially formed element fermium named in his honor, 1955. Died Chgo., Nov. 28, 1954.

FERNALD, CHARLES HENRY, zoölogist; b. at Mt. Desert, Me., Mar. 16, 1838; s. Eben and Sophronia (Wasgatt) F.; ed. at Me. Wesleyan Sem.; (hon. A.M., Bowdoin, 1871; Ph.D., Me. State Coll., 1886); m. Maria Elizabeth Smith, Aug. 24, 1862; father of Henry Torsey F. Served during Civil War as acting ensign U.S.N.; prin. Litchfield Acad., 1865, Houlton Acad., 1866-71; prof. natural history, Me. State Coll., 1871-86; prof. zoölogy, Mass. Agrl. Coll., and dir. Grad. Sch., 1886-1910. Entomologist to State Bd. of Agriculture. Mem. many scientific socs. U.S. and Europe. Home: Amherst, Mass. Died Feb. 22, 1921.

FERNALD, HENRY TORSEY, entomologist; b. Litchfield, Me., Apr. 17, 1866; s. Prof. Charles Henry and Maria Elizabeth (Smith) F.; B.S., U. Me., 1885, M.S., 1888; Ph.D., Johns Hopkins, 1890; m. Minna R. Simon, of Baltimore, June 9, 1890; children—Helen Elizabeth, Charles Henry, Ruth Louise (Mrs. C. B. Stone). Prof. zoology Pa. State Coll., 1890-99; prof. entomology Mass. Agrl. Coll., 1899-1930, also chmn. sch. sci., 1913-27, dir. grad. sch., 1927-30, retired 1930. State zoologist Pa., 1898-99; state nursery insp. Mass., 1902-18; entomologist Mass. Agrl. Expt. Sta., 1910-30. Fellow A.A.A.S.; mem. Assn. Econ. Entomologists (a founder, pres. 1914), Entomol. Soc. Am., Boston Soc. Natural History, Phi Beta Kappa, Phi Kappa Phi. Mem. Congl.-Christian Ch. Club: Men's University (Winter Park, Fla.). Author: Applied Entomology; also bulls., pamphlets, on zoology and entomology. Address: 1128 Oxford Rd., Winter Park, Fla. Died July 15, 1952; buried Palm Cemetery, Winter Park, Fla.

FERNALD, MERRITT LYNDON, botanist; b. Orono, Me., Oct. 5, 1873; s. Merritt Caldwell and Mary Lovejoy (Heywood) F.; B.S., Harvard, 1897; hon. D.C.L., Acadia U., N.S., 1933; D.Sc., U. Montréal, 1938; m. Margaret Howard Grant, Apr. 15, 1907; children—Katharine, Mary (dec.), Henry Grant. Asst. in Gray Herbarium, Harvard, 1891-1902, curator, 1935-36, dir., 1937—, instr. botany, 1902-05, asst. prof., 1905-15, Fisher prof. natural history 1915-49, prof. emeritus, 1947—. Asso. editor of Rhodora (jour. of N.E. Bot. Club), 1899-1928, editor in chief, 1924—. Writer about 899 bot. papers and monographs. Editor: Gray's Manual of Botany, 7th edit. (with Benjamin L. Robinson). Hon. pres. Internat. Botanical Congress, Stockholm, 1950. Fellow Am. Acad. Arts and Scis. Bot. Soc. American (pres. 1942), A.A.A.S. (v.p. 1941); mem. Societas pro Fauna et Flora Fennica, Am. Soc. Plant Taxonomists (pres. 1938), Am. Philos. Soc., Nat. Acad. Science, N.E. Bot. Club (pres. 1911-14), Acad. Natural Scis. Phila., Conn. Bot. Soc., Phila. Bot. Club, Bot. Soc. and Exchange Club of British Isles, Norske Videnskaps Akademi, Société Linnéane de Lyon, Societas Phytogeographica Suecana (hon.), Royal Soc. Scis. Uppasal (Sweden), Franklin Inst., Phila. (hon.). Pa. Hort. Soc. (hon.), Assn. Am. Geographers, Josselyn Bot. Soc. Me.; fgn. mem. Linnean Soc., London. Recipient Leidy gold medal Acad. Scis. Phila., 1940; gold medal Mass. Hort. Soc., 1944; Marie-Victorin medal la Fondation Marie-Victorin for outstanding services to botany in Can., 1950. Author: Edible Wild Plants of Eastern North America (with Alfred C. Kinsey); Gray's Manual of Botany, 8th and Centennial edit., 1950. Home: 14 Hawthorn St., Cambridge, Mass. Died Sept. 22, 1950; buried Mt. Auburn Cemetery, Cambridge.

FERNALD, ROBERT HEYWOOD, engineer; b. Orono, Me., Dec. 19, 1871; s. Merritt Caldwell and Mary Lovejoy (Heywood) F.; B.M.E., Me. State Coll., 1892; Mass. Inst. Tech., 1892-93; M.E., Case Sch. Applied Science, 1918; A.M., Columbia, 1901, Ph.D., 1902; Sc.D., U. of Pa., 1924; m. Catherine Mason Coupland, June 27, 1905; children—Merritt Caldwell, Frances Mason (dec.), Mason. Instr., 1893-96, asst. prof., 1896-1901, Case Sch. Applied Science, dir. dept. mech. engr., 1907-12; dir. dept. mech. engring., Washington U., 1902-07; Whitney prof. dynamical engring., and dir. dept. mech. engring., U. of Pa., 1912—, dean Towne Scientific Sch. same univ., 1930—. Conducted investigations for U.S. Geol. Survey and Bur. of Mines in U.S. and Europe; engr. in charge technologic branch, U.S. Geol. Survey, Sept. 1, 1904-July 1, 1910; cons. engr. Pub. Service Commn. of Pa., 1913-15; cons. engr., fuel div. Bureau of Mines, 1910-20. Formulated rules and regulations for gas, heating and water utilities of Pa., 1914. President Cleveland Engring. Soc., 1912; mem. bd. dirs. Sesquicentennial Internat. Expn. at Phila.; engr. mem. Giant Power Survey Bd. of Pa.; mem. science advisory com. (mech. engring. dir.), Century of Progress Expn., Chicago; mem. exec. com. Traffic Commn. of Phila., 1930—; engring. mem. advisory com., Phila. Agency of Reconstruction Finance Corp., 1932—; mem. exec. com. 3d World Power Conf., 1935-36; chmn. exec. com. Tech. Advisory Council affiliated with Phila. Chamber of Commerce, Jan. 1936—. Author: Engineering of Power Plants (with George A. Orrok), 1916, 3d edit., 1927. Home: Haverford, Pa. Died April 24, 1937.

FERNBACH, R(OBERT) LIVINGSTON, chemist; b. New York, Sept. 18, 1876; s. Henry and Henriette (Michaelis) F.; B.S., Coll. City of New York, 1896; post-grad. New York U.; m. Gertrude Rich White, of Bangor, Me., Apr. 30, 1906. In chem. work, 1898—; established Fernbach Lab., Paterson, N.J., 1910. Chemist to Broad Silk Mfrs.' Assn. Lecturer industrial chemistry, Brooklyn Poly. Inst., and Brooklyn Inst. Arts and Sciences, 1908-9. Member Soc. Chem. Industry. Republican. Author: Glue and Gelatine, 1907; Chemical Aspects of Silk Manufacture, 1910; Silk Dyeing, 1911. Contbr. to chem. jours. Home: Ridgewood, N.J. Office: Romaine Bldg., Paterson NJ

FERREE, CLARENCE ERROL, (fer-re'), psychologist; b. Sidney, O., Mar. 11, 1877; s. Jeremiah Dixon and Arvesta (Line) F.; B.S. and A.M., Ohio Wesleyan U., 1900, M.S., 1901; Sage fellow in psychology, Cornell U., 1902-03, Ph.D., 1909; D.Sc. Ohio Wesleyan U., 1939; m. Gertrude Rand, Sept. 28, 1918. Assistant in psychology, Cornell U., 1903-05, 1906-07; instr. in physics and psychology, U. of Ariz., 1905-06; lecturer in exptl. psychology, 1907-09, asso., 1909-12, asso. prof., 1912-17, prof., 1917-28, dir. Psychol. Lab., 1912-28, Bryn Mawr Coll.; dir. Research

Lab. Physiol. Optics, and resident lecturer in ophthalmology, 1928-32, prof. physiol. optics and dir. Research Lab. Physiol. Optics, 1932-36, Wilmer Ophthal. Inst., Johns Hopkins Med. Sch.; dir. Research Lab. Physiol. Optics, Baltimore, since 1936. Fellow A.A.A.S.; mem. Am. Psychol. Assn., Illuminating Engring. Soc., Optical Soc. Amer., Franklin Inst., Phi Gamma Delta, Sigma Xi, P.B.K. (hon.). Apptd. mem. Engr. Reserve Corps Com., May 1917. Inventor (with G. Rand) various lighting appliances, apparatus for measuring speed of accommodation and convergence of the eye, apparatus for testing visual acuity and the light and color sense, perimeter, pupilometer, centralvision scotometer and other optical and ophthalmic instruments. Author: Radiometric Apparatus for Use in Psychological and Physiological Optics, 1917; Studies in Physiological Optics, 2 volumes (with G. Rand), 1934; The Light Sense, Chapter XV, Modern Trends in Ophthalmology, London, 1940. Editor and author: Studies in Psychology, 3 volumes, 1916, 1922, 1925. Contbr. more than 275 articles in scientific, technical and ophthal. jours. on lighting in its relation to the eye, hygiene of the eye, methods and apparatus for refracting the eye, etc. Contbr. (with same) of apparatus and research, air service of army and lookout and signal service of navy. Contbr. Fourth Internat. Congress Sch. Hygiene, 1913, Internat. Congress of Ophthalmology, 1922. English-speaking Congress of Ophthalmology, London, 1926, Joint Discussion on Vision, The Physical and Optical Societies, London, 1932. Member committee of 4 on standards of field taking in study of eye diseases, Internat. Congress of Opthalmology, 1922, Nat. Research Council's Com. on Industrial Lighting, 1924, Inter Soc. Com. on Color, 1931. Granted several patents on illuminating devices and optical instruments. Home: 2609 Poplar Drive, Baltimore. Address: Research Laboratory of Physiological Optics, Baltimore, Md. Died July 26, 1942.

FERRIS, CHARLES EDWARD, mech. engr.; b. Napoleon, O., Sept. 23, 1864; s. George Nathaniel and Adelia (Harris) F.; B.S., Mich. Agrl. Coll., 1890; post-grad. work, McGill U., Montreal, Can.; m. Lillian LaCore, 1892; children—George Marvin, Georgia May; m. 2d, Katherine Stollzfus, 1904; children—Mary Elizabeth, Katherine Holly. Instr. engring., 1890-1900, prof. mech. engring., 1900-10; became dean of engring., 1910, U. of Tenn., now dean emeritus. Del. to Am. Engineering Council; mem. Tenn. Highway Commn. Mem. Am. Soc. M.E., Soc. Promotion Engring. Edn.; Am. Soc. M.E. (hon.). Republican. Presbyterian. Mason. Author: Elements of Descriptive Geometry, 1907; Manual for Engineers. Home: Kingston Pike Knoxville TN

FERRIS, EUGENE B(EVERLY), JR., physician; b. McNeill, Miss., June 24, 1905; s. Eugene B. and Martha (Reynolds) F.; B.S., Miss. State Coll., 1925; M.D., U. of Va., 1930, M.S. (Dupont fellow, 1930-31). 1931; m. Charlotte Gordon Hopkins, June 6, 1936; children—Charlotte Beverly, Ann Gordon, Eugene Beverly. Interne, Boston City Hosp., 1931-33; resident U. of Mich. Hosp., 1933; asst. resident Thorndike Meml. Lab. and research fellow, Harvard Med. Sch., 1933-35; mem. faculty, U. of Cincinnati Coll. of Medicine, 1935-52, asso. prof. of medicine and asst. dir., dept. internal medicine, Cincinnati Gen. Hosp., dir. psychosomatic teaching program, 1947-51, prof. of medicine, 1951-52; prof. of medicine Emory U., chief of med. services Grady Hosp., 1952—, Cons. in mental health and mem. com. on research of mental hygiene council, USPHS, 1946-51, cardiovascular study section, 1952-57; med. dir. Am. Heart Assn., 1957—. Member of the medical teaching mission to Poland and Finland (sponsored by Unitarian Service Com. and World Health Orgn.), 1948. Dir. research project on aviation medicine for Office Scientific Research and Development, 1942-45; mem. sub. com. on decompression sickness, Nat. Research Council, 1942-46. Recipient Horsley prize for research from U. of Va., 1936; Certificates of appreciation from the War Dept., The Navy Dept., and Office of Scientific Research and Development for med. research (as civilian), World War II. Fellow A.A.A.S., A.C.P. (regent); mem. Am. Soc. for Clin. Investigation (mem. council, v.p., 1949, pres., 1950), Assn. Am. Physicians, Am. Psychosomatic Soc. (mem. council, sec., 1947, pres., 1950), A.M.A., Am. Heart Assn. (v.p., bd. govs. 1955-57), Council High Blood Pressure Research (chmn. 1955-56), Ohio Med. Assn., Cin. Acad. Medicine, Central Soc. Clin. Research, Phi Beta Kappa, Sigma Xi, Alpha Omega Alpha, Beta Theta Pi. Editor-in-chief, Cincinnati Journal of Medicine, 1945-47, Journal of Clinical Investigation, 1947-52, mem. editorial bd., 1952—, Annals of Internal Medicine, Am. Jour. Medicine, Jour. Psychosomatic Medicine. Home: 1035 Park Av., N.Y.C. 28. Office: 44 E. 23d St., N.Y.C. Died Sept. 26, 1957; buried Holly Springs, Miss.

FERRIS, HARRY BURR, prof. anatomy; b. Old Greenwich, Conn., May 21, 1865; s. Samuel Holmes and Mary F. (Clark) F.; B.A. Yale, 1887, M.D., 1890; m. Helen Whiting, June 23, 1892; children—Helen Millington (Mrs. Davenport Hooker), Henry Whiting. Instr. in anatomy, 1891, asst. prof. 1892, prof. of anatomy, 1895-1933, Yale U., prof. emeritus, 1933—. Conglist. Author: The Indians of Cuczo and the Apurimac, 1916; The Quichua and Machiganga Indians, 1921. Home: New Haven, Conn. Died Oct. 12, 1940.

FERRY, ERVIN SIDNEY, physicist; b. Croydon, N.H., June 14, 1868; s. Harvey S. and Hattie W. (Eastman) F.; B.S., Cornell, 1889, grad. student, 1891-93, fellow in physics, 1902-03; grad. student, Upsala, Sweden, 1897-98; grad. student and fellow in physics Johns Hopkins, 1893-94; m. Ruth M. White, Aug. 21, 1900; 1 dau., Priscilla Grace. Prof. physics Purdue U., 1899—. Mem. Am. Physical Soc., Am. Electro-chem. Soc., Astron. and Astrophys. Soc. Am., Société Française de Pshysique, Delta Kappa Epsilon, Sigma Xi. Author: Elementary Dynamics, 1906; Practical Physics (with A. T. Jones), 1907; Pyrometry (with others), 1917; General Physics and Its Application to Industry and Everyday Life, 1921; (with others), Physics Measurements (2 vols.), 1929; Applied Gyrodynamics, 1931. Home: Lafayette, Ind. Died Oct. 8, 1956. *

FESSENDEN, EDWIN ALLAN, professor mech. engring.; b. Seven Mile, Butler County, O., Aug. 14, 1882; s. Timothy Dwight and Mary Jeannette (Snively) F.; student Washington U. Sch. of Engring.; B.S., U. of Mo. Sch. of Engring., 1904, M.E., 1906; m. Abigail Sayward Roper, Dec. 26, 1906 (died 1916); m. 2d, Louise French Matheny, June 28, 1917; children—Mary Elizabeth (Mrs. Newell R. Washburn), James Dwight, Eleanor Ray (Mrs. James W. Squires). Draftsman various cos., St. Louis and Springfield, until 1906; instr. mech. engring., U. of Mo., 1905-07, asst. prof., 1907-12, asso. prof., 1912-16, also dean Sch. of Engring. and dir. Engring. Expt. Sta. 1 1/2 yrs.; prof. mech. engring. and head of dept., Pa. State Coll., 1916-22; prof. mech. engring., Rensselaer Poly. Inst. from 1922, head of dept. from 1922, professor emeritus also consulting practice. Designed and equipped Mechanical Laboratory Bldg. at Pa. State Coll. Mem. Am. Soc. M.E., Am. Society for Engring. Edn., Soc. Engrs. Eastern N.Y., Sigma Xi, Alpha Tau Omega, Tau Beta Pi, Pi Tau Sigma. Republican. Presbyterian. Mason (K.T.), Rotarian. Author: Problems in Thermodynamics and Steam Power Plant Engineering (with Prof. Thos. G. Estep); The Fessenden Family in America, pub. posthumously. Home: Troy NY Died Nov. 22, 1967; buried Greenwood Cemetery, Hamilton OH

FESSENDEN, REGINALD AUBREY, physicist, engr.; b. of New England parentage at Milton, P.Q., Can., Oct. 6, 1866; s. Rev. E. J. and Clementina (Trenholme) F.; ed. Bishop's Coll., P.Q.; m. Helen May Trott, 1889; 1 son, Reginald Kenneley. Prin. Whitney Inst., Bermuda, 1885-86; insp. engr. Edison Machine Works, 1886-87; head chemist Edison Lab., 1887-90; electrician Westinghouse Electric & Mfg. Co., 1890-91; prof. elec. engring., Purdue U., 1892-93; prof. same, Western U. of Pa. (U. of Pittsburgh), 1893-1900; spl. agt. U.S. Weather Bur., 1900-02; gen. mgr. Nat. Elec. Signaling Co., 1902-10; cons. engr. Submarine Signal Co., 1910. Home: North Newton, Mass. Died July 22, 1932.

FETHERSTON, JOHN TURNEY, engineer; b. New Brighton, N.Y., Oct. 31, 1874; s. John Jay and Katharine (Turney) F.; B.S., New York U., 1897, C.E., 1898; hon. Sc.D., Fordham, 1919; m. Edith Hedges Kelly, June 14, 1917. Engr. Pub. Wks. Dept. Borough of Richmond, N.Y. City, 1898-1913; engr. Efficiency Staff, Bd. of Estimate and Apportionment, N.Y. City, 1913; commr. street cleaning under Mayor Mitchel, N.Y. City, 1914-18; v.p. Air Nitrates Corp., 1918-21; v.p. Sterling Salt Co., 1921-30, Genesee Valley Nat. Bank, 1928-30; pres. The Selden Co. and Selden Engring. Research Co., 1930-33; vice-pres. Filtration Equipment Corp., 1933-35; mem. bd. of dirs. Catalytic Process Corp., 1933-35; cons. engineer since 1935. In charge, for agt. of U.S. Govt., of constrn. and operation of Muscle Shoals Nitrate Plant No. 2, World War I; instr. engring. economy, Navy Training course, Bucknell University, World War II. Director Warsaw Hospital, 1926-30; trustee Wadsworth Library, 1928-30. Member American Soc. C.E., Am. Inst. Mining and Metall. Engrs., Am. Chem. Soc., A.A.A.S., N.Y. State Hist. Assn., Livingston County Hist. Soc. (pres. 1926-30), Genesee County Assn. (v.p. 1926-30), Iota Alpha (hon.), Delta Phi. Catholic. Writer of newspaper columns "Time and Tide" and " Quo Vadis." Research on the Basic Laws of the Universe; Justice at the Summit in United Nations. Contbr. to tech. jours. Home: Packwood House. Office: 12 Market St., Lewisburg, Pa. Died Oct. 9, 1962; buried Lewisburg Cemetery.

FEWKES, J(ESSE) WALTER, ethnologist; b. Newton, Mass., Nov. 14, 1850; s. Jesse and Susan E. (Jewett) F.; A.B., Harvard, 1875, A.M., Ph.D., 1877; student of Louis and Alexander Agassiz, student of zoölogy, U. of Leipzig, Germany, 1878-1880; LL.D., U. of Ariz., 1915; m. Harriett O. Cutler, Apr. 4, 1893. Asst. in Mus. Comparative Zoölogy, Harvard, 1881-89; editor Journal of Ethnology and Archaeology, 1890-94; field dir. Hemenway Southwestern Archaeol. Expdn. field work in Ariz., 1891-94; ethnologist Bur. Am. Ethnology, 1895-1918; chief Bur. Am. Ethnology, 1918-28. Mem. for 30 yrs. of Com. of the Overseers to visit Peabody Mus. of Harvard Coll. In charge excavation and repair Casa Grande, Ariz., Spruce Tree House, Cliff Palace, Sun Temple, Fire Temple, Far View House, Pipe Shrine House, Mesa Verde Nat. Park, Colo., Wupatki, Elden, Pueblo, Ariz., Weden Island near Tampa, Fla., 1908-26. Fellow Am. Acad. Arts and Sciences, A.A.A.S. (v.p. 1911-12), Am. Anthrop. Soc. (pres. 1911, 12), Anthrop. Soc. Washington (pres. 1909-10), Am. Folk-Lore Soc. (v.p.), Washington Acad. Sciences. Knight Order of Isabella the Catholic, Spain, 1892. Author: Snake Ceremonials at Walpi, 1894; Archaeological Expedition to Arizona in 1895; Two Summers' Work in Pueblo Ruins, 1897; Aborigines of Puerto Rico and Neighboring Islands, 1907; Casa Grande, Arizona, 1913. Home: Forest Glen, Md. Died May 31, 1930.

FIELD, ALLAN BERTRAM, engineer; b. New Barnet, Hertfordshire, Eng., Dec. 28, 1875; s. James John and Sarah S. (Dodd) F.; ed. Highgate Grammar Sch., London; Finsbury Tech. Coll., London, 1890-93; B.A., St. John's Coll., Cambridge, 1899, M.A., 1903 (mathematical tripos); B.Sc., London U. (1st Class Honors), 1900; m. Virginia W. Pearne, of Cincinnati, O., Sept. 8, 1911; children—Caroline Pearne, Ellen Kate, Virginia, Allan James Michael. With British Thomson-Houston Co. and Gen. Electric Co. (of U.S.A.), 1900-04; with Bullock Electric Mfg. Co., and Allis-Chalmers Co., 1905-08, and chief asst. on alternating current work to Mr. B.A. Behrend, chief engr. Professionally associated with Mr. Behrend subsequently for several yrs.; engr. with Westinghouse Electric & Mfg. Co., Pittsburgh, 1909-13; cons. engr. and prof. mech. engring., U. of Manchester, Eng. and mem. Univ. Senate, 1914-17; with Messrs. Vickers, Ltd., London, 1917-20; consulting engr. to Metropolitan-Vickers Elec. Co., Ltd., Manchester, since 1920. Temporarily apptd. by British Admiralty 1st tech. dir. of (anti-submarine) Admiralty Expt. Sta., Shandon, N.B., 1918. Fellow Am. Inst. E.E.; mem. Am. Soc. M.E., Instn. Elec. Engrs. London, Inst. Mech. Engrs. London. Home: Marple Cheshire England

FIELD, CROSBY, inventor, engr., mfr.; b. Jamestown, N.Y., Mar. 12, 1889; B.S., N. Y. U., 1909; M.E., Cornell U., 1912; M.S. in Elec. Engring., Union Coll., Schenectady, N.Y., 1914; m. Ethel Henriksen, Nov. 23, 1916; children—Margaret Roberta, Dorothy Henrietta, Patricia Crosby. With Gen. Electric Co., 1912-14; in private practice as cons. engr., 1914-15; chief engr., Standard Aniline Products, Inc., 1915-17; engring. mgr., Nat. Aniline & Chem. Co., in charge all engring. including constrn., maintenance, power plant operating, appraisal and engring. research, 1919-23; v.p., dir. and sec., Brillo Mfg. Co., 1923-45; also with FlakIce Corp., 1923-72. Chem. Machinery Corp., 1923-37. Reserve officer. Army Ordnance Dept., Jan., 1917-72; served as 1st lt., capt., maj., U.S. Army, 1917-19, acting chief, explosives and loading sect. Inspection Div.; in active service, col., Army Ordnance Dept., AUS, 1942-45, assigned as asst. dir. Safety Office of Chief of Ordnance. Decorated Legion of Merit. Registered profl. engr. Fellow Am. Soc. M.E. (medalist 1953, hon. mem.), I.E.E.E., A.A.A.S., Am. Soc. Heating, Refrigerating and Air Conditioning Engrs. (past pres., hon. mem.); mem. Am. Chem. Soc., Am. Inst. Chem. Engrs. (past mem. council), Am. Inst. Chemists, Nat., N.Y. socs. profl. engrs., Am. Ordnance Assn., Sigma Xi, Phi Beta Kappa Alumni Assn., Phi Beta Kappa Assos., Pi Kappa Alpha, Tau Beta Pi, Pi Tau Sigma. Mason. Republican. Episcopalian. Clubs: Andiron, Engineers, Chemists (N.Y.C.); Union League (Chgo.). Contbr. numerous papers on engring. specialties to sci. orgns. Inventor of the Oxide Film Lightning Arrestor, 1912, and continuous ice ribbon freezing process, 1916, continuous steel wool mfg. process, 1923; over 140 U.S. patents including elec., chem., mech. and refrigeration processes and equipment. Home: Brooklyn NY Died Sept. 20, 1972.

FIELD, CYRUS WEST, mcht., promoter 1st Atlantic cable; b. Stockbridge, Mass., Nov. 30, 1819; s. David Dudley and Submit (Dickinson) F.; A.M. (hon.), Williams Coll., 1859, LL.D., 1875; m. Mary Stone, 1840, 7 children. Asst. to his brother (a paper mfr.), 1837; started paper mfg. bus., Westfield, Mass., 1839; became partner wholesale paper firm E. Root & Co. (firm failed, 1840); built up firm of Cyrus W. Field & Co.; ret. from bus., formed (with a group of prominent New Yorkers) co. to build cable communication between Newfoundland and Ireland; copper wire 1950 miles long and 2 miles deep connected Trinity Bay, Newfoundland and Valentia, Ireland, Aug. 5, 1858, stopped working after 3 weeks of operation; engaged the Great Eastern (world's largest steamer) to lay new cable, successfully laid, 1866; helped establish elevated trains in N.Y.C.; participated with Jay Gould in devel. of Wabash R.R. and control of newspaper Mail and Express, N.Y.C. Died Ardsley, N.Y., July 12, 1892; buried Stockbridge.

FIELD, GEORGE WILTON, consulting biologist; b. N. Bridgewater, Mass., Sept. 29, 1863; s. Charles Copeland and Lucy Cobb (Cross) F.; A.B., Brown U., 1887 (Phi Beta Kappa), A.M., 1890; Ph.D., Johns Hopkins, 1892; postgrad. work, Smithsonian Table, Naples Zool. Sta., and Munich, 1892-93; m. Mary Bell, d. Hon. J. W. Bacon, of Natick, June 9, 1892; children—Bernice, John Bacon, Lucy Amelia, Margaret, Daniel Bacon. Asst. in biology, Johns Hopkins, 1891-92; asso. prof. cellular biology, Brown U., 1893-96; biologist, R.I. Agrl. Expt. Sta., 1896-1901; instr. economic biology, Mass. Inst. Tech., 1902;

biologist, Mass. Commission on Fisheries and Game, 1903 (chmn., 1904-16); in charge mammal and bird reservations of Bur. Biol. Survey, U.S. Dept. Agr., 1916-19; adviser on fisheries, Brazilian Govt., 1919-21; mem. advisory com., Dept. of Biology and Public Health, Mass. Inst. Tech.; mem. com. on regulation of the pollution of pub. waters, Nat. Conf. on Outdoor Recreation; 1st Internat. Conf. on Pollution of Water by Oil. Fellow A.A.A.S.; mem. Soc. Natural History, Soc. Zoologists, Mass. Audubon Soc. (v.p.), Brit. Assn. Adv. Sci., Am. Ornithologists' Union, pres. Nat. Shellfish Assn., 1911; sec. Nat. Assn. Game and Fish Commrs., 1910-15; corr. sec. Am. Fisheries Soc., 1912 (pres. 1916-17); mem. exec. com. Mass. Fish and Game Protective Assn.; mem. Delta Phi, Sigma Xi; pres. Nat. Assn. Conservation Commrs., 1913-16. Club: Cosmos (Washington, D.C.). Author of reports on numerous original biol. investigations; collaborateur, Annales de Biologie lacustre, Brussels. Home: Sharon, Mass. Office: 3 Joy St., Boston, Mass. *

FIELD, HERBERT HAVILAND, zoölogist; b. Brooklyn, Apr. 25, 1868; s. Aaron and Lydia Seaman (Haviland) F.; Poly Inst. Brooklyn, 1882-85; A.B., Harvard, 1888, A.M., 1890, Ph.D., 1891; univs. of Frieburg, Leipzig and Paris, 1891-95; m. Nina Eschwege, of London, Eng., Apr. 25, 1903. Founder, and dir. concilium Bibliographicum, Zürich, Switzerland, 1895—. Hon. asst., Mus. Comparative Zoölogy, Harvard, 1902—; an editor Zoölogischer Anzeiger, Leipzig, 1903—. Trustee Internationale de Bibliographie, Brussels; hon. mem. Leipzig Naturalists' Soc. Died Apr. 5, 1921.

FIELD, HUGH W(ILLIAM), chem. engr.; b. Indianapolis, Aug. 21, 1906; s. Frederick Hugh and Sadie (Ehrich) F.; B.S., U. of Pa., 1928; D.Sc., (honorary), Drexel Institute Tech., 1952; m. Mildred Mosser, Aug. 2, 1930; children—Frederick Hugh, Patricia. Jr. engr. Atlantic Refining Co., Phila., 1928-30, asst. engr., 1930-35, sr. engr., 1935-38, supervising engr., 1938-40, asst. mgr. research and development dept., 1940-47, gen. mgr. dept. since 1947, dir. since 1946; v.p. since 1949; petroleum consultant, Glen Mills, Pa., 1959—. Member Am. Petroleum Inst., Am. Inst. Chem. Engrs., Am. Chem. Soc., Phila. C. of C., Am. Soc. for Testing Materials, Inst. Petroleum, Alpha Chi Sigma, Tau Beta Pi. Clubs: Union League of Philadelphia, Exchange. Home: Glen Mills, Pa. 19342. Office: Springlawn Rd., Glen Mills, Pa. Died Aug. 28, 1960.

FIELD, ROBERT PATTERSON, mining engr.; b. Phila., Nov. 19, 1850; s. Samuel and Mary Gray (Patterson) F.; A.B., U. of Pa., 1872, A.M., 1875; m. May P. Trumbull, of Phila., Oct. 17, 1878. Mem. Robert P. Field & Co., bankers, Phila., Mar. 1908—; treas. Armstrong Engring. Co. Mem. Am. Philos. Soc., Actuarial Soc. America. Home: Hamilton Court. Office: Franklin Bank Bldg., Philadelphia. *

FIELD, STEPHEN DUDLEY, inventor; b. Stockbridge, Mass., Jan. 31, 1846; s. Jonathan Edwards and Mary Ann (Stuart) F.; nephew of late Cyrus W. F. and David Dudley F.; ed. Williams Acad. and Reid Hoffman's Sch., Stockbridge and Dutchess Co. Acad., Poughkeepsie, N.Y.; m. Celestine Butters, Sept. 30, 1871. Invented multiple call dist. telegraph box, 1874, electric elevator, 1878; pioneer of modern trolley ry., 1878-79; made 1st application of dynamo machines to telegraphy, 1879; invented dynamo quadruplex telegraph, 1880, fast stock ticker, 1884; made 1st application of quadruplex telegraph on ocean cable (Key West to Havana), 1909. Home: Stockbridge, Mass. Died May 18, 1913.

FIELDNER, ARNO CARL, chem. engr.; b. Ney, O., Dec. 12, 1881; s. Charles and Ellen (Ginther) F.; B.Sc. in Chem. Engring., Ohio State U., 1906, Chem. Engr., 1923; D.Sc., 1944; D.Sc., U. Ala., 1936, U. N.D., 1954. Indsl. fuel engr. Denver Gas & Electric Co., also chemist Am. Zinc & Chem. Co., Denver, 1906-07; with U.S. Bur. Mines, 1910-55, became chief engr., expt. stas. div., Washington, 1927, chief technol. br. and chief engr. coal div., 1936-42, chief, fuels and explosives div., 1942-51, chief fuels technologist, 1951-54, staff advisor, 1955-56. Served as maj. CWS, 1918-19, chemist in charge gas mask research sect. of Research Div., Washington; developed Am. methods of testing gas masks and gas absorbents; methods of testing and analyzing coal, coke and gas; had charge research on ventilation of Hudson River Vehicular Tunnel. Mem. Am. Chem. Soc., Am. Inst. Chem. Engrs.; Am. Inst. Mining and Metall. Engrs., Am. Soc. for Testing Materials (pres. 1937), Am. Gas Assn., Sigma Xi, Tau Beta Pi. Clubs: Coal Research (London); Cosmos (Washington); Chemists (N.Y.). Received Lamme and Sullivant medals from Ohio State U., 1931 and 1940; Melchett Medal, Inst. of Fuel, 1942; Percy Nicholls award Am. Inst. Mining and Metall. Engrs., 1946; award of Merit, Am. Gas Assn., 1955; Engring. Achievement award, Washington Soc. Engrs., 1951; D.S.M., U.S. Dept. Interior, 1949. Author monographs and tech. articles. Address: Cosmos Club, Washington 8. Died July 14, 1966; buried Bryan, O.

FIGGINS, JESSE DADE, museum dir.; b. Jefferson, Md., Aug. 17, 1867; s. James Ludwig and Letitia Aiken (Orr) F.; ed. pub. schs., Frederick, Md., and prep. course for ministry; spl. studies in biology, ornithology and mammalogy; m. Jane Marr, of Washington, D.C., Dec. 28, 1893 (now deceased); children—Marien Lee (Mrs. M. N. Lincoln), Frank Marr, Barbara Jane (Mrs. F. W. Miller), James Marr (deceased); m. 2d, Mrs. Helen M. Haskell. Engaged in biological survey of the Dismal Swamp, Virginia, 1896, 98; naturalist with the 6th and 7th R.E. Peary expeditions to North Greenland, 1896-97; became connected with Am. Mus. Natural History, New York, 1897, specializing in phases of exhibition and in field expdns. to Alaska, etc.; dir. Colo. Mus. Natural History, 1910-36, Bernheim Foundation Mus. (Louisville) since 1936; interest centered during recent yrs. in vertebrate palaeontology. Fellow A.A.A.S. Methodist. Club: Cactus Club. Author of description and naming (Homonovusmundus) of oldest and most primitive man in America; also author of numerous archaeological papers. Address: Louisville Trust Bldg., Louisville, Ky. *

FILLION, FRANCIS, entomologist; b. Angouléme, France, Feb. 20, 1851; ed. there and in Paris; has written numerous papers on entomology; employed by U.S. Dept. Agr., 1885, to investigate natural history of buffalo gnats of La. and Miss.; discovered 2 new species, described in report; mem. Am. and European scientific socs. By profession, teacher of the French language. Address: 101 Green St., New York. *

FINCH, JAMES KIP, ret. dean and prof.; b. Peekskill, N.Y., Dec. 1, 1883; s. James Wells and Winifred Florence Louise (Kip) F.; grad. Trinity Sch., N.Y., 1902; C.E., Columbia, 1906, A.M., 1911; m. Lolita Pauline Mollman, June 25, 1910; 1 son, Edward Cornell Kip, Asst. engr. Tompkins Engring. Constrn. Co., N.Y., 1906; instr. civil engring., Lafayette Coll., Easton, Pa., 1907; asst. engr. John B. Snook's Sons, architects, N.Y., 1907-08; engr. D. J. Ryan, contractor, Bklyn., 1908-09; List & Rose, contractors, N.Y., 1909; 10; partner on irrigated ranch, Mont., 1910; with civil engring. dept., Columbia, since 1910, as instr., 1910-15, asst. prof. 1915-17, asso. prof., 1917-27, prof., 1927-30, Renwick prof. since 1930, head dept. 1932-46, asso. dean, Sch. Engring., Columbia, 1941, dean, 1946-51, emeritus. Awarded Class of 1889, Columbia, gold medal for "outstanding services to university, to students and to profession," 1944, Egleston medal, Columbia Engring. Sch. Alumni Assn. for "distinguished engineering achievement," 1946. Trustee Bronx Savs. Bank; trustee, v.p. White Meml. Found., Litchfield, Conn. Organized and directed officers training course, Camp Columbia, 1917; instr. S.A.T.C., 1918. Mem. Am. Soc. Civil Engrs. (dir. 1934-36, v.p. 1943-44), Litchfield Hist. Soc. (trustee since 1932), Am. Soc. for Promotion of Engring. Edn., Newcomen Soc. Eng. (Am. br.), Tau Beta Pi, Sigma Xi; French Acad. Edn. (Order des Palmes Academiques). Republican. Episcopalian. Clubs: Columbia University, Century (New York), The Sanctum (Litchfield, Conn.), Faculty Club of Columbia University (pres. 1944-46). Author: Plane Surveying, 1918; Topographic Maps and Sketch Mapping, 1920; Early Columbia Engineers, 1929; Trends in Engineering, 1948. Contbr. of sects. on "Elements of Structural Design." "Elements of Hydraulics," to Mining Engineers Pocketbook, 1918. Editor in chief Columbia Univ. Quarterly, 1934-39. Contbr. to tech. jours. Home: 417 W. 117th St., N.Y.C. Died Apr. 1967.

FINCH, JOHN WELLINGTON, geologist, engineer; b. Lebanon, N.Y., Nov. 3, 1873; s. DeLoss S. and Mary Elizabeth (Lillibridge) F.; A.B., Colgate, 1897, A.M., 1898; fellow U. of Chicago, 1898-99, D.Sc., 1913; LL.D., U. of Alabama, 1936; D.Engring., Colorado School of Mines, 1938; m. Ethel Ione Woods, 1901; children—Ione Lillibridge (Mrs. George M. Nye), Nancy Allen. Instr. in geology and physics, Colgate, 1898, in geology, U. of Chicago, 1899; state geologist of Colo., 1901-02; consulting engr. at various times for Guggenheim Exploration Co., Venture Corp. (London, Eng.), Amalgamated and Anaconda copper cos., Hayden, Stone & Co., J. P. Morgan & Co., William Boyce Thompson, Newmont Corp., etc., v.p. and gen. mgr. N.Y. Orient Mines Co., 1916-22; dir. Anglo-Am. Corp. of S. Africa, 1921-22. Exploration in China, Siam and India, 1916-20, Africa, 1921, Turkey and Near East, 1922; v.p. Yunnan Ming Hsing Mining Co., Ltd., since 1920. Industrial adviser to gov. of Yunnan, China, 1922-25. Prof. economic geology, Colo. Sch. of Mines, 1926-30; dean of Sch. of Mines, U. of Ida., 1930-34. Director Ida. State Bureau of Mines and Geology, 1930-34; director United States Anaconda Copper Mining Co., Bureau of Mines, 1934-40; consulting engineer, New York, 1940-45; mem. Assn. of State Geologists, 1930-34, Fellow Geological Society of America; member American Institute Mining and Metallurgical Engineers, Society Economic Geologists, Am. Assn. Petroleum Geologists, Colo. Scientific Soc. (pres. 1929-30), Sigma Xi, Sigma Gamma Epsilon, Sigma Tau, Delta Kappa Epsilon. Author of various scientific articles. Address: 1711 E. Fifth Av., Denver 3 CO

FINCH, ROYAL GEORGE, civil engr.; b. Eagle Bridge, N.Y., Aug. 17, 1884; s. George Nelson and Helen (Hunt) F.; C.E., Rensselaer Poly. Inst., 1906; m. Jessie Lewis Weller; 1 dau., Mary Lewis (Mrs. Denny D. Williams). With the state engring. dept., in various capacities, 1908-18; dep. state engr., 1919-22; pvt. practice, 1923-24; state engr. and surveyor N.Y. 1925-26; now in pvt. practice; dir. Nat. Comml. Bank & Trust Co.; apptd. mem. Inter-oceanic Canal Bd., 1930. Vice pres., trustee Rensselaer Poly. Inst., Mem. Am. Soc. C.E., Albany Soc. Engrs., N.Y. State Soc. Profl. Engrs., Newcomen Soc., Delta Kappa Epsilon. Republican, Episcopalian. Mason (K.T.). Clubs: University, Fort Orange. Home: 634 Western Av., Albany, N.Y. Died Mar. 4, 1959; buried Granville, N.Y.

FINCH, RUY HERBERT, vocanologist; b. Sunbury, O., Aug. 31, 1890; s. Thacker Webb and Ida (Hubbard) F.; ed. George Washington U., U. Chgo.; independent studies in meteorology, seismology, volcanology with Dr. W. J. Humphreys and Dr. T. A. Jaggar, Jr.; m. Margaret Helena Harvey, Oct. 12, 1923; children—Robert H., Harvey E., Amy Jean. With U.S. Weather Bureau, 1910, meteorologist, 1919; asst. to Dr. Jagger, dir. Hawaiian Volcano Obs., 1919; asso. volcanologist U.S. Geol. Survey, 1924. Established obs. for study of Cascade Volcanoes at Lassen Peak, Cal., 1926, orchardist Watsonville, Cal., 1936-39; volcanologist Nat. Park Service, Hawaii, 1940-47, now U.S. Geol. Survey. Instr. meteorology USN, forecast at Naval Air Sta., Ireland, during World War I; del. 4th Pacific Sci. Congress, Java, 1929, 7th Congress, New Zealand, 1949. Fellow A.A.A.S., Geophysical Union, Geol. Soc., Am.; mem. Seismol. Soc. Am. Presbyn. Contbr. on sci. topics to various publs. Address: Watsonville, Cal. Died Mar. 15, 1957; buried Golden Gate Nat. Cemetery, San Bruno, Cal.

FINESINGER, JACOB ELLIS, physician; b. New Castle, Pa., Oct. 28, 1902; s. Hyman Joseph and Fannie M. (Kaplan) F.; A.B., Johns Hopkins, 1923, A.M., 1925, M.D., 1929; studied psychoanalysis in Vienna, 1933-34, conditioned reflex activity in Leningrad. under Professor Pavlov, 1934; married to Grace Lubin, June 24, 1932; children—Ruth Joan (Mrs. Sheppard Kellam), and Joe Lubin. Intern neurology Boston City Hosp., 1929, resident neurologist, 1930, jr. vis. neurologist, 1930-32; Commonwealth fellow Boston Psychopathic Hosp., 1932-35; asst. in neuropathology Harvard Med. Sch., 1930-32, research fellow in psychiatry, 1932-35, asso. in psychiatry, 1935-36, asst. prof. psychiatry, 1936-49; asst. psychiatrist Mass. Gen. Hosp., 1936-39, psychiatrist, 1939-49; prof. psychiatry and head dept. U. Md. Sch. Medicine since 1949, psychiatrist in chief U. Hosp. since 1949. Port exec., port of Boston, U.S. Shipping Bd., 1941-45; prin. investigator on studies on selection of air-craft pilots, U.S. Navy and Nat. Research Council, 1941-45; consultant to Surgeon Gens. Office, U.S. Army; mem. study health sect. for mental health, U.S.P.H.; mem. com. on psychiatry Nat. Research Council; mem. dean's subcom. for psychiatry U.S. V.A. and research council U.S. Army Chem. Center. Mem. A.M.A., Am. Psychiat. Assn., Am. Neurol. Assn., Am. Soc. for Clin. Investigation (editorial bd. Jour. Clin. Investigation, 1948-54, mem. adv. editorial bd. Human Relations), American Psychoanalytic Assn., Assn. for Research in Nervous and Mental Disease, Am. Acad. Neurology, Soc. Biol. Psychiatry, also local and state profl. socs. Tech. adviser series of sound films on therapeutic interviewing. Contbr. to monographs; author papers on neurol., psychiatric tonics. Editor in chief Journal Nervous and Mental Disease, 1958—. Home: 4512 N. Charles St., Balt. 10. Office: Department of Psychiatry, U. Md. Sch. of Medicine, Balt. Died June 19, 1959.

FINGER, HENRY JAMES, apothecary, chemist; b. San Francisco, Mar. 19, 1853; s. Theodore and Wihelmina (Kock) F.; ed. pub. schs.; Calif. Coll. of Pharmacy, 1871, 72; m. Ella Chase Hentley, of New Haven, Conn., June 9, 1866. Clk. in drug store, Redwood City, Calif., 1869; removed to Santa Barbara, 1872. Mem. Calif. State Bd. of Pharmacy almost continuously, 1891-1922 (ex-pres.); author of California's pharm. law, act regulating sale of poisons, act regulating itinerant vendors of drugs, and Calif. laws relating to detention and cure of inebriates and drug victims (resigned from bd. 1922). Apptd. by Pres. Taft del. Internat. Opium Conf., The Hague, 1911, 12 (mem. tech. com. and signed treaty in behalf of U.S. Govt.). Mem. Calif. Pharm. Assn. Progressive Republican. Unitarian. Author of numerous papers and published addresses concerning narcotic and other habit-forming drugs; regarded as an authority on these subjects. Home: Santa Barbara, Calif. *

FINK, ALBERT, railroad engr., exec.; b. Lauterbach, Germany, Oct. 27, 1827; s. Adres S. and Margaret (Jacob) F.; grad. in engring. and architecture Darmstadt schs., 1848; m. Sarah Hunt, Apr. 14, 1869. Came to U.S., 1849; invented bridge truss that bears his name; became constrn. engr. L. & N. R.R., 1857, chief engr., 1860, gen. supt., 1865; wrote The Fink Report on Cost of Transportation, (regarded as basis of Am. ry. econs.), 1874; exec. dir. So. Ry. & S.S. Assn.; organized Trunk Line Assn., 1877, became commr. Died Sing Sing (now Ossining), N.Y., Apr. 3, 1897.

FINK, BRUCE, botanist; b. Blackberry, Ill., Dec. 22, 1861; s. Reuben and Mary Elizabeth (Day) F.; B.S., U. of Ill., 1887, M.S., 1894; A.M., Harvard, 1896; Ph.D., U. of Minn., 1899; studied U. of Chicago, 1903; m. Ida May Hammond, Jan. 9, 1888; children—Mrs. Lois Honberger, Hugh Willard, Ruth Elizabeth. Principal of high schools, 1887-92; prof. biology, Upper Iowa University, 1892-1903; prof. botany, Grinnell Coll.,

1903-06; prof. botany, Miami U., 1906—. Mem. Minn. Bot. Survey, 1896-1903; in charge of botany, U. of Wash. Marine Sta., 1906. Asso. editor Micologia, 1908—. Author: Tobacco, a book on the tobacco problems, 4 revised edits.; The Lichens of Minnesota, 1910; Laboratory Exercises in Plant Physiology and Ecology, 1911. Mem. Ohio Biol. Survey Bd. Bot. editor Ohio Jour. of Science. Taxonomic studies of lichens. Home: Oxford, O. Died July 10, 1927.

FINK, COLIN GARFIELD, electrochemist; b. Hoboken, N.J., Dec. 31, 1881; s. Frederick William and Minnie (Spengeman) F.; B.A., Columbia, 1903; M.A., Ph.D., Leipzig, 1907; hon. Sc.D., Oberlin Coll., 1936; m. Charlotte K. Muller, June 6, 1910; children—Frederick William, Ernest Arthur (dec.), Harold Kenneth. Asst. in electrochemistry U. Leipzig, 1906-07; research engr. Gen. Electric Co., Schenectady, 1907-10, Edison Lamp Works, Harrison, N.J., 1910-17; head research lab. Chile Exploration Co., N.Y.C., 1917-21; head div. electrochemist, Columbia, 1922-50. also metall. and art research; cons. practice, 1922-50. Chmn. tungsten com. U.S. Munitions Board, 1939. Fellow A.A.A.S.; mem. Electrochem. Soc. (past pres., past sec.), Am. Chem. Soc., NRC, Am. Inst. Mining and Metall. Engrs., Met. Mus. Art. Sigma Xi, Phi Lambda Upsilon (asso.), Tau Beta Pi (hon.). Republican. Club: Faculty (N.Y.C.). Editor "Electrochemistry" of Chem. Abstracts, 1907—; contbg. editor Mineral Industry. Originator of the drawn tungsten filament; platinum substitute for tungsten lamps and radio tubes; insoluble anode for copper; process for tin smelting and refining; corrosion resistant metals; commercial chromium and tin plating; aluminum plate on steel, etc. War Work, Time Bomb, S.A.M. Labs.; govt. cons. on metals. Recipient of Edward Goodrich Acheson gold medal for outstanding accomplishments in electrochemistry; Perkin medal, 1934; Modern Pioneer Award, 1940. Home: 440 Riverside Dr., N.Y.C. 27. Died Sept. 16, 1953.

FINKLE, FREDERICK CECIL, cons. engr.; b. Viroqua, Wis., May 3, 1965; s. Thurston and Sophia Amelia (Michelet) F.; student pvt. and high schs. and spl. course in engring. U. Wis.; m. Henrietta Catherine Billette, Oct. 10, 1924; children—Frederick Cecil, Yvette Catherine. Settled in Cal., 1887; chief engr. Jurupa Land & Water Co., and N. Riverside Land & Water Co., San Bernardino County, 1887-90; city engr. San Bernardino, 1890-92; chief engr. water supply Cal. State Instns., 1892-94; chief engr. E. Riverside Irrigation Dist. (later changed to Riverside Highland Water Co.) and Graepland Irrigation Dist., 1894-97; chief engr. Redlands Electric Light & Power Co., Cal. Power Co., 1897-1901; chief hydraulic engr. and geologist So. Cal. Edison Co., Los Angeles, 1901-07, cons. engr., 1907-13; cons. engr., gen. practice 1913—. Mem. Rapid Transit Commn., Los Angeles, 1925-26. Has served as cons. engr. on many projects and for many domestic water supplies, among them Denver Union Water Co. and cities of San Bernardino, Long Beach, Ontario, Glendale, Burbank, Beverly Hills, Cal.; chief engr. of cons. engr. for eighteen important storage reservoir dams; had charge of flood protection works in Palo Verde Valley on Colorado River after overflow in 1922; has constructed many dams and hydro-electric power plants; designed Arrowhead Lake Dam, Boulder Creek Power Plant, others; now in practice as cons. engr. specializing in water supply for domestic and irrigation uses, and hydroelec. power development; large land owner, also owner Finkle Arms Apts., Finkle Manor Apts., and York Apts. (Los Angeles), Savoy Hotel (Burbank, Cal.). Mem. Am. Soc. M.E., Am. Assn. Engrs., Am. Inst. E.E., Am. Water Works Assn., Southside, Harbor Dist. (pres. 1941) C.'s of C., Wis. Alumni Assn. Republican. Roman Catholic. Elk. Club: California. Home: 805 N. Crescent Drive. Office: Lomitas Av. & Crescent Dr., Beverly Hills, Cal. Died Apr. 7, 1949; buried Calvary Cemetery, Los Angeles.

FINKLER, RITA V. SAPIRO, endocrinology cons.; b. Kherson, Russia, Nov. 1, 1888; d. Woolf and Sara (Hoppner) Sapiro; came to U.S., 1910, naturalized, 1913; B.A., U. Petersburg, Leningrad, U.S.S.R., 1908; M.D., Woman's Med. Coll. Pa., 1915; m. Samuel Finkler, July 6, 1913 (dec. 1941); 1 dau., Sylvia (Mrs. Marvin C. Becker). Intern, Polyclinic Hosp. U. Pa., Phila.; practice medicine specializing in endocrinology Newark, 1919-62, Millburn, N.J., 1962-68; chief endocrine clinic Beth Israel Hosp., Newark, 1934-68, chief dept. endocrinology, 1950-68, chief emeritus, cons., 1960-68. Recipient Woman's Coll. Med. Pa. Gold certificate 50 yrs. in practice, 1965, Achievement award, 1967. Mem. N.J., Woman's Med. Assn. (Woman of Year 1956), Am., N.J., Israel, World med. assns., Am., Internat., N.J. (pres. 1934) woman's med. assns., Endocrine and Sterility-Fertility Assn., Jerusalem Acad. Medicine, UN Am. Assn. Contbr. articles to profl. jours. Home: Short Hills NJ Died Nov. 8, 1968.

FINLAY, GEORGE IRVING, geologist; b. Marlboro, N.Y., July 9, 1876; s. David James and Ella (Peck) F.; A.B., Harvard, 1898; Ph.D., Columbia, 1903; m. Margaret H. Curtin, of New York, July 19, 1905. Asst. geologist, U.S. Geol. Survey, 1901—; prof. geology, Colo. Coll., Colorado Springs, Colo., 1903-13; asst. prof. geology, New York U., Sept., 1913. Republican. Epsicopalian. Mem. New York Acad. Science, Kappa Sigma. Author: Guide Book to Colorado Springs Rock Formations, 1907; Introduction to the Study of Igneous Rocks, 1913. Address: 134 W. 75th St., New York

FINLAY, JAMES RALPH, mining engr.; b. Blenheim, Ont., Can., Sept. 30, 1869; s. Ralph Spence and Anna (Rankin) F.; Colo. Coll., Colo. Springs; A.B., Harvard, 1891; m. Edith D. Adams, of Spokane, Wash., Aug. 10, 1904. Continuously occupied in the management, examination and appraisal of mining properties since 1891. Chief employments: mgr. Portland Gold Mining Co., Cripple Creek, Colo., 1902-03; Goldfield Consolidated Mines Co., 1910; appraisal mining properties of Mich., 1911; appraisal for state of copper mines of Arizona, 1931-32. Lecturer on economics of mining, Harvard and Columbia univs. Mem. Am. Inst. Mining and Metall. Engrs., Mining and Metall. Soc. America (v.p.), Soc. Harvard Engrs. (v.p.). Republican. Clubs: Harvard, University. Author: Cost of Mining, 1909; Appraisal of Mining Properties, 1911; also many brochures and articles on economic mining. Engr. or adviser in many projects of mining, consolidations, etc.; appraised mines of New Mexico for the State. Home: South Av., Redlands, Calif. Address: 20 Exchange Pl., New York NY

FINLEY, JAMES, bridge designer; judge Ct. Common Pleas, also justice of peace Fayette County, Pa.; designed cast iron eye-bar chain suspension bridge with suspended level roadway (important feature of modern suspension bridge); his 1st bridge (70 foot span, 12 1/2 feet wide) was built over Jacob's Creek on contract to Fayette and Westmoreland counties, 1801; patented his design, 1808; 40 of his bridges built in Am. in next 7-8 years, most famous being Newburyport Bridge (by John Templeman) over Merrimack River, 1810; 1 bridge fell at Brownsville, Pa., winter 1820.

FINLEY, SOLOMON HENDERSON, civil engr.; b. Lincoln County, Mo., Oct. 10, 1863; s. Andrew Ramsey and Caroline (Gibson) F.; A.B., Monmouth (Ill.) College, 1886, A.M., 1889; m. Ida Hedges, Jan. 8, 1891; children—Gailene (Mrs. Donald Mynard Swarthout), Malcolm Hedges, Knox Henderson, Wendell William, Rhodes Andrew. Began practice as civ. engr., Santa Ana, Calif., 1886; city engr. (installed original municipal water system), 1891-97; planned and built Modjeska Dam for Madam Modjeska, 1900; planned and built agrl. drainage systems for 5 dists., Orange County, Calif., 1889-1905; as chief engr. built Santa Ana Newport R.R., 1891-99; mem. bd. trustees, Santa Ana, 1900-02, mayor, 1902-04; chief engr. Orange County Highway Commn., 1915-16; supervisor of Orange County, 1916-28; an organizer, 1928, since sec., and dir. from Santa Ana, The Met. Water Dist. of Southern Calif. Mem. Nat. Guard of Calif., 1890-1908; capt. 7th Calif. Vols., Spanish-Am. War; col. 7th Regt. Nat. Guard of Calif., 1904-08; assigned for duty with Red Cross in France, 1918, war closed before reaching front. Apptd. by Gov. Young as mem. Calif. com. to adjust Colorado River water claims with Ariz. and Nev. Mem. S.R., Spanish War Vets. Democrat. Presbyterian. Club: Rotary. Home: 1633 E. 4th St., Santa Ana, Calif. Died Dec. 4, 1944.

FINLEY, WILLIAM HENRY, civil engr.; b. Delaware City, Del., Jan. 22, 1862; s. William F. and Mary (McDonough) F.; ed. pub. schs. and by pvt. tutelage; m. Sarah H. Furry. Worked in office of Delaware Gazette, 1878-82; engring. dept. Edge Moor Iron Co., 1882-87; in engring. dept., C.,M.&St.P. Ry., 1887-92; entered service of C.&N.W. Ry. Co., May 1892; engr. of bridges, 1892-1900, prin. asst. engr., 1900-05, same rd. v.p. and mgr. Widell-Finley Co., engrs. and contractors, 1905-06; asst. chief engr. C.&N.W. Ry., 1906-13, chief engr., 1913-18, and pres., June 1918—, also pres. C.,St.P.,M.&O. Ry. Co., Sept. 19, 1922—. Home: Wheaton, Ill. Died Mar. 17, 1926.

FINLEY, WILLIAM LOVELL, naturalist; b. Santa Clara, Cal., Aug. 9, 1876; s. John Pettis and Nancy Catherine (Rucker) F.; A.B., U. Cal., 1903; D.Sc., Ore. State Coll., 1931; m. Irene Barnhart, Feb. 21, 1906; children—Phoebe Katherine (Mrs. Arthur N. Pack), William Lovell. Writer Review of Reviews Co., 1904-05; lectr. Nat. Assn. Audubon Socs., N.Y.C., 1906-25; mem. Bd. of Fish and Game Commrs., Ore., 1911; state game warden, Ore., 1911-15; state biologist, 1915-19; mem. Ore. Game Commn., 1925-27. Mem. adv. bd. U.S. Dept. Agr., Migratory Bird Treaty Act; mem. Adv. Council on Outdoor Recreation. Republican. Methodist. Hon. pres. Ore. Audubon Soc.; mem. Am. Ornithologists' Union, Outdoor Writers Assn. Am. (dir.), Nat. Parks Assn. (adv. council), Wildlife Soc. (trustee), Sigma Xi; charter mem. Am. Soc. Mammalogists, Cooper Ornithol. Club, Pacific Northwest Bird and Mammal Soc. Author: American Birds, 1907; (with wife) Little Bird Blue, 1915, Wild Animal Pets, 1928; also many sci. papers on bird life and 2 bulls. on Ore. birds. Producer of Finley nature films (motion pictures). Asso. editor The Condor, 1906-09. Editorial staff Nature Mag., 1923-37; v.p. Izaak Walton League Am., Nat. Wildlife Fedn. Home: R.F.D. 10, Portland, Ore. Died June 29, 1953; buried Riverview Cemetery, Portland.

FINNELL, WOOLSEY, civil engr.; b. Tuscaloosa, Co., Ala., Oct. 24, 1866; s. Adoniran Judson and Narsissa (Durrett) F.; prep. edn., Pleasant Hill Acad. (Jefferson Co., Ala.) and Tuscaloosa Mil. Acad.; C.E., U. of Ala., 1887; m. Margaret Hagler, of Tuscaloosa Co., Oct. 21, 1890; children—Edward Judson, Lillian Margaret (dec.), Julia Judson (Mrs. Joseph J. Wode), Newbie (Mrs. Charles Livingston), Susie (Mrs. C.W. Gross), Woolsey, Mary-Jessie, Harriett M. Began in Jefferson Co. as axeman on K.C., M.&B.R.R. (now St. Louis-San Francisco Ry.), 1887, continuing as asst. engr., resident engr., locating engr. and division engr. several railroads; served as chief engr. various ry. projects; opened office as cons. engr., at Tuscaloosa, Ala., 1894; served as judge of probate, Tuscaloosa Co.; became dir. State Highway Department, Ala., Feb. 1, 1927; now with United States Department of Justice, Bureau of Prisons. Commd. maj. engrs., U.S.A., June 19, 1917; sailed for France with 501st Engrs. and later made engr. officer of Intermediate Sect., in command of 18,000 men; lt. col. Sept. 14, 1918; duty at Paris, 1919, with War Damage Bd. of Peace Conf., later field executive of Army Ednl. Corps; hon. discharged, Sept. 16, 1919; col. Engr. Res. Corps, Jan. 20, 1920. Charter mem. Am. Soc. Mil. Engrs., Am. Soc. C.E. Awarded citation by Gen. Pershing "for extremely meritorious service"; Legion of Honor (French). Democrat. Missionary Baptist. Mason (33 deg., Scottish Rite; Shriner); in York Rite has held offices of Eminent Comdr. of Commandery, Grand Comdr. K.T. of Ala., v.p. Order of High Priesthood of Ala.; Most Puissant Sovereign Red Cross of Constantine and many others; organized the first Masonic Club in France, Apr. 1918. Home: Tuscaloosa, Ala. *

FIPPIN, ELMER OTTERBEIN, agronomist; b. Columbus, O., Sept. 18, 1879; s. John and Sidney A. (Holt) F.; B.Sc. in Agr., Ohio State U., 1900; postgrad. Cornell U., 1904; m. Florence E. Postle, Nov. 21, 1901; children—Walter Russell, Robert Allen (dec.), William Howard, James Elmer (dec.), Julia Anne, Elizabeth Carol. Asst. in soil survey U.S. Bur. Soils, 1900-04; asst. prof., prof. soil technology Cornell U., 1905-19; dir. agrl. dept. Nat. Lime Assn., 1920, gen. mgr., 1921-22; cons. practice, Washington, 1923-24; dir. agrl. expt. stas., Republic of Haiti, 1924-26; exec. sec. and treas. State Conservation and Development Commn. of Va., 1926-30; N.E. rep. Fed. Farm Bd., 1931-32; economist A.A.A., 1933-34; agrl. adviser TVA, 1935-47, ret. Fellow A.A.A.S.; charter mem. Am. Soc. Agronomy; mem. Soil Science Soc. Am., Am. Farm Mgmt. Assn., Alpha Zeta. Author: Rural New York, 1921; First Principles of Cooperation in Buying and Selling in Agriculture, 1934; (with T. L. Lyon) Principles of Soil Management, 1909, Soils—Their Properties and Management, 1914: also five chapters on soils in Farmers' Handbooks of Knowledge, and various articles and repts. Home: 223 E. 6th Av., Fountain City, Tenn. Died Dec. 26, 1949.

FIREMAN, PETER, chemist; b. Lipovetz, Russia, Apr. 4, 1863; grad. Gymnasium Charkov, Russia, 1881; came to U.S., 1882; studied at U. of Odessa, Königsberg, Zürich and Berne; Ph.D., Berne, 1893. Asst. in chemistry, Columbia U. (now George Washington U.), 1892, 94, instr., 1894-98, asst. prof., 1898-1901; prof. chemistry, Mo. Sch. of Mines, 1901-02; chem. geologist, U.S. Nat. Museum, 1901; in charge Chem. Research Lab., Alexandria, Va., 1904-06; mfg. chemist since 1906; pres. Magnetic Pigment Co., 1911-42; chmn., Adv. Com. of Magnetic Pigment Co., Div. Columbian Carbon Co. (since 1943). Mem. A.A.A.S., Am. Philos. Assn., Chemists' Club. Club: Cosmos (Washington). Author: Sound Thinking and Perceptualistic Theory of Knowledge. Address: P.O. Box 116, Lambertville, N.J. Died Apr. 27, 1962; buried Ewing Cemetery, Trenton, N.J.

FIRM, JOSEPH LANNISON, inventor; b. at Brooklyn, Mar. 19, 1839; s. John and Judith (Morrell) F.; ed. Brooklyn pub. schs. Served apprenticeship in press room of Harper & Bros.; was 22 yrs. supt. of Frank Leslie's press room; now in charge of patent dept., Goss. Printing Press Co. Has secured and perfected many patents on printing presses, including the "straight-line" newspaper press, the automatic "set-off," etc. Was pres. bd. of edn. Jersey City; 2 yrs. past master Amity Lodge, Jersey City; past high Priest of Amity Chapter, Jersey City, and a 32 deg. Mason. Address: 1535 S. Paulina St., Chgo. *

FISCHER, ARTHUR FREDERICK, museum adminstr.; b. Chgo., Feb. 6, 1888; s. Joseph and Mary Anna (Ehert) F.; C.E., Ohio No. U., 1909; M.F., Yale, 1911; grad. U.S. War Coll., 1927; hon. M.A., Yale, 1939; m. Helen Wyly Campbell, June 21, 1911; children—Arthur Frederick, Ruth Winifred (dec.), Alan Campbell. Asst. to state forester of Ohio, 1910; forester Bureau of Forestry, P.I., 1911-16, acting dir., 1916-17, dir., 1917-36; asst. prof. forest engring. U. Philippines, 1912-17, dean Sch. Forestry, 1917-36, prof. tropical forestry, 1917—; now dir. Natural History Mus. San Diego, adviser on natural resources, Commonwealth Govt. of P.I., 1937-41, Bataan Corregidor campaign, 1941-42; exec. dir. Am. Cinchona Plantations U. S. Com. Co., 1943-46; established U.S. Govt. Quinine Plantation in Costa Rica; col. M.I., S.G.O., AUS, now ret. Fellow Soc. Am. Foresters, San Diego Soc. Natural History (sec.-treas.). Awarded Legion of Merit, Distinguished Service Star (Philippines), Merite-Agricol (France), Green Dragon Annam. Fellow Soc. Am. Foresters, San Diego Soc. Natural History (sec.-treas.). Presbyn. Clubs: Rotary (pres. 1934-35), Army and Navy, Manila, Polo, Cosmos,

Army and Navy (Washington). Home: 1746 Warrington St., San Diego 92107. Office: Natural History Mus., Balboa Park, San Diego 1. Died Oct. 31, 1962; buried Ft. Rosecrans Nat. Cemetery.

FISCHER, EARL BRITZIUS, pharmacognocist-biochemist; b. Winona, Minn., Aug. 27, 1892; son John Henry and Charlotte (Britzius) F.; B.S., U. of Minn., 1919, Ph.D., 1940; m. Merry Christmas Mueller, Oct. 15, 1921; children—James R., Charlotte Ann, Mary Jean, Elizabeth Foote. Asst. chemist McLaughlin, Gormley, King & Co., Minneapolis, 1919-22; instr. in pharmacognosy Coll. of Pharmacy U. of Minn., 1922-26, asst. prof., 1926-30, asso. prof., 1930-40, prof. of pharmacognosy and head dept. of pharmacognosy since 1940. Served as sergt., Chem. Warfare Service, U.S. Army, 1917-19. Mem. bd. management Univ. branch Minneapolis Y.M.C.A. since 1944, chmn. bd. since 1946. Mem. Am. Pharm. Assn., Am. Chem. Soc., Am. Assn. Univ. Profs., Minn. Acad. Sci., Nat. Plant Sci. Seminar, Kappa Sigma, Alpha Chi Sigma, Sigma Xi, Rho Chi, Phi Lambda Upsilon, Tau Beta Pi, Kappa Psi, Phi Delta Chi, Scabbard and Blade, Crotchets and Quavers. Republican. Conglist. Clubs: Evergreen, Campus, Faculty Dining. Mem. com. on botany U.S. Pharmacopoeia XII, XIII, XV, XVI (revision com.) since 1930; mem. com. on botany Nat. Formulary Revision com. for National Formulary VII and VIII since 1930. Mem. editorial bd. Kraemer's Scientific and Applied Pharmacognosy, 1928. Contbr. to scientific jours. Home: 4921 Fremont Av. S., Mpls. 9. Died Mar. 5, 1961.

FISCHER, ERNST GEORG, mech. engr.; b. Baltimore, Md., Aug. 6, 1852; s. Georg Ernst and Caroline (Schmidt) F.; ed. Zschogg's Real Schule, Dresden, Germany, 1865-67; Engring. Works of Moritz Kleber, Dresden, 1867-70; subsequently under pvt. tutors; m. Julia Frances Lawson, Apr. 26, 1878 (died 1915). With U.S. Coast and Geod. Survey, June 1, 1887—, chief of Instrument Div., Mar. 1, 1898—. Has made many improvements in the instrumental equipment and devised and constructed new apparatus and instruments as follows: Improvements in plane table alidade; base bars; spring balance for base tape measurement; tape stretching apparatus; tide gauge and tide indicator; photographic camera; compass declinometer; interferometer for measuring flexure of gravity pendulum supports; electric signal lamp for triangulation; magnetometer; transit micrometer; pendulum apparatus for determination of gravity; plane table; direction theodolite for primary triangulation; astronomical transit. Designed and constructed, after principles taken from Sir William Thomson and Dr. William Ferrel, U.S. Coast and Geod. Survey tide predicting machine No. 2, the geodetic or precise level, geodetic invar level rod, a new type of pressure sounding tube, a new artificial horizon for sextants, etc. Retired Aug. 22, 1922. Home: Washington, D.C. Died Sept. 1935.

FISCHER, HERMANN OTTO LAURENZ, biochemist; b. Wurzburg, Bavaria, Dec. 16, 1888; Ph.D. in Chemistry, Jena, 1912; hon. degree Giessen (Germany) U., 1959; m. 1922; 3 children. Asst. prof. organic chemistry U. Berlin, 1922-32; asso. prof. U. Basle, 1932-37; prof. chemistry, Toronto, 1937-48; lectr. biochemistry U. Cal., 1948—, chmn. dept. biochemistry, 1953-56, prof. biochemistry, emeritus, 1956—. Recipient Sugar Research award Am. Chem. Soc., 1949; Adolf-von-Baeyer Meml. Gold medal, Soc. German Chemists, 1955. Fellow Chem. Inst. Can.; mem. Soc. Biol. Chemists, Royal Canadian Inst., Nat. Acad. Sci., other profl. assns. Home: 829 Regal Rd., Berkeley, Cal. Died Mar. 9, 1960.

FISCHER, MARTIN HENRY, M.D.; b. at Kiel, Germany, Nov. 10, 1879; s. Rudolph Henry and Theresa (Beuthien) F.; came to U.S., 1885; grad. S. Div. High Sch., Chicago, 1897; M.D., Rush Med. Coll., Chicago, 1901; hon. Pharm. D., Cincinnati Coll. of Pharmacy, 1925; hon. Sc.D., Wittenberg Coll., 1932; LL.D., U. of Cin., 1951; Holmes scholar, summers, Woods Hole, Mass., 1900-01; post-grad. studies in Germany and Austria, 1905-06; m. Charlotte Rust Leonard, May 6, 1903 (died June 14, 1960). Asst. in pathology, 1898-1901, physiology, 1900-01, Rush Med. Coll.; asso. in physiology, U. of Chicago, 1901-02; asst. prof. physiology, U. of Calif., 1903-05; prof. pathology, Oakland Coll. of Medicine and Surgery, 1905-10; prof. physiology, U. Cin., 1910-50, emeritus, 1950-62; Cutter lectr. Harvard, 1917; lectr. fine arts, New York U., 1931. Hatfield prize, College Physicians, Phila., 1909; Cartwright prize, Alumni of Coll. of Physicians and Surgeons, New York, 1911; gold medal for research, A.M.A., 1913, diploma, 1915, silver medal, 1916, diploma, 1920; merit award Miami chapter Am. Inst. Chemists, 1946; gold medal Am. Artists Professional League, 1947. Internat. prize, Kolloid Gesellschaft, 1924. Fellow A.A.A.S., Am. Inst. Chemists, (Ohio award 1952); mem. A.M.A., Soc. Exptl. Biology and Medicine, Am. Physiol. Soc., Am. Assn. Biol. Chemists, Am. Artists Professional League (hon. chmn. com. technic), Cincinnati Research Soc. (pres. 1912), Am. Chem. Soc. (president Cincinnati section, 1922; Eminent Chemist award, 1952 from Cin. sect.); foreign mem. Kolloid-Gesellschaft, Leopold-Carl German Acad. Scientists, Societas Spinozana, Czechoslovakian Botanical Society, History of Science Society, and others. Author several profl. books, latest being: Der kolloide Aufbau der lebenden Substanz, 1951. Translator books in field of chemistry. Contbr. numerous papers in field. Home: 2236 Auburn Av., Cin. 19. Died Jan. 19, 1962; buried Spring Grove Cemetery, Cin.

FISH, EDWARDS R., mech. engr.; b. Stone Mountain, Ga., Aug. 4, 1870; s. Laurens B. and Amelia R. (Whitman) F.; student St. Louis Manual Training Sch., 1884-87; M.E., Washington U., St. Louis, Mo., 1892; m. Ida M. McBride, Apr. 29, 1902; children—Laurens B., Marjorie, Janet (Mrs. Richard A. Waite), Edwards R. Draughtsman, Lewis Valve Gear Co., 1892; supt. Washington Univ. Testing Lab., 1892-93; asst. engr. Heine Boiler Co., 1893-97, sec. 1897-1914; vice pres. and chief engr., 1914-30; chief engr. boiler div. Hartford Steam Boiler Inspection and Insurance Co., 1930-44; engring. consultant since 1944. Fellow Am. Soc. M.E., Am. Welding Soc. Clubs: Engineers (St. Louis) (sr. mem.); Hartford (Conn.) Engineers. Home: 30 Laurel Av., Windsor CT

FISH, FRED ALAN, prof. electrical engring.; b. Milan, Erie Co., Ohio, Feb. 21, 1875; s. Albert M. and Emily Marie (Graves) F.; grad. High Sch., Milan, 1893; science course, Buchtel Coll., Akron, O., 1893-95; M.E. in E.E., Ohio State U., 1898; hon. fellowship in electrical engring., U. of Wis., 1900-01; m. Annie Knower Caulkins (B.S., U. of Wis., 1901), of Troy, N.Y., Aug. 14, 1901; children—Frances Louise, Elizabeth Harriet. Asst. prof. elec. engring., Ohio State U., 1901-05; prof. elec. engring., Ia. State Coll., since 1905. Fellow Am. Inst. Elec. Engrs., 1913; mem. Soc. Promotion Engring. Edn., Nat. Electric Light Assn., Sigma Xi, Tau Beta Pi, Phi Kappa Phi, Phi Delta Theta, Eta Kappa Nu. Home: 503 Ash Av., Ames IA

FISH, JOHN CHARLES LOUNSBURY, civil engineer; b. Townsend Twp., Huron County, O., June 3, 1870; s. Job and Annie Elizabeth (Peabody) F.; C.E., Cornell U., Ithaca, N.Y., 1892; m. Ethelwyn Rebecca Slaght, July 31, 1894; children—Job (dec.), Lounsbury S., Frances C. (Mrs. Garth L. Young). Asst. to city engr., Sandusky, O., 1886-88; instr. civ. engring., Cornell U., 1892-93; instr. Stanford, 1893-94, asst. prof., 1894-98, asso. professor, 1898-1905; res. engineer L.S.& M.S. Ry., 1905-07; div. engr., same, 1907-09; prof. railroad engring., 1909-25, prof. civil engring., 1925-35, exec. head civil engring. dept., 1928-35, emeritus prof. civil engring, since 1935, Stanford U. Health commr. and mem. Bd. Pub. Safety. Palo Alto, 1909-24. Mem. Am. Soc. C.E., Am. Ry. Engr. Assn., Sigma Xi, Alpha Tau Omega; hon. mem. Sigma Delta Pi. Awarded Fuertes gold medal for original research, Cornell U., 1915. Author: Lettering of Working Drawings, 1894; Linear Drawing & Lettering, 1901; Descriptive Geometry, 1903; Earthwork Haul and Overhaul, 1913; Engineering Economics, 1915, 23. Technic of Surveying Instruments, and Methods, 1917; The Engineering Profession (with T. J. Hoover), 1941. Home: 1336 Emerson St., Palo Alto CA

FISH, WALTER CLARK, electrical engr.; b. at Taunton, Mass., Aug. 25, 1865; s. Frederick L. and Mary (Jarvis) F.; A.B., Harvard, 1886; B.S. in Elec. Engring., Mass. Inst. Tech., 1887; m. Martha Brewster, of Taunton, Mass., Aug. 7, 1890. Mgr. Lynn Works Gen. Electric Co. for many yrs.; now mgr. Internat. Gen. Electric Co., Boston (an affiliation of Gen. Electric Co.); dir. Campagnie Francaise Thomson Houston (Paris), British Thomson Houston Co. (London), Société d' Electricite et de Mecanique (Brussels). Mem. Am. Inst. Elec. Engrs. Address: Care V. McGuffin, Gen. Electric Co., West Lynn, Mass. *

FISHER, ALBERT KENRICK, biologist; b. Sing Sing (now Ossining), N.Y., Mar. 21, 1856; s. Hiram and Susan E. (Townsend) F.; ed. Holbrook's Mil. High Sch., Sing Sing; M.D., Coll. Phys. and Surg. (Columbia U.), 1879; m. Alwilda Merritt; children—Harry Townsend (dec.), Walter Kenrick, Mrs. Ethel Merriam White (dec.), and Mrs. Alberta Merritt Marble (twins). Was with Death Valley Expdn., 1891, sent out by Dept. Agr., made biol. survey of portions of Calif., Nev., Ariz. and Utah; also made biol. survey in various other western states, 1892-98; member Harriman (Alaska) Expdn., 1899; member Pinchot South Sea Expdn., 1929. In charge econ. investigations U.S. Biol. Survey; collaborator U.S. Nat. Museum. One of founders of the Am. Ornithologists' Union (pres.); hon. mem. Am. Game Protective Assn.; corr. mem. Linnaean Soc. N.Y., Nuttall Ornithol. Club; hon. mem. Cooper Ornithol. Club, Delaware Valley Ornithol. Club; Internat. Assn. Game and Fish Commissioners; member Biological Society of Washington, Washington Biological Field Club; associate Boone and Crockett Club; president Baird Ornithol. Club. Club: Cosmos. Author: Hawks and Owls of the United States, 1893; Ornithology of the Death Valley Expedition of 1891, 1893; also 160 shorter papers. Address: Cosmos Club, Washington 5, D.C. Died June 12, 1948.

FISHER, EMORY DEVILLA, educator, chemist; b. Walker, Ia., May 4, 1908; s. Frank Ray and Clara (Shaffer) F.; B.S., Dakota Wesleyan U., 1931; Ph.D., U. Wis., 1935; m. Marie Elsie Michaelis, Oct. 26, 1935; children—Lawrence Wayne (dec.), Michael Emory, Mary Ellen (Mrs. George Minkevich), Frank Ray. Instr. chemistry Kan. State U., 1935-40, U. Tex., 1940-41; asso. prof. E. Tex. State Coll., 1941-46; prof. U. Mo. at Rolla, 1946-63; prof. chemistry, chmn. dept. U. Wis. Center System, 1963-69. Mem. Am. Chem. Soc., Sigma Xi, Gamma Alpha, Alpha Chi Sigma, Phi Kappa Phi. Home: Madison WI Died Aug. 25, 1969; buried Middleton Junction Cemetery, Dane County WI

FISHER, HARRY LINN, chemist; b. Kington, N.Y., Jan. 19, 1885; s. George Edwin and Emma Adelia (Bray) F.; A.B., Williams Coll., 1909, D.Sc. (hon.), 1953; A.M., Columbia U., 1910, Ph.D., 1912; m. Nellie Edna Andrews, June 7, 1910; children—Helen, Ruth (Mrs. Francis B. Roseyear), Robert Andrews. Instr. chemistry Cornell, 1911-12; instr. organic chemistry Columbia, 1912-19; research chemist B. F. Goodrich Co. Akron. O., 1919-26, U.S. Rubber Co., N.Y.C., Passaic, N.J., 1926-36; dir. organic chem. research Air Reduction Co., 1936-44, U.S. Indsl. Chemicals, Inc., Stamford, Conn., 1936-49, Balt., 1949-50; organizing sec. 12th Internat. Congress Pure and Applied Chemistry, N.Y.C., 1950-51, arranging sec. 16th Conf., N.Y.C., Washington, 1950-51, administrative asst. div. chemistry NRC, Washington, 1950-51; tech. synthetic rubber div. RFC, Washington, 1951-52; prof. rubber tech., sch. engring. U. So. Cal., 1953-56; western tech. dir. Ocean Minerals, Inc., 1957-58, v.p., 1958—. Sch. bd. Leonia, N.J., 1929-36, v.p., 1931-36; tech. cons. Office Rubber Dir., 1943-44, Office Rubber Research, 1944-51. Recipient Nat. Assn. Mfrs. Mod. Pioneer award for devels. attaching rubber to met., 1940; Am. Chem. Soc. Chas. Goodyear medal, 1949. Fellow A.A.A.S., Am. Inst. Chemists (nat. pres. 1940-42), Inst. Rubber Industry Gt. Brit.; mem. Am. Soc. Testing Materials, Am. Chem. Soc. (chmn. rubber div. 1927-28; pres. 1954), Phi Beta Kappa, Sigma Xi, Phi Lambda Upsilon. Clubs: Chemists, Cosmos (Washington). Author: Laboratory Manual of Organic Chem., 1920, rev. edits. 1924, 31, 38; Rubber and its Use, 1941; Chemistry of Natural and Synthetic Rubbers, 1957. Contbr. articles profl. jours. Patentee processes for attaching rubber to metal, non-sulphur vulcanization, synthesis organic chem. compounds, methionine, others. Address: 524 E. Football Blvd., Claremont, Cal. Died Mar. 19, 1961; buried Forest Lawn Hollywood Hills, Los Angeles.

FISHER, IRVING, polit. economist; b. Saugerties, N.Y., Feb. 27, 1867; s. Rev. George Whitefield and Ella (Wescott) F.; A.B., Yale, 1888, Ph.D., 1891; LL.D., Rollins Coll., 1932, University of Athens and U. of Lausanné, 1937; studied Berlin and Paris, 1893-94; m. Margaret, d. Rowland Hazard, June 24, 1893 (dec.); children—Margaret (dec.), Caroline (Mrs. Carol Fisher Baumann), Irving Norton. Tutor math., 1890-93, asst. prof., 1893-95, asst. prof. polit. economy, 1895-98, professor political economy, 1898-1935, now prof. emeritus, Yale Recuperating health in Colorado, California, 1898-1901. One of editors Yale Review, 1896-1910; Hitchcock lecturer, University of California, 1917; lecturer University of London School of Economics and Polit. Science, 1921, Geneva School of Internat. Studies, 1927. Gave lectures on income tax reform, U. of Southern Calif., Feb.-Apr. 1941. President for U.S. of Third Internat. Commn. on Eugenics; mem. Theodore Roosevelt's Nat. Conservation Commn.; chmn. Hygiene Reference Bd. of Life Extension Inst. since 1914; chmn. sub-com. on Alcohol of Council Nat. Defense, 1917-18; pres. Citizens' Com. on War-Time Prohibition, 1917; pres. Com. of 60 on Nat. Prohibition, 1917; chmn. bd. scientific dirs. Eugenics Record Office, 1917; dir. of Cowles Com. for Econ. Research. Vice pres., dir. Gotham Hosp., Gotham Med. Center. Chmn. bd. and dir. Check Master Plan, Inc., Gyrobalance Corp., Automatic Signal Corp.; dir. and mem. exec. com. Remington Rand Inc., dir. Buffalo Elec. Furnace Corp., Sonotone Corp., Latimer Lab., Life Extension Inst. President American Assn. Labor Legislation, 1915-17, Nat. Institute Social Sciences, 1917, Am. Econ. Assn., 1918, Eugenics Research Assn., 1920, Pro-League Independents, 1920, Econometric Soc. 1931-33, Am. Statis. Assn., 1932; founder and 1st pres. Am. Eugenics Soc., 1923-26; founder Vitality Records office, 1937; founder Stable Money Assn.; fellow Royal Statis. Soc., A.A.A.S. (chmn. com. of 100 to promote pub. health and to advocate establishing a nat. dept. of health); rec. sec. New Haven County Anti-Tuberculosis Assn., 1904-14; mem. editorial bd. of Econometrics; mem. Phi Beta Kappa, Sigma Chi. Royal Econ. Society, Conn. Acad. Arts and Sciences, Am. Acad. Polit. and Social Science, Am. Statis. Assn., Am. Ethnographical Soc., N.E. Free Trade League, Internat. Free Trade League, Nat. Assn. Study and Prevention Tuberculosis, Am. Assn. for Study and Prevention Infant Mortality, Nat. Consumers League, League of Nations Assn., Am. Philos. Soc., Reale Accademia dei Lincei (Rome), Institut Internat. Statisque, Norwegian Acad. of Sci. and Letters, Instituto Lombardo (Milan, Italy), Com. for the Nation. Conglist. Club: Cobden (hon.), Civic, Yale, Reform (New York); Faculty Graduate (New Haven). Published weekly index number of wholesale prices in business jours. since 1923, founded Index Number Institute. Author: Mathematical Investigations in the Theory of Value and Prices, 1892, transl. into French, 1917, into Japanese, 1925; Elements of Geometry (with Prof. A. W. Phillips), 1896 (transl. into Japanese, 1900); Bibliography of Mathematical Economics in (and asst. in translating and editing) Cournot's Mathematical Theory of Wealth, 1897; A

Brief Introduction to the Infinitesimal Calculus, 1897 (transl. into German, 1904, Italian, 1909); The Nature of Capital and Income, 1906, transl. into French, 1911, Japanese, 1913, Spanish, 1921, Italian, 1922; The Rate of Interest, 1907, transl. into Japanese, 1912; National Vitality, 1909; The Purchasing Power of Money, 1911, transl. into Japanese, 1911, transl. into German, 1916, and transl. into Russian, 1926; Elementary Principles of Economics, 1910; Why is the Dollar Shrinking?, 1914; How to Live (with Dr. E. L. Fisk, in collaboration with 93 members of hygiene reference board of Life Extension Institute, 1915, translated into Japanese, 1917, Spanish, 1918, Chinese, 1919, Norwegian 1929, 20th rev. ed., with Dr. Haven Emerson 1938, 21st edition appeared, 1945. Stabilizing the Dollar, 1920; The Making of Index Numbers, 1922, trans. into Russian; League or War?, 1923; America's Interest in World Peace, 1924; Prohibition at Its Worst, 1926; The Money Illusion, 1928 (transl. into German, French, Dutch, Polish, Italian, Greek); Prohibition Still at Its Worst (with H. B. Brougham) 1928; The Theory of Interest, 1930 (trans. into German); The Noble Experiment (with H. B. Brougham), 1930; The Stock Market Crash, 1930; Booms and Depressions, 1932; Inflation, 1933; Stamp Scrip, 1933; After Reflation, What?, 1933; Stable Money, a History of the Movement, 1934; 100% Money, 1935, revised edit., 1936; Constructive Income Taxation, 1942; World Maps and Globes (with O. M. Miller), 1944; also numerous articles, monographs, etc, Home: 113 Park Av., Hamden, Conn., Post Office Box 1825, New Haven, Conn. Died Apr. 29, 1947; buried in Evergreen Cemetery, New Haven.

FISHER, JAMES MAXWELL MCCONNELL, naturalist, writer; b. Clifton, Eng., Sept. 3, 1912; s. Kenneth and Constance Isabel (Boyd) F.; King's scholar Eton Coll., 1926-31; M.A., Magdalen Coll., Oxford U., 1935; m. Margery Lilian Edith Turner, Sept. 16, 1936; children—Edmund Boyd, Crispin James, Selina Toussaint (Mrs. Randal Charlton), Adam J. Kenneth, Anstice Rosina, Clemency Thorne. Asst. master Bishop's Stortford Coll., 1935-36; asst. curator Zool. Soc. London, 1936-39; with Bur. Animal Population, Oxford U., 1940-43, Edward Grey Inst. Field Ornithology, 1944-46; editor William Collins, Sons & Co., 1946-56; dir. Rathbone Books Ltd., 1956-64, Aldus Books Ltd., 1962-64; writer, broadcaster for BBC, 1939—. Dep. chmn. Countryside Commn., 1966—; chmn. Northamptonshire Naturalists Trust; mem. council Royal Soc. Protection of Birds; mem. survival service commn. Internat. Union Conservation Nature and Natural Resources. Recipient Gold medal Royal Soc. Protection Birds; Tucker medal British Trust for Ornithology; Union medal Brit. Ornithologist's Union; Arthur A. Allen award Cornell Laboratory of Ornithology; Silver Medal, Zoological Society of London. Corr. fellow Am. Ornithol. Union; hon. mem. Danish Ornithol. Soc.; mem. Arctic Club (past pres.), Linnean Soc. (past council), British Ornith. Union (past council), British Ornith. Club, British Trust for Ornithology (past hon. sec., treas., vice chmn.), Wildfowl Trust (past council), Nat., Canadian Audubon socs., Cooper, Wilson ornithol. socs., Northeastern Bird Banding Assn., numerous other British and fgn. conservation socs. Author: Birds as Animals, 1939; (with Margaret Shaw) Animals as Friends and How to Keep Them, 1939; (with Julian Huxley) The Living Thoughts of Darwin, 1939; Watching Birds, 1940; The Birds of Britain, 1942; Birds of the Village, 1945; Bird Recognition, 1947—; The Fulmar, 1952; Birds of the Field, 1953; (with others) Fine Bird Books, 1953; (with Peter Scott) A Thousand Geese, 1952; (with R. M. Lockley) Sea-Birds, 1954; A History of Birds, 1954; The Wonderful World, 1954; (with Roger T. Peterson) Wild America, 1955; Rockall, 1956; The Wonderful World of the Sea, 1957, The Wonderful World of the Air, 1958; (with Margery Fisher) Shackleton and the Antarctic, 1958; (with Roger T. Peterson) The World of Birds, 1964; The Migration of Birds, 1966; Shell Nature Lovers' Atlas, 1966; The Shell Bird Book, 1966; Zoos of the World, 1967; Thorburn's Birds, 1967; (with others) Wildlife in Danger, 1969; also numerous articles. Home: Northampton Eng Died Sept. 29, 1970.

FISHER, JOHN DIX, physician; b. Needham, Mass., Mar. 27, 1797; s. Aaron and Lucy (Stedman) F.; grad. Brown U., 1820, Harvard Med. Sch., 1825. One of 1st in America to utilize auscultation (an aid to diagnosis); pioneer in use of etherization in childbirth; acting physician Mass. Gen. Hosp.; mem. Mass. Med. Soc., introduced in Am. movement for educating the blind, largely responsible for creation Perkins Instn., Mass. Sch. for Blind, 1829, v.p., dir., 1829-50. Author: Description of the Distinct, Confluent, and Inoculated Smallpox, 1829. Died Mar. 3, 1850.

FISHER, ROBERT JOSEPH, mfr., inventor; b. Athens, Tenn., Jan. 23, 1857; s. Richard M. and Ann M. (Gettys) F.; ed. E. Tenn. Wesleyan U.; m. Alice M. Gauche, June 9, 1892. Teller Cleveland (Tenn.) Nat. Bank, 1880-83; organized First Nat. Bank, Athens, Tenn., and cashier same, 1884-96. Inventor Fisher Book Typewriter (N.Y. and Pa.), and has taken out numerous patents; awarded John Scott Medal by City of Phila. on recommendation of Franklin Inst. for meritorious invention, 1899. Home: Athens, Tenn. Died May 1, 1932.

FISHER, SAMUEL BROWNLEE, civil engr.; b. Cherry Fork, O., Oct. 24, 1846; s. Rev. Jacob Piper and Jane Thompson (Brownlee) F.; B.S., Washington and Jefferson Coll., 1868, M.S., 1871 (D.Sc., 1909); m. Agnes Crooks, Feb. 8, 1881 (died 1906); children—Brownlee, Ann Palmer. With Rogers Locomotive Works, Paterson, N.J., 1869-71; engring. dept. Pa. lines Pittsburgh, from chainman to asst. engr., 1873-85; chief engr. Milwaukee & Northern R.R., 1885-90, Minneapolis, St. Paul & Sault Ste. Marie Ry., 1890-92, Everett & Monte Cristo Ry., Everett, Wash., 1893-94, M.,K.&T. Ry., 1895-1913; chmn. valuation com., M.,K.&T. Ry., 1913-16, cons. engr. same, 1916—. Republican. Presbyn. Home: Parsons, Kan. Died July 9, 1926.

FISK, HAROLD N(ORMAN), geologist; b. Medford, Ore., Aug. 31, 1908; s. George Norman and Lulu Blanche (McPherson) F.; B.S., U. of Ore., 1930, M.A., 1931; Ph.D., U. of Cincinnati, 1935; m. Emma Allen Ayrs, June 8, 1935; children—George Ayrs, Norma Jean. Research asst., U. of Ore., 1930-31; lab. asst., U. of Cincinnati, O., 1931-33; lab. instr., Northwestern U., Evanston, Ill., 1933-35; instr. mineralogy, La. State U., 1935-38, asst. prof., 1938-41, asso. prof., 1941-45, prof. geology, 1945-48; research geologist La. Geol. Survey, 1935-40; cons. Miss. River Commn., 1941—; chief geologic research sect. Humble Oil & Refining Co., Houston, 1948—. Recipient award as distinguished lecturer, Am. Assn. Petroleum Geologists, 1946; James Laurie Prize, Am. Soc. C.E., 1953. Mem. Am. Assn. Petroleum Geologists, Am. Geophys. Union, Geol. Society of Am. (mem. council 1958-60), Soc. Econ. Paleontologists and Mineralogists (hon. mem.; pres. 1953-54), Sigma Xi. Author: Geological Investigation of the Alluvial Valley of the Lower Mississippi River (Mississippi River Commn., Vicksburg, Miss., 1944); other publs. on geology and Cenozoic stratigraphy of La. and Gulf Coast region in Bulls. of La. Geol. Survey and other sci. jours. Home: 1936 Swift Blvd., Houston 77025. Office: Humble Oil & Refining Co., P.O. Box 2180, Houston, Tex. Died Oct. 3, 1964.

FISKE, BRADLEY ALLEN, naval officer; b. Lyons, N.Y., June 13, 1854; s. Rev. William Allen and Susan (Bradley) F.; grad. U.S. Naval Acad. (2d in class), 1874; m. Josephine, d. Joseph Wesley Harper, 1882; 1 dau., Caroline Harper. Ensign, July 17, 1875; promoted through grades to rear-adm., Aug. 3, 1911; retired June 13, 1916. Served on various duties and stations; was on "Yorktown," under Commander Robley D. Evans, in Valparaiso, during critical times following the "Baltimore" incident; on board Admiral Benham's flagship, "San Francisco," in Rio, in 1894, when the U.S. fleet cleared for action, and enforced neutral rights; navigator of "Petrel" at battle of Manila; reported by capt. of "Petrel" for "eminent and conspicuous conduct in battle," and by Admiral Dewey for "heroic conduct" at battle of Manila; navigator of monitor "Monadnock" during 4 mos. following outbreak of the Filipino insurrection; took part in bombardments of Parañaque and Malabon; as exec. officer of "Yorktown" took part in bombardment of San Fernando, Aug. 1899; comd. the Minneapolis, the Arkansas and the Tennessee; comd. 5th, 3d and 1st divs. Atlantic Fleet, 1912; aid for operations, Navy Dept., 1913, till May 1915, when resigned. Mem. 1st Electrical Conf., Phila., 1884; mem. naval wireless telegraph bd., 1904-05; mem. Gen. Bd. of Navy, also Joint Bd. Army and Navy, 1910-11 and 1913-15. Invented boat detaching apparatus, system of elec. communication for interiors of warships, stadimeter, an electric range finger, an electric ammunition hoist, a range indicator, a battle-order telegraph, an elec. engine telegraph, a helm-indicator, a speed and direction indicator, a system of turning turrets of war ships by electricity, the naval telescope mount, the naval telescope sight, gun director system, wireless control of moving vessels, the torpedo-plane, system for detecting submarines, prism system of target practice, electro-magnetic system for exploding torpedoes under ships, and also the reading machine. The naval telescope sight has been adopted by all the navies of the world, and is the main cause of the recent great improvement in the accuracy of naval gunnery; the torpedoplane has been adopted by all the leading navies. Awarded Elliott Cresson gold medal by Franklin Institute, 1893; gold medal for prize essay by U.S. Naval Institute, 1905; gold medal by Aero Club of America for invention of torpedoplane, 1919. Pres. U.S. Naval Inst., 1911-23. Club: Army and Navy of New York (hon. pres.). Author: Electricity in Theory and Practice, 1884; 10 edits.; War Times in Manila; The Navy as a Fighting Machine, 1917, 2d edit., 1918; From Midshipman to Rear Admiral, 1919; The Art of Fighting, 1920; Invention, 1921; also numerous articles on elec. and naval subjects. Home: Waldorf Astoria, New York. N.Y. Died Apr. 7, 1942.

FISKE, WILLIAM F., entomologist; b. Webster, N.H., Mar. 20, 1876; s. Friend F. and Jane B. (Smith) F.; spl. course N.H. Coll. Agr. and Mech. Arts; unmarried. Asst. entomologist N.H. Expt. Sta., 1897-1901; asst. entomologist for state of Ga., 1901-3; asst. in forest investigations, 1903-6; in charge Gypsy Moth Lab., Melrose Highlands, Mass., May, 1906-Jan., 1913. U.S. Dept. Agr.; spl. investigator of sleeping sickness in Africa for joint commn. of Royal Soc. and British Colonial Office, 1913—. Mem. A.A.A.S., American Society Economic Entomology, Boston Soc. Natural History, Cambridge Entomol. Soc., Entomol. Soc. Washington, etc. Club: Cosmos (Washington, D.C.). Address: Bur. of Entomology, Dept. of Agr., Washington

FISKEN, JOHN BARCLAY, electrical engr.; b. Helensburgh, Dumbartonshire, Scotland, Nov. 2, 1861; s. Archibald and Sarah A. (Kerr) F.; grad. Coll. of Science and Arts, Glasgow, Scotland, 1886 (1st class honor diploma); m. Helen Kyle Binnie, of Barassie, Ayrshire, Scotland, June 4, 1889 (died June 30, 1901); children—Mary Carolyn (Mrs. Louis Kapek), Ruth Kerr (Mrs. Thomas Large), James Binnie; m. 2d, Eva Jane Weymouth, Sept. 3, 1907. With office of Anchor Line Steamship Co., Glasgow, Scotland, 4 yrs.; came to U.S., 1886; with Washington Water Power Co. and its predecessors since 1887, except 1 yr., chief engr. same, 1918-20, and consulting engr. from 1920 until date of retirement, December 31, 1942. Fellow Am. Inst. Elec. Engrs. (v.p. 1919-20); mem. Associated Engineers of Spokane. Republican. Conglist. Clubs: Tesemini Outing, Spokane Country, Spokane City and University, Seniors North West Golf Assn., Rotary (Spokane). Home: W. 28 28th Av., Spokane 9, Wash. Died June 6, 1946; buried in Fairmount Memorial Park, Spokane.

FISTELL, HARRY, musician, educator, inventor, bus. exec.; b. Beaver Falls, Pa., Jan. 16, 1907; s. Abraham Isaac and Ella (Pitler) F.; B.A., U. Denver 1930; B.Mus. Edn., Am. Conservatory Music, 1939; m. Marian Leah Wolf, Jan. 13, 1934; 1 son, Ira Jacob. Orch. leader, 1925-33; high sch. tchr., 1931-33; tchr. WPA sch. programs, Chgo., 1933-41; founder, owner pres. Chgo. Music Sales (Ill.). 1941-71, Toneline Mfg. Co., Chgo., 1941-71; pres. Allied Affiliates Inc., Chgo., 1970-71; mgrs. rep. and sales rep., 1941-71, Lowenthal Mfg. Co., Chgo., 1967-71; appraiser, cons. mediator for music industry. Mem. Am. Fedn. Musicians, Fretted Instrument Guild Am.; Nat. Assn. Music Mchts., Ill. Mfg. Assn., U. Denver Alumni Assn., Nat. Band Assn. Mem. B'nai B'rith. Designed and implemented course of music instrn. for individual and class participation (strings, brass and reeds). Home: Chicago IL Died Dec. 28, 1971.

FITCH, ASA, entomologist; b. Fitch's Point, Salem, N.Y., Feb. 24, 1809; s. Dr. Asa and Abigail (Martin) F.; grad. Vt. Acad. of Medicine, Castleton, 1829; m. Elizabeth McNeil, Nov. 15, 1832. Asst. prof. natural history Rensselaer Poly. Inst., Troy, N.Y., 1830; practiced medicine, Fort Miller, N.Y., 1831-38; moved to Salem, N.Y., 1838; commd. to categorize insects of N.Y. State by N.Y. State Cabinet of Natural History; state entomologist, N.Y., 1854-71. Died Apr. 8, 1879.

FITCH, CHARLES HALL, engineer; b. Manitowoc, Wis., Sept. 12, 1854; s. Charles Walton and Mary F. (Warbasse) F.; ed. pvt. schs. Wis. and Md. and Georgetown (D.C.) Acad.; studied engring. under pvt. tutors; m. Mary C. H. Stevens, of Washington, Apr. 26, 1882. Aid, U.S. Coast Survey, 1873-76; mining and pub. land surveys, N.M., 1876-84; topographer, U.S. Geol. Survey, 1884-93; Gen. Land Office, 1893-95; topographer and engr., U.S. Geol. Survey, 1895-1902; topographer in charge Indian Ty. surveys, 1895-99; engr. U.S. Reclamation Service, 1902-09; mgr. Ida. Irrigation Co., Ltd., Richfield, Ida., 1909-10; project engr., U.S. Reclamation Service in charge Salt River Valley project, Mar. 15, 1911-13; project mgr. same, Nov. 1, 1913-15; chief clerk U.S. Reclamation Service since 1916. Address: U.S. Reclamation Service, Washington, D.C. *

FITCH, JOHN, metal craftsman, inventor, steamboat developer; b. Windsor, Conn., Jan. 21, 1743; s. Joseph and Sarah (Shaler) F.; m. Lucy Roberts, Dec. 29, 1767, 1 child. Established brass shop, East Windsor, Conn., 1764; in charge of Trenton Gun Factory during Revolutionary War; surveyed lands along Ohio Valley and N.W. Territory, 1780-85; organized co. to acquire and exploit lands in N.W. Territory, 1782; invented steamboat successfully launched and operated, 1787; launched 60-foot steam paddle propelled boat used to carry passengers from Phila. to Burlington, N.J., 1788; received French and U.S. patents for steamboat, 1791; lost financial support through inefficient handling of financial affairs, even though he had perfected and constructed 4 steamboats. Died Bardstown, Ky., July 2, 1798.

FITCH, JOSEPH HENRY, civil engr.; b. Burlington, Ia., Feb. 12, 1861; s. David and Sarah M. (Williams) F.; ed. common schs., Lexington, Mass., and Mass. Inst. Tech.; civil engr. Arlington Mills since 1885. Home: Andover, Mass. *

FITCH, WILLIAM EDWARD, physician, author; b. Burlington, N.C., May 29, 1867; s. William James and Mary Elizabeth (King) F.; M.D.; Coll. Physicians and Surg., Baltimore, Md., 1891; m. Minnie Crump, Oct. 5, 1892; children—Lucille, Elizabeth, William Edward. Specialist in diseases of metabolism, med. hydrology and dietotherapy; lecturer on principles of surgery, Fordham U. Sch. Medicine, 1907-09; attending physician Vanderbilt Clinic; attending gynecologist outpatient dept. Presbyn. Hosp.; asst. in surg. clinic, St. Luke's Hospital; med. dir. and cons. med. hydrologist at French Lick (Ind.) Springs, 1931; cons. med. hydrologist Crazy Hotel and Spa Mineral Wells, Tex.

Served as editor Gaillard's Southern Medicine, 1900-09; editor Pediatrics, 1908-17; co-editor and pub. Am. Jour. Electrotherapeutics and Radiology, 1918-19. Served as acting asst. surg. U.S.P.H. and M.H. Service, Spanish-Am. War, 1898; commd. 1st lt. Med. R.C., U.S. Army, July 3, 1912; capt., July 16, 1917; maj., Sept. 25, 1917; comdg. officer hosp. at Ft. Terry, N.Y., 18 mos., later at Ft. Totten and Ft. Schuyler, N.Y., and chief nutrition and dir. mess, Base Hosp., Camp Jackson, S.C.; later adviser to camp surgeon's office; hon. disch., Dec. 3, 1918. Mem. Hudson-Fulton Celebration Commn. Pres. Alamance Battle Ground Commn. Mem. med. soc. states of Va., Ind., Am. Med. Editors' and Authors' Assn., Med. Assn. Greater N.Y., Nat. Soc. Advancement Gastroenterology. Am. Soc. Balneology, Internat. Soc. Med. Hydrology (London), N.Y. Soc. Founders and Patriots Am. (council, gen. court), Soc. Cincinnati, Soc. Fgn. Wars, Soc. Am. Wars, Soc. Vets. World War, Southern Soc. (New York). Democrat. Episcopalian. Clubs: Lotos (New York); Burlington Country. Author: Fitch's Medical Pocket Formulary, 1914, now in 7th edit.; Dietotherapy (3 vols.), 1918, now in 3d edit.; Mineral Waters of the U.S. and Greater American Spas, 1926; Diseases of Metabolism; The Battle of Alamance; also various writings on early history of N. Carolina. Address: 3707 Segovia St., Coral Gables, Fla. Died Sept. 12, 1949; buried Burlington, N.C.

FITTERER, J(OHN) C(ONRAD), engr. and mathematician; b. at Clyde, Ohio, Dec. 15, 1871; s. Jeremiah S. and Rosena E. (Mook) F.; B.Sc., Ohio State U., 1898; B.S. in C.E., U. of Colo., 1904, C.E., 1912; m. Lucy E. Kamp, Dec. 27, 1899. In charge dept. Am. Clay Machinery Co., Bucyrus, O., 1898-1903; with U.S. Reclamation Service, various projects, until 1908; prof. civ. and irrigation engring., U. of Wyo., 1908-28, also irrigation engr. Agrl. Expt. Sta., and acting dean Coll. Engring., 1922-24; prof. math., head dept. Colo. Sch. Mines, Golden; cons. practice, Mem. Am. Soc. C.E., Am. Math. Soc., Math. Assn. America, Soc. for Promotion Engring. Edn., A.A.A.S., N.E.A., Tau Beta Pi, Phi Kappa Phi. Republican. Presbyterian. Wrote: Reclamation by Drainage, 1911; co-author of Meteorology for Twenty Years, 1913. Home: 1620 Maple St., Golden, Colo. Died Mar. 1947; buried Crown Hill Park, Denver.

FITZGERALD, DESMOND, civil engr.; b. Nassau, New Providence, May 20, 1846; s. Capt. Lionel C. W. H. and Caroline (Brown) F.; ed. Phillips Acad., Andover, Mass.; m. Elizabeth P. C. Salisbury, June 21, 1870. For 40 yrs. practice as hydraulic engr., principally in connection with construction maintenance of Boston water-supply system. Dept. engr. Met. Water Bd., Boston; was chmn. of the Topographical Survey Commn. of Mass.; chmn. Brookline Park Commn.; mem. Met. Improvement Commn. of Mass.; cons. engr., water supply and sewage systems, Manila, P.I., 1904. Fellow Am. Acad. Arts and Sciences. Home: Brookline, Mass. Died Jan. 12, 1928.

FITZGERALD, THEODORE CLINTON, veterinarian, educator; b. Green Springs, O., Mar. 25, 1903; s. Albert Daniel and Maud (May) F.; student Heidelberg U., Tiffin, O., 1922-23; D.V.M., Ohio State U., 1928, M.S., 1933; m. Frances Clement Bailey, June 27, 1929; children—Robert Theodore, Ivan Dale (dec.). Mem. bur. animal industry Ohio Dept. Agr., also engaged in gen. practice vet. medicine, Ohio, 1928-30; instr. anatomy Ohio State U., 1930-40; prof., head dept. anatomy and histology Auburn U., from 1940. Served with Vet. Corps, AUS, World War II. Grantee NSF, 1961, Mem. Am., Ala., Central Ala. vet. med. assns., Am. Assn. Vet. Anatomists (pres. 1960-61), Animal Disease Research Workers So. States, Ala. Edn. Assn., Phi Zeta, Omicron Delta Kappa, Omega Tau Sigma (Leta award 1958). Author: Anatomy and Histology Coturnix Quail, 1968. Contbr. articles profl. jours. Instituted saliva testing race horses in Ohio. Home: Auburn AL Died Oct. 17, 1967.

FITZ-PATRICK, GILBERT, obstetrician; b. Columbiana Co., O., Jan. 19, 1873; s. Thomas C. and Mary J. (Gilbert) F.; ed. Ohio Northern U., Ada; M.D., Chicago Homoe. Med. Coll., 1896; m. Elizabeth Sanford, May 1913. Interne Silver Cross Hosp., Joliet, Ill., 1897; house surgeon, Garfield Park Hosp., Chicago, 1898-99, Rotunda Hosp., Dublin, Ireland, 1902, Sloane Maternity Hosp., New York, 1903; formerly head dept. of obstetrics, Hahnemann Med. Coll. and Hosp., and attdg. obstetrician Cook Co. Hosp.; cons. obstetrician, Ill. Masonic Hosp.; attdg. obstetrician Chicago Polyclinic and Henrotin hosps.; mem. visiting staff Passavant Hosp.; trustee Ill. Masonic Hosp. Mem. Ill. State Med. Exam. Bd. Mem. bd. Gorgas Memorial Inst. of Tropical Medicine; fellow and gov. Am. Coll. Surgeons; chmn. Ill. Cancer Committee. Colonel Med. R.C., U.S.A.; chief of surgery, Base Hosp., Camp Gordon, Atlanta, Ga., World War; now comdg. officer U.S. Gen. Hosp. No. 110; del. from Assn. Mil. Surgeons, U.S.A., to Royal Inst. of Pub. Health, Ghent, Belgium, 1927; U.S. del. to 1st Internat. Congress of Pub. Health and Hygiene, Cairo, Egypt, 1928. Republican. Mason. Home: Chicago, Ill. Died Nov. 15, 1936.

FLAD, EDWARD, civil engr.; b. Arcadia, Mo., Nov. 23, 1860; s. Henry and Caroline (Reichard) F.; C.E., Washington U., 1881; m. Emilie E. Speck, Feb. 10, 1890 (died 1935); 1 dau., Virginia S. (Mrs. H. Towner Deane). Draftsman and mech. engr. St. Louis Water Works, 1883-88; Johnson & Flad, consulting engrs., 1889-92; gen. consulting engr., 1892-99; water commr. City of St. Louis and mem. Bd. Pub. Improvements, 1899-1903; consulting engr. since 1903. Mem. Bd. of Freeholders that drafted the charter adopted by the City of St. Louis, June 30, 1914. Special master in Pulaski Chancery Court on Little Rock, Ark., water works case, 1914. Asso. mem. Naval Consulting Bd. of U.S.; mem. Pub. Service Commn. of Mo., 1917-21, consulting engr. since 1921; mem. Miss. River Commn. since 1924. Republican. Mem. Am. Soc. C.E., Am. Soc. M.E., Loyal Legion. Clubs: University, Engineers, Noonday. Home: 17 Lenox Pl. Office: 828 U.S. Court House St Louis MO

FLAD, HENRY, engr., inventor; b. Rennhoff, Germany, July 30, 1824; s. Jacob and Franziska (Brunn) F.; grad. U. Munich (Germany), 1846; m. Helen Reichard, 1848; m. 2d, Caroline Reichard, Sept. 12, 1855 6; 3 children. Served as capt. co. of army engrs. in Bavaria during German Revolution 1848; fled to U.S., 1849; ry. constrn. engr., 1849-60; served from pvt. to col. U.S. Army during Civil War; asst. to James B. Eads in constrn. Eads Bridge over Mississippi River; mem. bd. water commrs. St. Louis 1868-76 (during which time city water-works were completed); mem. Am. Soc. C.E., pres., 1866; founder Engrs. Club of St. Louis, pres. 1868-80; pres. St. Louis Bd. Pub. Improvements, 1877-90; mem. Mississippi River Commn., 1890-98; patented filters, water meters, methods of preserving timber and sprinkling streets, systems rapid transit and cable rys.; devised hydrostatic and hydraulic elevator, deep-sea sounding apparatus, pressure gauges, pile driver. Died Pitts., June 20, 1898.

FLAGG, JOSIAH FOSTER, civil engr.; b. Dedham, Mass., Sept. 4, 1835; s. Josiah Foster and Mary (Wait) F.; ed. in common, high and Latin schs., Boston; S.B., summa cum laude, Harvard, 1854; m. Emma A. Wiggin, Apr. 13, 1858 (died 1888); m. 2d, Florence N. Dukes, Dec. 3, 1903. Had charge of important engring. works in Mexico, S. America and the W.I., as well as in New York, and other parts of U.S. Home: Santa Barbara, Calif. Died Apr. 13, 1928.

FLAGG, PALUEL JOSEPH, physician; b. Yonkers, N.Y., Aug. 22, 1886; s. Howard W. and Lilli (de Marmon) F.; M.D., Fordham U. Med. Sch., 1909; m. Stella Robblee, Oct. 8, 1910; 1 dau., Sister Virginia Marie; m. 2d, Dorothy Ritter, Sept. 12, 1916; children—Jane Dorita (Mrs. Joseph Richardson), Paluel Venard, Alfred Dante, James Anthony, Dorothy Byrne (Mrs. George Webster), Francis Mercier, Peter Guerin, Paul Martin, Mary Ann (Mrs. James Wilson), Noel Morrow, Thomas Aquinas; m. 3d, Marcella V. Devlin, June 27, 1945. Practiced medicine, 1909-70; cons. pneumatologist, Manhattan Eye and Ear, New York City Eye and Ear Hospitals; Queens Hospital, and St. Francis Hospital, Honolulu, Hawaii. Founder Catholic Med. Missions, N.Y.C. Decorated knight Grand Cross Holy Sepulchre. Fellow Nat. Acad. Scis.; mem. Soc. for the Prevention of Asphyxial Death, Inc. (founder; pres.), Med. Surgical Soc., Med, Jurisprudence, Med. Mission Bd. (founder), Phi Alpha Sigma. Author: Patient's Viewpoint, 1923; Art of Anaesthesia, 1916, 1944; Art of Resuscitation, 1944. Inventor of apparatus for anaesthesia and resuscitation. Home: Yonkers NY Died Jan. 17, 1970; buried Vinalhaven ME

FLANAGAN, JAMES WAINWRIGHT, mining engr.; b. Henderson, Tex., Oct. 26, 1872; s. Robert Buck and Anna Bell (Cornelius) F.; ed. pub. schs. and pvt. study; m. Panchita G. Love, Jan. 1902; 1 son, James W. (dec.); m. 2d, Hazel B. Brown, Dec. 10, 1913; 1 dau., Diva B. Railroad work and mining, 1888-1912, in Cuba, Mexico and U.S.; foreign financial assn., 1913-19, with Sir Herbert Holt, pres. Royal Bank of Can.; organized, 1919, Andian Nat. Corp., of Toronto, Can., to build 615 miles petroleum pipe line from Cartagena to Barranca Bermeja in Colombia, S.A., and to purchase wharf and terminals at Cartagena; obtained concession from Colombian Govt. and completed construction; was 1st v.p. and gen. manager Andian National Corp., Ltd., pres., 1925-42; spl. asst. to exec. officer of petroleum for war, serving Puerto Rico, Cuba and West Indies, Nov. 1942-44. dir. International Petroleum Corp.; dir. Macassa Mines, Ltd., Toronto, Ont., 1930. Served as lieut. col. Cuban Army, 1896-97; awarded Medal of Mil. Merit; spl. assignment on staff of Brig. Gen. W. W. Gordon, U.S. Army, 1898; commd. hon. lt. col., 2d Bn., Irish Regt. of Canada, Dec. 1940, and of 1st Bn., Irish Regt. of Canada, July 1941. Hon. mem. Cuban Expn. at St. Louis, Mo., 1904. Democrat. Roman Catholic. Decorated by Pope Pius XI, as Comdr. Order of St. Gregory, 1926; decorated Cross of Boyacá, in the official and military class, Colombia, 1933. Clubs: Bankers, New York Athletic, India House, Canadian Club, Army and Navy, Catholic (New York); Denver Country; Jockey (Lima, Peru); Jockey, Anglo-American (Bogota, Colombia); Cartagena (Cartagena). Address: Waldorf Astoria Hotel, New York, N.Y.; also Shamrock Hotel, Houston, Tex. Died July, 1950.

FLANDERS, RALPH EDWARD, mech. engr., ex.-U.S. senator; born Barnet, Vermont, September 28, 1880; son of Albert W. and Mary L. (Gilfillan) F.; graduate high school Central Falls, Rhode Island; International Corr. Schs.; hon. degrees: M.A., Dartmouth, 1932, LL.D., 1951; M.E. Stevens Inst., 1932; D.Sc., Middlebury (Vermont) College, 1934, Rose Polytechnical Institute, 1935, Univ. of Vermont, 1935; Northwestern U., 1940; LL.D., Harvard University, 1950; also Poly. Inst. Bklyn., 1934, Northeastern University, 1942, Clarkson Inst. Tech., 1949, Marlboro Coll., 1949, Allegheny Coll., 1953, Rollins Coll., 1954, Allegheny Coll., U. R.I.; married Helen E. Hartness, Nov. 1, 1911;children—Helen Elizabeth Ballard, Anna H. Balivet (dec.), James Hartness. Machinist apprentice and draftsman, Providence and Woonsocket, 1897-1901; designer Internat. Paper Box. Mach. Co., Nashua, N.H., 1903; asso. editor Mach., New York, 1905-10; engr. Fellows Gear Shaper Co., Springfield, Vt., 1910; became dir. and mgr. Jones & Lamson Mach. Co., Springfield, 1912, pres., 1933-46; president of Bryant Chucking Grinder Co., 1934-46; dir. Nat. Life Ins. Co.; pres. Fed. Reserve Bank of Bos., 1944-46. Pres. Am. Research & Devel. Corp., 1946, now dir.; U.S. Senator from Vt., 1946-58. Godkin lectr. Harvard, 1949. Trustee St. Johnsbury (Vt.) Academy, Sterling School; member of corp. Mass. Inst. Tech.; mem. bus. adv. and planning council of U.S. Dept. Commerce, 1933; also mem. Indsl. Advisory Bd. of NRA, Advisory Bd. for the Subsistence Homestead Adminstrn.; adminstr. Machine Tool Priorities, Office of Production Management, Washington, D.C., 1941; mem. Economic Stabilization Bd., 1942-44; chmn. Machine Tool Com. of Combined Prodn. and Resources Bd., 1943; chmn. Screw Thread Standardization Bd. of Am. Standards Assn. until 1944; chmn. research com. and trustee Com. for Economic Development. Mem. Nat. Screw Thread Commn., 1920-24; dir. Social Science Research Council, 1932-36; mem. Am. Engring. Council (v.p. 1937; Hoover medal, 1944). Pres. New England Council, 1941-42; mem. American Society Mechanical Engineers (pres. 1934; Worcester-Warner medal, 1938), Franklin Inst. (Edward Longstreth medal with Ernest V. Flanders), Nat. Machine Tool Builders (pres. 1923), Acad. Polit. and Social Science, Am. Econ. Assn. Hon. mem. M.I.T. Chapter of Tau Beta Pi, Phi Beta Kappa (Dartmouth College, 1948). Republican. Congregationalist. Clubs: Engineers' (New York City, N.Y.); Union (Boston, Mass.); Cosmos (Washington). Author: Gear Cutting Machinery, 1909; Taming Our Machines, 1931; Platform for Am., 1936; The American Century; Letter To A Generation, 1956; Senator from Vermont, 1960.; Models for Living, 1967. Co-author: Toward Full Employment, 1938; also tech. papers. Home: Springfield VT Died Feb. 19, 1970; buried Summer Hill Cemetery, Springfield VT

FLATH, EARL HUGO, elec. engr., educator; b. Dayton, O., June 5, 1895; s. Andrew Jackson and Cora Helen (Sigler) F.; E.E., U. of Cincinnati, 1919; M.S., Georgia Sch. of Tech., 1926; m. Ruth Lovertia Riley, June 5, 1920; children—Earl Hugo, Joseph Clarence Andrew. Began as office boy Nat. Cash Register Co., Dayton, 1913; university apprentice same company, 1914-19, asst. elec. engr., 1919; asso. prof. elec. engring., U. of Ala., 1919-20; development and research engr., Bell Telephone Labs., 1920-22; asso. prof. elec. engring. and dir. coop. courses, Georgia Sch. Tech., 1922-25; dean of engring., Southern Methodist University, Dallas, 1925-60, dean emeritus from 1960; prof. elec. engring. Tenn. Poly. Inst., from 1961. Served as 2d lt. inf., U.S. Army, 1918; 1st lt. Ordnance Res. to 1933. Trustee Highland Park Ind. Sch. Dist., 1935-44. Fellow I.E.E.E. (chairman N. Tex. sect., 1944); member Am. Soc. Engring. Edn., Nat. Soc. Profl. Engrs., Am. Legion, Sigma Tau, Phi Kappa Phi, Tau Beta Pi, Eta Kappa Nu, Alpha Tau Omega. Methodist. Club: Dallas Technical. Home: Cookeville TN Deceased.

FLEISHER, WALTER LOUIS, engr.; b. Phila., Pa., July 18, 1880; s. Simon and Rosa Wolf F.; B.S., Univ. of Pa., 1900, M.S. 1901, M.E. (hon.) 1931; m. Marcia Garrick 1938 (died 1947); children—Walter L., Anna (Mrs. Jerome Shore), Jeffrey. Engr.-in-chief firm of Francis Bros. and Jellett, N.Y. City, 1903-11; formed W. L. Fleisher & Co., Inc., 1911 and served as pres., treas. and chief engr. until merger with 2 other cos. under name of The Cooling and Air Conditioning Corp. and served as vice pres. and chief engr. to 1930; established consulting office Walter L. Fleisher, N.Y.C., 1930, since served as pres. and treas.; pres. Air & Refrigeration Corp. since 1934. Life mem. Am. Soc. Heating and Air Conditioning Engrs., Inc. (2d v.p., 1939, pres., 1941; chmn. com. on air conditioning in industry). Recipient F. Paul Anderson award, 1953; citation U. Pa., 1955. Fellow Am. Soc. Heating and Air Conditioning. Am. Soc. Refrigerating Engrs.; mem. Am. Soc. Bakery Engrs., A.S.M.E. (life), Heating, Piping and Air Conditioning Contractors Nat. Assn. (hon. mem., chmn. standards com.); mem. Princeton U. Adv. Council Dept. of M.E., since 1940. Club: Princeton. Editor-in-chief ASHVE Guide, 1932-33; mem. bd. cons. and cont. editors of Heating, Piping and Air Conditioning since 1929. Contbr. chpts. to tech. publs. Mem. ASHVE Speakers Bur. Holder 100 Am. and fgn. patents. Home: Saw Mill Farm, New City, N.Y. Address: 439 Madison Av., N.Y.C. 22. Died Apr. 18, 1959.

FLEMER, JOHN ADOLPH, topographical engr.; b. New York, Apr. 1, 1859; s. Charles H. and Martha (Lindenkohl) F.; ed. Latin sch., 1870-74; grad. Poly. Sch., Cassel, Germany, 1878; course in civ. engring., Royal Tech. High Sch., Berlin, 1878-81; m. Cornelia Chaplin Matthews, Mar. 22, 1887; children—Martchen Lindenkohl (Mrs. James Latane), Ellen Bagby Matthews (dec.), Cornelia Chaplin Matthews (Mrs. Julian Hungerford Griffith). With topog. survey of D.C., 1882-86; asst. U.S. Coast and Geod. Survey, 1886-1900; with F. and F. Nurseries, Springfield, N.J., 1900-03; engr. to commr. for demarcation of Alaskan boundary, 1904-06. Topog. engr. to Commn. on Improvement and Development of Jamaica Bay, N.Y., 1909-10. Fellow A.A.A.S., Am. Geog. Soc.; mem. Washington Soc. Engrs. U.S. Naval Inst.; Soc. of Am. Mil. Engrs., Am. Soc. of Engrs., Va. Acad. of Science; asso. mem. Am. Museum of Natural History, Societe Academique d'Histoire Internationale. Contbr. of articles on photographic surveying to scientific jours., U.S. Coast and Geod. Survey reports, etc. Author: Treatise on Photo-topographic Methods and Instruments, 1906. Home: Oakgrove VA

FLEMING, JOHN ADAM, magnetician, geophysicist; b. Cincinnati, O., Jan. 28, 1877; s. Americus V. and Catherine B. (Ritzmann) F.; B.S., U. of Cincinnati, 1899, D.Sc., 1933; D.Sc., Dartmouth Coll., 1934; m. Henrietta C. B. Ratjen, June 17, 1903 (died Mar. 26, 1912); 1 dau., Margaret Catherine; m. 2d, Carolyn Ratjen, Oct. 30, 1913. Aid, U.S. Coast and Geod. Survey, 1899-1903, asst., 1903, magnetic observer, 1904-10; chief magnetician of the dept. of terrestrial magnetism, Carnegie Institution, Washington, 1904-46, chief observatory div., 1915-18, chief magnetic survey div., 1919-21, assistant director, 1922-29, acting director 1929-34, director 1935-46, retired in 1946; adviser of Carnegie Institution, Washington, in international scientific relations, 1946-54. Trustee of Woods Hole Oceanographic Institute, 1930-50, Washington Biophysical Institute, 1940-46; president Temporary Commission on Liquidation of International Polar Year, 1932-33, 1948-50. President Assn. Terrestial Magnetism and Elec. International Union of Geodesy and Geophysics, 1930-48; mem. Internat. Commn. Terrestrial Magnetism and Atmospheric Electricity, 1930-46; mem. International Commission for Polar Year, 1931-47; member of executive council Internat. Council of Scientific Unions, since 1937 (president 1946-49); member National Research Council, del. to assemblies of Internat. Union Geodesy and Geophysics; acting chairman, American section Aeroartic, 1929-33. del. from Nat. Research Council to Stockholm Assembly, 1930, Lisbon Assembly, 1933, Edinburgh Assembly, 1936, Washington Assembly, 1939, of Internat. Union Geodesy and Geophysics. Fellow A.A.A.S., Washington Academy Sciences, American Physical Society, American Geog. Soc.; mem. Nat. Acad. Sciences (chairman section on geophysics, 1951-54), American Institute of Mining and Metallurgic Engineers, American Geophysical Union (gen. sec., 1925-47, hon. president since 1947), Seismol. Soc. of America, Md. Acad. Science, Philos. Soc. Washington (sec. 1913-16, pres. 1925), Nat. Inst. of Social Sciences, Sigma Xi; hon. mem. State Russian Geog. Soc., Royal Soc. of New Zealand, corr. mem. Michelsen Inst. Science and Intellectual Freedom of Norway, Geophysical Society of Finland; mem. Norwegian Acad. Sciences and Letters, Geological Soc. of Peru, Geographical Soc. of Lima. Awarded William Bowie medal of Am. Geophysical Union, 1941; Charles Chree medal and prize of The Physical Soc. (London) 1945; certified effective service O.S.R.D., 1945; certificate exceptional service, Bureau of Ordnance, United States Navy, 1945; Commander of the Order of St. Olav of Norway, 1948. Republican. Presbyterian. Club: Cosmos. Editor and co-author: Scientific Results of the Ziegler Polar Expedition of 1903-05, 08. Co-author of vols. II to VII, Researches of Department of Terrestrial Magnetism, Carnegie Institution, Washington, 1915, 17, 21, 25, 27, 46; Scientific Results of Cruise VII of the Carnegie during, 1928-29, 1943-46. Editor of Journal Terrestrial Magnetism and Atmospheric Electricity, 1927-49. Contributor numerous articles and reviews on geophysics. Address: The Cosmas Club, Washington. Died July 29, 1956; buried Woodlawn Cemetery, Nashville.

FLEMING, SAMUEL WILSON, JR., cons. engr.; b. Harrisburg, Pa., July 7, 1885; s. Samuel Wilson and Mary (deSausser) F.; B.A., Princeton, 1906; M.E., Lehigh U., 1909; m. Sarah Fullerton Hastings, Jan. 8, 1918; children—Barbara (Mrs. George W. Reily III), Frances (Mrs. George B. Barnard), Samuel Wilson III: m. 2d, Nancy Robinson Simmons, Aug. 23, 1948. Engr., Central Hudson Gas & Electric Co., Newburgh, N.Y., 1909-15; partner, treas. Gannett Fleming Corddry & Carpenter, Inc., engrs., Harrisburg, 1915—, now chmn., treas.; pres. Owego Waterworks; dir. Cayuga Rock Salt Co., Nat. Central Bank & Trust Co., Gen. Waterworks Corp. Trustee Temple U. Served as maj. 315th Inf., 79th Div. AEF, World War I; lt. col. 104th Cav., Pa. N.G. Decorated D.S.C., Order Purple Heart, Legion of Honor, Croix de Guerre (France). Mem. Am. Soc. French Legion of Honor, Engrs. Soc. Pa. (pres.), C. of C. (pres.) Presbyn, (trustee). Home: 104 South St. Office: 600 N. 2d St., Harrisburg, Pa. Died Apr. 16, 1966.

FLEMING, WILLIAMINA PATON, astronomer; b. Dundee, Scotland, May 15, 1857; d. Robert and Mary (Walker) Stevens; ed. there; married. Taught at Dundee, 1871-76; asst. Harvard Coll. Obs., 1879—; apptd, 1898, curator astron. photographs. Has charge of Astrophotographic Bldg., Harvard, and is assisted by more than a dozen women computers; known to astronomers as a discoverer of new stars, variables, etc. Hon. mem. Royal Astron. Soc. (London), 1906; hon. asso. in astronomy, Wellesley Coll., 1906. Home: Cambridge, Mass. Died 1911.

FLETCHER, ALICE CUNNINGHAM, ethnologist; b. Boston, 1845; ed. pvt. schs. Devised system for loaning of small sums of money to aid Indians to buy land and build houses for themselves; instrumental in securing land in severalty to Omaha tribe by Act of Aug. 7, 1882, and apptd. spl. agt. to allot the Omaha tribe, 1883-84; apptd. spl. agt. under Severalty Act of Feb. 1887; allotted the Winnebago tribe, 1887-88; Nez Perces tribe, 1889-92; connected with anthrop. dept. of Chicago Expn., 1893. Asst. in ethnology, Peabody Mus. Am. Archaeology and Ethnology, 1882—; holder Thaw Fellowship, 1891—. Author: Indian Story and Song from North America, 1900. Home: Washington, D.C. Died Apr. 1923.

FLETCHER, AUSTIN BRADSTREET, civil engr.; b. Cambridge, Mass., Jan. 19, 1872; s. Ruel Haseltine and Rebecca Caroline (Wyman) F.; student Lawrence Scientific Sch., 1889-93; S.B. in C.E., Harvard, 1893; m. Ethel Hovey, Mar. 1, 1894; children—Dorothy (Mrs. Laurence H. Chapman), Norman (dec.). Sec. and exec. officer Mass. Highway Commn., 1893-1910; sec. and engr. San Diego County (Calif.) Highway Commn., 1910-11; state highway engr. of Calif., 1911-23; highway engr. Joint N.E. R.R. Com., Jan.-May 1923; cons. highway engr. U.S. Dept. Agr., Bur. of Pub. Roads, 1923—. Acting chief engr. U.S. Bur. of Pub. Roads, assisting in formulation of new federal aid road policies during leave of absence, 1916. Pres. State Reclamation Bd., Calif., 1917-23; dir. State Dept. of Pub. Works, Calif., 1921-23. Del. from Mass. to 1st Internat. Road Congress, 1908, del. from Calif. to 3d congress, 1913; pres. 4th Nat. Road Congress, 1914. Mem. exec. com. State Council of Defense, Calif., World War. Fellow Am. Geog. Society. Republican. Conglist. Home: Chevy Chase, Md. Died Mar. 8, 1928.

FLETCHER, PAUL FRANKLIN, gynecologist; b. Sheridan, Wyo., Dec. 24, 1903; s. Thomas Isaac and Margaret (Collins) F.; B.S., U. Santa Clara, 1926; M.D., St. Louis U., 1932, M.S., 1936; m. Margaret Elizabeth Mudd, Feb. 10, 1938; children—Paul Dayton, Margaret Ann, Elizabeth Gay, Nancy Joan, Thomas Gerard, Robert Joseph. Intern St. Luke's Hosp., San Francisco, 1932-33; practice of gynecology, St. Louis, 1936—; asst. gynecologist and obstetrician St. Mary's Group Hosps., 1940-45, asso., 1945; attending gynecologist Barnard Free Skin & Cancer Hosp., 1945—, charge cancer cytology lab., 1951-54; cons. obstetrician and gynecologist Incarnate Word Hosp., Fairfield Meml. Hosp., Fairfield, Ill.; vis. staff St. Louis City Hosp.; sr. instr. obstetrics and gynecology St. Louis U. Sch. Medicine, 1946—, asso. dir. Cancer Cytology Center, dept. pathology, 1951—. Served as lt. col., M.C., AUS; flight surgeon USAAF. Diplomate Am. Bd. Obstetrics and Gynecology, also Internat. Bd. Surgery. Fellow A.C.S., American Geriatrics Society, International College Surgeons (founder American chapter), American College Obstetrics and Gynecology (founder); mem. A.M.A., St. Louis Gynecol. Soc. (pres. 1951-52), St. Louis Surg. Soc., Central Assn. Obstetricians and Gynecologists (exec. com. 1952-55, v.p. 1955-56), Pan-Pacific Surg. Assn., N.Y. Acad. Scis., Inter-Soc. Cytology Council (mem. founders exec. com.; sec.-treas. 1952-58; clin. representative on exec. committee 1958-60, president, 1961-62), American Academy of Obstetricians and Gynecologists (mem. pub. relations com. 1953-54), St. Louis Medical Soc., Am. Radium Soc., Mo. Med. Assn., Endocrine Soc., Mo. Hist. Soc., St. Louis Zool. Soc., St. Louis Acad. Scis. Clubs: Missouri Athletic, University, Old Warson Country, Harbor Point Yacht, St. Louis Sailing, St. Louis Revolver, Green Head Duck, Missouri Duck Hunters Assn., Ducks Unlimited (St. Louis). Editor St. Louis Med. Soc. Bull., 1946-48. Contbr. sci. articles med. publs. Home: 7345 Westmoreland Dr., University City. Mo. Office: 634 N. Grand Blvd., St. Louis 3. Deceased.

FLETCHER, ROBERT, engr.; b. New York, Aug. 23, 1847; s. Edward H. and Mary (Hill) F.; student Coll. City of New York, 3 yrs.; grad. U.S. Mil. Acad., 1868; hon. A.M., 1871, Ph.D., 1881, D.Sc., 1918, Dartmouth Coll.; m. Ellen M. Huntington, July 2, 1872. Commd. 2d lt., 1st U.S. Arty., June 1868; instr. mathematics, U.S. Mil. Acad., Sept. 1869-Dec. 31, 1870; sr. prof. and dir., Thayer Sch. of Civ. Engring., Dartmouth Coll., Jan. 1871-July 1918, dir. emeritus and overseer, 1918—. Cons. engr. for steel bridges over White River, at Hartford, N.H.; engr. Enfield (N.H.) Waterworks, 1902; pres. and engr. Hanover Water Works Co.; served many yrs. as mem. and pres. N.H. Bd. of Health, also in charge N.H.-Vt. boundary survey. Republican. Baptist. Home: Hanover, N.H. Died Jan. 7, 1936.

FLETCHER, STEVENSON WHITCOMB, horticulturist; b. Littleton, Mass., Sept. 10, 1875; s. Charles Kimball and Anna (Holton) F.; B.Sc., Mass. Agrl. Coll., 1896; M.S., Cornell, 1898, Ph.D., 1900; m. Margaret Rolston, June 28, 1905; children—Robert Holton, Richard Rolston, Stevenson Whitcomb, Peter Whitcomb, John Emmett, Margaret, Emmett Hine. Prof. horticulture and horticulturist, Expt. Sta. of Wash. Agrl. Coll., Pullman, 1900-02; same, W.Va. U., 1902-03; asst. prof. extension teaching in agr., Cornell U., 1903-05; prof. horticulture. Mich. Agrl. Coll., 1905-08; dir. Va. Agrl. Expt. Sta., 1908-16; prof. horticulture, Pa. State Coll., 1917-37; also vice dean and dir. research, 1927-39, dean Sch. Agr., 1939-46, dean emeritus since 1946. Mem. Phi Kappa Phi (Mass. Agricultural College), Alpha Gamma Rho, Alpha Zeta, Sigma Xi. Republican. Baptist. Author: How to Make a Fruit Garden, 1906; Solls-How to Handle and Improve Them. 1907; Strawberry Growing, 1917; The Strawberry in North America, 1917; A History of Fruit Growing in Pennsylvania, 1933; Pennsylvania Agriculture and Country Life (1640-1840), 1950; Pennsylvania Agriculture and Country Life (1840-1940), 1955. Home: State College PA Died Feb. 10, 1971.

FLEXNER, SIMON, physician; b. Louisville, Ky., Mar. 25, 1863; s. Morris and Esther (Abraham) F., ed. Louisville pub. schs.; M.D., U. of Louisville, 1889; post-grad. student Johns Hopkins, univs. of Strassburg, Berlin, Prague and Pasteur Inst.; D.Sc., Harvard, 1906, Yale, 1910, Princeton, 1913, U. of Pa., 1929, Nat. U. of Ireland, 1936, U. of Louisville, 1937; LL.D., U. of Md., 1907, Washington U., Brown, Johns Hopkins—all 1915, Cambridge U. (England), 1920, Western Reserve, 1929; Doctor, Univ. of Strassburg, 1923, Univ. of Louvain (Belgium), 1927, Univ. Libre, Brussels, 1930; M.A., Oxford U.; Fellow, Balliol Coll., Oxford, U., 1937; m. Helen Whitall Thomas, 1903; children—William Welch, James Carey Thomas. Asso. prof. pathology, 1895-98, prof. pathol. anatomy, 1898-99, Johns Hopkins; prof. pathology, U. of Pa., 1899-1903; dir. Ayer Clin. Lab., 1901-03; pathologist, Univ. Hosp., Phila. Hosp., 1900-03; dir. laboratories Rockefeller Inst., Med. Research, 1903-35, dir. Inst., 1920-35, emeritus since 1935; Eastman prof., Oxford U., 1937-38. Col., O.R.C., United States Army. Trustee Carnegie Instn. Washington, 1910-14., Rockefeller Foundation, 1913-28, Johns Hopkins University, 1937-42. Chairman Public Health Council of New York. Chevalier Legion of Honor, France, 1914, Officer, 1919, Commander, 1923; Order of the Sacred Treasure, Japan, 1915. Fellow American Academy Arts and Sciences (Boston). Academy Medicine, A.A.A.S.; member National Acad. Sciences, Assn. Am. Physicians, Am. Philos. Soc., Am. Assn. Pathologists and Bacteriologists, A.M.A., Harvey Soc.; corr. mem. Medico-Chirurgical Soc. of Bologna, Reale Instituto Lombardo di Scienza e Lettere, Milan, Soc. Path. Exotique (Paris), Academy of Medicine (Paris), Academy of Sciences, Inst. of France (Paris, foreign associate), Gesellschaft d. Aerzte in Wien, Wiener Gesellschaft für Mikrobiologie, Berliner Medical Gesellschaft, Academy Medicine Caracas, Society Med. Chirg. del. Guyas, Guyaquil, Ecuador; hon. mem. Inst. for Exptl. Therapy, Frankfurt am M., Deutsche Akademie Naturforscher, Halle, Swedish Medical Society, Société Med. des Hôpitaux, Paris, Société de Biologie, Paris; fgn. mem. Royal Soc. (London); hon. fellow Royal Society of Medicine (London); fgn. mem. Royal Soc. Trop. Med. and Hygiene, Brit. Med. Assn., Soc. belge de. Med. Trop., Soc. belge de Biol., Royal Acad. Medicine, Brussels, Soc. Royale des Sciences Med. et Nat., Brussels, Bataafsch Genootschap d. Proefonder-vindelijke Wijsbegeerte, Rotterdam, Copenhagen Medical Soc., Royal Danish Scientific Soc., Soc. Argentina de Biol. (Buenos Aires), Microbiol. Soc., Leningrad. Author of many papers and monographs relating to bacterial and pathol. subjects, including: The Pathology of Toxalbumin Intoxication; biochemical constitution of snake venoms, experimental pancreatitis and fat necrosis; epidemic cerebrospinal meningitis, and its serum treatment; poliomyelitis, its cause, mode of transmission, and prevention; epidemic encephalitis; experimental epidemiology, etc. Author: (with James Thomas Flexner) Biography of William Henry Welch, 1941. Home: 530 E. 86th St., New York, Died May 2, 1946.

FLINT, ALBERT STOWELL, astronomer; b. Salem, Mass., Sept. 12, 1853; s. Simeon and Ellen Rebecca (Pollard) F.; A.B., Harvard, 1875; A.M., U. of Cincinnati, 1880; m. Helen A. Thomas, Oct. 22, 1884. Computer U.S. Naval Obs., 1881-83, 1888-89; asst., U.S. Transit of Venus Commn., 1883-88; asst. astronomer, 1889, astron., 1904-19 (emeritus), Washburn Obs., U. of Wis. Coöperated with the dir. of the obs. and others in producing several of the publs. of The Washburn Obs. Fellow A.A.A.S. Author: Meridian Observations for Stellar Parallax, 1st series (Vol. XI, Publ. Washburn Obs.), 1902; 2d series, Vol. XIII, Part I, 1919. Home: Madison, Wis. Died Feb. 22, 1923.

FLINT, AUSTIN, physician; b. Northampton, Mass., Mar. 28, 1836; s. Austin (physician) and Anne (Skillings F.; ed. pvt. schs., Buffalo, and Harvard, 1852-53; studied medicine in office, and med. dept. U. of Louisville, 1854-56; M.D., Jefferson Med. Coll., 1857 (LL.D., 1885; hon. A.M., Princeton, 1894) m. Elizabeth B.

McMaster, Dec. 23, 1862. Practiced in Buffalo, 1857-59; editor Buffalo Med. Journal, 1857-60; prof. physiology, med. dept., U. of Buffalo, 1858-59; visiting surgeon, Buffalo Gen. Hosp., 1858; removed to New York, 1859; prof. physiology, N.Y. Med. Coll., 1859-60, New Orleans Sch. of Medicine, 1860-61; acting asst. surgeon, U.S.A., at Gen. Hosp., New York, 1862-65; a founder and prof. physiology, 1861-98, Bellevue Hosp. Med. Coll.; prof. physiology, L.I. Coll. Hosp., 1862-68, Cornell U. Med. Coll., 1898— (emeritus prof.). Visiting phys. 1869, cons. phys., 1896, visiting phys. Insane Pavilion, 1896, Bellevue Hosp.; surgeon-gen. N.Y., 1874-78; cons. phys. Manhattan State Hosp. for Insane, 1896 (pres. cons. bd., 1899). Decorated 3d class Order of Bolivar, Venezuela, 1891. Mem. exec. com. N.Y. Prison Assn., 1896. Author: Text-Book of Human Physiology (4 edits.), 1875-88. Died Sept. 23, 1915.

FLOOD, HENRY, JR., cons. engr.; b. Elmira, N.Y., Feb. 9, 1887; s. Henry and Ella Louise (Seeley) F.; grad. Elmira Acad., 1904; grad. Wertz Sch., Annapolis, Md., 1905; M.E., Cornell U., 1909; m. Iona Grace Sandford, Apr. 6, 1912; 1 dau., Iona Sandford. Chief engr. Central Hudson Gas & Electric Co., 1909-17; mech. engr. Am. Smelting & Refining Co., 1917-19; associated in practice with Dr. John Price Jackson, New York, 1920; engineers secretary U.S. Super-power Survey, 1920-21; president and director M. & F. Management Corp., Murray and Flood, Inc.; chmn. and dir. Lanova Corp.; pres. Flood & Watson, cons. engs. Fellow Am. Inst. E.E.; mem. Am. Soc. M.E., Phi Gamma Delta; asso. mem. Soc. Automotive Engrs. Episcopalian. Club: Engineers. Home: 36 Riverside Av., Red Bank, N.J. Died June 17, 1948; buried in Fairview Cemetery, Red Bank.

FLOREY, LORD HOWARD WALTER, scientist, college provost; b. Sept. 24, 1898; s. Joseph Florey; ed. St. Peter's Collegiate Sch.; M.D., Adelaide U., Magdalen Coll., Oxford; Rhodes Scholar for S. Australia, 1921; John Lucas Walker student, Cambridge, 1924; Rockefeller Travelling Fellow, U.S., 1925; Freedom Research Fellow, London Hosp., 1926; Fellow Gonville and Caius College, Cambridge, 1926; Fellow, Lincoln College, Oxford; held degrees Bachelor of Medicine, Bachelor of Surgery, M.A., B.Sc., Ph.D.; L.H.D. (hon.), Georgetown University, 1965; D.Sc. (hon.), Harvard Univ., 1967; m. Mary Ethel Reed, 1926 (dec. 1966); 1 son, 1 dau.; m. 2d, Margaret Jennings, 1967. Huddersfield lect. in spl. pathology Cambridge, 1927; Joseph Hunter prof. of pathology, U. of Sheffied, 1931-35; prof. pathology, Oxford, 1935-62; provost Queen's College, Oxford, from 1962. Charles Mickle fellowship, Toronto Univ., 1944. Awarded Cameron Prize, Edinburgh U., 1945; Lister Medal, R.C.S., Eng., 1945; Berzelius Silver Medal, Swedish Med. Soc., 1945; Nobel Prize for Physiol. and Med., 1945; Harmsworth Memorial Award, 1946 Albert Gold Medal, Royal Soc. Arts, 1946; Medal in Therapeutics, Soc. Apothecaries of London, 1946; Gold Medal, Royal Soc. Med., 1947, Royal Medal, 1951; Comdr. Legion d'Honneur, 1948; United States Medal for Merit, 1948; Addingham Gold Medal, 1949; Copley Medal, Royal Society, 1957; Gold medal Brit. Med. Assn., 1964; Lomonossov medal USSR Academy of Sciences, 1964. Fellow of the Royal Soc. (pres. 1960), Royal Coll. Physicians; Am. Acad. Arts and Scis. (fgn. hon. mem.). Pioneered devel. of penicillin for clin. use. Author: Antibiotics (with others), 1949. Editor and part author: General Pathology, 1958. Home: Oxford Eng Died Feb. 21, 1968.

FLOWERS, ALAN ESTIS, engineer; b. St. Louis, Mo., Oct. 4, 1876; s. William Pitts and Mary Emnia (Cummins) F.; M.E., Cornell U., 1902, M.M.E., 1914, Ph.D., 1915; m. Ida Vandergrift Burns, June 29, 1907; children—George Schlnederberg, Nancy Holmes, Priscilla (dec.). Engr. apprentice with Westinghouse Electric & Mfg. Co., 1902-04; instr. and asso. prof. elec. engring., U. of Mo., 1904-12; with Gen. Electric Co., 1912-13; prof. elec. engring., Ohio State U., 1913-18; appraisal engr., Columbus Electric Power & Light Co., 1917-18; capt. Signal Corps, U.S. Army, on duty in radio development sect., Washington, D.C., Mar. 31, 1918-Mar. 8, 1919; test engr. engring. dept., Nat. Aniline & Chem. Co., New York, 1919-20; research engr. in charge of Research Engring. Sect., 1921-22; mgr. and cons. engr. Chem. Machinery Construction Co., 1922-23; engr., in charge development, De Laval Separator Co., 1923-43, research engr. since 1943; dir. Flakice Corp. since 1943. Mem. Am. Inst. Elec. Engrs., Am. Soc. Mech. Engrs. (mem. spl. research com. on lubrication), Am. Soc. for Testing Materials (chmn. sub-com. on sampling and gaging), Am. Phys. Soc., Am. Soc. Metals, Am. Assn. Univ. Profs., Phi Mu Alpha, Lambda Phi Rho, Sigma Xi, Tau Beta Pi. Conglist. Developed apparatus for measuring cylinder friction and lubrication in steam engines, also invented a viscosimeter; developed processes for oil reclamation, improvements in centrifugal separators and ultra high speed test tube centrifuge. Contbr. on tech. topics.; chapter on "Centrifuges" in Chemical Engineers' Handbook. Home: 148 College Av., Poughkeepsie, N.Y. Died Dec. 4, 1945.

FLOY, HENRY, engr.; b. Elizabeth, N.J., Sept. 19, 1866; s. James and Sarah A. F.; A.B., Wesleyan U., 1889, A.M., 1892; M.E., Cornell U., 1891; m. Alice Van Benschoten, 1895. Engaged as consulting engr. with office in New York, spl. reputation as elec. engr. in connection with hydraulic and high tension long-distance transmission work, valuation of utility properties. Mem. Internat. Com. of Awards, and elec. juror, St. Louis Expn., 1904. Spl. engr., Dept. of the Interior; appraiser, apptd. by U.S. Circuit Ct. Fellow Am. Inst. Elec. Engrs. Republican. Author: Valuation of Public Utility Properties. Died May 5, 1916.

FLUG, SAMUEL S., indsl. engr., lawyer; b. Warsaw, Poland, Feb. 28, 1905; s. Harry and Fannie (Szuch) F.; brought to U.S., 1907, naturalized, 1916; B.C.S., N.Y.U., 1926; LL.B., Bklyn. Law Sch., 1929; m. Evelyn C. Raphael, June 3, 1929; children—Martin R., James F., Barbara R., Robert K., Victoria M. Admitted to N.Y. bar, 1930, since practiced in N.Y.C.; partner Flug, Strassler Assos. (and predecessor firms), 1930—. Chmn. bd. dirs. Am. Type Founders Co., Inc., Elizabeth, N.J., 1956—; pres., dir. Ames Iron Works, Oswego, N.Y., 1942—; treas., dir. Billings & Spencer Co., Hartford, Conn., 1950—, Peck, Stow & Wilcox Co., Southington, Conn., 1954—; asst. treas., dir. Servus Rubber Co., Rock Island, Ill., 1938—; dir., mem. exec. com. Lafayette Nat. Bank, Bklyn., 1955—; dir. Lumber and Millwork Co. Phila., Namm-Loeser's, Inc. (Bklyn.), Sidney Blumenthal & Co. (N.Y.C.), Landis Machine Co. (St. Louis). Home: 78 Exeter St., Bklyn. 35; also Easton Rd., Westport, Conn. Office: 60 E. 42d St., N.Y.C. 10017. Died Oct. 10, 1952.

FLYNN, JOHN E(DWARD), biologist; b. Friendsville, Pa., Aug. 19, 1897; s. William M. and Mary (Murphy) F.; B.S., Pa. State, 1922; M.S., U. Md., 1924; Ph.D., Cornell, 1929; m. Elizabeth Helen Schunk, Nov. 12, 1933; children—Barbara, Patricia. Asst. in botany U. Md., 1922-24; instr. in mycology and plant pathology Cornell, 1924-28; asst. editor Biol. Abstracts, Phila., 1929-37, editor-in-chief, 1938-53; biologist Office Naval Research, N.Y.C., 1954-62, chief scientist, 1962—, spl. cons. biophysics, 1958—. Editor: The New Microbiology. Fellow N.Y. Acad. Sci.; mem. Biophys. Soc., Sigma Xi. Roman Catholic. Home: 22 Rockland Pl., New Rochelle, N.Y. Office: 207 W. 24th St., N.Y.C. 11. Died Sept. 22, 1965.

FOCKE, THEODORE MOSES, (fok), mathematician; b. near Massillon, O., Jan. 3, 1871; s. Theodore H. and Katherine M. (Brown) F.; B.S. in C.E., Case Sch. of Applied Science, Cleveland, O., 1892; Ph.D., U. of Göttingen, Germany, 1898; Sc.D. (hon.), Case Sch. of Applied Science, 1944; m. Anne L. Bosworth, Aug. 7, 1901 (died 1907); children—Helen Metcalf, Theodore Brown, Alfred Bosworth. Instr. mathematics, Case Sch. Applied Science, 1892-93; tutor in physics and chemistry, Oberlin Coll., 1893-96; instr. mathematics and civ. engring., 1898-1902; asst. prof. mathematics, 1902-08, Kerr prof. and head of dept. mathematics, 1908-44, dean of the faculty, 1918-44, dean emeritus Case Inst. Tech., since 1944. Fellow A.A.A.S., mem. Am. Math. Soc., Math. Assn. America, Am. Society for Engring., Sigma Xi, Phi Kappa Psi, Tau Beta Pi. Republican. Episcopalian Home: 2517 Wellington Rd., Cleveland Heights 18, O. Died Mar. 2, 1949.

FOERSTER, OTTO HOTTINGER, dermatologist; b. Milw., May 19, 1876; s. Erwin and Sophia (Hottinger) F.; M.D., U. Pa. 1898; grad. student U. Vienna, 1900-01; m. Louise Leidersdorf, June 18, 1907; children—Frances (wife of Dean H. Echols, M.D.), Frederick Erwin (M.D.). Intern, Howard Hosp., Phila., 1899; asst. demonstrator physiology, med. sch. U. Pa., vol. asso. William Pepper Lab. Clin. Medicine, asst. surgeon Genito-Urinary Dispensary, Univ. Hosp., also asst. in medicine Poly-clinic Hosp., Phila., 1902; practice of dermatology and syphilology, Milw., 1902—; prof. dermatol., Med. School, U. Wis., 1925-46; prof. emeritus, 1946; dermatologist State of Wis. Gen. Hosp., Madison, 1926-46; past chief of staff, Columbia Hosp., Milw. (10 yrs.); dermatologist Milw., Columbia and Children's hosps. Served as hosp. steward, 4th Wis. Vol. Inf., 1898; capt., med. corps, U.S. Army 1918-19. Mem. Am. Dermatol. Assn. (v.p. 1926, 27, pres. 1928), Am. Acad. Dermatology and Syphilology, Am. Roentgen Ray Soc., Soc. Investigative Dermatology, A.M.A. (chmn. sect. on dermatology 1919), Chgo. Dermatol. Soc. (pres. 1912, 1937), Milw. Acad. Medicine (pres. 1911; hon. mem. 1938). Milw. Surg. Soc., Mil. Order Fgn. Wars, Phi Gamma Delta, Alpha Mu Pi Omega. Corr. mem. Vienna Dermatol. Soc. Clubs: University Milwaukee, Chicago. Home: 3333 N. Sheppard Av., Milw. 53211. Office: 111 E. Wisconsin Av., Milw. 53202. Died July 18, 1965.

FOGG, LLOYD CLARKE, zoologist; b. West Canaan, N.H., Apr. 10, 1899; s. Allen Ira and Drusilla Adeline (Clarke) F.; B.S., Dartmouth, 1922, M.S., 1924; Ph.D., Columbia, 1930; m. Mildred Cass, June 5, 1926; children—Lyman Babcock, Richard Lloyd. Instr. zoölogy Dartmouth, 1922-24, Washington Sq. Coll., N.Y. U., 1924-31; cytologist USPHS, Harvard Med. Sch., 1932-36; research fellow in preventive medicine and hygiene, Harvard Med. Sch., 1932-36; instr. zoölogy, U. N.H., 1937, asst. prof., 1937, asso. prof., 1938-40; asst. prof. histology and embryology, Boston U. Sch. Medicine, 1940-41, asso. prof. 1945-46, registrar, 1946. Cancer research, Pondville State Cancer Hosp. (chief of research lab.); dir. Isle of Shoals Marine Biol. Lab. Mem. A.A.A.S., Am. Soc. Zoölogists, Am. Assn. Anatomists, Am. Assn. Cancer. Writer of many articles and reports in sci. mags. Home: 17 Glenwood Av., Newton Centre, Mass. Died Feb. 29, 1960; buried Newton Cemetery.

FOHS, FERDINAND JULIUS, oil geologist; b. N.Y.C., Mar. 1, 1884; s. Mark E. and Fredericka (Baum) F.; ed. high sch. and home study; postgrad. course Columbia, 1909; D.Sc. in Tech., Israel Inst. Tech., 1957; m. Cora Bladauf, 1908; children—Ella B. (dec.), Frances Sohn. Mine supt. in Ky., 1901; field asst. geologist U.S. Geol. Survey, 1902; engr. in charge of mines in Ky., 1902-05; asst. state geologist of Ky., 1905-12; lectr. Sch. Mines, State U. of Ky., 1906-08; spl. lectr. oil geology Columbia U., 1927, 47; recommended in advance and assisted in devel. of more than 80 important oil and gas pools; investigated natural and water resources of Palestine and directed devel. of water, 1919, 30, 36, 37; investigated oil possibilities of Sicily, 1927; has made maps and private report on natural resources of Palestine in behalf of World Zionist Organization and Brit. War Office, 1919, which led to devel. cement plant, Dead Sea potash and bromine plant, etc. Actively identified with Humphreys-Fohs group of cos. 1914-31, serving as consulting geologist and v.p. Humphreys Corp.; pres. Fohs Oil Co., 1932-46; ind. oil operator, 1946—; pres., dir. Whitclay Oil Operators, Inc., 1952—; v.p., mgr., dir. Dakamont Exploration Corp., 1952-58. Chmn., Fohs Found., 1937—; with wife founded Ella Fohs Camp for underprivileged children, 1927—. Follow Geology Soc. Am.; mem. Ind. Petroleum Assn. Am. (dir. 1937-53), Am. Inst. Mining Metall. and Petroleum Engrs. (v.p. 1927-30, chmn. petroleum div. 1925-26, certificate of service award 1949, Legion of Honor, 1954), Am. Assn. Petroleum Geologists, A.A.A.S., Brit. Inst. Petroleum Tech., Houston Contemporary Arts Assn. (dir. 1952-53). Clubs: Engineers (N.Y.); Houston Petroleum. Author reports and papers water, natural resources and oil fields, also papers on Russian stamps and cancellations. Home: Lamar Hotel. Office: San Jacinto Bldg., Houston, Died. Jan. 19, 1965.

FOKKER, ANTHONY H(ERMAN) G(ERARD), airplane designer and mfr.; b. of Dutch parents, Kediri, Dutch East Indies, Apr. 6, 1890; ed. Haarlem, Holland; m. Viola Lawrence, Feb. 8, 1929 (died 1929). Began flying, 1911; head of important aircraft concerns in Germany during World War; came to U.S., 1922. Former pres. Fokker Aircraft Corp. of America. Home: Alpine, N.J. Died Dec. 23, 1939.

FOLEY, ARTHUR LEE, physicist; b. Hancock County, Ind., Feb. 22, 1867; s. Mansfield Calvin and Clara Alice (Myers) F.; student Central Normal Coll., Danville, 1882-84 (Litt.D., 1941), Hayward Coll., Fairfield, Ill., 1886-87; A.B., Ind. U., 1890, A.M., 1891; University of Chicago, 1894; Ph.D., Cornell, 1897; European univs., 1908; m. Lorettie Hayworth, Apr. 15, 1885; children—Ernest Lee, Mrs. Eupha May Tugman. Teacher pub. sch., Vivalia, Ind., 1884-85; prin. pub. sch., Cleveland, Ind., 1885-86, Johnsonville, Ill., 1887-88; instr. physics, Ind. U., 1890-91, asso. prof., 1891-97, prof. and head of dept. of physics, 1897-1938, emeritus prof. since 1938, Waterman research prof., 1917-25, also chmn. Bur. of Science Service, 1926-35. Dir. of physics research, Affiliated Coll. of Ind., 1917-25; chmn. research com. Ind. State Council of Defense, 1915-18; dir. U.S. Radio Sch., Ind. U., 1918. Mem. Nat. Research Council. Republican. Methodist. Fellow A.A.A.S., Ind. Acad. Science (pres. 1909; chmn. research com. since 1924), Am. Phys. Soc., Acoustical Soc. America; mem. Am. Assn. Physics Teachers, Sigma Xi (pres. 1892), Phi Beta Kappa (pres. 1914). Acoustical engineer, inventor, investigator, author of 90 scientific papers and 4 editions of a physics text. Home: Bloomington, Ind. Died Feb. 13, 1945.

FOLEY, FRANCIS B(ENEDICT), exec. metall. engr.; b. Germantown, Pa., July 7, 1887; s. Dennis J. and Margaret A. (Gribbon) F.; student Girard Coll.; m. Anne M. Flaherty, Apr. 20, 1915 (died 1936); 1 son, Gerard Moylan; m. 2d, Katherine Campbell, Aug. 8, 1938; 1 dau., Frances Campbell. Various positions Midvale Co., 1905-17, dir. research, 1926-49; asst. metallography U. Minn., 1917-19; metallurgist U.S. Bur. Mines, 1919-24, Lucy Mfg. Corp., Chattanooga, 1924-26; cons. metallurgist Internat. Nickel Co., 1950-57; executive metallurgical engineer Pencoyd Steel and Forge Company, Phila., 1957-65; cons., 1965-73. Dollar a year tech. cons. W.P.B.; adviser, research projects Nat. Def. Research Council; com. for investigation prodn. ferromanganese, collaborator Ordnance Dept. on ordnance steels, World War I. Fellow Am. Inst. Chemists; mem. Am. Ordnance Assn., Franklin Inst. (chmn. com. sci. and arts 1956-57). Acid Open Hearth Research Assn. (dir., trustee, pres. 1947), Am. Iron and Steel Inst., Iron and Steel Inst. (London), Alloy Casting Inst. (dir., chmn. tech. com.), Am. Soc. Metals (pres. 1947; Sauveur lectr. 1950), Am. Inst. Mining and Metall. Engrs. (dir.; Howe lectr. 1950), Am. Chem. Soc., Am. Soc. Testing Materials (chmn. joint ASTM-ASME com. on effect of temperature on properties of metals), Girard Coll. Alumni Assn. (pres.), Nat. Acad. Econs. and Polit. Sci. Club: Metals Science (N.Y.C.). Author tech. papers, metallurgy of steel. Home: Philadelphia PA Died Feb. 27, 1973.

FOLEY, JAMES OWEN, anatomist; b. Erie, Kan., Mar. 1, 1897; s. Patrick William and Mary Katherine (Carroll) F.; B.S., Ore. State Coll., 1919, Ph.G., 1919, Ph.C., 1921, M.S., 1921; Ph.D., U. of Wis., 1925; Doctorate of Science, University of Alabama, 1960; m. Neva Helen Drummond, June 19, 1926; children—Mary Luella, Patricia Helen. Grad. asst. zoology, Ore. State Coll., 1919-21, U. of Wis., 1921-25; instr. anatomy, Tulane U. of La. Sch. of Med., 1925-28, asst. prof., 1928-30; asst. prof. anatomy, U. of Ala. Sch. of Medicine, 1930-34, asso. prof., 1934-45; asso. prof., Med. Coll. of Ala., 1945-47; prof. and chmn. dept. anatomy of Med. Coll. and School of Dentistry of U. of Ala., since 1947; associate dean, Med. Coll. of Ala., 1951. Served in Coast Artillery, 5th Co., C.A.C., 1919. Rockefeller research fellow, Cornell Med. Coll., 1938; Guest research fellow, Neurol. Inst., Northwestern U., 1932-33. Fellow Ala. Acad. Neurology and Psychiatry (pres. 1954), Ala. Acad. Sci. (treas. 1947); mem. New York Academy of Science, American Association of Anatomists, Soc. for Exptl. Biology and Medicine, Sigma Xi, Rho Chi, Gamma Alpha, Phi Sigma, Beta Beta Beta. Home: 409 Sunset Dr., Vestavia Hills, Birmingham, Ala. 35216. Died Feb. 28, 1961, buried Elmwood Cemetery, Birmingham.

FOLEY, MAX HENRY, engr., architect; b. Norwich, Conn., Nov. 9, 1894; s. Michael James and Ann Elizabeth (Garvey) F.; Ph.B., Yale, 1914; m. Gwendolyn Powell, Feb. 3, 1917 (dec.); 1 son, Max Henry; married second Kathryn McTigue, October 18, 1828; children—Mary Ada (Mrs. William Pedrick), John, Frank, Jean (Mrs. Thomas Rizzo). Associate partner of the firm Voorhees, Gmelin & Walker, 1928-38; partner Voorhees, Walker, Foley & Smith, 1938-54; pvt. practice, 1954-68; cons. N.Y. Housing Commission; mng. partner in Trinidad of Caribbean Architect-Engineer; dir. Fedn. Bank & Trust Co. of N.Y. Mem. engring bd. Port of N.Y. Authority; prin. works include Western Union Hdqrs. Bldg., N.Y.C., Library, Dining halls Coll. New Rochelle, N.Y., N.J. Bell Telephone Bldg., Newark, Gen. Electric Research Lab., Schenectady, N.Y., also Army Air Bases, Trinidad, Antigua, St. Lucia, Brit. Guiana, Dutch Guiana; Loyola Sem., Shrub Oak, N.Y.; AFL hdqrs., Washington; Travelers Insurance Co. office building, Hartford. Trustee American Architectural Found., Inc.; chmn. Architects' Emergency Committee. Chmn. bldg. trades apprenticeship; dir. Greater N.Y. Safety Council; mem. Cardinal's Com. of Laity, N.Y. Chmn. Board of Standards and Appeals, N.Y.C. Profl. engr., N.Y., Ohio, Del. Recipient Sydney Strauss Meml. Award, N.Y. State Soc. Architects, 1961. Fellow A.I.A. (chmn. com. on costs, labor relations, chmn. joint com. A.I.A.-Am. Gen. Contractors Assn.), Am. Soc. C.E., mem. N.Y. Bldg. Congress (past pres., gov.), Liturgical Arts Soc. (treas.), Archtl. League N.Y. (past treas.), Yale Engring. Assn., Nat. Soc. Profl. Engrs., Beaux Arts Inst., Am. Soc. Mil. Engrs., Nat. Sculpture Soc., Am. Inst. Cons. Engrs., Municipal Art Soc., Sigma Xi, Alpha Chi Rho. Clubs: Yale, Canadian (N.Y.C.); Edgartown Yacht. Home: New York City NY Died Dec. 1968.

FOLGER, WALTER, congressman, scientist; b. Nantucket, Mass., June 12, 1765; s. Walter and Elizabeth (Starbuck) F.; m. Anna Ray, Dec. 29, 1785. Exhibited Folger's astronomic clock, 1790; discovered a process of annealing wire; admitted to Mass. bar, 1807; mem. Mass. Gen. Ct. from Nantucket, 1808; mem. Mass. Senate, 1809-14, 22; established cotton and woolen mill, Nantucket, 1812; mem. U.S. Ho. of Reps. (Democrat) from Mass., 15th-16th congresses, 1817-21; judge Nantucket Ct. Common Pleas and Sessions, 1828-34. Author: Description of Nantucket, 1794; Observations of the Solar Eclipse of 1811. Died Nantucket, Sept. 8, 1849; buried Friend's Burying Ground, Nantucket.

FOLIN, OTTO, chemist; b. Asheda, Sweden, Apr. 4, 1867; s. Nils Magnus and Eva (Olson) F.; came to America, 1882; B.S., U. of Minn., 1892; Ph.D., U. of Chicago, 1898, Sc.D., 1916; univs. in Sweden and Germany, 1897, 1898; M.D., U. of Lund (Sweden), 1918; Sc.D., Washington U., 1915; m. Laura Churchill Grant, Sept. 11, 1899; children—Joanna (dec.), Grant, Teresa. Asst. prof. physiol. chemistry, U. of W.Va., 1899-1900; research chemist, McLean Hosp., Waverley, Mass., 1900-08; prof. biol. chemistry, Harvard Med. Sch., 1907—. Home: Brookline, Mass. Died Oct. 25, 1934.

FOLK, MARION HAYNE, JR., botanist, coll. dean; b. Pomaria, S.C., Feb. 9, 1899; s. Marion Hayne and Carrie M. (Setzler) F.; B.S. (4 yr. scholar) Clemson Agrl. Coll., 1919; M.S., La. State U., 1929, student, summers 1942, 49; m. Juanita Blanche Coates, Aug. 9, 1923. Vocational agr. tchr., asst. prin. Choudrant (La.) High Sch., 1919-21; asst. supt. East Carroll Parish schs., also prin. Lake Providence (La.) High Sch., 1921-25; faculty Columbia High Sch., 1925-26; asst. prof. dept. biology, La. oly. Inst. 1926-36, asso. prof., 1936-42, prof., 1942-47, prof., head dept. botany, dean Sch. of Agr. and Forestry, 1947—. Chief air raid warden, Rushton, World War II. Chmn., Lincoln Parish Folk Sch., 1936; exec. sec. N. La. High Sch. Rally Assn., 1933-46. Bd. dirs. N. La. State Fair. Mem. Ruston C. of C. (agrl. com.), Am. Legion, La. Acad. Scis., La. Tchrs. Assn., La. Fruit Growers Assn., La. Jersey Cattle Club, La. Artificial Breeders Assn., N. La. Poultry Growers Assn., La. Farm Bur. Fedn., La. Forestry Assn., A.A.A.S., N.E.A., Phi Kappa Phi, Omicron Delta Kappa, Lambda Chi Alpha. Democrat. Methodist. Clubs: Lions (1st v.p. 1945-47), Louisiana Tech. Men's Faculty (pres. 1948-49). Author: Methods of Delinting Cotton Seed for Early Germination, 1919; A New Method for Preparing Sulfonphthalein Indicators, 1929; History of the North Louisiana High School Rally, 1936. Home: 406 S. Sparta St., Ruston, La. Died Aug. 23, 1964.

FOLLANSBEE, ROBERT, hydraulic engr.; b. Mpls., June 7, 1879; s. Thomas M. and Nellie (Woodruff) F.; C.E., Cornell U., 1902; m. Isabelle A. Gold, Apr. 6, 1904; children—Robert Ashby, Elizabeth Noyes Funkhouser. Engr. for L. P. & J. A. Smith Co., Cleve., 1902-03; recorder U.S. Lake Survey, on resurvey of Gt. Lakes, 1903; with U.S. Geol. Survey since 1904, in charge various dists., for purpose of studying surface run-off for power, irrigation, flood protection and municipal water supply, Minn., Mont., Colo., Wyo., Neb., and S.D., 1906—; fed. rep. Wyo.-Ida. Boundary Commn., 1931; spl. investigation, 1948—. Mem. Am. Soc. C.E., Colo. Soc. Engrs., Wyo. Engring Soc. Club: University. Author of hydraulic reports and tech. articles. Home: 2040 Ash St., Denver 80207. Office: 126 New Custom House, Denver 2. Died July 17, 1952.

FOLLETT, WILLIAM W., civil engr.; b. New Sharon, Me., Sept. 22, 1856; s. William T. and Julia (Merrill) F.; C.E., U. of Mich., 1881 (M.Engring., 1914); m. Helen Jordan, June 13, 1888. In practice as civil engr., 1881—; cons. engr. Internat. Boundary Commn. U.S. and Mexico, 1897-1900, and again, Feb. 1, 1902-July 1, 1914; cons. engr. to U.S. Reclamation Service in the drainage of the Rio Grande, Apr. 1906-Nov. 1914; also cons. engr. for some pvt. irrigation projects. Home: El Paso, Texas. Died Dec. 28. 1915.

FOLSOM, JUSTUS WATSON, entomologist; b. Cambridge, Mass., Sept. 2, 1871; s. James Nelson and Charlotte Elizabeth (Watson) F.; Sc.B., Harvard, 1895, Sc.D., 1899; unmarried. Won Bowdoin prize and was lab. asst. in botany and zoölogy, at Harvard; prof. natural sciences and physiology, Antioch Coll., O., 1899-1900; instr., 1900-06, asso., 1906-08, asst. prof. entomology, 1908-23, U. of Ill.; asso. entomologist, 1925-27, entomologist, 1927-28, sr. entomologist, 1928—, U.S. Bureau of Entomology. Fellow A.A.A.S., Entomol. Soc. America (pres. 1931), Republican. Author: Entomology, with Special Reference to Its Biological and Economic Aspects, 1906. Home: Tallulah, La. Deceased.

FOLWELL, AMORY PRESCOTT, civil engr.; b. Kingston, N.Y., Jan. 15, 1865; s. Rev. G. W. and Mary P. F.; A.B., Brown U., 1885; studied civil engring. at Mass. Inst. Tech.; Sc.D., Lafayette Coll., Easton, Pa., 1907; m. Helen P. Peck, Dec. 4, 1894. Engaged in practice as cons. municipal engr., asso. prof. municipal engring., 1896-1904, prof. 1904-06, Lafayette Coll.; editor Municipal Journal and Engineer (now Public Works) since 1906. Mem. New Eng. Water Works Assn., American Water Works Assn., Am. Society C.E., Beta Theta Pi, Sigma Xi; ex-pres. Am. Soc. Municipal Improvements. Contbr. to engring. jours. Author: Sewerage, 1897, 11th edit., 1935; Water Supply Engineering, 1900; 3d edit., 1917; Municipal Engineering Practice, 1916; Practical Street Construction, 1916. Home: Montclair, N.J. Office: 310 E. 45th St., New York NY

FONT, PEDRO, missionary. Franciscan missionary in charge Indian mission San Jose de los Pimas, Sonora, Mexico, before 1774 until 1781; apptd. cartographer of Juan Bautista de Anza's expdn. to establish mission and presidio on Bay of San Francisco, 1774-76, determined elevation of Farallon Islands, figured latitude of entrance to San Francisco Bay, made extensive sketches and maps of Bay area, aided in selecting site on which presidio and mission were later built; wrote diary which contains a graphic account of expdn. resulting in selection of site for San Francisco. Died Pitique, Sonora, Mexico, Sept. 6, 1781.

FOOT, NATHAN CHANDLER, pathologist; b. N.Y. City, July 27, 1881; s. James Dwight and Ellen Bellows (Chandler) F.; A.B., Harvard, 1903; M.D., Columbia, 1907; m. Emma May Cobb, Jan. 11, 1910; children—Louise K. Foot Besson, Dr. Ellen B. Foot Neumann. Surg. intern, N.Y. Hospital, 1908-10; assistant instructor and instr. pathology, Harvard Medical Sch., 1912-19; instructor comparative pathology, 1919-22; assistant professor, associate professor, and prof., pathology, Coll. of Medicine, U. of Cincinnati, 1922-32; prof. surg. pathology, Cornell Med. Coll. and surg. pathologist, N.Y. Hosp. 1932-48; prof. emeritus surg. pathol.; cons. surg. pathol., N.Y. Hosp., since July 1948; consulting path., Armed Forces Inst., Washington. Research in cancer detection, dept. pathology, med. coll. Cornell U. Diplomate Am. Bd. Pathology (pres.). Fellow Coll. Am. Pathologists; mem. Intersociety Cytologie Com., Am., N.Y. Co. med. socs., Pathol. Society of Argentina (corr.), N.Y. Acad. Medicine, Am. Assn. Pathologists and Bacteriologists, Am. Soc. Exptl. Pathology, N.Y. Pathol. Soc., Harvey Soc., A.A.A.S., Phi Rho Sigma, Sigma Xi, Alpha Omega Alpha. Unitarian. Clubs: Century Assn., New York Practitioners' Soc. Editor: Studies on Tsutsugamushi Disease (by Dr. Rinya Kawamura). Author papers on pathology, experimental pathology and morphology; Pathology in Surgery, 1945; Identification of Tumors, 1948. Home: 106 Tanglewylde Av., Bronxville, N.Y. Address: 1300 York Av., N.Y.C. 21. Died Sept. 4, 1958.

FOOTE, HARRY WARD, chemist; b. Guilford, Conn., Mar. 21, 1875; s. Christopher Spencer and Hannah Jane (Hubbard) F.; Ph.B., Yale, 1895, Ph.D., 1898; studied in Leipsic and Munich, 1899-1900; m. Martha Babcock Jenkins, June 22, 1904; children—William Jenkins, Mary, Margaret Spencer. Instr. in chemistry, Sheffield Scientific Sch., Yale, 1898-1904. asst. prof., 1904-12, prof. physical chemistry since 1912. Fellow Royal Geog. Soc., mem. Conn. Acad. Science, Am. Chem. Soc. Episcopalian. Address: 209 Livingston St., New Haven, Conn. Died Jan. 14, 1942.

FOOTE, JOHN A., M.D.; b. Archbald, Pa., June 9, 1874; s. John (M.D.) and Margaret (McAndrew) F.; Georgetown Coll., 1900-04; M.D., Georgetown U., Washington, 1906; post-grad. work, Berlin, 1913; m. Lois Gibson Dyer, Oct. 12, 1910; children—Mary Virginia, William Dyer. Practiced in Washington, 1906—; asst. prof. therapeutics and materia medica, 1906-08, asst. prof. anatomy, 1908-10, asso. prof. therapeutics and pharmacology, 1911-17, asso. prof. clin. medicine and diseases of children, 1917-20, prof. diseases of children, 1920—, Georgetown U., also dean of faculty of medicine, 1929—; pediatrist to Providence and Children's hosps.; cons. pediatrist to Foundling and Gallinger hosps. Mem. sub-com. to Gen. Med. Bd., Council Nat. Defense; also lecturer on social hygiene for Bur. of Training Camp Activities and U.S. Pub. Health Service, 1918. Del. Internat. Med. Congress, London, 1913; trustee Nat. Geog. Soc., 1924—. Author; Essentials of Materia Medica and Therapeutics, 1910; State Board Questions for Nurses, 1916; Diseases of the New-Born, 1925; Diseases of Bones and Joints in Childhood, 1926. Official del. from U.S. to Pan Am. Child Conf., Havana, 1927. Home: Washington, D.C. Died Apr. 12, 1931.

FOOTE, PAUL D(ARWIN), physicist; b. Andover, O., Mar. 27, 1888; s. Howard Spencer and Abbie Lottie (Tourgee) F.; A.B., Western Res. U., 1909, D.Sc., 1961; A.M., U. Neb., 1911; Ph.D. U. Minn., 1917; D.Sc., Carnegie Institute of Technology, 1953; m. Berenice C. Foote, Feb. 3, 1913 (died June 10, 1939); children—Mrs. C. Jane Halliwell, William Spencer; m. 2d, Miriam Sage, June 26, 1940; stepchildren—Robert Land, Evan T. Sage. Asst. physicist, U.S. Bureau of Standards, 1911, sr. Physicist, 1924-27; exec. v.p. Gulf Research & Development Co. (Pittsburgh, Pa.); v.p. Gulf Oil Corp., Gulf Refining Co., retired all positions with Gulf, 1954; assistant sec. def., research and engring., Dept. of Def., 1957-58; exec. sec., chmn. Nat. Acad. Sci. Panels adv. to Bur. Standards, 1960-71. Recipient Achievement medal University Minn., 1951; Jr. C. of C. science award, 1953; Pitts. award, 1954; Meritorious Civilian Service medal Dept. Def., 1958. Sr. fellow Mellon Inst. Indsl. Research, 1927-29; fellow Am. Physical Soc. (pres. 1933), A.A.A.S.; mem. Optical Soc. Am., Am. Philos. Soc. (sec. 1956-59), Nat. Acad. Sci., Washington Acad. Scis. (v.p. 1936), Am. Inst. Mining and Metall. Engrs., Am. Geophysical Union, Phi Beta Kappa, Sigma Xi, Sigma Pi Sigma, Sigma Tau, Tau Beta Pi. Club: Cosmos (Washington, D.C.). Author: Pyrometric Practice (with others), pub. 1921; (with Fred Loomis Mohler) The Origin of Spectra, 1922; (with others) Physics in Industry, 1937. Editor in chief Jour. Optical Soc. America, Rev. of Scientific Instruments, 1921-32; asso. editor Jour. Franklin Inst. Home: Washington DC Died Aug. 2, 1971; buried Nat. Meml. Park, Falls Church VA

FORBES, ALEXANDER, (forbs), physiologist; b. Milton, Mass., May 14, 1882; s. William Hathaway and Edith (Emerson) F.; student Milton (Mass.) Acad., 1889-99; A.B., Harvard, 1904, A.M., 1905, M.D., 1910; Sc.D., Tufts Coll., 1952, Johns Hopkins 1954; married Charlotte Irving Grinnell, June 9, 1910; children—Lawrence Irving (dec.), Robert Grinnell (dec.), Katharine (Mrs. Katharine F. Goodhue), Janet (Mrs. Joseph R. Frothingham), Florence Emerson (Mrs. W. Andrew Locke), Alexander Irving. Began career as instructor of physiology Harvard U. Med. Sch., 1910-11; research student, U. of Liverpool (Eng.), 1911-12; instr. physiology, Harvard University Medical School, 1912-21, associate prof. physiology, 1921-36, prof. physiology, 1936-48, professor emeritus, 1948—. Served as lieutenant, j.g., U.S. Navy Res., 1917-19. On active duty as comdr. Med. Corps, U.S.N.R., World War II; disch. Dec. 1945; retired as capt., May 1946. Trustee Geo. Junior Republic (pres. bd.). Mem. Am. Physiol. Soc., Am. Acad. Arts and Sciences, Am. Philos. Soc., Nat. Acad. Sciences. Unitarian. Clubs: St. Botolph, Tavern (Boston). Home: Harland St., Milton, Mass. Died Mar. 27, 1965; buried Milton.

FORBES, ERNEST BROWNING, physiologist, nutritionist; b. Normal Ill., Nov. 3, 1876; s. Stephen Alfred and Clara Shaw (Gatson) F.; B.S., U. Ill., 1897, B.S. in Agr., 1902; Ph.D., U. Mo., 1908; m. Lydia M. Mather, Aug. 18, 1903; children—Lydia Frances, Winifred Mather, Stephen Alfred, II, Rosemary, Richard Mather. Zool. asst., Ill. Biol. Sta., 1894-96; asst. to state entomologist of Minn., 1897-98; zool. asst. Ill State Lab. Natural History, 1899; acting state entomologist of Minn., 1901; asst. animal husbandry Ill.

Agrl. Expt. Sta., 1901-02; instr. in animal husbandry U. Ill., 1902-03; asst. prof. animal husbandry U. Mo., 1903-07; chief Dept. Nutrition, Ohio Agr. Expt. Sta., 1907-20; specialist in nutrition, United Chem. and Organic Products Co., 1921, Inst. Am. Meat Packers, 1922; dir. Inst. Animal Nutrition, prof. animal nutrition Pa. State Coll., 1922-46, prof. emeritus animal nutrition, 1946—. Fellow A.A.A.S.; mem. Am. Chem. Soc., Am. Physiol. Soc., Am. Soc. Animal Production (pres. 1914, 15), Am. Inst. Nutrition, Delta Tau Delta, Sigma Xi, Alpha Zeta, Phi Lambda Upsilon, Gamma Sigma Delta; fgn. me. L'Academie Royale D'Agriculture De Suéde. Republican. Unitarian. Author: Phosphorus Compounds in Animal Metabolism (with M. Helen Keith), 1914; also numerous reports of research on energy, protein and mineral metabolism. Home: State College, Pa. Died Sept. 9, 1966.

FORBES, JOHN SIMS, mech. engr.; b. Phila., Pa., May 7, 1866; s. William Smith and Celanire Bernoudi (Sims) F.; A.B., U. of Pa., 1887; m. Martha Jane Ayers Falls, of Lancaster Co., Pa., Nov. 8, 1900 (dec.). Practiced at Phila. since 1888. Awarded Elliott Cresson medal and Edward Longstreth medal, by Franklin Inst. Home: Wynnewood Rd., Overbrook, Pa. *

FORBES, ROBERT HUMPHREY, agrl. science; b. Cobden, Ill., May 15, 1867; s. Henry Clinton and Laura Jane (Gorham) F.; B.S., U. of Ill., 1892; M.S., 1897; spl. courses in research work, Harvard, 1893-94; Ph.D., U. of Calif., 1916; hon. Sc.D., U. of Ariz., 1925; m. Georgie Hazel Scott, Jan. 16, 1902. Instr., U. of Ill., 1891-93; prof. chemistry, U. of Ariz., and chemist of Ariz. Agrl. Expt. Sta., 1894-99; dir. and chemist, Ariz. Expt. Sta., 1899-1911; dir. Ariz. Expt. Sta., and of agrl. instrn., U. of Ariz., 1912-15; dean and dir. Coll. of Agr. and Agrl. Experiment Sta., U. of Ariz., 1915-18; sec. Ariz. Commn. of Agr. and Hort., 1909-18; agronomist, Societe Sultanienne d'Agriculture, of Egypt, 1918-22; chief engr. Etudes Agronomiques Mission Niger, and counselor tech. Office du Niger, French West Africa, 1922-1939; also dir. expt. stations, Service Technique d'Haiti, 1927-29; rep. Ariz. State Legislature since 1939. Author numerous reports and bulletins on chemistry of soils and water supplies, date palm culture, toxic effects of copper on crops and the agronomy of cotton in Egypt, French West Africa and Haiti; also descriptive articles in mags. Home: 105 Olive Rd., Tucson AZ

FORBES, STEPHEN ALFRED, naturalist; b. Silver Creek, Ill., May 29, 1844; s. Isaac Sawyer and Agnes (Van Hoesen) F.; ed. at Beloit Acad. and Rush Med. Coll.; Ph.D., on exam. and thesis, Ind. U., 1884; (LL.D., U. of Ill., 1905); m. Clara Shaw Gaston, Dec. 25, 1873; children—Bertha Van Hoesen, Ernest Browning, Winifred, Ethel Clara, Richard Edwin (dec.). Capt. 7th Ill. Vol. Cav. in Civil War; prisoner 4 months; curator Mus. of Ill. State Natural History Soc., 1872-77; taught zoölogy, Ill. State Normal U., 1875-78; founded, 1877, and dir. Ill. State Lab. of Natural History to 1917; since chief of natural history survey of Ill.; state entomologist, 1882-1917; prof. zoölogy, 1884-1909, prof. of entomology, Sept. 1, 1909-21, dean Coll. of Science, 1888-1905, Univ. of Ill. Awarded first class medal of Société d'Acclimatation de France for scientific publs., 1886; organized Internat. Congress Zoölogists, Chicago Expn., 1893; dir. aquarium of U.S. Fish Commn. and prepared natural history exhibit of Ill. at same. Was founder of and has been editor and contbr. to Bulletins of Illinois State Lab. of Natural History, 1877— (now Bulletin Ill. State Nat. Hist. Survey). Author: Biennial Reports as State Entomologist, 1883-1916; Studies of the Food of Birds, Fishes and Insects; Contagious Diseases of Insects. Final Report on the Fishes of Illinois and Studies on the Biology of the Illinois River (with R. E. Richardson). Home: Urbana, Ill. Died Mar. 13, 1930.

FORD, ARTHUR HILLYER, prof. elec. engring.; b. Chicago, Feb. 6, 1874; s. Charles Henry and Edna Coe (Hillyer) F.; B.S. in E.E., U. of Wis., 1895, E.E., 1896, fellow, 1895-97; fellow Columbia, 1897-98; m. Sadie Murray Hess, June 18, 1908; children—Ellen, Edwin Hillyer, Robert Murray. Engr. with Western Electric Co., Chicago, 1899-1900; acting prof. elec. engring., U. of Colo., 1900-01; prof. same, Ga. Sch. of Tech., 1901-05, State U. of Ia., Sept. 1905—. Fellow Am. Inst. Elec. Engrs., 1912. Congregationalist. Home: Iowa City, Ia. Died Feb. 16, 1930.

FORD, FRANCIS CHIPMAN, anatomist; b. Niles, Mich., June 26, 1865; s. Henry Allen and Emily F. (Chipman) F.; desc. on mother's side of four Mayflower passengers; A.B., U. of Mich., 1888; M.D., Homoe. Med. Dept., U. of Mich., 1890; m. Ida Harriet Larimore, July 15, 1890. Practiced, Niles, Mich., 1890-91, Chicago, 1891-93, Los Angeles and Pasadena, Calif., 1893-96; removed to Chicago, 1897; anatomist in Chicago med. colls., 1897-1906; prof. and head dept. of anatomy, Hahnemann Med. Coll., Chicago, 1906—; chmn. com. of management, Hahnemann dept., Chicago Y.M.C.A. Mem. Vol. Med. Service Corps, 1918-19. Republican. Presbyn. Home: Chicago, Ill. Died May 9, 1922.

FORD, FRANK RICHARDS, cons. engr.; b. Phila., Pa., 1871; s. Henry C. and Emilie C. (Richards) F.; B.S. and M.E., U. of Pa., 1890; m. Sunshine H. Donaldson, 1898 (died 1923); 4 children; m. 2d, Ethelwyn Linnell, 1927. Mem. Ford, Bacon & Davis, cons. engrs., 1894—. Dir. L. C. Smith & Corona Typewriters, Inc., Lackawanna & Wyo. Valley R.R. Corp., Syracuse Washing Machine Corp. Mem. New York, New Jersey Port and Harbor Development Commn., 1917-21; mem. Port of New York Authority, 1921-23. Trustee Washington Square Assn. Republican. Episcopalian. Homes: Roseland, N.J., and New York City. Died Sept. 17, 1930.

FORD, HENRY, automobile manufacturer; b. Dearborn Township, Wayne County, Mich., July 30, 1863; s. William and Mary (Litogot) F.; ed. in dist. sch., Dearborn, Mich., D.Eng., U. of Mich., 1926; LL.D., Colgate U., 1935; m. Clara J. Bryant, Apr. 11, 1888; 1 son, Edsel Bryant. Learned machinist's trade; in Detroit since 1887; was chief engr. Edison Illuminating Co.; organizer, 1903, pres. many yrs. Ford Motor Co. (largest mfr. of automobiles in the world, employing over 100,000 persons). Announced, 1914, plan of profit-sharing involving distribution of ten to thirty millions of dollars annually to employees. Mem. Soc. Automotive Engrs., Detroit Board of Commerce. Clubs: Detroit, Detroit Athletic. Country, Detroit Boat, Automobile of America. Chartered ship, and at own expense conducted party to Europe, leaving New York, Dec. 4, 1915, with object of organizing a conf. of peace advocates to influence belligerent govts. to end the war; returned home after reaching Christiania, Norway, but members of the party preceeded to Stockholm, Sweden, and Copenhagen, Denmark, and through Germany to The Hague. Built Henry Ford Hosp. at cost of $7,500,000. Apptd. by Pres. Wilson mem. Wage Umpire Bd., July 13, 1918; Dem. candidate for U.S. Senate against Truman H. Newberry, 1918. Author: My Life and Work, 1925; Today and Tomorrow, 1926; Moving Forward, 1931. Home: Dearborn, Mich. Died Apr. 7, 1947. *

FORD, RICHARD, physician, educator; b. Cambridge, Mass., Jan. 31, 1915; s. Jeremiah D.M. and Anna (Fearns) F.; A.B., Harvard, 1936, M.D., 1940; m. Hope Cullinan, Jan. 23, 1942; children—Hope, Faith, Cathleen Charity, Lucy Ann. Intern pathology Peter Bent Brigham Hosp., 1940-41, cons. in pathology, 1953—; intern surgery Boston City Hosp., 1941-42; research fellow legal medicine and pathology, med. sch. Harvard, 1945-49, acting head dept. legal medicine, asst. prof. legal medicine, 1949-61, asst. clin. prof. legal medicine, chmn. dept., 1961-65; lectr. legal medicine Harvard, Yale, Tufts, and Boston univs. med. schs.; hon. lectr. forensic medicine U. Southern Cal. School of Medicine, 1953; Rockefeller traveling fellow, 1953. Pathologist to State Police, Commonwealth of Mass., 1949-65; asso. med. examiner Suffolk Co. (Boston), 1946-50, med. examiner, 1950-70; cons. in pathology Peter Bent Brigham Hosp., 1953-70; cons. in forensic pathology Mass. Gen. Hosp., 1959-70, Armed Forces Inst. Path., 1959-70, Fed. Aviation Agy., 1960. Served from 1st lt. to maj. AUS, 1942-45. Certified in Forensic Pathology by Am. Bd. Pathology. Decorated Legion of Merit. Fellow Coll. Am. Pathologists; mem. A.M.A., Am. Assn. Pathologists and Bacteriologists, Am. Acad. Forensic Scis., Am. Assn. Neuropathologists (asso.). Home: Peterborough NH Died Aug. 3, 1970; buried Peterborough NH

FORD, WALTER BURTON, mathematician; b. Oneonta, N.Y., May 18, 1874; s. Sylvester and Emogene (Burton) F.; student Amherst, 1893-95; A.B., Harvard, 1898; Ph.D., 1905; studied in Europe, 1903-04; m. Edith W. Banker, Oct. 20, 1900 (dec. 1959); children—Sylvester (dec.), Clinton B. Instr. math. U. Mich., 1900-03, Williams Coll., 1904-05; again with U. Mich., 1905-39, prof. math., 1917-39. Mem. Am. Math. Soc., Math. Assn. Am. (pres. 1926-28). Societe Mathematique de France, Delta Upsilon. Unitarian. Author: Studies on Divergent Series and Summability, 1916; also various math. texts and research publications. Editor-in-chief Math. Monthly, 1923-27. Home: Ovid NY Died Feb. 24, 1971; buried Ovid NY

FORD, WILLIAM EBENEZER, mineralogist; b. Westville, Conn., Feb. 18, 1878; s. William Elbert and Caroline Aby (Bishop) F.; Ph.B., Yale, 1899, Ph.D., 1903; m. Mary Treat Jennings, 1920. Asst. in mineralogy, 1899-1903, instr., 1903-06, asst. prof., 1906-20, prof., 1920—, Sheffield Scientific Sch., Yale. Fellow Am. Acad. Arts and Sciences. Editor: Second and Third Appendices to Dana's System of Mineralogy, 1909 and 1915; New Edition of Dana's Manual of Mineralogy, 1912, 29; Dana's Text Book of Mineralogy (new edits.), 1921, 32. Home: New Haven, Conn. Died Mar. 23, 1939.

FORD, WILLIAM HENRY, mechanical engr.; b. Paterson, N.J., May 17, 1852; s. John and Phoebe T. (Flaville) F.; ed. pub. schs. Chester and Phila., Pa., and Chester Acad.; m. Agnes L. Burgess, of Providence, R.I., Sept. 6, 1881. Mech. engr. Hinkley Locomotive Works, 1879-89; chief drafting dept. New York Air Brake Co., 1890-1900; now in business for self. P.G. and P.D.D. Grand Master Odd Fellows of New York. Author: Boiler Making for Boiler Makers, 1885; Symbolism of Odd Fellowship, 1903. Address: Niagara Falls, N.Y. *

FORNEY, JOHN H., civil engr.; b. Lincoln Co., N.C., Aug. 12, 1829; s. Jacob and Sabina Swope (Hoke) F.; moved to Jacksonville, Ala., 1835; apptd. cadet. U.S. Mil. Acad., June 1848; bvt. 2d lt., 1852; 1st lt., 1855; staff officer to Col. Charles F. Smith on exploring expdn. to Pembina, 1855; comd. pioneer corps with Gen. A. S. Johnson in Utah Campaign, 1857; instr. West Point, 1860; 1st lt. 10th inf.; resigned to accept service as col. and aide to gov. Ala., Jan. 23, 1861; apptd. col. arty., Army of Ala., March 1861, comdg. at Pensacola, Fla.; resigned to accept capt. arty., C.S. army and insp. gen. with Gen. Bragg; apptd. col. 10th Ala. regt.; mustered for war June 4, 1861; brig. gen., C.S.A., March 10, 1862, comdg. Dept. Gulf, hdqrs. Mobile; maj. gen., Oct. 27, 1862, comdg. dist. of Vicksburg; comd. parole camp, Enterpise, Miss., July 1863; ordered July 1864 to Trans-Mississippi Dept. to bring East a div. of troops; 4 large brigades were concentrated at Hempstead, Tex., preparatory to running blockade from Galveston to St. Mark's, Fla., when Gen. Lee surrendered; paroled at Galveston, and returned to home in Ala.; m. Septima Sexta Middleton Rutledge, great g.d. Edward Rutledge, Feb. 5, 1863. Home: Jacksonville, Ala. Died 1902.

FORSTALL, ARMAND WILLIAM, coll. prof.; b. Chaumont, France, July 5, 1859; s. Eugene Forstall and Armande (Carette) F.; ed. Jesuit College, Dole-Jura, France, 1870-72, Amiens, Somme, 1872-78; B.A., U. of Douai (North), 1877; student St. Stanislaus Coll., Paris, 1878-79, Tronchiennes (Belgium) Sem., 1880-82, Jesuit Sem., Louvain, 1882-85; A.M., Woodstock (Maryland) College, 1894; student Angers Seminary, Angers (Maine et Loire), France, 1894-95; D.Sc., U. of Denver, 1935. Came to U.S., 1885. Ordained to ministry R.C. Ch., 1892; instr. mathematics, Coll. of Sacred Heart, Morrison, Colo., 1885-86, instr. in physics, chemistry, mathematics, Las Vegas (N.M.) Coll., 1886-88, Regis Coll., Denver, 1888-90, and 1898-99; instr. physics, Georgetown U., 1895-96 and 1900-02, Holy Cross Coll., Worcester, Mass., 1899-1900; prof. of chemistry, Woodstock Coll., Md., 1902-04; prof. of mathematics, physics, chemistry, Regis Coll., 1904-25, prof. of physics and chemistry, 1904-23, prof. of physics and engring. drawing, 1904-31, prof. engring. drawing, 1923-32, also head of dept., 1923-32, prof. of analytic chemistry since 1932, and dir. Seismic Station, 1909-34. Mem. Seismol. Soc. of America, Jesuit Seismol. Assn., Soc. for Research on Meteorites. Has written many reports on mining resources of Colo., especially uranium, molybdenum and tungsten; also publs. of Observatory—U.S. Weather Review to 1921, U.S. Geodetic Survey Publications, 1922-26; publs. of St. Louis Univ. on Geophysics, etc. Address: Regis College, Denver. Died Apr. 21, 1948; buried in Regis College Cemetery, Denver.

FORSTER, ALEXIUS MADOR, physician; b. Lexington, Va., Sept. 27, 1880; s. Charles Warham and Inda Carey (Payne) F.; M.D., U. Louisville, 1904; m. Liane Raymonde Queffelec, May 1, 1919; children—Josianne Liane, Evelyn Fairfax. Asst. resident physician French Lick Springs Hotel, Ind., 1904; asst. Adirondack Cottage Sanitarium, N.Y., 1904-05; asst. Gaylord Farm Sanitarium, 1905-06; resident physician Endowed Sanitarium, Towson, Md.; asst. in medicine, Johns Hopkins, 1906-09; directed Tb. work in Louisville, 1910; physician in chief Cragmor Sanatorium, Colorado Springs, Colo., 1910—. For many years engaged in the rehab. of tuberculous. Commd. 1st lt. Med. R.C., 1917, capt., 1917, maj., 1918, lt. col., 1918. Mem. Nat. Tuberculosis Assn. (1st v.p. 1925). Address: Cragmor Sanatorium, Colorado Springs, Colo. Died Mar. 23, 1954; buried Evergreen Cemetery, Colorado Springs.

FORT, MARION KIRKLAND, JR., mathematician, educator; b. Spartanburg, S.C., Mar. 5, 1921; s. Marion Kirkland and Emily (Connor) F.; A.B., Wofford Coll., 1941; M.A., U. Va., 1944, Ph.D., 1948; m. Doris Marie Lowe, Apr. 7, 1945; children—Mary Susan, John Kirkland. Instr. U. Va., 1945-48; instr. U. Ill., 1948-49, asst. prof., 1949-53; mem. faculty U. Ga., 1953—, prof. math., 1956—, chmn. dept., 1959-63, Barrow prof. of mathematics, 1963-64. Named Ford Found. fellow, 1952-53; Sloan fellow, 1958-61. Served with AUS, 1944-45. Mem. Am., Indian math. socs., Math. Assn. Am., Phi Beta Kappa, Pi Mu Epsilon (councilor gen. 1960-63), Sigma Xi. Presbyn. Clubs: Exchange (past pres.), City (past pres.). (Athens). Author research papers. Editor: Topology of 3-Manifolds and Related Topics. Home: 145 Meadowview Rd., Athens, Ga. 30601. Died Aug. 2, 1964; buried Evergreen Meml. Park, Athens.

FORTH, EDWARD WALTER, research and engring. co. exec.; b. Syracuse, N.Y., Sept. 2, 1919; s. Walter Dallas and Cecilia (Trinkhaus) F.; B.S., U.S. Naval Acad., 1940; grad. U.S. Naval Post-grad. Sch., 1942; M.S., Mass. Inst. Tech., 1947; m. Bernice Sherarer, Dec. 24, 1940; children—Douglas S., Gerald E., Michael F., Kathleen M., Cecilia A., Christine M. Commd. ensign U.S. Navy, 1940, advanced through grades to lt. comdr., 1944; engaged in design, constrn., repair naval vessels and equipment; resigned, 1946; with Am. Machine and Foundry Co., 1946-53, asst. works mgr., 1950-53; v.p. mfg. DeWalt, Inc., Lancaster, Pa., 1953-56; v.p., gen. mgr. AMF Cycle Co., E. Longmeadow, Mass., 1956-57; v.p., dir. engring. Packaging Machinery Co., 1957-60, v.p. research and engring. plumbing and heating div.

Am. Radiator & Standard San. Corp., 1960-64, pres. Am. Standard Indsl. div., 1964—. Active Little League Baseball, Boy Scouts Am., Mem. Am. Mgmt. Assn., Soc. Plastics Industry, Soc. Die Casting Engrs., Western Mass. Engring. Soc. Republican. Roman Cath. Patentee automatic machinery. Home: Ponus Ridge, New Canaan, Conn. Office: 40 W. 40th St., N.Y.C. 18. Died Oct. 1967.

FORTIER, SAMUEL, engineer; b. Leeds, P.Q., Can., Apr. 24, 1855; s. Leandre and Ann (Reid) F.; grad. McGill Normal Sch., Montreal, Can., 1880; B.Sc., McGill U., 1885, M.E., 1896, D.Sc., 1907; m. S. B. Helena Macleay, of Danville, P.Q., Oct. 17, 1888; children—Roy Macleay, Winifred R., Ernest Cleveland. First asst. engr., Denver Water Co., 1886-90; chief engr. and supt. Ogden Water Works and Bear River Canal & Irrigation Co., 1890-93; prof. civ. and hydraulic engring., Agrl. Coll. of Utah, 1893-97, also acting as hydrographer U.S. Geol. Survey and cons. engr. for irrigation enterprises; dir. Montana Expt. Station, 1899-1903, also resident hydrographer of U.S. Geol. Survey in Mont., and irrigation engr. U.S. Dept. Agr.; in charge Pacific Coast Dist. of irrigation investigations of U.S. Office of Expt. Stas., 1903-07, and delivered lectures on irrigation, U. of Calif.; chief of irrigation investigations, 1907-15; adviser to govt. to B.C. on irrigation law and its administration, 1912; chief of division of irrigation investigations, U.S. Bureau Public Roads, 1915-22; asso. chief Div. Agrl. Engring., 1922-24, sr. irrigation engr., 1924-27, prin. irrigation engr., 1927-30; retired 1930. Awarded Gowski medal, 1896, by Canadian Soc. C.E., for paper on storage of water. Author: Use of Water in Irrigation. Home: Berkeley, Calif. Died Aug. 17, 1933.

FORTUNE, J(OHN) ROBERT, mechanical engr.; b. Detroit, Aug. 1, 1871; s. Thomas Jenkins and Mary (Buckley) F.; ed. Detroit pub. schs. and by pvt. study; m. Nettie E. Thomas, of Detroit, June 6, 1898. Engr. Murphy Iron Wks., Detroit, 1890-8, Am. Stoker Co., New York, 1898-1900, Automatic Furnace Syndicate, London, Eng., 1900-1; chief engr., Underfeed Stoker Co., London, 1901-3; European mgr. Murphy Iron Wks., London, 1903-5; chief engr., Murphy Iron Wks., Detroit, 1905-15; mech. engr. Dodge Bros., Detroit, 1915-17; works mgr. Bunting Brass & Bronze Co., Toledo, 1917-18. Mem. Am. Soc. M.E., Engrs. Soc. Western Pa., Detroit Engineering Soc., Ohio Soc. Mech., Elec. and Steam Engrs., Am. Foundrymen's Assn. Inventor and patentee many improvements in mech. stoking apparatus. Club: Ingleside. Home: 3Harold Arms, Toledo OH

FOSS, FEODORE FEODOROVICH, mining and metall. engr.; b. Odessa, Russia, Dec. 29, 1874; s. Feodore A. and Olga A. (Mansfield) F.; grad. Classical Gymnasium. St. Petersburg, 1893; entered through competitive exam. (60 out of 1,000) Imperial Mining Inst. and grad. M.E., cum eximia laude, 1898; m. Zenaida M. Magula, Apr. 28, 1899. Came to U.S., 1917, naturalized citizen 1926. Asst. prof. metallurgy, Mining Inst. of St. Petersburg, 1900-02; as chief engr., later mng. dir. Lyssva Mining Dist., developed iron and steel industry there by introduction of mfr. of tin plate, galvanized sheet iron, hollowware, etc.; developed platinum mining of same district to output of nearly 2 tons per yr.; tinplate produced in the plants under his management was only resource for canning food for Russian armies; during World War built new plants employing 15,000 men to supply Russian armies with shells, fuses, powder boxes, soldiers' canteens and trench instruments; awarded hon. degree in engring. by Imperial Russian Govt.; former pres. and dir. Lyssva Mining Dist., Inc., Russia, Urals, vice chmn. bd. Verch-Issetsk Mining Dist., dir. Bogoslovsk Mining Dist.; col. Russian Mining Corps; came to U.S., 1917, as chmn. industrial commn. to study Am. methods of developing natural resources; severed connection with Russia on account of Bolshevik upheaval; now retired, after 21 years service with Wheeling Steel Corporation as asst. to president, asst. to chairman and director of research and metallurgy. Mem. Am. Inst. Mining and Metall. Engrs., Am. Soc. M.E., Am. Soc. for Metals. Am. Economic Soc., Am. Acad. Polit. Science, Am. Geog. Soc., Army Ordnance Assn., Assn. Iron and Steel Engineers, Am. Polit. Science Assn., Am. Academy Polit. and Social Science. Republican. Unitarian. Home: 1857 E. Las Tunas Rd., Santa Barbara CA

FOSTER, ALBERT DOUGLAS, med. dir., U.S. Pub. Health Service (retired); b. Detroit, Mich., Feb. 13, 1875; s. Edward Dwight and Marian (Langley) F.; M.D., U. of Mich., 1899; m. Hilda Ann Mitcham, Dec. 27, 1911; children—Edith Frances (Mrs. Alfred Leighton Gibson), Albert Douglas, Florence Mitcham (Mrs. Robert Lewis Berg), Theodore Tillinghast. Interne U.S. Marine Hosp., Cleveland, O., 1899; commd. asst. surgeon in U.S. Pub. Health Service, 1902, passed asst. surgeon, 1907, surgeon, 1914, med. dir., 1930; retired from active duty, 1939. Am. vice and dept. consul at Amoy, China, 1909. Fellow Am. Coll. of Physicians; mem. A.M.A., Me. State Med. Soc. Mason (32 deg.). Clubs: Portland Medical, National Sojourner, Torch of Western Maine. Author of monographs, Railway Car Sanitation, School Hygiene, Interstate Migration of Tuberculosis Persons. Home: Bay Shore Dr., Falmouth Foreside ME

FOSTER, ERNEST LE NEVE, mining engr.; b. London, Eng., Jan. 23, 1849; s. Peter and Georgiana Elizabeth (Chevallier) Le Neve F.; edn. followed by courses at Royal Sch. of Mines, London, and Bergakademie, Freiberg, 1866-69; m. Charlotte Teal, 1875 (died 1906); 2d, Mrs. Marion C. (Wright) Fulton, of Mich., Feb. 20, 1909. Began practice in Italy; practiced in Colo. since 1872; State geologist, Colo., 1883-84. Fellow Geol. Soc. London; pres. Colo. Scientific Soc., and mem. several Other scientific socs. Home: Perrenoud Apartments. Office: 412 Nassau Block, Denver. *

FOSTER, GEORGE SANFORD, surgeon; b. at Barrington, N.H., Apr. 20, 1882; s. George Sanford and Etta Frances (Moulton) F.; student Harvard Summer Sch. of Physical Edn., 1900, Harvard Summer Sch. of Obstetrics, 1905; M.D., cum laude, Tufts Coll. Med. Sch., 1906 (pres. of class); post grad. study in Europe; m. Elizabeth Russell Danforth, Dec. 27, 1905; children—Clayton Reginald, Virginia Frances, George Sanford, Jr., Russell Danforth. Athletic dir. various high schs. and Y.M.C.A.'s for several years; interne Children's Hosp., Boston, Boston City Hosp., Sacred Heart Hosp., Manchester, N.H., 1905-07; began practice at Manchester, Feb. 1, 1907; surgeon and pathologist to Notre Dame Hosp., Manchester, N.H., 1907-25; surgeon Lucy Hastings Hosp., Manchester, 1925-38; cons. surgeon Peterboro (N.H.) Hosp. Trustee Manchester Boys' Club (pres. 12 yrs.). Founded clin. lab. and training school for nurses, Notre Dame Hosp., Manchester; founded Lucy Hastings Hosp., also training schools for nurses and technicians and cancer research lab. at same, Manchester. Served as capt. Med. Corps, U.S. Army, during World War I. Now serving at lt. comdr., Med. Corps, U.S.N.R. Fellow Internat. Coll. Surgeons (Geneva). Mem. N.H. Surg. Club, Manchester Med. Soc. (past pres.), Hillsboro County Med. Soc., N.H. Med. Soc., Am. Med. Assn., Am. Assn. for Study of Neoplastic Diseases (founder Northern New England Assn.), Am. Med. Editors and Authors Assn., Wild Life Soc., Am. Forestry Assn., Nat. Assn. Audubon Socs., Mass. Audubon Soc., Northern New England Bird Banding Assn. (treas.), Fed. Boys' Clubs of Am. (exec. com. New Eng. div.), Clin. Congress Surgeons of N. America (rep. from N.H., 1908-11; sen. from N.H., 1911-14), Manchester Hist. Assn., N.H. Hist. Soc., N.H. S.A.R., Manchester Inst. Arts and Sciences, Phi Chi (ex-pres. Delta Chapter), Mil. Order of the World War, Mil. Order of Foreign Wars, Assn. Mil. Surgeons of U.S., Am. Legion, Res. Officers Assn. of U.S. Army, Eugene Field Soc. (hon.). Mason. Odd Fellow. Clubs: Manchester Country, Y.M.C.A. (Manchester); University (Boston); Army and Navy (Washington). Author: Post Operative Treatment; Qualifications of a Model Nurse; Health Day by Day; Health; Art of Living; Birds and Bird Clubs; They Know Not; Why I Believe in God and Immortality; Trapping the Common Cold; Our Youth (Helping Them to Help Themselves); also numerous monographs, brochures and articles on med. subjects, etc. Home: Manchester, N.H. Died Aug. 13, 1945.

FOSTER, HORATIO ALVAH, electrical engr.; b. Phila., Pa., Jan. 12, 1858; s. Edward Vose and Martha Allis (Smith) F.; ed. Northampton (Mass.) High Sch.; m. Florence Louise Root, Dec. 22, 1893. Installed first commercially operated electric ry. in U.S., in Baltimore, 1885; engr. for Thomson-Houston Electric Co., 1886-91, and of Central Sta., New York, for same co., 1890-91; elec. expert for U.S. Census Office, 1891-92; editor "Electrical Industries," Chicago, during World's Fair; 1st asst. to Prof. George Forbes, of London; elec. consulting engr., Niagara Falls Power Co., 1895-1900; federal receiver Consumers Brewing Co., Phila., 1901-06; with L. B. Stillwell, engrs., 1906-08; with Bion J. Arnold, Chicago, 1908-11; J. G. White & Co., New York, 1912—. Fellow Am. Inst. Elec. Engrs., 1912. Republican. Unitarian. Author: Electrical Engineers' Pocket Book, 1901; Engineering Valuation of Public Utilities and Factories, 1912. Home: Yonkers, N.Y. Deceased.

FOSTER, JOHN WELLS, geologist; b. Petersham, Mass., Mar. 4, 1815; s. Festus Foster; grad. Wesleyan U., Middletown, Conn., 1833; studied law, Zanesville, O.; m. Lydia Conerse, Oct. 24, 1838. Practiced law for time, Zanesville; asst. Ohio Geol. Survey, 1837; asso. U.S. geologist, 1847-52; a founder Native Am. Party in Mass., 1852; an organizer Republican Party in Mass., 1855; land commr. I.C. R.R., 1858-63; lectr. geology U. Chgo., 1863-65; pres. A.A.A.S. Author: The Mississippi Valley: Its Physical Geography, Including Sketches of the Topography, Botany, Climate, Geology and Mineral Resources; And of the Progress of Development in Population and Material Wealth, 1869; Prehistoric Races of the United States of America, 1873. Died June 28, 1873.

FOSTER, ROBERT ARNOLD, mining engr.; b. Sacramento, Calif., Jan. 19, 1877; s. John Curry and Mary Starkweather (Patterson) F.; B.S., Coll. of Mines, U. of Calif., 1898; m. Katherine Lucretia Fairchild, of Canton, O., Aug. 3, 1901; children—Lucretia Mary, Katherine Wilhelmenia. Const. engr., Ariz. Copper Co., Ltd., Clifton, Ariz., 1898-1901; chief engr. and gen. mgr. Mining Corpn., Ltd., Portland, Ore., 1901-03; pres. Alaska-Peninsular Coal & Coke Co., 1903-10; pres. Lewiston-Clarkston Improvement Co., 1913-31; pres. Mexican Coal & Coke Co. Mem. Am. Soc. C.E., Sigma Alpha Epsilon, Sigma Xi. Episcopalian. Mason (33 deg. hon., Shriner). Clubs: University, Mexico City. Home: Las Esperanzas, Coahuila Mexico*

FOSTER, RUFUS JAMES, mining engr.; b. at Minersville, Pa., Oct. 10, 1856; s. Clement Storer and Rebecca (McCamant) F.; grad. Ashland High Sch., 1874; m. Jane Bennett Taylor, of Minersville, Pa., Sept. 9, 1884. With engring. dept. Phila. & Reading Coal & Iron Co., 1874-87; mng. editor The Collier Engineer from 1887—; a founder, 1891, and v.p. Internat. Textbook Co. and allied corps. Mem. Am. Inst. Mining Engrs., Am. Soc. Mech. Engrs., Engineers' Soc. of N.E. Pa., Pa. Soc. S.R., New England Soc. of North Eastern Pa. Republican. Episcopalian. Clubs: Scranton, Engineers', Country. Home: 807 Clay Av. Office: 424 Wyoming Av., Scranton, Pa. *

FOSTER, WILLIAM, chemist; b. Hartford, Ky., May 15, 1869; s. William and Sarah Jane (Carson) F.; A.B., Hartford Coll., 1892; B.S. Vanderbilt U., 1893; A.M., Princeton, 1896, Ph.D., 1899; m. Helen Dunham Steward, Sept. 3, 1902; children—Katharine Sutliff, Helen Stewart, Wilhelmina. Prof. chemistry, Central U. of Ky., 1899-1900; instr. chemistry, 1900-05, asst. prof., 1905-10, prof., 1910—, Princeton. Formerly chief examiner in chemistry, Coll. Entrance Examination Bd. Fellow A.A.A.S. Democrat. Presbyn. Author: A Laboratory Manual in General Chemistry, 1905; Introduction to General Chemistry, 1922, 31; The Elements of Chemistry, 1925, 32; Experiments in General Chemistry (with H. W. Heath), 1925; The Romance of Chemistry, 1927, German edit. of same as Welt und Wunder der Chemie, 1931; Inorganic Chemistry for Colleges, 1929; A Laboratory Course of General Chemistry, 1930. Home: Princeton, N.J. Died May 24, 1937.

FOSTER, WILLIAM JAMES, retired elec. engr.; b. Argyle, N.Y., Sept. 17, 1860; s. James and Martha (Dobbin) F.; A.B., Williams Coll., Williamstown, Mass., 1884, A.M., 1885, D.Sc., 1923; M.S., Cornell, 1891; m. Caroline McEachron, Sept. 16, 1896; 1 son, William James. Instr. mathematics, William Coll., 1885; asst. prin. Burr & Burton Sem., Manchester, Vt., 1885-86; tchr. sci. and mathematics, Hill Sch., Pottstown, Pa., 1886-90; engr. Thomson-Houston Co., Lynn, Mass., 1891-94; asst. engr. Gen. Electric Co., Schenectady, N.Y., 1894-1925, cons. engr., 1925-29 (now retired). Fellow Am. Inst. E.E., A.A.A.S.; mem. Acad. Polit. Sci., Phi Beta Soc. Hudson Valley Soc. Recipient medals for machine design by St. Louis, San Francisco, and other expns., Lamme medal of Am. Inst. E.E., 1931. Republican. Mem. Ref. Church of Am. Clubs: Mohawk Golf; Williams (New York); Taconic Golf (Williamstown, Mass.). Contbr. articles to tech. publs.; also wrote Descendants of John Dobbin of Connagher. Home: 2 Douglas Rd., Schenectady. Died July 2, 1943; buried Argyle (N.Y.) Cemetery.

FOULK, CHARLES WILLIAM, (fulk), chemist; b. Warren, O., Apr. 26, 1869; s. Elias James and Louisa (Paltzgrove) F.; A.B., Ohio State U., 1894; grad. study Mass. Inst. Tech., summer, 1897, Physico-Chem. Inst., Leipzig, Germany, 1899-1901; D.Sc., Mt. Union Col., Alliance, O., 1934; m. Elma Brooks Perry, Sept. 12. 1905. Asst. to chemist O. State Bd. Agr., 1894-96; prof. analytical chemistry, Ohio State U., 1908—, emeritus prof., 1939; cons. chem., Geol. Survey of O., 1914-16. Past chmn. tech. com. no. 3, joint research on boiler feed water studies (Am. Boiler Mfrs. Assn., Am. Ry. Engring. Assn., Am. Water Works Assn., Nat. Electric Light Assn., Am. Soc. Testing Materials, Am. Soc. M.E.). Fellow A.A.A.S.; mem. Am. Chem. Soc., Sigma Xi, Phi Beta Kappa, Phi Lambda Upsilon. Clubs: University Faculty, Torch. Author: Introductory Notes on Quantitative Chemical Analysis, 2d edit., 1910; General principles and Manipulation of Quantitative Chemical Analysis, 1913; Industrial Water Supplies of Ohio, 1925. Contbr. jours. of Am. Chem. Soc., Jour. Am. Water Works Assn. Inventor of density measuring apparatus. Home: 275 East Lane Av., Columbus, O. Died Dec. 15, 1958; buried Piqua, O.

FOUNTAIN, CLAUDE RUSSELL, prof. physics; b. Ashland, Ore., Nov. 2, 1879; s. James Davis and Grace (Russell) F.; A.B., U. of Ore., 1901; univ. scholar in mathematics, Columbia, 1901-02, Ph.D. in physics, 1908; m. Lucy E. Landru, June 16, 1914; children—Betty Grace Edwards, Margaret Louise Pinkston. Asst. in physics, Columbia, 1902-05, also assistant in Columbia Summer School of Practical Astronomy and Geodesy; associate professor physics, University of Idaho, 1905-06; instructor physics, Williams Coll., 1906-09; asst. prof. physics, Kenyon Coll., Gambier, O., 1909-13; adj. prof. physics, U. of Ga., 1913-18; prof. physics and astronomy, Mercer U., 1918-26; prof. mathematics and physics, 1926-27, prof. teaching of physics, 1927-40, George Peabody Coll. for Teachers; also prof. physics, same instn., summers 1915-19, 1923-26; prof. of Aeronautics (teaching all courses at Ground Sch. of the Civil Aeronautics Authority), Southwestern Coll., Memphis, summer, 1940; prof. applied science and mathematics Hume-Fogg Technical High Sch., 1940-41; vis. prof. physics, Amherst Coll., 1941-42; vis. prof. of physics, Mass. Inst. of Technology, 1942-43; senior physicist U. S. Signal Corps, ground signal service, Camp Evans,

Belmar, N.J., 1943-46; research physicist Naval Research Lab. since 1946. Assistant district ednl. dir. Dist. 5, S.A.T.C., 1918. Fellow A.A.A.S.; mem. Am. Physical Society, Am. Meteorol Society, Am. Assn. Physics Teachers, Tenn. Acad. of Sciences (pres. 1936), Kappa Delta Pi. Club: Freolac. Democrat. Conglist. Author: Laboratory. Manual of Practical Physics, 1925. Inventor of simplified types of laboratory apparatus and devices in automechanics, heat and radio. Developed a lab. course in which the student is led to discover the fundamental laws instead of trying to verify them. Home: 4708 Nichols Av. S.W., Washington 20. Office: Naval Research Laboratory, 4th St. near Chesapeake S.W., Washington, D.C. Died Nov. 28, 1947.

FOWKE, GERARD, archeologist; b. Maysville, Ky., June 25, 1855; s. John D. and Sibella (Mitchell) Smith; present name adopted; unmarried. Was engaged in explorations and surveys of aboriginal remains in eastern half of U.S. in connection with Bur. of Am. Ethnology, 1885-88, and 1891-93; also under other auspices at various times; excavations among Norse remains near Boston, 1894 and 1896; explorations on Vancouver Island, B.C., and lower Amoor River in Siberia, for Am. Mus. Natural History, New York, 1898; examinations at Kimmswick, Mo., and Lansing, Kan., of geol. deposits containing prehistoric human remains of aboriginal flint quarries and of caves for early human remains, in Ky., Ind., Ill., Mo., Tenn., and Ala., 1902-04; geol. and archaeol. investigations in Mo., 1905-08; investigated glacial deposits and traced pre-glacial channels, in entire length of Ohio valley, within above dates, and later; with Mo. Hist. Soc., St. Louis, 1911-16. Explored caves in Ozark mountain region for Bur. of Ethnology, 1918-23; preliminary ethnologic examination of Hawaiian Island group, 1920; mound explorations around Portsmouth, O., 1921, mound explorations vicinity of Muscle Shoals, 1924; investigation of mounds and villagesites along Red River in La. and in western Ark., and examination of flint quarries in S.W. Mo., 1925; archaeol. work in La. and Mexico, 1926; in Ohio and Ky., 1927; with Mo. Hist. Soc., 1930; investigations in Ohio Valley, Cincinnati to Cairo, 1931. Author: Archaeological History of Ohio (Ohio Archaeol. and Hist. Soc.), 1902. Home: Madison, Ind. Died 1933.

FOWLE, FRANK FULLER, consulting electric engineer; b. San Francisco, Calif., Nov. 29, 1877; s. Edward Osborne and Helen (Fuller) F.; S.B. in E.E., Mass. Institute of Technology, 1899; m. Alice Edna, d. William H. and Ida Thomas Cowper, October 17, 1905 (died March 17, 1944); children—Frank Fuller, William Cowper. With Am. Telephone & Telegraph Co., N.Y. City engineering department, 1892-1903, special agent. ry. dept., 1903-06, mgr. Chicago operating district (long lines dept.), 1906-08; cons. engr., Chicago, 1908-12; asso. editor in joint charge of Electrical World, 1912-13; cons. engr., 1913-14; receiver Central Union Telephone Co., an associated co. of Bell System operating in Ohio, Ind. and Ill., 1914-19; mem. Fowle & Cravath, cons. engrs., Chicago, 1919-20; head of Frank F. Fowle & Co., cons. elec. and mech. engrs. since 1920; practice covers electric power and telephone utilities and allied industries; cons. engr. Nat. Elec. Light Assn., 1920-32; expert in numerous court and commn. cases. Editor-in-chief Standard Handbook for Electrical Engineers, 1913-38; dir. Ill. Engring. Council since 1938, pres. 1943-44; mem. Am. Inst. E.E. (mgr. 1919-23), Western Soc. Engrs. (pres. 1935-36), Washington Award Commn., 1938-41 (chmn. 1940-41), Illuminating Engring. Soc., Am. Soc. for Testing Materials, Assn. Am. R.R.s, Am. Soc. for Metals, Winnetka (Ill.) Zoning Commn. and Bd. of Zoning Appeals, Newcomen Soc., Indiana Soc. Professional Engrs., Ry. and Locomotive Hist. Soc., N.E. Historic Geneal. Soc., Art Inst. Chicago (life), Ill. State Hist. Soc. (life), Wis. State Hist. Society (life). Member Winnetka Conglist Church. Clubs: University, Engineers (Chicago); Engineers (New York). Author: Transmission Line Crossings, 1909; numerous professional papers. Home: 233 Ridge Av., Winnetka, Ill. Office: 25 E. Wacker Drive, Chicago. Died Jan. 21, 1946; buried at Hancock, N.H.

FOWLER, CHARLES EVAN, civil engr.; b. Bartlett, Washington County, O., Feb. 10, 1867; s. Chalkley T. and Phebe W. (Hobson) F.; Ohio State U.; Master C.E.; m. Lucille H. Doyle, Dec. 4, 1890; children—Harold D., Louise H., Margaret E., Robert C. In practice as civ. engr. since 1886; bridge engr. Hocking Valley (O.) Ry., 1887; designing engr. Berlin (Conn.) Iron Bridge Co., 1889; engr. Bear Valley (Calif.) Irrigation Co., 1891; chief engr. Youngstown (O.) Bridge Co., 1891-98; built Knoxville (Tenn.) cantilever and Youngstown arch. also bridges for 60 American rys.; consulting engr., New York, 1898-1900, erection Williamsburg suspension 1,600 ft. span, numerous other bridges and bldgs. U.S. and Can.; pres. and chief engr. constrn. cos., 1900-13; built White Pass (Alaska) arch and navy coaling plant; asso. on Manila (P.I.) harbor; filling Seattle tide flats and dredging contracts 20 million yards; asso. in planning Seattle park system and Seattle port improvements; foundations 42 story bldg. and 600 ft. brick chimney; plans for three 2,000 ft. spans, three 2,400 ft. sus. spans, San Francisco-Oakland Bay bridge, 1915, and 4,850 foot suspension; cons. engr. N.Y. City, 1917-41; rebuilt Niagara Ry. arch, 1919, receiving Rowland prize Am. Society Civil Engrs.; plans for Detroit, 1,850 ft. suspension bridge, 1920-21, for 1,650 ft. arch bridge, Sydney, Australia, foundations 34 story bldg., Detroit; 24 mile causeway over Lake Pontchartrain at New Orleans, Narrows Bridge, N.Y. City, 4,550 ft. suspension, Mackinac Cantilever Bridge and Causeway, 25 miles, Soo Internat. Bridge, 2,000 ft. suspension; cons. engr. other long span bridge projects, plans 1,500 ft. high bldg., N.Y.; 2,500 ft. television tower, N.Y.; harbor work including 50 mile ship canal and 24 mile ry. and hy. bridge and causeway, U.S., Mexico and Cuba; 250-ft. piers, Tacoma-Lincoln bridge, and others; consulting engineer in defense work, 1941-43. Past president bd. park commrs. Madrona Heights Improvement Club; trustee Seattle Chamber Commerce, 10 yrs., Seattle Expn., 1909. Mem. Inst. Am. C.E., Engring. Inst. of Can., Pacific Northwest Soc. Engrs. (past pres.), Soc. of Terminal Engrs. Author: Cofferdam Process for Piers, 1898; Ordinary Foundations, 1904; General Specifications for Steel Roofs and Buildings, 1894; Engineering Studies (12 parts), 1899; Contracts and Specifications, 1907; Law and Business of Engineering and Contracting, 1909; Sub-Aqueous Foundations, 1913; Seaport Studies, 1913; San Francisco-Oakland Bridge, 1915; Engineering and Building Foundations, 1919; World Ports and Harbor Data, 1921; The Ideals of Engineering Architecture, 1929; The Mississippi Flood Problem, 1929; Fowler Family, 1937; Engineering Epics. Owner of large Napoleon collection. Contbr. to engring. jours. Home: Everett Av. N., Seattle, Wash. Office: 92 Liberty St., New York, N.Y. Died 1944.

FOWLER, EDMUND PRINCE, otologist; b. N.Y.C., Dec. 19, 1872; s. George Bingham (M.D.) and Anna (Prince) F.; student Coll. City of N.Y., 1889-92; M.D., Coll. Phys. and Surg., Columbia U., 1900; m. Mabel Denman, 1900; children—George B., Edmund P., Benjamin P., Mary, Denman; m. 2d, Dorothy Kenney, May 27, 1932. Post-grad. tng. in otolaryngology Manhattan Eye, Ear & Throat Hosp., Nose and Throat Clinic of Dr. Knight, 1903-06, Ear Service under Dr. Wendell Phillips; chief of heart and lung clinic Bellevue Hosp., 1901-03; eye, ear, and throat surgeon, several hosps., 1902-32. Mem. or past mem. several spl. consultative coms. of govtl. agys. and profl. orgns. in field of hearing. Recipient award of merit, bronze medal Am. Otol. Soc., 1952. Fellow A.C.S., N.Y. Acad. Medicine; hon. mem. Royal Soc. Medicine (Eng.), Otol. Study group Am. Acad. Ophthal. and Otolaryngology; mem. local, state, nat. and internat. profl. and sci. socs. in gen. and spl. fields of medicine, has served as officer many of them, also vets. orgns. Served to lt. col. N.Y. N.G.; served on Mex. border and A.E.F. Republican. Dutch Reformed Ch. Clubs: Columbia Yacht, Nipnichsen, D.K.E. Patentee many medical devices. Author profl. publs. Home: 319 E. 50th St. Office: 140 E. 54th St., N.Y.C. 22. Died Oct. 6, 1966; buried Green-Wood Cemetery, Bklyn.

FOWLER, EDMUND P(RINCE), JR., physician; b. N.Y. City, Feb. 16, 1905; s. Edmund Prince and Mabel (Denman) F.; B.S. cum laude, Storm King Sch., Dartmouth Coll., 1926; M.D., Columbia, 1930, Med. Sc.D., 1934; m. Olivia Jarrett, May 21, 1938; children—Heather, Edmund Prince. Med. interne Presbyterian Hosp., 1931-33; resident, ear, nose and throat Presbyn. Hosp., 1934-35; research fellow in ear, nose and throat, 1933-34; asst. surgeon Manhattan Eye and Ear Hosp., 1931-45; attending otolaryngology Presbyn. Hosp. since 1937; prof. otolaryngology and dir. of Ear, Nose and Throat Service, Columbia-Presbyn. Med. Center, 1947—. Past pres. Audiology Found.; president Microcirculatory Conference, 1959. Served as captain, 2d Gen. Hosp. Unit, U.S. Army, 1942; consultant to 8th Air Force, 1944; consultant to air surgeon, 1945; disch. with rank of lt. col., Oct. 1945. Awarded Legion of Merit. Fellow Royal Soc. of Medicine; hon. fellow Royal Coll. of Surgeons (Ireland); mem. Am. Otol. Soc., Trilogical Soc., Am. Acad. of Ophthalmology and Otolaryngology, N.Y. Acad. of Medicine, Collegium Otolaryngolicum, Nat. Research Council Com. on Hearing and Bio-Acoustics, Zeta Psi, Nu Sigma Nu, Sigma Xi, Alpha Omega Alpha. Clubs: University, Omega, Riverdale Yacht, Garison Highlands. Editor: Medicine of the Ear, 1947. Mem. editorial board of Annals of Otology, also of Rhinology and Laryngology, Excerpta Medica, Practica Oto-Laryngologica. Contbr. articles on diseases of ear to med. jours.; research in disease of ear, nose and throat, psychosomatic medicine and microcirculation. Died Jan. 13, 1964.

FOWLER, FREDERICK HALL, civil engr.; b. Fort Custer, Mont., Mar. 30, 1879; s. J. L. and Marion (Hall) F.; A.B., Stanford, 1905; m. Elsie Branner, Dec. 20, 1909. Engr. in charge constrn. Calif. sect. Laguna dam, Colo. River, 1905-06; engr. on surveys for proposed American River water supply for San Francisco, 1906-07; instr. in civ. engring., Stanford, 1907-08; in Europe and Egypt, 1908-09; engr. on topographic surveys, Mich., 1909; same on sewer constrn., Calif., 1910; hydro-electric engr. and dist. engr. U.S. Forest Service, San Francisco, 1910-22; engring. rep. in Calif. and Nev. of Federal Power Commn., 1920-22, and cons. civ. engr., San Francisco, since 1922. Adviser for U.S. Fuel Administration, Calif., 1917-18; capt. and topographic officer 211th Engrs., U.S. Army, Camp Meade, Md., 1918. Has made valuations for oil corporations to amount of 75 millions; reported to American Petroleum Institute on power requirements of 7 western states. Mem. cons. bd. San Gabriel River Flood Control, 1927, financial com. Sewage Disposal Research Com., northern Calif.; mem. Calif. Forest Research Adv. Com.; mem. Governor's Commn. to Investigate Causes Leading to Failure of St. Francis Dam, 1928; mem. State Com. on Water Resources Investigation of Southern Calif., 1929-30; mem. Tech. Board of Review, Federal Emergency Adminstrn. of Public Works, 1933-35, with spl. cons. assignment by Public Works Adminstrn. on Fort Peck, Grand Coulee and Bonneville dams, Casper-Alcova Project, and on Platte Valley Pub. Power and Irrigation, and Loup River Pub. Power dists.; mem. President's Bd. of Review, Atlantic-Gulf (Fla.) Ship Canal, 1934; mem. San Luis Valley Drain Com. (Rio Grande Basin) 1935; cons. engr. Federal Emergency Adminstrn. of Pub. Works, 1935-36; consultant to Corps of Engrs., U.S. Army, on dams on Yuba, Bear and Am. rivers, Calif., and on power on the Yuba, 1934; consultant to Flood Protection Planning Com. Greater Kansas City, 1935-41; dir. Nat. Drainage Basin Study, Nat. Resources Com., 1936, and water consultant thereafter; consultant Dept. of Water and Power, City of Los Angeles, 1938-41; chief civil engring. group, Construction Div., Office of the Q.M. General, 1941; chief consulting civil engr., Office of Chief of Engrs., Power Procurement officer, War Dept., 1943; valuations for Federal Works Agency, Puerto Rico, July-Dec. 1943; resumed private practice, San Francisco, Feb. 1944; consultant Dept. of Water and Power, City of Los Angeles, and State of California, Colorado River and Mexican Treaty matters, 1944-45. Mem. Am. Society C.E. (dir. 1928-30; pres. San Francisco Section, 1939; nat. pres. 1941), Society American Military Engineers (dir. 1941, pres. 1943-44), Seismological Society of America, American Ornithologists Union, Cooper Ornithological Club, Calif. Acad. of Sciences, Newcomen Society, Stanford Alumni Association (ex-pres.), Delta Upsilon. Clubs: Engineers. (San Francisco); Cosmos, Army and Navy (Washington). Author: Hydro-electric Power Systems of California, 1923, also of various papers on power development, flood control, dam design, Colo. River, etc., and on ornithol. subjects. Home: 360 Forest Av., Palo Alto, Calif. Office: 1300 Crocker First Nat. Bank Bldg., San Francisco 4, Calif. Died Nov. 7, 1945.

FOWLER, GEORGE LITTLE, mech. engr.; b. Cherry Valley, N.Y., Aug. 9, 1855; s. Jonathan A. and Eliza O. F.; A.B., Amherst, 1877; m. Harriet F. Goldie, Oct. 17, 1882. In practice as consulting mech. engr., 1899—, previous to that in ry. service. U.S. commr. to Ry. Expn., Paris, 1887. Author of a number of books on engring. matters. Editor Locomotive Dictionary; asso. editor Railway & Locomotive Engineering. Home: New York, N.Y. Died July 2, 1926.

FOWLER, RUSSELL STORY, surgeon; b. Brooklyn, N.Y., May 1, 1874; s. George Ryerson and Louise Rachel (Wells) F.; grad. Brooklyn Polytechnic Inst., 1891; M.D., Coll. Physicians and Surgeons (Columbia) 1895; grad. study, Allegemeine Krankenhaus, Vienna, 1900-01; m. Rose Blanche Beauchesne, Aug. 11, 1933; children—Rachel Story, George Ryerson, and (by former marriage) Russell Story. Held various minor hosp. and dispensary positions, 1895-96; adjunct surgeon Brooklyn Hosp., 1896-1906; acting attending surgeon 2d Div., Meth. Episcopal Hosp., 1898-99, asst. surgeon, 1898-1906, attending surgeon, 1906-27, cons. surgeon, 1927-29, sr. surgeon, 1929-34, cons. surgeon, 1934—; asst. surgeon German Hosp. of Brooklyn, 1899-1906; chief surgeon German Hosp. (Wyckoff Heights Hospital of Brooklyn), 1906-48, chief consultant surgeon, 1948—, now hon. dir. emeritus surgery; lecturer New York Polyclinic, 1896-97; former consultant surgeon Huntington Hospital and Hebrew Orphan Asylum Brooklyn; former cons. surgeon Beth Moses Hosp. and Bay Ridge hospitals, Brooklyn. Member N.Y. State Com. Council Nat. Defense, 1917, 18; chmn. Auxiliary Med. Defense Com. of Kings County, 1917, 18; organizer of Kings County and Long Island Med. Advisory Bd.; mem. Med. Advisory Bd. No. 17, Censor Med. Soc. County of Kings, 1909, v.p., 1914, pres., 1915, trustee, 1916-20 and 1927-33, chmn. Centenary Celebration Com., 1921-22; mem. Joint Com. on Graduate Edn. of Med. Soc. County of Kings and L.I. Med. Coll., 1925-29. Licentiate (founders group) Am. Bd. Surgery. Fellow Am. Coll. Surgeons (one of founders; gov. several times), N.Y. Acad. Medicine, Societe Internationale de Chirurgie; sr. fellow Brooklyn Surg. Soc. (past pres.), A.M.A., Am. Med. Editors' and Authors' Assn., Med. Soc. of State of N.Y., N.Y. Physicians Mutual Aid Assn., Am. Geog. Soc., Nat. Geog. Soc. N.Y. Zoöl. Soc. Brooklyn Inst. Arts and Sciences, Brooklyn Museum, Am. Mus. Natural History, etc.; founder and past pres. Clin. Soc. of Wyckoff Heights Hosp.; hon. mem., one of founders and former concillor Trail Riders Assn. of Canadian Rockies. Republican. Episcopalian (trustee Ch. of the Messiah 1922-26). Clubs: Montauk (Brooklyn); Nassau Country, Alpine of Canada, Campfire of America, Brooklyn Hosp. No. 1. Author: Surgery of the Spleen, and Operations Upon the Small Intestine, Mesentery and Omentum (Johnson's Operative Therapeusis); The Operating Room and the Patient, 3 edit.; Minor Surgery in Bryant & Buck System, 1906. Collaboraor in G. R. Fowler's Surgery, 1906. Contbr. to surgery mags.

Home: 155 Stratford Rd., Bklyn. 18. Died Jan. 5, 1959; buried Greenwood Cemetery.

FOX, HENRY, biologist; b. Germantown, Pa., Feb. 18, 1875; s. William and Elizabeth Ellen (Saylor) F.; B.S. in Biology, U. of Pa., 1899, M.A., 1903, Ph.D., 1905; m. Adelaide Townsend Godfrey, June 27, 1906; 1 dau., Emily Elizabeth (Mrs. George Alfred Clark). Instructor biology, U. of Wis., 1902-03; prof. biology, Temple U., Phila., 1903-05; instr. natural science, Manual Training High Sch., Phila., 1905-07; prof. biology, Ursinus Coll., 1907-12; field investigator U.S. Bureau of Entomology, 1912-18; prof. biology, Mercer U., Macon, Ga., 1918-24; asso. entomologist (Japanese Beetle project), U.S. Bureau Entomology, 1925-36; teaching fellow New York U., 1936-39, 1941-43; instr. in entomol., Brooklyn Coll., 1940, retired since 1943. Fellow A.A.A.S.; mem. Am. Entomol. Soc., Phila. Acad. of Natural Science, N.Y. Entomol. Soc., Sigma Xi; pres. Ga. Soc. Biologists, 1923; sec. Ga. Acad. Sciences, 1922-24. Contbr. on professional topics. Address: R. 1, Cape May Court House NJ

FOX, HERBERT, pathologist; b. Atlantic City, N.J., June 3, 1880; s. Samuel Tucker and Hannah Ray (Freas) F.; A.B., Central High Sch., Phila., 1897; M.D., Med. Dept., U. of Pa., 1901; studied U. of Vienna; m. Louise Carr Gaskill, Nov. 9, 1904 (died Nov. 16, 1933); children—Margaret, John Freas (dec.), Samuel Tucker; m. 2d, Mary Harlan Rhoads, Dec. 3, 1938. Volunteer asso. in William Pepper Clin. Lab. 1903-06; pathologist to Rush Hosp., since 1904; pathologist to Phila. Zoöl. Soc., since 1906; chief of Labs., Pa. Dept. of Health, 1906-11; dir. William Pepper Lab. of Clinical Medicine, Hosp. U. of Pa., since 1911; pathologist to the Children's Hosp., 1915-26; prof. comparative pathology, U. of Pa., since 1927. Mem. Coll. of Physicians, Am. Philos. Society, Acad. of Natural Sciences, County Med. Soc., Pathol. Society (all of Phila.), A.M.A., Am. Assn. Pathologists and Bacteriologists; fellow A.A.A.S. Served as chief cantonment lab., Camp Zachary Taylor, Ky., 1917-19; maj. M.C. U.S. Army. Republican. Author: Elementary Bacteriology and Protozoölogy, 1912, 5th edit., 1931; Text Book of Pathology (with Alfred Stengel), 8th edit., 1927; Disease in Captive Wild Mammals and Birds, 1923. Home: Hamilton Court, 39th and Chestnut Sts., Philadelphia, Pa. Died Feb. 27, 1942.

FOX, PHILIP, astronomer; b. Manhattan, Kan., Mar. 7, 1878; s. Simeon M. and Esther (Butler) F.; B.S., Kan. State Agrl. Coll., 1897, M.S., 1901; B.S., Dartmouth Coll., 1902; Univ. of Berlin, 1905-06; grad. Army Gen. Staff Coll., Langres, France, 1918; LL.D., Drake Univ., 1929; D.Sc., Kans. State, 1931; m. Ethel L. Snow, Aug. 28, 1905; children—Stephen Snow, Bertrand, Gertrude, Robert Temple. Commandant and teacher of math., St. John's Mil. Sch., Salina, Kan., 1899-1901; asst. in physics, Dartmouth, 1902-03; Carnegie research asst., Yerkes Obs., U. of Chicago, 1903-05; instr. astro-physics, Univ. of Chicago, 1907-09; prof. astronomy and dir. Dearborn Obs., Northwestern Univ., 1909-29; dir. of Adler Planetarium and Astron. Museum, Chicago, 1929-37; dir. Museum of Science and Industry, Chicago, 1937-40. In active duty as col. Inf. since Mar. 21, 1941. Fellow American Academy Arts & Sciences, A.A.A.S., Royal Astron. Soc.; mem. Am. Astron. Soc. (v.p.), Société Astronomique de France, Astronomische Gesellschaft, Alpha Delta Phi, Phi Beta Kappa, Phi Kappa Phi, Sigma Xi. Mason. Served as 2d lt. 20th Kan. Inf., U.S. Vols., in P.I., 1898-99; maj. inf., May 1, 1917-Sept. 23, 1919; in France, asst. chief of staff, 7th Div.; col. inf., R.C. Officier de l'ordre du Sauveur (Greece); Chevalier Legion d'Honneur. Author: Annals of the Dearborn Observatory (vols. I, II and III), also scientific brochures and contbns. to astron. jours., principally on double stars, stellar parallax and solar physics. Home: 816 Milburn St., Evanston, Ill. Died July 21, 1944.

FOX, WALTER GORDON, civil engineer; b. Hoboken, N.J., May 8, 1863; s. Conrad and Susan Eliza (Golding) F.; grad. in civ. engring. Lycée Henri IV, Paris, France, 1880; m. May Frances McDonald, of New York, Sept. 28, 1889. Various engring. position with C.,R.I. & P.Ry., C. & O. R.R., Norfolk & Western, N.Y.C. & H.R. rys., Hudson River Tunnel, etc., 1880-99; went to Ecuador, S.A., 1899, and had charge of location and constrn. of a div. of Guayaquil & Quito Ry., the rd. starting at sea level and rising to elevation fo 11,000 feet; returned to U.S., 1903, and as. div. engr. located and constructed a part of the White River Ry. in Ark.; in employ of govt. of Ecuador, surveying a line to the Curaray River, 1905-06; in charge constrn. of extension of Mexican Southern Ry., state of Oaxaca, Mex., 1910-11; now dir. engring. and constrn. of Curaray R.R., Ambato, Ecuador. Republican. Episcopalian. Author: Transition Curves, 1893; also published pamphlets on field engring. and stresses in bridges and roofs. Home: 764 West End Av., New York. Address: Ambato, Ecuador, S.A.

FRACKER, STANLEY BLACK, entomologist; b. Ashton, Ia., Apr. 8, 1889; s. George H. and Nettie (Black) F.; A.B., Buena Vista Coll., Storm Lake, Ia., 1910; student Lakeside Lab. of U. of Ia., summer 1909, U. of Mich., 1910-11, Cornell U., summer 1911; M.S., Ia. State Coll. Agr. and Mech. Arts, 1912; Ph.D., U. of Ill., 1914; Sc.D., Buena Vista College, Storm Lake, Ia., 1941; m. Grace E. Parker, Sept. 10, 1914; children—Mrs. Doris F. Hoard, Alice Lorraine (Mrs. Philip A. Randall, Jr.), Janet Marie (Mrs. John S. Watson). Asst. state nursery insp. Ia., 1912-13; asst., acting, and state entomologist Wis., 1915-34; charge plant disease control. Bur. Entomol. and Plant Quarantine, 1934-42; research coordinator, Agr. Research Adminstrn., U.S. Dept. Agr., 1942-51, assistant to the adminstr., 1951-58; asst. to dir. Office Sci. Personnel, Nat. Acad. Sci., 1959—. Agrl. research cons. Research and Development Bd. Department of Def., 1948-54; mem. govt. patents board, 1950-57; mem. National Forest advisory board, 1950-54; U.S. rep. Internat. Phytopathol. Conf., Hague, Netherlands, 1950; mem. U.S. delegation F.A.O. conf., Washington, 1949, Rome, 1953, 57, F.A.O. council, Rome, 1950, 52; chmn. plant protection com. FAO, Rome, 1955; Washington representative Agricultural Research Administration on research in Alaska, 1948-53. United States representative at quarantine conference, Suva, Fiji, 1951. Recipient distinguished service gold medal and award from Dept. of Agriculture, 1957; Verdienstkreuz Ester Klasse, West Germany, 1959; honor award Orgn. Profl. Employees of Dept. of Agr., 1960. Fellow A.A.A.S., Entomol. Soc. Am.; mem. Am. Assn. Econ. Entomol. (chmn. sect. plant quarantine and inspection, 1935), Entomol. Soc. Washington (pres. 1936), Internat. Entomol. Congress, Orgn. of Professional Employes of Department of Agriculture (president 1935-37), American Phytopathol. Society, Wisconsin State Hort. Society, Potomac River Power Squadron, Sigma Xi, Phi Kappa Phi. Presbyn. Clubs: Cosmos, Fossils (Washington). Author: Classification of Lepidopterous Larvae, 1915. Contributor technical and popular articles on entomology and on prevention of spread of plant diseases and bee diseases to profession jours., Bulls. of Wis. State Dept. of Agr. Yearbook of U.S. Dept. Agr., etc. Home: Washington DC Died June 15, 1971; buried Parklawn, Inc., Rockville MD

FRACKLETON, SUSAN STUART (MRS.), artist, inventor; b. Milwaukee, June 5, 1848; d. Edwin H. and Mary Stewart (Robinson) Goodrich; ed. pvt. schs. and studios, Milwaukee and New York prominent as ceramic artist; has taken numerous prizes, including medal at Antwerp Expn., 1894 and in various European, Am., Canadian and Mex. competitions; declined offer of Mexican govt. of place at head of a nat. sch. of ceramic decoration. Invented and patented gas-kilns for firing decorated china and glass; founded and was 1st pres. Nat. League of Mineral Painters. Medal at Paris Expn., 1900, when the exhibit of potting was made by invitation of U.S. Commn. Lectured on arts and crafts topics. Mem. Am. Civic Assn., D.A.R., Chicago Arts and Crafts Soc. Clubs: Chicago Woman's, Chautauqua Woman's (N.Y.). Author: Tried by Fire (work on china painting), 1885. Address: 6030 Jackson Park Av., Chicago, Ill.

FRANCIS, EDWARD, bacteriologist; b. Shandon, O., Mar. 27, 1872; s. Abner and Martha Ann (Vaughan) Francis; B.S., Ohio State U., 1894; hon. D.Sc., 1933; M.D., U. of Cincinnati, 1897; LL.D., Miami U., 1929; unmarried. In U.S. Pub. Health Service since 1900, asst. surgeon, 1900-05, passed asst. surgeon, 1905-13, surgeon, 1913-30, med. dir. since 1930. Member American Medical Association, Assn. Am. Physicians, Association Military Surgeons, Phi Delta Theta and Sigma Xi fraternities. Awarded gold medal by Am. Med. Assn. for contributions to knowledge of tularaemia, 1928. Republican. Conglist. Author: Tularaemia Francis, 1921, a New Disease of Man. (bull.), 1922; also bulls. and papers on yellow fever, pellagra, tetanus, filariasis, rat-bite fever, undulant fever, relapsing fever, athlete's foot and tularaemia. Address: National Institute of Health, Bethesda MD

FRANCIS, GEORGE BLINN, civil engr.; b. W. Hartford, Conn., Jan. 31, 1857; s. Blinn and Lucy (Hart) F.; ed. Hartford High Sch.; (hon. A.M., Brown U., 1905); m. Florence Louise Green, Apr. 11, 1882. Began civ. engring. in 1874; identified with numerous important works; in st. ry. engring. and other railroad work. Mason. Home: New York. Died June 9, 1913.

FRANCIS, JAMES BICHENO, hydraulic engr.; b. Southleigh Eng., May 18, 1815; s. John and Eliza (Bicheno) F.; m. Sarah Brownell, July 12, 1837, 6 children. Arrived in N.Y.C., 1833; chief engr. group known as "Proprs. of the Locks & Canals on the Merrimack River," 1837-1840; chief engr., gen. mgr. devel. water-power facilities, Lowell, Mass., 1845; began constrn. of Northern Canal, 1846; following trip to Eng., 1849, built machines for timber preservation; devised water supply for fire protection, Lowell, 1850's; designed and constructed hydraulic lifts for guard gates of Pawtucket Canal, 1870; original mem. Boston Soc. Civil Engrs., pres. 1874, 80; pres. Stonybrook R.R., 20 years; dir. Lowell Gas Light Co., 43 years. Author: Lowell Hydraulic Experiments, 1855, 68, 83; Strength of Cast Iron Columns, 1865. Died Boston, Sept. 18, 1892.

FRANCIS, JOHN MILLER, chemist; b. Jacksonville, Ala., Oct. 25, 1867; s. Miller W. and Julia (Clark) F.; M.A., U. of Ala., 1887; grad. work in organic chemistry Johns Hopkins University, 1889-90; m. Evie E. Harris, 1891. Adj. prof. chemistry, U. of Ala., 1887-92; chemist, Parke, Davis & Co., Detroit, Mich., 1892—, chief chemist, Aug. 1904—. Mem. Com. Revision U.S. Pharmacopoeia. Republican. Presbyn. Home: Detroit, Mich. Died Jan. 8, 1924.

FRANCIS, JOSEPH, inventor, mfr.; b. Boston, Mar. 12, 1801; s. Thomas and Margaret F.; m. Ellen Creamer. Produced a wooden boat that withstood severest tests; constructed life boats for U.S. vessels Santee and Alabama, 1829; all U.S. Govt. ships equipped with boats of his invention by 1841; contracted with Novelty Iron Works of N.Y. to manufacture the boats; granted patent for corrugated metal boat, 1845; constructed fleet of light-draft corrugated iron steamers for Russian govt., sometime between 1855-63. Recipient medal Franklin Inst., 1854, Gold medal King Ferdinand III of Sicily, gold snuffbox from Napoleon III, 1856, Congressional medal presented by Pres. Harrison, 1890; named to Royal Order Knighthood St. Stanislaus by Czar of Russia. Died Cooperstown, N.Y., May 10, 1893; buried Mpls.

FRANCIS, MARK, veterinarian; b. Shandon, O., Mar. 19, 1863; s. Abner and Martha Ann (Vaughan) F.; D.V.M., Ohio State U., 1887; 1 yr. at Am. Vet. Coll., New York; some time at U. of Mich.; Berlin and Munich, 1904; LL.D., Miami U., 1929; m. Anna J. Scott, Sept. 10, 1890; children—Andrew Jones (dec.), William Bebb. Professor veterinary science from 1888, dean Sch. Vet. Medicine, 1916—, Agrl. and Mech. Coll. of Texas. Veterinarian to Tex. Expt. Sta. and introduced methods of producing immunity to Texas fever by subcutaneous injections with infected cattle blood. Home: College Station, Texas. Died June 28, 1936.

FRANCIS, SAMUEL WARD, physician, inventor; b. N.Y.C., Dec. 26, 1835; s. John W. and Maria (Cutler) F.; B.A., Columbia, 1857; M.D., U. City N.Y., 1860; m. Harriet McAllister, June 16, 1859. Patented printing machine which anticipated the typewriter, 1860; invented heating and ventilating device for railroad cars, 1868; developed a sewing machine, 1875; devised signal for telephone and telegraph lines, 1879; active in Sanitary Protection Assn. (founded 1878). Author: Report of Valentine Motts' Surgical Cliniques in the University of New York, 1859-60, pub. N.Y., 1860; Inside and Out, 1862; Biographical Sketches of Distinguished Living New York Surgeons, 1866; Life and Death, 1871. Died Newport, R.I., Mar. 25, 1886.

FRANCIS, THOMAS, JR., physician, coll. prof.; b. Gas City, Ind., July 15, 1900; s. Thomas and Elizabeth Ann (Cadogan) F.; B.S., Allegheny Coll., 1921; M.D., Yale Univ., 1925, honorary M.S., 1941; honorary Sc.D., Allegheny College, 1941. U. Freiburg (Germany), 1968; m. Dorothy Packard Otton, June 29, 1933; children—Mary Jane, Thomas, 3d. Interne in medicine New Haven (Conn.) Hosp., 1925-26, prof. bacteriology, director bacteriol labs., coll. medicine N.Y.U., vis. physician Third med. div. Bellevue Hosp., 1938-41; vis. physician Willard Parker Hosp., 1940-41; Henry Sewall U. prof. epidemiology and chmn. dept. epidemiology, school public health also prof. epidemiology, med. school U. Mich. 41-69. Mem. Armed Forces Epidemiology Bd. 1955-68 (pres., 1958-60), dir. Influenza Commn. 1941-55; cons. Sec. Def., USPHS, Michigan State Department of Health. Mem. Sci. adv. council Am. Cancer Soc.; dir. Poliomyelitis Vaccine Evaluation Program; bd. sci. advisers, bd. dirs. Jane Coffin Childs Meml. Fund for Med. Research. Member of the Lobound Advisory Board, 1958-69. Served as pvt. S.A.T.C., 1918. Awarded Medal of Freedom, AUS, 1946; Lasker Award, Am. Public Health Assn., 1947; Howard Taylor Ricketts award and medal, U. Chgo., 1952; James D. Bruce Meml. medal A.C.P., 1953; Bristol award Infections Disease Soc., 1969; Kovalenka award Nat. Acad. Sci.; Distinguished Service award Japanese Nat. Inst. Health. Fellow A.A.A.S., Am. Pub. Health Assn. (mem. governing council), Am. Acad. Arts and Scis.; mem. Nat. Acad. Scis. (mem. governing council 1958-61), Soc. Am. Bacteriologists (pres. 1947), Am. Society Clin. Investigation (pres. 1945-46), Assn. Am. Physicians, A.M.A., Harvey Society (sec. 1938-40), N.Y. Acad. Medicine, History of Science Society, Am. Soc. Immunologists, Am. Epidemiol. Soc. (pres. 1954-55), Am. Philos. Soc., Constantinian Soc., N.Y. Acad. Sci., Soc. Exptl. Pathology, Soc., for Experimental Biology and Medicine, Phi Delta Theta, Nu Sigma Nu, Sigma Xi, Alpha Omega Alpha, Delta Omega, Phi Kappa Phi. Club: Cosmos (Washington). Home: Ann Arbor MI Died Oct. 1, 1969; buried Forest Hill Cemetery, Ann Arbor MI

FRANCK, JAMES, prof. phys. chemistry; b. Hamburg, Germany, Aug. 26, 1882; s. Jacob and Rebecca (Drucker) F.; student U. of Heidelberg, 1901-02; Dr. of Phil., U. of Berlin, 1906; LL.D., U. of Calif., Berkeley, 1928, Sc.D., Technion, Haifa, Israel, 1954; Dr. rer. nat. Univ. of Heidelberg, Germany, 1957; Sc.D., Humboldt Univ. Berlin, 1960, U. Kiel, Germany, 1960, U. Giessen, Germany, 1962, Gustavus Adolphus Coll., St. Peter, Minn., 1963, Duke, 1964; m. Ingrid Josephson, Dec. 1906 (dec. 1942); children—Dagmar (wife of Dr. Arthur Von Hippel), Elisabeth (wife of Dr. Herman Lisco); m. Hertha Sponer, June 29, 1946. Came to U.S., 1935. Asst. in phys. lab. U. of Berlin, 1906, pvt. docent 1911-16, associate professor of physics, 1916-18; head of physics division Kaiser Wilhelm Institute of Phys. Chemistry, 1918-20; prof., dir. Phys. Inst., U. Göttingen, 1920-33, now prof. emeritus; guest prof.,

Univ. of Copenhagen, 1934; prof. physics, Johns Hopkins U., 1935-38; prof. physical chemistry, U. of Chicago, since 1938, now professor emeritus. Hitchcock professor at University of California in 1941. Shared 1925 Nobel prize in physics; awarded Max Planck medal German Physical Society, 1953; Rumford Medal, Am. Acad. Arts and Scis., 1955. Mem. Research Institutes University of Chicago. Am. Philos. Soc., Acad. Arts and Scis., Boston, Nat., Washington acads scis., Royal Soc. (fgn. Eng.), several European academies and other learned societies. Jewish religion. Author: Anregung von Quantensprüngen, 1926; also scientific articles on molecular physics and its application to chemistry. Address: care Dept. of Physics, Duke U., Durham, N.C. Died May 21, 1964.

FRANDSEN, PETER, biologist; b. Vislev, Denmark, Sept. 27, 1876; s. Soren Johansen and Lena Maria (Buck) F.; A.B., U. of Nev., 1895, LL.D., 1924; A.B., Harvard, 1898, A.M., 1899; studied abroad, 1909-10; m. Alice Sheldon Moreland, June 10, 1902 (died Mar. 19, 1907); 1 dau., Edith; m. 2d, Jane Elliott Higham, Jan. 1, 1913; 1 son, John H. (dec.). Teacher, pub. schs., 1895-96; asst. in zool., Harvard, 1898-1900, Radcliffe Coll., 1899-1900; asst. prof. zool. and bacteriology, U. of Nev., 1900-02, asso. prof., 1902-03, prof., 1903-06, prof. biology since 1906. Republican. Fellow A.A.A.S.; mem. Phi Kappa Phi, etc. Author of Laboratory Manual of General Zoology, Manual for Physiology, Topical Outlines for General and Personal Hygiene, and various bulls. and articles on biol. subjects. Home: 210 Maple St., Reno NV

FRANK, ALFRED, mining engr.; b. Cincinnati, O., Jan. 27, 1879; s. Charles and Amalia (Binger) F.; student U. of Cincinnati, 1895-96; C.E., Cornell U., 1898; unmarried. Mine engr. and surveyor, Butte, Mont., 1900-02; mine foreman, 1903; chief engr., mines of F. Aug. Heinze, 1904-07; supt., Davis-Daly Copper Co., 1907-09; gen. mgr. Ohio Copper Co., Salt Lake City, Utah, 1910-14; cons. engr., Stewart Mining Co., 1910-15; mgr. mining properties since 1915; pres. and gen. mgr. Nat. Parks Airways, 1928-37; v.p. Keystone Mining Co.; pres. The Exploration Syndicate; dir. Western Air Lines, Inc., 1937-42. Mem. Am. Inst. Mining Engrs. Clubs: Alta, Commercial, Country (Salt Lake City); Silver Row, Country (Butte). Home: Walker's Lane, Halloday. Office: Continental Bank Bldg., Salt Lake City, Utah. Deceased.

FRANK, ISAAC WILLIAM, machinery mfg.; b. Pittsburgh, Pa., Dec. 2, 1855; s. William and Paulina (Womser) F.; prep. edn., Newell Inst., Pittsburgh; C.E., Rensselaer Poly. Inst., 1876; m. Tinnie Klee, Nov. 15, 1883; children—Mrs. Bessie Anathan, William K., Robert J. Draftsman Keystone Bridge Co., 1876-77; insp. materials New York Elevated R.R. Co., 1877; asst. engr. on Mississippi River improvement, 1878; dep. U.S. mineral surveyor, 1879-80; sec. and engr. Lewis Foundry & Machine Co., of Pittsburgh, 1880-92; organizer, 1892, and pres. Frank-Kneeland Machinery Co., 1892-1901; organizer, 1901, and thereafter pres. United Engring., 1921—. Trustee, Rensselaer Poly. Inst., U. of Pittsburgh. Mem. Rodolf Shalom Congregation, Y.M. and Y.W. Hebrew Assn., etc. Republican. Home: Pittsburgh, Pa. Died Dec. 1, 1930.

FRANKEL, MAX, organic chemist; b. Czechoslovakia, Oct. 31, 1900; s. Siegfried and Rose (Chajes) F.; student tech. U., U. Vienna; Dr.phil., U. Vienna (Austria), 1923; m. Helen Hammermann, 1930. Asst., Inst. Chemistry, also Inst. Chem. Tech., Vienna U., 1920-24; sr. research chemist Verein fuer Chemische und Metallurgische Produktion, Aussig, Czechoslovakia, 1924-25; faculty Hebrew U., Jerusalem, Israel, 1925-71, prof. organic chemistry, dir. dept., 1953-71. Fellow Chem. Soc. London; mem. Am. Chem. Soc., Chem. Soc. Israel. Author numerous books, monographs and articles on topics in chemistry. Research on amino acids, synthesis of polypeptides, polymers and organometallic compounds, sterochemistry. Home: Jerusalem Israel Died Apr. 27, 1971.

FRANKFORTER, GEORGE BELL, chemist; b. Potter, O., Apr. 22, 1859; s. Andrew and Elizabeth (Clunk) F.; A.B., U. Neb., 1886, A.M., 1888; chem. course Bergakademie, Berlin; Ph.D., U. Berlin, 1893; m. Mary Spalding Carter, 1898; children—Alice Sylvia, Mary Elizabeth (Mrs. Charles Christian Hewitt), Eleanor Evans (dec.), George William Carter. Instr. chemistry U. Neb., 1885-87, prof. chemistry, 1893-94; high sch., Lincoln, Neb., 1887-88; dean Sch. Chemistry and dir. Chem. Lab., U. Minn., 1894-1917, prof. organic and indsl. chemistry, 1920-25, prof. emeritus, 1927—. Prof. chemistry, Stanford, 1925-26. Mem. State Council Def. Maj., Ordnance Dept. U.S.A., 1918; chief chem. supervisory br. of inspection div.; dir. Ordnance Technol. and Officer's Tng. Sch., at DuPont Powder Plant, Carney's Point, N.J.; dir. supervisory and control lab., Phila.; examiner, explosives, chemicals and loading, Ordnance Claims Bd.; tech. adv. War Claims Bd., 1919-20. U.S. Mint commr., 1900. Fellow A.A.A.S.; mem. Am. Chem. Soc., Am. Electrochem. Soc., Soc. Chem. Industry, Ordnance Assn., Mil. Order World War, Asso. Tech. Adv. Corpn., Phi Beta Kappa, Sigma Xi, Gamma Alpha, Phi Lambda Upsilon. Republican. Conglist. Clubs: Chemists', Skylight. Author numerous papers on chem. subjects; also series of bulls. on explosives. Home: 525 East River Rd., Mpls. Died Sept., 1947.

FRANKLAND, FREDERICK HERSTON, consulting engr.; b. Wellington, New Zealand, May 6, 1882; s. Frederick William and Miriam (Symons) F.; came to U.S., 1893, naturalized, 1900; ed. private schs., Eng. and U.S.; m. May Jeanette Scott, Dec. 10, 1904; children—John Middleton, Eleanor Margaret. Began as engineer, 1902. Technical dir., chief engr. and dir. engring. (in charge research and development), Am. Institute of Steel Construction, 1928-44; mem. firm Frankland & Lienhard; has served individually or with firm as designer, engr. or consultant numerous constrn. projects including spl. indsl. plants for cement mills, strip mills; primary field has been hwy. and ry. bridge design including expressways, also harbors and river control works in U.S., S.A., C.A., New Zealand, Australia, Cuba, Dominican Republic, Siam; research cons. Bur. Ships, Navy Dept. Licensed profl. engr., N.Y., N.J., Conn. Fellow Royal Society Arts (London); member Am. Inst. Cons. Engrs., Internat. Soc. Soil Mechanics and Found. Engring., Am. Soc. C.E., Am. Soc. for Testing Materials (mem. various committees), Am. Railway Engring. Assn., Am. Welding Soc., Soc. Am. Mil. Engrs., Welding Research Council, Column Research Council, Engring. Foundation, Internat. Assn. Bridge and Structural Engrs. Episcopalian. Author Suspension Bridges of Short Span, 1934; Structural Steel, 1938; The Comparative Economics of Bridges and Tunnels, 1939; The Manufacture of Iron and Steel, 1940. Contbr. tech. jours. Home: 200 E. End Av., N.Y.C. 28. Office: 156 William St., N.Y.C. 10038. Died Oct. 31, 1959; cremated Ferncliffe Cemetery, Ardsley, N.Y.

FRANKLIN, BENJAMIN, statesman, scientist, philosopher; b. Boston, Jan. 17, 1706; s. Josiah and Abiah (Folger) F.; self-educated; M.A. (hon.), Yale, 1753, Harvard, 1753, Coll. William and Mary, 1756; LL.D., St. Andrews Coll., 1759; D.C.L. (hon.) Oxford (Eng.) U., 1762; took Deborah Read as common law wife, Sept. 1, 1730, later married, 2 children—Francis Folger, Sarah; 2 illegitimate children including William. Contbr. articles to New Eng. Courant (newspaper pub. and printed by his bro. James to whom he was apprenticed), Boston, until 1723; in London, 1724-26; owner Pa. Gazette, 1730-50; established 1st circulating library in Am. at Phila., 1731; wrote and pub. Poor Richard's Almanac (one of 1st Am. lit. prodns. to attain internat. renown, largely because of his common-sense philos. aphorisms), 1732-57; clk. Pa. Assembly, 1736-51, mem. from Phila., 1751-64; dep. postmaster Phila., 1737-53; aided Brit. in French and Indian War; founder Am. Philos. Soc., 1743, Phila. City Hosp., 1751; a founder Acad. for Edn. of Youth, 1751, inc., 1753 (later Coll. of Phila., now U. Pa.); joint dep. postmaster gen. Am. colonies, 1753-74; Pa. rep. at Albany (N.Y.) Congress, 1754; submitted "Plan of Union" adopted by Congress but vetoed by colonial legislatures (later important in drafting Articles of Confedn. and U. S. Constn.); polit. agt. Pa. Assembly, sent to Eng. to present case against Penn family for refusing to support defense expenditures, 1757-62, returned to Eng. to obtain recall of Pa. Charter, 1766; questioned before Ho. of Commons during debates on repeal of Stamp Act, 1766; colonial agt. of Ga., 1768, N.J., 1769, Mass., 1770; aided William Pitt in fruitless conciliation efforts, in Eng.; mem. 2d Continental Congress, 1775, sketched plan of union for colonies, organized post office, became 1st postmaster gen.; mem. com. to draft Declaration of Independence, also a signer, 1776; del. of mission to persuade Can. to join Am. cause; commr. to negotiate treaty with France (only Am. with whom French Prime Minister Vergennes would deal), 1776, signed final commerce and defense alliance treaties, 1778; apptd. minister to France, 1778; apptd. a commr. to negotiate peace with Gt. Britain, 1781, assumed responsibility for preliminary talks, peace treaty signed, 1783; returned to Phila., 1785; pres. Pa. Exec. Council, 1785-87; mem. U. S. Constl. Conv., 1787, largely responsible for representation compromise actually incorporated in Constn.; signed meml. to Congress for abolition of slavery (last public act), Feb. 12, 1790. Named charter mem. Hall Fame for Gt. Ams., 1900. Mem. French Acad. Scis. (1st Am. fgn. mem.); Fellow Royal Soc., (Copley medal 1753). Author: Experiments and Observations on Electricity, 1750; Opinions and Conjectures concerning the Properties and Effects of the Electrical Matter, 1750; Experiments and Observations on Electricity carried out at Philadelphia, 1751; Edict by the King of Prussia, Rules by Which a Great Empire May be Reduced to a Small One (both satires), early 1770's; Observations on the Increase of Mankind, of the Peopling of Countries, 1775; Autobiography (never finished); also essays (some of earliest signed Silence Dogood). Convinced himself of identity of lightning with electricity and suggested kite expt., 1752; from his expts. with Leyden jar (from 1747), deduced that lightning conductor could be used for safe discharge of low thunderclouds (1st mentioned, 1749, recommended to pub., 1753); developed duFay's discovery that there are 2 kinds of electricity; formulated influential one fluid theory of electricity, according to which all bodies possess normal quantity of an electric fluid and are able to produce elec. effects whenever this normal quantity is decreased or increased; suggested that an excess (or deficiency) of fluid be called positive (or negative) electricity, and held that electric fluid flows from positive to negative; implied important principle of conservation of charge; attempted to work out course of storms over N. Am.; 1st to study Gulf Stream; early investigator of population growth; early advocate of fresh air as adjunct to hygiene; inventor Pa. Fireplace (known as Franklin stove), circa 1727, Fergusson's clock, circa 1744, also bifocals. Died Phila., Apr. 17, 1790.

FRANKLIN, EDWARD CURTIS, chemist; b. Geary City, Kan., Mar. 1, 1862; s. Thomas Henry and Cynthia Ann (Curtis) F.; B.S., U. of Kan., 1888, M.S., 1890; student U. of Berlin, 1890-91; Ph.D., Johns Hopkins, 1894; D.Sc., Northwestern, 1923; D.Sc. from Western Reserve U., 1926; LL.D., Wittenberg Coll., O., 1927; m. Effie June Scott, July 22, 1897; children—Mrs. Anna Comstock Barnett, Charles Scott (dec.), John Curtis. Assistant in chemistry, 1888-93, asso. prof., 1893-99, prof. physical chemistry, 1899-1903, U. of Kan.; asso. prof., 1903-06, prof. organic chemistry, 1906-29 (emeritus), Stanford Univ. Professor chemistry and chief div. chemistry, U.S. Pub. Health Service, 1911-13. Mem. U.S. Assay Commn., 1906. Mem. Advisory bd. U.S. Bur. Mines, 1917-18; phys. chemist U.S. Bur. Standards, 1918; consulting chemist Ordnance Bur., U.S.A., 1918. Fellow A.A.A.S., Am. Acad. Arts and Sciences. Was guest British Assn. Advancement Science, Capetown and Johannesburg, 1929. Awarded Nichols medal, 1924; Willard Gibbs medal, 1931. Home: Stanford University, Calif. Died Feb. 13, 1937.

FRANKLIN, PHILIP, prof. mathematics; b. New York, N.Y., Oct. 5, 1898; s. Benjamin and Isabelle (Phelps), F.; B.S., Coll. City of New York, 1918; M.A., Ph. D., Princeton U., 1921; m. Constance Wiener, June 14, 1924; children—David, Janet (Mrs. Vãclav E. Benes), Hope (Mrs. Barrett O'Neill), Ballistic computer, 1918-19; instr. mathematics, Princeton U., 1921-22; Benjamin Pierce instr., Harvard U., 1922-24; instr. mathematics, Mass. Inst. Tech., 1924-25, asst. prof., 1925-30, asso. prof., 1930-37, prof. since 1937; consultant instrumentation Laboratory, 1944-46; lecturer on mathematical physics, Harvard U., 1948. Guggenheim fellow, 1927-28. Fellow A.A.A.S., American Acad. Arts and Sciences; mem. Am. Math. Soc., Math. Assn. America, Phi Beta Kappa, Sigma Xi. Mem. Inst. for Advanced Study at Princeton, 1935-36. Editor of Journal of Mathematics and Physics since 1929. Awarded Townsend Harris Medal, Coll. City of New York, 1943. Author: Differential Equations for Electrical Engineers, 1933; a Treatise on Advanced Calculus, 1940, The Four Color Problem, 1941, Methods of Advanced Calculus, 1944; Fourier Methods, 1949; Differential and Integral Calculus, 1953; Functions of Complex Variables, 1958; Compact Calculus, 1963. Contbr. to math. jours. Home: 312 Pleasant St., Belmont 78, Mass. Died Jan. 27, 1965; buried Pawlet, Vt.

FRANKLIN, WALTER SIMONDS, civil engr.; b. York, Pa., Mar. 1, 1836; s. Walter Simonds and Sarah (Buel) F.; B.S., summa cum laude, Lawrence Scientific Sch. (Harvard), 1857; m. Mary Campbell Small, Dec. 13, 1866. Began work in wholesale store in New York, 1850; chainman and rodman in engring. party of Pa. R.R., 1852; studied, 1854; entered engring. sch., Harvard; on Fernandina & Cedar Keys R.R., Fla., 1857-88; in Europe, 1859; apptd. 1st lt. 12th U.S. Inf., May 1861; served in Army of the Potomac in McClellan's campaign; afterward under Sheridan in Shenandoah Valley, and with Grant until surrender of Lee; on staff of Gen. Sedgwick until he was killed, then with Wright as insp.-gen. 6th Army Corps, with rank of lt. col.; bvtd. maj. and lt. col. U.S.A., and col. U.S.V.; returned to regt. as capt., 1865, and resigned, 1870. Gen. mgr. Ashland Iron Co., Md., till 1887, then with Md. Steel Co. till 1894 (dir.); pres. Baltimore City Passenger R.R. till consolidation of all the roads; v.p. of the consolidated roads till 1903; retired. Mem. U.S. Lighthouse Bd., 1884—. Presbyn. Democrat. Home: Baltimore, Md. Died 1911.

FRANKLIN, WILLIAM BUEL, engr., soldier; b. York, Pa., Feb. 27, 1823; s. Walter Simonds and Sarah (Buel) F.; grad. West Point, 1843; m. Anna L. Clarke, July 7, 1852 (died 1900). Assigned to topog. engrs.; served through Mexican war and engaged in engring. service, becoming col. 12th inf., May 14, 1861; brig. gen. vols., May 17, 1861; maj. gen. vols., July 4, 1862, and afterwards received bvt. rank of brig. gen. and maj. gen. U.S. Army; resigned March 15, 1866; became v.p. Colts Patent Fire Arms Mfg. Co., Hartford; widower. Was pres. of commn. for laying out Long Island City, 1871-72; pres. of commn. for building new State house at Hartford, Conn., 1872-73; cons. engr. of same, 1874; U.S. commr. gen. for Paris Expn., 1889; grand officer French Legion of Honor, Oct. 1889; pres. Bd. Mgrs. Nat. Soldiers' Home until 1899. Hartford, Conn. Died 1903.

FRANKLIN, WILLIAM SUDDARDS, physicist; b. Geary City, Kan., Oct. 27, 1863; s. Thomas Henry and Cynthia Ann (Curtis) F.: B.S., U. of Kan., 1887, M.S., 1888; student Cornell, winters 1892-96, D.Sc., 1901; student U. of Berlin, 1890-91; holder Morgan fellowship, Harvard, 1891-92; m. Hattie F. Titus, Aug. 14, 1888; children—Curtis, Kellogg. Asst. prof. physics, U. of Kan., 1887-90; prof. physics and elec. engring., Ia. State Coll., 1892-97, Lehigh U., 1897-1903; prof.

physics, Lehigh, 1903-15; prof. physics, Mass. Inst. Tech., 1917-29; prof. physics, Rollins Coll., Winter Park, Fla., 1929—. Hon. mem. Kan. Acad. Sciences. Joint author: Elements of Physics, 3 vols.; Elements of Alternating Currents; Elements of Electrical Engineering, 2 vols., 1906; Dynamo Laboratory Manual; Elements of Electricity and Magnetism; Practical Physics, 3 vols.; Electric Waves. Died June 6, 1930.

FRANTZ, VIRGINIA KNEELAND, physician, educator; b. N.Y.C., Nov. 13, 1896; d. Yale and Anna Ilsley (Ball) Kneeland; A.B., Bryn Mawr Coll., 1918; M.D., Columbia, 1922; m. Angus Macdonald Frantz, Dec. 29, 1920; children—Virginia Hathaway (Mrs. Virginia Moriconi), Angus Macdonald, Andrew Gibson. Surg. intern Presbyn. Hosp., N.Y. City, 1922-24, asst. surgeon, out-patient dept., 1924-27, asst. attending surg. pathologist, 1931-40, asso. attending surg. pathologist, 1940-51, attending surg. pathologist since 1951; instr. surgery Coll. Phys. and Surg. Columbia, 1924-30, asso. surgery, 1930-36, asst. prof., 1936, asso. prof., 1948, prof. surgery, 1951-62, prof. emeritus, 1962; cons. surgery Presbyn. 1962—; cons. Roswell Park Meml. Inst., Buffalo, N.Y. Responsible investigator development oxidized cellulose Office Sci. Research and Development Contract, World War II. Awarded honorable mention for exhibits on use and evaluation of absorbable hemostatics in modern surgery, San Francisco, Cin. and Mexico City; recipient Elizabeth Blackwell award N.Y. Infirmary, 1957. Mem. com. library N.Y. Acad. Medicine Library. Mem. Thyroid Assn. (pres. 1961-62), N.Y. Path. Soc. (pres. 1949-51), N.Y. Acad. Medicine, Harvey Soc., A.M.A., N.Y. State and Co. med. socs. Clubs: Colony, Cosmopolitan (N.Y.C.). Contbr. med. jours. Home: 1185 Park Av., N.Y.C. 28. Office: 630 W. 168th St., N.Y.C. 32. Died Aug. 23, 1967.

FRAPS, GEORGE STRONACH, agrl. chemist; b. Raleigh, N.C., Sept. 9, 1876; s. Anton Wenzel and Margaret Elizabeth Lumley (Stonebanks) F.; B.S., N.C. Coll. of Agr. and Mechanic Arts, 1896; fellow Johns Hopkins, 1898-99, Ph.D., 1899; m. Ellen Hale Saunders, June 17, 1903; children—George Saunders, Mary Brandon Tinns, Richard Benbury Saunders (dec.). Asst. chemist, N.C. Expt. Sta., 1899-1903; asst. prof. chemistry, N.C. Coll. of Agr. and Mechanic Arts, 1899-1903; asst. chemist, 1903-04, asso., 1904-05, chemist, 1905-18, chief Div. of Chemistry, 1918-45, collaborating chemist, 1945-47, Texas Agricultural Experiment Station; associate prof. chemistry, 1903-05, acting prof. 1905-06, asso. prof. agrl. chemistry, 1906-12, Tex. Agrl. and Mech. Coll.; state chemist of Tex., 1904-45. Delegate for U.S. to 1st Internat. Congress of Soil Science, 1927. Fellow A.A.A.S.; member American Chemical Society, Am. Society Agronomy, Assn. Official Agrl. Chemists (pres. 1913), Phi Kappa Phi, Phi Beta Kappa. Episcopalian. Author Principles of Dyeing, 1903; Principles of Agricultural Chemistry, 1913; also over 400 bulls. and articles in science jours. Retired since 1947. Address: College Station TX

FRASCH, HERMAN, chem. engr., inventor; b. Würtemberg, Germany, Dec. 25, 1851; son of Johannes Frasch; m. Romalda Berks; m. 2d, Elizabeth Blec. Came to U.S., 1868, worked for Phila. Coll. of Pharmacy; moved to Cleve., 1877, opened chem. lab. to study petroleum refining; organized Empire Oil Co., London, Ont., Can., 1885; developed Frasch process for desulfurization of crude petroleum oil; received 21 U.S. patents for refining of petroleum 1887-94, sold patents to Standard Oil Co.; received patent for mining of sulfur by means of superheated water, 1891; organizer, pres. Union Sulfur Co., 1892; recipient Perkin Gold medal in chemistry, 1912. Died Paris, France, May 1, 1914.

FRASER, HORACE JOHN, mining geologist; b. Girvin, Sask., Can. Nov. 27, 1905; s. Frederick Brisbin and Jennie (Macklin) F.; B.S., U. Manitoba, 1925, M.S., 1927; M.A., Harvard, 1928, Ph.D., 1930; LL.D., Queens U., 1958; m. Catherine W. Cheek, June 4, 1932; children—Ian Bruce, Malcolm Bradley. Travelling fellow sci. U. Manitoba, 1927-28; instr. econ. geology Harvard, 1928-30, research asso. engring sch., 1931-32; fellow geology NRC, 1930-31; geologist Internat. Nickel Co. Can., 1932-35; asst., asso. prof. Cal. Inst. Tech., cons. mining geologist for various cos., 1935-42; asst. divisional chief ferro alloys Fgn. Econ. Adminstrn., Washington, 1942-45; mgr. Falconbridge Nickel Mines, Ltd., 1945-47, gen. mgr., 1948-57, pres., managing director, 1957-69, director of associate and subsidiary companies; member board directors Canadian Imperial Bank of Commerce, Crown Trust Company, United Accumulative Fund Ltd., McIntyre Porcupine Mines Limited. Chairman of the board Laurentian University, Sudbury, Ont., Canada. Fellow Royal Soc. Can., Geol Soc. Am., Mineral. Soc. Am.; mem. Ontario Mining Assn. (pres. 1953), Canadian Metal Mining Assn. (pres. 1954-56), Am. Inst. Mining, Metall. and Petroleum Engrs., Canadian Inst. Mining and Metall. (pres. 1957), Soc. Econ. Geologists, Assn. Profl. Engrs. Ont., Sigma Xi, Gamma Alpha. Clubs: York, Toronto. Home: Palgrave ON Canada Died Feb. 2, 1969; buried Baltimore, Ont., Canada

FRASER, HORATIO NELSON, manufacturing chemist; b. Providence, R.I., Nov. 30, 1851; s. Edward Simon and Mary (Waller) F.; grad. Davenport (Ia.) High Sch., 1867; Ph.G., Phila. Coll. of Pharmacy, 1872, Ph.M., 1908; M.D., St. Louis Coll. Phys. and Surg., 1909; m. Nellie Davis, of Davenport, Ia., Oct. 31, 1876. Engaged in business as mfg. chemist; now pres. The Fraser Tablet Co. Office: 5 E. 47th St., New York.

FRAZER, JOHN, chemist; b. Paris, France, Feb. 5, 1882 (parents Am. citizens); s. Persifor and Isabella Nevins (Whelen) F.; B.S. in chemistry, U. Pa., 1903, A.M., 1904, Ph.D., 1907; m. Mary Foxley Tilghman, June 9, 1915; children—Tilghman (dec.), Isabel, John, Tench. Instr. chemistry, 1904-06, 07-09, assistant professor 1909-18, 19-21, professor, 1921-33, dean Towne Science School, 1912-18, 19-28, secretary board of deans, 1921-22, chmn. faculty policy com., 1920-21, U. Pa.; Am. exchange prof. applied sci. to French univs., 1922-23; rep. U. Pa. on Coll. Entrance Exam. Bd., 1912-18, 19-21; sec. com. on sci. and arts Franklin Inst., Phila., 1936-56. Active mem. 1st Troop, Phila. City Cav., 1903-16, hon. roll, 1921; commd. capt. Chem. Warfare Service, U.S. Army, Aug. 9, 1918; trained in France and detailed as asst. gas officer 1st A.C., and later with 78th and 6th divs. in Argonne, A.E.F., and at Hdqrs. C.W.S., at Tours, France; hon. discharged Jan. 10, 1919; lt. col. O.R.C., C.W.S., U.S. Army, 1921-29. Fellow, life mem. A.A.A.S.; life member Pennsylvania Prison Society; member American Chem. Soc., Franklin Inst. (asst. sec. 1941-56). Franklin Inst. (asst. editor Jour. 1941-48), Hist. Soc. Pa., Soc. War of 1812, Loyal Legion (sr. vice comdr. Pa. 1945), Delta Psi, Sigma Xi, Phi Beta Kappa. Republican. Clubs: St. Anthony, Phila., Mask and Wig (Philadelphia); St. Anthony (N.Y.). Home: 8015 Navajo St., Chestnut Hill, Phila. 18. Office: Franklin Inst., Phila. 3, Pa. Died June 7, 1964; buried Laurel Hill Cemetery, Phila.

FRAZER, JOHN FRIES, scientist, univ. ofcl.; b. Phila., July 8, 1812; s. Robert and Elizabeth (Fries) F.; grad. U. Pa., 1830, M.A., 1833; LL.D., Harvard, 1857; m. Charlotte Cave, Sept. 1, 1838, 3 children including Persifor. Experimented (with Alexander Dallas Bache) on determination of daily variations of magnetic needle in Am., circa 1828; participated in geol. survey of Pa., 1836; prof. chemistry and natural philosophy U. Pa., 1844-72, vice provost, 1855-68; lectr. Franklin Inst., editor its journal, 1850-66; a founder Nat. Acad. Scis., 1863. Died Phila., Oct. 12, 1872.

FRAZER, JOSEPH CHRISTIE WHITNEY, prof. chemistry; b. Lexington, Ky., Oct. 30, 1875; s. Joseph George and Mary Jane (Filson) F.; B.S., Ky. State U., 1897, M.S., 1898; Ph.D., Johns Hopkins, 1901; Sc.D., Kenyon Coll., 1926; m. Grace Carvill, Sept. 16, 1903; children—Joseph Hugh, Grace Carvill, Jean Cameron (dec.), Jeanne Henry. Asst. and asso. in chemistry, Johns Hopkins, 1901-07; chemist, U.S. Bur. of Mines, 1907-11; prof. chemistry since 1911, chmn. dept. of chemistry, 1916-36, B.N. Baker, prof. since 1921, Johns Hopkins. Foreign mem. Soc. of Arts and Sciences, Utrecht; mem. Kappa Alpha, Phi Beta Kappa, Tau Beta Pi (hon.). Democrat. Presbyterian. Research work on osmotic pressure and vapor tension of solutions, catalysis and the chem. behavior of surfaces. Address: 3937 Cloverhill Rd., Baltimore, Md. Died July 28, 1944.

FRAZER, PERSIFOR, geologist, chemist, bibliote; b. in Philadelphia, July 24, 1844; s. John Fries (LL.D.), and Charlotte (Cave) F.; grad. Univ. of Pa., 1862 (A.M., 1865); was aide U.S. Coast Survey in S. Atlantic squadron, 1862-63; then in the cav. through Gettysburg campaign, 1863; actg. ensign U.S.N., in Mississippi squadron till hon. disch., Nov. 1865; studied Saxon Sch. Mines, Freiberg, Germany, 1866-69; mineralogist and metallurgist U.S. Geol. Survey, 1869-70; instr. and prof. chemistry, Univ. of Pa., 1870-74; asst. geol. survey, Pa., 1874-82; received degree of Docteur ès-Sciences Naturelles, Université de France, being the first, not a native of France, to whom this degree was ever awarded; m. Isabella Nevins Whelen. Fellow Geol. Soc. of America, A.A.A.S. Officer de l'Instruction Publique (France); corr. k. k. Reichsanstalt, Vienna. Author: Tables for the Determination of Minerals (5 edits.), 1874-1901; Reports of Sub-com. of the Am. Committee, Internat. Geol. Congress, 1888; Bibliotics, or the Study of Documents (3 edits.), 1894-1901. Received from City of Phila. the John Scott legacy medal "for his system of colorimetry and contbns. to the science of Bibliotics," 1905. Home: Philadelphia, Pa. Died 1909.

FRAZIER, CHESTER NORTH, prof. dermatology; b. Portland, Ind., Jan. 27, 1892; s. Luther Melanchthon and Etta (North) F.; student Wooster Coll., 1911-13; B.S., Ind. U., 1915, M.D., 1917; Dr. P.H., John Hopkins, 1947; grad. study U. of Paris, 1927, U. of Munich, 1931; A.M. (honorary) Harvard University, 1948; married Sally Harmon, Aug. 3, 1918; 1 son, Philip North. Asst. in dermatology and syphilology, Ind. U., 1919-22, asso. in dermatology, Peiping (China) Union Med. Coll., 1922-26, asso. prof. dermatology and syphilology, 1927-31, professor, 1932-42, librarian, 1937-11, acting dir., 1939-40; head dermatol. service Hosp. of Peiping Union Med. Coll., 1922-42; asst. vis. physician Johns Hopkins Hosp., 1942; prof. dermatology and syphilol., U. of Tex., 1943-48; Edward Wigglesworth prof. dermatol., Harvard U., since 1948; dermatologist-in-chief John Sealy Hospital, 1942-48; consultant in dermatology, M.D. Anderson Hosp. for Cancer Research, 1944-48; cons. Children's Hospital, Boston, 1948; chief dermatol. service Mass. Gen. Hosp. since 1948; cons. Mass. Eye and Ear Infirmary, Army Med. Library (hon.). Served as 1st lt. med. corps, U.S. Army, 1918-19. Chmn. bd. dirs. Peking (China) Am. Sch., 1927-31; vice pres. Internat. Congress Dermatology and Syphilology, Copenhagen, Denmark, 1930; chmn. United China Relief, Galveston, Tex., 1945-46; nat. consultant in dermatology Wartime Post-grad. Meetings, 1945-46; consultant to surgeon gen., U.S. Army, 1945-46. Diplomate, Am. Board of Dermatology and Syphilology. Fellow A.A.A.S., American College of Physicians; member Soc. Exptl. Biology and Medicine, N.Y. Acad. Sci., Hungarian Dermatol. Soc. (corr. mem.), Soc. Investigative Dermatology (dir.), Mass. Soc. for Social Hygiene (president), Swedish Dermatological Society (corr. mem.). Dallas Acad. Ophthalmology (hon.), Human Genetics Soc., Am. Dermatol. Assn. (corr. mem.). Tex. Acad. of Science, Soc. Investigative Dermatology, Assn. Am. Physicians, Am. Assn. History of Med., Am. Acad. Dermatology and Syphilology, N.E. Dermatol. Society, Am. Venereal Disease Assn., Alpha Omega Alpha. Episcopalian. Clubs: Johns Hopkins (Baltimore, Md.); Harvard (Boston); Peking (China). Mem. bd. editors, Jour. Investigative Dermatology; contbr. articles in Am. and Chinese jours. concerning nutritional dermatoses, cutaneous aspects of vitamin deficiency, sex and immunity to syphilis and mode of action of penicillin. Co-author (with H. C. Li): Racial Variation in Immunity to Syphilis; A Formulary for External Therapy of the Skin (with I. H. Blank). Home: Cambridge MA Died Feb. 14, 1973.

FREAR, WILLIAM, chemist; b. Reading, Pa., Mar. 24, 1860; s. Rev. George and Malvina (Rowland) F.; A.B., U. of Lewisburg (now Bucknell U.), 1881; Ph.D., Ill. Wesleyan U., 1883; m. Julia Reno, July 18, 1900. Asst. in sciences, Bucknell U., 1881-83, asst. chemist U.S. Dept. of Agr., 1883; prof. agrl. chemistry, 1885-1907, exptl. agrl. chemistry, 1907—, Pa. State Coll. Vice-dir. and chemist Pa. Agrl. Expt. Sta., 1887—; chemist to Pa. State Bd. Agr., 1888-1919; chemist Pa. Dept. of Agr., 1895-1916; spl. agt., U.S. Dept. of Agr., 1900—; chief chemist, Pa. Bur. of Foods. Writing exclusively communications to scientific periodicals and expt. station and state reports. Editor and prop. of "Agricultural Science," 1892-94. Pres. Assn. of Official Agrl. Chemists of U.S.; pres. Soc. for Promotion Agrl. Science; fellow A.A.A.S.; chmn. Nat. Food Standards Commn., 1902-07; mem. Joint Com. on Food Definitions and Standards, 1914—; mem. Assn. Am. Dairy Food and Drug Officials (pres. chem. sect. 1911-13), Franklin Inst., Washington Acad. Sciences. Mason. Dir. First Nat. Bank. Died Jan. 7, 1922.

FREAS, THOMAS BRUCE, prof. chemistry; b. nr. Newark, O., Nov. 2, 1868; s. Andrew and Mary (Bruce) F.; A.B., Stanford, 1896; Ph.D., U. of Chicago, 1911; m. Mary Kuhn, Dec. 28, 1898; children—Royal Bruce, Joseph Kuhn (dec.). Prin. high sch., Hiawatha, Kan., 1896-97; chemist, Western Electric Co., Chicago, 1897-98; asst. in chemistry and grad. student, U. of Chicago, 1898-1903; mgr. Ernst Leitz apparatus house, Chicago, 1903-04; instr. chemistry, U. of Chicago, 1904-11; successively asst. prof., asso. prof. and prof. chemistry, Columbia, 1911—; pres. Thermo Electric Instruments Co., Irvington, N.J. Fellow A.A.A.S., Am. Geog. Soc., N.Y. Acad. of Sciences. Republican. Presbyn. Home: Leonia, N.J. Died Mar. 15, 1928.

FREE, EDWARD ELWAY, chemist; b. Dagus Mines, Pa., May 3, 1883; s. Spencer Michael (M.D.) and May Irene (Elway) F.; grad. Bellefonte (Pa.) Acad., 1902; A.B., Cornell U., 1906; Ph.D., Johns Hopkins, 1917; m. Marion Allen, Apr. 28, 1922. Asst. chemist Agrl. Expt. Sta., U. of Ariz., 1906-07; physicist and scientist U.S. Dept. Agr., Washington, D.C., 1907-12; cons. chemist, and physicist, 1912—, head E.E. Free Laboratories, New York. Editor Scientific American, 1924-25; owner and editor "The Week's Science" (a news service). Lecturer on Outlines of Science, New York U., 1926-34. Served as capt. Ordnance Dept., U.S.A., 1917-18; maj. C.W.S., 1918-19. Fellow A.A.A.S., Wash. Acad. of Science, Acoustical Soc. America (treas. 1930-34). Died Nov. 24, 1939.

FREEBORN, STANLEY B., medical entomologist; b. Hudson, Mass., Dec. 11, 1891; s. Franklin K. and Addie M. (Houghton) F.; B.S., Mass. Arg. Coll., 1914, Ph.D., 1924; Sc.D., U. Mass., 1949; LL.D., U. of Cal., 1959; m. Mary B. Chase (died), Mar. 15, 1917; children—Stanley B. Joyce; m. 2d Marion Gay Maclise, December 16, 1949. Asst. dean Coll. of Agr. U. of Calif. and dir. Calif. Agr. Expt. Sta. since 1934 (on leave 1942-44, as sr. malariologist (R), U.S.P.H.S.), now chancellor Davis Campus U. Cal.; research worker on mosquitoes and malaria; mem. Fed. Water Pollution Control adv. bd., 1949-51. Unitarian. Contbr. articles on med. and vet. parasitology to tech. jours. Home: 16 College Park. Office: U. California, Davis, Cal. Died July 17, 1960.

FREEDMAN, WILLIAM HORATIO, elec. expert; b. New York, Dec. 28, 1867; s. John Joseph and Agnes (Roessel) F.; ed. Coll. City of New York, 1882-85; C.E., Columbia Sch. of Mines, 1889, E.E., 1891; post-grad. physics and mathematics, and fellow Columbia, 1891-92, M.S., U. of Vt., 1908; m. Lillian Augusta

Wilson, Jan. 30, 1895. Instr. elec. engring., Columbia, 1892-99; prof. elec. engring., U. of Vt., 1899-1910; head of dept. applied electricity, Pratt Inst., Brooklyn, 1910-13; prof. elec. engring., U. of Vt., 1913-20; tech. employment rep. Am. Telephone & Telegraph Co., Apr. 1, 1920-Sept. 1, 1922; research dept. Bonded Products Corp., 1923. Ednl. dir. U.S. Signal Corps schs. at U. of Vt., Sept. 1917-Jan. 1919. Fellow A.A.A.S., Am. Inst. E.E. Home: Nyack, N.Y. Died Dec. 11, 1940.

FREEMAN, EDWARD MONROE, plant pathologist, botanist; b. St. Paul, Feb. 12, 1875; s. Henry Jacob and Sybilla Jenny F.; B.S., U. Minn., 1898, M.S., 1899; Ph.D., 1905; student U. Cambridge, Eng., 1 yr.; m. Grace D. Studeman, Aug. 19, 1902; children—Monroe, Edward. Prof. botany and plant pathology, head div. U. Minn., 1907-40; dean Coll. of Agr., Forestry and Home Econs., 1917-43, dean and prof. emeritus since 1943. Fellow A.A.A.S.; mem. Bot. Soc. Am., Am. Phytopathol. Soc., Am. Soc. Naturalists, Phi Beta Kappa, Sigma Xi, Gamma Sigma Delta, Alpha Zeta. Club: Campus. Author: Minnesota Plant Diseases, 1905. Home: 2196 Carter Av., St. Paul. Died 1954.

FREEMAN, ERNEST HARRISON, elec. engr., educator; b. Topeka, Kan., Sept. 26, 1876; s. Harrison and Marinda D. (Hunter) F.; B.S., Kan. State Coll., 1895; D.Eng., 1935; grad. Kan. State Tchrs. Coll., 1897, Eng. D. (hon.), 1935; B.S., Armour Inst. Tech., 1902, E.E., 1906; married. Taught sch. in Kan., 1897-99; tchr. Armour Inst. Tech. (now Ill. Inst. Tech.), 1902—, prof. and head dept. elec. engring., 1909-41, prof. elec. engring., 1941—, prof. emeritus elec. engring., 1944—; inventor, cons. elec. engr. Mem. Am. Inst. E.E., Eta Kappa Nu, Tau Beta Pi, Phi Kappa Phi. Home: 601 Laurel Av., Wilmette, Ill. Address: 3300 Federal St., Chgo. Deceased.

FREEMAN, FRANCIS BREAKEY, ry. official; b. Dublin, Ireland, Apr. 2, 1867; s. William and Anne (Breakey) F.; ed. Rathmines Sch. and Royal Coll. of Science, Ireland; come to U.S., 1892; m. Mary Louisa Brewer, Nov. 1893; children—Ellen Breakey (dec.), William Morten Breakey. Mech. apprentice, later constrn. engr. and sub. agt. various rys. in Ireland; asst. engr. Kingsley & Brewer, civil engrs., New York, 1892-94; with S. Orange & Maplewood St. Rys., 1894; asst. engr. bridge dept. Erie R.R., 1894-1900; chief draftsman, later asst. engr., N.Y.C. & H.R. R.R., 1900-02; supt. constrn. Catawba Power Co., S.C., 1902-03; with H. DeB. Parsons, civil engr., New York, 1903; asst. engr. joint facilities and agreements, N.Y.C. & H.R., R.R., 1903-05, continuing with same rd. as designing engr., 1905-07, and engr. of constrn., 1907-09; chief engr. B. & A. R.R., at Boston, 1909-27; chief engr. N.Y.C. R.R. Co. (Buffalo and East). Mem. A.R. Engrs. Assn. Republican. Clubs: St. Andrew's Golf (New Brunswick); Siwanoy Country. Home: 145 E. 52d St. Address: 466 Lexington Av., New York. Died June 14, 1934.

FREEMAN, GEORGE FOUCHE, plant geneticist; b. Maple Grove, Ala., Nov. 4, 1876; s. George W. and Laura C. (Nuckols) F.; B.S., Ala. Polytechnic, 1903; Sc.D., Harvard, 1917; m. L. Adelle Blachly, Kan., 1906; children—Eleanor Adelle (Mrs. G. C. Wilson), George Donald. Principal Downer Inst., Beech Island, S.C., 1899-1901; asst. instr. in botany, Mass. Coll. of Agr., 1903-04; asso. botanist, Kan. State Agr. Coll., 1904-06; plant breeder, Ariz. Agr. Expt. Sta., 1906-18; acting dean, Coll. of Agr. and dir. Expt. Sta., Ariz., 1915-16; chief plant breeding, Soc. Sultanienne d'Agr., Cairo, Egypt, 1918-22; chief Dept. of Cotton Breeding, Tex. Agrl. Expt. Sta., 1922-23; official agriculturist and economist mission for French Govt. to Indo-China, 1923; dir. gen. Service Technique d'Agriculture et de l'Enseignement Professionnel, Republic of Haiti, 1923—. Mason. Home: Tucson, Ariz. Died 1930.

FREEMAN, HADLEY FAIRFIELD, engineer and patent lawyer; b. Sandusky, O., June 27, 1893; s. Thomas Edward and Mary Ann (Talbot) F.; B.S., Case Sch. Applied Science, Cleveland, 1914; LL.B., George Washington U., Washington, D.C., 1918; m. Gertrude Veronica Browne, Aug. 10, 1918; children—Thomas Hadley, James Janvrin. Examiner U.S. Patent Office, 1915-18. Air Service, U.S. Army, 1918; patent and trademark lawyer and engineer, New York, 1919-20, Milwaukee, 1920-23, 1931-34, Cleveland, 1923-46, Chicago, 1929-43, Pittsburgh since 1946. Dir. Research, Edwin L. Wiegand Co. Mem. Am. and Allegheny Co. bar assns., Am. and Pittsburgh patent law assns., Internat. Assn. for Protection of Industrial Property, Am. Inst. E.E., Engring. Soc. of W. Pa., Am. Soc. for Metals, Patent Inst. of Canada, Eta Kappa Nu. Clubs: Cosmos (Washington, D.C.), University Club of Pittsburgh. Home: 4735 Bayard St. Office: 7500 Thomas Blvd., Pitts. Died May 28, 1951; buried Lakewood, O.

FREEMAN, JOHN RIPLEY, civil and mech. engr.; b. W. Bridgeton, Me., July 27, 1855; s. Nathaniel D. and Mary Elizabeth (Morse) F.; B.S., Mass. Inst. Tech., 1876; hon. Sc.D., Brown U., 1904, Tufts, 1905, Sachs Tech. Hochschule, 1926, U. of Pa., 1927, Yale, 1931; m. Elizabeth Farwell Clark, Dec. 27, 1887. Prin. asst. engr. Water Power Co., Lawrence, Mass., 1876-86; prin. asst. to Hiram F. Mills, consulting engr., 1878-86; chief engr. Associated Factory Mut. Ins. Cos., 1886-96; cons. engr. on water power and mill construction to sundry large mfg. corps., 1886—. Made extensive studies of water supply for Greater New York, for finance dept., 1899-1900; chief engr. investigations, Charles River Dam, Boston Harbor, 1903; cons. engr. Boston Met. Park Commn. on sanitary and drainage problems, 1903-04. Water Commr., Winchester, Mass., 1882-86; engr. mem. Mass. Met. Water Bd., 1895-96; mem. R.I. Met. Park Commn., 1904; mem. spl. commn. additional water supply, New York. Was civilian engr. mem. spl. bd., gun carriage tests, War Dept., 1902. Pres. Mfrs., R.I. Mechanics, State, Enterprise and Am. Factory Mut. Ins. cos. Planned water power developments Feather River, Calif., 1904-05, St. Lawrence River, Long Sault, 1905, regulation of Great Lakes, 1924-26; cons. engr. water supplies of Nashua, Los Angeles, San Diego, Baltimore, City of Mexico; cons. engr. New York Bd. of Water Supply since 1905; in charge water power investigations N.Y. State Water Supply Commn., 1906-07; cons. engr. on Isthmian Canal locks and dams, 1907 and 1909; cons. engr. San Francisco water supply, 1910— (planned Hetch Hetchy water supply now bldg.); to Canadian Govt. on water power conservation, etc., 1910. Trustee of Mass. Inst. Tech., 1895—. Twice received Normal medal, Am. Soc. C.E., for best engring. paper contributed to its Transactions during year. Fellow Am. Acad. Arts and Sciences. Chmn. Nat. Advisory Com. for Aeronautics, 1918-19; cons. engr. for Chinese Govt., Grand Canal Improvement Bd., 1917—. Unitarian. Republican. Home: Providence, R.I. Died Oct. 6, 1932.

FREEMAN, THOMAS, civil engr., explorer; b. Ireland. Came to Am., 1784; surveyor for new capitol of U. S., 1794-96, surveyed entire No. portion of the dst.; started 1st topographic survey of Washington, D.C., resigned to accept. commn. as U. S. surveyor to chart boundary between U.S. and Spain; explored Red and Arkansas rivers, 1806; surveyed boundary between Tenn. and Ala., 1807; commd. U.S. surveyor pub. lands South of Tenn., 1811; 1st to accurately chart course of lower Red River. Died Huntsville, Ala., Nov. 8, 1821.

FREEMAN, THOMAS J. A., S. J., clergyman, prof. physics and chemistry, St. Peter's Coll., Jersey City, N.J., 1900—; b. Colchester Co., Nova Scotia, April 5, 1841; s. James and Mary (Marr) F.; student Montreal Coll., 1859-63; taught there, 1863-65; made a yr. of divinity studies in Montreal Sem.; entered Jesuit novitiate at Sault-au-Récollet, nr. Montreal, Sept. 1866; treas. St. Francis Xavier's Coll., New York, 1868-70; one year's spl. study, chemistry, Columbia Coll.; studied divinity 2 yrs. at Louvain, Belgium; has been prof. physics and chemistry St. Francis Xavier's Coll., and St. John's Coll., Fordham, N.Y., and Woodstock Coll., Md.; treas. St. John's Coll., 1899-1900; was prof. physics, Boston Coll. Home: Jersey City, N.J. Died 1907.

FREEMAN, WALTER, neurologist; b. Philadelphia, Pa., Nov. 14, 1895; s. Walter Jackson and Corinne (Keen) F.; A.B., Yale, 1916; M.D., U. of Pa., 1920; grad. study in neurology, Paris and Rome, 1923-24; M.S., Georgetown U., 1929, Ph.D., 1931; diplomate Nat. Bd. Med. Examiners and Am. Bd. Psychiatry and Neurology; m. Marjorie Lorne Franklin, Nov. 3, 1924; children—Marjorie Lorne (Mrs. Donald Canter), Walter Jackson III, Franklin, Paul, William Williams Keen (deceased), Robert Fitz Randolph. Med. practice, Washington, 1926; dir. labs. St. Elizabeths Hosp., Washington, 1924-33; prof. neurology George Washington U., 1927-54; specialist neurology, 1926-72; medical practice, Sunnyvale, Cal., 1961-72. Served as private Medical Corps, U.S. Army, Camp Dix, N.J., summer 1918. Fellow A.M.A. (chmn. sect. nervous and mental diseases 1930-31), Am. Neurol. Assn., Am. Bd. of Psychiatry and Neurology (president 1946-47), Santa Clara County Med. Soc., American Association Neuropathologists (president 1944-45), Philadelphia Neurological Society (pres. 1945), Am. Psychiatric Assn., Med. Soc. Dist. Columbia (president, 1949-50), Academia das Ciencas, Lisbon (corr. mem.); mem. Santa Clara-Monterey Counties Psychiatric Soc. (pres. 1958-59), Royal Medico-Psychol. Assn. (corr. mem.), Sigma Xi. Author: Neuropathology, 1933; Psychosurgery (with J. W. Watts), 1942, also 1950; Psychosurgery and the Self (with M. F. Robinson), 1954; The Psychiatrist, 1967. Contbr. to sci. publs. Home: Los Altos CA Died 1972.

FREER, PAUL CASPAR, chemist; b. Chicago, Mar. 27, 1862; s. Joseph Warren (M.D.) and Catharine (Gatter) F.; bro. of Otto Tiger F.; M.D., Rush Med. Coll., Chicago, 1882; Ph.D., U. of Munich, 1887; m. Agnes May Leas, June 1891. Asst., with Dr. Perkin, in Owens Coll., Manchester, 1887; asst. and instr. Tufts Coll., 1887-89; lecturer, 1889-90, prof. gen. chemistry, 1889-1903, U. of Mich.; supt. Govt. Laboratories, Manila, P.I., 1901-05; dir. Bur. Science, Manila, P.I., 1905—; dean P.I. Med. Sch. (now Coll. Medicine and Surgery), 1906—; prof. chemistry, U. of Philippines; editor Philippine Jour. of Science. Author: A General Inorganic Descriptive Chemistry, 1895; The Elements of Chemistry, 1896. Home: Manila, P.I. Died Apr. 17, 1912.

FREESE, JOHN HENRY, lawyer, astronomer, writer; b. Bangor, Me., Mar. 4, 1876; s. Andrew Jackson and Harriet (Langdon) F.; ed. Bangor High Sch. and pvtly., Harvard Coll. 1902, Harvard Law Sch. Asst. clerk Supreme Court Me., 1893-6; observer at Harvard Coll. Observatory in 1901; successfully photographed for the first time a spectrum of lightning at the Harvard Coll. Observatory, giving new data about the elements of the atmosphere; (described in "Making of the Universe," Century Mag., Dec., 1902). Contb'r to mags. and newspapers. Mem. Am. Social Science Assn., Delta Upsilon, Harvard Union, S. A. R., S. R., Harvard Club, etc. Home: Bangor, Me. Address: 25 W. 42d St., NY

FREITAG, JOSEPH KENDALL, civil engr.; b. New York, Sept. 12, 1869; s. F. D. and Annie F. (Kendall) F.; student U. City of New York, 1886; B.S., U. of Mich., 1890, C.E., 1894; married, 1891. Associated as engr. with Burnham & Root, architects, Chicago, 1890-1; asst. gen. supt. Chicago Expn., 1891-3; asst. engr., Met. Elevated Ry., Chicago, 1893-5; civ. engr. and agt. in bldg. constrn. at Boston, 1895-1907; associated with Hecla Iron Works, Brooklyn, to 1907; now sec. and treas. of the Norfolk Iron Co., Norfolk Downs, Mass. Asso. mem. Am. Soc. C.E.; mem. Loyal Legion, Nat. Fire Protection Assn., British Fire Prevention Com. Author: Architectural Engineering, 1895, 2d edit. (revised and extended), 1901; The Fireproofing of Steel Buildings, 1899; Fire Prevention and Fire Protection, 1912. Contbr. to mags. Address: 166 Devonshire St., Boston

FRENCH, AARON, mfr., inventor; b. Wadsworth, O., Mar. 23, 1823; s. Philo and Mary (McIntyre) F.; m. Euphrasia Terrill, 1848; m. 2d, Caroline B. Speer. Learned blacksmith trade, 1835; with Ohio Stage Co., Cleve., 2 years, Gayoso House, Memphis, Tenn., 1 year; lived in St. Louis, 1844-45; built wagons for Peter Young, Carlyle, Ill., 1845; became ill, returned to Ohio as semi-invalid, 1845-49; with Cleve. & Pitts. R.R., 1853; supt. blacksmithing Racine & Miss. R.R., Racine, Wis., until 1861; sheriff Racine County, 1861-62; partner (with Calvin Wells) in manufacture of 1st steel springs for railroad cars, Pitts., 1862; invented coiled and elliptic springs (revolutionized railroad industry); owned A. French Spring Co. (merged with Ry. Steel Spring Co.), Pitts.; left some money to Ga. Sch. Tech. Died Mar. 24, 1902.

FRENCH, ARTHUR WILLARD, civil engr.; b. Battle Creek, Mich., July 13, 1868; s. Willard and Elmira (Holt) F.; student Dartmouth Coll., 1887-90; C.E., Thayer Sch. Civ. Engring. (Dartmouth), 1892; m. Carrie Viola Kyte, of Denver, Colo., July 2, 1895; children—Willard Kyte, Robert Fletcher, Frederick Arthur, Walter Horace. Civ. engr. Platte River Paper Mills, Denver, 1892-94, asst. U.P., Denver & Gulf Ry., 1894-95; asst. prof. civ. engring., Thayer Sch. Civ. Engring., 1895-98; prof. civ. engring., Worcester Poly. Inst., 1899-1938, prof. emeritus since 1938. Mem. bd. overseers Thayer Sch. of Civil Engring., 1925-39. Mem. Am. Soc. C.E., Soc. Promotion Engring. Edn., Boston Soc. C.E. Author: Stereotomy (with H. C. Ives), 1902. Home: 202 Russell St., Worcester, Mass.

FRENCH, HOLLIS, consulting engr.; b. Boston, Mass., June 26, 1868; s. John James and Frances M. (Stratton) F.; B.S., Mass. Inst. Tech., 1889; m. Helen Goodwin, June 3, 1896; children—Alden, Stanley Goodwin, Hollis Stratton, Rue Elizabeth. Cons. engr., alone, 1895-98; mem. Hollis French & Allen Hubbard, 1898-1930; office of Hollis French, 1931—; v.p. Exolon Co. Episcopalian. Author: American Silversmiths and Their Marks, 1917; The Thatcher Magoun, An American Clipper Ship, 1934; Jacob Hurd and His Sons, 1939. Home: Boston, Mass. Died Nov. 21, 1940.

FRENCH, LEIGH HILL, engineer; b. Dover, N.H., Oct. 1, 1863; s. George F. and Clara Shackford (Hill) F.; ed. Portland (Me.) High Sch.; M.D., U. of Minn., 1894. Practiced medicine in Washington, 1897. Capt. and insp. rifle practices, Washington, 1898; maj. 3d Cav. U.S.V. ("Rough Riders"), 1898. Admitted to bar, 1902. Prominent in development of Alaska, building ry., and hydraulic mining waterways. Mem. Loyal Legion, Arctic Brotherhood, Am. Inst. Mining Engrs. Pres. Tex. Boy Scouts, 1920. Clubs: Cosmos, Chevy Chase, Army and Navy (Washington, D.C.); Worcester (Worcester, Mass.). Apptd. lt. comdr. U.S.N. and assigned to Am. Embassy, Paris, France, as asst. naval attaché, 1918; trans. to U.S. Army Air Service as capt., Aug. 1918. Big game hunter in India, Africa, Alaska, etc. Author: Sanitary Conditions at Camp Thomas During 1898, 1898; Nome Nuggets, 1902; Seward's Land of Gold, 1905; also medical books and brochures. Home: Flintridge, Pasadena, Calif.

FRENCH, OWEN BERT, geodesist; b. nr. Cleveland, O., Dec. 7, 1865; s. Marshall and Melissa A. (Harris) F.; B.S., Case Sch. Applied Science, 1888, C.E., 1905; m. Marie Wilhelmine Schott, of Washington, May 27, 1907. In charge of scientific work on Wellman's 1st Polar trip, 1894; asst. U.S. Coast and Geod. Survey, 1889-1915; consulting geodesist and engr., Washington, since 1915. Comd. several Coast and Geod. Survey ships; has worked nearly whole length of coasts of U.S., Hawaii and Alaska, and also in interior of U.S.; determined astron. positions for Mexican and N.W. boundaries of U.S.; engr. for U.S. on location of provisional boundary bet. British Columbia and Alaska, 1900; with another observer determined latitudes and longitudes of U.S. Naval Obs., Yerkes Obs., and Presidio Astron. Sta. and many other stations. Made 1st investigations of invar (nickel steel) tapes for use in the measurement of distances and used these tapes on the measurement of 6 primary base lines, proving them to be the most accurate form of base measuring apparatus. Prof. geodesy and geodetic astronomy, Inst. of Mil. Surveying, for Chinese Govt., 18 months; prof. surveying and astronomy, George Washington U., 1920-33. Awarded Wheat decoration by China. Mem. Geodetic Conf., Washington, 1893-94. Fellow A.A.A.S.; mem. Am. Soc. C.E., Washington Soc. Engrs., Philos. Soc. Washington, Washington Acad. Sciences, Washington Bd. of Trade, Am. Geophysical Union. Club: Cosmos. Joint Author: Gillespie's Higher Surveying, 1897. Contbr. to reports and tech. jours. Home: 3420 36th St., Washington, D.C.

FRESEMAN, WILLIAM LANGFITT, engring. exec.; b. Pitts., Dec. 1, 1901; s. William Luther and Irma L. (Gunther) F.; B.S., U.S. Naval Acad., 1922; M.S., Harvard, 1929; certificate, U.S. Naval War Coll., 1935; m. Barbara Rice, Aug. 8, 1947. Enlisted as midshipman, USN, 1918, advancing through ranks to rear adm., 1947; dir. Radar Research Lab., Univ. Miami, 1951-57; dir. Internat. Tel. & Tel. Corp. Projects Group, also v.p. Internat. Standard Engring., Inc., 1957-61; asst. to pres. Radio Engring. Labs., Inc., 1961—; asst. to exec. v.p. Dynamics Corp. Am., 1963—. Decorated Legion of Merit with gold star, Bronze Star; War Medal (Brazil); Croix de Guerre (France). Fellow Radio Club Am.; mem. Navy League of the United States, I.E.E.E., United States Naval Inst., Armed Forces Communication and Electronic Assn. (nat. v.p.), Am. Humane Soc. Clubs: University Yacht (Miami); Army-Navy Country (Arlington, Va.). Author: (with others), Radar Meteorology, 1955. Patentee electronic devices. Home: New York City NY Died Jan. 1971.

FREUD, SIGMUND, psychoanalyst, psychiatrist; b. Freiberg, Moravia, May 6, 1856; s. Jacob and Amalia (Nathanson) F.; M.D., U. Vienna, 1881; LL.D., Clark U., 1909; m. Martha Bernays, 1886; 6 children including Anna. Studies psychol. aspects of hysteria under Jean Charcot, Paris, 1885-86; with physiol. lab. of Ernst Bruck, 1876-82, Inst. Cerebral Anatomy, Vienna Gen. Hosp.; lectr. U. Vienna, from 1885; studied nervous diseases of children, Kassowitz Inst., Vienna; specialist on nervous diseases, Vienna, from 1886; collaborator (with Josef Breuer) on use of hypnosis for treatment of hysteria; founder (with Eugen Bleuler and C. G. Jung) Jahrbuch für psychoanalytische und psychopathologische Forschungen, 1908; lectr. Clark U., Worcester, Mass., 1909; formed Internat. Psychoanalytical Assn., 1910; recipient Goethe prize, 1930; Fellow Royal Soc., 1936; moved to London after annexation of Austria by Germany, 1938. Author: On the Psychological Mechanism of Hysterical Phenomena, 1893; (with J. Breuer) Über Hysteria, 1895; Die Traumdeutung, 1900; The Psychopathology of Everyday Life, 1904; Totem and Taboo, 1913; The History of the Psychoanalytic Movement, 1914; Thoughts for the Times on War and Death, 1915; Beyond the Pleasure Principle, 1921; Group Psychology and the Analysis of the Ego, 1922; The Ego and the Id, 1923; Inhibitions, Symptoms and Anxiety, 1925; Autobiography, 1925; The Future of an Illusion, 1927; Civilization and its Discontents, 1929; (with A. Einstein) Why War? 1933; Moses and Monotheism, 1939. Father of psychoanalytic sch. of psychiatry; evolved concepts of dynamic subconscious, resistance and repression; discovered aetiological significance of sexual life and importance of infantile experiences in human devel.; stated that fundamental rule of psychoanalysis is to bring into consciousness repressed material held back by resistances; developed psychotherapy based on free association, interpretation of dream symbolism and patient-doctor transference; propounded theories of Odeipus complex and guilt; later divided mental apparatus into id (instinctive urges), ego, and superego (ethical standards derived from Oedipus complex); introduced concept of libido (energy of sexual instincts); conceived idea of self-preservation (eros) and death instincts; applied his theories to analyses of artistic creativity, folk culture, religion, war. Died London, Sept. 23, 1939.

FRIDEN, JOHN H(ARRY), engr.; b. Sweden, Apr. 23, 1896; s. Gustaf Fredrik and Augusta Lovisa (Peterson) F.; ed. pvt., pub. schs.; m. Hildur Teglund, Oct. 29, 1923; children—Brit, John Frederick. Asst. to city engr., Vesteras, Sweden, 1916; design engr. E. W. Bliss Co., 1920, staff engr., 1923-1925; chief engr. Sun Tube Corp., 1925-28, exec. v.p., dir., 1928-48; v.p., dir. engring. Bristol-Myers Co. 1948-54, ret.; dir. Hillside Nat. Bank, Hillside, N.J. Served on numerous govt. technol. coms. during World War II. Mem. N.J. Soc. Profl. Engrs., Am. Soc. Swedish Engrs., John Ericson Soc., Swedish Colonial Soc. (mem. bd. govs.). Republican. Lutheran. Mason (32 deg.). Home: 25 Clinton Av., Maplewood, N.J. Died Dec. 30, 1962; buried Gunnebobruk, Sweden.

FRIEDEN, ALEXANDER, chemist; b. Lithuania, Oct. 5, 1895; s. Abraham and Sarah (Rubin) F.; B.S., U. Va., 1919, M.S., 1919; M.A., Columbia, 1920, Ph.D., 1923; m. Evelyn Gutman, Nov. 13, 1920; children—Dr. Julian, Dr. Carl. Came to U.S., 1912, naturalized, 1919. Tchr. Charlottesville (Va.) High Sch., 1917-18, Columbia, 1920-23; with cons. labs. of Dr. Raymond F. Bacon, 1923-33; ind. cons., 1933-36; lectr. food and nutrition coll. New Rochelle (N.Y.), 1935-36; tech. dir. food products dept. Stein, Hall & Co., Inc., N.Y.C., 1936-39, tech. dir., 1939-41, v.p., 1941-46; dir. research Pabst Brewing Co., Milw., 1946-53, v.p. research, 1953—. Mem. food engring. council Ill. Inst. Tech., 1949—; bd. visitors Agrl. Research Inst., N.R.C. Served with C.W.S., U.S. Army, 1918. Mem. Cerevisiae Yeast Inst. (dir.), Am. Chem. Soc., A.A.A.S., Am. Soc. Cereal Chemists, Am. Soc. Brewing Chemists, Inst. Food Technologists, Textile Research Inst., Tech. Assn. Pulp and Paper Industry, Am. Soc. Textile Chemists and Colorists, N.Y. Acad. Sci., Chemists Club N.Y., Sigma Xi. Mem. Ethical Culture Soc. Contbr. sci. and tech. publs., chpts. sci. books. Patentee in field. Home: 746 E Beaumont Av., Milw. 17. Office: 1037 W. McKinley Av., Milw. 3. Died Apr. 21, 1956.

FRIEDENWALD, JONAS STEIN, ophthalmologist; b. Baltimore, Md., June 1, 1897; s. Harry and Bertha (Stein) F.; A.B., Johns Hopkins, 1916, M.D., 1920; A.M., Harvard, 1922; m. Marie Louise Sherwin, Aor. 19, 1925. Instr. ophthalmic pathology, Johns Hopkins, 1923-29, asso. in clin. ophthalmology, 1929-31, asso. prof. since 1931; asst. visiting ophthalmologist, Johns Hopkins Hosp., 1929-31, visiting ophthalmologist since 1931; ophthalmic surgeon, Baltimore Eye and Ear, Union Memorial, Women's Sinai and Provident hosps. Fellow Am. Coll. Surgeons; mem. A.M.A., Am. Ophthal. Soc., Am. Optical Soc., Am. Acad. Ophthalmology and Otolaryngology, Am., Assn. Clin. Investigation, Ophthal. Soc. United Kingdom, Awarded medal research ophthalmology A.M.A., 1935, Lucien Howe medal, Am. Ophthal. Soc., 1951; Howe prize in ophthalmology U. Buffalo, 1948; Proctor award medal, 1949; Donders award medal, Dutch Ophthal. Soc., 1952. Jewish religion. Club: University. Author: Pathology of the Eye, 1929. Contbr. to profl. jours. Address: 1212 Eutaw Pl., Balt. 17. Died Nov. 5, 1955.

FRIEDMAN, FRANCIS LEE, physicist; b. N.Y.C., Sept. 5, 1918; s. Harry George and Adele (Oppenheimer) F.; grad. Phillips Exeter Acad., 1935; B.A., Harvard, 1939, M.A., 1940; Ph.D., Mass. Inst. Tech., 1949; m. Betty Anthony, Aug. 27, 1944; children—Gweneth, Karen, Seth. Grad. asst. physics U. Wis., 1941; asst. physicist atomic energy project Nat. Bur. Standards, 1941-42; physicist Manhattan Dist. Plutonium Project, U. Chgo., 1942-46; research asso. Mass. Inst. Tech., 1946-49, A.D. Little postdoctoral fellow, 1949-50, asst. prof., 1950-54, asso. prof. physics, 1954-58, prof., 1958—, dir. sci. teaching center, 1960—; guest Inst. Theoretical Physics, Copenhagen, Denmark, 1955-56; chief scientist phys. sci. study com., 1956-60; v.p. Ednl. Services, Inc., 1959—, trustee, 1961—; cons. Oak Ridge, Brookhaven Nat. labs.; cons., dir. Nuclear Devel. Corp. Am., 1948-51; participant govt. projects. Mem. Am. Phys. Soc., Am. Acad. Arts and Scis. Author articles on atomic energy; nuclear reactor theory, nuclear physics. Home: 149 Brattle St., Cambridge 38, Mass. Died July 5, 1962.

FRIEDMAN, WILLIAM FREDERICK, cryptologist; b. Kishinev, Russia, Sept. 24, 1891; s. Frederick and Rosa (Trust) F.; brought to U.S. 1893; B.S., Cornell U., 1914, grad. study, 1914-15; m. Elizabeth Smith, May 21, 1917; children—Barbara, John Ramsay. Asst. dept. genetics Cornell U., 1913-15; field asst. Sta. Exptl. Evolution, Carnegie Inst., 1913-14; dir. dept. genetics Riverbank Labs., Geneva, Ill., 1915-18, dir. dept. ciphers, 1917-21; chief cryptanalyst War Dept., Washington, 1921-47; chief Signal Intelligence Service, 1930-40; dir. communications research Army Security Agy., 1942-49; chief tech. div. Armed Forces Security Agy., 1949-50, chief tech. cons. 1950-52; spl. asst. to the dir. Nat. Security Agy. 1953-55; cryptologist Dept. Def., 1947-55, cons., 1955-69; cryptologic cons., lectr. Armed Forces Service Schools and RCA, Washington, D.C.; member sci. adv. bd. Nat. Security Agy., 1957-61. Recipient 100,000 Congressional award for cryptologic inventions and patents, 1956; Medal for Merit, 1946; National Security medal, 1955; War Dept. Exceptional Service award, 1944; (with wife) Fifth Annual award Am. Shakespeare Festival Theatre and Acad. Served as 1st lt. mil. intelligence, U.S. Army, 1918-19; capt. Signal Corps Res., 1924-26, maj., 1926-36, lt. col., 1936-51. Mem. Sigma Xi. Clubs: Cosmos, Ft. Lesley J. McNair Officers' (Washington). Author War Dept. publs.; (with wife) The Shakespearean Ciphers Examined (May 1958 selection Readers' Subscription; lit. prize Folger Shakespeare Library 1955). Contbr. sci. and lit. jours., encys. Inventor many cryptographic devices and machinery. Home: Washington DC Died Nov. 12, 1969; buried Arlington National Cemetery, Arlington VA

FRIEDMAN, WILLIAM HENRY, tunnel commr., indsl. engr., printer; b. Poland, July 15, 1886; s. Pinkus and Rachel (Forlager) F.; came to U.S., 1888, naturalized 1896; E.E., Columbia, 1907, A.M., 1909; student Tchrs. Coll., Columbia, 1909-11, Poly. Inst. of Brooklyn, 1914-15, Coll. City N.Y., 1916-17; m. Gertrude Markowitz, June 25, 1913; children—Leonard, Harry Jay, Authur Stanley, Paul Harvey (dec.). Printer's apprentice Carey Press Corp., 1903-05, pres., dir. since 1921; pres., dir. Carey Craft Press, Inc., Mag. Art Press, Inc., Bank Advt. Corp., Ready Reference Pub. Co., Diary Splty. Co.; cons., indsl. engr. since 1911; commr. Queens Mid-town Tunnel Authority, 1935-36; commr. N.Y.C. Tunnel Authority, 1936-45 (chmn. labor and pub. relations com.). Mem. Municipal Com. for Relief Home Owners, Mayor's Com. on Traffic Regulation, City of N.Y. George Washington Bi-centennial Com.; mem. adv. com. Bur. Indsl. Edn. of N.Y. State Dept. Edn., mem. Printing Edn. Commn., N.Y.C. Bd. Edn.; chmn. Benj. Franklin's Birthday Celebration, 1936-53; commr. Boy Scouts Am., nat. merit badge counsellor in printing, mem. Nat. council. Spl. arbitrator for mayor N.Y.C. Mem. Conf. on Fgn. Relations; mem. Nat. Council, Joint Distbn. Com.; mem. Golden Jubilee Celebration Com., N.Y.C., 1948. Dir. N.Y. Employing Printers' Assn.; chmn. Graphic Arts Commn. on Vocational Edn. N.Y.C.; Sch. for Printers' Apprentices, Sch. for Printing Pressmen, Sch. for Machine Composition, N.Y. Sch. of Printing; mem. adv. bd. Indsl. Edn. for Printing Industry; mem. Joint apprenticeship com. Printing Industry, N.Y.C.; gen. chmn. Com. on Apprenticeship Edn., Printers League, N.Y.C.; sponsor ann. Harry J. Friedman Award for distinguished service in cause of printing edn.; chmn. adv. bd. N.Y. Evening Sch. of Printing; vice chmn. Am. Arbitration Assn.; charter mem. Am. Jewish Congress, Council of Industries and Professions; trustee Temple Ansche Chesed, dir. Jewish Club N.Y.; dir. Men's Club of Temple; mem. High Sch. Tchrs. Assn., Tchrs. Guild Assos. Mem. Internat. Graphic Arts Ednl. Assn., United Typothetae Am., Nat. Printers Assn., advt. Fedn. Am., Mchts. Assn., Broadway Assn., Typog. Union, Elec. Engring. Soc. Columbia, Soc. Older Graduates Columbia, N.Y. Credit Men's Assn. (adv. bd.); mem. N.Y. Acad. Sci.; mem. Printing Industries Am., Inc. Democrat. Jewish religion. Clubs: Printing Crafts, Grand Street Boys' Assn., Advertising, Civitan (N.Y.); Old Oaks Country. Author and lectr. Home: 225 W. 106th St. Office: 406 W. 31st St., N.Y.C. 10001. Died Apr. 17, 1963.

FRIEL, FRANCIS DE SALES, civil engr.; b. Queenstown, Md., Feb. 24, 1894; s. John and Avis (Whiting) F.; C.E., Drexel Inst. Tech., 1916, D.Eng., 1949; LL.D., U. of Scranton, 1958, Pa. Military Coll., 1959; D.E. Sc., Lafayette College, 1960; D.Sc., Villanova U., 1961; m. Sarah Gertrude Scanlan, Oct. 17, 1921. Pres. Albright & Friel, Inc., cons. engrs., 1931-62, chmn. bd., 1962—, specializing in water, sewage, indsl. wastes, power plants, incineration, city planning, hwys., bridges, airports, flood control, dams, Army and Navy installations, financial studies and reports. Registered engr., Pa. (mem. state registration bd. 1952-58), N.Y., N.J., Md., Del., Va., W.Va., N.C., Ohio. Bd. dir. Beneficial Saving Fund Bank Phila.; vice chmn. bd. trustees Drexel Inst. Tech.; member of board trustees Trinity College. Served as major C.E., U.S. Army, WW I. Recipient medal Am. Pub. Works Assn., 1948; named Engr. of Year, Engring. Socs. of Phila., 1956. Diplomate Am. Acad. San. Engrs. Mem. Am. Soc. C.E. (nat. pres. 1958-59), Am. Inst. Cons. Engrs. (pres. 1955-56), Internat. Commn. on Large Dams (v.p. 1958-61, chmn. U.S. com. 1955-58), Am. Water Works Assn. (chmn. Pa. sect. 1955-58, recipient of the Fuller award 1959), Water Pollution Control Federation (president 1946-47), American Concrete Institute Am. Public Works Assn., Pa. Soc. Profl. Engrs., Am. Pub. Health Assn., Internat. Assn. Hydraulic Research, World Power Congress, Am. Road Builders Assn., Tau Beta Pi, Chi Epsilon, Pi Kappa Phi. Papal Knight of the Holy Sepulchre, Ky. col., 1959. Clubs: Engineers, Philadelphia Country, Skytop, Union League (Phila.). Contbr. engring. jours. Home: 611 Carisbrooke Rd., Bryn Mawr, Pa. Office: 3 Penn Center Plaza, Phila. 2, Pa. Died Feb. 11, 1964; buried St. Peter's Cemetery, Queenstown.

FRIEND, ALBERT WILEY, cons. engr., physicist; b. Morgantown, W.Va., Jan. 24, 1910; s. Lemuel Ellsworth and Louisa Gertrude (Michael) F.; B.S. in Elec. Engring., W.Va. U., 1932, M.S., 1936; S.D., Harvard 1948; m. Evelyn Augusta Hall, Aug. 6, 1931; children—Albert Wiley, Evelyn Joyce (Mrs. William C. Everett), John Robert. Engr., Ohio Power Co., 1933-34; from instr. to asst. prof. physics W.Va. U., 1934-44; instr., research fellow, instr. Harvard (on leave W.Va. U.), 1939-42, 46-47; research asso., staff Radiation Lab., Radar Sch., tech. dir. Heat Research Lab., Mass. Inst. Tech., 1941-44; research staff RCA, 1944-51; dir. engring. Daystrom, Inc., 1951; dir. engring. Magnetic Metals Co., 1951-53; cons. engr., physicist, 1953-72; pres. Amicon Corp., Acoustex, Inc., 1968-72, A.W. Friend Engrs. Lectr., U. Pa., 1965. Cons. controls, electromagnetic isolation, tropoopheric radio echo phenomena; research and devel. electronic color TV system and equipment, also radar, guided missiles, telemetering, electronic computer components, magnetic materials and componenets, weather radar, lunar exploration communications, satellite communications systems, noise abatement, archtl. acoustics, vibration etc. Recipient award for outstanding research RCA Labs., 1950; award for contbns. to advancement electronic art Nat. Electronics Conf., 1955. Fellow I.E.E.E. (chmn. tech. com. recording and reproducing), A.A.A.S., Am. Phys. Soc.; mem. Acoustical Soc. Am., Am. Geophys. Union, Air Force Assn., Am. Inst. Physics, Am. Meteorol. Soc., Am. Ordnance Assn., Harvard Engrs. Soc., Am. Ordnance Assn., Harvard Engrs. Soc. N.Y., Electrochem. Soc., Franklin Inst., Nat., Pa. socs. profl. engrs., Tau Beta Pi, Sigma Xi, Sigma Pi Sigma. Clubs: Engineers (Phila.); Cosmos (Washington). Author numerous tech. papers and reports. Contbg. author:

Magnetic Recording in Science and Industry. Holder U.S. and fgn. patents. Home: Bethesda MD Died Sept. 27, 1972; interred Morgantown WV

FRIES, J(OENS) ELIAS, engr.; b. Frinnaryd, Sweden, Apr. 6, 1876; E.E. and M.E., Kongl, Tekiuska Hogskolan, Stockholm, 1898; m. Annerika Bjerkander, Vestergotl, Sweden; 1 son, Erik Fritiof Bjerkander. Came to U.S. 1903; with Westinghouse, Church, Kerr & Co., New York, 1903-05, Allis-Chalmers Co., 1905-07, Canadian Gen. Electric Co., 1907-08, Crocker-Wheeler Co., advancing to asst. chief engr., 1908-16; chief elec. engr., Tenn. Coal, Iron & R.R. Co., 1916-20; chief engr. same, 1920—, and Chickasaw Shipbuilding & Car Co. Fellow Am. Inst. E.E., A.A.A.S. Unitarian. Author: Einstein's Theory of Relativity, 1921. Translator: Death and Resurrection (by G. Bjorklund), 1910; The Destinies of the Stars (by Arrhenius), 1918. Home: Birmingham, Ala. Died Jan. 23, 1932.

FRINK, FRED GOODRICH, civil engr.; b. Pilot Grove, Ill., Apr. 16, 1862; s. Morey French and Ellen E. (Goodrich) F.; B.S. in Civ. Engring., U. of Mich., 1886; M.S., U. of Chicago, 1902; spl. student in sanitary engring., Mass. Inst. Tech., 1900-01; m. Mae Beadle, July 10, 1888. Asst. engr. Big 4, C.&A. and C.&N.W. rys., 1886-88; computer and supt. Vierling & McDowell, and Snead & Co. iron works, Chicago, 1888-90; instr. archtl. drawing, Manual Training High Sch., Chicago, 1890-97; in charge drawing, Chicago Athenaeum, 1893-97; prof. civ. engring., U. of Ida., 1897-1900; in pvt. bus., 1900-02; taught engring. classes of the late Dean C. E. Greene, U. of Mich., 1902-04; asst. prof. civ. engring., U. of Ill., 1904-06; pres. Lake Constrn. Co., Hammond, Ind., 1906-08; prof. of engring., U. of Ore., 1908-15; cons. practice, 1915—. Republican. Episcopalian. Mason. Author: Trigonometry (Hall and Frink), 1909. Home: Palo Alto, Calif. Died Sept. 30, 1929.

FRISCH, MARTIN, engring. exec.; b. Csebze, Hungary, Nov. 22, 1899; came to U.S., 1909, naturalized, 1917; student Washington U., 1917-19; B.S., U. Ill., 1921; m. Anita Laurence Barnard, Apr. 3, 1937. With Combustion Engring. Corp., N.Y. City, successively as field research engr., asst. mgr. service and erection dept. and mgr. field engring. dept., 1923-29; with Foster Wheeler Corp., N.Y. City, since 1929, successively chief engr. pulverizer div. chief engr. steam div., dir. engring. and dev., 1940-47, v.p. and chief engr., 1947-52, v.p., general mgr. equipment div. since 1953, dir. since 1948, member executive com. since 1944. Instr. mechanics and strength of materials U. Wis., 1922. Served as 2d lt. F.A., O.R.C., U.S. Army, World War I. Fellow Am. Soc. M.E. (boiler code com.); mem. Am. Soc. Naval Engrs., Am. Soc. Testing Materials, Pi Tau Sigma, Tau Beta Pi, Sigma Xi (asso.). Republican. Unitarian. Mason. Clubs: Lawyers, Engineers (N.Y. City). Numerous patents in pulverization, steam generation, combustion. Author articles and papers in tech. jours. Home: 65 Central Park W., N.Y. City 23. Office: 666 Fifth Av., N.Y.C. 19. Died June 16, 1959.

FRISON, THEODORE HENRY, (fri-sun), entomologist; b. Champaign, Ill., Jan. 17, 1895; s. Joseph and Helen (O'Neal) F.; B.A., U. of Ill., 1918, M.A., 1920, Ph.D., 1923; m. Ruby Gertrud Dukes, Aug. 22, 1919; children—Theodore Henry, Jr., Patricia Ann. Began as asst. Wis. state entomologist, 1920; asst. entomologist U.S. Bur. Entomology, 1921-22; asst. in dept. of entomology, U. of Ill., 1922-23; systematic entomologist Ill. State Natural History Survey, 1923-30, also acting chief of same, 1930-31, chief of Ill. State Natural History Survey since July 1, 1931. Dir. Central States Forest Exptl. Sta., Central States Forestry Congress. Entered U.S. Army, Apr. 1918; commd. 2d lt., Aug. 1918; resigned, Dec. 1918. Fellow A.A.A.S., Entomol. Soc. America (v.p. 1936); member American Association Economic Entomologists (1st vice president 1945). Ecol. Society Am. (rep. on Nat. Research Council, 1937), Ill. Audubon Soc. (dir. 1942), Limnological Soc. America, Soc. Wildlife Specialists, Am. Wildlife Inst., Am. Soc. Naturalists, Wilderness Soc., Ill. State Florists Assn., Conservation Council of Ill., Ill. Hort. Soc., Ill. State Nurserymen's Assn. (hon.), Ill. State Acad. Science (2d vice-president 1929-30; 1st vice-president 1939-41; president 1941-42), Izaak Walton League of America, Alpha Sigma Phi and Sigma Xi fraternities. Methodist. Club: Urbana Golf and Country. Author: Fall and Winter Stoneflies, or Plecoptera, of Illinois, 1929; The Plant Lice, or Aphiidae, of Illinois (with Frederick Hottes), 1931; The Stoneflies, or Plecoptera, of Illinois, 1935; and over eighty other scientific articles. Compiler: List of Insect Types in the Collections of Illinois State Natural History Survey and University of Illinois, 1927. Editor of Journal of Economic Entomology, 1936-40; mem. editorial board of Ecology, 1938-40. Mem. Thomas Say Foundation Bd., 1942-44. Home: 1005 S. Douglas St. Address: Natural Resources Bldg., Urbana, Ill. Died Dec. 9, 1945.

FRITCH, LOUIS CHARLTON, engineer; b. Springfield, Ill., Aug. 11, 1869; s. Joseph and Margaret (Mather) F.; engring. course U. of Cincinnati; m. Frances Myers Fritch, of Jeffersonville, Ind., Apr. 1904. Div. engr., 1892-99, supt., 1899-1904, B.&O. R.R., at Cincinnati; asst. to gen. mgr., 1904-1906, asst. to pres., 1906-09, consulting engr., 1909, I.C. R.R., at Chicago; chief engr. C.G.W. Ry., Chicago, Nov. 15, 1909-Apr. 1, 1914; asst. to the president Canadian Northern Ry. and gen. mgr. eastern lines, same, Toronto, Can., 1914-17; gen. mgr. S.A.L. Ry., Norfolk, Va., June 15, 1917-Aug. 19, 1918; v.p. C.,R.I. & P. Ry., in charge constrn., maintenance and capital expenditures, 1918-23, v.p. in charge of operation, 1923-36. Mem. Am. Ry. Engring. Assn. (ex-pres.), Am. Soc. C.E., Western Soc. C.E., Sigma Alpha Epsilon. Republican. Methodist. Clubs: Union League, South Shore Country, Rock Island Country. Home: 1648 E. 50th St. Office: 30 N. La Salle St., Chicago IL

FRITTS, CARL EMERSON, highway engr.; b. Hemlock, N.C., Jan 9, 1900; s. Elzie K. and Sevilla E. (Graybeal) F.; student Wash. State Coll., 1918-21; m. Jean Lauder, June 9, 1947; 1 son, Carl Emerson. Various positions constrn., maintenance, traffic engring., planning, adminstrn. Wash. State Hwy. Dept., 1922-42; traffic engr. Hwy. Traffic Adv. Com., War Dept., 1942; hwy. engr. Automotive Safety Found., 1946-49, dir. hwys. div., 1950, v.p. in charge engring., 1951—. Mem. national advisory com. road test Am. Association of State Highway Ofcls. Mem. hwy. research bd. dept. econs., finance and adminstrn. Served as col. Transportation Corps, AUS, 1942-45. Decorated Legion of Merit. Registered engr., Ida., Ky., D.C., La., Me., Minn. Miss. N.M., N.D., R.I., Ore., Tenn., Va., Wash., W.Va., Montana, D.C., Province of Ontario (Canada), National Bur. of Engring. Registration. Fellow Am. Society C.E. (president of national capital section); member Inst. Traffic Engrs., Sigma Chi. Episcopalian. Club: Cosmos (Washington). Home: Silver Spring MD Died Sept. 1970.

FRITZ, JOHN, mech. engr.; b. Chester Co., Pa., Aug. 21, 1822; ed. common schs.; (hon. A.M., Columbia, 1898; Sc.D., U. of Pa., 1906; Temple U., 1911; D.Eng., Stevens Inst. Tech., 1907). Apprenticed to blacksmith trade, 1838; employed in Norristown (Pa.) Iron Works, where soon became mill foreman; with others started small machine shop, 1852; made gen. supt. Cambria Iron Works, Johnstown, Pa., 1854; entered service of Bethlehem Iron Co. as gen. supt. and engr., 1860, and built works of co.; retired in 1892. Received complimentary resolution from Am. Soc. Mech. Engrs., 1892 (hon. mem.); elected, 1893, hon. mem. Iron and Steel Inst. of Great Britain, from which received Bessemer gold medal for services in advancement of steel mfrs. (hon. v.p. same, 1909). Selected by Armor Plate Bd., 1897, to make plans and estimates for a Govt. armor plate works. Republican; presdl. elector, 1896. Mem. Group I, Centennial Expn., Phila., 1876; hon. expert on iron and steel, St. Louis Expn., 1904; awarded John Fritz medal, United Engring. Socs., 1902; Elliott Cresson medal, Franklin Inst., 1910. Home: Bethlehem, Pa. Died Feb. 13, 1913.

FRIZELL, JOSEPH PALMER, civil engr.; b. Barford, Quebec, Mar. 13, 1832; s. Oliver and Mary S. (Beach) F.; ed. in Can.; spl. studies in civ. engring.; m. Julia A. Bowes, Oct. 1864. Was engaged in constrn. of fortifications on Gulf Coast during Civil War; later employed in pub. service in improvement of rivers and harbors; especially in charge system of reservoirs on head waters of the Mississippi; chief engr. bd. pub. works, Austin, Tex., 1890; from 1892 in Boston engaged in hydraulic engring., mainly in line of water power. Home: Boston, Mass. Died May 4, 1910.

FROEHLICH, JACK E(DWARD), aero. engr.; b. Stockton, Cal., May 7, 1921; s. Adolph Henry and Maude Leon (Gillespie) F.; student U. Cal. at Los Angeles; B.S., Cal. Inst. Tech., 1947, M.S. in Aero. Engring., 1948, Ph.D., 1950; m. Marion Louise Crofts, June 22, 1946; children—John Howard, Mark Edward. Research engr. Jet Propulsion Lab., Cal. Inst. Tech., 1949-53, chief guided missiles engring. div., 1953-55, head design and power plants dept., 1955-59, also satellite project dir.; tech. dir. electronic systems engring. div., v.p. Alpha Corp., subsidiary Collins Radio Co., 1959-60; gen. mgr. applied sci. div. Space Electronics Corp., subsidiary Aerojet-Gen. Corp., 1960, v.p. Space-Gen. Corp. (subsidiary), 1960-62, exec. v.p., 1962—. Mem. panel on fuels and lubricants Dept. Defense; research adv. com. chem. energy processes NASA. Served to capt. USMC, 1942-46; test pilot. Mem. Am. Inst. Aeros. and Astronautics (sr.), I.E.E.E., Armed Forces Communication and Electronics Assn., Am. Astronautical Soc., Sigma Xi. Home: 621 Foxwood Rd., Pasadena 3, Cal. Office: 9200 E. Flair Dr., El Monte, Cal. Died Nov. 24, 1967.

FROHMAN, PHILIP HUBERT, architect; b. N.Y.C., Nov. 16, 1887; s. Gustave and Marie (Hubert) F.; ed. Throop Poly. Inst., Pasadena, Cal., 1899-1903, Throop Coll. Engring. (now Cal. Inst. Tech.), specializing in art, archtl. engring. and civil engring., 1903-07; m. Olivia Avery, July 15, 1922 (dec. Apr. 1955); children—Mary, Alice; m. 2d, Mary Ann Evans, Feb. 27, 1957 (dec. Mar. 1970). Began practice as architect at Pasadena, Cal., 1908; mem. Frohman & Martin, 1909-17; opened office in Boston, 1919; mem. Frohman, Robb & Little, 1920-34; pvt. practice 1934-72; opened office in Washington, 1924, continuing assn. with former partners in Boston and Cal. on certain projects; specializes in church architecture; architects of Nat. Episcopal Cathedral, Washington, Md. Cathedral, Balt., Trinity Coll. Chapel, Hartford, Conn., Catholic Cathedral, Los Angeles, and other monumental churches; cons. architect Kent Sch. Chapel, also various chs.; cons. architect cathedral projects. Served with U.S. Army, 1917-19; assigned to Ordnance Constrn. Sect. and Supply Div.; designed bldgs. at Rock Island Arsenal and Aberdeen Proving Grounds. Decorated Medal Pro Ecclesia et Pontifix (Pope John). Fellow A.I.A. (mem. Washington chpt.); mem. Nat. Cathedral Assn., Guild Religious Architecture, Liturgical Art Soc., The Restorers of Mount Carmel in Md., Am. Ord. Assn. (life). Republican. Catholic. Club: Gibson Island. Specialist in structural engring. as applied to cathedrals, etc. Regarded as an authority on Romanesque and Gothic architecture, stained glass, and also on design and voicing of ch. organs and in field of sci. of mus. sounds. Inventor electric organs and various apparatus for elec. reproduction of mus. sounds. Writer on ecclesiastical art and architecture. Home: Washington DC Died Aug. 7, 1972.

FRONING, HENRY BERNHARDT, (fro'ning), professor chemistry; b. Sebastian, O., Sept. 7, 1884; s. John Bernard and Mary (Rose) F.; A.B., St. Joseph's Coll., Rensselaer, Ind., 1908; M.A., Ohio State U., 1912; student Johns Hopkins U., 1912-13; hon. LL.D., St. Vincent Coll. (Latrobe, Pa.), June 1940; m. Mary Mildred Cain, June 23, 1915; children—Joseph Fendall, Mary Mildred, Laura Harvey, Ned Cain, Henry Bernhardt. Instr. chemistry, Catholic U. of America, 1909-11; instr. and asst. prof. bacteriology, Ohio State U., 1914-18, asst. prof. biochemistry, 1918-19; research chemist and bacteriologist Nizer Labs., Inc., Detroit, Mich., 1919; prof. chemistry and head depts. of chemistry and chem. engring., U. of Notre Dame, since 1920; dean, Coll. of Science, same univ., 1940-43; dean emeritus since 1943. Mem. Am. Chem. Soc., Phi Lambda Upsilon, Sigma Xi. Roman Catholic. Died 1960.

FROST, EDWIN BRANT, astronomer; b. Brattleboro, Vt., July 14, 1866; s. Carlton P. and Eliza A. (DuBois) F.; A.B., Dartmouth, 1886, A.M., 1889, D.Sc., 1911; hon. D.Sc. Cantab., 1912; studied physics and astronomy, Princeton, Strassburg (Germany), and Astrophys. Observ., Potsdam, Germany; m. Mary E. Hazard, Nov. 19, 1896; children—Katharine Brant, Frederick Hazard, Benjamin DuBois. Instr. physics and astronomy, 1887-90, asst. prof. astronomy and dir. of obs., 1892-95, prof. astronomy, 1895-98, nonresident instr. 1898-1902, Dartmouth; prof. astrophysics, 1898—, dir. Yerkes Observatory, 1905-32, director emeritus, U. of Chicago. Assistant editor, 1895-1901, editor, 1902, Astrophysical Journal. Fellow Am. Acad. Arts and Sciences, A.A.A.S. Translated, revised and enlarged, A Treatise on Astronomical Spectroscopy, by Dr. J. Scheiner, 1894. Author: An Astronomer's Life, 1933. Died May 14, 1935.

FROST, WILLIAM DODGE, bacteriologist; b. Lake City, Minn., Sept. 13, 1867; s. Benjamin Cutler and Lucy Jane (Dodge) F.; B.S., U. of Minn., 1893, M.S., 1894; Ph.D., U. of Wis., 1903; Dr. P.H., Harvard, 1913; m. Jessie H. C. Elwell, of Minneapolis, Jan. 1, 1895; children—Herbert Cutler (dec.), Russell Elwell, Theodore Dodge. Biologist in lab., Minn. State Bd. Health, 1894-95; asst. in bacteriology, 1895-98; instr., 1898-1902, asst. prof., 1902-07, asso. prof., 1907-15, prof. agrl. bacteriology, 1916-38, U. of Wis. Trustee Congl. Sum. Assembly, Frankfort, Mich. Fellow A.A.A.S., Am. Pub. Health Assn.; associate fellow A.M.A.; member American Association Medical Milk Commissions (pres.), Society American Bacteriologists, Nat. Soc. Study and Prevention Tuberculosis, Wis. Anti-Tuberculosis Assn. (dir.), Madison Anti-Tuberculosis Assn. (dir.), Wis. Acad. Sciences, Royal Inst. Pub. Health (London), Sigma Xi, Alpha Zeta, Farm House; life mem. Am. Missionary Assn. Pres. The Morningside Sanatorium. Author: Laboratory Guide in General Bacteriology, 1901; General Bacteriology (with E. G. McCampbell), 1911; The streptococci (with Mildred A. Englebrecht), 1940; also collaborator, Marshall's Microbiology. Originator of "cellular test" for pasteurized milk and "little plate" method of counting bacteria in milk. Contbr. tech. jours. on bacteriology, especially the hemolytic streptococci of milk. Address: 1010 Grant St., Madison, Wis. Died Jan. 25, 1957; buried Forest Hill Cemetery, Madison.

FROTHINGHAM, ARTHUR LINCOLN, archeologist; b. Boston, June 21, 1859; s. Arthur Lincoln and Jessie (Peabody) F.; bro. of Jessie Peabody F.; early edn. Acad. Christian Bros., Rome, Italy, 1868-73; spl. courses in Oriental langs., Catholic Sem., S. Apollinare and Royal U., Rome, 1875-81; A.M., Ph.D., U. of Leipsiz, 1883; (hon. A.M., Princeton U., 1896); m. Helen Bulkley Post, Jan. 27, 1897. Fellow in Semitic langs., and lecturer in archaeology, Johns Hopkins, 1882-86; prof. archaeology and history of art, 1887-98, ancient history and archaeology, 1898-1906, Princeton. Founded, 1885, editor and propr., 1885-96, Am. Jour. of Archaeology; founded Princeton College Bulletin; asso. dir. Am. Sch. Classical Studies, Rome, 1895-96. Author: A History of Sculpture; Mediaeval Art Inventories of the Vatican; Monuments of Christian Rome, 1908; Roman Cities of Italy and Dalmatia, 1910; A History of Architecture, III-IV (sequel to vols. I-II by Russell Sturgis), 1915; Handbook of War Facts and Peace Problems; Simplified Italian Manual, etc.,

1918-19. Co-Author (with A. E. Stevenson) of 4 vols. Report on Revolutionary Radicalism of the Joint Legislative Com. of State of N.Y. (Lusk Com.), 1921. Home: Princeton, N.J. Died July 28, 1923.

FRY, ALFRED BROOKS, engineer; b. New York, Mar. 3, 1860; s. Maj. Thomas William Gardiner (U.S.V.) and Frances (Olney) F.; g.g.s. Capt. Benj. F., Continental Army; ed. pvt. schs. and Morse's Sch., New York; engring. sch. Columbia Coll.; m. Emma V., d. Brig. Gen George A. Sheridan, U.S.V., 1890; 1 son, Sheridan Brooks. Marine and mech. engr., 1879-86; acting asst. engr. U.S. Treasury service, 1886, advanced through grades to supervising chief engr., supervising engr., duty at Port of New York, 1924-26; chief inspection engr. for supervising architect U.S. pub. bldgs., etc., on Pacific Coast, Aug. 1926-Mar. 1927; consulting engr., 1927—; engr. lt. and engr. lt. comdr. naval militia, 1892-1910; comdr. and chief of staff, naval militia, New York, 1910—; acting chief engr. U.S.N., Spanish-Am. War, 1898; chief engr. and supt. constrn., etc., U.S. pub. bldgs., New York, 1899-1917; engr. aide to Admiral Burd, industrial mgr. Navy Yard N.Y., and 3d Naval Dist., Mar. 1917. Capt. U.S. N.N.V., 1917; capt., U.S.N.R., July 1, 1918; duty in Navy Yard, New York, at sea and French and English ports. Mem. bd. consulting engrs. for improvement of state canals, 1904-11; consulting engr. to Assn. for Protection of the Adirondacks, 1908—, Congressional Commn. of 1913 on mech. transmission of mails; mem. com. on waterways Merchants' Assn., New York; cons. engineer, Dept. Water Supply, Gas and Electricity, City of New York, 1914; mem. com. of engrs. representing Nat. Engring. Socs. at N.Y. Constl. Conv., 1915; mem. Special Panama Canal Commn., 1921; cons. engr. U.S.A., transport service, 1922. Commodore, comdg. Naval Militia, N.Y., 1923; retired as rear adm. Feb. 27, 1924. Mem. Harbor Com. of San Diego Chamber of Commerce, 1929; mem. City Council, Coronado, Calif., 1929-30, mayor pro tem., 1930-31; elected mayor for term, 1932-34. Pres. San Diego County League of Municipalities, 1932-33; mem. Engrs. Employment Com. of Southern Calif., 1931. Home: Coronado, Calif. Died Dec. 4, 1933.

FRY, HARRY SHIPLEY, prof. chemistry; b. Cincinnati, Oct. 24, 1878; s. Harry Oliver and Emma Elizabeth (Richards) F.; B.A., U. of Cincinnati, 1901, M.A., 1902, Ph.D., 1905; m. Corinne Angele Lacroix, June 16, 1904; 1 son, Harry Lacroix (M.D.). With faculty Univ. of Cincinnati since 1901, professor and head department of chemistry since 1918. Professor emeritus 1945. Former mem. Nat. Research Council (div. chemistry and chemical technology), Nederlandsche Chemische Vereeniging, Nat. Inst. of Social Sciences. Fellow A.A.A.S.; mem. Am. Chem. Soc., Sigma Xi, Phi Lambda Upsilon. Protestant. Author: The Electronic Conception of Valence and the Constitution of Benzene, 1921. Contbr. many articles in Am. and foreign tech. publs. First to propose and apply the term "electromer" and "electronic tautomerism" as fundamental concepts in the development of the electronic conception of valence and explanation of chem. reactions of compounds of carbon. Home: 6371 Grand Vista Av., Cincinnati. Died May 18, 1949; buried Spring Grove Cemetery, Cincinnati.

FRY, LAWFORD H., mech. engr.; b. Richmond, P.Q., Can., June 16, 1873; s. Howard and Eliza Tyrell (Lawford) E.; brought to U.S., 1873, naturalized, 1929; ed. Bedford (Eng.) Grammar Sch.; City and Guilds Tech. Inst., London; U. of Goettingen and Hannoversche Technische Hochschule (Germany); m. Marjorie Stockton Canan, Sept. 9, 1905 (died Sept. 1932); children—Frances Elizabeth, Lucy Howard, Humphrey Lawford, Christopher Arthur, Alison Marjorie (Mrs. Nelson Orr Wieman); m. 2d, Mildred Lucinda Kolb, Dec. 2, 1935. Engr., Baldwin Locomotive Works, 1897-1913; metall. engr., Standard Steel Works, 1913-30; railway engr., Edgewater Steel Co., 1930-43; dir. of research The Locomotive Inst., New York, N.Y., since 1943. Mem. Inst. Civil Engrs., Inst. Mech. Engrs. (Bernard Hall prize 1927), Inst. Locomotive Engrs., Am. Soc. M.E. (Warner Reed Medal 1938), Am. Soc. Testing Materials, Newcomen Soc. of England; affiliated mem. mech. div., A.A.R. Author: A Study of the Locomotive Boiler, 1924; Contbr. papers and articles to tech. socs. and jours. Home: 15 Wales Place, Mt. Vernon, N.Y. Office: 60 E. 42d St., New York 17, N.Y. Died July 10, 1948.

FRYE, THEODORE CHRISTIAN, botanist; b. Washington, Ill., Sept. 15, 1869; s. Joseph and Catherine (Kinzinger) F.; B.S., U. of Ill., 1894; Ph.D., U. of Chicago, 1902; married Else Marie Anthon, June 30, 1908; children—Elizabeth Anthon, Joanne Anthon (dec.). Prin. High Sch., Monticello. Ill., 1894-96; supt. schs., Batavia, 1897-1900; fellow in botany, U. of Chicago, 1901-02; prof. biology, Morningside College, Iowa, 1902-03; professor botany, 1903-46, professor emeritus since 1946; acting dean, College of Science, 1913-15, University of Washington. In charge Puget Sound Biol. Sta., summers, 1905, 07, 08, 09; dir. same, 1913-30; in charge Kelp Expdn. to Southeastern Alaska, for U.S. Bur. of Soils, summer, 1913. Instr. R.O.T.C., U. of Wash., with rank of capt., 1917. Mem. A.A.A.S., Bot. Soc. America. Sigma Xi. Author: (with George B. Rigg) Laboratory Excercises in Elementary Botany, 1910; Northwest Flora, 1912; Elementary Flora of the Northwest (with same), 1913; (with Lois Clark) Liverworts of the Northwest (article), 1929; Ferns of the Northwest. 1934; The Hepaticae of North America (with Lois Clark), 1937-1947. Home: 18237 40th Av. N.E., Seattle 55 WA

FTELEY, ALPHONSE, civil engr.; b. Paris, France, April, 1837; several yrs. in engring. offices in Europe; came to U.S., 1865; was draftsman and asst. until 1870, then in general practice. In 1873-80 resident engr. in charge of investigation and construction for Sudbury River Water Works system, at Boston; chief asst. city engr., Boston, 1880-84; principal asst. engr., 1884-86; consulting engr., 1886-88, and chief engr. Aqueduct Commn. of New York, 1888-1900. Identified with many water supply, sewerage, rapid transit and other engring. projects. Died 1903.

FULLER, GEORGE WARREN, engineer; b. Franklin, Mass., Dec. 21, 1868; s. George Newell and Harriet (Craig) F.; S.B., Mass. Inst. Tech., 1890; post-grad. course U. of Berlin; m. Miss Goodloe, Nov. 1899 (died 1907); m. 2d, Mrs. Charlotte Bell Todd, June 1913 (divorced 1918); m. 3d, Mrs. Eleanor Todd Burt, Oct., 1918. With Mass. State Board of Health, at Lawrence Expt. Sta., 1890-95 (in charge 1893-95); in charge of elaborate tests for cities of Louisville, Ky., and Cincinnati, O., on most feasible method of purifying water, 1895-99; in pvt. practice, 1899—, as hydraulic and sanitary engr. Has been expert adviser for filtration plants for New York, Baltimore, Washington, New Orleans, Montreal, etc. Home: New York, N.Y. Died June 1934.

FULLER, LEVI KNIGHT, inventor, mfr., gov. Vt.; b. Westmoreland, N.H., Feb. 24, 1841; so. Washington and Lucinda (Constantine) F.; m. Abby Estey, May 8, 1865. Self-taught in practical science, telegraphy, and electricity; mech. engr. J. Estey & Co., 1860, v.p., 1866-68; holder about 50 patents on inventions, most of which were appliances for organs; mem. Vt. Senate, 1880-82; lt. gov. Vt., 1886; gov. Vt. (Republican), 1892-94; trustee Shaw U.; adoption of internat. pitch for mus. instruments due largely to his efforts; mem. A.A.A.S., Soc. Am. Engrs. Died Brattleboro, Vt., Oct. 10, 1896.

FULLER, MYRON LESLIE, geologist; b. Brockton, Mass., Apr. 19, 1873; s. Albert Henry and Phoebe Ann F.; S.B., Mass. Inst. Tech., 1896; m. Lillian A. Gayner, Apr. 26, 1897. Did pvt. field work on pegmatics of N.H., 1895, and in pleistocene deposits of Cape Cod, 1896, field work on copper range, Keweenaw Point, for Mich. Geol. Survey, 1897; asst. in geology, 1897-99, instructor, 1899-1900, Mass. Inst. Tech.; field work in Pa., Ind., Ill., for United States Geol. Survey, 1900-02; organized Eastern sec. of div. of hydrology, Jan. 1, 1903; chief of sect., 1903-06; in charge coastal plain investigations, 1907. U.S. explorations in China, Manchuria and Mongolia, 1913-15; has done much field work in coal, oil and gas fields and on glacial and artesian water problems in U.S. and gen. field work in Alaska, Northern Canada, West Indies, and Brazil. Received Walker prizes of Boston Soc. Natural History, 1897 and 1905; gold medal for govt. exhibit of building stones at Paris Expn., 1900. Extensive contbr. to tech. jours. and to publs. of U.S. Geol. Survey. Mem. Geol. Soc. America, A.A.A.S., Seismological Soc. Address: 60 Main St., Brockton MA

FULMER, (HENRY) ELTON, chemist; b. Marcellus, N.Y., Feb. 6, 1864; s. David Morgan and Ellen Elizabeth (Longstreet) F.; bro. of Clark Adelbert F.; B.S., U. of Neb., 1887, A.M., 1889; m. Helen Barbara Aughey, Dec. 25, 1889. Instr. chemistry, U. of Neb., 1888-93; prof. chemistry, 1893—, dean of faculty, 1908—, State Coll. of Wash. State chemist of Wash., 1900—. Republican. Methodist. Home: Pullman, Wash. Died 1916.

FULTON, CHARLES HERMAN, metallurgist; b. of Am. parents, at Ludwigshafen am Rhein, Germany, July 16, 1874; s. Albert Charles and Bertha Anne (Arzberger) F.; prep edn., Pratt Inst., Brooklyn, N.Y.; E.M., Sch. of Mines (Columbia), 1897; hon. D.Sc., U. of S. Dak., 1911; m. Marion Cunninghame, Sept. 19, 1898; children—Bertha Isabelle, Marion Emily (dec). Asst. in assaying, Columbia, 1898-99; instr. in metallurgy, U. of Wyo., 1899-1900; prof. metallurgy, S. Dak. State Sch. of Mines, Rapid City, S.D., 1900-05, pres., 1905-11; prof. metallurgy, Case Sch. Applied Science, 1911-20; dir. Mo. Sch. of Mines and Metallurgy, U. of Mo., 1920-37, research prof. of metallurgy, 1937-39, acting prof. metallurgy, Montana School of Mines, since 1942; Consulting metallurgical engineer. Member Missouri Academy Science (president 1938-39), American Institute Mining and Metall. Engrs., Theta Delta Chi, Sigma Xi, Tau Manual of Fire Assaying, 1907.

FULTON, JOHN FARQUHAR, physiologist, med. historian; b. St. Paul, Nov. 1, 1899; s. John Farquhar and Edith Stanley (Wheaton) F.; student U. Minn., 1917-18; B.S., Harvard, 1921, M.D., 1927; Rhodes scholar, Oxford U., 1921-23, Christopher Welch scholar, 1923-25, B.A., 1923, M.A., D.Phil., 1925, D.Sc., 1941; fellow Magdalen Coll., Oxford, 1928-30; M.A. (hon.), Yale, 1929; LL.D., Kenyon Coll., 1938, U. Birmingham, 1948; M.D. (hon.), U. Oslo, 1951, U. Louvain, 1951, U. Uppsala, 1956; D.Sc., Boston U., 1952, Emory University, 1954; Litt.D., Oxford, University, 1957; married Lucia Wheatland, Sept. 29, 1923. Demonstrator physiology Oxford U., 1923-25, 28-30; asso. neurol. surgery Peter Bent Brigham Hosp., Boston, 1928; Sterling prof. physiology Yale, 1929-51, Sterling prof. history of medicine 1951—; has been spl. named lectr. in field various univs. and colls., 1947—. Trustee Inst. Advanced Study, Princeton, 1942—. Chmn. com. on hist. records NRC, 1940-46, com. on aviation medicine, 1940-46, vice chmn. div. med. scis., 1943. Recipient Order Cultural Merit Class II, 1932 (Rumania); Hon. Officer, Civil Div., Order Brit. Empire; President's Certificate of Merit (U.S.), 1948; Officer Legion of Honor (France); gold medal U. Liége, 1951; Comdr. Order Leopold II (Belgium), 1951; Orden de Mérito, Carlos J. Finlay (Cuba), 1954; Sarton medal History of Science, 1958. Member foreign, local, state, nat., internat. profl. orgns. in both spl. and gen. med. field; also Phi Beta Kappa, Chi Psi, Alpha Omega Alpha; hon. or corr. mem. several fgn. nat. professional societies, including Royal College of Physicians and Royal Society of Medicine (London), Deutsche Gesellschaft für Neurologie. Clubs: Graduate, Lawn (New Haven); Century (N.Y.C.). Author several tech. books including: Frontal Lobotomy and Affective Behavior, 1951; The Great Medical Bibliographers, 1951; Humanist and Martyr, 1953. Editor A Textbook of Physiology, 1955; Journal of Neurophysiology, 1938—, Jour. of History of Medicine, 1951—. Home: Mill Rock, 100 Deepwood Dr., Hamden 17, Conn. Office: 333 Cedar St., New Haven 11. Died May 29, 1960; buried Grove St. Cemetery, New Haven.

FULTON, ROBERT, civil engr., inventor, artist; b. Little Britain, Pa., Nov. 14, 1765; s. Robert and Mary (Smith) F.; m. Harriet Livingston, Jan. 8, 1808; 4 children. Devised successful manually operated mechanism to propel a boat by paddle wheels, 1779; engaged in a variety of engring. ventures connected with devel. of inland waterways; went to Eng.; worked and lived in Europe, 1786-1806; secured British patent for "double inclined plane" for raising and lowering canal boats; patented machine for sawing marble for which he received medal Soc. for Encouragment of Arts, Commerce and Mfg.; invented dredging machine or power shovel for cutting canal channels; published A Treatise on the Improvement of Canal Navigation, 1796; proposed constrn. of cast iron aqueducts to Bd. Agr. Gt. Britain, 1796, ultimately used; experimented unsuccessfully with self-propelling torpedo; painted what is "L'Incendie de Moscow (thought to be 1st panorama), Paris, France; built diving boat Nautilus, 1800-01, to prove its worth he was to destroy Brit. shipping, but was unsuccessful in sinking ships, later attempted to prove worth to Brit., failed to sink French ships (torpedo failure), 1801-03; entered legal agreement with Robert Livingston (minster to France), to construct steamboat for purpose of navigating Hudson River between Albany (N.Y.) and N.Y.C., 1802; successful in experiments in France, 1803; returned to U.S., 1806; Steamboat Clermont began voyage up Hudson River, Aug. 17, 1807; engaged in establishment, mgmt. steamboat lines, constrn., 1807-15; constructed steam war vessell authorized by U.S. Congress, 1814; dir. company which produced a commercially successful steamboat; ensured introduction, continued operation of steamboats. Died N.Y.C., Feb. 24, 1815; buried Old Trinity Churchyard, N.Y.C.

FULTON, WESTON MILLER, SR., inventor; b. Stewart, Ala., Aug. 3, 1871; s. William Frierson II and Mary Brown (Hudson) F.; student Howard Coll., Birmingham, 1887-89; B.S. with highest honors, U. Miss., 1892; postgrad. in engring., Tulane U., 1896-98; M.S., U. Tenn., 1902; m. Barbara S. Murrian, Aug. 17, 1910; children—Weston Miller, Jr. (dec.), Barbara Alexander (Mrs. Fenton Gentry), Robert William, Jean Hudson (Mrs. James Talley III), Mary Helen (Mrs. C. J. Hartley). With U.S. Weather Bur., Vicksburg, Miss., 1892-98, Knoxville, Tenn., 1898-1903; inventor Sylphon (a seamless metal bellows now used in radiators, refrigerators, atomic plants, diesel, automobile and airplane engines; used in anti submarine depth bombs World War I), 1904; organizer (to produce the Sylphon) The Fulton Co. (later became Fulton Sylphon Co., now Fulton Sylphon div. Robertshaw Fulton Controls Corp.), Knoxville, 1904, prin. owner, 1904-28; pres., owner W. J. Savage Co., 1930-36, Tenn.-Odin Ins. Co. (name now So. Fire & Casualty Ins. Co.), 1935-46, Royal Mfg. Co., 1940-45 (all Knoxville). Prof. meteorology U. Tenn., 1898-1903. Recipient Modern Pioneer award N.A.M., 1940; certificate of appreciation Pres. Roosevelt, 1945. A separate sect. U.S. Patent Office set aside to house his 125 patents which include the sylphon and other thermostatic devices. Died Knoxville, May 16, 1946; buried Highland Meml. Cemetery, Knoxville, Tenn.

FUNK, CASIMIR, biochemist; b. Warsaw, Poland, Feb. 23, 1894; s. Jacques and Gustawa (Zysan) F.; student, Gymnasium, Warsaw, 1894-1900, U. of Geneva, 1900-01; Ph.D., U. Berne, 1901-04; post grad. work Inst. Pasteur, Paris, 1904-06, Univ. of Berlin, 1906-07; U. of London, D.Sc., 1913; m. Alix Denise Schneidesch, June 19, 1914; children—Ian Casimir, Doriane Jacqueline. Biochemist Wiesbaden Municipal Hosp., 1907-08; biochemist, Huntington Cancer

Research Fund, Cornell Med. Sch., 1915-16; research head Metz & Co., N.Y. City, 1917-23; asso. in biochemistry, Coll. Phys. and Surgs., Columbia, 1921-23; head biochem. dept., Warsaw Sch. of Hygiene, Rockefeller Found., 1923-27, Rueil Research Lab., France, 1928-39; cons. U.S. Vitamin Corp., N.Y.C., since 1936. Pres. Funk Found. for Medical Research. Mem. British Biochem. and Physiol. Socs., French Biochem. Soc., Am. Chem. Soc., Soc. for Exptl. Biology and Medicine, Am. Soc. Biol. Chemists. Author books. Address: U.S. Vitamin Corp., 800 2d Av., N.Y.C. 10017. Died Nov. 19, 1967.

FUNKHOUSER, WILLIAM DELBERT, zoölogist; b. Rockport, Ind., Mar. 13, 1881; s. Hugh Clark and Laura Josephine (Mobley) F.; A.B., Wabash Coll., Crawfordsville, Ind., 1905, Sc.D., 1929; M.A., Cornell U., 1912, Ph.D., 1916, honor fellow, 1916-17; m. Josephine H. Kinney, June 29, 1910. Instr. biology, high sch., Brazil, Ind., 1905-07; high sch., Greencastle, Ind., 1907; headmaster, high sch., Ithaca, N.Y., 1908-14; prin. Cascadilla Sch., July 1, 1915-Aug. 15, 1918; head dept. zoölogy and entomology since 1918, prof. of anthropology and dean of Grad. Sch. since 1925, U. of Ky. Fellow A.A.A.S., Entomol. Soc. Am. (pres. 1940); mem. New York and Brooklyn entomol. socs., Ky. Acad. Sciences, Ky. Ednl. Assn., Wilson Orinthol. Club, Am. Zoöl. Soc., Am. Anthrop. Soc., Kappa Sigma (past dist. grand master Ky. and Tenn.), Phi Beta Kappa, Sigma Xi (pres. Ky. Chapter, 1923-24); pres. Ky. Research Club, 1922-23, pres. Rotary Club (Lexington), 1925-26; pres. Ky. Archaeol. Soc., 1933; sec. of Southeastern Athletic Conf. since 1934; president Conference of Deans of Southern Graduate Schools, 1944-45 (secretary 1935-40); mem. com. on instns. of higher edn. 1941-43; mem. com. on grad. instrn., Southern Univ. Conf., 1940-44. Mem. exec. com. Oak Ridge Inst. Mem. Filson Club, Bradford Soc., Ky. Hist. Soc. Republican. Conglist. Rotarian. Author: Biology of Membracidae of Cayuga Lake, 1917; Outlines of Zoölogy, 1919; Wild Life in Kentucky, 1923; Birds of Kentucky, 1925; Catalogue of Membracidae, 1927; Kentucky Prehistory, 1931; Autobiobraphy of an Old Man, 1940; Ethnology Behind the War, 1943; Portraits of Kentuckians, 1943; Dead Men Tell Tales, 1944; The Days That Are Gone, 1945; also about 300 articles in entomol. jours. Home: 468 W. Second St. Lexington, Ky. Died June 9, 1948.

FURER, JULIUS AUGUSTUS, naval officer; b. Mosel, Wis., Oct. 9, 1880; s. Rev. Edmund E. and Caroline Louisa (Wedemeyer) F.; B.S., U.S. Naval Acad., 1901; M.S., Mass. Inst. Tech., 1905; m. 2d, Helen Carlin Emery, May 12, 1927; 1 dau., (by 1st marriage), Helen C. (Mrs. Clifton Toal). Commd. lt., USN, 1903, advanced through grades to rear adm. 1941; midshipman U.S.S. Indiana, U.S.S. Shubrick, 1901-03; transferred to constrn. corps, 1903; duty at navy yards, N.Y., Charleston (S.C.), Phila., Pearl Harbor (T.H.), 1905-15; planned and supervised raising of submarine F-4 from depth of 304 feet (greatest depth from which any ship has been raised), Honolulu, 1915; with Bur. Constrn. and Repair, USN Dept., designing submarine chasers and supervising building program for small craft, 1915-19; mem. staff comdr.-in-chief, Pacific fleet, 1919-21; with Bur. Constrn. and Repair, 1921-23; mem. U.S. Naval Mission to Brazil, 1923-27; mgr. Navy Yard, Cavite, P.I., 1928-30, Phila., 1930-35; tech. asst. to naval attaches, London, Paris, Berlin, Rome, 1935-38; gen. insp. Bur. Ships, USN Dept., 1938-40; head Compensation Bd., Navy Dept., 1941; coordinator research and devel. Navy Dept., 1941-45; ret. from active duty, Nov. 1945; recalled to active duty 1951—, engaged in writing History of Adminstrn. of Navy Dept. in World War II. Cons. Brazilian govt. on laying out naval yard, Rio de Janeiro, 1923-27; tech. adviser Naval Limitations Conf., London, 1936. Trustee Naval Hist. Found., supervised constrn. naval Mus., Washington. Awarded Navy Cross, Legion of Merit, various campaign and victory medals (U.S.), Legion of Honor (France), Order of Crown (Belgium). Mem. Soc. Naval Architects and Marine Engrs., Am. Soc. Naval Engrs., U.S. Naval Inst., Chi Phi. Clubs: Chevy Chase, Army-Navy (Washington), Yacht (N.Y.C.). Contbr. numerous articles to Ency. Americana, Naval Inst., other tech. jours. Invented submersible pontoons for raising sunken ships, 1915, adopted as standard salvage equipment for submarine bases. Home: 2101 Connecticut Av., Washington 8. Died June 5, 1965; buried Arlington Nat. Cemetery.

FURLONG, CHARLES WELLINGTON, explorer, writer, painter, soldier, ethnologist, lectr.; b. Cambridge, Mass., Dec. 13, 1874; s. Atherton Bernard and Carletta Eleanor (Wellington) F.; student pub. schs., Boston, also pvt. schs., U.S. and Eng.; grad. Mass. Normal Art Sch., 1895; student Cornell U., Harvard Ecole des Beaux Arts, Acad. Julian (Paris), 1901-02; m. Eva C. Earll, June 20, 1899; children—Ruth Earll, Roger Wellington; m. 2d, Edith Virginia Calista Spinney, Mar. 31, 1933. Faculty Cornell U., 1896-1904, 06-10, also Clark U., Boston U.; paintings in leading Am. art exhibits, life drawings of now extinct Ona and Yahgen Indians in permanent collection Smithsonian Inst., lectr. ednl. instns. and before learned socs. in U.S. and Eng. Leader expdns. and explorations in Africa, Near East, S.A., C.A., Tierra-del-Fuego and Patagonia; discovered sunken wreck of U.S. frigate Philadelphia in Tripoli Harbor, (sunk by Lt. Decatur 1804), 1904; also new Columbus date, 1915; now cons. to Stefansson Collection Baker Library, Dartmouth Coll., Hanover, N.H. Served mil. service Army of U.S., 34 yrs.; from pvt. to maj. Gen. Staff, World War I; commd. col., 1929, expert cons. M.I., World War II, 1943; ret. from Honorary Reserve, 1943. Member American Peace delegation, Paris, 1918, special military aide to Pres. Wilson; military observer and intelligence officer in Balkans and Near and Middle East, 1919. Twice was cited for D.S.M.; recipient Croix de Gueer (Greek); Medal for Bravery (Montenegro) and other U.S. and fgn. honors, including palms of French Acad. Fellow Royal Geog. society, Mil. Order World Wars (lion, life mem., d.s.m.), Order of Lafayette, Naval Inst., Cannon Hunters Assn.; Epsilon Alpha, Sigma Xi. Clubs: Ends of Earth, Explorers, Harvard Travelers. Author: The Gateway to the Sahara, 1909, 12; Tripoli in Barbary, 1911; Let'er Buck, 1921. Contbr. to ethnol. collections various museums and edns. instns. Records of expdns. to Tierra-del-Fuego and Patagonia (including the only song, speech and hand and footprint records extant of now extinct Ona and Yahgan Fuegian tribes) acquired by Stefanson Collections, Dartmouth Coll., 1960. Address: Dartmouth Coll., Hanover, N.H. Died Oct. 9, 1967.

FURNAS, CLIFFORD COOK, univ. pres., author; b. Sheridan, Ind., Oct. 24, 1900; s. Thomas Chalmers and Clara Evana (Spray) F.; B.S., Purdue U., 1922, D.Eng. (hon.), 1946; graduate work Carleton College, 1923-24; Ph.D., U. Mich., 1926, D.Eng., 1957; LL.D., Alfred U., 1958; D.Sc., Theil Coll., 1960; Dr. Honoris Causa, University de Paraguay, 1963; m. Sparkle Moore, Apr. 12, 1925; 1 daughter, Beatrice Louise. Teacher of mathematics, Shattuck School, 1922-24; research chemist with U.S. Steel Corp., 1924-25; phys. chemist with U.S. Bur. of Mines, 1926-31; asso. prof. of chem. engring., Yale U., 1931-42; tech. aide, Nat. Defense Research Com., 1941-43; director research, Curtiss-Wright Airplane Div. 1943-46; exec. v.p., Cornell Aeronautical Lab., 1946-54; now dir.; industrial cons.; chancellor University Buffalo, 1954-62, pres. State Univ. of New York at Buffalo, 1962-66, pres. emeritus, 1966-69; pres. Western N.Y. Nuclear Research Center; research asso. Bur. Ednl. Research in Science, summer, 1938; lectr. Bur. of Ednl. Research in Science for Tchrs. Coll., Columbia, summer, 1939. Research chem. engring. and metallurgy; chmn. guided missile com., Research and Development Bd., 1952-53; NACA, 1955-57; chmn. Air Navigation Devel. Bd., 1956-57; chmn. advisory panel on aeros. Dept. of Defense, 1954-55; asst. sec. of def. for research and devel. 1955-57; member of the science advisory panel of the United States Army; chairman New York Adv. Council Industrial Research and Devel., 1961-69; member Defense Science Board, 1957-69, chmn., 1961-65; mem. Naval Res. Adv. Com., 1958-69. Mem. board of directors of Carborundum Hooker Hooker Chem. Co., Mfrs. & Traders Trust Co., Aerospace Corp. Awarded Big 10 Conf. medal for best combined scholastic and athletic record, 1922; mem. 1920 Am. Olympic Team. Decorated gold cross Order of Phoenix (Greece); recipient Vincent Bendix award Am. Soc. Engring. Edn., 1956; Western N.Y. honor scroll Am. Inst. Chemists; gold medal Buffalo Club. Charles M. Schwab Meml. lectr., 1958; Schoellkopf medal, 1962; Fairchild award Arnold Air Soc., 1963; citation Nat. Conf. Christians and Jews, 1965; Chancellor's medal U. Buffalo, 1968. Fellow A.A.A.S., Inst. Aero. Scis. (hon. v.p.); mem. Am. Inst. Chem. Engrs., Nat. Acad. Engring., Am. Chem. Soc., Newcomen Soc., Sigma XI, Phi Beta Kappa, Tau Beta Pi, Phi Lambda Upsilon, Theta Chi. Clubs: Fort Orange (Albany, N.Y.); Chemists (New York); Buffalo, Buffalo Country, Saturn, Aero, Thursday, (Buffalo); Cosmos (Washington). Author: America's Tomorrow, 1932; The-Next Hundred Years, 1936; Man, Bread and Destiny, 1937; section on metallurgy in Technological Trends and National Policy, 1937; The Storehouse of Civilization, 1939; The Engineer, 1966; also author sects. on sci. in various publs. Editor: Roger's Manual of Industrial Chemistry, 1941; Industrial Research: Organization and Management, 1948. Contbr. sect. on sci. and technology Modern World Politics, 1953. Home: Buffalo NY Died Apr. 27, 1969; interred Memorial Chapel, Forest Lawn Cemetery, Buffalo NY

FURNESS, CAROLINE ELLEN, prof. astronomy; b. Cleveland, O., June 24, 1869; d. Henry Benjamin and Caroline Sarah (Baker) F.; A.B., Vassar, 1891; Ph.D., Columbia, 1900. Began as asst., Vassar Coll. Obs., promoted instr., asso. prof., and has been Alumnae Maria Mitchell prof., 1915—. Vol. research asst., Yerkes Obs., and research worker, Groningen, Holland. Unitarian. Author: Catalog of Stars Within 1 deg. of North Pole, 1900; Catalog of Stars Within 2 deg. of North Pole, 1906; Introduction to Study of Variable Stars, 1915. Editor Observations of Variable Stars Made at Vassar College (1901-12), 1913. Visited Japan, 1918-19, in interest of Am. and Japanese women, and organized Japan br. Asso. Coll. Alumnae, Travelled around world, 1926-27, visiting oriental scientific instns. Del. 3d Pan-Pacific Congress in Japan, 1926. Home: Poughkeepsie, N.Y. Died Feb. 9, 1936.

FURNESS, JAMES WILSON, mining engr.; b. Phila., Pa., June 5, 1874; s. Frank and Fannie (Fassitt) F.; prep. edn., William Penn Charter Ch., Phila., 1883-91; B.S., Pa. Mil. Coll. 1895, B.M.S., 1927; m. Adeline E. Brown, Oct. 25, 1899; 1 dau., Adeline Fassitt. Assayer and metallurgist in Colo., 1895-1900; asst. to D.M. Barringer, mining engr., Phila., in examining mining properties in Can., western U.S. and Mexico, 1904-08; operator of mines, 1908-09; asso. with O.A. Robertson in chge. mining properties in Can., Calif., Colo. and Nevada, also visited mines in Belgium, 1910-18; operated mines in Colo. and Ariz., 1919-22; investigated manganese situation in Georgia, Russia, 1920; with U.S. Bur. of Mines, 1922-26; chief of mineral div. U.S. Bur. Foreign and Domestic Commerce. Dept. of Commerce, 1927-34; chief of economics br. Bur. of Mines, 1934-40; retired. Served as officer Ordance Dept., U.S. Army, Aug. 1918-Jan. 15, 1919; lieut. colonel Special Res., U.S. Army, 1937; member Minerals Advisory Com. to War Dept.; mem. Mineral Policy Committee, 1935. Mem. Washington Geol. Soc. Dem. Unitarian. Clubs: Civitan, Down Town (Asheville). Author of many government publications on mineral economics. Home: 76 North Griffing Boulevard, Asheville NC

FURNISS, HENRY DAWSON, gynecologist; b. Selma, Ala., Mar. 25, 1878; s. John Perkins and Elizabeth Matthews (Dawson) F.; student U. of Ala., 1894-96, LL.D., 1928; M.D., U. of Va., 1899; m. Ruth Kellogg Pine, Nov. 18, 1912; children—Henry Dawson, James Pine, Warren Todd. Interne N.Y. Post-Grad. Hosp., 1894-1901; in practice of gynecology and urology, 1903—; prof. gynecology, N.Y. Post-Grad. Med. Sch., 1917-27; attending gynecologist N.Y. Post-Grad. Hosp., 1917-27, cons. gynecologist, 1927—; cons. gynecologist Broad St. Hosp., N.Y. City, St. Luke's Hosp., Newburgh, N.Y., Holy Name Hosp., Teaneck, N.J., Hackensack (N.J.) Hosp., All Souls Hosp., Morristown, N.J.; cons. cystoscopist N.Y. Infirmary for Women and Children; surgeon Flower-Fifth Av. and Metropolitan hosps., N.Y. City. Served as capt. Med. Corps, U.S. Army; chief surgeon Camp Hancock, 1918. Fellow Am. Coll. Surgeons. Home: New York, N.Y. Died Jan. 25, 1942.

FURRER, RUDOLPH, consultant; born Union City, N.J., Apr. 14, 1893; s. Rudolph and Bertha (Hardmeier) F.; ed. in pub. schs., Union City; m. Leone Barbara Peters, Oct. 19, 1921; children—John Rudolph, Barbara Christine. With Allis-Chalmers Mfg. Co., Milwaukee, 1907-17; mech. engr., chief of field inspection, and purchasing engr. A.O. Smith Corp., Milwaukee, 1918-26, chief engr. and dir. research, 1926-32; asst. to vice presidents Nat. Tube Co., Pittsburgh, 1933-35; v.p. A. O. Smith Corp., Milwaukee, 1936-47; became v.p. American Car and Foundry Co., N.Y.C., 1947, formerly pres. Nuclear Energy Products div., pres. Advanced Products div.; v.p., dir. ACF Industries Inc., until 1959; mgmt. cons., 1959-60; spl. asst. to dir. def., research and engring., Washington, 1960; sr. cons. Lockheed Missile & Space Co., 1961-62. Member of Committee on Ordnance, Joint Research and Development Board, Washington. Served with Aviation Division, United States Naval Reserve Forces, World War I; member War Metallurgy Com., 1943-45; spl. cons. Army Ordnance Research Com., 1944-45. Awarded certificate of appreciation, Bureau of Ordnance, U.S. Navy, 1946, Ordnance Dept., U.S. War Dept., 1945. Mem. Am. Ordnance Assn. Republican. Unitarian. Mason. Clubs: Milwaukee, Milwaukee University; Oconomowoc (Wis.) Lake; Rockefeller Center Luncheon. Helped develop mass prodn. auto frames with 1st automatic auto frame system, 1920s; major role in develop. flash welding large diameter pipes; supr. design and constrn. A. O. Smith Bldg., Milw. Home: 1000 Harbor Rd., Southport, Conn. Died Jan. 19, 1965; buried Wisconsin Meml. Park, Milw.

FUSSELL, LEWIS, prof. electric engring.; b. Media, Pa., Apr. 22, 1882; s. Henry Moore and Mary (Townsend) F.; grad. Friends' Central Sch., Phila., 1899; B.S., Swarthmore Coll., 1902, M.S., 1903; E.E., and Ph.D., U. of Wis., 1907; m. Margaret Hardy Lewis, Dec. 28, 1907; children—Lewis, Morris Hardy. Joshua Lippincott fellow, Swarthmore Coll., 1905-06; with Swarthmore Coll., 1907—, prof. electric engring. and head of dept., 1920--; has served, summers and part time, with Gen. Electric Co., Bell Telephone Co. of Pa., Phila. Electric Co., Westinghouse Electric & Mfg. Co., United Gas Improvement Co., R.C.A. Victor Co., electrolysis surveys, cons. elec. engineer. Republican. Mem. Soc. of Friends. Author: The Self Excited Polyphase Asynchronous Generator, 1907. Home: Swarthmore, Pa. Died July 15, 1935.

FUSSELL, M(ILTON) HOWARD, physician; b. Belvidere, Pa., Nov. 24, 1855; s. Milton and Tamar (Haldeman) F.; ed. Friends' Central Sch., Phila., until 1872; U. of Pa. med. dept., 1875-76; taught pub. sch., Radnor, Pa., 1876-81; U. of Pa., 1881-84, grad. M.D., 1884; m. Sarah E. Entwisle, May 3, 1884. Entered pvt. practice, Manayunk, Phila., July 1884; in fall of 1884, apptd. asst. in med. dispensary, U. of Pa., later instr. clin. medicine and phys.-in-chief, med. dispensary, and asst. phys. to hosp., and asst. prof. medicine, 1901—, consultant to med. dispensary, 1909—, phys. to hosp., and asst. prof. medicine, 1901, consultant to medical dispensary, 1909—; mem. council of Med. School, U. of Pa., 1904—; prof. applied therapeutics, June 1911—, U. of Pa. Phys. and dir. pathol. lab., St. Thimothy's Hosp.; phys. to Episcopal and Chestnut Hill hosps. Mem. Soc. of Friends. Republican. Editor: Tyson's Practice of

Medicine. Author of Differential Diagnosis of Internal Diseases, in Monographic Medicine. Home: Philadelphia, Pa. Died Oct. 15, 1921.

FUTCHER, THOMAS BARNES, M.D.; b. St. Thomas, Ont., Jan. 1, 1871; s. Thomas and Susan (Northwood) F.; ed. Ontario pub. schs.; grad. U. of Toronto Med. Sch., 1893; house officer, Toronto Gen. Hosp., 1893-94; asst. resident physician, 1894-98, resident physician, 1898-1901, Johns Hopkins Hosp., Baltimore; student U. of Graz, Austria, 1896, U. of Strassburg, 1898; m. Gwendolyn Marjorie Howard, Nov. 24, 1909. Inst. medicine, 1896-97, asso., 1897-1901, asso. prof. medicine, 1901-14, asso. prof. clinical medicine, 1914-32, asso. prof. medicine, 1932—, Johns Hopkins U.; visiting physician, Johns Hopkins Hospital; chief consultant in medicine, Johns Hopkins Dispensary; cons. practice in internal medicine, Baltimore. Episcopalian. Lt. col. Canadian Army Med. Corps and in charge of med. div. of No. 16, Canadian Gen. Hosp., Orpington, Kent, Eng., Sept. 1917-Apr. 1918. Home: Guilford, Baltimore, Md. Died Feb. 25, 1938.

GABB, WILLIAM MORE, paleontogologist; b. Phila., Jan. 20, 1839; s. Joseph H. and Christiana Gabb; B.A., Central High Sch., 1857; studied with James Hall, Albany, N.Y., 1857-60; became mem. Acad. Natural Scis., 1860; paleontologist Geol. Survey cal., 1861-67, classified cretaceous, tertiary fossils; recognized as Am.'s leading expert on cretaceous marine paleontology (at age 22); made report on area of Lower Cal., made geol. map which gave true structure on Mexican peninsula, 1867; made topog. and geol. survey of Santo Domingo, 1868-71, Province of Talamanca (for Costa Rica), 1873-76; mem. Nat. Acad. Scis. Author: sects. 1, 4 of 1st vol., and entire 2d vol. of Whitney's Geological Survey of California, 1864; On the Topography and Geological Survey of San Domingo, 1873; On the Indian Tribes and Languages of Costa Rica, 1876; also monographs, papers on gen. paleontol. studies. Died Phila., May 30, 1878.

GAENSLEN, FREDERICK JULIUS, orthopedic surgeon; b. Milwaukee, Wis., Dec. 7, 1877; s. Julius and Mathilda (Hummel) G.; B.S., U. of Wis., 1899; M.D., Johns Hopkins, 1903; student summer sch., Harvard, 1901; m. Clara F. Schock, June 17, 1909; children—Eleanor Flora, Gustave Frederick. Interne, German Hosp. (now Lennox Hill Hosp.), N.Y. City, 1903-06; gen. practice, Milwaukee, 1906-12; specializing in orthopedic surgery, 1912—; orthopedic surgeon Milwaukee Children's Hosp., Milwaukee Hosp., Columbia Hosp.; asso. prof. orthopedic surgery, Marquette U., 1918; prof. orthopedic surgery, U. of Wis., 1925—. Home: Milwaukee, Wis. Died Mar. 11, 1937.

GAERTNER, WILLIAM, instrument maker; b. Merseburg, Germany, Oct. 24, 1864; s. Karl and Louise (Pippel) G.; ed. pub. sch. and Tech. Sch. for Instrument Makers, Berlin; m. Belva Eleanora Boosinger, June 14, 1917. Apprentice in instrument shop, Halle, at 16; worked for various firms in Germany, later in London, and Vienna; came to U.S., 1889, naturalized citizen, 1896; instrument maker for Coast and Geodetic Survey, 1890-93; with Smithsonian Instn., 1893-96; opened shop in Chicago, Ill., 1896, later William Gaertner & Co. and since 1924, Gaertner Scientific Corp., of which is pres. and treas.; mfr. of the "interferometer," for Prof. Albert A. Michelson; the photographic zenith tube, for the Internat. Geodetic Assn., to determine variations of latitude, etc.; has practically solved the problem of eliminating error in accurate precision screws. Awarded Howard N. Potts gold medal, "for notable achievements as a designer and maker of scientific instruments," by the Franklin Inst., 1924. Mem. Am. Astron. Soc., Army Ordnance Assn., Chicago, Assn. Commerce. Lutheran. Club: Press. Active in developing new instruments and improving old designs for U.S. Air Corps. Home: 115 Garrison St., Wilmette, Ill. Office: 1201 Wrightwood Av., Chicago, Ill. Died Dec. 3, 1948. *

GAGE, HOMER, surgeon; b. Worcester, Mass., Oct. 18, 1861; s. Thomas Hovey and Annie M. (Lane) G.; A.B., Harvard U., 1882, A.M., M.D., 1887; Dr. Engring., Worcester Poly. Inst., 1929; LL.D., Clark U., 1937; m. Mabel Reynolds Knowles, June 15, 1893. Cons. surgeon Worcester City and St. Vincent's hosps.; retired. Pres. Crompton & Knowles Loom Works. Commd. major, Med. R.C., 1917, lt. col., 1919. Trustee and treas. Worcester Poly Inst.; pres. bd. trustees Memorial Hosp.; pres. Community Chest of Worcester. Fellow Am. Surg. Assn., Am. Coll. of Surgeons. Comdr. Legion of Honor (France); v.p. Conseil d'Administration de Fondation des États Unis, U. of Paris. Home: Worcester, Mass. Died July 3, 1938.

GAGE, SIMON HENRY, biologist; b. Otsego County, N.Y., May 20, 1851; s. Henry V. and Lucy (Grover) G.; B.S., Cornell U., 1877; studied in Europe, 1889; m. Susanna Phelps, Dec. 15, 1881 (died Oct. 5, 1915); 1 son, Henry Phelps; m. 2d, Clara C. Starrett, Apr. 14, 1933. Instructor, 1878-81, asst. prof., 1881-89, asso. prof. physiology, 1889-93, asso. prof. anatomy, histology and embryology, 1893-95, prof., 1895-96, prof. histology and embryology, 1896-1908, Cornell; apptd. prof. histology and embryology, emeritus, June 1908, after 25 yrs'. service to undertake spl. investigations, on an allowance from Carnegie Foundation for the Advancement of Teaching; resumed teaching, 1918-19, to take place of instrs. who entered military service. Co-editor Am. Jour. Anatomy, 1901-21; pres. Comstock Publishing Co., Inc., 1932-44. Chmn. section embryology, Internat. Congress Arts and Sciences, St. Louis, 1904; fellow A.A.A.S. (v.p., 1885, 1892, 1899); mem. Assn. Am. Anatomists, Am. Soc. Naturalists, Am. Micros. Soc., Am. Soc. Zoölogists, Am. Soc. of Amateur Microscopists (pres. 1939), Royal Soc. of Arts, London. Mem. advisory bd. Wistar Inst. Anatomy since 1905; trustee Cornell U., 1921-22. Author: The Microscope and Microscopic Methods, 17th Edit., 1941; History of Microscopy in America, 1943 (in manuscript); Anatomical Technology (with Prof. Burt G. Wilder); Optic Projection with the Magic Lantern, the Reflecting Lantern, the Projection Microscope, and the Moving Picture Machine (with Henry Phelps Gage, Ph.D.), 1913-14; also numerous papers on biol. subjects; collaborator or contbr. to Foster's Encyclopaedie Medical Dictionary, Wood's Reference Handbook of the Medical Sciences, Johnson's Cyclopedia. Editor and contbr. Record of the Class of 1877, Cornell U., 1923; librarian Van Cleef Memorial Library, Cornell U., 1921-40; life sec. Class of 1877, Cornell. Home: Interlaken, N.Y. Office: Stimson Hall, Ithaca, N.Y. Died Oct. 20, 1944; buried at Worcester, Otsego County, N.Y.

GAGEL, EDWARD, civil engr.; b. Mt. Hope, N.Y., Oct. 25, 1858; s. Christian J. and Anna M. (Aulinger) G.; ed. Cooper Inst., New York; m. Jennie Field Smith, Oct. 14, 1885. Began with Dennis & Mairs, civ. engrs., New York, 1876; draftsman and engr. in charge constrn., Brooklyn, Flatbush & Coney Island R.R., 1877-79; draftsman and asst. engr. in charge constrn., Met. Elevated R.R., N.Y. City, 1879-80; draftsman West Side & Yonkers Ry., Jan.-Mar. 1880; leveler, draftsman and on constrn. extension to Hudson River, of N.Y.&N.E. R.R., 1880-82; transit man on location Erie & Wyo. Valley R.R., Jan.-July 1882; contractor's engr. on constrn. Pittsburgh, McKeesport & Youghiogheny R.R., July-Sept. 1882; draftsman, N.Y.C.&H.R. R.R., Sept.-Dec. 1882; with N.Y.,N.H.&H. R.R., 1882-1929, successively draftsman, engr. in charge constrn., div. engr., prin. asst. engr., dist. engr. and chief engr., 1905-29. Conglist. Home: West Haven, Conn. Died Feb. 11, 1931.

GAGER, C(HARLES) STUART, botanist; b. Norwich, N.Y., Dec. 23, 1872; s. Charles Carroll and Leora Josephine (Darke) G.; A.B., Syracuse U., 1895; Pd.B. and Pd.M., N.Y. State Normal Coll., Albany, 1897; Harvard summer, 1898; Ph.D., Cornell U., 1902; D.Sc., Syracuse, 1920; Pd.D., N.Y. State Coll. for Teachers, 1921; m. Bertha Woodward Bagg, June 25, 1902; children—Benjamin Stuart (dec.), Ruth Prudence (Mrs. Kenneth G. Bucklin). Laboratory asst., Syracuse U., 1894-95; vice-principal, Ives Sem., Antwerp, N.Y., 1895-96; prof. biol. sciences and physiography, N.Y. State Normal Coll., 1897-1905; dir. labs., N.Y. Bot. Garden, 1906-08; prof. botany, U. of Mo., 1908-10; dir. Brooklyn Botanic Garden since 1910. Asst. in botany, 1901-02, instr., 1904, Summer Sch., Cornell; lab. asst., N.Y. Bot. Garden, 1904-05; acting prof. botany, Rutgers Coll., 1905; teacher botany, Morris High School, New York, 1905; prof. botany, summer session, New York U., 1905-06. Editor Brooklyn Botanic Garden Record since 1912; bus. mgr. Am. Jour. Botany, 1914-35, Ecology since 1920, Genetics since 1922. Mem. com. on plant quarantines and their adminstrn. of Merchants Assn. of N.Y. City since 1922, chmn. since 1933; mem. com. on bot. exhibits, A Century of Progress, Chicago, 1933; v.p. Hortus, Inc. (hort. section, N.Y. World's Fair, 1939, 40): mem. various commns. Nat. Research Council; chmn. sub-com. on edn. and public relations, U.S. Botanic Garden; mem. and dir. Corp. of Bermuda Biological Station for Research; member board directors N.J. Federation of Shade Tree Commissions; trustee Adelphi College, 1932-40. Honorary life mem. Pa. Hort. Soc.; fellow A.A.A.S. (v.p. and chmn. of Sect. G, 1917), N.Y. Acad. Sciences, Brooklyn Inst. Arts and Sciences; mem. Bot. Soc. America (pres. 1936), Soc. Exptl. Biology and Medicine, Torrey Bot. Club (sec. 1905-08; v.p. 1911, 1917-31), Am. Soc. of Biol. Chemists, Am. Soc. Naturalists, Nat. Inst. Social Sciences (vice pres. 1928-31 and since 1935; pres. 1932-35), Sch. Garden Assn. America (hon.), Horticultural Soc. of N.Y. (vice chmn. board since 1937), Internat. Flower Show Commn. since 1932; N.J. Federation of Shade Tree Commissions since 1934; Svenska Linné Sällskapet, Société Linnéene de Lyon, Royal New Zealand Inst. of Horticulture, Phi Beta Kappa, Sigma Xi, Delta Upsilon, Gamma Sigma Delta. Clubs: Century, N.Y. Bird and Tree Club (dir.), Twentieth Century of Brooklyn (pres. 1933-35). Author: Errors in Science Teaching, 1901; Effects of the Rays of Radium on Plants, 1908; Fundamentals of Botany, 1916; Laboratory Guide for General Botany, 1916; Heredity and Evolution in Plants, 1920; The Relation between Science and Theology, 1925; General Botany with Special Reference to Its Economic Aspects, 1926; The Plant World, 1931; also numerous papers in scientific and ednl. jours. Abstractor Biol. Abstracts, 1926-31; bot. editor and contbr. Nat. Cyclo., 1932. Contbr. Ency. Brittanica, Standard Cyclo. Horticulture, Cyclo. Edn. Translator: (from the German of de Vries) Intracellular Pangenesis, 1910. Home: 29 Linden Blvd., Brooklyn, N.Y. Died Aug. 9, 1943.

GAILLARD, EDWIN SAMUEL, surgeon, editor; b. Charleston S.C., Jan. 16, 1827; grad. S.C. Coll. (now U.S.C.), 1845; M.D., Med. Coll. State of S.C., Charleston M.A. (hon.) also LL.D. (hon.), U.N.C., 1873; m. Jane Marshall Thomas, 1856; m. 2nd, Mary Elizabeth Gibson, 1865; 4 children. Practiced medicine, Fla., 1855-57; after trip to Europe settled in Balt., 1861; became asst. surgeon 1st M. Regt., Confederate Army, 1861; mem. examining bd. Army of Va., 1861; lost right arm at Battle of Seven Pines, 1862; apptd. mem. dir. mil. hosps., Va. and N.C., 1862, insp. gen. Confederate hosps., 1863-65; prof. principles and practice medicine and gen. pathology Med. Coll. Va., Richmond, 1865; founded Richmond Med. Journal (changed name to Richmond and Louisville Med. Journal 1868), publisher, 1865-79; prof. medicine Ky. Sch. Medicine, 1868; an organizer, 1st dean, prof. gen. medicine and pathology Louisville (Ky.) Med. Coll., 1869; established Am. Med. Weekly, Louisville, 1874, editor, 1874-83; moved to N.Y.C., 1879; published Gaillard's Med. Jour., until 1883. Author numerous papers including Ozone: Its Relation to Health and Disease (received Fiske Fund prize 1861), essay on diphtheria (received Ga. Med. Assn. prize 1866). Died Feb. 1885.

GAINES, EDWARD FRANKLIN, prof. genetics in agronomy; b. Avalon, Mo., Jan. 12, 1886; s. Charles Samuel and Mattie (Millay) G.; grad. State Normal Sch., Cheney, Wash., 1907; B.S., State Coll. of Wash., 1911, M.S., 1913; Sc.D., Harvard, 1921; m. Xerpha McCulloch, June 6, 1912; children—Edward McCulloch, Xerpha Mae, John Charles, Irene (dec.), Grant Robert. Instr. in agronomy, State Coll. of Wash., 1911-17, asst. prof. farm crops, 1917-21, asso. prof., 1921-30, prof. genetics in agronomy since 1930; cerealist, Washington Expt. Station, since 1917. Fellow A.A.A.S., Am. Soc. Agronomy; mem. Am. Phytopathol. Soc., Am. Bot. Soc., Northwest Scientific Assn. (pres. 1939), Alpha Gamma Rho, Alpha Zeta, Phi Kappa Phi, Phi Beta Kappa, Sigma Xi. Contbr. agrl. publs. Home: Pullman, Wash. Died Aug. 17, 1944.

GAINES, PASCHAL CLAY, educator, chemist; b. St. John, Wash., Mar. 7, 1898; s. Robert Bruce and Anna (Hamilton) G.; B.S., Washington State Coll., 1919, M.S., 1931; m. Blanche B. Henry, Mar. 10, 1919 (dec. Aug. 1954); children—Jeanne (Mrs. D. L. Wood), Gladys (Mrs. K. A. Eggensperger), Janice (Mrs. C. F. Fox), Jack, Robert; m. 2d, Mrs. Vina Ruth Denever, Feb. 21, 1956. Worked as a chemist Three Forks Portland Cement Company, Hanover, Montana, 1919-23; assistant chief chemist, Cowell Portland Cement Co., Cowell, Calif., 1923; mem. faculty Mont. State Coll. since 1923, prof. chemistry since 1941, head, dept. chemistry, 1946-57, v.p., 1945—, acting president 1951-53, dean faculty 1954—. Mem. Am. Chem. Society, Chem. Soc. London, Sigma Xi, Phi Kappa Phi, Lambda Chi Alpha, Alpha Chi Sigma, Fangs. Club: Kiwanis (past pres.). Author: Introduction to Modern Chemistry (with L. O. Binder and R. A. Woodriff), 1951; Experiments in General Chemistry (with L. O. Binder, R. A. Woodriff, A. R. Johansson), 1951. Home: 411 W. Koch St., Bozeman, Mont. Deceased Oct. 9, 1966; buried Sunset Hills Cemetery.

GAINEY, PERCY LEIGH, bacteriologist; b. Fayetteville, N.C., March 9, 1887; s. Abraham and Amelia (McNab) G.; B.S., N.C. State Coll., 1908, M.S., 1910; A.M., Washington Univ., 1911, Ph.D., 1926; m. Grace Trueman Deaton, Dec. 25, 1913; children—Janis Leigh, Phillip McNab. Teacher U. of Mo., 1911-14; teacher, Kan. State Coll., Manhattan, head dept. bacteriology 1946-57, soil bacteriologist, Kan. Agrl. Expt. Sta., 1914-57. Received Chilean Nitrate Ednl. award for research in soil sci., 1929. Mem. Kan. Acad. of Sci., Soc. Am. Bacteriologists, Phi Kappa Phi, Sigma Xi, Gamma Alpha, Gamma Sigma Delta, Alpha Zeta. Author books, latest: Biology in Relation to Man (with H.H. Haymaker, E. J. Wimmer, M. J. Harbaugh), 1945; Microbiology of Water and Sewage (with Thomas H. Lord), 1952; Laboratory Manual for Microbiology of Water and Sewage (with Thomas H. Lord), 1952; Fundamentals of Biology (with others), 1953; Basic Bacteriology Laboratory Manual (with Thomas H. Lord and W. A. Miller), 1953; also sci. and tech. papers. Address: Manhattan KA Died Oct. 1972.

GALE, ARTHUR SULLIVAN, mathematician; b. Appleton, Wis., June 26, 1877; s. Rev. Sullivan French and Elizabeth Taylor (Felt) G.; B.A., Yale, 1899, Ph.D., 1901; m. Mary Cotton-Walker Tuke, June 29, 1901; children—Marland, Arthur, Polly Anne; m. 2d, Katharine Bowen, June 26, 1939. Instructor mathematics, Yale, 1901-05; asst. prof. of mathematics, 1905-06, Fayerweather prof., 1906-45, freshman dean, 1921-36, dean Coll. for Men, 1936-39, Univ. of Rochester. Member Nat. Institute Social Sciences, Am. Math. Society, Am. Math. Assn., A.A.A.S., Phi Beta Kappa, Sigma Xi. Author: (Smith and Gale) Elements of Analytic Geometry, 1905; (same) Introduction to Analytic Geometry, 1905; (Gale and Watkeys) Elementary Functions, 1920. Home: 93 Bellevue Drive, Rochester 7 NY

GALE, BENJAMIN, physician, author; b. Jamaica, L.I., N.Y., Dec. 14, 1715; s. John and Mary Gale; M.A., Yale, 17; studied medicine and surgery with Dr. Jared Eliot; m. Hannah Eliot, June 6, 1739, 8 children. Began practice of medicine, Killingworth, Conn., circa 1739, became highly respected for abilities as physician; mem. Conn. Gen. Assembly, 1747-67; helped devise the Am. Turtle (a depth bomb); Author: The Present State of the Colony of Connecticut Considered, 1755; Historical Memoirs, Relating to the Practice of Inoculation for the Small Pox, in the British American Provinces, Particularly in New England, 1765; A Brief Essay, or, An Attempt to Prove, from the Prophetick Writings of the Old and New Testaments, What Period of Prophecy the Church of God is Now Under (his chief theol. work), 1788. Died Killingworth, Conn., May 6, 1790; buried Conn.

GALE, HENRY GORDON, physicist; b. Aurora, Ill., Sept. 12, 1874; s. Eli Holbrook and Adelaide (Parker) G.; A.B., U. of Chicago, 1896, grad. student, 1896-97, fellow in physics, 1897-99, Ph.D., 1899; m. Agnes Spofford Cook, Jan. 5, 1901; 1 dau., Beatrice Gordon. Asst. in physics, 1899-1900, asso., 1900-02, instr., 1902-07, asst. prof., 1907-11, asso. prof. physics, 1911-16, prof., 1916-40, dean in Junior Colls., 1908-40, dean of science in the Colls., 1912-40, dean of Ogden Grad. Sch. Science, 1922, chmn. dept. of physics, 1925, dean div. of phys. sciences, 1931, emeritus, Univ. of Chicago. Physicist, Solar Observatory, Mt. Wilson, Calif., 1906; research associate of Carnegie Inst. at Mt. Wilson, 1909, 10, 11; editor Astrophys. Jour. since 1912. Capt. of Inf., N.A., 1917; maj. Sig. Corps, Jan. 1918, lt. col., Mar. 1919; in charge spl. service div., Tours, France, 1918-19. Cited by comdr.-in-chief A.E.F. for "especially meritorious and conspicuous service"; Chevalier Legion of Honor, France. Mem. bd. John Crerar Library. Fellow A.A.A.S. (v.p. 1934), Am. Physical Soc. (v.p. 1927-29; pres. 1929-31), Am. Optical Society; mem. Delta Kappa Epsilon, Sigma Xi and Gamma Alpha fraternities. Clubs: Quadrangle, Wayfarers, University, Lake Zurich (Ill.) Golf. Republican. Author: (with R. A. Millikan) A First Course in Physics, 1906; A Laboratory Course in Physics, 1906; Practical Physics, 1920; Elements of Physics, 1926; (with R. A. Millikan and C. W. Edwards) A First Course in College Physics, 1928. Vice chmn. div. of phys. sciences, Nat. Research Council, 1920-21, chmn., 1921-22. Home: 5646 Kimbark Av., Chicago, Ill. Died Nov. 16, 1942.

GALE, HOYT STODDARD, geologist; b. Cleveland, O., Dec. 9, 1876; s. George Rodney and Helen Maria (Richardson) G.; A.B., Harvard, 1900, S.B., 1902; m. Almira Miller, June 18, 1902; 1 son, Hoyt Rodney. Asst. Geologist, U.S. Geol. Survey, 1902-10, geologist since 1910; in charge section of non-metalliferous deposits, 1912-20; chief geologist of the various foreign subsidiaries of Gulf Oil Corp., 1921-23; in charge Gulf Co.'s operations in Calif. and on Pacific Coast, 1923-29; survey oil possibilities S. Africa, 1938-39; now geologist in cons. practice. Fellow Geol. Society America (mem. of council 1937-39), Soc. Economic Geologists, A.A.A.S. Unitarian. Author of U.S. Geol. Survey bulletins on coal fields, of northwestern Colorado, borax, potash and nitrate deposits in the U.S., and miscellaneous contbrns. on geologic subjects, including Geology of Southern California, guidebook for 16th Internat. Geological Congress, 1933, Geology of the Kramer borate deposits, Calif., 1945, etc. Home: 1775 Hill Drive, Eagle Rock, Los Angeles 41, Cal. Died July 6, 1952.

GALLANT, ALBERT ERNEST, surgeon; b. June 27, 1861; s. Rev. Walter and Sarah (Horsley) G.; common sch., edn.; M.D., Coll. Phys. and Surg. (Columbia), 1890; interne Sloane Maternity Hosp., 1891, New York Cancer Hosp., 1892; m. Eudora Milroy Elliott, Jan. 1, 1895; m. 2d, Mary Claire Parsons, June 14, 1920. Instr. surgery, N.Y. Post-Grad. Med. Sch., 1894-96, N.Y. Polyclinic Med. Sch. and Hosp., 1897-99; asst. surgeon, Lebanon Hosp., 1894-95; med. dir. Miss Helen Gould's War Relief Assn. and Soldiers' Comfort Com., 1898; prof. gynecology, N.Y. Sch. Clin. Medicine, 1901-06; was attending gynecologist, McDougal Mem. Hosp., Metropolitan Hosp. and Dispensary, and cons. surgeon Bapt. Deaconess Home and Training Sch., Jamaica Hosp., and Eastern L.I. Hosp.; asst. surgeon, Med. Reserve Corps U.S.N.; operating surgeon 1st Gen. (mil.) Hosp., Birmingham, Eng., 1917-18. Republican. Home: Sarasota, Fla. Deceased.

GALLATIN, (ABRAHAM ALFONSE) ALBERT, senator, U.S. sec. of treasury; b. Geneva, Switzerland, Jan. 29, 1761; s. Jean and Sophie Albertine (Rolaz) G.; grad. Geneva Acad., 1779; m. Sophie Allegre, 1789; m. 2d, Hannah Nicholson, 1793; at least 2 sons, Albert, Francis. Came to U.S., 1780; tutor French, Harvard, 1781; leader of settlers to Western Pa., 1784; mem. Harrisburg Conf. to revise U.S. Constn., 1788; mem. Pa. Constl. Conv., 1789; mem. Pa. Ho. of Reps. from Fayette County, 1790-93, instrumental in establishing state system of publ. edn., proposed establishment of state paper money and a Bank of Pa.; chiefly responsible for quelling Whiskey Rebellion of 1794 (thus preventing civil war in Pa.); mem. U.S. Ho. of Reps. from Pa., 4th-6th congresses, 1795-1801, Republican minority leader, caused creation of standing com. on finance (now ways and means com.); U.S. sec. treasury under Jefferson and Madison, 1801-14, favored natural growth of industry, opposed excessive govt. taxation, reduced mil. appropriations and public debt, believed that Fed. money should be used to further an expanding internal economy; changed policies when they became unpopular during War of 1812, revived internal taxes visited St. Petersburg (Russia) to attempt to secure Russian mediation to end war with Eng., 1813; peace commr. to Eng. negotiating Treaty of Ghent, 1814, concluded (with Adams and Clay) favorable comml. treaty with British, 1815; U.S. minister to France, 1815-23, to Eng., 1826-27; pres. Nat. (later Gallatin) Bank of N.Y.C.; a founder, 1st pres. council U. City N.Y. (now N.Y.U.), 1831; founder Am. Ethnol. Soc., 1842; pres. N.Y. Hist. Soc., 1843. Author: Considerations on the Currency and Banking System of the United States, 1831; Memorial of the Committee Appointed by the "Free Trade Convention" Held in Philadelphia in . . . 1831, published 1832. Died Astoria, L.I., N.Y., Aug. 12, 1849; buried Trinity Churchyard, N.Y.C.

GALLAUDET, BERN BUDD, surgeon; b. New York, N.Y., Feb. 11, 1860; s. Thomas (D.D.) and Elizabeth (Budd) G.; A.B., Trinity Coll., Conn., 1880, A.M., 1883; M.D., Coll. Phys. and Surg. (Columbia), 1884; interne New York Hosp., 1884-86; student medicine, Vienna, 1886-87; m. Elise G., d. late Col. William A. Elderkin, U.S.A., June 4, 1894. Engaged in practice of surgery, 1887-1909; surgeon to Vanderbilt clinic, 1888-90; asst. demonstrator anatomy, 1887-91, clin. lecturer on surgery, 1890-97, demonstrator anatomy, 1891-1905, instr. surgery, 1897-1909, asst. prof. anatomy, 1905-29, asso. prof., 1929—, Coll. Phys. and Surg.; visiting surgeon, 1890-1909, cons. surgeon, 1909—, Bellevue Hosp., N.Y. City. Author: Surgery, Quiz Compends, 1892. Editor: Gray's Anatomy, 1897. Died Mar. 30, 1934.

GALLOWAY, BEVERLY THOMAS, botanist; b. Millersburg, Mo., Oct. 16, 1863; s. Robert M. and Jane (McCray) G.; B.Agr.Sc., U. of Mo., 1884, LL.D., 1902; m. Agnes S. Rankin, Sept. 5, 1888; children—Robert Rankin, Alexander Gordon, Beverly Stewart. Asst. in hort. dept., U. of Mo., 1884-86; asst. pathologist, 1887-88, pathologist and chief Div. Vegetable Pathology and Physiology, 1888-1900, chief Bur. Plant Industry, 1901-12; asst. sec. of agr., U.S., 1913-14; dean State Coll. Agr., Cornell U., 1914-16; pathologist, Office Foreign Plant Introduction of U.S. Dept. Agr., 1916-33; now collaborator U.S. Dept. of Agriculture. Home: Takoma Park, D.C. Died June 13, 1938.

GALLOWAY, J(ESSE) J(AMES), educator; b. Cromwell, Ind., Aug. 23, 1882; s. George and Mary (Archer) G.; A.B., Ind. U., 1909, A.M., 1911, Ph.D., 1913; m. Clara Beswick Davis, Sept. 14, 1913; 1 dau., Priscilla Sarah (Mrs. P. T. Sgro). Tchr. Ligonier (Ind.) High Sch., 1909-10; instr. geology Ind. U., 1913-16, curator paleontology, 1916-17, instur. 1917-21, asst. prof., 1921-31, prof. geology and paleontology, since 1931; asso. prof. Columbia U., 1931; instr. and br. head geology Biarritz Am. U., U.S. Army U., 1945-46. Field asst. U.S. Geol. Survey, 1907, 1908, 10, 14; cons. geologist for Tenn., N.Y., Ind., Mex.; cons. geologist and research micro-paleontologist for petroleum cos., summers 1915-49. Fellow Geol. Soc. Am., Paleontology Soc. Am. (v.p. 1931), A.A.A.S., Ind. Acad. Sci.; mem. Am. Assn. Petroleum Geol., Soc. Econ-Paleontologists and Mineralogists (pres. 1927), Sigma Xi, Phi Beta Kappa, Sigma Gamma Epsilon. Corr. etranger Soc. Geol. de France. Author: A Manual of Foraminifera, 1933, Tertiary Foraminifera of Porto Rico (with Caroline E. Heminway), 1941. Contbr. articles on geology and paleontology to prof. jours. Home: 420 E. 6th St., Bloomington, Ind. Died Apr. 10, 1962; buried Rose Hill Cemetery, Bloomington.

GALLOWAY, THOMAS WALTON, biologist; b. Columbia, Tenn., Nov. 2, 1866; s. William T. and Elizabeth Rebecca (Smith) G.; A.B., Cumberland U., Tenn., 1887, A.M., 1889, Ph.D., 1892; A.M., Harvard, 1890; m. Mary L. Armstrong, Dec. 22, 1892; 1 dau., Mrs. Elizabeth Joan Woods. Prof. natural history, Baird Coll., Clinton, Mo., 1887-89; grad. student, Harvard, 1889-91; prof. biology, 1891-1902, dean, 1899-1902, Mo. Valley Coll.; prof. biology James Millikin U., Decatur, Ill., 1902-15; prof. zoölogy, Beloit (Wis.) Coll., 1915-19; asso. dir. Dept. of Edn., Am. Social Hygiene Assn., 1919—. On leave of absence at Harvard, 1897-98, won Bowdoin prize. Sec. Am. Micros. Soc. and editor Quarterly Transactions; fellow A.A.A.S. Author: Biology of Sex for Parents and Teachers; Reproduction, 1916; Motivation in Moral Education; Sex and Life, 1919; Sex Factor in Human Life; The Father and His Boy; The Dramatic Instinct in Religious Education; Sex and Social Health; Love and Marriage; Parenthood and the Character Education of Children, etc. Home: New York, N.Y. Died July 16, 1929.

GALLUP, JOSEPH ADAMS, physician; b. Stonington, Conn., Mar. 30, 1769; s. William and Lucy (Denison) G.; M.D., Dartmouth, 1798; m. Abigail Willard, Sept. 1792. Active in formation of med. socs. including Vt. Med. Soc., 1813, pres., 1818-29; prof. theory and practice of medicine Vt. Acad. Medicine 1821-25, pres. corp., 1822; prof. materia medica med. sch. Burlington, Vt., 1825; founded a clinical sch. of medicine, Woodstock, Vt., 1827; published Domestic Medical and Dietetical Monitor or Journal of Health, 1815. Author: Sketches of Epidemic Diseases in the State of Vermont, 1815; Pathological Reflections on the Supertonic State of Disease, 1822; Outlines of the Institutes of Medicine, 1839. Died Woodstock, Oct. 12, 1849.

GAMBEL, WILLIAM, ornithologist; b. N.J., circa 1819. Protege of Thomas Nuttall (for whom he named Nuttall's woodpecker 1843); crossed continent via Santa Fe Trail, 1841, then went with Workman party over Mormon Trail to Cal.; his writings are most important of early works on birds of Cal.; Gambel's quail named in his honor. Died of typhoid fever on Feather River, Cal., Dec. 1849.

GAMBLE, JAMES LAWDER, pediatrician; b. Millersburg, Ky., July 18, 1883; s. Edwin and Elizabeth (Lawder) G.; A.B., Stanford U., 1906; M.D., Harvard U. Med. Sch., 1910; M.S. (hon.), Yale, 1930; M.D. (hon.), U. Zurich, 1950; Sc.D., U. Chgo., 1952; m. Elizabeth Chafee, Apr. 26, 1916; children—Jane, Sheila, James Lawder, Edwin Francis, John. Instr. pediatrics, Johns Hopkins U. Med. Sch., 1915-22; asst. prof. pediatrics, Harvard U. Med. Sch., 1922-29, prof., 1929-50, emeritus since 1950. Served as physician A.R.C. France, 1917-19. Borden Award, Am. Acad. Pediatrics, 1946, Chapin Award, R.I. Med. Soc., 1950, Kober Award, Assn. Am. Physicians, 1951; Moxon Award Royal Coll. Physicians, 1954; Howland award, American Pediatric Society, 1955. Member American Pediatric Soc., Assn. Am. Physicians, Am. Soc. Biol. Chemists, Am. Academy of Arts and Sciences, Nat. Acad. Sciences, Société de Pediatrie de Paris. Clubs: Century Association (New York); Harvard, Tavern (Boston). Contbr. papers reporting researches in body fluid physiology. Editor: Am. Jour. Clinical Investigation, 1941-47. Home: 33 Edge Hill Rd., Brookline, Mass. Office: Children's Hosp., Boston. Died May 28, 1959.

GAMBLE, WILLIAM ELLIOTT, oculist, aurist; b. Palermo, Carroll Co., O., Apr. 9, 1860; s. G.W.C. and Margaret (Cotter) G.; ed. Hyatt's Acad., Iowa City, Ia., 1883; med. dept. U. of Ia., 1884; M.D., Rush Med. Coll., 1886; B.S., Iowa State Coll., 1886; m. Clara Daisy Bixby, 1889 (died 1930); children—Celia Martin (Mrs. Edwin H. House), Raleigh Welch, Richard Cotter, Josephine Margaret (Mrs. C.P.L. Nicholls), Elisabeth (Mrs. Donald Troller); m. 2d, Fern-Dell Hunt, 1931. Practiced at What Cheer, 1887-92, Chicago, since 1892; limited practice to diseases of the eye and ear since 1898; long served as acting head of dept. of ophthalmology and prof. clin. ophthalmology, med. dept., U. of Ill., (now emeritus); formerly ophthalmic surgeon to Cook Co. Hosp., also asst. surgeon Ill. Charitable Eye and Ear Infirmary; oculist and aurist University Hosp.; oculist St. Anne's Hosp. Fellow Am. Coll. Surgeons, Inst. of Medicine, Chicago; mem. A.M.A., Chicago Med. Soc., Chicago Ophthal. Soc. (ex-pres.), Chicago Alumni Assn. of Ia. State Coll. (ex-pres.). Republican. Mason. Club: University. Home: 2201 Malaga Road, Los Angeles, Calif.

GAMOW, GEORGE, author, educator; b. Odessa, Russia, Mar. 4, 1904; s. Anthony and Alexandra (Lebedinzeva) G.; student Normal Sch., Odessa, 1914-20, U. Leningrad, 1922-26 (Ph.D., 1928); m. Loubov Wochminzewa, Nov. 1, 1931 (div.); 1 son, Igor; m. 2d, Barbara Perkins, Oct. 11, 1958. Fellow U. Gottingen, Germany, summer, 1928, U. Copenhagen, Denmark, 1928-29; Rockefeller fellow, Cambridge, Eng., 1929-30; asst. U. Copenhagen, 1930-31; master in research Acad. Scis., Leningrad, 1931-33; lectr. U. Paris and London, 1933-34, U. Mich., 1934; prof. physics George Washington U., 1934-56, U. Colo., 1956-68; lectr. Stanford, 1936; vis. lectr. Venezuelian Assn. for Advancement Sci., 1956. Participated Convegnio Fisica Nucleare, Rome, 1931; Solvay Congress, Brussels, 1933; Internat. Phys. Congress, London, 1934, Warsaw, 1938. Recipient Kalinga Price award UNESCO, 1956. Mem. Am. Phys. Soc., Washington Philos. Soc., Internat. Astron. Union, Am. Astron. Soc., Nat., Royal Danish acads. scis. Author numerous books, latest being: Atomic Energy in Cosmic and Human Life, 1946; One, Two Three. . . Infinity, 1947; Creation of the Universe, 1952; Mr. Tompkins Learns the Facts of Life, 1953; The Moon, 1953; Puzzle-Math, 1958; Matter, Earth and Sky, 1958; (with J. Cleveland) Physics: Foundations and Frontiers, 1960; Biography of Physics, 1961; Gravity, 1962; A Planet Called Earth, 1963; A Star Called the Sun, 1964; Thirty Years That Shook Physics, 1965; Mr. Tompkins in Paperback, 1965; Mr. Tompkins Inside Himself, 1967; articles. Research in problems of nuclear physics. Home: Boulder CO Died Aug. 20, 1968; buried Green Mountain Cemetery Boulder CO

GANONG, WILLIAM FRANCIS, botanist; b. St. John, N.B., Can., Feb. 19, 1864; s. James H. and Susan E. (Brittain) G.; A.B., U. of N.B., 1884, A.M., 1886; A.B., Harvard, 1887; Ph.D., U. of Munich, 1894; Ph.D., ad eundem, U. of N.B., 1898, LL.D., 1920; m. Jean M. Carman, Apr. 4, 1888 (died 1920); m. 2d, Anna Hobbet, June 20, 1923; children—William Francis, Ann Hobbet. Asst. and instr. botany, Harvard, 1887-93; prof. botany and dir. Bot. Garden, Smith Coll., 1894-1932; prof. emeritus. Author: The Teaching Botanist, 1899, 2d edit., 1910; Laboratory Course in Plant Physiology,

1901, 2d edit., 1908; The Living Plant, 1913, 23; Textbook of Botany for Colleges, 1917. Home: Northampton, Mass. Died Sept. 7, 1941.

GANTT, HENRY LAURENCE, mechanical engr.; b. Calvert Co., Md., May 20, 1861; s. Virgil and Mary Jane (Steuart) G.; McDonogh Sch., Baltimore Co., Md.; A.B., Johns Hopkins, 1880. Teacher, McDonogh Sch., 1880-83; M.E., Stevens Inst. Tech., 1884; m. Mary Eliza Snow, of Fitchburg, Mass., Nov. 29, 1899. Mech. engr., 1884—; specializes in installing modern methods of mfg. Mem. Am. Soc. Mech. Engrs., Soc. Naval Architects and Marine Engrs., Am. Geog. Soc., Beta Theta Pi. Clubs: Engineers', Machinery (New York,) Johns Hopkins (Baltimore). Author: Work, Wages and Profits, 2d edit., 1913; Industrial Leadership, 1915; Organizing for Work, 1919. Home: Montclair, N.J. Office: Singer Bldg., New York, N.Y.

GANZ, ALBERT FREDERICK, educator, electrical engr.; b. Elberfeld, Germany, Apr. 25, 1872; s. Albert and Helene Theresa (Brinkmann) G.; ed. Coll. City of New York, 1886-87; Cooper Inst. Night Sch., New York, 1887-91; M.E., Stevens Inst. Tech., 1895; m. Antonia Christina Stursberg, June 21, 1902. Instr. gen. physics and applied electricity, 1895-97, asst. prof., 1897-1902, prof. elec. engring., and head dept. of elec. engring., 1902—, Stevens Inst. Tech. Patent expert and cons. engr., specializing in electric lighting and investigation of and remedies for electrolysis from stray electric currents. Fellow Am. Inst. Elec. Engrs., A.A.A.S. Home: Hoboken, N.J. Died July 27, 1917.

GARCIA, FABIAN, (gär-se'a), horticulturist; b. Chihuahua, Mex., Jan. 20, 1871; s. Ricardo and Refugio (Rivera) G.; brought to U.S. in 1873, naturalized 1889; B.S., N.M. Agrl. Coll., 1894, M.S.A., 1906, D.Agr., 1927; spl. work, Cornell U., 1899-1900; m. Julieta J. Amador, Aug. 14, 1907 (died Dec. 5, 1920). Asst. in agr. N.M. Agrl. Coll., 1894-1906, prof. horticulture, 1906—, horticulturist Expt. Sta., 1906-13, dir., 1913—, extension lectr. in horticulture, gen. agr., rural edn., English, Spanish, 1918—. Pres. Dona Ana County Fair, 1912; dir. Dona Ana County Fair Assn. Mem. Am. Pomol. Soc., Am. Hist. Assn., A.A.A.S., Alpha Zeta, Epsilon Sigma Phi. Catholic. Rotarian. Contbr. numerous articles and bulls. on agrl. and other sci. topics. Home: Las Cruces, N.M. Address: State College, N.M. Died Aug. 6, 1948; buried Las Cruces, N.M.

GARDEN, ALEXANDER, naturalist, physician; b. Aberdeenshire, Scotland, circa 1730; s. Rev. Alexander Garden; M.D., Marischal Coll., Aberdeen, Scotland, 1753; m. Elizabeth Peronneau, Dec. 24, 1755; 1 son, Maj. Alexander. Came to U.S., 1754; discovered vermifugal properties of pink-root (Spigelia marilandica); discovered Congo snake, mud eel; corresponded with various Am. and European naturalists and was instrumental in sending 1st electric eels to Europe; mem. Royal Soc. Upsula (Sweden), 1763; became fellow Royal Soc. London (Eng.), 1773; sided with King in Am. Revolution; banished, property confiscated by Act of Feb. 26, 1782; v.p. Royal Soc., Eng.; flower gardenia named after him. Died London, Apr. 15, 1791.

GARDINER, JAMES TERRY, civil engr.; b. Troy, N.Y., May 6, 1842; ed. Rennselaer Poly Inst. and Sheffield Scientific Sch.; (hon. Ph.B., Yale, 1868); m. a d. of William Croswell Doane. Became sub-asst. engr. Brooklyn Water Works; insp. U.S. ordnance corps, 1861-62; constructing earthworks around harbor, San Francisco, 1863-64; topog. asst. geol. survey of Calif., 1864-67; with Clarence King, 1867-72, and 1872-75 under Ferdinand V. Hayden, in U.S. Geol. Survey; dir. state survey of N.Y., 1876-86; mem. State Bd. of Health, 1880-86; afterward in practice as cons. engr.; pres. St. R.R. and Lighting Co., St. Joseph, Mo., 1892-95; v.p. coal cos. of Erie R.R. Co., 1895; pres. Mexican Coal & Coke Co., 1899—, Coahuila Coal Ry., Northeast Harbor Water Co. Home: New York, N.Y. Died Sept. 1912.

GARDNER, FRANK DUANE, agronomist; b. Gilman, Ill., Nov. 19, 1864; s. Isaac James and Invern (Bennett) G.; B.S., U. Ill. Coll. of Agr., 1891; postgrad. George Washington U., 1895-96; m. Ellen P. Crum, June 6, 1894; children—Matthias Bennett, Frank Easter, Reina Elisa. Agriculturist, U. Ill., 1891-95; soil expert U.S. Dept. Agr., 1895-1901; dir. P.R. Agrl. Expt. Sta., 1901-04; in charge soil mgmt. investigations U.S. Dept. Agr., 1904-08; prof. agronomy Pa. State Coll. and Expt. Sta., 1908-37, now prof. agronomy emeritus. Propr. Pleasant View Farms. Fellow Am. Soc. Agronomy (pres. N.E. sect. 1932-33); mem. Am. Farm Econs. Assn., Am. Assn. U. Profs., Pa. State Edn. Assn., Gamma Sigma Delta, Republican. Presbyn. Club: University (State College, Pa.). Author: Successful Farming, 1916; Soils and Soil Management, 1918; Farm Crops, Their Cultivation and Management, 1918. Contbr. to Rural Pennsylvania, also to The Book of Rural Life; writer many bulls. on soil and crop investigations. Home: State College, Pa. Died Oct. 1963.

GARDNER, HORACE CHASE, engineer, architect; b. Bentonsport Ia., Oct. 3, 1856; s. David Noble and Susan (Kuhn) G.; ed. pub. sch.; studied engring. under father; m. Nellie Gray, Jan. 5, 1888; 1 dau., Ruth (Mrs. Robert M. See). Came to Chicago in 1884 and entered employ of Swift & Co., later becoming mgr. constrn. and mech. depts.; began practice as architect, 1897; mem. Gardner & Lindberg, indsl. engrs. and architects, 1913-31, retired. Republican. Conglist. Home: Evanston, Ill. Died Sept. 20, 1936.

GARDNER, IRVINE C(LIFTON), optics physicist; b. Idaville, Ind., Sept. 19, 1889; s. James Wilson and Sarah Jane (Irvine) G.; A.B., DuPauw U., 1910, Sc.D. (hon.), 1938; A.M., Harvard, 1912, Ph.D. (Whiting fellow and Tyndall fellow), 1915; m. Merriel Pratt Maslin, June 30, 1927. Cutting research fellow Harvard, 1916, instr., 1915-17; chief optical instruments sect. Nat. Bur. Standards, 1921-50, chief div. optics and metrology, 1950-59; leader National Geog. Soc.-Nat. Bur. Standards Eclipse Expdn., Ak Bulaak, Russia, 1936, Patos, Brazil, 1940; mem. eclipse U.S.N.-Nat. Geog. Soc., Canton Island, 1937, A.A.F.-Nat. Geog. Soc., Bocaiuva, Brazil, 1947. Del. to Internat. Commn. Optics, London, Eng., 1950, Madrid, Spain, 1953, Boston Massachusetts, 1956. Served with Ordnance Dept., U.S. Army, mil. optical fire control instrument design and development, 1917-21; Ordnance Dept. rep. to visit German optical plants, 1945. Awarded Abrams award, Am. Soc. Photogrammetry, 1950. Fellow Am. Phys. Soc., Soc. Photog. Engrs.; mem. Optical Soc. of America (president 1958; council 1930-31; Frederic Ives Medal 1954), American Soc. Photogrammetry (dir. 1948-50, v.p. 1951, hon. mem.), A.A.A.S., Washington Academy Sci., Washington Philos. Society, Am. Soc. Optics (exec. v.p. 1955-56, president 1958), Sigma Xi, Phi Beta Kappa, Delta Kappa Epsilon. Clubs: Explorers, Harvard, Cosmos (Washington). Author articles in sci. jours. Holder patents. Home: Gaithersburg MD Died Dec. 29, 1972.

GARDNER, JAMES AUGUSTUS, surgeon; b. Poughkeepsie, N.Y., Oct. 28, 1870; s. La Vergne F. and Frances (McNutt) G.; student New York U., leaving in sophomore yr.; M.D., Coll. Phys. and Surg. (Columbia), 1895; m. Mary Louise Everett, Jan. 21, 1898; children—Helen Louise, James MacDowell. Intern, Bellevue Hosp., New York, 1895-98; practiced at Buffalo, 1898—; cons. urologist, Millard Fillmore Memorial Hosp. Fellow Am. Coll. Surgeons. Republican. Mason. Writer on prostatechtomy, post-operative treatment of same, and kindred topics. Home: Buffalo, N.Y. Died Sept. 13, 1926.

GARDNER, JAMES HENRY, geologist; b. Sonora, Ky., Apr. 25, 1883; s. Martin Roof and Bellona (Brown) G.; B.S., U. of Ky., 1904; M.S., 1906; Ph.D., George Washington U., 1910; m. Willie Wilkerson Spiers, Apr. 20, 1910; children—Martin, James Henry, Judith. Employed by Ky. Geol. Survey, 1904-06 and 1910-12, Geol. Survey, 1906-10, Pa. Geol. Survey, 1912; cons. geologist, 1913-19; pres. Gardner Petroleum Co., 1919-63 (merged with Goff Oil Co.) vice pres. Goff Co., 1963—. Mem. Geol. Soc. Am., Am. Assn. Petroleum Geologists (ex-pres.), Tulsa C. of C. (ex-dir.), Tulsa Aududon Soc., Alpha Tau Omega. Ind. Democrat. Methodist. Mason (32 deg.). Home: 1624 E. 31st Av. 74105. Office: Mayo Bldg., Tulsa. Died Sept. 1, 1964.

GARDNER, LEROY UPSON, physician; b. New Britain, Conn., Dec. 9, 1888; s. Irving Isaac and Inez Baldwin (Upson) G.; B.A., Yale, 1912, M.D., 1914; graduate study Boston City Hospital and Harvard Medical School, 1914-17; honorary M.S., Yale, 1940; m. Carabelle McKenzie, June 22, 1915; children—Margaret, Dorothy. Instructor in pathology, Harvard Medical School, 1916-17; asst. prof. pathology, Yale Sch. of Medicine, 1917-18; pathologist Trudeau Foundation, Saranac Lake, N.Y., 1919-27, director of same since 1936; director Saranac Lab. for Study of Tuberculosis since 1927. Lecturer in medicine, U. of Rochester. Served as lt. Med. Corps, U.S. Army, 1917. Trustee Village of Saranac Lake, 1932-33; mem. water bd., same, 1929-30; mem. Village Planning Commn.; trustee of Trudeau Sanatorium; dir. Trudeau Foundation since 1938. Mem. Corr. Com. on Silicosis, Internat. labor Office, 1930. Fellow A.A.A.S.; mem. Am. Assn. Pathologists and Bacteriologists, Nat. Tuberculosis Assn. (bd. dirs.), A.M.A. (Council Industrial Health), Beta Theta Pi, Nu Sigma Nu. Republican. Presbyterian. Author: Tuberculosis—Bacteriology, Pathology and Laboratory Diagnosis (with S. A. Petroff), 1927. Contbr. to med. publs. on silicosis and related disease due to dust. Home: 36 Old Military Rd.; Saranac Lake, N.Y. Died Oct. 24, 1946.

GARLAND, FRANK MILTON, inventor; b. Hennaker, Merrimac Co., N.H., 1855; s. Moses and Cevalla (Bean) G. At 17 became employe of Winchester Arms Mfg. Co., New Haven, learning trade of machinist and gun-maker. Later in other employments; visited China. Inventor of Garland Rapid Fire Gun, an automatic gun capable of discharging 300 shots per minute. Address: New Haven, Conn.

GARLAND, LANDON CABELL, univ. chancellor; b. Nelson County, Va., Mar. 21, 1810; s. Spotswood and Lucinda (Rose) G.; grad. Hampden-Sydney Coll., 1829; m. Louisa Garland, Dec. 1835. Prof. natural science Washington Coll. (now Washington and Lee U.), 1829-32; prof. natural philosophy Randolph-Macon Coll., 1832-36, pres., 1836-46; became prof. U. Ala., 1847, pres., 1855-65; prof. physics and astronomy U. Miss., 1866; wrote a series of articles for Christian Advocate, Nashville, Tenn.; resulted in plan for sectionwide Methodist univ. to be established, Nashville, 1868; 1st chancellor Vanderbilt U., Nashville, 1875-93, Author: Trigonometry, Plane and Spherical, 1841. Died Nashville, Feb. 12, 1895.

GARLAND, L(EO) HENRY, physician, educator; b. Dublin, Ireland, Mar. 30, 1903; s. John Peter and Mary M. (Martin) G.; student Belvedere and Castleknock Coll., 1911-19; M.B., B.Chir., B.A.O., U. Coll. Med. Sch., 1924; grad. study London, Eng., 1924-25, San Francisco, 1925-27; M.D., U. Coll. Dublin, 1960; m. Edith Isabel Dohrmann, July 6, 1928; children—Edith M. (Mrs. J. Merrifield, Jr.), Isabel A. (Mrs. V. E. Caglieri), Judith M. (Mrs. R. Harrington), Michael H., Sheila E. (Mrs. E. Reeves). Came to U.S., naturalized, 1931; Intern. Richmond and Rotunda hosps., Dublin, 1924; radiologist St. Mary's Hosp., San Francisco, 1927-29; clin. instr. Stanford, 1929-32, asst. prof., 1932-43, clin. prof. radiology, 1948-60; clin. prof. radiology U. Cal., 1960—; cons. Armed Forces Inst. Pathology, USPHS, Army, Navy, VA. Chmn. com. cancer diagnosis and therapy NRC. Served as comdr. USNR, 1942-46. Recipient distinguished service award Am. Cancer Soc., 1954; gold medal Am. Coll. Radiology, 1960; gold medal Radiology Soc. N.Am., 1961. Diplomate Am. Bd. Radiology. Past fellow Am. Coll. Radiology (pres. 1961-62); mem. Cal. Acad. Med. (pres. 1957-58), Cal. Radiol. Soc. (hon. sec.), Cal. and Am. med. assns., Radiol. Soc. N.A. (pres. 1948), Am. Roentgen Ray Soc., A.M.A. Club: Bohemian (San Francisco). Author sects. med. books and articles in med. jours. Home: 2853 Green St., San Francisco 94123. Office: 450 Sutter St., San Francisco 8. Died Oct. 31, 1966; buried Holy Cross Cemetery, Colma, Cal.

GARLICK, THEODATUS, surgeon, sculptor; b. Mar. 30, 1805; s. Daniel and Sabra (Kirby) G.; grad. U. Md. Med. Sch., 1834; m. 3d, Mary Chittenden, 1845. Practiced surgery, Youngstown, O., 1834-52, had reputation as plastic surgeon; inventor new splints, surg. instruments; made models of surg. and pathol. anatomy; sculpted bas-reliefs of Andrew Jackson, Henry Clay, full length miniature of Chief Justice John Marshall; constructed camera which took daguerreotypes (photographing a person not in direct sunlight for 1st time), 1840; did experiments in artificial trout-breeding (1st of kind in Am.). Died Dec. 9, 1884.

GARMAN, HARRISON, naturalist; b. Lena, Ill., Dec. 27, 1856; s. Benjamin and Sarah A. (Griffith) G.; ed. pub. schs. of Normal, Ill., Ill. State Normal University, and Johns Hopkins U.; m. Rosalie Miller, of Hatfield, Mass., Oct. 30, 1883. First asst. Ill. State Lab. of Natural History, 1883-89; asst. Ill. state entomologist, 1883-85; asst. prof. zoology, U. of Ill., 1885-89; entomologist and botanist, Agrl. Expt. Sta. of U. of Ky., since 1889. Prof. zoology and entomology, U. of Ky., 1892-96, now emeritus prof. entomology, same; state entomologist of Ky., 1897-1929. Mem. Assn. Econ. Entomologists (pres.), Soc. Promotion Agrl. Science, Am. Soc. Naturalists, Am. Soc. Zoologists, Am. Acad. Polit. and Social Science, Nat. Geog. Soc., Am. Genetic Assn., Ky. Acad. Science, Am. Assn. Univ. Profs.; fellow A.A.A.S., Am. Ecol. Soc., Am. Soc. Botanists; late chmn. entomol. sect. Am. Assn. Agrl. Colls. and Expt. Stas. Home: 638 S. Limestone St., Lexington, Ky.

GARMAN, RAYMOND LEROY, corp. ofcl.; b. Schoeneck, Pa., July 21, 1907; s. Albert and Amelia (Wagner) G.; B.S., Franklin and Marshall Coll., 1929; M.Sc., N.Y.U., 1931, Ph.D., 1932; m. Grace Ross, July 1933; children—Elizabeth, Robert. Instr. N.Y.U., 1932, asst. prof. chemistry, 1932-34; instr. Washington Sq. Coll., 1934-41, asst. prof., 1941-42; research group leader Mass. Inst. Tech., 1943-45 v.p. charge research Gen. Precision Lab., Inc., Pleasantville, N.Y., 1945-52, v.p., mng. dir., 1952-56, exec. vice pres., tech. dir., N.Y.C., 1956-57, chmn. bd. and tech. dir. in charge of research and development, 1957-59; v.p. engring. and research General Precision Equipment Corp., 1958-66, senior vice pres. for technology, 1966-68; v.p. chief scientist Gen. Precision, Inc., 1959-68; v.p. charge advanced tech. Singer Co., 1968-70. Cons. sci. adv. bd. USAF. Mem. bd. trustees Franklin and Marshall College. Recipient Presidential Certificate Merit, 1946; Alumni citation Franklin and Marshall Coll., 1963, Alumni medal, 1970. Fellow Soc. Motion Picture & Television Engineers, Institute of Electrical and Electronic Engineers, New York Academy of Sciences; mem. Am. Chem. Soc., Am. Phys. Soc., Optical Soc. Am., Acoustical Soc. Am., Instrument Soc. Am., Inst. Navigation. Author: (with Muller, Droz) Experimental Electronics, 1940. Contbr. articles profl. jours. Home: Hastings-on-Hudson NY Died Jan. 20, 1970; buried Kensico Cemetery, Valhalla NY

GARMAN, SAMUEL, naturalist; b. Indiana Co., Pa., June 5, 1843; s. Benjamin and Sarah Ann (Griffith) G.; grad. Ill. State Normal U., 1870; hon. S.B., Harvard, 1898, A.M., 1899; m. Florence, d. R. Sands Armstrong (barrister and M.P.), of St. John, N.B., Sept. 2, 1895. Prin. Miss. State Normal Sch., 1870-71; prof. natural sciences, Ferry Hall Sem., Lake Forest, Ill., 1871-72; spl. pupil of Louis Agassiz in natural history, 1872-73; asst. in herpetology and ichthyology, Mus. of Comparative Zoölogy, Harvard, 1873—. Was with

Major Powell's 1st expdn. in Colo.; with Alexander Agassiz in South Am. expdns. Author: Deep Sea Fishes, 1899; The Chimaeroids, Chismopnea, 1904; New Plagiostomia, 1906; New Plagiostomia and Chismopnea, 1907: The Reptiles of Easter Island, 1908; Plagiostomia (sharks, skates and rays), 1913. Home: Arlington Heights, Mass. Died Sept. 30, 1927.

GARNER, JAMES BERT, chem. engr.; b. Lebanon, Ind., Sept. 2, 1870; s. James Washington and Orrah Jane (Shepard) G.; B.Sc., Wabash Coll., Crawfordsville, Ind., 1893, M.Sc., 1895, D.Sc., 1950; Ph.D., magna cum laude, University of Chicago, 1897; married Glenna May Greene, December 31, 1900 (died Dec. 7, 1918); children—Mrs. Lura Faulkinbury (died October 15, 1946), Mrs. Marjorie Schmeltz, James Herbert, Mrs. Eleanor Shannon, Mrs. Mildred Beckwith, Mason (dec.), Jean Hale, Harry F., Mrs. Glenna MacGregor, Mrs. Ruth Kindelin; m. 2d, Margaret Martin, June 30, 1923 (died Sept. 19, 1932); 1 son, William Jenkins; m. 3d, Sarah Elizabeth Harold, May 12, 1934; 1 dau., Sarah Elizabeth. Teacher chemistry, Bradley Poly. Inst., and Wabash Coll., 1897-1914; fellow and professor Mellon Inst. (U. of Pittsburgh), since 1914, administrative fellow since 1950, director natural gas investigations same, since 1915; dir. research Chem. Storage Fellowship in Mellon Inst. for Pitts.-Des Moines Steel Co. Inventor of gas mask Apr. 1915. Metall. research. Fellow Am. Assn. Advancement of Science, mem. Am. Chem. Soc., Phi Delta Theta, Phi Beta Kappa, Alpha Chi Sigma, Phi Sigma, Sigma Xi. Mem. United Presbyn. Ch. Mason (32 deg.). Home: 54 Lebanon Hills Drive, Mt. Lebanon, Pitts 28

GARNER, WIGHTMAN WELLS, chemist, plant physiologist; b. Timmonsville, S.C., July 15, 1875; s. James Nathaniel and Joanna (Wright) G.; S.C. Mil. Acad., 1892-93; A.B., U. of S.C., 1896; Ph.D., Johns Hopkins, 1900; Sc.D., Clemson Coll., and N.C. State Coll., 1937; m. Judith Goode, Nov. 8, 1905. Instr. chemistry, and pvt. asst. to Prof. A. Michael, Tufts Coll., Mass., 1900-03; scientific asst. Bur. Chemistry, Dept. Agr., 1904; scientific asst. in tobacco investigations, 1905-08, physiologist in charge, tobacco and plant nutrition investigations, 1909-40, principal physiol. in charge, tobacco investigations, Bureau of Plant Industry, Dept. of Agriculture, 1941-45; retired. Fellow A.A.A.S.; member American Chemical Society, Am. Genetic Assn., Bot. Soc. America, Am. Soc. Naturalists, Washington Acad. Sciences, Am. Soc. Plant Physiologists (Stephen Hale's award 1930), Am. Soc. Agronomy, Sigma Alpha Epsilon, Phi Beta Kappa. Episcopalian. Author scientific papers in American and foreign jours., and bulls., particularly on photoperiodism in plants, mineral nutrition of plants and tobacco production; The Production of Tobacco, 1946. Home: 1367 Parkwood Pl. N.W., Washington 10

GARRETT, JOHN WORK, railroad exec., banker; b. Balt., July 31, 1820; s. Robert and Elizabeth (Stouffer) G.; attended Lafayette Coll. (Pa.), 2 years; m. Rachel Harrison. Became pres. B.&O. R.R., 1858 (after stockholders' challenge to mgmt., which he led); managed road successfully, improved earnings, freed bd. of dirs. from polit. control; instrumental in preventing Md. Confederates from taking Washington (D.C.) during Civil War; continued railroad service throughout war, although line twice crossed Confederate territory; obtained direct routes to Chgo. and Pitts., after war, also acquired independent line to N.Y.C.; arranged for N. German Lloyd line to unload ships at Balt., re-establishing city as major seaport; built B.&O. R.R. into integrated co. by having line build its own cars and operate its own express and telegraph cos.; solved problem of rate wars by formation of pools; attempted to manipulate state legislature (because of charges of discrimination), 1870's. Died Deer Park, Garrett County, Md., Sept. 26, 1884.

GARREY, WALTER EUGENE, (gar'e), physiologist, educator; b. Reedsville, Wis., Apr. 7, 1874; s. John Eugene and Harriet (Anderson) G.; B.S., Lawrence U., 1894; studied U. Berlin, 1898; Ph.D., U. Chgo., 1900; M.D., Rush Med. Coll., 1909; m. Charlotte Eaton, Dec. 31, 1901; 1 son, Walter Eaton. Extension instr. in zoölogy U. Chgo., 1894-98, fellow in physiology, 1898-1900; prof. physiology Cooper Med. Coll., San Francisco, 1900-10; asso. prof. physiology Washington U., 1910-16; prof. physiology Tulane U., 1916-25; prof. physiology Vanderbilt U. Med. Sch., 1925-44, prof. emeritus, 1944. Lectr. on gen. physiology Marine Biol. Labs., Woods Hole, Mass., also mem. research staff. Mem. bd. trustees Marine Biol. Lab., Nat. Bd. Med. Examiners. Mem. A.M.A., A.A.A.S., Am. Physiol. Soc. (pres. 1937, 1938), Am. Soc. Biol. Chemists, NRC, San Francisco Acad. Medicine (hon.), Phi Beta Kappa, Alpha Omega Alpha, Sigma Xi. Contbr. many articles, original research, chiefly on the heart. Address: Vanderbilt Hospital, Nashville 4. Died June 15, 1951; buried Woods Hole, Mass.

GARRIGUES, HENRY JACQUES, physician; b. Copenhagen, Denmark, June 6, 1831; s. Jacques Louis and Cecelia Olivia (Duntzfelt) G.; A.B., Metropolitan Coll., Copenhagen, 1950, A.M., 1863; M.D., U. of Copenhagen, 1869; m. Louise Riemer, 1868. In U.S., 1875—; obstetric surgeon N.Y. Maternity Hosp., 1881, Infant Asylum, 1884; gynecologist to German Hosp., 1885; prof. obstetrics, Post-Grad. Med. Sch. and Hosp., 1886; gynecologist St. Mark's Hosp., 1890; cons. surgeon Maternity Hosp., 1892; prof. gynecology and obstetrics, Sch. of Clin. Medicine, 1898. Hon. fellow Am. Gynecol. Society, 1901, Obstet. Soc. (Edinburgh), 1902. Author: Text-Book of Obstetrics, 1902, 1907; Gynecology,' Medical and Surgical, 1905. Died Aug. 1913.

GARRIOTT, EDWARD BENNETT, meteorologist; b. Lockland, O., Mar. 17, 1853; ed. pub. schs. and Washington U., St. Louis; m. Gertrude L. Dewey, Jan. 12, 1882. Asst. observer, 1874-75, observer, 1876-87, meteorol. clerk, 1888-91, chief Div. Meteorology, 1892-93, forecaster, 1893-94, supervising forecaster and prof. meteorology, 1895—, U.S. Weather Bureau, Washington, D.C. Writer and lecturer on meteorology, Died 1910.

GARRISON, F(RANK) LYNWOOD, mining engr.; b. Philadelphia, Pa., Jan. 12, 1862; s. David Rea and Maria Morgan (Pleiss) G.; ed. Rittenhouse and Rugby acads., Phila.; B.S., U. of Pa., mining and civ. engring. metallurgy, chemistry and geology, 1883; Royal School of Mines of London, England, 1884-85; m. Adele Mary Dwight, Nov. 21, 1894 (died Sept. 1929); children—Dwight, Elizabeth D., Laura D.; m. 2d, Mrs. Edith Brinton McKenna, Oct. 17, 1931. Was in Russia investigating methods of making iron during years, 1887-88; commr. Paris Expn., 1889; practiced profession U.S., Alaska and Canada, 1890-99, in China, 1900; chief engr. Empire Lumber and Mining Co., Johnson County, Tenn., 1902-04; in cons. practice S. America, S. Africa and U.S. since 1904. Mem. Soc. Economic Geologists, Am. Inst. Mining and Metall. Engineers, Franklin Institution, Academy Natural Sciences Philadelphia, Instn. Mining and Metallurgy (London), Newcomen Soc., The Champlain Soc. of Canada, Zeta Psi. Chmn. Nat. Manganese Commn., 1917. Episcopalian. Mason. Club: Union League. Author Kerl's Assaying, 1889; also many tech. papers. Home: 1019 Clinton St., Philadelphia PA

GARVEY, JOHN L(OUIS), physician; b. Oconto, Wis., Jan. 16, 1895; s. John M. and Marie L. (Hoeffel) G.; M.D., U. of Mich., 1920; m. Catherine Anne Cudlip, May 8, 1943. Intern U. of Mich. Hosp., 1920-21, resident, 1921-22; instr. neurology, U. of Mich. Med. Sch., 1922-25, asst. prof., 1925-29, asso. prof., 1929; prof. neurology, Marquette Sch. of Medicine, Milwaukee, since 1929, dir. Div. of Neurology, 1933-61; pvt. practice neuropsychiatry, Milwaukee since 1929; chief of staff Columbia Hosp., 1952-58, Milw. County Gen. Hosp., 1947; area cons. neurology, Wis., Ill. Fellow A.C.P., Am. Acad. Neurology; mem. Harvey Cushing Soc., Wisconsin State, Milwaukee County medical societies, Central Neuropsychiatric Assn. (emeritus), Chicago Neurol. Soc. (hon.), Milw. Neuropsychiatric Soc., A.M.A., Milw. Surg. Soc. (pres. 1957), Milw. Acad. Medicine (hon.), Milw. Neurol. Club, K.C. Clubs: Chippewa, University (Milw.). Home: 1260 N. Prospect Av. 53202. Office: 208 E. Wisconsin Av., Milw. 2. Died Mar. 31, 1964; buried Cemetery Park, Iron Mountain, Mich.

GASKILL, HARVEY FREEMAN, inventor, engr.; b. Royalton, N.Y., Jan. 19, 1845; s. Benjamin F. and Olive G.; grad. Comml. Coll., 1866; m. Mary Moore, Dec. 25, 1873. Designed revolving hay-rake, 1858; mem. clock mfg. firm Penfield, Martin & Gaskill; draftsman Holly Mfg. Co., 1873; engr., supt., 1877, dir., v.p., 1885; invented Gaskill pumping engine (1st crank and fly-wheel high duty pumping engine built as standard for waterworks service), 1882; mem. Am. Soc. M.E. Died Apr. 1, 1889.

GASSER, HERBERT SPENCER, physician; b. Platteville, Wis., July 5, 1888; s. Herman and Jane Elizabeth (Griswold) G.; A.B., U. Wis., 1910, A.M., 1911, D.Sc., 1941; M.D., Johns Hopkins, 1915; postgrad. in Europe, 1923-25; many hon. degrees. Asst. and instr. in physiology U. Wis., 1911-13; instr. pharmacology Washington U., St. Louis, 1915-16; instr. in physiology, 1916-18, asso., 1918-20, asso. prof., 1920-21; prof. pharmacology, 1921-31; prof. physiology, Cornell Univ. Med. Coll., N.Y., 1931-35; dir. Rockefeller Inst., 1935-53, mem. emeritus, 1953—. Recipient (with Erlanger) Nobel prize in physiology, 1944; Kobr medal Assn. Am. Physicians, 1954. Fellow A.A.A.S., Am. Acad. Arts and Scis., fellow Royal Soc. Edinburgh (hon.); mem. Royal Soc. London (fgn.), Nat. Acad. Scis., Am. Physiol. Soc., Am. Soc. Pharmacology and Exptl. Therapeutics, Soc. Exptl. Biology and Medicine, Am. Neurol. Assn., Assn. for Research in Nervous and Mental Disease, Harvey Soc., Am. Philos. Soc., Assn. Am. Physicians, Physiol. Soc. Eng. (hon.), Sigma Xi, other fgn. sci. socs. Editor Jour. Exptl. Medicine, 1936—. Author: (with J. Erlanger) Electrical Signs of Nervous Activity, 1937; also papers. Research on blood coagulation; investigated (with Joseph Erlanger) electrophysiology of nerves, especially action currents of phrenic nerve, also discovered conductivity difference of different groups of nerve cells, by combining electronic amplifiers and cathode-ray oscillographs, 1924. Died N.Y.C., May 11, 1963.

GASTON, JAMES MCFADDEN, physician; b. nr. Chester, S.C., Dec. 27, 1824; s. John Brown and Polly (McFadden) G.; grad. S.C. Coll., 1843; M.D., same, 1846; (M.D. ad eundem Univ. of Brazil, 1854); m. Sue G. Brumby, Nov. 2, 1852. Practiced Chester dist., S.C., 1846-52, Columbia, S.C., 1852-61; surgeon and med. director C.S. army, 1861-65; practiced in province of São Paulo, Brazil, 1867-73, Campinas, Brazil, 1874-83; at Atlanta, Ga., 1883—. Prof. principles and practice of surgery, Southern Med. Coll., Atlanta, 1884—. Honorary mem. Am. Assn. Obstetricians and Gynecologists, Southern Surg. and Gynecol. Assn. Asso. editor Annual of the Universal Medical Sciences and Sajous' Annual and Analytical Cyclopaedia of Practical Medicine. Home: Atlanta, Ga. Died 1903.

GATES, FANNY COOK, prof. physics; b. Waterloo, Ia., Apr. 26, 1872; d. John Cook and Adelia (St. John) G.; B.S., Northwestern U., 1894, M.S., 1895; grad. scholar in mathematics, Bryn Mawr Coll., 1895-96, grad. fellow, 1896-97; European fellow Asso. Coll. Alumnae, at U. of Göttingen, and Zurich Polytechnic, 1897-98; studied U. of Chicago, McGill U., U. of Cambridge, U. of Pa., Ph.D., 1909; unmarried. Head Dept. of Physics, Woman's Coll. of Baltimore (now Goucher Coll.), 1898-1911; prof. physics and dean of women, Grinnell (Ia.) Coll., 1913-16; dean of women, U. of Ill., 1916-18; gen. sec. Y.W.C.A., N.Y. City, 1918-19; head mistress, Model School of Bryn Mawr Coll., 1922-23; spl. teacher physics, Lincoln and Brearley Schs., N.Y. City, 1920-22 and 1923-28. Was chmn. edn. com. Md. State Fedn. of Women's Clubs, 1909-11. Home: New York, N.Y. Died Feb. 24, 1931.

GATES, JOSEPH WILSON, mechanical engr.; b. Cincinnati, Feb. 6, 1862; s. DeWitt Clinton and Annie (Williams) G.; ed. Cincinnati High Sch.; m. Isabel Gibson, of Chicago, Feb. 2, 1892. With William Deering & Co., harvesting machinery, Chicago, 1882-92, Gates Iron Works, Chicago, 1892-1900, The Mine & Smelter Supply Co., Salt Lake and Denver, 1900-10; in business on own account, coal mining equipment, 1910—. Democrat. Episcopalian. Mem. Am. Inst. Mining Engrs., 1903. Club: Salt Lake Commercial. Home: 923 3d Av. Office: 503 Dooly Blk., Salt Lake City, Utah.

GATES, ROBERT MCFARLAND, mech. engr.; b. O'Brien County, Ia., Sept. 7, 1883; s. Charles and Minnie Choate (Richardson) G.; B.S. in Mech. Engring., Purdue U., 1907; D.Engring., 1944; LL.D. (hon.), Alfred U., 1953; m. May Leuty, Dec. 25, 1912; children—Robert McFarland (dec.), Marjorie Gates Woodrow. Practiced as cons. engr., Cleve., 1909-15; eastern mgr. Thew Shovel Co., Lorain, O., 1915-18, Lakewood Engring. Co., Cleve., 1918-21; v.p. Superheater Co., N.Y., 1923-35; v.p. Combustion Engring. Co., 1933-40; pres., dir. Air Preheater Corp., 1940—, chmn. bd. 1956—; dir. Apra Precipitator Corp. Trustee village and town of Scarsdale, N.Y., 1945-47. Formerly mem. exec. com. U.S. Nat. Commn. for UNESCO. Past mem. Engrs. Joint Council; mem. adv. com. on internat. technologic assistance NRC. Mem. Am. Soc. M.E. (pres. 1943-44, now hon. mem.), Am. Inst. E.E., Am. Iron and Steel Inst., Instn. Mech. Engrs. (Gt. Britain), Newcomen Soc.; Am. Soc. for Engring. Edn., Nat. Soc. Profl. Engrs., Am. Standards Assn. (dir.), Am. Arbitration Assn., Tau Beta Pi, Pi Tau Sigma. Republican. Baptist. Mason. Clubs: Engineers, Union League, Purdue (N.Y.); Scarsdale Golf, Manursing Island. Home: 45 Birchall Dr., Scarsdale, N.Y. Office: 60 E. 42d St., N.Y.C. 10017. Died Nov. 9, 1962.

GATEWOOD, ARTHUR RANDOLPH, marine engr.; b. Phila., Nov. 6, 1899; s. William and Mary Edwin (Hartzell) G.; B.S. in Civil Engring., Va. Mil. Inst., 1918; S.B. in Naval Architecture and Marine Engring., Mass. Inst. Tech., 1921. Apprentice to chief engr. Merchant Marine, 1921-29; surveyor Am. Bur. Shipping, N.Y.C., 1929-47, chief engr. surveyor, 1947-57, vice president, 1957-62, president, 1963, chairman of the board 1964-66. Engring. spokesman U.S. delegation Safety of Life at Sea Conf., London, 1948, U.S. del., chmn. conf. com. on safety of nuclear ships, 1960, mem. U.S. adv. com. Safety of Life at Sea, 1960-64; U.S. del. Internat. Electrotechnical Commn., 1948-60, Internat. Inst. Welding, 1956-62, Internat. Standards Orgn., 1959-64; mem. U.S. sec. of treas. Com. on Tanker Hazards, 1962-63. Served as 2d lt., inf., U.S. Army, 1918. Recipient David W. Taylor gold medal Society of Naval Architects and Marine Engineers, 1963. Fellow Am. Inst. Elec. Engrs.; mem. Am. Soc. M.E., Am. Soc. Refrigerating Engrs., Soc. Naval Architects and Marine Engrs., Am. Standards Assn., Am. Nuclear Soc., Am. Welding Soc., Inst. Mech. Engrs. (London), Inst. Elec. Engrs. (London), Inst. Marine Engrs. (v.p.; London), Soc. Naval Architects and Marine Engrs. N.Y. (v.p.), Soc. Marine Port Engrs. N.Y., Kappa Sigma, Theta Tau. Episcopalian. Clubs: Whitehall, Engineers, India House (N.Y.C.). Author and composer: Noel, Noel, Our Saviour is Born. Home: New York City NY Died Jan. 15, 1970.

GATHMANN, LOUIS, inventor; b. Province of Hanover, Germany, Aug. 11, 1843; s. Turgen Heinrich and Magdalena G.; ed. Luneberg, Hanover, pub. schs.; studied engring.; came to U.S.; m. Henriette Ehlert, Chicago. Inventor of the Gathmann gun; is engaged on improvements of the telescope, flying-machines (mechanical), and refining crude petroleum by a new method. Address: 2017 Kalorama Av., Washington.

GATLING, RICHARD JORDAN, inventor; b. Hertford Co., N.C., Sept. 12, 1818. As a boy assisted his father in perfecting machine for sowing cotton-seed; later invented machine for sowing rice; adapted it to sowing wheat and patented it. Grad. Ohio Med. Coll., 1850, but never practiced. Invented, 1862, the revolving gun known as the "Gatling gun"; invented, 1886, a new gun metal, composed of steel and aluminum. Congress voted him $40,000 for proof experiments in a new method of casting cannon. Also invented hemp-breaking machine, a steam plow, etc. Home: Hartford, Conn. Died 1903.

GATY, LEWIS RUMSEY, elec. engr.; b. West Orange, N.J., Aug. 21, 1902; s. Theodore Emmett and Cornelia (Pomeroy) G.; E.E., Cornell U., 1924; m. Katharine Morris Fleischmann, Mar. 16, 1929; children—Lewis Rumsey, Joan P. Engring. asst. Sioux City Gas & Electric Co., 1924-26, Counties Gas & Electric Co., 1926-27; electric supt. Phila. Suburban Counties Gas & Electric Co., 1927-29; with Phila. Electric Co., 1929—, successively electric supt., gas supt., supt. overhead lines, asst. to gen. supt. electric transmission and distbn., asst. electric engr., elec. engr., mgr. engring. dept., 1929-56, v.p. research and development, 1956-59, b.p. engring. and research, 1959—; vice pres., dir. Atomic Power Development Associates, Inc.; director Phila. Electric Power Co., Susquehanna Power Co., Susquehanna Electric Company; vice president and trustee High Temperature Reactor Development Assos., Inc. Fellow Am. Inst. E.E. (chmn. mgmt. com. 1955-57; chmn. of publ. dept. 1957-59); mem. Am. Society M.E., Am. Soc. Engring. Edn., Franklin Inst., Assn. Edison Illuminating Cos. (chmn. switching and switchgear com. 1950-52), Edison Electric Inst., Am. Gas Assn., Cornell Soc. Engrs., Nat. Soc. Profl. Engrs., Newcomen Soc., Internationale des Grands Reseaux Electriques. Clubs: Union League, Cornell, Engineers (Phila.); Merion Cricket; Cosmos (Washington). Home: 729 Waverly Rd., Bryn Mawr, Pa. 19010. Office: 1000 Chestnut St., Phila. 5. Died Aug. 29, 1961; buried Church Yard, St. Christopher's Episcopal Ch., Gladwyne, Pa.

GAULT, JAMES SHERMAN, elec. engr.; b. Detroit, June 23, 1899; s. James Robert and Etta May (Eby) G.; student Detroit City Coll. (now Wayne U.), 1917-19; B.S., U. of Mich., 1921, M.S., 1924; m. Wilma Hazel Smith, June 14, 1924; children—Margaret, Marian, Madelaine. Test dept. Gen. Elec. Co., Schenectady, N.Y., 1921-22, turbine engring. dept., Lynn, Mass., May-Sept. 1922; mem. faculty U. of Mich. since 1922, prof. elec. engring. since 1946, in charge of A-C machinery and indsl. control courses since 1944; elec. engr. Holland, Ackerman & Holland, Chicago, and Ann Arbor, Mich., 1926-48. Fellow Am. Inst. E.E. (chmn. com. on indsl. power systems), Alumni Assn. U. of Mich. (past dir.). Sigma Xi, Iota Alpha, Eta Kappa Nu (asso.). Club: Exchange (Ann Arbor). Author: Alternating-Current Machinery (with Benj. F. Bailey), 1951. Died Nov. 16, 1951.

GAY, FREDERICK PARKER, pathologist, bacteriologist; b. Boston, July 22, 1874; s. George Frederick and Louisa Maria (Parker) G.; A.B., Harvard, 1897; M.D., Johns Hopkins, 1901; Sc.D. George Washington U., 1932; m. Catherine Mills Jones, Oct. 18, 1904; children—Louisa Parker, Lucia Chapman, Frederick P. (dec.), William. Asst. on Johns Hopkins Med. Commn. to Philippines, 1899; asst. demonstrator pathology U. Pa., 1901-03; fellow Rockefeller Inst. for Med. Research, 1901-03; research student Pasteur Institute, Brussels, 1903-06; bacteriologist Danvers Insane Hosp., 1906-07; asst. and instr. in pathology Harvard Med. Sch., 1907-10; prof. pathology, U. Cal., 1910-21, prof. bacteriology, 1921-23; prof. bacteriology, Columbia, 1923—. Maj., M.C., U.S.A., 1918-19; mem. med. sct. NRC, 1917-24, chmn., 1922-23, chmn. Med. Fellowship Bd., 1922-26; C.R.B. exchange prof. to Belgian univs., 1926-27. Fellow A.M.A., A.A.A.S.; mem. Nat. Acad. Science, Assn. Am. Physicians, Am. Assn. Pathologists and Bacteriologists, Soc. Experimental Biology and Medicine Assn. Am. Bacteriologists, American Assn. Immunologists. Comdr. Order of Crown of Belgium. Republican. Clubs: Faculty (Columbia and U. Cal.); Century (N.Y.C.). Author: Studies in Immunity, 1909; Typhoid Fever, 1918; Agents of Disease and Host Resistance (with others) 1935; The Open Mind—a Life of Elmer Ernest Southard; also contbr. scientific jours. on bacteriology, immunology and pathology. Home: New Hartford, Conn. Office: 630 W. 168th St., N.Y.C. Died July 14, 1939; buried Old Town Hill Cemetery, New Hartford, Conn.

GAY, GEORGE WASHINGTON, surgeon; b. Swanzey, N.H., Jan. 14, 1842; s. Willard and Fanny (Wright) G.; acad. edn., Swanzey, N.H., and Bernardston, Mass.; M.D., Harvard, 1868; hon. A.M., Dartmouth, 1895; m. Mary E. Hutchinson, Nov. 1868 (died 1873); m. 2d, Grace Greenleaf Hathorne, Nov. 1875. Surgeon Boston City Hosp. many years; instr. clin. surgery, 1888-1900, lecturer, 1900-07, Harvard Med. School. Trustee Wrentham State Sch. for the Feeble Minded. Retired after practicing 55 yrs. Home: Chestnut Hill, Mass. Died May 30, 1931.

GAY, NORMAN RUSSELL, coll. dean; b. Cortland, N.Y., Aug. 17, 1919; s. Clarence Nathaniel and Agatha Emma (Smith) G.; B.S. in Mech. Engring., U. Rochester, 1941; M.S. in Mech. Engring., Cornell U., 1946; Ph.D., Purdue U., 1960; m. Mary Barbara Feinberg, Sept. 6, 1941; children—Barbara, Virginia, Lucinda, Leslie Ann. Indsl. engr. Eastman Kodak Co., 1939-41; John Edson Sweet research asso. Cornell U., 1941, prof. mech. engring., 1946-56; staff engr. Bendix-Westinghouse Co., 1956-58; G. Stanley Mickle research asso. Purdue U., 1958-60; dir. Tex. Engring. Expt. Sta., 1960-61; dean Coll. Engring., U. Notre Dame, 1961—; cons., 1947—. Served to lt. USNR, World War II. Registered profl. engr., N.Y. Mem. Am. Soc. Engring. Edn., Am. Soc. Heating, Refrigerating and Air Conditioning Engrs., Phi Beta Kappa, Sigma Xi, Tau Beta Pi, Psi Upsilon, Pi Tau Sigma, Atmos Soc. Contbr. articles to profl. jours. Home: 1238 E. Wayne S., South Bend, Ind. 46615. Died Oct. 31, 1966; buried Notre Dame U.

GAYLORD, TRUMAN PENFIELD, electrical engr.; b. Shelby, Mich., Feb. 15, 1871; s. Edward B. and Maranda G.; prep. edn. Allen Acad., Chicago, 1886-89; studied U. Mich., 1889-92; B.S. in Elec. Engring., Armour Inst. Tech., 1894; m. Helen Ross-Lewin, 1903; children—Katharine (dec.), Marion Helen. Asst. prof. of elec. engring., Armour Inst. Tech., 1894-98; engr., Commonwealth Edison Co., 1898-1900; engr. sales, later acting v.p., Westinghouse Electric & Mfg. Co., 1900-29, v.p., 1929—; v.p. Interboro Improvement Co. Mem. Pittsburgh Chamber Commerce (pres.), Pa. State Chamber Commerce (dir.). Republican. Presbyn. Home: Pittsburgh, Pa. Died July 5, 1931.

GEAR, HARRY BARNES, ret. elec. engr.; b. Marietta, O., Mar. 6, 1872; s. George Rufus and Julia (Barnes) G.; A.B., Marietta Coll., 1892; M.E., Cornell, 1895; m. Bertha Riley, Jan. 4, 1897; children—Margaret (Mrs. Roland H. Lawrence), Robert Barnes. Insp., Commonwealth Edion Co., Chgo., 1895-1900, chief insp., 1900-11, engr. distbn., 1911-21, asst. to v.p., 1921-35, v.p. operating and engring., 1936-44, ret., 1944. Fellow Am. Inst. E.E.; mem. Western Soc. Engrs. Republican. Baptist. Home: 10018 Bell Av., Chgo. 43. Died Mar. 27, 1959; buried Marietta, O.

GEBHARDT, GEORGE FREDERIC, cons. mech. engr.; b. Salt Lake City, Utah, Mar. 1, 1874; s. Henry Andrew and Wilhelmina (Schuster) G.; A.B., Knox Coll., 1895, M.S., 1897; M.E., Cornell, 1897; m. Edith M. Jensen, Sept. 1, 1914. Professor mech. engring. Armour Inst. Technology, 1902-34, prof. emeritus since 1934; consulting practice. Mem. Am. Society M.E., Western Soc. Engrs., Nat. Assn. Power Engrs., Phi Delta Theta, Tau Beta Pi, Pi Tau Sigma. Republican. Presbyterian. Club: University (Chicago). Author: Combustion, 1925; Steam Power Plant Engineering, 1927. Home: 469 N.E. 69th St., Miami FL

GEDDES, JAMES, congressman, civil engr.; b. Carlisle, Pa., July 22, 1763; m. Lucy Jerome, 1799, 1 child. Began production of salt, Liverpool, N.Y., 1794; admitted to N.Y. bar, 1800; justice of peace, Onondaga County, N.Y., 1800-04; mem. N.Y. State Assembly, 1804-22, asso. justice Onondaga County Ct., 1809; judge Ct. Common Pleas, Onondaga County, 1809; mem. U.S. Ho. of Reps. (Federalist) from N.Y., 13th Congress, 1813-15; mem. N.Y. Assembly 1822; one of prin. engrs. engaged by N.Y. Canal Commn. to construct Erie and Champlain canals, 1816-22; surveyed canal from Ohio River to Lake Erie for State of Ohio, 1822; chief engr. Chesapeake and Ohio Canal, 1827. Died Geddes, N.Y., Aug. 19, 1838; buried Oakwood Cemetery, Syracuse, N.Y.

GEDDES, NORMAN BEL, (ged'es), designer, author, theatrical producer; b. Adrian, Mich., Apr. 27, 1893; s. Clifton Terry and Lulu (Yingling) G.; student Cleve. Sch. of Art, Art Inst. Chgo.; M.A., U. Mich., 1937; LL.D., Adrian College, 1936; B.F.A., Syracuse U., 1940; m. Helen Belle Sneider, Mar. 9, 1916 (dec.); children—Joan, Barbara; m. 2d, Frances Resor Waite, Mar. 3, 1933 (dec.); m. 3d, Ann Howe, 1944 (div.); m. 4th, Edith Luytens, 1953. Pioneer in Am. stage design, 1914, in present day methods of stage lighting, 1916; designer, dir., co-author or producer of more than 200 plays, musicals, operas, motion pictures, and for the circus; planner or designer numerous theatres in U.S. and Europe, including Theatre Guild, Roxy Theatre (N.Y.C.), Ukrainian State Opera House (Karov, USSR), Copa City (Miami, Fla.); designer Gen. Motors Corp. bldg. and exhibit, Futurama, N.Y. World's Fair, 1938, master plan for City of Toledo, 1944, NBC studios, 1955; asso., archtl. commn., Century of Progress Expn., Chgo., 1938; indsl. designer, 1927—; pioneer designer indsl. products, including streamlined automobiles, 1928, railways trains, 1931, ocean liner, 1932, airplane interiors, 1933, electric typewriter, 1946; originator methods and techniques for use by U.S. Army, USN, USAF, OSS, as techniques for ship identification, aircraft recognition, "natural" camouflag (Corps Engrs.,) model constrn. and photograph (USN), Mark IV submarine trainer, stop motion tng. films, rubber mat processes, psychol. warfare weapons (OSS), method, equipment and bldg. Air Force Strategic Command trainer; ofcl. record Battle of Midway (sec. of def.); mem. Inventors Council; adviser QMG, U.S. Army, also OWI. Exhibitor in museums in U.S., Europe, Africa, Asia, 1912—; represented in collections of museums in U.S., Europe, Asia. Mem. NRC, Authors League Am., United Scenic Artists Union, Illuminating Engring. Soc., Archtl. League of N.Y., U.S. Naval Inst., Mediaeval Acad. Am., Royal Soc. Arts (London), (hon.) Arquitectura de Mexico. Clubs: Players, Coffee House, North American Yacht Racing Union. Author: Theatrical Presentation of the Divine Comedy of Dante, 1923; Horizon, 1932; Magic Motorways, 1940. Contbr. encys. and mags. Address: 350 Park Av., N.Y.C. 22. Died May 8, 1958.

GEDDES, WILLIAM FINDLAY, prof. of biochemistry; b. Manotick, Ont., Can., Aug. 18, 1896; s. Thomas Henry and Wilhelmina (Mansfield) G.; B.S.A., Univ. of Toronto, 1918, A.M., 1925; M.S., Univ. of Minn., 1928, Ph.D., 1929; married Florence May Clayton, September 1, 1920; children—Mary Catherine (Mrs. Warren Randall), Richard, Dorothy (Mrs. William Longley), Barbara (Mrs. Douglas Hagg). Came to U.S., 1938, naturalized, 1944. Explosives chemist, British Chem. Co., Ont., 1918-19; prof. agrl. biochemistry Univ. of Minn., 1939—, head dept. of agrl. biochemistry since July 1945. Mem. com. on food research Office of Q.M. General, 1945-48; mem. subcom. on Foods, Com. on Q.M. Problems, National Research Council, 1948-54, collaborator Northern Utilization Research Branch, 1944—. Awarded Coronation medal by King George VI; Osborne medal, Am. Assn. Cereal Chemists, 1950; Nicholas Appert medal, Inst. Food Technologists, 1958. Fellow A.A.A.S.; mem. Am. Assn. Cereal Chemists (chmn. com. on standardization of lab. baking, 1932-34, vice pres., 1937-38, pres. 1938-39), Am. Chem. Soc. (councillor for Minn. 1940-42, 47-48, chmn. Minn. sect., 1943-44), Am. Oil Chemists' Soc., Inst. Food Technologists (mem. com. on edn., 1946-47); Sigma Xi (president of the Minnesota chapter 1947-48), Phi Lambda Upsilon. Episcopalian. Mason (hon. life mem. past master). Clubs: Science of Winnipeg, Science of Univ. of Minn. Author numerous chpts. on food chemistry. Editor Cereal Chemistry since 1943; associate editor Cereal Chemistry, 1936-42; editor Cereal Science Today, 1956-57. Author research and tech. papers. Home: 2141 Doswell Av., St. Paul 8. Died Mexico City, Mexico, Jan. 7, 1961.

GEE, WILSON, educator; b. Union, S.C., Sept. 18, 1888; s. Reuben Thompson and Gertrude (Gist) G.; B.S., Clemson Agrl. Coll. of S.C., 1908, hon. D.Sc., 1937; M.A., U. S.C., 1910; postgrad. U. Chgo., U. Wis., 1909-11; Ph.D., U. Cal., 1913; LL.D., U., Ala., 1938; m. Mary Gaston, June 7, 1921; children—Mary Wilson (Mrs. William Carroll Tuthill), Williford Gaston. Instr. biology U. S.C. 1908-09; asst. in zoology U. Wis., 1909-11; asst. prof. zoology and asso. entomologist Expt. Sta., Clemson Coll., 1911-12; fellow in zoology U. Cal., 1912-13; acting prof. biology U. S.C., 1913-14; prof. biology Emory U., Oxford, Ga., 1914-17; asst. dir. agrl. extension service Clemson Coll., 1917-18; prof. rural econs., rural sociology U. S.C., 1919-23, U. Va. since 1923, also editor U. Va. News Letter since 1925, dir. U. Va. Inst. for Research in Social Scis. since 1926; mem. So. Regional Com. Social Sci. Research Council, 1929-34; mem. Gov's Adv. Commn. on Unemployment Ins., Va., 1933-34; exec. dir. Edn. Commn. (legislative), 1944-45. Served as technician U.S. M.C., Central Med. Dept. Lab., Dijon, France, 1918-19. Mem. Am. Econ. Assn., Am. Sociol. Soc. (exec. com. 1937-39), Am. Farm Econ. Assn., Am. Assn. U. Profs., So. Sociol. Soc. (1st v.p. 1936; pres. 1937), Rural Sociol. Soc., Theta Chi, Sigma Xi, Phi Kappa Phi. Democrat. Methodist. Club: Colonnade. Author: The Place of Agriculture in American Life, 1930; The Social Economics of Agriculture, 1932, rev. edit., 1942; Research Barriers in the South 1932; The Cotton Cooperatives in the Southeast (with E. A. Terry), 1933; Social Science Research Organization in American Universities and Colleges, 1934; American Farm Policy, 1934; The Gist Family of South Carolina, 1934; The Virginia Public School System; Report of the Virginia Education Commission, 1944; Social Science Research Methods 1950; also pamphlets and articles on econ. and social problems of rural life. Home: 225 Montebello Circle, Charlottesville, Va. Died Feb. 1, 1961; buried U. Va. Cemetery, Charlottesville.

GEER, WILLIAM CHAUNCEY, research chemist; b. Ogdensburg, N.Y., June 17, 1876; s. Charles Pease and Lucy Ann (Guernsey) G.; grad. Potsdam (N.Y.) State Normal Sch., 1897; A.B., Chemistry, Cornell, 1902, Ph.D., Chemistry and Physics, 1905; m. Effie Aurelia Work, Dec. 29, 1908; children—Aurelia Henrietta (Mrs. John H. Stresen-Reuter), Margery Lucy (Mrs. John M. Allen). Sci. high tchr. Nyack, N.Y., 1898-99; asst. instr., scholarship, 1902-03, fellow in chemistry, 1904-05, instr. chemistry, 1904-06, Cornell U.; expert in wood distillation U.S. Forest Service, 1906-07; actively identified with B. F. Goodrich Co., Akron, 1907-25, advancing to v.p. in charge research and devel.; ret. from exec. work to spend time in research and travel. Chmn. Gas Def. Div. War Service Com., Rubber Assn. Am., World War. Received Modern Pioneer award N.A.M., 1940. Ex-pres. Akron YMCA; pres. Ithaca (N.Y.) Meml. Hosp., 1930-32. Fellow A.A.A.S.; fellow and hon. mem. Instn. Rubber Industry (Eng.), Am. Inst. Chemists; asso. fellow Inst. Aero. Scis. Mem. Am. Chem. Soc., Inst. Chem. Engrs., Am. Phys. Soc., Sigma Xi. Republican. Episcopalian. Clubs: Chemists (N.Y.);

Rotary (pres. 1946-47), Country (Ithaca). Author: The Reign of Rubber, 1922. Inventor many processes in mfr. rubber goods, notably golf ball covers and airplane de-icer. Contbr. tech. and ednl. articles. Died Sept. 9, 1964.

GEHRING, JOHN GEORGE, M.D.; b. Cleveland, O., July 4, 1857; s. Karl August and Wilhelmina (Vetter) G.; M.D., Western Reserve U. Sch. of Medicine, 1885, D.Sc., 1913; post-grad. work, U. of Berlin, 1891; LL.D., Bates Coll., 1923; m. Marian True Farnsworth, Oct. 20, 1888. Began practice at Cleveland, 1885, practiced at Bethel, Me., specializing in functional nervous diseases, 1895—; dir. Bethel Nat. Bank; pres. Gould's Acad., Bethel. Author: The Hope of the Variant, 1923. In recognition of his work in neurology, a gift of $200,000 was made by William Bingham, II, of Bethel, Me., in 1927, for the construction of one of the two large wards in the New Neurol. Inst. of New York, 168th St. and Broadway, and named "The Gehring Ward and Rooms." Home: Bethel, Me. Died Sept. 1, 1932.

GEHRMANN, ADOLPH, hygienist, bacteriologist; b. Decatur, Ill., July 19, 1868; s. Theodore A. and Emelie (Jehnke) G.; M.D., Chicago Med. Coll., 1890; m. Albertina Marianne Weinstein, Dec. 24, 1910. Interne Cook Co., Hosp., 1890-92; established Chicago Bur. of Food Inspection, 1893; apptd. prof. bacteriology and hygiene, Coll. Phys. and Surg. (U. of Ill.), 1894 (emeritus); supt. food inspection, and bacteriologist Health Dept., City of Chicago, 1884-1903; organizer and pres. Columbus Med. Laboratory. Presbyn. Home: Chicago, Ill. Died Oct. 3, 1920.

GEIST, EMIL SEBASTIAN, orthopedic surgeon; b. St. Paul, Minn., May 9, 1878; s. Smil and Anna (Erd) G.; ed. U. of Minn., M.D., same, 1900; interne, St. Joseph's Hosp., 1900-01; post-grad. work, Paris, Bresslau, Vienna, 1901-04; m. Augusta Ohage, May 9, 1911. Practiced, Minneapolis, 1904—; asst. prof. orthopedic surgery, U. of Minn.; orthopedic surgeon, St. Mary's, St. Barnabas, Abbott, Asbury, Swedish, Northwestern hosps.; cons. orthopedist, Minn. State Hosp. for Crippled Children. Fellow Am. College Surgeons, Minn. Acad. Medicine. Maj. Med. R.C., U.S.A., 1915-18. Home: Minneapolis, Minn. Died May 14, 1933.

GELLERT, N(ATHAN) HENRY, (gel'lert), management cons.; b. Balt., Sept. 7, 1889; s. Horace and Minna (Goldmann) G.; B.A., Yale, 1910; Ph.B., Sheffield Sci. Sch. (Yale), 1915, C.E., 1916; m. Edna Louise Smith, June 18, 1912 (dec.); children—Nathan Henry, Eleanor Louise, Helen Elizabeth, Edward Bradford; m. 2d, Georgia Marrs Barber, March 12, 1954. Cadet engr. Am. Gas Co., 1910-11; chief engr. Pub. Service Constrn. Co., 1912-14; v.p. several gas cos., 1916-20; cons. engr. and v.p. Atlantic Gas Co., 1920-30, pres., 1930-38; pres. Southern California Water Co., 1941-47; chmn. bd dirs. Edison Sault Electric Co., 1941-47; president board of dirs. Seattle Gas Company, 1941-55; executive partner, Gellert, Griffin, Harrigan & Associates, consulting engineers; lecturer San Diego State College, Loyola U., U. Ariz., Ariz. State College, University of New Mexico, U. of Southern California, Los Angeles State College Pepperdine and Occidental Colleges; formerly president Great Lake Utilities Co., Atlantic Gas Corp., Pa. and Southern Gas Co.; past chmn. Manufactured Gas Industry Code Com.; mem. nat. defense and par coms. Am. Gas Assn.; formerly chief bus. cons. power div. W.P.B.; past v.p. and director United Defense Fund; former pres. exec. bd. Valley Forge Council, vice chmn. Region III, mem. exec. bd. Seattle area council Boy Scouts of Am.; mem. exec. committee, Region II, Boy Scouts of Am.; received Silver Beaver Award, Nat. Council, Boy Scouts of Am.; mem. bd. director Greater Seattle, Inc. Mem. bd. of trustees Pacific Coast Gas Assn. (past pres.). Mem. Am. Soc. Civil Engrs., Am. Soc. Mech. Engrs., Am. Gas Assn., Sigma Xi. Republican. Episcopalian. Clubs: Yale (N.Y.); Washington Athletic, Broadmoor Golf, Rotary, Tennis, Rainier (Seattle). Designer and builder 1st electric blast furnace gas cleaners in U.S. Author tech papers. Home: 476 Lake Washington Blvd. E. Seattle 98102. Died Nov. 14, 1959.

GELLHORN, ERNST, prof. physiology; b. Breslau, Germany, Jan. 7, 1893; s. Moritz and Hulda (Stein) G.; student Univ. of Berlin, 1910-14; Ph.D., Univ. of Muenster, 1919; M.D., Univ. of Heidelberg, 1919; m. Hilde Obermeier, Aug. 1, 1925; children—Irene Florence (deceased), Helen, Ernest Albert Eugene, Joyce Geraldine. Came to U.S., 1929, naturalized, 1935. Began as instr. physiology, Halle Univ., 1919; asso. prof. physiology, Univ. of Halle, 1925-29; asso. prof. physiology, Univ. of Oregon, 1929-31, prof., 1931-32; prof. physiology, Univ. of Ill. Coll. of Medicine, 1932-43; prof. neurophysiology, U. of Minn. from Sept. 1943. Mem. Am. Physiol. Soc., Soc. Exptl. Biology and Medicine, Central Soc. Electroencephalographers, A.A.A.S., N.Y. Acad. Scis., Sigma Xi. Awarded A Cressy Morrison prize by New York Acad. Sciences, 1930, Alvarenga prize, Coll. of Physicians, Phila., 1934. Author several books and papers, including: Physiological Foundations of Neurology and Psychiatry, 1953; Autonomic Imbalance and the Hypothalmus, 1957. Co-editor Acta Neurovegetativa. Address: Charlottesville VA Died Apr. 13, 1973.

GELLHORN, GEORGE, gynecologist; b. Breslau, Germany, Nov. 7, 1870; s. Adolph and Rosalie (Pincus) G.; ed. Gymnasium, Ohlau, Germany, 1876-90; M.D., U. of Würzburg, 1894; m. Edna Fischel, Oct. 21, 1903; children—George, Walter F., Martha E., Alfred A. Asst. in clinics at univs. of Berlin, Jena and Vienna, 1895-99; came to America, 1899; practiced, St. Louis, 1900—; prof. of gynecology and obstetrics, and dir. of dept., St. Louis U. Sch. of Medicine, 1922-32; professor clin. obstetrics and gynecology, Washington U. Sch. of Medicine, 1932—; gynecologist, Barnard Free Skin and Cancer Hosp.; gynecologist and obstetrician, St. Luke's and City hosps., asso. gynecologist and obstetrician, Barnes and St. Louis Maternity hosps.; cons. gynecologist and obstetrician, Jewish and St. Louis County hosps. Home: St. Louis, Mo. Died Jan. 25, 1936.

GEMMELL, ROBERT CAMPBELL, mining engr.; b. Port Matilda, Pa., July 5, 1863; s. Robert Brown and Anna Eliza (Campbell) G.; B.S. in Civ. Engring., U. of Mich., 1884, C.E., 1895, Master Engring., 1913; m. Belle E. Anderson, Oct. 17, 1888. Engr. surveys and constrn., A.,T.&S.F., R.R., 1884-90; civ. and mining engr. in Ore., Wash. and Utah, 1890-96; mining engr. in Utah, Nev., Ida. and Calif., and engr. of De LaMar's mines, 1896-1901; mgr. Mexican Mining Syndicate, Mex., 1901-03; supt. of mines for Guggenheim Exploration Co., in Mexico, 1903-05; examining mines in Spain, 1905; gen. supt., 1906-09, asst. gen. mgr., 1909-13, gen. mgr., 1913—, Utah Copper Co.; gen. mgr. Bingham & Garfield Ry. Co.; from Aug. 1, 1919, asst. mng. dir. Utah, Chino, Ray Consol. and Nevada Concol. copper cos. Republican. Presbyn. Home: Salt Lake City, Utah. Died Oct. 25, 1922.

GEMUNDER, AUGUST MARTIN LUDWIG, violin maker; b. Ingelfingen, Wurtemberg, Germany, Mar. 22, 1814; s. Johann Georg Heinrich Gemunder. Specialized in copying violins of old Italian masters before 1840's succeeded in producing an entirely original violin, after 1844, used by internationally known artists; came to U.S., 1846; opened shop (with his brother George), N.Y.C., 1852; pioneer quality violin building in U.S.; made reprodns. of 18th century violins of greatest Italian violin makers; submitted a model so skillfully made that experts believed it to be a genuine Guarnerius, at Vienna Exposition, 1873; won medals all over world, circa 1860-80. Author: Fine Violins, 1884. Died N.Y.C., Sept. 7, 1895.

GENTH, FREDERICK AUGUSTUS (original name Friedrich August Ludwig Karl Wilhelm Genth), chemist; b. Wachtersbach, Hesse-Cassel, Germany, May 17, 1820; s. George Fredrich and Karoline (Freyin von Swartzenau) G.; attended U. Heidelberg, U. Giessen (both Germany); Ph.D., U. Marburg (Germany), 1845; m. Karolina Jager, 1847, 3 children; m. 2d, Minna Fischer, 1852, 9 children. Became asst. to Robert Wilhelm Bunsen in Europe; came to U.S., 1848; opened analytical chem. lab. in Phila., 1848; prof. chemistry U. Pa., 1872-88; re-opened pvt. lab., 1888; chemist to Pa. Bd. Agr., 1877-84; expert in mineral chemistry, discovered 23 new mineral species, genthite (nickelgymnite) named in his honor; best example of work is paper "Corundum, its Alterations and Associated Minerals," 1873; did study ammonia-cobalt bases, 1847-56; wrote most important paper; mem. Nat. Acad. Scis., 1872, A.A.A.S., 1875. Died Feb. 2, 1893.

GENTH, FREDERICK AUGUSTUS, JR., chemist; b. Phila., Pa., Feb. 12, 1855; s. Frederick A. and Minna P. (Fischer) G.; B.S., U. of Pa., 1876, M.S., 1878; (Pharm. Dr. Medico-Chirurg. Coll., Phila., 1909); m. Louise Thekle Raht, Sept. 8, 1881 (died 1889); m. 2d, Miriam Stoddard Du Bois, Apr. 30, 1890. Asst. in chemistry, Pa. Geol. Survey, 1877-80; instr., 1881-83, asst. prof. chemistry, 1883-88, U. of Pa.; chemist of Dairy and Food Commn., Dept. of Agr. of Pa., 1897-1903; state pharm. examining bd. of Pa., 1901-03; prof. mineralogy and assaying, dept. pharm. chemistry, Medico-Chirurg. Coll., Pa., 1908—; also in gen. practice as analytical and expert chemist. Home: Lansdowne, Pa. Deceased.

GENTRY, THOMAS GEORGE, educator; b. Holmesburg (Phila.), Pa., Feb. 28, 1843; s. Alfred and Caroline G.; ed. pub. schs., Phila., and Central High Sch. to 1859; D.Sc., Chicago Coll. of Science, 1888; spl. studies, botany and zoology; m. Dec. 27, 1864, Mary Shoemaker, Lewisburg, Pa. First began teaching, 1861; now in U.S. Grant Sch., Phila. Mem. Phila. Acad. Sciences; Davenport Acad. Sciences; Canadian Entomol. Soc., Franklin Literary Soc. of Univ. of Pa. Author: Life Histories of Birds of Eastern Pennsylvania (2 vols.), 1876-77 01; The House Sparrow at Home and Abroad, 1878 01; Nests and Eggs of Birds of the United States, 1882 01; Family Names, 1892 01; Pigeon River and Other Poems, 1892 01; Life and Immortality—or Soul in Plants and Animals, 1897; Intelligence in Plants and Animals, 1900 D6. Contbr. on biol. subjects to scientific jours. Residence: 1950 N. 19th St., Philadelphia.

GEORGE, HAROLD COULTER, engineer; b. Oil City, Pa., May 24, 1881; s. Wesley and Belle (Coulter) G.; B.S. in Mining, Pa. State Coll., 1904; E.M., U. of Pittsburgh; 1906; m. Laura Holland Painter, June 25, 1908; children—Richard Painter, Julia Elizabeth. Instr. in mining and metallurgy, U. of Pittsburgh, 1904-07; mgr. Columbia Mining Co., Platteville, Wis., 1907-08; dir. Wis. State Mining Sch., 1908-11; chief engr. Wis. Zinc Co., Platteville, 1911-16 and 1918-21, gen. mgr., 1916-17; pres. Platteville Gas Co., 1913-20; cons. practice, 1917-18; oil recovery engr., U.S. Bur. Mines, San Francisco, 1921-23, petroleum engr. in charge Ardmore (Okla.) office, 1923-24; dir. Sch. of Petroleum Engring., U. of Okla., 1924-33; head dept. of oil and gas production, U. of Pittsburgh, 1933—; cons. petroleum engr., U.S. Bur. Mines. Mem. com. which drew up Brief of Zinc Producers of U.S., 1913; com. which drew up Safety Rules for Wis. Zinc Mines, 1915; com. which drew up Safety Order for Drilling and Production in Oil Fields of Calif., 1924. Author: Oil Well Completion and Operation, 1931. Home: Pittsburgh, Pa. Died Sept. 23, 1937.

GEORGE, HENRY, economist, reformer; b. Phila., Sept. 2, 1839; s. Richard Samuel Henry and Catherine (Vallance) G.; m. Annie Fox, Dec. 3, 1861. Compositor on Home Jour., c. 1860; a founder and publisher Evening Jour.; returned to San Francisco as printer on newly established Times, 1866, became reporter editorial writer, then mng. editor; 1st of his articles appeared in Overland Monthly, Oct. 1868; revisited East as agt. for San Francisco Herald, late 1868; established independent news service; returned to Cal., became editor Oakland Transcript, 1869; became partner and editor Daily Evening Post, 1871; state insp. of gas meters, 1876; advanced theory of the single tax on unearned increment of land values in book Progress and Poverty, 1879; became leader of reform element in Am. and traveled throughout country; founded single tax party; probably most important polit. reformer of early 1880's; pub. The Irish Land Question (became very popular, had heavy influence on Fabian Socialists), 1881; correspondent for Irish World in N.Y., 1881-82; lectured in Gt. Britain under auspices of Land Reform Union, 1883-84, for Scottish Land Restoration League, 1884; ran for mayor of N.Y.C. on social reform platform, lost to Tammany leader Abrams Hewitt (but ran ahead of Theodore Roosevelt) 1886; ran for mayor again, 1897; published weekly Standard, 1887-92; lectured in Gt. Britain, 1888, 89, Australia, 1890; The Science of Political Economy, 1897. Author: Our Land and Land Policy (contained essentials of econ. philosophy which he later expanded), 1871; Progress and Poverty, 1879; Social Problems (originally series of articles in Frank Leslie's Newspaper), 1883; Protection or Free Trade, 1886; An Open Letter to the Pope, 1891; A Perplexed Philosopher, 1892. Died N.Y.C., Oct. 29, 1897; buried Bklyn.

GEORGE, RUSSELL D., geologist; b. Claremont, Ont., Can., May 5, 1866; s. Frederick and Mary A. (Palmer) G.; A.B., McMaster University, Toronto, Canada, 1897, A.M., 1898, LL.D., 1923; m. Marcia Chipman, of Chicago, June 1908. Mem. field staff Ontario Bur. of Mines, 1898; fellow in geology and instr. in mineralogy, U. of Chicago, 1898-1901; with U.S. Geol. Survey, 1899; instr. geology, 1900, asst. prof., 1901, prof. econ. geology, 1902, State U. of Ia.; instr. geology, summer quarters, U. of Chicago, 1900, 01, 02; head of dept. of geology, U. of Colo., 1903-34, emeritus since 1934; now cons. geologist, mining engr.; state geologist, Colo., 1907-28. Fellow A.A.A.S., Colo. Scientific Soc.; mem. Am. Inst. Mining and Metall. Engrs., Geol. Soc. America, Am. Mining Congress, Soc. of Econ. Geologists, Am. Assn. Petrol. Geologists, Sigma Xi. Author: First Report of Geological Survey of Colorado, 1909; Topographic Map of Colorado, 1913; Geologic Map of Colorado, 1913; Common Minerals and Rocks, 1917; Mineral Waters of Colorado, 1920; Oil Shales of Colorado, 1921. Joint author: Shale Oil, 1925; Geology and Natural Resources of Colorado, 1927. Contbr. to jours. Republican. Conglist. Home: 845 11th St., Boulder, Colo.

GERDINE, THOMAS GOLDING, engineer; b. West Point, Miss., June 2, 1872; s. John and Susan (Golding) G.; B.E., U. of Ga., 1891; m. Frances E. Bishop, 1907; m. 2d, Marguerite N. Rowell. Topographic engr. U.S. Geol. Survey, 1893-1907; geographer in charge Pacific div. topographic survey, 1907-11, Northwestern div., 1912-16; major Eng. O.R.C., in charge mil. mapping Tex. and N.M., 1917; geographer in charge Northwestern and Rocky Mountain divs., topographic surveys, 1917-19; topographic engr. in charge Rocky Mountain Div. Topographic Surveys, 1920-21, in charge Pacific Div., Sacramento, Calif., 1922—. Author many maps published by the Survey, Deceased.

GERHARD, WILLIAM PAUL, sanitary engr.; b. Hamburg, Germany, July 30, 1854; s. Bernhard and Mathilda (Hühn) G.; grad. Poly. Sch., Carlsruhe, Baden, 1875; served as 1-yr. vol. in railroad regt., Berlin, 1875-76; passed exam. as lt. of the reserve; worked 6 weeks at the Gen. Staff under Gen. Helmuth Moltke; civil engr. in Hamburg, 1876-77; came to U.S., 1877, settling in St. Louis; hon.D. Engring., Tech. U., Darmstadt, 1911; m. Selma Weiskirch, May 10, 1881 (dec.); children—Hans W., Norman P. Asst. engr. Dept. Pub. Works, St. Louis, 1877-79; in Capt. James B. Eads' office, 1880; chief asst. engr. to Col. George E. Waring, Newport, R.I., 1881-83; engaged in New York as cons. sanitary expert. Editor Building (archtl. jour.), 1885-86; sanitary engr. on staff state architect of N.Y., 1892-99. Author: Recent Practice in Sanitary Drainage of Buildings, 1890; Gas Lighting and Gas Fitting, 1894; Sanitary Engineering, 1898; Sanitary Engineering of

Buildings, 1899; Theatres—Their Safety from Fire and Panic, 1900; The Superintendence of Piping Installations in Buildings, 1907; The Sanitation of Public Buildings, 1907; American Practice of Gas Piping and Gas Lighting in Buildings, 1908; Guide to Sanitary Inspections, 4th edit., 1909; The Sanitation, Water Supply and Sewage Disposal of Country Houses, 1909, 2d edit., 1914; Sanitation and Sanitary Engineering, 1909; The Water Supply, Sewerage and Plumbing of Modern City Buildings, 1909. Naturalized citizen of U.S. Home: Scarsdale, N.Y. Died July 8, 1927.

GERHARD, WILLIAM WOOD, physician; b. Phila., July 23, 1809; s. William and Sarah (Wood) G.; A.B., Dickinson Coll., Carlisle, Pa., 1826; M.D., U. Pa., 1830; m. Miss Dobbyn, 1850, 3 children. Wrote thesis on endermic application of medicaments, 1830; went to Paris to study Asiatic cholera epidemic of 1831-32; published paper on pathology of smallpox, 1833, pneumonia in children 1834; wrote On Cerebral Affections of Children (study of tuberculosis meningitis), 1834; published his most important paper, On the Typhus Fever, which Occurred at Philadelphia in 1836. . .showing the Distinction between this Form of Disease and. . .Typhoid Fever with Alteration of the Follicles of the Small Intestine (clearly distinguished typhus from typhoid fever for 1st time; 1837; published paper on epidemic meningitis, 1863; resident physician Pa. Gen. Hosp., Phila., 1834-68; prof. physiology U. Pa., 1838-72. Author: Lectures on the Diagnosis, Pathology, and Treatment of the Diseases of the Chest, 1842; Diagnosis of Thoracic Diseases, 1835. Editor: Grave's System of Clinical Medicines. Died Phila., Apr. 28, 1872.

GERIG, WILLIAM, civil engr.; b. Columbia, Boone County, Mo., Mar. 25, 1866; s. Francis Joseph and Caroline (Degen) G.; B.S., U. of Missouri, 1885, C.E., 1886, hon. LL.D., 1938; m. Fannie Crow, Jan. 21, 1890; children—Frank Austin, Mildred. Asst. engr. St. Louis & San Francisco R.R., 1886-89; U.S. asst. engr. Miss. River Commn., 1889-90; asst. engineer Chicago Drainage Canal, 1890-1900; chief engr. Southwest Ark.&I.Ty. Ry., 1890-91; U.S. asst. engr. Miss. River Commn., 1891-1905; div. engr. Panama Canal, 1905-08; pvt. practice, 1908-09; v.p., treas., chief engr. and gen. mgr. Pacific & Eastern Ry., cons. engr. Spokane, Portland & Seattle Ry. and St. Paul Union Depot, and consulting highway engr. Jackson County, Ore., 1909-15; cons. engr. N.Y. Barge Canal, etc., 1916; engr. Alaskan Engring. Commn., 1917; engr. and engr. in charge Anchorage div., Alaska R.R., 1918; asst. chief engr., Alaskan Engring. Commn., 1919-23; U.S. asst. engr., 1923, asso. engr., 1926, later sr. engr., head engr. Office of Chief Engrs. U.S. Army, 1923-38; retired Apr. 1, 1938. Mem. bd. engrs. Saluda Dam and cons. engr. Fort Peck Dam on Mo. River; cons. engr. Muskingum River Dams, Tygert Dam, Conchos Dam, etc. Mem. Am. Soc. C.E., Soc. Am. Mil. Engrs., Phi Beta Kappa, Tau Beta Pi. Presbyn. Mason. Contbr. to periodicals. Home: 9th and Pine St., Arkadelphia, Ark. Died Apr. 3, 1944.

GERLAUGH, PAUL, (ger'lâ), animal science research; b. near Osborne, O., April 21, 1891; s. Charles Lewellen and Julia Alnetta (Hower) G., S.B., O. State U., 1913; S.M., Pa. State Coll., 1917; m. Anna Rebecca Brosey, Feb. 7, 1914; children—Julia Ann (Mrs. Richard B. Bogner), Donald Brosey. Instr., Pa. State Coll., 1913-17; county agrl. agent, Wood County, O., 1917-21; livestock extension specialist, O. State U., 1921-28; chief, dept. of animal industry, O. Agrl. Exptl. Sta., 1928-47; asso. in animal science since 1948. Mem. Am. Soc. of Animal Prodn. (pres. 1948), Alpha Zeta, Gamma Alpha Delta, Sigma Xi. Presbyterian. Home: 1019 Forest Dr. Office: Ohio Agriculture Experimental Station, Wooster, O. Died Aug. 10, 1951; buried Wooster Cemetery.

GERMER, LESTER HALBERT, physicist; b. Chgo., Oct. 10, 1896; s. Dr. Hermann G. and Marcia (Halbert) G.; A.B., Cornell U., 1917; M.A., Columbia, 1922, Ph.D., 1927; m. Ruth Woodard, Oct. 2, 1919; children—Emily (Mrs. V. W. Samms), John Halbert G. Engring. dept. Western Electric Co., 1917-25, research physicist, 1925-53; tech. staff, research physicist Bell Telephone Laboratories, 1925-61, Cornell University, New York, 1961-71. Served as second lt. 139th aero squadron, A.E.F., 1918. Received Elliot Cresson medal, 1931. Fellow A.A.A.S., N.Y. Acad. Sci., Am. Phys. Soc. (chmn. N.Y. sect. 1944); mem. Soc. X-Ray and Electron Diffraction (v.p. 1943, president 1944), American Crystallographic Society, also Sigma Xi. Republican. Club: Appalachian Mountain of Boston (chmn. N.Y. chpt. 1951-52). Author sci. articles. Discoverer (with Dr. C. J. Davisson) of diffraction of electrons by crystals, 1927. Home: Millington NJ Died Oct. 3, 1971.

GERMUTH, FREDERICK GEORGE, research chemist; b. Baltimore, Md., Apr. 6, 1891; s. Ferdinand J. H. and Magdalena (Schlickenmaier) G.; student City Coll., Baltimore, 1907-08, Blue Ridge Coll., New Windsor, Md., 1908-10, Johns Hopkins, 1910-14, 1921-23, U. of Maryland, 1929-30; Sc.D., U. of Maryland, 1937; m. Anna Elizabeth Brown, May 18, 1910; children—Viola Anna, Gorden Henry, Bertha May, Laura Marie, Ruth Elizabeth, Frederick G., Donald F., Roland F., Ferne Elizabeth, Jeanne Magdalena, Ferdinand, Shirley Mae, Betty Lee, Leonore. In tin-testing div. Crown Cork & Seal Co., Balt., 1916-18; chemist, Wilson Martin Co., 1918-20, Bur. Water Supply, Baltimore, 1921-25; research chemist, Baltimore Bur. Standards since 1925; research consultant McCormick & Co., Inc., since 1933; cons. chemist; consultant to Sheppard-Enoch Pratt Hosp., Towson, Bur. of Tests, Balt. Fellow Am. Inst. Chemists, Chemical Society (London); member American Chemistry Soc., A.A.A.S., American International Acad. (awarded double wreath 1930), Maryland Acad. of Sciences, Soc. of Hygiene of Johns Hopkins U. Republican. Mem. Ref. Church. Contbr. to Jour. Am. Chem. Soc., Jour. Industrial and Engring. Chemistry, Jour. Am. Water Works Assn., The Analyst, Indian Med. Gazette, etc. Abstractor for Chem. Abstracts and Biol. Abstracts. Co-discoverer with Dr. Clifford Mitchell of new reagent for detection of uranium and other metallic elements. Licensed professional engr., State of Md., 1943. Home: 5704 Second Av., Halethorpe, Md. Office: Municipal Office Bldg., Balt. Died Feb. 17, 1964; buried London Park Cemetery, Balt.

GEROULD, JOHN HIRAM, zoölogist; b. Stoddard N.H., Oct. 2, 1868; s. Samuel Lankton and Laura Etta (Thayer) G.; Litt.B., Dartmouth, 1890; A.B., Harvard, 1892, A.M., 1893, Ph.D., 1895; studied and traveled in Europe, 1898-99 and 1925-26, in Trinidad, 1937; m. Adah May Hasbrook, July 2, 1902; children—Mary Foster (Mrs. Troyer S. Anderson), Elisabeth (Mrs. T. Avery Chadwick), Virginia (Mrs. Thomas K. Macdonald). Tchr. natural scis. Burr and Burton Sem., Manchester, Vt., 1890-91; instr. and prof. biology (zoölogy), Dartmouth, 1894-1938, prof. emeritus since 1938. Fellow A.A.A.S.; mem. Am. Soc. Zoölogists, Am. Soc. Naturalists (v.p. 1919), Genetics Soc. Am., N.H. Acad. Sci. (pres. 1929). Phi Beta Kappa, Kappa Kappa Kappa, Casque and Gauntlet (Dartmouth). Author: numerous papers on marine zoölogy, genetics and insect physiology; editor various biol. publs. Home: Hanover, N.H. Died July 15, 1961.

GERRISH, FREDERIC HENRY, surgeon; b. Portland, Me., Mar. 21, 1845; s. Oliver and Sarah (Little) G.; A.B., Bowdoin, 1866, A.M., 1869, M.D., 1869; (LL.D., U. of Mich., 1904, Bowdoin, 1905); m. Emily Manning Swan, Dec. 31, 1879. Lecturer therapeutics, materia medica and physiology, 1873-74, prof., 1874-75, U. of Mich.; prof. materia medica and therapeutics, 1873-82, anatomy, 1882-1904, surgery, 1904-11, medical ethics, 1911-15, emeritus prof. surgery, 1911—, Bowdoin Coll. Pres. Me. State Bd. of Health, 1885-89; Shattuck lecturer, Mass. Med. Soc., 1910; cons. surgeon and dir. Me. Gen. Hosp. Fellow Am. Surg. Assn., Am. Acad. Medicine (pres. 1887-88), Am. Coll. Surgeons. Governor State of Me. Soc. Colonial Wars, 1916—. Author: Prescription Writing, 1878. Home: Portland, Me. Died Sept. 8, 1920.

GERRISH, WILLARD PEABODY, engineer, astronomer; b. Roxbury, Mass., Aug. 31, 1866; s. William Hamilton and Eliza Ann (Willoby) G.; ed. Roxbury Latin Sch. and Mass. Inst. Tech.; m. Mary M. Wylie, Oct. 24, 1896. Opened Blue Hill Meteorol. Obs., Milton, Mass., as observer in charge, 1885; joined staff of the Obs. of Harvard U., 1886; asst. in Obs. Harvard, 1892-1913; asst. prof. mech. engring., Harvard U., 1913-38, emeritus, 1938; consulting engr. since 1902. Mem. Amherst Eclipse Expedn. to Japan, 1896. Designer of large telescopes at Harvard U., Amherst Coll. and elsewhere. Author of the Telegraphic Cipher Code in internat. use for dissemination of astron. information. Address: Frankland Rd., Ashland MA

GERRY, MARTIN HUGHES, JR., (ger'l), electrical engr.; b. Boston, Mass., October 16, 1868; s. Martin Hughes and Mary (Kernan) G.; grad. University of Minnesota, mechanical and electrical engineer, 1890; M.M.E., Cornell University, 1894; m. Altha Child, September 1900. In employ Sprague Elec. Ry. Co., and Thomson-Houston Co., and later with Gen. Elec. Co.; later at work on construction Met. Elevated Ry. of Chicago, and its supt. of motive power until 1898, when went to Mont. to take charge of engring. and construction for Helena Water & Elec. Power Co. (Missouri River Power Co.) in building dams and power plants for transmission of power to Helena, 18 miles, Butte, 65 miles, and Anaconda, 100 miles, upon completion of which he became its chief engr. and gen. mgr.; also consulting engr. Mont. Power Co., operating lighting plants in all large Mont. towns and power plants at Great Falls and Thompson Falls, 250,000 h.p.; also constructed elec. pumping plants for irrigation at Helena and other points in Mont. During World War served as Federal Fuel Administrator for Mont. Chief engr. and agent, St. Anthony Falls Water Power Co. and Minneapolis Mill Co. until 1924; Am. rep. Benguet Consolidated Mining Co., Manila, P.I.; now consulting engr. Address: 1107 Hobart Bldg., San Francisco, Calif. Died Dec. 30, 1941.

GERSHON-COHEN, JACOB, radiologist, educator; b. Phila., Jan. 9, 1899; s. Abraham and Dora (Starkman) Cohen; M.D., U. Pa., 1924, D.Sc. in Medicine, 1936; m. Sara Eskin, Mar. 26, 1921. Intern Jewish Hosp., Phila, 1924-25; resident X-ray dept. U. Pa. Hosp., 1926-28; practice medicine specializing in radiology, Phila., 1929-71; asst. prof. radiology U. Pa. Grad. Med. Sch., 1941-68; dir. div. radiology Albert Einstein Med. Center, Phila., 1949-65; prof. radiology Hahnemann Med. Coll., 1952-59; prof. research radiology Temple U. Med. Sch., 1965-71; cons. various area hosps., 1929-71; Served to comdr., M.C., USNR, 1942-46. Recipient Alvarenga prize Internat. Coll. Radiology, Gold medal award, 1937; Clement Cleveland award Am. Cancer Soc., 1968. Diplomate Am. Bd. Radiology. Fellow Am. Coll. Radiology, Gerontol. Soc.; mem. Am. Roentgen Ray Soc., Radiol. Soc. N.Am., Inter-Am. Coll. Radiology, Soc. Nuclear Medicine, Fedn. Am. Socs. Exptl. Biology, A.M.A., Med. Soc. Pa., Am. Cancer Soc., N.Y. Acad. Sci., Coll. Physicians Phila., Phila. County Med. Soc., Laennec Soc., Pa. Radiol. Soc., Phila. Roentgen Ray Soc. (v.p. 1964-65, pres. 1965-66). Author numerous articles in field. Home: Philadelphia PA Died Feb. 1971.

GERST, FRANCIS JOSEPH, prof. mathematics; b. Cincinnati, O., June 29, 1882; s. Frank Joseph and Caroline (Goessling) G. A.B., Xavier U., Cincinnati, 1902; A.M., St. Louis U., 1909, M.S., 1911; post grad. work, St. Louis U., 1906-09, 1910-11, 1914-18, U. of Mich., 1920-21; Ph.D., Johns Hopkins, 1923. Ordained priest R.C. Ch., 1917; instr. mathematics, U. of Detroit, 1909-10, John Carroll U., Cleveland, O., 1911-14; asst. prof. mathematics, Loyola U., Chicago, 1918-19, prof., 1931-62, emeritus, dean graduate sch., 1933-46; prof. mathematics, St. Louis Univ., 1924-31. Mem. Am. Math. Soc., Math. Assn. of America. Mem. Soc. of Jesus. Address: Chicago IL Died Sept. 30, 1968; buried All Saints Cemetery, Desplaines IL

GESELL, ARNOLD, (ge-sel'), child specialist; b. Alma, Wisconsin, June 21, 1880; s. Gerhard and Christine (Giesen) G.; student State Normal Sch., Stevens Point, Wis.; B.Ph., U. of Wis., 1903; Ph.D., Clark U., 1906, Sc.D., 1930; M.D., Yale U., 1915; Sc.D., University of Wisconsin, 1953; married Beatrice Chandler, Feb. 18, 1909; children—Gerhard Alden, Katherine Chandler. Teacher dept. of psychology, Los Angeles State Normal Sch., 1908-10; asst. prof. edn., Yale, 1911-15; prof. child hygiene, Yale School of Medicine, 1915-48. Asso. several yrs. in sch. of spl. training in psychology and pedagogy, for defective children, summers, New York U.; established, 1911-48, dir. Yale Psycho-Clinic (now Clinic of Child Development, Yale Sch. Med.); research associate Child Vision Research Yale Sch. Med., 1948-50; research consultant Gesell Institute of Child Development, 1950-58; lecturer School for Social Research since 1950; associate Harvard Pediatric Study, since 1948; school psychol. Connecticut State Board Education, 1915-19; member Conn. Commission on Child Welfare, 1919-21; attending pediatrician, New Haven Hospital, 1928-48; mem. Inst. of Psychology, Yale, 1925-29. Recipient Laureate, Kappa Delta Pi, 1958. Fellow A.A.A.S.; mem. Conn. Soc. Mental Hygiene (exec. com.), A.M.A., Am. Orthopsychiatric Assn., American Academy Pediatrics); mem. Am. Psychological Assn., Am. Acad. for Cerebral Palsy (pres. 1952-53), American Psychiatric Association, American Pediatric Society, Conn. Child Welfare Assn. (executive committee), Association Internationale pour la Protection de l'Enfance (vice president), Nat. Acad. of Sciences, Phi Beta Kappa, Sigma Xi, Alpha Omega Alpha; associate member Child Study Association of America. Member White House Conference on Child Health and Protection, White House Conference on Children in a Democracy; mem. Nat. Research Council, 1937-40. Author: The Normal Child and Primary Education (with wife), 1912, and many others, including: Foundations of Experimental Psychology (in part), 1929; Guidance of Mental Growth in Infant and Child, 1930. Established the photographic library of the Yale Films of Child Development, 1925; produced scientific and educational motion pictures since 1930; An Atlas of Infant Behavior (2 vols., in collaboration), 1934; How a Baby Grows (book), 1945; The Embryology of Behavior, 1945; The Child From Five to Ten (with F. Ilg), 1946; Studies in Child Development, 1948; Vision: Its Development in Infant and Child (with F. Ilg and G. Bullis), 1949; Infant Development, 1952. Produced The Embryology of Human Behavior for Med. Film Inst., 1949-50; Youth: The Years from 10 to 16 (with Ilg and Ames), 1956. Home: 185 Edward St. Office: 310 Prospect St., New Haven 11. Died May 29, 1961.

GESELL, ROBERT, neurophysiologist; b. Alma, Wis., June 23, 1886; s. Gerhard and Christina (Geisen) G.; A.B., U. Wis., 1910; M.D., Washington U., 1914; m. Cora Lees, 1912; 1 dau., Christine (Mrs. Roger Stevens). Asst. zoology U. Wis., 1909-10; asst. physiology Washington U., 1910-12, instr., asso. and asso. prof. physiology, 1912-19; prof. physiology U. Cal., 1919-22, U. Mich. since 1923. Mem. Am. Physiol. Soc., Am. Soc. Exptl. Biology. Contbr. med. articles profl. publs. Home: 3 Ridgeway, Ann Arbor, Mich. Died Apr. 19, 1954.

GESSLER, A(LBERT) E(DWARD), chemist; b. Metzingen, Wurtt, Germany, May 8, 1885; s. Edward Albert and Marie Louise (Leuze) G.; B.S., U. of Stuttgart, 1905; Ph.D., U. of Berlin, 1907; m. Mildred B. Murray, Feb. 2, 1915; children—Isolde (Mrs. Craig P. Smith), Albert; married 2d, Helen Yarnall, Mar. 31, 1932; 1 daughter Sally (Mrs. F. G. Appleton). Came to United States, 1908, became naturalized, 1922. Chemist, G. Siegle Co., Rosebank, N.Y., 1908, vice pres. and mem. bd., 1914-18; partner and vice pres. Ultro Chem. Corp., 1918, firm consol. with Zinsser & Co., 1926; chief chemist, mem. bd. and exec. com. Zinsser & Co., 1926-34; dir. research Interchem. Corp., N.Y. City, 1934-44, vice pres. and dir. research, 1944-52, director emeritus of research from 1952; engaged in private practice as chemical cons. Recipient certificate awarded for effective research in connection with atomic bomb, 1945; certificate awarded for effective service in work on camouflage organized through Nat. Defense Research Council, Mar. 1, 1945; recipient grant for cancer research from Lillia Babbitt Hyde Found., 1944-53; Ault Award. National Assn. Printing Ink Makers. Fellow N.Y. Acad. Sci.; mem. Am. Chem. Soc. (councilor), Am. Assn. Cancer Research, A.A.A.S., Electron Microscope Society, Assn. Research Dirs. Rep. Luth. Club: University (Winter Park, Florida). Contributor of papers to chemical and to medicial publications. Holder chemical patents. Full family name—Gessler von Braunegg with hereditary rank of Knight decreed by Emperor Charles VI of Austria, 1726. Home: Sarasota FL Died Dec. 3, 1969; buried Saint Boniface Columbarium, Sarasota FL

GETMAN, FREDERICK HUTTON, chemist; b. Oswego, N.Y., Feb. 9, 1877; s. Charles Henry and Alice (Peake) G.; ed. Rensselaer Poly. Inst., Troy, N.Y., and Lehigh U.; grad. chem. dept., U. of Va., 1896; Ph.D., Johns Hopkins, 1903; m. Ellen M. Holbrook, Nov. 26, 1906. Instr. chemistry and physics, Stamford High Sch., 1897-1901; fellow physical chemistry, 1902-03, fellow by courtesy, 1903-04, Carnegie research asst. in phys. chemistry, 1903-04, Johns Hopkins; lecturer in phys. chemistry, Coll. City of New York, 1904-05; instr. in phys. science, Stamford High Sch., 1905-1906; lecturer physics, Columbia, 1907-08; asso. prof. chemistry, Bryn Mawr (Pa.) Coll., 1909-15; dir. Hillside Laboratory, Stamford, Conn.; dir. Stamford Trust Co.; pres. The Getman & Judd Co. Dir. and v.p. Ferguson Library; v.p. Stamford Hosp. Fellow A.A.A.S., Am. Inst. of Chemists; mem. Am. Chem. Soc., Am. Electrochem. Soc., History of Sciences Soc., London Chem. Soc., Nederlandsche Chemische Vereeniging, Phi Beta Kappa. Club: Chemists (New York). Presbyterian. Republican. Author: Blow-pipe Analysis, 1899; Laboratory Exercises in Physical Chemistry, 1904; Introduction to Physical Science, 1909; Outlines of THeoretical Chemistry, 1913; Electrochemical Equivalents (with Dr. Carl Hering); Life of Ira Remsen; also scientific papers on various problems in phys. chemistry and chem. biography. Died Dec. 2, 1941.

GHERARDI, BANCROFT, telephone engr.; b. San Francisco, Apr. 6, 1873; s. Bancroft (rear adm. U.S.N.) and Anna Talbot (Rockwell) G.; B.Sc., Poly. Inst. Brooklyn, 1891, Dr. Engring. from same institute, 1933; M.E., Cornell U., 1893, M.M.E., 1894; m. Mary Hornblower Butler, June 15, 1898. Began as engr. asst., N.Y. Telephone Co., 1895; traffic engr. same, 1900; chief engr. New York and New Jersey Telephone Co., 1901-06; asst. chief engr. N.Y. Telephone Co., and N.Y. and N.J. Telephone Co., 1906-07; equipment engr. Am. Telephone & Telegraph Co., 1907-09, engr. of plant same, 1909-18; acting chief engr. same co., 1918-19, chief engr., 1919-20, v.p., chief engr., 1920-38, retired. Trustee Cornell U. Republican. Episcopalian. Awarded Edison Medal, 1932, "for contributions to the art of telephone engineering and the development of electrical communication." Home: Short Hills, N.J. Died Aug. 14, 1941.

GIAVER, JOACHIM G., civil engr.; b. in Norway, Aug. 15, 1856; s. Jens H. and Hanna Birgitte (Holmboe) G.; came to America, 1882; C.E., Throndhjems Tech. Coll., Throndhjem, Norway, 1881; m. Louise C. Schmedling, Throndhjem, Norway, Sept. 3, 1885. Draftsman bridge dept. N.P. R.R., St. Paul, Minn., 1882-83; draftsman, 1883-85, chief engr., 1885-90, Shiffler Bridge Co., Pittsburgh; asst. chief engr. World's Columbian Expn., Chicago, 1891-93; gen. contracting, 1893-96; bridge designer for Sanitary Dist., Chicago, 1896-98; chief engr., D. H. Burnham & Co., Chicago, 1898-1915; cons. engr., Chicago, 1915— mem. Giaver & Dinkelberg. Trustee Norwegian Am. Hosp. Decorated by the King of Norway with Order of St. Olaf, first grade, 1921. Home: Chicago, Ill. Died May 29, 1925.

GIBBES, ROBERT WILSON, physician, scientist, mayor; b. Charleston, S.C., July 8, 1809; s. William Hassell and Mary (Wilson) G.; grad. S.C. Coll., Charleston, 1827; M.D., S.C. Med. Coll., 1830; m. Carolina Guignard, Dec. 20, 1827, 12 children. Asst. prof. chemistry, geology and mineralogy S.C. Coll., 1827-35; wrote article "On Typhoid Pneumonia, as it Occurs in the Neighborhood of Columbia, S.C.," (revolutionized treatment of the disease), 1842; took over, edited The South Carolinian (Democratic paper), 1852-58; edited Weekly Banner, 1852-60; mayor Charleston, 2 terms; surgeon gen. S.C. during Civil War; owned Saluda factory mfg. cotton shirting. Author: Monograph on Fossil Squalidae; Memoir on Monosaures and the Three Allied New Genera, 1849; Documentary History of the American Revolution, 3 vols., 1853-57. Died Columbia, S.C., Oct. 15, 1866.

GIBBS, ALFRED WOLCOTT, mech. engr.; b. Fort Fillmore, N.M., Oct. 27, 1856; s. Gen. Alfred Gibbs (U.S.A.) and Peggy F. (Blair) G.; student Rutgers Coll., 1873-74; M.E., Stevens Inst. Tech., 1878. Apprentice in Altoona shop of Pa. R.R., 1879-81; draftsman, 1881-86; master mechanic, 1886-90, 1892-93, Richmond & Danville R.R.; supt. motive power, Central of Ga. Ry., 1890-92, 1893-1902; asst. mech. engr., Pa. R.R., and supt. motive power, Phila., Wilmington & Baltimore R.R., 1902-03; gen. supt. motive power, 1903-11, chief mech. engineer, July 1, 1911—, Pa. R.R. Mem. bd. of mgrs. Franklin Inst., Phila. Home: Wayne, Pa. Died May 19, 1922.

GIBBS, GEORGE, mineralogist; b. Newport, R.I., Jan. 7, 1776; s. George and Mary (Channing) G.; M.A., R.I. Coll. (now Brown U.), 1800; attended Yale, 1808; m. Laura Wolcott, children include George, Oliver Wolcott, Alfred. Amassed collection of minerals by 1805 (largest and most valuable yet seen in U.S.), offered to deposit collection at Yale, 1810, sold collection to Yale, 1825; initiated suggestion for founding Journal of Science; v.p. N.Y. Lyceum of Natural History, 1822. Died Astoria, L.I., N.Y., Aug. 5, 1833.

GIBBS, GEORGE, enthnologist, geologist; b. Astoria, L.I., N.Y., July 17, 1815; grad. Harvard, 1838; m. Mary Gibbs, 1871. Collector, Port of Astoria, 1850-53; geologist U.S. Govt. commn. laying N.W. boundary; mem. N.W. boundary survey, 1857; important mem. Loyal Nat. League and Loyal Publication Soc., at outbreak of Civil War; contbd. to study of Indian langs., specialized in N.W. Indian langs. and customs. Author: Memoirs of the Administrations of Washington and John Adams (of great importance for history of Federalist Party), 1846; Instructions for Research Relative to the Ethnology and Philology of America. Died New Haven, Conn., Apr. 9, 1873.

GIBBS, GEORGE, consulting engr.; b. Chicago, Apr. 19, 1861; s. Francis S. and Eliza G. (Hosmer) G.; grad. Stevens Inst. Tech., 1882, Dr. Engineering, 1931. Engineer of tests and chemist, C.,M.&S.P. Ry., 1888-97; mech. engr. same road and Milwaukee & Northern Railroad; cons. engr. Baldwin Locomotive Works and Westinghouse Electric & Mfg. Co., 1897-1902, also chief engr. Brit. Westinghouse Electric & Mfg. Co., and Continental Westinghouse cos.; 1st v.p. Westinghouse, Church, Kerr & Co., 1901-05; cons. engr. Interborough Rapid Transit Co., Pa. R.R., and elec. engr. L.I. R.R.; mem. elec. traction commn. N.Y.C.&H.R. R.R., 1902-05; chief engr. electric traction and sta. constrn. Pa. R.R., N.Y. terminal, 1905-12; chief engr. electric traction L.I. R.R., 1912—, also cons. elec. engr. Pa. R.R.; cons. engr. Chicago Assn. Commerce Com. on Smoke Abatement and Electrification of Ry. Terminals, N.Y. Connecting R.R., N.&W. Ry., Pa. R.R., Pub. Service Commn. 1st Dist. State of N.Y., I.C. R.R., Transit Commn. State of N.Y., D.,L.&W. R.R., N.Y.,N.H.&H. R.R., Virginia Ry. Confidential adviser on engineering, Carnegie Instn. of Washington, D.C. Mem. U.S. Govt. Commn. of Ry. Experts to Russia, 1917. Trustee Stevens Inst. Tech., Presbyn. and Woman's hosps., New York. Fellow Am. Institute Electrical Engineers. Reporter on electric traction to Internat. Railway Congress, session, 1910, and pres. at Rome session, 1922. Awarded Norman medal, Am. Soc. C.E., 1911; Wellington prize, 1930. Home: New York, N.Y. Died May 19, 1940.

GIBBS, HARRY DRAKE, chemist; b. Cincinnati, Mar. 10, 1872; s. William Henry and Emma A. (Drake) G.; student Rose Poly. Inst., Terre Haute, Ind., 1890; B.S., Cornell, 1894; Ph.D., Stanford, 1913; m. Camille Lafayette Hopper, Nov. 1, 1909; children—Edward H. D., Emma Carroll, Helen Barbara, William Eric. Asst. prof. chemistry, Ore. Agrl. Coll., 1901-03; research asst., Stanford U., 1904; chief chemist, San Francisco Bd. of Health, 1905-07; chief, div. of organic chemistry, Bur. of Science, Manila, 1907-14, also chief, Food and Drug Inspection Lab. and asst. to dir. of bur.; asso. prof. chemistry, 1910-12; chief Dept. of Chemistry, 1912-14, U. of Philippines; asst. chief eastern food inspection dist. Bur. of Chemistry, 1914-15, and chemist in charge of color lab., 1915-19; head of chem. dept. science and research div. of Bur. of Aircraft Production, 1918; mem. Nat. Research Council, 1918; chemist E. I. duPont de Nemours & Co., 1919-22; senior chemist Hygienic Lab., U.S. Pub. Health Service, 1922-29; cons. chem. engr. Presbyn. Home: Hyattsville, Md. Died Dec. 28, 1934.

GIBBS, JAMES ETHAN ALLEN, inventor; b. Rockbridge County, Va., Aug. 1, 1829; s. Richard and Isabella (Poague) G.; m. Catherine Givens, 1883; m. 2d, Margaret Craig, 1893; at least 3 children. Asso. with father's machine carding bus., Rockbridge County, until 1846; made unsuccessful attempt to establish wool-carding bus. utilizing machine of own design, Mill Point, Pocahontas County, W. Va., 1846; engaged in agr., 1846-50; built a sewing machine (from pictures of sewing machines appearing in advertisements), patented 2 improvements (a forerunner of automatic tensions system and a material feeding device), 1856; patented several chain and lock stitch machines, 1857; invented twisted loop rotary hook machine, 1857; formed partnership with James Willcox, introduced Willcox and Gibbs sewing machine, 1858; patented a lock and clutch driven bicycle; mfr. gunpowder for Confederate Army during Civil War; ret. from bus., 1890; traveled around U.S. and to Europe; gave name to Town of Raphine (from Greek: to sew), Rockbridge County. Died Raphine, Nov. 25, 1902.

GIBBS, JOSIAH WILLARD, mathematical physicist; b. New Haven, Conn., Feb. 11, 1839; s. Prof. Josiah Willard and Mary Anna (Van Cleve) G.; grad. Yale U., 1858; Ph.D., Yale U., 1863; studied in Paris, 1866-67; Berlin, 1867, Heidelberg, 1868; hon. doctorates from Erlangen, 1893; Williams Coll., 1893; Princeton, 1896; tutor in Latin, 1863-65, tutor in natural philosophy, 1865-66, Yale College; prof. of mathematical physics, Yale, 1871-1903. Mem., Nat. Acad. Scis.; Fellow Royal Soc., 1897 (Copley medal, 1901); elected to Hall of Fame for Great Americans, 1950. Author: Graphical methods in the thermodynamics of fluids, 1873; A method of geometrical representation of the thermodynamic properties of substances by means of surfaces, 1873; On the equilibrium of heterogeneous substances, 1876-78; Elementary principle in statistical mechanics, 1902. Applied thermodynamics to chemistry (by application of 1st and 2nd laws of thermodynamics to heterogeneous substances, he established theoretical basis for physical chemistry); discovered Gibbs phase rule; began development of vector analysis and applied it to problems of crystallography and to computation of planetary and cometary orbits; also conducted research in optics and statistical mechanics; patented railroad brake. Died New Haven, Conn., Apr. 28, 1903.

GIBBS, (OLIVER) WOLCOTT, chemist; b. New York, Feb. 21, 1822; s. George and Laura (Wolcott) G.; A.B., 1841, A.M., 1844, Columbia; M.D., Coll. Phys. & Surg., New York, 1843; studied at Univ. of Berlin and under Liebig at Giessen, and at Coll. of France, Paris; (LL.D., Columbia, 1873, Harvard, 1888, Columbian, 1895; U. of Toronto, 1897, U. of Pa., 1902). Delivered lectures at Delaware Coll., Newark; prof. physics and chemistry, Coll. City of New York, 1849-63; Rumford prof. and lecturer on the application of science to the useful arts, 1863-87, prof. emeritus, Harvard, Mem. exec. com. U.S. Sanitary Commn., New York, during Civil War; U.S. commr. Vienna Expn., 1873. Home: Newport, R.I. Died 1908.

GIBBS, WILLIAM FRANCIS, naval architect, marine engr.; b. Phila., Pa. Aug. 24, 1886; s. William Warren and Frances Ayers (Johnson) G.; student Harvard, scientific, 1906-19; LL.B. and M.A., Columbia, 1913; E.D. (hon.), Stevens Inst. Tech., 1938, N.Y.U., 1955; D.Sc. (hon.), Harvard, 1947, Bowdoin Coll., 1955; m. Mrs. Vera Cravath Larkin, 1927; children—Francis C., Christopher L.; (step-son) Adrain C. Larkin. Organizer Gibbs Bros., Inc., Feb. 1922, Gibbs & Cox, Inc., 1929 (pres.). Controller of shipbuilding WPB, Dec. 1942-Sept. 1943. Chmn. Combined Shipbuilding Com. of Combined Chiefs of Staff, 1943; rep. Office War Mobilization on Procurement Rev. Bd. of Navy, 1943. Recipient Am. Design award, 1943, David W. Taylor gold medal Soc. Naval Architects and Marine Engrs., 1946. Presdl. Certificate of Merit, 1947, Holland Soc. of N.Y. Distinguished service gold medal, 1951, Franklin Medal (gold) from Franklin Inst., 1953; Elmer A. Sperry Award, 1955; Michael Pupin medal, Columbia Engring. Alumni Assn., 1959; Allied Professions medal, A.I.A., 1960; William S. Newell Meml. award, United Seaman's Service, 1962. Fellow Royal Soc. Arts. Arts, Am. Soc. M. E. (hon.), (asso.) Inst. Aeronautical Scis.; mem., Soc., N.Y. Acad. Scis., Naval Architects and Marine Engrs. (v.p.), Instn. Naval Architects, Am. Soc. Naval Engrs., Am. Bur. Shipping (tech. com.), N.E. Coast Inst. Engrs. and Shipbuilders, U.S. Naval Inst., Nat. Acad. Scis., N.Y. Bar, Phi Beta Kappa. Clubs: University, Century, Broad Street, Piping Rock, India House, N.Y. Yacht. Home: 945 5th Av. Office: 1 Broadway, N.Y.C. 4. Died Sept. 1967.

GIBNEY, VIRGIL PENDLETON, surgeon; b. Jessamine Co., Ky., Sept. 29, 1847; s. Dr. Robert A. and Amanda (Weagley) G.; A.B., Ky. U., 1869, A.M., 1872, LL.D., 1899; M.D., Bellevue Hosp. Med. Coll. (New York U.), 1871; m. Charlotte L. Chapin, Dec. 1883; m. 2d, Julia Trubee, June 20, 1893. Asst. phys., 1871, resident house surgeon, 1871-84, surgeon-in-chief, 1887—, Hosp. for Ruptured and Crippled; prof. orthopedic surgery, N.Y. Polyclinic, 1882-94; clin. lecturer orthopedic surgery, 1894-95, clinical prof., 1895-1904, prof., 1904-17, Coll. of Phys. and Surg. (Columbia). Fellow Am. Coll. Surgeons. Democrat. Author: The Hip and Its Diseases, 1884. Died June 16, 1927.

GIBSON, CHARLES BROCKWAY, chemist, metallurgist, mining engr.; b. Massena, N.Y., Aug. 6, 1854; s. Otis and Chloe (Brockway) G.; B.Sc., U. of Ill., 1877; M.D., Coll. Phys. and Surg. same univ., 1885; student U. of Berlin, Royal Mining Acad., Royal Agrl. Acad., 1891-93; m. Eva Katherine Clapp, June 29, 1891 (now dec.); m. 2d, Susie Irene Gibson, of Chester, Vt., July 3, 1917; children—Theodore Otis, Conrad Bradley. With G.A. Mariner and C. G. Wheeler, chemists, until 1882; professor chemistry College of Physicians and Surgeons, Chicago, 1882-90; professor chemistry and metallurgy, Chicago Coll. Dental Surgery, 1888-96, and prof. 1 yr. each at Hahnemann Med. Coll. and Northwestern Dental Coll.; in Chicago since 1879; has done much expert and legal work; devoted attention principally to mining engring. and metallurgy since 1906. Former mem. Vt. N.G.; capt., acting maj., Ill.

N.G.; 1st lt. Med. R.C., U.S.A., 1917; sanitary officer Ft. Sheridan (Ill.) T.C.; served as 1st lt. and sanitary officer, Am. Red. Cross Commn. in Greece and Bulgaria, 1918-19; chemist U.S. Naval Ordnance Plant, Charleston, W. Va., 1919. Spl. com. to Germany, Chicago Expn., 1891-93. Mason (32 deg., K.T., Shriner). Mem. Writer's Guild, Lit. Guild. Author: (brochures) Recovery of Poisons in the Presence of Organic Matter, 1883; Analysis of Urine for Clinical Indications, 1884; State University Ideals, 1896; Universal Military Training, 1915. Translator of Tuedorff's Leitfaden zur Chem. Anal., 1896. Contbr. papers on chem. and metall. topics. Has traveled widely in U.S., Can. Mexico, Europe and the Orient, and has written and lectured on subjects bearing on those countries. Home: 6912 N. Ashland Blvd., Chicago, Ill.; and Altadena, Cal.

GIBSON, JAMES LAMBERT, mathematician; b. Kamas, Utah, Mar. 10, 1873; s. William and Mary Adelia (Lambert) G.; B.S., U. of Utah, 1895; A.M., Columbia, 1898; Ph.D., Vienna, 1923; studied Cambridge U., Eng., 1902-03, Bonn., Germany, 1922, Vienna, 1922-23, Paris, 1923, Göttingen, 1931; m. Sarah Pope, Feb. 11, 1904; children—Marl D., Rhea, James L., Vera, Keath P., Earle. Prof. mathematics, University of Utah, 1904-41, dean School of Arts and Sciences, 1915-41, now emeritus. Pres. Utah Conservation and Research Foundation since 1937. Fellow A.A.A.S., Utah Acad. of Sciences, Arts and Letters; mem. Am. Math. Soc., Math. Assn. America, Phi Kappa Phi, Sigma Xi. Home: 1337 Harrison Av., Salt Lake City 3, Utah. Died Feb. 10, 1945. *

GIBSON, LORENZO P., physician; b. Little Rock, Ark., Aug. 18, 1855; s. Lorenzo and Caroline Louisa (Thomas) G.; Ph.B., St. John's Coll., Little Rock, 1875; M.D., Jefferson Med. Coll., Phila., 1877; m. Mary Johnson Jordan, Apr. 18, 1883. In practice at Little Rock, Ark., 1877—; demonstrator anatomy U. of Ark., 1878-1903; acting asst. surgeon, U.S. Pub. Health Service, 1882—. Chief med. staff, St. Vincent's Infirmary. Sec. Ark. State Bd. Health. Editor Journal Ark. Med. Soc., 1890-95. Died Dec. 31, 1919.

GIBSON, WILLIAM, surgeon, educator; b. Balt., Mar. 14, 1788; s. John Gibson; ed. St. John's Coll., Annapolis; M.D., U. Edinburgh (Scotland), 1809; studied with Sir Charles Bell in Eng.; m. Sarah Hollingsworth, 8 children including Charles Bell. Prof. surgery U. Md., 1811-19; tied common iliac artery for aneurism (1st time done in Am.), 1812; prof. surgery U. Pa., 1819-55; did much to advance knowledge and practice surgery; performed Caesarean section twice on same patient who lived 50 years after 1st operation (most striking surg. success). Author: The Institutes and Practice of Surgery (prin. publ.), 1824. Died Savannah, Ga., Mar. 2, 1868.

GIDEON, PETER MILLER, pomologist; b. Woodstock, O., Feb. 9, 1820; s. George and Elizabeth (Miller) G.; m. Wealthy Hull, Jan. 2, 1849. Moved to land claim "Gideon's Bay," Lake Minnetonka Minn., 1858; engaged in developing varieties of fruit to withstand Northern climates for 41 years; developed "Wealthy" apple from seeds of Siberian crabtree; head of Minn. state exptl. fruit farm, 1878; originated new varieties of crab apples. Author: Growing Hardy Fruits, 1885; Our Seedling and Russian Apples, 1887. Died Oct. 27, 1899.

GIES, WILLIAM JOHN, (giz), biological chemist; b. Reisterstown, Md., Feb. 21, 1872; s. John Jr., and Ophelia Letitia (Ensminger) G.; B.S., Gettysburg, 1893, M.S., 1896, Sc.D., 1914, LL.D., 1924; Ph.B., Yale, 1894, Ph.D., 1897; LL.D., Baylor Univ., 1924; Sc.D., Temple Univ., 1938; Sc.D., U. of Maryland, 1940; studied U. of Berne, 1899; Marine Biol. Lab., Woods Hole, Mass., 1901, 1902; m. Mabel Loyetta Lark, May 24, 1899; children—John, James Tressler, Robert Henry, Mary. Asst. in physiol. chemistry, 1894-98, in zoölogy, 1895, tutor in physiology, 1896-98, Yale; instr. physiol. chemistry, 1898-1902, adj. prof., 1902-05, prof., 1905-07, prof. biol. chemistry, 1907-55, Columbia. Sec. of faculty of Coll. Phys. and Surg. (Columbia), 1905-21; prof. physiol. chemistry, New York Coll. of Pharmacy, 1904-22, Teachers Coll. (Columbia), 1909-28; cons. chemist New York Bot. Garden, 1902-21, and mem. board of scientific directors, 1911-28; consulting pathol. chemist, Bellevue Hosp., 1910-22. Pres. Ann. Conf. of Biol. Chemists, 1917-18; dir. Lutheran Hosp., 1917-19; chmn. exec. com. N.Y. Sch. of Dental Hygiene, 1916-17; sec. administrative bd. Sch. of Dentistry, Columbia U., 1917-21; chmn. Dental Adv. Board N.Y. Dept. of Health, 1926-35; mem. com. New York State Department of Health on fluoridation of Water Supplies since 1944. In charge study of dental education for Carnegie Foundation, 1921-31. Fellow A.A.A.S. (organizer, sec. sect. K, 1905-09), Am. Coll. Dentists (asst. sec. 1933-43; chmn. N.Y. sect. 1939-40, hist., 1947), Am. Acad. Periodontol., N.Y. Acad. Dentistry (v.p. 1938-40, pres. 1940-41, first hon. fellow, 1945); asso. fellow N.Y. Acad. Med., mem. Am. Philos. Soc., Soc. Exptl. Biol. and Med. (sec. 1903-09, v.p. 1909-10, 1914-15, pres. 1917-19), Am. Soc. Biol. Chemists (sec. 1906-10), Internat. Assn. Dental Research (hon. pres. 1922-28; sec. 1928-38; pres. elect 1938-39; pres. 1939-40), Am. Assn. Dental Editors (pres. 1935-36), Pan-Am. Odontol Assn. (pres. 1943-44); N.Y. State Dental Society (hon.), Allied Dental Council (hon.), American Physiological Society, Soc. Pharmacology and Exptl. Therapeutics, Phi Beta Kappa, Phi Sigma Kappa, Sigma Xi, Nu Sigma Nu, Omicron Kappa Upsilon, Theta Kappa Psi; hon. member Austrian and Danish dental societies. Choice of alumni for pres. of Gettysburg Coll., 1904, alumni trustee, 1908-20; trustee Irving Coll., 1900-10. Author: Biochemical Researches (8 vols.), 1903-27; Text-Book of General Chemistry, 1904; Text-Book of Organic Chemistry, 1905, 09; Laboratory Work in Biological Chemistry, 1906; Bull. on Dental Edn., for Carnegie Foundation, 1926. Editor Am. Dental Assn. vol. on Dental Caries, 1939, 2d edit., 1941, Wells Memorial vol., 1948. Editor Am. Coll. of Dentists volume on Dental Care Under Clinical Conditions, 1943; editor vol. for N.Y. Inst. Clin. Oral Path., on Fluorine in Dental Public Health, 1945. Founder, editor Proc. Soc. Exptl. Biology and Medicine, 1904-10, Proc. Am. Soc. Biol. Chemists, 1907-10, Bio-chem. Bull., 1911-16; Jour. Dental Research, 1919-36, editor emeritus since 1936; Jour. Am. Coll. of Dentists, 1934-38; asst. editor, 1938-40; editor dept. of biol. chemistry in Chem. Abstracts, 1911-21; asso. editor New York Jour. of Dentistry, 1935-36; contbg. editor Annals of Dentistry, 1936-42, mem. editorial bd., 1947-52; editor History of First Three Decades of N.Y. Acad. of Dentistry 1953. Past director research under auspices National Dental Research Commn., N.Y. State Dental Soc., First Dist. Dental Soc. State of N.Y. and N.Y. Sabbath Com.; chmn. Research Council of N.Y. Acad. Dentistry, 1927-41. Collaborator for various chemical, medical, and biological journals since 1895. Award of merit Rhode Island State Dental Soc., 1927; Callahan medal of Ohio State Dental Soc., 1928; permanent ann. fellowship in biol. chemistry, Columbia, founded in his honor, 1928, by pupils and colleagues; permanent dental research awards and fellowships founded in his honor, 1937, by Am. Coll. Dentists. Recipient of distinguished service award, Gettysburg Coll., 1938, Alpha Omega Frat., 1940, Sigma Epsilon Delta, 1948. Gies Found. for Advancement of Dentistry established by dentists, 1951; Spenadel and Burkhart awards by N.Y.C. and State dental socs., 1951, 52; Pa. ambassador (Manheim), 1951; inscribed bas-relief portrait-plaque erected 1952, as founder Columbia U. Dental Sch. Address: 502 W. Orange St., Lancaster, Pa. Died May 20, 1956.

GIESECKE, FREDERICK ERNEST, engineer; b. Washington County, Tex., Jan. 28, 1869; s. Julius and Wilhelmine (Groos) G.; M.E., Tex. A. and M., Coll., 1890; student Cornell, 1893-94; S.B. Architecture, Mass. Inst. Tech., 1904; student Tech. Hochschule, Charlottenburg, 1906-07; Ph.D., Univ. of Ill., 1924, C.E., 1943; m. Hulda C. Gruene, Mar. 5, 1891; children—Bertram E., Alma (Mrs. McCloud B. Hodges,) Linda (Mrs. Preston M. Geren), Minnie (Mrs. Edward A. Wight). Instr. in shop work and drawing, Tex. A. and M. Coll., 1886-88, prof. of drawing 1888-1906, prof. of archtl. engring., 1906-12; prof. archtl. engring., head div. engr. research, Univ. of Tex., 1912-27; dir. expt. sta. and coll. architect, Tex. A and M. Coll., 1927-39, prof. emeritus, 1939-45; cons. engr., New Braunfels, Tex., since 1945. Served as maj. engr. reserves, U.S., 1926-42. Awarded the F. Paul Anderson medal by Am. Soc. Heating and Ventilating Engrs., 1942. Mem. Am. Soc. E.E. (charter and life mem.), Am. Soc. C.E. (life mem., past pres. Tex. sect.), Am. Soc. Heating and Ventilating Engrs. (life mem., past pres. Tex. chapter, nat. pres. 1940), Am. Soc. M.E., A.A.A.S., Am. Soc. Engring. Edn., (past pres. Tex. chapter), Tau Beta Pi, Sigma Xi. Mason (32 deg.). Author: Gravity-Circulation Hot-Water Heating Systems, 1926; Descriptive Geometry and Descriptive Geometry Problems (with A. Mitchell), 1921; Technical Drawing and Technical Drawing Problems (with A. Mitchell and H. C. Spencer), 1933; Hot-Water Heating, Radiant Heating, and Radiant Cooling, 1947. Contbr. about 75 tech. articles in engring. pubs. and bulls. Home: New Braunfels TX*

GIFFORD, HAROLD, ophthalmic surgeon; b. Milwaukee, Oct. 18, 1858; s. Charles and Mary Caroline (Child) G.; B.Sc., Cornell, 1879; M.D., U. of Mich., 1882, hon. M.A. from same univ., 1912; LL.D., U. of Neb., 1918; post-grad. studies, New York, Erlangen, Vienna, Zurich; m. Mary Louise Millard, Dec. 30, 1890. Began practice as ophthalmic and aural surgeon, Omaha, 1886; prof. emeritus of ophthalmology, U. of Neb.; ophthalmic and aural surgeon to Methodist Hosp. Home: Omaha, Neb. Died Nov. 28, 1929.

GIFFORD, ROBERT LADD, cons. engr.; b. Smithfield, O.; s. William and Lydia (Ladd) G.; Chemical Engineer also Mechanical Engineer Cornell U.; L.H.D., U. So. Cal.; m. Evelyn A Brooks; 1 son, Brooks. Chmn. bd. or pres. Ill. Engring. Co., 1900-53; pres. G. & C. Patents Co., ret. 1953; cons. engr.; inventor and patentee of numerous automatic steam devices, locomotive boiler washout system and industrial processes. Trustee Whittier College; trustee U. So. Cal. Fellow Royal Hort. Soc., London; member Honolulu Orchid Society (life member), Am. Society Civil Engrs., Am. Soc. Mech. Engrs., Am. Soc. Heating & Ventilating Engrs., Western Soc. Engrs., Pasadena Humane Soc. (past pres., treas.), Soc. Mayflower Descendents, Boys Club (director), Am. Orchid Soc. Republican. Quaker. Clubs: University (Chicago); University (Pasadena); Alpha Delta Phi; Atheneum; Valley Hunt. Home: 1231 S. El Molina Av., Pasadena 5. Died Jan. 10, 1963; buried Inglewood Park Cemetery.

GIFFORD, SANFORD ROBINSON, ophthalmologist; b. Omaha, Neb., Jan. 8, 1892; s. Harold and Mary (Millard) G.; A.B., Cornell U., 1913; M.A. and M.D., U. of Nebr., 1918; m. Alice Carter, July 11, 1917; children—Sanford R., Carter. Bacteriologist, rank of 1st lt. U.S. Army Base Hosp., in France, 1918-19; in practice with father, Omaha, 1919-29; instr. in ophthalmology, U. of Neb. Med. Sch., 1919-24, asst. prof. ophthalmology, 1924-29; prof. ophthalmology, Northwestern U. Med. Sch., also ophthmologist to allied hosps. since 1929; attending ophthalmologist Cook County Hosp. since 1932. Mem. Am. Ophthal. Soc., Am. Acad. Ophthalmology and Oto-Rhino.-Laryngology, Chicago Inst. Medicine, Phi Rho Sigma, Alpha Omega Alpha and Sigma Xi fraternities. Clubs: Tavern, University, Saddle and Cycle, Bohemian (San Francisco, Calif.). Author: Handbook of Ophthalmic Therapeutics, 3d edit., 1942; Textbook of Ophthalmology, 2d edit., 1941, Asso. editor Archives of Ophthalmology since 1928. Contbr. to Am. Jour. Ophthalmology, 1919-28. Corr. editor Klinische Monatsblätter für Augenheikunde, 1928-40. Author of articles on bacteriology of the eyes, especially diseases due to fungi and higher bacteria. With Dr. J. M. Patton reported probable etiological agent of hitherto unknown disease, agricultural conjunctivitis. Home: 1430 Lake Shore Drive. Office: 720 N. Michigan Av., Chicago, Ill. Died Feb. 25, 1944.

GIHON, ALBERT LEARY, med. dir. U.S.N., retired; b. Phila., Sept. 28, 1883; A.B., Phila. High School, 1850; M.D., Coll. of Medicine and Surgery, 1852; A.M., Princeton, 1884; m. Clara Montfort Campfield, Apr. 3, 1860. Prof. chemistry and toxicology, Phila. Coll. Medicine and Surgery, 1853-54; asst. surgeon U.S.N., May 1, 1855; served at attack and capture barrier forts, nr. Canton, China, Nov., 1856; on Paraguay expdn., 1858-59; during Civil war, 1861-65; received thanks of British govt. of comdr.-in-chief French Asiatic squadron, and made Knight of the Portuguese Mil. Order of Christ, for services to British, French and Portuguese men-of-war while senior med. officer of Idaho (1st hosp. ship in U.S.N.); sr. med. dir., U.S.N., May 1, 1895; retired by operation of law, Sept. 28, 1895, with rank of commodore. Fellow and pres. Am. Acad. of Medicine. Was editor Annual of the Medical Sciences 6 yrs. Died 1901.

GILBERT, CHARLES HENRY, zoölogist; b. Rockford, Ill., Dec. 5, 1859; s. Edward and Sarah (Bean) G.; B.S., Butler U., 1879; M.S., Ind. U., 1882, Ph.D., 1883; m. Julia R. Hughes, Aug. 7, 1883. Asst. in natural sciences and modern langs., Ind. U., 1880-84; prof. natural hist., U. of Cincinnati, 1884-89; prof. zoölogy, Ind. U., 1889-91; prof. zoölogy, Stanford, 1891—. Asst. to U.S. Fish Commn., 1880-98; naturalist in charge U.S. Fish Commn. steamer Albatross, 1889-90; naturalist in charge Hawaiian Explorations of U.S. Fish Commn. steamer Albatross, 1902, and explorations in northwest Pacific and Japan, 1906; asst., Internat. Fisheries Commn., 1909; in charge expert salmon investigations for U.S. Bur. of Fisheries and British Columbia Fisheries Dept., 1909-27. Author: Synopsis of the Fishes of North America (with David Starr Jordan), 1882; The Deep-Sea Fishes (of the Hawaiian Islands), 1905. Home: Stanford University, Calif. Died Apr. 20, 1928.

GILBERT, EARL C., chemist, educator; b. Palmyra, O., Feb. 2, 1895; s. Henry Warner and Lily Belle (Turnbull) G.; B.S., Hiram (O.) Coll., 1916; M.S., 1917; Ph.D., U. Chgo., 1922; m. Annette Leonard, June 5, 1918; children—Henry Leonard, Allan Earl. Prin. Brimfield (O.) High Sch., 1917; jr. gas chemist Bur. of Mines, Washington, 1918; mem. faculty Ore. State Coll., since 1917, prof. chemistry, 1930—, chmn. dept. chemistry 1940-56. Pvt. Chem. Warfare Service, 1918; chief chem. warfare def. Ore. State Civil Def., 1949-50. Guggenheim fellow, Copenhagen and Berlin, 1928-29. Fellow A.A.A.S.; mem. Am. Chem. Soc. (pres. Ore. sect. 1932, councilor 1933), Electrochem. Soc. (pres. 49, Ore. Acad. Sci. (v.p. 1956, pres. 1957); Sigma Xi, Phi Kappa Phi, Phi Lambda Upsilon. Republican. Mem. Christian Ch. Mason. Contbr. articles sci. jours. Home: 210 N. 29th St., Corvallis, Ore. 97300. Died Jan. 13, 1964.

GILBERT, EDWARD MARTINIUS, prof. botany; b. Blair, Wis., Sept. 20, 1875; s. Thomas J. and Julia (Jahr) G.; grad. Normal Sch., Stevens Point, Wis., 1901; Ph.B., U. of Wis., 1907, Ph.D., 1914; m. Esther Montogomery Lowry, June 15, 1910; children—Jane, Thomas Lowry, Edward Everett. Teacher biology, State Normal Sch., Superior, Wis., 1907-10; with U. of Wis. since 1912 as asst. prof. botany to 1917, prof. botany, 1923-46, emeritus, 1946. Mem. Botanical Society of America, American Phytopathol. Society, American Microscopical Society, Wisconsin, Academy Science, Am. Mycol. Soc., Am. Society Taxonomists, Sigma Xi, Gamma Alpha, Phi Sigma. Club: University. Joint Author: Text-book of Botany for High Schools (with C.E. Allen), 1915; Text-book of General Botany (with Allen, Bryan, Duggar, Evans and Smith), 1924, new edit., 1943. Home: 2120 Chamberlain St., Madison WI

GILBERT, GROVE KARL, geologist; b. Rochester, N.Y., May 6, 1843; s. Grove Sheldon and Eliza (Stanley) G.; A.B., U. of Rochester, 1862, A.M., 1872 (LL.D., 1898, U. of Wis., 1904, U. of Pa., 1907); m. Fannie L. Porter, Nov. 10, 1874. Asst. in Ward Mus., Rochester, 1863-68; geologist in Ohio survey, 1868-70, Wheeler survey, 1871-74, Powell survey, 1875-79, U.S. Geol. Survey. 1879—(chief geologist, 1889-92). Spl. lecturer, Cornell, 1886, Columbia, 1892, Johns Hopkins, 1895 and 1896. Walker grand prize, Boston Soc. Natural History, 1908. Editor geol. and phys. geography depts., Johnson's Encyclopaedia. Author: Introduction to Physical Geography, 1902; Glaciers and Glaciation, vol. 3, Harriman Alaska Expdn., 1904. Died May 1, 1918.

GILBERT, RUFUS HENRY, physician, inventor; b. Guilford, N.Y., Jan. 26, 1832; s. William Dwight Gilbert; attended Coll. Phys. and Surg., N.Y.C.; m. Miss Maynard; m. 2d, Miss Price; 2 children. Began practice medicine, Corning, N.Y., circa 1853; went to Europe, circa 1857, became convinced that public health problems could best be solved by building rapid transp. facilities to permit urban residents to live outside cities in cleaner atmosphere; surgeon to Duryée Zouaves, 1861, later served as med. dir. XIV Corps, U.S. Army; to implement his ideas on rapid transp., became asst. supt. Central R.R. of N.J.; obtained patents for pneumatic tube system, 1870; instrumental in incorporation of Gilbert Elevated R.R. Co., 1872 (opened for travel, 1878), forced out of mgmt. of co., circa 1878. Died N.Y.C., July 10, 1885.

GILBREATH, JAMES RICHARD, sci. research adminstr.; b. Seattle, Apr. 27, 1918; s. James Alvin and Matilda (Karrer) G.; B.S. in Chemistry, U. Wash., 1939, M.S., 1941; Ph.D., U. Chgo., 1952; (div.); 1 son, James Michael. Chemist uranium project OSRD, U. Chgo., 1942-43; engaged in Signal Corps project, U.S. Army-U. Chgo., 1943-44; with metall. lab. Manhattan Project, 1944-46; mem. staff Argonne Nat. Lab., 1946—, asso. dir. chemistry div., 1953-57, asst. dir. lab., 1957-65. Fellow A.A.A.S.; mem. Research Soc. Am., Am. Chem. Soc., Am. Nuclear Soc., Phi Beta Kappa, Sigma Xi, Phi Lambda Upsilon, Pi Mu Epsilon. Home: 5433 Dorchester Av., Chgo. 60615. Office: 9700 S. Cass Av., Argonne, Ill. 60440. Died July 8, 1965.

GILBRETH, FRANK BUNKER, cons. engineer; b. Fairfield, Me., July 7, 1868; s. John Hiram and Martha (Bunker) G.; grad. English High Sch., Boston, 1885; LL.D., U. of Me., 1920; m. Lillian Evelyn Moller (B.L., M.L., U. of Calif.; Ph.D., Brown U.), Oct. 19, 1904. Contracting engr., Boston, 1895-1904, New York, 1904-11; consulting engr., 1911—; pres. Frank B. Gilberth (Inc.). Commd. maj., Engrs., July 1917; on active duty Gen. Staff Coll., Washington, Dec. 1917. Lecturer at 20 Am. and European univs.; dir. Summer Sch. of Management for Professors of Engineering, Psychology and Economics; organized Soc. Promotion Science of Management (afterwards Taylor Soc., the first of its kind); founder internat. museums for elimination of unnecessary fatigue of workers in the industries; inventor of the micro-motion and chronocyclegraph processes for determining fundamental units and methods of industrial edn., and of methods for fitting crippled soldiers for industrial life. Author: Field System, 1908; Concrete System, 1908; Bricklaying System, 1909; Motion Study, 1911; Primer of Scientific Management, 1911; also with wife, Time Study; Fatigue Study, 1916; Applied Motion Study, 1917; Motion Study for the Handicapped, 1919. Home: Montclair, N.J. Died June 14, 1924.

GILBRETH, LILLIAN MOLLER, cons. engr.; b. Oakland, Calif., May 24, 1878; d. William and Annie (Delger) Moller; B.Litt., U. of Calif., 1900, M.Litt., 1902, LL.D., 1933; Ph.D., Brown, 1915, Sc.D., 1931; M. Engring., U. Mich., 1928; Dr. Engring., Rutgers Coll., 1929, Stevens Inst. Tech., 1950, Syracuse U., 1952; Sc.D., Russell Sage Coll., 1931, Colby Coll., 1951, Lafayette Coll., 1952; LL.D., Smith Coll., 1945, Mills Coll., 1952; Dr. Humane Letters, Temple U., 1949, Alfred U., 1948; Dr. Indsl. Psychol., Purdue U., 1948, hon. degrees from Milw. Downer, Washington Univ., Princeton, Skidmore Coll., U. Wis., Pratt Inst., U. Mass., Western Coll. Women; Doctor of Laws, Arizona State Univ., 1964; m. Frank Bunker Gilbreth, October 19, 1904; children—Anne Moller (Mrs. Robert E. Barney), Mary Elizabeth (dec.), Ernestine Moller (Mrs. Charles E. Carey), Martha Bunker (Mrs. Richard E. Tallman) (dec.), Frank Bunker, William Moller, Lillian Moller (Mrs. Donald D. Johnson), Frederick Moller, Daniel Bunker, John Moller, Robert Moller, Jane Moller (Mrs. G. Paul Heppes, Jr.). Pres. of Gilbreth, Inc., cons. engrs. in mgmt., Montclair, N.J., from 1924; dir. courses in motion study, 1925-32; prof. mgmt. Purdue U., 1935-48; chmn. dept. of personnel relations Newark Coll. Engring., 1941-43; univ. teaching P.I., Formosa, 1953-54; prof. mgmt. U. Wis., 1955; lectr. on tech. and human relations problems in mgmt. in Asia, Australia, Can., Europe, Mexico, U.S.A., from 1955. Mem. U.S. Govt. coms. on civil def., also state and local coms. Trustee Russell Sage Coll., 1943-45, Montclair Library, 1944-54; mem. Essex County Vocational Bd. Recipient Henry Lawrence Gantt medal (with Frank Gilbreth), Nat. Inst. Social Scis., Wallace Clark International award, gold medal Comite Internat. de l'Orgn. Scientifique, Washington award; Allan R. Cullimore medal, 1959; Hoover medal American Society Civil Engrs., 1966. Mem. Housing Com., 20th Century Fund; mem. N.J. State Bd. Regents, 1929-33; mem. Essex Co. Vocational Bd. Hon. fellow British Institute of Management, 1951; member American Association University Women, American Management Assn. (hon.), Institute of Management, Soc. for Advancement of Management (hon.), Acad. Masaryk, Am. Psychol. Assn., A.S.M.E. (hon. mem. 1950), Engring. Inst. Can. (hon. mem. 1949), Am. Home Econs. Assn. (honorary member 1952), Soc. Indsl. Engrs. (hon.), Inst. for Scientific Management of Poland, Women's Engring. Soc. of London. Nat. Acad. Engring., Internat. Acad. of Mgmt., Phi Beta Kappa. Author: (with Frank B. Gilbreth) Fatigue Study, 1911. Applied Motion Study, 1917, Motion Study for the Handicapped, 1919; The Psychology of Management, 1921; Living with Our Children, 1928; Normal Lives for the Disabled (with Edna Yost), 1945; The Foreman and Manpower Management (with Alice Rice Cook), 1947; Management in the Home (with O.M. Thomas, Eleanor C. Clymer), 1954, 59. Contbr. Indsl. Engring. Handbook. Home: Upper Montclair NJ also Nantucket MA Died Jan. 2, 1972.

GILCHRIST, T(HOMAS) CASPAR, M.D.; b. Crewe Cheshire, Eng., June 15, 1862; s. Robert and Emma (Weiss) G.; ed. Owen's Coll. (Victoria U.), Eng.; intermediate M.B., U. of London, 1886; M.R.C.S., London, 1887; licentiate in medicine, surgery and midwifery, London, 1887; hon. M.D., U. of Md., 1907; m. Annie McKerrow Hall, 1894. Came to America, 1890; clin. prof. dermatology, U. of Md., 1897—; clin. prof. dermatology, Johns Hopkins U. and dermatologist, Johns Hopkins Hosp., 1898—. Presbyn. Home: Roland Park, Md. Died Nov. 14, 1927.

GILE, JOHN MARTIN, physician; b. Pembroke, N.H., Mar. 8, 1864; s. Brainerd and Mary (Kimball) G.; A.B. Dartmouth, 1887; M.D., 1890; m. Vesta Grace Fowler, June 8, 1892. Began practice at Tewksbury, Mass., 1890; prof. practice of medicine, 1896-1910, dean and prof. clin. surgery, 1910—, Dartmouth Med. Sch. Fellow Am. Coll. Surgeons. Member Governor's Council, 4th dist., 1911, 1912. Commd. lt. Med. R.C., and med. aide to the gov., 1917-18. Trustee Dartmouth Coll. Home: Hanover, N.H. Died July 15, 1925.

GILL, AUGUSTUS HERMAN, prof. chemistry; b. Canton, Mass., Aug. 1, 1864; s. Augustus and Hannah P. (Drake) G.; S.B., Mass. Inst. Tech., 1884; Ph.D., U. of Leipzig, 1890; Sc.D., Rhode Island State Coll., 1923; m. Mabel F. Shepard, Sept. 2, 1897; children—Helen (Mrs. Charles McKay Welling), Paul Herman. Became assistant, 1884, instr., 1886-87, and 1890-94, asst. prof. gas analysis, 1894-1906, asso. prof. tech. analysis, 1906-09, prof., 1909-34, professor emeritus, Mass. Inst. of Technology. Lecturer Wellesley Coll., 1892-93. Unitarian. Republican. Mason. Author: Gas and Fuel Analysis for Engineers, 1896; A Short Handbook of Oil Analysis, 1897; Engineroom Chemistry, 1907; Automobile Gasoline, 1923; Power Plant Chemistry, 1935. Home: Belmont, Mass. Died Nov. 11, 1936.

GILL, ELBYRNE GRADY, physician; b. Bedford, Va., Oct. 21, 1891; s. Stonewall Jackson and Mittie Lillian (Page) G.; M.D., Vanderbilt U., 1916; postgrad., U. Pa., 1930, N.Y. Eye and Ear Infirmary, 1917-19; Berlin, Vienna, and London, 1936; m. Ruth Houck Meals, June 16, 1923; children—Edith (Mrs. Stanley Breakell), Jean (Mrs. W. Courtney King), Betty (Mrs. John M. Chaney). Began practice 1919; founded Gill Meml. Eye, Ear, and Throat Hosp., 1926; founded ann. spring seminar course for grads. in medicine specializing in eye, ear, nose, and throat, 1927; founder Elbyrne G. Gill Eye and Ear Found. Mem. bd. visitors Va. Sch. for Deaf and Blind, 1936-44; chmn. Bd. Health, Roanoke, Va., 1937—; mem. council Nat. Eye Bank, N.Y.C.; ophthalmologist, Norfolk & Western Ry. Past mem. bd. trustees Roanoke City Pub. Library. Pres., Roanoke Acad. Medicine, 1950-51. Dir. Eye Bank and Sight Conservation Soc. Va., 1956—; pres. Elbyrene G. Gill Eye and Ear Found. Diplomate Am. Bd. Otolaryngology. Fellow A.C.S.; mem. A.M.A., Internat. Coll. Surgeons, Am. Tri-O-Logical, Am. Acad. Ophthalmology and Otolaryngology, S.W. Va. Med. Soc., Am. Bronchoscopic Soc., Oxford Congress Opthalmology (Eng.), Alumni; Assn. N.Y. Eye and Ear Infirmary (past pres.), William and Mary Alumni Assn. Omicron Delta Kappa, Omega, Alpha, Alpha Tau Omega, Alpha Kappa Kappa. Clubs: Lions (internat. past pres., past dist. gov., dir.), Roanoke Country, Shenandoah, Roanoke German, Farmington Country, Virginia Seniors Golf Assn. (dir.). Democrat. Baptist. Mason (Shriner). Home: 2506 Cornwallis Av., South Roanoke, Va. 24014. Office: 711 S. Jefferson St., Roanoke, Va. Died Sept. 30, 1966; buried Evergreen Cemetery, Roanoke.

GILL, HENRY Z., physician; b. on farm, Richboro, Pa., Oct. 6, 1831; s. Henry and Mary (Fretz) G.; ed. in public schools and private acad. (A.M., McKendree Coll., 1875; LL.D., U. of Wooster, 1885); taught school, 1853-54; read medicine under physicians and at Starling Med. Coll., Columbus, O.; grad. Jefferson Med. Coll., Phila., 1857; m. Mattie W., d. Timothy R. Carpenter, Columbus, O., April 21, 1869. Practiced at Columbus, O., until 1861; asst. surgeon 11th regt., 1861, and later surgeon 95th regt., Ohio vols.; surgeon U.S. vols. from June, 1864-65 (surgeon-in-chief 1st div., 20th army corps, during Atlanta, Savannah and Carolina campaigns); 2 yrs. in European hosps.; later 3 yrs. asst. St. Louis Eye and Ear Infirmary; lecturer on pathology, St. Louis Med. Coll.; asso. editor and prop. St. Louis Med. and Surg. Jour.; pres. St. Louis Micros. Soc.; physician Southern Ill. penitentiary, 1881-83; prof. operative and clinical surgery, med. dept. Wooster Univ., 1883-86; resigned and removed to Kan.; some time prof. history, microscopy and bacteriology, Kan. Med. Coll., Topeka; sec. State bd. of health, Kan., 1897-99. Author: Gill's Sanné on Diphtheria, Croup and Tracheotomy. Home: Long Beach, Calif. Died 1907.

GILL, JAMES PRESLEY, metallurgist; b. Montgomery City, Mo., Jan. 21, 1896; s. James William and Julia (Kirn) G.; B.S., U. of Mo. Rolla Sch. of Mines, 1918, M.S. in Metall. Engring., 1919; grad. study Columbia U. Sch. of Mines, 1918-20; Dr. Engring. (hon.) University of Missouri, 1946; m. Clarice Powell, July 14, 1922; children—James Powell, Mary Julia. Began as metallurgist Anaconda Copper Co., 1918; research metallurgist, Vanadium Alloys Steel Co., 1920, chief metallurgist since 1921; chief metallurgist Anchor Drawn Steel Co. since 1926, and Colonial Steel Co., 1928—; dir. Vanadium Alloys Steel Co., v.p., 1943, chmn. exec. com., 1945, pres., 1953, chmn. 1958—; chmn. bd. Vanadium Alloys Steel Can., Ltd., 1954; v.p. Anchor Drawn Steel Co., 1945-58, pres., 1958—; pres. Colonial Steel Co., 1949—; chmn. Vanadium Alloys & Finance Co., Ltd., Eng., 1959—; dir. Societe Commentryenne des Aciers Fins Vanadium Alloys, France; v.p., dir. Vanadium-Alloys Steel Societa Italiana per Azioni, Italy. Dir. Council of Profit Sharing Industries; bd. mgrs. Trade Relations Council. Councilman of Latrobe, Pa., 1938-39. Pres. Am. Soc. for Metals, 1939-40, trustee since 1937. Mem. Nat. Commn. Celebration Sesquicentennial Founding of Patent Office. Mem. adv. com. on metals and minerals Nat. Acad. Sciences and Nat. Research Council, 1941; mem. Nat. Inventors Council, 1942; mem. com. Fgn. Econ. Adminstrn. to investigate German steel industry, 1945. Mem. Am. Inst. Mining & Metall. Engrs., Am. Soc. for Testing Materials, Am. Standards Assn., Am. Soc. Testing Engrs., Am. Soc. Tool Engrs., British Iron & Steel Inst., Am. Iron and Steel Inst., Tau Beta Pi, Pi Kappa Alpha, Theta Tau. Republican. Presbyterian. Mason (32 deg., Shriner). Clubs: Country (Latrobe, Pa.); University, Duquesne (Pittsburgh); Seven Springs (Champion, Penna.). Author: Tool Steels, 1934. Co-author: Modern Steels, 1939; Tool Steels, 1944. Mem. editorial bd. Metals Handbook, 1936, 1939. Contbr. over 40 articles on metall. subjects; has delivered over 200 different lectures on metall. subjects. Campbell Memorial lecturer, Am. Soc. for Metals, 1936. Inventor of compositions of special steels (10 patents). Home: 850 Weldon St. Office: Vanadium-Alloys Steel Co., Latrobe, Pa. Died Oct. 30, 1961; buried Unity Cemetery, Latrobe, Pa.

GILL, JOE HENRY, electric engr.; b. Kerrville, Tex., Sept. 25, 1886; s. Wm. Francis and Miriam (Fort) G.; E.E., U. of Tex., 1910; m. Mabel Jenkins, Oct. 2, 1918; 1 son, Wm. Haywood. With Gen. Electric Co., Schenectady, N.Y., 1910-12; with Tex. Power & Light Co., Dallas, 1912-17, advancing to gen. supervision design and constrn. of elec. distribution and transmission systems; with Dallas Power & Light Co., 1919-25, beginning as salesman and advancing to asst. gen. mgr. design, construction and operation of co.'s plants and systems; with Fla. Power & Light Co., Miami, 1925-35, pres. and gen. mgr., 1929-33; pres. Electric Power & Light Corp. since 1935. Served as pvt., later 2d and 1st lt. C.A.C., U.S. Army, 1917-20. Asso. mem. Am. Inst. E.E.; mem. Kappa Sigma. Democrat. Presbyterian. Club: Round Hill (Greenwich). Home: 5108 Gaston Av., Dallas, Tex. Office: 2 Rector St., New York, N.Y. Died June 16, 1944.

GILL, RICHARD C(OCHRAN), research-explorer, author; b. Washington, Nov. 22, 1901; s. Dr. William Tignor Gill and Flora May (Allen) G.; B.A., Cornell U., 1924; grad. student Columbia, N.Y.U., 1926-27; m. Ruth Lenfest, Apr. 19, 1926. Instr. English, Lafayette Coll., Easton, Pa., 1925-28; field mgr. in Ecuador, Peru, Bolivia, S.A., B. F. Goodrich Rubber Corp., 1928-30; pres. Gill, Miller Co., ranching, Ecuador, 1930—; pres. Gill, Dundas and Co., Palo Alto, Cal., leader Gill-Merrill expdn., other S.A. (upper-Amazonian) expdns. in ethno-botany, tropical Am. pharmacognosy, etc.; ethnographic exploring chiefly in ethnobotany of drug curare, and clin. application to spastic paralysis, and its accepted clin. application in shock-therapy method of treating mental diseases, more recently its use as an adjuvant in anesthesia and an anti-convulsant in other fields; pvt. research in evolution and clin. application of new therapeutic curare variant of higher alkaloidal potency; evolution of economical prodn. technique for chem. pure d-tubocurarine, its clin. uses in acute anterior poliomyelitis, obstet. anaesthesia, allied gynecologic employments, recent easier co-adminstrn. with intravenous anaesthetics; writer, lectr., 1930—; acting adviser on tropical Am. def. commodities and drugs, def. facilities and terrain; pres. Gill-Merrill Participants; bot. collections N.Y. Bot. Garden, Arnold Arboretum (Harvard), Kew Gardens (London), referable elsewhere; pres., founder S.A. mfg. base, Transandino Co., curare and other tropical drugs;

founded tech. library, over 5000 items on history, botany, pharmacognosy, pharmacology and clin. reprints and curare, curare synthetics, anti-curare agts. Recipient 2 citations from Republic of Ecuador. Fellow Am. Geog. Soc., Am. Polar Soc.; mem. Hakluyt Soc. (Great Britain), Explorers Club, A.A.A.S., Am. Acad. Polit. and Social Sci.; Cal. Acad. Scis., Am. Pharm. Assn., Torrey Bot. Club, Sigma Phi Sigma. Baptist. Author: Manga, 1937; Volcano of Gold, 1938; Kalu, 1939; White Water and Black Magic (a history of curare), 1940; Paco Goes to the Fair (a Jr. Lit. Guild book), 1940; The Other America, 1941; The Flying Death (Curare): A Manga Book, 1942; Francisco de Oreliana, a Biography (in prep.); Scientific Bibliography of Curare (1595-1945) (in prep.); Clinical Employments and History of Modern Curarization (in prep.); Physico-Chemical Determination of d-Tubocurarine in Therapeutic Formulations in prep.); South American juvenile books, Contbr. articles to Ency. Britannica; Saturday Evening Post, Yale Rev., Nat. Geographic, Technology Rev., Natural History sci., med. publs. Home: Presque Isle, Me.; also P.O. Box 281, Palo Alto, Cal. Died July 7, 1958; buried Rock Creek Cemetery, Washington.

GILL, THEODORE NICHOLAS, zoölogist; b. New York, N.Y., Mar. 21, 1837; s. James Darrell and Elizabeth (Vosburgh) G.; ed. in pvt. schs. and under spl. tutors; (hon. A.M., Columbian [now George Washington U.], 1865, M.D., 1866, Ph.D., 1870, LL.D., 1895); unmarried. Adj. prof. physics and natural history, 1860-61, lecturer on natural history, 1864-66 and 1873-84, prof. zoölogy, 1884-1910, emeritus, George Washington U. Librarian, Smithsonian Instn., 1865-67; asst. librarian, Library of Congress, 1866-75; asso. in zoölogy, U.S. Nat. Mus. Pres. A.A.A.S., 1897. Author: Parental Care Among Fresh-Water Fishes, 1906; contributions to the Life-histories of Fishes, Vol. I, 1909. Asso. editor Johnson's New Univ. Ency., Century Dictionary and Standard Dictionary. Home: Washington, D.C. Deceased.

GILLAN, SILAS LEE, mining engr.; b. Danville, Ill., Apr. 17, 1883; s. Silas Y. and Elizabeth (Harned) G.; student U. Wis., 1903; E.M., U. Minn. Sch. of Mines, 1907; m. Emily Norwood Crosby, Jan. 1, 1908; children—Crosby Lee (dec.), Emily (Mrs. Stuart Collins), Adelaide (Mrs. Edw. P. Leveen, Jr.), Mary Jane (Mrs. Robert M. Norman). Mining engr. with U.S. Forest Service and Dept. Interior, 1908-20, engaged chiefly in exam. Cal. oil fields, also mining dists. Ariz., N.M., others; valuation engr. Income Tax Unit, Oil and Gas Sect., Washington, 1920-21; pvt. practice, Los Angeles since 1921. Del. to World Engring. Congress, Tokyo, Japan. Fellow A.A.A.S.; mem. Cal. Acad. Scis., Am. Soc. Profl. Engrs., Am. Inst. Mining and Metall. Engrs. (chmn. So. Cal. sect.), Am. Assn. Petroleum Geologists, Sch. of Mines Soc. U. Minn., Sigma Alpha Epsilon. Democrat. Conglist. Elk. Clubs: Adventures, Engineers' (pres.), Branner, University (Los Angeles). Home: 230 Webb Dr., Glendale 6, Cal. Office: 614 S. Hope St. Los Angeles 14. Died Nov. 9, 1954.

GILLES, VERNER ARTHUR, (gil'es), geologist; b. Kirwin, Kan., Jan. 3, 1886; s. Arthur William and Sarah (Weaver) G.; B.S., U. of Ore., 1911; m. Eva Kathleen Norris, Sept. 20, 1920. Began as mining engr., June 1911; const. engr. N.P. Ry. Co., 1911-16; intermittently with several mining companies, 1916-21; cons. engr. Lewisohn Bros., 1921; geologist N.P. Ry. Co., 1921-26, asst. chief geologist, 1926-40, chief geologist 1940-54. Mem. Am. Inst. Mining and Metall. Engrs., Am. Assn. Petroleum Geologists, Delta Tau Delta, Acacia. Clubs: Hilands Golf (Billings, Mont.). Mason (K.T., Shriner). Home: Western Apts., 33rd and Division Sts. Office: 201 Yale Bldg., Billings, Mont. Died Nov. 9, 1954.

GILLESPIE, WILLIAM, mathematician; b. Hamilton, Ont., Can., Nov. 1879; s. George Hamilton and Elizabeth Agnes G.; B.A., Toronto U., 1893; Ph.D., U. of Chicago, 1900; unmarried. Teacher of mathematics, Princeton U., since 1897, prof., 1905-39, emeritus prof., 1939. Presbyterian. Address: 160 Springdale Rd., Princeton, N.J. Died Sept. 13, 1947.

GILLESPIE, WILLIAM MITCHELL, civil engr., educator; b. N.Y., 1816; s. James and Ann (Waldron) G.; grad. Columbia, 1834, LL.D. (hon.) 1859; studied at Ecole des Ponts et Chaussees, France; m. Harriet Emily Bates, Apr. 7, 1864, at least 1 son, T. Waldron. First prof. civil engring. Union Coll., Schenectady, N.Y., 1845-68, stressed importance of humanities to engring.; after trip to France lost voice and lectured by whispering to an asst., 1867. Author: Rome: As Seen by a New-Yorker in 1843-44, published 1845; A Manual of the Principles and Practice of Road-Making, 1847; The Philosophy of Mathematics, 1851; A Treatise of Land-Surveying, 1855. Died N.Y., Jan. 1, 1868.

GILLETTE, CLARENCE PRESTON, entomologist; b. Lyons, Mich., Apr. 7, 1859; s. William Henry and Larissa Esther (Preston) G.; B.S., Mich. Agrl. Coll., 1884, M.S., 1887; spl. work in entomology, U. of Ill., 1885, D.Sc., 1917; embryology, Woods Hole, Mass., 1900; m. Clara M. Smith, Mar. 3, 1886. Asst. entomologist and physiologist, Mich. Agrl. Coll., 1886-87; entomologist, State Expt. Sta., Ames, Ia., 1888-90; head dept. of zoölogy and entomology, and entomologist, Expt. Sta., Colo. Agrl. Coll., 1891-1933; dir. Colo. Expt. Sta., July 1, 1910-33; prof. and dir. emeritus, 1933—. Expert entomologist, St. Louis Expn., 1904. Presbyn. Home: Ft. Collins, Colo. Died Jan. 4, 1941.

GILLETTE, KING CAMP, mfr.; b. Fond du Lac, Wis., Jan. 5, 1855; s. George Wolcott and Fanny Lamira (Camp) G.; mother author of the White House Cook Book; ed. public schools, Chicago; m. Alanta Ella Gaines, July 2, 1890; 1 son, King G. Inventor Gillette razor; organizer Gillette Safety Razor Co., 1901, pres. until 1931, now dir. Republican. Mason. Address: Los Angeles, Calif, Died July 9, 1932.

GILLHAM, ROBERT, civil engr.; b. New York, Sept. 25, 1854; ed. Classical and Math. Inst., Hackensack, N.J.; studied engineering; engaged in practice at Hackensack; invented furnace for desulphurizing zinc ores; constructed cable road in Kansas City; became v.p. and chief engr. Kansas City Elevated Ry.; constructed cable railways in Omaha, Denver and Cleveland, O.; afterward with numerous companies; now gen. mgr. and chief engr. Kansas City, Pittsburgh and Gulf Ry. Home: Kansas City, Mo. Died 1899.

GILLIAM, DAVID TOD, surgeon; b. Hebron, O., Apr. 3, 1844; s. William and Mary Elizabeth (Bryan) G.; ed. pub. schs., and Bartlett's Commercial Coll., Cincinnati; M.D., Med. Coll. of Ohio, 1871; m. Lucinda E. Mintun, of Nelsonville, O., Oct. 7, 1866. Enlisted 2d Va. (Union) Cav., Aug., 1861; elected corporal Co. I; with Garfield in march against Humphrey Marshall on Big Sandy River, Ky.; sent to Wheeling, W. Va., as recruiting officer; later ascended Kanawha River and took part in many skirmishes; with Crook in battle of Lewisburg, Va.; wounded and taken prisoner nr. Gauley, Va., by Gen. Loring; escaped 5 weeks later; sent to parole camp; discharged spring of 1863. In practice of medicine, Columbus, O., since 1868; emeritus professor of gynecology, Medical Department of Ohio State University (trustee same since 1905); gynecologist to St. Anthony's and St. Francis hospitals. Originated operations for suspension of uterus, for cystocele, for incontinence of urine in the female; devised many surg. instruments and the Gilliam operating table. Hon. fellow Am. Assn. Obstetricians and Gynecologists (v.p., 1905-06); mem. A.M.A., Ohio State Med. Assn., Columbus Acad. Medicine; ex-pres. Franklin Co. Med. Soc.; hon. mem. Northwestern Ohio Med. Assn.; mem. Pan-Am. Med. Congress, World's Med. Congress. Congregationalist. Republican. Author: Pocket Book of Medicine, 1882; Essentials of Pathology, 1883; Practical Gynecology, 1903; The Rose Croix, 1906; The Righting of Richard Devereux. Collaborator, Randall & Ryan's History of Ohio, 5 vols., 1912. Home: 1819 Franklin Park, S. Office: 333 E. State St., Columbus, O.

GILLIARD, E(RNEST) THOMAS, naturalist; b. York, Pa., Nov. 23, 1912; s. Ernest Theodore and Marie Thérèse (Waelchli) G.; student Deep Springs Coll., 1931-32, U. Santo Tomas, 1945; Sc.D., Wagner Coll., 1959; m. Margaret Fitzell Tifft, Apr. 6, 1940; children—Thomas Chapman, Suzanne Thérèse, James Fitzell. Volunteer dept. ornithology Am. Museum Natural History, N.Y.C., 1932-40, asst. curator, 1940-50, associate curator, 1950-62, curator, 1962—; scientific expeditions to Canada, 1934, Newfoundland, 1936; to S. America, Panama, 1936, Venezuela, 1937, Colombia, 1941, Brazil, 1941; to Brit. Guiana, 1961; to Philippines, 1947; to New Guinea: Owen Stanley Mountains, 1948, Hagen and Bismarck Mountains, 1950, Kubor Mountains, 1952; Victor Emanuel and Hindenberg Mountains, 1953-54, Finisterre Mountains, 1956, Adelbert Mountains, 1959; to Whiteman Mountains, New Britain, 1958-59 Schrader Mountains, New Guinea, Batanta Island, 1964. Fellow Am. Ornithologists Union; mem. Brit. Ornithologists Union, Biol. Soc. Wash. Am. Geog. Soc., Wilson, Cooper ornithol. socs., Linnaean Soc. Club: Explorers (2d v.p.) (N.Y.C.). Author: Living Birds of the World, 1958; Birds of Paradise and Bower Birds; (with others) Handbook of the Birds of New Guinea; also articles. Has discovered and named 55 subspecies, 6 species and 1 genus of birds. Home: 75 Belvedere Dr., Yonkers, N.Y. Office: Am. Museum Natural History, Central Park W. at 79th St., N.Y.C. 24. Died Jan. 26, 1965.

GILLISS, JAMES MELVILLE, naval officer, astronomer; b. Georgetown, D.C., Sept. 6, 1811; s. George and Mary (Melville) G.; attended U. Va., 1833; m. Rebecca Roberts, Dec. 1837. Entered U.S. Navy, 1826; commd. midshipman, 1833; studied in Paris for 6 months, 1835, ordered back to Washington (D.C.), assigned to Depot of Charts and Instruments; in charge of depot, 1837; commd. to make astron. observations in Washington necessary for evaluation of longitude observation of Lt. Charles Wilkes' expdn., 1838; pointed out inadequacy of existing building and equipment for astron. research to Bd. Naval Commrs., 1841 (led to act of Congress providing for establishment U.S. Naval Observatory at Washington); visited Europe in interests of observatory, circa 1842-1843, authorized by Congress to go to Santiago (Chile) to observe Venus and Mars, 1849-52; became supt. U.S. Naval Observatory, 1861; mem. Nat. Acad. Sci. Died Feb. 9, 1865.

GILLMAN, HENRY, scientist; b. Kinsale, Ireland, Nov. 16, 1833; s. Edward and Eleanor Mandeville (Hackett) G.; desc. from Adam Winthrop, lord of the manor, of Groton, Suffolk, grandfather of Gov. Winthrop of Mass., 1630; acad. edn.; m. Mary Julia, d. Hiram Reeve Johnson, of Detroit, Dec. 7, 1858. Came with his parents to Detroit, 1850; was 1st asst. U.S. Geod. Survey of Great Lakes, in charge of a topog. and hydrographical party, 1851-69; asst. supt. construction 10th and 11th lighthouse dists. on Northern lakes, 1870-76; supt. and librarian Detroit Pub. Library, 1880-85; U.S. consul, Jerusalem, 1886-91. Took such a stand against expulsion of Jews from Palestine by Turks that his position was upheld by several European powers and exclusion laws were modified by the sultan. Known for his researches in archeology and botany and his procurement and publication of photograph fac-similes of texts of early Christian MSS., including the Didache. Home: Detroit, Mich. Died July 30, 1915.

GILLSON, JOSEPH LINCOLN, geologist; b. Evanston, Ill., Feb. 12, 1895; s. Louis K. and Ida (Bartholomew) G.; B.S., Northwestern, 1917, A.M., 1920; M.S., Mass. Inst. Tech., 1921, D.Sc., 1923; m. Grace Brown, Sept. 13, 1918; children—Joseph L., Jane (Mrs. William G. Langton), Patricia (Mrs. John Baker). Instr. Harvard, 1920-22; faculty mem. Mass. Inst. Tech., 1922-28; geologist E.I. duPont de Nemours & Co., Wilmington, Del., 1928-60; Crosby lectr. econ. geology, Mass. Institute Tech., 1961-62, vis. lectr. dept. geol. and geophysics, 1961-63; prof. geology Arizona State U., 1963-64. Member U.S. delegation UN Conf. on Application Sci. and Tech. Underdeveloped Nations, 1963. Recipient D. C. Jackling award Am. Inst. Mining, Metall. and Petroleum Engrs., 1957, Hal Williams Hardinge award, 1963; Distinguished alumnus Northwestern U., 1961. Fellow Geol. Soc. Am., Mineral. Soc. Am.; mem. Soc. Econ. Geologists (v.p. 1955, pres. 1959), Am. Geol. Inst. (v.p. 1955, pres. 1956-57), Am. Inst. Mining, Metall. and Petroleum Engrs. (v.p., dir. 1951-54, 56-58, pres. 1960-61). Editor-in-chief 3d edit. Industrial Minerals and Rocks, 1959-60. Home: 109 Mullin Rd., Wilmington, Del. 19809. Office: Ariz. State U. Died Aug. 4, 1964; buried Carlsbad, N.Mex.

GILMAN. ALBERT FRANKLIN, chemist; b. Hallowell, Me., Sept. 9, 1871; s. William Franklin and Julia Ann (Gordon) G.; grad. Kent's Hill (Me.) Acad., 1892; student, Wesleyan U., Conn., 1893-94; S.B., Amherst Coll., 1897, A.M., 1901; postgrad. U. Tenn., 1902, Harvard 1903, U. Chgo., 1905, 1906; Ph.D., U. Denver, 1913; m. Agnes Geneva McGlynn, Sept. 28, 1899 (dec.); children—Albert Franklin, Gertrude Marcelle. Tchr. sci., Farmington, Me., 1897-98; prof. science Dow Acad. Franconia, N.H., 1898-99; prof. chemistry and physics Maryville (Tenn) Coll., 1900-06; prof. chemistry and physics Maryville (Tenn) Coll., 1906-17, Huron (S.D.) Coll., 1917-18, Ill. Wesleyan U., 1918-20, Carroll (Wis.) Coll., 1920-21, Central YMCA Coll. of Arts and Scis., Chgo., 1921-42. Toured Europe during 1910 to study methods used in chemical labs. Fellow A.A.A.S.. Royal Soc. Arts, Am. Inst. Chemists, Inst. Am. Genealogy; mem. Am. Chem. Soc., Wis., S.D., Ill. acads. sci., Delta Tau Delta, Phi Lambda Upsilon. Republican, Mason. Author: A Laboratory Outline Quantitative Analysis, 1908; Laboratory Outline Qualitative Analysis, 1908; (brochure), Origin of the Republican Party, 1915; Organic Reactions (with son), 1931. Collector of statistics and sociol. data for Dietary Studies in Rural Regions of Eastern Tenn., U.S. Bull. No. 221. Writer various chem. papers. Home: 948 Chicago Av., Oak Park, Ill. Died May 18, 1951; buried Forest Home Cemetery, Forest Park, Ill.

GILMAN, JOHN ELLIS, physician; b. Harmar, suburb of Marietta, O., July 24, 1841; s. Dr. John Salvin and Elizabeth C. (Fay) G.; ed. schs. of Marietta; student medicine and surgery under his father and brother, and Dr. George Hartwell, of Toledo, O.; M.D., Hahnemann Med. Coll., Chicago, 1871; m. Mary D., d. William Johnson, 1860. Was the first physician to offer his services for relief of sufferers at time of Chicago Fire, 1871, and apptd. by the Relief and Aid Soc. as sec. of its com. on sick and hosps.; prof. physiology, sanitary science and hygiene, and later prof. materia medica, Hahnemann Med. Coll., Chicago, 1884-1904 (emeritus). Introduced X-ray in therapeutic use, 1906; afterwards used it in treating cancers. Home: Chicago, Ill. Died June 21, 1916.

GILMORE, CHARLES WHITNEY, vertebrate paleontologist; b. Pavilion, N.Y., Mar. 11, 1874; s. John Edward and Caroline M. (Whitney) G., B.S., U. of Wyo., 1901; m. Laure Coutant, Oct. 22, 1902; children—Eloise Elizabeth (dec.), Dorothy Caroline (dec.), Helen Rosalie Collector dept. vertebrate paleontology, Carnegie Mus., 1901-04; with U.S. Nat. Museum since 1904, as preparator dept; vertebrate paleontology until 1908, custodian, 1908-11, asst. curator, 1911-18, asso. curator, 1918-23, curator since 1923. Specialized in extinct reptiles. Served as sergt. Spanish-American War. Mem. Paleontol. Soc. (pres. 1938), Biol. Soc. Washington, Geol. Soc. Washington, Geol. Soc. of America, Paleontol. Soc. Washington (pres. 1935), Soc. Vertebrate Paleontol. (pres. 1943). Presbyterian. Club: Explorers. Home: 451 Park Rd. N.W., Washington, D.C. Died Sept. 27, 1945.

GILPIN, JOSEPH ELLIOTT, prof. chemistry; b. Baltimore, Md., Nov. 21, 1866; s. Albert G. and Fannie (Elliott) G.; A.B., Johns Hopkins, 1889, Ph.D., 1892; m.

Katharine Pleasant, 1895 (died 1903); m. 2d, Olive Russell, Nov. 18, 1904. Instr. chemistry, 1892-95, associate, 1895-1911, asso; prof., 1911-13, collegiate prof., 1913—, Johns Hopkins. Christian Scientist. Died Aug. 25, 1924.

GILTNER, WARD, dean of veterinary medicine; b. Ithaca, N.Y., Apr. 5, 1882; s. Richard Dana and Frances Victoria (Knickerbocker) G.; D.V.M., Cornell U., 1906; M.S., Ala. Poly. Inst., 1908, Dr. P.H., U. Mich., 1933; m. Mabel A. Decker, Dec. 20, 1902; children—Dorothy (Mrs. Charles Parrish), Alice (Mrs. Richard Teel), Elizabeth (dec.), William Ward, David. Asst. in vet. sci. Ala. Polytech. Inst., 1906-08; research asst. in bacteriology Mich. State Coll., 1908-12, prof., 1912-23, dean vet. medicine, 1923—, also dir. biol. scis.; dir. East Lansing State Bank, East Lansing Bldg. & Loan Assn. Fellow A.A.A.S., Am. Pub. Health Assn.; mem. Soc. Am. Bacteriologists, Am. Assn. Pathologists and Bacteriologists, Am. Chem. Soc., Mich. Acad. Sci., Am., Mich. vet. medicine assns., Sigma Xi, Phi Sigma, Delta Omega. Clubs: Wranglers (Lansing), Mich. State Coll. Faculty. Home: 652 Hillcrest Av., East Lansing, Mich. Died July 14, 1950; buried Evergreen Cemetery, Lansing, Mich.

GIMSLEY, GEORGE PERRY, geologist; b. Granville, O., Feb., 1868; s. Carson PPorter and Mary E. G.; grad. Ohio State Univ., 1890 (A.M., 1891; Ph.D., Johns Hopkins, 1894). Asst. geologist, Ohio geol. survey of Kan., since 1896. Prof. geology and natural history, Washburn Coll., Topeka, Kan., 1894-1904; asst. geologist, Mich. Geol. Survey, 1902; asst. State geologist, W.Va. Geol. Survey, since 1904; chief Kan. mineral exhibit, St. Louis Expn., 1903-04. Fellow Geol. Soc. America, Geol. Soc., Washington; hon. mem. Kan. Acad. Science Clara M. Spencer. Author: Study of Granites of (sec. 1901-04); m. Brooklyn, Ia., Dec. 25, 1901, Cecil Co., Md.; Gypsum Deposits of Kansas; Microsopical Study of Limestones of Ohio; Mineral Resources of Kansas; Gypsum and Cement Plasterers, 1899; The Gypsum of Michigan and the Plaster Industry, 1905; etc. Address: Morgantown, W.Va.

GINGRICH, CURVIN HENRY, (ging'rik), astronomer; b. York, Pa., Nov. 20, 1880; s. William Henry and Ellen (Kindig) G.; B.A., Dickinson Coll., Pa., 1903, M.A., 1905; U. of Chicago, summers, 1909-12, Ph.D., 1912; Yerkes Observatory (Univ. of Chicago), 1911-12; Sc.D., from Dickinson College, 1941; m. Mary Ann Gross, Aug. 10, 1915; 1 daughter, Gertrude. Teacher of mathematics, Maryville Sem., Mo., 1903-05, Northwest Mo. Coll., Albany, 1905-07, Baker Univ., Baldwin, Kan., 1907-09; instr. mathematics, 1909-12, prof. mathematics and astronomy since 1912, acting dean, 1914-15, dean, 1915-17; asst. to the pres., and registrar, 1917-19. Carleton Coll.; at Mt. Wilson Obs., 1921-22; in charge courses in astronomy, Columbia, summers, 1929, 30; lecturer Adler Planetarium, summers, 1931, 32, 33; research asst. at McCormick Obs., summer 1935. Asso. editor Popular Astronomy, 1912-26, editor since 1926. Astron. work at Goodsell Obs., Carleton Coll., principally micrometric measures of comet positions and double stars, also celestial photography and photographic determinations of positions of asteroids; stellar photometry. Mem. Am. Astron. Soc., Math. Assn. America, Phi Beta Kappa, Sigma Xi, Kappa Sigma. Mason. Methodist. Home: Northfield, Minn. Died June 17, 1951; buried Oak Lawn Cemetery. Northfield, Minn.

GINTER, LEWIS, tobacco mfr.; b. N.Y.C., Apr. 4, 1824; s. John and Elizabeth Ginter. Founded retail merchandise firm, Richmond, Va., 1842; partner (with John F. Alvey) in import drygoods firm, Richmond, circa 1851-61; served as q.m. under Gen. J.R. Anderson of Confederate Army of Northern Va., 1861-65; his activity in battle gave him title of "fighting commissary"; asso. with a brokerage business, N.Y.C., 1865-69; returned to Richmond, 1869, established tobacco firm Allen & Ginter (mfg., selling smoking and chewing tobacco) 1872; introduced manufacture of cigarettes, 1875 (1st manufacturer to use Va. tobacco successfully produced); "Richmond Gem" and other brands of cigarettes, which led to expansion of firm and its absorption into Am. Tobacco Co. in 1890; realized large fortune in this transaction, devoted wealth to civic improvements and projects in Richmond. Died Richmond, Oct. 2, 1897; buried Hollywood Cemetery, Richmond.

GIPPRICH, JOHN L., clergyman, physicist; b. Balt., Jan. 5, 1880; s. Anton and Mary (Hopf) G.; A.B., Loyola Coll., 1900; studied Johns Hopkins, 1908-09. Joined Soc. of Jesus (Jesuits), 1900; ordained priest R.C. Ch., 1913; prof. physics, Holy Cross Coll., 1903-05, Boston Coll., 1906-07; prof. mathematics, Fordham, 1907-08; prof. physics, Georgetown U., 1914-29; became regent Med. and Dental schs., same univ., 1929; prof. physics St. Joseph's Coll., Phila., 1935-36; pastor Southern Md. Chs., 1936-44; mem. faculty Georgetown U., 1944—. Mem. Washington Acad. Sci., Royal Astron. Soc., London. Author: Laboratory Manual of Mechanics, Heat and Sound, 1927. Address: Georgetown U., Washington. Died Mar. 7, 1950; buried Georgetown U.

GIRARD, CHARLES FREDERIC, zoologist; b. Mulhausen, Upper Alsace, France, Mar. 9, 1822; ed. Sch. at Neuchatel (Switzerland), circa 1843-47; M.D., Georgetown (D.C.) Coll., 1856. Came to U.S. with Louis Agassiz, 1847, lived in Cambridge (Mass.) until 1850, published papers on flatworms and fish; moved to Washington (D.C.), 1850, served as asst. to Spencer Baird at Smithsonian Instn. until 1860, in this capacity helped plan U.S. Nat. Museum, 1857; published many reports on fish and reptiles, especially dealing with collections made by exploring and survey parties in Far West during 1850's; went to France, 1860; became Confederate sympathizer, 1861, travelled through Va. and Carolinas as Confederate agt. for drug and surg. supplies, 1863; practiced medicine, Paris, France, 1865-85; published "Herpetology" of Wilkes expdn., 1858; published essay on fish in reports of the railroad explorations to the Pacific (Vol. X), 1859; published paper on typhoid fever during Franco-Prussian War, 1872, paper on fishes, also bibliography of his works, 1888, paper on N.Am. flatworms, 1891. Died Neuilly-sur-Seine, France, Jan. 29, 1895.

GIRDNER, JOHN HARVEY, physician, surgeon; b. Cedar Creek, Greene Co., Tenn., Mar. 8, 1856; s. William and Mary Ann (Link) G.; A.B., Tusculum Coll., Tenn., 1876; M.D., Univ. Med. Coll., New York U., 1879; m. Adela Pratt of Opelousas, La., Sept. 23, 1886. Interne, Bellevue Hosp., 1879-80; lecturer on surgery, New York Post-Grad. Med. Sch. and Hosp. (mem. corp.). Was 1st to graft skin successfully from dead body onto the living; inventor of telephonic bullet probe, 1887, and phymosis forceps. Fellow New York Acad. Medicine. Democrat. Author: "Newyorkitis," 1901; also contbr. many essays on med. and other subjects. Home: 47 W. 71st St., New York. Died Nov. 25, 1933.

GIRSCH, FREDERICK, engraver; b. Budingen, Hesse, Germany, Nov. 14, 1825; attended Royal Acad. of Darmstadt, circa 1845-48. Came to U.S., 1849, became engraver for New-Yorker Criminal Zeitung, N.Y.C.; became well-known bank note engraver, during Civil War; work includes head of Liberty on many small bills, proposed Legion of Honor (which Pres. Lincoln had planned to give to Civil War vets.; widely-known engravings included Grand Ma's Toast, The Gypsy Girl; large engraving Niagara now in collection of N.Y. Hist. Soc. Died Dec. 18, 1895.

GLADDING, ERNEST KNIGHT, chemist; b. Newport, R.I., Aug. 16, 1888; s. Henry and Mary Elizabeth (Dennis) G.; B.S., Worcester Poly. Inst., 1910; m. Elizabeth Boss Congdon, Oct. 10, 1914; children—Prescilla C. (Mrs. Victor J. D. Moore), Elizabeth K. (Mrs. Weston J. Donehower), Anne (Mrs. Oscar N. Stern), Thomas C., Marcia (Mrs. John C. Guthrie). Chemist eastern lab. DuPont Powder Co., 1910, Kenvil lab., 1910, DuPont, Wash., 1910-15, E. I. duPont de Nemours & Co., Inc., Parlin, N.J., 1915, acid supt., later asst. plant supt., Hopewell, Va., 1915-18, plant supt., Old Hickory, Tenn., 1918-19, chem. dir. dye works, 1919-20; supt. royal plant DuPont Fibresilk Co., Buffalo, 1920-24, asst. prodn. mgr., 1924-25; prodn. mgr. DuPont Rayon Co., Buffalo, 1925-28, gen. mgr. tech. dept., N.Y.C., 1928-30, Buffalo, 1930-32, asst. gen. mgr., 1932-36; asst. mgr. tech. div. rayon dept. E. I. duPont de Nemours & Co., Inc., Buffalo, 1936-38, mgr. nylon div. rayon dept., Wilmington, Del., 1938-44, dir. development dept., 1944-51, ret. 1951. Dir. Chem. Fund. Mem. A.A.A.S., Army Ordnance Assn., Am. Chem. Soc., Am. Geog. Soc. Home: 913 Stuart Rd., Wilmington 67, Del. Died July 16, 1958.

GLADSON, WILLIAM NATHAN, electrical engr.; b. Corning, Ia., Feb. 22, 1866; s. James Marion and Elmyra (Newcomb) G.; B.M.E., Ia. State Coll., Ames, 1888, E.E., 1911; Ph.D., McLemoresville College, Tenn., 1898; special work, University of Chicago, summer, 1899; D.Eng., Univ. of Arkansas, 1937; m. Edna L. Wade, of Mt. Vernon, Ia., Mar. 16, 1890; children—Hazel Wade (Mrs. Charles Baker), Marion Leonore (Mrs. A. E. Brown). Asst. prof. elec. engring., Ohio State U., 1902-03; professor electrical engineering, U. of Arkansas, 1904-37; v.p. U. of Ark. and dean Coll. of Engring., 1913-37, dean emeritus since 1937. Engr. in charge water power survey of Ark. (in cooperation with U.S. Geol. Survey), 1909, 1910; pres. State Board for Engineering Registration, 1938. Progressive Democrat. Charter mem. Am. Electrochem. Soc.; mem. Am. Inst. Elec. Engrs., Soc. Promotion Engring. Edn. Author: Water Powers of Arkansas (preliminary report of State Geol. Survey), 1911. Asso. mem. Naval Consulting Bd. for State of Ark., 1917. Home: Fayetteville, Ark.

GLASER, OTTO (CHARLES), (glä'ser), biologist; b. Wiesbaden, Germany, Oct. 13, 1880; s. Charles and Eleanore (Blum) G.; brought to U.S. in infancy; A.B., Johns Hopkins, 1900, Ph.D., 1904; studied U. Budapest, 1911-12; m. Dorothy Gibbs Merrylees, Sept. 1, 1909; children—Comstock, Victoria; m. 2d, Anita Gibson Glaenzer, 1934 (died 1940); m. 3d, Dorothy Wrinch, Aug. 20, 1941. Demonstrator in comparative anatomy, embryology and biology Coll. Phys. and Surg. (now University Maryland), Baltimore, 1901-03; fellow Johns Hopkins, 1903-05; investigator oyster culture North Carolina Geological Survey and U.S. Bureau Fisheries, 1901-02; in charge oyster culture Gulf Biol. Station, La., 1903-04; instr. zoölogy and embryology Marine Biol. Lab., Woods Hole, Mass., 1905-07; with U. Mich., 1905-08, advancing to asso. prof. biology; prof. biology Amherst (Mass.) Coll., 1918—, Harkness prof., 1939—; lectr. on biology New Sch. for Social Research, N.Y.C. Trustee clk. of corp. Marine Biol. Lab., Woods Hole. Fellow A.A.A.S.; mem. Am. Soc. Naturalists, Am. Soc. Zoölogists, Am. Physiol. Soc., Soc. Exptl. Biology and Medicine, N.Y. Acad. Science, Soc. Growth and Development, Phi Beta Kappa, Sigma Xi. Contbr. to sci. jours. on developmental physiology and growth. Home: 33 Kendrick Pl., Amherst, Mass. Died Feb. 7, 1951.

GLASGOW, HUGH, entomologist; b. Tennessee, Ill., Nov. 17, 1884; s. Douglass and Margaret Matilda (Walker) G.; A.B., U. of Ill. 1908; Ph.D., 1913; m. Beulah P. Ennis, Dec. 28, 1935. Asst. entomologist, U. of Ill., 1912-13, instr. entomology, 1913-14; asst. in research, N.Y. Agrl. Experiment Station (Cornell University), Geneva, N.Y., 1914-20, asso. in research, 1920-26, chief in research, 1926-38, professor of entomology and chief division of entomology since 1938. Member A.A.A.S., American Association of Econ. Entomologists, Entomological Soc. of America, Sigma Xi. Author: Experiment Sta. Bulls. on Applied Entomology and articles in Jour. of Econ. Entomology. Home: 665 Castle St. Office: 630 W. North St., Geneva, N.Y. Died July 16, 1948.

GLASS, JAMES H., surgeon; b. Mohawk, N.Y., June 15, 1854; s. Robert and Emily Lowell (Merrill) G.; student U. of Mich., 1874-75; M.D., Bellevue Med. Coll. (New York U.), 1877; (hon. A.M., Hamilton); m. Anna Wells, May 31, 1882. Attending surgeon, St. Luke's Hosp., Utica, N.Y., 1882-90; phys. and surgeon in charge Utica City Hosp., 1886-91; attending surgeon St. Elizabeth's Hosp., 1890-93; surgeon in charge Faxton Hosp., 1893-1922; consulting surgeon Utica State Hosp., Rome City Hosp. many yrs.; pres. bd. trustees Utica City Dispensary from 1895; retired. Trustee Hamilton Coll. Home: Trenton Falls, N.Y., and Benson Springs, Fla. Died Aug. 4, 1931.

GLASSER, OTTO, biophysicist; b. Saarbruecken, Germany, Sept. 2, 1895; s. Alexander and Lina (Gentsch) G.; Ph.D., U. Freiburg, 1919; m. Emmy von Ehrenberg, July 19, 1922; 1 dau., Hannelore. Came to U.S., 1922, naturalized, 1929. Asst., instr. radiol. inst. U. Freiburg, 1919-21; asst., instr. inst. phys. found. medicine U. Frankfurt, 1921-22; biophysicist Howard Kelly Hosp., Balt., 1922-23, Cleve. Clinic, 1923-25; asst. prof. biophysics N.Y. Postgrad. Med. Sch., Columbia, 1925-27; head dept. biophysics Cleve. Clinic Found., 1927—; prof. biophysics Frank E. Bunts Ednl. Inst., Cleve., 1937-60, emeritus prof. biophysics, 1961—; curator Roentgen-Mus., Lennep, 1950—. Served with German Army, World War I. Received spl. certificate honor for roentgen exhbn. A.M.A., Detroit, 1930, gold medal achievement award Radiol. Soc. N.A., 1936, Olympia Decoration, 1938; Janeway medal Am. Radium Soc., 1950; Honor-Roentgen plaque, Roentgen-Mus., Lennep, 1951; John Stanley Coulter plaque Am. Congress Phys. Medicine, 1953; Comdrs. Cross Order of Merit (Germany), 1960. Diplomate Am. Bd. Radiology. Fellow Ohio Acad. Sci., A.A.A.S., Am. Phys. Soc., Am. Coll. Radiology; mem. Cleve. Radiol. Soc. (hon.), Deutsche Roentgen Gesellschaft (hon.), Am. Roentgen Ray Soc., Am. Radium Soc., A.M.A. (vice chmn. council med. physics 1956-62), Detroit Roentgen and Radium Soc. (hon.), Radiol. Soc. N.Am., Cleve. Acad. Medicine, Sigma Xi. Author: Wilhelm Conrad Roentgen, 1931, 33, 34; Science of Radiology, 1934; Dr. W. C. Roentgen, 1945. Collaborator, editor: Physical Foundations of Radiology, 1944, 2d edit., 1952, 3d edit., 1961. Compiler, editor: Medical Physics, 1944, vol. 2, 1950, vol. 3, 1960. Contbr. sci. articles profl. jours. Inventor condenser dosemeter for measurement x-rays and radiation from radioactive substances. Home: 2289 Chatfield Dr. Office: 2040 E. 93d St., Cleve. 6. Died Dec. 11, 1964.

GLEASON, ELLIOTT PERRY, mfr., inventor; b. Westmoreland, N.H., June 27, 1821; common school edn.; one of the pioneers in the mfr. of gas burners in early stages of the industry; inventor of regulating argand burner and many other standard devices; also identified with development of electric lighting. Pres. and prin. owner E. P. Gleason Mfg. Co., New York, mfrs. gas and electric lighting appliances, also Gleason & Bailey Mfg. Co., Seneca Falls, N.Y., mfrs. fire dept. rolling stock. Home: Brooklyn, N.Y. Died 1901.

GLEASON, JAMES E., machinery mfr.; b. Rochester, N.Y., Nov. 25, 1868; s. William and Ellen (McDermott) G.; student Hale Acad., M.E., Cornell U., 1892; m. Miriam Blakeney, Oct. 18, 1899 (dec.); 1 son, E. Blakeney (dec.). Designer, builder lathes and planers Gleason Tool Co., Rochester; former chmn. bd. Gleason Works. Awarded Civic medal Rochester Mus. Arts and Scis. for notable achievements in field in indsl. sci., 1939; Medal for Service to cause of safer and better transp. Am. Soc. M.E., 1939; award for far-reaching inventions of machines to make new types of gears Nat. Modern Pioneers Com., N.A.M., 1940. Chmn. bd. Rochester Inst. Tch. Trustee U. Rochester. Mem. Soc. Automotive Engrs., Nat. Machine Tool Builders Assn. (pres., 1926-27), Am. Soc. M.E., U.S. C. of C., Army Ordnance Assn., Rochester C. of C. (pres. 1922-23), Rochester Bur. Municipal Research, Rochester Engring. Soc., Sigma Xi, Newcomen Soc. Club: Rochester, Genesee Valley, Country of Rochester, Oak Hill Country, Cornell. Holder patents on two-tool bevel gear generators. Home: 766 East Av., Rochester 7.

Office: 1000 University Av., Rochester 3. Died Feb. 10, 1964.

GLEASON, WILLIAM PALMER, steel mfr.; b. Chicago, Ill., Feb. 12, 1865; s. Martin Francis and Alice (Simmes) G.; ed. pub. schs., Joliet, Ill.; m. Elizabeth Harvey, 1890 (died 1895); 1 dau., Mary Louise (dec.); m. 2d, Ann Knowlton, 1898; 1 dau., Eleanor May. Began as chem. apprentice Ill. Steel Works, 1880, foreman machine shop, 1887; master mechanic Joliet Works, same co., 1892-1900; master mechanic Colo. Fuel & Iron Works, Pueblo, Colo., 1900-01; asst. mgr. Clairton Works of Carnegie Steel Co., 1901-06; gen. supt., gen. mgr. constrn. Gary Works, U.S. Steel Corporation, 1906-08, gen. mgr., 1908-35, retired; dir. Gary State Bank, Ind. Steel Co. Mem. bd. trustees Ind. World War Memorial; mem. Nat. Council Boy Scouts America; dir. Ind. Tuberculosis Assn.; pres. Lake County Tuberculosis Assn.; v.p., bd. mgrs., Lake County Tuberculosis Sanatorium (Crown Point, Ind.); chmn. Gary Chapter, Am. Red Cross; pres. W. P. Gleason Welfare Center. Republican. Catholic. Home: Gary, Ind. Died June 14, 1936.

GLENN, LEONIDAS CHALMERS, geologist; b. Crowder's Creek, N.C., Sept. 9, 1871; s. William Davis and Sarah P. (Torrence) G.; A.B., U. of S.C., 1891; Ph.D., Johns Hopkins, 1899; m. Nellie Louise McCullough, Sept. 12, 1900; children—William David, Hugh Wilson. Taught in secondary schs., 1891-94; supt. town schs., Darlington, 1894-96; student Harvard Coll., summer, 1895; Johns Hopkins, 1896-99; adj. prof. biology and geology, S.C. Coll., Columbia, 1899-1900; adj. prof. geology, Vanderbilt University, 1900-03, professor, 1903-42, head of division of science, 1928-42, professor emeritus since 1942. Recently engaged in work for North Carolina, Kentucky, Tennessee, and U.S. geol. surveys and U.S. Forest Service; mem. faculty George Peabody Coll. for Teachers, 1914-15; oil geologist, Sinclair Oil Co., 1916-17 and 1918; actg. state geologist of Tenn., 1918; spl. agt. U.S. Internal Revenue Dept., oil and gas valuation works 1918-19; investigated changes in Red River, Tex. Okla. boundary, for U.S. Dept. Justice, 1919-21; studied mining for oil and oil shale industry in Europe, 1923. Mapping W. Ky. coal field for Ky. Geol. Survey since 1924; cons. geologist Tenn. Valley Authority and U.S. Army Engrs. Fellow A.A.A.S.; Geol. Soc. Washington, Am. Inst. Mining and Metall. Engrs., Geol. Soc. America, Seis. Soc. Am., Tenn., Ky. Acads. Science, Phi Beta Kappa, Sigma Xi, Kappa Sigma. Contbr. to scientific periodicals. Presbyterian. Democrat. Address: 2111 Garland Av., Nashville 5. Died Jan. 11, 1951.

GLICKMAN, IRVING, educator, periodontist; b. N.Y.C., Jan. 17, 1914; s. Nathan and Rose (Gurland) G.; B.S., Bklyn. Coll., 1933; D.M.D., Tufts U., 1938, postgrad. dept. pathology Med. Sch., 1939-40; m. Violeta Arboleda, Mar. 13, 1954; children—Alan, Denise. Faculty, Tufts U. Sch. Dental Medicine, Boston, 1938-72, prof. oral pathology, 1948-72, research prof. oral pathology, 1960-72, prof. periodontology, 1948-72, chmn. dept., 1960-72, dir. div. grad. and postgrad. studies, 1951-60. Mem. Army Med. Service Adv. Com. on Preventive Dentistry; mem. adv. group Cambridge (Mass.) Health Dept.; lectr. dental pathology Boston U. Sch. Medicine; cons. in periodontology Forsyth Dental Center, Boston, VA Hosp., Boston; cons. Armed Forces Inst. Pathology; dental cons. U.S. Naval Hosp., Chelsea, Mass.; asso. staff New Eng. Center Hosp.; staff Brookline Hosp.; cons. in oral pathology Grove Manor Hosp.; periodontist Boston City Hosp.; dir. Berkshire Conf. on Periodontology and Oral Pathology, 1950-72. Chmn. alumni council Tufts U., 1963-64. Trustee, Combined Jewish Philanthropies, Boston. Recipient numerous awards including Samuel Charles Miller Meml. award in oral medicine, 1965, award for basic research in periodontology Internat. Assn. for Dental Research, 1966. Diplomate Am. Bd. Periodontology, Am. Bd. Oral Medicine, Am. Bd. Oral Pathology. Fellow Am. Acad. Dental Sci., A.A.A.S., Am., Internat. colls. dentists; mem. Am. Acad. Periodontology (Gold Medal award 1972), Am. Acad. Dental Medicine, Am. Assn. Dental Schs., Am. Assn. Anatomists, New Eng. Soc. Pathologists, Internat. Assn. for Dental Research, Internat. Acad. Oral Pathology, Tissue Culture Assn., Am. Dental Assn., Mass. Dental Soc., Tufts U. Dental Alumni Assn. (pres. 1966-67), Sigma Xi, Omicron Kappa Upsilon; also hon. mem. fgn. socs. Jewish religion (trustee temple). Author: Clinical Periodontology, 4th edit., 1972; Periodontal Disease, 1972. Guest editor Symposium on Preventive Dentistry, 1972. Contbr. numerous articles to profl. jours., also chpts. to books. Home: Newton Center MA Died Oct. 2, 1972.

GLICKMAN, MENDEL, educator, cons. archtl. engr.; b. Vitebsk, Russia, Dec. 25, 1895; s. Ezekiel and Sara (Shefrin) G.; brought to U.S., 1905, naturalized, 1915; B.S., Tri-State Coll., Angola, Ind., 1921; m. Babette Spitz, July 1, 1922; children—Iris Ann (Mrs. John Richard Herzfeld), David Moohr, Jean (Mrs. Frederick Schuster). Instr., Marquette U., 1921-22; plant engr. Internat. Harvester Co., Milw., 1922-29; chief Am. engr., tractor plant in Stalingrad, USSR, 1929-31; charter mem. Frank Lloyd Wright fellowship, 1931-32; supervising engr. WPA, Milwaukee County, 1933-36, also asso. on housing devel.; asso. Darby, Bogner & Assos., engrs. and architects, 1930-42; engr. procurement div. USAAF, 1942-45; cons. practice, 1942-45, independent cons. engr., 1945-49; prof. architecture and engring. U. Okla. Sch. Architecture, 1949—, also chmn. school; cons. engr. on bldgs. for Frank Lloyd Wright, Frank Lloyd Wright Found., 1932—; vis. lectr. applied engring. Nat. Tech. U. Sch. Architecture, Athens, Greece, 1955-56 (Fulbright grant). Served to sgt., 6th Engrs., U.S. Army, World War I. Decorated Silver Star. Mem. A.I.A., Am. Soc. C.E., Am. Concrete Inst., Nat. Soc. Profl. Engrs., Am. Soc. Mil. Engrs. Home: 1411 Jenkins Av., Norman, Okla. Died May 16, 1967.

GLIDDEN, JOSEPH FARWELL, farmer, inventor, mfr.; b. Charleston, N.H., Jan. 18, 1813; s. David and Polly (Hurd) G.; attended sem., Lima, N.Y.; m. Clarissa Foster, 1837; m. 2d, Lucinda Warne, 1851; at least 1 child. Worked his way West from N.H. as thresher, 1842-44; purchased land in De Kalb County (Ill.), a cattle ranch in Tex.; sheriff of De Kalb County, 1852-53; patented improvement on barb wire fences, 1874; organized (with Isaac L. Ellwood) Barb Wire Fence Co., De Kalb County, 1875; sold his half interest to Washburn & Moen Mfg. Co., 1876, lived on royalties. Died Oct. 9, 1906.

GLOVER, TOWNEND, entomologist; b. Rio de Janeiro, Brazil, Feb. 20, 1813 (parents English citizens); s. Henry and Mary (Townend) G.; ed. in Eng.; m. Sarah T. Byrnes, Sept. 1840, 1 adopted dau.; studied art in Germany under Mattenheimer (insp. Munich Art Gallery), 1834-35; came to New Rochelle, N.Y., 1836; took his collection of modelled fruits to Washington, D.C., 1853-54, resulted in appointment by Bur. Agr., U.S. Patent Office until 1878; had plans for work illustrating insects of U.S., never completed; ret. to Balt. due to ill health, 1878. Died Balt., Sept. 7, 1883.

GLUHAREFF, MICHAEL E., aero. engr., designer; b. St. Petersburg, Russia, Sept. 17, 1892; s. Eugene and Iraida (Borisoff) G.; grad. (gen. scis.) Imperial Coll. Commerce, 1910, (mech. engring.) Poly. Inst. Tech., 1914, (mil. engr.) Imperial Mil. Engring. Coll., 1916, (mil. pilot) Mil. Aviation Sch., 1917; m. Antonina Gretzkoff, Apr. 21, 1915; children—Eugene, Alexander; m. 2d Anastasia Gartwig, Oct. 1947. Came to U.S., 1924, naturalized, 1937. Began as designer, builder and test pilot sailplanes of original types, Finland, 1920-24; designer 1st non-spinnable airplane, U.S., 1925; chief engr., Sikorsky Aviation Corp., 1925-35, in charge all models in regard to gen. structural aerodynamic and hydrodynamic design, developed wings known as G.S. airfoils with which all types of Sikorsky land planes, amphibions and flying boats were equipped; chief design, Vought-Sikorsky Aircraft, div. United Aircraft Corp., 1935-42, charge complete design of large flying boats which made 1st non-stop Pacific and Atlantic flights with Am. mail and passengers, inauguration of Pan-American Airways; also in charge design 1st successful helicopter, which set new world's records, 1942; chief engr. Sikorsky Aircraft div. United Aircraft Corp., in charge design research and development, Sikorsky Helicopters, 1943-57, engring. mgr. Sikorsky Aircraft div., 1957-60, engineering consultant to the division, 1960—. Mem. tech. adv. panel Office Asst. Sec. Def., 1954-58; mem. Army scientific advisory panel, 1959-61. Awarded Certificate of Merit, American Helicopter Soc., 1948, Dr. Alex Klemin award, 1954; Chrysler Award, as outstanding world designer, 1954; Elmer A. Sperry award for transportation, 1964. Fellow Am. Inst. Aeros. and Astronautics, Soc. Automotive Engrs. (hon.), Am. Helicopter Soc. (hon.); mem. Soaring Soc. Am. Holds patent of first Dartshaped airplane. Home: Hoyden Hill Rd., Fairfield, Conn. Office: N. Main St., Stratford, Conn. Died Sept. 4, 1967; buried St. Joseph's Cemetery, Stratford, Conn.

GODDARD, CALVIN LUTHER, inventor; b. Covington, N.Y., Jan. 22, 1822; s. Levi and Fanny (Watson) G.; grad. Yale, 1845; m. Gertrude Griggs Quimby, Dec. 19, 1846, 4 children. Tchr. in classical sch., N.Y.C., 1846; clk. in burring-machine mfg. firm, 1846-54; worked on machine that efficiently removed dust, burs, other extraneous matter from wool, 1854-66, patented machine, 1866, organized firm to manufacture burring machines, N.Y.C., moved business to Worcester, Mass., 1875-95; received Gold medal for invention at World's Fair, London, Eng., 1862, Paris, France, 1867. Died Mar. 29, 1895.

GODDARD, CHRSITOPHER MARSH, engineer; b. Claremont, N.H., Apr. 16, 1856; s. Edward L. and Elizabeth P. (Marsh) G.; ed. Stevens High Sch., Claremont; Episcopal Acad., Cheshire, Conn.; B.S., Dartmouth, 1877; m. Emilie Georgette Brandner, of Brooklyn, Feb. 14, 1882. Teacher natural sciences, Episcopal Acad., 1877-80; with Hatch & Foote, bankers, New York, 1880-85; elec. engr., Plainfield, N.J., 1885-90; sec. and treas. N.E. Ins. Exchange, 1890-1925 (retired). Originator of movement which resulted in the adoption of the "Nat. Elec. Code," and has been especially prominent in ins. rating fire prevention work. Republican. Conglist. Hon. life mem. Nat. Fire Protection Assn. (pres. 1908, 09; exec. com., 1902-15); mem. Am. Inst. E.E. Mason. Home: 19 Prospect St., Summit, N.J.

GODDARD, PAUL BECK, physician, photographic pioneer; b. Balt., Jan. 26, 1811; grad. Washington (now Trinity) Coll., Hartford, Conn., 1828; M.D., U. Pa., 1832. Practiced medicine, Phila.; asst. to Dr. Robert Hare (prof. chemistry U. Pa.), circa 1833, later prof. anatomy med. dept.; began experimenting with photography after Louis Daguerre's discovery that pictures could be produced with sun and sensitized plate as agt.; later discovered that process could be accelerated by using vapor of bromide on silvered plate, presented his discoveries before Am. Philos. Soc., 1839, elected mem., 1840; his discovery ignored by some Brit. writers and credit erroneously given to John Frederick Goddard (London optician). Author: Plates of the Cerebro-Spinal Nerves with References, 1837; Plates of the Arteries, with References, 1839. Died Phila., July 3, 1866; buried Laurel Hill Cemetery, Phila.

GODDARD, ROBERT HUTCHINGS, physicist; b. Worcester, Mass., Oct. 5, 1882; s. Nahum Danford and Fannie Louise (Hoyt) G.; B.Sc., Worcester Poly. Inst., 1908; A.M., Clark U., 1910, Ph.D., 1911, Sc.D., 1945; m. Esther Christine Kisk, June 21, 1924. Instr., Worcester Poly. Inst., 1909-11, Princeton, 1912-13; instr. and fellow, physics Clark U., 1914-15, asst. prof., 1915-19, prof., 1919-43, also dir. phys. labs.; leave of absence, 1930-32, 34-42, engaged in rocket research, under Daniel and Florence Guggenheim Found. grants; dir. research, bur. aeros. Navy Dept., 1942-45; cons. engr. Curtiss-Wright Corp., 1943-45. Fellow A.A.A.S.; mem. Am. Phys. Soc., Am. Meteorol. Soc., Inst. Aero. Scis., Nat. Aero. Assn., Geophys. Union, Sigma Xi, Sigma Alpha Epsilon. Author: A Method of Reaching Extreme Altitudes, 1914; Rocket Development: Liquid-Fuel Rocket Research, 1929-41 (pub. posthumously, 1948). Elaborated the fundamental theory of rocket flight, 1914-16; built 2-stage solid fuel rocket, 1914; developed rocket engine fueled with gasoline and liquid oxygen, 1923; launched 1st liquid fuel rocket (4 feet high, 6 inches diameter), 1926; launched 1st rocket to carry instruments (barometer, thermometer, camera), 1929; engaged in rocket research for reaching high altitudes, developed self-cooling combustion chambers, 1st automatic steering systems, multistage rockets, 1924-42; designed small rockets to help Navy airplanes take off from carriers, during World War II; developed 1st smokeless powder rocket; proved experimentally efficiency of rocket propulsion in vacuum; an early invention perfected as the bazooka; holder 214 patents in rocketry. Died Balt., Aug. 10, 1945.

GODLOVE, ISAAC HAHN, color physicist; b. St. Louis, June 13, 1892; s. Lewis and Lillie G.; B.S., M.A., Washington U., 1915; Ph.D., U. Ill., 1926; m. Esther Alice Hurlbut, Dec. 22, 1923; 1 son, Terry Francis; m. 2d, Margaret Noss, Aug. 6, 1949. Prof. chemistry Mo. State Normal Sch., 1915-16; asso. prof. U. Okla., 1921-26; research dir. Munsell Color Co., 1926-30; dir., exhbn. color N.Y. Mus. Sci. and Industry, 1930-31; color editor Webster's New Internat. Dictionary, 1931-32; propr. Color Service Labs., 1932-35; chemist and physicist DuPont Co., 1935-43, Gen. Aniline & Film Corp., 1943—. Trustee Munsell Color Found. Mem. Optical Soc. Am. (com. colorimetry), Am. Assn. Textile Chemists and Colorists (chmn. color com.), Inter-Soc. Color Council (chmn. 1948-49, editor), Wash. Oratorio Soc. (v.p.), Sigma Xi, Alpha Chi Sigma. Author articles on color physics and psychology. Joint author: The Science of Color, 1953. Co-author: The Smithsonian Tables of Physical Constants, 1954. Home: 127 Spring Garden St. Office: General Aniline & Film Corp., Easton, Pa. Died Aug. 14, 1954; buried Greenwood Cemetery, Lancaster, Pa.

GODMAN, JOHN DAVIDSON, naturalist, anatomist; b. Annapolis, Md., Dec. 20, 1794; s. Capt. Samuel and Anna (Henderson) G.; studied medicine; M.D., U. Md., 1818; m. Angelica Kauffman Peale, Oct. 6, 1821. Practiced medicine, New Holland, Pa.; moved to village nr. Balt.; gave series of lectures on anatomy and physiology, Phila.; became prof. surgery Med. Coll. of Ohio, Cincinnati; editor 1st issue of Quarterly Reports of Med., Surg. and Natural Science (1st med. jour. published West of Allegheny Mountains), 1822. Mem. editorial bd. Phila. Jour. of Med. and Phys. Scis. (became Am. Jour. Med. Scis., 1827), 1825-27; prof. anatomy Rutgers Med. Coll., N.Y.C., 1826-27; suffered attack of tuberculosis; ret. to Germantown, Pa., devoted remainder of his life to naturalist studies and writing. Author: American Natural History, 3 vols., 1826-28; Rambles of a Naturalist, 1833. Died Apr. 17, 1830.

GODSHALL, LINCOLN DERSTINE, mining engr., metallurgist; b. Lansdale Pa., Nov. 26, 1865; s. Abraham C. and Anna (Derstine) G.; B.S., Lafayette Coll., Pa., 1887, M.S., Ph.D., 1890; m. Estelle B. Hall, Mar. 30, 1889 (died Feb. 10, 1920); children—Clarence Hall, Leon Deane, William Arthur, Harold Lincoln; m. 2d, Mrs. Laura Chambers Smith, Oct. 8, 1923. Supt. and metallurgist, Colo., 1888-93; sulpt. Puget Sound Reduction Works, Wash., 1894-99; supt. Boston-Wyo. Smelting, Power & Light Co., 1900-02; v.p. and mng. dir. Ariz.-Mexican Mining & Smelting Co., 1904-10; v.p. and mgr. Cocopah Copper Co.; mgr. Needles Mining & Smelting Co. (a subsidiary of U.S. Smelting, Refining & Mining Co.), Nov. 1909-Jan. 1911; v.p. in charge Tecopa (Calif.) Consol. Mining Co., and Tecopa R.R. Co., 1912-28, pres. Ivanpah Copper Co., Los

Angeles. Regent U. of Wash., 6 yrs. Republican. Club: Los Angeles Country. Contbr. to engring. and mining jours. Home: 722 S. Oxford Av. Office: Standard Oil Bldg., 605 W. Olympic Blvd., Los Angeles CA

GOERTZ, RAYMOND C., engr.; b. Clearwater, Kan., Mar. 12, 1915; s. Norman E. and Flora (Saint) G.; B.S., Mont. State Coll., 1940; grad. study, Poly. Institute of Brooklyn, 1942-46, Illinois Institute of Technology, 1947-49; m. Helen Boula, September 2, 1950;children—Alan, Jean, and Linda. Jr. engr., project engr. Servomechanisms Lab., Sperry Gyroscope Co., 1940-47; formerly group leader Argonne Nat. Lab., Lemont, Ill., sr. engr. remote control engring. div. U.S. del. 1st and 2d Internat. Confs. on Peaceful Uses of Atomic Energy, Geneva, Switzerland, 1955, 58. Recipient Edward Longstreth medal Franklin Inst., Phila., 1967; Radiation Industry award Am. Nuclear Soc., 1969. Mem. Am. Nuclear Soc., Research Soc. Am., Am. Inst. Chem. Engrs., I.E.E.E., Am. Nuclear Soc., Research Soc. Am. Contbr. articles to profl. jours. Patentee in field. Home: Downers Grove IL Died June 4, 1970; buried Clarendon Hills Cemetery, Clarendon Mills IL

GOETZ, GEORGE WASHINGTON, metallurgist; b. Milw., Feb. 17, 1856; s. August W. and Augusta (Stottyr) G.; attended U. Wis., Sch. Mines, Berlin, Germany; m. Elsie Luedecke, 1886, 3 children. Telegraph operator Milw. Iron Co., 1870; began metall. studies with Otis Steel Co., 1881, in charge of open hearth steel dept.; became foremost iron and steel metallurgist in Am.; established metall. lab., Milw., 1890, cons. metallurgist Ill. Steel Co., Westinghouse Co., others. Died Jan. 15, 1897.

GOFF, EMMET STULL, horticulturist; b. Elmira, N.Y., Sept. 3, 1852; s. Gustavus A. and Mary (Stull) G.; m. S. Antoinette Carr, Oct. 2, 1880. Fruit grower and farmer, nr. Elmira, 13 years; horticulturist N.Y. Exptl. Sta., Geneva, 1882-89, experimented on culture of many economically important plants; 1st prof. horticulture U. Wis., 1889-1902; did his most notable research in field of differentiation of flower buds of fruit plants. Author: Principles of Plant Culture, 1897; Lessons in Commercial Fruit Growing, 1902. Died June 6, 1902.

GOFFE, J(AMES) RIDDLE, surgeon; b. Kenosha, Wis., Aug. 10, 1851; s. William and Betsy D. (Riddle) G.; Ph.B., U. of Mich., 1873, Ph.M., 1876, A.M., 1916; M.D., Bellevue Hosp. Med. Coll. (New York, U.), 1881; Woman's Hosp., N.Y., 1883; studied Paris and Vienna; m. Eleanor Taylor, Sept. 29, 1890 (died 1908). Attending surgeon Polyclinic Hosp., 1894—, Woman's Hosp., 1902—; consulting surgeon, St. Joseph's Hosp., Yonkers, N.Y., Mt. Vernon (N.Y.) Hosp., New York City Hosp., Lawrence Hosp., Bronxville. Prof. diseases of women, New York Polyclinic Med. Sch. and Hosp., Dartmouth Med. Sch. Trustee New York Polyclinic Med. Sch. and Hosp. Republican. Home: New York, N.Y. Died Dec. 24, 1931.

GOFORTH, WILLIAM, physician; b. N.Y.C., 1766; s. Judge William and Catharine (Meeks) G.; studied medicine under Drs. Joseph Young and Charles McKnight, N.Y.C.; m. Miss Wood, circa 1790. Went to Ky., 1788, to Cincinnati, 1800; probably 1st to vaccinate West of Alleghanies; made 1st vaccinations in N.W. Territory, 1801; commd. surgeon-gen. 1st Div., Ohio Militia, 1804; at Big Bone Lick (Ky.) dug up collection of prehistoric fossils of interest to natural science, 1803; signed 1st med. diploma given in N.W. Ty. (given Daniel Drake), 1805; considered leading physician of Cincinnati, 1800-07; went to New Orleans as parish judge, 1807; mem. La. Constl. Conv.; served as surgeon in a volunteer regt. during Brit. attack on New Orleans. Died Cincinnati, May 12, 1817.

GOLD, HARRY, pharmacologist, cardiologist; b. Russia, Dec. 25, 1899; s Samuel and Naomi (Katz) G.; A.B., Cornell, 1919, M.D., 1922; m. Bertha Goldman, 1926; children—Naomi, Stanley, Muriel. Came to U.S., 1903, naturalized, 1910. Instr. pharmacology Cornell, 1922-29, asst. prof., 1929-44, asso. prof., 1944-47, prof. clin. pharmacology, 1947-65, emeritus, 1965-72; attending-in-charge cardiovascular research unit, Beth Israel Hosp., 1931-65, cons. cardiology, 1965-72; attending cardiologist, chmn. med. adv. bd. hosp. Joint Diseases, 1933-65, cons. cardiologist, 1965-72; mem. med. bd. Doctors Hosp., 1950-63, honorary member of attending staff, 1963-72; consulting cardiologist at St. Vincent's hosps. S.I., Army Med. Center Richmond Meml. Hosp., S.I.; civilian instr. and cons. U.S. Naval Hosp., St. Albans; lectr. therapeutics Post Grad. Extension div. Rutgers U. Mem. revision com. U.S. Pharmacopoeia, 1940-57. Recipient award of distinction as father clin. pharmacology Cornell U. Med. Coll., 1971. Fellow N.Y. Acad. Scis., N.Y. Acad. Medicine, A.A.A.S.; mem. A.M.A., Am. Heart Assn. (sci. council), Am. Soc. Pharmacology and Exptl. Therapeutics, mem. N.Y. Heart Assn. (bd. dirs.), Harvey Soc., Am. Coll. Clin. Pharmacology and Chemotherapy (charter mem. bd. regents), Poison Control Center N.Y.C., Alpha Omega Alpha, Phi Beta Kappa; honorary member of Argentine Med. Assn., Cardiological Soc. Brazil. Democrat. Jewish religion. Mng. editor Cornell Confs. on Therapy, 1949-55; asso. editor Am. Jour. Medicine, 1947-57, Am. Jour. Medical Sci., 1944-72; editorial bd. Jour. Clin. Pharmacology, 1963-72. Author: Quinidine in Disorders of the Heart, 1950. Asso. editorial bd. N.Y. State Jour. of Medicine. Contbr. sci. articles Am., European med. jours. Home: New York City NY Died Apr. 21, 1972.

GOLDBECK, ALBERT THEODORE, engr.; b. Phila., Mar. 1, 1885; s. George E. and Clara (Rowley) G.; B.S., U. Pa., 1906, C.E., 1923; m. Alice Lucile Davis, Aug. 30, 1916; children—Page, Clara Gale. Instr. civil engring. U. Pa., 1906-08, Lafayette Coll., 1908-10; engr. tests U.S. Office Pub. Rds., 1910-13, City of Phila., 1913-15; engr. tests, chief div. tests U.S. Bur. Pub. Rds., 1915-25; engring. dir. Nat. Crushed Stone Assn., 1925-56, cons., 1956—. Mem. steering com. First Internat. Skid Prevention Conf., chmn. com. on effect of rd. surface. Recipient Distinguished Service award. Hwy. Research Bd., 1951; Turner Award, 1957. Mem. Am. Soc. C.E. (life), Am. Concrete Inst. (pres. 1952), Am. Soc. Testing Materials (hon.; 1st recipient Frank E. Richart award; chmn. long range planning com. on standardization procedure), Am. Inst. Mining Engrs., Am. Ry. Engring. Assn. Joint Com. (concrete and reinforced concrete), Asphalt Paving Technologists, Sigma Xi. Clubs: Cosmos, Capital Yacht (Washington). Author tech. papers bulls. Home: 7105 Beechwood Dr., Chevy Chase 15, Md. Office: 1415 Elliot Pl., Washington 7. Died Aug. 19, 1966.

GOLDBERGER, ISIDORE HARRY, physician, educator, author; b. N.Y.C., Aug. 24, 1888; s. Herman and Rose (Weiss) G.; grad. N.Y.U. Med. Coll., 1910; m. Minnie Snow, Feb. 12, 1913; children—Eleanor (Mrs. Robert S. Frank), Marjorie (Mrs. Edmund Grasheim). Clin. prof. pediatrics N.Y.U. Med. Coll., 1911-41, spl. lectr. Sch. Edn., also Columbia U. Sch. Pub. Health, Coll. City N.Y.; dir. health edn. Bd. Edn., N.Y.C., 1914-58; dir. emeritus, 1958-67; co-founder Sch. Oral Hygiene, Columbia U. Coll. Phys. and Surg., mem. faculty, 1915-45; vis. pediatrician Willard Parker Hosp., 1915-48; v.p. med. bd., 1934-40; co-founder Morrisania City Hosp., 1929, dir. pediatrics, 1929-41, now consulting dir.; college medical consultant Bronx Community, Board of Higher Education, City of New York; with Dr. William H. Park; introduced diphteria toxoid, 1917; collaborated in discovery process to incorporate Vitamin D in milk for prevention and cure of rickets; originator School Health Day program for health care of children; founder Let's See Movement, project to furnish free eyeglasses to needy children, 1924. Board of directors N.Y.C. unit Am. Cancer Soc.; past mem. Nat. Com. Child Health and Protection; mem. bd. trustees Lavelle School for the Blind. Recipient award for services to children N.Y. State Assn. Health, Phys. Edn. and Recreation, 1958; trophy for promotion mutual goodwill and understanding Interfaith Movement, 1958; plaque for years distinguished and exceptional pub. service, City N.Y.; Dr. William G. Anderson award, Am. Assn. Health, Physical Education and Recreation, 1963. Diplomate Am. Bd. Pediatrics Fallon N.Y. Acad. Medicine, A.M.A., Am. Pub. Health Assn., Royal Soc. Promotion of Health (Eng.); mem. Am. Health, Phys. Edn. and Recreation (Dr. William G. Anderson award 1963), Medical Society State N.Y., Bronx County Med. Soc. (past v.p.), Bronx Pediatric Soc. (founder, mem. governing council), Am. Sch. Health Assn., N.Y. Acad. Pub. Edn. Rotarian (pres. Bronx 1933-34). Co-author: Health for Life, 1962; textbooks on child health; also articles profl., popular mags. Home: Bronx NY Died May 9, 1967; buried Ferncliff, Ardsley NY

GOLDBERGER, JOSEPH, medical research; b. Austria-Hungary, July 16, 1874; s. Samuel and Sarah (Gutman) G.; ed. Coll. City of New York, 1890-92; M.D., Bellevue Hosp. Med. Coll. (New York U.), 1895; m. Mary Humphreys Farrar, Apr. 19, 1906; children—E. Farrar, Joseph H., B. Humphreys, Mary Humphreys. Resident physician Bellevue Hosp., 1895-97; pvt. practice, Wilkes-Barre, Pa., 1897-99; commd. asst. surgeon U.S. Pub. Health Service, 1899; passed asst. surgeon, 1904; surgeon, 1912. Chief work, research in preventive medicine, infectious diseases; now dir. field nutrition investigations. Mason. Contbr. results of original investigations of trematodes, the straw itch, yellow fever, dengue fever, measles, typhus fever, cholera media, diphtheria carriers and pellagra. Home: Washington, D.C. Died Jan. 17, 1929.

GOLDMAN, EDWARD ALPHONSE, naturalist; b. Mt. Carroll, Ill., July 7, 1873; s. Jacob Henry and Laura Carrie (Nicodemus) G.; ed. pub. schs. and under pvt. tutors; m. Emma May Chase, June 23, 1902; children—Nelson Edward, Orville Merriam, Luther Chase. With U.S. Biol. Survey since 1892; much of time, 1892-1906, in biol. investigations in Mexico; in biol. survey of Panama, 1911-12, of Ariz., 1913-17; in charge div. of biological investigations, 1919-25; in charge div. of game and bird reservations, 1925-28; senior biologist since 1928. Fellow A.A.A.S.; mem. Am. Ornithologists' Union, Am. Soc. Mammalogists, Washington Acad. of Science, Biol. Soc. of Washington (pres. 1927-29), Am. Forestry Assn., Cooper Ornith. Club of Calif., Washington Biologists' Field Club. Commd. major, Sanitary Corps N.A., 1918, and with A.E.F. in France; maj. Sanitary Officers' Res. Corps, 1921-37, now retired. Clubs: Cosmos (Washington), Explorers (New York). Author: Revision of Wood Rats of Genus Neotoma, 1910; Revision of Spiny Pocket Mice (Heteromys and Liomys), 1911; Plant Records of an Expedition to Lower California, 1916; Rice Rats of North America (Oryzomys), 1918; Mammals of Panama, 1920; The Wolves of North America (with Stanley P. Young); also numerous shorter papers, mainly on mammals and birds and conservation of wild life. Home: 2702 17th St. N.E. Office: U.S. National Museum, Washington, D.C. Deceased.

GOLDMAN, HETTY, archaeologist; b. N.Y.C., Dec. 19, 1881; d. Julius and Sarah (Adler) Goldman; A.B., Bryn Mawr Coll., 1903; student Columbia, 1903-04, 06-07; A.M., Radcliff Coll., 1910, Ph.D., 1916; Norton fellow of Harvard, Am. Sch. Classical Studies, Athens, 1910-12. Manuscript reader Macmillan Co., 1903-04; excavator, Halae in Greece, 1911-14, 21, 31; dir. of excavations for Fogg Mus. of Harvard at Colophon, Asia Minor, 1922, 25, Eutresis, Greece, 1924-27; vis. lectr. archaeology Johns Hopkins, 1928; mem. representing Fogg Museum of Harvard Archaeological Expdn. to Yugoslavia, 1932; archaeol. reconnaissance for Bryn Mawr Coll. in ancient Cilicia, Turkey, 1934; excavator at Tarsus, Turkey, for Bryn Mawr Coll., Harvard and Archaeol. Inst. of Am., 1935-38, 47, 48; prof., Sch. of Humanistic Studies of Inst. for Advanced Study, Princeton, N.J., 1936-47, emeritus professor, 1948-72. Trustee Archaeol. Inst. Am. Served with Am. Red Cross in Greece, 1918-19; visited Balkan States for Jewish Joint Distribution Com., 1918-19, Paris office, 1920. Recipient Distinguished Achievement medal, Grad. chpt. Radcliffe Alumnae Soc., 1953. Mem. Am. Acad. Arts and Scis., Archaeol. Soc. Am. Am. Numismatic Soc., Am. Assn. U. Women (mem. com. on fellowship award 1936-41), Phi Beta Kappa; corresponding member German Archaeol. Inst. Club: Cosmopolitan (N.Y.C.). Author: Excavations at Eutresis in Beotia, 1931. Editor and co-author: Excavations at Gozlu Kule Tarsus, Vol. I., Vol. II, 1956. Contbr. articles on archaeology to profl. jours.; revised sect. on archaeology of Turkey for Ency. Brit. Home: Princeton NJ Died May 4, 1972.

GOLDSBOROUGH, W(INDER) ELWELL, engr. and economist; b. Balt., Oct. 10, 1871; s. Washington Elwell and Martha Pierce (Laird) G.; M.E., Cornell U., 1892; m. Charlotte Poole Wallace, Dec. 20, 1899; children—Winder Elwell (dec.), Laird Shields. Engr. Colliery Engring. Co., Scranton, Pa., 1892-93; prof. elec. engring., Ark. U., 1893-94; cons. engr., Edison Elec. Illuminating Co., Balt., 1894-96; prof. elec. engring., Purdue, 1894-1905, also dir. Sch. Elec. Engring., 1896-1905; asst. to pres., 1905-06, bus. mgr. engring. dept., 1906-07, J. G. White & Co., N.Y.C.; dir., v.p. and gen. mgr. Denver (Colo.) Reservoir Irrigation Co., 1907-10; pres. Platte Valley Land Co., 1908—; pres. the Goldsborough Co., engrs., 1910-23; gen. mgr. Laramie (Wyo.) Water Co., 1910-13; gen. and financial mgr. New Home Sewing Machine Co., 1918-20; cons. engr., N.Y. City, 1914-23; with Henry L. Doherty & Co., N.Y., 1923-32; mgr. and dir. research Power Div. Labs., Combustion Utilities Corp., New York, 1924-32; cons. engr. and economist, 1932—. Major, Cornell Univ. Cadet Corps, 1892; maj. Ark. State Guards, 1893-94; comdt. cadets Ark. U., 1893-94. Mem. or del. to Internat. Elec. congresses, Chicago, 1893, Paris, 1900, St. Louis (v.p.), 1904; chief of dept. electricity, St. Louis Expn., 1902-05; mem. jury of awards, Buffalo Expn., 1901; mem. superior jury Internat. Jury of Awards, St. Louis Expn., 1904; mem. com. com. of Nat. Electric Light Assn. on Arc Light Photometry, 1900-03; chmn. exec. com. Electric Ry. Test Commn., 1903-07. Commerative Medal Univ. Expn., 1904. Decorated Order of Crown (Italy), 1904. Fellow A.A.A.S., Am. Inst. E.E. (v.p. 1901-05); asso. fellow American Electro-Therapeutic Assn.; mem. or past mem. Am. Soc. M.E., Inst. Elec. Engrs. of England, Franklin Inst., Internat. Assn. Testing Materials, Sco. Promotion Engring. Edn., Nat. Inst. Social Sciences, Ind. Acad. Science, Am. Electro-Chem. Soc., New York Southern Soc., Beta Theta Pi. Clubs: (mem. or past mem.): Denver, University, Country, Transportation (Denver); St. Louis, Mercantile (St. Louis); Lawyers, Engineers, Nat. Arts, Cornell, Purdue (New York); Country (South Norwalk). Inventor and patentee of numerous machines and devices. Author of ednl., literary, scientific, econ. and engring. books, monographs, papers and reports. Home: Bonniebrook Rd. and Richards Av., Norwalk, Conn. Died Jan. 12, 1957.

GOLDSCHMIDT, RICHARD BENEDICT, zoologist; b. Frankfurt on Main, Germany, Apr. 12, 1878; s. Solomon and Emma (Flürscheim) G.; Ph.D., U. Heidelberg, 1902; also student U. Munich; M.D. (hon.), U. Kiel, 1929; D.Sc. (hon.), U. Madrid, 1934; Dr. (hon.), Berlin, 1953; m. Elsa Kühnlein Mar. 15, 1906; children—Ruth Emma (Mrs. H. Williams), Hans. Came to U.S., 1936. Asst. U. Heidelberg, 1900; lectr., asst. and asso. prof. U. Munich, 1903-14; mem. and dir. Kaiser Wilhelm Inst. for Biol. Research, Berlin, 1914-36; prof. zoölogy Imperial U., Tokyo, 1924-26; prof. zoölogy U. Cal., 1936-48, emeritus; Silliman lectr. Yale, 1939-40. Mem., hon. mem., fgn. mem. numerous academies, learned socs. in 12 different countries. Author: The Mechanism and Physiology of Sex Determination, 1923; Physiological Genetics, 1938; Ascaris: The Biologist's Story of Life, 1937; The Material Basis of Evolution, 1940; Understanding Heredity, 1952; Theoretical Genetics, 1955; Portraits from Memory, 1956; 12 books in German on genetics, sex, travel, popular sci., pub. Germany, many trans. other langs. Contbr. articles on biology to tech. jours. U.S. and Europe. Home: 590 Arlington, Berkeley, Cal. Died Apr. 24, 1958.

GOLDSMITH, MIDDLETON, surgeon; b. Port Tobacco, Md., Aug. 5, 1818; s. Dr. Alban and Talia Ferro (Middleton) Smith; attended Hanover (Ind.) Coll.; grad. Coll. Physicians and Surgeons, N.Y.C., 1840; m. Frances Swift, June 1843, 2 daus. Introduced (with his father) the practice of lithority (method of crushing bladder stones) in Am. A founder 1st Alumni Assn. Coll. Physicians and Surgeons, N.Y. Path. Soc., 1844; prof. surgery Castleton (Vt.) Med. Coll., 1844-45; pres. Vt. Med. Soc., 1851; prof. surgery Ky. Sch. Medicine, Louisville, 1856; brigade surgeon Army of Cumberland; med. dir. U.S. Army under Gen. Buell at Battle of Shiloh; insp. hosps. under Gen. Grant at Battle Corinth; surgeon gen. Ky. and Dept. of Ohio mil. hosps.; in charge of Gen. Army Hosp., Jeffersonville, Ind.; wrote pamphlet A Report on Hospital Gangrene, Erysipelas, and Pyaemin as Observed in the Departments of the Ohio and the Cumberland: With Cases Appended, 1863; pioneer in antiseptic surgery; established Rutland (Vt.) Free Dispensary; spl. commr. to investigate state insane asylum, Vt., which resulted in its improvement and reform; drew up game laws of Vt. Died Nov. 26, 1887.

GOLDSPOHN, ALBERT, physician; b. Dane County, Wis., Sept. 23, 1851; B.S., Northwestern Coll., Naperville, Ill., 1875; M.D., Rush Med. Coll., Chicago, 1878; studied in Germany 2 yrs.; m. Cornelia E. Walz, (died 1901). Resident physician and surgeon, Cook County Hosp., Chicago, 1878-79; practiced at Des Plaines 6 yrs.; settled in Chicago; attending surgeon former German Hosp., 1888-1904; prof. diseases of women and abdominal surgery, Post-Grad. Med. Sch. and Hosp., 1890-1922; surgeon in chief Evang. Deaconess Hosp. Trustee Northwestern Coll., 1889— (donated abt. $40,000 to this instn.). Republican. Mem. Evangelical Ch. Devised a fundamental operation for injuries sustained during childbirth, and two major operations for displacements and prolapse of the womb. Home: Naperville, Ill. Died Sept. 1, 1929.

GOLDSTEIN, MAX AARON, M.D., oto-laryngologist; b. St. Louis, Mo., Apr. 19, 1870; s. William and Hulda (Loewenthal) G.; M.D., Mo. Med. Coll., 1892; LL.D.; study in oto-laryngology, Strassburg, Berlin, Vienna and London, 1893; m. Leonore Weiner, June 4, 1895; 1 dau., Helen (Mrs. Norman C. Wolff). Began practice oto-laryngology, St. Louis, 1894; prof. otology and laryngology, Beaumont Hosp. Med. Coll., 1896-1900, St. Louis U., 1900-12; founder, 1914, and dir. Central Inst. for Deaf, St. Louis; dir. dept. otology and laryngology, Jewish Hosp. of St. Louis. Founder, 1896, and editor The Laryngoscope (monthly mag.); founder, 1922, and editor Oralism and Auralism (semi-annual jour.). Served as maj., Med. Corps, U.S. Army, World War; head of dept. head surgery, Camp Dodge, Ia.; mem. com. on reconstrn. for deal and defective speech soldiers. Democrat. Mem. Jewish Ref. Ch. Author: Problems of the Deaf; The Acoustic Method for Training the Deaf and Hard of Hearing Child, 1939. Home: Clayton, Mo. Died July 27, 1941.

GOLDTHWAIT, JAMES WALTER, prof. geology; b. Lynn, Mass., Mar. 22, 1880; s. James Wesley and Olive Jane (Parker) G.; A.B., Harvard, 1902, A.M., 1903, Ph.D., 1906; D.Sc. (hon.) Univ. of New Hampshire, 1945; married Edith Dunnels Richards, June 25, 1906; children—Richard Parker, Lawrence. Asst. prof. geology, Northwestern U., 1904-08; asst. prof. geology, 1908-11, prof. geology since 1911, Dartmouth. Engaged during summers in geologic field work for state surveys of Wis. and Ill., for U.S. Geol. Survey and for Geol. Survey of Can. Served as capt. U.S. Army, Apr. 8-Dec. 31, 1918, in charge of map room, Office Chief of Staff, Washington. Geologist, N.H. State Highway Dept. since 1917. Fellow Geol. Soc. America, Am. Acad. Arts and Sciences; mem. Phi Beta Kappa, Sigma Xi, Gamma Alpha fraternities. Conglist. Author: Abandoned Shorelines of Eastern Wisconsin (Wis. Geol. Survey), 1906; Physiography of Nova Scotia (Geol. Survey of Can.), 1925; Geology of New Hampshire (N.H. Acad. Science Handbook No. 1), 1925; also numerous reports and papers, dealing with extinct shorelines, earth movements, river floods, glacial and physiographic studies in N.E. and Can. Home: Hanover, N.H. Died Dec. 31, 1947.

GOLDTHWAITE, GEORGE EDGAR, cons. engr.; b. Marion, Ind., Oct. 18, 1889; s. Edgar Louis and Candace (Zombro) G.; B.S. in elec. engring., Purdue U., 1911; m. Emily Jack Duncan, May 30, 1925; 1 son, Duncan. Engring. apprentice Westinghouse Electric Co., East Pittsburgh, 1911-12; load dispatcher and asst. to elec. engr. Pittsburgh Rys. Co., 1912-14; chief operator electrified div. Norfolk & Western Ry. Co., 1914-16; asso. editor Ry. Age Gazette and Ry. Elec. Engr., 1916-17; elec. constrn. engr. and foreman, 1919; asso. with Milo R. Maltbie, public utility investigations, reports, etc., 1919-29; mem. firm Hine & Goldthwaite, public utility consultant, since 1930; cons. engr. for Pub. Service Commn. and other N.Y. State depts.; spl. cons. to various cities and states, U.S. P.O. Dept. and other govtl. bodies, Montreal, Can., Que. Hydro-Elec. Commn., Republic of Cuba. Mem. exec. com. Citizens Union. Served as 1st lieut. (pilot and flight comdr.). 24th Aero Squadron, U.S. Army, with A.E.F., 1918. Decorated D.S.C. for action in Argonne-Meuse offensive, Oct. 15, 1918. Mem. Amer. Inst. E.E. Republican. Congregationalist. Clubs: Engineers, City (New York); Appalachian Mountain (Boston); Adirondack Mountain (pres. 1950-52), American Alpine, Alpine of Canada. Contbr. to jours. Home: 3328 81st St., Jackson Heights, N.Y. 11372. Office: 7 Dey St., N.Y. Died Jan. 10, 1960; buried Marion, Ind.

GOLOVIN, NICHOLAS ERASMUS, govt. exec.; b. Odessa, Russia, Mar. 18, 1912; s. Erasm N. and Galina A. (Kharchenko) G.; A.B., Columbia, 1933, M.A., 1936; Ph.D., George Washington University, 1955; m. Anne Castrodale, December 30, 1966; children by former marriages—Paul Nicholas, Karl Nicholas, Theresa (Mrs. William J. B. Trittipoe Jr.), Natalie (Mrs. King Nelson). Began as a research statistical analyst for R. H. Macy & Company, 1934-38, dept. mgr., 1938-43; chief prodn. and requirements analysis sect. tool div., WPB, 1943-43; asso. supt. electricity div. Naval Research Lab., 1946-48; head mgmt. div. staff Naval Ordnance Test Sta., Cal., 1948-49; cons. to dir. Nat. Bur. Standards, 1949, exec. asst. to dir., 1949, asso. dir. adminstrn., 1953-55, asso. dir. planning, 1955-58; became chief scientist White Sands Missile Range, N.M., 1958; dir. tech. operators div. Advanced Research Projects Agy., Dept. of Def., 1959; dep. asso. adminstr. NASA, 1960, tech. asst. to asso. adminstr. NASA and dir. NASA-DOD large launch vehicle planning group 1961-62; tech. adviser Office of the Spl. Asst. to Pres. for Sci. and Tech., 1962-69; v.p., gen. mgr. Rabinow Engring. Co., Inc., 1960-61. Mem. Am. Inst. Aeros. and Astronautics, Inst. Elec. and Electronic Engrs., Am. Phys. Soc., Am. Nuclear Soc., A.A.A.S., Philos. Soc. Wash., Am. Ordnance Assn., Phi Beta Kappa, Sigma Xi. Home: Washington DC Died Apr. 27, 1969.

GOLTRA, EDWARD FIELD, iron metallurgy; b. Jacksonville, Ill., Dec. 29, 1862; s. Moore Compton and Evelina (Parsons) G.; Ill. Coll.; A.B., Princeton, 1887; m. Kate Mary Brown, May 31, 1888. Began in iron business at St. Louis, 1889; organized and operated various iron and steel properties. Mem. Dem. Nat. Com. for Mo., 1911—; chmn. Municipal Commn. on Tuberculosis, St. Louis; mem. Bd. of Edn., St. Louis; trustee Ill. Coll. Address: St. Louis, Mo. Died Apr. 2, 1939.

GOMBERG, MOSES, chemist; b. Elizabetgrad, Russia, Feb. 8, 1866; s. George and Marie Ethel (Resnikoff) G.; ed. Elizabetgrad Gymnasium, 1878-84; B.S., U. of Mich., 1890, M.S., 1892, Sc.D., 1894; studied at U. of Munich, 1896-97, U. of Heidelberg, 1897; hon. Sc.D., U. of Chicago, 1929, Poly. Inst., Brooklyn, 1932; LL.D., U. of Mich., 1937; unmarried. Instr. chemistry, 1893-99; asst. prof. organic chemistry, 1899-1902, jr. prof., 1902-04, prof., 1904-36; also chmn. dept. of chemistry, 1927-36, Univ. of Mich., prof. emeritus since 1936. Consulting chemist, Bureau of Mines, 1917-18; maj. Ord. Department, North America, July 1918. Contbr. to various chemical jours. Awarded Nichols medal, Am. Chem. Soc., 1914, Willard Gibbs medal, 1925, Chandler medal, 1927; fellow A.A.A.S. (vice-pres. and chmn. sect. C, 1935); mem. Nat. Acad. Sciences, Am. Philos. Soc., Am. Chem. Society (pres. 1931); hon. mem. Netherlands Chem. Soc., Am. Inst. of Chemists. Home: 712 Onondaga St., Ann Arbor, Mich. Died Feb. 12, 1947.

GONCE, JOHN EUGENE, JR. (gons), pediatrician; b. Elkton, Md., Oct. 17, 1893; s. John Eugene and Eliza (Bratton) G.; A.B., U. of Del., 1913; M.D., U. of Pa., 1918; m. Louise Allyn, Sept. 3, 1927; children—John Eugene III, Allyn. Interne U. Hosp., Phila., Pa., 1918-19; instr. clinical medicine, U. of Wis., 1919-25; interne Children's Hosp., Phila., Pa., 1922-23; asso. in pediatrics, U. of Wis., 1925-26, asst. prof. pediatrics, 1926-30, asso. prof. pediatrics, 1930-32, prof. pediatrics, since 1932; pediatrician to Wis. Gen. Hosp., since 1925. Fellow Am. Coll. Physicians; mem. Dane County Med. Soc. (pres., 1945-46), Wis. Med. Assn., A.M.A., Am. Acad. Pediatrics, Sigma Xi, Sigma Sigma, Kappa Alpha. Club: Blackhawk Country. Contbr. to med. jours. and Grulee and Eley's textbook of pediatrics. Home: 2221 Chamberlain Av., Madison 5. Office: 1300 University Av., Madison 6, Wis. Died Mar. 25, 1956.

GOOCH, FRANK AUSTIN, chemist; b. Watertown, Mass., May 2, 1852; s. Joshua Goodale and Sarah Gates (Coolidge) G.; A.B., Harvard, 1872, A.M., Ph.D., 1877; hon. M.A., Yale, 1887; m. Sarah Elisabeth Wyman, Aug. 12, 1880; 1 dau., Meredyth (Mrs. John Downes Whiting). Asst. in chem. lab. under Prof. Josiah P. Cooke until 1875; studied with Prof. Wolcott Gibbs, and in Europe until 1878; engaged in analytical work at Newport for U.S. 10th Census, 1879-81, chemist on Northern Transcontinental Survey, 1881-84, and U.S. Geol. Survey, 1884-86; prof. chemistry, Yale, 1885-1918, and dir. Kent Chem. Lab.; emeritus. Investigator of inorganic and analytical chemistry. Author: Analyses of Waters of the Yellowstone Park (with J. E. Whitfield), 1888; Research Papers from the Kent Chemical Laboratory of Yale Univ. (2 vols.), 1901; Outlines of Inorganic Chemistry (with C. F. Walker), 1905; Laboratory Experiments (with C. F. Walker), 1905; Outlines of Qualitative Chemical Analysis (with P. E. Browning), 1906; Methods in Chemical Analysis, 1912; Representative Procedures in Quantitative Chemical Analysis, 1915. Home: New Haven, Conn. Died Aug. 12, 1929.

GOOD, CHARLES WINFRED, educator, research exec.; b. Saginaw, Mich., May 17, 1893; s. Charles Henry and Mary Winnifred (Farrar) G.; B.S., U. of Mich., 1918; m. Vera L. Tibbetts, Apr. 8, 1923; children—Martha Ann (Mrs. F. C. Vibrans), Phoebe J. (Mrs. D. L. Trezise), Charles Hansen. Instr., auto mechanics, U. of Mich., 1918, in mech. engring., 1918-25. asst. prof., 1925-33, asso. prof., 1933-43, prof. of mech. engring. since 1943, on leave as engring. cons. Am. Car & Foundry Co. in its Albuquerque, N.M. operations for AEC until 1953; asst. to dir., dept. of engring. research (changed to Engring. Research Inst., 1948), 1923-36, asst. dir., 1936-51; cons. mech. engr. since 1925; cons., indsl. research and development div., Office of Tech. Service, 1946-47. Mem. A.S.M.E. (life mem.; chmn. profl. divs. com.), Society Automotive Engineers, American Society Engineering Education, Engineering Society of Detroit, Gamma Alpha, Delta Alpha Epsilon, Tau Beta Pi. Clubs: University, Michigan Union (Ann Arbor). Author: Internal Combustion Engines (with Lay and Vincent), 1931. Contbr. articles to tech. publs. Home: 2307 Hill St., Ann Arbor, Mich. Died Sept. 6, 1956.

GOOD, EDWIN STANTON, animal husbandman; b. Clarence Center, N.Y., Mar. 16, 1871; s. John and Esther (Hummel) G.; B.S., Mich. Agrl. Coll., 1903; M.S., U. of Ill., 1906; m. Louise A. Millikan, June 24, 1908; children—John Wolcott, Edwin Millikan. Sec. to pres. Mich. State Agrl. Coll., East Lansing, Mich., 1897-99; instr. and investigator in animal husbandry, U. of Ill., 1903-06; head dept. animal husbandry, Ky. Agrl. Expt. Sta., since 1906; prof. animal husbandry, University of Kentucky, since 1912; also chairman of animal industry group and leader in animal husbandry extension, 1919-43, professor emeritus since 1943. Investigated live stock conditions in Eng., Scotland, Holland, France and Belgium, 1905. Isolated and named the bacillus causing infectious abortion in mares, and perfected a vaccine which immunizes mares against this disease. Mem. Ky. Live Stock Sanitary Bd. Mem. A.A.A.S., Am. Soc. Animal Production, Assn. Southern Agrl. Workers, Ky. Acad. Science, Am. Assn. Univ. Profs., Alpha Zeta, Sigma Alpha Epsilon, Sigma Xi. Presbyterian. Club: Kiwanis. Author of animal husbandry section in Hallegan's Fundamentals of Agriculture, 1911; also numerous articles in agrl. periodicals, scientific journals, and bulletins Ky. Agrl. Expt. Sta. Home: 238 Tahoma Rd. Address: Ky. Experiment Sta., Lexington KY

GOODALE, CHARLES WARREN, mining engr.; b. Honolulu, Hawaii, Sept. 6, 1854; s. Warren and Ellen R. (Whitmore) G.; grad. English High Sch., Boston, 1871; S.B., Mass. Inst. Tech., 1875; unmarried. With the Boston & Colorado Smelting Co., at Boston, 1875-76, at Black Hawk, Colo., 1876-80; supt. and mgr. Boston & Ariz. Smelting & Reduction Co., Tombstone, Ariz., 1880-85; supt. mining dept., Colo. Smelting & Mining Co., at Butte, 1885-98; with Boston & Mont. Consolidated Copper & Silver Mining Co. (now Boston and Mont. dept. of Anaconda Copper Mining Co.), 1898-1914, Great Falls, Mont., 1898-1901, asst. mgr. and mgr. at Butte, 1901-18; chmn. bur. of safety Anaconda Copper Mining Co., 1914-20. Alderman, 2d Ward, City of Butte, 1888-90. Republican. Episcopalian. Home: Butte, Mont. Died Apr. 11, 1929.

GOODALE, GEORGE LINCOLN, botanist; b. Saco, Me., Aug. 3, 1839; s. Stephen Lincoln and Prudence Aiken (Nourse) G.; A.B., Amherst, 1860, A.M., 1866; M.D., Harvard, 1863; Bowdoin, 1863; hon. A.M., Bowdoin, 1869; LL.D., Amherst, 1890, Bowdoin, 1894, Princeton, 1896; m. Henrietta Juel Hobson, 1866; 1 son, Joseph Lincoln. Practiced medicine, Portland, Me., 3 yrs.; Josiah Little prof. natural science and prof. mineralogy, botany and applied chemistry, Bowdoin, 1868-72; instr. botany and lecturer on vegetable physiology, 1872-73, asst. prof., 1873-78, prof. botany, 1878-88, Fisher prof. botany, 1888-1909, Fisher prof. natural history emeritus, 1909, curator Bot. Mus., 1879-1909, hon. curator, 1909—, Harvard. Home: Cambridge, Mass. Died Apr. 12, 1923.

GOODALE, STEPHEN LINCOLN, agriculturist; b. South Berwick, Me., Aug. 14, 1815; s. Enoch and Lucy (Lincoln) G.; m. Prudence Nourse, Sept. 23, 1838. Moved with family to Saco, Me., 1816; bought a place in Saco, began cultivating and studying trees and shrubs, 1841; 1st sec. Me. Bd. Agr., 1856-73; founder, trustee State Coll. of Agr. and Mech. Arts (later U. Me.); pres. Saco & Biddeford Savs. Instn.; pres., mgr., chemist Cumberland Bone Co. Author: The Principles of Breeding: or, Glimpses at the Physiological Laws Involved in the Reproduction and Improvement of Domestic Animals, 1861. Died Saco, Nov. 5, 1897.

GOODE, GEORGE BROWN, naturalist, govt. ofcl.; b. New Albany, Ind., Feb. 13, 1851; s. Francis Collier and Sarah (Crane) G.; grad. Wesleyan U., Middletown, Conn., 1870; m. Sarah Lamson Ford Judd, 4 children. Moved to N.Y., 1857; in charge Orange Judd Mus. Natural History, 1871-77; mem. staff Smithsonian

Instn., 1873, asst. sec., 1887; employed in Atlantic Coast explorations of Fish Commn.; U.S. commr. fish, 1887-88; supervised Smithsonian exhibits at Phila. Centennial Expn., 1876; U.S. commr. at fisheries exhbns., Berlin, Germany, 1880, London, Eng., 1883; conducted survey Am. fisheries for 10th census, 1880. Author: Catalogue of the Fishes of the Bermudas, 1876; Oceanic Ichthyology (added 156 new species of fish from Atlantic), 1895; An Account of the Smithsonian Institution, 1895, and The Smithsonian Institution 1846-96, 1897 (best known hist. treatises); Virginia Cousins (his own family record), 1887; The Game Fishes of North America; American Fishes, 1888; The Beginnings of American Science; The Origin of the Scientific and Educational Institutions of the United States, 1890; The Museums of the Future, 1891. Died Washington, D.C., Sept. 6, 1896.

GOODE, RICHARD URQUHART, geographer; b. Bedford, Va., Dec. 8, 1858; s. John and Sally (Urquhart) G.; student Norfolk, Va., Hanover Acad. Va., and U. of Va.; m. Sophie J. Parks, Jan. 2, 1889. Asst. engr. army engr. corps, 1877-78; topographer U.S. Geol. Survey, 1879-82; engr. and topographer Northern Transcontinental Survey, 1882-84; engr. and astronomer Panama Canal Co., 1888; geographer U.S. Geol. Survey, 1889—. Lecturer. Home: Washington, D.C. Died 1903.

GOODENOUGH, GEORGE ALFRED, college prof.; b. Davison, Mich., May 3, 1868; s. James Webster and Eliza (Gifford) G.; B.S., Mich. Agrl. Coll., 1891; grad. student, U. of Mich., 1892-93; M.E., U. of Ill., 1900; m. Elizabeth Clara Kitzmiller, Sept. 27, 1894. Instr. mechanics, Mich. Agrl. Coll., 1891-93; text book writer, Internat. Corr. Schs., Scranton, Pa., 1893-95; instr. mech. engring., U. of Ill., 1895-97; editor, Internat. Corr. Schs., 1897-99; asst. prof. mech. engring., 1899-1906, asso. prof., 1906-11, prof. thermodynamics, 1911—, U. of Ill. Author: First Course in Calculus, 1908; Essentials of Calculus (with E. J. Townsend), 1910; Principles of Thermodynamics, 1911; Properties of Steam and Ammonia, 1915. Home: Urbana, Ill. Died Sept. 29, 1929.

GOODFELLOW, EDWARD, scientist; b. Philadelphia, Pa., Feb. 23, 1828; grad. U. of Pa., 1848; m. Julia C. Smiley, 1871. Entered service of U.S. Coast Survey as aid; in 1860 became asst. in U.S. Coast and Geodetic Survey and executive asst. in 1861-62, and again from 1875-82; then became editor of the Annual Reports of the Survey and other publications relating thereto. Home: Washington, D.C. Died 1899.

GOODHUE, WILLIAM JOSEPH, physician; b. Athabaskaville, P.Q., Can., Oct. 4, 1869; s. James and Mariam Miranda (Emerson) G.; bro. of E. S. Goodhue; High Sch., Rochester, N.Y., 1882-4; M.D., Rush Med. Coll., Chicago, 1897; (D.Sc., from Milton U., Baltimore, 1913); m. Christina Meyer, of Kalae, Molokai, H.I., Oct. 23, 1905. Surgeon to McBryde Sugar Co., Koloa, H.I., 1902-4; chief surgeon Eleele Hosp., 1902-4; surgeon Molokai Leper Clinic, 1904—; med. supt. Molokai Leper Settlement; mem. Govt. exec. staff segregation of lepers. Author of reports on phases of leprosy, 1906, 8, 10, 12, Hawaiian Bd. of Health, Honolulu. Author section on leprosy in the Sajous Analytic Cyclopaedia of Practical Medicine, 1914. Republican. Unitarian. Address: Kataupapa, Molokai HI

GOODKIND, MAURICE LOUIS, M.D.; b. Chicago, Ill., Nov. 14, 1867; s. Louis G.; Williams Coll., 1885-86; M.D., Coll. Phys. and Surg. (Columbia), 1889; post-grad. work, Vienna and Munich; m. Rose S. Snydacker, 1896; children—G. L., Ruth, M. Lewis. Attending physician Cook County Hosp., 14 yrs., Michael Reese Hosp., 29 yrs.; prof. clin. medicine, U. of Ill. Coll. of Medicine; specializes in internal medicine. Was chief of med. service, Base Hospital 53, U.S. Army, Langres, France; col. Med. R.C. Officier the French Acad., silver palm, for services during war. Republican. Mason. Home: Chicago, Ill. Died Jan. 4, 1939.

GOODMAN, CHARLES, surgeon; b. Hungary, June 14, 1871; s. Albert and Frances (Richman) G.; brought to U.S., 1874; M.D., Western Reserve U., 1892; post-grad. work, Berlin, Goettingen and Halle; m. 2d, Adele Frederica Prauger, July 11, 1923; 1 dau., Jane Helen. On staff Lying-in Hosp., N.Y. City and City Hosp., Blackwell's Island, 1892; mem. resident staff, surg. div., Mt. Sinai Hosp., 1893-96, chief of surg. dept., 1896-1916; attending surgeon Sydenham Hosp. 3 yrs., Montefiore Hosp. 15 yrs., Beth Israel Hosp. 20 yrs.; clin. prof. surgery, N.Y. Univ. and Bellevue Hosp. Med. Coll. since 1914; cons. surgeon Rockaway Beach Hosp., Beth Israel Hosp.; surgeon Park West Hosp.; asso. surgeon, Polyclinic Hospital. Member of Nobel Prize nominating committee in medicine, 1936. Successively capt. U.S. Med. Reserve Corps, comdg. officer of reinforcement of Presbyn. Hosp. (Gen. Hosp. No. 1, A.E.F.), major, head of operating team, Paschendale offensive, dir. Field Hosp. Sect., 42d Div., 1917-19; lt. col. Med. Res., U.S. Army. Cons. vascular surgeon to U.S. Veterans Facilities, II Corps Area, U.S. Veterans Hosp., No. 81. Fellow Am. Coll. Surgeons; mem. A.M.A., Acad. Medicine, Internat. Surg. Soc., N. Y. State and N.Y. Co. med. socs., Metropolitan, Harlem and Riverside med. socs., Harvey Soc., Eastern Med. Soc. (ex-pres.), Assn. Alumni of Mt. Sinai Hosp. (ex-sec.), Physicians' Mut. Aid Assn., Am. Legion, Mil. Order World War, Reserve Officers' Assn., Assn. Mil. Surgeons, Am. Public Health, Internat. Med. Club (v.p.), Union Médicale Latine. Republican. Clubs: Army and Navy, Central Park Riding, Lakeville Golf and Country. Author of 64 reprints of med. articles pub. in various scientific journals on file at N.Y. Acad. of Medicine. Home: 125 E. 72d St., New York 21. Address: 745 5th Av., New York 22, N.Y. Died May 23, 1945.

GOODPASTURE, ERNEST WILLIAM, pathologist; b. Montgomery County, Tenn., Oct. 17, 1886; s. Albert Virgil and Jennie Willson (Dawson) G.; B.A., Vanderbilt, 1907; hon. M.S., Yale; M.D., Johns Hopkins U., 1912; D.Sc. (hon.), U. Chgo., Wash. U.; LL.D., Tulane, 1957; m. Sarah Marsh Catlett, Aug. 11, 1915; 1 dau., Sarah; m. 2d, Frances Katharine Anderson, May 23, 1945. Rockefeller fellow in pathology Johns Hopkins, 1912-13, asst. and acting resident pathologist, instr., 1913-15; resident pathologist Peter Bent Brigham Hosp., Boston, 1915-18; asst. prof. pathology, Harvard, 1918-21; chief dept. pathology, bacteriology U. Philippines, Manila, 1922; dir. William H. Singer Meml. Research Lab., Pitts., 1922-24; scholarship Gen. Edn. Bd. of Rockefeller Found., at Inst. for Gen. and Exptl. Pathology, Vienna, 1924-25; prof. pathology, Vanderbilt U. since 1924, dean sch. medicine, 1945-50; mem. Army Epidemiol. Bd., 1941-46; cons. Health Div. TVA, since 1942; sci. dir. Internat. Health Div. Rockefeller Found., 1938-40, 1942-44; bd. dirs. Oak Ridge Inst. Nuclear Studies since 1946; mem. adv. bd. Life Ins. Med. Research Fund, 1945-50; Com. on Growth, Panel on Virus, NRC, 1946-48; mem. NIH virus and rickettsia sect., 1946-49. Adv. com., div. biology, medicine AEC, since 1947. Recipient Kappa Sigma Man-of-the-Year award, 1946; John Scott award City of Philadelphia, 1945; Passano Found. award, 1946; Ricketts award U. Chgo., 1955, Kovalenko medal Nat. Acad. Scis., 1958. Served as lt. (j.g.) USNRF, 1918-19. Fellow A.A.A.S. (v.p 1940); mem. Nat. Acad. Scis., (council, 1944-48), Am. Philos. Soc., Assn. Am. Physicians (Kober medalist 1943), So. Med. Assn. (research medalist 1937), Gorgas Soc. (hon. Ala.), Am. Assn. Pathol. and Bacteriol. (council since 1942; pres. 1948-49), Am. Soc. Exptl. Pathol. (pres. 1939-40), Am. Soc. for Control Cancer (dir.), A.C.P. (John Phillips award, lectr. 1948). Harvey Soc., Sedgwick Meml. medalist, A.P.H.A., 1944; Kappa Sigma, Nu Sigma Nu, Alpha Omega Alpha, Phi Beta Kappa, Sigma Xi. Home: 408 Fairfax Av., Nashville. Died Sept. 20, 1960.

GOODRICH, ERNEST PAYSON, cons. engr.; b. Decatur, Mich., May 7, 1874; s. Edward Payson and Mary Isabelle (Hall) G.; B.Pd., Michigan Normal College, 1898; B.S., in C.E., U. of Mich., 1898, C.E., 1901, hon. D.Eng., 1935; hon. M.Ed., Michigan Normal Coll., 1936; D.Eng., Polytechnic Institute, 1955; married to Mildred Louise Weed, May 18, 1899; 1 son, Ernest Weed (dec.). Commd. civ. engr. (lt. jr. grade), U.S. Navy, 1899; resigned, 1903; chief engr. Bus Terminal Co. and affiliated cos., New York, 1903-07; pvt. practice since 1907, designing harbors in many parts of world, surveying zoning and planning cities and regions, including new capital of Nanking Whampoa, port of Canton, China, Bogota, Colombia, S.A., Los Angeles, Portland, Ore., Newark, N.J., etc.; cons. engr. N.Y. City Govt., 1910-16; managing director N.Y. Bureau Municipal Research; N.Y. City dir. Mil. census and inventory, 1917-18; cons. Regional Plan of N.Y. and Environs, also Cincinnati, Norfolk, Newark, Springfield, and New Haven; deputy commissioner and chief engr. Dept. of Sanitation, N.Y. City, later commr., 1933-34; port engr. and subsequently consultant, Albany Port Commn., 1924-1933; prof. engring. economics, N.Y. Univ., 1934-35; mem. tech. adv. com. War Claims Bd. after World War I; mem. Price Adjustment Bd., U.S. Navy, 1943. Past pres. Inst. Traffic Engrs.; trustee Brooklyn Poly. Inst., Packer Collegiate Inst. Lecturer and writer on tech. subjects, Inventor of the progressive system of electric light signal street traffic control; discoverer of laws of population distribution; made extended studies of the application of sunlight to building orientation and city planning. Fellow A.A.A.S.; mem. (life) Am. Soc. Civil Engrs. (past dir.; Collingswood prize, 1905), Am. Inst. Cons. Engrs. (pres. 1951), Soc. Terminal Engrs. (past dir.), Am. Inst. of Planning (past dir.), Phi Gamma Delta and Tau Beta Pi fraternities. Conglist. Clubs: Engineers, Univ. of Michigan Club, Rembrandt. Translator; Der Eisenbetonbau (Concrete Steel Construction), by Prof. Emi Mörsch, 1909. Home: 161 Henry St., Brooklyn 2, N.Y. Office: 115 Broadway, N.Y.C. 6. Died Oct. 7, 1955; buried Forest Hill Cemetery, Ann Arbor, Mich.

GOODRICH, HALE CALDWELL, civil engr.; b. Upper Sandusky, O., May 19, 1904; s. George E. and Carrie C. (Hale) G.; B.C.E., Ohio State U., 1926; B.B.A., So. Meth. U., 1946; m. Flora Virginia Forehand, Mar. 26, 1933; children—Roy Gordon, Gary Wayne. Rodman, levelman N.Y.C. R.R. and Hocking Valley Ry. Co., asst. erector Western Gas Constrn. Co., Ft. Wayne, Ind., engr. Miss. River bridge constrn., Cape Girardeau, Mo., 1926-28; draftsman Cleve. Union Terminals Co., 1928-31; engr. United Gas Pipe Line Co., Houston, dist. engr., Dallas, gen. office Shreveport, La., 1931-68; noise cons. Active Boy Scouts Am. Registered profl. engr., Tex., La., Miss., Ala. Mem. Am. Gas Assn., Soc. for Exptl. Stress Analysis. Democrat. Methodist. Home: Shreveport LA Died Jan. 15, 1968; buried Centuries Meml. Park Cemetery Park Cemetery Shreveport

GOODRICH, HUBERT BAKER, zoologist; b. Salem, Mass., Sept. 11, 1887; s. Arthur Lewis and Mary Eastman (Bachelder) G.; B.S., Amherst, 1909, Sc.D. (hon.), 1954; M.A., Columbia, 1914, Ph.D., 1916; fellow biology Princeton, 1914-15; Sc.D. (hon.), Hamline U., 1952; m. Clara Crosby Ware, Aug. 23, 1917; children—Mary Ware, Arthur Lincoln. Instr. biology Union Coll., 1915-16; instr. zoology Wesleyan U., 1916-17, asso. prof., 1917-23, prof. biology 1923—; program dir. NSF, Washington, 1953-54; instr. embryology Marine Biol. Lab., Woods Hole, Mass., 1917-21, in charge, 1922-1941. Instr. S.A. T.C., World War. Trustee Corp. Marine Biol. Lab., 1931-49; trustee Biol. Abstracts, 1937-42; dir. Conn. State Forest and Park Assn., 1947-51. Fellow A.A.A.S.; mem. Am. Soc. Zoologists (sec. 1934-36, v.p. 1939), Soc. Am. Naturalists, Am. Assn. U. Profs., Genetics Soc. Am., Am. Assn. Anatomists, Sigma Xi, Phi Beta Kappa, Beta Theta Pi. Conglist. Club: Appalachian Mountain. Author: (with R. H. Knapp) Origins of American Scientists, 1952; also various papers. Home: 2 Miles Av., Middletown, Conn. Died Sept. 26, 1963; buried Newton (Mass.) Cemetery.

GOODRICH, WILLIAM MARCELLUS, organ maker; b. Templeton, Mass., July 21, 1777; s. Ebenezer and Beulah (Childs) Goodridge (later changed his name to Goodrich); m. Hannah Geald, on February 1822. Employed in shop of Benjamin Crekor, Milton, Mass., 1798; established himself in organ-bldg. bus., Boston, 1799; constructed duplicate of J. M. Maelyel's panharmonicon, sent to Europe for exhbn. after Maelyel's was lost at sea, 1809; moved factory to East Cambridge, Mass., 1809, asso. with Thomas Appleton (a cabinetmaker); directed bldg. of organ for Catholic Cathedral, Franklin Street, Boston; built some organs which are still in use. Died Sept. 15, 1833.

GOODRIDGE, MALCOLM, physician; b. Flushing, N.Y., Feb. 28, 1873; s. Edwin Alonzo and Anna Margaret (Field) G.; A.B., Princeton, 1894; M.D., Coll. Physicians and Surgeons (Columbia), 1898; m. 2d, Elizabeth C. Stone, Aug. 11, 1930; children of 1st marriage—Malcolm, Edwin Tyson. Practiced at N.Y.C. since 1899; former prof. clin. medicine, Cornell U., Med. Coll.; cons. physician New York Hosp. (hon. mem. bd. govs.), Bellevue Hospital, Neurological Institute (New York); Mercy Hosp. (Hempstead). Trustee Home for Old Men and Aged Couples, New York. Fellow A.M.A., N.Y. Acad. Med. (hon.; p. pres.; chairman committee on med. and the changing order); member Nu Sigma Nu. Republican. Clubs: University, Century, Grolier. Contributor chapter on The Treatment of Arteriosclerosis in George Blumer edition of Billings-Forchheimer's Therapeusis of Internal Diseases; chapter on Diseases of the Arteries, in a Textbook of Medicine by Russell L. Cecil, M.D.; contbr. chapter "General Principles Involved in Treatment of Infectious Diseases," in Therapeutics of Internal Diseases by George Blumer. Home: 333 E. 57th St., N.Y.C. 22; also The Ugly Duckling, Woodstock, Vt. Died July 16, 1956; buried Woodstock, Vt.

GOODSPEED, ARTHUR WILLIS, physicist; b. at Hopkinton, N.H., Aug. 8, 1860; s. Obed and Helen B. (Morse) G.; A.B., Harvard Univ., 1884; Ph.D., U. of Pa., 1889; m. Annie H. Bailey, of Hyde Park, Mass., June 24, 1896; children—Frederick Long, Willis Bailey, Helen Gertrude; m. 2d, Ethel W. Mitchell, Aug. 19, 1913; 1 son, Arthur Willis. Assistant in physics, 1884-85, instr., 1885-89, asst. prof., 1889-1904, prof. physics, 1904-31, now emeritus, U. of Pa. Mem. Jury Awards, Nat. Export Expn., 1899. Fellow A.A.A.S.; mem. Am. Röutgen Ray Soc. (pres. 1902-03), Royal Soc. Arts, Am. Philos. Soc. (sec. 1900-35, editor publs.), Am. Phys. Soc., N.H. Antiq. Soc. (v.p. 1901-14, pres. 1914—), Société francaise de Physique. Mem. Jury of Awards, Sesquicentennial, Phila., 1926. Has written numerous articles on Röntgen Rays and other scientific subjects. Home: 4623 Sansom St., Philadelphia, Pa.

GOODSPEED, THOMAS HARPER, botanist; b. Springfield, Mass., May 17, 1887; s. George Stephen and Florence Duffy (Mills) G.; student College Gaillard, Lausanne, Switzerland, 1902-03; advanced study Stockholms Hogskölan, 1922-23, Kaiser Wilhelm Gesellschaft, Berlin-Dahlem, 1930-31; A.B., Brown U., 1909; Ph.D., U. Cal., 1912; Doctor honoris causa U. La Plata, 1939; D.Sc. honoris causa, Brown, 1940; m. Florence Spencer Beman, June 6, 1911 (dec. Apr. 1950); m. Elizabeth Bibbons Noack, Feb. 5, 1954; desc. Roger Goodspeed, Barnstable, Mass., 1639; children—Stephen Spencer, Ellen Strutt (Mrs. J. D. Ainsworth). Faculty, U. Cal., 1909—, prof., 1928—; curator U. Cal. Bot. Garden, 1926-34, dir. 1934—; hon. dir. Jardin Botanique de Lima (Peru), Jardin Botanico Nacional, Chile; hon. mem. faculty, various agrl. colls.; collaborator various orgns.; adv. on establishment bot. gardens; organizer and leader bot. expdns.; del. internat. congresses. Fellow John Simon Guggenheim Meml. Found., Europe, 1930-31, S.Am., 1935. Comdr. Orden All Mérito Bernardo O'Higgins (Chile). Fellow Linnean Soc. (London), A.A.A.S.; hon. mem. Nat. Acad. Scis.

Argentina, Argentine Anat. Soc., Biol. Soc. of Montevideo; mem. U.S., State and S.A. profl., sci. assns. and socs., including Sigma Xi and local spl. hort. socs. Clubs: Authors (London); Bohemian (San Francisco); Faculty (Berkeley). Author books including: The Genus Nicotiana, 1953. Editor: Essays in Geobotany, 1935; also editor U. Cal. publs. in botany, 1930-38. Contbr. sci. articles. Home: 2480 Virginia St., Berkeley 9, Cal. Died May 1966.

GOODWIN, HANNIBAL WILLISTON, clergyman, inventor; b. Taughannock, N.Y., Apr. 30, 1822; s. George and Cynthia Williston (Gregory) G.; grad. Union Coll., Schenectady, N.Y., 1848; grad. Gen. Theol. Sem. of Episcopal Ch., N.Y.C., 1851; attended Yale Law Sch.; m. Rebecca Goodwin, 2 children. Apptd. rector Christ Ch., Bordentown, N.J., 1851-54; pastor St. Paul Ch., Newark, N.J., 1854-59; moved to San Francisco to regain health, 1860-67; rector House of Prayer, Newark, 1867-87; studied photography to find substitute for glass negatives; applied for patent for "Photographic Pellicle," 1887, however Henry M. Reichenback of Eastman Dry Plate Co. also applied and received patent for "manufacture of flexible photographic films," 1889, patent contested 12 years, obtained patent just before his death. Died Dec. 31, 1900.

GOODWIN, HARRY MANLEY, physicist, educator; b. Boston, Apr. 18, 1870; s. Richard D. and Sarah (Clisby) G.; S.B., Mass. Inst. Tech., 1890; student Harvard Grad. Sch., 1890, 1891; Ph.D., U. Leipzig, 1893; U. Berlin, 1894; m. Mary B. Linder, Apr. 16, 1906; 1 son, Richard Hale. Asst. in physics, Mass. Inst. Tech., 1890-92, instr., 1892-97, asst. prof., 1897-1903, asso. prof. physics, 1903-06, prof. physics and electrochemistry in charge dept. of electrochemistry, 1906-34, dean of Graduate School 1932-40, prof. emeritus, 1940—. Fellow Am. Acad. Arts and Sciences, Washington Acad. Sciences, A.A.A.S., Am. Physical Soc.; mem. Am. Astron. Soc., Sigma Xi. Clubs: Harvard Club of Boston, Harvard Travellers, The Country Club. Author: Physical Laboratory Manuals; The Precision of Measurements and Graphical Methods. Contbr. of papers on physics and electrochemistry to scientific jours. Home: 424 Walnut St., Brookline, Mass. Died June 26, 1949.

GOODYEAR, CHARLES, inventor; b. New Haven, Conn., Dec. 29, 1800; s. Amasa and Cynthia (Bateman) G.; m. Clarissa Beecher, Aug. 24, 1824; m. 2d, Fanny Wardell, 1854; 7 children. Began expts., 1834; obtained 1st patent for acid and metal coating to destroy the adhesive properties of rubber, 1837; discovered (with N.M. Hayward, whom he employed to expt. with effects of sulphur on rubber) what became vulcanization process, patented 1844; went to Europe to extend his patent, 1851; recipient Grand Medal of Honor and cross of Legion of Honor (France), 1855; obtained fgn. patents in all countries but Eng.; sold mfg. licenses and thus was largely responsible for establishment of rubber industry in Europe. Died N.Y.C., July 1, 1860.

GORDIN, HARRY MANN, chemist; b. in Russia, Aug. 16, 1855; ed. Gymnasium; grad. in pharmacy at U. of Moscow; came to U.S., 1882; engaged in drug business at San Francisco till 1893; studied chemistry in France, Germany and Switzerland; Ph.D., U. of Berne, 1897. Research chemist for U.S. Pharmacopoeia at U. of Mich., 1897-1900; head chemist William S. Merrell Chem. Co., Cincinnati, 1900-02; prof. chemistry, schs. of dentistry and pharmacy, Northwestern U., 1902—. Spl. subjects alkaloids and drug assaying. Home: Chicago, Ill. Died July 5, 1923.

GORDON, ARTHUR HORACE, physician; b. Calais, Me., Oct. 23, 1863; s. David and Mary Brooks (Keen) G.; ed. Calais Acad.; M.D., Hahnemann Med. Coll., Chicago, 1887; m. Julia Agnes Cavanaugh, Dec. 30, 1891; 1 dau., Jewel M. Practiced, Chicago, 1887—; prof. internal medicine Hahnemann Med. Coll., 1898-1922; head of dept., 1921-22; attending physician same hosp., 1902-22; prof. internal medicine, Gen. Med. Coll., 1922-24; mem. gen. staff Ill. Masonic Hosp.; mem. staff Edgewater Hosp.; pres. Hahnemann Instns., Inc., 1928—. State med. examiner, The Maccabees; trustee New York Homoe. Med. Coll. and Flower Hosp., 1928-29; mem. exec. com. Med. Inter-Fraternity Congress, 1928-30, vice-chmn., 1932-34. Mason (32 deg., Shriner). Home: Chicago, Ill. Died Dec. 2, 1938.

GORDON, CHARLES HENRY, geologist; b. Caledonia, N.Y., May 10, 1857; s. John and Ann (McKinnon) G.; B.S., Albion, Coll., 1886, M.S., 1890; fellow, U. of Chicago, 1893-95, Ph.D., 1895; U. of Heidelberg, 1897-98; m. Mary E. Hydorn, June 22, 1887; children—Irene Hydorn (Mrs. Burton Ashton Gaskill), Helen Garnett (Mrs. Don Carlos Ellis), Isabel (Mrs. Hugh Sevier Carter). Instr. high sch., Keokuk, Ia., 1886-87; prin. Wells Sch., Keokuk, 1887-90; instr. natural history, Northwestern U., Ill., 1890-93; supt. schs., Beloit, Wis., 1895-97, Lincoln, Neb., 1899-1903; lecturer, U. of Neb., 1901-03; acting prof. geology, U. of Wash., 1903-04; prof. geology and mineralogy, N.M. Sch. of Mines, 1904-05; field asst., 1905-06, asst. geologist, 1906-13, U.S. Geol. Survey; prof. geology, U. of Tenn., 1907-31, emeritus, 1931. Asso. state geologist, Tenn., 1910-14; dir. and supt. Dept. of Minerals, Nat. Conservation Expn., Knoxville, 1913. Home: Anna Maria, Fla. Died June 12, 1934.

GORDON, CLARENCE MCCHEYNE, physicist; b. Fannettsburg, Pa., Apr. 14, 1870; s. Rev. Jeremiah Smith and Margaret Beatty (Kyle) G.; A.B., Princeton, 1891, A.M., 1893; Ph.D., Gottingen, 1897; m. Amie Baker Lanier, July 17, 1909; 1 dau., Margaret Lanier. Math. fellow Princeton, 1891-92; instr. physics, Williams Coll., 1893-95; instr. physical chemistry, Harvard, 1897-98; prof. physics, Centre Coll., Ky., 1898-1909, Lafayette College, 1909-47, emeritus since 1947; prof. physics, Davis and Elkins Coll., since 1948. Optical engr., Wollensak Optical Company, Rochester, New York, 1918-19; electrical engineer Western Electric Company, New York, 1920; prof. physics, Temple U., summer 1923, Muhlenberg Coll., summer 1924, 27. Fellow A.A.A.S., Am. Physical Soc. Republican. Presbyterian. Author: Experiments in General Physics, 1922; also articles in Physical Rev., Jour. Am. Chem. Soc., etc. Address: Davis and Elkins Coll., Elkins WV

GORDON, GEORGE PHINEAS, inventor; b. Salem, N.H., Apr. 21, 1810; s. Phinias and Mary (White) G.; m. Sarah Cornish, 1846; m. 2d Lenore May, 1856; 1 child. Apprenticed to printer, N.Y.C.; opened small job-printing office, N.Y.C.; began experimenting on improved press for card printing, 1835; obtained 1st patent for "Yankee" job press, 1851; introduced "Firefly" job press, 1854, turned out 10,000 cards per hour; built more than 100 kinds of presses; established factory in Rahway, N.J., with offices in N.Y.C., 1872. Died Norfolk, Va., Jan. 21, 1878.

GORDON, HIRSCH LOEB, neuropsychiatrist; b. Wilno, Lithuania, Nov. 26, 1896; s. Rabbi Elijah and Malcah (Katzenellenbogen) G.; prep. edn. Wolozhin Yeshivah Gymnasium, Odessa, Russia, 1911-14; Ph.D., in Semitic Langs., Yale, 1922; L.H.D. in Egyptology, Cath. U., 1923; A.M. in Diplomacy, American U., 1924; A.M., in Edn., Teachers Coll., Columbia, 1926; D.H.L., Jewish Theol. Sem. of Am., 1928; A.M. in Fine Arts, N.Y.U., 1928; U. Berlin, 1931; Litt.D. in Classical Archaeology, Royal U. Rome, Italy, 1931, M.D., Sc.D., Diplomate Royal Inst. of Legal Medicine, Rome, 1934; m. Tamara L. Liebowitz. Came to U.S., 1915, naturalized, 1922. Lectr. in instructor, tchrs. colls., 1920-27; with neurol. clinic of Mt. Sinai Hosp., N.Y.C., 1935, Maimonides Hosp., Bklyn., 1935-37, physician skin and syphilis clinic, Mt. Sinai Hospital, 1937-40, surgery, 1940-41; member of psychiatric staff of Pilgrim State Hosp., Brentwood, N.Y., 1941-42; Cornell Div. Neurology, Bellevue Hospital, N.Y.C.; Kings County Psychiatric Hospital, Bklyn., 1934-44; Bellevue Psychiatric Hospital, 1944; qualified psychiat., State of New York, 1944; chief, shock therapy, U.S. Vets. Hosp., Northport, N.Y., 1944-46; chief neuropsychiat., U.S. Vets. Adminstrn., Jacksonville, Fla., 1947; neuropsychiat. consultant Div. U.S. Surgeon Gen., U.S. Army, Washington, 1947-48; sr. surgeon (comdr.) USPHS, also chief neuropsychiatry div. U.S. Marine Hosp., S.I., 1948-50; with neuropsychiat. div. Met. Hosp., N.Y.C., 1951-69, now asso. psychiatrist; asso. vis. psychiatrist Bird S. Coler Meml. Hosp., Met. Hosp.; adjunct in neuropsychiatry Beth Israel Hosp.; asso. in psychiatry, N.Y. Med. Coll.; lectr. N.Y.C. Cancer Com., 1935-69, N.Y.C. Dept. Health, 1937-69, L.I. Inst. 1951-53. Member board of appeal New York State SSS, 1951-69. Sgt. Royal Fusiliers, B.E.F., Palestine front, 39th R.F., 1918-19; maj., M.C., AUS, 1944-46. Recipient Maimonides award Michael Reese Med. Center, 1967, Am. Univ. Alumni Recognition award, 1968. Fellow Am. Geriatric Soc., Am. Psychiatric Assn., A.C.P.; mem. numerous medical, psychiatric, other orgns. Mason. Author several books, 1926-69, including Objectors to Electric Shock, 1946; Fractures in Electric Shock, 1946, 50; Shock Therapy Theories, 1946; The Maggid of Caro; Psychiatric Concepts in the Bible, Talmud and Zohar; contbr. literary and scientific monographs in Amer. and foreign reviews. Address: New York City NY Died Jan. 19, 1969; buried Cedar Park NJ

GORDON, LOUIS, tech. inst. dean; b. N.Y.C., Sept. 3, 1914; s. Harry and Gussie (Feinstein) G.; B.S., U. Ky., 1937; M.S., U. Mich., 1939, Ph.D., 1947; m. Ruth Levy, June 13, 1940; 1 son Michael Gordon. Prof. chemistry Ohio State U., 1946-48, Syracuse U., 1948-57; mem. faculty Case Inst. Tech., 1957—, prof. chemistry, 1957—, dean grad. studies, 1961—. Served to maj., chem. warfare service, AUS, 1942-46. Mem. Am. Chem. Soc., Internat. Union Pure and Applied Chemistry (sec. analytical chem. sect. 1959-61), Am. Assn. U. Profs., Sigma Xi, Phi Lambda Upsilon, Sigma Pi Sigma. Co-author: Precipitation from Homogeneous Solution, 1959; also articles. Co-editor: Internat. Series Monographs on Analytical Chemistry, 50 vols., 1957—. Died Oct. 21, 1966.

GORDON, NEIL ELBRIDGE, chemist; b. Spafford, N.Y., Oct. 7, 1886; s. William James and Ella C. (Mason) G.; Ph.B., Syracuse U., 1911, M.A., 1912, Pd.B., 1921; Ph.D., Johns Hopkins, 1917; m. Hazel A. Mothersell, June 29, 1915; children—Neil Elbridge, Fortuna Lucille. Asst. prof. chemistry, Goucher Coll., Baltimore, Md., 1917-19; prof. phys. chemistry, U. of Md., 1919-21, dir. chem. dept., 1921-28; state chemist of Md., 1921-28; Francis P. Garvan prof. chemical edn., Johns Hopkins U., 1928-36; head chemistry dept., Central Coll., Fayette, Mo., 1936-42; chmn. chemistry dept., Wayne University since Sept. 1942; dir. Nat. Fellowships, Johns Hopkins, 1930-36. Organizer and editor Jour. of Chem. Edn., 1924-33. Dir. Hooker Scientific Library, 1936-46; dir. Friends of the Kresge-Hooker Scientific Library, since 1946. Organizer and editor, Record of Chemical Progress, since 1939. Fellow A.A.A.S. (organizer and director Gibson Island Research Conferences, 1938-46; mem. Am. Chem. Soc., Mo. Acad. Science, Faraday Soc., Royal Soc. Arts and Sciences, Sigma Xi, Alpha Chi Sigma. Methodist. Author: Project Study of Chemistry, 1925; Introductory College Chemistry, 1926, 2d edit., 1941; Introductory Chemistry, 1927, revised 1940; College Chemistry, 1928; Record Book for Introductory Chemistry, 1928. Contbr. numerous articles in scientific jours. Home: The Wardell Sheraton Hotel, Detroit 2. Died May 20, 1949.

GORDON, SETH CHASE, physician; b. Fryeburg, Me., Aug. 17, 1830; s. Stephen and Lydia (Chase) G.; ed. Fryeburg Acad., M.D., Bowdoin, 1855; LL.D., Dartmouth, 1905. Practiced at Gorham, Me., 1855-61, Portland, Me., 1865—; served as asst. surgeon, 13th Me. Vols., and surgeon, 1st La. Vol. Inf. in Union Army; has been mem. common council, and of sch. com., Portland; mem. Dem. Nat. Com. for Me., 1896-1900. Surgeon Me. Gen. Hosp., 1874-94. Home: Portland, Me. Died June 22, 1921.

GORDON, WILLIAM ST. CLAIR, physician; b. Raleigh, N.C., Mar. 28, 1858; s. James and Mary St. Clair (Cooke) G.; prep. edn. University Sch., Richmond, Va.; M.D., Med. Coll. of Va., 1879; spl. courses, Jefferson Med. Coll., Phila., and med. dept., U. of Pa.; m. Kate Blanks Gordon, Oct. 16, 1890. Practiced at Richmond, Va.; a founder University Coll. of Medicine, Richmond, 1893, and prof. physiology, later asso. prof. clin. medicine, same; prof. medicine, Med. Coll. of Va., 1913-14, emeritus; physician and mem. bd. dirs. Laurel (Va.) Reformatory. Democrat. Presbyn. Author: Recollections of the Old Quarters (dialect, prose and verse), 1902. Investigated outbreak of typhoid in Richmond, 1884, and subsequently, and submitted extensive rept. on same, 1893. Home: Richmond, Va. Died Apr. 24, 1924.

GORE, ELBERT BRUTUS, civil engr.; b. Sinking Springs, Adams Co., Ohio, Mar. 21, 1867; s. Charles Henry and Hester Ann (Burbage) G.; ed. Ohio U., Athens (left coll. in jr. yr.); m. Edith Virginia Kimball, of Ogden, Utah, July 23, 1912. In gen. engring. practice, Brown Co., Ohio, 1891-98; irrigating engring., Crowley, La., 1898-1900 (built canal system for Messrs. Hurd & Wright); chief engr. Brownsville Land & Irrigation Co., 1901-03; chief engr. in survey of Brownsville, Hidalgo & Northern Ry. (300 miles), 1905-06; chief engr. Hartingen Land & Water Co., and other cos., from 1908, also consulting engr. various large irrigation projects, including Hidalgo Co., Rio Grande Irrigation Co.; was engr. in charge La.-Rio Grande Canal Co.; mem. Bd. Water Engrs. for Texas, 1913-17; mgr. Panama-Pacific Products Co., Anton, Panama, Nov. 1, 1917—. Single Taxer. Mem. Am. Soc. C.E., Phi Delta Theta. Home: Pharr, Tex. Address: Anton, Provincia de Cocle, Republica de Panama.

GORE, HERBERT CHARLES, chemist, inventor, consultant; b. N.Y. City, June 19, 1877; s. Charles Willard and Anna Isabella (Guild) G.; B.S., U. of Mich., 1899; M.S., Ohio State U., 1901; m. Mella Taylor, July 7, 1903; children—Harriet Willard Looney, Richard Taylor, Winifred Loewen, William Robert. Asst. chemist, Ohio State U., 1900-01; teacher of science, high sch., Freeport, Ill., 1901-02; scientific asst., 1902-12, chemist, fruit and vegetable utilization, 1912, Bureau of Chemistry, Dept. of Agr., Washington; research chemist, Fleishmann Labs., New York, until 1942. Inventor of maltose sugar process. Member Am. Chem. Soc. Republican. Congregationalist. Author of numerous papers on chem. technology of fruits, vegetables, cereals and their products. Address: 5301 27th Av., St Petersburg, FL

GORE, JAMES HOWARD, univ. prof.; b. Frederick Co., Va., Sept. 18, 1856; s. Mahlon and Sidney S. (Cather) G.; Richmond Coll., Va., 1874-77; B.S., Columbian (now George Washington) U., 1879, Ph.D., 1888; studied Leyden, Berlin, Brussels; LL.D., Georgetown, 1910, Richmond, 1911; Litt.D., George Washington U., 1918; m. Miss Sparendahl, of Stockholm, Sweden, June 20, 1888 (now deceased); 1 son, Sidney S. (dec.). Tutor mathematics, 1878-81, adj. professor, 1881-83, professor, 1883-1909, professor emeritus, 1909, George Washington Univ. Astronomer U.S. Geol. Survey, 1880-83; civilian expert U.S. Coast and Geol. Survey, 1888-90; lecturer on trusts, Yale, Princeton, and Copenhagen. Was commr.-gen. to internat. expns. at Antwerp, Amsterdam, Brussels, St. Louis and Liège; juror-in-chief, Paris Expn., 1900; U.S. del. at 6 internat. congresses. Decorated by Belgium, Bulgaria, Holland, France, Roumania, Siam, Spain and Sweden. Mem. bd. dirs. Dupont Bank. Life trustee National Geographical Society; dir. Nat. Lib. for the Blind; fellow Actuarial Soc. America; mem. Am. Meteorol. Soc., Philos. Soc. Washington (pres. 1904), Imperial Russian Geog. Soc. Clubs: Cosmos, Chevy Chase. Author: Elements of Geodesy, 1886;

Bibliography of Geodesy, 1889; History of Geodesy, 1890; Manual of Geography, 1897; German Science Reader, 1891; American Members of Foreign Orders, 1910; American Legionnaires of France, 1920; My Mother's Story, 1923. Also series of math. text-books. Editor various German texts; contbr. to European and Am. mags. Address: 221 Prospect St., Chevy Chase, Md. *

GORGAS, JOSIAH, army officer, educator; b. Dauphin County, Pa., July 1, 1818; s. Joseph and Sophia (Atkinson) G.; grad. U.S. Mil. Acad., 1841; went abroad to study ordnance and arsenals of European armies, 1845; m. Amelia Gayle, Dec. 1853; children—William C., Jesse, Mary, Amelia, Maria, Richard H. Served as lt. Ordnance, Mexican War, 1847-48, commd. capt., 1855; commd. maj., chief of ordnance Confederate Army, 1861; established armories for making arms, Richmond, Va., and Fayetteville, N.C.; set up arsenals throughout South; responsible for founding a cannon foundry and central lab. at Macon, Ga.; brought about steady improvements in products of foundries and armories despite difficulties of Confederate system; brig. gen., by Nov. 1864; became mgr. Brierfield Iron Works in Ala. after war; became headmaster jr. dept. U. of South, Sewanee, Tenn., 1869, prof. engring., 1870, vice chancellor, 1872; pres. U. Ala., 1878-79, librarian of univ., 1879-82. Died Tuscaloosa, Ala., May 15, 1883.

GORGAS, WILLIAM CRAWFORD, surgeon gen. U.S. Army; b. Mobile, Ala., Oct. 3, 1854; s. Gen. Josiah (C.S.A.) and Amelia (Gayle) G.; A.B., U. of the South, 1875; M.D., Bellevue Hosp. Medical College (New York U.), 1879; interne, Bellevue Hosp., 1878-80; hon. Sc.D., U. of Pa., 1903, U. of the South, 1904. Harvard, 1908, Brown, 1909, Jefferson Med. Coll. 1909; LL.D., U. of Ala., 1910, Tulane, 1911; m. Marie Cook Doughty, Sept. 15, 1885. Apptd. surgeon U.S. Army, June 16, 1880; capt. asst. surgeon, June 16, 1885; maj. brigade surgeon vols., June 4-July 6, 1898; maj. surgeon, July 6, 1898; chief sanitary officer of Havana and in charge of sanitary work there, 1898-1902; applied methods of combating yellow fever which eliminated that disease in Havana; col. asst. surgeon gen., by spl. act of Congress, for yellow fever work at Havana, Mar. 9, 1903; surgeon gen. U.S. Army, with rank of brig. gen., Jan. 16, 1914; major gen., surgeon gen., U.S. Army, Mar. 4, 1915; retired, Dec. 1, 1918; director yellow fever research, Rockefeller Foundation. Apptd. chief sanitary officer Panama Canal, Mar. 1, 1904; mem. Isthmian Canal Commn., Mar. 4, 1907—; permanent dir. Internat. Health Board of Rockefeller Foundation. Recipient of Mary Kingsley medal from Liverpool School of Tropical Medicine, May 27, 1907; gold medal Am. Museum of Safety, 1914. Awarded D.S.M., 1918; comdr. Legion of Honor (French), 1919; Grand Officer Order of the Crown of Italy, 1918. Died July 4, 1920.

GORHAM, FREDERIC POOLE, biologist; b. Providence, R.I., Apr. 29, 1871; s. Samuel and Abby Harding (Fish) G.; A.B., Brown U., 1893, A.M., 1894; spl. studies in bacteriology, Harvard Med. Sch.; m. Emma Mary Lapham, June 24, 1897 (died 1913); children—Mary Emma, Sayles, Nancy, Hope; m. 2d, Ruth Elizabeth Björkdahl, Jan. 1, 1917; 1 dau., Ruth. Instr. biology, 1893-99, asst. prof., 1899-1901, asso. prof., 1901-13, prof. bacteriology, 1913—, Brown U. Bacteriologist, Providence Health Dept., 1899; bacteriologist and biologist, R.I. Shellfish Commn., 1913—; deputy insp. milk, City of Providence, 1914—. Sec. trustees R.I. State Sanatorium, 1908—. Author: Laboratory Guide to the Dissection of the Cat (with R. W. Tower), 1895; Laboratory Course in Bacteriology, 1897, 1901. Home: Providence, R.I. Died June 4, 1933.

GORHAM, JABEZ, silversmith, mcht.; b. Providence, R.I., Feb. 18, 1792; s. Jabez and Catherine (Tyler) G.; m. Amey Thurber, Dec. 4, 1816; m. 2d, Lydia Dexter, Apr. 16, 1822. Apprenticed to Nehemiah Dodge, 1807; mem. jewelry firm, 1813-18; in jewelry firm with Stanton Beebe, 1818-31; began making spoons, forks and thimbles, 1831 (1st silversmiths to use machinery), bought silverware part of bus., 1842, formed new firm (origin of Gorham Mfg. Co.); mem. R.I. Gen. Assembly from Providence; mem. Providence Common Council, 1842-44; capt. of a co. R.I. Militia. Died Providence, Mar. 24, 1869.

GORHAM, JOHN, physician, chemist; b. Boston, Feb. 24, 1783; s. Stephen and Molly (White) G.; B.A., Harvard, 1801, M.B., 1804, M.D., 1811; studied exptl. chemistry under Friedrich Accum, London, Eng.; m. Mary Warren, June 2, 1808. Adjunct prof. chemistry and materia medica Harvard, 1809-15, Ewing prof. chemistry and mineralogy, 1815-27; librarian Mass. Med. Soc., 1814-18; fellow Am. Acad. Arts and Scis.; ret., 1827. Author: The Elements of Chemical Science (1st systematic chemistry textbook written by an Am. and published in this country), 2 vols., 1819-20; contbr. articles on medicine and chemistry to profl. jours., including New Eng. Jour. of Medicine, New Eng. Jour. of Medicine and Surgery. Died Mar. 27, 1829.

GORRELL, EDGAR STALEY, (gor'rel), industrial engr.; b. Baltimore, Md., Feb. 3, 1891; s. Charles Edgar and Pamelia Stevenson (Smith) G.; ed. Baltimore City Coll., 1904-07; B.S., U.S. Mil. Acad., 1912; M.Sc., Mass. Inst. Tech., 1917; D.Sc., Norwich Univ., Northfield, Vt., 1937; m. Ruth Maurice, Dec. 10, 1921; children—Mary (dec.), Edgar Staley; m. 2d Mary Frances O'Dowd Weidman, Feb. 22, 1945. Served in inf., 1912-14; trans. to Aviation Sect. Signal Corps (now Army Air Corps), 1914; joined 1st Aero Squadron, as lt., San Antonio, Tex., Jan. 1916; participated in Punitive Expdn., Mexico, under General Pershing; detailed to Mass. Inst. Tech., then at hdqrs., Washington, D.C.; promoted to capt., 1917; sent to Europe by Pres. Wilson, as mem. Bolling Mission; to visit Allies to determine what aerial material should be produced in United States and what purchased in Europe; served as chief engr. officer of Air Service, A.E.F.; promoted to colonel, October 28, 1918; later assistant chief of staff, Air Service; representative of U.S. at more than 200 internat. confs.; participated in campaigns on all five fronts during war; chief of staff of Air Service, A.E.F., with rank of col.; resigned from army, Mar. 1920. With the Nordyke & Marmon Co., 1920-25, vice-pres., 1923-25; with Stutz Motor Car Co., 1925-39, dir., v.p. and gen. mgr., 1925-29, dir. and pres., 1929-35, also chmn. board; pres., dir. and chmn. of bd. Edgar S. Gorrell Investment Co. since 1935; pres. and dir. Air Cargo, Inc., since 1940; apptd. mem. Army Air Service Investigating Com., Mar. 1934; now mem. Transportation Advisory Group, U.S. Army. Mem. bd. of trustees Norwich U. since 1935; pres. Air Transport Assn. of America since 1936; mem. visitors com. Mass. Inst. of Tech. since 1936; mem. com. of nat. sponsors Air Youth of America, 1940; mem. Aeronautical Advisory Council, 1940. Mem. Soc. Automotive Engineers, Nat. Aeronautic Assn.; mem. Inst. of Aeronautical Science, Am. Meteorological Soc. Awards: medal, Mexican Punitive Expdn., 1916; Victory medal, 1918; Distinguished Service medal (U.S.); British D.S.O.; Legion of Honor (French). Presbyterian. Clubs: Country (Indianapolis); Racquet and Tennis, Wings (New York); The Attic (Chicago); Winter Lake (Lake Forest); Conquistadores del Cielo, New Mexico. Author of Study in Aerofoils, 1917. Member editorial board Journal of Air Law and Commerce, Northwestern U., Jan. 1939. Home: 777 N. Washington Rd., Lake Forest, Ill. Office: 1515 Massachusetts Av. N.W., Washington. Died Mar. 5, 1945; ashes scattered by Army Air Corps over West Point.

GORRIE, JOHN, physician, mayor, inventor; b. Charleston, S.C., Oct. 3, 1803; grad. Coll. Physicians and Surgeons, N.Y.C., 1833; m. Caroline (Myrick) Beeman, May 1838. Postmaster, Apalachicola, Fla., 1834-38, mem. city council, 1835-36, treas., 1835-36, mayor, 1837; received patent on mech. refrigeration, 1851 (discovery was result of plan to cool hospital rooms). Died Apalachicola, June 16, 1855.

GORTNER, ROSS AIKEN, (gort'ner), biol. chemist; b. nr. O'Neill, Holt County, Neb., Mar. 20, 1885; s. Rev. Joseph Ross and Louisa E. (Waters) G.; B.S., Neb. Wesleyan U., 1907; M.A., U. of Toronto, 1908; univ. fellow in chemistry, Ph.D., Columbia University, 1909; hon. Sc.D., Lawrence Coll., 1932; m. Catherine V. Willis, Aug. 4, 1909 (died 1930); children—Elora Catherine, Ross Aiken, Willis Alway, Alice Louise; m. 2d, Rachel Rude, Jan. 12, 1931. Research asst. in agrl. chemistry, U. of Neb., 1906-07; asst. in chemistry, Faculty of Arts, U. of Toronto, 1907-08; resident investigator in biol. chemistry, Sta. for Exptl. Evolution of the Carnegie Instn. of Washington, Cold Spring Harbor, N.Y., Sept. 1, 1909-Aug. 1, 1914; asso. prof. soil chemistry, 1914-16, asso. prof. agr. biochemistry, 1916-17, Coll. of Agr. of U. of Minn.; prof. agrl. biochemistry and chief of div. of agrl. biochemistry, Coll. of Agr. of U. of Minn. and Minn. Agrl. Expt. Sta., since Aug. 1, 1917. Consultant Chem. Warfare Service, U.S. Army, since 1926. Asso. editor Jour. Am. Chem. Soc., Jour. Physical Chemistry, 1929-30 and 1934-35; asst. editor of Chemical Abstracts (zoölogy). Mem. Nat. Research Council (div. chemistry and chem. technology, 1930-33; div. biol. agr., 1930-33; mem. exec. com. 1931-32); chmn. U.S. com. of Internat. Com. on Biochem. Nomenclature of Union of Pure and Applied Chemistry, 1930-37. Wis. Alumni Foundation lecturer, 1930; George Fisher Baker non-resident lecturer Cornell U., 1935-36 (1st sem.). Priestly lecturer, Pa. State Coll., 1934. Mem. jury Willard Gibbs medal award, Am. Chem. Soc., 1933-39; mem. jury Borden medal award, Am. Chem. Soc. since 1939. Fellow A.A.A.S.; mem. Am. Chem. Society (councillor 1918-25, 1929-39; v. chmn. and sec., 1919; chmn. biol. div., 1920; sec. colloid div., 1929; chmn. 1931), Nat. Acad. of Sciences, Am. Soc. Biol. Chemists, Soc. Exptl. Biology and Medicine, Am. Society Naturalists (pres. 1932), Sigma Xi (exec. com. 1936-40), Phi Lambda Upsilon (nat. pres. 1921-26; hon. mem. 1939), Gamma Sigma Delta, Gamma Alpha, Phi Kappa Phi; hon. mem. Des Moines Acad. Medicine, Eugene Field Society (hon.), Alpha Zeta, Alpha Chi Sigma. Author: Outlines of Biochemistry, 1929, 2d edit., 1938; J. Arthur Harris, Botanist and Biometrician (with others), 1936; Selected Topics in Colloid Chemistry, 1937; also extensive contbr. on topics pertaining to biol. chemistry. Home: 1460 Raymond Av., St. Paul, Minn. Died Sep. 30, 1942.

GOSLEE, HART JOHN, dental surgeon; b. St. Joseph, Mo., Apr. 30, 1871; s. James Wilder and Katherine Ryland (Todhunter) G.; D.D.S., Chicago Coll. Dental Surgery, 1895; B.S., Marquette U., 1910; m. Edith Pearl Blakemore, Nov. 26, 1891. Practiced at Chicago. Fellow Am. Coll. Dentists. Republican. Episcopalian. Author: Principles and Practice of Crowning Teeth, 1903; Principles and Practice of Crown and Bridgework, 1907, 5th edit., 1925. Home: Chicago, Ill. Died May 31, 1930.

GOSS, HARVEY THEO, exec. engr.; b. El Campo, Tex., Oct. 6, 1900; s. John Harvey and Mary Elizabeth (Thomas) G.; B.S., Tex. A. and M. Coll., 1922; m. Helen Rowe, July 24, 1927; children—Emily Caroline, Robert Warren, Jr. Engr. Empire Cos., Bartlesville, Okla., 1922-23, engr., 1923-24; natural gas engr. Cities Service Gas Co., 1924-29; engr. Ark. Natural Cos., Shreveport, La., 1929-32, chief engr., 1932-45, v.p., chief engr., 1945—; v.p. Ark. Natural Gas Corp., Ark. Fuel Oil Co., Ark. La. Gas Co. Ark. Pipeline Corp.; sec., adv. chief engr. Cities Service Def. Corp.. 1941—. Councilman Eagle Dist. Boy Scouts. Mem. Am. Gas Assn., So. Gas Assn., So. Gas Assn., Am. Petroleum Inst. (councilor), Mid-Continent Oil and Gas Assn. (exec. com. La.-Ark. div.), Army Ordnance Assn., Shreveport C. of C. Mason. Clubs: Pipeliners, Shreveport Country. Shreveport Riding, Shreveport. Home: 251 Patton Av. Office: P.O. Box 1734, Shreveport, La. Died Feb. 10, 1959.

GOSS, WILLIAM FREEMAN MYRICK, engineer; b. Barnstable, Mass., Oct. 7, 1859; s. Frank B. and Mary Gorham (Parker) G.; Mass. Inst. Tech., Boston, 1877-79; M.S., Wabash, 1888; D.Engring., U. of Ill., 1904; m. Edna D. Baker, Aug. 22, 1884. Organized dept. of practical mechanics, Purdue U., 1879; instr. practical mechanics, 1879-83, prof., 1883-90, prof. exptl. engring., dean schs. of engring. and dir. engring. lab., 1890-1907, Purdue U.; dean Coll. of Engring., dir. Sch. of Ry. Engring. and Adminstrn., and prof. ry. engring., U. of Ill., 1907-17, and dir. Engring. Expt. Sta., 1909-17; pres. Railway Car Mfrs. Assn., New York, 1917-25. Mem. Jury of Awards, Chicago Expn., 1893; chmn. advisory com. of Pa. Ry Co., charged with testing locomotives, St. Louis Expn., 1904; chief engr., com. of investigation on somke abatement and electrification of ry. terminals, Chicago, 1913-15. Author: Bench Work in Wood, 1890; Locomotive Sparks, 1902; Locomotive Performance, 1907; High Steam Pressures in Locomotive Service, 1907; Superheated Steam in Locomotive Service, 1910. Home: Barnstable, Mass. Died Mar. 23, 1928.

GOTSHALL, WILLIAM CHARLES, engineer and scientist; b. St. Louis, May 9, 1875; s. Daniel H. and Minnie Wortmann Gotshall. Began as an elec. expert with Mo. Electric Light & Power Co.; U.S. Govt. engr. in charge of work of riprapping and protecting banks of 150 miles of Mississippi River; in charge location St. Louis & Eastern R.R.; rebuilt and operated Cairo (Ill.) Electric Ry.; built Belleville (Ill.) Electric Ry.; built Marshalltown (Ia.) ry. and lighting plant, Muncie (Ind.) Electric Ry., Grand Av. Ry., St. Louis; apptd. chief engr. Union Depot Ry. Co., St. Louis, and rehabilitated entire system and made pioneer introduction of and operated 3-wire system on electric rys.; converted 2d Av. (horse) Ry., New York, into a conduit electric ry., 1897-98; was pres. and chief engr. New York & Portchester, R.R. Co., in the development of which the pioneer work in the design and development of high-speed electric traction was done—first high speed electric ry. in U.S. located entirely on a private right of way, with no grade crossings whatever, and cost about $25,000,000. Now engaged in design and development of new and in purchase and rehabilitation of existing railroads in U.S., Europe, the Near and Far East and Africa. Commd., Engr. R.C., 1917, and in active service. Author: Electric Railway Economics (text-book), 1914. Active in organizing and directing Near East archaeol. excavations. Address: New York, N.Y. Died Aug. 20, 1935.

GOTWALS, JOHN C., civil engr.; b. Norristown, Pa., Nov. 4, 1884; s. Abraham G. and Mary (Logan) G.; grad. Pa. State Coll., 1906, C.E., 1907; m. Muriel C. Clemens, Nov. 10, 1927; children—Katharine, Mary Muriel. Engring. work with Pa. R.R. and Catskill Aqueduct, N.Y., until 1913; commd. 2d lt. engrs., U.S.A., Mar. 8, 1913; capt., July 1, 1916; maj. (temp.), Aug. 5, 1917; lt. col. (temp.), 1918-20; maj. engrs., U.S.A., July 1, 1920. Organized and comd. 56th Engrs. in France; in charge searchlight operations, A.E.F., Aug. 1917, to close of war; apptd. chief engr. Alaska Rd. Commn., July 1, 1920; v. chmn. Alaska R.R., Apr. 1-Sept. 30, 1923, chief engr. since Oct. 1, 1923-Mar. 15, 1924; U.S. dist. engr., St. Louis, Mo., 1924-30; engr. commr. Dist. of Columbia, 1930-34; ret. as lt. col., 1934. Mem. Am. Soc. Mil. Engrs., Delta Upsilon; asso. mem. Am. Soc. C.E. Presbyn. Address: 11321 Conway Rd., St. Louis 31. Died Jan. 15, 1946; buried Calvary Cemetery.

GOULD, AUGUSTUS ADDISON, physician, conchologist; b. New Ipswich, N.H., Apr. 23, 1805; s. Nathaniel Duren and Sally (Prichard) G.; grad. Harvard, 1825, M.D., 1830; m. Harriet Sheafe, Nov. 25, 1833. Became one of leading physicians in Mass.; influential in devel. of conchology in Am.; wrote Report on the Invertebrata of Mass., 1841, Mollusca and Shells, 1852 (his most important contbns. to Am. science); editor The Terrestrial-Air-Breathing Mollusks of the United States and the Adjacent Territories of North America; introduced such subjects as principles of classification, geog. distbn. of genera and species, geol. relationships, and anatomical structures; mem. Boston

Soc. Natural History, Pres., several years; an original mem. Nat. Acad. Arts and Scis. Author: Invertebrate Animals of Mass., 1841; Mollusca and Shells of the United States Exploring Expedition under Capt. Wilkes, 1852; A System of Natural History Containing Scientific and Popular Descriptions of Various Animals, 1833; (with Louis Agassiz) Principles of Zoology, 1848. Died Boston, Sept. 15, 1886.

GOULD, BENJAMIN APTHORP, astronomer; b. Boston, Sept. 27, 1824; s. Benjamin Apthorp and Lucretia (Goddard) G.; grad. Harvard, 1884, LL.D. (hon.), 1885; Ph.D., U. Gottingen (Germany), 1848; LL.D. (hon.), Columbia, 1887; m. Mary Quincy, 1861, 5 children. Established and conducted Astronomical Journal, 1849-51, re-established, 1886; in charge of longitude dept. U.S. Coast Survey, 1852-67; organized and directed Dudley Observatory, Albany, N.Y., 1855-59; gauged (by aid of submarine cable) difference in longitude between Am. and Europe, 1860; prepared "standard catalogue," applying for 1st time systematic corrections to various star catalogues, 1862; built pvt. observatory, nr. Cambridge, Mass., 1862; dir. Nat. Observatory, Cordoba, Argentina, 1870-circa 1884, did greatest work in observation of stars of So. hemisphere; 1st astronomer to use telegraph in geodetic work, made 15 determinations before method introduced in Europe. Fellow U. Chile, Royal Soc., London, Acad. of Sci., Paris, Imperial Acad., St. Petersburg, Bureau des Langitudes, Paris, Astronomical Gesellschaft, Berlin, v.p. Am. Acad. Arts and Scis., recipient Watson medal; charter mem. Nat. Acad. Scis.; pres. Colonial Soc. of Mass., 1892; hon. prof. U. Argentine Republic; created knight Order Pour le merite by Emperor of Germany. Author: Investigation of the Orbit of the Comet U., 1847; Reports on the Discovery of the Planet Neptune, 1850; Uranometria Argentina, 1879; Resultados Del Observatorio Nacional Argentino en Cordoba (most important work, contains zone catalogues giving positions of 73,160 stars and gen. catalogue of 32,448 stars in So. hemisphere), 1879-96. Died Cambridge, Nov. 26, 1896.

GOULD, CHARLES NEWTON, geologist; b. Lower Salem, O., July 22, 1868; s. Simon G. and Arvilla A. G.; grad. Southwestern Coll., Winfield, Kan., 1899; special studies geology and paleobotany; A.M., U. of Neb., 1900, Ph.D., 1906, hon. D.Sc., 1928; hon. LL.D., Oklahoma City Univ., 1933; m. Nina Leola Swan, Sept. 24, 1903; children—Lois Hazel, Donald Boyd. Prof. of geology U. of Okla., 1900-11; resident hydrographer U.S. Geol. Survey, 1902-06; dir. Okla. Geol. Survey, 1908-11; consulting geologist, engaged chiefly in petroleum investigations, 1911-24; director Okla. Geol. Survey, 1924-32, with rank of dean in Univ. of Oklahoma. Chmn. of Am. Com. on Revision of Rules of Stratigraphic Nomenclature, 1929-33. Member Am. Inst. Mining and Metall. Engrs., Geol. Soc. America, Am. Assn. State Geologists, Paleontol. Soc. America, A.A.A.S., Internat. Geol. Congress, Inst. Patroleum Technologist, Sigma Xi, Phi Beta Kappa, Sigma Gamma Epsilon, Phi Sigma, Pi Gamma Mu. Okla. Acad. Science (twice pres.), Am. Assn. Petroleum Geologists, Royal Soc. Arts, Okla. Bd. of Geographic Names; past vice pres. American Mining Congress; member American Geophysical Union; Oklahoma Hall of Fame. Methodist. Clubs: University, Rotary, Men's Dinner. Author: Geology and Water Resources of Oklahoma, 1905; Geography of Oklahoma, 1909; Petroleum and Natural Gas in Oklahoma, 1912; Index to the Stratigraphy of Oklahoma, 1926; Travels Through Oklahoma, 1928; Humanizing Geology, 1928; Oklahoma Place Names, 1933; Covered Wagon, Geologist, 1947; also numerous bulletins and articles. Director structural materials survey Oklahoma State, Federal Emergency Relief Administration, 1934; state director mineral survey, Oklahoma Geology Survey, Works Progress Adminstrn., 1935; hon. member Am. Assn. of Petroleum geologists, 1944; regional geologist Nat. Park Service, 1936-40; Am. Geographical Union, 1947. Home: 420 Chautauqua St., Norman, Okla. Died Aug. 13, 1949; buried in I.O.O.F. Cemetery, Norman.

GOULD, EDWARD SHERMAN, civ. engr.; b. New York, Aug. 13, 1837; s. Edward Sherman and Mary Elizabeth (Du Bois) G.; ed. pvt. tutors and pvt. schs., New York; Ecole des Mines, St. Etienne, France; m. Arabella Duncan Ludlow, 1868. Sec. to Hon. John Bigelow, U.S. Consul Gen. at Paris, France, 1862-65. Began practice, 1865; asst. engr. U.S. Corps of Engrs., 1872-76; asst. engr. Croton Aqueduct, div. engr. New Croton Aqueduct, 1879-86; built Scranton, Pa., water works, 1886-90, Havana (Cuba) water works, 1890-94, etc. Received Venezuelan decoration "El Busto del Libertador." Author: Practical Hydraulic Formulae, 1889; Elements of Water Supply Engineering (3d edit.) 1899; Arithmetic of the Steam Engine, 1897. Home: Yonkers, N.Y. Died 1905.

GOULD, GEORGE MILBRY, physician; b. Auburn, Me., Nov. 8, 1848; s. George Thomas and Eliza A. (Lapham) G.; drummer boy, 63d Ohio Vols., 1861-62; enlisted in 141st Ohio Vols., 1864-65; A.B., Ohio Wesleyan U., 1873, A.M., 1892; Harvard Div. Sch., 1873; M.D., Jefferson Med. Coll., Phila., 1888; m. Harriet Fletcher Cartwright, Oct. 15, 1876; m. 2d, Laura Stedman, Oct. 3, 1917. Began practice, Phila., 1888, splty. ophthalmology; ophthalmologist, Phila., Almshouse, 1892-94. Editor Medical News, 1891-95, Philadelphia Medical Journal, 1898-1900, American Medicine, 1901-06. Speaker Congress Arts and Sciences, St. Louis Exposition, 1904. Received first Doyne medal, Ophthalmological Congress, at Oxford, England. Author (in collaboration) of many med. books and dictionaries. Address: Atlantic City, N.J. Died Aug. 8, 1922.

GOULD, HARRIS PERLEY, horticulturist; b. North Bridgton, Me., Sept. 6, 1871; s. Charles Henry and Bethia Spring (Wadsworth) G.; B.S., U. of Maine, 1893; M.S. in Agr., Coll. of Agr., Cornell U., 1897; m. Alice Hewes Peabody, Apr. 24, 1905; children—Lawrence P., Stanley W. (dec.). Asst. in horticulture, Me. Expt. Sta., 1892-96; asst. in Cornell U. Expt. Sta., 1897-98; state nursery insp., N.Y., 1898; asst. entomologist and asst. horticulturist, Md. Agrl. Coll. Expt. Sta. and Md. State Hort. Dept., 1899-1900, and acting state entomologist, Jan.-June, 1901; asst. pomologist and pomologist, U.S. Dept. of Agr., 1901-28, sr. pomologist, 1928-38, prin. horticulturist in charge Div. Fruit and Vegetable Crops and Diseases, Bur. Plant Industry, U.S. Dept. of Agr., 1938-1941, retired as Collaborator, 1941. Conglist. Fellow A.A.A.S.; mem. Am. Pomol. Society, Am. Soc. Hort. Science, Bot. Soc. of Wash., Phi Kappa Phi, Beta Theta Pi. Author many circulars, bulls. and pub. addresses on pomol. subjects. Author: Peach-Growing (in Rural Science Series), 1918. Home: 3909 13th St. N.W. Office; Bureau of Plant Industry, Station, Beltsville, Md. Died Oct. 31, 1946.

GOURLEY, JOSEPH HARVEY, (gor'le), horticulturist; b. Homer City, Pa., July 1, 1883; s. John and Elizabeth Anna (Harvey) G.; B.S., Ohio State U., 1908, also M.S., 1915; Ph.D. from U. of Chicago, 1931; m. Lucy M. Kinney, June 7, 1911; children—Margaret Cruickshank, Elizabeth. Asst. horticulturist Ohio Agrl. Expt. Sta., 1908-10; asst. prof. horticulture, Ohio State U., 1910-12; prof. horticulture, N.H. Coll., and horticulturist, N.H. Agrl. Expt. Sta., 1912-20 (v. dir. 1920); prof. horticulture W.Va. U. and horticulturist W.Va. Agrl. Expt. Sta., 1920-21; horticulturist, Ohio Agrl. Expt. Sta., since 1921; chmn. dept. of horticulture, Ohio State U., since 1929. Fellow A.A.A.S. (v.p. sect. O), Ohio Acad. Science; hon. mem. Ohio Nursery Assn., Columbus Hort. Soc.; mem. Am. Soc. Hort. Science (president 1923), Ohio State Hort. Soc. (pres. 1940-41), Alpha Zeta, Sigma Xi, Alpha Tau Omega, Gamma Alpha, Pi Alpha Xi, Phi Upsilon Phi. Republican. Presbyterian. Mason. Grange. Clubs: Wooster Country, Century. Author: Text-Book of Pomology, 1922; Orchard Management, 1924; Modern Fruit Production (with F. S. Howlett), 1941. Cons. editor Am. Fruit Grower Mag. Home: Wooster, O. Died Oct. 7, 1946.

GOW, CHARLES R(ICE), engineering; b. Medford, Mass., Dec. 5, 1872; s. Robert M. and Cordelia (Flynn) G.; B.S., Tufts Coll., 1893, D.Sc., 1919; hon. Dr. Engring., Northeastern Univ., 1932; same, Worcester Poly. Inst., 1935; m. Jeannette A. Weaving, June 12, 1900; children—Ralph F., Arthur R., Jeannette (dec.), Charles R., Grace A. Asst. supt. water dept., Medford, 1893; asst. city engr., Medford, 1895; supt. for contractor in sewer and subway constrn., 1895; asst. engr. Boston Transit Commn., 1895-98; contractor, pub. works and engring. constrn., 1899-1922; cons. engr., Boston, 1922-30; pres. Warren Bros. Co. since 1930; chairman of the board since November 30, 1942. Lecturer on foundations, Mass. Inst. of Tech., 1912-18, prof. of humanics, 1928-30. Postmaster Boston Postal Dist. (25 cities and towns), 1929-30. Served as pvt., advancing to lt. col. engrs., Mass. Nat. Guard, 1889-1908; sergt. maj., later 2d lt. and 1st lt., 5th Mass. Vols., Spanish-Am. War; maj., later lt. col., Constrn. Div., U.S. Army, World War. Mem. commn. on water needs of cities and towns of Ipswich River Valley, 1911-12; chmn. Boston Licensing Bd., 1915-16, Joint N.E. Commn. on St. Lawrence Waterway, 1924-25, Met. Water Supply Investigating Commn., 1924-25, Met. Planning Div., 1928-34. Mem. Am. Soc. C.E., Boston Soc. C.E. (pres. 1915); pres. Associated Industries of Mass., 1921-23. Republican. Conglist. Author: Fundamental Principles of Economics, 1922; Foundations for Human Engineering, 1930; Elements of Human Engineering, 1931. Home: 1751 Beacon St., Brookline, Mass. Office: 38 Memorial Drive, Cambridge MA

GOWDY, ROBERT CLYDE, physics; b. Springfield, O., Mar. 10, 1886; s. William Fishell and Rhoda Elizabeth (Vose) G.; B.A., U. of Cincinnati, 1906, M.A., 1907, Ph.D., 1909; studied Trinity Coll. (U. of Cambridge), Eng., 1909-10, College de France, Paris, 1910-11; D.Sc. (honorary), University of Cincinnati, 1947; m. Mabel Greely, Dec. 19, 1914; 1 son, William Robert. Instr. physics, Lehigh U., 1911-12; instr. physics, U. of Cincinnati, 1912-16; asst. prof., 1916-19, asso. prof., 1919-20, prof. since 1920, also acting dean Grad. Sch., 1924, asst. dean Coll Engring. and Commerce, 1925-28 and since Sept. 1932, acting dean, 1928-32, and 1939-40, dean, Jan. 1940, to Sept., 1946, dir. Sch. Applied Arts, 1940-46, dean emeritus, Coll. of Engineering since Sept. 1946. Commd. 1st lt. Ordnance Dept., U.S. Army, Jan. 1918; capt. Chem. Warfare Service, July 1918. Mem. A.A.A.S., Am. Physical Soc., Societe Physique, Phi Beta Kappa, Sigma Xi, Tau Beta Pi, Omicron Delta Kappa, Delta Tau Delta. Republican. Presbyterian. Club: Literary. Home: 2111 Auburn Av., Cincinnati 19. Died Mar. 27, 1950

GOWDY, ROY COTSWORTH, civil engr.; b. Washington, Ia., Sept. 3, 1878; s. L. H. and Anna L. (Reid) G.; ed. pub. and high schs., Colorado Springs, Colo.; Colo. Coll., 1 yr.; m. Emma L. Malden, June 27, 1905; 1 son, Joseph Scott. Rodman and asst. engr. on location and constrn., Colo. Springs & Cripple Creek Dist. Ry., 1899-1900; draftsman and instrument man, Denver & Northwestern Ry. (Moffatt Line), 1902-03, draftsman and clk. to E. C. von Diest, Colorado Springs, 1905-06; resident engr. and later chief engr., Ft. Worth & Denver City Ry., and Wichita Valley Lines, 1906-18; corporate chief engineer, C.&S. Ry. Co., Fort Worth & Denver City Ry. Co., and Wichita Valley Lines, 1918-20; chief engr. C.&S. Ry. Co., Fort Worth & Denver City Ry. Co., and Wichita Valley Ry. Co., 1920—. Home: Denver, Colo. Died June 10, 1939.

GOWEN, JOHN WHITTEMORE, biologist; b. Evinston, Fla., Sept. 5, 1893; s. Charles Hayes and Gertrude (Whittemore) G.; B.S., U. of M., 1914, M.S., 1915; Ph.D., Columbia, 1917; m. Marie Helena Stadler, 1917; children—Elaine Stadler, Helen Marie. Biologist, Me. Agrl. Expt. Sta., 1917-26, Rockefeller Inst. for Med. Research, 1926-37; prof. genetics, Ia. State Coll., 1937-64, head genetic dept., 1948-59; prof. radiology and radiation biology Colo. State U., Fort Collins, Colo., 1964—. Mem. med. zoology, tropical medicine and morphology, and genetics study sects. Nat. Insts. Health, 1953-57, genetics tng. sects., 1957-61, mem. of the program-project committee, 1961—. Mem. Biometric Soc., Am. Genetic Assn., Inst. of Mathematical Statistics, A.A.A.S., Am. Naturalists, Genetics Soc. America, Am. Soc. Zoologists, Radiation Research Soc., Gerontological Soc., Sigma Xi, Phi Kappa Phi, Phi Beta Kappa. Author: Milk Secretion, 1924; Manual of Dairy Cattle Breeding, 1925. Editor: Heterosis, 1952; Statistics and Mathematics in Biology, 1954. Contbr. sci. articles to jours. Home: 1430 W. Oak St., Fort Collins, Colo. Died Sept. 14, 1967.

GOWEN, ROBERT FELLOWS, cons. engr.; b. Lowell, Mass., Dec. 30, 1883; s. Charles Sewell and Alice J. (Fellows) G.; grad. Mt. Pleasant Mil. Acad., Ossining, N.Y., 1902; A.B., Harvard, 1906, post-grad., 1906-07; m. Grace Marie, d. Thomas T. Chadeayne, Oct. 7, 1921; children—Mary Elizabeth, Charles Allen. Lab. asst. to Prof. T. Lyman, Harvard, 1907-08; with engring. dept. Am. Tel. & Tel. Co., 1909-12; partner Ednl. Exhibit Co., Providence, 1912-16; radio engr. De Forest Radio Tel. & Tel. Co., 1916, apptd. chief engr. and plant mgr., Jan. 1, 1921; dir. Robert F. Gowen Labs., Ossining, specializing in receiver design and constrn., 1922-30; attained record, N.Y. to Chgo. 900 miles (300 watts), and N.Y. to Valley City, N.D., 1,500 miles (500 watts), in long distance radio telephone transmission on low power, Jan. 1920. Founder 1st coll. radio club Harvard, 1906. Since 1928, producer 16 mm. non-theatrical motion-picture prodns. documentary indsl., comml., ednl.); winner 4 "10 Best" awards; "The Birth of St. Mary's," an hist. film, granted 2d place in 1937; "Ossining in Wartime." A Pictorial Document of the Home Front during World War II, 1946 (selected for preservation in Library of Congress). Mem. Kappa Gamma Chi. Republican. Episcopalian. Club: Harvard (N.Y.). Home: Overton Rd., Ossining-on-Hudson, N.Y. Died June 2, 1966.

GRABAU, AMADEUS WILLIAM, palaeontologist; b. Cedarburg, Wis., Jan. 9, 1870; s. Prof. William and Maria (von Rohr) G.; S.B., Mass. Inst. Tech., 1896; S.M., Harvard, 1898, S.D., 1900; m. Mary Antin, of Boston, Oct. 6, 1901; children—Josephine, Esther. Prof. geology, Rensselaer Poly. Inst., Troy, N.Y., 1899-1901; adj. prof. palaeontology, 1905-19, Columbia U.; consulting geologist, New York, 1919-20; prof. palaeontology Nat. U., Peking, China, and chief palaeontologist Chinese Geological Survey, 1920—; dean Peking Lab. of Natural History since 1925. Research asso. in palaeontology, 3d Asiatic Expdn. of Am. Mus. Natural History. Fellow Geol. Soc. America, Palaeontol. Soc. America, New York Acad. Science, A.A.A.S., Geol. Soc. China (v.p. 1925-26; 1st award Grabau gold medal), Peking Soc. Natural History; hon. mem. China Inst. Mining and Metallurgy, Science Soc. of China. Author: North American Index Fossils (with H. W. Shimer), 2 vols., 1909-10); Principles of Stratigraphy, 1913, 2d edit., 1921; Geology of the Non-Metallic Minerals Other than Silicates, Vol. I, 1920, Vol. II, 1922; Text Book of Geology, Vol. I, 1920, Vol. II, 1921; Palaeogoeic Corals of China, 1921, 28; Silurian Fossils of Yunnan, 1926; also many other contbns. on Am., European and Chinese Geology and Palaeontology; Ordovician Fossils of North China, 1921; Evolution of the Earth and Its Inhabitants (in Chinese trans.), 1921; Stratigraphy of China, Vol. I, 1924-25. Address: Geological Survey of China, Peiping China*

GRABAU, MARTIN, scientist; Ph.D., Harvard, 1931; married Catharine Yale Knock. Executive director committee on basic physical sciences Research and Development Bd., Dept. Defense, 1948-51; sr. staff mem. Operations Research Office U.S. Army, of Johns Hopkins 1951-56; operations research duty with U.S. Army in Korea, 1951; also dir. operations research office, Tokyo, Japan; supr. thermodynamics sect., research in space problems Von Karman Hypervelocity br. Arnold Engring. and Devel. Center, also prof. Space Inst., Tullahoma, Tenn., 1956-65. Home: Point Circle, Route 2, Tullahoma, Tenn. 37388. Died Dec. 26, 1965.

GRACE, JAMES THOMAS, JR., physician, surgeon; b. Troy, Ala., July 16, 1923; s. James Thomas and Anna (Salter) G.; B.S., Yale, 1945; M.D., Harvard, 1948; m. Betty Bryant Thornton, Nov. 21, 1951 (dec.); children—Elizabeth Anne, Mary Day, John Bryant, Patricia Merrill. Practiced medicine, specializing in surgery, Huntsville, Ala., 1950-51; asst. resident surgery Vanderbilt-VA Hosp., Nashville, 1953-56, resident surgeon, 1956-57; mem. staff Roswell Park Meml. Inst., Buffalo, 1957-70, asst. dir., 1959-67, dir. viral oncology sect., 1963-70, dir. inst., 1967-70; faculty Vanderbilt U., 1956-57; faculty U. Buffalo Sch. Medicine, 1958-70, asso. research prof. surgery, 1962-70; research prof. microbiology State U. N.Y., Buffalo, 1964-70. Mem. cancer virology panel NIH, 1961-62; mem. human cancer virus task force USPHS, 1962-64. Recipient Billings medal A.M.A., 1961. Diplomate Am. Bd. Surgery. Mem. A.M.A., Soc. U. Surgeons, A.C.S., Halsted Soc., N.Y. Acad. Scis., Am. Fedn. Clin. Research (councillor Eastern sect. 1960-62), Soc. Exptl. Biology and Medicine (councillor Western N.Y. sect. 1959-64), A.A.A.S., Am. Assn. Cancer Research (dir. 1966-70), Am. Soc. Mammalogists, Surg. Investigators Exchange, Am. Cancer Soc. (pres. Erie County div. 1965-70), Nat. Inst. Gen. Med. Scis. (clin. research tng. com. 1965-70), Sigma Xi, Editor surg. sect. Yearbook of Cancer, 1960-70; editorial bd. Rev. Surgery, 1964-70. Contbr. articles surg. jours. Studies of host defense factors in cancer; immunology of cancer; relationship of viruses to malignancy; surg. physiology; devel. of surg. techniques for management of cancer. Established immunological relationship between cancer and coexisting dermatomysoitis. Home: Clarence NY Died Aug. 13, 1971; buried Huntsville AL

GRAFF, FREDERIC, civil engr.; b. Phila., May 23, 1817; s. Frederick and Judith (Swyer) G.; m. Elizabeth Mathieu. Asst. engr. Phila. Water Dept., 1842-47, chief engr., 1847-56, 66-62, reorganized dept. by combining dist. works with prin. city works, planned and directed constrn. of 3 reservoirs and 1 dam, modernized Phila. water system; park commr. City of Phila., 1851, established Fairmount Park System; experimented with pumping machinery, suggested water-supply systems for many of larger cities in East; pres. Am. Soc. Civil Engrs., 1885, dir. several years; pres. Engrs. Club of Phila., 1880, pres. Franklin Inst. Died Phila., Mar. 30, 1890.

GRAFF, FREDERICK, engr.; b. Phila., Aug. 27, 1774; s. Jacob Graff; m. Judith Sawyer, 1 son Frederic. Draftsman, Phila. Water Works (1st steam-powered water works in U.S.) 1797, apptd. supt., 1805; selected (with John Davis) Mt. Morris (now Fairmount), Pa. as site for new reservoir, 1810; designed mains (over 113 miles of which were laid by 1842), connections, stipcocks, and fire plugs for water system of Phila. (1st efficient hydraulic water system in nation), chief engr. for Phila. Water Dept. until 1847; mem. Franklin Inst., 1826. Died Apr. 13, 1847.

GRAHAM, ALEXANDER WILLIAM, (gra'am), civil engr., postmaster; b. Mineola, Mo., Aug. 6, 1884; s. William A. and Epsey Ann (McGhee) G.; student William Jewell Coll., 1902-04; B.S., U. of Mo., 1908; m. Edna Grace Ramsey, Aug. 4, 1912; 1 son, William Alexander. Gen. engring. work, 1908-17; state highway engr. of Mo., 1917-22; dealer in heavy constrn. machinery, 1922-27; pres. Graham-Hobson Tractor Co., 1927-33; postmaster at Kansas City, Mo., since 1933; served as asst. resident engr. on constrn. of Armour Swift Burlington Bridge, Kansas City; Miss. River bridges near Keithsburg, Ill.; Yellowstone River bridge near Fairview, Mont. Pres. Nat. Assn. of Postmasters, 1936-37. Mem. Kansas City Safety Council (dir.), Better Business Bur. (dir.), Chamber of Commerce. Democrat. Clubs: Automobile of Mo., Indian Hills Country. Home: 11 East Winthrop Rd. Office: U.S. Post Office, Kansas City, Mo. Died Jan. 30, 1949.

GRAHAM, CLARENCE HENRY, psychophysiologist; b. Worcester, Mass., Jan. 6, 1906; s. Robert Samuel and Ann Jane (Gillespie) G.; A.B., Clark Univ., Worcester, 1927, A.M., 1928, Ph.D., 1930; M.A. (ad eund.), Brown U., 1943, D.Sc., 1958; Guggenheim fellow, Imperial College, London, England, 1959; m. Elaine R. Hammer, September 6, 1949. Instructor, psychol., Temple U., 1930-31; National research fellow, Johnson Foundation for Medical Physics, U. of Pa., 1931-32; asst. prof., Clark U., 1932-36; asst. professor psychol., Brown U., 1936-37, asso. prof. 1937-41, prof., 1941-45; prof., Columbia U., since 1945; on leave as sci. liaison officer, Office Naval Research, London, 1952-53; member of the Applied Psychology Panel of National Defense Research Com., 1942-46; mem. Physiological Psychology Panel, Office of Naval Research, 1947-55; participant Kyoto Seminars in Am. studies, Kyoto, Japan, summer 1952; survey Japanese psychology labs. under State Dept. and Nat. Sci. Found. grants, summer 1960; v.p. section of Exptl. Psychology and Animal Behavior, Internat. Union Biological Scis., 1956-60; mem. Armed Forces, NRC Vision Com., 1946-58, exec. council, 1956-58, U.S. Nat. Com. of Internat. Commn. on Optics, 1957-59. Awarded Howard Crosby Warren medal by Soc. Exptl. Psychologists, 1941; Presdl. Certificate of Merit, 1948; Tillyer medal Optical Soc. Am., 1963; award for distinguished sci. contribution Am. Psychol. Assn., 1966. Mem. American Psychological Assn. (director, 1946-49; policy and planning bd., 1946-49), Am. Physiol. Society, Optical Soc. America, Society Exptl. Psychologists, Am. Acad. Arts and Sciences, A.A.A.S., (vice president, chmn. section I, 1956), Nat. Acad. Scis., Am. Philos. Soc., Nat. Acad. Scis. (sect. chmn. 1953-56), Sigma Xi. Editor, contbr. Vision and Visual Perception, 1965, cons. editor profl. jours. Home: New York City NY Died July 25, 1971.

GRAHAM, EVARTS AMBROSE, surgeon; b. Chicago, Ill., Mar. 19, 1883; s. David Wilson and Ida Anspach (Barned) G.; A.B., Princeton, 1904; M.D., Rush Med. Coll., 1907; Sc.D., Cincinnati, 1927; LL.D., Central Coll., 1927; hon. M.S., Yale, 1928; Sc.D., Princeton Univ. 1929; Sc.D., Western Reserve University, 1931; Sc.D., U. of Pa., 1940; Sc.D., U. of Chicago, 1941; Sc.D., McGill, U., 1944, Emory University, 1954, New York University, 1955; LL.D. University of Glasgow, 1951, Johns Hopkins U., 1952. Washington U., 1952, U. Leeds (England), 1954; special student chemistry, University Chgo., 1913, 14; m. Helen Tredway, January 29, 1916; children—David Tredway, Evarts Ambrose. Interne Presbyn. Hosp. Chgo., 1907-08; asst., also instructor surgery, Rush Medical College, 1909-15; asst. attending surgeon, Presbyterian Hosp., Chgo., 1912-15; mem. staff Otho. S. A. Sprague Meml. Inst., Rush, Chgo., 1912-15; chief surgeon Park Hosp., Mason City, Ia., 1915-17; professor surgery Washington U. Sch. of Medicine, 1919-51, prof. emeritus since 1951; emeritus surgeon in chief Barnes Hosp. and St. Louis Children's Hosp.; mem. Presidents Commn. on Health Needs of Nation, 1952; apptd. by Rockefeller Foundation to investigate teaching of surgery in British medical school, 1922; Harvey Soc. lecturer, 1924 and 1934; Mütter lecturer, 1924; McArthur lecturer, 1926; Shattuck lecturer, 1928; Alvarez lecturer, 1930; Joyce lecturer, 1931; Bevan lecturer, 1932; Caldwell lecturer, 1933; Balfour lecturer, 1934; Judd lecturer, 1937; Lister orator, London, 1947; Fraser lectr., Edinburgh, 1954; surgeon in chief Peter Bent Brigham Hosp., 1925; temp. prof. surgery St. Bartholomew's Hosp., London, 1939. Mem. Nat. Research Council (med. fellowship bd.), 1925-39; chmn. com. on surgery, 1940-46. Captain Medical Corps, U.S. Army, Jan. 1918; maj. May 1918; served with Sch. of Neurol. Surgery, Chicago, later as mem. Empyema Commn., Camp Lee, Va.; spl. lab. research on empyema, at Baltimore, Md.; comdg. officer Evacuation Hosp. No. 34, in France, Sept. 1918-May 1919; hon. discharged, 1919. Mem. com. apptd. by sec. of war to study activities of Medical Department of U.S. Army, 1942. Pres. bd. trustees John Burroughs School, St. Louis, 1930-37; mem. Nat. Bd. Med. Examiners, 1924-33. Chairman Am. Board of Surgery (1937-41); fellow Am. Coll. Surgeons (pres. 1940-41); Am. Med. Assn. (chmn. sect. gen. and abdominal surgery, 1925); mem. Am. Surg. Assn. (pres. 1937), Soc. Clin. Surgery, Am. Assn. Thoracic Surgery (pres. 1928), St. Louis Assn. Surgeons (pres. 1925), Soc. for Clin. Research. Société Internationale de Chirugie; Kaiserlich Deutsche Akad, d. Naturforscher (1932); National Academy Sciences (1941), Am. Philos. Soc. (1941); hon. fellow Assn. of Surgeons of Great Britain and Ireland, Royal College of Surgeons (London, Eng.); honorary mem. Society of Thoracic Surgeons of Great Britain and Ireland, Sociedad Argentina de Cirujanos Royal Society of Sciences, Uppsala, Sweden, others; mem. Nu Sigma Nu, Alpha Omega Alpha fraternities. Author: Empyema Thoracis, 1925; Diseases of the Gall-Bladder and Bile Ducts, 1928. Editor: Surgical Diagnosis, 1930. Wrote sect., "Treatment of the Acute Empyema," for Medical and Surgical History of World War (published by Surgeon General's Office), 1924. Editor, Year Book of Surgery. Awarded Gross prize in surgery, 1920; Leonard prize by American Roentgen-Ray Society, 1925; gold medal by the American Radiol. Soc., 1925, for the development of cholecystography; gold medal and certificate of merit from St. Louis Medical Society, 1927, for development of cholecystography; gold medal by Southern Medical Association, 1934, for scientific research; John Scott medal by City of Philadelphia, 1937; received St. Louis Award, 1942; Lister Medal of Royal Coll. Surgeons, Eng., 1942; Roswell Park medal, 1949; American College Chest Physician medal, 1949; Miss. Valley Med. Soc. medal, 1949; distinguished service medal of A.M.A., 1950; Bigelow Medal of Boston Surgical Soc., 1951, Charles Mickle Fellowship, Univ., Toronto, 1943. Gave expositions of disturbed mechanics of respiration and circulation when normal intrathoracic pressures are altered; developed method for cholecystography, or the X-ray visualization of the gall-bladder; new treatment for chronic abscess of the lung; contbns. to pathology and treatment of carcinoma of bronchus, explanation of particular, toxicity of choloroform and similar anaesthetic agents; etc. Co-editor Archives of Surgery, 1920-45 and of Annals of Surgery, 1935-45; editor Journal of Thoracic Surgery since 1931; editor Year Book of Surgery, 1926-27. Home: Old Jamestown Rd., R.R. 2, Box 256, Florissant, Mo. Office: Barnes Hospital, 600 S. Kingshighway, St. Louis 10. Died Mar. 4, 1957.

GRAHAM, JOHN HOWARD, (gra'am), chemist; born Phila., Pa., Dec. 29, 1880; s. Jonathan Wesley and Anna Elizabeth (Mifflin) G.; A.B., Central High Sch., 1898; B.S., U. of Pa., 1902, A.M., 1927; m. Lillian Mae Cogswell, June 19, 1906; children—Marguerite Rae (Mrs. Robert G. Wetmore), Dorothy Cogswell (Mrs. David C. Miller), Ruth Eleanor (Mrs. Herbert S. Simons), Lois Adele (Mrs. Roy G. Anderson), Janet Mae. Began as chief chemist, Spanish-American Iron Company, Daiquiri, Cuba, 1902; teacher chemistry, Central High School, Philadelphia, also Drexel, Central, Frankford, Mastbaum, and Germantown evening schools and Central High Summer Sch., 1903-30; chemist, Smith, Kline, French Co., Henry K. Wampole Co., Rohm and Haas Co.; consultant Central Railway Signal Co. Professor and head dept. organic chem., Temple U. Pharmacy Sch. since 1930; business manager, the Catalyst. Dir. Westminster Cemetery. Mem. A.A.A.S., Am. Assn. Univ. Profs., Pa. Acad. Science, Am. Chem. Soc., Pa. Bee Assn., Sigma Xi. Republican. Presbyterian (elder). Mason (32 deg., Shriner). Home: 113 Cliveden Av., Glenside, Montgomery County, Pa. Office: 3223 N. Broad St., Phila. 40. Died Oct. 5, 1951.

GRANGER, ARMOUR TOWNSEND, engring. educator, b. Austin, Tex., Mar. 21, 1898; s. John and Jane Rebecca (Baker) G.; B.S., U. of Tex., 1918, C.E., 1921; m. Willoughby Crawford, June 15, 1920; children—Amy Jane (Mrs. William A. Haldeman), Charlotte Emily (Mrs. William B. Hinman). Detailer and structural designer, Harrington, Howard & Ash, consulting engrs., Kansas City, Mo., 1919-20; instr., adjunct prof., asso. prof. civil engring., U. of Tex., 1920-28; asst. engr., Ash-Howard-Needles & Tammen, consulting engrs., Kansas City-N.Y. City, 1928-39; asso. prof., U. of Tenn., 1939-40, prof. and head of the department of civil engineering, 1940-56, dean engring., 1956-66; consulting services on unusual or complicated structures, 1940-66. Mem. Tenn. Bd. Archtl. and Engring. Examiners, 1957-63. Registered profl. engr., Tenn. and N.Y. State. Mem. Am. Soc. C.E. (pres. Tenn. Valley sect. 1951), Am. Railway Engr. Assn., Soc. Profl. Engrs., Soc. Am. Mil. Engrs., Am. Soc. for Engring. Edn., Tenn. (pres. 1955), Nat. socs. profl. engrs., Tenn. Acad. Sci., Tenn. Education Association, Knoxville Tech. Soc. (pres., 1946), International Association of Bridge and Structural Engineers, Omicron Delta Kappa, Sigma Xi, Phi Kappa Phi, Tau Beta Pi, Chi Epsilon. Presbyn. Contbr. articles in field to jours. Designer portions of the athletic stadiums of U. of Tex. and U. of Tenn. Home: Knoxville TN Died Sept. 16, 1966; buried Highland Meml. Cemetery, Knoxville TN

GRANT, DAVID NORVELL WALKER, physician; b. Richmond, Va., May 14, 1891; s. Percival Stuart and Avis Barney (Walker) G.; M.D., U. Va., 1915; grad. Army Med. Sch., 1917, Sch. of Aviation Medicine, San Antonio, 1931, Air Corps Tactical Sch., 1937, Chem. Warfare Sch., 1939; Sc.D., Hahnemann Med. Coll., 1944; m. Dorothy Krayenbuhl, May 14, 1917; 1 son, David Norvell Walker. Res. officer, M.C., U.S. Army, 1916; commd. 1st lt., U.S. Army, 1917, and advanced through grades to maj. gen., 1943; ret. for physical disability, 1946; served in Panama and Occupation of Germany, World War I; became chief med. service AAF, 1939, The Air Surgeon, 1941-46, duties including responsibility for all med. research, such as devel. of oxygen equipment and clothing for altitude flight; inaugurated rehab. program (later adopted by Army and Navy); established aviation psychology program, also introduced organized air evacuation of casualties on mass scale; now med. dir., dir. blood program A.R.C. Decorated D.S.M.; hon. mem. mil. div. Order of the Bath. Fellow A.C.S.; mem. Assn. Mil. Surgeons U.S., A.M.A., Assn. Aviation Medicine, D.C. Med. Soc., Academia Brasileira de Medicina Militar, Delta Kappa Epsilon, Theta Nu Epsilon, Phi Rho Sigma. Club: Army and Navy (Washington). Contbr. articles to med. publs. Home: 3134 Ordway St. Office: care A.R.C. 17th and D Sts., Washington. Died Aug. 1964.

GRANT, GEORGE BARNARD, inventor, mech. engr.; b. Gardiner, Me., Dec. 21, 1849; s. Peter and Vesta (Capen) G.; B.S., Harvard, 1873; never married. Obtained patents for calculating machine, 1872, 73; exhibited his calculator "Grant's Difference Engine" at Phila. Centennial Expn., 1876; opened gear-cutting machine shop, Charleston, Mass., 1873; established Grant Gear Works, Inc., Boston. Author: Chart and Tablets for Bevel Gears, 1885; A Handbook on the Teeth of Gears . . . with Odontographs, 1885. Died Pasadena, Cal., Aug. 16, 1917.

GRANT, HENRY HORACE, surgeon; b. Petersburg, Ky., Dec. 12, 1853; s. Dr. Elijah Lane and Jane Rebecca (Prest) G.; A.B., Centre Coll., Danville, Ky., 1875, A.M., 1884; M.D., Jefferson Med. Coll., Phila., 1878; m. Leila Owsley, Aug. 3, 1886. Prof. surgery, Hosp. Coll. of Medicine, 1893-1909; prof. principles of surgery and oral surgery, Louisville Coll. Dentistry, 1893—; prof. surgery, med. dept. U. of Louisville, 1909—. Author: Principles of Surgery and Diseases of the Mouth and Jaws, 1902. Editor of Louisville Monthly Journal of Medicine and Surgery. Home: Louisville, Ky. Died Jan. 1921.

GRANT, JOHN PRESCOTT, surgeon; b. New Glasgow, N.S., Can., Oct. 31, 1872; s. Donald Cameron and Mary (Fraser) G.; M.D., McGill U., Montreal, 1895; Kings Coll. Hosp., London, 2 years, 1899, 1900; house surg. Royal United Hosp., Bath, Eng., 1901; m. Edith G. Quirk, 1901. Came to U.S., 1902, naturalized, 1917. Chief of surg. clinic Cornell Med. Coll., 1907-12; instr. in operative and clin. surgery, Cornell U. Med. Coll., 1906-12; adj. prof. surgery, New York Polyclinic Med. Sch., and Hosp., 1912-14, clin. prof. surgery, 1914-17, prof. surgery, 1917-38, emeritus since 1938, pres. of faculty, 1924-26; dir. Dept. of Surgery, 2 yrs., cons. surgeon, 1938; surgeon to Polyclinic Hosp.; cons. surgeon N.Y. City Hosp., Midtown Hosp. (New York); dir. surgery Long Beach (N.Y.) Hosp.; cons. surg. Peoples Hosp. and Bronx Maternity Hosp. (New York). Fellow N.Y. Acad. Medicine, Nat. Soc. Advancement of Gastroenterology, Am. Coll. Surgeons; mem. Royal Coll. Surgeons, A.M.A., Gastro-enterol. Soc. of New York, Alpha Mu Pi Omega. Republican. Presbyn. Clubs: Lotus (New York); Yacht (Wayne, Me.). Author of surg. sect. in Dr. Samuel Weiss' textbook, Diseases of the Stomach, Liver and Pancreas, 1935. Home: "Sunnycroft," Wayne, Me.; (winter) 2901 Columbus Blvd., Coral Gables, Fla. Office: 27 W. 55th St., New York. Died May 27, 1946; buried in Woodlawn Cemetery, Coral Gables, Fla.

GRANT, LESTER STRICKLAND, mining engr.; b. New Haven, Conn., Oct. 31, 1877; s. Charles Alfred and Mary J. (Strickland) G.; E.M., Colo. Sch. of Mines, 1899; m. Chloe Ella Thornton, 1900; children—Robert Waltman, Richard Thornton. Engr. Isabella Gold Mining Co., Cripple Creek, Colo., 1899-1901, Isabella Mines Co., 1901-03; supt. Isabella Lease, 1904; engr. and assayer, Findley Consol. Mining Co., Cripple Creek, 1905-06; metallurgist and engr. Inca Mining Co., Peru, S.A., 1906-09; asst. supt. Roosevelt Drainage Tunnel, Cripple Creek, 1909-10; supt. Isabella Mines Co., 1910-13; gen. mgr. Jumper, Calif., Gold Mines. Co., Stent, Calif., and v.p. and gen. mgr. Contention Mining Co., Knight Creek, Tuolumne Co., Calif., 1913-19; treas. Ajax Mine Lease Co., Victor, Colo., 1921-22; mgr. and vice president McElroy Ranch Co., Crane, Tex., 1927-49 (ret.); v.p., dir. Franco Wyoming Oil Co., McElroy Royalty Corp. Professor mining, 1919-28, dean, 1921-28, Colo. Sch. of Mines. Served as captain, engineer, Officer Reserve Corps (now retired). Distinguished Achievement Medal, Colo. Sch. of Mines, 1949. Mem. Inst. Mining and Metall. Engrs., Am. Petroleum Inst., Theta Tau, Tau Beta Pi. Republican. Episcopalian. Mason. Clubs: Teknik (Denver); Rotary (Midland, Tex.). Home: 1613 Palmer Park Blvd., Colorado Springs, Colo. Address: P.O. Box 912, Midland TX

GRANT, ROBERT JOHN, mining engr.; b. Pictou County, N.S., Nov. 12, 1862; s. Peter J. and Christy Ellen G.; ed. pub. schs., N.S.; Boston Evening High Sch.; m. Leslie Hayden, June 14, 1894. Mining, Colo. and Ariz., 1889-1902, in Mexico, 1903, Australia, 1904-05; mine engr. and mgr. since 1906; supt. U.S. Mint, Denver, 1921-23; dir. of Mint, Washington, D.C., 1923-33; adviser Central Mint, Shanghai, China, since 1933. Executive mgr. U.S. Food Administration for Colo., 1917-19. Republican. Presbyterian. Mem. Am. Inst. Mining and Metall. Engrs. Clubs: Denver Country; American, Columbia Country (Shanghai). Address: 832 Equitable Bldg., Denver, Colo. Died Nov. 24, 1949.

GRASTY, JOHN SHARSHALL, geologist, mining engr.; b. Versailles, Ky., Mar. 15, 1880; s. Thomas Percy and Mattie Virginia (White) G.; A.B., Johns Hopkins, 1902, Ph.D., 1908; studied Washington and Lee U. and Mass. Inst. Tech.; Sc.D., Washington Coll., Md., 1912; m. Elizabeth Montgomery Cochran, Nov. 9, 1909; children—Thomas P., John Sharshall. Asst., U.S. Geol. Survey, 1905; geologist, Md. Geol. Survey, 1906-08; asst. state geologist, Va., 1909-16; adj. prof. econ. geology, 1908-13, asso. prof., 1913-16, U. of Va.; prof. mining geology, Washington and Lee U., 1916-18 (on leave); investigations for B.&O. Ry., Southern Ry. and C.&O. Ry.; spl. geologist, Ala. Geol. Survey; chem. engr. Ordnance Dept., U.S. Army, 1918; oil geology, Mid-Continent Fields, 1919-20. Inventor "fire sentinel" apparatus; specialist on rock slides and foundations. Author: Limestones of Maryland, 1909; The Slate Deposits of Virginia, 1917; Origin of Caverns in Relation to Structure, 1925. Home: Charlottesville, Va. Died June 5, 1930.

GRAVE, CASWELL, biologist; b. Monrovia, Ind., Jan. 24, 1870; s. Thomas C. and Anna (Hubbard) G.; B.S., Earlham Coll., Richmond, Ind., 1895; awarded LL.D. from same college, 1928; scholar and fellow and Adam T. Bruce fellow, Johns Hopkins Univ., 1898-1901, Ph.D., 1899; m. Josephine Grave, Sept. 24, 1896; 1 son, Thomas Brooks. Temporary asst., U.S. Fish Commn., 1899-1900; asst. in zoölogy, 1901-02, asso., 1902-06, asso. prof., Johns Hopkins; Rebstock prof. zoölogy and head dept., Washington U., 1919-40, emeritus prof. of zoölogy since 1940. Dir. U.S. Fisheries Lab., Beaufort, N.C., 1902-06; shellfish commr., Md., 1906-12; instr. in charge course in invertebrate zoölogy, Marine Biol. Lab., Woods Hole, Mass., 1912-19. Capt. Chem. Warfare Service, U.S. Army, 1918-19. Fellow A.A.A.S. (ex-v.p. sect. F); mem. Am. Soc. Zoologists (sec.-treas. 1913-18; v.p. 1920; pres. 1928), Am. Soc. Naturalists, Phi Beta Kappa, Sigma Xi. Trustee Marine Biol. Lab., 1936-40, emeritus trustee since 1940; mem. Bd. Nat. Research Fellowship in the Biol. Sciences, 1935-38. Club: University (Winter Pk.). Author scientific papers. Home: Winter Park, Fla. Died Jan. 8, 1944.

GRAVES, ALVIN C(USHMAN), physicist; b. Washington, Nov. 4, 1909; s. Herbert C. and Clara Edith (Walter) G.; B.S., U. Va., 1931; postgrad. Mass. Inst. Tech., 1932; Ph.D., U. Chgo., 1939; m. Elizabeth Riddle, Sept. 27, 1937; children—Marilyn Edith, Alvin Palmer, Elizabeth Anne. Instr. physics U. Tex., 1939-41, asst. prof., 1941, asso. prof. (on leave), 1942-60; with U. Chgo. Metall. Lab., 1942-43; staff mem. Los Alamos (N.M.) Sci. Lab., U. Cal., 1943-45, group leader, 1945-47, asso. div. leader, 1947-48, div. leader, 1948—; dep. sci. dir. Pacific Proving Grounds operations, 1947-48, sci. dir., 1948-55; test dir. Nev. Proving Grounds operations, 1951-54, sci. adviser Nev. Test Site, 1955—, Eniwatok Proving Ground operations, 1955-60. Chmn. Com. Sr. Reviewers, AEC; AEC rep. Conf. on Discontinuance Nuclear Weapons Tests, and Tech. Working Group on Detection and Identification High-Altitude Nuclear Explosions, Geneva, Switzerland, 1959-60; chmn. Nev. planning bd. (AEC), 1961; mem. Pacific planning bd. (AEC), 1963, also joint nuclear test plan group, 1964; cons. Army Science Adv. Panel. Organizer, dir., chmn. bd. Los Alamos Nat. Bank, 1963—. Mem. past pres. Los Alamos School Board. Recipient Exceptional Civilian Service award, Air Force, 1951, Certificate of Achievement, Army, 1954; Distinguished Service award, FCDA, 1955. Fellow American Physical Society; member American Institute Physics, Sigma Xi, Gamma Alpha, Delta Sigma Phi, Tau Beta Pi. Home: 277 Andanada. Office: P.O. Box 1663, Los Alamos Sci. Lab., Los Alamos, N.M. Died July 28, 1965; buried Guaje Pines Cemetery, Los Alamos, N.M.

GRAVES, GRANT OSTRANDER, educator, physician; b. Columbus, O., Jan. 21, 1905; s. Henry and Kathleen (Ostrander) G.; B.A., Ohio State U., 1926, M.A. in Anatomy, 1929, M.D., 1932; m. Helen Louise Pierson, July 18, 1940; children—Scott, Heather, Holly. Intern Duke U. Hosp., 1932-33; resident Univ. Hosp., Columbus, 1933-34; mem. faculty Ohio State U., from 1935, prof. anatomy, from 1959, chmn. dept., from 1962, asst. clin. prof. medicine, from 1947, asst. prof. radiology, from 1947, med. sci. bldg. named Grant O. Graves Hall in his honor, 1968. Mem. exec. bd. Central Ohio Blue Cross, 1960-65. Diplomate Am. Bd. Internal Medicine. Life fellow A.C.P.; mem. A.M.A., Ohio Med. Assn., Columbus Acad. Medicine (pres. 1951), Alpha Omega Alpha (bldg. named in his honor 1972). Home: Columbus OH Died Feb. 7, 1972.

GRAVES, HERBERT CORNELIUS, civil engr.; b. Alexandria, Va., Aug. 17, 1869; s. Willard Purdy and Lucy Malvina (Libby) G.; C.E., U. of Va., 1889; m. Clara Edith Walter, Sept. 4, 1894. Railroad surveyor, N.C., 1889-90; railroad, land and townsite surveys, Va., 1890-91; city surveyor, Alexandria, Va., 1891-95; nautical expert, Hydrographic Office, U.S. Navy, Cleveland, O., 1895-98; nautical expert and asst., 1898-1917; apptd. chief Div. of Hydrography and Topography, U.S. Coast and Geodetic Survey, 1915. Compiler of "Coast Pilots," relative to coasts of U.S. and Alaska (pub. by Coast and Geodetic Survey). Home: Washington, D.C. Died July 26, 1919.

GRAVES, WILLIAM WASHINGTON, neuropsychiatrist; b. La Grange, Ky., Nov. 13, 1865; s. David William and Julia Ann (Crockett) G.; M.D., St. Louis Coll. Phys and Surg., 1888; post graduate work London, Heidelberg, Berlin and Vienna, 1901-04; m. Helena J. Sessinghaus, June 9, 1891; 1 dau., Helen (dec.). With St. Louis U. Med. Sch., 1905—, prof. nervous and mental diseases, 1914—, dir. of dept., 1923—. Mem. A.M.A., A.C.P., St. Louis Med. Soc., Am. Neurol. Assn., Am. Psychiatric Assn., Alpha Kappa Kappa, Alpha Omega Alpha. Awarded Certificate of Merit and gold medal for scientific accomplishment based on his classification of scapulae and his discovery of the age-incidence principle of investigation, St. Louis Med. Soc., 1939. Democrat. Baptist. Mason (32 deg.), Elk. Home: 5136 Enright Av. Office: 1402 S. Grand Blvd., St. Louis, Mo. Died Apr. 18, 1949.

GRAWE, OLIVER RUDOLPH, (graw), educator, geologist; b. St. Louis, Nov. 26, 1901; s. Louis Christ and Charlotte Catharine (Sommerkamp) G.; A.B., Washington U., 1922, M.S., 1924; Ph.D., U. of Iowa, 1927; m. Sarah Catharine Hillard, Dec. 23, 1941; 1 son, Oliver Rupert. Teaching fellow, Washington U., 1922-24; grad. asst., U. of Iowa, 1924-26; instr. in geology, U. of Nev., 1926-28; mineralogist Nev. State Mining Lab., 1926-28; asst. prof. of mineralogy, U. Mo. at Rolla, 1928-35, asso. prof., 1935-46, prof. of geology since 1946, chmn. geology dept., 1945-57. Cons. geologist, mineralogist, 1945—; geologist Mo. Geol. Survey, summers, 1937-45; metallurgist U.S. Bureau of Mines, 1956—; Nat. Research fellow geology 1925-26. Fellow Geol. Soc. of Am., Mineral Soc. of Am., A.A.A.S.; mem. Am. Chem. Soc., Association of Geology Teachers (president central section 1958-59), Am. Assn. Petroleum Geologists, Soc. Econ. Geologists, Am. Soc. Engring. Edn., Am. Inst. Mining and Metall. Engrs., Geochemical Society, Assn. Missouri Geologists (organizer, pres. 1954-55), Am. Assn. Univ. Profs., Phi Beta Kappa, Sigma Gamma Epsilon (asso.), Phi Kappa Phi, Sigma Xi, Gamma Alpha. Meth. Author articles on mineralogy, sedimentary petrology, economic geology to profl. pubs. Home: 671 Salem Av., Rolla, Mo. Died Mar. 22, 1965; buried Valhalla Cemetery, St. Louis.

GRAY, ALEXANDER, engineer; b. Edinburgh, Scotland, Mar. 9, 1882; s. James and Christina (Seton) G.; diploma in engring., Heriot Watt Coll. (night sch.), Edinburgh, 1904; B.Sc. in Engring., Edinburgh U., 1904; B.Sc. in Elec. Engring., McGill U., Montreal Can., 1906, M.Sc., 1916; m. Margaret Annandale Low, Oct. 11, 1906. Machinist, 1897-1900; draftsman and erection engr., Edinburgh, 1900-04; elec. designer with Bullock Elec. Co. and Allis-Chalmers Co., 1905-10; asst. prof. elec. engring., McGill U., 1910-15; head of elec. engring. dept., Cornell U., 1915—. Presbyn. Author: Electrical Machine Design, 1913; Principles and Practice of Electrical Engineering, 1914. Wrote Sect. 8 of Standard Handbook for Electrical Engineers. Home: Ithaca, N.Y. Died Oct. 13, 1921.

GRAY, CHESTER EARL; b. Columbus Junction, Ia., May 16, 1881; s. James Edward and Margaret Jane (Dawdy) G.; B.S., Ia. State Coll., 1901, M.S., 1924; m. Rachel L. Mosier, Apr. 25, 1905; children—Catherine Jane, Annabel. Asst. in agrl. chemistry, Ia. State Coll., 1901-02; chemist Continental Creamery Co., Topeka, Kan., 1902-03, Beatrice (Neb.) Creamery Co., 1904-05; chemist in charge Research Lab., Dairy Div. Bur. of Animal Industry U.S. Dept. Agr., 1905-08; asst. gen. mgr. Central Creamery Co. (now Golden State Co., Ltd.), Eureka, Calif., 1908-15; gen. mgr. Calif. Central Creameries (now Golden State Co., Ltd.), San Francisco, 1915, pres., 1915-33; chmn. bd. Golden State Co., Ltd., 1931-37, now dir. Mem. Calif. State Board of Agr., 1929-40; mem. com. advisory to dir. Giannini Foundation of Agrl. Economics, University of California; dir. Am. Dry Milk Institute (chairman board), California Dairy Council, Pacific Slope Dairy Show. Inventor and patentee processes and apparatus for desiccating and for mfg. of products from milk and cream. Republican. Mem. Am. Chem. Soc., Am. Dairy Science Assn., A.A.A.S. Clubs: Commonwealth, Commercial (San Francisco); Athens Athletic (Oakland); Univ. of Calif. Club (Berkeley). Author of bulls. pub. by Dept. of Agr., Dry Milk Inst., to encourage outstanding contbns. and meritorious achievements in dry milk production, distribution and research established the C. E. Gray Award in his honor, Apr. 1943. Home: 6263 Chabot Rd., Oakland, Calif. Office: 425 Battery St., San Francisco, Calif. Died Sep. 19, 1944.

GRAY, ELISHA, electrician, inventor; b. Barnesville, O., Aug. 2, 1835; m. M. Delia Shepard, 1862. Learned blacksmithing, carpentry and boat-building; then pursued special studies in physical science at Oberlin Coll., supporting himself by working at his trade. Invented, 1867, a self-adjusting telegraph relay; established as mfr. of electric apparatus at Cleveland, 1869; perfected the type-writing telegraph, the telegraph repeater, telegraphic switch, annunciator, etc. Organized, 1872, Western Electric Mfg. Co., but retired from it in 1874. Invented the speaking telephone, 1876; telautograph, 1893; established the Gray Electric Co., Highland Park. Organized the Congress of Electricians, in connection with World's Columbia Expn., 1893, and was its chmn. Author: Experimental Researches in Electro-Harmonic Telegraphy and Telephony; Elementary Talks on Science. Home: Highland Park, Ill. Died 1901.

GRAY, GEORGE EDWARD, civil engr.; b. at Verona, N.Y., Sept. 12, 1818; s. Joel and Betsey R. G.; pub. sch. edn.; studied civil engring. under Peletiah Rawson; m. Lucina S. Corning, of Syracuse, N.Y. (now deceased). Asst. and resident engr. on N.Y. state canals, also N.Y. & Harlem R.R.; chief engr. New York Central R.R., 1853-65; consulting engr. Central Pacific R.R., 1865-71; chief engr. S.P.R.R., 1871-85, and engr. of various other roads comprised in the S.P. system. Trustee Leland Stanford Jr. U.; mem. Cal. Acad. Sciences; mem. Instn. Civ. Engrs. of Great Britain; hon. mem. Am. Soc. C.E., etc. Address: Care Wells, Fargo & Co.'s Express, San Francisco.

GRAY, HOWARD KRAMER, surgeon; b. St. Louis, Mo., Aug. 28, 1901; s. Carl Raymond and Harriette (Flora) G.; B.S., Princeton U., 1923; student U. of Neb., Coll. of Med., 1923-25, D.Sc. (honorary); M.D., Harvard, 1927; M.S., in surgery, Univ. of Minn., Mayo Foundation, 1932; D.Sc. (hon.), Lafayette College; married Lila DeWeenta Conrad, September 2, 1925; children—Howard Kramer, DeWeenta Russell (Mrs. Walter I. Bones, Jr.). Fellow in surgery, Mayo Foundation, 1928-32; jr. surgeon, Mayo Clinic, 1932-35, surgeon and head of a sect. in surgery since 1935; professor, Mayo Foundation, Graduate Sch., U. of Minn., since 1935. Captain U.S. Naval Med. Corps Res. Fellow A.C.S., So. Surg. Assn. A.M.A.; mem. Am. Surg., Assn., Am. Assn. Thoracic Surgery, Western Surgical Assn., Soc. of Clinical Surgery, Surgeons' Club, Minn. State Med. Assn., Minn. Surg. Assn., Southern Minn. Med. Assn., Nu Sigma Nu. Independent. Baptist. Clubs: Ivy (Princeton. N.J.); Rochester Country, Rochester Tennis. Contbr. to med. jours. Home: 612

10th Av., S.W. Office: Mayo Clinic, Rochester, Minn. Died Sept. 6, 1955; buried Rochester, Minn.

GRAY, J(ACQUES) P(IERCE), physician; b. Redkey, Ind., July 17, 1900; s. James E. and Laura Jane (Reeves) G.; A.B., Grinnell Coll., 1922; M.D., Johns Hopkins, 1928; M.P.H., Harvard, 1935; m. Amy Hannah Williams, Aug. 12, 1925; 1 dau., Virginia Williams (Mrs. R. A. Garrett). Began as instructor of physics, Newton (Iowa) High School, 1922-24; jr. bacteriologist, Baltimore City Hosp., 1925, Md. State Health Dept., 1926; asst. surgeon U.S.P.H.S., New Orleans, 1928-29; dep. health officer Sonoma County, Calif., 1929; jr. epidemiologist Calif. Dept. of Pub. Health, 1930; epidemiologist, acting health officer, asst. dir. of pub. health, City and County of San Francisco, Calif., 1930-37, dir. of pub. welfare, 1937-39; lecturer, U. of Calif., 1939-40; associate clin. prof. of preventive medicine and pub. health, Stanford U., Sch. of Medicine, 1937-40; dir. Hillsdale County (Mich.) Health Dept., W. K. Kellogg Foundation Mich. Community Health Project, 1940-42; vis. prof. Sch. Pub. Health, Grad. Sch. U. of N.C., 1942; dean, Sch. of Med. and prof. of preventive and pub. health medicine, Med. Coll. of Va., 1942-46; dean, Sch. of Medicine, U. of Okla.; also supt. hospitals, prof. pub. health medicine, 1946-47; med. cons., Parke Davis & Co., Detroit Labs., 1947—, director spl. med. services, 1953—. Recipient Distinguished Service award American Medical Writers Association, 1959. Diplomate American Board of Preventive Medicine and Public Health (founders group). Mem. A.M.A., Am. Pub. Health Assn., Mich. State, Wayne Co. med. socs., Assn. Am. Med. Colls., Am. Med. Writers' Assn. (visiting lecturer medical writing 1954—). Association Tchrs. Preventive Med., Am. Coll. Preventive Medicine, Delta Omega, Phi Beta Kappa, Phi Beta Pi, Alpha Omega Alpha. Presbyn. Contbr. articles to profl. jours. Home: 8900 E. Jefferson, Detroit 48214. Office: Parke Davis & Co., Detroit 48232. Died Oct. 13, 1961; buried White Chapel Cemetery, Detroit.

GRAY, JOHN PURDUE, physician, alienist; b. Center County, Pa., Aug. 6, 1825; s. Peter B. and Elizabeth (Purdue) G.; A.M., Dickinson Coll., 1846; M.D., U. Pa., 1849; LL.D., Hamilton Coll., 1874; m. Mary B. Wetmore, Sept. 6, 1854. Resident physician Blockley Hosp., Phila., 1849; 1st asst., acting med. supt. N.Y. State Lunatic Asylum, Utica, 1853; med. supt. Mich. State Lunatic Asylum, 1853; full editor Am. Jour. of Insanity, 1854; prof. psychol. medicine and med. jurisprudence Bellevue Hosp. Med. Coll., 1874-82, Albany Med. Coll., 1876-82; pres. Assn. Med. Supts. of Am. Instn. for the Insane; revolutionized asylum construction, introduced steam heat and ventilation; abolished as far as possible mechanical restraint and solitary feeding for patients. Died Utica, Nov. 29, 1886.

GRAYDON, JAMES WEIR, engineer, inventor; b. in U.S., of American parents, Jan. 18, 1848; grad. U.S. Naval Acad.; served in vol. army in Civil War under Grant and Sherman; apptd. midshipman, 1865; served on various stations and became lt. U.S.N.; resigned. Inventor Graydon Dynamite Gun, Graydon Gigantic Wheels (exhibited at Paris, Vienna, Madrid, Rome, Blackpool, England, etc.). Graydon Aerial Torpedo, Graydon Cable System of Torpedoes, Graydon Ry. Carriage Heater, Graydon High Velocity Projectiles, Graydon Compound Rotary Turbine Engines, etc. Address: Care Jensen & Son, 77 Chancery Lane, W.C., London.

GREAVES, JOSEPH EAMES, biochemist; b. Logan City, Utah, Nov. 2, 1880; s. Joseph C. and Catherine (Eames) G.; B.S., Utah Agrl. Coll., 1904; M.S., U. of Ill., 1907; Ph.D., U. of Calif., 1911; m. Pernecy Dudley, June 10, 1907 (died May 9, 1918); children—Joseph D., Florence D., Pernecy D., Vera D., Mary Oretta; m. 2d, Ethelyn Oliver, May 5, 1920; children—Marguerite Oliver, Thelma Mae, Oliver. Began as instructor in chemistry, Utah Agrl. Coll., 1907, asst. prof., 1908-10, asso. prof. physiol. chemistry, 1911-13, professor bacteriology and physioligical chemistry, 1913-27, professor bacteriology and public health, 1927-29, professor bacteriology and biochemistry since 1929; also bacteriologist Utah Experimental Sta. Member Logan City Bd. of Health. Mem. Am. Chem. Soc., Am. Bacteriol. Soc., A.A.A.S., Am. Public Health Assn., Am. Soc. Biochemists, Utah Acad. Science Arts and Letters (pres. 1947). Latter Day Saint. Author: Agricultural Bacteriology, 1922; Bacteria in Relation to Soil Fertility (with E. O. Greaves), 1925; Elementary Bacteriology (with same), 5th edit., 1945; also over 100 articles in professional jours. Cons. editor Soil Science; contributing editor Americana Annual. Home: 445 North 3 E., Logan City, Utah. Died June 6, 1954; buried Logan City, Utah.

GREELEY, SAMUEL ARNOLD, cons. engr.; b. Chicago, Ill., Aug. 20, 1882; s. Frederick and Florence Morehouse (Arnold) G.; A.B., Harvard, 1903; B.S. in Sanitary Engring., Mass. Inst. Tech., 1906; m. Dorothy Coffin, Oct. 4, 1913; children—Samuel Sewall, Frederick, Lois, Dorothy. Assistant engineer Hering & Fuller of N.Y. City, 1904-09; was resident engr. in charge construction and supt. in charge operation Milwaukee Refuse Disposal Plant, 1909-11; investigation and report on water supply and sewage treatment, Caracas, Venzuela, 1911; engr. with Sanitary Dist. of Chicago, 1912-15; supervising engr. Camp Custer, Mich., 1917-18, also sanitary engr. U.S. Shipping Bd., operations on Pacific Coast, N.E. Coast and Great Lakes; cons. engr. on sanitary engring. projects for New York, Los Angeles County, Buffalo, Hampton Roads, Minneapolis-St. Paul, Milwaukee, Madison (Wis.), Dallas, Chicago, Phila., Boston, Washington, Toronto, Toledo, Miami, New Bedford, Kansas City, Grand Rapids, Worcester, Peoria, Rockford, and over 200 other cities; mem. Greeley and Hansen, cons. engrs. Chicago. Served as spl. cons. constrn. Div., and Corps Engrs.; gen. charge layout and constrn. camp Forest, Tenn.; World War II. Recipient Brown medal, Franklin Inst., 1951, Charles Alvin Emerson medal, Water Pollution Control Fedn., 1961. Mem. Am. Soc, C.E. (hon. mem.; dir. 1947-50), Am. Water Works Assn., Am. Pub. Health Assn., Am. Assn. Engrs., N.E. Water Works Assn., Am. Pub. Works Assn. (honorary member), Ill. Soc. Engrs., Western Soc. Engrs., etc. Mem. Council and Bd. Local Improvements, Winnetka, Ill., 1916-18. Episcopalian. Clubs: Univ., Engrs., Cosmos. Author: (with Rudolph Hering) Collection and Disposal of Municipal Refuse, 1921. Home: Winnetka IL Died Feb. 3, 1968.

GREEN, ARTHUR LAURENCE, chemist; b. Newark, O., Sept. 18, 1857; s. Jesse Stoneman and Mary Jane (Conine) G.; Ph.C., U. of Mich., 1882; M.D., Ind. Med. Coll., 1894; Ph.D., Franklin (Ind.) Coll., 1895; m. Fannie E. Smith, of Newark, Aug. 24, 1880. Prof. chemistry and dean Sch. Pharmacy, Purdue U., 1886-1910; now in charge of Prof. Green's State Board Sch. of Pharmacy, Indianapolis. Fellow A.A.A.S. Address: 18 N. Ritter Av., Indianapolis.

GREEN, CHARLES HENRY, inventor, promoter; b. Dayton, O., Oct. 21, 1837; grad. Miami U., 1856; in produce commn. business, New York, 1863-70; organized, 1879, Hektograph Co., mfg. a device for reproducing drawings, writings, etc., pres., 1879—; also pres. Columbia Navigation Commercial Co., Washington City & Point Lookout (Md.) Ry. Co.; dir. other corps.; m. Lilla A. Wightman, 1872. Home: New York, N.Y. Died 1908.

GREEN, DARRELL BENNET, prof. elec. engring.; b. Martinsville, Ill., Feb. 11, 1893; s. Henry Alvarado and Catherine Anne (Bennett) G.; student, Central Normal Coll., 1912-19; A.B., A.M., Ph.D., Ind. Univ., 1921-37; student U. of Wis., 1925, Ohio State, 1931, Ia. Univ., 1929; m. Minnie Jean Lotich, 1917; children—Ursula Kathryn, Nona Jean. Became public sch. teacher, 1912, high sch. teacher, 1916; coll. prof. since 1925. Director of engring. Ohio Univ., 1943-47, chairman electrical engring., 1937-57. Mem. Internat. Illuminating Commn., Zurick, 1955. Licensed professional engineer, Ohio, 1946. Mem. Inst. of Radio Engrs., Am. Inst. E.E. Illuminating Engrs. Soc., Phi Delta Kappa, Sigma Xi. Home: 5 Arden Place, Athens, O. Died Feb. 20, 1959; buried West Union St. Cemetery, Athens.

GREEN, HORACE, laryngologist; b. Chittenden, Vt., Dec. 24, 1802; s. Zeeb and Sarah (Cowee) G.; M.D., Castleton Med. Coll., 1825; m. Mary Butler, Oct. 20, 1829; m. 2d, Harriet Douglas, Oct. 27, 1841; 11 children. First Am. physician to specialize in diseases of the throat; wrote Treatise on Diseases of the Air Passages: Comprising an Inquiry into the History, Pathology Causes and Treatment of those Affectations of the Throat Called Bronchitis, Chronic Laryngetis, Clergyman's Sore Throat (advocated application of local medication in the larynx, created a controversy; this was before invention of laryngscope); prof. medicine and pres. Castleton Med. Coll., 1840-43; a founder N.Y. Med. Coll., 1850, prof. medicine, 1850-60; founded Am. Med. Monthly, 1854; contbr. numerous articles to med. jours. Died Ossining, N.Y., Nov. 29, 1866.

GREEN, JEROME JOSEPH, electrical engr.; b. nr. Somerset, O., Dec. 26, 1865; s. Joshua and Emily (Flowers) G.; M.E., Ohio State U., 1893; studied at U. of Paris and at Technische Hochschule, Berlin, 1907-08; m. Elizabeth Feeney, of Rochester, Minn., June 20, 1899; 1 son, Francis E.; m. 2d, Mabel G. Cortis, of London, Eng., Sept. 3, 1908; children—Winifred D., Jerome J. Did testing of elec. apparatus for bur. of awards, Chicago Expn., 1893; engaged at installation of elec. apparatus, Atlanta Expn., 1895; with Chicago Edison Co. and chief instr. in the Nat. Sch. of Electricity, Chicago, until 1895; prof. physics and elec. engring. U. of Notre Dame, Ind., 1895-1915; head of technical dept. and director of vocational education, Junior College and High School, San Diego, Calif., 1915-20; head sci. dept. Moorpark Memorial Union H.S., 1921—; prof. elec. engring. U. of Southern Calif., 1922-23; science dept., San Diego High School, 1926-27; prof. elec. engring. and dean of faculty, Pacific Technical University, San Diego, since 1927. Designer radio sets; instructor in radio receiving. Conducted experiments in wireless telegraphy, April 1899, first sending signals from one room to another in Science Hall at Notre Dame Univ. with apparatus made up in the laboratories and shops of the instn. The distance was increased, till signals were distinctly received at a distance of half a mile; afterward, with improved apparatus, dots and dashes were sent to St. Mary's Acad., a mile and a half; last trial at Notre Dame was for distance of 3 miles; the signals were received; a series of tests were next made in the down-town dist. of Chicago, where conditions were quite different; also on the lake, where words were sent about a mile and a half. Mem. A.A.A.S., International Elec. Congress, St. Louis, 1904. As supervisor for western dept. K. of C. Welfare Activities, established schs. for ex-service men at Spokane, Salt Lake City, San Diego, and Nogales and Douglas, Ariz., 1920-21. Home: 1028 N. Hudson Av., Pasadena, Calif.

GREEN, ROBERT GLADDING, prof. bacteriology; b. Wadena, Minn., Jan. 11, 1895; s. George Henry and Ella Augusta (Banta) G.; student Valparaiso (Ind.) U., 1914-16; A.B., U. of Minn., 1919, A.M., 1920, M.B., 1921, M.D., 1922; m. Beryl Bertha Sparks, Apr. 7, 1917 (died Apr. 23, 1941). Asst. in bacteriology, U. of Minn., 1918, instr., 1921, asst. prof., 1922-25, asso. prof., 1925-29, became prof. 1929, head dept. of bacteriology, Univ. of Minn. 1946-47. Served in Med. R.C., 1917, Students' Army Training Corps, 1918-19, World War I. Capt. and Med. Officer, Civil Air Patrol, Wing No. 71, Air Corps, Minnesota State Guard, 1942-43. Fellow N.Y. Zoöl. Soc.; mem. A.A.A.S., Soc. Am. Bacteriologists, Am. Assn. Pathologists and Bacteriologists, A.M.A., Society for Exptl. Biology and Medicine, Am. Soc. Mammalogists, Am. Assn. of Immunologists, American Legion, Sigma Xi, Alpha Omega Alpha. Republican. Episcopalian. Mason. Club: Minneapolis Athletic. Author of many scientific publs. and contbr. numerous tech. articles. Home: 3948 1st Av. S. Office: 223 Millard Hall, Dept. of Bacteriology, University of Minnesota, Minneapolis. Died Sept. 6, 1947.

GREEN, SETH, fish culturist; b. Monroe County, N.Y., Mar. 19, 1817; s. Adonijah Green; m. Helen M. Cook, Feb. 14, 1848. Established fish stall in city market, Rochester, N.Y.; began experimenting on artificial hatching of salmon and trout, 1837, resulted in location of trout ponds nr. Caledonia, N.Y., 1864; apptd. to N.Y. State Fish Commn., 1868, later became supt. of fisheries; established hatchery adjacent to his own which had been acquired by the state, 1875; noted for expts. with hatching shad, sturgeon and white fish; contbr. many articles on fish culture to sportsman's periodicals. Author: Trout Culture, 1870. Died Aug. 20, 1888.

GREEN, WALTER LAWRENCE, engr., shipbuilder; b. Bklyn., July 9, 1894; s. Walter Lawrence and Emily (Schnibbe) G.; student Pratt Inst. Tech., 1913; D.Sc., Wagner Coll., 1958; m. Isabel Macilravey, June 27, 1916; children—Doris Elizabeth (Mrs. Fred Searls), Ethel Emily (Mrs. Robert J. Searls); m. 2d, Stella Atchison, Nov. 4, 1940; 1 son, Walter L. With Luckenbach Steamship Co., Inc., N.Y.C. and Seattle, 1914-38, designer, 1914-20, supt. engring., 1920-28, mgr. engring., 1928-38; v.p., gen. mgr. Seattle-Tacoma Shipbldg. Corp. plant, Todd Shipyards Corp., 1939-42, v.p., gen. mgr. New Eng. Shipbldg. Corp. plant, Portland, Me., 1943-47; v.p. Am. Bur. Shipping, N.Y.C., 1938-39, 1947-50, pres., 1950-52, chmn. bd., pres., 1952—. Recipient Admiral Land medal, Society of Naval Architects and Marine Engrs. Mem. Welding Research Council (chmn.), Soc. Naval Architects and Marine Engrs. (v.p., treas.), A.S.M.E., Inst. Marine Engrs. (Brit.), Northeast Coast Inst. Engrs. and Shipbuilders (Brit.). Clubs: India House; Metropolitan; Whitehall (N.Y.C.); Stamford Yacht. Home: Emery Dr., Westover Park, Stamford, Conn. Office: 45 Broad St., N.Y.C. 4. Died Mar. 26, 1962.

GREENBAUM, SIGMUND SAMUEL, dermatologist; b. Philadelphia, Pa., Mar. 17, 1890; s. Joseph and Sarah (Klein) G.; B.S., Central High Sch., Phila., 1909; M.D., Jefferson Med. Coll., 1913; certificate from U. of Paris, faculty of medicine Hosp. St. Louis Clinic of Skin Diseases and Syphilis, 1919; married Rae Refowich, Nov. 30, 1922; children—Charles, Edwin, Carol (dec.), Janet. Practiced Phila. since 1913; professor clinic dermatology and syphilology, University of Pennsylvania; graduate School of Medicine since 1935; attending dermatologist, Philadelphia General Hospital since 1922; dermatologist Graduate Hosp. University of Pennsylvania, Rush Hosp., Phila. Psychiatric Hosp., Med. Adv. Bd. 1 of Pa. Selective Service; lecturer on skin and social diseases, Phila. Occupational Sch. of Therapy; cons. dermatologist, Bamberger Home and Betty Bacharach Home, Atlantic City, N.J., Eagleville Sanitarium, Camden (N.J.) General Hospital; fellow in research, Inst. of Cutaneous Medicine; director Bankers Securities Corporation. Trustee National Farm School. Diplomate Am. Bd. Dermatology and Syphilology. Fellow Am. Acad. Dermatology and Syphilology. Served as capt. Med. Corps, U.S. Army. Mem. A.M.A., West Phila. Med. Assn., Med. Club of Phila., A.A.A.S., Northern Med. Assn. of Phila., Phila. Dermatol. Soc., Phila. Defense Council (venereal disease sub-com.), Med. Soc. State of Pa., Phila. County Med. Soc. (chmn. com. on cutaneous and social diseases), Am. Coll. of Physicians, Phila. Coll. of Physicians, Am. Legion, Phi Delta Epsilon. Author: (with H. Prinz) diseases of the Mouth, 1935; Dermatology in General Practice, 1947. Contbr. to med. jours. Home: 320 S. 18th St., Philadelphia. Died Oct. 3, 1949; buried Roosevelt Cemetery, Philadelphia.

GREENE, ARTHUR MAURICE, JR., mech. engr., educator; b. Phila., Pa., Feb. 4, 1872; s. Arthur Maurice and Eleanor J. (Lowry) G.; B.S., U. of Pa., 1893; M.E., 1894, Sc.D., 1917; D.Eng., Rensselaer Polytech. Inst., 1922; studied in Germany, summers, 1896 and 1905; LL.D., U. of Mo., 1940; m. Mary Elizabeth Lewis, June 12, 1906. In charge of apprentice sch., Franklin Sugar Refinery, Phila., 1892-94; instr., Drexel Inst., 1894-95, U. of Pa., 1895-1902; prof. mech. engring., U. of Mo., 1902-07, and jr. dean Sch. of Engring., 1906-07; prof. mech. engring., Rensselaer Poly. Inst., 1907-22; dean Sch. of Engring., prof. mech. engring., Princeton U., 1922-40, dean emeritus since 1940. Consultant engr. for power plants and mfg.; expert in patent causes; consultant Coordinator of Inter-American Affairs; consultant to chmn. War Production Board, February-June 1942. Expert cons. Army Specialized Training Div., U.S. Army. Member World Power Conferences, 1930 and 1936. Former member Board of Education, Princeton, New Jersey. Member National Research Council (engineering division); chairman power plant committtee United States Fuel Adminstrn. for Rensselaer County, N.Y.; "Four Minute Man"; mem. War Service League of Troy; mem. engring. council, war com. of tech. socs. Trustee Princeton Hosp.; formerly trustee Troy Public Library and v.p. Troy Y.M.C.A. Mem. Govs. Highway Safety Council of N.J.; mem. N.J. State Board of Professional Engrs. and Land Surveyors. Member War Price and Rationing Board, Princeton, N.J.; mem. Belgian American Ednl. Foundation. Fellow A.A.A.S.; life member Am. Ordnance Assn.; honorary mem. Am. Soc. M.E. (former mgr. and v.p.; chmn. research com.; mem. boiler code com.; chmn. com. on awards); member American Society for Engineering Education (pres. 1919-20), Soc. Engrs. Eastern N.Y. (ex-pres.), Am. Engring. Council, Princeton Engring. Assn. (hon.), Newcomen Soc., Guild of Brackett Lectures of Princeton Univ., Kappa Sigma, Sigma Xi, Phi Beta Kappa, Tau Beta Pi, Mu Phi Alpha. Awarded silver medal by Jugo-Slovakian Red Cross Soc. Republican. Baptist. Mason. Clubs: Nassau (Princeton); University (Columbia, Mo., life); Princeton (N.Y.). Author: Elements of Steam Engineering (with H. W. Spangler and S. M. Marshall), 1902; Pumping Machinery, 1911; Elements of Heating and Ventilation, 1912; Heat Engineering, 1914; Elements of Refrigeration, 1916; Elements of Power Generation, 1933; Elements of Hydraulic Power Generation, 1934; Principles of Heating, Ventilating and Air Conditioning, 1936; Principles of Thermodynamics, Part I, 1938, Part II, 1939. Contbr. to Mech. Engineering American Year Books, 1941. Has traveled widely in America and Europe. Home: 19 Maple St., Princeton NJ

GREENE, CHARLES WILSON, univ. prof.; b. Crawford Co., Ind., Aug. 12, 1866; s. William Henry and Mary (Pence) G.; grad. De Pauw U. Normal Sch., 1889; studied De Pauw U., 1889-91; A.B., Stanford U., 1892, A.M., 1893; Ph.D., Johns Hopkins, 1898; m. Flora Hartley, of Yankeetown, Ind., Aug. 7, 1895; children—Carl Hartley, Helen Hartley, Harold Hartley. Began teaching 1886; instr. in geography DePauw Normal Sch. 1880-90, and in physiology, De Pauw Prep. Sch., 1890-91; asst. and instr. physiology, 1891-98, asst. prof., 1898-1900, Stanford U.; prof. physiology and pharmacology, University of Missouri, 1900-36; prof. physiological research, 1936-37; lecturer in physiology, Stanford University, 1939-40; retired as emeritus in physiology, 1936. Mem. jury, Forestry, Fish and Game Division, St. Louis Expn., 1904; carried on physiol. investigations for U.S. Bur. of Fisheries, summers, 1901-17. Student and investigator, Zool. Sta., Naples and U. of Strassburg, 1910. Maj. Sanitary Corps U.S.A., in charge dept. of physiology, Med. Research Lab., Air Service, Hazelhurst Field, November 5, 1918-September 4, 1919; maj. Sanitary Reserve Corps U.S.A., 1919-30. Member exec. com. Union of Am. Biol. socs.; mem. American Physiological Society (secretary 1914-23; president 1933-34), American Society Pharmacology and Therapeutics, Am. Soc. Biol. Chemists, Am. Chem. Soc., Am. Assn. Anatomists, Anesthesia Research Soc., Bot. Soc. America, Indiana Acad., A.M.A., A.A.A.S., Phi Beta Kappa (Johns Hopkins), Sigma Xi, Alpha Kappa Kappa. Club: University. Author: Experimental Pharmacology (3d edit.), 1909; Handbook of Pharmacology, 1914. Editor Kirke's Handbook of Physiology (6th to 10th Am. edit.). Contbr. many scientific research papers in physiology, biology, and preclinical med. sciences. Research in European heart clinics, 1927. Address: 814 Virginia Av., Columbia, Mo.

GREENE, DAVID MAXSON, consulting engr.; b. Brunswick, N.Y., July 8, 1832; s. Joseph Langford and Susanna (Maxson) G.; grad. Rensselaer Polytechnic Inst. (C.E.), 1851; took private course, topog. engring., West Point, 1856; instr. Rensselaer Polytechnic Inst., 1851-52; asst. engr., enlargement Erie Canal, 1852-53; on railroads in Ohio and Ind., 1853-54; prof. geodesy and topog. drawing, Rensselaer Polytechnic Inst., 1855-61, dir. same, 1878-91; in corps of engrs., U.S.N., 1861-69; then in general practice, div. engr. and deputy State engr., New York, 1874-78; col. engrs., Nat. Guard, N.Y., 1872-93. Home: Troy, N.Y. Died 1905.

GREENE, EDWARD LEE, botanist; b. Hopkinton, R.I., Aug. 20, 1843; s. William M. and Abby (Crandall) G.; Ph.B., Albion (Wis.) Coll., 1866; LL.D., U. of Notre Dame, Ind., 1895; unmarried. Was Episcopal clergyman, 1871-85; then R.C. layman; prof. botany, U. of Calif., 1885-95, Catholic U. of America, 1895-1904; asso. in botany, Smithsonian Instn., 1904—. Pres. Internat. Congress of Botanists, Chicago Expn., 1893. Author: Manual of Botany for the region of San Francisco Bay, 1894; West American Oaks, 1887; Flora Franciscana, 1891; Plantae Bakerianae, 1901; Pittonia (5 vols.), 1887-1903; Leaflets of Botanical Observation (2 vols.), 1903-09; Landmarks of Botanical History, 1909. Address: Washington, D.C. Died Nov. 10, 1915.

GREENE, GEORGE SEARS, army officer, engr.; b. Apponaug, R.I., May 6, 1801; s. Caleb and Sarah (Robinson) G.; grad. U.S. Mil. Acad., 1823; m. Elizabeth Vinton, July 14, 1828; m. 2d, Martha Barrett Dana, Feb. 21, 1837; 3 children. Taught mathematics U.S. Mil. Acad., 1823-27; served in various arty. posts throughout New Eng., 1827-36; promoted 1st lt., 1829; became engr. after leaving army; engr. in charge of Croton water-works extension and Croton Reservoir, Central Park, N.Y., at outbreak of Civil War; apptd. col. 60th N.Y. Volunteers, 1862, served at Washington, D.C., 1862, apptd. brig. gen. volunteers serving in Shenandoah Valley; fought in battles of Antietam, Chancellorsville and Gettysburg (where he commanded defense of Culp's Hill); transferred to Tenn., 1863, wounded at Battle of Wauhatchie, 1863; resigned commn., 1866, resumed engring. work, N.Y.C., did notable work in other Eastern cities; planned sewerage system for Washington, extension of water system in Detroit, Troy and Yonker, N.Y.; a founder Am. Soc. C.E., pres., 1875-77; returned to U.S. Army as lt. by spl. act of Congress, placed on retired list, 1894. Died Morristown, N.J., Jan. 28, 1899; buried Warwick, R.I.

GREENE, GEORGE SEARS, JR., civil engr.; b. Lexington, Ky., Nov. 26, 1837; s. Gen. George Sears and Martha (Dana) G.; entered Harvard, 1856, but left before grad. to study civil engring. under father; m. Susan Moody, d. James Dana, Apr. 23, 1862 (died 1881). Asst. engr. on Croton Aqueduct, on various Cuban railroads and Lake Superior copper mines; conducted topog. surveys in 1868; introduced valuable improvements in instruments, some of which were adopted by U.S. Coast Survey. Became engr.-in-chief, dept. of docks, New York, 1875; consulting engr. in New York, 1898; advisory engr. on Barge Canal, N.Y., 1911-14. Home: South Orange, N.J. Died Dec. 23, 1922.

GREENE, HARRY SYLVESTRE NUTTING, pathologist; b. Woonsocket, R.I., Sept. 22, 1904; s. George Wellington and Gertrude (Earl) G.; student Wilbraham (Mass.) Acad., 1917-21; student Brown U., 1921-25; M.D., C.M., McGill U., 1930; A.M. (hon.), Yale, 1943; m. Helen May Davis, Sept. 27, 1930; 1 dau., Judith Ann; m. 2d, Jean Barnes, Dec. 18, 1954; 2 daus., Susan, Melissa. Instr. pathology, Path. Inst., McGill U., 1930-31; asst. in pathology, Rockefeller Inst. for Med. Research, N.Y. City, 1931-35; asso. in pathology, Rockeffer Inst., Princeton, N.J., 1935-41; asso. prof. of pathology and surgery, Yale U. Sch. of Medicine, 1941-43, prof. of pathology, 1943-50, Anthony N. Brady prof. of pathology, 1950-69. Recipient Borden award, 1956. Mem. Am. Assn. Advancement Sci., Am. Assn. Pathologists and Bacteriologists, Am. Genetic Assn., Soc. for Exptl. Biology and Medicine, Soc. for Study of Growth and Development, Am. Assn. for Cancer Research, Harvey Soc. of N.Y., Am. Acad. of Arts and Scis., N.E., Cancer Soc., Sigma Xi, Theta Delta Chi, Alpha Kappa Kappa, Alpha Omega Alpha. Clubs: Interurban Pathological, Faculty, Graduates (Yale). Home: Guilford CT Died Feb. 14, 1969; buried North Smithfield RI

GREENE, JAMES SONNETT, physician; b. N.Y.C., Dec. 25, 1880; s. Jacob J. and Doris (Harrow) G.; M.D., Cornell U., 1902; post grad. studies at Univ. Berlin, Allerheilegen Hosp. (Breslau), Univ. Jena, 1906-12; m. Emilie Josephine Wells, Aug. 27, 1919. Began practice at N.Y.C., 1902; founded Nat. Hosp. for Speech Disorders (devoted solely to diagnosis and treatment of voice and speech disorders), N.Y.C., 1916, and since med. dir.; prof. of speech, Coll. of Dental and Oral Surgery, N.Y.C., 1916-18; lectr. on voice and speech disorders, Grad. Sch. Med., U. Pa. Cons. on speech disorders, N.Y. Eye and Ear Infirm., Meml. Hosp., N.Y.C. Awarded spl. gold medal by Am. Laryngol., Rhinol. and Otol. Soc., 1940. Fellow N.Y. Acad. Medicine; mem. Med. Soc. Co. of N.Y., A.M.A., Am. Acad. Ophthalmology and Otolaryngology, Am. Laryngol., Rhinol. and Otol. Soc., Am. Group Therapy Assn., A.A.A.S.; sustaining mem. Nat. Assn. Teachers Speech; mem. Am. Soc. for Research in Psychosomatic problems. Clubs: Cornell Lotos (N.Y.). Author: The Cause and Cure of Speech Disorders (with E.J. Wells), 1927; I was A Stutterer, 1932; Straight Talk (essays) 1948, also many monographs on speech and voice disorders. Editor of Talk (published by National Hospital for Speech Disorders); asso. editor of Better English in Speech and Writing. Contbg. editor to Year Book of the Eye, Ear, Nose and Throat, 1938. Contbr. to med. jours. Address: 61 Irving Place, N.Y.C. Died Sept. 17, 1950.

GREENE, SAMUEL STILLMAN, educator; b. Belchertown, Mass., May 3, 1810; s. Ebenezer and Sybil (Hitchcock) G.; grad. Brown U., 1837; m. Edna Amelia Bartlett, Aug. 29, 1839; m. 2d, Mary Adeline Bailey, Aug. 10, 1854. Taught at Worcester (Mass.) Acad., 1837-40, public schs., Boston, 1842-49; apptd. supt. public schs., Springfield, Mass., 1840-42; agt. Mass. Bd. Edn. (1st office of its kind in U.S.), 1849-51; supt. schs., Providence, R.I., 1851; prof. didactics Brown U., 1851, prof. mathematics and civil engring., 1855, prof. natural philosophy and astronomy, 1864-75, prof. mathematics and astronomy, 1875; opened pvt. normal sch., Providence, 1852, later taken over by state, now R.I. Coll. Edn.; pres. Nat. Tchrs. Assn., 1856-60, Am. Inst. Instrn., 1864-65, 69-70. Author: Greene's Analysis: A Treatise on the Structure of the English Language, 1848; The Elements of English Grammar, 1853; An Introduction to the Study of English Grammar, 1868. Died Jan. 24, 1883.

GREENHOW, ROBERT, physician, linguist, historian; b. Richmond, Va., 1800; s. Robert and Mary Ann (Wills) G.; grad. Coll. William and Mary, 1816; studied medicine under John W. Francis, N.Y.C.; M.D., Coll. Physicians and Surgeons, N.Y.C., 1821; m. Rose O'Neil, 4 children. Went to Europe, 1821-25; practiced medicine, N.Y.C., 1825-28; lectr. chemistry to a N.Y. literary and scientific soc.; translator Dept. of State, Washington, 1828-50; moved to Cal., 1850; with law office U.S. Land Commn. in Cal., 1852-54; used original sources such as jours. of explorers in Spanish, English, French, in addition to literary and hist. works, did all translating himself. Author: The History and Present Condition of Tripoli, 1835; The History of Oregon and California, 1844, English edit., 1844 (written at request of Senator Lewis F. Linn, head Congressional com. on Am. claims to Ore. Territory, 1839). Died San Francisco, Mar. 27, 1854.

GREENLEAF, BENJAMIN, educator; b. Haverhill, Mass., Sept. 25, 1786; s. Caleb and Susanna (Emerson) G.; grad. Dartmouth, 1813; m. Lucretia Kimball, Nov. 20, 1821, 9 children. Taught sch., 1805-10; prin. grammar sch., Haverhill, 1813; preceptor Bradford (Mass.) Acad., 1814-36; mem. Mass. Legislature, 1837-39, advocated normal schs., chmn. com. which recommended geol. and natural history surveys of state which were later made; founded, became head Bradford Tchrs. Sem., 1839-48; spent last years in making calculations for almanacs and in gen. activities on behalf of edn. Died Oct. 29, 1864.

GREENLEAF, MOSES, cartographer; b. Newburyport, Mass., Oct. 17, 1777; s. Moses and Lydia (Parsons) G.; m. Persis Poor, Feb. 11, 1805. Kept gen. store, New Gloucester, Bangor, Me., 1799-1806; entered into real estate partnership with William Dood of Boston; helped settle what is now Williamsburg (Me.); spent rest of his life in furthering settlement interior of Me.; surveyed roads, located stone and mineral deposits, secured charter for Picataquis Canal and R.R. Co., 1833, provided valuable information to miners, purchasers and legislators through his publications and maps. Author: Map of the District of Maine from the Latest and Best Authorities, 1815. Died Mar. 20, 1834.

GREENMAN, JESSE MORE, botanist; b. North East, Pa., Dec. 27, 1867; s. James William and Clarissa (More) G.; B.S., U. Pa., 1893; M.S., Harvard, 1899; Ph.D., U. Berlin, 1901; m. Anne Louise Turner, Sept. 20, 1902; children—Jesse More, Milton Turner. Asst. in botany, 1890-92, instr., 1893-94, U. of Pa., asst. Gray Herbarium, Harvard, 1894-99; Kirkland fellow from Harvard at U. Berlin, 1899-1901; asst. Gray Herbarium; instr. Harvard, 1902-05; asst. curator botany, Field Museum, Chgo., 1905-13; asst. prof. bot., U. Chgo., 1908-13; asso. prof. bot., 1913-16, prof., 1917-45, prof. emeritus 1945—; in charge grad. Henry Shaw Sch. Botany, 1927, Washington U.; emeritus curator herbarium, Mo. Bot. Garden, 1948—. Editor taxonomy vascular plants, Bot. Abstracts, 1917-27. Hon. chmn. U. of Pa. Bicentennial Com. St. Louis Dist. Fellow A.A.A.S. (chmn. sect. G 1936-37); mem. Bot. Soc. Am., Ecol. Soc. America, Am. Soc. Naturalists, N.E. Bot. Club, Germanistic Soc. St. Louis, Am. Assn. University Professors, New York Academy of Science, St. Louis Acad. Sci., Ill. Acad. Science, Sigma Xi, Phi Beta Kappa (pres. Washington U. chapter 1936-37), Phi Sigma, Sigma Alpha Epsilon; corr. mem. Phila. Acad. Natural Sciences. Democrat. Presbyn. Clubs: University, Harvard (St. Louis); Faculty (Washinton U.). Contbr. numerous articles on flora of N. America and Mexico, also monograph on Genus Senecio. Home: 4129 Magnolia Av. Address: Missouri Botanical Garden, St. Louis, Mo. Died Jan. 20, 1951; buried West Laurel Hill Cemetery, Bala-Cynwyd, Pa.

GREENOUGH, GEORGE GORDON, army officer; b. Washington, Dec. 8, 1844; s. John James and Mary Frances Ascough (Cushing) G.; ed. pvt. and pub. schs. to 1857, Paris, France, 1857-60, pvt. sch., Baltimore, 1860-61; grad. U.S. Mil. Acad., 1865; unmarried. Commd. 2d lt. and 1st lt. 12th Inf., June 23, 1865; transferred to 21st Infantry; Sept. 21, 1866; assigned to 4th Arty., Dec. 15, 1870; grad. Arty. Sch., 1882; capt., Dec. 1, 1883; maj. 7th Arty., Mar. 8, 1898; lt. col. Arty. Corps, July 1, 1901; col., Feb. 21, 1903; brig. gen. and retired, Dec. 8, 1908. Instr. asst. prof. and acting prof. of French, U.S. Mil. Acad., 1868-73; served in 3d Army Corps, 1863; in Modoc Indian campaign, 1873; Nev. expdn., 1875, and in Powder River expdn., 1876-77; mil. instr. U. of Calif., 1877-78; was one of the pioneers in range-finding work, 1882-98; sharp shooter for 5 yrs.; comd. arty. defenses of Washington, 1898; served in Cuba, 1898-99, and in P.I., 1900-02. Inventor of various devices for arty. operations. Died June 27, 1912.

GREENSFELDER, ALBERT PRESTON, constrn. engr.; b. St. Louis, Mo., July 6, 1879; s. M. B. and Carrie G.; B.S. in C.E., Washington U., St. Louis, 1901; m. Blanche Younker, Jan. 24, 1909. Engr. on constrn. Kan. Interurban Ry., 1901-02; asst. engr. with Terminal R.R. Assn., St. Louis, 1902-05; constrn. supt., 1906, sec. Fruin Colnon Contracting Co., 1908-27, pres. 1927-40, chmn.. 1940-50. cons. constructor, 1950; dir. Mercantile Trust Co., Mo. Portland Cement Co. Past chmn. Univ. City Planning Commn.; past mem. Nat. Capital Planning Commn.; pilot Miss. River Parkway Planning Commn. former vice chairman Mo. Conservation Commn. and dir. City of St. Louis and U.S. chambers of commerce. Hon. chmn. Cons. Constructors Council of A.; dir. Asso. Gen. Contractors of America (ex-pres.); mem. Business Advisory Council of Dept. of Commerce; hon. mem. A.S. Civil Engrs., Engrs. Club at St. Louis. Mason. Clubs: University, Engineers (ex-pres.), Circle, Mo. Athletic (St. Louis); Engineers (N.Y.C); Cosmos (Washington); Westwood Country. Home: 7041 Lindell Av., St. Louis, 5. Office: 1706 Olive St., St. Louis 3. Died Apr. 11, 1955.

GREENSTEIN, JESSE P(HILIP), biochem. research; b. N.Y.C., June 20, 1902; s. Louis and Lena (Birnbaum) G.; B.S., Polytech. Inst. Bklyn., 1926; Ph.D., Brown U., 1930; m. Lucy Louise Mitchell, May 19, 1933; children—Louise (Mrs. Warren Brill), Michael Efrem. NRC fellow Harvard, 1930-31. instr., 1933-39; NRC fellow Kaiser Wilhelm Inst., Dresden, Germany, 1931-32; instr. U. Cal., 1932-33, vis. prof., 1948; chief biochemist National Cancer Inst., Nat. Insts. of Health, Bethesda, Md., 1939—, chief biochemistry lab., 1945—. Mem. com. sci. advisors Inst. Microbiology, Rutgers U., 1958-59; mem. Am. delegation Cancer Colloquium, Rome, 1949. Recipient Neuberg medal in biochemistry, 1950; Distinguished Service award U.S. Dept. Health, Edn. and Welfare, 1954; Hillebrand prize from Wash. chpt. Am. Chem. Soc., 1957. Hon. mem. Japanese Found. for Cancer Research, Japanese Biochemical Society; member American Chem. Society (chmn. div. biol. chemistry), Am. Soc. Biol. Chemistry, Am. Assn. Cancer Research, Nat. Research Council (mem. com. biochemistry, 1957-59, chmn. sub-com. on amino acids). Author: Biochemistry of Cancer, 2d edit. 1954. Editor Cancer Research Advances in Cancer Research, Archives of Biochemistry; co-author: Chemistry of the Amino Acids, 1960. Home: 1606 Highland Dr., Silver Spring, Md. Office: Nat. Cancer Inst., Bethesda, Md. Died Feb. 12, 1959; buried King David Meml. Garden, Falls Church, Va.

GREENWAY, JOHN CAMPBELL, mining engr.; b. Huntsville, Ala., July 6, 1872; s. Gilbert Christian and Alice (White) G.; student U. of Va.; Ph.B., Yale U., 1895 (pres. of class); LL.D., U. of Ariz.; unmarried. Began as helper, Duquesne (Pa.) furnaces, Carnegie Steel Co., 1895; pvt. U.S. Volunteer Cavalry (Roosevelt's Rough Riders), Spanish-Am. War, 1898; commd. 2d lt. and promoted 1st lt. "for gallantry in action," at Battle of San Juan Hill; recommended to Congress by Col. Roosevelt for bvt. of capt. Asst. supt. mines of U.S. Steel Corp., Ishpeming, Mich., 1899-1906; gen. supt. Oliver Mining Co., Mesaba Range, Minn., 1906-10; gen. mgr. Calumet & Ariz. Mining Co.; gen. mgr. New Cornelia Copper Co., Tucson, Cornelia & Gila Bend Ry. (v.p.). Commd. maj. engrs. 1st and 26th divs., A.E.F., France; lt. col. 101st Inf., 26th Div.; in action on Cantigny, Chateau Thierry, St. Mihiel, Argonne and Meuse fronts; awarded D.S.C. (U.S.), Croix de Guerre with two Palms, Order Legion of Honor and Croix de l'Etoile Noire (France). Mem. bd. regents U. of Ariz.; chmn. defense com. Council of Defense of Ariz. Episcopalian. Address: Warren, Ariz. Died Jan. 19, 1926.

GREENWOOD, ALLEN, surgeon; b. Chelsea, Mass., Mar. 1, 1866; s. William Allen and Caroline (Carleton) G.; M.D., Harvard, 1889; house officer, Boston City Hosp., 1888-90; m. Bertha Underhill, June 23, 1892 (dec.); m. 2d, Hope Whipple, Mar. 8, 1917 (dec.); children—Allen, Carolyn; m. 3d, Marion Tucker, Aug. 16, 1924; 1 dau., Grace Tucker. Instructor Waltham Training Sch., 1890-1901; bacteriologist, Waltham Bd. of Health, 1894-98; asst. instructor in ophthalmology, Harvard Med. Sch., 1904-05; ophthalmic surgeon to the Boston City Hosp., 1901-18, since consulting ophthalmologist; visiting surgeon, 1895-1900, visiting ophthalmic and aural surgeon since 1900, Waltham Hospital; now cons. ophthalmic surgeon, Mass. Eye and Ear Infirmary, Beth Israel Hosp. (Boston); Union Hosp. (Framingham), Milford Hosp., lecturer in ophthalmology, Harvard Graduate Sch. of Medicine; prof. emeritus ophthalmology, Tufts Med. Sch. Apptd. acting asst. surgeon U.S. Army, Aug. 22, 1898, and assigned to 19th U.S. Inf., Ponce, P.R.; hon. disch., Oct. 19, 1898; hon. lt. col. Royal Army Med. Corps, with B.E.F. in France, summer 1916; mem. sub-com. on ophthalmology Gen. Med. Bd. of Council Nat. Defense, Apr. 26, 1917; commd. maj. Med. R.C., 1917, and on duty surgeon gen.'s office, Washington; lt. col. Med. Corps, sr. consultant in ophthalmology for A.E.F., 1918; col. Med. R.C. U.S. Army, 1919. Mem. A.M.A. (chmn. ophthal. sect.), Mass. Med. Soc., Am. Ophthalmology Society (president), American Academy Ophthalmology and Oto-Laryngology (president 1918), New England Ophthalmology Society (president 1913), Waltham Med. Club, Waltham Edn. Soc. (pres. 1904-05), etc. Club: Harvard. Home: 84 Commonwealth Av. Office: 82 Commonwealth Av., Boston, Mass. Died Oct. 24, 1942.

GREENWOOD, ISAAC, mathematician; b. Boston, May 11, 1702; s. Samuel and Elizabeth (Bronsdon) G.; grad. Harvard, 1721; m. Sarah Clarke, July 31, 1729, 5 children. Influenced by lectures on exptl. philosophy John T. Pesaguliers while in London (Eng.); prof. mathematics Harvard, 1728-38. Author: Experimental Course on Mechanical Philosophy, 1726; Arithmetic, Vulgar and Decimal: with the Application Thereof to a Variety of Cases in Trade and Commerce (1st textbook of its kind by an American), 1729. Died Charlestown, Mass., Oct. 12, 1745.

GREENWOOD, JOHN, dentist; b. Boston, May 17, 1760; s. Isaac and Mary (I'ans) G.; m. Elizabeth Weaver, Mar. 22, 1788. Apprenticed to a cabinetmaker; served as rifleman and scout during Revolutionary War; became dentist, N.Y.C., 1785; credited with originating foot-power drill, also springs which held plates of false teeth in position, and use of porcelain in manufacture of false teeth; George Washington was one of his patients, (found Greenwood to be most satisfactory of his numerous dentists). Died N.Y.C., Nov. 16, 1819.

GREENWOOD, MILES, ironmaster; b. Jersey City, N.J., Mar. 19, 1807; s. Miles Greenwood; m. Miss Mills, 1832; m. 2d, Phoebe Hopson, 1836. Moved with family to Ind., 1825; in charge of a foundry under exptl. colony led by Robert Owen, New Harmony, Ind., 1828; established (with Joseph Webb) Eagle Iron Works, Cincinnati (became largest iron-mfg. concern in old West), 1832; mem. Cincinnati City Council, 1840; built 1st steam fire engine in U.S. for use by Cincinnati Volunteer Fire Dept.; an organizer 1st paid fire dept. in Cincinnati, 1853; manufactured 1st steam engine in U.S., put in use, 1852; his factories were burned 3 times by So. sympathizers during Civil War; dir. Cincinnati So. Ry., pres. bd., 1869. Died Cincinnati, Nov. 5, 1885.

GREGERSEN, MAGNUS INGSTRUP, prof. of physiology; b. Kimballton, Ia., Jan. 27, 1903; s. Rev. Jens Moller and Sofie (Madsen) G.; A.B., Stanford U., 1923; A.M., 1924; student Mass. Inst. Tech., 1925-26; Ph.D. in Physiology (division medical sciences), Harvard, 1930; m. Charlotte Kennedy, May 30, 1931 (divorced); children—Kirsten, Sofia, Charlotta; m. 2d Georgiane Schenck, Nov. 27, 1948; son, Peter. Austin teaching fellow in physiology, Harvard Med. Sch., 1925-27; instr. physiology, 1927-35; professor physiology, University of Maryland Med. Sch., 1935-37, head dept., 1935-37; prof. physiology and exec. officer dept., Coll. Phys. and Surg., Columbia, 1937-61, Dalton prof. physiology, 1945-69; pres. Am. Bureau Medical Aid to China, 1947-56, (honorary president, 1956-69); medical teaching mission, Poland, 1946, China, 1948; special consultant E.C.A., Taiwan, 1951; trustee China Internat. Found., 1952, pres., 1954-69; chmn. bd. Ingalls-Taiwan Shipbuilding & Drydock Co., 1956-62; vice chmn. Am. Emergency Com. for Tibetan Refugees; exec. com. Aid to Refugee Chinese Intellectuals; nat. adv. council Thomas A. Dooley Found.; trustee Mannes College of Music. Member subcomittee on shock, Division Medical Scis. of the Nat. Research Council, World War II. Recipient Special Cravat of the Order of Brilliant Star, Republic of China, 1956. Fellow New York Academy of Sciences, asso. fellow New York Acad. Med., mem. Am. Physiological Society, A.A.A.S., Soc. Exptl. Biology and Medicine, Soc. Rheology, Harvey Soc., Phi Beta Kappa, Sigma Xi. Clubs: 14 W. Hamilton Street (Balt.); Englewood, Englewood Field; University (N.Y.C.). Home: Englewood NJ Died Aug. 26, 1969; buried Solvang CA

GREGG, ALAN, physician; b. Colorado Springs, Colo., July 11, 1890; s. James Bartlett and Mary (Needham) G.; prep. edn., Cutler Acad., Colorado Springs; A.B., Harvard, 1911; M.D., Harvard Med. Sch., 1916; m. Eleanor Agnes Barrows, July 2, 1923; children—Peter Alan, Nancy Barrows, Richard Alexander, Michael Barrows. Interne, Mass. Gen. Hosp., Boston, 1916-17; served with Royal Army Med. Corps. B.E.F., 1917-19; field staff mem. internat. health bd. Rockefeller Foundation, 1919-22, asso. dir. div. med. edn., 1922-28, asso. dir. med. sciences, 1929-30, dir. med. sciences, 1930-51, vice pres., 1951-56. Decorated Chevalier Legion d'Honneur, 1951; recipient Lasker award Am. Pub. Health Assn., 1957. Fellow A.A.A.S., Am. Acad. Arts and Scis., N.Y. Acad. Medicine, American Coll. Surgeons; hon. member Alpha Omega Alpha, American Association Physicians; mem. Am. Philosophical Society, Phi Beta Kappa (1936). Club: Century (N.Y.C.); Cosmos (Washington). Home: Big Sur, Cal. Died June 9, 1957; buried Westwood Cemetery, Oberlin, O.

GREGG, JOHN B., physician; b. Gladbrook, Ia., Sept. 28, 1888; s. Daniel and Lillie A. (Sharp) G.; A.B., State U. of Ia., 1915, M.D., 1915, M.S., 1916; m. A. Elida Bailey, Aug. 10, 1921; children—John Bailey, Charles Dan, Mary Elida, Elizabeth Ann, Margaret Jane. Sr. clinical assistant oto-laryngology; State University of Ia., 1915-17; maj. Medical Reserve Corps, U.S. Army, assigned to British Royal Army Medical Corps, 1917-19; asso. prof. oto-laryngology, State U. of Ia., 1919-20; private practice, specializing in oto-laryngology, Sioux Falls, S.D., since 1920. Fellow Am. Coll. Surgeons; mem. A.M.A., S.D. State Med. Soc., Am. Acad. Ophthalmology and Otolaryngology, Am. Laryngol., Rhinol. and Otol. Soc., Newcomen Soc. of England, Alpha Omega Alpha, Sigma Xi, Phi Rho Sigma. Decorated British Mil. Cross, 1918. Republican. Episcopalian. Mason (Shriner). Club: Minnehaha Country. Home: 309 N. Duluth Av. Office: Security Nat. Bank Bldg., Sioux Falls, S.D. Died Mar. 3, 1954; buried Woodlawn Cemetery, Sioux Falls, S.D.

GREGG, WILLIS RAY, meteorologist; b. Phoenix, N.Y., Jan. 4, 1880; s. Willis Perry and Jennie E. (Ray) G.; A.B., Cornell U., 1903; Sc.D., Norwich U., 1937; m. Mary Chamberlayne Wall, Oct. 15, 1914; 1 dau., Ruth Marguerite. With U.S. Weather Bur., 1904—; at Mt. Weather Obs., Va., 1907-14, Washington, D.C., 1915—; in charge Aerological Div. of Weather Bur., 1917-34; chief of U.S. Weather Bureau, 1934—; spl. meteorol. adviser trans-Atlantic flight for NC seaplanes (U.S.N.) at Trepassey, Newfoundland, May 1919, and for British dirigible R34, at Mineola, N.Y., July 1919, engaged in organizing weather service for commercial airways activities, 1926—. Mem. Nat. Advisory Com. for Aeronautics (chmn. exec. com. and of subcom. on meteorol. problems), Internat. Meteorol. Orgn., Internat. Meteorol. Com. (pres. commn. on projections of meteorol. maps), Daniel Guggenheim Com. on Aeronautical Meteorology, Interdepartmental Com. on Co-ordination of Meteorol. Service for Aeronautics, etc. Fellow Am. Meterol. Soc. (treas. 1923-35). Mason (Past Master). Co-Author: Introductory Meteorology, 1918; Meteorology, 1931. Author: Aeronautical Meteorology, 1925, 2d edit., 1930; Aerological Survey of the United States (monograph), 1922 and 1926. Home: Takoma Park, Md. Died Sept. 14, 1938.

GREGORY, HERBERT E(RNEST), geologist, educator; b. Middleville, Mich., Oct. 15, 1869; s. George Albert and Anne (Bross) G.; A.B., Yale, 1896, Ph.D., 1899; D.Sc. hon., Doane Coll., 1934; m. Edna Earle Hope, June 30, 1908; 1 dau., Anne Cutts (Mrs. John L. Scarlett). Asst. in botany Yale, 1896-98, instr. phys. geography, 1899-01, asst. prof. physiography, 1901-04, Silliman prof. geology, 1904-36, emeritus since 1936; asst. geologist U.S. Geol. Survey, 1900-09, geologist, 1909-48; supt. Conn. Geol. and Natural History Survey, 1916-20; acting dir. Bernice P. Bishop Museum, Honolulu, T.H., 1919-20, dir., 1920-36. emeritus dir. since 1936; chmn. bd. regents U. Hawaii, 1937-42; organized 1st Pacific Sci. Congress, 1920; del. European sci. congresses, 1948, 1950. Mem. bd. water supply, Honolulu, 1928-36. Trustee Palama Settlement, Honolulu, 1934-42. Served as maj., supervisor sci., com. edn. and special training War Dept., 1918. Fellow Geol. Soc. Am., Assn. Am. Geographers, Am. Acad. Arts and Scis., Washington Acad. Sci., Am. Philos. Soc.; mem. Nat. Research Council. Author geol. articles profl. jours. Asso. editor Am. Jour. Sci., 1904-28. Home: 3066 Wailani Rd. Office: Bishop Museum, Honolulu 17, Hawaii. Died Jan. 23, 1952; buried Honolulu, Hawaii.

GREGORY, LUTHER ELWOOD, b. Newark, Jan. 9, 1872; s. A. Belknap and Susan (Montrose) G.; C.E., Sch. of Mines, Columbia, 1893; hon. D.Eng., Rensselaer Polytechnic Inst., 1938; m. Anna R. Roome, Dec. 26, 1894 (dec. Feb. 1904); 5 daughters; m. 2d, Pauline E. Turner, Nov. 12, 1918 (dec. Jan. 1936); one son; m. 3d, Ethel B. Nelson, June 20, 1947. Became civil engineer, U.S. Navy, 1898; served as public works officer at U.S. naval stas.; mem. Alaskan Coal Commn., 1919; chief of Bur. Yards and Docks, Navy Dept., 1922-29; mem. bd. location San Francisco-Oakland bridge; cons. engr. Lake Washington pontoon bridge, Seattle, foundations and piers of Puget Sound Bridge, Tacoma; ret. as rear admiral. Chmn., Wash. Liquor Control Bd., 1934-42, 1945-49. Mem. Am. Soc. C. E., Soc. Am. Mil Engrs. (trustee, dir.), Mil. Order of World War (comdr. Seattle chapter), Beta Theta Pi. Mason (33 deg., K.T., Shriner). Clubs: Army and Navy, National Sojourners, Rainier and Washington Athletic of Seattle. Home: 310 W. Prospect St., Seattle. Died Nov. 14, 1960.

GREGORY, WILLIAM BENJAMIN, engineer; b. Penn Yan, N.Y., Mar. 13, 1871; s. Ezra Eugene and Mary Elizabeth (Bush) G.; grad. Penn Yan Acad., 1890; M.E., Cornell, 1894, post-grad. work, 1907-08, master mech. engring., 1908; m. Selina Elizabeth Bres, June 21, 1898; children—Elizabeth (Mrs. Henry S. Ferris, now deceased), William Bres, Angela. Instructor drawing, Tulane University, 1894-97, asst. prof. exptl. engring., 1897-1902, asso. prof., 1902-05, prof. 1905-38, prof. emeritus experimental engineering and hydraulics since 1938. Irrigation engr., U.S. Dept. Agriculture; summer vacations devoted largely to the latter work and to drainage work (specialty rice irrigation) since 1902; cons. engineer Mississippi River Commn., in tests of hydraulic dredges, 1903; cons. engr. to U.S. Army Engineers in hydraulic tests, Bonnet Carré Spillway, 1928-29. Pres. New Orleans Acad. Sciences, 1914. Awarded Warner medal by Am. Soc. M.E., 1940 for distinguished work in hydraulic engineering. Major engrs., U.S.R.; service with A.E.F. in France, Oct. 1917-Jan. 1919; col. (inactive), U.S. Engrs. Res. Corps. Decorated Order of Purple Heart and awarded citation.

Mem. Engring. Com., "Safe River," New Orleans. Mem. adv. com. Nat. Hydraulic Lab. Fellow Am. Soc. M.E. (council 1916-19; v.p. 1920-21); mem. Am. Soc. C.E. (life), La. Engring. Soc. (pres. 1910; hon. life mem.). New Orleans Acad. Sciences (past pres., hon. mem.); Am. Soc. for Testing Materials, Sigma Xi (pres. Tulane chapter), Tau Beta Pi; formerly mem. Soc. des Ingenieurs Civils de France. Unitarian. Club: Round Table (hon. 1942). Contbr. to trans. engring. socs. and bulls. on engring. Inventor Tulane Pitot Tube used to measure flow of water. Home: 630 Pine St., New Orleans. Died Jan. 29, 1945; buried in Cypress Grove Cemetery, New Orleans.

GREGORY, WILLIAM K(ING), palentologist, morphologist; b. N.Y.C., May 19, 18976; s. George and Jane (King) G.; student Sch. of Mines, Columbia, 1894-96; A.B., Columbia, 1900, A.M., 1905; Ph.D., 1910; D.Sc., Witwatersrand, 1938; m. Laura Grace Foote, Dec. 4, 1899; m. 2d, Angela DuBois, 1938. Research asst. to Henry Fairfield Osborn, 1899-1913; asst. curator dept. vertebrate paleontology Am. Museum Natural History, 1911-14, asso. in paneontology, 1914-26, curator department comparative anatomy, 1921-44, emeritus, 1944-70, curator dept. ichthyology, 1925-44, emeritus, 1944-70; lecturer, asst. and asso. prof., prof. vertebrate paleontol., Da Costa prof., Columbia, 1943-45, emeritus, 1945-70. Fellow N.Y. Acad. Sciences (pres. 1932-33), N.Y. Zool. Soc., A.A.A.S. (v.p. sect. H, 1931); mem. Am. Soc. Naturalists (v.p. 1936). Am. Assn. Anatomists, Geol. Soc. America, Paleontol. Soc. America, Am. Soc. Mammalogists, Am. Philos. Society, Nat. Acad. Sciences, Am. Acad. Arts and Sciences, Am. Assn. Physical Anthropology (pres. 1941-42), Am. Soc. Ichthyology and Herpetology (pres. 1936-38); fgn. fellow London Zool. Soc.; fgn. fellow Geol. Soc. London, Linnean Society London, Royal Soc. of Queensland, Royal Soc. Science of Upsala, State Russian Paleontological Soc. of Leningrad, Acad. Hon., Museo de la Plata. Clubs: Explorers, Boone and Crockett, Faculty of Columbia Univ. Author: The Orders of Mammals, 1910; On the Structure and Relations of Notharctus, an American Eocene Primate, 1920; The Origin and Evolution of the Human Dentition, 1922; Our Face from Fish to Man, 1929; Fish Skulls—A Study of the Evolution of Natural Mechanisns, 1933; A Half Century of Trituberculy—The Cope-Osborn Theory of Dental Evolution, 1934; In Quest of Gorillas, 1937; Studies on the Origin and Early Evolution of Paired Fins and Limbs, Parts I-IV (with H.C. Raven) 1941; The Monotromes and the Palimpest Theory, 1947; Evolution Emerging also numerous revs. and tech. papers. Home: Kingston NY Died Dec. 1970.

GREHAN, BERNARD H(ENRY), civil engr.; b. New Orleans, Sept. 4, 1893; s. Bernard and Caroline (Simon) G.; B.C.E., Tulane Univ., 1915, C.E., 1923; m. Marie Louise LeMore, Aug. 25, 1917; children—Gloria Marie (Mrs. William C. Ellis), Bernard Albert, Patricia Ann (Mrs. J. W. Pou), Marie Le More (Mrs. Luther E. Hall III). With U.S. Engrs., in charge of hydrog. and topographic surveys, 1915-16; asso. with J. F. Coleman, cons. engrs., 1916-17; in gen. contracting bus., constrn. of bldgs. and foundations with George J. Glover Co., Inc., 1919—, v.p. and dir., 1925-47; asso. with Boh Bros. Construction Co., 1949—. Mem. La. State Bd. of Engring. Examiners, mem. bd. of adminstrs., Louise S. McGehee Sch. for Girls, 1941-49, Tulane U., 1949—, v.p. 1951. Served as 1st lt. U.S. Engrs. Corps, 1917-19; A.E.F., 1918-19. Mem. Am. Soc. Civil Engrs. (pres., La. sect., 1928), La. Engring. Soc. (pres. 1938), Asso. Gen. Contractors of Am. (pres., New Orleans chapter, 1946-47), Tau Beta Pi, Phi Kappa Sigma. Roman Catholic. Clubs: Louisiana, Recess, Boston (New Orleans). Home: 1670 Soniat St., New Orleans 15. Office: 2400 Cypress St., New Orleans 19. Died Dec. 15, 1952.

GREINER, JOHN E., (grin'er), consulting engr.; b. Wilmington, Del., Feb. 24, 1859; s. John and Annie (Steck) G.; B.S., Delaware Coll., 1880, later C.E., Sc.D.; Dr. Engring., Johns Hopkins U., 1937; m. Lily F. Burchell, Dec. 16, 1886; children—Lillian Burchell, Gladys Houston. Practiced, Baltimore, since 1908; has served as cons. engr. B.&O. R.R., Erie R.R., Norfolk&Southern R.R., State of Pa., State of Md., etc.; designed and built nine bridges across the Ohio River and many others east of the Mississippi River; also railroad ocean terminals, dams and highways; now mem. J. E. Greiner Co., consulting engrs. Mem. Am. Ry. Commn. to Russia, 5 months, 1917. Chmn. Port Development Commn., authorized to expend $50,000,000 in improving the port of Baltimore. Mem. Am. Inst. Consulting Engrs., Am. Soc. Testing Materials, Am. Ry. Engring. Assn. (chmn. com. which adopted specifications for iron and steel structures); hon. mem. Am. Soc. C.E. Clubs: University, Elkridge Fox Hunting. Home: Ruxton, Md. Office: 1201 St. Paul St., Baltimore, Md. Died Nov. 15, 1942.

GRESS, ERNEST MILTON, botanist; b. Fulton County, Pa., Aug. 1, 1876; s. George B. and Rebecca (De Shong) G.; M.E., Shippensburg (Pa.) Normal Sch., 1896; Ph.B., Bucknell U., Lewisburg, Pa., 1907; M.A., U. of Pittsburgh, 1912, Ph.D., 1920; m. Nora Booth Gress, May 16, 1901; children—LaRue Ernestine (Mrs. George Lehman), Margaret Rebecca (Mrs. Thomas R. Tatnall), Dorothy Evelyn (Mrs. Russel Dougherty). Teacher pub. and high schs., Pa., 1893-1920; state botanist of Pa. since 1920. Mem. Bot. Soc. America, A.A.A.S., Pa. Acad. Science. Methodist. Mason. Author: Grasses of Pennsylvania, 1924; Common Wild Flowers of Pennsylvania, 1928; Poisonous Plants of Pennsylvania, 1934; also bulls. and mag. articles. Home: Camp Hill, Pa. Address: 2000 Hight St., Camp Hill PA

GREW, THEOPHILUS, mathematician; M.A. (hon.), Coll. and Acad. of Phila., 1757; m. Elizabeth Cosins, 1735; m. 2d, Frances Bowen, 1739; m. 3d, Rebecca Richards, 1747. Published widely circulated almanacs in N.Y.C., Phila., Annapolis, Md., Williamsburg, Va., 1732-57; headmaster Kent County (Md.) Pub. Sch., 1740-42; conducted pvt. sch. for study of mathematics, Phila., 1742-50; cons. for Pa. in survey to determine boundary between Pa. and Md., 1750; apptd. 1st prof. mathematics Coll. and Acad. of Phila., 1750. Died Phila., 1759.

GRICE, DAVID STEPHEN, orthopedic surgeon; b. Chgo., July 9, 1914; s. John and Margaret (Frey) G.; A.B., U. Rochester, 1935, M.D., 1938; m. Mary Burns, Mar. 30, 1940; children—Patricia Ann, Martha Mary, Constance. Intern surgery Strong Meml. Hosp., 1938-40, asst. resident surgery, 1940-41; asst. resident orthopedic surgery Children's Hosp., Boston, 1941-43, resident orthopedic surgery, 1943-44, orthopedic surgeon, 1949-58; asst. resident orthopedic surgery Mass. Gen. Hosp., Boston, 1941-43; asso. dir. Mass. Infantile Paralysis Clinics, 1944-58; lectr. anatomy, orthopedic surgery Simmons Coll., 1948-51; asst. clin. prof. orthopedic surgery Harvard Med. Sch., 1954-58; orthopedic surgeon Peter Bent Brigham Hosp., 1956-58; prof. orthopedic surgery Med. Sch., U. Pa., 1958—, chmn. dept. orthopedic surgery Hosp. U. Pa., 1958—. Diplomate Am. Bd. Orthopedic Surgeons. Mem. A.M.A., Am. Acad. Orthopaedic Surgeons, Am. Orthopedic Assn., Orthopedic Research Soc., Soc. Internal. de Chirurg. et de Traumatologie, Phila. County Med. Soc., Med. Soc. Pa., Phila. Orthopedic Club. Home: 1311 Hillside Rd., Wynnewood, Pa. Office: 3400 Spruce St., Phila. 19104. Died Oct. 4, 1960.

GRIDLEY, RICHARD, army officer, mil. engr.; b. Boston, Jan. 3, 1711; s. Richard Gridley; m. Hannah Deming, Feb. 25, 1730, 9 children. Served as engr. during Siege of Louisbourg, 1745; drew plans for battery and other fortifications Boston Harbor, 1746; built Ft. Western (Augusta, Me.) and Ft. Halifax, 1752; commd. col. Brit. Army, served under Winslow in expdn. to Crown Point, 1756, under Amherst, 1758, under Wolfe in expdn. to Quebec, 1759; commanded Mass. arty., 1759; commd. chief engr., comdr. arty. Continental Army at Cambridge, Mass., 1775; commd. maj. gen., 1775, planned defensive works of Bunker Hill on the night before battle, 1775; commd. col., 1775; engr. gen. Eastern Dept., 1777-80. Died Stoughton, Mass., June 21, 1796.

GRIER, NORMAN MACDOWELL, biologist, educator; b. Pittsburgh, Pa., June 12, 1890; s. James B. and Marian (Gibson) G.; B.S., U. of Pittsburg, 1911, M.A., 1912, Ph.D., 1919; studied Cold Spring Harbor Biol. Lab., 1911, Yale, 1912-14, Harris Teachers' Coll., 1914-18, U. of Paris, 1919, Columbia, 1928-31; m. Margaretta Gibson, Aug. 30, 1915; 1 dau., Elizabeth Frances; m. 2d, Christine Ruth, Feb. 21, 1925; children—John James, Benjamin. Instr. physiology, Central High Sch., St. Louis, Mo., 1914-18; prof. zoology, Hollins Coll., 1919-20, Washington and Jefferson Coll., 1920-23; asst. prof. evolution Dartmouth Coll., 1923-26; prof. and head of dept. biology, Des Moines U., 1926-27; head dept. science, and prof. biology, Westchester (Pa.) State Teachers Coll., 1927-28; prof. biology, Elizabethtown (Pa.) Coll., 1928-30, also head science dept.; prof. zoology, Evansville (Ind.) Coll., 1930; prof. biology, Wagner Coll., S.I., N.Y., 1930-33; research in higher edn. and Inst. of Edn., New York U., 1933-34; dir. Industrial Survey Lebanon County, 1934; area dir. for Pa., Nat. Youth Adminstrn., 1935-36; founder and chmn. Lebanon County Mental Health Clinic, Lebanon. Pa., 1936—; personnel expert, Pa. Social Security Adminstrn., 1937; mem. Pa. State advisory board Fed. Writers' Project, 1938-39; mem. Nat. Committee for Planned Parenthood since 1939; with Veterans Adminstrn., Washington, D.C., 1944; exec. officer, Veterans Adminstrn. Guidance Center, U. of Pa., 1945. Asso. Am. Psychol. Assn., 1945. Lecturer at Hahnemann Med. Coll., 1945-46; prof. histol. and embryol. Pennsylvania State Coll. Optometry, Phila., 1946-49; lecturer Philadelphia Junto since 1949. Member Committee on Religion and Health, Fed. Council, Churches of Christ in Am. since 1943. Instr. Biol. Lab., Cold Spring Harbor, N.Y., summers 1921, 22, in charge field systematic botany, 1923-26; lecturer Wagner Free Inst. of Science, Phila., 1928, Coll. of New Rochelle, 1932-33; Columbiona fellowship, 1929. In charge of mussel survey of Upper Miss. River, U.S. Bur. of Fisheries, 1920, 25; Commd. 2d lt. inf., Pa. N.G., 1911; 1st lt. C.W.S., U.S. Army, Aug. 1918; asst. gas. officer 5th A.C., A.E.F., 1918-19. Fellow A.A.A.S. (com. on place of science in edn. 1925-32), Ia. Acad. Science, 1927; mem. St. Louis Acad. Science (sec. 1916-18), Paleontol. Soc. America, Am. Eugenics Soc. (Pa., com. 1929), Am. Soc. Zoologists, Ecol. Soc. America, Bot. Soc. America (sec. syst. sect. 1932), Am. Assn. Univ. Profs., Pa. State Edn. Assn., State Conservation Assn., Pa. State Acad. Science, L.I. Biol. Assn., Am. Acad. Polit. and Social Science, Geographic Players (advisory bd.), Phi Delta Theta, Phi Sigma, Pi Delta Epsilon, Pi Gamma Mu, Phi Delta Kappa, Am. Legion, Vets. Fgn. Wars. Chmn. Lancaster County (Pa.) Wild Flower Preservation Soc. America, 1929; local chmn. United Welfare Fund of Lebanon County; member executive com. Lebanon County Boy Scouts. Mem. Disciples of Christ Ch.; mem. bd. ednl. survey Colls. of Ch. of the Brethren, 1932. Author of various tech. papers and book reviews in biol. subjects and higher edn. Asso. editor Am. Midland Naturalist, 1923-35; editorial staff Biological Abstracts since 1950. Lecturer. Home: 207 Hathaway Park, Lebanon, Pa. Died Dec. 26, 1951; buried Mt. Lebanon Cemetery, Lebanon.

GRIFFIN, EUGENE, soldier, elec. engr.; b. Ellworth, Me., Oct. 13, 1855; s. George K. and Harriet J. G.; grad. West Point, 1875; m. Allie Hancock, April 24, 1889. Served 2d lt., 1st lt. and capt. corps of engrs., 1875-89; resigned Oct. 5, 1889; col. 1st U.S. col. engrs., May 24, 1898; brig. gen. vols., Jan. 21, 1899. In regular army, served on various surveys until 1883; was asst. prof. civil and mil. engring. and the art of war, West Point, 1883-85; a.-d.-c. staff of Maj. Gen. Winfield Scott Hancock, 1885-86; chief engr. div. Atlantic and dept. of the East, 1885-86; asst. engr., commr. Dist. of Columbia, 1886-88; in volunteer service, organized 1st regt. U.S. vols., engrs., serving with it in Puerto Rico, 1898-99. Gen. mgr. ry. dept., and 2d v.p. Thomson-Houston Elec. Co., 1888-91; 1st v.p. Gen. Elec. Co., 1892—; pres. Thomson-Houston Internat. Elec. Co., 1893—; dir. British-Thomson-Houston Co. and of the Cie. Français pour l'Exploitation des Procédés Thomson-Houston, Paris, 1893—. Home: New York, N.Y. Died 1907.

GRIFFIN, FRANK LOXLEY, college pres.; b. Topeka, Kan., Aug. 19, 1881; s. James Franklin and Hetty Rhess (Parsons) G.; B.S., U. of Chicago, 1903, M.S., 1904, fellow in astronomy, 1904-06, Ph.D., magna cum laude, 1906; biomathematic, econometric study in Europe, 1931; LL.D. (honorary), Reed College, 1956; married Mary Louisa Chambers, August 7, 1905; children—Helen Chambers, Ruth Hardy, Frank Loxley, Alice Rhees. On staff Yerkes Obs., Williams Bay, Wis., summer, 1905; instr. mathematics, 1906-09, asst. prof., 1909-11, Williams Coll., prof. mathematics, Reed Coll., Portland, Ore., 1911-52, mem. adminstrn. com. 1920-21, 24, president 1954-56; dir. Mathematics Teaching Seminar, Reed Coll., 1939-40; lectr. U. So. Cal., summer 1937; vis. prof. Weselyan U., 1952-53; vis. prof. Newcomb Coll., 1953-54; lectr. confs. on mathematics, U. of N.C. and Univ. Wash., 1954; member commn. on Place of Mathematics in Secondary Schs.; mem. bd. regents Multnomah Coll., v.p., 1952. Citation for public service, U. Chgo., 1949; citation for service to sci., Oregon Academy Science, 1949. Fellow A.A.A.S.; mem. Am. Math. Soc., Mathematic Assn. Am. (govs. 1940-42, v.p. 1952-53), Nat. Council Teachers of Math., Circolo Matermatico di Palermo, Northwest Sci. Assn., Am. Assn. Univ. Profs. (v.p. 1944-45), Econometric Society, Oregon Academy Sci. (pres. 1950), Sons of Am. Revolution, Sigma Xi, Phi Beta Kappa. Republican. Baptist. Club: City (board govs. 1941-44). Author: Introduction to Mathematical Analysis, 1921, enlarged edit., 1936; Periodic Orbits (with F. R. Moulton, et al.), 1920; Mathematical Analyiss—Higher Course, 1926; Introduction to Spherical Trigonometry (pamphlet), 1943. Contbr. scientific papers and articles on mathematics, astronomy, and population. Foreign corr. Comitati Italiano per lo studio dei problemi delle popolazione. Home: Portland OR Died Nov. 9, 1969.

GRIFFIN, JAMES H., engr.; b. Ft. Edward, N.Y., Sept. 3, 1889; s. James J. and Sarah (Stevens) G.; B.E., Union Coll., 1912; m. Dorothy Van Valkenburgh, May 25, 1918; 1 dau., Janet (Mrs. Robert J. O'Connell). Surveyor and field engr., barge canal dept. State of N.Y., Waterford, 1912-13; with Pub. Service Commn., 1st dist., State N.Y., and successor bodies, Transit Commn. and Bd. Transportation, City of N.Y., 1913—, jr. engr., 1913-17, asst. engr., 1917-39, div. engr., 1939-45, dep. chief engr., 1945. chief engr., 1945—. Served as capt. 5th U.S. Engrs., 1917-18; maj. Engrs. Res. Corps, 1924-40. Mem. Am. Assn. Engrs. (nat. pres., 1931-32), Am. Soc. C.E., Soc. Am. Mil. Engrs. (pres., N.Y. City post), Am. Legion (past comdr.), Phi Gamma Delta. Clubs: The Engineers, N.Y. Railroad. Home: Hillcrest Av., Darien, Conn. Office: 370 Jay St., Bklyn. 1. Died Sept. 17, 1955.

GRIFFIN, JOHN JOSEPH, chemist; b. Corning, N.Y., June 24, 1859; s. Jeremiah and Mary G.; A.B., Ottawa (Can.) U., 1881, A.M., 1883; entered Ottawa Diocesan Sem., 1883. Ordained R.C. priest, May 1, 1885; instr. physics, Ottawa U., 1885-86; instr. chemistry, St. Thomas Aquinas Coll., Cambridgeport, Mass., 1886-87; prof. chemistry, Ottawa U., 1887-90; grad. student chemistry, physics and mathematics, Johns Hopkins, 1890-95, Ph.D., 1895, at same time conducting classes in chemistry, St. Joseph's Sem. and Notre Dame of Md.; prof. chemistry, 1895—, dean faculty philosophy, 1903-05, dean faculty science, 1908-11, Catholic U. of America. Home: Washington, D.C. Deceased.

GRIFFIN, LAWRENCE EDMONDS, zoologist; b. Dalton, N.Y., Sept. 10, 1874; s. Milton Joseph and Dona (Edmonds) G.; B.A., Ph.B., Hamline U., 1895; post-grad. study, U. of Minn., 1895-98; Ph.D., Johns Hopkins, 1900; m. Estelle Edwards, of Hamline, Minn., Jan. 1, 1901; children—Curtis Edwards, Lawrence Milton, Richard Edmonds. Instr. in biology, Western Reserve U., 1900-02; prof. biology, Mo. Valley Coll., Marshall, Mo., 1902-08; research asst., Carnegie Inst., 1904-05; asst. and asso. prof. zoology, U. of Philippines, 1908-13, also dean Coll. of Liberal Arts, 1910-13; prof. zoology, U. of Pittsburgh, 1914-20; prof. biology, Reed Coll., Portland, Ore., since 1920; custodian Dept. of Herpetology, Carnegie Mus. Fellow A.A.A.S.; mem. Soc. Am. Zoologists, Am. Micros. Soc. (pres.), Am. Ecol. Soc., Am. Soc. Herpetology, Phi Beta Kappa, Sigma Xi, Omicron Delta Kappa. Republican. Unitarian. Author of numerous papers on zool. subjects. Home: 1325 E. 31st St., Portland OR

GRIFFIN, MARTIN LUTHER, cons. chem. engr.; b. Northampton, Mass., May 21, 1859; s. John and Naomi (Estabrook) G.; A.B., Amherst, 1883, A.M., 1886; m. Ada Riggs, Mar. 28, 1894; children—Artcher Estabrook, Carroll Riggs. Expert in pulp and paper-making processes and raw materials therefor, also in textile finishing of cotton, silk and woolen fabrics, combustion of fuels, destructive distillation, deportment of gases, processes of evaporation and drying, the electrolytic cell for the production of caustic soda and chlorine and the application of their products to industry, the treatment of water and trades wastes in industry. Mem. various chem. socs. and author of tech. papers. Home: 4 Prospect Pl., Taunton, Mass. Died Aug. 28, 1942.

GRIFFITH, FREDERIC RICHARDSON, surgeon; b. Phila., Sept. 17, 1873; s. David R. and Sarah Jane (Richardson) G.; ed. Friends, schs., Phila., and Camden, N.J., grad., 1892, Pa. Nautical Sch., Phila., 1892; M.D., U. of Pa., 1897; m. Lucile Andrews Menken, of New York, Dec. 12, 1900. Surgeon since 1897; surgeon Bellevue Dispensary, 1899-1904; pub. lecturer, on practical surgery, under direction New York City Bd. Edn., 1904-5; examiner First Aid to the Injured Soc., New York, since 1904; lecturer and examiner on first aid to New York City police and fire depts. since 1905. Acting asst. surgeon, 3d Regt. Inf. N.G., Pa., 1897-8. Fellow N.Y. Acad. Medicine; mem. N.Y. Hist. Soc. Sculptor since 1905; studied France, Italy; served in studio C. Daal Magelssen; executed 4 groups. Mem. Friends Meeting. Inventor; chloroform inhaler; eyed grooved dir.; modern enclosed ambulance; instruments to increase safety of anaesthetics, to increase scope of cocaine surgery, and to diagnosticate hydrocele; combination gas and liquid anaesthetizing inhaler; new surg. mallet, chisel, operating table bed, med. chart, and various other devices. Del. 13th Internat. Peace Congress, Lucerne, 1905. Author: Wounds (pamphlet), 1902; Handbook of Surgery, 1904; revised edit. Stoney's Bacteriology and Surgical Technic for Nurses, 1905. Contbr. in surgery to Internat. Clinics, and more than 150 articles in professional and scientific jours. Address: 49 E. 64th St., New York NY

GRIFFITH, IVOR, educator, pharmacist, chemist; b. Rhiwlas, Wales, Jan. 3, 1891; s. Rev. John William and Anne (Hughes) G.; came to U.S., 1907; Ph.D., Phila. Coll. Pharmacy and Science, 1912, Ph.M., 1920; Sc.D. honoris causa, Bucknell U., 1930; m. Carolyn Amanda Hobson, Mar. 28, 1914 (died Feb. 26, 1938); children—Doris Anne, Gwen Ivora; m. 2d, Hilda MacDonald, September 27, 1947 (deceased on April 5, 1961); 1 son, John MacDonald. Dir. Labs., Stetson Hosp., Phila., 1916-42; instr. math., Phila. Coll. Pharm. and Sci., 1916-17, instr. pharmacy, 1917-22, prof. and dean pharm. div., 1936-40, pres. since 1940; mem. Pa. State Board of Health since 1939; chmn. Pa. State Venereal Disease Council; chmn. Pa. State Lab. Accreditment Com.; special lecturer Brooklyn Inst. Arts and Sciences; hon. prof. organic chemistry, Wagner Inst. of Science, Philadelphia, director research, John B. Stetson Co., 1924-41, Frank H. Lee Co., Danbury, Conn., since 1943. Editor Am. Jour. of Pharmacy, 1921-41. Pres. Gt. Fifth B. & L. Assn.; Chem. investigations for Med. Supply Depot, Phila., during World War. Mem. com. on pharm., Nat. Research Council, 1943-46. Founder Nat. Quinine Pool. War Prodn. Bd., 1942. Pres. St. David's Soc. (Phila.) since 1928; pres. Science Teachers Assn. Middle States; pres. Am. Pharmaceutical Assn., 1943-44. Fellow Am. Inst. Chemists, Royal Soc. of Arts, London; mem. Am. Pharm. Assn. (editor Formula Book, 1926; Procter Gold Medalist, 1945), S.A.R. (Continental chpt. medalist 1953), A.A.A.S., Am. Chem. Soc., Am. Soc. Bacteriologists, Pa. Acad. Sci., Welsh Soc. Phila., Kappa Psi, Rho Chi. Republican. Presbyterian. Mason. Clubs: Union League, Penn, Rotary. Author: Recent Remedies, 1927; "Lobscows," a science miscellany; To the Lilacs, poems and essays. Collab. editor United States Dispensatory, 1936; editor of Science Talks (14 vols.). Home: Stafford House, Phila. Office: Philadelphia Coll. of Pharmacy and Science, 43d and Woodland Av., Phila. Died May 16, 1961; buried Whitemarsh Meml. Park, Prospectville, Pa.

GRIFFITH, WENDELL HORACE, scientist; b. Churdan, Ia., Nov. 7, 1895; s. George William and May Elizabeth (Fowler) G.; B.S., Greenville (Ill.) Coll., 1917; M.S., U. of Ill., 1919, Ph.D., 1923; m. Harriet Isabel Leas, Aug. 31, 1922; 1 son, Wendell Horace. Instr., Cooper Coll., Sterling, Kan., 1919-20, U. of Mich., 1922-23; dept. of biol. chemistry, St. Louis U., 1923-48, prof., 1940-48; chmn., prof. dept. biochem. and nutrition, U. Tex. Med. Sch., 1948-51; chmn., prof. dept. physiol. chemistry U. Cal., 1951-63, prof. emeritus, 1963-68; Gen. Edn. Bd. fellow, Oxford Eng., 1936-37; mil. leave absence, 1941-45; leave absence as FAO nutrition advisor in India, 1959-60, as dir. Life Scis. Research Office, Fedn. Am. Socs. for Experimental Biology, 1962-68; consultant Office Surgeon Gen., Army, 1946-68; cons. Office Surgeon Gen., USPHS, 1949-53, 55-68. Mem. Food and Nutrition board, NRC, 1950-61. Served with U.S.A., 1918-19; col. Sanitary Corps. U.S.A., 1941-46; nutrition officer, chief nutrition br., European Theater Operations, 1942-45. Decorated Legion of Merit, Bronze Star (World War II); recipient Outstanding Civilian Service award Dept. Army, 1966. Fellow Am. Public Health Assn., A.A.A.S., N.Y. Acad. Sci.; mem. Am. Soc. Biol. Chemists, Am. Inst. Nutrition (pres. 1950-51), Am. Chemical Soc., Soc. for Exptl. Biol. and Medicine. A.M.A. (council on Foods and Nutrition, 1953-59), Inst. Food Technologists, Sigma Xi, Alpha Omega Alpha, Phi Lambda Upsilon. Club: Cosmos, Asst. editor: Nutrition Reviews, 1946-50, editorial com., 1952-68. Editorial bd., Jour. Biol. Chemistry, 1949-59. Home: Bethesda MD Died Feb. 5, 1968; buried Oak Hill Cemetery, Kirkwood MO

GRIFFITH, WILLIAM, editor, author; b. Memphis, Mo., Feb. 15, 1876; s. Samuel P. and Minerva (Downing) G.; pub. sch. edn.; m. Florence Vernon, June 25, 1909. On staffs of New York newspapers, 1901-06; mng. editor Hampton's Mag., 1906-09; editor, dir. and sec. Travel Mag., 1910; editor McCall's Mag., 1911-12; editor, dir. and treas. National Sunday Mag., 1912-16; editor Current Opinion, 1917-25; editor William H. Wise & Co., 1925-29; editor Forum Press, Inc., 1929; editor The Authors Digest, 1931—. Pres. Poetry Soc. of America, 1929-31. Author: History of Kansas City and the Louisiana Purchase, 1899; Loves and Losses of Pierrot, 1916, revised and completed edit., 1924; Candles in the Sun, 1921; Selected Pierrot Lyrics, 1923. Editor: Life, Meaning, and Messages of Theodore Roosevelt, 1919; Great Painters and Their Famous Bible Pictures, 1925. Asso. editor, with Edwin Markham, of The Book of Poetry, 1926; The Book of Elbert Hubbard, 1934; Bermuda Troubadours, 1934. Editor American Scrap Book and European Scrap Book, 1928-29. Home: New York, N.Y. Died Apr. 1, 1936.

GRIFFITHS, DAVID, botanist; b. Aberystwith, Wales, Aug. 16, 1867; s. David and Rachel (Lewis) G.; B.S., Agrl. Coll., Brookings, S.D., 1892, M.S., 1893; Ph.D., Columbia, 1900; married; children—Elizabeth L., John D. Prin. or teacher in S.D. schs., 1889-98; prof. botany, U. of Ariz., 1900-01; asst. agrostologist, 1901-07, agriculturist, 1907-18, horticulturist, 1918—, U.S. Dept. Agriculture. Author: Torrey Bot. Club monograph on North Am. Sordariaceae. Home: Takoma Park, D.C. Died Mar. 1935.

GRIFFITHS, JOHN WILLIS, naval architect; b. N.Y.C., Oct. 6, 1809; s. John Griffiths. Wrote series of articles on naval architecture in portsmouth Advocate, 1836; delivered 1st formal lecture on naval architecture, N.Y.C.; editor American Ship, 1878-82; one of 1st to specialize in designing; designed Rainbow (1st "extreme clipper ship"); designed Sea Witch; developed improved form of rivet; invented machine for bending timber into crooked forms used in shipbldg.; designed New Era (1st ship with mechanically bent timber), 1870. Author: Treatise on Marine and Naval Architecture, 1850; Ship Builder's Manual, 1853; Progressive Ship-Builder, 1875. Died Bklyn., Mar. 30, 1882.

GRIMSHAW, ROBERT, engineer; b. Phila., Pa., Jan. 25, 1850; s. William and Marie Caroline (Delacroix) G.; prep. edn., Taylor's Acad., Wilmington, Del.; grad. Andalusia Coll., Pa., 1869; studied under Profs. Alexander and Guyot, Princeton, and in Paris, France; Ph.D.; m. Margaret Morton Dillon, of Wilmington, Del., Apr. 2, 1872 (died 1877); children—Charlotte (Mrs. Malcolm MacLear), Mary Morton (Mrs. Cornelius B. Hite), Edith Dillon (Mrs. Adolf Stelling); m. 2d, Marta Scharstein, of Kappeln, Schleswig-Holstein, Germany, May 15, 1914. Began practice, 1873; was mem. faculty New York U., Coll. City of N.Y. and Rutgers Univ.; served as consulting engr. for U.S. Govt., and various European govts. A founder Am. Soc. Mech. Engrs.; corr. sec. Polytechnic Soc.; ex-pres. James Watt Association Stationary Engineers; member National Institute of Social Sciences. Founder of "Blindaid," furnishing Braille printed matter. Republican. Episcopalian. Odd Fellow. Author: Why Manufacturers Lose Money, 1922; The Modern Foreman, 1923; Shop Kinks (6th edit.); Machine Shop Chat, 1923; The Locomotive Catechism (30th edit.), 1923; also many other tech. works in English, German and French. Home: 321 Sylvan Av., Leonia, N.J.

GRINDLEY, HARRY SANDS, chemist; b. Champaign, Ill., Apr. 13, 1864; s. Joseph S. and Sarah E. (Sands) G.; B.S., U. of Ill., 1888; Harvard U. scholarship, 1892-93, Morgan fellowship, Harvard, 1893-94, Sc.D., Harvard, 1894; m. Anna Eaton, of Champaign, July 2, 1896. Asst. in chemistry, Ill. Agrl. Expt. Sta., 1888-89, U. of Ill., 1889-92, Harvard U., 1892-93; instr. in chemistry, 1894-95, asst. prof., 1895-99, asso. prof., 1899-1904, prof. gen. chemistry and dir. Chem. Lab., 1904-07, prof. animal nutrition and chief in animal nutrition, since 1907, U. of Ill. Dir. investigations of saltpeter in meat, 1907-10. Mem. Am. Chem. Soc., A.A.A.S., Am. Soc. Biol. Chemists, Am. Soc. Animal Production, Am. Pub. Health Assn., Soc. Promotion Agrl. Science, Sigma Xi, Phi Lambda Upsilon. Conglist. Author of more than 110 bulls., reports, mag. articles, etc., presenting results of effects of methods of cooking, preservatives, animal nutrition, etc. Home: 1010 W. Green St., Ubana, Ill.

GRINDON, JOSEPH, SR., dermatologist; b. St. Louis, Mo., Aug. 20, 1858; s. Arthur St. Leger and Kelis (Chérot-Dupavillon) G.; educated St. Louis public schools, 1868-74; M.D., St. Louis Medical Coll., 1879; Ph.B., St. Louis U., 1884; Sc.D., St. Louis U., 1943; m. Lina Boislinière, Sept. 30, 1903 (deceased); children—Pauline C., Joseph B. (deceased), Dorothy M. (Mrs. A. B. Murphy, Jr.), Joseph B. (M.D.). Began practice, 1879; lecturer on diseases of the skin, 1886-95, prof. physiology, 1894-95, prof. dermatology, 1895-1900, St. Louis Med. Coll.; prof. clin. dermatology and syphilology, Washington U., 1900-12; prof. dermatology, St. Louis U., 1912-44; prof. emeritus since 1944; physician to St. Louis Smallpox Hosp., 1881-83; formerly dermatologist to O'Fallon Dispensary; dermatologist to St. John's, St. Mary's, Desloge and St. Louis City hospitals. Diplomate Am. Bd. Dermatology and Syphilus. President Medical Soc. of City Hosp. Alumni, 1897, St. Louis Med. Soc., 1899, St. Louis Dermatol. Soc., 1914-24; fellow A.M.A.; mem. Am. Dermatol. Assn. (pres. 1928), Mo. State Medical Assn. (v.p. 1931-32), Chicago Dermatol. Society, Dermatol. Conf. Mississippi Valley, Am. Acad. of Dermatology, Soc. for Investigative Dermatol., Archaeol. Inst. Am., St. Louis Acad. Scis., Mo. State Acad. Sci.; corr. mem. Société Francaise de Dermatologie et de Syphiligraphie. Author: Diseases of the Skin, 1902; also several chapters in American Text-Book of Genito-Urinary Diseases, Syphilis and Diseases of the Skin, 1898; Handbook of Cutaneous Therapeutics (with Dr. W. A. Hardaway), 1907. Contbr. to med. jours. Home: 7029 Westmoreland Av., St. Louis 5. Died Apr. 1, 1950; buried Calvary Cemetery, St. Louis.

GRINNELL, FREDERICK, mech. engr., inventor; b. New Bedford, Mass., Aug. 14, 1836; s. Lawrence and Rebecca S. G.; prep. edn. Friends' Acad., New Bedford; grad. Rensselaer Poly. Inst., Troy, 1855, as civ. and mech. engr.; m. Mary B. Page, Feb. 17, 1874. Was successively supt. Corliss Steam-engine Works, Providence; mgr. Jersey City Locomotive Works; supt. motive power Atlantic & Great Western R.R.; from 1869, pres., mgr. and mech. engr. Providence Steam and Gas Pipe Co. Introduced and has done much to perfect automatic fire exteinguisher and alarm, taking out about 40 patents in connection with it. Home: New Bedford, Mass. Died 1905.

GRISCOM, JOHN, educator, chemist; b. Hancock's Bridge, N.J., Sept. 17, 1774; s. William and Rachel (Denn) G.; m. Abigail Hoskins, 1800; m. 2d, Rachel Denn, Dec. 13, 1843; children—Abigail, John. First Am. educator to teach chemistry and give lectures on subject to classes, 1803; prof. chemistry and natural history Queens Coll. (now Rutgers U.), 1812-28; organized N.Y. High Sch. for Boys 1825; instituted Lancasterian system of monitorial instrn.; prin. Friends' Sch., Providence, R.I.; prof. chemistry Columbia; made known med. properties of cod-liver oil and value iodine in treatment of goiter; a founder N.Y. Soc. for Prevention Pauperism, Soc. for Reformation Juvenile Delinquents; prin. founder House of Refuge (1st reformatory in U.S.). Author: Year in Europe, 2 vols., 1823; Discourse on Character and Education, 1823; Monitorial Instruction, 1825. Died Burlington, N.J., Feb. 26, 1852.

GRISCOM, LUDLOW, (gris'kum), ornithologist; b. N.Y.C., June 17, 1890; s. Clement Acton and Genevieve Sprigg (Ludlow) G.; A.B., Columbia, 1912; A.M., Cornell U., 1915; m. Edith Sumner Sloan, Sept. 14, 1926; children—Edith Rapallo (Mrs. P. O. Daley), Andrew, Joan Ludlow. Instr. elementary biology, Cornell U., 1915-16; asst. in Am. Mus. Natural History, 1917-20, asst. curator ornithology, 1921-27; research curator zoölogy, Mus. Comparative Zoölogy, Harvard, 1927-48, and research ornithologist, 1948—. Mem. zool. exploration parties in Panama, 1924, 27, Yucatan, 1926, Nicaragua, 1917, Guatemala, 1930; vol. asst. with Gray Herbarium Expdn. to Arctic Newfoundland, 1925, and Gaspé Peninsula, 1923. Served as 2d lt. U.S. Army, 1917-19; U.S. del. 2d Interallied Propaganda Conf., London, 1918. Del. 8th Internat. Ornithol. Congress, Oxford, Eng., 1934. Recipient Conservation medal, 1956. Fellow A.A.A.S., Am. Ornithologists Union (pres. 1956), N.Y. Acad. Scis., Linnaean Soc. N.Y. (pres. 1927); mem. Ecol. Soc. Am. British Ornithologists Union, Nat. Audubon Soc. (chmn. bd. dirs.), Boston Soc. Natural History (trustee, pres. 1948, hon. curator birds), Children's Mus. of Boston (trustee). Mass. Fish and Game Assn. Am. Mus. Natural History, Mass. Audubon Soc. (dir.), Colonial Soc. Mass., Sigma Xi. Protestant. Clubs: Union, Harvard (Boston); Faculty (Cambridge); Union, Century (N.Y.C.); Cosmos (Washington). Author: Birds of the N.Y. City Region, 1923; Distribution of Bird Life in Guatemala, 1932; Ornithology of the Republic of Panama, 1935; A Monographic Study of the Red Crossbill, 1937; Modern Bird Study, 1945; Birds of Nantucket, 1948; Birds of the Concord Region, a Study in Population Trends, 1949. Origin and Distribution Birds of Mexico, 1940; Distributional Check-List Birds of Mexico, Part I, 1940. Birds of Massachusetts, 1955, Annotated and Revised Checklist, with Dorothy E. Snyder, 1955. Contbr. articles to ornithol. and bot. jours.; spl. field of research birds of C.A., field identification of N. Am. birds, conservation. Contbg. editor Nat. Audubon Mag.; asso. editor, Audubon Field Notes. Home: 21 Fayerweather St., Cambridge 38, Mass. Died May 28, 1959; buried Mt. Auburn Cemetery, Cambridge.

GRISSOM, VIRGIL IVAN, astronaut; b. Mitchell, Ind., Apr. 3, 1926; s. Dennis D. and Cecil (King) G.; B.S. in Mech. Engring., Purdue U., 1950; student aero. engring., Air Force Inst. Tech., 1955, Test Pilot Sch., Edwards AFB, 1956; m. Betty L. Moore, July 6, 1945; children—Scott, Mark. Aviation cadet USAAF, 1944-45; commd. 2d lt. USAF, 1951, advanced through grades to lt. col.; fighter pilot 75th Fighter-Interceptor Squadron, Presque Isle, Me., 1951; combat pilot 334th Fighter-Interceptor Squadron, Korea, 1951-52; test pilot Fighter Br., Wright-Patterson AFB, 1957-59; astronaut Project Mercury, 1959—; made 2d Project Mercury Flight, July 1961, Gemini two-man 3 orbital flight, Mar. 1965. Decorated D.F.C., Air. Medal with cluster. Home: 211 Pine Shadows, Seabrook, Tex. Office: Project Mercury, Nat. Aeronautics and Space Administration, Washington. Died Jan. 27, 1967.

GRISWOLD, LEON STACY, mining geologist; b. Boston, July 30, 1865; s. Henry A. and Lucy A. (Milliken) G.; A.B., Harvard, 1889. Asst. geol. survey of Ark., 1889-91; asst. U.S. Geol. Survey, 1893-94; asst. and inst. geol. dept., Harvard, 1893-96; engaged in mining in Mont., 1896-99; consulting geologist, Boston, 1899-1903; asst. prof. geology and mineralogy, Mo. Sch. of Mines, since Jan. 1, 1904. Published Vol. III, 1890, Report of Geol. Survey of Arkansas; also papers in publs. of Geol. Soc. of America, Mus. of Comparative Zoology, Boston Soc. Natural History, etc. Mem. Geol. Soc. America, A.A.A.S., Boston Soc. Natural History, Nat. Geog. Soc., Am. Forestry Assn., Am. Inst. Mining Engrs., Boston Soc. Civ. Engrs. Address: Rolla, Mo.

GRISWOLD, THOMAS, JR., civil engr., cons. engr.; b. Ashtabula, O., Sept. 29, 1870; s. Thomas and Ruth Coleman (Hubbard) G.; B.S. in C.E., Case Sch. Applied Science, 1896, C.E., 1908; m. Helen Josephine Dow, of Cleveland, O., Nov. 25, 1897 (died 1918); children—Josephine (Mrs. Louis Henry Ashmun), Nelson Dow, Lelia Ruth (Mrs. E. Rex Edick); m. 2d, Vera Ann Hadsall, of Midland, Mich., Oct. 17, 1918; children—Catherine Ann, Grant Hadsall. Chief engr. Dow Chem. Co., Midland, Michigan, 1897-1926, chief of patent department, 1927-37; cons. engineer since 1937; dir. Chem. State Savings Bank. Mem. Am. Inst. Chem. Engrs., Am. Chem. Soc., Am. Soc. Mech. Engrs., Phi Delta Theta, Tau Beta Pi, Sigma Xi. Episcopalian. Clubs: Saginaw Valley Torch, Midland Country. Home: Midland MI

GROAT, BENJAMIN FELAND, (grot), cons. engr., patent atty.; b. Hannibal, Mo., Oct. 18, 1867; of Colonial and Revolutionary ancestry; s. Peter Benjamin and Ann Garnett (Ritter) G.; B.Sc. in Engring., U. of Minn., 1901, LL.B., 1908, LL.M., 1910; m. Harriet Grace Mitchell, June 25, 1906; 1 dau., Lucy Mitchell (Mrs. George Ashmun Morton). Identified with railroad service, various branches, for a number of yrs.; instr. physics, 1895, prof. in charge mechanics and mathematics, U. of Minn. Sch. of Mines, 1898-1910, admitted to bar, 1908; hydro-electric engr. Aluminum Co. of America, 1910-20; cons. practice since 1910; made alloy lead pipe coupling with adjusted expansion properties; developed precise turbine tests, measuring water chemically, 1914; planned and directed dredging and power improvements of Grasse River, N.Y., 1914; inventor-patentee method of automatic ice diversion; originated plan and wrote application for permit to install ice diversion, St. Lawrence River, which was granted by Internat. Joint Commn.; advocate of Nat. Hydraulic Laboratory (citing its value in planning means to stop erosion of soils); advocate of a "standard-of-living-wage-price-dollar"; etc. Awarded silver medal, Engrs.' Soc. Western Pa., 1915; Norman medal, Am. Soc. Civil Engrs., 1917. Former fellow A.A.A.S.; mem. Am. Soc. Civil Engrs., Soc. for Promotion Engring. Edn., Am. Math. Soc., Sigma Xi; former mem. Am. Soc. Mech. Engrs.' Soc., Western Pa.; asso. Am. Inst. Elec. Engrs. Protestant. Author of scientific papers relating to force of New Richmond tornado; summation of differences; inversions and determinants; back-water slopes; chemihydrometry; ice diversion; rod float theory and tables; dimensional theory; similarity and models (founding a proposed new branch of accurate engring. design); gas flow with frictional and received (rejected) heat; rules of quadrature, Generalized Maxwell's Viscosity Theory, disclosing an error not previously recognized. Address: Emlen Arms, Philadelphia 19. Died June 16, 1949; buried in Princeton Cemetery, Princeton, N.J.

GROAT, WILLIAM AVERY, physician; b. Canastota, N.Y., Nov. 9, 1876; s. William Robert and Elizabeth Morgan (Avery) G.; B.S., Syracuse U., 1897, M.D., 1900; m. Nellie Nichols Bacon, Oct. 2, 1901; children—William Avery, Robert Andrews, Elsie (Wade). In practice Syracuse, N.Y., since 1901; mem. faculty, Coll. of Medicine, Syracuse U., since 1902, prof. clin. pathology since 1911; sr. attending physician and dir. Hazard Lab., Memorial Hosp.; sr. attending physician diseases of metabolism and dir. Jacobson Memorial Lab., St. Joseph Hosp.; consultant University, City and Psychopathic hosps. and Syracuse Free Dispensary. Chmn. advisory com. on pub. health, City of Syracuse. Served as capt., later maj., M.C., U.S. Army, World War; lt. col. Med. O.R.C. Mem. Am. Pharmacopaeia Convs., 1910, 20, 30, 40 (com. on constl. revision, 1940). Trustee Syracuse Univ. Fellow American College Physicians, A.A.A.S. Diplomate and member exec. committee American Board Internal Medicine, A.M.A. (delegate), N.Y. State Medical Society (chmn. bd. trustees, ex-president and member house of delegates; ex-chairman committee on scientific work; ex-president 5th district branch), American Assn. Immunologists, Am. Assn. Clin. Pathologists, Am. Assn. for Study of Goitre, Am. Assn. for Diseases of Internal Secretions, Delta Kappa Epsilon, Nu Sigma Nu, Sigma Xi, Alpha Omega Alpha, Phi Kappa Phi, Phi Kappa Alpha. Republican. Episcopalian. Clubs: Faculty, Onondaga Golf and Country, Thousand Island Park Golf; Holland Society of N.Y. (ex-v.p.). Contbr. articles and reports of researchers, particularly diseases of the blood and metabolism, to med. publs. Cons. editor N.Y. State Med. Jour. Home: 1352 Teall Av., Syracuse; (summer) Cedar Island, Fishers Landing, N.Y. Died Sept. 9, 1945.

GROEDEL, FRANZ MAXIMILIAN, (gro'del), physician; b. Bad Nauheim, Germany, May 23, 1881; s. Maximilian J. and Rosa (Klopfer) G.; ed. Univs. of Munich, Giessen and Leipzig, 1899-1904 (M.D., U. of Leipzig, 1904); unmarried. Came to U.S. 1934, naturalized, 1939. Chief X-ray dept., Holy Ghost Hosp., Frankfurt am Main, Germany, 1910-34; instr. U. of Frankfurt, 1919-34, prof. on med. faculty, since 1929; director Kerckhoff Heart Research Institute, Bad Nauheim, since 1929; cardiologist Heart Sanitarium, Bad Nauheim, 1904-34; licensed to practice medicine in New York State, 1934; now practicing in New York City; cons. cardiologist Lenox Hill Hosp.; attending cardiologist Beth David Hosp.; cardiol. St. Anthony's Hosp.; research fellow Biological Inst., Fordham Univ. Formerly pres. Deutsche Röntgengesellschaft and Frankfurter Röntgengesellschaft; formerly bd. dirs. German Heart Assn., Deutsch Balneologische Gesellschaft, etc. Founder Am. Coll. Cardiology; mem. Am. Physiol. Soc., Am. Heart Assn., New York Heart Assn., N.Y. Cardiol. Soc., A.M.A., N.Y. County Medical Soc., N.Y. State Med. Society, Am. Assn. History of Medicine, New York Phys. Therapy Soc., N.Y. Med. Union, Internat. Soc. Med. Hydrology; honorary member X-ray Society of Chicago, Ill., Detroit Roentgen Ray Society, American College Radiology, Med. Soc. Bologne, Italy, Hessian Roentgen Soc., Deutsche Kreislanfforsching Ges. Served as mil. surg. during World War. Author of many books, also brochures and articles on X-ray and diseases of the heart. Address: 829 Park Av., N.Y.C. Died Oct. 12, 1951.

GRONWALL, THOMAS HAKON, cons. mathematician; b. Axberg, Sweden, Jan. 16, 1877; s. Carl T. G.; student U. of Upsala and U. of Stockholm, Ph.D., Upsala, 1898; C.E., U. of Berlin, 1902. Asst. in mathematics, U. of Stockholm, 1897; practiced civ. engring., 1902-13; instr. mathematics, Princeton, 1913-14, asst. prof., 1914-15; math. expert. Ordnance Dept., U.S.A., 1918-22; cons. mathematician, 1922—. Naturalized citizen of U.S., 1922. Editor Annals of Mathematics, 1913—. Died 1933.

GROSS, ALFRED OTTO, biologist; b. Atwood, Ill., Apr. 8, 1883; s. Henry and Sophia (Gross) G.; A.B., U. of Ill., 1908; research scholarship, Bermuda Biol. Sta., 1910-11; Edward Austin research fellow, Harvard, 1911-12, Ph.D., 1912; D.Sc. (honorary), Bowdoin College, 1952; married Edna Grace Gross, July 2, 1913; children—William Albert, Thomas Alfred, Edna Louise (Mrs. Otis N. Minot). Ornithologist, Illinois Natural History Survey, 1906-08; instructor in biology, Bowdoin College, 1912-13, asst. prof. biology, 1913-22, prof., 1922-53, emeritus, 1953; Joshiah Little prof. natural sci. Bowdoin, 1950. Ornithologist, Roosevelt Wild Life Experiment Sta., 1924; in charge Heath Hen Investigation, 1923-27; in charge N.E. Ruffled Grouse Investigation, 1925-35; research at Barro Colorado Island, Panama, 1925, Ecuador and Costa Rica, 1927-28; in charge Prairie Chicken Investigation, Research Bureau, State of Wisconsin, 1929-30; dir. Ornithol. Expdn. to Labrador, 1931; orinthologist in charge Bowdoin-MacMillan Artic Expdn., 1934; mem. Ornithol. Expdn., Cuba, 1947, Panama, 1949, Alaska, 1951; ornithol. investigation around the world, 1953, 56, 58, Africa, 1959, Hawaiian Islands, 1960; official U.S. delegate Internat. Ornighol. Congress, Sweden, 1950, Switzerland, 1954; dir. Bowdoin Biol. Station, 1935; biologist, U.S. Fish and Wildlife Service, 1944; councilor Fedn. of Bird Clubs of New England, Inc.; Me. state adviser National Association of Audubon Societies; advisor to State of Maine dept. of fish and game. Trustee Am. Wild Life Inst. Fellow Am. Zoologists, Am. Ornithologists' Union (council), A.A.A.S., Am. Geog. Soc.; mem. N.E. Bird Banding Assn., (pres.) Boston Soc. Nat. Hist., British Ecol. Soc., Me. Audubon Soc. (pres.), Am. Wildlife Soc., Sigma Xi, Alpha Tau Omega, Gamma Alpha. Republican. Congregationalist. Club: Harvard Travellers. Editor, Maine Audubon Society Bulletin, 1945. Author: The Heath Hen, 1928. Contributor 150 papers on birds and biology to Auk, Jour. Exptl. Zoology, Bull. U.S. Nat. Museum, Wilson Bull., Condor. Home: Brunswick ME Died May 9, 1970; buried Pine Grove Cemetery, Brunswick, Brunswick ME

GROSS, SAMUEL DAVID, surgeon, educator; b. Easton, Pa., July 8, 1805; s. Philip and Johanna (Brown) G.; grad. Jefferson Med. Coll., 1828; D.C.L., Oxford (Eng.) U.; LL.D., Cambridge (Eng.) U., U. Edinburgh (Scotland), U. Pa.; m. Louisa Weissell, 1828. Apptd. demonstrator anatomy Med. Coll., Ohio, 1833; prof. pathological anatomy Cincinnati Med. Coll., 1835; prof. surgery U. Louisville, 1840; Jefferson Med. Coll., 1856; a founder A.M.A.; founder Phila. Path. Soc., Phila. Acad. Surgery, Am. Surg. Soc.; established Acad. Surgery prize for original articles; presided over Internat. Congress Surgeons, 1876; v.p. German Surg. Soc.; inventor numerous instruments; translator from French and German med. texts. Author: Elements of Pathological Anatomy (1st work on subject in English lang.), 1839; A Practical Treatise on Foreign Bodies in the Air Passages, 1854; A System of Surgery, Pathological, Diagnostic, Theraputive and Operative, 1859. Died Phila., May 6, 1884.

GROSS, SAMUEL WEISSELL, surgeon; b. Cincinnati, Feb. 4, 1837; s. Samuel David and Louisa (Weissell) G.; grad. Jefferson Med. Coll., 1857; m. Grace Linzee Revere, Dec. 28, 1876. Served as surgeon U.S. Army during Civil War; commd. lt. col. Med. Corps, 1865; surgeon Phila. Hosp.; surgeon hosp. of Jefferson Med. Coll.; founded, developed present-day radical operation for cancer; prof. principles of surgery and clin. surgery Jefferson Med. Coll., 1882; one of 1st physicians in Phila. to use antiseptic surgery. Author: Practical Treatise on Tumors of the Mammary Gland, 1880; Practical Treatise on Impotence, Sterility and Allied Disorders of the Male Sexual Organs, 1881. Died Phila., Apr. 16, 1889.

GROSVENOR, WILLIAM MASON, (gro've-nor), cons. chem. engr.; b. St. Louis, Mo., Oct. 5, 1873; s. Col. William and Ellen (Sage) G.; father was econ. editor N.Y. Tribune and Dun's Weekly Rev.; prep. edn. Roots Acad., Greenwich, Conn.; B.S., Polytechnic Inst., Brooklyn, 1893; Johns Hopkins Univ., Baltimore; Ph.D., U. of Pa., 1898; m. Marie Dexter, Apr. 9, 1901; children—Mary Dexter (Mrs. Ralph O. Ellsworth), William Mason. Served as industrial investigator for New York Tribune, 1895; was chemist Mathieson Alkali Works, 1896; Millview Mining Co., 1898; engr. and asst. treas. Ampere Electrochem Co., 1899; asst. supt. Gen. Chem. Co., 1900-02; asst. mgr. investigating dept. same, 1903-04; supt. Contact Process Co., Buffalo, N.Y., 1905; engr., treas. George F. Westcott Co., 1906; engr., sec. Dryer Engring. Co., 1907; cons. practice and chem. expert since 1907. Mem. Textile Com., Council of Nat. Defense, World War. Mem. Am. Chem. Soc., Soc. Chem. Industry (chmn. 1915), Am. Inst. Chem. Engrs. (charter mem.), Electrochem Soc., Am. Institute of Chemists, Professional Engrs. Assn., A.A.A.S., Soc. de Chimie et Industrie. Presbyterian. Clubs: Chemists' of New York (charter mem.), Lawrence Beach, Lido. Contbr. to professional jours. First to introduce high speed moving picture and projection to analysis of rapid motion in industrial work; etc. Holder of numerous U.S. patents. Home: R.F.D. No. 1, New Canaan, Conn. Office: Chemists' Bldg., 50 E. 41st St., New York, N.Y. Died May 30, 1944. *

GROVER, FREDERICK ORVILLE, botanist; b. Bangor, Me., July 31, 1868; s. Nahum Wesley and Frances Elizabeth (Osgood) G.; A.B., Dartmouth, 1890, A.M., 1893; A.B., Harvard, 1895, A.M., 1896; m. Ruth Havergal Creighton, Sept. 3, 1925. Instr. St. James Mil. Acad., Macon, Mo., 1890-92, Western Mil. Acad., Upper Alton, Ill., 1892-94; grad. student in botany, Harvard, 1894-98, asst. in botany, 1895-96; asst. in botany, Radcliffe Coll., 1895-97; asso. prof. botany, Oberlin (O.) Coll., 1898-1900, prof., 1900-33, emeritus 1933—; engaged in bot. research. Mem. adminstrv. bd. Orio Biol. Survey 1913—. Trustee Oberlin Kindergarten Tng. Sch., 1911-33; sec. Oberlin Improvement Soc. 1938—. Mem. Oberlin Park Bd., 1941—. Collaborator U.S. Dept. Agr., Div. Forage Crops, 1932-44. Served at Nat. Red Cross Hdqrs., in charge of forwarding Red Cross workers to Europe by Troop Ships, World War I. Republican. Congregationalist. Fellow, Ohio Acad. Scis. (v.p. 1912-13, 1914-15, 1940-41; pres. 1916-17); mem. A.A.A.S., N.E. Bot. Soc., Am. Genetic assn. (life), Soc. Linnéenne de Lyon (life), Am. Soc. Plant Taxonomists, Am. Soc. Naturalists, Botanists U.S., Prehistoric Soc (England), Phi Delta Theta, Phi Beta Kappa, Sigma Xi. Home: 180 Morgan St., Oberlin, O. Died June 2, 1964.

GROVER, NATHAN CLIFFORD, civil engr.; b. Bethel, Me., Jan. 31, 1868; s. Daniel Barker and Martha Matilda (Eames) G.; B.C.E., U. Me., 1890, C.E., 1897, D.Eng., 1930; B.S., Mass. Inst. Tech., 1896; m. Anna Allen, June 14, 1900; children—Dorothy Allen, Mary Hamilton (Mrs. John Douglass Fitch). Instr. civil engring. U. Me., 1891-94, asst. prof., 1894-95, asso. prof., 1895-97, prof., 1897-1903; engr. U.S. Geol. Survey, 1903-07; hydraulic, constrn. and irrigation engr. with J. G. White & Co., N.Y.C., 1907-11; chief engr. Land Classification Bd., 1911-13, chief hydraulic engr. charge water resources br. U.S. Geol. Survey, 1913-39; ret. 1939. Conglist. Mem. Am. Soc. C.E., Washington Soc. Engrs., Washington Acad. Scis., Phi Kappa Phi, Tau Beta Pi, Beta Theta Pi. Club: Cosmos (Washington). Author: River Discharge (with J. C. Hoyt), 1907; Notes on Framed Structures (with H. S. Boardman), 1902. Home: 4505 Dexter Road, Washington. Died Nov. 29, 1957; buried Rock Creek Cemetery, Washington.

GRUBBE, EMIL HERMAN, physician, radiologist; b. Chgo., Jan. 1, 1875; s. Albert and Bertha (Reets) G.; tchrs. and pharmacy degrees Valparaiso (Ind.) U.; 1890-92, B.S., 1893, A.M., 1894, Ph.D., 1895, chemist and physicist, 1895-96; M.D., Gen. Med. Coll., Chgo., 1898, Chicago Coll. Medicine and Surgery, 1910; postgrad. Bellevue Hosp., N.Y.C., 1901. Specialist x-ray therapy, 1896—; pioneer application x-ray for treatment of disease, for cure recurrent carcinoma; treatment cancer with x-ray, Jan. 28, 1896. Tb of the skin, Jan. 29, 1896; pioneered use of lead as protection untoward effects x-ray; pioneered design, establishment of hosp. x-ray dept.; dir. Ill. X-Ray and Electro-Therapeutic Lab.; lectr. chemistry and physics Gen. Med. Coll., 1895, adj. prof. chemistry, physics and x-rays, 1896-97, prof. roentgenology, electrotherapeutics dept. Hahnemann Hosp., Chgo., 1896-1919; prof. radiology, x-ray therapeutics and electrophysics Ill. Postgrad. Sch. Electro-Therapeutics, 1899-1921; roentgenologist Chgo. Bapt. Hosp., 1900-16, Pine Sanitarium, 1911-16; cons. staff Peekskill Sanitarium, 1900-06; prof., head dept. roentgenology and electrotherapeutics Chgo. Coll. Medicine and Surgery, 1910-20; cons. physician Frances E. Willard Hosp., 1910-24; prof. roentgenology, phys. therapeutics Jenner Med. Coll., 1914-17; hon. cons. roentgenologist Streeter Meml. Hosp., Chgo., 1938. Del. Internat. Elec. Congress, St. Louis, 1904. Mem. citizens bd. U. Chgo. Recipient award for pioneer work x-ray therapy and electrotherapy Am. Inst. Medicine; citation Chgo. Med. Soc., 1946; award Walter Reed Soc., 1952; citation scroll Chgo. Roentgen Soc., 1956. Diplomate Am. Bd. Radiology, 1937. Fellow A.C.P.; mem. Am. Roentgen Ray Soc., Radiol. Soc. N.A. (founder mem.), A.M.A., Assn. Am. Physicians, Nat. Acad. Scis., Am. Assn. Cancer Research, Nat. Soc. Phys. Therapeutics (pres. 1912), Ill., Chgo. med. socs., Chgo. Roentgen Soc., A.A.A.S., Assn. Approved Radiology, Am. Philos. Soc., North Shore (pres. 1939), Am. philatelic socs.; hon. mem. Pioneer Philatelic Soc., Pioneer Philatelic Phalanx. Clubs: Press, Hamilton. Author: A System of Inorganic Chemical Analysis, 1898; X-Ray Treatment—Its Origin, Birth and Early History, 1949. Editor Archives of Electrology and Radiology, 1904-08; asso. editor Am. Electro-Therapeutic and X-Ray Era, 1901-13. Author numerous med. articles, monographs. Home: 1205 Sherwin Av., Chgo. Died. Mar. 26, 1960.

GRUBBS, SAMUEL BATES, pub. health service; b. Indianapolis, Ind., Feb. 11, 1871; s. Daniel Webster and Matilda (Miller) G.; prep. edn., Boys Classical Sch., Indianapolis, and Abbott Sch., Farmington, Me.; grad. Hogsetts Acad., Harrodsburg, Ky., 1888; A.B., U. of Mich., 1893; M.D., Coll. Physicians and Surgeons, Columbia, 1896; grad. study, Paris, 1900-01, Vienna, 1908; m. Mary Evelyn Noble, June 17, 1903; 1 son, Daniel Dean. In United States Public Health Service since 1897, specializing in yellow fever, bubonic plague, typhus fever and meningitis prevention, advanced through ranks to med. dir. retired, Sept. 1, 1933; service in Europe, Mexico, South America, P.I. and Orient; was chief quarantine officer, Porto Rico, 1908-12; visiting physician, Presbyn. Hosp., San Juan, Porto Rico, 1910-12; chief of extra cantonment sanitary area, Newport News, Va., 1917-18, and sanitary inspector U.S. Army, post of embarkation, N.Y.; served in France; chief quarantine officer, Panama Canal, 1919-20; health officer, Port of New York, 1921-25; chief of foreign quarantine div., 1925-27; dir. Great Lakes dist., 1928; adviser to Los Angeles Health Dept., 1929; chief quarantine officer, Hawaiian Islands, 1929-33. Sanitary insp. on board transport Sedgwich, Spanish-Am. War. Am. del. orgn. office Internat. d'Hygiene Publique. Mem. A.M.A., A.A.A.S., Nu Sigma Nu, Delta Upsilon. Republican. Clubs: University (Washington); Delta Upsilon (New York); Columbia, Indianapolis Literary (Indianapolis). Contbr. to Pub. Health Reports. Originator of vacuum cyanide method of disinfecting clothing, ratproofing of ships and cheopis index for bubonic plague. Home: Carmel, Ind. Address: U.S. Public Health Service, Washington, D.C. Died Sep. 19, 1942.

GRUEHR, ANATOLE RODOLPH, engr., economist, educator; b. Istanbul, Turkey, Feb. 20, 1897; s. Rodolph and Vera Cecile (DuBois) G.; student Eidgenossische Technische Hochschule, Zurich, Switzerland; B.S. in Elec. Engring., Mass. Inst. Tech., 1924; M.B.A., N.Y.U., 1932, Ph.D., 1943; m. Meta Florence Ward, Sept. 4, 1931; children—Rodolph Anatole, Constance Milan, Meta Christine. Came to U.S., 1921, naturalized, 1929. Dir. transportation Constantinople unit Near East Relief, 1919-21; water power constrn., electrician Mich. and Ky., also field engr., Mich., Tenn., Fla.; div. engr. Manhattan distbn. Consol. Edison Co. of N.Y., 1929-45, rate engring., 1945-47, staff engr. system engring., 1947-50, sr. engr., 1950-55; lectr. Stevens Inst. Tech., 1951-52, vis. asso. prof. indsl. engring., 1952-56; adj. prof. econs. Grad. Sch., Bklyn. Poly. Institute, 1951-55, Charles S. Baylis professor economics and head department of economics & history, 1955—. Director Ramado Valley Coop., 1937-42, pres., 1942-44. Mem. bd. edn., Ridgewood, N.J., 1949-52. Profl. engr., N.Y. Recipient outstanding service award N.Y. chpt. Profl. Engrs., 1952. Fellow Am. Inst. E.E.; mem. Nat. Soc. Profl. Engrs. (pres. N.Y. chpt. 1947-49, zone dir. 1953-59, pres. N.Y. State, 1959-60, nat. dir. 1955—), Am. Soc. Engring. Edn., A.A.A.S., Am. Econ. Assn. Mason. Clubs: Appalachian Mountain (Boston); Mass. Institute Technology (N.Y.C.; No. N.J.); Brooklyn. Home: 161 Prospect St., Ridgewood, N.J. 07450. Office: 333 Jay St., Bklyn, 11201. Died Jan. 17, 1963.

GRUENER, HIPPOLYTE, chemist; b. New Haven, Conn., Feb. 23, 1869; s. Leopold and Katharine (Kern) G.; A.B., Yale, 1891, Ph.D., 1893; post-grad. studies, univs. of Munich and Berlin; m. May Cole, of Cleveland, June 21, 1899; children—Theodore, Katharine Lange, James Cole. Instr. chemistry, 1895-1903, asst. prof., 1903-07, Adelbert Coll.; asso. prof. chemistry, 1898-1907, prof., 1907-39, emeritus prof. since 1939, Mather College, Western Reserve U. Republican. Protestant. Fellow A.A.A.S., Am. Pub. Health Assn.; mem. Am. Chem. Soc., Deutsche Chemische Gesellschaft. Club: University. Contbr. tech. papers to scientific publs. Author: Organic Chemistry (with H. P. Lankelma); also vol. on chemistry in Popular Science series. Home: 2324 Coventry Rd., Cleveland Heights, Cleveland OH

GRUNSKY, CARL EWALD, civil engr.; b. San Joaquin Co., Calif., Apr. 4, 1855; s. Carl Albert Leopold and Clotilde Josephine Frederica (Camerer) G.; grad. Realschule, Stuttgart, Germany, 1872-74; Polytechnikum, Stuttgart, 1874-77, grad., 1877, Dr. Ing., 1910; D.Eng., Rensselaer Poly. Inst., 1924; m. Mattie Kate Powers, Mar. 12, 1884 (died 1921); children—Carl Ewald, Kate Louise (Mrs. B. Grant Taylor), Eugene Lucius, Clotilde. First work as topographer with river surveying party of State Engring. Dept. of Calif., 1878; asst. and chief asst. state engr. of Calif., 1879-88; in pvt. practice, largely in irrigation work, sewerage and drainage, 1887-99, located at Sacramento and San Francisco; at work on river rectification and drainage problems as mem. Examining Commn. on Rivers and Harbors of Calif., 1889-90, and as cons. engr. to commr. of public works of Calif., 1893-94; mem. San Francisco Sewerage Commn., 1892-93; city engr., San Francisco, 1900-04; mem. Isthmian Canal Commn., 1904-05; cons. engr. U.S. Reclamation Service, 1905-07; in pvt. practice as cons. engr., New York and San Francisco, 1907-09; at San Francisco, 1910—; now sr. mem. C. E. Grunsky Co. and acting dir. Calif. Acad. of Sciences. Author: Valuation, Depreciation and the Rate-Base (with son), 1916; Topographic Stadia Surveying, 1917; Public Utility Rate Fixing, 1918; Ways to National Prosperity, 1929. Home: Berkeley, Calif. Died Jan. 9, 1934.

GRUNWALD, KURT, cons. agrl. engr.; b. Russia-Poland, Aug. 18, 1881; s. Ferdinand and Ottilie (Joerdens) G.; grad. College Graudenz, West Prussia, 1900; served agrl. apprenticeship 1 1/2 yrs.; m. Mabel Lester Townsend; 1 son by previous marriage, James F. Came to U.S. in 1901, naturalized, 1908. With Am. Beet Sugar Co., Colo., 1903-05; foreman constrn., Am. Falls Canal & Power Co., Ida., 1905-06; field supt. Holly Sugar Co., Colo., 1906-07; cons. practice, 1908—, also supervision farms and ranches; investigations and reports on agrl. conditions Atlantic States, 1923—; asst. dir. agr., L.I. R.R., 1925-27. Mem. Colo. N.G., 1910-12. Nat. Farm Chemurgic Council, Am. Farm Congress (bd. govs.) Internat. Farm Congress (v.p. 1912-17), Internat. Irrigation Congress (v.p.), A.A.A.S., Am. Acad. Polit. and Social Sci. Am. Geog. Soc., Farmers' Independence Council Am. (dir.), Am. Soybean Assn., Am. Soc. Sugar Beet Technologists, Patrons of Husbandry (Grange). Republican. Protestant. Elks. Widely known as speaker on agrl. topics. Home: Bayport, L.I., N.Y. Died Aug. 11, 1958.

GUCKER, FRANK THOMSON, chemist; b. Phila., Apr. 8, 1900; s. Frank Thomson and Louise Dliphant (Fulton) G.; B.A., Haverford Coll., 1920, A.M., 1921, LL.D., 1966; Ph.D., Harvard U., 1925; m. Eleonore Dubois Harris, 1925; children—Frank Fulton, Katharine Harris (Mrs. Herbert H. Hand). Research asst. Harvard U., 1924-25; nat. research fellow. Cal. Inst. Tech., 1925-27; research fellow, Harvard U., 1927-28; research chemist, duPont Co., 1928-29; asst. prof. Northwestern U., 1929-36, asso. prof., 1936-42, prof. 1942-47; prof. and chmn. dept. of chemistry Ind. U., 1947-51, dean Coll. Arts and Scis., 1951-65, research prof. chemistry, 1965-70, research prof. emeritus chemistry, 1970-73, dir. research on phys. chemistry aerosols, 1970-73. Chief tech. aide Nat. Def. Research Com., 1941-42; mem. com. phys. Chemistry NRC, 1951-54; regional councilor Office Ordnance Research, 1951-54, mem. com. on awards in Chemistry under the Fulbright Act, 1954, chmn., 1955-59. Cons. Nat. Sci. Found. (mem. adv. panel chemistry div. math., phys., engring. scis., 1957-60, chmn. 1958-59); cons. Ford Found. Latin Am. Program, 1965; exec. com. Inter-Univ. Com. Travel Grants, 1966-69. Mem. Oak Ridge Nat. Lab. Adv. Com., Reactor Chemistry, 1961-63. Mem. exec. com. Am. Council Academic Deans, 1961-65; mem. commn. on liberal learning Assn. Am. Colls., 1966-68, chmn. 1968, exec. com. spl. com. liberal studies, 1968. Mem. alumni council Haverford Coll., 1957-60. Fellow Carnegie Instn., 1940-50. Fellow A.A.A.S., Ind. Acad. Sci.; Am. Soc. Testing Materials (instrumentation subcom. com. methods atmospheric sampling and analysis), Am. Assn. U. Profs., Am. Chem. Soc. (asso. editor Chem. Revs. 1950-53; sec.-treas. 1952-53, chmn. elect 1953-54, chmn. div. phys. and inorganic chemistry 1954-55; councilor, chmn. council policy com. 1959-61, mem. com. nominations and elections 1963-68, sec. 1964-66, chmn. 1967-68), Phi Beta Kappa (chpt. pres. 1965-66), Alpha Chi Sigma, Sigma Xi, Phi Lambda Upsilon. Presbyn. Club: Faculty Men's (Ind. U.). Author: (with Ralph L. Seifert) Physical Chemistry, 1966; textbooks; also articles assn. jours. Home: Bloomington IN Died Mar. 6, 1973.

GUDAKUNST, DONALD WELSH, (good'a-koonst), med. dir.; b. Paulding, O., Aug. 18, 1894; s. William Edward and Fannie May (Welsh) G.; B.S., U. of Mich., 1917, M.D., 1919; Dr. P.H., Wayne U., 1937; m. Jen Fray, June 20, 1921; 1 dau., Betty Sue; m. 2d, Bernice Drahner, Sept. 16, 1932. Industrial physician Solway Process Co., Detroit, Mich., 1920; county health officer, Roswell, N.M., 1921-23; dir. sch. health service, Detroit Dept. of Health, 1924-37; prof. pub. health and preventive medicine, Wayne Univ., 1937-41; dep. health commr. Detroit Dept. of Health, 1932-37; state health commr., Mich. State Dept. of Health, 1938-39; sr. surgeon (R.), U.S.P.H.S., 1939; med. dir., Nat. Foundation for Infantile Paralysis since Jan. 1, 1940. Fellow Am. Pub. Health Assn., N.Y. Acad. of Medicine, A.M.A.; mem. Alpha Kappa Kappa, Delta Omega. Contbr. to med. jours. Home: North Av., Westport, Conn. Address: 120 Broadway, New York, N.Y. Died Jan. 20, 1946.

GUDGER, EUGENE WILLIS, (gud'jer), ichthyologist; b. Waynesville, N.C., Aug. 10, 1866; s. James Cassius Lowry and Mary Goodwin (Willis) G.; student Emory & Henry Coll., Va., 1883-87; B.S., U. of Nashville, 1892, M.S., 1893; Ph.D., Johns Hopkins, 1905; unmarried. Instr. science high sch., Asheville, N.C., 1893-94, Asheville Coll., 1894-59, Peabody High Sch., Little Rock, Ark., 1895-1901; lab. asst. Gen. Biol. Lab., Johns Hopkins, 1902-04; prof. biology, N.C. Coll. for Women, Greensboro, N.C., 1905-19; investigator U.S. Bur. Fisheries, Beaufort, N.C., 1902-11; research asso., Tortugas Lab., Carnegie Inst., 1912-15; editor Vol. III, Bibliography of Fishes (Am. Museum), 1919-23; asso. in ichthyology, Am. Museum, 1921, bibliographer in ichthyology, 1923-38, associate curator, 1935-38; now hon. associate in ichthyology, Am. Museum and librarian Dean Memorial Library. Fellow A.A.A.S., New York Zoöl. Society; mem. Am. Museum of Natural History (life), Am. Soc. Zoölogists, Am. Soc. Naturalists, History of Science Soc., N.C. Acad. Science (sec. 1907-18; pres. 1918; life mem.); hon. corr. mem. Salmon-Trout Association of Gt. Britain; corr. mem. Zoöl. Soc. of London, 1939. Mason. Author: (brochures) Breeding Habits of Segmentation of Egg of Pipe Fish, 1908; Habits and Life History Toadfish, 1910; History of the Spotted Eagle Ray, 1914; Natural History of the Whale Shark, 1915; Structure and Habits of Barracuda, 1918; Use of the Sucking Fish for Catching Fish, 1919; Myth of Ship-holder, 1919; Rains of Fishes, 1921; Smallest Shark-suckers, 1926; Live Fishes in Throat of Man, 1926; Nesting Habits of Gunnell, 1927; A Three-eyed Haddock, 1928; Nicolas Pike's Fishes of Mauritius, 1929; The Candiru, the Only Vertebrate Parasite of Man, 1930; Fishes with Two Mouths, Some Spider Fishermen, Fourth Florida Whale Shark and Model in American Museum, The Opah on the California Coast, 1931; Cannibalism among Sharks, Dolphin on Coast of North Carolina, 1932; Abnormal Dentition in Rays, 1933; Ambicoloration in Flatfishes, 1934; Geographical Distribution of the Whale Shark; Breathing Valves in Sharkes and Telcosts, 1935; Reversal in Flatfishes, 1935; Beginnings of Fish Teratology (15S5-1642), 1936; Natural History and Geographical Distribution of the Pointed-tailed Ocean Sunfish, Abnormal Dentition in Sharks, 1937; Two-headed Trout, 8 inches long—the Record Size, 1938; A School of Whale Sharks in the Bahama Islands, 1938; Whale Sharkes in Gulf of Mexico, 1938; Whale Sharks Rammed by Steamers, Pugnacity of Swordfish Shown in Attacks on Vessels, Swordfishing in the Strait of Messina, Breeding Habits and Embryology of Frilled Shark (all 1940); Feeding Organs and Food of Whale Shark, Behavior of Whale Shark, Quest of Smallest Fish (all 1941): Giant Fresh Water Fishes of North America, Swordfishing with Harpoon in New England Waters, 1942; Fish-Eating Bats of India and Burma, 1943; The Stingray's Sting Poisonous to Man; The Earliest Winged Fish-catchers; Fishes That Play Leapfrog, Fishes That Swim Tandem-fashion, 1944; Fish-eating Bats of the Caribbean Region, The Frogfish (Antennarius) and the Anglerfish Use Their Lures in Fishing, 1945; Oral

Breathing Valves in Fishes (1685-1935), 1946; Pomacentrid Fishes Symbiotic with Giant Sea Anemones, Utricularia, the only known Fish-Catching Plant, 1947; The Tiger Shark on the N.C. Coast and its Food there, 1948. Editor of Bashford Dean Memorial Volume; editor for ichthyological terms in 2d edit. Webster's New Internat. Dictionary, 1935. Home: Waynesville, N.C. Address: American Museum of Natural History, N.Y.C. 24. Died Feb. 19, 1956.

GUENTHER, AUGUST ERNEST, physiologist, educator; b. Sandusky, O., Jan. 20, 1874; s. August and Sophie (Kolbe) G.; grad. Sandusky High Sch., 1892, Univ. of Mich., S. B., 1898; unmarried. Asst. in Univ. of Mich. Mus., 1894-7; asst. in physiology, med. dept. Univ. of Mich., 1897-1901; fellow in physiology, 1903-4, asst. in physiology since 1904, Johns Hopkins Univ. Author: (with Dr. T. C. Guenther) volume on Physiology (in Epitome of Medicine), 1903 L12. Residence: 1818 N. Broadway, Baltimore

GUESS, HARRY ADEIBERT, mining engr.; b. Hartington, Ont., Can., Nov. 21, 1875; s. Charles Wellington and Augusta (Shorey) G.; M.A., Queen's Univ., Kingston, 1895, LL.D., 1926; m. Eva Young, Winnipeg, Can., June 19, 1901 (died Mar. 13, 1935); 1 son, Shorey Cameron; m. 2d, Vista Brabham, Mar. 18, 1936 (died Dec. 24, 1940); 1 son, Harry Adelbert Jr. Came to United States, 1901, naturalized citizen, 1923. Has been connected with the American Smelting & Refining Co. since 1901, as manager various mines, in charge metal mining explorations and operations, v.p. since 1917, in charge of mining operations and explorations; chmn. Big Bell Mines, Ltd. (Western Australia); pres. Neptune Gold Mining Co., Buchans Mining Co., Ltd., Premier Gold Mining Co., Ltd. (Can.), Montezuma Lead Co. and Cia Metalurgica Mexicana, Silbak Premier Mines, Ltd. (Can.), Toburn Gold Mines Co. (Can.); v.p. Northern Peru Mining & Smelting Co., Federal Mining & Smelting Co., N.Y. and Honduras Rosario Mining Co.; dir. Compania Minera Asarco (Mexico), Revere Copper & Brass Co., Inc., Towne Mines, Inc., Gen. Cable Corp. Mem. Am. Inst. Mining & Metall. Engrs., Mining and Metall. Soc. America. Republican. Presbyterian. Clubs: University, Bankers. Home: 8 Markwood Rd., Forest Hills, L.I., N.Y. Office: 120 Broadway, New York, N.Y. Died Apr. 11, 1946.

GUION, CONNIE M., physician; b. Lincolnton, N.C., Aug. 29, 1882; d. Benjamin Simmons and Catherine (Caldwell) Guion; student Kate Ship Sch., Lincolnton, Northfield (Mass.) Sem.; A.B., Wellesley Coll., 1906, D.Sc. (hon.), 1950; A.M., Cornell, 1913, M.D., 1917, D.Sc. (hon.), Women's Medical Coll. of Pa., 1953; D.Sc. (honorary), Queen's College, Charlotte, N.C., 1957; Doctor of Laws, Univ. of North Carolina, 1965. Successively instr. of chemistry, Vassar Coll., prof. of chemistry and head dept., Sweet Briar (Va.) Coll., asst. attdg. physician, Bellevue Hosp., Cornell U. div. and N.Y. Infirmary for Women and Children; chief med. clinic, Cornell U. Med. Coll., 1929-32; clinic became part of New York Hosp., 1932, and since served as chief med. clinic; asst. prof. medicine, Cornell U. Med. Coll., 1929-36, asso. prof., 1936-46, prof. of clinical medicine, 1946-52, professor of clinical medicine emeritus, 1952-71; asst. attending physician, N.Y. Hosp., 1932-42, asso. attending physician, 1942-43, attending physician, 1943-50, cons. pvt. practice med. N.Y.C. specialist in internal medicine. Recipient Elizabeth Blackwell citation, N.Y. Infirmary for Women and Children, Jan. 1949. Mem. bd. dir., 1956, Sweet Briar Coll. Served as mem. indsl. council, Dept. of Labor of State of N.Y. Formerly chmn. Med. Appeals Unit. Mem. adv. com., Nat. Health and Safety Council of Girl Scouts. Recipient, Award of Distinction, Cornell U. Medical College, 1951, Northfield Award for distinguished service, 1951, Jane Addams medal for distinguished service Rockford Coll., 1963. Diplomate American Bd. Internal Medicine. Member New York Academy of Medicine, New York State Medical Assn., Med. Women's Assn., Shakespeares Soc., Phi Beta Kappa, Sigma Xi, Alpha Omega Alpha. Club: Wellesley (N.Y. City), Cosmopolitan. Contbr. numerous papers on med. subjects. Home: New York City NY Died Apr. 30, 1971; buried Charlotte NC

GUITERAS, JUAN, physician; b. Matanzas, Cuba, Jan. 4, 1852; s. Eusebio and Josefa (Gener) G.; ed. at La Empresa, Matanzas; M.D., U. of Pa., 1873 (Ph.D.); m. Mrs. Dolores Guiteras, née Gener, of Matanzas, May 5, 1883. Resident and visiting phys. to Phila. Hosp., 1873-79; marine hosp. service, 1879-89; served as expert in yellow fever in all epidemics, 1881—; prof. medicine, Charleston Med. Sch., 1884-88; prof. pathology, U. of Pa., 1889-99; on staff Gen. Shafter as yellow fever expert in Santiago campaign, 1898; prof. gen. pathology and tropical diseases, U. of Havana, 1900-21; dir. of pub. health, Cuba, 1909-21, and pres. Nat. Bd. of Health; sec. Public Health and Charities, Cuba, 1921-22, resigned. Prominent in Cuban politics in this country. Editor La Revista de Medicina Tropical. Pres. 2d Nat. Med. Congress of Cuba; v.p. Assn. of Health Officers of N. America, Am. Public Health Assn.; mem. Yellow Fever Commn. of Internat. Health Bd. of the Rockefeller Foundation, 1916—. Discovered filaria Bancrofti in the U.S. and uncinaria in Cuba. Home: Benavides, Cuba. Died Oct. 28, 1925.

GUMMERE, JOHN, educator, mathematician; b. Willow Grove, Pa., 1784; s. Samuel and Rachel (James) G.; m. Elizabeth Bugby, 1808, at least 1 son Samuel James. For most part self-educated; taught mathematics, Horsham, Pa., 1803-05; taught in Rancocas, N.J., 1806-11; opened, operated boarding sch., Burlington, N.J., 1814-33; elected to Am. Philos. Soc., 1814, began contbg. articles to their Transactions; taught mathematics Haverford (Mass.) Sch., 1833-44, supt., several years; reestablished (with son Samuel James) sch., Burlington, 1843-45; recognized as one of ablest mathematicians in U.S. at that time. Author: A Treatise on Surveying, 1814; Elementary Treatise on Astronomy, 1822. Died May 31, 1845.

GUMPERT, MARTIN, (goom'pert), physician; b. Berlin, Germany, Nov. 13, 1897; s. Ely and Elise (Abraham) G.; studied medicine Univ. of Heidelberg; M.D., U. of Berlin, 1923; m. Charlotte Blaschko, Jan. 27, 1923 (died 1933); 1 dau., Nina. Came to U.S., 1936, naturalized, 1942. Resident asst. Rudolf Virchow Hosp., Berlin, 1923-27; dir. city clinic for skin and venereal diseases, Berlin-Wedding, 1927-33; engaged in practice as physician, also writer, New York, New York, 1936—; staff member Goldwater Memorial Hosp. research service; chief of Geriatric Clinic, Jewish Memorial Hospital; medical adviser Time Magazine, 1943-45. Fellow American Geriatric Soc., A.M.A.; mem. Gerontological Soc.; New York Medical Society, American Public Health Association, Am. Authors League. Author: Verkettung, 1916; Heimkehr des Herzens, 1921; Venereal Diseases in Childhood, 1926; Handbook of Deformity Diseases, 1931; Hahnemann Biography, 1934; Life for the Idea, 1935; Trailblazers of Science, 1936; Dunant, Story of the Red Cross, 1938; Hell in Paradise: Autobiography, 1939; Heil Hunger! Health under Hitler, 1940; First Papers, 1941; You Are Younger Than You Think, 1944; Birthday (novel), 1949; Reports from Abroad, 1949, The Prejudice Against Old Age, 1951, Anatomy of Happiness, 1951. Contbr. articles to mags., including Readers Digest, Red Book, Coronet, Nation, Survey Graphic. Home: 315 E. 68th St. N.Y.C. Died Apr. 18, 1955.

GUNDER, DWIGHT FRANCIS, engineer; b. Ames, Ia., Dec. 11, 1905; s. F. E. and Catherine (Cooney) G.; B.S., Ia. State Coll., 1925, M.S., 1926; Ph.D., U. Wis., 1933; m. Kathryn Mae Lamb, 1932. Prof., Colo. A. and M. Coll., 1926-47; prof. and head dept. engring. mechanics and engring. materials Cornell since 1947-56; cons. Hercules Powder Company, Rohm & Haas Company, Project Lincoln (Massachusetts Institute of Technology), Project Rand, Rock Island Arsenal. Spl. advisor Bur. Ordnance, USN (rockets, missiles). Served as engr., U.S. A.S.F., 1943-45. Mem. Am. Soc. M.E., Am. Soc. C.E., Am. Soc. Engring. Edn., Am. Soc. for Metals, Am. Soc. Testing Materials, Math. Assn. Am., Sigma Xi, Phi Kappa Phi, Tau Beta Pi, Sigma Tau. Author: Engineering Mechanics (with D. A. Stuart), 1959. Home: 463 W. 5th St., Loveland, Colo. 80537. Died Oct. 21, 1964; buried Loveland Burial Park, Loveland, Colo.

GUNLOCK, V(IRGIL) E(MMETT), profl. engr.; b. New Canton, Ill., May 18, 1905; s. John and Elta (Gard) G.; student James Millikin U., 1924; B.S. in Civil Engring., U. Ill., 1927; m. Drew Chenoweth, May 18, 1940; children—Karen Ann, George Warren. Asst. engr. San Dist. of Chgo., 1927-38; resident engr. Chgo. Subways, 1938-41; engr. subway constrn., Chgo., 1941-43, chief subway engr., 1943-45, commr. subways and superhighways, 1945-52, commr. pub. works, 1952-54; chmn. Chgo. Transit Bd., 1954—. Trustee McCormick Theol. Sem., Chgo. Mem. Chgo. Plan Commn., Am. Soc. C.E., Western Soc. Engrs., Nat. Soc. Profl. Engrs., Tau Beta Pi. Presbyn. Home: 525 Arlington Pl., Chgo. 60614. Office: Merchandise Mart, Chgo. 60654. Died Mar. 21, 1963.

GUNN, JAMES NEWTON, indsl. engr.; b. Springfield, O., 1867; s. Rev. James and Mary (Johnson) G.; m. Mabel Scott, 3 daus. With Library Bur. of Boston, circa 1892-1901, developed use of comml. card indexes, patented tab index card and vertical file; early worker in field of indsl. and prodn. engring.; organized Gunn, Richards & Co., Bus. Consultants, 1901; cons. for Campbell's Soup Co., Pa. Steel Corp., Studebaker Corp., 1901-11; pres. U.S. Tire Co., also asst. to pres. U.S. Rubber Co., 1915-23; an organizer Harvard Grad. Sch. of Bus. Adminstrn.; represented Rubber Assn. on War Industries Bd., 1917-18; pres. Lincoln Hwy. Assn. Died Nov. 26, 1927.

GUNN, ROSS, research physicist; b. Cleve., May 12, 1897; s. Ross Delano Aldrich and Lora Arletta (Conner) G.; B.S. in E.E., U. Mich., 1920, M.S., 1921; Ph.D., Yale, 1926; m. Gladys Jeannette Rowley, Sept. 8, 1923; children—Ross, Andrew Leigh, Charles Rowley, Robert Burns. Instr. engring. physics, U. Mich., 1920-22; radio research engr. U.S. Air Service, 1922-23; instr. physics, Yale, 1923-27; research physicist U.S. Naval Research Lab., 1927-33, tech. adviser, 1933-47, supt. mechanics and electricity div. 1938-46; supt. aircraft elec. div., 1943-46; supt. physics div., 1946-47; tech. dir., Army-Navy Precipitation Static Project, 1943-46; Amry-Navy Atmospheric Electricity Project, 1946-47; cons. NACA, 1943-59, NDRC, 1942-43; Research and Development Bd., 1946-48. Dir. phys. research, U.S. Weather Bur., 1947-57; also asst. chief, 1955-56; research prof. physics, Am. U., 1958—; cons. AEC, 1958-60; dir. Air-Force-Weather Bur. Cloud Physics Project physics, Am. U., 1958—; cons. AEC, 1958-60; A.F., 1948-53; cons. C.F. Kettering Found. 1951-54. Inventor instruments and specialized devices, several fundamental contbns. Served in U.S. Signal Res. Corps, World War I. Cited by sec. of navy for exceptionally distinguished service in connection with devel. of atomic bomb, 1945; Distinguished Service award, Flight Safety Found., 1951, Robert M. Losey Award, Inst. of Aero. Scis., 1956, also recipient Gold medal for Exceptional Service U.S. Dept. Commerce, 1957, Distinguished Alumnus award U. Mich., 1953. Fellow Am. Phys. Soc., I.E.E.E., Geophys. Union; mem. Nat. Acad. Scis., Am. Meterol. Soc., Sigma Xi, Tau Beta Pi. Author more than 100 sci. and tech. articles. Inventor, organizer 1st work on atomic powered submarine. Patentee in field. Address: American University, Washington. Died Oct. 15, 1966; buried Bethesda Methodist Church Cemetery.

GUNTHER, CHARLES OTTO, prof. mathematics and ordnance engring.; b. N.Y.C., May 21, 1879; s. Otto and Anna (Eybel) G.; M.E., Stevens Inst. Tech., 1900, D.Sc., 1950; m. Beatrice Disbrow, Feb. 19, 1901; children—Beatrix (Mrs. Fred B. Llewellyn), Jack Disbrow. With Stevens Inst. of Tech. 1900—, as instr. in mathematics, 1900-02, asst. prof., 1902-03, asst. prof. mathematics and mech. drawing, 1903-04, mathematics and mechanics, 1904-08, prof. and head of dept., 1908-36, prof. mathematics and ordnance engring., 1936-50, emeritus prof. mathematics and engring., 1950—, dean of student activities, 1920-25, dean of sophomores, 1927-28. Served with Ordnance Dept., U.S. Army, 1918-19; now lt. col. Ordnance Dept. Army U.S., inactive duty. Recipient of Stevens Honor Award, 1947; Stevens Alumni award, 1957. Fellow A.A.A.S.; mem. Army Ordnance Assn., Assn. Mathematics Teachers of New Jersey (past president, member council), Am. Soc. Civil Engrs. (life member), Am. Society Mech. Engrs., Soc. Am. Mil. Engrs., Societe Astronomique de France, Tau Beta Pi, Sigma Nu. Club: Officers of Army and Navy (New York). Author: Integration by Trigonometric and Imaginary Substitution, 1907; The Identification of Firearms from Ammunition Fired Therein, 1935. Contbr. to jours. Home: Grand View-on-Hudson, Nyack 9, N.Y. Office: Stevens Institute of Technology, Hoboken, N.J. Died June 8, 1958.

GUTENBERG, BENE, (goo'ten-berg), prof. geophysics; b. Darmstadt, Germany, June 4, 1889; s. Hermann and Pauline (Hachenburger) G.; student Technische Hochschule, Darmstadt, 1907-08; Ph.D., U. of Göttingen, 1911; Ph.D. (honorary), U. Uppsala, Sweden, 1955; m. Hertha Dernburg, Aug. 17, 1919; children—Arthur, Stephanie. Came to U.S., 1930, naturalized, 1936. Began as asst. in central office Internat. Seismol. Assn., Strasbourg, 1913; prof. geophysics, U. Frankfurt am Main, 1926-30; professor geophysics, Cal. Inst. Tech., Pasadena, since 1930. Pres. Internat. Assn. for Seismology and Physics of Interior of Earth, 1951-54. Awarded Prix de Physique du Globe, Acad. Royal de Belgique. Served in German Army, World War, 1914-18. Recipient William Bowie Medal, 1953; Wiechert Medal 1956. Fellow Royal Astronomical Society; foreign member Geological Society, London; member Seismol. Soc. Am. (pres. 1945), Geol. Soc. Am., Am. Geophys Union, A.A.A.S., Soc. Exploration Geophysicists, Nat. Acad. Sci.; hon. mem. Royal Soc. New Zealand; corr. mem. Finnish Geog. Soc.; foreign mem. Academy Lincei, Rome; Swedish Acad. Sci.; Finnish Acad. Letters and Science. Author: Seismicity of the Earth (with C. F. Richter), 1949. Author, co-author or editor several books pub. in Germany; also more than 150 scientific papers. Editor: Internal Constitution of the Earth. Made first exact determination of radius of earth's core; regarded as authority on earthquakes. Home: 526 S. Sierra Vista Av., Pasadena 10. Office: Seismological Laboratory, 220 N. San Rafael Av., Pasadena 2, Cal. Died Jan. 1960.

GUTERMAN, CARL EDWARD FREDERICK, (goot'er-man), plant pathologist; b. West Springfield, Mass., Oct. 27, 1903; s. Hans Wilhelm and Edith Arbella (Williams) G.; B.Sc., Mass. State Coll., 1925; Ph.D., Cornell, 1930; m. Hilda La Verne Kelly, July 7, 1926; children—Phyllis May, Donald Carl; m. 2d Mary M. Wetzsteon, July 21, 1949; step-children—Ross D. Wetzsteon, R. Scott Wetzsteon. Asst. plant pathology, Cornell, 1925-27, lily disease investigation fellow, 1927-30, asst. prof., 1930-36, prof., 1936—, asst. dir. Agr. Expt. Sta., 1936-42, dir. 1942—; dir. research, N.Y. State Coll. Agr. and N.Y. State Coll. Home Econs. (Cornell), 1942—. Mem. food protection com. Nat. Research Council 1950-53, N.Y. State Council, U.S. Dept. Agr., 1948—, N.Y. State Agr. Mobilization Commn., 1951-54. Dir. Cornell Research Found. Fellow A.A.A.S.; mem. Am. Inst. Biol. Scis., Am. Phytopath. Soc. (plant disease prevention com. 1944-48), Forest City Grange, N.Y. State Agr. Soc., Land Grant College Assn. (chmn. expt. sta. sect. 1952-53, sec. div. agr. 1952-53), Kappa Sigma, Gamma Alpha, Phi Kappa Phi, Sigma Xi. Unitarian. Clubs: Cornell of Ithaca, Statler. Contbr. articles on plant diseases and adminstrn. of agrl. research. Home: "The Byway," Forest Home, Ithaca, N.Y. Died Mar. 27, 1957; buried East Lawn Cemetery, Ithaca.

GUTHE, KARL EUGEN, physicist; b. Hanover, Germany, Mar. 5, 1866; s. Otto and Anna (Hanstein) G.; ed. Gymnasium, Hanover, Hanover Tech. Sch., univs. of Marburg, Strassburg and Berlin; passed state exam., Marburg, 1889, Ph.D., 1892; m. Clara Belle Ware, 1892. Came to U.S., 1892; instr. physics, 1893-1900, asst. prof., 1900-03, U. of Mich.; asso. physicist, Bur. of Standards, 1903-05; prof. physics, State U. of Iowa, 1905-09; prof. physics, 1909—, dean of Grad. Dept., 1912—, U. of Mich. Mem. jury of awards (electricity) St. Louis Expn., 1904. Fellow A.A.A.S. (v.p. 1908). Author: Manual of Physical Measurements (with J. O. Reed), 1902, 07, 12; Laboratory Exercises with Primary and Storage Cells, 1903; Textbook of Physics (joint author), 1908, 1909; College Physics (with J. O. Reed), 1911; Definitions in Physics, 1913. Home: Ann Arbor, Mich. Died Sept. 10, 1915.

GUTHRIE, ALFRED, engr.; b. Sherburne, N.Y., Apr. 1, 1805; s. Dr. Samuel and Sybil (Sexton) G.; studied medicine and chemistry under his father; m. Nancy Piper, Oct. 2, 1823; m. 2d, Phoebe Guthrie, Mar. 31, 1857. Moved West due to financial distress, 1845; engr., designed and constructed hydraulic works on Ill. and Mich. Canal in order to carry Chgo. sewerage to Mississippi River; aided devel. of fed. system of steamship inspection, inspected over 200 vessels and determined their defects, succeeded in having bill introduced into Congress providing for regulation, 1851, placed at head of enforcement bureau when bill passed, 1852, number of steamboat accidents steadily decreased under his leadership. Died Chgo., Aug. 17, 1882.

GUTHRIE, CHARLES CLAUDE, physiologist; b. nr. Wentzville, Mo., May 13, 1880; s. Robert McCluer and Fannie (Hall) G.; grad. Woodlawn Inst., O'Fallon, Mo., 1897; M.D., U. Mo., 1901, Sc.D., 1962; Ph.D., U. Chgo., 1907; Sc.D., U. Pitts., 1935. Instr. U. Mo., 1901-02; demonstrator physiology, Western Res. U., Cleve., 1902-03; instr. physiology, U. Chgo., 1903-06; prof. physiology and pharmacology, Washington U., 1906-09; prof. physiology and pharmacology, U. Pitts., 1909-49, emeritus 1949-63. Served to maj. Med. Res. Corps, Dept. of War, 1917-43. Recipient award Am. Assn. Plastic Surgeons, 1962. Mem. Am. Physiol. Soc., Soc. Pharmacology and Exptl. Therapeutics, Soc. Exptl. Biology and Medicine, Sigma Xi, Alpha Omega Alpha. Author: Blood Vessel Surgery and Its Applications, 1912; also contbr. articles on physiol. and other med. problems to profl. jours. Home: 814 Hitt St., Columbia, Mo. 65201. Died June 16, 1963; buried Columbia Cemetery.

GUTHRIE, DAVID VANCE, astronomer; b. nr. Staunton, Va., Oct. 15, 1884; s. Walter Craig and Sallie Lyle (Gilkeson) G.; B.A., Washington and Lee U., 1903, M.A., 1904; Ph.D., Johns Hopkins, 1908; m. Hallie McPheeters See, June 30, 1914; children—Elizabeth See, David Vance. Vol. research asst. Yerkes Obs., Wis., 1908; instr. physics U. Va., 1908-10, adj. prof., 1910-11; prof. physics and astronomy La. State U., 1912-55, emeritus, founder, dir. Astron. Obs., 1939-55; head dept. physics Emory and Henry Coll., Emory, Va., 1955-58; professor of physics and astronomy and head department of physics Catawba Coll., Salisbury, N.C., 1958-59. Mem. Am. Assn. Physics Tchrs., Am. Astron. Soc., Phi Beta Kappa, Phi Kappa Phi (pres. La. State U. chpt., 1946-47). Democrat. Presbyn. Contbr. numerous articles on electromagnetic theory of light to sci. publs. Address: Fort Defiance, Va. Died Dec. 4, 1962; buried Tinkling Spring Presbyn. Ch. Cemetery, nr. Staunton, Va.

GUTHRIE, JOSEPH EDWARD, prof. zoölogy; b. York, N.Y., Sept. 24, 1871; s. James F. and Agnes (McCracken) G.; B.S., U. of Minn., 1900, M.S., 1901; m. Emma Florence Brooks, Dec. 28, 1904; children—Charles Francis, Jean Brooks. With Ia. State Coll. Agr. and Mechanic Arts, 1901—, consecutively asst. in zoölogy until 1904, asst. prof., 1904-14, asso. prof., 1914-17, prof., 1917—. Conglist. Author: The Collembola of Minnesota, 1903; The Snakes of Iowa, 1926. Home: Ames, Ia. Died Apr. 16, 1935.

GUTHRIE, SAMUEL, chemist; b. Brimfield, Mass., 1782; s. Samuel and Sarah Guthrie; attended Coll. Physicians and Surgeons, N.Y.C., 1810-11, U. Pa., 1815; m. Sybil Sexton, 1804, 4 children including Alfred, Edwin. Moved from Sherburne (N.Y.) to Sacketts Harbor, N.Y., 1817, practiced medicine, set up exptl. chem. lab.; said to have invented an effective priming powder called "percussion pill" and punch lock for exploding it which together made the flintlock musket obsolete; devised process for rapid conversion of potato starch into molasses, 1830; made "chloric ether" by distilling chloride of lime with alcohol in copper (proved to be chloroform). Author: The Complete Writings of Samuel Guthrie (collection of letters and comments), 1832. Died Sacketts Harbor, Oct. 19, 1848.

GUY, WILLIAM EVANS, retired mining and civil engr.; b. Cincinnati, Dec. 22, 1844; s. Alexander (M.D.) and Susan Ann Livingston (Wade) G.; Miami U., Oxford, O., 1860-62, 1863; A.B., Princeton, 1865, A.M., 1868; U. of Heidelberg, Germany, 1865-66; Freiberg Sch. of Mines, 1866-69; Collége de France, Paris, 1869; LL.B., Cincinnati Law Sch., 1879; LL.D., Westminster Coll., Fulton, Mo., 1917; m. Katharine, d. of Dr. E. S. Lemoine, of St. Louis, Mar. 13, 1894; children—Katherine Lemoine (Mrs. Henry S. F. Cooper), William Edwin, David Wade, Evelyn Spotswood. Asst. supt., Stewart Silver Reduction Works, Georgetown, Colo., 1870-71; asst. geologist, Mo. State Geol. Survey, 1872; one of 3 founders, and v.p. St. Louis Bolt & Iron Co., 1872-81; also organized, and was pres. Tudor Iron Works, 1879-81; consolidated the two as Tudor Iron Works, of which was v.p., 1881-86; organized, built and was pres. of St. Louis & Eastern Ry., 1889-95; organized, and was pres. Madison Coal Co., 1889-99; organized, built and was pres. and gen. mgr. St. Louis, Peoria & Northern Ry., 1895-99, when it became part of the I.C. system; organized, built and was pres. and gen. mgr. St. Louis Valley Ry., 1901-03 (now part Mo.P. Ry.), also St. Louis & Gulf Ry., 1902-03 (now part Frisco system); retired. Pvt. and 1st sergt. 86th Ohio Inf., 1862. Nominated for pres. City Council, St. Louis, 1900; mem. exec. com. Civil Service Reform Assn. 20 yrs. Presbyn. Home: St. Louis; (summer) Cooperstown, N.Y. Died July 24, 1928.

GUYER, MICHAEL FREDERIC, zoologist; b. Plattsburg, Mo., Nov. 17, 1874; s. Michael and Sarah J. (Thomas) G.; U. of Mo., 1890-92; B.S., U. of Chicago, 1894; A.M., U. of Neb., 1897; Ph.D., U. of Chicago, 1900; LL.D., U. of Mo., 1924; Paris and Naples, 1908-09 (Smithsonian table, at Naples); m. Helen M. Stuaffer, Dec. 21, 1899 (died Nov. 4, 1948); 1 son, Edwin Michael Cooley. Asst. in zoology, U. of Neb., 1895-96; teacher biology, Lincoln (Neb.) High Sch., 1896-97; fellow zoology, U. of Chicago, 1897-1900; head dept. biology, U. of Cincinnati, 1900-11; professor zoology, University of Wisconsin, 1911-45; professor emeritus since 1945. Member National Committee on Medical Education, 1928-32. Fellow A.A.A.S. (vice-pres. sec. F 28); mem. Am. Soc. Naturalists, Assn. American Anatomists, Soc. American Zoologists (pres. 1923), Ohio Acad. Sciences, Wis. Acad. Sciences, Am. Micros. Soc. (pres. 1916-18), Soc. Exptl. Biology and Medicine, Wis. Basic Science Board, Acad. Natural Science of Phila, Sigma Xi, Phi Kappa Phi, Phi Beta Pi; corr. mem. Peiping Soc. of Natural History. Clubs: University, Chaos. Author: Animal Micrology, 1906, revised edits., 1917, 30, 36; Being Well Born, 1915, revised edit., 1927; Animal Biology, 1931 (rev. edit. 1948); Speaking of Man, 1942. Also various tech. biol. researches. Address: 138 N. Prospect Av., Madison 5 WI

GUYOT, ARNOLD HENRY, geographer, educator; b. Boudevilliers, Switzerland, Sept. 28, 1807; s. David Pierre and Constance (Favarger) G.; grad. Coll. of Neuchatel, 1825; Ph.D., U. Berlin, 1835; LL.D. (hon.), Union Coll., 1873; m. Sarah Doremus Haines, July 2, 1867. Prof. history and phys. geography Acad. of Neuchatel, 1839-48; 1st to formulate laws of structure and movement of glaciers; came to U.S., 1848; published The Earth and Man; lectured under Mass. Bd. Edn. 6 years; published geography textbooks, 1866-75, made 1st definite attempt at scientific presentation of geography in Am. schs.; prof. phys. geography and geology Princeton, 1854-84; founded museum at Princeton; selected and equipped weather observation stations in N.Y. and Mass. Died Princeton, N.J., Feb. 8, 1884.

GWATHMEY, JAMES TAYLOE, physician; b. Norfolk, Va., Sept. 10, 1863; s. William Watts and Margaret (Tayloe) G.; ed. Norfolk Male Acad., Va. Mil. Inst.; M.D., Vanderbilt U. Med. Dept., 1899; m. Margaret L. Riddle, Dec. 1890. Practiced in N.Y. City, since 1902; anesthetist New York Skin and Cancer Hosp., People's Hosp., Mem. A.M.A., Am. Assn. Anaesthetists, N.Y. Acad. Med., N.Y. Anes. Soc., Kappa Alpha, Southeast. Episcopalian. Club: New York Athletic. Author: Anaesthesia, 1914. Read paper "An Attempt to Abolish Inhalation Anaesthesia" (by mixing ether and oil and placing in lower bowel), before Internat. Med. Congress, London, Eng., 1913; contbr. results of original research in anaesthetics. Introduced (with Capt. Howard T. Karsner) method of giving ether and oil by mouth for painful dressings; with Asa B. Davis, instituted "Obstetrical Analgesia" at Lying-in Hosp., New York, 1923. Home: New York Athletic Club, 180 Central Park S. Office: 133 E. 58th St., New York. Died Feb. 1944.

HAAG, HARVEY B(ERNHARDT), (hag), pharmacologist; b. Richmond, Va., Sept. 16, 1900; s. Georg N. and Anna Louisa Anderson (Lund) H.; Ph.G., sch. of pharmacy, Med. Coll. of Va., 1923, M.D., 1928, S.B., 1931; student, Coll. of William and Mary, 1923-24; m. Gladys Vaden, Sept. 25, 1926. Asst. physiology and pharmacology Med. Coll. of Va., 1924-28, asst. prof. of physiology and pharmacology, 1929-31, aso. prof. 1932-36, prof. of pharmacology since 1936, dean, sch. medicine, 1947-50. Mem. American Soc. Pharmacology and Exptl. Therapeutics (past pres.), So. Soc. Clin. Research, Nat. Safety Council (com. on tests for intoxication), A.M.A., Virginia Medical Society, Richmond Academy of Medicine, So. Med. Association, A.A.A.S., Soc. for Exptl. Biology and Medicine, Am. Pharm. Assn., Am. Therapeutic Soc. (p.p.), Alpha Omega Alpha. Democrat. Contbd. many sci. articles to journals. Home: 603 N. Davis Av., Richmond 20, Va. Died Oct. 14, 1961.

HABER, ERNEST STRAIGN, horticulturist; born near Cleveland, Feb. 7, 1896; s. William Henry and Ellen (Straign) H.; B.S., Ohio State U., 1918; M.S., Iowa State Coll., 1922, Ph.D., 1928; m. Helen Reece Barrett Sept. 1, 1918. Asst. prof. horticulture, Iowa State Coll. 1920-32, asso. prof., 1932-40, prof. of horticulture 1940—, head dept., 1947—. Mem. Am. Soc. Hort Science (pres. 1954-55), Sweet Corn Breeders Assn Am. (pres. 1953-54), Iowa Acad. of Sci., Iowa Hort Soc. (dir.), Fed. Gardens Clubs of Iowa (dir.), Sigma Xi Gamma Sigma Delta. Episcopalian. Clubs: All-Breed Dog (past pres., Des Moines), Tallcorn Cocker Spaniel (past pres.). Author: Laboratory Manual in Horticulture (with Nichols), 1948; Plant Propagation (with Mahlstede); also numerous Iowa Agricultural Experimental Sta. bulletins (noted for sweet corn hybrid introductions). Contbr. articles in horticultural and biological jours. Home: 2125 Country Club Rd., Ames Iowa. Died Mar. 11, 1961; buried Ames.

HABERMAN, SOL, microbiologist, educator; b Chgo., Jan. 15, 1914; s. Nathan and Eva (Yankovitch) H.; A.S., N. Tex. Agrl. Coll., 1934; So. Meth. U., 1935 A.B., U. Tex., 1936, M.A., 1937; Ph.D., Ohio State U. 1941; m. Carleta Jeanne Rambo, May 14, 1948; 1 son Hardy Kemp. Bacteriologist, immunologist Baylor U Hosp., from 1939; instr. Coll. Medicine, Baylor U. 1941-43, prof. Coll. Dentistry, 1947, Grad. Sch., from 1950; asso. prof. Southwestern Med. Coll., 1943-52 lectr. bacteriology So. Meth. U.,1947-50; asst. dir Wadley Research Inst. and Blood Center, 1952-56; dir microbiology dept. pathology, Baylor U. Med. Center now dir. grad. studies Dallas div. Grad. Sch. Coll Dentistry. Pres. immuno-hematology sect. 5th Congress Internat. Soc. Hematology, Paris, France, 1954; med adv. bd. Leukemia Soc. Recipient of award of merit Tex Soc. Pathology. Diplomate Am. Bd. Microbiology Fellow Am. Acad. Microbiology, Am. Coll, Dentists Am. Assn. Advancement Sci.; mem. Internat. Soc Hematology (past sec.-gen. Western Hemisphere), Soc Am. Bacteriologists, Am. Assn. Immunologists, Am Assn. U. Profs., Am. Soc. Human Genetics, American Academy of Forensic Science, Sigma Xi, Omicron Kappa Upsilon, also Sigma Pi Sigma, Beta Beta Beta Phi Delta Epsilon. Author: Laboratory Manual for Dental Bacteriology, 1953. Asso. editor various proc Internat. Soc. Hematology; editor newsletter Am. Bd Microbiology. Contbr. profl. publs. Home: Dallas TX Died Apr. 17, 1968.

HACKETT, LEWIS WENDELL, hygienist; b. Benicia Calif., Dec. 14, 1884; s. Hannibal Eugene and Abigail (Sanborn) H.; A.B., Harvard, 1905, M.D., 1912, Dr P.H., 1913; m. Hazel Swinburne Woods, July 1, 1912 (died 1950); children—David, Robert. Teacher Belmont (Calif.) Sch., 1905-08; asst., Harvard Med Sch., 1912-13, instr. in preventive medicine, 1913-14 field staff International Health Division, Rockefeller Foundation, C. and So. Am. 1914-23, Italy and Albania 1924-39, Egypt, 1940, Rio de la Plata and Andean Region, 1940-49 asst. dir., 1927-45, asso. director 1945-49, ret. 1949; lectr. U. of Calif. Sch. of Pub Health, 1950-51, vis. prof. pub. health, 1951-57; lecturer Harvard School of Pub. Health, 1950-56. Formerly engaged investigation of malaria in Mediterranean area Corr. mem. expert com. on malaria, WHO. Heath Clark lecturer, London University, 1934; Lowell lecturer Boston, 1937; v.p. Malaria Commn., Health Orgn. of League of Nations; charter mem. Am. Academy of Tropical Medicine (president 1943); honorary member National Malaria Com. Recipient Walter Reed medal American Soc. of Tropical Medicine and Hygiene 1953; Bernhard Nocht Medal, Tropeninstitut Hamburg, 1957. Fellow of Am. Public Health Assn. Am. Soc. Tropical Medicine and Hygiene (pres. 1958) Royal Soc. Tropical Medicine and Hygiene (hon.) mem. founders' group Am. Bd. Prev. Med. and Pub Health; mem. Harvard Med. Alumni Assn. (president 1953-54), Nat. Malaria Soc., A.A.A.S., Soc. de Path Exotique, Soc. per gli Studi della Malaria, Academia Medicina (Brazil, Argentina), Argentine Soc. Pathol and Epidemiol. (charter mem.), Phi Beta Kappa, Alpha Omega Alpha, Delta Omega. Decorated by Italy Ecuador, Bolivia, Chile, hon. mem. Faculty, Nat. U Chile. Clubs: Aesculapean (Boston); Harvard (San Francisco). Author: Malaria in Europe, 1937 Co-author: Human Malaria, 1941; Malariology, 1949 Editor in chief Am. Jour. of Tropical Medicine and Hygiene, 1951-57. Contbr. to sci. jours. Home: 267 Hillcrest Rd., Berkeley 5, Cal. Died Apr. 28, 1962.

HACKH, INGO W(ALDEMAR) D(AGOBERT) prof. chemistry; b. Stuttgart, Germany, Mar. 25, 1890 s. Eugen and Frieda (Hack) H.; preparatory edn Real-gymnasium and Technische Hochschule Stuttgart; student Drogisten Akademie, Braunschweig Germany; A.B., U. of Calif., 1918; A.M. from the same university, 1933; m. Vera Eliot, Feb. 11, 1919. Came to U.S., 1912, naturalized citizen, 1921. Chemist, control lab., E. de Haen, Germany, 1908-10, Abbott Labs. Chicago, 1912-13, Research Lab. for Tuberculosis Asheville, N.C., 1913-15; lecture and lab. asst., U. of Calif., 1916-18; prof. chemistry, Coll. Phys. and Surg. San Francisco, 1918—. Fellow A.A.A.S., Am. Inst Chemists, Royal Soc. of Arts (London). Lutheran Author: Chemical Reactions and Equations, 1921, 28 A Chemical Dictionary, 1929, 35; Structure Symbols of Organic Compounds, 1931. Home: San Francisco, Calif Died Oct. 19, 1938.

HADEN, RUSSELL LANDRAM, med. educator; b. Palmyra, Va., May 22, 1888; s. Clifton James and Nicie Delima (Landram) H.; A.B., U. of Va., 1910, A.M., 1911; M.D., Johns Hopkins, 1915; m. Isabel McLeod Smith, Oct. 6, 1917; children—Russell Landram, James Coke. Resident house officer, Johns Hopkins Hosp., 1915-16; asst. resident physician, Henry Ford Hosp., Detroit, Mich., 1916-17; dir. of labs., same hosp., 1917-18, 1919-21; asso. prof. medicine, U. of Kan., 1921-23, prof. exptl. medicine, 1923-30; head of dept. medicine, Cleveland (O.) Clinic, 1930-49, ret. 1949, now consultant in medicine and research. First lt. Med. Corps, U.S. Army, asst. chief med. service, base hosp., Camp Lee, Va., 1918-19. Fellow Am. Coll. of Physicians; mem. A.M.A., Am. Assn. of Pathologists and Bacteriologists, Am. Soc. for Clin. Investigation. Am. Clin. and Climatol. Assn., Assn. Am. Physicians, Central Soc. for Clin. Research, Society for Experimental Medicine and Biology, American Society of Clinical Pathologists, Phi Beta Kappa, Sigma Xi, Theta Delta Chi, Nu Sigma Nu, Alpha Omega Alpha, Pithotomy, Rowfant and Pasteur clubs. Democrat. Methodist. Author: Clinical Laboratory Methods, 1923; Dental Infection and Systemic Disease, 1928; Principles of Hematology, 1939. Awarded gold medal by Radiol. Soc. America for contributions to dental roentgenology, 1929. Contbr. on diseases of the blood, focal infection and intestinal obstruction. Home: Brightberry Farm, Crozet, Va. Died Apr. 26, 1952; buried Monticello Meml. Park, Charlottesville, Va.

HADLEY, EVERETT ADDISON, chief engr. Mo. P. Ry.; b. Lowell, Mass., Nov. 19, 1879; s. Frank Milan and Susan Lillian (Eastman) H.; grad high sch., Lowell, 1897; m. Lilla May Sturtevant, Feb. 5, 1902; children—Carleton Sturtevant, Raymond Everett (dec.). Engring. apprentice with Smith & Brooks, Lowell, 1897-1900; with engring. dept. B.&M. R.R., at Boston, 1900-10; engr. of design, with Mo. P. Ry., 1910-15; chief engr. same rd., 1915-18; engr. asst. to regional dir., U.S.R.R. Administration, at St. Louis, 1918-20; again chief engr. Mo. P. Ry., Mar. 1; 1920—. Republican. Conglist. Mason. Home: St. Louis, Mo. Died Nov. 11, 1932.

HADSALL, HARRY HUGH, engr., contractor; b. Wilmington, Ill., July 9, 1875; s. Kittie (Townsend) H.; B.S. in C.E., U. of Ill., 1897; m. Jean Stewart, of Wilmington, July 1, 1903; children—Harry Stewart (dec.), John McIntyre. With Leonard Constrn. Co., Chicago, builders of ry. structures, mfg. plants, hotels, office bldgs., warehouses, etc., since 1907, v.p. and sec. since 1913. Mem. Am. Soc. C.E., Western Soc. Engrs., Kappa Sigma. Clubs: Chicago Engineers', University, South Shore Country, Flossmoor Country. Home: 1121 E. 49th St. Office: 37 S. Wabash Av., Chicago IL

HAERTLEIN, ALBERT, (hart'lin), prof. civil engring.; b. Alton, Ill., Aug. 9, 1895; s. John George and Emma (Elbe) H.; A.B., Harvard, 1916, B.S., Mass. Inst. Tech., 1918, B.S., Harvard, 1918; D.Eng. (honorary), Northeastern University, 1949; m. Ethel Eleanor Lacey, Sept. 17, 1919; children—John Belford, James Allen. Instr. civil engring., Harvard, 1919-23; structural engring., Dwight P. Robinson & Co., N.Y., and Duquesne Light Co., Pittsburgh, 1923-28; lecturer civil engring., Harvard, 1928-29, asso. prof., 1929-40, Gordon McKay prof., 1940—, also associate dean of applied science, 1951—. Served as 1st lt. Corps Engrs., A.E.F., 1918-19; mem. Bd. Registration of Professional Engrs., Commonwealth of Mass., since 1942. Awarded Desmond Fitzgerald Medal, Boston Soc. of Civil Engrs. Fellow Am. Acad. Arts and Sciences; mem. Am. Soc. of Civil Engineers, Newcomen Society, American Concrete Institute, American Railroad Engineering Association, Phi Beta Kappa, Sigma Xi, Tau Beta Pi. Clubs: Harvard (Boston, New York); Harvard Faculty (Cambridge). Contbr. to Sections in Mark's Mech. Engrs. Handbook of 1941. Home: 44 Marion Rd., Watertown 72, Mass. Office: Pierce Hall, Oxford St., Harvard Univ., Cambridge 38, Mass. Died June 7, 1960; buried Mt. Auburn Cemetery, Watertown, Mass.

HAGAN, WILLIAM ARTHUR, veterinarian; b. Fort Scott, Kan., Oct. 14, 1893; s. Arthur Edward and Ann (Hunter) H.; D.V.M., Kan. State Coll., 1915, hon. D.Sc., 1938; M.S., Cornell U., 1918; Doctor of Laws, University Toronto, 1962; m. Esther Grace Lyon, Aug. 29, 1917; children—William Lyon, Janet Ann, Margaret Elaine. Instr. in vet. pathology, Kan. State Coll., 1915-16; with N.Y. State Vet. Coll. at Cornell U., successively as instr. of pathology and bacteriology, asst. prof. and prof., 1916-59, head of dept., 1926-46, dean of college, 1932-59: dir. National Animal Disease Laboratory U.S. Department of Agriculture, Ames, Iowa, 1960—; assistant, Rockefeller Inst. for Med. Research, 1921-22; European fellow Internat. Edn. Bd., 1925-26; special consultant to chief of bureau of animal industry, U.S. Dept. of Agriculture 1944-45; consultant, Div. Public Health and Welfare, U.S. Group Control Council, Germany, 1945-46; advisor to dir. U.S. S.S.S. since 1948; mem. Agrl. Bd., NRC, 1948-55; adv. council Chem. Corps, 1956—; cons. Dept. of Agr., 1947—; fgn. corr. l'academie Nationale de Medicine (France) 1952, Académie Vétérinaire de France, 1959. Honorary Asso., Royal College of Vet. Surgeons (Gt. Brit.); hon. mem. Royal Acad. of Medicine (Gt. Brit.). Fellow A.A.A.S., New York Academy of Sciences; member of World Veterinary Association (vice pres. 1959), American Veterinary Medical Association (ex-pres.), Soc. Am. Bacteriologists, Am. Assn. Pathologists and Bacteriologists, U.S. Pub. Health Assn., Societe Nationale Veterinaire Helenique (Greece; hon.), Swedish Nat. Vet. Med. Assn. (hon.), Sigma Xi, Phi Kappa Phi, Phi Zeta, Alpha Psi, Alpha Sigma Phi. Mason. Author books including: The Infectious Diseases of Domestic Animals, 1943; rev. edit., 1960. Mem. editorial bd. Cornell Veterinarian. Contbr. profl. jours. Home: 2004 Greenbriar Circle. Office: Nat. Animal Disease Lab., Box 70, Ames, Ia. Died Feb. 1, 1963; buried Pleasant Grove Cemetery, Ithaca, N.Y.

HAGEMAN, HARRY ANDREW, design engr.; b. Niagara Falls, N.Y., July 25, 1877; s. Henry Charles and Kate (Frambach) H.; M.E., Cornell U., 1899; m. Evelyn Chase, Sept. 11, 1926; 1 son, John Andrew. Rodman and chainman Cataract Construction Co., 1894-95; draftsman and insp., Cornell Univ., 1894-96, 1897-99, Niagara Falls Power & Allied Companies, 1899-1906; asst. hydraulic engr. I. P. Morris Co., Phila., 1906-08; asst. mech. engr. Niagara Falls Power & Allied Cos., 1908-10; hydraulic engr. Stone & Webster Engring. Corp., Seattle, Wash., and Boston, 1910-17; mech. engr. Bethlehem Shipbuilding Corp., 1917-21; chief hydraulic engr. Stone & Webster, Boston, 1921-31, pub. bldg. commr., Newton, Mass., 1931-36; chief hydraulic engr. and chief design engr. Tenn. Valley Authority, 1936-41. Mem. American Soc. Civil Engrs., Boston Soc. Civil Engrs. Conglist. Mason (K.T., Shriner). Club: Knoxville (Tenn.) Technical Society. Home: 137 Allerton Rd., Newton Highlands MA

HAGER, ALBERT DAVIS, geologist; b. Chester, Vt., Nov. 1, 1817. Asst. geologist of Vt. under Edward Hitchcock, 1857-61; curator Vt. Cabinet of Natural History, 1862-70; geologist Mo., 1870-72; librarian Hist. Soc., Chgo., 1877-88. Contbr. to Report on the Geology of Vermont, 2 vols., 1861, Annual Report of Vermont Fish Commission, 1866-69. Died Chgo., July 29, 1888.

HAGGARD, HOWARD WILCOX, educator, author; b. La Porte, Ind., July 19, 1891; s. William Henry and Elsie (Wilcox) H.; prep. edn., Phillips Exeter Acad.; Ph.B., Yale, 1914, M.D., 1917; m. Josephine Foley, Sept. 9, 1916; children—Howard Wilcox (dec.), William Henry, Marjorie Marie (Mrs. William F. Bigoney, Jr.). Physiologist United States Bureau Mines, 1917; capt. Chem. Warfare Service, U.S. Army, 1917-18; cons. physiologist U.S. Bur. Mines, 1919-22; instr. physiology, Med. Sch., Yale, 1919-23, asst. prof., 1923-26, asso. prof. applied physiology, Sheffield Scientific Sch., Yale, 1926-38; prof. and dir. Lab. of Applied Physiology, Yale, since 1938, director of the office of U. Development, 1948-51. Physiologist N.Y. and N.J. Tunnel Commn.; mem. 3d Resuscitation Commn. Mem. Am. Soc. of Biol. Chemists, Am. Physiol. Soc., Internat. Anaesthesia Soc., Am. Soc. Hygiene Association, Connecticut Medical Society, Connecticut Academy of Arts and Sci., Nu Sigma Nu, Phi Sigma Kappa, Sigma Psi, Aurelian Soc. (Yale). Clubs: Elizabethan, Beaumont, New Haven Yacht, Essex Yacht. Author: Are You Intelligent?, 1926; Noxious Gases and the Principles of Respiration Influencing Their Action (with Yandell Henderson), 1927; The Science of Health and Disease, 1927; What You Should Know About Health and Disease, 1928; Devils, Drugs and Doctors, 1929; Schädliche Gase, 1931; The Lame, the Halt and the Blind, 1932; Mystery, Magic and Medicine, 1933; The Doctor in History, 1934; Diet and Physical Efficiency, 1935; The Anatomy of Personality, 1935; Staying Young Beyond Your Years, 1937; Man and His Body, 1938; Alcohol Explored (with E. M. Jellinek), 1942. Editor, Quarterly Journal of studies on Alcohol; mem. editorial bd. Personnel Journal. Contbr. numerous papers on physiological subjects. Pres. Nat. Com. for Edn. on Alcoholism. Research work on noxious gases, alcohol, physiology of industrial fatigue and effiency. Home: Plantation Key, Fla. Died Apr. 22, 1959.

HAGGARD, WILLIAM DAVID, surgeon; b. Nashville, Tenn., Sept. 28, 1872; s. William David and Jane (Douglass) H.; M.D., U. of Tenn., 1893; D.C.L., U. of the South, 1931; m. Mary Laura Champe, Jan. 18, 1898 (died 1920); m. 2d, Lucile Holman, July 27, 1926. Practiced, 1893—; prof. gynecology and abdominal surgery, U. of Tenn., 1899-1912; prof. surgery and clin. surgery, Vanderbilt U. Med. Dept., 1913—; surgeon, president staff, St. Thomas Hosp.; visiting surgeon Vanderbilt U. Hosp. Served as major and lt. colonel Med. Corps, U.S.A.; surgeon Evacuation Hosp. No. 1, Toul, France, 1918-19, also consultant in surgery, Mesves Hosp. Center, France, Was chmn. med. sect. Council Nat. Defense, State of Tenn.; maj. and med. aide to gov. of Tenn.; mem. advisory bd. div. of surgery, Surgeon General's Office, Washington, D.C. Fellow Am. Coll. Surgeons (regent; pres. 1933), Am. Surg. Assn. Democrat. Episcopalian. Home: Nashville, Tenn. Died Jan. 28, 1940.

HAGUE, ARNOLD, geologist; b. Boston, Dec. 3, 1840; s. Rev. Dr. William and Mary Bowditch (Moriarty) H.; Ph.B., Sheffield Scientific Sch. (Yale), 1863; studied at univs. of Göttingen and Heidelberg and at Freiberg Sch. of Mines, 1863-66; (Sc.D., Columbia, 1901; LL.D., Aberdeen, 1906); m. Mary Bruce Howe, Nov. 14, 1893. Asst. geologist, U.S. Geol. Exploration, 40th parallel, and made investigations of mines and mining processes in Nevada, etc., 1867-77; govt. geologist, Guatemala, 1877-78; examining mines in northern China for the govt., 1878-79; geologist of U.S. Geol. Survey, 1879—. Mem. commn. apptd. by Nat. Acad. Sciences at request of U.S. Govt., 1896, to prepare plan of Nat. forest reserves; v.p. Internat. Geol. Congresses, Paris, 1900, Stockholm, 1910, Toronto, 1913. Author: Geology of the Yellowstone National Park (with others), 1899; Atlas of Yellowstone National Park (27 plates), 1904; The Origin of the Thermal Waters in the Yellowstone National Park, 1911. Died May 14, 1917.

HAGUE, JAMES DUNCAN, cons. mining engr.; b. Boston, Feb. 24, 1836; s. Rev. Dr. William and Mary Bowditch (Moriarty) H.; ed. private schools; studied at Lawrence Scientific Sch., Harvard, 1854; Georgia Augusta Univ.; Göttingen, Germany, 1855; Royal School of Mines, Freiberg, Saxony, 1856-58; m. Mary Ward Foote, Apr. 1872 (died 1898). Exploring in South seas, 1859-61; brief service in U.S.N., 1862-63; mgr. copper mines at Lake Superior, participating in early development of Calumet mine, 1863-66; first asst. geologist, U.S. Geol. Survey, 40th parallel, 1867-70; cons. mining engr. in Calif., 1871-78; U.S. commr. to Paris Expn., 1878. Resident of New York, 1879; pres. and mgr. of mining companies. Home: New York, and Stockbridge, Mass. Died 1908.

HAHN, CONRAD VELDER, consulting engr.; b. Phila., Pa., May 9, 1890; s. John G. and Elizabeth (Velder) H.; B.S., U. of Pa., 1908, M.E., 1912; studied Temple U. (Phila.), D.Eng., Ph.D.; U. of San José (Costa Rica), Oxford U. (Eng.); married. Consulting practice, 1910—; mng. dir. The Hahn Co. (cons. engrs.); dir. and asso. engr. Internat. Development Co., Washington, D.C.; cons. mech. engr. Turbo Motor Co., East Radford, Va.; mem. N. T. Whitaker & Co., Washington, D.C.; mem. faculty, civ. engring. dept., Temple U., 1910-12, and of mech. engring. dept. U. of Pa., 1912-14; dir. mech. engring. dept. of evening schs., Drexel Inst., Phila., 1919—. 1st lt. and capt. Ordnance Dept., U.S.A., 1917-19; maj. Ordnance R.C.; spl. mention for tech. service, Am. Ordnance Base Depot, France, and Aberdeen Proving Ground, Scotland, World War. Mason. Republican. Baptist. Home: Aberdeen, Md. Died Dec. 3, 1933.

HAHN, OTTO, scientist; b. Frankfurt on the Main Germany, Mar. 8, 1879; s. Heinrich and Charlotte (Giese) H; student U. Marburg, 1897, U. Munich, 1898, Dr. deg., 1901; U. Coll., London, winter 1904-05, Phys. Lab. McGill U., Montreal, Can., winter 1905-06; m. Edith Junghans, Mar. 22, 1913 (dec. 1968); 1 son, Hanno (dec. 1960). Mem. faculty U. Berlin, 1907, prof. chemistry, 1910-33; mem. Kaiser Wilhelm Inst. Chemistry, 1912-28, dir., 1928-45; pres. Max Planck Soc. for Advancement of Sci. (formerly Kaiser Wilhelm Society), 1946-60, hon. pres., 1960-68. Recipient Nobel prize for chemistry for splitting uranium atom, 1944; Enrico Fermi award Atomic Energy Commn., 1966. Mem. Berlin, Goettingen, Munich, Stockholm, Vienna, Madrid, Helsinki, Lissabon. Mainz, Rome (Vatican). Allahabad, Copenhagen, Boston, Indian, Halle, Bukarest acads. sci. Lutheran. Home: Goettingen Germany Died July 28, 1968; buried Stadtfriedhof, Goettingen West Germany

HAINES, JOHN PETER, humanitarian; b. New York, N.Y., Dec. 17, 1851; s. William Augustus and Emily S. H.; ed. by pvt. tutors and spl. course, Columbia; m. Mary, d. George Merritt, Irvington-on-Hudson, 1873 (died 1911). Prominently identified with humane and benevolent movements for many yrs.; pres. Am. Soc. for Prevention of Cruelty to Animals, 1889-1906 (resigned); during his administration the operations of the soc. were extended, new laws for protection of animals enacted, reforms in transportation of animals instituted, brutal and demoralizing "sports," pigeon shooting, rabbit coursing, suppressed, and many forms of cruelty checked or abolished. Life mem. Am. Soc. for Prevention Cruelty to Animals (was editor Our Animal Friends, official organ of the soc.). Owner of celebrated Cranmoor Farm, Toms River, N.J. Invented and patented the Haines' electric log, by means of which the speed of vessels is indicated and registered in any part of a vessel. Homes: Toms River, N.J., and N.Y. City. Died June 26, 1921.

HAINES, WALTER STANLEY, toxicologist; b. Chicago, Ill., Sept. 27, 1850; s. John C. and Emma A. (Adams) H.; Mass. Inst. Tech., 1869-71; M.D., Chicago Med. Coll. (Northwestern U.), 1873; (hon. A.M., Monmouth, 1881). Prof. chemistry, Chicago Med. Coll., 1872-76; student Paris and London, 1875-76; prof. chemistry and toxicology, 1876-85, chemistry, pharmacy and toxicology, 1885-1905, chemistry, materia medica and toxicology, 1905—, Rush Med. Coll. (U. of Chicago); professorial lecturer on toxicology, U. of Chicago, 1901—. Mem. Com. of Revision of U.S. Pharmacopoeia, 1900-20; mem. Ill. State Food Standard Commn., 1909—. Author: A Text-Book of Legal Medicine and Toxicology, 1903, 04, 22; also chapters on alkaloidal poisons in Hamilton's System of Legal Medicine, 1894. Died Jan. 27, 1923.

HAISH, JACOB, inventor, mfr.; b. Baden, Germany, Mar. 9, 1826; s. Christian and Christina (Layman) H.; m. Sophia Brown, May 24, 1847. Came to U.S. with parents, 1836; worked on farm, Pierce, Ill., 1849-51; applied for patent for his improvements in barbed wire, 1873, found that a similar patent had been applied for by J. F. Gilden; patented "S" barbed wire, 1875; his patents purchased by Washburn & Moen Mfg. Co. (which soon controlled prodn. of barbed wire in U.S.), 1876; fought ultimately unsuccessful ct. battle to retain sole right to manufacture barbed wire, 1876-92; founder Barb City Bank, DeKalb, Ill. Died Feb. 19, 1926.

HALBERSTADT, BAIRD, engineer, geologist; b. Pottsville, Pa., Jan. 26, 1860; s. Andrew Howell (M.D.) and Augusta Mary (Baird) H.; U. of Pa.; Internat. Inst., Paris, France; m. Ida Ray Smith, Oct. 15, 1918; children—Lesley Richards, Anne Josephine. Aid, Geol. Survey of Pa., 1881-86; engr. and supt. Tazewell Coal & Iron Co., 1887; asst. to Dr. Charles A. Ashburner, coal expert, 1889; spl. agt. and expert, 11th U.S. Census, 1889-91; asst. geologist, Pa. Geol. Survey, 1891-93; spl. tech. corr. and representative mining jours., 1893-98; geol. expert for large coal cos. before important commns. and in local cts., 1902; consulting geologist, State Bd. Agr., 1909-19. Capt. Signal and Telegraph Corps, attached (but not mustered) Pa. N.G., 1893-95; 1st lt. and insp. 4th Regt. Inf., 1897; 1st lt. and regimental q.m. 4th Regt., 1898; 1st lt. and regimental q.m. Pa. Inf. U.S.V., Spanish-Am. War, 1898; capt. and regimental q.m. 4th Reg. Pa. N.G., 1899; maj. and a.d.c. on staff nat. comdr. Soc. P.R. Expdn. Mem. Advisory Commn. for Preservation of Pub. Records of Pa., 1918; chmn. Local (state) Armory Bd., 1916-22. Federal fuel adminstr. for Schuylkill Co., 1917-19; chmn. com. on materials and mem. com. on mil. of Com. Pub. Safety of Pa. Republican. Episcopalian. Home: Pottsville, Pa. Died Sept. 13, 1934.

HALDEMAN, SAMUEL STEMAN, scientist, philologist; b. Locust Grove, Pa., Aug. 12, 1812; s. Henry and Frarce (Steman) H.; attended Dickinson Coll., Carlisle, Pa.; m. Mary A. Hough, 1835. Operated sawmill, Locust Grove, 1831-36, at same time studied natural history; asst. to Darwin Rodgers (geologist of Pa.), 1836-42; prof. natural history U. Pa., 1851-55, 1st prof. comparative philology, 1868-80; prof. chemistry Pa. Agrl. Coll., 1853-58; prof. natural scis. Del. Coll., 1853-58; made study of Am. Indian dialects, became expert in field. Author: Monograph on the Freshwater Mollusca of the United States, 1842; Elements of Latin Pronunciation, 1851; Outlines of Etymology, 1877; Word Building, 1881. Died Chickies, Pa., Sept. 10, 1880.

HALE, ALBERT CABLE, chemist; b. Adams, N.Y., Sept. 2, 1845; s. Abner Cable and Sally Ann (Barton) H.; A.B., U. of Rochester, 1869, A.M., 1872, E.M., 1881; Ph.D., U. of Heidelberg, 1880; m. Carrie Helen Angell, Dec. 23, 1889. Vice prin. high sch., Jersey City, N.J., 1873-77; commr. for ednl. exhibit of N.J. at U.S. Centennial Expn., 1876; pres. State Sch. of Mines, Colo., 1880-83; head teacher, physical science dept., Boys' High Sch., Brooklyn, 1883-1912; pres. dept. chemistry, Brooklyn Inst. of Arts and Sciences, 1890. Dir., 1887-1902, v.p., 1889, sec., 1889-1903, councilor, 1893-1909, Am. Chem. Soc.; councilor A.A.A.S., 1901, 1902; v.p. N.E. Assn. Chem. Teachers, 1901-02; examiner in chemistry, Coll. Entrance Bd., 1902-06; life mem. Chemists' Club, New York. Home: Brooklyn, N.Y. Died Apr. 24, 1921.

HALE, ENOCH, physician, author; b. Westhampton, Mass., Jan. 19, 1790; s. Rev. Enoch and Octavia (Throop) H.; M.D., Harvard, 1813; m. Almira Hooker, 1813; m. 2d, Sarah Hooker, 1822; m. 3d, Jane Murdock, 1829. Practiced medicine Gardiner, Me., 1813-18, Boston, 1818; taught medicine, Boston, 1818; apptd. dist. physician Boston Dispensary, 1819; won Boylston prize for med. dissertations, 1819, 21; a founder Boston Soc. for Med. Improvement, 1828; recording sec. Mass. Med. Soc., 1832-35. Author: History and Description of an Epidemic Fever, Commonly Called Spotted Fever (observations on meningitis), 1819; Observations on the Typhoid Fever of New England, 1839. Died Nov. 12, 1848.

HALE, GEORGE ELLERY, astronomer; b. Chicago, Ill., June 29, 1868; s. William Ellery and Mary S. H.; S.B., Mass. Inst. Tech., 1890; studied Harvard College Obs., 1889-90, Univ. of Berlin, winter 1893-94; hon. Sc.D., U. of Pittsburgh, 1897, Yale, 1905, Victoria U., Manchester, 1907, Oxford, 1909, Cambridge, 1911, Chicago, 1916, Columbia, 1917, Harvard, 1921; LL.D., Beloit, 1904, U. of Calif., 1912, Princeton, 1917; Ph.D., Berlin, 1910; m. Evelina S. Conklin, June 5, 1890; children—Margaret, William Ellery. Dir. Kenwood Astrophys. Obs., 1890-96; asso. prof. astrophysics, 1892-97, prof., 1897-1905, organizer, and dir. Yerkes Obs., 1895-1905, U. of Chicago; organizer, and dir. Mount Wilson Obs. of Carnegie Instn. of Wash., 1904-23, hon. dir., 1923—. Trustee Calif. Inst. Technology (chmn. observatory council), Huntington Library and Art Gallery. Principal scientific researches have been made in solar stellar spectroscopy. Joint editor Astronomy and Astrophysics, 1892-95, Astrophysical Journal, 1895-1935. Janssen medal, Paris Acad. Sciences, 1894; Rumford medal, 1902; Draper medal, 1903; gold medal, Royal Astron. Soc., 1904; Bruce medal, Astron. Soc. of the Pacific, 1916; Janssen medal, Astron. Soc. of France, 1917; Galileo medal, Florence, 1920; Actonian prize, Royal Instn., 1921; Arthur Noble medal for civic service (Pasadena), 1927; Cresson and Franklin medals, Franklin Inst., 1926, 27; Holland Society medal, 1931; Copley medal, Royal Society, London, 1932; awarded Ives medal by Optical Soc. of America; Commander Order of Leopold II (Belgium); Commander Order of the Crown (Italy). Mem. com. on intellectual cooperation League of Nations, 1922. Author: The Study of Stellar Evolution; Ten Years' Work of a Mountain Observatory; The New Heavens; The Depths of the Universe; Beyond the Milky Way; Signals from the Stars. Died Feb. 21, 1938.

HALE, HUGH ELLMAKER, cons. engr.; b. Minomen, Minn.; s. William Wilberforce and Ann Graham (Patterson) H.; prep. edn. Selwyn Hall, Reading, Pa., Bethlehem (Pa.) Prep. Sch.; C.E., Lehigh U., 1897; m. Marianna Buckner Clark, June 27, 1904. Asst. engr. Pa. R.R., Phila., 1896-98, Altoona, Pa., 1898-99, asst. supr. signals, Jersey City, 1899-1901, supr. signals, Camden, N.J., 1901; div. engr. B.&O. R.R., Phila., 1902, supt., Butler, Pa., 1903-05, engr. maintenance of way, Balt., 1905-08; engr. of design, Mo.Pac. R.R., St. Louis, 1908-10, prin. asst. engr., 1910, engr. maintenance of way, Little Rock, Ark., 1911-14; engr. Eastern group, Pres.' Conf. Com., Fed. Valuation of R.R.'s in U.S., 1914-26, vice chmn. 1926-31; sr. mem. H. E. Hale & Co. cons. engrs., 1931-36; investment dept. Equitable Life Assurance Soc. of U.S., 1936-45; cons. engr., 1945—. Mem. Am. Soc. C.E., Am. Ry. Engring. Assn., Soc. Am. Mil. Engrs., Sigma Phi. Republican. Episcopalian. Mason. Contbr. to tech. papers, etc. Home: 1165 5th Av. Office: 1165 Fifth Av., N.Y.C. 29. Deceased.

HALE, WILLIAM J., chemist; b. Ada, O., January 5, 1876; s. James Thomas and Emma Elizabeth (Ogle) H.; A.B., A.M., Miami U., 1897, LL.D., 1937; A.B., Harvard Univ., 1898, A.M., 1899, Ph.D., 1902; traveling fellow in chemistry, Technische Hochschule, Berlin, and U. of Göttingen, 1902-03; m. Helen, d. Herbert H. Dow, Midland, Mich., Feb. 7, 1917 (died Oct. 16, 1918); 1 dau., Ruth Elizabeth (Mrs. Wiley T. Buchanan, Jr.). Research assistant, University of Chicago, 1 term, 1903; instructor, chemistry, 1904-08, asst. prof., 1908-15; asso. prof., 1915-19, U. of Mich.; dir. organic chem. research, Dow Chem. Co., Midland, Mich., 1919-1934, research consultant since 1934; president Verdurin Co., Detroit and Midland, Mich., since 1951. Chairman division of chemistry and chemical technology, Nat. Research Council. Washington, D.C., 1925-27; vis. prof. chemurgy, Conn. Coll., 1936-39. Fellow A.A.A.S., London Chem. Soc.; mem. American Chem. Soc., Société Suisse de Chimie, Société Chimique de France, Deutsche Chemische Gesellschaft, Phi Beta Kappa, Sigma Xi, Phi Lambda Upsilon, Alpha Chi Sigma. Author: A Laboratory Outline of General Chemistry (with Alexander Smith). 1907; The Calculations of General Chemistry, 1909; A Laboratory Manual of General Chemistry, 1917, 2d edit. with Wm. G. Smeaton, 1930; Chemistry Triumphant, 1932; The Farm Chemurgic, 1934; Prosperity Beckons, 1936; Farmward March, 1939; Farmer Victorious, 1949; Chemivision, 1952; papers organic chem., addresses chemurgic development for industrialization agr. Patentee of new process for mfr. of phenol, aniline, acetic acid, butadiene and their derivatives. Clubs: Detroit Club; Chemists (New York); Cosmos (Washington). Home: Midland, Mich. Office: The Dow Chemical Co., Midland, Mich. Died Aug. 8, 1955.

HALL, ANSEL FRANKLIN, naturalist, forester; b. Oakland, Calif., May 6, 1894; s. Charles and Laura V.C. (Crocker) H.; B.S., U. of Calif., 1917; m. June I. Alexander, Jan. 12, 1923; children—Knowles, Roger, Merrie, Sylvia, Laurel, Robin. Ranger and other positions Nat. Park Service, 1917-23; chief naturalist Nat. Park Service, 1923-30, sr. naturalist and chief forester, 1930-32, chief div. edn. and forestry, 1932-33, chief of field div. of edn., 1933-37; gen. mgr. Mesa Verde Nat. Park, Colo., 1937—; pres., gen. mgr. Mesa Verde Enterprises, Inc., 1954; president Anasazi Assos., Incorporated; Executive American Association Museums, 1924-25, Nat. Acad. Sci. (Grand Canyon com.), 1929-32, Nat. Academy Sciences (Crater Lake com.), 1924-37; sec. recreation sect., First Pan Pacific Conf. on Edn., Rehabilitation, Reclamation and Recreation, Hawaii, 1927; organizer and dir. scientific field expdns., 1929, 30, 31, 32; organizer, gen. dir. Rainbow Bridge-Monument Valley Expdn., 1933-38; director of Alaska-Yukon Expdn., 1936; research director Navajo Trail Assn., since 1939. Served as 2d lt., U.S. Engring. Corps, 1917-18, with A.E.F. in France, 19 mos.; instr. forestry, A.E.F. Univ., Beaune, France, 1918. Mem. Society American Foresters, American Association Museums, Calif. Acad. Sciences, Explorers' Club, Am. Alpine Club, Sierra Club. Author: books including Guide to Mesa Verde National Park, 1937; Mesa Verde, 1952. Editor of Yosemite Nature Notes (serials), 1919-25. Home: 2811 Kearney St., Denver 7. Address: Mesa Verde National Park, Colo. 81330. Died Mar. 28, 1962.

HALL, ASAPH, prof. astronomy, Harvard, 1895—; b. Goshen, Conn., Oct. 15, 1829; ed. common school; worked at farming and carpentry; spl. studies at Norfolk Acad. and Univ. of Mich. (LL.D., Yale, Harvard; Ph.D., Hamilton). Taught school; became student and, 1857-62, asst. Harvard Coll. Observatory. Aide, 1862, prof. mathematics (relative rank of capt.), 1863, U.S. Naval Observatory. Has headed many govt. astron. expdns.; made numerous important discoveries, notably that of the two moons of Mars, which he named "Deimos" and "Phobos." Mem. from 1875, Nat. Acad. Sciences; foreign mem. Royal Astron. Soc.; m. Angeline Stickney. Home: Norfolk, Conn. Died 1907.

HALL, ASAPH, JR., astronomer; b. Cambridge, Mass., Oct. 6, 1859; s. Asaph and Angeline (Stickney) H.; A.B. Harvard, 1882; Ph.D., Yale, 1889; m. Mary Estella Cockrell, July 14, 1897. Asst., U.S. Naval Obs., Washington, D.C., 1882-85; asst. astronomer, Yale Obs., 1885-89, Naval Obs., 1889-92; prof. astronomy and dir. of the obs., U. of Mich., 1892-1905; asst. Naval Obs., 1905-08; prof. mathematics, U.S.N., rank of lt., 1908; now comdr. U.S.N., retired. Died Jan. 12, 1930.

HALL, BENJAMIN MORTIMER, civil and mining engr.; b. Fairfield Co., S.C., Jan. 31, 1853; s. Dr. Nathaniel Barber and Nancy (Boulware) H.; moved to Ga., 1854; reared on father's plantation Webster Co., Ga., to age 16, when father moved to Floyd Co.; B.E., U. of Ga., 1876, C. and M.E., 1885, D.Sc., 1921; m. Kate Chamberlin, Jan. 5, 1881; children—Warren Esterly, Gertrude (Mrs. Brainard Clapp), Benjamin Mortimer. Prof. mathematics, N. Ga. Agrl. Coll., Dahlonega, 1876-80; engr. water supply investigations, construction and operation of Ga. gold mines, 1880-85; constrn. and operation, Southern Marble Co., Pickens Co., Ga., 1887-90; sr. mem. Hall Bros., civil and mining engrs., Atlanta, 1890-1903; consulting engr. U.S. Geol. Survey, 1896-1903; supervising engr. U.S. Reclamation Service for N.M., Tex., and Okla., 1904-07; constructed Hondo, Carlsbad and Leasburg projects; negotiated terms of Mexico-Rio Grande treaty, at El Paso, Tex.; made original plans Elephant Butte dam and Rio Grande project and supervised the settlement of all water rights disputes on Rio Grande; organized Puerto Rico Irrigation Service and was chief engr., Mar. 1908-July 1910; reconstructed and operated the plant of Amicalola Marble Co., Pickens Co., Ga., 1910-12; senior mem. B. M. Hall & Sons, cons. engrs., civil, mining and hydraulic, Atlanta; mem. Bd. Consulting Engrs., City of Atlanta. Mem. arbitration bds., Raleigh, N.C., Durham, N.C., New York and Washington, D.C.; was chmn. water power com., Nat. Conservation Congress. Democrat. Methodist. Home: Atlanta, Ga. Died Nov. 19, 1929.

HALL, CHARLES EDWARD, mining engr., geologist; b. Albany, N.Y., Aug. 12, 1852; s. Prof. James H. (geologist); ed. Albany Acad. and Feldkirch-Voralberg, Tyrol, Austria; spl. studies in geology, chemistry, mineralogy, physics, engring., mining, etc., at Munich, Bavaria. Asst. in charge geol. survey of Texas, 1873; in charge Eastern (Phila.) Dist.; Geol. Survey of Pa., 1875-83; removed to City of Mexico. Mem. Am. Philos. Soc., Phila., Acad. Natural Sciences, Phila., A.A.A.S. Wrote reports on the geology of the Phila. Dist.; Notes on Glacial Deposits (Am. Philos. Soc.); Laurentian Magnetic Ore Deposits (N.Y. Regent's Reports); Notes on Geology and Mining in Lower Calif.; etc. Address: Blake-Calle Gante 8, City of Mexico, Mex.

HALL, CHARLES FRANCIS, explorer; b. Rochester, N.H., 1821. As a restless youth held various jobs; became interested in fate of Arctic explorer Sir John Franklin and his party, left New London, Conn. in search of relics and survivors of expdn., May 1860; landed alone at Frobisher Bay in Arctic region, July 1860; lived with and gained help of Eskimos until his return to New London, Sept. 1862, having found relics of Frobisher's expdn. of 1577-78 but none of Franklin expdn.; made similar journey, 1864-69, during which he found relics of Franklin expdn. as well as traces of possible survivors; on June 29, 1871, with backing of U.S. Congress, he undertook last voyage to North in command of ship Polaris, penetrated to 82 deg. 11′ N and 61 deg. W, the farthest point attained up to that time by vessel; Hall died on trip, but crew members survived extremely severe winter to return to U.S.; trip proved to have important geographic results. Author: Arctic Researches and Life Among the Esquimaux, 2 vols., 1865. Died Thank God Harbor, Greenland, Nov. 8, 1871.

HALL, CHARLES MARTIN, inventor; b. Thompson, O., Dec. 6, 1863; s. Rev. Heman B. and Sophronia (Brooks) H.; A.B., Oberlin, 1885, A.M., 1893 (LL.D., 1910); unmarried. Invented the electrolytic process for the mfr. of aluminum now universally used, Feb. 1886; commenced commercial manufacture of aluminum with Pittsburgh Reduction Co., 1888 (now Aluminum Co. of America), v.p. same, 1890—; U.S. court sustained the Hall patent and conceded priority of invention, 1893. Hall process has so reduced price of aluminum as to make it a common metal of commerce, whereas it was formerly as costly as silver and little used. Trustee Oberlin Coll. Awarded Perkin medal, for work in chemistry, Jan. 1911. Home: Niagara Falls, N.Y. Died Dec. 27, 1914.

HALL, CHRISTOPHER WEBBER, geologist; b. Wardsboro, Vt., Feb. 28, 1845; s. Lewis and Louisa (Wilder) H.; A.B., Middlebury Coll., 1871, A.M., 1874; m. Nellie A. Dunnell, July 26, 1875; 2d, Sophia L. Haight, Dec. 26, 1883. Prin. Glens Falls (N.Y.) Acad., 1871-72, high sch., Mankato, Minn., 1872-73; supt.

schs., Owatonna, 1873-75; student U. of Leipzig, 1875-78; instr. geology, 1878-79, asst. prof., 1879-80, prof. geology, mineralogy and biology, 1880-90, geology and mineralogy, 1890—, dean Coll. Engring., Metallurgy and Mechanic Arts, 1892-97, U. of Minn. Asst. geologist, Minn. Geol. Survey, 1878-80, U.S. Geol. Survey, 1883—. Fellow A.A.A.S., Geol. Soc. America, Am. Geographers' Assn., Minn. Acad. Sciences (editor, 1888—, pres. 1900-01). Author: Syllabus of Physical Geography (with Prof. Kunze), 1897; Geography of Minnesota, 1903. Home: Minneapolis, Minn. Died 1911.

HALL, DAVID, printer; b. Edinburgh, Scotland, 1714; m. Mary Lacock, Jan. 7, 1748. Learned printing trade, London, Eng.; came to Phila. as journeyman in office of Benjamin Franklin, 1743, became partner under name Franklin & Hall, 1748, sole owner, 1766, then took in partner. Died Phila., Dec. 24, 1772; buried Christ Ch. Graveyard, Phila.

HALL, EDWIN HERBERT, physicist; b. Gorham, Me., Nov. 7, 1855; s. Joshua E. and Lucy Ann (Hilborn) H.; A.B., Bowdoin, 1875, A.M., 1878; Ph.D., Johns Hopkins, 1880; LL.D., Bowdoin, 1905; m. Caroline Eliza Bottum, August 31, 1882 (dec. 1921); 1 dau., Constance Huntington. Instr. physics Harvard, 1881-88, asst. prof., 1888-95, prof. 1895-1921, emeritus prof., 1921. Recipient medal Am. Assn. of Physics Teachers, 1937. Fellow Am. Acad. Arts and Scis.; corr. mem. Brit. Assn. Adv. Science; fgn. mem. Société Hollandaise des Sciences. Author: A Textbook of Physics (with J. Y. Bergen), 1891, 3d edit., 1903; Lessons in Physics, 1900; The Teaching of Chemistry and Physics (with Alexander Smith), 1902; College Laboratory Manual of Physics, 1904; Elements of Physics, 1912; Dual Theory of Conduction in Metals, 1938. Discovered the shifting of equipotential lines of electric current under influence of magnetic field (Hall effect), 1879; contbd. to theory of thermo-electric and thermal conduction in metals; studied thermomagnetic and electromagnetic effects in soft iron. Died Nov. 20, 1938.

HALL, GENE W., engr.; b. Bklyn., Nov. 25, 1898; s. George Fowler and Lucy (Holmes) H.; m. Marguerite Mars, June 27, 1923; 1 dau., Jean Lois. With Parsons, Brinckerhoff, Hall & MacDonald, N.Y.C., 1919—, mem. firm, 1932—, pres. subsidiary, Parklap Nat. Builders, 1936—; pres. Housing Co. of Dundalk, Linden Housing Corp., Liberty Park Housing Corp.; pres. Cornwall Manor, Inc., 142 Maiden Lane Corp. Commd. brig. gen., U.S. Army, 1945. Elk. Home: 168 West Blvd., Bay Park, N.Y. Office: 51 Broadway, N.Y.C. 6. Died Nov. 30, 1951.

HALL, GEORGE MARTIN, geologist; b. Baltimore, Md., Sept. 13, 1891; s. George Arlow and Alice Josephine (Higgins) H.; A.B., Johns Hopkins 1915, Ph.D., 1923; unmarried. Clerk and stenographer for city engr., Baltimore, 1910-11; inspector State Roads Commn. of Md., summers 1912-14; geol. aid Md. Geol. Survey, summer 1915; asst. geologist Md. Geol. Survey, part time, 1916-26, Roxana Petrol Corp., summer, 1917; asst. geologist U.S. Geol. Survey, part time, 1921-38, asso. geologist, part time, 1938—; instr. in geology, Johns Hopkins, 1923-26; asso. prof. of geology, U. of Tenn., 1926-29, prof. Served as private Signal Corps, U.S. Army, 1918, 2d lt., 1918-20. Author: Ground Water in Yellowstone and Treasure Counties, Mont. (with Howard), 1929; Geology of Big Horn County, Mont. (with others), 1935; Ground Water in Southeastern Pa., 1934. Home: Knoxville, Tenn. Died Apr. 28, 1941.

HALL, GEORGE WASHINGTON, neurologist; b. Crawfordsville, Ind., June 18, 1869; s. Y. P. and Martha E. (Stillwell) H.; A.M., Wabash Coll., 1890; M.D., Rush Med. Coll., 1893; special post-grad. studies Nat. Hosp. for Paralyzed and Epileptics, London, Eng., and in Berlin, Germany, 1904; post-grad. work in Vienna and Munich, 1907; m. Neil Nicholson, June 5, 1894; children—Martha Nadine, Bertram Brower. Formerly prof. medicine, Rush Med. Coll.; sr. neurologist St. Luke's Hosp.; clin. prof. meurology, U. of Chicago (Rush Med. Coll.); formerly attending psychiatrist, Psychopathic Hosp. Fellow Inst. of Medicine (Chicago). Home: Chicago, Ill. Died Oct. 25, 1941.

HALL, G(RANVILLE) STANLEY, univ. president; b. Ashfield, Mass., Feb. 1, 1846; s. Granville Bascom and Abigail (Beals) H.; A.B., Williams, 1867, A.M., 1870; student Union Theol. Sem., 1867-68, Berlin and Bonn, 1868-71, Berlin and Heidelberg, 1871-72; Ph.D., Harvard, 1878; Leipzig, Berlin, London, 1878-81; (LL.D., U. of Mich., 1888, Williams, 1889, Johns Hopkins, 1902); married. Prof. psychology Antioch Coll., 1872-76; instr. English, Harvard, 1876-77; lecturer, psychology, Harvard and Williams, 1880-81; prof. psychology, Johns Hopkins, 1881-88; pres. and prof. psychology Clark U., 1888-1920. Founder and editor Am. Jour. Psychology, 1887-1921; editor Pedagogical Sem., 1892—, Am. Jour. Religious Psychology and Edn., 1904-15, Jour. Applied Psychology, 1917—. Author: Adolescence (2 vols.), 1904; Youth—Its Education, 1907; Educational Problems (2 vols.), 1911; Founders of Modern Psychology, 1912; Jesus the Christ, in the Light of Psychology, 1917; Morale: The Supreme Standard of Life and Conduct, 1920; Recreations of a Psychologist, 1920; Senescence, 1922; Life and Confessions of a Psychologist, 1923. Home: Worcester, Mass. Died Apr. 24, 1924.

HALL, HARVEY MONROE, botany; b. Lee Co., Ill., Mar. 29, 1874; s. Reuben and Martha (Leist) H.; B.S., U. of Calif., 1901, M.S., 1902, Ph.D., 1906; m. Carlotta Case, Feb. 23, 1910; 1 dau., Martha. Asst. in botany, U. of Calif., 1903, instr., 1903-08, asst. prof., 1908-16, asso. prof., 1916-19; also asst. botanist, Agrl. Expt. Sta., U. of Calif., 1902-19, and instr. in botany, mountain lab., U. of Colo., 1917; investigator in exptl. taxonomy, div. plant biology, Carnegie Instn. of Washington, D.C., 1919—. Fellow Am. Acad. Arts and Sciences, A.A.A.S., Bot. Soc. America, Calif. Acad. Science. Hon. curator Herbarium, U. of Calif.; acting prof. botany, Stanford U. Author: Botanical Survey of San Jacinto Mountain, 1902; Compositae of Southern California, 1907; Yosemite Flora (with wife), 1912; Rubber Content of North American Plants (with F. L. Long), 1921; Phylogenetic Method in Taxonomy (with F. E. Clements), 1923, Haplopappus, 1928. Died 1932.

HALL, JAMES, geologist; b. Hingham, Mass., Sept. 12, 1811; s. James and Susanna (Dourdain) H.; grad Rensselaer Poly. Inst. (then Rensselaer Sch.), 1832; A.M. (hon.), Union Coll., 1842; M.D. (hon.), U. Md., 1846; LL.D. (hon.), Hamilton Coll., 1863, McGill U., 1884, Harvard, 1886; m. Sarah Aiken, 1838, 4 children. Asst. prof. chemistry Rensselaer Poly. Inst., 1832-36, prof. geology, 1836; began explorations, Western N.Y., 1838; state geologist Ia., 1855-58, Wis., 1857-60; dir. N.Y. State Museum, 1866-98; recipient Wollaston medal of Geol. Soc. of London, 1858, Walker prize of Boston Soc. Natural History, 1884, Hayden medal from Acad. Natural Scis. of Phila., 1890; 1st pres. Geol. Soc. Am.; v.p. Internat. Congress of Geologists, Paris, 1878, at Bologna, 1881, at Berlin, 1885; charter mem. Nat. Acad. Scis. Author: The Paleontology of New York, Part IV Comprising the Survey of the Fourth Geological District, 1843, (classic of early geol. lit.); New York State Natural History Survey: Paleontology, 8 vols., 1847-94. Died Albany, N.Y.; Aug. 7, 1898.

HALL, JAMES ALEXANDER, prof. mech. engring.; b. Berlin, Vt., July 26, 1888; s. John Joseph and Agnes Brock (Hardie) H.; A.B., Brown U., 1908, Sc.B. in M.E., 1910; m. Leila Tucker, June 21, 1919; children—James Alexander, Flora, Margaret. Asst. and instr. in mech. engring., Brown U., 1910-14; with engring., dept. Link-Belt Co., Phila., 1914-15; with Brown U., 1915—, asst. prof., asso. prof. to 1925, prof. mech. engring., 1925; also cons. engr. Brown & Sharpe Mfg. Co., 1926—. Republican. Conglist. Co-author: (with D. T. Farnham, R. W. King and H. E. Howe) Profitable Science in Industry, 1925. Home: Providence, R.I. Died Oct. 29, 1936.

HALL, LLOYD AUGUSTUS, chemist; b. Elgin, Ill., June 20, 1894; s. Elisha A. and Isabel (French) H.; Ph.C., B.S., Northwestern U., 1916; grad. student U. Chgo., 1917; Sc.D., Va. State Coll., 1944, Tuskegee Inst., 1947, Howard U., 1959; m. Myrrhene E. Newsome, Sept. 23, 1919; children—Dorothy Ann (Mrs. Lloyd Powell), Kenneth Lloyd. Chemist, Dept. Health Labs., Chgo., 1916, sr. chemist, 1917; chief chemist John Morrell & Co., Ottumwa, Ia., 1919-21, Boyer Chem. Lab. Co., Chgo., 1921; pres., chem. dir. Chem. Products Corp., Chgo., 1922-25; chem. cons., chief chemist, dir. research The Griffith Labs., Inc., Chgo., 1925-46, tech. dir., 1946-59, tech. cons., from 1959; research adv. bd. Tuesdail Labs., Inc., from 1960; v.p. Pilot Chem. Co., Santa Fe Springs, Cal. Mem. food commn. Ill. Dept. Agr., 1944-49; cons. George Washington Carver Found., 1946-48; mem. food protection ind. liaison com. NRC; mem. Chgo. exec. com. N.A.A.C.P., mayor's commn. on Chgo. House of Correction, 1955; Hyde Park-Kenwood Conservation Community Council, 1956-58; adviser Los Angeles County Air Pollution Control Dist., Los Angeles County Water Resources Com., UN, Am. Food for Peace Council, 1965-71; mem. adv. bd. Los Angeles State Coll.; cons. United Cal. Bank, Los Angeles. Mem. bd. Chgo. Urban League, 1935-36, Wabash Av., Washington Park YMCA's, 1935-55, Kenwood Neighborhood Redevelopment Corp., 1954, S. E. Chgo. Com., 1959. Asst. chief insp. powder and explosives Ordnance Dept., U.S. Army, 1917-19; sci. adv. bd., com. on food research Q.M.C., War Dept., 1943-48. Trustee Adler Planetarium, Hull House Assn. Recipient achievement award Phi Beta Sigma, 1952, honor scroll Chgo. chpt. Am. Inst. Chemists, 1956, Brotherhood award Chgo. Conf. on Brotherhood, 1957. Fellow Am. Inst. Chemists (hon.; chmn. Chgo. 1954-55, chmn. com. on econ. status of chemists 1952-53, nat. councilor-at-large, mem. bd. from 1962), A.A.A.S.; mem. Inst. Food Technologists (councilor Chgo. sect. 1950-52, nat. councilor-at-large 1951-53, nat. exec. bd. 1951-52, 54-55), Am. Pub. Health Assn., N.Y. Acad. Sci., Am. Chem. Soc., Am. Assn. Cereal Chemists, Am. Oil Chemists Soc., Ill. Acad. Sci., Soc. Chem. Industry, Pasadena C. of C., Sigma Xi, Phi Tau Sigma, Beta Kappa Chi, Alpha Phi Alpha. Baptist. Clubs: City, Pobla (pres. 1948), Druids (pres. 1945-47) (Chgo.). Asst. editor Beta Kappa Chi Jour., 1948-49; editor The Vitalizer (Chgo. sect. Inst. Food Tech.), 1948; cons. editor, 1949-50; editorial adv. bd. Food Processing mag., 1952-56; adv. bd. Chem. and Engring. News, 1957-60. Patentee in field, also lectr. Home: Altadena CA Died Jan. 2, 1971; buried Forest Lawn Cemetery, Glendale CA

HALL, MAURICE CROWTHER, zoölogist; b. Golden, Colo., July 15, 1881; s. George Hemingway Birtby and Marion Wallace (Crowther) H.; S.B., Colo. Coll., Colorado Springs, 1905, hon. D.Sc., 1925; M.A., U. of Neb., 1906; Ph.D., George Washington U., 1915, D.V.M., 1916; m. Lola May Davis, June 18, 1906; children—Marion Millicent, Winifred Lois, Margaret Lola. Instr. botany and physiology, Cutler Acad., Colorado Springs, 1904-05; instr. biology and chemistry, Cañon City (Colo.) High Sch., 1906-07; jr. zoölogist, 1907-11, asst. zölogist, 1911-16, U.S. Bur. Animal Industry; asst. zoölogist, U.S. Insecticide and Fungicide Bd., 1915-16; prof. zoölogy and parasitology, Coll. of Vet. Medicine, George Washington U., 1914-16; parasitologist, research lab. of Parke, Davis & Co., Detroit, 1916-18; 2d lt. and 1st lt. Vet. Corps, U.S.A., 1918-19; sr. zoölogist U.S. Bur. Animal Industry, 1919-36, chief of zoöl. div., 1925-36; asst. custodian Helminthol. Collection, U.S. Nat. Museum, 1925-31, custodian, 1931—. Pres. Permanent Internat. Commn. on Parasitology of Internat. Zoöl. Congress, 1930—; pres. Internat. Commn. on Control of Parasites of Internat. Veterinary Congress, 1934—. Mem. Nat. Research Council; prof. zoölogy and chief div. of zoölogy, Nat. Inst. of Health, U.S. Pub. Health Service, Apr. 1936—. Proposed the carbon tetrachlorid treatment, and, with Dr. J. E. Schillinger, the tetrachlorethylene treatment for hookworm disease. Home: Chevy Chase, D.C. Died 1938.

HALL, ROBERT WILLIAM, biologist; b. Cincinnati, O., Aug. 17, 1872; s. Ephraim Gaylord and Alice Cogswell (Crossette) H.; Ph.B., Yale, 1895; A.B., Harvard, 1897, A.M., 1898, Ph.D., 1901; m. Mary Alice Bowers, of Saco, Me., Aug. 4, 1908; children—Mrs. Roberta Bowers McLean, Marjorie Crossette, Roscoe Bowers. Asst. in zoology, Harvard, 1896-99, Yale, 1899-1901; instr., Yale, 1901-02, Woods Hole, 1899-1901; head of dept. of biology, Lehigh Univ., 1902-37, prof. biology since 1937. Fellow A.A.A.S.; mem. Pa. Forestry Assn. (life), Sigma Xi (Yale Chapter). Home: 37 E. Church St., Bethlehem PA

HALL, RUFUS BARTLETT, gynecologist; b. at Washington Co., O., May 15, 1849; s. Joseph B. and Irene (Bartlett) H.; M.D., Miami Med. Coll. (now Ohio-Miami Med. Coll.), Cincinnati, 1872; m. Margaret Chancellor, of Lower Salem, O., Mar. 14, 1872; children—Joseph Arda, Mrs. Anna Park, Lydia (dec.), Ruufs Bartlett. Practiced in Cincinnati since 1888; gynecologist, Presbyn. Hosp., 1894-1904; prof. gynecology, and clin. gynecology, Ohio-Miami Med. Coll., 1898-1917, now emeritus prof.; gynecologist, Cincinnati Hosp. Mem. Am. Assn. Obstetricians and Gynecologists (pres. 1900), A.M.A., Ohio State Med. Soc. (pres. 1900), Acad. Medicine of Cincinnati (pres. 1909). Republican. Presbyn. Club: Business Men's Home: 723 Ridgeway Av. Office: 628 Elm St., Cincinnati, O.

HALL, SAMUEL, shipbuilder; b. Marshfield, Mass., Apr. 23, 1800; s. Luke and Anna (Tuels) H.; m. Christina Kent; m. 2d, Huldah B. Sherman; 2 sons including Samuel, Jr., 6 daus. Established shipbldg. yard, East Boston, Mass., 1839; launched 110 clipper ships from yard including Surprise (1st clipper built in Mass.), Game Cock, Race Horse (all 1850), RB Forbes, 1851; John Gilpin, Flying Children, Hoogby, Polynesia (all 1852), Amphitrite, Mystery, Wizard, Oriental (all 1853); set style for New Eng. fishing schooners with Express, Telegraph; instrumental in having water piped to East Boston, 1851; pres. East Boston Ferry Co., Dry Dock Co., Maverick Nat. Bank (all Boston). Died Princeton, Ind., Nov. 13, 1870.

HALL, THOMAS, inventor; b. Phila., Feb. 4, 1834; ed. U. of Lewisburg, Pa. Devised mechanism for printing by touching keys, and in 1867 exhibited a keyed typewriter at Paris Expn.; later studied mechanics in Europe; invented and, 1881, placed on the market the Hall typewriter; has also invented several successful sewing machines, drill-grinding and other machinists' tools; now patent atty. Home: Brooklyn. Died 1911.

HALL, THOMAS SEAVEY, mfr. automatic railroad and highway signal devices; b. Upper Bartlett, N.H., Apr. 1, 1827; s. Elias and Hannah (Seavey) H.; m. Sarah C. Phillips, 1 son. A prominent woolen mfr. in New Eng.; a victim of a railroad accident, 1866, led to interest in signal devices to avoid such accidents; patented electric automatic signals, 1867; organized Hall Drawbridge & Signal Co., Stamford, Conn., 1867; 1st signal installed, Stamford, 1868; devised electric enclosed disc or "banjo" signal, 1869; 1st automatic block signalling system installed, 1871; patented highway-crossing signal, 1879. Died Meriden, Conn., Dec. 1, 1880.

HALL, WILLIAM SHAFER, mathematician; b. Chester, Pa., June 27, 1861; s. Stephen Cloud and Mercie Emma (Baker) H.; C.E., Lafayette Coll., 1884 (Phi Beta Kappa Fraternity), M.E., 1885, M.S., 1887, LL.D. from the same college, 1934; Sc.D., Gettysburg Coll., 1922 (Tau Beta Pi); m. Rachel Estelle Kline, Aug. 11, 1891; children—Rachel Elizabeth, Margaret (dec.), Mary Estelle, William Arthur (dec.), Eleanor Bassett.

Tutor in Eng. and graphics, 1884-88, adj. prof. mining engring. and graphics; 1890-98, prof., 1898-1912, prof. tech. mathematics, 1912-14, prof. mathematics and head dept., 1914-34, emeritus professor of mathematics since 1938, Lafayette College, also secretary of faculty. Fellow A.A.A.S.; mem. Math. Assn. of America, Am. Assn. Univ. Pros., Math. Assn. Middle States and Md., Pa. Soc. S.R. Republican. Presbyterian. Elder. Mason (Past Eminent Comdr. K.T.). Author: Mensuration, 1893; Descriptive Geometry, 1904; Differential and Integral Calculus, 1897; Mine Surveying, 1911. Address: 310 March St., Easton, Pa. Died Dec. 17, 1948.

HALL, WILLIAM THOMAS, chemist; b. New Bedford, Mass., Aug. 4, 1874; s. Anthony D. and Mary E. (Soule) H.; S.B., Mass. Inst. Tech., 1895; studied U. of Gottingen, 1895-97; m. Agnes D. Allen, Apr. 17, 1901; children—Catharine S., Mary E., Margaret D., William A., Constance D. Asst. in chemistry, 1898-1900, instr., 1900-11, asst. prof., 1911-18, asso. prof., 1918-40, prof. emeritus since 1940, Mass. Inst. Technology; head of science department, Thayer Academy, South Braintree, Mass., 1942-43. Assistant editor Chemical Abstracts. Member American Chemical Soc., Mass. Congregational Laymen's Council (since 1946), A.A.A.S., Sigma Alpha Epsilon. Congregationalist. Republican. Author; The Chemical and Metallographic Examination of Iron, Steel and Brass (with R. S. Williams), 1921; Textbook of Quantitative Analysis, 1930. Editor: Moore's History of Chemistry, 1931; Moore's Organic Chemistry, 1933. Translator from the German: (of F. P. Treadwell) Analytical Chemistry (2 vols.), 1903; (of H. Classen) Beet-sugar Manufacture (with G. W. Rolfe), 1906; (of E. Abderhalden) Text-book of Physiological Chemistry (with George Defren), 1908; (of H. and W. Blitz) Laboratory Methods of Inorganic Chemistry (with A. A. Blanchard), 1909; (of H. Blitz) Introduction to Experimental Inorganic Chemistry (with J. W. Phelan), 1909; (of Wilhelm Ostwald) Introduction to Chemistry (with R. S. Williams), 1910; (of W. Borchers) Metallurgy (with C. R. Hayward), 1910; (of A. Classen) Quantitative Chemical Analysis by Electrolysis, 1913; (of Bauer-Deiss) Sampling and Chemical Analysis of Iron and Steel (with R. S. Williams), 1915. Home: Snipatuit Road, Rochester MA

HALL, WINFIELD SCOTT, M.D., author, lecturer; b. Batavia, Ill., January 5, 1861; s. Albert Nelson and Adelia (Foote) H.; B.S., Northwestern U., 1887, M.D., 1888, M.S., 1889; M.D., U. of Leipzig, Germany, 1894, Ph.D., 1895; m. Jeannette Winter, of Juniata, Neb., Oct. 11, 1888; children—Albert Winter, Ethel Louise, Reymond Ludwig, Murill Jeannette. Interne Mercy Hosp., Chicago, 1888-89; prof. biology, Haverford Coll., Pa., 1889-93; prof. physiology, Northwestern U. Med. Sch., 1895-1919, prof. emeritus since 1919, and jr. dean med. faculty, 1901-13; lecturer on dietetics, Mercy Hosp. Sch. for Nurses, 1896-1918; lecturer on physiology, Y.M.C.A. Coll., Chicago, 1898-1917; lecturer on dietetics, Wesley Hosp. Sch. for Nurses, 1903-18; med. dir. Bureau of Social Hygiene, Board of Christian Edn., Presbyterian Church of U.S.A., 1919-29; exchange prof. Université Internationale, Brussels, Belgium, 1921-27; retired, 1929. Mem. Phi Beta Kappa (Northwestern, 1892), Sigma Xi; fellow American Acad. Medicine (pres., 1904-05), Chicago Acad. Sciences, A.A.A.S.; mem. Am. Physiol. Soc., A.M.A. (chmn. sect. pathology and physiology, 1905); pres. Am. Med. Soc. for Study of Alcohol and Other Narcotics, 1903-10; pres. of Alpha Omega Alpha (hon. med. soc., internat.), 1904-13; mem. Internat. Congress on Tuberculosis; mem. Research Council of Nat. Health League; mem. hygiene reference board, Life Extension Inst. of America, 1920—; dir. Life Conservation League of America, 1922—; mem. Authors' League. Counsel for Northwestern U., Internat. Academic Commn.; pres. Health League, Chicago, 1913; mem. Nat. Council Boy Scouts of America, Chicago Council Boy Scouts of America; pres. Child Conservation League America; mem. med. service Nat. War Work Council of Internat. Y.M.C.A.; with U.S. Volunteer Medical Service, 1918-19; with U.S. Public Health Service, 1919-29. Author: Laboratory Guide in Physiology, 1897; Anatomy of the Central Nervous System in Man and in Vertebrates, 1899; Text-Book of Physiology, 1899; Elementary Anatomy, Physiology and Hygiene, 1900; Intermediate Physiology and Hygiene, 1901; Manual of Experimental Physiology, 1904; Text-Book of Normal and Pathologic Physiology, 1905; The Biology, Physiology and Sociology of Reproduction; also Sexual Hygiene, 1906; Essentials of Physiology and Hygiene, 1908; From Youth into Manhood, 1909; Nutrition and Dietetics, 1909; The Strength of Ten, 1909; Instead of Wild Oats, 1911; Sexual Knowledge, 1913; Manual of Instruction in Sex Hygiene, 1913; Life Problems, 1913; The Doctor's Daughter, 1913; John's Vacation, 1913; Chums, 1913; Constructive Eugenics, 1915; A Physician's Counsel to Parents, 1916; The Intimate Life, 1925; The Book of Our Own Life, 1925; Man and Woman—In the Family and in Society, 1927; Love and Marriage, 1929. Extensive contbr. to med. and ednl. jours. Home: 3202 Clinton Av., Berwyn, Ill.; (summer) Wynnewood, Grand Haven, Mich.

HALLER, H(ERBERT L(UDWIG JACOB), chemist; b. Cincinnati, Aug. 15, 1894; s. Andreas and Gretchen (Hock) H.; Chem.E., U. Cin., 1918; Ph.D., Columbia, 1926; m. Iva M. Shanabrook, May 11, 1921. Jr. chemist Dept. of Agr., 1919-21, asso. chemist, 1921-23, Rockefeller Inst., 1923-29; sr. chemist, insecticide div. Bur. Chemistry and Bur. Entomology and Plant Quarantine, Dept. of Agr., 1929-40, prin. chemist, 1940-47, asst. chief Bur., 1947-53, asst. director crops research, 1954-57, assistant to administrator farm research, 1957-62, assistant administrator farm research, 1962-64; cons. Nat. Agrl. Chems. Assn., 1964-71. Mem. Am. Chem. Soc., Entomol. Soc. Am., A.A.A.S., Chem. Soc. of Washington (treas. 1935, pres. 1941; awarded Hillebrand prize 1933), Entomol. Soc. Washington, Washington Acad. Arts and Scis., Insecticide Soc. Washington (pres. 1941), Sigma Xi, Alphia Chi Sigma. Home: Washington DC Died Nov. 1, 1972.

HALLETT, GEORGE HERVEY, mathematician; b. Manchester, Me., Dec. 30, 1870; s. James Hervey and Sarah Louise (Hawkes) H.; student Lehigh U., 1889-90; A.B., U. of Pa., 1893, A.M., 1894, Ph.D., 1896; m. Gertrude Amy Hawkes, Feb. 21, 1894; children—George H., Henry M., Mrs. Rebecca Richie, Margaret E. (Mrs. Margaret Pittman), Winslow N. Instructor in mathematics, 1894-1904, asst. prof., 1904-09; prof. 1909-33, Thomas A. Scott prof. of mathematics, 1933-41, emeritus since Jan. 1, 1942, University of Pa. Mem. Assn. Teachers of Math. Middle States and Md., Pa. State Ednl. Assn. (ednl. council 1910-16), Am. Math. Soc., Pi Mu Epsilon, Sigma Xi, Phi Beta Kappa. Club: Meridian (Philadelphia). Author: (with Robert F. Anderson) Elementary Algebra, 1917. Home: West Chester, Pa. Died Aug. 12, 1947.

HALLETT, ROBERT LEROY, engr.; b. Estes Park, Colo., July 13, 1881; s. William Leroy and Elvena Ada (Sessions) H.; E.M., Colo. Sch. of Mines, 1935; m. Phebe Louise James, June 10, 1911 (died 1933); 1 dau., Frances (Mrs. Arthur A. Denton, Jr.); m. 2d, Ann Elizabeth Beyer, Oct. 24, 1942. Chemist, Selby Smelting & Lead Co., Selby, Calif., 1905-08; mill supt., Midas Gold Mining Co., Knob, Calif., 1908-09; chemist and engr., Consolidated Arizona Smelting Co., Humboldt, Ariz., 1909-11; chemist and engr., Nat. Lead Co., New York, 1911-48, chief chemist, 1938-48; cons. mining and indsl. engr., New York, since 1949. Chmn. sub com. on tin, Army and Navy Munitions Bd., 1939; adviser on tin, Council of Nat. Defense, Washington, D.C., 1940-41. Member Mining and Metall. Soc. of Am. (pres. 1947), Am. Inst. of Mining and Metall. Engrs., Am. Chem. Soc., Am. Soc. Testing Materials. Republican. Protestant Episcopalian. Club: Mining of New York (pres. 1949-50). Author: chapter on Paint Industry, Warshow's Representative Industries in the United States, 1928; section on Lead, Ency. Britannica, 1929 and 1947; sect. on Tin Industry, Metals Handbook, 1939; chapter on Tin, Liddell's Handbook of Nonferrous Metallurgy, 1945. Examined and investigated mining properties particularly those containing lead, tin, titanium and antimony for Nat. Lead Co. Made many mine examinations in the United States from 1911-46, in Brazil, 1924, Spain, 1926 and 1929, Norway, 1927, Germany, 1926, 1928 and 1929, Canada, 1927. Home: 49 E. 19th St., Brooklyn 26, N.Y. Office: 132 Nassau St., N.Y.C. 7. Died May 17, 1952.

HALLIDIE, ANDREW SMITH, engr., inventor; b. London, Eng., Mar. 16, 1836; s. Andrew and Julia (Johnstone) Smith; m. Martha Elizabeth Woods, Nov. 1863, 1 child. Adopted godfather's name Hallidie (legalized by Cal. Legislature); came to Cal. in search of gold, 1853; constructed flume across Middle Fork of American River, 1855; built various flumes and suspension bridges along Pacific coastal area, 1855-circa 67; became mfr. wire rope, circa 1857, constructed 1st wire rope factory on West Coast, 1858; invented rigid suspension bridge, 1867, perfected means of transporting freight over canyons and difficult areas by use of endless wire rope (Hallidie ropeway); devised method to pull streetcars up a steep slope by means of underground endless moving cable, 1871, made 1st installation in San Francisco, 1873; regent U. Cal., 1868-1900, chmn. finance com., 1874-1900, also acting pres.; pres. Mechanics Inst. of San Francisco; v.p. James Lick Sch. Mech. Arts; a founder San Francisco Public Library and Art Soc.; mem. exec. com. World's Columbian Expn., 1892-93. Died San Francisco, Apr. 24, 1900.

HALLOCK, CHARLES, journalist, author, scientist; b. New York, 1834; s. Gerard and Eliza (Allen) H.; A.B., Amherst, 1854, A.M., 1871; m. Amelia J. Wardell, Sept. 10, 1855. Editor New Haven Register, 1855-56, New York Journal of Commerce, 1856-61, St. John (N.B.) Telegraph and Courier, 1863-65; broker at St. John and Halifax, N.S., 1865-66; financial editor Harper's Weekly, 1868; founded Forest and Stream, 1873; editor Nature's Realm, 1890; editor Northwestern Field and Stream, 1896-97. Was 1st sec. Blooming Grove Park Assn., New York, 1870-72; dir. Flushing and Queens Co. Bank, 1873; founded Internat. Assn. for Protection of Game, 1874; formulated uniform game laws, 1875; founder town of Hallock, Minn., 1880. Has done collecting and field work for Smithsonian Instn., 1860—. Author: Camp Life in Florida, 1876; Sportsman's Gazetteer, 1877; Vacation Rambles in Michigan, 1877; American Club List and Glossary, 1878; Dog Fanciers' Directory and Medical Guide, 1886; Our New Alaska, 1886; The Salmon Fisher, 1890; Hallock Ancestry, 1906; Peerless Alaska, 1908. Died Dec. 2, 1917.

HALLOCK, FRANK KIRKWOOD, M.D.; b. Oyster Bay, L.I., Aug. 18, 1860; s. Winthrop Bailey (M.D.) and Mary Kirkwood (Kent) H.; A.B., Wesleyan U., 1882, A.M., 1885; M.D., Coll. Phys. and Surg. (Columbia), 1885; interne New York Hosp., 1885-87; student in Germany, 1887-89; m. Kate Camp Avery, May 7, 1890 (died 1930); children—Winthrop Avery (dec.), Abraham Avery, Mary (Mrs. S. W. Armstrong), Leonard Avery, Elizabeth (Mrs. J. G. Vermillion). Specialist in neurology, 1890—; med. dir. Cromwell Hall Health Sch., 1898—; established an instn. for the treatment of nervous invalidism on an educational basis, combining medical, physical, occupational and nature agencies with the psychological analysis and interpretation of the individual. Pres., now dir. Savings Bank (Cromwell); dir. Rand Avery Supply Co. (Boston), Industrial Securities Corp. (Middletown). Mem. bd. trustees Wesleyan U. (Middletown, Conn.); dir. Middlesex Hosp. (Middletown). Mason. Home: Cromwell, Conn. Died Apr. 29, 1937.

HALLOCK, WILLIAM, physicist; b. Milton, N.Y., Aug. 14, 1857; s. Isaac S. and Phoebe (Hull) H.; A.B., Columbia, 1879; Ph.D., U. of Würzburg, 1881 (hon. D.Phar., Nat. Coll. Pharmacy, Washington, 1892); m. Georgianna B., d. Charles Henri Ames, of Keesville, N.Y., Oct. 15, 1885. Asst. in physical lab., Würzburg, 1881-82; physicist, U.S. Geol. Survey, 1882-91; prof. physics, Corcoran Scientific Sch., Washington, 1884-86; prof. chemistry and toxicology, Nat. Coll. Pharmacy, 1889-92; asst. in charge, Astrophysical Obs., Smithsonian Instn., 1891-92; adj. prof., 1892-1902, prof. physics, 1902—, dean faculty of pure science, 1906-09, Columbia. Home: New York, N.Y. Died May 20, 1913.

HALPERN, JULIUS (JULES), physicist, educator; b. Norfolk, Va., Feb. 4, 1912; s. Jacob and Lena (Kanter) H.; B.S., Carnegie Inst. Tech., 1933, M.S., 1935, Sc.D., 1937; m. Phyllis E. Melnick, Feb. 4, 1940; children—Paul Joseph, Sydney Ann. Nuclear physics research U. Mich., 1937-40, U. Cal., 1940-41; staff Mass. Inst. Tech., 1941-46, asso. dir. Brit. br. Radiation Lab., tech. advisor USAAF, 1944-45, physics research Mass. Inst. Tech. Research Lab. Electronics, 1946-47; asst. prof. U. Pa., 1947, asso. prof., 1948-52, prof. from 1952. Chmn., organizer biennial Internat. Conf. on Exptl. Meson Spectroscopy, Phila., 1968, 70, 72. Sr. postdoctoral fellow Nat. Sci. Found., Paris, France, 1956-57; recipient Alumnus Merit award Carnegie-Mellon U., 1970. Fellow Am. Phys. Soc.; mem. Fedn. Am. Scientists (sec. treas. 1951, chmn. 1952, exec. com. 1953), Sigma Xi, Tau Beta Pi, Pi Delta Epsilon, Beta Sigma Rho. Contbr. profl. publs. Home: Philadelphia PA Died May 13, 1972; buried Shalom Meml. Park, Philadelphia PA

HALSTEAD, WARD CAMPBELL, psychologist; born Sciotoville, O., Dec. 31, 1908; s. Ward Beecher and Fannie (Campbell) H.; student Miami U., 1925-27; A.B., Ohio U., 1930; A.M., Ohio State U., 1931: Ph.D., Northwesktern U., 1935; Nat. Research fellow, U. of Chicago, 1935; m. Elizabeth Lee, Dec. 6, 1932; 1 son, Mark Beecher. Instr. in exptl. psychology, dept. of medicine, U. of Chicago, 1936-39; asst. prof. and asso. mem. Otho S.A. Sprague Meml. Inst., U. of Chicago, 1939-43, asso. prof., 1943-46, prof. exptl. psychology, dept. of medicine, 1946-69, dir. psychology sect., chmn. sect. biopsychology, 1953; consultant in neurology and blindness Nat. Insts. of Health, 1953-69; vis. prof. psychology, U. of Calif., Los Angeles, 1947, Berkeley, 1949. Spl. lectureships: Hixon Symposium on Brain Mechanisms, Calif. Inst. Tech., 1948; Nineteenth James Arthur lecture, Am. Museum of Natural History, 1950. Mem. com. on psychiatry, Nat. Research Council, 1947-53; cons. Nat. Inst. Neurol. Diseases & Blindness, 1954-69. Mem. Am. Psychol. Assn., A.A.A.S., Am. Physiol. Soc., Am. Neurol. Assn., Soc. of Biological Psychiatry, Midwestern Psychol. Assn. Chicago Neurol. Assn. Chgo. Inst. of Medicine Author: books include Brain and Intelligence, 1947; The Frontal Lobes (with J. F. Fulton, editor), 1948; Brain Mechanisms and Behavior, 1951. Home: Chicago IL Died Mar. 25, 1969.

HALSTED, BYRON DAVID, botanist; b. Venice, N.Y., June 7, 1852; s. David and Mary (Mechem) H.; B.S., Mich. Agrl. Coll., 1871, M.S., 1874; Sc.D., Harvard, 1878; m. Susan E. Howe, Jan. 7, 1883. Mng. editor Am. Agriculturist, 1880-85; prof. botany, Ia. Agrl. Coll., 1885-89. Rutgers Coll., 1889—. Asso. editor Bull. of Torrey Bot. Club, 1890-93, Systematic Flora of N. America, 1905—. Silver medal, Mass. Hort. Soc., 1877. Home: New Brunswick, N.J. Died Aug. 28, 1919.

HALSTED, THOMAS HENRY, otologist; b. Listowel, Ontario, Canada, July 8, 1865; s. James Addison and Jane (Hacking) H.; Toronto U., 1883; M.D., Toronto Med. Sch., Toronto U., 1887; mem. Coll. Physicians and Surgeons, Ont., 1887; studied New York, Vienna, Heidelberg, Berlin, Budapest and London; m. Lola B. Bridgford, 1889 (died 1895); m. 2d, Charlotte C. Palmer, Oct. 7, 1897 (died 1932); m. 3d, Maida Lawrence Smyth, Sept. 30, 1933. In practice at Syracuse, 1889-1937; laryngologist and otologist, Syracuse Meml., St. Joseph's hosps.; became prof. laryngology and otology, Syracuse U., 1899, now emeritus. Unitarian. Fellow A.C.S., Am. Laryngol. Assn. (ex-pres.), Am. Otol. Soc., Am. Laryngol. Rhinol. and Otol. Soc., Am. Bronchoscopic Soc.; mem. A.M.A., N.Y. State Med. Soc. (ex-pres.), Onondaga County Med. Soc., Syracuse Acad. Medicine, Nu Sigma Nu, Alpha Omega Alpha. Mason. Home: Engelwood, N.J. Office: 475 Fifth Av., N.Y.C. Died Nov. 20, 1956. *

HALVERSON, WILTON L., physician, educator; b. Litchfield, Minn., June 30, 1896; s. Halver L. and Mary (Westman) H.; B.A., Union Coll. (Neb.) 1919; M.D., Coll. Med. Evangelists, 1929; Dr. P.H., Yale Univ., 1932; m. Hazel Richardson, July 22, 1920; children—Robert Lee, Harold Wilton. Dist. health officer, Los Angeles Co. (Calif.), 1929-34; health officer, Pasadena, Calif., 1934-41, lecturer, U. of Calif. at Los Angeles, 1934-37; dir. pub. health, Cal., 1943-54; asso. dean sch. of pub. health and chairman dept. preventive medicine U. Cal. Med. Sch. at Los Angeles; cons. physician Huntington Memorial Hosp., Pasadena, since 1935, sr. attending physician, Los Angeles Co. Hosp., since 1936, prof. pub. health, Coll. Medical Evangelists, since 1937; health officer for Los Angeles County, 1941-43. Sci. dir., internat. health div., Rockefeller Foundation. Mem. adv. com. Fgn. Operations Adminstrn.; member International Development Advisory Board. Diplomate Am. Bd. Preventive Medicine and Public Health. Life fellow Am. Pub. Health Assn. (past v.p., chmn. com. adminstrv. practice 1945-51, pres. 1953); mem. A.A.A.S., Assn. Am. Med. Colls., Assn. Tchrs. Preventive Medicine, So. Cal. Pub. Health Assn. (past pres.), Los Angeles Co. Med. Assn., Delta Omega (past pres.). Home: 2301 E. Glenoaks Blvd., Glendale, Cal. Office: University of Cal., Los Angeles 24. Died June 8, 1961.

HAMAKER, JOHN IRVIN, biologist; b. Elizabethtown, Pa., Nov. 29, 1869; s. Jacob and Martha (Gish) H.; A.B., U. Kan., 1893; A.B., Harvard, 1894, A.M., 1895, Ph.D., 1897; studied U. Berlin, 1910-11; m. Ray Parker, Aug. 12, 1914; children—Madeline, Marjorie Love, Templin (dec.), Richard Franklin. Prof. biology Trinity Coll., Durham, N.C., 1897-1904; prof. biology Randolph-Macon Woman's Coll., 1904-45, emeritus, 1945—. Fellow A.A.A.S.; mem. Am. Soc. Zoölogists, Pa. German Soc. Methodist. Author: A Compend of the Principles of Biology, 1905; The Principles of Biology, 1913; The Elements of Biology, 1929; Matthias Gish of White Oak—The History of an American Family, 1940. Home: 223 S. Princeton St., Lynchburg, Va. Died July 24, 1956.

HAMBLEN, EDWIN CROWELL, gynecologist and endocrinologist; b. Greenville, Miss., Aug. 23, 1900; s. Reuben McPherson and Zoula Lee (Crowell) H.; B.S., U. Va., 1921; student So. Med. U., 1923, Baylor U. Sch. Medicine, 1923-25; M.D., U. Va., 1928; m. Agnes Morton Baptist, Dec. 27, 1930; children—Agnes Crowell (Mrs. Paul G. McDonald), Margaret Lewis (Mrs. Robert W. Wynne III). Assistant and instructor in biochemistry and pharmacology, Baylor University, Coll. of Medicine, 1922-24 and 1925-26; interne U. of Va. Hosp., 1928-29, resident in obstetrics and gynecology, July-Dec. 1929; asst. in surgery and gynecology Gamble Bros. and Montgomery Clinic, Greenville, Miss., Dec. 1929-Apr. 1930; clin. instr. and asst. in obstetrics and gynecology and asst. obstetrician and gynecologist U. of Va. Hosp., Apr. 1930-July 1931; asso. prof. obstetrics and gynecology Duke University since July 1931, clinical professor of endocrinology, 1944-47, professor of endocrinology since 1947; associate obstetrician and gynecologist Duke U. Hosp., 1931-37; chief endocrine div. and endocrinologist Duke U. Hospital, 1937-55; sometime lecturer and professor endocrinology S.A. univ. Mem. S.A.T.C., Oct.-Dec. 1918. Fellow Am. Coll. Surgeons; diplomate Am. Bd. Obstetrics and Gynecology; mem. A.M.A., Am. Therapeutic Soc. (v.p. 1939-40; mem. council 1942-50), Assn. for Study Internal Secretions (vice pres. 1936-37; mem. council 1937-40; mem. publ. bd. and com. on awards, 1940-44), Am. Soc. Clin. Investigation, Am. Soc. Anatomists, South Atlantic Assn. Obstetrics and Gynecology, Southern Med. Assn. (chmn. sect. on gynecology 1940-41), Am. Soc. for Study Sterility (mem. bd. dirs. 1944-49), Durham-Orange Co. Med. Soc., N.C. Med. Assn. (chmn. sect. on obstetrics and gynecology, 1933-34), N.C. Obstetrical and Gynecological Society (pres. 1935-37), Durham Rose Society (president 1948-49), Am. Rose Soc. (dir. 1951-53, 61—), Internat. Corrs. Soc. Obstetricians & Gynecologists; hon. mem. Sociedad Antiquena Columbia, corr. mem. Sociedad Columbiana de Obstetricia y Ginecologia, Sigma Xi, Alpha Omega Alpha, Phi Beta Pi. Author: Endocrine Gynecology, 1939; Facts for Childless Couples, 1942; Endocrinology of Woman, 1945; Facts About the Change of Life, 1949. Member editorial committee Jour. Clinical Endocrinology, 1941-46 and 1951-55; editor Am. Lectures in Obstetrics and Gynecology since 1950. Contbr. to med. jours., books. Office: Duke Hosp., Durham, N.C. Died Nov. 24, 1963.

HAMERSCHLAG, ARTHUR ARTON, educator, engr.; b. Neb., Nov. 22, 1867; s. William and Francesca H. (Brummel) H.; ed. pub. schs., Omaha and New York, and pvt. tutors; (Sc.D., Lehigh U., 1907, Western U. of Pa., 1907; LL.D., Trinity Coll., Conn., 1912, Allegheny Coll., Pa., 1915); m. Elizabeth Ann Tollast, Dec. 23, 1901. In engring. field work U.S., Cuba, Mex., 1888-92; supt. St. George's Evening Trade Sch., New York, 1892-1904; pres. Carnegie Inst. Tech., Pittsburgh, 1903-22; dir. industrial research, Office of Maj. Gen. George W. Goethals; pres. Research Corp. New York, 1923—. Consulting engr. New York Trade Sch., Boys' Prep. Trade Sch., New York, Highland Falls (N.Y.) Evening Trade Sch., etc., until 1904. During same period in independent practice as consulting elec. and mech. engr. for numerous corps. and industries; mem. Smoke and Dust Abatement League of Pittsburgh (pres.), Schenley Memorial Commn., Pittsburgh Chamber of Commerce; mem. Internat. Jury of Award of Dept. of Edn., Pamana P.I. Expn., 1915. Home: Pittsburgh, Pa. Died July 20, 1927.

HAMILL, SAMUEL MCCLINTOCK, pediatrician; b. Oak Hall, Pa., Nov. 3, 1864; s. Robert and Margaret E. (Lyon) H.; student Princeton, 1886; M.D., U. of Pa., 1888; hon. D.Sc., U. of Pa., 1940; m. Lila Clarke Kennedy, Apr. 17, 1895; children—Kennedy, Samuel McClintock, Hugh Maxwell. Practiced in Phila. since 1890; demonstrator physical diagnosis, 1892-94, instr. medicine, 1894-1901, U. of Pa.; prof. diseases of children, Phila. Polyclinic and Coll. for Graduates in Medicine, 1901-19; prof. same, Post-Graduate Dept. of Medicine, U. of Pa., 1919-20; cons. pediatrician, Presbyn. Hosp.; formerly visiting pediatrician to St. Christopher's Hosp. for Children and Phila. Polyclinic; chmn. sect. I, med. service, and chmn. follow-up com. of sect. I, White House Conf. on Child Health and Protection. Mem. bd. mgrs. Babies' Hospital of Phila. Mem. exec. com. of Pa. mental hygiene com. of Public Charities Assn. Mem. Am. Med. Assn. (chmn. sect. on diseases of children, 1911), Am. Academy Pediatrics (pres. 1932), Am. Pediatric Soc. (pres. 1913-14), Med. Soc. State of Pa. (1st chmn. sect. on pediatrics), Phila. Pediatric Soc. (pres. 1901-02), Phila. Pathol. and Neurol. socs., Coll. of Physicians of Phila. Chmn. Pa. Emergency Child Health Com., 1933-39; mem. Gen. Med. Bd. and chmn. Nat. Child Welfare Com. of Council Nat. Defense; dir. child welfare for State of Pa., 1917-18; del. Cannes Med. Conf. of Red Cross Socs., 1919; pres. dirs. of Phila. Child Health Soc., 1919-42; mem. Am. Assn. Study and Prevention Infant Mortality (pres. 1915-16), Am. Child Health Assn. (pres. 1931-35); former mem. trustees Lawrenceville Sch. Republican. Presbyterian. Home: 1822 Spruce St., Philadelphia. Died May 3, 1948.

HAMILTON, ALBERT HINE, micro-chem. investigator; b. Weedsport, N.Y., Dec. 10, 1859; s. James Theodore and Clarissa (Hine) H.; Ph.G., Coll. of Pharmacy of City of New York (now dept. Columbia U.), 1885; specialized later with expert tutors; m. Jessie Eccles, Feb. 1, 1888. Pharmacist, 1887-1911; formerly chemist, Auburn Bd. of Health; frequently called as expert chemist in legal proceedings, appearing in upwards of 300 homicide cases and hundreds of cases pertaining to forgery, arson, burglary, bomb assaults, etc. Discovered by test shots into human bodies, how to identify the "contact shot" in homicide cases; originated a system of examination of exhibits in circumstantial evidence cases whereby the exhibits reveal the truth, regardless of claims to the contrary; discovered by test shots, that the fine scratches on murder bullets which have been relied upon by forensic ballistics to identify a suspected firearm, are not made by the barrel interior but by the crimping of the cartridge shell and the hot escaping exploding powder. Republican. Presbyn. Mason. Home: Auburn, N.Y. Died July 1, 1938.

HAMILTON, DONALD ROSS, physicist; b. Hartford, Vt., Sept. 5, 1914; s. Rollo Albert and May Davina (Ross) H.; A.B., Princeton, 1935; Ph.D., Columbia, 1939; m. Eileen Mary Clare-Patton, Aug. 20, 1938;children—Erica Lynn (Mrs. Richard S. Weeder), Eleanor Patton (Mrs. Stanley Sienkiewicz), David Ross. Jr. fellow Soc. of Fellos, Harvard, 1939-42; staff Mass. Inst. Tech. Radiation Lab., 1940-46; project engr. Sperry Gyroscope Co. Research Labs., Garden City, N.Y., 1941-42, research engr., 1942-45; asst. prof. physics Princeton, 1946-48, asso. prof., 1948-55, prof. from 1955, dean of the graduate school, 1958-65; member of the Inst. for Advanced Study, 1952; vis. sr. physicist Brookhaven Nat. Lab., 1953. Fellow Am. Phys. Soc., Fedn. Am. Scientists. Author: Klystrons and Microwave Triodes (with J.B.H. Kuper and J.L. Knipp), 1947. Trustee Princeton U. Press, from 1956, mem. editorial bd., 1956-60. Home: Princeton NJ Died Jan. 4, 1972; buried Fairview Cemetery, Tyler County WV

HAMILTON, GEORGE ANSON, electrical engr.; b. Cleveland, O., Dec. 30, 1843; s. Daniel and Elizabeth A. (Beardsley) H.; ed. pub. schs.; m. Nellie F. Park, Dec. 15, 1880; children—Corinne F. (Mrs. R. H. Smith), Edith A. In telegraph and ry. signaling service, 1860-73; asst. to Prof. Moses G. Farmer, a pioneer elec. inventor of New England, 1873-75; asst. engr. and engr. Western Union Telegraph Co., at N.Y. City, 1875-89; engr., Western Electric Co., N.Y. City, 1889-1909 (retired). Fellow Am. Inst. Elec. Engrs. (treas., 1895-1930). Republican. Presbyterian. Home; Elizabeth, N.J. Died Jan. 10, 1935.

HAMILTON, GEORGE HALL, astronomer; b. of Am. parents, London, Eng., Jan. 31, 1884; s. John McLure and Clara Augusta (Raiguel) H.; brought to U.S. in infancy; M.A., Trinity Coll., Cambridge U., Eng., 1911; m. Elizabeth Langdon Williams, June 2, 1922. Prof. astronomy, Bellevue (Neb.) Coll., 1910-14; astronomer Lowell Obs., 1917-22; astronomer Jamaica br. Harvard Coll. Obs., 1922-24; working privately, 1924—. Fellow, Royal Astron. Soc. (Eng.). Republican. Episcopalian. Author: Mars at Its Nearest, 1925. Died Aug. 4, 1935.

HAMLIN, EMMONS, inventor, mfr.; b. Rome, N.Y., Nov. 16, 1821; s. Henry and Laura (Munson) H.; m. Elvira J. Patrick, Feb. 12, 1843. With George A. Prince & Co., melodeon mfrs., Buffalo, N.Y., circa 1840-52; discovered means of perfecting melodeon by clearing up thin nasal tones, 1850; went to Boston, became partner Mason & Hamlin Organ Co., 1854-85, new co. made its 1st Organ-Harmonium, 1855, this instrument (with improvements) became popular as Am. Cabinet Organ, 1861; Mason and Hamlin Organs won 1st prize at Paris Expdn., 1876; took up art of violin-making in later years. Died Boston, Apr. 8, 1885.

HAMMER, EDWIN WESLEY, cons. engr.; b. Newark, N.J., Dec. 16, 1867; s. William Alexander and Anna Maria Nichols (Lawton) H.; descendant on maternal side of Michael Hillegas, of Phila., first treas. of United States, and the Pilgrim, John Howland, on paternal side of George Frederick Hammer of Pa.; ed. pub. schs.; m. Emily Augusta Thompson, May 28, 1890; 1 son, Wesley Thompson. With Thomas A. Edison and Edison Cos., 1884-87; mgr. Edison Elec. Illuminating Co., Fall River, Mass., 1887-88; asst. engr. New York Edison Co., 1888-89; with Thomas A. Edison at Paris Expn., 1889-90, Northwestern Expn., 1890-91; engr. for legal dept. Edison Electric Light Co. and Gen. Electric Co., 1891-96; engr. Bd. of Patent Control, Gen. Electric Co., and Westinghouse Electric & Mfg. Co., 1896-1911; cons. practice, 1911—; professional engr., State of N.Y. Served as commr. water supply East Orange, N.J.; consultant to U.S. Navy, 1917-18. Fellow Am. Inst. Elec. Engrs.; mem. Am. Soc. Mech. Engrs., N.Y. Elec. Soc., Franklin Inst., Am. Water Works Assn.; asso. Am. Electro-Therapeutic Assn. (founder mem.), Edison Pioneers (pres. 1941-42). Mem. Society Colonial Wars, S.R., New Eng. Soc. of Oranges. Republican. Presbyterian. Club: Bankers. Co-Author: The X-Ray, or Photography of the Invisible, 1896; Cataphoresis, 1898. An inventor and patentee and has had much to do with patents and inventions as technician and patent expert. Home: 10 Crestmont Rd., Montclair, N.J. Died Oct. 11, 1951; buried Fall River, Mass.

HAMMER, WILLIAM JOSEPH, cons. engineer; b. Cressona, Pa., Feb. 26, 1858; s. William Alexander and Martha A. (Beck) H.; ed. pub. schs. and high schs., Newark, N.J.; m. Alice Maude White, Jan. 3, 1894; 1 dau., Mabel White (Mrs. Thomas Cleveland Assheton). Asst. to Edward Weston in Weston Malleable Nickel Co., Newark, N.J., 1878; became asst. in lab. of Thomas A. Edison, Menlo Park, N.J., Dec. 1879; chief engr. Edison Lamp Works, 1880-81; sent to Eng. by Mr. Edison in fall of 1881 and became chief engr. English Edison Co., and established in London 1st central sta. in world for incandescent elec. lighting; chief engr. German Edison Co. (now Allfemeine Elektricates Gesellschaft), 1883-84; had charge of interests of Mr. Edison and 8 Edison interests at Franklin Inst. Elec. Expn., 1884; represented Mr. Edison's interests Crystal Palace Elec. Expn., 1882, and Paris Expn., 1889; at close of latter expn. made balloon flight over France; chief insp. central stas., Edison Elec. Lab. Co., 1884-85; became confidential asst. of pres. of parent Edison Co., 1884, and incorporator and trustee Sprague Elec. R.R. & Motor Co.; installed the 8,000-light plant of Ponce de Leon Hotel at Augustine, Fla., 1887, and acted at cons. and contracting engr. in connection with the elaborate elec. effects at Cincinnati Expn., 1888; chief engr. and gen. mgr. Boston Edison Co., 1886-87; cons. practice as elec. engr., 1890—. Rep. of Am. Inst. E.E. at Hall of Fame ceremonies, 1901-07. Received 2 medals abroad for professional work, and John Scott Legacy medal and premium from Franklin Inst.; grand prize, St. Louis Expn., 1904, for hist. collection of incandescent elec. lamps; gold medal, St. Louis Expn., and Elliot Cresson gold medal, Franklin Inst., 1906; World War medal (U.S.), 1920; World War Medal, N.Y. State, 1920; Chevalier Legion of Honor (France), 1925. Past v.p. Am. Inst. Electrical Engrs. (life mem., fellow), N.Y. Elec. Soc. Aeronautical Soc.; pres. Edison Pioneers, 1920-21; pres. Franklin Exptl. Club; pres. Nat. Conf. on Standard Elec. Rules ten years; fellow Am. Physical Soc. A.A.A.S., Am. Inst. E.E., Am. Acoustical Soc.; chmn. Jamestown Expn. Aeronautical Congress, 1907; sec. and expert Aeronautics Com., Hudson Fulton Celebration, 1909. Served as maj., Gen. Staff, U.S.A., Inventions Sec. of War Plans Div., and later Operations Div., Army War College, Washington, D.C., after entrance of U.S. into World War; in charge elec. and aeronautical war inventions. Invented the radium luminous preparations used for watches, clocks, airplane and automobile instruments, etc.; brought 9 tubes of radium from Curie labs., 1902, and delivered 88 lectures on radium; first suggested and used radium for cancer and tumor treatment; inventor of motor-driven flashing electric sign. Republican. Episcopalian. Home: New York, N.Y. Died Mar. 24, 1934.

HAMMOND, ALONZO JOHN, civil engr.; b. Thorntown, Ind., Apr. 23, 1869; s. John W. and Mary Ann (Padgett) H.; B.S., Rose Poly. Inst., 1889; M.S., 1894, C.E., 1898, Dr. Engring., 1933; grad. study, Mass.

Inst. Tech., 1891; m. Flora Troll, May 23, 1893; children—Alonzo John, Mary A. (Mrs. George E. Davies). City engr. Frankfort, Ind., 1888-98; asst. engr. Terre Haute & Ind. R.R., 1898-1901; city engr. South Bend, Ind., 1901-09; cons. engr., Chicago, since 1910; chief engr. Bur. Public Efficiency, Chicago, 1911; engr. of bridges and harbors, Chicago, 1912-13; asst. chief engr. Chicago Union Station Co. (in charge engring. design and constrn. $75,000,000 station), 1914-22; asso. with James O. Heyworth, 1922-25, constructing hydroelectric plants and bridges; with Mellon-Stuart Co., 1926-27, rep. of company in negotiations for $130,000,000 internal improvement program for Cuba; since 1927 in cons. engring. practice (City of Chicago on river straightening, viaducts and bridges; Des Moines and Sioux City, Ia., union stations; vehicular tunnel under Delaware River; high level bridge Pittsburgh and report on Minneapolis and St. Louis R.R.). Mem. Building Code Com., Chicago; gen. chmn. Construction League of U.S., 1933-34; pres. Am. Engring. Council, 1940-41; mem. bd. mgrs. Rose Poly. Inst., mem. advisory com. Army and Navy Munitions Bd. on engring. and construction; consulting engr. construction div. of War Dept. on all field operations; now member construction contract board of construction division, War Department, Washington. Vice-president Am. Inst. Consulting Engrs., 1943. Member American Society of Civil Engineers (pres. 1933; elected hon. mem. Jan. 1943), Western Soc. Engrs., Am. Ry. Engring. Assn., Am. Inst. Cons. Engrs. Republican. Presbyterian. Mason (Shriner). Clubs: Chicago Engineers, Shawnee Country. Home: Hotel Claridge, 820 Conn. Av. N.W., Washington, D.C. Office: 120 S. La Salle St., Chicago, Ill. Died Dec. 2, 1944.

HAMMOND, EDWIN, sheep breeder; b. Middlebury, Vt., May 20, 1801; s. Elnathan and Deborah (Carr) H.; m. Alpha Olmstead, Dec. 29, 1828, 3 children. Foremost contbr. to improvement of breed Merion sheep (one of most profitable branches of animal husbandry in Northern New Eng. at the time); founder Vt. State Agrl. Soc., 1851, pres., several years; aided and advised in formation New Eng. Agrl. Soc.; mem. exec. com. Nat. Woolgrowers Assn., asso. with Nat. Mfrs.' Assn. in framing schedule on wool and woolens in connection with tariff of 1867; mem. Vt. Legislature, 1858, 59; del. Republican Nat. Conv., 1864; trustee Middlebury Coll. Died Dec. 31, 1870.

HAMMOND, JAMES BARTLETT, inventor, mfr.; b. Boston, Apr. 23, 1829; s. Thomas and Harriet (Trow) H.; grad. U. Vt., 1861, Union Theol. Sem., 1865; never married. Reported Henry Ward Beecher's sermons for Boston Daily Traveller, 1861; with N.Y. Tribune, 1862-63, started working on devel. of typewriter, circa 1871, patented typewriter, 1880; his machine won Elliott Cresson Gold medal when publicly demonstrated at New Orleans Centennial Expn., 1884; pres. Hammond Co., typewriter mfg. firm, N.Y., 1884-1909; left his large fortune to Met. Mus. Art, N.Y.C. Died St. Augustine, Fla., Jan. 27, 1913.

HAMMOND, JOHN HAYS, mining engr.; b. San Francisco, Calif., Mar. 31, 1855; s. Richard Pindell and Sarah Elizabeth (Hays) H.; ed. pub. and pvt. schs.; Ph.B., Sheffield Scientific Sch. (Yale), 1876, A.M., Yale, 1898; mining course at Royal Sch. of Mines, Freiberg, Saxony; D.E., Stevens Inst., Tech., 1906; LL.D., St. John's Coll., 1907, Yale, 1925; Dr. Engring., U. of Pennsylvania, 1928; m. Natalie Harris, Jan. 1, 1881; children—Harris John Hays, Richard Pindell, Natalie Hays. Spl. expert U.S. Geol. Survey, 1880, examining Calif. gold fields; later in Mexico and afterward consulting engr. Union Iron Works, San Francisco, and to Central and Southern Pacific rys.; has examined properties in all parts of world; became consulting engr. for Barnato Bros., 1893, and later for Cecil Rhodes, of whom he became a strong supporter; consulting engr. Consolidated Gold Fields of S. Africa, British South Africa Co. and the Randfontein Estates Gold Mining Co. Was one of four leaders in reform movement in the Transvaal, 1895-96; after Jameson Raid (with which he was not in sympathy), was arrested and sentenced to death; sentence was afterward communted to 15 yrs. imprisonment; and later was released on payment of fine of $125,000; went to London and became interested in many mining cos.; returned to U.S., 1900, and became associated with some of most important financial groups in this country, purchasing and promoting several of largest and most valuable mining properties in U.S. and Mexico; cons. engr. Guggenheim Exploration Co., 1903-07; has also been very active in various interests outside of mining, including hydro-electric enterprises, irrigation projects, etc. Has lectured at Columbia, Harvard, Yale and Johns Hopkins univs. Apptd. by Pres. Taft as spl. ambassador and rep. of the President to the coronation of King George V, 1911. Pres. Panama-Pacific Expn. Commn. to Europe, 1912; chmn. World Court Congress, 1914-15. Chmn. U.S. Coal Commn., 1922-23. Fellow A.A.A.S., Am. Acad. Arts and Sciences. Home: Gloucester, Mass. Died June 8, 1936.

HAMMOND, JOHN HAYS, JR., inventor; b. San Francisco, Apr. 13, 1888; s. John Hays and Natalie (Harris) H.; B.S., Sheffield Sci. Sch., Yale, 1910; Sc.D., Geo. Washington U.; m. Irene Fenton (dec.). Pioneer in systems radio control of moving objects (torpedoes, ships, airplanes, rockets) since 1910; demonstrated target seeking controls, 1914, also prins. proximity fuse for torpedo control; pres. Radio Engring. Co. of N.Y., Hammond Research Corp. of Mass.; dir., cons. engr. Radio Corp. Am. Curator Hammond Medieval Mus., Gloucester, Mass., since 1926; improved methods of phonographic reprodn.; constructed organ 150 stops and new system electronic control; fundamental patents cover Intermediate Frequency Selective Receivers; has applied for over 800 patents in U.S., Europe, relating to radio telephony and telegraphy, wirelessly controlled torpedoes, unicontrol superheterodynes, multiplex telephony, privacy systems of telephony, frequency modulation, picture transmission, vol. expansion and compression, nav. aids for aircraft, selective radar system, multiplex radio systems, and various improvements in pipe organ mechanisms. Inventor: aluminothermic incendiary projectiles used by allies in World Wars I and II; radio control ships used on U.S.S. Iowa, Utah and Stoddart targetships, airplane drone targets, radio control boats and planes carrying instruments into radio-active areas at Bikini tests; new type reflecting modulator for pianos, presented on tour with Phila. Symphony Orch., Mpls. Symphony Orch.; Pirafon, a combination piano, radio and phonographic reprodn.; Telespot, a new high speed method of transmitting intelligence over tv channels, demonstrated to reps. U.S. Dept. Def., Civil Def., FCC; Dynamic Accentor, device to accent and clarify organ tone demonstrated Am. Guild Organists, 1952. U.S. del. Radio Telegraphic Conv., London, 1912; apptd. by Pres. Coolidge del. Radio Conf., Washington, 1927. Grand officer Crown of Italy. Former mem. adv. bd. USN Bd. Inventors; mem. adv. com. Langley Aerodynamic Lab. Smithsonian Instn., cooperating with 3d Naval Dist.; mem. conf. com. Nat. Preparedness. Received Elliott Cresson medal Franklin Inst., 1959; Medal of Honor award for pioneering contbns. to circuit theory and practice, to radio control of missiles and basic communications methods I.R.E., 1962; Medal of Honor, I.E.E.E., 1963. Mem. bd. govs. Aero Club Am., v.p. Am. Soc. Aero. Engrs. Fellow Am. Geog. Soc., I.R.E. (past treas.); mem. Am. Inst. E.E., Royal Soc. Arts (London), Am. Soc. M.E. (assoc.), Nat. Inst. Inventors (hon.), Harvard Aero. Soc. (hon.). Clubs: University, Explorers. Home: Hesperus Av., Gloucester, Mass. Died Feb. 12, 1965.

HAMPTON, AUBREY OTIS, physician; b. Copeville, Tex., Sept. 10, 1900; s. Calvin Wade and Mary Catherine (Hornbuckle) H.; student Ride Inst., 1918-19, Baylor U., 1919-21; M.D., Baylor Coll. Medicine, 1925; m. Marian Greene, May 30, 1928, remarried Apr. 23, 1955; 1 son, Aubrey Otis; m. 2d, Mrs. Astrid Young, Sept. 16, 1946; 1 dau., Julie Astrid. Intern St. Pauls Sanitarium, Parkland Hosp., Dallas, 1925; city physician, Ft. Worth, 1926; asst. resident radiology Mass. Gen. Hosp., Boston, 1927-28, radiologist, 1928-40, radiologist-in-chief, 1941-46; also asst. prof. radiology med. sch. Harvard; sr. partner Groover, Christie and Merritt, radiologists, Washington, 1946—; chief dept. radiology Garfield Meml. Hosp., Washington, 1946—; chief cons. radiology VA.; con radiology Dept. Army, Walter Reed Gen. Hosp., Armed Forces Inst. Pathology. Rep. Am. Roentgen Ray Soc. and V.A. to Nat. Research Council. Served as col., chief, sect. radiology, Walter Reed Gen. Hosp., Med. Corps, U.S. Army, 1942-45. Decorated Commendation Ribbon, Am. Campaign Medal, Victory Medal. Awarded Gold medal sci. exhibit by Am. Roentgen Ray Soc., 1936. Fellow Am. Coll. Radiology; mem. A.M.A., Am. Roentgen Ray Soc., Radiol. Soc. North Am., Med. Soc. D.C., S.E. Surg. Congress, Clinico-Path. Soc., Hippocrates-Galen Soc., Phi Beta Pi, Theta Nu Epsilon. Clubs: Army-Navy, Congressional Country. Rotary, (Washington); Aesculapian (Harvard). Editor of Am. lectr. series roentgenology. Contbr. med. jours. Home: South Weare, Mass. Died July 17, 1955; buried South Weare Cemetery.

HANCHETT, GEORGE TILDEN, electrical engineer; b. Hyde Park, Mass., Sept. 4, 1871; s. George W. and Augusta L. (Tilden) H.; S.B., Mass. Inst. Tech., 1893; m. Dorothy A. Lewis, of Cleveland, Nov. 29, 1894. Worked in factory Brush Elec. Co., Cleveland, later was with E.P. Roberts & Co., Cleveland, laying out plans, designing switch boards and in other consulting engring. work; later in same work at Providence, R.I.; had charge elec. work for Collyer Machine Co., Pawtucket, R.I. Moved to New York, 1895, and was on editorial staff Electric Railway Gazette; afterward on staff Electrical World and Engineering. Inventor various elec. devices; specialist in improved machine design; consulting engr. for numerous corpns. Fellow Am. Inst. Elec. Engrs.; mem. Illuminating Engring. Soc. Author: Modern Electric RailwayMotors; Alternating Currents.*

HANCOCK, H(ARRIE) IRVING, chemist, author; b. Waltham, Mass., Jan. 16, 1868; s. William Henry and Laura (Oakes) H.; ed. pub. schs. and spl. courses at colls. and tech. schs.; m. Nellie Stein, Dec. 21, 1887. Was with Boston Globe, 1885-90, New York Journal, etc.; war corr. in Cuba and Philippines; asst. editor Leslie's Weekly, 1900-01; edited revised edition Collier's Cyclopaedia, 1901. Organized Ferguson-Hancock Laboratories, with Prof. George A. Ferguson, 1906. Author: Detective Johnson of New Orleans; His Evil Eye; Inspector Henderson; Life at West Point, 1902; Physical Training for Women by Japanese Methods, 1904; Jiu-jitsu Combat Tricks, 1904; The Physical Culture Life, 1905; Dave Darrin at Vera Cruz, 1914; Physical Training for Business Men, 1917; The Motor Boat Club Series, The High School Series, The Grammar School Series, The Annapolis Series, The West Point Series, The Boys of the Army Series, The Young Engineers Series, The Square Dollar Boys Series. Home: Blue Point, N.Y. Died Mar. 12, 1922.

HANCOCK, HARRIS, univ. prof.; b. Ellerlie, Albemarle Co., Va., May 14, 1867; s. Richard J. and Thomasia (Harris) H.; grad. Sch. of Mathematics, U. of Va., 1886; A.B., Johns Hopkins, 1888; postgrad. in mathematics, physics and astronomy, same, 1888-91; hon. scholar, same, 1887-91; student, Cambridge, Eng., 1891, Berlin, 1891-92 and 1893-94, Sorbonne (U. of Paris), 1899-1900; A.M., Ph.D., Berlin, 1894; D.Sc., U. of Paris, 1901; m. Belle, d. Brutus J. Clay and Pattie A. (Field) Clay, of Richmond, Ky., and g.d. Cassius M. Clay, Sept. 30, 1907; children—Thomasia (Mrs. Hugh Spencer), Belle Clay (Mrs. Asa Atkins). Instructor, University of Chicago, 1892-93 and 1894-99; prof. mathematics, U. of Cincinnati, 1900-37. Author courses of lectures on the higher branches of mathematics, including Maxima and Minima of Functions of Several Variables, the Calculus of Variations and the Theory of Elliptic Functions (3 vols.), Vol. I, Analysis, 1910; Elliptic Integrals; The Foundations of the Theory of Algebraic Numbers, Vol. I; Introduction to the General Theory; Vol. II, the General Theory; Development of the Minkowski Geometry of Numbers; also articles in leading math. jours. of America and Europe. Mem. various math. and scientific socs., U.S. and abroad; treas. Am. Assn. Univ. Profs., 1917-21; fellow A.A.A.S. (v.p. sect. A, 1923). Democrat. Presbyn. Address: University Station, Charlottesville, Va.

HAND, GEORGE TROWBRIDGE, civil engr.; b. Elizabeth, N.J., Dec. 1, 1872; s. James A. and Harriet M. (Trowbridge) H.; ed. pub. schs. and business sch.; m. Margaret Healy, May 10, 1897 (died 1928); children—George Kenneth (died 1936), Margaret Jean, James Donald, Frederick Gordon. Rodman, Nat. Docks Ry. (now Lehigh Valley R.R.) at Jersey City, N.J., 1889; prin. asst. engr. Lehigh Valley's Jersey City terminals at Nat. Docks; asst. engr., terminal engr., div. engr., in charge Morris and Essex divs., D., L. & W. R.R., 1891-97; chief engr. Lehigh Valley R.R., 1917-37, cons. engr., 1937-38, now retired. Mem. Am. Soc. C.E. Home: Denville NJ

HAND, WILLIAM FLOWERS, chemist; b. Shubuta, Miss., Dec. 1, 1873; s. Albert Powe and Florence May (Flowers) H.; B.S., Mississippi State Coll., 1893, M.S., 1895; Ph.D., Columbia, 1903. Asst. in chemistry, Miss. State Coll., 1893, prof. chemistry since 1899, v.p. since 1935, also dean Science Sch., 1916-46; state chemist, Miss., 1899-1946 (now emeritus). Pres. Assn. Feed Control Officials of U.S., 1922. Mem. Am. Chem. Soc., Assn. Official Agrl. Chemists of North America (pres. 1921), Sigma Alpha Epsilon. Democrat. Address: State College, Mass. Died Sept. 25, 1948.

HANDLEY, CARROLL ALFRED, pharmacologist; born Ceres, Cal., Aug. 30, 1911; s. James and Dorothy Marie (Gripenstroh) H.; A.B., U. Cal., 1934, Ph.D., 1940; m. Zella Katherine Dunlop, Aug. 25, 1940 (div. 1956); children—Barbara Lorene, John Steven; m. 2d, Louise Moody, January 2, 1960. Asst. prof. pharmacology U. S.D. Sch. Medicine, 1940-41, prof., 1942-44; asso. pharmacology Western Regional Research Lab., U.S. Dept. Agr., 1941-42; asso. prof. physiology and pharmacology Baylor U. Coll. Medicine, 1944-47, prof., 1947-60, chmn. dept., 1942-60; director of pharmacology New England Institute for Medical Research, Ridgefield, Conn., 1961—. Mem. Am. Soc. Pharmacology and Exptl. Therapeutics, Soc. Exptl. Biology and Medicine, A.A.A.S., Am. Chem. Soc., N.Y. Acad. Sci., Sigma Xi. Author: Pharmacology and Clinical Use of Diuretics. Contbr. chpt. Pharmacology in Medicine (Victor A. Drill), 1954. Contbr. articles med. jours. Home: Florida Hill Rd. Office: New Eng. Inst. for Med. Research, Ridgefield, Conn. Died July 24, 1961.

HANDY, HENRY HUNTER SMITH, civ. engr., mfr.; b. Phila. Pa., Nov. 30, 1856; s. Edward Smith and R. A. Virginia (Bryan) H.; spl. student in civ. engring., U. of Pa., 4 yrs.; m. Caroline Templeman Craighill, Jan. 6, 1886. Ry. work, principally with Norfolk & Western R.R., engring. and operating depts., advancing to div. supt. and supt. terminals, at Norfolk, Va., until 1899; entered employ Solvay Process Co., Syracuse, N.Y., 1901, later pres. Semet-Solvay Co. (and chmn. By Products Coke Corp.); dir. First Trust & Deposit Co., Syracuse. Assisted in establishing the first large industry in U.S. for production of aniline dyes, and in merger of Gen. Chemical, Solvay Process, Semet-Solvay Barrett, and Nat. Aniline and Chem. cos. into the Allied Chem. and Dye Corp.; retired from these industries in 1921. Republican. Episcopalian. Home: Syracuse, N.Y. Died Aug. 9, 1935.

HANES, FREDERIC MOIR, physician; b. Winston-Salem, N.C., Sept. 18, 1883; s. John Wesley and Anna (Hodgin) H.; A.B., Univ. of N.C., 1903; A.M., Harvard, 1904; M.D., Johns Hopkins, 1908; m. Elizabeth Peck, Dec. 16, 1913. Interne Johns Hopkins Hosp., 1908-09; asso. prof. of pathology, Columbia, and pathologist, Presbyn. Hosp., New York, 1909-12; asso.

Rockefeller Inst., 1912-13; asso. prof. of medicine, Washington U. Med. Dept., 1913-14; asst. in neurology Queen Square Hosp., London, 1914; prof. of therapeutics, Med. Coll. of Va., 1914-16; internist, Winston-Salem, N.C., 1918-31; physician Duke Hosp., 1931, prof. of medicine since 1933. Served as lt. col., Med. Corps, U.S. Army, Comdg. Base Hosp. 65, A.E.F., 1917-19. Fellow Am. Coll. Physicians; mem. Assn. Am. Physicians, A.M.A., Clin. and Climatol. Assn., N.C. State Med. Soc., Sigma Alpha Epsilon, Nu Sigma Nu, Phi Beta Kappa, Alpha Omega Alpha. Contbr. to med. jours. Home: Campus Road, Durham, N.C. Died Mar. 25, 1946.

HANGER, FRANKLIN M(CCUE), physician and educator; b. Staunton, Va., Sept. 5, 1894; s. Frank M. and Martha (McDowell) H.; B.S., U. of Va., 1916; M.D., Johns Hopkins U., Baltimore, Md., 1920; m. Harriet Echols Ewing, Apr. 15, 1942; 1 dau., Harriet Echols. Interne and resident Presbyn. Hosp., New York, N.Y., 1920-26, attending physician since 1945; asso. in medicine Columbia, 1926-27, asst. prof., 1928-31, asso. prof., 1931-47, prof. medicine, 1947-60, emeritus, 1960-71; sr. med. cons. Vets. Kingsbridge Hosp., N.Y.C., 1948-61. Emeritus mem. bd. examiners Am. Bd. Internal Medicine. Fellow of American Coll. Physicians (regent; pres. 1962-63); mem. N.Y. Clin. Soc., Assn. Am. Physicians, Am. Assn. Study Liver Diseases (pres. 1954-55), Am. Soc. Clin. Investigation, Am. Assn. Immunologists, Soc. Exptl. Biol. and Med., Harvey Soc., Phi Beta Kappa, Alpha Omega Alpha, Sigma Xi. Democrat. Episcopalian. Club: Century. Contbr. to Nelson System of Medicine, Oxford loose leaf medicine, Cecil Textbook of Medicine. Originator of Cephalin Floculation Test for disorders of the liver. Home: Staunton VA Died Oct. 10, 1971; buried Thornrose Cemetery, Staunton VA

HANKS, ABBOT ATHERTON, chem. engr.; b. San Francisco, Calif., 1869; s. Henry G. and Ellen F. (Barker) H.; student U. of Calif.; m. Vesta L. Jordan, 1900. Pres. Abbot A. Hanks, Inc., chemists, assayers, engineers, San Francisco. Served as member California National Gd. 13 yrs., retiring as major. Unitarian. Home: San Francisco, Calif. Deceased.

HANKS, HENRY G., chemist, geologist; b. Cleveland, O., 1826; went to Calif., 1852; established Pacific Chemical Works, 1866; has made important geol. and chem. investigations; mineral Hanksite named for him by its discoverer, W. E. Hidden; 6 yrs. State mineralogist of Calif.; Calif. commr. to Paris Expn., 1878, and supt. U.S. Mineral sect. at that expn. Fellow Am. Geol. Soc. (resigned, 1899); fellow Geol. Soc. of London. Home: San Francisco, Calif. Died 1907.

HANLEY, HERBERT RUSSELL, professor of metallurgical engineering, metallurgical engineer; born Paxton, Illinois, September 18, 1874; son of John M. and Jennie (Byers) H.; Ph.G., Northwestern Univ. Sch. of Pharmacy, 1895; B.S., Mo. Sch. Mines and Metallurgy, 1901, Metall. Engr., 1918; Doctor Engineering (honoris causa), Nov. 1946; m. Bertha M. Miles, May 1905; 1 son, John Miles. Chem. and mining engr. Bully Hill Copper Mining and Smelting Co., 1901-03, supt. copper smelter and mines, 1903-16 (in charge metall. research on electrolytic zinc, 4 years); development and supt. of process and plant production electrolytic zinc and cadmium, U.S. Smelting, Refining and Mining Co., Calif., 1916-20; cons. engr., San Francisco, 1920-23; asso. professor metallurgical engineering, Missouri School of Mines and Metallurgy, 1923-26; prof. 1926-46; prof. emeritus metall. engring. since Aug. 1946; consulting engineer since 1918. Mem. American Inst. Mining and Metall. Engrs., Mining and Metall. Soc., Electrochem. Soc., Tau Beta Pi. Sigma Xi, Phi Kappa Phi. Developed electrolytic zinc and cadminm process, special alloy anodes for electrolytic zinc, etc.; holds several patents on processes. Contbr. to scientific journals. Home: 606 West Eighth Street, Rolla MO*

HANLEY, WILLIAM ANDREW, mech. engr.; b. Greencastle, Ind., Dec. 13, 1886; s. Michael T. and Catherine (Connell) H.; student St. Joseph's Coll., Rensselaer, Ind., 1901-02, 07-08, LL.D., 1956; B.S., Purdue U., 1911, D.Eng. (hon.), 1937; Dr. Engring. (hon.), Rosepolytech. Inst., 1954; m. Irma McGrath, 1914; children—Mrs. Robert W. Smith, Mrs. H. J. Noel, William Andrew, Robert Edward. With Eli Lilly and Co. since 1911, now dir., v.p.; dir. Indpls. Water Co., Indpls. Power & Light Co., Flanner House Homes, Indpls., Fed. Res. Bank, Chgo. Chmn. bd. Indpls.-Marion Bldg. Authority. Mem. adv. bd., v.p. St. Francis Hosp., Indpls.; dir. Indpls. Hosp. Assn.; chmn. bd. trustees Purdue U.; mem. lay bd. trustees St. Joseph's Coll.; mem. bd. trustees St. Joseph's Coll.; mem. bd. trustees Saint Mary of Woods Coll.; dir. Bd. for Fundamental Edn.; trustee Associated Catholic Charities of Indpls.; director U.S. C. of C., 1947-53, Indpls. C. of C. Civilian aide to USAAF, 1942, Office of Naval Officer Procurement, U.S. Navy, 1942-45. Fellow A.A.A.S., Am. Soc. Mech. Engrs. (ex-mgr., ex-v.p., pres. 1941); mem. Ind. Engring. Council (ex-pres.), Newcomen Soc. (Eng.), Tau Beta Pi (hon.), Pi Tau Sigma (hon.), Sigma Phi Epsilon (nat. trustee). Catholic. Clubs: Columbia, Highland Golf and Country. Chicago. Writer and speaker on engring. and econ. subjects. Address: Box 618, Indpls. 6. Died Nov. 10, 1967.

HANLON, THOMAS J., JR., engr.; b. Boston, Oct. 18, 1884; grad. Lawrence Sci. Sch., Harvard, 1907; m. Blanche Arbuckle, Nov. 11, 1916; m. 2d, Rose C. Eggers, May 30, 1942. Employe, Stone & Webster orgn., Dallas, 1907-14; mgr. Pensacola Electric Co., 1914-19; v.p. and gen. mgr. Tampa Electric Co., 1919-31; v.p. Engrs. Pub. Service Co., N.Y.C., 1931-47; chmn. bd. dirs. Gulf States Utilities Co., Baton Rouge, since 1917. Roman Catholic. Home: Prairieville, La. Office: Gulf States Utilities Co., Baton Rouge. Died Sept. 1960.

HANNA, FRANK WILLARD, water supply engr.; b. Geneseo, Ill., Sept. 16, 1867; s. James Steel and Harriet Louise (Hunt) H.; B.S., Highland Park Coll., Des Moines, Ia., 1893, M.S., 1898, C.E., 1902; m. Frances Grace Gore, Aug. 28, 1901; 1 son, John Alden. Dean of civ. engring. dept., Highland Park Coll., 1895-1902; hydrographer U.S. Geol. Survey, 1903-05; tech. engr. U.S. Reclamation Service, Washington, D.C., 1906-08, project engr., Boise, Ida., 1909-12, tech. engr., Washington, 1913, supervising engr., Phoenix, Ariz., 1914-15, cons. engr., Ankney, Ia., 1915-17, 1919-21, engr., Soldier Settlement investigations, northern div., 1918-19; gen. mgr. Canada Land & Irrigation Co., Medicine Hat, 1921-23; hydraulic and designing engr., East Bay Municipal Utility Dist., Oakland, Calif., 1924-28, chief engr. and gen. mgr., 1929-34; cons. engr. since 1934. Mem. Am. Soc. C.E. Republican. Methodist. Clubs: Lions, Oakland Engineers' Lunch. Author: Logical Methods in Arithmetic, 1900; Tables for Reinforced Concrete, 1913; Measurement of Irrigation Water, 1913; Agriculture by Irrigation, 1913; The Agricultural Value of Peat Soils, 1919; The Design of Dams (with R. C. Kennedy), 1931. Contbr. to Engring. News Record, Western Constrn. News. Inventor of an angle multisector, irrigation water meter, automatic stop and relief valves. Home: Webster City, Ia. Died Jan. 26, 1944.

HANNA, JOHN HUNTER, civil engr.; b. Henderson, Ky., Dec. 9, 1871; s. William M. (M.D.) and Mary Virginia (Matthews) H.; C.E., Princeton, 1892; m. Jane Edwards Soaper, Nov. 18, 1896; children—Nancy P., William M., John H., Robert C., Francis H., Jane E. Ry. constrn. in Ky., 1892-94; with Washington & Georgetown R.R. Co., 1894, and continued with its successor, the Capital Traction Co., chief engr., 1908-16, v.p., 1916-26, pres. since 1926; pres. Capital Transit Co., a new corp. organized to take over all st. ry. and bus lines in D.C., 1933-37, chairman board since 1937; director Capital Transit Company. Member American Society Civil Engring., Am. Transit Assn. (ex-pres.), Washington Soc. Engrs., Washington Bd. of Trade, Columbia Hist. Soc. Presbyn. Clubs: Cosmos, Columbia Country (Washington); Blue Ridge Rod and Gun (Harpers Ferry, W.Va.). Home: 3009 Q St. N.W. Office: 36th and M St. N.W., Washington, D.C. Died June 28, 1947.

HANOVER, CLINTON DEWITT, JR., cons. civil engr.; b. Groton, Conn., Apr. 4, 1901; s. Clinton DeWitt and Emma Caroline (Nordfeldt) H.; B.S., Sheffield Sci. Sch., Yale, 1922; m. Irma Ianthe Smith, Dec. 22, 1924; children—Marion Virginia (Mrs. Henry C. Meyer, Jr.), Barbara Louise, Carole Ianthe, Clinton DeWitt III. Designer, engr., fixed and movable bridges, N.Y.C. firms, 1924-36; also engr. charge mech. and elec. sect., bur. bridges Dept. Pub. Works, City N.Y., 1936-39, chief bur. bridge design, 1939-45; partner Hardesty & Hanover, N.Y.C., 1945—, now sr. partner specializing design and supervision constrn., govtl. agys., tollroads, railways. Recipient award for movable bridge over Miami Canal, Am. Inst. Steel Constrn., 1952; silver medal of honor in engring. Archtl. League N.Y., 1954. Profl. engr. Fellow Yale Engring. Assn. (past dir.), Am. Soc. C.E. (past dir.); mem. Am. Inst. Cons. Engrs. (v.p. 1955). Am. Ry. Engring. Assn. (chmn. com. movable bridges), Soc. Am. Mil. Engrs., Am. Soc. Testing and Materials, Am. Welding Soc., Column Research Council, Sigma Xi, Chi Epsilon (hon.). Clubs: Yale, Engineers (N.Y.C.); Camp Fire Am. Inventor Hanover Skew Bascule for use at skewed waterway crossings. Home: 8 Gedney Way, Chappaqua, N.Y. Office: 101 Park Av., N.Y.C. 10017. Died July 7, 1965; buried Nassau Knolls Meml. Park, Port Washington, L.I., N.Y.

HANRAHAN, EDWARD MITCHELL, surgeon; b. Binghamton, N.Y., Oct. 16, 1892; s. Edward M. and Julia (Stack) H.; A.B., Cornell, 1915; M.D., Johns Hopkins, 1919; m. Evelyn Barton Randall, Feb. 3, 1923; children—Julia Stack, Edward Mitchell. Intern, asst. resident Johns Hopkins Hosp., 1919-21; asst. resident Union Meml. Hosp., Balt., 1921-22; grad. study surgery, Vienna, Austria, 1922; instr. surgery and anatomy med. sch., Johns Hopkins, 1923-36, asso. surgery, 1936-45, asst. prof., 1945-49, asso. prof. plastic surgery since 1949; vis. surgeon plastic surgery Johns Hopkins Hosp., 1926-49, plastic surgeon in charge since 1949; vis. plastic surgeon Union Meml. Hosp., Balt. City Hosp., U.S. Marine Hosp., Balt.; cons. plastic surgery Hanover (Pa.) Gen. Hosp. Served with S.A.T.C., Med. Officers Res. Corps. Diplomate Am. Bd. Surgery (fdr.), Am. Bd. Plastic Surgery. Fellow A.C.S.; mem. A.M.A., So. Surg. Assn., Brit. Assn. Plastic Surgeons, So. Med. Assn., Am. Soc. Plastic and Reconstrn. Surgery, Alpha Delta Phi. Democrat. Episcopalian. Club: Halsted. Contbr. to med. books and encys., also articles to jours. Home: Cambridge Arms Apt., Balt. 18. Office: 1201 N. Calvert St., Balt. Died 1952.

HANSEL, CHARLES, cons. engr.; b. Peoria, Ill., July 31, 1859; s. John W. and Mary (Tillitson) H.; grad. high sch., Peoria, Ill.; studied civ. engring. under pvt. tutor; m. Frances Parker, 1887; children—Charles Francis, Anna Virginia Joy. Locating engr. D.&R.G. R.R. 4 yrs., and div. engr. in charge of building the first div. of D.&R.G. into New Mexico; chief engr. Wabash Ry., 1884-89; 1st cons. engr. Railroad and Warehouse Commn. of Ill., sent to Europe by state of Ill. to report on European railroads. Commd. to Europe, 1892, by dir. gen. Chicago Expn. to aid in getting exhibits of English equipment for railroads; apptd. by gov. of Mich. mem. Bd. of Review, 1901, to adjudicate problems in connection with valuation of railroads in that state; cons. engr. Indiana Harbor Ry., Ind., 1904-06, building 110 miles of double track; expert in charge valuation of railroads and canals of N.J., 1909; apptd., 1912, to make valuation Duluth, South Shore & Atlantic R.R.; made valuation of Reading System for Anthracite Rate Case, 1913; mem. Presidents' Conf. Engring. Com. of Railroads, 1913—; chmn. Valuation Com. of P.&R. Ry. Co., Central R.R. Co. of N.J., Phila. Rapid Transit Co., Internat. Ry. Co.; cons. valuation engr. Pa. System; etc.; head of Charles Hansel Cons. Specialists, practice in engring., law and economics in problems arising under Interstate Commerce Act and Federal Income Tax laws. Pres. Union County (N.J.) Park Commn. Author: Report on Revaluation Railroads and Canals of New Jersey, 1911. Home: Cranford, N.J. Died Dec. 24, 1936.

HANSEN, ARILD EDSTEN, pediatrician; born Minneapolis, Minn., June 2, 1899; s. Carl G. O. and Amelia Marie (Edsten) H.; B.S., U. of Minn., 1923, M.B., 1924, M.D., 1925, Ph.D., 1934; grad. work Yale, 1934-35; m. Margaret Day, Aug. 28, 1926. Interne Minneapolis Gen. Hosp., 1925; asst. pediatrics, U. of Minn., 1926-30, U. of Heidelberg and U. of Vienna, 1929-30; instr. pediatrics, U. of Minn., 1930-34, asst. prof., 1935-37, asso. prof., 1937-42, acting head of dept., 1939-40, prof., 1943-44, mem. Grad. Sch. faculty, 1937-44; pediatric consultant, Fairview Hosp., Minneapolis, Minn., 1935-44; prof. and chmn. dept. pediatrics, Sch. of Medicine, and dir. child health program, U. of Tex., 1944-59; dir. Children's Hosp., Galveston, Tex., 1944-59; dir. research Bruce Lyon Meml. Research Lab., Children's Hosp. of East Bay, Oakland, Cal., 1959—; lectr. dept. nutritional scis. Sch. Pub. Health, U. Cal. at Berkeley, 1961—; clin. prof. pediatrics U. Cal. Sch. Medicine, San Francisco, 1962—. Received research grants from Mead, Johnson & Co., Nat. Research Council, Nat. Livestock and Meat Bd., Sharp and Dohme, Inc., Hoffman La Roche Co., Bur. Home Econ. and Nutrition, Gerber Products Co., Baker Labs., Wyeth, Inc., Nat. Insts. Health, U.S. Dept. Agr., Central Soya Co., Am. Heart Assn., others. Distinguished achievement award, U. of Minn., 1951; Borden Award, Am. Academy of Pediatrics, 1957; Hektoen Bronze medal, A.M.A., 1959. Diplomate Am. Bd. Pediatrics (sec.-treas. 1961-62). Mem. American Medical Association (Cert. of Merit for original investigation, 1948, chmn. sect. pediatrics 1961-62). Asso. mem. council on foods and nutrition, A.M.A., 1939-40; vice pres. Soc. Pediatric Research, 1940-41; pres. N.W. Pediatric Soc., 1943-44; hon. mem. Omaha Midwest Clin. Soc.; mem. Am. Pediatric Soc., Am. Acad. Pediatrics, Am. Pub. Health Association, American Soc. Exptl. Pathology, Am. Soc. Clin. Investigation, Am. Inst. Nutrition, Soc. Exptl. Biology and Medicine, Southern Medical Assn. (chmn. sect. pediatrics), A.A.A.S., Am. Assn. U. Profs., Minn. Acad. Sci., Sigma Xi, Phi Beta Pi. Mem. editorial bd. Pediatrics, Jour. of Am. Acad. Pediatrics (formerly Jour. Pediatrics). Contbr. numerous articles med. jours. Address: 1512 W. View Dr., Berkeley, Cal. Died Oct. 16, 1962; buried Lakewood Cemetery, Mpls.

HANSEN, AUGIE LOUIS, mfg. exec., inventor; b. Viborg, Denmark, Aug. 3, 1879; s. Lebrath Winkleman and Clara (Halle) H.; student pub. schs.; m. Agnes Hildegard Stark, Aug. 14, 1906; children—Virginia, William Stark, Betty Jane, Jack Augie. Apprentice Western Electric Co., Chgo., 1893; tool and die apprentice E. W. Bliss, Bklyn., 1897-1900; exptl. engr. Greise Mfg. Co., New Haven, 1900-05; works mgr. Acorn Brass Mfg. Co., Chgo., 1905-09; founder Justrite Mfg. Co., Chgo., v.p., gen. mgr., 1909-20; founder A. L. Hansen Mfg. Co., auto hardware, metal spltys., Chgo., 1920—, now chmn. bd., pres. Mem. Ill. Mfrs. Assn. Republican. Lutheran. Mason (K.T., Shriner). Inventor, patentee in field. Home: 117 DeWindt Rd., Winnetka, Ill. Office: 5037 Ravenswood Av., Chgo. 40. Died Nov. 5, 1965.

HANSEN, NIELS EBBESEN, horticulturist; b. nr. Ribe, Denmark, Jan. 4, 1866; s. Andrew and Bodil (Midtgaard) H.; came to U.S. with parents, 1873; B.S., Ia. Agrl. Coll., 1887; M.S., 1895; Sc.D., U. of S.D., 1917; m. Emma Elise Pammel, Nov. 16, 1898 (died Dec. 16, 1904); children—Eva Pammel (Mrs. David L. Gilkerson), Carl Andreas; m. 2d, Dora Sophie Pammel, Aug. 27, 1907. In practical horticulture, commercial Iowa nurseries, 1888-91; asst. prof. horticulture, Ia. Agrl. Coll., 1891-95; prof. horticulture, S.D. Agrl. College and Expt. Station, 1895-1937, prof. emeritus of horticulture since 1937. Spent 4 months, 1894, in hort. study in 8 countries of Europe, including Russia; made

10 months' exploration trip, 1897-98, for U.S. Dept. Agr., collecting new economic seeds and plants in Russia, Turkestan, Western China, Siberia, Transcaucasia; made 6 months' exploration, 1906, for U.S. Dept. Agr. around the world through Lapland, Finland, Russia, Siberia, Manchuria and Japan; made 9 months' exploration, 1908-09, for U.S. Dept. Agr. to Siberia, Mongolia, Manchuria, Turkestan, Transcaucasia and N. Africa; went to North China (Manchuria) for State of S.D., 1924; del. Internat. Congress Horticulture, London, 1930; originator new fruits, especially the Hansen hybrid plums, now extensively grown in the West; introduced the Turkestan, Siberian and many other alfalfas; also introduced and named the Cossack alfalfa, now widely grown in the prairie Northwest, developing from a spoonful of seed in 1906 to over one thousand bushels of seed in 1916; originated a method of field hybridization of hardy alfalfas by transplanting; made 5 months' exploration for alfalfa for S.D. in Siberia, 1913; also imported the Siberian fat-rumped sheep from which Director James W. Wilson developed a tailless breed of sheep; made exploration tour of 4 mos., 1934, at invitation of the Soviet govt., to East Siberia, with son, Carl A., as tech. asst.; a program of experiments in horticulture and agriculture, covering 100 points, was completed Mar. 1935, and published in 4000 copies by the U.S.S.R., 1937. Awarded George Robert White gold medal of honor "for eminent service in horticulture," by Mass. Hort. Soc., 1917; Marshall P. Wilder silver medal, Am. Pomol. Soc. (for new fruits), 1929; Cosmopolitan gold medal "for public service," Sioux Falls, 1933; awarded A. P. Stevenson gold medal by the Manitoba Hort. Soc. (for new fruits), 1935; Alumni Merit Award, Chicago Alumni Assn., 1942; Medal of Honor, Iowa, Iowa State Horticultural Soc., 1944; Medal of Honor, S.D. Hort. Soc., 1946. Sec. S.D. State Hort. Soc., 1895-1929, pres., 1929-32, pres. emeritus, 1936. Life mem. (hon.) Saskatchewan Hort. Soc., 1946. Mason. Author: Handbook of Fruit-culture and Tree-Planting (in Danish-Norwegian), 1890; Systematic Pomology (with J. L. Budd), 1903. Writer on horticulture. Home: Brookings, S.D. Died Oct. 5, 1950; buried Brookings.

HANSEN, PAUL, engineer; b. Arlington, Va., Aug. 9, 1879; s. John and Pauline (Meyenberg) H.; grad. in sanitary engring., Mass. Inst. Tech., 1903; m. Alison May Scott, Oct. 3, 1905; children—Elizabeth Scott (Mrs. Henry Pope, Jr.), Dr. Paul Scott. Mem. U.S. Geol. Survey party, Ind., summer, 1901; in engring. dept. Mass. State Bd. of Health, summer, 1902, June 1903-May 1904); on water supply and sewerage improvements, Columbus, O., May-Dec. 1904; chief engr. Pittsburgh (Pa.) Filter Mfg. Co., Jan.-Oct. 1905; 1st asst. and later chief engr. Ohio State Board of Health, 1906-10; state sanitary engr. of Ky., Aug. 1910-Oct. 1911; chief engr. Ill. State Waterway Survey, 1911-15, Ill. State Bd. of Health, 1915-17 and 1919-20; member Greeley & Hansen, Chicago, since May 1920. Engaged in design and constrn. of numerous water supply and drainage works, including projects for New York, Boston, Washington, Chicago, Buffalo, etc. Spent 19 mos., 1917-19, with A.E.F. in France as staff officer with Gen. Persing. Mem. Am. Soc. C.E., Western Soc. Engrs., Am. Soc. Municipal Improvements, Boston Soc. C.E., Am. Pub. Health Assn., Am. Water Works Assn., N.E. Water Works Assn., Sigma Xi, Theta Xi. Author of numerous engring. and tech. reports and papers. Home: 223 E. Delaware Place. Office: 6 N. Michigan Av., Chicago, Ill. Died Feb. 1944.

HANSEN, WALTER WILLIAM, educator; b. Hartford, S.D., July 30, 1901; s. Jurgen August and Sara M. (Rannoü) H.; A.B., Peru State Coll., 1927; A.M., U. Mich., 1929; Ph.D. in Botany, Neb. U., 1942; m. Gertrude Louise Zabel, Aug. 4, 1929; children—Philip, Thomas, Lynda, Mark. Tchr., prin., secondary schs., Neb., 1920-40, supt. 1942-46; instr. botany U. Neb., 1940-42; asst. prof. ecology U. Ida., 1946-47; mem. faculty Okla. State U., 1947; —, prof. botany, head dept., 1948—, vice dean Coll. Arts and Sci., 1952—. Mem. exec. bd. Central States Synod United Lutheran Ch., 1960—. Mem. Soc. Range Mgmt., Okla. Ednl. Assn., Sigma Xi, Phi Kappa Phi. Author articles. Home: 2116 W. Sunset Dr., Stillwater, Okla. Died Jan. 16, 1967.

HANSEN, WILLIAM W(EBSTER), physicist; b. Fresno, Calif., May 27, 1909; s. William George and Laura Louise (Gillogly) H.; m. Betsy Ross, Oct. 18, 1938; A.B., Stanford, 1929, Ph.D., 1932. Instr. in physics, Stanford, 1930-34; Nat. Research fellow, 1932-34; asst. prof. of physics, Stanford U., 1935-37; asso. prof., 1937-42; prof., 1942—; research engr., Sperry Gyroscope Co., Garden City, N.Y. cons. to Nat. Def. Research Com., 1941-45. Recipient Liebmann prize of Inst. Radio Engrs. for work in electromagnetic theory, 1945. Fellow Am. Phys. Soc., Inst. Radio Engrs., A.A.A.S.; mem. Am. Assn. Physics Tchrs., Phi Beta Kappa, Sigma Xi. Contbr. articles to sci. jours. Specialist in physics, microwaves, nuclear induction. Home: 515 Gerona, Stanford University, Cal. Died May 23, 1949.

HANSON, FRANK BLAIR, zoologist; b. Bloomington, Ill., July 15, 1886; s. Warren John and Lùzetta (Adrean) H.; A.B., George Washington U., 1913; A.M., U. of Ill., 1916; Ph.D., Am. U., 1919; m. Harriet R. Cavender, June 21, 1910; children—Betty Blair, Phyllis Claire, Frank Blair (dec.) Instr. zoology, Washington U., 1916-18, asst. prof., 1918-20, asso. prof., 1919-24. Prof., 1924-33; fellowship administrator for Natural Sciences of Rockefeller Foundation in Europe, 1930-32, asst. dir. in New York City, 1933-35, asso. dir., 1935. Received traveling fellowship, Am. U., 1915-16. Fellow A.A.A.S., Mem. Am. Soc. Naturalists, Am. Soc. Zoologists, Am. Assn. Anatomists, Genetics Soc. of Am., Phi Beta Kappa, Sigma Xi. Contbr. articles to professional jours. Home: 8 McKinley St., Bronxville 8, N.Y. Office: 49 W. 49th St., New York 20, N.Y. Died July 21, 1945.

HANSON, O(SCAR) B(YRAM), engr., broadcasting exec.; b. Huddersfield, Eng., Feb. 11, 1894; s. Benjamin Byram and Lavinia (Butterworth) H.; came to U.S., 1896, naturalized, 1917; student Hillyer Inst., Hartford, Conn., 1911-13, Marconi Sch., N.Y.C., 1914-15. With Underwood Typewriter Co., 1911-15; ship radio operator, 1915-17; with engring. dept. Marconi Wireless Telegraph Co., 1917-20, chief test engr., 1918-20; own automotive electric bus., 1921; chief engr. radio sta. WAAM, Newark, 1922; staff engr. radio sta. WEAF, N.Y.C., 1923-26, plant mgr., 1924-26, plant mgr. NBC, 1926-34, chief engr., 1934-37, v.p., chief engr., 1937-54; v.p. engring. services RCA, 1955—. Served as capt., specialist res. AAC, 1933; adv. council chief signal officer U.S. Army, 1939. Fellow I.R.E., Acoustical Soc. Am., Soc. Motion Picture and TV Engrs. Mason. Clubs: Rockefeller Center Luncheon (N.Y.C.); Cedar Point Yacht (Westport, Conn.). Patentee in field. Author articles. Home: 107 S. Compo Rd., Westport, Conn. Office: 30 Rockefeller Plaza, N.Y.C. 20. Died Sept. 26, 1961.

HANZLIK, PAUL JOHN, prof. pharmacology; born Shueyville, Ia., July 24, 1885; s. Martin and Mary (Kreysa) H.; Ph.G., State U. of Ia., 1902, Ph.C., 1908; A.B., U. of Ill., 1908, A.M., 1911; M.D., Western Reserve U., 1912; m. Bertha Shimek, Aug. 1909; children—Harold, Dorothy. Demonstrator in pharmacology, Western Reserve U., 1912-13, instr., 1913-15, asso., 1915-17, asst. prof., 1917-20, asso. prof., 1920-21; prof. pharmacology Stanford Univ., 1921-50, prof. emeritus since 1950; cons. pharmacologist San Francisco Dept. Health, since 1934. U.S. Dept. Agriculture, 1936-44. With Pharmacological Inst. and Physico-Chemical-Biological Inst., U. of Vienna, 1913-14. Served as capt. Med. Corps, U.S. Army, attached to Chemical Warfare Service, 1918. Mem. Am. Med. Assn., Am. Physiol. Soc., Soc. Pharmacology and Exptl. Therapeutics, Soc. Exptl. Biology and Medicine, A.A.A.S., Calif. Acad. Medicine, Calif. Med. Assn., Com. on Research on Syphilis, Inc., Internat. Assn. Dental Research. Sigma Xi, Phi Rho Sigma, Alpha Omega Alpha; fellow Am. Coll. Physicians, Am. Coll. Dentists (hon.), Am. Social Hygiene Assn., Inc. Republican. Author: Actions and Uses of the Salicylates and Cinchophen in Medicine, 1927; (with Prof. T. Sollman), Fundamentals of Experimental Pharmacology, 1928, 2d ed., 1939; Handbook of Accepted Remedies, Symptoms and Treatment of Poisoning, Diagnostic Procedures and Miscellaneous Information, 1940, 3d edit. Contbr. to med. and scientific periodicals. Home: 303 Franklin St., San Mateo, Calif. Office: 2398 Sacramento St., S.F. 15. Died Feb. 1, 1951; buried Columbarium, Cypress Lawn.

HARDEN, JOHN HENRY, mining engr.; b. Leicester, England, Dec. 15, 1836; s. John W. and Mary H.; academic edn. at private school; in service Nerbudda Coal and Iron Co., Central India, 1861-65; came to U.S., 1866; in professional work, 1873; asst. dept. geology and mining, Univ. of Pa., 1879; gen. mining engr., Phoenix Iron Co.; real estate agent, 1899. Address: Phoenixville, Chester Co., Pa.

HARDESTY, IRVING, anatomist; b. Beaufort, N.C., Oct. 8, 1866; s. Washington Irving and Katherine (Harrell) H.; A.B., Wake Forest College, N.C., 1892; Ph.D., Univ. of Chicago, 1899; D.Sc., Wake Forest Coll., 1918; m. Anne Myatt Kinnard, Dec. 21, 1904, children—Mary (Mrs. William Larkin Duren, Jr.), Katharine (Mrs. Chester McArthur Destler), Irving. Prin. Wakefield Acad., 1892-03; asst. in biology, U. of Mo., 1895-96; asso. in anatomy (neurology), U. of Chicago, 1899-1900; instr. and asst. prof. anatomy, 1901-06, asso. prof., 1906-09, U. of Calif.; prof. anatomy and head of dept., Tulane U., 1909-34, prof. emeritus since 1934. Mem. Assn. Am. Aanatomists, A.A.A.S., Society of Exptl. Biology and Medicine, Sigma Xi, Nu Sigma Nu. Democrat. Baptist. Author: Neurological Technique, 1902; The Nervous System (Part III of Morris's Human Aanatomy), 1907, 14, 21, 33; A Laboratory Guide for Histology, 1908. Contbr. to jours. involving research of nervous system, including organ of hearing. Home: 1301 Pine St., New Orleans. Died Nov. 7, 1944; buried in Metairie Cemetery, New Orleans.

HARDESTY, SHORTRIDGE, civil engr.; b. Weston, Mo., Sept. 13, 1884; s. John H. and Bertie Malin (Railey) H.; A.B., Drake University, Des Moines, Ia., 1905, LL.D., from same, 1928; C.E., Rensselaer Poly. Inst., 1908, D.E., 1951; D.E., Union College, 1949; married Adelia V. Ferrell, August 20, 1910; children—Julia H. Davidson, Egbert Railey. Draftsman and designer, Waddell & Harrington, Kansas City, Mo., 1908-15; designing engr., Waddell & Son, 1916-17; mem. Waddell & Son, Inc., 1918-19; asso. engr. with J. A. L. Waddell, N.Y. City, 1920-26; partner Waddell & Hardesty, New York City, 1927-38; in practice as Waddell & Hardesty, 1938 to 1945; partner Hardesty & Hanover, 1945—; in charge work 1920—, including Washington Bridge over Housatonic River, Missouri River Bridge at Lexington, Mo., Goethals Bridge and Outerbridge Crossing for Port of New York Authority, North End Bridge, Springfield, Mass., four vertical lift spans in Jersey Central Bridge over Newark Bay, Kennebec bridge at Bath, Maine, Mississippi River bridge at Cairo, Ill., Standard Highway bridge plans for the Cuban Government, Cooper River Bridge at Charleston, S.C., lift span in Suisin Bay Bridge of Southern Pacific Ry., Anthony Wayne River Bridge at Toledo, O., Hudson River bridges at Albany and Troy, N.Y., Grand Island bridges over Niagara River, Pa. R.R. bridges over Passaic and Hackensack rivers, Marine Parkway Bridge over Rockaway Inlet, Allegheny County Bridges, Pittsburgh, Flushing River Bridge of Bronx-Whitestone Bridge Project, Perisphere and Trylon for New York World's Fair, 1939, bridges on Cross Bay Parkway and Circumferential Parkway in New York City, Rainbow Arch Bridge at Niagara Falls, Res. Basin bridge, Phila. Navy Cross Bronx Expressway and Van Wyck Expressway, in New York City, bridges for Virginia Highway Dept.; Captree State Parkway, Atlantic Beach Bridge, Niagara Thruway in Buffalo, Ohio Turnpike, Garden State Parkway in New Jersey, Cuyahoga River Bridges in Cleveland for W.&L.E. Ry., Nickel Plate Ry., and B.&O. Ry.; Jamaica Bay Bridges in N.Y.C.; Bd. Transportation. Chmn. Column Research Council; mem. Am. Soc. Civil Engrs., Am. Inst. Consulting Engineers, Society Am. Military Engrs., Am. Ry. Engring. Assn., Am. Soc. for Testing Materials, Am. Concrete Inst., Am. Toll Bridge Assn., Internat. Assn. for Bridge and Structural Engring., Rensselaer Soc. Engrs., Rensselaer Tech. Soc., Phi Beta Kappa, Sigma Xi, Tau Beta Pi. Democrat. Mem. Christian (Disciples) Ch. Club: Winged Foot Golf, Engineers. Home: 12 Cambridge Court, Larchmont, N.Y. Office: 101 Park Av., N.Y.C. 17. Died Oct. 16, 1956; buried Kensico Cemetery, Valhalla, N.Y.

HARDIN, WILLETT LEPLEY, chemist; b. S. Warsaw, O., Dec. 8, 1868; s. John and Elizabeth (Jacobs) H.; B.S., Buchtel Coll., O., 1893; Ph.D., U. of Pa., 1896; m. Isabella M. Green, of Akron, O. 1903. Asst. in chemistry and instr. physics, Buchtel Coll., 1893-94; fellow in chemistry and lecturer in physical chemistry, U. of Pa., 1896-99; instr. physical and tech. chemistry, same univ., 1899-1900; gen. mgr. Symmes Valley Coal Co., 1903-07; with Mexican Nat. Gas Co., 1908-11; consulting chemist, 1911-30; editor Quarterly Jour. Science, Religion and Philosophy, 1930-32, World Affairs Interpreter since 1932. Fellow A.A.A.S.; mem. Am. Chem. Soc., Nat. Plant, Flower and Fruit Guild (pres. Los Angeles br.), Calif. Avocado Assn. (pres. 1922-23); corr. mem. Masaryk Sociol. Soc., Czechoslovakia. Author: The Rise and Development of the Liquefaction of Gases; Democracy—Its Problems and Its Strength. Address: 4171 Central Terrace, Los Angeles, Calif.

HARDING, C(HARLES) FRANCIS, electrical engr.; b. Fitchburg, Mass., Sept. 11, 1881; s. Charles Theodore and Ellen (Lane); B.S. in E.E., Worcester Polytechnic Inst., 1902, E.E., 1910, hon. Dr. Engring., 1931; post-grad. work, Dartmouth Coll. and Cornell U.; m. Mabelle C. Brooks, July 14, 1903. With testing dept. Gen. Electric Co., Schenectady, N.Y., 1902; elec. engr. Worcester & Southbridge St. Ry. Co., Worcester, 1903-04, D.&W. Fuse Co., Providence R.I., 1904-05; asst. prof. elec. engring., Cornell U., 1905-06; elec. engr. Stone & Webster Engring. Corp., Boston, 1906-08; head prof. elec. engring. and dir. Elec. Lab., Purdue U., 1908—; also consulting engr. Fellow Am. Inst. E.E. (v.p. 1937-38); mem. Soc. Promotion Engring. Edn. (v.p. 1931), Am. Assn. Univ. Profs., Sigma Xi, Tau Beta Pi, Eta Kappa Nu, Alpha Tau Omega, etc. Presbyn. Clubs: Rotary (past pres.), Country. Author: Electric Railway Engineering, 1911; Business Administration for Engineers; Legal and Ethical Phases of Engineering, 1936; also over 50 articles in tech. jours. Home: 503 University St., West Lafayette, Ind. Died Apr. 13, 1942.

HARDING, HARRY ALEXIS, bacteriologist; b. Oconomowoc, Wis., Nov. 28, 1871; s. Joseph and Elizabeth A. (Dean) H.; B.S., U. of Wis., 1896, M.S., 1898; studied in Europe and at Mass. Inst. Tech.; Ph.D., Cornell U., 1910; m. Esther Gordon, of Brodhead, Wis., Aug. 31, 1899; children—Harry Gordon, Esther M., Helen A., Ruth. Fellow U. of Wis., 1897-98; bacteriologist, N.Y. Agrl. Expt. Sta., 1899-1913; prof. dairy bacteriology, U. of Ill., 1913-21; chief of dairy research div. Mathews Industries, Inc. Fellow A.A.A.S., Am. Pub. Health Assn.; mem. Soc. Am. Bacteriologists, Am. Dairy Science Assn., Royal Inst. Pub. Health, Eng. Republican. Conglist. Author and joint author numerous agrl. bulls. and articles on bacteriol. topics. Home: Urbana, Ill. Office: 685 Mullett St., Detroit MI

HARDING, HENRY, civil engr.; b. Hartland, Vt., Dec. 10, 1837; s. Dr. John H.; academic edn. with Job Atkins, mining engr., Richmond, Va., 1859-60; unmarried. One of pioneer civ. engrs. on surveys, construction, etc., U.P. Ry., 1865-70; employed at intervals, 1871-95, by U.S. engr. corps. on river and harbor improvements; engaged on fortifications, Ft. Adams, Newport, R.I., 1872-73; in private practice, 1895—. Home: Hartland (Four Corners), Vt. Died 1910.

HARDING, LOUIS A., cons. engr.; b. Factoryville, Pa., Oct. 16, 1876; s. Henry L. and Luzette I. (Maynard) H.; student Keystone Acad., 1890-91; Centenary Collegiate Inst., 1893-95; B.S. in M.E., Pennsylvania State Coll., 1899; m. Charlotte Hanes Phelps, Oct. 6, 1923. Engr., Dickson Mfg. Co., Scranton, Pa., 1899, Lackawanna Steel Co., 1900; instr. machine design Cornell U., 1900-01; supt. coal washeries Lackawanna Coal & Coke Co., 1901-02; mgr. Pa. Engring. Co., 1902-03; br. mgr. Armstrong Cork Co., 1903-05, chief engr., 1906-09; partner Cumming's-Harding, Inc., 1909-10; head dept. mech. engring., Pa. State Coll., 1910-13; cons. engr. N.Y., 1913; prof. expert mech. engr. U. Ill.; 1913-15; chief engr. John W. Cowper Co., 1915-21; pres.-treas. Harding & Crea, Inc., 1921-23; treas. Leach Steel Corp., fabricators, 1923—; pres. L.A. Harding Constrn. Corp., contractors, 1924-34; treas. Wilkeson Harding Corp., 1923—, also director; pres. Harding-Carlton Corp., 1934-36; commr. pub. works City of Buffalo, 1936-40; treas. and dir. N.Y., Leach Steel Corp., Rochester, N.Y. Fellow Am. Soc. M.E., 1943; mem. Am. Soc. C.E., Am.-Soc. Heating and Ventilating Engrs. (pres. 1930), Sigma Psi, Phi Kappa Sigma, Pi Tau Sigma. Mason. Clubs: Buffalo, Niagara Falls City. Contbr. to Kent's Mechanical Engineers' Pocket Book, 1916-45; written on Mechanical Equipment of Buildings, 1916; Heating, Ventilating and Air Conditioning, 1932; Steam Power Plant Engineers, 1932; Heating and Air Conditioning Manual, 1935; A Brief History of the Art of Navigation, 1952. Address: 85 Cleveland Av., Buffalo 22. Deceased.

HARDINGE, HAL WILLIAMS, cons. engr.; b. San Antonio, Tex., Sept. 30, 1855; s. George and Sarah A. L. (Bumstead) H.; E.M., Colo. Sch. of Mines, 1883; m. Bertha Wilson, Nov. 12, 1889; children—Mrs. Arlene H. Greening, Harlowe. Mgr. mines and smelters in West many yrs.; now chmn. bd. Hardinge Co., Steacy-Schmidt Mfg. Co., Ruggles-Coles Engring. Co. With Bur. of Mines, Washington, during World War, as "dollar-a-year man." Awarded John Scott medal, 1915, Franklin Inst., Phila., for inventions; also Longstreth medal, 1927; awarded James Douglas gold medal, 1938, for metall. inventions. Mem. Am. Inst. Mining and Metall. Engrs., Mining and Metall. Soc. of America, Tau Beta Pi. Republican. Mason (K.T., Shriner). Clubs: Engineers' Nat. Arts, Mining, Engineers Country. Home: 75 Greenway S., Forest Hill, L.I., N.Y. Office: 122 E. 42d St., New York, N.Y. Died Sept. 15, 1943.

HARDY, GEORGE FISKE, cons. engr.; b. Poquonock, Hartford County, Conn., Feb. 12, 1865; s. George F. and Jane (Smyth) H.; B.S., Dartmouth, 1888; hon. Sc.D. from same college, 1926; m. Johnetta Beall, Jan. 29, 1896; (died Nov. 3, 1925); children—George Fiske, John Alexander. Engr. in employ of D. H. & A. B. Tower, of Holyoke, Mass., specialists in pulp and paper mills, 1888-93; jr. mem. of firm under name of A. B. Tower & Co., 1893-96; resigned 1896, to build a mill for the Hudson River Pulp & Paper Co., Corinth, N.Y.; built mill for making news paper for the Laurentide Paper Co., Grand Mere, P.Q., 1897; was apptd. chief engr. Internat. Paper Co. (controlling prin. news paper mills of the country after they were combined), 1898, but resigned, 1901, to acquire Tower business, which had been moved to New York; now sr. partner George F. Hardy & Son; has built numerous paper and pulp mills and power plants since 1901, including 275,000 horsepower hydroelectric plant, Abitibi Canyon, Ont., 1930-32; since 1932 engaged in kraft pulp and paper development in Southern states (Savannah, Georgia, and St. Marys, Georgia, Fernandina, Florida, Port St. Joe, Florida, Bogalusa, La., Monroe, La.); first mill to make newsprint from Southern pine at Lufkin, Tex., later added Sulphate Pulp Mill; now engaged in work on kraft mill, Atenquique, Mex.; doubling newsprint capacity, Lufkin; liner board mill, Macon, Ga.; also work on improvements in pulp and paper industry; dir. St. Croix Paper Co. (Woodland, Maine). N.Y. dist. manager, div. of supply Emergency Fleet Corp., 1918. Republican. Episcopalian. Mem. Am. Soc. C.E., Am. Soc. M.E., Engring. Inst. of Can.; F.R.S.A. (Great Britain). Clubs: Union League, University (New York). Home: Cryders Point, Whitestone Landing, L.I., N.Y. Office: 441 Lexington Av., N.Y. City 17. Died Oct. 2, 1947.

HARDY, LE GRAND HAVEN, ophthalmologist; b. Provo City, Utah, June 13, 1894; s. Milton Henry and Elizabeth (Smoot) H.; A.B., Brigham Young U., 1916; grad. study, U. of Chicago, 1917; B.S., Columbia, 1919, M.D., 1921; m. Susanna Edwards Schuyler Haigh, July 9, 1923. Began practice as ophthalmologist at N.Y. City, 1922; asst. surgeon N.Y. Eye and Ear Infirmary, 1924-30; ophthalmologist Northern Dispensary, 1924-29, consultant since 1929; ophthalmic surgeon Midtown Hosp., 1925-29; dir. ophthalmology Fifth Avenue Hosp., 1929-36; prof. of clin. Ophthalmology Coll. P and S. Columbia U., attending ophthalmologist Presbyterian Hospital and Vanderbilt Clinic; staff member Inst. of Ophthalmology; dir. Functional Testing and Physiologic Optics Labs., Inst. of Ophthalmology. Fellow A.C.S., A.M.A., N.Y. Acad. Medicine, Am. Ophthalmol. Soc., N.Y. Ophth. Soc., Am. Acad. Ophthalmology and Otolaryngology, A.A.A.S., Association Research Ophthalmologists, American Orthoptic Council (pres. since 1938), Inter-Society Color Council. Author: History and Technic of Scotometry, published by American Ophthal. Society, 1931; also articles on illumination as it affects the eye, orthoptics, the bases of color vision, measurements of sight, etc. Co-author: The Geometry of Binocular Space Perception, 1953. Co-inventor: Hardy-Rand-Ritter Pseudoisochromatic Plates. Home: 21 E. 79th St., New York 21. Office: 23 E. 79th St. N.Y.C. Died Apr. 14, 1954.

HARE, HUGH F., radiologist; b. State Coll., N.M., Mar. 26, 1902; s. Raleigh Frederick and Adele (Nelson) H.; student, N.M. Agrl. and Mech. Coll., 1917-20, Stanford, 1920-21; S.B., Ala. Poly. Inst., 1924; S.B., U. Ala., 1926; M.D., Harvard, 1928; m. Louise Henderson, Dec. 11, 1933 (dec. Dec. 1957); children—Hugh Gerald, Carolyn Sue; m. 2d, Edna Katherine Druwing, Feb. 20, 1959. Asso. roentgenologist Children's Hosp., Boston, 1935-50, Peter Bent Brigham Hosp., Boston, 1932-52; cons. roentgenologist, New Eng. Deaconess Hosp., Boston, 1940-52; asst. roentgenologist, New Eng. Bapt. Hosp., Boston, 1940-52; chief radiologist, Lahey Clinic, Boston, 1934-53; research asso. Mass. Inst. Tech.; radiologist Los Angeles Tumor Inst. Mem. N.Y. Acad. Sci., Am. Radium Scoiety (sec. and past pres.), Mass. Med. Soc., A.M.A., New England Ray Soc., American Roentgen Ray Soc., Radiol. Soc. North America, Roentgen Soc., (hon., Colombia, S.A.) Tex., Rocky Mountain radiol. socs., Phi Delta Theta. Republican. Conglist. Club: Harvard. Contbd. many articles on radiology to profl. jours. Home: 619 S. Hill Av., Pasadena, Cal. Office: 1407 S. Hope St., Los Angeles 15. Died July 17, 1967; buried Rose Hills, Whittier, Cal.

HARE, ROBERT, chemist, educator; b. Phila., Jan. 17, 1781; s. Robert and Margaret (Willing) H.; studied chemistry under James Woodhouse; A.M., M.D. (both hon.), Yale, 1806; M.D. (hon.), Harvard, 1816; m. Harriett Clark, Sept. 11, 1811; 1 son, John Clark. Discovered oxy-hydrogen blow-pipe (source of highest degree of heat then known, which enabled him to fuse the most refractory substances and led to founding of platinum industry), 1801; prof. chemistry U. Pa.; inventor calorimeter, 1816; received 1st Rumford medal from Am. Acad. Arts and Scis., prof. chemistry Coll. William and Mary, 1818; prof. chemistry, med. dept. U. Pa., 1818-47; for discovery of mercury cathode in electrolysis of aqueous solutions of metallic salts, 1839; developed means of using tar for lighting; hon. mem. Smithsonian Instn.; inventor deflagrator, 1820; author chem. process for denarcotizing laundanum. Author: Brief View of the Policy and Resource of the United States, 1810; Chemical Aparatus and Manipulations, 1836; Compendium of the Course of Chemical Instruction in the Medical Department of the University of Pennsylvania, 1840. Died Phila., May 15, 1858.

HARGITT, CHARLES WESLEY, biologist; b. nr. Lawrenceburg, Ind., Mar. 28, 1852; s. Thomas and Mary Fisher (Lynas) H.; B.S., Moores Hill (Ind.) Coll., 1877; Ph.D., Ohio U., 1890; hon. Sc.D., Moores Hill Coll., 1908, Evansville Coll., 1920, Syracuse U., 1922; m. Susan E., d. Rev. Enoch G. Wood, of Moores Hill, Ind., July 26, 1877; children—Frank Wood, George Thomas, Charles Andrews. Prof. natural sciences, Moores Hill Coll., 1885-88; prof. biology and geology, Miami U., 1888-91; prof. biology, 1891, prof. embryology, Coll. of Medicine, 1898-1912, curator Biol. Mus. and dir. Zoöl. Lab., 1893—, Syracuse U.; research prof. of zoölogy, same univ., 1921—. Asst. dir. Cold Spring Biol. Lab., 1891-93; trustee Marine Biol. Lab., 1900-21; studied and traveled in Europe, 1894, 1903, 1910-11, investigations Naples Biol. Sta. Chmn. local com. Nat. Research Council. Author: Outlines of General Biology, 1901. Home: Syracuse, N.Y. Died June 11, 1927.

HARING, ALEXANDER, (har'ing), engineer, lawyer; b. Troy, New York, August 19, 1871; s. States S. and Anna M. (Alexander) Haring; C.E., from Rensselaer Polytechnic Institute, Troy, New York, 1895; LL.B., New York U., 1909, LL.M., 1910, J.D., 1911; m. Ethel Chapman, May 29, 1901; 1 son, Forrest Chapman. Began engring. practice, 1895; admitted to N.Y. Bar, 1909; prof. bridge and ry. engring., New York U., 1905-36, with N.Y. World's Fair, 1936-39; sec. Dept. of Public Works, N.Y.C., 1939-40; editor, Engr. Research Office, U.S. Army, 1943-45; private engring. and law practice, 1909—. Mem. Am. Soc. Civil Engrs.; Bronx Soc. Professional Engrs. (pres.), Bull-terrier Club of N.Y. (pres.), Phi Belta Phi. Presbyterian. Club: Rotary of the Bronx (pres.). Author: The Law of Contract, 1910. Home: 2489 Sedgwick Av., Bronx, New York. Died Mar. 14, 1960.

HARING, CLARENCE MELVIN, prof. veterinary science; b. Freeville, N.Y., June 1, 1878; s. Purley Work and Ellen Augusta (Ainsworth) H.; student Colgate Acad., 1897-98; D.V.M., N.Y. State Vet. Coll., Cornell U., 1904; m. Grace E. Moody, Aug. 22, 1908. Asst. in vet. anatomy, Cornell U., 1903-04; instr. vet. science, 1904-06, asst. prof., 1906-10, veterinarian and bacteriologist at Agrl. Expt. Sta. U. of Calif., 1910-13, dir. same, 1920-24; prof. veterinary science, U. of Calif., since 1913. Dir. Calif. anti-hog cholera serum lab., 1911-18. Consultant Calif. State Dept. Pub. Health since 1928; consultant War Manpower Commission, 1942-45. Second lieut. Vet. R.C., Feb.-Apr. 1918; 1st lt., Vet. Corps N.A., Apr.-June 1918; capt., Vet. Corps U.S. Army, July 1918-Jan. 1919. Baptist. Fellow A.A.A.S. Mem. Am. Vet. Med. Assn. (sec. 1915-16), Soc. Am. Bacteriologists, Sigma Xi, Alpha Zeta, Delta Omega, Phi Zeta. Mason. Club: Faculty. Contbr. to agrl. and vet. publs.; investigator of animal diseases. Home: 2405 Hillside Av., Berkeley 4, Cal. Died July 9, 1951; buried Riverside, Cal.

HARKINS, HENRY NELSON, surgeon; b. Missoula, Mont., July 13, 1905; s. William Draper and Anna Louise (Hatheway) H.; B.S., U. Chgo., 1925, M.S., 1926, Ph.D., 1928; M.D., Rush Med. Coll., 1931; postgrad. work, U. Edinburgh, and Nat. Hosp., London, 1933; Guggenheim Meml. fellow in surgery, U. Edinburgh, U. Ghent, U. Frankfurt-am-Main, U. Uppsala, 1938-39; m. Jean Hamilton Trester, June 19, 1937; children—Pamela Jean (Mrs. John Parr), Ellen Christine, Anne Wayne, Harriet Nelson. Interne, Presbyn. Hosp., Chgo., 1930-31; Douglas Smith fellow in medicine U. Chgo., 1926-28, in surgery, 1934, asst. resident in surgery, 1931-36, instr. in surgery, chief resident surgeon, 1936-38; asso. surgeon Henry Ford Hosp., Detroit, 1939-43; gen. surgeon Madigan Army Hosp.; cons. surgeon Seattle VA Hosp.; attending surgeon Univ. Hosp.; cons. surgeon King County Hosp. Sec. sub-com. shock OSRD, NRC, 1943-45; mem. hematology study sect. NIH 1948-49, mem. surgery study sect., 1950-55, mem. gen. med. study sect., 1960-65. Research asst., asst. prof. physiol. chemistry, Yale, 1943; asso. prof. surgery, Johns Hopkins U. Med. Sch., 1943-47; prof. surgery U. Wash., 1947—, chmn. dept. surgery, 1947-64; prof. surgery pro tem U. Cin., 1960, Marquette U., 1962; Ball vis. prof. surgery U. Ind., 1965; Sir. Edwin Tooth vis. prof. U. Queensland, Brisbane, Australia, 1965; 1st Swedish Govt. vis. prof. U. Lund, 1965, U. Gothenburg, 1966. McGraw lectr. Wayne State U., 1941; Trona lectr. U. Ariz., 1944; Clagett lect. U. Colo., 1955; Phemister lectr. U. Chgo., 1960; Hale-McMillan lectr. Meharry Med. Coll. 1962; Lee lectr. U. Pa., 1964; Judd lectr. U. Minn., 1964; Rives lectr. La. State Med. Sch., 1965. Editor-in-chief, Quar. Rev. Surgery, 1943-61, Rev. Surgery, 1962—. Regent, Nat. Library Med., 1962-65. Mng. editor, Bull. Johns Hopkins Hosp., 1944-47. Editorial bd. Pacific Medicine and Surgery, 1948—. First lt., Med. Res., 1931-36. Diplomate Nat. Bd. Med. Examiners, Am. Bd. of Surg. Fellow A.C.S.; mem. A.M.A., Am. Fedn. for Clin. Research, Am. Physiol. Soc., Inst. Medicine Chgo., Central Surg. Assn. (founder mem.), Soc. for Exptl. Biology and Medicine, Soc. for Surgery Alimentary Tract (founding), Phoenix (hon.), Tacoma (hon.) surg. socs., Soc. Grad. Surgeons Los Angeles County Hosp., Soc. U. Surgeons, Am., No. Pacific, Pacific Coast, Western surg. assns., Seattle Surg. Soc., King County, Wash. State med. socs., Société Internat. de Chirurgie, Alpha Omega Alpha, Tau Kappa Epsilon, Nu Sigma Nu, Sigma Xi. Author: The Treatment of Burns, 1942; The Billroth I Gastric Resection: With Particular Reference to the Surgery of Peptic Ulcer (with Horace G. Moore, Jr.), 1954. Co-editor: Surgery; Principles and Practice, 1957; Surgery of the Stomach and Duodenum, 1962; Geriatric Surgical Emergencies, 1963; Hernia, 1964. Contbr. articles to med. jours. Episcopalian. Home: 4416 50th N.E., Seattle 98105. Office: Dept. Surgery, U. Wash., Seattle 5. Died Aug. 12, 1967; buried Lakeview Meml. Cemetery, Seattle.

HARKINS, WILLIAM DRAPER, educator, cons. chemist; b. Titusville, Pa., Dec. 28, 1873; s. Nelson Goodrich and Sarah Eliza (Draper) H.; A.B., Stanford, 1900, Ph.D., 1907; post-grad. U. Chgo., 1901, 04, Stanford, 1905-06, Institut für Physikalische Chemie, Karlsruhe, Germany, 1909; research asso. Research Lab. Phys. Chemistry, Mass. Inst. Tech., 1909-10, 11; m. Anna Louise Hatheway, June 9, 1905; children—Henry Nelson, Alice Marion. Asst. and instr. chemistry Stanford, 1898-1900; prof., head dept. U. Mont., 1900-12; chemist in charge of smelter smoke investigation Anaconda Farmers's Assn., 1902-10, Mountain Copper Co. of Cal., 1904, U.S. Dept. of Justice, 1910-12; research work for Carnegie Instn., Washington, 1911; asst. prof. gen. chemistry U. Chgo., 1912-14, asso. prof., 1914-17, prof. physical chemistry 1917—, Andrew MacLeish Distinguished Service prof., 1935—, dir. rubber research, 1942—; professorial lectr. Mellon Inst. Indsl. Research, 1916-17; lectr. U. Ill., 1918-19; cons. chemist U.S. Bur. Mines, 1920-22; cons. engr. U.S. Air Service, 1924-27; cons. C.W.S., 1927—; cons. chemist Libbey-Owens-Ford Glass Co., 1929—, Universal Oil Products Co., 1930—, U.S. Rubber Co., 1939—, Nat. Def. Research Com., 1941—; George Fisher Baker lectr. Cornell Univ., 1936-37. Mem. Internat. Com. on Atoms, 1932—; Chgo. Commn. on Ventilation, 1916-28. Editor, sect. gen. and phys. chemistry Chem. Abstracts, 1912-16. Pres. Missoula (Mont.) City Bd. of Health, 1906-12. Fellow A.A.A.S. (v.p.); mem. Am. Chem. Soc. (chmn. Chgo. sect. 1915-16, chmn. div. phys. and inorganic chemistry 1919-20), Nat. Acad. Sciences, Am. Philos. Soc., hon. mem. Alpha Omega Alpha. Episcopalian. Awarded Willard Gibbs medal by Am. Chem. Soc., 1928. Author of over 200 papers on heat of sun and stars, stability of atomic nuclei and physics and chemistry of surfaces. Home: 5437 Ellis Av., Chgo. 15. Died Mar. 7, 1951; buried Chgo.

HARKNESS, WILLIAM, astronomer, rear admiral U.S.N.; b. Ecclefechan, Scotland, Dec. 17, 1837; s. James and Jane Weild H.; studied Lafayette Coll., Pa., 1854-56, Rochester Univ., 1856-58, A.B., 1858, A.M., 1861, LL.D., 1874, Rochester (A.M., Lafayette, 1865); studied medicine, New York, M.D., 1862. Served as surgeon, U.S. army, at second battle of Bull Run; also during attack on Washington, July 1864. Apptd. from N.Y. as aide U.S. Naval Observatory, Aug. 1, 1862; commd. prof. mathematics, with relative rank of lt. comdr., Aug. 24, 1863; served at Naval Observatory until Oct. 4, 1865. Served on U.S. monitor Monadnock, 1865-66; attached to U.S. Hydrographic Office, 1867; discovered the coronal line K 1474, during total solar eclipse of Aug. 1869; mem., 1871, and from 1882 exec. officer U.S. Transit of Venus Commn.; had charge of transit of Venus parties in 1874 at Hobart, Tasmania, and in 1882 at Washington, D.C. In 1879, discovered the theory of the focal curve of achromatic telescopes, now universally adopted. Attached to U.S. Naval Observatory most of the time from Aug. 1862; designed most of its large instruments; astron. dir. Naval Observatory, 1894-99, and dir. U.S. Nautical Almanac, 1897-99. Attained relative rank of comdr., May 31, 1872, capt., April 17, 1878, rear admiral, Dec. 15, 1899; unmarried. Home: Jersey City, N.J. Died 1903.

HARLAN, CAMPBELL ALLEN, elec. engr.; b. Columbia, Tenn., May 31, 1907; s. Alexander and Ellagreen (Pickard) C.; student coll. engring. U. Tenn., 1926-28; D.Sc. (hon.), U. of Detroit; m. Ivabell Campbell, June 29, 1932; children—John Marshall, Campbell Allen, Joyce Lily, James Gregory, Joseph Duncan, Jay Scott, Jeanne Marie. Engr., estimator Turner Engring. Co., Detroit, 1929-35, mgr., 1935-40; chmn. bd. Harlan Electric Co., v.p., dir. subsidiary and affiliated cos.; dir. Power Piping Co., Pitts., Liberty Mut. Co. City National Bank Detroit, Detroit Mortgage & Realty Co.; pres. Univ. House-Holiday Inn, Morgantown W.Va. Bd. dirs. Community Health Assn., Maryglade Coll.; vice chmn. Detroit com. Nat. Jewish Hosp.; mem. alumni bd. govs. U. Tenn.; v.p. dir. exec. com. United Found.; bd. dirs., past pres. Ednl. TV Found; trustee Burton Mercy Hosp., Bethany Coll., Fisk U., Hampton Inst.; trustee emeritus Mich. State U.; fellow Brandeis U.; hon. trustee Brandeis U. Assos. Served as lt. USNR, 1944-45. Mem. Engring. Soc. Detroit, Navy League U.S. (Detroit Council), Mich. Soc. Architects (hon.), Am. Assn. UN (bd. mem.), Detroit Bd. Commerce, Nat. Elec. Contractors Assn., Detroit Elec. Assn. (past pres.). Met Art Assn., Tau Beta Pi, Eta Kappa Nu. Clubs: Detroit Athletic, Recess, Economic (dir.) (Detroit). Home: Bloomfield Hills MI Died June 23, 1972.

HARLAND, THOMAS, watch and clock maker, silversmith; b. England, 1735; m. Hannah Leffingwell, 1779. Supposed to have come to Am. aboard a tea ship; opened shop as watch and clock maker and silversmith, Norwich, Conn.; superintended constrn. of fire engine, Norwich, 1788; became master craftsman by 1790; his shop produced some 200 watches and 40 clocks per year. Died Norwich, Mar. 31, 1807.

HARMAN, JACOB ANTHONY, civil engr.; b. Randolph County, Mo., Mar. 7, 1866; s. Jacob Madison and Emma (Cox), H.; C.E., Nat. Normal U., Lebanon, O., 1887; m. Emma Flagg, Mar. 4, 1889; children—Harris J., Howard W. County surveyor, Iroquois County, Ill., 1889-93; city engr., Peoria, Ill., 1893-95; cons. engr., Ill. State Bd. of Health, 1899-1903; pres. Jacob A. Harman Inc. (successor to Harman Engring Co., established 1892); cons. engr. hydraulic, municipal and drainage work. Pres. Illinois Engineering Council, 1938-39. Cons. Engr. State of Ill. (1944-45). Member American Society Civil Engineers, Western Soc. Engrs., Ill. Soc. Engrs. (pres. 1912); pres. Nat. Drainage Congress (1923). Republican. Mem. Disciples of Christ, Mason. (32 deg. Shriner). Club: Creve Coeur. Home: 1301 Glendale Av. Office: Apt. A., 144 Fredonia Av., Peoria IL

HARMAN, PINCKNEY JONES, educator, anatomist; b. Washington, Feb. 20, 1913; s. Pinckney Jones and Isabel (Zerega) H.; B.S., Georgetown U., 1934, M.S., 1935; postgrad. Cath. U., 1935-36; Ph.D. (Knight fellow 1939-40) Yale, 1941; m. Yvonne Richardson Smith, Jan. 31, 1942; 1 son, Pinckney Jones. Asst. biology Georgetown U., 1934-35, instr., 1935-37, instr. anatomy, 1940-46; asst. prof. N.Y.U., 1946-49, asso. prof., N.Y.U.-Bellevue Med. Center, 1949-56; summer investigator R. B. Jackson Meml. Lab., 1948-52, sci. asso., 1952—; prof., chmn. dept. anatomy Seton Hall Coll. Medicine and Dentistry (name changed N.J. Coll. Medicine and Dentistry, 1965), 1956—; Arthur lectr. Am. Mus. Natural Hist., 1956. Program com. Internat. Anat. Congress, 1960. Recipient Carroll award, 1959; Gaston award, 1964. Fell. A.A.A.S., N.Y. Acad. Medicine; mem. Assn. Am. Med. Colls., Am. Acad. Neurology, Am. Assn. Anatomists, Am. Genetics Assn., Am. Neurol. Assn., Am. Soc. Zoologists, Assn. Research Nervous and Mental Diseases, Phi Rho Sigma, Sigma Xi, Georgetown U. Alumni Assn. Roman Catholic. Club: Cajal (sec.-treas. 1947—). Asso. editor Jour. Comparative Neurology, 1955—. Home: 107 Kensington Av., Jersey City 4. Died May 13, 1966; buried Cedar Hill Cemetery, Washington.

HARMELING, STEPHEN JOHN, horticulturist; b. Sheboygan Falls, Wis., Mar. 8, 1951; s. Gerritt John and Everdinah (Hyink) H.; A.B. and A.M., Hope Coll., Holland, Mich.; B.D., Rutgers Theol. Sem.; m. Alida Maria Binnekant, Apr. 12, 1876; children—Stephen J., Gertrude Henrietta (Mrs. George Ensing), Emma Johannah (Mrs. S. W. Libbey), Henry, Geral Ridboeck, Kate (Mrs. Guy Bernisse), Philip, Margaret (Mrs. W. E. Gorsuch), Elmer, Edward Benjamin. Missionary Dutch Ref. Ch. in the states west of Mississippi River, 1882-1902, retiring on account of ill health; has devoted much time to horticulture and botany; propr. Island Nurseries, Vashon, Wash. Under commn. of Gov. Lister of Wash., organized and drilled 105 men for the war, 1918. Republican. Mason; Past Eminent Comdr. Vashon Island Commandery, K.T., also Past High Priest Chapter 48, Wash. Widely known as lecturer on hort. and landscape gardening subjects. Home: Vashon, Wash. Died Nov. 1940.

HARMON, PAUL M(ONTGOMERY), prof. physiology; b. Elwood, Ind., July 20, 1892; s. William Henry and Mary (Montgomery) H., A.B., Ind. U., 1914, A.M., 1915, Ph.D., 1920; m. Elizabeth Rose Dickerson, Nov. 14, 1914; 1 son, Philip W. Instr., physiology Ind. University, 1918-21, asst. prof., 1921-23, asso. prof., 1923-28, prof., 1938—, chmn., dept. physiology, 1941-58; department physiology, Harvard med. sch., 1926-27. Fellow, A.A.A.S.; mem. Am. Physiol. Soc., Phi Beta Kappa, Sigma Xi. Home: 505 Ballantine Rd., Bloomington, Ind. Died July 16, 1964; buried Rose Hill Cemetery, Bloomington.

HARPER, HENRY WINSTON, chemist, educator; b. Boonville, Mo., Sept., 20, 1859; s. James W. and Virginia (Crenshaw) H.; ed. Mound City Coll.; Ph.G., Phila. Coll. Pharmacy, 1881; M.D., U. of Va., 1892; spl. study with Dr. J. W. Mallet, U. of Va., summer 1894, and in Europe, summer 1897; LL.D., Baylor U., Waco, Tex., 1914; m. Susan Randolph West, July 9, 1895; children—Henry Winston, Virginia Randolph. Mfg. chemist and perfumer, Ft. Worth, Tex., 1881-84; chemist and metallurgist to mining cos. in Mex., 1884-86; chemist, Ft. Worth, Tex., 1887-90; asst. resident phys., Rockbridge Alum Springs, Va., 1892; adj. prof. chemistry in charge of Sch. of Chemistry, and dir. Chem. Lab., 1894-97, asso. prof., 1897-1903, prof. since 1903, chmn. grad. council, 1900-13, and dean Graduate Sch., 1913-36, U. of Tex., dean emeritus of Grad. Sch. since 1936. Chemist to U. of Tex. Mineral Survey, 1901-06. Has investigated and reported upon mining and reduction properties, U.S. and Mexico. Honorary chmn. 95th meeting Am. Chemical Society, Dallas, Tex., 1938. Fellow Chem. Soc. London, A.A.A.S. (emeritus life mem.), A.M.A., Tex. Acad. Sciences (pres. 1900-01), Am. Inst. of Chemists; mem. Am. Chem. Soc., 5th, 7th and 8th Internat. Congress Applied Chemistry, Soc. Chem. Industry (London, Eng.), Texas State Med. Assn., Southern Med. Assn., Philos. Soc. of Tex.; charter mem. Am. Assn. Univ. Profs.; mem. Beta Theta Pi, Phi Beta Kappa, Alpha Mu Pi Omega, Phi Lambda Upsilon, Pi Gamma Mu, Alpha Epsilon Delta; asso. mem. Am. Museum Natural History (New York), S.A.R. Member committee to draft ednl. plan for S.A.T.C., 1918; field aide to Texas dirs., Com. on Industrial Preparedness, Naval Consulting Bd., Southern Div., 1917-18, etc. Clubs: University, Town and Gown, University Science. Has written many articles on chem. and med. subjects in tech. jours. and proc. of learned socs. Home: 2216 Rio Grande St., Austin. Tex. Died Aug. 28, 1943.

HARPER, JOHN LYELL, mechanical engr.; b. Harpersfield, N.Y., Sept. 21, 1873; s. Joseph F. and Quintilla Keturah (Hendry) H.; M.E., Cornell U., 1897; m. Linda E. Wheeler, Sept. 12, 1898. Electrician, Union Electric Co., Seattle, Wash., 1897-98; constrn. and operating engr. Twin City Rapid Transit Co., Minneapolis, 1898-99, St. Croix Power Co. (Apple River development), 1899-1901; asst. engr. Niagara Falls Hydraulic Power & Mfg. Co., 1902-03; chief engr., same, 1903-18, and Cliff Elec. Distributing Co., 1910-18; v.p. and chief eng. Niagara Falls Power Co. (merger of all power plants on Am. side of Niagara River, 1918—, also chief engr. Canadian Niagara Power Co., and Niagara Junction Ry. Co.; gen. cons. practice. Mem. Industrial Commn. and Grade Crossing Commn., Niagara Falls. Fellow Am. Inst. E.E. Republican. Presbyn. Home: Lewiston, N.Y. Died Nov. 28, 1924.

HARPER, ROBERT ALMER, botanist; b. Le Claire, Ia., Jan. 21, 1862; s. Rev. Almer and Eunice (Thomson) H.; A.B., Oberlin, 1886, A.M., 1891; Ph.D., U. of Bonn, 1896; m. Alice Jean McQueen, June 25, 1899; m. 2d, Helen Sherman, Jan. 2, 1918; 1 son, Robert Sherman. Prof. Greek and Latin, Gates Coll., 1886-88; instr. in acad., 1889-91, prof. botany and geology, 1891-98, Lake Forest U.; prof. botany, U. of Wis., 1898-1911, Columbia U., 1911-30, now emeritus. Mem. Nat. Acad. Sciences. Am. Acad. Arts and Sciences, Am. Philos. Soc., Bot. Soc. America, A.A.A.S. Home: Route 5, Bedford, Va. Died May 12, 1946.

HARPER, ROLAND M(CMILLAN), geographer; b. Farmington, Me., Aug. 11, 1878; s. William and Bertha (Tauber) H.; B.E., U. Ga., 1897, hon. Sc.D., 1929; Ph.D., Columbia, 1905; m. Mary Susan Wigley, June 23, 1943. Was aid in U.S. Nat. Herbarium, 1901, 02; forestry collector Geol. Survey of Ga., 1903-04; botanist and geographer Geol. Survey of Ala., various periods since 1905; same Fla. State Geol. Survey, 1908-31; asst. in agrl. geography, U.S. Dept. Agr., 1917, 18; in charge of Fla. State Census, Feb.-June, 1925; with Ala. State Commn. of Forestry, 1927; research prof. econs. U. Ga., 1928-29. Formerly specialized in botany; discovered one genus and about 30 species flowering plants, mostly in Ga. Specialized in geography since 1911; has visited 41 states (and over 1000 counties), and published descriptions of vegetation or notes on flora of 17 states and Can., also statis. studies of population several states and fgn. countries. Fellow A.A.A.S.; mem. Ecol. Soc. Am., Assn. Am. Geographers, Soc., Ga. hist. socs., Population Assn. Am., Am. Eugenics Soc., Inter-Am. Soc. Anthrop. and Geog. Ala., Fla. acads. sci., Am. Soc. Plant Taxonomists, Assn. S.E. Biologists, N.E., Torrey, So. Appalachian bot. clubs. Publs. (beginning 1899) aggregate about 470 titles and 5200 pages. Home: University, Ala. Died Apr. 30, 1966; buried Tuscaloosa (Ala.) Meml. Park.

HARRINGTON, ARTHUR WILLIAM, civ. engr.; b. Watertown, N.Y., June 7, 1888; s. Ernest E. and Cora (Waddingham) H.; C.E., Cornell, 1909; m. Elsie I. Sutton, May 25, 1910; children—Fred H., Arthur W., Edith M. Engr. and supt. constrn. L.B. Cleveland, engr. and contractor, Watertown, N.Y., 1909-13; water resources investigation in Ida. with U.S. Geol. Survey, 1914-17; sec. B. B. Culture Lab., Yonkers, N.Y., 1917-20, v.p., 1933-40, pres., 1921-32, hydraulic engr. U.S. Geol. Survey, 1920-58; dist. engr. in charge water resources investigations, N.Y. State, 1922-58; private consultant in civil engineering, 1958-64; investigation of stream gaging possibilities in lower Miss. River basin, 1928; mem. com. investigating division of power profits at Minidoka Dam, Ida., 1929; mem. President's Tech. Com. on Water Flow, 1933; mem. Water Resources Com., N.Y. State Planning Bd., 1934. Served as 1st lt. Sanitary Corps, U.S. Army, in charge sanitation of various southern camps, designing drainage system for Ellington Field, Houston, Tex., 1918-20, World War I. Member Am. Soc. C.E. (dir. 1938-40; v.p. 1946-47, pres. Mohawk-Hudson sect. 1944). Nat. Soc. Professional Engrs., Albany Soc. Engrs. (pres. 1941). Cornell Soc. Engrs., Federal Business Assn. of Albany (pres. 1933), Nat. Fedn. of Federal Employes—Local 126 (pres. 1936), Engring. Inst. of Canada, Am. Geophysical Union, Military Order World Wars. American Water Works Association, New York Academy of Sciences. Presbyterian. Clubs: Statler (Cornell U.), University. Author: (with Nathan C. Grover) Stream Flow, 1943; also annual reports on surface-water supplies and misc. reports on stream flow. Address: 320 Elmwood Av., Ithaca, N.Y. 14850. June 29, 1964; buried Watertown, N.Y.

HARRINGTON, CHARLES, educator, physician; b. Salem, Mass., July 29, 1856; s. George and Delphine Rose Eugenie H.; student Bowdoin Coll., 1873-74; grad. Harvard Coll., 1878, Harvard Med. Sch., 1881; studied univs. of Leipzig, Strassburg, Munich, 1881-83; m. M. Josephine Jones, Feb. 25, 1884. Began as asst. in chemistry, 1883, later instr., asst. prof., 1899-1906, prof. hygiene, 1906—, Harvard Med. Sch. Formerly chemist to State Bd. of Health of Mass. 9 yrs.; in charge of bureau of milk inspection, Boston Bd. Health, 1889-1904; sec. Mass. State Bd. of Health, Dec. 1904—. Author: Practical Hygiene, 1901, 02, 05. Home: Jamaica Plain, Boston. Died 1908.

HARRINGTON, FRANCIS CLARK, commr. of work projects, army officer; b. Bristol, Va., Sept. 10, 1887; s. William Clark and Victoria (Gauthier) H.; B.S., U.S. Mil. Acad., 1909; student Engr. Sch., U.S. Army, 1910-11, Gen. Staff Sch., 1927-28, Army War Coll., 1928-29, Ecole Superieure de Guerre, 1933-35; m. Eleanor Crozier Reyburn, June 30, 1915 (died 1938); children—William Stuart, Mary Eleanor. Commissioned 2d lt., Corps of Engrs., U.S. Army, 1909, and advanced through the grades to col., 1938; during World War was instr. in officer training camps, also with 603d Engrs. and comdg. 215th Engrs. and special duty Hdqrs., A.E.F.; has served as asst. prof. of mathematics at U.S. Mil. Acad., dir. Engr. Sch. of U.S. Army, dist. engr., Baltimore, asst. engr. of maintenance at Panama Canal and on War Dept. Gen. Staff; assigned asst. adminstr. Works Progress Administration, 1935, apptd. adminstr., Dec. 24, 1938, commissioner of work projects, July 1, 1939; dir. Panama R.R. Co. Home: Washington, D.C. Died Sept. 30, 1940.

HARRINGTON, HENRY HILL, educator; b. Chicasaw Co., Miss., Dec. 14, 1859; s. Dr. J. T. and Margaret W. (Belk) H.; grad. Agrl. and Mech. Coll. of Miss., 1883; spl. work in chemistry, Mich. Agrl. Coll., 1882, Conn. Expt. Sta., New Haven, 1885, Rensselaer Poly. Inst., 1888, in Germany, 1903-04; (LL.D., Univ. of Miss., 1906); m. 1892, Florine Ross. Asst. prof. chemistry and physics, Agrl. and Mech. Coll. of Miss., 1882-88; prof. chemistry and mineralogy and chemist to Expt. Sta., 1888-1905, pres. since 1905, Agrl. and Mech. Coll. of Tex.; state chemist of Tex., 1899-1905. Author numerous papers on economic agr., and bulls. Tex. geol. survey on soils and water of West Tex. Address: College Station, Tex.

HARRINGTON, JOHN LYLE, cons. engr.; b. Lawrence, Kan., Dec. 7, 1868; s. Robert Charles and Angeline Virginia (Henry) H.; A.B., B.S., C.E., U. of

Kan., 1895; B.S., McGill U., Montreal, 1906, M.S., 1908; Dr. Engring., Case Sch. of Applied Science, 1930; m. Daisy June Orton, June 21, 1899; 1 son, Thomas Orton. With J. A. L. Waddell, Kansas City, 1895-96; with Elmira Bridge Co., 1896, Pencoyd Iron Works, Phila., 1896-97, Keystone Bridge Works, 1897-98, designing Monongahela R.R. bridge and other heavy structures for Pittsburgh, Bessemer & L.E. R.R.; asst. supt. structural dept. Cambria Steel Co., Johnstown, Pa., Jan.-Sept. 1898; asst. chief engr. and asst. supt. Bucyrus Co., Milwaukee, Sept. 1898-Mar. 1899; asst. to chief engr. Northwestern Elevated R.R. Co., Chicago, Mar.-Dec. 1899; designing engr. Berlin Iron Bridge Co., E. Berlin, Conn., 1899-1900; asst. engr. bldgs. and bridges, B.&O. R.R., 1900-01; with C.W. Hunt Co., New York, in charge engring., estimating and contracting, 1901-05; chief engr. and mgr. Locomotive & Machine Co., Montreal, Ltd., 1905-06; mem. firm Waddell & Harrington, cons. engrs., Kansas City, Mo., 1907-14, Harrington, Howard & Ash, 1914-28, Harrington & Cortelyou since 1928. Designed 6 bridges over Chesapeake and Del. Canal; 18 bridges over Welland Canal; bridge over San Francisco Bay; bridge over Mobile River; bridge over Ohio R. at Paducah, Ky., over Missouri R. nr. St. Louis, Mo., at Kansas City, Mo., at Blair, Neb., and at Rulo, Neb., over Mississippi River at Cape Girardeau and Louisiana, Mo., Alton, Ill., Vicksburg, Miss., and railway and highway at Baton Rouge, La.; railroad and highway bridge over Piscataqua River between New Hampshire and Maine; bridges over St. John's River at Jacksonville, Fal., and over Atchafalaya River at Simmesport, La., over Don River, Rostoff, Russia, Yalu River, Manchuria, docks at Beaumont, Tex., and water supply, Brownwood, Tex., etc. Mem. Engineers Advisory Board and chief engr., R.F.C. Has taken out many patents on movable bridges. Trustee Robert College, Turkey. Mem. Am. Soc. C.E., Am. Soc. M.E. (v.p. 1920-22, pres. 1923), Am. Railway Engring. Assn., The Newcomen Soc., Am. Soc. Testing Materials, Instn. Civ. Engrs. (Eng.), Engring. Inst. Can., A.A.A.S., Sigma Nu, Sigma Xi, Tau Beta Pi (pres. 1917), Theta Tau; mem. Am. Engring. Council, 1926-32. Presbyterian. Clubs: University, Engineers' (ex-pres.), Mission Hills Country (Kansas City); Cosmos (Washington, D.C.). Home: 4909 Belinder Terrace, Kansas City, Kan. Office: 1004 Baltimore Av., Kansas City, Mo. Died May 20, 1942.

HARRINGTON, JOSEPH, mechanical engr.; b. Reading, Mass., Apr. 28, 1873; s. Edward B. and Helen L. (Montgomery) H.; S.B., Mass. Inst. Tech., 1896; m. Cora A., d. James Dunlap, of Champaign, Ill., Oct. 6, 1904; children—Joseph, Jr., Dunlap. Prospecting and mining in Mexico, 1896-99; designer of special machinery for Stillwell-Bierce & Smith Vaile Co., Dayton, O., 1899-1900; became identified with the Green Engring. Co., 1900, and continued as designer, field supt., gen. supt. and chief engr. and sec. until 1913; consulting combustion engr. since 1913; pres. Joseph Harrington Co. (automatic stokers). Mem. Advisory Board of Engrs., Dept. Smoke Inspection City of Chicago. Mem. Bituminous Coal Code Authority, Div. 2. Inventor and patentee of devices for use in automatic stoking. Mem. Am. Soc. Mech. Engrs., Western Soc. Engrs. Republican. Unitarian. Clubs: Technology, Engineers' (New York). Home: Riverside, Ill. Office: 360 N. Michigan Boul., Chicago IL

HARRINGTON, LOUIS CLARE, mining engr., educator; b. Ludington, Mich., Oct. 28, 1880; s. Jackson Davis and Emma Ada (Ink) H.; student Mich. Coll. of Mines, Houghton, 1901-03, B.S. in civil engring., U. of Mich., 1908; E.M., Mich. Coll. of Mines, 1909; m. Alberta Harriet Amstein, June 13, 1912. Miner in Mich., 1902; mining engr., Bisbee, Ariz., 1903-06; prof. geology and engring., Western Md. Coll., 1909-12; with Univ. of N.D. since 1912, as instr. mining and metallurgy, 1912, asst. prof., 1913-20, asso. prof., 1920-21, prof. since 1921, dir. of civ. of mines and mining experiments since 1931, dean of Coll. of Engring. since 1932; summer work in mine examination in Nevada City, Calif., 1913, Jackson, Ky., 1915, Ketchikan, Alaska, 1916, survey of lignite mines for State of N.D., 1919, 20, 26, 28, 30, Hyder, Alaska, 1922, 24. Mem. Am. Inst. Mining and Metall. Engrs., Mining and Metallurgical Society of America, Am. Soc. Testing Materials, Am. Chem. Soc., Soc. for Promotion Engring. Edn., N.D. Acad. Science, Am. Assn. Univ. Profs., Sigma Xi, Sigma Tau, Lambda Chi Alpha. Republican. Presbyn. Mason. Club: Grand Forks Country. Author of reports on investigations of lignite. Home: 319 S. 6th St., Grand Forks, N.D. Died Feb. 3, 1951; buried Toledo.

HARRINGTON, MARK WALROD, astronomer, coll. pres.; b. Sycamore, Ill., Aug. 18, 1848; s. James and Charlotte (Walrod) H.; attended Northwestern U., 1864-66; grad. U. Mich., 1868, A.M. (hon.), 1870, LL.D. (hon.), 1894; attended U. Leipzig (Germany), 1876-77. Taught mathematics and geology U. Mich., 1868-71, 71-76, prof. astronomy, 1879-91; worked for U.S. Coastal Survey in Alaska, 1870-71; taught mathematics and astronomy at Fgn. Office Cadet Sch., Peking, China, 1877-78; prof. astronomy U. La., 1878-79; founder, editor Am. Meteorol. Jour., 1884-92; 1st civilian head U.S. Weather Bur., 1891-95; pres. U. Wash., 1895-97; mem. Imperial Anthrop. Soc. Moscow, Linnean Soc. of London, Austrian Meteorol. Soc.; corr. mem. Scottish Geog. Soc. discovered irregular periodic change of light in star Vesta, trifid character of Gt. Hercules nebula. Author: About the Weather, 1899; also many scientific papers. Died Oct. 9, 1926.

HARRINGTON, PHILIP, chmn. Chicago Transit Authority; b. Worcester, Mass., Jan. 28, 1886; s. Michael and Ellen (Ryan) H.; B.S., Armour Inst. Tech., 1906; LL.D., Kent Coll. of Law, 1915; Doctor Engring., 1944; children—Marjorie, Ann, Michael. Admitted to Illinois bar, 1916. Connected with Sanitary District of Chicago, Ill., 1906-35, beginning as rodman, chief engr. 1933-35; directed design and construction tunnels, bridges, pumping stations and sewage disposal works costing over $100,000,000; special traction engr., City of Chicago, 1935-38; author study and report of Comprehensive Transportation Plan for City of Chicago, Nov. 22, 1937; apptd. commr. of subways, City of Chicago, Nov. 3, 1938; designed and constructed first transportation subway, City of Chicago ($60,000,000); author comprehensive superhighway plan for City of Chicago, Oct. 30, 1939; apptd. commr. subways and superhighways, City of Chicago, Jan. 1, 1940; chmn. Chicago Transit Authority since 1945. Mem. Chicago Plan Commn. Chief Civilian Defense Communications and administrator of Defense Transportation for Chicago Metropolitan Area during World War II. Mem. Am. Soc. of Civil Engrs., Western Soc. Engrs. Clubs: Chicago Athletic Assn., Exmoor Country. Life mem. Art. Inst. of Chicago. Co-inventor system of flash-drying and incineration of sewage sludge and other waste materials. Alumni award of merit Ill. Inst. Tech., 1942. Home: 219 South Av., Glencoe, Ill. Office: 20 N. Wacker Dr., Chicago 6, Ill. Died Feb. 11, 1949.

HARRIS, CHAPIN AARON, dentist; b. Pompey N.Y., May 6, 1806; s. John and Elizabeth (Brundage) H. A.M., M.D.; m. Lucinda Heath Hawley, Jan. 11, 1826, 9 children. Licensed as dentist by Med. and Chirurg. Faculty of Md., Balt., 1833; editor Am. Journal Dental Science (1st dental periodical), 1839; organizer Balt. Coll. of Dental Surgery (world's 1st dental coll.), 1839, 1st dean, 1st prof. operative dentistry and dental prosthesis, 1840-44, pres., 1844-60; an organizer Am. Soc. of Dental Surgeons (1st nat. dental assn.), 1840, 1st corr. sec., pres. 1844; an organizer Am. Dental Conv., 1855, pres., 1856-57. Author: The Dental Art, a Practical Treatise on Dental Surgery, 1839; translator: A Treatise on Second Dentition (C.F. Delabarre), 1845; Complete Elements of the Science and Art of the Dentist (A.M. Desiraback), 1847; editor: Natural History and Diseases of the Human Teeth (Joseph Fox). Died Balt., Sept. 29, 1860; buried Mt. Olivet Cemetery, Balt.

HARRIS, DANIEL LESTER, engr.; b. Providence, R. I., Feb. 6, 1818; s. Allen and Hart (Lester) H.; grad. Wesleyan U., 1838; m. Harriet Corson, May 25, 1843, 11 children. Engr. for Erie R.R., also Troy-Schenectady R.R., 1839-43; mem. engring. firm Boody, Stone & Harris, Springfield, Mass., 1845-79; an owner Howe Truss patent, designed many railroad bridges for firm; pres. Conn. River R.R. 1856-79; mem. Mass. Legislature, 1857, 73; mayor Springfield, 1860; dir. U.P. R.R., from 1869; sec. Eastern R.R. Assn., 1866-78. Died Springfield, July 11, 1879; buried Springfield.

HARRIS, ELIJAH PADDOCK, chemist; b. Le Roy, N.Y., Apr. 3, 1832; s. Daniel and Mary (Paddock) H.; A.B., Amherst, 1855; Ph.D., U. of Göttingen, 1859; (LL.D., Victoria Coll., 1886); m. Ellen Park, July 26, 1860. Prof. chemistry, Victoria Coll., Can., 1859-66, Beloit (Wis.) Coll., 1866-68, Amherst, 1868-1907; retired under Carnegie Foundation, 1907. Congregationalist. Author: Qualitative Analysis, 1875 (10 edits.). Home: Warsaw, N.Y. Died Dec. 10, 1920.

HARRIS, FRANKLIN STEWART, coll. pres.; b. Benjamin, Utah, Aug. 29, 1884; s. Dennison Emer and Eunice (Stewart) H.; grad. Juarez Stake Acad., Mex., 1903; B.S., Brigham Young U., 1907, LL.D., 1945; Utah Agrl. Coll., 1907-08; Ph.D., Cornell, 1911; studied in Orient and Europe, 1926-27; m. Estella Spilsbury, June 18, 1908; children—Arlene, Franklin Stewart, Chauncy Dennison, Helen, Leah Dorothy, Mildred. Instr. sci. Juarez Stake Acad., 1904-05; asst. in agrl. chemistry Brigham Young U., 1906-07; asst. in chemistry Utah Expt. Sta., 1907-08; asst. in soil technology Cornell U., 1909-10, instr., 1910-11; prof. agronomy Utah Agrl. Coll., 1911-16, dir. Sch. Agrl. Engring., 1912-16; dir. Utah Expt. Sta., 1916-21, pres. Brigham Young U., 1921-45, Utah State Agrl. Coll., 1945-50; chmn. mission on tech. collaboration between govts. Iran and U.S. since 1950. Fellow A.A.A.S., Utah Acad. Sci. (pres.), Am. Geog. Soc., Am. Soc. Agronomy (pres. 1920-21); mem. Am. Farm Econ. Assn., N.E.A., Utah Dry Farmers' Assn. (sec.), Utah Irrigation and Drainage Congress (pres. 1923), Am. Asiatic Soc., Am. Oriental Soc., Am. Acad. Polit. and Social Sci., Acad. Polit. Sci., Philos. Soc. Gt. Britain, Acad. Western Culture, Newcomen Soc. Eng., Utah Mental Hygiene Assn. (dir.), Sigma Xi, Gamma Sigma Delta, Phi Kappa Phi, Pi Gamma Mu, Alpha Kappa Psi, Sigma Nu, Delta Phi. Author: The Principles of Agronomy (with George Stewart), 1915, rev., 1929; The Young Man and His Vocation, 1916; The Sugar Beet in America, 1918; Soil Alkali, 1920; Scientific Research and Human Welfare, 1924; The Fruits of Mormonism, 1925; also numerous sci. papers, bulls. Chmn. and agriculturist Siberian colonizing project Jewish Colonization Orgn. of Russia, 1929; chmn. U.S. agrl. mission to Middle East, 1946; chmn. UN FAO mission to Greece, 1946. Agrl. adviser to Iranian govt., 1939-40. Home: Logan, Utah. Died Apr. 18, 1960; buried Salt Lake City Cemetery.

HARRIS, GILBERT DENNISON, geologist; b. Jamestown, N.Y., Oct. 2, 1864; s. Francis E. and Lydia Helen (Crandall) H.; Ph.B., Cornell U., 1886; m. Clara Stoneman, Dec. 30, 1890; 1 dau., Rebecca Stoneman. On U.S., Tex. and Ark. geol. surveys, 1887-93; investigated tertiary deposits of Southern Eng. and Northern France, 1894; asst. prof. paleontology and strategraphic geology, 1894-1909, prof., 1909-35, now emeritus, Cornell; founder Paleontol. Research Instn., 1932. State geologist of La., 1899-1909. Editor and propr. Bulls. of Am. Paleontology, 1895—, and of Paleontographica Americana. Consulting geologist, Trinidad Petroleum Development Co., Trinidad, B.W.I., 1919-23; paleontologist to Standard Oil Co. of Venezuela, 1923-25; visiting grad. lecturer in Geology, Tex. State U., 1927; paleontologist to the Oldenbergische Erdölgesellschaft, Germany, 1929. Fellow Geol. Soc. Am. (v.p. 1937); Paleontological (pres. 1936); mem. Société Geologique de France, Palaeontologische Gesellschaft v. Deutschland, Société géologique de Suisse, Acad. Nat. Sci., Phi Beta Kappa, Sigma Xi. Home: 126 Kelvin Pl. Office: Paleontological Research Inst., 109 Dearborn Pl., Ithaca, N.Y. Died Dec. 4, 1952.

HARRIS, GUY W(ALTER), engineer; b. Neosho Falls, Kan., Mar. 7, 1878; s. A. G. and Hattie (Ricketts) H.; ed. high sch., Kansas City, Mo.; m. Maude Leslie, June 20, 1908. Began as rodman Santa Fe, Pacific R.R., Williams, Ariz., 1898; rodman, A.T.& F. Ry., Las Vegas, N.M., 1899-1900, and continued with same rd. as transitman, Pueblo, Colo., 1900-03, asst. engr., 1903-06; asst. engr. in charge constrn. Pecos & Northern Tex. Ry., and Southern Kan. Ry. of Tex., 1906-09; chief engr. constrn. Pecos & Northern Tex. Ry., 1909-12; chief engr. A.T.& F. Ry. Coast Lines, Los Angeles, Calif., 1912-18; corporate chief engr. same rd. Chicago, 1918-20, asst. chief engr. System, 1920-27, acting chief engr., Dec. 1927-Mar. 1928, chief engr. System since 1928. Mem. Am. Soc. C.E., Western Soc. Engrs., Am. Ry. Engring. Assn. Home: 6922 S. Jeffrey Av. Office: 80 E. Jackson Blvd., Chicago IL

HARRIS, J(AMES) ARTHUR, biologist, statistician; b. Plantsville, O., Sept. 29, 1880; s. Jordan Thomas and Ida Ellen (Lambert) H.; A.B., U. of Kan., 1901, A.M., 1902; Ph.D., Washington U., St. Louis, 1903; m. Emma Lay Apr. 20, 1910; children—James Arthur, Alanson Lay, Daniel Lambert, George Galton. Bot. asst., 1901-03, librarian, 1904-07, Mo. Bot. Garden, St. Louis; instr. botany, Washington U., 1903-07; bot. investigator, Sta. for Exptl. Evolution, Carnegie Instn., 1907-24; head dept. of botany, U. of Minn., 1924—. Studied U. of London, 1908, 09. Lecturer Grad. Sch. Agr., U. of Mo., 1914. An editor Bull. Torrey Bot. Club. Unitarian. Mem. Internat. Jury of Awards, St. Louis Expn., 1904. Author: Biometric Study of Basali Metabolism in Man (with F. G. Benedict). Collaborator Bur. Plant Industry, U.S. Dept. of Agr., 1918—. Awarded Weldon medal and Memorial prize by U. of Oxford, 1921. Home: St. Paul, Minn. Died Apr. 24, 1930.

HARRIS, JOHN WARTON, obstetrician, gynecologist; b. Reidsville, N.C., Jan. 12, 1891; s. Robert and Ella Kerr (Lea) H.; Reidsville Sem., 1898-1907; A.B., U. of N.C., 1911, A.M., 1912; M.D., Johns Hopkins U., 1916; m. Margaret Price Ivey, Sept. 14, 1921; children—John W., Jr., Thomas Ivey. Resident in obstetrics, Johns Hopkins Hosp., 1916-19, asst. obstetrician, 1920-25, asso. obstetrician, 1925-28, asst., 1916-18, instr., 1918-21, asso., 1921-25, asso. prof., 1925-28; prof. obstetrics and gynecology, U. of Wis., obstetrician and gynecologist in chief, State of Wis. Gen. Hosp., since 1928. Mem. A.M.A., Am. Gynecol. Soc., Wis. Soc. Obstetricians and Gynecologists, Central Assn. Obstetricians and Gynecologists (founder), Wis. Med. Soc., Dane County Med. Soc., A.A.A.S. (fellow), Sigma Chi, Sigma Xi. Club: University. Baptist. Home: 1713 Summit Av., Madison 5, Wis. Died Jan. 14, 1955; buried Reidsville, N.C.

HARRIS, JOSEPH SMITH, ry. official; b. Chester, Co., Pa., Apr. 29, 1836; s. Stephen (M.D.) and Marianne (Smith) M.; A.B., Central High Sch., Phila., 1853, A.M., 1855; (Sc.D., Franklin and Marshall Coll., 1903); m. Delia Silliman Broadhead, June 20, 1865. Entered ry. service Apr. 1853 to Oct. 1854, rodman and topographer, N. Pa. R.R.; officer U.S. Coast Survey, 1854-64; detached in 1856 with Ky. Geol. Survey to trace and mark parallel of latitude in Ky.; asst. astronomer N.W. Boundary Survey, 1857-64; while in this service was also, Feb. to Sept. 1862, 1st officer and later comdr. U.S. steamer "Sachem," attached to Farragut's Miss. River Squadron; assisted in reduction of Forts Jackson and St. Philip on Miss. River below New Orleans. In private practice as civ. and mining engr., Pottsville, Pa., 1864-68, and at same time engr. Lehigh & Mahanoy R.R.; chief engr. Morris & Essex R.R., 1868-70; engr. Phila. & Reading Coal and Iron Co., 1870-77; supt. and engr. Lehigh Coal & Navigation Co., 1877-80; gen. mgr. Central R.R. of N.J., 1880-82;

pres. Lehigh Coal & Navigation Co., 1882-93; also receiver and afterward v.p. Central R.R. of N.J., 1886-90; v.p. Phila. & Reading Coal & Iron Co., 1892; receiver and pres. Phila. & Reading R.R., 1893-96; pres. Reading Co., Phila. & Reading Ry. Co., and The Phila. & Reading Coal & Iron Co., 1896-1901; from 1901, mem. exec. com. of Reading Cos., Central R.R. of N.J., Lehigh & Wilkes-Barre Coal Co., Lehigh Coal & Navigation Co., and others, 1901—. Trustee U. of Pa., 1889—. Author: Record of the Harris Family, 1903; Record of the Smith Family, 1906; The Collateral Ancestry of Stephen Harris, M.D., and Marianne Smith, 1908. Home: Germantown, Philadelphia. Died 1910.

HARRIS, LESLIE HUNTINGTON, electrical engr.; b. nr. Bradford, Pa., Oct. 23, 1883; s. Fernando C. and Clara (Ingoldsby) H.; B.S. in E.E., Purdue U., 1907; m. Alma Woods Kerr, Sept. 3, 1914. Elec. engr. with Westinghouse Electric & Mfg. Co., 1907-08; with U. of Pittsburgh, 1908—, prof. elec. engring., 1914—; cons. elec. engr. Pub. Service Commn. of Pa., 1913—. Commd. capt. Engr. R.C., U.S.A., Apr. 1917; called into service, Aug. 6, 1917; maj. Q.-M.C., Mar. 19, 1918; served as asst. constructing q.-m., Camp Stuart, Newport News, Va., and later as port utilities officer. Republican. Presbyn. Home: Pittsburgh, Pa. Died Feb. 21, 1920.

HARRIS, ROLLIN ARTHUR, mathematician; b. Randolph, N.Y., Apr. 18, 1863; s. Francis E. and Lydia Helen (Crandall) H.; bro. of Gilbert Dennison H.; Ph.B., Cornell U., 1885, fellow in mathematics 1886-87, Ph.D., 1888; fellow Clark University, 1889-90; m. Emily J. Doty, June 13, 1890. On math. staff U.S. Coast and Geod. Survey, 1890—. Fellow A.A.A.S. Author of Manual of Tides, published in Coast Survey Reports for 1894, 97, 1900, 04, 07. Inventor of machines or instruments relating to tidal work. Died Jan. 20, 1918.

HARRIS, SEALE, physician; born Cedartown, Ga., Mar. 13, 1870; s. Charles Hooks and Margaret Ann (Monk) H.; U. Ga.; M.D., U. Va., 1894; grad. study N.Y. Polyclinic, 1898; U. Chgo., 1904, Johns Hopkins, 1906, U. Vienna and other European clinics, 1906; hon. LL.D., U. Ala.; m. Stella Rainer, on April 28, 1897 (dec. 1940); children—Seale (deceased 1943), Josephine Anne (Mrs. John J. Keegan). General private practice medicine, Union Springs, Ala., 1894-1906; physician-in-chief Mobile (Ala.) City Hosp., 1906-13; prof. medicine U. Ala., 1906-13, now prof. emeritus med. coll.; founder, dir. Seale Harris Clinic, 1922-56, ret. Served as maj., M.C. Res., U.S. Army, 1917; staff Surgeon Gen. Gorgas Hosp., 1918-19; sec. research com. A.R.C., France, 1918-19; investigated food conditions and nutritional diseases in Italy, Austria and Germany, Jan.-Feb. 1919; cons. physician Pres. Wilson's Party, Italy, Jan. 1919; col. (ret.), M.C. Res. Recipient Distinguished Service Medal, A.M.A., Research Medal, So. Med. Assn. for discovery (1923) of hyperinsulinism, 1949; citation by Gen. Pershing for conspicuous and meritorious service in France. Fellow A.C.P., Am. Geriatrics Soc.; mem. Jefferson Co. Med. Soc., Ala. Med. Assn., So. Med. Assn. (past pres. and sec.), A.M.A., Am., Ala diabetes assns., Jefferson Co. Diabetes Soc., Am. Therapeutic Soc., Am. Gastroenterological Assn., Am. Medical Editors Assn. (past pres.), Sigma Alpha Epsilon, Phi Chi. Independent Presbyn. Club: Mountain Brook. Author: Clinical Pellegra, 1940; Banting's Miracle, 1946; Woman's Surgeon, 1950. Editor-owner Southern Medical Journal, 1910-22; editor War Medicine, Paris, France, during World War I. Home: 3822 Jackson Blvd., Birmingham 13. Office: 2219 Highland Av., Birmingham, Ala. Died Mar. 16, 1957; buried Elmwood Cemetery, Birmingham.

HARRIS, THADDEUS WILLIAM, entomologist, librarian; b. Dorchester, Mass., Nov. 12, 1795; s. Thaddeus Mason and Mary (Dix) H.; grad. Harvard, 1815; med. degree, 1820; m. Catherine Holbrook, 1824. Librarian, Harvard, 1831-56; instr. in nat. history, 1837-42; mem. com. apptd. to make bot. and geol. survey of Mass., 1837. Author: A Treatise, Some of the Insects of New England Which are Injurious to Vegetation, 1842. Died Jan. 16, 1856.

HARRIS, TITUS HOLLIDAY, neuropsychiatrist; b. Fulshear, Tex., Nov. 11, 1892; s. Dr. Robert Locke and Sallie Bright (Holliday) H.; A.B., Southwestern U., 1915, Doctor of Science (honorary), 1960; M.D., University of Texas, 1919; m. Laura Hutchings, Dec. 17, 1927; children—Mary Elizabeth, Titus, Ann Hutchings, Edward Randall. Intern John Sealy Hosp., Galveston, Tex., 1919-20; practiced medicine, Galveston, Tex., since 1920; instr. medicine U. of Tex., 1920-25, asso. prof., 1925-26, prof. and head dept. neurology and psychiatry, from 1926; ret. chmn. dept. neurology and psychiatry U. Tex. Med. Br.; dir. div. psychiatric patients, John Sealy Hosp. since 1935; active in promoting mgmt. psychiatric patients in gen. hosps.; founder and editor nat. med. jour., Diseases of the Nervous System. Recipient Hogg Found. Award, 1955, E. B. Bowis award Am. Coll. Psychiatrists, 1965. Mem. Nat. Com. Alcoholism; dir. Med. Research Found. Tex. Mem. Nat. Multiple Sclerosis Soc. (med. adv. bd.), Am. Psychiatric Assn. (vice pres. 1960-61), Nat. Research Council (mem. of subcom. personnel training 1942-43, psychiatry, 1953-45), A.M.A., Central Neuropsychiatric Assn. (pres. 1936), Tex. State Med. Assn., Tex. Neuropsychiatric Assn. (pres. 1943-44), Tex. Soc. Mental Hygiene (pres. 1943), So. Psychiat. Assn. (president 1961-62), Am. Neurol. Assn. Democrat. Methodist. Asso. editor: Am. Jour. of Psychiatry. Contbr. articles to med. jour. Home: Galveston TX Died Apr. 22, 1969.

HARRIS, WALTER BUTLER, civil engr., educator; b. Princeton, N.J., July 13, 1865; s. Rev. William and Christina Van Alen (Butler) H.; C.E., Princeton, 1886; m. Anne L. Yeomans, Nov. 22, 1892; children—Dorothy C., Walter Butler, George Yeomans (dec.), Helen Boyd. With Wilkes-Barre & Scranton Ry., 1886-87, Lehigh Coal & Navigation Co., 1887-88, Central R.R. of N.J., 1888-89; instr. civ. engring., 1889-95; asst. prof., 1895-99, prof. geodesy, 1899-1934, emeritus, Princeton University. Engr. and architect The Prospect Co.; designed and constructed a system of jetties for protection of N.J. coast at Asbury Park and other places. Former borough engr. and township engr.; pres. Bd. of Health, Princeton. Republican. Presbyn. (elder). Home: Princeton, N.J. Died Nov. 20, 1935.

HARRISON, JAMISON RICHARD, prof. physics, radio communication; b. Boston, Sept. 26, 1903; son Herbert Spencer and Annie Clifton (Gorham) II; B.S., magna cum laude, Tufts Coll., 1925; A.M., Wesleyan U., 1927; m. Katherine Olivia Schucker, June 19, 1930; children—David Edward, Katherine Priscilla, Charles Richard. Asst. in physics, Wesleyan U., 1925-27, Charles A. Coffin fellow, 1927-29; instr. physics, U. Pitts., 1929-30; physicist Wired Radio, Inc., Newark, N.J., 1930-31; asst. prof. physics, Tufts Coll., 1931-36, asst. dean engring., 1933-36, prof. physics and radio communication, and head of dept., 1936-47, prof. emeritus since 1947, also dir. U.S. Army Signal Corps research on Piezo-Electricity, Tufts Coll., 1943-47; vis. prof. physics Brown U., 1949-51, Boston Coll. 1952-54; head physics dept. Franklin Inst. of Boston, 1954-60; lectr. in physics Fisher Coll., 1956-59; mem. research com. on undersea warfare, Nat. Research Council, 1949. Mem. A.A.A.S., Am. Optical Soc., Am. Physical Soc., Inst. of Radio Engrs., Am. Physics Teachers Assn., American Assn. U. Profs., Phi Beta Kappa, Sigma Xi; regional v.p. (N.E. div.) Am. Iris Soc. Republican. Contbr. on piezo-electricity and high frequency circuits to the proceedings of the Inst. of Radio Engrs. and Physical Review. Author: A Half Century of Iris, 1954. Editor Bull., Am. Iris Soc., 1954—. Home: 8 Old Billerica Rd., Bedford, Mass. Office: Franklin Inst. of Boston, 41 Berkeley St., Boston 16. Died Sept. 24, 1966; buried North Cemetery, Billerica, Mass.

HARRISON, JOHN, mfg. chemist; b. Phila., Dec. 17, 1773; s. Thomas and Sarah (Richards) H.; studied chemistry under J.B. Priestly; m. Lydia Leib, Nov. 27, 1802; 8 children, including George Leib, Thomas, Michael. Served as capt. Phila. Militia, 1792; 1st mfg. chemist in U.S., 1801; pioneer in manufacture of sulfuric acid, 1806; 1st to attempt prodn. of nitric acid; recorder City and County of Phila., 1821-24; mem. 1st bd. mgrs. Franklin Inst.; established firm Harrison & Sons, chem. mfrs., 1831. Died Phila., July 19, 1833.

HARRISON, JOSEPH, mech. engr.; b. Phila., Sept. 20, 1810; s. Joseph and Mary (Crawford) H.; m. Sarah Poulterer, Dec. 15, 1836, 7 children. Apprenticed to steam-engine builders, 1825; foreman Garrett, Eastwick & Co., mfrs. locomotives, 1835; designed locomotive "Samuel D. Ingham", became partner 1837; designed 1st practical 8-wheel engine with 4 driving and 4 truck wheels; patented method for equalizing weight on driving wheels, 1839; among first to successfully burn anthracite coal in locomotives; built Gowan and Marx locomotive which attracted attention of Russia, 1841; went to Russia to build 162 locomotives, 2500 freightcars, 1843; decorated by Czar Nicholas I; returned to Phila., 1852; patented Harrison Steam Boiler, 1859; mem. Am. Philos. Soc., 1864; recipient Gold and Silver Rumford medals Am. Acad. Arts and Scis., 1871. Author: An Essay on the Steam Boiler, 1867; (essay) The Iron Worker and King Solomon, 1869; (book) The Locomotive Engine and Philadelphia's Share in Its Early Improvements, 1872. Died Phila., May 27, 1874.

HARRISON, PERRY G(ALBRAITH), mining engr.; b. Mpls., Mar. 6, 1885; s. Hugh and Teresa V. (Scott) H.; student Columbia, 1909-10; E.M., Mich. Coll. Mines, 1909; m. Alice L. Smith, 1917 (dec.); 1 son, Hugh Howard; m. 2d, Virginia Climo, 1955. Mining engineer Meriden Iron Company, 1911-14; supt. Nat. Mines Co., 1911-17; cons. engr., geologist with H. V. Winchell, 1917-20; gen. supt. Campania Minera del Misrasol, Mexico, 1921; gen. mgr. Portland Gold Mining Co., 1922; mine supt. Smuggler Union, 1923; gen. mgr. Cusi Mining Co., 1924-27, North Range Mining Co., 1927-37; gen. mgr. Evergreen Mines Co., 1927-46, pres., 1937-46; v.p., dir. Hanna Coal & Ore Corp. since 1946 (also subsidiaries); ore sales manager M. A. Hanna Company, Cleve., 1946-57, now iron ore consultant; dir. Wheeling Steel Corp. Mem. Am. Iron and Steel Inst., Am. Mining Congress, Am. Inst. Mining and Metall. Engrs. Clubs: Kitchi Gammi (Duluth); Country, Union (Cleve.); Fort Henry (Wheeling, W.Va.). Home: 18000 S. Woodland Rd., Shaker Heights 22, O. Office: Leader Bldg., Cleve. 14. Died Nov. 11, 1959.

HARRISON, ROSS GRANVILLE, biologist; b. Germantown (Phila.), Pa., Jan. 13, 1870; s. Samuel and Katherine (Diggs) H.; A.B., Johns Hopkins, 1889, Ph.D., 1894, LL.D., 1942; M.D., U. Bonn, 1899; A.M. (hon.), Yale, 1907; D.Sc., U. Cin., 1920, U. Mich., 1929, U. of Dublin, 1932, Harvard, 1936, Yale, 1939, Columbia, 1940, U. Chgo., 1949; Ph.D. (hon.), U. of Freiburg, 1929; M.D. (hon.), U. of Budapest, 1935; Dr. Rev. Nat., University of Tübingen, 1953; m. Ida Lange, Jan. 9, 1896; children—Dorothea Katharine, Elizabeth Ross, Richard Edes, Eleanor Barrington (Mrs. Rufus Putney, Jr.), Ross Granviille. Lectr. on morphology Bryn Mawr Coll., 1894-95; instr. and asso. in anatomy Johns Hopkins, 1896-99; asso. prof. anatomy, 1899-1907; prof. comparative anatomy Yale, 1907-27, Sterling prof. of biology, 1927-38, prof. emeritus, 1938—. Chmn. NRC, Washington, 1938-46; pres. 6th Pacific Sci. Congress, 1939; Dunham lectr. Harvard, 1926; Croonian lectr. Royal Society, London, 1933; Linacre lectr. St. John's College, Cambridge, 1939; Silliman lectr. Yale, 1949. Mem. science com. Nat. Resources Planning Bd., 1938-43; mem. U.S. Nat. Com. for UNESCO, 1946-51. Conf. bd., Assoc. Research Councils (chmn., 1944—). Mng. editor Jour. Exptl. Zoology, 1903-46; trustee Marine Biol. Lab., Woods Hole, Mass., 1908-40, trustee emeritus, 1940—; bd. dirs. L.I. Biol. Sta.; trustee Bermuda Biol. Sta. (treas. 1930-46), Woods Hole Oceanographic Inst., Science Service. Mem. adv. bd. Wistar Inst.; bd. sci. dirs. Rockefeller Inst. Med. Research (v.p., 1939—); bd. sci. advisers, Jane Coffin Childs Fund for Med. Research. Fellow Am. Acad. Arts and Scis., A.A.A.S. (v.p. 1936); mem. Nat. Acad. Sciences (council 1932-46), Conn. Acad., Am. Philos. Soc. (council 1941-44, v.p. 1947-50), Am. Soc. Zoologists (pres. 1924), Soc. Study Development and Growth (pres. 1946-47), Beaumont Med. Club (pres. 1933), Am. Assn. Anatomists (pres. 1912-13), Anatomische Gesellschaft (pres. 1934-35), Royal Physiog. Soc. (Lund), Royal Soc. Science (Uppsala), Am. Soc. Naturalists (sec. 1902-04, pres. 1913), Am. Neurol. Assn., Soc. Exptl. Biology and Medicine; corr. member Göttingen Akad der Wissenshaften, Deutsche Acad. Sciences, Bavarian Acad. Science, Acad. Nat. Sci. Phila., Acad. des Sciences de l'Institut de France, Soc. de Biol., Paris; hon. mem. Conn. Med. Soc., Harvey Society, Royal Acad. Medicine, Turin, Royal Acad. Medicine, Belgium, N.Y. Acad. Science; fgn. asso. Acad. de Medecine, Paris; fgn. mem. Royal Netherlands, Norwegian, Royal Swedish acads. sci., Acad. Nazionale Lincei, Rome, Stockholm, Zool. Soc., London, Royal Society, London. Fgn. corr., Acad. Science of Institute of Bologna, Italy. Awarded (1914) The Archduke Rainer medal of Imperial Royal Zoölogical Botanical Soc. of Vienna, 1925; John Scott medal and premium, of the City of Philadelphia, "for the invention of devices for tissue grafting and for tissue culture." John J. Carty Medal, Nat. Acad. Sciences, 1947; Antonio Feltrinelli International prize Accademia Nazionale de'l Lincei, Italy, 1956. Author numerous scientific papers on development of fishes, nervous system, embryonic transplantation and cultivation of animal tissues outside the organism. In 1907 first adapted the hanging drop culture method to the study of embryonic tissues and demonstrated directly the outgrowth of the developming nerve-fiber. Home: 142 Huntington St., New Haven. Died Sept. 30, 1959.

HARRISON, WARD, consulting engr.; b. East Orange, N.J., May 16, 1888; s. George K. and Abby Augusta (Ward) H.; M.E., Stevens Inst. Tech., 1909; hon. D.I.Eng., Case School Applied Science, 1940; m. Dorothy Fuller, June 12, 1913; children—Dorothy (Mrs. Wm. R. Van Aken), Cornelia (Mrs. Wm. L. Schlesinger), John Ward. Was with General Electric Co., 1909-48, dir. engring., Lamp Dept., 1930-48; chairman of Curtis Lighting, Incorporated, 1955-59; member board of directors Thompson Electric Co.; inventor and designer many types lighting equipment for industrial, commercial and street lighting. Supervising engr., representing U.S. Fuel Adminstrn. in N.E. Ohio, World War I. Mem. advisory committee fluorescent lighting fixture industry, War Production Bd., World War II. Pres. Internat. Commn. on Illumination (24 countries), 1951-55; vice chmn. Adv. Com. on Fine Arts, Cleve.; mem. Cleve. Met. Service Commission, 1956-59. Gold medalist, Illuminating Engrs. Soc., 1949; Distinguished Service award Cleveland Tech. Socs. Council, 1950; Stevens Inst. Silver Medallion, 1950. Fellow Am. Inst. E.E., Illuminating Engring. Soc. (v.p., 1913-15; pres. 1922-23); mem. British Illuminating Engrs. Society (hon.), Assn. Francaise des Eclairagistes; Cleveland Engring Soc. (v.p. 1937), Sigma Xi, Tau Beta Pi. Rep. Presbyn. Author: Electric Lighting, 1921. Coauthor: Street Lighting Practice, 1929. Contbr. many tech. papers in Elec. World, Procs. Illuminating Engring. Soc., etc. Chmn. com. that prepared Charters on Light (text-book). Address: Shaker Heights OH Died Jan. 24, 1970; buried Lakeview Cemetery, Cleveland OH

HARRISON, WILLIAM HENRY, communications engr.; b. Bklyn., June 11, 1892; s. John and Ann (Terahin) H.; student Pratt Inst., 1913-15; D. Engring. (hon.), Polytech. Inst. Bklyn., 1938; LL.D. (hon.), Notre Dame U., 1939, Hofstra Coll., 1951; D. England (honorary) Renssalaer Poly. Inst., 1946, Manhattan College, 1950; Master of Procurement (hon.), Signal Supply Sch., Ft. Horabird, Md., 1952; married Mabel

Gilchrist Ouchterloney, Apr. 14, 1915, children—William Henry, John Grant. Repairman and wireman, N.Y. Telephone Co., 1909-14; in engring. dept., Western Electric Co., New York, N.Y., 1914-18; engineer equipment and bldg. engr., and plant engr., Am. Telephone and Telegraph Co., N.Y. City, 1918-33; v.p. and dir. The Bell Telephone Co. of Pa. and The Diamond State Telephone Co., 1933-37; asst. v.p., Am. Telephone and Telegraph Co., N.Y.C., 1937-38; v.p. and chief engr., 1938-45, v.p. department operational engineering, 1945-48, pres., dir., 1948—; chmn. divs. of Internat. Tel. & Tel. Corp., subsidiaries; dir. subsidiary cos. Chief Shipbuilding, Construction and Supplies Branch, Office of Prodn. Management, 1941-42; dir. of Production, W.P.B., 1942. Apptd. brig. gen., U.S. Army, 1942, maj. gen., 1943; director construction division National Defense council, 1940; dir. of procurement and distribution service, Office of Chief Signal Officer, 1943-45; adminstr. N.P.A., 1950-51, D.P.A., 1951. Awarded D.S.M., 1945; Hon. Comdr. Order British Empire, 1946; Hoover Medal, 1946; Cross French Legion of Honor (Officer) 1947. Dir. Nassau Hosp.; mem. bd. gov. N.Y. Hospital; trustee Pratt Institute, Manhattan Coll. Mem. Am. Inst. Electric Engrs. (ex-president), Newcomen Society, Eta Kappa Nu, Tau Beta Pi. Clubs: University, Downtown Athletic (New York); North Fork Country (Cutchogue, N.Y.); Garden City Golf, Cherry Valley (Garden City); Chevy Chase (Wash.); India House; Chgo. Home: 120 Kensington Rd., Garden City, N.Y. Office: 67 Broad St., N.Y.C. 4. Died Apr. 21, 1956.

HARROD, BENJAMIN MORGAN, civil engr.; b. New Orleans, La., Feb. 19, 1837; s. Charles and Mary (Morgan) H.; A.B., Harvard, 1856, A.M., 1859; (LL.D., Tulane, 1906); m. Eugenia Uhlhorn, Sept. 11, 1883, Pvt., lt. of arty., brigade and div. engr. and capt. engr. corps, C.S.A., in Civil War. Chief state engr. of La., 1877-80; mem. U.S. Miss. River Commn., 1879-1904; city engr. of New Orleans, 1888-92, chief engr. in charge of constructing drainage system, New Orleans, 1895-1902; mem. Panama Canal Commn., 1904-07. Home: New Orleans, La. Died Sept. 7, 1912.

HARROP, GEORGE ARGALE, JR., med. research; b. Peru, Ill., Nov. 5, 1800; s. George Argale and Mary Belle (Cole) H.; U. of Wis., 1908-10; A.B., Harvard, 1912; M.D., Johns Hopkins Univ., 1916; research U. of Copenhagen, 1920-21; m. Esther Caldwell, Mar. 16, 1924; children—George Argale III, William Caldwell, David Cole, Esther. Intern and asst. resident phys. Johns Hopkins Hosp., 1916-21; resident phys. and instr. in medicine, Columbia U., 1921-28; asso. prof. medicine, Peking U. Med. Coll., China, 1923-24; asso. prof. medicine, Johns Hopkins, 1925-38 in charge chem. lab. and work in diseases of metabolism and endocrinology; dir. of research Squibb Inst. for Med. Research, New Brunswick, N.J., since 1938; v.p., dir. of research, E. R. Squibb and Sons, N.Y., since 1943. Fellow Am. Scandinavian Foundation; mem. A.M.A., Assn. Am. Physicians, Am. Coll. Physicians, Am. Soc. for Clin. Investigation, Am. Soc. Biol. Chemists, Soc. for Exptl. Biology and Medicine, Société Biologique (Paris), Cosmopolitan Clinical Clubs, New York Academy of Medicine, American Clinical and Climatol. Association, Phi Beta Kappa, Alpha Omega Alpha, Phi Kappa Psi, Nu Sigma Nu, Sigma Xi. Clubs: Harvard University (New York); Nassau (Princeton); Maryland (Baltimore). Author: Management of Diabetes, 1925; Diet in Disease, 1930; also numerous articles on metabolism, diabetes, the use of diet in therapy, etc. Home: 33 Cleveland Lane, Princeton, N.J. Died Aug. 4, 1945.

HARROW, BENJAMIN, chemist; b. London, Eng., Aug. 25, 1888; s. Emil and Erna H.; student Finsbury Coll., London, 1904-06; B.S. (chem.), Columbia, 1911, A.M., 1912, Ph.D., 1913; m Carolyn Solis, July 1917; 1 dau., Margaret. Came to U.S., 1907, naturalized, 1913. Was assistant in organic chemistry, Clark U.; asst. physiol. chemistry, Columbia, 1912-13; asst. prof. biochemistry, Fordham Med. Sch., 1913-14, asso. in physiol. chemistry, Coll. Physicians and Surgeons (Columbia), 1914-28; asst. prof. chemistry, Coll. City of New York, 1928-33, asso. prof. of chemistry, 1933-39, professor since 1939, chairman of department since 1944. Instructor O.T.C., 1917-18. Mem. Am. Chemical Society, Am. Assn. Advancement of Science, Harvey Soc., Soc. for Exptl. Biol. and Med. N.Y. Acad. Med., Am. Society Biol. Chemists, Biochem. Society, Royal Society Arts (Eng.), Sigma Xi. Author books including: Laboratory Manual of Biochemistry (with Drs. G.C.H. Stone, H. Wagreich, E. Borek, A. Mazur), 1940, 2d edit., 1944; also research publs. Editor of Contemporary Sci. in Modern Library, 1921; A Text-Book of Biochemistry (with Dr. C.P. Sherwin), 1935; Casimir Funk, 1955. Home: New York City NY Deceased.

HARSHBARGER, WILLIAM ASBURY, prof. mathematics; b. Brandonville, Va. (now W.Va.), Sept. 1, 1862; s. Abner Gaines and Eleanor Jane (Guthrie) H.; student W.Va. U.; B.S., Washburn Coll., Topeka, Kan., 1893, Sc.D., 1919; studied U. of Chicago, 1895, 96; m. Lucy Stratton Platt, of Franklin, Neb., June 22, 1888; children—Eugene Lee, Frank Victor, Ralph Platt (dec.), Ray Stratton. Teacher in Acad. of Washburn Coll., 1893-95; prof. mathematics, Washburn Coll., since 1895, dir. dept. of science since 1915. Mem. Am. Math. Soc., Math. Assn. America (ex-v.p.), Kan. Math. Soc. (ex-pres.), A.A.A.S., Am. Genetic Assn., Kan. Acad. Science (ex-pres.), Kan. Hort. Soc., Am. Rose Soc. (v.p. for Kan.). Republican. Conglist. Mason (32 deg., K.T., Shriner). Club: Saturday Night. Home: 1401 College Av., Topeka, Kan.

HARSHBERGER, JOHN WILLIAM, botanist; b. Phila., Pa., Jan. 1, 1869; s. Dr. A. and Jennie (Walk) H.; A.B., Central High Sch., Phila., 1888; B.S., U. of Pa., 1892, Ph.D., 1803; spl. student Harvard, 1890; traveled and botanized in Europe, Brazil, Argentine, Chile, Mexico, Alaska, Ariz., Utah, Calif., Can., W.I., Southern Fla., Northwestern and Eastern states; m. Helen B. Cole, June 28, 1907 (died 1923); children—Jane Yard, Elyonta Cole. Instr. botany and zoölogy, 1892-1907, asst. prof. botany 1907-11, prof., June 21, 1911—, U. of Pa. Formerly lecturer Soc. for Extension of Univ. Teaching; lectured in farmers' insts. in Pa., 1904-06; in charge nature study, Pocono Pines Assembly, summers 1903-08; in charge ecology, Marine Biol. Laboratory, Cold Spring Harbor, Long Island, 1913-21; in charge botany, Nautucket Maria Mitchell Assn., 1914-15. Author: Maize, a Botanical and Economic Study, 1893; The Botanists of Philadelphia, and Their Work, 1899. Bot. editor Worcester's New English Dictionary; Student's Herbarium for Descriptive and Geographic Purposes, 1901; A Phytogeographic Survey of North America, 1911, for the series of monographs, "Die Vegetation der Erde," The Vegetation of South Florida, 1914. The Vegetation of the New Jersey Pine Barrens, 1916; A Text-Book of Mycology and Plant Pathology, 1917; Colored Wall Map Vegetation of North America, 1919; Pastoral and Agricultural Botany, 1920. Bot. editor new Funk & Wagnall's College Dictionary. Home: Philadelphia, Pa. Died Apr. 27, 1929.

HART, CHARLES ARTHUR, entomologist; b. Quincy, Ill., Oct. 12, 1859; s. William Henry and Janet Elizabeth (Hoffman) H.; student State Normal U., 1881-82. Entomologist of Ill. Biol. Sta., 1894—; specialist in aquatic insect life; asst. Ill. State Lab., 1884-1900; asst. entomologist State Ill., 1900—. Mem. Soc. Am. Zoologists, Assn. Econ. Entomologists, A.A.A.S. Author: Entomology of the Illinois River (bull. State Lab. of Natural History), and various other entomol. articles. Address: Urbana, Ill. Died Feb. 18, 1918; buried Quincy, Ill.

HART, EDMUND HALL, horticulturist; b. Poughkeepsie, N.Y., Dec. 26, 1839; s. Benjamin Hall and Elizabeth (Nichols) H.; m. Isabella Howland, Dec. 1, 1870, 3 children. Settled in Fla., 1867; imported and bred bananas; imported seeds and developed ornamental palm trees; introduced Valencia orange to Fla.; mem. Fla. Fruit Growers' Assn.; charter mem. Am. Pomological Soc.; chmn. Fla. State Fruit Com. Died Apr. 22, 1898.

HART, EDWARD, chemist; b. Doylestown, Pa., Nov. 18, 1854; s. George and Martha Longstreth (Wasson) H.; B.S., Lafayette Coll., 1874, LL.D., 1924; Ph.D., Johns Hopkins, 1878. Asst. and tutor chemistry, 1874-76, adj prof., 1876-82, prof., 1882-1924 (emeritus), Lafayette Coll., also dean Pardee Scientific Dept., 1909-24. Pres. Baker & Adamson Chem. Co., 1881-1913; propr. Chem. Pub. Co., 1892—. Has taken out 10 chem. patents (one awarded John Scott medal and premium by Franklin Inst., Phila.). Editor Jour. Analytical and Applied Chemistry, 1887-93, Jour. Am. Chem. Soc., 1893-1901. Pres. Easton City Improvement League, 1912—; chmn. City Planning Commn., 1913. Author: Text Book of Chemical Engineering, 1920; Our Farm in Cedar Valley, 1923; The Silica Gel Pseudomorph, 1924. Home: Easton, Pa. Died June 6, 1931.

HART, EDWIN BRET, biochemist; b. Sandusky, O., Dec. 25, 1874; s. William and Mary (Hess) H.; student U. of Mich., 1892-97; U. of Marburg, Germany; U. of Heidelberg, Germany, 1900-01; m. Ann Virginia De Mille, Nov. 18, 1903; 1 dau., Margaret Virginia. Asst. chemist, N.Y. Agrl. Exptl. Station 1897-1902, asso. chem., 1902-06; prof. agrl. chemistry, U. of Wis.; chemist, Wis. Exptl. Station since 1906. Fellow A.A.A.S.; mem. Nat. Acad. Science, Am. Chem. Soc., Soc. Biol. Chemists, Soc. Animal Production, Soc. Dairy Science. Home: 302 Lathrop. Office: Biochemistry Bldg., U. of Wis., Madison 6, Wis. Died Mar. 12, 1953; buried Forest Hill Cemetery, Madison.

HART, MARION WEDDELL, statistician; b. Rocky Mount, N.C., May 18, 1890; s. Richard Gatlin and Minnie Floy (Daughtridge) H.; grad. Tarboro (N.C.) Male Acad., 1907, Oak Ridge Inst., 1909, Eastman Business Coll., Poughkeepsie, N.Y., 1910; m. Carrie Sharp Shubrick, Sept. 16, 1912; children—Marion Weddell, Carrie Shubrick. Statistician with Atlantic Coast Line R.R. Co., 1910-18; with U.S. R.R. Labor Bd., 1918—, becoming chief statistician. Episcopalian. Mason. Home: Chicago, Ill. Died Mar. 28, 1938.

HART, THEODORE STUART, physician; b. Groving, Ill., Feb. 25, 1869; s. Charles Langdon and Sarah (Franks) H.; A.B., Yale, 1891, A.M., 1893; M.D., Columbia U. Coll. Phys. and Surg., 1895; m. Mary Robbins, June 12, 1901. Intern Presbyn. Hosp., N.Y.C., 1895-97; vis. physician Seton Hosp., 1901-11; instr. Coll. Phys. and Surg., 1903-13, asst. prof. clin. medicine, 1913-22; vis. physician Presbyn. Hosp., 1914-22, cons. physician, 1922—; cons. physician Manhattan Eye, Ear and Throat Hosp., 1922—, Neurological Inst., 1936—. Mem. Conn. N.G., 1891-92; cardio-vascular cons. to U.S. Army, 1917, N.Y. Draft Board, 1918. Mem. U.S. Citizens Defense Corps, Emergency Medical Reserve Pool, 1941—. Diplomate Am. Bd. Internal Medicine. Mem. Assn. Am. Physicians, Am. Soc. Clin. Investigation, A.M.A., N.Y. Acad. Medicine, N.Y. Heart Assn. (pres. 1920-24), Am. Heart Assn. (chmn. exec. com., 1924-31), N.Y. Tb and Health Assn. (director 1924-31), Harvey Soc., Zeta Psi, Chi Delta Theta, Elihu Club. Republican. Presbyn. Author: The Diagnosis and Treatment of Abnormalities of Myocardial Function, 1917; Taking Care of Your Heart, 2d edit., 1937. Contbr. many papers on metabolic disorders and diseases of the circulation to med. jours. Clubs: University (N.Y.C.); West Side Tennis (L.I.). Home: 410 Park Av., N.Y.C. Died Jan. 1, 1951.

HARTER, ISAAC, mech. engr.; b. Mansfield, O., Jan. 2, 1880; s. Michael Daniel and Mary Lucinda (Brown) H.; grad. Episcopal Acad., Phila., Pa., 1896, St. Paul's Sch., Concord, N.H., 1897; B.S., U. of Pa., 1901; m. Elizabeth Farrington, Mar. 15, 1904; 1 son, Isaac; married 2d, Alice Crane Howland, June 6, 1956. With Aultman & Taylor Machinery Co., Mansfield, O., 1901-05, The Stirling Co., Barberton, O., 1905-07; with The Babcock & Wilcox Co. as supt. Barberton Works, 1907-10, Bayonné (N.J.) Works, 1910-20, asst. to pres., 1920-25, v.p. and dir. 1924-47; exec. v.p. and dir. The Babcock & Wilcox Tube Co., 1924-47, chmn. bd., dir., 1947—. Mem. Am. Soc. M.E., Inst. of Metals (London), Ohio Society of New York, Am. Welding Soc., Sigma Xi, Phi Kappa Sigma. Republican. Episcopalian. Clubs: University, Engineers (New York); Piping Rock (Locust Valley, N.Y.); Seawanhaka-Corinthian Yacht (Oyster Bay, N.Y.). Address: 36 E. 72d St., N.Y.C. Died Aug. 22, 1957; buried Mansfield, O.

HARTIGAN, RAYMOND HARVEY, chemist; b. Rensselaer, N.Y., Sept. 2, 1915; s. Raymond A. and Nettie M. (Green) H.; B.S., Rensselaer Poly. Inst., 1937, M.S., 1939, Ph.D., 1941; m. Kathryn P. Comerford, Nov. 29, 1941; children—M. Janice, Donna M., Rana Rae. Asst. instr. chemistry Rensselaer Poly. Inst., 1937-41; indsl. fellow Mellon Inst., Pitts., 1941-47, sr. fellow, 1947-50, adminstrv. fellow, 1951-52, asst. dir. research, 1952-55, dir. research, 1955-58; vice president research and development Foster Grant Co., Inc., Leominster, Mass., 1958-61; dir. research div. Rensselaer Poly. Inst., 1961-65; v.p. research and devel. div. Nat. Dairy Products Corp., 1965, pres. of research and development division, 1965-71; v.p. Kraftco Corp., 1971; pres. Rensselaer Research Corp., 1964-65; instr. Pa. State U. Extension, evenings 1942-44, Carnegie Inst. Tech., evenings 1946-48; asst. mgr., mgr. lab. sect., research dept. Koppers Co., 1950. Alumni trustee Rensselaer Poly. Institute, 1958-61; mem. plastics engring. adv. com. Lowell Tech. Inst., 1958-61; food industries adv. com. Nutrition Found. Fellow N.Y. Acad. Sci.; mem. Am. Dairy Sci. Assn., Am. Chem. Soc., A.A.A.S., Rensselaer Alumni Assn. (past dir.), Soc. Chem. Ind., Inst. Food Tech., Ind. Research Inst., Nat. Conf. Adminstrn. Research, Sigma Xi, Phi Lambda Upsilon. Methodist. Clubs: Sunset Ridge Country (Winnetka, Ill.); Chemists, Engineers' (N.Y.C.). Home: Lake Forest IL Died July 28, 1971; buried Lake Forest Cemetery, Lake Forest IL

HARTLEY, LOWRIE C., civil engr.; b. Masontown, W.Va., Dec. 29, 1871; s. S. W. and Wilhelmina (Menear) H.; Ohio State U., 2 yrs., spl. course in engring.; m. Eva Grimes, of Uniontown, Ohio, 1900; children—Lois, Margaret, Wilma. Signalman, 1898-1900, asst. on engring. corps, 1900-04, asst. engr. maintenance of way, 1904-07, Pittsburgh, Cincinnati, Chicago & St. Louis Ry.; signal engr., 1907-10, engr. maintenance of way, 1910-11, chief engr., since July 1911, Chicago & Eastern Ill. R.R. Presbyn. Clubs: Chicago Engineers', Ridge Country. Home: 6731 Clyde Av. Office: 6600 So. Union Av., Chicago IL

HARTMAN, CARL G., zoologist; b. Reinbeck, Ia., June 3, 1879; s. Ossian W. and Sophia (Lemwigh) H.; student State U. Ia., 1896-97; B.A., U. Tex., 1902, M.A., 1904, Ph.D., 1915; m. Eva Rettenmeyer, June 23, 1919; children—Carl Frederick, Philip Emil, Paul Arthur and Bertha Grace. County supt. of schs., Travis County, Tex., 1904-09; mem. faculty U. Tex., 1912-25, prof. zoology, 1923-25; research asso. Lab. of Embryology, Carnegie Instn., Johns Hopkins Med. Sch., 1925-41; prof. zool., U. Ill., Urbana, 1941-47; dir. emeritus Ortho. Research Found., Raritan, N.J.; research cons. Margaret Sanger Research Bur., N.Y. Mem. Club Study of Ageing; mem. Ill. State Bd. Nat. Resources and Conservation, 1945-47; mem. bd. Biol. Abstracts, Phila. (pres. 1948-50). Mem. Nat. Acad. Sci., Am. Soc. Zoologists (pres. 1948), A.A.A.S. (v.p. sect. F. 19), Am. Assn Anatomists, Am. Physiol. Soc., Am. Soc. Mammalogists, Soc. Exptl. Biol. and Med., Am. Soc. of Naturalists, Am. Soc. Study Sterility (v.p. 1958-59), Inst. Internat. d'Embryologie; hon. mem. Pacific Coast Obstetrical and Gynecol. Soc. Central States Assn. Obstetrics and Gynecol., Chgo., Balt. gynecol. socs., Brazil Soc. Study Fertility, Anat. Soc. Gt. Britain and Ireland; mem. Sigma Xi, Phi Beta Kappa. Lutheran. Author Possums, 1952, and several others 1905-36; Science and the Safe Period, 1962; Mechanisms

Concerned with Conception, 1963. Home: 219 Norwood Av., N. Plainfield, N.J. Died Mar. 1, 1968.

HARTMAN, FRANK ALEXANDER, prof. physiology; b. Gibbon, Neb., Dec. 4, 1883; s. George Washington and Flora (Sprague) H.; A.B., U. of Kan., 1905, A.M., 1909; Ph.D., U. of Wash., 1914; m. Anna Caroline Botsford, Feb. 10, 1906; children—William Brewster, Warren Elmer, Donald George, Flora Lilian (Mrs. Milton Victor Jones), Mary Louise (Mrs. Merrill H. Barnebey). Teacher in high school, Beardstown, Illinois, 1906, Wichita, Kansas., 1906-08, Seattle, Wash., 1908-14; Austin teaching fellow, Harvard Med. Sch., 1914-15; lecturer in physiology, Toronto Univ., 1915-18, asst. prof., 1918-19; prof. physiology and head dept., U. of Buffalo, 1919-34; research professor, Ohio State Univ., from 1948. Awarded Chancellor's medal, U. of Buffalo, 1932; gold medal by A.M.A., 1932; Schoellkopf medal by Western N.Y. Sect. of Am. Chem. Soc. Fellow A.A.A.S.; mem. Am. Physiol. Soc. Soc. Exptl. Biology, Am. Soc. Zoologists, Am. Chem. Soc., Assn. for Study Internal Secretions (pres. 1935), A.M.A., Ohio Acad. Science, Sigma Xi, Phi Lambda Upsilon, Phi Beta Kappa, Alpha Omega Alpha. Unitarian. Co-author (book) The Adrenal Gland. Contbr. to scientific jours. Home: Columbus OH Died Mar. 21, 1971.

HARTMAN, HOWARD RUSSELL, physician; b. Toledo, Dec. 11, 1887; s. George D. and Emma Elizabeth (Fauster) H.; A.B., U. Mich., 1911, M.D., 1914; m. Ila Fern Alexander, January 27, 1915; 1 daughter, Ruth Forrest (Mrs. James S. Ross). Fellowship Mayo Clinic, 1914-19, member of the permanent staff, 1915—, asso. prof. medicine, Mayo Found., 1940-53, head of section in medicine, 1938-53, mem. emeritus staff, 1953—. Developed Latin Am. Clientele at Mayo Clinic. Decorated El Sol del Peru (Peru), La Orden de Bayaca (Colombia). Fellow A.C.P.; mem. Am., So. Minn. med. assns., Am. Gastro-Enterol. Assn., Nu Sigma Nu, Alpha Omega Alpha, Sigma Xi. Republican. Baptist. Home: 800 12th Av. S.W. Office: Mayo Clinic. Rochester, Minn. Died Oct. 6, 1959.

HARTMAN, LEON WILSON, univ. pres.; b. Downsville, N.Y., June 18, 1876; s. Henry and Sarah Eleanor (Wilson) H.; B.S., Cornell Univ., 1898, A.M., same, 1899; Ph.D., Univ. of Pa., 1903; Univ. of Göttingen, 1903-04; m. Edith Dabele Kast, July 31, 1907; children—Margaret Eleanor, Sara Louise (dec.), Paul Leon, Charles Frederick, David Kast. Asst. in physics, Cornell U., 1900-01; prof. physics, Kan. Agrl. Coll., 1901-02; Fraser fellow in physics, U. of Pa., 1902-03, Tyndale fellow, 1903-04; instr. physics, Cornell, U., 1904-05; asst. prof. physics, 1905-06, asso. prof., 1906-09, U. of Utah; prof. physics, U. of Nevada since 1909, acting pres., 1938, pres. since 1939. With Utah Power and Light Co., summer, 1906, U. of Utah summers, 1907, 08, 09, U. of Calif., summers, 1924, 25; investigator Nela Research Lab. of Gen. Electric Co., Cleveland, O., summer, 1916; with Pacific Telephone and Telegraph Co., summer, 1927, Leeds & Northrup Co., Phila., summers, 1928, 29, Bureau of Standards, Washington, D.C., autumn 1929 and summer 1930. Mem. A.A.A.S., Am. Phys. Soc., Utah Acad. Science, Illuminating Engring. Soc., Am. Assn. Univ. Profs., Sigma Xi, Phi Kappa Phi. Author: Laboratory Manual of Experiments in Pbysics, 1906; An Introduction to Electrical Measurements, 1930; Measurement of Coefficient of Self-Inductance in Terms of Resistance and Time (joint author), 1940. Contbr. to various scientific journals, articles on radiation, pyrometry, acetylene, Nernst lamp, spectro-photometry, visibility, etc. Home: Reno, Nev. Died Aug. 27, 1943.

HARTMANN, ALEXIS FRANK, pediatrician; b. St. Louis, Mo., Oct. 30, 1898; s. Dr. Henry Charles and Bertha (Griesedieck) H.; B.S., Washington U., 1919, M.S., 1921, M.D., 1921; m. Gertrude Krochmann, Aug. 9, 1922; children—Henry Carl, Alexis F. Interne St. Louis Children's Hosp., 1921-22, asst. resident, 1922-23, chief resident, 1923-24; instr. pediatrics, 1921. Mem. Am. Pediatric Soc., Am. Acad. asso. prof., 1930-36, prof. and head of dept. since 1936; physician-in-chief St. Louis Children's Hosp.; pediatrician-in-chief St. Louis Maternity Hosp. Mem. S.A.T.C., World War. Awarded Gill prize in pediatrics, 1921; Abraham Jacobi award in pediatrics A.M.A., 1963. Mem. Am. Pediatric Soc., Am. Acad. Pediatrics, Am. Soc. Biol. Chemists, Am. Med. Assn., St. Louis Med. Soc., Mo. Med. Soc., Soc. for Clin. Research, Alpha Tau Omega, Nu Sigma Nu, Sigma Xi, Alpha Omega Alpha. Writer many scientific articles and chapters in current text books. Home: 7433 Teasdale Av. Office: 500 S. Kingshighway, St. Louis 10. Died Oct. 1964.

HARTNESS, JAMES, governor; b. Schenectady, N.Y., Sept. 3, 1861; s. John Williams and Ursilla (Jackson) H.; ed. Cleveland pub. schs.; M.E., Univ. of Vt., 1910; M.A., Yale, 1914; LL.D., U. of Vermont, 1921; m. Lena Sanford Pond, May 13, 1885; children—Anna (Mrs. William H. Beardsley), Helen (Mrs. Ralph E. Flanders). Successively, 1890—, supt., mgr., pres., Jones & Lamson Machine Co., Springfield, Vt.; inventor and patentee of over 100 patents including Hartness flat turret lathe, Hartness automatic die, Turret equatorial telescope, Hartness screw thread comparator, etc. Chmn. Com. of Pub. Safety, Vt., war period, also federal food administrator for Vt.; gov. of Vt., term 1921-23. Mem. commn. that represented U.S. Air Bd. at Inter-Allied Air Craft Standardization Conf., London and Paris; v. chmn. Congressional Screw Thread Standardization Commn. Chmn. State Bd. of Edn., Vt., 6 yrs. Fellow A.A.A.S., Royal Astron. Soc. Awarded John Scott medal by bd. of dirs. of City Trusts of Phila., 1921; Edward Longstreth Medal by Franklin Inst., Phila. Home: Springfield, Vt. Died Feb. 2, 1934.

HARTNEY, HAROLD EVANS, tech. adviser in aviation; b. Packenham, Ont., Can., Apr. 19, 1888; s. James Harvey and Annie Evans (Cuthbert) H.; B.A., U. of Toronto, 1911; grad. U. of Saskatchewan, 1912; student Law Soc. of Saskatchewan, 1911-14; married to Irene McGeary, November 11, 1914; children—Mrs. Frederick Yeager, Mrs. Robert Gensel, Harold Evans (killed in action May 13, 1944), James Cuthbert. Came to United States, 1917, naturalized, 1928. Began with Royal Flying Corps, Canada; comdg. 1st Pursuit Group, U.S. Army Air Service, with A.E.F., 1917-19; chief of training, Washington, D.C., 1919-21; discharged with rank of lt. col. (Reserve); organizing sec. and 1st gen. mgr. Nat. Aeronautic Assn., 1921-22; tech. adviser to several aeronautic corps; tech. adviser to U.S. Senate Com. on Air Safety, 1935-38; tech. adviser Civil Aeronautics Adminstrn., 1938-41; active duty Ferrying Command Air Corps (lt. col.); mgr. Washington Bureau, Ziff Davis Publications, 1941-42; has been active in efforts to make air power recognized in war and industry. Decorated Distinguished Service Cross, Silver Star, Purple Heart (U.S.); Legion of Honor, Croix de Guerre (France); Silver Medal for Valor (Italy); Service Decoration (Brit.); Victory medals U.S. and Great Brit. Mem. Early Birds, Quiet Birdmen, Inst. Aeronautical Sciences, Am. Legion (past comdr. Aviators Post), Nat. Aeronautic Assn. Episcopalian. Author: Up and At 'Em, 1940; Complete Flying Manual, 1940; Aircraft Spotters' Guide, 1942; What the Citizen Should Know about the Air Force, 1942. Home: 3130 16th St., N.W., Washington, D.C. Died Oct. 5, 1945.

HARTREE, DOUGLAS RAYNER, educator; b. Cambridge, Eng., Mar. 27, 1897; s. William and Eva (Rayner) H.; B.A., M.A., Ph.D., St. Johns's Coll., Cambridge; M.Sc., U. Manchester; m. Elaine Charlton, Aug. 21, 1923; children—Nesta Margaret (Mrs. Edward L. Booth), Oliver Penn, John Richard. Research fellow St. John's Coll., Cambridge, 1924-27, Christ's Coll., Cambridge, 1928-29; prof. applied mathematics U. Manchester, 1929-37, prof. theoretical physics, 1937-45; prof. math. physics Cambridge U., 1946—, acting chief, Inst. Numerical Analysis, U.S. Bur. Standards, U. Cal., 1948; vis. prof. Princeton, 1955. Served with anti-aircraft exptl. sect. Munitions Inventions Dept., Ministry Munitions, 1916-19; with sci. research sect. Ministery of Supply, 1940-45. Recipient Rockefeller fellowship for study Inst. Theoretical Physics, Copenhagen, 1928. Mem. Royal Soc., Inst. Physics, Inst. Elec. Engrs., Cambridge Philos. Soc. Author: Calculating Instruments and Machines, 1949; Numerical Analysis, 1952. Home: 21 Bentley Rd. Office: Cavendish Laboratory, Cambridge, Eng. Died Feb. 12, 1958.

HARTSHORNE, HENRY, physician; b. Phila., Mar. 16, 1823; s. Dr. Joseph and Anna (Bonsall) H.; grad. Haverford Coll., 1839; M.D., U. Pa., 1845, LL.D. (hon), 1884; m. Mary Brown, Jan. 8, 1849. Resident physician Pa. Hosp., Phila., 1846-48; prof. insts. of medicine Phila. Coll. Medicine, 1853-54; lectr. natural history Franklin Inst., Phila., 1857-58; prof. theory and practice medicine Gettysburg (Pa.) Coll., 1859-61; prof. hygiene U. Pa., Phila., 1865; prof diseases of children, then prof. physiology and hygiene Woman's Med. Coll., Phila., 1867-76; instr., lectr. Phila. Central High Sch., Pa. Coll. Dental Surgery, Girard Coll., circa 1869-76; advocate of edn. of women, particularly right of women to study medicine; engaged in religious and missionary work in Japan, 1893-97; active in Am. Philos. Soc., Acad. Natural Scis.; a founder Am. Public Health Assn; Died Tokyo, Japan, Feb. 10, 1897; buried Tokyo.

HARTT, CHARLES FREDERICK, geologist; b. Frederickton, N.B., Can., Aug. 23, 1840; s. Jarvis William Hartt; grad. Arcadia Coll., N.S., Can., 1860. Studied at Mus. of Comparative Anatomy on invitation of Louis Agassiz, Cambridge, Mass., 1861-64; geologist on Thayer expdn. to Brazil, 1865-66; prof. geology Vassar Coll., 1866-67; prof. geology and phys. geography Columbia, 1868-75; chief Geol. Commn. of Brazil, 1875-78. Author: Geography of Brazil, 1870; Notes on the Modern Tupi of the Ana, 1872; Crustacea Collected on the Coast of Brazil, 1866-73. Died Rio de Janeiro, Brazil, Mar. 18, 1878.

HARTWELL, BURT LAWS, chemist; b. Littleton, Mass., Dec. 18, 1865; s. Charles Pollard and Lucinda (Laws) H.; B.Sc., Mass. Agrl. Coll., 1889, M.S., 1900; B.Sc., Boston U., 1889; Ph.D., Univ. of Pa., 1903; m. Mary Louise Smith, of Stow, Mass., Sept. 9, 1891; 1 dau., Gladys (Mrs. Leroy B. Newton). Asst. chemist, Mass. Agrl. Expt. Sta., 1889-91; 1st asst. chemist, 1891-1903, asso., 1903-07, chemist, 1907-23, dir., 1912-28, agronomist, 1913-28, Agrl. Expt. Station, R.I. State Coll.; also prof. agrl. chemistry, R.I. State Coll., 1908-28; now agrl. editor and lecturer. Fellow Am. Soc. Agronomy, A.A.A.S.; mem. Phi Kappa Phi, Sigma Xi, Pi Gamma Mu. Home: Auburndale, Mass.

HARTWELL, EDWARD MUSSEY, statistician; b. Exeter, N.H., May 29, 1850; s. Shattuck and Catherine Stone (Mussey) H.; A.B., Amherst Coll., 1873, A.M., 1876; Ph.D., Johns Hopkins, 1881; M.D., Miami Med. Coll., Cincinnati, 1882; (LL.D., Amherst, 1898); m. Mary Laetitia Brown, July 25, 1889. Vice prin. high sch., Orange, N.J., 1873-74; teacher Boston Latin Sch., 1874-77; student medicine, Cincinnati, 1877-78; fellow Johns Hopkins, 1879-80; asso. physical training and dir. gymnasium, same, 1883-91; dir. physical training, pub. schs., Boston, 1891-97; sec. statis. dept., City of Boston, from its establishment, 1897. Chmn. Mass. State Commn. for the Blind, 1906-08. Spl. expert agt., U.S. Dept. Labor in Europe, 1888-89; has studied in Berlin, Vienna and Stockholm, and made spl. investigations in hygiene, edn. and statistics in Great Britain, Germany, Russia and Scandinavia. Translator from Swedish; Kleen's Handbok i Massage. Mem. Med. and Chirurg. Faculty of Md. Home: Jamaica Plain, Boston. Died Feb. 19, 1922.

HARTZELL, J(OSEPH) CULVER, genealogist; b. New Orleans, Sept. 10, 1870; s. Joseph Crane and Jennie (Culver) H.; B.S., Chattanooga, 1892; M.S., Yale, 1899; M.D., Coll. Phys. and Surg., 1901; Ph.D., Munich, 1904; student. Harvard, 1896; Johns Hopkins, 1897-98; Pisa, 1903; Ohio-Miami Med. Coll., 1915; m. Helen Hitchcock Thresher, Aug. 31, 1893. Prof. of biology, Ill. Wesleyan U., 1899-1904; in Europe, 1903-04; prof. chemistry, U. of the Pacific, 1904-10; cons. engr. chemistry and metallurgy, 1910-13; Ill. Malleable Iron Co., 1913-14; research work, 1914-18; chief chemist, Cincinnati Milling Machine Co., 1918-19; cons. engr. to Dalton Adding Machine Co., 1920, to Victor Safe & Lock Div. of the Safe-Cabinet Co., and to the Hall's Safe Co., 1920-21; pres. and gen. mgr. Ohio Lesgas Co., 1921-25. Fellow Seismol. Soc. America, A.A.A.S.; charter mem. and chmn. exec. com. Cincinnati Chapter Am. Steel Treaters Society. Home: Blue Ash, O. Deceased.

HARVEY, ANDREW MAGEE, physician and surgeon; b. Galesburg, Ill., Jan. 14, 1868; s. William Nathaniel and Lovina (Brewer) H.; B.S., Knox Coll., 1889, M.S., 1892; M.D., Coll. of Physicians and Surgeons, 1893; D.Sc. (hon.), Knox Coll., 1939; m. Edith Dorset Earle, June 1, 1898; children—Andrew Magee, Lovina Brewer (Mrs. Lawrence A. Williams), John Earle. Interne, St. Elizabeth Hosp., Chicago, 1893-95; attending surgeon, West Side Free Dispensary, Frances Willard Hosp., Garfield Park Sanitarium, Chicago; asst. health offr., Long Beach Calif., since 1942; med. dir. and chief surgeon Crane Co. (retired); capt. No. 6 Calif. State Guard (retired), President of Grace Hospital, 1905-10, second section preventive medicine and public health, A.M.A., chief med. officer, Republican nat. convention, 1932. Dir. Nat. Safey Council; bd. dirs. The Edward Sanitarium, 1920-39; bd. edn., LaGrange, Ill. Fellow American College Surgeons, A.M.A.; honorary fellow (co-founder) Am. Assn. Indsl. Physicians and Surgeons, Tuberculosis Assn. Mem. Chicago Public Policy Com., Ill. State Med. Soc., Chicago Council for Indsl. Safety (first pres.), Alumni Assn. Coll. of Physicians and Surgeons (pres.), Alumni Assn. Knox Coll., (pres.) Chicago Med. Soc., Calif. State, Los Angeles County Med. Assns., Instructor for Traumatic Surgery, West Suburban Council Boy Scouts of Am. Health officer, Village LaGrange Park, Phi Gamma Delta, Nu Sigma Nu. Mason. Pioneered in systematically protecting eyes of indsl. workers, reducing eye injuries by placing safety glasses on those exposed to eye accidents. Home: 21 Redondo Av. Office: 218 E. 1st St., Long Beach, Calif. Died July 18, 1949; buried in Rose Hill Cemetery, Chicago.

HARVEY, BASIL COLEMAN HYATT, educator; b. Watford, Ont., Can., Jan. 16, 1875; s. Dr. Leander H. and Anne (Wilson) H.; A.B., U. Toronto, 1894. M.B., 1898; M.D., 1928; grad. Normal College of N.S., 1895; member College of Physicians and Surgeons, Ontario, 1898; student U. Basel, Switzerland, 1903; m. Janet Hinsdill Holt, Sept. 1, 1904. Demonstrator of anatomy U. Toronto, 1895-97; practiced medicine, Watford, Ont., 1898-1901; asst. in anatomy U. Chgo., 1901-02, asso., 1902-04, instr., 1904-08, asst. prof., 1908-11, asso. prof., 1911-17, prof., 1917-40, emeritus, 1940—, dean med. students, 1923-40, dean students of biol. science div., 1931-40; recalled as acting dean of med. students and students in biol. sciences, 1943-44. Served as maj. Med. Dept., U.S. Army, AEF, during World War. Treas. Assn. Am. Med. Colls., 1933-35. Vice pres. Inst. Medicine (Chicago), 1933; mem. Assn. Am. Anatomists, A.A.A.S., Sigma Xi, Alpha Kappa Kappa. Clubs: Quadrangle, University, Olympia Fields Country. Translator: The Inheritance of Acquired Characters, Rignano. Author: The Nature of Vital Processes According to Rignano; Simple Lessons in Human Anatomy. Asso. editor Anat. Record, 1928-40; Papers on Anatomy; article on anatomy, Ency. Britannica. Home: 1326 E. 58th St., Chgo. 37. Died Feb. 15, 1958.

HARVEY, EDMUND NEWTON, physiologist; b. Phila., Nov. 25, 1887; s. William and Althea Ann (Newton) H.; grad. Germantown (Pa.) Acad., 1905; B.Sc., U. Pa., 1909; Ph.D., Columbia, 1911; m. Ethel Nicholson Browne, Mar. 12, 1916; children—Edmund Newton, Richard Bennet. Instr. physiology Princeton,

1911-15, asst. prof., 1915-19, prof. 1919-33, H. F. Osborn prof., 1933—; vis. lectr. in biology Mass. Inst. Tech., 1940-41. Trustee Bermuda Biol. Sta.; v.p., trustee Marine Biol. Lab., Woods Hole, Mass. Vis. lectr. Inst. de Biofisica, Rio de Janeiro, 1946. Recipient John Price Wetherill medal Franklin Inst. Pa., 1934, Rumford medal Am. Acad. Arts and Scis., 1947; Certificate of Merit, U.S. Armed Forces; decorated Officer Nat. Order do Cruzerio do Sul (Brázil). Mem. A.A.A.S., Am. Soc. Naturalists, Am. Soc. Biol. Chemists, Am. Physiol. Soc., Soc. Exptl. Biology and Medicine, Am. Soc. Zoölogists, Growth Soc., Nat. Geog. Soc., Am. Assn. U. Profs., N.Y. Acad. Scis., Soc. Am. Bacteriologists, Bot. Soc. Am., Harvey Soc., Am. Philos. Soc., Nat. Acad. of Sciences, Am. Acad. Arts and Sciences Boston, Internat. Soc. of Cell Biology (v.p. 1947-50), Nat. Research Council, Sigma Xi. Author: The Nature of Animal Light, 1920; Laboratory Directions in General Physiology, 1933; Living Light, 1940. Has made special studies in bioluminescence, cell permeability, nerve conduction, regulation in plants, ultrasonic radiation, cell surface tension, brain potentials, decompression sickness, mechanism of wounding, etc. Editor Survey of Biological Progress. Asso. editor Biol. Bull., Biol. Abstracts; Jour. of Cellular and Comparative Physiology. Home: 48 Cleveland Lane, Princeton, N.J. Died July 21, 1959.

HARVEY, ETHEL BROWNE, research biologist; b. Balt., Dec. 14, 1885; d. Bennet Bernard and Jennie (Nicholson) Browne; A.B., Goucher Coll., 1906; D.Sc. (hon.), 1956; M.A., Columbia, 1907, Ph.D., 1913; Sarah Berliner fellow U. Cal., 1914-15; m. Edmund Newton Harvey, Mar. 12, 1916 (dec. 1959); children—Edmund Newton, Richard Bennet. Investigator Cold Spring Harbor, 1905, Marine Biol. Lab., Woods Hole, 1906-62; instr. sci. Bennett Sch., Millbrook, N.Y., 1908-11; asst. biology Princeton, 1912-13, ind. investigator biology dept., 1931-62; instr. biology Dana Hall, Wellesley, Mass., 1913-14; asst. histology Cornell Med. Coll., 1915-16; instr. biology Washington Sq. Coll., N.Y.U., 1928-31. Trustee Marine Biol. Lab., Woods Hole, Mass., 1950-58, trustee emeritus, 1958-65. Fellow A.A.A.S., N.Y. Acad. Sci., Inst. Internat. d' Embryologie Utrecht; mem. Am. Soc. Zoologists, Am. Soc. Naturalists, Am. Genetic Assn., Soc. Growth and Devel., Soc. Gen. Physiologists, Internat. Soc. Cell Biology, Soc. Ital. Biol Sper (hon.), Bermuda Biol. Sta., Biol. Photog. Assn., Phi Beta Kappa, Sigma Xi. Author: The American Arbacia and Other Sea Urchins, 1956; also articles on cell physiology and centrifuging marine eggs; article on fertilization Ency. Brit., 1960. Address: Marine Biol. Lab., Woods Hole, Mass. Died Sept. 2, 1965; buried Woods Hole Cemetery, Mass.

HARVEY, HAROLD BROWN, engr. and mfr. nonferrous forgings; b. Parkman, Me., June 20, 1884; s. Daniel Genthner and Ida Gertrude (Brown) H.; grad. high sch., Wakefield, Mass., 1902; Mass. Inst. Tech., 1905; lecturer courses Northwestern U. Sch. of Commerce; m. Alwilda Fritsch, May 20, 1911. Elec. engr. with Becker Bros., Chicago, and chief engr. Am. Maintenance Co., 1906; factory mgr. Henry Newgard & Co., elec. constrn. and mfg., 1910-15; founder 1915, and pres. until 1920, Marquette Electric Switchboard Co.; pres. Harvey Electric Co. (now Chicago Forging & Mfg. Co.), brass forgings, 1919-21; founder, 1923, and since pres., The Harvey Metal Corp., aluminum, brass and copper forgings for automotive, aircraft, railroad, and gen. industries; pres. Burr Oak Coal Co.; Fed. reorganization mgr. Interstate coal properties, 1941-46; mgr. Marquette Indsl. Bldgs. Inventor magnetic metal separator and early high voltage equipment; pioneer in aluminum and brass forging industry; originator of drop forgings of brass and various processes in the forging of nonferrous metals. Developed ins. plan maintaining elec. machinery. Pres., 1919-20, Rotary Club of Chicago, which originated and sponsored first Boys' Week in Chicago, also originated scholarship for city boys in agrl. course, U. of Ill. Charter mem. Nat. Assn. Brass Forging Industries, and dir., 1932-33; sec. Aluminum Forging Council, 1933. Under N.R.A., successively sec. code com. and chmn. Nat. Code Authority Brass Forging Industry; chmn. code com. and nat. chmn. Aluminum Forging Div.; dir. Alumninum Code Authority, Inc. Since N.R.A. chmn. com. to reorganize nationally the brass forging industry forming the Brass Forging Assn. of which was first pres.; also mem. com. to organize assn. for aluminum industry and first chmn. of the Aluminum Forging Div.; western vice pres. and dir. Assn. Mfrs. in Aluminum Industry, 1935. Mem. Aluminum Assn. (western v.p., dir. and mem. various cons.), Aluminum Forging Div. (chmn.) Brass Forging Assn. (pres. since 1936), Nat. Assn. of Mfrs. (com. on Nat. Defense), Army Ordnance (mem. nat. endowment com.), U.S. C. of C., Ill. Mfrs. Assn., Ill. C. of C., Soc. Automotive Engrs. (com. on nat. defense), Am. Soc. of Metals, Am. Soc. Mech. Engrs.; trustee mem. corp. Mass. Inst. Tech. (various coms.), Chicago Assn. of Commerce, Soc. for Oriental Research. Mason (32 deg., Shriner). Clubs: Rotary (past pres.), Technology (M.I.T. Alumni, past pres.), Chicago Motor; New York Athletic. Author of Rotary's Message to Garcia, Renaissance of the Bronze Age, and several statistical treatises on non-ferrous forgings. Home: 320 23d St., Santa Monica, Calif. Died Dec. 3, 1949; buried Forest Lawn Cemetery, Glendale, Calif.

HARVEY, HAYWOOD AUGUSTUS, inventor, mfr.; b. Jamestown, N.Y., Jan. 17, 1824; s. Thomas William and Melinda (Hayward) H.; m. Matilda Winant, Dec. 29, 1849, 1 child; m. Emily Halsey, June 21, 1865, 1 child. Patented corrugated blind staple; invented hay-cutter; joined Harvey Iron & Steel Co., Mott Haven, N.Y., 1852; patented ry. chair, 1859, peripheral grip bolt, 1874; original inventor of cold-forged screw; organized Harvey Steel Co., 1886; developed Harvey process of treating armour plate (to harden surface of steel for combat ships, adopted by U.S. and several European navies), became world famous. Recipient Silver medal Am. Inst. Fair, 1847. Died Aug. 28, 1893.

HARVEY, RODNEY BEECHER, prof. plant physiology; b. Monroeville, Ind., May 26, 1890; s. Aaron Lawrence and Mary Vandervort (Hester) H.; Ph.C., Purdue U., 1912, D.Sc. causa honoris, 1939; B.S., U. of Mich., 1915; Ph.D., U. of Chicago, 1918; student Cambridge (Eng.) U., 1927-28, U. of Bonn, Germany, summer 1928; m. Helen M. Whittier, June 17, 1916; children—Hale M. Whittier (dec.), Rodney Bryce, Rhoda Beatrice, Helen Elizabeth, Eleanor Whittier, Asst. botanist Eli Lilly Co., 1912-13; asst. pharmacognosist U.S. Bur. Chemistry, 1915; asso. pharmacognosist U.S. Bur. Plant Industry, 1918, plant physiologist, 1918-20; asst. prof. botany, U. of Minn., 1920-21, asso. prof. plant pathology and botany, 1921-31; prof. plant physiology, agrl. botany and horticulture since 1931; dir. Fla. Citrus Expt. Sta., 1936-37; dir. division of industrial microbiology, General Mills Research Laboratory, 1942-43. John Simon Guggenheim fellow, 1927-28. Fellow A.A.A.S.; mem. Bot. Soc. America, Am. Chem. Soc., Am. Soc. Plant Physiologists (pres. 1936-37), Minnesota Academy of Science (v.p. 1938-39, pres. 1942-43), Am. Phytopathol. Soc., Ecol. Soc. of America, Bot. Soc. of Czechoslovakia (corr. mem.), Phi Lambda Upsilon, Sigma Xi, Gamma Sigma Delta, Alpha Zeta, Gamma Alpha. Mason. Author: Plant Physiological Chemistry, 1930; A Textbook of Plant Physiology (with A. E. Murneek), 1930; An Annotated Bibliography of Low Temperature Relations of Plants, 1935; Plant Physiology (with A. E. Murneek), 1938. Discoverer of ethylene process of ripening fruits and holder of patents on fruit ripening and coloration. Home: R.F.D. 2, Box 116, Stillwater, Minn. Address: University Farm, St. Paul, Minn. Died Nov. 4, 1945.

HARZA, LEROY FRANCIS, engr.; b. Brookings County, S.D., Feb. 6, 1882; s. William Frederick and Clara Samantha (Jolley) H.; B.S. in M.E., S.D. State Coll., 1901, D.Eng., 1950; B.S. in C.E., U. of Wis., 1906, C.E., 1908; m. Zelma (Davidson) Hoffman, May 27, 1922; 1 son, Richard Davidson, and stepson, Arthur Charles Hoffman. Instr. mathematics, Mich. Agrl. Coll., 1902-04; hydraulic engring., U. of Wis., 1905-06. Cons. engineer investigation, design and construction of dams, hydraulic works, hydroelectric projects, bridges in U.S., Can., Uruguay, Argentina, El Salvador, India, Philippines, France, Iraq. Pres. Harza Engring. Co., Chgo. Awarded Citation, U. Wis., 1949; John Croes Medal, Am. Soc. C.E., 1950. Mem. Am. Soc. C.E., A.S.M.E., Am. Inst. Elec. Engrs., Western Soc. Engrs., Engring. Inst. Can., Tau Beta Pi. Presbyn. Mason. Club: Engineers. Author articles in tech. periodicals. Home: 215 Pierce Rd., Highland Park, Ill. Office: 400 W. Madison St., Chgo. 6. Died Nov. 22, 1953; buried Brookings, S.D.

HASBROUCK, CHARLES ALFRED, civil engr.; b. on farm at Forest Home suburb of Ithaca, N.Y., July 31, 1864; s. Alfred and Sarah (McKinney) H.; grad. Cornell, C.E., 1888; m. June 14, 1893, Mary Fobes, Cresco, Ia. Asst. engr. Detroit Bridge & Iron Co., 1884-88; engr. Am. Bridge Works, Chicago, 1888-1900; contracting mgr. R.R. dept. Western dist. of Am. Bridge Co. since 1900; specialist as bridge and structural engr. Mem. Am. Soc. Civ. Engrs. since 1887, Brit. Instn. Civil Engrs. since 1904. Residence: 4740 Madison Av. Office: 1315 Monadnock Blk., Chicago.

HASCHE, RUDOLPH LEONARD, cons., mfr.; b. Doon, Ia., June 20, 1896; s. Carl Harmann and Clara Belle (Lemon) H.; B.S., Tarkio (Mo.) Coll., LL.D., 1953; M.S., Washington and Jefferson College, 1919, Ph.D., Johns Hopkins, 1924; fellow U. Cal., 1924-25, univs. Berlin and Vienna, 1925-26; m. Blanche Knox, Aug. 25, 1920; 1 dau., Blanche Geraldine (Mrs. Richard P. Clarke). Research chemist for Am. Smelting & Refining Co., 1926-30, supt. research, 1930-31; dir. chem. research A. O. Smith Corp., 1931-34; supt. research and development div. Tenn. Eastman Corp., 1934-43, sci. counsel, 1943-52; pres., chmn. bd. Carbonic Development Corp., 1931—; pres. Hasche Engring. Co., 1950—, Hasche Process Co., 1958—; also pvt. cons. Cons. WPB, 1943, F.E.A., 1945, investigator chem. plants in Germany, 1945. Technical Deferment Com., WPB, 1943. Served in poison gas research dept., C.W.S., U.S. Army, World War. Nat. Research fellow of Rockefeller Found., 1924-25; Internat. Edn. Bd. fellow, 1925-26. Recipient certificate of appreciation Dept. of Army, 1951. Fellow A.A.A.S.; mem. Am. Gas Assn., Am. Inst. C.E., Am. Chem. Soc., Soc. Chem. Industry (London), Am. Petroleum Inst., Am. Soc. Refrigerating Engrs., Phi Beta Kappa, Sigma Xi, Gamma Alpha. Republican. Episcopalian. Clubs: University, Chemists. Author: Plastics, Theory and Practice, 1947. Contbr. to chem. jours. Holder of patents on Hasche process for mfg. dry ice, gas reforming and other chem. and liquefaction process. Home: 1107 Southwest Av. Office: P.O. Box 384, Johnson City, Tenn. Died Jan. 8, 1959.

HASEMAN, CHARLES, prof. mathematics; b. Linton, Ind., Sept. 27, 1880; s. John Diederich and Elizabeth (Schultz) H.; A.B., Ind. U., 1903, A.M., 1906; Ph.D., U. of Göttingen, Germany, 1907; m. Lucile Bernice Ulery, May 28, 1917. Teacher of mathematics, pub. sch., Linton, Ind., 1898-1901; same, high sch., Elwood, Ind., 1904-05; student asst. in mathematics, Ind. U., 1905-06, instr., 1907-08, asst. prof., 1908-09; asso. prof. mathematics and mechanics, U. of Nev., 1909-10, prof. 1910—; dean of men, same university, 1929—. Dir. U. of Nev. Glee Club, 1910-27. Republican. Mason. Rotarian. Author of General Mathematical Analysis, Analytic Geometry, Differential Calculus, Integral Calculus, Applied Mechanics—all mimeographed textbooks. Home: Reno, Nev. Died July 9, 1931.

HASKELL, EUGENE ELWIN, civil engr.; b. Holland, N.Y., May 10, 1855; s. Addison Wells and Sarah (Colby) H.; ed. Forestville, N.Y., Acad.; B.C.E., Cornell, 1879, C.E., 1890; m. Lettie E. Wright, Feb. 4, 1880. With U.S. Lake Survey, Detroit, 1879; Sioux City & St. Paul R.R., 1880; Miss. River Commission, St. Louis, 1880-85; U.S. Coast and Geod. Survey, Washington, 1885-93; U.S. Lake Survey, Detroit, 1893-1906; dean Coll. Civil Engring., Cornell, 1906-21, emeritus; hon. chmn. Engring. Bd. of Review, Sanitary Dist. of Chicago, 1924-25. Mem. Am. Sect. Internat. Waterways Commn., 1906-15. Home: Hamburg, N.Y. Died Jan. 29, 1933.

HASKINS, CARYL DAVIS, electrical engr.; b. Waltham, Mass., May 22, 1867; s. John F. (mech. engr.) and Helen P. (Davis) H.; ed. in U.S. and Eng., including spl. work in London U.; E.E., U. of Vt.; m. Frances J. Parker, Nov. 1894. Elec. engr. with Ferranti, 1888, Gen. Electric Co., 1889, now mgr. lighting dept., Gen. Electric Co. Inventor auto-dirigible torpedo, 1896; volunteered for Spanish War and placed 2d in charge of submarine mining operations in Boston Dist., comdg. vol. electric corps, Boston battalion, 1898. Home; Schenectady, N.Y. Deceased.

HASKINS, CHARLES NELSON, mathematician; b. New Bedford, Mass., May 7, 1874; s. Herbert Kinsley and Sarah Kinsley (Nelson) H.; B.S., Mass. Inst. Tech., 1897; M.S., Harvard Univ., 1899, M.A., 1900, Ph.D., 1901; hon. Sc.D. from Dartmouth College, 1928; m. Edith Delano Dexter, Sept. 4, 1909. Asst. in physics, 1897-98, instr. mathematics, 1902-03, Mass. Inst. Tech.; instr. mathematics, Yale, 1903-04, Cornell, 1904-06; asst. prof. mathematics, U. of Ill., 1906-09; asst. prof. mathematics, 1909-16, prof. since 1916, Dartmouth. Fellow A.A.A.S.; mem. Am. Math. Soc. Republican. Club: Harvard (Boston). Contbr. Trans. Am. Math. Soc., Annals of Mathematics and bulletins of U.S. Govt. Home: Hanover Rd., Lebanon, N.H. Died Nov. 13, 1942.

HASLAM, ROBERT THOMAS, chem. engr.; b. North Adams, Mass., Apr. 3, 1888; s. Robert Henry and Emma Dawson (Lynch) H.; B.S., in Chemical Engring., Mass. Inst. of Tech., 1911; LL.D., University South Carolina, 1953. Asst. in qualitative and quantitative analysis, Mass. Inst. Tech., 1911-12; with Nat. Carbon Co., Cleveland, O., in Research Lab. and as asst. supt., 1912-20; prof. chem. engring., Mass. Inst. Tech., 1920-27, also dir. Research Lab. of Applied Chemistry and dir. Sch. of Chem. Engring. Practice, in charge of course in gas and fuel engrings., 1927-35; v.p. and gen. mgr. Standard Oil Development Co. (subsidiary of Standard Oil Co., N.J.), 1931-35; v.p. Hydro Engring. & Chemical Co.; gen. sales manager, Standard Oil Co. of N.J., 1935-42; v.p., 1937-42; director Plantation Pipe Line Co., 1940-42; dir. Standard Oil Co. (N.J.), 1942-50, v.p., 1945-50; dir., mem. exec. com. Am. Electric Co.; dir. W. R. Grace & Co., Tropical Gas Co., Eurofund, Inc. Mem. Army Sci. Adv. Panel, 1952—. Mem. Corp. Mass. Inst. Tech., 1949—, life mem. 1954—. Decorated Chevalier, French Nat. Order Legion of Honor, 1947. Fellow Inst. of Fuel (Gt. Britain); mem. Am. Inst. Chemical Engrs. (v.p. 1927; dir. 1928-31), Am. Petroleum Inst., Soc. Auto. Engrs., Alpha Chi Sigma, Tau Beta Pi. Clubs: University, 29 (N.Y.); Gatineau Fish and Game, Canada; Baltusral Golf (Springfield, New Jersey); Sarasota Yacht (Sarasota, Florida). Author: Fuels and Combustion (with R. P. Russell), 1926; and one of co-authors of Britain's Fuel Problems. Contbr. Jour. Industrial Engineering and Chemistry, etc. Home: St. Armand's Key, Sarasota, Fla. Office: 7 Hanover Square, N.Y.C. 5. Died Apr. 4, 1961.

HASSELBRING, HEINRICH, botanist; b. at Flint, Mich., Jan. 12, 1875; s. Bernhardt and Augusta (Lange) H.; S.B., in Agr., Cornell U., 1899; Ph.D., U. of Chicago, 1905; unmarried. Asst. in botany, Cornell U., 1899-1900; asst. horticulturist, N.Y. Expt. Sta., 1900-1; plant pathologist, U. of Ill., 1901-3; asst. in botany, U. of Chicago, 1903-7; chief dept. of botany, Estacion Central Agronomica, Santiago de las Vegas, Cuba, 1907-9; with Bur. Plant Industry, U.S. Dept. of Agr., since Apr. 12, 1909. Mem. A.A.A.S., Sigma Xi. Author various articles in Bailey's Cyclopedia American Horticulture, scientific papers on plant physiology and pathology, mag. articles, etc. Address: Bureau of Plant Industry, Dept. of Agr., Washington

HASSKARL, JOSEPH F., engineer; b. Hazleton, Pa., June 23, 1863; s. Rev. William R. (D.D.) and Elizabeth (Lang) H.; student Elmhurst (Ill.) Coll., 1880-83; m. M. Clara Baggy, June 17, 1913. Began as civ. and hydraulic engr., at Chicago, 1884; served as principal or chief engr., Phila. Dist., U.S. Engr. Dept.; dir. Dept. of Wharves, Docks and Ferries, Phila., 1909-12; commr. new water supply for Phila., 1920-24; chmn. Harbor and Navigation Com. of Philadelphia Chamber Commerce. Had charge various dredging enterprises, requiring removal of more than 50,000,000 cubic yds. of material from rivers and harbors; designed and built breakwater at entrance of Delaware Bay; first reinforced concrete pier (fireproof) in America. Republican. Lutheran. Mason. Home: Philadelphia, Pa. Died Mar. 5, 1926.

HASSLER, FREDINAND RUDOLPH, geodesist, mathematician; b. Aarau, Switzerland, Oct. 7, 1770; s. Jakob Hassler; m. Marianne Gaillard, 1798, 9 children. Acting prof. mathematics U.S. Mil. Acad., 1807-09; prof. natural philosophy and mathematics Union Coll., 1809-11; 1st supt. U.S. Coast Survey, 1816-18, 32-43; U.S. supt. weights and measures, 1830-32. Died Phila., Nov. 20, 1843.

HASTINGS, CHARLES SHELDON, physicist; Ph.B., Yale, 1870, Ph.D., 1873. Instr. physics, Yale, 1871-73; later asso. prof. physics, Johns Hopkins; prof. physics, Sheffield Scientific Sch. (Yale), 1884—. Mem. Nat. Acad. Sciences; fellow A.A.A.S. Author (with F. E. Beach) Text-Book on General Physics, 1899; Light—A Consideration of the More Familiar Phenomena of Optics, 1901. Home: New Haven, Conn. Died Feb. 1, 1932.

HASTINGS, EDGAR MORTON, civil engr.; b. Lutherville, Md., May 5, 1882; s. Robert John and Ada (Heilig) H.; student Baltimore City Coll., 1899-1900, Balt. Poly. Inst., 1901-02; hon. alumnus Va. Mil. Inst.; m. Carmen Robertson, Feb. 27, 1908; children—Edgar M., David C. Rod and instrument man, B.&O. R.R., Western Pa. and W.Va., 1901-03; R.F.&P. R.R. Co., Va., 1903-06, resident engr., 1906-20, prin. asst. engr., 1920-22, chief engr. in charge of all engring., design, constrn. signals, communications, 1922—. Dir. Richmond Land Corp. Cons. China Aid Program, Survey Mission to China, 1948. Past chmn. Richmond planning com. and bd. of zoning appeals. Mem. Nat. Tech. Adv. Com., 1940—. Dir. and pres. Richmond Home for Ladies, 1935—. Mem. Am. Soc. C.E. (pres. 1947), Am. Ry. Engr. Assn. (pres. 1939-40), Am. Soc. Testing Materials, Nat. Soc. Profl. Engrs., Engrs. Joint Council (1947-48). Democrat. Methodist. Mason. Clubs: Engineers, Hampton Roads, Central Va. (past pres.), Va. Peninsula, Lions. Home: 515 N. Boulevard, Richmond 20. Office: Broad St. Sta., Richmond 20, Va. Deceased.

HASTINGS, EDWIN GEORGE, bacteriologist; b. Austinburg, O., Aug. 11, 1872; s. of Oramel Pierce and Susan Elizabeth (Rose) H.; B.S., Ohio State U., 1898; M.S., U. of Wis., 1899; Royal Vet. Sch., Munich, Germany; m. Elvira J. Waters, of Austinburg, O., Sept. 16, 1902. Began as teacher and researcher, U. of Wis., 1899, prof. agrl. bacteriology, 1913; bacteriologist, Expt. Sta. Mem. Wis. State Live Stock Sanitary Bd. Conglist. Fellow A.A.A.S.; mem. Soc. Am. Bacteriologists, Sigma Xi, Sigma Alpha Epsilon. Club: University. Author: Agricultural Bacteriology, 1909; Experimental Dairy Bacteriology, 1909; Dairy Bacteriology, 1910. Contbr. to microbiology, 1911. Home: 1906 West Lawn Av., Madison WI

HASTINGS, REUBEN C. M., inventor; b. Hibbardsville, Athens Co., O., May 27, 1867; s. of Prof. William and Mary Jane (Miller) H.; ed. Ohio University, Athens; m. Elizabeth Fuller, of Chauncey, O., Apr. 27, 1892. Inventor Automatic Selective System of Telephony (U.S. patents issued May, 1913, patents also issued in Argentine Republic, Australia, Austria, Belgium, Cape Province, Chile, Denmark, Dominion of Canada, France, Germany, Great Britain, Hungary, Italy, Sweden and Switzerland) whereby inventor claims that 2 persons, by the action of a selecting or master key, may be connected and signaled on a party line circuit for conversation, to exclusion of all others; pres. and gen. mgr. The Internat. Telephone Co. Member Church of Christ. Member Delta Tau Delta Fraternity (Beta Chapter); non-resident mem. of The Franklin Inst. Mason. Home: 1502 Belmont Av. Office: Columbus Savings and Trust Co., Columbus, O.

HASWELL, CHARLES HAYNES, civil, marine and mech. engr.; b. New York, May 22, 1809 (English parentage); grad. Collegiate Inst. of Joseph Nelson; entered engine works of James P. Allaire; designed engines and boilers for U.S. steam frigate Fulton; was 1st chief engr. and engr. in chief U.S.N., 1836-51; designed and operated 1st steam launch; first to introduce zinc in marine boilers and in bottom of iron vessels to arrest oxidation of the plates; mem. navy bd. that designed 6 steam frigates; retired and began private practice; built merchant vessels; designed and constructed ballasted crib, Hart Island; was engr. health dept., Dept. Charities and Correction, trustee New York and Brooklyn bridge; from 1898 cons. engr. bd. public improvements New York, and engr. in charge extension and improvement Riker's Island, L.I. Sound; asst. engr. Bd. of Estimate and Appropriation. Mem. 1855-58, pres., 1858, New York Bd. Councilmen. Author: Mechanics' and Engineers' Book, 1842 (69th edit., 1903); Mechanics' Tables, 1854; Mensuration and Practical Geometry, 1856. Home: New York, N.Y. Died 1907.

HATCH, EDWIN GLENTWORTH, engr.; b. Brooklyn, N.Y., Mar. 25, 1886; s. Edwin Austin (M.D.) and Emilie Jane (Pesinger) H.; M.E. Stevens Inst. of Tech., Hoboken, N.J., 1907; m. Amalia Riches, Apr. 5, 1920; 1 son, Edwin Pesinger. Held engineering position successively with Lackawanna Steel Co., Oakland Chem. Co., Safety Car Heating & Lighting Co., N.Y.C.&H.R. R.R. Co. until 1910; treas. and mgr. Clark Electric & Mfg. Co., 1910-15; cons. engr., Victoria Falls & Transvaal Power Co., serving the Rand Mines in S. Africa, 1915-24; pres. Edwin G. Hatch & Co., Inc., industrial engrs. and financial council specializing in corp. financing. Home: Brooklyn, N.Y. Died Jan. 24, 1933.

HATCH, FREDERICK THOMAS, civil engr.; b. Haverhill, Mass., Nov. 21, 1855; s. Nathaniel and Catherine P. (Harbach) H.; ed. Phillips Acad., Andover, Mass.; m. Alice Gertrude Hill, Aug. 13, 1884; m. 2d, Mrs. Nola P. Underwood, May 9, 1916. Began with engr. corps Pittsburgh, Cincinnati & St. Louis Ry., 1880; became connected with Vandalia R.R. Co., 1894, as supt. Terre Haute & Logansport R.R.; chief engr. Vandalia Line, 1905-17; chief engr. maintenance of way, St. Louis System P.,C.,C.&St.L. R.R., consolidation of Vandalia with P.,C.,C.&St.L. R.R., Jan. 1, 1917, cons. engr. same. Republican. Conglist. Mason. Home: St. Louis, Mo. Died Mar. 9, 1920.

HATCH, JAMES NOBLE, consulting engr.; b. St. Helena, Cal., Jan. 3, 1868; s. Lucius Lucian and Sarilda Berry (Hornback) H.; B.S. in C.E., U. of Mich., 1892, M.E., 1909; m. Lufanna Barber, of Ann Arbor, Mich., Sept. 14, 1893; children—Marion Abagail, James Hadley, Esther Louise. Practiced engring. since 1892; supt. constrn. U.S. pub. bldgs. (post office structures), Treasury Dept., Washington, D.C., 1900-02; engr. in charge of building design and construction, for Sargent & Lundy, Chicago, 1903-14; consulting engr. for pub. utility properties, 1914-21; mem. Chicago Engineering Associates since 1921; dir. and sec.-treas. Electro-Magnetic Tool Co. Mem. Am. Soc. C.E., Western Soc. Engrs., Structural Engrs. Assn. of Ill. (dir.), Chicago Assn. Commerce. Republican. Protestant. Club: Chicago Engineers'. Home: 216 Kedzie St., Evanston, Ill. Office: 717 Mondanock Blk., Chicago, Ill.

HATCH, LLOYD A., chem. engr.; b. Howard. S.D., Mar. 31, 1901; s. Erwin S. and Anna B. (West) H.; Chem. E., U. Minn., 1923; m. Edith L. Munns, Dec. 29, 1924; children—Alice, Meredith, Richard, Shirley. Chief chemist Minn. Mining & Mfg. Co., St. Paul, 1923-28, supt., mineral dept., 1928-32, plant mgr., Wausau, Wis., 1932-35, gen. mgr. Roofing Granules div., 1935-45, v.p. same div., 1945-49, v.p. charge research and product devel., 1949-59, v.p. new product devel., 1959-62, v.p. long range planning, since 1962. Recipient Outstanding Achievement award U. Minn., 1954. Fellow Am. Inst. Chemists; mem. Am. Inst. Chem. Engrs., Am. Soc. Testing Materials, Am. Chem. Soc. A.A.A.S. Club: Engineers (N.Y.C.). Home: 1131 Scheffer, St. Paul 55116. Office: Minnesota Mining & Mfg. Co., St. Paul 55119. Deceased.

HATCHER, ROBERT ANTHONY, pharmacologist; born New Madrid, Mo., Feb. 6, 1868; s. Richard H. and Harriet Hinton (Marr) H.; Ph.G., Phila. Coll. Pharmacy, 1889, Pharm.M., 1929; M.D., Tulane, 1898; D.Sc. in Pharmacy, Columbia, 1929; m. Mary Q. Burton, Dec. 28, 1904; 1 son, Robert Lee. Prof. materia medica, Cleveland Sch. Pharmacy, 1899-1904; demonstrator pharmacology, Western Reserve Medical Coll., 1901-03; instr. pharmacology, Cornell U. Med. Sch., 1904-06; asst. prof. pharmacology and materia medica, 1906-08, prof., 1908-35, prof. emeritus pharmacology, , since 1935. Mem. A.M.A. (mem. council on pharmacy and chemistry), Am. Physiol. Soc., Am. Soc. Biol. Chemists, Am. Soc. Pharmacology and Exptl. Therapeutics, Am. Pharm. Assn., Harvey Soc., N.Y. Acad. Medicine. Republican. Author: (with Torald Sollmann) Textbook of Materia Medica, 1904; (with M. I. Wilbert) Pharmacology of Useful Drugs, 1915. Editor: Useful Drugs, 1934. Contbr. to med. and scientific jours. Home: Flushing, L.I. Office: 1300 York Av., New York. Died Apr. 1, 1944.

HATHAWAY, KING, cons. engr.; b. San Francisco, Calif., Apr. 9, 1878; s. John Dudley and Susan (King) H.; ed. pub. schs. of San Francisco, Calif.; m. Ethel Cramer, in Paris, France, Aug. 12, 1929; children—Pierre, Taylor, Joan. With Midvale Steel Works, Phila., 1896-1901; supt. Payne Engine Co., 1902-04; supt., v.p., mgr. Tabor Mfg. Co., 1904-16; asso. with Dr. F. W. Taylor, 1904-15; lecturer on scientific management, Harvard Grad. Sch. of Business Adminstrn., 1912-17, Wharton Sch., U. of Pa., 1921-22; cons. engr. in foundry operation Industrial Assn. of San Francisco, 1923-26; gen. mgr. Schlage Lock Co., 1927-28; cons. work in Japan and Europe, 1929; cons. engr. Manning, Maxwell & Moore and gen. mgr. Consol. Ashcroft Hancock Co., 1930-32; consultant in orgn. and management, 1906-17, 1919-22, and since 1932; also cons. prof. of scientific management, Stanford U., since 1937. Served as capt. and lt. col. Ordnance Dept., U.S. Army, with A.E.F., 1917-18. Decorated Officier de l'Ordre de l'Etoile Noir. Mem. Masaryk Acad. of Work (Prague), Soc. for Advancement of Management, Am. Soc. Mech. Engrs. Republican. Episcopalian. Contbr. articles to professional societies and jours. Home: 200 Lowell Av., Palo Alto, Calif. Died June 12, 1944.

HATT, WILLIAM KENDRICK, cons. engr.; b. Fredericton, Can., Oct. 10, 1868; s. George and Sarah Elizabeth (Clark) H.; B.A., Univ. of N.B., 1887, M.A., 1898, Ph.D., 1901; C.E., Cornell U., 1891; m. Josephine Appleby, 1897 (died Nov. 18, 1910); children—Kendrick Appleby, Elise, Robert Torrens, Wilhelmina (dec.). Prof. civ. engring., Univ. of N.B., 1891-92; instr. civ. engring., Cornell U., 1892-93; asso. prof. civ. engring., 1893-95, asso. prof. applied mechanics, 1896-1901, prof., 1902-06, prof. civ. engring. and dir. Material Testing Lab., 1907-38, research prof., 1938-39, emeritus since 1939, Purdue. Fuertes Gold Medalist, Cornell Univ., 1903; Turner Medalist, American Concrete Institute, 1929. Mem. Am. Soc. for Testing Materials, Am. Ry. Engring. Assn., Am. Soc. Civil Engrs., Alpha Tau Omega, Chi Epsilon, Sigma Xi and Tau Beta Pi fraternities; pres. Ind. Engring. Soc., 1907-08; pres. Am. Concrete Inst., 1917-19; dir. Advisory Bd. on Highway Research of Nat. Research Council, 1921-23; state engr., Ind. Conservation Dept., 1921-39; mem. Com. on Building Codes Dept. of Commerce, Washington, D.C., 1921-27, chmn., 1928-32. Episcopalian. Author: Manual of Testing Materials (with H. H. Scofield), 1908; Concrete Work (with W. C. Voss), 1921; also about 100 scientific papers on engring. and structural materials. Home: 402 Observatory Lodge, Ann Arbor MI

HATTON, T. CHALKLEY, sanitary engr.; b. Avondale, Pa., Aug. 11, 1860; s. Chalkley and Hannah H.; ed. Maplewood Inst., Delaware Co., Pa.; hon. M.C.E., Pa. Mil. Coll.; m. Catharine E. Hinkson, 1888; 1 dau., Anna Elizabeth (Mrs. R. Horton Norris, Jr.). With engring. dept. S.P.,M.&M. Ry., 1878-82; hydraulic surveys, Dept. of Pub. Works, Dominion of Can., 1882-83; asst. engr. City of Wilmington, Del., 1883-89; chief engr. street and sewer dept., Wilmington, 1890-1900; cons. practice, water works, sanitation and street improvements, 1898-1914; chief engr. Sewerage Commn., City of Milwaukee, Wis., 1914-27; chief engr. Metropolitan Sewerage, County of Milwaukee, 1921-27; private practice as consulting engr., 1927—. Republican. Episcopalian. Home: Milwaukee, Wis. Deceased.

HAUPT, HERMAN, engr.; b. Phila., Mar. 26, 1817; s. Jacob H.; grad. West Point, 1835; entered army but resigned, Oct. 1835; prof. civil engring., Pa. Coll., 1844-47; gen. supt. chief engr. and dir. Pa. R.R. and engr. Hoosac Tunnel, 1847-61; col., brig. gen. and chief of bureau, U.S. Mil. Rys., in Civil War; gen. mgr. Piedmont Air Line, 1875; later engr. Tide-Water Pipe Line Co. and gen. mgr. Northern Pacific R.R. Author: General Theory of Bridges, 1852; Military Bridges, 1863. Died 1905.

HAUPT, LEWIS MUHLENBERG, civil engr.; b. Gettysburg, Pa., Mar. 21, 1844; s. Gen. Herman and Ann Cecilia (Keller) H.; ed. Lawrence Scientific Sch. (Harvard); grad. U.S. Mil. Acad., 1867; hon. M.A., U. of Pa.; Sc.D., Muhlenberg; LL.D., Pa. Coll.; m. Isabella Christiana Cromwell, June 26, 1873 (died 1912); children—Eva Ruth (dec.), Elsie Catherine (dec.), Walter Cromwell (dec.), Bessie May, Eleanor (dec.), Florence Belle, Susan Gertrude, Edna Schaeffer, Lewis Herman. Second lt. engrs. U.S.A., June 17, 1867; engr. officer, survey of Great Lakes, till Feb. 1869; 5th mil. dist. Texas, 1869; resigned, Sept. 20, 1869; topog. engr. Fairmount Park, Phila., to 1872; prof. civ. engring., U. of Pa., 1872-92; practices his profession in Phila. In charge of hydrog. survey of Delaware River, 1873, Franklin Inst. Drawing Sch., 1874-79, triangulation of Eastern Pa., 1875-80. Member of Nicaragua Canal Commn., 1897-99, Isthmian Canal Commn., 1899-1902; pres. Colombia-Cauca Arbitration, 1897; chief engr. survey for ship canal across N.J., 1894; consulting engr. Lake Erie & Ohio River Ship Canal, etc.; prof. civil engring., Franklin Inst. Editor of Am. Engineering Register, 1885-86. Inventor of "Reaction Breakwater" for creating channels through ocean bars, 1887, successfully applied by the U.S. Premiums: Magellanic, by Am. Philos. Soc., 1887; Nat. Export Expn., 1899; Paris Expn., 1900; Elliott Cresson gold medal, Franklin Inst., 1901; also was awarded gold and silver medals, St. Louis Expn., 1904. Patented automatic devices for reclaiming eroded beaches by hooked jetties, 1911, since applied on the L.I. and N.J. coasts. Saved Barnegat Light, 1920, by two pile jetties, also beaches at Sea Isle City, Cape May Point, Surf City, Stone Harbor, Townsend's Inlet, Beach Haven, etc. Author: Physical Phenomena of Harbor Entrances (prize essay American Philos. Society), 1887; Canals and Their Economic Relation to Transportation, 1890; A Move for Better Roads, 1891; The Nation and the Waterways; The Miss. River Problems; Opening of

Aransas Pass, Tex.; The New York Entrance. Home: Bala-Cynwyd, Pa. Died Mar. 10, 1937.

HAUSER, ERNST A(LFRED), educator, consultant; b. Vienna, Austria, July 20, 1896; s. Alfred C. (dec.) and Alice (Sobotka) H.; ed. K.K. Akademisches Gymnasium (Vienna); Ph.D., U. of Vienna, 1921; Sc.D. (hon.), Worcester Polytech. Inst., 1952; m. Vera M. Fischer, Apr. 8, 1922; children—Ernst F., Wolf Dieter, George W. Came to U.S., 1935, naturalized, 1940. Asst., U. Goettingen, 1921-22. res. chemist, 1922-25; chief chemist, Colloid Labs., Metallges, A.G., Frankfurt am Main, Germany, 1925-32, Semperit, Vienna, 1932-35; non-res. asso. prof. chem. engring. Mass. Inst. Tech., 1928-29, res. asso. prof. chem. engring., 1935-48, prof. chem. engring. 1948-56, dir. Div. Cooloid Chemistry, Dept. Chem. Engring.; vis. prof. colloid chemistry Worcester Poly. Inst. 1948-52. Served as capt., Austrian Army, 1914-18; recipient citations and honors. Fellow Am. Inst. Chemists, A.A.A.S., Royal Inst. Rubber Industry (London, Eng.); mem. Am. Chem. Soc. (past chmn. Div. Colloid Chemistry), Nat. Research Council. Am. Inst. Chem. Engrs., Soc. Chem. Industry, Sigma Xi, Alpha Chi Sigma. Episcopalian. Club: Chemists (N.Y.C.). Author: Latex, 1927; The Colloid Chemistry of the Rubber Industry, 1928; Handbook of Rubber Technology, 1925; Colloidal Phenomena, 1939; Experiments in Colloid Chemistry, 1940; Silicic Science, 1955; also many sci. publs. in fields of rubber, clays, theoretical and applied colloid science. Home: 15 Robinson St., Cambridge 38, Mass. Died Feb. 10, 1956; buried Cathedral of the Pines, N.H.

HAUSMAN, LEON AUGUSTUS, educator, ornithologist, trichologist; b. New Haven, Nov. 9, 1888; s. Augustus C. and Ella Amanda (Allen) H.; ed. Mt. Hermon Sch., 1910; A.B., Cornell U., 1914, A.M., 1916, Ph.D., 1919; m. Ethel Hinckley, June 1915. Instr. biology Cornell, 1941-42; instr. zoöl. Rutgers, 1922-25; prof. zool. N.J. Coll. Women (Rutgers), 1925-55 emeritus prof. zoology, 1955; cons. ornithologist N.J. Exptl. Sta. (Rutgers) since 1928; lectr. ornithology, biology since 1922; tchr. biology, ornithology, Bates Coll., summer sessions, 1927-32. Mem. Allegheny Sch. Nat. History (bd. advisors 1939), Phi Beta Kappa, Sigma Xi, Am. Soc. Zoöl., Am. Ornith. Union, N.J. Audubon Soc., S.A.R., Monadnock Region Assn. (N.H.). Republican. Episcopalian. Clubs: Appalachian Mountain (Boston), Stanton Bird (Lewiston, Me.); Harvard Faculty. Author: latest publs.: Beginner's Guide to the Seashore, 1949, to Freshwater Life, 1950, to Attracting Birds, 1951; Bird Hiking, 1954; Birds of Prey, 1966; Big Book of Stars, 1955; The Bird Book, 1955; Illustrated Book of the Sea, 1959; La Mer, French edit. 1960; contbr. profl. jours., Ency. Brit.; contbg. editor Compton's Ency. Home: Fitzwilliam, N.H. Died Feb. 2, 1966; bequeathed body to Dartmouth Med. Coll.

HAUSMAN, LOUIS, physician, educator; born N.Y.C., Apr. 30, 1891; s. Joseph and Fannie (Dalmatz) H.; M.D., Cornell U., 1916; m. Esther May Hausman, Jan. 14, 1925. Intern Mt. Sinai Hosp., 1916-18, Manhattan State Hosp. Ward's Island, 1920; asst. psychiatrist Phipps Psychiatric Clinic, Johns Hopkins Hosp., Balt., 1921-22; asso. neuroanatomist Cornell, 1922-39, prof. clin. medicine (neurology) med. sch., 1945-58, prof. clin. medicine (neurology) emeritus, 1959-72; dir. neurological service 2d (Cornell) Med. Div. Bellevue Hosp., 1950-56; asso. attending physician N.Y. Hosp., 1945-56; clinical prof. neurpsy med. coll. N.Y.U. since 1945. Mem. Assn. Research Nervous and Mental Disease, Am. Assn. Anatomists, Harvey Soc., Am. Psychiat. Assn., New York Neurological Society (pres. 1961-62), A.M.A., Am. Neurological Assn. Author: Clinical Neuroanatomy, Neurophysiology and Neurology with a Method of Brain Reconstruction, 1958; Atlas III: Illustrations of the Nervous System, 1961. Home: New York City NY Died Dec. 7, 1972.

HAUSMANN, ERICH, educator, coll. dean; b. Solingen, Germany, Feb. 27, 1886; s. Hugo and Anna (Reutershan) H.; B.S., Cooper Union, N.Y., 1907, E.E., 1914; E.E., Poly. Inst. Bklyn., 1908; M.S., N.Y. U., 1910, Sc.D., 1911; m. Augusta C. Kohlhaas, Nov. 27, 1911; 1 dau. Helen H. Thurber. Electrician with Willyoung & Gibson Co. Elec. Testing Labs. and Nat. Electric Signal Co., 1904-07; instr. physics and elec. engring., 1908-12, asst. prof., 1912-15, asso. prof., 1915-18, prof. elec. communication, 1918-37, prof. physics since 1918, sec. faculty, 1917-23, dean grad. study, 1929-44, registrar, 1944-49, dean coll. since 1944, Poly Inst.; v.p. dept. electricity, Bklyn. Inst. Arts and Scis., 1909-21, pres., 1921-29; mem. grad. faculty N.Y. U., 1911-16, and in charge dept. of physics, summer 1912. Fellow Am. Inst. E.E., A.A.A.S., Am. Phys. Soc.; mem. N.Y. State and Nat. Socs. Profl. Engrs., N.Y. Elec. Soc. (pres. 1924-25), Soc. for Promotion Engring. Edn. Conglist. Author: Electric Wave Propagation and Distortion Along Conductors, 1911; Telegraph Engineering, 1915; Dynamo Electric Machinery, 1924; Elements of Electricity, 1943. Joint Author: Alternating Current Machines, 1908; Direct Current Machines, 1910; Electric Traction and Transmission Engineering, 1912; Physics Laboratory Experiments, 1917; Physics, 1935. Editor Swoope's Lessons in Practical Electricity since 1920, Radio Phone Receiving, 1922. Mem. State Bd. Examiners for Profl. Engrs. Home: 1405 Dorchester Rd., Bklyn. Died Feb. 22, 1962.

HAUSSMANN, ALFRED CARL, physicist; b. Phila., Pa., Oct. 11, 1897; s. Carl Christian and Martha Louisa (Kaiser) H.; A.B., Lehigh U., 1919; A.M., U. of Rochester, 1922; Ph.D., U. of Chicago (fellow, 1926), 1927; m. Marie Cameron Roberts, Apr. 27, 1920; children—Winifred Anne, Martha Agnes, Alfred Carl II. Instructor Lehigh U., 1919-20; assistant professor physics, Hobart Coll., Geneva, N.Y., 1920-22, chairman science div.; Prendergast professor physics and astronomy since 1922; consultant and physicist, Naval Research Lab., Anacostia, summer 1940. Supervisor of radio, Geneva Police Dept., since 1937. Fellow A.A.A.S.; mem. Am. Assn. Physics Teachers, Am. Assn. Univ. Profs., Physical Soc., Optical Soc.; Phi Beta Kappa, Sigma Xi. Republican. Presbyterian. Club: University. Contbr. articles on spectroscopy, properties of matter and electronics to sci. jours. Home: 214 White Springs Rd., Geneva, N.Y. 14456. Died Mar. 30, 1963; buried Glenwood Cemetery, Geneva.

HAUT, IRVIN CHARLES, scientist; b. Mitchell, S.D., June 7, 1906; s. Adolph and Adeline (Sieg) H.; B.S., U. Ida., 1928; M.S., State Coll. Wash., 1930; Ph.D., U. Md., 1933; m. Marie K. Mahlandt, Dec. 26, 1935 (div. 1961); 1 son, William Frederick; m. 2d, Mary Jane Hurt Noonan, Apr. 16, 1966; step-children—Richard, Thomas, Douglas. Asst. prof., asst. horticulturist Okla. A. & M. Coll., 1933-36; asso. prof., asso. horticulturist Agrl. Expt. Sta., U. Md., 1936-46, prof., head dept. horticulture, horticulturist Agrl. Expt. Sta., U. Md., 1946-72, asst. dir. Expt. Sta., 1950-51, dir., 1951-72, state horticulturist, Md., 1954-72. Mem. A.A.A.S., Am. Soc. Hort. Sci., Wash. Acad. Scis., Sigma Xi, Alpha Zeta, Pi Alpha Xi, Phi Sigma, Phi Kappa Phi (past pres. Md.). Lutheran. Home: Silver Spring MD Died Aug. 21, 1972; buried Montgomery PA

HAVAS, GEORGE, engineer; b. Budapest, Hungary, Nov. 12, 1903; s. Emil and Sara (Fisch) H.; diploma engring. Technische Hochschule, Stuttgart, Germany, 1924; Dr. Engring., Rensselaer Polytechnic Inst., 1959; m. Judith Berta Dobai, Sept. 23, 1926; children—Eva Judith (Mrs. Donald E. Robinson), George Paul, Judith Anne. Came to U.S., 1931, naturalized, 1938. Asst. engr. Gen. Sugar Corp., Cuba, 1925; resident engr. Eastern Cuba Sugar Corp., Central Velasco, Cuba, 1926-28; office engr., chief engr. Kaiser Paving Co., Cuba, 1929-31; estimator Six Companies, Inc., Hoover Dam., 1932-34; chief engr. Columbia Constrn. Co., Bonneville Dam, 1935; chief engr. Henry J. Kaiser Co., Oakland, 1935-42, v.p. since 1944; chief engr. Kaiser Co., Inc., 1942-44; gen. mgr. Overseas Constrn. div., 1958—; v.p., dir. engring. Kaiser Industries Corp., 1960—; v.p., dir. Consol. Builders, Inc., 1952—. Fellow Am. Soc. C.E.; mem. Am. Assn. Engrs., Soc. Am. Mil. Engrs., Am. Ordnance Assn., Am. Iron and Steel Inst., Am. Inst. Mining, Metall. and Petroleum Engrs., Assn. Iron and Steel Engrs. Presbyn. Mason. Clubs: Commonwealth, Engineers (San Francisco). Home: 21 Sharon Av., Piedmont 11, Cal. Office: 300 Lakeside Dr., Oakland 12, Cal. Died Mar. 16, 1962; buried Oakland.

HAVENHILL, L.D., (ha'ven-hill), educator; b. Newark, Ill., Apr. 5, 1870; s. Asher D. and Ermina (Crum) H.; Ph.C., U. Mich., 1893, Ph.M., 1894, M.S. (hon.), 1940; B.S., U. Kan., 1903; m. Myra Buck, June 8, 1897; children—Marshall Asher, Robert Samuel. Pharm. chemist, Honolulu, Hawaii, 1894-95; chemist Chgo. & Aurora Smelting & Refining Co., 1896-99; asst. prof. pharmacy U. Kan., 1899-1906, asso. prof., 1906-07, prof. pharmacy, 1908-25, 40-45, also acting dean, 1925-26, dean, prof. pharmacy and materia medica, 1926-40, prof. emeritus, 1945—; fed. food and drug inspection chemist N.Y.C., 1907-08; chief drug lab. Kan. Bd. Health, 1909-25, dir., 1925-40. Mem. 10th and 11th revision coms. U.S. Pharmacopoeia, auxiliary mem. 12th rev. com. Pres. Am. Assn. Colls. of Pharmacy, 1933-34. Mem. Am. Chem. Soc. (pres. Kansas City sect. 1914), Am. (v.p. 1914), Kan. (hon.) pharm. assns., Kan. Acad. Sci. (pres. 1918), Phi Delta Chi, Sigma Xi. Republican. Conglist. Author: Essentials of Pharmacy (Sayre and Havenhill), 1918; Pharmaceutical Arithmetic, 1912; State Boards of Pharmaceutical Questions, 1917. Home: 1539 Vermont St., Lawrence, Kan. Died Apr. 29, 1950.

HAWES, HARRIET BOYD (MRS. CHARLES HENRY HAWES), archaeologist; b. at Boston, Oct. 11, 1871; d. Alexander and Harriet Fay (Wheeler) Boyd; A.B., Smith Coll., 1892, M.A., 1901, L.H.D., 1910; student, 1896-97, fellow, 1898-1900, Am. Sch. of Classical Studies, Athens, Greece; m. Charles Henry Hawes, Eng., Mar. 3, 1906; children—Alexander Boyd, Mary Nesbit. Began archaeol. explorations in Greece, 1896, under fellowship of Am. Sch. of Classical Studies, Athens; excavated citadel and tombs of Iron Age (1000 B.C.) at Kavousi, Crete, 1900; as rep. Am. Exploration Soc., Phila., discovered and excavated town and palace of Bronze Age (1600 B.C.) at Gournia, Crete, 1901, 03, 04. Red Cross nurse in Turko-Grecian War, 1897, Spanish-Am. War, 1898; conducted relief work amont Serbians, in Corfu, 1915-16; organizer and first dir. of Smith College Relief Unit in dept. of Somme, France, 1917. Life mem. Archaeol. Inst. America. Red Cross decoration from Queen Olga of Greece. Episcopalian. Author: Gournia, Vasiliki and Other Prehistoric Sites on the Isthmus of Hierapetra, Crete (with others), 1908; Crete, the Forerunner of Greece (with C. H. Hawes), 1909. Lecturer in pre-Christian art, Wellesley Coll., 1920-36; active in work for New Economics, 1937—. Home: 2 Belfield Rd., Alexandria, Va. Died Mar. 31, 1945.

HAWGOOD, HARRY, hydraulic engr.; b. Derbyshire, Eng., Apr. 28, 1853; s. William and Sarah A. (Pike) H.; ed. City of London Sch.; studied civ. and mech. engring. as student on municipal water works and in shipbuilding yard; m. Harriet E. McWain, 1887 (died 1927). Came to U.S., 1880, naturalized citizen, 1895. Asst. engr. maintenance and constrn. govt. rys., Cape of Good Hope, S. Africa, 1874-79; asst. engr. of constrn., C.&N.W. Ry., Madison, Wis., 1880-81; locating engr., Utah Northern Ry., 1881-83; resident engr. Ore. Ry. & Navigation System, 1884-85; in pvt. practice, Portland, Ore., 1885-88; resident engr., S.P. Ry., 1888-95; chief engr. of location and constrn., San Pedro, Los Angeles & Salt Lake R.R., 1900-04; cons. hydraulic engr., Los Angeles, 1895—. Republican. Episcopalian. Home: South Pasadena, Calif. Died Jan. 3, 1931.

HAWK, PHILIP BOVIER, chemist; b. East Branch, N.Y., July 18, 1874; s. Ransom Riant and Ellen (Miller) H.; B.S., Wesleyan U., Conn., 1898, Sc.D. (hon.), 1949; M.S., Yale 1902; Ph.D., Columbia, 1903; m. Ellen Henrietta Moore, 1905 (div.); children—Ellen M., Philip Bovier; m. 2d, Gladys Taylor Lynch. Asst. to Prof. W. O. Atwater, Wesleyan U., 1898-1900; to Prof. W. J. Gies, Coll. Phys. and Surg. (Columbia), 1901-03; demonstrator physiol. chemistry, dept. medicine U. Pa., 1903-07; prof. physiol. chemistry U. Ill., 1907-12; prof. same and toxicology Jefferson Med. Coll., Phila., 1912-22; lectr. nutrition U. Cal., summer 1924; dir., 1925-26, pres. 1926-58 Food Research Labs., Inc., N.Y. Mem. 1st Conn. Vol. Inf., Spanish-Am. War; served on coast def., Ft. Preble, Me., later, Camp Alger. Lawn tennis champion, Del., 1905, Conn., 1907-09, Central N.J., 1907-09; vet. lawn tennis champion U.S., 1921, 22, 23; chmn. ranking com. U.S. Lawn Tennis Assn., 1908-09, 30, mem. exec. com., 1909, internat. play com., 1930, Davis Cup com., 1931. Mem. A.M.A., A.A.A.S., Am. Chem. Soc., several other nat., state and local profl. and sci. assns., orgns. Del. to U.S. Pharmacopoeial Conv., 1930. Mason. Clubs: West Side Tennis, Cynwyd (Phila.); Surf, La Gorce Country, Yale (Miami Beach). Author books, research reports, abstracts, sects. books, primarily in field biochemistry. Asst. editor Chem. Abstract. Contbr. to many sci., popular jours. Home: 750 W. 50th St., Miami Beach, Fla. Died Sept. 13, 1966.

HAWKESWORTH, ALAN SPENCER, clergyman; b. New Orleans, Aug. 10, 1867; s. William Colomb and Gertrude (Victor) H.; taken to England at 4 yrs. of age; ed. Ch. Missionary Coll., London; unmarried. Went to San Antonio, Tex., 1891; ordained deacon P.E. Ch., 1892; went to Buenos Aires, S.A.; ordained priest, 1894; English chaplain, Sao Paulo and Santos, Brazil, 1893-97; rector, Georgetown, St. Vincent, British W.I., 1897, Sheridanville, Pittsburgh, 1905-17. Mathematician in Bur. of Ordnance, Navy Dept., 1917-23. Has traveled extensively in nearly all countries of world; passed through 4 revolutions in S.A., and saw heavy fighting in W.I. (Spanish Main) and China Seas. Fellow A.A.A.S.; perpetual fellow Circolo Matematico di Palermo, 1923; life fellow Royal Society of Arts (England); mem. of Philosophical Society of Washington, Washington Soc. Engrs.; mem. 4th Internat. Math. Congress, Rome, 1908. Mason. Author: Identity of Hebrew and Aryan Roots, 1896; De Incarnatione Verbi Dei, 1897; also various brochures on theol. subjects. Lecturer on philosophy. Has discovered and published nearly 100 new theorems in geometrical conics. Address: 1216 Madison St. N.W., Washington, D.C. Died Oct. 31, 1942.

HAWKINS, J(OHN) DAWSON, chemist, metallurgist; b. Phila., Pa., Jan. 13, 1868; s. Edward Hunter and Mary Anne (Cover) H.; B.S. and P.C., U. of Pa., 1887; m. Mary Salisbury Robbins, of Denver, Colo., Nov. 15, 1898; children—Jeannette Salisbury, John Dawson. Chemist, Globe Smelting & Refining Co., Denver, Colo., 1888-92; supt. Holden Smelting & Milling Co., Aspen, 1892-93, Lawrence Gold Extraction Co., Cripple Creek, 1894, El Paso Reduction Co., Cripple Creek Dist., 1894-96, Colo.-Phila. Reduction Co., Colorado Springs, 1896-1901, Standard Milling & Smelting Co., Colo. Springs, 1899-1901; gen. supt., 1901-06, gen. mgr., 1906-07, pres. 1907-12, U.S. Reduction & Refining Co., Colorado Springs. Mem. Am. Inst. Mining Engrs., Franklin Inst. (Phila.). Republican. Unitarian. Clubs: El Paso (Colorado Springs); Denver (Denver). Home: Broadmoor Hotel. Office: Mining Exchange Bldg., Colorado Springs, Colo.

HAWKINS, LAURENCE ASHLEY, elec. engr.; b. Pittsfield, Mass., Mar. 22, 1877; s. William J. and Harriet E. (Foxcroft) H.; B.A., Williams Coll., Williamstown, Mass., 1897, Sc.D., 1944; B.S., Mass. Inst. Tech., 1899; m. Florence Kellogg, June 12, 1902; children—Laurence K., Elizabeth (Mrs. Raymond E. Booth); m. 2d, Ruth Kellogg, Aug. 10, 1910; m. 3d, Ann D. Krebs, Dec. 16, 1931. Elec. engr. Stanley Elec. Mfg. Co., Pittsfield, Mass., 1899-1903; asst. patent atty., patent dept. Gen. Electric Co., Schenectady, 1903-08, engr. ry. signal dept., 1908-11, exec. engr. research lab., 1912-45, cons., 1945-48, retired; pres. Mahwak Development Service, Inc. Mem., past pres. Boy Scouts Council. Mem. Am. Inst. E.E. (life), Illuminating

Engring. Soc., Theta Delta Chi, Phi Beta Kappa, Sigma Xi. Clubs: Mohawk, Mohawk Golf, Rotary (Schenectady). Awarded Order of Ky. Colonels. Contbr. articles and lectures on indsl. research. Home: 1130 Wendell Av., Schenectady. Died May 15, 1958; buried Pittsfield, Mass.

HAWLEY, JOHN BLACKSTOCK, hydraulic engr.; b. Red Wing, Minn., May 27, 1866; s. Augustine Boyer (M.D.) and Harriet Bowman (Blackstock) H.; B.S., U. of Minn., 1887; M.S., Tex. Christian U., 1926, hon. D.Sc., 1938; m. Sue A. Terrell, Apr. 11, 1895; children—Judith Terrell, John Blackstock, Harriet Elizabeth, George Maxwell Blackstock. Engr., Water Bd., St. Paul, Minn., 1887-89; pvt. practice, Ft. Worth, 1890-97; city engr., Ft. Worth, 1897-1907; pres. Gen. Construction Co., 1909-17, also cons. engr.; pvt. practice, 1920-22; mem. Hawley & Sands, water supply and sanitary engrs., 1923, alone, 1923-27; mem. Hawley & Freese, 1927-29, Hawley, Freese & Nichols, 1930-38; consulting hydraulic and san. engr., 1938—. Major engrs., World War, comdg. 503d Engrs., A.E.F., in France, hdqrs. St. Nazaire; also engr. in charge water supply and sanitation, Base Sect. No. 1; hon. discharged Apr. 1919. Mem. Governor's Advisory Council Engrs. (Tex.), 1922-24; mem. Engineering Board of Review, Sanitary District of Chicago, 1924-25; mem. engr. advisory bd., 1924, asso. in biol. research, 1926-29, Texas Christian U., Fort Worth. Mason. Home: Ft. Worth, Tex. Died Jan. 9, 1941.

HAWORTH, ERASMUS, geologist; b. on farm nr. Indianola, Ia., Apr. 17, 1855; s. Elwood and Matilda (Folger) H.; B.S., U. of Kan., 1881, M.S., 1884; Ph.D., Johns Hopkins, 1888; m. Ida E. Huntsman, Mar. 26, 1889; children—Henry Huntsman, Paul Eugene, Rose Elizabeth, Margaret Josephine. Teacher in coll., 1883—, except 1 yr., 1887-88; prof. geology and mineralogy, U. of Kan., 1892-1920; doing commercial expert work in geology. Organized Kan. State Geol. Survey, 1894, state geologist to 1915; has done much professional work for U.P. R.R. Co. in Wyo. and Kan., and for pvt. cos. in Mo., Kan., Ark., Oklahoma, etc.; connected with U.S. Geol. Survey for yrs.; recently has devoted much time to economic geology. Fellow and life mem. Geol. Soc. America; life mem. Kan. Acad. Science. Wrote vols. 1, 2, 3, 8, and Bulletin 1 on Well Waters of Kansas, 1895-1904, and parts volumes 5 and 9, Reports Kan. State Geol. Survey, and ann. reports Mineral Statistics of Kan., 1897-1904. Home: Ridgewood, N.J. Died Nov. 17, 1932.

HAWXHURST, ROBERT, JR., mining engr., geologist; b. San Francisco, Calif., June 19, 1875; s. Robert and Kate (Stephens) H.; both parents of English descent, and of American Colonial ancestry dating from 1636; ed. U. of Calif., Stanford U. Engr., geol. with various mining, oil and ry. cos., in Central and South America, Hawaii, China, Malay States and East Indies, 1894-1905; gen. mgr. Eden Mining Co., Nicaragua, 1916-19; cons. engr. and geologist, San Francisco, since 1919. Fellow A.A.A.S.; mem. Am. Soc. Civil Engineers, Am. Inst. Mining and Metall. Engineers (past chmn. San Francisco Sect.), San Francisco Engring. Council (1938-41), Seismol. Soc. America, California Academy Sciences, Am. Geophysical Union, Society of California Pioneers, Society Geologie de France, Le Conte Geologists Club. Republican. Episcopalian. Mason. Club: Engineers of San Francisco (past pres.). Home: 2 Presidio Terrace. Office: Crocker First National Bank Building San Francisco

HAY, EARL DOWNING, prof. engring.; b. New Goshen, Ind., Sept. 19, 1886; s. Walter Bruce and Valora Adela (Downing) H.; student Ind. U., 1905-06; B.S., Rose Poly. Inst., Terre Haute, Ind., 1910, M.S., 1915, M.E., 1921; grad. student U. of Wis., 1911-12; m. Bessie Louise Whipp, Aug. 14, 1913; children—Flavia Valora (Mrs. Charles Hazen), Charrie Anne (Mrs. Thurman Kepner), Helen Louise (Mrs. Jack Richardson), David Earl. Designer Nat. Malleable Castings Co., Indianapolis, 1910-11; design instructor, Univ. of Wis., Coll. of Engring., 1911-13; head dept. of design, Oshkosh (Wis.) State Teachers Coll., 1913-18; asso. in design, U. of Ill. Coll. of Engring., 1918-20; dean, Coll. of Engring., Des Moines (Ia.) U., 1920-24; dean, Coll. of Engring. Univ. of Wyo., 1924-28; head depts. of mechanics and industrial engineering, University of Kansas, 1928-46; head design dept. of mechanical engring., Iowa State Coll. since 1946. State representative to World Power Conf., Washington, D.C., 1936; mem. Airport Bd., Lawrence, Kan. Sec., mem. State Registration Board for Professional Engrs. Licensed professional engr., Kan. and Iowa. Mem. Am. Soc. Mech. Engrs. (chairman Kansas City Sect., 1939-40), secretary-treasurer, Central Iowa Section, 1946-47, chairman, Central Iowa section, 1948-49), Soc. for Engineering Education (pres. Kan.-Neb. section, 1935, 1941), Engrs. Council Professional Development (mem. accrediting com.), Kan. Engring. Society, Tau Beta Pi, Phi Kappa Phi, Pi Tau Sigma, Tau Omega, Theta Tau. Republican. Methodist. Co-author: Trade Foundations, 1918; Education Through Woodworking, 1923. Contbr. articles and fiction to popular science publs., also tech. jours. Home: 523 Beech Av., Ames, Ia. Died Jan. 1, 1953.

HAY, OLIVER PERRY, vertebrate paleontologist; b. Saluda, Ind., May 22, 1846; s. Robert and Margaret (Crawford) H.; A.B., Eureka (Ill.) Coll., 1870, A.M., 1873; Yale, 1876-77; Ph.D., Ind. U., 1884; m. Mary Emily Howsmon, of Eureka, Ill., June 30, 1870; children—William Perry, Mrs. Mary Minnick, Frances Steele, Robert Howsmon. Prof. natural sciences Eureka Coll., 1870-72, Oskaloosa (Ia.) Coll., 1874-76; prof. biology and geology, Butler Coll., Indianapolis, 1879-92; asst. curator zoölogy, Field Mus. Natural History, Chicago, 1895-97; asst. and asso. curator vertebrate paleontology, Am. Mus. Natural History, New York, 1901-07; engaged in pvt. investigations in vertebrate paleontology, 1907-11; research asso., 1912-17, and associate, 1917—, retired, Carnegie Institution of Washington, investigating history of Pleistocene vertebrata of N. America. Asst. Geol. Survey of Ark., 1884-88, of Ind., 1891-94, 1911-12, of Ia., 1911-13; asso. editor American Geologist, 1902-05. Author: Bibliography and Catalogue of the Fossil Vertebrata of North America, 1902; The Fossil Turtles of North America, 1908; Pleistocene Period in Indiana and its Vertebrates, 1912; Pleistocene Mammals of Iowa, 1914; Pleistocene and its Vertebrates, East Mississippi River, 1923; and of Middle Region of N.A., 1924; Pleistocene of Western Region, 1927; Second Bibliography and Catalogue of the Fossil Vertebrata of North America, Vol. I, 1929, Vol. II, 1930. Home: Washington, D.C. Died Nov. 2, 1930.

HAY, WILLIAM PERRY, biologist; b. Eureka, Ill., Dec. 8, 1872; s. Oliver Perry and Mary Emily (Howsmon) H.; B.S., Butler U., Ind., 1890, M.S., 1891; nr. Annie Aletha McKnew, Dec. 19, 1902. Teacher zoölogy, Central High Sch., Washington, 1892-98, biology, 1898-99; head dept. biology, Washington high schs., 1899-01; asst. prof. zoölogy, Columbian, 1898-99; prof. biology and geology, Howard U., 1901-07; head dept. biology and chemistry, Washington high schs., since Sept., 1907. Lecturer on zoölogy, Georgetown U., 1898; engaged in investigations for U.S. Bur. of Fisheries, 1900-15. Contbr. to various publs. on zoöl. subjects. Fellow A.A.A.S.; mem. Biol. Soc. Washington (pres. 1916-17), Washington Acad. Sciences, Nat. Fisheries Soc., Washington Biologists' Field Club (pres. 1901-04, 1915-16). Home: Kensington, Md. Died Jan. 26, 1947.

HAYDEN, ARTHUR GUNDERSON, cons. civil engr.; b. Akron, O., Oct. 10, 1874; s. Charles Albert and Helen M. (Genderson) H.; A.B., Ripon Coll., 1898, hon. D.Sc., 1951; S.B., Mass. Inst. Tech., 1901; m. Florence Ketcham, June 1, 1905; children—Helen Gertrude, George Gunderson, Robert Riggs. Structural detailer Am. Bridge Co. and McClintic-Marshall Constrn. Co., Pitts., 1901-04; structural designer and asst. engr. N.Y. State Barge Canal, 1904-20; devised method of reinforcing the Mohawk River Bridge dams without building falsework; chief designing engr. Bronx Pkwy. Commn., 1920-1926 and Westchester County Park Commn., 1925-37, in charge designing dept.; cons. civil engr. engaged in design of bridges and grade separation projects. Developed design and constrn. of rigid frame bridge. Chmn., N.Y. Engrs. Com. Student Guidance 1937-42; mem. com. student guidance and selection Engrs. Council for Profl. Devel., 1940-1947. Mem. Am. Soc. C.E. (dir. met. sect. 1933-35; mem. various coms.), Nat. Soc. Profl. Engrs., N.Y. State Soc. Profl. Engrs. past pres. Ripon College Club of N.Y. Episcopalian. Author: The Rigid Frame Bridge, 1932; also sects. books. Contbr. to engring. mags. Lectr. Home: St. Michaels, Md. 21663. Died Mar. 18, 1964.

HAYDEN, EDWARD EVERETT, naval officer; b. Boston, Apr. 14, 1858; s. William and Louise Annie (Dorr) H.; grad. U.S. Naval Acad., 1879; m. Kate Reynolds, Dec. 12, 1882; children—Reynolds, Herbert Bainbridge, William (dec.), Dorothy, Alfred Dorr, Mary Bainbridge. Promoted through grades to rear adm., retired, June 30, 1921. Asst. geologist, U.S. Geol. Survey, 1885; marine meteorologist, U.S. Hydrographic Office, and editor pilot chart, 1886-92; in charge Naval Obs., Mare Island, Calif., 1898, branch hydrographic office, Manila, 1899; in charge, dept. chronometers and time service, U.S. Naval Obs., Washington, 1902-10, comdt. U.S. Naval Sta., Key West, Fla., 1910-15; pres. Gen. Court Martial, Navy Yard, Norfolk, Va., 1916-21. Republican. Episcopalian. Died Nov. 17, 1932.

HAYDEN, FERDINAND VANDIVEER, geologist; b. Westfield, Mass., Sept. 7, 1829; s. Asa and Melinda (Hawley) H.; A.B., Oberlin Coll., 1850; M.D., Albany Med. Coll., 1853; LL.D., U. Rochester, 1876, U. Pa., 1887; m. Emma Woodruff, Nov. 9, 1871. Went to Badlands of S.D. on collecting trip, 1853; 1st contbn. to geology was a vertical geol. sect. showing order of superposition of the strata; geologist on staff Lt. G. K. Warren of Topog. Engrs. in the surveying expdn. of Yellowstone and Missouri rivers and Badlands of S.D., 1856-57; with F. B. Meek in explorations in Kan. Territory, 1858; explored Yellowstone and Missouri rivers with Capt. W. F. Raynolds, 1859-62; served as surgeon U.S. Army, 1861-65, promoted to lt. col., 1864; prof. geology U. Pa., 1865-72; entered upon a survey of Neb. Territory in 1867 which laid foundation for U.S. Geol. Survey as it exists today; his work resulted in the setting aside of land for Yellowstone Nat. Park. Mem. Acad. Natural Scis. of Phila., Nat. Acad. Scis., Geol. Socs. of London and Edinburgh, Geologosche Reichsanstalt of Vienna, Société Impériale of Moscow. Died Phila., Dec. 22, 1887.

HAYDEN, HORACE H., dentist, geologist, coll. pres.; b. Windsor, Conn., Oct. 13, 1769; s. Thomas and Abigail (Parsons) H.; received D.D.S. as mem. Am. Soc. Dental Surgeons, 1840; M.D. (hon.), Med. Sch., U. Md., 1840; m. Marie Robinson, Feb. 23, 1805, 6 children including Handel. Licensed as dentist by Med. and Chirurgical Faculty of Md., 1810; asst. surgeon, sgt. Md. Militia, 1814; 1st sec. Balt. Phys. Assn., 1818; pres. Md. Acad. Scis. and Lit. 1826; prin. founder Balt. Coll. Dental Surgery (world's 1st dental coll.), 1840, 1st pres., 1st prof. principles of dental science, prof. dental physiology and pathology until 1844; influenced orgn. of Am. Soc. Dental Surgeons, N.Y.C., 1840; discovered nr. Balt. a form of chalazite (named Haydenite after him. Author: Geological Essays; or An Inquiry into Some of the Geological Phenomena to be Found in the Various Parts of America and Elsewhere, 1820. Died Balt., Jan. 26, 1844.

HAYDEN, JOSEPH, inventor, mfr.; b. Foxborough, Mass., July 31, 1802; s. Daniel and Abigail (Shepard) H.; m. Ruhamah Guilford, 1819, 1 son, Hiram Washington. Started in mech. work with his father in Mass.; moved to Waterbury, Conn., entered brass industry; invented machine to manufacture cloth-covered buttons, 1828; patented invention of wire-eyed buttons, also machines for making them, 1830. Died Feb. 17, 1877.

HAYES, ANSON, chemist; b. Sigourney, Ia., Jan. 31, 1882; s. Daniel Webster and Kate Lee (Richardson) H.; B.S., Drake U., 1908; M.S., Ia. State Coll., 1917; Ph.D. in chemistry, U. Chgo., 1921; m. Phebe McClaran, June 23, 1909; children—Dan McClaran, Anson Mack, Ted. R. Began as high sch. tchr., 1908; asst. in chemistry Ia. State Coll., 1915-17, prof. phys. chemistry, 1921-28, now chmn. adv. com. to chemistry dept.; chief chemist Am. Rolling Mill Co., Middletown, O., 1928-29, dir. research labs., 1929-46, v.p., 1946-47; dir. emeritus research, since 1947. Capt. civil air patrol and squadron comdr. Bd. dirs. Ohio State U. Research Found. Fellow A.A.A.S.; mem. Am. Chem. Soc., Am. Electrochem. Soc., Am. Foundrymen's Assn., Am. Inst. Mining and Metall. Engrs., Am. Soc. for Metals, Brit. Iron and Steel Inst., West of Scotland Iron and Stel Inst., Brit. Inst. Metals, Am. Soc. for Testing Materials, Nat. Farm Chemurgic Council, Ohio Chemurgic Commn., Gamma Sigma Delta, Phi Beta Kappa, Phi Kappa Phi, Phi Lambda Upsilon, Sigma Xi. Clubs: Engineering (Dayton); Chemists' (N.Y.); Forest Hills Country, Middletown Aviation. Contbr. sci. articles to tech. mags. Operator of large livestock farm. Home: 311 Stanley St., Middletown, O. Died July 1960.

HAYES, AUGUSTUS ALLEN, chemist; b. Windsor, Vt., Feb. 28, 1806; s. Thomas Allen and Sophia (West) H.; attended med. sch. Dartmouth, M.D. (hon.), 1846; m. Henrietta Bridge Dana, July 13, 1836. Published account of he isolation of alkaloidal compound which he called sanguinaria; 1825; investigated certain chromium compounds, 1826-28; became dir. of large plant mfg. colors and other chemicals, Roxbury, Mass.; consulting chemist for several large dyeing, bleaching, gas-making and smelting establishments in New Eng.; state assayer Mass.; devised methods for shortening the time needed in smelting iron and refining copper; work led to fundamental improvements in constrn. of furnaces and arrangement of steam boilers; conducted investigation of water supply, Charlestown, Mass., 1859-60; devised and used simple elec. method of detecting the limits of slight impurities in drinking water; 1st to suggest application of oxides of iron in refining of pig iron mem. Am. Acad. Arts and Scis., contbr. scientific papers to its Proceedings, also to Am. Jour. of Science. Died Brookline, Mass., June 21, 1882.

HAYES, C(HARLES) WILLARD, geologist; b. Granville, O., Oct. 8, 1859; s. Charles C. and Ruth (Wolcott) H.; bro. of Ellen H.; A.B., Oberlin Coll., 1883; fellow chemistry and geology, Johns Hopkins, 1884-87, Ph.D., 1887; (LL.D., Oberlin, 1908); m. Rosa Paige, Mar. 22, 1894. Prin. Brecksville (O.) High Sch., 1883-84; apptd. asst. geologist, 1887, geologist, 1894, chief geologist, 1902-11, U.S. Geol. Survey; 1st v.p. and gen. mgr. Cia Mex. de Petrolea "El Aguila," S.A., Oct. 16, 1911—. Geologist to Nicaraguan Canal Commn., 1898-99. Home: Washington, D.C. Died Feb. 8, 1916.

HAYES, HAMMOND VINTON, engr.; b. Madison, Wis., Aug. 28, 1860; s. William Allen and Elisabeth (Vinton) H.; A.B., Harvard, 1883, A.M., Ph.D., 1885; Mass. Inst. Tech., 1884-85; unmarried. Entered employ Am. Bell Telephone Co., 1885, in charge of lab. and later was made elec. engr., asst. chief engr. and chief engr., Am. Telephone & Telegraph Co., 1902-07; consulting engr., 1907-24; pres. Submarine Signal Corp., 1925-30. Fellow Am. Inst. E.E., Am. Acad. Arts and Sciences; mem. A.A.A.S. Republican. Episcopalian. Clubs: Union (Boston); University (New York). Author: Public Utilities—Their Cost New and Depreciation; Public Utilities—Their Fair Present Value and Return. Assisted in development of telephony and infra-red signaling. Home: 48 Beacon St. Office: 253 Summer St., Boston, Mass. Died Mar. 22, 1947.

HAYES, HARVEY CORNELIUS, research physicist; b. North Fenton, N.Y., Nov. 2, 1878; s. William Henry and Edith Marion (Reynolds) H.; grad. Normal Sch., Oneonta, 1900; A.B., Harvard, 1907, A.M., 1908, Ph.D., 1911; m. Marjorie Dodge Wood, 1909; children—Shirley Wood, Harvey Cornelius, Gordon Brewster, Benjamin Osgood; m. 2d, Katherine Moore. Research fellow, Harvard, 1911-13; prof. physics, Swarthmore (Pa.) Coll., 1913-17; research physicist U.S. Navy, at New London, Conn., 1917-19, Annapolis, Md., 1919-23, Washington, from 1923. In cooperation with others during World War I, developed methods and apparatus for locating submerged submarines. Fellow Am. Physical Soc.; mem. Washington Acad. Sciences, Geophysical Union, Philos. Soc. of Washington, Phi Beta Kappa. Republican. Club: Cosmos. Awarded Levy gold medal and John Scott medal, by Franklin Inst., Phila., for development of method for measuring ocean depths by means of sound waves, also Cullom geog. medal for same, by Am. Geog. Soc.; Distinguished Service Citation, by Sec. of Navy for service in anti-submarine campaign. Home: Peterboro NH Died July 9, 1968; buried Dublin NH

HAYES, JOSEPH, soldier, mining engr.; b. S. Berwick, Me., Sept. 14, 1835; s. William Allen H.; ed. S. Berwick, Me., and Phillips Acad., Andover, Mass.; grad. Harvard, 1855; unmarried. Apptd. maj., 18th Mass. Regt., July 26, 1861, lt.-col., Aug. 25, 1862, col., Nov. 20, 1862, brig.-gen. vols., May 12, 1864; comd. 1st div., 5th Army Corps; taken prisoner by Confederates, and confined for several months in Libby Prison; apptd. U.S. commr. of supplies in seceded States, Jan., 1865; bvtd. maj.-gen. vols., Mar. 13, 1865; mustered out of service, Aug. 24, 1865. Later engaged as mining engr.; introduced Am. system of hydraulic mining into United States of Colombia, 1877. Address: Care J. E. Kelly, 318 W. 57th St., New York.

HAYES, MONTROSE W(HITE), meterologist; b. Charlotte, N.C., Nov. 21, 1874; s. Junius W. and Lucie Connor (Morrow) H.; ed. pub. schs.; m. Marie C. Leuschen, Mar. 18, 1908; children—Idelia A., Montrose H. Observer, U.S. Weather Bur., 1892-1903; organizer nat. weather forecasting service, Argentina, 1904-06; in charge various offices of U.S. Weather Bur., 1907-09; in charge St. Louis (Mo.) office, 1910-29; chief of river and flood div., Weather Bur., Washington, D.C., 1930—. Home: Washington, D.C. Died Nov. 16, 1936.

HAYES, STEPHEN QUENTIN, electrical engr.; b. Washington, D.C., Dec. 17, 1873; s. Henry Gillespie and Maria Louisa (Hogan) H.; A.B., Georgetown U., 1892; E.E., Johns Hopkins, 1894; m. Helen Grace Buck, Nov. 6, 1901 (died 1931); children—Helen Grace (Mrs. R. J. Peterman), Jane Louise (Mrs. L. J. Hartman), Stephen Quentin, Charles Joseph, John Henry, Isabel Gillespie. With Westinghouse Electric & Mfg. Co., on students' course, 1894-95; draftsman, 1895-98, designing engr., 1898-1906, estimating and commerical engr., 1906-09, gen. and commercial engr., 1909-33. Temporarily with Westinghouse European cos. part 1917-18, with U.S. Govt. part 1919; in Australia and Japan, 1921-22; cons. engr. Japanese Imperial Govt. rys., 1922; in Colombia, Panama and Ecuador, 1928-31; cons. engr., Municipality of Quito, Ecuador, 1928; cons. engr., Quito Electric Light & Power Co., 1931. Lecturer U. of Pittsburgh and Carnegie Inst., 1933-36. Hon. Ecuadorean vice consul for Pittsburgh, 1931-35; sec. and treas. Consular Assn. of Pittsburgh, 1932-35. Fellow Am. Inst. E.E. Republican. Catholic. Author: Switching Equipment for Power Control. Asst. editor switchgear and control sect. Am. Elec. Engineers' Handbook, 1913-35; asst. editor E.M.F. (Electrical Year Book), 1920-26. Home: Pittsburgh, Pa. Died Apr. 4, 1936.

HAYFORD, JOHN FILLMORE, civil engr.; b. Rouse's Point, N.Y., May 19, 1868; s. Hiram and Mildred Alevia (Fillmore) H.; C.E., Cornell Univ., 1889; Sc.D. from George Washington Univ., 1918; m. Lucy Stone, Oct. 11, 1894. Apptd. computer U.S. Coast and Geod. Survey, June 1889; asst. astronomer to Internat. Boundary Commn. U.S. and Mexico, in charge of one of field parties, 1892-93; aid and later asst. U.S. Coast and Geod. Survey, 1894-95; instr. civ. engring., Cornell U., 1895-98; expert computer and geodesist, U.S. Coast and Geod. Survey, 1898-99, and inspr. of geodetic work and chief of computing div., 1900-09; dir. Coll. Engring., Northwestern U., Sept. 1, 1909—. Mem. Nat. Advisory Com. for Aeronautics, 1915-23. Research asso. Carnegie Instn. of Washington, D.C. Author: Geodetic Astronomy, 1898. Home: Evanston, Ill. Died Mar. 10, 1925.

HAYHURST, EMERY ROE, cons. indsl. hygienist; b. St. Louis, June 28, 1880; s. John Emery and May Eva (Roe) H.; A.B., U. Ill., 1903, A.M., 1905, M.D., 1908; Ph.D., U. Chgo., 1916; m. Isabelle Norris, 1910 (died 1918); children—Roe Norris, Cuthbert Newton, James Dwight; m. 2d, Jessie Ives, 1919; children—Wallace Ives, Jessie Mae. With Am. Can Co., 10 summers, to 1905; instr. physiology, U. Ill., 1903-08; resident physician Cook County Hosp., 1908-10; Ill. Survey occupational diseases, 1910; pathologist U. Hosp., Chgo., 1910-13; dir. occupational disease clinic Rush Med. Coll., and fellow in occupational diseases Sprague Meml. Inst., U. Chgo., 1911-13; dir. occupational disease survey, Ohio, 1913-15; dir., later cons., div. indsl. hygiene, Ohio Dept. Health, 1915-32; asst. prof. hygiene and dir. dispensaries, 1915-20, prof. hygiene, chmn. dept. pub. health, 1920-31, Ohio State U. Chief div. hygiene, cons. in occupational diseases Ohio Dept. of Health, 1932-37. Sec. com. on factory sanitation Council of Nat. Def., 1917-18; prof. mil. hygiene, S.M.A., 1918; surgeon USPHSR, 1919-24, cons. hygienist, 1924-37, spl. cons., 1942-47. Mem. com. on nutrition in industry NRC, 1941-45. Fellow A.M.A., Am. Assn. Indsl. Phys. and Surgeons, A.A.A.S., Ohio Acad. Sci., Am. Pub. Health Assn. (various appts. and elections, to mem. exec. bd., chmn. ventilating com., indsl. hygiene sect. 1931-45), Inst. Am. Genealogy; mem. Am. Chem. Soc., Ohio Archeol. and Hist. Soc. Royal Inst. Pub. Health, Friends of Land, Alpha Omega Alpha, Sigma Xi. U.S. del. Interntional Congress on Indsl. Accidents and Diseases, Budapest, 1928; chmn. Am. Com. same Congress, 1925-38. Pres., Columbus Council Social Agys., 1931, 32. Mem. Community Ch. Clubs: Optimists, Torch (pres. 1937-38). Author: Survey of Industrial Health Hazards and Occupational Diseases, Ohio, 1915; "Occupations" in Craig's Diseases of Middle Life, 1923; Industrial Health (with Geo. M. Kober), 1924; Personal Health, 1927, et al. to 1938. Editorial bds. Am. Jour. Pub. Health, (1918-34), Jour. Indsl. Hygiene, Indsl. Medicine, Ohio Jour. Sci. Address: 1925 Concord Rd., Columbus, O. 43212. Died Oct. 17, 1961; buried Eastlawn Cemetery, Columbus.

HAYLER, GUY WILFRID, planning engr.; b. Hull, Eng., Feb. 5, 1877; s. Guy and Elizabeth (Harriss) H.; ed. Collegiate House Sch. (Hull) and Rutherford Coll. (Newcastle); trained as municipal engr. and architect; special study city planning, housing, etc., Great Britain and Continental Europe; married Mollie Beddow, December 13, 1913; children—Guy Beddow, Joan Marylyn (Mrs. Curt Demele). Worked on Further Strand Improvement plans, London; municipal engineer, Gateshead, 1908-09; town planning, western Canada, 1912-13; senior designer South Parks Commissioners, Chicago, 1913-19; made city plans for Richmond, California, 1922; chief engr. Regional Plan for San Francisco Bay Counties, 1926-28; regional planning consultant, Golden Gate Bridge, 1930; city plan cons. for Burlingame and Menlo Park; mgr. land program projects U.S. Dept. of Interior, 1934-35. Asst. engr. U.S. Farm Security Adminstrn., 1942-45. Civil Engineer, U.S. Engrs., San Francisco, 1945-47; research engr., joint Army-Navy Bd. on so. crossing of San Francisco Bay, 1947. Exhibited at 1st Inter Town Plan Exhibition, Royal Academy, London, 1910; made first city planning aeroplane flight over an American City, 1920; directed "The Pay Roll Dollar" (city planning motion picture), 1926. Connected during World War I with U.S. Hosp., Div., the War Recreation Bd., and made social surveys for Treasury Department; during World War II, with War Prodn. Bd. War Manpower Com. and War Food Adminstrn. Office of Labor. Mem. Am. Soc. C.E., Royal Sanitary Inst., Instn. Municipal Engrs. (London), Am. Statis. Assn. Author of several booklets on city planning; contbr. to Am. Rev. of Revs. Am. City. Am. Architect, British Architect, etc. Home: 453 34th Av., San Francisco CA

HAYNES, ELI STUART, astronomer; b. Trenton, Mo., July 12, 1880; s. Aaron and Philena (Biggs) H.; A.B., U. of Mo., 1905, A.M., 1907; Ph.D., U. of Calif., 1913; m. Mamie Ruth Mode, May 20, 1908 (died Feb. 1934); children—Charles Mode, Willis Stuart, Mary Ruth (dec.); m. 2d, Nola Lee Anderson, July 9, 1938. Asst. in mathematics, Univ. of Mo., 1905-06; research asst. Laws Obs., same univ., 1906-08; instr. in astronomy, U. of Mo., 1908-11, in charge dept., 1909-11; fellow in astronomy, 1911-12, instr., 1912-13, U. of Calif.; Martin Kellogg fellow, Lick Obh., 1913-14; asso. prof. astronomy, 1914-15, prof. 1915-23, Beloit Coll., also dir. Smith Obs.; prof. astronomy and dir. Laws Obs., U. of Mo., 1923-50, professor emeritus of astronomy, 1950—. Member board of trustees Christian College, Columbia, Mo., 1937-54. Fellow A.A.A.S. (mem. council 1935-38); mem. Am. Astron. Soc., Phi Beta Kappa, Sigma Xi, Delta Tau Delta. Mem. Christian (Disciples) Church. Mason (grand treas. Grand Chap. R.A.M., Mo., 1945—). Contbr. on variable star photometry, orbits of comets and asteroids and orbits of spectroscopic binaries. Home: 1408 Rosemary Lane, Columbia, Mo. Died Sept. 13, 1956; buried Memorial Park Cemetery, Columbia.

HAYNES, ELWOOD, inventor; b. Portland, Ind., Oct. 14, 1857; s. Jacob March and Hilinda Sophia (Haines) H.; B.S., Worcester Poly. Inst., 1881; Johns Hopkins, 1884-85; m. Bertha Beatrice Lanterman, Oct. 21, 1887. Teacher sciences, Eastern Ind. Normal Sch., Portland, 1885-86; mgr. Portland Natural Gas & Oil Co., 1886-90; field supt. Ind. Natural Gas & Oil Co., 1890-1901; pres. Haynes Automobile Co., 1898—. Discovered tungsten chrome steel, 1881, alloy of chromium and nickel, 1897, alloy of cobalt and chromium, 1900; developed latter alloy for cutting instruments, 1910; designed and constructed a horseless carriage, 1893-94, which is the oldest American automobile in existence and is on exhibition at Smithsonian Instn.; first to introduce aluminum in automobile engine, 1895; invented and built rotary valve gas engine, 1903. Prohibitionist. Presbyn. Discovered alloys of cobalt, chromium, and tungsten, also alloys of cobalt, chromium and molyhdenum, 1911-12, and pres. The Haynes Stellite Co., mfg. tool metals of same, 1912-20; discovered "stainless steel," 1911 (patented 1919). Trustee Western Coll., Oxford, O., Winona Assembly and Bible Conf., Winona Lake, Ind. Home: Kokomo, Ind. Died Apr. 13, 1925.

HAYNES, IRVING SAMUEL, physician; b. Saranac, N.Y., Aug. 29, 1861; s. Samuel and Phebe (Ayre) H.; Ph.B., Wesleyan, 1885; M.D., University Med. Coll. (New York U.), 1887; (Sc.D., Wesleyan U., 1915); m. Charlotte E. Scribner, Mar. 19, 1890 (died Dec. 7, 1897); m. 2d, Laura C. Marsh, July 5, 1899 (died July 26, 1935); children—Harriett Marsh, Dorothy Helen, Irving Samuel (dec.). Interne Bellevue Hosp., 1887-88; visiting surgeon Harlem Hosp., 1895-1922, cons. surgeon since 1922; visiting surgeon New York Park Hosp., 1909-17; cons. surgeon Reconstruction Hosp., Glens Falls Hosp.; supt. Physicians Hospital (Plattsburg), 1931-1943; prof. practical anatomy, Univ. Med. Coll., 1888-98; prof. applied anatomy, 1898-1917, prof. clin. surg., 1911, now emeritus, Cornell U. Med. Coll. Fellow Am. Coll. Surgeons; mem. A.M.A., Clinton County Med. Soc., N.Y. Surg. Soc., D.K.E., S.A.R.; hon. Phi Beta Kappa (Wesleyan, 1914). Pres. trustees Park Av. M.E. Ch., 1900-28; mem. bd. govs. Lake Champlain Assn., 1909-28; mem. bd. dirs. Physicians Hosp. since 1944. Author: Practical Guide for Beginners to the Dissection of the Human Body, 1893; Manual of Anatomy, 1896. Contbr. to various med. jours. Home: Plattsburg, N.Y. Died Oct. 9, 1946.

HAYS, ISAAC, ophthalmologist, med. editor; b. Phila., July 5, 1796; s. Samuel and Richea (Gratz) H.; B.A., U. Pa., 1816, M.D., 1820; m. Sarah Minis, 1834, 4 children including Isaac Minis. One of first to study colorblindness and astigmatism; invented spl. knife for cataract operations; mem. staff Infirmary for Diseases of the Eye and Ear, Phia., 1822-27; surgeon Wills' Ophthalmic Hosp., Phila., 1834-54; fellow Coll. of Physicians, Phila., 1835-79; editor-in-chief Am. Jour. Med. Scis., 1827-79; established Med. News, 1843; published Monthly Abstract of Med. Science, 1874-79; a founder Franklin Inst., A.M.A.; mem. Acad. Natural Scis. of Phila., pres., 1865-69. Died Phila., Apr. 13, 1879.

HAYS, WILLET MARTIN, agriculturist; b. in Hardin Co., Ia., Oct. 19, 1859; s. Silas and Christena (Lepley) H.; student Oskaloosa (Ia.) Coll., 1878-81; freshman Drake U., 1882-83; B.Agr., Ia. Agrl. Coll., 1885; M.Agr., 1896; m. Clara Shepperd, of Chariton, Ia., July 25, 1885 (died 1892); 2d Ellen Beach of Cortland, N.Y., Apr. 22, 1897. Asst. in agr., Ia. Agrl. Coll., 1886; asso. editor Prairie Farmer, Chicago, 1887; asst., 1888-89, prof. agr., 1890-91; Agrl. Coll., and agriculturist, Expt. Sta. U. of Minn.; prof. agr. and agriculturist, Expt. Sta. N.D. Agrl. Coll., 1892-93; prof. agr., Agrl. Coll., and agriculturist, Expt. Sta., U. of Minn., 1893-04; asst. sec. of agr., U.S., Jan. 1, 1905-March 4, 1913; consulting agriculturist, Washington, 1913—. Republican. In Minn. Expt. Sta. devised and published methods of breeding wheat, corn, flax, alfalfa and other field crops, now widely used, and produced new and valuable varieties; prominently connected with movement for organization of agrl. high schs.; adviser to the Sec. of Agr. of Argentine Rep., 1913. Organizer, and sec. Minn. Field Crop Breeders' Assn., 1903, 04; organizer, and sec. Am. Breeders' Assn., 1903-13, and was editor of its reports and Am. Breeders' Mag., organized 1910. Hon. mem. Minn. Edn. Assn. fellow A.A.A.S.; mem. Am. Assn. Adv. Agrl. Science, Am. Assn. Advt. Hort. Science, N.E.A., Am. Soc. Agronomistes. Clubs: Commercial (Minneapolis), Cosmos (Washington) Mem. Christian (Disciples) Ch. Author of various books, monographs and papers on efficiency, farm organization, genetics, and edn. Address: Washington.

HAYWARD, NATHANIEL MANLEY, inventor, mfr.; b. Easton, Mass., Jan. 19, 1808; s. Jerahmeel Hayward; m. Louisa Buke, 7 children. Discovered that sulphur is agt. which prevents rubber from softening when warm; successfully produced rubber which would not become soft and sticky in summertime, 1835; result of discovery, employed as gen. supt. Eagle India Rubber Corp., Woburn, Mass., 1835, became co-owner, 1836, sole owner, 1838, sold factory to Charles Goodyear, 1838; brought about superficial vulcanization; granted patent on volcanization, 1839; discovered method of giving rubber shoes a luster; mgr. Hayward Rubber Co., Colchester, Conn., 1847-54, pres. co., 1855-65, obtained large govt. contracts during Civil War. Died Colchester, July 18, 1865.

HAYWOOD, JOHN KERFOOT, chemist; b. Raleigh, N.C., Dec. 19, 1873; s. Edward Graham and Margaret (Henry) H.; B.S., Cornell U., 1896; M.D., George Washington U., 1907; m. Margaret O'Brien Palmer, June 19, 1912; children—Walker H. (dec.), John H. Instr. in chemistry, Cornell U., 1897; became connected with Bur. of Chemistry, U.S. Dept. of Agr., 1897; chief of Miscellaneous Div., same bur., 1904-27, and chmn. Insecticide and Fungicide Bd., 1912-27; chief of office of insecticide, fungicide and caustic poison supervision in Food, Drug and Insecticide Administration, 1927—. In charge of enforcement of Federal Insecticide Act of 1910, also Federal Caustic Poison Act. Episcopalian. Specialist on insecticides, fungicides, disinfectants, caustic poisons. Home: Washington, D.C. Died Nov. 30, 1928.

HAZARD, DANIEL LYMAN, magnetician; b. Narragansett Pier, R.I., Aug. 26, 1865; s. Thomas George and Mary King (Brooks) H.; student Brown U., 1880-81: A.B., Harvard, 1885. Bookkeeper and land surveyor until 1889; computer Mass. Topog. Survey Commn. on triangulation of Mass., 1889-92; apptd. computer U.S. Coast and Geod. Survey, 1892, later chief magnetician Div. Terrestrial Magnetism and Seismology until retirement, 1936. Fellow A.A.A.S.; mem. Am. Geophys. Union, Washington Acad. Sciences, Washington Soc. Engrs., Philos. Soc. Washington (pres. 1924). Unitarian. Club: Cosmos. Author: Directions for Magnetic Measurements, 1911, 31; The Earth's Magnetism, 1925; U.S. Magnetic Tables and Magnetic Charts for 1925, 1929. Contbr. to Jour. Terrestrial Magnetism, also article for Am. Year Book, 1915-19, 25-31. Editor of most of the publs. connected with magnetic work of the bur., 1908-35. Home: Narragansett, R.I. Died Sept. 21, 1951.

HAZELTINE, ALAN, cons. engr.; b. Morristown, N.J., Aug. 7, 1886; s. Louis Rawson and Henrietta Maud (Ahern) H.; M.E., Stevens Inst. Tech., 1906, Sc.D., 1933; A.M., Columbia, 1938; m. Elizabeth Barrett, Jan. 16, 1931; children—Barrett, Patricia (Mrs. Alan Duhnkrack), Maud Denise (Mrs. Ansel Chaplin), Esther (Mrs. Jeffery Kramer), and Richard Deimel. Tester Gen. Electric Co., 1906-07; asst. Stevens Inst. Tech., 1907, successively instr. asst. prof., prof., prof. phys. mathematics, chmn. physics dept., 1943-44; cons. Hazeltine Corp., 1945—, dir., 1949-63. Member of the National Conference, 1922-24. Cons. radio engineer Washington Navy Yard, 1918-19; with OSRD, 1944-45. Fellow Am. Inst. E.E., Inst. Radio Engrs. (pres. 1936), A.A.A.S.; mem. Math. Assn. Am., Radio Club of Am. (pres. 1946-47; recipient Armstrong Medal 1937), Tau Beta Pi. Author: Electrical Engineering, 1924. Inventor neutrodyne radio receiver. Address: 15 Tower Dr., Maplewood, N.J. Died May 24, 1964; buried Madison, N.J.

HAZEN, ALLEN, civil engr.; b. Hartford, Vt., Aug. 28, 1869; s. Charles D. and Abbie (Coleman) H.; ed. Hartford, Vt., and at Mass. Inst. Tech.; hon. Sc.D., N.H. and Dartmouth Colls.; m. Elizabeth McConway, Jan. 1, 1903. In charge of State Bd. of Health Expt. Sta., Lawrence, Mass., 1888-93; in charge sewage disposal, Chicago Expn., 1893; in private practice, Boston, 1894-97, New York, 1897—; work mainly on city water supplies. Author: The Filtration of Public Water Supplies, 1895, 1900; Clean Water, 1907; Meter Rates for Water Works, 1917. Home: Dobbs Ferry, N.Y. Died July 26, 1930.

HAZEN, HENRY ALLEN, prof. meteorology, U.S. Weather Bureau, July 1, 1891—; b. Serur, India (where his father was missionary); grad. Dartmouth, 1871; 1 year in Thayer School of Civil Engring.; asst. in drawing, 1873-76, Sheffield Scientific Sch., Yale; private asst. to Prof. Elias Loomis in physics and meteorology, 1877-80. Joined U.S. Signal Service (now Weather Bur.), May 1, 1881. Devised sling psychrometer, 1884; established tables for reduction of barometric readings to sea-level; devised thermometer shelter, etc.; author numerous meteorol. papers; has made five balloon ascensions (one to 16,000 feet) for meteorol. research. Home: Washington, D.C. Died 1900.

HAZEN, HENRY HONEYMAN, dermatologist; b. Oldswick, New Jersey, July 21, 1879; s. David Henry and Emma Louise (Honeyman) H.; A.B., Johns Hopkins, 1902, M.D., 1906; A.M., Georgetown University, 1925; Dr. Science, Howard University, 1944; m. (Miss) Laura Mae Ross, June 1, 1908 (dec.); m. 2d, Anita Burt, July 20, 1922; 1 son, Henry H. Began practice at Washington, 1908; prof. dermatology, Howard U., 1911-44; same, Georgetown U., 1913-34; cons. dermatologist, U.S. Pub. Health Service, since 1926 (com. for evaluation of serodiagnostic tests for syphilis), spl. cons., U.S.P.H.S., since 1918; dir. post-grad. course in venereal disease control, Howard U., 1937-42; attending physician, D.C. Health Dept., 1942-46; cons. syphilol., D.C. Health Dept.; chmn. Nat. Prophylactic Com.; pres. Social Hygiene Soc. of Dist. of Columbia; chmn. advisory com. on public edn. for the prevention of venereal diseases, U.S.P.H.S., since 1943. Certified by Am. Bd. Dermatol. and Syphilol., 1939. Fellow A.M.A.; member Am. Dermatol. Assn., Am. Roentgen Ray Soc., Social Hygiene Soc. of D.C. (pres., 1937-45), Am. Social Hygiene Assn. (hon. life). Club: Cosmos. Author: Diseases of the Skin, 1915, 3d ed., 1927; Skin Cancer, 1916; Syphilis, 1919, 2d ed., 1928; Cutaneous X-ray and Radium Therapy, 1931; Syphilis in the Negro, 1942. Contbr. to Jour. A.M.A., Archive of Dermatology and Syphilology, Am. Jour. of Syphilis, Am. Jour. Roentgenology. Home: 3708 Ingomar St., Washington 15. Died May 1, 1951.

H'DOUBLER, FRANCIS TODD, (do-bler), surgeon; b. Beloit, Kan., Apr. 22, 1887; s. Chas. Wright and Sarah Emerson (Todd) H'D.; student Beloit (Wis.) Coll., 1903-05; A.B., U. of Wis., 1907, A.M., 1908, Ph.D. in Mathematics, 1910; student Med. Sch., U. of Wis., 1911-12, Med. Sch., U. of Chicago, 1912, Med. Sch., U. of Philippines, Manila, 1912-13; M.D., Harvard, 1915; m. Alice Louise Bemis, Aug. 5, 1922; children—Alice Margaret, Francis Todd, Louise Emerson, Peter Bemis, Charles Edward. Asst. in mathematics, U. of Wis., 1907-10; asst. prof. mathematics, Miami U., Oxford, O., 1910-11; intern Augustana Hosp., Chicago, and Peter Bent Brigham Hosp., Boston, 1915-18; Mosley traveling fellowship from Harvard in research at U. of Berne (Switzerland), de Quervain Clinic, Insel Spital, Physiol. Inst. and European clinics, 1920; spl. resident Lakeside Hosp., Cleveland, O., 1921; surg. resident Augustana Hosp., 1921-22, jr. attending surgeon, 1922-23; pvt. practice with A. J. Ochsner and N. M. Percy Clinic, Chicago, 1922-23; instr. in pathology and surgery, U. of Ill. Med. Sch., Chicago, 1922-23; practice in Springfield, Mo., since 1923; mem. surg. staffs of St. John's Hospital, Burge Deaconess Hospital, Springfield Bapt. Hosp.; surg. consultant Mo. State Tuberculosis Hosp., Mt. Vernon, Mo.; organized classes and taught bacteriology, Southwest Teachers Coll., Springfield, Mo., 1924-27; patron Smithsonian Institution. Member board directors Springfield (Mo.) Chamber of Commerce; pres. Greene County Welfare Bd., 1935-37; mem. bd. dirs. Community Chest; exam. physician, local bd. S.S.S., Green Co., Mo., 1942-47. Served as lt. M.C., U.S. Army, with A.E.F., 1917-19; disch. grade capt. Diplomate Am. Bd. Surgery (founders group). Fellow A.C.S., A.A.A.S., Am. Geog. Soc.; mem. Mo. State Bd. Med. Examiners (v.p. 1951-52, pres. 1952-53). Fellow, Am., So., Mo. (v.p. 1941, speaker 1949) med. assns., S.W. Surg. Congress (founders group), Mo., Greene County med. socs., Am. Assn. for Study of Goiter, Assn. for Study Internal Secretions, Am. Math. Soc., Math. Assn. Am., N.Y., Mo. acads. sci., Mo., Alpha Epsilon Delta, Sigma Nu, Phi Rho Sigma, Phi Beta Kappa (assoc. 1948), Gamma Alpha, Alpha Omega Alpha, Sigma Xi. Republican. Mason. (Shriner). Clubs: University, Hickory Hills Country (Springfield); Automobile of Missouri (bd. govs.). Contbr. med. jours. Home: Route 7, Box 207. Office: 609 Cherry St., Springfield, Mo. Died June 18, 1962; buried Springfield.

HEADLEE, THOMAS J., entomologist; b. at Headlee, Ind., Feb. 13, 1877; s. Josephus and Ruann (Mattix) H.; grad. State Normal Sch., Terre Haute, Ind., 1900; A.B., Ind. U., 1903, A.M., 1904; Ph.D., Cornell U., 1906; m. Blanche Ives, Oct. 11, 1903; children—Mary Ruanna, Josephine (dec.), Miriam Esther, Ruth Margaret. Asst. entomologist, 1906-07, asso., July-Sept. 1907, State Agrl. Expt. Sta., N.H.; head dept. of entomology and zoölogy, State Agrl. Coll. and Expt. Sta., Kan., 1907-12; prof. entomology. Rutgers U., and entomologist N.J. Expt. Sta., and state entomologist, Oct. 1912-Dec. 31, 1943, emeritus professor of entomology since Jan. 1, 1944. Fellow A.A.A.S. (council, 1920-24); mem. Am. Assn. Econ. Entomologists (pres. 1929), Entomol. Soc. America (charter mem.), Sigma Xi, Phi Beta Kappa. Author: The Mosquitoes of New Jersey and Their Control, 1945; of repts., bulls. and articles in tech. jours. Home: Dayton, N.J. Office: New Brunswick, N.J. Died June 14, 1946; buried in Masonic Cemetery, Delphi, Ind.

HEALD, FREDERICK DE FOREST, botanist; b. Midland City, Mich., July 23, 1872; s. Henry Francis and Hettie (Charles) H.; grad. prep. dept. U. S.D., 1891, B.S., U. Wis., 1894, fellow in botany, 1895-96, M.S., 1896; Ph.D., U. Leipzig, 1897; m. Nedre Townley, Dec. 27, 1899 (died 1939); children—Doris Adelaide, Henry Townley, Marian Bessey; m. 2d, Mrs. Charlotte Chamberlin, Nov. 5, 1942. Prof. biology Parsons Coll., Fairfield, Ia., 1897-1903; adj. prof. plant physiology U. Neb., 1903-06; asso. prof. botany, botanist, Neb. Expt. Sta., 1905-06; prof. agrl. botany, botanist, Neb. Expt. Sta., 1906-08; head botany U. Tex., 1908-12; pathologist Pa. Chestnut Tree Blight Commn. U. Pa., agent in forest pathology U.S. Dept. Agr., 1912-14; prof. plant pathology, Wash. State Coll., and plant pathologist Wash. State Expt. Sta., 1915-17; head dept. plant pathology, Wash. State Coll., Pullman, Wash., 1917-41, prof. emeritus, 1941—. Collaborator, 1905-08, 15, expert, 1909-10, Bur. Plant Industry, Washington; state botanist, Neb., and asso. chief Neb. State Insect Pest and Plant Disease Bur., 1907-08. Spl. research work in plant physiol. and pathol.; asso. editor Phytopathology, 1911-16, 19-21, 31-33. Fellow A.A.A.S.; mem. Bot. Soc. Am., Am. Phytopathol. Soc., Am. Forestry Assn., Am. Micros. Soc. (pres. 1912), Wash. Hort. Assn., N.W. Sci. Assn. (sec. 1923-26), Sigma Xi, Phi Beta Kappa, Phi Kappa Phi, Alpha Zeta, Phi Sigma, sec. Neb. Acad. Sciences, 1904-06. Conglist. Republican. Author: Revision of Analytic Keys to Genera and Species of North American Mosses, by C. R. Barnes, 1897; Laboratory Manual in Elementary Biology, 1902; Symptoms of Disease in Plants, 1909; Experiments in Plant Physiology (with I. M. Lewis), 1910; Manual of Plant Disease, 1926, 2d edit., 1932; Introduction to Plant Pathology, 1937, 2d edit., 1943; Bunt or Stinking Smut of Wheat, a World Problem (with C. S. Holton), 1941; also Neb., Tex. and Wash. agrl. expt. sta. bulls. and reports. Editor Plant Pathology and Mycology, Webster's New Internat. Dictionary, 2d edit., 1935. Contbr. to bot. mags. 1894—, cyclopedias. Address: 312 Howard St., Pullman, Wash. Died Apr. 24, 1954; buried Riverside Park Mausoleum, Spokane, Wash.

HEALD, KENNETH CONRAD, geologist; b. Bennington, N.H., Mar. 14, 1888; s. Josiah Heald and Mary Katharine (Pike) H.; U. N.M., 1907-08; B.S. in Engring., Colorado Coll., 1912; studied Yale, 1912-14; D.Sc., U. Pitts., 1928; LL.D., Colo. Coll., 1955; m. Mary Marguerite Drach, Dec. 26, 1914; children—Mary Katherine (dec.), Kenneth Conrad. Field work, summers, U.S. Geol. Survey, until 1914, and full time, 1914-24, except 1918; chief of Sect. of Oil Geology, U.S. Geol. Survey, 1919-24; asso. prof. petroleum geology, Yale, 1924-25; geologist with Gulf Oil Cos. 1925-53, v.p. 1945, dir. 1950; dir. and v.p. various Gulf Oil subsidiaries; now owner Heald & Heald, geology and engring. cons.; petroleum cons Lectured on petroleum geology, U. Chicago and Johns Hopkins, 1923, 24, U. of Pitts. 1926-53; spl. lecturer, Texas Christian University, Director of Texas Christian U. Research Found. Director Goodwill Industries, Ft. Worth. Capt. engrs., U.S. Army, unattached, staff geologist, 1918. Awarded certificate of appreciation by Am. Petroleum Inst., 1952; Sydney Powers Meml. Award by Am. Assn. Petroleum Geologists, 1952; Metcalf award Engrs. Soc. Western Pa., 1966. Member at large Nat. Research Council, 1925-26; member American Assn. Petroleum Geologists hon. mem.; rep. NRC 1925-25), Geol. Soc. Can., Geol. Society Am. (rep. Nat. Research Council 1927), Soc. Economic Geologists, Am. Inst. Min. and Metall. Engrs., Geol. Soc. Washington, Engrs. Soc. Western Pa., American Petroleum Institute; fellow Am. Association Advancement of Sci., Geological Soc. of Fort Worth. Conglist. Clubs: Cosmos, Mid-River (Washington, D.C.); Fort Worth, Petroleum (Ft. Worth). Author: (bulls.) Geologic Structure of the Pawhuska Quadrangle, Okla., 1918; Structure and Oil and Gas Resources of Osage Reservation, Okla., 1922; Healdton Oil Field, Oklahoma, 1915; Eldorado Oil Field, Arkansas, 1925; Geology of Ingomary Anticline, Mont., 1926. Contbr. papers dealing with geology, geophysics and oil field technology. Home: Fort Worth TX Died Oct. 18, 1971; buried Pittsburgh PA

HEALY, DANIEL JOSEPH, physician; b. Toronto, Can., Mar. 26, 1873; s. William and Ellen (McCarthy) H.; student De LaSalle Coll., Toronto, 1886-89; M.D., C.M., McGill U., 1896; m. Louise Susette Bergmann (M.D.), June 26, 1902. Settled at Lexington, Ky., 1896; visiting physician, House of Mercy, 1896-99; pathologist Eastern Ky. Asylum for the Insane, 1897-99, Central Ind. Asylum for the Insane, 1899-1900; health officer City of Lexington, 1900-01; anatomist, office of Surgeon-Gen. U.S. Army, 1904-07; supt. Ky. Instn. for Feeble Minded Children, 1909-10; prof. bacteriology, 1910-19, prof. agrl. bacteriology, 1919—, U. of Ky., and research bacteriologist, Expt. Sta., 1910—. Mem. Vol. Med. Service Corps. Democrat. Home: Lexington, Ky. Died Nov. 24, 1935.

HEATH, FRED H(ARVEY), chemist; b. Warner, N.H., Feb. 25, 1883; s. Benjamin Franklin and Julia Augusta (Wadleigh) H.; B.S., U. of N.H., 1905; Ph.D., Yale, 1909; grad. student U. of Marburg, Germany, 1909; m. Winnifred A. Grant, Apr. 20, 1911 (died 1918); 1 son, Frank Harvey; m. 2d, Mrs. Ida M. Erickson, Sept. 7, 1921 (died 1928); m. 3d, Mrs. Errah Shannon Schindler, June 8, 1932. In chem. analysis of waters and water problem research N.D. State Biol. Station, 1914-16; investigation on platinum ores of Washington, 1921-22; invented seleniam mustard gas, 1918. Instr. phys. chemistry Mass. Inst. Tech., 1909-10; instr. gen. chemistry Case Sch. of Applied Sci., 1910-11; instr. Wesleyan U. Conn., 1911-12; instr. and asst. prof. U. of N.D., 1912-17; asst. prof. U. of Washington, 1917-23; prof. U. of Fla. since 1923. Gas consultant to Fla. Defense Council, World War II, reserve officer Chem. Corps since 1924. Mem. several years of com. on examinations, div. of chem. edn., Am. Chem. Soc. Mem. Am. Chem. Soc. (pres. Puget Sound sect., 1919; sec. Florida sect. 1924-26, pres. 1943), Fla. Acad. Sci., Alpha Chi Sigma, Phi Lambda Upsilon, Gamma Sigma Epsilon. Democrat. Baptist. Mason. Club: Rotary (Gainesville). Author: Laboratory Manual of Quantitative Analysis, 1910, 1921-22, Laboratory Manual of General Chemistry (with W. H. Beisler), 1926, 1934, General Chemistry Text Book (with others), 1926, 2d edit., 1927. Contbr. chem. research articles to professional jours. Special work in photography. Home: 561 N.E. 7th Av., Gainesville, Fla. Died Jan. 26, 1952.

HEATH, HAROLD, zoölogist; b. Vevay, Ind., June 5, 1868; s. Charles Wesley and Sarah Ann (Cowgill) H.; A.B., Ohio Wesleyan U., 1893, Sc.D., 1919; Ph.D., U. Pa., 1898; m. Elsie Hjerleid Shelley, May 13, 1897; children—Ronald Wayland, Phyllis Thoburn, Sivert H. (dec.), James Procter. Asst. in biology Ohio Wesleyan, 1891-93; prof. biology U. of Pacific, 1893-94; instr. zoölogy Stanford, 1894-98, asst. prof., 1898-1904, asso. prof., 1904-09, prof., 1909-33, now emeritus. Mem. Ohio Wesleyan U. expdn. to Fla., 1890; naturalist, U.S. Fish Commn. Str. Albatross, 1904, exploration Cal. coast, summer, 1905, Japanese expdn., summer, 1906; naturalist on Pribilof Islands, summers 1910, 17; zoölogist, Stanford expdn. to Brazil, summer 1911; naturalist on Forrester Island, Alaska, summer 1913. Fellow Cal. Acad. Sci.; mem. Am. Soc. Zoölogists, A.A.A.S., Western Soc. Naturalists, Phi Beta Kappa, Sigma Xi. Home: care Hopkins Marine Station, Pacific Grove, Cal. Died Apr. 22, 1951.

HEBDEN, JOHN CALDER, chemical engr.; b. Colgate, Wis., Dec. 22, 1862; s. John and Mary (Calder) H.; prep. edn., Mt. Plesant Acad., Providence, R.I.; A.B., Brown U., 1885 (Phi Beta Kappa); post-grad. work, same univ., 1901-03; m. Lucie A. Mann, Nov. 2, 1898 (dec.); 1 dau., Ruth Dunham; m. 2d, Gertrude S.

Beard, Oct. 8, 1919. Chemist and dyer Nat. & Providence Worsted Mills, and Silver Spring Bleachery, 1885-87; resident agt., technician and chemist, William J. Matheson & Co., and Cassela Color Co., 1887-1904; chemist and technician, A. Klipstein & Co., 1904-09; v.p. F. E. Atteaux & Co., 1909-10; v.p. and gen. mgr. Franklin Process Co., 1910-13, Federal Dyestuff & Chem. Corp., 1915-17; pres. and gen. mgr. Dyeing Processes Corp., v.p. Hebden Sugar Process Corp.; also practicing as consulting chemist and chem. engr. Republican. Baptist. Mason. Home: Brooklyn, N.Y. Died June 3, 1929.

HECHT, HANS H., physician, physiologist, educator; b. Basel, Switzerland, Jan. 23, 1913; s. Hans and Hannah (Meinhold) H.; came to U.S., 1937, naturalized, 1942; M.D., U. Berlin (Germany), 1936, U. Utah, 1946; sr. yr. certificate, U. Mich., 1944; m. Ilse Wagner, Nov. 8, 1937; children—Hannelore (Mrs. David R. Ebel), Frank Thomas, Susan. Intern, then resident Wayne County Gen. Hosp., Detroit, 1942-44; research fellow U. Mich., 1937-44; from instr. to asso. prof. medicine U. Utah Coll. medicine, 1944-58, L.E. Viko prof. cardiology, 1957-65, prof. medicine, 1958-65, chmn. div. cardiology, dept. medicine, 1944-65; dir. heart sta. Salt Lake County Gen. Hosp., 1944-65; cons. VA hosps., Salt Lake City and Grand Junction, Colo., 1946-64; prof. medicine and physiology U. Chgo. Med. Sch., 1964-71, Blum-Riese prof. medicine and physiology, 1968-71, chmn. cardiology dept. med., 1964-71, chmn. dept. medicine, 1966-69. Mem. tng. grant com. USPHS, 1959-62, mem. cardiovascular study sect., 1965-71; pres. Utah Heart Assn., 1957. Diplomate Nat. Bd. Med. Examiners, Am. Bd. Internal Medicine (subspeciality cardiovascular medicine; vice chmn. cardiovascular bd. 1961-66). Fellow A.C.P., Am. Coll. Chest Physicians, Pan-Am. Med. Assn., N.Y. Acad. Sci.; mem. Am. Heart Assn., Western Soc. Clin. Research (past pres., sec.), Am. Fedn. Clin. Research (western chmn. 1946), Assn. Am. Physicians, Am. Physiol. Soc., Am. Soc. Clin. Investigation, Western Assn. Physicians (councilor 1957-60, 64-65), I.R.E., Inst. Advancement Med. Communication. Royal Soc. Medicine, Assn. Univ. Cardiologists. Mem. editorial bd. Circulation, Diseases of Chest, Excerpta Medica: Cardiovascular Disease, Am. Jour. Medicine, Malatti Cardiovasculari. Home: Chicago IL Died Aug. 12, 1971.

HECHT, SELIG, prof. biophysics; b. Glogow, Austria, Feb. 8, 1892; s. Mandel and Mary (Mresse) H.; brought to U.S., 1898; B.S., Coll. of City of N.Y., 1913; Ph.D., Harvard, 1917; m. Cecilia Huebschman, June 3, 1917; 1 dau., Maressa. Research asst. U.S. Bureau Fisheries, 1912-13; asst. pharmacologist Bureau of Chemistry, 1913-14; Austin teaching fellow, Harvard, 1915-17; asst. prof. physiology, Creighton Med. Coll., Omaha, 1917-21; nat. and internat. research fellow at Liverpool, Harvard, Naples, Cambridge (Eng.), 1921-26; prof. biophysics, Columbia University, since 1926; lectureships at Cornell, 1929, Harvard, 1930, Harvey Society, 1937; lecturer, New Sch. for Social Research, since 1935; national lecturer, Sigma Xi, 1944; research in chemistry and physics of the processes involved in vision and light reception since 1917. Official investigator, Nat. Defense Research Com., and with Office of Scientific Research and Development (Office of Emergency Management); mem. sub-committee on visual problems, Nat. Research Council; mem. com. Army-Navy Office of Scientific Research and Development Vision Com. Mem., Army-Navy Nat. Research Council Vision Com. Awarded Frederic Ives medal, Optical Soc., 1941; Townsend Harris Medal, Associate Alumni City Coll. of N.Y., 1942. Fellow A.A.A.S.; mem. Am. Soc. Naturalists, Am. Society Zoölogists, Am. Physiol. Society, Optical Society of America, Harvey Society, Phi Beta Kappa, Sigma Xi (v.p. 1940-41, pres. 1941-42, Kappa Chapter), Nátional Academy of Sciences. Editor of Columbia Biological Series, Monographs on Experimental Biology, Biological Bulletin. Asso. editor Journal Optical, Society of America. Author: The Retinal Processes Concerned with Visual Acuity and Color Vision, 1931; La Base Chimique et Structurale de la Vision, 1938; Explaining The Atom, 1947. Contbr. articles to scientific jours. Home: 35 Claremont Av., New York 27. Died Sept. 18, 1947.

HECK, NICHOLAS HUNTER, hydrog. and geodetic engr.; b. Heckton Mills, Pa., Sept. 1, 1882; s. John Lewis and Mary Frances (Hays) H.; B.A., Lehigh, 1903, C.E., 1904. D.Sc., 1929; D.Sc., Fordham University, New York, N.Y., 1941. With U.S. Coast Survey, 1904-45; in charge wire drag parties, Atlantic Coast, 1906-16, comdr. schooner Mathlcess, 1917; lt. and lt. comdr. USNRF, New London, Conn., London, Eng., 1917-19, in charge location of submerged forest in Lake Washington, nr. Seattle, 1919-20; comdr. steamer Explorer, 1920-21; chief div. geomagnetism and seismology Coast and Geodetic Survey, 1921-42, asst. to dir., 1942-45, ret. 1945. Recipient William Bowie medal, Am. Geophys. Union, 1942. Fellow A.A.A.S., Am. Geog. Soc., Philos. Soc. Washington (pres. 1938), Washington Soc. Engrs., Wash. Acad. Sci., Am. Geophys. Union (chmn. 1935-38), Geol. Soc. Am.; mem. Am. Soc. C.E., Geol. Soc. Washington, Seismol. Soc. Am. (pres. 1936-39), Soc. Am. Mil. Engrs., Internat. Seismol. Assn. (pres. 1936-45), Tau Beta Pi, Phi Beta Kappa, Sigma Xi. Presbyn. Club: Cosmos. Author: Earthquakes; also govt. publs. concerning wire drag and sweep work of Coast and Geodetic Survey; compensation of the magnetic compass; velocity of sound in sea water; radio acoustic method of determining position in hydrography; earthquake history of U.S. and articles relating to magnetism and seismology. Home: 3421 Northampton St., Washington 15. Died Dec. 21, 1953; buried Arlington Nat. Cemetery.

HECK, ROBERT CULBERTSON HAYS, mechanical engr.; b. Heckton Mills, Pa., Oct. 30, 1870; s. John Lewis and Mary Frances (Hays) H.; M.E., Lehigh U., 1893, hon. D.Eng., 1927; m. Anna Wilson, Sept. 10, 1902; children—Margaret Wilson, Robert C. H., Mary Hays. Instr. mech. engring., 1893-1903, asst. prof., 1903-07, prof. exptl. engring., 1907-08, Lehigh U.; prof. mech. engring., Rutgers Coll., 1908-35, research prof. of mechanical engring., 1935-41, now emeritus, but teaching Army spl. training students, 1943. Republican. Presbyn. Fellow A.A.A.S.; mem. Am. Soc. Mech. Engrs., 1906, Soc. Promotion Engring. Edn., Nat. Research Council (1932-37), Tau Beta Pi, Phi Beta Kappa, Sigma Xi. Author: Notes to Supplement Holmes' Steam Engine, 1902; Manual for Course in Engineering Laboratory, Lehigh Univ., 1903; The Steam Engine and other Steam Motors, Vol. 1, 1905, Vol. II, 1907; Notes on Elementary Kinematics, 1910; Notes on the Graphics of Machine Forces, 1910; The Steam Engine and Turbine, 1911; Steam Formulas, 1920; Mechanics of Machinery—Mechanism, Kinematics and Dynamics, 1925; Ideal Combustion-Engine Cycles, 1926; New Specific Heats, 1940. Home: 51 Adelaide Av., New Brunswick, N.J. Died Sept. 22, 1951; buried Riverview Cemetery, Heckton, Pa.

HECKEL, NORRIS JULIUS, urol. surgeon; b. Winthrop, Ia., Dec. 16, 1896; s. Joseph and Elizabeth Maxine (Crowder) H.; B.A., U. Ia., 1922; M.D., Rush Med. Coll., U. Chgo., 1926; m. Eileen Valleye McMains, Aug. 19, 1922. Physician, engaged in practice urology and genito-urinary surgery, Chgo., since 1928; prof. urology, dept. surgery Coll. of Medicine, U. Ill.; chmn. dept. Urology Presbyn. Hosp. since 1946; attending Urol-Surgeon Ravenswood Hosp. since 1933. Fellow A.C.S.; mem. Inst. Medicine, Chgo. Soc. Internal Medicine, Soc. Exptl. Biology and Medicine, Am. Bd. Urology, Am. Assn. Genito-Urinary Surgeons (past pres.), Am. Geriatrics Soc. (past pres.), Internat., Am., Chgo. urol. assns., A.M.A., Ill. Med. Soc., Chgo. Med. Soc. (pres. elect), Am. Assn. for Study Internal Secretions, Central Soc. for Clin. Research, Miss. Valley Med. Soc., Western Surg. Assn., Nu Sigma Nu, Phi Kappa Sigma, Sigma Xi. Republican. Club: University (Chgo.). Home: 60 E. Cedar St. Office: 122 S. Michigan Av., Chgo. Died May 28, 1966.

HEDGCOCK, GEORGE GRANT, plant pathologist; b. Augusta, Ill., Oct. 5, 1863; s. Barnett and Sarah Lutitia (Haines) H.; B.Sc., U. of Neb., 1899, A.M., 1901; m. Loura Ladelle Merrill, of Nelson, Neb., June 29, 1892; children—Elaine Ruthe, Leland Merrill, Margaret Lutitia. Teacher, pub. schs., Neb., 1882-91; prin. graded schs., Neb., 1891-95; scholar in botany, 1898-99, fellow, 1899-1901, U. of Neb.; scientific aid, 1901-02, asst. in pathology, 1902-05, plant pathologist, 1905-06, forest pathologist, 1907—, U.S. Dept. Agr. Fellow A.A.A.S.; mem. Bot. Seminar U. of Neb., Bot. Soc. of America, Bot. and Geog. socs. of Washington, Phyto-Pathological Soc. of America, Sigma Xi. Author: Studies in the vegetation of the state, II (Neb.), 1902; Studies upon some chromogenic fungi which discolor wood, 1906; numerous publs. on plant and tree diseases. Home: 110 Maple Av., Takoma Park, Md.

HEDGES, JOSEPH HAROLD, mining engr., govt. ofcl.; b. Lansing, Mich., June 9, 1882; s. Hiram C. and Louise (Gibson) H.; B.S., Mich. State Coll., 1903; E.M., Mich. Coll. Mines, 1905; m. Ethel Adams, Sept. 5, 1916; children—Dorothy, Florence (Mrs. P. L. Norton), Charles. Engr. Copper Range Cons. Mines Co., 1905; engr., mine supt. Mex. Cons. Mining and Smelting Co., 1906-11, Guanajuato Development Co., 1912; chief engr. Moctezuma Copper Co., 1913-16; asst. mgr. Utah Minerals Concentrating Co., 1917; mine foreman United Verde Extension Mining Co., 1918; gen. supt. Prince Cons. Mining and Smelting Co., 1918-22; field engr. Mining Corp. Can., Ltd., 1923-25; asst. to dir. U.S. Bur. Mines, 1926-40; sr. mining engr. U.S. Bur. Mines, College Park, Md., 1940-42; chief Tucson div., 1942-49, chief minerals division, Washington, 1949-50, special assistant to the director since 1951. Minerals advisor Military Govt., Germany, 1945. Mem. Am. Inst. Mining and Metall. Engrs., Tau Beta Pi. Club: Cosmos. Home: 4809 De Russey Parkway, Chevey Chase 15. Md. Office: U.S. Bureau Mines, Washington 25. Died Jan. 12, 1956.

HEDGES, SAMUEL HAMILTON, civil engr.; b. Ira, N.Y., Apr. 18, 1866; s. David Talmadge and Jane (Hamilton) H.; M.S. in C.E., Ia. State Coll. Agr. and Mechanic Arts, 1886; m. Jessie Jackson, June 29, 1892. Began as rodman with Cedar Rapids & Manchester R.R., 1887; asst. city engr. Cedar Rapids, 1887-88; contracting engr. Clinton Bridge & Iron Works, 1888-92; partner John Ward & Co., bridge builders, 1892-93; northwestern agt. Chicago Bridge & Iron Works, at St. Paul, Minn., 1893-99; contracting and designing engr., same, at Chicago, 1899-1905; pres. Puget Sound Bridge & Dredging Co., 1905-28. Mem. Seattle Chamber of Commerce (pres. 1920; trustee, 1921-24). Mem. Am. Soc. C.E. (dir. 1913-16), Western Soc. Engrs., Engineers' Club of Seattle, Sigma Nu. Mason (32 deg., K.T., Shriner). Clubs: Rainier, Broadmoor Golf. Home: 702 14th Av. N. Office: 2929 16th St. S.W., Seattle, Wash. Deceased. *

HEDRICK, EARLE RAYMOND, college prof.; b. Union City, Ind., Sept. 27, 1876; s. Simon and Amy Isabella (Vail) H.; A.B., U. of Mich., 1896, hon. D.Sc., 1936; A.M., Harvard, 1898; Ph.D., U. of Göttingen, 1901; École Normale Supérieure, Paris, 1901; LL.D., U. of Mo., 1939; m. Helen Breeden Seidensticker, Oct. 21, 1901; children—Edith Vail, Helen Breeden, Dorothy Janet, Earle R., Amy Isabella, Rachel Esther (dec.), Clyde Lewis, Frank Jerome, Marjorie Bertha (dec.), Elisabeth Busch, Marjorie Janet (adopted daughter). Instr. mathematics, Sheffield Scientific Sch. (Yale), 1901-03; prof. mathematics, U. of Mo., 1903-24; prof. mathematics, U. of Calif. at Los Angeles, since 1924, provost since 1937 and v.p. U. of Calif. Dir. mathematics, Army Ednl. Corps, A.E.F., Jan.-June 1919. Editor in chief Bull. of Am. Math. Soc., 1921-37. Mem. Am. Math. Soc. (v.p. 1916; pres. 1929-30), Math. Assn. of America (pres. 1916), Nat. Research Council (div. of physical sciences, 1921-24 and 1929-32), Société Mathématique de France, Circolo Matematico di Palermo, Am. Soc. Mech. Engrs., Am. Inst. E.E., A.A.A.S. (v.p.; chmn. Sect. A 1931; sec. Sect. A 1933-40), Soc. for Promotion of Engring. Edn., Am. Assn. Univ. Profs., Deutsche Mathematiker Vereinigung, Phi Beta Kappa, Sigma Xi. Decorated Officier d'Academie (France), 1932. Clubs: University (Los Angeles); Faculty (Berkeley); Bohemian (San Francisco). Author: A Course in Mathematical Analysis (Goursat and Hedrick), 1904; An Algebra for Secondary Schools, 1908; Applications of the Calculus to Mechanics (with O. D. Kellogg), 1909; also articles in math. and educational jours. Editor for the Macmillan Company, of A Series of Mathematical Texts, and of the Engineering Science Series. Address: Univ. of Calif. at Los Angeles, Los Angeles. Died Feb. 3, 1943; buried in Forest Lawn Memorial Park, Glendale, Calif.

HEDRICK, IRA GRANT, civil engr.; b. W. Salem, Ill., Apr. 6, 1868; s. Henderson and Mary Ann H.; C.E., U. of Ark., 1892; B.S., McGill U., Can., 1898, M.S., 1899, D.Sc., 1900; m. Louise Luther, Feb. 10, 1889. Established practice as civ. engr., Oct. 1892; has been identified with many large and important engring. works; pres. Kansas City Viaduct & Terminal Ry. Co., 1907-09; later mem. firm of Hedrick & Cochrane. Address: Kansas City, Mo. Died Dec. 28, 1937.

HEDRICK, ULYSSES PRENTISS, author, horticulturist; b. Independence, Ia., Jan. 15, 1870; s. Benjamin Franklin and Mary Catherine (Myers) H.; B.S., Mich. Agrl. Coll., 1893, M.S., 1895; D.Sc., Hobart Coll., 1913; LL.D., Utah Agrl. Coll., 1938; m. Amy Willis Plummer, June 23, 1898; children—Catherine Layton, Penelope (dec.), Ulysses Prentiss (dec.). Asst. horticulturist, Mich. Agrl. Coll., 1893-95; prof. botany and horticulture Ore. Agrl. Coll., 1895-97, Utah Agrl. Coll., 1897-99; prof. horticulture Mich. Agrl. Coll., 1899-1905; horticulturist N.Y. Agrl. Expt. Sta., 1905-30, dir. 1928-37, emeritus. Fellow A.A.A.S., N.Y. Hist. Assn.; mem. Am. Soc. for Hort. Sci., Am. Pomol. Soc., Sigma Xi, Kappa Alpha, Alpha Zeta. Democrat. Episcopalian. Author: Grapes of New York, 1908; Plums of New York, 1910; Cherries of New York, 1915; Peaches of New York, 1917; Manual of American Grape Growing, 1919; Sturtevant's Notes on Edible Plants, 1919; Cyclopedia of Hardy Fruits, 1921; The Pears of New York, 1922; Systematic Pomology, 1925; Small Fruits of New York, 1925; The Vegetables of New York, 1929; A History of Agriculture in the State of New York, 1933. Fruits for the Home Garden, 1944; Grapes and Wines from Home Vineyards, 1945; Land of the Crooked Tree, 1948; History of Horticulture in America to 1860, 1950. Home: 600 S. Main St., Geneva, N.Y. Died Nov. 14, 1951; buried Geneva, N.Y.

HEDRICK, WYATT CEPHAS, architect, engr.; b. Chatham, Va., Dec. 17, 1888; s. Washington Henry and Emma Cephas (Williams) H.; B.A., Roanoke Coll., 1910, Washington and Lee U., 1910; m. Pauline Stripling, June 17, 1918; 1 dau., Pauline (Mrs. William Robert Coffey); m. 2d, Mildred Sterling, Dec. 17, 1925; children—Mildred (Mrs. Howard Martin Fender), Jean (Mrs. William E. Darden). Engr., Lane Bros., Alta Vista, Va., 1910-13; asso. offices Dallas and Ft. Worth, Stone & Webster Engring. Corp. of Boston, 1913; mgr. W. C. Hedrick Constrn. Co., 1914-21; mem. firm Saguinet, Staats & Hedrick, Ft. Worth, Houston, 1921-25; architect, engr. Wyatt C. Hedrick, Inc., 1925-35, Wyatt C. Hedrick, Ft. Worth, Dallas, Houston, since 1935; architect on projects including: air and naval base Keflavik, Iceland; Shamrock Hotel, Houston; campus bldgs. Tex. Tech. Coll., Lubbock; naval base, Trinidad, B.W.I; extrusion plant Aluminum Co. Am., Phoenix, others. Mem. Am. Soc. C.E., A.I.A. Mason (Shriner), Elk. Clubs: Ft. Worth; Houston; Dallas Athletic; Country (Dallas, Houston, Rivercrest). Died May 5, 1964.

HEDSTROM, CARL OSCAR, inventor; b. Smoland, Sweden, Mar. 12, 1871; s. Andrew P. and Caroline (Danielson) H.; ed. pub. schs., Brooklyn, N.Y.; m. Julia Anderson, of Portland, Conn., Nov. 12, 1898. Early became expert tool maker, later designer and builder of racing bicycles; connected with Hendee Mfg. Co. since 1901; invented the Indian Motorcycle for which was awarded silver medal and high diploma of merit, St. Louis Expn., 1904. Founder mem. Federation Am. Motorcyclists; mem. Soc. Automotive Engrs. K.P. Clubs: New York Athletic; Hartford Gun; Portland; Middletown Yacht. Home: Portland CT

HEERMANN, ADOLPHUS L., physician, ornithologist; b. S.C., circa 1827; M.D., U. Md., 1846. Joined Phila. Acad. Natural Scis., 1845; made trip to Cal., 1849-52, collected many specimens of birds, nests and eggs; apptd. acting asst. surgeon U.S. Army on railroad survey of So. Cal., 1853; used word oology for his collection of birds' nests and eggs (possibly 1st usage of term in Am. Ornithology); Heermann's gull named in his honor, 1852. Died nr. San Antonio, 1865.

HEGNER, ROBERT WILLIAM, zoölogist; b. Decorah, Ia., Feb. 15, 1880; s. Charles G. and Wilhelmina (Busch) H.; B.Sc., U. of Chicago, 1903, M.S., 1904; Ph.D., University of Wisconsin, 1908; hon. Sc.D., Mt. Union College, 1939; m. Jane Zabriskie, Sept. 12, 1906; children—Janette La Tourette Zabriskie, Mary Elizabeth (dec.), Isabel McKinney (dec.). Instr. and asst. prof. zoölogy, U. of Mich., 1908-18; asso. prof. protozoölogy, Sch. of Hygiene and Pub. Health, Johns Hopkins, 1918-20; prof. and head of dept. med. zoölogy, same univ., since 1922; visiting prof. of parasitology, Sch. of Hygiene and Pub. Health, U. of the Philippines, 1929-30, London Sch. of Tropical Medicine, 1926. Mem. scientific expedition to Mexico, 1903; del. to Royal Inst. Pub. Health, Brussels, Belgium, 1920; in chg. expdn. for study of tropical medicine, Porto Rico and Venezuela, 1921; del. to Internat. Congress on Health Problems in Tropical America, Jamaica, 1924; mem. Scientific Board of Gorgas Memorial Institute. Fellow A.A.A.S., Royal Inst. Pub. Health (London), Royal Soc. Tropical Medicine; mem. American Soc. Zoölogists, Am. Soc. Parasitologists, Am. Soc. Naturalists, Sigma Xi, Phi Beta Kappa, Delta Omega, Alpha Pi Lambda; corr. mem. Belgium Soc. of Tropical Medicine. Unitarian. Author: Introduction to Zoölogy, 1910; College Zoölogy, 1912; Germ Cell Cycle in Animals, 1914; Practical Zoölogy, 1914; Diagnosis of Protozoa and Worms Parasitic in Man (with Dr. W. W. Cort), 1921; Outlines of Medical Zoölogy (with Dr. Cort and Dr. F. M. Root), 1923; Human Protozoölogy (with Dr. W. H. Taliaferro), 1924; Host-Parasitic Relations between Man and His Intestinal Protozoa, 1927; Animal Parasitology (with Dr. F. M. Root and D. L. Augustine), 1929; Problems and Methods of Research in Protozoölogy (with Dr. Justin Andrews), 1930; Invertebrate Zoölogy, 1933; Parade of the Animal Kingdom, 1935; Big Fleas Have Little Fleas, 1938. Editor of Century Biol. series; contbg. editor Quarterly Rev. of Biology; mem. editorial board, Jour. of Morphology, Am. Jour. of Hygiene, Jour. of Parasitology; hon. editor Revista di Malariologia. Contbr. to mags. Home: 218 Hawthorne Rd., Baltimore, Md. Died Mar. 11, 1942.

HEIKES, VICTOR CONRAD, statistician; b. Dayton, O., May 21, 1867; s. William Fletcher and Lettie (Conard) H.; grad. as assayer and chemist, Colo. State Sch. of Mines, 1889; m. Anna Sellier, Oct. 25, 1899; 1 son, George Conrad. Railroad surveys, Wyo., 1886; chemist, spl. mining investigation for Rio Grande Western Ry., 1890; chemist, La Gran Fundicion Nacional Mexicana, Monterey, Mex., 1891; asst. and chief, Colo. mining dept., Chicago Expn., 1892-93; curator economic geology, Field Columbian Museum, Chicago, 1894; supt. of mill, Sunshine Gold Mining Co., Utah, 1895-96; chemist, Mingo Smelter, Utah, 1896; mem. firm Watts & Heikes, assayers and chemists, Boulder, Colo., 1897-99; spl. agt., asst. and acting dir. mines and metallurgy, U.S. Commn. to Paris Expn., 1899-1900; field asst. Div. of Mineral Resources, U.S. Geol. Survey, 1901; chief clk., 1902, asst. chief, 1903-04, Dept. Mines and Metallurgy, St. Louis Expn.; statistician in charge Salt Lake Region branch U.S. Geol. Survey, 1904-25; engr. in charge Salt Lake sect. mineral resources and statistics, including Ariz., Ida., Mont., Nev., Utah and Wash., 1925-27; in charge mine production statistics of Calif. and Ore., San Francisco office of U.S. Bur. of Mines, 1928-33 (retired). Mem. Am. Inst. Mining and Metall. Engrs. Author (with G. F. Loughlin) of treatises on arsenic, bismuth, selenium, tellurium; also on platinum and allied metals. Mason. Home: Carmel, Calif. Died June 29, 1948; buried Piedmont Cemetery, Oakland, Calif.

HEILAND, CARL AUGUST, geophysicist; b. Hamburg, Germany, July 16, 1899; s. Carl Heinrich and Emilie (Gruetter) H.; grad. Wilhelm Gymnasium, Hamburg, 1917; Dr. rer. nat., U. of Hamburg, 1923; student U. of Hamburg, 1918-22, U. of Heidelberg, 1922-23. Came to United States, 1925, naturalized, 1935. Married Peggy Johnston, May 24, 1947; one daughter, Ann, one son John Thomas. Geophysical field work State of Hamburg, 1921-22, A. Raky Drilling Company, 1922-23; in charge geophys. dept. Askania Werke, Berlin, 1924-25, Am. rep., 1925-26; prof. of geophysics and head dept., Colo. Sch. of Mines, 1926-48; pres. Heiland Research Corp., Denver, pres. div. of Minneapolis-Honeywell Regulator Co. Collaborator in seismology, U.S. Coast & Geodetic Survey. Fellow Geol. Society of America; Mem. Am. Geophys. Union, Soc. Exploration Geophysicists, Am. Inst. Mining and Metall. Engrs., Seismol. Soc. Am., Am. Assn. Petroleum Geologists. Republican. Lutheran. Clubs: Teknik, Denver (Denver). Author: Geophysical Exploration, 1940. Contbr. many geophys. and geol. articles to tech. jours. Home: 935 Field St., Lakewood, Colo. Office: 130 E. Fifth Av., Denver. Died Feb. 23, 1956.

HEILBRUNN, LEWIS VICTOR, biologist; b. Bklyn., Jan. 24, 1892; s. Victor and Matilda (Biedermann) H.; A.B., Cornell U., 1911; Ph.D., U. Chgo., 1914; m. Marion Applebee Kerr, Jan. 13, 1923 (dec.); 1 dau., Constance; m. 2d, Ellen Donovan, June 3, 1932. Asso. in zoölogy, U. Chgo., 1914-16; instr., U. of Ill., Med. Sch., 1916-17; instr. of zoölogy, U. of Mich., 1919-21, asst. prof., 1921-29; Guggenheim Meml. Found. fellow, 1927-28; asso. prof. zoölogy, U. Pa., 1929-43, prof. 1943—. Mem. Nat. Research Council (Div. of Biology and Agriculture), 1935-38; trustee Marine Biol. Lab., Woods Hole, Mass., 1931—. Served as 1st. lt. Air Service, U.S. Army, 1917-19; later capt., Air Corps Res., 1919-29. Awarded Silver Star with 2 oak leaf clusters. Fellow A.A.A.S.; mem. Am. Soc. Zoölogists (v.p. 1932), Am. Soc. Naturalists, Amer. Physiol. Soc., Soc. for Exptl. Biology and Medicine, Soc. Gen. Physiologists (pres., 1946). Author: The Colloid Chemistry of Protoplasm, 1928; An Outline of General Physiology, 1937; 2d ed., 1943. Former mng. editor Protoplasm monographs; mem. editorial bd. Physiol. Zoölogy. Address: Zoöl. Laboratory, Univ. of Pa., Phila. 4. Died Oct. 1959.

HEILMAN, FORDYCE R(USSELL), physician; b. Austin, Minn., June 16, 1905; s. Oliver Charles and Emma (Larson) H.; student N.D. Agrl. Coll., 1923-26; B.S., Northwestern U., 1930, M.D., 1931; fellow Mayo Foundn. Grad. Sch., U. of Minn., 1932-35, M.S., 1938, Ph.D. 1940; m. Dorothy Henderson, Aug. 10, 1934 (div. 1953). Intern St. Luke's Hosp., Chicago, 1930-31, resident physician, 1931-32; 1st asst. Mayo Foundn., 1935-39, cons. physician Mayo Clinic since 1939, head sect. on bacteriology since 1945; instr. in bacteriology Mayo Foundn. Grad. Sch., U. of Minn., 1939-41, asst. professor bacteriology, 1941-45, asso. prof., 1945-46, professor bacteriology since 1946. Mem. A.M.A., A.A.A.S., Am. Soc. Bacteriologists, Am. Assn. Cancer Research, Am. Soc. Clin. Pathologists, Soc. Exptl. Biology and Medicine, Am. Pub. Health Assn., N.Y. Academy Sciences, American Academy of Microbiology, Society for General Microbiology, Phi Rho Sigma, Sigma Xi, Alpha Omega Alpha. Conbr. to med. and sci. jours. Research in chemotherapy of infectious disease. Home: 1516 3d Av. N.E. Office: Mayo Clinic, Rochester, Minn. Died Aug. 15, 1960.

HEILMAN, RUSSELL HOWARD, engr.; b. Ford City, Pa., Nov. 30, 1893; s. William Thompson and Anna Louise (Montgomery) H.; B.S., U. Pitts., 1921, E.E., 1923, M.E., 1927; m. Olive I. Butler, Jan. 8, 1916; children—Helen Claire (Mrs. E. D. Greer, Jr.), Betty Louise (Mrs. R. L. Watterson, Jr.). Asst., Mellon Inst., Pitts., 1917-19, fellow, 1920-25, sr. fellow since 1925. Recipient jr. award Am. Soc. M.E. for papers on heat transmission, 1922 and 1924. Profl. engr., Pa., since 1946. Mem. Am. Soc. M.E., Am. Soc. Heating and Ventilating Engrs., Am. Soc. for Testing Materials, Am. Standards Assn., Sigma Xi. Republican. Methodist. Mason (Shriner). Specialist on heat-insulation and heat and vapor transmission; contbr. papers on heat transmission to tech. publs. Home: 113 Mason Dr., Glenshaw, Pa. Office: Mellon Inst., Pitts. 13. Died May 1, 1966.

HEILNER, VAN CAMPEN, editor, author, explorer; b. Phila., July 1, 1899; s. Samuel and Adelaide Lincoln (Breese) H.; studied Phillips Acad., Andover, Mass.; grad. Lake Placid-Florida Sch., 1918; M.S., Trinity Coll., Hartford, Conn., 1927; studied ichthyology under Dr. J. T. Nichols, Am. Mus. Natural History; m. Mary La Vie, June, 1919 (divorced 1951); children—Mary, Samuel; married second, Raquel Romero, February 19, 1950. Asso. editor Field and Stream; field representative in ichthyology of American Mu. of Natural History, ichthyologist expdn. to Peru and Ecuador, 1924-25, Alaska, 1927, Cuba, 1934-35; Peabody Mus. of Yale expdn. to Tiena del Fuego and Straits of Magellan, 1948. First naturalist to make motion pictures successfully of the roseate spoonbill in its nat. haunts; disc. several new species of West Indian fishes. Fellow Royal Geog. Soc., Royal Anthropol. Inst. (London), Am. Geog. Soc.; mem. Am. Mus. Natural History (hon. life), American Soc. of Mammalogists, Am. Soc. Ichthyologists and Herpetologists, Society of Colonial Wars, Sons of Revolution, Huguenot Soc., Bombay Natural History Soc.; asso. Am. Ornithologists' Union; hon. mem. British Sea Anglers Soc. Republican. Presbyn. Mason (32 deg.). Clubs: Explorers (life); Phlia. Gun. Author books. Master smallest motor boat ever to go from Atlantic City to Venezuela, 4000 miles. Decorated Order of Carlos Manuel de Cespedes (Cuba), 1937. Photographer and dir. short and feature subjects for motion picture companies. Home: Hampton Bays LI NY Deceased.

HEILPRIN, ANGELO, naturalist; b. Sátoralja-Ujhely, Hungary, March 31, 1853; s. Michael and Henrietta H.; came to U.S., 1856; ed. in Europe, making spl. study of natural history. Successively prof. invertebrate paleontology and geology, 1880-1900, and exec. curator, 1883-92. Acad. Natural Sciences, Phila.; prof. geology, Wagner Free Inst., 1885-90; pres. for 7 yrs. Geog. Soc., Phila.; v.p. Am. Alpine Club, 1903. Leader Peary Relief Expdn., 1892. Exhibited paintings several exhbns. Author: The Animal Life of our Seashore, 1888 L5; The Bermuda Islands; A Contribution to the Physical History and Zoölogy of the Somers Archipelago, 1889 A7; Principles of Geology, 1890 O1; Peary Relief Expedition, 1893 O1; The Earth and Its Story, 1896 S6; Alaska and the Klondike, 1899 A2; Mont Pelée and the Tragedy of Martinique, 1903; Tower of Pelée, 1905 L5. Died 1907.

HEINICKE, ARTHUR JOHN, pomologist; St. Louis, Mo., Oct. 23, 1892; s. Martin Theodore and Magdalena (Beckert) H.; B.S.A., U. of Mo., 1913, M.A., 1914; Ph.D., Cornell U., 1916; m. Marguerite Eva Riemann, Sept. 15, 1917; 1 son, Arthur John. Fellow in horticulture, U. of Mo., 1913-14; with Cornell U. from 1914, instr. in pomology until 1917, asst. prof., 1917-20, prof., 1920-60, head dept., 1921-60, head div. pomology, 1942, dir. N.Y. State (Geneva) Agrl. Expt. Sta., 1942-60, prof. emeritus, from 1960. Fellow A.A.A.S.; mem. Am. Soc. Hort. Science (pres. 1937), Am. Bot. Soc., Am. Soc. of Plant Physiologists, Sigma Xi, Gamma Alpha, Phi Kappa Phi, Gamma Sigma Delta. Ind. Republican. Lutheran. Author of various research bulls. issued by Cornell U. also articles in profl. jours. Home: Ithaca NY Deceased.

HEINRICH, EDWARD OSCAR, (hin'rich), chemical-legal expert; b. Clintonville, Wis., Apr. 20, 1881; s. August Frederick and Albertina Otilla (Zempel) H.; licentiate in pharmacy, Wash., 1899; B.S., U. of Calif., 1908; m. Marion Allen, Sept. 28, 1908; children—Theodore Allen, Mortimer Allen. Began as pharm. chemist, at Tacoma, Wash., 1899; chem. and sanitary engring. practice, Tacoma, 1908-17; also served as city chemist, engr. of tests and as expert in criminal investigations; chief of police, Alameda, Calif., 1917; city mgr., Boulder, Colo., 1918-19; practice, San Francisco, since July 1919. Lecturer on criminal investigation, University of California, 1917-25, 1938-39; research asso. in police science, 1930-31, lecturer in polit. science, 1943, lecturer in industrial plant protection, Engineering, Science, and Management War Training, 1943. Expert on questioned documents and other scientific evidence in Hindu-Ghadr revolution plot trials, San Francisco, 1917, also in cases of United States vs. William (Jack) Dempsey, United States vs. Levin (income tax frauds), People vs. Roscoe Arbuckle, People vs. William Hightower, the d'Autremont train bandits, Ore., St. Francis Dam failure, Los Angeles, 1928, U.S. vs. Germany (Black Tom cases, 1930-34), U.S. in re Harry Bridges, 1939, and other celebrated cases. Participant XVth International Criminal Police Commission Conference, Berlin, 1939, Captain Engineer Res., U.S. Army, 1917-32. Mem. Am. Inst. Criminal Law and Criminology, Am. Chem. Soc., Soc. Am. Mil. Engrs., Soc. of Pub. Analysts (Eng.), L'Académie Internationale de Criminalistique, Acacia, Phi Lambda Upsilon; hon. fellow Internat. Medico-Legal Assn. Democrat. Protestant. Mason (K.T.). Clubs: Hillside (Berkeley); Faculty (University of California); Engineers (San Francisco). Author: Introduction to Signature Inspection and Authentication, 1947; Flow Sheet for Criminal Investigation, 1953; articles and reports on subjects pertaining to detection of forgery, criminal investigation, city management, etc. Home: 1001 Oxford St., Berkeley 7, Calif. Office: Marvin Bldg., 24 California St., San Francisco 11. Died Sept. 28, 1953; inurned Chapel of the Chimes, Columbarium, Oakland, Cal.

HEINZ, JOHN BERNARD, pharmacist; b. Petersburg, Neb., Sept. 25, 1890; s. Lawrence and Wilhelmina (Radfeski) H.; Ph.G. Creighton U., 1912, LL.D., 1955; Pharm.M., Phila. Coll. Pharmacy and Sci., 1954; m. F. Dorothy Hieber, Aug. 12, 1913 (dec. June 1958); children—Jack Donald, Kennth; m. 2d, Ethel Hanson, Apr. 18, 1960. Pharmacist Parchen Drug Co., Helena, Mont., 1912; lab. technician Starz Pharmacy, Helena, 1912-17; founder Heinz Drug Co., Laurel, Mont., 1917-30, Heinz Drug, Salt Lake City, 1930-44; founder, pres. Heinz Apothecaries, Inc., Salt Lake City, 1944—; head Am. delegation Pan-Am. Congress Pharmacy and Biochemistry, Sao Paulo, Brazil, 1954, Internat. Fedn. Pharmaeutique, London, Eng., 1955. Pres. Utah State Bd. Pharmacy, 1953-54; dir. Utah chpt. Am. Cancer Soc. Mem. Nat. Pharm. Council (adv. com.), Am. (pres.), Utah (past pres., dir.) pharm. assns., Nat. Assn. Retail Druggists, Am. Coll. Apothecaries (past pres.; Leon Lascoff award 1956), C. of C. (adv. council), Phi Delta Chi, Rho Chi. K.C. (4 deg.), Elk. Clubs: Rotary, Salt Lake Country, Ambassador Athletic. Office: 508 E. South Temple St., Salt Lake City 2. Died Apr. 29, 1965.

HEINZE, F. AUGUSTUS, mining engr.; b. Brooklyn, N.Y., Dec. 5, 1869; s. Otto and Lida M. (Lacey) H.; ed. Poly. Inst., Brooklyn; E.M., Columbia Sch. of Mines, 1889; studied in Germany; unmarried. Engaged in mining and smelting in Mont., 1889—; pres. United

Copper Co.; dir. Montana Ore Purchasing Co. Active in Mont. politics as Democrat. Home: Butte, Mont. Died Nov. 4, 1914.

HEISER, VICTOR GEORGE, hygienist; b. Pennsylvania, 1873; s. George and Mathilde H.; M.D., Jefferson Medical College, Philadelphia, 1897, Sc.D., 1911; Sc.D., Rutgers Coll., N.J., 1917; LL.D., Temple U., 1939; Sc.D., Thiel Coll., 1939; m. Marion Phinny, April 20, 1940. Entered U.S. Marine Hosp. Service, 1898; spl. detail to Europe to report upon emigration to U.S., 1899; spl. detail to Egypt to study plague, 1899; del. Internat. Congress on Tuberculosis, Naples, 1900; to Canada with regard to emigration, 1901; del. Internat. Congress on Med., Egypt, 1902; chief quarantine officer, P.I., 1903-15, and dir. of health, 1905-15; asso. dir. Internat. Health Div., Rockefeller Foundation, 1915-34 (retired); formerly mem. adv. council, Nat. Health Adminstrn., China; pres. Internat. Leprosy Assn., 1931-38; consultant in pub. health administration and industrial medicine; chmn. med. advisory com., New York World's Fair of 1939; consultant on Healthful Working Conditions, National Association of Mfrs., since 1938; mem. bd. directors American Museum of Health. Connected with work of stamping out plague, cholera, smallpox, etc., also the building of the Philippine Gen. Hosp., Coll. Medicine and Surgery, and many hosps. throughout the Philippines; served as prof. hygiene, Coll. Medicine and Surgery, P.I. Received Trimble Lecture Medal, 1935; award for distinguished service in public health by Holland Soc. of N.Y., 1939; gold medal of Pa. Soc. Mem. A.M.A., Am. Acad. Tropical Medicine, Am. Pub. Health Assn., Far Eastern Assn. of Tropical Medicine, J. Aitken Meigs Med. Assn., A.A.A.S., Am. Philos. Soc., Pa. Society. Member committee on nutrition of industrial workers, National Research Council. Clubs: Army and Navy (Manila, Philippine Islands, and Washington, D.C.); Century, New York Athletic (New York City). Author: An American Doctor's Odyssey, 1936; You're the Doctor, 1939; Toughen Up, America!, 1941; Industrial Health Practices, 1941; Health on the Production Front, 1943; Vision in Industry, 1947. Sanitary Code, Manila, Manual Bur. Health, Manila. Co-Author: Handbook of Medical Treatment, 1918; Oxford System of Medicine, 1921; Practice of Medicine in the Tropics, 1922; A System of Pediatrics, 1924; A Text-Book of Medicine by American Authors, 1926; Cyclopedia of Medicine, 1932; Encyclopedia Americana, 1943-46. Mem. American Red Cross Commission to Italy, 1917; mem. com. on health and med. relief, U.S.R.R. Administration, 1918-20. Home: Bantam CT

HEISING, RAYMOND ALPHONSUS, cons. engr., patent agt.; b. Albert Lea, Minn., Aug. 10, 1888; s. Charles and Anna A. (Fitzgerald) H.; E.E., U. N.D., 1912; M.S., U. Wis., 1914; D.Sc., 1947; m. Teresa A. Coneys, Nov. 25, 1920; children—William P., Charles R., Mary Ellen. Engr. radio research engr. Western Electric Co. Inc., N.Y., 1914-25; radio research engr. Bell Telephone Lab. Inc., 1925-44, patent engr., 1945-53, ret.; cons. engr., patent agt., 1953—. Developed radio telephone transmitters for naval ships and army airplanes, World War, 1917-18; aided in devel. trans-Atlantic long wave telephone circuit, 1922-29, short wave transoceanic circuits, 1925-29, ship-shore telephone circuit, 1929. Awarded Modern Pioneer award, N.A.M., 1940, Armstrong medal, Radio Club Am., 1953. Fellow I.R.E. (past pres., Morris Liebmann Meml. Prize, 1921, Founder's medal 1957), A.A.A.S., Am. Phys. Soc., Am. Inst. E.E. Republican. Catholic. K.C. Author: Quartz Crystals for Elec. Circuits, 1946. Contbr. articles to engring. socs. Over 100 U.S. patents. Address 232 Oak Ridge Av., Summit, N.J. Died Jan. 16, 1965.

HEISKELL, HENRY LEE, meteorologist; b. Washington, Oct. 17, 1850; s. Maj. Henry Lee (U.S.A.) and Elizabeth K. (Gouverneur) H.; g.g.s. President James Monroe; Rock Hill Coll., Ellicott City, Md.; U.S. Naval Acad., 1866-69 (resigned); spl. course in meteorology under Prof. Frank H. Bigelow and Prof. Cleveland Abbe; m. Emma L. Heiskell, Oct. 16, 1878 (died 1890); m. 2d, Henrietta Brent, Oct. 12, 1892. In mercantile business, St. Louis and Yazoo City, Miss., 1869-76; pvt. and sergt., U.S. Signal Corps, 1876, until that service was transferred to Agrl. Dept. as U.S. Weather Bur., 1888; clk., chief of div., marine meteorologist, and from Mar. 1, 1913, prof. meteorology, U.S. Weather Bur. Democrat. Catholic. Died Jan. 28, 1914.

HEKTOEN, LUDVIG, (hek'ton), pathologist; b. Westby, Wis., July 2, 1863; s. Peter P. and Olave Hektoen; A.B., Luther Coll., Ia., 1883, A.M., 1896; studied U. of Wis.; M.D., Coll. Phys. and Surg., Chicago, 1887; interne, Cook County Hosp., Chicago, 1887-89; studied Upsala, Prague, Berlin, 1890, 94, 95; M.D., ad eundem, Rush Med. College, 1896; hon. M.D., U. of Norway, 1911; Sc.D., U. of Mich., 1913. U. of Wis., 1916; U. of Chicago, 1940; LL.D., U. of Cincinnati, 1920. Western Reserve U., 1920, and Luther Coll., Decorah, Ia., 1936; m. Ellen Strandh, July 7, 1891; children—Aikyn (dec.), Josef Ludvig, Pathologist to Cook County (Ill.) Hosp., 1889-1903; lecturer pathology, Rush Med. Coll., 1890-92; physician to coroner's office, Chicago, 1890-94; prof. pathology, Coll. Phys. and Surg., Chicago, 1892-94; prof. morbid anatomy, Rush Med. Coll., 1895-98, prof. pathology, 1898-1933, prof. emeritus since 1933; prof. and head dept. pathology, U. of Chicago, 1901-32; dir. John McCormick Inst. for Infectious Diseases, 1902-39. Mem. Occupational Diseases Commission of Illinois, 1909-11. President Chicago Tumor Institute since 1938. Editor Journal of Infectious Diseases, 1904-40, Archives of Pathology, 1926-49. Chmn. div. of med. sciences, Nat. Research Council, 1924-25, 1926-27, 1929-30; chmn. Nat. Research Council, 1936-38; mem. Nat. Advisory Health Council, U.S.P.H.S., 1934-38; exec. dir. Nat. Advisory Cancer Council, U.S.P.H.S. 1937-1944. Received Centennial Award, Wis. State Medical Society, 1941, Distinguished Service medal, American Medical Association, 1942. Gold-headed cane, Association American Pathologists and Bacteriologists, 1944; Howard Taylor Ricketts award, U. of Chicago, 1949. Mem. National Acad. Sciences, Assn. Am. Phys., A.M.A., Chicago Med. Soc. (pres. 1919-21), Chicago Pathol. Soc. (pres. 1898-1902), Assn. Am. Pathologists and Bacteriologists (pres. 1901), Soc. Am. Bacteriologists (pres. 1929), Soc. Immunologists (pres. 1927), Inst. of Medicine of Chicago (pres. 1929), A.A.A.S. (v.p. 1909); hon. mem. Norwegian Med. Soc., Am. Soc. of Clinical Pathologists; mem. Norwegian Acad. of Sciences; honorary member Philadelphia Pathological Society, Swedish Medical Society (Stockholm), Norwegian Pathological Society, Vienna Microbiologie Society, American Society of Bacteriologists, Academy of Medicine, Washington, College of American Pathologists (honorary member). Decorated Order of St. Olaf (Norway). Club: University (Chicago, Illinois). Author: Post-mortem Technique, 1894; Introduction to Study of Infectious Diseases. Editor: Durck's Pathologic Histology; Collected Works of Christian Fenger: Contributions to Medical Science, by Howard Taylor Ricketts. Co-editor and contributor to American Text-Book of Pathology, 1902; has written numerous articles on pathology, bacteriology and immunology. Co-compiler: A Bibliography of Infantile Paralysis, 1789-1944, 1946. Home: 5650 Dorchester Av. Address: 21 W. Elm St., Chicago 10. Died July 5, 1951; buried Rosehill Cemetery, Chgo.

HELLBAUM, ARTHUR ALFRED, pharmacologist; b. Latah, Wash., June 22, 1904; s. Frederick Erick and Emma Elizabeth (Herrmann) H.; A.B., St. Olaf Coll., 1930; D.Sci. (hon.), 1964; A.M., U. Wis., 1932, Ph.D., 1934; M.D., U. Chgo., 1943; m. Halcyon Woodward Lallier, June 17, 1933; children—Lois Mae, Dorothy Ann, Richard Frederick. Teaching asst. zoology St. Olaf Coll., 1928-30; grad. asst. U. Wis., 1930-34, instr., 1934-36; asst. prof. physiology Okla. Sch. Medicine, 1936-39, asso. prof., 1937-43, prof. pharmacology, 1943—, chmn. dept., 1943—, asso. dean Med. Sch., 1947-52, asso. dean grad. Coll. Okla. U. in charge grad. work Sch. Medicine 1947-54; practice limited to arthritis and related diseases, 1960—; adminstr. personnel for research Am. Cancer Soc., 1958-60; cons. Bone and Joint Hosp., Oklahoma City. Mem. Am. Soc. Pharmacol. and Exptl. Therapeutics, Am. Physiol. Soc., Am. Zool. Assn., A.M.A., Am. Assn. Anatomists, Soc. Exptl. Biology and Medicine, Endocrine Soc., Am. Assn. Cancer Research, Geriatrics Soc., Am. Rheumatism Assn., A.A.A.S., American Diabetes Assn., Okla. Acad. Sci., Gerontology Soc., Alpha Omega Alpha, Phi Beta Pi, Sigma Xi, Gamma Alpha. Lutheran. Contbr. research papers sci. jours., books fields endocrinology, metabolism, gastrointestinal physiology, protein metabolism, arthritis. Home: 1713 3d S.W. Office: 207C N.W., Ardmore, Okla. Died Sept. 4, 1964; buried Meml. Park Cemetery, Oklahoma City.

HELLER, A(MOS) ARTHUR, botanist; b. Montour Co., Pa., Mar. 21, 1867; s. Amos and Susan H.; A.B., Franklin and Marshall Coll., 1892, A.M., 1898 (Sc.D., 1911); m. E. Gertrude Halbach, of Lancaster, Pa., Apr. 8, 1896. On bot. explorations in South and West, 1892-94, in H.I., 1895, Ida., 1896; instr. botany, U. of Minn., 1896-98; on bot. exploration in Wash., 1898, Cal., 1902 and 1908, Porto Rico, 1898-99, 1900-2-3; asst. botanist, Nev. Agrl. Expt. Sta., 1908; asst. prof. botany, horticulture and forestry, U. of Nev., 1910-13. Wrote about 20 papers in Bull. Torrey Bot. Club, 1892-99; Memoirs Torrey Bot. Club, 1892; 3 papers in Minn. Bot. Studies, 1897-98; Catalogue of North American Plants, 1898, 2d edit., 1900. Editor and publisher of "Muhlenbergia," a Journal of Botany. Address: Chico, Cal.

HELLER, EDMUND, naturalist; b. Freeport, Ill., May 21, 1875; s. Edward and Mary Ann (Schottle) H.; A.B., Stanford U., 1901. Stanford Zoölogy Expdn. to Galapagos Islands, 1898-99; asst. naturalist, U.S. Biol. Survey, Alaska, 1900; naturalist, Field Mus., Chicago, exploration in Calif., Mexico, Guatemala and E. Africa, 1901-07; curator of mammals in U. of Calif. Mus. of Natural History, 1907-08; naturalist, Smithsonian African Expdn. under direction of Col. Theodore Roosevelt, E. Africa, 1909-10, Rainey African Expdn., E. Africa, 1911-12; Peruvian Expdn., 1915, under auspices of Yale U. and Nat. Geog. Soc.; exploration in S.W. China on Tibetan and Burma borders for Am. Mus. Natural History, 1916-17; photographic staff of the Czecho-Slovak army, with Paul J. Rainey in Siberia, 1918; Cape to Cairo African Expdn. of Smithsonian Instn., 1919-20; investigation big game animals, Yellowstone Nat. Park, 1921; expdn. across Peru and down Amazon to its mouth, 1922-23; expdn. Central Africa Mountains of Moon, Gorilla Volcanoes, 1924-26; served as asst. curator mammals, Field Museum, Chicago; dir. Milwaukee Zoöl. Gardens, 1928-35, Fleishhacker Zoo, San Francisco, 1935—. Joint author: (with Theodore Roosevelt) Life Histories of African Game Animals. Died July 18, 1939.

HELLMAN, MILO, orthodontist; b. Jassy, Roumania, Mar. 26, 1872; s. Wolf and Fanny (Hellman) H.; came to U.S., 1888, naturalized, 1893; prep. edn., New York Prep. Sch.; D.D.S., University of Pennsylvania, 1905; hon. Sc.D., 1933; graduate student Angle School of Orthodontia, N.Y. City, 1908; hon. Sc.D., Witwatersrand Univ., Johannesburg, South Africa, 1938; m. Helen Michelson, Nov. 30, 1905; children—Doris, Edith (Mrs. John L. Bull Jr.), Marion (Mrs. William T. Sandalls). Practiced dentistry N.Y. City, 1905-08; in practice of orthodontia 1908-42, consultant since 1942; lecturer in orthodontia, Univ. of Pa. School of Dentistry, 1924-26, Harvard Dental Sch., 1927-28; prof. comparative dental anatomy, New York U. Coll. of Dentistry, 1927-28, prof. of orthodontia, 1928-29; prof. of dentistry, Sch. Dental and Oral Surgery, Columbia U., since 1932; research associate in phys. anthropology, Am. Museum of Natural History since 1917. Mem. com. on growth and development, White House Conf. on Child Health and Protection, 1930. Participated in Internat. Symposium on Early Man, Phila., 1937, Symposium on Development of Occlusion at Bicentennial Celebration U. of Pa., 1940, Orthodontic Conf., U. of Southern Calif., 1940; hon. pres. 1st Internat. Orthodontic Congress, N.Y. City, 1926, 2d, London, 1931; mem. exec. group of coms. for standardization of anthrop. techniques, Internat. Congress Anthropologists and Ethnologists, 1937-38; mem. S. African Expdn. of Am. Mus. of Nat. History, 1938; consultant Bur. of Med. Information, N.Y. Acad. of Medicine. Received hon. citation by Assoc. Founds. in Lab. of Anatomy, Western Reserve Univ., Cleveland O., 1937; Albert H. Ketcham Memorial award, 1939. Fellow N.Y. Acad. Science (v.p. 1932, 33), A.A.A.S., Am. Coll. of Dentists, N.Y. Acad. Dentistry, Odontological Soc. Union of S. Africa; asso. fellow N.Y. Acad. Med.; mem. Am. Dental Assn. (life), N.Y. State Dental Soc. (Scientific research com). 1st Dist. Dental Soc., Internat. Assn. Dental Research (pres. N.Y. Sect. 1933), Soc. for Research in Child Development (mem. field com. on physical environment and nutrition), Am. Association Physical Anthropologists (life), American Assoc. Mammalogists, Am. Ethnol. Soc., N.Y. Soc. of Orthodontists, Am. Assn. Orthodontists (exec. and research coms.; v.p. 1941), Eastern Assn. Grads of Angle Sch. of Orthodontia (president 1911), American Association of Dental Editors, Delta Sigma Delta, Sigma Xi, Omicron Kappa Upsilon; hon. mem. Southern Soc. of Orthodontists, Mexican Orthodontic Soc.; charter mem. Soc. of Vertebrate Paleontology. Author: The Dentition of Dryopithecus and the Origin of Man (with W. K. Gregory), 1926; Fossil Anthropoids of the Yale-Cambridge Expedition of 1935 (with others), 1938. Mem. editorial board Archives of Clinical and Oral Pathology. Editor American Orthodontist, 1910-12. Contributor of chapter "The Evidences of the Dentition on the Origin of Man" in Early Man, 1937; chaper "The Face in Its Developmental Career" in The Human Face, 1935; chapter "The Factors Influencing Occlusion" in Development of Occlusion, 1941; chapter "White House Conf. on Child Health and Protection, Part II." 1931. Contributor over 70 articles to scientific and dental journals. Home: 49 Merrall Road, Far Rockaway, N.Y. Died May 11, 1947.

HELLMUND, RUDOLPH EMIL, electrical engr.; b. Gotha, Germany, Feb. 2, 1879; s. Louis and Katharina (Wenzel) H.; grad. realschule, Gotha, 1895; studied Tech. Coll., Ilmenau, and U. of Charlottenburg, 1896-99 and 1902-03; m. Hetty Borgmann, May 24, 1913. Came to U.S., 1903, naturalized citizen, 1920. Asst. to William Stanley, Great Barrington, Mass., 1904-05; designing engr. Western Electric Co., Chicago, 1905-07; with Westinghouse Electric & Mfg. Co. since 1907; apptd. chief engr., 1933, responsible for adequacy of company's engring. and design work, covering all branches of the orgn., also chmn. ednl. com., etc. Inventor elec. devices covered by more than 250 U.S. and foreign patents. Fellow Am. Inst. of E.E. (bd. dirs.; chmn. standards com.); mem. standards council, Am. Standards Assn. Lutheran. Mason (K.T., Shriner). Awarded Benjamin Lamme medal, Am. Institute Electrical Engineers, 1929. Club: Pittsburgh Athletic. Writer of numerous papers and articles in American and European publications. Home: Swissvale, Pa. Died May 16, 1942.

HELLSTROM, CARL REINHOLD, engr., bus. exec.; b. Stockholm, Sweden, Jan. 29, 1895; s. Carl Malmros and Emma Carolina (Reinholde) H.; grad. Tensta Sch., Uppsala, Sweden, 1910; C.E., Christiania Coll., Christiania, 1914; post grad. Univ. of Paris, 1915-16; Doctor of Science (honorary), Lafayette Coll., 1950; m. Lois Allison, Nov. 24, 1932; 1 son, Douglas Reinhold. Mem. French engring. commn. to U.S., 1916-17; discharged with hon. S.C.D. from U.S. Army, 1919; engr. Eastern Coal & Mining Corp., Washington, 1919-20; chief engineer American Rack Co., Washington, 1920-22, president 1922-31; research engr., general supt., works manager, Smith & Wesson, Springfield, Mass., 1931-40, dir., v.p. plant operations, 1940-46, pres., 1946—, chmn. bd. Mem. of council

American Ordnance Assn. Life trustee Lafayette Coll. Awarded Citation by U.S. Ordnance Dept., 1947. Mem. Newcomen Soc. Eng. (vice chmn. N.E. Com.), Acad. Polit. Sci., Nat. Inst. Social Scis. Clubs: Economic, Metropolitan (N.Y.); Colony (Springfield); Stonehorse Yacht (Cape Cod). Home: 38 Maugus Av., Wellesley Hills, Mass.; also Harwich Port, Mass. Office: 2100 Roosevelt Av., Springfield, Mass. Died Apr. 6, 1963; buried Harwich Port, Mass.

HEMINGWAY, ALLAN, physiologist, biophysicist; B. Leeds, Eng., Jan. 25, 1902; s. Arthur and Eleanor (Eastwood) H.; B.A., U. B.C., 1925; Ph.D., U. Minn., 1929; Sterling fellow, Yale, 1936-37; m. Gayle Shirey, Nov. 9, 1929, (dec.); 1 dau., Eleanor; m. 2d Claire Conklin Carr, July 5, 1951. Instr., asst. prof. physiol. chemistry U. Minn., 1930-36, asst. prof., asso. prof. physiology, 1936-48, prof. physiology 1948-51; prof. physiology Med. Sch., U. Cal. at Los Angeles, 1951-72; chief cardiopulmonary lab. San Fernando VA Hosp. (Cal.). Served as maj. USAAF, 1943-45; chief lab. biophysics Sch. Aviation Med., Randolph Field, Tex., 1942-45. Mem. Am. Physiol. Soc., Am. Phys. Soc., Am. Chem. Soc., Soc. Exptl. Biology and Medicine, Am. Assn. U. Profs., Sigma Xi, Gamma Alpha, Phi Beta Pi. Contbr. articles to physiol. and biochem. jours. Home: Los Angeles CA Died Apr. 22, 1972.

HENCH, PHILIP SHOWALTER, physician; b. Pitts., Feb. 28, 1896; s. Jacob Bixler and Clara John (Showalter) H.; A.B., Lafayette Coll., 1916, Sc.D., 1940; M.D., U. Pitts., 1920, Sc.D., 1951; postgrad. study U. Freiburg and Ludwig-Maximilians-Universitat, Munich, 1928-29; M.S. in Internal Medicine, U. Minn., 1931; Sc.D., Lafayette Coll., 1940, Washington and Jefferson Coll., 1940, Western Res. U., Nat. U. Ireland, 1950, University of Pittsburgh, 1951; LL.D., Middlebury (Vt.) Coll., 1951; m. Mary Genevieve Kahler, July 14, 1927; children—Mary Showalter, Philip Kahler, Susan Kahler, John Bixler. Intern St. Francis Hosp., Pitts., 1920-21; with Mayo Found., Mayo Clinics, Grad. Sch., U. Minn., 1921—; cons. head sect. rheumatic diseases, Mayo Clinic, 1926—; prof. medicine Mayo Found. and Grad. School, University of Minnesota, 1947—. Vice president Kahler Corporation, Rochester, Minn. Chmn. arthritis and rheumatism study sect. Nat. Insts. of Health, U.S.P.H.S., 1949-50; mem. adv. council Nat. Inst. Arthritis and Metabolic Diseases, U.S.P.H.S., 1950-53; mem. med. and sci. com. Arthritis and Rheumatism Found.; mem. adv. com. Nat. Research Council. Vice pres. bd. mgrs. Walter Reed Meml. Assn. Chmn. Am. com of Ligue Internat. Contre le Rhumatisme; titulate to Central Com. of Pan Am. League Against Rheumatism. Recipient Herberden Medal (London), 1942, spl. citation Am. Rheumatism Assn., 1951, Pa. Ambassador award Pa. State C. of C., 1951, Northwestern U. Centennial award, 1951; recipient (with Edward C. Kendall, Ph.D.) Lasker award Am. Pub. Health Assn., 1949, Page One award Newspaper Guild of N.Y. (for discovery and development of cortisone), 1950, Passano Found. award, 1950, Award of Merit of Masonic Found. Med. Research and Human Welfare, 1951, Criss Award, 1951, spl. citation from Regents of U. Minn., 1951; recipient (with Prof. George Thorn, Harvard) scientific award Am. Pharm. Mfrs. Assn., 1950; recipient (with E. C. Kendall and Tadeus Reichstein) Nobel prize for physiology and medicine, 1950, honor award Miss. Valley Med. Soc., 1952; decorated Order of Carlos Finlay, Orden Nacional de Merito Carlos Manuel de Cespedes (Cuba). Served with Med. Enlisted Res. Corps, 1917-19; from lt. col. to col. AUS, 1942-46; on active duty, expert civilian cons. to surgeon gen. U.S. Army, 1946—. Fellow A.M.A., A.C.P.; mem. internat., nat., state and local profl. socs. and assns.; fgn. mem. or foreign corr. Several profl. assns. Republican. Presbyn. Chief editor Am. Rheumatism Reviews (Am. Rheumatism Assn.), 1932-48; asso. editor Annals of Rheumatic Diseases (London). Contbr. about 200 articles to med. jours. Home: 517 Fourth St. S.W. Address: Mayo Clinic, Rochester, Minn. Died Mar. 30, 1965; buried Oakwood Cemetery, Rochester.

HENCK, JOHN BENJAMIN, electric ry. engr.; b. Dedham, Mass., Aug. 14, 1854; s. civ. engr. of same name; grad. Mass. Inst. Technology, S.B., 1876; m. Dec. 1, 1887, Winnifred Wadsworth, Malden, Mass. (she died May 23, 1921). Taught in the physical laboratory, Massachusetts Institute of Technology, 1876-80; in experimental work and patent investigation with Bell Telephone Co., 1880-81; represented Bell Telephone Co. at Paris Electrical Exps., 1881; in experimental and patent work for London and Globe Telephone Co., London, 1881-83; editor and pub. Florida Republican, Longwood, Fla., 1886-87; continued printing business until 1890; sec. faculty Mass. Inst. Technology, 1890-91. From 1892 in electric ry. engring.; retired 1902. Mem. City Council, Santa Barbara, 1912-13; bd. of freeholders which prepared new city charter for Santa Barbara, 1915. Mem. Bd. of Freeholders for county charter, 1916; mem. Bd. of Park Commrs., Santa Barbara, 1917-23 (pres. 1920-23); trustee Santa Barbara Truth Center. Mem. A.A.A.S., Am. Acad. Polit. and Social Sciences, Seismol. Soc. America, Nat. Economic League, etc. Home: 1505 Santa Barbara St., Santa Barbara, Calif.

HENDERSON, ARCHIBALD, educator; b. Salisbury, N.C., June 17, 1877; s. John Steele and Elizabeth Brownrigg (Cain) H.; A.B., U. N.C. (head of class, winner Holt Math. medal), 1898, A.M., 1899, Ph.D., 1902; fellow and tutor math. U. Chgo., 1902-03, Ph.D., 1915; student Cambridge U. (Eng.), U. Berlin, Sorbonne (Paris), 1910-11; research student on Kenan Research Found., Cambridge, U. Berlin, 1923-24; U.C.L., U. of South, 1917; LL.D., Tulane U., 1922, Coll. William and Mary, 1932; Ltt.D., Catawba Coll., 1932, Oglethorpe U., 1932; Litt.D., University of North Carolina, 1961; m. Minna Curtis Bynum, June 23, 1903; children—Mary Curtis, Elizabeth Brownrigg, Barbada Gray, Archibald, John Steele; m. 2d, Lucile Kelling, June 15, 1957. Instr. math., 1899-1902, asso. prof., 1902-08, prof. pure math. 1908, head math. dept., 1920, U. N.C. emeritus prof. since 1948. So. U. Exchange U. Va., 1925-26. Mem. N.C. Acad. Sci. (ex-pres.); pres. Elisha Mitchell Sci. Soc., 1908-09, Mod. Lit. Club, 1906-07, State Lit. and Hist. Assn. N.C., 1913-14; v.p. Drama League Am. Fellow Royal Soc. Lit. U.K., A.A.A.S., Soc. Am. Historians; mem. Poetry Soc. Am., Am. Scandinavian Found. Am. Acad. Polit. Sci., Am. Math. Soc., Math. Assn. Am., Am. Antiquarien Soc., Lloyd Fam. Assn. (historian), Ohio Valley, Miss. Valley hist. assns., Va. Ky. State, Henderson County (Ky.), Rowan County, Clark County (Ky.) hist. socs., Boone Fam. Assn., Boone Trail Hwy. and Meml. Assn., Filson Club, Soc. of Cin., Soc. Transylvanians (pres.), Omicron Delta Kappa, Sigma Xi, S.A.R., pres. N.C. State Soc. of S.R., Phi Beta Kappa, Sigma Nu. Club: Authors' (London). Author: Lines on the Cubic Surface, 1911; Interpreters of Life, 1911; Mark Twain, 1911; George Bernard Shaw, His Life and Works, 1911; Forerunners of the Republic, 1913; The Life and Times of Richard Henderson, 1913; European Dramatists, 1913; The Changing Drama, 1914; "O. Henry," 1914; The Star of Empire, 1919; The Conquest of the Old Southwest, 1920; The Teaching of Geometry, 1921; Relativity Relativity—a Romance of Science, 1923; Washington's Southern Tour, 1923; The Theory of Relativity (in collaboration), 1924; Table Talk of G.B.S., 1925; Is Bernard Shaw a Dramatist?, 1929; Contemporary Immortals, 1930; Washington the Traveler, 1931; Bernard Shaw—Playboy and Prophet, 1932; The Chapel of the Cross, 1938; also chpt. on math. in Roads to Knowledge, 1932; Old Homes and Gardens of N.C., 1940; The Old North State and New, 2 vols., 1914; A New Geometrical Interpretation of Einstein's Special Relativity Theory, 1941; The Campus of the First State University, 1949; George Bernard Shaw, Man of the Century, 1956. Translator (with Barbara Henderson) of E. Boutroux's William James, 1911. Contbg. editor Modern Drama and Opera, 1915; Francois de Curel's A False Saint, 1916. Editor Thomas Godfrey's The Prince of Parthia, 1917; Foreword to American Folk Plays, 1939. Guest editor The Carolina Playbook (Koch Memorial); Pioneering a People's Theatre 1946. Contbr. to sci., hist. and lit. periodicals; pub. lectr. Home: 721 E. Franklin St., Chapel Hill, N.C. Died Dec. 6, 1963.

HENDERSON, CHARLES WILLIAM, mining engr.; b. Valley City, N.D., Sept. 10, 1885; s. David and Jane Louise (Morton) H.; A.B., in geology and mining, Stanford Univ., Calif., 1910; D.Sc., Colo. Sch. of Mines, 1930; unmarried. Statistical and geological work, San Francisco, 1907-08, in charge, Denver, 1908-25, U.S. Geol. Survey; in charge Denver office economic br. U.S. Bur. of Mines, 1925-35; supervising engr. of field offices, mineral production and economics div., U.S. Bur. of Mines, 1935—, acting asst. to dir., bureau, Feb. 5-Apr. 18, 1940. Cons. engr. U.S. Geol. Survey on Colo. Coöp. Geol. Survey since 1925. Chmn. Colo. sect. 16th Internat. Geol. Congress, 1932-33; v.p. Colo. Engring. Council, 1932-34. Advisor on copper, lead and zinc codes, NRA, 1933-34; mem. sub-com. on vanadium, mineral advisory com., Army and Navy Munitions Board, 1939-40. Fellow Am. Assn. for Advancement of Science; mem. Am. Assn. Petroleum Geologists, Am. Inst. Mining Metall. Engrs. (ex-sec. and chmn. Colo. sect.); Mining and Metall. Soc. of America, Colo. Scientific Soc. (pres. 1931-43), Teknik Club (Denver), Sigma Xi, Phi Gamma Delta, Sigma Gamma Epsilon. Clubs: University (Denver, Washington D.C.), Phi Gamma Delta (New York). Author: History of Mining in Colorado (U.S. Geological Survey); Gold and Silver Am. Year Book, 1928-36; History and Influence of Mining in the Western United States, Lindgren vol. (A.I.M.M.E.), 1933. Author of ann. reports on mineral resources (U.S. Geol. Survey and Bur. of Mines), 1908-43; also articles in mining jours. and U. of Ore. Bull. Home: University Club. Office: Custom House Bldg., Denver, Colo. Died Jan. 26, 1945.

HENDERSON, EDWARD, physician; b. Hendersonville, N.C., Dec. 16, 1896; s. Edward Everett and Muriel Lee (Bell) H.; M.B., B.Chir., M.D., Glasgow U., 1922; Ph.D., Oxford U., 1932; postgrad. Yale, 1937-38; diploma tropical medicine, Tulane U., 1944; m. Kathryn Silverthorne, 1944; children—Edward Bell, Susan Lee (Mrs. Catani). Intern Royal Infirmary, 1922-23; med. officer sci. expdns. Malay archipelago, 1927, China, India, 1929, Central Africa, 1935, Amazon region, 1938-39; med. research div. Schering Corp., Bloomfield, N.J., 1939-62, sec., 1940-52, v.p., 1952-62, dir., 1940-43, dir. div. clin. research, 1945-62; cons. tropical medicine Med. Soc. N.J., 1945; research cons. Mound Park Hosp. Found., St. Petersburg, Fla., from 1955; pres. Ellis Bell & Co., Inc., N.Y.C., from 1967, Bansen, Inc., N.Y.C., from 1967, Henderson Safety Closure Co., Inc., N.Y.C., from 1969; chmn. bd. Elbesa Ltd., London, Eng., from 1970. Bd. dirs. Liberian Inst., Am. Found. Tropical Medicine, 1951; trustee Aging Research Inst., Inc., from 1953, pres., from 1953; pres. Pneumonia Research Found., from 1969. Served as lt., inf., U.S. Army, 1917, capt. Intelligence Corps, 1918. Recipient Willard O. Thompson award, 1961; Malford W. Thewlis gold medal award, 1967. Mem. Internat. Soc. Tropical Dermatology, Pan Am. Med. Assn. (pres. sect. geriatrics and gerontology from 1967), A.A.A.S., Am. Soc. Tropical Medicine, Endocrine Soc., Gerontological Soc., Am. Geriatrics Soc. (dir. from 1952, pres. 1955, editor-in-chief jour. from 1954, exec. dir. from 1962), Am., N.J. rheumatism assns., Assn. Med. Dirs. (pres. 1949-50), N.Y. Acad. Scis. Clubs: New York Athletic; Graduates (New Haven); Columbia University (N.Y.C.). Author: Sixteenth Century Literature and Its Influence on Modern Civilization, 1932; Disorders of Calcium Metabolism, 1952; Section on Cholera, Clinical Tropical Medicine, Gradwohl, Benitex Soto, Felsenfeld, 1951. Contbr. articles sci. jours. patentee chemistry, sci. instruments, safety devices. Home: New York City NY Died Jan. 5, 1973; buried Mill Hill, London England

HENDERSON, ELDON HAZELTON, engr., mfg. exec.; b. Memphis, Mich., July 20, 1908; s. Charles W. and Mary (Haselton) H.; student Detroit City Coll., 1927; m. Alene Zimmerman, Aug. 30, 1934; children—Jane S., John E., Lynn L. Mgr. warehouse control Detroit br., Continental Rubber Works, 1927-29, sales engr., 1929-45; founder Yale Rubber Mfg. Co., Sandusky, Mich., 1945, pres., gen. mgr., 1945-65, chairman of the board, from 1965; mem. bd. dirs. Mich. Mutual Liability Co., Yale Auscao Co., Lima Peru, Info Data, Inc., Trustee Manitou Island Assn.; v.p. Wm. R. Angell Found. Mem. Am. Chem. Soc. Mason, Lion, Rotarian. Clubs: Huron Shores Golf, Horton Ranch, Kingston Hunt. Home: Sandusky MI Deceased.

HENDERSON, GEORGE LOGAN, civil engr.; born Alameda, Cal., Oct. 14, 1891; s. George Logan and Bessie B. (Graves) H.; B.S. with honors in Civil Engring., U. Cal. at Berkeley, 1919; m. Florence E. Redpath, Mar. 30, 1921; 1 son, Richard L. Hydroelectric power, drainage and irrigation engring., Cal. and Ariz., 1919-28; with Kern County Land Co., Bakersfield, Cal., 1928-59, beginning as asst. engr., successively engr., chief engr., 1928-54, v.p., 1954-59; v.p. Kern County Canal and Water Co., Bakersfield, 1954-59; practice as consulting civil engineer, 1960—. Vice pres. Nat. Water Conservation Conf., 1953-61; mem., pres. bd. dirs. Belridge Water Storage Dist., 1962—; dir. Arvin-Edison Water Storage Dist., 1942-58; mem. engring. adv. com. Feather River Project Aqueduct Routes, 1956-59; mem. adv. council, water resources center U. Cal., 1958—. Dir. Bakersfield Savs. & Loan Assn. Fellow Am. Soc. C.E.; mem. Nat. Reclamation Assn. (chairman agrl. research com.), Cal. C. of C., Water Assn. Kern County (dir.), Am. Legion (past commdr.), Sigma Xi, Theta Xi, Tau Beta Pi. Clubs: Stockdale Country; Bakersfield Kiwanis (past pres.). Home: 6605 Mt. Whitney Dr. Office: P.O. Box 6, Bakersfield, Cal. Died Oct. 1, 1965.

HENDERSON, YANDELL, physiologist; b. Louisville, Ky., Apr. 23, 1873; s. Isham and Sally Nielson (Yandell) H.; B.A., Yale, 1895, Ph.D., 1898; univs. of Marburg, 1899, and Munich, 1900; m. Mary Gardner Colby, Apr. 2, 1903; children—Malcolm Colby, Sylvia Yandell (Mrs. G. McL. Harper, Jr.). Instr. physiology, 1900-03, asst. prof., 1903-11, prof., 1911-21, prof. applied physiology, 1921-38, prof. emeritus since 1938, Yale. Cons. physiologist, U.S. Bur. of Mines, 1913-25. Mem. Naval Militia, C.N.G., 1897-99; ensign U.S. Navy, during Spanish-American War; served on U.S.S. Yale in Cuban waters and on 1st expdn. to P.R. Chief of physiol. sect. U.S. war gas investigation, 1917-18; chmn. Med. Research Bd., Aviation Sect., Signal Corps, U.S. Army, 1917-18. Mem. Charter Revision Commn., New Haven, Conn. V.-chmn. Conn. delegation to 1st Prog. Nat. Conv., 1912; Prog. candidate for Congress, 3d Conn. Dist. Mem. A.M.A., Am. Physiol. Soc. Am. Pharm. Soc., Nat. Soc. Anaesthetists, Physiol. Soc. (Gt. Britain), A.A.A.S., Nat. Acad. Sciences, Am. Philos. Soc.; hon. mem. Am. Climatol. Assn., Assn. Physicians of Vienna, Austria, Coal Mining Inst. America. Clubs: Graduate (New Haven); Yale (New York). Honorary M.D., Conn. State Med. Soc., 1942. Home: 440 Prospect St., New Haven, Conn. Died Feb. 18, 1944.

HENDRICK, CALVIN WHEELER, civil and sanitary engr.; b. Paducah, Ky., June 21, 1865; s. Rev. Calvin Stiles and Elizabeth Winston (Campbell) H.; ed. pub. schs. until 16; learned civil engring. by pvt. study and practice; m. Sarah Rebecca Herring, of New York, Nov. 29, 1892; children—Calvin W. (dec.), Herring de-la Porte, John Vivian. Rodman engring. corps, C. & O. Southwestern R.R., 1881-83, asst. div. engr., 1883-85; asst. city engr., Louisville, 1883-85; engr. Chess Carley Oil Co., Ky., 1885-86; asst. to chief engr. Ga. Southern & Fla. R.R., 1886-87; city engr., Macon, Ga., st. ry. engr. and receiver Macon, Savannah & Dublin R.R., 1887-92; consulting engr., div. engr., New York subway, 1892-98; chief engr., commn. for sewering and draining Baltimore, 1905-15; chief engr. City of Baltimore, 1914-18; cons. engr. for the city; chmn. com. to revise building code of Baltimore; mem. City Planning Com. and Smoke Commn. of Baltimore; president Automatic Train Control Corp.; now gen. cons. engr.; elected pres. W.Va. Coal & Lumber Co., 1919. President Nat. Assn. for Preventing Pollution of Rivers and Waterways; mem. Com. of 100 on Nat. Health, A.A.A.S., Am. Soc. C.E., Soc. Colonial Wars, Southern Soc. Democrat. Presbyn. Clubs: Batchelor Cotillion, Maryland Club, Baltimore Club, Merchants, University, Baltimore Country, Greenspring Valley Club. Home: 12 E. Mt. Vernon Pl., Baltimore, Md.; also Miami Beach, Fla. Office: 128 N.E. 1st St., Miami, Fla.

HENDRICK, ELLWOOD, author, chemist; b. Albany, N.Y., Dec. 19, 1861; s. James and Anna (Wands) H.; student U. of Zürich, Switzerland; hon. Sc.D., Franklin and Marshall Coll., 1921; m. Josephine Pomeroy, Nov. 15, 1897; children—Grace V. Pomeroy (Mrs. George W. Patterson), James Pomeroy. Mgr. Albany Aniline & Chemical Works, 1881-84; engaged in fire ins. until 1900, then in stock brokerage in New York, until 1915. With indsl. research establishment of Arthur D. Little, Inc., Cambridge, Mass., 1917-22; cons. editor Chem. and Metall. Engring., 1918-23; now curator Chandler Chem. Mus. of Columbia U. Trustee, mem. exec. com. Research Corp. Author: Everyman's Chemistry, 1917; Opportunities in Chemistry, 1919; Percolator Papers, 1919; Life of Lewis Miller, 1925; Modern Views of Physical Science, 1925. Home: New York, N.Y. Died Oct. 29, 1930.

HENDRICK, IVES, psychiatrist; b. New Haven, Conn., Mar. 10, 1898; s. Burton J. and Bertha Jane (Ives) H.; student Phillips Andover Acad., 1913-16, Williston Acad., 1916-17; A.B., Yale, 1921, M.D., 1925; grad. student Psychoanalytical Inst., Berlin, 1928-30; m. Martha Marie Crawford McClung, Nov. 14, 1934 (div. 1945); children—Ives, Jr. (dec.), Bertha-Jane (Mrs. James Rumsey), and Martha (Mrs. Robert Rusnak). Served internship Lenox Hill Hospital, New York City, 1925-26; asst. in the dept. of psychiatry, med. sch., Harvard, 1930-34; instr., 1943-47, asso., 1947-48, asst. clin. prof., 1948-51, associate clinical professor, 1951-54, clin. prof., 1954-65, emeritus, 1965-72; clin. dir. emeritus Mass. Mental Health Center, chief Harvard Teaching Unit, Southard Clinic, 1943-64; dir. med. edn., Boston Psychopathic Hosp., 1949-56; consultant McClean and Mass. Gen. Hosps., 1930-33; pvt. practice psychoanalysis and psychiatry from 1930. Fellow Am. Psychiatric Assn.; mem. Am. Psychoanalytic Assn. (pres.-elect. chmn. bd. prof. standards, 1951-53, pres. 1953-55) Boston Soc. Psychiatry and Neurology, Soc. Research in Psychosomatic Problems, Group for Advancement in Psychiatry, Nu Sigma Nu, American Medical Association, Massachusetts Psychiatric Soc., Mass. Med. Assn., Macy Found. Conf. on Infancy, Boston Psychoanalytic Soc. and Inst. (pres. 1944-45). Clubs: Yale (N.Y. City); Harvard, Harvard Music Association (Boston, Mass.); Harvard Faculty (Cambridge, Mass.). Author: Facts and Theories of Psychoanalysis, 1934, revised edition pub., 1958; (Spanish transl., 1951); Psychiatric Education Today, 1965. Author and editor: Birth of an Institute, 1961. Contbr. sci. publs. Contbg. editor Ency. Brit.; editorial bd. Jour. Am. Psychoanalytic Assn., 1952-56. Address: Boston MA Died May 28, 1972; buried Evergreen Cemetery, New Haven CT

HENDRICKS, ALLAN BARRINGER, JR., electrical engr.; b. Red Hook, N.Y., Jan. 28, 1874; s. Allan Barringer and Anna (Rodgers) H.; student Lawrence Scientific Sch. (Harvard), 1897-1900; m. Sallie Fox Acken, Feb. 8, 1908 (dec. Aug. 12, 1947); children—George Bartlett, Dorothea Brooks, Sylvia Acken. With Stanley Electric Mfg. Co., Pittsfield, Mass., 1900; when this company was absorbed by the General Electric Co., continued as employee in the same plant, until retirement, 1944; organized Testing Laboratory, then became asst. engr. Power Transformer Dept. Specialized in invention and design of apparatus for high voltage and current, both alternating and continuous; first to produce 1,000,000 volts above ground, 1,000,000 volts three phase, 2,100,000 volts single phase, and 1,200,000 volts three phase, at commercial frequency; 20 patents granted. Designed high potential equipment for million volt three phase arc exhibit at New York World's Fair, 1939; now independent designing engr. Home: 115 Wendell Av., Pittsfield MA

HENDRICKSON, WILLIAM WOODBURY, prof. mathematics, U.S.N.; b. Mt. Joy, Pa., June 21, 1844; s. James W. and Ellen (Woodbury) H.; grad. U.S. Naval Acad., 1863; m. Eleanor M. Burnham, Apr. 18, 1867. Apptd. acting midshipman from Ohio, 1860; ensign, 1863; served in Lancaster, Portsmouth and Plymouth; instr. mathematics, U.S. Naval Acad., 1870-73; resigned commn. as lt. comdr. to accept commn. as prof., Mar. 1873; head dept. mathematics, U.S. Naval Acad., 1873-90, and 1897-1907; in office Nautical Almanac, 1890-97; retired June 21, 1906, with rank of rear admiral. Home: Annapolis, Md. Died June 1, 1920.

HENDRIXSON, WALTER SCOTT, chemist; b. Felicity, O., Jan. 11, 1859; s. Eber Adkins and Sarah (Hoover) H.; B.S., Union Christian Coll., Merom, Ind., 1881; A.M., Harvard, 1889, Ph.D., 1903; univs. of Berlin and Göttingen, 1894-95; m. Bessie Bradley, Apr. 18, 1906. Instr., 1882-85, prof. chemistry and physics, 1885-88, Antioch Coll., O.; asst. in chemistry, Harvard, 1889-90; prof. chemistry, Ia. (now Grinnell) Coll., 1890—. Prof. chemistry, State U. of Ia., summer, 1902; lecturer chemistry, U. of Ill., on leave, 1917; research fellow, Johns Hopkins U., 1920-21; connected with water resources branch U.S. Geol. Survey, 1905-09. Pres. Ia. Acad. of Science, 1899, Assn. of Ia. Colls., 1900; mem. council for Ia. of Am. Chem. Soc. Home: Grinnell, Ia. Deceased.

HENNESSY, WILLIAM THOMAS, civil engr.; b. Ft. Smith, Ark., June 5, 1887; s. Thomas Abraham and Eula (Tatum) H.; student U. Ark., 1908-10; m. May Pitman, Apr. 28, 1915; 1 son, William Thomas (dec.). U.S. govt. worker constrn. Panama Canal, 1911-12; civil engr. Guantanamo Sugar Co., Cuba, 1912-13, Central Aquirre Sugar Co., P.R., 1913-17; supt. constrn. South Puerto Rico Sugar Co., 1917-26, mgr. Central Santa Fe, Republic of Santo Domingo, 1926-39, gen. mgr., v.p. control Romana and Santa Fe, Republic Santo Domingo, 1939-48, pres., 1948-54, chmn. bd., 1954—. Home: 575 Park Av., N.Y.C. Died July 1962.

HENNY, DAVID CHRISTIAN, hydraulic engr.; b. Arnhem, The Netherlands, Nov. 15, 1860; s. David and Berendina (Lorentz) H.; C.E., Poly. U., Delft, 1881; Dr. Engineering, Oregon State Coll., 1933; m. Julia A. H. Wetzel, 1893; children—George Christian, Frances Berendina, Arnold Lorentz. Railroad location, Holland, 1881-84; came to U.S., 1884, naturalized citizen, 1894; engaged in ry. waterworks and irrigation constrn., 1884-91; gen. mgr. Excelsior Redwood Pipe Co., San Francisco, 1892-1902, Redwood Mfrs. Co., 1902-05; supervising engr. U.S. Reclamation Bur. (Pacific Coast dist.), 1905-09; cons. engr. with U.S. Reclamation Service, 1909—, also pvt. practice, Portland, Ore., 1910—. Introduced wooden stave pipe on Pacific Coast, and built many pioneer lines; built first large factory in U.S. with individual motor drive, Pittsburgh, Calif., 1902; connected with constrn. and maintenance of many western irrigation projects and dams; cons. engr. various cities and states, irrigation dists. and power cos., also govts. of Puerto Rico and Cuba. Mem. Am. Concrete Inst. on Mass Concrete; mem. U.S. Reclamation Bd. on Hoover Dam. Home: Portland, Ore. Deceased.

HENRICH, V.C., chem. engr.; b. Allentown, Pa., Nov. 5, 1899; s. G. and Sallie Ann (Lynn) H.; grad. Lehigh U., 1921; m. Isabell C. Wirt, May 29, 1919; children—Vincent, Gustav J., Betty A. (Mrs. Wallace DeWitt), Barbara (Mrs. Richard Ewing). Chemist Robesonia Iron Co., 1921-22; supr. Rohm & Haas Co., 1922-39, then supt. and plant mgr., v.p., plant mgr. Tex. div., 1947—, dir.; dir. Pasadena State Bank. Trustee San Jacinto Jr. Coll. Mem. bd. Salvation Army, Houston chpt. A.R.C.; trustee Harris County United Fund. Mem. Tex. Chem. Council, Am. Chem. Soc., Am. Inst. Chem. Engrs. Presbyn. (elder). Address: City Line Av., Lower Merion Phila. Died June 29, 1966.

HENRICI, ARTHUR TRAUTWEIN, (hen-re'se), bacteriologist; b. Economy, Pa., Mar. 31, 1889; s. Jacob Frederick and Viola (Irons) H.; M.D., U. of Pittsburgh, 1911; m. Blanche Ressler, Aug. 7, 1913; children—Carl Ressler, Ruth Elizabeth, Hazel Jean. Pathologist St. Francis Hosp., Pittsburgh, 1912-13; instr. in pathology and bacteriology, U. of Minn., 1913-16, asst. prof. bacteriology, 1916-20, asso. prof., 1920-25, prof. since 1925; Walker-Ames Prof., U. of Wash., 1941. Served as capt. Med. Corps, U.S. Army, 1917-19. Mem. Soc. Am. Bacteriologists (pres. 1939), Soc. Exptl. Biology and Medicine, Limnological Soc. of America, Mycological Soc. of Am., Sigma Xi, Gamma Alpha, Alpha Omega Alpha. Author: Morphologic Variation and the Rate of Growth of Bacteria, 1928; Molds, Yeasts and Actinomycetes, 1930; The Biology of Bacteria, 1934, 2d edit., 1939. Contbr. to bacteriological jours. Home: 130 Arthur Av. S.E., Minneapolis, Minn. Died Apr. 23, 1943.

HENRY, ALFRED JUDSON, meteorologist; b. New Bethlehem, Pa., Sept. 1, 1858; s. John McConnell and Nancy (Reid) H.; ed. Reid Inst., Pa., 1871-73; studied telegraphy; student Columbian (now George Washington) U., 1885-86; spl. studies also, 1897-98; m. Jessie Holbrook Ide, July 25, 1883; 1 dau., Helen Hall (dec.). Signal Service of U.S.A., 1878; chief of the div. Meteorol. Records, 1895-1900; prof. meteorology, U.S. Weather Bureau, 1900-17, senior and principal meteorologist, Nov. 1917—; exec. officer Mount Weather Research Obs., May 1908-12. Editor Mo. Weather Review, 1921—. Home: Washington, D.C. Died Oct. 5, 1931.

HENRY, GEORGE FREDERICK, prof. chemistry; b. Ainsworth, Ia., Nov. 20, 1870; s. William and Margaret (Frederick) H.; student Albion (Mich.) Coll., 1895-96; B.S., Wash. State Coll., 1903; M.S., Northwestern U., 1915; studied U. of Chicago, 1915; m. Julia M. Reeve, Oct. 31, 1903 (died 1914); children—Dorothy Eleanor, George Frederick; m. 2d, Louise McIntosh, June 5, 1927. Teacher rural schs. until 1900; teacher high sch. Lewiston, Wash. 1903-06; head dept. science, Lucknow (India) Christian Coll., 1906-14, v. prin., 1912-14; prof. chemistry and physics, Mt. Union Coll., 1915-16, Fargo (N.D.) Coll., 1916-21, asst. dean, 1919-21; prof. chemistry, Coll. of Puget Sound, 1921-38, prof. emeritus since 1938, dean, 1922-26. Fellow of A.A.A.S., Am. Inst. of Chemists; mem. Am. Chem. Soc., Pi Kappa Delta, Phi Kappa Phi, Phi Beta Kappa. Republican. Methodist. Author: Laboratory Manual of General Chemistry, 1911. Home: 1011 11th St., N.W., Puyallup, Wash. Died May 9, 1945.

HENRY, GEORGE WILLIAM, psychiatrist; b. Oswego, N.Y., June 13, 1889; s. Charles and Ann Amelia (Wallace) H.; A.B., Wesleyan U., Middletown, Conn., 1912; M.D., Johns Hopkins, 1916; postgrad. U. Berlin, 1929, U. Amsterdam, 1930; m. Eleanor Anne Siebert, Nov. 2, 1927; children—Barbara Anne (Mrs. Allan Kern), Sarah (Mrs. R. Kitchen). (dec.), Jane (Mrs. James D. Hunt). Asst. psychiatry Johns Hopkins, 1917, intern, asst. physician, dir. lab., 1922, sr. physician, 1923; dir. psychiat. clinic N.Y. Hosp., 1924-29; instr. to asso. prof. psychiatry Cornell U.; now in pvt. practice psychiatry, N.Y.C.; attending psychiatrist N.Y. Hosp.; cons. psychiatrist United Hosp., Port Chester, N.Y.; med. dir. Brooklea Farm Sanitarium. Fellow A.M.A., Am. Psychiat. Assn.; mem. N.Y. Psychiat. Soc. (pres.), Assn. Research Nervous and Mental Disease, N.Y. Soc. Clinical Psychiatry, Phi Beta Kappa. Methodist. Author: Essentials of Psychiatry, 1925; Essentials of Psychopathology, 1935; Sex Variants, 1941; History of Medical Psychology, 1941; All the Sexes, a Study of Masculinity and Femininity, 1955. Contbr. articles sci. jours. Home: Brooklea Farm, Greenwich, Conn. Office: 580 Park Av., N.Y.C. 21. Died May 23, 1964.

HENRY, HOWARD JAMES, engring. exec.; b. Grand Forks, N.D., Nov. 11, 1911; s. John Dan and Olean (Stennes) H.; B.S. in Mech. Engring., U. N.D., 1933; M.S. in Mech. Engring., U. Kan., 1941; M.E., Mass. Inst. Tech., 1951; Ph.D., State U. Ia., 1952; m. Norma A. Higgins, Dec. 28, 1938; children—John George, Lucinda Scott (Mrs. Richard N. Lapp). Instr. mech. engring. U. N.D., 1936-37; design engr. Fairbanks Morse Co., Beloit, Wis., 1937-38; instr. mech. engring. U. Kan., 1938-41, Carnegie Inst. Tech., 1941-43; design engr. Chgo. Pneumatic Tool Co., Franklin, Pa., 1946-47, dir. engring., 1951-60; prof. mech. engring. Ia. State U., 1947-51; dean Sch. Engring., So. Methodist U., Dallas, Texas, 1960-64; v.p. engring. pneumatic equipment division of the Westinghouse Air Brake Company, Sidney, O., 1964-69. Pres. United Fund Franklin, 1958, Franklin C. of C., 1959; chairman Franklin Planning Commn., 1959-60, Franklin Sch. Authority, 1958. Served to lt. (s.g.) USNR, 1943-46; ret. comdr. Recipient Citizenship award Franklin, 1959. Registered profl. engr., Ia. Mem. Am. Soc. M.E. (vice chmn. N. Tex. sect. 1962-63, rep. dir. to Engrs. Council for Profl. Devel. 1968), American Society for Engineering Education, Sigma Tau, Pi Tau Sigma. Methodist (ofcl. bd.). Elk. Home: Sidney OH Died Aug. 13, 1969; buried Franklin Cemetery, Franklin PA

HENRY, JOSEPH, scientist; b. Albany, N.Y., Dec. 17, 1797; s. William and Ann (Alexander) H.; received numerous hon. degrees including A.M., Union Coll., 1829; LL.D., S.C. Coll. (now U. S.C.), 1838, U. State N.Y., 1850, Harvard, 1851; m. Harriet Alexander, May 1830, 6 children. Conducted research in self-induction; 1st to detect the induced current, 1832; invented an electromagnetic motor; prof. natural philosophy Coll. of N.J. (now Princeton), 1832-46; did research which anticipated some of the modern developments in science of electricity, 1838-42; invented low and high resistance galvonometers; 1st sec. and dir. Smithsonian Instn., 1846-78, (instn. as known today largely a result of his work); initiated system of basing weather forecasts on weather reports received by telegraph, 1850; became mem. Light House Bd., 1852, pres., 1871-78; became mem. Am. Philos. Soc., 1835; an organizer A.A.A.S., pres. 1849; a founder Philos. Soc. of Washington 1871, pres. 1871-78; charter mem. Nat. Acad. Scis., v.p., 1866, pres., 1868-78; scientific unit of self-induction named "Henry" in his honor. Died Washington, D.C., May 13, 1878.

HENRY, MORRIS HENRY, physician; b. London, Eng., July 26, 1835; s. Henry A. Henry; M.D., U. Vt., 1860; m. Elizabeth Hastings, 1872; m. 2d, Mrs. Harrison Everett Maynard, 1880; survived by 1 child. Came to N.Y.C., 1852; surgeon Northern Dispensary, 1864; surgeon N.Y. Dispensary, 1869; surgeon-in-chief N.Y. State Emigrant Hosp., 1873-80; chief police surgeon of N.Y.C., 1872-84, organized ambulance service; founder, editor Am. Jour. Syphilography and Dermatology, 1870-75; published Am. edit. Skin Diseases: Their Description, Pathology, Diagnosis, and Treatment (W.T. Fox), 1871; invented numerous instruments including forceps, scissors for many purposes; decorated by sovereigns of Greece and Turkey. Died May 19, 1895.

HENRY, PHILIP WALTER, consulting engr.; b. Scranton, Pa., Mar. 24, 1864; s. Eugene Thomas and Emma Elizabeth (Walter) H.; C.E., Rensselaer Poly. Inst., 1887; m. Clover Cox, Jan. 22, 1906; children—Clover Eugenia. With Barber Asphalt Paving Co., 1887-1902, becoming v.p. and gen. mgr.; v.p. Medina Quarry Co., 1902-04; v.p. A. L. Barber Asphalt Co., and Pan Am. Co. of Del., 1904-09; pres. S. American Constrn. Co., 1907-09; pres. Central R.R. Co., of Haiti, 1909-17; v.p. Am. Internat. Corp., 1916-23, Siems-Carey Ry. & Canal Co., 1921-23. Mem. Tech. Bd. Review, Public Works Adminstrn., 1933-35.

V.p. Rensselaer Poly. Inst. Has been identified with engring. and constrn. work in Mex., Haiti, Venezuela, Peru, Boliva, Argentine, Spain and China. Dir. N.Y. City Mission Soc. Mem. Am. Soc. Civil Engrs., American Institute Consulting Engrs. (past president; secretary since 1924), American Inst. Mining Engrs., Am. Geog. Soc. (councillor), Pan-Am. Soc., (hon.) Assn. Chinese and Am. Engrs. Republican. Presbyn. Clubs: University, Engineers', Century (New York). Author of various articles and papers. Home: Scarborough, N.Y. Office: 75 West St., New York. Died Nov. 7, 1947.

HENRY, SAMUEL CLEMENTS, pharmacist, mem. Nat. Recovery Review Bd.; b. Washington, D.C., Oct. 5, 1872; s. James and Rachel Amelia (Clements) H.; ed. pub. schs., Washington; Pharm. M., Phila. Coll. Pharmacy, 1924; m. Mary Elizabeth Young, 1893; 1 dau., Mary Elizabeth (dec.). Apprentice in Pharmacy, and pharmacist, 1886-91; opened retail drug store in West Phila., 1891, later acquired 2 add. stores; pres. Nat. Assn. Retail Druggists, 1914-15, sec., 1917-33; pres. Nat. Drug Trade Conf., 1920-30, Chicago Veteran Druggists Assn., 1933-34; sec. bd. trustees U.S. Pharmacopoeial Conv. (trustee since 1926); became mem. National Recovery Review Bd., Mar. 6, 1934; asso. editor Am. Druggist, 1934-36; asso. ed. and Western mgr. of Drug Store Retailing Mag.; sec. and treas. Rigidtest Products, Inc. Republican. Presbyterian. Home: 412 N. Maple, Oak Park, Ill. Office: 318 W. Randolph St., Chicago IL*

HENRY, WILLIAM, gunsmith, Continental congressman, inventor; b. West Caln Twp., Pa., May 19, 1729; s. John and Elizabeth (DeVinne) H.; m. Ann Wood, Jan. 1755, 7 children including William, Joseph. Went to Lancaster, Pa., 1744, apprenticed to gunsmith; formed partnership with Joseph Simon for making of firearms, prin. armorers of colonial troops during French and Indian Wars, 1750; went on business trip to Eng., 1761, learned from James Watt about his steam engine; aided Robert Fulton and Benjamin West in their youth; pioneer steam propulsion in Am.; built stern-wheel steamboat (1st in U.S.) 1762-63; joined Am. Philos. Soc., 1768; credited with invention of a screw auger; perfected steam-heating system; justice of peace, Pa., 1758; asst. burgess of Lancaster, 1765-75; del. to Pa. Assembly, 1776; mem. Pa. Council of Safety, 1777; treas. Lancaster County, 1777-86; elected by Assembly as del. Continental Congress, 1784; asst. commissary gen. and disbursing officer U.S. Govt. for dist. of Lancaster, 1775-81. Died Lancaster, Dec. 15, 1786.

HENRY, WILLIAM ARNON, agriculturist; b. Norwalk, O., June 16, 1850; s. William and Martha Haines (Condict) H.; student Holbrook Normal Sch., Lebanon, O.; Ohio Wesleyan U., 1870-71; B.S. Agr., Cornell U., 1880; (D. Agr., U. of Ill., 1904; D.Sc., U. of Vt., 1904, Mich. Agrl. Coll., 1907); m. Clara Roxanna Taylor, Aug. 19, 1881. Prin. New Haven (Ind.) High Sch., 1871-73, Boulder (Colo.) High Sch., 1873-76; prof. botany and agr., U. of Wis., 1881, prof. agr., 1883; dir. Agrl. Expt. Sta., 1887, dean Coll. Agr., 1891-1907, emeritus prof. agr., 1907—, U. of Wis. Had charge from beginning Agrl. Coll. and Expt. Sta. U. of Wis. Author: Feeds and Feeding, 1898 (17th edit., revised, with F. B. Morrison, 1917, and abridged edit., 1917). Home: San Diego, Calif. Died 1932.

HENSHAW, HENRY WETHERBEE, naturalist; b. Cambridge, Mass., Mar. 3, 1850; s. William and Sarah (Holden) H.; ed. Cambridge pub. schs.; ed. as naturalist, chiefly by outdoor study; unmarried. Joined Wheeler Survey, 1872, as naturalist, and explored the West and made reports thereon until 1879, when began work with Bur. of Ethnology, with which was connected, chiefly in administrative capacity, until 1893, part of which time was editor American Anthropologist; administrative biologist, Biol. Survey, U.S. Dept. Agr., June 1, 1905—; Chief of Biol. Survey, June 1, 1910—. Was in H.I., 1894-1904, devoting much time to the study of biology. Author: Report on Ornithology of Nev., Utah., Calif., Colo., N.Mex., and Ariz., 1875; Birds of the Hawaiian Islands, 1902. Home: Washington, D.C. Died Aug. 1, 1930.

HENSHAW, SAMUEL, zoölogist; hon. A.M., Harvard, 1903. Dir. Mus. Comparative Zoölogy, Harvard, 1911-27. Fellow Am. Acad. Arts and Sciences; mem. Am. Soc. Naturalists, Am. Soc. Zoölogists. Address: 28 Fayerweather St., Cambridge, Mass. Died Feb. 5, 1941.

HENYEY, LOUIS G(EORGE), astronomer; b. McKees Rocks, Pa., Feb. 3, 1910; s. Bela and Mary (Floszmann) H.; B.S., Case Inst. Tech., 1932, M.S., 1933; Ph.D., U. Chgo., 1937; m. Elizabeth Rose Belak, Apr. 29, 1934; children—Thomas Louis, Francis Stephen, Elizabeth Maryrose. From instr. to asst. prof. Yerkes Observatory, U. Chgo., 1937-47; from asst. to asso. prof. U. Cal., Berkeley, 1947-56, prof., 1956-70, dir. Computer Center, 1956-60, chmn. astronomy dept., 1959-64; research asso. Princeton, 1951-52; prin. investigator optical project NDRC. Guggenheim fellow, 1940-41. Mem. Am., Royal astron. socs., National Academy of Sciences, Astron. Society of the Pacific (president 1964-66), Sigma Xi. Home: El Cerrito CA Died Feb. 18, 1970; buried Sunset Cemetery, El Cerrito CA

HERBERT, ALBERT, cons. business engr.; b. Shrewsbury, Eng., Feb. 29, 1856; s. Thomas and Elizabeth (Norris) H.; ed. in Eng.; m. Jennie Wyatt, of Leamington, Eng., 1881; children—Harold (dec.), Major Wilwyn, Gladaid (dec., Mrs. Edward Neville Stent), Serval. Came to U.S., 1880; pres. Hub Gore Makers, mfrs. rubber elastic products, Boston, 1882-1900; pres., treas. Leolastic, Bayonne, Port of New York, 1903-13; dir. Everlastik Corp., rubber textile products, New York. Chmn. Carnegie Metric Com. of Nat. Assn. Mfrs., 1898, which reported unanimously for metric units; chmn. U.S. Am. Standardization Com., Internat. Chamber of Commerce, 1920 (Paris, London). Home: New York, N.Y. Deceased.

HERBERT, FREDERICK DAVIS, engineering; b. Brooklyn, N.Y., Oct. 16, 1873; s. Wilbur F. and Charlotte Amelia (Weekes) H.; M.E., Cornell U., 1897; m. Jane Whittlesey Mitchell, Sept. 16, 1903; children—Emily Whittlesey (Mrs. W. Almon Stopford), Charlotte Weekes (Mrs. Philip L. DuQuesnay), Frederick Davis, John Mitchell, Sidney Pembroke, Wilbur Fisk. Draftsman, Harlan & Hollingsworth Co., shipbuilders, Wilmington, Del., 1897-1900; editor Marine Engineering, 1900-04; with Allis Chalmers Co., 1904-07, Terry Steam Turbine Co., 1908-40; pres. Kearfott Engring. Co., Inc., N.Y. City, 1918-46; director Kearfott Mfg. Corp., since 1947; pres. Kearfoot Co., Inc., since 1946. Fellow American Society Mechanical Engineers; member Society of Naval Architects and Marine Engrs. (ex-council), Shipbuilders Council of America, Am. Soc. Naval Engrs., Montclair Soc. Engineers (past president), Instn. Naval Architecture (London), N.E. Coast Engrs. and Shipbuilders (Newcastle-on-Tyne), Maritime Assn. of N.Y., Propellers Club of U.S., Chamber Commerce, State of N.Y., Nat. Assn. Mfrs., U.S. Chamber of Commerce, Sigma Chi. Clubs: Cornell, Engineers, India House, Railway (New York); Appalachian Mountain (Boston); Upper Montclair County. Home: 27 Norwood Av., Upper Montclair, N.J. Office: Little Falls, N.J. Died Aug. 4, 1955; buried Highland Heath, West Milford, N.J.

HERDIC, PETER, lumberman, inventor; b. Ft. Plains, N.J., Dec. 14, 1824; m. Amand Taylor, Dec. 25, 1849; m. 2d, Encie E. Maynard, Jan. 12, 1860; at least 2 children. Worked for lumberman, Pipe Creek, N.Y., 1844-46; operated shingle mill, Williamsport, Pa. (town which he had built by purchasing land surrounding his original lumber mill and developing it), 1846-78; obtained patent for improved vehicle running gear, 1880, later patented fare-collecting box to be used on coach or cab; organizer, operator Herdic Coach Co., Phila., 1880's. Died Williamsport, Mar. 2, 1888; buried Williamsport.

HERING, CARL, electrical engr.; b. Phila., Mar. 29, 1860; s. late Dr. Constantine and Therese (Buchheim) H.; B.S., U. of Pa., 1880, M.E., 1887, hon. D.Sc., 1912; post-grad. studies at Darmstadt, Germany, 1883-84; married; 1 dau., Mary Truesdell. Instr. several yrs., U. of Pa., and Polytechnikum, Darmstadt; practiced elec. engring. in Frankfort (Germany), 1884, and Phila. to date; splty. elec. furnaces, electrochemistry, physical research, and patent litigation. Del. and juror of wards at 12 expns.; U.S. juror, Paris expns., 1889, 1900; U.S. del. Internat. Elec. Congress, Paris, 1900; Am. delegate several internat. conferences. Decorated Légion d'Honneur, 1901; Officier de l'Instruction Publique, 1889, both by French Govt. Pres. Am. Inst. Elec. Engrs., 1900-01, Am. Electrochem. Soc., 1906-07, Engrs'. Club, Phila., 1904, Phys. Club of Phila., 1918; fellow Am. Institute Electrical Engineers, Physical Society, A.A.A.S. Formerly compiler of "Digest of Electrical Literature." Author: Conversion Tables, 1904; Tables of Electrochemical Equivalents, 1917, etc. Home: Philadelphia, Pa. Died May 10, 1926.

HERING, RUDOLPH, hydraulic and sanitary engr.; b. Phila., Feb. 26, 1847; s. Dr. Constantine and Theresa (Buchheim) H.; grad. Dresden Poly. (Germany), 1867; asst. engr. Prospect Park, Brooklyn, 1868; asst. engr. Fairmount Park, Phila., 1869-71; astronomer Yellowstone Nat. Park, 1872; asst. city engr. Phila., 1873-80; from then in private practice. Investigation for new water supply of Phila., 1883-86; chief engr. Chicago Drainage and Water Supply Commn., 1886-88; cons. engr., dept. of public works, New York, 1889; m. Hermine, d. Prof. Dr. Buchheim, govt. councilor of Giessen, Germany, 1894. Consulting engr. for water supply and sewerage works, Phila., Baltimore, Washington, Buffalo, Cleveland, Atlanta, Montgomery, New Orleans, Los Angeles, Tacoma, Victoria, San Francisco, Honolulu, Columbus, O., and now for Dept. of Water Supply, Gas and Electricity, New York; etc. Home: Montclair, N.J. Died May 30, 1923.

HERLY, LOUIS, surgeon; b. Vienna, Ill., Aug. 11, 1881; s. Leopold and Regina (Popper) H.; student Coll. City N.Y., 1894-97; Columbia Coll., 1897-99; M.D., Columbia, 1903; m. Queenie Brown, Dec. 15, 1928; children—Irene Winifred (Mrs. Robert C. Wilson), Lillian Isabelle. Gen. surgery at St. Marks, Lincoln, Community, Lenox Hill, Flower, Sydenham, Flower-Fifth Av. Hospitals, N.Y. City, since 1908; staff mem. Fordham Med. Coll. Hosp. for Women since 1911; cancer research, Inst. for Cancer Research, Columbia U., Memorial Hospital, N.Y. City, since 1920; collaborated in cancer work at Radium Hemmet, Stockholm, and Radium Inst., Copenhagen, 1923; extensive study trips to European med. centers and research insts., 1904, 1913, 1922-23; asso. in cancer research, Columbia U., since 1946. Mem. N.Y. County and State med. socs., N.Y. Acad. Medicine, Am. Med. Assn., N.Y. Pathol. Soc., Am. Cancer Research Asso. Internat. Cancer Congress. Author articles including: A Critical Investigation of the Freund-Kaminer Reaction, 1920; Adenomyoma of the Uterus: Relation to Malignancy, 1924; Experimental Production of Tumor in White Rat, 1926. Studies in Selective Differentiation of Tissues by Means of Filtered Ultra-violet Light, 1944, A Simple Diagnostic Blood Test for Cancer, 1947. Early investigator of tar cancers in animals; discovered new method of diagnosing malignancy of breast tumors by means of filtered ultra-violet light; producted sarcoma in mice by means of sterile and cell free ascitic fluid; exhibited blood test for early cancer at 4th Internat. Congress of Cancer Research, St. Louis, 1947. Home: 440 West End Av., N.Y.C. Died July 14, 1952; buried Mount Pleasant Cemetery, Pleasantville, N.Y.

HERMANN, EDWARD ADOLPH, civ. engr.; b. Washington Co., Ark., Dec. 28, 1856; s. Charles F. and Lena D. (Wilhelmi) H.; prep. edn. St. Louis pub. schs. and prep. dept. Washington Univ., St. Louis; grad. Rensselaer Polytechnic Inst., C.E., 1879; m. St. Louis, Apr. 30, 1896, Florence Pitzman. Employed as civil engr. on R.R. construction work (principally on Pa. and Big 4 lines), 1879-99; since 1899 mem. bd. pub. improvements, and sewer commr., St. Louis; Republican. Mem. Am. Soc. Civ. Engrs., St. Louis Civ. Engrs. Club. Club: Republican. Author: Steam Shovels and Steam Shovel Work, 1894 E15. Residence: 1921 Virginia Av. Office: City Hall, St. Louis

HERMS, WILLIAM BRODBECK, prof. emeritus; born Portsmouth, O., Sept. 22, 1876; s. Carl Julius Herman and Rosa Emma (Brodbeck) H.; B.Sc., Baldwin-Wallace Coll., 1902, hon. D.Sc., 1935; studied Western Reserve U., 1905; Ohio State U., Lake Lab., Sandusky, Ohio, summers 1903, 04, 05; M.A., Ohio State U., 1906; Harvard, 1907-08; m. Lillie (Carrie) Magly, June 14, 1902; children—William Magly, Herbert Parker, George Walter. Head of Sch. of Commerce and prof. theory and practice of domestic commerce, 1902-05, instr. biology, 1904-05, Baldwin-Wallace Coll.; teaching fellow zoölogy, 1905-06, instr. exptl. zoölogy and invertebrate zoölogy, summer sessions, 1907-08, Ohio State U.; acting head dept. zoölogy, Ohio Wesleyan U., 1906-07; Edward Austin fellow in zoölogy, Harvard, 1907-08; asst. prof. parasitology, 1908-15, asso. prof., 1915-20, prof., 1920-46, prof. parasitol. emeritus, 1946; head div. entomology and parasitology, 1923-46; U. of Calif. visiting prof. med. entomol., Ohio State U., summer 1930. Officer in charge malaria investigations, Calif. Bd. Health, 1910-13; consulting entomologist and parasitologist, Calif. Bd. of Health, since 1913; made malaria-mosquito survey of Calif. Del. from Ohio Wesleyan U. to 7th Internat. Zoöl. Congress, Boston, 1907; from Calif. and U. of Calif. to Internat. Hygiene Exhibit, at Dresden, Germany, 1911; from U. of Calif. to Pan Pacific Food Conservation Congress, Honolulu, 1924; from U. of Calif. to 4th Internat. Congress of Entomology, Ithaca, N.Y., 1928. Capt. Sanitary Corps, U.S. Army, Feb. 5, 1918; maj., Aug. 14, 1918; attached to dept. lab., Fort Sam Houston, Tex., Feb. 18-April 17, 1918; thence to office of surgeon, Hdqrs. Port of Embarkation, Newport News, Va., Apr. 23, 1918-Feb. 20, 1919; in charge of malarial drainage operations, chief of insect control and asst. sanitary insp.; hon. disch., Feb. 20, 1919; lt. col., San. Res. Corps, Apr. 21, 1924-Sept. 22, 1940; Inactive Res. until called to active duty, Carlisle Barracks, Pa., Jan.-Sept. 1943. Investigated coconut pests of Fanning and Washington Island, 1924. Awarded rank of Chevalier du Mérite Agricole (France), 1935; Benj. Ide Wheeler distinguished citizenship medal (Berkeley), 1937. Chmn. draft bd. No. 70, Calif., Oct. 1940-Jan. 1943. Fellow A.A.A.S.; fellow Calif. Acad. of Science, Entomological Soc. Am. (v.p. 1933, pres. 1941); hon. mem. Nat. Malaria Com. Helminthological Soc. Washington, Am. Assn. Econ. Entomologists (pres. 1928), Pacific Coast Entomol. Soc. (chmn. 1925-26), Western Soc. Naturalists, Am. Soc. Parasitologists (v.p. 1936), Am. Soc. Naturalists, Am. Soc. Tropical Medicine, Ohio Acad. of Science, Scabbard and Blade, Sigma Xi, Alpha Zeta, Phi Sigma, Delta Omega, Alpha Kappa Lambda, Am. Legion. Pres. Bd. of Edn., Berkeley, Calif., 1915-18 and 1921-25; pres. Berkeley-Contra Costa (Calif.) Area Council Boy Scouts Am., since 1928; dir. Am. Auto. Assn., 1946; pres. Calif. State Auto Assn., 1947. Republican. Mason. Clubs: Faculty, Lions. Author: Malaria, Cause and Control, 1913; Laboratory Guide to the Study of Parasitology, 1913; Textbook in Medical and Veterinary Entomology, 1915-23, 3d edit., 1939, 4th edit., 1949; Mosquito Control (with H. F. Gray), 2d edit., 1944. Home at 2032 Del Norte St., Berkeley, Calif., sold, Apr. 1951. Died May 9, 1949; buried Sunset View Cemetery, Berkeley.

HERON, S(AM) D(AIZIEL), engr.; b. Newcastle on Tyne, Eng., May 18, 1891; s. Walter Daiziel and Isabelle Ann (Coxon) H.; student Alleyn's Sch., Dulwich, London, also London U. Naturalized 1940. Engr., air-cooled aircraft engines, aviation fuels; now cons. engr. Home: 415 Burns Dr., Det. 14. Died July 10, 1963.

HEROY, WILLIAM BAYARD, geologist; b. N.Y. City, Oct. 9, 1883; s. Newman Lounsberry and Mary Louise (Totten) H.; Ph.B., Syracuse, 1909, Sc.D., 1958; LL.D., Southern Methodist University, 1964; m. Jessie M. Page, June 10, 1909; children—John Newman Heroy, Laura Page (Mrs. Jack S. Guyton), Frances Totten (Mrs. C. J. Kirkland, Jr.), William Bayard; m. second, Mrs. Monroe G. Cheney, Dec. 31, 1960. With U.S. Geol. Survey, 1908-19; asst. geologist, 1910-12, geologist and chmn. water power section Land Classification Board, 1912-13; chmn. irrigation section same board, 1913-15; geologist-in-charge, sect. hydrographic classification, same board, 1915-18; chief division of power resources, 1918-19; advisory engr. Bur. of Conservation, U.S. Fuel Administration, 1918-19; asso. editor Elec. World, New York, 1919; geologist, foreign mgr. Sinclair Consol. Oil Corp., Nov. 1919-28, chief geologist, 1929; chief geologist Consolidated Oil Corp., 1933-39; pres. and mem. bd. dirs. Pilgrim Exploration Co., 1939-42; consultant, Bd. of Economic Warfare, 1942; dir. div. of Reserves, Office of Petroleum Adminstrn. for War, 1942-43; dir. Division of Fgn. Production, 1943-46; spl. asst., Sec. of Interior, 1946; mem. firm Beers & Heroy, 1946-56; mem. adv. com. U.S. Geol. Survey, from 1946; member Sec. Interior's Survey Com. Geol. Survey, 1953-54; v.p. The Geotechnical Corp., 1946-52, pres., 1952-61, chmn., 1961-66; dir. Inst. Study of Earth and Man, So. Meth. U., from 1966. Author articles and reports on conservation, devel. and use of fuels and water resources for power, petroleum geol. and engring. Recipient Powers medal Am. Assn. Petroleum Geologists, 1966. Fellow Of Geological Soc. of America, A.A.A.S.; mem. Am. Inst. Mining, Metallurgical and Petroleum Engrs. (v.p. 1939-42, mem. board directors 1935-39, 1942-45, Legion of Honor 1969), American Association Petroleum Geologists (hon. mem.; pres. 1934-35), Soc. Econ. Geologists (treas. 1935-39, pres. 1942), Am. Petroleum Inst., Am. Geophys. Union, Soc. Exploration Geophysicists, Geol. Soc. Washington, Dallas Geol. Soc., Am. Geog. Soc., Am. Geol. Inst. (v.p., 1948, pres. 1949-51), Am. Assn. Petroleum Geol. (hon.), Paleontological Research Instn. (v.p. 1967), Zeta Psi, Methodist. Clubs: Cosmos (Washington); Mining (N.Y.); Petroleum (Dallas). Home: Dallas TX Died Sept. 23, 1971; buried Fantinekill Cemetery, Ellenville NY

HERR, EDWIN MUSSER, electrical and mech. engr.; b. Lancaster, Pa., May 3, 1860; s. Theodore W. and Annie (Musser) H.; Ph.B., Sheffield Scientific Sch. (Yale), 1884; D.Sc., Franklin and Marshall Coll., Pa., 1911; A.M., Yale, 1915; m. Mary Forsyth, June 14, 1900. Engr. of tests, supt. telegraph and div. supt. C.,B.&Q. Ry., 1886-1900; div. master mechanic, C.,M.&St.P. Ry., 1891; gen. supt. Grant Locomotive Works, Chicago, 1892-93; gen. mgr. Gibbs Electric Co., Milwaukee, 1894; asst. supt. motive power C.&N.W. Ry., 1895; supt. motive power, N.P. Ry., 1896-98; gen. mgr., Westinghouse Air Brake Co., 1898-1905; 1st v.p., 1905-11, pres., Aug. 1911-May 1929, now vice-chmn. Westinghouse Electric & Mfg. Co. Republican. Home: New York, N.Y. Died Dec. 24, 1932.

HERR, HERBERT THACKER, mech. engr.; b. Denver, Colo., Mar. 19, 1876; s. Theodore Witmer and Emma (Musser) H.; grad. East Denver High Sch., 1895; Ph.B., Yale, 1899; m. Irene Viancourt, Feb. 10, 1896; children—Herbert Thacker, Muriel Viancourt. Began with D.&R.G. R.R., 1899, later with C.G.W. Ry., and Norfolk & Western R.R.; apptd. gen. supt. D.&R.G. R.R., 1906; closely associated with George Westinghouse during the last 7 yrs. of his life, 1907-14; v.p., gen. mgr., Westinghouse Machine Co., 1908-15; v.p. Westinghouse Electric & Mfg. Co., 1915—; v.p. Westinghouse Gear & Dynamometer Co. Inventor locomotive air brake equipment (Westinghouse Air Brake Co.), improvements in turbines, oil and gas engines, remote control for marine steam turbines (in electrically propelled U.S. battleships), etc. Awarded Longstreth Medal by Franklin Inst., 1914; John Scott medal by Bd. of Dirs. of City Trusts, Phila., for sundry inventions, discoveries and improvements in mechanical apparatus, 1931. Republican. Episcopalian. Home: Philadelphia, Pa. Died Dec. 19, 1933.

HERR, HIERO BENJAMIN, mining engr.; b. Lancaster Co., Pa., Nov. 12, 1842; s. Benjamin G. and Mary Emma (Witmer) H.; grad. U.S. Mil. Acad., 1866; m. Martha A. Shenk, June 25, 1868. Second lt. and 1st lt., U.S. Arty.; resigned May 15, 1870; in charge mathematics, etc., Lehigh U., Bethlehem, Pa., 1870-74; supt. silver mines in Colo., 1874-78; in charge engring. parties in Miss., for U.S. Govt., 1879-82; made survey for location Miss. and Ill. Canal, 1882; in charge dept. civ. engring., U. of Calif., 1883-84; engring. business, Chicago, as Hiero B. Herr & Co., 1884-95; pres. Chicago Star Constrn. Co., 1895-1900; cons. mining engr., 1911—. Republican. Home: Carlisle, Pa. Died Sept. 3, 1920.

HERRE, ALBERT W. C. T., naturalist; b. Toledo, O., Sept. 16, 1868; s. John and Marilda (Kirkman) H.; A.B., Stanford, 1903; A.M., 1905, Ph.D., 1908; m. Clara Mendonsa, Sept. 16, 1891 (died 1905); children—Inez Constance (Mrs. Andrew Kallstead), Dorothy Anderson (Mrs. Walter Crabtree), Helen Hiller (Mrs. Stephen Tarr), Marion Kirkman (dec.), Albert Lawrence; m. 2d, Mrs. Lizzie Bailey, 1907; children—Verne, Geraldine (Mrs. Lawrence Keplinger). Engaged in newspaper work, 1888-1902; curator and ichthyologist Natural History Mus., Stanford, 1928-47; sci. cons. Philippine Fisheries Project, U.S. Fish and Wild Life Service, 1947; ichthyologist and curator tropical Pacific fishes, Sch. Fisheries, U. Washington, since 1948. Mem. various sci. expdns., latest to Philippines, Malaya, Burma, India, 1940-41; monographing Genus Usnea in U.S., Can. Del. Pan-Pacific Sci. Congress, Tokyo, 1926. Fellow A.A.A.S., Cal. Acad. Sci. (hon.); mem. Biol. Soc. Wash., Cal. Bot. Soc., Inst. Pacific Relations, Am. Soc. Ichthyologists and Herpetologists (pres. Western div.), Am. Bryological Soc., San Francisco Aquarium Soc., Western Soc. Natualists, Soc. Systematic Zoology, Phi Beta Kappa, Sigma Xi. Author: A Check List of Philippine Fishes, 1951; also articles sci. jours. Home: 507 Caledonia St., Santa Cruz, Cal. 95060. Office: U. Wash. Sch. Fisheries, Seattle. Died Jan. 16, 1962.

HERRESHOFF, CHARLES FREDERICK, cons. engr., naval architect; b. Nice, France, May 28, 1876; s. James Brown and Jane Brown H.; student Glasgow (Scotland) U.; m. Edna M. Burt, 1912 (dec. 1937); m. 2d, Virginia Townsend, May 26, 1943. Chief engr. Am. & British Mfg. Co., Bridgeport, Conn., 1904-08; v.p. and chief engr., Herreshoff Motor Co., Detroit, 1908-09, pres., 1909-10, v.p. and gen. mgr., 1910-14. Invented an engine to run by superheated steam up to 800 degrees Fahrenheit; center control for automobile; electric switch for electric horn on steering gear of automobile, etc. A leader in originating improvements in automobiles and steam yachts; designer of Alabama, motor yacht champion of America, 1907, 08, 09; of Vim, winner interstate races, New York to Poughkeepsie, 1908, 09; of Chickadee, winner of Mass. Yacht Assn. cup; of Vivian, winner Hudson-Fulton Celebration races, etc. World's record holder for mile championship, U.S. Navy Course, Hudson River, 1907; winner of Canad's cup, with Iroquois, etc. Herreshoff motor car won gold medal of Am. Automobile Assn., 1910, and same yr. won more prizes than any other car. Designer of Nevada, 65 Rater, 1901, winner of Glasgow, Scotland, internat. expn. races, also largest winner of any Am. designed yacht in foreign waters. Mem. Soc. Automotive Engrs. Republican. Episcopalian. Home: 924 Scott St., Yacht Club Terrace, San Diego, Cal. Died Jan. 30, 1954.

HERRESHOFF, JAMES BROWN, inventor; b. Bristol, R.I., Mar. 18, 1834; s. Charles Frederick and Julia Ann (Lewis) H.; student Brown U., 1853-56; m. Jane Brown, of Dromore, Ireland, 1875; children—James Brown, Charles Frederick, William Stuart, Jane Brown, Ann Frances. Supt. Rumford (R.I.) Chem. Works, 1858-63; mfr. fish oil, Prudence Island, R.I., 1863-69. Resided in Europe, much of time since 1869, giving attention to inventions, among the more important of which are: first naphtha driven motorcycle of internal combustion type in America (1870); coil boiler; fin-keel for sailing yachts; mercurial anti-fouling paint; sliding-seat for rowboats; thread-tension regulator for sewing machines; apparatus for measuring specific heat of gases; sounding apparatus, etc. Home: New York, N.Y. Died Dec. 5, 1930.

HERRESHOFF, J(OHN) B(ROWN) FRANCIS, chemist; b. Bristol, R.I., Feb. 7, 1850; s. Charles Frederick and Julia Ann (Lewis) H.; student Brown U., class of 1870, Ph.B., by spl. vote, 1905, hon. A.M., 1890, Sc.D., 1909; m. Grace Eugenia, d. John Dyer, of Providence, R.I., Feb. 9, 1876; m. 2d, at Phila., Emily Duval, d. Dr. Richard Henry Lee, Oct. 25, 1882; m. 3d, Carrie Ridley Enslow, d. Dr. James Lucas Ridley, of Hoboken, N.J., June 9, 1919 (died 1924); m. 4th, at Chattanooga, Tenn., Irma Grey, d. Dr. James Lucas Ridley, Apr. 14, 1925. Prof. analyt. chemistry, Brown U., 1869-72; supt. Laurel Hill Chem. Works, L.I., 1876; invented process for mfg. sulphuric acid; now v.p. and trustee Nichols Copper Co.; dir. Granby Consol. Mining, Smelting & Power Co.; hon. v.p. Gen. Chem. Co. Awarded Perkin medal (1st time awarded in America) for work in chem. and metall. industries. Home: New York, N.Y., and Atlanta, Ga. Died Jan. 30, 1932.

HERRICK, ALBERT BLEDSOE, consulting elec. engr.; b. Bergen Point, N.J., March 31, 1862; 1879-80. Edison's laboratory; was asst. in perfecting the incandescent lamp under Edison; took physical, chem. and mech. course, Stevens Inst. Technology, Hoboken (did not remain for degree); was patent expert for Brush-Swan Co., then chief electrician for Bergmann & Co., then for Edison Co., then the Edison Gen. Electric Co., then the Gen. Electric Co.; since 1894 has been a consulting elec. engr. for street ry. and lighting plants and tech. expert; edits "Date Sheets" in The Electrical Engineer; writes on elec. engring. topics. Office: 120 Liberty St., New York,

HERRICK, CHARLES JUDSON, univ. prof.; b. Minneapolis, Oct. 6, 1868; s. Rev. Henry Nathan and Anna (Strickler) H.; B.S., U. Cin., 1891, Sc.D., 1926; M.S., Denison U., 1895, Sc.D., 1930; Ph.D., Columbia, 1900, Sc.D., 1931; m. Mary Elizabeth Talbot, Aug. 17, 1892; 1 dau., Ruth. Instr. natural sciences, Granville Acad., 1891-92; prof. natural sciences, Ottawa U., 1893-93; fellow in biology, 1893-95, instr., 1895-96, Denison U.; univ. scholar biology, Columbia, 1896; asso. in comparative neurology, Pathol. Inst. of N.Y. State Commn. in Lunacy, 1897-1901; prof. zoology, Denison, 1898-1907; prof. neurology, U. Chgo., 1907-34, emeritus, in residence, 1934-37, emeritus 1937, chmn. dept. anatomy, 1933; visiting prof. anatomy, emeritus, U. Mich., 1942. Fellow A.A.A.S. (secretary zool. sect. 1902-07, chmn. 1908); pres. Ohio Acad. Science, 1903. Author many books and papers on biol. and neurol. subjects. Editor Journal Comparative Nuerology since 1894. Commd. maj., Sanitary Corps, N.A., 1918. Mem. Nat. Acad. Sciences, Kon. Akademie von Wetenschappen te Amsterdam, Norwegian Acad. of Science and Letters; Royal Acad. Science of Sweden; honorary member American Neurol. Assn., Société Scientifique "Antonio Alzate," Mexico; corr. mem. Académie Royale de Medicine de Belgique. Home: 236 Morningside Drive, Grand Rapids 6, Mich. Died Jan. 29, 1960.

HERRICK, EDWARD CLAUDIUS, scientist, librarian; b. New Haven, Conn., Feb. 24, 1811; s. Claudius and Hannah (Pierpont) H.; A.M. (hon.), Yale, 1838. Clk. in bookstore at age 16; advanced theory of periodic occurance of large number of meteors, 1837; contbr. to Am. Jour. of Sci., 1837-62; published A Brief Preliminary Account of the Hessian Fly and Its Parasites, 1841; 1st to find and describe parasites of eggs of spring canker-worm moth; one of best early econ. entomologists; librarian Yale, 1843-58. Died New Haven, June 11, 1862.

HERRICK, FRANCIS HOBART, biologist; b. Woodstock, Vt., Nov. 19, 1858; s. Rev. Marcellus Aurelius and Hannah Andrews (Putnam) H.; A.B., Dartmouth, 1881; Ph.D., Johns Hopkins, 1888; Sc.D., Western U. of Pa., 1897, Western Reserve U., 1936; m. Josephine Herkomer, Eng., June 24, 1897; children—Agnes Elizabeth (Mrs. Hans Platenius), Francis Herkomer. Instr. biology, 1888-91, prof., 1891-1929, prof. emeritus, 1929, Adelbert Coll., Western Reserve U. Fellow A.A.A.S., Am. Ornithologists' Union. Trustee Cleveland Mus. of Natural History, 1920—, v.p., 1928—. Author: Audubon the Naturalist, 2 vols., 1917, 1 vol. edit., 1938; The American Eagle on the Shores of Lake Erie, 1925, 27; The American Eagle—A Study in Natural and Civil History, 1934; Wild Birds at Home, 1935. Home: Cleveland Heights, O. Died Sept. 11, 1940.

HERRICK, GLENN WASHINGTON, entomologist; b. Otto, N.Y., Jan. 5, 1870; s. Stephen M. and Marion (Botsford) H.; Fredonia State Normal Sch.; B.S.A., Cornell U., 1896; post-grad. work, Cornell and Harvard, 1896-97; m. Nannie Young Burke, Aug. 17, 1898; children—Marvin Theodore, Stephen Marion, Ann Bertha (Mrs. John M. Raines). Professor biology, Mississippi Agricultural and Mechanical Coll., 1897-1908; v.dir. Miss Agrl. Expt. Sta., 1906-08; prof. entomology, Tex. Agrl. and Mech. Coll., 1908-09; asst. prof. economic entomology and entomologist to Expt. Sta., Cornell U., 1909-12, prof. and entomologist, 1912-35, prof. emeritus since 1935. Mem. Am. Palestine Com. Fellow Entomol. Society of America, A.A.A.S.; member American Association Econ. Entomologists (pres. 1915). Biol. Soc., Washington. Acad. Polit. Sci., Am. Assn. Univ. Profs., New York Acad. of Scis., Sigma Xi, Alpha Gamma Rho, Pi Gamma Mu; hon. mem. Eugene Field Soc. Republican. Episcopalian. Author: Text-book General Zoology, 1907; Laboratory Exercises in General Zoology, 1907; Insects Injurious to the Household and Annoying to Man, 1914; Insects of Economic Importance, 1915; Manual of Injurious Insects, 1925; Manual for Study of Insects (with J. H. Comstock and A. B. Comstock), 20th edit., 1930; Insect Enemies of Shade-trees, 1935; also numerous papers and bulls. Contbr. to Ency. Britannica Yearbook. Home: 219 Kelvin Place, Ithaca NY

HERRING, SILAS CLARK, safe mrf.; b. Salisbury, Vt., Sept. 7, 1803; s. Otis and Mary (Olds) H.; m. Mary Draper, 1831; m. 2d, Caroline Trabell, May 9, 1843; at least 1 child, Francis. Apptd. paymaster and col. 5th regt. N.Y. Arty.; began building Salamander safes (1st fire-proof safes in U.S.), constructed of metal with plaster of paris lining (mfg. rights for lining purchased from patentee Enos Wilder, who received 1 cent per pound royalty), 1840; added improvements to makes safes burglarproof; eventual fire and burglar-proof Herring Champion safe awarded 1st Prize at World's Fair, N.Y.C., also at Exposition Universelle, Paris, 1862. Died Plainfield, N.J., June 23, 1881.

HERRMANN, HENRY FRANCIS, chemist; b. Wehlau, East Prussia, July 2, 1890; s. Rev. Albert E. and Friedericke (Wiechmann) H.; cmae to U.S., 1897, naturalized, 1907; B.Sc., Coll. City N.Y., 1913; post grad. Bklyn. Poly. Inst.; m. Charlotte A. Dougherty, Sept. 28, 1918; children—Robert H., William E. With Cassella Color Co., agt. in U.S. for Leopold Cassela, Germany, aiding devel. dyestuff industry, N.Y.C., 1913-16; developer dyes Century Color Co., Nutly, N.J., 1916-18; mgr. dye application lab. Nat. Aniline & Chem. Co., N.Y.C., 1918-28; with Gen. Dyestuff Corp., N.Y.C., since 1928, mgr. N.Y. sales dist., 1928-40, prodn. mgr. and gen. exec., 1940-52, market mgr., 1952-55, cons., 1955-56; exec. sec. Vat Dye Inst.,

1956-59. Mem. Am. Assn. Textile Chemists and Colorists (pres. 1947-50), Textile Research Inst. (dir. 1947-51), Sales Assn. Am. Chem. Industry, Republican. Episcopalian. Clubs: Long Island Golf Association (sec.); Garden City Country (v.p., dir.). Home: 32 Whitehall Blvd., Garden City, N.Y. 11530. Office: 435 Hudson St., N.Y.C. 14. Died Oct. 12, 1964.

HERRON, JAMES HERVEY, cons. engr.; b. Girard, Pa., Jan. 4, 1875; s. James Hervey and S. Josephine (Fuller) H.; student U. of Mich., 1897-99, B.S. in Mech. Engring., 1909; student Grad. Sch., U. of Mich., 1916-17, 1920-21; Dr. of Engring. (hon.) 1943, Case Sch. of App. Sci.; m. Cora El Lewis, June 19, 1900. Apprentice, Stearns Mfg. Co., Erie, Pa., 1889-95; asst. and chief engr. Erie City Iron Works, 1895-97; draftsman and asst. engr. Cambria Steel Co., Johnstown, Pa., 1899-1902; v.p. and chief engr., Bury Compressor Co., Erie, Pa., 1902-05; mgr. Motch and Merryweather Machinery Co., Detroit, 1905-07; chief engr. and works mgr. Detroit Steel Products Co., 1907-09; pres. The James H. Herron Co., cons. engrs., Cleveland, O., since 1909; dir. Forest Glen Estate, Youngstown, O. Pres. Bd. of Edn., Cleveland Heights, 1914-20. Life mem. Cleveland Engring. Soc. (pres. 1917-18, hon. mem. 1940); fellow Am. Soc. M.E. (mgr. 1922-25; v.p. 1934-36; pres. 1936-37), A.A.A.S., Am. Inst. Elec. Engrs.; mem. Am. Soc. Civil Engrs. (pres. Cleveland sect. 1935), Am. Inst. Mining and Metall. Engrs., American Chemical Society, Am. Soc. for Testing Materials, Brit. Iron and Steel Inst., Am. Concrete Inst., Tau Beta Pi. Christian Scientist. Mason. Club: Mid-Day (Cleveland). Asso. editor and contbr. chapter on "Iron and Steel" to Hool and Johnston, Handbook of Building Construction; Hool and Kinne, Bldg. Constrn. Home: 17612 Winslow Rd., Shaker Heights 20, O. Died March 29, 1948.

HERSCHEL, CLEMENS, hydraulic engr.; b. Mar. 23, 1842; S.B., Lawrence Scientific Sch. (Harvard), 1860; m. Grace D. Hobart, May 12, 1869 (died 1898); children—Arthur Hobart, Winslow Hobart, Clementine (Mrs. Hobart Rawson); m. 2d, Jeannette B. Hunter, Mar. 5, 1910; 1 son, Clemens. Hydraulic engr., Holyoke (Mass.) Water Power Co., 1879-89; engr. and supt. E. Jersey Water Co., 1889-1900; r.r. commr. of Mass., 1881-83. Awarded Elliott Cresson gold medal of Franklin Inst., Phila., for his Venturi Water Meter. Author: Continuous Revolving Draw Bridges, 1875; 115 Experiments, 1897; Frontinus and the Water Supply of the City of Rome, 1899. Home: Glen Ridge, N.J. Died Mar. 3, 1930.

HERSEY, HENRY BLANCHARD, meteorologist and balloonist; b. Williamstown, Vt., July 28, 1861; s. Joel and Recta Wheelock (Blanchard) H.; B.S., Norwich U., Vt., 1885, M.S., 1906; course at U.S. Signal Service Tech. Sch., Va.; m. Mrs. Laura A. Saunier, Mar. 13, 1926 (died 1940). Service of U.S. Weather Bur., 1885-1932. Maj. 1st U.S. Vol. Cav. ("Roosevelt's Rough Riders"), Spanish-Am. War; exec. officer Wellman Chicago Record-Herald Polar Expdn., 1906-07; experienced meteorologist and balloonist, being a licensed aeronautic pilot of the Aero Club of France, and of the Aero Club of America. Assisted Lt. Frank P. Lahm, U.S. Army, in the internat. balloon race at Paris, 1906, helping to win the James Gordon Bennett cup; sailed the balloon "United States" in the internat. race at St. Louis, 1907, crossing lakes Michigan, St. Clair and Erie, and landing in Canada. Apptd. maj., Aviation Sect., Signal Corps, May 1917, and placed in command U.S. Army Balloon Sch., Ft. Omaha, Neb.; rated as jr. mil. aeronaut, July 24, 1917; promoted lt. col. Signal Corps, U.S. Army, Sept. 27, 1917; served with balloon div., Air Service, in France, Oct. 1918-Mar. 1919. Fellow Royal Meteorol. Soc., London; mem. Southern Calif. Acad. Sciences, A.A.A.S., etc. Elected permanent hon. comdr. Los Angeles Bd. No. 4, Am. Balloon Corps Vets. Mason (32 deg.). Club: Cosmos (Washington). Contbr. on aeronautical subjects to Century Mag. Home: 135 East Laurel Av., Sierra Madre, Calif. Died Sept. 24, 1948.

HERSH, A(MOS) H(ENRY), biologist; b. Lancaster, Pa., Nov. 2, 1891; s. George and Margaret (Rudy) H.; A.B., Franklin and Marshall Coll., 1914, A.M., 1915, Sc.D., 1946; student Princeton, 1915-16; Ph.D., U. of Ill. (fellow in zoology, 1919-22), 1922; m. Roselle Karrer, Aug. 19, 1922; children—Charles Karrer, Robert Tweed. Grad. asst. in biology Princeton, 1915-16; instr. in zoology Kan. State Coll., 1916-18; instr. in biology Marquette U., 1918-19; instr. in zoology U. of Mich., 1922-23; instr. biology Western Res. U., 1923-25, asst. prof., 1925-36, asso. prof., 1936-46, prof. biology, 1946—. Fellow Ohio Acad Sci., A.A.A.S.; mem. Am. Soc. Zoologists, Am. Soc. Naturalists, Genetics Soc. of Am., Am. Soc. Human Genetics, Soc. for Study Development and Growth; Am. Assn. U. Profs., Gamma Alpha, Sigma Xi, Phi Kappa Sigma. Contbr. articles on genetics and relative growth to sci. jours.; Blakiston's New Gould Medical Dictionary, 1949. Home: 1937 Parkway Dr., Cleveland Heights 18, O. Office: Western Reserve University, Cleve. 6. Died Aug. 28, 1955.

HERSHEY, J(OHN) WILLARD, chemist; b. Gettysburg, Pa., Feb. 6, 1876; s. Abraham and Hosie (Eyster) H.; B.S., Gettysburg Coll., 1907, M.S., 1910; student Harvard, 1907-08, Johns Hopkins, 1910-11; Ph.D., U. of Chicago, 1924; m. Effie Bowman, Aug. 24, 1916; 1 son, Ardys Willard. Taught 5 yrs. in Pa. pub. schs.; prof. chemistry, Bridgewater (Va.) Coll., 1908-10, Defiance (O.) Coll., 1911-18, McPherson (Kan.) Coll. since 1918. Fellow A.A.A.S., Internat. Coll. of Anesthetists (life); mem. Am. Chem. Soc. (councilor 1930-32; pres. Wichita sect. 1937-39), Am. Inst. Chemists, Kan. Acad. Science (pres. 1933-34), Physical Science Teachers Soc. (pres. 1933-37), Sigma Xi, Phi Beta Kappa. Democrat. Mem. Ch. of Brethren. Rotarian. Author: A Laboratory Guide to Study of Qualitative Analysis, 1927; (with L. A. Enberg) Laboratory Manual for General Chemistry, 1933; The Book of Diamonds, 1940; also research papers on synthetic diamonds and components of the atmosphere and snythetic gases in relation to animal life. Home: McPherson, Kan. Died Sept. 27, 1943.

HERSHEY, OSCAR H., mining geologist; b. Blue Rock, Pa., Mar. 27, 1874; s. Urias H. and Susan Ida (Hengst) H.; ed. high sch., Lebanon, Pa.; m. Mabel E. Zollers, Sept. 29, 1923. Began study of geology in the field, 1896; prospected in Calif. and Isthmus of Panama much of time until 1904; with U.S. Geol. Survey, Clear Creek Quadrangle, Colo., summer 1904; examining mines and prospects, 1904-08; mem. Burch, Caetani & Hershey, later Hershey & White; cons. geologist to Bunker Hill & Sullivan Mining and Concentrating Co. Fellow A.A.A.S. and Geol. Soc. of America. Republican. Home: Oakland, Calif. Died Dec. 11, 1939.

HERTY, CHARLES HOLMES, chemist; b. Milledgeville, Ga., Dec. 4, 1867; s. Bernard R. and Louisa T. H.; student Ga. Mil. and Agrl. Coll., 1880-84; Ph.B., U. of Ga., 1886; Ph.D., Johns Hopkins, 1890; at univs. of Berlin and Zürich, 1899, 1900; hon. Ch.D., U. of Pittsburgh, 1917; D.Sc., Colgate U., 1918, Oglethorpe U., 1934, U. of Fla., 1937; LL.D., U. of Ga., 1928, Univ. of N.C., 1933; m. Sophie Schaller, Dec. 23, 1895 (died 1929); children—Charles Holmes, Frank Bernard, Sophie Dorothea. Asst. chemist, Ga. State Expt. Sta., 1890-91; instr., 1891-94, adj. prof. chemistry, 1894-1902, U. of Ga.; collaborator, 1901-02, expert, 1902-04, Bur. of Forestry, U.S. Dept. of Agr.; with Chattanooga Pottery Co., 1904-05; prof. chemistry U. of N.C., 1905-16; editor Jour. Industrial and Engring. Chemistry, 1917-21; pres. Synthetic Organic Chemical Mfrs.' Assn., 1921-26; advisor to The Chemical Foundation, Inc., 1926-28; became industrial consultant, N.Y. City, 1928; dir. div. pulp and paper research, Ga. State Dept. Forestry and Geol. Development, 1932-33; dir. Pulp and Paper Lab. of Industrial Com. of Savannah, Ga. Fellow A.A.A.S., Chemical Society (London). Home: Savannah, Ga. Died July 27, 1938.

HERTY, CHARLES HOLMES, JR., metallurgist; b. Athens, Ga., Oct. 6, 1896; s. Charles H. and Sophie (Schaller) H.; B.S., U. of North Carolina, 1918; M.S., Mass. Inst. Tech., 1921, D.Sc., 1924; m. Kathleen Malloy, Nov. 13, 1929; children—Dorothea, Charles H. III, Kathleen, Timothy. Research asso., Sch. of Engring. Practice, Mass. Inst. Tech., at Lackawanna plant of Bethlehem Steel Co., 1924-26; in charge ferrous metall. research, U.S. Bur. of Mines, 1926-31; dir. research Metall. Advisory Bd., Pittsburgh, Pa., 1931-34; research engr. Bethlehem Steel Co., 1934-42, asst. to vice pres. in charge of operations since 1942. Served as sergt. Ordnance Dept., U.S. Army, 1918-19. Mem. Am. Iron and Steel Inst., Am. Inst. Mining and Metall. Engrs. (Hunt medalist; Howe lecturer), Am. Soc. for Metals (Campbel lecturer, Saveur Award), Am. Chem. Soc., Nat. Acad. Sciences, Engineers Club of Lehigh Valley, Phi Beta Kappa, Sigma Xi, Delta Kappa Epsilon, Alpha Chi Sigma. Republican. Episcopalian. Author of about 81 tech. papers for various societies. Home: R.D. No. 1, Hellertown, Pa. Office: Bethlehem Steel Co., Bethlehem, Pa. Died Jan. 17, 1953; buried Nisky Hill Cemetery, Bethlehem, Pa.

HERZIG, CHARLES SIMON, mining engr.; b. New York, Jan. 28, 1874; s. Simon and Anna (Schanzer) H.; Coll. City N.Y., 1891; E.M., Sch. of Mines (Columbia), 1895; m. Mae Rose Sullivan, May 12, 1903; m. 2d, Florence F. Upmeyer, of Minneapolis, Oct. 13, 1917. Served various capacities in mines and smelting works, U.S. and Mexico; became rep. and local partner, 1903, in eastern Australia for Bewick, Moreing & Co., mining engrs., of London, Eng., at the time when Herbert C. Hoover was a mem. of that firm, and had charge of a number of cos. as mgr. and dir.; in gen. practice London, 1906-15; returned to U.S., 1915. Has visited most of the principal mining districts of the world. Republican. Mem. Instn. Mining and Metallurgy, London, Am. Inst. Mining Engrs., Tau Beta Pi. Author: Mine Sampling and Valuing. Contbr. to tech. magazines and socs. Home: Ansonia Hotel, New York. Office: 27 William St., N.Y. City, and Boston Bldg., Salt Lake City UT

HESS, ELMER, physician; b. Millville, N.J., May 31, 1889; s. Frederick and Mary (Theise) H.; prep. edn. Peddie Sch., Hightstown, N.J., 1903-07; M.D., U. of Pa. Med. Sch., 1911; grad. study, Johns Hopkins U., 1919-21; grad. study in Europe, 1919, 1925; D.Sc., Allegheny Coll., Meadville, Pa., 1956; m. Edna Africa, June 26, 1911; children—Celeste Remle (wife of Capt. P. W. Cann, USN, ret.), Hope (Mrs. John W. Luther). Physician Indian Service U.S., 1911-12, in pvt. practice of medicine and surgery at Erie, Pa., 1912—, specializing in urology, 1920—; consultant urologist numerous hospitals Pennsylvania. Surveyed med. installations in Israel for Hadassah, 1956. Chmn. health resources adv. com. Office Civil and Def., Exec. Office of President, Washington. Served from lt. to capt. M.C., U.S. Army, 1917-19, with 15th F.A., 2d Div., A.E.F. Decorated Croix de Guerre, Verdun medal, Chateau Thierry medal (France); 3 army citations (Silver Star), Victory medal with 5 clasps (U.S.). Rep. nominee for mayor, Erie, 1919; pres. Erie Boys Club, 1919-39; mem. bd. trustees, Pa. Soldiers and Sailors Home 1940-56; mem. Pa. State Board of Medical Education and Licensure, 1946-57. Mem. of governing com. Gorgas Memorial Inst. Certified by Am. Bd. Urology, 1935. Fellow Am. Coll. Surgeons, Internat. Coll. Surgeons, Academy-Internat. of Medicine; member A.M.A. (pres. 1955-56), Pa. State Medical Society (pres. 1947-48), Erie County Med. Soc. (pres. 1938), Am. Urol. Assn. (pres. 1952), Western N.Y. and Ontario Urol Assn. (pres. 1941), Canadian Urol. Assn., World Med. Assn., Pan-Am. Urol. Assn., Pan.-Am. Med. Assn. (trustee since 1937; pres. urol. sect. 1937), Newcomen Soc. of England, Am. Legion, Forty and Eight; hon. mem. Detroit Urol. Soc., Western Branch Soc. Am. Urology Assn.; corr. mem. Cuban and Argentine urol. socs.; hon. mem. Colegio Brasileiro de Urologistas. Republican. Episcopalian. Mason. Clubs: Erie, Kahkwa, Rotary (pres. 1943-44), Lake Shore Golf, Aviation Country. Contributor medical jours.; urol. editor Cyclopedia of Medicine, Revision Service for Sajou's System of Medicine, 1933-40, 1942-54. Home: 4819 Highview Blvd. Office: 8 E. 12th St., Erie, Pa. Died Mar. 29, 1961; buried Wintergreen Gorge Cemetery, Erie.

HESS, FRANK L., geologist; b. Streator, Ill., Sept. 4, 1871; s. Jesse M. (M.D.) and Mary (Brown) H.; A.B. in geology and mining, Stanford, 1903; m. Eva Roseberry, May 25, 1903. With U.S. Geol. Survey, 1903-25, U.S. Bur. Mines, 1925-44, profl. work in Alaska, Bolivia, Burma, Can., Ceylon, Chile, China, Federated Malay States, India, Italy, Mex., and in nearly all the mining states of U.S., now ret., lectr. on geology U. Md., 6 yrs. Hon. custodian of rare earths and rare metals, U.S. Nat. Museum. Former mem. of Com. on Determination of Geologic Age, Nat. Research Council, A.A.A.S., Soc. Econ. Geologists, Washington Acad. Sciences, Geol. Soc. of Washington, Petrologist Club, Geol. Soc. Am. (fellow), Mineral. Soc., Phycol. Soc. of the Americas. Methodist. Author papers on rare metals and their deposits, pegmatites and other geol. subjects. Address: 5509 Roosevelt St., Bethesda, Md. Deceased.

HESS, HARRY HAMMOND, geologist; b. N.Y.C., May 24, 1906; s. Julian S. and Elizabeth (Engel) H.; B.S., Yale, 1927; Ph.D., Princeton, 1932; D.Sc. (hon.), Yale, 1969; m. Annette Burns, Aug. 15, 1934; children—George Burns, Frank Deming Mather. Geologist Loangwa Concessions, Ltd., N. Rhodesia, 1928-29; geologist gravity measuring cruises U.S. submarines S-48 and Barracuda, 1931, 36; asst. instr. Rutgers U., 1932-33; research asso. geophys. lab. Carnegie Instn., Washington, 1933-34; instr. Princeton U., 1934-37, asst. prof., 1937-46, asso. prof., 1946-48, prof., 1948-69, Blair prof. geology, 1964-69, chmn. dept., 1950-66; vis. prof. U. Cape Town, 1949-50, Cambridge U., 1965. Chmn. Space Science Bd., 1962-69; mem. U.S. nat. com. geology Internat. Union Geol. Scis., 1961-69, chmn., 1961-62; mem. div. com. math., phys. and engring. scis. NSF, 1960-64; cons. U.S. Navy Oceanographic Office, 1966-69, Nat. Council Marine Resources and Engring. Devel., 1967-69; mem. Pres.'s Com. Nat. Medal Sci., 1967-69; mem. sci. and tech. adv. com. manned space flight NASA, 1964-69, mem. lunar and planetary missions bd., 1967-69, mem. lunar sample analysis planning team, 1967-69. Served comdr. USNR; commanding officer U.S.S. Cape Johnson, 1945; rear adm. USNR. Recipient Penrose medal Geol. Soc. Am., 1966; Feltrinelli prize Accademia Nazionale dei Lincei, 1966; Distinguished Pub. Service medal NASA, 1969. Fellow Geol. Soc. Am. (pres. 1962), Mineral Soc. Am. (pres. 1954-55); mem. Nat. Acad. Sci. (chmn. sect. geology 1960-63), Mineral Soc. London, Geol. Soc. S. Africa, Soc. Econ. Geologists, Am. Geophys. Union (pres. sect. geodesy 1951-53, pres. sect. tectonophysics 1956-58), NRC (chmn. division of earth sciences 1956-58, chmn. committee on disposal radioactive waste 1955-62), Geol. Soc. London, Am. Soc. Oceanography (dir. 1966-69), Sociedad Venezolana de Geologos (hon.), Am. Philos. Soc., Accademia Nazionale dei Lincei, Am. Acad. Arts and Scis. Clubs: Cosmos (Washington); Nassau (Princeton). Author articles in science journals. Discoverer greatest depth in oceans, 1945. Home: Princeton NJ Died Aug. 25, 1969; buried Arlington National Cemetery, Arlington VA

HESS, HENRY, mech. engr.; b. Darmstadt, Germany, 1863; s. George and Louise (Hess) H.; brought to America in infancy; ed. Heidenfeld's Inst., and under Dr. Douai, New York, and high sch., Germany; m. Caroline Annie Serle, of London, Eng., 1886. Served as designer with Pond Machine Tool Co., Watervliet Arsenal (U.S.A. heavy ordnance), Niles Tool Works Co., Bur. Constrn. and Repair, U.S. Navy; consulting engr. and mng. dir. German Niles Tool Works, Berlin; founder, and pres. Hess-Bright Mfg. Company, 1904-02, Hess Steel Co., Hess-Ives Co. Special lecturer, Columbia U. Home: Philadelphia, Pa. Died Mar. 22, 1922.

HESS, VICTOR FRANCIS, educator; b. Waldstein, Austria, June 24, 1883; s. Vincens and Seraphine (Grossbauer) H.; student U. Graz, 1901-05, U. Vienna, 1905-08; Ph.D., 1906; Sc.D., Fordham U., 1946, U. Chgo., 1956; m. Mary Bertha Warner (Breisky), Sept. 6, 1920 (dec. 1955); m. 2d, Elizabeth M. Hoenke, 1955. Prof. physics U. Vienna, Graz and Innsbruck, Austria, 1919-38; chief physicist U.S. Radium Corp., N.Y.C., Orange N.J., 1921-23; prof. physics Fordham U., 1938-56, prof. emeritus, 1956—. Recipient Nobel prize in physics for discovery cosmic rays, 1936. Fellow Am. Phys. Soc., Sigma Xi; mem. Pontifical Acad. Sci. Rome, Acad. Sci. Vienna (life), Am. Geophys, Union. Catholic. Author: Conductivity of the Atmosphere and Its Causes, 1928; Ionization Balance of the Atmosphere, 1933; Cosmic Rays and Their Biological Effects, 1949. Extensive research in cosmic rays atmospheric electricity and radioactivity. Home: 20 William St., Mt. Vernon, N.Y. Died Dec. 17, 1964; buried Mount Cavalry Cemetery, White Plains, N.Y.

HESS, WENDELL FREDERICK, educator, research dir.; b. Troy, N.Y., Jan. 1, 1903; s. Wendell, Jr. and Anna Marie (Beiermeister) H.; E.E., Rensselaer Polytech. Institute, Troy, N.Y., 1925, Dr. Engring., 1928; m. Grace Eleanor Towne, Feb. 4, 1933; children—Wendell Towne, Eleanor Sylvia, Frederick W., John. Instr. Rensselaer Polytech. Inst., 1928-30, asst. prof. elec. engring. and physics, 1930-37; asst. prof. metall. engring., 1937-38; asso. prof. and head of welding lab., 1938-45; prof. and head welding lab., 1945-47, head department of metallurgical engring. 1947—, dir. research, 1952—, tchr. course in welding to U.S.N. Annapolis grads., sent by Bur. of Yards and Docks, 1929-47. Fellow Am. Inst. Elec. Engr.; mem. Am. Inst. Mining and Metall. Engrs., Am. Welding soc. (pres., hon. life mem.; Samuel Wylie Miller Meml. medallist, 1949), Am. Soc. for Engring. Edn., Am. Soc. Metals, Am. Soc. Testing Materials, Sigma Xi. Awarded Lincoln Gold Medal by Am. Welding Soc.; University Award of the Resistance Welder Mfrs. Assn., 1944, 1945, 1947, 1948; Am. Iron and Steel Inst. Medal, 1944; John Price Weatherill Medal of Franklin Inst., 1948. Home: 25 Hawthorne Av. Office: Rensselaer Polytechnic Inst., Troy, N.Y. Died Apr. 21, 1954; buried Oakwood Cemetery, Troy.

HESSE, BERNARD CONRAD, chemist; b. East Saginaw, Mich., Oct. 3, 1869; Ph.C., U. of Mich., 1889, B.S., 1893; Ph.D., U. of Chicago, 1896. Asst. in chemistry, U. of Mich., 1890-93; research chemist at Ludwigshafen-on-Rhine, Germany, 1896-1906; consulting practice, New York, 1906—; consulting mem. General Chemical Co., N.Y. City. Died Apr. 1934.

HETERICK, ROBERT HYNTON, med. dir. USPHS (ret.); b. Georgetown, O.; s. Robert Grant and Martha Bell (Cooper) H.; student U. Cin., M.D., Med. Coll. of Ohio, 1906; grad. U.S. Army Med. Sch., 1911; m. Frances Susan Felker, Feb. 8, 1908. Resident physician Ohio Maternity Hosp., 1906, Hosp. of Good Samaritan, Cin., 1907; commd. 1st lt., Med. Dept., U.S. Army, 1909; commd. asst. surgeon, USPHS, 1911, passed asst. surgeon, 1915, surgeon, 1923, sr. surgeon, 1931; served in Iloilo, Manila, Batan, P.I., 1912-15; instr. pub. health U. of Philippines, 1914-15; assigned to U.S. Naval Forces in European waters during World War I; med. dir., 3d Dist. U.S. Indian Service, 1935-36, commd. med. dir., 1937; formerly sr. med. officer Ellis Island Hosp., exec. officer Marine Hosps. at Chgo., Cleve. and San Francisco; former comdg. officer Vineyard Haven, Savannah and Louisville Marine hosps. and USPHS Hosp. 30, Chgo.; mem. surg. staff. San Pedro Gen. Hosp., Cal. Hosp., French Hosp., Cal. and Hollywood hosps., Los Angeles; chief quarantine officer, Port of Los Angeles, 1941-46; supr. ports of Hueneme, Port San Luis, Santa Barbara, Newport, San Diego, quarantine affairs; dist. med. officer, War shipping Adminstrn., Los Angeles Dist., 1944-45; cons. in pub. health and sanitation to port surgeon, U.S. Army, Los Angeles, to sr. med. officer of U.S. Naval Bases at San Diego and Terminal Island, 1941-45; cons. in pub. health to State of N.M., City of Albuquerque; lecturer in pub. health U. So. Cal. Med. Sch., U. of N.M. Recipient medal S.A.R., 1948; hon. mem. Indian Medical Service, third district. Fellow A.C.S.; mem. A.M.A., Med. Officers of World War Vets. Fgn. Wars of America, Assn. Mil. Surgeons, S.A.R., Wanderers and Sojourners, Omega Upsilon Phi. Mason (32 deg., Shriner). Author: articles on public health in various med. jours.; Health Hints for Primary Teachers, 1949. Also short stories for children. Address: 605 Ridgecrest Dr., Albuquerque, N.M. Died Sept. 14, 1957.

HETLER, DONALD MCK(INLEY), univ. prof.; born Osage City, Kan., Feb. 19, 1896; s. Thomas Jefferson and Katharine (Slusser) H.; A.B., Univ. Kan., 1918, A.M., 1923; Ph.D., Yale (Nat. T.B. Assn. fellow, 1924-26), 1926; m. Rossleene Merle Arnold, Jan. 1, 1928 (dec.); 1 d., Katharine Jane. Chemist Hercules Powder Co., Parlin, N.J., 1918-21; grad. asst., dept. chemistry, Univ. Kan., 1921-24; asst., Rockefeller Inst., 1926-28; instr., Washington Univ. Sch. Med., 1928-31, asst. prof., 1931-37; asso. prof., dept. bacteriology, Mont. State Univ., 1937-38, prof. and chmn., dept. bacteriology since 1938. Fellow A.A.A.S. Mem. Am. Chem. Soc., Alpha Chi Sigma, Sigma Xi, Phi Sigma, Acacia. Gamma Alpha. Republican. Methodist. Mason. Research work in field of chem. studies of bacteria, immune sera, bacteriophage, immunity in cancer. Home: 322 E. Beckwith Av., Missoula, Mont. Died Sept. 1, 1956.

HETTINGER, FREDERICK C(ARL), chem. engr.; b. Phila., Mar. 15, 1891; s. Carl Frederick and Ida Frederica (Pohl) H.; student U. Me., 1910-13, Mass. Inst. Tech., 1913, Lowell Inst., 1915; B.S., Sch. Indsl. Foremen, 1916; m. Sophora Louise Bliss, Nov. 15, 1916; children—Carl F., Ora Louise (Mrs. Paul Brayton) (dec.), Ruth Evelyn (dec.). Plant mgr. U.S. Indsl. Chem. Co., 31 yrs.; chmn., vis. prof., prof. chem. engring. Johns Hopkins, 1949-57; now sr. engring. supr. Balt. City Health Dept. Mem. Am. Inst. Chem. Engrs., Am. Chem. Soc., Sigma Xi. Home: 2608 Goodwood Rd., Balt. 14. Died Feb. 1, 1959.

HEUSER, EMIL, (hoi'zer), educator, research asso.; b. Stralsund, Germany, Sept. 15, 1882; s. Karl Ludwig and Olga (Oborn) H.; student Tech. U. Munich, Germany, 1903-05, Tech. U., Karlsruhe, 1905-07, U. of Graz, Austria, 1907-09; Dr. Engring. Sci., Tech. Univ., Karlsruhe, 1909; m. Frieda Thiele, July 2, 1910; children—Heinrich, Dietrich, Klaus, Andreas. Came to Canada, 1926; naturalized British subject. Mill chemist various German and Austrian pulp and paper mills, 1909-12; prof. cellulose chemistry Tech. U., Darmstadt, 1912-23; dir. research Glanzstoff-Werke (rayon), Seehof nr. Berlin, 1923-26; dir. research Canadian Internat. Paper Co., Hawkesbury, Ont., Can., 1926-38; research asso. Inst. Paper Chemistry, Appleton, Wis., 1938-47, ret. Mil. service with Red Cross, 1916-18. Mem. govt. com. for utilization of cellulose waste (alcohol, furfural, fodder). Mem. Am. Chem. Soc. (chmn. cellulose div. 1937), Tech. Assn. Pulp and Paper Industry, Wis. Acad. Letters and Science. Sec. German Assn. Pulp and Paper Chemists and Engrs., 1918-26; hon. prof. cellulose chemistry, Tech. Univ., Berlin, Charlottenburg, 1923-26. Editor: Papierfabrikant, 1918-23; founder and editor: Cellulose-Chemie, 1920-26. Author: Das Farben des Papiers auf der Papiermachine (Berlin), 1913; Lehrbuch der Cellulose-Chemie (Berlin), 3d edit., 1927; translation into Russian (L. K. Lepin and N. A. Shilova), Moscow, 1923. Textbook of Cellulose Chemistry (translation C. J. West and G. J. Esselen), 1924; The Chemistry of Cellulose, 1944. Contbr. to sci. publs., Germany and U.S., and to sci. vols., chiefly on pulp and paper, cullolose, non-cellulosic carbohydrates, lignin, and wood. Home: 339 Vista de la Playa, La Jolla, Cal. Died Dec. 24, 1953.

HEVESY, GEORGE DE, chemist; b. Budapest, Hungary, Aug. 1, 1885; s. Louis; ed. U. Budapest; D. Natural Philosophy, U. Freiburg, 1908; studied in Germany and Switzerland, 1908-10; research fellow U. Manchester (Eng.), 1911; hon. degrees Cape Town, Uppsala, Freiburg, Copenhagen, Sao Paulo, Rio de Janeiro, Turin; m. Pia Riss, 1924; 4 children. Asst., tech. high sch., Zurich, Switzerland, 1910; lectr. U. Budapest, 1913, became full prof., 1918; joined staff Inst. for Theoretical Physics, U. Copenhagen (Denmark), 1920; prof. phys. chemistry U. Freiburg, 1926; Baker lectr. Cornell U., 1930; became prof. Research Inst. for Organic Chemistry, U. Stockholm (Sweden), 1943. Recipient Canizzaro prize Acad. Scis., Rome, 1939; Nobel prize in chemistry for work on use of isotopes as tracer elements in researches on chem. processes, 1943; Copely medal Royal Soc., 1950; Faraday medal, 1951; Baily medal London Coll. Physicians, 1952; Silvanus Thompson medal Brit. Inst. Radiology, 1956; Atoms for Peace award, 1959. Hon. mem. chem. socs. of London, Helsinki, Royal Inst. London, Royal Soc., sci. acads. of Copenhagen, Goteborg, Stockholm, Brussels, Rome, Heidelberg. Author: Das Element Hafnium, 1927; Quantitative Analysis by X Rays, 1932; Praktikum der Rontgenspektroskopischen Analyse, 1932; Radioactive Indicators, 1948; also many papers. Noted for work in fields of radioactivity, physiol. chemistry, organic chemistry. Died July 5, 1966. *

HEWE, LAURENCE ILSEY, civil engr.; b. Dover, N.H., Sept. 28, 1876; s. Horace Greeley and Helen Ilsley (Jones) H.; B.Sc., Dartmouth, 1898; Ph.D., Yale, 1901; m. Agnes Danforth June 1901; 5 children. With Mass. Hwy. Commn., 1897-99; prof. mathematics and engring. R.I. State Coll., 1901-05; instr. mathematics Yale, 1905-09; with U.S. Pub. Rd. Adminstrn., 1911—; successively chief of econs., dist. engn., gen. insp., dep. chief engr., chief Western Region Hdqrs., San Francisco. Cons. to government of Saudi Arabia, 1946-47. Chmn. Am. delegation Internat. Rd. Congress Munich, 1934. Mem. Am. Soc. C.E., Am. Assn. Highway Ofcls., Am. Math. Soc. (1901-31), Sigma Xi, Casque and Gauntlet; fellow A.A.A.S. Clubs: Cosmos (Washington), Commonwealth (San Francisco). Author: (with Prof. Jas W. Glover) Highway Bonds, 1913; (with Prof. H. L. Seward). Design of Diagrams for Engineering Formulas, 1924; American Highway Practice (2 vols.), 1941. Contbr. tech. articles in math. and engring. publs.; tech. and popular articles in World's Work, Nat. Geog. Mag., Collier's, etc. Home: 114 Edgewood Av. Office: Phelan Bldg., San Francisco. Died Mar. 2, 1950; buried Goodnoe Hills, Washington.

HEWES, ROBERT, mfr.; b. Boston, 1751; son of Mr. and Ann (Frye) Hewes. Made unsuccessful attempt to start glass factory, Temple, N.H., 1780; organized Essex Glass Works, Boston, 1787 (name changed to Boston Crown Glass Co. 1809); granted patent on manufacture of glass in Mass., 1787-1802; retired, 1824; part owner of a glue factory, a soap-works, a slaughter-house; taught fencing to Boston elite. Author: Rules and Regulations for Sword Exercise of Cavalry, 1802; On the Formation and Movements of Cavalry, 1804. Died Boston, July 1830; buried burying ground on Boston Common.

HEWETT, DONNEL FOSTER, geologist; b. Irwin, Pa., June 24, 1881; s. George Claude and Hetty Barclay (Foster) H.; student Georgia School of Technology, Atlanta, Ga., 1895-97; Metall. Engr., Lehigh University, 1902; D.Sc. (honorary), 1942; graduate student Yale, 1909-11, Ph.D., in Geology, 1924; m. Mary Amelia Hamilton, Jan. 14, 1909. Asst. in dept. of metallurgy, Lehigh U., 1902-03; mining practice, Pittsburgh, Pa., 1903-09; geologist vanadium at Mina Raqre, Peru, 1906; geologist U.S. Geol. Survey 1911-71, in charge section of metalliferous deposits 1935-44, strategic mineral investigations, 1939-44, geologist rare earths Mt. Pass, Nev., 1946, research geologist, 1963; research asso. Stanford Univ., Stanford, Cal. Recipient D.S.M., Dept. Interior; Penrose medal Soc. Economic Geologists, 1956; award American Acad. of Achievement, 1965. Mem. Geological Soc. Am. (council 1931-33; v.p. 1935, 45, Penrose medal 1964), Nat. Acad. of Scis., Am. Chem. Soc., Mineral. Soc. Am., Am. Inst. of Mining and Metall. Engrs., Am. Assn. Advancement Sci., American Acad. Arts and Sciences, the Society of Economic Geologists (president 1936), also Tau Beta Pi, Sigma Nu, Sigma Xi, Phi Beta Kappa. Conglist. Clubs: Cosmos. Author: Anticlines of the Bighorn Basin, Wyo. (with C. T. Lupton), 1916; Geology, Oil and Coal Resources in the Oregon Basin, Meeteetse, and Grass Creek Basin Quadrangles, Wyo., 1926; Geology and Ore Deposits of the Goodspring Quad., Nevada, 1931; Geology and Ore Deposits of the Ivanpah Quadrangle, Nev.-Calif., 1956; also numerous smaller sci. reports on mineralogy and ore deposits. Home: Palo Alto CA Died Feb. 5, 1971; buried Palo Alto CA

HEWITT, EDWARD RINGWOOD, engr., inventor, author; b. Ringwood Manor, N.J., June 20, 1866; s. Abraham Stevens and Sarah Amelia (Cooper) H.; g.s. of Peter Cooper; A.B., Princeton, 1889, A.M., 1892; U. of Berlin 1890-91; m. Mary E. Ashley Sept. 7, 1892; children—Candace (Mrs. Gordon Stevenson), Ashley C., Lucy (Mrs. Guido Pantalconi), Abram. Chemist, Peter Cooper Glue Factory, 1901-02; designed automobiles, established one design, in Eng., known as the "Adams-Hewitt"; dir., engr. Metzger Motor Car Co.; built motor trucks under name of Hewitt Motor Co., which was absorbed by Internat. Motor Co., of which became cons. engr., dir. Mem. Am. Soc. M.E., Am. Assn. Auto Engrs. Clubs: Century, Anglers, Dutch Treat, Players, Tuxedo. Author: Secrets of the Salmon; Telling on the Trout; Trout Streams; Handbook of Stream Improvement; Handbook of Fly Fishing; Trout Raising and Stocking; Those Were the Days, 1943. Address: 48 Gramercy Park, N.Y.C. Died Feb. 1957. *

HEWITT, OGDEN BLACKFAN, engr.; b. Trenton, N.J., Feb. 24, 1893; s. Charles Edward and Eva (Blackfan) H.; B.S., Worcester Poly. Inst., 1915; m. Margaret Middleton, Apr. 29, 1916; children—Cynthia (Mrs. J. W. Correll), Charles E. Began in constrn. and mining engring.; pres. and dir. Gauley Mountain Coal Co., N.Y.C., since 1941, Ringwood Co., since 1941, Green & Hewitt Inc., since 1949. Electric Ferries, Inc., since 1949; dir. Wood Newspaper Machinery Corp., Marion Power Shovel Co., Lehigh Coal & Nav. Co. Mem. Phi Gamma Delta. Clubs: Union League, Downtown Athletic (N.Y.C.). Home: Ringwood, N.J. Died Oct. 17, 1963; buried Valleau Cemetery, Ridgewood, N.J.

HEWITT, PETER COOPER, scientist, inventor; b. New York, N.Y.; s. late Hon. Abram Stevens H. (congressman and mayor of New York) and Sarah Amelia (Cooper) H.; g.s. Peter Cooper, philanthropist; (hon. Sc.D., Columbia University, 1903, and Rutgers College, 1916); m. Lucy Work; m. 2d, Mrs. Maryon J. Bruguiere. Dir. N.Y. & Greenwood Lake Ry., Cooper, Hewitt & Co., Midvale Water Co., Hexagon Realty Co., Ringwood Co., Hewitt Realty Co., Lehigh & Oxford Mining Co. First v.p. Naval Consulting Board, 1915—. Trustee Cooper Union for Advancement of Science and Art, Hosp. House of Rest for Consumptives. Home: Ringwood Manor, N.J. Died Aug. 25, 1921.

HEWITT, WILLIAM, mech. engr.; b. Trenton, N.J., Oct. 26, 1853; s. Charles and Anna (Conrad) H.; student Lehigh U., 1869-71; M.E., Stevens Inst. Tech., Hoboken, N.J., 1874; m. Josephine H. Walker, Dec. 11, 1878. Connected with Trenton Iron Co., 1874-1913, v.p., 1879-1903; estimating engr. and wire rope expert, tramway dept. Am. Steel & Wire Co., Trenton, 1903—. Inventor of machinery for mfr. of wire rope. Mem. Co. A, 7th Regt. N.J.N.G., 1874-82. Episcopalian. Home: Trenton, N.J. Died Aug. 3, 1922.

HEXAMER, CHARLES JOHN, civil engr.; b. Phila., Pa., May 9, 1862; s. Ernest and Marie (Klingel) H.; B.S., U. of Pa., 1882, A.M., 1884, Ph.D., 1886; (LL.D., Nat. U., 1899); m. Annie Josephine Haeuptner, Jan. 7, 1891. In practice, Phila., 1882-1917 (retired). Awarded Scott legacy medal and premium by Franklin Inst. for inventions. Republican. Lutheran. Author: Spontaneous Combustion, 1885; Fire Hazards in Textile Mills, Mill Architecture and Means for Extinguishing Fire, 1895; Finely Divided Organic Substances and Their Fire Hazard, 1896. Home: Atlantic City, N.J. Died Oct. 15, 1921.

HEYL, PAUL RENNO, physicist; b. Phila., Pa., June 30, 1872; s. Henry Renno and Mary Clarena (Knauff) H.; B.S., U. of Pa., 1894, Ph.D., 1899; grad. study, Harvard; m. Lucy Knight Daugherty, July 26, 1899; children—Marian (dec.), Alice, Dorothy. Teacher of physics, high sch., 1898-1910; physicist with Commercial Research Co., New York, 1910-20; physicist U. S. Bur. Standards, 1920, until retirement. Mem. Am. Physical Soc., A.A.A.S., Philos. Soc. of Washington, Washington Acad. Science. Awarded Boyden premium, Franklin Inst., 1907. Author: The Common Sense of the Theory of Relativity, 1925; Fundamental Concepts of Physics, 1926; The Philosophy of a Scientific Man, 1933. Contbr. to Scientific Monthly. Inventor (with Dr. L. J. Briggs) of Earth Induction compass. Home: 2800 Ontario Road N.W., Washington DC

HEYROVSKY, JAROSLAV, phys. chemist; b. Prague, Czechoslovakia, 1890; D.Sc., U. London; Ph.Dr., Prague U.; Dr. Rer. Nat. (hon.), Technische Hochschule, Dresden; Dr. Chem. Sci. (hon.), Warsaw; Dr. honoris causa U. Acad. Aix-Marseille, U. Paris; Dr. Med. h.c., U. Vienna, 1965; Dr. Sc. honoris causa, Univ. Prague, 1965; Dr. Phil. Nat., Frankfurt/Main; children—Judith, Michael. With Charles U., Prague, 1919-54, lectr., 1920-22, asso. prof., 1922-26, prof. phys. chemistry, 1926-54; dir. Polarographic Inst., Czechoslovak Acad. Scis., Prague, 1950-63, dir. emeritus, 1963—; Carnegie vis. prof. U. Cal., 1933; inventor polarography. Recipient Nobel prize in chemistry, 1959. Hon. mem. chem. Soc. London, Am. Acad. Arts and Scis., Hungarian Acad. Sci., Indian Acad. Sci. Author: Application of the Polarographic Method in Practical Chemistry, 1933; Polarographie, 1941; Oscillographic Polarography, 1953; Polarographisches Praktikum, 1948; Principles of Polarography, 1959. Co-editor: Collection of Czechoslovak Chemical Communications, 1929-48. Home: Na Stáhlavce 6, Prague 6. Office: J. Heyrovsky Polarographic Inst., Czechoslovak Acad. Scis., Vlasska 9, Prague 1, Czechoslovakia. Died Mar. 27, 1967; buried Prague.

HEYWOOD, LEVI, mfr., inventor; b. Gardner, Mass., Dec. 10, 1800; s. Benjamin and Mary (Whitney) H.; m. Martha Wright, Dec. 29, 1825; 5 children. Became mfr. wooden chairs, Gardner, 1826; formed partnership (with brother and friend) to start sawmill, Charlestown, Mass., 1831; invented method for sawing veneers from maghony and other woods; partner Heywood Bros. & Co., chair mfg. firm, 1835-41, became sole owner, 1841; invented many furniture mfg. devices including rattan-processing machine, wood-bending machine; partner (with W. B. Washburn) in chair and wooden ware mfg. firm, Erving, Mass.; a major stockholder Am. Rattan Co., 1876; erected foundry to make various iron posts used in chair mfg., 1876; del. Mass. Const. Conv., 1853; mem. lower house Mass. Legislature, 1871. Died Gardner, July 21, 1882.

HIBBARD, ANGUS SMITH, elec. engr.; b. Milwaukee, Feb. 7, 1860; s. William B. and Adaline H.; ed. Milwaukee Acad. and Racine Coll.; D.Sc., Carleton Coll., Northfield, Minn., 1939; m. Lucile Ray, Dec. 4, 1884; 1 dau., Janet (Mrs. Janet H. Henneberry). Began bus. experience in railroading; later sec. to gen. supt. Northwestern Telegraph Co.; studied telephony; supt. Wis. Telephone Co., 1881-86; first gen. supt. Am. Telephone & Telegraph Co., 1886-93, inaugurating their long-distance lines; gen. mgr. Chicago Telephone Co., 1893-1911, later also 2d v.p.; adviser to exec. dept. Am. Telephone & Telegraph Co., New York, 1911-16; now cons. engr. Invented and patented many improved devices for use with telephone. Designer of the "Blue Bell" sign of the telephone, used throughout the world. Editor emeritus The Diocese Magazine, since 1937. Mem. Am. Inst. Elec. Engrs., Wis. Soc. of Chicago (pres. 1911), Chicago Assn. of Commerce (hon.). Republican. Episcopalian. Clubs: Union League, University, Industrial, Glen View (hon.). Composer of song, The U.S.A. Forever, music for song, Hail Chicago, etc. Capt. Am. Red Cross, with A.E.F. in France, June-Dec. 1918. Chmn. Camp Roosevelt Assn., 1919-23. Home: 2440 Lake View Av. Office: 212 W. Washington St., Chicago. Died Oct. 21, 1945.

HIBBARD, H(ERBERT) WADE, mech. engr.; b. Maulmain, Burma, India, Sept. 10, 1863; s. Rev. Charles and Susan Ann (Robinson) H.; A.B., Brown U., 1886, A.M., 1899; M.E., Cornell, 1891; (1st Sibley prize man, 1890); m. Mary Coleman Davis, Aug. 20, 1896; children—Hope, Ruth (Mrs. Alfred S. Romer), Harlan Davis, Jeanne. With R.I. Locomotive Works, Providence, 1886-89; mech. dept., Pa. R.R., 1891-94; chief mech. engr., Lehigh Valley R.R., 1894-95; prof. machine design and locomotive engring., U. of Minn., 1895-98; prof. ry. mech. engring., and prin. Grad. Sch. Ry. Mech. Engring., Cornell U., 1898-1909; prof. mech engring., U. of Mo., 1909—. Engring. work in Europe, 1892, 1900; engring. expert, N.Y. State Civ. Service Commn., 1904, 05, 08; smoke expert, 1908; cons. engr. on president's staff, Wabash Ry. War organizing work Council of Nat. Defense, Washington, May-Aug. 1917; U.S. dist. engr. in charge 18 Mo. counties, on power-plant fuel conservation, 1918-19. Presbyn. Member Internat. Jury Awards, San Francisco Expn., 1915. Home: Columbia, Mo. Died May 25, 1929.

HIBBARD, RUFUS PERCIVAL, botanist, plant physiologist; b. New Haven, Conn., Apr. 2, 1875; s. Rufus Piercy and Sarah Amelia (Brown) H.; A.B., Williams, 1899; Harvard, summer 1901; University of Chicago, summer of 1902; Woods Hole, Mass., 3 summers; fellow U. of Mich., 1904-06, Ph.D., 1906; married; children—John Sidney, William Thomas. Teacher of science, Kiskiminetas Springs Acad., Saltsburg, Pa., 1900-01; teacher of biology, Blair Academy, Blairstown, N.J., 1901-04; asst. Woods Hole, Marine Biol. Lab., summers 1903, 04; scientific asst. Bureau Plant Industry, U.S. Department Agr., 1906-08; bacteriologist and plant pathologist, Miss. Agrl. Expt. Sta., 1908-11; collaborator plant disease survey, Bur. Plant Industry, Dept. Agr., Washington, 1908-11; research asso. plant physiology, Mich. Agrl. Expt. Sta. and asso. prof., 1911—. Republican. Conglist. Fellow A.A.A.S.; mem. Am. Genetic Assn., Am. Soc. Plant Physiologists (pres. 1925-26), Bot. Soc. America, Am. Chem. Soc., Sigma Xi. Author various articles and bulls. Home: 512 Hillcrest Av., East Lansing MI

HIBBEN, SAMUEL GALLOWAY, engr. elec. illumination; b. Hillsboro, O., June 6, 1888; s. Joseph M. and Henriette (Martin) H.; B.Sc., Case Institute Tech., 1910, E.E. (hon.), 1915, D.Eng., 1952; student U. of Paris, Sorbonne, France, 1918; m. Ruth Rittenhouse, April 14, 1923; children—Eleanor Rittenhouse, Stuart Galloway, Barry Cummings, Craig Rittenhouse. Began as electrician, 1906; illuminating engineer Macbeth Evans Glass Company, Pittsburgh, Pennsylvania, 1910-15; consulting engr., Pittsburgh, 1915-16; with Westinghouse Lamp Co. from 1916, dir. of lighting from 1933. Served as 2d and 1st lt. U.S. Army, searchlight design Washington, D.C., and capt. sound ranging, A.E.F., World War I; U.S. Strategic Bombing Survey, Germany, World War II. Mem. Am. Inst. E.E., Soc. Am. Mil. Engrs., Illuminating Engring. Soc. (p. pres), Am. Soc. Agrl. Engrs., Illuminating Engrs. London, Sigma Nu. Republican. Presbyn. Clubs: Engineers, Ohio Soc. of New York. Contbr. tech. articles. Credited with designing 1st mobile anti-aricraft searchlight, 1917; pioneered marine illumination; designed floodlight displays illuminating Washington Monument, Holland Tunnel, Natural Bridge and Endless Caverns in Va., Carlsbad Caverns, N.M., Crystal Cave, Bermuda. Home: Montclair NJ Died June 9, 1972.

HICKENLOOPER, ANDREW, engr., soldier; b. Hudson, O., Aug. 10, 1837; s. Andrew and Abigail H. (Cox) H.; removed to Cincinnati, 1844; ed. Woodward Coll.; practiced as civ. engr.; was chief engr., City of Cincinnati; entered army, 1861; capt. 5th O. battery; promoted to brig. gen., comdg. 3d brigade, 4th div., 17th army corps. For 5 yrs. U.S. marshal, Southern dist., O.; lt. gov. O., 1880-81; pres. Cincinnati Gas Light & Coke Co., 1872—. Author: Street Lighting, 1899; Fairy Tales, or Romance of an Arc Electric Lamp, 1901; Competition in the Manufacture and Delivery of Gas, 1881; Incandescent Electric Lights for Street Illumination, 1886. Home: Cincinnati, Ohio. Died 1904.

HICKERNELL, LATIMER FARRINGTON, engring. and research exec.; b. Middletown, Pa., Mar. 22, 1899; s. Harry O. and Eva (Farrington) H.; A.B. in Math., Physics, Grinnell Coll., 1920, D.Sc., 1962; B.S. in Elec. Engring., Mass. Inst. Tech., 1922 D.Eng., Polytechnic Inst., Bklyn., 1961; m. Estelle M. Cummings, Oct. 24, 1927. Electrician, Ia. Light Heat & Power Co., Grinnell, 1916-20; elec. contractor, Grinnell, 1921; grad. student engr. Gen. Electric Co., 1922-23; instr. elec. engring. Ia. State Coll., 1923; asst. investigations engr. Consumers Power Co. and Commonwealth Power Corp., Jackson, Mich., 1922-27; gen. engr. Stevens & Wood, Inc. and Allied Engrs., Inc., Jackson, 1927-31; elec. engr. Anaconda Wire & Cable Co., Hastings-on-Hudson, N.Y., 1931-33, chief engr., 1933-57, v.p. engring., 1957—. Served with U.S. Army, 1918. Profl. engr., Mich., N.Y. Fellow Am. Inst. E.E. (pres. 1958-59); mem. United Engring. Trustees (bd. dir.), Engring. Found., (dir.), Elec. Hist. Found. (dir.), Instn. Elec. Engrs. (asso.), Insulated Power Cable Engrs. Assn., Am. Soc. Testing Materials, Conf. Internationale des Grands Reseaux Electriques (U.S. nat. com.). Clubs: M.I.T., Engineers (N.Y.C.). Editor: Current Ratings for Electrical Conductors, 1942. Contbr. handbooks, ref. books. Holder patents on magnetic mine sweeping, high voltage cables. Home: 11 Birch Lane, Dobbs Ferry, N.Y. Died Dec. 16, 1963; buried Woodland Cemetery, Jackson.

HICKS, LAWRENCE EMERSON, biologist; b. Fredericktown, O., Oct. 22, 1905; s. Earl H. and Floy (Coe) H.; B.S., Otterbein Coll., 1928; M.S., Ohio State U., 1929, Ph.D., 1933; m. Thyra Jane Bevier, June 27, 1931; children—Jane Ann, Thomas Edward Deam. Biol. asst., Otterbein Coll., 1926-28; bot. asst. Ohio State Univ., 1928-30, instr., 1930-34; game ecologist Ohio Div. Conservation, 1929-31; forester and wildlife conservationist in charge Region 3, U.S. Soil Conservation Service, 1934-36; biol. U.S. Fish and Wildlife Service; asst. prof. zoölogy, entomol., and dir. Ohio Wildlife Research Sta., 1936-45; summers: New England Camps, U.S. Bur. Plant Industry, instr. field ecol. U. of Buffalo, N.Y. State Museum; ecol., Ohio Conservation Lab.; owner Buckeye Apiaries; dir. Ohio Apiaries Co-operative. Chmn. tech. com. Columbus Metropolitan Parks; U.S. del. to Internat. Ornithol. Congress, Rouen, France, 1938. Fellow Am. Ornithol. Union (sec. 1937-45), A.A.A.S., Ohio Acad. Science; mem. Wilson Ornithol. Soc. (sec. 1931-36, v.p., 1937-39, pres. 1940-41), Inland Bird Banding Assn. (v.p.), Wheaton Club (pres.), Cooper Ornithol. Club, Ecol. Soc., Wildlife Soc., Am. Soc. Mammalogists, Biol. Soc. Washington, Limnol. Soc., Ohio Beekeepers Assn. (v.p.), Nat. Outdoors Writers, Sigma Xi, Gamma Alpha, Gamma Sigma Alpha, Theta Alpha Phi. Co-author: The Pheasant in North America (Am. Wildlife Inst., 1945; won Wildlife Soc. Award for 1945); author: Breeding Birds of Ohio (Ohio biol. survey, 1935), Ohio Game and Song Birds in Winter (Ohio div. conservation, 1931), numerous scientific papers; contbr. articles on natural hist. to newspapers and jours.; lecturer on animal and plant life; collector: biol. specimens and rare books on natural history, plant and animal specimens for Herbaria, museums and labs. Home: 8 Chatham Rd., Columbus 14, O. Died Jan. 20, 1957; buried Fredericktown, O.

HIDDEN, WILLIAM EARL, mineralogist; b. Providence, R.I., Feb. 16, 1853; s. James Edward and Abbie S. (Angel) H.; ed. pub. schs., Providence, New York and Washington; m. Josephine W. Morton, Oct. 30, 1883. Engaged as mineralogist, 1872—; discovered, 1880, mine producing emeralds and a transparent emerald-green gem, variety of spodumene (now known as hiddenite) in Alexander Co., N.C.; sent out by Edison, 1879, on a 5 months' search for platinum mines in Appalachian belt of N.C., S.C., Ga. and Ala.; discovered monazite (thought to be excessively rare) in commercial quantities in N.C., and this mineral now furnishes thoria for incandescent gas lights. Describer of iron meteorites known as the Lick Creek Iron (N.C.), the Chulafinnee (Ala.), Laurens Co. (S.C.), Elmo (Ark.), Maverick Co. (Tex.), and the thought-to-be "bielid" of Mazapil, Mex., in Am. Journal of Science. Co-discoverer and co-describer (with late Dr. James B. Mackintosh) of minerals hanksite, sulphohalite, yttrialite, thorogummite, nivenite; also (with late Samuel L. Penfield) of hamlinite; (with Dr. W. F. Hillebrand) of rowlandite and mackintoshite; (with Dr. J. H. Pratt) of the new gem rhodolite, and its associated minerals; discovered the 2d known locality for sperrylite (the only known ore of platinum) in Macon Co., N.C.; with Prof. John W. Judd of London discovered and described new mode of occurrence of ruby in Cowee Mountains of N.C.; discovered new mineral Yttrocrasite, a new yttrium-thorium-uranium titanate, from Burnet Co., Tex., an analysis by Prof. C. H. Warren, Am. Jour. Science, Dec. 1906. Solving the mineral. and geol. problems of Cobalt, Ont., 1906—. In Aug. 1911, traced the occurrence of the rich ore of thorium, auerlite, to its source in the Green River Zircon belt of Henderson Co., N.C., and found it in place there and mined several tons of zircons which were used in electric light glowers and in making "zircon-glas." Consulting mining geologist to Sunshine Copper Co. of Lavic, Calif., where is pursuing a mineral reconnaissance. Fellow Geol. Soc., London. Home: Ocean Grove, N.J. Died June 1918.

HIDER, ARTHUR, engineer; b. London, Eng., Feb. 29, 1844; s. James and Maria H.; ed. in London, Can., and Cleveland, O., pvt. pupil, 1864-66, Peter Emslie, C.E. (dec.). Draftsman and asst. city engr., Louisville, Ky., 1866-74; prin. asst. city engr., Louisville, 1874-76; consulting engr., 1876-78; in charge surveys and physical exams. lower Mississippi, under U.S. Engrs. Corps, 1878-81; prin. engr. in local charge improvements on Mississippi River, 3d dist., under Mississippi River Commn., 1881—. Home: Grenville, Miss. Died July 28, 1916.

HIGGINS, GEORGE FREDERICK, consulting engr.; b. Mancheser, N.H., June 8, 1862; s. Freeman and Mary Wilson (Dennett) H.; S.B. and M.E. in mech. engring., Worcester Poly. Inst., 1885; m. Mary Peabody Clark, of Manchester, Dec. 29, 1886. Practiced at Boston and in Mass. since 1892; treas. Gem Stamped Steel Co., Chelsea. Designed water works power plant of Winnipeg, Man.; power plants of Manchester, N.H., Worcester, Mass., Winchester, N.H., Peabody, Mass., Chelsea, Mass., etc. Mem. Am. Soc. M.E., Boston Engring. Soc., Soc. Mayflower Descendants, S.A.R. Republican. Conglist. Clubs: Engineers (New York), University, Congregational, Rotary (Boston). Developed 16 original patents and 7 more in Patent Office, Washington. Home: Melrose, Mass.

HIGLEY, HENRY GRANT, biometrician; b. Lima, Peru, June 11, 1903 (parents Am citizens); s. Henry Grant and Rosario (Andrade) H.; student U. Guadalajara, 1920-24, Ratledge Chiropractic Coll., 1934-37, U. So. Cal., 1953-57; M.S., U. Nuevo Leon, 1957; m. Mary Bavin, Aug. 1931; 1 son, Henry. Research dir. Los Angeles Coll. Chiropractic, 1948-69, also chmn. dept. physiology; dir. dept. research, statistics Am. Chiropractic Assn., 1958-69; statis. analyst Ghormley & Assos., Los Angeles, 1952-56;

statis. analyst Vitaminerals, Inc., Glendale, Cal., 1956-57. Mem. Am. Inst. Biog. Scis., Inst. Math. Statistics, Biometric Soc., Am. Documentation Inst., Am. Statis. Assn. Author: (with Haynes) General Chemistry, 1938. Contbr. articles to profl. jours. Home: Alhambra CA Died May 18, 1969; interred Resurrection Cemetery South San Gabriel CA

HILDEBRAND, H(ENDRICK) EDWARD, engr.; b. Sandstedt, Germany, Jan. 25, 1895; s. Edward Christian and Elise (Ratjen) H.; came to U.S., 1904, naturalized, 1916; M.E., Columbia, 1917; m. Marion B. Gross, Nov. 23, 1918; children—H. Edward, Ruth Elsa. Asst. chief engr. Newburgh (N.Y.) shipyards, 1917-22; engr. Continental Baking Co., 1922-26, dir. engring., 1926-63, v.p., 1944-63; v.p. Morton Frozen Foods, Inc., 1956-63; cons. Continental Baking Co., 1963—, Office Def. Transp., 1942-43. Mem. Am. Soc. M.E., Am. Soc. Bakery Engrs., Soc. Automotive Engrs. Republican. Mem. Dutch Reformed Ch. Mason. Mem. Phi Kappa Sigma. Club: Larchmont (N.Y.) Shore. Professional engr., N.Y. Home: 133 Douglas Pl., Mt. Vernon, N.Y. Office: Halstead Av., Rye, N.Y. Died July 22, 1965.

HILDRETH, DAVID MERRILL, civil engr.; b. Haverhill, N.H., Jan. 15, 1862; s. Sylvester Levi and Teressa (Nelson) H.; B.S., Dartmouth, 1887, M.S., 1894; LL.M., Columbian (now George Washington) U. Law Sch., 1896; m. Cleora H. DeCoster, Jan. 1, 1889. Asst. on New Hampshire Mass. boundary survey, 1887-88; topo. draftsman, Coast and Geodetic Survey, 1888-12; topographer Post Office Dept., Mar. 6, 1912-June 15, 1920; mem. U.S. Geographic Bd., Oct. 1912-Oct. 1920. Universalist. Mason. Home: Hanover, N.H. Died June 2, 1923.

HILDRETH, SAMUEL PRESCOTT, physician, historian; b. Methuen, Mass., Sept. 30, 1783; s. Dr. Samuel and Abigail (Bodwell) H.; studied medicine with father, then with Dr. Thomas Kittredge, Andover, Mass.; M.D., Med. Soc. of Mass., 1805; m. Rhoda Cook, Aug. 19, 1807, 6 children. Practiced medicine, Hampstead, N.H., 1805; moved to Marietta, O., 1806, practiced medicine, 1806-61; recorded discoveries of curative effect of malaria on epilepsy and value of charcoal and yeast in malignant fevers; mem. Ohio Legislature, 1810-11, secured passage of law providing for med. socs. and regulating practice of medicine; wrote med. papers on epidemics, especially great epidemic of 1822-23; as naturalist contbd. articles to Am. Jour. Science, 1826-33, wrote one of earliest papers of presence of petroleum in salt springs; pres. 3d Med. Conv. of Ohio; hist. writings include: "A Brief History of the Floods of the Ohio River from the Year 1772 to the Year 1832" (in Jour. of Hist. and Philos. Soc. Ohio, Vol. I), 1838; Genealogical and Biographical Sketches of the Hildreth Family, 1840; Pioneer History, 1848; Biographical and Historical Memoirs of the Early Pioneer Settlers of Ohio, 1852; reports of meteorol. observations published in Smithsonian. Contributions to Knowledge, Vol. XVI, 1870. Died Marietta, July 24, 1863.

HILGARD, EUGENE WOLDEMAR, prof. agr.; b. Zweibrücken, Rhenish Bavaria, Jan. 5, 1833; s. Theodore Erasmus and Margaretha (Pauli) H.; emigrated, 1836; ed. Belleville, Ill.; Ph.D., Univ. of Heidelberg, 1853 (re-conferred honoris causa, 1903); studied, also Zürich and Freiberg, Saxony; (LL.D., U. of Miss., 1882, Columbia and U. of Mich., 1887); m. J. Alexandria Bello, of Madrid, Spain, 1860. State geologist of Miss., 1855-73; prof. chemistry, U. of Miss., 1866-73; prof. geology, zoölogy and botany, 1873-74, mineralogy, geology and zoölogy, 1874-75, U. of Mich.; prof. agr., 1874-1904, prof. emeritus, 1904—; U. of Calif.; dir. Calif. Agrl. Expt. Sta., 1888-1904. Spl. agt. cotton production reports 10th U.S. Census, 1879-83; in charge agr. div. Northern Transcontinental Survey, 1881-83. Specialist in direct investigation of soils in connection with their native vegetation; of the influence of climate upon the formation of soils, and of "alkali lands." Received Liebig medal for distinguished achievements in agrl. sciences from Acad. of Sciences, Munich; also gold medal, Paris Expn., 1900, as collaborator in agrl. science. Fellow Am. Acad. Arts and Sciences, A.A.A.S. Author: Soils of the Arid and Humid Regions, 1906; Agriculture for Schools of the Pacific Slope (with W. J. V. Osterhout), 1909. Author and editor: Cotton Culture in the U.S., 10th Census, 1880. Home: Berkeley, Calif. Died Jan. 8, 1916.

HILGARD, JULIUS ERASMUS, geodesist; b. Zweibrucken, Bavaria, Jan. 7, 1825; s. Theodor Erasmus and Margaretha (Paule) H.; m. Katherine Clements, Aug. 1848, 4 children. Chief bur. U.S. Coast Survey under Alexander Bache, 1856; made 1st reliable determination of differences of longitude between Washington, Greenwich and Paris, 1872; U.S. del. to Internat. Bur. Weights and Measures 1872; dir. Office Weights and Measures; charter mem. Nat. Acad. Scis., pres., 1875; mem. A.A.A.S.; supt. U.S. Coast Survey, 1881-85. Died Washington, D.C., May 8, 1891.

HILL, ARTHUR EDWARD, chemist; b. Newark, N.J., Mar. 20, 1880; s. Charles Edward and Caroline Greenwood (Hill) H.; B.S., New York U., 1901, M.S., 1903; Ph.D., U. of Freiburg, 1904; m. Grace L. Kent, Aug. 12, 1904; children—Douglas Greenwood, Dorothy Kent; m. 2d, Bess J. Talmadge, 1925. Fellow in chemistry, New York U., 1901-02; teacher, Newark High Sch., 1903-04; instr. chemistry, 1904-05, sec. Sch. Applied Science, 1906-19, asst. prof., 1906-08, asso. prof., 1908-12, prof. chemistry, and head dept., 1912—, New York U., acting dean, 1932, also acting dean College of Arts, 1935-36; prof. chemistry, N.J. Coll. Pharmacy, 1906-19; research chemist, Chem. Warfare Service, 1918-19; asso. editor Jour. of Am. Chem. Soc., 1923-33. Republican. Presbyn. Author: Laboratory Guide for Qualitative Analysis, 1910; chapter on Heterogeneous Equilibrium in Taylor's Treatise on Physical Chemistry, 1924. Died Mar. 16, 1939.

HILL, BANCROFT, cons. engr.; Balt.; May 5, 1887; s. Charles Ebenezer and Kate Watts (Claymon) H.; student Johns Hopkins, 1906-07, B.S., Mass. Inst. Tech., 1911; m. Frances G. McCoy, May 5, 1915. Began as draftsman, 1915; successively civil engr., harbor engrs., pres. Harbor Bd. of Balt., engr. Port Development Commn., 1919-25; valuation engr. United Rys. & Electric Co., Balt., 1925-35; exec. v.p. Baltimore Transit Co., 1935-36, pres., 1936-45. Devoted last 8 yrs. life making appliances to aid crippled children. Author articles on costs, depreciation, valuation and earnings of pub. utilities. Home: 1812 Sulgrave Av., Mt. Washington, Balt. 9. Died Jan. 5, 1957; buried Druid Ridge Cemetery, Balt.

HILL, EBEN CLAYTON, M.D., roentgenologist; b. Baltimore, Md., Oct. 9, 1882; s. Charles Ebenezer and Kate Watts (Clayton) H.; A.B., Johns Hopkins, 1903, M.D., 1907; matriculate research student, U. of Freiburg, Germany, 1904, 05; graduate of Army Medical School, 1909; m. Carolyn Sherwin Bailey, Oct. 14, 1936. Assistant in anatomy, Johns Hopkins U. Medical Sch., 1907-08; practiced, Baltimore, 1907-08, Poughkeepsie, N.Y., 1913-20; pathologist and radiologist, 1911-13, Roentgenologist, 1912-20, Vassar Hosp. and Dispensary. Instr. 1920-21, asso. in Roentgenol. anatomy, 1921—2, now lecturer roentgenology, Johns Hopkins. Roentgenologist U.S. Med. Advisory Bd., U.S.A., for N.Y., 1917-19. First lt. and capt., Med. Corps, U.S.A., 1908-13 (retired). Fellow A.A.A.S.; fellow and life mem. Am. Coll. Physicians, A.M.A. Republican. Episcopalian. Contbr. research X-ray technic for studying collateral circulation, sacroiliac injuries and effects of rays on cellular life. Proved the necessity in 1909, of massive doses of diphtheria antitoxin in laryngeal and other serious cases of dihptheria; proved the importance, 1910, of carriers in the spread of diphtheria, and the relative unimportance of disinfection and fumigation; showed, 1912, that salvarsan, even in frequent dosages, is not specific in action, and is not the complete curative drug as supposed; invented radiopaque injection method, etc. Completed in 1937 anatomical-surgical studies of sacro-iliac joint. Author of Cross Roads of the Mind, 1939. Died June 15, 1940.

HILL, EDWARD CURTIS, clin. and analyt. diagnostician; b. Cleveland, Ill., Oct. 5, 1863; s. William and Mary M. (Garrison) H.; B.S., Northwestern Normal and Scientific Sch., Geneseo, Ill., 1886; M.D., Gross Med. Coll., Denver, 1891; m. Phoebe Elliott, of Denver, 1893; children—Mary Beatrice, Frederic Henry, Kenneth Alfred, Flora Kathleen, John Elliott, Paul Victor. Practicing medicine in Denver since 1891; prof. chemistry Gross Med. Coll. and med. depts. Denver U., and U. of Colo., 1892-1912; state chemist, 1907-11; city chemist of Denver, 1917-23. Pres. Denver Clin. and Pathol. Soc., 1905-06; pres. Denver Med. Club, 1920-21. Author: Text-book of Chemistry for Students of Medicine, Pharmacy and Dentistry, 1903, 11; Pain and Its Indications, 1904; The Reasons Why, 1907. Home: 1101 E. Alameda Av., Denver, Colo.

HILL, EDWARD LLEWELLYN, chemist; b. Carthage, Ill., Jan. 19, 1900; s. William Kuhns and Katharine (Griffith) H.; A.B., Carthage College, 1922, Doctor of Science (honorary), 1955; M.S., University of Ill., 1925 Ph.D., State U. of Ia., 1930; m. Mary Lucille Mullen, Aug. 15, 1935; children—Katharine Lucille, David Llewellyn. Instr., Carthage Coll., 1925-27, asst. prof., 1928-29, asso. prof., 1930-32, prof. and head chemistry dept., 1933-42; prof. chemistry, Augustana Coll., Rock Island, Ill., since 1947; research chemist, Armour Research Foundn., Ill. Inst. Tech., Chicago, 1942-47, supervisor organic chemistry research, 1945-47; exec. and research dir., Augustana Research Foundn. since 1947. Fellow A.A.A.S.; mem. American Society Heating and Ventilating Engrs., Am. Chem. Soc., Am. Oil Chemists Soc., Ill. Acad. Sci., Theta Chi Delta, Beta Beta Beta, Phi Lambda Upsilon, Sigma Xi. Contbr. to jours. organic chemistry. Home: 3909 8th Av. Office: 35th St. and 7th Av., Rock Island, Ill. Died June 6, 1958; buried Moss Ridge Cemetery, Carthage, Ill.

HILL, E(RNEST) ROWLAND, consulting engr.; b. Pompton, N.J., Jan. 29, 1872; s. Benj. Rowland, Jr., and Hetty M. (Van Duyne) H.; prep. edn., Pratt Inst., Brooklyn, N.Y.; M.E. and E.E., Cornell U., 1893; m. Grace G. Crider, June 1, 1904; 1 dau., Jean S. (Mrs. E. C. Johnson). Gen. shop training, Westinghouse Electric & Mfg. Co., 1893-95; special engr. same co., 1895-1901; engr. in chief British Westinghouse Electric & Mfg. Co., London, in charge of all elec., steam, mech. and gen. engring. work of the co., design and constrn. stations, lines, etc., in Gt. Britain, 1901-06; asst. to chief engr. of electric traction in electrification of New York Terminal and tunnels of Pa. R.R. and extension of electrification L.I. R.R., 1906-12; partner Gibbs and Hill, cons. engrs., 1912-24; now pres. Gibbs & Hill, Inc., engaged in gen. consulting engring. practice, designing construction, including electrification work on Pa. R.R., New York-Washington-Harrisburg electrification, Norfolk & Western Railway and Virginian Railway electrification; changes and additions in Cos Cob Power House and other electric power equipment of N.Y., N.H.&H. R.R.; electrification of N.Y. Connecting R.R., I.C. R.R. (Chicago, Ill.), Broad St. Subway, Philadelphia, Pa.; engaged in consulting, designing, construction, general practice, power plants, Army and Navy bases, industrial plants, etc. Dir. Ampere Bank & Trust Co.; mem. bd. Orange Memorial Hosp. Mem. and past pres., Am. Inst. Cons. Engrs. Fellow Am. Inst. Electrical Engrs., mem. Am. Soc. C.E., Am. Soc. M.E., Inst C.E. (London), S.A.R. Presbyterian. Clubs: Cornell, Bankers, Rock Spring Country. Home: 111 S. Munn Av., East Orange, N.J. Office: Pennsylvania Station, 7th Av. and 32d St., New York, N.Y. Died Aug. 25, 1948.

HILL, FREDERICK THAYER, physician; b. Waterville, Me., June 14, 1889; s. James Frederick and Angie (Foster) H.; B.S., Colby Coll., Waterville, Me., 1910, D.Sc., 1936; M.D., Harvard, 1914; D.Sc. (honorary) University of Maine, 1942; m. Ruby Winchester Choate, June 16, 1924; children—Virginia, Barbara, Joan, Marjorie. Resident in otolaryngology, Mass. Eye and Ear Infirmary, Boston, Mass., 1915-16, mem. staff, 1919-20; engaged in pvt. practice as otolaryngologist, Waterville, Me., from 1920; mem. staff Sisters Hosp. (Waterville), 1920-30; mem. staff Thayer Hosp. since 1930; mem. cons. staff Central Maine Gen. Hosp., St. Marie's Hosp. (Lewiston), Augusta (Me.) Gen. Hosp., Gardiner (Me.) Gen. Hosp., Redington Hosp. (Skowhegan), Knox County Hosp. (Rockland), Waldo County Hosp. (Belfast), Miles Memorial Hosp. (Damariscotta), St. Andrews Hosp. (Boothbay Harbor), Central Maine Sanatorium (Tb); v.p. planning and devel. Trayer Hospital; member consulting staff, Bath Memorial Hospital, Franklin Co. Hosp., Farmington, U.S. V.A. Hosp. Togus. Served as lt. Med. Corps, U.S. Army, 1918-19; instr. Army Sch. of Otolaryngology, Gen. Hosp. No. 14. Mem. Council for Health and Welfare, State of Maine; chmn. Me. Adv. Hosp. Commn. Dir. Am. Bd. Otolaryngology (pres., 1953-54); past mem. Federal Hospital Council; past president of Me. Hosp. Assn.; mem. bd. of directors Me. Heart Assn. Former trustee Colby Coll. Recipient Newcomen award American Laryngological Association, 1953, Roaldes award, 1961; received Roselle W. Huddilston award Me. Tb Association. Fellow A.C.S., Am. College of Hospital Administrators (hon.); mem. Am. Laryngol. Assn. (pres. 1948), Internat. Congress Otolaryngology (treas. 1957), Me. Med. Assn. (past pres.), New England Otolaryngol. Soc. (past pres.), Am. Otol. Soc. (pres. 1953), N.E. Hospital Assembly (pres. 1953), Am. Laryngol., Rhinol. and Otol. Soc., Am. Broncho-Esophol. Assn., American Academy of Ophthalmology and Otolaryngology (1st v.p. 1961), Am. Coll. Chest Physicians, Am. Cancer Soc., Zeta Psi, Alpha Kappa Kappa, Mason (33 deg.), Rotarian. Club: Harvard (Boston). Mem. editorial bd. Annals of Otology, Rhinology and Laryngology. Contbr. to Military Surgical Manual, Otolaryngology, 1942; also numerous articles to professional jours. and med. publs. Home: Waterville ME Died April 1969.

HILL, GEORGE ANDREWS, astronomer; b. Elizabeth, N.J., Apr. 11, 1858; s. late Rev. I. N. and Annie M. H.; ed. pvt. sch. and Columbia Coll.; married; children—George Cooper, Edgar Montgomery (dec.). An astronomer U.S. Naval Obs., 1893—. Spl. work has been in line of fundamental determination of star positions, determination of longitude by wireless, astronomical constants, and upon subject of variation of latitude. Died Aug. 29, 1927.

HILL, HAROLD O(TTO), engr.; b. Stouffville, Ont., Can., Nov. 17, 1887; s. Rev. Lewis Warner and Margaret Matilda (Long) H.; B. Applied Sci., U. Toronto, 1908; m. Dorothy Isabele Beatty, Oct. 18, 1919; children—Lewis Warner, Henrietta Jane (Mrs. R. Dean Coddington). Came to U.S., 1908, naturalized, 1919. Engr., Riter-Conley Co., Pitts., 1908-27, chief engr., 1928-29; asst. chief engr. McClintic-Marshall Co., 1930-38; asst. chief engr. fabricated steel constrn. Bethlehem Steel Co., 1934-56; ret. Mem. Am. Welding Soc. (pres. 1947-48), Am. Soc. C.E., Am. Soc. M.E., Am. Inst. E.E., Am. Waterworks Assn., Am. Petroleum Inst., Am. Soc. for Testing Materials, Republican. Methodist. Mason. Rotarian (pres. 1942-43). Holder patents on elec. transmission lines and steel pipes. Home: Wesley Manor, Jacksonville, Fla. 32223. Office: Bethlehem Steel Co., Bethlehem, Pa. Died. Feb. 1963.

HILL, HARRY HARRISON, petroleum engr.; b. Rushville, Neb., June 21, 1888; s. James Ross and Mary Elizabeth (Marshall) H.; A.B. in Chemistry, U. Wyo., 1911; A.M., U. Wash., 1913; m. Natalie West Berry, May 4, 1916. Plant chemist Canadian Mineral Rubber Co., Vancouver, B.C., 1912; jr. and asst. chemist U.S. Bur. Mines, Pitts., 1913-18; with Bur. of Mines, successively as chem. engr., Washington, 1918-19, refinery engr., Bartlesville, Okla., 1920; supt. petroleum expt. sta., Bartlesville, 1921-22; supr. oil gas operations, Denver, 1922-23; asst. chief petroleum engr.,

Washington, 1923-24; chief petroleum engr., 1925-28; dir. prodn., research and engring. Standard Oil Devel. Co., 1928-34; mem. coordination com. Standard Oil Co. (N.J.), July 1934-Mar. 1943 and Jan. 1945-July 1948; v.p. Eurogas Co., 1935. Bur. of mines rep. on Com. for Standardization of Petroleum Specifications during World War; mem. tech. adv. com. Fed. Oil Conservation Bd., 1925-28, chmn. sub-com. on Micromovements of fluids through rocks NRC, 1925-28. Mem. Am. Inst. Mining and Metall. Engrs. (chmn. engring. research, petroleum div., 1928-30), Am. Petroleum Inst. (chmn. central com. on drilling and prodn. practice, 1930-31), Delta Theta Kappa, Phi Lambda Upsilon. Mason. Author several sci. articles on oil and gas, and co-author with E. W. Dean various publs. Bur. of Mines. Home: 16 Canterbury Rd., Bellair, Charlottesville, Va. Died July 14, 1965; buried Woodbine Cemetery, Harrisonburg, Va.

HILL, HENRY BARKER, chemist; b. Waltham, Mass., April 27, 1849; s. Thomas H. (pres. Harvard, 1862-68) and Anne Foster (Bellows) H.; grad. Harvard, 1869; studied chemistry, Univ. of Berlin, 1869-70; m. Ellen Grace Shepard, Sept. 2, 1871. Asst. in laboratory, 1870-74, asst. prof., 1874-84, and from 1884 prof. chemistry, Harvard; 1894, dir. chem. laboratory. Mem. Nat. Acad. Sciences, 1883—. Author: Notes on Qualitative Analysis; etc. Home: Cambridge, Mass. Died 1903.

HILL, JOHN EDWARD, civil engr.; b. N.Y. City, Nov. 9, 1864; s. Edward and Harriet (Smith) H.; B.S., Rutgers Coll., 1884, M.S., 1887, C.E., 1892 (D.Sc., 1905); M.C.E., Cornell, 1895; m. Jessie Louise Gould, Dec. 19, 1894; children—Berenice Gould, Audrey Chapman, Elsbeth, Jessica (Mrs. Eugene A. Bond). Instr. civ. engring., Cornell, 1890-94; instr., asso. prof. and prof. civ. engring., Brown, 1894—. Engaged in various branches civ. engring., 1884—. Fellow A.A.A.S. Home: Providence, R.I. Died Nov. 2, 1934.

HILL, JOHN ETHAN, engr., educator; b. Mystic, Conn., Oct. 15, 1865; s. Mason Crary and Margaret (Wheeler) H.; grad. Yale, 1885 (Ph.D., Clark Univ., 1895). Resident engr., Chicago, Milwaukee & St. Paul R.R. Co., 1885-90; prof. mathematics, Highland Park Coll., Ia., 1890-92, Columbia, 1895-99, W.Va. Univ., 1898-1904; asst. city engr., New York, since 1904. Mem. Am. Math. Soc., A.A.A.S., The Scientific Alliance, Am. Soc. Civ. Engrs. Author: Quintic Surfaces, 1896; Three Septic Surfaces, 1897; Bibliography of Surfaces and Twisted Curves, Bull. Am. Math. Soc., 1898; also various monographs upon Surfaces of Higher Order; contbr. to Math. Rev. and Am. Jour. Mathematics. Clubs: Yale, University (New York), Brooklyn Engineers. Address: 25 Herkimer St., Brooklyn.

HILL, JOSEPH ST. CLAIR, engineer; b. Smyrna, Del., Jan. 22, 1860; s. Charles and Marie Theresa (Bosselle) H.; ed. pub. schs.; m. Leonore Caldwell Benson, of Baltimore, Nov. 29, 1891. In employ various cos. until 1891; gen. mgr. Lafayette St. Ry. Co., 1891-94; supt. overhead constrn., West Side, Chicago, for J. R. Chapman (now of London Tube System), 1894-95; constrg. engr. and supt., Los Angeles Traction Co., 1895-96; constrg. engr. Pasadena St. Ry., 1897; entered govt. service, 1898; instr. engring., Wind-River Sch., 1898-1900; transferred to Washington, D.C., in 1900, as consulting and constructing efficiency engr. in charge Department of Interior bldgs., Patent Office, Land Office, Pension Bldg., Freedman's Hosp., Howard U. heat, light & power plant, etc. Mem. Am. Inst. Elec. Engrs., Washington Soc. Engrs., California Soc. Clubs: Home, Maryland Automobile. Inventor and patentee various mech. devices for st. rys., automobiles, etc. Home: "Cedar Lodge," The Hills, Montgomery Co., Md.

HILL, LOUIS CLARENCE, engineer; b. Ann Arbor, Mich., Feb. 22, 1865; s. Alva Thomas and Frances (Bliss) H.; B.S. in Civ. Engring., U. of Mich., 1886; reëntered 1889, B.S. in elec. engring., 1890, hon. Master of Engring., 1911; m. Gertrude B. Rose, Aug. 26, 1890; children—Raymond Alva, Margaret. Asst. engr. Duluth, Red Wing & Southern R.R., 1887-88; asst. engr. U.S.A. (summer), 1887; div. engr. G.N. R.R., 1888-89, prof. hydraulic and elec. engring., Colo. Sch. of Mines, 1890-1903; engr. U.S. Geol. Survey, 1903-04, in charge Roosevelt Dam; supervising engr. U.S. Reclamation Service, in charge of all work in Ariz., Southern Calif., N.M., Texas and Utah, 1905-14. U.S. commr., div. of water of Rio Grande between U.S. and Mex., and for division of water of Colorado River; cons. engr. Boulder Canyon Dam, All American Canal, U.S. Reclamation Service, Los Angeles Co. Flood Control, Bouquet Canyon Dam, San Gabriel Dams Nos. 1 and 2, Bonneville Dam, El Capitan Dam, Long Valley Dam, Fort Peck Dam, Tygart Dam, Conchas Dam, Sardis Dam, and 10 dams of Muskingum Conservancy Dist. for War Dept.; cons. engr. Internat. Boundary Commission; mem. Quinton, Code, Hill, Leeds & Barnard, Los Angeles. Was cons. engr. for Camp Kearney. Mem. Jury Awards, Chicago Expn., 1893. Home: Hollywood, Calif. Died Nov. 5, 1938.

HILL, NATHANIEL PETER, metallurgist, senator; b. Montgomery, N.Y., Feb. 18, 1832; s. Nathaniel P. and Matilda (Crawford) H.; grad. Brown U., 1856; m. Alice Hale, July 1860; 2 daus., 1 son. prof. chemistry Brown U., 1860-64; mem. commn. of Mass. and R.I. mfrs. to investigate mineral deposits in Colo., 1864; studied metallurgy in Europe, 1865-66, 66-67; organized Boston & Colo. Smelting Co. (introduced smelting process increasing gold ore yield), 1867; mayor Blackhawk (Colo.), 1871; mem. Colo. Territorial Council, 1872-73; developed refining process for separating precious metals from copper, 1873; mem. U.S. Senate from Colo., 1879-85; propr. Denver (Colo.) Republican, 1886; mem. Internat. Monetary. Commn. (studying question of internat. metal currency), 1891; del. Bimetallic Conf., 1893. Died Denver, May 22, 1900; buried Fairmount Cemetery, Denver.

HILL, REUBEN L(ORENZO), coll. prof., chemist; b. Ogden, Utah, Mar. 24, 1888; s. George Richard and Elizabeth Nancy (Burch) H.; student Brigham Young U., 1908-11; B.S., Utah State Agrl. Coll., 1912; Ph.D., Cornell U., 1915; m. Mary Theresa Snow, Oct. 11, 1911; children—Reuben Lorenzo, Cornella (Mrs. MacNovak), Richard Snow, Theresa Marie (Mrs. Donald Ashdown), Wesley Sherwin, Alwyn Spencer, Edward Eyring, Carl David. Instr. in biochem. Cornell U., 1914-16; biochemist, Bureau of Chemistry, U.S. Dept. Agr., Washington, 1916; biochemist Md. Agr. Expt. Sta., 1916-18; head dept. chemistry Utah State Coll. of Agr. since 1919, human nutritionist, expt. sta., 1919-41. Commd. 1st lt., San. Corps, U.S.A., 1918; in Med. Officers Training, Camp Greenleaf, 1918, 2 mos.; nutrition officer, Camp Upton, L.I., 1918-19, 6 mos.; capt. Gen. Res. Corp, U.S. Army, 1927-41; recalled to active duty as maj., U.S. Army, 1941; completed Army Nutrition course, Army Med. Center, Washington, 1941, 2 mos.; nutritionist and chief Nutrition Service, 5th Service Command, U.S. Army, 1941-44, 34 mos.; apptd. lt. col., San. Res. Corps, 1946. Mem. Am. Chem. Soc., Am. Assn. Univ. Profs., A.A.A.S., Utah Acad. Arts, Sci. and Letters, Res. Officers Assn., Sigma Xi. Republican. Mem. Ch. of Jesus Christ of Latter-Day Saints. Author of research papers and bulls. on milk secretion, soft curd milk. Holder patent on original equipment used in Hill Curd Test. Home: 645 N. 8th East St., Logan, Utah. Died Jan. 22, 1953; buried Logan (Utah) City Cemetery.

HILL, ROBERT THOMAS, geologist; b. Nashville, Tenn., Aug. 11, 1858; B.S., Cornell, 1886; LL.D., Baylor, 1920; m. Justina Robinson, Dec. 28, 1887. Asst. paleontologist Smithsonian Instn., 1885; geologist U.S. Geol. Survey, 1885-1904; asso. geologist Ark. Geol. Survey, 1888-90; prof. geology, U. of Tex., 1890-91; geologist in charge U.S. investigation underground water and arid regions, 1891-92; cooperator with Prof. A. Agassiz in W. Indian and Central Am. explorations, 1895-1905; contract work, Geol. Survey of Southern Calif., U.S. Geol. Survey, 1911-17; lecturer various colleges and univs.; explored for first time great canons of the Rio Grande; spl. commr., Martinique eruptions for Nat. Geog. Soc.; etc.; cons. practice, 1918—. Fellow Am. Geol. Soc., A.A.A.S. Expert for State of Tex. in Okla.-Tex. boundary suit, U.S. Supreme Court, 1921. Home: Glendale, Calif. Died July 28, 1941.

HILLE, HERMANN, chemist; b. Moelln, Germany, June 7, 1871; s. Hermann and Charlotte (Beckman) H.; Ph.G., Univs. of Kiel and Würzburg, 1896, with Prof. Roentgen during his discovery of X-Rays; Ph.D., U. Heidelberg, 1900; m. Christina Aaronson, June 16, 1906; 1 dau., Mona Wandanita. Came to U.S., 1900; lifelong student sci., philosophy and religion; adv. primitive Christianity. Mem. A.A.A.S. (life), Am. Chem. Soc., Am. Pharm. Assn., German Med. Soc., Med. Round Table Chgo.; hon. mem. S.W. Mo. Med. Soc. Author: Ueber das primäre und sekundäre symmetrische Hydrazid der propionsäure und Valeriansäure (Heidelberg), 1900; Facts of Modern Science and Their Value in the Prevention and Cure of Disease, 1912; The New Chemistry and the New Materia Medica, 1913; Colloids and Their Relation to Medicine, 1914; Colloidal Chemistry, 1919-20; A History of Colloids in Medicine, 1925, enlarged, 1930; Colloidal Sulphides in Medicine, 1927; Colloids—Just What Are They?, 1930. Discoverer of Argyrol, Lunosol, Mervenol, Armervenol, Aurol, Aurol-Sulfide, Colloidal Mercury Sulphide-Hille, Bismo-Rhodanol and other well known chemico-med. products; pres. Hille Labs. Home: Wilmot Rd., Deerfield, Ill. 60015. Office: 6007 N. Lincoln Av., Chgo. 60645. Died Apr. 28, 1962.

HILLEBRAND, WILLIAM FRANCIS, chemist; b. Honolulu, H.I., Dec. 12, 1853; s. Dr. William and Anna (Post) H.; ed. there and at Oakland, Calif.; attended Cornell, 1870-72; studied 6 yrs. in Germany; Ph.D., U. of Heidelberg, 1875; studied at U. of Strassburg and Mining Acad., Freiberg, Saxony; m. Martha May Westcott, Sept. 6, 1881. Assayer, Leadville, Colo., 1879-80; chemist U.S. Geol. Survey, 1880-1908; chief chemist Bur. of Standards, Washington, June 1908—. Prof. gen. chemistry and physics, Nat. Coll. of Pharmacy, 1892-1910. Author: Some Principles and Methods of Rock Analysis (2 edits.), 1900, 1902; Methods of Silicate and Carbonate Analysis, 1907, 10, 19. Home: Washington, D.C. Died Feb. 7, 1925.

HILLIARD, CURTIS MORRISON, prof. biology and pub. health; b. Dorchester, Mass., Aug. 5, 1887; s. Aubrey and Anna G. (Morrison) H.; prep. edn., Chauncey Hall Sch., Boston; A.B., Dartmouth, 1909; grad. study, Mass. Inst. Tech., 1909-10; m. Helen A. Nixon, June 30, 1914; children—Albert N., Elizabeth. Instr. in biology, Coll. City N.Y., 1910-12; asst. prof. sanitary science, Purdue, 1912-14; asso. prof. and head of dept. biology and health, Simmons Coll., Boston, 1914-18, prof. 1918-52; emeritus prof. biol. and pub. health, 1952, Supervisor bds. of health of Wellesley, Needham and Weston, Mass. Director Moseley Health Fund, Newburyport, Mass., since 1937; dir. Boston and Wellesley chapters Am. Red Cross, chmn. Health Edn. Com.; dir. health div. Mass. Com. Pub. Safety, 1941-44; consultant field training Mass. Dept. Pub. Health from 1950; dir. Nat. Tuberculosis Assn. from 1948. Served as first lieutenant Sanitary Corps, United States Army, 1918-19. Member administrative committee Massachusetts Civic League, executive committee Massachusetts Central Health Council (ex-pres.); vice pres., Mass. Tuberculosis League, 1945. Fellow Am. Pub. Health Assn., A.A.A.S.; mem. Soc. Am. Bacteriologist, Mass. Pub. Health Assn. (ex. pres.), Lemuel Shattuck Medal for Outstanding Service Pub. Health, N.E., Sigma Nu, Sigma Psi, Delta Omega. Mem. Governor's Commn. to Study Health Practice, Mass., 1935. Republican. Unitarian. Author: Bacteriology and its Application, 1928; Prevention of Disease in the Community, 1931. Home: Wellesley Hills MA Died May 14, 1969.

HILLMAN, JOHN WILLIAM, orthopaedic surgeon; b. Dante, Va., Jan. 9, 1921; s. Rolfe L. and Edith H.; M.D., Johns Hopkins U., 1945; m. Virginia Swindler, 1949; children—Ellen (Mrs. Horace Moore), Mary (Mrs. Michael Trueblood), Jayne, Nancy. Intern, Johns Hopkins Hosp., Balt., 1945-46, asst. resident and resident orthopaedic surgeon, 1948-51; visiting orthopaedic surgeon Vanderbilt Hosp., Nashville. Instr. orthopaedic surgery Johns Hopkins U., 1951-52, asst. prof Vanderbilt U., Nashville, 1952-54, asso. prof., 1954-58, prof., 1958-70, chmn. dept., 1962-70. Cons. orthopaedic surgeon Tenn. Crippled Children's Service, Nashville, 1952-70, Ft. Campbell Hosp., 1964, Thayer VA Hosp., Nashville, Sewart AFB, Tenn., 1958-64, Alaska Crippled Children's Com., 1963-66, Am. Bd. Prosthetics and Orthotics, 1967-70; chmn. med. adv. com. Medicenter, Nashville; med. adv. Bd. Edn. Film Prodn.; chmn. profl. services program com. United Cerebral Palsy Assns.; mem. Gov.'s Com. On Employment of the Handicapped; pres. med. staff Jr. League Home for Crippled Children, 1962-63; sci. program com. 3rd, 4th Internat. Confs. on Congenital Malformations. Bd. dirs. Bill Wilkerson Hearing and Speech Center, 1962-70, med. staff, 1958-70; exec. com. Tenn. Council for Handicapped Children, 1962-65, Mid-Cumberland Region Health Planning Council, 1968-70. Diplomate Am. Bd. Orthopaedic Surgeons (dir.). Fellow A.M.A. (orthopaedic residency review com., 1963-70), So. Med. Assn., Am. Coll. Surgeons, Am. Acad. Orthopaedic Surgeons (chmn. rehab. com. 1966-68); mem. Am. Orthopaedic Assn., Tenn., Nashville-Davidson County med. assns., Tenn. Orthopaedic Soc., Am. Acad. Cerebral Palsy (pres. 1969), Clin. Orthopaedic Soc., Internat. Soc. Orthopaedic Surgery and Traumatology, Orthopaedic Research Soc., Am. Assn. Rehabilitation Facilities, Soc. Med. Cons. Armed Forces, Internat. Soc. Rehab. of Disabled, A.A.A.S., Nashville Surgical Soc. (pres. 1968), Nat. Acad. Scis., Am. Physical Therapy Assn. (adv. bd.), World Commn. Cerebral Palsy, Volunteer State Rehab. Assn., Johns Hopkins Tenn. Alumni Assn., Sigma Xi; asso. mem. Am. Acad. Neurology. Asso. editor Jour. Bone and Joint Surgery, 1962-64. Home: Nashville TN Died Mar. 7, 1970; buried Emory VA

HILLS, JOSEPH LAWRENCE, univ. dean; b. Boston, Mass., Mar. 2, 1861; s. Thomas and Amelia Ellen (Drew) H.; B.S., Mass. Agrl. Coll. (now Univ. of Mass.), 1881; B.S., Boston U., 1881; post-grad., Mass. Agrl. Coll., 1881-84; D.Sc. (hon.), Rutgers, 1903, Mass. State Coll., 1931; R.I. State Coll. of A. and M. Arts, 1942, Vt., 1943; m. Kate Conover, Sept. 1888 (dec.). Asst. chemist, Mass. Agrl. Expt. Sta., Amherst, 1882-83, N.J. Agrl. Expt. Sta., New Brunswick, 1884-85; chemist Phosphate Mining Co., Ltd., Beaufort, S.C., 1885-88; chemist, 1888-98, dir., Vt. Agrl. Expt. Sta., 1893-42, emeritus since 1942, prof. agronomy, U. of Vt., 1893-1933, dean, Coll. of Agr. same, 1898-42, emeritus since 1942. Mem. Assn. Land-Grant Colleges and Universities (sec.-treas. 1904-27; pres. 1928); fellow A.A.A.S.; mem. Soc. Colonial Wars, Kappa Sigma, Alpha Zeta, Phi Kappa Phi, Sigma Xi. Episcopalian. Republican. Home: Burlington VT

HILLS, RICHARD CHARLES, geologist; b. Ewhurst, Surrey, Eng., Feb. 5, 1848; s. Richard C. and Emily (Cooper) H.; ed. at Ewhurst and Shoreditch, London; m. Louise A. Bruce, Mar. 7, 1901. Came to U.S., July 1865; went to Calif., 1867, to Nev., 1869, and to Ida., 1870, to Colo., 1877; engaged for several yrs. in expert examinations of mines in the Western States and Territories and Mexico; geol. expert for the Colo. Fuel & Iron Co., 1883-1904; at intervals engaged on field work for U.S. Geol. Survey; now geol. expert for Victor-Am. Fuel Co. Hon. curator geology and mineralogy, Colo. Mus. Natural History. Fellow Geol. Soc. London, Geol. Soc. America. Home: Denver, Colo. Died Aug. 14, 1923.

HILLS, VICTOR GARDINER, mining engr.; b. Nunda, N.Y., Jan. 21, 1855; s. Milton Tyler and Mary Jane (Gardiner) H.; B.A., Highland (Kan.) Coll., 1877, M.A., 1880; spl. study in mining and assaying, Colo. Coll., 1879; m. M. Adaline Flick, Jan. 1, 1883. Began at Leadville, Colo., 1879; city engr., Pueblo, Colo., 1885, 86; co. surveyor, Pueblo Co., 1885-90; city engr., Cripple Creek, Colo., 1893; consulting engr., Portland Gold Mining Co., etc., at Cripple Creek; mgr. and consulting engr., Colo. Tungsten Corp., 1905-07; consulting engr. and mgr., Sheelite Mines, Ltd., N.S., 1910-12. Home: Denver, Colo. Died July 13, 1930.

HILLYER, HOMER WINTHROP, chemist; b. Waupun, Wis., Jan. 26, 1859; s. Edwin and Angeline C. (Coe) H.; B.S., U. of Wis., 1882; Ph.D., Johns Hopkins, 1885; m. Hariet A. Robbins, July 12, 1887. Asst. instr. and asst. prof. organic chemistry, U. of Wis., 1885-1905; with research dept. Gen. Chem. Co., 1907-17, Nat. Aniline & Chem. Co., 1917-25. Conglist. Author: Laboratory Manual of General Chemistry. Inventor fungicide known as atomic sulfur. Home: Farmington, Conn. Died Jan. 3, 1949.

HILPRECHT, HERMAN VOLRATH, educator; b. Hohenerxleben, Germany, July 28, 1859; s. Robert and Emilie (Wielepp) H.; grad. Herzogl. Gymnasium, Bernburg, Germany, 1880; studied, 1880-85, theology, philology and law, U. of Leipzig, Ph.D., 1883 (D.D., U. of Pa., 1894; LL.D., Princeton, 1896); "repetent" of O.T. theology, U. of Erlangen, Bavaria, 1885-86; m. Miss S. C. Haufe, 1886 (died 1902); m. 2d, Mrs. Sallie Crozer Robinson, d. Samuel Aldrich Crozer, Apr. 24, 1903. Curator Semitic sect. of mus., U. of Pa., 1887-1911, containing over fifty thousand original Babylonian antiquities, for the greater part presented by him; Clark research prof. Assyrian and prof. comparative Semitic philology, U. of Pa., 1886-1911. Assyriologist and from 1895 also scientific dir., U. of Pa. expdn. to Nippur, Babylonia (4 campaigns), and editor-in-chief of its publs., The Babylonian Expdn. of U. of Pa., 4 series; reorganized Babylonian sect., Imperial Ottoman Mus., Constantinople, 1893-1909; made frequent scientific explorations in Asia Minor and Syria, and trips to India, Ceylon, China, Japan and Korea, 1911-12. Leading authority in cuneiform research. Knight of first class, 1893, commander, 1898, Crown of Comthur of II class, 1909; Star of the Comthur I class, 1915; Albrecht der Baer (German decoration); comdr. Turkish Osmanië Order, 1895; comthur with star, same, 1897; comdr. Danish Order of Danebrog, 1898; German Order Frederika, 1901; Lucy Wharton Drexel Medal, 1902; Golden Liakat Medal, 1905. Author: Business Documents of Murashû Sons of Nippur, dated in the Reign of Artaxerxes I (with A. T. Clay); Mathematical Metrological and Chronological Texts from the Temple Library of Nippur, Part 1, 1906; Assyriaca, Eine Nachlese auf dem Gebiete der Assyriologie. Died Mar. 20, 1925.

HILTON, DAVID CLARK, surgeon; b. Saline County, Neb., Apr. 22, 1877; s. John Bulin Whitehead and Mary Elizabeth (Redgate) H.; A.B., U. of Neb., 1900, A.M., 1901; M.D., Rush Med. Coll., Chicago, 1903; m. Sarah Luella O'Toole, Aug. 23, 1900; children—Blossom Virginia (Mrs. Harold Stanley Gish), Ruth Acacia (Mrs. Woodward Burgert), Hiram David (M.D.). Practice Lincoln, Neb., since 1903; head of science depts., Cotner U., 1904-05; demonstrator in anatomy, U. of Neb., 1903-05; attending surgeon St. Elizabeth's Hosp. since 1905; attending surgeon Bryan Memorial Hosp. since 1926; consultant-surgeon U.S. Vets. Bur. Hosp. since 1930. Served as captain Med. Corps, U.S. Army, World War; col. comdg. 110th Med. Regt., Neb. N.G. 1925-40; div. surgeon, 35th Div., N.G., 1927-40; brig. gen. of the line, Neb. N.G., since Sept. 1940 (unassigned). U.S. del. to 5th Internat. Congress of Mil. Medicine and Pharmacy, Warsaw, Poland, 1927, VIth, London, Eng., 1929. Awarded cross of the Army Med. Sch. (Poland), 1927. Fellow A.A.A.S., Am. Coll. Surgeons; mem. A.M.A., S.A.R., Soc. Colonial Wars, Lancaster County Medical Soc., Inter-Professional Men's Inst., Neb. Ornithol. Union, The Audubon Soc., Neb. Geneal. Soc., Lincoln Chamber of Commerce, Acacia, Sigma Xi. Republican. Anglican. Mason (33 deg., K.T., R.C. of Constantine). Author of various papers on med., mil. and ornithol. subjects. Home: 2500 Woodscrest Blvd. Office: Continental Bldg., Lincoln Neb. Died Dec. 12, 1945.

HIMES, CHARLES FRANCIS, physicist; b. Lancaster County, Pa., June 2, 1838; s. Wilviam D. H.; A.B., Dickinson Coll., 1955, A.M., 1858, LL.D., 1896; Ph.D., U. Giessen, 1865; m. Mary E. Murray. Prof. mathematics Troy (N.Y.) U., 1860-63; prof. natural sci. Dickinson Coll., 1865-85, physics, 1885-96, acting pres., 1888-89. Author numerous lectures and addresses on sci. and ednl. subjects; editor chem. textbooks. Has made specialty of photographic investigation. Address: Carlisle, Pa. Died Dec. 6, 1918.

HIMMELWRIGHT, ABRAHAM LINCOLN ARTMAN, civil engr.; b. Milford Sq., Pa., Feb. 7, 1865; s. Charles Reller and Susan (Artman) H.; C.E., Rensselaer Poly. Inst., Troy, N.Y., 1888; m. Harriet Sage Hamlin, of Albany, N.Y., Jan. 21, 1895 (died, 1897); 2d Adeline Dagmar Neilson, Oakland, Cal., May 3, 1916. In ry. engring. work, 1888-90; in mining engring., bituminous coal fields of Pa., 1891, and later extensively identified with limestone, granite and phosphate properties of the East and Fla.; has made spl. study of fireproof constrn. and is a recognized authority on the subject; gen. mgr. Roebling Constrn. Co., 1895-1909; consulting engr., 1909—. Republican. Lutheran. Pres. U.S. Revolver Assn., 1904-10; life mem. N.Y. State Rifle Assn.; mem. Am. Soc. C.E., Am. Geog. Soc. (life), Nat. Geog. Soc., Chi Phi. Club: Engineers'. Author: In the Heart of the Bitter Root Mountains, 1895; Tests of Fire Proof Construction, 1899; The San Francisco Earthquake and Fire, 1906; A Model Fire-Proof Farm House, 1913; Pistol and Revolver Shooting, 1914. Home: Stockholm, N.J. Office: Masonic Hall Annex, 23d St. and 6th Ave., New York.

HINDERLIDER, MICHAEL CREED, civil engr.; b. Medora, Ind., May 19, 1876; s. Daniel Peck and Ann Eliza (Wilson) H.; B.S. in C.E., Purdue Univ., 1897; m. Caroline Kirk, Oct. 31, 1900, children—Ruth (Mrs. James Thomas Mac Cluskey), Clyde Kirk, Michael Creed (dec.), Daniel Peck (dec.). Civil engineer on public land surveys in Colo., 1897; draftsman Bd. Pub. Works, Denver, 1899-1900; hydrographer state engr.'s office, Denver, 1901-02; dist. engr. U.S. Geol. Survey, in charge of hydrographic work in Colo., and later in seven states, 1902-07; engr. for U.S. Reclamation Service in charge of surveys, designs and estimates of cost for a 60,000 acre project in Southern Colo. and Northern N.M., 1903-04; engr. in charge of surveys, location and constrn. of a 28,000 horsepower hydro-electric installation on Colo. River, near Glenwood Springs, 1906-07; designed and engr. on constrn. of hydro-electric power plants, dams, irrigation projects in Colo., Calif., Wyo., Ariz., N.M., etc., 1907-23; cons. engr. for State of Calif. on San Gabriel and Pine Canyon dams; state engr. of Colo. since 1923, with supervision over all water supplies and construction of all dams and reservoirs; chmn. State Irrigation Dist. Commn.; sec. and treas. State Bd. of Examiners for Engrs. and Land Surveyors, official in charge of negotiation and administration of all interstate river compacts; interstate river commr. since 1932. Mem. State Planning Commn., State Water Conservation Bd. Consulting engr. for U.S. Corps of Engrs. Mem. Am. Soc. C.E., Colo. Soc. Engrs. Democrat. Presbyn. Mason (32 deg.). Author articles on engring. subjects. Home: 4037 E. 17th Av. Office: State Capitol Bldg., Denver CO*

HINDLE, NORMAN FREDERICK, engr., educator; b. Ft. Wayne, Ind., Apr. 9, 1902; s. Edmund William and Caroline Dorothea (Kley) H.; B.S. in Chem. Engring., Purdue U., 1925, Met.E., 1949; B.S., U. Ida., 1949; m. Jeannette Beatrice Merillat, Sept. 6, 1925; 1 dau., Barbara Jane (Mrs. Douglas Lee Ellis). Various positions Gen. Electric Co., Ft. Wayne, 1920-21; spl. apprentice Am. Steel Foundries, Chgo., 1925-26, asst. chief chemist and metallurgist East Chicago plant, 1926-29, process insp. Hammond (Ind.) plant, 1932-33; asso. editor The Foundry Mag., Cleve., 1929-32; with Am. Foundryman's Soc., Chgo., 1933-47, successively editorial asst., asst. to tech. sec., asst. tech. sec., tech. sec., asst. sec., tech. dir.; associate prof. mech. engring. dept. U. Ida., 1947-49, prof., head dept., 1949—. Chmn. engring council Ida. Profl. Guidance Com. 1952-55. Profl. engr., Ill. Mem. Am. Soc. M.E. (chmn. Inland Empire sect. 1951-52), Am. Soc. Engring. Edn., Am. Soc. Metals, Am. Foundrymen's Soc., Sigma Xi, Phi Lambda Upsilon, Kappa Phi Sigma. Mason, Kiwanian. Editor: Cast Metals Handbook, Alloy Cast Irons, Standards and Tentative Standards of Foundry Sands and Clays, Handbook of Cupola Operation, Am. Foundryman mag., 1934-47, Transactions of Am. Foundrymen's Assn., 1934-47. Contbr. profl. publs. Home: 122 East A St., Moscow, Ida. Died 1960.

HINDS, HENRY, petroleum geologist; b. Helena, Mont., Oct. 12, 1883; s. Henry and Augusta A. (Robertson) H.; A.B., U. N.D., 1906; Rhodes scholar Oxford U., Eng., 1904-07, B.A., 1906; fellow U. Chgo., 1907-09; m. Beulah Schield, 1918. Asst. geologist N.D. Geol. Survey, 1903; gen. mgr. Venezuelan Pantepec Co., 1923-24, chief geologist, 1924-26, chief geologist, v.p., dir. Pantepec Oil Co. of Venezuela and Pantepec Consol. of Venezuela, 1926-33; now cons. geologist. Coordinator petroleum geology Fuel Adminstrn. and U.S. Capital Issues Com., World War, 1918. Fellow Am. Assn. Rhodes Scholars, Am. Assn. Petroleum Geologists; mem. Gamma Alpha, Sigma Xi. Author: Numerous books on coal deposits, Geology and Coal Resources of Buchanan County, Va., 1918; also numerous articles and reports. Home: Greenwich Towers, Greenwich, Conn. Died Aug. 5, 1964.

HINDS, WARREN ELMER, economic entomologist; b. Townsend, Mass., Sept. 20, 1876; s. Warren David and Mary Persis (Colby) H.; B.S., Mass. Agrl. Coll. (Boston U. Agrl. Dept.), 1899, Ph.D., 1902; m. Edith Goddard Gary, Mar. 4, 1903. Asst. in entomology, Mass. Expt. Sta., 1899; expert asst. U.S. Bur. Entomology, 1901, spl. field agent, 1902-07; prof. entomology, Ala. Poly. Inst., and entomologist, Ala. Expt. Sta., 1907-24; extension entomologist, Ala. Poly. Inst. Extension Service, 1914-24; entomologist La. Expt. Sta. and Extension Service, 1924-29; entomologist, La. Expt. Sta., 1929—; summer lecturer, U. of Md., 1901; in charge lab. work on Mexican boll weevil, 1902-07; studied cotton pest problems of Peru, S.A., 1926. Mem. City Council, Auburn, Ala., 1921-23; v.p. exec. com., La. State Schs. for Blind and Deaf, 1932—. Del. from Am. Assn. Econ. Entomologists to Centennial of French Entomol. Soc., and to 5th Internat. Congress of Entomology, Paris, 1932. Mason. Kiwanian (pres. Baton Rouge, La., Club, 1932). Author: The Boll Weevil, 1920. Died Jan. 11, 1936.

HINES, HARRY MATLOCK, physiologist; b. Spencer, Ia., Feb. 16, 1893; s. Lafayette and Clara May (Logan) H.; A.B., State U. Ia., 1916, M.S., 1917, Ph.D., 1922; m. Leona Grace Fisher, Mar. 29, 1920; children—Howard Harry, Eileen Barbara. Instr. in physiology State U. Ia., 1919-22, asst. prof., 1922-26, asso. prof., 1926-38, prof., 1938-61, emeritus, 1961-63, head dept. physiology since 1944; research asso. Cornell Med. Coll., 1939-40. Served as 2d lt. San. Corps, U.S. Army, 1918. Mem. Am. Physiol. Soc., Soc. Exptl. Biology and Medicine, Harvey Soc., Ia. Acad. Sci.; fellow AAAS, Am. Coll. Cardiology, N.Y. Acad. Sci.; mem. Am. Coll. Phys. Medicine, Am. Assn. U. Profs., Am. Inst. Gerontology, A.M.A. (affiliate), Assn. for Higher Edn., Sigma Xi, Gamma Alpha, Alpha Omega Alpha. Methodist. Club: Triangle (Iowa City). Home: 1480 Grand Av., Iowa City. Died Apr. 1, 1963.

HINES, LAURENCE EDWARD, physician; b. Livermore, Ia., June 8, 1896; s. Edward J. and Clara Helen (Knowles) H.; student Creighton Coll., Omaha, Neb., 2 yrs.; M.D., Northwestern Univ., 1919, B.S., 1925; m. Dorys Elizabeth Zinn, June 29, 1921; children—Laurence Edward, John Richard, David Winslow, James Jordan, Anne, George. Resident physician Michael Reese Hosp., Chicago, 1919, Cook County Hosp., 1920-21, research, John McCormick Inst. Infectious Diseases, 1921-24; dir. pathol. lab., St. Joseph Hosp., since 1922, pres. of staff, 1934; attending staff Passavant Hosp.; formerly attending physician Cook County Hosp.; prof. medicine Northwestern U. Licentiate Am. Bd. Internal Medicine; fellow Am. Coll. of Physicians; mem. Chicago Soc. of Internal Medicine, A.M.A., Chicago Med. Soc., Chicago Pathol. Soc., Inst. Medicine, Chicago, Sigma Xi, Nu Sigma Nu. Catholic. Clubs: University, Edgewater Golf. Contbr. to Archives Internal Medicine, Jour. Am. Med. Assn., Archives of Pathology. Home: 5322 Lakewood Av. Office: 104 S. Michigan Av., Chgo. Died May 13, 1955.

HINRICHS, GUSTAVUS DETLEF, chemist; b. Lunden, Holstein, Denmark, Dec. 2, 1836; s. Johan Detlef and Caroline C. E. (Andersen) H.; studied 8 yrs. in Poly. Sch. and U. of Copenhagen, Denmark; m. Auguste S. F. Springer, of Marne, Holstein, Apr. 1861 (died 1865); m. 2d, Anna C. M. Springer, July 1867; (died 1910); father of Carl Gustav H. Was 25 yrs. prof. physical science, State U. of Ia.; prof. chemistry, Coll. Pharmacy, St. Louis, 1889-1903; prof. chemistry, med. dept., St. Louis U., 1903-07. Originated graded courses in lab. work, mng. classes of several hundred students, about 1870; founded, 1875, and sustained, 1st state weather service in U.S.; has done practical scientific work for U.S. and state authorities; served as expert chemist before state and federal courts. Hon. and corr. mem. many scientific socs. in Austria, Eng., France, Germany and U.S. Author of 40 vols. and many scientific memoirs in German, Danish, English, French, main object of which is math. demonstration of Unity of Matter, by quantitatively determined physical, chem. and crystallographical properties of all chem. compounds known; many of his memoirs published in Trans. Acads. of Sciences of Vienna and Paris; also in Proc. Am. Philos. Soc., Philadelphia. Author: The Proximate Constituents of the Chemical Elements (32 plates), 1904; The Amana Meteorites (16 plates), 1905 (German edit., Berlin, 1906); La Matière est Une, Paris, 1906; Absolute Atomic Weights now confirmed; 60 articles in Comptes Rendus, Acad. Sciences, of Paris; from 1906, over 100 pp. in Moniteur Scientifique, Paris. Home: St. Louis, Mo. Died Feb. 14, 1923.

HINSHELWOOD, SIR CYRIL (NORMAN), scientist; b. London, Eng., June 19, 1897; s. Norman Macmillan and Ethel (Smith) H.; M.A., Balliol. Coll., Oxford U., 1924, D.Sc., 1947, D.C.L., 1960; D.Sc., univs. Dublin, 1936, London, 1947, Leeds, 1952, Sheffield, 1954, Cambridge, 1955, Bristol, 1956, Hull, 1957, Wales, 1958, Ottawa, 1961, Southampton, 1965. Fellow, tutor Trinity Coll., Oxford, 1921-37; Dr. Lees prof. chem. Oxford, 1937-64; sr. research fellow Imperial Coll., London, 1964—; fellow Exeter Coll., 1937—. Chmn. Fuel Research Bd., 1950-55; mem. adv. council sci. policy Brit. Govt., 1953-56; hon. adv. sci. com. Natl. Gallery. Created Knight, 1948; recipient Lavoisier medal French Chem. Soc., Guldberg medal Oslo; Davy and Royal Medalist Royal Soc.; Longstaff and Faraday medalist Chem. Soc.; co-winner Nobel prize for chemistry, 1956; Grand Officer Order of Merit (Italy), 1956; Avogodro medal Acad. dei XL, Rome, 1956. Fellow Royal Soc. (past pres.); mem. Nat. Acad. of Sciences, Pontifical Acad., Chem. Soc. (pres. 1946-48); hon. mem. French, Belgian, Swiss, Italian chem. socs., Spanish Soc. Physics and Chemistry; fgn. mem. Accademia dei XL Rome, U.S.S.R. Academy of Scis., Accademia Nazionale dei Liucei (Rome), Real Academia de Ciencias Madrid, A.A.A.S. Author: Kinetics of Chemical Change, 1946; Chemical Kinetics of the Bacterial Cell, 1946; The Structure of Physical Chemistry, 1951; also papers in sci. jours. Home: Exeter College, Oxford, Eng. Office: Imperial Coll., London S.W. 7, Eng. Died Oct. 1967.

HINSON, NOEL BERTRAM, engr.; b. Evansville, Ind., Dec. 25, 1885; s. John Thomas and Sally Margaret (Vick) H.; grad. Los Angeles High Sch.; student Internat. Corr. Sch.; m. Ethel Florence Adland, June 20, 1911 (dec. Nov. 28, 1929); 1 dau., Barbara Jane (Mrs. Burton Cliffe Kaye); m. 2d Lois Myerhoff, June 18, 1931. With So. Calif. Edison Co. and its predecessor, Edison Electric Co., 1906-51, v.p., exec. engr., 1945-51, ret. Jan. 1, 1951. Mem. elec. power survey com. Edison Electric Inst., 1948-52; chmn. Pacific S.W. Power Interchange Com., 1943-52. Registered professional engineer, California. Fellow Am. Inst. E.E. (v.p. 1935-37, dir. 1949-53); mem. A.A.A.S., Astron. Soc. Pacific, Pacific Coast Elec. Assn., Tau Beta Pi (hon. mem.). Mason. Clubs: Univ., Electric (Los Angeles); Oneonta (South Pasadena). Contbr. articles population growth, planning electric utilities. Home: 1709 Marengo Av., South Pasadena, Cal. Died Apr. 16, 1958.

HINTON, JAMES WILLIAM, surgeon; b. Reedville, Va., Mar. 12, 1894; s. John Braxton and Anne Augusta (Crosswell) H.; student Cluster Springs Acad., Va., 1910-13; M.D., U. Va., 1919; LL.D., Hampden Sydney Coll., 1961; m. Jannett Lord, May 19, 1951. Intern surg. service Boston City Hosp., 1917. U. Va. Hosp., 1918-19, N.Y. Post-Grad. Hosp., 1919-21, Sloane's Hosp. for Women, 1921-22; former dir. fourth surg. service, dir. children's surg. service Bellevue Hosp., N.Y.C.; prof., chmn. dept. surgery Post Grad. Med. Sch., N.Y.U., 1949-60; former dir. surg. service Univ. Hosp.; attending surgeon Beekman Downtown Hosp., N.Y.C., Gouverneur Hosp.; cons. surgery N.Y. Women's Infirmary, Jersey City Med. Center, Norwalk (Conn.) Gen. Hosp., Southampton (N.Y.) Hosp., Jamaica (N.Y.) Hosp., St. Agnes Hosp., White Plains, N.Y., Good Samaritan Hosp., Suffern, N.Y., United Hosp., Portchester, N.Y., Nassau Hosp., Mineola, N.Y., Central Suffolk Hosp., Riverhead, N.Y., Elizabeth A. Horton Meml. Hosp., Middletown, N.Y., Wyckoff Height Hosp., Bklyn., Bellevue Hosp., University Hosp., Manhattan VA Hosp., Sherbrooke Hosp.; cons. Columbus Hosp., Manhattan State Hosp. Pres., trustee Royal Coll. Surgeons Found., 1967-73. Diplomate, founders group Am. Bd. Surgery. Fellow Royal Coll. Surgeons Eng. (hon.), Royal Coll. Edinburgh (hon.), A.C.S. (chmn. credentials com.), Am. Surg. Assn., Royal Coll. Surgeons in Ireland (hon.), Internat. Surg. Soc., N.Y. Acad. Medicine (v.p. 1944-46); mem. N.Y. (past pres.), Eastern surg. socs., Am. Gastroenterological Soc., Pan Pacific, So. surg. assns., N.Y. Cardiovascular Surgery, James IV Assn. Surgeons (foundeer, sec. 1957-67), Hon. Company Edinburgh Golfers, Alpha Omega Alpha. Club: Links (N.Y.C.). Home: New York City NY Died Apr. 18, 1973.

HIRES, CHARLES ELMER, soft drink mfr.; b. nr. Roadstown, N.J., Aug. 19, 1851; s. John Dare and Mary (Williams) H.; m. Clara Kate Smith, 1875; children—Linda Smith John Edgar, Harrison Streeter, Charles Elmer, Clara Sheppard; m. 2d, Emma Waln, 1911. Worked in drug store, Bridgeton, N.J., 1863-67; moved to Phila., 1867; became propr. pharmacy, Phila., 1869; experimented with sarsaparilla root, developed drink which he named Hires Root Beer, 1875, sold drink at Centennial Expn., Phila., 1876; at 1st sold root beer as a package of dried roots and herbs to be brewed at home, later sold it in form of concentrated extract; organized Charles E. Hires Co., 1890; pioneer in processing of condensed milk (taken over by Nestlé Co. 1918). Died Haverford, Pa., July 31, 1937; buried Westminster Cemetery, nr. Cynwyd, Pa.

HIRSCH, ALCAN, chem. engineer; b. Corpus Christi, Tex., Feb. 1, 1885; s. David and Olivia (Benedict) H.; A.B., U. of Tex., 1907; M.S., U. of Wis., 1908, Chem. Engr., 1909, Ph.D., 1911; m. Murilla Polakoff, Mar. 30, 1930; children—Alcene, (3 adopted daughters) Helene, Shirley and Audrey. Research asso. in chem. engring., Mass. Inst. Tech., 1909-10; established lab., New York, 1911; consultant to various indsl. corps., 1912-16; consultant to Japanese Govt. in chem. development, 1916-18; pres. Hirsch Labs., 1917—; formed Rector Chemical Co., 1917, consultant Bayer Co., 1918-20, and to various other cos., 1920-27; one of founders of Molybdenum Corp. of America, 1920, consultant, 1920—; part owner New Rochelle Research Labs., Inc., 1927—; chief consultant to Soviet Govt. in heavy chem. industry, 1931-33; chief consultant Giprokhim, U.S.S.R. 1932; cons. engr., 1911—; formerly chem. dir. J. P. Devine Co. (Buffalo, N.Y); consultant Treadwell Engring. Co. (New York); v.p. and chmn. bd. Hirestra Laboratories; started the pyrophoric alloy industry in U.S., 1915. Carnegie award of Iron and Steel Inst. of Gt. Britain, 1913. Mem. Am.-Russian Chamber of Commerce, Am.-Russian Inst. (dir.). Jewish religion. Author: Industrialized Russia, 1934. Home: New Rochelle, N.Y. Died Nov. 24, 1938.

HIRSCH, GUSTAV, cons. engr.; b. Columbus, O., Nov. 4, 1876; s. Leonhard and Charlotta (Meyer) H.; M.E. in Elec. Engring., Ohio State U., 1897; m. Aletta Kremer, Aug. 12, 1899; 1 dau., Irene Dorothea. Cons. engrs., builder or engr. of utility properties in all states, 1902—; v.p. and dir. Conneaut Telephone Co.; pres., dir. Warren Telephone Co., Gustave Hirsch Orgn., Skyway Broadcasting Co.; v.p., dir. Mansfield Telephone Co., United Utilities, Inc.; dir. Elyria Telephone Co., Cosmo Investors Corp., Jaeger Machine Co. Dir. Ohio Mental Health. Served from pvt. to capt. O.N.G., 1893-96, 1899-1901; 2d lt., Signal Corps, U.S. Army, Spanish-Am. War; maj. and lt. col., Signal Corps, U.S. Army, 1917-19, now lt. col. U.S. Army retired. Decorated French Verdun medal. Registered engr., Ohio. Fellow Am. Geog. Soc.; mem. Am. Soc. M.E., Am. Inst. E.E., Am., Ohio socs. profl. engrs., A.A.A.S., Ind. Telephone Pioneers, Am. Legion, U.S. Veteran Signal Corps Assn., United Spanish War Vets. (dir.), Ohio Independent Telephone Assn., Independent Telephone Pioneers of America, Tau Beta Pi. Elk. Clubs: Columbus Athletic, Scioto Country, Columbus Riding (Columbus). Home: 2459 Tremont Rd. Office: 1347 W. 5th Av., Columbus 12, O. Died Jan. 7, 1959; buried Green Lawn Cemetery, Columbus.

HIRSCHFELDER, ARTHUR DOUGLASS, prof. pharmacology; b. San Francisco, Calif., Sept. 29, 1879; s. Joseph Oakland and Clara (Honigsberg) H.; B.S., U. of Calif., 1897; student Pasteur Inst., Paris, 1898-99, U. of Heidelberg, 1899; M.D., Johns Hopkins, 1903; m. May R. Straus, June 26, 1905; children—Rosalie Claire (Mrs. Gosta C. Akerlof), Joseph Oakland. Resident house officer Johns Hopkins Hosp., Baltimore, 1903-04; asst. in medicine, Cooper Med. Coll., San Francisco, 1904-05; successively vol. asst., instr., asso. in medicine Johns Hopkins, 1905-13; prof. pharmacologist, U. of Minn., since 1913. Served as pharmacologist, War Dept., 1918. Fellow A.A.A.S.; mem. A.M.A. (chmn. sect. on pharmacology 1917-18), Am. Soc. Clin. Investigation, Soc. Exptl. Biology and Medicine, Am. Soc. Pharmacology and Exptl. Therapeutics, Am. Physiol. Soc., Am. Soc. Biol. Chemistry, Am. Chem. Soc., Minn. Acad. Science, Sigma Xi, Gamma Alpha. Club: Campus (Minneapolis, Minn.). Author: Diseases of the Heart and Aorta, 1910; An Investigation of the Louse Problem (with Wm. Moore), 1918. Contbr. professional jours. Home: 2364 Lake of the Isle Blvd., Minneapolis, Minn. Died Oct. 11, 1942.

HIRSHBERG, LEONARD KEENE, M.D.; b. Baltimore, Md., Jan. 9, 1877; s. Isidore Nathan and Fannie (Thalheimer) H.; A.B., Johns Hopkins, 1898, M.D., 1902; univs. of Berlin and Heidelberg, 1902, 03, Harvard Summer Sch., 1903; hon. A.M., Loyola Coll., Md., 1913; m. Edna Dalsemer, of Baltimore, Nov. 25, 1904; children—Leonard Keene Dalsemer, Gordon Henry Dalsemer. Instr. neuro-pathology and asso. in bacteriology, Coll. Phys. and Surg., Baltimore, 1904; visiting phys., Mercy, Baltimore City, Md. Gen. and St. Agnes hosps.; research worker, Johns Hopkins; lecturer, Loyola Coll., Baltimore; physician in chief Nat. Health Service, 1926. Chmn. com. scientific research Am. Assn. Clinical Research (pres. 1914-15); mem. A.A.A.S., Am. Neurol. Soc., Soc. of Biologists, Am. Acad. Sciences, etc.; pres. Physicians' Civic Club; v.p. Direct Legislation League. Mason (32 deg., Shriner), Elk, K.P., etc. Clubs: Royal Societies Club (London); Johns Hopkins, Charcoal, Press, Lauraville Country, Bohemians. Author: Collected Humor, Poetry and Philosophy, 1898; Practical Bacteriology, 1904; Action of Light, 1904; What You Ought to Know About the Baby, 1909, 26; Researches in Anaphylactic Medicine, 1911; How to Have a Beautiful Complexion, 1918, 26; Secrets of Health, 1926; The Book of Health, 1926. Contbr. Scientific American, Beautiful Motherhood, Physical Health, Brain Power, Harper's Bazar, and over 100 other Am., English, Canadian and Australian mags., also syndicate artilces in over 600 daily newspapers; owner and pub. Popular Medicine; asso. editor Med. Review of Reviews and other mags. Winner of Fisk Fund prize (R.I. Med. Soc.), N.Y. Med. Jour. prize, etc. Home: 422 National Boul., Long Beach, N.Y. Office: 17 W. 60th St., New York NY

HIRSHFELD, CLARENCE FLOYD, engineer; b. San Francisco, Calif., Jan. 30, 1881; s. Charles and Lotta (McCarthy) H.; B.S. in Elec. Engring., U. of Calif., 1902; M.M.E., Cornell U., 1905; Dr. Engring., Rensselaer Poly. Inst., 1932; m. Elizabeth Bishop Winslow, June 16, 1906; children—John Winslow, James Floyd. Successively instr., asst. prof. and prof. of mech. engring., Sibley Coll. (Cornell U.), 1903-14, also cons. practice, 1903-14; chief of research dept., Detroit Edison Co., 1913— (absent on leave 1918-19); cons. engr., 1919—; chief engineer Transit Research Corp. Major and lt. colonel Ordnance Dept., U.S.A., 1918-19. Mem. Am. Com. of World Power Conf.; mem. bd. nat. councillors, Purdue Research Foundation; mem. advisory council Yenching Univ. Mem. U.S. Bur. of Mines Advisory Bd., Ohio State Univ. Research Foundation. Republican. Episcopalian. Author: Engineering Thermodynamics, 1913; Farm Gas Engines (with T. C. Ulbricht), 1913; Steam Power (with same), 1913; Elements of Heat Power Engineering (with W. N. Barnard), 1915; Economic Operation of Steam-Turbo-electric Stations (with C. L. Karr), 1918; Elements of Heat Power Engineering (with W. N. Barnard and F. O. Ellenwood), 1933. Home: Detroit, Mich. Died Apr. 19, 1939.

HITCHCOCK, ALBERT SPEAR, botanist; b. Owosso, Mich., Sept. 4, 1865; B.S., Iowa Agricultural College, 1884, M.S., 1886, D.S., 1920; m. Rania Belle Dailey, Mar. 16, 1890; children—Horace Dailey, Frank Harold, Elizabeth Hortense, Helen Esther, Albert Edwin. Asst. in chemistry, State U. of Ia., 1886-89; asst. Mo. Bot. Garden, St. Louis, 1889-91; prof. botany, Kan. Agrl. Coll., 1892-1901; asst. agrostologist, 1901-05, systematic agrostologist, 1905-24, prin. botanist in charge systematic agrostology, 1924—, U.S. Dept. of Agr. Home: Washington, D.C. Died Dec. 16, 1935.

HITCHCOCK, CHARLES BAKER, geographer; b. Boston, Mar. 16, 1906; s. John and Esther Mary (Baker) H.; A.B., Harvard Univ., 1928; M.A., Columbia, 1933; D.Sc. (honorary), Temple University, 1954; m. Agnes Murchie, Dec. 3, 1931; children—Gail, Suzanne, Esther Lee; married second, Anita Kincaid, January 19, 1957. Joined Am. Geog. Soc., N.Y. City, 1930, chief dept. Hispanic Am. research and assistant director, 1943-48, acting dir., 1949, exec. sec., dir., 1956-66, research asso., 1967-69, chmn. advisory committee Am. cartography, 1948-69, research and devel. bd., 1949; mem. adv. com. Am. Geography Pan Am. Inst. Geog. and History; mem. nat. atlas com. Nat. Research Council; mem. adv. com. census atlases Bur. Census; expdns. Am. Mus. Natural History, So. Venezuela, 1929, Phelps Venezuela, 1947-49, 51-53, U.S. del. to Internat. Geog. Congress, Amsterdam, 1938, Rio de Janeiro, 1956, London, England, 1964. United States delegate Pan American Inst. Geography and History, Lima, 1941, Caracas, 1946, Buenos Aires, 1948, Santiago, Chile, 1950, Dominican Republic, 1952, Mexico, 1955, Ecuador, 1959, Stockholm, Sweden, 1960; alternate U.S. delegate to the Commn. Cartography, from 1957. Mem. Assn. Am. Geographers (treas., 1948-49), Arctic Institute, N.Y. Acad. Scis., Soc. Geog. de Lima (corr. mem.), Soc. Venezolana de Ciencias Naturales (honorary), Scottish Geographical Society (honorary), A.A.A.S., Geol. Soc. Am., Nat. Geog. Soc. (hon.). Editor Map of Hispanic America, 1938-47. Contbr. articles tech. publs. Recipient Morse medal Am. Geog. Soc., 1966; Explorers Club medal, 1967. Home: Pound Ridge NY Died Mar. 26, 1969.

HITCHCOCK, CHARLES HENRY, geologist; b. Amherst, Mass., Aug. 23, 1836; s. late Edward (pres. Amherst Coll.) and Orra (White) H.; brother of Edward H.; A.B., Amherst Coll., 1856, A.M., 1859; student Yale Div. Sch. and Andover Theol. Sem.; Royal Sch. Mines, London; (Ph.D., Lafayette, 1870; LL.D., Amherst, 1896); m. Martha Bliss, d. Prof. E. P. Barrows, June 19, 1862. Lecturer zoölogy, Amherst Coll., 1858-64; non-resident prof. geology and mineralogy, Lafayette Coll., 1866-70; prof. geology and mineralogy, Dartmouth, 1868-1908, emeritus prof., 1908—. Asst. state geologist, Vt., 1857-61; state geologist, Me., 1861-62, N.H., 1868-78; prof. geology, Va. Agrl. and Mech. Coll., 1880; prof. natural history, Williams Coll., 1881; lecturer geology, Mt. Holyoke Coll., 1870-96. Headed expdn. occupying Mt. Washington, N.H., in winter of 1870-71, the 1st high mountain observatory in the U.S.; best known as compiler of several geol. maps of U.S., and for researches in ichnology, geology of the crystalline schists, and glacial geology. Author: Elementary Geology (with Edward Hitchcock), 1861; Mt. Washington in Winter, 1871; Report on Geology of New Hampshire (3 vols.), 1873-78 (state publ.); Geological Map of the United States, 1881; Hawaii and Its Volcanoes, 1909. Home: Honolulu, T.H. Died Nov. 5, 1919.

HITCHCOCK, EDWARD, geologist, coll. pres.; b. Deerfield, Mass., May 24, 1793; s. Justin and Mercy (Hoyt) H.; grad. Yale Theol. Sem., 1820; m. Orra White, 1821, 6 children including Charles Henry, Edward. Prin, Deerfield Acad., 1815-19; pastor Congregational Ch., Conway, Mass., 1821-25; prof. chemistry and natural history Amherst (Mass.) Coll., 1825-45, pres., 1845-54, prof. theology and geology, 1854-64; made 1st complete geol. survey of Mass., 1830; state geologist Vt., 1857-61. Author: Geology of Connecticut Valley, 1823; Elementary Geology, 1840; Fossil Footsteps, 1848; Religion of Geology, 1851; Illustrations of Surface Geology, 1857. Died Amherst, Feb. 27, 1864.

HITCHCOCK, EMBURY ASBURY, engineer, educator; b. Henrietta, N.Y., June 26, 1866; s. Julius Charles and Finett Rosett (Potter) H.; student Syracuse U., 1885; M.E., Cornell U., 1890; m. Hattie Isabel Mortimore, July 7, 1896 (died 1933); children—Isabelle, Mortimore, Harriett; m. 2d, Florence Estelle Mortimore, Apr. 27, 1940. Designer Corliss Steam Engine Co., Providence, R.I., 1890-93; mem. faculty, Ohio State U., 1893-1912; engr. with E. W. Clark Co. Management Corp., 1912-19; v.p. Bailey Meter Co., Cleveland, O., 1919-20; dean Coll. of Engring., Ohio State U., 1920-36, dean emeritus since 1936. Represented Appalachian Power Co. at First World Power Conf., London, 1924. Member American Society Engineering Education (v.p. 1929-30), National Soc. Professional Engrs., Sigma Xi, Tau Beta Pi, Scabbard and Blade, Triangle. Chmn. engring. section Association Land-Grant Colleges, 1925-26; vice-president Columbus Chamber Commerce, 1926-27; hon. judge Fisher Body Craftsmen's Guild, 1930-37. mem. nat. council Boy Scouts America, 1937-45. Republican. Methodist. Author: My First Fifty Years in Engineering. Conducted first complete heat balance tests of locomotives on road. Home: 348 W. Eighth Av., Columbus, O. Died April 29, 1948; buried in Amaranth Abbey, Columbus, O.

HITCHCOCK, FRANK LAUREN, mathematician; b. N.Y.C., Mar. 6, 1875; s. Elisha Pike and Susan Ida (Porter) H.; A.B., Harvard, 1896, Ph.D., 1910; student U. of Paris, France, 1897-1903, U. Cin., 1906-07; m. Margaret Johnson Blakely, May 25, 1899;

children—Lauren B., George B. Asst. in chemistry. Harvard, 1895-96; instr. chemistry, Milton (Mass.) Acad., 1896-97; prof. chemistry Fargo (N.D.) Coll., 1903-06; instr. chemistry, Franklin Sch., Cin., 1906-07; asst. prof. physics, Kenyon Coll., 1907-09; instr. mathematics, Mass. Inst. Tech., 1910-17, asst. prof., 1917-49, ret. 1949. Fellow Am. Acad. Arts and Sciences; mem. Internat. Soc. for Promotion Study of Quaternions and Allied Branches, Sigma Xi. Author: (with Clark S. Robinson) Differential Equations in Applied Chemistry. Conglist. Home: Hillside Terrace, Belmont, Mass. Died May 29, 1957.

HITCHCOCK, FREDERICK COLLAMORE, engr., contractor; b. Toledo, O., Sept. 19, 1864; s. Bailey Hall and Sarah Hatch (Collamore) H.; ed. high sch., Toledo, and preparatory sch., Ann Arbor, Mich.; studied engring. under father; unmarried. Engr. on constrn. of rys., 1883-92; gen. mgr. and partner George S. Good & Co., ry. contractors, Lock Haven, Pa., 1893-1905; v.p. and gen. mgr. Construction Co. of S. America, 1906-07; built Nat. Railways of Bolivia; v.p. and gen. mgr. MacArthur Bros. Co., New York and Chicago; engaged in bldg. rys., dams, docks, subways, tunnels, etc., including Ashokan Dam, N.Y., 1908-16; also as mgr. MacArthur, Perks & Co., built piers at Havana, Cuba; pres. Equipment Co. of America, 1908-16; in China as v.p. and gen. mgr. Siems, Carey & Co., holding contracts for 2,600 miles of railroads, and rehabilitation of Grand Canal, 1916-19; pres. Carey, Campbell & Co., highway contractors, 1919-22; v.p. W. F. Carey Co., building dam in Vt., 1921-22; pres. Hitchcock & Tinkler, Inc., 1923—; built Moffat Tunnel, Colo.; made reports on reclamation project in Greece, 1929; consultant of Soviet Govt. on 1,000,000 acre irrigation project, Turkestan, 1930; v.p. Ambursen Engineering Corp.; consultant. Republican. Unitarian. Home: New York, N.Y. Died June 28, 1937.

HITCHCOCK, LAUREN BLAKELY, cons. chem. engr., educator; b. Paris, France (parents U.S. citizens), Mar. 18, 1900; s. Frank Lauren and Margaret Johnson (Blakely) H.; S.B. in Chem. Engring., Mass. Inst. Tech. 1920, S.M., 1927, Sc. D., 1933; m. Eleanor M. Mulhern, Sept. 22, 1920 (dec. Aug. 1963); children—Eleanor M. (Mrs. John R. Higgins) (dec.), Patricia (Mrs. Peter Malof), Jacquelyn I. (Mrs. K. E. Aamodt), Hope M. (Mrs. J. A. Maurice Cantin), John; m. 2d, Lusyd Wright Smith, Mar. 1, 1966 (dec. Feb. 1971). Chemist, H. P. Hood & Sons, Boston, 1920; prof. chem. engring. U. Va., 1928-35; cons. chem. engr., research exec., mgr. sales devel. Hooker Electro-Chem. Co., Niagara Falls, 1935-44; mgr. chems. dept. Quaker Oats Co., Chgo., 1944-46, v.p. charge, 1946-49; dir. research and devel. Nat. Dairy Products Corp., also pres. Nat. Dairy Research Labs., Inc., N.Y.C., 1949-53; mgmt. cons., N.Y.C., 1953; pres., mng. dir. Air Pollution Found., Los Angeles, 1954-56; cons. chem. engr. Lauren B. Hitchcock Assos., 1957-63; prof. engring. State U. N.Y. at Buffalo, 1963-72; dir. grad. engring. Mgmt. TV Network, 1969-72; dir. devel. Ecology & Environment, Inc., Buffalo, 1972. Served with U.S. Naval Aviation Corps, 1918; officer U.S. Army, 1921-28. Registered profl. engr., Cal., N.Y., Va. Mem. Am. Soc. Engring. Edn., Am. Inst. Chem. Engrs. (Profl. Achievement award Western N.Y. sect. 1971), Am. Chem. Soc., Soc. Chem. Industry (chmn. Am. sect. 1953-54), Air Pollution Control Assn., Comml. Chem. Devel. Assn. (pres. 1947-49), Niagara Frontier Assn. Research and Devel. Dirs. (pres. 1970-71), Sigma Xi, Alpha Chi Sigma. Clubs: Cosmos (Washington); M.I.T., Chemists (N.Y.C.); Saturn (Buffalo). Author numerous sci. articles field chem. technology and research mgmt. Home: Buffalo NY Died Oct. 16, 1972; buried Belmont MA

HITCHCOCK, ROMYN, chemist; b. St. Louis, Dec. 1, 1851; s. Alonzo and Hannah Ethloine (Hallenbeck) H.; student Cornell, 1868-71, Columbia Sch. of Mines. 1872; m. Emma Louise Bingham, of Ithaca, N.Y., Apr. 21, 1875. Asst. in chemistry, Lehigh U., 1873-75; prof. chemistry, med. coll., Chicago, 1876-77; prof. Koto Chiu Gakko, Osaka, Japan, 1887-89; curator Nat. Mus., Washington, 1884-99; consulting chemist and technologist, 1899—. Editorial staff American Chemist, 1872-76; editor and pub. American Quarterly Microscopical Journal, 1878-79, American Monthly Microscopical Journal, 1880-87; judge of awards London Fisheries Exhbn. for U.S. com., 1883; on U.S. Eclipse expdn. to Japan in charge of photographic work, 1887; U.S. commr. to China for Chicago Expn., 1890-92; expert on Pa. com. to arrange state mining exhibit, and judge awards, Dept. of Mfrs., same, 1893; judge of awards, St. Louis Expn., 1904. Student of economic effects of prevailing methods of corporate organization; lecturer on promotion methods and capitalization and taxation of resources. Fellow A.A.A.S.; sec. 1877-78, pres. 1878-79, N.Y. Micros. Soc.; mem. Am. Chem. Soc., Cornell Chapter Delta Upsilon. Author of numerous contbns. on scientific subjects and reports on travels and observations in the Orient. Address: New York City.

HITCHENS, ARTHUR PARKER, health commissioner; b. Delmar, Delaware, Sept. 14, 1877; s. William Smith and Fannie (Parker) H.; Prep. Sch., Temple Coll., Phila.; M.D., Medico-Chirurg. Coll., Phila., 1898; studied U. of Pa., St. Mary's Hosp. (London), Woods Hole, Mass.; grad. Army Med. Sch., 1923; also grad. course preventive medicine; m. Ethel Mary Bennett, June 20, 1906. Dir. biol. labs., Glenolden, Pa., 1900-18; commd. maj. M.C., U.S. Army, 1920, lt. col. 1937; spl. lecturer on infection and immunity, Sch. for Grads., Dept. of Agr., 1922; advisory prof. bacteriology, Am. Univ., Washington; inrst. Army Med. Sch.; tech. adviser to gov. gen. P.I. in pub. health matters, 1925-29; professorial lecturer on epidemiology, Sch. Hygiene and Pub. Health, U. of Philippines, 1928-29; in charge Corps Area Lab., Fort Sheridan, Ill., 1929-33; instr. in bacteriology and chief dept. bacteriology, Army Medical Sch. Washington, 1935-38; asst. prof. military science and tactics, U. of Pa., 1938, prof. of public health and preventive medicine, 1939-44; commissioner of health, Wilmington, Del., since 1944; staff mem. Wilmington General Hospital, since 1945; dir. State of Pa. Bur. of Labs., 1948-49. Mem. Phila. City Bd. of Health, 1940-43. Editor Abstracts of Bacteriology; chmn. editorial bd., sect. on microbiology, Biol. Abstracts, 1937-45; member exec. com. Union of Am. Biol. Societies, Fellow A.M.A., Phila. Coll. Physicians, Am. Public Health Assn. (chmn. laboratory sect. 1923-24; chairman coordinating com. on standard methods, lab. sect., 1931-46); mem. Soc. Am. Bacteriol. (sec. 1912-22, v.p. 1923, pres. 1924; pres. Washington local 1936-37), Am. Assn. Immunologists, North Shore Science Club (founded 1931, pres.). Episcopalian. Mason. Clubs: Union League (Phila.); Cosmos (Washington); Army and Navy, Manila; Polo (Manila, P.I.); Laboratory (founder 1944), Torch, Rotary, Masonic (Wilmington). Address: 906 S. 48th St., Phila. 43. Died Dec. 10, 1949.

HITE, BERT HOLMES, chemist; b. Morgantown, W.Va., Aug. 18, 1866; s. Isaac and Catherine (Hennen) H.; M.S., W.Va. U., 1890; student Johns Hopkins U., 1891-95; m. Evelyn Pratt, Nov. 2, 1898. Fellow in chemistry, Johns Hopkins, 1893-95; chemist W.Va. Agrl. Expt. Sta., 1895—, v.dir., 1902—; prof. organic chemistry, 1895-98, prof. agrl. chemistry, 1898—, W.Va. U.; chemist W.Va. Geol. Survey, 1898—; chemist W.Va. Dept. Agr.; consulting chemist U.S. Ordnance Dept., B.&O. R.R. Co. Republican. Episcopalian. Home: Morgantown, W.Va. Died Oct. 6, 1921.

HLAVATY, VACLAV, mathematician; b. Louny, Czechoslovakia, Jan. 27, 1894; s. Hlavaty and Laura (Feltl) V.; Ph.D., Prague U., 1922; grad. study Delft, Rome, Paris, Oxford, 1924-30; m. Olga Neumann, Jan. 10, 1931; 1 dau., Olga (Mrs. Yusufzai). Came to U.S., 1948, naturalized, 1956. Prof. math. Prague U., 1930-48; vis. prof. Princeton, also Inst. Advanced Study, 1937-38; exchange prof. Sorbonne, Paris, 1948; prof. Ind. U., 1948-69, Distinguished Service prof., 1962. World lecture tour on math., U.S., Japan, Hongkong, India, Afghanistan, Iran, Israel, Italy, France, Belgium, Eng., Ireland; co-editor Tensor (Japan), Rendiconti Circ. Mat. (Palermo, Italy). Bd. reviewers Math. Rev., Jour. Math. and Mechanics. Bd. trustees Masaryk Fund. Mem. Soc. Roy. des Sci Liege, Ac. Intern. Libre des Sci Paris, Czechoslovak Soc. Art and Sci. of U.S. (past pres.), Ind. Acad. Sci. Sigma Xi, Mu Epsilon. Author numerous books, latest being Geometry of Einstein's Unified Field Theory, 1958. Contbr. numerous articles tech., profl. jours., U.S. and fgn. countries. Home: Bloomington IN Died Jan. 11, 1969.

HOAD, WILLIAM CHRISTIAN, (hōd), engineer; b. Lecompton, Kan., Jan. 11, 1874; s. Francis Dearing and Gertrude Millicent (Evans) H.; B.S., Lane Univ., 1896; B.S. in C.E., U. of Kansas, 1898; m. Louise Green, August 7, 1901; children—Hortense (Mrs. John Russell) (dec.), William Marvin, John Green. Engaged in railroad location and maintenance, 1898-1900; assistant prof., associate prof. and prof. civil engineering, University of Kansas, 1900-12; chief engr. Kan. State Bd. of Health, 1907-12; prof. municipal and san. engring., U. of Mich., 1912-37, prof. civil engring., 1937-44, prof. emeritus since 1944; mem. firms Hoad and Decker; Hoad, Decker, Shoecraft and Drury; Drury, McNamee and Porter; mem. engring. firm McNamee, Porter & Seeley, consultants in gen. field of municipal and sanitary engring. since 1912; has served more than fifty cities and industries in solving major problems related to water supply, sanitation, drainage, steam control, etc. Maj. and lt. col. engring. div. Sanitary Corps, U.S. Army, 1918-19; lt. col. Engr. R.C., 1919-26. Fellow Am. Pub. Health Assn.; mem. American Society C.E., American Water Works Association, N.E. Water Works Association, Sigma Xi, Theta Xi. Republican. Presbyn. Clubs: Union, Rotary. Author reports and articles in field. Home: 2114 Devonshire Rd., Ann Arbor, Mich. Died July 2, 1962.

HOADLEY, JOHN CHIPMAN, civil engr., mfr.; b. Martinsburg, N.Y., Dec. 10, 1818; s. Maj. Lester and Sarah (Chipman) H.; m. Charlotte Kimball, Aug. 24, 1847; m. 2d, Catherine Melville, Sept. 15, 1853. Moved to Utica, N.Y., 1824; held various surveying and engring. jobs in youth; helped form McKay and Hoadley, firm mfg. mill machinery, steam engines and water wheels, 1848; also engaged in constrn. railroad locomotives; developed 1st single valve automatic steam engine; in charge constrn. with McKay Sewing Machine Assn., 1868; organizer Clinton Wire Cloth Co.; pres. Archibald Wheel Co.; mem. Mass. Legislature, 1858; founder Am. Soc. M.E.; original trustee Mass. Inst. Tech. Author various papers for sci. and engring. socs., best known being The Portable Steam Engine, 1863; Steam Engine Practice in the United States, 1884. Died Oct. 21, 1886.

HOAG, WILLIAM RICKETSON, drainage engr.; b. Sumner, Minn., Feb. 25, 1859; s. Milton John and Catharine (Everitt) H.; grad. Rochester (Minn.) High Sch., 1878; B.C.E., U. of Minn., 1884, M.C.E., 1888; m. Annie L. Lawrence of Minneapolis, 1885. Instr., asst. prof. and prof. civ. engring., U. of Minn., 1885-1907. Acting asst. U.S. Coast and Geod. Survey, 1888-95; state topographer in charge state triangulation, Minn., 1892-95; engr. State Drainage Commn., 1897-1905; resident hydrographer, U.S. Geol. Survey, 1902. Mem. Jury of Award, Chicago Expn., 1893, Paris Expn., 1900, St. Louis Expn., 1904. Mem. Surveyors and Engrs.' Soc. of Minn. (pres. 1898-99), Minn. State Engrs.' Soc., Engrs.' Club, Minneapolis (pres. 1900-01), Phi Beta Kappa, Sigma Xi, Delta Kappa Epsilon. Conducted a "Good Roads" column in Minneapolis Times, 1896-1902; also contbr. numerous papers to engring. jours. and proceedings, etc. Home: 1320 7th St., S.E., Minneapolis. Office: Fram, Minn.

HOAGLAND, DENIS ROBERT, (hog'land), prof. plant nutrition; b. Golden, Colo., Apr. 2, 1884; s. Charles Breckenridge and Lillian May (Burch) H.; A.B., Stanford, 1907; A.M., U. Wis., 1913; m. Jessie A. Smiley, May 1, 1920 (dec.); children—Albert Smiley, Charles Rightmire, Robert Charles. Asst. and instr. agrl. chemistry U. Cal., 1907-10, asst. prof. agrl. chemistry, 1913-20, asso. prof. plant nutrition, 1920-25, prof., 1927—, faculty research lectr., 1942, head div. of plant nutrition, 1921—, chmn. dept. botany, 1934-36, asso. chemist Agrl. Expt. Sta., 1920-25, chemist, 1925—; research chemist U.S. Dept. Agr., 1910-12. Received Stephen Hales prize Am. Soc. Plant Physiologists, 1930; joint recipient A.A.A.S. prize, 1940. Fellow A.A.A.S. (pres. Pacific div., 1941), Am. Acad. Arts and Scis.; mem. Western Soc. Soil Science (pres. 1924), Am. Soc. Hort. Science, Am. Soc. Agronomy, Internat. Soc. Soil Science, Nat. Acad. Science, Am. Chem. Soc., Am. Soc. Naturalists, Bot. Soc. Am., Am. Soc. Plant Physiologists (pres. 1932), Western Soc. Naturalists (pres. 1931). Club: Faculty (U. of Calif.). Cons. editor Soil Science; mem. bd. editors Ann. Rev. Biochemistry. Contbr. sci. articles on results of research on mineral nutrition on plants. Home: 839 Indian Rock Av., Berkeley, Cal. Died Sept. 5, 1949.

HOBART, FRANKLIN GATFIELD, cons. engr.; b. Oak Creek (now S. Milw.), Wis., Jan. 31, 1864; s. Adin P. and Clarissa A. (Beckwith) H.; B. Mech. Engring., U. Wis., 1886, M.E., 1890; m. Bertha C. Lewis, Oct. 14, 1891; m. 2d, Daisy M. Buckeridge, Sept. 12, 1918; children—Charles F., Carolyn F. (Mrs. Walter L. Brooks); m. 3d, Ida E. Schaub, Mar. 6, 1937. Began as draftsman, successively with Sweets Mfg. Co., Syracuse, N.Y.; Babcock & Wilcox Co., N.Y.C.; Carnegie, Phipps Steel Co., Beaver Falls, Pa.; E. P. Allis Co., Milw.; New Castle (Pa.) Steel Co.; chief engr. Williams Engine Works, Beloit, Wis. (this firm later absorbed by Fairbanks, Morse & Co.), 1889-1929, and as cons. engr. with interest chiefly in gas and oil engines for pumping oil wells, since 1929. Mem. Beloit Common Council, 1 term; mem. Beloit Sch. Bd., 1 term. Fellow Am. Soc. M.E. Has held and assigned to Fairbanks, Morse & Co., about 45 U.S. patents. Home: 732 Hobart Pl., Beloit, Wis. 53511. Died Oct. 2, 1960.

HOBART, HENRY METCALF, engr.; b. Boston, Mass., Nov. 29, 1868; s. Arthur William and Martha Lambard (Nichols) H.; B.S. in E.E., Mass. Inst. Tech., 1889; m. Edith Walpole, Aug. 26, 1909. With Thomson-Houston Electric Co., and its successor, the Gen. Electric Co., 1889-94, British Thomson-Houston Co., London, 1894-99; cons. engr., Union Elektricitäts Gesellschaft, Berlin, 1900-03; independent cons. practice, London, Eng., 1903-11; cons. engr. Gen. Electric Co. of America, 1911-40; consulting engineer since 1940. Fellow Am. Inst. Elec. Engrs.; mem. Inst. Civil, Mech. and Elec. Engrs. (England), Am. Soc. M.E. Author: Electric Motors, 1904, 2d edit., 1910, 3d edit., 1923; Continuous Current Dynamo Design, 1906; Heavy Electrical Engineering, 1908; Electricity, 1909; Electric Trains, 1910; Design of Static Transformers, 1911; Electric Propulsion of Ships, 1911; Design of Polyphase Generators and Motors, 1913; also other books with collaborators. Editor: Dictionary of Electrical Engineering, 1910. Office: 10 Balltown Rd., Schenectady, N.Y. Died Oct. 11, 1946. *

HOBBS, ALFRED CHARLES, mfr.; b. Boston, Oct. 7, 1812; 2 children. Apprenticed to glass-cutting works Boston & Sandwich Glass Co., 1834-36; invented and patented new cutglass doorknob with new attachment to door socket; partner Jones and Hobbs, lockmakers; became salesman of safes for Edwards & Holman Co., later Day & Newell Co., became expert lock picker to demonstrate uselessness of his competing locks; partner firm Hobbs, Ashley Co., 1851-60; recipient Telford medal from Inst. Civil Engrs. for his paper On the Principles and Construction of Locks, 1854; engr., supt. for Elias Howe Jr. Sewing Machine Co., 1860-66; supt. Union Metallic Cartridge Co., Bridgeport, Conn., 1866-90. Died Bridgeport, Nov. 5, 1891.

HOBBS, PERRY L., prof. chemistry, Western Reserve Univ., since 1889; b. Cleveland, O., Sept. 10, 1861; s. Caleb S. and Ada Antoinette (Lynes) H.; grad. Case School Applied Science (B.S.), 1886; post. grad. Univ. of Berlin (Ph.D.); m. Apr. 6, 1892, Mary L. Marshall, Cleveland, O. Chemist for Ohio Dairy and Food Commn.; analyt. and consulting chemist. Contributor to periodicals on scientific subject. Address: 1420 Euclid Av., Cleveland, O.

HOBBS, WILLIAM HERBERT, geologist; b. Worcester, Mass., July 2, 1864; s. Horace and Mary Paine (Parker) H.; S.B., Worcester Poly. Inst., 1883, D.Engring., 1929; fellow geology, Johns Hopkins, 1887-88, A.M., Ph.D., 1888; student U. of Heidelberg, 1888-89; LL.D., U. of Michigan, 1939; m. Sara K. Sale, June 23, 1896; 1 dau., Winifred (Mrs. J. N. Lincoln). Curator Geol. Mus., 1889-90, asst. prof. mineralogy and metallurgy, 1890-99, prof. mineralogy and petrology, 1899-1906, U. of Wis.; prof. geology and dir. Geol. Lab., U. of Mich., 1906-34, prof. emeritus since 1934; Russel lecturer, 1931. With U.S. Geol. Survey, 1886-1906; U.S. asst. geologist, 1896. Lectured on World War I, summer sch., U. of Pittsburgh, 1918; extended cruises to mandated Pacific Islands, 1921; exch. prof. Technische Hoogeschool, Delft, 1921-22. Dir. Greenland expdns., U. of Mich., 1926-31, hon. director 1932-33. Vice-pres. Internat. Glacier Com., 1930-36. Fellow A.A.A.S. (v.p. 1932), Geol. Soc. America (first v.p. 1922); mem. Am. Philos. Soc. (mem. council 1930), Assn. Am. Geographers (first v.p. 1917; pres. 1936), Mich. Acad. Science (pres. 1917). Chevalier Legion Honor, France, 1924. Club: Explorers (New York). Author: Earthquakes, 1907 (German transl. 1910); Characteristics of Existing Glaciers, 1911; Earth Features and Their Meaning, 1912; The World War and Its Consequences (with Introd. by Theodore Roosevelt), 1919; Leonard Wood Administrator, Soldier and Citizen, 1920; Earth Evolution and Its Facial Expression, 1921; Cruises Along By-ways of the Pacific, 1923; The Glacial Anti-cyclones, 1926; Exploring About the North Pole of the Winds, 1930; Peary, 1936; Explorers of the Antarctic, 1941; Fortress Islands of the Pacific, 1945; Glacial Studies of the Pleistocene of N. Am., 1947; (autobiography) An Explorer-Scientist's Pilgrimage 1952. Adv. mem. O.S.S., 1941-45. Designer project for combined open-cut and tunnel sea-level ship-canal across Tehuantenec Isthmus in Mexico, sea level ship-canal across Honduras, 1952. Home: 1005 Berkshire Road, Ann Arbor, Mich. Died Jan. 1, 1953.

HOBSON, JESSE EDWARD, consultant, university adminstr; b. Marshall, Ind. May 2, 1911; s. Clayton Arthur and Alice N. (Newlin) H.; B.S. in Electrical Engineer, Purdue University, 1932, M.S., 1933, Doctor of Engring., 1957; Ph.D., Cal. Inst. Tech., Pasadena, 1935; m. Anne Warren, July 8, 1934 (div., Dec., 1949); 1 dau., Carolyn Jean; m. 2d, Louise Smith Taylor, June 30, 1950. Assistant prof. mathematics, Earlham Coll., Richmond, Ind., 1935-36; instr. elec. engring., Armour Inst. Tech., Chicago, 1936-37; central station engr., Westinghouse Elec. & Mfg. Co., Pittsburgh, Pa., 1937-41; dir. and prof. elec. engring., Ill. Inst. Tech., Chicago, 1941-44; director of Armour Research Foundation, 1944-48; dir. Stanford Research Inst., 1948-56; v.p. United Fruit Co., Boston, 1957-61, director of research, 1958-61; v.p. So. Meth. U., 1963-65; pres. Heald Hobson & Assos., 1966-70; exec. dir. Tager (Dallas), 1966-67; cons. in research mgmt. and planning; dir. planning and devel. Southwest Research Institute, San Antonio, Tex.; Tau Beta Pi. Research Fellow, 1932-33; Charles Coffin Found. Research Fellow, 1933-34. Exec. chmn. 1st Nat. Electronics Conf., 1944; chmn. bd. Nat. Electronics Conf., Inc., 1945; bd. adv. Purdue Research Found. Recipient Outstanding Young Elec. Engrs. Award, 1940. Fellow I.E.E.E.; mem. Western Soc. Engrs., Am. Soc. Engring. Edn., N.Y. Acad. Scis., Tau Beta Pi, Sigma Xi, Eta Kappa Nu (nat. pres. 1954-55). Episcopalian. Mason. Clubs: University (Chgo.); Engineers (N.Y.C.); California (Los Angeles). Home: Los Angeles CA Died Nov. 5, 1970; buried Popular Grove Cemetery, Marshall IN

HOBSON, ROBERT LOUIS, indsl. psychologist; b. Blountstown, Fla., Aug. 15, 1918; s. Claude C. and Lenna S. (Van Gundy) H.; A.B., Grinnell Coll., 1940; M.S., Purdue U., 1943, Ph.D., 1948; m. Elizabeth A. Maxwell, Aug. 15, 1941; children—Barbara L., James A., Caroline A., Henry C., Linda S., William T. Lab. instr. Grinnell Coll., 1940-41; pvt. practice indsl. psychology cons., 1941-72; purchasing and materials control Nat. Homes Corps., 1942-44; vocational appraiser Purdue U., 1946-47, test editor div. edn. reference, 1947-48; tng. cons., maintenance Am. Airlines, 1955-57; with psychology dept. U. Tulsa, 1946-73, head dept., 1956-70; personnel cons. Skelly Oil Co., 1965-73. Dir. research Nat. Tng. Dirs. Joint Elec. Apprentice Programs. Served with USAAF, 1944-45. Mem. Am., Midwest, S.W. psychol. assns., Grinnell Friars, Tulsa Personnel Group, Tulsa Tng. Group, Sigma Xi, Psi Chi. Mason. Contbr. articles to profl. publs. Inventor flexible gunnery trainer. Home: Tulsa OK Died Jan. 8, 1973.

HOCH, PAUL H., psychiatrist, educator, state ofcl.; b. Hungary, Oct. 31, 1902; s. Hugh Henry and Olga (Pollach) H.; M.D., U. Goettingen, (Germany), 1926; m. to Barbara Griffiths, November 24, 1960. Came to U.S., 1933, naturalized, 1939. Intern U. Goettingen, 1927-28; asst. physician Psychiat. Clinic, Zurich, Switzerland, 1928-30; first asst. physician charge brain research div. U. Goettingen, 1930-33; asst. physician Manhattan State Hosp., N.Y.C., 1933-42; cons. psychiatry USPHS, 1942-43; asst. clin. psychiatrist N.Y. State Psychiat. Inst., N.Y.C., 1943-46, sr. clin. psychiatrist, 1946-48, prin. research psychiatrist, 1848—; asso. attending psychiatrist Frances Delafield Hosp., N.Y.C., 1952—; commr. mental hygiene State of N.Y., Albany, 1955—; asst. prof. psychiatry and neurology U. Goettingen, 1932; with Columbia, 1944—, beginning as instr. psychiatry, successively teaching and research collaborator Psychoanalytic Clinic, asso. psychiatry Coll. Phys. and Surgs., asst. prof. psychiatry, prof. clin. psychiatry, Coll. Phys. and Surg., Columbia, 1956—, attending psychiatrist Psychoanalytic Clinic, 1951—. Diplomate Am. Bd. Psychiatry and Neurology. Fellow N.Y. Acad. Medicine, Am. Psychiat. Assn., A.M.A.; mem. N.Y. County, N.Y. State med. socs., Am. Psychopath. Assn., Am. Acad. Neurology, Soc. Biol. Psychiatry, N.Y. Neurol. Soc., N.Y. Soc. Clin. Psychiatry, N.Y. Acad. Scis. Author: (with others) Shock Treatment, Psychosurgery and Other Somatic Treatments in Psychiatry, 1952. Asso. editor of Am. Jour. Psychiatry, Psychosomatic Medicine; editor: (with others) Anxiety, 1950; (with others) Failures in Psychiatric Treatment, 1948. Contbr. articles sci. publs. U.S., Germany, S.A. Home: 65 E. 96th St., N.Y.C. Office: N.Y. State Psychiatric Institute, N.Y.C.; also Dept. Mental Hygiene, Gov. Alfred E. Smith Bldg., Albany, N.Y. Died Dec. 15, 1964.

HOCHSTETTER, ROBERT WILLIAM, chemist; b. Cincinnati, Aug., 1873; s. William and Agnes (Hartmann) H.; early edn. Cincinnati pub. schs.; grad. U. of Cincinnati, 1895; postgrad. studies at Federal Polytechnic, Zurich, Switzerland; unmarried. Pres. Am. Chem. Soc., 1902; v.-p. Ault & Wiborg Co. Home: Oak St., Mt. Auburn, O. Office: 7th and Culvert St., Cincinnati OH

HOCHWALD, FRITZ G(ABRIEL), chemist; b. Berlin, Germany, July 23, 1897; s. Moritz and Elsa (Stahl) H.; grad. Berlin Inst. Tech., 1923, Dr. Chem. Engring., 1925; patent law exam., Germany, 1928, U.S., 1945; m. Ilse Eva Wolfsberg, Dec. 29, 1943. Came to U.S., 1943, naturalized, 1947. Admitted to patent law practice, 1928; research chemist Bavarian Cyanamid Co., 1923-28; head central patent dept. German Cyanamid Cos., 1928-38; practice before U.S. and Canadian patent offices, 1945-68, before German Patent Office, 1967-68. Served as lt., Signal Corps, German Army, 1915-19. Mem. Am. Chem. Soc., Washington Acad. Scis., Botanical Society of Washington, New York Patent Law Assn., Internat. Patent and Trademark Assn. Contbr. profl. publs., Germany. Patents cyanamid and accumulator fields. Home: Washington DC Died May 6, 1968.

HODGDON, FRANK WELLINGTON, civil engr.; b. West Cambridge (now Arlington), Mass., Jan. 12, 1856; s. Richard Lord and Maria (Wellington) H.; B.S. in C.E., Mass. Inst. Tech., 1876; m. Grace M. Plumer, Oct. 1886. Engr., Harbor and Land Commrs. of Mass. until 1912; chief engr. Dirs. of Port of Boston, 1912-16; engr. Commn. on Waterways and Pub. Lands, Mass., 1916-20; chief engr. Mass. Dept. of Pub. Works, div. of waterways and pub. lands, 1920—. Republican. Unitarian. Home: Arlington, Mass. Died Jan. 25, 1923.

HODGE, CLIFTON FREMONT, biologist; b. at Janesville, Wis., Oct. 16, 1859; s. Nelson Wellington (of St. Martin's Island, W.I.) and Mary E. (Merrill) H.; A.B., Ripon Coll., 1882; Ph.D., Johns Hopkins, 1889; m. at Ripon, Wis., Thekla Johanna Eversz, of Wesel, Germany, Sept. 25, 1888. Civil engr., Mont., 1882-86; instr. in biology, U. of Wis., 1891-92; asst. prof. biology, 1892, and prof. biology, Clark U. and collegiate dept. same, 1902-14; later prof. civic biology, Univ. of Ore. Mem. American Physiol. Soc., Assn. Am. Anatomists, Am. Soc. Naturalists, Mass. Forestry Assn., Am. Forestry Assn., Am. Ornithologists' Union; pres. Am. Nature-Study Soc., 1909. Author: Nature Study and Life, 1902. Contbr. to scientific jours. on fatigue of nerve cells, physiology of alcohol, dynamic biology, domestication of ruffed grouse and Bobwhite, and other biol., morphol. and physiol. subjects. Address: 125 Buffalo Av., Takoma Park, D.C.

HODGE, HENRY WILSON, civil engr.; b. Washington, Apr. 14, 1865; s. John Ledyard and Susan Savage (Wilson) H.; C.E., Rensselaer Poly. Inst., 1885; m. Sarah Cunningham Mills, Dec. 14, 1897. Asst. engr. Phoenix Bridge Co., Phila., 1885-91; chief engr. Union Iron Works, New York, 1891-93; mem. Boller, Hodge & Baird, consulting engrs., 1899—; pres. The Porterfield Construction Co. Designed municipal bridge over Miss. River, at St. Louis, G.N. R.R. bridge, Duluth, Minn., C.,R.I.&P. bridge, Little Rock, Ark., all bridges for Choctaw, Okla. & Gulf R.R., Nat. R.R. Co. of Mex., and for Wabash-Pittsburgh Terminal Co., including the large cantilever bridges over Monongahela River and Ohio River, the former the largest R.R. bridge in U.S. Engr. for City of New York for Melrose Av. viaduct, 96th St. bridge; commr. for Blackwell's Island bridge and Manhattan Suspension bridge over East River; cons. engr. for Brooklyn Rapid Transit Co., N.Y. and N.J. Interstate Bridge and Tunnel Commn., and many other corps., etc. Apptd. pub. service commr., State of N.Y., Jan. 1916, resigned July 1917; commd. major Engr. R.C.U.S.A., and dir. of rys. in France, July 1917—. Presbyn. Republican. Home: New York, N.Y. Died Dec. 21, 1919.

HODGE, WALTER ROBERTS, mining engr.; b. Kirkwood, Mo., Apr. 1, 1884; s. Clarence Walcot and Mary (Roberts) H.; B.S. and E.M., Mich. Coll. of Mines, 1907; m. Olive C. Croze, June 29, 1908. Engr. and mill supt. for Carpenter, Brennon & Ryan, Salinas, Mex., 1907-10; exploration work in Shining Tree Dist., Ont., Can., 1911, 12; chief engr. mines dept., Tenn. Copper Co., Jan. 1913-20; private practice, 1920-21; inspector Minn. State Highway constrn., 1921-22; mining engr. Mariska Mine, 1922-23; supt. Delta Mine, 1923-24; mng. editor Skillings Mining Review, 1924—. Republican. Sigma Rho. Home: Duluth, Minn. Died Apr. 24, 1940.

HODGE, WILLIAM IRVINE, engr.; b. Salt Lake City, Jan. 7, 1905; s. Robert Henderson and Margaret (Irvine) H.; student U. Utah, 1924-26, Columbia, 1928-30; m. Doris Magee, Apr. 16, 1943. Design engr. Gibbs & Hill, cons. engrs., N.Y.C., 1927-28, Amalgamated Sugar Co., Ogden, Utah, 1933-43; v.p. Utah-Ida. Central R.R., Ogden Transit Co., Ogden, 1944-45, bd. dir.; chief engr. Vitorio-minas R.R. project in Brazil, Raymond-Morrison-Knudsen, 1946-47; prin. engr. Bechtel Corp., Los Angeles, 1948-50; West Coast mgr. Bulkley Dunton Processes, Inc., Los Angeles, 1951-53; supr. N. Am. Aviation, Los Angeles, 1953-58; project engr. Gen. Dynamics-Convair, San Diego, 1958-70; dir. Yucca Mut. Irrigation Dist., Fallbrook, Cal. Mem. Nat., Cal., Ida. socs. profl. engrs., Soc. Am. Mil. Engrs., Phi Delta Theta, Nat. Mgmt. Assn., C. of C. Clubs: Kiwanis, Ogden Weber, Ogden Country, Ogden Gun, Convair Gun. Home: San Diego CA Died Mar. 3, 1970.

HODGES, HARRY FOOTE, army officer; b. Boston, Mass., Feb. 25, 1860; s. Edward Fuller and Anne Frances (Hammatt) H.; Boston Latin Sch. and Adams Acad., Quincy, Mass.; grad. U.S. Mil. Acad., 1881; m. Alma L'Hommedieu Raynolds, Dec. 8, 1887 (died 1926); children—Antoinette (dec.), Frances (widow of Col. A. H. Acher), Alma Louise (Mrs. G. L. Dickson), Duncan. Additional 2d lt., June 11, 1881; promoted through grades to maj. gen. N.A., Aug. 5, 1917; maj. gen. regular army, Dec. 21, 1921; retired Dec. 22, 1921. Lt. col. 1st U.S. Vol. engrs., June 10, 1898; col., Jan. 21, 1899; hon. mustered out. Jan. 25, 1899. Served with battalion of engrs. and on river and harbor duty, 1881-88; instr. and asst. prof. engring., U.S. Mil. Acad., 1888-92; river and harbor, and fortification duty, 1892-98; in field in P.R., 1898-99; river and harbor duty, 1899-1901; chief engr. Dept. of Cuba, 1901-02; in office of chief of engrs., U.S.A., 1902-07; gen. purchasing officer, asst. chief engr. and mem. Isthmian Canal Commn., 1907-14; in charge design of locks, dams and regulating works, Panama Canal; engr. of maintenance, Panama Canal, 1914-15; given thanks of Congress and advanced in rank Mar. 4, 1915; comdg. N. and Middle Atlantic Coast Arty. dists., 1915-17; comdg. 76th Div., U.S.A., Aug. 25, 1917-Jan. 1, 1919, at Camp Devens, Mass., and with A.E.F. in France; comdg. 20th Div., Camp Sevier, S.C., and Camp Travis, Tex., Jan. 1-July 1, 1919; comdg. N. Pacific and 3d Coast Arty. districts, July 1, 1919-Dec. 21, 1921. Awarded D.S.M. Episcopalian. Home: Lake Forest, Ill. Died Sept. 24, 1929.

HODGKINS, WILLIAM CANDLER, geodesist; b. Boston, Mass., Oct. 21, 1854; s. William E. and Ann M. (Bubier) H.; C.E., Lawrence Scientific Sch. (Harvard), 1877; m. Mary L. von Dodt, 1880. Aid and asst., 1871-1917, hydrographic and geodetic engr., July 1, 1917, U.S. Coast and Geod. Survey. Service has covered many parts of Atlantic, Gulf and Alaskan coasts, besides numerous spl. duties; relocated, 1892, circular boundary bet. Pa. and Del., originally surveyed for William Penn, 1701; took part in joint Am. and Canadian survey along Alaskan boundary, 1893; relocated part of boundary bet. Ia. and Mo., 1896; inspected survey of line bet. Greenville and Sparttanburg cos., S.C., 1896; engr. for Md. in joint marking of water boundary bet. Md. and Va., 1897; in charge survey Puerto Rico and in command U.S.S. Blake, 1898-1900; chairman commn. apptd. by Supreme Ct. of U.S. to relocate boundary bet. Va. and Tenn., 1900-02; engr. in charge resurvey "Mason and Dixon's line" bet. Pa. and Md., 1900-03; cartographer to U.S. agency before Alaskan Boundary Tribunal, London, 1903; in command U.S.S. Patterson, on Alaska sta., 1905-08; in command U.S.S. Bache, Atlantic Coast and P.R., 1909-13; dir. coast surveys in P.I., 1914-Mar. 1916; insp. in charge of Boston Field Sta., June 25, 1919—. Author: An Historical Account of the Boundary Line Between Pennsylvania and Delaware, 1894. Deceased.

HODGKINSON, FRANCIS, mech. engr., inventor; b. London. Eng., June 16, 1867; s. Francis Otter and Margaret H.; ed. Royal Naval Sch., New Cross, London; night courses, Durham U.; m. Edith Marion Kate Piercy, June 1, 1897; children—Francis Piercy, George Arthur, William Sampson. Apprentice Clayton & Shuttleworth, Agrl. engrs., 1882-85; with C. A. Parsons Co., advancing to supt. field work, 1885-90; engr. Chilean Navy, 1890-92, later identified with telephone and elec. light engring. in Peru; with C. A. Parsons & Co., 1894-96; with Westinghouse Electric & Mfg. Co. since 1896, cons. mech. engr. of its South Phila. and East Pittsburgh works on retirement in 1936; appointed hon. prof. mech. engring., Columbia U. Widely known as designer and builder of steam turbines. Awarded Elliott Cresson gold medal, Franklin Inst., 1925; Holley gold medal, Am. Soc. Mech. Engrs., 1938; awarded 101 patents, principally in field of steam turbines. Mem. Am. Soc. Mech. Engrs., Am. Inst. E.E., Engrs. Soc. of Western Pa., Inst. of Mech. Engrs. of Great Britain. Clubs: Engineers' (New York). Contbr. many articles on tech. subjects. Home: 138 E. 36th St., New York, N.Y. Died Nov. 4, 1949. *

HODGSON, ALBERT JAMES, (hod'sun), surgeon; b. Waukesha, Wis., Nov. 9, 1858; s. John and Hannah (Seller) H.; student Carroll Coll., Waukesha, 1872-77; M.D., Rush Medical Coll., Chicago, 1886 Sc.D., Carroll Coll., 1916; m. 2d, Flora Christensen, Nov. 3, 1925. In gen. practice in Waukesha, 1886-92; specialized in treatment of diabetes and Bright's disease since 1892 (recognized as an authority on the subjects); founder Still Rock Hosp. for treatment of diabetes mellitus and Bright's disease, 1909, Still Rock Spa, 1912, inc. as Waukesha Spa Co., of which is ex-pres. Mem. Am., Wis. State and Waukesha County med. socs. Republican. Has read various papers on treatment of kidney diseases before A.M.A. and Can. Med. Assn. Home: Jupiter, Fla. Died Oct. 5, 1943.

HODGSON, CAREY VANDERVORT, geodetic engr.; b. Wilmington, O., July 11, 1880; s. Lorenzo Dow and Clara Emma (Hyatt) H.; B.S., Wilmington Coll., 1902; B.S., Haverford Coll., 1903; m. Edith Hockett, Apr. 17, 1916; 1 son, William Hockett. With Coast and Geodetic Survey, 1904—, except when in mil. service; on geodetic work, 1911—; field observations for first order triangulation, astronomic latitudes and longitudes, 1911-20; asst. chief Div. of Geodesy, 1920—. Capt. and maj. Corps of Engrs., U.S.A., 1917-19; served overseas with 29th Div. Quaker. Mason. Author: Utah-Washington Arc of Primary Triangulation, 1922; Manual of First Order Triangulation, 1926; Manual of Third Order Triangulation and Traverse, 1928. Home: Washington, D.C. Died May 19, 1929.

HODGSON, JOSEPH PARK, mine mgr.; b. Swathrmoor, Lancashire, Eng., Aug. 19, 1869; s. Wilson Park and Jane H.; ed. night schs., Ishpeming, Mich., 2 yrs., and corr. course Alexander Hamilton Inst., New York; married Ellen Jewell, Apr. 19, 1890; married 2d, Clara W. Naylor, July 2, 1932. Came to U.S., 1889, naturalized citizen, 1894. Miner, timberman, foreman, Lake Superior Iron Co., and Oliver Mining Co., Ishpeming, 1889-1907; asst. supt., supt. and gen. supt. Breitung Mines, Negaunee, Mich., 1907-12; supt. mines Copper Queen Consol. Mining Co., Bisbee, Ariz., 1912-16; apptd. cons. engr. mining dept., Phelps Dodge Corp., Ariz. and New York, 1918, also mgr. mines and reduction plants, same corp., Morenci and Bisbee, Ariz.; became cons. mining engr. Phelps Dodge Corp.; now retired. County supervisor Marquette County, Mich., 6 yrs.; formerly regent, U. of Ariz. Mem. Am. Inst. Mining and Metall. Engrs., Lake Superior Mining Inst., Am. Mining Congress. Republican. Presbyn. Mason (32 deg., K.T., Shriner). Contbr. on mining topics to tech. publs. Home: 1228 Selby Av., Los Angeles 24 CA

HODGSON, ROBERT WILLARD, educator; b. Dallas, Apr. 3, 1893; s. Mark and Olivia (Rice) H.; B.S., U. Cal., 1916, M.S., 1917, LL.D., 1865; m. Evelyn Mitchell, Aug. 20, 1930; children—Robert Willard, Richard Warren. Asst. in botany U. Cal., 1916-17, instr. citriculture, 1917-19; asst. farm adviser, Los Angeles County, 1918-19, farm advisor, 1919-24; asso. prof. subtropical horticulture U. Cal., 1924-34, prof. since 1934; asso. citriculturist in Expt. Sta., 1924-29, subtropical horticulturist since 1929; asst. dir. Br. Coll. Agr. in So. Cal., U. Cal., Los Angeles, 1932-38, asst. dean 1943-52, dean Coll. Agr. (Los Angeles br.), asst. dir. expt. sta., 1952—; chmn. Walnut Control Bd., 1950—; vice chmn. Navel Orange Adminstrn. Com., 1953—; mem. adminstrn. com. Inter-Am. Inst. Agrl. Scis., Costa Rica, 1955—; adv. to govt. Tunsia, govt. Egypt, govt. Patiala (India) and to citrus and subtropical fruit growers in Palestine, Morocco and Central Am.; cons. in agrl. edn. U. Concepcion, Chile, cons. in sub-tropical horticulture Ministry of Agr., Chile, 1957. Decorated Officier de Merite Agricole (France); Fulbright Research Award Egypt, 1951-52. Fellow A.A.A.S.; mem. Am. Soc. Hort. Sci., Assn. Am. Geographers, N.Y. Acad. Sci., Phi Beta Kappa, Sigma Xi, Phi Delta Kappa, Phi Sigma, Alpha Zeta. Decorated Nichan Iftikhar (Tunisia), Ouissam Alaouite (Morroco); awarded Aztec emblem, Cal. Avocado Soc., 1940, others. Republican. Methodist. Home: 601 Bonhill Rd., Los Angeles 90049. Office: U. Cal., Los Angeles 24. Died May 17, 1966; buried Forest Lawn Meml. Park, Glendale, Cal.

HOE, RICHARD MARCH, inventor, mfr.; b. N.Y.C., Sept. 12, 1812; s. Robert and Rachel (Smith) H.; m. Lucy Gilbert; m. 2d, Mary Gay Corbin; 5 children. Patented new method of grinding circular saws; designed and put into prodn. single large cylinder press (1st flat bed and cylinder press ever used in U.S.); introduced rotary press which remained world leader for 25 years, 1847; introduced stop cylinder press, 1853; built web press, 1871; his printing inventions (by increasing speed and volume) made possible modern day journalism and immense circulation of daily newspapers. Died Florence, Italy, June 7, 1886.

HOE, ROBERT, mfr.; b. Hoes, Eng., Oct. 29, 1784; s. Thomas and Elizabeth H.; m. Rachel Smith, 3 children including Richard M. Came to N.Y., 1803; with Smith, Hoe & Co., carpentry firm specializing in printer's presses, 1805-23; began mfg. power press, circa 1830; improved upon Napier's cylinder press which soon replaced all English presses. Died Jan. 4, 1833.

HOEN, AUGUST, lithographer, cartographer; b. Nassau, Germany, Dec. 28, 1817; s. Martin and Eliza (Schmidt) H.; m. Caroline (Muth) Weber, Feb. 1849, at least 1 son, Albert B. Came with his family to U.S., 1835; worked for E. Weber & Co. (lithography firm operated by his cousin), Balt., circa 1837, name changed to A. Hoen & Co. upon Weber's death, 1849, printed 1st color show cards in U.S., 1830; printed lithographed maps illustrating Fremont's expdn. in 1840's; patented method of reproduction known as Lithpkaustic, 1860; developed method of map symbolism making it possible to differentiate subdivisions of geol. periods. Died Sept. 20, 1886.

HOERR, NORMAND LOUIS, anatomist; b. Peoria, Ill., May 3, 1902; s. Christian J. and Lydia (Dallinger) H.; student Bradley U., 1919-21; A.B., Johns Hopkins, 1923; Ph.D., U. Chgo., 1929, M.D., 1931; m. Virginia Collier Gale, Sept. 10, 1927. Chemist, Dupont Co., 1923-24; instr. anatomy U. Chgo., 1926-33, asst. prof., 1933-39; prof. anatomy Western Res. U., 1939—, now found. prof. and dir. anatomy dept. Mem. A.A.A.S., Am. Assn. Anatomists (sec.-treas. 1946—), Soc. Exptl. Biology and Medicine, Cleve. Acad. Medicine, Sigma Xi, Alpha Omega Alpha, Phi Beta Pi. Republican. Baptist. Editor: Frontiers in Cytochemistry, Biological Symposia X, 1943; asso. editor: Gary's Anatomy, 1942, Medical Physics, 1944; co-editor: Blakiston-Gould Medical Dictionary, 1949. Home: 2792 Scarborough Rd., Cleveland Heights 18, O. Office: 2109 Adelbert Rd., Cleve. 6. Died 1958.

HOFF, JOHN EDWARD, educator, civil engr.; b. Comanche, Tex., Mar. 12, 1906; s. John Peter and Emma Sophia (Rea) H.; A.S. in Civil Engring., John Tarleton Agrl. Coll., 1924; B.S. in Civil Engring., U. Tex., 1927, M.S., 1929; m. Johnnie A. Durst, May 16, 1936; children—Barbara (Mrs. Donald Woodsmall), Candy. Researcher, insp. concrete pavement Tex. Hwy. Dept., 1927-29; chief engr. lease, surveys and gen. constrn. Lloyd Oil Corp., Ft. Worth, 1929-30; bridge designer, estimator Tex. Hwy. Dept., 1930-31; pres., gen. mgr. Comanche Milling co., 1931-40; engr. design and estimates on constrn. Camp Bowie, Tex. for Koch & Fowler Co., 1940-41; faculty U. Houston, 1941—, prof. civil engring., 1949—, chmn. dept., 1950-64, varsity tennis coach 1946—. Mayor, Comanche, 1935-39. Registered profl. engr., Tex. Mem. Nat., Tex. socs. profl. engrs., Am. Soc. C.E. Am. Soc. Engring. Edn., Houston Engring. and Sci. Soc., Tau Beta Pi, Omicron Delta Kappa. Lion (past pres. Comanche). Home: 4380 Varsity Lane, Houston 4. Died Dec. 8, 1966.

HOFF, OLAF, civil engr.; b. Smaalenene, Norway, Apr. 2, 1859; s. Martin C. and Gunhild (Smaadal) H.; grad. in engring., Poly. Inst., Christiania, 1879, and came to America same yr.; m. Josie Johnson, June 25, 1885. Engr. with Keystone Bridge Co., Pittsburgh, Pa., 1880; with Mexican Central Ry., 1881-83, Shiffler Bridge Works, Pittsburgh, 1883-85; cons. and contracting engr., Minneapolis, 1885-1901; in charge of bridges and bldgs., N.Y.C.&H.R. R.R., 1901-05; v.p. and chief engr. Butler Bros.-Hoff Co., gen. contractors, 1905-08; consulting engr., New York, 1908—; mem. Arthur McMullen & Hoff Co. Devised and executed method for tunneling Detroit River at Detroit, 1906-09, also the subway tunnel under Harlem River at N.Y. City, 1912-15, by constructing the tunnels from the water's surface; chief consultant to Cunard Steamship Co., Ltd., in connection with proposed steamship terminal in port of N.Y. Home: Montclair, N.J. Died Dec. 24, 1924.

HOFFMAN, FREDERICK LUDWIG, statistician; b. Varel, N. Germany, May 2, 1865; s. Augustus Franciscus and Antoinette (von Laar) H.; common school and private education in Germany; LL.D., Tulane U., 1911; m. Ella G. Hay; children—Ella, Frances, Armstrong, Virginia, Gilbert Hay, Barbara, Victoria. Cons. statistician of Prudential Ins. Co. of America, 1894-1934; cons. statistician Biochemical Research Foundation of Franklin Institute, Phila., to 1938; retired. Ex-pres. Am. Statis. Assn.; fellow A.A.A.S., Royal Statis. Soc., Royal Anthropol. Inst.; hon. corr. mem. Actuarial Soc. Switzerland; asso. fellow A.M.A.; asso. mem. Am. Acad. Medicine; hon. mem. Nat. Inst. Homoeopathy, German Cancer Research Soc.; charter mem. Nat. Tuberculosis Assn.; dir. Am. Public Health Assn., Am. Society Control of Cancer; mem. Nat. Safety Council, Safety Inst. of America, Am. League to Abolish Capital Punishment (v.p.); hon. pres. Nat. Malaria Soc., 1944; dir. Nat. Foundation for Care of Advanced Cancer Patients, 1944. Awarded Clement Cleveland medal by Am. Soc. for Control of Cancer, 1943. Dir. Health Survey of the Printing Trades; dir. San Francisco Cancer Survey; mem. London Cancer Conf., 1928. Author of numerous brochures, books, etc., some of which are The Race Traits and Tendencies of the American Negro, 1896; History of the Prudential Ins. Co. of America, 1900; Insurance Science and Economics, 1911; Facts and Fallacies of Compulsory Health Insurance, 1917; Annual Record of Homicide and Suicide (Spectator, N.Y.), 1910-23; Cancer and Civilization, Belgian Nat. Cancer Congress, 1923; also in 1926, Cancer in Canada; Cancer in Native Races; The Homicide Problem; Windstorm and Tornado Insurance; and in 1927, Cancer and Overnutrition; Industrial Insurance; fourth to seventh reports on San Francisco Cancer Survey, 1928-31; Suicide Problem, 1928; Earthquake, Hazards and Insurance, 1928; Problems of Longevity, 1929; also repts. and papers; Malaria in Mississippi and Adjacent States, 1931; 9th and final San Francisco Cancer Rept., 1934; Final Results of the San Francisco Cancer Survey, 1932; Malaria in India and Ceylon, 1933; Cancer in British Malaya and the Philippine Islands, 1933; Cancer in Spain, 1933; Cancer in Iceland, Cancer and Diet, 1937; Deaths from Lead Poisoning, 1943 and Earlier Years. Was v.p. Congress of Royal Inst. of Pub. Health, Ghent, Belgium; mem. 8th Internat. Actuarial Congress, London; mem. 1st Internat. Civil Aeronautics Congress, Washington, D.C., 1928; speaker on cancer before Pan Pacific Surg. Conf., Honolulu, H.T. Home: 1978 Sunset Blvd., San Diego, Calif. Died Feb. 24, 1946.

HOFFMAN, GEORGE MATTHIAS, army engr.; b. Wilkes-Barre, Pa., June 15, 1870; s. Matthias and Margaretha (Schwab) H.; grad. U.S. Mil. Acad., 1896; grad. Army War Coll., 1921; m. Ruth Thompson, Dec. 5, 1901; children—George Matthias, Richard Thompson, Mary. Commd. 2d lt., May 18, 1896; promoted through grades to col. engrs., July 1, 1920. Served in Span.-Am. War and World War; served on Panama Canal and various river and harbor works; apptd. mem. Miss. River Commn., 1927. Awarded D.S.M. (U.S.). Died Nov. 1, 1936.

HOFFMAN, JAMES DAVID, practical mechanics; b. Auburn, Ind., Jan. 23, 1868; s. Daniel Zinn and Rachael Catharine (Goetschius) H.; B.M.E., Purdue, 1890, M.E., 1893; m. Kate Blanche Peterson, Aug. 7, 1890 (died 1902); m. 2d, Zoelah M. Burroughs, Aug. 3, 1913; 1 son, James David. Apprentice machinist with Auburn Foundry and Machine Co., 1883-86; draftsman and designer Buckeye Engine Co., Salem, O., summer 1890; became connected with Purdue U., 1890, successively instr. and asst. prof. in practical mechanics, asst. prof. machine design, asso. prof. and prof. engring. design until 1911; prof. mech. engring. and practical mechanics, U. of Neb., 1911-17; again with Purdue U. as prof. practical mechanics, 1917—, also head of dept., dir. practical mechanics lab. and dir. curriculum of industrial education. Presbyn. Author: Hand Book for Heating and Ventilating Engrs., 1910, 3d edit., 1920; (with C. H. Benjamin) Machine Design, 1913; Elements of Machine Design (with L. A. Scipio), 1928. Home: West Lafayette, Ind. Died Aug. 15, 1938.

HOFFMAN, JAMES I., chemist; b. Enterline, Pa., Oct. 26, 1893; s. Peter and Ida Elizabeth (Shoop) H.; A.B., Franklin and Marshall Coll., 1918, Sc.D., 1943; M.S., George Wash. U., 1921; Ph.D., Am. U., 1930; m. Mabel Hemminger, Dec. 16, 1921; 1 son, John Drake. Tchr. pub. schs. Pa., 1913-16; tchr. grad. schs., dept. agr. George Wash. U., 1936-47. Am. U., 1931-36; chief, sect. surface chemistry Nat. Bur. Standards, 1947-56, asst. chief chemistry div., 1952-56, chief metallurgy div., 1956-61, cons. to dir., 1961-62. Army as sgt. in inf. and chem. warfare, World War I. Awarded Hillebrand prize in chemistry for work on atomic energy and aluminum from clay, 1947; Fisher award Am. chem. Soc., 1959. Mem. Am. Soc. for Metals, Wash. Acad. Scis. (editor), Am. Chem. Soc. (councilor), Sigma Xi, Alpha Chi Sigma, Phi Beta Kappa. Club: Cosmos. Author books including: Outlines of Methods of Chemical Analysis (with G. E. F. Lundell). Contbr. articles. Died Jan. 1964.

HOFFMAN, JOHN WESLEY, agriculturist, educator; b. Charleston, S.C., Aug. 11, 1870; s. Henry and Barbara H.; is a colored man; ed. Avery Normal Sch., Charleston, S.C., Albion Coll., Mich., Mich. Agr'l Coll.; grad. Howard Univ., Washington, 1889, D.Sc., State Univ. of Ky.; sp'l studies in agriculture and biology; prof. agr. and biology, Tuskegee Inst., 1894-6, State A. & M. Coll., Orangeburg, S.C., and Florida State Industrial Coll.; now prof. agriculture, Lincoln Inst., Jefferson City, Mo. Originated a new strawberry called the "Hoffman Seedling Strawberry"; demonstrated that a grade of tea can be grown in Florida that would be superior in every way to imported teas; prepared for U.S. Dept. Agr. a dietary study of the kind and quality of food used by the Negro of the "Black Belt" of the South, which has been translated into several languages for use by scientists; introduced farmers' insts. among colored people of South. Fellow Royal Micros. Soc. of England, fellow Royal Agr'l Soc., Am. Geog. Soc.; mem. A.A.A.S. At Lagos, West Africa, 1903-4, in service of British Colonial Dept. of Agr., as dir. of the cotton industry, engaged in introducing cotton growing into that country. Home: Charleston, S.C. Address: Lincoln Institute, Jefferson City MO

HOFFMAN, RALPH, ornithologist; b. Stockbridge, Mass., Nov. 30, 1870; s. Ferdinand and Caroline (Bullard) H.; A.B., Harvard, 1890; m. Gertrude, d. Dr. Walter Wesselhoeft, of Cambridge, Mass., June 23, 1894. Teacher since 1891; at Browne & Nichols Sch., Cambridge, since 1891. Mem. Am. Ornithologists' Union; hon. mem. Phi Beta Kappa; mem. N.E. Bot. Club; dir. Mass. Audubon Soc. Author: Guide to the Birds of New England and Eastern New York, 1904; (joint author) Birds of Berkshire County (Berkshire Hist. and Scientific Soc., Vol. 3). Home: Belmont, Mass.

HOFMAN, HEINRICH OSCAR, metallurgist; b. Heidelberg, Germany, Aug. 13, 1852; s. Prof. Carl and Sophia (Proctor) H.; ed. U. of Heidelberg; E.M., Met.E., Sch. of Mines, Clausthal, 1877; Ph.D., Ohio U., 1889; m. Fanny E. Howell, Aug. 5, 1902. Came to U.S., 1881; practiced metallurgy, 1881-87; prof. metallurgy, Dak. Sch. of Mines, 1887-89, Mass. Inst. Tech., 1898—. Author: Metallurgy of Lead, 10th edit., 1918; Metallurgy of Iron and Steel, 2d edit., 1904; General Metallurgy, 3d edit., 1918; Metallurgy of Copper, 2d edit., 1917. Home: Jamaica Plain, Mass. Died May 28, 1924.

HOGAN, GEORGE ARCHIBALD, surgeon; b. Bibb County, Ala., Jan. 24, 1871; s. Rev. James and Margaret Elizabeth (Marshall) H.; B.S., Howard Coll., Birmingham, 1893; M.D., U. of Ala., 1896; post-grad. work, New York, 1900; m. Myra Clark Gaines, Jan. 25, 1904; children—George Archibald, Ann Marshall, James Thomas (deceased). Interne Davis Infirmary, Birmingham, 1896-98; professor chemistry, Birmingham Medical College, 1896-97; surgeon Tennessee Coal & Iron Company, 1899-1907; professor in minor surgery, Birmingham Medical College, 1907-14; member surgical staff, Hillman Hospital, 1907-28; examiner U.S. Marine Service, 1910-19; coroner Jefferson County, Ala., by apptmt., 1916-20; formerly asso. mem. Hogan Clinic; with Tenn. Coal & Iron Co., now retired. Apptd. convict surg., State of Ala., by Gov. Emmett O'Neal, 1912; report on convict camps resulted in end of convict leasing to pvt. industries in Ala. Mem. A.M.A., Ala. Med. Soc., Jefferson County Med. Soc. (v.p. 1905, 06), Phi Chi. Democrat. Baptist. Mason (Shriner), K.P., Elk, Woodmen of the World. Contbr. to Am. Medicine. Address: 1901 Bessemer Rd., Birmingham 8 AL

HOGAN, JOHN PHILIP, engr.; b. Chgo., June 12, 1881; s. Denis John and Mary A. (Duhey) H.; grad. Chgo. U. Sch., 1899; A.B., Harvard, 1903, S.B., 1904; hon. D.Engring., N.Y. U., 1940; m. Helen Scott Fargo, Oct. 4, 1929. Engr. N.Y. Rapid Transit Commn., 1904-06; asst. and div. engr. constrn. Catskill Aqueduct, 1906-17; acting dep. chief engr. N.Y. Bd. Water Supply, 1919-20; dir. N.Y. Water Power Investigation under William Barclay Parsons, 1920-23; cons. engr. Parsons, Klapp, Brinckerhoff & Douglas, now Parsons Brinckerhoff, Hogan & MacDonald, 1923-25, mem. firm since 1926; chief engr. and dir. constrn., then v.p. and chief engr. N.Y. World's Fair 1939; chmn. constrn. adv. com. Army and Navy Munitions Bd., 1940. Served in U.S. Army, May 1917-July 1919, two yrs. in France, grades from capt. engrs. to lt. col. Gen. Staff. Trustee United Engring. Socs. Mem. John Fritz Medal Bd. of Award. Mem. Am. Soc. C.E. (past pres., past v.p.), Am. Soc. M.E., Am. Inst. E.E., Soc. Am. Mil. Engrs. (1st v.p.), Harvard Engring. Soc., A.A.A.S.; gen. chmn. Constn. League of U.S.; mem. Tau Beta Pi. Awarded D.S.M., Purple Heart (U.S.); citation A.E.F.; Conspicuous Service Cross (N.Y. State); Chevalier Legion d'bonneur (French); Officer of Order of Crown of Home: 225 E. 73d St. Office: 142 Maiden Lane, N.Y.C. Died June 1966.

HOGAN, JOHN VINCENT LAWLESS, consulting engr.; b. Phila., Pa., Feb. 14, 1890; s. John Lawless and Louise Eleanor (Shimer) H.; grad. University Sch., New Haven, Conn., 1908; student Sheffield Scientific Sch. (Yale), 1908 to 1910; D.Eng., Polytechnic Institute of Brooklyn, 1957; m. Edith MacLennan Schrader; 1 son, John Vincent. With Nat. Electric Signaling Co., later Internat. Radio Telegraph Co., 1909-21, advancing to chief research engr. and mgr.; also spl. consultant to R.C.A., G.E. Co., Westinghouse Electric & Mfg. Co., etc.; now practicing on own account, engaged in applying facsimile techniques to military, indsl. and broadcast uses; special asst. to dir. of Office of Scientific Research and Development, 1943-45; pres., dir. Hogan Labs., Inc., Faximile, Inc., 1929—. Mem. Joint Tech. Adv. committee Institute Radio Engineers—E.I.A. Member patent compensation bd. A.E.C., 1949—. Decorated King Christian X's medal of Liberation, 1946; Armstrong medal, 1950; Medal of Honor, Inst. Radio Engineers, 1956. Fellow Inst. Radio Engineers (ex-pres.), Acoustical Soc. of Am., American Institute Elec. Engrs.; mem. Society American Mil. Engineers, A.A.A.S., Radio Club America, Alpha Sigma Phi. Republican. Episcopalian. Clubs: Yale, Players, Dutch Treat (N.Y.C.); Cosmos (D.C.). Author: The Outline of Radio, 1923, 25, 28. Lecturer on technical subjects. Inventor radio devices. Home: 239 Greenway S., Forest Hills 75, L.I., N.Y. Office: 155 Perry St., N.Y.C. 14. Died Dec. 29, 1960.

HOGELAND, ALBERT HARRISON, civil engr.; b. Southampton, Pa., Jan. 10, 1858; s. John and Keziah D. (Willard) H.; C.E., Lafayette Coll., Pa., 1877; m. Elizabeth T. Trego, Jan. 10, 1889; 1 dau., Anna Trego (wife of Dr. John de J. Pemberton). Rodman and leveler, St. Paul & Pacific R.R., Minn. and Dak., Apr.-Sept. 1879; leveler surveys for new ry. bet. Chicago and St. Paul, 1879-80; leveler, transitman and topographer, 1880-82, asst. engr., 1882-84, N.P. Ry.; asst. engr. St. Paul, Minneapolis & Manitoba, constrn. new lines in N.D., Apr.-Sept. 1884; asst. engr. constrn., Wis., N.P. Ry., 1884-85; with St. Paul, Minneapolis & Man. R.R. and its successor the G.N. Ry., July 1885—, as asst. engr. constrn. and maintenance lines in Minn., N.D., S.D., and Mont., 1885-90; engr. maintenance of way, Eastern dist., 1890-96; resident engr. Eastern dist., 1896-1902; asst. chief engr., 1902-03; chief engr., 1903-13, chmn. valuation committee, 1913-28, cons. engr., 1913-14, again chief engr., 1914-25, consulting engr., May 1, 1925—, G.N. Ry. Co. Presbyn. Home: St. Paul, Minn. Died May 14, 1930.

HOHMAN, LESLIE B., physician; b. Columbia, O., July 23, 1891; s. Lee and Hennie (Schlesinger) H.; A.B., U. Mo., 1912; M.D., Johns Hopkins, 1917; grad. student U. Vienna, 1924. Psychiat. tng. and residency Phipps Clinic, Johns Hopkins Hosp., 1917-22; instr. psychiatry Johns Hopkins Med. Sch., 1920-22, asso. psychiatry, 1922-43, asst. prof., 1943-46; prof. of psychiatry sch. medicine Duke, 1946-60, prof. psychiatry emeritus, 1960-72, director child guidance clinic, 1946-53; pvt. practice psychiatry, 1924-72; cons. dept. of psychiatry Duke Medical Center, Veterans Administration, U.S. Army, U.S.N. Served as 1st lt. M.C., U.S. Army, 1917-19; comdr. M.C., U.S.N., 1943-46. Mem. Am. Acad. Cerebral Palsy (past pres.), Am. Psychiat. Assn., A.A.A.S., A.M.A., Am. Neurol. Assn., Am. Psychopath. Association (councillor, past president), North Carolina, Southern medical assns., So. Psychiat. Assn. Author: As the Twig is Bent, 1939. Contbr. articles popular mags., profl. jours. Home: Durham NC Died Jan. 28, 1972; buried Druid Ridge Cemetery, Baltimore MD

HOLBROOK, FREDERICK, engineer, contractor; b. Lynn, Mass., July 20, 1861; s. Franklin F. and Anna E. (Nourse) H.; ed. pub. schs. and under pvt. tutors; m. Grace Cabot, Apr. 12, 1887. With engr. dept. U.P. R.R., 1880-88, N.Y.,N.H.&H. R.R., 1888-92; supt. for Dwight & Daly, contractors, Boston, 1902-04; an organizer Holbrook, Cabot & Rollins Corp., contractors, 1894, becoming v.p.; pres. Am. Internat. Shipbuilding Corp., 1918; pres. Grace Am. Internat. Corp.; v.p., Am. Internat. Corp. Large contractor for subway and aqueduct work for N.Y. City, also for extensive improvements for N.Y.,N.H.&H. R.R. Home: Brattleboro, Vt. Died Feb. 3, 1920.

HOLBROOK, JOHN EDWARDS, physician, zoologist; b. Beaufort, S.C., Dec. 30, 1794; s. Silas and Mary (Edwards) H.; grad. Brown U., 1815; M.D., U. Pa., 1818; m. Harriott Pinckney Rutledge, May 1827. A founder Med. Coll. of S.C., 1824, prof. anatomy, 1824-54; med. officer Confederate Army, head S.C. Examining Bd. of Surgeons, 1861-65; specialized in study of Am. reptiles and fishes; considered most important Am. zoologist of his time. Author: American Herpetology: or a Description of Reptiles Inhabiting the United States, 1842; Ichthyology of South Carolina, 1855, 2d edition., 1860. Died Norfolk, Mass., Sept. 8, 1871.

HOLCH, ARTHUR EVERETT, educator, plant ecologist; b. Gilman, Ill., Apr. 18, 1891; s. Frederick Godfrey and Mary Elizabeth (West) H.; B.Mus. with spl. honors, U. Ill., 1913; A.B., U. Colo., 1913, A.M., 1924; Ph.D., U. Neb., 1931; m. Hazeldean Shirley, June 8, 1915; children—Mary Shirley (Mrs. William L. Jacobs), Arthur Everett. Supt. schs., Cortez, Colo., 1913-14; prin., sci. instr. Cripple Creek (Colo.) High Sch., 1914-18; prin. Scottsbluff (Neb.) High Sch., 1918-19; asst. prof. biology, dir. band and orchestra Neb. State Tchrs. Coll., 1919-21, chmn. biology dept., 1921-32; instr. botany U. Neb., 1930-31; chmn. botany dept. Denver U., 1932—. Fellow A.A.A.S. (council 1931-32); mem. Ecol. Soc. Am., Brit. Ecol. Soc., Bot. Soc. Am., Neb. (pres. 1930-31), Colo-Wyo. acads. sci., Sigma Xi, Phi Delta Kappa, Kappa Delta Pi, Phi Sigma, Delta Sigma Rho, Pi Kappa Lambda, Pi Gamma Mu. Episcopalian. Contbr. articles profl. jours. Home: 140 Krameria St., Denver 20. Died Mar. 12, 1958.

HOLCOMB, AMASA, telescope maker; b. Southwick, Mass., June 18, 1787; s. Elijah and Lucy (Holcomb) H.; m. Gillett Kendall, 1808; m. 2d, Maria Holcomb, circa 1861. Began mfg. telescopes, circa 1825, his telescopes described as being same quality as more expensive European makes; recommended by com. on science and arts of Franklin Inst. (Phila.) for award and medal from John Scott Legacy Fund, 1835; mem. Mass. Ho. of Reps. from Southwick, 1832-33; justice of peace for Hampden County (Mass.), 1834-75. Died Southwick, Feb. 27, 1875.

HOLDEN, CHARLES ARTHUR, civil engr.; b. Hudson, Mass., July 14, 1872; s. Charles William and Martha Stearns (Willard) H.; B.S., Dartmouth, 1895, C.E., Thayer Sch. Civil Engring., 1901; m. Gertrude May Robinson, June 19, 1900. Civil engr. B. & A. R.R. Co., 1895-98; instr. civ. engring. Worcester Poly. Inst., 1898-1900; resident hydrographer U.S. Geol. Survey, 1900-04; with Thayer Sch. Civil Engring. (Dartmouth), 1900-25, prof. civil engring., 1904-25, acting dir. 1918-19, dir., 1919-25; prof. civil engring., Dartmouth, 1925-37, prof. emeritus, since July 1, 1937. Engr. for State of N.H., N.H.-Vt. boundary case, 1916-37; exec. sec. sub-com. Emergency Help and Equipment Com. N.H. Pub. Safety Com. 1917; supr. mil. tng. Dartmouth Coll. Tr. Detachment, N.A., June-Dec. 1918; mem. Mary Hitchcock Meml. Hosp. Corp. (Hanover, N.H.), Dartmouth Says. Bank Corp.; chmn. Village Precinct Commrs., Hanover, 1913-16; mem. Bd. Selectmen, Aug. 1923-Dec. 1938, chmn. bd., Jan. 1930-Dec. 1938; mem. N.H. Ho. of Rep., 1925-26, and 1941-56. Mem. N.H. Constl. Conv., 1938, 1941, 1948; proposer and sponsor resolution to prohibit diversion of motor vehicle revenues to other than hwy. purposes; passed conv. and adopted by voters of state, 1938; sponsor resolution to provide proposed constn. for a fedn. of world and a bill for jury service by women, both adopted by legislature; chmn. N.H. Hwy Conf. until 1944; dir. N.H. div., Am. Automobile Assn.; N.H. legislative rep., Regional Continuing Com. on Hwy. and Bridges Postwar Program. Mem. Thayer Soc. Engrs., U.S., N.H. good roads assns., Am. Soc. C.E., Soc. Am. Mil. Engrs., N.H. Hist. Soc., Bunker Hill Monument Assn., N.H. Assessors Assn. (pres. 1938-39), S.A.R. (pres. N.H. 1926-37), Phi Beta Kappa (Dartmouth). Clubs: Hanover Republican, Rotary (pres. 1936-37). N.H. del. Rep. Nat. Conv., 1944, 48. Author pamphlets on world fedn. Expert in ct. cases; contbr. to tech. press. Registered profl. engr. N.H. Home: 10 Occom Ridge, Hanover, N.H. Died Oct. 12, 1960.

HOLDEN, EDWARD SINGLETON, astronomer; b. St. Louis, Nov. 5, 1846; s. Edward and Sarah Frances (Singleton) H.; B.S., Washington U., 1866, A.M., 1879; grad. U.S. Mil. Acad., 1870; LL.D., U. of Wis., 1886, Columbia, 1887; Sc. D., U. of the Pacific, 1896; Litt.D., Fordham U., 1910; m. Mary Chauvenet, May 8, 1871. Lt. engrs., U.S. Army, 1870-73; prof. mathematics, U.S.N., 1873-81; dir. Washburn Obs., Wis., 1881-85; pres. U. of Calif.; 1885-88; dir. Lick Obs., 1888-98; librarian U.S. Mil. Acad., 1901—. Mem. Nat. Acad. Sciences. Knight Order of the Danebrog (Denmark); Knight Comdr. Ernestine Order of Saxony; etc. Author: Bastian System of Fortification, 1872; Index Catalogue of Nebulae, 1877; Life of Sir William Herschel, 1881; Writings of Sir William Herschel, 1881; Astronomy (with Simon Newcomb), 1887; Hand-book of the Lick Observatory, 1888; Briefer Astronomy (with Simon Newcomb), 1892; Mogul Emperors of Hindustan, 1895; Mountain Observatories, 1896; Memorials of W. C. and G. P. Bond, 1897; Pacific Coast Earthquakes, 1898; Earth and Sky, 1898; Our Country's Flag, 1898; Primer of Heraldry, 1898; Elementary Astronomy, 1899; Family of the Sun, 1899; Essays in Astronomy, 1900; Stories of the Great Astronomers; Real Things in Nature, 1903; The Sciences, 1903. Editor: Publications Washburn Observatory, 4 vols., 1881-85; Publications Lick Observatory, 3 vols., 1888-94; Centennial U.S. Military Academy, 1902 (2 vols.). Address: West Point, N.Y. Died Mar. 16, 1914.

HOLDEN, EDWIN CHAPIN, mining engr.; b. New York, Nov. 8, 1872; s. Albert James and Henrietta V. (Chambers) H.; B.S., Coll. City of New York, 1893; E.M., Sch. of Mines (Columbia), 1896; m. Grace E. Morgenroth, Sept. 19, 1908; children—Florence, Edwin C. Mining engr., supt. and mgr. various properties in British Columbia and U.S., 1897-1903; cons. mining engr., New York, 1903-08, with work in U.S., Can., Mex. and W.I.; prof. mining and metallurgy, U. of Wis., 1908-16; gen. mgr. Davison Sulphur & Phosphate Co., 1916-19; cons. engr., Davison Chem. Co. and Silica Gel Corp., 1919-32; developing mines in British Columbia, 1930-34, and in Colo. since 1934. Mem. Am. Inst. Mining and Metall. Engrs., Mining and Metall. Soc. America, Phi Gamma Delta, Sigma Xi. Unitarian. Co-author Mining Handbook. Home: 202 E. Chase St., Baltimore, Md. Deceased.

HOLDEN, ROY JAY, geologist; b. Sheboygan Falls, Wis., Oct. 21, 1870; s. Harvey J. and Sarah Diana (Danforth) H.; prep. edn., high sch., Sheboygan Falls and Wayland Acad.; B.S., U. of Wis., 1900, Ph.D., 1915; m. Elizabeth Virginia Evans, June 29, 1915; children—Sarah Virginia, Elizabeth Flora, Roy Jay. Teacher country schs., 1892-95, high sch., Sheboygan Falls, 1895-97; science teacher high sch., Beloit, Wis., 1900-02; with Va. Poly. Inst. since 1905, successively asso. in geology and mineralogy, asso. prof. and prof. geology; also consulting commercial geologist. Determined geological structure of the Valley Coal Field of Va., adding 100 sq. miles to the previously known coal-bearing territory; located the first gas well in Virginia. Fellow A.A.A.S., Geological Society America; member American Inst. Mining and Metall. Engrs., Am. Assn. of Petroleum Geologists, Soc. of Economic Geologists. Va. Acad. of Science, Phi Kappa Phi, Sigma Xi. Baptist. Author of various articles and reports on geological resources in Wis., Va., etc. Home: Blacksburg, Va. Died Dec. 16, 1945. *

HOLDER, FRANCIS JEROME, mathematician; b. Santa Fe, Fla., Aug. 11, 1876; s. Ivin and Priscilla (May) H.; B.S., Nat. Normal U., Lebanon, O., 1896; grad. Massey's Business Coll., Jacksonville, Fla. 1900; A.M., Yale, 1905, Ph.D., 1908; m. Isabella Leffingwell Pierson, June 17, 1908; children—Lois Rosalind, Mildred Louise, Curtis Raymond (dec.), Gladys May, Floyd

Pierson. Prin. high sch., Alachua, Fla., 1896-1900; v.p. and mgr. King's Business Coll., Raleigh, N.C., 1901-03; prin. Sch. of Commerce, U. of Wyo., 1908-09; head dept. of mathematics, Colby Coll., Waterville, Me., 1909-11, Buchtel Coll., Akron, O., 1911-12, U. of Pittsburgh, 1912-18; established Sch. of Commerce, Mercer U., 1918, becoming dean and head dept. of mathematics. Democrat. Missionary Baptist. Home: Macon, Ga. Died Dec. 30, 1931.

HOLDER, JOSEPH BASSET, physician, naturalist; b. Lynn, Mass., Oct. 26, 1824; s. Aaron Lummus and Rachael (Bassett) H.; m. Emily Augusta Cove, at least 1 child, Charles Frederick. City physician, Lynn; surgeon-in-chief to U.S. Engrs. on Fla. reef, 1859; studied reef formation, plant and animal life; health officer, surgeon mil. prison Ft. Jefferson, Fla., 1861-65; curator zoology sect. Am. Mus. Natural History, N.Y.C., 1881. Author: The Florida Reef; (with H.G. Wook) Our Living World. Died N.Y.C., Feb. 27, 1888.

HOLGATE, THOMAS FRANKLIN, (hol'gat); univ. prof.; b. Hastings County, Ont., Apr. 8, 1859; s. Thomas and Eleanor (Wright) H.; A.B., Victoria College, Toronto, 1884, A.M., 1889; fellow Clark University, 1890-93, Ph.D., 1893; LL.D., University of Ill., 1905, Queen's University, 1919, Northwestern University, 1937; married Julia Caroline Sharp, Aug. 12, 1885 (died 1887); m. Georgina Angela Burdette, July 23, 1890 (died 1934); children—Eleanor (Mrs. Owen Lattimore), Robert Burdette, Barbara, Frances Burdette. Prof. mathematics, Northwestern U., 1893-1934, retired 1934; dean of coll., 1902-19, acting pres., 1904-06 and 1916-19; visiting prof. U. of Nanking, China, 1921-22. Sec. Internat. Congress of Mathematicians, Rome, 1908. Mem. Chicago Pub. Library Commn., 1909; pres. North Central Assn. Colls. and Secondary Schs., 1917-18; mem. Bd. Edn. for Negroes, M.E. Ch., 1920-24; mem. Bd. of Edn., 1924-44, treas., 1934-38; pres. Chicago Ch. Fed., 1923-25. Mem. Gen. Conf. M.E. Ch., 5 times, 1920-36. Fellow A.A.A.S.; mem. Am. Math. Soc. Clubs: University (Chicago and Evanston). Author: Elementary Geometry, 1901; Projective Pure Geometry, 1930. Translator: Reye's Geometry of Position, 1898. Home: 617 Library Pl., Evanston, Ill. Died April 11, 1945.

HOLL, DIO LEWIS, math. prof.; b. North Canton, O., Jan. 7, 1895; s. of Samuel J. and Emma (Swartz) H.; ed. Canton (Ohio) high sch.; A.B., Manchester Coll., 1917; M.A., Ohio State U., 1920; Ph.D., U. of Chicago, 1925; m. Irma Nauman, Aug. 1924; children—Bruce R. William W., Barbara Elizabeth. High sch. principal, 1917; grad. asst., instr., dept. of math. Ohio State U., 1919-22; grad. fellow U. Chgo. dept. math., 1922-23; asst. prof. math. Ohio Wesleyan U., 1923-25; asst. prof. math. Iowa State Coll., 1925-30, asso. prof. math., 1930-34, prof. math., 1934—, now also head dept. math., research prof. applied math., 1937—. Abstractor of papers in applied elasticity for Zentrablatt fur Mechanik, 1934-39; in applied elasticity for Mathematical Reviews since 1940. Has published many research articles in applied mathematics. Soldier, U.S. Army, Base Hospital, Camp Sherman, Ohio, 1918-19. Mem. Am. Math. Soc., Am. Soc. M.E. (mechanics sect.), Delta Sigma Phi, Pi Mu Epsilon, Sigma Xi (sec.-treas. Iowa State Coll. chpt., 1936-41, pres. 1941-42). Presbyn. Contbr. articles to research publs. Home: 2323 Donald St., Ames, Ia. Died May 20, 1954; buried College cemetery, Ames, Ia.

HOLLADAY, WALLER, mathematician; b. Ooroomiah, Persia, April 7, 1840; s. Rev. Albert Lewis and Anne Yancey (Minor) H., Am. missionaries; grad. B.S., C.E. and M.E., Univ. of Va., 1872; (studied there, 1857-59, 1860-61 and 1871-72); m. June 24, 1873, Kate Minor Emerson (died, Aug. 25, 1891). Served in C.S.A. under Gens. Lee and Jackson; surrendered at Appomattox; was for yrs. prof. mathematics and physical sciences in Va. institutions; conducted a boys' school preparatory to college in New York, 1873-87; mathematician Equitable Life Asurance Soc., 1887-1903; became instr., 1873, and prof. mathematics, 1884-1901, now emeritus prof., Cooper Inst. Address: Fredericksburg, Va.

HOLLAND, CLIFFORD MILBURN, civil engr.; b. Somerset, Mass., Mar. 13, 1883; s. Edward John and Lydia Francis (Hood) H.; A.B., Harvard, 1905, S.B. in C.E., 1906; m. Anna Coolidge Davenport, Nov. 5, 1908. Asst. engr. East River tunnels, Rapid Transit Commn., New York, 1906-07; asst. engr. East River Tunnels and 4th Av. Subway, Pub. Service Commn., New York, 1907-15; div. engr. East River Tunnels, Public Service Commn., New York, 1915-19; chief engr. Hudson River Vehicular Tunnel, N.Y. State Bridge & Tunnel Commn. and N.J. Interstate Bridge & Tunnel Commn., 1919—. Home: Brooklyn, N.Y. Died Oct. 27, 1924.

HOLLAND, JOHN PHILIP, inventor; b. Liscanor, County Clare, Ireland, Feb. 29, 1840; s. John and Mary (Scanlon) H.; m. Margaret Foley, Jan. 17, 1887, 4 children. Taught sch., Ireland 1858-72; came to U.S., 1873, taught sch., Paterson, N.J.; offered design of submarine to U.S. Navy, 1875 (offer rejected); constructed his 1st submarine with financial backing of revolutionary Fenian Soc. (sank on 1st trial, 1878; launched Fenian Ram, 1881 (proved impractical); contracted to build submarine Plunger for U.S. Navy, 1895, but his designs were radically altered; launched his own submarine the Holland, 1898 (1st submarine equipped to move underwater by electric power and on surface by gasoline engine; 1 of 1st designed to dive by inclining its axis); sold Holland, with 6 sister ships to U.S. Navy, 1900; also built submarines for Russia, Japan, Gt. Britain; invented respirator for escape from disabled submarines 1904. Died Newark, N.J., Aug. 12, 1914.

HOLLAND, LAURIER FOX-STRANGWAYS, mining engr.; b. London, Eng.; s. Lt. Col. F. Holland (Indian Staff Corps) and Lily Mary (Everett) H.; ed. King's Coll., London; Sch. of Mining, Queen's U., Ont., Can., 1898; m. Lillian Harris, Halifax, N.S. Was metallurgist of Black Eagle Mine, Ont.; mine capt., Belmont Mine, Ont.; mill supt., Waverley Mines, N.S.; mgr. Evangeline Gold Mine, N.S.; supt. of mines for Smuggler Union Mining Co., Telluride, Colo., 1905-13; also examining engr. New England Exploration Co.; research work in rare metals, especially molybdenum, to 1916; field engr. Consol. Ariz. Smelting Co., Humboldt, Ariz., 1916-17; cons. engr. Ariz. Mines & Reduction Co., Wickenburg, Ariz., and Rare Metals Refining Co., Pasadena, Cal., 1917-19; mgr. for U.S. Smelting, Refining & Mining Co. of the Crater Mining Co., Ariz., 1920-21; research work in flotation processes, 1924; micro-paleontologist for Cal. Petroleum Corp. and the Tex. Co. (Cal.), 1925-29; pres. and gen. mgr. Golden Horseshoe Mining Corp., Ltd., to 1933; gen. mgr. Guildford Mine, Placerville, Cal., 1934; now gen. mgr., sec. Pacific Mines, Oregon Mine, Rose Mine, Texas Hill Placer, Harmon Mine, Excelsior, Epley Mine and the Missouri Flat Placer; sec. and treas. Placerville Gold Mining Co. (all at Placerville, Cal.); cons. engr. Mem. Am. Inst. Mining and Metall. Engrs., Am. Assn. Petroleum Geologists, Soc. Economic Paleontologists and Mineralogists, Legion of Honor of Am. Inst. Mining Engrs. Episcopalian. Mason. Clubs: Peter Pan Woodland (Cal.); Royal Socs. (London). Address: Placerville, Cal. Died Nov. 13, 1957; buried East Lawn Cemetery, Sacramento.

HOLLAND, MADELINE OXFORD (MRS. JOHN N. MCDONNELL), editor, cons.; b. Bangor, Pa., Aug. 3, 1916;3d. Raymond and Bertha (Oxford) Holland; B.Sc., Phila. Coll. Pharmacy and Sci., 1937, M.Sc., 1938, D.S.C., 1940; m. Dr. John N. McDonnell, Aug. 9, 1941. Instr. pharmacy Phila. Coll. Pharmacy and Sci., 1937-42; chief pharmacist McDonnell's Inc., Jenkintown, Pa., 1937-41; editor Am. Profl. Pharmacist, 1937-60; owner Sci. Adv., 1937-68; cons. pharm. marketing, pharmacology, 1937-68; sci. editor Med. Times, 1937-52; editor El Farmaceutico, 1937-52; corr. editor Pharm. Jour., London, 1960-68. Mem. bd. Women's Med. Coll. of Pa. and Hosp. Recipient ann. alumni award Alumni Assn. Phila. Coll. Pharmacy and Sci., 1957. Fellow Am. Inst. Chemists, A.A.A.S.; mem. Am. Pharm. Assn., Am. Soc. Microbiologists, Am. Chem. Soc., Fedn. Internat. Pharm., Am. Soc. Hosp. Pharmacists, Phila. Club. Advt. Women, Franklin Inst., Bus. and Profl. Women's Club (past pres. Phila.), Pa. Fedn. Bus. and Profl. Women's Clubs (past pres.), Alumni Assn. Phila. Coll. Pharmacy and Sci. (pres. 1956, dir. 1953-68), Women's Club Columbia U. Coll. Pharmacy (v.p. 1962-63), Am. Assn. U. Women, Clubs: Soroptimist (past pres. Phila., past pres. Old York Rd.); Huntingdon Valley Country (Abington, Pa.). Author numerous articles profl. jours.; also editorials in U.S. and fgn. jours. Home: Meadowbrook PA Died Oct. 1, 1968.

HOLLAND, WILLIAM J(ACOB), zoölogist, paleontologist; b. of Am. parents, Jamaica, W.I., Aug. 16, 1848; s. F. R. and Eliza Augusta (Wolle) H.; grad. Moravian Coll. and Theol. Sem., Bethlehem, Pa., 1867; A.B., Amherst, 1869, Phi Beta Kappa, A.M., 1872; grad. Princeton Theol. Sem., 1874; Ph.D., 1886, Sc.D., 1902, Washington and Jefferson; D.D., Amherst, 1888; LL.D., Dickinson, 1896, New York U., 1897, Bethany Coll., 1905, St. Andrew's, 1905; L.H.D., U. of Pittsburgh, 1928; m. Carrie T., d. John Moorhead, Jan. 23, 1879; children—Moorhead Benezet, Francis Raymond. Prin. high school, Amherst, Mass., 1860-70, Westboro, Mass., 1870-71; ordained Moravian ministry, 1872; pastor Phila., 1872-74, Bellefield Presbyn. Ch., Pittsburgh, 1874-91; chancellor of the Western U. of Pa. (now U. of Pittsburgh), 1891-1901; dir. Carnegie Inst., Pittsburgh, 1898-1922, dir. emeritus, 1922—. V.p. Carnegie Hero Fund Commn., 1904-22, pres., 1922—; mem. Carnegie Corp., 1922—. Naturalist U.S. Eclipse Expdn. to Japan, 1887, to West Africa, 1889. Ritter d. Kön. Preuss. Kronen-Ordens, III Kl.; Officier de la Légion d'Honneur, 1908; Offizier d. K.K. Franz Josefs Orden, 1909. Comdr. d. Corona d'Italia, 1910; Knight (II cl.) Order of St. Stanislas, Russia, 1911; Comdr. Ord. Civil Alfonzo XII, Spain, 1913; Comdr. Order of Crown of Belgium, 1919; was Belgian consul for Western Pa., 1918-22; authority upon zoölogy, paleontology and museum administration. Sr. trustee U. of Pittsburgh, Western Theol. Sem. Author: The Butterfly Book, 1898; The Moth Book, 1903; To the River Plate and Back, 1913; The Butterfly Guide, 1915. Editor "Annals" and "Memoirs" Carnegie Mus. Has traveled extensively in North and South America, Europe, Asia and Africa. Home: Pittsburgh, Pa. Died Dec. 13, 1932.

HOLLANDER, FRANKLIN, physiologist; b. N.Y. City, Jan. 19, 1899; s. Louis and Annie (Oshinsky) H.; B.S. magna cum laude, Columbia, 1919, Ph.D., 1924; m. Muriel Kornfeld, June 20, 1926; children—John, Michael. Med. fellow Nat. Research Council, Yale, 1925-27; asst. prof. physiology N.Y. Med. Coll., 1927-32; mem. research staff biol. lab., Cold Spring Harbor, L.I., N.Y., 1928-32; research asso., sec. dental carries research group dental sch. Columbia, 1932-36, lectr. medicine, 1947-51, asst. clin. prof. physiology Coll. Phys. and Surgs. since 1951; chief of the gastrointestional physiology research laboratory at the Mount Sinai Hospital, New York City, 1936—; mem. gen. medicine study sect., div. research grants Nat. Insts. Health, 1960—; cons. gastrointestinal research VA Hospital, Washington, 1962—; cons. gastric physiol. Cancer Control Division, Dept. Health, N.Y.C. Fellow A.A.A.S., N.Y. Acad. Medicine (asso.), N.Y. Acad. Scis.; mem. Am. Gastroenterol. Assn. (chmn. com. standardization lab. procedures; recipient Julius Friedenwald medal 1965), American Soc. Biol. Chemists, Am. Physiol. Soc., Am. Statis. Assn., Soc. Exptl. Biology and Medicine, Am. Assn. Cancer Reserach, Am. Chem. Soc., Harvey Soc., Phi Beta Kappa, Sigma Xi, Phi Lambda Upsilon. Author articles sci., med. jour. Abstract editor Gastroenterology; gastrointestinal physiology sect. Am. Jour. Physiology. Jour. Applied Physiology. Home: 120 E. 81st St., N.Y.C. 28. Office: 1 E. 100th St., N.Y.C. 29. Died Mar. 24, 1966.

HOLLERITH, HERMAN, inventor, mfr.; b. Buffalo, N.Y., Feb. 29, 1860; s. George and Franciska (Brunn) H.; grad. Columbia U. Sch. of Mines, 1879; m. Lucia Beverly Talcott, Sept. 15, 1890; children—Lucia, Nannie, Virginia, Herman, Richard Charles. Asst. to statistician William Petit, Columbia, 1880; instr. mech. engring. Mass. Inst. Tech., 1882; went to St. Louis, 1883; with Patent Office, Washington, D.C., 1884-90; invented tabulating machine which worked on principle of punched holes in non-conducting material (counting took place as electric current passed through holes); his tabulating machine used for Census of 1890; read paper concerning his invention before Berne session Internat. Statis. Inst., 1895; founded Tabulating Machine Co., N.Y., 1896, merged with 2 other cos. to become Computing-Tabulating-Recording Co., 1911, later became IBM. Died Washington Nov. 17, 1929.

HOLLEY, ALEXANDER LYMAN, mech engr.; b Lakeville, Conn., July 20, 1832; s. Alexander H. and Jane (Lyman) H.; grad. Brown U., 1853; m. Mary Slade, 2 children. With N.J. Locomotive works, Jersey City, 1855, published Holley's Railroad Advocate, N.J., 1855-57; mem. staff N.Y. Times, 1858-75; tech. editor Am. Ry. Review; chiefly responsible for introducing Bessemer process in U.S.; designer and builder Bessemer plant, Harrisburg, Pa., 1867; became leading engr. and designer of steel plants in U.S., including Edgar Thomeson Works, Pitts; patentee 5 mech. improvements on Bessemer process; mem. Am. Soc. C.E., U.S. Bd. for Testing Structural Materials; pres. Am. Inst. Mining Engrs., 1876; a founder Am. Inst. Mech. Engrs.; trustee Rensselaer Poly. Inst.; mem. Instn. Civil Engrs. (Eng.), 1877. Author: American and European Railway Practice, 1860. Died Bklyn., Jan. 29, 1882.

HOLLICK, (CHARLES) ARTHUR, botanist, geologist; b. on Staten Island, N.Y., Feb. 6, 1857; s. Frederick and Eleanor Eliza (Bailey) H.; Ph.B. Columbia Sch. Mines, 1879; Ph.D., Columbian (now George Washington) U., 1897; m. Adeline Augusta Talkington, Sept. 19, 1881; children—Eleanor Adeline, Roger Frederick (dec.), Grace Eaton. Sanitary engr., later insp. and spl. insp. N.Y. City Health Dept., 1881-92; spl. insp. N.Y. State Bd. of Health, 1883-93; fellow, asst. tutor, Geol. Dept. Columbia, 1890-1900; curator dept. fossil botany, 1900-13, hon. curator, 1914-21, paleobotanist, 1921—, New York Bot. Garden. Sr. geologist U.S. Geol. Survey. Dir. Pub. Museum, Staten Island Inst. Arts and Sciences, 1914-June 30, 1919. Mem. Bd. of Health, New Brighton, N.Y., 1886-92; commr. and pres. Port Richmond, N.Y., boulevard commn., 1896; commr. and pres. Richmond Co. (N.Y.) park commn., 1897-1904; mem. Bd. of Edn., City of New York, 1907-10. Has written numerous works upon geology and botany. Article "Palaeobotany," New Internat. Ency., 1903; "Palaeobotany or Fossil Botany," Ency. Americana, 1904. Home: New York, N.Y. Died 1933.

HOLLIS, HENRY LEONARD, mining engr.; b. Boston, Feb. 17, 1866; s. John Henry and Esther (Harlow) H.; student Bklyn. Poly. Inst.; E.M., Sch. of Mines, Columbia, 1885; m. Jane Dustin Grannis, Nov. 9, 1892 (dec.); 1 dau., Mrs. Clara Hollis McLean. Profl. work, 1889—, has been examination and management of mining properties, and consultation work in connection with development and operation of mines, gas and petroleum properties and metall. plants; dir. Libby-Owens-Ford Co., Electric Bond & Share Co. Unitarian. Mem. Am. Inst. Mining and Metall. Engrs. Clubs: Chicago, Saddle and Cycle, Old Elm (Chgo.). Home: 1242 Lake Shore Dr. Office: 224 S. Michigan Av., Chgo. 4. Died Nov. 1958.

HOLLIS, IRA NELSON, engineer; b. Mooresville, Ind., Mar. 7, 1856; s. Ephraim Joseph and Mary (Kerns) H.; grad. U.S. Naval Acad., 1878; (hon. A.M., Harvard, 1899; L.H.D., Union Coll., 1899; Sc.D., U. of Pittsburgh, 1912); m. Caroline Lorman, Aug. 22, 1894;

children—Janette Ralston, Oliver Nelson, Elinor Vernon, Carolyn. Commd. asst. engr., U.S.N,, 1880; passed asst. engr., 1888; resigned from Navy, Oct. 1, 1893; prof. engring., Harvard, 1893-1913; pres. Worcester Poly. Inst., 1913-25. Fellow Am. Acad. Arts and Sciences. Author: War College Lectures on Naval Ships, 1892; History of the Frigate Constitution, 1900. Home: Worcester, Mass. Died Aug. 15, 1930.

HOLLISTER, NED, zoölogist; b. Delavan, Wis., Nov. 26, 1876; s. Kinner Newcomb and Margaret Frances (Tilden) H.; ed. high sch., Delavan, and pvt. studies in zoölogy, 1896-1901; m. Mabel Pfrimmer, Apr. 15, 1908. Field work in vertebrate zoölogy, U.S. Biol. Survey, in Tex., N.M., Alaska, B.C., Wash., Ore., Calif., Utah, Nev., La. and Ariz., 1902-09; asst. curator of mammals, U.S. Nat. Mus., 1910-16; mem. Canadian Alpine Club expdn. to explore Mt. Robson region of B.C. and Alberta, 1911; mem. Smithsonian-Harvard expdn. to Altai Mountains, Siberia and Mongolia, 1912; supt. Nat. Zoöl. Park, Smithsonian Instn., Washington, 1916—. Author: The Birds of Wisconsin, 1903; A Systematic Synopsis of Muskrats, 1911; Mammals of the Philippine Islands, 1912; Mammals of Alpine Club Expedition to Mount Robson, 1913; Philippine Land Mammals in the U.S. National Museum, 1913; A Systematic Account of the Grasshopper Mice, 1914; A Systematic Account of the Prairie-dogs, 1916; East African Mammals in the U.S. National Museum, vol. 1, 1918, vol. 2, 1919. Home: Washington, D.C. Died Nov. 3, 1924.

HOLLMANN, HARRY TRIEBNER, (hol'man), physician; b. Phila., Pa., Dec. 13, 1878; s. Harry and Mary (Thomas) H.; M.D., Medico-Chirurg. Coll., Phila., 1898; m. Amelia Thomas Duncalfe, Apr. 17, 1900; m. 2d, Bonita Clarke, July 12, 1929; children—Bonita L., Pamela Jane, Harry Triebner. Instr. in pathology, Medico-Chirurg. Coll., 1903-05; physician to Dept. of Charities, Phila., 1903-06; asst. eye, ear, nose and throat surgeon, Phila. Gen. Hosp., 1905-06; with U.S. Public Health Service, 1907-18. On duty at Leprosy Investigation Sta., Honolulu, 1907-18; med. supt. Kalihi Hosp.; supt. Queen's Hosp., 1918, 19. Chmn. Territorial Radio Commn. (Hawaii). First lt. Med. Corps, Hawaiian Nat. Guard. Mem. Ky. State Med. Soc., Hawaiian Territorial Med. Soc., W. E. Hughes Med. Soc. Baptist. Mason, Odd Fellow. Club: Commercial. Author of various bulls. setting forth original research on leprosy; specialist in diseases of the skin. Home: 2154 Atherton Road. Office: 1124 Miller St., Honolulu, T.H. Died Dec. 13, 1942.

HOLLOWAY, JOSEPH FLAVIUS, mech. engr.; b. Uniontown, O., Jan. 18, 1825; s. Joseph T. Holloway. Worked for Cuyahoga Steam Furnace Co., 1846; designed machinery for screw-propelled boat Niagara, 1847; designed equipment for iron steamers, 1851; supt., later pres. Cuyahoga Steam Furnace Works, 1857-87; v.p. H. R. Worthington firm of hydraulic engrs., 1887-94. Died Sept. 1, 1896.

HOLM, GEORGE ELMER, biochemist; b. Cokato, Minn., Jan. 20, 1891; s. John and Anna Sophia (Jonsson) H.; B.S., Carleton Coll., 1914; M.S., U. Minn., 1916, Ph.D., 1919; m. Julia M. Zanger, June 22, 1918; children—Helen Marie (Mrs. William W. Bedsworth), Julianne (Mrs. Lewis B. Timberlake). Principal of the high school in Dawson, Minn., 1914-15; instr. dept. agrl. biochemistry U. Minn., 1919, asst. prof., 1919-20; biochemist bur. dairy industry U.S. Dept. Agr., 1920-42, head dairy products research div. since 1942. Ofcl. U.S. del. Internat. Dairy Congress, Berlin, 1937, Stockholm, 1949. Served as 1st lt. C.W.S., U.S. Army, 1917-19. Received Borden award Am. Chem. Soc., 1942, superior service award U.S. Dept. Agr., 1948. Mem. Am. Chem. Soc., Am. Dairy Sci. Assn., Washington Acad. Sci., A.A.A.S., Sigma Xi, Gamma Sigma Delta, Phi Lambda Upsilon, Alpha Chi Sigma, Gamma Alpha. Club: Cosmos (Washington). Contbr. articles profl. publs. Home: 3513 R St., Washington 7. Office: Bureau of Dairy Industry, U.S. Dept. of Agriculture, Washington. Died Nov. 11, 1955; buried Arlington Nat. Cemetery.

HOLM, (HERMAN) THEODOR, botanist; b. Copenhagen, Denmark, Feb. 3, 1854; s. Christian and Amalie H.; grad. U. of Copenhagen, 1880; Ph.D., Catholic U. of America, 1902; unmarried. Arrived in U.S., Apr. 12, 1888, naturalized citizen, 1893. Botanist and zoölogist, Danish North Pole Expdn., 1882-83; traveled in West Greenland as botanist and zoölogist for the Danish Govt., summers of 1884-86; explored the high alpine flora of Colo., 1896-99; was for about 8 yrs. bot. asst. Smithsonian Instn. and U.S. Dept. Agr. Home: Clinton, Md. Died 1932.

HOLMAN, MINARD LAFEVER, mech. engr.; b. Oxford County, Me., June 15, 1852; s. John Henry and Mary Ann (Richards) H.; A.B., Washington U., 1874, hon. A.M., 1905; m. Margaret H. Holland, Sept. 7, 1879. In supervising architect's office, U.S. Treasury Dept., 1874-76; with Flad & Smith, engrs., 1876-77; asst. engr., St. Louis Water Works, 1877-87; water commr., St. Louis, 1887-99; in gen. engring. work, 1899-1900; gen. supt. Mo. Edison Electric Co., 1900-04; sr. mem. Holman & Laird, consulting engrs., St. Louis, 1904—. Home: St. Louis, Mo. Died Jan. 4, 1925.

HOLMAN, RUSSELL LOWELL, physician, educator; b. Conway, Ark., Jan. 29, 1907; s. Lloyd Cooper and Maude Della (Freeman) H.; A.B., Washington U., 1927; M.D., Vanderbilt, 1931; m. Sara del Valle, Aug. 15, 1938; children—Russell Lowell, Mary Esther. Asst. pathology U. Rochester, 1931-33; instr. pathology Columbia, 1933-37; asst. prof. to prof. pathology U. N.C., 1937-46; prof., head dept. pathology La. State U. Sch. Medicine, pathologist-in-chief La. State U. div. Charity Hosp. of La., New Orleans, 1947—. Cons. pathology study sect. Nat. Insts. Health, 1948-53; mem. NRC, 1952—, exec. com. div. med. scis., 1958—; resident cons. Armed Forces Inst. Pathology, 1952-54; pres. New Orleans Assn. Retarded Children, 1956-58. Diplomate pathologic anatomy and clin. pathology Am. Bd. Pathology. Mem. Am. Soc. Study Arteriosclerosis (pres. 1954), Am. Soc. Exptl. Pathology (pres. 1956), Am. Assn. Pathologists and Bacteriologists (sec. 1957—), Internat. Acad. Pathology, Am. Soc. Clin. Pathology. Home: 1505 Audubon St., New Orleans 18. Died May 5, 1960; buried Garden of Memories, New Orleans.

HOLMES, CHAMPNEYS HOLT, physician; b. Macon, Ga., Jan. 30, 1894; s. John Champneys and Pearl (Lewis) H.; B.S., U. of Ga., 1915; M.D., Johns Hopkins U., 1919; m. Jacqueline Swift, Aug. 25, 1938. Began private practice of medicine, 1922; specialized in diseases of the chest, 1931—; mem. staff, Emory U. Med. Sch., 1922—. Mem. staff Atlanta Tb Assn., 1922—, pres., 1939—. Mem. Planning Council. Fellow A.C.P.; mem. A.M.A., Fulton County Med. Soc., Ga. State Med. Assn., Nat., So. Tb assns., Am. Coll. Chest Physicians (pres. 1938-39), Trudeau Soc., Phi Delta Theta, Phi Chi. Episcopalian. Club: Presidents, Piedmont Driving (Atlanta). Contributor many articles and editorials on chest diseases. Mem. editorial staff Diseases of the Chest. Died June 12, 1950. *

HOLMES, EZEKIEL, agriculturalist; b. Kingston, Mass., Aug. 24, 1801; s. Nathaniel and Asenath (Chandler) H.; grad. Brown U., 1821; M.D., Bowdoin Coll., 1824; m. Sarah E. Benson, Aug. 14, 1825, 2 children. Practiced medicine in Me.; discovered great tourmaline desposit on Mt. Mica, Me., 1823; instr. in agr. Gardiner Lyceum, 1825-29, prin., 1829-32; lectr. chemistry, mineralogy, botany and geology Colby Coll., 1833-37; founder and editor Kennebec Farmer and Jour. of the Useful Arts (1st newspaper in Me. devoted to sci. study of agr.), 1833-65; a founder Me. Bd. Agr., 1852, sec., 1852-55; a founder Me. Agrl. Soc., 1855, sec., 1855-65; mem. Me. Legislature, 1835-39, 50, Me. Senate, 1840-41; a founder U. Me., 1865. Author: Report of an Exploration and Survey of the Territory on the Aroostook River during the Spring and Autumn of 1838. Died Feb. 9, 1865.

HOLMES, FREDERICK S., bank-vault engr.; b. Boston, Aug. 27, 1865; s. George Washington and Frances Ann (Stacy) H.; high sch. edn.; m. Katharine Vincent, of Berlin, N.H., Mar. 27, 1886. Engaged in pattern and machine work, 1879-83; machine draftsman, 1883-87; supt. vault factories at Boston and Chicago, 1887-95; professional vault engr. Mem. N.Y. State Soc. of Professional Engrs. Club: N.Y. Athletic. Office: 2 Rector St., New York, N.Y.

HOLMES, GEORGE KIRBY, statistician; b. Great Barrington, Mass., May 10, 1856; s. Harvey and Mary J. (Kirby) H.; ed. com. and high schs., Great Barrington; studied law; m. Lillian C. Hunter, Apr. 27, 1898; children—Emma Biscoe (Mrs. Harold C. Taylor), Mary Kirby, George Kirby, John Hunter. Admitted to Mass. bar, 1877; spl. agt. in charge Div. of Farms, Homes and Mortgages, U.S. Census of 1890; agrl. statistician; mem. Crop Reporting Bd. of U.S. Dept. Agr., 1905-24, writer of interpretive comment concerning its reports to the press. Del. Gen. Assembly of Internat. Inst. of Agr., Rome. Fellow Am. Statis. Assn. Author: Farms and Homes; Real Estate Mortgages (both Census of 1890); numerous publs. of Dept. of Agr. Home: Washington, D.C. Died Feb. 1, 1927.

HOLMES, HOWARD CARLETON, civil engr.; b. Island of Nantucket, Mass., June 10, 1854; s. Cornelius and Maria (Folger) H.; removed with parents to San Francisco, Calif., 1860; ed. pub. schs.; tech. training in office of city engr., Oakland, Calif.; m. Josephine Bauer, 1883. Asst. engr. to State Bd. of Harbor Commrs. of Calif. until 1883; consulting engr., 1883—; built ferry terminal at Alameda, cable rys., Portland, Spokane, Seattle, San Francisco, also elec. rys. in various cities on Pacific Coast; chief engr. State Bd. Harbor Commrs. of Calif., 1892-1901; designed and built ferry terminus of the S.F., Oakland & San Jose R.R., pleasure pier at Long Beach, Calif.; designed yacht harbor and marine works, etc., for San Francisco Expn., also all ferry slips in Bay of San Francisco; completed largest graving dock in the world, at Hunter's Point, San Francisco Bay, for Bethlehem Steel Corp.; inventor of cylinder pier of San Francisco water front; chief engr. San Francisco Dry Dock Co., S.F.O.&S.J. R.R.; constructing engr., docks and wharfs Western Pacific Ry., A.,T.&S.F., and Calif. & N.W. rys.; consulting engr. Union Iron Works, etc. Republican. Unitarian. Home: San Francisco, Calif. Died Oct. 30, 1921.

HOLMES, ISRAEL, brass mfr.; b. Waterbury, Conn., Dec. 19, 1800; s. Israel and Sarah (Judd) H.; m. Ardelia Hayden, 6 children. Became partner (with Horace Hotchkiss) in mfg. hats, Augusta, Ga., circa 1818; became one of 7 partners firm Holmes & Hotchkiss, mfrs. of sheet brass and wire (1st venture of its kind in U.S.), 1830; went to Eng., 1831, returned with 1st wire drawing and tube-making machinery seen in U.S.; founder Wolcottville Brass Co. (1st U.S. firm to employ battery process in mfg. brass kettles), 1833; pres. Waterbury Brass Co., 1845-53; organizer Holmes, Booth & Haydens (1st U.S. co. to both roll and manufacture brass on large scale), 1853-69; leader in constrn. Naugatuck R.R.; mem. Conn. Legislature from Torrington, 1839, from Waterbury, 1870. Died July 15, 1874.

HOLMES, JAMES THOMAS, engring.-constrn. co. exec.; b. Kansas City, Mo., Dec. 1, 1890; s. Robert James and Elizabeth (Vacoe) H.; B.S., Mass. Inst. Tech., 1914; m. Ester Roen, Jan. 25, 1922. Jr. engr. D.C. &W.B. Jackson Co., Boston, 1914-16; from sr. elec. engr. to chief elec. engr. Schofield Engring. Co., Phila., and subsidiary, 1916-20; partner Holmes & Sanborn, Los Angeles, 1920-31; fgn. travel, 1931-33; pres. Holmes & Narver, Inc., Los Angeles, 1933-70, chmn. bd., 1970, also dir. Registered profl. engr., Cal., Nev., Ariz. Fellow Am. Soc. C.E.; hon. mem. Am. Soc. M.E.; mem. Am. Soc. Testing and Materials, Atomic Indsl. Forum, U.S., Los Angeles chambers commerce, Def. Orientation Conf. Assn., Beta Theta Pi. Episcopalian. Clubs: Engineer's, California, Wilshire Country (Los Angeles); Mass. Inst. Tech. Southern California. Home: Los Angeles CA Died Dec. 11, 1970.

HOLMES, JOSEPH AUSTIN, geologist; b. Laurens, S.C., Nov. 23, 1859; s. Z. L. and N. Catherine (Nickles) H.; B.S., Cornell U., 1881; D.Sc., U. of Pittsburgh; LL.D., U. of N.C.; m. Jeanie I. Sprunt, Oct. 20, 1887. Prof. geology and natural history, U. of N.C., 1881-91, lecturer on geology, 1891—; state geologist of N.C., 1891-1904; in charge U.S. Geol. Survey laboratories for testing fuels and structural materials, St. Louis, 1904-07, and Pittsburgh, 1908; chief technol. branch, U.S. Geol. Survey, in charge investigation of mine accidents, 1907-10; dir. Bur. of Mines, Dept. of the Interior, since its creation, July 1, 1910—. Chief dept. mines and metallurgy, St. Louis Expn., 1904; mem. Mining Legislation Commn. of Ill., Nat. Conservation Commission. Died July 12, 1915.

HOLMES, OLIVER WENDELL, physician, author; b. Cambridge, Mass., Aug. 29, 1809; s. Rev. Abiel and Sarah (Wendell) H.; grad. Harvard, 1829, M.D., 1836; hon. degrees, Edinburgh, Harvard, Cambridge (Eng.) U, 1887, Oxford (Eng.) U., 1887; m. Amelia Lee Jackson, June 15, 1840; children—Amelia (Mrs. Turner Sargent), Edward Jackson, Chief Justice Oliver Wendell. Wrote poem Old Ironsides which caused preservation of U.S.S. Constitution, 1830; winner Boylston prize for med. essay, 1836; prof. anatomy Dartmouth, 1838-40; Parkman prof. anatomy and physiology Harvard Med. Sch., 1847-82, dean, 1847-53, prof. emeritus, 1882-94. Elected to Hall of Fame for Great Americans, 1910. Established Atlantic Monthly, 1857, contbd. essays noted for humor and common sense later published as The Autocrat of the Breakfast-table, 1858, The Professor at the Breakfast-table, 1860, The Poet at the Breakfast-table, 1872, Pages from an Old Volume of Life, 1883, Over the Teacups, 1891; mem. Saturday Club (also included James Russell Lowell, Louis Agassiz, William Wadsworth Longfellow, Ralph Waldo Emerson, others); poems The Chambered Nautilus, The Deacon's Masterpiece or, The Wonderful One-Hoss Shay included in Poems, 1836; other works include Songs in Many Keys, 1862; Songs of Many Seasons, 1875; The Iron Gate and Other Poems, 1880; Before the Curfew and Other Poems, 1887. Author: novels including Elsie Venner, 1861; The Guardian Angel, 1867; A Mortal Antipathy, 1885 (novels were anti-Calvinist, dealt with med. problems, were ahead of their time in understanding of psychology); sci. writings include Lectures on Homeopathy and Its Kindred Delusions, 1842; The Contagiousness of Puerperal Fever, 1843; Currents and Counter Currents in Medical Science, 1861; Border Lines in Some Provinces of Medical Science, 1862; Medical Essays (reissue), 1883. Promoted exploratory surgery as means of diagnosis; 1st to recognize contagiousness of puerperal fever, 1843, recommended aseptic methods to prevent it; introduced aseptic techniques in obstetrics and surgery; devised term anesthesia to describe process of using either to induce unconsciousness. Died Boston, Oct. 7, 1894.

HOLMES, RUDOLPH WIESER, physician; b. Chgo.; s. Edward Lorenzo and Paula (Wieser) H.; student Harvard, 1888-90; M.D., Rush Med. Coll., Chgo., 1893; postgrad. work hosps. at Vienna and Prague, 1900-01; m. Maria Baxter, May 5, 1898. Specialist in obstetrics and gynecology; prof. emeritus of obstetrics and gynecology Rush Med. Coll. at U. Chgo.; formerly asso. prof. obstetrics Northwestern U. Med. Sch.; chief dept. obstetrics Passavant Meml. Hosp. Dir. Am. Com. on Maternal Welfare, Inc.; former mem. adv. com. Childrens Bur. Treas. 1st Am. Congress on Obstetrics and Gynecology, Cleve., 1939. Fellow A.C.S., Inst. Medicine Chgo., Am. Gynecol. Soc., Central Assn. Obstetricians and Gynecologists (pres.

1931-32); mem. A.M.A., Ill., Chgo. med. socs., Chgo. Gynecol. Soc. (past pres.). Republican. Unitarian. Club: University. Home: University, Va. Died Apr. 25, 1953; buried Rosehill Cemetery, Chgo.

HOLMES, SAMUEL JACKSON, zoologist; b. Henry, Ill., Mar. 7, 1868; s. Joseph and Avis Folger (Taber) H.; B.S., U. of Calif., 1893, M.S., 1894; fellow in zoology, University of Chicago, 1895-97, Ph.D., 1897; LL.D., University of California, 1943; D.Sc. (hon.), University of Michigan, 1948; married Cecelia Warfield Skinner; children—Samuel Jackson, Marion Virginia, Avis Cecelia, John Warfield, Joseph Edward. Assistant in zoology, Univ. of California, 1893-95; teacher San Diego (Calif.) High Sch., 1898; instr. U. of Mich., 1899-1905; asst. prof. zoology, U. of Wis., 1905-12; asso. prof. zoology, U. of Calif., 1912-17, prof. since 1917. Fellow A.A.A.S. (pres. Western div.); mem. Am. Soc. Zoologists (pres.), Wis. Acad. of Sciences, Am. Psychol. Assn., Am. Soc. Naturalists (pres.), Calif. Acad. of Sciences, Soc. Exptl. Biology and Medicine, Am. Genetics Assn., Eugenics Soc. (pres.), Eugenics Research Assn., Population Assn. of America, Am. Acad. of Arts and Sciences. Democrat. Author: Synopsis of California Stalk-eyed Crustacea, 1900; The Biology of the Frog, 1906; The Evolution of Animal Intelligence, 1911; Studies in Animal Behavior, 1916; The Elements of Animal Biology, 1918; The Trend of the Race, 1921; Studies in Evolution and Eugenics, 1923; Louis Pasteur, 1924; A Bibliography of Eugenics, 1924; Life and Evolution, 1926; The Eugenic Predicament, 1933; Human Genetics and Its Social Import, 1936; The Negro's Struggle for Survival, 1937; Organic Form and Related Biological Problems, 1948; Life and Morals, 1948. Home: 2821 Regent St., Berkeley CA

HOLT, ANDREW HALL, prof. civil engring.; b. Sunderland, Vt., Aug. 23, 1890; s. Winfield Selah and Effie Ida (Andrew) H.; student Burr & Burton Sem., Manchester, Vt., 1904-08; B.S. in C.E., U. of Vt., 1912, C.E., 1922; M.S., State U. of Ia., 1920, J.D., 1931; m. Ruth E. Brownson, Jan. 1, 1915; children—Elisabeth Ursula, Barbara Ruth, Winfield Andrew, Nancy Fay. Began 1911, surveying and engring., summer work with Am. Bridge Co., Ia. Ry. & Light Corp., U.S. Dist. Engr. and others; engr. in chg. river improvements, Iowa City; instr. U. of Vt., 1912-14; instr. civil engring., State U. of Ia., 1914-17, asst. prof, 1919-21, asso. prof., 1921-34, prof., 1934-37; prof. civil engring., and head of dept. of civil engring., Worcester Poly. Inst., since 1937. Served as capt. engrs., U.S. Army, A.E.F., World War I; col., Corps Engineers, commanding 361st Engineer Regiment, Pacific and European Theaters, World War II; Colonel, Corps of Engineers Reserve, ret. Member Iowa, Massachusetts and Federal bars. Member Am. Soc. Civil Engrs., Am. Society for Engineering Edn., Soc. American Military Engrs., Worcester Society of Civil Engineers, Scabbard and Blade, Order of Coif, Phi Beta Kappa, Tau Beta Pi, Sigma Xi, Theta Tau, Alpha Tau Omega. Republican. Conglist. Mason. Author: Manual of Field Astronomy, 1916, 2d edit., 1927; (with B. J. Lambert) Elementary Structures in Steel and Concrete, 1929; also papers on surveying and the law of boundaries. Home: 10 Germain St., Worcester, Mass. Died Nov. 22, 1956; buried Ira Allen Cemetery, Sunderland, Vt.

HOLT, LEE CONE, chemist; b. Harlan, Ia., Feb. 19, 1880; s. Lee Elwood and Eva Boise (Collier) H.; B.S., Pomona Coll., Cal., 1901; Ph.D., U. Mich., 1905; grad. study, U. Berlin, 1907-08; m. Daisy Ellen Ben Oliel, June 18, 1907 (dec.); children—Florence Lee (dec.), Helen Agnes (dec.); Lee Elbert; m. 2d, Maud N. Rogers, July 1939. Instr. in chemistry Pomona Coll., 1901-02, Carnegie research asst., 1903-05; instr. in organic chemistry U. Mich., 1905-08, asst. prof., 1908-13, asso. prof., 1913-16; with Dow Chem. Co., Midland, Mich., 1916-17, Semet Solvay Co., Syracuse, N.Y., 1917-18; with Nat. Aniline & Chem. Co., Buffalo, 1918-29, in charge research and development work, 1921-29, v.p., 1922-29; with Jackson Lab. of Du Pont Co., 1929-45, retired, 1945—. Mem. Am. Chem. Soc., Phi Beta Kappa, Sigma Xi. Republican. Contbr. articles to German and Am. chem. jours. Home: "Holthaven," Preston, Md. Died May 27, 1957.

HOMBERGER, ALFRED WILLIAM, (hom'bûrg-er), prof. chemistry; b. Prairie du Sac, Wis., May 18, 1887; s. Robert and Anna (Schoenburg) H.; A.B., U. of Wis., 1905 (honors in chemistry); M.S., U. of Ill., 1908, Ph.D., 1910; studied U. of Göttingen and Columbia; m. Iva Lucille Ward, 1915. Instr. in chemistry, Rose Poly. Inst., Terre Haute, Ind., 1905-07; asst. prof. chemistry, Ill. Coll., Jacksonville, Ill., 1910-11; prof. chemistry, dir. of chemistry, Illinois Wesleyan U., 1911-18; prof. chemistry and head of department, U. of Louisville, 1918-42, prof. physiol. chemistry and nutrition and head of dept., School of Medicine, U. of Louisville 1942-52, ret. June 1952, prof. nutrition Sch. Dentistry. Mem. executive com. Louisville Presbyn. Seminary since 1950. Fellow A.A.A.S.; mem. Am. Chem. Society (councillor for Louisville sect.), 1920-45, Ky. Acad. Science (pres. 1939-40), American Association of University Professors, Alpha Tau Omega, Gamma Alpha, Sigma Xi, Phi Lambda Upsilon, Theta Chi Delta, Alpha Epsilon Delta. Contbr. papers on research. Home: 2368 Carlton Terrace, Louisville. Died Sept. 11, 1952.

HONNOLD, WILLIAM LINCOLN, (hon'nold), mining engr.; b. Oconee, Ill., Apr. 16, 1866; s. Rev. Robert and Sarah (Ernest) H.; Knox Coll., Galesburg, Ill., 1886-87, LL.D., 1927; U. Mich., 1887-88; E.M., Mich. Coll. of Mines, Houghton, 1895; D.Sc., Claremont Coll., 1936; D.Eng., Mich. Coll. Mining and Tech., 1937; m. Caroline Burton, Nov. 12, 1895. Successively foreman, supt., mgr. and cons. engr. of mines, in Minn. and Cal., 1895-1902; went to S. Africa, 1902, as cons. engr. Consolidated Mines Selection Co. (London) and subsidiary cos., becoming mng. dir., 1912, also chmn. Transvaal Coal Trust, Brakpan Mines, Springs Mines and The New Era Co.; retired from S. Africa, 1915. Was mem. Council of Edn. and v.p. Chamber of Mines, Johannesburg, S.A. Apptd. dir. in London of Commn. for Relief in Belgium, 1915; trans. to New York, as dir. in America, 1916, continuing until armistice; now dir. Commn. for Relief in Belgium, Ednl. Found. Spl. rep. in Europe of Guaranty Trust Co. of New York, 1919; dir. (permanent) Anglo-Am. Corp. of South Africa, Ltd. Trustee Cal. Inst. Tech., Claremont Colleges; hon. trustee Pomona Coll. Mem. Am. Inst. Mining and Metall. Engrs., Mining and Metall. Soc. Am. Decorated Comdr. Order of the Crown, Médaille Commemorative du Comite Nat. (Belgian); Médaille Reconnaissance Française (French). Mem. Phi Delta Theta, Tau Beta Pi, Phi Beta Kappa, Phi Beta Kappa Associates. Republican. Mason. Clubs: California, Los Angels Country, Bel-Air Country, Sunset (Los Angeles). Home: Bel-Air, Los Angeles 24. Office: Pacific Mutual Bldg., Los Angeles 14. Died May 6, 1950; buried Oak Park Cemetery, Clearmont, Cal.

HOOBLER, B(ERT) RAYMOND, (ho'bler), pediatrist; b. Standish, Mich., May 5, 1872; s. Saml. R. and Mary Roselia (Worth) H.; B.S., Wabash Coll., Ind., 1901, M.A., 1903; M.D., Cornell U., 1905; studied in Europe, 1914; m. Madge Sibley, Oct. 15, 1906; m. 2d, Icie G. Macy, June 11, 1938. Practiced at N.Y. City, 1905-14, also teaching in Cornell U. Med. Coll.; prof. diseases of children, Wayne U., 1914-37, emeritus since 1937; cons. Children's Hosp. of Mich. Mem. A.M.A., Am. Pediatric Soc., Phi Beta Kappa, Sigma Xi, Phi Gamma Delta, Nu Sigma Nu. Republican. Presbyterian. Mason (K.T.). Author of numerous papers on nutrition of children. Home: 805 Three Mile Drive, Grosse Pointe, Mich. Died June 11, 1943.

HOOD, J(OSEPH) DOUGLAS, biologist; b. Laramie, Wyo., Nov. 29, 1889; s. Thomas Henry and Eva Maria Josephine (Dickson) H.; A.B., U. Ill., 1910; M.A., George Washington U., 1913; Ph.D., Cornell U., 1932; m. Helen Madge Hincher, 1930; 1 dau., Barbara. Asst. instr. in mil. sci. and tactics, U. Ill., 1909-10; instr. biology U. Rochester, 1922-25, asst. prof., 1925-28, prof., 1928-37; Cornell U. resident dr., 1937-38, asst. prof., biology, 1939-43, asso. prof. 1943, prof., 1948; cons. U. Fla. Brevet capt. Ill. N.G., 1910; served as 2d lt. D.C. N.G., Mexican Border, 1916-17; 1st lt. Ordnance Dept., U.S. Army, 1917-18, capt., 1918-20; supervised procurement all gun carriages for ry., seacoast and improvised field arty., World War. Fellow A.A.A.S., Entomol. Soc. Am. (charter mem.), Royal Entomol. Soc. London; mem. N.Y. Entomol. Soc., Entomoly Soc. Washington, Bklyn. Entomol. Soc., Bol. Soc. Washington, Natural History Soc. C.Z. (hon.), Entomol. Soc. Brazil, Sigma Xi, Phi Kappa Phi, Alpha Sigma Phi (nat. sec. 1910-13), Theta Nu Epsilon, Scabbard and Blade (nat. sec. and treas. 1910-13). Republican. Unitarian. Mason. Rifle and pistol expert; mem. D.C. rifle team, 1914, 15, U.S. N.G. team, 1915; winner 2d pl. Boyle Match and Reading Matches, Sea Girt, N.J., 1914. Contbr. articles to sci. jours. Home: 207 Cobb St., Ithaca, N.Y. Died Oct. 22, 1966.

HOOD, OZNI PORTER, mechanical engr.; b. Lowell, Mass., June 14, 1865; s. Harrison Porter and Vesta (Merrill) H.; Worcester Poly. Inst., 1882-83; B.S. in mech. engring., Rose Poly. Inst., 1885, M.S., 1895, M.E., 1898, Dr. Eng., 1933; m. Gertrude Benight, July 31, 1884; children—Ben Benight, Karl Kedzie, Harrison Porter. Began as pattern maker, 1885; supt. shops, 1886-89, supt. shops and prof. engring., 1889-98, Kan. State Agrl. Coll., Manhattan; prof. mech. and elec. engring., Mich. Coll. of Mines, 1898-1911; consulting engr. in mech. engring. relating to mines, 1900-11; chief mech. engr., U.S. Bur. Mines, 1911-26; chief of technologic br. U.S. Bur. of Mines, 1926—. Home: Washington, D.C. Died Apr. 22, 1937.

HOOD, WASHINGTON, topog. engr.; b. Phila., Feb. 2, 1808; s. John McClellan and Eliza Forebaugh) H.; grad. U.S. Mil. Acad., 1827. Commd. 2d lt. 4th Inf., U.S. Army, 1827, on topog. duty, 1831-36, commd 1st lt., 1835, capt. Topog. Engrs., 1837; drew (with Robert E. Lee) boundary line between Ohio and Mich., 1835; drew map of Ore. which was used as part of basis for U.S. claims to that territory. Died Bedford Springs, Pa., July 17, 1840.

HOOD, WILLIAM, civil engr.; b. Concord, N.H., Feb. 4, 1846; s. Joseph Edward and Maria (Savage) H.; B.S., Chandler Scientific Dept., Dartmouth, 1867; D.Sc., Dartmouth, 1923. With field engring. party, 1867-68; asst. engr., 1868-72, Central Pacific Ry.; asst. engr., 1872-75, chief asst. engr., 1875-83, S.P. R.R.; chief asst. engr., June-Oct. 10, 1883, chief engr., 1883-85, Central Pacific Ry.; chief engr. Southern Pacific Co. until May 3, 1921, retired. Home: San Francisco, Calif. Died Aug. 26, 1926.

HOOK, JAMES WILLIAM, engr.; b. near Hedrick, Ia., Jan. 9, 1884; s. James and Virginia (Eller) H.; B.M.E., Ia. State Coll., 1905, M.E., 1912; m. Hattie Rosamond Bechtel, Sept. 17, 1907; children—James William, Rose Virginia. Editor and pub. Cody (Wyo.) Enterprise, 1905-06; sales engr. Globe Machinery & Supply Co., Des Moines, Ia., 1906-09; sales mgr. and later gen. mgr. C. A. Dunham Co., Marshalltown, Ia., 1909-16; pres. and dir. Allied Machinery Co. of America, New York, also dir. other corps. in New York, 1916-23; pres. and treas. Geometric Tool Co., New Haven, Conn., 1923-44; pres. and director United Illuminating Company of New Haven, Conn., 1939-42, chairman of Board, 1942—; director Acme Wire Co., of New Haven. Mem. Connecticut Emergency Relief Commission, 1933-36; resident industrial advisor NRA, 1933; member Industrial Advisory Board NRA, 1934-35; vice chairman Durable Goods Industries Com. NRA, 1934-35; mem. Bd. of Edn., Tarrytown, N.Y., 1922-23; distribution com., New Haven Foundation; 1928-38; pres. N.E. Council, 1937-38; mem. President Hoover's Nat. Orgn. on Unemployment Relief, 1931-33; chmn. Conn. Unemployment Commn., 1931-33; awarded the Marston medal by Iowa State Coll., 1940, for achievement in engineering; mem. Bus. Adv. Council for the U.S. Dept. of Commerce, 1939—. Trustee University of Connecticut, 1935-53, chairman, 1949-53; trustee New Haven YMCA (chmn.); member Citizens Action Commission of New Haven; mem. New England Regional Manpower Committee, 1943-44; v.p. Mfrs. Assn. of Conn., 1941-46. Member A.A.A.S., Am. Soc. M.E., Academy Political Science, Society of Colonial Wars, Tau Beta Pi, Kappa Sigma. Republican. Mason (32 deg.). Clubs: University (New York City); Graduate, Quinnipiack, Lawn, Country (New Haven). Author: Industry's Obligation to the Unemployed, 1938. Co-author: The New Outlook in Business, 1940; wrote genealogies, James Hook and Virginia Eller, 1925; Judge Karl Bechtel, of Hanau, Germany, 1936; George Michael Eller and Descendents of His in America, 1957. Home: 56 Mulberry Hill St., Hamden 17, Conn. Office: 80 Temple St., New Haven 6. Died Oct. 21, 1957; buried Evergreen Cemetery, New Haven.

HOOKER, DONALD RUSSELL, physiologist; b. New Haven, Conn., Sept. 7, 1876; s. Frank Henry and Grace (Russell) H.; B.A., Yale, 1899, M.S., 1901; M.D., Johns Hopkins, 1905; student U. of Berlin, 1906; m. Edith Houghton, June 14, 1905; children—Donald Houghton, Russell Houghton, Edith Houghton, Elizabeth Houghton, Beatrice Houghton. Asst. instr. and asso. in physiology, 1906-10, asso. prof. 1910-20, Johns Hopkins Med. Sch.; lecturer on physical hygiene, Johns Hopkins U. Mng. editor Am. Journal Physiology, since 1914; also mng. editor Physiological Revs. Mem. Am. Physiol. Soc. Home: 1016 St. George's Rd. Office: 19 W. Chase St., Baltimore, Md. Died Aug. 1, 1946.

HOOKER, ELON HUNTINGTON, civil engr.; b. Rochester, N.Y., Nov. 23, 1869; s. Horace B. and Susan (Huntington) H.; direct descendant of Thomas Hooker, founder, at Hartford, of the Colony of Connecticut, 1638; A.B., U. of Rochester, 1891, A.M., 1894; C.E., Cornell U., 1894, Ph.D., 1896 (European fellowship); post-grad. work Zürich (Switzerland) Polytechnicum, École des Ponts et Chaussées, Paris; m. Blanche Ferry, Jan. 25, 1901. Engring. work, 1888-98; mem. pvt. commn. inspecting Panama and Nicaragua Canal routes, 1898; deputy supt. pub. wks., N.Y., under Gov. Roosevelt, 1899-1900, under Gov. Odell, 1901; resigned, 1901, to engage in timber, mining and r.r. enterprises in the Southwest; organizer and pres. Hooker Electrochem. Co. (Niagara Falls and Tacoma). Pres. Mfg. Chemists' Assn. of the U.S., 1923, 24, 25; chmn., former pres. and dir. Research Corporation; mem. Nat. Industrial Conf. Bd. (exec. com.). Trustee U. of Rochester. Chmn. Am. Defense Soc.; treas. Progressive Nat. Com., 1912, also chmn. finance com., 1913; member Roosevelt Memorial Assn. (exec. com.). Baptist. Died May 10, 1938.

HOOPER, EVERETT (DENNISON), chemist; b. Riverdale, Mass., Sept. 16, 1868; s. Dennison and Emma (Hodgkins) H.; A.M., Tufts Coll., 1888; M.D., Coll. Phys. and Surg., Boston, 1891; Ph.D., Harvard, 1905. Instr. chemistry, 1890-91, asst. prof., 1892-93, prof. since 1893, Coll. Phys and Surg. Asst. surgeon U.S.V., 1898; mem. Mass. State Bd. Health since 1902. Mem. Am. Chem. Soc., Nat. Geog. Soc., A.A.A.S., and med. socs. Home: Gloucester, Mass. Address: Warren Chambers, Boston.

HOOPER, STANFORD CALDWELL, rear admiral USN, ret., electronics consultant; b. Colton, Cal., Aug. 16, 1884; s. William Swayze and Mary (Caldwell) H.; B.S., U.S. Naval Academy, 1905; m. Margaret Nye, May 27, 1915; 1 dau., Elizabeth. Commd. ensign, USN, 1907, advanced through grades to rear adm., 1938; first U.S. Fleet radio officer, 1912; head of Radio Div., Navy Dept. during 3 tours of shore duty beginning 1915; comd. destroyer Fairfax during World War I; chief engr. Fed. Radio Commn., 1927-28; dir. Naval Communications, 1928-34; dir. Tech. Div., Naval Operations, and chmn. Naval Research Com., 1934-39; dir. Radio Liaison Div., 1940-43, ret. Hooper Trophy awarded annually to outstanding electronics div. USNR. Decorated World War I medal Navy Cross, Mexican Campaign medal (United States); Legion of Honor (France); awarded gold medal Institute Radio Engineers, 1934, Marconi Medal of Merit, 1939, Elliot Cresson Medal (Franklin Institute), 1945, U.S. delegate to International Radio Confs. at The Hague, Bucharest, Lisbon, Cairo, Chile. Episcopalian. Clubs: Army and Navy, Army and Navy Country, Chevy Chase, Sulgrave (Washington, D.C.); New York Yacht; Bath (Miami Beach, Fla.). Editor of Robinson's Manual of Radio Telegraphy and Telephony. Address: 4425 Garfield Street N.W., Washington; also 6320 Alton Rd., Miami Beach, Fla. Died Apr. 6, 1955; buried Arlington Nat. Cemetery.

HOOPER, WILLIAM LESLIE, electrical engr.; b. Halifax, N.S., Aug. 2, 1855; s. Rev. William and Anne Jane (Whytal) H.; A.B., Tufts Coll., 1877, A.M., 1878, hon. Ph.D., 1898; m. Mary E. Heard, July 9, 1879. Instr. mathematics and sciences, 1878-80, prin., 1882, Bromfield Acad., Harvard, Mass.; asst. prof. physics, 1883-90, prof. elec. engring., 1890—, actg. pres., July 1, 1912-Nov. 15, 1914, Tufts Coll. Author: Electrical Problems, 1902. Address: Tufts College, Mass. Died Oct. 3, 1918.

HOOPES, JOSIAH, botanist, nurseryman; b. West Chester, Pa., Nov. 9, 1832; s. Pierce and Sarah (Andrews) H.; ed. public schools and Friends' Central High School, Phila.; m. Ellen A. Morgan, founder of the Maple Avenue Nurseries, in 1853, now Hoopes, Bro. & Thomas, Mar. 17, 1898. One of founders and pres. Hort. Soc. of Pa., 1869-79. Trustee West Chester State Normal School, 13 yrs. Author: Book of Evergreens, 1868. Address: West Chester, Pa. Died 1904.

HOOTON, EARNEST ALBERT, (hoo'tun), anthropologist; b. Clemansville, Wis., Nov. 20, 1887; s. William and Margaret Elizabeth (Newton) H.; B.A., Lawrence Coll., Appleton, Wis., 1907, Sc.D., 1933; M.A. University of Wisconsin, 1908, Ph.D., 1911; also LL.D. (honorary), 1954; Rhodes Scholar at Oxford U., 1910-13, diploma in anthropology, 1912, B.Litt., 1913; m. Mary Beidler Camp, June 3, 1915; children—Jay Camp, William Newton, Emma Beidler. Instr. anthropology, 1913, asst. prof., 1921, asso. prof., 1927, prof. since 1930, Harvard. Asst. curator somatology, Peabody Museum, 1913-14, curator since 1914. Fellow A.A.A.S. (v.p. sect. H, 1923-24), Royal Anthropol. Inst., Am. Acad. Arts and Sciences; mem. Am. Anthropol. Assn., Am. Assn. Phys. Anthropol., Am. Genetic Assn., Am. Philos. Soc., Am. Soc. Naturalists, Nat. Acad. Sci., Phi Beta Kappa; hon. fellow Am. Acad. Dental Science. Author: Ancient Inhabitants of the Canary Islands, 1925; The Indians of Pecos, 1930; Up from the Ape, 1931; rev. ed., 1946; Apes, Men and Morons, 1937; Crime and the Man, The American Criminal, Vol. I, Twilight of Man, 1939; Why Men Behave Like Apes and Vice Versa, 1940; Man's Poor Relations, 1942; "Young Man, You are Normal," 1945; also papers on physical anthropology. Home: 13 Buckingham St., Cambridge, Mass. Died May 3, 1954; buried Mt. Auburn Cemetery.

HOOVER, C(HARLES) R(UGLAS), chemist; b. Oskaloosa, Ia., Sept. 30, 1885; s. Hiram Alonzo and Edith Adaline (Crane) H.; Ph.B., Penn Coll., Oskaloosa, Ia., 1906; B.S., Haverford, 1907, M.A., 1908; Ph.D., Harvard, 1915; m. Anna Mary Johnson, Sept. 7, 1912; children—Albert Charles, John Crane. Prof. chemistry, Penn Coll., 1909-10; Austin fellow in chemistry, 1910-12, Carnegie research fellow in chemistry, 1912-13, Harvard; asso. prof. chemistry, Syracuse U., 1913-15; asso. prof. chemistry, 1915-18, prof. since 1918, v.p., 1926-27, Wesleyan U., Conn. Gas chemist research div. C.W.S., U.S. Army, 1918; cons. chemist same, 1917-19; cons. chemist, State Water Commn. and State Commn. Fisheries and Game, Conn., since 1928. Consultant Nat. Defense Research Com. Mem. Conn. State Board of Registration for Engineers; mem. State Flood Control and Water Policy Commn. Mem. of committees of Nat. Research Council and Assn. Harvard Chemists; fellow Am. Inst. Chemists, A.A.A.S.; mem. Am. Chem. Soc. (councillor, also pres. Conn. Valley sect.). Conn. Soc. Civil Engrs., New England Sewage Works Assn., Soc. Chem. Industry, Am. Public Health Assn., N.E.A., Sigma Xi, Phi Beta Kappa, Alpha Chi Sigma. Conglist. Rotarian. Inventor of gas absorbent and gas detector. Author: Laboratory Construction and Equipment; contbr. on chem. topics. Home: 10 Wesleyan Pl., Middletown, Conn. Died June 8, 1942.

HOOVER, HERBERT, thirty-first U.S. Pres.; b. West Branch, Ia., Aug. 10, 1874; s. Jesse Clark and Hulda Randall (Minthorn) H.; A.B. in Engring., Stanford, 1895; hon. degrees from 81 instns. in U.S. and abroad; 296 medals, awards, honors including 61 gold medals from Am., fgn. orgns. and socs. Hon. citizen of 24 European cities; 56 hon. memberships in sci. and tech. socs.; m. Lou Henry, 1899 (died Jan. 7, 1944); children—Herbert, Allan Henry. Profl. work in mines, r.r.'s, metall. works, U.S., Mexico, Can., Australia, Italy, Gt. Britain, South Africa, India, China, Russia, etc., 1895-1913. Represented Panama-Pacific Internat. Expn., in Europe, 1913-14; chmn. Am. Relief Com., London, Eng., 1914-15; chmn. Commn. for Relief in Belgium, 1915-19; U.S. food adminstr., June 1917-July 1, 1919; served as mem. War Trade Council; was chmn. U.S. Grain Corp., U.S. Sugar Equalization Bd., Interallied Food Council, Supreme Econ. Council, European Coal Council; chmn. Am. Relief Adminstrn. since 1919; v. chmn. Pres. Wilson's 2d Indsl. Conf., 1920; chmn. European Relief Council since 1920; apptd. sec. commerce by Pres. Harding, Mar. 5, 1921, reapptd. by Pres. Coolidge. Chmn. Pres.' Conf. on Unemployment, Sept. 20, 1921; mem. adv. com. Limitation of Armaments Conf., Nov. 1921, World War Debt Com., etc.; chmn. Colo. River Commn.; chmn. Spl. Miss. Flood Relief Commn., 1927; Pres., U.S., term 1929-33; renominated for Pres.; Rep. Nat. Conv., 1932. At request of Pres. Truman undertook coordination of world food supplies of 38 countries, March-June 1946; at request of Pres. Truman, undertook a study of econ. situation in Germany and Austria, 1947; chmn. Commn. On Orgn. Exec. Br. of Govt., 1947-49, also chmn. second commn., 1953-55; guest of Fed. Rep. of Germany at invitation Chancellor Adenauer, 1954; mem. adv. bd. World Bank Reconstrn. and Devel. Trustee Stanford U., Mills Coll., Carnegie Inst. of Wash., Henry E. Huntington Library and Art Gallery; chmn. C.R.B. Ednl. Fund, Am. Children's Fund, Boys' Clubs of Am., Finnish Relief Fund, Inc., Robt. A. Taft Meml. Found.; hon. mem. Woodrow Wilson Centenniel Celebration Commn.; hon. chmn. Nat. Fund Med. Edn., Hith. Information Found. Recipient John O'Hara Cosgrave gold medal award Dutch Treat Club of N.Y.; Gold medal Internat. Benjamin Franklin Soc., 1954. Mem. Am. Inst. Mining and Metall. Engr. (pres. 1920), Am. Engring. Council (pres. 1921), Am. Child Health Assn. (pres. 1922). Author: Am. Individualism, 1922; The Challenge to Liberty, 1934; America's First Crusade, 1941; The Problems of Lasting Peace, 1942; Addresses on American Road, 7 vols., 1938-55; Memoirs, Vols. I, II, III, 1951-52; The Ordeal of Woodrow Wilson, 1958. Translator (with Mrs. Hoover) Agricola de Ré Metallicca. Home: Waldorf Astoria Towers, N.Y.C. Died Oct. 1964.

HOOVER, HERBERT, JR., consulting engineer; born at London, England, August 4, 1903; son of Herbert (31st President of the United States) and Lou (Henry) H.; B.A., Stanford U., 1925; M.B.A., Harvard, U. 1928; hon. degrees N.Y.U., Rutgers, Temple U., 1956, U. So. California, Claremont Men's Coll., 1957; m. Margaret Watson, June 25, 1925; children—Margaret Ann (Mrs. Richard Tatem Brigham), Herbert, III, Joan Ledlie (Mrs. William Leland Vowles). Mining engineer, 1925; member research staff, Harvard Business School, 1928-29; communications engineer Western Air Express, 1929-31, Transcontinental & Western Air (T.W.A.), Incorporated, 1931-34; teaching fellow, at the California Institute Technology, 1934-35; president of the Consol. Engring. Corporation, 1936-46, consultant to govts. of Venezuela, Iran, Brazil, Peru, etc., 1942-52; pres., gen. mgr. United Geophysical Co., 1935-52, chmn. bd., 1952-53; under sec. of state, 1954-57; cons. engr., Los Angeles, 1957-69; dir. So. Cal. Edison Co., Monsanto Co., Am. Mut. Fund, Investment Co. Am., Hanna Mining Co., Pacific Mutual Life Ins. Co., Automobile Club So. Cal. (pres. 1965-67). Trustee Claremont Men's College, U. So. Cal., Boys Clubs Am., Freedoms Found. Appointed spl. adviser on worldwide petroleum matters to sec. of state, 1953. Decorated by Venezuela, Chile, Peru; Kemp Medalist, Columbia, 1956; Hoover Medalist, Am. Inst. Mining Engrs., Am. Soc. Mech. Engrs., Am. Inst. E.E., Am. Soc. C.E., 1957. Mem. Am. Inst. Mining, Metall. and Petroleum Engrs., Am. Assn. Petroleum Geols., Society Exploration Geophysicists, Am. Radio Relay League (pres. 1962-66). Cal. C. of C. (dir.). Republican. Clubs: Century, University (N.Y.C.); Bohemian (San Francisco); California (Los Angeles); Metropolitan (Washington); Chevy Chase Country; Eldorado (Palm Desert). Home: Pasadena CA Died July 9, 1969.

HOOVER, THEODORE JESSE, mining engr.; b. West Branch, Ia., Jan. 28, 1871; s. Jesse Clark and Huldah Randall (Minthorn) H.; A.B., Stanford, 1901; m. Mildred Crew Brooke, 1899 (died 1940); children—Louis Brooke (Mrs. William Havselt), and Mrs. Cornelius Willis, Mrs. Charles McLean, Jr. Manager of the consulting engineers of mines in Cal., Mex., Russia, Burma, Australia and Alaska, 1903-19; prof. mining and metallurgy Stanford, 1919—, dean of engring., 1925-36, now dean of engring. emeritus. Mem. Am. Inst. Mining and Metall. Engrs., Cooper Ornithol. Club. Author: Concentrating Ores by Flotation, 3d edit., 1916; Economics of Mining, 1933; 3d ed., 1947; The Engineering Profession, 1941; 2d ed., 1947. Home: Rancho del Oso, Davenport, Santa Cruz County, Cal. Died Feb. 5, 1955.

HOPKINS, ANDREW DELMAR, bioclimatist; b. Jackson Co., W.Va., Aug. 20, 1857; s. Andrew Evans and Miriam Florence (Evans) H.; early edn. at Jackson C.H., W.Va.; hon. Ph.D., W.Va. U., 1893; m. Adealia S. Butcher, of Wood Co., W.Va., Nov. 18, 1880; children—Roy Samuel, Edwin Butcher, Louise (dec.), Herbert Evans. Entomologist W.Va. Agrl. Expt. Sta., 1890-1902; v. dir. same, 1897-1902; prof. econ. entomology, W.Va. U., 1896-1902; apptd. forest entomologist in charge forest insect investigations, Division of Entomology, U.S. Department of Agriculture, July 1, 1902; senior entomologist, 1904-23; spl. research in bioclimatics, 1923-31; collaborator in charge of bioclimatics, 1931. Fellow A.A.A.S. (mem. 1893-1938, emeritus life mem. since 1938); former fellow Entomol. Soc. of America; former mem. Assn. Econ. Entomologists (v.p. 1900, pres. 1902), W.Va. Acad. Sciences (1st pres.), Entom. Soc. Washington (pres.), Biol. Soc. Washington (pres. 1920), Washington Acad. Sciences (v.p.), life mem. Am. Meteorol. Soc.; hon. mem. Soc. Econ. Biologists (Eng.). Author of numerous bulls., principally on forest tree insects and Scolytidae and bioclimatics, including development of the bioclimatic law and science of bioclimatics; results pub. as Bioclimatics. Club: Cosmos. Home: 1708 Washington Av., Parkersburg, W.Va.

HOPKINS, B. SMITH, chemist; b. Owosso, Mich., Sept. 1, 1873; s. Loren Hopkins and Clara Sibley (Norgate) H.; A.B., Albion (Mich.) Coll., 1896, A.M., 1897, Sc.D., 1926; studied Columbia, 1900-01; Ph.D., Johns Hopkins, 1906; LL.D., Carroll Coll., 1940; m. Maude Childs, June 25, 1901; children—Harvey Childs, B. Smith; m. 2d, May L. Whitsitt, Dec. 17, 1942. Began with pub. schs., Menominee, Mich., 1897; prin. high school, 1898-1900, supt. schs., 1901-04; prof. chemistry Neb. Wesleyan U., 1906-09. Carroll Coll., Waukesha, Wis., 1909-12; with U. Ill., 1912—, prof. inorganic chemistry, 1923—, dir. sci. Gen. Studies Div., 1941-42, dir. chemistry teaching Army Specialized Tng. Program, 1942-43; spl. summer lectr. Northwestern U., 1910-11, Western Reserve U., 1929, emeritus, 1941. Pres. Urbana Bd. Edn., 1932-44. Fellow A.A.A.S.; mem. Am. Chem. Soc., Am. Electrochem. Soc., Ill. Acad. Science (pres. 1933-34), Central Assn. Science and Mathematics Tchrs., Am. Philos. Soc., Sigma Xi, Phi Beta Kappa, Phi Lambda Upsilon, Alpha Chi Sigma, Alpha Tau Omega. Conglist. Clubs: Exchange; Chaos (Chgo.). Author: Exercises in Chemistry (with W. A. Noyes), 1917, 19; Chemistry of the Rarer Elements, 1923; Laboratory Exercises in General Chemistry (with H. A. Neville), 1925, 26, 31; General Chemistry for Colleges, 1930 (rev. 1937, 42); Essentials of College Chemistry, 1932; with J. C. Bailar, Jr. 1945; Laboratory Exercises in General Chemistry (with M. J. Copley), 1937, (with M. J. Copley and F. B. Schirmer, Jr., 1942); (with T. Moeller and F. B. Schirmer, Jr., 1946). Co-author: Chemistry and You, 1939, 44, 49; chapters in Chemistry of Less Familiar Elements, 1940. With colleagues discovered element 61, named it illinium, 1926. Home: 402 W. Florida Av., Urbana, Ill. Died Aug. 27, 1952.

HOPKINS, EDWIN BUTCHER, petroleum geologist; b. Evans, W.Va., Oct. 25, 1882; s. Andrew Delmar and Delia (Butcher) H.; student W.Va. U., 1899-1901, George Washington U., 1903-04; m. Amy Longcope, June 20, 1913; children—Mrs. Ted Fitch, Mrs. Jack Munger, Louise, Madeleine, Edwin. With U.S. Geol. Survey, 1906-09; geologist Mexican Eagle Petroleum Co., 1909-13; mgr. Cuban Oil Co., 1913-14; mgr. Internat. Petroleum Co., 1914-16; cons. petroleum geologist, 1916—; pres. Delta Petroleum Co.; v.p. and gen. mgr. Am. Maracaibo Co.; v.p. Drilling and Exploration Co., Inc.; dir. Santa Fe Corp., Petroleum Finance Corp. Home: Dallas, Tex. Died July 5, 1940.

HOPKINS, ERASTUS, chemist; b. Greenfield, Mass., June 9, 1867; s. W. S. B. and E. S. (Peck) H.; grad. Williams Coll., 1890, A.M., 1893, postgrad. studies Worcester Poly. Inst., B.Sc., 1893, M.Sc., 1900; m. Sept. 17, 1902, Anna L. Colvin, Enfield, Conn. Engaged in practice as chemist since 1893; spl. examiner for U.S. and chemist in charge U.S. laboratories (customs) at Boston, 1897-1900; now gen. mgr., sec. and treas. Lake Helen Mfg. Co., mfrs. Cassava and comptie flour starches. Mem. Sigma Phi, Soc. Chem. Industry, Am. Chem. Soc. Mayor Lake Helen since 1905. Author: Oil Chemists' Hand-Book, 1900 W9. Address: Lake Helen, Fla.

HOPKINS, GRANT SHERMAN, anatomist; b. Westfield, N.Y., Sept. 23, 1865; B.S., Cornell, 1889, Sc.D., 1893; D.V.M., N.Y. State Veterinary Coll., 1900; married; children—Ellen C., Florence M. (dec.), Stephen J. (dec.). Instr. history and embryology, 1889-96, asst. prof. anat. methods and comparative vet. anatomy, 1896-1903, prof. vet. anatomy, 1903-34, prof. emeritus since 1934, N.Y. State Vet. Coll. of Cornell U. Fellow A.A.A.S.; mem. Assn. Am. Anatomists, N.Y. State Vet. Med. Soc. Home: Ithaca, N.Y.

HOPKINS, JOSEPH GARDNER, physician; b. Brooklyn, June 30, 1882; s. George Gallagher and Alice (Gardner) H.; student Adelphi Acad., Brooklyn, 1890-98; A.B., Columbia, 1902; M.D., Johns Hopkins, 1907; unmarried. Interne Johns Hopkins Hosp., 1907-08; resident pathologist St. Luke's Hosp., New York, 1908-10; bacteriologist, 1910-13; asst. instr. clinical pathol. Columbia, 1911-13, asso. in bacteriol., 1913-14, asst. prof. bacteriol., 1915-17, asso. instr. in dermatology, 1920-26; prof. dermatol., 1925-47, prof. emeritus since 1947; dir. Dermatology Vanderbilt Clinic, 1926-47, Presbyn. Hosp., 1936-47; practicing physician New York City since 1921. Served as bacteriol. Am. Red Cross Commn. to Serbia, 1915. Served as lt., capt. U.S. Army Med. Corps, 1917-19; investigator com. on med. research, Office Scientific Research Development, 1941-46, tech. observer, consultant Office of Field Service, 1945-46; civilian cons. to surgeon gen. (Army), 1945-46; cons. Veterans Hosp., Bronx, N.Y., since 1946. Mem. Am. Bd. Dermatol. and Syphilol., 1938-47. Mem. Am.

Dermatol. Assn., Am. Acad. Dermatol., Soc. Investigative Dermatol., New York Dermatol. Soc., Am. Soc. Pathol. and Bacteriol., Soc. Am. Bacteriol., Am. Mycological Soc., Torrey Botanical, Soc. Pithotomists, Royal Soc. Medicine, Austrian Dermatol. Soc. (hon. mem.), Swedish Dermatol. Soc. (corr. mem.), Phi Beta Kappa, Alpha Omega Alpha. Republican. Episcopalian. Clubs: Century Assn., Columbia University. Home: 217 Haven Av., New York 33. Office: 102 E. 78th St., N.Y. City 21. Died Feb. 27, 1951; buried Washington St. Cemetery, Geneva, N.Y.

HOPKINS, NEVIL MONROE, engineer, educator; b. Portland, Me., Sept. 15, 1873; s. Francis Nevil and Frances Anna (Monroe) H.; B.S., Columbian (now George Washington) U.; 1899, M.S., 1900, Ph.D., 1902; grad. student, Harvard, 1901; m. Katherine Guy, Jan. 5, 1897; children—Anne Dorsey (Mrs. James W. Allison), Frances Monroe (Mrs. Horace W. Peaslee); m. 2d, Raymonde Briggs, June 22, 1932. Instr. chemistry, Columbian Univ., 1899-1902; asst. prof. chemistry since 1902, George Washington U.; professional engr. lecturer, Coll. of Engring., New York U., since 1934; mem. faculty Institute for Industrial Progress; mem. Munroe, Hall & Hopkins, cons. engrs. Electrician, Gen. Electric Co., Schenectady, N.Y.; editorial rep. Electrical World and Engineer, N.Y.; trustee and in charge div. elec. engring., Inst. of Industrial Research; v.p. and elec. engr. Electric Tachometer Co. Elec. engr. Navy Dept. in charge power plant design and constrn. at all navy yards and stas., 1905-08; expert engr. U.S. Office of Public Roads, Washington, D.C., since 1909. Inventor of electric and mech. devices, instruments for high temperature measurements, etc.; awarded John Scott medal, Franklin Inst., 1900. Temporary asst. Am. Embassy, Paris, during outbreak European war; vol. to French Red Cross and with French army in retreat from Mons to Paris. Lectured in Am. theatres on European war for benefit of Belgian destitute; chmn. Belgian Scholarship Com., for bringing to America worthy Belgian professors and scholars and providing funds for their support with free use of Am. univs. Lecturer on the navy and national defense, auspices of Navy League U.S. Tech. adviser, design sect. of gun div. Bur. of Ordnance, since 1917; maj. of ordnance, U.S. Army, 1917. Consulting engr. Rys. Electric Equipment Co., Philadelphia; cons. engr. Aircraft Fireproofing Corp., New York, also of Union Carbide and Carbon Co., New York, and in charge dept. of mech. research, Union Carbide and Carbon Research Labs., Long Island; dir. research Burnot Fireproofing Products; pres. New-Mix Products, Inc., Internat. Tube Co. Inventor and developer "Televotes," "Radiovotes"; also submersible battle cruiser and long range naval and antiaircraft guns, high explosive antiaircraft shells and battleship wrecking bombs; new blast meter and system for U.S. Army for measuring force of high explosives in the field; new electro chronograph for ballistic measurements; inventor Synchronous Electric Registration and Voting System, and Home Registration Voting Stations therefor, making possible mass voting by radio and newspaper announcement; automatic radio-electric survey system showing the number of radio receiving sets tuned in to any particular broadcasting station wave lenth, at any time; inactivators for destroying criminal time bombs and infernal machines; designer of torpedo and magnetic-mine protection equipment for freighters at sea; also super rocket guns and rocket missiles. President National Electric Ballots, Inc. Consultant in high explosives in regard to bomb-proofs and shelters for animals to American Society for Prevention of Cruelty to animals. Recipient of George Washington U. Alumni Award for notable achievement in science and conspicuous service, June 1942. FEllow A.A.A.S., American Institute Mech. Engrs., mem. Am. Chem. Soc., Am. Electrochem. Soc., Am. Soc. Testing Materials, Am. Soc. M.E., Am. Inst. Chem. Engrs., Soc. Am. Mil. Engineers, Army Ordnance Assn., Inst. of Social Sciences, Military Order of World War, Master Marines' Assn. (Gloucester, Mass.), Loyal Legion, United States Power Squadron, S.R., Society Colonial Wars (lt. gov. and gov.). Clubs: Metropolitan, Cosmos, Chevy Chase, Adventurers, Corinthian Yacht (Washington, D.C.); MacDowell, National Arts (v.p.), New York Yacht (New York). Author: Model Engines and Boats, 1898; Twentieth Century Magic, 1904; Experimental Electro-Chemistry, 1905; The Strange Cases of Mason Brant, 1916; The Racoon Lake Mystery; Over the Threshold of War; The Outlook for Research and Invention; The Inventor and His Workshop; The Horrors in the Grew Mystery; also over 100 articles in scientific and engring. jours., and short stories in mags. Home: 12 Washington Square N., New York. Died Mar. 26, 1945; buried in Rock Creek Cemetery, Washington.

HOPKINS, THOMAS CRAMER, geologist; b. Center County, Pa., May 4, 1861; s. Isaac Cramer and Mary Ann (Glenn) H.; B.S., De Pauw U., 1881; M.S., 1890; A.M., Leland Stanford Jr. U., 1892; Ph.D., U. Chgo., 1900; D.Sc., Colgate U., 1923; m. Edistina Farrow, Jan. 8, 1890 (dec. May 1907); m. 2d, Elizabeth G. Hendrix, Mar. 31, 1909. Prin. high sch., Rising Sun, Ind., 1887-88; instr. in chemistry De Pauw U., 1888-89; asst. geologist Ark. Geol. Survey, 1889-92, Ind. Geol. Survey, 1895, 96, 1901; prof. geology Pa. State Coll., 1896-99, Syracuse U., 1900-32. Mem. Geol. Soc. America, Washington Geol. Soc., Sigma Xi, Phi Beta Kappa, Phi Kappa Phi, Phi Delta Theta. Republican. Methodist. Clubs: Faculty, Current Events, Onondaga, Geology. Author: Marble and Other Limestones, 1893; Brownstones of Pennsylvania, 1896; Clays and Clay Industries of Pennsylvania, 1898; Elements of Physical Geography (text-book), 1908; Laboratory Manual on Physical Geography, 1909; also numerous papers on geol. subjects pub. in tech. jours. and in various state reports. Home: 114 Victoria Pl., Syracuse, N.Y. Died Apr. 3, 1935.

HOPPER, DAVID CLAUDE, cons. engr.; b. Caddo Gap, Ark., Nov. 2, 1888; s. John Franklin and Martha (Burke) H.; B.S., U. Ark., 1915; student Chgo. Central Sta. Inst., 1915-16, U. Pitts., 1927; m. Ida Middlebrooks, Dec. 4, 1918; children—Mary Jean (Mrs. K. L. Wommack), Martha Doris (Mrs. Courter D. Mills), Engr. Union Switch & Signal Co., Pitts., 1914; engr. Commonwealth Edison Co., Chgo., 1915-18; engr. Am. Internat. Shipbuilding., Phila., 1918; engr. Va. Power Co., Newport News, 1919-20; engr. No. Ohio Power & Light Co., Akron, 1920-23; engr. Duquesne Light Co., Pitts., 1923-54; instr. Pa. State U., 1954-59; cons. prof. engr., 1959-68. Served as cadet lt. F.A., U.S. Army, World War I. Decorated Legion of Honor. Profl. licensed elec. engr., Pa. Mem. I.E.E.E., Tau Beta Pi, Tau Epsilon Chi. Republican. Mem. Christian Ch. Mason (Shriner). Club: Winston-Salem Engineers. Author tech. articles engring. jours. Home: Winston-Salem NC Died Apr. 29, 1968; buried Winston-Salem NC

HOPPES, JOHN J., mechanical engr., mfr.; b. Circleville, O., 1857; s. Daniel and Helen (Stanton) H.; ed. pub. schs.; m. Hattie Merrell, of Auburn, N.Y., Dec. 29, 1890. Entered manufacturing business at Springfield, O., 1886; inventor of Hoppes system of heating and purifying water for steam boilers, also Hoppes system of deaërating water; designer of Hoppes hydro-electric plant for small streams; holder of 45 patents; now pres. Hoppes Mfg. co., Everwear Mfg. Co., Hoppes Water Wheel Co. Mem. City Council, Springfield, 1887-88; mem. Bd. Fire and Police Commrs., 1895-96; city commr. under commission manager form of govt., 1913-19 (originator of this form of govt.). Mem. Am. Soc. M.E. Mason, Shriner, Club: Springfield Country, Home: Springfield, O.

HORN, FRANK CHURCHILL, consulting engr.; b. Macomb, Ill., Jan. 8, 1861; s. Adam E. and Martha P. (Naylor) H.; ed. pub. and high schs. and under pvt. instruction; m. Margaret K. Ferguson, of Guelph, Ont., Can., June 24, 1888 (died 1899). Asst. engr., St.L.&S.F. R.R., in charge heavy mountain work and building bridges in western Ark., 1881-82; in gen. engring. practice and contr. water works sewerage systems, foundations, bldgs., rys., sts. and rds. until 1894; in charge constrn. of regulating work, Chicago Drainage Canal, Lockport, Ill., 1895; asst. chief engr. Denver Union Water Co., and built system of gravity filtration beds at Platte Canon, Colo., for purification of water supply for Denver, later built masonry dam for conserving water supply for Denver; constructing engr. U.S. Reclamation Service, 1905-08; apptd. spl. consulting engr., same, 1911. Invented pneumatic system for placing concrete in large units. Home: Boise, Ida. Died Feb. 16, 1919.

HORN, GEORGE HENRY, physician, entomologist; b. Phila., Apr. 7, 1840; s. Philip Henry and Frances Isabella (Brock) H.; M.D., U. Pa., 1861. Served as mil. surgeon U.S. Army, Civil War, regtl. surgeon Cal. Volunteers, 1864; mem. Entomol. Soc. of Phila., 1860, pres., 1866; vice dir. Acad. of Natural Scis., 1876-83, dir. entomol. sect., 1883-97; prof. entomology U. Pa., 1889; prin. contbr. to study and classification of Coleoptera, responsible for naming and describing more than 1,550 species; pres. Am. Entomol. Soc., 1883-97; hon. mem. Entomol. Soc. France. Author papers: "Description of New North American Coleoptera in the Cabinet of the Entomological Society of Philadelphia," 1860; The Classification of the Coleoptera of North America, 1883. Died Beesley's Point, N.J., Nov. 24, 1897.

HORNADAY, WILLIAM TEMPLE, zoölogist; b. Plainfield, Ind., Dec. 1, 1854; s. William and Martha (Varner) H.; ed. Ia. State Coll.; studied zoölogy and museology in U.S. and Europe; Sc.D., U. of Pittsburgh, 1906; A.M., Yale, 1917; Ph.M., Ia. State Coll., 1923; m. Josephine Chamberlain, Sept. 11, 1879; 1 dau., Helen Ross (Mrs. George T. Fielding). As collecting zoölogist visited Cuba, Fla., the W.I., S. America, India, Ceylon, the Malay Peninsula and Borneo, 1875-79; chief taxidermist U.S. Nat. Mus., 1882-90; in real estate business, Buffalo, N.Y., 1890-96; dir. New York Zoöl. Park, 1896-1926 (retired). Gold medalist Republic of France; British Royal Soc. for Protection of Birds, Royal Zoöl. Soc. of Antwerp; New York Zoöl. Soc.; Camp Fire Club of America; Inter-Nat. Congress for Study and Protection of Birds; silver medalist Société Nationale d'Acclimatation of France; holder of Cross of Crown of Belgium. Active in promoting game preserves and new laws for the protection of wild life generally; took initiative in creation of Mont. Nat. Bison Range, Wichita Nat. Bison Range, and Elk River Game Preserve (Mont.); the Bayne law to prohibit the sale of native game; and new tariff law to prohibit all importations of wild birds' plumage into U.S. for millinery purposes (1913); organized Permanent Wild Life Protection Fund, 1913-14. Author: Two Years in the Jungle, 1885; Taxidermy and Zoölogical Collecting, 1892; The American Natural History, 1904; Camp-Fires in the Canadian Rockies, 1906; Camp-Fires on Desert and Lava, 1908; Wild Life Conservation in Theory and Practice, 1914; Minds and Manners of Wild Animals, 1922; Tales from Nature's Wonderlands, 1924; A Wild-Animal Round-Up, 1925; Wild Animal Interviews, 1928; Thirty Years War for Wild Life, 1931. Home: Stamford, Conn. Died Mar. 6, 1937.

HORNER, LEONARD SHERMAN, elec. engr.; b. Marshall, Va., Mar. 26, 1875; s. Frederick (U.S. Navy) and Maria Elizabeth H.; prep. edn. Bethel Mil. Acad., Warrenton, Va.; E.E., Lehigh U., 1898; m. Julia Stuyvesant Barry, Nov. 8, 1902; children—H. Mansfield, Helen N. Began with engr. constrn. dept., Am. Telephone & Telegraph Co., New York, 1898; with Crocker-Wheeler Co. as sales engr. and mgr. for Conn., 1900-08; v.p. Acme Wire Co., 1908-26, now dir.; pres. Niles-Bement-Pond Co., 1926-30; v.p. and dir. The Bullard Co. Chmn. com. on census of mfrs., Dept. Commerce, 1931-32, chmn. Nat. Research Council Com., 1929-30, in preparation of aircraft prodn. study and report, which study covered factors affecting increased output and reduced cost of prodn. and embodied recommendations in methods, etc.; dep. adminstr. National Recovery Administration, 1933-34; now active in estate management and supervision of investments; also active on indsl. surveys and as indsl. advisor to mfrs. With troop A, New York Cavalry, in Puerto Rico, Spanish-Am. War, 1898; with Air Service at Washington, D.C., World War, 1917-18, as chief of staff, Bureau Aircraft Production, rank of maj.; promoted to lt. col. Mem. U.S. Chamber Commerce (dir. 1929, 30), Chamber Commerce of New Haven (v.p.; dir.). Mem. Nat. Industrial Conf. Bd., Nat. Assn. Mfrs., New England Council, Va. Hist. Soc., New Haven Hist. Soc., Sigma Chi, Am. Legion. Republican. Episcopalian. Clubs: Graduate, New Haven Country (New Haven); Army and Navy (Washington, D.C.). Home: 870 Prospect St., New Haven, Conn. Died Aug. 1, 1943.

HORNER, WESLEY WINANS, consulting engr.; b. Columbia, Mo., Sept. 22, 1883; s. William A. and Minnie (Winans) H.; B.S.E., Washington U., 1905, D.Eng. (hon.), 1952; post grad. deg. in C.E., 1909; m. Elinor Alice Hall, June 16, 1908; children—Frederic Winans, John Linscott, Richard William, David Alan. Asst. engr. 1905-19, engring. service City of St. Louis, chief engr., 1919-32, cons. engr. since 1932; in gen. personal cons. engring. practice, 1916-32; sr. partner Horner & Shifrin, cons. engrs., St. Louis, since 1933; faculty Washington Univ. as lecturer and prof. sanitary and hydraulic engring. 1934-42. Mem. tech. bd. of rev. P.W.A., 1933-35; water consultant and mem. nat. water com. Nat. Resources Planning Bd., 1936-43; bd. cons. engrs. Dept. of Agr., 1940-43, mem. adv. com. on research, 1952-55; mem. engring. adv. com. AEC, 1949-54. Mem. task force on water and power 2d Hoover Commn., 1953-55. Recipient Rudolph Hering Medal, Am. Soc. C.E., 1937. Mem. St. Louis C. of C. (com. chmn.), U.S. C. of C. (natural resources com.), Fedn. Civic Improvement Assns. (officer), Smoke Abatement League (pres.), State Bd. of Registration for Architects and Profl. Engrs. of Missouri, Am. Geophysical Union, Am. Pub. Works Assn. (past pres.), Am. Inst. Cons. Engrs., Am. Soc. C. E. (dir. 1933-35, pres., 1946). Sigma Xi, Tau Beta Pi, Sigma Chi. Clubs: Engineers, Missouri Athletic (St. Louis); Cosmos (Washington). Republican. Conglist. Contbr. to tech. pubs. Home: 64 Broadview Dr., Clayton 5, Mo. Office: 803 Shell Bldg., St. Louis 3. Died Sept. 22, 1958.

HORNER, WILLIAM EDMONDS, anatomist; b. Warrenton, Va., June 3, 1793; s. William and Mary (Edmonds) H.; grad. U. Pa., 1814; m. Elizabeth Welsh, Oct. 26, 1820, 10 children. Adj. prof. anatomy U. Pa., 1819, later prof., dean med. dept., 1822-52; described for 1st time tensor tarsi, spl. muscle connected with lachrymal apparatus, 1824; a founder St. Joseph's Hosp. Author: The American Dissector, 1819; A Treatise on Pathological Anatomy for the Use of Dissectors, 1823; Treatise on Special and General Anatomy, 2 vols., 1826; Treatise on Pathological Anatomy (1st path. text pub. in America), 1829. Died Phila., Mar. 13, 1853.

HORNEY, KAREN, psychiatrist; b. Hamburg, Germany, Sept. 16, 1885; dau. Berndt and Clotilde (Von Ronzelen) Danielson; M.D., Univ. Berlin, 1913; m. Oscar Horney, Oct. 1909; children—Brigitte (Mrs. K. Tschetwerikoff), Marianne (Mrs. W. von Eckardt), Renate (Mrs. F. Crevenna). Came to U.S., 1932, naturalized, 1938. Instr. Inst. for Psychoanalysis, Berlin, 1920-32; asso. dir., Chicago Inst. for Psychoanalysis, 1932-34; lecturer New Sch. for Social Research, New York City, since 1935; dean Am. Inst. for Psychoanalysis since 1941. Mem. Assn. for Advancement of Psychoanalysis, Am. Psychiatric Assn. Author: The Neurotic Personality of Our Time, 1936; New Ways in Psychoanalysis, 1939; Self-Analysis, 1942; Out Inner Conflicts, 1945; Neurosis and Human Growth, 1950. Most important contbns. were emphasis on cultural and social factors in personality devel. and growth of neurosis which differed from Freudian emphasis on biol. factors, and research in area of feminine psychology; described anxiety as failure of neurotic defense mechanisms in helping individual to cope with world. Died N.Y.C., Dec. 1952.

HORRAX, GILBERT, (ha'rux), neurosurgeon; b. Glen Ridge, N.J., Apr. 9, 1887; s. Edwin and Mary Alice (Gilbert) H.; A.B., Williams Coll., 1909, Sc.D., 1936; M.D., Johns Hopkins, 1913; m. Geraldine Kemmis Martin, June 29, 1921 (dec.); children—Trudeau Martin, Elizabeth Daintry; m. 2d, Helen Anne Pagenstecher (Mrs. S. S. Tregellas), July 19, 1938; 1 step-son, S. Staley Tregellas. House officer Peter Bent Brigham Hosp., Boston, 1913-14, neurol. resident, 1915-16, jr., later sr. asso. in neurol. surgery, 1919-32; Arthur Tracy Cabot fellow Harvard Med. Sch., 1914-15, successively asst., instr., faculty instr. and asst. prof. surgery, 1919-32, instr. in neurology courses for graduates, 1935-41; resident surgeon Mass. Gen. Hosp., 1916-17; neurosurgeon N.E. Deaconess and N.E. Bapt. Hosps., 1932—; in charge dept. neurosurgery The Lahey Clinic, Boston, 1932—; cons. to U.S. Vets. Hosp., W. Roxbury, Mass., 1944-46; cons. in neurosurgery Cushing Gen. Hosp., Framingham, Mass. Served from 1st lt. to maj. M.C., U.S. Army, France, 1917-19; USPHS Res., 1944—. Diplomate Am. Bd. of Surgery and Am. Bd. Neurol. Surgery. Fellow A.C.S.; mem. Soc. Neurol. Surgeons (pres. 1937-39), Am. Neurol. Soc. (v.p. 1940-41), Assn. for Research in Nervous and Mental Diseases (v.p. 1936), Am. Surg. Assn., N.E. and Boston surg. socs., Harvey Cushing Soc., Boston Soc. Psychiatry and Neurology (pres. 1939), Mass. Med. Soc., A.M.A., Royal Soc. of Med. (hon. mem. sect. of neurology); corrs. mem. Société de Neurol., France; hon. mem. La Societe de Neuro-chirurgie de la langue Française; mem. Phi Delta Theta, Gargoyle. Trustee Met. State Hospital (Waltham, Mass.), Lawrence Acad. (Groton, Mass.). Clubs: Harvard (Boston); Williams (N.Y.C.); The Country, Longwood Cricket (Brookline, Mass.); Orleans Fish and Game (Quebec, Can.). Contbr. numerous sci. articles to med. and surg. publs. Home: 30 Cedar Rd., Chestnut Hill, Mass. Office: 605 Commonwealth Av., Boston 15. Died Sept. 28, 1957; buried Forest Hills Cemetery.

HORSFALL, FRANK LAPPIN, JR., physician; b. Seattle, Dec. 14, 1906; s. Frank L. and Jessie Laura (Ludden) H.; B.A., U. Wash., 1927; M.D., C.M., McGill U., 1932; Ph.D., Uppsala Univ., 1961; LL.D., U. Alberta, 1963; D.Sc., McGill University, 1963; m. to Norma E. Campagnari, July 1, 1937; children—Frank III, Susan, Mary. House officer pathology Peter Bent Brigham Hosp., Boston, 1932-33; resident physician Royal Victoria Hosp., Montreal, 1933-34; resident surgeon Montreal General Hosp., 1934; asst. The Rockefeller Inst., 1934-37, member, 1941-57, mem., prof., 1957-60, v.p. clin. studies, 1955-60, asst. resident physician Hosp. The Rockefeller Inst., 1934-36, resident physician, 1936-37, physician, 1941-55, physician-in-chief, 1955-60; staff mem. Internat. Health Div., The Rockefeller Found., 1937-41; pres., dir., trustee Sloan-Kettering Institute Cancer Research, 1960-71; director research Memorial Sloan-Kettering Cancer Center, 1965-71, Memorial Hospital Cancer and Allied Diseases, 1965-71; professor of medicine Cornell U. Med. Coll., 1960-71, dir., prof. microbiology Sloan-Kettering Div. Grad. Sch. Med. Scis., 1960-71; cons. to Surgeon Gen. U.S. Army, mem. commn. immunization Army Epidemiol. Bd., 1947-55; cons. USPHS, 1948-53; mem. nat. research council com. adv. U.S. Army Chem. Corps, Washington, 1957-59; chmn. research and engring. adv. panel Def. Dept., 1960-61, vice chmn., 1959-60, mem.-at-large Def. Sci. Bd., 1957-62; vice chmn. Biol. and Chem. Def. Planning Bd., 1959-61; mem. U.S. Panel, U.S.-Japan com. Sci. Coop., 1962-63, Human Cancer Virus Task Force, NIH, 1962-64, Pres.' Commn. Heart Disease, Cancer, Stroke, 1964-65. Chmn. vis. com. Med. Dept. Brookhaven Nat. Lab., Upton, L.I., N.Y., 1955-57; mem. sci. adv. comm. Inst. Microbiology Rutgers U., 1955-62; mem. expert adv. panel virus diseases WHO, Geneva, Switzerland, 1956-71; director of Public Health Research Institute City of New York, Incorporated, 1956-71, chairman research council, 1956-57; special cons. N.Y.C., Dept. Health, 1956-71; member nat. adv. com. Okla. Med. Research Found., Oklahoma City, 1957-71; mem. bd. sci. dirs. Roscoe B. Jackson Meml. Lab., Bar Harbor, Me., 1958-61; mem. exec. com. Health Research Council City N.Y., 1958-68, vice chairman, 1962-66; member panel of advisers New York State Committee for Medical Edn., 1962-63; sci. adv. com. Inst. Cancer Research, 1962-71; sci. adv. council N.Y. State Legislature, 1963-71; mem. Commn. Health Services City New York, 1959-71; member committee respiratory diseases, National Tb Association, 1959-60; chairman program committee 5th Internat. Poliomyelitis Conf., Denmark, 1960; gen. chmn. 2d Internat. Conf. Congenital Malformations. N.Y. 1963; mem. com. virus research and epidemiology Nat. Found., 1956-58, com. on research basic scis., vaccine adv. com., 1959-71; adv. com. electronic computers biology and medicine Nat. Acad. Scis.-NRC, 1959-60; com. sci. and pub. policy Nat. Acad. Scis., 1963-66. Trustee Internat. Med. Congress, Ltd., 1959-71, v.p., 1962-71; trustee Internat. Poliomyelitis Congress Ltd., 1959-71, So. Research Inst., 1960-71, Memorial Sloan-Kettering Cancer Center, N.Y., 1960-71, bd. govs. Weltzmann Inst. Sci., Rehovoth, Israel, 1964-71; trustee Med. Library Center N.Y., 1959-71. Served to comdr. M.C., USNR, 1942-46. Recipient Banting research fellow, McGill U. Med. Sch., 1930-32; Holmes gold medal, 1932; Eli Lilly award bacteriology and immunology, 1937; Casgrain and Charbonneau award in medicine McGill U., 1942; John F. Lewis prize Am. Philos. Soc., 1959; Alumnus Summa Laude Dignatus award Alumni Assn. U. Wash., 1962; gold medal award Peter Bent Brigham Hosp., 1963. Fellow Montreal Medico-Chirurgical Soc.; mem. Am. Assn. Immunologists (councillor 1962-66, v.p. 1966-67, pres. 1967-68), A.M.A., Am. Philos. Soc., Am. Pub. Health Assn. (mem. Lasker awards committee 1958-60), Assn. of Am. Cancer Insts. (president 1968-71), Royal Society Medicine (affiliate), National Institutes Health (member virus and rickettsial study section 1948-53), International Board Editors Excerpta Medica (U.S. sect. rep.), American Soc. Clin. Investigation (past v.p.), N.Y. Acad. Medicom. 1957-58, editorial bd. Bull. 1969-71), Nat. Acad. Scis., Assn. Am. Phys., A.A.A.S., Harvey Soc., Practitioners' Soc. (president 1969-71), Am. Assn. Cancer Research, American Assn. Pathologists and Bacteriologists, Am. Soc. Microbiology, Soc. Exptl. Biology and Medicine, Am. Acad. Arts and Scis., Royal Coll. Physicians and Surgeons Can. Mem. bd. editors Jour. Immunology, 1950-62; asso. editor Virology, 1954-60, co-editor, Journal of Experimental Medicine, 1958-60, adv. editor, 1963-71; mem. editorial bd. World Wide Abstracts Gen. Medicine, 1958-71, Am. Jour. Pub. Health, 1958-60; mem. editorial adv. bd. Med. World News, 1959-61. Home: New York City NY Died Feb. 1971.

HORSFALL, R(OBERT) BRUCE, (hors'fal), artist, naturalist; b. Clinton, Ia., Oct. 21, 1868; s. John Tomlin and Anne (Battersby) H.; ed. pub. schs.; studied Cincinnati Art Acad., 1886-89; awarded European scholarship and studied at Art Acad., Munich, and at Paris, France, 1889-93; m. Carra Elisabeth Huntting, May 27, 1906; 1 son, R. Bruce. First exhibited at Chicago, Ill., in 1886; also at Chicago Expn., 1893, and at Midwinter Expn., San Francisco, 1893-94; scientific illustrations for Am. Museum Natural History, New York, 1898-99, for Princeton Patagonian Report, 1904-14; illustrator for Century and St. Nicholas, 1899-1921; illustrated Land Mammals of the Western Hemisphere, 1912-13; also many natural history books. Permanently represented by backgrounds for Habitat Groups, Am. Museum Natural History, Peabody Museum (Yale), Kent Scientific Museum (Grand Rapids, Mich.), State Museum (Springfield, Ill.), Zoöl. Museum (U. of Minn.); life size paintings of Great Auk, Calif. condor, Pallas cormorant in Adminstrn. Bldg., New York Zoöl. Park; Great Auk, Dinosaur, in U.S. Nat. Museum; by portraits of Dr. William John Sinclair and Alexander H. Phillips in Guyot Hall, Princeton University. Asst. biologist, Oregon Fish and Game Commn., 1914-16. Mem. Am. Ornithologists' Union, Cooper Ornithological Club, Northwest Bird and Mammal Soc., Am. Soc. Mammalogists, Am. Museum Natural History. Address: Route No. 2, Fairport, N.Y. Died Mar. 24, 1948.

HORSFIELD, THOMAS, naturalist, physician; b. Bethlehem, Pa., May 12, 1773; s. Timothy and Juliana Sarah (Parsons) H.; M.D., U. Pa., 1798. Surgeon, Dutch Colonial Army, Java, 1801; joined Brit. East India Co., 1811; went to London with collections of Java flora, 1819; curator East India Co. Museum, 1820-59. Author: An Experimental Dissertation on Rhus Vernix, Rhus Radicans and Rhus Glabrum (pioneer contbn. to study of poison ivy and sumac in exptl. pharmacology), 1798; Plantae Javanicae Rariores, 5 vols., 1838-52. Died July 24, 1859.

HORSFORD, EBEN NORTON, chemist; b. Moscow, N.Y., July 27, 1818; s. Jerediah and Charity (Norton) H.; grad. Rensselaer Poly. Inst., 1838; A.M., Harvard, 1847; studied analytical chemistry with Liebig, Giessen, Germany, 1844-46; m. Mary L'Hommedieu Gardiner, 1847, 4 daus.; m. 2d, Phoebe Dayton Gardiner, 1857, 1 dau. Prof. mathematics and natural scis. Albany (N.Y.) Female Acad., 1840-44; taught chemistry, research Lawrence Scientific Sch. (now part of Harvard), Cambridge, Mass., 1847-63; pres. bd. visitors Wellesley Coll.; early mem. Am. Chem. Soc. Author: The Theory and Art of Breadmaking, 1861; contbr. many articles to scientific jours. Died Cambridge, Jan. 1, 1893.

HORSLEY, JOHN SHELTON, (hors'le), surgeon; b. Lovingston, Va., Nov. 24, 1870; s. John and Rose Evelyn (Shelton) H.; student acad. dept. U. of Va., 1889-90, M.D., 1892; post-graduate courses, New York; LL.D., U. of Richmond; D.Sc., Medical Coll. of Va.; m. Eliza Braxton, Feb. 14, 1899; children—John Shelton (dec.), Elizabeth Braxton (dec.), Caperton Braxton, Guy Winston, Mary Caperton, Braxton, Frederick, Alice Cabell. Began practice in Nelson County, Va.; moved to Staunton, 1894; asst. to Dr. John A. Wyeth, of New York, 1896; editor New York Polyclinic Med. Jour., 1897-98; at El Paso, Tex., 1898-1903; propr. and surgeon in chief St. Lukes's Hosp., El Paso, 1899-1903; prof. principles of surgery, Med. Coll. of Va., Richmond, 1903-12; surgeon in charge St. Elizabeth's Hospital. Certified by American Board of Surgery. Fellow American Surg. Assn., Southern Surg. Assn., Am. Med. Assn., hon. mem. Soc. of Alumni of Bellevue Hosp.; mem. Internat. Soc. of Surgery; Richmond Acad. Medicine (former president), Phi Beta Kappa, Alpha Omega Alpha, Sigma Xi; honorary member N.M. Medical Soc., St. Louis Med. Soc.; ex-pres. Med. Soc. of Va.; ex-pres. Southern Med. Assn.; ex-pres. Va. Acad. of Science. Democrat. Unitarian. Clubs: Commonwealth, Country of Va.; Colonnade. Author: Surgery of Blood Vessels; Operative Surgery; Surgery of Stomach and Small Intestines; Research and Medical Progress; Surgery of Stomach and Duodenum. Associate editor of Lewis Practice of Surgery. Contbr. to medical press on surgical subjects. Home: Westmoreland Pl. Office: 617 W. Grace St., Richmond, Va. Died Apr. 7, 1946.

HORSTMANN, WILLIAM H., inventor, mfr.; b. Cassel, Germany. Came to Am., 1815; became silk goods mfr., Phila.; invented and patented various machines and improvements for silk goods manufacture; introduced Jacquard loom into Am.; founder firm William H. Horstmann & Sons (oldest silk mfg. firm in U.S.). Died Phila., 1852.

HORTENSTINE, RALEIGH, civil engineer, consultant; born at Abingdon, Va., July 12, 1887; s. Joel Wilson and Mary Virginia (Campbell) H.; B.S. in C.E., Va. Poly. Inst., 1906; grad. student Cornell U., 1906-07; m. Helen Buchanan Grant, June 26, 1912; 1 son, Raleigh. Engr. and supt. Penn Bridge Co., Beaver Falls, Pa., 1907-12; contracting engr. Va. Bridge & Iron Co., Dallas, Tex., 1912-18, plant mgr. Memphis, Tenn., 1918-23; v.p., gen. mgr. Wyatt Industries, Inc. (formerly Wyatt Metal & Boiler Works), Dallas, 1923-38, pres. 1938-55, chmn. bd., 1955-61, sr. chmn. bd., 1961-68; consultant Wyatt division U.S. Industries, Inc., 1968-69; dir. Lone Star Steel Co., Dallas; dir. Republic Nat. Bank of Dallas. Mem., past chmn. bd. trustees Tex. A and M Research Found. Mem. N.A.M. (past dir.), Am. Soc. C.E., Tau Beta Pi. Presbyn. Clubs: Country, Petroleum. Home: Dallas TX Died Nov. 15, 1969; buried Hillcrest Mausoleum, Dallas TX

HORTON, ELMER GRANT, M.D., educator; b. Horton Hill, Erie County, N.Y., May 22, 1868; s. Lorenzo Lincoln and Phila Ann (Chase) H.; B.S., Cornell U., 1892; fellow U. of Pa., 1895-96; M.D., Ohio Med. U., Columbus, 1906; grad. study, Harvard, 1912-14; m. Belle Fisher, Sept. 4, 1894; children—Vivian Fisher, Mildred Mae (Mrs. Harry R. Ansel). Teacher dist. schs., 1885-88, Cornell U. Summer Sch., 1892; instr. in sciences, Detroit School for Boys, 1892-93; prof. hygiene and physical culture, Wabash Coll., 1893-95; instr. in hygiene U. of Pa., 1896-98; bacteriologist and chemist in charge Ohio State Bd. of Health labs., 1898-1907; health commr., Columbus, O., 1907-09; practice in pediatrics since 1912; pediatrist and asst. chief of staff Children's Hosp.; head of pediatric dept. University Hosp.; in charge Isolation Hosp.; lecturer on communicable diseases, Grant Hosp. Prof. hygiene, Ohio Med. U., 1902-07, prof. pediatrics 1912-14; prof. pediatrics, Starling Ohio Med. Coll., 1907-12; asst. prof. pediatrics, Ohio State U., 1914-24, prof., 1924-37, clin. prof. of pediatrics, 1937-39, emeritus prof. of pediatrics since 1939. Recalled 1940 to active duty as professor and in charge of Isolation Hospital. Member Franklin County Board of Health, 1928-33. Member A.M.A., American Academy of Pediatrics, Ohio State Medical Assn., Columbus Acad. Medicine (pres. 1935; hon. life mem. since 1941), Alpha Mu Pi Omega, Nu Sigma Nu. Republican. Methodist. Clubs: University Faculty, Lions (past pres., zone-chmn., Ohio, 1938-39; deputy dist. gov., 1939-40, dist. gov., 1940-41; internat. counselor, 1941), Columbus Automobile. Contbr. to med. publs. Home: 285 E. Lane Av. Office: 350 E. State St., Columbus, O. Died May 30, 1949.

HORTON, GEORGE TERRY, civil engr., mfr.; b. Waupun, Wis., 1873; s. Horace E. and Emma (Babcock) H.; C.E., Rensselaer Poly. Inst., 1893; m. Hazel Heath, Nov. 27, 1907; 1 dau., Florence (Mrs. Arnold Gillatt). Became identified with the Chicago Bridge & Iron Works, 1893, pres. and mgr. since 1912. Chairman Chicago Plan Commission; life trustee Rensselaer Poly. Inst. Lt. comdr. U.S.N.R., retired. Mem. Am. Soc. C.E., Western Soc. Engrs., Chicago Hist. Soc., Am. Welding Soc. (pres.), Am. Soc. for Testing Materials, Soc. Naval Architects and Marine Engrs., Chicago Engrs., New Eng. Historic Geneal. Soc., Art Inst. of Chicago, Am. Petroleum Inst., Am. Water Works Assn., Delta Kappa Epsilon. Clubs: Engineers', University, South Shore Country, Commercial Club, Aero Club of Illinois (Chicago). Home: 4940 Woodlawn Av. Office: 1305 W. 105th St., Chicago, Ill. Died Mar. 19, 1945.

HORTON, J(OSEPH) WARREN, acoustical engr.; b. Ipswich, Mass., Dec. 18, 1889; s. Benjamin R. and Susan Elizabeth (Tower) H.; B.S. in Electrochemistry, Mass. Inst. Tech., 1914, D.Sc. in Elec. Engring., 1935; m. Adelina C. Doucet, Sept. 4, 1916; 1 son, Peter. Asst. physics and electrochemistry Mass. Inst. Tech., 1914-16, research asso., 1933-37, asso. prof. biol. engring., 1937-45, asso. prof. elec. communication, dept. elec. engring., 1945-49; tech. staff Bell Telephone Labs., N.Y.C., 1916-28; chief engr. Gen. Radio Co., Cambridge, Mass., 1928-33; tech. expert Naval Expt. Sta., Nahant, Mass., also Naval Hdqrs., London, 1917-18; spl. adviser Nat. Def. Research Com., also OSRD, 1941-45; chief research cons. U.S. Navy Underwater Sound Lab., New London, Conn., 1949-59, technical director, from 1959; lecturer in electrical engineering University Conn., from 1950. Trustee, mem. corp. Cable Meml. Hosp., Ipswich, Mass., from 1940. Served as lt. comdr. USNR, inactive, 1936-51. Recipient best research of year award Am. Inst. E.E., 1927, distinguished civilian service award U.S. Navy,

1958. Fellow A.A.A.S., Acoustical Soc., Am. Inst. E.E. (bd. examiners from 1950), Inst. Radio Engrs. (adminstrv. com. profl. group ultrasonics engring. from 1958), Am. Phys. Soc.; mem. N.E. Soc. Anesthetists (hon.), Newcomen Soc., Audio Engring. Soc. (hon.), Sigma Xi, Eta Kappa Nu. Club: Thames (New London). Author: Fundamentals of Sonar, 1957. Contbr. tech. articles profl. jours. Drafted safe practice recommendations operating rooms for Nat. Fire Protection Assn. Holder 56 patents, including submarine detectors, frequency standardizing systems, picture transmission and TV systems, carrier current and radio secrecy systems. Home: New London CT Died May 10, 1967.

HORTON, ROBERT ELMER, hydraulic engr.; b. Parma, Mich., May 18, 1875; s. Van Rensselaer W. and Rowena Spencer (Rafter) H.; B.Sc., Albion Coll., 1897, Sc.D., 1932; m. Ella H. Young, June 19, 1901. Asst. on U.S. Deep Waterways Survey, 1898-99; dist. engr. U.S. Geol. Survey, 1900-06; engr. in charge Bur. Hydraulics, N.Y. State Barge Canal, 1906-11; cons. practice since 1911; hydraulic expert Dept. Pub. Works and Atty. Gen.'s Dept., State of N.Y., 1911-25; engr. in charge Del. River Case before Supreme Court of U.S., for State of N.J., 1922-30; cons. engr. Bd. of Water Supply, Albany, N.Y., 1924-32; cons. engr. The Power Authority, State of N.Y., 1932-33; mem. advisory council of Federal Board Surveys and Maps, 1918-39, and Engring. Board of Review, Sanitary Dist. of Chicago, 1925-27; engineer consultant, Nat. Resources Com., 1934-37; cons. U.S. Soil Conservation Service, 1939-41; consultant Tenn. Valley Authority, 1942-44, City of Rochester, N.Y., 1942-43; dir. Horton Hydrologic Lab. Member Am. Society C.E., Am. Water Works Assn., N.E. Water Works Assn., Am. Geophys. Union, Sigma Nu, Inst. C.E. (London), Instn. of Water Engrs. (England); fellow Am. Meteorol. Soc. (pres. 1939), Royal Meteorol. Soc., Am. Geog. Soc. Republican. Author: Weir Experiments, Coefficients and Formulas, 1905; Turbine Water Wheel Tests and Power Tables, 1906; Water Wheels, 1907; Determination of Stream Flow during the Frozen Season (with H. K. Barrows), 1907; Hydrography of N.Y. State (N.Y. State Annuals) 1900-11; Hydrology of the Gt. Lakes (with C.E. Grunsky), 1926; Rainfall Runoff and Evaporation (with L. K. Sherman), 1933; Surface Runoff Phenomena, 1935; Apples from Eden (stories), 1938; also numerous scientific papers. Inventor water level gauge; joint for wood stave pipe. Home: Voorheesville, N.Y. Died Apr. 22, 1945.

HORTON, VALENTINE BAXTER, bituminous coal operator, towboat builder; b. Windsor, Vt., Jan. 29, 1802; s. Zenas and Nancy (Seaver) H.; grad. Norwich (Vt.) Acad., 1825; m. Clara Pomeroy, 1833, 6 children including Clara Pomeroy, Frances Dabney, Samuel Dana. Admitted to Conn. bar; designed "Condor" towboat to tow barges back up Ohio River in early shipping of coal from Ohio mines; mem. Ohio Constl. Conv., 1850; organizer Pomeroy Salt Co. (O.), 1851; reorganizer, pres. Ohio River Salt Co.; mem. U.S. Ho. of Reps. from Ohio, 34th-35th, 37th congresses, 1855-59, 61-63; trustee Ohio U., Athens. Died Pomeroy, Jan. 14, 1888.

HORWITZ, PHINEAS JONATHAN, med. dir. U.S.N.; b. Baltimore, March 3, 1822; ed. St. Mary Coll., Baltimore; grad. Univ. of Md., M.D., 1845; apptd. asst. surgeon, U.S.N.; Nov. 8, 1847; served in Mexican war, in charge of hosp. at Tampico; asst. surgeon gen., 1859-65; surgeon gen., 1865-69; med. insp., March 3, 1871; med. dir., Dec. 19, 1873, with relative rank of capt. While asst., 1859-65, and chief, 1865-69, of Bur. of Medicine and Surgery, had entire charge of tabulating casualties of war, indexing books of reference, etc.; had charge Naval Asylum, Phila., 1877-83; pres. examining bd., 1883-84; retired. Died 1904.

HORWOOD, MURRAY PHILIP, pub. health engr.; b. N.Y.C., Dec. 31, 1892; B.S., Coll. City N.Y., 1913; S.M., Mass. Inst. Tech., 1916, Ph.D., 1921; Harvard Tech. Sch. Pub. Health, 1917-18; m. Louise van Valkenburgh Peirce, Dec. 25, 1919; children—Louise van Valkenburgh (Mrs. Charles S. Alden), Charlotte Peirce, Sargent Peirce. Chemist, bacteriologist Bklyn. Sewage Expt. Station, 1913-15; Mass. Inst. Tech., 1916—, asso. prof., 1929-37, prof. bact. and pub. health, 1937-44, prof. sanitary science, 1944—; instr. advanced bacteriology Wellesley College, 1918-19; lectr. bacteriology, and public health, Boston U. Med. Sch., 1920-21; instr. hygiene Tufts Med. Sch., 1921-25, 1928-29. Conducted pub. health and Tb surveys in Me., Mass., R.I., Conn., N.J., Pa., Ind. and Okla.; dir. New England Health Surveys for Am. Child Health Assn., 1924; dir. investigation into bacteriology of household dusts, 1930; cons. in bacteriology, sanitation and biology for Atlantic Gelatin Co. (Gen. Foods Corp.), 1921-52; apptd. dir. M.I.T. Ednl. Project at College of Engring., U. Rangoon, Burma, 1952-54; cons. in pub. health engring. Boston Health Dept., 1941—; cons. for Salem Civic Action Com. on pollution of North River, 1944; dir. sanitation of Mass. Inst. Tech. dining services, 1944—. Author Sanitary Code, Arlington, 1937. Mem. bd. dirs. Housing Assn. Met. Boston, 1940-44; mem. exec. com. Mass. Tb League, 1942-48, Cambridge Tb and Health Assn. (pres. 1944-46); chmn. Health Com., Cambridge community Council, 1946-48; mem. adv. com. sch. hygiene, Boston Pub. Schs., 1927—; mem. nutrition com., Cambridge Red Cross, 1947-50. Apptd. WHO fellow, 1951. Fellow Am. Public Health Assn., A.A.A.S., Am. Acad. Arts and Sciences; mem. Am. Soc. Bacteriol., Boston Bacteriol. Club: Mass. Pub. Health Assn. (chmn. health officers sect. 1941-43; organizer and chmn., sect. on sanitation, 1944-45), Conf. Municipal Pub. Health Engrs., Inst. Food Technologists, Assn. Food and Drug Officials, Delta Omega, Sigma Xi. Author: Public Health Surveys, 1921; Sanitation of Water Supplies, 1932; Sedgwick's Principles of Sanitary Sci. and Public Health (with S. C. Prescott), 1935; Public Health in Burma, 1956; A Natural Scientist Looks at America's Foreign Economic Aid Program, 1957, also various papers on bacteriology, sanitation and pub. health. Home: 8 Craigie St., Cambridge 38, Mass. Died June 4, 1957.

HOSACK, ALEXANDER EDDY, surgeon; b. N.Y.C., Apr. 6, 1805; s. Dr. David and Mary (Eddy) H.; M.D., U. Pa., 1824; studied under Dupuytren, France; m. Celine B. Hosack. Introduced Syme's operation for exsection of elbow to Am.; known for his improvements in cleft palate operation by 1833; a pioneer urological surgeon; 1st N.Y. surgeon to use ether as anesthetic; author paper on removal tumors in female uretha in New York Jour. Medicine and Surgery, 1839. Died Mar. 2, 1871.

HOSACK, DAVID, physician; b. N.Y.C., Aug. 31, 1769; s. Alexander and Jane (Arden) H.; attended Columbia, 1786; grad. Princeton, 1789; m. Catharine Warner, 1792; m. 2d, Mary Eddy, 1797; m. 3d, Magdalena Coster; 10 children including Alexander Eddy. Began med. practice Alexandria, Va., 1791; prof. botany Columbia, 1795-1811, prof. materia medica, 1795-1811, prof. materia medica Coll. Phys. and Surg., 1807-08, prof. theory and practice of physic, 1811; attending surgeon at Burr-Hamilton duel, 1804; 1st American to litigate femoral artery for aneurysm, 1808; an incorporator Am. Acad. Fine Arts, 1808; a founder Rutgers Med. Coll., pres. until 1830; a founder Bellevue Hosp., N.Y.C., 1820; a founder N.Y. Hist. Soc., pres., 1820-28; established Am. Med. and Philos. Register, editor, 1810-14. Author: A Tribute to the Memory of the Late Caspar Wistar, M.D., 1818; A System of Practical Nosology, 1819; Memoir of DeWitt Clinton, 1829. Died N.Y.C., Dec. 22, 1835.

HOSKIN, ARTHUR JOSEPH, mining engr.; b. Shopiere, Wis., Jan. 4, 1869; s. Albert A. and Eliza M. (Taylor) H.; B.M.E., U. of Wis., 1890, M.E., 1905; m. Mary Margaret Allen, July 27, 1893; children—Elizabeth Louise (Mrs. A. S. Irvine), Margaret Jane. Began as mining engr., Idaho Springs, Colo., 1890; assayer, Omaha & Grant Smeltery, Denver, 1891-95; U.S. surveyor-gen.'s office, Denver, 1895; ore broker, Central City, 1896; mine engr., Cripple Creek, 1896-97; ore agencies, Florence, Leadville, Pueblo, Denver, 1897-99; U.S. sur.-gen.'s office, Denver, 1900-01; mine engr., Leadville, 1902; chief engr., Leyden Coal Co., Denver, 1903-06; asst. prof. and prof. mining, Colo. Sch. of Mines, Golden, 1905-11; editor, Mining and Metallurgical Jour., 1908; on Colo. Geol. Survey, 1910-11; western editor, Mines and Minerals, 1912-13; mgr., Square Deal G.M. Co., 1912-13; mine engr., consulting practice, 1913-16; mine engr., Leadville, 1916-17; editor The Mining American, Denver, 1917-18, oil-shale and consulting engr., 1918-21; research asst. prof. mining, 1921-23, research asso. prof. mining, 1923—, acting head of mining dept., 1923-24, U. of Ill. Research for Am. Ry. Assn. and asso. in geology and mineralogy, Purdue, 1926-29; editor Pit and Quarry, 1929—. Mason. Author: The Business of Mining, 1912. Home: Chicago, Ill. Died Mar. 13, 1935.

HOSKINS, JOHN HOBART, educator; b. Carmel, Ind., Jan. 17, 1896; s. John B. and Cicely (Lancaster) H.; B.S., Earlham Coll., 1919; M.S., U. Chgo., 1920, Ph.D. summa cum laude, 1924; m. Gertrude Louise Keller, June 18, 1931; children—John, William, Robert. Prof. biology Whittier Coll., 1920-22; fellow biol. sci. NRC, Eng., France and Belgium, 1924-25; vis. prof. U. Notre Dame, summers 1925-33; with dept. botany and bacteriology U. Cin., 1925—, head dept., 1928—; dir. The Valley Shopping Center. Dir. Lloyd Library and Mus., Cin.; trustee Cin. Country Day Sch., U. Cin. Research Found. Tng. specialist OQMG, World War II. Mem. A.A.A.S., Bot. Soc. Am. (past chmn. paleobot. sect.), Paleontog. Soc., Am. Phycol. Soc., Phytomorphol. Soc., Ohio, Ind. acads. scis., Phi Beta Kappa, Sigma Xi, Alpha Tau Omega. Club: Cincinnati Country. Editor paleobotany Am. Midland Naturalist, 1934-55; co-founder, asso. editor Lloydia, a Quarterly Jour. Biol. Sci., 1938—. Contbr. articles profl. jours. Home: 3566 Raymar Dr., Cin. 8. Died Feb. 7, 1957; buried Spring Grove Cemetery, Cin.

HOSKINS, JOHN K., sanitary engr.; b. New Holland, Pa., July 12, 1884; B.C.E., Pa. State Coll., 1905, C.E., 1910; student U. Berlin, 1908-09; m. Mattie Sublette, Apr. 30, 1913. With cons. engrs. 1905-08, 10-13 water works design and constrn.; with USPHS as san. engr. principally in research activities relating to water supply and sewage disposal since 1913, in charge of stream pollution investigations sta. of the Service at Cin., 1924-40; head san. engring. activities of Service since 1940, asst. surgeon gen. USPHS, Washington, 1944-48, ret. 1948. Mem. bd. consultants Nat. Sanitation Found. Mem. bd. Washington Housing Assn., 1948. Former mem. Inst. Sewage Purification, Federal Sewage Research Assn. (pres. 1933-34), Fedn. Sewage Research Assn. (pres. 1945-46), Am. Pub. Health Assn. Home: 6318 Woodside Pl., Chevy Chase 15, Md. Died May 16, 1958; buried Arlington Nat. Cemetery.

HOSKINS, WILLIAM, chemist; b. Covington, Ky., July 15, 1862; s. John and Mary Ann (Hoskins) H.; grad. Chicago High Sch., 1879, followed by chemical and other instrn.; m. Ada May Mariner, Dec. 8, 1885; children—Minna, Edna (Mrs. Fred Scheele), William, Florence (Mrs. Harvey Melcher). Joined Prof. G. A. Mariner in his analyt. chem. lab., 1880, and became partner, 1885, Mariner & Hoskins; sole propr., 1890—; pres. Mariner & Hoskins, Inc. Associate mem. Naval Consulting Bd., 1917, and mem. sub-com. in charge Chicago office; mem. advisory com. U.S. Bureau of Mines. Republican. Unitarian. Died May 19, 1934.

HOSMER, RALPH SHELDON, forester; b. Deerfield, Mass., Mar. 4, 1874; s. Rev. George Herbert and Julia West (Sheldon) H.; B.A.S., Harvard, 1894; M.F., Yale, 1902; m. Jessie Nash Irwin, Dec. 30, 1913; children—David Irwin, Jane Sheldon (Mrs. Robert Hall Llewellyn), Emily Frances (Mrs. Marc Daniels). Asst. Div. of Soils, Dept. Agr., 1896-98; field asst. Bur. Forestry, 1899-1903; collaborator in U.S. Forest Service, supt. forestry, Hawaii, 1904-14; prof. forestry Cornell U. and head dept. forestry N.Y. State Coll. Agr., 1914-42, emeritus, 1942—. Chmn. Territorial Conservation Commn. of Hawaii, 1908-14. Mem. research council Northeastern Forest Expt. Sta., 1926-42; sec. Forestry sect. Internat. Congress Plant Scis., 1926; mem. N.Y. State Conservation Adv. Council, 1932-41; mem. City Planning Commn., Ithaca, N.Y., 1928-38; mem. exec. com. Celebration of N.Y.'s Fifty Years of Conservation, 1935, commemoration com. 75th Anniversary N.Y.'s Forest Preserve. Recipient Sir William Schlich Meml. Forestry medal, 1950; given spl. introduction for five decades of service at golden anniversary dinner U.S. Forest Service, 1955. Fellow A.A.A.S., Soc. Am. Foresters (pres. 1923), Forest History Found.; mem. Am. Forestry Assn., Empire State Forest Products Assn. (hon. life), Alpha Zeta, Phi Kappa Phi. Republican. Unitarian. Club: Statler (Cornell U.). Author: Impressions of European Forestry, 1922; The Cornell Plantations, a History, 1947; The Society of American Foresters; an Historical Summary, 1950; Forestry at Cornell, 1950; also articles in profl. jours.; writer concerning geneal. history. Home: 209 Wait Av., Ithaca, N.Y. 18450. Died July 19, 1963; buried Sleepy Hollow Cemetery, Concord, Mass.

HOSTER, HERMAN ALBERT, (hä'ster), univ. prof. (oncology); b. Columbus, O., Mar. 5, 1912; s. Herman Albert and Martha (Welle) H.; student Hill Sch., Pottstown, Pa., 1927-30; A.B., Yale, 1934; M.D., Johns Hopkins, 1938; m. Margaret Prentiss, March 23, 1938 (divorced); children—Frederick William, Albert Stanton; m. 2d, Miriam E. Shanley, Aug. 26, 1947. Interne, resident staff Jefferson Med. Coll. Hosp., Phila., June 1938-Sept. 1940; research fellow dept. biochemistry, Yale Sch. of Medicine, 1940-41; instr. medicine, Ohio State U. Coll. Med., 1941-44, asst. prof., 1944-46, asso. prof., 1946-47; prof. and coordinator oncology, prof. med., 1947; asso. dir. Div. Cancer Research since 1945; research dir. Ohio State Univ. Tumor Clinic and Columbus Cancer Clinic since 1947; pres. Hodgkin's Disease Research Found., Inc.; vice chmn. cancer com., Metropolitan Health Council (Columbus, O.) since 1947; vice chmn. and sec. of research Adv. Com. on Cancer, Ohio State U. Mem. Am. Assn. for Advancement Science, A.M.A., Ohio State Med. Assn., Columbus Acad. Medicine, Am. Assn. for Cancer Research, Am. Chem. Soc., Alpha Sigma Phi, Sigma Xi. Mem. Conglist. Ch., Columbus, O. Contbr. articles to scientific jours. Address: 2173 Bryden Rd., Columbus, O. Died May 14, 1951; buried Greenlawn, Columbus.

HOTCHKISS, BENJAMIN BERKELEY, inventor, mfr.; b. Watertown, Conn., Oct. 1, 1826; s. Asahel A. and Althea (Guernsey) H.; m. Maria Bissell, May 27, 1850. Inventor (with his brother) new form of cannon projectile, demonstrated at Washington (D.C.) Navy Yard, 1855; made gift of some projectiles to liberal govt. of Mexico, 1859; furnished several hundred projectiles to Japanese, 1860, succeeded in getting small order from U.S., 1860; founder factory, N.Y.C., when Civil War produced demand for projectiles; patentee practical machine gun, 1872; inventor magazine rifle, 1875, exhibited in Phila., sold patent rights to Winchester Repeating Arms Co., New Haven, Conn. (rifle used by U.S. Army, then by U.S. Navy); organizer Hotchkiss & Co., with hdqrs. in U.S., factories in Eng., Germany, Austria, Russia and Italy, 1882; other patents include an explosive shell and packing for projectiles. Died Paris, France, Feb. 14, 1885; buried Sharon, Conn.

HOTCHKISS, WILLIAM OTIS, coll. pres., geologist; b. Eau Claire, Wis., Sept. 17, 1878; s. Lyman Palmer and Almeda E. (Smith) H.; B.S. in Engring., U. Wis., 1903, C.E., 1908, Ph.D., 1916; D.Sc., Lafayette Coll., 1929; LL.D., Middlebury Coll., 1936; LL.D., U. Wis., 1937; D.Sc., Columbia, 1940; m. Edith Rachel Balsley, Sept. 20, 1904; children—Eugene Bishop, Edwin Lyman, Nancy (Mrs. Henry C. Boschen). Mining engr. Donora Mining Co., Duluth, 1902; exploration and geology work, Ontario, Can., 1903; cons. engr. Madison, 1904;

inst. petrography and mineralogy U. Wis., 1904-07; exploration and geol. work, Cobalt, 1905; state geol. survey of Wis., 1906-08, in charge econ. geology, 1907; state geologist of Wis., 1909-25; dir., 1919-25, chmn., 1923-25, State Highway Commn.; pres. Mich. Coll. of Mining and Technology, 1925-35; pres. Rensselaer Poly. Inst. 1935-43, emeritus pres., 1945—; cons. engr. N.J. Zinc Co., 1944—. Dept. dir., brig. gen. Army Specialist Corps, June-Dec. 1942, in charge of Bureau of Engring. and Tech. Personnel. Started state hwy. work in wisconsin and succeeded in having a hwy. commn. formed. Mem. Science Advisory com. of Century of Progress Expn., Chgo., also chmn. geology subcom. Chmn. N.Y. State Regents Council on Apprentice Training. Fellow Geol. Soc. Am. (mem. council, treas.); mem. Assn. Am. State Geologists, Society Econ. Geologists (pres. 1946), Am. Inst. Mining Engrs., Am. Soc. C.E., Lake Superior Mining Inst., A.A.A.S., Wis. Acad. Sci., Arts and Letters, Wis. Hist. Soc., Sigma Nu, Tau Beta Pi, Sigma Xi, etc. Club: Cosmos (Washington). Author: Rural Highways of Wisconsin, 1906; Limestone Road Materials of Wisconsin (joint author); Mineral Lands of Northern Wisconsin; The Story of a Billion Years—in Century of Progress Science Series; Minerals of Might, 1945. Home: Two Tudor Lane, Scarsdale, N.Y. Died June 20, 1954.

HOTTES, CHARLES FREDERICK, botanist; b. Mascoutah, Ill., July 8, 1870; s. Frederick and Barbara (Dathan) H.; B.S., U. of Ill., 1894, M.S., 1895; M.A., Ph.D., U. of Bonn, 1901; m. Flora Guth, Aug. 25, 1895; 1 dau., Flora Emily. Asst. in botany, U. of Ill., 1895-98, instr., 1901-02, asst. prof., 1902-13, prof. plant physiology, 1913-38, cons. plant psychologist in agronomy, and head of dept. of botany, 1928-38, prof. emeritus since 1938. Unitarian. Fellow A.A.A.S., Bot. Soc. America; mem. Am. Genetic Assn., Ill. Acad. Science, Acacia, Alpha Zeta, Sigma Xi, Gamma Sigma Delta. Mason (K.T., 32 deg., Shriner), Red Cross of Constantine. Clubs: University, Kiwanis, Chaos. Home: 406 W. Iowa St., Urbana IL

HOUDINI, HARRY, magician; b. Appleton, Wis., Apr. 6, 1874; s. Rev. Dr. Mayer Samuel and Cecelia (Steiner) Weiss, but name legally changed to Houdini; ed. pub. schs.; m. Wilhelmina Rahner, June 22, 1894. Began as trapeze performer, 1882; has made several tours of the world, performing before many rulers and notables. Inventor of a diving suit. Pres. Weehawken St. Corp., Film Developing Corp., Houdini Picture Corp. Awarded prize by Australian Aeronautic League, 1910, as being the first successful flier in Australia. Author: The Right Way to Do Wrong, 1906; Unmasking of Robert Houdini, 1908; Miracle Mongers, Paper Prestidigitation; Rope Ties and Escapes; A Magician Among the Spirits, 1924. Home: New York, N.Y. Died Oct. 31, 1926.

HOUGH, GEORGE WASHINGTON, prof. astronomy, Northwestern Univ., and dir. Dearborn Observatory, 1887—; b. Montgomery Co., N.Y. Oct. 24, 1836; s. William and Magdalene (Selmser) H.; grad. Union Coll., 1856 (A.M., LL.D.); m. Emma C., d. Jacob H. Shear, Albany, N.Y., 1870. Asst. astronomer, Cincinnati Observatory, 1859-60; astronomer and dir. Dudley Observatory, Albany, N.Y., 1860-74; dir. Dearborn Observatory and prof. astronomy Chicago Univ., 1879-87; discovered more than 600 new double stars and made a systematic study of the planet Jupiter; invented many instruments pertaining to astronomy, meteorology and physics. Died 1909.

HOUGHTON, DOUGLASS, geologist, mayor Detroit; b. Troy, N.Y., Sept. 21, 1809; s. Jacob and Maria (Douglas) H.; grad. Rensselaer Poly. Inst., Troy, 1829; m. Harriet Stevens, 1833, 2 daus. Asst. prof. chemistry and natural history Rennselaer Poly. Inst., 1829; Lectured on biology, geology and chemistry, Detroit, 1830; licensed as med. practicioner, 1831; apptd. surgeon and botanist H.R. Schoolcraft's expdn. to find sources of Mississippi River, 1831; practicing physician and surgeon, Detroit, 1832-37; prof. geology and mineralogy U. Mich. 1838-45; mayor Detroit, 1842-43; mem. Literary and Hist. Soc. of Que., Boston Soc. Natural History. Drowned in Lake Superior, Oct. 13, 1845.

HOURWICH, ISAAC A., statistician, lawyer; b. Wilno, Russia, Apr. 26, 1860; s. Adolph and Rebecca (Sheveliovich) H.; grad. Classical Gymnasium, Minsk, 1877; St. Petersburg Acad. Med. and Surg.; U. of St. Petersburg; LL.M., Demidov Juridical Lyceum, Yaroslavl, 1887; Seligman fellow, Columbia, 1891-92, Ph.D., 1893; m. Helen Kushelevsky, of Minsk, Russia, 1881; m. 2d, Louise Joffe, 1893. Admitted to bar, Russia, 1887, Chicago, 1893, New York, 1896. Docent in statistics, U. of Chicago, 1893-95; translator, Bur. of the Mint, Washington, 1900-02; expert spl. agt. Bur. of the Census, 1902-06; statistician Pub. Service Commn., New York, 1908-09; expert spl. agt. on mining, Bur. of the Census, 1909-13. Lecturer on comparative commercial law, George Washington U., 1902-03. Author: Immigration and Labor, 1912, 2d edit., 1922; Mooted Questions of Socialism (in Yiddish), 1917. Editor Yiddish translation of "Capital," by Karl Marx, 1919. Died July 9, 1924.

HOUSE, HENRY ALONZO, inventor, mfr.; b. Bklyn., Apr. 23, 1840; s. Ezekial Newton and Susan (King) H.; attended primary sch., Pa.; studied architecture with father; m. Mary Elizabeth House, Nov. 24, 1861; 1 son, 2 daus. Worked in architect's office, Chgo., 1857-59; returned to Bklyn.; received 1st patent for partly self-operating farm gate, 1860; obtained (with brother James) several patents for devel. and improvement buttonhole-making machine, 1862-63, sold machine to Wheeler & Wilson Sewing Machine Co., Bridgeport, Conn., worked as experimenters and inventors for co., developing many sewing machine innovations, until 1869; designed 12 horse power Horseless Carriage, 1866; awarded gold medals for their inventions at Paris Expn., 1867; organized Armstrong and House Mfg. Co. to produce his numerous patented devices, 1869, continued mfg. until factory destroyed by fire, 1889; cons. to Hiram and Percy Maxim in Eng., others. Mem. Bridgeport Common Council, 1872. Died Bridgeport, Dec. 18, 1930. *

HOUSE, HOMER DOLIVER, botanist; b. Oneida, N.Y., July 21, 1878; s. Doliver E. and Alice J. (Petrie) H. B.S., Syracuse U., 1902; M.S., Columbia, 1903, Ph.D. 1905; m. Erma N. H. Hotaling, Dec. 21, 1908. Prof. botany and bacteriology, Clemson Coll., S.C., 1906-07; asso. dir. and lecturer botany and dendrology, Biltmore (N.C.) Forest Sch., 1908-13; asst. state botanist, N.Y., 1913-14, state botanist since 1914. Mem. Torrey Bot. Club, Am. Bot. Soc., Am. Mycolo. Soc., Am. Fern Soc. Author: North American Species of Ipomoea, 1908; Wild Flowers of New York, 1923; Annotated List of Ferns and Flowering Plants of New York State, 1924; Wild Flowers, 1935; also ann. repts. of State Botanist of N.Y. State since 1915. Contbr. bot. articles. Home: Loudonville, N.Y. Address: N.Y. State Museum, Albany, N.Y. Died Dec. 21, 1949.

HOUSE, JAMES ALFORD, inventor; b. New York, N.Y., April 6, 1838; ed. as architect, but became mech. engr. for the Wheeler & Wilson Sewing Machine Co. Inventor of buttonhole attachments and other sewing machine devices, and other useful articles. Home: Bridgeport, Conn. Died 1906.

HOUSE, ROBERT ERNEST, M.D.; b. Dallas, Tex., Aug. 3, 1875; s. John Ford and Marguerite Janie (Harper) H.; student U. of Tex., 1896-98; M.D., Tulane U., 1899; post-grad. work, New Orleans Polyclinic, Chicago, New York, etc.; m. Mary Alma Orr, Feb. 28, 1900; children—John Ford, Samuel David. House surgeon City Hosp., Dallas, 1897-98; practiced at Ferris, 1899—, specializing in obstetrics. Democrat. Presbyn. K.P. Originated the Florence-Rosser method in obstetrics; introduced the use of scopolamin to determine guilt or innocence of an individual charged with crime; also for the diagnosis and treatment of insanity by determining the cause of delusions. Home: Ferris, Tex. Died July 15, 1930.

HOUSE, ROYAL EARL, inventor; b. Rockland, Vt., Sept. 9, 1814; s. James N. and Hepsibah (Newton) H.; m. Theresa Thomas, 1846, no children. Patented machine to saw barrel staves, 1839; worked on electric telegraph of teletype model, 1840-44; exhibited his printing telegraph at Am. Inst. Fair, N.Y., 1844, patented it, 1846; telegraph lines equipped with printing telegraph constructed from N.Y. to Boston, Washington, Cleve. and Cincinnati, 1847-55; spanned Hudson River with his telegraph lines, established permanent telegraphic communication between N.Y. and Phila., 1849. Died Feb. 24, 1895.

HOUSER, GILBERT L(OGAN), biologist; b. on farm, Lee County, Ia., July 9, 1866; s. David L(ogan) and Malvina (Saxe) H.; B.S., State U. Ia., 1891, M.S., 1892; studied U. Chgo., and Marine Biol. Lab., Woods Hole, Mass.; Ph.D., Johns Hopkins, 1901; m. Hattie Riggs, June 21, 1899; children—Arthur R., Harold S., Paul C., Ralph L., Mark R. Instr. animal biology State U. Ia., 1892-95, asst. prof., 1895-97, prof. and dir. Labs. of Animal Biology, 1897—. Mem. biol. expdn. to W.I., summer 1893; investigator Marine Biol. Lab., Woods Hole, Mass., 4 seasons. Fellow A.A.A.S., Ia. Acad. Science (pres. 1910-11); mem. Am. Soc. Naturalists, Am. Soc. Zoölogists, Sigma Xi (corr. sec. Ia. chpt., and pres. 1917-18). Republican. Presbyn. Author of papers and articles on biol. science. Home: Iowa City, Ia. Died July 1951.

HOUSER, KARL MUSSER, physician, educator; b. Pennsylvania Furnace, Pa., Sept. 30, 1893; s. Luther Murray and Anna Catherin (Musser) H.; Ph.B., Franklin and Marshall Coll., 1915, D.Sc.; M.D.,U. Pa., 1921, M.Sc., 1925; m. Grace Ellen Shipley, Sept. 22, 1926; children—Karl Musser, Luther Murray. Tchr. grade sch., Clifton, Ariz., 1915-16, Mercersburg Acad., 1916-17; intern U. Pa. Hosp., 1921-23, chief resident physician, 1923-24; prof. otolaryngology U. Pa., 1925-59, now emeritus. Mem. A.M.A., Coll. Physicians Phila., Am. Laryngol. Assn., Am. Otol. Soc., Am. Laryngol., Rhinol. and Otol. Soc., Am. Acad. Otology, Sigma Xi, Phi Kappa Sigma, Phi Alpha Sigma. Presbyn. Home: 838 Bryn Mawr Av., Narberth, Pa. Office: 2035 Delancey St., Phila. 3. Died Jan. 5, 1967.

HOUSER, SHALER CHARLES, civil engr.; b. Lincolnton, N.C., June 7, 1879; s. Thomas Lawson and Elizabeth (James) H.; B.S., U. of Ala., 1898, C.E., 1899; hon. D.Sc., 1938; m. Mary George Cruikshank, June 11, 1911 (died Mar. 8, 1918); 1 son, Shaler Charles; m. 2d, Anna Taylor Donoho, July 16, 1927 (died May 26, 1928); m. 3d, Martha Warren Parham, Aug. 5, 1930; 1 dau., Mattha Parham. Began as asst. engr., City of Mobile, Ala., 1899; gen. contractor Anniston, Ala., 1900-01; designing engr. Stewart Coal Washer and engr. Mobile & Ohio R.R. and coal mines, Ala.. 1901-04; engr. in charge Marx & Windsor, Cuba, on railroad location, irrigation and constrn. work, 1904-11; chief engr. Guantanamo & Western R.R., 1912; prof. engring., supervising engr. and treas., U. of Ala., since 1912. Mem. Am. Soc. C. E., Am. Soc. for Engring. Edn., Phi Beta Kappa, Omicron Delta Kappa, Alpha Tau Omega. Clubs: Rotary, Country of Tuscaloosa. Democrat. Presbyterian. Home: 154 The Highlands, Tuscaloosa, Ala. Died Jan. 11, 1948.

HOUSSAY, BERNARDO ALBERTO, scientific investigator; b. Buenos Aires, Argentina, Apr. 10, 1887; s. Alberto and Clara (Lafont) H.; Pharmacist, 1904; M.D., Buenos Aires, 1911; Dr. Honoris causa in medicine, universities Paris, 1935, Montreal, 1946, Lyon, 1946, Geneva, 1946, Asuncion, 1943, Catholic (Chile), 1942, Montevideo, 1948, Brussels, Catholique of Louvain, 1949, Strasbourg, 1949, also Duseldorf, Montpellier, Alger, Brazil, Venezuela, also Salamanco, hon. degrees in science, Harvard, 1936, Sao Paulo, 1936, Oxford, 1947, Mexico, Toronto, Columbia, New York, Cambridge (England) University, 1961; L.H.D. (hon.), Georgetown U., Washington; LL.D., (hon.), Glasgow; Dr. honoris causa med. scis. U. Orienta; Dr. honoris causa chemistry U. Nacional del Sud; married Maria Angelica Cata, Dec. 22, 1920; children—Alberto Bernardo, Hector Emilio Jose, Raul Horacio. Prof. physiology Vet. Faculty, Buenos Aires, 1910-19, Faculty Medical Scis., 1919-43, 45-46, 55-57; hon. prof. faculties of med. univs. of Montevideo, Santiago, Bogota, Lima, Brazil, Bahia, Porto Alegre, Recife, La Habana Concepcion (Chile), Venezuela, Minas Gerais, San Carlos, de Guatemala, Veterinary Sch., Buenos Aires and Lima; faculty sci., Lima; Hitchcock prof. U. Cal., 1948; dir. Inst. Bilogy and Exptl. Medicine, was research prof. Physiology Faculty Med. Scis., Buenos Aires. Decorated Order Merit of Chile, grand officer Order Merit (Italy), Belgian Crown Order, grand cross Order Merit of Germany, Isabel la Catolica, comdr. Legion of Honor, Officer Order of Leopold; Order de San Gregorio Magno (Vatican); Gran Cruz al merito con placa de la Orden Militar Soberanade Malta; gran oficial Order Holandesa de Orange y Nassau; Segunda clase Orden Sol Naciente del Japan; also numerous other decorations and awards; recipient Nat. Award Scis., Buenos Aires, 1923; Charles Mickle Fellowship, Toronto, 1945; Banting medal Am. Diabetes Association, 1946; research award Am. Pharm. Mfrs. Assn., 1947; Baly medal Royal Coll. Physicians, London, 1947; Nobel Prize for Physiology and Medicine, 1947; James Cook medal, Sidney, 1948; Dale medal Soc. for Endocrinology, London; Weizmann prize in scis. and humanities. Foreign associates mem. Nat. Acad. Scis. U.S.A., Royal Soc. London, Am. Philos. Soc., Swedish Acad. Scis., Acad. Medicine Paris, Acad. Sciences, Paris, Deutsche Akdemie fur Naturforschung, Royal Acad. Medicine Belgium, Academia Nazionale dei Lincei (Italy), Academia Inst. Egypt, Ciencias Exactas, Fiscias y Naturales, Lima; hon. mem. academies of medicine of Rio de Janeiro, Madrid, Mexico, N.Y., Lombardia, Bogota, Washington; hon. mem. Am. Physiol. Soc., Physiol. Soc. (Gt. Britain), Italian Soc. Physiology, Royal Soc. Edinburgh, Harvey Soc. N.Y., Mus. de la Plata Argentina, Academy Scis. Cordoba, honorary mem. numerous sci. socs.; pres. Argentine Soc. Biology; past pres. Argentine Assn. Advancement Sci., Nat. Acad. Medicine Buenos Aires, Internat. Union Philosophy of Scis., Physiology and Pharmacology Soc. Israel, Weizmann Inst. Scis., Assn. Am. Physiocians. Author numerous sci. papers. Home: Buenos Aires Argentina Died Sept. 21, 1971.

HOUSTON, EDWIN JAMES, electrical engr.; b. Alexandria, Va., July 9, 1847; s. John Mason and Mary (Larmour) H.; A.B., Central High Sch., Phila., 1864, later A.M.; (hon. Ph.D., Princeton). One of inventors of Thomson-Houston System of arc lighting; emeritus prof. physical geography and natural philosophy, Central High Sch.; emeritus prof. physics, Franklin Inst.; prof. physics, Medico-Chirurg. Coll.; elec. expert and consulting engr. Mem. U.S. Elec. Commn. and chief electrician, Internat. Elec. Exhbn., Phila., 1884. Author: Elements of Physical Geography (9 edits.), 1878, 1904; Dictionary of Electrical Word Terms and Phrases (4 edits.), 1894; The Boy Electrician, 1907; In Captivity in the Pacific, 1907; Wonder Book of Magnetism, 1908; Five Months on a Derelict, 1908; The Land of Drought, 1910; The Jaws of Death, 1910; The Yellow Magnet, 1911; Elements of Physics (with A. N. Seal), 1912. Home: Philadelphia, Pa. Died Mar. 1, 1914.

HOUSTON, GEORGE HARRISON, (hous'tun), industrial consultant; b. Covington, Ky., Jan. 4, 1883; s. Charles R. and Elizabeth (Mapes) H.; ed. Cincinnati Tech. Inst.; m. Mary Stuart Hoge, Apr. 29, 1909. Began with Houston, Stanwood & Gamble Co., Cincinnati, O.; asso. with Root and Vandervoort Engring. Co., Moline,

Ill., 1910-15; became partner, Jamieson and Houston, cons. industrial engrs., N.Y. City, 1915; firm succeeded by George W. Goethals & Co., in which was partner, retiring from latter in 1922; pres. Wright-Martin Aircraft Corp. 1917-19, Wright Aeronautical Corp., 1919-22, Marlin Rockwell Corp., 1920-22; with others organized General Sugar Co., 1922, to engage in reorganizing group of West Indian sugar properties; completed this work, and resumed gen. cons. work, 1927; pres. Baldwin Locomotive Works, 1929-38; mem. Houston & Jolles (name later changed to Geo. W. Houston & Co.), consultants on indsl. management, financing and reorgn.; dir. Causejero Delegado and Financiera Técnica de Mexico, S.A. Mem. Soc. Automotive Engrs., Am. Soc. Mech. Engrs. Clubs: Metropolitan, Knickerbocker, City Midday, Broad Street (New York); Rittenhouse (Phila.); Round Hill (Greenwich, Conn.); Metropolitan (Washington); Chicago (Chicago); Bankers (Mexico City). Address: care Financiera Técnica de Mexico, S.A., Venustiano Carranza 944, Mexico, D.F. Died July 10, 1949; buried at Louisville, Ky.

HOVEY, CHARLES MASON, horticulturist; b. Cambridge, Mass., Oct. 26, 1810; s. Phineas and Sarah (Stone) H.; m. Ana Chaponil, Dec. 25, 1835. Established nursery, Cambridge, 1832; developed Hovey strawberry (1st variety of fruit to be developed by planned breeding in N. Am.), 1834; founder, editor, Mag. of Horticulture, Botany, and All Useful Disconeries and Improvements in Rural Affairs, 1835-68; mem. Am. Pomol. Soc.; pres. Mass. Hort. Soc., 1863-66. Author: Fruits of America, 3 vols., 1847-56. Died Sept. 2, 1887.

HOVEY, EDMUND OTIS, geologist; b. New Haven, Conn., Sept., 15, 1862; s. Horace Carter and Helen Lavinia (Blatchley) Hovey; A.B., Yale, 1884, Ph.D., 1889, U. of Heidelberg, 1890-91; m. Esther A. Lancraft, Sept. 13, 1888 (died 1914); m. 2d, Dell G. Rogers, Oct. 23, 1919. Prin. and supt. schs., Janesville, Minn., 1884-85, Elk River, Minn., 1885-86; asst. mineral. lab., Sheffield Scientific Sch., 1886-87; asst. prin., 1888-91, prin., 1891-92, high school, Waterbury, Conn.; supt. of Mo. mineral exhibit, Chicago Expn., 1892-93; asst. curator, 1894-1900, asso. curator, 1901-10, curator, 1910—, geol. dept., Am. Mus. Natural History. Asst. on U.S. Geol. Survey, 1890, 1901-06; in the Far Arctic of Greenland with the Crocker Land Expdn., winters of 1915-17. Fellow Geol. Soc. America (sec. 1907-22), N.Y. Acad. Sciences, Am. Geog. Soc. Compiled (with R. P. Whitfield) Catalogue of the Types and Figured Specimens of Geol. Dept., Am. Mus. Natural History. Home: Yonkers, N.Y. Died Sept. 27, 1924.

HOVEY, OTIS ELLIS, civil engr.; b. E. Hardwick, Vt., Apr. 9, 1864; s. Jabez Wadsworth and Hannah Catherine (Montgomery) H.; B.S., Dartmouth Coll., 1885; C.E., Thayer School of Civil Engring., Dartmouth, 1889; D.Eng., Dartmouth Coll., 1927; D.Sc., Clarkson Coll., 1933; m. Martha W. Owen, Sept. 15, 1891; children—Otis Wadsworth, Mrs. Ellen Catherine Davis. Engr. Hoosac Tunnel and Wilmington R.R., Vt., 1885-86; draughtsman Edge Moor Iron Co., Wilmington, Del., 1887; asst. engr. for D.H.&A.B. Tower, Holyoke, Mass., in charge of Dam at Chicopee, Mass., and various improvements in paper mills, 1888; instr. civ. engring., Washington U., St. Louis, 1889-90; asst. engr. with George S. Morison, engaged on bridge designs, in Miss. valley and other engring. work, 1890-96; engr. Union Bridge Co., New York, and Athens, Pa., 1896-1900; in engring. dept. since 1900; asst. chief engr., 1907-31, cons. engr., 1931-34, Am. Bridge Co.; private practice since 1934. Dir. The Engring. Foundation since 1937. Mem. bd. overseers Thayer Sch. of Civ. Engring. (Dartmouth), Mem. Am. Soc. C.E. (hon.), Am. Soc. Mech. Engrs., Am. Soc. Testing Materials, Am. Ry. Engring. Assn., Am. Welding Soc., Am. Inst. of Consulting Engrs., Beta Theta Pi, Phi Beta Kappa. Republican. Presbyterian. Club: Engineers. Author: Movable Bridges (2 vols.), 1926, 27; Steel Dams, 1935. Home: 425 Riverside Drive. Office: 11 W. 42d St., New York, N.Y. Died Apr. 15, 1941.

HOWARD, BURTON JAMES, microscopist; b. Ionia, Mich., Sept. 17, 1872; s. William H. and Helen L. (Butler) H.; B.S., U. of Mich., 1897, post-grad. work, 1900-01; m. Gertrude Louise Peck, June 28, 1899; 1 dau., Bertha Helen. Asst. in chemistry, U. of Mich., 1895-96, asst. in pharmacognosy, 1901; microscopist in charge of Microchem. Lab., Bur. of Chemistry, U.S. Dept. of Agr., Washington, 1901-27; sr. microscopist, Bur. Chemistry and Soils, 1927-28; with Food, Drug and Insecticide Adminstrn., 1928-42, in charge Micro-analytical Lab., retired Sept. 1942. Prof. of microscopy, evenings, Nat. Coll. of Pharmacy, 1904-17. Mem. Am. Chem. Soc., A.A.A.S., Washington Bot. Soc. Republican. Methodist. Home: 1212 Decatur St. N.W., Washington, D.C. Died Feb. 4, 1950.

HOWARD, CHARLES DANFORTH, chemist and sanitarian; b. Westford, Mass., July 31, 1873; s. Calvin L. and Mary Jane (Hale) H.; B.S., Worcester Poly. Inst., 1893; m. Ada Yates, Aug. 5, 1901; children—John Adams, Charlotte Danforth. Pvt. asst. to Dr. Wolcott Gibbs, at his lab., Newport, R.I., 1893-94, to Prof. L. P. Kinnicutt, Worcester Poly. Inst., 1894-95; asst. chemist, N.H. Expt. Sta., Durham, 1895-98; asst. and asso. chemist, W.Va. U. Expt. Sta., 1898-1905; chemist and sanitarian, N.H. Bd. of Health, since 1905, dir. div. of chemistry and sanitation since 1920. State water coordinator; chmn. N.H. Commn. on Stream Classification. Mem. federal Com. on Definitions and Standards for Foods, 1918-42. Fellow Am. Pub. Health Assn.; mem. Am. Chem. Soc., Am. Water Works Assn., N.E. Water Works Assn., N.E. Assn. Dairy Food and Drug Officials (ex-pres.), N.H. Acad. Science (pres. 1942), Sigma Xi; hon. mem. N.H. Med. Soc., N.H. Pharm Assn. Conglist. Author of numerous articles in bulls. and scientific jours.; various sanitary and related legislation. Editor: N.H. Health News. Home: Concord, N.H. Died Oct. 29, 1944.

HOWARD, EDGAR BILLINGS, archaeologist; b. New Orleans, La., Feb. 28, 1887; s. Frank Turner and Emma Cora (Pike) H.; prep. edn. St. Paul's Sch., Concord, N.H., 1900-06; Ph.B., Yale (Sheffield Scientific Sch.), 1909; M.S., U. of Pa., 1930, Ph.D., 1935; m. Elizabeth Newhall, Oct. 1, 1910; children—Edgar Billings, Frank Turner, Charles Newhall Willing, Robert Pike. Bond salesman, 1910-11; export-import business with Wharton, Sinkler & Robert Toland, 1922-28; scientific work as archaeologist since 1928; research asso. U. Museum, Phila., since 1929, Carnegie Inst. of Washington, D.C., since 1934, Lab. of Anthropology, Santa Fe, N.M., 1939. Served as capt. Hdqrs. Co., 313th Inf., U.S. Army, with A.E.F., during World War; hon. mem. 1st City Troop, Phila. Former pres. Sch. Bd., Radnor Twp., Pa.; former trustee Acad. Natural Sciences, Phila. Mem. Am. Anthropol. Soc., Am. Mus. Natural Hist., Anthropol. Society Phila., Society Pa. Archaeology, Archaeol. Soc. of N.M., Soc. for Am. Archaeology (former pres.), Museum Stone Age Antiquities, Sigma Xi, Delta Psi. Republican. Episcopalian. Clubs: Yale (Phila.); Boston (New Orleans). Writer of articles and bulletins pertaining to archeology. Home: Bryn Mawr, Pa. Died Mar. 18, 1943.

HOWARD, ERNEST E(MMANUEL), cons. engr.; b. Toronto, Can., Feb. 29, 1880; s. Rev. Henry Augustus and Emma (Skipp) H.; came to U.S. at early age; B.S., U. of Texas, 1900, C.E., 1900, Dr. Engring. honoris causa, U. of Nebraska, 1939; D.Sc. (honorary), University of Missouri, 1952; married Josephine Tiernan, June 6, 1942. Instructor in engineering, University of Texas, 1901; bridge engineering, with J.A.L. Waddell and partners, 1901-14; partner successive firms, Harrington, Howard & Ash., 1914-28, now Howard, Needles, Tammen & Bergendoff; designers of bridges in 40 of the 48 States; various govtl. units and pvt. corps., incl. more than 20 railroads; Canada, Mexico, China, Russia, Etc. Work includes bridges across Mobile Bay, Fraser, Columbia, Willamette, Sacramento, Colorado, Neches, Mo. (15), Mississippi (9) (including bridges at Vicksburg, Natchez, Greenville, Miss., Rock Island, Ill., Dubuque, Ia., St. Mary's at Soo, O., Hudson, Delaware (incl. bridge being built at Wilmington) and other rivers and waterways; Welland Canal (18 bridges), Chesapeake & Delaware Canal (6 bridges), Harlem River and Bronx Kill spans of Triborough Bridge, N.Y.; Potomac River twin bridges at 14th St., Washington, D.C. (winner design competition); consultant service for New Jersey on Pulaski Skyway Viaduct and Raritan River Bridge; also various large viaducts; designer important bridge and viaduct structures for states of Del., Va., W.Va., Ala., Ark., Ill., Neb., Ky., Wis., Mo., Kan., Ia., Tex., and N.J.; engrs. for Maine Turnpike Express Highway, Denver-Boulder Turnpike, New Jersey Turnpike, bridges and express highways Akron and Toledo; cons. engineer Commission Renovation White House. U.S. war work, architect-engr. S.W. Proving Ground, Bluebonnet Ordnance Plant, Army Post Facilities, Ft. Riley, Internment Camp, Concordia; spl. design work for U.S. Engring. Bd.; compiled War Dept. Technical Manual TMS-286. Mem. Mo. State bd. of registration for architects and professional engrs., 1941-45. Received 5 of the 9 A.I.S.C. awards for the most beautiful bridges built in United States, 1942-48. Awarded Thomas Fitch Rowland Prize, A.S.C.E., 1921. Commd. Capt. Engrs. U.S. Army, 1918-19. Chmn. bd., U. of Kansas City since 1930. Fellow Am. Soc. M.E., A.A.A.S.; mem. Am. Inst. Cons. Engrs., Am. Soc. C.E. (dir., 1941-44, v.p., 1945-46, pres. 1950), Engring. Inst. Can., Am. Soc. Testing Materials Internat. Assn. Bdge. and Structl. Engrs. (U.S. del. 2d Internat. Cong., Berlin, 1926; chmn. Am. del. to 3d Cong., Liege, 1948, 4th Cong., Cambridge, London, 1952; U.S. rep. London Conf. Engring. Socs., 1948). Archaeological Institute of America, Military Order of World War, Tau Beta Pi, Phi Beta Kappa. Presbyterian. Clubs: Engineers, University, Country. Author: Documents Governing Bridge Construction, 1916; also tech. papers. Awarded Thomas Fitch Rowland prize, Am. Soc. C.E., 1921. Home: 5708 State Line Rd., Kansas City 2. Office: 1805 Grand Av., Kansas City 6, Mo.; and 99 Church St., N.Y.C. 7. Died Aug. 19, 1953; buried Kansas City, Mo.

HOWARD, FRANK ATHERTON, research cons.; b. Danville, Ill., Jan. 5, 1890; s. James W. B. and Mary (Atherton) H.; B.S. in Mechanical Engineering, George Washington U., 1911, LL.B., 1914, Sc.D., 1961; married Almeda Barr, 1915 (deceased 1934); children—Almeda B., Mary A., Frank A., Barr, James W. B.; m. 2d Irma Amelie Osborne (Duchess of Leeds), 1947. President Standard Oil Development Company, now Esso Research & Engineering Co., active research exec. and inventor in development oil refining processes and prodn. of tetraethyl lead, petroleum chem. and synthetic rubber, 1919-1944, v.p. Standard Oil Co. (N.J.), 1940-1945; dir. Ethyl Corp., Minerals & Chemicals Phillipp Corp. Chmn. Sloan-Kettering Inst. for Cancer Research; trustee George Washington U., Meml. Sloan-Kettering Cancer Center, N.Y., Woods Hole Oceanographic Instn.; trustee, v.p. Alfred P. Sloan Found. Decorated chevalier Legion of Honor (French); Kettering Award, Patent, Trademark and Copyright Found. Mem. Am. Inst. Mining, Metall. and Petroleum Engrs., A.A.A.S., Am. Chem. Soc., Am. Patent Law Assn., Soc. Automotive Engrs., Sigma Chi, Theta Tau. Republican. Episcopalian. Clubs: University (N.Y.C.). Author: Buna Rubber, 1947. Home: 920 Fifth Av., N.Y.C. 21; also 4 Av. Matignon, Paris 8. Office: 30 Rockefeller Plaza, N.Y.C. 20. Died Sept. 25, 1964.

HOWARD, FREDERIC HOLLIS, prof. physiology; b. Newburyport, Mass., Sept. 3, 1876; s. Eugene and Susan Ella (Nash) H.; M.D., U. of Pa., 1898; m. Mary Malleville McClellan, of Lakewood, N.J., Apr. 9, 1901; children—Edgerton McClellan, Paul Malleville, Caroline. Began teaching at U. of Pa. (med. dept.), 1899; prof. physiology, Williams Coll., since 1900. Mem. A.M.A. Conglist. Mem. M.C.U.S.A., June 1, 1917. maj., Sept. 3, 1918; with A.E.F., Jan. 7, 1918-Apr. 18, 1919; hon. discharged, May 6, 1919; now lt. col., Med. R.C. Address: Williamstown MA

HOWARD, GUY C(LEMENS), chemist and chemical engineer; born at Batavia, New York, August 26, 1878; son of Thomas Mentor and Frances Athalia (Rudgers) H.; B.S., University of Nebraska, 1900; A.M., Columbia, 1906; m. Mildred Jane Horan, July 5, 1916; children—John Rudgers, Elizabeth Ann. Chemist for various companies, 1901-03; head chemist Am. Smelting & Refining Co., Perth Amboy, N.J., 1903-05; chief chemist El Cobre Mines, Ltd., Santiago, Cuba, 1906, Am. Smelting & Refining Co., Salt Lake City, Utah, 1907-09; investigations in utilization of wood waste in lumber industry, Seattle, Wash., 1909-11; developments in utilization of pulp mill waste, Everett (Wash.) Pulp & Paper Co., 1911-16; chem. engr. in copper smelting plant Am. Smelting & Refining Co., Tacoma, Wash., in charge recovery sulphur products from metall. gases, 1916-20; cons. chem. engr. in utilization of industrial wastes, Seattle, Wash., 1920-27; at Marathon Paper Mills Co., Rothschild, Wis., pioneering the recovery and utilization of lignin and asso. materials since 1927, and as chemical counsellor. Me. Am. Inst. Chem. Engrs., Am. Chem. Soc., Tech. Assn. of Pulp and Paper Industry, A.A.A.S. Republican. Conglist. Clubs: Wausau, Wausau Country (Wasau, Wis.); Chemists (New York). Contbr. to tech. jours. Address: 922 Franklin St., Wausau, Wis. Died Dec. 19, 1943.

HOWARD, HENRY, chem. engr.; b. Jamaica Plain, Mass., July 5, 1868; s. Alonzo Potter and Emma (Babcock) H.; ed. Boston Latin Sch., Mass. Inst. Tech., 1885-89; m. Alice Sturtevant, Sept. 5, 1896; children—Katharine (Mrs. Charles Townsend), Henry Sturtevant, Thomas Clark, John Babcock, Robert Sturtevant (dec.). Became chemist 1889, supt. 1896, v.p., 1902-20, Merrimac Chem. Co., Boston, mfrs. of heavy chemicals; joined Grasselli Chem. Co., Cleveland, Ohio, 1920, and in charge of research and development work 6 years, now cons. chem. engr. Largely interested in public welfare; organized and directed dept. of U.S. Shipping Bd. which provided and trained personnel for new Am. Merchant Marine. Mem. Mfg. Chemists' Assn. of U.S. (pres. 3 yrs.; chmn. exec. com. 22 yrs.), Am. Inst. Chem. Engrs. (ex-pres.), Am. Chem. Soc. (mem. patent com.), Am. Electrochem. Soc. (past v.p.), Soc. Chem. Industry; mem. Joint Com. of U.S. and Canadian Chambers of Commerce. Republican. Episcopalian. Clubs: Union (Boston); India House, New York Yacht, Cruising Club of America; Club Nautico (San Sebastian, Spain); Porcupine (Nassau); Clambake, Spouting Rock Beach Assn. (Newport, R.I.). Home: Paradise Rd., Newport, R.I. Died Aug. 26, 1951.

HOWARD, JAMES E., engineer-physicist; b. Palmer, Mass., June 26, 1851; s. Sanford and Charlotte (Tupper) H.; ed. Nichols Acad., Dudley, Mass., Highland Mil. Acad., Worcester; hon. M.S., Dartmouth, 1910; m. Annie B. Potter, Aug. 23, 1882; 1 dau., Marion P. Engr. of tests, Watertown Arsenal, Mass., 1880-1910; engr. physicist, Bur. Standards, Washington, Mar. 1, 1910-Feb. 1914, Interstate Commerce Commn., 1914—. Home: Cohasset, Mass. Deceased.

HOWARD, JOSEPH WHITNEY, prof. chemistry; b. Dixon, Ill., June 18, 1889; s. John Fleming and Martha Elizabeth (Regan) H.; A.B., Shurtleff Coll., 1912; fellow U. of Ill., 1912-15, A.M., 1913, Ph.D., 1915; m. Guyda Lang, Sept. 4, 1918; children—Robert Randolph, Guyda Leone. Instr. in chemistry, State U. of Mont., 1915-19, asst. prof. chemistry, 1919-24, asso. prof., 1924-27, prof., from 1927. Mem. Am. Chem. Soc., Sigma Xi, Phi Lambda Upsilon, Gamma Alpha. Awarded Osborne scholarship medal, Shurtleff Coll., 1912. Republican. Baptist. Mason. Club: Authors. Contbr. to Jour. Am. Chem. Soc., Jour. Am. Pharm. Soc., Jour. Chem. Edn. Home: Missoula MT Died Sept. 30, 1968.

HOWARD, LELAND OSSIAN, entomologist; b. Rockford, Ill., June 11, 1857; s. Ossian Gregory and Lucy Dunham (Thurber) H.; B.S., Cornell, 1877, M.S., 1883; Ph.D., Georgetown U., 1896; M.D. (hon.), George Washington U., 1911; LL.D., U. Pitts., 1911, U. Cal., 1929; Sc.D., U. Toronto, 1920; Rutgers U., 1930; m. Marie T. Clifton, Apr. 28, 1886; children—Lucy Thurber, Candace Leland (Mrs. Edward De Mille Payne), Janet Moore. Asst. entomologist Bur. of Entomology, U.S. Dept. Agr., 1878-94, chief of bur., 1894-1927, prin. entomologist, 1927-31, ret. Hon. curator dept. of insects, U.S. Nat. Museum, 1895—; cons. entomologist USPHS 1904—, sr. entomologist with grade of sr. surgeon in Res., 1919. Mem. com. on agr. Nat. Council Defense, 1917; chmn. sub-com. on med. entomology NRC, 1917. Trustee Cornell U., 1900-05. Permanent sec. A.A.S.S., 1898-1920; pres. Assn. of Econ. Entomologists, 1894, Biol. Soc. Washington, 1897-98, Cosmos Club, 1909, Washington Acad. Sciences, 1916, A.A.A.S., 1920; v.p. Internat. Congress of Agr., Paris, 1923; hon. pres. Internat. Conf. of Phytopathologists and Econ. Entomologists, Holland, 1923; chmn. Pan-Pacific Food Conservation Congress, Honolulu, 1924; pres. sect. econ. zoölogy Internat. Congress of Zoölogy, Budapest, 1927; pres. Internat. Congress Entomology, Ithaca, N.Y., 1929. Fellow Am. Acad. Arts and Scis.; mem. Am. Philos. Soc., Nat. Acad. Sciences; hon. mem. many fgn. sci. socs. Decorated Chevalier Legion of Honor, 1925, Officier, 1929, and Officier Order of Agricultural Merit (both of France), 1925; Medalist Holland Soc. of New York, 1924; 2d Capper award, 1931. Author: Mosquitoes—How They Live, Etc., 1901; The Insect Book, 1901; The House-Fly—Disease Carrier, 1911; monograph, Mosquitoes of North America, Carnegie Instn., 1912-17; History of Applied Entomology (Smithsonian Inst.), 1930; The Insect Menace, 1931; Fighting the Insects—The Story of an Entomologist, 1933. Home: 45 Pondfield Rd. W., Bronxville, N.Y. Died May 1, 1950.

HOWARD, LOUIS ORRIN, mining engr.; b. Thompson, Conn. Feb. 27, 1884; s. Mart A. and Azora (Cummings) H.; A.B., Harvard, 1907, M.E., 1909; m. Muriel Burnet Crawford, Aug. 28, 1908; children—Lydia Wadsworth, Betty Burnet, Louise Orrin, Muriel Crawford, Sylvia May; m. 2d, Nellie Barker Jacobs, Nov. 25, 1925. Instr. ore treatment and metallography, Case Sch. Applied Science, Cleveland, O., 1909-11; mgr. Phila. syndicate, later organized as Radium Co. of America, Green River, Utah, 1912; asso. editor Salt Lake Mining Review, 1913-14; consulting practice, 1913-17; erected mill for Edison Tungsten Mines, Lucin, Utah, 1916; prof. mining and metallurgy, State Coll. of Wash., 1917-26, also dean Sch. of Mines and Geology; acting prof. metallurgy, S. Dak. State Sch. of Mines, Rapid City, 1926-27; same at U. of Ida., Moscow, 1928-29; cons. mining and metall. engr. since 1927. Unemployment relief work with Red Cross, County Welfare Board, and Nat. Reemployment Service as supervisor, welfare commr. and mgr. respectively, 1932-34; chief engr. Whitman County Wheat Production Control Assn., 1934-35; pvt. practice since 1936; wage, social security, unemployment and tax consultant since 1937; exec. sec. War Price and Rationing Bd., Pullman, since Oct. 1942. Mem. Sigma Tau, Sigma Gamma Epsilon, Phi Kappa Phi, Theta Xi. Republican. Episcopalian. Club: Harvard. Author: Cyanidation in the Mercur District of Utah, 1915; also 53 titles in professional jours. Home: Pullman, Wash. Died May 14, 1944.

HOWARD, WALTER LAFAYETTE, horticulturist; b. nr. Springfield, Mo., May 12, 1872; s. Henry Tate and Nancy Elizabeth A. (Cooper) H.; B.Agr. and B.S., U. of Mo., 1901, M.S., 1903; studied U. of Leipzig, 1905; Ph.D., U. of Halle-Wittenberg, 1906; studied at East Malling Research Sta., Eng., 1930; m. May Belle Cooper, June 25, 1908; children—Thomas Henry (dec.), Robert Cooper, Edwin Lewis, Walter Egner. Asst. and asst. horticulturist, Expt. Sta., U. of Mo., 1901-03, instr. 1903-04, asst. prof., 1905-08, prof. horticulture, 1908-15; asso. prof. pomology, U. of Calif., 1915-18, prof., 1918, head div. of pomology, 1922-29, acting dir. Br. of Coll. of Agr., 1924-25, dir., 1925-37, professor emeritus since 1942. Investigated horticultural problems in France and contiguous countries, 1921-22. Secretary Missiouri State Bd. of Horticulture, 1908-12; mem. Jury of Awards, San Francisco Expn., 1915. Fellow A.A.A.S.; mem. Am. Genetic Assn., Am. Pomol. Soc., Am. Soc. Hort. Science, Soc. Promotion Agrl. Science, Am. Eugenics Soc., Sigma Xi, Alpha Zeta, Sigma Kappa Zeta, Gamma Sigma Delta. Clubs: Faculty (Berkeley and Davis); Commonwealth (San Francisco). Author of Luther Burbank, A Victim of Hero Worship, 1946, and various bulls. and pamphlets. Home: 24 College Park, Davis, Calif. Died Oct. 17, 1949.

HOWARD, WILLIAM TRAVIS, pathologist; b. Sans Souci, Statesburg, S.C., Mar. 13, 1867; s. John and Mary Catherine (Macleod) H.; student U. of Va., 1885-87; M.D., U. of Md., 1889; grad. student Johns Hopkins, 1889-93; m. Mary Cushing Williams, Aug. 15, 1896. Engaged in teaching and research in pathology since 1892; prof. pathology, Western Reserve U., Cleveland, 1894-1914; asst. commr. of health, Baltimore, 1915-19; lecturer vital statistics and biometry, Sch. Hygiene and Pub. Health, Johns Hopkins, 1919-25, asso. mem. Inst. of Biol. Research, 1926; voluntary asso. in biology, 1930. Former bacteriologist Cleveland Bd. of Health. Pres. Am. Assn. Pathologists and Bacteriologists, 1902; mem. Assn. Am. Physicians. Author numerous papers on pathology, bacteriology and vital statistics, including Public Health Administration and The Natural History of Disease in Baltimore, Md., 1797-1920, 1924. Home: 835 University Parkway, Baltimore MD*

HOWE, CARL ELLIS, educator, physicist; b. Maitland, Pa., May 16, 1898; s. Edward Martin and Della (Greninger) H.; A.B., Juniata Coll., 1919; Ph.D., U. Chgo., 1929; m. Nettie Gregory, Aug. 24, 1920; children—Robert M., Virginia (Mrs. Roger McCaig). Instr. Blue Ridge Coll., 1920-22, Juniata Coll., 1922-24; asst. prof. Oberlin Coll., 1924-26, asso. prof., 1929-45, prof., 1945—, chmn. dept. physics, 1957—; asst. U. Chgo., 1926-29; research engr. Princeton, summer 1945, physicist U. Mich., summers 1947-57. Mem. Am. Assn. Tchrs. Physics, I.R.E., Am. Phys. Soc., Am. Assn. U. Profs., Sigma Xi. Author: (with Taylor, Watson) General Physics for the Laboratory, rev. edit., 1942. Home: 182 Shipherd Circle, Oberlin, O. Died Aug. 1, 1966.

HOWE, CLARENCE DECATUR, cons.; b. Waltham, Mass., Jan. 15, 1886; s. William Clarence and Mary (Hastings) H.; B.Sc., Mass. Inst. Tech., 1907, LL.D., Dalhousie U., 1939; D.E., Clarkson Coll., 1942; LL.D., Queens U., 1942, Harvard, 1945, U. N.B., 1948, U. Toronto, 1952, U. Melbourne (Australia), U. Ottawa (Ont.), 1955; D.E. (hon.), N.S. Tech. Coll., 1948, Northeastern U., 1953; D.Sc. (hon.), U. B.C., 1950, Laval U., 1952, St. Francis Xavier University, 1954; D.C.L. (honorary), Bishop's University, 1951; married Alice Martha Worcester, Sept. 16, 1916; children—William Hastings, Elisabeth, John Worcester, Barbara, Mary. On staff of Mass. Inst. Tech., 1907-08; prof. civil engring., Dalhousie U., Halifax, N.S., 1908-13; chief engr. Bd. Grain Commnrs., Can., Ft. William, Ont., 1913-16; established C. D. Howe & Co., cons. engrs., 1916, specializing in the design and constrn. of terminal grain elevators; elected to the House of Commons, general election, 1935, and appointed the minister of railways and canals and minister of marine; became 1st minister of transport, 1936; minister of munitions and supply, 1940-44; minister of reconstruction, 1944, of reconstruction and supply, 1946, trade and commerce, 1948-51, defense production, 1951-57; chmn. bd. Price Bros. & Co., Ltd., 1957—, Ogilvie Flour Mills Co., Ltd.; dir. Bank of Montreal, Province Quebec. Appointed to the Imperial Privy Council, carrying the designation Right Honourable Recipient Medal for Merit. U.S. Govt., 1947; Award of Merit, Am. Inst. Cons. Engrs., 1952; Hoover Medal, Am. Soc. C.E., 1952; Daniel Guggenheim Medal and Certificate, 1954 Member American Soc. Civil Engrs., Association Professional Engrs. Home: 3468 Drummond St., Montreal 25, P.Q. Office: Sun Life Bldg., Montreal 2, P.Q., Can. Died Dec. 31, 1960; buried Montreal.

HOWE, ELIAS, inventor sewing machine; b. Spencer, Mass., July 9, 1819; s. Elias and Polly (Bemis) H.; m. Elizabeth J. Ames, Mar. 3, 1841; married a 2d time. Invented sewing machine that equated speed of 5 of swiftest hand sewers, making 250 stitches per minute, 1844-45, granted patent, 1846; made and marketed a number of sewing machines, N.Y.C.; royalties reached $4,000 a week; organized Howe Machine C., Bridgeport, Conn., 1865; won Gold medal for Howe Machine at Paris Exhbn., 1867. Died Bklyn., Oct. 3, 1867.

HOWE, ERNEST, geologist; b. N.Y. City, Sept. 28, 1875; s. Walter and Mary Bruce (Robins) H.; A.B., Yale, 1898; A.M., Harvard, 1899, Ph.D., 1901; m. Anne Wilson, June 7, 1905; children—Walter, Margaret Bruce. Asst. geologist U.S. Geol. Survey, 1900-08; geologist 1st Isthmian Canal Commn., 1906-07; cons. geologist, 1908—; chief of inspection labs., Air Service, aircraft production, 1918; mem. Conn. Gen. Assembly, 1921, State Senate, 1925; editor Am. Jour. Science, 1926—; pres. First Nat. Bank, Litchfield. Fellow Geol. Soc. America. Home: Litchfield, Conn. Died Dec. 18, 1932.

HOWE, FREDERIC WILLIAM, educator; b. Westford, Mass., Sept. 30, 1872; s. Adonijah Woodbury and Martha Dunster (Butterfield) H.; student Worcester Poly. Inst.; B.S. in Chemistry, U. of N.H., 1894; spl. student Mass. Inst. Tech.; m. Flora Folger Haynes, June 21, 1900; children—Olive Haynes (Mrs. William G. Lossone, dec.), Elizabeth (Mrs. Wm. D. Middleton); m. 2d, Mrs. Jennie Barnard Bartlett (Tufts), Apr. 2, 1910. Asst. in chemistry Govt. Expt. Sta., Durham, N.H., 1894-95; chemist D. Whiting & Sons, Boston, Jan.-Oct. 1895; asst. in chemistry Mass. Inst. Tech., 1894-98; dir. Dept. of Chemistry and Dietetics, State Normal Sch., Framingham, Mass., 1898-1921; sci. dir., and dir. Walker Gordon Lab. Co., New York and Boston, 1902-41; dir. Food Lab. of Boston Floating Hosp., 1906-21, Food Lab. Infants' Hosp., 1907-21; dir. Sch. of Household Science and Arts of Pratt Inst., Bklyn., 1921-38; pres. Nat. Acilophilus Milk Coöp. Assn., 1923-43; Sewing Inst., Inc., mem. corp. Garland Sch. of Homemaking, Boston; trustee Geo. H. and Irene L. Walker Meml. Home for Children, St. Peter's Episcopal Church (Ogunquit, Me.). Mem. Food Conservation Commn., State of Mass., World War. Mem. White House Conf. on Child Health and Protection. Mem. 7th Internat. Mgmt. Congress. Fellow Am. Pub. Health Assn.; mem. New York Nutrition Council, Certified Milk Producers' Assn. of America. Republican. Episcopalian. Clubs: Church (dir.), Cliff Country of Ogunquit, Me. (dir.). Author of numerous papers read before sci. socs., also article in mags. Home: Ogunquit, Me. Died Nov. 27, 1957.

HOWE, FREDERICK WEBSTER, machine tool mfr.; b. Danvers, Mass., Aug. 28, 1822; s. Frederick and Betsey (Dale) H.; m. Anna Clafton, 1 dau. Asst. machine tool designer Robbins, Kendall & Lawrence, 1847, plant supt., 1848-54; designed profiling machine (became widely used in gun shops), 1848; built plain milling machine (forerunner of Lincoln type miller), 1849; designed 1st comml. universal milling machine, 1850; operated own armory, Newark, N.J., 1856-58, Middletown, Conn., 1858-60; supt. armory Providence Tool Co. (R.I.), 1861-65; sewing machine mfr., Bridgeport, Conn., 1865-68; pres. Brown & Sharpe Mfg. Co., 1868-76; aided in devel. Wilcox and Gibbs sewing machine; built (with Charles Goodyear, Jr.) Shoe-making machinery. Died Apr. 25, 1891.

HOWE, HARLEY EARL, educator; b. Linneus, Mo., Aug. 26, 1882; s. Isaiah E. and Mary E. (Homan) H.; B.S., U. Mo., 1906; A.M., Cornell, 1909, Ph.D., 1916; m. Eva Belle Rich, Aug. 21, 1913; 1 dau., Marion Louise, Grad. student, instr. in physics Cornell, 1908-12; prof. physics, astronomy Randolph-Macon Coll., 1912-18; asst. prof. and prof. physics Cornell, 1918-50, prof. physics emeritus, since July 1950. Author: Introduction to Physics, 1942, rev., 1948. Home: 108 Brandon Pl., Ithaca, N.Y. Died Aug. 18, 1965; buried Pleasant Grove Cemetery, Ithaca.

HOWE, HARRISON ESTELL, chemist, editor; b. Georgetown, Ky., Dec. 15, 1881; s. of William James and Mary (Scott) H.; B.S., Earlham Coll., Ind., 1901; U. of Mich., 1901-02; M.S., U. of Rochester, 1913, Sc.D., 1927; LL.D., Southern Coll., 1934; Eng.D., Rose Poly. Inst. 1936, S.D. State Sch. of Mines 1939; m. May McCaren, Oct. 17, 1905; children—Mary, Betty. Chemist, Sanilac Sugar Refining Co., Croswell, Mich., 1902-04; chemist, office mgr. and editor Bausch & Lomb Optical Co., Rochester, N.Y., 1904-16; chem. engr. with Arthur D. Little, Inc., Boston, 1916; asst. to pres., Arthur D. Little, Ltd., Montreal, Can., 1916-17; mgr. commercial dept. Arthur D. Little, Inc., Cambridge, Mass., 1917-19; chmn. div. research extension, Nat. Research Council, 1919-22; editor Industrial and Engineering Chemistry, Washington, since Dec. 1, 1921. Trustee Science Service; mem. Purdue Research Foundation; chmn. Chemicals Group, and chmn. Chemicals Priority Com., Priorities Div., Office of Production Management, Feb.-July 1941, now chmn. adv. com. Chemical Sect. Cons. chemist nitrate div., Ordnance Bureau, U.S. Army, World War; col. R.O.C., C.W.S. Fellow A.A.A.S.; mem. Am. Chem. Soc., Am. Inst. Chem. Engrs. (dir., and its rep. in Am. Engring. Council 1921-32), Am. Engring. Council (treas. 1923-30); round table and gen. conf. leader Inst. of Politics, Williamstown, Mass., 1926-29. Decorated Officer Crown of Italy, 1926. Republican. Baptist. Mason (K.T.). Clubs: Cosmos, Rotary, Torch, Chemists' (New York). Author: The New Stone Age, 1921; Profitable Science in Industry, 1924; Chemistry in the World's Work, 1926; Chemistry in the Home (with F.M. Turner), 1927; Series of six Nature and Science Readers (with E. M. Patch). Editor: Chemistry in Industry, Vol. I, 1924, Vol. II, 1925. Contbr. numerous articles in scientific jours.; a leader in organizing industrial groups for research. Home: 2702 36th St. N.W., Washington, D.C. Office: 1155 16th St. N.W., Washington, D.C., and 332 W. 42nd St., New York. Died Dec. 10, 1942; buried in Ft. Lincoln Cemetery, Washington.

HOWE, HENRY MARION, metallurgist; b. Boston, Mar. 2, 1848; s. Dr. Samuel Gridley and Julia (Ward) H.; bro. of Florence Marion Howe Hall, Laura Elizabeth Richards and Maud Howe Elliott; A.B., Harvard, 1869, A.M., 1872; B.S., Mass. Inst. Tech., 1871; (LL.D., Harvard U. and Lafayette Coll., 1905; Sc.D., U. of Pittsburgh, 1915)); m. Fannie Gay, Apr. 9, 1874. Now consulting metallurgist; prof. metallurgy, Columbia, 1897— (emeritus). V.p. Taylor-Wharton Iron & Steel Co. Bessemer medalist, Brit. Iron and Steel Inst., 1895; gold medalist, Verin zur Beförderung des Gewerbfleisses, 1895; Elliott Cresson gold medalist, Franklin Inst. Phila., 1895; gold medal, Société d'Encouragement pour l'Industrie Nationale, 1916; John Fritz gold medal, 1917. Pres. jury mines and mining, Chicago Expn., 1893; mem. jury, Paris expns., 1889. 1900. Chevalier Légion d'Honneur, France; Knight with star of 1st Order of St. Stanislas, Russia, 1906. Fellow Am. Acad. Arts and Sciences, N.Y. Acad. Sciences. Author: Metallurgical Laboratory Notes, 1902; Iron, Steel and Other Alloys, 1903; Metallography of Steel and Cast Iron, 1916. Hon. chmn. engring. div. Nat. Research Council; consulting metallurgist, U.S. Bur. of Standards. Home: Bedford Hills, N.Y. Died May 14, 1922.

HOWE, HERBERT ALONZO, astronomer; b. Brockport, N.Y., Nov. 22, 1858; s. Alonzo J. and Julia M. (Osgood) H.; A.B., U. of Chicago, 1875; A.M., U. of

Cincinnati, 1877; Sc.D., Boston U., 1884; LL.D., U. of Denver, 1910, Colo. Coll., 1913; m. Fannie McClurg Shattuck, Dec. 23, 1884; children—Julian Osgood, Hubert Shattuck, Warren Francis, Ernest Joseph. Student and asst., Cincinnati Obs., 1875-80; prof. astronomy, U. of Denver, 1880—; dean Coll. Liberal Arts and dir. Chamberlin Obs., University Park, Denver, 1891—. Author: A Study of the Sky, 1896; Elements of Descriptive Astronomy, revised, 1909. Designed an impersonal micrometer for equatorial telescopes. Home: Denver, Colo. Died Nov. 2, 1926.

HOWE, JAMES LEWIS, chemist; b. Newburyport, Mass., Aug. 4, 1859; s. Francis A. and Mary F. (Lewis) H.; A.B., Amherst, 1880; A.M., Ph.D., Göttingen, 1882; hon. M.D., Hosp. Coll. of Medicine, Louisville, 1886; Sc.D., Washington and Lee Univ., 1946; married Henrietta Leavenworth Marvine, Dec. 27, 1883 (died October 11, 1943); children—Guendolen, Frances Ray (dec.), James Lewis. Prof. chemistry, Central University, 1883-86; scientist and lecturer, Polytechnic Society of Kentucky; 1886-94; professor chemistry and head department chemistry, Washington and Lee University, 1894-1938, emeritus prof. of chemistry and university historian, since 1938; also dean of School of Applied Science, 1921-32. Chmn. bd. Peoples Nat. Bank, Lexington, Va. Chairman Finance Com., Lexington (Va.) Town Council, Fellow A.A.A.S. (sec. chem. section, 1893, secretary council, 1894, gen. sec., 1895, v.p. chem. sect., 1900); mem. Am. Chem. Soc., Va. Acad. Sci. (pres. 1924), Nat. Inst. Social Science, Soc. Chem. Industry, Washington Acad. Sciences, Deutsche Chemische Gesellschaft, Chemical Society (London); mem. special committee on platinum, National Research Council, 1917. Recipient Herty Medal for advancement of chemistry in the Southeastern states, April 1937. Life trustee of United Society Christian Endeavor; moderator of Lexington Presbytery, 1945; Commissioner to General Assembly, Presbyterian Ch. United States, 1893, 1918, 25, 34, 39, 46, 47; member of advisory council, Simplified Spelling Bd., Va. Philatelic Federation; member, Phi Beta Kappa, Omicron Delta Kappa, Delta Kappa Epsilon. Mason (Knights Templar, Shriner); past lt. governor Kiwanis. Member Rockbridge County Defense Council. Author: A Bibliography of the Metals of the Platinum Group, 1897; Inorganic Chemistry According to the Periodic Law (with Francis Preston Venable), 1898, revised as Inorganic Chemistry for Schs. and Colleges, 3d edit., 1921; Brief History of Missions, 1913; (with staff of Baker & Co., Inc. A Bibliography of the Metals of the Platinum Group, 1749-1917, 1919; A Bibliography of the Metals of the Platinum Group, 1918-30 (with addenda to edit. of 1919), 1947; A Bibliography of the Metals of the Platinum Group (1931-40), 1953, (1941-50) (in press). Numerous papers in Jour. Am. Chem. Soc., Science, Virginia Mag. of History and Biography, etc. Translator. Home: 30 University Pl., Lexington, Va. Died Dec. 20, 1955; buried Lexington, Va.

HOWE, JOHN IRELAND, inventor, mfr.; b. Ridgefield, Conn., July 20, 1793; s. William and Polly (Ireland) H.; grad. Coll. Physicians and Surgeons, N.Y.C., 1815; m. Cornelia Ann Ireland (cousin), May 20, 1820. Practiced medicine, N.Y.C., 1815-29; resident physician N.Y. Alms House; gave up practice, 1829, started experimenting in mfr. of rubber; set up rubber mfg. plant, North Salem, N.Y., 1829-30; attempted to find mech. way of making straight pins, 1830-31, designed successful pin-making machine, 1832; obtained fgn. patents for machine in England, France, Scotland, Ireland, 1832-33; manufactured pins, North Salem, 1835-38, Darby, Conn., 1838-68; lived in retirement, Birmingham, Conn., 1868-76. Died Birmingham, Sept. 10, 1876.

HOWE, MALVERD ABIJAH, civil engr.; b. at Northfield, Vt., Dec. 9, 1863; s. Dr. Asa and Lucy Ann Frances (Cummings) H.; B.S., Norwich University, 1882, M.S.; C.E., Thayer Sch. of C.E. (Dartmouth), 1886; m. Jessie White, of Emporia, Kansas, June 25, 1888. Professor civ. engineering, 1887-1916, emeritus prof. since 1916, Rose-Poly. Inst. Mem. Am. Soc. C.E., Permanent Internat. Assn. Navigation Congresses. Author: Sabula Draw by Graphics, 1887; Theory of the Continuous Girder, 1889; Tables for Use in Application of the Method of Least Squares, 1890; Retaining Walls for Earth, 1897; 6th edit., 1913; A Treatise on Arches, 1897, 2d edit., 1907; Design of Simple Roof Trusses in Wood and Steel, 1902, 3d edit., 1912; Symmetrical Masonry Arches, 2d edit., 1913; Foundations, 1914; Masonry, 1915. Also pamphlets and numerous papers in engring. jours. and trans. Address: The Hermitage, Northfield, Vt.

HOWE, MARSHALL AVERY, botanist; b. Newfane, Vt., June 6, 1867; s. Marshall Otis and Gertrude (Dexter) H.; Ph.B., U. of Vermont, 1890 (Sc.D., 1919); Ph.D., Columbia U., 1898; m. Edith Morton, d. of Rev. Edward N. Packard, D.D., June 8, 1909 (died 1928); children—Gertrude Dexter, Prentiss Mellen. Instr. cryptogamic botany, U. of Calif., 1891-96; curator herbarium, Columbia, 1899-1901, prof. botany, 1935—; asst. curator, New York Bot. Garden, 1901-06, curator, 1906-23, asst. dir., 1923-35, acting dir. in chief, 1929, dir., Oct. 1935—. Editor of Torreya, 1901-07; asso. editor, 1898-1907, editor, 1908-10, again asso. editor, 1911, Bull. of the Torrey Bot. Club. Mem. scientific expdns. to Newfoundland, the W.I., and Panama, 1901-15. Home: Pleasantville, N.Y. Died Dec. 24, 1936.

HOWE, PERCY ROGERS, dental research; b. Providence, R.I., Sept. 30, 1864; s. James Albert and Elizabeth Rachel (Rogers) H.; grad. Nichols Latin Sch., Lewiston, Me., 1883; A.B., Bates Coll., 1887, Sc.D., 1927; D.D.S., Philadelphia Dental College, 1890; LL.D., Harvard University, 1941; m. Rose Alma Hilton, December 21, 1891 (died 1942); children—James Albert, John Farwell; m. 2d, Ruth Loring White, 1943. Began practice at Auburn, Maine, 1890; moved to Lewiston, 1891, to Boston, 1898; chief of research labs., Forsyth Dental Infirmary for Children, since 1915, dir. since 1927; asso. prof. dental research, Harvard, 1915-25, Thomas Alexander Forsyth prof. dental science; instr. in pathology, Harvard Medical School, 1925-40, now emeritus. Fellow dental surg., Royal Coll. Surgeons (Eng.); honorary fellow Internat. College Dentists, 1947. Member American Dental Association (pres. 1928-29), American Academy Arts and Sciences, Am. Acad. Dental Sci., Hist. Science Soc., New Eng. Pediatrics Soc., Norwegian Dental Soc., Acad. Internacional de odontologia, Fedn. Dentaire Internat., Sociedad Cubana de Odontologia Infantil, Sigma Xi, Phi Beta Kappa, Delta Sigma Delta. Awarded Jarvie medal by New York State Dental Society, 1926; Callahan medal, Columbus Dental Society, 1926; Newell Sill Jenkins medal, Conn. Dental Society, 1927; R.I. State Dental Soc. medal, 1929. Granted hon. award of American Dental Assn., 1945. Republican. Mason. Club: Harvard. Research in nutrition; originator of silver reduction treatment for infected dentine and septic roots, used extensively in the Army, World War; isolated group of bacteria from dental caries. Home: Belmont, Mass. Office: 140 The Fenway, Boston, Mass. Died Feb. 28, 1950.

HOWE, REGINALD HEBER, naturalist; b. Quincy, Mass., Apr. 10, 1875; s. Reginald Heber and Susan (Adams) H.; ed. at home and at Noble's Sch., Boston; grad. spl. course Lawrence Scientific Sch. (Harvard), 1901; Docteur de l'Université, Sorbonne, Paris, 1912; S.M., Harvard, 1922; m. Marion Appleton Barker, Sept. 19, 1904; children—Susan Appleton, Richard Ollerton. Curator Thoreau Museum of Natural History; instr. natural sciences, Middlesex Sch., Concord, Mass., 1901-20; dir. of rowing and instr. Dept. Physical Edn., Harvard, 1919-23; research scholar, Bussey Instn., Harvard, 1921-23; headmaster, Belmont Hill Sch., Belmont, Mass., 1923—. Curator David Mason Little Memorial Mus. of Natural History. Writer serial "Contributions to North American Ornithology," containing Birds of Vermont, Index to Ornithologist and Oölogist, and The Birds of Florida (unfinished); Common and Conspicuous Lichens of New England in parts I-V, 1908; Education of the Modern Boy (co-author), etc. Died Jan. 28, 1932.

HOWE, WILLIAM, inventor; b. Spencer, Mass., May 12, 1803; s. Elijah and Fanny (Bemis) H.; m. Azubah Towne Stone, Mar. 12, 1828. Commd. to construct bridge at Warren, Mass., 1838, devised 2 features which he later patented, designed bridge as a truss with wooden diagonals and vertical iron ties in single or double systems; spent last years building bridges in Mass. Died Springfield, Mass., Sept. 19, 1852.

HOWELL, A(LFRED) BRAZIER, anatomist; b. Catonsville, Md., July 28, 1886; s. Darius Carpenter and Katherine Elinor (Hyatt) H.; studied Sheffield Sci. Sch. (Yale), 1908; m. Margaret Gray Sherk, Apr. 14, 1914; children—Elinor Gray, Margaret Travers, John Brazier, Jane. Spl. investigations in geog. variation and comparative anatomy of mammals; with U.S. Biol. Survey, 1918, sci. asst., 1923-27; collaborator U.S. Nat. Mus. since 1926; lectr. comparative anatomy Johns Hopkins Med. Sch., 1928-32, asso. prof. anatomy, 1932-43. Mem. Am. Ornithologists' Union, Cooper Ornithol. Club (sec. 1913; trustee, 1920; v.p. 1921), Am. Soc. Mammalogists (corr. sec. 1925-31, editor 1936-38, v.p. 1938-42, pres. 1942-44), Am. Assn. Anatomists, Council for Conservation of Whales (exec. sec.); fellow A.A.A.S.; corr. mem. Internat. Office for Protection Nature. Club: St. Elmo, Author 4 books and 180 contbns. on mammals, birds, anatomy, others. Home: Alna, Me. Died Dec. 23, 1961.

HOWELL, ARTHUR HOLMES, naturalist; b. Lake Grove, N.Y., May 3, 1872; s. Elbert Richard and Anne Judson (Holmes) H.; ed. pub. schs., Brooklyn, N.Y.; m. Grace Bowen Johnson, June 20, 1900; children—Ruth Alden (Mrs. E. E. Stansbury), Elizabeth Carolyn, Elbert Jerome. Biologist of the U.S. Biological Survey, Dept. of Agriculture, 1895—; in charge explorations in Tex. and N.M., 1903, Tex. and La., 1905-07, Ga. and Tenn., 1908, Mo., Ill. and Ky., 1909, Mont. and Ark., 1910, Ala., 1911-16, Fla., 1918-39, Ga., 1927-33, N.C., 1928-30. Fellow Am. Ornithol. Union. Conglist. Author: Birds of Arkansas, 1911; Biological Survey of Alabama, 1921; Birds of Alabama, 1924; Florida Bird Life, 1932. Home: Washington, D.C. Died July 10, 1940.

HOWELL, JOHN WHITE, electrical engr.; b. New Brunswick, N.J., Dec. 22, 1857; s. Martin A. and Abby Lucetta (Stout) H.; Coll. City of New York, 1874-76; Rutgers, 1876-78, Sc.D., 1925; Stevens Inst. Tech., 1878-81, hon. E.E., 1899, hon. Sc.D., 1932; m. Frederica Burckle Gilchrist, Apr. 23, 1895; children—Frederica B., John White, Jane Augusta, Cornelia Margaret, Robert G. With engring. dept., Edison Lamp Works, 1881-93; became chief engr. Lamp Works of Gen. Electric Co., 1893; retired 1931; mem. Research Council of Gen. Electric Co., Schenectady, 1900—. Mem. bd. mgrs. Howard Savings Instn. Trustee Newark Mus. Assn. Fellow Am. Inst. E.E. Awarded Edison medal by Am. Inst. E.E., 1924. Episcopalian. Home: Newark, N.J. Died July 28, 1937.

HOWELL, WILLIAM HENRY, prof. physiology; b. Baltimore, Feb. 20, 1860; s. George Henry and Virginia Teresa H.; A.B., Johns Hopkins, 1881, Ph.D., 1884; hon. M.D., U. of Mich., 1890; LL.D., Trinity, 1901, U. of Mich., 1912, Washington U., 1915, U. of Edinburgh, 1923; Sc.D., Yale, 1911; m. Anne Janet Tucker, June 15, 1887; children—Janet Tucker (Mrs. Admont H. Clark), Roger, Charlotte Teresa (Mrs. Edward O. Hulburt). Asso. prof. physiology, Johns Hopkins, 1888-89; prof. physiology and histology, U. of Mich., 1889-92; asso. prof. physiology, Harvard, 1892-93; prof. physiology Johns Hopkins U., 1893-1931, dean med. faculty, 1899-1911, asst. dir. Sch. Hygiene, 1917-26, dir., 1926-31, emeritus since 1931. Chmn. Nat. Research Council, 1932-33. Mem. Nat. Acad. Sciences, Am. Philos. Soc., etc.; hon. mem. English Physiol. Soc. Author: Text-book of Physiology, 1905. Editor of An American Text-book of Physiology, 1896. Home: 112 St. Dunstan's Rd., Baltimore, Md. Died Feb. 6, 1945.

HOWER, HARRY (SLOAN), prof. physics; b. Parker, Pa., July 24, 1877; s. William H(enry) and Rebecca (Sloan) H.; B.S., Case Sch. Applied Science, 1899, M.S., 1907; grad. study, U. of Berlin, 1903-05; m. Sara Chester, June 23, 1909; children—Thomas Chester, Harry Sloan, Sara, William Henry II. Teacher physics, high sch., Conneaut, O., 1 yr., 1899-1900; instr. in physics, Case Sch. Applied Science, 1900-03, 1905-06; with Carnegie Inst. Tech. since 1906, prof. physics and head of dept. since 1915; cons. physicist. Designer of lenses for range lights for Panama Canal Commn., U.S. Light House Bd., U.S. Navy submarines, U.S. Army searchlight, Norwegian merchant marine, etc. Fellow Am. Physical Soc., A.A.A.S.; mem. Am. Optical Soc., Soc. Promotion Engring. Edn., Am. Ceramic Soc., Illuminating Engring. Soc., English Soc. Glass Technology, Pa. Acad. Science, Sigma Xi, Tau Beta Pi, Theta Xi. Republican. Episcopalian. Mason. Club: University. Home: 5709 Solway St., Pittsburgh, Pa. Died Oct. 10, 1941.

HOWES, BENJAMIN ALFRED, (houz), engr.; b. Keene, N.H., Aug. 4, 1875; s. Benjamin Thomas and Maria Adelaide (Holt) H.; B.S., Mass. Inst. Tech., 1897; m. Ethel D. Puffer, Aug. 5, 1908; children—Ellen Dench (Mrs. J. A. R. Pimlott), Benjamin Thomas. With Frank Sprague, Sprague Multiple Unit System, N.Y., 1897-1900; mining equipment, design and constrn., with Randfontein Estates, S. Africa, and Thomas Robins, Paris and London, 1900-03; research and constrn., sand-lime brick, 1903-05; pvt. practice, N.Y., 1905-33; spl. problems, reinforced concrete, power plants, electro-metallurgy (including microanalysis in such investigations), coal mining, oil prodn. and transport, power and pub. utilities, sch. and camp planning and operation; staff engr. Fed. Emergency Relief Adminstrn., 1934; sr. engr., chief of Materials Intake Sect., Resettlement Adminstrn., 1934-38; sr. engr., chief specifications and materials sect. U.S. Housing Authority, 1938-42; sr. archl. engr., chief materials sect., Fed. Pub. Housing Adminstrn.; developed specifications for 2 1/2 billion dollars of govt. and war housing. Mem. Am. Soc. for Testing Materials, Soc. Am. Mil. Engrs., Nat. Soc. Profl. Engrs., Assn. Fed. Architects, Soc. Mass. Inst. Tech. Author: Building by a Builder, 1914; tech. articles on concrete bldg. construction. Home: 4911 V St., N.W., Washington 7. Died Jan. 9, 1952.

HOWEY, WALTER CRAWFORD, (hou'e), editor, inventor; b. Ft. Dodge, Ia., Jan. 16, 1882; s. Frank Harris and Rosa (Crawford) H.; ed. Ft. Dodge pub. schs.; student Chicago Art Inst., 1899-1900; m. Elizabeth Board, 1900 (died 1935); m. 2d, Gloria Ritz, Sept. 1, 1936; 1 son, William Randolph. Reporter Ft. Dodge (Ia.) Messenger, 1902, Des Moines (Ia.) Daily Capital, 1902, Chicago American, 1904; city editor Chicago Inter Ocean, 1906-07, Chicago Tribune, 1907-17; editor Chicago Herald Examiner, 1917-22, Boston American, 1922-24; founder New York Mirror, 1924; assistant to William Randolph Hearst; editor Boston Record-American, 1939; editor Chicago Herald-American, 1942; supervising editor American Weekly, New York; Hearst newspapers, Boston and Chicago; president Internat. Research Laboratory, Lee Electric Company. Inventor of sound photo wire and radio transmission, photo electric engraving system, cold light photograph system, photo electric pantagraph and high speed code transmission. Home: The Eliot, 370 Commonwealth Av., Boston. Died Mar. 21, 1954.

HOWLETT, FREEMAN S(MITH), horticulturist; born Jordanville, N.Y., June 15, 1900; s. William Jacob and Anna Belle (Smith) H.; B.S., Cornell, 1921, Ph.D., 1925; D.Sc. (honorary), Wooster College, 1968; student University London, Nat. Research Council Fgn. fellowship, biol. sci. John Innes Hort. Institute, London,

England, 1932-33; Doctor Science, Wooster College, 1968; m. Jean Margaret Waterbury, Sept. 26, 1925. Instr. in agrl. economics, Cornell, 1921, instr. pomology, 1922-24; asst. horticulturist, Ohio Agricultural Research and Development Center, Wooster, 1924-27, asso. horticulturist. 1924-27, professor and chmn. department horticulture, since 1947; asst. prof. horticulture, Ohio State Univ., 1929-37, asso. prof., 1937-42, prof., 1942-71, chmn. dept. horticulture and forestry, 1947-70; guest lectr. horticulture Agr. Colls. Yugoslavia, 1951, Slovak Academy of Sciences, Czechoslovakia, 1966, Bulgarian Acad. of Sciences, 1962; cons. U.S. AID, Punjab Agr. U., India, 1967. Fellow Royal Hort. Soc. London (England), A.A.A.S., Ohio Academy of Science (past vice president), Am. Soc. Hort. Sci. (president 1958-59); mem. American Institute Biol. Sci. (past gov.), Botanical Soc. Am., Am. Soc. Plant Physiol., Genetics Soc. Am., Ohio State Hort. Soc., Ohio Vegetable and Potato Growers Association, Ohio Forestry Assn., Internat. Soc. Horticultural Science, Sigma Xi, Gamma Sigma Delta, Phi Kappa Phi. Independent. Presbyterian. Author: Modern Fruit Production (with Joseph H. Gourley), 1941. Home: Wooster OH Died Nov. 18, 1970; buried Wooster Cemetery.

HOXIE, GEORGE LUKE, engr. b. Leonardsville, Madison County, N.Y., May 14, 1872; s. Luke and Harriet Ellen (Parker) H.; ed. pub. schs., Leonardsville, Ilion and Utica, N.Y.; M.E. Cornell U., 1892, M.M.E., 1897, Ph.D., 1902; m. Mary Coleta Osborn, June 29, 1896; children—Dorothy E., Robert O., Stephen P., Henry L. Instr., U. of Ariz., 1892-93; acting prof. mechanics and industrial drawing, 1893-94, prof. physics and mechanics, 1894-96; instr. in elec. engring., Cornell U., 1898-1901; engr. Westinghouse, Church, Kerr & Co., 1901-04; cons. engr. in independent practice since June 1, 1904. Mem. Am. Soc. Mech. Engrs.; fellow Am. Inst. E.E. Author: (with Profs. Ryan and Norris) Test-book of Electrical Machinery, Vol. I, 1903; Stock Speculation and Business, 1930; Men, Money and Mergers, 1932. Home: 605 S. Lucerne Blvd., Los Angeles CA*

HOXIE, SOLOMON, agriculturist; b. Brookfield, N.Y., July 29, 1829; s. Nathan B. and Eliza (Langworthy) H.; ed. McGrawville Coll. and Madison (now Colgate) U.; m. Lucy P. Stickney, Sept. 22, 1859. Layman pastor Freewill Bapt. Ch., 8 yrs., Columbus, N.Y., 1868-76. One of first importers of Holstein Cattle in America; sec. Unadilla Valley Dutch Stock Breeders' Assn., 1876-85; sec. Dutch-Friesian Cattle Breeders' Assn. of America, 1878-85; originator of the earliest system for registering dairy cattle on the basis of product and supt. Advanced Registry of Holstein-Friesian Cattle Breeders' Assn., 1885-1904, emeritus, 1906—. Author: Holstein-Friesian Herd Book, 4 vols., 1880-85; Advanced Register Holstein-Friesian Cattle Breeders' Association, 14 vols., 1887-1903. Home: Edmeston, N.Y. Died Apr. 11, 1917.

HOYNE, ARCHIBALD LAWRENCE, pediatrician; b. Chgo., Apr. 4, 1878; s. Thomas Maclay and Jeanie Thomas (Maclay) H.; grad. Lake Forest Acad., 1897; A.B., Williams Coll., 1901; B.S., U. Chgo., 1902; M.D., Rush Med. Coll., 1904; m. Mary Alicia Williams, Mar. 25, 1908; children—Mary Williams (Mrs. Archibald T. Olmsted), Susan Dayton, Archibald Thomas. Clin. prof. pediatrics, emeritus U. Chgo.; prof. pediatrics Chgo. Med. Sch.; attending physician Cook County Hosp., chief contagious disease dept.; attending physician Children's Meml. Hosp.; cons. St. Vincent's Infant and Maternity Hosp.; former med. supt. Municipal Contagious Disease Hosp., Isolation Hosp.; attending pediatrician, former chmn. pediatric dept. St. Joseph Hosp.; cons. staff (pediatrics) St. Mary of Nazareth Hosp. Fellow Am. Coll. of Physicians, Am. Acad. of Pediatrics, A.M.A.; mem. Ill. State and Chicago med. socs., Inst. of Medicine, A.A.A.S., Chicago Pediatric Soc. (past pres.), Chicago Soc. of Med. History, Chicago Soc. Internal Medicine, Soc. of Ill. Bacteriologists, Am. Assn. Univ. Profs. Hon. mem. Sociedad Mexicana de Pediatria, Sociedad Cubana de Pediatria. Home: 428 Oakdale Av., Chgo. 60614. Died Mar. 3, 1963.

HOYT, CREIG SIMMONS, coll. dean; b. Auburn, N.Y., Feb. 27, 1894; s. Rev. Frank and Florence (Simmons) H.; ed. Unadilla (N.Y.) Acad.; B.S., Grove City Coll., 1913; A.M., Cornell U., 1917; Ph.D., U. Pitts., 1933; Sc.D., Grove City (Pa.) Coll., 1943; m. Matilda Thompson, July 22, 1915; children—Dr. Creig, Margaret. Successively instr. to prof. chemistry Grove City Coll., head dept. chemistry 1925—, dean, 1950—; cons. field of chemistry; mem. Grove City Bd. Edn., 1933-40; mem. Am. Chem. Soc., Am. Inst. Chemists, Sigma Xi, Phi Lambda Upsilon. Mason, Rotarian. Author: numerous papers in field of chemistry. Presbyterian. Republican. Home: 631 S. Center St., Grove City, Pa. Died May 9, 1957; buried Grove City, Pa.

HOYT, JOHN CLAYTON, civil engr.; b. Lafayette, N.Y., June 10, 1874; s. Newton O. and Mary E. (Ford) H.; C.E., Cornell U., 1897; m. Jennie F. King, Oct. 31, 1900; 1 son, Kendall King. With Cornell Hydraulic Lab. Constrn. Co., U.S. Deep Waterways Commn. and Bur. Yards and Docks, Navy Dept., 1897-99; U.S. Coast and Geod. Survey, 1900-02; with U.S. Geol. Survey since 1902; hydraulic engr. in charge Surface Water Div., 1911-30; cons. engr. since 1931. Professional work for Geol. Survey in various states and Hawaii and Alaska. U.S. del. 13th and 14th Internat. Navigation Congress, London, 1923, Cairo, 1926; mem. Am. com. representing U.S. Dept. of Interior, World Power Conf., London, 1924; delegate to World Engring. Congress, Tokyo, Japan, 1929. Mem. Am. Soc. C.E. (dir. 1920-22; v.p. 1927-28), Washington Sco. of Engrs. (sec. 1908-15; pres. 1916), Washington Acad. Sciences (v.p. 1916), Sigma Xi. Congregationalist. Mason. Clubs: Cosmos (pres. 1921), Chevy Chase. Author: (with Nathan C. Grover) River Discharge, 1907; Droughts of 1930-34 and 1936; also of various other U.S. Geol. Survey reports and articles in tech. papers. Home: 4749 MacArthur Blvd. N.W. Office: Cosmos Club, Washington, D.C. Died June 21, 1946.

HOYT, WILLIAM DANA, prof. biology; b. Rome, Ga., Apr. 16, 1880; s. (Dr.) William Dearing and Florence West (Stevens) H.; A.B., University of Georgia, 1901; M.S., 1904; Ph.D., Johns Hopkins, 1909; studied University of Heidelberg, 1909-10; research work, Naples, 1910; m. Margaret Howard Yeaton, Dec. 27, 1910 (died Sept. 26, 1943); children—William Dana, Southgate Yeaton, Robert Stephens. Tutor in biology, U. of Ga., 1901-04; fellow Johns Hopkins, 1908-09; scientific asst. U.S. Bur. Fisheries, Beaufort, N.C., 1902-09; Adam T. Bruce fellow, Johns Hopkins, 1909-10; instr. in botany, Rutgers Coll., 1910-12; fellow Johns Hopkins, 1912-15; asso. prof. biology, Washington and Lee U., 1915-20, prof. since 1920; instr. in botany, Marine Biol. Lab., Woods Hole, Mass., 1917-19. Fellow A.A.A.S.; mem. Bot. Soc. America, Am. Forestry Assn., Am. Genetic Assn., Am. Eugenic Soc., Am. Soc. Naturalists, Assn. Research Human Heredity, Va. Acad. Science, Chi Psi, Phi Beta Kappa. Democrat. Presbyterian. Club: Fortnightly. Author: Marine Algae of Beaufort, N.C., and Adjacent Regions, 1920; also articles on life habits and physiology of algae; proved alternation of generations in algae. Chmn. advisory Council on State Parks and Forests, 1930-33. Home: 5 Lewis St., Lexington, Va. Died Sept. 24, 1945.

HRDLICKA, ALES, (hûr'dlich-ka), anthropologist; b. Humpolec, Bohemia, Mar. 29, 1869; s. Maxmilian and Karolina H.; M.D., N.Y. Eclectic Coll., 1892, New York Homoe. Coll., 1894; Md. Allopathic State Bd., 1894; hon. Sc.D., Prague U., 1920, Brno U., 1929; investigator among insane and other defective classes, N.Y. State Service, 1894-99; asso. in anthropology, N.Y. State Pathol. Inst., 1896-99; studied in Paris U. and Anthrop. Sch., first half 1896; married 1896. Tour over European prisons, insane asylums and museums, 1896; in charge phys. anthropology of Hyde expdns. for Am. Mus. Natural History, 1899-1903; asst. curator in charge div. phys. anthropology, 1903-10, curator since 1910, U.S. Nat. Museum. Anthrop. expdns. to many countries throughout period since 1898. Author exhibits phys. anthropology and prehistoric Am. pathology, San Diego Expn., 1915-16. Asso. editor Am. Naturalist, 1901-08; founder, and editor Am. Jour. Phys. Anthrop. since 1918. Sec. gen. XIX Internat. Congress Americanists, 1915, sec. Sect. 1, anthropology, 2d Pan-Am. Scientific Congress, 1915-16; sec. com. on anthropology, Nat. Research Council, 1917-18; etc. Fellow Am. Acad. Arts and Sciences, A.A.A.S. (life); mem. Assn. Am. Anatomists, Am. Anthrop. Assn. (pres. 1925-26), Nat. Acad. Sciences, Am. Philos. Soc., Washington Acad. Sciences (pres. 1928-29), Archaeol. Inst. America, Am. Assn. Physical Anthropology (pres. 1928-32; founder and life mem.); hon. and corr. member various foreign acads. and socs. Huxley medal lecturer, London, 1927. Author of numerous books and papers on anthropology and related subjects. Home: 2900 Tilden St., N.W. Address: U.S. National Museum, Washington, D.C. Died Sept. 5, 1943.

HSIA, DAVID YI-YUNG, physician, educator; b. Shanghai, China, Aug. 22, 1925; s. Ching-Lin and Wai-Tsung (New) H.; came to U.S., 1940, naturalized, 1960; A.B., Haverford Coll., 1944; M.D., Harvard, 1948; m. Hsio-Hsuan Shih, July 23, 1949; children—David, Judith Ann, Lisa, and Peter. Intern Charity Hosp., New Orleans, 1948-49; asst. resident pediatrics, Childrens Hosp., Phila., 1949-50; asst. resident pediatrics New York Hosp., 1950-51; research fellow pediatrics Harvard Med. Sch., 1951-53, instr. pediatrics, 1953-56; research asst. Galton Lab., Univ. Coll., London, 1956-57; faculty Northwestern U., 1957-69, prof. pediatrics, 1960-69, now lectr.; prof. and chmn. dept. pediatrics Loyola U.-Stritch Sch. Medicine, 1969-72; chief pediatrics Loyola University Hospital, 1969-72; consultant pediatrics at Children's Meml. Hosp., Chgo.; attending physician Evanston, Cook County hosps. Bd. dirs. Am. Bur. Med. Aid to China, 1965-72; Cook County chpt. Nat. Found., 1959-72, Chgo. Cystic Fibrosis Found., 1961-72. Recipient Mead Johnson award pediatric research, 1965, City of Hope award, 1971. Mem. Soc. Pediatric Research, Central Soc. Clin. Research, Soc. Exptl. Biology and Medicine, Am. Pediatric Soc., Phi Beta Kappa, Alpha Omega Alpha. Author: Inborn Errors of Metabolism, 2d edit., 1966; Human Developmental Genetics, 1968. Home: Evanston IL Died Jan. 27, 1972; buried Ferncliff, Hartsdale NY

HUBBARD, CHARLES J., explorer; b. Kansas City, Mo., June 25, 1902; s. Charles J. and Alice (Davis) H.; A.B. cum laude, Harvard, 1924, S.B. magna cum laude, 1925; m. Anna Fuller, 1925; 1 son, Charles J.; m. 2d, Dorothy Speare, 1934; m. 3d, Harriet Bissell, Jan. 18, 1943; children—Aries B., Hamal, Dana. Engr. Stone & Webster, Inc., 1925-28; v.p. George B. H. Macomber Co., Boston, 1929-31; made aerial surveys with N. Labrador Expn. of Forbes and Grenfel, 1931-35; freelance exploration and journalism, 1935-40; now chief Arctic Sect. U.S. Weather Bur., mng. U.S. interests in network internat. Arctic sci. stas. Served as lt. comdr. USNR, 1941-42; lt. col. USAAF, 1942—. Condr. surveys and airfield construction in Greenland, N. Labrador, Hudson Bay area, etc., in development of northern airways through Greenland and eastern Canadian arctic for U.S. Army Air Transport Command; established first Arctic weather sta. network by airplane. Recipient medal, U.S. Dept. Agr., 1950. Mem. Am. Geographical Soc. Geophys. Inst. Clubs: Explorers, Cruising Club of America, Delphic, Varsity (Harvard). Contbr. articles and fiction to numerous popular mags. Navigator, aviator, comml. license. Office: Arctic Section, U.S. Weather Bureau, Washington. Killed in air crash at Alert, Ellesmere Island, July 31, 1950; buried Alert Ellesmere Island, N.W.T., Can.

HUBBARD, GARDINER GREENE, telephone pioneer; b. Boston, Aug. 25, 1822; s. Samuel and Mary Anne (Greene) H.; grad. Dartmouth, 1841; m. Gertrude McCurdy, Oct. 21, 1846, children include Mabel G. (wife of Alexander Graham Bell). Introduced gas lighting into Cambridge (Mass.), 1857, also secured fresh water supply for city and built one of earliest U.S. street-car lines between Cambridge and Boston; leader movement which incorporated Clarke Instn. for Deaf Mutes, Northampton, Mass., 1867, pres., 1867-77; mem. Mass. Bd. of Edn., 12 years; became interested in elec. work invention of telephone, 1875; became exec. of 1st telephone orgns. (became Bell Telephone Co.), directed early bus. devel., his system of renting (rather than selling) phones led to present federated structure of Bell System; mem. commn. to investigate transp. of the mails and make recommendations for improvement to Congress, 1876; trustee Columbian (now George Washington) U., 12 years; founder (with Alexander Graham Bell) Science (organ of A.A.A.S.), 1883; asso. with Bell in founding Am. Assn. to Promote Teaching of Speech to the Deaf, 1890, v.p., 1890-97; interested in Alaskan explorations, Hubbard Glacier named for him, 1890; became regent Smithsonian Instn., 1895; pres., joint commn. of scientific socs. of Washington (D.C.) which later organized Washington Acad. of Scis., 1895-97; founder Nat. Geog. Soc., 1888, 1st pres., 1888-97; Hubbard Hall (home of Nat. Geog. Soc.), Washington, named for him. Died Washington, Dec. 11, 1897.

HUBBARD, GEORGE DAVID, geologist and geographer; b. Tolono, Champaign County, Ill., May 12, 1871; s. Linus Green and Helen Lorena (Stanard) H.; B.S., University of Illinois, 1896, M.S., 1898; A.M., Harvard, 1901; Ph.D., Cornell University, 1905; m. Edna Almira Rugg, Sept. 10, 1901; children—Ruth Marilla, Oscar Edwin, Dorothy Hope (dec.), Marjorie Helen. Fellow in science and acad. teacher of physics, University of Illinois, 1896-97; asst. in geology, same, 1897-1900; professor geography, Eastern Illinois State Normal School, 1901-03; instructor physiography, Cornell U., 1903-05; temp. asst. U.S. Geol. Survey, 1903-05; asst. prof. geology, Ohio State U., 1905-10; acting prof. geology, Oberlin Coll., 1910-12, prof., 1912-17, prof. geology and geography, 1917-36, emeritus, 1936—; prof. geology and geography, Harvard Univ., summer, 1937, Berea (Ky.) College, 1941; visiting prof. geography, Univ. of Missouri, 1942-44 and 1946-48. Assistant geologist Ohio Geol. Survey, 1906-26; geologist S.D. Geol. Survey, summer 1945, 49. Fellow A.A.A.S., Geol. Soc. Am., Am. Geog. Soc., Assn. Am. Geographers, American Soc. Professional Geographers; member Academy Polit. Science, International Council of Religious Education, Ohio Acad. Sci. (pres. 1917), Sigma Xi. Republican. Conglist. Joint Author: Ednl. Bulletin (Ohio Geol. Survey), 1912; Columbus Folio (U.S. Geol. Survey), 1914. Author: Geography of Europe (Textbook), 1937; Geographical Influence of Gold and Silver Mining on United States, 1912. Contbr. about 100 papers on geol., geog. and ednl. subjects, also lecturer. Consulting practice. Home: 279 Oak St., Oberlin, O. Died June 11, 1958; buried in Oberlin.

HUBBARD, HENRY GRISWOLD, inventor, mfr.; b. Middletown, Conn., Oct. 8, 1814; s. Elijah and Lydia (Mather) H.; attended Wesleyan U., Middletown, Conn.; m. Charlotte Rosella Macdonough, June 19, 1844. Clk., J.&S. Baldwin's store, Middletown, 1831-33; owner, operator dry goods store, Middletown, 1833-37; perfected 1st successful elastic web woven on power looms, 1841; purchased control of Russell Mfg. Co., 1850, began mfg. elastic and non-elastic webbing; mem. Conn. Senate, 1866-67; dir. Middletown Bank; trustee Middletown Savs. Bank. Died July 29, 1891.

HUBBARD, HENRY GUERNSEY, entomologist; b. Detroit, May 6, 1850; s. Bela and Sarah (Baughman) H.; grad. Harvard, 1873; m. Kate Laiser, 1887, 4 children, Started museum for study of entomology, Detroit, 1874;

took several expdns. with E.A. Schwartz to Lake Superior Region in search for Coleoptera, 1877-78; naturalist Geol. Survey of Ky., 1879-80; agt. U.S. Entomol. Commn. of Dept. Agr., 1880-84; engaged in research of insects attacking orange trees for U.S. Dept. Agr., 1894-99. Died Jan. 18, 1899.

HUBBARD, JOHN CHARLES, physicist; b. Boulder, Colo., Apr. 16, 1879; s. James Edwin and Rhoda Maude (Duke) H.; B.S., U. of Colo., 1901; Ph.D., Clark Univ., 1904; LL.D., Loyola Coll., Baltimore, 1938; m. Gertrude L. Pardieck, Feb. 9, 1929. Instr. in physics at Simmons Coll., Boston, 1904-05; asst. prof. physics, New York U., 1905-06, Clark U., 1906-11; prof. physics Clark Coll., 1911-16; prof. and head of physics dept., N.Y. Univ., 1916-27; prof. same, Johns Hopkins Univ., 1927-46; physicist, Radiation Lab., Johns Hopkins Univ., 1946-47; research prof. physics, Catholic U. of Am., 1947—. Dir. summer work in physics, New York Univ., 1906, U. of Colo., 1912, 14; research engr., Western Electric Co., summer, 1917. Commd. capt. Signal Corps, U.S.R., Div. Research and Insp., Sept. 29, 1917; active service in France, information sect. Office of Chief Signal Officer, A.E.F.; official historian, Signal Corps, A.E.F.; maj., Oct. 4, 1918; discharged, May 20, 1919. Awarded Mendal medal, Villanova College, 1946. Officier d'Académie Instruction Publique, 1919. Fellow A.A.A.S., Am. Acad. Arts and Sciences, Am. Physical Soc.; mem. Beta Theta Pi, Phi Beta Kappa, Sigma Xi; rep. of Am. Inst. of Physics on Am. Engring. Standards Com.; mem. at large Div. of Physical Sciences of Nat. Research Council, 1931-33; sec. member National Defense Research Committee. Clubs: Johns Hopkins (Baltimore); Andiron (New York). Author various papers giving results of original physical research. Asso. editor Physical Rev., 1933-35. Roman Catholic. Address: 4304 13th Place N.E., Washington. Died Aug. 2, 1954; buried Richmond, Ind.

HUBBARD, JOSEPH STILLMAN, astronomer; b. New Haven, Conn., Sept. 7, 1823; s. Ezra Stiles and Eliza (Church) H.; grad. Yale, 1843. Asst. to Sears C. Walker at High Sch. Observatory, Phila., 1844-45; prof. mathematics U.S. Naval Acad., stationed at U.S. Naval Observatory, 1845-63; especially interested in question of parallax of Alpha Lyrae; contbr. numerous articles to Astron. Jour.; calculated orbit of comet of 1843. Deid Aug. 16, 1863.

HUBBARD, LUCIUS LEE, geologist; b. Cincinnati, Aug. 7, 1849; s. Lucius Virgilius and Annie Elizabeth (Lee) H.; A.B., Harvard, 1872; LL.B., Boston U., 1875; Ph.D., U. of Bonn, 1886; m. Frances Johnson Lambard, Sept. 29, 1875; children—Charlotte Armitage (Mrs. H. S. Goodell), Lucius Lambard (dec.), Frances Johnson (Mrs. R. J. Flaherty), Julia Lambard (Mrs. Platt Adams). Asst. Mich. Geol. Survey and instr. mineralogy, Mich. Coll. Mines, 1891-93; state geologist, 1893-99. Mem. bd. control Mich. Coll. of Mines, 1905-17; regent U. of Mich., 1911—. Author: Woods and Lakes of Maine, 1884; A Dutch Source for Robinson Crusoe—The Narrative of El-ho, "Sjouke Gabbes," 1921. Compiler: The University of Michigan—Its Origin, Growth, and Principles of Government, 1923. Home: Houghton, Mich. Died Aug. 3, 1933.

HUBBARD, S(AMUEL) DANA, dermatologist; b. Montgomery, Ala., Mar. 19, 1869; s. Samuel Dana and Mary C. (Taylor) H.; preo. edn., pvt. high sch., Montgomery; student U. of Ala., 1886; M.D., Bellevue Hosp. Med. Coll., N.Y. City, 1891; m. Armilla Monell, Oct. 23, 1895; children—Aileen (Mrs. Harry Chapin), Beryl. Interne, Bellevue Hosp., 1891-92; resident phys. Riverside Hosp., N.Y. City, 1892-95; began practice at N.Y. City, 1895; former dermatologist N.Y. City Children's Hosp. and attending dermatologist Letchworth Village. Maj. and surgeon, N.G.N.Y., 1891-98; maj. and surgeon, U.S. Vol. Inf., Spanish-Am. War. Presbyn. Author: Sex Facts, 1927; Diseases of Scalp and Hair, 1928. Home: Freeport, L.I., N.Y. Died July 12, 1937.

HUBBARD, WYNANT DAVIS, writer, naturalist; b. Kansas City, Mo., Aug. 28, 1900; s. Charles and Alice (Field) H.; ed. Christchurch, Bournemouth, Eng., Seligs, Montreux, Switzerland; student Milton (Mass.) Acad., 1918, Harvard, 1921; m. Margaret Carson, 1921; children—Charles Joseph, Margaret Carson; m. 2d, Isabella Menzies, 1928; 1 son, Wynant Davis; m. 3d, Loyala Bradley Lee, June 10, 1950. In gold, silver mining, Ont., 1920, asbestos, Que., 1921; profl. hunter, British Central Africa, 1922-24; leader First Nat. Motion Picture expdn. to No. Rhodesia 1925-26; rancher Ibamba, No. Rhodesia, 1929-35; war corr. Ethiopian side Italo-Ethiopian War, 1935-36; pres. The Africa Co., export, 1938-39; chief livestock Development Dept. of Interior, St. Croix, Virgin Islands, 1943; prin. agrl. economist Office Fgn. Agrl. Relations, 1943; acting dir. div. agr. and fisheries UNRRA, Cairo, 1943-44; acting chief UNRRA Mission, Ethiopia, 1944-45; export-import in mineral bus. Matavic Corp., 1948-49; v.p., gen. mgr. El Ghedem Mining Corp., also El Ghedem Mining Corp., S.A., Asmara, Eritrea, East Africa, 1950-51, dir., 1950—. Served as lt., Air Force, USN, 1917; master Benedict Field airforce crashboat, served in G-2 in anti-submarine warfare and intelligence, World War II. Fellow Zool. Soc. (London), Am. Geog. Soc.; mem. Am. Soc. Mammalogists, Soc. Preservation Fauna of the Empire, Zool. Soc. Fla. (founder, exec. v.p., dir.), Humane Society of Greater Miami (dir. 1958—). Clubs: Delphic, S-K, Institute-Hasty Pudding, Varsity (Harvard). Author: Wild Animals, 1925; Bong'-kwe, 1930; The Thousandth Frog, 1934; Fiasco in Ethiopia, 1936; Wild Animal Hunter, 1958; also articles sci. nat., lit. publs. Home: 1890 N.W. 43d St., Miami, 42, Fla. Died Dec. 9, 1961; buried Petersham, Mass.

HUBBELL, CLARENCE W., civil engr.; b. Cole County, Mo., Apr. 10, 1870; s. John James and Sarah Maria (Huntington) H.; B.S. in Civil Engring., U. Mich., 1893, C.E., 1904; m. Winifred Temperance Waters, Dec. 31, 1895; children—Theodore H., Mrs. Albert Huntington, Roger S., George E., Harriet W. Junior engr. on railroad location and constrn., 1887-93; chief draughtsman Detroit Water Works Dept., 1893-98, engr. in charge, 1898-1907; prin. asst. engr. water supply of Manila, P.I., 1907-09, city engr., Manila, 1909-10; chief engr. pub. works, P.I., 1910-13; cons. engr. Pub. Utilities Commn., P.I., 1913-14; returned to Detroit, 1915; cons. engr. on Detroit pollution, internat. boundary waters, 1915-16; city engr., Detroit, 1917-22; mem. engring. firm Hubbell, Roth & Clark, pres. 1915-47; mem. bd. cons. engrs. Detroit Sewage Collection and Treatment Project, 1925-37; cons. engr. Wayne County Sewage Treatment plant, 1937-40. Served as engr. on design and reconstruction of sewer system of Detroit, 1916-22, involving outlay of about $40,000,000; bd. engring. rev. San. Dist. Chgo., 1924-25; member Rapid Transit Commn., Detroit, 1925-40; mem. Bd. Review Sewage Treatment, Toronto, Ont., 1939. Mem. Am. Soc. C.E., Am. Assn. Engrs., Am., N.E. water works assns., Mich. (pres.), Detroit engring. socs. Recipient Norman medal, Am. Soc. C.E., 1902. Republican. Conglist. Mason (Shriner). Home: Hill Hollow, Milford, Mich. Office: Buhl Bldg., Detroit. Died Feb. 1, 1950; buried Benzonia, Mich.

HUBBLE, EDWIN POWELL, (hub'b'l), astronomer; b. Marshfield, Mo., Nov. 20, 1899; s. John Powell and Virginia Lee (James) H.; B.Sc., U. of Chicago, 1910, Ph.D., 1917; Rhodes scholar from Ill. at Oxford U., Eng., 1910-13, B.A. in Jurisprudence, 1912; honorary D.Sc., Oxford, 1934, Princeton, 1936, Brussels, 1937; LL.D., Occidental, 1936; U. of Calif., 1949; m. Grace Burke, Feb. 26, 1924. Admitted to Ky. bar, 1913; research work, Yerkes Obs., Univ. of Chicago, 1914-17; astronomer on staff Mt. Wilson Obs., Pasadena, Calif., since 1919; chmn. research com., Mt. Wilson and Palomar Observatories; Hitchcock Lecturer, Univ. of Calif., 1948; Silliman lecturer, Yale University, 1935; Rhodes Memorial lecturer, Oxford Univ., 1936. Student 1st O.T.C., Fort Sheridan, Ill., 1917; capt. inf., Aug. 1917; maj., Dec. 1917; comdr. 2 Batt., 343d Inf., 86th Div., U.S. Army, Sept. 1917-Nov. 1918; with A.E.F., Sept. 1918-Aug. 1919; hon. disch. at Presidio, San Francisco, Aug. 1919. Chief ballistician and dir. of Supersonic Wind Tunnels Lab., Ballistic Research Lab., U.S. War Dept., 1942-46. Awarded Medal for Merit, 1946. Fellow Royal Astronomical Soc., Eng.; mem. Astron. Soc., Astron. Soc. of Pacific, Nat. Academy Sciences, 1927, Am. Philos. Soc., 1929; Sigma Xi, Kappa Sigma. Awarded Barnard medal for scientific service, 1935; Bruce medal, 1938, Franklin medal, 1939. Royal Astronomical Soc. medal, 1940; hon. fellow, Queen's Coll., Oxford, 1948; membre de l'Institut, Academie de France. Trustee Huntington Library and Art Gallery. Clubs: Athenaeum, Sunset, Author: The Realm of Nebulae, 1936; The Observational Approach to Cosmology, 1937; The Nature of Science. Home: 1340 Woodstock Rd., San Marino, Cal. Office: Mt. Wilson Observatory, Pasadena 4, Cal. Died Sept. 28, 1953.

HUBER, WALTER LEROY, civil engr.; b. San Francisco, Calif., Jan. 4, 1883; s. M. F. and Celia (Dill) H.; B.S. Civil Engring., U. Cal., 1905, LL.D., 1955; m. Alberta Mann Reed, November 11, 1941. Asst. engr. with J. D. Galloway, San Francisco, 1905-06; chief structural designer, Howard & Galloway, 1906-08; chief engr. for supervising architect, U. of Calif., 1908-10; dist. engr. (Calif. and Nev.), U.S. Forest Service, 1910-13; pvt. practice since 1913; in partnership with Edward M. Knapik since 1941; engaged in hydroelectric, hydraulic and structural work in Western United States; consultant on dams; consultant engr. State Department Public Works, California, on many projects, including San Gabriel Dam No. 1, and Central Valley Project; cons. engr. California Debris Commn. on arch dams; mem. bd. cons. engrs. U.S. War Department on flood control projects on Los Angeles, San Gabriel and Santa Ana rivers, including Prado, Sepulveda, Brea, Fullerton, Santa Fe, Whittier Narrows dams; in Central Valley, Isabella, Pine Flat. dams, also the Cherry Valley Dam & power projects San Francisco; structural engr. 4-story underground garage occupying all of Union Square, San Francisco; U. Cal. Med. Center including 2 15-story units; spl. cons. on the earthquake resistant design of many large structures; member advisory committee to Bureau of Building Inspection, San Francisco, Calif., 1930-37; regional engring. advisor R.F.C., 1932-33; spl. consultant U.S. War Dept. on structures, water supplies, etc.; engr. Hammond Gen. Hosp., DeWitt Gen. Hosp. and other mil. works, 1942-43; engr. buildings, Hunters Point Dry Docks, U.S. Navy, 1944, Fresno Vet. Adminstrn. Hosp., Letterman Gen. Hosp., U.S. Army. Mem. Calif. Forest Study Com., Calif. State C. of C., 1926-38; mem. Gov.'s Adv. Engring. Com. on Calif. State Water Resources Development, 1932; regional water consultant, Nat. Resources Planning Bd., 1934-43; spl. rep. President U.S. on Ark., White and Red River Basins Survey, 1954-55; mem. adv. bd. nat. parks, hist. sites, bldgs. and monuments U.S. Dept. Interior, chmn. 1956-59. Mem. engring. adv. council U. Cal. 1947-57. Recipient honor award Pacific Coast Building Industry Conf., 1953. Fellow California Acad. Scis. (v.p. 1953-57); mem. Am. Soc. C.E. (pres. 1952-53; del. European-U.S. Congress, Paris, 1953), Am. Inst. Cons. Engrs., Am. Concrete Inst., Seismol. Soc., Soc. Cal. Pioneers, Cal. Hist. Soc., Phi Sigma Kappa, Sigma Xi, Tau Beta Pi, Chi Epsilon. Clubs: Sierra (dir. 1915-48; v.p. 1922-24; pres. 1925-26, hon. v.p., 1948—), Commonwealth, Engrs., Am. Alpine. Chmn. adv. bd. Nat. Parks, Hist. Sites, Bldgs. and Monuments, U.S. Dept. Interior, 1953-59. Author numerous tech. papers. Home: 19 Presidio Terrace. Office: 57 Post St., San Francisco 4. Died May 30, 1960; buried St. Mary's Cemetery, Yolo, Cal.

HUBERT, CONRAD, inventor; b. Minsk, Russia, 1855; married, 1914. Owned distillery in Russia; came to U.S. to escape Russian persecution of Jews, 1890; invented elec. device for lighting gas, 1898; later invented electric time alarm; invented electric battery and small electric lamp (forming basis for modern flashlight); founder, pres. Am. Ever Ready Co., flashlight mfg. firm, N.Y.C., circa 1903-14, sold out to Nat. Carbon Co., 1914; founder, chmn. bd. Yale Electric Corp., 1914-28. Died Cannes, France, Mar. 14, 1928; buried N.Y.C.

HUBERTY, MARTIN R., irrigation engr.; b. San Andreas, Cal., May 16, 1894; s. August J. and Mary Ann (Donnallan) H.; B.S., U. Cal., 1920; Engr., Stanford, 1934; m. Gertrude E. Turner, July 5, 1930; children—Richard A., Mary Ann, Alice Turner, Frederick Turner, Elizabeth Lee. Tchr. grammar sch., 1912-14; draughtsman, 1920; asst. irrigation U. Cal., 1921-25, jr. irrigation engr., 1925-28, asst. irrigation engr., 1928-31, asso. irrigation engr., 1931-42, asso. prof., 1936-42, prof., irrigation engr., 1942—, chmn. dept. irrigation and soils, 1952, dir. Water Resources Center, 1957—, acting dean agr., Los Angeles, 1957, 59-60, 60—; irrigation and drainage engr. FAO, Rome, 1951-52. Mem. No. Cal. Airport Commn., U.S. Dept. Commerce, 1927; regional cons. engr. drought relief F.E.R.A., 1934; cons. U.S. Bur. Reclamation, 1938. Served with Air Corps, U.S. Army, 1917-19. Fellow A.A.A.S.; mem. Am. Geophys. Union, Am. Soc. Agrl. Engrs., Am. Soc. Soil Sci., Am. Soc. C.E. (asso.), Sigma Xi, Tau Beta Pi, Alpha Zeta. Editor: (with Warren Flock) Natural Resources. Contbr. articles on water supply and irrigation problems to tech. jours. Home: 826 Glenmont St., Los Angeles. Office: University of California Water Resources Center, Los Angeles 24. Died Dec. 12, 1960.

HUBLEY, GEORGE WILBUR, (hub'le), engr.; b. Pittsburgh, Pa., May 9, 1870; s. George W. and Fanny (McAlister) H.; prep. edn., high sch., Allegheny, Pa.; spl. courses in mathematics and engring. under pvt. tutors. Student with Westinghouse Electric & Mfg. Co., Pittsburgh, 1887-90; elec. supt. Citizens Traction Co., Pittsburgh, 1890-93; supt. Louisville Gas & Electric Co., 1893-1915; gen. mgr. Merchants Heat & Light Co., Indianapolis, 1915-18; administrative engr. and chief of conservation, U.S. Fuel Adminstrn. of Ky., 1918; cons. practice, Louisville, since 1918; cons. engr. Ky. State Bd. Charities and Corrections, 1920-25; engr. Public Utilities Bur., Louisville, 1923-35. Fellow Am. Inst. E.E.; mem. Am. Soc. M.E., Am. Gas Assn., Ind. Engring. Soc., Engineers and Architects Club of Louisville (ex-pres.), S.A.R. (pres. 1940). Republican. Presbyterian. Mason. Home: 2428 Longest Av. Office: Norton Bldg., Louisville, Ky. Died Apr. 8, 1944. *

HUDDLESON, I. FOREST, bacteriologist; b. Murphysville, Ky., Oct. 17, 1893; s. John W. and Molly (Linville) H.; B.S., Okla. Agrl. and Mech. Coll., 1915; M.S., Mich. State Coll., 1916; D.V.M., 1925, Ph.D., 1937; Dr. Honoris Causa, U. La Plata, Argentina, 1950; D.Sc. (hon.), University of Kentucky, 1961; m. Isabel Sieger, 1921; children—Lenore, John, Louise, Mary. Research prof., Mich. State Univ., 1937-64, prof. microbiology, public health, 1957-64, student of brucellosis in animals and man since 1915, in Tunis, 1929, Malta, 1937-38, Mexico, 1940. Served as pvt., 2d lt., 1st lt., Sanitary Corps, U.S. Army during World War I. Recipient Internat. Veterinary prize award, 1940, Borden Award from Am. Vet. Med. Assn., 1944. Sigma Xi award, M.S.C., 1944, Soc. Ill. Bacteriologists award, 1948, Michigan State Coll. Alumni award, 1948; Kimble award, 1960; Distinguished Professor award, Michigan State University, 1961. Fellow American Academy of Microbiologists, American Association for Advancement Science; mem. Soc. American Bacteriologists, Am. Vet. Med. Assn., Royal Acad. Medicine of Belgium (fgn. corr.), Sigma Xi. Author: several books 1934-43, also tech. papers. Home: 644 Sunset Lane, East Lansing, Mich. Died May 26, 1965.

HUDSON, CLAUDE SILBERT, chemist; b. Atlanta, Ga., Jan. 26, 1881; s. William James and Maude Celestia (Wilson) H.; B.S., Princeton, 1901, M.S., 1902, Ph.D., 1907; D.Sc. (hon.), 1947. Research asst. in phys. chemistry, Mass. Inst. Tech., 1903-04; instr. physics,

Princeton, 1904-05; same, U. of Ill., 1905-07; assistant physicist, United States Geological Survey, 1907-08; assistant chemist, Bureau of Chemistry, United States Department Agriculture, and later chief of Carbohydrate Laboratory, 1908-19; chemist Bureau of Standards, United States Department Commerce, 1923-28; professor chemistry, U.S.P.H.S., 1928-51; mem. exec. com., editor Advance in Carbohydrate Chemistry. Councillor Internat. Union of Chemistry, 1930. Mem. Am. Com. on Organic Chem. Nomenclature, 1912. Mem. Am. Chem. Soc. (Nichols medal, 1916; Gibbs medal, 1929; Hillebrand prize, 1930; Richards medal, 1940; Borden award, 1941; chmn. organic div. of same soc. 1933), Nat. Acad. Sciences, German Acad. Natural Scientists (Halle), Acad. of Medicine (Washington, D.C.). Asso. editor: Journal of Am. Chem. Soc., 1938. Author: Collected Papers of C. S. Hudson, 2 volumes, 1946, 1948. Recipient Cresson medal, Franklin Institute, 1942. Recipient of $10,000 Grand Prize by Sugar Research Found., Inc., 1950, First Fed. Security Agency Distinguished Service Award, 1950, Distinguished Service medal, U.S.P.H.S., 1951. Died Dec. 27, 1952; buried Presbyn. Cemetery, Princeton, N.J.

HUDSON, JOHN ROGERS, civ. engr.; b. at New York, 1859; s. John R. and Jane E. H.; ed. pub. and pvt. schs., New York, Washington Univ., St. Louis; unmarried. In ry. and city engring. in West since 1878. Served pvt. to sergt. in U.S. vol. engrs. and U.S. Vol. inf. in Cuba and the Philippines, 1898-1901. Mem. Am. Soc. Civ. Engrs. Author: Tables for Calculating the Cubic Contents of Excavations and Embankments, 1884 W9. Address: 1806 Locust St., St. Louis.

HUDSON, WILLIAM SMITH, mech. engr.; b. Derby, Eng., Mar. 13, 1810; s. Daniel Smith and Anne (Roper) H.; learned trade of machinist; m. Ann Elizabeth Cairns, Oct. 6, 1836; 1 child. Worked in locomotive shop, New Castle, Eng., 1830-35; came to Am., 1835; locomotive engr. Troy & Saratoga R.R., 1835-36; engr. Rochester & Auburn R.R., 1838-49; master mechanic Attica & Buffalo R.R., 1849-51; supt. locomotive works Rogers Locomotive & Machine Works, 1851-81; designed, patented unique feed water-heater, 1860; patented application of cast-iron thimbles to the ends of boiler tubes, 1861; invented an improved valve gear, safety-valves, levers, an equalizing lever, 1868-70. Died July 20, 1881.

HUGHES, CHARLES HAMILTON, physician; b. St. Louis, May 23, 1839; s. Capt. Harvey Jackson and Elizabeth Rebecca (Stocker) H.; student Ia. (now Grinnell) Coll., M.D., St. Louis Med. Coll., 1859; m. Addie Case, of St. Louis, 1862 (now deceased); 2d, Mattie Dye Lawther, of Fulton, Mo., 1873 (now deceased). Maj. of cav. and surgeon in charge hosps., in Civil War; former supt. Hosp. for Insane, Fulton, Mo.; ex-lecturer on medicine, ex-prof. nervous and mental diseases, and ex-pres. med. coll. faculties, St. Louis; a founder of Marion-Sims Med. Coll. (now med. dept. St. Louis U.); founder, 1880, and since editor, Alienist and Neurologist. Mem. A.M.A., Am. Acad. Medicine, Am. Medico-Psychol. Assn., Am. Electro-Therapeutic Assn., Assn. Mil. Surgeons of U.S., Miss. Valley Med. Assn. (ex-pres.), Mo. State Med. Assn., St. Louis Med. Soc.; hon. mem. British Medico-Psychol. Soc., Russian Soc. Neurology and Psychiatry, Italian Soc. Chemico-Physiol., Palermo, etc. U.S. Govt. del. Internat. Congress for Prevention of Alcoholism, Stockholm, 1907, and later, London, and 14th and 15th Internat. med. congresses, etc. Author: The Neurological Practice of Medicine. Deviser of Hughes' Asthesiometer; discoverer of virile reflex, etc. Address: 3858 W. Pine Boul., St. Louis, Mo.

HUGHES, CHARLES HAYNES, naval architect and engr.; b. Boston, Mass., Sept. 3, 1877; s. Richard and Mary H.; educated English High School, Boston, and Mass. Institute of Tech.; m. Grace F. Charles, Dec. 25, 1918; 1 son, Dr. Charles H. Jr. Held responsible positions with Bath Iron Works, N.Y. Shipbuilding Co., and Crescent Shipyard; tech. aid for U.S. Shipping Bd. during World War I; engaged in spl. engring. work and projects relating to ships, World War II. Mem. Soc. Naval Engrs., Mass. Inst. Technology Alumni Assn. Author: Motor Boats, 1915; Hughes' Handbook of Ship Calculations and Construction (3d edition); Standard Details, 1918. Contbr. to New International Year Book. Awarded prizes for papers on welding by Lincoln Electric Co. and Hobart Bros. Home: 2681 Amboy Rd., New Dorp SI NY

HUGHES, DAVID EDWARD, inventor; b. London, Eng., May 16, 1831; son of David Hughes; m. Anna Chadbourne. Came with parents to U.S., 1838; taught music and natural philosophy; became interested in telegraphic experimentation; settled in Bowling Green, Ky., 1853; supported his researches by giving music lessons; worked on improved methods of telegraphic printing, sold his still-uncompleted printing device to Comml. Printing Telegraph Co. for $100,000, 1855, patented invention, 1856; starting working for Am. Telegraph Co., 1856; went to Eng. in unsuccessful attempt to introduce his methods there, 1857-60; had his system adopted by France, 1861, also by all other major European countries, by 1869; lived in London, 1877-1900; considered to be inventor of microphone, 1878; did work in aerial telegraphy, never published results; fellow, v.p., recipient Gold medal Royal Soc.; recipient Albert medal Soc. of Arts. Died London, Jan. 22, 1900; buried London.

HUGHES, DONALD JAMES, physicist; b. Chgo., Apr. 2, 1915; s. William and Anna (Johnson) H.; B.S., U. Chgo., 1936, Ph.D., 1940; m. Emily Peterson, Aug. 6, 1943 (divorced, Jan. 1957); children—Bonita, Carolyn; married 3d, Valerie Turner, Feb. 15, 1957; children—Therese, Howard. Instr. Univ. Chgo., 1940-43; mem. cosmic ray expdn., S.A., 1941; sect. chief Naval Ordnance Lab., 1942-43; staff Manhattan Project, 1943-45; div. dir. Argonne Nat. Lab., 1945-49; sr. physicist Brookhaven Nat. Lab., 1949—, mem. nuclear cross sects. adv. group, also chmn., 1950-52; Fulbright prof. Oxford, Cambridge univs., 1953-54; lectr. U.S. Information Service, Denmark, Eng., Finland, Germany, Holland, 1954-56; Loeb lectr. Harvard, 1955. Chmn. Atoms for Peace Meeting, Geneva, 1955. Fellow Am. Phys. Soc.; mem. A.A.A.S., Franklin Inst., Fedn. Am. Scientists (chmn. 1955-56), Sigma Xi, Phi Beta Kappa, Tau Kappa Epsilon. Editorial bd. Science Mag., 1958—, editorial com. Annual Reviews of Nuclear Science, 1958—. Author: Pile Neutron Research, 1953; Neutron Optics, 1954; Neutron Cross Sections, 1955; On Nuclear Energy, 1957; The Story of the Neutron, 1959. Mng. editor Progress in Nuclear Energy, 1956. Home: 25 North Brewster Lane, Bellport, N.Y. Office: Brookhaven Nat. Lab., Upton, N.Y. Died Apr. 12, 1960.

HUGHES, HECTOR JAMES, civil engr.; b. Centralia, Pa., Oct. 23, 1871; s. James H. and Mary (Miller) H.; A.B., Harvard, 1894; S.B., Lawrence Scientific Sch. (Harvard), 1899; m. Elinor Lambert, Apr. 15, 1902; children—Katharine Porter, Elinor Lambert. In office of town engr., Brookline, Mass., 1894-98; asst. engr. maintenance, Chicago, 1899-1900, resident engr. in charge constrn. in Ia., 1900-02, C.,B.&Q. R.R.; designer, Am. Bridge Co., Pittsburgh, 1902; instr. civ. engring., 1902-03, asset. prof., 1903-13, asso. prof., 1913-14, prof., 1914—, Harvard; also prof. Mass. Inst. of Tech., 1914-18; dean Harvard U. Engring. Sch., 1920—. Fellow A.A.A.S., Am. Acad. Arts and Sciences. Unitarian. Author: (with A. T. Safford) A Treatise on Hydraulics, 1911; Roads and Toll Roads in America, 1913; Highway Engineering Education, 1914-27. Home: Cambridge, Mass. Died Mar. 1, 1930.

HUGO, TREVANION WILLIAM, mechanical engr.; b. Cornwall, Eng., July 29, 1848; s. Nicholas and Mary R. (Marks) H.; came to America in early life; acad. edn., Kingston, Can. Mech. engr. since 1862; went to Duluth, Minn., 1881; pres. Common Council, 1890-94, mayor 2 terms, 1900-04; pres. Bd. of Edn., Chamber of Commerce. Republican. Mem. Am. Soc. Mech. Engrs., A.A.A.S. Clubs: Kitchi Gammı, Commercial (chmn. pub. affairs com. since 1905), Garfield. Address: 221 W. 6th Av., Duluth, Minnesota.

HUIDEKOPER, RUSH SHIPPEN, physician; b. Meadville, Pa., May 3, 1854; s. Edgar and Frances (Shippen) H.; ed. Philips Acad., Exeter; grad. med. dept. Univ. of Pa., 1877; veterinarian, Nat. Veterinary School, Republic of France, Alfort, France, 1882, and following yr. in laboratories of Virchow, Koch, Chauveau and Pasteur; m. Anne P. Morris, 1877. Physician Phila. Dispensary; out-patient physician Children's Hosp.; asst. surgeon hosp., Univ. of Pa.; coroner's physician of Phila.; U.S. commr. gen., Agrl. Expn., Hamburg, Germany, 1883; dean veterinary dept. Univ. of Pa., and prof. internal pathology and contagious diseases, zoötechnics and hygiene, prof. comparative anatomy and veterinary surgery, New York Coll. Veterinary Surgery; maj. and a.d.c. Nat. Guard, Pa., 1874-78; maj. and brig. surgeon Nat. Guard Pa., 1878-91; acting asst. q.m. gen. Nat. Guard Pa., 1888 (Johnstown flood); late lt. col. and surgeon-in-chief, Nat. Guard Pa.; lt. col. and chief surgeon U.S. vols., 1898; chief surgeon 1st army corps and chief surgeon Puerto Rico; Pennsylvania Republican. Editor: Journal of Comparative Medicine and Veterinary Archives, Phila., 1889—. Died 1901.

HUIZENGA, LEE SJOERDS, (hi'zeng-a), leprologist; b. Lioessens, Friesland, Netherlands, June 28, 1881; s. Sjoerd Liebes and Harmke (Van Der Veen) H.; brought to U.S., 1883; student Calvin Coll. and Sem., Grand Rapids, Mich., 1902-09; M.D., Homoe. Med. Coll., New York, 1913; student N.Y. Ophthalmic Coll., 1915-16; C.P.H., Yale, 1928, Dr.P.H., 1930; married Matilda Vandyke, September 22, 1909; children—Dr. Ann Harriet, Myrtle Leonora, Hannah Eunice, Faith Lois, Philip Lee S. (adopted son). Ordained ministry Christian Reformed Church, 1909; pastor Englewood, N.J., later missionary to Navajo indians, N.M., and med. missionary to China, by apptmt. of Foreign Missionary Bd., Christian Ref. Ch.; med. adviser to Mission to Lepers, N.Y. City; hon. sec. Shanghai Anti-Tuberculosis Assn.; has specialized in treatment of leprosy. Fellow Am. Geog. Soc., Am. Pub. Health Assn., A.A.A.S., Royal Geog. Soc. (London); mem. Internat. Leprosy Assn., Am. Soc. Parasitology, Am. Tropical Disease Assn., Far Eastern Tropical Disease Assn., China Med. Assn., Delta Omega. Author: The Navajo Indian, 1910; Unclean, Unclean, 1927; Leprosy in Legend and History (in the Chinese), 1931; Leprosy Control in Countries Bordering on the Pacific (Shanghai), 1934; Anhydrosis in Leprosy, 1934; History of Leprosy in China, 1935; John and Betty Stam—Martyrs, 1935; Legislation and Leprosy, 1937; Sensation Disturbances in Leprosy, 1937; Development of Leprosy Control Clinics, 1936; Nestorian Advance in China in the 8th Century (in Holland), 1936; Missionary Significance of the Lord's Prayer, 1938; Leonard Brink, 1939; Miss Mary Reed—Forty years a missionary to the Lepers, 1938; Hair in Leprosy 1939; Men of Note in Chinese History of Leprosy, 1939; Lu Tsu and his Relation to Other Medicine Gods in Chinese Medical Lore, 1940; Tuberculosis control, 1941. Contbr. to religious and scientific periodicals; also to Triomfen Van Het Kruis, 1913. Home: Grand Rapids, Mich. Died July 1945; buried in Bubbling Well Cemetery, Shanghai.

HULETT, EDWIN LEE, (hu'let), chemist; b. Heuvelton, St. Lawrence County, N.Y., Apr. 30, 1870; s. Edwin Henry and Emma Catherine (Austin) H.; grad. Potsdam (N.Y.) State Normal Sch., 1896; New York U., summer sessions, 1899-1901; A.B., St. Lawrence U., 1903, A.M., 1904, LL.D., 1925; m. Minne A. Dollar, Feb. 5, 1896. Prin. high sch., Brushton, N.Y., 1896-1902; instr. chemistry, 1903-04, asst. prof., 1904-05, prof. and head dept. since 1905, head of dept. chemistry, 1905-29, St. Lawrence U.; registrar College of Arts and Sciences same, 1912-15, dean since 1915. Analyst for St. Lawrence County, N.Y., 1905-15. Mem. Am. Chem. Soc., Alpha Tau Omega. Republican. Mason. Club: Citizens'. Home: Canton, N.Y. Died Aug. 30, 1942.

HULETT, GEORGE AUGUSTUS, chemist; b. Will County, Ill., July 15, 1867; s. Frank Amos and Louise (Holmes) H.; Oberlin Coll., 1888-90; A.B., Princeton, 1892; Ph.D., U. of Leipzig, 1898; m. Dency Minerva, d. Dr. J. W. Barker, Aug. 15, 1904; 1 son, George Barker. Asst. in chemistry, Princeton, 1892-96; instr. phys. chemistry, 1899-1904, asst. prof., 1904-05, U. of Mich.; asst. prof. phys. chemistry, 1905-09, prof., 1909—, now emeritus, Princeton. Mem. U.S. Assay Commn., 1906; chief chemist U.S. Bur. Mines, 1912-13. Mem. Am. Chem. Soc., Am. Electro-chem. Soc., Am. Phys. Soc., Am. Philos. Soc., Nat. Acad. Sciences; mem. Nat. Research Council (vice chmn. division of chemistry and chem. technology, 1927-28; chmn. of div. at Washington, D.C., 1928-29). Clubs: Cosmos (Washington, D.C.); Chemists' (New York). Mem. foreign service com. of Nat. Research Council, 1917; spent 4 months, mostly at battle fronts of French and English, to study orgn. and development of scientific activities in connection with warfare; mem. N.J. Commn., Workman's Compensation for Occupational Diseases, 1923-24. Asso. editor Jour. Physical Chemistry, 1923-27. Home: 8 Greenholm, Princeton, N.J. Died Sept. 6, 1955; buried Princeton (N.J.) Cemetery.

HULICK, PETER VAUGHN, radiologist; b. Nanticoke, Pa., 1909; s. Timothy and Julia (David) H.; M.D., Jefferson U., 1936; m. Helen Barno, Apr. 19, 1935; children—Patricia Helen, Timothy Peter, Peter Richard. Intern Harrisburg (Pa.) Polyclin. Hosp., 1936-37; resident in radiology New Rochelle (N.Y.) Hosp., 1940; resident in radiology and radiotherapy Bellevue Hosp., N.Y.C., 1944-45; former mem. staff Phillipsburg State Hosp., Mercy Hosp., Altoona, Pa., Indiana (Pa.) Hosp., Miners Hosp., Spangler, Pa., later St. Mary's Hosp., Sparta, Wis.; founder sch. radiol. tech. St. Francis Hosp., LaCrosse, Wis., also mem. staff. Preceptor in radiology U. Wis. Active Community Chest. Diplomate Am. Bd. Radiology. Fellow Am. Coll. Radiologists; mem. A.M.A., Radiology Soc. N.Am., Flying Physicians Assn., Isaac Walton League. Elk. Home: LaCrosse WI Died Apr. 7, 1971; buried Woodlawn Cemetery.

HULL, ALBERT WALLACE, physicist; b. Southington Conn., Apr. 19, 1880; s. Lewis Caleb and Frances Reynolds (Hinman) H.; A.B., Yale, 1905, Ph.D., 1909; Sc.D., 1947; Sc.D., Union U., 1930; Middlebury Coll., 1931; Eng.D., Worcester Poly Inst., 1944; m. Mary Shore Walker, June 14, 1911; children—Robert Wallace, Harriet. Instr. physics Worcester Poly. Inst., 1909-11, assn. prof., 1911-13; research physicist Gen. Electric Co., Schenectady, 1914-50, asst. dir. research lab., 1928-50, cons. 1950—. Recipient Medal of Honor, I.R.E., 1958. Pres. Am. Phys. Soc., 1942. Mem. Nat. Acad. Sci., Phi Beta Kappa, Sigma Xi. Fellow Am. Phys. Soc., Inst. Rad. Eng. Presbyn. Awarded Potts' medal Franklin Inst., 1923, for work on X-ray crystal analysis; Morris Liebman prize I.R.E., 1930, for work on vacuum tubes. Contbr. to sci. publs. Home: 1435 Lowell Rd., Schenectady. Died Jan. 1966.

HULL, CLARK LEONARD, prof. psychology; b. Akron, N.Y., May 24, 1884; s. Leander G. and Florence L. (Trask) H.; grad. Alma (Mich.) Academy, 1905; student Alma College 2 years; A.B., U. of Mich., 1913; Ph.D., U. of Wis., 1918; m. Bertha E. Iutzi, 1911; children—Ruth Trask, Richard Hazard. Prin. pub. sch., Sickels, Mich., 1909-11; acting prof. psychology, Eastern Ky. State Normal Sch., Richmond, Ky., 1913-14; with U. of Wis. as instr. psychology, 1916-20, asst. prof., 1920-22, asso. prof. and dir. lab., 1922-25, prof., 1925-29; prof. psychology, Inst. Human Relations (Yale), 1929-47, Sterling professor of psychology, since July 1947. Fellow A.A.A.S.; member Am. Psychol. Assn. (council 1931-33, president 1935-36), Nat. Acad.

Sciences, Am. Acad. Arts and Sciences, Sigma Xi. Club: University. Author: The Evolution of Concepts, 1920; Influence of Tobacco Smoking on Mental and Motor Efficiency, 1924; Aptitude Testing, 1928; Hypnosis and Suggestibility—An Experimental Approach, 1933; (with Hovland, Ross, Hall, Perkins and Fitch) Mathematico-Deductive Theory of Rote Learning, 1940; Principles of Behavior, 1943; Essentials of Behavior, 1951; A Behavior System, 1952. Contbr. to psychol. jours. Home: 888 Ridge Road, Hamden 14. Address: 333 Cedar St., New Haven. Died May 10, 1952; buried Willington, Conn.

HULL, GORDON FERRIE, physicist; b. Garnet, Haldimand County, Ont., Oct. 7, 1870; s. John and Jane (Moore) H.; A.B., U. Toronto, 1892, fellow in physics, 1892-95; fellow and asst. in physics U. Chgo., 1895-97, Ph.D., 1897; Cambridge U., 1905-06; studied at English and German univs., 1928-29; m. Wilhelmine Brandt, Sept. 5, 1911; 1 son, Gordon Ferrie. Taught in Hamilton Collegiate Inst., 1890-91; instr. physics U. Chgo., 1897-98, and summers 1898-99; prof. physics Colby Coll., Me., 1898-99; asst. prof. physics Dartmouth Coll., 1899-1903, prof. 1903-40, prof. meritus, 1940—, active service, 1941-44; prof. physics Columbia, summer sessions 1909-15. Maj. Ordnance Dept., U.S. Army, 1918-19, head math. and dynamics sect., tech. staff Washington, and physics expert, tech. staff Ordnance Dept., 1919-20, cons. physicist, tech. staff, 1920—. Fellow Am. Acad. Arts and Sciences, A.A.A.S.; mem. Am. Phys. Soc., etc. Author: Survey of Modern Physics, 1936; Elementary Modern Physics, 1948. Contbr. various sci. jours. on radiation. Home: 5 Parkway, Hanover, N.H. Died Oct. 7, 1956.

HULSE, GEORGE EGBERT, mech. and elec. engr.; b. Bellport, L.I., N.Y., Jan. 21, 1877; s. Egbert Hampton and Mary Roe (Homan) H.; M.E., Stevens Inst. Tech., 1902; m. Mary L. Preston, Sept. 6, 1905; children—George E., Mary (Mrs. William A. Nyland), Barbara Ruth. With Safety Car Heating & Lighting Co., New Haven, since 1902, as asst. engr., later engr. tests, then chief engr. in charge design and quality control of all products, including gas and electric lighting equipment, heating and air conditioning equipment (all for ry. cars) since 1907. Pres. Am. Soc. Refrigerating Engrs., 1940; mem. council Am. Soc. M.E., 1940-43; chmn. Conn. Tech. Council, 1934-36. Home: 1628 Boulevard, New Haven 11. Office: Box 904, New Haven 4. Died May 14, 1965.

HULST, NELSON POWELL, mining engr.; b. East Brooklyn, N.Y., Feb. 8, 1842; s. Garret and Nancy (Powell) H.; A.B., Yale, 1867, Ph.B., 1869, Ph.D., 1870; m. Florence Terry, May 12, 1875. Engr. and chemist, Milwaukee (Wis.) Iron Co., 1870-76; engr. and gen. supt. Menominee (Mich.) Mining Co., 1876-81; gen. supt. Pewabic Iron Co., 1886-96; gen. mgr. iron mining interests of Carnegie Steel Co. in Wis., Mich. and Minn., 1896-1901; v.p. various mining cos. of U.S. Steel Corp., 1901-04 (retired); chmn. bd. dirs. Milwaukee Gas Light Co. Trustee Milwaukee Assn. Commerce (chmn. pub. charities com); dir. Asso. Charities of Milwaukee, Martha Washington Home, Free Employment Bur., Boys' Busy Life Club. Republican. Conglist. Home: Milwaukee, Wis. Died Jan. 11, 1923.

HUMASON, M. L., astronomer; b. 1891; Ph.D. (hon.), Lund U., Sweden. Asst. astronomer Mt. Wilson Obs., 1919-48, asst. astronomer, sec. Mt. Wilson and Palomar obs., 1948-54, astronomer and sec., 1954-57. Mem. Am. Astron. Soc., Astron. Soc. Pacific; asso. mem. Royal Astron. Soc. Address: Mendocino CA Died June 18, 1972; interred Mountain View Mausoleum, Altadena CA

HUME, EDGAR ERSKINE, army officer; b. Frankfort, Ky., Dec. 26, 1889; s. Enoch Edgar (M.D.) and Mary (South) H.; B.A., Centre Coll., Ky., 1908, M.A., 1909; M.D., Johns Hopkins, 1913, Dr.P.H., 1924; D.M., U. Munich, 1914, U. Rome, 1915; 1st honor grad. Army Med. Sch., 1917; M.P.H., Harvard and Mass. Inst. Tech., 1921; D.T.M., Harvard, 1922; grad. U.S. Infantry Sch., 1928; hon. degrees from Centre Coll., U. Ky., Georgetown U., William and Mary, Hampden-Sydney, Washington and Lee, Transylvania U., Dickinson, Louisville, Washington and Jefferson, univs. of Naples, Rome, Florence, Bologna, Modena, Milan, Pisa, Siena, Chile, San Marcos (Peru), Paris, Madrid, and Leon (Nicaragua); grad. U.S. Army Medical Field Service Sch., 1936; m. Mary Swigert Hendrick, 1918 (deceased); 1 son, Edgar Erskine. Commd. 1st lt. Med. Corps, U.S. Army, 1916; promoted through grades to maj. gen., 1949. Staff Johns Hopkins Hosp., 1913-14; med. dir. Am. Relief Expdn. to Italy after earthquake, 1915; dir. dept. sociology, Disciplinary Barracks, Ft. Leavenworth, Kan., 1917; executive, Div. of Sanitation in Surgeon Gen.'s Office, 1917-18; comdg. officer U.S. Army Hospitals, with Italian Army; with Brit. Expeditionary Forces, 1918; at Meuse-Argonne. St. Mihiel and Vittorio-Veneto (wounded); chief med. officer (dir. typhus fever campaign) and Am. Red Cross Commr. for Serbia, 1919-20; in charge Army Lab. for N.E., Boston, 1920-22; editor Index Catalog Army Med. Library, Washington, 1922-26; med. insp. Infantry Sch., Ft. Benning, Ga., 1926-30; insp. Mass. and N.H. Nat. Guards, 1930-32; librarian Army Med. Library, 1932-36; dir. of adminstrn. Med. Field Service Sch., Carlisle, Pa., 1937-42; comdg. officer, Winter Gen. Hosp., Topeka, Kan., 1942-43; in African, Sicilian and Italian invasions (wounded); chief of public health, Sicily, 1943; chief Allied Mil. Govt., 5th Army, Italy, 1943-45; chief Mil. Govt. U.S. Zone, Austria, 1945-47; chief reorientation br. Dept. of Army, 1947-49; chief surgeon Far East Command, 1949-51, U.N., Korea, 1950-51; ret. for age, Dec. 31, 1951. Editor Mil. Surg., 1922; lectr. in med. history Georgetown Univ. and Univ. of Kan.; U.S. Army del. to Internat. Congress of Mil. Medicine, Paris, 1925, London, 1929, The Hague, 1931, Madrid, 1933, Brussels, 1935, Mexico, 1936, Bucharest, 1937, Washington, 1939, Basle, 1947, Stockholm, 1948 (nat. corr. for these congresses). Awarded D.S.M. (three), Silver Star (four), Legion of Merit, Purple Heart (four) Bronze Star (four), Soldier's Medal, Commendation ribbon (four), Air Medal (two), Typhus Medal (U.S.); also decorations from France, Gt. Britain, Belgium, China, Turkey, Philippines, Jugoslavia, Brazil, Russia, Bolivia, Sweden, Ecuador, Bulgaria, Tunis, Nicaragua, Denmark, Peru, Lithuania, Colombia, Norway, Haiti, Vatican, Esthonia, Cuba, Hungary, Chile, Netherlands, Finland, Venezuela, Latvia, Italy, Serbia, Panama, Poland, Spain, Greece, Czechoslovakia, Portugal, Montenegro, Luxembourg, Roumania, Korea; Bali Grand Cross of Sovereign Mil. Order of Malta; Sir Henry Wellcome prize, 1933; Oberlaender fellow to Germany, 1937; Gorgas Medal, 1948; hon. prof. U. Warsaw; hon. col. Royal Serbian Army; hon. cpl. French Army; hon. citizen of 40 Italian and Austrian cities. Mem. Soc. of Cincinnati (pres. gen.), Aztec Club (pres.), Kappa Alpha, Phi Beta Kappa, Sigma Xi, Alpha Omega Alpha, Delta Omega (founder; nat. pres. 1926), Omicron Delta Kappa, etc.; fellow Am. Acad. Arts and Sciences, Royal Soc. of Edinburgh, Royal Soc. Tropical Med. and Hygiene, Am. Coll. Surgeons, Am. Pub. Health Assn. Am. Coll. Physicians, Royal Italian Soc. Hygiene, Soc. Antiquaries of Scotland, academies of science of Spain, Mexico and Philadelphia, Assn. of Mil. Surgeons (pres.), academies of medicine of Rome, Washington (charter), Mex., Rio, Lima, Madrid, Swedish Soc. Anthropology, Royal Soc. of Naples, Accademia Pontiniana (Naples). Diplomate Am. bds. Neurology, Preventive Medicine and Internal Medicine. Clubs: Union (Tokyo, Japan); Army and Navy, Cosmos, Chevy Chase (Washington); Lambs, Metropolitan, Union, Explorers (N.Y.); Pithotomy (Baltimore); St. Botolph (Boston); Caccia (Rome); Cercle Militaire (Paris); Royal Soc. (London). Author of about 400 books and papers, including The Med. Book of Merit; Pettenkofer's Theory; Military Operations on the Italian Front (also Italian transl.); A Colonial Scottish Jacobite Family; Sanitation in War Planning; various papers on the Soc. of Cincinnati, Fighting Typhus Fever in Serbia; Preparation of Potable Water for Field, Heros von Borcke, Italy's Part in World War, Theodore O'Hara, Sandfly Fever, History and Work of Army Med. Library, Med. Service in Combined Army and Navy Operations, Med. Work of Knights Hospitallers, Ornithologists of Army Med. Corps, General Washington's Correspondence, Victories of Army Medicine, War and Medicine, Vesuvius Eruption of 1944, Medicine Goes to War, etc. Asso. editor Annals of Medical History. Contbr. to Ency. Brit., Ency. Am., Tice's Practice of Medicine, Dictionary of Am. Biography. Believed to be most decorated soldier in U.S. history. Home: Frankfort, Ky. Address: care Soc. of the Cincinnati, 2118 Massachusetts Av., Washington 8. Died Jan. 24, 1952; buried Arlington Nat. Cemetery.

HUME, H. HAROLD, dean of agr.; b. Russell, Ont., Can., June 13, 1875; s. John and Esther (McIntyre) H.; B.S. in Agr., Iowa State Coll., 1899; M.S.A., 1901; hon. D.Sc., Clemson Coll., S.C., 1937; m. Emily Georgia Norman, Dec. 24, 1900; children—Edward Grisdale, Harold Norman. Came to U.S., 1898, naturalized, 1912. Asst. botanist, Iowa State Coll., 1898-99; head dept. botany and horticulture Fla. Agrl. Coll. and Fla. Expt. Station, 1899-1904; head dept. horticulture, N.C. State Dept. Agr., N.C. State Coll. and Expt. Station, 1904-06; v.p. and sec., Glen Saint Mary Nurseries Co., Glen Saint Mary, Fla., 1906-29, chairman board since 1929; pres. E. O. Painter Fertilizer Co., Jacksonville, Fla., 1918-29; inspector Fla. State Plant Bd., 1929-31; asst. dir. research, Fla. Agr. Expt. Station, and asst. dean Coll. of Agr., U. of Fla., 1931-38; dean Coll. of Agr., University of Florida since 1938. Provost for Agriculture. Awarded Jackson Dawson Memorial medal by Mass. Hort. Society, 1935; Achievement medal, Florida Academy Science, 1936; Arthur Hoyt Scott Garden Award, 1944. President Fla. State Hort. Soc., 1910-22. Mem. Phi Kappa Phi, Alpha Zeta, Phi Gamma Delta, Phi Sigma, Sigma Xi. Presbyterian. Author: Citrus Fruits and Their Culture, 1904; The Pecan and Its Culture, 1906; Cultivation of Citrus Fruits, 1926; Gardening in the Lower South, 1929; Azaleas and Camellias, 1931; Camellias in America, 1946; Azaleas, Kinds and Culture, 1947. Contbr. numerous articles to agrl. jours.; author agrl. bulletins; speaker at hort. meetings. Address: College of Agriculture, Univ. of Florida, Gainesville FL

HUMES, HAROLD LOUIS, metall. engr.; b. Marquette, Mich., Jan. 31, 1900; s. Louis Samuel and Virginia Lee (Meyers) H.; B.Sc., McGill U., 1922, M.Sc. in Metall. Engring., 1923; student Mass. Inst. Tech.; m. Alexandra Elizabeth MacGonigle, Sept. 27, 1923; 1 son, Harold Louis. Engaged in research and prodn. copper smelting Phelps Dodge Corp., 1923-33; research and prodn. copper and lead smelting and refining U.S. Metals Refining Co., 1933-40; with Baldwin-Ehret-Hill, Inc., Trenton, N.J., 1940—, v.p. mfg., 1942-59, v.p. internat., 1959—, also dir. Chmn. program com. Bldg. Research Inst. of Nat. Acad. Scis.-NRC, 1956-58, v.p., 1957-59, pres., 1959-61. Mem. edn. com. N.J. Taxpayers Assn., 1958—. Served with U.S. Army, 1918. Recipient Applied Sci. medal British Assn. Advancement Sci., 1922. Mem. N.A.M. (research com. 1958—), A.A.A.S., Indsl. Relations Research Assn. Rotarian. Clubs: Canadian (N.Y.C.); Nassau (Princeton); Mass. Inst. Tech. (N.Y.C. and Phila.). Home: Rosedale Rd., Princeton, N.J. Office: 500 Breunig Av., Trenton 2, N.J. Deceased.

HUMPHREY, GEORGE COLVIN, animal husbandman; b. Palmyra, Mich., Feb. 13, 1875; s. George and Sarah Celestina (Colvin) H.; B.S., Mich. Agrl. Coll., E. Lansing, Mich., 1901; m. Eva Doty, June 25, 1902 (died Mar. 12, 1941); children—Carolyn Elizabeth (dec.), George Doty, Sarah Katharine; m. 2d, Madge Herbison. Successively instr., asst. prof., asso. prof. and professor animal husbandry, professor dairy husbandry, U. of Wis., 1901-42, head dept. of animal husbandry, 1903-39, professor emeritus since 1942; continues to give active attention to practical dairy farming. Presbyterian. Mem. Am. Soc. Animal Production, Am. Dairy Science Assn., Alpha Zeta (Babcock Chapter), Alpha Sigma. Devotes spl. attention to dairy cattle improvement and research problems. Home: 407 E. Court St., Ludington, Mich. Died June 18, 1947.

HUMPHREY, HARRY BAKER, plant pathologist; b. Granite Falls, Minn., Aug. 4, 1873; s. John Wadsworth and Adeline (Regester) H.; B.S., U. Minn., 1899; Ph.D., Stanford, 1907; m. Olive Agatha Mealey, June 10, 1901; children—Llewellyn Mealey, Robert Regester, Helen Wadsworth (Mrs. John M. McLernon), Isabel Estella (Mrs. G. H. Godfrey), Harry Bartholomew, John William David. Secondary sch. tchr. and prin., 1899-1903; instr. botany and grad. student, Stanford, 1903-07; instr. marine botany Hopkins Marine Sta., Pacific Grove, 1906-08 (summers); bot. editor Cree Pub. Co., 1907-08; prof. botany Wash. State Coll., 1908-13, vice dir. agrl. exptl. sta., 1912-13; instr. marine botany U. Wash., 1912 (summer); pathologist in charge cereal disease investigations Bur. Plant Industry, U.S. Dept. Agr., 1913-19, sr. pathologist, 1919-22, prin. pathologist, 1922-43; retired, 1943; editor-in-chief Phytopathology, 1929-43. Fellow A.A.A.S.; mem. Can. Geog. Soc., Am. Phytopathol. Soc., Washington Bot. Soc., Wash. Biol. Soc., Wash. Acad. Sciences, Minn. Hist. Soc., Sigma Xi. Club: Cosmos. Author of several bot. papers: joint author of handbook of pisé de terre construction; contbr. bulls. and reports on researches of cereal diseases. Home: Cabin John, Md. Address: Cosmos Club, Washington. Died 1955.

HUMPHREY, HENRY H., cons. engr.; b. Coolville, O., June 23, 1862; s. Shepherd and Emily (Cole) H.; A.B., Ohio U., Athens, O., 1884; A.M., 1886; M.S., Cornell U., 1886; m. Louisa D. Richardson, Sept. 12, 1887; children—William Richardson, Harry Edward, Helen, Martha Blair, Arthur Cole, Mary Louise. With U.S. Coast and Geod. Survey, summers, 1884, 85; in employ Westinghouse, Church, Kerr & Co., 1886-87; supt. Buffalo Electric Light & Power Co., 1888, Brush Electric Light Co., Buffalo, 1889-90; agt. Edison Gen. Electric Co., Omaha and St. Louis, 1891; St. Louis mgr. Gen. Electric Co., 1892; engr. and salesman St. Louis Electric Supply, Co., 1893, Laclede Power Co., St. Louis, 1894-95; mem. Bryan & Humphrey, cons. engrs., 1896-1900; cons. elec. and mech. engr., 1900-17; v.p., treas. Flad-Humphrey Engring. Co., 1917-20; gen. cons. elec. and mech. engr., 1920-35; v.p. and mgr. Evens & Howard Sewer Pipe Co., 1935-41. Designed electric part of Imperial Electric Light, Heat & Power Plant (St. Louis), complete plant of De Beers Explosives Works (Cape Town, S. Africa), mech. and elec. equipment Ry. Exchange Bldg. (St. Louis), etc. Fellow Am. Inst. E.E. (life); mem. St. Louis Inst. Cons. Engrs., Beta Theta Pi. Democrat. Methodist. Mason. Clubs: Engineers, Cornell, Circle. Retired July 1, 1942. Home: 5596 Bartmer Av., St. Louis, Mo. Died Dec. 21, 1947.

HUMPHREY, RICHARD LEWIS, engineer; b. Marblehead, Mass., Oct. 19, 1869; s. Richard Henry and Caroline (Curtis) H.; A.B., Central High Sch., Phila., 1888, A.M., 1893; C.E., U. of Pa., 1891; m. Anna Kay Thompson, Apr. 30, 1904. With Phila. Municipal Testing Lab., 1892-99; engr. and gen. mgr. Buckhorn Portland Cement Co., 1899-1903; consulting expert for Pa. R.R. Co. and for other large corps. Engr. in charge Collective Portland Cement Exhibit and Model Testing Lab. of Assn. Am. Portland Cement Mfrs. at St. Louis Expn., 1904; has served as cement and concrete expert U.S. Geol. Survey; was mem. War Industries Bd. Republican. Home: Westtown, Pa. Died Nov. 2, 1928.

HUMPHREYS, DAVID CARLISLE, civil engr.; b. Chatham Hill, Va., Oct. 14, 1855; s. Dr. William Finley and Betsey (McFarland) H.; C.E., Washington and Lee U., 1878; m. Mary L., d. E. M. Sloan, Sept. 4, 1888. U.S. asst. engr. on improvement of Mo. River, 1879-85; adj. prof. applied mathematics, 1885-89, prof. civ. engring., 1889—, dean Sch. of Applied Science, 1904—, Washington and Lee U. Resident hydrographer, U.S.

Geol. Survey, 1895-1908; sec. building commn. and supt. heating and power plant, Washington and Lee U.; mem. gov.'s Bd. of Mech. Survey of Va. Pres. bd. deacons Presbyn. Ch. Home: Lexington, Va. Died Jan. 10, 1921.

HUMPHREYS, RICHARD F(RANKLIN), physicist, college president; born in Greenville, Ohio, May 16, 1911; son of Robert Thomas and Tunia Daisy (Cunningham) H.; A.B., DePauw University, 1933; M.A., Syracuse U., 1936; Ph.D., Yale, 1939. Instr. physics Syracuse (N.Y.) U., 1939-40; instr. Yale, 1940-42, asst. prof., 1942-47, asso. prof., 1947-49, acting dir. Sloan Lab., 1942-45; cons. physicist New Haven Clock Co., 1943-45; physicist in sonar Bur. Ships, 1945; asst. chmn. physics Armour Research Found., Chicago, 1949-51, chmn., 1951-56, asst. dir., 1956-59, v.p. 1959-61; pres. The Cooper Union, 1961-68. Bd. dirs. Washington Sq. Assn., Josiah Macy Jr. Found., Asso. Hosp. Service N.Y.; trustee Mills Coll. Edn. Mem. Am. Phys. Soc., A.A.A.S., Sigma Xi. Author: First Principles of Atomic Physics (with E. R. Beringer), 1950; also sci. papers. Home: New York City NY Died Aug. 1968.

HUMPHREYS, WILLIAM JACKSON, (hum'-frez), physicist; b. Gap Mills, Monroe County, W.Va., Feb. 3, 1862; s. Andrew Jackson and Eliza Ann (Eads) H.; A.B., Washington and Lee U., 1886, C.E. (valedictorian), 1888, Sc.D. (hon.), 1942, University of Virginia, 1888-89, graduated School of Physics and School of Chemistry, 1889; Johns Hopkins Univ., 1894-97, fellow in physics, 1895-96, Ph.D., 1897; m. Margaret Gertrude Antrim, Jan. 11, 1908. Prof. physics and mathematics, Miller Sch., Va., 1889-93; prof. physics and chemistry, Washington Coll., Md., 1893-94; instr. physics, U. of Va., 1897-1905; prof. meteorol. physics, U.S. Weather Bur., July 1, 1905-Dec. 31, 1935, when retired (collaborator since 1936); prof. meteorol. physics, George Washington Univ., 1911-34, now prof. emeritus. Dir. Research Sta., Mt. Weather, Va., 1905-08; mem. U.S. Naval Observatory's eclipse expdn. to Sumatra, 1901; sec. Physics of the Electron, Internat. Congress of Arts and Sciences, St. Louis, 1904. Asso. editor Jour. of Franklin Inst.; editor of Monthly Weather Review, 1931-35; spl. editor, Webster's New Internat. Dictionary, 2d edition. Fellow Am. Phys. Soc., Optical Soc. America, Astron. Soc. America, Seismol. Soc. America, A.A.A.S. (sec. sect. physics 1912-16, mem. com. on policy 1912-28; v.p., chmn. sect. B, 1917; gen. sec. 1924-28); mem. Am. Math. Soc., Am. Meteorol. Soc. (v.p. 1920-23; pres. 1928-29), Am. Acad. Arts and Sciences, Am. Philos. Soc., Am. Geophys. Union (sec. 1921-22; chmn. seismol. sect. 1922-24; chmn. 1932-35), Franklin Inst., Philos. Soc. Washington (pres. 1919), Washington Acad. Sciences (pres. 1922), Phi Beta Kappa, Sigma Xi, Raven Soc. (U. of Va.); corr. mem. Meteorol. Soc. of Hungary, State Russian Geog. Soc. Club: Cosmos (v.p. 1935; pres. 1936). Author: Physics of the Air, 1920, 2d edit., 1929, 3d edit., 1940; Weather Proverbs and Paradoxes, 1923, 2d edit., 1934; Rain Making and Other Weather Vagaries, 1926; Fogs and Clouds, 1926; Snow Crystals (with W. A. Bentley), 1931; Weather Rambles, 1937; Ways of the Weather, 1942; Fogs Clouds and Aviation, 1943. Of Me (autobiography), 1947. Special editor (meteorology) Webster's New Internat. Dictionary, 2d edit. Contbr. Dictionary of Am. Biography and tech. jours. Address: Cosmos Club, Washington 5, D.C. Died Nov. 10, 1949.

HUNGERFORD, CHARLES WILLIAM, plant pathologist; b. Fillmore County, Minn., Feb. 26, 1885; s. Judson Belee and Alice Helen (Moore) H.; B.S., Upper Ia. U., 1910; M.S., U. of Wis., 1915, Ph.D., 1925; m. Ruth Edna Patridge, June 11, 1913; children—Kenneth, Eugene, Doris Olive, Charles Roger. Prin. high. sch., Houston, Minn., 1910-11; supt. schs. same, 1911-13; asst. in botany, U. of Wis., 1913-14, asst. plant pathologist, 1914; scientific asst., cereal investigations, U.S. Dept. Agr., 1915-17, asst. pathologist, 1917-19; prof. plant pathology, U. of Ida., from 1919, asst. dean of Coll. Agr., 1927-35; vice-dir. Agrl. Expt. Station, 1927-47; also dean Graduate School 1931-51. Recipient award for work in hybridization of beans Bean Improvement Coop. Fellow A.A.A.S.; mem. Am. Phytopathol. Soc., Sigma Xi, Alpha Zeta. Republican. Methodist. Kiwanian. Contbr. articles on plant disease control. Home: Moscow ID Died Nov. 6, 1971; buried Moscow Cemetery, Moscow ID

HUNT, ALFRED EPHRAIM, metallurgist; b. East Douglas, Mass., Mar. 31, 1855; s. Leander and Mary (Hanchett) H.; grad. Mass. Inst. Tech., 1876; m. Maria McQuesten, Oct. 29, 1878, 1 son. Worked for Bay State Steel Co., 1876, helped build 2d open hearth furnace in U.S., South Boston; reported on iron fields of Northern Mich. and Wis., 1876, important in devel. of these regions; supt. steel dept. Nashua Iron & Steel Co. (N.H.), 1877-81; metall. chemist, supr. Park Bros. & Co., Pitts., 1881-83; established chem. and metall. lab. with George Clapp, 1883; organized Pitts. Reduction Co., company bought control patents for Hall process of reduction of aluminum; commanded Battery B of Pa. in Spanish-Am. War, contracted malaria in P.R. Died Phila., Apr. 26, 1899.

HUNT, ANDREW MURRAY, consulting engr.; b. Sioux City, Ia., Aug. 12, 1859; s. Andrew Murray and Marion (Kent) H.; grad. U.S. Naval Acad., 1879; unmarried. Engr. officer on several vessels of U.S. Navy; was instr. mech. engring., Orchard Lake Mil. Acad., Mich., 1 yr.; mem. Naval Steel Inspn. Bd., having charge of chem. work of inspn. and started the chem. lab. at Mare Island Navy Yard; chief engr. of U.S. Fish Commn. steamer Albatross, 1893, and detailed as chief of the Dept. Mech. Arts, Mid-winter Fair, San Francisco; resigned from Navy, July 1894, and engaged as consulting engr. in San Francisco. Built 4 steamers in Alaska, 1897-98, for service on Yukon River; resumed practice, San Francisco, 1899; was consulting engr. for Claus Spreckels in erection of plant of Independent Elec. Light and Power Co., of which became gen. mgr., also gen. mgr. Independent Gas and Power Co.; consulting engr. many important constructions on Pacific Coast; removed to New York, 1915; pres. Peyton Hunt Co., Inc., consulting engrs., N.Y. City, 1915—. Mem. Naval Consulting Bd., Sept. 4, 1915—; mem. ship protection gen. com. of U.S. Shipping Bd., 1917. Died Dec. 8, 1930.

HUNT, CHARLES WALLACE, engineer; b. Candor, N.Y., Oct. 13, 1841; s. William Walter and Elizabeth Bush (Sackett) H.; m. Frances Martha Bush, 1868; 2d, Katharine Humphrey, 1889; spl. agt. War Dept., 1864, to care for freedmen coming into the Union lines. V.p. Richmond County Savings Bank; engaged in engring. and mfg. Pres. Am. Soc. Mech. Engrs., 1898, United Engring Soc., 1909; mem. N.Y. Chamber of Commerce. Home: Stapleton, N.Y. Died 1911.

HUNT, CHARLES WARREN, civil engr.; b. New York, May 19, 1858; s. Charles Havens and Anna de Peyster (Livingston) H.; B.S. and C.E., 1876, LL.D., 1909, New York U.; m. Mary Osgood, d. George S. Riggs, of Baltimore, Sept. 8, 1883. Asst. sec., 1892-95, sec., 1895-1920 (emeritus), Am. Soc. Civil Engineers. Died July 23, 1932.

HUNT, FREDERICK VINTON, prof. applied physics, Harvard; born Barnesville, Ohio, February 15, 1905; s. Fred and Ella (Shipley) H.; B.A., Ohio State U., 1924, B.E.E., 1925, Master of Arts Harvard University, 1928, Ph.D., 1934, S.D. (hon.), 1945; married Katharine Buckingham, November 25, 1932; children—Thomas Kintzing. Graduate assistant physics, Ohio State University, 1924-25; assistant in physics, Harvard, 1927, 1928-29, instr., 1929-34, instr. physics and communication engring., 1934-37; tutor in div. physical sciences, 1931-38, asst. prof. physics and communication engring., 1937-40, asso. prof. 1940-46; Gordon McKay prof. applied physics, 1946-70, also Rumford prof. physics, 1953-70; director Underwater Sound Lab., 1942-46; chmn. Dept. Engring. Sci. and Applied Physics, 1946-49. Awarded Presdl. Medal Merit, 1947; Emile Berliner Award, 1954, Publs. award, 1956, John H. Potts medal, 1965 (all Audio Engring. Soc.); Pioneers Underwater Acoustics medal, 1965, Gold medal, 1969 (all Acoustical Society of America. Fellow of American Academy of Arts and Scis., Acoustical Society Am. (exec. council, 1938-41, editorial bd. 1940-45, pres. 1951-52), American Physical Society, Institute of Radio Engineers; Phi Beta Kappa, Tau Beta Pi, Sigma Xi, Eta Kappa Nu, Sigma Nu. Club: Cosmos (Washington). Author: Electroacoustics; also research papers on acoustics and applied electronics. Home: LaJolla CA Died Apr. 20, 1972.

HUNT, HARRY HAMPTON, elec. engr.; b. Melrose, Mass., Nov. 18, 1868; s. Harry and May Imogen (Covel) H.; S.B. in E.E., Mass. Inst. Tech., 1889; m. Louisa Cleaves Sargent, June 8, 1897; 1 dau., Helen. With Stone & Webster, Mar. 26, 1900—, admitted as member firm Jan. 1, 1920; v.p., May 26, 1920; chairman bd. Stone & Webster Service Corp.; dir. Stone & Webster Engring. Co., Stone & Webster Realty Corp., Tarrant County Traction Co., etc. Mem. Boston Chamber Commerce. Home: Melrose, Mass. Died Nov. 30, 1937.

HUNT, REID, pharmacologist; b. Martinsville, O., Apr. 20, 1870; s. Milton L. and Sarah E. (Wright) H.; A.B., Johns Hopkins, 1891, Ph.D., 1896; student U. of Bonn, Germany; M.D., U. of Md., 1896, Sc.D., 1925; student Ehrlich's Institut, Frankfort, 1902-04; m. Mary Lillie, d. Hannis Taylor, Dec. 12, 1908. Tutor in physiology, Coll. Phys. and Surg. (Columbia), 1896-98; asso. and asso. prof. pharmacology, Johns Hopkins, 1898-1903; chief of div. and prof. pharmacology, U.S. Pub. Health Service, 1904-13; prof. pharmacology, Med. Dept. Harvard, 1913-36; visiting prof. Peking-Union Med. Coll., 1923. Cons. pharmacologist Mass. State Dept. Pub. Health; mem. advisory bd. Hygienic Lab., U.S. Pub. Health Service. Mem. Permanent Standards Com. of League of Nations. Fellow Am. Acad. Arts and Sciences; mem. Nat. Acad. Sciences, Assn. Am. Physicians, Am. Physiol. Soc., Am. Soc. Pharmacology and Exptl. Therapeutics, A.M.A. (ex-chmn. council on pharmacy and chemistry), Am. Chem. Soc. (chmn. Northeastern sect. 2 yrs.), Leopold-Carol Akademie, Deutsch Pharmacologie Gesellschaft, Phi Beta Kappa, Alpha Omega Alpha. Pres. U.S. Pharmacopeia, 1920-30. Contbr. Am. and European med. jours. and govt. publs. Joint-Author: Non-Alkaloidal Organic Poisons, in Vol. II of Peterson, Haines and Webster's Text-Book of Legal Medicine and Toxicology, 1923; Studies in Experimental Alcoholism, 1907; Studies on the Thyroid (with A. Seidell), 1909; Effects of Various Diets Upon Resistance to Poisons, 1910; Effects of Derivatives of Choline and Analogous Compounds, 1911. Contbr. to Heffter's Handbuch der Exper. Pharmakologie, 1923. Home: 382 Commonwealth Av., Boston. Died Mar. 10, 1948.

HUNT, ROBERT WOOLSTON, metall. engineer; b. Fallsington, Pa., Dec. 9, 1838; s. Robert A. (M.D.) and Martha L. (Woolston) H.; ed. in Covington, Ky.; studied analyt. chemistry, Phila., 1859-60; (Dr. Engring., Rensselaer Poly. Inst., 1916); m. Eleanor Clark, Dec. 5, 1866. Worked in rolling mill at Pottsville, Pa.; chemist Cambria Iron Co., 1860-61; supt. steel works, Wyandotte, Mich., 1865-66, Cambria Iron Co., 1866-73, John A. Griswold & Co., Troy, N.Y., 1873-75, Troy Steel & Iron Co., 1875-88; head of Robert W. Hunt & Co., cons. engrs., iron insps., etc., 1888—. Served pvt. and sergt. Pa. Vols. and capt. in command Camp Curtin, Harrisburg, Pa., 1861-65. Trustee Rensselaer Poly. Institute. Awarded John Fritz Medal, 1912. Republican. Protestant. Home: Chicago, Ill. Died July 11, 1923.

HUNT, THOMAS STERRY, chemist, geologist; b. Norwich, Conn., Sept. 5, 1826; s. Peleg and Jane (Sterry) H.; attended Yale; m. 1877. Chemist, mineralogist Geol. Survey of Can., 1847-72; taught chemistry Laval U., Que., Can., McGill U., Montreal, Can. 1862-68; prof. geology Mass. Inst. Tech., 1872-78. Author: Chemical and Geological Essays, 1875, 78; A New Basis for Chemistry; A Chemical Philosophy, 1887; Systematic Mineralogy, 1891. Died Feb. 12, 1892.

HUNT, WESTLEY MARSHALL, otolaryngologist; b. Auburn, Me., Sept. 1, 1888; s. Edward Everett and Ellen Matilda (Anderson) H.; B.S., Dartmouth, 1910, M.D., 1913; grad. St. Luke's Hosp. and S.I. Hosp., N.Y.C.; post-grad. study, Vienna; m. Emily H. Callaway, Feb. 27, 1920. Instr. N.Y.U. and Bellevue Med. Coll., 1920-22, lectr., 1922-25, clin. prof. otology, 1925-30; dir. dept. otolaryngology Fifth Av. Hosp., 1924-35; attending otolaryngologist and bronchopist St. Luke's Hosp., N.Y.C.; surgeon, director Manhattan Eye, Ear, and Throat Hosp.; cons. otolaryngologist Woman's Hosp., Huntington Hosp., S.I. Hosp., Nat. Hosp. for Speech Disorders, Ruptured and Crippled Hosp. Dir. Am. Bd. of Otolaryngology. Served as lt. (s.g.) USNRF, and maj. U.S. M.C., comdg. head surgery operating team, France, 1917-18. Past pres. New York League for the Hard of Hearing. Fellow A.C.S., N.Y. Acad. Medicine (past chmn. otolaryngology sect.); mem. A.M.A., Am. Laryngol. Assn., Am. Otol. Soc., Am. Broncho-Esophogological Assn. Am. Laryngol., Rhinol. and Otol. Soc. (v.p. eastern sect.), Clin. Research Soc. (pres. 1924), New York Bronchoscopic Club (pres. 1932), N.Y. Laryngol. Soc. (pres. 1942), Am. Acad. Ophthalmology and Oto-Laryngology, N.Y. Oto-Laryngol. Soc. (pres.), Soc. Colonial Ward (lt. governor), S.R., S.A.R., Mil. Order Foreign Wars, New York Soc. Mil. and Naval Officers World War, Assn. Mil. Surgeons of U.S., Order Founders and Patriots (past gov.), Soc. Mayflower Descendants of N.Y. (past gov.), Am. Legion (past comdr. Fiji Post), Alpha Kappa Kappa, Phi Gamma Delta. Republican. Conglist. Mason. Clubs: Quill (pres. 1942), Sleepy Hollow, Megantic Fish and Game. Home: Northport, L.I. Office: 907 Fifth Av., N.Y.C. 21. Died June 28, 1950; buried Cathedral St., John Divine, N.Y.C.

HUNT, WILLIAM CHAMBERLIN, statistician; b. Charlestown, Mass., Dec. 20, 1856; s. Samuel C. and Sarah K. H.; grad. Charlestown High Sch., 1875. With Mass. State Census of 1875, 1875-77; with Boston Herald and Oliver Ditson Co., 1877-83; 2d clerk Mass. Bur. Statistics of Labor and Mass. Census of 1885, 1883-89; expert spl. agt. in charge of population, 11th U.S. Census, 1889-95; statis. expert, U.S. Dept. of Labor, 1895-99; chief statistician for population, U.S. Census, since 1899. Mem. Am. Econ. Assn., Am. Statis. Assn., Am. Assn. Labor Legislation. Address: Census Bureau, Washington, D.C.

HUNT, WILLIAM PRESCOTT, ordnance mfr.; b. Bath, N.H., Jan. 14, 1827; s. Caleb and Rebecca (Pool) H.; ed. Haverhill (N.H.) Acad.; m. Katherine Muller, of New York, 1856 (now deceased); 2d, Helen Summer Cummings, of New Bedford, Mass., 1871. Clerk S. Boston Iron Co., 1847, treas., 1863, pres., 1876-82 (the co. made the 11-inch Dahlgren gun which crippled the Merrimac in Hampton Roads, and same class of gun which sunk the Alabama); pres. S. Boston Iron Works 1883-90, continuing to furnish ordnance to U.S. Govt. and made several experimental cannons of over 50 tons finished weight; also designed, built and put on U.S. Monitor Terror, a pneumatic system for turning the turrets, taking up the recoil of the guns, hoisting the ammunition, and steering the ship; pres. Boston Machine Co., 1864-84, Forbes Lith. Mfg. Co., 1875-1909, Atlas Nat. Bank, 1878-82, Hunt-Spiller Mfg. Co., 1890-1909; and dir. and officer in many other cos. Home: 140 Salvin Hill Av. Office: 383 Dorchester Av., Boston.

HUNTER, GEORGE WILLIAM, biologist, author; b. Mamaroneck, N.Y., Apr. 7, 1873; s. George William and Emma Louise (Cartwright) H.; A.B., Williams, 1895, A.M., 1896; fellow in zoölogy, U. of Chicago,

1896-99; post-grad. work and lecturer in methods of teaching nature study and biology, N.Y. Univ., 1907-14, Ph.D., 1918; m. Emily Isabel Jobbins, June 19, 1899; children—George William III, Cartwright, Francis Robert. Teacher of biology at Hyde Park High Sch., Chicago, 1898-99; teacher biology at DeWitt Clinton High Sch., New York City, 1899-1906, head dept. biology, 1906-19; prof. biology, Carleton Coll., 1919-20; prof. biology, Knox Coll., 1920-26; adjunct prof. biology, Pomona Colls., 1926-29; lecturer in methods in science, Claremont Coll., since 1930. Asst. Marine Biol. Lab., Woods Hole, Mass., summers, 1900-10. Ednl. dir., Washington dist., War Work Council Y.M.C.A., 1918-19. Chairman War Finance Com., Claremont, since 1942. Fellow A.A.A.S.; mem. N.E.A., American Zoölogical Society, Calif. Assn. Secondary Edn., Nat. Assn. for Research in Science Teaching, National Society for Study of Edn., Phi Delta Kappa, Theta Delta Chi. Episcopalian. Clubs: Kiwanis, University. Author: Elements of Biology, 1907; Essentials of Biology, 1911, 23; A Civic Biology, 1914; Laboratory Problems in Civic Biology, 1916; History of Y.M.C.A. War Work in the Washington District, 1919; Laboratory Manual in Biology, 1923; New Civic Biology, 1926; Teachers Manual, 1927; New Laboratory Problems in Civic Biology, 1927; Problems in Biology, (4th edition, revised, 1940); Pupil's Workbook for Problems in Biology, 1932; Teacher's Manual for Problems in Biology, 1932; The Teaching of Science at the Junior and Senior High School Levels, 1934; Life Science, A Social Biology, 1941. Co-Author: Laboratory Manual of Biology, 1903; Civic Science in the Home, 1921; Civic Science in the Community, 1922; Civic Science in Home and Community, 1923; Civic Science Manual, 1924; Problems in General Science, (4th edit. rev., 1944); Teacher's Manual and Key for Problems in General Science, 1931; Readings in Science, 1931; Workbook in General Science, 1932; A Testing Program in General Science, 1933; A Testing Program in Biology, 1933; The March of Science Series (My Own Science Problems; Science in Our Social Life; Science in Our World of Progress), 1935; Biology, The Story of Living Things, 1937; Work book and testing program for life science, 1941-42; Doorways to Science, 1947; Work book, Doorways to Science, 1947. Contbr. numerous educational and scientific articles. Address: 466 W. 10th St., Claremont, Calif. Died Feb. 4, 1948.

HUNTER, JOHN, mechanical engr.; b. Girvan, Scotland, Aug. 11, 1866; John and Elizabeth (Templeton) H.; ed. Ayr Acad., and Hawthorne Acad., London; hon. M.E., Stevens Inst. Tech., Hoboken, 1933; m. Minnie L. Templeton, of Detroit, Mich., Jan. 18, 1899. Apprentice in mech. engring., Ayr, 1881-86; sea-going engr., 1886-95; sr. 1st asst. engr. steamship St. Louis, Am. Line, New York, 1895-98; chief engr. steamship St. Paul, 1898-1905; chief engr. Union Electric Light & Power Co., St. Louis, 1905-17; chief engr. Heine Boiler Co., 1921-24; cons. engr., specializing in combustion and smoke abatement; now retired. Chief engr., rank of lt. on steamship St. Paul, under Capt. Sigsbee, during Spanish-Am. War, May-Sept. 1898; awarded 3 medals. Apptd. rep. of Emergency Fleet Corp., Nov. 10, 1917, in charge building 150 5,000-ton vessels, Newark Bay, N.J.; naval constr., Standard Shipbuilding Corp., Shooters Island, N.Y., Jan. 1918—. Mem. jury of awards, San Francisco Expn., 1915. Mem. Am. Soc. M.E. (v.p.), Uniform Boiler Law Soc. Republican. Presbyn. Mason (32 deg., Shriner). Clubs: Circle, Engineers (ex-pres.), Caledonian Soc. (ex-pres.); University (Winter Park, Fla.). Home: 2346 Fairbanks Av., Winter Park, Fla.

HUNTER, OSCAR BENWOOD, pathologist, educator; b. Cherrydale, Va., Jan. 31, 1888; s. Montgomery and Lillian Theresa (Edmonston) H.; M.D., George Washington U., 1912, A.B., 1916, A.M., 1917; m. Sidney Sophia Pearson, Dec. 26, 1914; children—Oscar Benwood, Frances Elizabeth, Mary Ellen, Margaret Pearson. Instr. in anatomy, George Washington U., 1912, prof. histology and embryology, 1913-16, prof. bacteriology and pathology, 1916-32, acting dean Dental Sch., 1918, asst. dean Med. Sch., 1918-32; pathologist George Washington U. Hosp. and Dispensary, 1916-32; pathologist The Doctors' Hosp., Sibley Memorial Hosp.; cons. pathol., Montgomery County Gen. Hosp.; prof. sanitary science, Central Training Sch. for Nurses, 1932-40; lecturer, Kober Foundation, Georgetown U., 1926; professorial lecturer Georgetown U., 1935-45; Am. U.; sec. Wash. Med. Bldg. Corp., Columbia Med. Bldg. Corp., Columbia Operating Corp., Doctors' Hosp., Maj. Med. Reserve Corps. Asso. Internat. Coll. Surgeons; fellow Am. Coll. Physicians, Coll. of Am. Pathologists; mem. Am. Hosp. Assn., Wash. Heart Assn., Wash. Acad. Scis., Wash. Acad. Med., Internat. Assn. Med. Museums, D.C. Rheumatism Soc., Diabetes Assn. of D.C., Inc., American Heart Association, A.M.A., American Association Anatomists, American Society Bacteriologists, American Society Pathologists and Bacteriologists, Am. Therapeutic Soc. (pres. 1938-39; sec. 1934-38 and since 1939), A.A.A.S., Southern Medical Association (vice pres., 1946-47, president-1948-49), Tri-State Medical Society, also Galen-Hippocrates Society, Medical Society D.C. (pres. 1928), Washington Medical Surg. Soc., George Washington U. Med. Soc. (pres. 1918-19, re-elected 1938-39; sec. since 1941), Am. Soc. of Clinic Pathologists, Am. Assn. for Study of Neoplastic Diseases, Miss. Valley Med. Soc. (hon.), Am. Assn. of University Profs., Assn. of Military Surgeons of U.S., Reserve Officers Assn. of U.S., Washington Soc. of Pathologists (pres. 1937-38), Am. Pub. Health Assn., Nat. Safety Council, Alpha Kappa Kappa; pres. Gen Alumni Assn. of George Washington U., 1928-29 and 1929-30. Republican. Roman Catholic. Clubs: University, Corinthian Yacht, Kiwanis of Washington (pres. 1941), Cosmos, Internat. Medical. Contbr. Washington Med. Annals, Am. Jour. Clin. Pathology, Jour. A.M.A., Jour. Lab. and Clin. Medicine, etc. Home: 3815 Bradley Lane, Chevy Chase, Md. Office: 915 19th St. N.W., Washington 6. Died Dec. 19, 1951.

HUNTER, RUDOLPH MELVILLE, consulting engr.; b. N.Y. City, June 20, 1856; s. Robert (M.D.) and Sarah (Barton) H.; M.E., Polytechnic Coll. State of Pa., 1878; m. Emilie M. Phillips, Aug. 1879. Began in Cincinnati, O., making distillery plans for U.S. Govt., 1871; gen. engineering and patents, Ironton, Ohio, blast furnaces and steel works, 1874-75, Chicago, 1875-76, Phila., 1877; developed spl. process for mfg. gas at Coney Island, N.Y., 1878; organizer Atlantic & Pacific Electric Mfg. Co., 1879; developed and patented transformer system of electric power and lighting, 1879-86; developed complete electric railway systems, 1881-89; placed before Brit. Parliament elec. ry. plan for proposed tunnel, Dover to Calais, May 1883; developed submarine vessel, 1879-81, and pub. pamphlet on torpedo boats, 1882; sold telephone patents to Am. Bell Telephone Co., 1882; tests, smokeless powder for French Govt., 1883-84; demonstrated submarine inventions before members of Congress, 1885; sold electric transformer system inventions to Westinghouse Electric Co., 1886; organized Hunter Electric Co., 1886-87; organized Elec. Car Co. of America, 1887; sold many patents to Thomson-Houston Electric Co. and retained as elec. engr. and patent counsel by said co., 1889, and continued by General Electric Co. for 22 yrs; later licenses, covering about 300 patents, granted to General Electric Co. and to Westinghouse Elec. & Mfg. Co.; designed and built first moving picture projector in the world, 1894; organized Gen. Electric Automobile Co., 1898, Tractor Truck Automobile Co., 1899, etc.; inventor of many devices now in use by various corps.; pres. Electric Car Co. of America, U.S. Assay & Bullion Co., The Mirabile Corp., Hunter Pressed Steel Co.; dir. Herr Automatic Press Co., etc. Expert of Victor Talking Machine Co. with spl. reference to acoustics. Original research, 1902—, include breaking down and reconstruction of atomic matter; "growth" of cells, and discovering of nature's processes in multiplying atoms; causes for different members of the elements in various stars and sun from those of the earth; physical properties of atomic structure; has discovered and commercialized transmutation of the elements, duplicating nature's processes in creating the precious metals; cause of gravitation; etc. Republican. Episcopalian. Home: Philadelphia, Pa. Died Mar. 20, 1935.

HUNTER, SAMUEL JOHN, entomologist; b. Ireland, Nov. 11, 1866; s. Rev. James and Rebecca (Davison) H.; removed with parents to Iowa in infancy; A.B., A.M., U. of Kan., 1893; grad. student, Cornell U., 1896; investigator Marine Biol. Lab., 1901-02; m. Lida W. Campbell, June 16, 1897 (died June 1929); 1 dau., Geneva (Mrs. Edwin J. Simmons). Prin. Columbus (Kan.) High Sch., 1890-91, Atchison County High Sch., 1893-96; absent on leave, 1894, to visit zoöl. laboratories of Europe; asst. prof. entomology, 1896-99, asso. prof., 1899, asso. prof. comparative zoölogy and entomology, 1901, head dept. entomology, 1902, prof., 1906, curator entomol. collections, 1909, U. of Kan. State entomologist; mem. Kan. State Entomol. Commn., 1907, 24; collaborator Federal Bur. Entomology; mem. Nat. Com. on Unification of State and Federal Hort. Inspection Legislation; mem. City Planning Com.; mem. Nat. Com. on Real Estate Taxation. Mem. Kan. Council for Defense, World War. Pres. Eastern Kan. Teachers' Assn., 1894-95; fellow A.A.A.S.; mem. Kan. Acad. Science, Phi Beta Kappa, Sigma Xi. Author: Elementary Studies in Insect Life, 1902; An Account of Kansas Coccidae and Their Hosts, 1903; Morphology of Artificial Parthenogenesis, 1904; Insect Parthenogenesis, 1906; Problems in Parthenogenetic Parasites, Pathogenic Parasites, 1911; etc. Chmn. Science Bull. editorial com., 1916-24. Owner (50 acres) and developer West Hills Dist. and Country Club Terrace, Lawrence. Republican. Conglist. Pres. Sportsman's Club, 1933. Home: 1145 W. Campus Rd., Lawrence, Kan. Died July 10, 1946.

HUNTER, WALTER DAVID, entomologist; b. Lincoln, Neb., Dec. 14, 1875; s. Joseph H. and Mary Abbey (Crooker) H.; A.B., U. of Neb., 1895, A.M., 1897; (LL.D., Tulane U. of La., 1916); m. Mary P., d. of Dr. E. H. Smith, of Victoria, Tex., Mar. 1906. Asst. entomologist, U. of Neb., 1895-1900, Ia. Agrl. Expt. Sta., 1901; asst. entomologist in charge of boll weevil investigation, Bur. of Entomology, U.S. Dept. Agr., 1902-05; in charge southern field crop insect investigations and mem. Federal Hort. Bd., in charge field work against pink boll worm of cotton, 1908. Died Oct. 13, 1925.

HUNTER, WARREN CLAIR, physician; b. Dustin, Neb., Feb. 14, 1895; s. Joseph E. and Louisa J. Hunter; M.D., U. Ore., 1924; M.A. in Pathology, U. Mich., 1927; m. Martha Dorothy Schreiner, July 3, 1925;children—Ruth Mary (Mrs. Johannes Horst Max Meyer), Warren Clair. Intern, Multnomah Hosp., Portland, Ore., 1924-25; fellow in med. pathology NRC, 1926-27; dir. pathology lab. Portland Adventist Hosp., 1960-70; instr., asst. prof., asso. prof., prof. pathology U. Ore. Med. Sch., Portland, 1925-60, clin. prof., 1960-65, emeritus prof., 1965-70. Coroner's physician Multnomah County, 1924-60; acting dir. Ore. Police Crime Lab.; area counselor VA, 1945-66. Mem. regional com. Boy Scouts Am., 1941-45; mem. exec. com. Ore. div. Am. Cancer Soc., 1945, nat. bd. dirs., 1947-55, nat. v.p., 1952. Trustee, Lewis and Clark Coll., 1937-62, life trustee, 1962-70. Served with USN, 1917-18. Recipient Distinguished Alumnus award Lewis and Clark Coll., 1954, award for outstanding contbn. to control cancer Am. Cancer Soc., 1955. Diplomate Am. Bd. Pathology. Mem. A.M.A., Coll. Am. Pathologists, Am. Assn. Pathologists and Bacteriologists, Pacific N.W. Soc. Pathologists (pres. 1938-39, 62), Am. Soc. Clin. Pathology, Ore. Pathologists Assn., Ore., Multnomah County med. socs., Portland Acad. Medicine, Alpha Omega Alpha, Nu Sigma Nu. Republican. Presbyn. Contbr. numerous articles to med. jours. Research on hypothermia, origins of embolism, coronary arterial disease. Home: Portland OR Died July 6, 1970; buried Mausoleum, Riverview Cemetery, Portland OR

HUNTINGTON, EDWARD VERMILYE, mathematician; b. Clinton, Oneida County, N.Y., Apr. 26, 1874; s. Chester and Katharine Hazard (Smith) H.; A.B., Harvard, 1895, A.M., 1897; Ph.D., U. of Strassburg, Germany, 1901; hon. Sc.D., U. of San Marcos, Lima, Peru, 1925; m. Susie Edwards Van Volkenburgh, July 6, 1909. Instr. mathematics, Harvard, 1895-97, Williams Coll., 1897-99; in Europe, 1899-1901; instr. mathematics, 1901-05, asst. prof., 1905-15, asso. prof., 1915-19, prof. mechanics, 1919-41, emeritus since 1941, Harvard U. Western Exchange prof. from Harvard to Beloit, Carleton, and Knox Colls., 1925. Consultant, Nat. Defense Research Com. since 1942. Major, Gen. Staff, on statis. duty at Washington, 1918-19. Editor Annals of Mathematics, 1902-11. Fellow Am. Acad. Arts and Sciences (chmn. com. of pub., 1914-19), A.A.A.S. (vice pres. and chmn. section A, 1926), Am. Inst. of Math. Statistics; mem. Am. Philos. Soc., Am. Math. Soc. (v.p. 1924; rep. on National Research Council, 1923-26), Math. Assn. America (pres. 1918), Am. Statistical Assn., Am. Standards Assn. (mem. sectional com.; chmn. sub-committee on math. symbols, 1928), Assn. for Symbolic Logic, American Academy Political Science. Honorary member of Phi Beta Kappa. Author: Four-Place Tables of Logarithms and Trigonometric Functions, arranged for decimal division of the degree, 1907; Monograph IV on "The Fundamental Propositions of Algebra," in work entitled "Mathematical Monographs" (edited by J. W. A. Young), 1911; The Continuum and Other Types of Serial Order, 1917; Handbook of Mathematics for Engineers, 1918; chapters I and IV in "Handbook of Mathematical Statistics" (edited by H. L. Rietz), 1924; Survey of Methods of Apportionment in Congress (Senate Doc. No. 304), 1940. Contbr. to math. journals. Congregationalist. Devised the method of apportioning representatives in Congress which became law Nov. 15, 1941. Home: 48 Highland St., Cambridge 38, Mass. Died Nov. 25, 1952.

HUNTINGTON, ELLSWORTH, geographer; b. Galesburg, Ill., Sept. 16, 1876; s. Rev. Henry Strong and Mary Lawrence (Herbert) H.; B.A., Beloit (Wis.) Coll., 1897, D.Sc.; Harvard, 1901-03, M.A., 1902, non-resident fellow, 1906-07; Ph.D., Yale, 1909; D.Litt. Clark; m. Rachel Slocum Brewer, Dec. 22, 1917; children—Charles Ellsworth, Anna Slocum, George Herbert (dec.). Asst. to pres., instr. Euphrates Coll., Harput, Turkey, 1897-1901; explored cañons of Euphrates River, 1901, and was awarded Gill Memorial by the Royal Geog. Soc. of London; research assistant Carnegie Institution, Washington, D.C., and member Pumpelly expedition to Russian Turkestan, 1903-04 (spent 1 1/2 years in Turkestan and Persia); member Barrett expedition to Chinese Turkestan (spent 1 1/2 years in India, China and Siberia, 1905-06) and was awarded Maunoir Medal by Geographic Society of Paris, and club medal by Harvard Travelers Club. Instructor in geography, 1907-10, assistant prof., 1910-15, and research asso., Yale, 1917-45, emeritus since 1945. Made expdn., Syrian Desert, Palestine, and Asia Minor, 8 mos., 1909, as rep. of Yale U., and spl. corr. Harper's Magazine. Research asso. of Carnegie Instn., Washington, for climatic investigations in U.S., Mex. and Central America, 1910-13. Capt., Mil. Intelligence Div., U.S. Army, 1918-19; maj. O.R.C. Asso. editor Geog. Rev., Econ. Geography, Ecology and Social Philosophy. Chmn. com. on atmosphere and man, Nat. Research Council. Attended Pan-Pacific Scientific Congress, Australia, 1923. Fellow Geol. Soc. America, A.A.A.S., Am. Acad. Arts and Sciences; mem. Assn. Am. Geographers (pres. 1923), Ecol. Soc. America (pres. 1917), Population Assn. of America (dir.), Am. Eugenics Soc. (dir., treas., pres. 1934-38), Nat. Research Council (geol. and geog. div. 1919-23, 1935; biol. and agrl. div., 1921-24); hon. mem. and medalist Geog. Soc., Phila. (Award of Merit, Council Geog. Teachers, 1943), pres. New Haven Council Religious Education, 1925-29; pres. Conn. League of Nations Association since 1941-45. Conglist. Clubs:

Harvard Travelers (Boston); Ends of the Earth (New York). Author: Explorations in Turkestan, 1905; The Pulse of Asia, 1907; Asia—A Geography Reader, 1912; Palestine, and Its Transformation, 1911; The Climatic Factor, 1914; Civilization and Climate, 1915; World Power and Evolution, 1919; Red Man's Continent, 1919; Principles of Human Geography (with S. W. Cushing), 1920; Business Geography (with F. E. Williams), 1922; Climatic Changes (with S. S. Visher), 1922; Earth and Sun, 1923; The Character of Races, 1924; Modern Business Geography (with S. W. Cushing), 1924; West of the Pacific, 1925; Quaternary Climates, 1925; The Pulse of Progress, 1926; The Builders of America (with L. F. Whitney), 1927; The Human Habitat, 1927; Living Geography (with F. M. McMurry and C. F. Benson), 1932; Economic and Social Geography (with F. E. Williams and S. van Valkenberg), 1933; After Three Centuries (with Martha Ragsdale), 1934; Europe (with S. van Valkenberg) 1935; Tomorrow's Children—The Goal of Eugenics, 1935; Season of Birth, 1938; Principles of Economic Geography, 1940; Mainsprings of Civilization, 1945. Home: 38 Kildeer Road, Hamden, Conn. Address: Yale University, New Haven, Conn. Died Oct. 17, 1947.

HUNTINGTON, RICHARD LEE, prof. of chem. engring.; b. Blackwell, Okla., March 24, 1896; s. Richard Collier and Corda Ann (Townsend) H.; A.B., U. of Okla., 1917; student U. of Ill., 1920, Mass. Inst. of Tech., 1930-31; M.S., Ph.D., in Chem. Engring., U. of Mich., 1933; m. Ruth Williams, April 30, 1921; children—Helen Louise, Richard Lee. Chem. engr., The Texas Co., Tulsa, Okla., 1919-20, The Skelly Oil Co., 1920-30; consultant for Phillips Petroleum Co., prof. chem. engring., U. of Okla., 1933-43, chmn. sch. chem. engring., 1937-54, research prof. chem. engring., 1954-72, George Lynn Cross research prof., 1968-72. Served in Water Supply Regt. and C.W.S., U.S. Army, 1917-19; with A.E.F. 14 mos. Mem. Am. Inst. Mining Engr., Am. Chem. Soc., Am. Inst. Chem. Engrs., Alpha Chi Sigma, Sigma Xi, Tau Beta Pi, Sigma Chi. Mason. Club: Faculty (U. Okla.). Author: Natural Gas and Natural Gasoline, 1950. Home: Norman OK Died Oct. 9, 1972.

HUNTINGTON, WARNER DARE, mfg. chemist; b. Sandusky, O., Apr. 19, 1874; s. Henry Clay and Josephine Holden (Warner) H.; grad. Sandusky High Sch.; student Oberlin Coll. 3 yrs.; m. Ola Craige Gibbins, June 4, 1902; children—Josephine Warner (Mrs. Robt. P. Bradford), William Henry; m. 2d, Edna Alice Gery Thomas, May 13, 1933. In business with father until 1898; served in Spanish-Am. War, 1898; sales mgr. Jarecki Chem. Co., 1899-1903, Buffalo Fertilizer Co., 1903-09; mgr. Internat. Agrl. Corp., 1909-15; v.p. Davidson Chem. Co., fertilizer and chemicals, 1915—; dir. fertilizer sales, Am. Cyanamid Co., N.Y. City, 1932—; v.p. Silica Gel Corp., Southern Phosphate Co.—both of Baltimore; treas. Va. Barrel Co. Chmn. acid com. War Industries Board, 1917-18. Chmn. soil improvement com. Nat. Fertilizer Assn., 1915-29; v.p. Nat. Fertilizer Assn., 1916-18, pres., 1918-20. Presbyn. Died Nov. 26, 1938.

HUNTINGTON, WHITNEY CLARK, civil engr.; b. Denver, Sept. 29, 1887; s. Glen Wood and Jennie Bird (Whitney) H.; B.S. in Civil Engring., U. Colo., 1910, C.E., 1912, M.S., 1913, Sc.D., 1947; m. Vera Ruth Allison, June 16, 1913; children—Dorothy Allison, Ruth Allison. With Crocker & Ketchum, cons. engrs., Denver, 1910, engr. with M. S. Ketchum, cons. engr., part time, 1911-19; bridge designer, C.B.&.Q. Ry., summer, 1915; instr. in civil engring. U. Colo., 1910-14, asst. prof. civil engring., 1914-18, prof., acting head of dept., asst. dean, 1918-19, prof., head of dept., 1919-26, head constrn. dept., in charge preliminary planning, structural design and constrn. of Engring. Lab. Bldg., Liberal Arts Bldg., Men's Gymnasium, Stadium, Chemistry Bldg., and structural design of Med. Sch. and Hosp. group, 1917-26; prof. civil engring., head dept. U. Ill., 1926-56, emeritus bldg. cons., 1956—; planning cons. various constrn. projects; cons. on planning to USAF Acad., 1955. Chmn. engring. bd. Civil Works Adminstrn. for Ill., 1934; vice-chmn. state adv. com. work and rehab. div. Ill. Emergency Relief Commn., 1934-35. Awarded Alumni Norlin medal for distinguished achievement U. Colo., 1937. Mem. Am. Soc. C.E. (pres. Colo. sect. 1919-20, pres. Central Ill. sect. 1930), Am. Soc. Testing Materials, Am. Soc. Engring. Edn., Ill. Soc. Profl. Engrs., Tau Beta Pi, Sigma Xi, Phi Kappa Phi, Beta Theta Pi. Conglist. Author: Building Construction, 1929, 41, rev., 1963; Earth Pressures and Retaining Walls, 1957. Home: 708 W. Florida Av., Urbana, Ill. Died Mar. 31, 1967.

HUNTOON, LOUIS DOREMUS, (hun'toon'), mining engr.; b. Paterson, N.J., Jan. 28, 1869; s. Josiah Parmley and Sarah M. (Doremus) H.; grad. Paterson High Sch., 1887; Ph.G., N.Y. Coll. of Pharmacy, 1890; E.M., Columbia, 1895; (hon. M.A., Yale, 1908); m. Edmee B. Boynton, Oct. 7, 1903. Chemist and assayer in Colo., 1895-96; mining and metall. engr., New York, 1896-1903; asst. prof. mining and metallurgy 1904-08, prof., 1908-11, Sheffield Scientific Sch. (Yale); cons. engr., New York, since 1911. Mem. Am. Inst. Mining and Metall. Engrs., Mining and Metall. Soc. America, Canadian Mining Inst., Sigma Xi. Home: Pleasantville, N.Y. Office: 15 Park Row, New York, N.Y., and 156 Yonge St., Toronto, Can. Died Feb. 22, 1947.

HUNZIKER, OTTO FREDERICK, dairy scientist; b. Zürich, Switzerland, Dec. 25, 1873; s. Carl Otto and Louise (Pupikofer) H.; grad. agrl. sch., Zürich, 1892, Bryant & Stratton Bus. Coll., Providence, R.I., 1896; B.S.A., Cornell U., 1900. M.S.A., 1901; D.Sc., Purdue U., 1932; m. Florence Belle Burne, 1905; children—Thelma Belle, Florence Louise, Karl Otto (dec.), Walter Burne, Isabelle Mary, Otto Frederick. Came to U.S., 1893, naturalized citizen, 1904. Instr. in bacteriology, Cornell U., 1901-02; milk expert, Scranton Condensed Milk Co., 1902-05; prof. dairying, chief of dairy dept., Purdue U., and Ind. Expt. Sta., 1905-16; mgr. of mfrs. dir. research labs., Blue Valley Creamery Co. (23 factories) 1916-39. Dir. La Grange Fed. Savs. & Loan Assn., 1933-54. Del. U.S. Dept. Agr. to Internat. Dairy, Stockholm, 1911; London, 1928, Copenhagen, 1931, Berlin, 1937; Stockholm, Sweden, 1949, and The Hague, 1953; chmn. program com., Industry and Economics, World's Dairy Congress, Washington, 1923; mem. La Grange Bd. of Health (pres. 1926-27). Charter and life mem. Am. Dairy Sci. Assn. (pres. 1911-13), Nat. Dairy Council, Internat. Dairy and Food Sanitarians, Am.-Swiss C. of C., Sigma Xi, Gamma Alpha, Alpha Zeta. Winner Cornell-Ohio State U. essay contest, 1899; awarded Distinguished Service gold medal, Swiss Dairy Fedn., Berne, 1928. Protestant. Republican. Clubs: Cornell, Kiwanis. Author: Condensed Milk and Milk Powder, 1914, 18, 20, 26, 35, 46, 49; The Butter Industry, 1920, 27, 40. Dairy consultant, author and publisher dairy books, lectr. Invited to Australia and New Zealand, 1927, for investigations and recommendations as to dairy industry. Appointed dairy technologist by U.S. Dept. Agr. for dairy survey in Latin-Am. countries, 1942. Awarded diploma for sci. pubs., by Internat. Exposition, Milan, 1924. Home and Office: 103 Seventh Av., La Grange, Ill. Died Nov. 15, 1959.

HUPP, JOHN COX, M.D.; b. Donegal Tp., Washington Co., Pa., Nov. 24, 1819; s. John and Ann (Cox) H.; prepared at West Alexander acad.; grad. Washington Coll., Pa., 1844 (A.M., 1848); Jefferson Med. Coll., 1847; practices at Wheeling, W.Va.; m. 1853, Carolene L. Todd, Wheeling, W.Va. Brought Chloral-hydrate to the notice of the profession, Feb. 21, 1870. One of founders Med. Soc. State of W.Va.; mem. Am. Med. Assn., since 1858; mem. many other med. socs.; author many med. papers and contributions to hist. literature. Pres. bd. of U.S. Pension Examining Surgeons, 1862-85; State vaccine agt., 1863-87; pres. bd. of supervisors, Ohio Co., W.Va., 1863-66. Address: Wheeling. W.Va.

HURLEY, ROBERT AUGUSTINE, engineer, ex-governor; b. Bridgeport, Conn., Aug. 25, 1895; s. Robert Emmett and Sabina (O'Hara) H.; student The Cheshire Acad., 1914-15, Leghih U., 1915-17; m. Evelyn L. Hedberg, Jan. 22, 1925; children—Joan Elizabeth, Robert Emmett, Sally Ann. Began as asst. to father in constrn. business, Bridgeport, Conn., 1919; formed own firm, Leverty & Hurley, contractors and constrn. engrs., Bridgeport, 1921, and partner, 1921-34; dir. WPA, Fairfield County, Conn., 1935; spl. rep. of fed. govt. to co-ordinate relief activities, Hartford, during floods of 1936; state administrator for WPA., 1936-37; commr. State Dept. of Pub. Works, 1937-40, charged with constrn. of 5,000,000 institutional bldg. program, involving 150 bldgs. on 13 locations, which program completed at saving by 1940; elected Governor of Conn., 1940, for 2-yr. term. Served as radio electrician, Submarine Fleet (on fgn. service) and on U.S.S. Pennsylbania, U.S. Navy, during World War I. Mem. Conn. Soc. Professional Engrs., Am. Legion, Delta Fraternity (Lehigh U.). Democrat. Catholic. Club: Hartford. Sponsored pending legislation for Conn. State Labor Relations Bd. and Wages and Hours Law, patterned after fed. laws, and legislation for increased prices of milk to farmers with resultant less cost to consumers. Home: West Hartford CT Died May 4, 1968.

HURST, CLARENCE THOMAS, zoölogist and archaeologist; b. Kingston, Ky., June 20, 1895; s. Alexander Lusk and Margaret Katherine (Folkerts) H.; B.Pd., Colo. State Normal Sch., Gunnison, 1920, M.Pd., 1922; A.B., Western State Coll. of Colo., Gunnison, 1923, A.M., 1923; Ph.D., U. of Calif., 1926; m. Blanche Hendricks, June 1, 1919. Pub. sch. teacher, Colo., 1916-21; teaching fellow in zoölogy, U. of Calif., 1923-24, 1925-26, tech. asst., 1924-25; asst. prof. of zoölogy, Mills Coll., 1926-28; prof. of zoölogy, Western State Coll. of Colo., since 1928, head dept. since 1928 and dean Grad. Sch. since 1930; chmn. div. of natural science and mathematics since 1937; dir. Museum of Archeol., Western State Coll., since 1935, and director Art Assn. of same, 1938-46; director field expeditions in archaeology, Museum of Archaeology, Western State Coll., since 1939; research asso. in zoölogy, U. of Calif., 1933-34. Mem. Gunnison Chamber of Commerce. Fellow A.A.A.S.; mem. Am. Assn. of Univ. Profs., Am. Soc. of Zoölogists, Colo.-Wyo. Acad. of Science (treas. 1933-40; pres. 1940-41). Colo. Archaeol. Soc. (exec. sec. and dir. since 1935), N.E.A., Colo. Edn. Assn., State Historical Society of Colorado, American Association Museums, Am. Museum of Natural History, Soc. for Am. Archaeology, N.M. Archaeol. Soc., Phi Sigma, Beta Beta Beta (mem. editorial bd.), Kappa Delta Pi, Sigma Xi. Republican. Author: Hegner's Invertebrate Nomenclature—A Dictionary of Zoölogy, 1934; Colorado's Old-Timers; The Indians Back to 25,000 Years Ago, 1946. Contbr. numerous articles on biology and anthropology to Am. and European publs. Editor of Southwestern Lore (journ. Colo. Archeol. Soc.). Home: 420 N. Main St., Gunnison, Colo. Died Jan. 17, 1949.

HURWITZ, WALLIE ABRAHAM, mathematician; b. Fulton, Mo., Feb. 18, 1886; s. Harry and Emma (Mayfield) H.; A.B., B.S., A.M., U. of Mo., 1906; A.M., Harvard, 1907; Ph.D., Göttingen, 1910; unmarried. Asst. in mathematics, U. of Mo., 1905-06; instr. mathematics, Cornell U., 1910-14, asst. prof., 1914-24, prof., 1924—. Asso. editor Trans. Am. Math. Soc., 1914-26; editor Am. Math. Monthly, 1919-22; editor Bull. Am. Math. Soc., 1921-24. Fellow A.A.A.S.; mem. Am. Math. Soc., Math. Assn. America, Circolo Matematico di Palermo, London Math. Soc., Société Mathematique de France, Phi Beta Kappa, Sigma Xi. Jewish religion. Address: Cornell University, Ithaca, N.Y. Died Jan. 6, 1958.

HUSKINS, C. LEONARD, educator; b. Walsall, Eng., Nov. 30, 1897; s. William and Annie Clara (Darby) H.; student Sch. Agr., Olds. Alberta, 1915, 20; B.S.A., U. Alberta, 1923, M.S.A., 1925; Ph.D., U. London, Eng., 1927, D.Sc., 1934; m. Margaret Harman Villy, Aug. 18, 1923; children—Sheila Wijcot, Olwen Margaret, John Michael. Asso. prof. botany McGill U., Montreal Can., 1930-34, prof. genetics, 1934-45; prof. botany U. Wis., 1945—; prof. dept. botany U. Cal., 1938; Guggenheim fellow, dept. of zoology Columbia, 1942-43. Served with Canadian Inf., 1916; flying officer, pilot Royal Flying Corps and R.A.F., 1917-19. Fellow Royal Soc. Can.; mem. Genetics Soc. Am., Soc. for Study evolution, Am. Assn. U. Profs., Am. Naturalists. Contbr. research papers to various jours. Home: 965 University Bay Dr., Madison 5, Wis. Died July 26, 1953.

HUSS, GEORGE MOREHOUSE, civil engr.; b. Tiffin, O., July 14, 1857; s. John Thomas and Sophronia Gates (Morehouse) H.; ed. high sch., Heidelberg Coll. (Tiffin, O.), Ohio Business Coll. (Sandusky); lit. and civ. engring., Cornell U., 1875; m. Ella A. Scranton, Jan. 31, 1883; children—Grace Scranton, Helen (dec.), Marjorie (dec.), Dorothy (Mrs. W.E. Gollan), Genevieve, George M. (dec.). Civil engr. and ry. builder in West until 1890; engr. and builder Deming, Sierra Madre & Pacific Ry., in Mexico, 1890-94; cons. engr. Basra to Bagdad, and Beira Ry. in East Africa, 1894; built ry. from Haifa to Damascus, Palestine, 1895-96; pres. Northern Electric Ry., Chicago, 1897; built Cleveland, Painesville & Eastern Ry., Ohio, 1899; built rys. in Northern Wis., since 1900, establishing six towns; chief constrn. engr. M., St.P.&S.S.Marie R.R., 1906-17; built 2000 miles of ry. in western states; with U.S. R.R. Adminstrn., 1918-22, in charge additions and betterments, and as asst. dir.; mem. United States Real Estate Board, 1920-22; v.p. Mont. Ry. and Wyo. North & South R.R., 1923-24; consulting practice, and farming since 1924; expert engr. for C.B.&Q. Ry. on Miss. river dams, 1933-35; pres. G. M. Huss Land Co. Mem. Am. Soc. C.E., Am. Ry. Engring. Assn., S.A.R. Republican. Clubs: Chicago Athletic, Congressional Country, Fossils. Wrote: Syrian Letters, 1897. Contbr. on lit., tech., and farming topics. Home: Stone Lake, Wis. Died Feb. 22, 1947.

HUSSEY, OBED, inventor; b. Me., 1792; m. Eunice Starbuck, 1 dau. Began work on a grain cutting machine, Cincinnati, 1830, obtained patent for reaper, 1833; gave successful demonstration of reaper before Hamilton County (O.) Agrl. Soc., 1833; introduced reaper into Ill., N.Y., Md. and Pa., 1834-38; exhibited reaper along with McCormick reaper at London (Eng.) Exhbn., 1851; forced to sell his bus. because of competition with McCormick reaper, 1858. Died Aug. 4, 1860.

HUSSEY, RAYMOND, (hus'i), physician; b. Greensboro, N.C., Dec. 26, 1883; s. John Bryant and Sue Ann (Mallard) H.; M.D., U. of Md., 1911; A.M., (hon.) Yale, 1927; m. Edith Woodward, June 14, 1917. Resident physician Municipal Tuberculosis Hosp., Baltimore, Md., 1911-12, Md. Tuberculosis Sanatorium, 1912-14; in gen. practice of medicine, Baltimore, 1912-15, also vol. asst., med. clinic, Johns Hopkins Hosp. Outpatient Clinic, 1914-15, med. clinic Phipps Tuberculosis Clinic, Johns Hopkins Hosp., Outpatient Clin. and dept. pathology, Johns Hopkins Med. Sch., 1915-16; asst. in pathology, Johns Hopkins Med. Sch., also resident pathologist, Baltimore City Hosps., 1916-17; associate in pathology and biophysics, Rockefeller Inst. Med. Research, New York, N.Y., 1919-22; asst. prof. pathology, Sch. of Medicine, Cornell U., 1922-24; asso. prof. pathology, Sch. of Medicine, Yale, 1924-27, prof., 1927-35; asst. attending physician, cardiology, Baltimore City Hosps., 1937-39, cardiologist, 1939-45; in practice of medicine, field of cardiac diseases, Baltimore, Md., also asso. prof. medicine, U. of Maryland, instr. medicine, Johns Hopkins Med. Sch., mem. visiting staff Union Memorial Hosp., Church Home and Infirmary, attending physician University Hosp. (Baltimore), 1937-45; physician in chief, St. Joseph's Hosp., Baltimore, 1940-41 (on leave from all civilian activities); dean, Sch. of Occupational Health, Wayne U., Detroit, Mich., 1945-49; sci. dir. Council on Indsl. Health, A.M.A., since 1950. Vice chmn. and acting chmn. div. med. sciences Nat. Research Council, 1918-19. Spl.

investigator Md. Tuberculosis Commn., 1938-39; chmn. med. bd. adminstrn. of occupational disease law, Md., 1939-45. Served as lt., advancing to major, Med. Corps, U.S. Army, 1917-19; lt. col., Med. Reserve Corps, 1919-24; lt. col., Med. Corps, U.S. Army, 1943-45; assigned as sci. dir. Army Indsl. Lab., Baltimore, Md., Feb.-June 1943, comdg. officer and dir., 1943-45. Vice chmn. com. on blood transfusion Baltimore chapter Am. Red Cross, 1938-40, mem. bd. dirs. and mem. exec. com., 1939-44, chmn. Am. Red Cross Blood Donor Center, 1940-41. Mem. bd. govs., Am. Acad. Compensation Med., 1948. Mem. com. indsl. health Md. State Med. Soc., 1938-45, v. chmn., 1938-39, chmn., 1939-44; mem. med. com. Indsl. Hygiene Foundation America, Mellon Inst., Pittsburgh, Pa., since 1942; mem. professional adv. com. on physical restoration, Office Vocational Rehabilitation, Fed. Security Agency, since 1943. Fellow A.A.A.S., Am. Coll. Physicians, American Public Health Assn., Gerontological Society, Am. Med. Assn. (mem. council indsl. health since 1941); mem. Illinois State and Chicago med. socs., Am. Soc. Exptl. Pathology, Soc. Exptl. Biology and Medicine, Sigma Xi, Phi Sigma Kappa. Contbr. numerous articles to med. publs. Home: 105 E. Delaware Pl., Chicago 11. Office: 535 N. Dearborn, Chgo. 10. Died Apr. 15, 1953; Buried Balt.

HUSSEY, WILLIAM JOSEPH, astronomer; b. at Mendon, O., Aug. 10, 1862; s. John Milton and Mary Catherine (Severns) Hussey; B.S., Univ. of Michigan, 1889; Sc.D., Brown U., 1912; m. Ethel Fountain, June 27, 1895; children—Roland Fountain, Allis Fountain; m. 2d, Mary McNeal Reed, Sept. 1, 1917. Instr. in mathematics, U. of Mich., 1889-91; acting dir. Detroit Obs., 1891-92; asst. prof. astronomy, 1892-93, asso. prof., 1893-94, prof., 1894-96, Leland Stanford Jr. U.; astronomer in Lick Obs., 1896-1905; prof. astronomy and dir. obs., U. of Mich., 1905—; also prof. astronomia y geodesia, U. of La Plata, Argentina and dir. Observatorio Nacional de La Plata, La Plata, Argentina, Sept. 1, 1911-17. Expert on observatory sites in Southern Calif., Ariz. and Australia, to com. on observatories of Carnegie Instn., 1903; in charge of Lick Obs. eclipse expdn. to Egypt, 1905, of La Plata eclipse expedition to Brazil, 1912; discoverer of 1,650 double stars; awarded Lalande prize of French Acad., 1906, for double star discoveries and investigations. Foreign asso. Royal Astron. Soc.; hon. mem. Sociedad Astronomica de Mexico. Author: Logarithmic and Other Mathematical Tables, 1891, 1895; Mathematical Theories of Planetary Motions, 1892; Micrometrical Observations of the Double Stars Discovered at Pulkowa (Vol. V, Lick Observatory publ.), 1901. Home: Ann Arbor, Mich. Died Oct. 28, 1926.

HUSTED, LADLEY, biologist; b. Wayne County, N.Y., Sept. 30, 1906; s. Don Gordon and Ruth Lucinda (Tuttle) H.; A.B., Oberlin Coll., 1928; student Cornell U., 1928-29; Ph.D., U. Va., 1934; m. Kathryn Funkhouser, Dec. 26, 1934; 1 son, Robert Ladley. Instr. botany Oberlin Coll., 1929-30; gen. edn. bd. fellow U. Mo., 1934-35, Bussey Inst. of Harvard, 1935-36, John Innes Hort. Inst., London, 1936-37, Inst. Animal Genetics of U. Edinburgh, 1937; asst. prof. biology U. Va., 1937-46, asso. prof., 1946-53, prof., 1953-69, sec. Miller Sch. Biology, 1946-48, chmn. dept. biology, 1949-57. Fellow A.A.A.S.; mem. Am. Soc. Naturalists, Genetics Soc. Am., Bot. Soc. Am., Human Genetics Soc., Genetics Assn., Assn. Southeastern Biologists, Virginia Academy Science, American Association U. Profs., So. Applachian Bot. Club, Sigma Xi, Phi Sigma. Conservative. Episcopalian. Clubs: Colonnade (Charlottesville); Farmington (Albemarle, Va.). Author sci. articles. Home: Charlottesville VA Died Mar. 26, 1969; buried University Cemetery, Charlottesville, VA

HUSTON, HENRY AUGUSTUS, chemist; b. Damariscotta, Me., Apr. 20, 1858; s. Albion G. and Sally (Woodward) H.; A.B., Bowdoin, 1879, A.M., 1882; A.C. (analytical chemist), Purdue U., 1882, D.Sc., 1931; m. Alice Brownson Cooke, Nov. 22, 1899 (died Mar. 25, 1940). Asst. chemistry and physics Bowdoin Coll., 1879-80; sci. tchr., prin. Lafayette High Sch., 1880-84; prof. physics Purdue U., 1884-88; dir. Ind. Weather Service 1884-96; asst. state chemist State Ind., 1884-86, state chemist, 1886-1903; chemist Ind. Agrl. Expt. Sta., 1888-1903, dir., 1902-03; prof. agrl. chemistry Purdue, 1888-1903; mgr. soil and crop service of Potash Syndicate (Kalisyndikat), 1903-23; dir., sec., asst. treas. German Kali Works, N.Y.C., defeating attacks in Congress on Potash Syndicate, 1909-22; in Berlin, Germany, July 1919, arranged for resumption of potash shipment to U.S. suspended, Jan. 1915; cons. agrl. chemist since 1923. Fellow A.A.A.S., Ind. Acad. Sci.; mem. Am. Chem. Soc., Am. Soc. Agronomists, Zeta Psi. Mason. Author: Reports of Indiana Weather Service, 1884-96; Reports of Indiana State Chemist, 17 yrs.; also Descendants of James Huston, 9 generations. Has furnished numerous papers on agrl. chemistry, research work in Bulls. of Ind. Agrl. Expt. Sta., Bull. of Chem. Div., U.S. Dept. Agr. and Ind., Mich., Minn. Agrl. and Hort. Reports, etc. Address: Kew Hall, Kew Gardens 15, NY City

HUTCHINGS, LESLIE MORTON, univ. dean; b. Portland, Me., Sept. 13, 1915; s. Morton Belmont and Clare (Hammons) H.; B.S., U. Me., 1937, D.V.M., Mich. State Coll., 1940, M.S., 1942; Ph.D., Purdue U., 1947; m. Mary A. Bruce, July 1, 1939; children—Bruce Leslie, Alan M., John T. Asst. in pathology Mich. State Coll., 1937-40; research veterinarian, 1940-42; mem. faculty Purdue U. since 1942, head dept. vet. sci., 1950—, dean sch. vet. sci. and medicine, 1957—; cons. comml. concerns. Dir. Official Animal Disease Diagnostic Lab. of Ind.; mem. agricultural bd. NRC, 1957—; panel of experts on brucellosis World Health Orgn., Food Agr. Orgns. 1950—; chmn. nat. com. for eradication of hog cholera, 1951—; Ind. Veterinary examining bd. Voted Outstanding Young Man of Ind. by Jr. C. of C., 1947. Mem. Am. Vet. Med. Assn. (exec. bd. dist. III 1953—, council in education 1958—), United States Livestock Sanitation Assn., Ofcl. Conf. Research Workers in Animal Diseases in N.A., Ind. State Livestock San. Bd., Sigma Xi (recipient Research award, 1947). Club: Rotary. Home: 331 Hollowood Dr., West Lafayette, Ind. Office: Purdue U., Lafayette, Ind. Died July 22, 1959.

HUTCHINGS, RICHARD HENRY, physician; b. Clinton, Ga., Aug. 28, 1869; s. Richard H. and Cornelia (Greaves) H.; certificate Middle Ga. Mil. Coll., Milledgeville, Ga., 1887; student University of Georgia, 1 year; M.D., Bellevue Hospital Medical College (New York Univ.), 1891; D.Sc., Colgate Univ., 1940; m. Lillie Beall Compton, Sept. 6, 1893; children—Richard Henry, Charles Wyatt, Dorothy (Mrs. R. N. Alberts). Intern, Almshouse and Workhouse Hospital, Blackwell's Island, New York, 1891-92; entered New York State Hospital Service through competitive examination, 1892; served as asst. physician to 1903, med. supt., 1903-19, St. Lawrence State Hosp., Ogdensburg, N.Y.; med. supt. Utica (N.Y.) State Hosp., 1919-39. Prof. clin. psychiatry (emeritus), Syracuse U. Chief psychiatrist 81st Div., N.A., Camp Jackson, S.C., Sept. 1917-Jan. 1918; assigned duty, Jan. 28, 1918, at office Surgeon Gen., Div. of Spl. Hosps. and Reconstruction, representing neurology and psychiatry, rank maj. Med. R.C.; chief of Division of Neuro-psychiatry, G.H. No. 31, Plattsburg Barracks, July 1918-Feb. 1919; mem. Med. Advisory Board 37 (psychiatrist) for Selective Service System, U.S. Army, 1941; mem. bd. directors National Com. for Mental Hygiene. Member American Medical Assn., Oneida County Med. Soc. (pres. 1931), Am. Psychiatric Assn. (pres. 1938), Kappa Alpha, Alpha Omega Alpha. Clubs: Fort Schuyler, Torch (pres. 1931), Rotary. Investigated epidemic of typhoid fever, 1903, traced its origin to infected ice, a source of contagion not previously recognized; made study of the care of insane in State of Ga., at request of Gov. Harris, and filed rept. with recommendations. Author: A Psychiatric Word Book, 7th edit., 1943. Contbr. numerous articles on care and treatment of Nervous and Mental Diseases. Editor of Psychiatric Quarterly. Home: 52 Fountain St., Clinton, N.Y. Office: care Psychiatric Quarterly, 1213 Court St., Utica 2, N.Y. Died Oct. 28, 1947.

HUTCHINS, CHARLES CLIFFORD, physicist; b. Canton, Me., July 12, 1858; s. Cyrus and Abigail (Stowell) H.; A.B., Bowdoin Coll., 1883, A.M., 1884; student, Harvard, 1885-86, U. of Leipzig, 1899-1900; m. Helen M. Stone, of Templeton, Mass., June 17, 1887. Prof. physics, Bowdoin Coll., 1888—. Fellow Am. Acad. Arts and Sciences, A.A.A.S.; mem. Am. Phys. Soc. Home: Brunswick, Me.

HUTCHINSON, CARY TALCOTT, engineer; b. St. Louis, Mo., Mar. 4, 1866; s. Robert Randolph and Mary (Mitchell) H.; Ph.B., Washington U., 1886; fellow in physics, Johns Hopkins, 1888-89, Ph.D., 1889. With the Sprague Electric Ry. Co. and Edison Gen. Electric Co., 1889-90; mem. of Sprague, Duncan & Hutchinson, consulting elec. engrs., 1891-92, then alone. Chief engr., McCall Ferry Power Co., bldg. large hydro-electric plant on Susquehanna River; consulting engr. G.N. Ry., in charge of electrification of Cascade Tunnel, state of Wash. Sec. Engring. Foundation, and Nat. Research Council. Mem. Electrification Commn., Ill. Central R.R. Co., 1921; in charge Ry. Div., Superpower Report, 1921; cons. engr. with Sanderson & Porter, 1922-32; in private practice, N.Y. City, 1932—. Died Jan. 18, 1939.

HUTCHINSON, ELY CHAMPION, indsl. exec. and cons. engr.; b. San Francisco, Feb. 10, 1882; s. Frederick Winslow and Ellen Cass (Tripler) H.; student pub. schs.; self-taught tech. edn.; m. Florence A. Grant, Sept. 26, 1906; 1 dau., Janet (Mrs. H. C. Alexander). Began work in the pattern shop and in the drafting room Union Iron Works, San Francisco, 1898; installing and operation hydro-electric plant in B.C., 1902-03; asst. mgr. mining dept. Union Iron Works, 1903-07; Pacific Coast rep. of Power & Mining Machinery Co., Cudahy, Wis., 1907-08; with Pelton Water Wheel Co., San Francisco, 1908-29, v.p., gen. mgr., 1922-26, prs., gen. mgr., 1926-29; editor Power (mag.), 1929-33; pres. Edgemoor Iron Co., 1933-34; exec. NRA, Washington, 1935, then under U.S. Dept. Commerce; cons. engr. J. G. White Engring. Corp.; mgr. Alco Products, Inc., 1936-39; cons. engr. indsl. orgn. and mgmt., 1940—; gen. mgr. Cambridge Div., Research Constrn. Co., Inc., 1941—. Became dep. dir. Office Prodn. Research and Development, WPB, 1944; chief indsl. research and development div., Office Tech. Services, U.S. Dept. of Commerce, Washington, 1945-48; chief gen. indsl. equipment sect., Office International Trade, Dept. Commerce, 1949. Inventor of numerous devices used in power plants. Chmn. N.Y. Com. Third Internat. World Power Confs. Fellow Am. Soc. M.E. (v.p. 1933-35; chmn. hydraulic prime movers power test code com., 1931-38); mem. Am. Soc. C.E., (chmn. bd. on honors, 1949), S.A.R. (life member California chapter); New York Committee Order Fgn. Wars. Clubs: Engineers (San Francisco); Engineers (N.Y.C.); Azted Club of 1847, Cosmos (Washington). Contbr. many tech. articles. Home: 4801 Connecticut Av., Washington 8. Died Nov. 12, 1955; buried St. Mathews Ch., Bedford, N.Y.

HUTCHINSON, JOHN IRWIN, mathematician; b. Bangor, Me., Apr. 12, 1867; s. Rev. Henry H. and Bessie Jane (Frank) H.; A.B., Bates Coll., Lewiston, Me., 1889; Clark Univ., Worcester, Mass., 1890-92, U. of Chicago, 1892-94, Ph.D., 1896; m. Genevra Barrett, June 17, 1896. Instr. math., 1894-1903, asst. prof., 1903-10, prof., 1910—. Cornell U. Republican. Conglist. Author: Differential and Integral Calculus (with Prof. Virgil Snyder), 1902; Elementary Treatise on the Calculus (with same), 1912. Home: Ithaca, N.Y. Died Dec. 1, 1935.

HUTCHINSON, ROBERT ORLAND, educator; b. nr. Bedford, Ind., Jan. 15, 1889; s. Joseph and Elizabeth Ellen (McCleery) H.; student Marion (Ind.) Normal Coll., 1908-10; A.B., Ind. U., 1916; student U. Me., 1916-17; Ph.D., U. Chgo., 1923; m. Mona Marie Randolph, June 4, 1921. Tchr. Mecca (Ind.) High Sch., 1908-10; prin. Walnut Grove (Ind.), 1910-11, Versailles (Ind.), 1911-13, Orleans (Ind.), 1914-16; instr. in physics and meteorology U. Me., 1916-17; research asst. Bur. of Standards, Washington, 1919; instr. in physics Miss. A. and M. Coll., 1919-20, asst. prof., 1920-21; teaching asst. U. Chgo., 1921-23; asst. prof. State Coll. Wash., 1923-25, acting head dept., 1925-26, asso. prof., 1926-28; prof. and head dept. mathematics Lincoln Meml. U., Tenn., 1929-31, registrar, 1930-31; prof., head dept. mathematics Tenn. Poly. Inst., 1931—, also coordinator Civilian Pilot tng., 1940-42. Served in Meteorol. Service, U.S. Army, with AEF, 1917-19. Fellow A.A.A.S.; mem. Math. Assn. Am., Nat. Council Tchrs. Mathematics, Am. assn. U. Profs., Tenn. Acad. Science, Sigma Xi, Phi Kappa Phi. Democrat. Conglist. Contbr. to sci. jours. Author: Introduction to Business Mathematics. Home: 530 N. Cedar St., Cookeville, Tenn. Died Oct. 22, 1950; buried Cookeville City Cemetery.

HUTCHINSON, WILLIAM SPENCER, prof. mining; b. Boston, Mass., Oct. 9, 1870; s. William and Hannah Amanda (Skinner) H.; grad. Dorchester High Sch., Boston, 1888; B.S., Massachusetts Institute of Technology, 1892; m. Elizabeth E. Baker, Aug. 17, 1898 (died November 27, 1944); children—Alfred Baker (dec.), Elizabeth Baker (Mrs. Edwin Delamater Ryer), Ruth (Mrs. Jervis Jefferis Babb), William Spencer, Jr., Virginia Hope (Mrs. Bernard Joseph Corrow). Asst. to sec. Mass. Inst. Tech., 1892-93; mining engineer in Calif., Ida., and Mo., 1894-1903; practicing alone, headquarters in Boston; 1903-22; assignments in Australia, New Caledonia, Peru, Chile, Transvaal, and Southern Rhodesia, 1916-25; mem. firm Hutchinson and Livermore, 1923-39; now practicing alone as industrial minerals specialist; professor mining, Massachusetts Institute Technology, 1922-39, head department of mining and metallurgy, 1927-37, department department of mining engineering, 1937-39, now professor emeritus. Member engineering div. Nat. Research Council (1924-25 and 1928-30). Mem. Am. Inst. Mining and Metall. Engrs. (dir. 1926-28), Mining and Metall. Soc. America (mem. council 1930-34), Tau Beta Pi, Delta Upsilon, Sigma Xi. Awarded silver medal, San Francisco Expn., 1915. Republican. Conglist. Home: 45 Old Morton St., Dorchester 26, Mass. Office: 31 Milk St., Boston 9. Deceased.

HUTCHISON, MILLER REESE, inventor, engr.; b. Montrose, Baldwin County, Ala., Aug. 6, 1876; s. William Peter and Tracie (Magruder) H.; student Marion Mil. Inst., 1889-91, Spring Hill Coll., 1891-92, University Mil. Inst., Mobile, 1892-95; B.S. in E.E., Ala. Poly. Inst., 1897, E.E., 1913; Ph.D., Spring Hill Coll., 1914; attended Ala. Med. Coll.; m. Martha J. Pomeroy, May 31, 1901. Chief elec. engr. U.S. Light House Establishment, 7th and 8th dists., during Spanish-Am. War, engaged in laying submarine mines and cables, Gulf Harbors; established Hutchison Laboratory, New York, 1899; invented and marketed many elec. and mech. appliances among which are "Acousticon" for the deaf, "Dictograph," "Klaxon Horn"; has been granted several hundred patents. Presented with spl. gold medal by Queen of Eng. for exceptional merit in the field of invention, 1902; present at Coronation Edward VII and Alexandra, Westminster Abbey, 1902; awarded gold medals, St. Louis Expn., 1904 for Acousticon and commercially operated wireless telephone. Became associated with Thomas A. Edison, 1910, in spl. work on storage batteries; apptd. chief engr. Edison Laboratory and all affiliated Edison interests, chief engr. to and personal rep. of Thomas A. Edison, 1913, and in addition adv. mgr. Edison Storage Battery Co., 1912-17; engr. adviser Thomas A. Edison, 1917-18; formed Miller Reese Hutchison, Inc., Jan. 1, 1917, to act as sole distributors Edison Storage Batteries for all govt. purposes all nations, of which became pres.; sold rights back to Edison Co., June 5, 1918, to devote entire time to govt. service for period of war; propr. Hutchison Laboratory. Hon. commr. of Dept. of Electricity, St.

Louis Expn., 1904; mem. Internat. Elec. Congress, St. Louis, 1904, Internat. Engring. Congress, San Francisco, 1915; mem. Naval Consulting Bd. Mem. Am. Acad. Polit. and Social Science, A.A.A.S., Am. Inst. E.E., Am. Inst. Radio Engrs., Am. Soc. M.E., Am. Soc. Naval Engrs., Nat. Inst. Social Sciences, Navy League U.S., New York Elec. Soc., Soc. Automotive Engrs., Nat. Geog. Soc., Soc. Am. Mil. Engrs., U.S. Naval Inst., Optical Soc. Am., Kappa Alpha (Southern), Accademia Internazionale di lettre e Scienze (Napoli), Royal Soc. for Encouragement of Arts, Manufacture and Commerce (London). Awarded diploma of academic corr. by Internat. Acad. Letters and Science, Naples, 1922, also Cross of Honor "for scientific and literary achievements," by same, 1925. Address: Box 1703, 180 Central Park South, New York, N.Y. Died Feb. 16, 1944.

HUTTON, COLIN OSBORNE, educator; b. Dunedin, New Zealand, Jan. 10, 1910; s. John and Jessie Alexander (Holms) H.; M.S., U. Otago, 1934; Shirtcliffe fellow, external research student Emmanuel Coll., 1936-38; Ph.D., Cambridge, 1938, Sc.D., 1952; m. Mary Piggot, Dec. 26, 1940. Came to U.S., 1947. Acting lectr. geology U. Otago, 1934-36, sr. lectr., 1946-47; govt. mineralogist, petrologist, Wellington, New Zealand, 1938-46; hon. lectr. petrology Victoria U. Coll., 1943-46; asso. prof. Stanford, 1947-48, prof. mineralogy, 1948-72. Guggenheim fellow, 1953-54. Recipient Hamilton award, 1937; Sir Julius Von Haast prize. 1934: NSF award research, 1961-63, 64-66, 68-70. Fellow Geol. Soc. Am., Geol. Soc. London, Royal Soc. New Zealand, Mineral. Soc. Am., Cal. Acad. Scis.; mem. Mineral. Assn. Can., Mineral. Soc. Great Britain, Cambridge Natural History Soc., New Zealand Assn. Sci. Workers (hon. life), Sigma Xi. Contbr. sci. articles to profl. jours. Former asso. editor Royal Soc. New Zealand. Home: Portola Valley CA Died Dec. 13, 1971; buried Palo Alton CA

HUTTON, FREDERICK REMSEN, mech. engr.; b. New York, May 28, 1853; s. Mancius Smedes and Gertrude (Holmes) H.; brother of Mancius Holmes H.; A.B., Columbia, 1873, A.M., E.M., C.E., 1876, Ph.D., 1881 (Sc.D., 1904; Sc.D., Rutgers 1913); m. Grace Lefferts May 28, 1878. Asst. civ. and mech. engring., 1876-77, instr. mech. engring., 1877-82, adj. prof., 1882-91, prof., 1891-1907, prof. emeritus, 1907, dean faculty applied science, 1899-1905, Columbia. Consulting engr. Dept. Water, Gas and Electricity, City of New York, and of Automobile Club of America, 1911-12. Trustee Collegiate Sch., New York, 1885—. Asso. editor Engineering Mag., 1892, Johnson's Encyclopaedia, 1893, Century Dictionary, 1904, New Internat. Encyclopaedia, 1913. Fellow Am. Acad. Arts and Sciences. Author: Mechanical Engineering of Power Plants, 1897; Heat and Heat Engines, 1899; Machine Tools (U.S. Census, 1880); The Gas Engine, 1904. Died May 14, 1918.

HUXFORD, WALTER SCOTT, prof. physics; b. Neligh, Neb., Dec. 15, 1892; s. Herbert C. and Cora (Scott) H.; B.A., Doane Coll., Crete, Neb., 1917; M.S., U. of Neb., 1924; Ph.D., U. of Mich., 1928; m. Mary Bertha Whalen, Aug. 28, 1917; children—Sara May (Mrs. George Ball), Barbara Jane (Mrs. Joseph Nicol), Charles K., Mary Patricia. Engaged in elec. communications work, 1917-19; high sch. instr. physics, 1919-21; instr. later prof. physics Doane Coll., 1923-26 and 1928-29; physicist dept. of engring. research U. of Mich., 1930-32; asst. prof., later asso. prof. physics Northwestern U., 1932-39, professor since 1939; researches in gaseous electronics and infrared communication systems, methods of optical communications; director of research, Nat. Defense Research Council, 1943-45. Served as lt. 36th Inf., 12th Div., A.E.F., 1918-19. Awarded Army and Navy certificate of merit, 1947. Fellow Am. Phys. Soc.; mem. Optical Soc. Am., Ill. Acad. Sci., Sigma Xi. Conglist. Clubs: Physics, Chaos (Chgo.). Contbr. tech. articles profl. jours. Home: 3027 Thayer St., Evanston, Ill. Died Feb. 12, 1958; buried Meml. Park, Evanston.

HYATT, JOHN WESLEY, inventor; b. Starkey, N.Y., Nov. 28, 1837; s. John Wesley and Anne (Gleason) H.; common sch. edn. and 1 yr. at Eddytown Sem.; m. Anna E. Taft, July 21, 1869. Removed to Ill. at 16 and became a printer; subsequently gave whole attention to inventing; first patent, 1861, a knife-sharpener; new method of making dominoes and checkers, 1869; discovered method of dissolving pyroxylin under pressure and with his late brother I. Smith H., invented "celluloid"; established mfg. at Newark, N.J.; began mfg. of sch. slates, 1875; invented Hyatt billiard ball, both material and machinery; invented water purifying system, 1881, now in use in 1,000 places in the U.S.; about 1892 invented Hyatt Roller Bearing and organized Hyatt Roller Bearing Co., Harrison, N.J.; invented, 1900, lockstitch sewing machine, with 50 needles, for sewing belting; has also invented machine for squeezing juice from sugar cane, obtaining 8 per cent more sugar than former machines, and at less cost; has recently patented new method of solidifying Am. hard woods, from which bowling balls, golf heads, mallets, etc., are being made. Awarded Perkin medal of Soc. Chem. Industry, 1914. Home: Short Hills, N.J. Died May 10, 1920.

HYDE, EDWARD WYLLYS, mathematician; b. Saginaw, Mich., Oct. 17, 1843; s. Rev. Harvey and Julia Dwight (Taylor) H.; lt. 33d U.S.C.T. in Civil War; B.C.E., Cornell, 1872, C.E., 1874; m. Sarah J., d. James Rowe, Sept. 11, 1878. Instr. civ. engring., Cornell, 1871-73; prof. mathematics, Pa. Mil. Acad., 1873-74; asst. prof., 1875-78, prof. mathematics, 1878—, dean 1892-93 and 1898-1900, chmn. of faculty, 1894-95, U. of Cincinnati. Treas. and actuary Columbia Life Ins. Co., 1903—. Author: Skew Arches, 1875; Directional Calculus, 1890; A Portion of Higher Mathematics, 1896. Died Nov. 4, 1930.

HYDE, HOWARD ELMER, contracting engr.; b. Ithaca, N.Y., May 19, 1876; s. Orange Percy and Eloise (Davies) H.; C.E., Cornell U., 1900; m. Evangeline M. Manatt, June 1917. Engr. dept. of sewers, Havana, Cuba, 1900-01; resident engr. in charge constrn. of substructure Toledo Terminal R.R. Bridge over lower Maumee River, 1901-02; asst. and 1st asst., acting city engr. and mem. Municipal Bd., City of Manila, P.I., 1902-06; 1st engr. Dept. of Pub. Wks., U.S. Provisional Govt. of Cuba, 1907-08; designing and prin. asst. engr. Havana Sewerage and Drainage Contracts, 1908-14; asst. engr. Bd. of Water supply, Providence, R.I., 1915-16; mem. Young & Hyde, Inc., contracting engrs., New York, since 1912, pres., 1917-41; with U.S. Navy on construction of dry docks, Brooklyn Navy Yard, 1941-43, on construction of naval torpedo testing range, Montauk, L.I., 1943-44; with Public Works Dept. of Nassau County, N.Y., 1944-48; retired. Mem. Am. Soc. C.E., Cornell Soc. C.E. Home: R. 1, Lincolnville ME

HYDE, JAMES MACDONALD, mining engr.; b. Mystic Bridge, Conn., June 25, 1873; s. William Penn and Seraphine Smith (Carr) H.; A.B., Stanford, 1901; m. Bessie Lorrain Ransom, of North San Juan, Nevada Co., Calif., 1923; 1 dau., Helen Elizabeth. Curator Calif. State Mining Bur. Mus., 1901-02; asst. prof. mining and metallurgy, U. of Ore., 1903-06; metallurgist Guanajuato Cons. Mining & Milling Co., 1906; supt. Manhattan Ore Reduction & Refining Co., 1907; cons. practice and independent operator, 1907-19; field agt. Mexican Syndicate, 1910; prof. metallurgy, Stanford, 1919-26; engaged as mine operator and in oil production since 1926. Vice pres. Bd. Pub. Works, Los Angeles, Calif., 1929-30, mem. City Council 1931-39. Democrat. Conglist. Mason. Contbr. tech. articles and editorials. Inventor Hyde roughing and cleaning flotation process, Hyde pneumatic flotation machine, etc. Home: 2079 Mound St., Hollywood CA

HYDE, JESSE EARL, geologist; b. Rushville, O., May 2, 1884; s. Eber and Flora Belle (Johnson) H.; B.A., Ohio State U., 1906; M.A. Columbia, 1907; post-grad. work Columbia and Harvard; m. Edna M. McCleery, Aug. 1, 1911; children—William McCleery, Eber Johnson. Asst. in physiography, Harvard, 1908, in paleontology, Columbia, 1909-11; asst. prof. geology, Queen's U., Can., 1911-15; asso. prof. geology, Western Reserve U., 1915-21, prof., 1921—. Asst. geologist, Geol. Survey of Ohio, many summers; paleontologist Geol. Survey of Can., 1912-14; consulting practice, 1919—; curator of geology, Cleveland Mus. Natural History, 1922—. Fellow Geol. Soc. America, Ohio Acad. Science, A.A.A.S. Protestant. Author: Geology of Camp Sherman Quadrangle (Geol. Survey of Ohio), 1921. Home: Cleveland Heights, Cleveland, O. Died July 3, 1936.

HYDE, JOHN, statistician, geographer; b. Stalybridge, Eng., Dec. 16, 1848; s. Abel and Emily (Adshead) H.; ed. Stamford Acad., and Owens Coll. (now U. of Manchester); m. Emily Watson, of Leamington, Eng., 1874; children—Edith Emily, Elizabeth Adshead, Edward Alderson, John Lawrence, Mrs. (Mary) Winifred Lee. Began as clk. country bank; made researches into econ. effects of preventable disease; traveled in U.S. and Can., 1882-83; asso. editor Prairie Farmer, 1884-85, Bankers' Monthly, 1885-86; investigations of econ. conditions in U.S. and Can., 1886-90; spl. agent 11th U.S. Census, in charge agr., 1890-94; editor Nat. Geog. Mag., 1895-1901; chief Bur. of Statistics, Dept. of Agr., 1897-1905; mem. U.S. Geog. Bd., 1899-1905; cotton expert U.S. Commn. to Paris Expn., 1900 (grand prize for Am. cottons); mem. Jury of Awards, Trans-Miss. Expn., Omaha, 1898, St. Louis Expn., 1904. Studied Far Eastern problems in China and Japan, 1906-10; contrib. editor Japan Mail, 1908-09; Washington corr. N. China Daily News and Herald, 1911-24. Presented library of 4,000 vols. of statis. ("Hyde Library") to Tokyo Statis. Soc., 1913; presented collection N. Am. Indian ethnologica to Harris Mus., Preston, Eng., 1914. Home: Washington, D.C. Died Jan. 18, 1929.

HYDE, ROSCOE RAYMOND, prof. immunology; b. Cory, Ind., Mar. 23, 1884; s. John Andrew and Mary Ann (Michaelree) H.; A.B., Ind. State Teachers Coll., Terre Haute, 1908; A.B. and A.M., Ind. U., 1909; Ph.D., Columbia, 1913; m. Elsie A. Coss, Sept. 18, 1910; children—Dr. Gertrude Martina, Dr. Margaret Irene Moore, Edith Raymond. Asst in embryology, Ind. U., 1908-09; asst. prof., later prof. and head of dept. zoölogy and physiology, Ind. Teachers Coll., 1909-19; lecturer in pathology, Terre Haute Veterinary Coll., 1912-19; fellow, Johns Hopkins, 1918-19, asso., 1919-22, asso. prof. immunology, 1922-28, asso. prof. filterable viruses and head of dept., 1928-32, prof. immunology and dir. of laboratories of filterable viruses and immunology since 1932; visiting prof., U. of Chicago, 1930; mng. editor Am. Jour. Hygiene, 1927-32. Fellow A.A.A.S., Am. Soc. Zoölogists, Am. Soc. Immunologists, Am. Soc. Geneticists, Johns Hopkins U. Club, Am. Soc. of Naturalists, Nat. Geog. Society, Sigma Xi, Delta Omega (pres. Alpha chapter). Democrat. Contbr. to scientific publs. Home: 4101 Penhurst Av. Office: N. Wolf St., Baltimore, Md. Died Sep. 15, 1943.

HYLAND, WILLIAM A., surgeon; b. Grand Rapids, Mich., Apr. 26, 1892; s. Michael and Sophia Hyland; B.S., M.D., Georgetown U.; m. Edith Goodspeed, Oct. 20, 1923; 1 son, William Goodspeed. Pvt. practice, E. Grand Rapids, Mich. Mem. SSS med. adv. bd., Mich., World War II; nat. bd. Am. Cancer Soc. Dir. Lansing and Grand Rapids bds. Mich. Nat. Bank. Served to maj., M.C., U.S. Army, World War II. Mem. A.C.S., A.M.A. (chmn. constn. and by laws com.), Central Surg. Soc., Am. Goitre Soc. Author papers abdominal and surgery of thyroid gland. Home: 2311 Wealthy S.E. Office: Ramona Med. Bldg., East Grand Rapids, Mich. Died July 18, 1966.

HYMAN, ALBERT SALISBURY, cardiologist; b. Boston, Mass., Apr. 6, 1893; s. John Jacob and Caroline (Greenwood) H.; A.B., Harvard, 1915, M.D., 1918; Med. Sc.D., U. London, 1924; med. deg. cardiology U. Vienna, 1925; m. Lillian Edyth Levenson, Jan. 29, 1967. Resident physician Boston City Hosp., 1919-20; med. supt. Mt. Sinai Hosp., Phila., 1920-23; med. dir. Jewish Maternity Hosp., Phila., 1922-23; med. supt. Beth David Hosp., N.Y.C., 1923-24; cons. cardiologist VA, N.Y. City Hosp. div. Mt. Sinai Hosp., Manhattan Gen. Hosp. div. Beth Israel Hosp., Richmond Meml. Hosp. (S.I.), Hosp. for Aged (Bronx); cons. cardiologist Wolffe Clinic, Phila., U.S. Naval Hosp., St. Albans, N.Y., Valley Forge (Pa.) Heart Inst. and Hosp., Beth David Hosp., Jewish Meml. Hosp., N.Y.C. Hosp. at Elmhurst, Long Beach Meml. Hosp.; attending physician N.Y. City Hosp.; dir. Daitz Cardiovascular Research Fund, N.Y. Dir. Witkin Found. for Study and Prevention Heart Disease, Cordiosonic Research Found. Examiner, Nat. Bd. Med. Examiners, 1948. Founders trustee Am. Coll. Cardiology; pres. Am. Coll. of Sports Medicine. Served from lt. comdr. to capt., USN, 1934-46; PT., and base hosps. Received Presidential Unit Citation (1st Marine Div.), Navy Commendation Ribbon. Diplomate Am. Bd. Internal Medicine. Fellow A.C.P.; mem. numerous nat., state, local profl. socs. and affiliated orgns., former pres. several. Clubs: Harvard (N.Y.C.); Rod and Gun, Outboard (Fairfield, Conn.). Medical editor Greenwood Collegiate Press. Author several books in field of cardiology latest being: Practical Cardiology, 1958; Acute Medical Syndromes, 1959. Co-author: Medical Care of the Athlete. Editor: The Medical Emergencies, 1957; Practical Cardiology, 1958; Functional Capacity of the Heart in Health and Disease, 1959. Editor: Ency. of Sports Medicine. Contbr. articles to sci. publs. Inventor artificial pacemaker for resusciatation of dying heart and other life-saving apparatus. Home: New York City NY Died Dec. 7, 1972; buried L.I. Nat. Cemetery, Farmingdale NY

HYMAN, IRVING, neurologist, educator; b. Buffalo, Aug. 12, 1908; s. Max and Rose (Dickman) H.; B.S., U. Buffalo, 1929, M.D., 1935; m. Irma Cohen, Dec. 31, 1937; children—Susan (Mrs. Franklin E. Koven), Lisbeth, Mark. Intern, resident neurology Buffalo Gen. Hosp., 1935-37, chief neurology and electroencephalography, 1953—, attending neurologist. 1945—; resident neurology Montefiore Hosp., N.Y.C., 1937-38; resident psychiatry Maudsley Hosp., London, Eng., 1938-39; chief neurology and electroencephalography, attending neurologist Millard Fillmore Hosp.; Buswell research fellow, prof. neurology U. Buffalo, 1959-61, Buswell prof. neurology, chmn. dept., 1959—. Served to lt. col., M.C., AUS, 1942-45. Fellow Am. Psychiat. Assn.; mem. A.A.A.S., Am. Assn. Research Nervous and Mental Disease, Am. Acad. Neurology, Eastern Assn. Electroencephalographers. Jewish religion. Contbr. sci. articles to profl. publs. Home: 96 Leicester Rd., Tonawanda, N.Y. Office: 100 High St., Buffalo 3. Died Mar. 7, 1961.

HYMAN, LIBBIE HENRIETTA, zoologist; b. Des Moines, Ia., Dec. 6, 1888; d. Joseph and Sabina (Neumann) Hyman; S.B., U. Chgo., 1919, Ph.D., 1915, Sc.D., 1941; Sc.D., Goucher College, 1958, Coe Coll., 1959. Research appt. U. of Chicago, 1916-31, research on physiology and morphology of lower invertebrates; research appointment (hon.) Am. Mus. Natural History, N.Y.C., 1937—. Recipient Gold Medal, Linnean Soc. London, 1960. Mem. Am. Soc. Zoologists, Am. Micros. Soc., Am. Soc. Limnology and Oceanography, National Academy of Sciences, American Society of Naturalists, Soc. Systematic Zoology (past pres.), Phi Beta Kappa, Sigma Xi. Author: A Laboratory Manual for Elementary Zoology, 1919; A Laboratory Manual for Comparative Vertebrate Anatomy, 1922; Comparative Vertebrate Anatomy, 1942; The Invertebrates, 6 vols. 1940-67; also articles sci. jours. Recipient Elliot Gold Medal, 1951; gold medal for distinguished achievement in sci. Am. Mus. Natural History, 1969. Home: New York City NY Died Aug. 3, 1969.

HYSLOP, JAMES AUGUSTUS, (his'lup), entomologist; b. Chicago, Ill., July 7, 1884; s. Charles George and Mary Agnes (Garvey) H.; B.S., Mass. Agrl. Coll., 1908, Boston U., 1908; M.S., Washington State Coll., 1911; m. Grace Genevra Anderson, Oct. 7, 1911; children—Charles Douglas, James Anderson, Ryntha (Mrs. D. R. Geehring), Wynnifred (Mrs. R. J. Shields). In charge first gipsy moth eradication work in Conn., 1906; cotton boll weevil parasite work, U.S. Dept. Agriculture, 1907; cereal and forage insect investigation, Dept. Agr., 1908-17; entomologist in charge Div. of Insect Pest Survey and Information, Bur. of Entomology and Plant Quarantine, U.S. Dept. Agr., 1917-44; now retired. Fellow A.A.A.S., Am. Entomol. Soc.; mem. Am. Assn. Econ. Entomologists, Washington Acad. Science, Washington Entomol. Soc. Has specialized in Elateridae. Home: Stateside Dr., Silver Spring, Md. Died Jan. 16, 1953.

IBSEN, HEMAN LAURITZ, prof. genetics; b. Chicago, Ill., Sept. 16, 1886; s. Oluf August Martin and Gemaliah (Larsen) I.; B.S. in Agr., U. of Wis., 1912; M.S., in Genetics, 1913, Ph.D., 1916; m. Elma Ruth Stewart, Dec. 22, 1927; 1 dau., Jane Ruth. Asst. in genetics, U. of Wis., 1913-17, in zoölogy, 1917-19; professor genetics, Kan. State College since July 1919. Member of American Society of Animal Production and of American Dairy Science Association. With Chemical Warfare Service, U.S. Army, 1918. Fellow A.A.A.S.; mem. Am. Society Zoölogists, Am. Society Naturalists, Am. Genetic Assn., Sigma Xi, Phi Kappa Phi, Gamma Sigma Delta, Alpha Zeta. Republican. Has specialized in research on inheritance and physiology of reproduction in guinea pigs, rabbits, cattle, and rats. Home: 1811 Laramie St., Manhattan, Kan. Died Jan. 29, 1955; buried Sunset Cemetery, Manhattan, Kan.

IDDINGS, EDWARD JOHN, animal husbandman; b. Peru, Ind., Mar. 22, 1879; s. John Byron and Mary (Huber) I.; student Butler Coll., 1899-1901; B.S. in Agr., Colo. A.&M. Coll., 1907, M.S., 1922; LL.D. (honorary), University of Idaho, 1950; married Maud Augusta Rowell, June 24, 1908; children—Edward John (dec.), Catherine May (dec.). Spl. agt. Bureau of Plant Industry, U.S. Dept. Agr., 1906; asst. to dean of agr., Colo. A.&M. Coll., 1907-09; asst. in animal husbandry, same Coll., 1909-10; with U. of Idaho since 1910, prin. Sch. of Practical Agr. and asst. in animal husbandry, 1910-11, prof. animal husbandry, 1911-18, vice dean College of Agr., 1913-15, dean, 1915-18, dean of agr. and dir. Agrl. Expt. Sta., 1918-46; acting dir. extension service, 1923-24, emeritus since Nov. 1, 1946; on leave of absence director of extension, 1924-46; dean of agriculture on round-the-world tour, 1927, visiting leading farming and livestock producing countries; on sabbatical leave November 1, 1945-October 31, 1946. Fellow Am. Assn. for Advancement of Science, American Society of Animal Production, Delta Tau Delta, Alpha Zeta, Sigma Xi. Mason (K.T., Shriner). Author numerous bulletins and articles relating to live stock. Chosen Honor Grad., Colo. A. and M. Coll., 1947. Home: Moscow, Ida.; also San Jacinto, Cal. Deceased.

IDDINGS, JOSEPH PAXSON, geologist; b. Baltimore, Md., Jan. 21, 1857; s. William Penn and Almira (Gillet) I.; Ph.B., in engring. course, Sheffield Scientific Sch. (Yale), 1877, grad. student in chemistry and mineralogy, 1877-78; asst. in mech. drawing and surveying same, 1877-78; grad. student geology and assaying, Columbia Sch. of Mines, 1878-79; in microscopic petrography, Heidelberg, 1879-80; Sc.D., Yale, 1907. Asst. geologist, 1880-88, geologist, 1888-92, and again, 1895—, U.S. Geol. Survey; asso. prof. petrology, 1892-95, prof. 1895-1908, U. of Chicago. Silliman lecturer at Yale U. for 1914; hon. asso. in petrology, U.S. Nat. Museum, 1917—. Joint Author: Geology of the Yellowstone National Park, 1899; Quantitative Classification of Igneous Rocks, 1903. Translated and abridged H. Rosenbusch's Microscopical Physiography of the Rock-Making Minerals, 1898. Author: Rock Minerals, 1906; Igneous Rocks, 1909, Vol. II, 1913; The Problem of Volcanism, 1914. Address: Washington, D.C. Died Sept. 8, 1920.

IDE, JOHN JAY, (id), aeronautics; b. Narragansett Pier, R.I., June 26, 1892; s. George Elmore (rear adm. U.S. Navy) and Alexandra Louise (Bruen) I.; grad. Browning Sch., New York, 1909; Certificate of Architecture, Columbia, 1913; studied École des Beaux Arts, Paris, 1914; LL.D. (honorary), Hanover College, 1952; married Dora Browning Donner, February 12, 1940. Architect with H. T. Lindeberg, N.Y., 1916-17 and 1920-21; tech. asst. in Europe of Nat. Adv. Com. for Aeronautics, at American Embassy, Paris, 1921-40, 1949-50; consultant for Nat. Adv. Com. for Aeros., 1950-58; on active duty in Bur. Aeronautics, Navy Dept., Wash., D.C., 1940-43. Ensign lt. (j.g.) and lt. United States Naval Reserve Flying Corps, 1917-20. Assigned to staff, commander U.S. Naval Forces (Europe) as Tech. Air Intelligence Officer, 1943-46; temporary duty with Combined Intelligence Objectives subcom., Paris, Aug. 1944, U.S. Strategic Bombing Survey, Germany, June 1945; apptd. asst. Naval attaché for Air, Am. Embassy, London, Aug. 1945, advanced to capt. U.S.N.R., Nov. 1945; ended fgn. duty, Nov. 1946; del. Anglo-Am. Air Conf., 1947-59; spl. mission Europe USAF, 1951. Trustee French Institute of the United States, Museum of the City of N.Y.; fellow Pierpont Morgan Library. Awarded Commendation Ribbon by Commander of Twelfth Fleet. Recipient gold medal NACA, 1952; Chevalier Legion of Honor (France). Hon. fellow Smithsonian Instn., Washington; fellow Inst. Aero. Scis.; mem. Society Colonial Wars, Soc. Automotive Engrs., Nat. Aero. Assn., Council Fgn. Relations (dir.), Fedn. French Alliances in U.S. (pres. 1959-60), Naval Order U.S., Huguenot Soc., France-Am. Soc. (dir.), Am.-Italy Soc. (dir.), Pilgrims of U.S.; hon. mem. Royal Aero. Society (London); vice pres. Internat. Aero. Fedn., 1948-50, 58-60. Republican. Episcopalian. Clubs: Union, River, St. Nicholas, Wings (N.Y.C.); Metropolitan (Washington); Everglades, Bath & Tennis (Palm Beach). Author: Georgian Country Houses in Ireland, 1959. Home: 485 Park Av., N.Y.C. 10022. Died Jan. 12, 1962; buried Jay Cemetery, Rye, N.Y.

IHLSENG, AXEL OLAF, mining engr.; b. N.Y. City, Feb. 20, 1855; s. Lars and Anna M. (Anderson) I.; B.S., Coll. City of New York, 1874; E.M. and C.E., Sch. of Mines, Columbia, 1877; m. Susan M. Reston, Apr. 18, 1887; 1 dau., Ulga Kathryn (Mrs. Thomas Richard Nunan). Chemist, Havemeyer Sugar Refining Co., 1877-82; mgr. Mountain Queen Mining Co. and other mines, Silverton, Colo., and metallurgist, Martha Rose Smelter, Silverton, and La Plata Smelter, Leadville, Colo., 1882-89; operator of zinc mines (owner of Orinogo Circle, Pleasant Valley and other mines), Joplin (Mo.) dist., 1889-1908; cons. engr., 1908—; co-owner and cons. engr. Keystone (S.D.) Consol. Mines; engaged in examination of strip coal mines, 1920-26. Democrat. Episcopalian. Home: New York, N.Y. Died Dec. 9, 1934.

IHLSENG, MAGNUS COLBJORN, college pres.; b. Christiania, Norway, May 2, 1852; s. Lars C. and Anna M. (Anderson) I.; came to U.S. in childhood; grad. Brooklyn Poly. Inst., 1872; E.M., C.E., Columbia, 1875, Ph.D., 1877; m. Agnes Reaser, of Carthage, Mo., Dec. 19, 1888. Asst. in physics, Columbia, 1875-81; div. engr. New York, Pittsburg & Chicago R.R., 1880-83; prof. engring., Colo. Sch. of Mines, 1881-93; dean Sch. of Mines, Pa. State Coll., 1893-99, Brooklyn Poly. Inst., 1899-1906; now pres. Blairsville (Pa.) Coll. Mem. Am. Inst. Mining Engrs. Brooklyn Engrs.' Club, N.Y. Elec. Soc. Author: Manual of Mining, 1890; also 6 works on machinery for Internat. Correspondence Sch., Scranton, Pa., and various monographs and contbns. to engring. jours., and Nat. Acad. Sciences. Address: Blairsville, Pa.

IHRIG, HARRY KARL, (er' rig), engr.; b. Appleton, Wis., Apr. 16, 1898; s. George William and Mary (Wurl) I.; student Carleton Coll., 1915-16; B.S., U. N.D., 1919, M.S., 1920; Ph.D., U. Cal., 1923; m. Luella La Moure, June 4, 1924; children—Judson La Moure, Harry Karl. Supt. Diatome Products Co., 1923-25; research engr. Asso. Oil Co., 1925-28; v.p. Ralph E. Davis (cons. engr.), 1928-33; cons. engr. European Gas & Electric Co., 1933-34; dir. labs. Globe Steel Tubes Co., 1934-48, v.p., 1948-50; v.p. in charge research Allis-Chalmers Mfg. Co. since 1950; research prof. biophysics, grad. sch. Marquette U. since 1951; dir. Nuclear Instrument & Chem. Corp. 1952—. Bd. dirs. med. sch., Marquette U., Wisconsin Heart Assn. Adv. council, dept. mech. engring. Princeton; bd. trustees Nat. Fund. Med. Edn.; adv. council U.S. Naval Proving Ground. Received Robert W. Hunt medal, Am. Inst. Mining and Metall. Engrs., 1947; citation for profl. services, coll. engring. U. Wis., 1949. Mem. Am. Soc. Metals, Am. Inst. Chem. Engrs., Am. Soc. Mining and Metall. Engrs., Am. Chem. Society, Am. Electrochem. Soc., National Society of Professional Engineers, and also Sigma Xi, Tau Beta Pi, and Phi Lambda Upsilon, Delta Sigma Rho, Sigma Chi, Alpha Chi Sigma. Author: Outline of Metallurgy of Iron and Steel (rev. edit.), 1948. Contbr. sci. articles, chem. and med. jours. Holds patents on chem., metall. processes. Home: 2611 E. Beverly Rd., Milw. 11. Office: Allis-Chalmers Mfg. Co., Milw. 53201. Died Aug. 22, 1960.

ILES, MALVERN WELLS, metallurgist; b. Midway, Ky., Aug. 7, 1852; Ph.B., Columbia Sch. of Mines, 1875, Ph.D., 1876; fellow Johns Hopkins, 1875-77, making spl. chem. researches. Chemist and assayer, Utica Mining & Milling Co.; supt. and metallurgist, Omaha & Grant Smelting Co., then of Holden Smelting Co., and now of Globe Smelting & Refining Co., Denver. Expert authority upon smelting lead and silver. Contbr. to scientific jours. Address: "Ilesmere," The Palms, Cal.

IMLAY, LORIN EVERETT, elec. engr.; b. Guernsey County, O., Nov. 2, 1864; s. Thomas Johnson and Lavina Catherine (Conner) I.; B.C.E., Cornell Coll., Ia., 1888, C.E., 1892; post-grad. work, U. of Calif., 1892; m. Helen Maria Smith, Dec. 2, 1889; children—Helen Louise (dec.), Robert; m. 2d, Marie H. Rose, June 16, 1919; 1 son, Alexander Rose. In civ. engring. work Calif. and H.I., 1888-91; with San Antonio Light & Power Co., Pomona, Calif., 1891-94; engr. of constrn. Westinghouse Electric & Mfg. Co., Pittsburgh, 1894-1902; supt. Niagara Falls Power Co. and Canadian Niagara Power Co., 1902-19; became operating engr. Niagara Falls Power Co., 1920; engr. superpower survey, U.S. Geol. Survey, 1920-21; statis. engr., Buffalo, Niagara & Eastern Power Corp., 1926; dir. statistics Niagara-Hudson Power Corp., 1930; retired, 1938. Republican. Unitarian. Author: Mechanical Characteristics of Transmission Lines. Home: Niagara Falls, N.Y. Died June 9, 1941.

IMPERATORI, CHARLES JOHNSTONE, (im-per-a-to're), physician; b. N.Y.C., Jan. 20, 1878; s. Carlo and Sarah (Johnstone) I.; M.D., N.Y.U., 1899; m. Olga Gilbert, 1902; children—Charles Johnstone, Olga (Mrs. W. R. Wolfinbarger), Sarah (Mrs. William F. Farrell). Sub-externe Bellevue Hosp., 1899-1900, vis. surgeon, 1917-21, 30-35; prof. laryngology N.Y. Post-Grad. Med. Sch. and Hosp., Columbia, 1922-38; clin. prof. otolaryngology N.Y.U., 1932-35; cons. laryngologist Nyack (N.Y.) Gen. Hosp., Harlem Hosp., N.Y.; cons. bronchoscopist Manhattan Eye, Ear and Throat Hosp.; mem. div. med. scis. NRC, 1941-44. Served as lt. col., C.O. 309th Med. Regt., 84th Div., U.S. Army, 1917-19, AEF. Decorated Medaille D'Honneur Des Epidemies (France). Mem. Am. Laryngol. Assn. (pres. 1942-44), Am. Bronchoscopic Soc. (pres. 1928), N.Y. Acad. Med., Am. Rhinol. Otol. and Laryngol. Soc., A.M.A., A.C.S. (bd. govs. 1942-49), Alpha Delta Sigma, Phi Alpha Sigma. Republican. Episcopalian. Author: Diseases of Nose and Throat (with Dr. H. J. Burman), 1935, 2d edit., 1939, Spanish Am. edition, 1942. Address: Block House, Essex, N.Y. Died June 15, 1949.

INCE, CHARLES R., mining engr.; b. N.Y.C., Mar. 8, 1903; s. Edward Thomas and Katherine (Hensle) I.; grad. Columbia Coll., 1924. Columbia Sch. Mines, 1928; m. Moselle Byars, Oct. 19, 1928; children—Keren, Thomas. Faculty Columbia Sch. Mines, 1926-29; asst. sales mgr. St. Joseph Lead Co., 1929-48, sales mgr. since 1948, v.p. since 1950, also trustee. Staff W.P.B., World War II; industry adv. com. N.P.A., OPS. Mem. Am. Inst. Mining Engrs., Am. Soc. Metals, Am. Zinc Inst., Lead Industry Assn. (pres.). Clubs: Gipsy Trail, University. Home: Gipsy Trail, Carmel, N.Y.; also 1000 Park Av., N.Y.C. Office: 250 Park Av., N.Y.C. Died Apr. 11, 1964; buried Ferncliff Cemetery, Hartsdale, N.Y.

INFELD, LEOPOLD, physicist, author; b. Krakow, Poland, Aug. 20, 1898; s. Salomon Infeld; Ph.D., U. Krakow, 1921; m. Helen Schlauch, Apr. 12, 1939; children—Eric S., Joan M. Lectr. U. Lwow, Poland, 1929-34; fellow Rockefeller Found. at Cambridge, England, 1934-35; research Inst. for Advanced Study, Princeton, 1936-38; prof. applied mathematics, U. Toronto, Canada, 1939-50; now at U. Warsaw in Poland. Mem. praesidium Polish Acad. Sci. Fellow Royal Canadian Soc., American Phys. Soc. Author books including: Evolution of Physics With A. Einstein; Quest The Evolution of a Scientist, 1941 (awarded Annisfield prize $1,000); Albert Einstein, His Work and Its Influence on Our World, 1950. Contbr. numerous sci. papers. Address: Physics Institute, Hoza 69, Warsaw Poland. Died Jan. 16, 1968.

INGALLS, WALTER RENTON, cons. engr.; b. Lynn, Mass., Oct. 25, 1865; s. Jerome and Emma (Renton) I.; S.B., Mass. Inst. Tech., 1886; E.D., U. Mo., 1923; m. Ella Gordon, Oct. 26, 1898; children—Rosamond, Catherine (dec.), Hildegarde (dec.), Ursula. Mining and smelting, Leadville, Colo., 1886-89; asst. editor Engring. and Mining Jour., 1890-92; engr., supt. Pittsburgh & Mexican Tin Mining Co., Durango, Mex.; cons. mining engr., N.Y., 1893; mgr. Ill. Phosphate Co. (Ocala, Fla.), Brodie Gold Reduction Co. (Cripple Creek, Colo.), and metallurgist Gold & Silver Extraction Co., Ltd., Denver, 1894-95; supt. smeltery, Quien Sabe Mine, Durango, Mexico, 1896; asst. editor The Mineral Industry, 1897-99; acting editor Engring. and Mining Jour., part of 1897; metall. engr. Am. Zinc, Lead & Smelting Co., Columbia Lead Co., Laharpe Zinc Smelting Co., 1899-1904; chief commn. apptd. by Canadian govt. to report on zinc resources of B.C., 1905-06; editor Engring. and Mining Jour., 1905-19, The Mineral Industry, 1905-10. Cons. engr., N.Y.C., 1919-48. Dir. Am. Bur. Metal Statistics, 1920-47. Mem. Am. Inst. Mining and Metall. Engrs., Instn. Mining and Metallurgy (London), Mining and Metall. Soc. Am. (past prs.; elected hon. mem. 1946), Am. Inst. Weights and Measures (pres.). Clubs: Engineers, Lawyers. Author: Production and Properties of Zinc, 1902; Metallurgy of Zinc and Cadmium, 1903; Lead and Zinc in the United States, 1908; The Wealth and Income of the American People, 1922; Current Economic Affairs, 1923. Co-author: Report on the Zinc Resources of British Columbia, 1906; Notes on Metallurgical Mill Construction, 1906; Lead Smelting and Refining, 1906; Rules and Regulations for Metal Mines, 1915. Home: Ingaldsby, Boxford, Mass. Died Feb. 25, 1956; buried Pine Grove Cemetery, Lynn, Mass.

INGERSOLL, COLIN MACRAE, cons. engr.; born New Haven, Conn., Dec. 1, 1858; s. Colin Macrae and Julia H. (Pratt) I.; B.A., Yale, 1880; m. Theresa McAllister, May 25, 1889 (died in 1910); children—Theresa Van den Heuvel, Coline Macrae, Ralph McAllister; m. 2d, Marie Harrison, Feb. 5, 1916. Entered employ of M.P. Ry., St. Louis, 1881; became connected with N.Y., N.H. & H. R.R., 1882; had charge of double-tracking of the Shore Line, improvements on N.Y. div., and elevating the tracks through Boston; asst. to pres., in charge at Boston, 1897-1900; chief engr., 1900-06 (resigned). City engr., New Haven, 1892; chmn. Harbor Commn. of New Haven, 1895; pres. Union Freight Co., Boston, 1897-1900, Old Colony

Steamship Co., 1897-1900, etc. Chief engr. Dept. of Bridges, N.Y. City, 1906-08 (erection of Manhattan and Queensboro bridges and regulation on traffic of Brooklyn Bridge); cons. practice, N.Y. City, 1908-37; retired. Mem. Alaskan R.R. Commn., investigating transportation problems in Alaska, 1912-13. Mem. Am. Inst. Cons. Engrs., Am. Soc. C.E., Delta Psi. Club: University (New York). Home: Salisbury, Conn. Died Apr. 7, 1948.

INGERSOLL, ERNEST, naturalist, editor; b. Monroe, Mich., Mar. 13, 1852; s. Dr. T. Dwight and Eliza (Parkinson) I.; ed. Oberlin Coll. and Harvard Mus. of Comparative Zoölogy; m. Mary Scofield (died 1921); children—Helen, Geoffrey (dec.); m. 2d, Frances L. Buchanan (died 1929); m. 3d, Mrs. Vera Edmondson Nelson. Formerly connected with Hayden survey and U.S. Fish Commn.; later at Montreal as editor Canadian Pacific Ry. publications; lecturer zoölogy, U. of Chicago. Co-editor Standard Dictionary, New Internat. Cyclopedia, Cyclopedia Americana, and other reference books. Author: Oyster Industries, 10th Census; Friends Worth Knowing, last edit., 1901; Country Cousins; Knocking 'Round the Rockies; Crest of the Continent; Canadian Guide-Book, Part II; Down East Latch Strings, 1885; The Book of the Ocean, 1898; Nature's Calendar, 1900; Wild Life of Orchard and Field, 1902; The Life of Animals—the Mammals, 1906; Wit of the Wild, 1906; Birds in Legend, Fable and Folklore, 1923; Dragons and Dragon Lore, 1928; also The Ice Queen, An Island in the Air, and other juvenile novels. Conducted 1899-38, department of educational natural history in weekly edit. of Montreal Star. Retired, 1938. Mem. N.Y. Zoöl. Soc. and other scientific assns. Club: Explorers. Address: 404 W. 116th St., New York. Died Nov. 13, 1946.

INGERSOLL, SIMON, inventor; b. Stanwich, Conn., Mar. 3, 1818; s. Alexander S. and Caroline (Carll) I.; m. Sarah B. Smith, 1839; m. 2d, Frances Hoyt; 5 children. Farmer, L.I., N.Y., 1839-58; patented rotating shaft for steam engine, 1858; built steam propelled wagon; patented friction clutch, gate latch, spring scale in 1860's; engaged in farming, 1870; patented rock drill, 1871; organized Ingersoll Rock Drill Co.; patented 16 improvements of drill machinery and 4 patents for life line thrower, 1873-83. Died July 24, 1894.

INGHAM, LUCIUS EDWIN, engineer; b. Oil City, Pa., Jan. 6, 1892; s. Phineas Staunton and Matie (Wilson) I.; student pub. schs.; m. Ann Brainard, Aug. 21, 1916; 1 dau., Janet Ann (Mrs. Sprengle). Engring. dept. United Natural Gas Co., 1910-23, Iroquois Gas Corp., 1923-30, Columbia Engring. Corp., 1931-36, Mich. Gas Transmission Co., 1936-39, v.p. Ky. Natural Gas Corp., 1939-47; v.p. operations, Tex. Gas Transmission Corp., 1947—, dir., 1947—; v.p. La. Natural Gas Corp., Shreveport, 1951—, Tex. No. Gas Corp., 1951—. Profl. engr., Ohio. Mason (32 deg.). Home: 1922 Griffith Pl. E. Office: 416 W. Third St., Owensboro, Ky. Died Mar. 3, 1957; buried Oil City, Pa.

INGLESON, ROBERT G., engr.; b. Manchester, Eng., 1868; ed. pvt. acad. and S. Kensington Science and Art Schs., London. Served apprenticeship Walker Mfg. Co., in Cleveland, and Westinghouse Elec. Co., of Pittsburgh; now in practice as mech. elec. and consulting engr.; consluting engr. for the Perry-Payne estates. V.p., 1901, and pres., 1902, Nat. Assn. Stationary Engrs. Address: 201 Perry-Payne Bldg., Cleveland.

INGMANSON, WILLIAM LESLIE, chem. engr.; b. Chgo., May 10, 1924; s. Knute W. and Edna (Milne) I.; B.S., Tufts U., 1947; M.S., Inst. Paper Chemistry, Lawrence U., 1949, Ph.D., 1951; m. Natalie Joyce Taber, Oct. 28, 1944; children—Scott Taber, Leslie Lord, Lance Eric. With Inst. Paper Chemistry, 1951—, chmn. chem. engring. dept., 1956—. Mem. T.A.P.P.I., Phi Beta Kappa, Theta Delta Chi. Spl. research porous media. Home: 719 E. Byrd St., Appleton, Wis. 54911. Office: Inst. Paper Chemistry, Appleton, Wis. 54911. Died Nov. 6, 1966.

INGRAHAM, FRANC DOUGLAS, neurosurgeon; b. Mpls., Mar. 10, 1898; s. Alexander and Eliza Jane (Caldwell) I.; A.B., Harvard, 1922, M.D., 1925; m. Martha Wheatland, Nov. 24, 1931; children-Timothy Alexander, Alice. Surg. house officer, Peter Bent Brigham Hosp., Boston, 1925-26; fellow surgery Johns Hopkins, 1926-27; asst. res. surgeon, Peter Bent Brigham Hosp., Boston, 1927-28, resident surgeon, 1928, neurol. surgeon, 1945-64, neurosurgeon emeritus, 1964—; traveling fellow in surgery, dept. physiology at Oxford, 1928-29; vis. surgeon neurosurgery Children's Hosp., Boston, 1929; asst. surgery, Harvard, 1930-39, instr., 1939-41, asso., 1941-44, asst. prof., 1944-48, asso. prof. surgery, Med. Sch., 1948-64, emeritus, 1964—; cons. neurosurgeon, New Eng. Hosp. for Women and Children, Boston, also Heywood Meml. Gardner 1946—, New Eng. Center Hosp., 1949—; cons. neurosurgery, VA Hosp., West Roxbury, Mass., 1954—; neuro-surgeon Beverly Hosp., 1942—; chief surgeon Children's Hosp., 1945-47, chief neurosurgeon, chmn. Neurol. Inst., 1946—. Fellow A.C.S., Scandinavian Neurosurg. Soc.; mem. Boston Surg. Soc., Boston Soc. Neurol., Psychiatry, A.M.A., Harvey Cushing Soc., Assn. Research Nervous and Mental Diseases, Mass. Med. Soc., New Eng. Surg. Soc., Soc. Neurol. Surgeons, Brit. Soc. Neurol. Surgeons (hon.), Scandinavian Neurosurg. Soc., Am. Acad. Cerebral Palsy, Am. Pediatric Soc., Am. Surg. Assn., Am. Acad. Pediatricians. Internat. Society Surgery (Belgium), N.E. Pediatric Soc., Am. Neurol. Assn., N.E. Neurosurg. Soc., Soc. Am. Magicians, Am. Acad. Arts and Scis., Sigma Xi, Theta Delta Chi, Nu Sigma Nu. Clubs: Harvard, Somerset (Boston); Brookline (Mass.) Country; Myopia Hunt (Hamilton, Mass.); Essex County (Manchester, Mass.). Author: (with others) Spina Bifida and Carnium Bifidum, 1943; (with others) Neurosurgery in Infancy and Childhood, 1953. Contbr. articles profl. jours. Home: 106 Sargent Rd., Brookline, Mass. Office: 319 Longwood Av., Boston. Died Dec. 4, 1965.

INSLEY, WILLIAM HENRY, engineer, mfgr.; b. Terre Haute, Ind., Jan. 16, 1870; s. William Quinn and Celia (Whitmore) I.; student De Pauw U., 1889-92; B.Sc., Rose Poly. Inst., Terre Haute, Ind., 1900, M.S., 1902, C.E., 1910; m. Jane Williams, Jan. 1, 1903 (died Feb. 29, 1948); 1 son, Francis Henry. Founder, 1905, pres., gen. mgr. until retirement, 1940, Insley Mfg. Corp.; engrs. and mfrs. contractors' machinery, and structural iron work, especially concrete distbn. equipment and excavators; patentee of excavating equipment and equipment for distbn. of concrete by gravity; dir. Citizens Gas Co. Cons. engr. for Ind. of U.S. Fuel Adminstrn., World War I, also chmn. Ind. subregion, War Industries Bd. Mem. state com. Indiana Y.M.C.A.; pres. Soc. Ind. Pioneers' past pres. Indianapolis Community Fund; mem. Board Volunteers of America; past pres. Indianapolis Family Welfare Society; mem. Am. Soc. M.E. (organizer and 1st chmn. Ind. sect.), Am. Soc. C.E. (life). Republican. Methodist (trustee). Clubs: Indianapolis Literary, Irvington Dramatic. Home: 445 N. Audubon Rd., Indianapolis 19

IPATIEFF, VLADIMIR NIKOLAEVICH, prof. chemistry; b. Moscow, Russia, Nov. 9, 1867; s. Nicoay and Anna (Giyky) I.; student Artillery Academy, St. Petersburg, 1889-92; Ch.D., U. of St. Petersburg, 1907; hon. Dr., U. of Munich, Strasbourg, Sofia, Northwestern; m. Barbara Ermakoff, July 26, 1892; children—Nicolay, Vladimir, Anna, Dimitry. Came to U.S., 1931. Prof. of chemistry Artillery Academy, St. Petersburg, 1898-1906; prof. of chemistry, U. of St. Petersburg, 1906-15; mem. Acad. of Science, St. Petersburg since 1915; mem. Am. Nat. Acad. of Science since 1939; prof. chemistry, Northwestern U., 1931-35, prof. emeritus since 1935; dir. chemical research, Universal Oil Products Co. Lieut. gen. Russian Artillery and chmn. Chem. Com. of Russia, 1914-17. Decorated Comdr. Legion d'Honneur (France). Received Berthelot gold medal from French Chem. Soc., 1928, Lavoisier medal, 1939; silver medal from King Boris of Bulgaria, 1939; Palmes d'officier from French Acad. of Sci., 1939; awarded Willard Gibbs medal from Am. Chem. Assn., 1940; title "Modern Pioneer" by Am. Nat. Assn. Mfrs., 1940. Recipient Fawcett honor award for work on aviation gasoline, 1943. Mem. Am. Chem. Soc.; hon. mem. Deutsche Chemische Gesellschaft (Berlin), Acad. of Gottingen (Germany). Club: Chicago Chemist's. Author: Text Book Organic Chemistry, 1903-30; Aluminum Oxide as Catalyst, 1929; Catalytic Reactions, at High Pressures and Temperatures, 1936; The Life of One Chemist (memoirs), 1946; also over 300 articles on high pressure catalytic reactions, 1892-1939; holds more than 200 patents. Founded Leningrad. Inst. of High Pressures, 1927; founded Ipatieff Catalytic High Pressure Lab. at Northwestern Univ., 1940. Home: 195 E. Pearson St. Office: Universal Oil Products Co., 310 S. Michigan Av., Chicago IL

IRONS, ERNEST EDWARD, physician; b. Council Bluffs, Ia., Feb. 17, 1877; s. Edward and Mary J. (Sharp) I.; B.S., U. Chgo., 1900, fellow, 1900-01, Ph.D., 1912; M.D., Rush Med. Coll., 1903; m. Gertrude Thompson, 1908; children—Edwin Newton, Spencer E. Practiced Chgo., 1903—; asst. in pathology and bacteriology, U. Chgo., 1902-04; clin. prof. medicine, emeritus, U. Ill. Med. Sch.; cons. physician Presbyn. Hosp. Mem. Nat. Adv. Health Council; hon. cons. USN. Mem. Assn. Am. Physicians, A.C.P. (pres.), Am. Assn. Pathologists and Bacteriologists, Am. Bd. Internal Medicine, Am. Soc. Bacteriology, A.M.A. (trustee; pres. 1949-50) Ill., Chgo. med. socs., Chgo. Pathol. Soc., Chgo. Soc. Med. History. Clubs: University, Chicago (Chgo.). Home: 5830 Stony Island Av. Office: 122 S. Michigan Blvd., Chgo. Died Jan. 18, 1959.

IRVING, JOHN DUER, mining geologist; b. Madison, Wis., Aug. 18, 1874; s. Roland Duer and Abby Louise (McCulloh) I.; A.B., Columbia University, 1896, A.M., 1898, Ph.D., 1899; hon. A.M., Yale U., 1907); unmarried. Geologic aid, 1899-1900, asst. geologist, 1900-06, geologist, 1906-07, U.S. Geol. Survey; acting prof. mining and geology, U. of Wyo., 1902-03 (while on leave of absence); apptd. asst. prof. geology, 1903, prof. geology, 1906, Lehigh U.; prof. economic geology, Sheffield Scientific Sch. (Yale), 1907—. Geologist for Alaska Syndicate (N. Guggenheim Sons and J. P. Morgan & Co.) summer of 1907. Editor of the journal, Economic Geology. Wrote Economic Resources of the Northern Black Hills, etc. Capt. engr., O.R.C., in active service. Home: New Haven, Conn. Died July 27, 1918.

IRVING, ROLAND DUER, geologist; b. N.Y.C., Apr. 29, 1847; s. Pierre Paris and Anna Henrietta (Duer) I.; attended Columbia, 1863-64; grad. Columbia Sch. Mines, 1869; m. Abby Louise McCulloch, 1872, 1 dau., 2 sons including John Duer. Supt. smelting works, Grenville, N.J., 1879; prof. geology and mineralogy U. Wis., 1870; asst. geologist during geol. survey of 1873-76; sponsored by U.S. Geol. Survey to investigate geology of Lake Superior region, 1880-88. Author: Copper-Bearing Rocks of Lake Superior, 1833. Died May 27, 1888.

IRWIN, KILSHAW MCHENRY, mech. engr.; b. Waukesha, Wis., Sept. 19, 1893; s. Franklin Kilshaw and Mary (McHenry) I.; grad. Phillips Acad., Andover, Mass., 1912; Ph.B., Sheffield Scientific Sch., Yale, 1915; m. Katharine Edgar, May 31, 1919; children—Margaret Edgar, Thomas Kilshaw. Test. engr., B. F. Sturtevant Co., Hyde Park, Mass., 1915-16; mech. engr. United Gas Improvement Co., 1919-31; asst. to vice pres. in charge engring., Phila. Electric Co., 1931-45, mgr. engring. department, 1945-48; vice president in charge engineering, 1948; dir. other cos.; exec. dir. London staff Public Utility Com. of W.P.B., 1944. Served as chief machinists mate, United States Navy, 1918. Mem. United States coms. on steam turbines and Diesel engines. Internat. Electrochem. Conf., Holland, 1935; mem. U.S. nat. com. of World Power Conf., 1955—, chmn., 1958—, def. electric power dir. Area 3, 1958—. Fellow Am. Soc. M.E. (chmn. Phila. sect., 1930-31; chmn. fuels div., 1934-36; chmn. finance com., 1937-39, vice pres., 1939-42), (chmn. A.S.M.E., com. on standardizing steam turbines 1943-52, mem. exec. com., Nuclear Engring. div., 1955). Served chief machinists mate United States Navy 1918-19. Mem. A.I.E.E., Phila. Engrs. Club (pres. 1936-37), Edison Electric Inst. (chmn. gen. com. on interconnection, 1939, chmn. Task Group 2, sub-com. 5, com. 13, on Railway Electrification, 1955), Pa. Electric Assn., Franklin Institute, American Power Conference, National Exposition of Power and Mechanical Engineering, Assn. Edison Illuminating Cos. (chmn. generating com., 1944-46), Com. on Appraisal of Atomic Energy, Pa. Electric. Assn., (chmn. prime movers com., 1923-24), Yale Engring. Assn. (vice president 1942-49), Newcomen Soc., Chi Phi, Tau Beta Pi. Republican. Episcopalian. Clubs: Yale (Phila., N.Y.); Union League, Engineers (Phila., pres. 1936-37, trustee, 1952—); Merion Cricket (Haverford, Pa.). Contbr. to tech. jours. Home: 105 Cambria Court, St. Davids, Pa. Office: 1000 Chestnut St., Phila. 19105. Died Oct. 3, 1960; buried Valley Forge Cemetery, Valley Forge, Pa.

ISAACS, CHARLES APPLEWHITE, mathematician; b. Brownstown, Ind., Apr. 9, 1881; s. William MacKenzie and Martha Adeline (Robertson) I.; B.A., U. of Ind., 1905; M.A., Columbia, 1908; m. Harriett May McRae, Dec. 21, 1910; children—Catherine Mabel, Doris May, Harriett Marea. Instr. mathematics and civ. engring., State Coll. of Wash., 1905-07; asst. in mathematics, Columbia, 1907-09; prof. mathematics, 1909—, State Coll. of Wash. Served as asst. ednl. dir. S.A.T.C. in states of Wash., Ore., Ida., and Mont., Oct. 1-Dec. 31, 1918. Democrat. Mem. Christian (Disciples) Ch. Mason, K.P. Home: Pullman, Wash. Died Aug. 12, 1937.

ISAACS, JOHN DOVE, engineer; b. Richmond, Va., Oct. 6, 1848; s. William Bryan and Julia Lee (Dove) I.; student U. of Va., 1867-70; m. Emily Louise Collins, of Oakland, Cal., Dec. 13, 1881. Draftsman S.P. R.R., 1875-85; asst. supt. bridges and bldgs., 1885-90, acting supt., 1890-91, 2d asst. engr. maintenance of way, 1891-1900, asst. engr., 1900-05, S.P. R.R. Co., Pacific System and lines in Ore., also engr. bridges, Pacific and Atlantic systems of S.P. Co.; consulting engr. U.P. and S.P. systems, Dec. 1, 1905-Feb. 1, 1913; consulting engr. S.P. System since. Mem. Am. Soc. C.E., Am. Ry. Engring. Assn., Engrs. Club (Chicago), Ry. Signal Assn. Clubs: Athenian (Oakland, Cal.), Railroad (New York). Mason. Address: 112 W. Adams St., Chicago.

ISAACS, MOSES LEGIS, professor of chemistry; b. Cincinnati, O., June 3, 1899; s. Abraham and Rachel (Friedman) I.; A.B., U. of Cincinnati, 1920, A.M., 1921; Ph.D., 1923; grad. work Columbia, 1924-26; D.Sc. (hon.), Yeshiva U., 1967; m. Elizabeth Klein, May 2, 1926; children—Philip Klein, Nancy Julie (Mrs. Sidney B. Klein). Asst. in chemistry U. of Cincinnati, 1919-21; instr. sanitary sci. Columbia U., 1926-36, asst. prof., Columbia, 1936-42; prof. chemistry Yeshiva Univ., 1942-67, dean 1942-53. Research worker in disinfection process. Mem. Kasruth Bd. N.Y. State Department of Agriculture, 1934-70, vice chairman, 1934-62. Awarded Merrell fellow by U. of Cincinnati, 1921-24, Nat. Research F. at Columbia, 1924-26. Vice pres. Mordecai Ben David Foundation, Pres. N.Y. City br. S.A.B., 1941, f. A.A.A.S., mem. Harvey Soc., Am. Chemical Soc., Society of American Bacteriologists, Societe de Chimie Biologique of France (life mem.), Phi Beta Kappa. Member of the cultural committee Joint; Distbn. Com.; mem. bd. dirs. Union of Orthodox Jewish Congregations. Rep. Jewish religion. Author chpt. on disinfection Agents of Disease by F.B. Gay (Chas. C. Thomas), 1935. Contbr. articles on chemistry and bacteriology to tech. jours. Research in reconstitution of milk. Home: Northport NY Died Feb. 12, 1970; buried Cedar Park and Beth-El Cemetery, Westwood NJ

ISAACS, RAPHAEL, med. research; b. Cincinnati, O., Aug. 29, 1891; s. Abraham and Rachel (Friedman) I.; A.B., U. of Cincinnati, 1911, A.M., 1912; M.D., U. of Cincinnati Coll. of Medicine, 1918; Marine Biol. Lab., Woods Hole, Mass., 1911 and 1912; Harvard Med. Sch., 1922-23; m. Agnes Wolfstein, Oct. 11, 1923; 1 son, Roger David. Assistant in biology, University of Cincinnati, 1910-11, asst. in zoölogy, 1911-14, asst. in physiology, Coll. of Medicine, 1917-18; resident staff Cincinnati Gen. Hosp., 1918-22; instr. in medicine, U. of Cincinnati Coll. of Medicine, 1920-22; vol. asst. in medicine Peter Bent Brigham Hosp., Boston, 1922-23; instr. in medicine, Harvard Med. Sch., 1923-27; asst. physician, Huntington Memorial Hosp. of Harvard U., 1923-27; hematological consultant Beth Israel Hosp., Boston, 1926-27; asst. physician Boston Dispensary, 1926-27; asst. prof. medicine, U. of Mich., 1927-29, asso. prof., 1929-41; asst. dir. Simpson Memorial Inst. for Medical Research, University of Michigan, 1927-41; attending physician in hematology, Michael Reese Hosp., Chgo., 1940-52, sr. attending physician, 1952—; cons. staff Meml. Hosp. DuPage County; attending physician Weiss Meml. Hosp.; biological stain commn. Adv. bd. Hematol. Research Found., Leukemia Research Found., Leukemia League, Hemophilia Foundation. Served as private Medical Enlisted Res. Corps, 1917-19, 1st lt., 1919-21. Fellow Am. Coll. Phys., A.A.A.S., International Society for Hematology; mem. fgn., nat. and state profl. and scientific socs. Awarded Alvarenga prize, 1925; bronze medal Am. Med. Assn., 1930; Maimonides Citation, Jewish Theol. Sem. of Am., 1944. Secretary United States Pharmacopeia Anti Anemia Products Advisory Board, 1934-42. Jewish religion. Author several books; also chapters in 20 books by others. Contbr. med. jours. Asso. editor Folia Haematologica 1925-40; cons. editor Leukemia Abstracts; sect. editor, Biol. Abstracts; mem. editorial board "Harofe Haivri". Discoverer several medical items; author syndicated column. Home: 5052 Marine Dr., Chgo. 40. Office: 104 S. Michigan Av., Chgo. Died Oct. 1965.

ISELIN, COLUMBUS O'DONNELL, scientist; b. New Rochelle, New York, Sept. 25, 1904; s. Lewis and Marie (de Neufville) I.; A.B., Harvard, 1926, A.M., 1928; D.Sc., Brown U., 1947; m. Eleanor Emmet Lapsley, 1929; children—Eleanor Emmet, Columbus O'Donnell, Marie de Neufville, Victoria David, Thomas Howard. Phys. oceanographer Woods Hole Oceanography Instn., 1932-40, dir., 1940-50, 56-58, senior physical oceanographer, 1950-56, Henry Bryant oceanographer, 1958-70, mem. corp., trustee, 1936-70; professor phys. oceanography Mass. Inst. of Technology, Cambridge, 1959-70, Harvard, 1960-70. Mem. sci. com. ocean research, convenor working group Internat. Indian Ocean Expdn., 1958; mem. subcom. oceanographic research NATO; oceanwide surveys panel NASCO; com. on undersea warfare Nat. Acad. Scis.-NRC. Trustee Bermuda Biol. Sta. for Research, Inc., 1936-70, Marine Biol. Lab., Woods Hole, 1941-52. Recipient Medal for Merit, U.S. Govt., 1948; Henry Bryant Bigelow medal, 1966. Fellow N.Y. Acad. Scis.; mem. Nat. Acad. Scis. (Agassiz medal 1943), Am. Acad. Arts and Letters, Am. Geog. Soc., Am. Geophys. Union, Am. Philos. Soc. Contbr. articles on oceanography to various periodicals. Home: Vineyard Haven MA Died Jan. 5, 1971; buried Lambert's Cove Cemetery, West Tisburg, Martha's Vineyard Island MA

ISELY, FREDERICK B., biologist; born in Fairview, Kan., June 20, 1873; s. C. H. and Elise (Dubach) I.; grad. Hiawatha Acad., 1894; B.S., Fairmount Coll., Wichita, Kan., 1899; M.S., University of Chicago, 1909; Sc.D. (hon.), Trinity University, 1946; m. Mary E. Nickerson, May 8, 1901; children—Marion Frances, Harold Nickerson, Ralph Dubach, Frederick B. Prin. Central Sch., Hiawatha, 1899-1901; teacher biology, high sch., Wichita, 1901-06; State Prep. Sch., Tonkawa, Okla., 1906-12; scientific asst. U.S. Bur. Fisheries, summers, 1910-13; prof. biology, Central Coll., Fayette, Mo., 1912-20; instr. zoölogy, U. of Mo., summers, 1915-17; dean and prof. biology Culver-Stockton Coll., Canton, Mo., 1920-22, Texas Woman's Coll., 1922-31; prof. of biology, Trinity U., since 1931; instr. ecology, Rocky Mountain Biol. Lab., summer, 1932. Fellow A.A.A.S., Entomol. Soc. Amer., Okla. Acad. Science (sec. 1909-12), Tex. Acad. Science (v.p. 1936-37, pres. 1937-38); mem. Am. Soc. Zoölogists, Ecol. Soc. America, N. Tex. Biol. Soc. (pres. 1924-26), Phi Sigma. Presbyterian. Monographs and research papers, concerning fresh water mussels and ecology of orthoptera. Home: 2835 W. Gramercy Pl., San Antonio, Tex. Died Dec. 30, 1947.

ISHAM, ASA BRAINERD, physician; b. Jackson C.H., O., July 12, 1844; s. Chapman and Mary A. I.; ed. schs. of Jackson until 1857; Marietta Coll., 1857-59 (A.M., 1889); M.D., Med. Coll. of Ohio, 1869; m. Mary Hamlin Keyt, of Cincinnati, Oct. 10, 1870. Compositor and asso. editor Lake Superior Journal, Marquette, Mich., 1860-62; city reporter, Detroit Daily Tribune, 1862; enlisted pvt. 7th Mich. Cav., fall, 1862; promoted sergt. Co. I; severely wounded in action nr. Warrenton Junction, Va., May 14, 1863; promoted 1st lt. Mar. 21, 1864; slightly wounded and captured Yellow Tavern, Va., May 11, 1864; prisoner 7 months; paroled for exchange Dec. 11, 1864; hon. discharged on account of wound received in action Apr. 14, 1865; prof. physiology, materia medica and therapeutics, Cincinnati Coll. Medicine and Surgery, 1876-80; trustee Cincinnati Hosp.; pres. bd. med. dirs. Cincinnati Hosp. Ex-pres. Cincinnati Acad. Medicine; mem. A.M.A., Ohio State Med. Assn., G.A.R., 7th Mich. Cav. Assn., Custer's Mich. Cav. Brigade Assn.; comdr. Ohio Commandery Loyal Legion. Author: Prisoners of War and Rebel Prisons, 1890; Historical Sketch of the Seventh Michigan Volunteer Cavalry, 1893. Editor: Sphygmography and Cardiography, by Alonzo T. Keyt, M.D., 1887. Has written a number of papers in Sketches of War History (vols. 1, 2, 4 and 5); also many articles in med. jours. Address: 849 Oak St., Walnut Hills, Cincinnat.

ISHAM, MARY KEYT, (i'sham), neurologist; Cincinnati, O., Aug. 20, 1871; d. Asa Brainerd and Mary Hamlin Keyt Isham; A.B., Wellesley, 1894; M.A., U. of Cincinnati, 1898; work in psychology and physiology, Univ. of Chicago, 1898-99; fellow in philosophy and psychology, Bryn Mawr, 1899-1900; M.D., Laura Memorial Med. Coll. (later absorbed into med. dept. U. of Cincinnati), 1903. Gave first course in psychology ever given at a med. coll., 1901-03; interne Presbyn. Hosp., Cincinnati, 1903-04; gen. practice, Cincinnati, 1904-09; mem. staff Columbus (O.) State Hosp., 1908-15; settled in N.Y. City, 1915; formerly instr. psychiatry N.Y. Post-Grad. Med. Sch. and Hosp., and neurologist Cornell dispensary. Fellow A.M.A., New York Acad. Medicine; mem. Med. Soc. State of N.Y., N.Y. County Med. Soc., Woman's State Med. Soc., Am. Psychiatric Assn., N.Y. Soc. for Clin. Psychiatry, N.Y. Psychoanalytic Soc., Am. Psychoanalytic Assn., etc. Presbyterian. Republican. Clubs: Women's University, Wellesley; Nat. Club of Am. Assn. of Univ. Women (Washington, D.C.). Contbr. numerous tech. articles to med. jours., also articles on med. psychology in New York Times. Author: Cosmos Limited, 1928. Home: 2207 Upland Place, Cincinnati 6, O. Died Sept. 28, 1947.

ISOM, EDWARD WHITTEN, petroleum refining cons.; b. Toledo, O., Oct. 23, 1885; s. William Henry and Nettie (Whitten) I.; E.M., Colo. Sch. of Mines, 1907 (awarded Medal of Merit, 1949); m. Leila Gifford, May 20, 1911 (dec. 1951); children—William Gifford, Mary Elizabeth (Mrs. George Forsyth), Edward Whitten; m. 2d, Lancie Hawkins, Nov. 1951. Mining and constrn. Yukon (Ter.) Gold Co., 1906-11; refinery engr., asst. supt. Cudahy Refining Co., Coffeyville, Kan., 1911-16; asst. to pres. also v.p. in charge petroleum refinery constrn. and operation Sinclair Refining Co., Chgo., 1916-24; v.p. research and devel., also dir.; pres. Sinclair Rubber, Inc.; chmn. Sinclair Research Labs., Inc., Sinclair Chems., Inc., ret., 1955; now cons. in petroleum refining. Mem. Am. Inst. Mining and Metall. Engrs., Soc. Automotive Engrs., Am. Petroleum Inst. Episcopalian. Clubs: University (Chgo.); Scarsdale (N.Y.C.). Inventor or co-inventor, patentee in petroleum refining. Home: R.F.D. 2, Lake Rd., Newport, Vt. Office: Sinclair Refining Co., 600 Fifty Av., N.Y.C. 20. Died Jan. 22, 1962.

ITTNER, MARTIN HILL, (it'ner), chemist; b. Berlin Heights, O., May 2, 1870; s. Conrad Smithman and Sarah Content (Hill) I.; B.Ph., Washington U., 1892, B.Sc., 1894, LL.D., 1938; A.M., Harvard U., 1895, Ph.D., 1896; D.Sc., Colgate U., 1930; m. Emilie A. Younglof, Nov. 20, 1900 (died Dec. 11, 1933); children—Irving Hill, Lois Elizabeth (Mrs. Eldon Bisbee Sullivan); m. 2d, Hildegard Hirsche, July 21, 1934; 1 son, Robert Austen. Became private asst. to Dr. Wolcott Gibbs, Newport, R.I., Nov. 1896; chief chemist Colgate & Co., New York and Jersey City, Dec. 1896-July 1928, Colgate-Palmolive-Peet Co. since July 1, 1928; also served as chem. engr. and dir. of research of both cos. Delegate of U.S. Govt. to First World Chem. Engineering Congress, London, 1936. Received Modern Pioneer award, Nat. Assn. Mfrs., 1940; Perkin medal, Soc. Chem. Industry, 1942. Mem. Am. Inst. Chem. Engrs. (pres. 1936, 37; treas. 1925-35; dir. 1925-40), Am. Chem. Soc. (chmn. nat. com. on industrial alcohol 1920-42; chmn. N.Y. sect. 1925), Soc. Chem. Industry (England), Am. Inst. Chemists, Am. Oil Chemists Soc. Franklin Inst., Assn. Harvard Chemists. Republican. Clubs: Chemists (pres. 1935-36; trustee 1932-39), Harvard (New York); Harvard (N.J.). Holder many U.S. and fgn. patents. Home: Forest Edge Farm, Glendola, N.J. Office: 105 Hudson St., Jersey City, N.J. Died Apr. 22, 1945.

IVES, FREDERIC EUGENE, inventor; b. Litchfield, Conn., Feb. 17, 1856; s. Hubert Leverit and Ellen A. (Beach) I.; ed. pub. schs., Litchfield, Norfolk, Newtown, Conn.; m. Mary Elizabeth Olmstead, June 15, 1879 (died 1904); 1 son, Herbert Eugene; m. 2d, Mrs. Margaret Campbell Cutting, Nov. 15, 1913 (died 1928). In charge of photography laboratory, Cornell U., 1874-78; realized first practically successful process of orthochromatic photography, and invented 1st practically successful process of half-tone photo-engraving, 1878; invented the half-tone photo-engraving process now universally employed, 1886; (inscribed gold testimonial Internat. Photo-Engravers' Assn., 1911; gold medals United Typothetae of America, Printing House Craftsman, Poor Richard Club, 1926); experiments in color photography on the so-called trichromatic principle commenced in 1878, culminating in the three-color printing process in typographic press, now an important industry, and in "Kromskop," "Tripak," "Hicrom" and "1931 Polychrome" processes; and a successful process for moving pictures in natural colors; 70 U.S. patents granted. Awarded Cresson gold medal, Franklin Inst., Philadelphia; spl. gold medal, Photo. Society of Philadelphia, and Progress medal, Royal Photo. Society for work in color photography; Science medal, Royal Photo. Society, London, and Scott Legacy medal, Franklin Inst., for The Parallax Stereogram; Rumford medal, Am. Acad. Arts and Sciences, for inventions in color photography and photo-engraving; and 14 other medals by scientific socs. for various inventions and discoveries. Author: The Autobiography of an Amateur Inventor, 1928. Home: Philadelphia, Pa. Died May 27, 1937.

IVES, HERBERT EUGENE, physicist; b. Phila., Pa., July 31, 1882; s. Frederic Eugene and Mary Elizabeth (Olmstead) I.; B.S., U. of Pa., 1905; Ph.D., Johns Hopkins, 1908; hon. Sc.D., Dartmouth and Yale, 1928, Pa., 1929; m. Mabel Agnes Lorenz, Nov. 14, 1908; children—Ronald Lorenz, Barbara Olmstead (Madame Charles Beyer), Kenneth Holbrook Asso. with Ives Kromskop Company, Phila., 1898-1901; physicist, Bur. of Standards, Washington, 1908-09; physicist, Nat. Electric Lamp Assn., Cleveland, O., 1909-12, United Gas Improvement Co., Phila., 1912-18, Bell Telephone Laboratories, New York, 1919-47. Commissioned capt., Aviation Sect. Signal Corps, Jan. 1918, in charge exptl. work in airplane photography; discharged, 1919, and commd. maj. R.C. Contbg. editor Lightning Journal, New York, 1913-15; asso. editor Jour. of Optical Soc. America. Fellow A.A.A.S. (v.p. Sect. B, 1938), Am. Inst. E.E.; mem. Am. Philos. Soc., Am. Phys. Soc., Optical Soc. Am. (v.p. 1922-23, pres. 1924-25), Am. Astron. Soc., Franklin Inst., Am. Numis. Soc. (pres. 1942-47), Nat. Acad. Sciences, Phys. Soc. of London, Phi Beta Kappa, Sigma Xi; pres. Physics Club of Phila., 1917-18; v.p. Illuminating Engring. Soc., 1911-12; corr. mem. British Illuminating Engring. Soc. Section head, NDRC, 1941-46. Medals from Franklin Inst. for diffraction color photography, artifical daylight and studies of Welsbach mantle; John Scott medal and award, 1927, for electric telephotography and television; medal of the Optical Society for distinguished work in optics, 1937, U.S. Medal for Merit, 1948, Rumford Medal from Am. Acad. Arts and Sci., 1951. Inventor apparatus for testing visual acuity, various photometric instruments, illuminating devices, means for producing artifical daylight, relief pictures, electrical photoengraving apparatus for transmission of pictures over telephone lines; in charge of experimental and development work culminating in first demonstration of television by wire and radio, 1927; developed scientific trichromatic palette for artists' use. De Forest lecturer, Yale, 1928; Lowell lecturer, Boston, 1932; Thomas Young orator Physical Society, London, 1933; Traill-Taylor memorial lecture, Royal Photographic Soc., 1933. Clubs: Cosmos (Washington); Century, (New York). Author: Airplane photography, 1920. Contbr. to scientific journals, Ency. Britannica, etc. Home: 32 Laurel Pl., Montclair, N.J. Died Nov. 13, 1953; buried Litchfield, Conn.

IVES, HOWARD CHAPIN, civil engr.; b. Cheshire, Conn., Mar. 20, 1878; s. Howard C. and Julia (Dunham) I.; Ph.B., Sheffield Scientific Sch. (Yale), 1898; C.E., Yale, 1900; m. Mary B. Young, June 30, 1908. Civ. engr., 1899-1900; instr. in civ. engring., Worcester Poly. Inst., 1900-03; asst. prof. civ. engring., U. of Pa., 1903-06; asst. prof. railroad engineering, 1906-12, prof. 1912-25, Worcester Poly. Inst.; civil and cons. engr. since 1925. Mem. Soc. for Promotion Engring. Edn., Nat. Inst. Social Sciences, Sigma Xi; asso. mem. Am. Soc. C.E. Mason, Odd Fellow. Author: Stereotomy (with A. W. French), 1902; Problems in Surveying, R.R. Surveying and Geodesey (with H. E. Hilts), 1906; Surveying Manual, 2d edit., 1938; Field Engineering (with Wm. H. Searles), 21st edit., 1936; Seven Place Natural Trigonometrical Tables, 1929, rev., 1939; Highway Curves, 3d edit., 1941; Map Drafting and Lettering (with H.R. Saunders), 1931; Natural Trigonometric Functions to Ten Seconds of Arc, 1931, 2d edit., 1942; Mathematical Tables, 2d edit., 1934, rev. edit., 1943. Address: 226 Cliff Drive, Laguna Beach, Calif. Died Oct. 6, 1944.

IVES, JAMES EDMUND, physicist; b. London, Eng., Sept. 19, 1865; s. James Thomas Bostock and Mary Collins (Johns) I.; U. of Pa., 1888-89; Harvard U., 1894; U. of Cambridge, Eng., 1896; Ph.D., Clark U., Mass., 1901; m. Georgiana Luvanne Stone, June 25, 1903; 1 dau., Elizabeth Laura (Mrs. Ives Lowe). Asst. curator, Acad. Natural Sciences, Phila., 1887-93; instr. physics, Drexel Inst., 1893-97; scholar and fellow in physics, Clark U., 1897-1901; instr. physics, U. of Cincinnati, 1901-03; scientific expert with the DeForest Wireless Telegraph Co., New York, 1903-05; asst. prof. physics, 1905-09, asso. prof., 1909-12, U. of Cincinnati; lecturer and research asso. in physics, Clark U., 1912-21; physicist U.S.P.H.S., on duty with the Office of Industrial Hygiene and Sanitation, 1921-31, sr. physicist, 1931-36. Asso. physicist Dept. Terrestrial Magnetism, Carnegie Instn., Washington, June-Aug. 1921. In charge dept. electricity and signals of U.S. Naval Aviation Detachment, Mass. Inst. Tech., 1917; lt., 1918, capt., 1919, Signal Corps, U.S. Army; capt. Signal R.C., U.S. Army, 1921; capt. Auxiliary R.C., U.S.

Army, 1926 and 1931; capt., inactive, 1935. Awarded silver medal, St. Louis Expn., 1904, for work in wireless telegraphy. Episcopalian. Fellow Am. Acad. Arts and Sciences; mem. Acad. Natural Science Phila., Am. Phys. Soc., Illuminating Engring. Soc., Optical Soc. of America, Washington Acad. of Sciences, Philos. Soc. of Washington. Clubs: Cosmos, Chevy Chase (Washington). Author: An Annotated List of Experiments in Physics, 1912; also many papers in scientific journals and reviews. Address: care Cosmos Club, Washington, D.C. Died Jan. 2, 1943.

JACK, JOHN GEORGE, dendrologist; b. Chateaugay, Que., Apr. 15, 1861; s. Robert and Annie Linda (Hayr) J.; m. Cerise Emily Agnes Carman, June 14, 1907 (died Aug. 29, 1935). Lecturer Arnold Arboretum, 1891-1908; lecturer landscape horticulture, Mass. Inst. Tech., 1899-1908; instr. forest botany Harvard, 1903-28, asst. prof. dendrology, 1928-35, asst. prof. emeritus, 1935—. Spl. agent U.S. Geol. Survey in Colo., 1898, U.S. Forest Service in Wyo., 1900; examiner and adviser Mass. Met. Water Bd., 1897-98. Fellow A.A.A.S., Am. Acad. Arts and Sciences; mem. Am. Forestry Assn., Soc. Am. Foresters, Mass. Hort. Soc., Boston Soc. Natural History, N.E. Bot. Club, Bot. Soc. Am., others. Home: East Walpole, Mass. Died May 20, 1949.

JACKMAN, HOWARD HILL, civil engr.; b. E. Liverpool, O., Feb. 9, 1852; s. Stockdale and Narcissa P. (Hill) J.; studied 2 yrs. Alliance (O.) Coll.; C.E., Bethany Coll., W.Va., 1873; married; 3 children. Surveyor at East Liverpool, O., 1873-75; in city engring. dept., Cleveland, O., 1875-77; returned to East Liverpool, practicing as civil and mining engr., 1877-78; surveyor in Harper Co., Kan., 1878; county surveyor Harper Co., 1880; upon engring. force, construction dept., St. Louis, Ft. Scott & Wichita R.R. from Ft. Scott, through Wichita, to line of Indian Ty., 1882-83; city engr. Wichita, suptg. complete sewerage and paving systems, city hall, bridges, parks, etc., 1889-91; engr. on sewer constrn., Topeka, 1891-92; judge of awards, Chicago Expn., 1893; with harbor div., City of Chicago, 1894-95, bur. of engring., 1895-99; in charge of constrn. of 3 miles of 10-ft. water works tunnel and maintenance of the five city water works cribs and of div. of tunnel constrn. and pumping sta. repairs, 1900-01; engr. in charge location trunk line of ry. across the two Virginias, 1901-02; engr. and mgr. of coal mines and properties in the anthracite field of Ark., designing new methods and appliances for operating same, 1903-07; designed a sanitary sewer system of 77 miles for Wichita, Kan., 1908-09; chief engr. Joplin, Okla. & Western R.R., 1908-13; chief engr. Memphis, Ark. & Western R.R., 1913-18; engr. maint. way dept. M.K. & T. R.R., 1918-22; engr.-insp. constrn., "cannon ball" concrete surfaced highway from Wichita, Kan., west 15 mi., 1922; project engr. Mo. State Highway Commn., 1922-24; engr. insp. on constrn. federal aid highway bridges, Jefferson Co., Kan., since Jan. 1926. Home: Muskogee, Okla.

JACKSON, ARNOLD S(TEVENS), physician and surgeon; b. Madison, Wis., Apr. 26, 1893; s. James Albert and Syndonia (Hobbins) J.; A.B., U. Wis., 1916, B.S., 1917; M.D., Columbia, 1919; M.S., U. Minn., 1922; m. Lora Ziesel, Dec. 25, 1917; children—Virginia (Mrs. Jackson Pharich, dec.), Arnold, Joanne (Mrs. Jackson Russell), Eleanor (dec.), Marjorie (dec.). Intern Madison Gen. Hosp., 1919-20; resident Mayo Clinic, Rochester, Minn., 1920-22; staff Meth. Hosp., Madison, 1922—, chief of staff, 1951—; director of the Jackson Clinic, 1952—. Past president of the Four Lakes council Boy Scouts of America. Hon. mem. Golden Key Soc., Univ. Vienna, 1956. Diplomate Am. Board Surgery (founder mem.). Fellow A.C.S.; mem. A.M.A., Wis. State, Dane Co. med. socs., Western Surg. Assn., Am. Goiter Assn. (pres.), Internat. Coll. Surgeons (past president of United States section, vice president, 1956; member jour. editorial board), Wis. Surg. Soc. (pres.), Am. Ry. Surgeons, Am. Geriatrics Socs., Columbia Coll. Phys. and Surg. Alumni Assn., Mayo Clinic Found. Alumni Assn., Wis. Alumni Assn.; hon. mem. surg. socs. of St. Paul, Madrid, Sao Paulo, Rome, U. Bordeaux, Tosco-Umbra, Peru, Hong Kong, Chiba Med. Soc. Japan. Club: Madison (past president). Author: Goiter and Other Diseases of the Thyroid, 1926; The Answer Is—Your Nerves, 1940; also numerous sci. publs. Editor Jackson Clinic Bull.; asso. editor Am. Jour. Surgery. Home: 3515 W. Beltline Hwy., Madison 53713. Office: 30 S. Henry St., Madison, Wis. 53713. Died Aug. 30, 1964; buried Forest Hill Cemetery, Madison, Wis.

JACKSON, CHARLES LORING, chemist; b. Boston, Apr. 4, 1847; s. Patrick Tracy and Susan Mary (Loring) J.; A.B., Harvard, 1867, A.M., 1870; studied Heidelberg and Berlin, 1873-75; unmarried. Asst. in chemistry, 1868-71, asst. prof., 1871-81, prof., 1881-99, Erving prof. chemistry, 1899-1911, prof. emeritus, 1911—, Harvard. Author: Gold Point and Other Strange Stories, 1926. Address: Boston, Mass. Died 1935.

JACKSON, CHARLES THOMAS, geologist; b. Plymouth, Mass., June 21, 1805; s. Charles and Lucy (Cotton) J.; M.D., Harvard, 1829; studied at Sorbonne and École des Mines, Paris, France, 1829; m. Susan Bridge, Feb. 27, 1834, 5 children. Became interested in mineralogy after visiting and collecting mineral specimens in Nova Scotia, circa 1828; travelled through Europe studying geology, mineralogy and meeting leading med. men, 1829-32; practiced medicine, Boston, 1832-36; mem. survey team in Me., Mass., 1837-39; became state geologist of Me., 1837; surveyor of R.I., 1839-40; state geologist, N.H., 1840, surveyor of N.H., 1841-44. Involved in controversy with Samuel F. B. Morse over invention of telegraph, claimed to have made 1st working model, 1840; also claimed to have 1st developed surg. anesthesia, 1846; a U.S. geologist in survey of Lake Superior region, 1847-48; contbr. articles to Am. Jour. of Science, 1828-29. Author: A Manual of Etherization, Containing Directions for the Employment of Ether, Chloroform and other Anaesthetic Agents, 1861. Died Aug. 28, 1880.

JACKSON, CHEVALIER L., laryngologist; b. Pitts., Aug. 1900; s. Chevalier and Allice B. (White) J.; A.B., U. Pa., 1922, M.D., 1926, postgrad. laryngology and broncho-esophagology Grad. Sch. Medicine, 1927-28, M.S., 1930; m. Hilda B. Cowling, 1929; 1 dau., Joan Louise. Intern, Chestnut Hill Hosp., Phila., 1926-27; clin. prof. broncho-esophagology Temple U., 1929-38, prof., 1938-46, prof. laryngology and broncho-esophagology, 1946—; visiting lecturer at the Graduate School of Medicine University of Pa., 1954; prof. honoris causa Facultad de Medicine, Montevideo; hon. mem. faculty biol. and med. scis. U. Chile; mem. adv. bd. on Am. to Am. Hosp. in Paris. Del. 3d Internat. Congress Oto-Rhino-Laryngology and Broncho-esophagology, Berlin, 1936, 2d Pan-Am. Congress Oto-Rhino-Laryngology, Montevideo, 1944, 6th Pan-Am. Congress of Tuberculosis, Havana, 1945, other internat. congresses. Developer technics peroral endoscopy and laryngeal surgery; condr. postgrad. course broncho-esophagology in various fgn. cities. Pres. Phila. Grand Opera Co.; past pres. Internat. House Phila. Awarded Comdr. Order San Martin (Argentina), 1948, Chevalier Legion of Honor (France), 1955. Diplomate Am. Bd. Otolaryngology. Fellow Am. Acad. Ophthalmology and Otolaryngology (v.p. 1943), Am. Laryngol. Assn., Am. Laryngol., Rhinol. and Otol. Soc. (v.p. 1957), Am. Broncho-Esophagol. Assn. (pres. 1950-51), Am. Assn. Thoracic Surgery, A.C.S., Am. Coll. Chest Physicians (pres. 1951-52), Pan-Am. Med. Assn. (sec.), Internat. Broncho-Esophagol. Soc. (founder, exec. sec. 1952—), Coll. Physicians Phila. (chmn. sect. otolaryngology 1959), Phila. Laryngol. Soc. (pres. 1956-57), Laennec Soc. Phila. (pres. 1943-44), Pa. Acad. Ophthal. and Otolaryngol. (pres. 1956-57), Phila. Bronchoscopic Club (pres. 1957-58), World Med. Assn., Soc. Française d'Oto-Rhino-Laryngologie, Soc. deBroncho-Esophagol. et de Gastros. (pres. 1957), Soc. Med. de Photo-Cinematographic Endoscopique, other internat., nat., state and local profl., sci. socs.; mem. Phi Beta Kappa, Sigma Xi., Alpha Mu Pi Omega. Clubs: Union League (Phila.); Racquet, Art Alliance, Franklin Inn, Penn. Editor: Internat. Directory of Otolaryngology. Author numerous articles; contbr. to textbooks. Home: The Springs, Schwenksville R.D. 2, Pa. Office: 3401 N. Broad St., Phila. 19140. Died Jan. 13, 1961; buried West Laurel Hill Cemetery, Phila.

JACKSON, DANIEL DANA, prof. chem. engring.; b. Gloucester, Mass., Aug. 1, 1870; s. Daniel and Lucy Agnes (Langsford) J.; B.S., Mass. Inst. Tech., 1893; student Harvard Graduate School, 1896-97; M.S., New York U., 1908; hon. Sc.D., U. of Pittsburgh, 1924; m. Ella Howard Phillips, Nov. 26, 1902; children—Daniel Dana, Elizabeth Purdy. Began as chemist, Boston (Mass.) Water Works, 1893; biologist, Mass. State Bd. of Health and lecturer Mass. Inst. Tech., 1895-97; chief chemist Brooklyn Water Supply Dept., 1897-1904; dir. labs. New York dept. water supply, gas and electricity, 1904-12; lecturer on sanitary engring. and bateriology, Columbia, 1911-13, asst. prof. chem. engring., 1913-17, asso. prof., 1917-18, prof. and exec. officer, dept. chem. engring., 1918—; v.p. Leavitt-Jackson Engring. Co., 1912-20; tech. mgr. Permitut Co., 1912-17; dir. Chem. Treatment Co. Mem. advisory com. on training camps, office of sec. of war, dean Sch. of Mil. Photography, U.S. Signal Corps, prof. Sch. of Explosives, Ordnance Dept., World War. Mem. advisory com., New York Health Dept. Consultant for cities and companies on water and drainage, factory processes. Home: New York, N.Y. Died Sept. 1, 1941.

JACKSON, DUGALD CALEB, elec. engr.; b. Kennett Square, Pa., Feb. 13, 1865; s. Josiah and Mary Detweiler (Price) J.; B.S. in Civil Engring., Pa. State Coll., 1885, C.E., 1888; grad. study in elec. engring. Cornell U., 1885-87; D.Sc., Columbia U., 1932; hon. D.Eng., Northeastern U., 1938; m. Mabel A. Foss, Sept. 24, 1889; children—Catharine Emma (Mrs. Philip L. Alger), Dugald Caleb. Vice pres., engr. Western Engring. Co., Lincoln, Neb., 1887-89; asst. chief engr. Sprague Electric Ry. and Motor Co., 1889; chief engr. central dist. Edison General Electric Co. 1890; cons. engr. 1891-1931, sr. mem. firm D.C. and Wm. B. Jackson 1902-18, Jackson & Moreland, 1919-30; prof. elec. engring. U. Wis., 1891-1907; prof. elec. engring. and in charge dept. Mass. Inst. Tech., 1907-35, prof. emeritus, 1935-51; lectr. Inst. E.E. of Japan, Iwadare Foundation, 1935; lectured on engring. edn. to univs. in China, 1936. Lt. col. engrs. in France, chief engr. Power Bd., AEF; chief engring. estimates Bd. to Estimate War Damage in Allied Countries, Am. Peace Commn., 1918-19, after disch., in recognition of war accomplishments, promoted to col. Engr. Res. Mem. internat. jury, Chgo. Expn., 1893, Buffalo Expn., 1901. Chmn. Research Com. on Indsl. Illumination, 1926-36; U.S. Govt. del. to World Engring. Congress, Tokyo, 1929; chmn. div. engring. and industrial research NRC, 1930-33; trustee Mass. Inst. Tech. Pension Assn., 1926-35; mem. Engrs. Council for Profl. Development, 1932-38; chmn. Engrs. Joint Com. on Ethics, 1940-50. Decorated Chevalier Legion of Honor (France); personal letter of commendation from Gen. Pershing; recipient Lamme medal of Soc. promotion Engring. Edn. for tech. teaching, 1931; Edison medal of Amer. Inst. E.E., 1938. Fellow Am. Inst. E.E. (pres. 1910-11, hon. mem. 1944), Am. Academy Arts and Sciences (pres. 1937-39), A.A.A.S. (chmn. sect. M. 1932). Am. Phys. Soc., Am. Soc. M.E., (hon. mem. 1945); member Am. Philos. Soc., Am. Soc. C.E., Instn. E.E. (London), Société Française des Electriciens (Paris), Am. Soc. for Engring. Edn. (council 1902-03, 06-46, pres. 1905-06), Am. Inst. Cons. Engrs. (mem. council 1920-23, 1937, pres. 1938-40), Boston Soc. C.E. (pres. 1922-23), Newcomen Soc., Sigma Xi, Tau Beta Pi; hon. mem. Institut Scientifique d'Etudes des Communications and des Transports (Paris); hon. mem. Mass. Inst. Tech. Alumni Association. Author: Text-book on Electro-Magnetism and Construction of Dynamos, 1893; Electricity and Magnetism, a series of lessons, 1895; Alternating Currents and Alternating Current Machinery (joint author, 1896, rewritten and enlarged, 1913; An Elementary Book of Electricity and Magnetism and Their Applications (joint author), 1902, rewritten, 1919; Street Railway Fares, Their Relation to Length of Haul and Cost of Service (joint author), 1917; Engineering's Part in the Development of Civilization, 1939; Present Status and Trends of Engineering Education in the United States, 1939; Present-Day Salaries of Engineering Schools in the United States and Canada (with D. C. Jackson, Jr.), 1947; also about 180 papers on engring. and engring. edn. Patentee fields of electric rotating machinery and transformers, electric motors and instruments, electric motor starting devices, telephone equipment, train lighting. Home: 5 Mercer Circle, Cambridge 38, Mass. Died July 1, 1951.

JACKSON, GEORGE WASHINGTON, engineer; b. Chicago, July 21, 1861; ed. pub. schs. of Chicago and at Oxford, Eng.; m. Rose Tracy Casey, 1883 (died 1913); m. 2d, Pearl Monroe, Dec. 1914. Engaged in engring. and contracting, 1893—; contractor for the Strickler tunnel through Pike's Peak; for 14-foot subway at Reading, Pa.; pneumatic tube system for the Associated Press; Wentworth Av. drainage system, Chicago, and about 90 per cent of the entire underground system for Chicago Telephone Co., Postal-Telegraph Cable Co., and Western Union Telegraph Co.; also systems at Columbus, O., Indianapolis, Ind., Muscatine, Ia., Phila., etc.; engr. and contractor for the entire system of tunnels in Chicago for the Ill. Telephone Constrn. Co.; consulting engr. for the local transportation com. of Chicago in its study of the traction problem, and hydraulic engr. for the high pressure water commn. of the city; constructed sect. 3 of Southwest Land Tunnel for City of Chicago, as well as sect. of Yonkers (N.Y.) Pressure Tunnel, 21 feet in diameter through granite, 2 1/2 miles long, contract price, $2,000,000; was pres. George W. Jackson, Inc. Mason, Elk. Home: Chicago, Ill. Died Feb. 5, 1922.

JACKSON, HERBERT SPENCER, botanist; b. Augusta Center, N.Y., Aug. 29, 1883; A.B., Cornell U., 1905; Ph.D., U. of Wis., 1929; m. Eunice Edythe Doyle, Apr. 22, 1907; children—Kenneth Kendall, Dorothy. Asst. in mycology, Cornell U., 1904-05; asst. mycologist, and instr. botany, Delaware Coll. and Expt. Sta., 1905-08; Austin teaching fellow botany, Harvard, 1908-09; prof. botany and plant pathology, Ore. Agrl. Coll., 1909-15; chief in botany. Puedue U. Agrl. Expt. Sta., 1915-28; agt. Bur. Plant Industry, U.S. Dept. Agr., 1918-28; prof. of mycology, U. of Toronto, since 1929, head dept. of botany since July 1941; instructor botany, Harvard, summer, 1909; prof. plant pathology, Cornell U., summers, 1916, 17. Fellow A.A.A.S., Royal Soc. of Canada (pres. sect. V, 1944); mem. Bot. Soc. Am., Mycol. Soc. Am. (pres. 1934), Am. Phytopathol. Society (pres. Pacific div. 1915), Am. Soc. Naturalists, Can. Phytopathol. Soc., N.E. Bot. Club, Sigma Xi, Gamma Alpha, Phi Sigma. Republican. Presbyterian. Home: 75 Glenview Av., Toronto, Can. Died Dec. 14, 1951.

JACKSON, MERCY RUGGLES BISBE, homeopathic physician; b. Hardwick, Mass., Sept. 17, 1802; d. Constant and Sarah (Green) Ruggles; grad. New Eng. Female Med. Coll., 1860; m. Rev. John Bisbe, June 1823; m. 2d, Capt. Daniel Jackson, 1835; 11 children including Dr. Samuel H. Opened sch. for young ladies after death of 1st husband, Port-physician; b. Hardwick, Mass., Sept. 17, 1802; d. Constant and Sarah (Green) Ruggles; grad. New land, Me., 1832-35; became interested in study of homeopathy, 1848; mem. Am. Inst. Homeopathy, 1871-77; adjunct prof. diseases of children Boston U. Sch. Medicine, 1873-77. Died Dec. 13, 1877.

JACKSON, ROBERT TRACY, paleontologist; b. Dorchester, Mass., July 13, 1861; S. Dr. John Barnard Swett and Emily Jane (Andrews) J.; S.B., Lawrence Scientific Sch. (Harvard), 1884; Sc.D., Harvard, 1889; m. Fanny Esther Roberts, June 27, 1889;

children—Esther, Dorothy Quincy (Mrs. John E. Bastille). Instr. paleontology, Harvard, 1892-99, asst. prof., 1899-1909; asso. in paleontology, Museum of Comparative Zoology, Harvard, 1911-16; curator of fossil echinoderms, Museum of Comparative Zoology, 1928-39. Fellow Am. Acad. Arts and Sciences, A.A.A.S.; mem. Am. Soc. Naturalists, Geol. Soc. America. Author: Phyolgeny of the Pelecypoda, 1890; Studies of Melonites Multiporus (with T. A. Jaggar. Jr.), 1896; Studies of Palaechinoidea, 1896; Localized Stages in Development in Plants and Animals, 1899; Phylogeny of the Echini, 1912; Studies of Arbacia, 1927; Palaeozoic Echini of Belgium, 1929; The Status of Bothriocidaris, 1929. Address: Peterborough, N.H. Died Oct. 24, 1948.

JACKSON, V(ESTUS) T(WIGGS), chemist; b. Sandersville, Ga., Jan. 29, 1889; s. Vestus and Jennie Irene (Beasley) J.; A.B., B.S., Mercer U., 1912; M.S., U. Chgo., 1916, Ph.D. cum laude, 1921; postgrad. work on photochemistry U. Wis., summer 1935; m. Josephine Louise Stenhouse, Sept. 12, 1918; 1 dau., Betty (Mrs. John Stanley Livingstone, Jr.). Asst. in physics Mercer U., 1910-11, asst. in chemistry 1911-12; instr. chemistry Okla. A. and M. Coll., 1912-16; chmn. research Lindsay Light Co., Chgo., 1916-19; 2d rank, chemistry dept. Catholic U. of Am., 1921-22; chem. research Western Electric Co., 1922-23; acting head, dept. chemistry Heidelberg U., Tiffin, O., 1924; asst. prof. chemistry U. Fla., 1924-27, asso. prof. 1927-35, prof., 1935—. Active duty tng., Ft. Benning, summer 1932; instr. chem. warfare, Ft. Bragg, summer 1936; Edgewood Arsenal, 1940; major (inactive) C.W.S., U.S. Army, Res. Officers Assn. Recipient Blalock Science medal (Mercer U.). Mem. Am. Chem. Soc. (past pres. Fla. sect.), Sigma Xi, Gamma Sigma Epsilon, Delta Sigma Phi, Phi Kappa Phi. Democrat. Club: Athenaeum (U. Fla.; past sec. and treas. and pres.). Author numerous articles on chem. subjects. Home: 515 Boulevard, Gainesville, Fla. Died Nov. 25, 1950; buried Oakwoods Cemetery, Chgo.

JACKSON, WILFRID J(AMES), physicist; b. Jacksonville, Nova Scotia, May 11, 1900; s. Capt. William G. L. (master mariner) and Helen E. (Musgrave) J.; student Sydney (N.S., Can.) Acad., 1914-17; B.A., Dalhousie Univ., 1921, A.M., 1923; A.M., Princeton, 1926, Ph.D., 1927; married Mabel E. Mott, June 21, 1932; children—Charles Wilfrid, Marilyn Mott. Came to U.S., 1923, naturalized, 1939. Demonstrator in physics, Dalhousie U., 1921-22; Macgregor teaching fellow, 1922-23; instr. of physics, Princeton U., 1923-25; James W. Queen fellow, physics, 1925-26, research asst., 1926-27; interim lecturer, mathematics, physics, King's Coll., Dalhousie Univ., 1927-28, spl. lecturer, univs. training, summer 1941; instr. physics, Rutgers, 1928-29, asst. prof., 1929-43; associate prof., 1943-46, prof. since 1946, chmn. dept. of physics, Douglass College, Rutgers State U., 1946—; vis. lecturer, Mass. Inst. Tech. ESMDT, 1941-42, radar sch., 1942-44, vis. asso. prof. radar sch., 1944-46; chief scientist N.Y. br. office, Office of Naval Research, 1950. Fellow American Association Advancement Science; mem. Am. Physical Society, American Inst. Physics, Am. Assn. Physics Teachers, Am. Assn. Univ. Profs. (pres. Rutgers chapter, 1946-47), N.B. Science Society, Sigma Xi (president of Rutgers chapter, 1954-55). Rotarian. Clubs: Dalhousie of N.Y.; Red Pine of N.B. (pres. 1948, 49). Contbr. articles in physics jours. Home: 250 Lawrence Av., Highland Park, New Brunswick, N.J. Died Mar. 13, 1959.

JACKSON, WILLIAM, civil engr.; b. Brighton, Mass., Mar. 13, 1848; s. Samuel and Mary (Field) J.; ed. pub. schs. and Mass. Inst. Tech. (non-grad.); m. Mary Stuart MacCorry, Apr. 27, 1886. Rodman, in Boston city engrs. office, 1868; city engr. of Boston, 1885—. Home: Boston, Mass. Died 1910.

JACKSON, WILLIAM BENJAMIN, engineer; b. Kennett Square, Pa., June 23, 1870; s. Prof. Josiah and Mary Detweiler (Price) J.; B.S. in Mech. Engring., Pa. State Coll., 1890, M.E., 1895; m. Isabel Morrison West, Sept. 3, 1903; children—Isabel Morrison, Josiah Kennett, Mary Price, John West. In banking business, Colorado Springs, Colo., 1890-93; in charge Pa. mining exhibit, Chicago Expn., 1893; with United Electric Light & Power Co., New York, then asst. to chief engr. Stanley Electric Mfg. Co., Pittsfield, Mass., 1894-95, and engr. for the Northwest, at Chicago, for same, 1895-96; mgr. Lowell Water & Light Co., and Peninsular Light, Power & Heat Co., Grand Rapids, Mich., 1896-97; chief engr. and gen. supt. N.Y.&S.I. Electric Co., and consulting engr. S.I. Electric Ry. Co., 1897-99; chief engr. and gen. supt. Colo. Electric Power Co., Cripple Creek, Colo., 1899-1901; spl. engr. Stanley Electric Mfg. Co., including services in Eng., Germany, Austria, Hungary and Switzerland, 1901-02; mem. engring. firm of D. C. & Wm. B. Jackson, 1902-18; rate engr. and consultant New York Edison Co. and N.Y. Edison Co., Inc., 1919—. Major U.S. Army, officer in charge of utilities and constructing quartermaster, Camp Merritt, N.J., during 1918; lt. col. Engr. R.C.U.S.A. Fellow Am. Inst. E.E. (mgr. 1912-15; v.p. 1918). Home: Scarsdale, N.Y. Died Jan. 20, 1937.

JACOBS, CHARLES M., civil engr.; b. Hull, Eng., June 8, 1850; married June 1, 1876. First practiced in Eng.; consulting engr. Phila. & Reading Ry. Co., N.Y.&N.E. Ry. Co., L.I. R.R. Co.; chief engr. East River Gas Tunnel; designed tunnel plans for Pa. R.R., connecting Pa. and L.I. rys.; chief engr. N.Y.&N.J. R.R. Co.; in charge of North Tunnel; chief engr. Hudson Cos., etc. Designed complete system of ry. tunnels under Manhattan Island and vicinity, requiring outlay of $50,000,000, 1890; consulting engr. for constrn. of tunnel under River Seine, France, at Paris. Pres. Jacobs & Davies, Inc. Died Sept. 7, 1919.

JACOBS, ELBRIDGE CHURCHILL, univ. prof.; b. Ogunquit, Me., Feb. 15, 1873; s. Benjamin Franklin and Isabella Churchill (Toplis) J.; B.S., Mass. Inst. Tech., 1896; A.M., Columbia U., 1914; m. Mabel Nelson, June 22, 1905 (died July 19, 1913); children—Harold Nelson (dec.), Elbridge Nelson (dec.); m. 2d, Jessie Chapman Noble, Sept. 21, 1918. Asst. instr. mining and metallurgy, Mass. Inst. Tech., 1897-99; instr. analytical chemistry and minerology, U. of Vt., 1899-1901, asst. prof., 1901-03, prof., 1903-24, professor geology and minerology, 1924-44, professor emeritus since July 1, 1944; seismologist, Univ. of Vermont Seismograph Sta.; curator in geology, U. of Vermont Fleming Museum; Vermont state geol., 1933-47; state cons. geol. since 1947. Acting geol. United States Engineer Corps on geology of damsites for Vermont Flood Control, 1929. In charge geog. teaching, U.S. Air Corps Detachment, 1943-44. Fellow Geol. Soc. Am., A.A.A.S.; mem. Am. Assn. U. Profs., Minerol. Soc. America, Seismol. Soc. Am., Geophys. Union, Alpha Tau Omega. Republican. Conglist. Mason. Club: Ethan Allen. Author: Reports of the State Geologist, An Account of Vermont Geology; Geology of the Green Mountains of Northern Vermont; The Great Ice Age in Vermont; The Vermont Geological Survey, 1845-1946; The Physical Features of Vermont, 1948; also various shorter papers on Vt. geology. Home: 146 Williams St., Burlington VT

JACOBS, NATHAN BERND, civil engr.; b. Pittsburgh, Pa., Dec. 18, 1891; s. Benjamin N. and Lottie (Pichel) J.; B.S. in san. engring., U. of Pittsburgh, 1914, San. Engr., 1917; m. Marie F. Oberndorf, Sept. 17, 1918; 1 dau., Emily Nan (Mrs. C. Morton Bachrach, Jr.). Assistant engineer Morris Knowles Incorporated, 1914-17, division engineer, 1917-21, assistant chief engr., 1921-32, pres. and chief engr. since 1932, now also treas. and dir.; mgr. Knowles-Main Appraisal Bureau, Pittsburgh and New York, since 1919; cons. engr. Maurice R. Scharff, N.Y., 1933-41; water cons. Dist. No. 2, Drainage Basin Study, Nat. Resources Planning Board; same, Interstate Commission on Delaware River Basin, 1936-39; consultant for the Office of Fgn. Economics Adminstrn.; consulting engineer Philadelphia Water Works; general manager Lewistown Water authority. Studied development of utilities for houses in Europe for President's (Hoover) Conference on Home Building and Home Ownership, 1931. Mem. bd. Emma Farm Assn. (pres. 1942-46), Maurice and Laura Falk Found. (v.p.), Irene Kauffman Settlement (pres. 1946-53), Ohio Valley Conservation and Flood Control Congress, Federation of Social Agencies, also Pittsburgh Housing Assn., Montefiore Hosp., Federal Jewish Philanthropies of Pitts., Rodef Shalom Temple, Am. Arbitration Assn. (Nat. Panel of Arbitrators), Jewish Welfare Bd. (Midwest sect.). Mem. American Institute Consulting Engineers, Am. Soc. Civil Engineers, Am. Water Works Association, Pa. Water Works Assn. (v.p.), Am. Soc. for Testing Materials, Nat. Soc. Professional Engrs., Am. Public Health Assn., Am. Soc. of Appraisers, Engineers Soc. of Western Pa., Pi Lambda Phi. Mason. Jewish religion. Clubs: Westmoreland Country (Export, Pa.); Civic Club of Allegheny County (pres. 1936-38); Engineers (Phila.); Concordia (Pittsburgh). Writer various tech. articles and speeches. Home: 6329 Bartlett St., Pittsburgh 17. Office: Park Bldg., Pitts. 22. Died Feb. 14, 1956.

JACOBS, WALTER ABRAHAM, chemist; b. N.Y.C., Dec. 24, 1883; s. Charles and Elizabeth (Friedlander) J.; A.B., Columbia, 1904, A.M., 1905; Ph.D., U. Berlin, 1907; m. Laura F. Dreyfoos, Oct. 7, 1908; children—Walter C., Elizabeth R. Stiller. With Rockefeller Inst. Med. Research, 1907—, fellow, 1907-08, asst., 1908-10, asso., 1910-12, asso. mem., 1912-23, mem. 1923-49, emeritus, 1949—. Decorated Order of Leopold II, 1953. Fellow A.A.A.S.; mem. Am. Chem. Soc., Am. Soc. Biol. Chemists, Soc. Exptl. Biology and Medicine, Soc. Pharmacology and Exptl. Therapeutics, Nat. Acad. Scis., Harvey Soc. Contbr. monographs, reports on reseraches in organic chemistry. Home: 2548 Laurel Pass Rd., Los Angeles 90046. Office: Rockefeller Institute, York Av. and 66th St., N.Y.C. 10021. Died July 12, 1967.

JACOBSON, CARL ALFRED, prof. chemistry; b. Grantsburg, Wis., Jan. 25, 1876; s. Carl John and Anna Britta (Asp) J.; B.S., Carleton Coll., 1903, M.S., 1907; Ph.D., Johns Hopkins, 1908; spl. studies in 3 univs. of Europe, 1911, 12; m. Mary Edna Metzger, June 21, 1906; children—Ernest Howard (dec.), Alfred Marcel (dec.), Carl Metzger, John David, Joseph Edward (Marine pilot, killed in World War II), Samuel Odin, Robert Stanley. Fellow and research chemist, Rockefeller Inst. for Med. Research, New York, 1908-09; prof. agrl. chemistry, U. of Nevada, and chief chemist Nev. Agrl. Expt. Station, 1909-18; fellow Johns Hopkins U., 1919-20; prof. chem., W.Va. U., 1920-26; emeritus since 1946. Fellow A.A.A.S., mem. Am. Chem. Soc., Am. Assn. U. Profs., Phi Beta Kappa, Phi Kappa Phi, Phi Lambda Upsilon. Democrat. Methodist. Author: A Pronouncing Chemical Formula Speller and Contest Guide. Editor-in-chief Ency. of Chem. Reactions (vols. I, II, III). Contbr. on elec. conductivity, phosphatides, chlorophylls, alfalfa constituents, enzymes, poisonous principles, oils, saponins, fluosilicic acid, fluosilicates, silica black and silica fluff, chemical spelling, chemical shorthand, etc. Inventor of various lab. apparatus, a calculating machine, and a new method for determining the solubility of solids at different temperatures; granted U.S. patents on processes for treating powdered coal and on 'carburized silica." An organizer of Sealco By-Products Co. of W.Va. (by-products of coal), Bluefield (factory of Greer, W.Va.), 1938. Home: 447 Cedar St., Morgantown WV

JACOBSON, MOSES ABRAHAM, pathologist; b. Portsmouth, Va., 1896; Ph.D. in Bacteriology, U. Chgo., 1927; M.D., Rush Med. Coll., 1932. Rotating intern Mt. Sinai Hosp., Chgo., 1931-32; chief lab. service VA Hosp., Downey, Ill., 1946-63; Instr. bacteriology Purdue U., Lafayette, Ind., 1916-18; asst. prof. bacteriology and clin. pathology Med. Coll. Va., 1921-22; asso. prof. bacteriology and pub. health U. Tenn., 1922-24; extern instr. bacteriology and pub. health U. Chgo., 1924-27. Served to 2d lt. San. Corps, U.S. Army, 1918-19, to capt. M.C., USNR, 1942-46. Diplomate Am. Bd. Pathology. Mem. A.M.A., Am. Pub. Health Assn., Am. Soc. Bacteriology, Am. Soc. Clin. Pathologists. Home: Waukegan IL Died Aug. 1, 1970; buried Chicago IL

JACOBUS, DAVID SCHENCK, (ja-ko-'bus), engineer; b. Ridgefield, N.J., Jan. 20, 1862; s. Nicholas and Sarah Catherine (Carpenter) J.; M.E., Stevens Ins. Tech., 1884 (Dr. Engring., 1906); spl. mech. engring.; m. Laura Dinkel, Apr. 5, 1899; children—David D., Laura C. (Mrs. Fred A. Muschenheim). Instructor, Stevens Institute Technology, 1884-97, prof. experimental mechanics and engring. physics, 1897-1906; adv. engr. The Babcock & Wilcox Co., 1906-41; now ret. Hon. mem. Am. Soc. Mech. Engrs., Boiler Code Com. (chmn. 1940-41); chmn. 1938, 1942 editions of American Welding Soc. Welding Handbook. Awarded Morehead medal by International Acetylene Assn. for year 1935 for leadership in formulation codes and procedures; awarded Miller medal by Am. Welding Soc., 1943; selected a Nat. Modern Pioneer by the Nat. Assn. Mfrs., 1940. Trustee Stevens Inst. Tech. Has written many papers and is an authority in steam engring. Hon. mem. Am. Soc. Mech. Engrs. (pres. 1916-17); mem. Soc. Naval Architects and Marine Engrs., Am. Inst. Mining and Metall. Engrs., Am. Math. Soc., Am. Soc. for Engring. Edn., Am. Inst. Electric Engrs. (life), Am. Soc. for Testing Materials, Am. Soc. Refrigerating Engrs. (life), (pres. 1906-07), Am. Soc. Heating and Ventilating Engrs. (life), Am. Welding Soc. (hon.), pres. 1934-35, Petroleum Inst., American Society for Metals, Franklin Institute, Holland Soc. N. Y., Newcomen Soc. Eng.; fellow A.A.A.S. Club: Engineers, Stevens Metropolitan. Home: 93 Harrison Av., Montclair, N.J. Died Feb. 11, 1955; buried Montclair, N.J.

JACOBY, HAROLD, astronomer; b. New York, Mar. 4, 1865; s. Max and Eve M. (Jackson) J.; A.B., Columbia, 1885, Ph.D., 1895; m. Annie Maclear, Dec. 28, 1890; children—Maclear, Eve (Mrs. Edward Terhune Van de Water). Asst. and instr. geodesy and practical astronomy, Columbia, 1888-92, instr. astronomy, 1892-94, adj. prof., 1894-1904, prof., 1904-30, acting dir. Obs., 1903-06, dir., 1906-30. Asst. astronomer U.S. eclipse expdn. to W. Africa in U.S.S. Pensacola, 1889-90. Civilian instr. navigation Submarine Officers' Material Sch., Pelham Bay Naval Training Sta., 1918. Author: Practical Talks by an Astronomer, 1891; Astronomy, a Popular Handbook, 1913; Navigation, 1917. Home: Westport, Conn. Died 1932.

JACOBY, HENRY SYLVESTER, (ja-ko-'bi), civil engr.; b. Springtown, Pa., Apr. 8, 1857; s. Peter Landis and Barbara (Shelly) J.; ed. Excelsior Normal Inst., Carversville, Pa., and pvt. instr.; C.E., Lehigh U., 1877, E.D., 1941; m. Laura Louise Saylor, May 18, 1880; children—John Vincent, Hurlbut Smith, Freeman Steel. Chief draughtsman U.S. Engr. Office, Memphis, 1879-85; instr. civil engring. Lehigh U., 1886-90; prof. bridge engring Cornell, 1890-1922, ret. Fellow A.A.A.S. (v.p. Sect. D., 1901; hon. mem. Am. Soc. C.E.; mem. Soc. Promotion Engring. Edn. (sec. 1900-02, v.p., 1913-14, pres. 1915-16), Am. Ry. Engring. Assn., Washington Acad. Scis., Religious Edn. Assn., Hist. Soc. Pa., Lehigh County Hist. Soc., Pa.-German Soc., Nat. Geneal. Soc. (pres. 1930-34), Geneal. Soc. Pa., Washington Soc. Engrs. (hon.), Tau Beta Pi, Sigma Xi. Author: Notes and Problems in Descriptive Geometry, 1892; Outlines of Descriptive Geometry (3 parts), 1895-96-97; Textbook on Plain Lettering, 1897; Text-Book on Roofs and Bridges (4 parts), 1890-98 (with Prof. Mansfield Merriman); Structural Details, or Elements of Design in Timber Framing, 1909; Foundations of Bridges and Buildings (with Prof. Roland P. Davis), 1914; Timber Design and Construction (with Prof. Roland P. Davis), 1929; The Jacoby Family Genealogy, 1930; Supplement, 1941; also numerous papers tech. jours. Genealogist of the Jacoby Family. Address: 3000 Tilden St. N.W., Washington 8. Died Aug. 1, 1955.

JACQUES, WILLIAM WHITE, physicist; b. Haverhill, Mass., Aug. 30, 1855; s. John Thurston and Lucy (Withington) J.; S.B., Mass. Inst. Tech., 1876; A.M., Ph.D., Johns Hopkins, 1879; studied Berlin, Leipzig, Vienna, Göttingen, 1877; m. Kate Shakespeare Haman, Nov. 10, 1880; children—Helen Louise (Mrs. John Lawrence Miller), Margaret Howard (Baroness Margaret de Brueggen). Fellow Johns Hopkins, 1876-80; lecturer on elec. engring., Mass. Inst. of Technology, 1887-90; expert for Am. Bell Telephone Co., 1880-97; originator of many of the salient inventions and engring. devices that have made long-distance telephony practicable; expert for numerous elec. and chem. industries in Eng., France and America, 1897-1914, and originator of many processes and mechanisms therein used; expert for anit-submarine div. of British Admiralty during war; originator of device by which submarines were detected and located; engaged in scientific investigations. Home: Boston, Mass. Died June 23, 1932.

JADWIN, EDGAR, army officer; b. Honesdale, Pa., Aug. 7, 1865; s. Hon. C. C. and Charlotte E. (Wood) J.; student Lafayette Coll., Easton, Pa., 1884-86; grad. head of class, U.S. Mil. Acad., 1890; grad. Engr. Sch. of Application, 1893; hon. Dr. Engring., Lafayette, 1925; m. Jean Laubach, Oct. 6, 1891; children—Charlotte (Mrs. Thomas G. Hearn), Cornelius C. (U.S. Cav.). Apptd. add. 2d lt. engrs., June 12, 1890; promoted through grades to lt. col., Oct. 12, 1913; col. N.A., July 6, 1917; brig. gen. (temp.), Dec. 17, 1917-Oct. 31, 1919; col. engrs., Sept. 10, 1919; apptd. asst. to chief of engrs. with rank of brig. gen., 1924, chief of engrs. with rank of major gen., 1926; retired Aug. 7, 1929. In charge improvements, Ellis Island, 1890-91; duty, Office Chief of Engineers, Washington, D.C., 1897-98, Panama Canal, 1907-11, Office Chief of Engrs., Washington, D.C., 1911-16; dist. engr. in various engring. dists.; organized and comd. 15th U.S. Engrs. (Ry.), the first Am. regt. to pass under arms through England, 1917; dir. light rys. and roads, A.E.F., in France, later dir. constrn. and forestry, in charge gen. construction program, working 160,000 men in dredging, building railroads, barracks, hosps., warehouses, roads, lumbering, etc.; mem. Am. Mission to Poland, 1919; observer in Ukraine, 1919; engr. 8th Corps Area, San Antonio, Tex., 1920-22; div. engr. Southeast Div., Charleston, S.C., 1922-24. Served as sr. mem. Am. sect. Joint Engring. Bd. St. Lawrence Waterway Project and as sr. mem. Bd. of Engrs. for Rivers and Harbors; was mem. tech. advisory com. of Federal Oil Conservation Bd., and mem. Am. delegation to Internat. Conf. on Oil Pollution of Navigable Rivers; served as chmn. Nat. Capital Park and Planning Commn.; supervised, 1927, plan which was adopted by congress for control of floods in Mississippi Valley, etc.; appointed 1929, chmn. Interocean Canal Bd. Presbyn. Awarded D.S.M. (U.S.); Companion Order of the Bath (British); Comdr. Legion of Honor (French). Home: Honesdale, Pa. Died Mar. 2, 1931.

JAEGER, ALPHONS OTTO, (ya'ger), chemist; b. Bergzabern, Palatine, Germany, Oct. 14, 1886; s. Philip and Scholastica Adolphine Wilhelmine (Stoecker) J.; student Inst. Tech. of Friedberg (Germany), 1906-07; U. Zurich (Switzerland), 1907; U. Basel (Switzerland), 1911, B.S., M.A., Ph.D., 1913; m. Hedwig Maria Wuermell, Sept. 9, 1920; children—Carl Heinz, Raymond Alphons, Marian Scholastica, Lucia Constancia. Came to U.S. 1923, naturalized, 1929. Research chemist Badische Anilin & Soda Fabrik, Germany, 1914-23; group leader research dept. Nat. Aniline & Chem. Co., Buffalo, 1923-25; cons. chemist, 1925-26; tech. dir. The Selden Co., Bridgeville, Pa., 1926-29, v.p., 1929-34; gen. mgr., research dir. Selden div. Am. Cyanamid & Chem. Corp., 1934-38, chmn. development com. Am. Cyanamid Co., 1938—; mem. new projects and process development coms.; dir. gen. tech. div. Mem. Am. Assn. Textile Chemists and Colorists, Am. Chem. Soc., Am. Soc. for Testing Materials, Internat. Soc. Leather Trades Chemists, Chem. Soc. (Eng.); hon. mem. U.S. Vets. Fgn. Wars (Overbrook Post). Republican. Roman Catholic. Club: Chemists (New York). Awarded numerous patents relating to apparatus and catalysts for Selden and Monsanto contact sulfuric acid processes, and with catalytic processes, apparatus, and catlysts for organic oxidations, oil cracking, catalysts, ammonia and Co oxidation catalysts, etc., dye intermediates and dyes, numerous organic acids, wetting agents and other Textile chemicals, leather and paper chemicals, paint, lacquer, varnishes, terpenes. Talloil etc. Contbr. tech. publs. Home: 1 Spring Rd., Milbrook, Greenwich, Conn. Office: 30 Rokefeller Plaza, N.Y.C. Died July 21, 1953.

JAFFA, MYER EDWARD, chemist; b. Sydney, Australia, Oct. 6, 1857; s. H. S. and Rebecca S. J.; Ph.B., U. of Calif., 1877, M.S., 1896; m. Adele R. Solomons, Mar. 21, 1895; children—Edward Moss, Aileen Raby, Robert Leon (dec.). Asst. chemist, 10th U.S. Census, 1879-80; asst. agrl. dept., U. of Calif., 1880-81; asst. chemist, Northern Transcontinental Survey, 1881-83; 1st asst. and chemist, dept. of viticulture, 1883-89, 1st asst. chemist in charge lab. of agrl. chemistry, 1889-93, instr. agr., 1893-96, asst. prof. agr. in charge lab. of agrl. chemistry, 1896, asst. prof. nutrition, 1906, asso. prof., 1907, prof. nutrition, 1908-25, emeritus, U. of Calif.; chief Bur. Food and Drugs, Calif. State Bd. of Health, 1925—; dir. State Food and Drug Lab., 1908-15. Spl. agt. and food expert, U.S. Dept. Agr., 1900; consulting nutrition expert, Calif. State Bd. Health, 1915—. Jewish religion. Home: Berkeley, Calif. Died June 28, 1931.

JAGGAR, THOMAS AUGUSTUS, (jag'ger), geologist; b. Phila., Jan. 24, 1871; s. Bishop Thomas Augustus and Anna Louisa (Lawrence) J.; Bach. of Arts, Harvard, 1893, A.M., 1894, Ph.D., 1897; D.Sc., Dartmouth Coll., 1938; LL.D., University of Hawaii, 1945; student at Munich Univ., 1894, Heidelberg Univ., 1895; m. Helen Kline, Apr. 15, 1903; children—Kline, Eliza Bowne; m. 2d Isabel P. Maydwell, Sept. 17, 1917. Instr. geology, Harvard U., 1895-1903, asst. prof., 1903-06; prof. geology, Mass. Inst. Tech., 1904-17, head of dept., 1906-12. Asst. geologist U.S. Geol. Survey, 1898-1904, in charge of work in S.D., Ariz. and Mass.; conducted volcano expdns. to Martinique, 1902, Vesuvius, 1906, Aleutian Isls., 1907, Hawaii and Japan, 1909, Costa Rica, 1910, Sakurajima, Japan, 1914, New Zealand, 1920; investigated Tokyo Earthquake, 1923, Alaskan volcanoes, 1927; leader of Nat. Geog. Soc. Pavlof Expdn., 1928; directed Aleutian expeditions 1929, 1931, 1932; geologist of U.S. Naval Obs. Eclipse Expdn. to Niuafoou, Tonga, 1930; established volcano experiment staiton, Hawaii, 1911; volcanologist in charge Hawaiian Volcano Obs., U.S. Weather Bur., 1919-24, U.S. Geol. Survey, 1924-35, chief of sect. of volcanology, 1926-35, with stations in Hawaii, Calif. and Alaska; volcanologist U.S. Nat. Park Service, 1935-40; retired; now research asso. in geophysics, U. of Hawaii. Awarded Burr prize for development amphibian vehicles, Nat. Geog. Soc., 1945. Dir. expeditions through research fellows of Hawiian Volcano Research Assn., in Hawaii, also in Chile, 1929-30. Mem. Royal Soc. earthquake investigation, Montserrat, 1936. Fellow Am. Acad. Arts and Sciences, Washington Acad. Sciences (non-res. v.p., 1918). Author: Volcanology, 1931; Volcanoes Declare War, 1945; Origin and Development of Craters, 1947; Union through the ages, 1948; Steam Blast Volcanic Eruptions, 1949; Abrasion Hardness, 1950; My Experiments with Volcanoes, 1952. Contributor to memoirs of Geological Society of America, reports of U.S. Geological Survey, to scientific jours., reports and bulls. of Hawaiian Volcano Obs.; also editor of "Volcano Letter." Home: 34 Dowsett Av., Honolulu 17, T.H. Died Jan. 17, 1953.

JAKOSKY, JOHN JAY, (ja-kos' ki), cons. engr.; b. Vinita, Okla., Jan. 20, 1896; s. John Lewis and Jennie (Meyerhart) J.; B.S. in M.E., U. of Kan., 1920, M.E., 1926; student Carnegie Inst. of Tech., 1923-24; B.S. in E.E., U. of Pittsburgh, 1925; Sc.D., U. of Ariz., 1933; m. Katharine Fulkerson, Jan. 22, 1923; 1 son, John Jay. Asst. research engr., U.S. Bur. of Mines, 1920-25; with Western Precipitation Co., 1925-27; with Southwestern Engring Co., 1927-29; dir. of research Electroblacks, Inc., 1929-38; pres., tech. dir. since 1945; International Geophysics, Inc., since 1929; pres. Trija Co. since 1945; dir. U. of Kansas Research Foundation, dean Sch. of Engring. and Architecture, U. of Kan., 1940-43; dir. industrial research and asst. to pres., U. of Southern California, 1943-45, chief technical advisor, Kansas Industrial Development Commission, 1940-44; cons. research engr. since 1945; pres. Trija Mfg. Co. of Calif. since 1945; pres. Internat. Geophysics, Inc. President Electrophysics Corporation, 1960—. Registered professional mech., elec. and petroleum engr., Calif. Liaison officer, U.S. Army, 1917-18. Mem. Soc. Promotion of Engring. Edn., American Inst. of Mining Engineers Society of Exploration Geophysicists (v.p. 1945, pres. 1946), A.A.A.S., Am. Assn. Petroleum Geologists, Kan. Engring. Soc. Newport Chamber of Commerce (director), Delta Upsilon, Sigma Xi, Tau Beta Pi, Sigma Tau, Sigma Gamma Epsilon, Theta Tau, Pi Tau Sigma. Clubs: Kansas City Engineers (honorary member); Lawrence Country; University, Petroleum (Los Angeles); Kona Kai (San Diego); Newport Harbor Yacht; Irvine Coast Country. Author: Exploration Geophysics, 1941. Contbr. articles to tech. jours. Home: 1042 W. Bay Av., Newport Beach, Cal. Office: 898 W. 18th St., Costa Mesa, Cal. Died Sept. 8, 1964; buried Pacific View Meml. Park, Newport Beach, Cal.

JAMES, CHARLES TILLINGHAST, engr., senator, inventor; b. West Greenwich, R.I., Sept. 15, 1805; s. Silas and Phebe (Tillinghast) J.; A.M., Brown Coll., 1838; 4 children. Commd. maj. gen. R.I. Militia; supt. Slater Cotton Mills, Providence, R.I.; built early steampowered cotton mills; built Atlantic DeLaine Mill, Olneyville, R.I., 1849; mem. U.S. Senate (Democrat) from R.I., 1851-57, chmn. com. on patents, 34th Congress; perfected rifle-cannon, projectile. Died Sag Harbor, N. Y., Oct. 17, 1862; buried Swan Point Cemetery, Providence.

JAMES, EDWIN WARLEY, civ. engr.; b. Ossining, N.Y., Oct. 17, 1877; s. Edwin Thomas and Alice (Warley) J.; grad. Phillips Exeter (N.H.) Acad., 1897; A.B., cum laude, Harvard, 1901; grad. study Mass. Inst. Tech., 1905-07; m. Ethel Townsend, Mar. 4, 1907; 1 dau., Alice. Dist. engr., Bur. Pub. Works, P.I., 1907-09; mem. U.S. Engr. Corps, 1909-10; chief of Inter-American Regional Office, U.S. Public Roads Administration, 1910-39, technical adviser International Diplomatic Conference on Automobile Circulation, Paris, France, 1926; in charge surveys and construction of Inter-American Highway since 1930, as rep. U.S. Bur. Pub. Roads, Dept. of Commerce; mem. Consejo de Vias de Communicacion, Colombia, S.A., 1929; dir. Franklin Manor Beach Co. Recipient Belgian Foundation award, 6th Internat. Road Congress. U.S. del. Pan-Am. Hwy. Congresses, Chile, 1939, Mexico, 1941, 52; staff mem. on U.S. Brazilian Tech. Commn., 1948. Mem. Am. Soc. Civil Engrs., Am. Assn. State Highway Officials (chmn. com. on standards), Washington Soc. Engrs. Baptist. Clubs: Cosmos (Washington); Columbia Country (Chevy Chase, Md.). Author books. Contbr. about 175 tech. articles. Home: 6412 Beechwood Dr., Chevy Chase 15, MD. Office: Bureau of of Public Roads, Dept. of Commerce, Washington DC

JAMES, GEORGE, physician; b. N.Y.C., Nov. 15, 1915; s. Victor and Lillian (Gilman) J.; A.B., Columbia, 1937; M.D. cum laude, Yale, 1941; M.P.H., Johns Hopkins, 1945; m. Beatrice Lucille Kerner, Dec. 16, 1939; 1 dau., Barbara. Intern pediatrics New Haven Hosp., also asst. pediatrics Yale Sch. Medicine, 1941-42; dir. Obion Lake (Tenn.) Health Dist., 1942-44; mem. staff N.Y. State Dept. Health, 1945-55, regional health dir. liaison with N.Y.C., 1951-52, asst. commnr. program devel. and evaluation, also liaison with N.Y.C., 1952-55; lab. asst. biostatistics Johns Hopkins Sch. Hygiene and Pub. Health, 1946; asst. clin. prof. pub. health practice Yale Sch. Medicine, 1947-52; mem. faculty Albany Med. Coll. of Union U., 1949-55, asso. prof. preventive medicine and pub. health, 1949-55; dir. health Akron, (O.) City Dept. Health, 1955-56; mem. staff N.Y.C. Dept. Health, 1956-65, 1st dept. commnr., 1959-62, commnr. health, chmn. bd. health, 1962-65; adj. asso. prof., then adj. prof. Columbia Sch. Adminstrv. Medicine and Pub. Health, 1956-65; exec. v.p. Mt. Sinai Med. Center, 1965-68, pres. 1968-72, prof. dept. community medicine Mt. Sinai School of Medicine, City U. N.Y., 1965-72, dean, 1965-72; professorial lecturer preventive medicine St. John's Sch. Edn., 1957-63; vis. lectr. Harvard Sch. Pub. Health, 1962-63. Pres. N.Y. State Conf. County, City and Dist. Health Officers, 1961-62; exec. com. Health Research Council N.Y.C. 1962-72; mem. hosp. Rev. and Planning Council So. N.Y. and N.Y. State, 1962-65; bd. mgrs. State Communities Aid Assn.; subcom. Edn. and supply, Nat. Adv. Com. Health Manpower, 1966-67; mem. N.Y.C. Community Mental Health Bd., 1962-65; Nat. Health Council, Greater N.Y. Safety Council, Nat. Council Alcoholism, N.Y. Blood Center; consultant N.Y. State Joint Legislative Com. Problems Pub. Health and Medicare, 1966-72; ad hoc committee narcotic addiction President's Office Sci. and Tech., 1962-63; White House Conf. Narcotic Addiction, 1963; chmn. Pres.'s Nat. Task Force on Health, 1964; Wooldridge com. evaluation program NIH, 1964, chmn. study sect. regional medicare programs, 1966-72; chmn. nat. conf. pub. health training USPHS, 1967; Lasker Journalism Award Com., 1964-66; cons. USPHS, WHO; Sheckman lectr. Soc. Pub. Health Edn., 1962; Crocker lectr. Roosevelt Hosp., N.Y.C., 1964; sec. Health, Edn. &Welfare's Rev. Com. Prescription Drugs. Chmn. bd. Med. Library Center. Recipient Campbell Gold medal Yale School Medicine, 1941; Bronfman award Am. Pub. Health Assn., 1965; Meritorious Service award National Found. Neuromuscular Diseases, 1966; Herman M. Biggs Meml. award, N.Y. Pub. Health Assn. Diplomate Nat. Bd. of Medical Examiners, American Board Preventive Medicine. Fellow Royal Soc. Health, A.M.A., Am. Pub. Health Assn., N.Y. Acad. Sci.; member of N.Y. Acad. Medicine (anniversary discourse 1964), N.Y.C. Pub. Health Assn. (pres. 1961-62), N.Y. Diabetes Assn. (director 1963-67), American Hospital Association, New York State Acad. Preventive Medicine (exec. bd. 1956-62, pres. 1960-61), N.Y. State, N.Y. County med. socs., N.Y. State Epidemiological Soc. (pres. 1948-49), Hosp. Soc. N.Y., A.A.A.S., Am. Coll. Preventive Medicine (v.p. 1964), Asso. Hosp. Service N.Y. (bd. dirs.), Am. Thoracic Soc., Am. Nat. Council Health Edn. (bd. dirs.), Am. Assn. Pub. Health Physicians, Harvey Soc., Nat. Health Council (pres. 1965-66); Nat. Publicity Council (v.p. 1954-55, exec. bd. 1955-58), Assn. Tchrs. Preventive Medicine, Phi Beta Kappa, Alpha Omega Alpha. Clubs: Columbia Club, Yale Club (N.Y.C.). Presbyterian. Author numerous articles in field. Editorial bd. Med. Opinion & Review, Inc., 1965-72; adv. editor Parents mag. Home: Garden City NY Died Mar. 19, 1972.

JAMES, GEORGE OSCAR, mathematician; b. Bowers Hill, Va., Aug. 1, 1873; s. George W. and Augusta C. (Walker) J.; A.B., Johns Hopkins, 1895, scholar, 1895-96, 1897-98, fellow, 1898-99, Ph.D., 1899; unmarried. Instr. in physics, U. of Utah, 1896-97; examiner U.S. Civil Service Commn., 1900-01; instr. mathematics and astronomy, Lehigh U., 1902-03; instr. mathematics and astronomy, 1903-08, asst. prof. astronomy and mathematics, 1908-13, asso. prof. astronomy and mechanics and dean of coll., 1914-17, Thayer prof. applied mathematics and dean, 1918—, Washington U. Author: Elements of Rational Mechanics, 1905. Address: St. Louis, Mo. Died Nov. 24, 1931.

JAMES, JOSEPH HIDY, chemist; b. Jeffersonville, O., Nov. 3, 1868; s. John A. and Mary J. (Hidy) J.; B.S., Buchtel Coll., Akron, O., 1894; post-grad. work chemistry and physics, Columbia, 1897, chemistry, U. of Pa., 1898-99, Ph.D., 1899; m. Edith Mallison, Nov. 28, 1899; children—Mary Alice, Virginia, Josephine.

Asst. chemistry and physics, Buchtel Coll., 1894-97; chief chemist Lake Superior Power Co., Sault Ste. Marie, 1899-1902; asst. prof. textile chemistry, Clemson (S.C.) Coll., 1902-05; asst. prof. tech. chemistry, 1905-06, asst. prof. chem. practice in charge dept. of chemistry, 1906-07, asso. prof., 1907-08, prof. chemistry from 1908 until retired, Carnigie Inst. Tech., Pittsburgh. Research and patents on acetylene storage and on oxidation products of petroleum. Mem. Am. Chem. Soc., Am. Inst. Chem. Engrs. Home: 5868 Douglas Av., Pittsburgh. Died Feb. 12, 1948.

JAMES, THOMAS POTTS, botanist; b. Radnor, Pa., Sept. 1, 1803; s. Dr. Isaac and Henrietta (Potts) J.; m. Isabella Batchelder, 1851. In wholesale drug bus. with brother in Phila. from 1831 for 35 years; prof., examiner Phila. Coll. Pharmacy, many years; moved to Cambridge, Mass., devoted rest of life to study of mosses, 1866; conferred with W.Ph. Schimper, Europe, 1878, compared Am. and Old World species mosses; became recognized as foremost Am. specialist on mosses, began collaboration with Charles Leo Lesquereux on Manual of North American Mosses, died before its completion in 1884; contbr. to sci. mags including Proceedings Acad. of Natural Sciences of Phila.; mem. Am. Philos. Soc., A.A.A.S.; a founder Am. Pomol. Soc. Died Feb. 22, 1882.

JAMES, WILLIAM, psychologist; b. New York, Jan. 11, 1842; s. Rev. Henry J. and Mary R. (Walsh) J.; student Lawrence Scientific Sch. (Harvard), 1861-63; M.D., Harvard, 1869; Ph.D., and Litt.D., Padua, 1893; LL.D., Princeton, 1896, Edinburgh, 1902, Harvard 1903; D.Sc., Oxford, 1908; Litt.D., Durham, 1908; D.Sc., Geneva, 1909; m. Alice H. Gibbens, 1878. Instr. physiology, 1872-76, anatomy, 1873-76, asst. prof. physiology, 1876-80, philosophy, 1880-85, prof. same, 1885-89, prof. psychology, 1889-97, philosophy, 1897-1907, emeritus prof. 1907, Harvard. Gifford lecturer on natural religion, U. of Edinburgh, 1899-1901; Hibbert lecturer on philosophy, Oxford, 1908. Author: Principles of Psychology (2 vols.), 1890; Psychology—Briefer Course, 1892; The Will to Believe, and Other Essays in Popular Philosophy, 1897; Talks to Teachers on Psychology and to Students on Life's Ideals, 1898; Human Immortality—Two Supposed Objections to the Doctrine, 1899; The Varieties of Religious Experiences, 1902; Pragmatism—A New Name for Some Old Ways of Thinking, 1907; A Pluralistic Universe, 1908; The Meaning of Truth, 1909. Address: Cambridge, Mass. Died 1910.

JAMES, WILLIAM STUBBS, engineer; b. Asbury Park, N.J., Sept. 3, 1892; s. Joseph Francis and Sarah (Stubbs) J.; B.S., in M.E., (C.L.) George Washington U., 1917; m. Rose Ramsay, June 26, 1920; children—Patricia Barbara, William Ramsay. Lab. aid to physicist in charge power plant section, Bureau of Standards, heat div., 1911-24; testing engr., Hupp Motor Car Co., Detroit, 1924; asst. technologist, Asso. Oil Co., San Francisco, 1924-26; with Studebaker Corp., South Bend, 1926-45, as research engr., 1926-37, chief engr., 1937-45; research Ford Motor Co., 1945-48; v.p. research and engring. Fram Corp., 1948-55; owner William S. James & Assos. Research, engineering consultant, 1956—; consultant civilian advisory committee Ordnance Department, United States Army, 1958-63. Fellow Am. Phys. Soc. Mem. Am. Soc. Testing Materials, A.S.M.E. Soc. Automotive Engrs. (life mem.), American Society of Lubrication Engineers. Clubs: Bloomfield Open Hunt; Cosmos (Washington); Bloomfield Hills (Mich.) Country. Contbr. articles profl. mags. Home: 4805 N. Adams Rd. Office: Birmingham, Mich. Died Feb. 29, 1964; buried White Chapel, Birmingham, Mich.

JAMESON, HORATIO GATES, physician, educator; b. York, Pa., 1778; s. Dr. David and Elizabeth (Davis) J.; studied medicine under father; M.D., U. Md., 1813; m. Catherine Shevell, Aug. 3, 1797; m. 2d, Hannah (Fearson) Ely, 1852; 7 children. Practiced medicine, Somerset County, Pa., 1795-1810; moved to Balt., 1810; physician to fed. troops, 1812; surgeon Balt. City Jail, 1814-35; cons. physician Balt. Bd. Health, 1821-35; founder Washington Med. Coll., Balt., 1827, obtained univ. charter, built hosp. by 1835, forced to close schs. because of financial difficulties, 1851; prof. surgery Med. Co. of Ohio, Cincinnati, 1835-36; used animal ligature (his most famous contbn. to surgery). Author: Treatise on Epidemic Cholera, 1855; published accounts of his unusual operations in leading med. jours. including Am. Med. Recorder. Died N.Y.C., Aug. 26, 1855; buried Balt.

JAMESON, P. HENRY, physician; b. Marion Co., Ind., Sept. 9, 1848; s. Alexander and Lydia (Thompson) J.; B.S., Northwestern Christian U. (now Butler Coll.), 1869; M.D., Bellevue Hosp. Med. Coll. (New York U.), 1871; m. Gertrude, d Harvey G. Carey, of Indianapolis, Nov. 25, 1873. Was demonstrator chemistry, Ind. Med. Coll.; ex-prof. chemistry, materia-medica and therapeutics, Coll. Phys. and Surg., Indianapolis; prof. chemistry, practice of medicine and clin. medicine, lecturer obstetrics, and diseases of children, and dean of faculty since 1899, Med. Coll. of Ind. Mem. consulting staff of the St. Vincent, Deaconess and City hosps., and of the dispensary of the City of Indianapolis. Devised apparatus for illustrating the phenomena of the total reflection of light, device adopted by Stevens Inst. Tech. and other scientific schs. One of organizers Am. Soc. of Microscopists; mem. A.M.A. Address: 212 Newton Claypool Bldg., Indianapolis, Ind.

JAMISON, ALPHA PIERCE, mechanical engr.; b. Lafayette, Ind., Nov. 27, 1875; s. Albert Ringo and Zelina Matilda (Pierce) J.; B.E.E. Purdue U., 1895, M.E., 1897; m. Clara C. Rogers, Lafayette, Ind., July 10, 1901. Prof. in drawing, Purdue U., since 1896. Jr. mem. of Soc. Mech. Engrs.; mem. Kappa Sigma. Republican. Baptist. Author: Elements of Mechanical Drawing, 1901; Advanced Mechanical Drawing, 1905; Isometric Drawing, 1911. Address: Lafayette IN

JANE, ROBERT STEPHEN, indsl. chemist; b. Cornwall, Eng., Dec. 27, 1898; s. Alfred S. and Katherine (Hoskin) J.; B.A.Sc., U. B.C., Vancouver, 1922; M.Sc., McGill U., 1923, Ph.D., 1925; Wembley scholar U. London, 1925-27; D.Sc., honoris causa, McGIll Univ., 1958; m. Ada Lois Pirie, Aug. 3, 1928; children—Dorothy Katherine, Margaret Frances. Plant chemist, later mem. plant research dept. Canada Carbide Co., Shawinigan Falls, Que., 1927-36 (merged with Shawinigan Chemicals, Ltd., wholly owned subsidiary of Shawinigan Water & Power Co.); research and development dept. Shawinigan Chemicals, Ltd., Montreal, 1936-43, v.p. charge research and development, 1946-54, dir., 1946—, exec. v.p., 1954-56, pres., 1956—; charge indsl. research dept. Shawinigan Water & Power Co., 1943-46, director, 1956—; president, director of the B.A.-Shawinigan, Limited, Montreal, St. Maurice Chemicals, Ltd., Montreal; vice pres., dir. Canadian Resins & Chemicals, Ltd., Montreal; dir. Shawinigan Products Corp. (N.Y.), Shawinigan Resins Corp. (Springfield, Mass.), Gelvatex Coatings Corp. (Anaheim, Cal.), Hedon Chemicals, Ltd. (Hull, Eng.). Dir. YMCA, Montreal. Fellow Chem. Inst. Can. (pres. 1952-53); mem. Soc. Chem. Industry (chmn. Montreal sect. 1941-42), Compressed Gas Mfg. Assn. Home: 6 Holmdale Rd., Hampstead, Que. Office: 600 Dorchester St. W., Montreal, Can. Died 1958.

JANEWAY, EDWARD GAMALIEL, physician; b. in N.J., Aug. 31, 1841; A.B., Rutgers, 1860, A.M., 1863; acting med. cadet U.S. Army Hospital, Newark, N.J., 1862-63; M.D., Coll. Phys. and Surg. (Columbia), 1864, LL.D., 1904. Curator, 1868-72, prof. pathology and practical anatomy, 1872-79; diseases of the mind and nervous system, 1881-86, medicine, 1886-92, Bellevue Hosp. Med. Coll.; prof. medicine, 1898—, dean, 1898-1905, Univ. and Bellevue Hosp. Med. Coll. Has held many hosp. appmts.; health commr. New York, 1875-82. Address: New York, N.Y. Died 1911.

JANEWAY, THEODORE CALDWELL, physician; b. New York, Nov. 2, 1872; s. Edward Gamaliel and Frances Strong (Rogers) J.; Ph.B., Yale, 1892; M.D., Coll. Phys. and Surg. (Columbia), 1895; hon. A.M., Yale, 1912; Sc.D., Washington U., 1915; m. Eleanor C. Alderson, Sept. 27, 1898. Instr., then lecturer on med. diagnosis, New York U., 1898-1906; asso. in medicine, 1907-09; prof. practice of medicine, 1909-14, Coll. Phys. and Surg. (Columbia); prof. medicine Johns Hopkins U. and physician-in-chief Johns Hopkins Hosp., Baltimore, 1914—. Sec. Russell Sage Inst. Pathology, New York, 1907—; mem. editorial bd. Archives of Internal Medicine, 1908—; mem. bd. scientific dirs. Rockefeller Inst. for Med. Research, 1911—. Author: The Clinical Study of Blood-Pressure, 1904. Home: Baltimore, Md. Died Dec. 27, 1917.

JANVRIN, JOSEPH EDWARD, gynecologist; b. Exeter, N.H., Jan. 13, 1839; s. Joseph Adams and Lydia Ann (Colcord) J.; ed. Phillips Exeter Acad.; asst. surgeon 15th N.H. Vols., in Civil War; M.D., Coll. Phys. and Surg. (Columbia), 1864; m. Laura L. LaWall, Sept. 1, 1881. Asst. surgeon Woman's Hosp., State of N.Y., 1872-82; gynecologist, N.Y. Skin and Cancer Hosp., 1883—, also consulting surgeon same. One of founders Internat. Congress Gynecology and Obstetrics, 1893; pres. Am. Gynecol. Soc., 1902-03, N.Y. Obstet. Soc., 1890, 1891, New York County Med. Assn., 1896-97. Address: New York, N.Y. Died Dec. 21, 1911.

JAQUES, WILLIAM HENRY, engineer and naval architect; b. Phila., Dec. 24, 1848; ed. pub. schs., Newark, N.J.; grad. U.S. Naval Acad., 1867; remained in service until 1887; resigned, 1887, to inaugurate mfr. of heavy ordnance and armor at works of Bethlehem Iron Co. Has served as asst. in U.S. Coast and Geod. Survey; mem. and sec. gun foundry bd., sec. senate com. on ordnance and war ships. Introduced into U.S. the fluid compression and hydraulic forging of heavy masses of steel and invented reforging process; was mem. international jury on marine transportation and war material, Chicago Expn., 1893. Organized, and comd. N.J. Naval Reserve, 1895-98. Pres. Hampton (N.H.) Water Works Co. Civil War service medal; mem. Loyal Legion U.S.; decorated Naval Order of the United States, Order of the Rising Sun, Japan. Republican. Mem. bd. visitors U.S. Naval Acad., 1905. Author: The Establishment of Steel Gun Factories in the United States, 1884. Address: Little Boar's Head, N.H. Died Nov. 23, 1916.

JARDINE, JAMES TERTIUS, (jär'dīn), agriculturist; b. Cherry Creek, Oneida County, Ida., Nov. 28, 1881; s. William and Rebecca (Dudley) J.; grad. Utah Agrl. Coll., 1905; studied U. of Chicago, summers 1905, 06; D.Sc. (hon.), Kansas Agrl. Coll., 1935; D.Sc. (hon.), Clemson Agrl. College, 1937; D.Sc. (hon.), Utah Agrl. College, 1946; married Gladys E. Carroon, Aug. 19, 1922; 1 son, James Carroon. Instr. in English, Utah Agrl. Coll., 1905-07; spl. agt. U.S. Forest Service, 1907-08; dept. forest supervisor, 1908-10; insp. grazing, in charge Nat. Forest Range, investigations and range surveys, 1910-20; dir. Ore. Agrl. Expt. Sta., 1920-31; insp. secretary's office, Dept. of Agr., Washington, D.C., June-Aug. 1924, insp. agrl. expt. stas. in Alaska; specialist in research, U.S. Office of Education, Dec.-Feb., 1927-28, and Sept. 1929-Mar. 1930; chief Office of Experiment Stations, U.S. Dept. Agr. 1931-46 (ret) dir. research, Dept. Agr., 1936-41. Special lecturer Yale Univ., 1914-16. Delegate Nat. Agrl. Conf., Jan. 1922. Fellow A.A.A.S.; mem. Washington Acad. Science, Phi Kappa Phi, Sigma Xi, Lambda Chi Alpha, Gamma Sigma Delta. Presbyterian. Club: Cosmos. Home: 4334 P St. N.W., Washington. Died Oct. 24, 1954; buried Logan, Utah.

JARECKY, HERMAN, otologist; b. N.Y. City, June 14, 1863; s. Louis and H. J.; A.B., Coll. City of New York, 1883; M.D., Coll. Phys. and Surg. (Columbia), 1886; m. Lillian A. Amster, of N.Y. City, July 17, 1894; 1 dau., Felice H. (wife of Dr. Henry W. Louria). House surgeon, City Hosp., 1886-87; later asst. surgeon Manhattan Eye, Ear and Throat Hosp.; cons. otologist and laryngologist, Sydenham Hosp. Mem. Am. Acad. Ophthalmology and Oto-Laryngology, A.M.A., N.Y. Acad. Medicine, Med. Society State of N.Y., N.Y. County Med. Sco., Harlem Med. Assn., Alumni Assn. City Hosp. Hebrew. Author of various papers on diseases, operations and treatment of the eye, ear, nose and throat. Address: 120 W. 86th St., New York, N.Y. *

JARRETT, EDWIN SETON, civil engr.; b. Brooklyn, N.Y., Mar. 7, 1862; s. James M. and Sarah Olivia (Heather) J.; C.E., Rensselaer Poly. Inst., 1889; m. Cora Hardy, June 26, 1906; children—Edwin Seton, William Armistead, Olivia Heather. Began, 1889, as engr. with firm of Sooysmith & Co., foundation specialists, New York, continuing until 1900, consulting practice, 1900-02; an organizer, and v.p. The Foundation Co., 1902-14; pres. Jarrett-Chambers Co., 1914-28; cons. engr., 1928-37; exec. v.p., actg. pres. Rensselaer Poly. Inst., 1935-37, retired; trustee Rensselaer Poly. Inst., 1937—; has been connected with design and building of many notable structures throughout U.S., including bridges, docks, retaining walls, dams, etc. Unitarian. Home: Princeton, N.J. Died Dec. 26, 1938.

JARVIS, DEMING, inventor, mfr.; b. probably Boston, circa 1790 (baptized Dec. 9, 1790); s. John and Hannah (Seabury) J.; m. Anna Smith Stutson, 1815, 2 sons, John, James. Bought (with Amos Binney and Daniel Hasting) Boston Crown Glass Co., Cambridge, Mass., 1817, granted charter to manufacture flint and crown glass; constructed exptl. furnace in which he compounded litharge or red lead which enabled co. to compete with English glass cos.; broke with former assos. and organized Boston and Sandwich Glass Co., Sandwich, Mass., 1826, produced apothecary and chem. supplies in addition to glass products, tableware, chandeliers, mantle lamps; reproduced certain shades of English glass by using barytes earth in his mixture; compiled directions for bldg. kilns, 1828; withdrew from former firm and organized Cape Cod Glass Co., Sandwich, 1858. Author: Reminiscences of Glass Making, (pamphlet) 1854. Died Boston, Apr. 15, 1869.

JARVIS, WILLIAM CHAPMAN, physician, laryngologist; b. Fortress Monroe, Va., May 13, 1855; s. Nathan Sturges Jarvis; M.D., U. Mdd., 1875; attended Johns Hopkins. Practiced medicine, N.Y.C., 1877; worked as asst. in Prof. Frank H. Bosworth's Nose and Throat Service, Bellevue Hosp., N.Y.C.; published account of his "Snare" or cold wire eraseur which revolutionized treatment of intranasal tumors, 1881; offered lectureship in laryngology U. City of N.Y. (now N.Y.U.), prof., 1886-93, prof. emeritus, 1893; famous for innovations in diagnosis and treatment of nasal and laryngeal diseases such as use of local anesthetic; contbr. 31 papers to periodical literature on his spl. subjects, 1880-92. Died West Point, N.Y., July 30, 1895.

JAUNCEY, GEORGE ERIC MACDONNELL, (jon'sê), physics; b. Adelaide, Australia, Sept. 21, 1888; s. George and Agnes Binnie (Davis) J.; B.S., U. of Adelaide, Australia, 1910, D.Sc., 1922; M.S., Lehigh U., 1916; m. Ethel Sarah Turner, Jan. 16, 1913; 1 dau., Molly Horsfall. Came to U.S. 1914; asst. prof. physics, Washington U., St. Louis, 1921-24, asso. prof., 1924-30, prof. since 1930. Has made spl. researches in theory of Compton effect in X-rays and diffuse scattering of X-rays by crystals. Fellow American Physical Society, A.A.A.S.; member Sigma Xi, Phi Beta Kappa. Associate editor Physical Review, 1926-28. Author: Modern Physics, 1932 (revised 1937). Co-author: M.K.S. Units, 1940. Contbr. over 90 research papers and articles in scientific publs. on the scattering of X-rays. Home: 7310 Lindell Av., St. Louis, Mo. Died May 19, 1947. *

JEFFERSON, THOMAS, polit. theorist, zoologist, 3d Pres. U. S.; b. "Old Shadwell," Goochland (now Albemarle County), Va., Apr. 13, 1743; s. Peter and Jane (Randolph) J.; attended Coll. William and Mary, 1760-62; studied law under George Wythe; m. Martha

Wayles Skelton, Jan. 1, 1772; 6 children (only Martha and Marie attained maturity). County lt. Albemarle County, 1770, county surveyor, 1773; admitted to bar, 1776; mem. Va. Ho. of Burgesses, 1769-75; mem. com. which created Va. Com. of Correspondence; introduced (with others) resolution for a fast day in Va. in sympathy with Boston Port Bill (resolution resulted in dissolution of Ho. of Burgesses); wrote A Summary View of the Rights of British America, 1774 (not adopted by Va. Ho.); mem. Continental Congress, 1775-76; mem. com. of 5 to draw up Declaration of Independence, personally wrote declaration (with minor changes by John Adams and Benjamin Franklin and by Congress as finally adopted), signed declaration, 1776; mem. Va. Ho. of Dels., 1776-79; gov. Va., 1779-81, struck blow at vested privilege by initiating abolition of primogeniture (achieved in 1785) and entail; originated bill to establish freedom of religion and opinion (passed in 1786); urged public sch. and library system; a resolution calling for inquiry into his mil. conduct as gov. was found groundless by Ho. of Dels. and resolutions of thanks were adopted; went into semi-retirement and finished his scientific work Notes on the State of Virginia (privately printed 1785); again mem. Continental Congress, 1783-84, drafted com. report urging adoption of dollar as unit of money system based on decimal notation, 1784; drafted resolution known as Ordinance of 1784, providing for temporary govt. of western territory; named as commr. to help carry out his formula for negotiating treaties of commerce based on universal reciprocity; succeeded Benjamin Franklin as minister to France, 1785-89; 1st U. S. sec. of state under new constn., 1790-93, chief architect of policy of neutrality; became leader of Anti-Federalist forces (Republicans); resigned, retired to Monticello, 1793; vice pres. U. S., 1796-1801; wrote Ky. Resolutions in answer to Alien and Sedition Acts which grew out of Am.-French trouble of the time, 1798; pres. U. S., 1801-09; his 1st administrn. marked by La. Purchase, 1803; sent Lewis and Clark to explore new territory; his 2d adminstrn. beset with troubles stemming from English-French wars on the Continent; maintained Am. neutrality largely through econ. measures such as Non-Importation Act, 1806, Embargo Act, 1807; forced by econ. distress to ease embargo through Non-Intercourse Act, 1809; retired to Monticello for remainder of his life, 1809; an architect of renown, partly planned City of Washington (D.C.), designed and built Monticello; a prin. founder U. Va., mem. 1st bd. visitors, a rector (1819-26), also conceived univ.'s distinctive architecture and ednl. perspective, personally compiled several thousand titles in all academic fields as basis for its library; pres. Am. Philos. Soc., 1797-1815; maintained scientific interests which led him into studies and writings on paleontology, ethnology, geography and botany; writings include: Manual of Parliamentary Practice, 1801, thereafter used in U. S. Senate. Regarded as 1st great shaper of Am. democracy based on individual liberties, people's capabilities and checks on fed. power; believed the solution to democracy's shortcomings was greater democracy. Died Monticello, Albemarle County, July 4, 1826.

JEFFREY, EDWARD CHARLES, botanist; b. St. Catharines, Ont., May 21, 1866; s. Andrew and Cecilia Mary (Walkingshaw) J.: grad. Collegiate Inst., St. Catharines, 1879; A.B., U. of Toronto, 1888; fellow in biology, same, 1889-92, lecturer in biology, 1892-1902; Ph.D., Harvard, 1898; hon. D.Sc., Univ. Toronto, 1919; hon. LL.D., Acadia U., 1923; m. Jennette Atwater Street, of New York, June 25, 1901; 1 son, Charles Street. Asst. prof. vegetable histology from 1902-07, prof., 1907-33, emeritus prof. botany since 1933, Harvard. Mem. Bot. Soc. America; hon. mem. Bot. Soc. Japan. Author: Anatomy of Woody Plants, 1917; Coal and Civilization, 1925; also many scientific papers. Home: 47 Lakeview Av., Cambridge, Mass.

JEFFREY, WALTER ROLAND, civil engr.; b. Ainsworth, Ia., July 25, 1892; s. William Riley, Jr. and Jessie (Brenhoits) J.; student Willamette U., 1912-16; m. Mildred Keith Honey, June 8, 1918 children—Judith Anne (Mrs. Burr E. Lee, Jr.), John Roland. Resident engr., chief estimating engr. Sinclair Refining Co., 1920-24; mgmt. engr. Bus. Research Corp., Chgo., 1924-28; pvt. cons. mgmt. engr., 1929-39; area mgr. Ill. and Ind., U.S. Bur. Census, 1940; exec. accountiant OPS, Chgo., 1951-53; supervisory auditor 5th Army Area, Army Audit Agy., 1953-56; bus. adviser to comdr., staff and suppliers Hdqrs. Def. Subsistence Supply Center, Chicago, Illinois, 1957-63, consultant, from 1964; president, chmn. bd. Analytical Tabulating Mgmt., Inc., Chgo., from 1928; v.p. Bills Realty, Inc., Chgo., 1946-47. Dir. Army Emergency Relief, Chgo., 1942; soldiers bonus div. Office Ill. Auditor, 1947-48. Served as pvt. Mexican Border, 1916; to capt. U.S. Army, 1917-19, as col., 1941-45, 49-51. Registered profl. engr., Ill. Recipient certificate outstanding performance Mil. Subsistence Supply Agy., 1961. Mem. Am. Assn. Engrs. (pres., sr. mem.), Soc. Am. Mil. Engrs. (charter mil. mem., past pres. Chgo.), Fed. Govt. Accountants Assn. (past pres. Chgo.), Am. Soc. Mil. Comptrollers (pres. Chgo. 1963), Midwest Joint Small Bus Council (chmn. from 1961), Am. Legion, Res. Officers Assn., Mil. Order World Wars, Retired Officers Assn., Assn. U.S. Army. Def. Supply Assn. (v.p., chmn. membership com., recipient meritorious civilian service award 1963). Republican. Methodist. Club: Union League (Chgo.). Home: Chicago IL Died Jan. 19, 1971.

JEFFRIES, JOHN, physician, balloonist; b. Boston, Feb. 5, 1745; s. David and Sarah (Jaffrey) J.; grad. Harvard, 1763; M.D., Marischal Coll., U. Aberdeen (Scotland), 1769; m. Sarah Rhoads, 1770; m. 2d, Hannah Hunt, Sept. 8, 1787; 14 children. Asst. surgeon on Brit. naval vessel, 1771-74; surgeon maj. with Brit. troops, 1775-79; surgeon gen. of forces in N.S.; surgeon gen. Am. forces at Charleston, S.C., 1780; 1st to attempt to gather scientific data of free air; made 2 ascents, one over London, 1784, other over English Channel for scientific purposes, Jan. 7, 1785, balloon voyage successful, flew from Dover to Forest of Guines, Ardes, France, 1st crossing of English Channel by air; made baron of Cinque Ports; gave 1st public lecture on anatomy in New Eng., 1789. Author: Narrative of Two Aerial Voyages, 1786. Died Boston, Sept. 16, 1819.

JEFFRIES, ZAY, metall. engr.; b. Willow Lake, S.D., Apr. 22, 1888; s. Johnston and Florence (Sutton) J.; B.S. in Mining Engring., S.D. State Sch. of Mines, 1910, Metall. Engr., 1914, hon. Dr. of Engring., 1930; D.Sc., Harvard U., 1918; hon. D.Sc., Case Sch. of Applied Science, 1937; hon. D.Sc., Clarkson Coll. of Tech., 1950; m. Frances Schrader, Dec. 27, 1911; children—Elizabeth (dec.), Marian. Instr. metallurgy Case Sch. Applied Sci., 1911-16, asst. prof., 1916-17; consultant Nat. Lamp Works of Gen. Electric Co., 1914-25, incandescent lamp department, 1925-36, technical director lamp department, 1936-45, vice president General Electric, chem. dept. 1945-49, now ret.; dir. research Aluminum Castings Co. and its successor, the Aluminum Mfrs., Inc., 1916-20; consultant Aluminum Co. of America, 1920-36; special lecturer on nonferrous metals, Harvard, 1920; annual lecturer Inst. of Metals (div. of Am. Inst. Mining and Metall. Engrs.), 1924, A.S.M.E., 1925; dir. Berkshire Life Ins. Co. Cons. to metall. lab. Manhattan District; chmn. tech. adv. panel on materials Dept. Defense, 1954-59, now mem. Corp., hon. trustee Case Inst. Tech.; hon. chmn. bd. trustees Battelle Meml. Inst.; dir. Phila. Fund. Decorated Medal for Merit (United States), 1948. Director-general World Metall. Congress, 1951, 57. Awarded Annual Power Metallurgy medal of Stevens Inst. of Tech. (1st recipient), 1945; Francis J. Clamer Silver medal of Franklin Inst., 1945; John Fritz gold medal, 1946. Hon. mem. Cleve. Engring. Soc., Japan Institute of Metals, Am. Inst. Mining and Metall. Engineers (James Douglas medalist 1927), Am. Soc. Metals (Sauvuer award 1935; gold medal, 1943; Distinguished service award 1948; past pres.; hon. mem.), mem. Nat. Academy Sciences; vice chairman War Metallurgy committee, chmn. advisory div. of same com.; chmn. Metals Conservation and Substitution Group of advisory board on metals and minerals, (chmn.), all of Nat. Research Council, Nat. Acad. of Sciences. Fellow American Physical Society, American Institute Elec. Engrs.; mem. A.A.A.S., Am. Philosophical Society, Am. Chemical Soc. Club: Harvard (New York). Author: (with R. S. Archer), The Science of Metals, 1924; The Aluminum Industry (with J. D. Edwards and F. C. Frary), 2 vols., 1930; Business Ideals, Principles and Policies (with T. W. Frech); also chapters in Kent's Mech. Engrs. Handbook, 1923. Home: 280 Holmes Rd. Address: Chemical Dept., General Electric Co., 1 Plastics Av., Pittsfield, Mass. Died May 21, 1965.

JELKS, JOHN LEMUEL, surgeon; b. Bells, Tenn., July 5, 1870; s. Lemuel Marshall (M.D.) and Nannie (Lane) J.; student U. of Ark.; M.D., Memphis Hosp. Med. Coll., 1892; m. Minnie Rollwage, Oct. 14, 1903; m. 2d, Mrs. Louise Whitmire Speegle, Jan. 25, 1940. Practiced, Memphis, since 1893; specializes in enteroproctology; asst. surgeon in chief Sons of Confed. Vets.; comdr. Tenn. Dept., United Confed. Vets. (ex-surgeon). Fellow Am. Proctologic Soc. (ex-pres.), Am. Coll. Surgeons, Nat. Gastro-Enterol. Assn.; mem. A.M.A., Southern Med. Assn., Tenn. Med. Assn., Tenn. Acad. Science, A.A.A.S., Internat. Soc. Gastro-Enterology, Am. Med. Editors and Authors. Democrat. Mem. Christian (Disciples) Ch. Mason (K.T., Shriner). Author of the theory of intestinal parasitic infection as the etiology of pellagra; contbr. chapter on Dysentery in Hirschman's Diseases of the Rectum, Sigmoid and Colon; chapter on intestinal protozoa in man, The Cyclopedia of Medicine. Home: 276 S. Pauline St. Office: Med. Arts Bldg., Memphis, Tenn. Died 1945.

JELLIFFE, SMITH ELY, (jel'if), neurologist; b. New York, Oct. 27, 1866; s. William Munson and Susan E. (Kitchell) J.; A.B., Brooklyn Poly. Inst., 1898; M.D., Coll. Physicians and Surgeons (Columbia), 1889, Ph.D., 1899, A.M., 1900; post-grad. work, Europe, at various times since 1890; m. Helena Dewey Leeming, Dec. 20, 1894; children—Sylvia Canfield, Winifred, Smith Ely, Wm. Leeming (dec.), Helena; m. 2d, Bee Dobson, Dec. 20, 1917. Visiting neurologist, City Hosp., 1903-13; clin. prof. mental diseases, Fordham U., 1907-12; instr. materia medica and therapeutics, 1903-07, prof. pharmacognosy and tech. microscopy, 1897-1907, Coll. of Pharmacy, Columbia; adjunct prof. diseases of the mind and nervous system, Post-Grad. Hosp. and Med. Sch., 1911-17; cons. neurologist, Manhattan State Hosp., Kings. Park Hospital. Editor Med. News, N.Y., 1900-05; asso. editor New York Med. Journal, 1905-09; mng. editor Journal of Nervous and Mental Disease, 1902-45, editor (with Dr. W. A. White) Nervous and Mental Monograph Series, 1907-45, Psychoanalytic Review, 1913-45; now retired. Mem. Am. Neurol. Assn. (pres. 1929-30), N.Y. Neurol. Soc. (pres.). N.Y. Psychiat. Society (pres.), A.M.A., Am. Psychiatric Assn., Am. Psychopathol. Society (pres.), Am. Psychoanalytic Soc. (pres.), Phila. Neurol. Soc., N.Y. Acad. Med.; corr. mem. Neurol. Soc. Paris, Acad. Medicine of Brazil. Clubs; N.Y. Athletic. Author: Essentials of Vegetable Pharmacognosy, 1895; Morphology and Histology of Plants, 1899; also "Nervous Diseases" in Butler's Diagnostics, 1902; Outlines of Pharmacognosy, 1904. Reviser: Butler's Materia Medica, 1902; Shaw on Nervous Diseases, 1903. Editor and Translator: Dubois' Psychoneuroses, 1905; Grasset-Demi Fous, 1907; Payot, Education of Will; Paranoia; the Wassermann Serum Reaction in Psychiatry; Dejerine, Psychoneuroses and Psychotherapy; Rank, Myth of the Birth of the Hero; Eppinger and Hess, Vagotonia; Silberer, Problems of Mysticism and Its Symbolism; W. Hess, Vegetative Nervous System and Psyche; also Hysteria, Tetany, Migraine, in Osler's System of Medicine, etc. Co-editor: Ency. Americana, 1904, 18; (with Dr. W. A. White) Modern Treatment of Nervous and Mental Diseases, 2 vols.; Diseases of the Nervous System, 7 edits.; Technique of Psychoanalysis; Psychoanalysis and the Drama; Respiratory Disorders in Encephalitis; Oculogyric Crises and Encephalitis. Contbr. to medical press. Home: Huletts Landing, Washington County, N.Y. Address: 64 W. 56th St., New York, N.Y. Died Sept. 25, 1945.

JELLINEK, ELVIN M(ORTON), biometrician; b. N.Y.C., Aug. 15, 1890; s. Ervin Marcell and Rose (Jacobsen) J.; student U. Berlin, 1908-11, U. Grenoble, 1911; M.Edn., U. Leipzig, 1914, Sc.D., 1935; m. Thelma Pierce, Oct. 18, 1935; 1 dau., Ruth. Biometric cons., library and field research, 1914-19; biometrician elder plant research, Sierra Leone, West Africa, 1920-25; biometrician, later asst. dir. research, United Fruit Co., Tela, Honduras, 1925-30; chief biometrician, later asso. dir. research, Meml. Found. for Neuro-Endocrine Research, Worcester St. Hosp., 1931-39, dir. study of effects of alcohol, 1939—; asso. prof. applied physiology Yale 1941—, dir. Sch. Alcohol Studies, 1943—; vice-chmn. sci. com. Research Council on Problems of Alcohol, 1941—; chmn. survey com. on tests of intoxication, 1941—, asso. editor Quar. Jour. of Studies on Alcohol, 1941—. Fellow Am. Acad. Arts and Scis., A.A.A.S.; mem. Am. Statis. Assn., Am. Psychopathol. Assn. Author: (with H. W. Haggard) Alcohol Explored, 1942. Editor: The Effect of Alcohol on the Individual, 1942. Contbr. to sci. jours. Home: 205 Livingston St., New Haven. Died Oct. 1963.

JENKINS, CHARLES FRANCIS, physicist, inventor; b. nr. Dayton, O., Aug. 22, 1867; s. Amasa Milton and Mary Ann (Thomas) J.; prep. edn., high sch., Fountain City, Ind., and Spiceland (Ind.) Acad.; student Earlham Coll.; spl. lectures, Johns Hopkins; Sc.D., Earlham Coll., Richmond, Ind., 1928; m. Grace Love, Jan. 30, 1902. Inventor of projecting machine for motion picture theatres, spiral-wound paraffin paper box; granted 400 patents, foreign and domestic, on inventions in radio-photography, television, radio-movies; pres., Jenkins Laboratories; research v.p. Jenkins Television Corp.; dir. Park Savings Bank, Federal-Am. Bank & Trust Co. Medalist, Franklin Inst. and City of Philadelphia. Quaker. Author: Picture Ribbons, 1896; Animated Pictures, 1898; Motion Picture Handbook, 1908; Vision by Radio, Radio Photographs, 1925; Visual Radio and Television, 1928. Home: Washington, D.C. Died June 6, 1934.

JENKINS, DAVID RHYS, prof. elec. engring.; b. nr. Dover, N.J., Sept. 1, 1865; s. John Rhys and Mary (Griffith) J.; student Kan. State Agrl. Coll., 1881-83; B.S., in E.E., U. of Colo., 1904, E.E., 1907; m. Kate Belle Gordon, Aug. 12, 1892; children—Jane May (Mrs. Alfred C. Buck), Gordon Rhys. Teacher common schs. of Kan., 1883-86; editor, pub. newspaper at mining camp, Colo., 1891-96; prin. high sch., Coal Creek, Colo., 1896-1900; instr. in elec. engring., U. of Colo., 1905-08, asst. prof., 1908-19; became prof. elec. engring., Univ. of N.D., now retired. Mem. Am. Inst. E.E., Illuminating Engring. Soc., Inst. Radio Engrs., Soc. for Promotion Engring. Edn., A.A.A.S., Am. Assn. Univ. Profs., N.D. Soc. Engrs., Sigma Xi, Sigma Tau. Republican. Congregationalist. Mason. Club: Lions. Home: McDonald, Kan. Died Sept. 24, 1949; buried Grace Cemetery, McDonald.

JENKINS, EDWARD HOPKINS, chemist; b. Falmouth, Mass., May 31, 1850; s. John and Chloe (Thompson) J.; A.B., Yale, 1872, spl. studies in chemistry, 1872-75; U. of Leipzig, 1875-76; Ph.D., Yale, 1879; m. Elizabeth Elliot Foote, June 18, 1885. Chemist, 1877-1900, vice dir., 1882-1900, dir., 1900-23, treas., 1901-23, Conn. Agrl. Expt. Station. Chmn. State Sewage Commn., 1897-1903. Author of Connecticut Agriculture in History of Connecticut. Home: New Haven, Conn. Died Nov. 7, 1931.

JENKINS, FRANCIS A(RTHUR), educator; b. Nashville, June 2, 1899; s. Thomas A. and Marian (Magill) J.; B.S., U. Chgo., 1922, Ph.D., 1925; Nat. Research Council fellow, Harvard, 1925-27; m. Henrietta Beynon Smith, June 19, 1924; children—Thomas Llewellyn, Frederic Magill, Edward Beynon. Asst. prof. physics N.Y.U., 1927-29; asst. prof.

U. Cal., 1929-31, asso. prof., 1931-37, prof. physics, 1937—, dean, 1950-55; physicist Manhattan Dist. Project, 1941-45. Fellow Am. Phys. Soc.; mem. Optical Soc. Am., Am. Assn. Physics Tchrs., Am. Assn. U. Profs. Author: Fundamentals of Physical Optics (with H. E. White), 1938. Contbr. articles profl. publs. Home: 1476 Greenwood Terrace, Berkeley, Cal. 94708. Died Aug. 3, 1960.

JENKINS, HERBERT F(RANKLIN), publisher; b. Rockland, Mass., Oct. 3, 1873; s. Joseph H. and Emily (Clark) J.; grad. high sch., Rockland, 1891; student Harvard, 1891-93; m. Anne H. Bradford, of Abington, Mass., 1897 (died 1914); m. 2d, Bessie Clark Guptill, of Winthrop, Mass., 1921. Reporter Boston Traveler, 1893-96, Boston Herald, 1897-1901; advertising mgr. Little, Brown & Co., 1901-16, editorial dir., 1916-38, v.p., 1927-38. Republican. Clubs: Republican, Boston City (Boston). Home: 129 Dean Road, Brookline, Mass. Office: 34 Beacon St., Boston MA

JENKINS, HILGER PERRY, surgeon, educator; b. Chgo., Oct. 26, 1902; s. Harry Dodge and Caroline A. (Perry) J.; B.S., U. Chgo., 1923, M.D., 1927; m. Julia Dodge, May 20, 1933; children—Samuel Lincoln, Theodora Neil. Intern Presbyn. Hosp., Chgo., 1926-27; asst. resident surgery Billings Hosp., Chgo., 1927-30, resident, 1930-31; instr. U. Chgo., 1930-33, asst. prof., 1933-38, asso. prof., 1938-46, prof., 1960-68, prof. emeritus, 1968-70; clin. asso. prof. surgery U. Ill. at Chgo., 1947-58, clin. prof. surgery, 1958-60, lectr., until 1970. Recipient McClintock award U. Chgo. Sch. Medicine, 1967. Mem. A.C.S. (chmn. motion picture com. 1951-67, Distinguished Service award 1959), Am., Central (past pres). surg. assns., Chgo. Surg. Soc. (past pres.), Chgo. Med. Soc. (past pres. Jackson Park br.), Soc. U. Surgeons, Internat. Soc. Surgery, Soc. for Surgery Alimentary Tract. Research on absorption of catgut sutures in surgery, sponge (gelfoam) for control hemorrhage. Patentee rear view automobile mirror; producer films for med. edn. Home: Chicago IL Died Jan. 17, 1970; buried Mt. Auburn Cemetery, Cambridge MA

JENKINS, NATHANIEL, inventor, mfr.; b. Boston, June 7, 1812; s. Nathaniel and Mary (Wheeler) J.; m. Mary W Tucker, Oct. 4, 1835, 4 children including Charles, Alfred B. Founder Rice, Jenkins & Co., coppersmith bus. (name changed to Jenkins & Co. 1853), Boston, 1837; later became silversmith and clock maker, Boston; began work on inventing and producing water faucets with renewable rubber packings, 1864; patentee rubber compound that would with-stand both hot water and steam, 1866; inventor Jenkins (steam) valve, circa 1868. Died May 20, 1872.

JENKINS, PERRY WILSON, b. Mt. Carmel, Ind., Apr. 5, 1867; s. Wilson Ragsdale and Susan (Smith) J.; A.B., Miami U., Oxford, O., 1890, A.M., 1891; student Ohio Law Sch., 1891; A.M., Columbia, 1900; fellow in astronomy, U. of Chicago, 1904-05; LL.D. (hon.), University of Wyoming, 1955; m. Eva C. Smith, June 24, 1897; children—Miriam A. (Mrs. Norman W. Barlow), Lois E., Helen V. (Mrs. John S. Kvenild), Ruth E. (Mrs. R. W. Wilson). Professor of mathematics, Tennessee Military Academy, Sweetwater, 1892-93, Amity College, College Springs, Iowa, 1893-96; professor of mathematics and astronomy Simpson Coll., Indianola, Ia., 1896-99; prof. applied mathematics and dir. Underwood Obs., Lawrence U., Appleton, Wis., 1900-04; irrigation engr. since 1905, ranchman, cattle raiser since 1908. Exec. mgr Green River Basin Development Co., Inc. Mem. Pub. Service Commn., World War I. Mem. Wyo. Ho. of Rep., 1919-25, Wyo. State Senate, 1929 (pres.); mem. Com. on Conservation and Adminstration of Pub. Domain (U.S.), 1929-32; pres. Wyo. Reclamation Assn., 1933-40; v.p. Nat. Reclamation Assn., 1933; v.p. Wyo. State Planning and Water Conservation Board, 1939; mem. Colo. River Commn., 1936-40, Named and founded Sublette County, Wyo. Originator of The Producer, nat. livestock mag., 1919. Awarded the Bishop medal "for meritorious public service," Miami U., 1940. Mem. Soc. Am. Engrs., Nat. Econ. League, Am. Nat. Livestock Assn., Nat. St. Lawrence Assn. (regional v.p. since 1946), Colo. River Water Users Assn. (pres. 1946), S.A.R. (pres. Utah soc., 1943), Phi Beta Kappa (life mem. of associates), Delta Kappa Epsilon. Republican. Presbyterian. Mason (32 deg.); mem. Order Eastern Star. Contbr. tech. articles to mags. and newspapers. Home: Cora, Wyo. Office: 40 Virginia St., Salt Lake City 3. Died June 19, 1955; buried Pinedale, Wyo.

JENKINS, WILLIAM DUNBAR, civil engr.; b. Adams County, Miss.; ed. mil. schs., France and Belgium; studied civ. engring., Lexington, Va., 1870-72, engaged in practice. Has done some important bridge work, including Randolph bridge over Mo. River at Kansas City, Mo., etc.; work on Miss. levees; chief engr. of railroads in South and Southwest; chief engr. Aransas Pass harbor and jetty works, Tex.; maj. vol. engrs., and chief engr. officer, 1st Div. 2d Army Corps, 1898-99; chief engr. Chattanooga Station Co. Address: Chattanooga, Tenn. Died Mar. 12, 1914.

JENKS, JOHN WHIPPLE POTTER, zoologist; b. West Boylston, Mass., May 1, 1819; s. Nicholas and Betsey (Potter) J.; grad. Brown U., 1838; m. Sarah Tucker, Oct. 30, 1842. Operated sch., Americus, Ga., 1838-40; pastor Baptist Ch., Washington, Ga., 1840-42; headmaster Peirce Acad., Mass., 1842-71; founder natural history museum Brown U., Providence, R.I., 1871, curator, also prof. zoology, from 1872. Author: Fourteen Weeks in Zoology, 1876. Died Providence, 1895; buried Providence.

JENKS, JOSEPH, inventor; probably born Colnbrook, Eng., 1602; m. Elizabeth, 5 children including Joseph Jenckes. Came to Lynn, Mass. to work in 1st Am. iron works (established by Robert Bridges), 1642; had unusual inventive ability, worked on new and original products to improve the iron works; chosen to cut dies for 1st coins when new mint was erected at Boston; constructed 1st fire engine in Am., 1654; produced new type of scythe (improvement on an old Brit. model), 1655. Died Sangus, Mass., Mar. 1683.

JENNESS, LESLIE GEORGE, chem. engr., exec.; b. Danbury, N.H., Aug. 12, 1898; s. George Burns and Vina (Bean) J.; B.S., N.H. U., 1920; M.S., U. Me., 1924; Ph.D., Columbia, 1930; m. Betty Hooks, June 29, 1926. Tech. dir. Intermetal Corp., 1932-41; div. head Linde Air Products Co., 1941-47; dir. research HumKo Co., 1947-50; asst. to pres. in charge research Kennecott Copper Corp., 1950-51; dir. research 1951-52, v.p., 1952-63; dir. Quebec Iron & Titanium, Quebec, Columbiun Ltd. Civilian with Manhattan dist. AEC, during World War II. Mem. Am. Inst. Mining and Metall. Engrs., Am. Chem. Soc., Inst. Chemists, N.Y. Acad. Scis., Am. Oil Chemists Soc., Sigma Xi, Alpha Chi Sigma. Clubs: Pinnacle Chemists (N.Y.C.). Holder patents. Home: New York City NY Died July 2, 1968.

JENNEY, WILLIAM LE BARON, architect; b. Fairhaven, Mass., Sept. 25, 1832; ed. Phillips Acad., Andover, Harvard Scientific School; grad. Ecole Centrale des Arts et Manufactures, Paris, 1856; studied art and architecture in Paris studios, 1858-59; was capt., U.S. Army, assigned to engr. duty; on staff Gen. U. S. Grant, Cairo to Corinth; on staff Gen. W. T. Sherman, Corinth, until 1866; bvtd. maj., 1864; located in Chicago as architect, 1868; landscape engr. for West Chicago Parks, 1870-71; invented, 1883, and first used in Home Ins. Bldg., 1884, the skeleton construction now generally used for tall bldgs., in honor of which the Bessemer Steam Ship Co., named one of its vessels the W. L. B. Jenney; architect of Union League Club, Siegel & Cooper Bldg., Y.M.C.A. Bldg., New York Life Bldg.; The Fair, and the Horticultural Bldg. at World's Columbian Expn., etc., in Chicago. Address: Chicago, Ill. Died 1907.

JENNINGS, HENNEN, mining engr.; b. Hawesville, Ky., May 6, 1854; s. James R. and Katharine Sharpe (Hennen) J.; C.E., Lawrence Scientific School (Harvard), 1877; hon. M.A., Harvard U., 1918; m. Mary L. Coleman, Oct. 7, 1886. Identified with mining in Calif., 1877-87, in Venezuela, 1887-89; consulting engr. to H. Eckstein & Co., Johannesburg, and to many Transvaal gold mining cos., 1889-98; consulting engr. Wernher, Beit & Co., London, 1898-1905, Convey Placer Mining Co., Mont., U.S. Bur. of Mines. Mem. tech. edn. commrs. in Transvaal, 1902-04; pres. London Inst. Mining and Metallurgy, 1903-04. Home: Washington, D.C. Died Mar. 5, 1920.

JENNINGS, HERBERT SPENCER, naturalist; b. Tonica, Ill., Apr. 8, 1868; s. Dr. George N. and Olive Taft (Jenks) J.; B.S., U. of Mich., 1893; A.M., Harvard, 1895; Ph.D., 1896; studied Jena (Germany), 1896-97, LL.D., Clark University, 1909, University of Pa., 1940, University of California, 1943, S.D., University of Mich., 1918, U. of Pa., 1933, Oberlin Coll., 1933, University of Chicago, 1941; m. Mary Louise Burridge, 1898; 1 son, Burridge; m. 2d, Lulu Plant Jennings, 1939. Assistant professor botany, Texas Agricultural College, 1889-90; professor botany, Montana State Agrl. College, 1897-98; instr. zoölogy, Dartmouth Coll., 1898-99; asst. prof. zoölogy, U. of Mich., 1900-03; asst. prof. zoölogy, U. of Pa., 1903-05; prof. exptl. zoölogy, 1906-10, Henry Walters prof. zoölogy and dir. zoöl. lab., 1910-38, emeritus prof. since 1938, Johns Hopkins Univ.; research associate U. of Calif. at Los Angeles since 1939; visiting prof., Keio University, Tokyo, 1931-32, George Eastman visiting prof. and fellow of Balliol College, Oxford Univ., England, 1935-36; visiting prof. U. of Calif. at Los Angeles, 1939; Terry lecturer Yale, 1933; Vanuxem lecturer, Princeton, 1934; Leidy lecturer, University of Pa., 1940; Patten lecturer, University of Indiana, 1943; hon. fellow, Stanford, 1941. Specialist in research work on physiology of microorganisms, animal behavior, and genetics. Director U.S. Fish Commn. Biol. Survey of the Great Lakes, 1901; trustee Marine Biol. Lab., Woods Hole, Mass.; biometrician, U.S. Food Administration, 1917-18; mem. Nat. Research Council, 1922-25. Asso. editor Jour. of Experimental Zoölogy, of Genetics, and of Biol. Bulletin. Pres. Am. Zoöl. Society, 1908-09, Am. Society Naturalists, 1910-11; fellow Am. Acad. Arts and Sciences, A.A.A.S.; hon. fellow Royal Micros. Soc. Great Britain; mem. Nat. Acad. Sciences, American Philosophical Soc., Philadelphia Academy Natural Sciences; Royal Society of Edinburgh; corr. member of Russian Academy of Science, Société de Biologie de Paris. Author: Anatomy of the Cat (with Jacob Reighard), 1901; Behavior of Lower Organisms, 1906; Life and Death, Heredity and Evolution in Unicellular Organisms, 1919; Prometheus—or Biology and the Advancement of Man, 1925; The Biological Basis of Human Nature, 1930; Genetics of the Protozoa, 1929; The Universe and Life, 1933; Genetics, 1935; Genetic Variations in Relation to Evolution, 1935. Contbr. of numerous papers in zoöl. and physiol. jours. Home: 10531 Wellworth Av., Westwood Village, Los Angeles 24, Calif. Died Apr. 14, 1947.

JENNINGS, O(TTO) E(MERY), biologist; b. Olena, O., Oct. 3, 1877; s. Byron Emery and Jennie Ellen (Cowpe) J.; B.Sc. in Agri., Ohio State U., 1903; Ph.D., U. Pitts., 1911, Sc.D., 1930; LL.D., Waynesburg, 1947; m. Grace Emma Kinzer, June 30, 1906. Florist, 1901-02, in botany dept. Ohio State U., 1902-04; custodian sect. botany, 1904-08, assn. curator sect. botany, 1908, curator of botany, 1915—, also dir. edn., 1929-45; acting dir. Carnegie Mus., Pitts., 1945; dir., 1946-49, emeritus 1950—; lectr. botany, Pitts. and Allegheny Kindergarten Coll., 1910-12; instr. botany Lake Lab. Ohio State U. Sandusky, Ohio, summer 1905, in ecology, 1910, 11; instr. in paleobotany, 1911-12, prof. paleobotany, 1912-13, prof., botany, 1913-35, head dept., 1926-35, prof. biology, 1935-45, also head dept., 1935-45; dir. Lake Lab. 1931-45 U. Pitts. Mem. adv. bd. Allegheny Fed. Forest Expt. Sta., 1932-45; Northeastern Forest Expt. Sta., 1945-47. Fellow A.A.A.S. (gen. sec. 1918); mem. Pa. Forestry (exec. bd. 1942), Bot. Soc. Western Pa. (pres. 1936—), Pa. Acad. Sci. (pres. 1924-25), Ohio Acad. Sci., Pitts. Acad. Sci. and Art (pres. 1934—), Am. Feorn Soc., Am. Bryological Soc., Sigma Xi, Townshend chpt. Alpha Zeta, Assn. Am. Geographers, Bot. Soc. Am.; hon. mem. Garden Club Allegheny County. Club: Authors' of Pittsburgh (pres.). Unitarian. Editor: Bryologist, 1913-37. Author: Manual of Mosses of Western Pennsylvania (rev. edit., 1951); Wildflowers of Western Pennsylvania and the Upper Ohio Basin, 1953; also various sci. articles in Annals Carnegie Mus. and various periodicals. Address: 241 Oakland Av., Pitts. Died Jan. 29, 1964; buried Columbarium, Homewood Cemetery, Pitts. 15218.

JENNINGS, SIDNEY JOHNSTON, mining engr.; b. Hawesville, Ky., Aug. 13, 1863; s. James Rody and Katherine Sharp (Hennen) J.; early edn. Tours, France, and in Germany; C.E., Lawrence Scientific Sch. (Harvard), 1885; post-grad. course, U. of Calif.; m. Amy Florence (Horne) Valpy, Aug. 18, 1893; children—John Morris, Amy Sidney, Mary Agnes, Philip Hennen. Surveyor, New Alameda Quicksilver Mining Co., Calif., 1885-87, Anaconda Copper Co., Butte, Mont., 1887-89; mgr. Willow Copper Co., S. Africa, 1889-90; asst. gen. mgr. De Beers Consol. Mines, Kimberley, 1891-93; mgr. Crown Deep Mine, Ltd., Johannesburg, 1893-96; mgr. Crown Mines and consulting engr. H. Eckstein & Co., 1896-1907; v.p. U.S. Smelting, Refining & Mining Co., 1908—; dir. Cia de Real del Monte y Pachuca; pres. Hanover Bessemer Iron & Copper Co. Was chmn. works com. of Town Council, Johannesburg, after occupation of the city by the British, providing the city with electric trolley lines, adequate water supply and underground sewers. Pres. American Mining Congress, 1922-23. Democrat. Episcopalian. Home: New York, N.Y. Died Nov. 17, 1928.

JENNINGS, WALTER LOUIS, chemist; b. Bangor, Me., Nov. 15, 1866; s. Stephen and Ellen Giddings (Ingalls) J.; A.B., Harvard, 1889, A.M., 1890, Ph.D., 1892; m. Alice Emily Page, July 24, 1897; children—Ruth, Frances, Alice. Asst. instr. organic chemistry, 1889-90, qualitative analysis, 1890-92, Parker fellow, 1893-94, Harvard U.; asst. prof. of chemistry, 1894-1900, prof. organic chemistry, 1900-37, dir. dept. of chemistry, 1911-37, since emeritus Worcester Poly. Inst. Fellow Am. Acad. Arts and Sciences, A.A.A.S.; mem. Am. Chem. Soc., German Chem. Soc. Mem. Mass. Medico-Legal Society, Harvard Musical Assn. Mem. Worcester Med. Milk Commn. Clubs: Bohemian, Cosmopolitan, Sigma Xi, Worcester Tennis, Worcester, Harvard, Longwood Cricket. Contbr. to scientific mags. Home: 8-A Chauncy St., Cambridge 38, Mass. Died Sep. 2, 1944.

JENSEN, JOHN CHRISTIAN, educator; b. Utica, Neb., Oct. 19, 1880; s. Frantz Peter and Ellen (Jensen) J.; B.Sc., Neb. Wesleyan U., 1909; A.M., U. Neb., 1916, Ph.D., 1939; student U. Ia., summer 1916, U. Chgo., summer, 1921; m. Susan E. Allington, Aug. 25, 1909 (died Dec. 26, 1918); children—Robert Roderick, Margaret Ruth; m. 2d, Emma Wilhelmsen, Aug. 22, 1922. Instr. physics, Neb. Wesleyan U., 1907-09. prof., 1909-52, prof. physics and astronomy, 1939—, dean men, 1934-36, 38-46; prin. Acad. Neb. Wesleyan U., 1939-43; vis. prof. Cornell Coll., 1952-53, Doane Coll., 1955-56. Registered profl. engr. Chief radio instr. War Tng. Unit, U. Neb., 1918; coordinator Civil Aeros. Adminstrn., Neb. Wesleyan U., 1939-43; research cons. Curtiss-Wright Corp., 1943-45. Fellow A.A.A.S., Inst. Radio Engrs. (rep. council A.A.A.S.), Am. Phys. Soc.; mem. Am. Geophysical Union, Am. Meteorol. Soc., Neb. Acad. Sci. (twice pres.), Inst. Radio Engrs., Am. Assn. U. Profs., Am. Optical Soc., Am. Interprofl. Inst., Sigma Xi, Sigma Pi Sigma, Phi Kappa Phi. Republican. Methodist. Has published research reports on relation of weather to radio reception, polarity of thunderclouds, ball lightning, and precipitation from local thunderstorms. Home: 4926 Leighton Av., Lincoln, Neb. Died Oct. 19, 1957; buried Wyuka Cemetery, Lincoln.

JEPSON, IVAR PER, engr., mfg. exec.; b. Onnestad, Sweden, Nov. 2, 1903; s. Per and Maria (Lundgren) Jeppsson; M.E., Hassleholme Tekniska Skola, Sweden, 1922; student U. Berlin (Germany); m. Lillian Borgman, Dec. 21, 1929; children—Brit Marie, Bert. Came to U.S., 1925, naturalized, 1935. Practiced with Swedish, German companies, 1922-24; with Sunbeam Corp. (formerly Chgo. Flexible Shaft Co.), Chgo., 1925-64, beginning as draftsman, successively tool designer, product designer, development engr., mgr. development and research, 1925-52, v.p. charge product design, development and research, 1952-64. Served with Swedish Air Force, 1924-25. Mem. Swedish Engrs. Soc. Chgo. Clubs: Swedish (Chgo.); Oak Park (Ill.) Country. Patentee in field. Home: Oak Park IL Died Nov. 1968.

JERVIS, JOHN BLOOMFIELD, engr.; b. Huntington, N.Y., Dec. 14, 1795; s. Timothy and Phoebe (Bloomfield) J.; LL.D. (hon.), Hamilton Coll., Clinton, N.Y., 1878; m. Cynthia Brayton, 1834; m. 2d, Elizabeth Coates. Axeman and rodman on survey for Erie Canal under Benjamin Wright, in charge of constrn. 17 miles of canal, 1819, became supt. in charge of flow of traffic on 50 miles of completed canal, 1823; prin. asst. to Wright on Del. and Hudson Canal, 1825, became chief engr., 1827; became chief engr. Mohawk and Boston R.R., 1830; designed swivel truck which enabled locomotives to travel 60-80 miles per hour, 1832; chief engr. Schenectady & Saratoga R.R.; became chief engr. Chenango Canal, N.Y., 1833; chief engr. eastern half Erie Canal, 1836; became chief engr. Croton Aqueduct, N.Y., 1836, directed completion of dam, Ossining and Harlem River bridges; engr. in charge of new source of water supply for City of Boston, 1846-48; chief engr. for various railroads and canals, 1866 until retirement. Author: Description of the Croton Aqueduct, 1842; Railroad Property: A Treatise on the Construction and Management of Railroads, 1861; The Question of Labour and Capital, 1877. Died Rome, N.Y., Jan. 12, 1885.

JESSUP, JOSEPH JOHN, civil engr.; b. New Providence, Ia., Dec. 18, 1856; s. Elias and Mary Jane (Morris) J.; grad. New Providence Acad., 1886; B.S., Penn Coll., Oskaloosa, Ia., 1891, M.S., 1892; post grad., U. Cal., 1900-02; m. Melissa Hammar, Aug. 23, 1892; children—Mildred, John Herschel, Mary Helen. Prof. mathematics and sci., Pacific Coll., Ore., 1891-96; pres. Whittier (Cal.) Coll., 1896-1900; instr. U. Cal., 1900-03; dep. city engr., Berkeley, 1903-08, city engr., 1908-18, cons. engr., 1918-30; city engr., Los Angeles, 1930-34; cons. civil and mining engr., 1934-57. Mem. (life) Am. Soc. C.E., Am. Assn. Engrs. and Architects. Republican. Mem. Soc. Friends. Home: 1977 N. New Hampshire Av., Los Angeles. Died Oct. 27, 1957.

JETT, EWELL KIRK, radio engr.; b. Balt., Mar. 20, 1893; s. John Covington and Elizabeth Woodrow (Bangs) J.; student grade and high schs. and U.S. Naval schs.; m. L. Viola Ward, Dec. 15, 1915; children—Geraldine Viola (Mrs. Joseph Burk), Frances Elizabeth (Mrs. John E. Boothe, Jr.). Served in USN, 1911-20, radio electrician, 1912-17, warrant radio officer, 1917-19, ensign and lt., 1919-29, ret., 1929; asst. chief engr. Fed. Radio Commn., 1929-37; chief engr. FCC, 1938-44, commr., 1944—; v.p. and dir. TV Baltimore Sunpapers. U.S. rep. to internat. confs., Mexico City, 1933, Bucharest and Havana, 1937, Cairo, 1938, Santiago, Chile, 1940; chmn. N. Am. Broadcast Conf., Washington, 1946. Mem. Censorship Operating Bd., World War II, chmn. coordinating com. Bd. War Communications. Decorated Mexican compaign medal. Victory medal (U.S.). Fellow Inst. Radio Engrs. Methodist. Mason. Clubs: Rotary, Merchants, Advertising (Balt.) Home: 4546 N. Charles St. Office: WMAR-TV, Balt. 21203. Died Apr. 29, 1965.

JEWETT, ARTHUR CRAWFORD, mech. engr.; b. Bath, Me., Aug. 26, 1878; s. Edwin Hale and Lizzie L. (Chapman) J.; B.S., Mass. Inst. Tech., 1901; m. Blanche Lind von Beseler, May 7, 1903 (dec.); children—Roger, Helen Hale (Mrs. Robert L. Lepper). Instr. mech. engring. U. Me., 1903-05, prof. mech. engring., 1905-14; engring. mgr. Bird & Son, East Walpole, Mass., 1914-16; supt. various depts. Winchester Repeating Arms Co., 1916-24; mem. research staff Nat. Indsl. Conf. Bd., N.Y.C., 1924-25; dir. Coll. Industries, Carnegie Inst. Tech., 1925-34. Exec. sec., Regional Labor Bd., 1933-35; supr. labor mgmt. Pa. dist. 15, Works Progress Adminstrn., 1935-36; cons. Indsl. Relations and Tng., 1936-41, U.S. Office Edn., 1941-47. Mem. A.M. Soc. M.E. Address: 905 Maryland Av., Pitts. Died July 27, 1957.

JEWETT, CHARLES, physician; b. Bath, Me., Sept. 27, 1839; s. George and Sarah (Hale) J.; A.B., Bowdoin, 1864, A.M., 1867 (Sc.D., 1894); M.D., Coll. Phys. and Surg. (Columbia), 1871; m. Abbie E. Flagg, 1868 (dec.). Has practiced medicine at Brooklyn; prof. obstetrics, 1880-1900, gynecology and obstetrics, 1900—, and gynecol. surgeon, L.I. Coll. Hosp.; consulting obstetrician Kings Co. Hosp., 1893—; consulting gynecologist Bushwick, Swedish and German hosps.; consulting surgeon St. Christopher's Hospital; trustee Brooklyn Eye and Ear Hosp., 1887—. Was first in America to perform symphyseotomy. Pres. Medical Soc. County of Kings, 1878-80, Brooklyn Gynecol. Soc., 1893, New York Obstet. Soc., 1894. Author: Essentials of Obstetrics; Manual of Child-Bed Nursing. Editor Practice of Obstetrics, by Am. authors. Address: Brooklyn, N.Y. Died 1910.

JEWETT, FRANK BALDWIN, electrical engr.; b. Pasadena, Calif., Sept. 5, 1879; s. Stanley P. and Phebe (Mead) J.; A.B., Throop Poly. Inst. (now Calif. Inst. Tech.), 1898; Ph.D., U. of Chicago, 1902; D.Sc., New York U., Dartmouth, 1925, Columbia Univ. and Univ. of Wis., 1927, Rutgers University, 1928, U. of Chicago, 1929, Harvard, 1936, Univ. of Pa., 1940, Boston U., 1944; Dr.Eng., Case School of Applied Science, 1928; LL.D., Miami U., 1932, Rockford College, 1939; Norwich Univ., 1944, Yale, 1946; married Fannie C. Frisbie, Dec. 28, 1905; children—Harrison Leach, Frank Baldwin. Research assistant to Professor A. A. Michelson, Univ. of Chicago, 1901-02; instructor physics and electrical engineering, Mass. Institute of Technology, 1902-04; transmission engr. Am. Telephone & Telegraph Co., 1904-12; asst. chief engr., 1912-16, chief engr., 1916, vice-pres., 1922, Western Electric Co.; v.p. Am. Telephone & Telegraph Co., in charge development and research 1925-44; pres. Bell Telephone Laboratories, Inc., 1925-Oct. 1, 1940, chmn. bd. 1940-44. Maj. Signal Corps, U.S.R., 1917; lt. col. Signal Corps, A.U.S., Dec. 1, 1917; was advisory mem. Spl. Submarine Bd. of the Navy and mem. State Dept. Spl. Com. on Cables. Vice-chmn. Engring. Foundation, 1919-25; chmn. Div. of Engring. and Industrial Research, Nat. Research Council, 1923-27, now mem. com. on scientific aids to learning; mem. President Roosevelt's Science Advisory Board, 1933-35; mem. Nat. Defense Research Committee of Office of Scientific Research and Development; mem. coordination and equipment division, Signal Corps; consultant to Chief of Ordnance. President, Nat. Academy of Sciences, since 1939. Pres. and trustee, New York Museum of Science and Industry. Life mem. Mass. Inst. Tech. Corp.; pres. M.I.T. Alumni Association, 1939-40. Trustee Princeton U., Carnegie Instn. of Washington, Woods Hole Oceanographic Inst. Tabor Academy, Carnegie Inst. of Tech. Fellow Inst. Radio Engrs., A.A.A.S., Am. Physical Soc., Acoustical Soc. of Am., Acad. Arts and Sciences; mem. Am. Inst. Electric Engrs. (pres. 1922-23), Inst. Elec. Engrs. (Brit.), Am. Soc. for Engring. Edn., Am. Philos. Soc.; member (hon.) N.Y. Electrical Society, Delta Upsilon, Sigma Xi, Tau Beta Pi. Awarded D.S.M. (U.S.); 4th Order Rising Sun, 1923, 3d Order Sacred Treasure, 1930 (Japan); Edison medal, 1928; Faraday medal, 1935; Franklin medal, 1936; Washington award, 1938; John Fritz medal, 1939; Medal for Merit, 1946. Clubs: University, Engineers, Century Assn. (N.Y.); Short Hills (N.J.); Cosmos (Washington). Author brochures, articles and pub. addresses on physical and elec. subjects. Home: Brantwood, Short Hills, N.J. Office: 140 West St., New York, N.Y.; and 2101 Constitution Av. N.W., Washington, D.C. Died Nov. 18, 1949.

JEWETT, FRANK FANNING, chemist; b. Newton Corner, Mass., Jan. 8, 1844; s. Charles and Lucy Adams (Tracy) J.; A.B., Yale, 1870, A.M., 1873; univs. of Göttingen and Berlin, Germany; m. Frances Gulick (q.v.). July 30, 1880. Tchr. Norwich Free Acad., later pvt. asst. to Dr. Wolcott Gibbs, of Harvard; prof. chemistry, Imperial U. of Japan, 1877-80; prof. chemistry and mineralogy Oberlin Coll., 1880-12, prof. emeritus, 1912. Trustee Oberlin Missionary Home Assn. Mem. Am. Chem. Soc., A.A.A.S,, Deutsche Cehmische Gesellschaft, Alpha Delta Phi. Author: Tables for Qualitative Chemical Analysis, 1883; Laboratory Manual of Inorganic Chemistry, 1885. Republican. Conglist. Address: Oberlin, O. Died July 1, 1926; buried Oberlin.

JEWETT, STEPHEN PERHAM, physician; b. North Waterford, Me., Sept. 1, 1882; s. Stephen Perham and Ella Lucia (Hinman) J.; A.B., Clark U., Worchester, Mass., 1906; M.D., N.Y. Med. Coll. and Flower Hosp., 1910; grad. student Columbia U., 1911-12; D.Sc. (honorary), New York Medical College, 1960, Clark University, 1965; married to Caroline Winterton, June 1, 1910 (died Aug. 1915); 1 son, Stephen Perham; m. 2d, Elizabeth Plunkett, Jan. 25, 1917; children—Mary Rita (Mrs. Jeremiah Donovan), Elizabeth Plunkett (Mrs. Jewett Hayes), Annette Plunkett (Mrs. Jewett Mullen, Jr.), Stephanie Plunkett (Mrs. Richard Byran McCormick). Gen. practice, Buffalo, N.Y., 1912-16; attending physician, psychiatric service, Bellevue and Allied Hosps., New York, 1916-22; with med. examiner's office, N.Y. State Hosp. Commn., 1922-23; psychiatrist Bur. of Children's Guidance and lecturer in mental hygiene and psychiatry, N.Y. School for Social Work, 1922-26; dir. Mental Hygiene Clinic, Hudson Guild Soc. Settlement, 1923-25; cons. psychiatrist Edgehill School, Carmel, N.Y., 1924-32; attending neuro-psychiatrist U.S. Vet. Hosp. No. 81, N.Y. City, 1922-27; cons. psychiatrist and dir. of research, Berkshire Industrial Farm, Canaan, N.Y., 1926-30; cons. psychiatrist and med. dir. mental hygiene dept., Montclair (N.J.) State Teachers' Coll., 1929-33; research consultant in psychiatry and neuorology, Dept. of Correction, N.Y. City, 1932-33; attending psychiatrist, Flower-Fifth Av. Hosp., dir. neuropsychiatry, Metropolitan Hosp., Dept. of Hospitals, N.Y.C.; vis. psychiatrist and dir. of psychiatry Bird S. Coler Meml. Hosp. and Home, N.Y.C.; cons. in psychiatry, Paterson General Hospital (N.J.), Riverside Hosp., N.Y.C.; U.S.; consulting psychiatrist of Kings Park (N.Y.) State Hospital, 1958-71; psychiatrist-in-chief of East View Pavilion, New York City, 1958-71. Induction Service for Armed Forces; dir. neuopsychiatric dept., Murray Hill Hosp., N.Y.C.; chmn. deans; com. for neuropsychiatry, Lyons Hosp., N.J.; dean New York Post-Grad. Center psychotherapy; prof. medicine (psychiatry) emeritus N.Y. Med. Coll.; lectr. psychopathology, New York Sch. for Social Work; lectr. Education of the Handicapped, Columbia U. Fellow A.M.A., Am. Psychiatric Assn., Am. Orthopsychiatric Assn.; mem. Nat. Com. for Mental Hygiene, Am. Psychoanalytical Assn. Collaborator, Tices Practice of Medicine and author of many scientific articles and monographs. Clubs: Alpha-Sigma, Physicians. Home: West Falls NY Died Apr. 26, 1971; buried Griffins Mills Cemetery, West Falls NY

JOB, HERBERT KEIGHTLEY, lecturer, author; b. Boston, Nov. 29, 1864; s. Daniel Ward and Susan Grey (Adams) J.; A.B., Harvard, 1888; grad. Hartford Theol. Sem., 1891; m. Elsie Ann Curtiss, Sept. 10, 1891; children—George Curtiss, Muriel Marion. Congl. pastor, N. Middleboro, Mass., 1891-98, Kent, Conn., 1898-1908; state ornithologist of Conn. and mem. faculty Conn. Agrl. Coll., 1908-14; econ. ornithologist in charge dept. applied ornithology, 1914-24; dir. Summer Sch. and Ornithol. Expt. Sta., 1918—, of Nat. Assn. Audubon Socs., Amston, Conn.; field agent for S.C. of Nat. Assn. of Audubon Socs. and state dir. of nature and conservation education, South Carolina, 1926-30. Has made frequent scientific expeditions to wilder parts of Northwestern states, Canada and South; nature photographer, securing large series of photographs and motion pictures of wild birds from life. Author: Among the Water Fowl, 1902; Wild Wings (introduction by President Roosevelt), 1905; The Sport of Bird Study, 1908; How to Study Birds, 1910; Blue Goose Chase, 1911; The Propagation of Wild Birds, 1915. Home: West Haven, Conn. Died June 17, 1933.

JOB, ROBERT, chemist; b. Boston, Oct. 10, 1866; s. Daniel W. and Susan G. J.; prep. edn. Boston Latin Sch.; grad. Harvard, 1890; m. Reading, Pa., Sept. 2, 1897, Marguerite E. Maltzberger. Chemist Phila. & Reading Ry. Co. since 1897. Contbr. to tech. and scientific jours. Mem. Am. Chem. Soc., Soc. Chem. Industry, Franklin Inst., Am. Soc. Testing Materials, A.A.A.S. Residence: 109 Windsor St. Office: Care Philadelphia & Reading Railway Co., Reading Pa.

JOBLING, JAMES WESLEY, pathologist; b. Steubenville, O., Aug. 2, 1876; s. William J.; M.D., Tenn. Med. Coll., 1896; postgrad. work, Johns Hopkins Med. Sch., Inst. für Infectionskrankheiten, Berlin; m. Nora Counihan, Sept. 22, 1906. Dir. Serum Lab., Manila, P.I., 1901-03; asso. Rockefeller Inst., N.Y., 1906-09; pathologist Morris Inst. and Michael Reese Hosp., Chgo., 1909-13; asst. prof. pathology Columbia U., 1913-14; prof. pathology med. dept. Vanderbilt U., 1914-18; prof. pathology, Columbia, 1918-45, prof. emeritus, 1945—. Mem. Assn. Am. Physicians, Am. Assn. Pathologists and Bacteriologists, N.Y. Path. Soc., Soc. Exptl. Biology and Medicine, Am. Assn. Cancer Research, Soc. Harvey Soc., Am. Assn. Immunologists, A.A.A.S., Soc. for Exptl. Pathology. Home: Park Manor Hotel, San Diego, Calif. Died Nov. 1961.

JOERG, W(OLFGANG) L(OUIS) G(OTTFRIED), (yerg), geographer; b. Brooklyn, N.Y., Feb. 6, 1885; s. Oswald and Denise (Coulin) J.; grad. Poly. Prep. Sch. of Brooklyn, 1899, Thomas Gymnasium, Leipzig, Germany, 1904; student U. of Leipzig, 1904, Columbia, 1904-06, U. of Göttingen, Germany, 1906-11; m. Hannah Heaton, Nov. 14, 1911; children—Oswald Heaton, Norton Coulin. Mem. scientific staff Am. Geog. Soc. 1911-37—asst. editor of Bull., 1911-15, asso. editor Geog. Review, 1915-20, editor research series, 1920-25, research editor, 1925-37; apptd. chief Div. of Maps and Charts, The Nat. Archives, 1937; member Federal Bd. of Surveys and Maps, 1937-42; mem. div. of geology and geography Nat. Research Council, 1924-27, and of exec. com., 1931-36, vice chmn., 1933-36; sec. U.S. nat. com. Internat. Geog. Union, 1931-37, chmn., 1937-39; mem. advisory com. U.S. Geog. Bd., 1931-34, Com. on Mapping Services of the Federal Govt., 1934; mem. U.S. Bd. on Geog. Names, 1937-47 (chmn. exec. com. 1938-47, com. on Antarctic names, 1943-47, adv. mem. since 1947; cons. prof. hist. geog., Univ. of Maryland, since 1947. Fellow A.A.A.S.; mem. Assn. Am. Geographers (v.p. 1928; pres. 1937), Am. Geophys. Union, Am. Soc. of Photogrammetry, Nat. Congress on Surveying and Mapping (charter mem. 1941), Arctic Inst. of North American (charter mem. 1948), Soc. Am. Archivists, Am. Assn. for State and local history; hon. mem. Geog. Soc. Neuchâtel (Switzerland). Unitarian. Club: Cosmos (Washington, D.C.). Author: Recent Geographical Work in Europe, 1922; Brief History of Polar Explorations since the Introduction of Flying, 1930; Work of the Byrd Antarctic Expedition of 1928 to 1930, 1930; and numerous papers on cartography, the regional geography of N. America and land utilization. Editor: Problems of Polar Research, 1928; Pioneer Settlement 1932; (with W. A. Mackintosh) Canadian Frontiers of Settlement, 9 vols. since 1934; contbg. editor Geographical Review since 1937. Home: 6302 Ridge Dr., N.W. Office: The National Archives, Washington. Died Jan. 7, 1952.

JOESTING, HENRY ROCHAMBEÁU, geophysicist; b. Balt., Nov. 16, 1903; s. Henry Jr. and Rosa (Rochambeau) J.; B.S. in Chemistry, Johns Hopkins, 1923, Ph.D. in Geology, 1940; m. Dorothy Byrd Oldham, Oct. 6, 1934. Indsl. chemist, 1923-26; leader Arctic party Jan Mayen Island, 1927-28; field geologist Sinclair Oil Co., Venzuela, 1929-31; prospector, miner in Alaska, 1933-35; instr. U. Alaska, 1935-38; mining, geol. and geophys. research Ty. Dept. Mines, Alaska, 1938-44; supervising geophysicist U.S. Bur. Mines, 1944-46; chief geophysics br. U.S. Geol. Survey, 1946-53, staff geophysicist, Washington, 1954—. Distinguished Service medal Dept. Interior, 1965. Fellow Geol. Soc. Am.; mem. Am. Geol. Inst. (sec.-treas. 1954-56), Am. Geophys. Union (pres. sect ter. magnetism and electricity 1956-59), Soc. Exploration Geophysics, Am. Assn. Petroleum Geologists, Geochem. Soc., Geology Soc. Washington. Home: Route 2, Box 170, Marshall, Va. Office: U.S. Geological Survey, Washington. Died May 28, 1965; buried Balt.

JOHANNSEN, OSKAR AUGUSTUS, entomologist; b. Davenport, Ia., May 14, 1870; s. Christian and Caroline Marie (Sturk) J.; B.S., U. Ill., 1894; A.M., Cornell, 1902, Ph.D., 1904; m. Harriette Fuller, Sept. 23, 1896; children—Dorothea E., Laurence O., Robert A. Engr., draftsman, Chgo., 1894-99; instr., grad. student, Cornell U., 1899-1904, asst. prof., 1904-09; prof. entomology U. Me., 1909-12; asst. prof. entomology, Cornell U., 1912-14, prof. 1914-38, head dept. entomology, 1936-38, ret. 1938. Fellow A.A.A.S., Entomol. Soc. Am.; hon. mem. Internat. Congresses Entomology; mem. Am. Soc. Zoologists, Soc. Econ. Entomologists, Soc. Naturalists, Limnological Soc., Sigma Xi, Tau Beta Pi, Phi Kappa Phi, Gamma Alpha. Author: Aquatic Nematocerous Diptera, 1903; The Mycetophilidae, 1909; (with W. A. Riley) Handbook of Medical Entomology, 1915, rev., on Med. Entomology, 1932, 38; Aquatic Diptera, 1934-37; (with B. F. Kingsbury) Histological Technique, 1927; (with F. H. Butt) Embryology of Insects and Myriapods, 1941; also numerous bulls. issued by N.Y. State Mus. and Me. Agrl. Expt. Sta. Home: 712 N. Cayuga St., Ithaca, N.Y. 14850. Died Nov. 7, 1961; buried Ithaca.

JOHNS, CARL OSCAR, chemist; b. Sweden, Aug. 19, 1870; s. Andrew and Clara Sophia (Gabrielson) J.; came with parents to U.S., 1879; student Upsala Coll., Brooklyn, N.Y., 1894-95; A.B., Bethany (Kan.) Coll., 1899, A.M., 1902, D.Sc., 1922; Ph.B., Yale, 1904, Ph.D., 1906; m. Marie Eugenie Malmberg, 1908; children—Marie Louise, Margaret Loraine, Carl Oscar. Instr. in natural history, Bethany Coll., 1899-1902, prof. 1902-03, also treas., 1899-1903; asst. in chemistry, Sheffield Scientific Sch. (Yale), 1904-06, instr., 1906-11, asst. prof., 1911-14; organic chemist, U.S. Bur. Chemistry, Washington, D.C., 1914-15, in charge Protein Investigation Lab., 1915-20, also in charge scientific personnel, 1917-20, and of color investigation lab., 1920; lecturer in chemistry, Yale, 1920; dir. of research, development dept. Standard Oil Co. of N. J., 1920-27; dir. of research labs. and mem. bd. dirs. Standard Oil Development Co., 1927-30, chem. consultant since 1930. Chmn. Intersectional Petroleum Symposium, New York, 1924. Fellow A.A.A.S.; mem. Am. Chem. Soc. (councillor), Soc. Chem. Industry, Soc. Biol. Chemists, Am. Petroleum Inst., N.J. Chem. Soc. (dir.), Sigma Xi; pres. Washington (D.C.) Chem. Soc., 1920, Yale Chem. Soc. since 1930. Republican. Presbyterian. Club: Graduate (New Haven, Conn.). Contbr. some 80 research articles. Home: 32 Old Estate Road, Manhasset, L.I., N.Y. Died Apr. 17, 1942. *

JOHNSON, ADELAIDE MCFADYEN, physician; b. Rockford, Ill., Mar. 26, 1905; d. Joseph F. and Margaret (Porter) McFadyen; B.S., Rockford Coll., 1926, Sc.D., 1947; Ph.D., U. Chgo., 1930, M.D., 1932; m. Victor Johnson, June 11, 1930. Asst. physiciology U. Chgo., 1928-30, intern dept. medicine, 1932-33, asst. medicine, 1933-34, lectr. psychiatry, 1943-46; resident psychiatry Henry Phipps Inst., Balt., 1934-37; instr. psychiatry Johns Hopkins, 1934-37; asst. psychiatrist Inst. Juvenile Research, 1937-40, psychiatrist, 1940-42; asso. criminology U. Ill. Sch. Medicine, 1938-42, asst. prof. criminology, 1932-46; staff Inst. Psychoanalysis, Chgo., 1942—; cons. psychiatrist Family Service Bur., Omaha, Neb., 1943-47; lectr. psychodynamics U. Neb., 1944-47; cons. psychiatrist United Charities of Chgo., 1945-46; lectr. child psychiatry Smith Coll. Sch. Social Work, 1945-47; asso. clin. prof. psychiatry U. Minn., 1947-49, asso. prof. psychiatry, 1949-54, clin. prof. psychiatry, 1954—, prof. psychiatry, 1954—; cons. psychiatrist Mayo Clinic, 1948-56; asso. prof. psychiatry Mayo Found. Med. Edn. and Research, 1949-54, prof. psychiatry, 1954-56. Trustee Rockford College, 1946-51. Diplomate Inst. Psychoanalysis, Am. Bd. Psychiatry and Neurology. Mem. Am. Acad. Child Psychiatry, A.A.A.S., A.M.A., Am. Orthopsychiat. Assn., Am. Psychiat. Assn., Am. Psychoanalytic Assn., Am. Psychosomatic Soc., Chgo. Psychoanalytic Soc., Internat. Psychoanalytic Assn., Minn. Med. Assn., Olmsted-Houston-Fillmore-Dodge County Med. Soc., Sigma Xi, Alpha Omega Alpha. Contbr. articles profl. publs., chpts. in books. Address: 626 S.W. 5th St., Rochester, Minn. Died Nov. 20, 1960; buried Solvang, Cal.

JOHNSON, ALBERT RITTENHOUSE, prof. of structural design; b. Lambertville, N.J., Mar. 7, 1880; s. Clark B., and Sallie A. (Green) J.; ed. Delaware Twp. pub. schs.; N.J. State Normal Sch., Trenton, N.J.; B.S., Rutgers U., 1907, C.E., 1925; m R. Ethel Hughes, Aug. 16, 1911; children—Edna Rittenhouse, Elizabeth Ann. Taught in N.J. pub. schs., Jan. 1900 to June 1903; engring. dept. Hudson & Manhattan R.R., 1907-08; U.S. River and Harbor work, 1908; mem. faculty Rutgers U., 1908-50, ret. professor of structural design; worked with McClintic Marshall Constrn. Co., Pottstown, Pa., and N.Y. C., Hughes Foulkrod Constrn. Co., Phila., N.J. State Highway Dept., Trenton, N.J. Mem. Nat. Soc. Engrs., Phi Beta Kappa, Sigma Xi, Tau Beta Pi, Lambda Chi Alpha. Mason. Home: Stockton, Hunterdon Co., N.J. Died Mar. 15, 1960.

JOHNSON, ALFRED LE ROY, orthodontist; b. Shelburne Falls, Mass., Sept. 23, 1881; s. Willis Morris and Allie Flayilla (Bowen) J.; D.M.D., Tufts Coll. Dental Sch., 1904, D.Sc., (hon.), 1920; A.M. (hon.), Harvard, 1942; D.Sc. (hon.), U. Rochester, 1945; m. Alice Lenora Taylor, Sept. 20, 1910; children—Jane Taylor, Alfred Townshend. Practiced as dentist, Great Barrington, Mass., 1904-10; orthodontist since 1910; prof. of orthodontics, Tufts Coll., Dental Sch., 1918-23, U. of Mich., 1923-24, U. of Pa., 1924-28; research asso. of Charles R. Stockard in exptl. genetics, Cornell Med. Sch., since 1931; dean, Harvard Sch. Dental Medicine, 1942-47; cons. in dental edn. under Foundation Grant, since 1947; prof. clin. dentistry, Harvard; asso. dean of the Faculty of Medicine, Harvard Univ., 1942-47. Ednl. consultant under a found. grant, 1947. Trustee, Tufts College. Mem. Am. Dental Assn., Am. Assn. Orthodontists, Psi Omega. Unitarian. Mason. Clubs: Dutch Treat, Harvard (New York); Harvard (Boston). Author: Basic Principles of Orthodontics, 1923; The Constitutional Factor in Skull Form and Dental Occlusion, 1940. Collaborator with Dr. C. R. Stockard in Constitutional Basis of Form and Behavior, 1940. Contbr. to professional and ednl. jours. Home: Egremont Rd., Great Barrington, Mass. Died Jan. 26, 1967.

JOHNSON, ARTHUR MONRAD, botanist; b. Fredrikstad, Norway, Jan. 19, 1878; s. Christen and Ottomine Marie (Andersen) J.; brought to U.S., 1882; A.B., U. of Minn., 1904, Ph.D., 1919, grad. study, Harvard, 1924-25; m. Eleanor Adalyn Henderson, June 22, 1915. Teacher in high schs., 1904-15; teacher summer sessions—Washington State Coll., 1908, 09, U. of Washington 1913, 14, De Pauw U., 1917, 19; fellow in botany, U. of Minn., 1916-19, instr., 1919-24; lecturer economic botany, Boston Teachers Sch. of Science, 1926; U. of Wis., 1927; lecturer U. of Calif. at Los Angeles, 1927-28, asst. prof., 1929-37, associate professor and director Botanical Garden since 1937; lecturer in art since 1940. Studied art at University of Minnesota and San Francisco Art Inst.; paintings exhibited in Minneapolis, Chicago, Brooklyn, Los Angeles, San Francisco, Sacramento; 1st prize in drawing and water-color at Odin Club Art Exhbn., Minneapolis, 1923. Mem. A.A.A.S., Am. Soc. Plant Taxonomists, Botanical Soc. of America, Am.-Scandinavian Foundation, Calif. Water-Color Soc., Theta Chi, Sigma Xi, Varsity-Village Club, Los Angeles (Westwood). Author: A Revision of the North American Species of Saxifraga, Section Boraphila (Engler), 1923; Taxonomy of the Flowering Plants, 1931. Contbr. to scientific jours. Home: 10733 Wellworth Av., Los Angeles (Westwood), Calif. Died July 19, 1943.

JOHNSON, ARTHUR NEWHALL, civil engr.; b. Lynn, Mass., Nov. 11, 1870; s. David Newhall and Amanda Malvina (Richardson) J.; S.B. in civ. engring., Lawrence Scientific Sch. (Harvard), 1894; hon. Dr. Engring., U. of Md., 1924; m. May Louise Ash, Sept. 12, 1900. Instr. descriptive geometry, Harvard, 1895-96; asst. engr. Calumet and Hecla Mine, Calumet, Mich., 1896-97; asst. engr. Mass. Highway Commn., 1897-98; state highway engr. of Md., 1898-1905; chief engr. U.S. Office of Pub. Roads, Washington, 1905; state highway engr. of Ill., 1906-14; with Bur. Municipal Research of New York, 1914-16; consulting highway engr., Portland Cement Assn., Chicago, 1916-20; dean Coll. of Engring., U. of Md., 1920-36, emeritus. Chmn. Highway Research Bd., Nat. Research Council, 1923-26; del. to Pan Am. Road Congress, Buenos Aires, 1925. Received Bartlett award for outstanding contribution to highway progress, 1933. Home: Baltimore, Md. Died July 10, 1940.

JOHNSON, CARL EDWARD, physician; b. Denver, June 20, 1898; s. Swan and Sophia (Johnson) J.; A.B., Leland Stanford U., 1922; M.D., Harvard, 1926; m. Louise Harriet Sharpe, Oct. 16, 1934 (dec. July 1957); children—Carl Edward, William Swan; m. 2d, Ann Ekman Gaines, Jan. 4, 1958. Teaching fellow in comparative anatomy Harvard, 1922-23, instr. histology and embroyology, 1923-26; intern Yale-New Haven Hosp., 1926-28, asst. resident in surg. obstetrics and gynecology, 1928-30, resident in surgery, 1931-32, resident in gynecology, 1932-33, attending obstetrician and gynecologist, 1932-62; practice medicine specializing in obstetrics and gynecology, New Haven, 1932-70; NRC fellow in physiology Hamburg (Germany) U., 1930-31; chief obstetrician and gynecologist Hosp of St. Raphael, New Haven, 1946-60; cons. Milford (Conn.) Hosp., Griffin Hosp., Derby, Conn. instr. surgery Yale Sch. Medicine, New Haven, 1928-32, instr. obstetrics and gynecology, 1932-34, asst. clin. prof., 1934-49, asso. clin. prof., 1949-56. Surg. cons. to surgeon gen. U.S., Germany, Austria, 1950; mem. Conn. Med. Examining Bd., 1948-60. Served to surgeon USPHS, 1942-47. Diplomate Am. Bd. Obstetrics and Gynecology (chmn. 1952-59). Fellow A.C.S., Am. Coll. Obstetricians and Gynecologists; mem. A.M.A., Am. Soc. for Study Sterility (treas. 1952-59), Internat. Fertility Assn., Conn. Med. Soc., New Haven County, New Haven med. assns., New Eng. Obstet. and Gynecol. Soc., NRC Fellowship, Fedn. State Med. Bds. U.S.A. Contbr. articles to med. jours. Home: Hamden CT Died Nov. 23, 1970; buried Hamden CT

JOHNSON, CARL GUNNARD, educator; b. Worcester, Mass., Feb. 24, 1902; s. John Efram and Maria (Blomstrom) J.; ed. pub. schs., Worcester; m. Eleanor Harrington Fisher, Aug. 18, 1928; children—Richard Fisher, Marilyn Harrington (Mrs. Robert Henry Eager). Instr. mech. engring. Worcester Poly. Inst., 1921-38, asst. prof., 1938-43, asso. prof., 1943-57, prof., 1957—, John Woodman Higgins prof. engring., 1961—; lectr. Fitchburg State Tchrs. Coll., 1932-47; instr. Worcester Jr. Coll., 1938-43; operator evening sch. metallurgy Worcester Poly. Inst., 1938-48; cons. Mass. Steel Treating Corp., 1933-60; founder Presmet Corp., 1944, v.p., dir. research and devel., 1944—, also dir.; corporator Westboro Savs. Bank. Conferee 1st and 2d World Metall. Congress, 1952, 57. Recipient award for sci. achievement Worcester Engring. Soc., 1957. Mem. Am. Ordnance Assn., Am. Inst. Mining and Metall. Engrs., Worcester Engring. Soc. (past pres.), Am. Soc. Metals (past sec., treas., chmn. Worcester chpt.), Am. Soc. Testing Materials (award of merit 1964), Worcester Country Mechanics Assn. (past dir.), Am. Soc. Engring. Edn., Metal Powder Industries Fedn. (past dir., pres. 1965—), Am. Powder Metallurgy Inst., Skull Honor Soc., Sigma Xi (past pres. Worcester chpt.), Phi Gamma Delta, Phi Tau Sigma. Mason. Kiwanian. Author: Forging Practice, rev. edit., 1957; Metallurgy, rev. edit., 1957. Home: Chauncy St., Westborough, Mass. Office: Worcester Polytechnic Inst., Worcester 9, Mass. Died May 21, 1966.

JOHNSON, CHARLES EUGENE, prof. zoölogy; b. Oslo, Norway, Apr. 24, 1880; s. Capt. Christen and Ottomine Marie (Anderson) J.; brought to U.S., 1882, naturalized, 1886; A.B., U. of Minn., 1906, A.M., 1907, Ph.D., 1912; post-grad. work, U. of Wis., 1910, Harvard Med. Sch., 1911; m. Jane A. Wood, Dec. 20, 1914; children—Lucia Marie, Jane Louise. Began as instr. gen. zoölogy and histology, Hamline U., St. Paul, 1907; asst. and instr. in gen. zoölogy and comparative anatomy, U. of Minn., 1907-19; asst. prof. and asso. prof. zoölogy U. of Kan., 1919-23; prof. zoölogy, N.Y. State Coll. of Forestry, 1923—, head dept. forest zoölogy and dir. Roosevelt Wild Life Sta., 1926—. Republican. Home: Syracuse, N.Y. Died June 6, 1936.

JOHNSON, CHARLES WILLIAMSON, civil engr.; b. Johnstown, N.Y., Jan. 20, 1845; s. Dr. William H. and Harriet Livermore (McCarthy) J.; attended sch. in France nearly 2 yrs.; C.E., Union Coll., 1866; m. Maria C. Bronson, of Menasha, Wis., June 14, 1875; children—William Lobdell (dec.), Maria Louise (Mrs. George C. Stone), Harriet Livermore (Mrs. Fred Mahler), Mrs. Elizabeth Ker Weaver. Asst. in chief engrs.' office, L.S.&M.S. Ry., Chicago, 1867-70; asst. engr. constrn. C.,R.I.&P. Ry., 1870-71; asst. and div. engr. constrn. Wis. Central Ry., 1871-78; chief engr., Mar. 1, 1879-Nov. 1, 1913, consulting engr., Nov. 1, 1913-June 1, 1918, C.,St.P., M.&O. Ry. Retired on pension June 1, 1918. Mem. Delta Phi. Clubs: Engineers' (Chicago); Minnesota (St. Paul). Home: 188 Virginia Av., St. Paul, Minn.

JOHNSON, CHARLES WILLIS, chemist; b. Concord, Ind., Sept. 23, 1873; s. Frederick Angell and Marie Jane (Tustison) J.; Pharm. Chemist, U. of Mich., 1896; B.S., 1900, Ph.D., 1903; m. Parthenia Sykes, June 21, 1900 (died May 2, 1918); children—Lois Kathleen, Eloise Ruth, Frederick Francis; m. 2d, Frances Edith Hindman, June 22, 1920. Teacher in pub. schs., 1890-92; pharmacist, Ann Arbor and Detroit, 1896-98; asst. instr. chemistry, U. of Mich., 1898-1901; instr. chemistry, State U. of Ia., 1901-02; asst. prof. chemistry, 1903-04, prof. pharm. chemistry and dean Coll. of Pharmacy, 1904-39, prof. and dean emeritus since Sept. 1939, U. of Washington. Chemist State Dairy and Food Commn. of Wash., 1909-13; state chemist Dept. of Agriculture, Washington, 1913-43. Congregationalist. Mem. Am. Pharm. Assn. (pres. 1927-28), Wash. State Pharm. Assn., Kappa Psi, Sigma Xi, Rho Chi, Phi Delta Chi. Mason (K.T., 32 deg., Shriner). Mem. com. in charge revision of U.S. Pharmacopoeia X and XI; pres. Wash. State Pharm. Assn., 1915-17; pres. Am. Conf. of Pharm. Faculties (now Am. Assn. Colls. of Pharmacy), 1923-24. Home: 4337 15th Av. N.E., Seattle. Died Jan. 4, 1949.

JOHNSON, CHARLES WILLISON, zoölogist; b. Morris Plains, N.J., Oct. 26, 1863; s. Albert Fletcher and Sarah Elizabeth (Willison) J.; ed. pub. and pvt. schs., Morristown, N.J.; m. Carrie W. Ford, Jan. 14, 1897 (died 1931). Moved to St. Augustine, Fla., 1880, continuing studies in natural history, and making large collection of insects, mollusca and fossils. Curator Mus. of Wagner Free Inst. of Science, Phila., 1888-1903; curator Boston Soc. Natural History since Mar. 1903. Especially interested in study of mollusca and diptera, and contbr. to biol. jours. of papers relating to these splties.; asso. editor and mgr. The Nautilus since May, 1890. Fellow Am. Acad. Arts and Sciences, Entomol. Soc. Am. (pres. 1924), A.A.A.S.; mem. Phila. Acad. Natural Sciences, Entomol. Soc. Washington, Malacol. Soc. of London. Home: Brookline, Mass. Office: 234 Berkeley St., Boston. Died May 8, 1932.

JOHNSON, DOUGLAS WILSON, geologist; b. Parkersburg, W.Va., Nov. 30, 1878; s. Isaac H. and Jennie A. (Wilson) J.; Denison U., Granville, O., 1896-98; B.S., Univ. of N.M., 1901; Ph.D., Columbia, 1903, hon. D.Sc., 1929; Docteur, honoris causa, Univ. of Grenoble, France, 1924, Nancy, France, 1932, Montpelier, France, 1933; hon. D.Sc., Denison University, 1932; m. Alice Adkins, Aug. 11, 1903; m. 2d, Edith Sanford Caldwell, 1943. Teacher public schs., 1897-98; field asst., Univ. Geol. Survey, in N.M., 1899-1901; teacher in high sch., Albuquerque, N.M., 1900-01; asst. U.S. Geol. Survey, 1901, 03, 04, 05; instr. in geology, 1903-05, asst. prof., 1905-07, Mass. Inst. Tech.; asst. prof. physiography, Harvard, 1906-12; asso. prof. physiography, 1912-19, prof. since 1919, exec. officer, dept. of geology since 1937, Columbia U. Asst. N.J. Geol. Survey, 1911; dir. Shaler Memorial Expdn., 1911-12; geog. adviser U.S. Dept. State, 1919-20; cons. physiographer to Canadian govt. in Labrador boundary dispute, 1926. Maj. Intelligence Div., U.S. Army, Feb. 1918; chief of div. boundary geography, Am. Commn. to Negotiate Peace, Paris, 1918-19; exchange prof. to France, in engring. and applied science, 1923-24; pres. sect. of physical geography of Internat. Geog. Congress, Paris, 1931. Chmn. national committee United States International Geographic Union, 1933-37; president International Terrace Commission, 1934-38. Mem. Nat. Acad. Science, Geological Society America (president, 1942), American Academy Arts and Sciences, American Museum of Natural History, New York Academy Sciences, A.A.A.S., Am. Philos. Soc.; mem. Assn. Am. Geographers, Am. Geog. Soc., Nat. Research Council, Sigma Xi, Phi Beta Kappa; hon. mem. Russian Geog. Soc., Serbian Acad. Sciences, Swedish Soc. Geography and Anthropology, Geog. Soc. of Bordeaux, Geog. Soc. Belgrade, Société Belge de Géologie, Geol. Soc. China, Geol. Soc. London, Geol. Soc. Finland. Janssen medallist, Paris Geog. Soc., 1920; Elisha Kent Kane medallist, Geog. Soc., Phila., 1922, U. of Nancy medallist, 1924; A. Cressy Morrison prize, N.Y. Acad. Sci., 1924, 30; Gaudy medallist, Soc. de Geographie Commerciale de Paris, 1925; Cvijic medallist, Geog. Soc. of Belgrade, 1935; Cullum medallist, Am. Geog. Soc., 1935. Decorated Chevalier Legion of Honor (French), 1924; Order of St. Sava (Jugoslavia), 1934. Clubs: Century. Author: Lettre d'un Américain á un Allemand, 1916; Topography and Strategy in the War, 1917; Peril of Prussianism, 1917; My German Correspondence, 1917; Shore Processes and Shoreline Development, 1919; Battlefields of the World War, 1921; The New England-Acadian Shoreline, 1925; Paysages Américains et Problèmes Géographiques, 1927; Stream Sculpture on the Atlantic Slope, 1931; The Assault on the Supreme Court, 1937; The Origin of Submarine Canyons, 1939; The Origin of the Carolina Bays; also numerous scientific bulls., papers, etc. Editor of Jour. Geomorphology. Address: Columbia University, New York, N.Y. Died Feb. 24, 1944.

JOHNSON, DUNCAN STARR, botanist; b. Cromwell, Conn., July 21, 1867; s. Edward Tracy and Lucy Emma (Starr) J.; B.S., Wesleyan U., Conn., 1892, D.Sc., 1932; student, Yale, 1887; Ph.D., Johns Hopkins, 1897; U. of Munich, 1901; m. Mary E. G. Lentz, June 22, 1904; children—George Duncan, David Starr. Asst. in botany, 1898-99, asso., 1899-1901, asso. prof., 1901-06, prof., 1906—, dir. bot. garden, 1913—, Johns Hopkins U. In charge of botany, 1896-1900, cryptogamic botany, 1902-11, Cold Spring Harbor, L.I., N.Y.; botanical exploration and investigation, Jamaica, B.W.I., 6 times to 1932; investigator, Carnegie Institution, Washington, D.C., 1912, 15; in charge of inspection for disease of grain fields of Atlantic States for Bureau of Plant Industry, May-Aug. 1918; v.p. Mt. Desert Biol. Lab., 1921—; lecturer Mt. Lake Biol. Sta., U. of Va., summer 1935. Dir. 6th Bot. Expdn. of Johns Hopkins U. to West Indian tropics, and Guatemala, June-Aug. 1932, and of 7th Expdn. of Bot. Dept., Johns Hopkins, to Jamaica and Central America, summer 1936. Mgr. L.I. Biol. Assn., 1923-24. Mem. Nat. Research Council, 1927-1933, chmn. division biology and agr., 1931-32. Fellow A.A.A.S. (v.p. sect. G, 1912); mem. Bot. Soc. America (sec. 1907-09). Author: The Relation of Plants to Tide Levels (with H. H. York), 1915; The Fruit of Opuntia fulgida and Proliferation in Fruits of the Cactaceae, 1918 (monograph); Littoral Vegetation on Mt. Desert Island (with A. F. Skutch), 1928. Home: Roland Park, Md. Died Feb. 16, 1937.

JOHNSON, EDWIN FERRY, civil engr.; b. Essex, Vt., May 23, 1803; s. John and Rachel (Ferry) J.; ed. Am. Literary, Scientific and Mil. Acad., Middletown, Conn. (now Norwich U.); m. Charlotte Shaler, Sept. 7, 1830, 8 children. Instr. mathematics and asst. prof natural history Am. Lit., Sci. and Mil. Acad., 1825-26, prof. mathematics and civil engring., 1826-29; in charge of land surveys for Erie Canal, 1829, Champlain Canal, 1830-31, Morris Canal, 1831; asst. engr. in charge of surveys for Catskill & Canajoharie R.R., 1831; chief engr. or prin. asst. in location of 14 railroads, including N.Y. & Erie, N.Y. & Boston, Chgo, St. Paul & Fond du Lac, also 4 canals; pres. Stevens Assn. (railroad and steamship lines), Hoboken, N.J.; mem. Conn. Senate, 1856; mayor Middletown, 1856-57; chief engr. N.P. Ry., 1867, consulting engr., 1871; inventor, canal lock improvement, screw power press, 6-wheeled locomotive truck, 8-wheeled locomotive. Author: Report. . .upon the Defenses of Maine, 1862; Report of a General Plan of Operations to the Secretary of War, 1863 (both at request of U.S. War Dept.); Review of the Project for a Great Western Railway, 1831; The Railroad to the Pacific, Northern Route, Its General Character, Relative Merits, Etc., 1854. Died N.Y.C. Apr. 12, 1872.

JOHNSON, EMIL FRITIOF, chemist; b. Sweden, Sept. 9, 1864; s. August and Maria (Johnson) J.; Chem. Engr., Inst. of Technology, Stockholm, 1887; m. Hildegard Noring, Nov. 4, 1891 (died 1925); children—Ella (Mrs. Roland Lorich), Hildur (Mrs. Einar Sjogren), Egil F.; m. 2d, Mrs. Anna Sundin Ullman, 1930. Came to U.S., 1887, naturalized, 1895. Analytical and cons. chemist, N.Y.C., since 1891; chemist British and Scandinavian Woodpulp Assn., Assn. Am. Woodpulp Importers, Am. Paper and Pulp Assn.; chemist to French and Italian military and food commns., during and after World War, also to U.S. Food Administration. Mem. bd. dirs. Swedish Old Peoples Home. Former pres. United Swedish Socs., John Ericson Memorial Assn., Am. Soc. Swedish Engrs.; mem. Chem. Soc. and Engring. Soc., Stockholm. Decorated Knight Order of Vasa, Order of North Star (Sweden). Republican. Lutheran. Mason; mem. Grand Lodge of Masons State of N.Y. Home: 900 Riverside Drive. Office: 133 Front St., New York, N.Y.

JOHNSON, FRANCIS ELLIS, educator; b. Leroy, Mich., May 27, 1885; s. John William and Florence Estella (Ellis) J.; A.B., U. of Wis., 1906, E.E., 1909; m. Elizabeth Dale Trousdale, Mar. 8, 1910; children—Ellis Trousdale, Margaret Dale, Florence Whitney, Helen Laurence. Power plant constrn. in Northwest; instr. engring. Rice Inst., Houston, Tex., 1912-15; with U. of Kan., 1915-30, successively instr. engring. until 1916, asst. prof., 1916-18, asso. prof., 1918-21, prof., 1921-30, and head dept. elec. engring., 1928-30; head dept. elec. engring., Ia. State Coll., Ames, Ia., 1930-35; dean Coll. of Engring., U. of Mo., 1935-38; dean Coll. of Engring, U. of Wis., 1938-46; Ednl. dir. Gen. Elec. Co. Nucleonics Project (Hanford), 1946-50, ret. Cons. practice in acceptance tests on power plants, design of transmission lines, valuation of municipal electric systems, etc. Fellow Am. Inst. E.E.; Society for Promotion Engring. Edn., Sigma Xi, Tau Beta Pi, Phi Kappa Phi, Kappa Eta Kappa, Eta Kappa Nu. Republican. Address: Salem OR Died Dec. 2, 1968; buried Forest Hill Cemetery, Madison WI

JOHNSON, FRANKLIN PARADISE, anatomist, urologist; b. Hannibal, Mo., Jan. 7, 1888; s. Horace William and Lillie May (Paradise) J.; A.B., U. of Mo., 1908; A.M., Harvard, 1910, Ph.D., 1912; studied U. of Freiburg, Germany, summer, 1911; M.D., Johns Hopkins Univ., 1920; m. Juliette Omohundro, Sept. 4, 1923; children—Lillian Paradise, Virginia Martin, Louise Carter. Austin teaching fellow, Harvard Med. Sch., 1908-10; instr. histology and embryology, same sch., 1910-12; asst. prof. anatomy, 1912; asso. prof., 1913, prof., 1919-20, U. of Mo., interne New Haven Hosp., 1920-21; asst. resident in urology, 1921-22, resident, 1922-23, Johns Hopkins Hosp.; now practicing at Portland, Ore.; assistant clin. prof. urology, U. of Ore., since 1929. Member A.M.A., Am. Assn. Anatomists, Sigma Xi, Phi Beta Pi; fellow Am. Coll. Surgeons, Am. Urol. Association; diplomate Am. Bd. of Urology. Author various research papers on development of the digestive tract, embryology and histology of the liver, urethra, urol. subjects, etc.; collaborator Young's Practice of Urology, Nelson's Loose Leaf Surgery, Morris' Anatomy, 9th and 10th edits. Home: 2798 S.W. Talbot Rd. Office: Medical Arts Bldg., Portland, Ore. Died Feb. 12, 1943; buried in Riverwood Cemetery, Portland, Ore.

JOHNSON, JAMES MCINTOSH, chemist; b. Newberry, S.C., Aug. 15, 1883; s. William and Mary Eugenia (Kibler) J.; B.S., Newberry (S.C.) Coll., 1902, A.M., 1903; Ph.D., Johns Hopkins, 1908; m. Mabel Rebecca Earnshaw, Mar. 15, 1912; children—William Mercier, Mabel Eleanor, Phoebe Rebecca, Frances Lillian. Chemist, Johns Hopkins Hosp., 1908-09; chemist Bur. Chemistry, U.S. Dept. of Agriculture 1910-18; research chemist Hygienic Laboratory (now Nat. Inst. of Health), U.S. Pub. Health Service, Washington, D.C., since 1918. Mem. Am. Chem. Soc. Democrat. Lutheran. Co-discoverer of present method of making sulpharsphenamine. Contbr. to scientific jours. Home: 1333 Spring Rd. N.W. Office: 1339 H St. N.W., Washington. Died Mar. 2, 1953.

JOHNSON, JOHN MONROE, civil engr., r.r. exec.; b. Marion, S.C., May 5, 1878; s. John Monroe and Emma Crider (Richardson) J.; student U. of South Carolina, 1895-96, Furman U., 1896-97; m. Helen Barnwell, Nov. 15, 1900. In practice as civ. engr., mem. Johnson & Roberts, Marion, S.C., since 1898; prin. projects, Cow Castle Drainage Dist., Orangeburg, S.C., Catfish Drainage Dist., Dillon, S.C., Mars Bluff Bridge, Pee Dee, S.C., Society Hill (S.C.) Bridge, Godfreys Bridge, Gresham, S.C. Served as sergt. arty., U.S. Vols., Spanish-Am. War; maj., lt. col. and col., chief engr. Rainbow Div., U.S. Army, World War I; participated in all campaigns of the div. and was with Army of Occupation. Chief engr. and chmn. Marion County (S.C.) Highway Commn., 1912-14; chmn. S.C. State Highway Commn., 1916-17; apptd. boundary commr., S.C., 1928; asst. sec. of Commerce, 1935-40; apptd. mem. Interstate Commerce Commn., June 1940; apptd. Dir. Office of Defense Transportation, April 4, 1944; renominated by President Truman as interstate commerce commr., Jan. 1949, confirmed by Senate, Feb., term, 1949-55, chmn. 1950, 1953-56; became assistant to president A.C.L. R.R., 1956. Mem. Am. Soc. C.E., Am. Soc. Mil. Engrs. (pres. 1940-41), Mil. Order of World Wars, Am. Legion (mem. nat. exec. com. 1919-36), Sigma Nu. Omicron Delta Kappa. Awarded D.S.M. (U.S.); Verdun Medal, Legion of Honor (France), Order of Leopold II (Belgium). Received from President Truman, Medal for Merit, Mar. 8, 1946, in recognition of services to U.S. as dir. Office of Defense Transportation, Certificate of Appreciation, U.S. Navy, Sept. 12, 1946, in recognition of meritorious personal service during World War II. Mem. Newcomen Soc. in N.A., Order of Lafayette. Democrat. Baptist. Mason. Clubs: Army and Navy, Burning Tree, Post Mortem (Washington). Home: 3040 Idaho Av. N.W., Washington 25. Office: ACL R.R. Co., 1000 Connecticut Av. N.W., Washington. Deceased July 1, 1964.

JOHNSON, LEIGHTON FOSTER, otolaryngologist; b. Hingham, Mass., Nov. 30, 1891; s. Rev. Samuel F. and Dora Alice (Belcher) J.; M.D., Boston U., 1915; post grad. Harvard Med. Sch., 2 yrs.; m. Harriet Woodman, Nov. 28, 1917; children—Leighton Foster, David Stanton. Engaged in practice as physician, otolaryngologist, Boston, Mass., since 1923; prof. and head of dept. otolaryngology, Sch. of Medicine, Boston U., 1941-45; surgeon in chief, ear, nose, throat dept. Mass. Meml. Hosp., since 1941, pres. staff, 1952-53; consultant to Fitchburg, Natick, Norwood, Cape Cod, Marthas Vineyard and Nantucket hospitals; lecturer Wellesley College. Consultant to Guild for Hard of Hearing. Served as captain, Fourth Division, Medical Reserve Corps, United States Army, during World War I. Fellow American College Surgeons; mem. A.M.A. (pres. Norfolk Dist., 1935-36), Am. Bd. Otolaryngology, Am. Acad. Otolaryngology, Am. Bronchoscopic Soc., Am. Triological Soc., N.E. Otolaryngol. Soc. (pres.), Boston Surgical Soc., Am. Bronch-Aesophological Soc. (president elect), Psi Upsilon. Clubs: Algonquin (Boston); Wellesley (Mass.) Country; Wellfleet (Mass.) Country. Contbr. numerous articles to nat. sci. jours. Home: Longwood Towers, Brookline, Mass. Office: 203 Commonwealth Av., Boston. Died July 21, 1953.

JOHNSON, LEON H., coll. pres.; b. Hawley, Minn., Mar. 6, 1908; s. Hans L. and Petra (Solum) J.; B.A., Concordia Coll., Moorhead, Minnesota, 1932, Doctor of Humane Letters (hon.), 1966; Ph.D. in Biochemistry (Frasch research fellow 1940-43), U. Minn., 1943; m. Esther Pauline Evenson, June 6, 1936; children—Linda (Mrs. Louis Wendt), Vance (Mrs. Peter Anderson). High Sch. tchr., N.D., 1932-39; instr. agrl. biochemistry U. Minn., 1939-43; asso. prof. chemistry, research biochemist Mont. State Univ., Bozeman, 1943-48, prof. chemistry, 1948-69, dean grad. div. 1955-64, acting president, 1963-64, president, 1964-69, exec. dir. endowment and research found., 1947-65. Mem. Am. Chem. Soc., Sigma Xi, Phi Kappa Phi. Elk, Rotarian (pres. Bozeman 1950). Contbr. articles profl. jours. Home: Bozeman MT Died June 18, 1969; buried Bozeman MT

JOHNSON, L(EON) S(ANFORD), educator; b. Granger, Mo., Sept. 21, 1887; s. John Richard and Sarah Thorpe (Howard) J.; grad. Kirksville (Mo.) State Normal, 1907; B.S., U. Mo., 1916, A.M., 1918; postgrad. U. Chgo., 1924-30; m. Alice Helen Baker, Aug. 25, 1915; children—Sarah Alice (Mrs. J. C. Maycock), Harriet (Mrs. N. R. Arthur). High sch. mathematics tchr., Hannibal, Mo., 1908-09, Richmond, Mo., 1909-11, Lingayen, P.I., 1912-13; instr. mathematics U. Philippines, 1913-14, head math. dept. Wis. State Normal, La Crosse, 1917-19; instr. mathematics U.S. Naval Acad., 1919-22; asst. prof. mathematics Pa. State Coll. 1922-26, asso. prof., 1926-28; asso. prof. mathematics U. Detroit, 1928-31, prof. mathematics, 1931; civil engr., maintenance of way, C.B.&Q. R.R., hdqrs. Chgo., summers 1918, 19, 20, B.&O. R.R., summer 1922; surveyor, 1913-14. Mem. Math. Assn. Am. (chmn. Mich. sect. 1934-35), Phi Delta Kappa, Sigma Xi. Democrat. Baptist. Author: Elements of Nomography, 1936; Differential Equations (with Dr. L. E. Mehlenbacher), 1947-48. Contbr. numerous articles to Am. Math. Monthly, 1929—. Home: 16509 Wildemere Av., Detroit 21. Died Feb. 18, 1955.

JOHNSON, LEWIS JEROME, civil engr., publicist; b. Milford, Mass., Sept. 24, 1867; s. Napoleon Bonaparte and Mary Tufts (Stone) J.; A.B magna cum laude, Harvard, 1887; C.E., Lawrence Sci. Sch., 1888; student Federal Technische Hochschule, Zürich,

1888-89, and at École des Ponts et Chaussées, Paris, portion of 1889-90; m. Grace Allen Fitch, June 27, 1893 (dec.); children—Jerome Allen, Chandler Winslow. Instr. civil engring. Harvard, 1890-92; practiced at Chgo., 1892-94; instr. Harvard, 1894-96, asst. prof., 1896-1906, prof. civil engring., 1906-34, now prof. civil engring. emeritus; also prof. civil engring. Mass. Inst. Tech., 1914-19. Lectr. on applied econ. and polit. science Div. Unit. Extension, Mass. Dept. Edn., 1934—. Pres. Mass. Single Tax League, 1913-21, and of Nat. Single Tax League, 1918-20. Joint designer of Harvard Stadium. Fellow Am. Acad. Arts and Sciences; mem. Boston Soc. Civil Engrs., Am. Soc. C.E., Am. Assn. U. Profs., Porportional Representation Soc. (London), League of Nations Assn., Tau Beta Pi, Sigma Xi. Author: Statics by Algebraic and Graphic Methods, 1903; The Initiative and Referendum, An Effective Ally of Representative Government, 1909; The Cincinnati Plan (of city government) for American Cities, 1932; Undeveloped Possibilities of Democracy, 1932; Economic Taxes vs. Government Taxes, An Engineer's View of Taxation, 1934; other essays on generally overlooked fundamentals to polit. and econ. order. Joint author of proposed new charter (of 1911) for Cambridge, Mass.; collaborator with his son, Chandler, in the latter's drafting and securing the authorization of Plan E (Cincinnati Plan), optional for Mass. cities outside of Boston (chap. 378, Acts of 1938) and adopted by Worcester, Quincy, Medford and Revere. Contbr. to tech. jours. Home: 37 Kirkland St., Cambridge, Mass. Died Apr. 15, 1952; buried Milford, Mass.

JOHNSON, MARION ALVIN, coll. dean; b. nr. Oskaloosa, Ia., Aug. 27, 1901; s. Gilbert D. and Ora E. (Eckroat) J.; B.S., William Penn Coll., Oskaloosa, Ia., 1924; M.S., U. Chicago, 1926, Ph.D., (fellow botany, 1927-28), 1928; D.Sc. (honorary), William Penn Coll., 1959; m. Laura L. McKibben, June 18, 1928; children—Karl M., Bruce M., Ellen M. Prin., Searsboro (Ia.) Consol. High Sch., 1924-25; instr. botany Syracuse U., 1926-27; acting asso. prof. botany Ind. State Tchrs. Coll., Terre Haute, 1928-29; asst. prof. botany Rutgers U., 1929-41, asso. prof., 1941-47, prof. botany, 1947—, chmn. dept., 1945-54, dean grad. sch., 1954—. Mem. A.A.A.S., Bot. Soc. Am., Torrey Bot. Club, Phila. Bot. Club, Sigma Xi, Gamma Alpha. Home: 297 Franklin Rd., Colonial Gardens, North Brunswick, N.J. 08902. Died Nov. 9, 1964; buried Oskaloosa, Ia.

JOHNSON, MELVIN MAYNARD, JR., inventor, research cons., exec.; b. Boston, Aug, 27, 1909; s. Melvin Maynard and Ina Delphine (Freeman) J.; B.S., Harvard, 1931, LL.B., 1934; m. Virginia Bingham Rice, Oct. 10, 1934; children—Melvin Maynard, III, Edward Rice, Byron Bingham, Gail. Admitted to Mass. bar, 1935, bar of U.S. Ct., 1936; mem. Johnson and North, 1935-38; instr. Boston U. Law Sch., 1935-40. Invented Johnson semi-automatic rifle, 1936; Johnson light machine gun, 1937; Johnson light machine rifle, 1940; Johnson auto-carbine, 1941; Johnson Indoor Target-Gun, 1946, and other devices. Resigned as pres., dir. Johnson Automatics and subsidiaries to join Olin Industries, Inc., research-devel. div., 1949 as tech. dir., mgr. armament research, 1951-54; pres. Advanced Devels., Inc., New Haven, 1961—; cons. to Sec. of Def., Operations Research Office. Dept. of Army, Johns Hopkins, Fairchild Engines, research cons., and others; chmn. air weapons com. Research and Devel. Bd., ordnance cons., mem. gun panel; cons. munitions bd. Dept. Def. Commd. 2d lt. USMC Res., 1933, 1st lt., 1936, capt., 1938; served on Harvard Rifle Team, Harvard Varsity Crew, and Harvard R.O.T.C. field artillery; on inactive status 1942-45 by decision of Marine Corps; engaged in weapons devel.; transferred to Ordnance Corps inactive res. as col., 1949, ret., 1961. Awarded Army-Navy Certificate for Meritorious Service during World War II; DeMolay Legion of Honor. Mem. Am. Soc. M.E., Newcomen Soc., Nat. Rifle Assn., Am. Ordnance Assn. Marine Corps League. Episcopalian. Mason (32 deg.). Clubs: Hasty Pudding. Institute of 1770, D K E, Pi Eta (Harvard); The Brookline Country; New Haven Lawn; Boston Authors; River (N.Y.C.). Lectr. on weapons and nat. defense. Author: Automatic Arms; For Permanent Victory; Ammunition; Weapons for the Future; Rifles and Machine Guns; Practical Marksmanship; Automatic Weapons of the World; numerous articles in Ordnance, Marine Corps Gazette. Editor Weapons sect. Army World Book Ency., Grolier Ency. Home: 224 St. Ronan St. Died Jan. 8, 1965; buried Mt. Auburn Cemetery, Cambridge, Mass.

JOHNSON, OTIS COE, chemist; b. Kishwaukee, Ill., Sept. 11, 1839; s. William H. and Alma (Otis) J.; A.B., Oberlin, 1868, A.M., 1877; grad. Sch. of Pharmacy, U. of Mich., 1871; m. Katharine Crane, July 18, 1878. Instr., 1873-80, asst. prof., 1880-89, prof. qualitative chem. analysis, 1889-1911, emeritus prof. qualitative analysis, 1911—, U. of Mich. Author: Presscott's and Johnson's Qualitative Chemical Analysis (with A. B. Presscott), 1888, 1901. Wrote: Chemical Theory of Negative Bonds and Rule for Balancing Equations, Chemical News, 1880 (later incorporated in books of other authors). Home: Ann Arbor, Mich. Died June 6, 1912.

JOHNSON, PALMER O(LIVER), univ. prof.; b. Eagle Grove, Ia., Sept. 13, 1891; s. Nels Andrew and Elizabeth Ann (Osmundsen) J.; A.B., U. Wis., 1912; B.S., U. Minn., 1921, M.S., 1926, Ph.D., 1928; research studies, Galton Lab., U. London, 1934-35; m. Hildegard Binder, Aug. 20, 1936; children—Gisela, Karin. Teacher and adminstr. in pub. schs., Minn. and Ill., 1913-16, 1921-25; asst. prof. edn. U. Minn., 1928-34, asso. prof., 1934-36, prof. 1936—, chmn. dept. of statistics; vis. prof. U. W.Va., summer 1932. U. Tex., summer 1939; supt. animal breeding farms, 1917. Dir. Land-Grant Coll. Survey, Minn., 1928-30; specialist mem. survey commn. Higher Edn. Institutions, State of Ore., U.S. Office of Edn., 1929; prin. educationist and cons. Pres. Roosevelt's Adv. Com. on Edn., 1937-38; cons. Ednl. Policies Commn. since 1939; conferee research and statistics U.S. Office of Edn., 1947. Served as lt., Coast Arty., U.S. Army, 1918; coordinator and dir. Army Specialized Training Program of Exams, Minn., 1943-44. Fellow Am. Assn. Advancement of Sci. (v.p., chmn. Sect. Q, 1950), Am. Statistical Association (mem. council 1951-52); mem. Inst. of Math. Statistics, Psychometric Society, Biometric Society. Am. Ednl. Research Assn., Nat. Soc. for Study of Edn., N.E.A., Minn. Acad. Scis., Sigma Xi, Phi Delta Kappa, Gamma Sigma Delta, Alpha Zeta, Phi Kappa Sigma. Author: Curriculum Problems in Science, 1930; Aspects of Land-Grant College Education, 1934; (with O. L. Harvey) The National Youth Administration, 1938; (with others) The Effective General College Curriculum, 1937; (with others) An Evaluation of Modern Education, 1942; Statistical Methods in Research, 1949; (with others) Educational Research and Appraisal, 1953 (with R. W. B. Jackson) Introduction to Statistical Methods, 1953; Modern Statistical Methods: Inductive and Description (with R. W. B. Jackson), 1957; Modern Sampling Methods, 1959; articles profl., classical jours., yearbooks of national societies. Statistical editor Jour. of Exptl. Edn. Research in. statis. methods and exptl. designs, measurement, higher edn., science education. Home: 3312 Edmund Blvd., Mpls. 6. Died Jan. 1960.

JOHNSON, S(AMUEL) ARTHUR, zoologist; b. Morristown, N.J., Dec. 13, 1866; s. Charles Henry and Abigail Emily (Johnson) J.; B.S., Rutgers Coll., 1891, M.S., 1895; m. May Abigail Bice, of Elkhart, Ill., Jan. 15, 1896; children—Alice Mary (dec.), Miriam Abigail, Frederick Bice. Teacher pub. schs., Ill., 1892-95; instr. mathematics and science, West Side High Sch., Denver, Colo., 1896-1902; asst. in zoology, 1902-04, assistant professor, 1904-06, professor, 1906-35, dean, 1913-1935, Colorado State Agricultural College; retired, July 1, 1935. Mem. A.A.A.S., Assn. Econ. Entomologists, Colo. Teachers' Assn. (edn. council 1908-26), Nat. Council YMCA, Delta Kappa Epsilon, Alpha Zeta, Phi Kappa Phi, Pi Delta Epsilon, Scabbard and Blade. Presbyn. Mason. Rotarian. Home: Fort Collins, Colo.

JOHNSON, THOMAS HUMRICKHOUSE, civil engr.; b. Coshocton, O., Jan. 12, 1841; s. William Kerr and Elizabeth (Humrickhouse) J.; A.B., Jefferson (now Washington and Jefferson) Coll., Pa., 1861, A.M., 1866 (Sc.D., 1911); m. Martha E. Patterson, Oct. 28, 1868. Rodman on constrn. of Steubenville bridge, 1863, Marietta & Cincinnati R.R., 1864-65; asst. engr. Pana, Springfield & N.W. R.R., 1866-67, P.,C.C.&St.L. Ry., 1867-72; engr. Union Depot Co., Columbus, O., 1873-75; civil engr. and architect, Columbus, 1875-78; engr. for contractors, Ind. State House, 1878-83; prin. asst. engr., 1883-96, chief engr. Pa. Lines West of Pittsburgh, 1901—. Republican. Presbyterian. Home: Pittsburgh, Pa. Died Apr. 16, 1914.

JOHNSON, VIRGIL LAMONT, architect, engr.; b. Mannsville, Jefferson Co., N.Y., June 10, 1868; s. Levi and Harriet C. (Baker) J.; prep. edn., Adams (N.Y.) Collegiate Inst.; spl. course in architecture, U. of Pa., 1898; m. Elizabeth W. Johnson, of Phila., Pa., June 10, 1901; children—Katharine, Elenore, Harriette, Ruth, Virgil. Began in Buffalo, 1894; settled in Phila., 1901; chief structural engr. for over 160 public schs. bldgs. for Phila. Bd. of Edn. Mem. Am. Inst. Architects. Retired 1939. Home: 29 W. Upsal St., Germantown, Philadelphia, Pa.

JOHNSON, W. OGDEN, engring. and constrn. co. exec.; b. Austin, Pa., July 21, 1893; s. E. Randall and N. Ermina (Smith) J.; B.Mech. Engring., U. Mich., 1915, B.S. in Naval Architecture and Marine Engring., 1917; m. Agnes Lumbard, May 30, 1927 (dec. 1947); children—Suzanne (Mrs. Jacques T. Schlenger), Lucile (Mrs. Alan C. Holliday); m. 2d, Barbara Stanfield Dunn, June 17, 1950. Vice pres. La Rocca Constrn. Corp., subway constrn. N.Y.C., 1925-31, Hewitt Constrn. Corp., sewer and tunnel constrn., N.Y.C., 1931-33, Am. Sealcone Corp., N.Y.C., 1933-41; with Ford, Bacon & Davis, Inc., engrs., N.Y.C., 1941—, v.p., 1957-62, cons., 1962—. Served to lt. (j.g.) USNRF, 1917-19. Registered profl. engr., N.Y. Clubs: Huguenot Yacht (New Rochelle, N.Y.); Shenorock Shore (Rye, N.Y.); Downtown Athletic, Harbor View (N.Y.C.). Patentee culinary mixes, continuous mixing. Home: 47 Prescott Av., Bronxville, N.Y. Office: 2 Broadway, N.Y.C. 4. Died Jan. 1966.

JOHNSON, WALLACE CLYDE, civil engr.; b. Granville, Mass., May 21, 1859; s. James W. and Frances A. (Whitney) J.; ed. public and high schools to 1880; Williams Coll., 1880-82; grad. Worcester Polytechnic Inst., 1884; m. Eloise Gertrude Murlless, May 31, 1893. Asst. engr. Holyoke Water Power Co., 1884; chief engr. The Niagara Falls Hydraulic Power & Mfg. Co., 1886-1900; consulting engr., 1900—; also chief engr. Shawinigen Water & Power Co., Montreal; engr. mem. River Improvement Commission, State of N.Y. Home: Niagara Falls, N.Y. Died 1906.

JOHNSON, WILLIAM WOOLSEY, mathematician; b. Owego, N.Y., June 23, 1841; s. Charles Frederick and Sarah Dwight (Woolsey) J.; A.B., Yale U., 1862, A.M., 1868; LL.D., St. John's Coll., Md., 1915; m. Susannah Leverett Batcheller, Aug. 12, 1869 (died 1916). In U.S. Nautical Almanac Office, Cambridge, Mass., 1862-84; asst. prof. mathematics, U.S. Naval Acad., at Newport, R.I., and Annapolis, 1864-70; prof. mathematics, Kenyon Coll., Ohio, 1870-72, St. John's Coll., Md., 1872-81, U.S. Naval Acad., 1881—; prof. mathematics in the Navy, 1913—. Author: Differential Calculus (Rice and Johnson), 1879; An Elementary Treatise on the Integral Calculus, 1881; Curve Tracing in Cartesian Co-ordinates, 1884; The Theory of Errors and Method of Least Squares, 1890; Treatise on Differential Equations, 1889; Theoretical Mechanics, 1901; Treatise on Differential Calculus, 1904; Differential Equations (math. monographs), 1906; Treatise on Integral Calculus, 1907; an Elementary Treatise on the Differential Calculus, 1908. Home: Baltimore, Md. Died May 14, 1927.

JOHNSTON, CLARENCE THOMAS, civil engr.; b. Littleton, Colo., Oct. 23, 1872; s. James Albert and Melissa (Drummond) J.; B.S., U. of Mich., 1895, C.E., 1899; m. Bessie Vreeland, Oct. 20, 1897; children—Clarence Nettleton, Franklin Davis. In irrigation work with father, E. S. Nettleton, and Elwood Mead, 1890-1911; in employ state of Wyo., summers, 1891-96; asst. state engr., 1895-99; with U.S. Geol. Survey, 1896-98, and in irrigation and drainage work, U.S. Dept. Agr., 1899-1903 (made trip to Egypt and reported on Egyptian irrigation); state engr. of Wyo., 1903-11; became prof. surveying and geodesy, University of Michigan, 1911, now emeritus. Fellow A.A.A.S.; mem. American Society Civil Engineers (member executive committee div. surveying and mapping, 1926-31; Mich. Engring. Soc., Sigma Xi, Tau Beta Pi, Acacia. Conglist. Author reports, bulls. and papers relating to irrigation and drainage and the principles which should underlie legislation dealing with the use of water from streams and lakes, also contbr. on geodesy and surveying. Home: 1235 Hill St., Ann Arbor MI

JOHNSTON, FRANKLIN DAVIS, physician; b. Cheyenne, Wyo., June 23, 1900; s. Clarence Thomas and Bessie (Vreeland) J.; B.S., U. Mich., 1922, M.D.,1929; m. Margaret Newell Woodwell, June 10, 1926;children—Richard W., Robert F., Marjory A. Intern U. Mich. Hosp., 1929-30, resident, 1930-32; practice medicine, specializing in cardiology, Ann Arbor, Mich., 1932-71; with Heart Sta. U. Hosp., 1932-71; sec. Med. Sch. U. Mich., 1943-48, mem. exec. bd. Grad. Sch., 1959-64. Served with U.S. Army, 1918. Recipient Henry Russel award U. Mich., 1937-38; James B. Herrick award Am. Heart Assn., 1969. Mem. Assn. U. Cardiologists (past pres.), Central Soc. Clin. Research, N.Y. Acad. Scis., Am. Heart Assn. (served on research com. many years. Mem. editorial bd. Virculation. Home: Ann Arbor MI Died Apr. 8, 1971; buried Washtenong Meml. Park, Ann Arbor MI

JOHNSTON, HERRICK LEE, chemist; b. North Jackson, O., Mar. 29, 1898; s. Edgar Francis and Adelaide Sarah (Simpson) J.; A.B., Muskingum Coll., 1922, B.S., Wooster Coll., 1922, D.Sc., 1943; Ph.D., U. Cal., 1928; m. Margaret Gardner Vanderbilt, June 14, 1923; children—William Vanderbilt, Margaret Louise, Robert Edgar. Instr., Shiloh (O.) High Sch., 1916-17; grad. asst. chemistry Ohio State U., 1923-24; teaching fellow chemistry, U. Cal., 1925-28, instr., 1928-29; asst. prof. chemistry, Ohio State U., 1929-33, asso. prof., 1933-38, prof., 1938-54; fellow John Simmons Guggenheim Mem. Found., U. Goettingen (Germany), 1933; research engr. Gen. Electric Research Labs., Schenectady, 1937; dir. Manhattan Project Research, Ohio State U., 1942-46; dir. Cryogenic Lab., Ohio State U., also Rocket Motor Lab., 1946-51; 1942-54; pres. Herrick L. Johnston, Inc., Johnston Research and Devel. Labs., 1954—. Fellow Am. Phys. Soc., A.A.A.S.; mem. Internat. Inst. Refrigeration (tech. com., 1948), Internat. Union Pure and Applied Physics (com. low temperature physics 1948-51, internat. com. thermo-dynamics and electro chemistry), Am. Chem. Soc. (past nat. sec., nat. chmn., div. phys. and inorganic chemistry; past chmn. divisional officers group; past chmn. Columbus sect.), N.A.M., NRC (mem. com. deuterium research, 1934-37; com. thermodynamic constants, 1940—, com. on natural and phys. constants, com. on phys. chem., 1948—), Am. Soc. M.E. (com. properties of gases), Ohio Post War Planning comm. (sci. com.), Am. Soc. Refrigeration Engrs. (com. on Low Temperature Research), Am. Rocket Soc. Author: Titanium and Its Compound. Asso. editor Jour. Chem. Physics, 1935-38; contbr. technical articles to sci. publications. Home: 177 Brevoort Rd., Columbus, O. Died Oct. 6, 1965; buried Union Cemetery, Columbus.

JOHNSTON, IVAN MURRAY, botanist; b. Los Angeles, Feb. 28, 1898; s. William Murray and Etta (Farnsworth) J.; Pomona Coll., Clermont, Cal.,

1916-18; A.B., Cal. U. (Berkeley), 1919, M.A., 1922; Ph.D., Harvard, 1925; m. Mildred Semva Williamson, Apr. 2, 1932; children—Elizabeth Page, William Murray. Asst. Gray Herbarium, Harvard, 1922-31; research asso., Arnold Arboretum, 1931-38; superv. Herbarium and Library, Arnold Arboretum since 1946; asso. dir. Arnold Arboretum 1948-54; lectr. botany, 1934-38, asso. prof. since 1938. Fellow A.A.A.S.; mem. Am. Acad. Arts and Sciences, Bot. Soc. Am., Am. Soc. Naturalists, Am. Soc. Plant Taxonomists, New England Bot. Club, Sigma Xi, Gamma Alpha. Corr. mem. Argentine Soc. Natural Science, Chilean Soc. Natural Hist. Mason. Methodist. Republican. Club: Faculty (Cambridge). Contbr. many tech. papers on classification Am. flowering plants, specialty of U.S., Mexican, and S.Am. deserts. Home: 383 South St. Office: Arnold Arboretum, Jamaica Plain, Mass. Died May 31, 1960.

JOHNSTON, JOHN, agriculturist; b. New Galloway, Scotland, Apr. 11, 1791; m. 1818, several children. Came to U.S., 1821; bought farm nr. Geneva, N.Y., 1821; 1st in U.S. to drain farm land by burying tiles; one of 1st to use lime and plaster and surface application of manure to increase crop yield; his farm became model of advanced agrl. techniques. Died Geneva, Nov. 24, 1880.

JOHNSTON, JOHN, chemist; b. Perth, Scotland, Oct. 13, 1881; s. James and Christina (Leslie) J.; B.Sc., Univ. Coll. (U. of St. Andrews), Dundee, Scotland, 1903; work in chemistry, Univ. Coll., 1903-05, U. Breslau, Germany. Prof. Abegg, 1905-07; research asso. in phys. chemistry Mass. Inst. Tech., 1907-08; D.Sc., U. of St. Andrews, 1908; M.A. (hon.), Yale, 1919; D.Sc. (hon.), N.Y.U. 1928, Lehigh, 1929; m. Dorothy Hopkins, July 17, 1909; children—Helen Leslie, John Murray, William Valentine. On staff of Geophysical Lab., Carnegie Instn. of Washington, 1908-16; in charge research dept. for Am. Zinc, Lead and Smelting Co., St. Louis, 1916-17, U.S. Bur. of Mines, 1917-18; sec. NRC, Washington, 1918-19; prof. chemistry, chmn. chemistry dept. Yale, 1919-27; dir. of research U.S. Steel Inst., Am. Electrochem. Soc. (pres. 1933-34), British Iron and Steel Inst., Faraday Soc., Inst. Metals, Verein deutscher Eisenhüttenleute. Club: Century (New York). Address: Southwest Harbor, Me. Died Sept. 12, 1950; buried Southwest Harbor.

JOHNSTON, RICHARD HALL, laryngologist; b. Tarboro, N.C., Apr. 6, 1871; s. W. H. and Caroline J.; M.D., U. of Md. Sch. of Medicine, 1894; m. Mary Page Small, of Baltimore, Dec. 21, 1904. Practiced in Baltimore since 1897; clin. prof. largngology, U. of Md. Sch. of Medicine, since 1909; attending laryngologist, U. of Md. Hosp.; laryngologist, St. Joseph's German Hosp.; consulting laryngologist, South Baltimore Eye, Ear, Nose and Throat Hosp., Children's Hosp. Sch., James Lawrence Kernan Hosp.; visiting laryngologist, Havre de Grace Hosp., etc. Fellow Am. Coll. Surgeons; mem. Am. Acad. Ophthalmology and Oto-Laryngology, Am. Laryngol., Rhinol. and Otol. Soc. Democrat. Episcopalian. Address: 807 N. Charles St., Baltimore MD

JOHNSTON, SAMUEL, inventor; b. Shelby, Orleans Co., N.Y., Feb. 9, 1835; common school edn.; m. June 8, 1856, Arsula S. Vaughan, Cataraugus Co., N.Y. Inventor of corn planters, rotary and disk harrows, self-rakes for harvesters, mowing machines, corn harvesters, self-raking reapers, platform reapers and binders, cold rolling rolling-mills, roller reamers, roller forging mills. Also a metal working process by which finished articles are produced in duplicate; also a fuel burning device, etc. Address: 3 Oxford Av., Buffalo, N.Y.

JOHNSTON, WILLIAM ATKINSON, mech. engr.; b. South Boston, Mass., Aug. 31, 1868; s. Archibald and Mary (Watt) J.; B.S., Mass. Inst. Tech., 1892; m. Eleanor Chant, June 12, 1895 (died 1920); 1 dau., Ruth Stevens; m. 2d, Edith Crane Lanphere, Aug. 8, 1922. Prof. theoretical and applied mechanics, 1912-33, Mass. Inst. Tech., prof. emeritus, 1933—. Republican. Baptist. Co-Author: (with C. E. Fuller) Applied Mechanics, Vol. I, Statics and Kinetics, 1913; Applied Mechanics, Vol. II, Strength of Materials, 1919. Home: Belmont, Mass. Died Aug. 6, 1937.

JOHNSTON, WILLIAM DRUMM, JR., geologist; b. Garrett, Ind., Nov. 3, 1899; s. William Drumm and Jessie Mae (Kane) J.; B.S., U. Chgo., 1921; Ph.D., George Washington U., 1933; m. Madelene A. Thomas, 1931; children—William Drumm Iii, John Thomson, Richard Thomas, Elizabeth Louise. Faculty dept. geology U. Cin., U. Ky., N.M. Sch. Mines, 1922-28; geologist U.S. Geol. Survey, 1928-41, chief sect. fgn. geology, 1945-48, chief Alaskan and fgn. geology br., 1949-51, chief fgn. geology branch, 1951-64, staff geologist, 1965-70; with Bd. Econ. Warfare, Brazil, 1942-45. Del., 3d Pan-Am. Consultation on Cartography, Caracas, 1946; 2d Pan-Am. Congress Mining Engring. and Geology, Rio de Janeiro, 1946; U.S. govt. delegation Internat. Geol. Congress, Eng., 1948, Algiers, 1952, Mexico, 1956, Denmark, 1960, New Delhi, India, 1964, Prague, Czechoslovakia, 1968; del. to 4th Empire Mining and Metall. Congress, Eng., 1949; adv. Joint Brazil-U.S. Tech. Commn., Rio de Janeiro, 1948; chief U.S. Geol. Mission to Thailand, 1949-50; del. Indian Sci. Congress, Bangalore, 1951, centenary of Geol. Survey of India, Calcutta, 1951; adviser coms. on iron and steel and indsl. devel. Econ. Commn. for Asia and Far East, Lahore, 1951, chmn. U.S. delegation 1st Symposium on Devel. Petroleum in Asia, Delhi, 1958, adviser 2d Symposium, Tehran, 1962, 3d Symposium, Tokyo, Japan, 1965, Canberra, Australia, 1969; chmn. U.S. delegation Seminar on Devel. and Use Natural Gas in Asia, Tehran, 1964; del. working party geol. map Asia, ECAFE, Calcutta, 1957, Tokyo, 1960, Manila, 1963, Bangkok, 1966, Terhan, 1968; del. Nat. Acad. Sci., Pacific Sci. Congress, Bangkok, 1958, Tokyo, 1966; observer 4th Inter-Territorial Geol. Conf., Entebbe, 1951; Inter-Guianean Geol. Conf., Georgetown, 1959; adviser conf. on application sci. and tech. for benefit underdeveloped nations UN, Geneva, 1963; del. UNESCO Conf. on Application Sci. and Tech. to Devel. Latin Am., Santiago, Chile, 1965; v.p. for N.A., Internat. Geol. Congress Commn. for Geol. Map of World, 1956-66; mem. U.S. Commn. Geology, 1961-72; pres. sub-com. for Metallogenic Map of World, 1957-72; mem. NAS-NRC com. Inter-Am. Sci. Coop., 1960-62, Latin Am. Sci. Bd., 1963-69. Decorated Cruizeiro de Sul (Brazil), 1952; recipient Distinguished Service medal Dept. Interior, 1959; Jose Bonifacio de Andrade medal Geol. Soc. Brazil, 1959, Leipold von Buch medal German Geol. Soc. 1963; named prof. honoris causa Fed. U. Rio de Janeiro (Brazil), 1970. Fellow Am. Acad. Arts and Scis., Geol. Soc. Am., Mineral. Soc. Am.; mem. Soc. Econ. Geologist (sec. 1938-41, v.p. 1957), Geol. Soc. Washington (pres. 1957), Pan-Am. Inst. Mining, Engring. and Geology (chmn. U.S. sect. 1948-49), Am. Rhododendron Soc., Sigma Xi; corr. mem. geol. socs. Argentina, Brazil, W. Germany, Peru, Brazil Acad. Sci. Clubs: Cosmos (Washington); Engenharia (Rio de Janeiro). Contbr. articles on geology and ore deposits to tech. jours. Home: Washington DC Died Nov. 5, 1972.

JOHNSTONE, HENRY FRASER, educator, chem. engr.; b. Georgetown, S.C., Dec. 16, 1902; s. William Henry and Elise (Moore) J.; B.S., U. South, 1923, Sc.D. (hon.); M.S., U. Ia., 1925, Ph.D., 1926; m. Mary Lee, Aug. 28, 1926; 1 dau., Mary Lee (Mrs. Ronald DeWald). Grad. assistant in chemistry University of Iowa, 1923-24, research asst., 1924-25, research fellow, 1925-26; asst. prof. chemistry U. of Miss., 1926-28; spl. res. asst., engring. expt. sta., U. of Ill., 1928-30, spl. research asso., 1930-32, spl. research asst. prof., 1932-35, professor of chem. engring., 1939-56, research prof. chem. engring., 1956—. Chmn. Chem. Corps Research Council, 1948-52; sci. advisor L.A. Co. Air Pollution Control Dist., 1948—. Received Naval Ordnance award, 1946, President's Certificate of Merit, 1948, Walker medal Am. Inst. Chem. Engring., 1943. Mem. American Soc. Engring. Edn., Am. Chem. Soc., Am. Inst. Chem. Engring., Tau Beta Pi, Phi Beta Kappa, Sigma Xi, Sigma Nu, Alpha Chi Sigma, Tau Beta Pi. Episcopalian. Club: Cosmos (Washington). Contbr. sci. articles Indsl. Engring. Chemistry, Chem. Engring. Progress, Jour. Am. Chem. Soc. Developed methods for treatment of waste gases to prevent atmospheric pollution. Home: 802 Delaware Av., Urbana, Ill. Died Jan. 8, 1962; buried Mt. Hope Cemetery, Urbana, Ill.

JOHONNOTT, EDWIN SHELDON, physicist; b. Richmond, Ill., Nov. 9, 1868; s. Edwin Sheldon and Frances L. (Brown) J.; B.S., Rose Poly. Inst., Terre Haute, Ind., 1893, M.S., 1897; Johns Hopkins, 1895-96, U. of Chicago, 1896-99; Ph.D., 1898; m. Mabel M. Stevens, Aug. 22, 1900. Prof. mathematics, physics and astronomy, Drury Coll., 1894-95; asst. in lab., U. of Chicago, 1898-99; asso. prof. physics, 1899-1909, prof., 1909—, Rose Poly. Inst. Home: Terre Haute, Ind. Died Jan. 2, 1925.

JOLLIFFE, CHARLES BYRON, electronics exec.; b. Mannington, W.Va., Nov. 13, 1894; s. Charles E. and Sallie (Vandervort) J.; B.S., W.Va. University, 1915, M.S., 1920; Ph.D., Cornell University, 1922; LL.D., W.Va. U., 1942; m. Ola Kiser, Sept. 21, 1918 (dec.); children—Jane, Julia (dec.) (twins). Instr. physics, W.Va. U., 1917-20, Cornell U., 1920-22; with radio sect. Bur. of Standards, Wash., D.C., 1922-30, serving as asst. chief and actg. chief; chief engr. Federal Radio Commn. and Federal Communications Commn., 1930-35; engr. in charge RCA Frequency Bur., Radio Corp. of America, 1935-41; chief engr. RCA Laboratories, 1941; assistant to president, RCA, 1942, vice-president and chief engineer, RCA Manufacturing Co., Inc., 1942, chief engineer, RCA Victor Div., RCA, 1943-45; exec. v.p. RCA in charge RCA Labs. Division, 1945-51, vice pres. tech. dir. RCA, 1951-59, also mgr. special systems and development dept.; director of RCA, National Broadcasting Company, Inc., RCA Comunications, Inc.; developed frequency standards for measuring operating frequencies of radio stations; mem. 3d and 4th nat. radio confs.; tech. asst. U.S. del. Internat. Radio Conf., Washington, 1927; International Tech. Cons. Committee on Radio Meeting, The Hague, 1929; U.S. delegate to 2d meeting, Copenhagen, 1931, to Internat. Telecommunications Conf., Madrid, 1932; chief tech. adviser N. Am. Regional Radio Conf., Mexico City, 1933. RCA rep. to internat. radio conferences, Paris, 1936, Bucharest, 1937, Inter-Am. Radio Conf., Havana, 1937, Internat. Telecommunications Confs., Cairo, 1938, Atlantic City, 1947; chief electrical communications div., Nat. Defense Research Com., 1940-44; sec. Industry Adv. Com., Bd. of War Communications, 1941-47. Chmn., Allocations Panel, Radio Tech. Planning Bd., 1942-46. Profl. engineer, New York. Fellow A.A.A.S., American Institute Electric Engineers, Institute Radio Engineers; Radio Club of America; member Sigma Xi, Phi Beta Kappa. Presbyterian. Club: Cosmos (Washington). Home: Olney MD Died July 16, 1970.

JOLLIFFE, NORMAN H(AYHURST), (jolif), physician; b. Knob Fork, W.Va., Aug. 18, 1901; s. Clarence Franklin and Romanza (Hayhurst) J.; B.Sc., W.Va. U., 1923; M.D., Univ. and Bell Hosp. Med. Coll., 1926; m. Edna Suddaby, Aug. 15, 1929 (dec. 1938); 1 son, Norman; m. 2d, Lillian Lebowitz, June 5, 1939. Intern Bellevue Hosp., N.Y.C., 1927-28, resident, 1929-30, dir. med. services, psychiatric div., 1932-45; instr. physiology N.Y.U., 1930-32, instr., asst. prof., asso. prof. medicine, 1932-45; asso. prof. nutrition, sch. pub. health Columbia, 1945-59, lecturer in public health nutrition, 1959—; opened first nutrition clinic N.Y.C. Dept. of Health, 1945, dir. bur. nutrition, 1949—. Mem. Newfoundland internat. survey teams, 1944, 48; condr. nutrition status surveys in Brazil, Formosa, Cuba; mem. food, nutrition bd. Nat. Research Council, 1941-56, chmn. sub-com. med. nutrition, 1953—; mem. sci. adv. com. Williams-Waterman Fund of Research Corp. Gov. Nat. Vitamin Found.; cons. Interdeptl. Com. on Nutrition for National Defense. Recipient Carlos J. Findlay award pub. health work Republic Cuba, 1956; award, contbn. to enrichment of bread Am. Bakers Assn., 1956. Diplomate Am. Bd. Internal Medicine, Am. Bd. Preventive Medicine and Pub. Health. Fellow N.Y. Acad. Medicine, Harvey Soc., American Physiological Soc., Am. College Physicians. Author: Reduce and Stay Reduced, 1952, revised edition 1957; The Reducing Diet Guide, 1952. Co-editor: Clinical Nutrition, 1950. Contbr. profl. jours. Home: 910 Park Av., N.Y.C. 10021. Office: 125 Worth St., N.Y.C. 10013. Died Aug. 1, 1961; buried Knob Fork, W.Va.

JONES, AMANDA THEODOSIA, author; b. E. Bloomfield, N.Y., Oct. 19, 1835; d. Henry and Mary Alma (Mott) J.; grad. normal classes Aurora Acad., and High Sch., Buffalo; unmarried. Wrote for Methodist Ladies' Repository, 1853-62, Frank Leslie's Illustrated, 1861-65; lit. editor The Western Rural, 1869-70, The Bright Side, 1870-71. Author: Ulah and Other Poems (2 edits.), 1861; Atlantis and Other Poems, 1866; A Prairie Idyl, 1882; Flowers and a Weed (booklet), 1899; Rubaiyat of Solomon and Other Poems, 1905; Poems, 1854-1906, 1906; A Mother of Pioneers, 1908; A Psychic Autobiography, 1910 (republished in London). Inventor: Vacuum preserving processes for canning without cooking, canning with cooking and desiccation of fruits, meats, etc., without use of preservatives; appliances, retorts, etc., for carrying on vacuum processes; the Jones Direct Feed Safety Oil-Burning System; the Jones Protection Valve (all patented); also improvements upon protection valve and additions thereto, comprising a series of valves applicable to oil, air, vacuum, steam, gas, etc. Address: Junction City, Kan. Deceased.

JONES, BARTON MILLS, civil and hydraulic engr.; b. Parsons, Kan., Apr. 12, 1885; s. Robert Mills and Alice (Barton) J.; B.S. in Mech. Engring. and Elec. Engring., U. Cal., 1908; m. Mary Todd, June 2, 1914; children—Alice Barton (Mrs. Edward W. Burdge), Barton Mills II. Asst. engr. The Nevada California Power Co., 1904-05; part time draftsman Cory, Meredith & Allen, Pelton Water Wheel Co., and C. C. Moore, San Francisco, 1905-08; asst. engr. hydro-electric project on Rio Verde for Ariz. Power Co., 1908-10; chief engr., water power investigations, Boston-Colo. Power Co., 1910-12; hydraulic engr. Electric Bond & Share Co., New York, 1912-14; investigations and planning, also designing constrn. installations and equipment on flood control of Miami Valley, O., for Morgan Engring. Co. and Miami Conservance Dist., 1914-17, charge constrn. Lockington hydraulic fill dam, same, 1918-21; chief engr. flood control, Pueblo Conservancy Dist., Colo., 1921-26; pvt. cons. practice in irrigation, drainage, flood control, gold dredge mining, etc., 1926-29; oil field development, Petroleum Reclamation Co., Bradford, Pa., 1930; head Antioch Industrial Research Corp. and dept. engring. Antioch Coll., Yellow Springs, O., 1930-33; constrn. engr. in charge planning and building Norris Dam, TVA, 1933-36, head design dept., embracing all projects, same, 1936-39, cons. design engr., 1939-41, head planning engr., 1941-42; Ingeniero-Director, Central Hidroclectric Del Cañon Del Pato, Peru, S.A., 1942-48; pvt. cons. engr. 1949; chief engr., gen. mgr. Miami (O.) Conservancy Dist., 1950-56; pvt. cons. practice, 1956—. Mem. Edison Pioneers, Am. Soc. C.E., Colo. Soc. Engrs., Tau Beta Pi. Presbyn. Mason (32 deg. Shriner). Club: Technical (Knoxville, Tenn.). Contbr. to tech. jours. Home: 1642 Brandon Av., Cin. 30. Died Oct. 14, 1957.

JONES, BASSETT, elec. engr.; b. West Brighton, S.I., N.Y., Feb. 6, 1877; s. Bassett and Sarah Catherine (Oakley) J.; student Mass. Inst. Tech., 1896-99; m. Emma M. Starr, May 20, 1907 (dec.); m. 2d, Emily L. Warren, Mar. 11, 1922. Mem. Meyer, Strong & Jones, Inc., cons. engr., N.Y. City cons. on illumination N.Y. World's Fair, 1939. Fellow Am. Geog. Soc.; mem. Am. Standards Assn., (chmn. elevator standards com.; mem.

elevator safety code com.; chmn. sub-com. on elevator safety research); Archtl. League New York, Am. Soc. M.E., Am. Statistical Assn., Soc. Am. Foresters. Clubs: Century, Explorers, Cruising Club of America. Received hon. degree of M.E. from Stevens Inst. Tech. Home: Nantucket Island, Mass.; and 101 Park Av., New York, N.Y. Died Jan. 25, 1960.

JONES, CALVIN, physician; b. Great Barrington, Mass., Apr. 2, 1775; s. Ebeneezer and Susannah (Blackmer) J.; m. Temperance Williams, 1819. Licensed to practice medicine in Mass., 1792; practiced medicine, Great Barrington, 1792-95, Smithfield, N.C., 1795, Raleigh, N.C., 1803-32; a founder N.C. Med. Soc., 1799; mem. lower house N.C. Legislature, 1799, 1802, 07; co-owner newspaper Star, Raleigh, 1808-15; adjutant gen. N.C. Militia, 1808, maj. gen. N.C. Militia during War of 1812, organized coastal defenses of state; one of 1st physicians in state to urge use of inoculation against smallpox; active Freemason; retired, 1832, moved to estate nr. Bolivar, Tenn. Died at estate Pontine, nr. Bolivar, Sept. 20, 1846.

JONES, CHARLES COLCOCK, III, mining and metall. engr.; b. Augusta, Ga., July 28, 1865; s. Joseph and Caroline S. (Davis) J.; student U. of La. (now Tulane U.). New Orleans, 1882, La. State U., Baton Rouge, 1882-84; B.S., Lehigh U., Bethlehem, Pa., 1887; m. Elizabeth Clayton King, May 21, 1898. Asst. supt. blast furnace dept. Pa. Steel Co., Steelton, Pa., 1887-89; supt. and chemist Va. Nail and Iron Works. Reusens, Va., 1889-90; asst. engr., mine surveys corps. Flat Top Coal Land Assn. Pocahontas, 1890-91; mining and civil engr. Cranes Nest Coal and Iron Co. Dunn Coal Land Co., 1891-92; coal operator, Wise County, Va., 1892-96; examining engr. Southern States and Central America, 1896-98; operator of gold mine, Ga., 1897-99; cons. engr. and mine mgr. for Edward N. Breitung, Marquette, Mich. and v.p. and mgr. Mary Charlotte Co., 1899-1902; mining and examining engr., Mountain Copper Co., Keswick, Calif.; rehabilitated Iron Mountain Mine and controlled under ground fire conditions to permit of ore recovery and extraction, 1902-04; discovered and opened inter-mountain phosphate fields of Ida., Wyoming, and Utah, shipped first car of phosphate rock ever mined in west from Cokeville, Wyo., to Los Angeles; cons. engr. Salt Lake City, 1904-06. Moved to Los Angeles, 1906; associated with L.C. Dillman in Copper River, Alaska, properties; pres. and mgr. Compania Mexicana Pacifico de Fierro, iron property, in Michoacan, Mexico, also pres. and mgr. Frances Copper Mining Co., Calif.; owner Vulcan Iron Deposits, Kelso, Calif., until sold to Kaiser interests, June 1942, when its iron ore became initial supply for blast furnace of the Kaiser Co., Inc., Iron and Steel Div., Fontana, Calif. Mem. Am. Inst. Mining and Metall. Engrs., Mining Assn. of Southwest, Soc. Colonial Wars (Calif. chapter), Kappa Alpha (Southern), Sigma Xi. Episcopalian. Author of many articles in tech. publs., including Phosphate Rock in Ida. and Wyo., An Iron Deposit in the Calif. Desert Region, Iron Ores of the Southwest, The Discovery and Opening of a New Phosphate Field in the U.S. and The Pacific Coast Iron Situation; report on Western Phosphate Field, 1903-05, placed in National Archives on request of U.S. Dept. of Interior. Home: University Club of Los Angeles, 614 S. Hope St., Los Angeles 14

JONES, CHESTER MORSE, physician; b. Portland, Me., Mar. 29, 1891; s. Harry Lee and Maria Albertina (Morse) J.; B.A., Williams Coll., 1913, D.Sc., 1942; M.D., Harvard, 1919; m. Kathleen Holmes, June 7, 1920; children—Robert H., Elizabeth M. (wife of Dr. Sam L. Clark, Jr.), Anne K. (wife of Dr. Ward Stoops). Intern Mass. Gen. Hosp., 1918-19, various staff positions, 1919-57, bd. consultants, 1957-64, honorary physician, 1964-72; member of the faculty Harvard Med. Sch., 1921-72, clin. prof. medicine, 1940-57, prof. emeritus, 1957-72, also spl. cons. to dean; William O. Moseley Jr. traveling fellow (Harvard) to Strasbourg, France, 1924-25, Henry Pickering Walcott fellow clin. medicine, 1925-28; acting asso. prof. medicine Vanderbilt U., 1940-41; cons. medicine Surg. Gen. U.S. Army, 1944-46; mem. Unitarian Service Com., Med. Missions to Austria, Greece, Italy, 1947-48. Recipient Rogerson cup and medal Williams Coll., 1956; Shattuck lectr. Mass. Med. Soc., 1958. Diplomate Am. Bd. Internal Medicine (chmn. 1955-57), Fellow Royal Coll. Physicians and Surgeons of Can. (hon.); mem. Am. Soc. for Clin. Investigation, Assn. Am. Physicians, Harvard Med. Alumni Assn. (pres.-elect), Am. Gastroenterological Soc. (pres. 1936), Am. Clin. and Climatological Soc. (pres. 1951), A.C.P. (member of board of regents; mastership 1958; pres. 1961-62). Author: Digestive Tract Pain, 1938. Editorial bd. New Eng. Jour. Medicine, Gastroenterology, Annals of Internal Medicine. Author med. articles on digestive tract physiology and disease. Home: Boston MA Died July 1972.

JONES, CLEMENT ROSS, engineer; b. Knottsville, W.Va., Apr. 19, 1871; s. Uriah and Pernissa Jane (Ford) J.; B.S., C.E., W.Va. U., 1894, M.E., 1897; Worcester Poly. Inst., summer 1896; Stevens Inst. Tech., summer 1897; M.M.E., Cornell, 1900; m. Elizabeth Charles Gambrill, July 22, 1915; 1 son, Ross Gambrill. Mem. engring. firm Jones & Jenkins, 1894-98; asst. in mech. engring., 1895-97, instr., 1897-99, asst. prof., 1899-1901, prof. and head dept., 1901-11, dean Coll. Engring. and prof. steam and exptl. engring., W.Va. U., 1911-32, dean emeritus and prof. power engring., 1932—. Sec. engring. sect. Land Grant Coll. Assn., 1921-24, mem. com. on engring. expt. sta., 1924-27; chmn. engineering sect. of same assn., 1928-29. Editor Experiment Station Record, 1921-24. Chmn. fuel com., 1917-18. Grad. as No. 1, and 1st lt. adj. W.Va. Corps of Cadets, 1894; 1st lt. W.Va. N.G., 1894; capt. 1896. Republican. Methodist. Mason. Home: Morgantown, W.Va. Died Aug. 16, 1939.

JONES, DANIEL JONATHAN, geologist; b. German, N.Y., Jan. 16, 1889; s. Jonathan E. and Hannah E. (Fernalld) J.; B.S., Syracuse U., 1913, M.S., 1916; m. Matilda T. Gilcher, Aug. 1, 1923; 1 dau., Charlotte L. Price. Instr. geology U. Tex., 1914-17; geologist McMan Oil Co., 1917, Eastern Gulf Oil Co., 1917-30; state geologist, Ky., 1934-59. Mem. com. Interstate Oil Compact Commn. Recipient Ann. conservation award State of Ky., 1963; named Ky. col., 1959. Mem. Am. Assn. Petroleum Geologists, Soc. Econ. Geologists, Assn. Am. State Geologists (pres. 1955), Ky., Ind., Appalachian geol. socs., Ky. Acad. Sci., Sigma Pi. Presbyn. Mason. Clubs: Rotary, Associated. Contbr. articles profl. publs. Home: 1471 Tates Creek Rd., Lexington 40502. Office: 120 Graham Av., Lexington, Ky. Died Dec. 18, 1965; buried Woodlawn Cemetery, Syracuse, N.Y.

JONES, DONALD FORSHA, geneticist; b. Hutchinson, Kan., Apr. 16, 1890; s. Oliver Winslow and Minnie Wilcox (Bush) J.; B.S., Kan. State Coll., 1911; M.S., Syracuse University, 1916; Sc.D., Harvard, 1918; Sc.D., (hon.) Kansas State Coll., 1947; m. Eleanor March, Dec. 20, 1915; children—Loring March, Margaret Louise. Asst. plant breeder, Ariz. Agrl. Expt. Sta., 1911-13; instr. horticulture and genetics, Syracuse U., 1913-15; geneticist, Conn. Agrl. Expt. Sta., 1915-60, now emeritus, head dept., 1915-60; geneticist, U. Conn.; lectr. Yale, 1961; vis. prof. U. Washington, 1953 propr. Seed Producers Adv. Service. Awards from several orgns. include Distinguished Service Award Am. Farm Bur., 1950 and Award of Merit from Am. Seed Trade Assn., 1947; N.E. Fellowship of Agrl. Adventures, by N.E. Council and Govs. N.E. States, 1953. Mem. A.A.A.S., Am. Naturalists Soc.; American Genetic Assn., Genetic Soc. America, Bot. Soc. American, Am. Acad. Arts and Sciences, Nat. Acad. Sciences, Conn. Acad. Arts and Sciences, Nat. Grange, Societa Italiana Genetica Agraria, Sigma Nu. Alpha Zeta, Phi Kappa Phi, Sigma Xi. Conglist. Clubs: Yale Faculty, Graduates. Author books in field of genetics. Editor of Genetics, 1925-35, now mem. editorial bd. Address: Box 1106, New Haven. Died June 19, 1963.

JONES, EDWARD CAMPBELL, gas engr.; b. South Boston, Mass., Feb. 8, 1861; s. Edward and Hannah Frances (Campbell) J.; ed. Lowell (Mass.) Inst., and Hawes Sch. of Art; m. Mary Stratton Jones, Nov. 22, 1883 (died 1922); children—Edward Stratton, Leon Barrett, Dwight Williams; m. 2d, Florence C. Harris, May 19, 1926. Began in the employ of South Boston Gas Light Co., 1876, and became asst. supt. and clerk of corp.; with Boston Gas Light Co. as supt. North End Sta., and asst. engr., 1889-90; asst. engr., later chief engr., San Francisco Gas Light Co., 1891-1902; chief engr. Calif. Central Gas & Electric Co., 1902-04; chief engr. gas dept. Calif. Gas & Electric Corp., 1904-06; chief engr. gas dept. Pacific Gas & Electric Co., 1906-20; later cons. gas engr. Had charge of restoration of gas in San Francisco after earthquake, 1906; lecturer in gas engring., U. of Calif., 1913; advisory gas engr., U.S. Bur. Standards. Del. Am. Gas Assn. to U.S. Chamber of Commerce. Awarded medal of honor and gold medal, San Francisco Expn., 1915; gold medal, Pacific Coast Gas Assn. Republican. Conglist. Mason. Author of numerous professional papers relating to heating and gas. Inventor of Jones Oil Gas Process and Jones Jet Photometer. Home: Palo Alto, Calif. Died July 22, 1933.

JONES, E(RNEST) LESTER, hydrographic and geodetic engr.; b. E. Orange, N.J., Apr. 14, 1876; s. Charles Hopkins and Ada (Lester) J.; mem. class of 1898, Princeton, A.M., 1919; m. Virginia Brent Fox, Sept. 28, 1897; children—Mrs. Elizabeth Brent Barker, Cecil Lester. Business, research and secretarial work 10 yrs.; U.S. dep. commr. fisheries, 1913-15; apptd. supt. U.S. Coast and Geod. Survey, Apr. 1915, title changed to dir., 1919, and commd. dir., 1920. Commr. Internat. Boundary bet. U.S. and Can. (Alaska and Can.); mem. first Aerial Coastal Patrol Commn.; mem. Federal Bd. Surveys and Maps, Federal Personnel Bd. Served pvt. to maj., D.C. Militia; commd. lt. col. Signal Corps U.S.A., World War, later col. Div. Mil. Aeronautics; served with A.E.F. in France and Italy. An organizer and incorporator Am. Legion; organizer, 1st comdt. 1st American Legion Post (Pioneer Post) and 1st Am. Legion Dept. Diploma of Honor, Aerial League America; decorated Officer Order S.S. Maurizio e Lazzaro, by King of Italy, and Fatigue de Guerre (Italy); Officer Legion of Honor (France); Verdun medal. Cited for D.S.M. Author: Alaska Investigations, 1914; Hypsometry, 1915; Elements of Chart Making, 1915; Neglected Waters of the Pacific, 1916; Safeguard the Gateways of Alaska, 1917; Aerial Surveying, 1919; Earthquake Investigation in United States, 1925; Tide and Current Investigations of the U.S.C. and G.S., 1926—all Govt. publs.; Surveying from the Air, 1922; The Evolution of the Nautical Chart, 1924; Science and the Earthquake Perils, 1926. Called first meeting, Feb. 5, 1919, and first caucus World War Vets., at Washington, D.C., Mar. 7, 1919; wrote first draft Preamble and Constn. of Am. Legion, and presented same, St. Louis Conv., May 1919. Home: Rixeyville, Va. Died Apr. 9, 1929.

JONES, FORREST ROBERT, engineer; b. Cincinnati, Dec. 12, 1861; s. Martin Ryan and Susan (Hageman) J.; M.E., Cornell, 1888; m. Miss Johnnie House Fletcher, of Knoxville, Tenn., Oct. 17, 1892. Apprentice Niles Tool Works, 1881-84; designer and experimenter, Edison's lab. and phonograph works, Orange, N.J., 1888; in charge of electric ry. and lighting plant constrn., Western Engring. Co. and Edison General Co., 1889-90; supt. mech. dept., 1890-1901; prof. mech. arts, 1901-02, U. of Tenn.; prof. machine design, U. of Wis., 1892-99; prof. drawing and machine design, Worcester Poly. Inst., 1899-1903; prof. machine design, Sibley Coll., Cornell, 1903-05; pres. Manhattan Automobile Sch., New York, since 1905. Designed machinery for phonograph manufacture and for putting high resistance insulation on wires, 1888; visited the principal tech. schs., and many of the commercial mfg. establishments in Eng. and on the continent to study their methods, giving spl. attention to gas and oil engines and gas producers for power purposes, 1902-03. Mem. Am. Soc. Mech. Engrs., Soc. Promotion Engring. Edn., Sigma Xi. Author: Notes on Iron and Steel, 1895; Machine Design, Vol. I, 1898, Vol. II, 1899; Automobile Catechism, 1906; The Gas Engine, 1909; Electric Ignition for Combustion Motors, 1912; also contbns. to publs. of tech. socs., periodicals and correspondence schs. Home: 1702 Melrose Pl., Knoxville, Tenn. Office: 102 Liberty St., New York,

JONES, GEORGE WILLIAM, mathematician; b. E. Corinth, Me., Oct. 14, 1837; s. George William and Cordelia (Allen) J.; A.B., Yale, 1859, A.M., 1862; m. Caroline Tuttle Barber, Aug. 11, 1862. Teacher mathematics, Russell's Mil. Sch., New Haven, 1859-62, Del. Lit. Inst., Franklin, N.Y., 1862-68; prof. mathematics, Ia. State Coll., 1868-74; asst. prof., asso. prof., and prof. mathematics, Cornell, 1877-1907. Author: Treatise on Algebra (joint author), 1882; Treatise on Trigonometry (joint author), 1881; Logarithmic Tables, 1889; Drill-book in Algebra, 1892; Drill-book in Trigonometry, 1896; Five-place Logarithms, 1896; Four-place Logarithms, 1896; Some Proofs in Elementary Geometry, 1904. Address: Ithaca, N.Y. Died 1911.

JONES, GRINNELL, chemist; b. Des Moines, Ia., Jan. 14, 1884; s. Richard and Carrie Holmes (Grinnell) J.; S.B., Vanderbilt U., 1903, S.M., 1905; A.M., Harvard, 1905, Ph.D., 1908; m. Genevieve Lupton, Aug. 18, 1910; 1 son, Grinnell. Instr. chemistry, U. of Ill., 1908-12; instr. chemistry, 1912-16, asst. prof., 1916-21, asso. prof., 1921-34, prof. since 1934, Harvard. Chief chemist, U.S. Tariff Commn., 1917-19 (leave of absence from Harvard), cons. chemist same, 1919-26; detailed for several mos., 1918, to U.S. Shipping Bd. Mem. Am. Chem. Soc., Am. Acad. Arts and Sciences, Am. Assn. of Textile Chemists and Colorists, Am. Inst. of Chem. Engineers, Phi Beta Kappa, Sigma Xi, Sigma Nu, Alpha Chi Sigma, Phi Lambda Upsilon. Congregationalist. Developed fire-resistant paint, method of purifying salt water. Home: 90 Larchwood Dr., Cambridge 38, Mass. Died June 23, 1947.

JONES, HAROLD WELLINGTON, physician, ex-army officer, editor; b. Cambridge, Mass., Nov. 5, 1877; s. Frank Henry and Elizabeth Cook (Towne) J.; ed. Mass. Inst. Tech., 1894-97; M.D., Harvard, 1901; Army Med. Sch., 1905-06 (honor grad.), Army Med. Field Service Sch., 1930; LL.D., Western Res. U., 1945; m. Eva Ewing Munn, Jan. 1, 1910 (died 1936); m. 2d, Mary Winifred Morrison, May 1, 1937; 1 dau., Helen (Mrs. Clifford M. Esler); 1 stepson, Frank A. McGurk. Physician, Boston, 1901; house surgeon Children's Hosp., Boston, 1902-03; practicing physician, St. Louis, 1903-05; asso. prof. orthopedic surgery St. Louis U. Med. Sch., 1904-05; entered M.C., U.S. Army, 1906, capt., 1909 (temp. col. and col., 1918-19), col., 1932; served in Philippines, 1906-08, 20-23; charge of ambulance and evacuation service, Mexican campaign, 1916; prof., sec. faculty Army Med. Sch., 1917-18; comdr. Beau Desert Hosp. Center, AEF, France, 1918-19; chief surg. service Gen. Hosp. 41, N.Y., 1920, Ft. Sam Houston Hosp., 1927-33; comdg. officer Tripler Gen. Hosp., Hawaii, 1933-36; librarian Army Med. Library, Washington, 1936-43, dir., 1944-46. Sec. gen. 10th Internat. Congress Mil. Medicine, 1939; chief U.S. del. 9th Internat. Congress Mil. Medicine, Rumania, 1937; mem. Commn. Naval Experts revising Hague and Geneva Convs. (Red Cross), Geneva, 1937; v.p. Internat. Congress Air Relief, Budapest, 1937; hon. curator Osler Library, Montreal, 1936-46. Decorated Chevalier, Legion of Honor (France), 1918; Officer, l'ordre de la Sante Publique (France), 1939; Cross of Order of Merit (Poland), 1939; Rumania, 1940; Legion of Merit (U.S.) 1945; Philippine Insurrection, Mexican Expdn. and World War medals. Recipient Marcia C. Noyes award Med. Library Assn., 1956. Fellow A.C.S., A.A.A.S.; hon. fellow Cleve. Med. Library Assn., Beaumont Med. Club; hon. mem. Mexican Assn. Mil. Surgeons, Med. Library Assn. (pres. 1940, 41); mem. Boylston Med. Soc., A.C.S. (mem. com. on library).

Unitarian. Clubs: Harvard (N.Y.C.); Army and Navy (Washington). Author: Green Fields and Golden Apples. Editor: Proceedings fo 10th International Congress Mil. Medicine, 1939; Bulletin of Medical Library Assn., 1941-42; New Gould Medical Dictionary, 1946-56. Contbg., med. editor Ency. Americana. Contbr. about 600 articles to med. and hist. Jours. Mayo Found. lectr., 1942. Home: 1303 Chichester Av., Orlando, Fla. Died Apr. 5, 1958.

JONES, HARRY CLARY, chemist; b. New London, Md., Nov. 11, 1865; s. William and Joanna C. J.; A.B., Johns Hopkins, 1889, fellow, 1891-92, Ph.D., 1892; univs. of Leipzig, Amsterdam and Stockholm, 1892-94; m. Harriet Brooks, May 22, 1902. Instr. physical chemistry, 1895-98, asso., 1898-1900, asso. prof., 1900-04, prof., 1904—, Johns Hopkins. Asso. editor Journal de Chimie Physique, Journal of Franklin Inst., and Zeitschrift für physikalische Chemie. Langstreth medalist, Franklin Inst., 1913. Author: Freezing Point, Boiling Point, and Conductivity Methods, 1897; The Modern Theory of Solutions (Harper's Scientific Series), 1898. Translator: Biltz's Practical Methods for Determining Molecular Weights, 1899; The Theory of Electrolytic Dissociation, 1900; Outlines of Electrochemistry, 1902; Elements of Physical Chemistry, 1902 (translated into Russian, 1911, and Italian, 1912); Principles of Inorganic Chemistry, 1903; Elements of Inorganic Chemistry, 1903; The Electrical Nature of Matter and Radioactivity, 1906; Hydrates in Aqueous Solutions, 1907; Conductivity and Viscosity in Mixed Solvents, 1907; The Absorption Spectra of Solutions, 1909; Introduction to Physical Chemistry, 1910; The Absorption Spectra of Solutions, 1910, 11; Electrical Conductivity of Salts and Organic Acids, 1912; A New Era in Chemistry, 1913; Absorption Spectra Studied by Radiomicrometer, 1913; Freezing Points, Conductivities and Viscosities of Solutions of Salts in Mixed Solvents, 1913; The Absorption Spectra of Solutions; The Conductivities, Dissociations and Viscosities of Solutions of Electrolites in Aqueous, Nonaqueous and Mixed Solvents, 1915; Conductivities and Viscosities in Pure and in Mixed Solvents; Radiometric Measurements of the Formation Constants of Indicators, 1915. Address: Baltimore, Md. Died Mar. 19, 1916.

JONES, HILTON IRA, chemist, lecturer; b. Mankato, Minn., May 9, 1882; s. Addison Sprague and Alice Nancy (Hilton) J.; A.B., Parker Coll., Winnebago, Minn., 1903; A.M., Drake Univ., 1904; Harvard Univ., 1906-08; fellow in chemistry, University of Chicago, 1908-09; Ph.D., University of South Dakota, 1916; Doctor of Science, Dakota Wesleyan University, 1948; married Blanche Pinkerton, June 16, 1908; children—Eugenia (Mrs. Clyde E. Peaster), Haydn, Llewellyn, Virginia (Mrs. R. W. Burrill), Joan (dec.), Ernestine Harriette (Mrs. Thomas C. Shaw), Florice (Mrs. Howard Dellard). Teacher of science, East High School, Des Moines, Ia., 1904-06; chemist for B. O. and G. C. Wilson, manufacturing pharmacists, Boston, 1907; professor chemistry, Central High School, Muskogee, Oklahoma, 1909-12; professor chemistry, Dak. Wesleyan University, 1912-18; professor chemistry and chem. engring., Okla. Agrl. and Mech. Coll., 1918-22; dir. of scientific research, The Redpath Bureau, 1922-29; dir. div. of edn. and research, The Nat. Selected Morticians, 1929-34; mng. dir. The Naselmo Corp., Chicago, 1934-37; mng. dir. Hizone Products (successor to Naselmo Corp.), 1937—. Registered pharmacist. Fellow A.A.A.S., Am. Inst. Chemists (past chmn. Chicago Chapt.), Chem. Soc. (London), Inst. Am. Genealogy; mem. Am. Chem. Soc., Am. Assn. Engrs., Isaac Walton League, Soc. Mayflower Descs., S.A.R., Order of First Crusade, Baronial Order Magna Charta, Sigma Phi Epsilon, Phi Kappa Phi, Pi Kappa Delta (diamond eye), Kappa Kappa Psi, Kappa Delta Pi. Meth. Mason (K.T., Scottish Rite), Elk, K.P. Clubs: Rotary, Engineers, Executives (Chicago). Contbr. to scientific publs.; sci. lecturer. Award of Merit Certificate, 11th editorial competition. Home: 1538 Forest Av., Wilmette. Office: Hizone Research Laboratory, 1211 Washington Av., Wilmette, Ill. Died May 2, 1955; buried Meml. Park Cemetery, Evanston, Ill.

JONES, J. CLAUDE, geologist; b. Merrimac, Wis., July 2, 1877; s. John Dorence and Alberta Rosella (Van Sice) J.; A.B., U. of Ill., 1902; Ph.D., U. of Chicago, 1923; m. Belle McCurdy, June 23, 1904; children—Alberta Rosella, Ellen May (dec.), Claude Dorence, Dorothy Ellen. Instr. geology, U. of Ill., 1904-06; field asst., Ill. State Geol. Survey, 1906-09; research asst., U. of Chicago, 1906-09; prof. geology, U. of Nev., 1909—, dean of men, 1931—; also in practice as consulting geologist. In charge Nevada mining exhibit San Francisco Expn., 1915; geologist Nev. State Mining Lab.; has served as mem. Nev. Cement Commn. Universalist. K.P. Home: Reno, Nev. Died 1932.

JONES, J. SHIRLEY, agrl. chemist; b. Garrett, Ind, Feb. 14, 1876; s. Sidney P. and Mary (Ditmars) J.; B.S., U. Cal., 1903; M.S. in agr., Cornell, 1914; m. Tillie Browning, Sept. 1906; children William Shirley. Chemist, asst. supt., Giant Powder Co., San Francisco, 1904-06; chemist Ida. Expt. Sta., 1906-14, chemist, dir., 1914-18; operating chemist, U.S. Nitrate Plant No. 1, Sheffield, Ala., for Ordnance Div. War Dept., 1918; prof. agrl. chemistry and expt. sta. chemist, Ore. Agrl. Coll., 1919—. Mem. Ida. Com. Indsl. Preparedness of Naval Cons. Bd. Mem. Am. Chem. Soc., Soc. Chem. Industry, A.A.A.S., Sigma Xi, Phi Lambda Upsilon. Presbyn. Mason. Home: Corvallis, Ore. Died Jan. 24, 1954.

JONES, JONATHAN, engr.; b. Lewisburg, Pa., Jan. 28, 1882; s. Jonathan and Mary (Bliss) J.; A.B., U. Pa., 1903, B.S., 1905, M.S., 1906, C.E., 1920; D.Eng., Lehigh U., 1952; m. Dorothy Bovee, Jan. 22, 1924; children—Dorothy Bliss (wife of Dr. Paul Worthen Dale), Nancy Severn (Mrs. Charles Laurence Stevens, Jr.). Engr. bridges, City of Phila., 1913-20; resident mgr. McClintic Marshall Products Co., Jamshedpur, India, 1920-23; chief engr. McClintic-Marshall Co., Pitts., 1929-31; chief engr. fabricated steel constrn. Bethlehem Steel Co. (Pa.), 1931-52. Served as maj., U.S. Army, C.E., 1917-18; AEF. Mem. Am. Soc. Testing Materials, Soc. Am. Mil. Engrs., Am. Soc. C.E., Am. Ry. Engring. Assn., Am. Welding Soc. Club: Engineers (Phila.; Lehigh Valley). Home: Rest Harrow, R.D. 3, Bethlehem, Pa. Died June 25, 1960; buried Westminster Cemetery, Phila.

JONES, LAWRENCE E., builder, engr., collector; b. Stotts City, Mo., Feb. 26, 1888; s. Columbus D. and Katherine (Payne) J.; A.B., William Jewell Coll., Liberty, Mo., 1911, LL.D., 1940; m. Edna Withers, Sept. 26, 1914. Designed machinery which produced practically all cartridge clips for U.S. Army, World War I. Pioneer in development of co-operative apartments in America, among them Alden Park, Philadelphia; president Alden Park Corp., Chelten Avenue Building Corporation, Kenilworth Building Corporation, Cambridge Bldg. Corp., Phila.; The Medical Research Found., Phila., Hotel Mariemont Corp., Cin. Trustee William Jewell Coll., Liberty, Mo.; mem. bd. corporators Woman's Med. Coll. of Pa. Clubs: Racquet, Philobiblon (Phila.); Rose Tree Fox Hunting (Media, Pa.); Grolier, Turf and Field (N.Y.C.); Radnor Hunt (Malvern, Pa.). Address: Apt. 107, Kenilworth, Alden Park, Phila. 19144. Died.

JONES, LEWIS RALPH, botanist; b. Brandon, Wis., Dec. 5, 1864; s. David and Lucy (Knapp) J.; student Ripon Coll., 1883-86; Ph.B., U. of Mich., 1889, grad. studies, 1901, 1904, Ph.D., 1904; hon. Sc.D., U. of Vt., 1910, U. of Cambridge (Eng.), 1930, U. of Wis., 1936; LL.D., U. of Mich., 1935; has also carried out investigations in lab. of Bur. of Plant Industry, Washington, under direction of Dr. Erwin F. Smith, 1899, and in Europe, 1904; m. May I. Bennett, June 24, 1890; m. 2d, Anna M. Clark, July 27, 1929. Prof. botany, U. of Vt. and botanist Vermont Expt. Sta., 1889-1910; prof. plant pathology, U. of Wis., 1910-35, emeritus prof. since 1935. Collaborator of Bureau of Plant Industry, U.S. Dept. Agriculture; ex-sec. bd. park commrs., Burlington, Vt.; ex-sec. Vt. Bot. Club; ex-pres. Vt. Forestry Assn.; fellow A.A.A.S.; ex-pres. Bot. Soc. America; mem. Nat. Acad. of Sciences, N.E. Bot. Club, Wis. Acad. Arts and Sciences, Am. Soc. Naturalists, Am. Philos. Soc.; corr. Assn. of Applied Biologists, England, Société de Pathologie Végétale et d'Entomologie Agricole de France; hon. mem. Vereinigung für Angewandte Botanik, Japanese Phytopathol. Soc.; ex-chmn. div. of biology and agr. Nat. Research Council; ex-pres. Am. Phytopathol. Soc. Conglist. Republican. Joint author of "Flora of Vermont," and author bot. reports, bulls. and contbns. to scientific jours. Editor "Phytopathology" editor Am. Jour. Botany; editor bacteriol. terms, Webster's New Internat. Dictionary. Home: 146 N. Prospect Av., Madison, Wis. Died Mar. 31, 1945.

JONES, LOYD ANCILE, physicist; b. York, Neb., Apr. 12, 1884; s. Oscar Rodolph and Rocetha (Cottrell) J.; B.S. in E.E., U. of Neb., 1908, A.M., 1910; hon. D.Sc., Univ. of Rochester, N.Y., 1933; m. Lillian May Chaplin, Dec. 4, 1911. Lab. asst. in physics, Bur. of Standards, 1910-12; asst. physicist research lab., Eastman Kodak Co., 1912-16, head of physics dept., 1916—. Served as lt. Constrn. Corps, U.S.N.R.F., World War. Mem. Optical Soc. America (pres. 1929-31; Frederic Ives Medal, 1943), Soc. Motion Picture Engrs. (fellow; progress medal 1939; pres., 1923-26, engr. vice-pres., 1933-39, outstanding service award 1954), Illuminating Engineering Society, Am. Physical Soc., Royal Photo. Soc. (Hurter & Driffield Medal, 1949, progress medal, 1948), Photo. Society Am. (progress medal, 1949, American Journalistic award), A.A.A.S., Sigma Xi. Contbr. to magazines. Home: 22 San Rafael Dr. Office: Kodak Park, Rochester, N.Y. Died May 15, 1954; buried Pittsford, N.Y.

JONES, LYNDS, zoölogist; b. Jefferson, Ohio, Jan. 5, 1865; s. Publius Virgilius and Lavinia (Burton) J.; student Ia. Coll., 1888-90; A.B., Oberlin, 1892, Sc.M., 1895; Ph.D., U. Chgo., 1905; m. Clara Mabelle Tallman, Sept. 8, 1892; children—Lynds Leo, Theodore Burton (dec.), George Tallman, Beth, Harold Charles. Began asst. in zoology Oberlin Coll., before graduation, prof. animal ecology, 1922-30; also. curator Zoöl. Mus., ret. 1930; vis. lectr. Berry Coll., 1936-37, 39; tchr. summers, transcontinental automobile ecology classes. Fellow A.A.A.S., Am. Ornithol. Union; mem. Am. Soc. Zoologists, Am. Geog. Soc., Cooper Ornithol. Club, Wilson Ornithol. Club. Republican. Conglist. Author: Revised Catalogue of Birds of Ohio, 1903. Editor of The Wilson Bull., 1896-1924. Home: 352 W. College St., Oberlin, O. Died Feb. 11, 1951; buried Birmingham, O.

JONES, MARCUS EUGENE, botanist, geologist; b. Jefferson, O., Apr. 25, 1852; s. Publius Virgilius and Lavinia (Burton) J.; A.B., Ia. (now Grinnell) Coll., 1875, A.M., 1878; m. Anna E. Richardson, Feb. 18, 1880; children—Mabel Anna, Howard Marcus, Mildred Lavinia. Tutor, Ia. Coll., 1876-77; prin. Lemars (Iowa) Acad., 1877; prof. natural science, Colorado Coll., 1879; same at Salt Lake City, 1880-81; prin. Jones High Sch., Salt Lake City, 1884-86; spl. expert, U.S. Treasury Dept., 1889; geologist Rio Grande Western R.R., 1890-93; spl. field agt., U.S. Dept. Agr., 1894-95; botanist, geologist and mining expert. Pres. Utah Acad. Sciences. Hon. curator of botany, Pomona Coll. Author: Excursion Botanique, 1879; Ferns of the West, 1883; Salt Lake City, 1889; Some Phases of Mining in Utah; Utah supplement to Tarr and McMurry's Geography, 1902; Contbns. to Western Botany (18 parts), 1879-1934. Exploring in Mexico, 1924—. Home: Claremont, Calif. Died June 3, 1934.

JONES, MARVIN FISHER, physician; b. Spencer, N.Y., Mar. 10, 1889; s. George Edward and Sadie (Fisher) J.; M.D., U. of Buffalo, 1913; m. Jessie Hill, June 8, 1922; children—James McKernan, Beatrice Clair, Robert Marvin. Asst. surgeon, Lackawanna Steel Co., Buffalo, N.Y., 1913; resident surgeon eye, ear, nose and throat, N.Y. Post Grad. Sch. and Hosp., 1914; engaged in practice, specializing in otolaryngology, N.Y. City, since 1918; consulting otolaryngologist Welfare Island Hosp.; surgeon dir. otology and mem. bd. dirs. Manhattan Eye, Ear and Throat Hosp.; cons. otolaryngologist, Port Chester, N.Y., Tioga County Gen. Hosp. (Waverly, N.Y.), N.Y. Hosp. of Cornell Med. Center, N.Y. City; prof. otology N.Y. Post Grad. Med. Sch. and Hosp., 1927-31; prof. clin. otolaryngology Columbia, 1931-38. Served as 1st lt., Med. Corps, A.E.F., France and Italy (enlisted for overseas service with Base Hosp. No. 8) during World War I; 1st asst. to chief consultant otolaryngologist, Consultants Hdqrs., Neuf Chateau, France; in charge eye, ear, nose and throat, A.E.F., Italy; detached service Evacuation Hosp., Argonne. Fellow Am. Coll. Surgeons; mem. A.M.A., Am. Men of Science, N.Y. State Med. Soc. (past chmn. sect. otolaryngology), N.Y. County Med. Soc., Am. Acad. Ophthalmology and Otolaryngology (past mem. council), Am. Triol. Soc., Am. Otol. Soc., (pres., research fellow; mem. council; trustee otosclerosis research fund), American Laryngol. Soc., Acad. of Medicine (sect. of otolaryngology; past mem. council; past chmn.), N.Y. Otol. Soc. (past sec.), N.Y. Otolaryngol. Soc., Inc. (past pres.), N.Y. Laryngol. Soc. Protestant. Clubs: Salmagundi (New York). Mem. editorial bd. of Annals of Otology, Quar. Rev. of Otolaryngology. Contbr. numerous sci. articles to med. publs. Home: 215 E. 79th St., N.Y. City. Office: 121 E. 60th St., N.Y.C. 22. Died May 26, 1952.

JONES, REGINALD LAMONT, elec. engr.; b. New York, N.Y., Feb. 28, 1886; s. Albert Sinclair and Clara Evaline (Bishop) J.; B.S., Mass. inst. of Tech., 1909, M.S., 1910, Sc.D., 1911; m. Marion Elizabeth Babcock, Oct. 2, 1917; children—Elizabeth, Reginald Lamont, Jr., Peter Babcock. On research staff Western Electric Co., 1911-14 in charge transmission research dept., 1914-23, inspection engring. dept., 1923-25; inspection mgr., Bell Telephone Lab., 1925-27, outside plant development engineer, 1927-28, director apparatus development, 1928-1944, vice pres. since Oct. 1, 1944; director Summit Trust Co. Capt. Signal Reserve Corps, U.S. Army, 1917-18. Mem. Non-Ferrous Metall. Adv. Bd., Army Ordnance Dept., Mem. Standards Council of Am. Standards Assn. Mem. Nat. panel, Am. Arbitration Assn. Pres., Summit Bd. of Edn. Trustee, Summit Cooperative Service Assn. Mem. alumni vis. com. Mass. Inst. Tech. Fellow Am. Phys. Soc., Am. Inst. of Elec. Engrs. (chmn. standards com.), A.A.A.S., Acoustical Soc. of Am.; mem. Am. Soc. Engring. Edn. Republican. Conglist. Trustee, Central Presbyn. Ch. of Summit. Club: Salmagundi (N.Y. City). Home: 190 Oakridge Av., Summit, N.J. Office: 463 West St., New York 14. Died Jan. 14, 1949; buried at West Bridgeport, Mass.

JONES, RICHARD URIAH, chemist; b. Ottawa, Minn., Jan. 25, 1877; s. William R. and Mary (Hughes) J.; B.A., Macalester Coll., St. Paul, Minn., 1901, hon. D.Sc., 1926; student U. of Minn., 1901-02, U. of Chicago, summers 1908, 09; M.A., U. of Wis., 1916; m. Mary Helen Smith, Aug. 18, 1909; children—Richard Herbert, Donald Caldwell, George William. Prof. physics and chemistry, 1903, prof. chemistry, 1907—, dean of coll., 1917-36, Macalester Coll. Presbyn. Specialized in researches in organic chemistry, particularly sugars, starches and volatile oils. Author: The Scientific Eye of Faith. Home: St. Paul, Minn. Died July 9, 1941.

JONES, RICHARD WATSON, educator; b. Greensville County, Va., May 16, 1837; s. Mordecai and Martha Randolph (Grigg) J.; A.B., Randolph-Macon Coll., 1857; A.M., U. of Va., 1861; LL.D., U. of Miss., 1881; in C.S.A., 1861-65; m. Bettie S. Spratley, Jan. 6, 1864. Prof. mathematics, Randolph-Macon Coll., Va., 1866-68; pres. Petersburg (Va.) Female Coll., 1868-71, Martha Washington Coll., Va., 1871-76; prof. chemistry, U. of Miss., 1876-85; pres. Miss. State Instn. for Girls, 1885-88, Emory and

Henry Coll., 1888-90; prof. chemistry, U. of Miss., 1890—. Lit. editor Rural Messenger, Petersburg, Va., 1870, of Petersburg Courier, 1868-71; one of asso. editors People's Encyclopaedia, 1881-82. Wrote pamphlets on Cotton Army Worm, 1880, and Cotton Boll Worm, 1880; also various reports as coll. pres., papers before scientific and ednl. bodies, pub. lectures, addresses, etc. Del. Meth. Ecumenical Conf., London, 1818, to six gen. confs., M.E. Ch., South, etc. Trustee State Dept. Archives and History; dir. Miss. Orphans' Home. Address: University, Miss. Deceased.

JONES, SAMUEL AUGUSTUS, statistician; b. Genoa, Ohio, Jan. 25, 1874; s. Noah Scarfield and Josephine (Brunner) J.; ed. pub. schs.; M.D., George Washington U. Dept. of Medicine, 1904; m. Ada Ellen Yost, of Toledo, O., Oct. 9, 1901; children—Lincoln Samuel, Bernice Josephine, Katherine Sarah, Ruth Pauline. Accountant Navy Dept., Washington, D.C., 1899-1907; agrl. statistician, Dept. of Agr. since 1907. Presbyn. Home: 2594 Wisconsin Av. Address: Dept. of Agriculture, Washington DC

JONES, WALTER, physiol. chemist; b. Baltimore, Apr. 28, 1865; s. Levin and Zeanette J. (Bohen) J.; A.B., Johns Hopkins, 1888, Ph.D., 1891; m. Grace C. Clarke, Sept. 1, 1891; 1 dau., Marion E. (Mrs. Gilbert A. Jarman). Prof. chemistry, Wittenberg Coll., Springfield, O., 1891-92; prof. analyt. chemistry, Purdue U., 1892-95; asst., asso. prof., 1895-1908, and prof. of physiol. chemistry, 1908-27, prof. emeritus, 1927, Johns Hopkins. Author: Nucleic Acids, 1921. Home: Baltimore, Md. Died Feb. 28, 1935.

JONES, WASHINGTON, mech. engr.; b. Phila., Feb. 22, 1822; s. Thomas J. and Eliza (Ransted) J.; common sch. edn. until 1938; apprenticed Southwark Foundry, 1838-44; studied under pvt. instrs., 1849-56. Chief draughtsman Penn Works, marine engines; then until 1861 supt. Port Richmond Iron Works; asst. supt. Southwark Foundry, 1861-66; gen. supt. and constructing engr. Port Richmond Iron Works, 1866-91; dir. Am. Dredging Co. Address: Philadelphia, Pa. Deceased.

JONES, W(ELTON) PAUL, business exec., inventor, lecturer; b. Winslow, Ind., Oct. 25, 1901; s. Thomas Edward and Lydia Agnes (Welton) J.; student Oakland City (Ind.) Coll. (bus. and tech. sch.), 3 yrs.; m. Clesta Jean Walker, Jan. 16, 1925; 1 dau., Margaret Louise Theis. With Jones and Welton, cafe, Oakland City, Ind., while in college; service mgr. Frigidaire Corp., Indianapolis, 1920-23; sales mgr. Frigidaire Distributors A. F. Wood Co., Evansville, Ind., 1923-27; pres. and gen. mgr. Refrigeration Products Co., Evansville, 1928-29; ednl. dir. Servel, Inc., Evansville, 1929-30, advt. and sales promotion mgr., 1930-33, asst. gen. mgr. commercial div., 1933-34; exec. v.p. Fairbanks-Morse Home Appliances, Chicago, at Indianapolis, 1934-38; pres. Philco Refrigerator Co., Jan. 1939-Dec. 1940; v.p. Philco Corp., Phila., 1940-49, dir. 1942-49; dir. Kellett Aircraft Corp.; pres., gen. mgr., dir. Servel Inc., Evansville, Indiana, 1949-54, vice chmn. bd., spl. adviser, 1954—; pres. Kellett Aircraft Corp., 1954—. Inventor and patentee several developments and designs refrigeration methods and features; lecturer on sales principles, distribution economics and product design and adaptation. One of organizers and former trustee Nat. Sales Exec. Council; v.p. dir. Ind. Employers Assn., 1936-40; Indianapolis Chamber of Commerce, 1936-40. Former mem. W.P.B. elec. refrigeration industry adv. com.; chmn. O.P.A. industry adv. com. elec. refrigeration industry, 1942-46; mem. Am. Soc. Refrigeration Engineers. Mason. Methodist. Clubs: Huntington Valley Country, Union League (Phila.); Seaview Country (Atlantic City); Rotary, Country (Evansville). Home: R.R. 5, Hillsdale Rd. Office: 119 N. Morton Av., Evansville, Ind. Died Jan. 20, 1955; buried Oak Hill Cemetery, Evansville.

JONES, WILLIAM ALBERT, brigadier gen. U.S. Army; b. St. Charles, Mo., June 26, 1841; s. Stilman and Ann J. (Perkins) J.; grad. U.S. Mil. Acad., 1864; m. Louisa V. Test, Nov. 25, 1873. Commd. 1st lt. engrs., June 13, 1864; capt., Mar. 7, 1867; maj., June 30, 1882; lt. col., Oct. 2, 1895; col., Apr. 21, 1903; brig. gen. and retired by operation of law, June 26, 1905. Asst. prof. civil and mil. engring., law and ethics, and instr. practical mil. engring., and comdg. Co. A Battalion of Engrs., also treas., U.S. Mil. Acad., 1864-66; served in 6th Corps, Army of the Potomac, Civil War; comd. U.S. Army exploring expdn. in northwestern Wyo. and Yellowstone Park, 1873; discovered Two Ocean Pass, Togwotee Pass and Shoshone Mountains; served on constrn. of fortifications, harbors and lighthouses on Atlantic coast and Great Lakes, on improvement of rivers in northwest, Yellowstone Park, etc.; mem. commn. to investigate salmon fisheries of Columbia River; div. engr. of the Chesapeake, etc.; consulting engr. location and construction rys., mining and treating ores, bldg. dams and water works in various localities; consulting engr. state of Calif., Golden Gate Park, San Francisco; consulting engr. Commonwealth of Mass., Marine Park, Charles River Dam. Owner and manager 2,000 acres oyster plantation on eastern shore of Va. Protestant. Author: Report of Exploration of Northwestern Wyoming and Yellowstone Park, 1874; The Salmon Fisheries of the Columbia River. Home: Ft. Monroe, Va. Died Nov. 10, 1914.

JONES, WILLIAM JAMES, JR., chemist; b. Watseka, Ill., Dec. 9, 1870; s. William James and Sallie Davenport (Jones) J.; B.S., Purdue U., 1891, M.S., 1892, A.C., 1899; m. Nelle Parker, Dec. 25, 1894. Asst. in chemistry, Purdue U., 1891-92; asst. state chemist of Ind., 1892-1901, chief deputy state chemist, 1901-07, state chemist, 1907—; spl. observer U.S. Weather Bur., 1894—; asso. chemist, Purdue Expt. Sta., 1903-07; prof. agrl. chemistry, Purdue U., 1907—. Collaborating chemist, U.S. Dept. of Agr. Mason, Odd Fellow. Address: Lafayette, Ind. Died Aug. 31, 1917.

JONES, WILLIAM RICHARD, engr., steel co. exec.; b. Hazleton, Pa., Feb. 23, 1839; m. Harriet Lloyd Apr. 14, 1861, 4 children. Journeyman machinist, 1853; with Cambria Iron Co., Johnston, Pa., 1859; served with Co. A, 133d Pa. Volunteers, 1862-63, served in battles of Fredericksburg and Chancellorsville; served as capt. Co. F., 194th Pa. Regt. of Emergency Men (which he raised), 1864-65; gen. supt. Edgar Thomson Steel Co., Braddock, Pa., 1875-89; cons. engr. Carnegie, Phipps & Co., 1888-89; inventor and patentee numerous devices connected with prodn. steel, most important was Jones mixer (mixed molten iron from blast furnaces for converter), 1889; 1st American to be invited to see Krupp steel works at Essen. Died Pitts., Sept. 28, 1889.

JORDAN, CHARLES BERNARD, pharm. chemistry; b. Morrice, Mich., Nov. 7, 1878; s. John and Mary (McCarthy) J.; grad. Ypsilanti (Mich.) State Normal Coll., 1904; Ph.C. and B.S., U. of Mich., 1910, M.S., 1912; hon. D.Sc., Ohio Northern U., 1933; m. Helen Mary Byrnes, Aug. 20, 1907; children—Veronica Kathryn, Robert Edward, Charles Richard, Mildred Helen. Teacher pub. schs., Shiawassee County, Mich., 1897-1901; supt. schs., Morrice, 1904-08; prof. pharm. chemistry, Purdue, since 1910, dir. Sch. of Pharmacy, 1910-23, dean since 1923. Lecturer, St. Elizabeth Hosp., Lafayette, Ind., since 1915. Mem. com. of revision U.S. Pharmacopoeia since 1920, chmn. subcom. on crude drug assay since 1930. Mem. Am. Pharm. Assn. (chmn. house of delegates 1929-30), Am. Assn. Colls. Pharmacy (pres. 1918-19; chmn. exec. com., 1923-36), Am. Chem. Soc., Ind. Pharm. Assn., Ind. Acad. Science, Sigma Xi; fellow A.A.A.S. Catholic. Club: West Lafayette Country. Author: Qualitative Analysis for Students of Pharmacy and Medicine, 1928. Editor Am. Assn. Colls. of Pharmacy sect. of Jour. Am. Pharm. Assn., 1923-36. Contbr. on pharm. edn. and pharm. chemistry. Home: 409 Russell St., West Lafayette, Ind. Died Apr. 22, 1941.

JORDAN, DAVID STARR, educator, author, naturalist; b. Gainesville, N.Y., Jan. 19, 1851; s. Hiram and Huldah Lake (Hawley) J.; M.S., Cornell, 1872; M.D., Ind. Med. Coll., 1875; Ph.D., Butler U., 1878; LL.D., Cornell, 1886, Johns Hopkins, 1902, Ill. College, 1903, Ind. U., 1909, U. of Calif., 1913, Western Reserve U., 1915; m. Susan Bowen, Mar. 10, 1875 (died 1885); m. 2d, Jessie L. Knight, Aug. 10, 1887; children—Edith, Harold, Thora (dec.), Knight, Barbara (dec.), Eric (dec.). Instr. botany, Cornell, 1871-72; prof. natural history Lombard U., 1872-83; prin. Appleton (Wis.) Collegiate Inst., 1873-74; teacher Indianapolis High Sch., 1874-75; prof. biology, Butler U., 1875-79; prof. zoölogy, 1879-85, pres., 1885-91, Ind. U.; pres. Stanford, 1891-1913, chancellor, 1913-16, emeritus. Coöperating asst. to U.S. Fish Commn., 1877-91, 1894-1909; also U.S. commr. in charge of fur seal and salmon investigations; internat. commr. of fisheries, 1908-10. Chief dir. World Peace Foundation, 1910-14; pres. World's Peace Congress, 1915; v.p. Am. Peace Soc. Pres. A.A.A.S., 1909-10, N.E.A., 1915. Author: Manual of Vertebrate Animals of Northern United States, 1876-1929; Science Sketches, 1887; Fishes of North and Middle America, 4 vols. (with B. W. Evermann), 1896; Care and Culture of Men, 1896; The Innumerable Company, 1896; To Barbara (verse), 1897; Footnotes to Evolution, 1898; The Story of Matka, 1898; Book of Knight and Barbara (stories), 1899; Imperial Democracy, 1899; The Strength of Being Clean, 1900; Standeth God Within the Shadow, 1900; Animal Life (with V. L. Kellogg), 1900; The Philosophy of Hope, 1902; The Blood of the Nation, 1902; Animal Forms (with others), 1903; Voice of the Scholar, 1903; Food and Game Fishes of North America (with B. W. Evermann), 1905; A Guide to the Study of Fishes, 1905; The Call of the Twentieth Century, 1905; The Human Harvest, 1907; Evolution and Animal Life (with V. L. Kellogg), 1907; Fishes, 1907; Life's Enthusiasms, 1907; College and the Man, 1907; The Higher Sacrifice, 1908; Fish Stories (with C. F. Holder), 1908; The Religion of a Sensible American, 1909; The Stability of Truth, 1909; The Fate of Iciodorum, 1909; Unseen Empire, 1912; War's Aftermath (with Harvey E. Jordan), 1912; Eric's Book of Beasts (children), 1913; War and Waste, 1914; World Peace and the College Man, 1914; War and the Breed, 1915; Ways to Lasting Peace, 1915; Alsace-Lorraine, a Study in Conquest, 1915; The Genera of Fishes, 1918-20, 4 parts; Democracy and World Relations, 1918; Fossil Fishes of Southern California, 1919-26, 9 parts; The Days of a Man, 1922; Autobiography (2 vols.); Classification of Fishes, 1922; (with K. D. Cather) High Lights of Geography, North America, 1925, Europe, 1925; The Higher Foolishness, 1927; Your Family Tree (with S. L. Kimball), 1929; The Trend of the American University, 1929. Home: Stanford University, Calif. Died Sept. 19, 1931.

JORDAN, EDWIN OAKES, bacteriologist; b. Thomaston, Me., July 28, 1866; s. J. L. and E. D. (Bugbee) J.; S.B., Mass. Inst. Tech., 1888; Ph.D., Clark U., 1892; student Pasteur Inst., Paris, 1896; hon. Sc.D., U. of Cincinnati, 1920; m. Elsie Fay Pratt, June 16, 1893; children—Henry Donaldson, Edwin Pratt, Lucia Elisabeth. Chief asst. biologist Mass. State Bd. of Health, 1888-90; lecturer on biology, Mass. Inst. Tech., 1889-90; fellow in morphology Clark U., 1890-92; asso. in anatomy, 1892-93, instr., 1893-95, asst. prof. bacteriology, 1895-1900, asso. prof. 1900-07, prof., 1907-33, and chmn. dept. hygiene and bacteriology, 1914-33, emeritus, 1933—, U. of Chicago. Chief of serum div. and trustee McCormick Memorial Inst. for Infectious Diseases, Chicago, Ill. Editor of Journal of Preventive Medicine; joint editor (with L. Hektoen and W. H. Taliaferro) Jour. Infectious Diseases. Mem. Internat. Health Bd. of Rockefeller Foundation, Feb. 1920-27; mem. bd. scientific dirs., Internat. Health Div. of Rockefeller Foundation, 1930-33; mem. Med. Fellowship Bd. of Nat. Research Council. Author: General Bacteriology, 1908; Food Poisoning, 1917, 2d edit., 1931; A Pioneer in Public Health—W. T. Sedgwick (with G. C. Whipple and C. E. A. Winslow), 1924: Epidemic Influenza, 1927; (with I. S. Falk) The Newer Knowledge of Bacteriology and Immunology, 1928. Home: Homewood, Ill. Died Sept. 2, 1936.

JORDAN, FRANK CRAIG, astronomer; b. Cordova, Ill., Sept. 24, 1865; s. John Henry and Louisiana (Craig) J.; B.Ph., Marietta Coll., 1889, M.A., 1892; Ph.D., U. of Chicago, 1914; Sc.D., Marietta (Ohio) Coll., 1929; m. Cora A. Ross, June 22, 1893; 1 son, Frank Warren (dec.); m. 2d, Mrs. Harriet C. Roy, Nov. 25, 1909; 1 son, John William. Instr. astronomy and mathematics, Marietta Coll., 1889-1900, high sch., Portland, Ore., 1900-02, at Colorado Springs, Colo., 1902-05; fellow Yerkes Obs., Williams Bay, Wis., 1905-08; with Allegheny Obs., 1908—; asst. prof. astronomy U. of Pittsburgh, 1910-19, prof., 1919—; asst. dir. Allegheny Obs., 1920-30, dir., 1930—. Democrat. Presbyterian. Has specialized in photometry; determined and published light curves of many short period variable stars. Home: Pittsburgh, Pa. Died Feb. 15, 1941.

JORDAN, HARVEY HERBERT, prof. engring.; b. Waltham, Me., Mar. 7, 1885; s. Roland Herbert and Carrie Frances (Blake) J.; B.S. in C.E., U. of Me., 1910; grad. work U. of Ill., 1912-16; m. Sara M. Slater, Oct. 9, 1919; 1 dau., Donna Elizabeth. Asst. in civ. engring. U. of Me., 1910-11; with U. of Ill. since 1911 as instr., asso. and asst. prof. engring., drawing until 1921, prof. engring., drawing and head of dept. from 1922, asst. dean Coll. of Engineering, 1917-34, asso. dean from 1934. Alderman city of Urbana, Ill., 1921-27. Instr. schs. of Mil. Aeronautics and S.A.T.C., 1917-18. Mem. Am. Soc. C.E., A.A.A.S., American Soc. of Engring. Education (v.p. 1931-32), Ill. Soc. Prof. Engrs., Phi Eta Sigma, Tau Beta Pi, Phi Kappa Phi, Sigma Tau, Chi Epsilon, Triangle. Republican. Mason. Clubs: Kiwanis (Champaign-Urbana); University (Urbana). Author: Engineering Drawing (with R. P. Hoelscher), 1923; Descriptive Geometry (with F. M. Porter), 1929; also bull. The Pipe Orifice as a Means of Measuring the Flow of Water Through a Pipe (with R. E. Davis), 1918. Contbr. on engring. subjects. Home: Urbana ILDeceased.

JORDAN, MAHLON KLINE, chem. engr.; b. Phila., Dec. 13, 1911; s. T. Carrick and Elizabeth (Kline) J.; B.S. in Chem. Engring., U. N.C.; m. Nona McAdoo Martin, June 9, 1933; children—Nona McA., T. Carrick, Wendy E. With Smith Kline & French Labs., 1935—, v.p., 1945—, also dir., mem. exec. com.; pres., dir. Avoset Co., 1947—. Home: 55 Alvarado Rd., Berkeley, Cal. 94705. Office: 5131 Shattuck Av., Oakland, Cal. 94609. Died July 1, 1967.

JORDAN, WHITMAN HOWARD, agrl. scientist; b. Raymond, Me., Oct. 27, 1851; s. James and Sarah (Symonds) J.; B.S., U. of Me., 1875; M.S., Cornell, 1878; D.Sc., U. of Me., 1896; LL.D., Mich. Agrl. Coll., 1907, Hobart, 1911; m. Emma L. Wilson, Mar. 3, 1880. Asst., Conn. Agrl. Expt. Sta., 1878-79; instr. U. of Me., 1879-80; prof. agrl. chemistry, Pa. State Coll., 1881-85; dir. Me. Agrl. Expt. Sta., 1885-96; dir. N.Y. Agrl. Expt. Sta., 1896-1921. Author: The Feeding of Animals, 1901; Principles of Human Nutrition, 1912. Home: Orono, Me. Died May 8, 1931.

JOSEPH, DON ROSCO, physiologist; b. Chatsworth, Ill., Nov. 24, 1881; s. George and Electa (Combs) J.; B.S., U. of Chicago, 1904; M.S., St. Louis U., 1906, M.D., 1907; m. Lura I. Licklider, 1905; children—Don Roscoe, Evelyn. Fellow, Rockefeller Inst., 1907-08, asst., 1908-10, asso., 1910-12; asso. prof. physiology, Bryn Mawr Coll., 1912-13; prof. physiology and dir. dept., St. Louis U. Sch. of Medicine, 1913—, vice dean, 1919—. Capt. Med. R.C., 1918; maj. Med. Corps U.S.A., 1918-19. Home: Clayton, Mo. Died July 9, 1928.

JOSLIN, CEDRIC FREEMAN, civil engr.; b. Staten Island, N.Y., Apr. 12, 1889; s. William Carey and Elizabeth Florine (Freeman); J.; B.S. in C.E., Brown U., 1913; m. Elizabeth O'Neill, Mar. 8, 1919. Engr. with F. L. Dillon Constrn. Co., 1914-15; erection foreman, Aberthaw Constrn. Co., Boston, 1915-17; chief of physics dept. U. of Puerto Rico, 1917-19, prof. civ.

engring., 1921—. Student Officers' T.C., San Juan, 1918; coorganizer and capt. Mayaquez Home Guard, World War; served as chief Sanitary engr. Mil. Govt. of Santo Domingo, Dec. 1919-June 1921. Mason. Episcopalian. Address: Mayaguez, P.R. Died Sept. 10, 1922.

JOSLIN, ELLIOTT PROCTOR, physician; b. Oxford, Mass., June 6, 1869; s. Allen L and Sarah (Proctor) J.; B.A., Yale, 1890; Ph.B., Sheffield Scientific Sch. (Yale), 1891; M.D., Harvard Med. Sch., 1895; hon. M.A., Yale, 1914; D.Sc., Harvard, 1940, Toronto U., 1953; m. Elizabeth Denny, Sept. 16, 1902. Engaged in practice of medicine in Boston, 1895—; asst. physiol. chemistry, 1898-1900, asst. theory and practice of physic, 1900-05, instr., 1905-12, asst. prof. theory and practice of physics, 1912-21, clin. prof. medicine, 1922-37, since emeritus, Harvard Med. Sch.; cons. physician Boston City Hosp.; hon. physician in chief New Eng. Deaconess Hosp. Maj., M.C. U.S. Army, 1918, lt. col., 1918. Awarded Distinguished Service Medal by A.M.A., 1943. Fellow Am. Acad. Arts and Sciences; mem. Assn. Am. Physicians, A.M.A., Am. Philos. Soc., etc. Conglist. Republican. Author: The Treatment of Diabetes Mellitus, 1916, 10th edit., 1959; A Diabetic Manual, 1918, 10th edit., 1959. Home: 20 Chapel St., Brookline, Mass. Office: Joslin Clinic, 15 Joslin Rd., Boston 02115. Died Jan. 28, 1962; buried Oxford, Mass.

JOSLIN, HAROLD VINCENT, civil engr.; b. Belleville, N.Y., June 22, 1883; s. William Cary and Elizabeth Florine (Freeman) J.; A.B., Brown, 1904 (Phi Beta Kappa); m. Annie Devereux Hinsdale, Dec. 2, 1908; children—Harold V. (dec.), Nell Devereux, John Devereux, William, Elliott Hinsdale. Surveyor for White Mountain Lumber Co., N.H., 1904, engr. with Norfolk Southern Ry., N.C. and Va., 1905-10, Norfolk City Water Dept., 1910-11, Yadkin River Power Co., N.C., 1911-13, Phoenix Constrn. Co., Utah and Idaho, 1913-14. Carolina Power & Light Co., N.C., 1914-18, U.S. Housing Corp., Washington, D.C., 1918-19; engr., contractor, Wilson (N.C.) Housing Corp., 1919-20; asst. to chmn. and purchasing agt. N.C. State Highway Commn., 1921-23; asst. engr. in charge constrn. and surveys, Carolina Power & Light Co., 1923, later engr. Episcopalian. Mason. Home: Raleigh, N.C. Died Nov. 3, 1928.

JOSTES, FREDERICK AUGUSTUS (Jos'tes), physician and surgeon; b. St. Louis, Mo., Aug. 14, 1895; s. Clemense and Appolonia (Niederberger) J.; B.S., Washington U., St. Louis, 1918, M.D., 1920; grad. student, orthopedic clinics, Eng., France, Germany, Austria, Switzerland, Ireland, Italy, 1925-26; m. Barbara Mary Donohoe, Dec. 4, 1945. Interne, Barnes Hosp., St. Louis, 1921, asst. resident surgeon, 1922, surgical pathologist, 1923; resident fellow, med. sch., Washington U., 1924; resident surgeon, orthopedics, Shriner Hosp. for Crippled Children, St. Louis, 1925; prof. clinical orthopedic surgery, U. of Mo., 1927-29; asst. prof. clin. orthopedic surgery, Washington U., since 1935; mem. staff Barnes, Childrens, Maternity, Deaconess, Jewish, City, County, Barnard Skin and Cancer hosps., St. Louis. Served with U.S. Navy, chief of surgery at Naval Air Station, San Diego, Calif., Jan.-July, 1942; exec. officer, Mobile Hosp. No. 2, July-Nov. 1942; sr. med. officer, U.S.S. Mt. Vernon, Nov. 1942-Feb. 1944; with bur. medicine and surgery, Office of Rehabilitation, Feb.-Sept. 1944; chief orthopedic surgery, U.S. Naval Hosp., St. Albans, Long Island, N.Y., Sept-Nov. 1944; chief surgery and orthopedics, U.S. Naval Hosp., Great Lakes, Ill., Nov. 1944-Feb. 1946; dist. med. office, 12th Naval Dist., San Francisco; rank of capt., Naval Reserve. Member of the Baruch Committee on Phys. Medicine. Certified by Am. Bd. Orthopedic Surgery, 1934. Fellow Am. Coll. Surgeons; mem. St. Louis, Mo. State, Am. Southern and Miss. Valley med. assns., Clin. Orthopedic Assn., Am. Acad. Orthopedic Surgeons, Am. Orthopedic Assn., St. Louis Surg. Soc., Acad. Internat. of Medicine, La Societe Internationale de Chirurgie Orthopedique et de Traumatologie. Contbr. of articles to med. jours.; author chpts. in med. books. Home: River's Arm, St. Ferdinand de Fleurissant, St. Louis County, Mo. Office: 3720 Washington, St. Louis 8. Died May 19, 1952.

JOYCE, J(AMES) WALLACE, engr.; b. Cranston, R.I., July 8, 1907; s. James and Annie Josephine (Malkin) J.; B.Eng., Johns Hopkins, 1928, Ph.D., 1931; m. Edith Mae Clagett, June 25, 1932; 1 son, James Wallace. Applied geophysical prospecting U.S. Bur. Mines, 1931-35; observer-in-charge U.S. Coast and Geodetic Survey, Tucson Magnetic Obs., 1935-37, head magnetic sect., 1937-41; elec. engr. U.S. Naval Ordnance Lab., 1941-42; engr. Bur. Areonautics (electronics) U.S. Navy Dept., 1947-51; spl. assignments to Dept. State; mutual def. assistance program, Apr.-June 1949, internat. science policy survey group, 1949-50; deputy science adviser Department of State, 1952-53; asst. dir. electronics and guided missiles Office Sec. Def., 1953-55; head Office for the International Geophysical Year, Nat. Science Foundation, Washington, 1955-58, head Office Special International Programs, 1958-61; spl. asst. to the dir. of foundation, 1961-63; officer in charge general sci. affairs Office Internat. Sci. Affairs, Dept. State, 1963-65, acting dep. dir. internat. sci. and technol. affairs, 1965-67, dep. dir. internat. sci. and technol. affairs, 1967-70. Entered active duty as lt. USNR, 1942; discharged to inactive duty as comdr., 1947. Mem. Internat. Assn. Terrestial Magnetism and Electricity (sec. 1948-51), Am. Geophys. Union (pres. sect. terrestial magnetism and electricity, 1950-53), Seismol. Soc. Am., Washington Academy of Science, Sigma Xi, Tau Beta Pi. Club: Cosmos. Contbr. articles geophysical prospecting (magnetic methods) in pubs. Home: Washington DC Died Jan. 6, 1970.

JUDAH, THEODORE DEHONE, engr., railroad builder; b. Bridgeport, Conn., Mar. 4, 1826; s. Henry R. Judah; attended Rensselaer Poly. Inst., Troy, N.Y.; m. Anna Pierce, May 10, 1847. Built bridge, Vergennes, Vt., 1847-54; planned and built Niagara Gorge R.R.; in charge of constrn. for Buffalo & N.Y. R.R.; chief engr. Sacramento Valley R.R., 1854-56; published widely circulated pamphlet advocating constrn. of transcontinental railroad; 1857; agt. Pacific R.R. Conv., Washington, D.C., 1859 60; organized Central Pacific R.R. Co., 1861, sold his share in co. because of friction with partners, 1863. Died N.Y.C., Nov. 2, 1863.

JUDAY, CHANCEY, (ju-da'), zoölogist; b. nr. Millersburg, Ind., May 5, 1871; s. Baltzer and Elizabeth (Heltzel) J.; A.B., Indiana U., 1896, A.M., 1897, LL.D. from the same univ. in 1933; m. Magdalen Evans, Sept. 6, 1910; children—Chancey Evans, Mary, Richard Evans. Teacher of science, high sch., Evansville, Ind., 1898-1900; biologist, Wis. Geol. and Natural History Survey, 1900-01; acting prof. biology, U. of Colo., 1903-04; instr. in zoölogy, U. of Calif., 1904-05 biologist, Wis. Geology and Natural History Survey, 1905-31; lecturer in zoölogy, 1908-31, prof. of limnology since 1931, U. of Wis.; asst. U.S. Bur. Fisheries, summers, since 1907; dir. Trout Lake Limnological Lab. since 1925; mem. Nat. Research Council, Biology and Agrl. Div., 1940-43; asso. editor, Ecological Monographs, 1940-43. Fellow A.A.A.S.; mem. Am. Soc. Zoölogists, Am. Society Naturalists, Am. Micros. Society (pres. 1923), Ecol. Soc. America (pres. 1927), Internat. Limnol. Soc., Wis. Acad. Sciences (sec.-treas., 1922-30) (pres. 1937-39), Am. Limnol. Soc. (pres. 1935-36), Phi Beta Kappa, Sigma Xi. Author: Dissolved Gases of Wisconsin Lakes, 1911; Hydrography and Morphometry of Wisconsin Lakes, 1914; Plankton of Wisconsin Lakes, 1922—all with E. A. Birge; also papers dealing with the physics, chemistry and biology of lakes. Home: 1840 Summit Av., Madison, Wis. Died Mar. 29, 1944.

JUDD, DEANE BREWSTER, color scientist; b. South Hadley Falls, Mass., Nov. 15, 1900; s. Horace and Etta Lois (Gerry) J.; A.B., Ohio State U., 1922, M.A., 1923; Ph.D., Cornell U., 1926; m. Elizabeth Melamed, Aug. 7, 1926; children—Dean Burritt, Audrey Lois. Physicist optics Nat. Bur. Standards, Washington, 1927-70, guest worker, 1970-72; pres. Munsell Color Found., 1943-72. Am. rep. Internat. Commn. Illumination, 1931, 35, 48, secretariat dir., 1951; Am. rep. Internat. Commn. Optics, 1948; studies color measurement, color differences, color perception, color blindness; invited prof. Instituto de Optica, Madrid, 1956-57. Recipient Jour. award Soc. Motion Picture Engrs., 1936; Exceptional Service award Gold medal Dept. Commerce, 1950; Samuel Wesley Stratton award Nat. Bur Standards, 1966. Mem. Illuminating Engring. Soc. (Gold medal 1961), Optical Soc. Am. (Herbert E. Ives medal 1958, pres. 1953-55, asso. editor jour. 1936-60, editor 1961-63), Inter-Soc. Color Council (Godlove award 1957, chmn. 1940-44). Author: Color in Business, Science and Industry, 1952, (with G. Wyszeck) 2d edit., 1963; Home: Chevy Chase MD Died Oct. 15, 1972.

JUDSON, EGBERT PUTNAM, inventor, explosives mfr.; b. Syracuse, N.Y., Aug. 9, 1812; s. William and Charlotte (Putnam) J. Founder 1st assay works in San Francisco, 1852; an organizer San Francisco Chem. Works (later Judson & Sheppard), 1867; dir. Giant Powder Co.; founder Judson Power der Co., Kenvil, N.J.; patentee Giant Powder, No. 2, 1873, "gentle" blasting powder, 1876; founder Judson Fuse Works, Judson Iron Works, Judson Candle Works, Butterworth & Judson Chem. Works; pres. Judson Mfg. Co., Cal. Paper Co. Died San Francisco, Jan. 9, 1893.

JUDSON, WILBER, mining engr.; b. Lansing, Mich., July 26, 1880; s. James Bradford and Julia (Byrnes) J.; student Northwestern U., Evanston, Ill., 1897-98, U. of Mich., 1898-1900; S.B., Harvard, 1901; grad. study, Mich. Coll. of Mines, 1902-03; m. May E. Reynolds, Aug. 28, 1917. Began as mining engr., 1903; examining engr., mine and mill operations in U.S., Mexico and S.A., 1903-17; with W. B. Thompson interests, N.Y. City, as officer and dir. various mining and exploration projects, 1917-21; with Tex. Gulf Sulphur Co. since 1921, now v.p. and dir.; v.p., dir., Sulphur Export Corp.; dir. Mesabi Iron Corp. Member adv. com. on raw materials of U.S. Atomic Energy Commn.; mem. National Minerals Adv. Council. Mem. Am. Inst. Mining and Metallurgical Engineers. (ex-v.p.), Mining and Metallurgical Society of America (ex-v.p.). Clubs: Houston (Tex.); Union League, Harvard, University (all New York); Lawrence Beach; The Apawamis. Home: Newgulf, Tex. Office: 75 E. 45th St., N.Y.C. Died Aug. 9, 1951; buried Kinderhook, N.Y.

JUDSON, WILLIAM PIERSON, cons. engr.; b. Oswego, N.Y., May 20, 1849; s. John W. and Emily (Pierson) J.; ed. Oswego schs. and pvt. tuition; m. Mrs. Anna L. T. McWhorter, Oct. 9, 1888. U.S. asst. engr. on forts, rivers, and harbors, 1870-99; commr. Varick power canal, Oswego, 1876-1922; dep. state engr. N.Y., May 1899-1905; pres. Broadalbin (N.Y.) Electric Light & Power Co., 1905—; pres. Broadalbin Supply & Constrn. Co., Inc., 1919—; dir. Broadalbin Knitting Co., Broadalbin Bank; consulting engr., 1905—. Mason. Republican. Episcopalian. Author: City Roads and Pavements, 1894, 1902, 1906, 1909; Road Preservation and Dust Prevention, 1908; From the West and Northwest to the Sea by the Way of the Niagara Ship Canal, 1890; Lake Ontario to the Hudson River through the Oswego-Oneida-Mohawk Valley from Oswego to Troy, 1896; History of various projects for reaching the Great Lakes from Tide-water, 1768-1901, 1901; also many reports on harbors to engring. jours. Home: Broadalbin, N.Y. Died Feb. 12, 1925.

JUDSON, WILLIAM VOORHEES, col. Corps Engrs. U.S.A.; b. Indianapolis, Ind., Feb. 16, 1865; s. Charles E. and Abby (Voorhees) J.; ed. Harvard, 1882-84, M.A., 1911; grad. U.S. Mil. Acad., 1888, U.S. Engr. Sch. of Application, 1891; m. Alice Carneal Clay, Apr. 21, 1891. Additional 2d lt. Engr. Corps, June 11, 1888; 2d lt., July 23, 1888; 1st lt., May 18, 1893; capt., July 5, 1898; maj., Mar. 2, 1906; lt. col., Mar. 2, 1912; col., May 15, 1917; brig. gen. N.A., 1917-19. Recorder board of engineers U.S.A.; mem. U.S. bd. of engrs. for rivers and harbors; harbor improvements at Galveston, etc.; river improvements, Miss. River, etc.; instr. mil. engring., U.S. Engr. Sch.; asst. to chief of engrs.; mil. attaché with Russian Army during Russo-Japanese War; in charge of harbor improvements and light house constrn. on Lake Michigan; engr. commr. of D.C.; on duty with Panama Canal Commn.; in charge of river and harbor improvements, Chicago and vicinity. With Root mission to Russia, 1917; detached therefrom and remained in Russia as mil. attaché and chief of Am. Mil. Mission to Russia until spring 1918. Comd. 38th Div., Camp Shelby, Miss., until Aug. 1918; thereafter until after Armistice comd. Port of Embarkation, New York; div. engr., Northwestern Div. Awarded D.S.M. Address: Chicago, Ill. Died Mar. 29, 1923.

JULIEN, ALEXIS ANASTAY, geologist; b. New York, N.Y., Feb. 13, 1840; s. Pierre Denis and Magdalen (Cantine) J.; A.B., Union Coll., 1859, A.M., 1864; hon. Ph.D., New York U., 1881; m. Annie Walker, d. P. I. Nevius, June 1, 1882. Resident chemist, guano island of Sombrero, 1860-64; studied geology and natural history there; collected birds and land shells and made meteorol. observations on the island for Smithsonian Instn.; asst. analytical chemistry, 1865-85, instr. microscopy, microbiology, 1885-97, curator geology, 1897-1909, Sch. of Mines, Columbia. Connected with Mich. Geol. Survey, 1872, N.C. Geol. Survey, 1875-78; reported on bldg. stones of New York City, 10th U.S. Census. Address: South Harwich, Mass. Died May 7, 1919.

JUNG, FRANZ AUGUST RICHARD, physician; b. Suhl, Germany, Oct. 9, 1869; s. Herman and Marie J.; grad. Univ. of Leipzig (M. D.); m. July 23, 1896, Dr. Sofie A. Nordhoff. Is prof. diseases of stomach and intestines, Post-Grad. Med. Sch. of D. C. Mem. Med. Soc. D.C., Med. Assn., D. C., Am. Med. Assn., Washington Acad. Sciences; Knight Order of St. Stanislaus (conferred by Czar of Russia, Apr., 1902), Order of the Crown, conferred by German Emperor, 1905. Extensive contb'r to Am. and German med. jours. Address: 1229 Conn. Av., Washington

JUNKERSFELD, PETER, engineer; b. Champaign County, Ill., Oct. 17, 1869; s. Peter J. and Josephine (Schmitz) J.; B.S., U. of Ill., 1895, E.E., 1907; m. Anna Boyle, June 19, 1901; children—Florence Rita, Josephine. In charge engring. dept. Chicago Edison Co. and its successor, Commonwealth Edison Co., 1895-1909, asst. to v.p. same, 1909-17; engring. mgr. Stone & Webster, Boston, 1919-22; mem. firm McClellan & Junkersfeld, Inc., engrs. Commd. maj. engrs., U.S.R., Feb. 23, 1917; called to active service June 7, 1917, as supervising officer cantonment and other war constrn., hdqrs., Washington, D.C.; lt. col. Feb. 1918; col., Mar. 1918; hon. discharged, Mar. 4, 1919. Awarded D.S.M., Aug. 1919. Pres. Assn. Edison Illuminating Cos., 1916-17. Home: Scarsdale, N.Y. Died Mar. 18, 1930.

JUST, ERNEST EVERETT, prof. zoölogy; b. Charleston, S.C., Aug. 14, 1883; s. Charles Frazier and Mary (Mathews) J.; grad. Kimball Union Acad., Meriden, N.H., 1903; A.B., Dartmouth, 1907; Ph.D., U. of Chicago, 1916; m. Ethel Highwarden, June 26, 1912. With Howard U., Washington, 1907—, prof. zoölogy, 1912—. Author: (with others) General Cytology, 1924; The Biology of the Cell Surface, 1939; Basic Methods for Experiments on Eggs of Marine Animals, 1939. Contbr. papers on physiology of development, including results of research on fertilization, artificial parthenogenesis, cell division. Asso. editor Physiol. Zoölogy (Chicago) and The Biol. Bull. (Woods Hole, Mass.), Jour. Morphology. Home: Washington, D.C. Died Oct. 27, 1941.

JUST, THEODOR KARL, botanist; b. Gross Gerungs, Austria, Oct. 27, 1904; s. Alois and Anna (Traindl) J.; Ph.D., Univ. of Vienna, 1928; m. Mary Agnes McGarry, June 11, 1938; children—Anne Elizabeth, Mary Margaret, Jane Frances. Came to U.S., 1929, naturalized, 1938. Asst. Herbarium, Naturhistorisches Museum, Vienna, 1928-29; instr. biology, Notre Dame, 1929-32, asst. prof., 1932-35, asso. prof., 1935-41, prof., 1941-45, head of dept., 1940-45; J. A. Nieuwland Research prof. in botany, 1945-46; asst. curator, curator, Herbaria, 1929-46; asst. editor Am. Midland Naturalist, 1930-34, editor, 1935-47; founder, editor Am. Midland Naturalist Monographs, 1944-47; founder, editor Lloydia, since 1938; science dir. Lloyd Library of Botany, Pharmacy and Materia Medica, Cincinnati, O.; asso. curator dept. botany, Chicago Nat. History Museum, 1946, chief curator since 1947; cons. Europe-Africa Div. Office of Strategic Services; asst. editor Chronica Botanica, Waltham Mass., since 1940; research asso., dept. botany, Northwestern U., since 1947; lectr., dept. botany U. Chgo. since 1951. Chmn. com. paleobotany, div. geology and geography Nat. Research Council, 1951—, editor Palebotany Report div. of earth sciences, 1959—. Fellow New England Botanical Club; member of Conf. of Biol. Editors (v.p. 1959—), Bot. Soc. Am. (sec. paleobot. section 1945-47, chairman 1948), Torrey Bot. Club, Ind. Acad. Sci. (v.p. 1942; pres. 1943), Ecol. Soc., Soc. for Study of Evolution (sec. 1949-52), California Botanical Society, Sullivant Moss Society, Sigma Xi. Roman Catholic. Club: University (Chicago). Editor: Plant and Animal Communities, 1939; Symposium on Paleobotanical Taxonomy, 1946. Address: Chicago Natural History Museum, Chgo. 60605. Died June 14, 1960.

KAEDING, CHARLES DEERING, (ka'ding), cons. mining engr.; b. San Francisco, Calif., Aug. 5, 1880; s. Charles Van Buren and Frances Caroline (Ladd) K.; grad. Calif. Sch. Mech. Arts, San Francisco, 1900; student U. of Calif., 1900; m. Martha Vahey, 1912. Supt. Oriental Consol. Mining Co., Wunsan, Korea, 1901-03, gen. supt., 1903, asst. gen. mgr., 1903-07; mining engr. gen. practice, Central America, Mexico and Nev., 1907-11, asst. gen. mgr. Goldfield Consol. Mines Co., Nev., 1911-13; asst. supt., mines Internat. Nickel Co., Sudbury, Ont., 1913-14; v.p. and gen. mgr. Dome Mines Co., Ltd., South Porcupine, Ont., 1914-20; cons. mining engr. since 1920; pres. and dir. Sachigo River Exploration Co., Ltd.; dir. Pioneer Gold Mines of B.C., Steep Rock Iron Mines, Ltd.; mng. dir. Pacific Nickel Mines. Mem. Am. Inst. Mining and Metall. Engr., Psi Upsilon. Clubs: Wunsan Mines (Korea); Bohemian, Olympic (San Francisco). Home: Mississauga Rd., Port Credit, Ont., Can. Office: 25 King St. W., Toronto, Can. Died Sep. 9, 1942.

KAHLENBERG, LOUIS, chemist; b. Two Rivers, Wis., Jan. 27, 1870; s. Albert and Bertha (Albrecht) K.; B.S., U. of Wis., 1892, fellow chemistry, 1892-93, M.Sc., 1893; Ph.D., summa cum laude, U. of Leipzig, 1895; m. Lillian Belle Heald (B.L., U. of Wis., 1893), July 21, 1896; children—Hester (Mrs. Jas. R. Davidson), Herman Heald, Eilhard (dec.). Instr., 1895-97, asst. prof. physical chemistry, 1897-1900, prof., 1900-07, prof. chemistry, 1907—, chmn. chem. dept. and dir. course in chemistry, 1908-19, U. of Wis. Fellow A.A.A.S. (v.p. Sect. C, 1907-08). Engaged in study of the celluloses, the keratins, separation of crystalloids by dialysis, potentiometric titrations, gas electrodes, and nature of metallic state, activation of gases by metals; exptl. studies of elemental carbon and phosphorus; with Dr. Edward H. Ochsner, boric acid treatment of blood poisoning, also use of colloidal gold in cases of malignancy, and the introduction of the use of dichloracetic acid in med. practice. Author: Outlines of Chemistry, 1909, 15; Qualitative Chemical Analysis (with J. H. Walton), 1911; Chemistry and Its Relations to Daily Life (with E. B. Hart), 1914. Inventor of Equisetene, new skin suture material. Home: Madison, Wis. Died Mar. 18, 1941.

KAHN, JULIUS BAHR, JR., pharmacologist, educator; b. Chgo., July 7, 1921; s. Julius Bahr and Leona (Kline) K.; B.S., U. Chgo., 1946, M.S., 1947, Ph.D., 1949; m. Carolyn Shadley, Dec. 1, 1948; children—David, Robert, Richard, Deborah. Postdoctoral fellow U. Chgo., 1949; biologist Oak Ridge Nat. Lab., 1949-51; asst. prof., asso. prof. pharmacology U. Cin., 1951-61; vis. prof. Pharmakologisches Institut, U. Berne (Switzerland), 1958-59; asso. prof., prof. pharmacology Northwestern U., Chgo., 1961-68, chmn. pharmacology dept., 1965—; mem. PET-A study sect. USPHS, 1965-68. Mem. bd. United World Federalists, 1966-68. Served with M.C., AUS, 1942-46. John and Mary Markle scholar med. sci., 1954-59. Mem. Am. Soc. Pharmacology and Exptl. Therapeutics, A.A.A.S., N.Y. Acad. Scis., Red Cell Club, Soc. Exptl. Biology and Medicine, Chgo. Med. Soc., Soc. Young Med. Educators (past sec., chmn.), Am. Civil Liberties Union, Com. Sane Nuclear Policy, Sigma Xi. Editor-in-chief Jour. Pharmacology and Exptl. Therapeutics, 1965-68. Home: Winnetka IL Died Oct. 18, 1968.

KAHN, MAURICE GUTHMAN, surgeon; b. Morrison, Ill., Mar. 27, 1873; s. Isaac and Hermina (Guthman) K.; M.D., cum laude, Harvard, 1898; m. Gertrude Berryman, Jan. 21, 1907. Practiced as surgeon, Denver and Leadville, Colo., 1900-14, Los Angeles, 1915—; instr. in anatomy, Denver and Gross Sch. of Medicine, 1903-04, U. So. Cal. Sch. of Medicine, 1918-19; surgeon Hosp. of Good Samaritan, Los Angeles, 1917—; surgeon-in-chief Cedars of Lebanon Hosp., Los Angeles, 1932—, prof. clin. surgery, U. So. Cal., Sch. of Medicine, 1931—. Trustee Federated Welfare Orgns. of Los Angeles, 1918-46. Served as mem. Med. Bd. of Appeals So. Cal. during World War. Fellow Am. Coll. Surgeons (founder), A.M.A., Am. Bd. Surgery (founder); mem. Western Surg. Assn., Pacific Coast Surg. Soc., Los Angeles Surg. Soc. Republican. Jewish religion. Mason (32 deg.). Clubs: Jonathan, Harvard of Southern California, Hillcrest Country (Los Angeles). Contbr. to med. jours. Home: 450 N. Rossmore St. Office: 727 W. 7th St., Los Angeles. Died Sept. 12, 1950.

KAINS, MAURICE GRENVILLE, horticulturist; b. St. Thomas, Ont., Can., Oct. 10, 1868; s. John Alexander and Emma Elizabeth (Hughes) K.; B.S., Mich. State Coll., 1895; B.S.A., Cornell U., 1896, M.S.A., 1897; m. Jean Bell Hickey, June 1, 1913; children—Maurice Eugene, Louis Stanley. Spl. crop culturist, U.S. Dept. Agr., 1897-1900; prof. horticulture, Sch. of Practical Agr. and Horticulture, Briar Cliff Manor, N.Y. (sch. now extinct), 1900-02; an editor New Internat. Cyclo., 1902-03; contbr. to Cyclo. Americana, 1904; horticulture editor Am. Agriculturist, New York, 1904-14; prof. horticulture and head of dept., Pa. State Coll., 1914-16; consultant practice since 1916; lecturer on horticulture Columbia University, 1917-19; contributing editor of Farm Knowledge, 1918-19, National Encyclopedia, 1932-33; editor Your Home (magazine), 1926-27; horticulturist, Poultry Tribune since 1934. Member Sigma Xi, Alpha Zeta. Mason. Democrat. Author: Ginseng, 1899; Making Horticulture Pay, 1909; Culinary Herbs, 1912; Plant Propagation, Greenhouse and Nursery Practice, 1916; Principles and Practice of Pruning, 1917; Home Fruit Grower, 1918; Modern Guide of Successful Gardening, 1934; Gardening Short Cuts, 1935; Five Acres and Independence, 1935; Gardening Children's Adventures, 1937; Propagation of Plants (with L. M. McQuisten), 1938; Grow Your Own Fruit, 1940; We Wanted a Farm, 1941; Food Gardens for Defense, 1942; Fifty Years Out of College, 1944; also many hort. articles. Home: Suffern, N.J. Died Feb. 25, 1946.

KALLET, ARTHUR, exec. dir. Med. Letter, engr., editor; b. Syracuse, N.Y., Dec. 15, 1902; s. Barnett and Etta (Kaplan) K.; B.S., Mass. Inst. Tech., 1924; m. Opal Boston, Apr. 27, 1927 (dec. 1952); 1 son, Anthony; m. 2d, Mary R. Fitzpatrick, January 28, 1954; children—Cynthia, Lisa. Engaged in editorial work New York Edison Company, 1924-26, then assistant manager editorial bureau 1927; mem. staff Am. Standards Assn. and editor, Industrial Standardization, 1927-34; publicity dept. Regional Plan N.Y., 1929-32; founder, dir. Consumers Union U.S., 1936-57; exec. dir. The Med Letter Drugs and Therapeutics, from 1958; pres. Drug and Therapeutics Information, Inc., from 1958, Buyers Laboratory, Inc., from 1961. Author: 100,000,000 Guinea Pigs (with F.J. Schlink), 1933; Counterfeit, 1935. Home: New Rochelle NY Died Feb. 24, 1972.

KALMUS, HERBERT THOMAS, (kal' mus), physicist; b. Chelsea, Mass., Nov. 9, 1881; s. Benjamin G. and Ada Isabella (Gurney) K.; B.S., Mass. Inst. Tech., 1904; Ph.D., U. of Zurich, Switzerland, 1906; E.D., Northwestern U., 1951; m. Natalie Mabelle Dunfee, July 23, 1902 (div. 1921); m. 2d Eleanore King, Sept. 6, 1949. Prin. U. Sch., San Francisco, 1904-05, graduate fellow, Massachusetts Institute Technology, studying in Europe, 1905-06; research associate, 1906-07, instructor, 1907-10, M.I.T.; asst. prof. physics, 1910-12, prof. electrochemistry and metallurgy, 1913-15, Queen's U., Kingston, Ont.; dir. Research Lab. of Electrochemistry and Metallurgy, Canadian Govt., 1913-15; pres. Kalmus, Comstock & Westcott, Inc., 1912-25, Am. Protein Corp., Boston, 1920-25; v.p. The Exolon Co., Buffalo and Thorold, Ont., 1914-19, pres. 1919-23; pres., gen. mgr. Technicolor Corp. (motion pictures in natural color), 1915-59, pres. subsidiaries, 1956-59; pres., gen. mgr. Technicolor, Inc., 1922-59; chmn. Technicolor, Ltd., London, 1935-59. Dir. Stanford Research Institute, 1953—. Hon. fellowship British Kinematograph Soc. London, Eng., 1951; mem. Am. Inst. Chem. Engrs., Am. Physical Soc., Soc. Motion Picture Engrs. (N.Y.), A.A.A.S., Acad. of Motion Picture Arts and Sciences (Hollywood) Clubs: Masquers (Hollywood); Los Angeles Country, Bel Air Country (Los Angeles); Motion Picture Pioneers (N.Y.). Author: Mr. Technicolor. Contbr. about 50 articles to tech. jours. Home: 729 Bel Air Rd., Los Angeles 90024. Office: 6311 Romaine St., Hollywood 38, Cal. Died July 11, 1963.

KARAPETOFF, VLADIMIR, (kär-a-pet'of), elec. engr.; b. St. Petersburg, Russia, Jan. 8, 1876; s. Nikita Ivanovitch and Anna Joakimovna (Ivanova) K.; C.E., Inst. of Ways of Communication, St. Petersburg, 1897, M.M.E., 1902; Technische Hochschule, Darmstadt, Germany, 1899-1900; hon. Mus. Doc., N.Y. College of Music, 1934; hon. D.Sc., Poly. Inst. Brooklyn, 1937; m. Frances Lulu Gillmor, Aug. 2, 1904 (died 1931); m. 2d, Rosalie Margaret Cobb, Nov. 25, 1936. Consulting engr. for Russian Govt., and instr. elec. engring. and hydraulics in 3 colls., St. Petersburg, 1897-1902; spl. engring. apprentice with Westinghouse Electric & Mfg. Co., E. Pittsburgh, Pa., 1903-04; prof. elec. engring. Cornell U., 1904-39; prof. emeritus since 1939; visiting prof. for grad. students, Poly. Inst. of Brooklyn, 1930-32; lecturer Stevens Inst. Technology, 1939-40. Cons. engr. and patent expert to various enterprises; with J. G. White & Co., Inc., engineers and contractors, 1911-12. Inventor and patentee of several elec. devices and of five-stringed cello. Awarded Montefiore prize, 1923, and Elliot Cresson gold medal, Franklin Inst., 1927, both for kinematic models of elec. machinery. Lt. comdr. U.S. Naval Res. since 1933, assigned to engring duties for spl. service. Mem. bd. trustees, Ithaca Coll., 1932-39, chmn., 1933-36. Mem. U.S. Naval Inst., U.S. Naval Reserve Officers' Assn., International Jury Awards, Panama P.I. Expn., San Francisco, 1915; mem. advisory bd. U.S. Naval Acad., 1916. Christian. Fellow Am. Inst. E.E., A.A.A.S., Am. Physical Soc.; mem. Am. Assn. Univ. Profs. (charter), Am. Math. Soc., Math. Assn. America, Franklin Inst., Sigma Xi; hon. mem. Eta Kappa Nu, Tau Beta Pi, Phi Mu Alpha (Sinfonia), Theta Xi. Author: Ueber Mehrphasige Stromsysteme, 1900; Resistance of Ships to Propulsion (in Russian), 1st part 1902, 2d part 1911; Experimental Electrical Engineering, 2 vols., 1908; The Electric Circuit, 1910; The Magnetic Circuit, 1911; Engineering Applications of Higher Mathematics, part I, 1911; parts II to V, 1916; Rhythmical Tales of Stormy Years (poems), 1937; also numerous articles in engring. mags. and trans. Research editor of the Electrical World, 1917-26. Gave several series of public piano recitals; developed five-stringed cello and plays it in public; lecturer on engring., and on moral and psychol. topics. Chmn. com. on physics of Conf. on Electrical Insulation, National Research Council, 1928-35, chmn. com. on monographs, 1935-38. Consultant to U.S. Bd. of Economic Warfare, 1942-43; consultant to Bethlehem Steel Co. since 1944. Home: 39 Claremont Av., Apt. 84, New York 27. Died Jan. 11, 1948; buried in East Lawn Cemetery, Ithaca, N.Y.

KARPINSKI, LOUIS CHARLES, (kär-pin'ske), educator; b. Rochester, N.Y., Aug. 5, 1878; s. Henry H. and Mary Louise (Engesser) K.; grad. State Normal and Tng. Sch., Oswego, N.Y., 1897; A.B., Cornell U., 1901; Ph.D., U. Strassburg, Germany, 1903; m. Grace Maude Woods, Apr. 20, 1905; children—Robert Whitcomb, Mary, Louise, Ruth, Joseph Louis, Charles Elwin. Tchr. Berea (Ky.) Coll., 1897-99, Oswego Normal, 1903-04; in charge math. dept., Chautauquan Instn., Chautauqua, N.Y., 1905, 06, 07; Tchrs. Coll. fellow and univ. extension lectr., Columbia U., 1909-10; instr. mathematics, U. Mich., 1904-10, asst. prof., 1910-14, asso. prof., 1914-19, prof., 1919-48, emeritus. Mem. Am. Math. Soc., Math. Assn. Am., A.A.A.S., Deutsche Mathematiker Veriningung, Comité Internat. d'Histoire des Scis. Democrat. Conglist. Author: The Hindu-Arabic Numerals (with David Eugene Smith), 1911; Robert of Chester's Latin Translation of the Algebra of Al-Khowarizmi, 1915; Unified Mathematics (with H. Y. Benedict and J. W. Calhoun), 1918; History of Arithmetic, 1925; The Arithmetic of Nicomachus (with M. L. D'Ooge and F. Robbins), 1926; Bibliography of the Printed Maps of Michigan, 1804-1880, with Atlas, 1931; Early Maps of Carolina and Adjoining Regions, Charleston, S.C., 1937; Bibliography of Mathematical Works Printed in America through 1850, 1940; Early Military Books in the University of Michigan Libraries (with Col. Thomas M. Spaulding), 1941. Collector of maps and early Americana; authority on early maps of Am. Expert authority on gas and electric rates. Home: 1315 Cambridge Rd., Ann Arbor, Mich.; (winter) Winter Haven, Fla. Died 1956.

KARRER, ENOCH, (kär'rër), research physicist; b. Rich Hill, Mo., May 23, 1887; s. Frank Xavier and Theresa (Braun) K.; A.B., U. of Wash., 1911, A.M., 1912; Ph.D., Johns Hopkins U., 1914; m. Ethel Walther, Aug. 2, 1919; children—Enoch, Aurora, Ethelda, Rathe. Research asst. with United Gas Improvement Co., Phila., 1914-18; chief searchlight sect. U.S. Bur. of Standards, 1919-21; in General Electric Co.'s research lab., Cleveland, O., 1921-26; research associate Cushing Laboratory for Exptl. Medicine, Western Reserve U., Cleveland, 1923-31; research physicist B. F. Goodrich Co., 1926-31; cons. research engr., 1931-36; economics and govt. research, Washington, D.C., 1934-35; research biophysics Smithsonian Instn., 1935; tech. consultant Am. Instrument Co., 1936; sr. physicist, U.S. Dept. of Agr. since 1936, at Southern Regional Research Lab., New Orleans, since 1941. Served as pvt. 1st sergt. Med. Corps, 345th Engrs., later master engr., 447th Engrs., U.S. Army, World War; now capt. Engrs., O.R.C. Awarded James A. Moore prize in physics, Seattle, 1913, Longstreet medal (co-winner), Franklin Inst., 1918. Mem. Washington Philos. Soc., Sigma Xi, Phi Beta Kappa, and several tech. socs. Author 70 publications in sci. field. Holder of 6 patents. Contbr. of papers to tech. jours. Home: 7003 Broad Place. New Orleans 18. Died Mar. 27, 1946; buried in Garden of Memories, New Orleans.

KARSNER, HOWARD, pathologist; b. Phila., Pa., Jan. 6, 1879; s. Charles W. (M.D.) and Martha M. (Wright) K.; B.S., Central High Sch., Phila., 1897; Phila. Sch. of Pedagogy, 1899; M.D., Univ. of Pa., 1903; LL.D., Western Reserve University, Cleveland, 1949; m. Audrey W. Stanwood, Dec. 11, 1912 (died 1944); m. 2d Daisy Stanley-Brown, Mar. 12, 1946 (died 1949);

married 3d Jessie Spencer Beach, July 5, 1950. Demonstrator pathology, Univ. of Pannsylvania, 1908-11; asst. prof. pathology, Harvard Med. Sch., 1911-14; prof. pathology, Western Reserve U., 1914-49; med. research adviser to Bur. Medicine and Surgry, U.S. Navy, from 1949; dir. Inst. Pathology, 1929-49; dir. Pathology, University Hosps.; div. chief of labs., City Hosp., 1914-49; cons. to Surg. Gen., U.S.A. Mem. sci. adv. bd. Armed Forces Inst. Pathology, adv. med. bd. Leonard Wood Meml. for Eradication Leprosy. Served as capt., Med. R.C., with A.E.F. in France, 1917-Feb. 11, 1918. Awarded W.W. Gerhard Medal, Phila. Path. Soc., Centennial Award, Northwestern U., 1951; Capt. Robert Dexter Conrad award, U.S. Navy, 1961. Fellow Aero. Med. Assn. (hon.), N.Y. Acad. Scis.; mem. Nat. Bd. Med. Examiners (pres. 1951-54), A.M.A., Assn. American Physicians, Am. Coll. Physicians, Am. Soc. Exptl. Pathol., Internat. Soc. Geog. Path. (vice president, Assn. Pathologists and Bacteriologists Society Exptl. Biology and Med., A.A.A.S. (v.p. Sect. N, 1931), Sigma Xi, Alpha Omega Alpha; corr. mem. various orgns. Rep. Club: Army and Navy. Author: Human Pathology, 1926, 55. Editor Year Book of Pathology, 1941-53. Contbr. tech. jours. Chmn. div. med. sciences, Nat. Research Council, 1927-28, chmn. com. on Pathology 1948-58; consultant in pathology, Army Air Forces, Army Med. Mus. and Office Scientific Research and Development, 1943-46; spl. cons. Secretary of War, 1946. Home: Washington DC Died Apr. 8, 1970; buried Beiliel Cemetery, Beiliel MD

KASNER, EDWARD, (kas'ner), coll. prof.; b. New York, Apr. 2, 1878; B.S., Coll. City of New York, 1896; A.M., Columbia University, 1897, Ph.D., 1899, Doctor of Science (honorary), 1954; University of Göttingen, 1900; unmarried. Tutor mathematics, 1900-05, instr., 1905-06, adj. prof., 1906-10, prof. since 1910, Adrain prof. since 1937, Columbia U.; staff of trans. and bulletins, Am. Math. Soc., Revue Semestrielle des Mathématiques (Amsterdam). Speaker Internat. Congress of Arts and Sciences, St. Louis, 1904, Harvard, 1936; mem. Nat. Acad. Sciences, Am. Math. Soc. (v.p. 1908), A.A.A.S. (v.p. and chmn. Section Mathematics and Astronomy, 1909), Circolo Matematico di Palermo, Société Mathématique de France, Phi Beta Kappa. Mem. com. mathematics NRC. Author: Ivariants of the Inversion Group, 1900; Present Problems of Geometry, 1905; Differential-Geomeyric Aspects of Dynamics (Princeton Colloquium Lectures), 1913; Conformal Geometry, 1915; Einstein's Theory of Gravitation, 1920; Polygenic Functions, 1927; New Names in Mathematics, 1937; Isothermal Families (in Revista and Pastor vols.), 1943; (with James Newman) Mathematics and the Imagination, 1940, Swedish, Russian and Spanish trans. 1941, armed services edit 1945. Editor: Scripta Mathematics. Del. Internat. Mat. Congresses, Bologna and Zurich. Home: 430 W. 116th St., N.Y.C. 27. Died Jan. 7, 1955.

KASSABIAN, MIHRAN KRIKOR, physician; b. Cesaria, Asia Minor, Turkey, Aug. 25, 1868; ed. Argeus (Am. missionary) High Sch., Cesaria, taught there, 1887-90; came to America, 1894; M.D., Medico-Chirurg. Coll., Phila., 1898; married. Enlisted 1898, in hosp. med. corps U.S.A.; instr. electro-therapeutics and skiagrapher, Medico-Chirurg. Coll. and Hosp., 1899-1902; dir. Röntgen Ray Lab. and lecturer on the Röntgen ray, Phila. Gen. Hosp., 1903—. Del. to Internat. Congress, Physio-therapy and Internat. Congress, Radiology and Ionization, Liege, Belgium, 1905, to Am. Congress for Tuberculosis, 1902. V.p. Am. Electro-Therapeutic Assn. Republican. Conglist. Author: Electro-Therapeutics and Röntgen Rays with Chapters on Radium and Phototherapy, 1907. Home: Philadelphia, Pa. Died 1910.

KASTLE, JOSEPH HOEING, chemist; b. Lexington, Ky., Jan. 25, 1864; s. Daniel and Thane (Vallandingham) K.; B.S., State Coll. of Ky., 1884, M.S., 1886; post-grad. studies Johns Hopkins, 1884-88, Ph.D., 1888; m. B. Callie Warner, June 18, 1895. Prof. Chemistry, State Coll. of Ky., 1888-1905; chief div. chem. hygienic lab., U.S. Pub. Health and Marine Hosp. Service, 1905-09; prof. chemistry, U. of Va., 1909-11; research prof. chemistry, Ky. Agrl. Expt. Sta., State U. of Ky., July 1, 1911-12; dir. Ky. Agrl. Expt. Sta. and dean Coll. of Agr., State U., Lexington, 1912—. Author: The Chemistry of Metals, 1900; The Chemistry of Milk; Oxidases. Home: Lexington, Ky. Died Sept. 24, 1916.

KATTE, EDWIN BRITTON, electrical engr.; b. St. Louis, Oct. 16, 1871; s. Walter and Elizabeth Pendleton (Britton) K.; M.E., Cornell, 1893, M.M.E., 1894; m. Elva King, Jan. 26, 1907; children—Elizabeth, Edwin Britton. Apprentice and engring. student, H. R. Worthington shops, Brooklyn, 1894-96; asst. engr. Park Av. Improvement Commn., 1896-98; successively, 1898—, draftsman, asst. engr., mech. engr., elec. engr., and 1906—, chief engr. of electric traction N.Y. Central R.R., in charge of design, constrn. and operation of electric traction systems; consulting elec. engr. Cleveland Union Terminals Co. Democrat. Episcopalian. Home: Irvington, N.Y. Died July 19, 1928.

KATTE, WALTER, civil engr.; b. London, Eng., Nov. 14, 1830; s. Edwin and Isabella (James) K.; ed. King's Coll. Sch.; pupil in civil engr's. office, 1846-49. Came to U.S., May 1849; m. Elizabeth Pendleton Britton, Nov. 22, 1870. Entered ry. service, 1850; resident engr. state canals, Pa., 1857-58; afterward engr. of several rys.; in U.S. mil. engring. service, 1861-62; with Keystone Bridge Co., Pittsburgh, as engr., sec. and gen. Western agt., 1865-75; superintended erection St. Louis steel arch bridge; chief engr. New York Elevated R.R., 1877-80, New York, West Shore & Buffalo R.R., 1880-86, N.Y.C.&H.R., New York & Harlem, and West Shore railroads, 1886-99; retired. Home: New York, N.Y. Died Mar. 4, 1917.

KATZ, FRANK J(AMES), geologist; b. N.Y. City, Jan. 27, 1883; s. Edward Marc and Alice (Neustadt) K.; B.A., U. of Wis., 1905; fellow in geology, U. of Chicago, 1906-07; m. Martha Valiant Wills, Nov. 1, 1913. Pvt. geol. work, 1904-07; mem. U.S. Geol. Survey, 1907-25; successively jr. geologist, asst. geologist, asso. geologist, to 1918, geologist, 1918-24, geologist in charge Div. of Mineral Resources, 1924-25; engr. in charge Div. of Mineral Resources and Statistics, U.S. Bur. of Mines, July 1, 1925—. Expert spl. agt. for mines and quarries, U.S. Census, 1919-22; specialist on mineral abrasives and feldspar resources. Author: Mines and Quarries, 1922. Home: Washington, D.C. Died Aug. 1930.

KATZIN, EUGENE M(AURICE), physician; b. Newark, Nov. 4, 1904; s. Harry Samuel and Bessie V(iolet) (Samuels) K.; A.B. with honors, Cornell U., 1927, M.D. (honor roll), 1931; postgrad. U. Vienna, 1933-34; m. Ethel Rosa Burstiner, Oct. 12, 1933; 1 don, Dicker. House officer Harlem Hosp., N.Y.C., 1931-33; vol. in pathology, lab. of Harrison S. Martland, M.D., Newark City Hosp. since 1934; in charge research Blood Transfusion Betterment Assn. of N.Y.C., 1935-37, asst. med. dir., 1937-40; med. dir. Blood Transfusion Assn., N.Y.C., since 1940, collaborator in original work in establishment of role of Rh blood factor in etiology of erythroblastosis fetalis (hemolytic disease of newborn), 1940-42; acting asst. pathologist Newark City Hosp., 1942-46; mem. attending staff Newark City, Newark Beth Israel, and Newark Presbyn. hosps.; dir. research Theresa Grotta Home for Cardiac Children, Caldwell, N.J.; in med. practice internal medicine. Organizer and community blood banks: Blood Transfusion Assn., N.Y.C., 1943; free blood bank County of Essex, N.J., 1947. Commd. sr. surgeon (res., inactive) USPHS. Diplomate Bd. Internal Medicine, Nat. Bd. Med. Examiners, Fellow N.Y. Acad. Medicine, Acad. Medicine No. N.J., A.M.A.; asso. mem. A.C.P.; mem. Hist. Soc. of N.J., N.Y. Acad. Scis., Med. Soc. N.J., Essex County Med. Soc., Essex County Anat. and Path. Soc., Soc. for Study of Blood, Am. Heart Assn., Pi Lambda Phi, Chi Alpha, Phi Delta Epsilon, Alpha Omega Alpha. Jewish religion. Home: 81 Parker Av., Maplewood, N.J. Office: 50 Baldwin Av., Newark, N.J.; also 2 W. 106th St., N.Y.C. Died May 22, 1966.

KAUFFMAN, CALVIN HENRY, botanist, mycologist; b. Lebanon, Pa., Mar. 10, 1869; s. John Henry and Mary Ann (Light) K.; A.B., Harvard, 1896; student U. of Wis., 1900-01, Cornell U., 1902-04; Ph.D., U. of Mich., 1906; m. Elizabeth Catharine Wolf, Sept. 3, 1895. Teacher secondary schs. of Pa., Ind., and Ill. until 1900; asst. in botany, Cornell U., 1902-04; instr. botany, 1904-08, asst. prof., 1908-17, U. of Mich.; pathol. insp. (leave of absence from univ.), Federal Hort. Bd., U.S. Dept. Agr., 1917-19; asso. prof. botany and dir. Univ. Herbarium, 1920-23, prof. and dir., 1923—. Presbyn. Author: Agaricaceae of Michigan (2 vols.), 1918. Home: Ann Arbor, Mich. Died June 14, 1931.

KAUFMANN, PAUL, prof. bacteriology and pathology, Univ. of Mo., since Sept., 1898; b. Brooklyn, Sept. 1, 1862; s. Carl and Elisabeth K.; gymnasium edn., Charlottenburg and Griefswalde, Prussia; studied univs. Berlin, Strassburg, Zurich, 1883-89; grad. Strassburg, Alsace, M.D., and "Approbiertet-Arzt"; unmarried. For nearly a yr. asst. to Prof. Weigert, Franfort-on-Main, 1890; spl. studies on malaria in Clinica Medica, Rome, 1891; studies in Zoological Station, Naples; studied at Quarantine Station (Gebel-Tor, Sinai Peninsula) of Internat. Quarantine Bd. of Alexandria, Egypt, 1891; prof. pathology and bacteriology, Med. School, Cairo, Egypt, 1892-96; apptd. to Mo. chair on spl. recommendation Profs. Koch and Virchow of Berlin. Has written numerous papers and addresses in German and French on bacteriol. and pathol. subjects. Address: Columbia, Mo.

KAUFMANN, WILFORD E., (kof'man), chemist; b. Glenmont, O., Feb. 12, 1893; s. Christian and Eliza (Bohren) K.; student Houghton (N.Y.) Coll., 1913-16; A.B., Oberlin Coll., 1918, A.M., 1919; Ph.D., U. Ill., 1923; m. Selma Niedergesaess, June 14, 1924; children—Paul Edward, Ann Elizabeth, Donald. Research chemist Du Pont Co., Jackson Lab., Deepwater Point, N.J., 1919-21; grad. dept. of chemistry U. Ill., 1921-23; prof. chemistry Hiram (O.) Coll., 1923-24; research chemist, asst. dir. of research Du Pont Co., Newark, 1924-26; asst. prof. chemistry Williams Coll., Williamstown, Mass., 1927; head dept. chemistry Alma (Mich.) Coll., 1927-41, Carleton Coll., 1941-48; dean, v.p., Carroll Coll., Waukesha, Wis., 1948—; tchr. Mich. State Normal Coll., Ypsilanti, summer 1929; research chemist, organic lab. Dow Chem. Co., Midland, Mich., summers 1930, 31, 32, 33. Pres. Valley Trails council Boy Scouts Am., Saginaw, Mich., 1939-40. Served with 308th Inf., 77th Div., U.S. Army, 1918-19; with AEF, 1918-19. Mem. Am. Chem. Soc., A.A.A.S., Phi Lambda Upsilon, Sigma Xi. Republican. Presbyn. Club: Lions (Northfield, Minn.). Contbr. articles to Jour. Am. Chem. Soc. Home: 209 S. James St., Waukesha, Wis. Died Aug. 6, 1953.

KAVANAUGH, WILLIAM HARRISON, engr.; b. Williamsport, Pa., Aug. 19, 1873; s. Daniel and Emma (Ramsey) K.; M.E., Lehigh U., 1894; m. Julia Sara Vogt, Feb. 20, 1896; children—Emma Cosette (wife of William Harry Regelman, M.D.), William Ramsey. Prin. Miners and Mechanics Inst., Freeland, Pa., 1894-95; mercantile business, Williamsport, 1895-97; instr. mech. enging., U. of Ill., 1897-98; draftsman and chief draftsman Pa. R.R., 1898-1901; instr. mech. engring. and asst. prof. exptl. engring., U. of Minn., 1901-07, prof. exptl. engring., 1907-16; prof. exptl. engring., U. of Pa., 1916—, also cons. practice and servicing as engring. expert in many cases of patent and other litigation. Mem. Exam. Bd. Civil Service Commn., Minneapolis, 1913-16. Mem. Internat. Jury of Awards, Panama-Pacific Expn., San Francisco, 1915, and Sesquicentennial Expn., Phila., 1926; mem. commn., Chicago, to report on "mushroom" system of concrete constrn., 1913; designed Exptl. Engring. Lab., U. of Minn. Progressive Republican. Mason. Home: Philadelphia, Pa. Died May 6, 1939.

KAVELER, HERMAN HENRY, cons. engr.; b. St. Charles, Mo., Dec. 5, 1905; s. Herman F. W. and Meta (Hachtmeyer) K.; B.S., Mo. Sch. Mines and Metallurgy, 1927, M.S. in Chem. Engring., 1928; Ph.D. in Chemistry, U. Md., 1931; m. Ethel Marie Spreckelmeyer, Sept. 9, 1932; 1 dau., Elaine Ann (Mrs. Johnson Jr.). Instr. chemistry U. Md., 1928-31, George Washington U., 1931-35; asst. chemist U.S. Bur. Mines, Pitts., 1935-36; various positions, asst. to v.p., asst. mgr. prodn. Phillips Petroleum Co., Bartlesville, Okla., 1936-52; cons. engr. Herman H. Kaveler, petroleum engr., mgmt. consultant, Tulsa, 1952—; member of board of directors of Eason Oil Company. Adviser Oil and Gas Conservation Bd., Province of Sask., 1954—; engring. com. Interstate Oil Compact Comm.; adviser Petroleo Brasielero, 1954. Mem. Am. Chem. Soc., A.A.A.S., Am. Inst. Mining Metall. and Petroleum Engrs., Ind. Petroleum Assn. Am. Club: Petroleum. Home: 3480 S. Florence Pl., Tulsa 5. Office: Nat. Bank of Tulsa Bldg., Tulsa 3. Died June 4, 1966; buried Oak Grove Cemetery, St. Charles, Mo.

KAY, EDGAR BOYD, civil engr.; b. Warriors Mark, Pa., Jan. 15, 1860; s. Dr. Isaac Franklin and Catharine (Bell) K.; acad. edn., Bellwood and Birmingham, Pa., 1872-77; C.E., Rensselaer Poly. Inst., 1883; m. Florence Edna Means, Sept. 26, 1900. Instr. civ. engring., Rensselaer Poly. Inst., 1883-85, Union Coll., Schenectady, N.Y., 1896-97, Cornell U., 1897-1903; prof. engring., 1903-07, civ. engring. and dean Coll. Engring., 1907-12, U. of Ala. Consulting engr. Ala. R.R. Commn., 1903-15; chief engr. State Convict Bur. Ala. and for several steam and hydroelectric power cos., and cities; has desinged and built many water works, sewer and lighting systems, steam and electric rys.; pres. Mt. Union (Pa.) Water Co., Dillsburg (Pa.) Water Co.; consulting engr. City of Mobile, water works dept., 1912; chief engr. City of Winchester water works and hydro-electric plant. Inventor of U.S. Govt. incinerators; also municipal incinerator plants for Niagara Falls, Wellsville, Tonawanda, Valley Stream, N.Y.; Highlands, Long Branch, Hackensack, N.J.; Munhall, McKees Rocks, Homestead, Woodland, Easton, Wilson, Pa.; Steubenville, Martins Ferry, Mingo Junction, Ohio; La Grange, Ill.; Portsmouth, Va. Chief of hydraulic and sanitray div., Office Quartermaster Gen. U.S.A., 1918-27; consulting engr. Democrat. Episcopalian. Mem. Bd. of Trade and Chamber Commerce, Washington, D.C. Mason. Home: Washington, D.C. Died Apr. 20, 1931.

KAY, G(EORGE) F(REDERICK), (kä), geologist; b. Virginia, Ont., Can., Sept. 14, 1873; B.A., U. of Toronto, 1900, M.A., 1902; fellow, U. of Chicago, 1903-04, Ph.D., 1914; hon. D.Sc., Cornell Coll., Mt. Vernon, Ia., 1935; LL.D., U. of Toronto, 1936. Prin. pub. schs., Ont., 1892-94; geologist, Lake Superior Power Co., 1900-02; asst. geologist, Ont. Bur. Mines, 1903; asst. prof. geology and mineralogy, U. of Kan., 1904-07; prof. geology, State U. of Ia., since 1907, head of dept. geology, 1911-34, dean College of Liberal Arts, 1917-1941; jr. geologist U.S. Geol. Survey since 1907; state geologist of Ia., 1911-34. Fellow A.A.A.S. (v.p. 1929), Geol. Soc. America, Ia. Acad. Science (pres. 1929). Contbr. on Geology and mineral resources of southwestern Oregon and Bering Coal Field; Pleistocene geology; history of Pleistocene deposits; Gumbotil; pre-Illinoian Pleistocene geology of Iowa; ages of drift sheets; mapping the Aftonian and Yarmouth interglacial horizons in Iowa; significance of post-Illinoian, pre-Iowan loess; classification and duration of the Pleistocene period. Home: Iowa City, Ia. Died July 19, 1943.

KAYAN, CARL F(REDERIC), educator, engineer; born N.Y.C., July 24, 1899; s. John Adam and Johanna (Freund) K.; A.B., Columbia, 1922, M.E., 1924; m. Barbara Helen Sherman, June 24, 1931; children—Cynthia Sherman, Julia Helen. Asst. mech. engring. Columbia, 1924-26, instr., 1926-37, asst. prof., 1937-44, asso. prof., 1944-48, prof., 1948-65, Stevens professor mechanical engineering, 1965-68, Stevens prof. mech. engring. emeritus, 1968-70, exec. officer dept. mech. engring., 1948-55; visiting prof. Royal Sch. Technology, Stockholm, 1955; also cons. engr. Mem. bd. Air Poll. Cont. N.Y.C., 1953-68. Sci. adv. council Refrigeration Research Foundation. Great Tchr. award Soc. Older Grads. of Columbia, 1959. Registered profl. engineer, New York and Cal. Fellow Am. Soc. of Mechanical Engineers, American Society of Heating, Refrigerating and Air Conditioning Engrs. (dr. 1965-68, Outstanding Teacher award 1964, also Distinguished Service award 1968), Instrument Society of American (pres. 1949), A.A.A.S., N.Y. Acad. Scis., Metric Assn. (v.p.), Internat. Inst. Refrigeration (pres. Commn. 2, 1959-67, ancien pres. 1967-70 Paris); mem. Inst. Measurement and Control (London, hon.), United Engring. Center N.Y. (library bd. 1968-70), Institut International du Froid (Paris, hon. member), A.A.A.S., John Ericsson Soc. (hon. v.p.), Am. Soc. Engring. Edn., Deutscher Kaltetechnischer Verein (hon.), Societe d'Encouragement pour la Recherche et l'Invention (comdr.), Sigma Xi, Tau Beta Pi, Pi Tau Sigma, Phi Kappa Psi. Clubs: Cosmos (Washington); Men's Faculty, Columbia U. Contbr. articles on energy-flow analysis, heat transfer, unit systems to sci. jours; contbr. sects. to Kent's Mechanical Handbook, 1948, Perry's Chemical Engineers Handbook, 1962; Marks' Mechanical Engineering Handbook, 1966, Ency. Sci. and Tech., 1968. Inventor, patentee in field. Home: Katonah NY Died July 5, 1970.

KEALY, PHILIP JOSEPH, civil engr., ex-pres. Kansas City Rys. Co.; b. Bloomington, Ill., July 2, 1884; s. Patrik J. and Mary Agnes (Ryan) K.; Lewis Inst., Chicago; U. of Ill., 1905-09; m. Josephine Dynan, 1909 (dec.); 1 dau., Coaina A.; m. 2d, Josephine Helen Crowley, 1917 (dec.); 1 son, J. Gerald; m. 3d, Joyce M. Hutchins, 1925; children—Hutchins D., Philip H. With Bd. Supervising Engrs., Chicago, 1909-10, Bion J. Arnold, Chicago, 1910-13, receivers of Traction Co., Kansas City, Mo., 1913-15; pres. Kansas City Rys., 1915-21; City mem. Board of Supervising Engrs. Chicago Traction, 1934-42, chmn. since 1942; dir. Lewis Sch. of Aeronautics, Cath. Youth Orgn. Lt. col. 3d Mo. Infantry, 1915, col., 1916-17; col. 138th Inf., U.S. Army, 1917-18. Mem. Memorial Assn. of Kansas City. Mem. Am. Soc. Civil Engrs., Am. Legion, Delta Upsilon. K.C. Club: Chicago Athletic Assn. Home: 37 Indian Hill Rd., Winnetka, Ill. Office: 231 S. La Salle St., Chicago, Ill. Died Aug. 26, 1944.

KEARNEY, ERICK WILSON, engr.; b. Franklinton, N.C., Feb. 26, 1906; s. Isaac Henry and Ozella (Williams) K.; B.S., N.C. State U., 1928; certificate pub. health U. N.C., 1936; M. Margaret Louise Lewis, Nov. 23, 1932; children—Erick W., William Lewis, Kay (Mrs. Jerry Gilbert), City clk. Town of Franklinton, N.C., 1929; supt. water plant Town of Mt. Airy, N.C., 1929-36; asst. san. engr. State of N.C., 1936-41; gen. engr. U.S. VA, 1946-69. Served to maj. AUS, 1941-46. Registered profl. engr., N.C. Mem. Tau Beta Pi. Democrat. Baptist. Mason. Home: Jackson MS Died Sept. 18, 1969.

KEARNEY, THOMAS HENRY, botanist; b. Cin., June 27, 1874; s. Thomas H. and Lavinia A. (Miner) K.; student U. Tenn., 1889-91, Columbia (spl. course), 1893-94; LL.D., U. Ariz., 1920; unmarried. Asst. botanist Tenn. Agrl. Expt. Sta., 1892-93; asst. curator herbarium, Columbia, 1893-94; asst. agrostologist, 1894-97, asst. botanist, 1898-1900, asst. physiologist Bur. Plant Industry, U.S. Dept. Agr., 1900-02, physiologist, 1902, sr. physiologist, 1924-29, prin. physiologist, 1929-44 (retired June 30, 1944). Prin. work, study of the flora of Arizona. Fellow A.A.A.S. Cal. Acad. Sci.; mem. Bot. Soc. America, Washington Acad. Sciences, Bot. and Biol. socs., Washington, Cal. Bot. Soc. (pres. 1949). Club: Cosmos. Address: Cal. Acad. Sciences, San Francisco 18. Died Oct. 19, 1956; buried San Francisco.

KEATING, F(RANCIS) RAYMOND, JR., physician; b. Phila., May 20, 1911; s. F. Raymond and Metta (Schaaf) K.; A.B., Cornell, 1933, M.D., 1936; M.S., U. Minn., 1942; m. Marion S. Bright, June 17, 1936; children—Priscilla, Peter, Cynthia, Michael. Intern Phila. Gen. Hosp., 1936-38; specializing endocrine and metabolic diseases, 1940-69; cons. medicine Mayo Clinic, 1942-69, prof. medicine Mayo Found. Med. Edn. and Research, grad. sch. U. Minn., 1953-69. Diplomate Am. Bd. Internal Medicine. Fellow A.C.P.; mem. Am., Minn. State med. assns., Minnesota Society of Internal Medicine. Endocrine Soc., Central Soc. Clin. Research, Am. Thyroid Assn. (pres. 1964), Zumbro Valley Med. Soc., Am. Soc. Clin. Investigation, Assn. Am. Physicians, Sigma Xi, Alpha Omega Alpha. Author med. articles. Home: Rochester MN Died Sept. 13, 1969.

KEATING, JOHN MARIE, physician; b. Phila., Apr. 30, 1852; s. William Valentine and Susan (La Roche) K.; grad. med. dept. U. Pa., 1873; m. Edith McCall, 4 children. Vis. physician Phila. Hosp., 1873-80; prof. medicine Women's Med. Coll. of Phila.; gynecologist to St. Joseph's and St. Agnes hosps., asst. physician to Children's Hosp., in charge of children's depts. Howard Hosp. and St. Joseph's Female Orphan Asylum (all Phila.); med. dir. Pa. Mut. Life Ins. Co., 1881-91; visited Far East with Pres. Grant's party, 1879; founder, editor Internat. Clinics, 1891-93; editor Archives of Pediatrics; fellow Coll. Physicians Phila., 1887-93; mem. Am., Brit. gynecol. socs., Assn. Life Ins. Med. Dirs.; pres. Am. Pediatric Soc. Author: With Grant in the East, 1879; Mother's Guide in the Management and Feeding of Infants, 1881; Maternity, Infancy, and Childhood, 1887; Diseases of the Heart and Circulation in Infancy and Adolescence, 1888; Cyclopedia of Diseases of Children, 5 vols., 1889-99; How to Examine for Life Insurance, 1890; A New Pronouncing Dictionary of Medicine, 1892; Mother and Child, 1893. Died Colorado Springs, Colo., Nov. 17, 1893.

KEATING, WILLIAM HYPOLITUS, mineral, chemist; b. Wilmington, Del., Aug. 11, 1799; s. John and Eulalia (Deschapelles) K.; grad. U. Pa., 1816, A.M., circa 1820; m. Elizabeth Bollman. Prof. minerology and chemistry U. Pa., 1822-27; largely responsible for discovery of new minerals including red zinc ore, franklinite, dysulsite, zinc carbonate; geologist and historiographer of Maj. Stephen H. Lang's 2d expdn. of 1823; editor Conversations on Chemistry, etc., published 1824; founded Franklin Inst. of Pa., 1824; one of 1st mgrs., elected prof. chemistry; mem. Am. Philos. Soc., 1822, sec.; admitted to Phila. bar, 1834; mem. Pa. Ho. of Reps., 1834; a founder Phila. & Reading R.R. Died London, Eng., May 17, 1840.

KEBBON, ERIC, (keb' bon), architect; b. Brooklyn, N.Y., June 6, 1890; s. Gustave Adolph and Datie Louise (Eldridge) K.; B.S. in Arch., Mass. Inst. of Tech., 1912; m. Jane Holmes Jutte, June 5, 1921; children—Eric, Jane Fay. Architect with John R. Freeman, 1912-13, with Welles Bosworth, 1913-17; resident architect, new buildings for Mass. Inst. of Technology; jr. partner with Welles Bosworth, 1919-21; in private practice, 1921-38; consulting architect, U.S. Treasure Department, 1934-35; designed post office and court house, Tallahassee, Fla., and Greenville, S.C.; post offices in N.Y. City, Poughkeepsie, Bronxville, Far Rockaway (all New York); designed numerous educational bldgs. and country houses in various states. Architect in charge of design and construction of pub. schs., New York City Bd. of Edn., 1938-51; resumed general practice, 1952; associate of McKim Mead and White, 1956-58. Served as captain and major in the Corps of Engineers, U.S. Army, 1917-19. Received Certificate of Merit, N.Y. State Assn. Architects. Fellow A.I.A.; mem. Soc. of Am. Mil. Engrs., Architectural League of N.Y., National Academy of Design, Nat. Soc. Mural Painters, National Sculpture Society. Clubs: Century (N.Y.C.) Home: 1105 Park Av., N.Y.C. 10028. Died Apr. 18, 1964; buried Stonington Cemetery, Stonington, Conn.

KEBLER, LYMAN FREDERIC, chemist, physician; b. Lodi, Mich., June 8, 1863; s. George John and Sophi G. (Gumpper) K.; Ph.C., U. Mich., 1890, B.S., 1891, M.S., 1892; spl. student Jefferson Med. Coll., Phila., 1898, Temple U., 1899-1903; M.D., George Washington U., 1906; m. Ida E. Shaw, Aug. 10, 1893; children—Mrs. Mabel Alice Kohr, Victor Lyman, Mrs. Ruth Wilhelmina Mercurio. Chief chemist for mfg. drug firm, Phila., 1892-1903; chief drug lab., Bur. Chemistry, Washington, 1903-07, chief, drug div., 1907-23, chief, spl. collaborative investigations, 1923-29; special adviser to Post Office Dept. in medical schemes, etc., to defraud, 1903-29; resigned from Govt. service to engage in pvt. work; chem.-med. cons. on foods, drugs, cosmetics, and mail order bus.; asst. prof. pharmacology and materia medica, Georgetown (D.C.) Coll., 1912-32. Instr. in chemistry, Ia. Agrl. Coll., 1888-89, U. Mich., 1891-92; mem. jury awards, Nat. export Expn., 1898; mem. U.S. Pharmacopoeia Revision Com., 1910-20; sec. U.S. Pharm. Conv., 1920-30. Mem. Am. Chem. Soc. (v.p. 1917), A.M.A. (council pharm. chemistry, 1905-14), D.C. Med. Soc., Am. Pharm. Assn. (v.p. 1922, 23, 24; chmn. scientific sect. 1901-02; pres. Washington br. 1915; chmn. hist. sect. 1928-29), Kappa Psi, Theta Kappa Psi; fellow A.A.A.S.; hon. mem. Md. Pharm. Assn.; trustee Nat. Coll. Pharmacy, 1918-26; pres. chem. sect. Franklin Inst., Phila., 1902; pres. U. Mich. Alumni, Washington, 1917. Chmn. Employees Reclassification Com. Dept. Agr., 1920; formerly dir. of health, Columbia Heights Community Centre, Washington; mem. Businss Men's Assn. and various civic bodies. Pres. Forum, Columbia Heights; mem. D.C. Drug Vets. Assn. Appeared many times before Congressional coms. and in court cases of P.O. Dept. Royal Arch Mason; Past Patron O.E.S. Club: Lions. Author: Eat and Keep Fit. Contbr. to chemical, food and medical subjects, on public welfare, drug habituation, analytical methods, adulteration of medicines and chemicals, harmful drugs, history of the tablet industry, variation of tablet medication, the use of the mails to defraud, etc. Home-Office: 1322 Park Rd N.W., Washington. Died Mar. 4, 1955.

KEEFE, DAVID ANDREW, consulting engr.; b. Athens, Pa., Jan. 28, 1869; s. Marcus and Mary (Pyne) K.; ed. pub. schs. of Athens and Athens Acad.; m. Clara Angela Wingerter, Sept. 24, 1913; children—Mary Clare, David A. Practiced, Athens, since 1896; pres. Merchants & Mechanics Nat. Bank, Sayre, Pa.; dir. Athens Nat. Bank; cons. engr. for Bradford, Luzerne and Carbon counties, Pa.; designer of reinforced concrete pier at Atlantic City, etc. Del. Rep. State Conv., 1912. Catholic. Mem. Am. Soc. C.E., Engineers' Soc. Pa., etc. Club: Shepard Hills Country. Home: Athens PA

KEEFER, CHESTER SCOTT, physician; b. Altoona, Pa., May 3, 1897; s. John Henry and Gertrude (Scott) K.; B.S., Bucknell U., 1918, M.S., 1922, hon. D.Sc., 1944; M.D., Johns Hopkins University, 1922; D.Sc. (honorary), Boston University, 1944, Bates College, 1962; m. Jean Balfour, August 11, 1928 (dec. Apr. 1967); 1 dau, Ishbel McGill; m. 2d, Dorothy Campbell, Mar. 27, 1971. Resident house officer, Johns Hopkins Hosp., 1922-23, asst. resident physician, 1923-26; asst. in medicine, Johns Hopkins U., 1923-25, instr. in medicine, 1925-26; resident physician, Billings Hosp., Univ. Clinics, U. of Chicago, 1926-28; asso. prof. of medicine, Peiping Union Med. Coll., China, 1928-30; asst. prof. of medicine, Harvard Med. Sch., 1930-36, asso. prof., 1936-40; asso. physician, Thorndike Memorial Lab., Boston City Hosp., 1930-40, consulting physician from 1940; jr. visiting physician, Boston City Hosp. from 1937; dir. 2d and 4th Med. Services (Harvard), Boston City Hosp., also chief 4th Med. Service, 1939-40; Wade prof. of medicine, Boston University Sch. of Medicine, 1940-64, Wade professor of medicine emeritus, 1964-72; dir. Robert Dawson Evans Meml. Hosp., 1940-59; physician in chief Mass. Meml. Hosp., 1940-59; dir. Boston U. Sch. Medicine, 1955-59; dir. Boston U.-Mass. Meml. Hosps. Med. Center, 1959-60. Member board directors Merck &Co., Inc. Mem. Exec. com., div. med. sci. NRC, Med. adminstrv. officer Com. Med Research O.S.R.D., 1944, 46, spl. asst. to Sec. of Health, Education & Welfare. Decorated Medal of Merit (U.S.); His Majesty's Medal. Diplomate Am. Bd. Internal Medicine. Fellow A.C.P. (pres. 1960; regent), Am. Acad. Arts and Scis.; mem. Am. Soc. Clinic Investigation Assn. Am. Physicians, Am. Clin. and Climatol. Assn., A.M.A., Am. Phila. Soc., Interurban Clin. Club. Phi Beta Kappa, Phi Gamma Delta, Phi Chi, Alpha Omega Alpha. Repub. Presbyn. Clubs: Harvard, St. Botolph (Boston); Cosmos, Capitol Hill (Washington); Country (Brookline); Harvard (N.Y.); Hunt (London, Ont.). Home: Brookline MA Died Feb. 3, 1972; buried Walnut Hills Cemetery, Brookline MA

KEEGAN, HARRY JOSEPH, physicist; b. Washington, Oct. 11, 1903; s. Harry Michael and Mary C.F. (Turner) K.; B.Mech. Engring., George Washington U., 1940; student U. Cin., 1929-33, U. Mich., 1939; m. Ruth Elizabeth Parker, Dec. 28, 1935; children—Joanne Marie, Rosemary Elizabeth (Mrs. Mark M. Powdermaker). Physicist Nat. Bur. Standards, Washington, 1921-66, coordinator infrared optical measurements program, 1963-66; Sirrine chair textile sci. Sch. Indsl. Mgmt. and Textile Sci., Clemson (S.C.) U., 1966-68. Lectr. mech. engring. machine design George Washington U., Washington, 1942-47; Nat. Bur. Standards rep. to absorption spectroscopy com. Am. Soc. Testing Materials, 1966. Fellow Optical Soc. Am., A.A.A.S., Washington Acad. Sci.; mem. Inter-Soc. Color Council, Nat. Geographic Soc., Am. Chem. Soc., Soc. Applied Spectroscopy, Am. Phys. Soc., Am. Assn. Textile Chemists and Colorists (sr. mem.), Sigma Xi. Contbr. articles to profl. publs. Home: Clemson SC

KEELER, JAMES EDWARD, astronomer; b. La Salle, Ill., Sept. 10, 1857; ed. public schools; grad. Johns Hopkins, 1881 (Sc.D., Univ. of Calif.). Was with Mt. Whitney (Calif.) expedition for study of solar physics, 1881. Studied in Heidelberg and Berlin; asst. astronomer, 1886-88, astronomer, 1888-89, Lick Observatory; dir. Allegheny Observatory, 1889-98; dir. Lick Observatory, June 1898—. Foreign asso. Royal Astronomical Soc., etc.; m. Cora S. Matthews, June 16, 1891. Home: Mt. Hamilton, Calif. Died 1900.

KEEN, MORRIS LONGSTRETH, inventor; b. Phila., May 24, 1820; s. Joseph Swift and Ann (Longstreth) K. Organized (with his brother) mfg. firm specializing in flat-irons; secured 1st paper-making patent on a boiler for making paper pulp from popular wood, 1859; a founder Am. Wood Paper Co., Manyunk, Pa.; established the Experiment Mills, Stroudsburg, Pa. Died Highland Grove nr. Stroudsbury, Nov. 2, 1883.

KEEN, WILLIAM WILLIAMS, surgeon; b. Phila., Jan. 19, 1837; s. William W. and Susan (Budd) K.; A.M., Brown U., 1859; M.D., Jefferson Med. Coll., Phila., 1862, Sc.D., 1912; LL.D., Brown, 1891, Northwestern, and Toronto, 1903, Edinburgh U., 1905, Yale, 1906, St. Andrews U., 1911, and U. of Pa., 1919; Ph.D., U. of Upsala, 1907; Sc.D., Harvard, 1920; Dr., honoris causa, U. of Paris, 1923; asst. surgeon 5th Mass. Regt., 1861; acting asst. surgeon U.S.A., 1862-64; studied in Europe, 1864-66; m. Emma Corinna Borden, 1867 (died 1886); children—Corinne (Mrs. Walter J. Freeman), Florence, Dora (Mrs. Geo. W. Handy), Margaret (Mrs. Howard Butcher, Jr.). In practice at Phila., 1866—; conducted Phila. Sch. of Anatomy, 1866-75; lecturer pathol. anatomy, Jefferson Med. Coll., 1866-75; prof. artistic anatomy, Pa. Acad. Fine Arts, 1876-89; prof. surgery, Woman's Med. Coll., 1884-89; prof. surgery, 1889-1907, prof. emeritus, 1907, Jefferson Med. Coll. 1st lt. med. R.C. U.S.A., Dec. 28, 1909; maj., Apr. 16, 1917; hon. disch., Mar. 18, 1918. Mem. Nat. Research Council during World War. Trustee and fellow Brown U., 1873—. Pres. Am. Surg. Assn., 1899, A.M.A., 1900, Coll. Physicians, Philadelphia, 1900-01, Internat. Congress of Surgery, Paris, 1920, Congress Am. Physicians and Surgeons, 1903, Am. Philos. Soc., 1907-17; hon. fellow Royal College of Surgeons of England, Edinburgh, Italian Surgical Soc., Royal

College of Surgeons in Ireland, American Coll. Surgeons; asso. fellow Am. Acad. Arts and Sciences; hon. fellow Boston Surg. Soc. (awarded Bigelow gold medal); awarded Colver-Rosenberger medal of honor, Brown U.; gold medal by Pennsylvania Soc. of New York. Officer Order of the Crown of Belgium, 1920; Officier Légion d'Honneur, France, 1923. Author: Surgical Complications and Sequels of Typhoid Fever, 1898; Animal Experimentation and Medical Progress, 1914; Treatment of War Wounds, 1917; Surgical Operations on President Cleveland, 1917. Editor: Heath's Practical Anatomy, 1870; Diagrams of the Nerves of the Human Body, by W. H. Flower, 1872; American Health Primers, 1879-80; Holden's Medical and Surgical Landmarks, 1881; Gray's Anatomy, 1887; American Text-Book of Surgery, 1892, 1903; I Believe in God and in Evolution, 1922; Everlasting Life, 1924; Keen's System of Surgery, 8 vols., 1906-21. Home: Philadelphia, Pa. Died June 7, 1932.

KEENAN, GEO(RGE) M(UNGOVAN), utilities exec.; b. Indpls., Sept. 17, 1891; s. James H. and Bridget Ann (Mungovan) K.; B.S., Purdue U., 1913; m. Florence K. Patterson, Feb. 16, 1915; children—Margaret Elizabeth, Florence Katheryn, George M., Robert Edward, John H. Student engr. Westinghouse Elec. Co., East Pittsburgh, 1913-15, erection engr., Chgo., 1916-17; operating and efficiency engr. Mcht.'s Heat & Light Co., Indpls., 1915-16; asst. to supt. power Union Gas & Electric Co., St. Louis, 1917-18; supt. power Little Rock Ry. & Electric Co., 1918; supr. operation Lehigh Nav. Electric Co., Allentown, Pa., 1918-20; chief system operator Pa. Power & Light Co., Allentown, Pa., 1920-29, supt. Pa.-N.J. interconnection, 1929-32, gen. sales mgr., 1932-42, chief engr., 1944-48, v.p. since 1948, also dir.; dir. Palmerton Telephone Co. Served as Dollar-a-yr.-Man, WPB, World War II. Fellow Am. Inst. E.E.; mem. A.I.M., A.S.M.E., Nat. Soc. Profl. Engrs. Internat. Conf. Large Elec. High Tension System. Edison Elec. Inst., Atomic Indsl. Forum, Inc. Purdue Alumni Assn., Hon. First Defenders. Roman Catholic. Clubs: Livingston. Engineers of Lehigh Valley, Skytop. Home: 36 N. 16th St. Office: 901 Hamilton St., Allentown, Pa. Died Jan. 1962.

KEENE, AMOR FREDERICK, mining engr.; b. Minneapolis, Minn., Dec. 18, 1879; s. Albin and Maria (Jeschka) Kuehn; ed. pub. and high schs., Minneapolis; E.M., U. of Minn., 1904; m. Muriel Leslie Carmody, Jan. 2, 1915; 1 son, Frederick Arthur. Gen. mining engring., U.S. Peru, Chile and Mexico, 1904-09; consulting practice, New York, 1909-11, London, 1911-18, New York and London, 1919—; v.p. Mego Corp.; dir. Internat. Marble Corp. Mem. Am. Relief Com., London, 1914; mem. Col. House Com., Sept. 1918-Feb. 1919, on World's mineral resources. Spl. commendation from Pres. Wilson and Ambassador Walter Hines Page for work done for Am. Relief Commrs. in London. Republican. Lutheran. Home: Douglaston, N.Y. Died Sept. 25, 1940.

KEETON, ROBERT WOOD, physician; b. West Point, Miss., July 7, 1883; s. James Madison and Georgia (Brown) K.; A.B., Cumberland U., 1903; student James Millikin U., 1903-05; A.B., U. Chgo., 1907, M.S., 1914; student U. Ill., 1910-12; M.D., Northwestern U., 1916; m. Emily Alcorn, Nov. 1, 1922. Taught chemistry, biology and physiology, Ill. and Tex., 1903-12; in practice internal medicine, Chgo., 1918—; adj. prof. physiology and physiol. chemistry Albany (N.Y.) Med. Coll., 1912-14; asst. prof. pharmacology and therapeutics U. Ill., 1918-22; fellow Otho S. A. Sprague Meml. Inst., 1922-25; asso. prof. medicine Coll. Medicine, U. Ill., 1925-28, prof., 1928-51, prof. medicine emeritus, 1951, acting head of the department, 1933, head of the department, 1934-51. Chairman suburban Cook County tuberculosis sanitarium district, 1951—. Diplomate Nat. Bd. Med. Examiners. Fellow A.C.P.; mem. A.M.A., Inst. Medicine, Am. Soc. Pharmacology and Therapeutics, Am. Physiol. Soc., Chicago Soc. Internal Medicine, Central Soc. Clin. Research, Am. Soc. Heating and Ventilating Engrs., Assn. Am. Physicians, Am. Bd. Internal Medicine, Soc. Exptl. Biology and Medicine, Miss. Valley, Ill., Chgo. med. socs., Central Interurban Clin. Club, Chgo. Heart Assn. (bd. govs.), Am. Diabetes Assn., Sigma Xi, Alpha Omega Alpha, Pi Kappa Alpha, Alpha Kappa Kappa. Presbyn. Clubs: University, Evanston Golf. Home: 1500 Hinman Av., Evanston, Ill. Office: 8 S. Michigan Av., Chgo. Died Jan. 22, 1957; buried Rosehill Cemetery, Chgo.

KEEVIL, CHARLES SAMUEL, educator; b. Woodside, L.I., N.Y., Oct. 3, 1899; s. Charles James and Paulina (Harrer) K.; S.B., Mass. Inst. Tech., 1923, S.M., 1927, Sc.D., 1930; m. Charlotte W. Thropp, May 28, 1924 (dec. 1937); 1 son, Charles Samuel; m. 2d, Etta Belle Pence, Sept. 12, 1938. Instr. chem. engring. Mass. Inst. Tech., 1927-30; prof. chem. engring., chmn. dept. Ore. State Coll., 1930-36, Bucknell U., 1936-45; on leave with Nat. Def. Research Com., 1943-45; chem. engr., sr. staff mem. Arthur D. Little, Inc., 1945-59; prof. chem. engring. Northeastern U., from 1960. Recipient Army-Navy certificate of appreciation, 1948. Registered profl. engr., Mass., Cal. Mem. Am. Chem. Soc., Am. Inst. Chem. Engrs., Am. Assn. U. Profs., Sigma Xi, Phi Lambda Upsilon, Theta Delta Chi, Tau Beta Pi, Phi Kappa Phi, Omega Chi Epsilon. Home: Needham MA Died July 19, 1969; buried Urn Garden, Newton (Mass.) Cemetery.

KEGEL, ARNOLD HENRY, commr. of health, Chicago; b. Lenox, S.D., Feb. 21, 1894; s. Rev. Arnold and Amelia (Lageman) K.; grad. high sch., Lansing, Ia.; student Dubuque (Ia.) U.; M.D., Loyola U., 1916; spl. student in surgery, Mayo Clinic, Rochester, Minn., 1917-22; m. Marie V. Sahlin, of Chicago, Ill., Aug. 16, 1924; 1 son, Robert Arnold. Began practice at Chicago, Ill., 1922; attending surgeon John B. Murphy Hosp., Ill. Masonic Hosp. and West Suburban Hosp.; commr. of health, Chicago, since 1927. Mem. A.M.A., Chicago Med. Soc., Phi Delta. Mason. Clubs: Lake Shore Athletic, Chicago Yacht, Ridgemoor Country. Home: 2820 Pine Grove Av. Office: City Hall, Chicago IL

KEIM, FRANKLIN DAVID, agronomist; b. Hardy, Neb., Sept. 10, 1886; s. Dennis and Jennie (Cramer) K.; ed. Bethany Coll. Acad., Peru State Normal; B.Sc., U. Neb., 1914, M.Sc., 1918; Ph.D., Cornell U., 1927; m. Alice Mary Voigt, June 12, 1914; children—Virginia (Mrs. William Honstead), Wayne Franklin. Tchr. in schs. of Nuckolls and Thayer Counties, 1905-08; prin. Chester (Neb.) High Sch., 1909-10; supt. schs., Blue Springs, 1910-11; mem. faculty U. Neb., 1914—, asst. in agronomy dept., 1914-16, extension specialist in agronomy, 1917-18, prof. agronomy, 1918—, acting chmn. dept. agronomy, 1930-32, chmn. 1932-52, ret.; chief agrl. sect. Biarritz Am. Army U., France, 1945. Dir. Union Nat. Ins. Co. (mem. exec. com.), Farmers State Bank. Received Plaque, Neb. Crop Improvement Assn., 1950; certificate of appreciation, 36 yrs. loyal service, U. Neb. Mem. C. of C., Farm House Frat., N.S.T.A., Nat. Geog. Soc., Am. Soc. Agronomy (past pres.), North Central Weed Com. (past v.p.), A.A.A.S., N.E.A., Neb. Writers Guild, Sigma Xi (past pres.), Gamma Sigma Delta. Mason (Shriner). Author numerous publs. on grass and weed research. Attended Grasslands Conf., Wales, summer 1937. Home: 1400 North 37th St., Lincoln 3, Neb. Died Mar. 7, 1956.

KEISER, EDWARD HARRISON, chemist; b. Allentown, Pa., Nov. 20, 1861; s. Bernhard and Katharine (Pfeifer) K.; B.S., Swarthmore Coll., 1880, M.S., 1881; fellow Johns Hopkins, 1882-84, Ph.D., 1884; studied at Göttingen and Freiburg, Saxony; specialized in chemistry; m. Elizabeth Harris, of Bryn Mawr, Pa., June 18, 1886; children—Katharine, Bernhard, Stephen Harris, Edward Harrison, Henry Francis, John MacArthur. Inst. chemistry, Swarthmore, 1880-81, Johns Hopkins, 1884-85; prof. chemistry, Bryn Mawr Coll., 1885-99, Washington, U., 1899-1913, Nat. Univ. Arts and Sciences, St. Louis 1914-18. Mem. Am. Chem. Soc., Soc. Chem. Industry, Eng., Deutsche Chemische Gesellschaft, Acad. of Science, St. Louis, Am. Philos. Soc. Author: Laboratory Work in Chemistry, 1895. Contbr. scientific papers to chem. jours. Home: Clayton, Mo.

KEITH, ARTHUR, geologist; b. St. Louis, Mo., Sept. 30, 1864; s. Harrison Alonzo and Mary Elizabeth (Richardson) K.; A.B., Harvard, 1885, A.M., 1886; studied Lawrence Scientific Sch. (Harvard), 1887; m. Elizabeth Marye Smith (LL.B. and LL.M., Washington Coll. of Law), June 29, 1916. Mem. Mass. State Topog. Survey, 1886-87; asst., U.S. Geol. Survey, in Tenn. work, 1887; in charge mapping party, Tenn. 1888-95; apptd. geologist, 1895; placed in charge areal. and structural geology of U.S., and of Geologic Atlas of U.S., 1907, in charge East of 100th meridian, 1913-21; making special investigation in U.S. and Canada of Appalachian mountain structure, stratigraphy, and earthquakes. Prof. grad. dept., U. of Tex., 1926. Mem. Geol. Soc. of America (pres. 1927), Nat. Research Council (chmn. div. geology and geography, 1928-31; chmn. coms. on earthquakes and fellowships), Nat. Acad. Sciences (ex-treas.), A.A.A.S., Am. Assn. Petroleum Geologists, Am. Inst. Mining and Metall. Engrs., Seismol. Soc. America, Am. Acad. Arts and Sciences, Am. Assn. Geographers, Geol. Soc. Washington (ex-pres.), Washington Acad. Sciences (ex-v.p.), Am. Geophysical Union, Chi Phi, Soc. Colonial Wars, S.R., Delta Kappa Epsilon, Hasty Pudding Club (Harvard); U.S. del. to Internat. Congress Geologists, 1913, to Internat. Geophysical Union; del. of Nat. Acad. of Sciences to Centenary of Geol. Society of France, 1930. Unitarian. Clubs: Cosmos, Chevy Chase, Harvard (Washington, D.C.); Harvard Varsity (Cambridge, Mass.); Quincy (Mass.) Yacht. Author: Geologic Atlas of U.S., Harpers Ferry Folio, 1894, and other folios, 1896-1907 (U.S. Geol. Survey); also many geol. articles. Home: 2210 20th St., Washington, D.C. Died Feb. 7, 1944.

KEITH, NATHANIEL SHEPARD, electro-metallurgist; b. Boston, July 14, 1838; s. Bethuel (M.D.) and Elizabeth P. K.; ed. Dover, N.H., and New York; tech. edn. in mining and elec. engring.; ed. as physician but never practiced, Mining and metallurgical engr. in Colorado, 1860-69; then elec. and electro-metall. engr.; inventor, with many patents in these lines; scientific editor Electrical World, 1884-85. Mfr. elec. appliances, as applied to mining and metallurgy, San Francisco, 1884-93; expert in same line in England till 1897. Organizer and 1st sec. Am. Inst. E.E., 1884. Author: Magnetic and Dynamo-Electric Machines, 1884. Sec.-treas. Am. Venture & Mines Corp. and officer other cos. Home: Philadelphia, Pa. Died Jan. 28, 1925.

KEITT, GEORGE WANNAMAKER, plant pathologist; b. Newberry County, S.C., June 11, 1889; s. Thomas Wadlington and Annie Selina (Wannamaker) K.; B.S., Clemson Coll., 1909, Sc.D., 1937; M.S., U. of Wis., 1911, Ph.D., 1914; m. Carol Seaver Keay, Aug. 30, 1927; children—George Wannamaker, Jr., John Keay, Alan Seaver. Asst. in botany and plant pathology, S.C. Agrl. Expt. Station, 1909-10; spl. agt. fruit disease investigations, U.S. Dept. Agr., 1910, and scientific asst., summers; scholar in plant pathology U. of Wis., 1911, lectr., 1912-14, asst. prof., 1914-17, asso. prof., 1917-20, prof., 1920-59, emeritus prof., 1959-69, part-time research professor, 1959-61, chairman dept. plant pathology, 1930-55; lecturer Mycol. Soc. of Am., 1956. Served as 1st lt. and capt. U.S. Army, World War; instr. Sch. of Arms, Camp Lee; asst. div. gas officer, 32d and 37th divs., div. gas officer 36th div., and asst. gas officer 1st Army, in France; maj. C.W.S., O.R.C. Fellow A.A.A.S.; mem. Am. Soc. Naturalists, Am. Phytopathol. Soc. (v.p. 1934, pres. 1937), Bot. Soc. America, Mycol. Soc. of America, Soc. Exptl. Biology and Medicine, Wis. Acad. Sciences, Arts and Letters, American Assn. University Professors (pres. Wis. chapter 1943-44), Indian Phytopathological Society, Nederlandse Plantenziektenkundige Vereniging; 7th Internat. Bot. Cong. (v.p. phytopathol. sect., 1950); guest speaker Brit. Assn. Advancement Sci., Edinburgh, 1951), Phi Sigma (honorary), Sigma Xi (president Wisconsin chapter, 1928-29), Gamma Alpha, Phi Kappa Phi (president Wisconsin chapter 1936-37), Chaos Club. Episcopalian. Club: University. Author of bulletins, contributor to professional journals. Mem. editorial bd. Am. Jour. Botany, 1935-44. Co-discoverer antimycin. Home: Cambridge MA Died Nov. 18, 1969; buried Old St. David's Churchyard, Radnor PA

KELKER, RUDOLPH FREDERICK, JR., consulting engr.; b. Harrisburg, Pa., Aug. 5, 1875; s. Luther Reily and Agnes Keyes (Pearsol) K.; B.S., Pa. State Coll., 1896, E.E., 1897; m. Georgia Moore, of Rochester, N.Y., May 1911. Engr. with steam and electric rys., Buffalo, Cleveland and N.Y City, 1897-1907; with Bd. of Supervising Engrs. of Chicago, in charge reconstruction of ry. tracks, 1907-14; engr. for Local Transportation Com. of Chicago City Council, 1914—; mem. firm Kelker, DeLeuw & Co., engrs., 1919-29; chief engr. Bur. of Subways, City of Chicago, 1930—. Served in World War as capt., 311th Engrs., 86th Div., U.S.A., and as maj. camp adj., Camp Grant, Ill., and staff duty in France. Mem. Am. Soc. C.E., Western Soc. Engrs., Am. Electric Ry. Assn., Chicago Assn. Commerce, Pa. Soc. S.R. Presbyn. Clubs: Mid-Day, City, University, Westmoreland Country, Mo. Athletic. Author of various reports on traffic and transportation matters for Chicago, New York, Los Angeles, Baltimore, St. Louis and other cities. Home: 999 Michigan Av., Evanston, Ill. Office: 309 W. Jackson Boul., Chicago IL*

KELLER, EMIL ERNEST, engineer and mfr.; b. N.Y. City, Oct. 16, 1863; s. John B. and Susan (Brueck) K.; ed. pub. schs. and German-Am. Inst., Rochester, N.Y.; m. Ella Miller, of Attica, N.Y., Oct. 23, 1884 (died 1915); m. 2d, Corinne B. Bray, of Detoirt, Sept. 15, 1971; children—Anne McCurdy (dec.), William Bray (dec.), Suzanne Brueck, Emil Ernest. Learned machinist's trade and advanced to foreman of a dept. Yawman & Erbe, Rochester, 1883; in business on own account, 1885-86; supt. Clark Novelty & Machine Works, 1886-88; became connected with Westinghouse corps., Pittsburgh, Pa., in charge elec. constrn., 1888; later, same year, mgr. at Chicago was engr. and gen. supt. of World's Fair electric lighting plant for Westinghouse Co., also elec. engr. Dept. of Electricity, World's Fair, 1892-94; removed to Pittsburgh, 1894, and served simultaneously as v.p. and gen. mgr., 1894-1908, for Westinghouse Machine Co., Pittsburgh Meter Co., Nernst Lamp Co., Westinghouse Inter-works Ry., Security Investment Co. and Westinghouse Foundry Co.; also mng. receiver Westinghouse Machine Co., 1907-08; organized, and pres. Detroit Insulated Wire Co., 1906-14, Insulating Materials Co., 1911-14, Metal Products Co., 1909-14, all of Detroit, Mich.; pres. Standard Screw Products Co., Detroit, since 1914; executive director and v.p. Detroit Motorbus Co., 1926; dir. Mich. Terminal Warehouse Co., Central Detroit Warehouse Company, Detroit, 1928. Fellow Am. Soc. M.E. (v.p. 1914, 15); mem. Am. Inst. E.E., Soc. Automotive Engrs., Franklin Inst., Phila., Detroit Engring. Soc., Rochester Engring. Soc., A.A.A.S., Rochester Chamber Commerce, Detroit Bd. Commerce; life mem. Nat. Marine League. Clubs: Engineers (New York); Detroit, Detroit Athletic (charter mem.), Detroit Boat; Rochester, Rochester Automobile. Home: Bloomfield Hills, Mich.

KELLER, HARRY FREDERICK, chemist, educator; b. Philadelphia, Dec. 15, 1861; s. William C. C. and Augusta Maria (Cramer) K.; B.S., U. of Pa., 1881; Ph. Nat. D., Strassburg, 1888; studied in chem. labs., of Prof. Fresenius, Wiesbaden, and U. of Strassburg; (Sc.D., U. of Pennsylvania, 1915); m. Henrietta M. Hexamer, 1892. Assayer and chemist various iron and metall. works, 1881—; asst. chemistry, 1883-86, instr. organic chemistry, 1888-90, U. of Pa.; prof. chemistry, Mich. Coll. Mines, 1890-92; prof. chemistry,

1892-1915, head dept. science, 1908-15, Central High Sch., Phila.; prin. Germantown (Pa.) High School, 1915—. Author: Experiments in General Chemistry (with E. F. Smith), 1892. Editor: Greene's Lessons in Chemistry, 1900; Am. edit. Wurtz's Modern Chemistry, 1902. Asst. dir. of allied bodies, Dept. of Pub. Safety of Pa., 1917. Home: Philadelphia, Pa. Died Feb. 5, 1924.

KELLER, WILLIAM SIMPSON, civil engr.; b. Tuscumbia, Ala., Feb. 20, 1874; s. Arthur Henley and Sally (Simpson) K.; State Normal Coll., Florence, Ala., 2 1/2 yrs.; B.C.E., U. of Ala., 1893; m. Aileen Moore, May 18, 1904 (died 1912); m. 2d, Annie Searcy, Dec. 1913. Practiced at Tuscumbia, 1893-1900; asst. engr. Shiloh Nat. Mil. Park, 1900-05; asst. engr., Apr.-Oct. 1905, engr., 1905-07, Madison Co. (Tenn.) Good Roads Commn.; supt. road construction, Office of Pub. Roads, U.S. Dept. Agr., 1907-10; co. engr., Dallas Co., Ala., 1910-11; state highway engr. of Ala., May 1, 1911—. Democrat. Presbyn. Home: Montgomery, Ala. Died Sept. 9, 1925.

KELLERMAN, KARL FREDERIC, bacteriologist; b. of American parents, Göttingen, Germany, Dec. 9, 1879; s. William Ashbrook and Stella V. (Dennis) K.; student Ohio State U.; S.B., Cornell, 1900; D.Sc., Kans. Agrl. Coll., 1923; m. Gertrude Hast, Aug. 17, 1905; 1 son, Karl Frederic. Asst. in botany, Cornell, 1900-01; asst. physiologist Bur. of Plant Industry, U.S. Dept. Agr., 1901-04; physiologist in charge lab. plant physiology, 1905-06; physiologist in charge soil bacteriology and water purification investigations, 1906-14; asst. chief of bur., 1914-17; asso. chief of bureau, 1917-33; chief Div. of Plant Disease Eradication and Control, Bureau of Entomology, 1933—. Organized the Journal of Agricultural Research, 1913, and was chmn. editorial com., 1913-24; mem. Federal Hort. Bd., 1914-24; organized, 1915, and thereafter directed the cooperative campaign of the Gulf States and Bur. of Plant Industry to eradicate citrus canker, one of the most contagious of all known diseases of citrus trees. Designated by President Wilson, 1917, as mem. Nat. Research Council, serving as sec. agrl. com., 1918—, as mem. Div. of Biology and Agr. and Div. of Federal Relations. Republican. Clubs: Cosmos, Columbia Country, Federal. Home: Washington, D.C. Died Aug. 30, 1934.

KELLETER, PAUL DELMAR, (kel'le-ter), forester; b. St. Louis, May 1, 1881; s. Carl and Pauline Josephine (Thomas) K.; grad. Central High Sch., St. Louis, 1899; A.B., Washington U., 1902; M.F., Yale, 1904; m. Lucy Taber Pool, Oct. 21, 1908; children—Helen, Paul. Forest supervisor Black Hills Nat. Forest, S. Dak., 1909-18; spl. rep. of sec. of agr. and chmn. bd. of exchange of 60,000 acres sch. lands with S.Dak., 1910-12; duty with dept. at Washington, 1918-23; dir. purchases and sales, Office Sec. of Agr., 1923-25; dir. extension, N.Y. State College Forestry, 1925-29; administrative asst., Federal Farm Bd., Washington, 1929; conservation dir. State of Wis., 1930-34; forest supervisor Huron Nat. Forest, Mich., 1934, Clark Nat. Forest, Mo., 1935-45; U.S. forest coordinator for State of Mo., 1945-46. Pres. Columbia Social Service Society, 1948-49. Mem. U.S. Dept. Agr. State War Board, 1940-46. Sec. Lawrence County (S.Dak.) Fuel and Food Adminstrns., 1917, 18, World War; pres. Sch. Bd., Deadwood, 1917; mayor of Kensington, Md., 2 terms, 1922-25. Mem. State Commn. of Resources and Development, 1943-45; state-wide com. on forestry for Mo. Sr. mem. Soc. Am. Foresters (sec. and mem. exec. council, 1919-20, 21), Mo. Assn. Social Welfare, State Hist. Soc. of Mo., Phi Kappa Phi, Kappa Phi Kappa, Alpha Xi Sigma, Robinhood, Naturalists Club. Republican. Episcopalian. Mason (32 deg., Shriner). Writer and speaker on forestry topics. Address: 1405 Pratt St., Columbia, Mo. Died Mar. 19, 1950; buried Glenwood Cemetery, Washington.

KELLEY, HOWARD G., civil engr.; b. Phila., Jan. 12, 1858; s. Edwin A. and Mary B. (Peterson) K.; grad. Poly. Coll. Pa.; m. Cora J. Lingo, Jan. 11, 1899. Entered ry. service, 1881, being asst. engr. on location, bridge constrn. and harbor work and div. engr. in charge design and field constrn. of 250 miles of the original constrn. in Wash., Ida. and Mont. on west. and Pac. divs. of N.P. Ry. until 1884; supt. mines in Mont., 1884-87; resident engr. and supt. bridges and bldgs., St. Louis Southwestern Ry. System, 1887-90; chief engr. same, 1890-98; chief engr. Minneapolis & St. Louis R.R. Co., including Ia. Central Ry. and leased and operated lines, 1898-1907; also cons. engr. St. Louis S.W. Ry., Mar. 1, 1898-May 1899; chief engr., July 4, 1907-Oct. 1, 1910, v.p. in charge operation, constrn. and maintenance, Oct. 1, 1910-Aug. 31, 1917, pres., Sept. 1, 1917—, Grand Trunk Ry. System; also pres. Grand Trunk Pacific Ry. and chmn. bd. Central Vt. Ry., Sept. 1, 1917—. Received decoration Order of St. John of Jerusalem in England, June 1913. Home: Montreal, Can. Died May 15, 1928.

KELLEY, JAY GEORGE, mining engr.; b. Worcester, Mass., July 4, 1838; ed. common schools, Boston; m. Lida Elliott, 1870. Ran away from home, 1850, and as a stowaway on "Witch of the Wave" went to Calif.; pony express rider, 1860; capt. Co. C, Nev. Inf., during Civil War; member U.S. Assay Commn., 1883; admitted to bar Deadwood, S.D., 1877, but has never practiced. Author: The Boy Mineral Collectors. Home: Denver, Colo. Died 1899.

KELLEY, WALTER PEARSON, chemist; b. Franklin, Ky., Feb. 19, 1878; s. John William and Mahala Eliza (Mayes) K.; B.S., Ky. State U., 1904; M.S., Purdue, 1907; Ph.D., U. Cal., 1912, LL.D., 1950; D.Sc., U. Ky., 1958; m. Sue Katherine Eubank, Aug. 6, 1913. Asst. chemist Purdue Agrl. Expt. Sta., 1905-08; chemist Hawaiian Agrl. Expt. Sta., 1908-14; prof. agrl. chemistry U. Cal., 1914-38, prof. soil chemistry, 1938-48, prof. emeritus, 1948—; cons. Gulf Research and Devel. Co.; spl. commr. Am. Soc. Agronomists and U. Cal. to report on researches on nitrogen fertilizers in Europe, 1930; del. U. Cal. and U.S. Govt. to 3d Congress Internat. Soc. Soil Sci., Oxford, Eng. (chmn. alklai sub.-com), 1935. Fellow A.A.A.S., Am. Soc. Agronomists (pres. 1930), Am. Mineral. Soc.; mem. Am. Chem. Soc., Western Soc. Naturalists, Internat., Western socs. soil sci., Soil Sci. Soc. Am., Nat. Acad. Scis., Sigma Xi, Phi Beta Kappa, Phi Lambda Upsilon, Alpha Tau Omega. Mason. Author (monographs): Cation Exchange in Soils; Alkali Soils, their formation, properties and reclamation. Contbr. expt. sta. bulls., sci. jours. Home: 2450 Warring St., Berkeley, Cal. Died May 19, 1965.

KELLOGG, ALBERT, physician, botanist; b. New Hartford, Conn., Dec. 6, 1813; s. Isaac and Aurilla (Barney) K.; M.D., Transylvania U. First botanist resident in Cal.; surgeon, botanist U.S. Govt.'s 1st expdn. to Bering Sea; a founder Cal. Acad. Scis., 1853, contbr. to its Proceedings, 1855. Author: Forest Trees of California, 1882. Died Alameda, Cal., Mar. 31, 1887.

KELLOGG, ARTHUR REMINGTON, biologist; b. Davenport, Ia., Oct. 5, 1892; s. Rolla Remington and Clara Louise (Martin) K.; A.B., U. of Kansas, 1915, M.A., 1916; student U. of Calif., 1916-17, Ph.D., 1928; m. Marguerite Evangel Henrich, Dec. 21, 1920. Taxonomic asst., Mus. of Birds and Mammals, U. of Kan., 1913-16; teaching fellow dept. zoology, U. of Calif., 1916-19; field asst. Bur. Biol. Survey, U.S. Dept. Agr., summers 1915, 16, 17, asst. biologist, 1920-24, asso. biologist, 1924-28; asst. curator, div. of mammals, U.S. Nat. Museum, 1928-40, curator, 1941-48; dir. U.S. Nat. Museum, 1948-62; asst. sec. Smithsonian Instn., Wash., 1958-62, research asso., 1962-69; research asso. Carnegie Instn. of Wash., 1921-43. Member board govs. Crop Protection Inst., 1935-36, Nat. Research Council (div. biology and agr.), Washington, D.C., 1930-54 (vice-chmn. 1945-47). Advisory Committee Chemical-Biological Coordination Center, 1946-52; Pacific Science Board, 1946-52. Am. mem. com. of experts on whaling, League of Nations, Berlin, 1930; apptd. del. Internat. Conf. for Regulation of Whaling, London, 1937, Oslo, Norway, 1938, London, 1938. London, 1944-45 (chmn. Am. delegation), Washington, D.C., 1946 (chmn. Am. delegation and chmn. conf.); London, 1949 (chmn. Am. delegation); U.S. commr. Internat. Whaling Commn., Oslo, Norway, 1950, Capetown, 1951, chmn. of commn. (1952-54), London, 1952, 53, 56-63, Tokyo, 1954, Moscow, 1955, The Hague, 1958, Sandefjord, 1964; del. internat. com. establish Internat. Hylean Amazon Inst., Brazil, 1947. Spl. detail to Brazil, 1943; dir. Canal Zone biol. Area, 1945-46. Arctic Research Lab. Advisory Bd., Navy Dept., 1948-51. Mem. Am. Soc. Mammalogists (past pres.), Paleaobiol. Soc. of Washington (pres. 1935-36), Biol. Soc. Wash., Am. Soc. Naturalists, Am. Assn. Anatomists, Soc. Systematic Zoology, Soc. Study Evolution, Acad. Natural Sciences of Phila. (corr.), Nat. Parks Assn. (trustee, 1931-49), Geol. Soc. Am. (fellow), Nat. Acad. Sci., Zool. Society of London, Am. Philos. Soc., American Academy of Arts and Sciences, Nat. Geog. Soc. (com. research and exploration 1955-69), Sigma Xi. Conglist. Club: Cosmos. Contbr. sci. jours. Home: Washington DC Died May 8, 1969; buried Sunset View Cemetery, Berkeley CA

KELLOGG, HAROLD FIELD, architect; b. Boston, Jan. 26, 1884; s. Charles Field and Carrie I. (Masury) K.; S.B. in Architecture (cum laude), Harvard, 1906; A.D.P.G. in architecture Ecole des Beaux Arts, Paris (5 Govt. medals), 1910; m. Eleanor Wise, June 1, 1914; children—Charles Dare, Harold Field, Jr.; m. 2d, Joyce Bannerman, Dec. 5, 1948. Pvt. practice architecture since 1913, in Boston, Orlando, Fla., 1923-24; Athens, O., 1945-49, Los Angeles, 1947-49, Pasadena since 1950; asso. Ludlow & Peabody, N.Y.C., 1910-30, Harold Plummer & Asso., Buffalo, 1925-28, Thomas W. Worcester Inc., Boston, 1948-51; chief architect Forest Lawn Meml. Park, Glendale, Cal., 1950-51, Town of Fairless Hills, Pa., 1951; formerly pres. Tuttle-Kellogg Archtl. and Engring. Co., Inc.; now v.p., chief engr. Tuttle Engring., Inc. Archtl. cons. N.E. Power Co., Boston, Standard Oil Co. of N.J., Turner Constrn. Co., U.S. Army and U.S. Navy; chmn. bd. Boston Housing Authority, 1937-39, treas. 1939-1946; dir. def. housing Fed. Works Agency, 1941; housing specialist, New Eng. War Manpower Commn., 1943-44; cons. Fed. Pub. Housing Authority, 1942. Served as cons. architect Mass. Commn. on Pub. Safety for all hosps. in state; coordinating same with surgeon gens. office, World War I; cons. for camouflage to Army and Navy; World War II. Registered architect, Cal., Ariz., Hawaii, Nev., Wash., Mass., D.C. A writer Mass. Housing Law, 1938. Illustrator of Around the Clock in Europe, 1912, Charles Fish Howell; Round the World Jingle, 1918; Thoughts as They Came, 1918; My Christmas Wish, 1922; A Motor Ramble, 1929; all by Charlotte Davenport; Amateurs at War, 1943, Ben Ames Williams. Writer, illustrator mag. articles. Mural painter (76 murals), artist and sculptor; frequently combines these arts with archtl. plans. Awarded silver medal as sculptor; Bronze medal as etcher. Mem. A.I.A., Print Makers Soc. Cal. Home: 661 Pomander Pl., Pasadena 3, Cal. Office: 4251 E. Live Oak Av., Arcadia, Cal. Died Jan. 1964.

KELLOGG, JAMES LAWRENCE, biologist; b. Kewanee, Ill., Sept. 15, 1866; s. Hosmer L. and Emily (Platt) K.; B.S., Olivet (Mich.) Coll., 1888; Ph.D., Johns Hopkins, 1892; hon. A.M., Williams, 1900; m. Ida M. Archambeault, June 16, 1892; children—Emilie (Mrs. E. A. Carrier), Louise, Helena (Mrs. W. E. Wright), Margaret (Mrs. J. R. Nelson). Prof. biology, Olivet Coll., 1892-99; asst. prof. biology, 1899-1903, prof., 1903-34 (emeritus), Williams College. Specialized in anatomy and habits of Lamellibranchiate mollusks. Author: (brochure) Oyster Culture Experiments for State of Louisiana, 1904; Shell-Fish Industries, 1910. Home: Williamstown, Mass. Died July 8, 1938.

KELLOGG, JOHN HARVEY, surgeon; b. Tyrone, Mich., Feb. 26, 1852; s. John Preston and Ann Jeanette K.; ed. State Normal Sch.; M.D., Bellevue Hosp. Med. Coll. (New York U.), 1875; studied in Europe, 1883, 89, 99, 1902, 1907, 1911, 1925; LL.D., Olivet (Mich.) Coll. and Lincoln Memorial U.; Dr. Pub. Service, Oglethorpe U., 1937; m. Ella E. Eaton, Feb. 22, 1879. Has been in practice at Battle Creek, Mich., since 1875; supt. and surgeon Battle Creek (Mich.) Sanitarium since 1876. Mem. Mich. State Bd. Health, 1878-90, 1912-16. Inventor of improved apparatus and instruments for med. and surg. purposes; discoverer of the therapeutic value of the electric light and inventor of the electric light bath; discoverer of the sinusoidal current; founder health food industries of Battle Creek. Founder and pres. emeritus, Battle Creek (Mich.) Coll.; founder and med. dir. Miami-Battle Creek Sanitarium, Miami Springs, Fla. Fellow Am. Coll. Surgeons, A.A.A.S., Royal Society Medicine (England), A.M.A., Nat. Geog. Soc.; mem. Am. Pub. Health Assn.; corr. mem. Société d'Hygiène de France. Author: Plain Facts, 1877; Home Book of Modern Medicine, 1880; Man, the Masterpiece, 1885; Art of Massage, 1895; The Stomach, 1896; Rational Hydrotherapy, 1900; Light Therapeutics, 1910; Colon Hygiene, 1912; Neurasthenia, 1915; Health Series of Physiology and Hygiene (joint author), 1915; Health Question Box, 1917; New Method in Diabetes, 1917; Autointoxication, 1918; The Itinerary of a Breakfast, 1918; The New Dietetics, 1921; Tobaccoism, 1922; The Natural Diet of Man, 1923; How to Have Good Health, 1932; also many tech. papers and articles. Editor Good Health Magazine since 1873. Founder and pres. Race Betterment Foundation, 1906. Address: Battle Creek, Mich. Died Jan. 16, 1945.

KELLOGG, VERNON LYMAN, zoölogist; b. Emporia, Kan., Dec. 1, 1867; s. Lyman Beecher and Abigail (Homer) K.; A.B., U. of Kan., 1889, M.S., 1892; Cornell, 1891; U. Leipzig, 1893, 97; U. of Paris, 1904; LL.D., U. of Calif., 1919, Brown, 1920; Sc.D., Oberlin, 1922; m. Charlotte Hoffman, Apr. 27, 1908; 1 dau., Charlotte Jean. Asst. and asso. prof. entomology, U. of Kan., 1890-94; prof. entomology and lecturer bionomics, Stanford U., 1894-1920. Mem. Nat. Acad. of Science and various other American and European scientific societies. Officer Legion of Honor (France); Comdr. Order of Crown (Belgium); Comdr. Order of Leopold I (Belgium); Comdr. Order of Polonia Restituta (Poland); gold medal (Poland). Dir., in Brussels, of Am. Com. for Relief in Belgium, 1915-16; asst. to U.S. Food administrator, 1917-19; chief of mission to Poland, special investigator in Russia, and other service in Europe with Am. Relief Administrator, 1918-21; permanent sec. Nat. Research Council, Washington, 1919-31, and chmn. div. of endl. relations, 1919-29, sec. emeritus, 1932. Trustee Rockefeller Foundation (1922-33), Brookings Institution, Gallaudet Coll. (1925-32) and other organizations. Author: Am. Insects, 1904; Animal Studies (with D. S. Jordan and H. Heath), 1905; Evolution and Animal Life (with D. S. Jordan), 1907; Insect Stories, 1908; Scientific Aspects of Luther Burbank's Work (with D. S. Jordan), 1909; Economic Zoölogy and Entomology (with R. W. Doane), 1915; Losses of Life in Modern Wars and Race Deterioration (with G. Bodart), 1916; Headquarters Nights, 1917; The Food Problem (with A.R. Taylor), 1917; Fighting Starvation in Belgium, 1918; Germany in the War and After, 1919; Herbert Hoover—The Man and His Work, 1920; Nuova, the New Bee, 1921; Human Life as the Biologist Sees It, 1922; Mind and Heredity, 1923; Evolution, 1924; Reading with a Purpose—Biology, 1925. Died Aug. 8, 1937.

KELLY, EDWARD JOSEPH, ex-mayor of Chicago, consulting engineer; born Chicago, Illinois, May 1, 1876; son of Stephen and Helen (Lang) Kelly; educated in pub. and high schs., Chicago, and under pvt. tutors, LL.D., Notre Dame, 1928; m. Mary Edmunda Roche, Mar. 20, 1910 (died 1918); m. 2d, Margaret E. Kirk, Jan. 25, 1922; children—Edward Joseph (dec.), Joseph, Patricia, Stephen. Axman to chief engr. Sanitary Dist. of Chicago, 1894-1933; loaned to the State for work as Ill. Waterway commr.; appted. South Park commr. by

Circuit Court, May 1922, re-apptd. commr., Mar. 1922, and re-elected president of bd. to which office was elected annually, 1924-34, when the consolidation of park districts sponsored by him for economy abolished all bds.; bd. had charge of 70 miles of parks and boulevards, including Lake Front and Michigan Blvd., south of Chicago River, calling for expenditure of $30,000,000; appointed mayor of Chicago to fill the unexpired term of A. J. Cermak, 1933, and elected, 1935, by vote of almost 800,000; re-elected, 1939 by similar high vote again re-elected April 1943. Served as v.p. of United States Conf. of Mayors, now pres. Directed the improvement of Grant Park; completion of Stadium; establishment of boulevards to relieve traffic; active in promoting bridge connecting outer drives at mouth of Chicago River; establishment of many parks, including one of 26 acres in colored district of Chicago; co-operated with officials of Century of Progress Exposition, Chicago, 1933, 34, securing re-opening of same, 1934; restoration of Fine Arts Bldg. in Jackson Park, as a convention hall and industrial museum; supervised as chief engineer 20 years program for Sanitary District to cost $120,000,000. A leader in fight for 10,000 cubic feet of water per second through the Main Drainage Canal; brought to successful conclusion Chicago's 50-year fight for subways and started $40,000,000 subway program in 1938; secured $100,000,000 superhighway program for Chicago, 1939; focused Congressional attention on municipal problems of housing, relief, transportation, city planning, education and taxation, 1933-39; organized the "Keep Chicago Ahead Com." of business men to stimulate comml. activities. Co-operated with state's atty. in drive against Chicago hoodlums, gangsters and racketeers, settled Chicago milk strike, 1934; organized Chicago's Own Christmas Benefit in 1933 to clothe needy children yearly, which in 7 years gave clothing and shoe outfits to approximately 448,000 needy children; established "Keep Chicago Safe" Committee; appointed Chicago Recreation Commission; U.S. Coordinator of Civilian Defense for Chicago Metropolitan Area; chairman Chicago Commission on National Defense. Trustee Art Institute Chicago; ex-officio member Chicago Plan Commission. Elected Ill. Nat. Committeeman for the Dem. Party, 1940-44, 48. Mem. Am. Soc. Civil Engrs., Western Soc. Engrs., Chicago Assn. Commerce. Democrat. Clubs: Chicago, Chicago Athletic Assn., Beverly Country, Chicago. Home: 1301 N. State St. Office: 20 N. Wacker Drive, Chicago 6. Died Oct. 20, 1950; buried Mt. Calvary, Chicago.

KELLY, HARRY MCCORMICK, biologist; b. Harrisburg, Pa., May 27, 1867; s. George Correy and Susan Hauer (Bradley) K.; A.B., Bucknell U., Lewisburg, Pa., 1888, A.M., 1891; A.B., Harvard, 1891, A.M., 1893; LL.D., John B. Stetson U., DeLand, Fla., 1911; m. Caroline May Vanderslice, Dec. 27, 1894; 1 dau., Caroline. Prof. mathematics, Central Pa. Coll., 1888-90; asst. in zoölogy, Harvard, 1891-93; instr. biology, Northwestern U., 1893-94; prof. biology, Cornell Coll., Mt. Vernon, Ia., 1894—. Library trustee Mt. Vernon, 1903-23. Republican. Methodist. Died Apr. 10, 1936.

KELLY, HOWARD ATWOOD, surgeon; b. Camden, N.J., Feb. 20, 1858; s. Henry Kuhl and Louisa Warner (Hard) K.; B.A., U. of Pa., 1877, M.D., 1882; LL.D., Aberdeen, 1906, Washington and Lee U., 1906, U. of Pa., 1907, Washington Coll., 1933, Johns Hopkins Univ., 1939; m. Laetitia Bredow, June 27, 1889; children—Olga Elizabeth Bredow, Henry Kuhl, Esther Warner (Mrs. Henry G. Seibels), Freiderich Heyn, Howard Atwood, William Boulton, Margaret Kuhl (Mrs. Douglas Warner), Edmund Bredow, Laetitia Bredow (Mrs. Winthrop K. Coolidge). Founder of the Kensington Hosp., Philadelphia; asso. prof. obstetrics, U. of Pa., 1888-89; prof. gynecology and obstetrics, Johns Hopkins U., 1889-99, gynecology, 1899-1919, emeritus prof. since 1919; gynecol. surgeon, 1899-1919, cons. gynecologist since 1919, Johns Hopkins Hosp.; surgeon and radiologist Howard A. Kelly Hosp. since 1892; Hunterian lecturer Mansion of Lord Mayor of London, 1928; hon. curator Div. of Reptiles and Amphibians, U. of Mich. Hon. fellow Royal Coll. Surgeons (Edinburgh), Edinburgh Obstet. Soc., Glasgow Obstet. and Gynecol. Soc., Royal Acad. Medicine in Ireland, Obstetrico Gynecol. Soc. of Kiev (Russia), Obstet. Soc. of London; mem. Am. Gynecol. Soc. (pres. 1912), Chicago Gynecol. Soc., Am. Urol. Assn., Roentgenol. Soc., Seaboard Med. Assn., Va. and N.C. med. socs.; fellow Southern Surg. and Gynecol. Soc., Am. Radium Soc., Am. Coll. of Surgeons, A.A.A.S., Am. Geog. Soc., British Gynecol. Soc., Md. Acad. of Sciences (life), Natural History Soc. of Md.; mem. Nat. Assn. Audubon Socs., Phila. Acad. Natural Sciences, N.Y. Zoölogical Soc., N.Y., Bot. Gardens, Am. Mus. of Natural History, Am. Soc. Ichthyologists and Herpetologists, Assn. Française d'Urologie (Paris), Société Internationale d'Histoire de la Médecine, Philos. Soc. of Gt. Britain, British Mycol. Soc., Deutsche Gesellschaft für Pilzkunde; hon. mem. many fgn. med. socs. Comdr. Order of Leopold (Belgium), 1920; Order of Cross of Mercy (Serbia), 1922; Cross of Charity of the Kingdom of the Serbs, Croats and Slovenes, 1926. Author: Operative Gynecology (2 vols.), 1898, 1906; The Vermiform Appendix and its Diseases (with Elizabeth Hurdon), 1905; Walter Reed and Yellow Fever, 1906, 07, 23; Gynecology and Abdominal Surgery (edited with C. P. Noble), Vol. I, 1907, Vol. II, 1908; The Stereo Clynic, 84 sections, 1908—; Medical Gynecology, 1908, 1912; Appendicitis and Other Diseases of the Vermiform Appendix, 1909; Myomata of the Uterus (with T. S. Cullen), 1909; Cyclopedia of American Medical Biography (2 vols.), 1912; Some Am. Med. Botanists, 1913; Diseases of the Kidneys, Ureters, and Bladder (with C. F. Burnam—2 vols.), 1914, 1922; American Medical Biographies (with W. L. Burrage), 1920; A Scientific Man and the Bible, 1925; Gynecology, 1928; Dictionary of American Medical Biography (with W. L. Burrage), 1928; Electrosurgery (with Grant E. Ward), 1932; also some 500 scientific articles. Home: 1406 Eutaw Pl. Sanatorium: 1412-20 Eutaw Pl., Baltimore, Md. Died Jan. 12, 1943.

KELLY, JOHN FORREST, electrical engr.; b. Carrick-on-Suir, Ireland, Mar. 28, 1859; s. Jeremiah and Kate (Forrest) K.; B.S. in physics and chemistry, Stevens Inst. Tech., 1878, Ph.D., 1881; m. Helen Tischer, 1892. Chemist in lab. of Thomas A. Edison, 1879; electrician New York factory Western Elec. Co., 1879-82, asst. electrician U.S. Elect. Lighting Co., 1882; with Parker Electric Lighting Co., 1882-84; with U.S. Electric Lighting Co., 1884-86; electrician Newark shops of Westinghouse Elec. Co. until Jan. 1892; with Stanley Lab. Co., 1892-95; consulting engr. for Stanley Electric Mfg. Co., Pittsfield, and Stanley Instrument Co., Great Barrington, Mass., until 1905; founded Telelectric Co., 1905, pres. until 1910; introduced Cooke-Kelly food drying process which preserves primal freshness. Has received over 90 U.S. patents for utilization of electricity, covering apparatus for generating transmitting, distributing and measuring; first to produce stable iron for electromagnetic purposes; pioneer in long distance, high tension transmission work. Fellow Am. Inst. Elec. Engineers. Received John Scott medal of Franklin Inst., Phila., 1909, for electric piano-players. Home: Pittsfield, Mass. Died Oct. 15, 1922.

KELLY, MERVIN J., research engr.; b. Princeton, Mo., Feb. 14, 1894; s. Joseph Fenemore and Mary Etta (Evans) K.; B.S., Missouri Sch. of Mines and Metal, 1914; M.S., U. of Ky., 1915, D.Sc. 1946; Ph.D., U. Chgo., 1918; D.Eng., U. Mo., 1936, N.Y.U., 1955, Bklyn. Poly. Inst., 1955, Wayne State U., 1958, Princeton, 1959; LL.D., U. Pa., 1954; Dr. Honoris Causa, U. Lyons, 1957; D.Sc., U. Pitts., 1959, Case Inst. Tech., Stevens Institute Technology, 1959; m. Katharine Milsted, November 11, 1917; children—Mary (Mrs. Robert von Mehren), Robert Milsted. Physicist, research dept. of Western Electric Company, 1918-25; physicist, Bell Telephone Labs., New York, N.Y., 1925-28; dir, vacuum tube development, 1928-34, development dir. Transmission Inst. and electronics, 1934-36, dir. of research, 1936-44, exec. v.p., 1944-51, pres., 1951-58, chmn., 1959, dir., 1944-59, research mgmt. cons. IBM Corp., 1959-65, 68-71; research mgmt. cons., dir. Bausch & Lomb, Inc., 1959-62; dir. Tungsol Electric Incorporated, Prudential Insurance Co. of Am., Bausch & Lomb Optical Co. Chmn. com. Sec. Def. continental def.; spl. cons. Nat. Aeros. and Space Adminstrn.; mem. adv. com. Sci. Manpower; chmn. subcom. role industry coll. N.Y.C. bd. edn.; chmn. com. for Sec. Commerce on Nat. Bur. Standards, chairman of the visiting com., chairman com. evaluaiton of all research and engineering activities; chairman of the task force on research Hoover Commn.; chmn. Dept. of Air Force sci. adv. bd.; v. chmn. Dept. Navy naval research adv. com. Member bd. trustees Stevens Inst. Tech. Awarded Presdl. Certificate of Merit; Indsl. Research Inst. award, 1954; Christopher Columbus Internat. Communication prize, 1955; Air Force Assn. trophy award; James Forrestal medal Nat. Security Indsl. Assn., 1959; John Fritz medal for achievements in electronics, 1959; Mervin J. Kelly award in telecommunication, Am. Inst. E.E., 1960, Am. Inst. E.E. and NEMA Golden Omego Award, 1960, Joint Engring. Socs. Hoover Medal, 1961. Fellow Rochester Mus. Arts and Scis., 1960; mem. Am. Acad. Arts and Scis., Swedish Royal Acad. Sci., M.I.T. Crop.; chmn. adv. council, dept. elec. engring. Princeton; mem. advisory committee, department of electricity, University Rochester. Fellow Am. Physical Society, I.E.E.E., Institute Radio Engrs., Acoustical Soc. of Am., Am. Philos. Soc., Nat. Acad. Sci., Sigma Xi, Eta Kappa Nu, Sigma Nu, Tau Beta Pi. Rep. Episcopalian. Clubs: Baltusrol Golf (Springfield, N.J.); University (N.Y.C.). Home: Short Hills NJ Died Mar. 18, 1971.

KELLY, WILLIAM, inventor; b. Pitts., Aug. 21, 1811; s. John and Elizabeth (Fitzsimons) K.; m. Mildred A. Gracy, circa 1847. Jr. mem. firm McShane & Kelly, 1846; developer Suwanee Iron Works & Union Forge, mfg. sugar kettles; granted U.S. patent for original invention Bessemer process (a process of air-boiling of steel which made possible inexpensive soft steel), 1857; built 1st successful fitted converter at Cambria Iron Works, 1859; founder axe mfg. firm, Louisville, Ky., 1861; honored by Am. Soc. for Steel Treating with bronze tablet at site of Wyandotte Iron Works, 1925. Died Louisville, Feb, 11, 1888.

KELLY, WILLIAM, mining engr.; b. New York, N.Y., Apr. 17, 1854; s. Robert and Arietta A. (Hutton) K.; B.A., Yale, 1874; E.M., Columbia, 1877; D.Eng., Rensselaer Polytech. Inst., 1924; D.Sc., Mich. Coll. Mining and Technology, 1930; m. Annie Ashcom, June 24, 1886; 1 son, William Ashcom (dec.). Asst. supt. Chem. Copper Co., Phoenixville, Pa., 1876, 79, 80; chemist Himrod Furnace Co., Youngstown, O., 7 mos., 1878; supt. Kemble Coal & Iron Co., Riddlesburg, Pa., 1881-85, Glamorgan Iron Co., Lewistown, Pa., 1885, Kemble Iron Co., 1886-89; gen. supt., gen. mgr. Penn Iron Mining Co., Vulcan, Mich., 1889-1923; gen. mgr. Republic (Mich.) Iron Co., 1902-14; treas. Penn Store Co., 1902-23; v.p. Commercial Bank, Iron Mountain, Mich. Pres. Bd. Examiners Bituminous Mine Inspectors of Pa., 1885-89; chmn. Bd. County Road Commrs., Dickinson Co., Mich., 1904—; mem. Pub. Domain Commn. Mich., 1909-21, chmn., 1917-21; pres. Bd. Edn., Norway Twp., Mich. several yrs.; mem. 1897-1929, chmn., 1904-29, bd. control Mich. Coll. Mines. Mem. State Highway Advisory Bd., Mich., 1919-30. Fellow A.A.A.S., Nat. Inst. Social Sciences; hon. mem. Instn. Mining Engrs. (London). Home: Iron Mountain, Mich. Died Oct. 1, 1937.

KELSER, RAYMOND ALEXANDER, (kelz'er) bacteriologist and immunologist; b. Washington, Dec. 2, 1892; s. Charles and Josie Mary (Potter) K.; D.V.M., George Washington U., 1914; A.M., Am. Univ., 1922, Ph.D., 1923; diploma hon. asso. Royal Coll. Veterinary Surgeons, London; m. Eveline Harriet Davison, Sept. 5, 1914; 1 dau., Evelyn Rae (Mrs. John Andrew Allgair). Bacteriologist for H. K. Mulford Co., Glenolden, Pa., 1914, for U.S. Dept. Agr., 1915-18; served as lt. Veterinary Corps, U.S. Army, Mar.-Oct. 1918, capt., 1918-20; commd. capt. of same in regular army, 1920, maj., 1927, lt. col., 1933, col., 1939, brig. gen., 1942, retired 1946; chief of veterinary lab., Letterman hosp., San Francisco, 1918; comdg. officer Army Veterinary Lab., Philadelphia, 1919-20; chief Veterinary Lab. Sect. Army Med. Sch., Washington, 1921-24, instr. bacteriology same sch., 1922-24; mem. U.S. Army Med. Dept. Research Bd., Manila, P.I., 1925-28; chief of Veterinary Lab. Sect. and instr. bacteriology, Army Med. Sch., instr. in infectious diseases, serology and helminthology, Army Veterinary Sch., Washington, 1928-33; instr. in pathology and bacteriology, Grad. Sch. of Arts and Sciences, Am. Univ., 1930-33; research fellow in bacteriology, Harvard U. Med. Sch., 1933-35; mem. Army Med. Research Bd., Ancon, Canal Zone, 1935-38; director, Veterinary Div., Office of Surgeon Gen. U.S. Army, 1938-46. Professor bacteriology and dean of faculty, Sch. of Veterinary Med., U. Pa., Phila., 1946-52. Mem. A.A.A.S., Am. Acad. Tropical Medicine, Am. Pub. Health Assn. mem. Am. Vet. Med. Assn. (ex-v.p.), Am. Assn. Pathologists and Bacteriologists, Nat. Acad. of Sci., Soc. Am. Bacteriologists, Pa. State Vet. Med. Assn., Keystone Vet. Med. Assn., Am. Soc. Exptl. Pathology, Am. Soc. Tropical Medicine, Washington Acad. Sciences, Assn. of Mil. Surgeons of U.S., New York Academy of Science, Phi Zeta, Sigma Xi. Decorated D.S.M.; recipient of the Gorgas Medal; XII International Veterinary Congress prize; George Washington U. Alumni Achievement award. Methodist. Mason (32 deg.). Clubs: Army and Navy (Washington); Army and Navy Country (Arlington County, Va.); Lenape (Phila.). Author: Manual of Veterinary Bacteriology, 1927; also articles. Discovered transmission of encephalomyelitis by mosquitoes, developed vaccine for rinderpest, resulting in eradication of worst stock plague in Philippines. Home: 268 Kent Rd., Wynnewood, Pa. Address: U. of Pa., 39th and Woodland Av., Phila. Died Apr. 16, 1952; buried Arlington Nat. Cemetery.

KEMMLER, EDWARD ALBERT, civil engr.; b. Columbus, O., 1867; s. William F. and Barbara K.; C.E., Ohio State U., 1888; m. Thecla Corzilius, Aug. 17, 1898. Asst. engr. U.P. Ry., locating new line in So. Utah and Ariz., 1889-91; asst. prof. civ. engring. Ohio State U., 1891-95; became constructing engr. city of Columbus 1895; dep. county engr., Summit County, 1938-40; ret. 1941; engring and planning dept., Akron, O., 1943-45, ret. Mem. Am. Soc. C.E., Ohio Soc. Profl. Engrs. (pres. 1900), Izaak Walton League, Columbus Maennerchor (pres. 1903-06). Mason (past master, 32 deg., Shriner). Contbr. to proc. engring. socs. Home: 85 Deshler Av. Office: Chamber of Commerce, Columbus, O. Died May 19, 1955.

KEMP, HAROLD AUGUSTUS, engr.; b. Frederick, Md., Apr. 27, 1894; s. Robert Augustus and Daisy Alice (Birely) K.; B.S., Va. Poly. Inst., 1917; short courses Rutgers U., 1930; m. Helen Virginia Work, Apr. 27, 1918; children—Helen Work (Mrs. Frank H. Whitney), Robert Augustus II (dec.), Virginia Bruyere (Mrs. William H. Holcombe, Jr.) Asst. master mechanic Westinghoue, Church, Kerr & Co., construction at Rock Island Arsenal, 1917-18; lt., Ordnance Dept., U.S. Army, asst. insp. Nitrate Plan No. 2, Muscle Shoals, Ala., 1918-19, supt. of service dept., 1919-20; steam engr. Dunlop, Am., Ltd., Buffalo, N.Y., constrn. power plant, pumping station, 1920-21; constrn. engr. Dupont Engring. Co., Buffalo, 1921-24; cons. engr. for sewage treatment plants, water supply, bridges, etc., with George C. Diehl, Inc., Buffalo, 1924-31; v.p., sec. Civic Research Corp., Buffalo, 1929-31; sr. engr. U.S. Engr. Office, chief of design, Ill. Waterways, Chgo., 1931-33, Upper Miss. River Project, St. Paul, 1933-34; gen. supt. design and constrn. sewage treatment plant and rebuilding pumping station, Washington, 1934-37; prin. engr. N. Atlantic Div. office, U.S. Army Engrs., flood control, 1937-38; chief engr. Dept. San. Engring., Washington, 1938-40; head engr., chief of airport sect., mem. of staff Bd. Engrs. for Rivers and Harbors, Office, Chief of Engrs., U.S. Army, Washington, 1940-44; dir. of san. engring. including supervision of water, sewer, refuse, pub. convenience and sewage treatment divs., D.C., 1944—; cons. engr., Office Civil Def. Planning, U.S., 1947-48; asst. dir. engr. services and coordinator, Utility Services D.C. Civil Def., 1951—. U.S. mem. apptd. by pres. Potomac River Basin Commn. 1941-44, D.C. mem., 1944—, chmn. 1950-51; mem. coordinating com. of Nat. Capital Park and Planning Commn., Washington Bd. Trade. Registered profl. engr. and land surveyor. Mem. Am. Soc. M.E., Am. Soc. C.E., Am. Pub. Health Assn., Soc. Am. Mil. Engrs., Am. Water Works Assn., Am. Pub. Works Assn., Md.-Del. Water and Sewerage Assn., Washington Soc. Engrs., Wash. Housing Assn., Am. Philatelic Soc., S.A.R., Frederick County (Md.) Hist. Soc., Am. Legion. Mason. Clubs: Engineers of Washington; Collectors and Washington Philatelic Soc. (Washington); Rotary. Prepared book, Estimating Data for Bridges and Miscellaneous Engineering Structures, for U.S. War Dept. Numerous articles on Potomac River. Home: 1721 N. Huntington St., Arlington 5, Va. Office: Govt. of D.C., Washington 4. Died Feb. 16, 1953; buried Mt. Olive Cemetery, Frederick, Md.

KEMP, JAMES FURMAN, geologist; b. New York, N.Y., 1859; s. James Alexander and Caroline (Furman) K.; A.B., Amherst, 1881, hon. Sc.D., 1906; E.M., Columbia, 1884; LL.D., McGill, 1913; m. Kate Taylor, Sept. 5, 1889; children—James Taylor, Philip Kittredge, Katherine Furman. Instr. and asst. prof. geology, Cornell U., 1886-91; adj. prof. geology, 1891-92, prof., 1892—, Columbia. Mgr. and scientific dir. New York Bot. Gardens, 1898—; formerly geologist U.S. and N.Y. Geol. Surveys. Hon. mem. and res. Am. Inst. Mining and Metall. Engrs., Mining and Metall. Soc. America (gold medalist). Author of textbooks and many scientific papers. Home: Great Neck, N.Y. Died Nov. 17, 1926.

KEMPNER, AUBREY JOHN, prof. mathematics; b. London, Eng., Sept. 22, 1880; s. Nathan and Sophia (Allberry) K.; student U. of Berlin, 1906-07; Ph.D., U. of Gottingen, 1911; m. Kate Henschel, Mar. 29, 1906. Instr. in mathematics, U. of Ill., 1911-14, asso. 1914-19, asst. prof., 1919-25; prof. mathematics, head dept., U. of Colo., 1925-49, ret. past co-editor Am. Math. Monthly; past asso. editor Trans. Am. Math. Soc. Mem. Am. Math. Soc. (mem. council 1925-28). Math. Assn. America (trustee 1924-43; v.p. 1927, 28, 35; pres. 1937-38), Sigma Xi (pres. Colo. sect. 1929-30). Contbr. on math. subjects. Home: 956 13th St., Boulder CO

KEMPSTER, WALTER, physician; b. London, Eng., May 25, 1841; s. Christopher and Charlotte (Treble) K.; infancy in Syracuse, N.Y.; acad. edn.; M.D., L.I. Med. Coll., 1864; m. J. L. J. Poessel, June 28, 1913. Served in Civil War, May-Nov. 1861, in 12th N.Y. Inf.; then in 10th N.Y. Cav. to Nov. 1863; 1st lt., June 9, 1863; actg. asst. surgeon U.S.A., June 1864-July 1865; asst. supt. N.Y. State Asylum for Idiots, 1866-67; asst. phys. N.Y. Hosp. for Insane, Utica, 1867-73; supt. Northern Hosp. for Insane, Wis., 1873-84; asst. editor Am. Jour. of Insanity, 1874-84; commr. of health, Milwaukee, 1894-98; prof. mental diseases in Wis. Coll. Phys. and Surg. First phys. in U.S. to make systematic microscopic exam. of brains of insane, and first to photograph through microscope the actual disease (1867); has filled important spl. med. commns. for U.S. Govt. Author: Hospital Gangrene in Army Hospitals, 1866; Entero-Colitis in United States Army, 1866. Home: Milwaukee, Wis. Died Aug. 22, 1918.

KEMPTON, CHARLES WALTER, mining engr.; b. Fairhaven, Mass., Jan. 30, 1847; s. Capt. Charles W. and Lucinda (Tripp) K.; acad. edn.; engring., with spl. instrn. in mining branches; m. Emma P. Goodale, of Lawrence, Dec. 25, 1872. On staff of Essex Water Power Co., Lawrence, Mass., 1870-74; in charge explorations with Diamond drill in Eastern States, 1874-76; in charge mining operations Eastern States and Canada, 1877-80; engr. silver mines in Mexico, 1881-82; engaged in mining and metall. operations in U.S., Mex., Cuba and S. America, 1883-92; gen. mgr. of gold mine at Oro Blanco, Ariz., 1892-97; engr. and metallurgist New York and Honduras Rosario Mining Co. in Honduras, 1897-99, Darien Isthmus, 1902, Santo Domingo, 1903-04, Chile and Peru, 1906; now consulting engr. and sr. mem. Kempton & McCoy, mining engrs. Office: 42 Broadway, New York.

KENDALL, EDWARD CALVIN, biochemist; b. South Norwalk, Conn., Mar. 8, 1886; s. George Stanley and Eva Frances (Abbott) K.; B.S., Columbia, 1908, M.S., 1909, Ph.D., 1910, D.Sc., 1951; D.Sc. (hon.), U. Cin., 1922, Yale, Western Res., Williams Coll., Nat. U. Ireland, Columbia, 1951, Gustavus Adolphus Coll., St. Peter, Minn., 1963; m. Rebecca Kennedy, Dec. 30, 1915; children—Hugh, Roy (dec.) Norman (dec.), Elizabeth (Mrs. J.J. Steve). Research chemist Parke, Davis, and Co., Detroit, 1910-11; investigations on thyroid gland St. Luke's Hosp., N.Y. City, 1911-14; head sect. biochemistry Mayo Clinic, 1914, prof. physiologic chemistry Mayo Found., (U. Minn.), 1921-51; visiting prof. chemistry, James Forrestal Research Center, Princeton University, New Jersey, from 1952. Recipient: John Scott prize and Premium awarded by City of Phila., 1921 (researches in thyroxin); Chandler medal, Columbia U., 1925; Squibb award for outstanding research in endocrinology, 1945; Lasker award (jointly with Dr. Hench), Am. Public Health Assn., 1949; Page One award (jointly with Dr. Hench), Newspaper Guild New York, 1950; John Phillips Meml. award, Am. Coll. Phys. in Boston, 1950; Research Corp. award, by Research Corp. of N.Y., 1950; Remsen Meml. award, by Md. sect. Am. Chem. Soc., 1950; Research award, Am. Pharm. Mfrs. Assn., 1950; Passano award for 1950 (with Dr. Hench), Passano Found., San Francisco, 1950; Medal of Honour from Canadian Pharm. Mfrs. Assn., 1950; Nobel Prize in Physiology and Medicine (with Dr. Philip S. Hench and Dr. Tadeus Reichstein), 1950; Dr. C.C. Criss award (jointly with Dr. Hench), 1951, Award of Merit (with Dr. Hench) from Masonic Found. Med. Research and Humane Welfare, 1951; Cameron award (with Prof. Reichstein), U. Edinburgh, 1951; Heberden Soc. award, London, 1951; The Kober award, Association of American Physicians, 1952; Alexander Hamilton medal, Alumni of Columbia Coll., 1961; Sci. Achievement award Am. Med. Assn., 1965. Mem. Am. Philos. Soc., Am. Acad. Arts and Scis., Am. Soc. Biol. Chemists (pres. 1925-26), Am. Physiol. Soc., Am. Soc. Exptl. Pathology, Am. Soc. Exptl. Biology and Medicine, Am. Chem. Soc., Harvey Soc., A.A.A.S., Assn. Am. Physicians, Assn. Study Internal Secretions, Nat. Acad. Scis., New York Academy of Sciences, Swedish Society. Republican. Congregationalist. Contbns. include isolation of thyroxine, crystallization of glutathione and establishment of its chemical structure, separation and identification of a series of compounds from the adrenal cortex; prepared cortisone by partial synthesis (with Merck & Co., Inc.), investigated effects of cortisone and of ACTH on rheumatoid arthritis and in rheumatic fever (with Drs. Hench, Slocumb and Polley). Home: Princeton NJ Died May 4, 1972; buried Oakwood Cemetery, Rochester MN

KENDALL, HENRY MADISON, geographer; b. Chicopee, Mass., Dec. 15, 1901; s. Charles Francis and Mary Lucinda (Hotchkiss) K.; A.B., Amherst Coll., 1924; student U. Edinburgh, Scotland 1924-26; M.A., U. Mich., 1928, Ph.D., 1933; m. Margaret K. Copeland, Feb. 9, 1935. Part-time instr. geography U. Mich., 1928-33, instr., 1933-37, asst. prof., 1937-43; asso. prof., chmn. dept. Amherst Coll., 1943-48; prof. Syracuse U., 1948-52; prof., chmn. dept. Miami U. since 1952. Spl. cons. O.S.S., 1941; spl. cons. War Dept., 1942, head geographer topographic br. M.I. Service, G-2, 1942-43. Recipient fellowship to Belgium, Belgian-Am. Ednl. Found., 1936-37; Meritorious Contbn. award Assn.; Am. Geographers, 1955; Fulbright lectr. to United Kingdom, University of Southampton, 1960-61. Member of Association Am. Geographers (editor, 1948-55, mem. council 1957-60, chmn. honors com. 1965-66), Am. Geog. Soc., Royal Scottish Geog. Soc. 1950—, Ohio Acad. Sci., Sigma Xi, Theta Xi, Phi Kappa Phi. Episcopalian. Club: Torch. Author: Atlas of World Affairs (with C. H. MacFadden, G. F. Deasy), 1946; Introduction to Geography (with R. M. Glendinning, C. H. MacFadden), 1951, rev. 1962, 4th edit., 1967; Introduction to Physical Geography (with R. M. Glendinning, C. H. MacFadden), 1952. Home: Wespiser Place, Route 1, Oxford, O.; also Shaftsbury, Vt. Died Jan. 13, 1966; buried Oxford (O.) Cemetery.

KENDALL, JAMES, chemist; b. Surrey, Eng., July 30, 1889; s. William Henry and Rebecca (Pickering) K.; A.M., B.Sc., Edinburgh U., 1910, Sc.D., 1915; student at Heidelberg, Stockholm and Petrograd; m. Alice Tyldesley, of Victoria, B.C., Sept. 13, 1915; children—James Tyldesley, Isabella Jean, Alice Rebecca. Vans Dunlop scholar in chemistry, Edinburgh U., 1909-12, also 1851 exhibitioner in chemistry, 1912-13; instr. chemistry, 1913-15, asst. prof., 1915-16, asso. prof., 1916-22, prof., 1922-26, Columbia; prof. and chmn. dept. Washington Square Coll. (New York U.), 1926-27, also dean Grad. Sch., New York U., 1927-28; prof., U. of Edinburgh, since 1928. Acting prof. chemistry, Stanford, 1919, 23, U. of Calif., 1923, Pa. State Coll., 1927. Lt. U.S.N.R.F., 1917-19; spl. duty for Bur. of Ordnance as liaison officer with allied navies on Naval Gas Warfare. Lt. comdr. U.S.N.R.F., 1924-26. Fellow Royal Soc., Royal Soc. Edinburgh, A.A.A.S.; mem. Am. Chem. Soc. (chmn. New York sect., 1925), Am. Inst. Chemists (chmn. New York sect. 1926), London Chem. Soc., London Soc. Chem. Industry, Faraday Soc., Phi Beta Kappa, Sigma Xi, Alpha Chi Sigma, Phi Lambda Upsilon. Clubs: Century, Chemists'. Revised and rewrote Smith's Intermediate Chemistry, Smith's College Chemistry, Smith's Elementary Chemistry, Smith's Inorganic Chemistry, and lab. outlines of each, 1922-26. Author: College Chemistry Companion, 1924; Intermediate Chemistry Companion, 1925; General Chemistry and Laboratory Outline, 1927; At Home Among the Atoms, 1929. Home: 14 Mayfield Gardens, Edinburgh Scotland

KENDALL, WILLIAM CONVERSE, naturalist; b. Freeport, Me., Apr. 4, 1861; s. William Pote and Frances Ann (Carver) K.; A.B., Bowdoin College, Brunswick, Maine, 1885, A.M., 1890, Sc.D., 1935; M.D., Georgetown Univ., 1896; m. Ida W. Aschenbach, Apr. 3, 1893; 1 dau., Minerva Converse (Mrs. Harrison Warner). Taught sch. in Minn., 1885-87; prin. Patten (Me.) Acad., 1887-89; naturalist with U.S. Commn. of Fish and Fisheries, 1889-1921; ichthyologist, Roosevelt Wilf Life Forest Expt. Sta., 1921-23; ichthyologist, U.S. Bur. Fisheries, 1923-32. Has written papers and reports on fishes and other natural history subjects in bulls. and reports U.S. Fish Commn.; proc. of the U.S. Nat. Mus. and publications of Boston Soc. Natural History, Portland Soc. Natural History and Mus. of Comparative Zoölogy. Member MacMillan Arctic Expdn., summer, 1929. Mason. Home: Freeport, Me. Died Jan. 28, 1939.

KENDIG, H(ARVEY) EVERT, univ. dean; b. Newville, Pa., Oct. 22, 1878; s. William Henry and Elizabeth J. (Christian) K.; student Pa. State Tchrs. Coll., Shippensburg, 1897; Ph.G., Medico-Chirurg. Coll., Phila., 1901, M.D., 1905; Pharm.D., Temple U., 1910; m. Agnes Charlton Royal, June 2, 1906; children—Agnes Elizabeth (Mrs. Richard W. Churchman), Janet Royal (Mrs. S. Logan Kerr), Catherine Lilian (Mrs. John W. Clegg, Jr.), Josephine Evert (Mrs. John N. Costello). Instr. pharmacy Medico-Chirurg. Coll., 1901-04, asst. prof., 1904-05; dean and prof. pharmacy Fla. Coll. Pharmacy, 1906-07; prof. pharmacy, Temple U., 1907—, dean and prof. public health Sch. Pharmacy, 1932—, asso. prof. pharmacology Med. Sch., 1914-22; prof. pharmacology and toxicology Women's Med. Coll. Pa., 1922-26. Served as major and adjutant, Temple U. Profl. Schs. Tng. Corps, World War; also examining physician Germantown Draft Bd., mem. Mayor's Com. on Home Defense (Phila.); became capt. Pa. N.G., 1920; maj. Med. Corps, State Fencibles (inf. regt.), Phila. Mem. Am. Pharm. Assn. (past pres. Phila. br.), Pa. Pharm. Assn. (chmn. com. on edn.; mem. A.Ph.A. com. on U.S. Pharmacopoeia, 1934-43; chmn. Nat. Steering Com. for Pharmacy Corps Bill), Am. Assn. Colls. of Pharmacy (pres. 1940-41; mem. nat. com. on edn. and defense 1940-43; chmn. joint com. on status of pharmacists in govt. services), 1934-43, Temple U. Gen. Alumni Assn. (bd. dirs.); hon. mem. Phila. Assn. Retail Druggists; hon. life mem. Ida., Md., N.D., Pa. and Utah pharm. assns.; charter mem. and mem. bd. dirs. Am. Found. on Pharm. Edn. Inc.; mem. bd. dirs. Am. Found. on Pharm. Edn. Inc.; mem. Am. Council on Edn. for Pharmacy (mem. pharm. survey com.), Survey Organizer Nat. Scholarship Com., 1940; chmn. Am. Assn. Colls. of Pharmacy Com. on Scholarships, 1941 (chmn. com. on emergency problems). Am. Assn. Colls. Pharm. and Am. Pharm. Assn. rep. to Am. Council on Edn. Presbyn. (ruling elder, 1919—; treas. session funds, 1920—; former trustee—all First Presbyn. Ch. of Germantown). Com. on revision of Recipe Book III, 1934-43; adv. chmn. com. on status of pharmacists in govt. service, 1943. Remington medalist, 1944; medalist N.H. Pharm. Assn., 1946. Club: Union League (Phila.). Home: 8254 Crittenden St., Chestnut Hill, Phila. 18. Office: 3223 N. Broad St., Phila. 40. Died Apr. 18, 1950.

KENLY, RITCHIE GRAHAM, civil engr.; b. Ritchie Mines, W.Va., Mar. 13, 1866; s. William L. and Elizabeth Marion (Hook) K.; Baltimore City Coll., 1879-84; m. Grace I. Erdman, Oct. 16, 1888 (dec.); children—Ritchie Graham (dec.), Guy, Grace Marion (Mrs. John A. Buck), Allen Jackson, Katherine Erdman (deceased, wife of Dr. Paul G. Bovard), Grace Isabella (Mrs. Edgar R. Bjorklund), Edith Lilian (Mrs. C. Hume Ritchie); m. 2d, Mrs. Augusta Davidson Kenly, Oct. 1, 1932. Held minor railway positions, 1885-91; supervisor Radford division, 1891-93, asst. engineer, 1893-97, asst. trainmaster Radford and Pulaski divs., 1897-98, N.&W. Ry.; asst. to chief engr. W.Va. Central & Pittsburgh Ry., 1898-99; draftsman and constrn. engr. Phila. & Erie R.R. and Northern Central Ry. (Pa. R.R.), 1899-1900; supervisor Lehigh div., L.V. Ry., June 1900; div. engr. Lehigh & N.J. divs., same rd., 1900-04; trainmaster same divs., Easton, Pa., 1904-07; gen. supt. Lehigh & N.E. Ry., 1907-08; engr. maintenance of way, L.V. R.R., 1908-09; chief engr., 1909-17, gen. mgr., May 17, 1917, asst. to pres. and chief engr., Mar. 1920, later chief engr., Minneapolis & St. Louis R.R., retired 1939. Mason. Conglist. Home: Minneapolis, Minn. Died Nov. 15, 1939.

KENNEDY, CLARENCE HAMILTON, entomologist; b. Rockport, Ind., June 25, 1879; s. Albert Hamilton and Emma Dorinda (Tennant) K.; A.B., Indiana U., 1902, A.M., 1903; A.M., Stanford, 1915; Ph.D., Cornell U., 1919; D.Sc. (honorary), Indiana University, 1950; married Lydia June Findley, March 16, 1927; children—Bruce Albert Hamilton, Mary Janet. Began as instr. in embryology, Ind. U. Biol. Sta., 1902; asst. in biology, Cornell U., 1915, instr. in limnology, 1916-17; instr. zoölogy, N.C. State Coll., 1918-19; instr. entomology, Ohio State U., 1919-21, asst. prof., 1921-30, asso. prof., 1930-33, prof., 1933-49, ret.; mng. editor Annals of Entomol. Soc. America, 1929-45; member editorial bd. ecol. monographs pub. by Ecological Soc. of America, 1934-40. Fellow A.A.A.S., Entomol. Soc. Am. (pres. 1935), Royal Entomol. Soc. of London, Ohio Acad. Sci.; mem. Am. Assn. Econ. Entomologists, Ind. Acad. Sci., Ecol. Soc. America, Am. Soc. of Naturalists, Société Entomologique de France (Paris), Phi Delta Theta, Gamma Alpha, Sigma Xi (pres. Ohio Chapter 1926-27), Gamma Sigma Delta. Republican. Presbyterian. Club: Faculty (Ohio State U.). Author: Methods for the Study of the Internal Anatomy of Insects, 1933; Insects, Ency. Britannica, 1948; many articles in biol jours. Home: 389 W. 10th Av., Columbus 1, O. Died June 6, 1952.

KENNEDY, FOSTER, neurologist; b. Belfast, Ireland, Feb. 7, 1884; s. William Archer and Hessie Foster (Dill) K.; ed. Queen's Coll., Belfast; M.D., Royal University of Ireland, 1906; married Katherine Caragol de la Terga; 1 daughter, Hessie Juana Dill and 1 daughter by previous marriage, Isabel Ann Foster. Resident med. officer Nat. Hosp., London, 1906; became chief of clinic New York Neurol. Inst., 1910; now prof. neurology Cornell U. Med. Coll., New York; consulting physician in neuropsychiatry, Bellevue Hosp.; consulting physician Neurol. Inst.; attending neurologist to New York Hosp.; cons. neurologist to Gen. Memorial, Lennox Hill, Women's, Monmouth (Long Branch, N.J.) Nassau (Mineola, L.I.), Vassar Bros. hosps. Chmn. com. neurology, National Research Council, Washington, D.C. Chairman Federal Medical Com., Ellis Island. Served médecinchef Hôp. Militaire, V.R. 76, France; commd. lt. Royal Army M.C., Brit. Army in France; promoted capt. and maj. and mentioned in dispatches. Fellow Royal Soc. Edinburgh, Royal Soc. of Medicine, London; mem. Am. Neurol. Assn. (past pres.), N.Y. Acad. Medicine, N.Y. Neurol. Soc. (pres.), N.Y. Command Brit. Great War Vets. Am. (past pres.); hon. mem. Neurol. Soc. of Paris, Hungary, Cuba, Mexico and Sweden. Decorated Confiere la condecoracion de la Orden Nacional de Merito, Carlos F. inlay en el grado de Oficial, Cuba; Chevalier Legion of Honor (France). Protestant. Clubs: Century, River, Coffee House, Pilgrims. Contbr. to tech. jours. on neurol. and psychiat. subjects. Home: 14 Sutton Sq. Office: 410 E. 57th St., N.Y.C. 22. Died Jan. 7, 1952; buried Pendleton Hill Cemetery, R.I.

KENNEDY, HENRY L., architect, engr.; b. Medfield, Mass., Aug. 15, 1897; s. John T. and Katherine (Davitt) K.; grad. Northeastern U., Boston, 1919; grad. student Beane U., France, 1920, Wentworth Inst., Boston, 1923; m. Helen S. Lake, Sept. 2, 1924; 1 dau., Dorothy Helen. Practicing architect, 1926-36, 40—; cons. architect, engr., 1925—; instr. constrn. course Wentworth Inst., 1926-36; lectr. cement and concrete tech. Harvard Grad. Engring. Sch., 1946-52; div. mgr. in charge concrete research Dewey & Almy Chemical Co., Cambridge, 1934—. Mem. corp. Belmont Hill Sch. Profl. engr., registered architect, Mass. Mem. Am. Soc. Mil. Engrs., Am. Concrete Inst. (past pres.), Am. Soc. Testing Materials, A.I.A., Am., Boston (Herschel award) socs. civil engrs. Clubs: Union League (Chgo.); Harvard Faculty (Cambridge, Mass.). Author: Cement and Concrete Technology (with Dr. R. F. Blanks), 1955. Home: 69 Radcliffe Rd., Belmont 78, Mass. Office: 62 Whittemore Av., Cambridge, Mass. Died Sept. 10, 1957; buried Medfield, Mass.

KENNEDY, JOSEPH WILLIAM, chemist; b. Nacogdoches, Tex., May 30, 1916; s. Joseph William and Mattie Baxter (Wade) K.; A.B., Stephen F. Austin State Teachers Coll., 1935; A.M., U. of Kan., 1937; Ph.D., U. of Calif., 1939; m. Adrienne Rushton Clark, Aug. 9, 1942; children—Joseph Wade, Burton Mack, Jill. Instr. chemistry U. of Calif., 1939-43; chemistry and metallurgy div. leader Los Alamos Lab., 1943-45; prof. chemistry, chmn. dept. Washington U., St. Louis, 46—; Priestley Lectr. Pa. State Coll., 1952; co-discoverer element 94 (plutonium), 1940. Awarded Medal for Merit, 1946, Jr. C. of C. award, 1948. Mem. Am. Chem. Soc., Am. Phys. Soc., Sigma Xi. Co-author: Nuclear Radiochemistry, 1949. Contbr. articles profl. jours. Office: Chemistry Dept., Washington Univ., St. Louis 5. Died May 5, 1957.

KENNEDY, JULIAN, mechanical engr., inventor; b. Poland, O., Mar. 15, 1852; s. Thomas Walker and Margaret (Trusdale) K.; ed. Poland Union Sem.; Ph.B., Sheffield Scientific Sch. (Yale), 1875, A.M., 1900; D.Eng., Stevens Inst. of Tech., 1909; m. Jennie Eliza, d. Joseph Brenneman; children—Lucy Bell (Mrs. J. O. Miller), Joseph Walker, Julian, Hugh Truesdale (dec.), Eliza Jane (Mrs. R. T. Smith), Thomas Walker (dec.). Before going to Yale he had been draftsman, under his father, in the construction of the Struthers Iron Co., where he was employed three years; was supt. blast furnaces, 1876-85, at Briar Hill Iron Co.'s works, Struthers Iron Co.'s works, Morse Bridge Works, Edgar Thomson Steel Works and at the Lucy furnaces; gen. supt. for Carnegie, Phipps & Co., at Homestead, 1885-88; chief engr. Latrobe Steel Works, 1888; gen. consulting and contracting engr., 1890—; has been connected with nearly every important steel plant in U.S. and Europe. Home: Pittsburgh, Pa. Died May 28, 1932.

KENNEDY, MILES COVERDALE, consulting engr.; b. Beaver Falls, Pa., Feb. 12, 1893; s. George and Fannie Creighton (Coverdale) K.; A.B., Geneva (Pa.) Coll., 1912; A.B., Yale, 1915; m. Mrs. Michele Esquiva Walker, December 22, 1951. Engaged in r.r. location and constrn., Southwest, 1916-22; engring. dept. Pa. R.R. Co., Pitts., 1922-27; staff mem. Coverdale & Colpitts, cons. engrs., New York, N.Y., 1927-32; chief examiner r.r. div., R.F.C., Washington, D.C., 1932-33; exec. sec. eastern regional coordinating com., New York (under Emergency Railroad Transportation Act, 1933), 1933-35; eastern regional dir. Fed. Co-ordinator of Transportation, N.Y., 1935-36; mem. staff Coverdale & Colpitts, 1936-42, partner, 1943—. Republican. Episcopalian. Clubs: Down Town Assn., Yale (N.Y.C.). Author: Centennial History Pa. Railroad Co. (with Geo. H. Burgess). Home: 333 E 57th St., N.Y.C. 22. Office: 120 Wall St., N.Y.C. 10005. Died Mar. 6, 1965.

KENNEDY, ROGER L(OUIS) J(OSEPH), physician; b. St. Paul, Feb. 8, 1897; s. Thomas James and Regina (Moisan) K.; B.S., U. Minn., 1918, M.B., 1920, M.D., 1922, M.S., Mayo Foundn. Grad. Sch., 1929; m. Ellen McGinn, July 30, 1925; children—Margaret Regina, Roger Thomas, James Arthur, Michael. Interne, City and County Hosp., St. Paul, 1921-22; practiced gen. medicine, Belle Plaine, 1920-21, Pediatrics, St. Paul, 1922-23; fellow in pediatrics Mayo Found., 1923; first asst., 1924-26, cons. physician Mayo Clinic, 1926, asso. prof. pediatrics Mayo Found., 1933-47, prof. pediatrics since 1947. Certified as specialist in pediatrics Am. Bd. Pediatrics, 1934. Mem. Am., Minn., (pres. 1952), So. Minn. med. assns., Soc. Pediatric Research, Olmsted-Houston-Fillmore-Dodge County Med. Soc., Am. Acad. Pediatrics (pres. 1954), Northwestern, Am. pediatric socs. Alpha Omega Alpha, Sigma Xi, Roman Catholic. Home: 815 9th St. S.W. Office: 200 1st St. S.W., Rochester, Minn. Died Jan. 1966.

KENNEDY, SAMUEL MACAW, utility engr.; b. Toronto, Can., June 20, 1863; s. Warring and Jane (Macaw) K.; ed. Model Sch. Collegiate Inst., Upper Can. Coll., Toronto, and under pvt. tutors; m. Mattie, d. of late J. C. Wallace, of Alhambra, Calif., Oct. 1, 1902. Entered business of father, Samson, Kennedy & Co., wholesale importers, Toronto, 1882; resigned, 1894, on account of ill health, and settled in Calif.; apptd. asst. to pres. United Electric Power & Gas Co., Los Angeles, 1900, and has been closely identified with development of light and power utilities in Calif.; served as v.p. Southern Calif. Edison Co., Santa Barbara & Suburban Ry., Pacific Gasoline Co., and as dir. Alhambra Savings and Commercial Bank; owing to accident retired from active business, 1927. Republican. Episcopalian. Mason. Author: Winning the Public, 2 edits. Home: Alhambra, Calif. Died July 1929.

KENNELLY, ARTHUR EDWIN, electrical engr.; b. Bombay, East India, Dec. 17, 1861; s. Capt. David Joseph and Cathrine (Heycock) K.; ed. pvt. schs., France and England, Univ. Coll. Sch., London; hon. Sc.D., U. of Pittsburgh, 1895; hon. A.M., Harvard, 1906; hon. Sc.D., U. of Toulouse, France, 1922; hon. Dr.Engring., University of Darmstadt, 1936; m. Julia Grice, July 22, 1903; 1 son, Reginald Grice. Telegraph operator in Eng., 1876; asst. electrician in Malta, 1878; chief electrician of a cable repairing steamer, 1881; senior ship's electrician Eastern Tel. Cable Co., 1886; prin. elec. asst. to Thomas A. Edison, 1887-94; asso. with Edwin J. Houston in firm Houston & Kennelly, consulting elec. engrs., Phila., 1894-1901; prof. elec. engring., Harvard, 1902-30, now prof. emeritus same and Mass. Inst. Tech. prof. elec. engring., 1913-24, dir. elec. engring. research, and chmn. faculty, 1917-18, Mass. Inst. Tech. Exchange prof. to French univs. in applied science, 1921-22; research asso. Carnegie Instn., 1924-30. Engr. in charge laying Vera Cruz-Frontera-Campeche cables for Mexican Govt., 1902. Mem. Nat. Research Council. Pres. Am. Inst. E.E., 1898-1900, Soc. Promotion Metric System of Weights and Measures, 1904. Illuminating Engring. Soc., 1911, Inst. of Radio Engrs., 1916; a vice pres. Am. Acad. Arts and Sciences; chmn. Rumford Com. 1924; hon. pres. U.S. Nat. Com. of Internat. Elec. Commn. (chmn. adv. com. on elec. and magnetic magnitudes and units, 1930—). Elected juror at expns. of Phila., 1898, Buffalo, 1901, St. Louis, 1904. Author: The Application of Hyperbolic Functions to Electrical Engineering Problems, 1911; Artificial Electric Lines, 1917; Electrical Vibration Instruments, 1923; Vestiges of Premetric Weights and Measures Persisting in Metric-System Europe, 1926-27; Electric Lines and Nets, 1928. Recipient of the Institution and Fahie premiums from the British Institute E.E., Howard Potts gold medal and Edward Longstreth silver medal Franklin Institute for electrical research; gold medal, Inst. Radio Engrs., 1932; Edison gold medal, Am. Inst. Elec. Engrs., 1933. Civilian liaison officer, U.S.A. Signal Corps, 1918, A.E.F. Third Order Mejidieh, Egypt, 1885; Chevalier Légion d'Honneur, France, 1922; Mascart medal, 1936. Hon. mem. Tau Beta Pi. First visiting elec. engring. lecturer, Iwadare Foundation, Japanese univs., 1931. Home: Cambridge, Mass. Died June 18, 1939.

KENNICOTT, CASS (LANGDON), chemist; b. Chicago, Feb. 25, 1871; s. Ransom (U.S.A.) and Helen M. (Smith) K.; ed. Chicago pub. schs. and Case Sch. of Applied Science, Cleveland; m. Mary E. Barstow, June 6, 1894; children—Ruth Barstow (Mrs. C. R. McEldowney), Marjorie Barstow (Mrs. Robert Mount). Chief chemist Municipal Lab., Chicago, 1893-98; inventor Kennicott water softening machine and numerous other patented devices, and v.p. Kennicott Co., 1899-1916; former pres. Mariner and Hoskins, Inc., cons. chem. engrs., Chicago; later operated under name The Kennicott Co.; now retired. Fellow London (Eng.) Chemical Soc., mem. Chicago Acad. of Sciences. Club: Engineers' (Chicago). Author: Dust Explosions, 1894; Chicago's Milk Supply, 1895; Ice, 1896; Water Analysis, 1891; Food Adulteration, 1898. Home: "Donswood," R.F.D. 2, Chesterton IN

KENNON, WILLIAM LEE, physicist; b. Columbus, Miss., May 3, 1882; s. Woodson Hughes and Sarah (Voight) K.; B.S., Millsaps Coll., Jackson, Miss., 1900, M.S., 1901; Ph.D., Johns Hopkins University, 1906; married Emma Gerdine Sykes, Sept. 12, 1912; 1 son, Summerfield Sykes. Professor of chemistry and physics, Ky. Wesleyan Coll., 1901-03; univ. scholar, 1904-05; fellow in chemistry, 1905-06, Johns Hopkins; instr. chemistry, Williams, 1906-09; asst. prof. chemistry, 1909, acting prof. physics and astronomy U. Miss., 1911, prof., 1912—, chmn. dept., 1912-52. Alderman, Oxford, Miss., 1935-39. Kennon Obs., U. of Miss., named in his honor. Fellow American Assn. Advancement Science; mem. American Assn. Univ. Profs., Am. Physical Soc. (vice chmn. Southeastern Sect. 1935-36, chmn. 1942-43), Phi Beta Kappa, Omicron Delta Kappa, Kappa Alpha (Southern). Democrat. Mem. Meth. Ch. Author: Astronomy-a Textbook for Colleges, 1948. Home: 716 S. 8th St., Oxford, Miss. Box 116, University, Miss. Died Dec. 4, 1952; buried Greenwood Cemetery, West Point, Miss.

KENT, A(RTHUR) ATWATER, mfr., inventor; b. Burlington, Vt., Dec. 3, 1873; s. Prentiss J. (M.D.) and Mary Elizabeth (Atwater) K.; ed. Worcester Poly. Inst.; hon. E.E., U. of Vt., 1924; Dr. Engring., Worcester Poly. Inst., 1926; D.Sc., Tufts Coll., 1927; m. Mabel Lucas, 1906; children—Arthur Atwater, Elizabeth Brinton (Mrs. William Laurens Van Alen), Virginia Tucker (Mrs. Kent Catherwood) and Jonathan Prentiss (adopted.). Established, 1902, the Atwater Kent Mfg. Works, Philadelphia, for manufacture of telephones and small volt meters; added mfr. of the unisparker (for which John Scott Medal was awarded in 1914), panoramic sights, clinometers, fuse setters and angle of sights for the army during World War; business incorporated, 1919, as the Atwater Kent Mfg. Co., of which is pres.; started mfg. radio receiving sets, 1922. Mem. com. on general problems of radio broadcasting, 3d and 4th Nat. Radio Confs., 1924, 25; sponsored multi-station broadcasting of world's greatest musical artists, beginning Oct. 1925; sponsored Nat. Radio Audition to discover talented singer. Restored the Betsy Ross House, Phila., 1937, as it existed in Colonial Days, in recognition of which the S.A.R. presented him with a medal; acquired, restored and presented the historic Franklin Institute Building to the City of Phila. as a museum dedicated to the history of Phila., 1938, the City, in appreciation, naming it Atwater Kent Museum. Clubs: Bar Harbor (Me.); Corinthian Yacht, New York Yacht; Everglades (Fla.). Home: 801 Bel-Air Road, Los Angeles 24. Died Mar. 4. 1949; buried in Forest Lawn Memorial Park, Glendale, Calif.

KENT, DONALD PETERSON, educator, gerontologist; b. Phila., June 4, 1916; s. Ralph and Ida (Peterson) K.; B.S., Pa. State Coll., 1940; M.A., Temple U., 1945; Ph.D., U. Pa., 1950; m. Marion H. Clime, Aug. 30, 1941; children—Marion H., Martha H. Instr. sociology U. Pa., 1945-50; asso. prof. sociology U. Conn., 1950-57; dir. Inst. Gerontology, 1957-61; spl. asst. to sec. health, edn. and welfare, Washington, 1961-63; dir. U.S. Office Aging, Washington, 1963-65; prof., head dept. sociology and anthropology Pa. State U., University Park, 1965-72. Chmn., Conn. Commn. on Services for Elderly Persons, 1957-61; vice chmn. Pres.'s Council on Aging, 1961-63. Recipient Distinguished Service award Inst. for Ret. Profls. Fellow Gerontological Soc. (pres. psychol. and social sect. 1966-67), Am. Sociol. Soc. Author: The Refugee Intellectual, 1953. Editor-in-chief: Gerontologist, 1967-70. Contbr. articles profl. jours. Home: State College PA Died Mar. 20, 1972.

KENT, EDWARD MATHER, physician; b. Syracuse, N.Y., May 2, 1907; s. Edward Enos and Eunice (Mather) K.; B.S., Pa. State Coll., 1929; M.D., Syracuse U., 1932; M.Sc. in Surgery, U. Pa., 1940; m. Dorothy Jean Dearborn, June 17, 1935; children—Jean (Mrs. Jean McNutt), Brian Mather, Beth Anne. Intern, St. Mary's Hosp., Rochester, N.Y., 1932-33; postgrad. in gen. surgery Grad. Sch. U. Pa., 1934-37; resident in surgery Abington (Pa.) Meml. Hosp., 1935-37; resident in thoracic surgery Norwich (Conn.) State Tb Sanatorium, 1937-39; fellow in thoracic surgery Washington U., Barnes Hosp., St. Louis, 1939-40; resident Tb Sanatorium, Glendale, Md., 1941-42; attending surgeon Allegheny Gen. Hosp., Pitts., chmn. surg. div. med. staff, 1965-69, pres. staff, 1968; area cons. thoracic surgery VA, Pitts.; cons. staff Columbia, St. Francis, St. Margaret's, South Side hosps., also others; asst. prof. surgery U. Pitts. Sch. Med., 1946-51, asso. prof., 1951-54, clin. prof. surgery, 1954-70; mem. exec. com., 1959. Kellogg Meml lectr. in surgery George Washington U., 1952; Trudeau Meml. lectr. Trudeau Sanatorium, Saranac Lake, N.Y., 1954; mem. med. adv. bd. Heart House. Bd. dirs. Allegheny County unit Am. Cancer Soc., 1956-59. Served to comdr., M.C., USNR, 1942-46. Diplomate Am. Bd. Surgery, Am. Bd. Thoracic Surgery (founder mem., dir. 1955-60). Fellow A.C.S. (past gov.); mem. A.M.A., Pa., Allegheny County med. socs., Am. (council 1963-67, 69-70, pres. 1968-69), Pa. assns. thoracic surgery, Am. Coll. Chest Physicians (v.p. Pa. chpt. 1956), Am., Central surg. assns., Soc. Internationale de Chirurgie (titulaire), Am. Coll. Cardiology, Soc. Thoracic Surgeons, Pitts. Acad. Medicine, Pitts. Surg. Soc. (pres. 1963), Western Pa. Heart Assn. (dir.). Republican. Roman Catholic.

Contbr. articles to med. jours., chpts. to books. Home: Wexford PA Died June 6, 1970; buried Syracuse NY

KENT, NORTON ADAMS, physicist; b. New York, July 28, 1873; s. Elmore Albert and Mary Abbie (Holman) K.; A.B., Yale, 1891-95; grad. work, same univ., 1897-98, Johns Hopkins, 1898-1901, Ph.D., 1901; m. Margaret Crowninshield, Mar. 27, 1906; 1 dau., Margaret Crowninshield. Asst., Yerkes Obs., Williams Bay, Wis., 1901-03; prof. physics, Wabash Coll., Ind., 1903-06; asst. prof. physics, Boston U., 1906-10, prof., 1910-42, emeritus since June 30, 1942; visiting prof. physics Mass. Inst. of Tech. since 1942. Fellow Am. Acad. Arts and Sciences; mem. Phi Beta Kappa, Sigma Xi. Republican. Conglist. Writer of research articles on various subjects in spectroscopy. Home: 1 Waterhouse St., Cambridge, Mass. Died June 5, 1944.

KENT, R(OBERT) H(ARRINGTON), ballistician; born Meriden, Connecticut, July 1, 1886; s. Silas William and Mary Elizabeth (Chapman) K.; A.B., Harvard 1910, A.M., 1916, Sc.D. (hon.), 1953. Asst. instr. physics, part-time instr. maths. Harvard, 1910-16; instructor electrical engineering University Pa., 1916-17; civilian engaged in experimental and theoretical work in ballistics Office Chief Ordnance, Washington and Aberdeen (Md.) Proving Ground, 1919-36; asso. dir., ballistic research labs. Aberdeen Proving Ground, Ordnance Dept., U.S. Army, 1936-48, asso. tech. dir. 1948-56, consultant 1956—. Served from first lieutenant to captain Ordnance Department, U.S. Army, 1917-19, Offices Chief Ordnance and of Chief Ord. Officer, A.E.F., France. Decorated Medal for Merit; awarded Potts medal, Franklin Inst., 1947, Air Force Exceptional Civilian Service Medal, American Ordnance Association, Campbell Medal, Army Exceptional Civilian Service Medal. Fellow A.A.A.S., Am. Phys. Soc.; member Nat. Acad. Scis., Phi Beta Kappa. Home: 307 S. Union Av., Havre de Grace. Office: Ballistic Research Laboratories, Aberdeen Proving Ground, Md. Died Feb. 3, 1961.

KENT, ROBERT THURSTON, mech. engr.; b. Jersey City, N.J., July 17, 1880; s. William and Marion Weild (Smith) K.; M.E., Stevens Inst. Tech., 1902; m. Alice Palmatier Howard, July 6, 1905; 1 dau., Marion Weild (Mrs. Charles F. Amelung). Machinist apprentice, 1896-98; erecting engr., Robins Conveying Belt Co., N.Y. City, 1902-03; designer, Link-Belt Co., Phila., 1903-04; associate editor, Electrical Review, N.Y. City, 1904-05; engring. editor Iron Trade Review, Cleveland, O., 1905-09; editor, Industrial Engring., N.Y. City, 1909-15; cons. engr., New York, 1912-17; chief engr. Myer, Morrison & Co., N.Y. City, 1917-21; cons. engr., 1921-24; supt. prison industries, N.Y. State, 1924-27 (reorganized and modernized industries and instituted wage system); gen. mgr. Bridgeport (Conn.) Brass Co., 1927-28; vice pres. and dir. engring., Divine Brothers Co., Utica, N.Y., 1928-34; cons. engr., Montclair, N.J., 1934-38; gen. mgr. Wm. Sellers & Co., Phila., 1938-40; production mgr., Control Instrument Co., Brooklyn, N.Y., 1942; cons. engr. with Stevenson, Jordan & Harrison, N.Y. City, since 1942. Served as prin. prodn. engr., U.S. Army Ordnance Dept., 1940-41. Fellow Am. Soc. M.E., Masaryk Acad. of Work (Prague, Czechoslovakia), Delta Tau Delta. Club: Engineers (New York). Author: Power Transmission by Leather Belting, 1915; Calorific Power of Fuels (with Herman Poole), 1918; Kent's Mechanical Engineer's Handbook, 10th edit., 1923, 11th edit., 1938. Home: 3 Argyle Rd., Montclair, N.J. Office: 19 W. 44th St., New York 18, N.Y. Died May 23, 1947.

KENT, WALTER HENRY, chemist; b. Levant, N.Y., March 29, 1851; s. Ara W. and Lucy A. (Neate) K.; grad. Cornell, B.S., 1876 (M.S., 1880; Ph.D., Göttingen, Germany, 1884). Instr. chemistry Cornell, 1877-81; prof. chemistry Drake Univ., Des Moines, Ia., 1881-82; student at Göttingen, 1883-84; chemist Brooklyn Health Dept., through a civil service exam., 1885-94; chemist New York Navy Yard, 1895-99; asst. prof. Brooklyn Coll. of Pharmacy, 1900-02; m. Ann Elizabeth Hall, June 30, 1904. Home: Brooklyn, N.Y. Died 1907.

KENT, WILLIAM, engineer; b. Philadelphia, Mar. 5, 1851; s. James and Janet (Scott) K.; A.B., Central High Sch., Phila., 1868, A.M., 1873; M.E., Stevens Inst. Tech., 1876; (Sc.D., Syracuse U., 1905); m. Marion Weild Smith, Feb. 25, 1879. Editor of Am. Manufacturer and Iron World, Pittsburgh, 1877-79; held positions as mech. engr. and supt. in iron and steel works, steam boiler business and Torsion balance scale factory, 1879-90; consulting engr. (office practice), 1890—; asso. editor Engineering News, 1895-1903; dean L. C. Smith Coll. Applied Science, Syracuse U., 1903-08; editor Industrial Engineering, 1910-14. Lecturer steam engring., Newark Tech. Sch., 1888-95; has also lectured at Purdue, Brooklyn Inst., Franklin Inst. (Phila.), Worcester Poly. Inst., W.Va. U., U. of Ill., Cornell, Stevens Inst., etc. Mem. N.J. State Commn. on Pollution of Streams, 1898-99. Has taken out over 20 patents on weighing machinery, water-tube boilers, smokeless furnaces, etc. Author: The Strength of Materials, 1879; The Mechanical Engineer's Pocket Book, 1895, 9th edition, 1915; Investigating an Industry, 1915; Bookkeeping and Cost Accounting for Factories, 1918. Home: Montclair, N.J. Died Sept. 18, 1918.

KENYON, ALFRED MONROE, mathematician; b. Medina, O., Dec. 10, 1869; s. Charles Champlin and Lucy Elizabeth (Gouldin) K.; A.B., Hiram (O.) Coll., 1894; grad. student Western Reserve U., and Case Sch. Applied Science, Cleveland, O., 1896-97; A.M., Harvard, 1898; m. Grace Greenwood Finch, Sept. 1, 1897. Instr. mathematics, 1898, asso. prof., 1900, prof., 1905—, head of dept., 1908—, Purdue U., also registrar, 1900-08. Fellow Ind. Acad. Science. Progressive Rep. Presbyn. Author: (with Louis Ingold) Plane and Spherical Trigonometry, 1913; (with William V. Lovitt) Mathematics for Students of Agriculture and General Science, 1917; (with Louis Ingold) Elements of Plane Trigonometry, 1919. Home: Lafayette, Ind. Died July 27, 1921.

KEREKES, FRANK, coll. dean; b. Budapest, Hungary, Jan. 13, 1896; s. Louis and Emilia (Grabinsky) K.; came to U.S., 1903, naturalized, 1914; B.S., Coll. City N.Y., 1917; C.E., Columbia, 1920; m. Jessie McCorkindale, Sept. 9, 1922; 1 dau., Frances Emilia (Mrs. Harny H. Meyer, Jr.). Bridge engr. Robinson & Steinman, 1925; engr. N.Y.C. R.R., 1917, 26, 27; asst. prof. Ia. State Coll., 1920-25, asso. prof., 1925-30, prof., 1930-47, asst. dean engring., 1947-54; research Ia. Engring. Expt. Sta., summers 1921-24, bull. editor, 1928; dean faculty Mich. Technol. U., 1954—; cons. structural engr., 1920—; cons. USAF Spl. Weapons Center, 1962. Chmn. Ames City Plan Commn., 1937-54, Ia. Bldg. Code Council, 1947-49. Recipient John Dunlap award, Ia. Engring Soc., 1944, (Anson Marston award, 1954; Townsend-Harris medal, City Coll. N.Y., 1955; designated Second Century Leader, Des Moines Register and Tribune, 1948; certificate of appreciation Sec. Army 1959, Sec. Air Force, 1960. Registered profl. engr. Mem. Am. Soc. C.E. (hon., chmn. engring. edn. com., past pres. Ia. sect.), Ia. Engring. Soc. (pres. 1947; hon. mem.), Am. Soc. Engring. Edn. (past chmn. civil engring. div., mem. nat. council 1954), Am. Ry. Engring. Assn., Am. Concrete Inst. (pres. 1956, dir.; chmn. com. bldg. code requirements for reinforced concrete, mem. govs. sci. adv. bd., 1958-59), Acad. Polit. Sci., Knights St. Patrick, Sigma Xi, Tau Beta Pi, Chi Epsilon, Phi Kappa Phi, Phi Eta Sigma, Cardinal Key. Episcopalian. Clubs: Rotary (Houghton); Miscowaubic (Calumet, Mich.); Union League (Chgo.). Author: Engineering Drawing Theory with Applications, 1928; (with Dr. A. H. Fuller) Analysis and Design of Steel Structures, 1936; (with Robley Winfrey) Report Preparation, 1951; also tech. and research bulls. Contbr. engring. jours. Home: 208 Hubbell St., Houghton, Mich. Died Oct. 25, 1965; buried Ames, Ia.

KERLIN, ISAAC NEWTON, physician; b. Burlington, N.J., May 27, 1834; s. Joseph and Sarah (Ware) K.; M.D., U. Pa., 1856; m. Harriet C. Dix, 1865, 4 children. Pioneer in care and treatment of mentally deficient children and adults; asst. supt. Pa. Tng. Sch. for Feeble-minded Children at Elwyn, nr. Media, Pa., 1856-62, supt., 1864-93; served with U.S. San. Cmmn. in Army of Potomac, 1863; a founder Nat. Assn. Supts. of Instn. for Feeble-minded 1876, sec., 1876-93; framed draft of bill to provide instns. in Western part of Pa.; did important pioneer work in field of psycho-pathology. Author: The Manual of Elwyn, 1891. Died Oct. 25, 1893; buried Elwyn.

KERN, MAXIMILIAN, endocrinologist; b. Stanislau, Austria, Jan. 16, 1890; s. Disrael and Rosalie (Shleifer) K.; ed. Royal Imperial Gymnasium, Stanislau; M.D., Long Island Coll. Hosp., Brooklyn, N.Y., 1911; M.D., Chicago Coll. Medicine and Surgery (now Med. Sch. Loyola U.), 1915; m. Elaine Frances Hoexter, Mar. 10, 1923 (dec.); 1 dau., Janet R. Came to U.S. 1907, naturalized citizen 1912. Practiced, Chicago, 1916—, specializing in internal medicine; prof. of endocrinology, Gen. Med. Foundation Med. Coll., Chicago, since 1922; formerly attending internist John B. Murphy Hosp., now attending internist and sec. of staff Edgewater Hosp., Chicago, and Oak Park (Illinois) hospitals. Served as first lt. M.C., U.S. Army, 1917; med. consultant U.S. Marine Hosp. Hon. pres. Med. Round Table, Chgo. Fellow American Geriatric Society Am. Coll. Cardiology; mem. A.M.A., Ill., Chgo. med. socs., U.S.P.H. Assn., Soc. for Study of Goitre, Endocrine Society Am. Heart Assn., Am. Med. Writers Assn., Zeta Mu Phi, Phi Gamma Mu (nat. social science honor soc.). Author: (monographs) Psychology and Daily Life; Blindness of Pituitary Origin; Rôle of Endocrinology in Epilepsy, 1923; Endocrines in Ophthalmology and Otolaryngology, Crime and the Endocrines, 1924; Les Glandes Endocrines avant la Puberté (Paris), 1925; Studies of Endocrine Types, 1926; The Salle Turcica in Relation to Endocrinology, 1927; Endocrines and Physiotherapy, 1927; Relation of the Sella Turcica to Endocrine Disturbances, 1927; Dermagraphia in Relation to Dysthyrodism, 1927; The Status of Physical Therapy in the Treatment of Obesity, 1928; The Thyroid Gland and Menstrual Disorders, 1928; Obesity and the Endocrines, 1928; Further Studies in the Problems of Obesity, 1930; Pituitary Tumors, 1931; Hemolytic Streptococcus Bacteremia with Endocarditis and Arthritis Following Scarlet Fever, 1931; Clinical Application of Testosterone Propionate, 1940. A Quantitative Study of Saliva Glucose (co-author) 1945. The Role of Carbohydrates in Management of Obesity, 1946. Home: 925 Bluff, Glencoe, Ill. Office: 55 E. Washington St., Chgo. 60602. Died July 31, 1964.

KERR, ABRAM TUCKER, anatomist; b. Buffalo, N.Y., Jan. 7, 1873; s. Abram and Rebecca (Marshall) K.; B.S., Cornell, 1895; M.D., U. of Buffalo, 1897; grad. student Göttingen, 1899, Johns Hopkins Med. Sch., 1899-1900, U. of Freiburg, 1909; m. Agnes Rogers Sherman, July 10, 1895; children—Bruce Duncan, Cynthia Jean. Student asst. in histology and pathology, 1894-97, acting and adj. prof. anatomy, 1898-1900, U. of Buffalo; asst. prof. anatomy, 1900-04, prof. anatomy and sec., 1904—, acting prof. hygiene, 1920-22, acting prof. and dir. hygiene, 1935-37, Cornell U. Med. Coll., Ithaca. Ind. Democrat. Mason. Episcopalian. Home: Ithaca, N.Y. Died Aug. 15, 1938.

KERR, CHARLES VOLNEY, mech. engr.; b. Miami County, O., Mar. 27, 1861; s. George W. and Nancy K.; Ph.B., honors in philosophy, Western U. of Pa. (now U. of Pittsburgh), 1884, Ph.M., 1888, hon. Ph.D., 1898; M.E., Stevens Inst. Tech., 1888; m. Libbie Applebee, Dec. 25, 1888; children—Clifton A. (dec.), Vida A. (dec.), Delia A., Volney A., Marion A. (dec.). Instr. mathematics and science, Pratt Inst., 1888-89; asst. prof. mech. engring., Western U. of Pa., 1889-91; prof. engring., Ark. Industrial U., Fayetteville, 1891-96; prof. mech. engring., Armour Inst. Tech., 1896-1902; engr. Westinghouse, Church, Kerr & Co., New York, 1902-04; chief engr. Kerr Turbine Co., Wellsville, N.Y., 1904-10, McEwen Bros., Wellsville, 1910-14; pres. and engr. Kerr Auxiliary Co., Chicago, 1914-16; steam turbine engr. Am. Well Works, Aurora, Ill., 1916-21, Llewellyn Iron Works, 1921-23; pres. Nat. Pump and Motor Co., 1923-24; cons. mech. engr. and inventor of Kerr pumps and blowers and Kerr steam turbine. Mem. Am. Soc. M.E. Contbr. to proceedings of socs. and mags. Home: 418 Ulysses St., Los Angeles, Calif. Died Oct. 31, 1949.

KERR, EUGENE WYCLIFF, mech. engr.; b. McKinney, Tex., Feb. 16, 1874; s. J.L. and O.J.K.; M.E., Agrl. and Mech. Coll. of Tex., 1899; spl. courses in mech. engring. in Stevens Inst. of Tech., U. of Wis., and Purdue U.; m. Rita Sbisa, Sept. 5, 1900; children—Eugene James, Janet Katherine, William Ray. Asst. prof. mech. engring., Agrl. and Mech. Coll. of Tex., 1896-1903; instr. machine design, Purdue U., 1903-05; prof. mech. engring., La. State U., 1905-16; in charge of investigations in sugar engring., La. State Expt. Stations, 1908-16; engr. Cuba Cane Sugar Corp., 1916-31; cons. mech. engr. since 1931. Mem. Am. Soc. Mech. Engrs. Presbyterian. Mason. Author: Power and Power Transmission, 1902; also various papers and pamphlets on subjects pertaining to sugar engring. Home: 808 Lake Park, Baton Rouge LA

KERR, HENRY HAMPTON, elec. engr.; b. St. Peter, Minn., Apr. 12, 1864; s. Aaron Hervey and Elizabeth (Craig) K.; ed. high sch.; m. Jessie C. Smith, June 17, 1894; children—Henry H., Malcolm C. With Westinghouse, Church, Kerr & Co., 1886-1920, advanced to v.p.; company taken over, 1920, by the Dwight P. Robinson Co., Inc., of which was v.p.; company absorbed with others, 1928, now United Engineers & Constructors, of which is v.p. Republican. Episcopalian. Home: Evanston, Ill. Died July 1932.

KERR, MARK BRICKELL, mining engr.; b. St. Michaels, Md., June 28, 1860; s. John Bozman and Lucy Hamilton (Stevens) K.; ed. pub. schs. of Washington, and spl. edn. as civil engr. under pvt. instruction; m. Kate Shepard, June 5, 1889. Made ascent of Mt. Shasta, 1886; geographer of expdn. sent out in 1890 by U.S. Geol. Survey and Nat. Geog. Soc. Home: Berkeley, Calif. Died Mar. 15, 1917.

KERR, WALTER CRAIG, mechanical engr.; b. St. Peter, Minn., Nov. 8, 1858; s. Aaron H. and Elizabeth (Craig) K.; common sch. edn. there; B.M.E., Cornell, 1879; m. Lucy Lyon, Dec. 27, 1883. Asst. prof. Cornell, 1880-83; since then mech. engr. in the Westinghouse interests; pres. Westinghouse, Church, Kerr & Co., 1902—. Trustee Cornell, 1890—. Home: Dongan Hills, S.I., N.Y. Died 1910.

KERR, WASHINGTON CARUTHERS, geologist, educator; b. Guilford County, N.C., May 24, 1827; s. William M. and Euphence (Doak) K.; grad. U. N.C., 1850, Ph.D., 1879, LL.D., 1885; attended Lawrence Sci. Sch., Harvard; m. Emma Hall, 1853. Prof., Marshall U., Tex., 1851-52; with Nautical Almanac office, Cambridge, Mass., 1852; prof. chemistry and geology Davidson College, N.C., 1856-65; chemist, supt. Mecklenburg Salt Co., nr. Charleston, S.C., 1862; state geologist N.C., 1864-82; lectr. geology U. N.C., 1869-84; made map of N.C., published 1882; chief So. div. U.S. Geol. Survey, 1882-83; one of 1st to call prominently to attention phenomena soil creep. Author: Report of the Geological Survey of North Carolina, vol. 1, 1875, vol. 2, 1881; Minerals and Mineral Localities of North Carolina, 1881; Ores of North Carolina, 1888. Died Asheville, N.C., Aug. 9, 1885.

KESCHNER, MOSES (kesh'ner), neuropsychiatrist; b. Dobromil, Austria, Sept. 30, 1876; s. Leon and Lottie Taub K.; ed. Gymnasium, at Przemysl, Austria, Coll. City of N.Y.; M.D., Coll. Phys. and Surg. (Columbia), 1899; LL.B., New York Law Sch., 1909; m. Dorothea Jackson, Mar. 27, 1901; children—Myron, Sidney R., Harold W., Hortense. Practiced at N.Y. City, 1899—; visiting physician Dept. of Correction, New York,

1906-20; adj. neurologist Mt. Sinai Hosp., 1920-31; asso. neurologist Mt. Sinai Hospital, 1932-38; consulting neurologist Montefiore Hosp., Sydenham Hosp.; Beth Moses Hosp., Newark Beth Israel Hosp.; mem. med. advisory bd. National Jewish Hospital, Denver; former clinical professor neurology, Columbia University. Diplomate American Board Psychiatry and Neurology (1940). Fellow A.M.A., Am. Neurol. Assn., New York Acad. Medicine (chmn. of sect. neurology and psychiatry) Am. Acad. of Neurology; mem. Am. Assn. Advancement Sci., Med. Soc. State of N.Y., New York County Med. Soc., New York Neurol. Soc. (past president), American Psychiatric Association, Association for Research in Nervous and Mental Diseases, Eastern Medical Society (past president), Jewish Mental Health Society; New York Soc. for Clinical Psychiatry; mem. Grievance Com., Univ. of State of N.Y., 1926-1944; del. to Governor Lehman's Confs. on Crime. Cons. neuropsychiatrist, Induction Station, New York City, 1944-46. Democrat. Jewish religion. Contbr. of Dyskinesias, Tice's Practice of Medicine (Vol. X), Simulation and medicolegal aspects of injuries of skull, brain and spinal cord in Brock's Text Book, 1940. Home: 451 West End Av., N.Y.C. Died Aug. 31, 1956; buried Union Fields Cemetery.

KESTER, FREDERICK EDWARD, physicist; b. Eaton, O., Feb. 22, 1873; s. Henry and Wilhelmina (Kester) K.; M.E. in Elec. Engring., Ohio State U., 1895; A.M., Cornell, 1899, Ph.D., 1905; student U. Gottingen, 1903-04; m. Tamar Daker Whitmyre, June 8, 1907; children—Frederick Daker, Barbara (Mrs. Tom Page), William Henry, Elizabeth (Mrs. Robt. Holmer). Asst. in physics Ohio State U., 1895-98, instr., 1899-1901, asst. prof., 1901-07, asso. prof., 1907-09; prof. physics U. Kan., 1909—, chmn. dept. until 1941, emeritus, 1944. Fellow A.A.A.S. (emeritus life mem. 1948), Am. Phys. Soc.; mem. Am. Assn. U. Profs., Am. Assn. Physics Tchrs., Kan. Acad. Science, Sigma Alpha Epsilon, Sigma Xi, Kappa Eta Kappa. Club: University (Lawrence, Kan.). Contbr. sci. jours. on investigations in physics. Home: 1612 Louisiana St., Lawrence, Kan. Died Mar. 31, 1954.

KETCHUM, MILO SMITH, civil engr., educator; b. Burns, Ill., Jan. 26, 1872; s. Smith and Martha Ann (Clement) K.; grad. Elmwood (Ill.) High Sch., 1889; B.S., U. of Ill., 1895, C.E., 1900; Sc.D., Colo. Sch. Mines, 1926, U. of Colo., 1927; m. Mary Esther Beatty, Sept. 17, 1903; children—Martha Esther (Mrs. N. C. Debevoise), Elizabeth Jane, Milo Smith, Jr. Instructor in civil engineering, U. of Illinois, 1895-97; bridge and structural engr. Gillette-Herzog Mfg. Co., 1897-99; asst. prof. civ. engring., U. of Ill., 1899-1903; contracting mgr. Am. Bridge Co., Kansas City, 1903-04; prof. civ. engring., 1904-19, dean Coll. of Engring., 1905-19, U. of Colo., prof. civil engring. and dir. dept., U. of Pa., Sept. 1919-Sept. 1922; dean of Coll. of Engring. and dir. Engring. Expt. Sta., U. of Ill., Sept. 1922—. Asst. dir. U.S. Govt. explosives plants, in charge of constrn. of smokeless powder plant at Nitro, W.Va., Feb. 1918-19. Mem. Crocker and Ketchum, consulting engrs., Denver, Colo., 1909-10. Registered structural engr. state of Ill. Author: Surveying Manual (with Prof. W. D. Pence), 1900, 5th edit., 1931; Design of Steel Mill Buildings, and The Calculation of Stresses in Framed Structures, 1903, 4th edit., 1921; Design of Walls, Bins and Grain Elevators, 1907, 3d edit., 1918; Design of Highway Bridges of Steel, Timber and Concrete, 1908, 2d edit., 1920; Design of Mine Structures, 1912; Structural Engineers' Handbook, 1914, 3d edit., 1924. Presbyn. Home: Urbana, Ill. Died Dec. 19, 1934.

KETCHUM, RICHARD BIRD, coll. dean; b. Augusta, Ill., June 10, 1874; s. Andrew Jackson and Ann Elizabeth (Sickles) K.; B.S., U. Ill., 1896; C.E., 1900; m. Lulu Pierce, Sept. 10, 1901; 2 sons, Pierce Waddell, 1 son died in infancy. Machinist Ajax Forge Co., Chgo., 1896-97; instr. U. Ill., 1897-98; draftsman C.&W.I.& Belt R.R., summer 1898; steel detailer Pitts. Bridge Co., 1898-99; asst. engr. C.&W.I.Belt R.R., 1899, C.&A. R.R., 1899-1901; chief draftsman Ore. Short Line R.R., 1901-03; asst. engr. Mo.P. Ry., 1903; div. engr. Ore. Short Line R.R., 1903-06; chief engr. Independent Coal & Coke Co., Helper, Utah, 1906-08, Kan., Colo. R.R., 1908-09; asst. engr. Grays Harbor & Puget Sound Ry., 1909; instr. in civil engring. U. Utah, also cons. engr., 1909-18; supervising engr. U.S. Explosives Plant, Nitro, W.Va., 1918; chief engr. Salt Lake County Meml. Bridge, 1920; prof. civil engring. and head of civ. engring. dept. U. Utah, 1920-27, dean School of Mines and Engring., 1927-39, dean emeritus since 1939; asst. engr. D.&R.G. R.R., in charge constrn. shops and terminal improvements Salt Lake City, 1923-24; cons. engr. for Salt Lake City water works improvements, 1931. Trustee, mem. exec. com., chmn. tech. com., investigation and report to gov. legislature on low temperature carbonization of Utah coals, Utah Conservation and Reserach Found. 1938-39. Mem. Am. Soc. C.E. Mem. Soc. Am. Mil. Engrs., Theta Tau, Phi Kappa Phi, Tau Beta Pi. Democrat. Methodist. Contbr. tech. papers. Address: 803 W. Illinois St., Urbana, Ill. Died Nov. 3, 1952.

KETTERING, CHARLES FRANKLIN, engr., mgr., research cons.; b. nr. Loudonville, Ashland Co., O., Aug. 29, 1876; s. Jacob and Martha (Hunter) K.; E.E. in M.E., Ohio State U., 1904, E.D., 1929; honorary degrees from 29 other instns.; m. Olive Williams, August 1, 1905 (died, 1946); 1 son, Eugene Williams. Began with Star Telephone Co., Ashland, later with Nat. Cash Register Co., Dayton, O.; organized Dayton Engring. Labs. Co. (Delco) for mfg. own inventions; co-organizer The Dayton Metal Products Co. and Dayton-Wright Airplane Co., 1914; served for 27 yrs. as v.p. Gen. Motors Corp. and gen. mgr. research labs. div., now retired and serving as research cons. to co. and as dir.; dir. Nat. Cash Register Co., Ethyl Corp., Mead Corp., Moraine Development Co.; chmn. bd. Winters Nat. Bank and Trust Co., Flexible Co. Founded, 1927, and financed Charles F. Kettering Found., 1927, since served as chmn. of bd., giving active direction to researches in natural sciences, including work on chlorophyll and photosynthesis, artifical fever therapy, and cancer; pres. Thomas A. Edison Found.; dir. Sloan-Kettering Inst. for Cancer Research; co-founder Moraine Park Sch., Dayton; trustee Ohio State U., Antioch Coll., Coll. Wooster (O.), U. Miami (Fla.), So. Research Inst.; served as chmn. Nat. Inventors Council Nat. Patent Planning Com., and Engring. and Indsl. Research Div., Nat. Research Council and as mem. Sci. Adv. Bd., Nat. Research Council; chmn. exec. com., Centennial of Engring., 1952. Fellow Nat. Acad. Scis.; pres. Soc. Automotive Engrs., 1918, A.A.A.S., 1945, member several other scientific and engring. socs. Scientific work includes invention of automotive starting, lighting, and ignition systems, electrified cash register, credit systems, and accounting machines; invented and marketed small generating unit for lighting farmhouses, etc.; originated and guided researches resulting in higher octane gasolines, including tetraethyl lead, extraction of bromine from sea water, high compression automobile engines, improved automobile finishes, nontoxic and noninflammable refrigerant, improved Diesel engines (applications of which include powering of railroads; contributor to or responsible for other developments of industrial importance. Home: Ridgeleigh Terrace, Dayton, O. Died Nov. 25, 1958; buried Dayton.

KETTERING, EUGENE WILLIAMS, diesel engr.; b. Dayton, O., Apr. 20, 1908; s. Charles Franklin and Olive (Williams) K.; student Cornell U.; D. Sc., Fenn College; H.H.D., University of Dayton; m. Virginia Weiffenbach, Apr. 5, 1930; children—Charles Franklin II, Jane (Mrs. Richard D. Lombard), Susan (Mrs. Peter D. Williamson). With Winton Engine Co., Cleve., 1930-36, Detroit diesel div. Gen. Motors Corp., 1936-37, chief engr. Electro-Motive div., LaGrange, Ill., 1938-56, dir. research 1956-58, research asst. to gen. mgr., 1958-59, cons., 1959-60; chmn. bd. C. F. Kettering, Inc., Winters Nat. Bank; dir. Flexible Co. (Loudonville, O.), Chmn. bd. Air Force Mus. Found., Inc., Aviation Hall of Fame; founder Charles F. Kettering Meml. Hosp., Dayton, Hinsdale Med. Center, including Health Mus., Health Library; pres. Charles F. Kettering Found.; trustee Meml.-Sloan Kettering Cancer Center, Kettering Hosp., Loudonville, O.; v.p., dir. Thomas Alva Edison Found., Sloan-Kettering Inst.; bd. dirs. Monmouth Coll.; trustee Berea Coll., So. Research Inst. Ala. Recipient Elmer A. Sperry award. Mem. Aircraft Owners and Pilots Assn., A.A.A.S., Cornell Soc. Engrs., Def. Orientation Conf. Assn., Soc. Automotive Engrs., Chi Phi. Clubs: Oakbrook Polo, Moraine Country, Engineers, Buz Fuz, Dayton Bicycle (Dayton, O.); Hinsdale (Ill.) Golf: Cornell U. Home: Dayton OH Died Apr. 19, 1969; buried Dayton

KEW, WILLIAM S(TEPHEN W(EBSTER), petroleum geologist; b. San Diego, Cal., June 15, 1890; s. Michael and Mary White (Marston) K.; B.S., U. Cal., 1912, M.S., 1914, Ph.D., 1917; m. Emma F. Black, Dec. 22, 1917; children—Stephen M., Kenneth W. With U.S. Geol. Survey, 1915-24, Western Gulf Oil Co., 1924-25; with Standard Oil Co. Cal., 1925-51, chief geologist, 1944-51; geol. cons., 1951—; dir. East Puente Oil Co., 1952—. Fellow Geol. Soc. Am., A.A.A.S., Cal. Acad. Scis. (trustee); mem. Am. Assn. Petroleum Geologists, Am. Inst. Mining Engrs., Seismol. Soc. Geophys. Union, Soc., Econ. Geologists. Clubs: Bohemian (San Francisco); University (Los Angeles). Home: 1100 Union St., San Francisco 94109. Died June 4, 1961; buried Cypress Lane Cemetery, San Francisco.

KEYES, CHARLES ROLLIN, geologist; b. Des Moines, Ia., Dec. 24, 1864; s. Calvin W. and Julia (Davis) K.; B.S., State U. of Ia., 1887, A.M., 1890; Ph.D., Johns Hopkins, 1892; unmarried. Asst. U.S. Geol. Survey, 1889-90; palaeontologist of Mo., 1890-92; asst. state geologist of Ia., 1892-94; dir. Mo. Geol. Survey, 1894-97; geol. travel in Europe, Asia and Africa, 1897-98; pres. N.M. State Sch. of Mines, 1902-06; foreign travel, 1906-07, 1926; pres. and gen. mgr. mining cos. and other corps.; consulting mining engr. since 1890. Editor of Pan-American Geologists since 1922. Fellow Geol. Soc. America, A.A.A.S., Am. Inst. Mining Engrs., Mining and Metall. Soc. America, Ia. Acad. Sciences, St. Louis Acad. Sciences, etc. Dem. nominee for U.S. senator, 1918. Author: Geological Formations, 1892; Coal Deposits, 1893; Organization of Geological Surveys, 1894; Palaeontology of Missouri, 1894; Maryland Granites, 1895; Origin and Classification of Ore Deposits, 1900; Genesis of Lake Valley Silver Deposits, 1907; Ozark Lead and Zinc Deposits, 1909; Deflation, 1910; Mid-Continental Eolation, 1911; Bibliography of Geology, 1913; Mechanics of Laccolithic Intrusion, 1922; Orogenic Consequences of a Diminishing Rate of Earth's Rotation, 1922; Astronomical Theory of Glaciation, 1925; numerous memoirs and essays; also contributor to scientific, tech. and ednl. jours. Home: 944 5th Av., Des Moines, Ia.; (winter) Avalon, Oracle Rd., Tucson, Ariz. Died May 18, 1942.

KEYES, WINFIELD SCOTT, mining engr.; b. Brooklyn, N.Y., Nov. 17, 1839; s. Erasmus D. K. (maj. gen. U.S.A.); grad. Yale, 1860; studied 3 yrs. at School of Mines, Freiberg, Saxony; widower. Supt. of mines; joint inventor Keyes & Arent's automatic tap for molten metals; mem. bd. of judges, Centennial Expn., Phila., 1876; hon. commr. to Paris Expn., 1878; leading expert in many mining suits. Pres. trustees Calif. State Mining Bureau, 16 yrs.; mem. exec. com. Calif. Miners' Assn. Owns vineyards in Napa Co., Calif.; received gold medal for exhibit of wines, Paris Expn., 1900, grand prize, St. Louis Expn., 1904. V.p. Humboldt Bank, San Francisco; gen. mgr. Pan-Am. Development Co., operating mines in State of Sinaloa, Mex. Died 1906.

KEYSER, CASSIUS JACKSON, (ki'ser), mathematician; b. Rawson, O., May 15, 1862; s. Jacob B. and Margaret Jane (Ryan) K.; B.S., Ohio Normal U., 1883; studied law, Ann Arbor, Mich., and Kenton, O., 1883-85; B.S., U. of Mo., 1892; student summer sch., U. of Mich., 1894; A.M., Columbia, 1896; Ph.D., 1901; LL.D., U. of Mo., 1914; Sc.D., Columbia, 1929; L.H.D., Yeshiva Coll., 1942; m. Ella Maud Crow, Aug. 19, 1885; m. 2d, Sarah Porter Youngman, Apr. 26, 1929. Prin. and supt. pub. schs., Ohio and Mo., 1885-90; instr. mathematics, U. of Mo., 1891-92, State Summer Schools, Kirksville, Mo., 1892; apptd. Thayer scholar in mathematics, Harvard 1892; prof. mathematics, State Normal Sch., New Paltz, N.Y., 1892-94; instr. mathematics, Smith Acad., Washington U., St. Louis, 1894-95, Barnard Coll., 1897-1900, tutor, Columbia U., 1897-1900, instr., 1900-03, adj. prof., 1903-04, Adrain prof. mathematics, 1904-27, head of dept., 1910-16, Adrain prof. emeritus since 1927, instr., summer sessions, 1900-07; prof. mathematics, U. of Calif., 1911, 15, exchange prof., 1916. Fellow A.A.A.S.; mem. Am. Math. Soc. Author: Mathematical Philosophy, etc. Asso. editor of Scripta, Mathematica. Home: 50 Morningside Dr., New York, N.Y. Died May 8, 1947.

KEYT, ALONZO THRASHER, physician, physiologist; b. Higginsport, O., Jan. 10, 1827; s. Nathan and Mary (Thrasher) K.; M.D., Med. Coll. Ohio, 1848; m. Susannah Hamlin, 1848, 7 children. Inventor multigraph sphygmometer cardiograph; important contbr. to knowledge of circulation, perfected clin. methods of diagnosis of diseased conditions of circulation; papers published under title Sphygmography and Cardiography, Physiological and Clinical, 1887. Died Nov. 9, 1885.

KEZER, ALVIN, agronomist; b. Bower, Neb., Nov. 7, 1877; s. George E. and Clara E. (Bower) K.; B.S., U. of Neb., 1904, M.A., 1906; m. Harriet M. Mitchell, June 19, 1906; children—Munro, James. With U.S. Dept. Agr., 1904-06; in charge soils, U. of Neb., 1906-09; prof. agronomy, Colo. State Coll. of Agr. and Mechanic Arts, 1909-46; retired July 1, 1946; agrl. cons. in soils, crops and animal nutrition, since 1946. Chairman of seed committee Colorado Council of defense, 1917. Member Colorado State Planning Commn. President State Soil Conservation Board, Jan. 1945. Mem. Am. Chem. Soc., A.A.A.S., Am. Genetic Assn., Soc. Promotion Agr. Science, Am. Soc. Agronomy, Am. Farm Economics Assn., Alpha Zeta, Sigma Xi, Phi Kappa Phi. Mason. Unitarian. Author various bulls. and articles on agrl. subjects. Home: 515 Remington, Ft Collins CO

KIBLER, RAYMOND SPIER, physician; b. East Aurora, N.Y., Nov. 8, 1917; s. Michael and Rose (Spier) K.; M.D., U. Buffalo, 1941; M.Sc. in Medicine, U. Ill., 1948; m. Diana Duszynski, Mar. 8, 1943; 1 dau., Jacqueline Louise (Mrs. Byledbal). Intern, Buffalo Gen. Hosp., 1941-42, asst. resident in internal medicine, 1942-43, resident in internal medicine, 1943, jr. clin. med. asst. in hematology and clin. pathology, 1957-69; practice medicine, specializing in internal medicine, Buffalo; Med. fellow U. Buffalo, 1946-47, U. Ill., 1947-48; sr. cancer research intern dept. nuclear medicine Roswell Park Meml Inst.; instr. State U. N.Y. at Buffalo. Served from 1st lt. to capt. AUS, 1943-46. Diplomate Am. Bd. Internal Medicine. Mem. A.M.A., Am. Soc. Clin. Pathologists, Soc. Nuclear Medicine, Am. Soc. Hematology. Home: Buffalo NY Died June 4, 1969; buried Mt. Calvary Cemetery, Cheekborough NY

KIDDE, WALTER, (kid), mech. engr.; b. in N.J., Mar. 7, 1877; s. F. E. and Mary O. (Lang) K.; M.E., Stevens Institute of Technology, 1897; E.D., 1935; Sc.D., Rutgers University, 1941; m. Louise Carter, October 22, 1902; children—Walter Lawrence, John Frederick, Mary (Mrs. W. E. Morgan). Practiced engineering at New York City since 1900; now pres. Walter Kidde & Co., Walter Kidde Constructors; dir. Vreeland Corp., Hudson Trust Co., of Union City, N.J., Firemen's Ins. Co. of Newark, Prudential Ins. Co.; trustee N.Y., Susquehanna & Western R.R. since 1937. Chmn. joint water com. which originated a comprehensive plan for water supply for Northern N.J., 1908; mem. N.J. advisory bd. U. S. Pub. Works Adminstrn., 1933; mem. N.J. State Highway Commn., 1922-26. Trustee Stevens Inst. Tech. (chmn. bd. 1928-35); treas. N.J. Conf. Social Work, 1917-38; v.p. N.J. Welfare Council; mem. N.J.

State Sanatorium for Tuberculosis, 1914-18. Mem. Am. Soc. M.E., United Engring. Trustees (chmn. finance com.), Newcomen Soc. of Eng., N.Y. State Chamber Commerce (arbitration com.), N.J. State Chamber of Commerce (president 1935-37; vice-pres. and chmn. Cost of Govt. Com.; was chmn. State Com. to Make Zoning Effective, 1929). Episcopalian; sr. warden St. Luke's Ch., Montclair; v.p. Brotherhood of St. Andrew in U.S.A., 1900-38; mem. Nat. Council of P.E. Ch. (mem. trust fund com.). Clubs: Whitehall (New York); Essex (Newark, N.J.); Nat. Golf Links (Southampton); Yeaman Hall (Charleston, S.C.); Montclair Golf, Quantuck Beach. Home: 56 Gates Av., Montclair, N.J. Office: 140 Cedar St., New York, N.Y. Died Feb. 9, 1943.

KIDDER, WELLINGTON PARKER, engr., inventor; b. Norridgewock, Me., Feb. 19, 1853; s. Wellington and Annie (Winslow) K.; ed. dist. school and Eaton Prep. School; m. Emma Louise Hinckley, Sept. 4, 1878. Patented, 1868, when but 15 yrs. old, improvement in rotary steam engines; studied applied mechanics and drawing, Boston; invented web adjustable press, 1874, which received diploma Mass. Charitable Mechanics Inst., 1878; Kidder press now in large use, especially for printing consecutive numbering of railroad and other tickets from continous roll; invented many other improvements in presses, typewriters, automobile appliances, etc. Consulting engr. Rochester Industries, Inc., mfrs. of his later improvements in writing machines, 1923—. Home: Rochester, N.Y. Died Oct. 2, 1924.

KIER, SAMUEL M., industrialist; b. Livermore, Pa., 1813; s. Thomas Kier; m. Nancy Eicher; 4 children. Partner firm Hewitt & Kier, operator ry. express; organizer Kier, Royer & Co., owners, operators canal boats, 1838; established Independent Line (dealing in section boats which were boats combined with ry. car, could be placed on rails), 1846-54; pioneer in manufacture of firebrick; sold Kier's Rock Oil, 1846; 1st in Am. to produce refined oil (later known as kerosene). Died Pitts., Oct. 6, 1874.

KIERNAN, JAMES GEORGE, neurologist; b. New York, June 18, 1852; s. Francis and Mary (Aiken) K.; student Coll. City of New York, 1868-71; M.D., Univ. Med. Coll. (New York U.), 1874; m. Jane Ann Trumper, Feb. 10, 1881 (died 1903); m. 2d, Grace Cole, Dec. 11, 1917. Assistant physician Ward's Island (now New York State Insane) Hosp., 1874-78, and as officer N.Y. Neurol. Soc. was active in reforms brought about by that soc. in Am. psychiatry and neurology; asst. prof. nervous and mental diseases, Northwestern U., Ill., 1881-82; insp. Nat. Bd. Health, 1882; supt. Cook Co. Insane Hosp., Chicago, 1885-89, and forced investigation of co. charities, 1885, which led to the "boodle" trials and convictions of 1887; prof. forensic psychiatry, Kent Coll. of Law, Chicago, 1890-1902; prof. mental and nervous diseases, Milwaukee Med. Coll., 1894-97; prof. neurology, Chicago, Post-Grad. Sch., 1903-04; prof. med. jurisprudence, Dearborn Med. Coll., Chicago, 1904; prof. nervous diseases, Illinois Medical Coll., 1906-08; prof. mental and nervous diseases, Chicago Medical School. Was expert for the defense in Guiteau trial, 1881, Mooney trial 1884, and in many other criminal and civil cases involving medico-legal issues. Democrat. Home: Chicago, Ill. Died July 1, 1923.

KIERSTED, WYNKOOP, hydraulic engr.; b. Mongaup Valley, N.Y., Feb. 9, 1857; s. Wynkoop and Jane A. (Swan) K.; ed. at home to age of 20; C.E., Rensselaer Poly. Inst., 1880; m. Medora R. Smith; children—Martha (dec.), Jeanette, Wynkoop, Louise. Chief engr., 1892, in design and construction of new water supply of Galveston, Tex.; chief engr. Kansas City (Mo.) water works, Kansas City (Kan.) water works, and several pvt. water cos. Valued Los Angeles water works, 1898, Dubuque, Ia., water works, 1899, Oakland, Calif., water works, 1900; arbitrator at Eau Claire and Beloit, Wis., 1901, in valuation of water works property. Designed water supply systems for various cities and has been otherwise associated with over 50 water works in different parts of the country; supervising engr. for water works and sewerage of the U.S. Cantonment, Camp Funston, Fort Riley, Kan.; div. engr. U.S. Housing Corp.; mem. engring. bd. of review, sanitary problems of Chicago, Ill.; bd. of advisory engrs., new water works of Kansas City, Mo.; chief engr. Amarillo (Tex.) sewage disposal works and new water supply works; designed and supervised constrn. of new water supply works, Fort Collins, Colo., Abilene, Tex., Providence, Ky.; retired. Home: Liberty, Mo. Died Nov. 7, 1934.

KIESSELBACH, T(HEODORE) A(LEXANDER), agronomist; b. Polk County, Neb., Mar. 14, 1884; s. Alexander and Caroline (Bayrhoffer) K.; A.B., U. Neb., 1907, B.Sc., 1908, M.A., 1912, Ph.D., 1919; m. Hazel Hortense Hyde, June 30, 1908; children—Theodore J., Max R., Katharine (Mrs. W. V. Guthrie), Helen (Mrs. William H. Green). Grad. asst. U. Neb., 1907-08, instr. field crops, 1909, asst. exptl. agronomy, 1910, prof. exptl. agronomy, 1912, prof. agronomy since 1917, mem. grad. faculty since 1912. Mem. Am. Soc. Agronomy, A.A.A.S., Am. Soc. Naturalists, Genetics Soc. Am., Neb. Acad. Sci., Sigma Xi, Gamma Sigma Delta, Alpha Zeta. Home: 3211 Holdredge St., Lincoln 3, Neb. Died Dec. 1964.

KILBY, CLINTON MAURY, physicist; b. Suffolk, Va., Nov. 1, 1874; s. Wallace and Margaret (Tynes) K.; grad. Suffolk (Va.) Mil. Acad., 1892; A.M., Randolph-Macon Coll., Ashland, Va., 1896; studied U. of Chicago, summer, 1903, Columbia, summer, 1904; Ph.D., Johns Hopkins, 1909; m. Jean McDonald Graham, June 11, 1912. Instr. mathematics, Randolph-Macon Coll., 1894-96; prin. pub. schs., 1896-98; master in mathematics and physics, Woodberry Forest Sch., 1898-1905; lecture asst. in physics, Johns Hopkins, 1908-09; instr. physics, Lehigh U., 1909-10; prof. physics and astronomy, Randolph-Macon Woman's Coll., since 1910. Fellow A.A.A.S.; mem. Am. Assn. Physics Teachers, Am. Phys. Soc., Optical Soc. America, Va. Acad. of Science, Phi Beta Kappa, Phi Delta Theta, Gamma Alpha. Democrat. Methodist. Club: Sphex. Author: Laboratory Manual of Physics, 1912; The Constellations, 1918; Definitions and Fundamentals of Physics, 1921; Introduction to College Physics, 1929, Elements of Optics, 1943; Redetermination of Wave-lengths of the Arc and Spark Lines of Titanium, Manganese and Vanadium; The Effect of Capacity and Self-induction on the Wave-lengths of the Spark Lines. Author of Genealogy of Kilby, Tynes, etc. Home: 345 Norfolk Av., Lynchburg, Va. Died March 13, 1948.

KILGEN, EUGENE ROBYN, business exec.; b. St. Louis, Oct. 20, 1897; s. Charles C. and Louise (Robyn) K.; student St. Louis Acad., 1912-16, St. Louis U., 1917; m. Marie von Phul Michel, Oct. 29, 1931 (dec. Mar. 1969); children—Marie Michel (Mrs. Charles Michael Drain), Eugene Robyn Kilgen, Junior. Joined Kilgen Organ Co., St. Louis, 1919, apprentice, 1919-20, installation dept., 1921, engring. and sales, 1922-25, sec., 1925-35, v.p., 1935-39, pres. 1939-67; president Kilgen Aircraft, St. Louis, 1942-45, chmn. bd., 1956-67, dir. research, 1958-67; independent research and consulting, 1959-67. Mem. the bd. of control St. Louis Symphony Orchestra, 1936. Served as cadet pilot, U.S. A.A.F., 1917-18. Mem. Am. Guild Organists, Inst. Aero. Scis., St. Louis C. of C. (air bd.), St. Louis Academy of Sciences, Better Business Bureau (St. Louis). Club: University (St. Louis). Designer, collaborator in design of large organs as one in St. Patrick's Cathedral, Carnegie Hall, N.Y.C., St. Louis Cathedral. Invented Control Master for air traffic, 1953; Lightning Control System for TV studios, 1954. Home: University City MO Died Apr. 5, 1967.

KILLIAN, JOHN ALLEN, (kil'li-an), biochemist; b. Philadelphia, Pa., Jan. 4, 1891; s. Mark and Sarah Anne (Bradley) K.; A.B., Central High Sch., Phila., 1909, St. Joseph's Coll., Phila., 1913; A.M., Fordham U., N.Y. City, 1915, Ph.D., 1921; grad. study Columbia, 1915-16; m. Marie Frances Fitzpatrick, Sept. 1, 1917 (div.); children—Francis Mark, Joan Allen, Elizabeth Marie; m. 2d Josephine Gloria Castro; 1 son, Mark. Instr. chemistry, Fordham U., 1913-16; instr. in biochemistry, N.Y. Post Grad. Med. Sch. and Hosp., 1916-26, prof. 1926-33; established Killian Research Labs. for analytical and research work in biochemistry, bacteriology and pathology, 1933, pres. and dir. since 1933. Served as capt. Sanitary Corps, U.S. Army. Mem. Am. Chem. Soc., Am. Soc. Biol. Chemists, Soc. for Exptl. Biology and Medicine, Am. Gastro-Enterological Assn., Am. Urol. Assn., Am. Pub. Health Assn. Republican. Club: Chemists. Contbr. to tech. jours. Home: 425 E. 79th St. Office: 2 E. End Av., N.Y.C. Died Dec. 2, 1957.

KILMER, FREDERICK BARNETT, chemist; b. Chapinville, Conn., Dec. 11, 1851; s. Charles and Mary Ann (Langdon) K.; ed. Wyoming Sem., Kingston, Pa.; grad. New York Coll. Pharmacy, with spl. courses in chemistry, etc., at New York Coll., Columbia, and Rutgers; also spl. course under Hoffman; Pharm.M., Phila. Coll. Pharmacy and Science, 1920; m. Annie E. Kilbourn, Dec. 25, 1871 (dec.); 4 children (all dec.). Dir. scientific dept., Johnson & Johnson, chemists, New Brunswick, 1889—. Pres. Bd. Health, 1901-14; dean Nurses' Training Sch. of St. Peter's Hosp., New Brunswick. Warden Christ Episcopal Ch. Author: First Aid Manual, 1925. Editor Red Cross Notes, Messenger. Home: Brunswick, N.J. Died Dec. 28, 1934.

KIMBALL, ARTHUR LALANNE, physicist; b. Succasunna Plains, N.J., Oct. 16, 1856; s. Horace and Mary D. (Fisher) K.; A.B., Princeton, 1881, fellow in science, 1881-82; Ph.D., Johns Hopkins, 1884; m. Lucilla P. Scribner, 1884; m. 2d, Julia S. Scribner, June, 1913. Asso. in physics, 1884-88, asso. prof., 1888-91, Johns Hopkins; prof. physics, Amherst, 1891—. Author: The Physical Properties of Gases, 1890; College Physics, 1911. Home: Amherst, Mass. Died Oct. 22, 1922.

KIMBALL, DEXTER SIMPSON, univ. prof.; b. New River, N.B., Can., Oct. 21, 1865; s. William Henry and Jane (Paterson) K.; A.B., in engring., Stanford Univ., 1896, M.E., 1913; LL.D., from U. of Rochester, N.Y., 1926; D.Sc., Case School of Applied Science, 1930; Dr. of Engring., Kansas State Coll., 1933; Northeastern Univ., 1934, Lehigh U., 1939; m. Clara Evelyn Woolner, 1898; children—Isabella Jane, Dexter Simpson, George Norman. Apprentice and journeyman with Pope & Talbot, Port Gamble, Wash., 1881-87; in shops of Union Iron Works, San Francisco, 1887-93; in engring. dept. same, 1896-98; designing engr., Anaconda Mining Co., 1898; asst. prof. machine design, Sibley Coll. (Cornell U.), 1898-1901; works mgr. Stanley Electric Mfg. Co., 1901-04; prof. machine constrn., 1904-05, prof. machine design and constrn., 1905-15, prof. industrial engineering, 1915, Sibley Coll. of Cornell U. Actg. pres., July 1-Oct. 1, 1918 and Nov. 1929-Feb. 1930, dean of Coll. of Engring., 1920-36, now emeritus, Cornell. Brackett lecturer, Princeton, 1929; lecturer on industrial orgn., Stanford Grad. Sch. of Business, 1930; lecturer, Grad. School, U.S. Naval Acad., 1943-52. Receiver for Ithaca Traction Corp., 1925; dir. McGraw-Hill Publ. Co., 1930-48; dir. Ithaca Savings Bank, 1932-42, 1st v.p., 1938-42; dir. Ithaca Enterprises, Inc., 1936. Mem. Council Indsl. Edn. N.Y. State Dept. Edn., 1911. U.S. fuel adminstr. for Tompkins Co., N.Y., 1917-18; dir. Training Schs. for Army Mechanics, 1917-18. Mem. bd. of visitors U.S. Naval Acad., 1922. Apptd. by Sec. of Commerce Hoover chmn. organizing com. 2d Pan-Am. Standardization Conf., 1927; chmn. Priority Com. on Machine Tools and Equipment, Office of Production Management, 1941, chief of priority section, Machine Tool Division, War Production Board, 1942-43. Mem. of staff Alexander Hamilton Institute, 1922, chmn. bd., 1930-35; chmn. bd. Internat. Accountants Soc.; chmn. Commn. on Rochester Mechanics Inst., 1927; pres. Ithaca Chamber Commerce, 1935-36. Mem. Soc. Promotion Engring. Edn. (v.p. 1922-23, pres. 1929), Am. Soc. Mech. Engrs. (pres. 1921-22), Federated Am. Engring. Soc. (vice president 1920-22), American Engring. Council (pres. 1926-28), Nat. Econ. League, A.A.A.S., Newcomen Soc., Kappa Sigma, Phi Kappa Phi (pres. Cornell chapter 1922-23), Sigma Xi, Tau Beta Pi (pres. 1922-23); hon. judge Fisher Body of Craftsman's Guild. Honorary member Engineers Club of Philadelphia. Chmn. John Fritz Medal Bd., 1930, Hoover Medal Bd., 1930. Awarded Lamme medal by Soc. for Promotion of Engring. Edn., 1933; Worcester Reed Warner gold medal, Am. Society Mech. Engineers, 1933; H. L. Gantt gold medal American Management Assn. and Am. Soc. Mech. Engineers, 1943; Fred Winslow Taylor Key. Soc. for Advancement Management, 1948. Kimball Hall, Cornell U., named for him. Author: Elements of Machine Design (with John H. Barr), 1909; Industrial Education, 1911; Principles of Industrial Organization, 1913; Elements of Cost Finding, 1914; Plant Management; Industrial Economics, 1930; I Remember, 1952. Editor: The Book of Popular Science. Contbr. to scientific press. Home: Bellaeyre Apts., Ithaca. Died Nov. 1, 1952; buried Ithaca.

KIMBALL, GEORGE ALBERT, civil engr.; b. Littleton, Mass., May 14, 1850; s. William and Mary (Lawrence) K.; ed. Appleton Acad., New Ipswich, N.H.; studied engring. City engr. Somerville, 1876-86; mem. Somerville bd. of health, 1879-86; mem. Mystic water bd.; mem. Met. Sewerage Commn., 1896-1901; chief engr. elevated and subway construction, Boston Elevated Ry. Co. Home: Arlington, Mass. Died Dec. 3, 1912.

KIMBALL, GEORGE ELBERT, educator; b. Chgo., July 12, 1906; s. Arthur Gooch and Effie Gertrude (Smallen) K.; B.S., Princeton, 1928, A.M., 1929, Ph.D., 1932; m. Alice Thurston Hunter, June 22, 1936; children—Prudence Bradstreet, Thomas Redington, Susanna Goodhue, Martha Smallen. Nat. research fellow, Mass. Inst. Tech., 1933-35; instr. physics, Hunter Coll., 1935-36; instr. and asst. prof. chemistry, Columbia, 1936-46; asso. prof., 1946-47, prof. chemistry, 1947-56; sci. adv. Arthur D. Little, Inc., 1956-61, v.p. 1961—. Examiner, reader coll. entrance exam. bd. Fellow Operations Research Soc. of Am. Nat. Research Council com. on contract catalysis, in operations research since 1952. Dep. dir. Operations Research Group, Office Chief of Naval Operations; alternate mem. Joint Army-Navy Vision Com., 1945-46; mem. panel on underwater ord., 1945-51, Office Sec. of Def. since 1948; cons. Office Chief of Naval Operations since 1946, Office Sec. of Defense since 1949. Reilly lecturer, U. of Notre Dame, 1949. Fellow Am. Phys. Soc., N.Y. Acad. of Science. Mem. Operations Research Soc. Am. (pres. 1964-65), Nat. Acad. Scis., Am. Chem. Soc., U.S. Army Sci. Adv. Panel, Statis. Adv. Com. of U.S. Census, Phi Beta Kappa, Sigma Xi. Republican. Unitarian (trustee, pres. Hackensack Ch., 1948-51). Club: Cosmos (Washington). Author: Quantum Chemistry (with H. Eyring and J. Walter), 1944; Methods of Operations Research (with P. M. Morse), 1951. Asso. editor Jour. of Chemical Physics. Contbr. numerous articles to scientific jours. Home: 20 Everett Av., Winchester, Mass. Office: Arthur D. Little, Inc., 35 Acorn Park, Cambridge 40, Mass. Died Dec. 1967.

KIMBALL, GEORGE HENRY, consulting engr.; b. Newburyport, Mass., Dec. 8, 1849; s. Lafayette and Mary (Grover) K.; student Mass. Inst. Tech.; m. Emma A. Carpenter, Feb. 25, 1874. Supt. bridges and bldgs. Pittsburgh, Cincinnati & St. Louis Ry., 1876-79; supt. Columbus & Sunday Creek Valley Rd., 1879-80; engr. maintenance of way, Little Miami Rd., 1880-81; chief engr. southern extension, Toledo, Cincinnati & St. Louis Ry., 1881-82; supt. N.Y., C.& St.L. Rd., 1882-89; chief engr. L.S.&M.S. Ry., 1889-91; in gen. practice as consulting engr., 1891-98; supt. and chief engr.,

Columbus, Sandusky & Hocking Rd., 1898-99; chief engr. Pere Marquette R.R., 1899-1902, Central Electric Constrn. Co., New York, 1902-03; engaged in designing a system of freight terminals for trunk lines at Buffalo, N.Y., 1903-04; chief engr. C.&A. R.R., 1904-06; in gen. practice, 1906—. City commr., Pontiac, Mich., 1920-23, mayor, 1923-24. Mason. Home: Pontiac, Mich. Deceased.

KIMBALL, GILMAN, surgeon; b. New Chester, N.H., Dec. 8, 1804; s. Ebenezer and Polly (Aiken) K.; M.D., Dartmouth, 1827; studied surgery in Paris with Guillaume Dupuytren, 1829; m. Mary Dewar; m. 2d, Isabella Defries; 1 child. Surgeon, Lowell (Mass.) Corp. Hosp.; pioneer operations in gynecology; 1st surgeon to remove tumor of uterus by abdominal incision; performed 1st successful removal of ovarian tumor; prof. surgery Vt. Med. Coll., 1844; prof. surgery Berkshire Med. Coll., Pittsfield, Mass., 1845; served as brigade surgeon during Civil War; v.p. Mass. Med. Soc., 1878; pres. Am. Gynecol. Soc., 1882-83. Died July 27, 1892.

KIMBALL, HERBERT HARVEY, meteorologist; b. Hopkinton, N.H., Feb. 13, 1862; s. Elbridge Gerry and Mary (Butler) K.; B.S., N.H. Coll. Agr. and Mechanic Arts, 1884; M.S., Columbia (now George Washington) U., 1900; Ph.D., George Washington U., 1910; fellow U. of Pittsburgh, 1912-13; hon. LL.D., U. of N.H., 1921; m. Margaret Gertrude Cowling, Nov. 4, 1891; children—Mrs. Dorothy Lingenfelter, Herbert Cowling, Donald Butler. Meteorol. observer, 1884-85, clerk at central office, 1886-1900, asst. editor of Monthly Weather Review, 1901-03, editor same, 1918-19, librarian, 1904-08, in charge of solar radiation investigations, 1908-32, U.S. Meteorol. Service; research asso. Harvard, in charge solar radiation investigations at Blue Hill Obs., 1932-39. Mem. Philos. Soc. Washington, Am. Geophysical Union; fellow A.A.A.S., Am. Meteorol. Soc. (ex-pres.). Baptist. Home: 1819 Monroe St. N.W., Washington DC

KIMBALL, JAMES HENRY, meteorologist; b. Detroit, Mich., Feb. 12, 1874; s. Charles Henry and Alice (Jordan) K.; student Mich. Agrl. Coll., 1891-94, B.S., 1912; studied U. of Mich., 1894-95; M.A., U. of Richmond, Va., 1914; Ph.D., New York U., 1926; hon. Sc.D., Mich. State Coll., 1934; unmarried. With U.S. Weather Bureau since 1895, serving in all sections of U.S. and in West Indies; now in charge New York office, U.S. Weather Bureau; meteorol. adviser, New York, for French High Commn., and instr. for flying units, 1917-18; faculty lecturer on aeronautical meteorology, New York U., 1941. Fellow Am. Meteorological Society, Inst. of Aeronautical Sciences; member New York Acad. of Sciences, Nat. Institute of Social Sciences (v.p.), D'Honneur Liguè Internationale des Aviateurs. Awarded scroll of honor with gold medal, City of N.Y.; Officers Cross Order Polonia Restituta; Chevalier Legion of Honor, France; Commandatore of the Crown of Italy. Republican. Episcopalian. Prepared first North Atlantic weather maps for transatlantic flying; cons. meteorologist for Lindbergh and subsequent Am. and European transatlantic fliers. Home: 39 1/2 Washington Sq. Address: U.S. Weather Bureau, 17 Battery Pl., New York, N.Y. Died Dec. 21, 1943.

KIMBALL, JAMES PUTNAM, geologist; b. Salem, Mass., Apr. 26, 1836; s. James and Maria Grace (Putnam) K.; ed. Lawrence Scientific Sch. (Harvard), univs. of Berlin and Göttingen and Freiberg Sch. of Mining; m. Mary Elizabeth Farley, July 20, 1874 (new deceased). Geologist Wis. and Ill. State geol. surveys; prof. chemistry and economic geology, N.Y. Agrl. Coll., Ovid, 1861-62; capt. and asst. adj. gen. vols., 1862-63; on gen. staffs of McClellan, Burnside, Hooker and Meade; provost marshal, general's div.; bvtd. maj., Mar. 23, 1865, "for gallant and meritorious services." Resumed mining practice, New York, 1864-74; hon. prof. geology, Lehigh U., 1874-85; apptd. dir. of the Mint, 1885-88. Home: Cody, Wyo. Died Oct. 23, 1913.

KIMBROUGH, ROBERT ALEXANDER, JR., physician; b. Jackson, Tenn., Aug. 6, 1899; s. Robert Alexander and Martha (Conn) K.; A.B., Miss. Coll., 1918; M.D., U. Pa., 1922; m. Agnes McComb, July 12, 1928; children—Robert Alexander, William McComb. Intern, Hosp. U. Pa., 1922-24, resident gynecologist 1924-25; practice medicine, specializing obstetrics and gynecology, Phila., 1925-60; faculty U. Pa., 1925-60, prof., chmn. dept. obstetrics and gynecology, grad. sch. medicine U. Pa., 1946-60, prof. emeritus, 1966—; dir. obstetrics and gynecology Pa. Hosp., 1951-60; dir. Am. Coll. Obstetricians and Gynecologists, 1960-66. U.S. Army col. (ret. res.). Diplomate Am. Bd. Obstetrics and Gycecology (dir.). Fellow A.C.S., Am. Gynecol. Soc. (pres. 1962), Am. Assn. Obstetrics and Gynecology; mem. A.M.A., Obstet. Soc. Phila. (pres. 1939), Am. Coll. Obstetricians and Gynecologists (pres. 1953). Episcopalian. Co-author: Clinical Obstetrics. Editor: Gynecology. Contbr. med. jours. Home: 3819 Calle Guaymas, Tucson 85716. Died July 1, 1967; buried St. Philips in the Hills, Tucson.

KIMMELSTIEL, PAUL, physician; b. Hamburg, Germany, Mar. 21, 1900; s. Adolf and Ernestine (August) K.; M.D., Tubingen (Germany) U., 1923; m. Charlotte Rose van Biema, Feb. 22, 1924; children—Ruth (Mrs. Norbert Freinkel), Marion (Mrs. Norman Goldberg). Came to U.S., 1934, naturalized, 1940. Intern, Hosp. of St. George, Hamburg, 1924-25; fellow bacteriology and immunology dept. Allgemeines Krankenhaus Rudolf Eppendorf, Hamburg, 1925, resident dept. pathology, 1929-30, asso. prof., 1930-33; resident dept. pathology Allgemeines Krankenhaus St. George, Hamburg, 1925-27; instr. pathology Harvard, 1934-35; coroner City of Richmond (Va.), 1936-40; pathologist, dir. clin. labs. Charlotte (N.C.) Meml. Hosp., 1940-58; asso. prof. pathology Med. Coll. Va., Richmond, 1935-40; prof., pathology Marquette U. Med. Sch., Milw., 1958-64, research prof., 1964-66; distinguished prof. pathology U. Okla., Oklahoma City, until 1970. NIH grantee. Recipient medal Am. Cancer Soc., 1956, Elliott Proctor Joslin medal New Eng. Diabetes Assn., 1966, medal Japanese Soc. Nephrology, 1968. Diplomate Am. Bd. Pathology. Fellow A.C.P.; mem. A.M.A., Am. Soc. Clin. Pathologists, Coll. Am. Pathologists, Am. Assn. Pathologists and Bacteriologists. Discovered Kimmelstiel-Wilson disease, 1936. Home: Oklahoma City OK Died Oct. 7, 1970; buried Dresher PA

KINCAID, TREVOR, zoologist; b. Peterboro, Ont., Can., Dec. 21, 1872; s. Dr. Robert and Margaret K.; B.S., U. of Wash., 1899, A.M., 1901; m. Louise F. Pennell, Aug. 23, 1917; children—Marjorie Farrar, Dorothy Elizabeth, Barbara Louise, Thomas Farrar, Mary Pennella, Kathleen. Instr. of biology, U. of Wash., 1895-99; asst. Am. Fur Seal Commn., 1897, acting prof. entomology, Ore. Agrl. Coll., 1897-98; entomologist Harriman Alaska expdn., 1899; asst. prof. biology, 1899-1901, prof. zoology, U. of Wash., 1911-47; retired; professor emeritus of zoology, since 1947; Austin scholar, Harvard, 1905-06; special field agt., U.S. Dept. Agr., in Japan, 1908, in Russia, 1909 (investigation of parasites of gypsy moth). Mem. Am. Soc. Econ. Entomologists, Entomol. Soc. Washington. Contbr. to Entomological News and to other publs., various papers and reports relating to the entomology of the Pacific Coast and particularly to Alaska, and papers on the oyster industry of the Pacific Coast. Home: 1904 E. 52d St., Seattle WA

KINCER, JOSEPH BURTON, meteorologist; b. Wythe Country, Va., Nov. 15, 1874; s. Alonzo and Margaret (Hilton) K.; ed. in pvt. schs.; m. Cora Helen Lampe, Aug. 26, 1896; children—Lockie Inez (Mrs. J.W. Davies), Alice Ruth (Mrs. W.T. Webb). Pub. sch. teacher, Wythe County, Va., 1894-1901; dep. treas. Wythe County, 1901-04; entered U.S. Weather Bureau as asst. observer, 1904, and promoted successively through various grades to prin. meteorologist and chief division of climate and crop weather, Washington, D.C.; now retired. Fellow A.A.A.S., Am. Meteorol. Soc. (pres. 1936-37); mem. Assn. Am. Geographers, Am. Geophysical Union, Internat. Climatol. Commn., Internat. Commn. Agrl. Meteorology. Lutheran. Mason. Odd Fellow. Wrote sect. on climate in Atlas of American Agriculture, also numerous meteorol. bulletins pub. by U.S. Dept. of Agr. Editor of Weekly Weather and Crop Bulletin. Home: 4112 Fessenden St. N.W., Washington DC

KINDLE, EDWARD MARTIN, paleontologist, geologist; b. near Franklin, Ind., Mar. 10, 1869; s. Martin V. and Tabitha Ann K.; A.B., Ind. U., 1893, LL.D., 1939; M.S., Cornell, 1896; Ph.D., Yale, 1899; m. Margaret Ferris, Dec. 31, 1901; children—Winona Helen, Leroy Ferris, Cecil Haldane, Edward Darwin, Virginia Tomlinson, Margaret Crane, Madeleine Barton, Katharine, Charlotte. Instr. geology, Ind. U., 1894-95; mem. Cornell expdn. to Greenland, 1896; asst. geologist, Ind. Geol. Survey, 1898-1900; asst. geologist, 1900-08, paleontologist, 1908-10, geologist, 1911, U.S. Geol. Survey; paleontologist in charge of palcontology, Geol. Survey of Can., 1912-38. Spl. lecturer in geology, U. of London, Eng., 1928. Fellow Geol. Soc. America, Am. Geog. Soc., Royal Soc. of Can. Home: Ottawa, Can. Died Aug. 29, 1940.

KINEALY, JOHN HENRY, engineer; b. Hannibal, Mo., Mar. 18, 1864; s. Michael and Sarah (Briscoe) K.; M.E., Washington U., 1884; m. Grace Sampson Strong, June 26, 1890; children—Mrs. Winifred Bryan, Mrs. Grace Pierson, Mrs. Virginia Jackson, Mrs. Sarah Wentworth, J. Henry. Instr. Washington U., 1886-87; asso. prof. Agrl. and Mech. Coll. of Tex., 1887-89; prof. N.C. Coll. of Agr. and Mech. Arts, 1889-92; prof. mech. engring., Washington U., 1892-1902; consulting engr., Boston, 1902-04; mech. engr., St. Louis, 1904—. Patent expert; inventor of devices used in heating and ventilation. Active in Progressive Party, 1912, mayor of Ferguson, St. Louis Co., Mo., 1913-23, chmn. local exemption board, 1917-19; pres. League of Municipalities of St. Louis Co., 1918-23. Author: Steam Engines and Boilers, 1895, 4th edit., 1903; Mechanical Draft, 1906. Home: Ferguson, Mo. Died May 6, 1928.

KING, ADEN J(ACKSON), prof. chemistry; b. La Fayette, N.Y., Nov. 25, 1897; s. Newton Earl and Orpha Amanda (Hoyt) K.; B.S., Syracuse U., 1921, M.S., 1922, Ph.D., 1927; m. Gladys Susan Nutter, Dec. 6, 1917; 1 dau., Mary E. Kelly. Instr. chem., Syracuse U., 1921-27, U. of Ill., 1927-28; Nat. Research Fellow (chemistry), U. of Ill., 1928-29; prof. chemistry and x-ray crystallography. Syracuse U. from 1929, acting chmn. dept. chemistry 1949-50; sabbatical term study, U. of Manchester, England, 1935; co-founder and pres., King Labs., Inc., 1931. Mem. Am. Chem. Soc., Am. Constallographic Assn., Am. Orchid Soc., Sigma Xi, Phi Beta Kappa, Alpha Chi Sigma, Phi Lambda Upsilon. Club: Men's Garden of America (Syracuse). Inventions and patents on use of alkaline earth metals in electronic industry. Home: Syracuse NY Died Dec. 1971.

KING, ARTHUR S(COTT), physicist; b. Jerseyville, Ill., Jan. 18, 1876; B.S., U. Cal., 1899, M.S., 1901, Ph.D., 1903; married. Asst. physics U. Cal., 1901-03, instr. physics, 1905-08; Whiting fellow Bonn U., 1903-04; Carnegie research asst. U. Berlin, 1904-05; supt. phys. lab. Mt. Wilson Obs., Carnegie Instn., 1908-43; physicist Cal. Inst. Tech., 1944-46; mathematician Naval Ordnance Test Sta., Pasadena, Cal., 1946-54. Civilian, Nat. Def. Research Com., 1944. Fellow Am. Phys. Soc., Meteoritical Soc. (pres. 1946-50); mem. Nat. Acad. Sci., Am. Optical Soc., Astronomers Soc., Astron. Soc. Pacific (pres. 1941). Home: 925 Topeka St., Pasadena 6. Office: Mount Wilson Observatory, Pasadena 4, Cal. Died Apr. 25, 1957.

KING, CLARENCE, geologist; b. Newport, R.I., Jan. 6, 1842; grad. Sheffield Scientific School, Yale, 1862; crossed continent on horseback and joined Calif. geol. survey, 1863, working with it until 1866; made palaeontol. discoveries which furnished the evidence upon which the accepted age of gold-bearing rocks was determined. Originated the plan and comd. the expdn. for geol. survey of 40th parallel, under auspices of army engr. dept., 1867-72; exposed Arizona "diamondfields" fraud, 1872; suggested and organized U.S. Geol. Survey, of which he was dir., 1878-81; then in spl. investigations. Author: Systematic Geology (Vol. I, Professional Papers of Engr. Dept., U.S.A.); Mountaineering in Sierra Nevada, etc. Died 1901.

KING, EDWARD LACY, obstetrician; b. Mound, La., Oct. 1, 1884; s. Williams Boardman and Julia Priscilla (Frasier) K.; A.B., Tulane U., 1906, M.D., 1911; m. Edith Chalin Follett, June 23, 1915; children—Edward Lacy, John Alfred, Williams Follett. Practiced in New Orleans since 1911, specializing in obstetrics and gynecology; with obstet. dept. Tulane Med. Sch. since 1914, professor of obstetrics, 1928-50, emeritus professor of obstetrics since 1950. Served as capt. Med. Corps, U.S. Army, 1918-19; with Evacuation Hosp. No. 31, A.E.F., 8 months. Decorated Star of Solidarity, 3d class (Italy). Licentiate Am. Bd. Obstetrics and Gynecology. Fellow Am. Coll. Surgeons, Am. Coll. Obstetricians and Gynecologists; mem. A.M.A., Am. Gynecol. Soc., Central Assn. Obstetricians and Gynecologists, American Association of Obstetricians, Gynecologists, Society of Experimental Biology and Medicine, Southern Med. Assn., New Orleans and La. State obstet. and gynecol. socs., Orleans Parish and La State med. scos., corr. mem. Soc. Obstetrics and Gynecology, Panama, hon. mem. Soc. Obstetrics and Gynecology, Venezuela, Kappa Sigma, Alpha Kappa Kappa, Alpha Omega Alpha. Democrat. Episcopalian. Mason. Clubs: New Orleans Country, Round Table (New Orleans). Author: Occipito-Posterior Positions. Contbr. to med. jours. Home: 2120 Audubon St. Office: 3634 Coliseum St., New Orleans 70115. Died May 30, 1963; buried New Orleans.

KING, EDWARD S(KINNER), astronomer; b. Liverpool N.Y., May 31, 1861; s. Nathaniel and Cornelia C. (Skinner) K.; A.B. from Hamilton College, 1887, A.M., 1890, and Sc.D. from the same college, 1927; m. Kate Irene Colson, July 23, 1890; children—Harold Skinner, Margaret Wight, Everett Tryon (dec.). Connected from 1887, with Harvard Coll. Obs. (except 3 yrs. absent on account of ill health); observer in charge Harvard Sta. on Mt. Wilson, Calif., 1889; asst. prof. astronomy, 1913-26, Phillips prof., Harvard, 1926—. Obtained first photog. observation of the occultation of a star, also first photograph of spectrum of the aurora; perfected method of obtaining circular photographic images of the stars without visual guiding of the telescope; devised method of transforming prismatic to normal spectra, both photographically and mechanically; determined photographic magnitudes of bright stars and planets, from images photographed out of focus; made photographic measures of the light of the moon, also of the sun; has maintained systematic tests of photographic plates, 1896—; also determined photovisual magnitudes of stars, and derived color indices of planets; etc. Fellow Am. Acad. Arts and Sciences, A.A.A.S. Republican. Conglist. Home: Cambridge, Mass. Died Sept. 10, 1931.

KING, FAIN WHITE, archeologist; b. Paducah, Ky., Sept. 3, 1892; s. Charles Henry and Katie Andrews (Burnette) K.; ed. Ky. pub. schs. and U. Chgo; m. 2d, Blanche Black Busey, June 6, 1935. Owner King Mill and Lumber Co., from 1912, also K.R.B. Realty Co.; pres. Paducah Development Co.; treas. Three Rivers Oil Co.; dir. Associated Realty Co., Central Warehouse Co., Paducah Roofing Co. Co-owner, Natural Flourite Optical Co. In charge dist. inspection Constrn. Div., War Dept., 1917-19. Mem. bd. regents Ala. State Mus. Natural History; dir. Collectors and Dealers Nat. Assn. Indian Relics; mem. bd. dirs. Nat. Econ. League for Ky.; research dir. of archeology for Ky. under govs. Chandler and Johnson. Reapptd. state archaeologist for 4th time as dir. archaeology under Gov. Simeon Willis, dept. conservation. Dir., mem. exec. com. Ballard Co. of Ky.

Lake Assn. Mem. Mus. Natural History (N.Y.C.), Ill. State Archaeol. Soc., Ky., Tenn. acads. sci., Ky. Ornithol. Soc., Wis. Archeol; Soc., Am. Legion, Col. Gov. Laffoon's staff. Democrat. Episcopalian. Editor, Gems and Minerals dept. Hobbies mag. Contbr. Wis. Archeologist, Ky. mag.; mem. adv. bd. Ky. Nature mag. Discoverer and excavator ancient buried city in Ky., at junction of Ohio and Mississippi rivers; has broadcast from site of excavations over NBC network; also from Radio City, Chgo. Home: San Diego CA Died June 5, 1972; buried Oak Knoll Cemetery, Paducah KY

KING, GEORGE B., entomologist; b. at Lowell, Mass., Jan. 23, 1848; s. William and Elizabeth K.; attended country school, Fremont, N.Y., about 2 yrs.; m. Julia Eastman, of Lawrence, Mass., July 17, 1871. Has been janitor Superior Court House, Lawrence, Mass., since 1886. Self taught in entomology. Mem. A.A.A.S., Assn. Econ. Entomologists, Harris Entomol. Club, Boston, Lawrence Soc. Natural History. Determiner of scale insects for Germany, Switzerland, Brit. N. America, and many U.S. agrl. coll. profs. Has written about 57 scientific papers, including monograph of the genus Kermes of N. America; has described about 50 new species of Coccidae. Address: Lawrence, Massachusetts.

KING, HELEN DEAN, zoologist; b. Owego, Tioga County, N.Y., Sept. 27, 1869; d. George Alonzo and Leonora Louise (Dean) King's A.B., Vassar, 1892; fellow in biology, Bryn Mawr, 1896-97, A.M., Ph.D., 1899; univ. fellow for research in zoölogy U. Pa.; unmarried. Student asst. in biology Vassar, 1894-95; tchr. sci. Baldwin Sch., Bryn Mawr, Pa., 1899-1907; asst. in anatomy Wistar Inst., Phila., 1909-10, asso., 1910-13, asst. prof. embryology, 1913-27, mem. same, 1927—. Fellow A.A.A.S.; mem. Am. Soc. Zoölogists (v.p. 1937), Am. Soc. Naturalists, N.Y. Acad. Science, Wistar Inst. (mem. adv. bd.), Soc. Exptl. Biology and Medicine, Am. Assn. Anatomists, Marine Biol. Lab. Assn. (Woods Hole, Mass.), Am. Genetic Assn., Phi Beta Kappa, Sigma Xi. Republican. Episcopalian. Contbr. on regeneration, sex determination, inbreeding, domestication, etc. Home: The Fairfax, Locust at 43rd St., Phila. Died Mar. 9, 1955.

KING, HORACE WILLIAMS, engr.; b. Big Rapids, Mich., Feb. 10, 1874; s. Charles B. and Fannie L. (Williams) K.; C.E., U. of Mich., 1895; m. Mabel V. Jones, June 8, 1909. In gen. engring. practice, 1895-99; asst. engr., Nicaragua Canal surveys, 1899-1901; provincial supervisor Philippines, res. engr. Canton-Hankow R.R. and U.S. asst. engr. in charge constrn., Manila Harbor, 1901-04; engr. U.S. Reclamation Service, 1905-07; gen. practice, Ore., 1907-09; engr. in charge hydraulic dept., Arnold Co., Chicago, 1909-12; prof. hydraulic engring., U. of Mich., 1912-39, prof. emeritus since 1939. Republican. Mem. Am. Soc. C.E. (hon.), Sigma Xi; honorary member Mich. Engineering Soc., Chi Epsilon (Southern California chpt.). Author: Handbook of Hydraulics, 1917, 2d rev. edit., 1939; Manning Formula Tables, Vol. I, 1937; Vol. II, 1939; section, Irrigation and Drainage, Am. Civil Engineers Handbook, 5th edit., 1930; section on Hydraulics, Civil Engineers' Handbook, 1933, 2d edit., 1940. Co-Author: Elementary Hydraulics, 5th edit., 1948. Address: State Savings Bank Bldg., Ann Arbor, Mich. Died April 22, 1951; buried Pasadena, Cal.

KING, JAMES HAROLD, marine engring.; b. New Haven, July 17, 1892; s. John Joseph and Helen Josephine (Grady) K.; student N.Y. pub. schs., Yale, 1913; m. Dorothy MacIsaac, Dec. 7, 1918; children—James Harold, Doris E. (Mrs. Robert K. Coutlee). With The Babcock & Wilcox Co., 1914, assigned engring. sect. marine dept., 1917, asst. mgr. marine dept., 1928-31, mgr. dept., 1931, v.p., 1945, head boiler div., 1952, dir. 1953; dir. Diamond Power Specialty Co., Lancaster, O., Hooper Holmes Bureau, Inc., N.Y.C. Mem. Scarsdale (N.Y.) Planning Commn. Mem. Soc. Naval Architects and Marine Engrs. (pres. 1951-52), Inst. Marine Engrs. (v.p.), Am. Soc. Naval Engrs. (past council mem.), Am. Bur. Shipping, Engrs. Joint Council, Newcomen Soc., Alpha Chi Rho, Sigma Xi, Pi Tau Sigma. Republican. Roman Catholic. Clubs: India House, Cloud, Engrs., Yale (N.Y.C.); Met. (Washington); Winged Foot Golf. Author several tech. papers, articles. Home: 20 Bradford Rd., Scarsdale, N.Y. Office: 161 East 42d St., N.Y.C. 17. Died Nov. 1953.

KING, JAMES WILSON, chief engr. U.S.N., retired, 1880, with relative rank of capt.; b. Baltimore, 1818; apptd. to navy as 3d asst. engr., Sept. 2, 1884; served in 1st steamers owned by Navy; participated in capture of coast towns during Mexican war; passed 3 grades asst. engr.; promoted, 1852, to chief engr.; chief engr. 2 terms Brooklyn Navy Yard, and 1 term of Boston Navy Yard; chief engr. Atlantic fleet, 1861-62; took part in capture forts at Hatteras and Port Royal; later ordered as supt. of bldg. of all iron naval vessels west of Alleghenies; in 1865 ordered to examine and report condition of all iron vessels and machinery bldg. under contract outside of navy yards; chief Bureau of Engring., 1869-73; gen. insp. Engring. Works, 1873; made 3 trips to Europe to collect and furnish information useful to navy. Served on many bds. as pres. or mem.; invented and made first condenser for distilling seawater for domestic purposes on shipboard; also system of exhausting foul air from lower decks; first officer to advocate iron and steel for hulls of ships. Author: European Ships of War, 1878 U31; The War Ships and Navies of the World, 1880. Address: 3231 Powelton Av., Philadelphia.

KING, JOHN, eclectic physician; b. N.Y.C., Jan. 1, 1813; s. Harman and Marguerite (La Porte) K.; grad. Reformed Med. Coll. of City N.Y., 1838; m. Charlotte M. Armington, 1833; m. 2d, Phebe Rodman, 1853. Sec. 1st nat. conv. Reform Med. Practitioners, 1848; became prof. materia medica and therapeutics, Memphis, Tenn., 1849; prof. obstetrics Eclectic Med. Inst., Cincinnati, 1851; pres. Nat. Eclectic Med. Assn., 1878; 1st pres. Ohio Eclectic Med. Assn.; leader reform in Am. med. therapeutics; a founder eclectic sch. medicine; introduced to gen. use oleo-resin of iris (1st of resin class of drugs); introduced podophyllin, hydrastis, sanguinaria; most notable work was The American Dispensatory, 1852; an early abolitionist. Died North Bend, O., June 19, 1893.

KING, OSCAR A., neurologist; b. on farm nr. Peru, Ind., Feb. 22, 1851; s. Timothy Lewis and Mary M. (Wright) K.; M.D., Bellevue Hosp. Med. Coll. (New York U.), 1878; m. Minerva Guernsey, 1887. Second and 1st asst. phy. Wis. State Hosp. for Insane, 1879-82; attended lectures U. of Vienna and clinics in Allgemeinen Krankenhausen, 1880-81; sp. studies in neurology and psychiatry under Meynert, Leidersdorf, Weiss and Benedict. Prof. mental and nervous diseases, 1882, and later of neurology, Psychiatry and clin. medicine, sec., 1894; vice dean, 1900—, Coll. Phys. and Surg. (U. of Ill.), Chicago; pathologist and consulting alienist Wis. state charitable and penal instns., 1895; prof. neurology, Post-Grad. Med. Sch.; chief dept. of neurology West Side Free Dispensary; asso. mem. med. staff Cook Co. Hosp. Founded, 1883, the Oakwood Retreat, Lake Geneva, Wis., a private sanitarium for care of the insane, of which became pres. and chief of med. staff; founded, in 1896, Lake Geneva Sanitarium, and in 1901 the two sanitaria were united into one, of which remains dir. In 1896 applied the toxine of erysipelas effectively in the treatment of 23 nearly consecutive cases of mania and melancholia. Home: Lake Geneva, Wis. Died Sept. 11, 1921.

KING, ROY STEVENSON, mech. engr.; b. Xenia, O., Sept. 10, 1876; s. William Harrison and Bertha Louise (Ritter) K.; M.E., Ohio State U., 1902; M.S., U. of Minn., 1907, U. of Chicago, 1914; Sc.D., U. of Ga., 1922; m. Estalla Gertrude Peterson, Feb. 19, 1903. Constrn. foreman Aetna (Ind.) Powder Co., 1898-99; foreman Nat. Cash Register Co., 1902-03; instr. in mech. engring. dept., U. of Minn., 1903-05; asst. prof. exptl. engring., Ohio State U., 1905-07; gen. mgr. Hall-Cronan Co., Dayton, O., 1907-10; in engring. dept. Ind. Steel Co., Gary, 1910-12, engring. dept. Fairbanks, Morse & Co., 1912-14; asst. prof. mech. engring., U. of Ariz., 1914-17; prof. exptl. engring., Ga. Sch. Tech., Atlanta, 1917-23, head of mech. engring. dept. and supt. shops and power (plant), 1923-46; prof. emeritus mech. engring., Ga. Sch. Tech. since Sept. 1946; dir. Atlanta Fed. Savings & Loan Assn. Mem. Ga. State Bd. of Registration for Professional Engrs. and Surveyors. Chmn. Atlanta Smoke Abatement Bd.; vice pres. Ga. Soc. Professional Engrs., hon. mem. Ga. Engring. Soc. In engring. dept. picric acid plant, Picron, Little Rock, Ark., 1948. Fellow Am. Soc. M.E., mem. Am. Soc. Engring. Education (v.p. 1924-25), Newcomen Soc., Sigma Xi, Phi Kappa Phi, Pi Tau Sigma, Tau Beta Pi, fellow A.A.A.S. Methodist. Mason. Home: 1293 Oxford Rd. N.E., Atlanta 6. Died Oct. 12, 1956.

KING, SAMUEL ARCHER, balloonist; b. Tinicum, Pa., Apr. 9, 1828; s. Isaac B. King; m. Margaret Roberts, 2 children. Made 1st ascent in balloon, 1851; made career of ascending in balloons at fairs and celebrations; believed it possible to cross Atlantic ocean in balloon, but never made trip; made several ascents for experimenters of U.S. Signal Service. Died Phila., Nov. 3, 1914.

KINGMAN, LEWIS, civil engr., ry. official; b. Bridgewater, Mass., Feb. 26, 1845; s. Isaac and Sibel (Ames) K.; grad. Hunt's Acad., 1861; studied with J. Herbert Shedd, civ. engr. of Boston, 2 yrs.; m. Alice Newman, Jan. 20, 1887. Engring. and developing oil wells, Wilkes-Barré and Oil City, Pa., 1863-68; div. engr. on location surveys, Atlantic & Pacific Ry., 1868-71; on surveys and location, Maxwell Land Grant and U.P. Ry. from Kit Carson, Colo., to Cameron, N.M., 1871-72; on U.S. Govt. surveys under surveyor gen. of N.M., 1873-76; asst. and locating engr. A.,T.&S.F. Ry., 1884-88, at Topeka, and Atlantic & Pacific Ry., West of Albuquerque, N.M., 1881-82; chief engr. Atlantic & Pacific Ry., 1882-83; chief engr. Northern div. Mexican Central Ry. at Chihuahua, Mex., 1883-84; asst. chief engr. A.,T.&S.F. Ry., 1884-88, at Topeka, and constructed 1,348 miles in Kan., Ind. Ty. and Tex.; city engr. of Topeka, 1889-94; chief engr. Mexican Central Ry., 1895-1909; engr. maintenance of way, Nat. Rys. of Mexico. Died Jan. 23. 1912.

KINGSBURY, ALBERT, mechanical engr.; b. near Morris, Ill., Dec. 23, 1863; s. Lester Wayne and Eliza (Fosdick) K.; M.E., Cornell, 1889; studied mech. engring., Ohio State U. and Cornell; m. Alison Mason, July 25, 1893; children—Margaretta Mason, Alison Mason, Elisabeth Brewster, Katharine Knox, Theodora. Instr. in mech. engring. and physics, N.H. Coll., 1889-90; mech. engr., H. B. Camp Co., Cuyahoga Falls, O., 1890-91; prof. mech. engring., N.H. Coll., 1891-99; prof. applied mechanics, Worcester Poly. Inst., 1899-1903; mech. engr. Westinghouse Electric & Mfg. Co., E. Pittsburgh, 1903-10; consulting engr. since 1910; pres. Kingsbury Machine Works, Frankford, Phila. Fellow A.A.A.S.; mem. Am. Soc. Mech. Engrs. Contbr. to trans. of engring. socs. on subjects in mech. engring. Home: Greenwich, Conn. Died July 28, 1943.

KINGSFORD, HOWARD NELSON, pathologist; b. at Providence, R.I., Sept. 24, 1871; s. John C. and A. F. (Thatcher) K.; spl. student, chemistry, Brown, 1894-5; M.D., Dartmouth, 1896; grad. student, medicine, Harvard, 1898-9; (A.M., Dartmouth, 1907); m. Mabel P. Carpenter, Pawtucket, R.I., July 16, 1898. Instr. histology, bacteriology and pathology, 1898-1900, prof. pathology, 1906—, Dartmouth Med. Sch.; med. dir. Dartmouth Coll., 1902—; pathologist Mary Hitchcock Hosp.; state bacteriologist of N.H. Mem. Am. Assn. Pathologists and Bacteriologists, A.M.A., N.H. Med. Soc., N.H. Surg. Club, etc. Commd. capt., Med. R.C., 1917. Address: Hanover, N.H. Died Feb. 9, 1950.

KINGSFORD, THOMAS, inventor, mfr.; b. Wickham, Kent County, Eng., Sept. 29, 1799; s. George and Mary (Love) K.; m. Ann Thomson, 1818; m. 2d, Elizabeth Austen, 1839; 1 son, Thomson. Came to U.S., 1831; supt. starch factory William Colgate & Co., Harsimus, N.J., 1833-46, developed method of producing starch from corn (rather than wheat), 1842; manufactured starch in own plant, Bergen, N.J., 1846-48; founder, owner Oswego (N.Y.) Starch Factory, 1848-69; produced cornstarch suitable for food purposes, 1850. Died Oswego, Nov. 28, 1869.

KINGSLEY, CLARENCE DARWIN, ednl. engr.; b. Syracuse. N.Y., July 12, 1874; s. Edwin A. and Emma Howell (Garnsey) K.; student Syracuse High Sch., 1889-92; B.S., Colgate, 1897; M.A., Teachers Coll. (Columbia), 1904; studied summers at Cornell U., Harvard, New York Sch. of Philanthropy; m. H. Elizabeth Seelman, June 26, 1914. Instr. mathematics, Colgate, 1898-1902; teacher Manual Training High Sch., Brooklyn, 1904-12; state supervisor high schs., Mass. Dept. Edn., 1912-23; ednl. engr. specializing on sch. building programs and plans and serving as consultant in various cities, 1923—; teacher ednl. dept. Harvard Summer Sch., 1917-21, U. of Mich. Summer Sch., 1923. Chmn. commn. on reorganization of secondary edn., apptd. by N.E.A., 1912—. Editor of Reports on Commn. on Reorganization of Secondary Edn. (15 separate repts. on different subjects, pub. by U.S. Bur. Edn.). Home: Chicago, Ill. Died Dec. 31, 1926.

KINGSLEY, J(OHN) STERLING, biologist; b. Cincinnatus, N.Y., Apr. 7, 1853; s. Lewis and Julia A. (Kingman) K.; A.B., Williams Coll., 1875; Sc.D., Princeton, 1885; U. of Freiburg, 1891-92; m. Mary Emma Read, Jan. 31, 1882. Curator, Peabody Acad. Science, 1876-78; asst., U.S. Entomol. Commn., 1877-80; curator, Worcester Natural History Soc., 1881-82; prof. zoölogy, Ind. U., 1887-89; prof. biology, U. of Neb., 1889-91, Tufts Coll., 1892-1913; prof. zoölogy, University of Ill., 1913-21, now emeritus. Editor of Standard Natural History, 1882-86, Am. Naturalist, 1884-96, Journal of Morphology, 1910-20. Author: Elements of Comparative Zoölogy, 1896; Vertebrate Zoölogy, 1899; Guides for Vertebrate Dissection, 1907; Comparative Anatomy of Vertebrates, 1912, 3d edit., 1926; Vertebrate Skeleton, 1925. Translator: Hertwig's Manual of Zoölogy, 1902, revised 1912. Home: 2500 Cedar St., Berkeley, Calif. Died Aug. 29, 1929.

KINNEAR, WILSON SHERMAN, civil engr.; b. Circleville, O., May 25, 1864; s. Richard and Mary Hall (Crow) K.; A.B., U. of Kan., 1884, C.E., 1907; m. Carrie M. Nichols, Nov. 13, 1887; children—Mrs. Carmen Johnston, Lawrence Wilson. In ry. constrn. in Middle West and Chile, S.A., 1884-90; asst. engr., asst. chief engr., asst. supt., asst. gen. supt., chief engr. and asst. gen. mgr., M.C. R.R., 1890-1910; pres. Kansas City Terminal Ry. Co., Sept. 1, 1910-May 1, 1912; pres. U.S. Realty & Improvement Co., New York, 1912-17; sr. partner W. S. Kinnear & Co., cons. engrs., New York, 1918. While asst. gen. mgr. Michigan Central R.R.. as chief engr. Detroit River Tunnel Co., built electrically operated tunnel under Detroit River, between Detroit and Windsor, Can., 1 3/4 miles in length and has largest cross-sectional area of any sub-aqueous tunnel in the world. The method employed in constrn. of river section, 1/2 mile in length, was so novel and daring that its successful completion marked an epoch in engring. history, tending to revolutionize sub-aqueous tunnel constrn. Awarded Norman medal, Am. Soc. C.E., 1912. Retired. Home: Grosse Pointe, Mich. Died Aug. 8, 1941.

KINNERSLEY, EBENEZER, educator, elec. experimenter; b. Gloucester, Eng., Nov. 30, 1711; s. William Kinnersley; M.A. (hon.), Coll. of Phila., 1757; m. Sarah Duffield, 1739, 2 children. Came to Am., 1714; ordained to ministry Baptist Ch., 1743; asso. with Benjamin Franklin, Edward Duffield, Philip Synge,

Thomas Hopkins in experiments with elec. fire; rediscovered Dr. DuFaye's 2 contrary electricities of glass and sulphur (led to verification of truth of positive-negative theory); delivered 1st recorded exptl. lectures on electricity in Fanneuil Hall, Boston, 1751; elected chief master Coll. of Phila., 1753, prof. English and oratory, 1755-73; demonstrated heat could be produced by electricity, invented elec. air thermometer, 1755; mem. Am. Philos. Soc. Died Phila., July 4, 1778.

KINNEY, WILLIAM MORTON, engr.; b. Chgo., Mar. 3, 1885; s. William M. C. and Frances E. (Sollitt) K.; M.E., Lewis Inst., Chgo., 1906; m. Loretta M. Hollinger, Feb. 2, 1914. Began as draftsman in Portland, Ore., 1906; with Universal Portland Cement Co., 1907, engr. promotion bur., 1914-18; gen. mgr. and sec. Portland Cement Assn., 1918-30, v.p., gen. mgr., sec., 1930-46, v.p. (promotion and advt.), sec., 1946-49; ret. Mem. Am. Soc. Testing Materials, Western Soc. Engrs., Am. Rd. Builders' Assn.; asso. mem. Am. Soc. C.E. Republican. Baptist. Clubs: Chicago Athletic Assn., Skokie Country (Chgo.). Home: 126 Abingdon Av., Kenilworth, Ill. Died Dec. 1964.

KINNICUTT, LEONARD PARKER, chemist; b. Worcester, Mass., May 22, 1854; s. Francis Harrison and Elizabeth Waldo (Parker) K.; bro. of Francis Parker K.; B.Sc., Mass. Inst. Tech., 1875; univs. of Heidelberg and Bonn, 1875-79, Johns Hopkins, 1879-80; D.Sc., Harvard, 1882; m. Louisa Hoar, d. Dr. Henry Clarke, of Worcester, June 4, 1885 (died 1892); m. 2d, Frances Ayres, d. Josiah H. Clarke, of Worcester, July 8, 1898. Instr. chemistry, Harvard, 1880-83; asst. prof. chemistry, 1883-85, prof., 1885—, dir. Chem. Lab., 1890—, Worcester Poly. Inst. Consulting chemist Conn. Sewage Commn., 1903-05. Fellow Am. Acad. Arts and Sciences, A.A.A.S. (v.p. 1904). Home: Worcester, Mass. Died 1911.

KINSELL, LAURANCE WILKIE, physician; b. Landsdowne, Pa., Oct. 15, 1908; s. S. Tyson and Clementine Keyser (Lynd) K.; M.D., Hahnemann Medical Coll., Phila., 1932, D.Sc., 1965; D.Sc., Blackburn College, 1960; m. Martha L. Williams, September 15, 1934; children—Laura Anne, Judith Scott, Martha Lynd. Intern, resident, grad. work Hahnemann Hosp., Phila., and instns. affiliated with Columbia U., 1932-35; clin. medicine, 1935-39; research fellow Columbia U., 1939-40; research fellow (med. and pharmacology), Harvard U. and Mass. Gen. Hosp., 1941-43; research asso., U. of Cal., 1943-44; United States Navy, 1944-46; consultant in medicine and endocrinology U. Cal. and other hosps. since 1946; asso. clin. prof. medicine U. Cal. Med. Sch., San Francisco, 1948-50; dir. Inst. for Metablolic Research of Highland General Hosp., Oakland, since 1950. Diplomate Am. Bd. Internal Medicine. Fellow A.C.P.; mem. A.M.A., Cal., Alameda Co. medical assns., Endocrine Soc., Am. Diabetes Assn., Am. Fedn. Clin. Research, Western Soc. Clin. Research. Soc. Exptl. Biology and Medicine, Am. Soc. Clin. Nutrition, Am. Inst. Nutrition, Western Assn. Physicians, Alpha Omega Alpha. Asso. editor American Jour. Clin. Nutrition, Metabolism, Excerpta Medica; editor Hormonal Regulations of Energy Metabolism, 1956; Cardiovascular diseases. Author papers and chpts. on endocrinology and metabolism. Home: Oakland CA Died July 9, 1968; buried Mountain View Cemetery, Oakland CA

KINSELLA, THOMAS JAMES, physician; b. Grand Meadow, Minn., Oct. 9, 1895; s. William Dennis and Anne (Grimes) K.; student Mont. State Coll.; M.D., U. Minn., 1920; m. Sara Monahan, Jan. 28, 1924. Intern, Mpls. Gen. Hosp., 1919-20, later attending thoracic surgeon; fellow in medicine Mayo Found., Rochester, Minn., 1920-22; asst. med. dir. Glen Lake Sanatorium, 1925-28, head, dir. thoracic surgery, 1928-36, cons. thoracic surgeon, 1936-69; practice medicine specializing in thoracic surgery, 1936-65; clin. prof. surgery U. Minn., 1949-64, prof. emeritus, 1965-69; sr. cons. thoracic surgery VA Facility, Ft. Snelling, N.D. State Sanatorium; surgeon Minn. State Sanatorium; surg. staff St. Mary's, Abbott, Northwestern hosps.; cons. staff Mt. Sinai Hosp. Diplomate Am. Bd. Thoracic Surgery (founder). Fellow A.C.S., Internat. Coll. Surgeons; mem. A.M.A., Western Surg. Assn., Am. Assn. Thoracic Surgery, Am. Coll. Chest Physicians, Am. Thoracic Soc., Nat. Tb Assn., Alpha Omega Alpha. Author: Tumors of the Chest. Contbr. numerous articles to med. jours. Pioneer non-Tb chest conditions. Home: Minneapolis MN Died Nov. 12, 1969; buried Resurrection Cemetery, Minneapolis MN

KINSEY, ALFRED CHARLES, zoologist, biologist; b. Hoboken, N.J., June 23, 1894; s. Alfred Seguine and Sarah Ann (Charles) K.; B.S., Bowdoin Coll., 1916; Sc.D., Harvard, 1920, Sheldon traveling fellow, 1919-20; m. Clara Bracken McMillen, June 3, 1921; children—Don (dec.), Anne, Joan, Bruce. Asst. in zoology Harvard, 1917-18, in botany, 1918-19; asst. prof. zoology, Ind. U., Bloomington, 1920-23, asso. prof., 1923-29, prof., from 1929, also Waterman research asso.; in charge biol. exploration in Mexico and Central Am., 1931-32, 35-36; in charge study on human sex behavior, supported jointly by Ind. U., Rockefeller Found. and NRC, from 1942. Mem. A.A.A.S., Am. Entomol. Soc., Assn. Econ. Entomologists, Ind. Acad. Sci., N.E. Bot. Club, Am. Soc. Geneticists, Am. Soc. Naturalists, Am. Sociol. Soc., Am. Assn. Marriage Counselors, Acad. Natural Sci., Am. Zoöl. Soc., Am. Iris Soc., Phi Beta Kappa, Sigma Xi. Author: An Introduction to Biology, 1926; Field and Laboratory Manual in Biology, 1927; The Gall Wasp Genus Cynips—A Study in the Origin of Species, 1930; New Introduction to Biology, 1933 (revised 1938); Workbook in Biology, 1934; The Origin of Higher Categories in Cynips, 1936; Methods in Biology, 1937; Edible Wild Plants of Eastern North America (with M. L. Fernald), 1943; Sexual Behavior in the Human Male (with W. B. Pomerov and C. E. Martin). 1948; Sexual Behavior in the Human Female (with W. B. Pomeroy, C. E. Martin and P. H. Gebhard), 1953. Research in early career on gall wasps of Mexico and Central Am., with particular emphasis on life histories, gall formations, evolution, taxonomy and geog. distbn.; most widely known for his extensive studies investigating human sexual behavior, pub. 1948, 53; his program is being continued at Inst. Sex Research, Inc., Bloomington. Died Bloomington, Aug. 25, 1956.

KINSLEY, ALBERT THOMAS, veterinary pathologist; b. Independence, Ia., Feb. 26, 1877; s. John and Jane Elizabeth (Footitt) K.; B.Sc., Kan. State Agrl. Coll., 1899, M.Sc., 1901; U. of Chicago, summer, 1901; Kan. City Vet. Coll., 1902-04, D.V.S., 1904; m. Anna Louisa Smith, Sept. 4, 1901; 1 son, Albert Smith. Instr. bacteriology, Kan. State Agrl. Coll., 1899-1901; pathologist and dir. museum, Kansas City Vet. Coll., 1904-18; organizer, 1909, and pres. Am. Serum Co.; became pres. Kansas City Vet. Coll.; retired, 1941. Originator of use of bacteria in vet. medicine. Pres. Kan. State Coll. Alumni Assn., 1935; del. to Internat. Veterinary Congress, London, 1930. Mem. Am. Vet. Med. Assn. (v.p. 1909-10, pres. 1921-22), Mo. Valley Med. Assn. (pres. 1909-10), Mo. State Vet. Med. Assn.; asso. mem. Jackson County (Mo.) Med. Soc. Mem. Ch. of England. Author: Veterinary Pathology, 1910; Diseases of Swine, 1914; Swine Practice, 1920. Home: 616 E. 59th St., Kansas City, Mo. Died Dec. 8, 1941.

KINSLEY, CARL, elec. engr., physicist; b. Lansing, Mich., Nov. 25, 1870; s. William Wirt and Mary (Jewell) K.; A.B., Oberlin, 1893, A.M., 1896; M.E., Cornell U., 1894; scholar, Johns Hopkins, 1898-99; student Cavendish Lab., Cambridge, Eng., 1905; m. Harriet Buchly, June 1, 1901 (died Oct. 19, 1910); m. 2d, Prudence Ellis, June 7, 1913; children—Colony, Stephanie, Penelope, and Roger (dec.). Instr. in physics and elec. engring., Washington U., 1894-99; elec. expert for War Dept., 1899-1901; fellow in physics, 1901, instr., 1902, asst. prof., 1903, asso. prof., 1909-19, U. of Chicago. Served in U.S. Army, as maj. Signal Corps, Dec. 1917-Aug. 1919; detailed to Gen. Staff and made chief of Sect. 10 of Mil. Intelligence Division, for radio, telegraph and telephone operations; cons. engr. elec. research and development since 1919. Republican. Congregationalist. Fellow A.A.A.S., Am. Physical Soc., Am. Inst. Elec. Engrs.; mem. Am. Soc. Testing Materials, Sigma Xi. Club: Cosmos (Washington). Has invented methods and apparatus of printing telegraph systems, storage batteries, radio circuits and method for non-destructive testing of steel. Contbr. engring. jours. and scientific mags. on radio, telegraphy, alternating currents, testing of steel, etc. Address: Box 905, Falls Church, Va., and Cosmos Club, Washington DC

KINTNER, SAMUEL MONTGOMERY, elec. engr.; b. New Albany, Ind., Dec. 11, 1871; s. James Peter and Anna (Montgomery) K.; B.M.E., Purdue, 1894, hon. Dr. Engring., 1932; D.Sc., U. of Pittsburgh, 1930; m. Elizabeth Blanchard, Oct. 24, 1895 (now dec.); children—John Benham, Eleanor Magee (Mrs. George Constance); m. 2d, Almira Doherty, Jan. 1, 1916. Engr. Bell Telephone Co. of Ind., 1894-95; asst. prof. and prof., Western U. of Pa., 1895-1903; in research labs., Westinghouse Electric & Mfg. Co., 1903-07, in ry. engring. dept., 1907-11; gen. mgr. Nat. Electric Signaling Co., 1911-17, v.p., 1917-19, pres., 1919; in radio research, Westinghouse Electric & Mfg. Co., 1920-22, dir. research labs., 1922-30, asst. v.p., 1930-31, v.p., 1931—; dir. Westinghouse Electric Elevator Co., Westinghouse Lamp Co. Fellow Inst. Radio Engrs., Am. Phys. Society. Republican. Presbyn. Home: Pittsburgh, Pa. Died Sept. 28, 1936.

KIOKEMEISTER, FRED LUDWIG, mathematician, educator; b. Chgo., May 5, 1913; s. Bernhard and Marian (MacMillan) K.; B.A., U. Wis., 1935, M.A., 1937, Ph.D., 1940; m. Evelyn Elizabeth Sharp, Aug. 25, 1940;children—Karen, Elizabeth Ann. Instr. U. Wis., 1940-42, Cornell U., 1942-43, Purdue U., 1943-46; asst. prof. Mt. Holyoke Coll., 1946-48, asso. prof. 1948-56, John Stewart Kennedy Found. prof., 1956-69. Univ. of Wis. fellow, 1938-39, Ford Found. fellow, 1951-52. Mem. Math. Assn. Am., Am. Math. Soc., Sigma Xi, Phi Beta Kappa. author: (with R. E. Johnson) Calculus with Analytic Geometry, 1957, Calculus, 1959. Home: South Hadley MA Died May 26, 1969; buried Walworth WI

KIPP, ORIN LANSING, hwy engr.; b. Wing, Ill., Feb. 18, 1885; s. Dyer Egbert and Mary E. (Basset) K.; B.S., Cornell Coll., Mt. Vernon, Ia., 1909; m. Leona B. Chapman, Feb. 11, 1913; children—Harriet (Mrs. Seth R. Fisher), Dorothy (Mrs. Randall R. Hunt), Mary (Mrs. Edward C. Nicholson), Ralph, Margaret (Mrs. A. N. Felice), Paul, Louise (Mrs. Roal Schneider) (deceased Sept. 1, 1958). Engineer at Mitchell South Dakota, 1909-13; hwy. engr., Redwood Falls, Minn., 1914-16; constrn. engr. Minn. Hwy. Dept., 1916-35; constrn. engr., asst. chief engr., 1935-43, chief engr., asst. commr. hwys. 1943-55, hwy. engring. cons., 1955—. Exec. com. hwy. research bd. NRC. Mem. Am., Miss Valley (pres.) assns. state hwy. ofcls., Minn. Engrs. and Surveyors Soc. (pres.), St. Paul Engrs. Soc. Methodist (ofcl. bd.). Home: 1685 Englewood St. Office: 1246 University St., St. Paul 4. Died Feb. 17, 1958; buried Sunset Meml. Park, Mpls.

KIRBY, DANIEL BARTHOLOMEW, ophthalmologist; b. Cleveland, O., Apr. 12, 1891; s. Daniel Bartholomew and Esther A. Robinson (Whitaker) K.; A.B., John Carroll University, Cleveland, Ohio, 1912, A.M., 1914, LL.D. (honorary), 1948; M.D., Western Reserve University, 1916; post-graduate student at Harvard Pa. University, Cornell University; m. Cecilia Katherine Hahn, June 9, 1923; children—Mary Elizabeth (Mrs. J. Dukes Wooters, Jr.), Mother Joan Kirby, Cecilia (Mrs. Peter Mullen), Janet Whitaker. Resident surgeon Bellevue Hosp., N.Y. City, 1921-23; asso. of Dr. John M. Wheeler, 1923-28; in private practice of ophthalmology since 1923; former surgeon in chief, Dept. of Ophthalmology, Bellevue Hosp., N.Y.; prof. emeritus department of ophthalmology, Coll. of Medicine, New York U.; cons. Surgeon in ophthalmology N.Y. Eye & Ear Infirmary and Manhattan Eye, Ear & Throat Hospital, New Rochelle Hospital. Served as lieut. (s.g.) Med. Corps, U.S. Navy, 1917-19. Former chairman American Board of Ophthalmology. Mem. (hon.) Alumni Assn., N.Y. Eye and Ear Infirmary. Fellow N.Y. Acad. Med., Am. Coll. Surgeons; mem. A.M.A., N.Y. County & State med. societies, Am. and N.Y. ophthal. soc. Am. Acad. Ophthal. and Oto-Laryngol. (research fellow in ophthal., 1923-29), Harvey Society, ophthal. socs. of Brazil, Argentina, Chile, Peru, Cuba, France, Greece. Awarded Schneider prize in ophthalmology. Roman Catholic (K.M., K.H.S.). Clubs: Union (N.Y.C.); Pelham Country; Lippincott (Phila.). Author of "Diseases of the Crystalline Lens" in Eye and its Diseases, edited by Conrad Berens, 1936; "The Crystalline Lens and Cataract" in Diseases of the Eye. edited by George Blumer, 1937; Surgery of Cataract, 1950; Advanced Surgery of Cataract, pub. 1955. Contributed many articles to ophthalmological and med. jours., including The Development of a System of Intracapsular Cataract Extraction in American Journal Ophthalmology, March 1942. Home: 76 Mount Tom Road, Pelham Manor, New York. Office: 780 Park Ave., N.Y.C. Died Dec. 27, 1953; buried Gate of Heaven Cemetery, Hawthorne, N.Y.

KIRBY, EDMUND BURGIS, consulting mining engr.; b. Lyme, Conn.; s. Eliab Burgis and Caroline Lydia (Noyes) K.; E.M., Washington U., St. Louis, 1884; unmarried. Engaged in gen. consulting practice, with intervals of mine, mill or smelter management, 1885—. Home: New York, N.Y. Deceased.

KIRK, CHARLES TOWNSEND, geologist; b. Francisco, Ind., June 22, 1876; s. David Henry and Martha Jane (Townsend) K.; B.S., U. of Okla., 1904, A.M., 1905; Ph.D., U. of Wis., 1911; m. Bessie Keller, Aug. 22, 1906; children—Ora Jane, Betty Clare, David Keller, Florence Nell. Instr. in geology, State School of Mines, Butte, Mont., 1906-08; instr. in correspondence sch., U. of Wis., 1908-10; instr. and asst. prof. geology, Hunter College, New York City, 1910-13; prof. geology U. of N.M., and state geologist, 1913-17; field geologist, U.S. Geol. Survey, 1910-11, 1934-36, 1938-39. Examinations mining, petroleum and natural gas lands and dam sites in Rocky Mountains, Mid-Continent and Spanish America since 1909. Installed Okla. Mineral Exhibit, La. Purchase Expn., St. Louis, 1904; judge of exhibits Panama Pacific International Exposition San Francisco, California, 1915. Member A.A.A.S., Geological Society of America, Am. Inst. Mining and Metall. Engrs., Am. Assn. Petroleum Geologists, N.Y. Acad. Sciences (sec. geol. sect. 1913), N.M. Geog. Soc. (sec. 1916-17), N.M. Assn. Science (pres. 1916), Tulsa Geol. Soc. (pres. 1923), Sigma Xi, Phi Kappa Phi. Democrat. Mem. Christian (Disciples) Ch. Mason (32 deg.). Wrote: Pennsylvanian-Permian Contact through Oklahoma, 1904; Mineralization in the Copper Veins at Butte, Montana, 1912; The Geography of New Mexico, 1917; Significant Features in Western Coal Deposits; Steep Subsurface Folds versus Faults, 1926. Reviews and contbns. to scientific mags. Home: 1226 S. Newport Av., Tulsa, Okla. Died June 1, 1945.

KIRK, RAYMOND ELLER, chemist; b. Hamilton County, Neb., June 24, 1890; s. Joseph Alexander and Virginia Eads (Eller) K.; student Neb. State Normal, Kearney, 1910-13; B.S., U. of Neb., 1915; M.S., Ia. State Coll., 1917; Ph.D., Cornell, 1927; student U. of Chicago, summer 1919; m. Beth Sibley, June 30, 1920; children—Virginia, Josephine Alvira. Instr. in chemistry, Ia. State Coll., 1917-20; asst. prof. chemistry, U. of Minn., 1920-27, asso. prof., 1927-29; prof. and head dept. of chemistry, Mont. State Coll., and state chemist, 1929-31; prof. and head dept of chemistry, Poly. Inst., Brooklyn, N.Y., 1931-55; dir. Shellac Research Bureau, 1936-42; also dean of the graduate school, 1944—. Served as civilian insp. Ordnance Dept. United States Army, 1917-18; captain Ordnance Reserve, 1923-30; major 1930-42. Fellow Am. Inst. Chemists, A.A.A.S.; mem. Am. Chem. Soc., Am. Assn.

Univ. Profs., Sigma Xi, Phi Lambda Upsilon, Alpha Chi Sigma, Phi Kappa Phi, Gamma Alpha, Delta Sigma Rho. Author: Laboratory Manual in Inorganic Chemistry (with M. C. Sneed), 1927. Co-editor Encyclopedia of Chemical Technology (15 volumes), 1947-56). Medical bd. editors Inorganic Synthesis, 1939. Contbr. to sci. jours. Home: 9269 Shore Rd., Bklyn. 9. Died Feb. 6, 1957.

KIRKHAM, WILLIAM BARRI, biologist; b. at Springfield, Mass., Feb. 11, 1882; s. James Wilson and Fanny Curtis (Barri) K.; B.A., Yale, 1904, M.A., 1906, Ph.D. 1907; studied Harvard, 1904-05; m. Irma Chapman, June 25, 1910; 1 dau., Marguerite. Archaeol. trip around the world, 1907-08; instr. biology, Sheffield Scientific Sch. (Yale), 1908-16; asst. prof. biology, same, 1916-20; prof. biology, Internat. Y.M.C.A. Coll., Springfield, Mass., 1921-30, also dean freshmen until 1930; cons. dir. Museum Natural History, Springfield, from 1930; v.p. Springfield Library and Mus. Assn., 1934-41, and from 1959, pres., 1941-59. Dir. Springfield Safe Deposit & Trust Co. from 1938. President Oak Grove Cemetery Assn., 1947-51 Lectr. on scientific subjects. Recipient Pynchon medal, Springfield Advt. Club, 1958. Mem. Am. Assn. for the Advancement of Sci., American Assn. Anatomists. Am. Soc. Zoologists, Am. Anthrop. Assn., New York Zool. Soc., Sigma Xi. Beta Theta Pi. Republican. Conglist. Author: You and I and the Universe, 1948. Contbr. result of researches on embryonic development of mice. Home: Springfield MA Died May 14, 1969.

KIRKLAND, ARCHIE HOWARD, entomologist; b. Huntington, Mass., June 4, 1873; s. Charles Henry and Jane Elizabeth (Parsons) K.; B.S., Mass. Agrl. Coll., 1894, M.S., 1896; unmarried. Asst. entomologist, Mass. Hatch Expt. Station, 1892-94; asst. entomologist, Mass. Bd. Agr., Gypsy Moth Commn., 1894-1900; entomologist Bowker Insecticide Co., 1900-05; state supt. Gypsy Moth work, 1905-09; agt. and expert, U.S. Bur. of Entomology, 1911—. Home: Huntington, Mass. Died 1931.

KIRKLIN, BYRL RAYMOND, radiologist; b. Gaston, Ind., Sept. 22, 1888; s. John Walter and Sarah Lavina (McCreery) K.; B.S., Indiana U., 1926, M.D., 1914; m. Gladys Marie Webster, June 3, 1915; children—John Webster, Mary Webster. Radiologist Muncie (Ind.) Home Hosp. and private practice, 1916-25; radiologist Mayo Clinic, Rochester, Minn., 1926-54, chmn. sects. on Radiology, prof. radiology, Mayo Foundation, Univ. of Minn., 1936-54. Served as 1st lt., M.C., United States Army, World War I; col., M.C., U.S. Army, sr. X-ray consultant Office of Surgeon Gen., World War II; ret. col. M.C. Res.; sr. cons. to surgeon gen., U.S. Army and to USAF. Past pres. Muncie Home Hosp. staff, Diplomate and mem. bd. trustees Am. Bd. Radiology (sec.-treas.); mem. adv. bd. med. specialties (sec.-treas.). Fel. Am. Coll. Radiology (pres. 1942-43), Am. Coll. Physicians, A.M.A., hon. fel. Internat. Coll. Surgeons; mem. Am. Roentgen Ray Society (pres. 1937-38), Radiol. Soc. North America, Minn. State and Olmsted County med. assns., Minn. Radiol. Soc. (pres. 1930), Am. Assn. Gastro-enterologists, Central Soc. Clin. Research, Am. Assn. Ry. Surgeons, Southern Minnesota Medical Association; corresponding mem. Academia Nacional de Medicina Republic de Colombia; hon. mem. Die Deutsche Röntgen-Gesellschaft (Germany), Royal Soc. Medicine (Eng.). Assn. Gastroenterologists of Paris (France), Soc. Colombiana de Radiologia, Soc. Mexicana de Radiologia y Fisioterapia, Soc. de Radiologia y Fisioterapia de Cuba, Chicago Roentgen Soc., St. Louis Med. Soc., Muncie Acad. Medicine (pres. 1921, 22), Dallas Southern Clin. Soc., Miss Valley Med. Assn.; mem. Sigma Chi, Phi Rho Sigma, Sigma Xi. Republican Methodist. Mason. Clubs: Univ., Rochester Country, Rotary (Rochester, Minn.); Army and Navy (Washington). Contbr. to med. jours. Home: 725 11th St., S.W. Office: Kahler Hotel Bldg., Rochester, Minn. Died Mar. 2, 1957; buried Rochester.

KIRKPATRICK, ELBERT W., horticulturist; b. Whitesburg, Tenn., Oct. 12, 1844; s. Jacob M. and Sarah Jane (Campbell) K.; self educated; removed to Collin Co., Tex., 1854; m. Emily T. Clive, Nov. 5, 1874. Took charge of mother's farm at 13; pvt. in C.S.A., 1862-65, Martin's regt. Tex. Brigade, Trans-Miss. Dept.; in 8 battles; wounded at battle of Cabin Creek, Ind. Ty.; taught 1st pub. sch. in Collin Co., 1872; practiced land surveying, 1873, 74; established 1874, and became pres. of the Texas Nursery Co., Whitesboro Orchard & Fruit Co., Nueces Land & Immigration Co.; also farmer and fruit grower. Mem. State Council Defense; co. chmn. Y.M.C.A. War-Fund Com., and Food Conservation Com. Home: McKinney, Tex. Died Mar. 24, 1924.

KIRKPATRICK, SIDNEY DALE, chem. engr., cons.; born Urbana, Ill., Apr. 2, 1894; s. Frederick Dilling and Virginia Mae (Hedges) K.; B.S., U. of Ill., 1916, grad. study, 1916-17; Sc.D., Clarkson Coll. of Tech., 1946; D. Engring., Polytechnic Institute, Brooklyn, 1948; m. Bonnie Jean Hardesty, Aug. 6, 1919; children—Mary (Mrs. A. H. Gable), S. Dale, Chemist and editor Ill. State Water Survey, 1916-17; chem. adviser U.S. Tariff Commn., 1917-18, spl. expert with same, 1919-21; with McGraw-Hill Pub. Co., N.Y.C., 1921-59, as asst. editor Chemical & Metall. Engineering (mag.), 1921-25, asso. editor, 1925-28, editor, 1928-50; editorial dir. Chem. Engring. and Chemical Week, 1950-59; v.p., McGraw-Hill Book Co., ret. 1959; director General Aniline & Film Corp., Mich. Chem. Corp., 1960-61, Carus Chem. Co., Roger Williams Tech. & Econ. Services, Inc.; cons. engr., 1959-73. Served as 2d lt. and lst lt. S.C., A.E.F., 1918-19; chem. advisor Am. Commn. to Negotiate Peace, 1919; mem. referee bd., Office of Prodn. Research and Development, War Prodn. Bd., 1942-45; cons. on engring., W.M.C., 1942-45; member advisory bd. U.S. C.W.S., 1935-62; consultant on research to U.S.Q.M.C., 1943-45, to tech. indsl. intelligence com. investigating Germany, 1945, to sec. of war, Operations Crossroads, Bikini, 1946; consultant U.S. Atomic Energy Commission, 1950-55; chmn. AEC, adv. com. on information for industry, 1950-55, Recipient Founders award, Am. Inst. Chem. Engrs., 1958; Meml. award, Chem. Market Research Assn., 1959, Fellow Am. Institute Chemists, 1949, hon. member, 1952; mem. Am. Inst. Chem. Engrs. (dir. 1932-39, 1946-49; v.p. 1940-41; pres. 1942), Am. Electrochem. Soc. (dir. 1933-35; v.p. 1931-35; pres. 1944-45), Am. Chem. Soc. (councillor), Society Chemical Industry Great Britain (dir. 1942-44; chmn. 1946-47), A.A.A.S., Am. Soc. Engring. Edn., Sigma Xi, Phi Lambda Upsilon, Alpha Chi Sigma, Sigma Delta Chi, Pi Delta Epsilon, Omega Chi Epsilon, Theta Delta Chi. Awarded silver anniversary medal American Institute Chemical Engineers, 1932; Chemical Industry medalist, 1945. Republican. Methodist. Clubs: Chemists (trustee), Western Universities. Editor: Twenty Five Years of Chemical Engineering Progress. 1933. Co-editor: Perry's Chemical Engineers' Handbook, 1963; cons. editor Chem. Engring. series (36 titles). Contbr. to Chem. Engring. Address: Short Hills NJ Died Feb. 1973.

KIRKWOOD, ARTHUR CARTER, cons. engr.; b. Colorado Springs, Colo., June 17, 1900; s. Thomas Carter and Lillie Marie (Gard) K.; A.B. in Mech. Engring., Stanford U., 1923; M.S. in Elec. Engring., Mass. Inst. Tech., 1924; m. Frances Noble Tucker, June 20, 1925; children—Thomas C., Beverley John, Ann Marie (dec.), Jr. engr., field engr., Wood & Weber, Cons. Engrs., Denver, 1924-29; asso. engr., Burns & McDonnell Engring. Co., Cons. Engrs., Kansas City, Mo., 1930-40, prin. engr., 1940-47; founder, A.C. Kirkwood & Assos., Cons. Engrs., 1947, sr. partner 1951-70, pres., dir. Kirkwood Assos., Inc., Con. Engrs., 1955-70. Bd. Govs., adv. com. Kansas City Citizen's Assn., 1945-70; chmn. Mo. Adv. Com. for Sci. Engring. & Specialized Personnel of Selective Service System, 1955-70. Mem. adv. bd. Kansas City council Boy Scouts Am. Registered profl. engr., Kan., Mo., Colo., Okla., Ark., Ill., Mich., Ore. Mem. I.E.E.E. (life mem.), Engrs. Club Kansas City (pres. 1939, life mem.), Kan. Engring. Soc., Am. Soc. M.E. (life), Am. Inst. Cons. Engrs., Nat. (nat. dir. 1954-57, chmn. bd. Ethical Rev. 1965-66, v.p. 1966-70), Mo. (pres. 1956) socs. profl. engrs., Am. Water Works Assn., Nat. Assn. Housing and Redevel. Ofcls. Rotarian. Home: Kansas City MO Died Oct. 5, 1970; buried Kansas City MO

KIRKWOOD, DANIEL, astronomer, educator; b. Harford County, Md., Sept. 27, 1814; s. John and Agnes (Hope) K.; A.M. (hon.), Washington Coll., 1849; m. Sarah McNair, 1845. Prin., Lancaster (Pa.) High Sch., 1843-49, Pottsville Acad., 1849-51; prof. mathematics Del. Coll., 1851-56, pres., 1854-56; prof. mathematics Ind. U., 1856-65, 1867-86; prof. mathematics and astronomy Jefferson Coll., Canonsburg., Pa.; apptd. lectr. Leland Stanford Jr. U., 1891; mem. Am. Philos. Soc., 1852; published his formula for rotation periods of planets in Proceedings of A.A.A.S., 1849, article on comets and meteors in Danville Quarterly Review, 1861. Author: Meteoric Astronomy, 1867; Comets and Meteors, 1873. Died Riverside, Cal., June 11, 1895.

KIRKWOOD, JOHN GAMBLE, chemist; b. Gotebo, Okla., May 30, 1907; s. John Millard and Lillian (Gamble) K.; student Calif. Inst. of Tech., 1923-25; S.B., University of Chicago, 1926, D.Sci. (hon.), 1954; Ph.D., Massachusetts Institute of Tech., 1929; Sc.D. (honorary), University of Brussels, 1959; m. Lillian Gladys Danielson, Sept. 5, 1930 (div. 1952); married 2d, Platonia P. Kaldes, March 11, 1958. 1 son, John Millard. Nat. research fellow Harvard, 1929-30; internat. research fellow, Leipzig and Munich, 1931-32; research asso., Mass. Inst. of Tech., 1930-31, 1932-34; asst. prof. of chemistry, Cornell, 1934-37, asso. prof., U. of Chicago, 1937-38; Todd prof. of chemistry Cornell, 1938-47; former Arthur Ames Noyes prof. chemistry, Calif. Inst. Tech., Sterling Prof. and chmn. Dept. Chemistry, Yale, dir. division of science, 1956—; Lorentz professor theoretical physics, U. Leiden, 1959. Received Am. Chem. Soc. award in pure chem., 1936, Theodore William Richards medal of Am. Chem. Soc., 1950, Gilbert Newton Lewis Medal, 1953. Fellow American Academy of Arts and Sciences, American Phys. Society; mem. Am. Chem. Soc., Nat. Acad. Scis. (fgn. sec.), Am. Philos. Soc., N.Y. Acad. Sci., Sigma Xi, Sigma Chi. Contbr. articles to scientific jours. Address: Sterling Chemical Laboratory, 225 Prospect St., New Haven. Died Aug. 9, 1959; buried Grove St. Cemetery, New Haven.

KIRSCHBAUM, ARTHUR, anatomist; b. N.Y.C., Oct. 15, 1910; s. Morris Lyon and Etta (Rosenbloom) K.; B.S., N.Y.U., 1931; M.A., U. Minn., 1933, Ph.D., 1936, M.D., 1943; fellow anatomy Yale, 1937-38, 39-40; m. Nylene Elvira Eckles, Sept. 10, 1943; children—Lynn Arthur, Todd Bittner. Teaching asst. zoology U. Minn., 1931-34, teaching fellow anatomy, 1934-37, instr., 1941-42, asst. prof., 1942-45, asso. prof. anatomy, 1945-51; instr. anatomy Yale, 1938-39, 40-41; prof., head dept. anatomy U. Ill. Coll. Medicine, 1951-54; prof., chmn. dept anatomy Baylor U. Coll. Medicine, 1954—, U. Tex. dental br., 1954—; cons. exptl. hematologist U. Texas M.D. Anderson Hosp and Tumor Inst., 1954—; cons. VA Hosp., 1956—. Cons. USPHS, 1951-55, 56—, VA, 1956—; consultant to committee on growth NRC, 1955-56; chmn. Gordon Cancer Conf., 1957—. Recipient Am. Cancer Soc. award, Minn., 1951. Mem. Am. Assn. Cancer Research (sec. S.W. sect. 1955—), A.A.A.S., Am. Soc. Exptl. Pathology, Soc. Exptl. Biology and Medicine, Am. Assn. Anatomists, Internat. Assn. Dental Research, Sigma Xi, Phi Beta Kappa. Mem. adv. editorial bd. Cancer Research, 1949—. Home: 4055 Tartan Lane. Office: M. D. Anderson Blvd., Houston. Died May 28, 1958; buried Houston.

KIRWIN, THOMAS JOSEPH, urologist; b. Frederick, Md., 1891; s. James John and Margaret Mary (Surplus) K.; Ph.C., B.S., U. Mich., 1910; grad. student U. Wis. 1912-13; M.D., Tulane, 1916. Cornell, 1917; M.A. in anatomy, Columbia, 1923; M.S. in surgery, Yale, 1929; m. Margaret Hughes, Sept. 8, 1917; 1 dau., Ruth Ann (Mrs. William S. McLean). Instr. in urology, Cornell Med. Coll., 1920-22; instr. in embryology, histology, Columbia, 1921-23; chief of clinic, adjunct vis. urologist James Buchanan Brady Found., Dept. Urology, N.Y. Hosp.; attending genito-urinary surgeon, N.Y.C. Hosp., Welfare Island; cons. urologist Coney Island Hosp. (Bklyn.), Benedictine Hosp. (Kingston), Monmouth Meml. Hosp. (Long Branch, N.J.), South Nassau Communities Hosp.; prof. urology N.Y. Med. Coll.; dir. of urology Flower and Fifth Avenue Hosp., Met. Hosp.; dir. Bird S. Coler Hosp. Served as capt. M.C., U.S. Army, France, World War I (Arsne-Marne, Orse-Arsne, Saint Mihiel, Meuse-Argonne, Ypres-Lys). Certified by Bd. Urology. Fellow N.Y. Acad. Medicine, Am. Coll. Surgeons, Internat. Coll. Surgeons; mem. A.M.A., N.Y. State and County med. socs., Am. Urol. Soc., Italian Urol. Soc., Societa de Obstetrica Gynecology et Urology (Rumania), Internat. Urol. Soc., Societas Japonica Urologiae (hon.), Delta Tau Delta, Nu Sigma Nu, Sigma Zi. Clubs: University, Yale, University of Michigan (N.Y.C.). Author: (with Dr. O. S. Lowsley) Textbook of Urology, 1926, Urology for Nurses, 1936, Clinical Urology (2 vols.), 1940. Author Chpt. Oxford Loose Leaf Surgery; chpt., Diseases of the Ureter, in Ency. of Medicine; Diseases of the Ureter, in Cyclopedia of Medicine. Contbr. numerous articles on surg. subjects to sci. jours. Devised instruments known as the Kirwin vesical neck resector, Kirwin prostatic resector, Kirwin Lithrotrite, Kirwin radon seed implanter, Kirwin measuring device for bladder tumor, Kirwin Automatic resectoscope, Kirwin cystoscope. Home: 21 E. 90th St., N.Y.C. 28. Office: 1 E. 63d St., N.Y.C. 21. Died Aug. 18, 1959.

KITCHIN, THURMAN DELNA, physician, educator; b. Scotland Neck, N.C., Oct. 17, 1885; s. William Hodge and Maria Figus (Arrington) K.; grad. Vine Hill Male Acad., Scotland Neck, 1902; A.B., Wake Forest (N.C.) College, 1905; student U. of N.C., 1905-06; M.D., Jefferson Med. Coll., Phila., 1908; LL.D., Duke U., 1931, U. N.C., 1933, Davidson College, 1947; spl. student in physiology Columbia, summer 1921; m. Reba Calvert Clark, Nov. 3, 1908; children—Thurman Delna, Irwin Clark, William Walton. Practiced at Lumberton, N.C., 1908; moved to Scotland Neck, N.C., 1910; prof. physiology Wake Forest Coll., 1917, pres., 1930-50, prof. physiology and hygiene, 1950—, dean Sch. of Medicine, 1919-30. Apptd. by Governor McLean mem. spl. com. to study problem of feebleminded in N.C., 1925; mem. bd. dirs. N.C. Sanatorium for Tb. Mem. Vets. Adminstrn. spl. com. on rehabilitation and edn. problems; mem. N.C. adv. council on Unemployment Compensation Commn.; chmn. N.C. Adv. Council for Employment Security Commn.; rep. of the Am. Assn. of Colls. Adv. Council on Med. Edn. Fellow A.C.P., A.A.A.S.; mem. A.M.A., So. Med. Dist. (pres. 1926-27), Wake County med. socs., Assn., Tri-State (president 1928-29) 6th District (president 1926-27), Wake County medical socs., Am. Gastroenterological Assn., Omicron Delta Kappa, Delta Kappa Epsilon, Phi Chi, Phi Beta Kappa. Democrat. Baptist. Mason. Author: Lectures on Pharmacology, 1929; The Doctor and Citizenship, 1934; Doctors in Other Fields, 1938. Home: Wake Forest, N.C. Died Aug. 28, 1955; buried Trinity Cemetery, Scotland Neck, N.C.

KITTREDGE, GEORGE WATSON, civil engr.; b. N. Andover, Mass., Dec. 11, 1856; s. Joseph and Henrietta Frances (Watson) K.; B.S., Mass. Inst. Tech., 1877; m. Georgia Davis, Oct. 17, 1888. With Pa. Lines West of Pittsburgh, 1880-90; engr. Louisville Bridge Co., 1886-88; engr. maintenance of way and asst. chief engr., 1890-91, chief engr., 1891-1906, C.,C.,C.&St.L. Ry.; chief engr. Louisville & Jeffersonville Bridge Co., 1900-06; chief engr. N.Y.C.&H. R.R.R. and Terminal Ry. of Buffalo and of N.J. Shore Line R.R., 1906-14; chief engr. N.Y. Central R.R., 1914-27, also chief engr. Hudson River Connecting R.R., Am. Niagara R.R., 1914-27 (retired); cons. engr. since 1927. Mem. Corp. Mass. Inst. Tech., 1907-12. Fellow A.A.A.S.; hon. mem.

Am. Soc. C.E. (v.p. 1917-18), Am. Ry. Engring. Assn. (ex-pres.). Home: 592 N. Broadway, Yonkers, N.Y. Died Aug. 23, 1947.

KITTS, JOSEPH ARTHUR, (kitz), cons. engr. and concrete technologist; b. Nevada City, Calif., Apr. 14, 1881; s. James and Mary Alice (Rafford) K.; student U. of Calif., 1900-03, 1908-09; m. Alberta Waldo Hawley, Sept. 10, 1912; children—James Waldo, Mary Elisabeth, Jean Josephine. Mining, surveys and constrn., Nevada City Mines, 1900-05; engr. of constrn., Panama Canal, 1905-06; engr. and supt. constrn., C. A. Meusdorfer, Couchot & O'Shaughnessy and Union Constrn. Co., San Francisco, 1906-10; engr. of surveys, concrete tests, design and constrn., Panama Canal, 1910-15; resident and field engr. U.S. Steel Co., Sonoma County Highway Commn., Calif. Highway Commn., Portland Cement Co., 1915-24; cons. concrete technologist, operating as Joseph A. Kitts Co., San Francisco, since 1924. Served as capt. Engr. Corps, U.S. Army, in France, 1917-19. Mem. Alpha Tau Omega (pres. Gamma Iota Asso.), Calif. Alumni Assn., Am. Concrete Inst., Am. Legion, Am. Red Cross. Awarded Roosevelt Panama Canal medal and bars; Victory medal with France bar. Author: Coordination of Basic Principles of Concrete Mixtures, 1933; Specifications for Structural Concrete, 1937. Contbr. to Concrete (Mag.). Inventor erosion control, water conservation, irrigation system, in use in exptl. project, Town Talk, Calif., since 1944. Home: Nevada City, Calif. Office: Rialto Bldg., San Francisco. Died March 1947.

KJELLGREN, BENGT R. F., beryllium mfr.; b. Dalby, Sweden, July 19, 1894; s. Hugo and Hulda (Johanson) K.; student Swedish pub.; pvt. schs.; Chem.E., Royal Inst. Tech., Stockholm, 1918; grad. student Mass. Inst. Tech., 1923-24; m. Florence M. Gylfe, Oct. 3, 1925; 1son, Bengt Hugo. Asst. plant engr. Bergman Mfg. Co., Trollhattan, Sweden, 1918-20; asst. to chief engr. Hoganas-Billesholm Corp., Hoganas, Sweden, 1920-22; research engr. Uddeholms Corp., Skoghall, Sweden, 1922-23; research engr. Brush Labs. Co., Cleve., 1924-31, v.p., dir., 1931-68; v.p. Brush Beryllium Co., Cleve., 1935-48, pres., 1948-60, chmn. board, mem. exec. com. 1960-68; formerly chief exec. officer, also dir. Recipient Modern Pioneer award, 1940. Mem. Am. Chem. Soc., Electrochem. Soc., Inst. of Metals (London), Cleve. C. of C. Clubs: Mentor Harbor (O.) Yacht; University (Cleve.). Author tech. articles on beryllium and alloys. Holder patents on beryllium and alloys, on crystals prodn. piezoelectric. Home: Chagrin Falls OH Died Nov. 10, 1968; buried N. Rada, Varmland Sweden

KLAUBER, LAURENCE MONROE, elec. engr.; b. San Diego, Calif., Dec. 21, 1883; s. Abraham and Theresa (Epstein) K.; A.B., Stanford Univ., 1908; honorary LL.D., University of California, 1941; Westinghouse Grad. Apprenticeship Course, 1910; m. Grace Gould, Nov. 29, 1911; children—Alice Gould (Mrs. David M. Miller), Philip Monroe. With San Diego Gas & Electric Co. since 1911, successively salesman, engr., dept. supt., v.p. operation, v.p. gen. mgr., pres., 1946-49, chmn. bd., 1949-53, cons. 1953-65; member board of directors Klauber Wangenheim Co. Chmn. San Diego Pub. Library Commn.; chmn. citizens com. San Diego County Air Pollution Control Bd. Lectr. biology, Stanford U.; cons. curator of reptiles, San Diego Zool. Soc.; cons. curator of herpetology and patron San Diego Soc. Natural History. Fellow I.E.E.E., A.A.A.S., California Acad. Sciences (hon.), Am. Geog. Soc., Acad. Zoology of India (honorary), member American Soc. C.E., Am. Soc. M.E., Am. Chem. Soc., Pacific Coast Elec. Assn. (pres. 1923-24), Am. Gas Assn., Pacific Coast Gas Assn. (pres. 1927-28), Am. Math. Soc., Math. Assn. America, Seismol. Soc. Am., Am. Mus. Natural Hist. (corr. mem.), Am. Soc. Ichthyologists and Herpetologists (pres. 1938-40), San Diego Zool. Soc. (pres. 1949-51), Am. Meteorol. Soc., Am. and Cal. Folklore Socs., Cal. Hist. Soc., Am. Ecological Soc., So. Cal. Acad. Sci., Internat. Society Toxinology, Society Industrial and Applied Mathematics, Southern California Air Pollution Control Council, Western Soc. of Naturalists (pres. 1946), Am. Statist. Assn., Soc. Systematic Zoology, (pres. 1955) Inst. Math. Statistics, Herpetologists League, Am., California library associations, also Biometric Soc., Sigma Xi, Tau Beta Pi. Republican. Rotarian. Author various publs. on elec. distribution, also reptiles, including Rattlesnakes: Their Habits and Life Histories, 2 vols., 1956, rev. edit., 1972. Home: San Diego CA Died May 8, 1968; buried Home of Peace Cemetery, San Diego CA

KLEIN, JOSEPH FREDERIC, mechanical engr.; b. Paris, France, Oct. 10, 1849; Ph.B., Sheffield Scientific School (Yale), 1871, D.E., 1873; m. Ada Louise Warner, Dec. 30, 1879. Instr. mech. engring., Sheffield Scientific Sch., 1877-81; prof. mech. engring., 1881—, dean, Sept. 1, 1907—, Lehigh U. Author: Elements of Machine Design, 1889; Design of a High-Speed Steam Engine, 1892; Physical Significance of Entropy, 1910. Home: Bethlehem, Pa. Died Feb. 11, 1918.

KLEIN, SIMON ROBERT, M.D., pathologist; b. Teplitz, Hungary, Dec. 23, 1868; s. Jacob M. and Augusta (Pollatschek) K.; A.B., Ungvar Coll., 1886; M.D., Royal Univ., Budapest, 1892, Ph.D., 1895; M.D., Vienna U., 1900; M.D., Ch.D., Tubingen U., 1902; hon. D.P.H., Budapest U.; hon. Dr. Mus., Vienna Musical U.; m. Sophie J. D. Van Schack, of Bremen, Germany, Jan. 14, 1905; children—Arthur Lee, Erna Columbia, Harold James. Came to U.S. and naturalized, 1900. Served as adj. prof. pathology at Royal Univ. and as asst. prof. pathology at Tubingen U.; was prof. pathology, histology and embryology, Fordham U., New York; prof. biology and dean pre-med. dept., St. Mary's Coll., at Emmitsburg, Md., 1914-16; chief pathologist Norwich State Hosp. for the Insane, 1920-28; reserve surgeon Police Dept., N.Y.C.; head of Klein's Pathol., Bacteriol., Serol. and Biochemical Laboratory. Mem. N.Y. Pathol., Clin. Research Soc., Acad. of Medicine. Catholic. Contbr. papers and articles on med. and surg. subjects. Home: 2554 37th St., Astoria, Long Island City, N.Y.

KLEINER, ISRAEL S(IMON), educator; b. New Haven, Apr. 8, 1885; s. Isaac Lyon and Helen (Bretzfelder) K.; Ph.B., Yale, 1906, Ph.D., 1909; student Cambridge U., Eng., U. Berlin Germany, Copenhagen U., 1914; Sc.D., N.Y. Med., Coll., 1960; m. Alma Kempner, Mar. 27, 1912 (died May 1956); children—Ruth Alma (Mrs. Arnold Glantz), Richard. Asst. physiol. chemistry Yale, 1907-09; instr. chemistry Tulane U. Sch. Medicine, 1909-10; asst. physiology Rockefeller Inst. Med. Research, 1910-14, asso., 1914-19; prof. biochemistry N.Y. Med. Coll., 1919—, dean, 1921-25, dir. dept., 1948-60; staff biol. lab., Cold Spring Harbor, 1928-33; cons. chemist Flower and Fifth Av. Hosps., Met. Hosp., N.Y.C. Recipient Van Slyke award Am. Assn. Clin. Chemists, 1959; alumni award N.Y. Med. Coll., 1959. Diplomate Am. Bd. Clin. Chemistry, Fellow Am. Assn. Clin. Chemists, A.A.A.S., N.Y. Acad. Sci., N.Y. Acad. Medicine; mem. Harvey Soc., Am; Physiol. Soc., Am. Soc. Biol. Chemists, Am. Soc. Pharmacology, Am. Inst. Nutrition, Am. Assn. Clin. Chemists (chmn. N.Y. sect. 1951-52), Soc. Exptl. Biology and Medicine (exec. com. N.Y. sect. 1952-54), NRC (panel appraisers, handbook biol. data), Sigma Xi, Alpha Omega Alpha (hon.). Jewish religion. Mason. Author: Lab. Instructions in Biochemistry (with L. B. Dotti), 1940; Human Biochemistry, 1945, 6th edit. (with J. M. Orten) Biochemistry (new title), 1962; also sci. articles. Home: 27 W. 96th St., N.Y.C. 25; also New Preston, Conn. Office: 20 E. 106th St., N.Y.C. 29. Died June 10, 1966.

KLEINPELL, WILLIAM DARWIN, geologist; b. N.Y.C., Apr. 9, 1898; s. William Ernest and Alma (Wilke) K.; B.A., Stanford, 1921; m. Fay Baker, Dec. 1, 1927; children—Jean Fay (Mrs. C. Don Horton), Karoline Kay (Mrs. Harold Rosoff). Cons. petroleum geologist, 1932—; dir. Kern County Land Co., San Francisco, 1948—, Intex Oil Co., 1950—. Mem. Am. Assn. Petroleum Geologists, Am. Inst. Mining and Metall. Engrs., Am. Geog. Soc., A.A.A.S. Home: 809 Oleander St. Office: Haberfield Bldg., Bakersfield, Cal. Died Apr. 1959.

KLEMIN, ALEXANDER, aero. cons.; b. London, Eng. May 15, 1888; s. Albert and Dora (Clemens) K.; B.S., London U., 1909; S.M., Mass. Inst. Tech., 1915; LL.D., Kenyon College, 1934; D.Eng., N.Y.U., 1950; m. Ethel Murton, 1921; 1 dau., Diana. Came to U.S., 1913, naturalized, 1917. In charge aeronautics dept. Mass. Inst. Tech., 1916-17; officer in charge of Research Dept. Army Air Service, McCook Field, Dayton, O., during World War; cons. aero. engr., 1919-24; in charge Daniel Guggenheim Sch. of Aeronautics, N.Y.U., 1924-41; research prof. N.Y.U., 1942-44; lectr. aeros. Princeton, 1934-35; cons. engr. Aero. Br., Dept. of Commerce, 1927-29; designed first amphibian landing gear used in U.S., 1921. Mem. aerodynamics and rotation wing aircraft coms. NACA. Winner of army and navy airplane design competitions; Dr. Alexander Klemin ann. award established by Am. Helicopter Soc., 1951. Fellow Inst. Aero. Scis.; mem. Am. Soc. M.E., Soc. Automotive Engrs., Royal Aero. Soc., Am. Helicopter Soc. (pres. 1949-50). Helicopter editor Aero Digest; editor Handbook of Aeronautical Engineering. Episcopalian. Club: Wings. Author: Textbook of Aeronautical Engineering, 1918; If You Want to Fly, 1926; Simplified Aerodynamics, 1927; Airplane Stress Analysis, 1927; The Helicopter Adventure, 1947; (with A. T. McPherson) Engineering Uses of Rubber, 1956. Contbr. to tech. jours. Address: Anderson Road, Greenwich, Conn. Died Mar. 13, 1950; buried Arlington Nat. Cemetery.

KLEMME, ROLAND M., neurosurgeon; b. Belleville, Ill., May 17, 1896; s. G. D. and Margaret (Metzler) K.; M.D., Washington U., 1921; m. Virginia M. Knobeloch, Dec. 31, 1926; 1 son, Charles T. Rayhill (stepson). Intern Barnes Hosp., St. Louis, 1921-22; out-patient surgery, in charge surg. path. Barnes Hosp., 1911-24; fellow in neurosurgery Washington U., 1924; asso. with Dr. Ernest Sachs in neurol. surgery, 1925-34; instr. clin. neurol. surgery Washington U., 1927-41; pvt. practice of neurosurgery, 1934—; prof. surgery St. Louis U., 1942—, also head neurosurg. div.; cons. neurosurgeon several r.r. hosp. assns., state cancer hosp.; affiliated with St. Luke's, St. Louis City, St. Mary's, St. Louis County, St. John's, Jewish, DePaul Bethesda, Luth., St. Anthony's, Firmin Desloge, Shriner's, Mo. Bapt. hosps. (all St. Louis), Salinas Valley Meml., Montery County hosps. (Salinas, Cal.), Monterey (Cal.) Hosp. Pres. Playgoers St. Louis, Inc., 1942-43; chmn. Contemporary Club, 1938-39. Diplomate Am. Bd. Neurology. Fellow A.C.S., Internat. Coll. Surgeons (treas. 1948-50; trustee); mem. A.M.A., Mo., St. Louis, Frisco, Mo.-Pacific, Mo.-Kan.-Tex., Monterey County, Mississippi Valley (life) med. socs., St. Louis Surg. Soc., Am., So., Cal., World, Western Indsl. med. assns., St. Louis Neurosurg. Soc., St. Louis Soc. for Crippled Children, Pan-Pacific Surg. Assn., Am. Assn. Ry. Surgeons, Internat. Soc. Gen. Semantics, N.Y. Acad. Sci., Acad. Polit. Sci., Southwestern Surg. Congress, Harvey Cushing Soc. (co-founder), Terre Haute Acad. of Medicine (hon.), Gorgas Soc. (hon.), AM. Assn. Industrial Physicians and Surgeons, Am. Soc. for Control of Cancer, Am. Assn. Anatomists; hon. mem. Soc. of Surgery of La Paz, Soc. of Medicine of Argentina, Surgical Soc. of Argentina; Societe de Chirurgie de Bordeaux, Sociedad de Chirugia de Madrid, Turkish, Am.-Soviet med. socs., and others; asso. mem. Assn. Med. Illustrators; fgn. member Soc. of Medicine and Surgery of Sao Paulo. Clubs: Racquet, University (St. Louis); Lotos (N.Y.). Author: Nursing Care of Neurosurgical Patients, 1949; 25 articles in profl. jours. Home: Carmel, Cal. Office: 45 W. Romie Lane, Salinas, Cal. Died Nov. 21, 1957.

KLEPETKO, FRANK, consulting engr.; b. Bohemia, Austria, 1856; came to America, 1867; s. James and Antonie (Bleha) K.; M.E., Sch. of Mines (Columbia), 1880; m. Minnie Liebetrau, of Houghton, Mich., Feb., 1884. Began as engr. and bookkeeper, Delaware and Conglomerate mining cos., Mich., 1880; engr. various cos. until 1889; supt. smelting dept., Tamarack Osceola Copper Mfg. Co., 1890-91; supt. smelting dept., Boston & Mont. Copper Co., Mont., 1891-96; mgr. same co., and also of Butte & Boston Copper Co., 1896-1902; mgr. smelting plant, Anaconda Copper Co., Mont., 1900-02; built smelting plant of Highland Boy Mining Co. (Utah), Anaconda Copper Co., Cerrode Pasco Mining Co. (Peru, S.A.), Mich. Smelting Co.; has spent large part of time since 1906 in Peru, investigating mining properties. Mem. Am. Inst. Mining Engrs., Am. Chem. Soc., Instn. of Mining Engrs. (Eng.), Instn. of Mining and Metallurgy (Eng.), Sociedad de Ingenieros (Lima, Peru). Mason (K.T.). Clubs: Columbia University, Rocky Mountain (New York); Phoenix (Lima, Peru). Address: Care Lewisohn Bros., 11 Broadway, New York, N.Y.

KLIMM, LESTER E(ARL), geographer; b. Bklyn., June 6, 1902; s. George Stephen and Wilhelmina Alfreda (Rood) K.; student Middlebury Coll., 1920-22; B.S., Columbia, 1924; Ph.D., U. Pa., 1930; m. Mary Elizabeth Lee, Dec. 21, 1927; 1 dau., Elizabeth Lee (Mrs. Donald R. MacAfee). Reporter, deskman Hartford Post, 1918-20; instr. geography Wharton Sch. Finance and Commerce, U. Pa., 1924-30, asst. prof., 1930-36, asso. prof., 1936-46, prof., 1946—; faculty Columbia, summers 1927, 39, 40, Harvard, 1950; Social Sci. Research fellow Brit. Isles, 1933-34. With Office Chief of Staff, War Dept., 1942-45; com. geophysics and geography Research and Development Bd., Dept. of Def., 1948-53; official U.S. del. 17th Internat. Geog. Congress, 1952, and 18th Congress, 1956. Chairman environmental research subpanel, army scientific advisory panel for 1958—. Recipient Henry G. Bryant gold medal Geographical Society Philadelphia, 1956; commendation for meritorious civilian service War Dept. Fellow A.A.A.S. (councilor 1954-56); mem. Am. Geog. Soc. (councilor 1946—), Assn. Am. Geographers (councilor 1944-46, v.p. 1957-58, pres. 1958-59), Geog. Soc. Phila., Beta Gamma Sigma, Alpha Sigma Phi. Club: Lenape (Phila.). Home: 4609 Osage Av., Phila. 19143. Died Dec. 16, 1960; buried Phila.

KLINE, JOHN ROBERT, prof. mathematics; b. Quakertown, Pa., Dec. 7, 1891; s. Henry K. and Emma (Osman) K.; A.B., Muhlenberg Coll., Allentown, Pa., 1912, Sc.D., 1934; A.M., U. of Pa., 1914, Ph.D., 1916; Guggenheim fellow, U. of Göttingen, 1925-26; m. Anna B. Shafer, June 1, 1915 (deceased); 1 son, John Shafer; m. 2d Eunice Story Eaton, March 24, 1951. Instr. in math., U. of Pa., 1917-18, Yale, 1918-19; asso. in mathematics, U. of Ill., 1919-20; asst. prof. mathematics, U. of Pa., 1920-28, prof. since 1928, chmn. department of mathematics and Thomas A. Scott Professor of Mathematics since 1940; visiting professor, Bryn Mawr Coll., 1935-36, Swarthmore Coll., 1938-39; vis. prof. math. University of Colorado, summer 1949, U. Tubingen, Germany, first semester, 1952-53. Member board examiners mathematics College Entrance Examination Bd., mem. adv. council in mathematics Princeton since 1942. Sec. conf. for formation Internat. Math. Union, 1950; mem. div. mathematics Nat. Research Council, 1951. Mem. Am. Math. Soc. (asso. editor of bulletin; mem. council; sec.), A.A.A.S. (v.p. and chmn. Sec. A. 1938), Math. Assn. America, Am. Philos. Soc., Polish Math. Soc., Internat. Congress of Mathematicians (sec.), Soc. of Science and Letters of Warsaw, Alpha Tau Omega. Presbyterian. Mason. Contributor to Trans. Am. Math. Soc., Fundamenta Mathematicae, etc. Asso. editor Trans. Am. Math. Soc., also of Am. Jour. Mathematics. Home: 529 Riverview Av., Swarthmore, Pa. Died May 2, 1955; buried Quakertown, Pa.

KLINE, PAUL ROBERT, physician; b. Trenton, N.J., Apr. 1, 1907; s. Abraham and Celia (Budson) K.; M.D., N.Y. Med. Sch., 1930; m. Renee Kusselman, June 29, 1941; children—Victor, Peter. Intern, William McKinley Meml. Hosp., 1930-31; asso. attending in dermatology and syphilis N.Y. Skin & Cancer Unit Postgrad. Hosp., N.Y.C.; cons. dermatologist N.J. Neuropsyhiat. Inst., Skillman, Princeton Hosp., McKinley Meml. Hosp., Trenton; asso. in dermatology and syphilis Univ. Hosp.-Bellevue Med. Center. Served with USNR, 1942-46. Diplomate Am. Bd. Dermatology, Pan Am. Med. Assn. Mem. Am. Acad. Dermatology, A.M.A., Soc. Investigative Dermatology, A.A.A.S., N.Y. Acad. Scis., Argentine Assn. Dermatology and Syphililogy (hon.). Hon. editor Jour. Practica Medica, Barcelona, Spain. Contbr. articles to profl. jours. Home: Princeton NJ Died July 11, 1970; buried People of Truth Cemetery, Trenton NJ

KLOTZ, OSKAR, pathologist; b. Preston, Ont., Jan. 21, 1878; s. Otto (LL.D.) and Marie (Widenman) K.; M.B., Univ. of Toronto, 1902; fellow in pathology, McGill U., 1903-05; M.D., C.M., same univ., 1906; student U. of Bonn, 1904-05, U. of Freiburg, 1908; m. Stella M. Scovil, Mar. 4, 1908. Demonstrator and lecturer, McGill U., 1905-10; prof. pathology, and bacteriology, U. of Pittsburgh, 1910-20; prof. pathology, Sao Paulo, Brazil (Rockefeller Foundation), 1920-23; prof. pathology and bacteriology, U. of Toronto, 1923—. Dir. Magee Pathol. Lab., Pathology Labs., Toronto Gen. Hosp., 1923—; cons. pathologist, Hosp. for Sick Children, Toronto, 1923—; hon. consultant in pathology, Dept. of Health, Ontario, 1934—; mem. Yellow Fever Commn., 1926, 28. Author: Arteriosclerosis, 1912. Home: Toronto, Canada. Died Nov. 3, 1936.

KNABENSHUE, ROY, aëronaut; b. Lancaster, O., July 15, 1876; s. Samuel S (q.v.) and Salome (Matlack) K.; ed. at Toledo, O.; married. Has experimented with aërial navigation for several yrs.; made first airship flight in U.S. at St. Louis Expn., 1904; since then has made numerous successful flights in various parts of U.S. with airship constructed by himself. Address: 133 Melrose Av., Toledo, O. Died Mar. 6, 1960.

KNAPP, WALTER I(RVING), engineer; b. Austinburg, O., July 15, 1899; s. William G. and Laura I. (Tallman) K.; student Case Sch. Applied Sci., Cleve., 1919-20; B.S. in Elec. Engring., Ohio No. U., 1923; student design and lighting in architecture Cranbrook Acad. Art, 1935-36; m. Ruth L. Snyder, May 7, 1924; 1 dau., Margaret Louise. Jr. engr., elec. and sales engr. Wilson-Painter Elec. Co., Canton, O., 1923-26; lighting engr. and sales Netting Co., Detroit, 1926-32; pres., design engr. Lighting Corp., Detroit, 1932-34; lighting design engr. Detroit Edison Co., 1934-44; product design, development and Marketing, Detroit, from 1944; work includes sunray finishing machine for stainless steel ware, plastics top fillet, seaming bridge for plastic counter tops, door actuated elevator cabinet, V arm metal secondary electric pole design, vertirail mass. transit system also designed all-purpose assessory light stanchion, Met. Civic Centers; pvt. research, guided missile control and space techniques; collaborator on design of bi-level stabilized rapid transit system, 1971. Registered professional engineer, Mich. Mem. Engring. Soc. Detroit (dir. 1942-45), Delta Sigma Phi. Methodist. Mason. Address: Detroit MI Died Nov. 23, 1971; buried Woodlawn Cemetery, Ada OH

KNAUSS, HAROLD PAUL, physicist, educator; b. Seipstown, Pa., July 12, 1900; s. Henry Franklin and Martha Luzina (Leibold) K.; B.S., Muhlenberg Coll., 1922; M.S., N.Y.U., 1924; Charles A. Coffin Found. fellow, U. Leiden (Netherlands), 1925-26; Ph.D. in Physics, U. Cal. at Berkeley, 1928; m. Dorothy E. Schelly, Sept. 4, 1928; children—Diana (Mrs. M.G. Walls, Jr.), David S., Judith Ann. Instr., then asst. prof. physics Ohio State U., 1928-42; spl. research asso. Underwater Sound Lab., Harvard, 1942-45; physicist Submarine Signal Co., Boston, 1945-46; physicist, dir. research Dayton (O.) atomic energy plant Monsanto Chem. Co., 1946-48; prof. physics U. Conn., 1948—, chmn. dept., 1948-62. Fellow Am. Phys. Soc., A.A.A.S.; mem. I.R.E., Am. Assn. Physics Tchrs., United World Federalists, Sigma Xi, Phi Kappa Phi, Phi Kappa Tau, Sigma Pi Sigma. Author: Discovering Physics, 1951; also research publs. molecular spectra, acoustics, biphysics. Home: Standish Rd., Route 3, Coventry, Conn. Office: Univ. Connecticut, Storrs, Conn. Died Jan. 1, 1963.

KNEASS, STRICKLAND LANDIS, mech. engr.; b. Phila., Jan. 7, 1861; s. Strickland and Margaretta Sybilla (Bryan) K.; grad. Rugby Acad., Phila., 1876; C.E., Rensselaer Poly. Inst., 1880; m. Mary Stewart Edwards, Oct. 22, 1888; children—Strickland, Edward, George Bryan. With William Sellers & Co., Phila., 1883—, became mgr. injector dept., 1895, vice president, 1926—. Awarded diploma, Chicago Exposition, 1893, St. Louis Exposition, 1904; awarded John Scott medal and premium, Franklin Institute, Phila., 1900. Republican. Presbyterian. Author: Practice and Theory of the Injector. Home: Philadelphia, Pa. Died Nov. 24, 1928.

KNIGHT, CHARLES MELLEN, chemist; b. Dummerston, Vt., Feb. 1, 1848; s. Joel and Fannie Maria (Duncan) K.; grad. Westbrook Sem., Deering, Me., 1868; A.B., Tufts Coll., 1873; A.M., 1878; post-grad. Harvard and Mass. Inst. Tech., 1874; hon. Sc.D., Buchtel Coll., 1897; m. May Acomb, Aug. 31, 1882 (died Oct. 31, 1930); children—Maurice Acomb, Hal Greenwood, Helen Lillian. Prof. natural science, 1875-83, physical science, 1883-1907, chemistry, 1907-13, prof. emeritus since 1913, dean, 1902-13, Buchtel Coll.; acting pres. Buchtel Coll., 1896-97; Knight Chem. Lab. named for him, 1909. Established a course in rubber chemistry, the first in any Am. coll., 1909. Universalist. Fellow A.A.A.S. (emeritus); mem. Am. Chem. Soc., Phi Beta Kappa, Zeta Psi, Phi Sigma Alpha. Contbr. on sanitary science, chemistry of rubber. Clubs: University, Chemists (hon. mem.). Home: (summer) Akron, O., (winter) Coral Gables, Fla. Died July 3, 1941.

KNIGHT, GEORGE LAURENCE, mech. engr.; b. Haddonfield, N.J., Feb. 20, 1878; s. George Warren and Ada Danforth (Atkinson) K.; grad. William Penn Charter Sch., 1896; E.E. (diploma, before degrees were conferred), Drexel Inst. Tech., 1900; m. Evelyn Creveling Sharp, Nov. 23, 1904 (died May 10, 1941); children—George Laurence, Richard Bunting. Began as switch operator Philadelphia Electric Co., later became draftsman N.Y. Edison Co.; with Brooklyn Edison Co., 1905-42, successively as chief draftsman, designing engr., mechanical engr., v.p. retired Mar. 1942. Trustee and sec. Bay Ridge Savings Bank since 1946. V.p. Victory Memorial Hosp. Fellow Am. Soc. M.E. (mem. and past chmn. finance com.), Am. Inst. E.E.; mem. United Engring. Trustees (chmn. finance com.). Past pres. Brooklyn Engrs. Club. Mem. and clerk of vestry Christ Ch. (Episcopal), Bay Ridge Home: 1 Harbor Lane, Brooklyn, N.Y. Died March 27, 1948.

KNIGHT, HENRY GRANGER, chemist; b. Bennington, Ottawa County, Kan., July 21, 1878; s. Edwin Richard and Elva Maud (Edwards) K.; A.B. in chemistry, U. of Wash., 1902, A.M., 1904; student in chemistry, U. of Chicago, 1902-03, summer session, 1906; Ph.D., U. of Ill., 1917; m. Nelly Dryden, June 28, 1905; 1 son, Richard Dryden. Asst. 1900-01, instr., 1901-02, asst. prof. chemistry, 1903-04, U. of Wash.; asst. in chemistry, U. of Chicago, 1902-03, fellow-elect, 1903; prof. chemistry and state chemist, U. of Wyo., 1904-10; dir. Wyo. Expt. Sta., and Farmers' Insts., Wyoming, 1910-18, dean Coll. of Agr., 1912-18; dean and dir. Okla. Agrl. Coll., Stillwater, 1918-21; hon. fellow Cornell U., 1921-22; dir. and research chemist Expt. Sta. W.Va. U., 1922-27, dean Coll. of Agr., 1926-27; chief Bur. of Chemistry and Soils, 1927-39, chief Bur. Agrl. Chemistry and Engring. since 1939, U.S. Dept. of Agr. Chmn. Wyo. State Council Defense, 1917-18. Fellow Am. Inst. Chemists (pres. 1933-35); mem. Am. Chem. Soc., Phi Gamma Delta, Sigma Xi, Phi Beta Kappa, Alpha Zeta, Phi Lambda Upsilon, Phi Kappa Phi. Mason. Methodist. Clubs: Cosmos, Rotary. Writer of various monographs on qualitative analysis; research work on potable waters, effect of alkali upon seeds, food adulterations, Wyo. forage plants, soil nitrogen, wool, poisonous plants, effect of alkali upon cement drainage experiments, digestion experiments, soil acidity, etc. Address: 4436 Q St. N.W., Washington, D.C. Died July 13, 1942.

KNIGHT, JONATHAN, physician; b. Norwalk, Conn., Sept. 4, 1789; s. Dr. Jonathan and Ann (Fitch) K.; grad. Yale, 1808, M.A., 1811, M.D. (hon.), 1818; m. Elizabeth Lockwood, Oct. 1813. Licensed to practice medicine by Conn. Med. Soc., 1811; asst. prof. anatomy and physiology Yale, 1813, prof. surgery, 1838, founder Med. Sch.; sec. Conn. Med. Soc., 1817; pres. meetings of Nat. Med. Conv. which formed A.M.A., 1846, 47; pres. A.M.A., 1853; 1st surgeon to cure aneurisms by compression. 1848. Died New Haven, Conn., Aug. 25, 1864.

KNIGHT, MONTGOMERY, aeronautical engr.; b. Lynn, Mass., Feb. 22, 1901; s. Franklin and Gertrude Boucher (Mosher) K.; B.S., in Elec. Engring., Mass. Inst. Tech., 1922; grad. student, Harvard, 1922-23, Johns Hopkins, 1924-25; m. Emily Millner, Jan. 1, 1927; children—Margaret, Ann Bowler (dec.), Montgomery, Edward. Research engr. with Army Air Corps, Aberdeen, Md., 1923-24; elec. engring. research with Westinghouse Electric & Mfg. Co., East Pittsburgh, Pa., 1925-26; aeronautical research, Nat. Advisory Com. for Aeronautics, Langley Field, Va., 1925-30; dir. Daniel Guggenheim Sch. of Aeronautics, Ga. Sch. of Tech., Atlanta, since 1930. Commd. 2d lt., Air Corps, U.S. Reserve Army, 1922-32. Asso. fellow Inst. of Aeronautical Sciences. Registered aeronautical engr., Ga. Episcopalian. Author or co-author of 16 tech. reports on aeronautical research, pub. by Nat. Advisory Com. for Aeronautics. Contbr. to tech. jours. Engaged in development of helicopter under State Engring. Expt. State of Ga. Home: 3529 Ivy Rd., Atlanta, Ga. Died July 26, 1943.

KNIGHT, NICHOLAS, chemist; b. Mexico, N.Y., Apr. 2, 1861; s. George and Mary (MacDonald) K.; A.B., Syracuse U., 1882, A.M., 1885, A.M. and Ph.D., 1888; U. of Strassburg, 1892-94; Johns Hopkins, 1894-95, 1898-99; student summers Harvard Univ., 1884, Marthas Vineyard Summer School, 1885, Cornell Univ., 1886; m. Anna M. Audas, of Oneida, N.Y., Aug. 11, 1887; children—Harold Audas, Donald MacDonald. Prof. natural science, Cazenovia (N.Y.) Sem., 1882-92; prof. chemistry, Randolph-Macon Coll., Va., 1895-98, Cornell Coll., Ia., 1899-1933; retired. Studied lab. equipment and methods in European univs. and tech. schs., 1908-09. Asso. editor School Science and Mathematics. City chemist, Mt. Vernon, Iowa, Dec. 1913—. Chemist to Oneida (N.Y.) Water Commn. Speaker for Nat. Security League and chmn. of the "Four Minute Men" of the township; visited Europe, 1922, to study economic conditions, speaker for League of Nations Non-Partisan Assn. Fellow Faculty of Sciences (chmn. for the United States), Ia. Acad. Sciences; mem. Am. Chem. Soc., Deutsche Chemische Gesellschaft, Phi Beta Kappa, Phi Lambda Upsilon, Delta Upsilon. Author: A Course in Quantitative Analysis, 1899, revised and rewritten, 1915; Notes on Blow Pipe Analysis, 1905; Problems in Chemical Arithmetic, 1906; Chemistry of Colloids, 1915; bulletin on 30 years' analysis of the rains and snows of Mount Vernon, Ia. Contributor many articles to various chemical journals. Home: Mt. Vernon, Ia.

KNIGHT, ORA WILLIS, chemist, geologist; b. Bangor, Me., July 15, 1874; s. George Willis and Nellie Ada (Blood) K.; B.S. (in chemistry), Me. State Coll., 1895; post-grad. work, U. of Me., M.S., 1897; (hon. Sc.D., 1909); m. Minnie Gertrude McDonald, Aug. 11, 1899. Asst. in natural history, Me. State Coll., 1895-97; asst. chemist, Me. Expt. Sta., 1897-1903; state assayer and cons. chemist, 1903—. Chemist, Lackawanna Foundries; expert chemist and microscopist in criminal cases in the courts (in case of State vs. Alexander Terrio, convicted of murder, discovered evidence through which a new trial was granted and Terrio set free—the only new trail ever granted in a murder case in the State of Me.). Republican. Unitarian. Has a nearly complete herbarium of the plants of Me. Home: Portland, Me. Died Nov. 11, 1913.

KNIGHT, WILBUR CLINTON, geologist; b. Rochelle, Ill., Dec. 13, 1858; s. David A. K.; grad. Univ. of Neb., 1886 (B.Sc., A.M.); asst. territorial geologist, Wyo., 1886; chemist and assayer, Swan Sampling & Testing Co., Cheyenne, 1887; supt. of mines in Colo. and Wyo., 1888-93; prof. mining, 1893, and from 1894 prof. mining and geology, Univ. of Wyo.; also, from 1897, State geologist of Wyo.. 1898-99. Fellow Geol. Soc. of America; m. E. Emma Howell, 1889. Home: Laramie, Wyo. Died 1903.

KNIPP, CHARLES TOBIAS, (nip), physicist; b. Napoleon, Henry County, O., Aug. 13, 1869; s. Frederick F. and Pauline (Youche) K.; A.B., Indiana U., 1894, A.M., 1896; Ph.D., Cornell U., 1900; studied Cavendish Laboratory, Cambridge, Eng., 1910-11, 1926-27; m. Frances Winona Knause, June 25, 1896; children—Pauline Louise, Frances Mary, Julian Knause, Barbara Matilda. Instr. physics, Ind. U., 1893-1900, asst. prof. 1900-03; asst. prof. physics, U. of Ill., 1903-15, asso. prof., 1915-17, prof. experimental electricity, 1917-37, emeritus prof. experimental electricity since 1937; visiting professor of physics, Rollins College, Winter Park, Florida, 1942-1945. Member of advisory sub-committee on physics for Century of Progress Exposition, Chicago, 1933. Fellow A.A.A.S.; member American Physical Society, Am. Inst. E.E., Optical Soc. of America, Soc. for Promotion of Engring. Edn., Ill. State Acad. of Science (v.p. 1920-21, pres. 1921-22), Ind. State Acad., Sigma Xi (pres. 1930-31), Phi Beta Kappa (Indiana Univ., 1915); hon. mem. Tau Beta Pi, Eta Kappa Nu, Epsilon Chi, Synton. Republican. Presbyterian. Author monographs and articles on scientific subjects. Designer of demonstration apparatus in physics. Co-inventor, with H. A. Brown, of Alkali vapor detector tube for use in radio; inventor of simple alpha-ray track apparatus; also of efficient mercury vapor vacuum pumps, electrodeless elec. discharge, cold-cathode rectifier. Home: Box 3808, T.S. C. W. Station, Denton, Texas. Died July 6, 1948.

KNOPF, ADOLPH, geologist; b. San Francisco, Dec. 2, 1882; s. George Tobias and Anna (Geisel) K.; B.S., U. Cal., 1904, M.S., 1905, Ph.D., 1909; M.A. (hon.), Yale, 1923; m. Agnes Burchard Dillon, Jan. 21, 1908 (died Nov. 1918); children—Elsa (dec.), George D. (dec.), Agnes, Theresa Ann; m. 2d, Eleanora Frances Bliss, 1920. On staff U.S. Geol. Survey since 1906, geologist, 1912-41, 1942-45; asso. prof. geology, Yale, 1920-23, prof. geology, 1923-38, Sterling prof. geology, 1938-51, Sterling prof. emeritus since 1951, dir. grad. studies Dept. Geol. Scis., 1933-50; vis. prof. geology Stanford, 1951-57, cons. prof., 1957—. Penrose medalist Geol. Soc. Am., 1959. Mem. A.A.A.S., Am. Acad. Arts and Scis., Geol. Soc. Am. (pres. 1944), Soc. Econ. Geologists, Washington Acad. Scis., Mineral. Soc. Am., Sigma Xi; mem. NRC 1923-26, Nat. Acad. Scis., Peninsula Geog. Soc. (pres. 1955-56). Author: Age of the Earth, 1931; Textbook of Geology—Physical Geology (with C. R. Longwell, R. F. Flint), 1932, 39, 48; also reports and papers pub. by U.S. Geol. Survey. Contbr. articles on geology and petrology to jours. Editor Jour. Washington Acad. Scis., 1917-18; asso. editor Am. Jour. Sci. Home: 130 Hardwick Rd., Woodside, Cal. 94062. Office: Stanford U., Stanford, Cal. Died Nov. 23, 1966; buried Skylawn Meml. Cemetery, San Mateo County, Cal.

KNOPF, S. ADOLPHUS, M.D.; b. Halle-on-the-Saale, Germany, Nov. 27, 1857; s. Adolphus and Nanina (Bock) K.; A.B., U. of Paris (Sorbonne) 1890; M.D., Bellevue Hosp. Med. Coll. (New York University), 1888; Faculty of Medicine, Univ. of Paris, 1895; m. Perle Nora Dyar, Oct. 19, 1889 (died 1931); m. 2d, Julia Marie Off, Oct. 6, 1935;

children—Gertrude, Lucille, Adolphus. Professor of medicine, department phthisitherapy, N.Y. Post-Grad. Med. School, Columbia U., 1908-20; sr. visiting phys. Health Department's Riverside Tuberculosis Hosp., 1906-22; hon. dir. Gaylord Farm Sanitorium, Wallingford, Conn.; hon. pres. med. bd. Bruchesi Tuberculosis Inst., Montreal; attending tuberculosis specialist, ranking as maj., U.S.P.H.S., 1920-22; consulting phys. to Riverside Hosp. (N.Y.), St. Gabriel's (N.Y.) Sanatorium for Consumptives, West Mountain Sanatorium, at Scranton, Pa., etc. Fellow N.Y. Acad. Medicine, Assn. Mil. Surgeons U.S., Soc. Med. Jurisprudence, Am. Heart Assn., Am. Soc. for Psychical Research; hon. member Am. Assn. for Thoracic Surgery, Am. Tuberculosis Assn.; hon. vice pres. Brit. Congress on Tuberculosis; govt. del. Internat. Prison Congress, Budapest, Internat. Tuberculosis Congress, Paris; v.p. sect. V of Tuberculosis Congress. Washington, 1908; official del. 4th Internat. Congress on Sch. Hygiene, Buffalo, 1913; laureate French Inst. of Paris, 1896, Coll. Physicians of Phila., 1898, Internat. Congress for study of how best to combat tuberculosis as a disease of the masses, 1900, Institut de France, 1900, Internat. Tuberculosis Congress, Washington, 1908; apptd. rep. U.S. International Union Against Tuberculosis, The Hague, 1932. Founder N.Y. City and Nat. Tuberculosis Assns. Capt. Med. R.C., U.S. Army, 1917; maj. M.O.R.C. Mason. Home: New York, N.Y. Died July 15, 1940.

KNOPF, WILLIAM CLEVELAND, JR., univ. dean; b. Louisville, Dec. 13, 1910; s. William Cleveland and Anne (Flood) K.; B.S., Washington and Lee U., 1932; M.S., Vanderbilt U., 1941; Ph.D., Northwestern U., 1950; m. Mary Gene Herren, Jan. 18, 1941; children—Katherine Herren (Mrs. H. James Stadelman), Gene Miller (Mrs. Randolph N. Jonakait). Asst. dean Northwestern U., 1945-51; asst. dir. research Internat. Minerals and Chem. Corp., Skokie, Ill., 1951-59; dir. research U.S. Industries Tech. Center, Pompano Beach, Fla., 1959-61; prof. elec. engring. U. Fla., 1961-63; prof. elec. engring. and ocean engring. U. Miami (Fla.), 1963—, dean Sch. Engring., 1965-70; lectr., research asso. Ill. Inst. Tech., 1941-43; cons. to govt. and industry, 1945-70. Chmn. sci. and oceanography Dade County (Fla.) Com. 21, 1966-70; mem. Fla. Tech. Services Program, 1966-70, Fla. Articulation Com. Engring., 1965-70; chmn. oceanography Fla. Space Eta Study Task Force, 1962-63. Mem. A.A.A.S., I.E.E.E., Instrument Soc. Am. (chmn. marine sci. div. 1964-66), Am. Soc. Engring. Edn., Miami-Dade County C. of C., Sigma Xi, Tau Beta Pi, Eta Kappa Nu, Alpha Tau Omega. Rotarian. Club: Riviera Country. Contbr. profl. jours. Home: Coral Gables FL Died Feb. 6, 1970.

KNOTT, EMMET KENNARD, hemo-irradiologist; b. Cripple Creek, Colo., Jan. 31, 1897; s. Kennard and Emma Maria (Schlichtmann) K.; D.Sc., Hahnemann Hosp. and Med. Coll., Phila., 1940; m. Norma Irene Lean, Aug. 17, 1925; 1 son, Emmet Kennard; m. 2d, Ethel H. Smith Weeks, July 9, 1934 (dec. 1952); m. 3d, Virginia Jones White, Feb. 14, 1955. Inventor of procedure and equipment for ultraviolet irradiation of auto-transfused blood (hemo-irradiation), 1927; research in ultraviolet blood irradiation since 1933. Mason. Co-author (with G. J. P. Barger) of first published article on ultraviolet blood irradiation, Northwest Medicine, June, 1934; author Development of Ultraviolet Blood Irradiation, Am. Jour. of Surgery, Aug., 1948. Home: 7144 55th Av. S., Seattle 98108. Office: Prefontaine Bldg., Seattle 98104. Died Dec. 16, 1961; buried Acacia Meml., Seattle.

KNOWER, HENRY MCELDERRY, anatomist; b. Baltimore, Aug. 5, 1868; s. Capt. Edward C. K. (U.S.A.) and Mary D. (McElderry) K.; A.B., Johns Hopkins, 1890, asst. in biology, 1891-93; Adam T. Bruce fellow, 1895-96, Ph.D., 1896; m. Virginia DuBarry, Feb. 16, 1897; children—Henry DuB., Virginia (wife of William A. Moore). Instructor biology, Williams Coll., 1896-97; instr. anatomy, 1899-1908, asso., 1908-09, Johns Hopkins; lecturer anatomy, U. of Toronto, 1909-10; prof. anatomy, U. of Cincinnati, 1910-25; visiting prof. anatomy, U. of Ga., 1924-26; prof. anatomy, U. of Ala., 1926-29; guest in research, Wistar Inst. Anatomy, Phila., 1929-30; asso. prof. anatomy, Albany Med. Coll., 1930—; research fellow in biology, Yale U., 1932-33, research asso. in biology, 1933-37. Asst. in zoölogy, 1897, librarian. 1910-20, Marine Biol. Lab., Woods Hole, Mass.; one of founders and mng. editor Am. Jour. Anatomy, 1901-22; founder and first editor Anat. Record, 1906. Researches in embryology and anatomy of Termites; lymphatic and vascular systems of frog embryos, by experiment and injections; muscles of human heart. Home: Woods Hole, Mass. Died Jan. 10, 1940.

KNOWLES, LUCIUS JAMES, inventor, mfr.; b. Hardwich, Mass., July 2, 1819; s. Simeon, Jr. and Lucetta (Newton) K.; A.M. (hon.), Williams Coll., 1865; m. Eliza Adams; m. 2d, Helen Strong. Perfected Knowles Safety Steam-boiler feed regulator, 1840, began mfg., 1859; began daguerreotype bus., Worcester, Mass., 1841; inventor machine for spooling thread, 1843; engaged in mfg., New Wooster, Mass., 1843-45; partner (with Harrison H. Sibley) to operate Old Draper Mill, mfg. cotton warp, Spencer, Mass., 1846; extended activities to include woolen mill, 1853-59; patented improvements in looms, 1856; erected bldg. near cotton factory to manufacture boiler-feeder water regulator, 1862; mem. Mass. Ho. of Reps. from Warren, New Braintree and West Brookfield, 1862, 65; made steam pumps, exptl. looms, 1863; propr. Knowles Steam Pump Co., L.J. Knowles & Bro. Loom Works (consol. as Crompton & Knowles Loom Works, 1897); mem. Mass. Senate from 3d Worcester Dist., 1869; trustee Worcester Free Inst. Tech., 1871. Died Washington D.C., Feb. 25, 1884.

KNOWLES, MORRIS, consulting engr.; b. Lawrence, Mass., Oct. 13, 1869; s. Charles Edwin and Ellen B. (Richardson) K.; S.B., Mass. Inst. Tech., 1891; Dr. Engineering, University of Pittsburgh, 1929; m. Mina P. McDavitt, Apr. 25, 1893. Employed Mass. State Bd. of Health and Met. Water Commn., Boston, 1893-97; investigations, design and construction of filtration system and new water supply, Pittsburgh, Pa., 1897-1910; consulting engring. practice, 1903—; pres. Morris Knowles, Inc., and Morris Knowles, Ltd.; dir. Pittsburgh Aviation Industries Corporation. Designed water works system, T.,C.&I. R.R. Co., Birmingham, Ala., 1909-11; consultant numerous cities and industries on municipal problems and community planning. Mem. Pittsburgh Flood Commn.; mem. Bd. Advisory Engrs. Miami Conservancy Dist., 1914; chief engr., Essex Border Utilities Commn., Ont., Can., 1916-21; superv. engr. Camps Meade and McClellan, 1917; chief engr. Housing Div., U.S. Shipping Bd., 1918-19; mem. Engring. Bd. of Review of Chicago Sanitary Dist., 1924; consultant and adviser to atty. gen. Conn. in case of Conn. vs. Mass. before U.S. Supreme Court, 1928-30; mem. Zoning Commn. U.S. Dept. of Commerce; chmn. com. on utilities, President's Conf. on Home Building and Home Ownership; vice chmn. Pa. Commn. to Study Municipal Consolidation in Counties of Second Class; chmn. City Planning Commn. and chmn. Bd. of Zoning Appeals, Pittsburgh; mem. Pa. State Chamber Commerce; mem. bd. dirs. Pittsburgh Chamber Commerce. Republican. Author: Industrial Housing. Home: Pittsburgh, Pa. Died Nov. 8, 1932.

KNOWLTON, FRANK HALL, botanist, paleontologist; b. Brandon, Vt., Sept. 2, 1860; s. Julius Augustus and Mary Ellen (Blackmer) K.; B.S., Middlebury Coll., 1884, M.S., 1887, hon. Sc.D., 1921; Ph.D., Columbian (now George Washington) U., 1896; m. Annie Stirling Moorhead, Sept. 27, 1887 (died 1890); 1 dau., Margaret; m. 2d, Rena Genevieve Ruff, Oct. 3, 1893; 1 son, Frank Lester. Aid, 1884-87, asst. curator botany, 1887-89, asst. palaeontologist, 1889-1900, U.S. Nat. Mus.; palaeontologist, 1900-07, geologist, July 1907—, U.S. Geol. Survey, prof. botany, Columbain, 1887-96. Editor The Plant World, 1897-1904 (founder); asst. on Century Dictionary, writing definitions in botany; had whole charge of botany for Standard Dictionary, for which he prepared about 25,000 definitions; assisted in preparing bot. definitions for new edit. (1900) of Webster's Dictionary; prepared bot. matter for The Jewish Encyclopaedia. Fellow Geol. Soc. America (v.p. 1917-18), Palaeontol. Soc. America (v.p. 1910 and 1915, pres. 1917-18). Author: Catalogue Mesozoic and Cenozoic Plants of North America, 1919; Plants of the Past, 1926. Home: Ballston, Va. Died Nov. 22, 1926.

KNOX, SAMUEL LIPPINCOTT GRISWOLD, cons. engr.; b. New York, N.Y., Nov. 26, 1870; s. Andrew and Annabel Grace (Douglas) K.; student Coll. City of New York, 1885-87; M.E., Stevens Inst. Tech., Hoboken, N.J., 1891; m. Edith Somerville Rulison, Sept. 16, 1897 (died Nov. 24, 1936); children—Nelson Rulison, Alexander Douglas. Chmn. com. of mech. design and engr. in charge drafting dept. Gen. Electric Co., 1900-02; v.p., gen. mgr. and chief engr. Bucyrus Co., S. Milwaukee, Wis., mfrs. excavating machinery, 1902-10, designing and mfg. much of machinery used in constrn. of Panama Canal, also placer gold dredges of the period; cons. engr., later v.p. and gen. mgr. Natomas Consol., of Calif., gold dredging and land reclamation, also pres. Pacific Engring. & Constrn. Co. and Pacific Dredging Co., building jetties on Pacific Coast, river correction and levee bldg., Sacramento and San Joaquin rivers, 1911-17; chmn. mech. engring. div. Nat. Research Council, Washington, D.C., also chief cons. engr. U.S. Navy Anti-Submarine Base, New London, Conn., 1917-20, devised improvement of secondary and turret guns of battleships, also apparatus for enemy airplane location; scientific attaché Am. Embassy, Rome, Italy, 1918-19; consulting engineer; president Lombard Tractor Co., 1927-28; president Knox Engring. Co., developing high efficiency steam power plants; dir. and mem. exec. com. Lamson Corp. of Del. (pneumatic tube and other service conveyors); dir., mem. exec. com. Lamson Corp. of N.Y.; dir. Boston Pneumatic Transit Co., New York Mail & Newspaper Transit Co. Fellow Am. Soc. Mech. Engrs.; mem. Pilgrims of U.S., Kappa Alpha. Episcopalian. Club: University (New York). Author: The Mailed Fist—the Background of Hitlerism. Address: 115 E. Palisade Av., Englewood, N.J. Died May 8, 1947.

KNOX, THOMAS WALLACE, author, inventor; b. Pembroke, N.H., June 26, 1835; s. Nehemiah Critchett and Jane (Wallace) K. Established, became prin. acad., Kingston, N.H., 1857; spl. reporter, then city editor Denver Daily News, 1860; lt. col. on staff Cal. Nat. Guard in Civil War; war corr. N.Y. Herald; granted patent for transmitting plans of battle field by telegraph; explored many unfrequented parts of Orient, secured materials for large number of travel volumes, 1877; decorated Order of White Elephant by Siam. Author: Overland through Asia, 1870; The Boy Travelers in the Far East, 1881; Pocket Guide Around the World 1882; Life of Henry Ward Beecher, 1887, others. Died N.Y.C., Jan. 6, 1896.

KOBE, KENNETH ALBERT, (kobe), chem. engr.; b. Osakis, Minn., Mar. 19, 1905; s. Albert M. and Mildred (Stillwell) K.; B.S., with distinction, Univ. of Minn., 1926, M.S., 1928, Ph.D., 1930; m. Jeneva K. Holm, July 6, 1932; children—Donald, Jean. Chem. engr. Dupont Ammonia Corp., Wilmington, Del., 1930; instr. Univ. of Wash., Seattle, 1931-34, asst. prof. chem. engring., 1934-39, asso. prof., 1939-41; prof. chem. engring., Univ. of Texas, since 1941, asso. director Bur. of Indsl. Chemistry, 1946-54; ednl. adviser Petroleo Brasileiro, Brazil, So. Am., 1951—. Served as major, C.W.S., 1942-44, now lt. col. USAF Reserve. Recipient outstanding achievement award U. Minn., 1955. Mem. Am. Inst. Chem. Engrs., Am. Soc. Engring. Edn., Am. Chem. Soc., Sigma Xi, Tau Beta Pi, Phi Lambda Upsilon, Alpha Chi Sigma, Gamma Alpha, Omega Chi Epsilon (National pres., 1955—). Author: Inorganic Process Industries, 1948; Petroleum Refining With Chemicals, 1956; Chemical Engineering Reports, 1957: associate editor Journal Chem. Education, 1947—; co-editor Advances in Petroleum Chemistry and Refining, vol. I, 1958. Contbr. many articles to scientific, technical and trade publications. Holder several patents on tear gas, submerged combustion, recovery of manganese and sodium sulfate. Specialist in submerged combustion processes, unit chem. processes. thermodynamics. Home: 3305 Bowman Rd., Austin 78703. Office: Dept. of Chemical Engineering, U. Texas, Austin, Tex. Died Nov. 2, 1958; buried Sunset Meml. Park, Mpls.

KOBELT, KARL, govt. ofcl., engr.; b. St. Gall, Switzerland, Aug. 1, 1891; student Swiss Fed. Int. Inst. Tech., 1910-14; m. M. Gallman, 1927; children—Nelly, Johanna, Karl. Asst. á l'EPF, 1914-17; ingénieur, 1917; also in topographic service; civil enterprise, 1918-19; chief Fed. Water Service, 1919-23; counselor (chief dept. pub. works) State of Canton de St. Gall, 1933-40; fed. counselor since 1941; pres. Swiss Confederation, 1946, 52. Mem. Internat. Commn. of Rhone, Internat. Commn. of Rhine (between Baden and Switzerland). Internat. Commn. for Regulation of Lake Constance, Internat. Commn. for Regulation of Rhine. Home: Kirchenfeldstrasse 60. Office: Department militaire federal, Berne, Switzerland. Died Jan. 5, 1968.

KOCH, FRED CHASE, engring. exec.; b. Quanah, Tex., Sept. 23, 1900; s. Harry and Margaret (Mixson) K.; student Rice Inst., 1917-19; S.B., Mass. Inst. Tech., 1922; Doctor of Science (honorary), Park College; m. Mary C. Robinson, Oct. 22, 1932; children—Frederick R., Charles deG., David H., William I. Chief engr. Medway Oil & Storage Co., Ltd., Isle of Grain, Eng., 1924-25; v.p. Winkler-Koch Engring. Co., 1925-41; pres. Koch Engring. Co., Inc., Wichita, Kan., 1941-50, chmn. bd., 1950-67; pres. Wood River Oil & Refining Co., Inc., Wichita, 1944-59; pres. Rock Island Oil & Refining Co., Inc., Duncan, Okla., 1947-66, chmn. bd., chief exec. officer, 1966-67; pres. Koch Oil Corp., Inc., Wichita, 1943-67, Matador Cattle Co., 1964-67; director of the Minn. Pipe Line Co., S. Saskatchewan Pipe Line Co., Great No. Oil Co., St. Paul, Minn., also the Coleman Company, Inc.; builder oil refineries in Eng., France, Belgium, Germany, Russia, Rumania, Portugal, Italy, Near East, Burma, S. Africa, Canada. Member of American Petroleum Inst., Am. Chem. Soc., Am. Inst. Chem. Engrs. Clubs: Chicago (Chgo.); University (N.Y.C.); Wichita, Wichita Country, Rotary (Wichita); Bear River (Ogden, Utah). Author: A Business Man Looks at Communism. Home: Wichita KS Died Nov. 17, 1967.

KOCH, JULIUS ARNOLD, (koh), chemist; b. Bremen, Germany, Aug. 15, 1864; s. Arnold and Amanda (Wenke) K.; came to America with parents in infancy; grad. Pitts. Coll. Pharmacy, 1884, Pharm.D., 1895; studied U. Munich, 1896, U. Heidelberg, 1897; Ph.D., Scio (O.) Coll., 1905; D.Sc., Washington and Jefferson Coll., 1907; Ph.M., Phila. Coll. of Pharmacy and Sci., 1922; m. Albertine M. Strunz, Oct. 17, 1889 (died Feb. 28, 1900); children—Adele M. (dec.), Florence S., Elsa A.; m. 2d, Alice M. Cope, July 15, 1927. Entered drug bus. as apprentice, 1880, became propr., 1885, sold out bus., 1891; dean Pitts. Coll. of Pharmacy, 1891-1933, dean emeritus, 1933—; prof. pharmacy, 1891-99, prof. chemistry, 1899—; prof. chemistry, med. dept. U. Pitts., 1900-13. Chmn. exec. com. Am. Conf. Pharm. Faculties, 1908-20; ex-pres. Pa. Pharm. Soc.; pres. Am. Pharm. Assn., 1922-23; pres. Pitts. br. Am. Pharm. Assn.; mem. Deutsche Chemische Gesellschaft, Soc. Chem. Industry (London), Am. Chem. Soc., A.A.A.S. Author: Chemical Laboratory Tables, 1898; Laboratory Manual for Pharmaceutical Students, 1904. Reporter on the Progress of Pharmacy and editor Year Book of Am. Pharm. Assn. 1915-16; mem. Revision Com. U.S. Pharmacopoeia, 1910-20. Home: 921 East Laurel St., Ocala, Fla. Office: 1431 Blvd. of the Allies, Pitts. Died Feb. 10, 1956.

KOENIG, GEORGE AUGUSTUS, chemist; b. Willstätt, Grand Duchy of Baden, Germany, May 12, 1844; s. Johannes and Margaretha (Pfotzer) K.; ed. pub. sch.; progymnasium at Kork, 1854-57; sch. of Moravian Brothers, Lausanne, Switzerland, 1857-59; Poly. Sch., Karlsrühe, 1859-63, degree mech. engr.; U. of Heidelberg, 1863-65, U. of Berlin, 1865-67, A.M., Ph.D., Heidelberg, 1867; Mining Acad., Freiburg, Saxony, 1867-68; m. Wilhelmina Marquart, of Willsbätt, Oct. 7, 1869. Came to U.S., Oct. 1868; manufactured sodium stannate from tin scraps in Phila.; chemist Tacony Chem. Works, Phila., 1868-72; made exam. of old mines in Mexico, winter of 1870-71; asst. prof. chemistry and mineralogy, 1872-79, mineralogy and geology, 1879-92, Univ. of Pa.; prof. chemistry, Mich. Coll. of Mines, 1892—. Discoverer of new minerals: Hydrotitanite, Randite, Leydyite, Alaskaite, Beegerite, Bementite, Footeite, Paramelaconite, Mezapilite, Mohawkite, Keeweenawite, Stibiodomykite, Melanochalcite; has reëxamined may other minerals and discovered diamond in meteoric iron. In 1885 published chromometric methods, a development of blow-pipe analysis, and in 1897 a new way of assaying without muffle; patented an assay furnace to carry out the methods; took out patent, 1881, for chlorination of low-grade silver and gold ores; latest work has been preparation of artificial crystals of arsenides. Author: Chemistry Simplified, 1905. Home: Houghton, Mich. Died Jan. 15, 1913.

KOERNER, WILLIAM, mining engr.; b. Oregon City, Ore., Feb. 22, 1886; s. Rudolph and Mary (Koehnlein) K.; A.B., Stanford, 1908; m. Della U. Snow, July 18, 1923; children—Katherine, William, Mary. Engr. Ray Consol. Copper Co., 1909, Inspiration Copper Co., 1909-11; supt. Barker Mines Co., 1912-14, Grey Eagle Copper Co., 1916-19; engr. Mason Valley Mines Co., 1921-24; mgr. Flin Flon Syndicate, 1920-21; gen. mgr. Magma Copper Co., 1925—; v.p. and gen. mgr. Magma Ariz. R.R. Co. Dir. William Boyce Thompson Arboretum of Southwest. Home: Superior, Ariz. Died June 30, 1940.

KOESTER, FRANK (FRANZ KÖSTER), engineer, author; b. Sterkrade, Germany, Aug. 28, 1876; s. Johann and Henriette (Trill) K.; ed. in Germany; theoretical and practical training for 10 yrs. in Europe; unmarried. Planned electric central stas. shown at Paris Expn., 1900, for which was awarded gold medal; came to U.S., 1902; was engr. with New York Subway Constrn. Co., J. G. White & Co., Guggenheim Exploration Co., Am. Smelting & Refining Co.; consulting engr. and city planner, 1911—; engring. expert for civic improvements, City of N.Y. Has patented various devices in the field of power plant engring. and other lines. Became naturalized citizen of U.S., 1911. Author: Modern City Planning and Maintenance, 1914. Advisory city planner for Allentown, Bethlehem and Scranton, Pa., etc.; st. lighting expert for Allentown, Scranton, etc. Home: New York, N.Y. Died Oct. 6, 1927.

KOFFKA, KURT, prof. psychology; b. Berlin, Germany, Mar. 18, 1886; s. Emil and Luise (Levy) K.; Ph.D., U. of Berlin, 1908; student U. of Edinburgh, 1904-05, U. of Freiburg, 1908-09, U. of Würzburg, 1909-10; m. Elisabeth Ahlgrimm (Ph.D.) of Hamburg, Germany, July 21, 1923. Came to U.S., 1928. Asst. U. of Würzburg, 1909-10, Acad. (now Univ.) of Frankfort, 1910-11; privatdozent, U. of Giessen, 1911-18, prof., 1918-27; visiting prof. Cornell U., 1924-25, U. of Wis., 1926-27; William Allan Neilson Research prof., Smith Coll., 1927-32, prof. psychology, 1932—. Fellow Am. Acad. Arts and Sciences. Co-founder, 1922, and editor Psychologische Forschung until 1935; editor Smith Coll. Studies in Psychology. Author: Growth of the Mind, 1924, 2d edit., 1928; also trans. in Spanish, Chinese, Japanese and Russian; Principles of Gestalt Psychology, 1935. Home: Northampton, Mass. Died Nov. 22, 1941.

KOHLER, G.A. EDWARD, engineer, mfr.; b. Phila., Pa., Feb. 17, 1864; s. Ignatius and Anna C. (Fischer) Kohler; ed. U. of Pa., class 1886; m. Mary Ward Everett, Oct. 11, 1899; children—Franklin W., John Bowen. Moved to Chicago, 1887; in employ of U.S. Construction Co. until 1888; then with Peabody, Daniels & Co.; became sec. and gen. mgr. of a saw mfg. co.; entered electrical business, 1890, and in 1891 organized firm of Kohler Bros., of which became sole propr. in 1910; dir. Kohler Aviation Corporation. Invented and manufactures devices for operating newspaper presses, including magazine reels, known under the name "The Kohler System." Republican. Home: Chicago, Ill. Died Apr. 29, 1932.

KÖHLER, WOLFGANG, educator; b. Reval, Esthonia, Jan. 21, 1887; s. Franz and Minni (Girgensohn) K.; student Gymnasium, Wolfenbüttel, 1896-1905, Tübingen, Bonn and Berlin univs. Germany, 1905-09; came to U.S., 1935; m. Lili Harleman, July 9, 1927; 1 dau., Karin. Privatdozent, Frankfurt on Main, Germany, 1912-21; dir. anthropoid sta., Tenerife, Canary Islands, 1913-20; prof. psychology, Göttingen U., Germany, 1921-22; prof. psychology and philosophy Berlin U., Germany, 1922-35; prof. psychology Swarthmore Coll., 1935-58; research prof. Dartmouth, 1958—. Mem. Am. Psychol. Assn., Soc. Exptl. Psychologists, Acad. Arts and Scis. (hon.), Am. Philos. Soc., Nat. Acad. Scis. Author: Die Physischen Gestalten in Ruhe and im Stationären Zustand, 1920; Mentality of Apes, 1925; Gestalt Physchology, 1929; Place of Value in a World of Facts, 1938; Dynamics in Psychology, 1940. Home: Enfield, N.H. Died June 11. 1967.

KOINER, C. WELLINGTON, engr., city mgr.; b. Augusta County, Va., May 16, 1870; ed. pub. and pvt. schs.; m. Katie M. Bragunier, Sept. 25, 1895; children—Carl W., Audrey Kathleen, Sara Marie, Virginia. Gen. mgr. Laurel Electric Light, Power & Heat Co., 1892-98; became gen. mgr. Oneida (N.Y.) Light & Power Co., 1898, when this co. was consol., forming Madison County Gas & Electric Co., 1901, was made supt., later pres., gen. mgr.; sec.-treas. Nat. Light & Imp. Co., St. Louis, 1905-07, in charge properties controlled by co. in Wichita, Kan., Ft. Worth, and Waco, Tex.; served as gen. supt., engr. Los Angeles Gas & Electric Co., 1907; engaged by City of Pasadena to build and manage its electric utility, 1908-21; cons. engr. to other cities; city mgr., Pasadena, 1921-25, 33—; cons. practice, 1925-27; dist. mgr. So. Cal. Edison Co., Ltd. (South Bay terr), 1927-33; dir. Pasadena Bldg. & Loan Assn. Past pres. Internat. City Mgrs'. Assn. Fellow Am. Inst. E.E., Am. Soc. Mil. Engrs. Presbyn. Mason, Elk, Kiwanian. Served as power expert, engring., staff U.S. Shipping Bd., Phila., for period during World War. Cons. engr. with power div. Pub. Works Adminstrn., Washington, 1935. Home: 1912 N. Fair Oaks Av. Office: City Hall, Pasadena, Cal. Died Sept. 29, 1947; buried Mountain View Cemetery, Altadena, Cal.

KOKATNUR, VAMAN RAMACHANDRA, cons. chemist; b. Athani, Bombay Presidency, India, Dec. 16, 1886; s. Ramachadra A. and Krishnabai K.; B.Sc., Bombay U., 1911; studied U. Cal., 1912- 13; Shevlin fellow U. Minn., 1914-15, M.S., 1914, Ph.D., 1916; m. Helen Graber, Feb. 11, 1921; children—Urmila, Arvind. Came to U.S., 1912, naturalized, 1921. Chemist Ranade Indsl. Inst., Poona, Inda, 1911-12; research asst. U. of Minn., 1915-17; research chemist Matheison Alkali Works, 1917-18; chief of research dept. Niagara Alkali Co., 1918-20; asst. chief of vat dye group Nat. Aniline & Chem. Co., 1920-21; spl. chemist By-Products Steel Corp. and du Pont Co., 1921-22; cons. practice, 1922—, covering research, engring., development, new processes, litigation, etc.; director of research Antoxygen, Inc., 1934—, pres., 1942—; in India as technical adviser and consulting manager of the Sri Shakti Alkali Works, Dhrangadhra, 1930-31; hon. tech. adviser to Am. Trade Commrs., India, 1930-33; cons. expert to Russia on 5 Year Plan reg. chlorine and caustic soda, 1928; faculty mem. Inst. of Chemistry, Am. Chem. Soc., Northwestern University, 1928; consultant U.S. Navy, 1938. Holder of more than 30 chem. patents; first to make aeroplane dope solvent and vat dyes in Am.; inventor war gases; inventor M59 bomb and flame thrower. Served as capt. C.W.S., U.S. Army Res., active duty, 1942-44. Honored as outstanding inventor Sesquicentennial celebration, U.S. Patent Office, 1940; selected for Wall of Fame, New York World's Fair, 1940. Fellow A.A.A.S., Am. Inst. Chemists; mem. Am. Chem. Soc., History of Science Soc., Am. Electro-chem. Soc., Soc. Am. Mil. Engrs., Sigma Xi, Indian Science Congress. Unitarian. Club: Chemists. Home: 148-09 9th Av., Whitestone, L.I. Office: 114 E. 32d St., N.Y.C. Died Apr. 14, 1950.

KOLLE, FREDERICK STRANGE, plastic surgeon; b. Hanover, Germany, Nov. 22, 1871; s. John and Bertha (Schaare) K.; common sch. edn. in Germany; M.D., Long Island Coll. Hosp., 1893; (hon. M.E., Nat. Coll. Electro-therapeutics, 1897); m. Loretto Elaine Duffy, 1899. Asst. aural phys. Brooklyn Eve and Ear Hosp., 1892-93; interne Kings Co. Hosp., 1893-94; asst. phys. Contagious Disease Hosp., Brooklyn, 1894; in practice, Brooklyn, 1894—. One of 1st X-ray investigators in U.S., 1896; chief instr. dept. electro-therapeutics, Elec. Engring. Inst., New York, 1896-1900; asso. editor Electrical Age, 1897-1902; radiographer to M.E. Hosp., Brooklyn. Inventor: Radiometer; Kolle X-ray coil switching devices; dentaskiascope; oesophameter; folding fluoroscope; X-ray printing process; Kolle focus tube; direct-reading X-ray meter and many instruments used in plastic surgery, etc. Author: The Recent Roentgen Discovery, 1896; The X-Rays, Their Production and Application, 1896; Medico-Surgical Radiography; Subcutaneous Hydrocarbon Protheses, 1908; Plastic and Cosmetic Surgery; Hakon Jare, 1911. Died May 10, 1929.

KOLMER, JOHN ALBERT, (kol' mer), physician; b. Lonaconing, Allegany County, Md., Apr. 24, 1886; s. Leonard and Selma Louisa (Reichelt) K.; grad. Charlotte Hall Mil. Acad., 1904; M.D., U. of Pa., 1908, Dr.P.H., 1914; M.Sc., Villanova, 1915, D.Sc., 1921, LL.D., 1927; D.Sc., LaSalle Coll., 1935; L.H.D., St. Joseph's Coll., 1935; m. B. Cecilia Herron, Sept. 18, 1912. Prof. medicine, Temple U. Sch. of Medicine and School of Dentistry; dir. Inst. Public Health and Preventive Medicine; cons. pathologist St. Vincent's and Misericordia hosps. Fellow A.M.A., Coll. Physicians of Phila., Am. Coll. of Physicians; mem. Am. Assn. Immunologists (pres.), Am. Soc. Clin. Pathologists (pres.), Alpha Kappa, Sigma Xi, etc. Catholic. Author: Infection, Immunity and Biologic Therapy, 1915; Manual of Laboratory Diagnostic Methods, 1925; Chemotherapy and Treatment of Syphilis, 1926; Serum Diagnosis by Complement Fixation, 1928; Acute Infectious Diseases (with Jay Frank Schamberg), 1928; Approved Laboratory Technic (with Fred Boerner), 1931; Clinical Immunology, Biotherapy and Chemotherapy (with Louis Tuft), 1941; Clinical Diagnosis by Laboratory Examinations, 1944; Penicillin Therapy, 1945. Contbr. to Frazier's Spinal Surgery and Keen's Surgery. Home: Bala-Cynwyd, Pa. Office: 2101 Pine St., Phila. Died Dec. 11, 1962.

KOMAREWSKY, VASILI ILYICH, chemist; b. Moscow, Russia, Feb. 17, 1895; s. Ilya V. and Olga P. (Kindiakova) K.; grad. Moscow 9th Gymnasium, 1913; Ph.D., U. Moscow, 1925; m. Jessie Baxter, July 15, 1933. Came to U.S., 1932, naturalized, 1938. Research fellow Kaiser Wilhelm Inst., Berlin, 1926-30; research chemist Universal Oil Product Co., Chgo., 1932-41; prof. chem. engring., dir. catalysis lab. Ill. Inst. Tech., 1936—. Mem. Am. Chem. Soc., Ill. Acad. Sci., A.A.A.S., Am. Soc. Engring. Edn., Sigma Xi, Alpha Chi Sigma, Phi Lambda Upsilon. Author: Isomerization of Pure Hydrocarbons, 1942; Techniques of Catalytic Reactions, 1956. Editor Advances of Catalysis, 1948—. Patentee in field. Home: 5439 East View Park, Chgo. 15, Died June 21, 1957; buried New Milford, Ill.

KOMP, WILLIAM H. WOOD, entomologist; b. Yokohama, Japan, Mar. 16, 1893; s. Frederick and Carrie Joanna (Wood) K.; brought to U.S., 1895; derivative citizenship; student Mass. State Coll., 1911, N.Y.U., 1912; B.S., Rutgers U., 1916, M.S., 1917, D.Sc., 1955; fellow in agr. Cornell, 1917; m. Mildred Crowell, Sept. 1, 1914; 1 dau., Anita (Mrs. Harry M. Williams). Ensign, USPHS, 1918, advanced through grades to capt., 1944, malaria control; vis. staff mem. Gorgas Meml. Lab., Republic of Panama, 1931-47; traveling rep. Pan-Am. San. Bur., 1937; research in malaria, 1921—; loaned to Rockefeller Found. Internat. Health Div. for research on yellow fever, Colombia, 1936; consultant to Creole Petroleum Co., Venezuela, 1936. United Fruit Co., tropical divs., 1924-30, Inst. Inter-Am. Affairs (consultant malaria), 1942—. Chmn. com. on entomology Pan-Am. San. Conf., Rio, 1942. Fellow A.A.A.S., Am. Soc. Tropical Medicine and Hygiene; mem. Am. Mosquito Control Assn., Nat. Malaria Soc., Sociedad Venezolano de Ciencias Naturales (corr. mem.), Am. Acad. Tropical Medicine, Isthian Med. Soc. (Panama), Entomol. Soc. Wash., Washington Acad. Medicine, Chi Psi. Author: The Anopheline Mosquitoes of the Caribbean Region, bull., 1941; discovered Anopheles Darlingi (malaria mosquito) in Central Am., 1940. Home: 6906 Dartmouth Av., College Park, Md. Office: National Institutes of Health, Bethesda, Md. Died Dec. 7, 1955; buried Elmwood Cemetery, New Brunswick, N.J.

KOPETZKY, SAMUEL JOSEPH, (ko-pet'ski), surgeon; b. N.Y. City, Aug. 1, 1876; s. Joseph and Lena (Bernhardt) K.; student Coll. City of N.Y., 1894-96; M.D., Coll. Physicians and Surgeons (Columbia), 1898; m. Anah Doob, Apr. 2, 1903; children— Karl, Yvonne K. (Mrs. Robert Sterling). Prof. otology N.Y. Polyclinic Med. Sch. and Hosp. since 1920; cons. otolaryngologist, Beth Israel Hosp.; dir. of otolaryngology, United Israel Zion Hosp. (Brooklyn); cons. otologist Nyack (N.Y.) Hosp., Newark (N.J.), Beth Israel Hosp., Vassar Bros. Hosp. (Poughkeepsie, N.Y.). Served in Spanish-Am. War and World Wars I and II; colonel Med. Corps. Received the Legion of Merit and the Silver Star; Chevalier of the Legion of Honor (France). Fellow Am. Coll. Surgeons, A.M.A., New York Acad. Medicine, Am. Acad. Ophthalmology and Oto-laryngology, Am. Rhinol., Laryngol. and Otol. Soc. (pres. 1937-38), Med. Soc. of State of N.Y. (pres. 1941-42); corr. Société Laryngologie des Hospiteaux de Paris; formerly speaker House of Delegates, Medical Society State of N.Y. Author: Surgery of the Ear, 1908; Otologic Surgery, 1925, 2d edit., 1929; Deafness, Tinctus and Vertigo, 1948. Editor of New York Medical Week since its establishment, 1920-36; editor Surgery of the Ear. Home: 300 E. 57th St. Office: 30 E. 60th St., N.Y. City 21. Died Nov. 13, 1950.

KOPPIUS, O(TTO) T(OWNSEND), educator; b. Hettstedt, Germany, Dec. 24, 1889; s. Karl and Friederike (Boettcher) K.; B.S., Marion (Ala.) Mil. Inst., 1909; B.S., U. Chgo., 1913, Ph.D., 1920; m. Mary Townsend, Sept. 23, 1915 (dec. Nov. 1960); children—Mary (Mrs. R. W. Williams), Martha (Mrs. H. A. Miller), Joseph T. Came to U.S., 1906, naturalized, 1912. Instr. math., physics Marion Mil. Inst., 1909-12, 1913-14; fellow research asst. U. Chgo., 1914-16, instr. U. High Sch., 1917, instr. physics, 1917-20; asst. prof. physics Oberlin Coll., 1920-24; asso. prof. physics U. Ky., 1924-33, prof., 1933—; vis. prof. physics U. Tenn., summer, 1922-23; geophysicist Sun Oil Co., Dallas, 1928-29 Mem. Am. Phys. Soc., Am. Assn. Physics Tchrs., A.A.A.S., Ky. Acad. Scis., Am. Assn. U. Profs., Sigma Xi, Sigma Pi Sigma, Phi Kappa Tau. Democrat. Mem. Disciples of Christ Ch. Mason. Researcher in electronics and optics. Contbr. articles on spltys. to sci. jours. Home: 131 University Av., Lexington 44, Ky. Died Nov. 6, 1965.

KORSTIAN, CLARENCE FERDINAND, dean and prof. forestry; b. Saline County, Neb., June 26, 1889; s. John Weber and Mary Emma (Trout) K.; B.S.F., U. of Neb., 1911, M.F., 1913; M.A., Southeastern Christian

Coll., 1924; research fellow, Yale U., 1925-26, Ph.D., 1926; m. Catherine Dick, Nov. 25, 1914; children—Kenneth Clarence, Robert John, Grace K. Graham. Asst. in dendrology and silviculture, U. of Neb., 1909-10; field asst. in Forest Service, U.S. Dept. Agr., 1910-11; asst. pathologist Pa. Chestnut Tree Blight Commn., 1912; forest asst. Forest Service U.S. Dept. Agr., 1912-13, forest examiner, 1913-22, asso. silviculturist, Appalachian Forest Expt. Sta., 1922-27, silviculturist, 1927-28, sr. silviculturist, 1928-30; dir. Duke Forest and prof. silviculture, Duke U., since 1930, dean Sch. of Forestry since 1938. Mem. Nat. Research Council (adv. rep. div. biology and agr., 1935-41; mem. exec. com. 1939-40; vice chmn. 1944-45). Chmn. of the City Tree Commission of Durham, North Carolina, 1931-53, commission on forestry and related tng. So. Regional Edn. Bd. Fellow A.A.A.S. (mem. council, 1933-46); mem. Soc. American Foresters (sec. Intermountain sect. 1916-20); sec. Appalachian sect. 1921-25, chmn. 1928, 35; mem. exec. council, 1932-35; pres., 1938-41; Fellow, 1942), Utah Acad. Sciences (v.p., 1919-20; pres., 1920-21), Am. Forestry Assn. (vice-pres. 1939, 41), N.C. Forestry Assn. (pres., 1943-47), N.C. Forestry Council (chmn. 1949-51), N.C. Acad. Sci. (pres., 1949-50), Ecolog. Soc. of Am. (v.p., 1942), Southern Assn. Science and Industry (v.p. 1949-51), Xi Sigma Pi (hon.), Phi Sigma, Sigma Xi, Acacia. Presbyn. Mason, Rotarian. Author: Seeding and Planting in the Practice of Forestry, 3d edit. (with James W. Toumey), 1941; Foundations of Silviculture Upon an Ecological Basis (with James W. Toumey), revised edit. 1947. Co-editor: Naturalist's Guide to the Americas, 1926. Contbr. bulls., reports and articles on forestry. Mem. editorial bd. Ecology, 1923-30, 33-49; editor Ecological Monographs, 1933-49. Home: 4 Sylvan Rd., Durham N.C. Died Feb. 22, 1968.

KORZYBSKI, ALFRED HABDANK (SKARBEK), (kor-zib'ski), scientist, author; b. Warsaw, Poland, July 3, 1879; s. Ladislas Habdank K. and Countess Helena (Rzewuska) K.; ed. Warsaw Realschule and Warsaw Poly. Inst.; grad. study in Germany, Italy, U.S.; m. Mira Edgerly, Jan., 1919. Came to U.S. 1916, naturalized, 1940. Managed family estates in Poland; teacher of mathematics, physics, French and German in Warsaw, Poland; served with cav. and bodyguard heavy arty., also attached to Intelligence Dept., Russian Gen. Staff; sent to U.S. and Canada as artillery expert; sec. Polish-French Mil. Commn. in U.S., 1918; recruiting officer Polish-French Army, U.S. and Can., 1918; war lecturer for U.S. Govt.: sec. Polish Commn. (Labor Sect.), League of Nations, 1926; writer and lecturer; became pres. and dir. Inst. of General Semantics, Chicago, 1938, now Lakeville, Conn. Fellow American Assn. Advancement Sci.; member Am. Math. Soc., Chicago Soc. for Personality Study, Assn. for Symbolic Logic, N.Y. Acad. Sciences, Soc. for Applied Anthropology. Author: Manhood of Humanity—The Science and Art of Human Engineering, 1921; Science and Sanity, An Introduction to Non-aristotelian Systems and General Semantics, 1933, 3d edit., 1948; also many scientific papers. Address: Institute of General Semantics, Lakeville, Conn. Died Mar. 1, 1950.

KOSER, STEWART ARMENT, bacteriologist, educator; b. Harrisburg, Pa., Mar. 30, 1894; s. Alexander Stewart and Ella Lucretia (Arment) K.; Ph.B., Yale, 1915, M.A., 1917, Ph.D., 1918; m. Hilda Marion Croll, Aug. 23, 1927; 1 dau., Marion Aimee (Mrs. Armstrong). Asst. in bacteriology, Yale, 1916-18; bacteriologist U.S. Bur. Chemistry, 1919-23; asst. prof. bacteriology, U. Ill., 1923-28; asst. prof. bacteriology U. Chicago, 1928-36, asso. prof., 1936-43, prof. bacteriology, 1943-59, professor of bacteriology, emeritus, 1959-71; mem. adv. com. lab. standards Ill. State Health Dept., 1943-47; chmn. Lilly award com. (bacteriology), 1940-42. Served as sgt., U.S. Army, World War I; adv. to pre-med. students war training program, 1943-44. Awarded Pasteur award by Soc. Ill. Bacteriologists, 1949. Mem. Soc. Am. Bacteriologists (councilor 1934-36, 38-40, dir. local brs. 1936-39), Soc. Ill. Bacteriologists (pres. 1943-44); Soc. Exptl. Biology and Medicine, Am. Pub. Health Assn., A.A.A.S., Internat. Assn. Dental Research, Sigma Xi, Gamma Alpha, Alpha Chi Sigma. Club: Quadrangle (Chicago). Author: Vitamin Requirements of Bacteria and Yeasts, 1968. Mem. editorial bd. Jour. Bacteriology, 1935-51, Jour. Infectious Diseases since 1941. Contbr. sci. jours. Home: Red Bank NJ Died Apr. 15, 1971; buried Womelsdorf PA

KOSMAK, GEORGE WILLIAM, (kos'mak), obstetrician, gynecologist, editor; b. New York, N.Y., July 24, 1873; s. Emil H. and Louise (Wack) K.; A.B., Columbia, 1894; M.D., Coll. Physicians and Surgeons, Columbia, 1899; m. Florence Fischer, Feb. 5, 1902; children—George William, Katherine Louise, Beatrice Florence. Physician, New York, 1902—; attending surgeon New York Lying-In Hosp., 1904-26; cons. obstetrician Caledonian, Woman's Infirmary, Fifth Av. and Nyack hosps.; med. dir. emeritus Booth Memorial; cons. Fed. Children's Bureau, New York State Dept. of Health; editor Am. Jour Obstetrics, 1909-19; founder and editor Am. Jour. Obstetrics and Gynecology, 1920—; pres. Fischer Realty Co., editor N. Y. State Journal of Medicine. Chmn. med. bds. of Maternity Center Assn., Visiting Nurses Association. Editor New York State Journal of Medicine. Hon. fellow Royal Coll. Obstetricians and Gynecologists; mem. American Medical Association, Am. Gynecol. Soc. (former pres.), Am. Assn. Obstetricians and Gynecologists, N.Y. Acad. Medicine, Med. Soc. State of N.Y. (treas. 1937-41; trustee), Theta Delta Chi. Clubs: Century, University (N.Y.C.). Author: Toxemia of Pregnancy, 1922. Contbr. to numerous med. jours. Address: 610 Park Av., N.Y.C. 21. Died July 10, 1954; buried Woodlawn Cemetery.

KOSZALKA, MICHAEL FRANCIS, physician; b. Bklyn., May, 25, 1911; s. John and Mary (Wojtas) K.; B.S., St. Bonaventure Coll., 1935; M.D., Georgetown U., 1938; m. Helen Charlotte Groniak, Aug. 14, 1942; children—Michele (Mrs. Gustav Massee), Michael Francis, Pamela. Intern, Kings County Hosp., Bklyn., 1938-40; practice medicine specializing in internal medicine, Woodhaven, N.Y., 1940-41; resident in internal medicine Norwalk (Conn.) Gen. Hosps., 1941-42, Mpls., 1949-50; resident in internal medicine VA Hosp., Wood, Wis., 1946-48, chief sect. gastroenterology, 1948-49; chief med. service VA Hosp., Fargo, N.D., 1950-69, chief staff, Hosp., 1969-70; teaching asst. Marquette U. Sch. Medicine, Milw. 1948, clin. instr. med., 1949; clin. asst. dept. medicine U. Minn., Mpls., 1949-50; asso. teaching staff U. N.D. Sch. Medicine, Fargo, 1954-68, asst. clin. prof. medicine, 1969-70, asso. prof. clin. medicine, 1970; adj. prof. pharmacology N.D. State U., 1969. Mem. Fargo-Moorhead Fed. Exec. Council, 1968-70; mem. med. subcom. N.D. Council for Safety, 1961; chmn. bus. sect. Cass County chpt. Am. Cancer Soc., 1963; mem. N.D. Com. on Mental Health with Spl. Interest in Alcoholism, 1969. Bd. dirs. Fargo VA Employees Credit Union, 1962-70, v.p., 1963, pres., 1963-70; trustee United Fund of Fargo, 1963-65. Served to maj., M.C., AUS, 1942-46. Diplomate Am. Bd Internal Medicine. Fellow A.C.P.; mem. A.M.A., Am. Soc. for Gastrointestinal Endoscopy, Am. Gastroscopic Soc., Am. Thoracic Soc., 1st Dist. Med. Soc. N.D. (asso.), Assn. U.S. Army, Res. Officers Assn., Am. Legion, Catholic War Vets. Elk. Contbr. articles to med. jours. Home: Fargo ND Died Nov. 11, 1970; buried Nat. Cemetery Ft Snelling St Paul MN

KOTH, ARTHUR WILLIAM, engr.; b. Wishek, N.D., Dec. 20, 1907; s. John William and Christina (Herr) K.; B.S. in Chem. Engring., U. N.D., 1931, M.S. 1932; m. Mildred F. Lewis, June 7, 1952. Indsl. fellow U. N.D., 1931-32, fuel technologist, 1932-35, instr. chem. engring., 1935-36; asst. prof. chem. engring. U. N.D., 1937-41, asso. prof., 1941-46, prof. chem. engring., acting head mining and metallurgy dept., 1946, prof. chem. engring., acting head mining engring. dept., 1946-48, prof. metallurgy and acting head mining engring. dept., 1948-50, prof. metallurgy, head mining engring. dept., 1950-60, prof. metallurgy, chmn. mining engring. dept., 1960-62, prof. gen. indsl. engring., chmn. dept., 1962—; research engr. welding dept. A. O. Smith Corp., Milwaukee, 1936-37. Chem. engr. U.S. Bur. of Mines, in charge coop. studies and operation of pilot plants on lignite drying and gasification, 1939-48. Registered profl. engr., N.D. Mem. Am. Inst. Mining and Metall. Engrs., Am. Chem. Soc., Am. Soc. Engring. Edn., Am. Assn. U. Profs., N.D. Soc. Profl. Engrs., Sigma Xi, Sigma Tau. Author tech. articles in field. Home: 706 N. 25th St., Grand Forks, N.D. Died Dec. 9, 1966; buried Meml. Park Cemetery, Grand Forks, N.D.

KOVACS, RICHARD (IGNATIUS), (ko'vach), physician; b. Nagybecskerek, Hungary (now Jugoslavia), May 5, 1884; s. Ignatius Marton and Irene (Korn) K.; student Kaiser Wilhelm U., Berlin, Germany, 1903-04; M.D., Royal Hungarian U., Budapest, 1901-03, 1904-06; m. Ina Claire Nickel, June 6, 1922. Came to U.S., 1909, naturalized, 1915. Interne, St. Rockus (City) Hosp., Budapest, 1907, 1st Mil. Hosp., Vienna, 1907; ship's surgeon Cunard Line, 1906 and 1909; clin. training U. of Vienna, 1907 and 1909; ship's surgeon Hamburg Am. Line, 1908; clin. asst. outpatient dept. Lenox Hill Hosp., New York, 1910-23, also Presbyn. Hosp., 1912-16; gen. practice of medicine, N.Y. City, 1910-20; phys. therapist Reconstruction Hosp., N.Y. City, 1920-29; adjunct prof. phys. medicine Polyclinic Med. Sch. and Hosp., N.Y. City, 1926-30, clin. prof., 1930-40, prof., 1940; attending phys. therapist Manhattan State Hosp. since 1929, Harlem Valley State Hosp., 1932, Dept. of Correction Hosp., 1938, Columbus Hosp., 1943; consultant Mary Immaculate Hosp., Jamaica, L.I., St. Charles Hosp., Pt. Jeffers, L.I., Alexian Bros. Hosp., Elizabeth, N.J., also Vets. Adminstrn., Branch No. 2, N.Y., surgeon gen. of the Army; U.S. del. to 5th Internat. Congress on Phys. Medicine, London, 1936; sec. Am. com. 5th and 7th Internat. Congress on Indsl. Accidents and Occupational Diseases. Vice chmn. Yorkville Dist. Charity Orgn. Soc., 1928-29. Examining physician Selective Service, World War I; instr. mil. postgrad. med. courses, World War II. Diplomate Am. Bd. Physical Medicine. Mem. Lenox Hill Neighborhood Assn., Hungarian Relief Soc. of N.Y. (dir.), Soc. Med. Jurisprudence (treas.), A.M.A. (consultant, council on phys. medicine), N.Y. Co. and N.Y. State Med. Soc., N.Y. Acad. Medicine (consultant, phys. medicine), Am. Therapeutic Soc., Am. Congress Phys. Medicine (sec., received Golden Key Award, 1948), N.Y. Soc. Phys. Medicine (past pres., treas.), Royal Soc. Medicine of London. Republican. Roman Catholic. Clubs: Internat. Med. of N.Y. (pres.), Liederkranz of N.Y. (trustee), Catholic of N.Y. Author: Electrotherapy and Light Therapy (Lea & Febiger, 1st edit. 1932, 6th revised edit. 1949), Manual of Physical Therapy (Lea & Febiger, 1935, 4th rev. edit. 1949); Nature—M.D. (Appleton-Century, 1934). Editor: Year Book of Physical Medicine, 1938-47; mem. editorial bd. Archives of Physical Medicine. Contbr. of numerous articles on phys. medicine. Home: 1150 Fifth Av. Office: 2 E. 88th St., N.Y. City 28. Died Dec. 29, 1950; buried Woodlawn Cemetery, N.Y.

KOYL, CHARLES HERSCHEL, engineer; b. Amherstburg, Ont., Aug. 14, 1855; s. Rev. Ephraim Lillie and Frances (Culp) K.; A.B., Victoria Coll., Cobourg, Ont., 1877; post-grad. student Johns Hopkins, 1879-81, fellow in physics, 1881-83; m. Georgiana Thacher Washburn, Nov. 6, 1885; m. 2d, Adéle T. Sanford, Apr. 27, 1901. Physical science master Wesleyan Coll., Stanstead, Que., 1877-79; head dept. mathematics and physics, high sch., Washington, 1885-87; prof. physics, Swarthmore Coll., 1887-89; v.p. Nat. Switch & Signal Co., 1889-91; pres. Nat. Drying Co., 1891-93; scientific asst. to Col. Waring, commr. street cleaning, New York, 1895-96; mgr. Automatic Banjo Co., New York, 1896-99; mgr. Industrial Water Co., 1899-1902; cons. practice; engr. water service G.N. Ry., 1912-19, and of C.,M.&St.P. Ry., 1919—. Delegate to Internat. Congress of Electricians, Phila., 1884. John Scott Legacy Medal, Franklin Inst., for invention of the parabolic semaphore, 1889. Home: Chicago, Ill. Died Dec. 18, 1931.

KRACKE, ROY RACHFORD, coll. dean; b. Hartselle, Ala., Dec. 5, 1897; s. Henry August and Carrie Camilla (Puryear) K.; student Ala. Poly. Inst., 1913-14; B.S., U. Ala., 1924; M.D., U. Chgo., 1927; m. Virginia Carolyn Minter, Oct. 17, 1925; children—Roy Rachford, Rachel Rebecca, Henry Minter, William Gunter, Robert Russel, Virginia Carolyn. Instr. in pathology U. Ala., 1925-26; successively instr. in pathology, asst. prof., asso. prof. and prof. of pathology, bacteriology and lab. medicine Emory U., 1926-44; pathologist Emory U. Hosp., 1930-44; now dean and prof. medicine (hematology), U. Ala. Sch. Medicine. Served with Hosp Corps., USN, 1917-21; lt. (j.g.) M.C., USN, 1927-28; lt. M.C., USNR, 1928-38. Recipient certificate of merit by A.M.A. for med. research, 1934; gold medal by Am. Soc. Clin. Pathologists, 1935. Mem. Am. Bd. Pathology, A.M.A. (chmn. sect. of pathology 1938), So. Med. Assn. (chmn. sect. of pathology 1940), Med. Assn. of Ala., Jefferson County Med. Soc. of Ala., Am. Soc. Clin. Pathologists (past pres.), Sigma Xi, Phi Beta Pi, Phi Beta Kappa, Alpha Omega Alpha. Democrat. Presbyn. Club: Rotary. Author: Diseases of the Blood and Atlas of Hematology, 1937, 2d edit., 1941. Editor: Textbook of Clinical Pathology, 1938, 2d edit., 1940; Laboratory Manual of Bacteriology, 4th edit., 1941; Color Atlas of Hematology, 1947. Contbr. articles to med. jours. Address: Medical College of Alabama, 620 S. 20th St., Birmingham, Ala. Died June 27, 1950; buried Oak Hill Cemetery, Birmingham.

KRAEMER, HENRY, scientist; b. Phila., Pa., July 22, 1868; s. John Henry and Caroline K.; parents died when he was 3 yrs. old; student Girard Coll., 1877-83; Ph.B., Columbia, 1895; Ph.G., Phila. Coll. Pharmacy, 1889; Ph.D., U. of Marburg, 1896; (hon. Pharm.M., Phila. Coll. of Pharmacy, 1912); m. Minnie A. Behm. Instructor in pharmacognosy, Coll. Pharmacy of City of New York, 1890; prof. botany and pharmacognosy, Sch. of Pharmacy, Northwestern U., 1896-97; prof. botany and pharmacognosy and dir. micros. lab., Phila. Coll. Pharmacy, 1897-1917; prof. pharmacognosy, U. of Mich., 1917-20; dir. Kraemer Scientific Lab., 1920—; dir. Era courses in pharmacy, 1921—. Editor Am. Jour. Pharmacy, 1898-1917. Member committee of revision of U.S. Pharmacopoeia and chairman sub-committee botany and pharmacognosy, 1900—. Mem. council on pharmacy and chemistry A.M.A., 1913-21; pres. Am. Conf. Pharm. Faculties, 1917, Phila. Author: A Text-book of Botany and Pharmacognosy, 1902, 07, 08, 10; Applied and Economic Botany, 1914, 16; Scientific and Applied Pharmacognosy, 1915, 20. Home: Mt. Clemens, Mich. Died Sept. 9, 1924.

KRAFKA, JOSEPH, JR., (kräf'ka), prof. micro-anatomy; b. Ottumwa, Ia., Aug. 14, 1890; s. Joseph and Anna Marie (Huber) K.; B.S., Lake Forest (Ill.) Coll., 1914, M.A., 1915; Ph.D., U. of Ill., 1919; M.D., U. of Ga., 1933; m. Bessie Belle Harsch, June 25, 1916; children—Katherine, Joseph Franklyn. Prof. zoölogy, and head of dept., U. of Ga., 1919-26; prof. micro-anatomy, med. dept. same univ., since 1926. Mem. Am. Soc. Zoölogists, Entomol. Soc. America, Ga. State Acad. Science, Am. Soc. Anatomy, Sigma Xi, Phi Pi Epsilon. Democrat. Methodist. Contbr. series of papers dealing with med. history of Ga., arteriosclerosis and human embryology. Wrote textbooks in histology and human embryology. Home: Lakemont Drive, Augusta, Ga. Died Nov. 5, 1946.

KRAFT, JAMES LEWIS, b. Stevensville, Ont., Can., Dec. 11, 1874; s. George Franklin and Minerva (Tripp) K.; ed. common schs.; m. Pauline Elizabeth Platt, June 2, 1909; 1 dau., Edith Lucile. Came to U.S., 1903, naturalized citizen, 1911. Settled in Chicago, 1905, and became identified with cheese business; organized corporation, 1909; now chmn. bd. Kraft Foods Corp., Chgo. (became div. Nt. Dairy Products Corp.), v.p., dir.

Invented pasteurizing process as applied to cheese industry. Trustee Baptist Theol. Sem., Chgo. Recipient of Horatio Alger award. Republican. Baptist. Clubs: Mid-Day, Lake Shore Athletic. Home: 1426 Chicago Av., Evanston, Ill. Office: 500 Peshtigo Court, Chgo. Died Feb. 16, 1953; buried Meml. Park Cemetery, Evanston, Ill.

KRAMER, ANDREW ANTHONY, mfr., inventor; b. Kansas City, Kan., June 4, 1867; s. Frederick and Margaret (Hartman) K.; ed. pub. schs.; m. Ella Mary Conway, Nov. 27, 1890; children—William Francis, Clarence Anthony (dec.), Walter Andrew, (dec.), Helen Ione, Joseph Michael. Founder, 1893, since pres. Columbian Steel Tank Co., mfrs. sheet steel products and metal specialties, Kansas City; Pres. Steel Mfg. & Warehouse Co. Mem. Am. Soc. M.E. (awarded 5 gold medals for excellence of manufactured products), Kansas City Chamber Commerce, St. Vincent de Paul Soc. Democrat. Mem. Knights of Columbus. Clubs: Kansas City, Blue Hills Country. Inventor of appliances for safe handling, transportation and storage of gasoline and other inflammable liquids; holder of nearly 300 patents. Home: 6700 Elmwood Av. Office: 1509 W. 12th St., Kansas City MO

KRAMER, HANS, (kra'mer), cons. engr.; b. Magdeburg, Germany, Dec. 12, 1894; s. Adolf and Toni Kramer; came to U.S., 1902, naturalized, 1913; student U. Mich., 1912-13; B.S., U.S. Mil. Acad., 1918; grad. Engr. Sch., 1927, 1929; M.S., U. Pa., 1928; D.Eng., Tech. U. of Dresden, Germany, 1932; m. Alice Elizabeth Harvey, May 20, 1939; 1 son, Hans Harvey. Commd. 2d lt. C.E., U.S. Army, 1918, advanced through grades to brig. gen., 1942, ret. from service, 1945; now in practice as cons. engr. Recipient Freeman Travelling Scholarship, Am. Soc. C.E., 1930-31. Mem. Soc. Am. Mil. Engrs., Am. Soc. C.E., Permanent Internat. Assn. Nav. Congresses, Am. Geophys. Union, Am. Inst. Cons. Engr., Internat. Assn. Hydraulic Structures Research, Tau Beta Pi. Rep. of U.S. on Ark. River Compact between Colo. and Kans.; mem. bd. of cons. engrs. for the Panama Canal. Author: Modellgeschiebe und Schleppkraft, 1932. Address: 462 Nevada Av., San Mateo, Cal. Died Feb. 16, 1957; buried Golden Gate Nat. Cemetery, San Bruno, Cal.

KRAMER, SIMON PENDLETON, surgeon; b. Cincinnati, Jan. 1, 1868; s. Jacob and Emma (Bloom) K.; grad. Woodward High Sch., Cincinnati, 1885; M.D., Med. Coll. of Ohio, 1888; post-grad. work U. of Göttingen, 1889, U. of Berlin, 1890, Univ. Coll., London, 1893; m. Minnie Halle; children—Victor Horsley, Simon Paul. Engaged in practice of medicine, Cincinnati, 1888—; prof. principles of surgery, U. of Cincinnati, Oct. 1909—; surgeon to Cincinnati Hosp., Nov. 1910—. Maj. and brigade surgeon, U.S.V., in Spanish-Am. War, Aug. 11, 1898-Oct. 31, 1899; served in Havana, during Am. occupation as comdg. officer Mil. Hosp., etc. Pres. Acad. Medicine of Cincinnati, 1904-05; 1st pres. Cincinnati Soc. Med. Research; mem. Am. Neurol. Assn. Author: of various memoirs on Surgery and Physiology of Central Nervous System. Maj. M.C., U.S.A., World War. Office: 826 Glenwood Av., Cincinnati, Ohio.

KRASIK, SIDNEY, physicist, mfg. co. exec.; b. Brownsville, Pa., Mar. 26, 1911; s. Samuel and Sophia (Podolny) K.; B.S., Carnegie Inst. Tech., 1932; Ph.D., Cornell U., 1947; m. Frances Goldberg, June 28, 1936; children—Carl, Sophie Ann. With Westinghouse Electric Corp., 1940—, tech. dir. astronuclear lab., 1959-61, project engr. Nerva rocket, 1961-62, v.p., 1963—; spl. research gaseous electronics, devel. microwave electronic devices, nuclear reactor devel. Fellow Am. Nuclear Soc. (dir.), Am. Phys. Soc., I.R.E.; mem. A.A.A.S., Am. Rocket Soc., Inst. Aerospace Scis. Home: 2081 Beechwood Blvd., Pitts. 17. Office: P.O. Box 10864, Pitts. 36. Died Oct. 1965.

KRATHWOHL, WILLIAM CHARLES, educator; b. Buffalo, N.Y., Oct. 10, 1882; s. Charles Gottlieb and Minnie (Stutzriem) K.; A.B., Harvard, 1907, A.M., Columbia, 1910; Ph.D., U. of Chicago, 1913; married Sarah H. Reading, July 14, 1917 (deceased); one son, David R.; married 2d, Marie A. Reimold, June 3, 1922 (dec.). Instr., Barnard Coll., Columbia U., 1907-11, Washington U., St. Louis, Mo., 1911-12; prof. mathematics, Ripon (Wis.) Coll., 1913-14; asst. prof. of mathematics, Armour Inst. Tech. (now Ill. Inst. Tech.), 1914-19, asso. prof., 1919-31, prof. since 1931, chmn. dept. of mathematics, 1931-34, dir. dept. educational tests and measurements 1938-45, dir. of tests, Inst. for Psychol. Services, 1945-69. Diplomate Am. Bd. Examinations in Professional Psychology; fellow A.A.A.S.; mem. Am. Math. Society, Math. Assn. of America, Am. Soc. for Engring. Edn., Central Assn. of Science and Mathematics Teachers, Nat. Vocational Guidance Assn., Am. Psychol. Assn., Midwest Psychol. Assn., Ill. Psychol. Assn., Chicago Psychol. Club, Phi Delta Kappa, Sigma Chi. Co-author: Analytic Geometry, 1921. Office: Chicago IL Died Apr. 16, 1969; buried Riverview Cemetery, South Bend IN

KRAUS, CHARLES AUGUST, chemist; b. Knightsville, Ind., Aug. 15, 1875; s. John H. and Elizabeth (Schaefer) K.; B.S., U. Kan., 1898; Ph.D., Mass. Inst. Tech., 1898; Sc.D., Kalamazoo Coll., 1933. Colgate U., 1939, Brown U., 1946, Clark U., 1949; m. Frederica Feitshans, June 9, 1902; children—Charles N., Mary E., Philip B., Douglas L. Research asso. Mass. Inst. Tech., 1908-12; asst. prof. chemistry research, 1912-14; prof. chemistry, dir. chem. research Brown U., 1924-46, now emeritus; cons. Metcalf Research Lab. Cons. Bur. of Mines, 1918. C.W.S., 1918-19. Recipient Nichols medal, 1924, Franklin medal, 1938, Priestly medal, 1950. Hon. fellow Franklin Inst.; mem. Am. Chem. Soc. (past pres.), Am. Phys. Soc., Am. Assn. U. Profs., A.A.A.S., Faraday Soc., Washington and Am. acads. scis., Am. Philos. Soc., Nat. Inst. Social Scis., Sigma Xi, Phi Beta Kappa, Phi Lambda Upsilon, Alpha Chi Sigma. Contbr. to sci. jours. Home: 92 Keene St., Providence 6. Died June 27, 1967.

KRAUS, EDWARD HENRY, educator, mineralogist; b. Syracuse, N.Y., Dec. 1, 1875; s. John Erhardt and Rosa Kocher (Knobel) K.; B.S., Syracuse U., 1896, M.S., 1897, Sc.D. (hon.), 1920, LL.D., 1934; Ph.D., U. Munich, 1901; Sc.D., U. Mich., 1967; m. Lena Margaret Hoffman, June 24, 1902; children—Margaret Anna (Mrs. Edward T. Ramsdell) (dec.), Edward Hoffman (dec.), John Daniel. Asst. in mineralogy and German, Syracuse U., 1896, instr., 1897-99, 1901-02, asso. prof. mineralogy, 1902, prof. geology and chemistry, summers, 1903, 04; head, dept. sci. Central High Sch., Syracuse, 1902-04; asst. prof. mineralogy U. Mich., 1904-06, jr. prof., 1906-07, mineralogy and petrography, 1907-08, prof. and dir. mineral lab. 1908-19, prof. crystallography and mineralogy, and dir. Mineral Lab., 1919-33, prof. crystallography and mineralogy, 1933-46, sec., 1908-10, acting dean, 1911-15, dean summer session, 1915-33, acting dean, 1920-23, dean Coll. Pharmacy, 1923-33, and Coll. of Lit., Sci. and Arts, 1933-45, dean emeritus 1945-73; Henry Russel lectr. U. Mich., 1945; Orton lectr. Am. Ceramic Soc., 1954. Recipient Roebling medal Mineral. Soc. Am., 1945. Fellow Geol. Soc. Am., A.A.A.S. Mineral Soc. Am. (pres. 1920, hon. pres. 1955-73), Am. Coll. Dentists (hon.), Optical Soc. Am.; mem. Am. Gem Soc. (hon. certified gemologist 1954), German Mineral. Soc. (hon.), Am. Chem. Soc., Mich. Acad. Sci. (pres. 1920), Am. Inst. Mining and Metallurgy Engrs., Am. Pharmacy Assn., Mich. Schoolmasters Club (pres. 1943-44), Gemological Assn. Gt. Britain (hon., v.p. 1956-73), German Gemological (hon.), Gemological Inst. Am. (pres. 1948-70), Phi Beta Kappa, Sigma Xi, Phi Kappa Phi. Author: Essentials of Crystallography, 1906; Descriptive Mineralogy, 1911; Tables for the Determination of Minerals (with W.F. Hunt) 1911; Mineralogy (with W.F. Hunt), 1920; Gems and Gem Materials (with E.F. Holden), 1925, 5th edit. (with C.B. Slawson), 1947; also numerous articles in scientific and ednl. jours., U.S. and abroad. Home: Ann Arbor MI Died Feb. 3, 1973.

KRAUSE, ALLEN KRAMER, M.D., medical research; b. Lebanon, Pa., Feb. 13, 1881; s. George Derr and Jeanie Julia (Kramer) K.; A.B., Brown U., 1901; grad. student in biology, same univ., 1901-03, A.M., 1902; M.D., Johns Hopkins, 1907; Litt.D. (hon.), Norwich U., 1935; m. Clara Fletcher, Oct. 10, 1906; children—Gregory, Francis, Fletcher. Asst. and instr. pathology, Johns Hopkins, 1907-09; asst. dir. Saranac (N.Y.) Lab., 1909-16; asso. prof. medicine and dir. Kenneth Dows Tuberculosis Research Labs., Johns Hopkins, 1916-29; in charge Tuberculosis Dispensary, Johns Hopkins Hosp., and asso. phys. Johns Hopkins Hosp., 1916-29; pres. The Desert Sanatorium, Tucson, Ariz., 1929-37; clin. prof. medicine, Stanford U., 1929-37; clin. prof. medicine, U. of Southern Calif., 1932-37. Lecturer in medicine, Johns Hopkins. Managing editor Am. Rev. of Tuberculosis, 1916, editor, 1922—; editor Am. sect. of "Tucercle" (London), 1924—; collaborator, Zeitschrift für Tuberkulose (Berlin), Arch. Med.-Chirurg. de l'Appareil Respiratoire (Paris); lecturer Trudeau School of Tuberculosis, 1916-29; counsellor Med. Council U.S. Vets. Bur., 1924—. Awarded Trudeau Medal, 1931. Fellow Am. Coll. Phys., A.A.A.S., American Geographical Soc.; mem. numerous med. societies. Democrat. Protestant. Author: Rest and Other Things, 1922; Environment and Resistance in Tuberculosis, 1923; The Evolution of Tubercle, 1927. Home: Baltimore, Md. Died May 12, 1941.

KRAVCHENKO, VICTOR A., metall. engr.; b. Ekaterinoslav, Russia, Oct. 11, 1905; s. Andrei F. and Tatiana (Kalyadina) K.; grad. Metall. Inst., Dniepropetrovsk, U.S.S.R., 1934; student Kharkov Tech. Inst. and War Coll. of Moscow Province; div. Came to U.S., 1943. Active as metall. engr., exec. in large indsl. trust and enterprises in Russia; lectr. politics, until 1943; mem. Communist Party 1929-44, held post in Soviet of Peoples Commissars, 1942-43. Served as capt. Red Army, World War II. Author: I Chose Freedom, 1946; I Chose Justice, 1950. Contbr. arts. to mags. Address: care Charles Scribner's Sons, 597 Fifth Av., N.Y.C. Died Feb. 25, 1966.

KRAYBILL, HENRY REIST, biochemist; b. Mount Joy, Pa., May 1, 1891; s. Samuel Snyder and Mary Garber (Reist) K.; B.S., Pa. State Coll., 1913; M.S., U. of Chicago, 1915, Ph.D., 1917; m. Ruth Grove, June 9, 1916; children—Henry Lawrence, Richard Reist, Robert Grove (killed in action serving in South Pacific area), Donald Philip. Assistant chemist Pa. State Coll. Agrl. Expt. Sta., 1913-15; instr. in agrl. chemistry, Pa. State Coll., 1915-17; teaching fellow, U. of Chicago, 1916-17; asst. physiologist U.S. Dept. Agr., 1917-19; prof. agrl. chemistry and head of dept., Univ. of N.H., 1919-24; also state chemist, N.H., 1919-24; biochemist, Boyce Thompson Inst. for Plant Research, 1924-26; prof. agrl. chemistry, Purdue, 1926-43 and head of dept. of agrl. chemistry, 1934-43; also state chemist and seed commr. of Indiana, 1926-43. Scientific adviser to Frasch Foundn. Research in Agrl. Chemistry, 1939-47; dir. research and edn. Am. Meat Inst. Found., 1947-55, vice president and director research and education, 1955—, also director dept. scientific research, 1941—; professorial lectr. dept. of biochem., U. of Chgo., since 1941; cons. E.C.A. Mission to Greece, 1949. Fellow A.A.A.S., Am. Inst. Chemists; mem. Am. Inst. of Nutrition, Am. Chem. Soc. (div. of agr. and food chemistry 1934-35, chmn. 1936-38), Bot. Soc. America, Am. Soc. Plant Physiologists (sec.-treas. 1928-29; pres. 1930; v.p. 1933), Am. Soc. Hort. Science, Assn. Official Agrl. Chemists (vice-pres. 1937; pres. 1938), Am. Assn. Feed Control Officials (pres. 1932), Institute of Food Technologists, American Association Cereal Chemists, American Oil Chemists Society, American Society of Biological Chemists, Ill., Ind. acads. sci., Am. Assn. U. Profs., Am. Dietetics Assn., Am. Pub. Health Assn., Am. Soc. Animal Prodn., Am. Soc. Naturalists, Am. Soybean Assn., Assn. Food and Drug Ofcls., Fed. Am. Soc. Exptl. Biology, Nat. Assn. Commrs. Agr., Nat. Farm Chemurgic Council, Nat. Research Council, Soc. Chem. Industry, Soc. Exptl. Biology and Medicine, Alpha Zeta, Sigma Xi, Phi Kappa Phi, Alpha Chi Sigma, Phi Lambda Upsilon, Phi Tau Sigma, Gamma Sigma Delta. Baptist. Mason. Clubs: Quadrangle, Chaos, Chicago Chemists. Contbr. on agrl. biochemistry. Home: 5720 Woodlawn Av. Address: Am. Meat Inst. Found., U. Chgo., Chgo. Died Sept. 30, 1956; buried Mt. Joy (Pa.) Cemetery.

KREISINGER, HENRY, (kri'sing'er), mech. engr.; b. Radnice, Czechoslovakia, Feb. 17, 1876; s. Emanuel and Maria (Milota) K.; came to U.S., 1891; prep. edn. Lewis Inst., Chicago; B.S. in M.E., U. of Ill., 1904, M.E., 1906; m. Ella M. Zaloudek, May 6, 1905; children—Robert Henry, Helen Catharine, Elizabeth Caroline, Emily Mildred (dec.). Asst. engr. U.S. Geol. Survey, technologic br., 1904-10; fuel engr. Clinchfield Fuel Co., Spartanburg, S.C., 1910-13; fuel engr. U.S. Bur. Mines, 1913-20; research engr. Combustion Engring. Corp., New York, since 1920. Assisted in developing the use of powdered coal for steam boilers. Received Percy Nicholls award for 1943 for scientific and industrial achievements in solid fuels. Mem. Am. Soc. M.E., Am. Inst. Mining and Metall. Engrs., A.A.A.S., Sigma Xi. Awarded Chanute medal for best paper on a mech. engring. subject, Western Soc. Engrs., 1907. Republican. Free Thinker. Author of abt., 20 bulls. and tech. papers pub. by U.S. Geol. Survey and U.S. Bur. Mines; also numerous papers on engring. subjects. Home: Piermont, N.Y. Address: Combustion Engineering Company, 200 Madison Av., New York, N.Y. Died May 7, 1946.

KREJCI, MILO WILLIAM, (kra' che), metall. engr.; b. Cleveland, Mar. 4, 1876; s. Martin and Laura (Wiesenberger) K.; B.S. in Mining and Metallurgy, Case Sch. of Applied Science, Cleveland, 1898; m. Hildagarde H. S. Johnson, June 18, 1902; children—Laura Emily, Edith Helen (Mrs. Emmons Bulson). Began career with National Gold Extraction Company, Florence, Colorado, 1899; Delamar Mercur Mines Co., Mercur, Utah, 1899-1900; assayer, Northern Light Mining Co., Ophir, Utah, 1900; chemist, foreman of various depts., gen. foreman of smelter and metall. investigator, Boston & Mont. Consolidated Copper & Silver Mining Co., Great Falls, Mont., 1900-10; chief metallurgist, 1910-15, asst. supt., 1915-18, Ananconda Copper Mining Co. and Boston & Mont. Reduction Works, Great Falls, Mont.; Supt. Internat. Lead Refining Co. and Anaconda Lead Products Co., E. Chicago, Ind., 1918-20; mgr. Parish-Pool Co., Cleveland, 1920-21; v.p. and general mgr. Butterworth-Judson Corp., New York, 1921-23; cons. engring. practice since 1923; consultant engineer U.S.S.R., 1930-32; metallurgist R.F.C., 1941-53. Patentee in field. Republican. Presbyn. Mem. Am. Inst. Mining and Metall. Engrs., Am. Electrochem. Soc. Mason. Address: 247 Haines St., Newark, Del.; (summer) Worcester, N.Y. Died June 24, 1963; buried Maple Grove Cemetery, Worcester, N.Y.

KRESS, DANIEL H., M.D.; b. St. Jacobs, Ont., Can., June 27, 1862; s. Anthony and Eva Katherine (Hartman) K.; prep. edn., high sch., Port Elgin, Ont., and Jones Business Coll., London, Ont.; M.D., U. of Mich., 1894; m. Lauretta Eby, of Flint, Mich., July 9, 1884; children—Eva Lauretta (dec.), Ora Hannah (wife of Dr. William H. Mason), John Eby. Came to U.S., 1886. With Battle Creek (Mich.) Sanitarium as gastro-intestinal specialist, 1894-98; med. supt., sanitarium, Medvale, Eng., 1898-1900. Warhronga Sanitarium, Sydney, Australia, 1900-07; med. supt. Washington (D.C.) Sanitarium and Hosp., 1907-11, neurologist 1919-39, was also med. dir.; now retired. Editor "Life and Health" (Eng.), 1898-1900, Good Health (Australia), 1900-07. Mem. A.M.A., Am. Pub. Health Assn. Seventh Day Adventist. Contbr. to The Watchman, Life and Health. Author: The Cigarette as a Physician Sees It, 1932; Under the Guiding Hand, 1933; also numerous leaflets on health topics. Home: 405 Niblic Av., Orlando, Fla.

KRESS, GEORGE HENRY, M.D.; b. Cincinnati, O., Dec. 23, 1874; s. Henry and Selma (Kern) K.; B.S., U. of Cincinnati, 1896; M.D., Med. Coll. of Ohio (U. of Cincinnati), 1899; post-grad. work Phila., Berlin, London and Vienna; m. Elizabeth Hamilton Hill, June 16, 1903. Asst. surgeon Nat. Soldiers' Hosp., Dayton, O., 1900-03; removed to Los Angeles, 1903; formerly specialized in diseases of eye, ear, nose and throat; dean Los Angeles Med. Dept. U. of Calif., 1914-38; was chief staff Graves Memorial Dispensary, and eye clinician; chief of the eye staff, Los Angeles County Hosp., 1910-38; was sec. faculty and prof. hygiene, University of Southern Calif. Coll. Medicine; emeritus prof. ophthalmology, Coll. of Med. Evangelists; sr. surgeon, U. of Southern Calif., S.A.T.C., World War I; ex-chmn. Los Angeles County Health Department Board; was member of Calif. State Bd. of Health; was chmn. Eye and Ear Com., Los Angeles City Schs.; was mem. Exec. Med. Group, Major Disaster Council, City of Los Angeles. Ex-president Calif. State Commn. to Investigate Tuberculosis of Calif. and Los Angeles tuberculosis assns., Los Angeles Acad. Ophthalmology and Oto-laryngology. Fellow Am. Coll. Surgeons, A.M.A. (past v.p.); mem. Los Angeles County Med. Assn. (past pres., past sec.-treas.), Calif. Med. Assn. (sec.-treas.; past pres.), Am. Acad. Ophthalmology and Otology, Pacific Coast Eye and Ear Soc., So. Calif. Hist. Soc., Calif. Hist. Soc., Sigma Alpha Epsilon (past honorary president), Phi Rho Sigma. Mason (32 deg.). Clubs: The Family (San Francisco), Scribes (Los Angeles); Authors (Hollywood, California). Author: Historical Manual of Sigma Alpha Epsilon Fraternity, 1903; A History of the Medical Profession of Southern California, 1910. Editor Calif. and Western Medicine, 1927-1946. Historian, Calif. Med. Assn.; sec'y, Med. Soc. State of Calif. Editor Jour. of Phi Rho Sigma. Home: 131 South Rampart Blvd., Los Angeles 4. Died Jan. 18, 1954; buried Forest Lawn, Los Angeles.

KRILL, ALEX EUGENE, ophthalmologist, educator; b. Cleve., Oct. 20, 1928; s. Samuel and Bertha (Rosner) K.; B.S., Western Res. U., 1950; M.D., Ohio State U., 1954; m. Suzanne Altschui, May 31, 1964; 1 dau., Eileen. Intern, Phila. Gen. Hosp., 1954-55; resident ophthalmology U. Ill., 1958-60, USPHS spl. trainee ophthalmology, 1960-61; postgrad. fellow in visual physiology U. Mich., 1961; asst. prof., research asso. in ophthalmology U. Chgo., 1961-65, asso. prof. 1965-68, prof., 1968-72, mem. com. on genetics, 1967-72. Served with USNR, 1955-57. Recipient award of merit Am. Acad. Ophthalmology and Otolaryngology, 1970; certificate of merit A.M.A., 1970. Diplomate Am. Bd. Ophthalmology. Mem. Am. Acad. Ophthalmology and Otolaryngology (sect. chmn.), A.C.S., Am. Ophthal. Soc., Internat. Congress Neuro-ophthalmology (sec. Western Hemisphere), Internat. Soc. Clin. Electroretinography (v.p. Western Hemisphere), Phi Beta Kappa, Sigma Xi, Alpha Omega Alpha. Chief editor Ophthalmology Digest, 1970-72; mem. editorial bd. Am. Jour. of Ophthalmology, 1966-72, Investigative Ophthalmology, 1969-72, Documents Ophthalmologica, 1970-72, Survey of Opthalmology, 1970-72. Contbr. articles to profl. jours. Home: Chicago IL Died Dec. 8, 1972.

KROEBER, ALFRED L., (kro'ber), anthropologist; b. Hoboken, N.J., June 11, 1876; s. Florence and Johanna (Mueller) K.; A.B., Columbia U., 1896, A.M., 1897, Ph.D., 1901, Sc.D. Yale, 1946; LL.D., California, 1951; D.H.L. (honorary), Harvard University, 1952, Columbia, 1953; married Henriette Rothschild, May 24, 1906 (dec.); m. 2d Theodora Kracaw Brown, Mar. 26, 1926; children—Clifton, Theodore (stepsons), Karl, Ursula. Asst. in English, 1897-99, fellow in anthropology, 1899-1900, Columbia U., anthropological expedns., 1899-1901, New Mexico, 1915-20, Mexico, 1924, 30, Peru, 1925, 26, 42; instr. anthropology, 1901, asst. prof., 1906, asso. prof., 1911, prof. 1919-46, curator, 1908-25, dir., 1925-46, Anthropol. Museum, U. of Calif. Ethnol. exploration in Calif. since 1900; curator anthropology, 1900, and 1903-11, Calif. Acad. Sciences; research asso. Chgo. Natural History Mus., 1925—; vis. prof. Harvard, 1947-48, Columbia, 1948-52, Brandeis, 1954, Yale, 1958; fellow Center for Advanced Study Behavioral Sciences, 1955-56. Founder and president, 1917, Am. Anthrop. Assn.; pres. Am. Folk Lore Society, 1906. Mem. Linguistic Soc. of America (pres. 1940), Nat. Acad. Sciences, Am. Philos. Soc., Am. Academy Arts and Sciences, American Ethnological Society. Recipient of the Huxley Medal, Royal Anthropological Institute, 1945; Viking Medal, 1946. Author: Zuni Kin and Clan; Peoples of the Philippines; Anthropology 1923, 1948; Handbook of Indians of Cal.; Cultural and Natural Areas; Peruvian Archaeology; Configurations of Culture Growth; The Nature of Culture; Style and Civilization, 1957. Home: 1325 Arch St., Berkeley 94708. Office: Univ. of Calif., Berkeley, Cal. 94704. Died Oct. 5, 1960; buried Berkeley, Cal.

KROECK, LOUIS SAMUEL, biologist; b. Dayton, Ia., June 13, 1872; s. Louis F. and Charlotte (Veith) K.; B.S., Coll. of the Pacific, 1895, M.S., 1898; A.M., Stanford University, 1897; Sc.D., Coll. of the Pacific, 1931; research work, Hopkins Biol. Lab. (Stanford) 3 summers, Calif. Acad. Sciences, 2 summers; m. Bertha Graff, of San Jose, Calif., June 30, 1904; children—Graf Louis (dec.), Margarethe Etamina, Bertha Louise, Theodora Wilhelmina, Barbara Fourth, Louis Graf. Instr. biology, 1896-99, prof. biology and geology, 1899-1904, prof. biology, 1904-32, Coll. of the Pacific, now emeritus. Fellow A.A.A.S., Calif. Acad. Sciences; mem. Am. Genetic Assn., Save the Redwood League. Methodist. Specilizes in micro-biology. Home: 205 Euclid Av., Stockton CA

KRUM, HOWARD LEWIS, (kroom), elec. engr.; b. Minneapolis, Minn., Nov. 15, 1883; s. Charles Lyon and Ella (Lewis) K.; B.S., Armour Inst. Tech., Chicago, 1906, E.E., 1910, hon. Dr. Engring., 1939; m. Fay Wilson, Oct. 29, 1919; children—Charles Wilson, Shirley Jean, Marjorie Lyon. Engaged in invention and development of teletype since 1906; cons. engr. Teletype Corp., mfrs. printing telegraph equipment, Chicago. Received Distinguished Service Award from Alumni Assn. of Armour Inst. Tech.; John Price Wetherill medal, Franklin Inst.; spl. award as "modern pioneer," Nat. Assn. Mfrs. Trustee Armour Inst. Tech. Fellow Am. Inst. Elec. Engrs.; mem. Tau Beta Pi. Clubs: University (Chicago), New York Athletic; Los Angeles Country (Beverly Hills). Address: 85 Robsart Rd., Kenilworth, Ill.; also 5480 N. Bay Rd., Miami Beach, Fla. Died Nov. 13, 1961; buried Forest Lawn Cemetery, Los Angeles.

KRUMB, HENRY, cons. mining engr.; b. Bklyn., Nov. 15, 1875; s. Faustus and Elizabeth (Geiss) K.; E.M., Columbia Sch. of Mines, 1898; D.Sc. (hon.), Columbia, 1951; m. LaVon Duddleson, Dec. 9, 1914. Draftsman and assayer, N.Y.C., 1898; supt. New St. Elmo Mine, mgr. No. Belle and Abe Lincoln mines, Rossland, B.C., Can. 1899-1902; chief engr. Camp Bird Mine, Ouray, Colo., 1902-03; examining engr. Guggenheim Exploration Co., 1903-07; cons. mining engr. since 1907; cons. engr. in examination and devel. porphyry copper mines; v.p. Hudson Bay M. & S. Co.; dir. Newmont Mining Corp., Churchill River Power Co., O'Kiep Copper Co., Ltd., Newmont Oil Co. Dollar a year man, mem. priorities com. War Industries Bd., World War I. Trustee Columbia, 1941-47. Recipient Egleston medal for engring. achievement. Fellow A.A.A.S.; mem. Am. Inst. Mining and Metall. Engrs. (became hon. mem. 1940). Republican. Mason. Clubs: Bankers, Columbia University, Westchester Country, University (N.Y.C.); Alta Salt Lake City, Utah; California, Los Angeles Country (Los Angeles). Home: 730 Park Av., N.Y.C. 21. Office: 300 Park Av., N.Y.C. 22; also Pacific Mutual Bldg., Los Angeles 14. Deceased.

KRUMBHAAR, E(DWARD) B(ELL), physician, pathologist; b. Phila., Aug. 1, 1882; s. Charles Hermann and Mary Ellis (Bell) K.; prep. edn. DeLancey Sch., Phila., 1894-95, Groton (Mass.) Sch., 1895-1900; A.B., Harvard, 1904; M.D., U. Pa., 1908, Ph.D., 1916; D.Honoris causa, Alcala, 1925; m. Helen Dixon, Mar. 14, 1911; children—Peter, David. Res. ident pathologist Pa. Hosp., 1908-09; instr. medicine U. Pa., 1912-15, asso., 1915-16, asst. prof. research medicine, 1916-20, asso. prof. Grad. Sch. Medicine, 1920-27, prof. pathology, 1927-48, emeritus; dir. labs. Phila. Gen. Hosp., 1920-27, cons. pathologist, 1927-47, Bryn Mawr Hosp. since 1921; editor Am. Jour. Med. Scis. "Clio Medica." Served as lt., later capt. and maj. M.C., U.S. Army, France, 1917-19, lt. Col. M.R.C. Mem. A.M.A., A.A.A.S., Assn. Am. Physicians, Am. Soc. Exptl. Pathology, Am. Assn. Pathology and Bacteriology, Am. Assn. Med. History; hon. fellow Royal Soc. Medicine (London). Sigma Xi, Alpha Omega Alpha, Delta Kappa Epsilon. Democrat. Episcopalian. Clubs: Whitemarsh Hunt. Harvard of Philadelphia. Author: Spleen and Anemia, 1917; History of Pathology, 1937; Castiglioni's History of Medicine (Eng. edit.), 1940, 47 about 170 med. articles and chpts. in med. books. Address: Chestnut Hill, Phila. Died Mar. 16, 1966.

KRUMWIEDE, CHARLES, M.D., bacteriologist; b. N.Y. City, Sept. 9, 1879; s. Charles and Johannah (Freese) K.; B.A., Columbia, 1902; M.D., Coll. Phys. and Surg. (Columbia), 1905; m. Ellen Louise Lipps, Nov. 20, 1907; children—Helen Louise, Elma. Began practice in N.Y. City, 1905; asst. dir. Bur. of Laboratories, Dept. of Health, N.Y. City; prof. bacteriology and immunology, Univ. and Bellevue Med. Coll. and New York U. College of Dentistry. Republican. Episcopalian. Home: Bronxville, N.Y. Died Dec. 1930.

KUCZYNSKI, ROBERT RENÉ, (koo-zin'ski), statistician; b. Berlin, Germany, Aug. 12, 1876; s. Wilhelm and Lucy (Brandeis) K.; ed. univs. of Freiburg, Munich, Strassburg, Berlin; m. Berta Gradenwitz, Dec. 1, 1903 (died 1947); children—Jurgen, Ursula (Mrs. L. Beurton), Brigitte (Mrs. Anthony Lewis), Barbara (Mrs. D. B. Macrae Taylor), Sabine (Mrs. Francis Loeffler), Renate (Mrs. Arthur Simpson). Mem. staff div. of methods and results, Census Office, Washington, D.C., 1900-01; dir. municipal statis. office, Elberfeld, Germany, 1904-05, Berlin-Schoeneberg, 1906-21; lecturer, Berlin Commercial High Sch., 1911-21; council mem., Brookings Inst., Washington, 1926-32; research fellow London School of Economics, 1933-38; reader in demography, U. of London, 1938-41; demographic adv. Colonial Office, London, since 1944. Author: Der Zug nach der Stadt, 1897; Loehne und Arbeitzeit in Europa und Amerika, 1913; Post-War Labor Conditions in Germany, 1925; Deutschlands Versorgung mit Nahrungsmitteln, 1926; American Loans to Germany, 1927; The Balance of Births and Deaths, vol. I, 1928, vol. II, 1931; Fertility and Reproduction, 1932; The Measurement of Population Growth, 1935; Population Movements, 1936; Colonial Population, 1937; The Cameroons and Togoland, 1939; Demographic Survey of the British Colonial Empire, 1947. Home: 12 Lawn Road, London, N.W. 3, Eng. Died Nov. 25, 1947.

KUEBLER, JOHN R(ALPH), chemist, editor, business exec.; b. Evansville, Ind., July 8, 1890; s. Henry and Isabelle (Fischer) K.; A.B., Ind. U., 1912, A.M. (fellowship, 1914-15), 1915; m. Ethel B. Smith, Sept. 15, 1917; 1 son, John R. Instr. physics and chemistry Butler Coll., 1912-14; secondary sch. teacher of chemistry Shortridge High Sch., Indpls., 1915-17, 1919-42; dist. officer Alpha Chi Sigma, 1917-22, asst. editor The Hexagon, 1920-22, editor, 1922-59, mem. nat. bd. officers, 1922-59, sec.-treas., editor, 1926-59, historian, 1958—, hon. pres., 1960—, nat. sec.-treas. emeritus. Served sgt. 1st cl. Research Div., Chem. Warfare Service, U.S. Army, 1917-19. Mem. Am. Chem. Soc. (pres. Ind. sect. 1944-45), Ind. Chem. Soc. (pres. 1945-46). Prof. Interfrat. Conf. (sec.-treas. 1948-52), A.A.A.S., Ind. Acad. Science; Nat. Conf. Coll. Frats. and Socs. (treas. 1949-52), Interfrat. Research and Advisory Council (treas. 1950-52). Republican. Home: 304 Burgess Av., Indianapolis 19. Office: 5503 E. Washington St., Indpls. Died June 17, 1967; buried Washington Park East Cemetery, Indpls.

KUEHNE, HUGO FRANZ, architect and engr.; b. Austin, Tex., Feb. 20, 1884; s. Franz Conrad and Clara (Langer) K.; C.E., U. Tex., 1906; A.B. in Architecture, Mass. Inst. Tech., 1908; m. Sybil Glass, Dec. 25, 1923; children—Hugo Franz, Frances Lorraine. Prof. architecture U. Tex., 1910-15; engaged in practice architecture, Austin, Tex., since 1915; mem. firm Kuehne, Chasey & Giesecke, 1915-17, Kuehne & Chasey, 1917-19, alone as H. F. Kuehne, architect and engr., 1919-42; partner Kuehne, Brooks and Barr, 1942-60; mem. firm Giesecke, Kuehne & Brooks since 1942; dir. Fidelity State Bank, Mut. Savs. Inst. (both Austin). Past vice chmn. parks and playground commn. City of Austin; past chmn. zoning com. City of Austin; chmn. City Planning Commn., 1931-48, Zoning Bd. of Adjustment since 1932. Fellow A.I.A. (twice pres. Central Tex. chpt.); mem. Nat., Tex. socs. profl. engrs., Tex. Soc. Architects (dir.), Am. Civic Assn., Am. Soc. Planning Ofcls., Nat. Assn. Housing Ofcls., Austin C. of C., Sigma Chi. Democrat. Conglist. Rotarian (past dir.). Home: 500 E. 32d St., Austin 78705. Office: 121 E. 8th St., Austin 15, Tex. Died Nov. 23, 1963; buried Austin Meml. Park, Austin, Tex.

KUETHER, FREDERICK WILLIAM, research physicist; b. Fon du Lac, Wis., June 19, 1922; s. Frederick Charles and Laura (Stoltz) K.; B.S., Miami (O.) U., 1944; M.S., Mich. State U., 1946, Ph.D., 1951; m. Dorothy A. Tyrrell, Sept. 20, 1947; children—Charles W., Richard A., Thomas B. Cottrell fellow, Mich. State U., 1949-50, instr. physics, 1950-51, sr. physicist Honeywell Research Center, Mpls., 1951-55, prin. scientist, 1955-60, sr. prin. scientist, 1960-69. Active Boy Scouts Am. Mem. Am. Phys. Soc., Electro Chem. Soc. Patentee in field. Home: Minneapolis MN Died Mar. 18, 1969.

KUICHLING, EMIL, civil engr.; b. Kehl, Germany, Jan. 20, 1848; s. Louis and Marie (von Seeger) K.; A.B., U. of Rochester, N.Y., 1868, C.E., 1869; student, Carlsruhe (Germany) Polv. Sch., 1870-73; m. Sarah L. Caldwell, Jan. 28, 1879. Asst. engr., western div. N.Y. State canals, 1869, 1873; asst. engr., 1873-85, chief engr., 1890-1900, Rochester water works; consulting engr. N.Y. State Bd. Health, 1881-91; mem. exec. bd., Rochester, 1885-87; consulting engr., New York, N.Y., 1900—. Died Nov. 9, 1914.

KUMMEL, HENRY BARNARD, geologist; b. Milwaukee, Wis., May 25, 1867; s. Julius M. F. and Annie (Barnard) K.; A.B., Beloit Coll., 1889, A.M., 1892; A.M., Harvard, 1892; Ph.D., U. of Chicago, 1895; m. Charlotte F. Coe, June 20, 1899 (dec.); children—Charlotte Proctor, Lucy Barnard; m. 2d, Mrs. Anna G. Williams, Sept. 1, 1934. Instr. Beloit Coll. Acad., 1889-91; asst. in geology, Harvard U., 1891-92; fellow geology, U. of Chicago, 1892-95; asst. geologist, N.J. State Geol. Survey, 1892-98; asst. prof. physiography, Lewis Inst., Chicago, 1896-99; asst. state geologist, 1899-1902, state geologist, New Jersey, 1902-37; dir. Conservation and Development of New Jersey, 1922-37; retired, 1937; exec. officer, Forest Commn. of New Jersey, 1905-15. Asso. editor Journal of Geography, 1897-1901. Fellow Geol. Soc. Am., A.A.A.S.; pres. Assn. Am. State Geologists, 1908-13; v.p. Geol. Soc. Am., 1931. Contbr. numerous papers to geol. jours. and reports. Home: 100 Abernethy Drive, Trenton, N.J. Died Oct. 23, 1945.

KUNESH, JOSEPH FRANCIS, civil engr.; b. Kewaunee, Wis., June 16, 1890; s. John P. and Kristina (Nemetz) K.; B.S., U. Wis., 1914; C.E., 1930; m. Anne Elizabeth Cabalek Apr. 12, 1921; children—Robert Joseph, Donald Francis. Draftsman and computer state hwys. Wis. Hwy. Commn., Madison, 1912; instrumentation C.&E.I. R.R., Villa Grove, 1912; engr. in charge irrigation Tex. Land & Devel. Co., Plainview, 1913-14; asst. irrigation and drainage engr. U.S. Dept.

Agr., Billings, Mont., Mercedes, Tex., 1915; jr. and asst. engr. U.S. Geol. Survey, San Francisco, 1916-18; asso. engr., Tucson, 1918-20; resident engr. in charge N.E., U.S.A., Layne & Bowler Co., N.Y., 1920-22; chief hydraulic engr. Republique d'Haiti, Port-au-Prince, 1922-24; asst. engr. Alexander Potter, cons. engr., N.Y.C., 1924; concrete and steel designer subways Bd. Transp., N.Y.C., 1925; chief water supply engr. Fla. East Coast Ry., St. Augustine, 1925; asst. engr. subways N.J. Transit Commn., 1926; asst. engr., Dept. Water Supply, Gas & Electricity, N.Y.C., 1927; sr. hydraulic engr. U.S. Geol. Survey in cooperation with Honolulu Sewer and Water Commn., also dept. engr. and asst. chief engr., water works Bd. Water Supply, Honolulu, 1927-38; dir.-engr. territorial planning, Territorial Planning Bd., 1938-41; chief engr. (World War II) Dept. Pub. Works, City and County of Honolulu, 1941-47; prof. civil engring. U. Hawaii, and dean Coll. Applied Sci., 1947-51; indsl. specialist water resource div.; nat. prodn. authority, Dept. Commerce, 1951-53; chief engr., exec. v.p. Layne Pacific, Inc., Seattle, 1953-56. Registered profl. engr. Ty Hawaii, D.C., Wash. Mem. Bd. Registration of Engrs. Architects and Surveyors of Hawaii, 1939-41; mem. Bd. Water Supply of Honolulu, 1941-47; exec. sec. Honolulu Sewerage Com., 1944-47; mem. Bd. Health, C. of C., Gov.'s Postwar Planning Bd. Mayor's Maj. Disaster Council (1941). Life mem. Am. Soc. C.E. (past pres. Hawaii sect.); mem. Am. Pub. Works Assn. (chmn. Hawaii sect. 1945-50), Hawaii Engring Assn. (past pres.), Wis. Alumni Assn. (past pres. Hawaii sect.), Am. Water Works Assn., Triangle. Author govt. reports, bulls. Home: 15524 Bothell Way, Seattle 55. Died Oct. 24, 1959.

KUNKEL, BEVERLY WAUGH, biologist; b. Harrisburg, Pa., Oct. 27, 1881; s. Charles A. and Eliza B. (Waugh) K.; grad. Lawrenceville (N.J.) Sch., 1898; Ph.B., Yale, 1901, Ph.D., 1905; studied U. of Freiburg, 1911-12; studied in London, 1925; m. Caroline T. Jennings, June 24, 1908; children—Mary T., Sarah W. Asst. in biology, 1901-05, instr., 1905-12, Yale; prof. zoology, Beloit (Wis.) Coll., 1912-15; prof. biology, Lafayette Coll., 1915-69. Fellow A.A.A.S.; mem. Am. Soc. Zoologists, Am. Assn. Anatomists, Am. Assn. Univ. Profs., Sigma Xi, Delta Phi. Conglist. Contbr. numerous papers chiefly on vertebrate embryology and the relations of the colleges to intellectual leadership. Home: Easton PA Died Mar. 6, 1969; buried Yelping Hill, West Cornwall CT

KUNKEL, LOUIS OTTO, botanist; b. Mexico, Mo., May 7, 1884; s. Henry and Katie Price (Spencer) K.; B.S. in Edn., U. Mo., 1909, A.B., 1910, A.M., 1911; student Henry Shaw Sch. Botany, St. Louis, 1911-12; Ph.D., Columbia, 1914; grad. study U. Freiburg, Germany, 1915-16; m. Johanna Caroline Wortmann, Sept. 4, 1915; children—Henry George, Otto Wortmann, Walter Relph, Paul Spercer. Asst. in botany U. Mo., 1908-11, Columbia, 1912-13, research asst., 1913-14; pathologist U.S. Dept. Agr., 1914-20; asso. pathologist expt. sta. Hawaiian Sugar Planters Assn., 1920-23; pathologist Boyce Thompson Inst. Plant Research, Yonkers, N.Y., 1923-32; mem. Rockefeller Inst. Med. Research, 1931-49, mem. emeritus, 1949—. Fellow A.A.A.S.; mem. Nat. Acad. Sci., Am. Philos. Soc., Bot. Soc. Am, Am. Phytopathological Soc., Phi Beta Kappa, Sigma Xi, Alpha Zeta, Phi Delta Kappa. Joint author: Filter Viruses, 1928. Home: 122 Voorhees St., Pennington, N.J. Office: Rockefeller Inst. Medical Research, 66th St. and York Av., N.Y.C. 21. Died Mar. 20, 1960.

KUNSTADTER, RALPH HESS, pediatrician; b. Chgo., Oct. 6, 1905; s. Samuel and Theodora (Hess) K.; B.S., U. Ill., 1927, M.D., 1930; m. Marjorie Lyon Solomon, June 21, 1928; 1 dau., Susan Lyon (Mrs. Walter Dewees). Intern, Michael Reese Hosp., Chgo., 1929-31, acting chmn. dept. pediatrics, 1955-56, vice chmn. dept., 1956—, attending pediatrician, chief children's endocrine clinic; asso. prof. pediatrics Northwestern U. Med. Sch.; pediatric courtesy staff Chgo. Lying-In Hosp.; cons. pediatrics Rehab. Inst. Chgo.; pvt. practice, Chgo. Am. Acad. Pediatrics rep. at Conf. Emergency Med. Identification, A.M.A., 1961. Vice chmn. Ill. Commn. on Children; exec. com. White House Conf. Children and Youth, 1960; med. adv. com. Cook County chpt. Nat. Found.; med. adv. bd. Chgo chpt. Muscular Dystrophy Assn. Am., Cook County Welfare Dept., Ill. Epileptic League; alternate rep. Ill. Joint Commn. Sch. Health; chmn. profl. adv. council Nat. Soc. for Crippled Children and Adults. Served to lt. col. M.C., AUS, World War II. Diplomate Am. Bd. Pediatrics. Fellow Am. Acad. Pediatrics (chmn. com. handicapped children Ill. chpt. 1957; exec. com. Ill. chpt. 1958-59; pres. Ill. chpt. 1964—; liaison to Nat. Soc. Crippled Children and Adults), A.C.P.; mem. A.M.A. (chmn. pediatric sect, 1954-55), Ill. State (chmn. com. on child health 1962), Chgo. med. socs., A.A.A.S., Endocrine Soc., Am. Chgo. heart assns., Ill. Acad. Sci., Chgo. Diabetic Assn., Chgo. Pediatric Soc. (pres. 1957-58), Inst. Medicine Chgo. (bd. govs.), Am. Pediatric Soc., Sigma Xi, Alpha Omega Alpha. Clubs: Key, Barclay, Executive's, Adventurer's (Chgo.). Author: (with Evelyn C. Lundeen, R.N.) Care of the Premature Infant, 1958. Abstract writer Excerpta Medica. Contbr. numerous med. articles to jours. Home: 900 N. Michigan Av. Office: 664 N. Michigan Av., Chgo. 60611. Died Nov. 1965.

KUNTZ, ALBERT, (koontz), professor of anatomy; b. Batesville, Ind., Mar. 19, 1879; s. Andrew and Barbara (Butz) K.; A.B., Morningside Coll., Ia., 1904; Ph.D., State U. of Ia., 1910; M.D., St. Louis U. Sch. of Medicine, 1918; m. Emma S. Magdsick, August 28, 1912; 1 daughter, Elizabeth Louise (Mrs. R. Hollis Hamstra). Professor science, Charles City (Ia.) College, 1905-08; fellow State Univ. of Ia., 1909-11, instr. in animal biology, 1911-13; asst. prof. anatomy, St. Louis U. Sch. of Medicine, 1913-16, asso. prof. 1916-19, prof. anatomy, 1919-30, prof. microanatomy, dir. of dept., 1930-46; professor anatomy, director of department since 1946. Mem. A.A.A.S., Am. Soc. Zoölogists, Am. Assn. Anatomists, Soc. Exptl. Biology and Medicine, Sigma Xi, Alpha Omega Alpha, Pi Gamma Mu; associate member American Neurological Society. Presbyterian. Author: The Autonomic Nervous System, 1929, 4th edit., 1953; Neuro-Anatomy, 1931, 5th edit., 1950; The Neuroanatomic Basis of Surgery of the Autonomic Nervous System, 1949; Visceral Innervation and Its Relation to Personality, 1951. Contbr. to med. jours. Home: 7355 Pershing Av., University City, Mo. Office: 1402 S. Grand Blvd., St. Louis. Died Jan. 19, 1957; buried Charles City, Ia.

KUNZ, ADOLF HENRY, prof. chemistry; b. Leavenworth, Kan.; s. Albert Louis and Bertha Louise (Holbein) K.; A.B., William Jewell Coll., Liberty, Mo., 1923; M.S., U. of Iowa, 1926, Ph.D., 1928; m. Bernice Madeline Bullock, July 26, 1927; 1 son, Alan Adolf. Teacher, high sch. science, Marshall, Mo., 1923-26; asst. lab. instr., U. of Ia., 1926-28; asst. prof. chemistry, U. of Ore., 1930-32, 1934-36, asso. prof., 1936-43, prof., 1943-66, acting head, dept. of chemistry, 1941-42, head of dept., 1942-66; asst. prof. chemistry, Ore. State Coll., 1932-34. Nat. research fellow in chemistry, Calif. Inst. Tech., 1928-29. Member State of Ore. Basic Science Com. since 1941. Mem. Am. Chem. Soc., A.A.A.S., Am. Assn. Univ. Profs., Phi Gamma Delta, Pi Kappa Delta, Pi Mu Epsilon, Sigma Xi, Phi Lambda Upsilon. Home: Eugene OR Died Oct. 14, 1966.

KUNZ, JAKOB, prof. mathematical physics; b. Brittnau Aargau, Switzerland, Nov. 3, 1874; s. Jakob and Anna Maria (Weber) K.; B.S., Polytechnicum, Zurich, Switzerland, 1897; Ph.D., U. of Zurich, 1902; m. Anna Bolliger, July 24, 1913; children—Annamarie, Margaret Rosa. Chemist, Gesellschaft für Chemische Industrie, Basel, 1897-1900; instr. and pvt. docent in physics, Polytechnicum, 1900-07; came to U.S., 1908; instr. in physics, U. of Mich., 1908; asst. and asso. prof. physics, U. of Ill., 1909-23, prof. mathematical physics, 1923—. With solar eclipse expdns. to Green River, 1918, Middletown (Conn.), 1925, Lancaster (N.H.), 1932. Served in Swiss Army, 1894-1900. Methodist. Author: Theoretische Physik auf mechanischer Grundlage, 1907. Home: Urbana, Ill. Died July 18, 1939.

KURCHATOV, IGOR V(ASLL'EVICH), nuclear physicist; b. Russia, 1903; grad. Crimean U., Simferopol; student Baku Polytechnical Inst. Joined staff Physico-Technical Inst., Acad. Scis. of USSR, 1925, dir. nuclear physics lab. Physico-Technical Inst., supervised building of cyclotrons; research elec. relations in materials which possess quality of spontaneous polarization; observed nuclear fission provoked by neutron bombardment, 1933; research spontaneous fission of uranium. Became mem. Communist Part, 1948, elected to Supreme Soviet, 1950. Dir. Atomic Emergy Inst., Acad. Scis. USSR. Decorated Order of Lenin; recipient Stalin prize. Mem. Acad. Scis. of USSR (presidium of the acad.). Author: Splitting the Atomic Nucleus, 1935. Address: care Academy of Sciences of USSR, B. Kaluzhskaya 14, Moscow, Russia. Died Feb. 1960. *

KURTZ, FORD, civil engr.; b. East Stroudsburg, Pa., Feb. 23, 1885; s. Nathaniel Pearson and Hannah (Morgan) K.; C.E., Cornell U., 1907; m. Gladys Chappell, June 28, 1917; 1 son, Peter. Aide, U.S. Coast and Geodetic Survey, 1907-09; asst. to hydraulic engr. J.G. White & Co., Inc., 1910-12, 1914-15, hydraulic design engr., successor firm J. G. White Engring. Corp., 1920-22, chief hydraulic design engr., 1923-27, hydraulic engr. since 1928, engring mgr. 1940-49, member board of directors, 1948—, vice president in charge engring., 1949-53, president, 1953—; resident engr. Parr Shoals Power Company, Parr, S.C., 1913-14; resident engr. Caibarien-Remedios Waterworks Co., Caibarien, Cuba, 1916-17, dir., 1931-42, sec. 1933-42; designing engr. Langley Field, Hampton, Va., 1917-18; resident engr. U.S. Nitrate Plant No. 2, Muscle Shoals, Ala., 1918-19. Exec. mem. U.S. com. on large dams World Power Conf. Awarded Fuertes Medal for highest scholastic record in civil engring. Cornell U. Mem. Am. Soc. C.E., S.R. Presbyn. Clubs: Cornell (N.Y.); India House. Licensed profl. engr., N.Y., Pa. Home: 8876 Crestwood Av., Hollis 23, N.Y. Office: 80 Broad St., N.Y.C. 4. Died Aug. 9, 1956; buried Rosemont Cemetery, Newberry, S.C.

KYLE, LAURENCE HARWOOD, physician, educator; b. Huntington, Mass., Apr. 16, 1916; s. Clayton Harwood and Alice Margaret (Millea) K.; B.S. U. Mass., 1937; M.D., Boston U., 1941; m. Margaret Ann Stringer, May 13, 1944; children,Margaret Alice, Patricia Adelaide, Laurence Harwood. Intern Nassau County Pub. Gen. Hosp., Hempstead, N.Y., 1941-42; resident medicine Boston City Hosp., 1946-47; sr. research fellow NIH, 1947-48; William Wade Hinshaw research fellow Georgetown U. Sch. Medicine, 1948-50, mem. faculty, 1948-71, prof. medicine, chmn. dept., 1958-71; dir. dept. medicine Georgetown Univ. Hosp., 1958-71. Cons. medicine Walter Reed Army Med. Center, Bethesda Naval Med. Center, Clin. Center of NIH, Mt. Alto VA Hosp.; cons. metabolism Walter Reed Army Inst. Research. Served with AUS, 1942-45. Recipient Raskob award research Georgetown U. Sch. Medicine, 1959. Diplomate Am. Bd. Internal Medicine. Master A.C.P.; member A.M.A. (del. to house of delegates 1964), Association of Am. Physicians, Am. Soc. Clin. Investigation, Am. Fedn. Clin. Research (chmn. Eastern sect. 1955), So. Soc. Clin. Investigation (counselor 1957-60, pres. 1960), Endocrine Soc., Soc. Exptl. Biology and Washington DC

LA BACH, JAMES OSCAR, chemist; b. Newcastle, Ind. Apr. 22, 1871; s. James Mayer (D.D.) and Cornelia Esther (Ryker) L.; Carleton Coll., 1 yr.; B.S., U. of Tenn., 1895, M.S., 1897; m. Mary Shepherd Parker, Oct. 10, 1917. Asst. chemist, food nutrition work, U. of Tenn., 1895-97; chemist, Procter & Gamble Co., Cincinnati, O., 1897-1901; chief chemist, Ky. Food and Drug Control Labs., at Ky. Agrl. Expt. Sta., U. of Ky., Lexington, 1901—, also head of food and drug control dept., 1916-18: dir. labs., Ky. State Bd. Health, 1918—. Mem. Lexington Bd. of Health, 1917-19; collaborating chemist, U.S. Bur. Chemistry. Democrat. Presbyn. Home: Lexington, Ky. Died Aug. 31, 1922.

LABBERTON, JOHN M(ADISON), prof. cons. engr.; b. nr. Hillsboro, N.C., Apr. 22, 1893; s. Herman H. and Mary (Efland) L.; B.S., U. of N.C., 1913; m. Mary Holton, 1917; 1 dau., Mary Holton; m. 2d, Victoria Dittler, 1938. Elec. mech. engr. Westinghouse Elec. Corp., 1913-35; mech. and marine engr., U.S. Navy, 1935-37; prof. N.Y. Univ. since 1937; cons. engr. for mfrs. of elec. and mech. apparatus since 1937. Civil Service Examiner, N.Y. City. Lt. comdr., U.S.N.R. Mem. Am. Soc. M.E., Am. Soc. Naval Engineers, Society of Naval Architects and Marine Engineers. Mason. Member of Phi Beta Kappa, Tau Beta Pi, Sigma Xi, Pi Tau Sigma. Author of many tech. papers and articles; many patents in elec. and mech. field. Author: Marine Engineering, 1943. Editor-in-chief Marine Engineers Handbook, 1946. Home: 114 W. 183d St., N.Y.C. 53. Died Oct. 6, 1953.

LA CAUZA, FRANK EMILIO, educator; b. Novara di Sicilia, Italy, Nov. 22, 1900; s. Carmelo and Angelina (Bertolami) LA G.; B.S., Harvard, 1923, M.S., 1924, M.A., 1929; grad. student Mass. Inst. Tech., 1926-27; grad. Sperry Gyro Sch., N.Y., 1930; m. Mary Ann Hunter, Mar. 16, 1935. Came to U.S., 1905, naturalized, 1926. Mem. engring. test dept. Gen. Electric Co., Schenectady, 1924; instr. elec. engring. Harvard, 1924-26; asst. prof. U.S. Navy Postgrad. Sch., Annapolis, 1929-39, asso. prof., 1939-45, prof., 1945-47; organized elec. engring., mathematics depts. Naval Schs. Gen. Line, Newport, R.I., Monterey, Cal., 1946-47, prof., head dept. elec. engring., mathematics Gen. Line Sch., Monterey, 1947-58, academic chmn. U.S. Gen. Line and Naval Sci. Sch., 1958-59. Vice president Interservice Fund. Member United States Naval Postgrad. Sch. Selection Bd., 1961. Mem. bd. trustees Monterey Library, 1956-57; mem. planning commn., Monterey, 1958-59; mem. City Council, Monterey, Cal., 1959-61. Served from lt. to lt. comdr., USNR, 1942-45; capt. Res. Decorated Knight Officer, Order of Crown (Italy), 1930. Profl. engr., Md., Cal. Mem. Am. Inst. E.E., Am. Soc. Engring. Edn., Am. Assn. U. Profs., Naval Res. Assn. (pres. Monterey chpt. 1961-62). Clubs: Officers, University, Harvard (Annapolis); Officers (Postgrad. Sch., Monterey). Contbr. Gyro Compass sect. Knights Modern Seamanship. Contbr. articles profl. publs. Home: 110 Monte Vista Dr., Monterey, Cal. 93940. Died July 25, 1964; buried Arlington Nat. Cemetery.

LACHMAN, ARTHUR, chemist; b. San Francisco, Calif., Dec. 4, 1873; s. Abraham and Marie (Lazarus) L.; B.S., U. of Calif., 1893; Ph.D., summa cum laude, U. of Munich, 1895; m. Bertha Nathan, June 28, 1898; children—Gertrude (Mrs. F. Eberson), Ruth (Mrs. J. Colyer). Asst. in chemistry, U. of Mich., 1896, instr., 1896-97; prof. U. of Ore., 1897-1902; cons. chem. engr., 1902-06; mfr., 1906-18; research asso. U. of Calif., 1920. Fellow A.A.A.S.; mem. Am. Chem. Soc. Author: Spirit of Organic Organic Chemistry, 1899; also numerous papers on pure and applied chemistry. Received various patents in petroleum technology. Address: Hotel Shattuck, Berkeley 4 CA

LADD, GEORGE EDGAR, econ. geologist; b. Haverhill, Mass., July 23, 1864; s. George W. and Eliza A. (Priest) L.; A.B., Harvard, 1887, A.M., 1888, Ph.D., 1894; studied German univs. 2 yrs.; m. Mary O. Hammond, May 24, 1889. Asst., and asst. geologist, U.S., Mo. and Tex. Geol. surveys, 1887-92; asst. in geology, Harvard, 1892-94; asst. geologist and chemist, Ga. Geol. Survey, 1895-96; dir. and prof. geology and mining, Sch. of Mines and Metallurgy, U. of Mo., 1897-1908; pres. Okla. Sch. of Mines and Metallurgy, 1908-13; pres. N.M. Coll. Agr. and Mech. Arts, 1913-17; economic geologist, Bur. of Pub. Roads, U.S. Dept. Agr., Sept. 1, 1917—. Lecturer on engring. geology, U. of Md., 1921. Died Dec. 23, 1940.

LADD, GEORGE TALLMAN, mech. engr.; b. Edinburgh, O., May 17, 1871; s. George Trumbull and Cornelia Ann (Tallman) L.; student Sheffield Scientific Sch. (Yale), 1891; M.E., Cornell, 1895; m. Florence Ewing Barrett, Sept. 2, 1910. With P.&L.E. Ry. Co., Pittsburgh, 1891-93; designer Brooks Locomotive Works, Dunkirk, N.Y., 1895-98; mech. engr. in charge engine and boiler sales, Bass Foundry & Machine Co., Ft. Wayne, Ind., 1898-1909; consulting engr., Pittsburgh, 1909-10; pres. and treas. The George T. Ladd Co., engrs., Pittsburgh, 1910-25; pres. Ladd Water Tube Boiler Co., 1925-1928; pres. and gen. mgr. United Engineering & Foundry Co., Pittsburgh, since 1928; pres. Ladd Securities Co., Ladd Equipment Co.; chmn. Pittsburgh Testing Laboratory, Woodings-Verona Tool Works; v.p. Davis Brake Beam Co., Johnstown, Pa.; dir. Columbian Enameling & Stamping Co. (Terre Haute, Ind.), United Engring. & Foundry Co., Combustion Engring. Co., Inc. (New York), Heyl & Patterson, Inc., First Nat. Bank (Pittsburgh), Pa.-Central Airlines Co., Flannery Bolt Co., Pittsburgh Steel Co., Pittsburgh Br. Federal Reserve Bank of Cleveland, Nat. Supply Co. (N.Y.), Peoples-Pittsburgh Trust Co., Tristate Industrial Assn., Follansbee Steel Corp., Westinghouse Electric & Mfg. Co., Union Switch & Signal Co. Dir. Elizabeth Steel Magee Hosp., Allegheny Gen. Hosp., Pittsburgh Chamber of Commerce; pres. Pittsburgh Diagnostic Clinic; trustee Bucknell University, Carnegie Inst., Carnegie Inst. Tech., Pittsburgh. Lt. comdr. U.S.N.R.F., in charge construction 14-inch naval railway mounts and 7-inch caterpillar mounts, which were in service in France, August 1918, with naval railway batteries, World War; was mem. advisory bd. Pittsburgh District, U.S. Fuel Administration; now mem. advisory bd. Pittsburgh Ordnance Dist. Designed and built largest water tube boilers in world, operating at Fordson Plant, Ford Motor Co., Detroit. Mem. Am. Soc. M.E., Engrs. Soc. of Western Pa. (ex-pres.), Am. Iron and Steel Inst., U.S. Naval Inst., American Geog. Soc., Pa. Soc. Mason (32 deg., K.T., Shriner). Republican. Clubs: Duquesne, Pittsburgh Athletic, Montour Heights Golf, Harvard-Yale-Princeton; Edgeworth (Sewickley, Pa.); Chicago Athletic (Chicago); Cornell, Yale, Lotos, Engineers' (New York); Youngstown (O.) Country Club. Home: Coraopolis Heights, Pa. Office: First Nat. Bank Bldg., Pittsburgh, Pa. Died Oct. 3, 1943.

LADD, WILLIAM SARGEANT, med. coll. dean; b. Portland, Ore., Aug. 16, 1887; s. William Mead and Mary Lyman (Andrews) L.; B.S., Amherst Coll., 1910; M.D., Columbia U., 1915; m. Mary Richardson Babbott, June 5, 1913; children—Frances Wood, William Sargent, Anthony Thornton, John. Interne, Peter Bent Brigham Hosp., Boston, 1915-17; asst. phys. Presbyn. Hosp., N.Y. City, 1917-19, 1924-31; instr. Columbia, 1917-19, 1921-24, asso. 1924-31; instr., Johns Hopkins U. and asst. in medicine Johns Hopkins Hosp., 1919-21; asst. prof. medicine, Cornell, 1931-32, professor medicine, 1932-42, associate dean Medical College, 1931-35, dean 1935-42 professor of clinical medicine since 1942, assistant visiting physician Bellevue Hospital, 1932-35; asst. attending phys. N.Y. Hosp., 1933-35, attending phys. since 1935; cons. staff Dept. of Medicine, Nassau Hosp. Association, since 1929. Director Seaboard Surety Co. Served as 1st lt. Med. Reserve Corps, 1917-18. Trustee American U. of Beirut, Syria, 1924-41, Amherst Coll., 1936-41, Memorial Hosp., N.Y., N.Y. Acad. Med. since 1934. Mem. A.A.A.S., A.M.A., N.Y. State and County med. soc., Soc. for Exptl. Biology, Soc. of Mammalogists, Harvey Soc., Alpha Omega Alpha, Alpha Delta Phi. Clubs: Century Association, University, American Alpine (pres. 1929-32), Alpine (London, Eng.); Alpine Française (hon.; Paris). Contbr. of articles to med. jours. and mountaineering mags. Home: Cold Spring, N.Y. Died Sep. 16, 1949.

LADD-FRANKLIN, CHRISTINE, scientist; b. Windsor, Conn., Dec. 1, 1847; d. Eliphalet and Augusta (Niles) Ladd; grad. Vassar College, 1869, LL.D., 1887; studied at Johns Hopkins, 1878-82, under Prof. Sylvester and others, also at Göttingen and Berlin; held fellowships, mathematics, at Johns Hopkins, 1879-82; m. Fabian Franklin, Aug. 24, 1882; 1 dau., Margaret. Her theory of color-vision, published 1892, known as the Ladd-Franklin theory; contributed the doctrine of antilogism to logic. One of asso. editors Baldwin's Dictionary of Philosophy and Psychology, 1901-02; lecturer in logic and psychology, Johns Hopkins, 1904-09, Columbia U., 1910—. Author: Colour and Colour Theories (collected papers), 1928. Home: New York, N.Y. Died Mar. 5, 1930.

LADENBURG, RUDOLF WALTER, (la'den-burg), prof. physics; b. Kiel, Germany, June 6, 1882; s. Albert and Margarete (Pringsheim) L.; Ph.D., U. of Munich, 1906; post. grad. work, Cambridge, Eng., 1906-07; m. Else Uhthoff, Aug. 15, 1911; children—Margarete (Mrs. Fritz Eichenberg), Kurt, Eva Marie (Mrs. Ewald Mayer). Came to America, 1931. Univ. instr. and prof. at Breslau, 1908-25; scientific honorary mem. Academy Goettingen, at U. of Berlin, 1925-31; Brackett research prof. physics, Princeton U., 1931-50. Contbr. scientific books and articles. Home: 55 Princeton Av. Address: Palmer Physical Laboratory, Princeton, N.J. Died Apr. 3, 1952.

LA DU, DWIGHT B., civil engr.; b. Van Buren, N.Y., 1876; s. J. Sears and Julia E. (Warner) La D; ed. pub. schs. Began with the engring. dept. State of N.Y., 1896, advanced to resident engr., 1911; apptd. dir. engr. Eastern div., laster spl. dep. state engr. in charge all canal and terminal work in the state of N.Y., resigned, 1918, engaged in contracting and as cons. engr.; state engr. of N.Y., 1923, 24. Mem. N.Y.-N.J. Bridge and Tunnel Commn., supervising constrn. Holland Tunnel; mem. Albany Port Comm., 1928-45, named chmn. 1934. Mem. Am., Eastern, Albany socs. Civil Engrs. Democrat. Mason (K.T., Shriner). Clubs: Ft. Orange, Albany Country, Wolferts Roost Country (Albany); Rochester (Rochester); Scranton Country. Home: 399 State St., Albany, N.Y. Died Aug. 16, 1954.

LA FORGE, LAURENCE, (lä-fôrj), geologist; b. N.Y. City, Sept. 17, 1871; s. Abiel Teeple and Margaret Swain (Getchell) L.; A.B., Harvard, 1899, A.M., 1900, Ph.D., 1903; m. Fannie Agnes Carryer, June 28, 1893 (died July 13, 1924); 1 dau., Helen Grace (Mrs. Henry Gilmore Brousseari); m. 2d, Kate Louise Harbaugh, Sept. 8, 1930. Began as astronomer, 1894; instr. astronomy, Alfred Univ., 1896-97; Austin teaching fellow, Harvard, 1902-03; geologist U.S. Geol. Survey, 1901-05, 1914-27; aid in geology, U.S. Nat. Museum, 1905-08; research asso., Harvard, 1932-38; prof. geology Suffolk Univ., 1939-40; prof. of geology, Teachers Sch. of Science, 1934-48; also professor of geology, Tufts Coll., 1942-45; cons. geologist, 1908-14, and 1927—. Fellow American Geog. Society, N.Y. Acad. Sciences; mem. Am. Geophys. Union, Am. Forestry Assn., Nat. Geog. Soc., Geol. Soc. of Boston, A.A.A.S., U.S. Infantry Assn., Soc. Am. Military Engrs., Am. Museum of Natural History, Boston Mineral Club, Mt. Washington Observatory. Republican. Conglist. Clubs: Harvard Faculty (Cambridge). Home: 8 Shepard St., Cambridge, Mass. Died May 29, 1954; buried Newton (Mass.) Cemetery.

LA GARDE, LOUIS ANATOLE, surgeon U.S.A.; b. Thibodaux, La., Apr. 15, 1849; s. Jules Adolph and Aurelia (Daspit) L.; student Louisiana Mil. Acad., 1866-68; M.D., Bellevue Hosp. Med. Coll., 1872; m. Frances Neely, Mar. 4, 1879. Interne Roosevelt Hosp., New York, 1872-74; apptd. actg. asst. surgeon U.S.A., Apr. 1, 1874; asst. surgeon, June 6, 1878; capt. asst. surgeon, June 6, 1883; maj. surgeon, Nov. 13, 1896; lt. col. dep. surgeon gen., and lt. col., Med. Corps, Mar. 17, 1906; col., Jan. 1, 1910; retired Apr. 15, 1913; recalled to active duty and served during World War. Participated in Sioux Indian War, 1876; comd. Divisional Reserve Hosp., 5th Army Corps, Siboney, Cuba, 1898; in charge evacuation of sick and wounded to Northern hosps.; prof. mil. surgery, New York U., 1900—; comdt. U.S. Army Med. Sch., 1910-13; mem. Nat. Bd. Med. Examiners. Mutter lecturer, Coll. Physicians, Phila., 1902. Author: (text book) Gunshot Injuries, 2d edit., 1916. Has carried on extensive research work with septic bullets and septic powders; demonstrated ineffective material not destroyed by firearms. Home: Washington, D.C. Died Mar. 7, 1920.

LAHEY, FRANK HOWARD, (la'he), surgeon; b. Haverhill, Mass., June 1, 1880; s. Thomas and Honora Frances (Powers) L.; M.D., Harvard, 1904; hon. Sc.D., Tufts, 1927, Boston University, 1943, Northwestern U., 1947; LL.D. (honorary) University of Cincinnati 1951; m. Alice Wilcox, Apr. 15, 1909. Surgeon Long Island Hosp., 1904-05, Boston City Hosp., 1905-07; resident surgeon Haymarket Sq. Relief Sta., 1908; instr. in surgery, Harvard Med. Sch., 1908-09, 1912-15; asst. prof., later prof. surgery, Tufts Med. Sch., 1913-17; prof. clin. surgery, Harvard Medical School, 1923-24; surgeon in chief N.E. Baptist hospitals; director of surgery The Lahey Clinic, Boston. Served as major, Medical Corps, U.S. Army. World War; dir. surgery Evacuation Hosp. No. 30, A.E.F.; now hon. consultant to Medical Dept., U.S.N. Fellow Am. Coll. Surgeons (bd. govs.); honorary fellow Royal Coll. of Surgeons, England; mem. Am. and Internat. surg. assns., Am. Assn. for Study of Goitre, A.M.A. (pres. 1942), Société des Chirurgiens de Paris, Theta Delta Chi. Republican. Mason. Clubs: Harvard, Algonquin. Author of Lahey Clinic Number (Surg. Clinics of N. America), pub. yearly. Contbr. numerous articles on surg. subjects. Chmn. Procurement and Assignment Service for Med. Personnel for the Armed Forces. Home: 118 Bay State Rd. Office: 605 Commonwealth Av., Boston. Died June 27, 1953.

LAHM, FRANK PURDY, army officer; b. Ohio, Nov. 17, 1877; grad. U.S. Mil. Acad., 1901; grad. Mounted Service Sch., 1911; m. Gertrude Jenner, Oct. 18, 1911. Commd. 2d lt. 6th Cav., Feb. 18, 1901; capt. Aviation Sect. Signal Corps, Apr. 1, 1916; lt. colonel, July 2, 1920; promoted colonel Air Corps, Oct. 7, 1931. Made many experiments with balloons for war purposes and participated in nat. and internat. races; won James Gordon Bennett cup in Internat. Balloon Race, Paris, France, Sept. 30-Oct. 1, 1906. Organized aviation service in Philippine Islands, 1912, conducting training on airplanes and seaplanes there, 1912-13; sec. Signal Corps Aviation Sch., North Island, San Diego, Calif., 1916-17; ordered to command Balloon Sch., Ft. Omaha, Neb., Apr. 1917, to England, Aug. 1917, thence to France, inspecting balloon services; organized Lighter than Air Service in A.E.F.; on duty Hdqrs. Chief of Air Service to Feb. 1918, Hdqrs. Zone of Advance Air Service to May 1918, Hdqrs. First Army Air Service to July 1918; air officer in G-3, 1st Army, to Oct. 1918; organized and commanded 2d Army Air Service, Oct. 1918; disbanded May, 1919; spl. student Army War Coll., 1919-20; G-3, War Dept. Gen. Staff, 1920-24; 9th Corps Area Air Officer, 1924-26; apptd. brig. gen. for period of 4 yrs., and asst. to chief of Air Corps, to organize and command Air Corps Training Center, 1926-30; air officer 9th Corps Area to July, 1930; apptd. air attache, Am. Embassy, Paris, France, July 1931. Awarded D.S.M. First airship pilot and first balloon pilot in U.S. Army. Address: War Department, Washington DC

LAKE, MARSHALL E(DGAR), exec. engr.; b. Washington, Nov. 26, 1900; s. Marshall Beverly and Eleanor Gibson (Harper) L.; B.S., U. of N.C., 1922; m. Mabel Lina Foster, June 12, 1924; children—Mary (Mrs. James Austin), Eleanor (Mrs. Russell Garrison), John. With Westinghouse Elec. Corp., E. Pitts. summers 1920, 21; indsl. power sales engr. Duke Power Co., 1922-44, mgr. indsl. power sales program since 1944, supervision of comml. power sales since 1948, member board of directors, 1946—, vice president, 1954—. Member Bd. Sch. Commrs., Charlotte, N.C., 1941-46, chmn. bd., 1945-46; dir. Charlotte Y.M.C.A., 1936-41; dir. Salvation Army, Charlotte, 1949—. Head Mecklenburg County, N.C., Civilian Defense Utilities Div., World War II. Registered professional engineer. Member of the American Inst. E.E. (co-organizer and sec. N.C. sect., 1929; sect. chmn. 1938), N.C. Soc. Engrs. (dir. 1945-46), Phi Beta Kappa. Baptist. Clubs: Engineers (pres. 1938), Rotary (Charlotte). Home: 926 Henley Pl., Charlotte 7. Office: 422 S. Church St., Charlotte 2, N.C. Died Nov. 16, 1958; buried Ever Green Cemetery Charlotte.

LAKE, SIMON, naval architect, mech. engr.; b. Pleasantville, N.J., Sept. 4, 1866; s. John Christopher and Miriam M. (Adams) L.; ed. Clinton Liberal Inst., Fort Plain, N.Y., and Franklin Inst., Phila.; m. Margaret Vogel, June 9, 1890. Inventor of even keel type of submarine torpedo boats; built first experimental boat, 1894; built Argonaut 1897 (first submarine to operate successfully in the open sea); has designed and built many submarine torpedo boats for U.S. and foreign countries; spent several yrs. in Russia, Germany and England, designing, building and acting in an advisory capacity in construction of submarine torpedo boats. Also inventor submarine apparatus for locating and recovering sunken vessels and their cargoes, submarine apparatus for pearl and sponge fishing, heavy oil internal combustion engine for marine purposes, etc. Pres. The Lake Submarine Co., The Lake Engring. Co., Merchant Submarine Co., Lake Submarine Salvage Corp., Industrial Submarine Corp., Lake Torpedo Boat Co. (also consulting engineer). Mem. Soc. Naval Architects and Marine Engrs., Am. Soc. M.E., Am. Soc. Naval Engrs., Instn. of Naval Architects (London), Soc. Founders and Patriots of America, Soc. Colonial Wars, S.A.R. Mason. Clubs: Engineers (New York); Algonquin (Bridgeport, Conn.). Home: Milford, Conn. Died June 23, 1945. *

LAKES, ARTHUR, mining engr.; b. at Martock, Somersetshire, Eng., Dec. 21, 1844; s. Rev. John and Catherine (Arthur) L.; ed. at Queen Elizabeth Coll., Guernsey, and at Queen's Coll., Oxford, Eng.; came to U.S., 1862; m. Edith Slater, of Trinidad, Colo. Prof. geology, Colo. Sch. of Mines, 1882-94; engaged as mining engr. since 1894. Western editor Mines and Minerals, 1895-1904. Made many new discoveries in palaeontology, notably of the atlantosaurus, a huge fossil lizard or dinosaur, the largest land animal ever, to that time, discovered. Author: Geology of Colorado Coal Fields, 1889; Geology of Colorado and Western Ore Deposits, 1893; Prospecting for Gold and Silver in North America, 1895; Geology of Cripple Creek Ore Deposits, 1896; Geology of Western Ore Deposits, 1905. Contbr. to various mining and scientific mags. on econ. geology. Home: 1569 St. Paul St., Denver.

LAMB, ALBERT RICHARD, prof. emeritus; b. Waterbury, Conn., Apr. 22, 1881; s. George Burton and Idabelle (Johnson) L.; prep. edn., Taft Sch., Watertown, Conn., 1895-99; A.B., Yale, 1903; M.D., Coll. Physicians and Surgeons, Columbia, 1907; m. Helen Foster, Jan. 4, 1910; children—Mary Nightingale, Albert Richard, Priscilla Foster, Helen. Interne Presbyn. Hosp., N.Y.C., 1908-10, resident bacteriologist, 1910-11, resident pathologist, 1911-13, chief of out patient dept. and asst. visiting physician, 1913-17, visiting physician since 1918; instr. of medicine, Coll. Physicians and Surgeons, 1913-18, became prof. clin. medicine, 1918, now prof. emeritus; pres. med. board Presbyn. Hosp., 1940-46; now consulting physician; cons. physician Englewood (N.J.) Hosp. Chmn. Med. Adv. Bd. No. 22, N.Y.C.; mem. emergency med. service Office Civilian Def., N.Y. Served as maj., M.C., U.S. Army, World War; attached to Am. Commn. to Negotiate Peace. Recipient D.S.M., Columbia U., 1956. Fellow A.C.P.; mem. A.M.A., Soc. Internal Medicine, N.Y. Acad. Medicine, N.Y. State Med. Soc., N.Y. Clin. Soc., Cosmopolitan Med. Club, Psi Upsilon, Skull and Bones. Republican. Episcopalian. Club: Century. Home: Pine Orchard, Conn. Office: Presbyn. Hosp., 622 W. 168th St., N.Y.C. Died Nov. 1959.

LAMB, ARTHUR BECKET, prof. chemistry; b. Attleboro, Mass., Feb. 25, 1880; s. Louis Jacob and Elizabeth Camerden Townsend (Becket) L.; A.B., A.M., Tufts, 1900, Ph.D., 1904, D.Sc., 1922; A.M., Harvard, 1903, Ph.D., 1904; univs. of Leipzig, 1904, Heidelberg, 1905; m. Blanche Anne Driscoll, Dec. 27, 1923. Instr. Electrochemistry, Harvard, 1905-06; asst. prof. chemistry, N.Y.U., 1906, asso. prof., 1907, prof., 1909-12, also dir. Havemeyer Chem. Lab.; asst. prof. chemistry, Harvard, 1912-20, prof., 1920-48, prof. emeritus, 1949-52, dir. chem. lab., 1912-47, dean Grad. Sch. Arts and Sciences, 1940-43. Editor Jour. Am. Chem. Soc., 1917-49. Served as lt. col. Research Div. Chem. Warfare Service, U.S. Army, 1918-19, in charge defense chem. research; mem. U.S. Fixed Nitrogen Mission, 1919; dir. Fixed Nitrogen Research Lab., Washington, 1919-21. Awarded Am. Chem. Soc., Nichols Medal, 1943, Priestly Medal, 1949, Austin M. Patterson Award, Dayton Sect., 1951; Ballou Medal, Tufts Coll., 1944. Hon. Fellow The Chem. Soc. London, 1951, Fellow A.A.A.S. (v.p. 1933); mem. Am. Chem. Soc. (pres. 1933), Am. Acad. Arts and Scis., Am. Philos. Soc., Am. Electrochem. Soc., Washington Acad. Scis., Nat. Acad. Sci., Deutsche Chemische Gesellschaft, Deutsche Bunsen-Gesellschaft, Delta Upsilon, Phi Beta Kappa, Alpha Chi Sigma, Phi Lambda Upsilon. Clubs: Faculty (Cambridge, Mass.); Harvard (Boston); Chemists (N.Y.); Country (Brookline). Home: 121 Colbourne Crescent. Brookline, Mass. Died May 15, 1952; buried Attleboro, Mass.

LAMB, ISAAC WIXOM, inventor, clergyman; b. Hartland, Mich., Jan. 8, 1840; s. Rev. Aroswell and Phebe (Wixom) L.; m. 2d, Mrs. Elizabeth Phelps. Invented a machine for braiding whiplashes and patented it in 1859; invented and patented, 1863-65, the Lamb Knitting Machine, which was also patented and introduced into many foreign countries; has since patented many improvements. Was ordained to Bapt. ministry, 1869; in active pastorate up to May 1899. Now pres. and supt. Perry Glove and Mitten Co. Address: Perry, Mich. Died 1906.

LAMB, JOSEPH F., mech. engr.; b. New York, N.Y., June 12, 1892; s. Joseph F. and Rose (Hannan) L.; B.S. in Mech. Engring., Cooper Union Inst. Tech., 1914; M.M.E., Columbia, 1916; student Fordham University, 1916-17; LL.D., Manhattan Coll., N.Y.C., 1947; m. Elizabeth Marie Gerety, Nov. 19, 1919 (dec.); children—Richard, David Joseph, Mary (Mrs. John Wilson Duffy) (dec.), Joseph Francis, Ann (dec.), Andrew William. With Third Av. Railway System, New York, N.Y., 1911-18 and 1919-24, beginning as student of elec. railway maintenance and construction of car equipment and advancing to equipment engr., mech. dept.; staff engr. and territorial engr. of lubricants and lubrication, The Texas Co., 1924-39; supreme sec. Supreme Council, Knights of Columbus, New Haven, Conn., since 1939, mem. bd. dirs., mem. exec. and finance com. Served with 39th Engineers, A.E.F., 1918-19. Grand Officer Order of St. Gregory the Great conferred by Pope Pius XII, 1946; 1st Cl. Order San Raimundode Penafort (Spain), 1956. Mem. executive committee, bd. dirs. Nat. Cath. Community Service of Archdiocese of N.Y.; State Deputy, Knights of Columbus, New York State 1937-40; Pres. Grand Jurors Assn. of Bronx County, N.Y., 1936-37; pres. Bronx County chapter N.Y. State Soc. Professional Engrs., 1934-35. Mem. Am. Soc. M.E., Soc. Am. Mil. Engrs., Fordham Alumni Assn., Holy Name Soc., Order of Alhambra, Tau Beta Psi, Am. Legion. Club: Union League (New Haven). Home: 1201 Shakespeare Av., N.Y.C. 52. Office: 71 Meadow St., New Haven. Died Feb. 2, 1964; buried Calvary Cemetery, Queens, N.Y.

LAMBERT, AVERY ELDORUS, anatomist, educator, author; b. Waldoboro, Me., Oct. 31, 1873; s. Ellison and Angouleme (Lambert) Maddocks (obtained right to use mother's maiden name, 1892); prep. edn., pub. schs., Waldoboro, Me., and Tabor Acad., Marion, Mass.; grad. Bangor (Me.) Theol. Sem., 1896; B.S., Dartmouth, 1902, Ph.D., 1906; grad. study, Harvard, 1917, U. of Chicago, 1920-22; m. Dora L. Hersom, 1896; 1 son. G. Hersom; m. 2d, Irene Lamson Adams; children—Mary Lamson, Adams. Ordained ministry Congl. Ch., 1896; pastor, Lebanon, Me., 1896-98, Thetford, Vt., 1898-1900; instr. zoology, Dartmouth, 1902-04; instr. biology, Framingham (Mass.) Normal Sch., 1904-10; prof. biology, Middlebury (Vt.) Coll., 1911-16, also dean, 1912-14; prof. of anatomy, U. of Vt., 1917-19; prof. anatomy and head of dept., U. of Ala., 1920-25; prof. histology and microscopical anatomy, State University of Iowa, 1925-1944; retired 1944. Fellow A.A.A.S.; member American Assn. Anatomists, Sigma Xi, Phi Beta Pi, Ia. Acad. Sci., Am. Geog. Soc. Clubs: Iowa Authors, Kiwanis, Triangle. Author: A New Trilobite from the Littleton Formation, 1905; History of the Procephalic Lobes of Epeira Cinerea, 1909; Guide to the Study of Histology, 1931; Poems of the Air (broadcast series), 1935; Introduction and Guide to the Study of Histology. Contributor to scientific and other periodicals. Asso. dir. of Morning Chapel, Radio Station, WSUI. Home: 1416 E. College St., Iowa City IA

LAMBERT, BYRON JAMES, civil engr., educator; b. Argyle, Wis., Apr. 25, 1874; s. Furniss and Mary Wasley (Reynolds) L.; B.Di., State Teachers Coll., Cedar Falls, Ia., 1896, M.Di., 1897; Ph.B., State U. of Ia., 1900, B.S. in C.E., 1901, C.E., 1906; m. Helen Leavitt Davison, Nov. 8, 1902; children—James Leavitt, Robert Davison, Mary Louise, Richard Hooker, Edward Reynolds. City engr. Cedar Falls and Waterloo, Ia., 1899-1901; chief engr. Waterloo, Cedar Falls & Northern Ry. during constrn., 1901-02; successively instr., prof., and head dept. civ. engring., State U. of Ia., 1902-50, acting dean of Engring. Coll., 1935-36. Cons. practice also gen. contractor; cons. engr. Moline Airport, Ia. City Municipal Swimming Pool. Major of engrs., U.S. Army, Nov. 1917; comdg. officer 3d Batt., 23d Engrs., in France, Mar.-Dec. 1918; engr. of bridges with 1st Army; hon. discharged, Jan. 6, 1919; lt. col. Engr. O.R.C. Mem. Am. Soc. C.E., Ia. Engring. Soc., Am. Soc. Millitary Engineers, Society Promotion Engineering Education, Iowa City Engrs.' Club, Scabbard and Blade, Sigma Xi, Tau Beta Pi, Sigma Tau, Chi Epsilon, etc. Republican. Methodist. Mason. Clubs: Triangle, Rotary. Joint author of Lambert and Holt's Elementary Structures in Steel and Concrete. Author: High Masonry Dams, Airport Engineering. Contbr. on engring. topics. Invented and patented all-steel stadium, 1923 and 1939. Course supervisor "Airport Engineering" in Nat. Defense Training, 1941. Home: 4 Melrose Circle, Iowa City, Ia. Died Oct. 29, 1952.

LAMBERT, FRED DAYTON, botanist; b. Muscatine, Ia., Oct. 28, 1871; s. Daniel Meader and Ellen (Scudder) L.; Ph.B., Tufts Coll., 1894, A.M., Ph.D., 1897; student U. of Freiburg, Germany, winter 1910-11; student Naples Zoöl. Sta., 1911; m. Mary Anna Ingalls, June 6, 1903; 1 dau., Elizabeth Allen. Asst. in biology, 1896-97, instr., 1897-98, Tufts Coll.; submaster Edward Little High Sch., Auburn, Me., 1898-99; instr. natural history, 1899, asst. prof. biology, 1904, prof. botany, 1913—, Tufts Coll. Home: Tufts College, Mass. Died Feb. 21, 1931.

LAMBERT, ROBERT ARCHIBALD, pathologist, educator; b. Lamison, Ala., Oct. 3, 1883; s. Joe and Lily (George) L.; prep. edn., South. Ala. Inst., Thomasville, Ala., 1897-1900; A.B., Howard Coll., Birmingham, Ala., 1902, A.M., 1903; M.D., Tulane, 1907, LL.D., 1949; grad. study Johns Hopkins and Berlin; Academico Honorario, U. of Salvador, 1922; Dr. honoris causa, U. of Sao Paulo, Brazil, 1948. Asst. in pathology, Coll. Phys. and Surg. (Columbia), 1909-11, asso., 1911-17, acting head dept., 1917-18; visiting pathologist Montefiore Hosp., New York, 1914-15, 1917-18; resident pathologist Presbyn. Hosp., 1915-16, visiting pathologist, 1917-18; mem. Rice scientific expdn. to Brazil, 1916-17; dir. labs. Near East Relief, Turkey and Syria, 1919-20; asst. prof. pathology, Yale, 1919-23; asso. and res. pathologist and bacteriologist, New Haven Hosp.; prof. pathol. anatomy Faculdade de Medicine de São Paulo, Brazil, 1923-25; prof. pathology and dir. Sch. Tropical Medicine, Univ. of Puerto Rico, under auspices Columbia Univ., 1926-28. Asso. dir. for the Med. Sciences, The Rockefeller Foundation, 1928-48. Cons. Pan-Am. Sanitary Bur., Regional Office World Health Organization, Washington, 1949-52; chmn. interim com., acting president Meharry Med. Coll., 1950-52, vice chmn. board trustees, 1952-53, chmn., 1953—; sent by Rockefeller Found. to Central America, summer 1922, to deliver series of lectures at U. of Salvador and make a survey of med. schs. in C.A. Mem. bd. visitors Tulane U. Decorated Chevalier de la Legion D'Honneur, 1951; named to Meth. Hall of Fame in Philanthropy, 1955. Member A.M.A., Am. Assn. Pathologists and Bacteriologists, Am. Assn. Cancer Research, Am. Soc. Tropical Medicine, Am. Society Parasitologists, Soc. Explt. Biology and Medicine, Soc. Explt. Pathology, Yale Med. Soc. (ex-sec.; ex-pres.), N.Y. Academy Medicine, N.Y. Pathol. Soc., Harvey Soc., Internat. Assn. Med. Museums (v.p. 1922), Sigma Xi, etc. Author or co-author abt. 70 papers and articles on med. topics. Address: 67 Magnolia Av., Fairhope, Ala. Died Nov. 20, 1960; buried Fairhope Cemetery.

LA MER, VICTOR KUHN, educator, chemist; b. Leavenworth, Kan., June 15, 1895; s. Joseph Seondule and Anna Pauline (Kuhn) La M.; A.B., U. Kan., 1915; Ph.D., Columbia, 1921; student U. Chgo., 1916, Cambridge U., Eng., 1922-23, Copenhagen, Denmark, 1923; Sc.D. (hon.), Clarkson Coll., 1962; m. Ethel Agatha McGreevy, July 31, 1918; children—Luella Belle (Mrs. A. P. Slaner), Anna Pauline (Mrs. Alex Burgo), Eugenia Angelique (dec.). Chemist, high sch. tchr. chemistry, 1915-16; research chemist Carnegie Inst. of Washington, 1916-17; asst. chemistry Columbia, 1919-20, successively instr., asst., asso. prof., prof., 1935-61, prof. emeritus, 1961—, sr. researcher mineral engring., 1963—, Fulbright prof. U. Copenhagen, 1953; vis. prof. Stanford, 1931, Northwestern U., 1928. Priestley lectr. Pa. State Coll., 1932; Fulbright lectr., Australia, 1959; distinguished lectr. Shell Devel. Co., 1963; lectr. NSF Colloid Sch., U.S.C., 1962-63, NSF Colloid Sch. Lehigh U., 1965. Recipient Presdl. Certificate of Merit, 1948; Kendall award Am. Chem. Soc., 1956. Mem. Royal Danish Acad. Sch., Nat. Acad. Scis., div. mem. Nat. Def. Research Com. Mem. Jury of Award, Nichols medal, 1934-38 (chmn. 1934, 37); pres. Leonia Civic Conf. 1941. 1st lt. San. Corps, U.S. Army, 1917-19. Hon. prof. San Marcos U., Lima, Peru; mem. Royal Belgian Acad. Arts Letters and Sci. Fellow N.Y. Acad. Sci. (v.p. 1939-41, treas. 1943, pres. 1949); mem. Am. Chem. Soc., Am. Phys. Soc., Faraday Soc. (Eng.), Sigma Xi, Phi Lambda Upsilon, Phi Chi, Epsilon Chi; pres. Leonia Rep. Assn., 1940-41. Conglist. Clubs: Cosmos (Washington); Faculty (Columbia). Translator, editor Fundamentals of Physical Chemistry by Arnold Eucken (with Eric Jette), 1925. Asso. editor Jour. Chem. Physics, 1933-36; editor-in-chief Jour. Colloid Sci. Editor: Retardation of Evaporation by Monolayers. Contbr. sci. jours. Home: 353 Moore Av., Leonia, N.J. 07605. Office: Columbia, N.Y.C. 27. Died Sept. 26, 1966; buried St. Joseph Cemetery, Hackensack, N.J.

LAMME, BENJAMIN G., elec. engr.; b. Clarke County, O., Jan. 12, 1864; M.E., Ohio State U., 1888; s. James G. and Sarah A. L.; unmarried. With Westinghouse Elec. & Mfg. Co., 1889—, chief engr., 1903—. Pioneer in development of direct current apparatus for ry. lighting and power; widely known for part in development of alternating current apparatus; has taken out many elec. patents. Mem. Naval Consulting Bd., 1915—. Edison medal, 1919. Author: Electrical Engineering Papers, 1919. Awarded Jos. Sullivant medal, Ohio State U., 1923 (first recipient), for engring. Work. Home: Pittsburgh, Pa. Died July 8, 1924.

LAMOUNTAIN, JOHN, balloonist; b. Wayne County, N.Y., 1830. Began experimenting with balloons, 1850's; made balloon ascension (with O. A. Gager) from Bennington, Vt., circa 1858; planned (with Gager and John Wise) balloon for trans-Atlantic use, 1859; travelled in balloon Atlantic (with Gager and Wise) from St. Louis to Henderson County, N.Y. (1,000 miles, longest air trip on record to that date), July 1, 1859; performed aerial reconnaissance missions for Gen. McClellan in balloon, passed behind Confederate lines, Aug. 1861; later supervised several ascensions for mil. reconnaissance purposes. Died Feb. 14, 1870.

LAMPLAND, CARL OTTO, astronomer; b. Dodge County, Minn., Dec. 29, 1873; s. Ole Helleckson and Beret (Skartum) L.; B.S., Valparaiso (Ind.) Univ., 1899; A.B., Indiana U., 1902, A.M., 1905, LL.D., 1930; m. Verna Basil Darby, Feb. 8, 1911. Prin. Bloomfield (Ind.) High Sch., 1902; astronomer Lowell Obs., Flagstaff, Ariz., since 1903; member Lowell Obs. Eclipse Expdn. to Kan., 1918, also solar eclipse expdn. to Ensenada, Mexico, 1923. Was asst. to late Dr. Percival Lowell in visual observations of the planets Venus, Mars, Jupiter and Saturn; has given much attention to development of photography of delicate detail on planetary surfaces; prin. work of recent yrs. photographic observations of planets, satellites, comets, nebulae, novae, and star fields; has discovered many variable stars and changes in nebulae; measurements of radiation from planets and determination of planetary temperatures (early work) with W. W. Coblentz, continued and extended in recent years with the assistance of V. D. Lampland); transmission of the earth's atmosphere (with A. Adel); investigation in connection with trans-Neptunian planet Pluto. Exchange professor astronomy, Princeton, 1929. Fellow Am. Acad. Arts and Sciences, A.A.A.S.; mem. Am. Astron. Society (council), Internat. Astron. Union (com. on planets and nebulae), Astron. Soc. Pacific, Société Astronomique de France, Astronomische Gesellschaft, Am. Physical Soc., Math. Assn. America, Am. Philos. Soc., Am. Math. Soc., Soc. for Research on Meteorites, Northern Ariz. Soc. of Science and Art (v.p. and trustee), Sigma Xi, Phi Beta Kappa; hon. mem. Sociedad Astronomico de Mexico. Medalist Royal Photographic Soc. of Grt. Britain, 1907, for photographs of planet Mars. Contbr. to astronomical journals. Address: Lowell Observatory, Flagstaff, Ariz. Died Dec. 14, 1951; buried Fairview Cemetery, Hayfield, Minn.

LAMSON, CHARLES HENRY, inventor; b. Augusta, Me., Sept. 17, 1847; s. Joseph S. and Eunice E. (Winslow) L.; ed. Exeter, N.H.; m. Elizabeth H. Cox, July 27, 1874. Engaged in business as watchmaker and optician. Inventor of luggage carriers for bicycles and of novel types of kites and aeroplanes for use in meteorological observations; also of flying machine; was the first to obtain an Am. patent for a method of tilting or warping the wings of kites and aeroplanes for the purpose of balancing the same in flight. Home: Oxnard, Calif. Died May 1930.

LAMSON, PAUL DUDLEY, educator; b. Charlestown, Mass., 1884; s. Charles Dudley and Annie (Knowles) L.; A.B., Harvard, 1905, M.D., 1909; postgrad. U. London, Eng., 1912; m. Alice Daland, 1919; children—Elliot Daland, Paul Dudley. House officer Mass. Gen. Hosp., 1909-10; asst. in pharmacology U. Wurzburg, Germany, 1911; asst. resident physician Peter Bent Brigham Hosp., Boston, 1912-14; asst. to asso. prof. pharmacology Johns Hopkins, 1914-25; prof pharmacology Vanderbilt U. Sch. Medicine since 1925. Mem. sub-com. on shock NRC. Fellow A.M.A.; mem. Am. Pharmacol. Soc., Am. Physiol. Soc., Assn. Am. Physicians, A.A.A.S. (chmn. sect. N), Sigma Xi. Author: The Heart Rhythms. Contbr. articles on blood vol., polycythaemia, carbon tetrachloride, anthelmintics, anesthesia, shock. Former editor Jour. Pharmacology and exptl. Therapeutics. Home: Stanford Dr., Nashville 37215. Died Oct. 3, 1962.

LAMSON-SCRIBNER, FRANK, agrostologist; b. Cambridgeport, Mass., Apr. 19, 1851; s. Joseph S. and Eunice E. (Winslow) L.; adopted at age of 3 by family named Scribner, living nr. Augusta, Me.; B.S., Me. State

Coll. of Agr., 1873; LL.D., U. of Me., 1920; m. Ella Augusta Newmarch, Dec. 25, 1877; children—Allen, Frank, Louise; m. 2d, Marjorie Fleming Anderson, Aug. 12, 1913. Teacher, public schools, Maine; clerk to secretary Maine State Board of Agriculture 2 yrs.; officer Girard Coll. Phila., 1876-85; taught botany in summer schs. of sciences; spl. agt. in charge mycol. sect., bot. div., U.S. Dept. of Agr., 1885-86, chief sect. of vegetable pathology, 1887-88; prof. botany, U. of Tenn., 1888-94; dir. Tenn. Agrl. Expt. Sta., 1890-94; chief div. of agrostology, U.S. Dept. Agr., 1894-1901; chief Insular Bur. of Agr., P.I., 1901-04. As spl. agt. and expert on exhibits had charge of the preparation and display of exhibits at a large number of fairs and expns. made by the Agrl. Dept., 1904-22, including the St. Louis Expn., 1904; Portland, Ore., 1905; Seattle, Wash., 1909; Buenos Aires, Argentina, 1910; Turin, Italy, 1911; Lethbridge, Can., 1912; Inter. Refrigeration Expn., Chicago, 1913; San Francisco Expn., 1915, at which served as mem. Govt. Exhibit Bd. by presdl. apptmt. Conducted series of war-time exhibits for food conservation in coöperation with the State Fairs throughout the country, 1917-20; apptd. by sec. of state, director of exhibits for U.S. Com. to Brazilian Centennial Expn., Rio de Janeiro, 1922-23; personal asst. to dir. Commercial Museum, Phila., 1924; spl. asst. to U.S. Com. and supervisor of U.S. Govt. Exhibits, Sesquicentennial Expn., Phila., 1926-27; dir. Hist. Museum of Cumberland County Hist. Soc., Carlisle, Pa., 1927-28; advisory mem. science planning com. of "Chicago Century of Progress Exposition 1933." Decorated Chevalier du Mérite Agricole (France), 1889. Author: Weeds of Maine, 1869; Fungus Diseases of the Grape and Other Plants, 1890; Grasses of Tennessee, 1894; American Grasses (3 vols.), 1897-1900. Translator: (with E. A. Southworth) The True Grasses (from the German), 1890. Home: Washington, D.C. Died Feb. 22, 1938.

LANCASTER, WALTER, B., ophthalmic surgeon; b. Newton, Mass., May 11, 1863; s. Charles Bartlett and Mary Elizabeth (Brackett) L.; A.B., magna cum laude, Harvard, 1884, M.D., 1880; grad. work, Vienna, London, Edinburgh; D.Sc. (hon.), Dartmouth Coll., 1939; m. Emma Winter, Dec. 15, 1885; 1 dau., Julia Elizabeth. Practice ophthalmology, Boston, Mass., since 1890; ophthalmic surgeon, Mass. Eye and Ear Infirmary, Mass. Gen. Hosp., Boston City Hosp.; chief staff eye clinic Dartmouth Coll., 1940-42; teacher med. sch. Harvard since 1898. Exec. officer, Ophthal. Study Council. Clerk, Foundation for Vision, Inc. Awarded ophthalmic research medal A.M.A., 1941, 5th De Scheinitz lecture Coll. Physicians, Phila., 1942, Leslie Dana medal for prevention of blindness, 1943; International Ophthalmic Medal of A.O.S., 1944; Lucien Howe Medal by American Ophthal. Soc., 1945. Served as major in the medical corps United States Army Air Force, 1918-19, in charge ophthalmology, research lab., Mineola. Mem. Am. Orthoplic Council; chmn. Am. com. on optics and visual physiol., since 1930. A founder, Lancaster course in ophthalmol. for graduate students. Mem. and past pres. Am. Ophthal. Soc., Am. Acad. Ophthal. and Otol., New England Ophthal. Soc., Am. Bd. Ophthal., A.M.A. (sect. on ophthal.); mem. A.A.A.S., A.C.S., Assn. Research in Ophthal. (mem. council); del. Internat. Congress Ophthal., 1929. Contbr. 75 papers to med. jours. Home: 374 Commonwealth Av. Office: 520 Commonwealth Av., Boston. Died Dec. 9, 1951.

LAND, WILLIAM JESSE GOAD, botanist; b. Alton, Ind., Dec. 2, 1865; s. James Glenn and Amanda (Goad) L.; Rome (Ind.) Acad., 1888-92; S.B., U. of Chicago, 1902, Ph.D., 1904; m. Estella Little, Feb. 8, 1890. Prin. Rome Acad., 1893-94; prin. high sch., Grand Rivers, Ky., 1894-95; supt. city schs., Ashley, Ill., 1895-1901; fellow, U. of Chicago, 1903, asst. in morphology, 1904-06, asso., 1906-08, instr. botany, 1908-11, asst. prof., 1911-15, asso. prof., 1915-28, prof. since 1928. Fellow A.A.A.S.; mem. Bot. Soc. America, Ill. Acad. Science, Am. Micros. Soc., Deutsche Botanische Gesellschaft, Tex. Geog. Society, Tex. Acad. of Science, Phi Beta Kappa, Sigma Xi, Alpha Sigma Phi. Contbr. numerous monographs, as results of original investigations in botany; bot. exploration in Mexico, 1906, 08, 10, in South Seas, especially western Polynesia, 1912. Life mem. Nat. Rifle Assn. America. Botanical exploration in tropical and neo-tropical America, 1932-34, 1935-36, 1937-38, 1939-40. Home: Brownsville, Tex.; (summer) Rome, Ind. Died Aug. 1, 1942.

LANDACRE, FRANCIS LEROY, anatomist; b. Hilliards, O., Feb. 13, 1867; s. Joseph Perry and Sarah Jane (Dobyns) L.; student Ohio Wesleyan U., 1887-91; A.B., Ohio State U., 1895; Ph.D., U. of Chicago, 1914; m. Frances Ward Yeazell, Dec. 17, 1901; children—Katharine Anita, Elizabeth Wade. Prof. embryology, Ohio Med. U., 1896; prof. histology and embryology, Ohio Med. U. and Starling-Ohio Med. Coll., 1902-14; asst. in zoölogy and entomology, 1895-1900, asso. prof., 1902, prof., 1908, prof. anatomy, 1914—, Ohio State U.; lecturer on Neurology, U. of Calif., 1924-27. Conglist. Author: A Laboratory Guide in Zoölogy, 1904; A Laboratory Guide for Vertebrate Dissections, 1918. Home: Columbus, O. Died Aug. 23, 1933.

LANDES, HENRY, geologist; b. Carroll, Ind., Dec. 22, 1867; s. Samuel and Lydia (Duncan) L.; A.B., Indiana U., 1892; A.B. and A.M., Harvard U., 1893; m. Bertha Ethel Knight, Jan. 2, 1894; children—Katherine (dec.), Kenneth. Asst. to state geologist of N.J., 1893-94; prin. Rockland (Me.) High Sch., 1894-95; prof. geology, 1895—, acting pres., 1914-15, also dean Coll. of Science, 1912—, U. of Wash. State geologist of Wash., 1901-21. Editor of and contbr. to Annual Reports and bulletins, Wash. Geol. Survey, 1901, 1902, 1909-21. Home: Seattle, Wash. Died Aug. 23, 1936.

LANDES, HERBERT ELLIS, urologist, educator; b. Greencastle, Ind., Oct. 5, 1894; s. Albert and Mary Louise (Ellis) L.; A.B., De Pauw U., 1917; M.S., U. Chgo., 1919; M.D., Rush Med. Coll., 1922; grad. study U. Vienna, 6 mos. 1930, Johns Hopkins Hosp., 1930-32; m. Wyota Ann Ewing, Sept. 4, 1918; children—Mary Louise, John Ewing. Intern Presbyn. Hosp., 1921-22; clin. prof. urology, sch. medicine Loyola U., 1932, prof. 1934—, chmn. dept. urology, 1939—; sr. attending urologist Mercy Hosp., 1932, chmn. dept. urology, 1939—; cons. urologist Chgo. Municipal TB Sanitarium, Elgin (Ill.) State Hosp., Little Co. of Mary Hosp., Chgo., Burlington R.R., Lewis Meml. Hosp., Chgo. Diplomate Am. Bd. Urology. Fellow A.C.S.; mem. A.M.A., Ill. State Med. Soc., Inst. Medicine, Am., Chgo. urology assns., Sigma Xi, Phi Beta Kappa, Nu Sigma Nu, Phi Gamma Delta, Alpha Omega Alpha. Clubs: South Shore Country, University (Chgo.). Contbr. textbooks on urology; also articles. Home: 6901 Oglesby Av. Office: 30 N. Michigan Av., Chgo. Died Sept. 24, 1959.

LANDIS, CHARLES WILLIAM, cons. engineer; b. Sacramento, Calif., Aug. 9, 1877; s. Leonidas Hamilton and Lovica (Smith) L.; B.S. in C.E., U. of Calif., 1902; m. Louise Coan, July 26, 1910; 1 dau., Mary Louise. Associated in practice with A. J. Cleary, San Francisco, since 1921; in analysis of Muscle Shoals project and preparation of bids for its operation, 1921; a designer, with Mr. Cleary, of Rincon Hill-Oakland Bridge across San Francisco Bay, 1926; asso. engr. for Pacific Gas & Electric Co. in underground water supply studies on Mokelumne River in Calif., 1930-31; consulting engr. on water supply problems with Cyril Williams, Jr., San Francisco, 1933-34; pioneer in development of Mokelumne River Water Supply project, American River project, etc. Mem. Am. Soc. Civil Engrs. Republican. Presbyn. Home: 2606 Harrison St., Oakland, Calif. Office: 269 Pine St., San Francisco CA

LANDRETH, DAVID, agriculturist; b. Phila., Sept. 15, 1802; s. David and Sarah (Arnell) L.; ed. common schs., Phila.; m. Elizabeth Rodney, 1825; m. 2d, Martha Burnet, 1842. Became propr. of his father's nursery and seed bus., Phila., 1828; a founder Pa. Horticultural Soc., v.p., 1829-36; became publisher Illustrated Floral Mag., 1832; constructed nursery and arboretum, Bristol, Pa., 1847; a founder Farmers' Club of Pa., 1847; active in agrl. experimentation, cattle breeding, 1850's, 60's; pres. Phila. Soc. for Promotion of Agr., 1856; experimented with steam plowing, digging and chopping, 1870's; published Am. edit. Dictionary of Modern Gardening (George W. Johnson), 1847. Died Bristol, Feb. 22, 1880; buried Bristol.

LANDRETH, OLIN HENRY, engineer; b. Addison, N.Y., July 21, 1852; s. Rev. James and Adelia (Comstock) L.; C.E., Union Coll., 1876, A.B., 1877, A.M., 1887, D.Sc., 1905; m. Eliza Taylor, Aug. 20, 1879 (dec.); children—William Comstock (dec.), Olin Henry (dec.), Mrs. Mary Eliza Parker, Helen Adelia, James Taylor (dec.), Robert Nelson. Asst. astronomer, Dudley Obs., Albany, N.Y., 1877-79; prof. engring., 1879-94, dean engring. dept., 1886-94, Vanderbilt U., Nashville, Tenn.; prof. engring., Union Coll., 1894-1917, emeritus prof. engring., 1917—; consulting engr., also chief engr. of Eastern Potash Corp., New York, 1919-21. Consulting engr. N.Y. State Bd. of Health, 1896-1906; mem. N.Y. State Water Storage Commn., 1902, N.Y. State Bay Commn., 1903; mem. Met. Sewerage Commn. of New York. Mech. engr., Ordnance Dept., Washington, 1918-19; consulting practice. Author: Metric Tables; contributor to scientific and tech. jours.; prepared civil engring. terms for new edit. Century Dictionary. Mem. N.Y. Constl. Conv., 1915. Home: Mount Vernon, N.Y. Died Nov. 6, 1931.

LANDRETH, WILLIAM BARKER, engineer; b. Rushville, Yates Co., N.Y., Aug. 3, 1857; s. James and Sarah (Barker) L.; A.B., C.E., Union Coll., 1881; m. Amelia T. FitzGerald, of Schenectady, N.Y., May 7, 1881. Asst. engr. Sinaloa & Durango R.R., Mex., 1881-84; city engr., Schenectady, N.Y., 1884-87; engr. Bd. Pub. Works, Amsterdam, N.Y., 1887-89; in charge city work at White Plains, Port Jervis and Jamestown, N.Y., Athens, Pa., and Waverly, N.Y., 1889-97; asst. engr. N.Y. State canals, 1897-1900; spl. resident engr. N.Y. State canals, 1900-09; spl. deputy state engr. of N.Y., 1909-10; consulting engr., 1910—. Mem. Am. Soc. C.E., Rensselaer Soc. Engrs., Mass. Highway Assn., Engrs. Soc. of Eastern New York. Republican. Episcopalian. Contbr. tech. papers in Trans. Am. Soc. C.E. Address: 20 Gillespie St., Schenectady, New York.

LANDRUM, ROBERT D(ALLAS), chemical engr.; b. Terre Haute, Ind., Feb. 8, 1882; s. James Wesley and Kate (Tolbert) L.; B.S., Rose Poly. Inst., Terre Haute, 1904, M.S., 1909, Ch.E., 1914; m. Ethel Price Sherwood, Sept. 1, 1908 (died 1935); children—Sherwood, Robert James, Kate Tolbert; m. 2d, Margaret Elizabeth Carr, 1937; 1 dau., Peggy Ann. Chemist and enameler, Columbian Enameling & Stamping Co., 1904-07; asst. prof. chemistry, U. of Kansas, 1907-10; chem. engr. Lisk Mfg. Co., Canandaigua, N.Y., 1910-13; cons. engr. Mich. Enameling Works, Kalamazoo, Mich., Gen. Stamping Co., Canton, O., 1913-14; chem. engr. and mgr. service dept. Harshaw Fuller & Goodwin Co., mfrs. industrial chemicals, Cleveland, O., 1914-22; v.p. Vitreous Enameling Co., also Vitreous Steel Products Co., Cleveland, 1922-25; gen. mgr. Ceramic Materials Div. Titanium Alloy Mfg. Co., Cleveland, 1925-32; sales mgr. Harshaw Chemical Company, Chicago, 1932-35, manager special products division, 1935-42, manager technical sales 1942 to date. Fel. A.A.A.S., Am. Ceramic Soc. (chmn. war service com., 1917-19, trustee, 1918-20, v.p., 1923-24, pres., 1924-25, trustee ex officio 1925-27); mem. Am. Chem. Soc. (sec. Cleveland sect. 1919-20), Am. Inst. Chem. Engrs., Soc. Chem. Industry, Keramos, Pi Gamma Mu, Acacia, Société de Chimie Industrielle, France. Mem. Chicago Drug and Chem. Assn. (dir. 1935-36), Chicago Assn. Commerce, Central Dist. Enamelers Club (pres. 1937-39). Republican. Methodist. Mason. Clubs: Cleveland, University, Chagrin Valley Country, Chemists' (New York). Author: Enamel, 1918; Bibliography and Abstracts of Literature on Enamels, 1929; also numerous articles and tech. papers. Mem. Nat. Tech. Salvage Advisory Com., War Prodn. Bd. Home: 3558 Bainbridge Rd. Office: Harshaw Chemical Co., 1945 E. 97th St., Cleveland 6, O. Now deceased.

LANDSTEINER, KARL, (land'stin-er), medical research; b. Vienna, Austria, June 14, 1868; s. Leopold and Fanny (Hess) L.; M.D., U. of Vienna, 1891; D.Sc., U. of Chicago, 1927; hon. D.Sc., Cambridge U., England; hon. M.D., Université Libre de Bruxelles, Belgium; D.Sc., Harvard; m. Helene Wlasto, 1880; 1 son, Earnest. Pathologist, U. of Vienna, 1909-19; mem. Rockefeller Inst. for Med. Research, 1922-39, now emeritus. Winner Nobel prize, for discovery of human blood groups, 1930; Paul Ehrlich medal, 1930; Chevalier Legion of Honor (France); Dutch Red Cross medal, 1933. Member Nat. Acad. Sciences, Royal Swedish Academy Science, Danish Academy Science, Deutsche Akademie Naturforscher (Halle, Germany), Am. Assn. Immunologists (pres. 1929), Swedish Med. Soc., Harvard Soc., Am. Philos. Soc., Société Belge de Biologie (Bruxelles), Am. Soc. of Naturalists; hon. mem. Pathol. Soc. of Gt. Britain and Ireland, Vienna Med. Soc.; fellow New York Acad. Medicine; hon. fellow Royal Soc. of Medicine (London); hon. mem. Pathol. Soc. of Philadelphia, Reale Academia delle Scienze (Modena, Italy); corr. mem. Med. Chirurgical Soc., Edinburgh. Contbr. papers on immunology, bacteriology and pathology, especially: Chemistry of Antigens; Human Blood Groups; Etiology of Poliomyelitis; Etiology of Paroxysmol Hemoglobinuria; Studies on Syphilis; etc. Home: 25 E. 86th St. Office: 66th St. and York Av., New York, N.Y. Died June 26, 1943.

LANE, ALFRED CHURCH, geologist; b. Boston, Mass., Jan. 29, 1863; s. Jonathan A. and Sarah D. (Clarke) L.; A.B., Harvard U., 1883, A.M., Ph.D., 1888; student U. of Heidelberg, 1885-87; Sc.D., Tufts Coll., 1913; m. Susanne Foster Lauriat, Apr. 15, 1896; children—Lauriat, Frederic Chapin, Harriet Page (Mrs. C. D. Rouillard). Instr. mathematics, Harvard, 1883-85; petrographer, Mich. State Geol. Survey and instr., Mich. Coll. of Mines, 1889-92; asst. state geologist of Mich., 1892-99, state geologist, 1899-1909; Pearson prof. geology and mineralogy, Tufts Coll., 1909-36, retired on account of teachers oath, elected prof. emeritus, 1936. Spl. lecturer on econ. geology, U. of Mich., 1904; first consultant in science, Library of Congress, 1929. Mem. com., apptd. by bd. overseers, to visit Harvard Observatory since 1924. Fellow A.A.A.S. (v.p. sect. E 1907), Geol. Soc. America (pres. 1931); mem. Nat. Research Council (com. on measurement of geologic time), Am. and Boston mineral socs., Am. Inst. Mining and Metall. Engrs. (pres. Boston Sect. 1918-19), Harvard Engring. Soc., Thomas Dudley Family Association (president tercentennial year), N.E. Historical and Genealogical Society; fellow Am. Academy Arts and Sciences (librarian 1929-36, vice president 1944-46), member Boston Natural History Soc., Am. Forestry Assn., Bond Astronomical Club (pres. 1933-35), Navy League, U.S. Naval Institute, Lake Superior Mining Inst. (treas. 1893); pres. Mich. Acad. Science, 1905-06, Mich. Engring. Soc., 1908-09, Lansing Law and Order League, 1904, Geol. Soc. Boston, 1919 and 1937; corr. mem. Canadian Mining Inst.; hon. mem. Geol. Soc. of Belgium; hon. life member of Harvard Engineering Society; del. Internat. Geol. Congress, 1913, 1933, 1937. With Y.M.C.A. and head dept. of mining, A.E.F. Univ., Beaune, France, 1919. Awarded Silver Beaver, Boy Scouts of America. Hon. and corporate mem. A.B.C.F.M. Mem. Mass. Civic League, Civil Liberties Union, com. of Moral and Social Welfare Suffolk North Conference, Boston Chapter United National Assn., Phi Beta Kappa, Sigma Xi. Conglist. Republican. Club: 20th Century Associates. Editor and part author books, also reports of Geol. Survey of Mich., Canada and U.S. Author: Die Korngrosse der Auvergnosen. Home: 22 Arlington St., Cambridge, Mass. Died Apr. 16, 1948.

LANE, CLARENCE GUY, physician; b. Billerica, Mass., Oct. 21, 1882; s. Albert Clarence and Estella Josephine (Davis) L.; A.B., Harvard, 1905, M.D., 1908; m. Mary Rivers McHarry, May 31, 1919; 1 son, Robert. Intern Worcester City Hosp., 1908-10; in gen. practice, Woburn, Mass., 1910-14; specializing in dermatology, Boston, 1914—; mem. dept. dermatology Mass. Gen. Hosp., 1920-47, chief of dept., 1936-47, teaching in dept. dermatology Harvard Med. Sch., 1922-47, head of dept., 1936-47; clin. prof. dermatology, 1939-47, emeritus, 1947—. On editorial bd. N.E. Jour. of Medicine, Archives of Dermatology and Syphilology cons. in dermatology at a number of hosps. Served from lt. to capt. M.C., U.S. Army, 1918-19. Awarded Cutter medal, Phi Rho Sigma, 1948. Mem. A.M.A. (mem. council on planning and chemistry), Am. Bd. Dermatology and Syphilology (dir. and sec., 1932-43; pres. 1944-45; sec. Adv. Bd. for Med. Specialties 1941-43), Nat. Com. on Indsl. Dermatoses, Am. Dermatol. Assn. (dir. 1927-35, pres. 1935, sec. 1925-30), N.E. Dermatol. Soc., N.Y. Acad. of Medicine. Republican. Protestant. Mason (K.T., Shriner). Clubs: Harvard (Boston); Faculty Editor: Vol. X of Practitioners Medical Library, 1935; contbr. about 70 articles to med. jours. Lecturer on dermatology A.M.A., 1949. Home: 220 Marlborough St., Boston. Died Mar. 12, 1954; buried Mt. Auburn Cemetery, Cambridge, Mass.

LANE, HENRY MARCUS, mech. engr.; b. Cincinnati, Aug. 15, 1854; s. Philander Parmelee and Sophia Rebecca (Bosworth) L.; Mass. Inst. Tech., 1873; m. Blanche A. Conkling, Feb. 4, 1903; 1 dau., Geneva. With Lane & Bodley, engine bldrs., Cincinnati, 1878-79; constructing engr. Elm St. Inclined Plane Ry., 1875, Mt. Adams Inclined Plane Ry., 1879-80; built Gilbert Av. Cable Ry. (1st in Ohio), 1885-86, Vine St. (Cincinnati) Cable Ry., 1887, Denver Tramway, 1888 (1st cable ry. in Colo.), Providence Cable Tramway, 1889 (1st and only cable ry. built in N.E.); consulting engr. St. Louis Cable Ry. Co., Western Ry. Co., St. Paul, Boston Tramway Co., 1885-89; pres. Lane & Bodley Co., 1890—. Independent Republican. Presbyn. Home: Cincinnati, O. Died May 15, 1929.

LANE, JAMES H., prof. civil engring. and drawing, Ala. Poly. Inst.; b. Mathews Court House, Va., July 28, 1833; s. Walter G. and Mary A. H. L.; grad. Va. Mil. Inst. and U. of Va.; Ph.D., W.Va. U.; LL.D., Trinity Coll., N.C.; m. Charlotte Randolph Meade, Sept. 13, 1869 (dec.). Before the Civil War was apptd. prof. mathematics and instr. in tactics in Va. Mil. Inst.; prof. of mathematics and commandant in the State Sem. of Fla., at Tallahassee; prof. natural philosophy and instr. in tactics, N.C. Mil. Inst. at Charlotte; served in Civil War as maj. and lt. col. 1st N.C. vols. and col. 28th N.C. troops; apptd. brig. gen. C.S.A. for gallantry; was in all large battles fought by army of Northern Va. and many of the minor ones. Became prof. natural philosophy and commandant in Va. Agrl. and Mech. Coll. after war; prof. mathematics Mo. School of Mines and Metallurgy; supt. Va. Mining and Mfg. Co.; prof. civil engring. and commandant in Ala. Agrl. and Mech. Coll.; later prof. engring. and drawing, Ala. Poly. Inst. Address: Auburn, Ala. Died 1907.

LANE, JOHN EDWARD, physician; b. Whately, Mass., Feb. 12, 1872; s. Rev. John William and Mary (Haynes) L.; B.A., Yale, 1894, M.A., 1897, M.D., 1903; studied univs. Göttingen, Berlin, Geneva and Paris abt. 2 yrs.; m. Alice Treat Rogers, May 19, 1909. Began practice, New Haven, 1903; specializes in dermatology and syphilology; clin. prof. dermatology, Yale U. Sch. of Medicine, 1920-22 (resigned). Fellow New York Acad. Medicine (chmn. sect. dermatology and syphilis, 1919 and 1920); mem. A.M.A. chmn. sect. dermatology and syphilis, 1924-25), Am. Dermatol. Assn. (v.p. 1922-23), New York Dermatol. Soc. (pres. 1927-28), Conn. State Med. Soc. (sec. 1917-20), New Haven Med. Assn. (pres. 1922), Beaumont Med. Club (pres. 1922-23). Home: New Haven, Conn. Died Oct. 17, 1933.

LANE, WILLIAM CARR, physician, mayor St. Louis; b. Fayette County, Pa., Dec. 1, 1789; s. Presley Carr and Sarah (Stephenson) L.; attended Jefferson Coll., Chambersburg, Pa.; grad. Dickinson Coll., Carlisle, Pa.; postgrad. Med. Dept., U. Pa.; m. Mary Ewing, Feb. 26, 1818; 2 children. Served as surgeon's mate at Ft. Harrison during Creek War, 1813; post surgeon, 1816; resigned from army, 1819; became q.m. gen. of Mo., 1822; 1st mayor St. Louis, 1823-29, 38-40; mem. Mo. Legislature (Democrat), 1826; served as surgeon with rank brig. gen. in Black Hawk War, 1832; a founder Mo. Med. Coll., 1840, also prof. obstetrics; apptd. gov. N.M. Territory by Pres. Fillmore, 1852; returned to practice medicine, St. Louis, 1853. Author: Water for the City (advocated municipal waterworks for St. Louis), 1860. Died St. Louis, Jan. 6, 1863; buried Bellefontaine Cemetery, St. Louis.

LANEY, FRANCIS BAKER, geologist; b. nr. Springfield, Mo., Apr. 9, 1875; s. John Baker and Jane (Alexander) L.; B.S., Drury Coll., Springfield, 1902; M.A., U. of Wis., 1905; Ph.D. in Geology, Yale, 1908; m. Minnie D. Towner, Sept. 1910; 1 son, Francis T. Began as asst. geologist, N.C., 1903; asst. curator applied geology, Nat. Museum, Washington, D.C., 1908-10; geologist U.S. Geol. Survey, 1914—; microscopist and mineralogist U.S. Bur. Mines, 1914-19; metallographist Central Checking Lab. of Ordnance Dept. U.S. Army, Pittsburgh, Pa., 1917-18; head dept. of geology, U. of Ida., 1920—. Unitarian. Home: Moscow, Ida. Died Apr. 23, 1938.

LANFORD, JOHN ALEXANDER, pathologist; b. Gainesville, Ala., June 19, 1881; s. John Bibb and Maria Adeline (Rogers) L.; Ph.G., Ala. Poly. Inst., 1900; M.D., U. of Ala., 1905; unmarried. Pharmacist (while studying medicine), Mobile, Ala., 1900-05; instr. in surg. pathology, Tulane, 1911-14, asst. prof. pathology and bacteriology, 1914; pathologist Touro Infirmary, New Orleans, La., 1912—; cons. pathologist U.S. Marine Hosp., 1928—; pathologist New Orleans Dispensary, 1926—. Mem. bd. dirs. Am. Soc. for Control of Cancer, 1939—. Served as captain Medical Reserve, U.S.A., 1917; laboratory officer, Justice and Perigueux Hosp. Centers, France, 1918-19; major Medical Reserve Corps, 1919-24, lt. col., 1924-32, col., 1932—; comdg. officer 312th Med. Regt. Res., 1932—. Mem. Southern Med. Assn. (chmn. pathol. sect. 1927), La. State Med. Soc. (chmn. cancer com., 1932—), Orleans Parish Med. Soc. (pres. 1932). Democrat. Methodist. Mason. Home: New Orleans, La. Died July 2, 1940.

LANGENBECK, KARL, ceramic engr.; b. Cincinnati, O., Oct. 7, 1861; s. Adolf and Emma (Roelker) L.; studied under Victor Meyer, Zürich, and Carl Liebermann, Berlin; m. Mildred Roelker, of Washington, Feb. 4, 1899; 1 dau., Elizabeth Leib. Supt. of Rookwood Pottery, Cincinnati, 1885-90, and originator of "Rookwood" faience and aventurine pottery glazes; consulting chemist and mgr. several potteries, tile and mosaic works. Prof. chemistry, Miami Med. Coll., 1888-90; research chemist for non-metallic mineral industries; chief ceramist, U.S. Tariff Commn., for cement, pottery and glass manufactures, 1922-24; consulting ceramic engr., U.S. Bur. Standards since 1924. Conducts pvt. research lab. for determining physical constitution of domestic clays and ceramic materials in relation to kiln reactions; tech. dir. Mosaic Tile Co., Zanesville, O. Fellow A.A.A.S. Author: Chemistry of Pottery, 1895. Club: Arts (Washington, D.C.). Address: 2218 Wyoming Av. N.W., Washington, D.C.

LANGFITT, WILLIAM CAMPBELL, army officer; b. Wellsburg, Va., Aug. 10, 1860; s. Obadiah and Virginia (Tarr) L.; grad. U.S. Mil. Acad., 1883, Engr. Sch. of Application, Willetts Point, N.Y., 1886; m. Anne St. John Bemis, Dec. 4, 1886; 1 dau., Dorothy. Commd. 2d lt. engrs., June 13, 1883; brig. gen. N.A., Aug. 5, 1917; maj. gen. N.A., Dec. 17, 1917; major gen. U.S.A., retired, June 21, 1930. Engr. office Dept. of Columbia, 1886-88; river and harbor improvements, Galveston, Tex., 1888-93; improvement of Ohio River and tributaries, 1893-95; instr. Engr. Sch., 1895-98; comd. U.S. forces in H.I., 1898-99; in charge river and harbor improvements, defenses, and engr. 13th Light House Dist., Portland, Ore., 1899-1905; comdr. Engr. Sch. and Depot, Washington Barracks, D.C., 1905-06 and 1907-10; chief engr. Army of Cuban Pacification, 1906-07; river and harbor improvements and water supply, Washington, D.C., 1910-14; river and harbor improvements and div. engr., S.E. Div., Savannah, Ga., 1914-16; chief engr. officer, Southern Dept., including ry. operations, 1916-17; organized 13th Engrs., May-Aug. 1917; joined A.E.F. in France, Aug. 1917; chief of staff, Aug. 24, 1917; apptd. mgr. light rys., Sept. 14, 1917; in charge of all Am. forces on duty with British Army, Oct. 15, 1917; chief of utilities, in charge of transportation, Dept. of Constrn. and Forestry, Dept. of Light Rys. and Roads, and Motor Transportation Dept., Mar. 12, 1918; chief engr. A.E.F., in charge of mil. engring. and engr. supplies, constrn. and forestry, light rys. and roads, July 10, 1918; dist. engr., 2d N.Y. Dist. and Puerto Rico Dist., Aug. 5, 1919; div. engr., N.E. Div., N.Y. City, Aug. 14, 1919-20. D.S.M. (U.S.); Comdr. Legion of Honor (French); Companion Most Honorable Order of the Bath (English); Comdr. Order of Crown (Belgian). Home: Geneva, N.Y. Died Apr. 20, 1934.

LANGLEY, SAMUEL PIERPONT, astronomer and physicist, Sec. the Smithsonian Instn., 1887—; b. Roxbury, Boston, Aug. 22, 1834; grad. Boston High School; D.C.L., Oxford; D.Sc., Cambridge, Eng.; LL.D., Harvard, Princeton, Yale, U. of Wis.; U. of Mich.; Ph.D., Stevens Inst. Tech. Practiced architecture and civ. engring.; asst. Harvard Observatory, 1865; later asst. prof. mathematics U.S. Naval Acad.; dir. Allegheny Observatory, 1867, where, 1869, he founded the system of railway time service from observatories, which has since become general, and where he devised the bolometer, now in general use, and other apparatus. Organized expdn. to Mt. Whitney, 1881, where he reëstablished the solar constant and discovered an entirely unsuspected extension of the invisible solar spectrum. Has carried out extended expts. on the problem of mech. flight. Established Astrophysical Observatory and the Nat. Zoöl. Park, Washington. Mem. Nat. Acad. of Sciences. Has been awarded Janssen medal, Inst. of France; Rumford medal of the Royal Soc. of London, and of Am. Acad. Arts and Sciences; Henry Draper medal, Nat. Acad. Sciences, etc., and numerous others. Author: The New Astronomy; Researches on Solar Heat; Experiments in Aërodynamics; Internal Work of the Wind; On the Possible Variation of the Solar Radiation, 1905. Trustee Carnegie Instn. Address: Washington, D.C. Died 1906.

LANGMUIR, IRVING, chemist; b. Brooklyn, N.Y., Jan. 31, 1881; s. Charles and Sadie (Comings) L.; Met. E., Columbia Sch. of Mines, 1903; Ph.D., U. of Göttingen, 1906; D.Sc., Northwestern, 1921, Union U., 1923, Columbia, 1925, Kenyon Coll., 1927, Princeton, 1929, Lehigh U., 1934, Harvard, 1938, Oxford, 1938, Rutgers, 1941, Queen's Coll. (Canada), 1941; D.Ing., Tech. Hochschule, Berlin, 1929; LL.D., Edinburgh, 1921, Johns Hopkins, 1936, U. of Calif., 1946; m. Marion Mersereau, Apr. 27, 1912; children—Kenneth, Barbara. Instr. chemistry, Stevens Inst., Hoboken, N.J., 1906-09; physical chem. research, Research Lab. of Gen. Electric Co., Schenectady, N.Y., since 1909, now consultant of Research Lab.; engaged in development of gas filled tungsten lamps, electron discharge apparatus, condensation high vacuum pump, atomic hydrogen welding, work on monomolecular films and surface chemistry, cloud physics, including weather modification, etc.; also in 1917-18, on devices for submarine detection at Naval Exptl. Sta., Nahant, Mass. Lecturer, London, 1938, Hitchcock Foundation lecturer, U. of Calif., 1946; mem. bd. trustees, State U. of N.Y., Sept. 1948-50. Fellow A.A.A.S. (president 1941), Am. Physical Soc., Indian Acad. Sci. (hon.); mem. Am. Philosophical Soc., Am. Chemists Society (pres. 1929), Nat. Acad. Sciences, Am. Acad. Arts and Sciences, Royal Soc. Upsala, corresponding mem. Académie des Sciences, Paris, 1951, Tau Beta Pi, Phi Lambda Upsilon, Sigma Xi; also hon. mem. Royal Instn., Chem. Soc. of London, Royal Soc. (London), Royal Physiog. Soc. (Lund), Academia Brasileria de Sciencias (Brazil), Société de Chimie Industrielle. Was awarded Nichols medal by N.Y. sect. of American Chem. Soc. for researches on chem. reactions at low pressures, 1915; Hughes medal, Royal Soc. London, for researches in molecular physics, 1918; Nichols medal for researches on atomic structure, 1920; Rumford medal, Am. Acad. Arts and Sciences, for researches on thermionic phenomena, 1920; Cannizzaro prize, Royal Acad. of Lincei (Rome), 1925; Perkin medal, 1928; Sch. of Mines medal, Columbia U. in recognition of achievements in science and invention, 1929. Chandler medal, 1930; Willard Gibbs medal, 1930; Popular Science Monthly prize, 1932; Nobel prize in Chemistry, 1932, for work in surface-chemistry; Franklin medal by the Franklin Institute, 1934; Holly medal, by American Society of Mech. Engrs., 1934; award under John Scott Medal Fund, 1937, by Board of City Trusts, Phila., Egleston medal Columbia Engring. Schs. Alumni Assn., 1939; Nat. Pioneer award Nat. Assn. Mfrs., 1940; Faraday Medal award Elec. Engrs. of Gt. Britain, 1943; Medal for Merit, U.S. Army and Navy, 1948; John Carty Medal Nat. Acad. Scis., 1950. Clubs: Chemists (N.Y.); Mohawk. Contbr. to jours. Home: 1176 Stratford Rd., Schenectady. Died Aug. 17, 1957.

LANGSDORF, ALEXANDER SUSS, engineer; b. St. Louis, Mo., Aug. 31, 1877; s. Adolph and Sarah (Suss) L.; B.S. in Mech. Engring., Washington U., 1898; M.M.E., Cornell U., 1901; m. Elsie H. Hirsch, June 26, 1906; children—Helen (Mrs. L. Shiman), Alexander, Jr. Instr. in physics, Washington U., 1898-99, 1899-1900, asst. prof. electric engring. in charge of dept., 1901-04, prof., 1904-20, dean Schs. of Engring. and Architecture, 1910-20; engr. sec. Crunden Martin Mfg. Co., 1920-22; alumni rep., Washington U., 1922-23; v.p. and chief engr., Alvey Mfg. Co., 1923-26; dir. Dept. Industrial Engring. and Research, Washington U., 1926-1944, acting dean Schs. of Engring. and Architecture, Jan. 1928-June 1929, dean, 1929-48, dean emeritus since 1948; prof. of applied mathematics, 1932-38, prof. of elec. engring., 1938-48, prof. emeritus since 1948; lecturer in elec. engineering, Mass. Institute Tech., summer 1927. Mem. Jury of Awards (elec. sect.) St. Louis Exposition, 1904; mem. City Plan Commn., 1915-35 (v. chmn. 1917-35); mem. Mo. State Planning Bd., 1933-35; regional adviser, Region 16, Engineering Science, Management War Training Program, 1940-45. Served as public panel member, Regional War Labor Board (VII). Chmn. bd. dirs. Met. Planning Assn. of St. Louis. Fellow A.A.A.S., American Institute Electrical Engineers (secretary St. Louis section, 1905-08; chmn. St. Louis section 1908-10). Mem. Am. Soc. Mech. Engrs., Am. Inst. Architects (hon.), Am. Soc. Engring Edn., Engineers Club of St. Louis (sec. 1908-10, 1st v.p. 1911, pres. 1912), Acad. Science St. Louis (sec. 1929-32, v.p. 1932-37), Am. Arbitration Assn., Ethical Soc. St. Louis (pres. bd. trustees 1930-37), Am. Ethical Union, Fraternity of Leaders, Mo. Academy Science (1st president 1934-35), Sigma Xi, Tau Beta Pi, Theta Ix (pres. Grand Lodge 1922-28). Club: Town and Gown. Author: Principles of Direct Current Machines, 1915, 5th edit., 1940; Theory of Alternating Current Machinery, 1937; (with G.E.M. Jauncey) M.K.S. Units and Dimensions. Contbr. to tech. jours. Home: 5187 Cabanne Av., St Louis MO

LANGSTROTH, LORENZO LORRAINE, educator, apiarist; b. Phila., Dec. 25, 1810; s. John G. and Rebekah (Dunn) L.; grad. Yale, 1831; m. Anne Tucker, Aug. 22, 1836, 3 children. Prin., Abbot Acad., Andover, Mass., 1838-39; prin. High Sch. for Young Ladies, Greenfield, Mass., 1838-44; prin. school for young ladies at Phila., 1848-52; invented movable-frame beehive. Author: Langstroth on the Hive and the Honeybee, 1853. Died Oxford, O., Oct. 6, 1895.

LANGWORTHY, CHARLES FORD, chemist; b. Middlebury, Vt., Aug. 9, 1864; s. Charles Parker and Ann Elizabeth (Ford) L.; A.B., Middlebury Coll., 1887, A.M., 1890, D.Sc., 1912; Ph.D., Emperor Wilhelm U., Strassburg, 1893; unmarried. Asst. and instr. chemistry, Wesleyan U., Conn., 1893-95; asso. editor Experiment Station Record, 1895-1924; chief of nutrition investigations, Dept. of Agr., 1905-15; chief of Office of Home Economics, 1915-23, specialist Bur. of Home Economics, 1923, 29, U.S. Dept. of Agr. Author: Digest of Metabolism Experiments (with late W. O. Atwater); Occurrence of Aluminium (with late Peter T. Austen). Writer of and contbr. to bulls. Dept. Agr.; contbr. to New Internat. Ency., 1902-03; Ency. Americana, etc. Home: Washington, D.C. Died 1932.

LANIER, ALEXANDER CARTWRIGHT, (la-ner), engr.; b. Nashville, Tenn., June 3, 1878; s. Louis Henry and Lamiza (Cartwright) L.; B.S. in E.E., U. of Tenn., 1900, M.E., 1905; M.E.E., Harvard U., 1909; unmarried. Electrical practice, 1900-02; instr. mech. engring., U. of Tenn., 1902-05; asst. prof. elec. engring., U. of Cincinnati, 1905-08; designing elec. engr., Westinghouse Electric & Mfg. Co., East Pittsburgh, Pa., 1909-11, sect. engr. in charge design of direct current industrial motors and generators, 1911-15; prof. elec. engring. and chmn. dept., U. of Mo., since 1915, acting dean Coll. of Engring., July 1, 1939-Oct. 1, 1939. Fellow Am. Inst. Elec. Engrs.; mem. Soc. Promotion Engring. Edn. Engineers' Club (St. Louis), Kappa Sigma, Phi Kappa Phi, Tau Beta Pi, Eta Kappa Nu, Sigma Xi. Democrat. Presbyn. Home: 310 Thilly Av., Columbia, Mo. Died Feb. 26, 1942.

LANNEAU, JOHN FRANCIS, college prof.; b. Charleston, S.C., Feb. 7, 1836; s. Charles Henry and Sophia (Stephens) L.; grad. S.C. Mil. Acad., Charleston, 1856; A.M., Baylor U., Waco, Texas, 1869; (LL.D., Furman University, S.C., 1915); m. Louise Skinner Cox, of Greenville, S.C., 1869. Tutor mathematics, 1857, prof. physics and chemistry, 1858-61, Furman U., Greenville, S.C.; capt. cav., then lt. and capt. engrs., 1861-64; teacher pvt. sch., 1865; prof. mathematics and astronomy, Furman U., 1866-68; prof. mathematics, William Jewell Coll., Mo., 1869-73; pres. Alabama Central Female Coll., Tuscaloosa, 1873-79, Bapt. Female Coll., Lexington, Mo., 1879-88, Pierce City Bapt. Coll., Mo., 1888-90; prof. physics and applied mathematics, 1890-99; applied mathematics and astronomy since 1899, Wake Forest Coll., N.C. Mem. N.C. Acad. Science, N.C. Nature Study Soc., Astron. Soc. Pacific. Invented, 1907, the cosmoid (a model of the celestial sphere, easily adjusted to illustrate astron. conceptions and motions). Address: Wake Forest, N.C.

LANSING, JOHN ERNEST, chemist; b. Brookline, Mass., June 3, 1878; s. John Arnold and Florence (Stetson) L.; A.B., Harvard, 1898, A.M., 1900; traveled in Europe, 1898-99; m. Lucy Caroline Wells, June 27, 1907 (died Oct. 14, 1916); m. 2d, Josephine Camp Belcher, July 3, 1918; children—John Belcher, Edward Stickney, Marion Frances. Instr. natural sciences, Phillips Acad., Andover, Mass., 1901-05; asst. prof. chemistry, 1905-06, prof., 1906—, Hobart Coll., also registrar, 1914-21, acting pres., 1941-42. Mem. Am. Chem. Soc. Republican. Presbyn. Author: Laboratory Experiments in Chemistry, 1908, revised, 1944; A Short Course in Qualitative Analysis, revised, 1948; retitled Lansing's Qualitative Analysis, revised, 1958. Home: Geneva, N.Y. Died Sept. 28, 1958.

LANTZ, DAVID ERNEST, biologist; b. Thompsontown, Pa., Mar. 1, 1855; s. John King and Margaret (Fry) L.; ed. State Normal Sch., Bloomsburg, Pa.; m. Clara Deen, Mar. 5, 1878. Prin. schs., Mifflintown, Pa., 1876-78; supt. schools, Manhattan, Kan., 1878-83; prof. mathematics, Kan. State Agrl. Coll., 1883-97; prin. Dickinson Co. (Kan.) High Sch., 1898-1900; field agt. Kan. Agrl. Expt. Sta., 1901-04; asst. biologist, U.S. Dept. of Agriculture, 1904—. Methodist. Life mem. Kan. Acad. of Science (sec., 1899-1901, pres., 1898-99). Mason. Home: Washington, D.C. Died Oct. 7, 1918.

LANZA, ANTHONY JOSEPH, physician; b. N.Y.C., Mar. 8, 1884; s. Manfredi and Clara (Hammond) L.; M.D., George Washington U., 1906; m. Laura Kate Thomas, Nov. 18, 1913; children—Mary Bianca (Mrs. W. Gregory Maue, Jr.), Elizabeth (Mrs. Gordon H. Felton). With USPHS, 1907-20; spl. staff mem. Rockefeller Found., adviser to Commonwealth Govt. of Australia on indsl. hygiene, 1921-24; exec. sec. Nat. Health Council, N.Y.C., 1924-26; asso. med. dir. Met. Life Ins. Co., 1926-49; chmn. Inst. Indsl. Med., Bellevue Med. Center; prof. indsl. medicine, 1947-54, prof. emeritus, 1954-64. Chief surgeon U.S. Bur. Mines, 1914-19; med. cons. Gen. Motors Corp., 1931-32. Served as sr. surgeon in charge indsl. hygiene USPHS, during World War I; col. M.C., AUS, 1942-45; dir. div. occupational health, preventive medicine service Office of Surgeon Gen. Decorated Legion of Merit. Recipient Adolph Kammer Merit-in-Authorship award Indsl. Med. Assn. Trustee and chmn. med. com. Indsl. Hygiene Found. Trustee Trudeua Found., N.Y. U. Mem. A.M.A. (mem. council on indsl. health), N.Y. Acad. Medicine (chmn. com. on indsl. health), Am. Pub. Health Assn., Nat. Tb Assn., Am. Social Hygiene Assn., N.Y. Tb and Health Assn., Kappa Sigma, Alpha Kappa Kappa, Sigma Xi. Clubs: Cosmos (Washington); Sleepy Hollow Country (N.Y.). Editor: Siliconsis and Asbestosis, 1938; Industrial Hygiene (with Jacob Goldberg), 1939; The Pneumoconioses, 1963; editor-in-chief Modern Monographs in Industrial Medicine; adv. editorial bd. History of Preventive Medicine in World War II. Contbr. articles on indsl. medicine and hygiene to med. publs. Establishment by N.Y. U. of Anthony J. Lanza Research Labs., 1964. Home: 441 E. 20th St., N.Y.C. 16. Office: 550 1st Av., N.Y.C. 16. Died Mar. 23, 1964; buried Arlington Nat. Cemetery.

LANZA, GAETANO, engineer, b. Boston, Mass., Sept. 26, 1848; s. Gaetano and Mary Ann (Paddock) L.; C.E., 1869, B.Sc., 1870, C.E., M.E., 1870, U. of Va.; m. Jennie D. Miller, Jan. 27, 1891 (died 1923). Asst. instr. mathematics, U. of Va., 1870-72; instr. and asst. prof., 1872-75, prof. theoretical and applied mechanics, 1875-1911, in charge dept. mech. engring., 1883-1911, prof. emeritus, 1911, Mass. Inst. Tech.; special consultant Baldwin Locomotive Works. Fellow Am. Acad. Arts and Sciences. Created Cavaliere dell Ordine dei Santi Maurizio e Lazzaro of Italy, 1907. Author: Applied Mechanics, 1885-1905; Dynamics of Machinery, 1911. Home: Philadelphia, Pa. Died 1928.

LAPHAM, INCREASE ALLEN, scientist, state ofcl.; b. Palmyra, N.Y., Mar. 7, 1811; s. Seneca and Rachel (Allen) L.; m. Ann Alcott, 1838, 5 children. Asst. engr. on Ohio Canal, 1829-33; sec. Ohio Bd. Canal Commrs., 1833; published Wisconsin: Its Geography and Topography, History, Geology and Mineralogy (1st good maps of Wis. and Milw. vicinity), 1844; published The Antiquities of Wisconsin, 1855; sch. commr. Milw., aided in establishing Milw.-Downer Coll. (normal sch. for girls), pres. bd. trustees, many years; charter mem. Wis. Acad. of Scis., Arts and Letters; influential in obtaining passage of law which established U.S. Weather Bur., 1869; state geologist Wis., 1873-75; v.p., pres. Wis. Hist. Soc. Died Oconomowoc, Wis., Sept. 14, 1875.

LAPHAM, JOHN RAYMOND, prof. civil engring.; b. West Medway, Mass., Apr. 1, 1886; s. Frank D. and Alfarata (Scott) L.; B.S., Brown U., 1909; M.S., Pa. State Coll., 1916; m. Evelyn M. Ayres, Aug. 16, 1916; children—Evelyn, John R. In construction department N.Y.,N.H.&H. R.R., 1901-11; asst. to instr. in civil engring., Pa. State Coll., 1911-16; asst. prof. civil engring., George Washington U., 1916-19, prof., 1919—, dean Sch. of Engring., 1927—. Home: Washington, D.C. Died Oct. 2, 1939.

LAPORTE, OTTO, physicist, educator; b. Mainz, Germany, July 23, 1902; s. Wilhelm and Anna Laporte; Ph.D., U. Munich (Germany), 1924; m. Eleanor Anders (dec. 1957); m. 2d, Adele Pond, Oct. 6, 1959; children—Claire, Irene, Marianne. Naturalized United States citizen, 1935. International Edn. Board Fellow National Bureau Standards, 1924-26; mem. faculty U. Mich., 1926-28, 29-71, prof. physics, 1937-71; lectr. Kyoto (Japan) Imperial U., 1928-29, U. Munich, 1937; intelligence analyst U.S. Army, Europe, 1949-50; sci. attache Am. embassy, Tokyo, Japan, 1954-56, 61-63, spl. research fluid dynamics at very high temperatures. Mem. Am. Phys. Soc., Nat. Acad. Scis. (posthumously elected). Author numerous articles in field. Home: Ann Arbor MI Died Mar. 28, 1971.

LARDNER, HENRY ACKLEY, engr.; b. Oconomowoc, Wis., Oct. 1, 1871; s. Richard and Catharine (Breck) L.; B.S. in E.E., U. of Wis., 1893, E.E., 1895; m. Ethel Anne Elmore, Sept. 17, 1902; children—Dorothy Ann, Richard Penn. V.p. J. G. White Engring. Corp., N.Y. City. Mayor of Montclair, N.J., 1924-28. Past pres. N.J. State League of Municipalities, Montclair Community Chest, United Engineering. Trustees, 1939-41. Fellow Am. Inst. E.E., Am. Soc. M.E.; mem. Montclair Soc. Engrs. (pres. 1930-31), S.A.R., Sigma Chi. Episcopalian. Club: Lawyers (New York). Home: 9 Bradford Av., Upper Montclair, N.J. Office: 80 Broad St., N.Y.C. 4. Died Dec. 27, 1952.

LARIMORE, JOSEPH WILLIAM, physician; b. Greenfield, Ind., Apr. 5, 1887; s. James Madison and Florence Clementine (Taylor) L.; A.B. DePauw U., 1908; M.D., Washington U. Med. Sch., St. Louis, Mo., 1913; m. Ruth Evans, Mar. 1, 1928; children—Ann Evans (Mrs. John F. Kolars), and Joseph William, Jr. Served as intern at Washington U. Med. Sch. Hosp., 1913-14; asst. physician, Barnes Hosp., 1915; instr. clin. med., Washington U. Med. Sch., 1915-28; asst. roentgenologist for gastro-enterology, Washington U. Med. Sch. Edward Mallinckrodt Inst. of Radiology, 1925-52; asso. prof. clin. medicine, Washington U. Med. Sch., 1928-52; emeritus associate prof. clinical med.; asst. roentgenologist, St. Louis Children's Hosp., 1930-52; gastro-enterologist staff, Missouri Pacific Hospital, 1928; staff. St. Luke's Hospital, since 1930. Lieutenant, later captain, Med. Corps, U.S. Army, 1917-19; served U.S. Base Hosp. No. 21, British Gen. Hosp. No. 12, and Am. Red Cross Hosp. No. 9, Paris. Diplomate Am. Bd. Internal Med. (gastroenterology), 1937; fellow Am. Coll. Physicians; mem. A.A.A.S., A.M.A., Southern Med. Assn., Am. Gastroenterol. Assn., Am. Roentgen Ray Soc., Radiol. Soc. N. Am., Mo. Hist. Soc., Sigma Xi, Alpha Omega Alpha, Sigma Chi. Mason (Scottish Rite). Club: University (St. Louis, Mo.). Contbr. med. papers on clin. and roentgenological gastroenterology. Home: St Louis MO Died Mar. 22, 1971.

LARK-HOROVITZ, KARL, (lärk'hôr'ô-vitz), prof. physics; b. Vienna, Austria, July 20, 1892; s. Moritz and Adelle (Hofmann) Horovitz; Ph.D., U. of Vienna, 1919; m. Betty Friedlaender, July 26, 1916; children—Caroline Betty, Karl Gordon. Came to U.S., 1925, naturalized, 1936. Asst. teacher of physics, U. of Vienna, 1919-25; internat. research fellow, U. of Toronto, 1925-26, U. of Chicago, 1926, Rockefeller Inst., 1926-27, Stanford U., 1927-28; prof. physics, Purdue U., since 1928, dir. Phys. Lab. since 1929, head dept. of physics since 1931. Served in Austrian Army, 1914-18. Fellow Am. Phys. Soc., A.A.A.S. (chmn. co-op. com. 1947-51, gen. sec. 1948-51); mem. Am. Assn. Physics Teachers, Sigma Xi, Sigma Pi Sigma, V.A.A.U.P., S.P.E.E. Lutheran. Contbr. articles to scientific jours. Home: 509 Lingle Av., Lafayette, Ind. Died Apr. 14, 1958.

LARKIN, EDGAR LUCIEN, astronomer; b. La Salle County, Ill., Apr. 5, 1847; s. Herman I. and Jane L.; ed. La Salle Co., Ill.; m. Alice A. Everman, Apr. 29, 1869. Opened, and dir. New Windsor (Ill.) Obs., 1880-88, Knox Coll. Obs., 1888-95; dir. Lowe Obs., Echo Mountain, Calif., 1900—. Author: Radiant Energy, 1903; Within the Mind Maze, 1911; The Matchless Altar of the Soul, 1916; Popular Studies in Recent Astronomy. Address: Mount Lowe, Calif. Died Oct. 11, 1924.

LARKIN, FRED VIALL, educator, industrial management engr.; b. Verona, Wis., April 2, 1883; s. Edwin Newcomb and Eudora (Viall) L.; B.S., U. of Wisconsin, 1906, M.S., 1915; Dr. Engring., Stevens Institute, 1948; married Nell Grant Wright, June 30, 1910; children—Franklin Jonathan, Richard Newcomb. Engr. and supt. Telluride (Colo.) Power Co., 1906-09; asst. and supt. Bargn Canal Contract No. 60, Empire Engring. Corp., N.Y. City, 1909-11; engr. Terry & Tench Co., N.Y. City, 1911-12; instr. later asst. prof. mech. engring., Lehigh U., 1912-15, prof. mech. engring. and head dept., 1919-27, dir. indsl. and mech. engring., 1927-48; asst. gen. supt. Harrisburg (Pa.) Steel Corp., 1915-19; cons. engr., 1919—. In charge plant producing army-navy ordnance, 1915-18; lecturer indsl. management, U.S. Navl Acad., 1942, cons. engr. Army Ordnance Dept., 1944—. Mem. Am. Soc. M.E. (mem. publ. com. council, relations colls. com.), Am. Management Assn., Soc. Promotion of Engring. Edn. (mem. council, vice pres.), Newcomen Soc. of Eng. (vice chmn. com.), Pi Tau Sigma (nat. vice pres.), Tau Beta Pi, Sigma Xi, Lambda Chi Alpha. Republican. Methodist. Clubs: Rotary, Chemists (N.Y.), Saucon Valley Country. Contbr. to tech. publs. 2 patents granted 1933. Visited colleges and industries in Orient and Europe on trip around the world, 1932-33. Retired, 1948. Home: 135 Wall St. Office: Lehigh U., Bethlehem, Pa. Died May 23, 1954.

LARKIN, THOMAS B., army officer; b. Louisburg, Wis., Dec. 15, 1890; s. Thomas and Dorothy (Donders) L.; B.A., summa cum laude, Gonzaga U., Spokane, 1910., hon. D.Sc., 1936; B.S., U.S. Mil. Acad., 1915; grad. Engr. Sch., 1916, Army Industrial Coll., 1927, Command and Gen. Staff Sch., 1929, Army War Coll., 1938, Naval War Coll., 1939; m. Mary Regina Irwin, April 16, 1917; children—Thomas B., Elizabeth Barbour, Harrison, Mary Virginia. Commd. 2d lt. Engrs. Corps, 1915; promoted through grades to lt. gen., 1949; on Mexican campaign, 1916-17; overseas, 1917-19; with Office Chief of Engrs., Washington, 1920-21; asst. mil. attache, Tokyo, 1921-23; asst. dist. engr., Pittsburgh, 1923-25; with Office Chief Engrs., 1925-28; asst. dist. engr. and engr., Vicksburg, Miss., 1929-33; in charge Ft. Peck Project, Mont., 1933-37; in charge 3d Locks Project, Panama Canal, 1939-42; chief engr. and chief of staff, Services of Supply, 1942-43; comdg. gen. Services of Supply and Communications Zone, N. Africa, 1943-44; Commd. hdqrs., dep. comdr. and chief of staff, Communications Zone, ETO 1943-44; comdg. gen., 2d Service Comd., Govs. Isl., N.Y., 1945-46; Q.M.G., rank of Major General; dir. logistics div., Gen. Staff, Dept. Army, 1949-52, ret., 1952; made econ. survey Dominican Republic, 1953; asst. in econ. survey West Berlin, 1953; cons. to asst. sec. def. on facilities assistance progress, Europe and Near East, 1953-60; dir. mut. weapons devel. team Dept. Def., 1955-60; project dir. transp. survey Argentine Govt.-World Bank, 1960-62; cons. Blauvelt Engring. Co., N.Y.C., 1962, Colfax Chem. Co., Cal., 1962-68. Decorated Silver Star (three bronze stars), Distinguished Service Medal (two oak leaf clusters), Legion of Merit, Bronze Star, Brazilian Military Order of Merit, Grand Officer, Order of Crown of Italy, Comdr. Honorable Order of the Bath; Grand Officer, Order of Ouissan Alouit Cherifils (Sultan of Morocco, 1945); Grand Officer 1st class, Order of Nichantan Ikhar (Bey of Tunis, 1945); Comdr. French Legion of Honor, Croix de Guerre with Palms (1945). Mem. Am. Soc. Civil Engrs., Soc. Mil. Engrs. Clubs: Chevy Chase; The American (London). Contbr. to engring. jours. Home: Washington DC Died Oct. 17, 1968; buried Arlington Nat. Cemetery, Arlington VA

LARNED, JOSEPH GAY EATON, inventor; b. Thompson, Conn., Apr. 29, 1819; s. George and Anna (Spalding) L.; grad. Yale, 1839; m. Helen Lee, May 9,

1859. Tchr. classics Chatham Acad., Savannah, Ga., 1839; pvt. tchr., Charleston, S.C., 1840; took charge of academy in Waterloo, N.Y., 1841; tutor Yale, 1842; wrote articles for New Englander, Conn., 1845-46; studied law at home, admitted to Conn. bar, 1847; moved to N.Y.C., 1854; in partnership with Wellington Lee to manufacture steam fire engines at Novelty Iron Works, N.Y., 1855-63; invented steam fire engine and demonstrated it in N.Y.C. and other cities; became asst. insp. of ironclads for Navy Dept. in charge of work at Green Point, Bklyn., 1863; returned to law practice, N.Y.C., after Civil War. Author: A Quarter-Century Record of the Class of 1839, Yale College, 1865. Died N.Y.C., June 3, 1870.

LARRABEE, WILLIAM CLARK, clergyman, educator; b. Cape Elizabeth, Me., Dec. 23, 1802; grad. Bowden U., Brunswick, Me., 1828; m. Harriet Dunn, September 28, 1828, 4 children. Licensed to preach by Methodist Ch., 1821; prin. Alfred Acad., Me., 1828-30; apptd. tutor of prep. sch. (later became Wesleyan U.), Middletown, Conn., 1830; prin. Oneida Conf. Sem., Cazenovia, N.Y., circa 1831-32; admitted to Oneida Conf., Meth. Episcopal Ch., 1832; assisted in 1st geol. survey of N.Y., 1837-38; del. Gen. Conf., Meth. Episcopal Ch., Balt., 1840; prof. mathematics and natural sci. Indiana Asbury U. (now De Pauw U.), Greencastle, 1841-50, pres., 1849-50; editor Ladies Repository, Cincinnati, 1852; 1st supt. pub. instrn. State of Ind., 1852-54, 56-59. Author: Lectures on the Scientific Evidences of Natural and Revealed Religion, 1850; Wesley and his Coadjutors, 2 vols., 1851; Asbury and his Coadjutors, 1 vols., 1853; Rosabower, 1854. Died Ind., May 5, 1859.

LARSEN, ESPER SIGNIUS, JR., geologist; b. Astoria, Ore., Mar. 14, 1879; s. Esper Signius and Louisa (Pauly) L.; B.S., U. of Calif., 1906, Ph.D., 1918; m. Eva Audrey Smith, Nov. 21, 1910; children—Clark Smith (deceased), Esper Signius III (dec.). Asst. petrographer Geophysical Laboratory, 1907-09, assistant geologist, United States Geological Survey, 1909-14, geologist, 1914-58, in charge section of petrology, 1918-23; acting prof. geology, U. of Calif., 1915-16; prof. petrography, Harvard, 1923-49. Recipient Roebling Medal, 1941, Penrose Medal, 1953. Member Nat. Acad. Sci., Geol. Soc. of Am., Mineral. Soc. of Am., Mineral. Soc. of Great Britain, Am. Acad. Arts and Sciences, Am. Inst. Mining and Metallurgical Engineers, Society of Econ. Geologists, London Geological Society (honorary). Republican. Congregationalist. Author: The Microscopic Determination of the Nonopaque Minerals, 1921; (with S. F. Emmons) Geology and Ore Deposits of the Creede District, Colorado, 1928; (with Whitman Cross) A Brief Review of the Geology of the San Juan Mountains of Southwestern Colorado; (with others) Igneous Rocks of the Highwood Mountains, Montana; Batholith of Southern California; Geology and Petrology of the San Juan Mountains, Colorado. Contbr. Am. Mineralogist, American Journal of Sci., Econ. Geology, etc. Home: 3930 Connecticut Av., N.W., Washington 8. Died Mar. 8, 1961.

LARSEN, MERWIN JOHN, educator, elec. engr.; b. Spencer, Iowa, Nov. 20, 1909; s. John A. and Emma L. (Cook) L.; B.S., State U. Ia., 1933, M.S., 1934, Ph.D., 1937; m. Janet Julia Seger, Dec. 11, 1935; children—Mernet Ruth, Lyndell Louise, Jnaeen Jess. Instr. Mich. Coll. Mining and Tech., 1937-39, asst. prof., 1940-43; sr. engr. research lab. Stromberg Carlson Co., 1943-47; chief engr. electronics Central Comml. Industries, Chgo., 1947-51; prof., head dept. elec. engring. U. Fla., 1951—. Registered profl. engr., Fla. Mem. I.R.E., Am. Inst. E.E, Am. Soc. Engring. Edn., Newcomen Soc. N.A., Sigma Xi, Eta Kappa Nu, Sigma Tau. Clubs: Rotary; U. Fla. Athenaeum. Contbr. articles on psychophys. measurements, TV, circuits to profl. jours. Patentee in field. Home: 805 N. W. 20th Terrace, Gainesville, Fla. Died Mar. 28, 1965.

LARSON, CARL W., dairy technologist; b. St. Ansgar, Ia., May 29, 1881; s. Henry and Minnie (Hansen) L.; B.S., in Agr., Ia. State Coll., 1906; M.S., Pa. State Coll., 1911; Ph.D., Columbia U., 1916; m. Nellie C. Wallace, Sept. 7, 1911; 1 dau., Eileen (Mrs. Charles A. Brady). Studied creamery and cheese factory methods in Minn. and Wis., 1906-07; instr. dairy husbandry 1907-11, asst. prof., 1911-13, prof. in charge dairy husbandry dept., Pa. State Coll., 1913-15; asst. prof. agr. and agrl. economics, Columbia, 1916-17; was with Dairy Div. Bur. Animal Industry, U.S. Dept. Agr., as dairy expert, asst. chief of Dairy Div., chief of Dairy Div., later chief of new Bureau of Dairy Industry; mng. dir. Nat. Dairy Council, 1928-29, Gen. Ice Cream Corp., 1930-36; pres. Whiting Milk and Bushway-Whiting Ice Cream Co., Boston, 1936-41; pres. and gen. mgr. The Bryant and Chapman Milk Co. and R. G. Miller & Sons, Hartford, Conn., 1942-44; mgr. and dir. West N.Y. div. Gen. Ice Cream Corp., Buffalo, N.Y., 1944-46; sec. and mng. dir. Dairy Prod. Improve, Inst., Inc., 1947-53. Sent by Red Cross to France, 1918, to develop and improve milk supplies for hospitals. U.S. del. Internat. Dairy Fedn., Stockholm, 1911; official del. Internat. Dairy Congress, London, 1928. Fellow A.A.A.S.; mem. Am. Dairy Science Assn., Alpha Zeta, Sigma Psi, Gamma Sigma Delta. Republican. Lutheran. Clubs: Cosmos, Rotary, Athletic. Author: Principles and Methods of Milk Cost Accounting, 1916; Dairy Cattle Feeding and Management (part author), 1916. Home: Tudor Plaza Apt., 731 W. Ferry St., Buffalo 22, Died June 13, 1954; buried Mount Olivet Cemetery, Kenmore, N.Y.

LARSON, GUSTUS LUDWIG, cons. engr.; born Werpinge, Lund, Sweden, June 30, 1881; s. Ole and Ingrid (Sjostrom) L.; came to U.S., 1890, naturalized, 1902; B.S. in elec. engring., U. of Ida., 1907; M.E., U. of Wis., 1915; m. Marion Frances Anthony, June 30, 1914; children—Dorothy Alida, Foster Anthony. Test engr. Gen. Elec. Co., Schenectady, N.Y., 1907-09; asso. prof. mech. engring., U. of Ida., 1909-11, prof., 1911-14; with U. of Wis., 1914-51, as asst. prof. of steam and gas engring., 1914-15, asso. prof., 1915-20, prof. and chmn. dept. mech. engring., 1920-43; cons. engr. U. of Wis. and other clients in Wis. since 1915. Apptd. by Wis. Indsl. Commn. to assist in drafting heating and ventilating code for State of Wis., 1925, also air conditioning, 1936; mem. Pres. Roosevelt's Conf. on Home Bldg. and Ownership, Washington, D.C., 1931; mem. advisory com. 12th Nat. Expn. of Power and Mech. Engring., New York, 1936, 13th, 1937. Grad. mgr. athletics, U. of Ida., 1909-14. Served as cons. engr. Ordnance Div., U.S. War Dept., 1917-18. Mem. Am. Soc. Mech. Engrs. (chmn. Rock River Valley Sect., 1939), Am. Soc. Heating and Ventilating Engrs. (mem. council 1929-33; chairman, Committee on Research, 1932 and 1933; v.p. 1934-36; pres. 1936; chmn. exec. com. 1937), Engring. Soc. of Wis. (pres. 1933), Soc. for Promotion Engring. Edn., Am. Assn. Univ. Profs., Nat. Assn. Power Engrs., Engrs. Soc. of Milwaukee, Tech. Club of Madison, Tau Beta Pi, Sigma Xi, Pi Tau Sigma (nat. pres. 1926-29), Phi Kappa Phi, Gamma Alpha, Phi Delta Theta, Triangle. Republican. Presbyterian (elder; trustee Presbyn. Student Center). Contbr. articles to Trans. Am. Soc. Heating and Ventilating Engrs.; editor of Heating, Ventilating and Air Conditioning Guide, 1936. Designed heating, ventilating and air conditioning for many bldgs. in Wis. including Union Bldg. and Field House (U. of Wis.), Wis. Gen. Hosp., Wis. Power & Light Bldg. (Madison), high schs. in Madison, Stevens Point, Janesville, Beloit, etc. Home: 1213 Sweet Briar Rd., Madison, Wis. Died Aug. 16, 1953.

LARSON, JOHN AUGUSTUS, psychiatrist; b. Shelbourne, N.S., Can., Dec. 11, 1892; s. Lars and Lucina Antonina (Mack) L.; A.B., Boston U., 1914, Am., 1915; Ph.D., U. Cal., 1920, grad. Sch. of Criminology, 1923; M.D., Rush Med. Coll., 1928; m. Margaret Steele Taylor, Aug. 9, 1922 (dec. 1960); 1 son, John William Earle. Came to U.S., 1892, naturalized, 1910. Asst. in biology Boston U., 1914-15; instr. U. So. Cal., 1915-16; asst. instr. later instr. physiology U. Cal., 1916-20; research in criminology with Berkeley (Cal.) Police Dept., 1920-23; research psychologist State of Ill., 1923-27; med. house officer Johns Hopkins Hosp., 1927-28, asst. resident in psychiatry, 1928-29; asst., later instr. in psychiatry Johns Hopkins Med. Sch., 1928-29; psychiatrist Ia. Psychopathic Hosp., and asso. in psychiatry U. Ia. Med. Sch., 1929-30; instr., later asst. clin. prof. in psychiatry Rush Med. Coll., 1930-36; asst. state criminologist State of Ill., 1930-36; research on validity of lie detector U. Chgo., 1931; supr. psychiat. fellows Mandel Clinics, U. Chgo., 1932-36; neurologist central Free Dispensary, Chgo., 1931-36; became asst. dir. Psychopathic Clinic, City of Detroit, 1936; physician in charge drastic therapy 1 yr. clin. dir. L.I.; lectr. forensic psychiatry Honolulu Police Dept., dir. Seattle Mental Hygiene Clinic; psychiatrist, Blythewood, Greenwich, Conn., 6 mos., 1944; chief psychiatrist N. Mex. State Hosp., Jan. 1946-Mar. 1947; supt. Ariz. State Hosp., Phoenix, 1947-49, Logansport (Ind.) State Hosp., 1949; clin. dir. and dir. research Wabash Valley Sanitarium Hosp., Lafayette, Ind., 1955-57; supt. Maximum Security Hosp., Nashville, also prison psychiatrist Tenn. State Prison, Nashville, 1957-61; psychiat. dir. Huron Mental Health Center (S.D.), 1961-63. Mem. bd. Ariz. Hosp. Adv. Survey and Constrn. Council Life fellow Am. Psychiat. Assn. (chmn. ct. com.), Am. Orthopsychiat. Assn.; life mem. A.M.A., Am. Med. Writers Assn.; mem. Ariz., Maricopa County med. socs., Ariz. Psychiat. Assn., Internat. Assn. Police Psychiatry (mem. exec. com.). Johns Hopkins Med. and Surg. Assn., Internat. Soc. of Identification, Norse Civic Assn. (chmn. civic affairs com.), Sigma Psi, Alpha Kappa Kappa. Developer, Larson Polygraph test in correlating several forms of apparatus, a decided modification of the Marston lie detection test was introduced into police and criminological procedure in 1921; spl. study tatoo symbolization, modus operandi and psychobiol. analysis with special respect to diagnosis and parole or furlough prediction. Club: Swedish-American. Author books including Larson Single Fingerprint System, 1923; Lying and its Detection (with George W. Harry and Leonardo Keeler), 1932. Contbr. sci. articles to med. jours. and police mags. Address: 1295 Vine St., Albany, Ore. Died Sept. 21, 1965.

LARSON, WINFORD PORTER, prof. bacteriology; b. Poy Sippi, Wis., Mar. 7, 1880; s. Charles J. and Mary (Peterson) L.; student Milton (Wis.) Coll., 1896-97, Union Coll., at Lincoln, Neb., 1897-99; M.D., U. of Ill. Coll. of Medicine, 1904; grad. study, U. of Berlin, 1906-08, Sorbonne, Paris, 1909-10; m. Alma E. Meldal, Apr. 4, 1908; children—Lorna G., Douglas M. Instr. in bacteriology, U. of Minn., 1911-12, asst. prof. bacteriology, 1912-15, asso. prof., 1915-18, prof. and head of dept. since 1918. Mem. Soc. Am. Bacteriologists, Am. Soc. Immunologists, Assn. Pathologists and Bacteriologists, Soc. Exptl. Biology and Med., Am. Assn. Univ. Profs., Nu Sigma Nu; asso. mem. N.Y. Acad. of Sciences. Club: Minneapolis Athletic. Contbr. on bacteriology. Home: 516 9th Av. S.E., Minneapolis, Minn. Died Jan. 1, 1947.

LA RUE, CARL DOWNEY, botanist; b. Williamsville, Ill., April 22, 1888; s. Abraham Chronister and Charlotte Parthena (Bates) La R.; B.S., Valparaiso U., 1910, A.B., 1911; A.B., U. of Mich., 1914, A.M., 1916, Ph.D., 1921; research, Harvard, 1936-37; m. Evelina Brown Forman, June 1, 1914; children—Adrian Jan Pieters, Anna Virginia, Charlotte Evelina, Carl Forman. Instr. botany, Syracuse U., 1916-17, botanist, Hollandsch-Amerikaansche Plantage Maatschappij, Sumatra, 1917-20; instr. botany, asst., asso. prof., U. of Mich., 1920-44, prof., 1944—; mem. Mich. Biol. Sta. staff, 1925-50; research Fed. Expt. Sta., Puerto Rico, 1951; specialist, rubber investigation, in charge S. American rubber expdn., U.S. Dept. Agr., 1923-24; specialist, co-dir., Ford Motor Amazon-Tapajos Expdn., 1926-27; agent, rubber investigations, in charge expdns., Bolivia, Nicaragua, Mexico, U.S. Dept. Agr., 1940-41, prin. specialist, U.S. Dept. Agr., 1943-44, Fellow A.A.A.S., Mem. Am. Soc. Naturalists, Bot. Soc. Am., Sullivant Moss Soc., Torrey Bot. Club, Mich. Acad. Sci., Arts, Letters (sec., 1923), Sigma Xi. Author: Agrl. Dept. bulls.; contbr. tech. articles to bot. jours. Home: 2940 Fuller Rd., Ann Arbor, Mich. Died Aug. 19, 1955.

LASHLEY, K(ARL) S(PENCER), psychologist; b. Davis, W.Va., June 7, 1890; s. Charles Gilpen and Margaret Blanche (Spencer) L.; A.B. in Zoology, W.Va. U., 1910; M.S. in Bacteriology (teaching fellow 1910), U. Pitts., 1911, D.Sc., 1936; Ph.D. in Genetics (fellow 1913, Bruce fellow 1914), Johns Hopkins, 1914, Johnston scholar, 1915-16, LL.D., 1953; M.A. (hon.) Harvard, 1942; D.Sc., U. Chgo., 1941, Western Res. U., 1951, U. Pa., 1955; m. Edith Ann Baker, 1918 (dec. 1948); m. 2d, Dr. Claire Imredy Schiller, 1957. Instr. psychology U. Minn., 1917-18, asst. prof. psychology, 1920-21, asso. prof., 1921-24, prof., 1924-26; investigator U.S. Interdepartmental Social Hygiene Bd., 1919-20; acting prof. psychology U. Chgo., summer 1925, prof. psychology, 1929-35; acting prof. psychology Columbia, summer 1926; research psychologist Behavior Research Fund of Inst. for Juvenile Research, Chgo., 1926-29; lectr. univs. London, Berlin, Moscow, 1932; prof. psychology Harvard, 1935-37, research prof. neuropsychology, 1937-55, emeritus, 1955-58; dir. Yerkes Labs. of Primate Biology, 1942-55, emeritus, 1955-58. Hughlings Jackson Meml. lectr. Montreal Neurol. Clinic, 1937; Vanuxem lectr. Princeton, 1952. Recipient Howard Crosby Warren medal in psychology Soc. Exptl. Psychologists, 1937; Daniel Giraud Elliot Medal in zoology Nat. Acad. Scis., 1943; William Baly Medal in physiology Royal Coll. Physicians, 1953. Mem. Nat. Acad. Scis., Am. Philos. Soc., Am. Acad. Arts and Scis., Am. Psychol. Assn. (pres. 1929, pres. eastern br. 1937), Soc. Am. Naturalists (pres. 1947), Am. Soc. Zoologists, Am. Physiol. Soc., Soc. Exptl. Psychologists, Am. Soc. Human Genetics, NRC (div. anthropology and psychology 1927-30, 32-35), Fla. Psychol. Assn.; hon. mem. Am. Neurol. Assn., Harvey Soc., N.Y. Acad. Scis., Brit. Assn. Study Animal Behavior; fgn. mem. Royal Soc. London, Brit. Psychol. Assn. Author more than 100 articles and monographs (including Brain Mechanisms and Intelligence, U. Chgo. Press, 1929) on the Structure and functions of the brain, comparative psychology, animal behavior, instincts of birds and primates, learning, and genetics. Home: 3936 McGirts Blvd., Jacksonville 10, Fla. Died Aug. 7, 1958.

LASKY, WAYNE EDWARD, chem. engr.; b. Normal, Ill., Nov. 8, 1902; s. Walter E. and Effie (Deal) L.; B.S., Ill. Wesleyan U., 1924; m. Lucille Dickinson, Aug. 4, 1926; 1 dau., Mary Lu (Mrs. Dwight Ostrowski). Tchr. pub. schs., Joy, Ill., 1924-25; engr. Electric Refrigeration, Evanston, Ill., 1925-26, Chgo., 1926-29; pres. Lasky-Jones, Inc., Bloomington, Ill., 1930-34; mgr., owner Lasky Grocery, Normal, 1931-48; chem. engr. Kankakee Ordinance (Ill.), 1942-43; chief chemist Alton R. R. (Ill.), 1943-48; engr. tests G.M.&O. R.R., Bloomington, 1948-68. Trustee Town of Normal, 1929-33. Fellow Am. Inst. Chemists; mem. Am. Soc. Lubrication Engrs. (nat. dir. 1954-57), Soc. Automotive Engrs., Am. Assn. R.R. (chmn. lubrication com. 1964-67), Nat. Assn. R.R. Engrs. of Tests (chmn. 1952-53), Nat. Ry. Lubrication Council (founder, chmn. 1955-58), Am. Soc. Testing Materials, Am. chem. Soc., Tau Kappa Epsilon. Mem. Christian Ch. Clubs: Optimist, Lakeside Country (Bloomington). Contbr. articles to profl. jours. Patentee in field. Home: Bloomington IL Died Aug. 8, 1968.

LATCH, EDWARD BIDDLE, chief engr. U.S.N.; b. Lower Merion Twp., Pa., Nov. 15, 1833; s. Gardiner and Henrietta (Wakeling) L.; ed. pub. schs.; studied mech. engring. Norris Locomotive Works, Phila., 1851-57; unmarried. Began service as asst. engr. U.S.N., Sept. 20, 1858; chief engr. with rank of comdr., Mar. 21, 1870; retired, Nov. 22, 1878. During Civil War was attached to the flagship Hartford (Admiral Farragut); took part in engagements at Fts. Jackson and St. Philip and Confederate fleet Mississippi River, Chalmette,

New Orleans, Vicksburg, Port Hudson, Grand Gulf, Warrenton, Grand Gulf and Fts. Morgan, Gaines and Powell; also with the ram Tennessee at the battle of Mobile Bay. Developed the Mosaic system of chronology. Extensive writer of elucidations of scripture and universal history by the Mosaic system of chronology. Editor The Greater Light (Phila. monthly). Author: A Review of the Holy Bible, 1884; Indications of the Book of Job, 1889; Indications of Genesis, 1890; Indications of Exodus, 1892; also serials in The Greater Light—Indications of Romans, 1900-01; Indications of the Revelation of St. John the Divine, 1901-03; Indications of Leviticus, 1905; Indications of Numbers, 1906-07; etc. Address: Academy P.O., Pa. Died 1911.

LATHAM, VIDA A., educator, microscopist; b. England, Feb. 4, 1866; ed. in Norwich, Manchester, Cambridge and London, England, and Mich. and Northwestern univs.; grad. Mich. Univ. Dental Dept., 1892; Northwestern Univ. Woman's Med. Dept., 1895. Has practiced medicine and dentistry at Ann Arbor, Mich., and Chicago; best known as teacher of sciences and microscopy in particular. Has been prof. histology Am. Dental Coll.; lecturer pathology and histology, dir. micros. laboratories and curator museum Northwestern Univ. Woman's Med. School. Mem. Am. Med. Assn., A.A.A.S., Am. Micros. Soc., Ill. State Micros. Soc., Chicago Acad. Sciences, Chicago Patholog. Soc.; fellow Royal Micros. Soc. Contributor to med. and scientific publications in England and U.S. Residence: 808 Morse Av., Chicago.

LATIMER, CLAIBORNE GREEN, educator, mathematician; b. Hyattsville, Md., Sept. 23, 1893; s. John Edward and Kate Mason (Green); L.; grad. Central Mo. State Tchrs. Coll., 1917; B.S., U. Chgo., 1920, M.S., 1921, Ph.D., 1924; m. Frieda Hildebrandt, Aug. 30, 1924; 1 son, Paul Henry. Instr. mathematics Swarthmore Coll., 1921-22; instr. mathematics Tulane U., 1923-24, asst. prof., 1924-27; prof. mathematics U. Ky., 1927-47; prof. mathematics Emory U., 1947—, chmn. dept., 1948-56; vis. prof. U. Wis., spring 1938; tchr. Am. U. Shrivenham, Eng., 1945; vis. prof. Northwestern U., summer 1947. Served in AS, U.S. Army, 1917-19. Mem. Am. Math. Soc. (mem. council 1930-31, 40-42), Math. Assn. Am. (bd. govs. 1942-45), Am. Assn. U. Profs., Ky. Soc. S.R. (treas. 1943-45), Sigma Xi, Pi Mu Epsilon. Democrat. Episcopalian. Asso. editor Duke Math. Jour., 1938-41. Contbr. math. jours. Home: 2098 Black Fox Dr. N.E., Atlanta 30329. Died Feb. 3, 1960; buried Westview Cemetery, Atlanta.

LATIMER, WENDELL MITCHELL, chemist; b. Garnett, Kan., Apr. 22, 1893; s. Walter and Emma (Mitchell) L.; A.B., U. of Kan., 1915, U. of Calif., 1918; m. Bertha Eichenauer, Aug. 1, 1917; 1 son, Walter R.; m. 2d, Glatha Hatfield, June 16, 1926; children—Eleanor Ann, Robert Milton. Lecturer and demonstrator in chemistry, U. of Calif., 1918-21, asst. prof., 1921-23, asso. prof., 1924-31, prof., 1931—; asst. dean Coll. Letters and Science, U. of Calif., 1923-24, dean College of Chemistry, 1941-50, associate director radiation laboratory, 1949—. Official investigator National Defense Research Com., 1942-43; mem. War Dept. Mission to England, 1943; mem. div. 10 com., Nat. Defense Research Com., technical observer and sci. expert G.H.Q., Southwest Pacific Area, 1944. Director Manhattan Eng. District Contract on Chemistry of plutonium, 1943-47. Member Chemical Corps Research Council, 1947-51, Commn. of Electrochemistry of Internat. Union of Pure and Applied Chemistry. Academy Polit. Sci., National Academy Sciences, American Chemistry Society, A.A.A.S., Electrochem. Soc., Sigma Xi, Alpha Chi Sigma. Guggenheim Foundation fellow, Munich, 1930. Recipient, Distinguished Service Award, Univ. of Kansas, 1948, Presidential Certificate of Merit, 1948, Nichols award N.Y. sect. Am. chem. Soc., 1955. Clubs: Bohemian, Orinda Country, Faculty. Author: A Course in General Chemistry (with W. C. Bray), 1923; Reference Book of Inorganic Chemistry (with J. H. Hildebrand), 1929; Oxidation Potentials, 1938. Contbr. to chem. publs. Editor of Prentice-Hall chemistry series. Asso. editor Jour. Chem. Phys., 1933, Chem. Review, 1940. Home: 810 Euclid Av., Berkeley 8, Cal. Died July 6, 1955; buried Woodlawn Cemetery, Kansas City, Kan.

LA TOUR, LE BLONDE DE, engr., army officer; b. France. A draftsman in Portugal, 1702, engr., 1703; served in Spanish Army, 1704-08, taken prisoner, 1705, exchanged, 1706; served in various battles in War of Spanish Succession (1701-04), decorated Cross of Royal and Mil. Order of St. Louis, 1715; reserve capt. Piedmont Regt., then cpl. His Majesty's Engrs.; apptd. engr.-in-chief Province of La., arrived in La. to superintend constrn. of public buildings, 1720; supervised building of capital of La. Province, New Biloxi (now Biloxi), 1721; claimed to have drawn up plans for building of New Orleans (claims false); left New Biloxi to supervise building of new capital in New Orleans, 1722; lt. gen. Province of La. Died New Orleans, Oct. 14, 1723.

LATROBE, BENJAMIN HENRY, engr., architect; b. Fulneck, Eng., May 1, 1764; s. Benjamin and Anna Margaret (Antes) L.; studied architecture under Samuel Pepys Cockerell (pioneer in Green revival), Eng., 1788-89; m. Lydia Sellon, 1790, 4 children including Henry, Lydia; m. 2d, Mary Hazlehurst, May 2, 1800, children—John, Benjamin Henry. Executed his 1st independent archtl. work "Hammerwood Lodge." East Grinstead, Sussex, Eng., circa 1787; later became surveyor of police force of London (Eng.); came to Am., 1796; cons. on improvement of navigation on James River, 1796; designed prison on principle of solitary confinement, Richmond, Va., 1797; completed exterior of Va. State Capitol (designed by Jefferson); designed Bank of Pa., Phila., 1798; designed and engineered project for pumping Phila.'s water supply from Schuylkill River by using pumps operated by steam engines, 1799; undertook improvement of navigation on Susquehanna River; designed several houses in Phila. including "Sedgby" for William Cramond, the Burd House at Chestnut and 9th Streets; apptd. surveyor of public bldgs. by Pres. Jefferson, 1803; commd. to design South Wing of Capitol Bldg. which would contain U.S. Ho. of Reps.; commd. by Bishop John Carroll to design cathedral for Diocese of Balt., 1804, executed in Gothic revival style; did much work on Washington and N.Y.C. naval yards, 1804; designed 1st bldg. at Dickinson Coll., Carlisle, Pa., 1804, bldg. for Pa. Acad. Fine Arts, Phila., 1805; apptd. engr. Chesapeake and Del. Canal, 1804; became partner of Robert Fulton, Robert R. Livingston and Nicholas J. Roosevelt to build steamboat to navigate Ohio River, 1812 (project collapsed after Fulton's death, 1815); worked on reconstrn. of Capitol Bldg. and White House, Washington, D.C. (after destruction by British), 1815-17; adviser to Thomas Jefferson on design of Pavillions V and III for U. Va., 1817; after death of son Henry, completed building of water works, New Orleans, 1817. Author: View of the Practicability and Means of Supplying the City of Philadelphia with Wholesome Water, 1799. Died of yellow fever, New Orleans. Sept. 3, 1820.

LATROBE, BENJAMIN HENRY, civil engr.; b. Phila., Dec. 19, 1806; s. Benjamin Henry and Mary (Hazlehurst) L.; m. Maria Eleanor Hazlehurst, Mar. 12, 1833, 5 children including Charles Hazlehurst. Mem. engr. corps B. & O. R.R., 1831-35, in charge of survey locating line from Balt. to Washington, 1832, built Thomas Viaduct (outstanding piece of railroad architecture); became chief engr. Balt. & Port Deposit R.R., 1835, directed survey of line from Point of Rocks to Harpers Ferry (Md.), 1836, built road through mountains from Harpers Ferry to Cumberland; apptd. chief engr. B. & O. R.R., 1842, completed survey of line from Wheeling, Va. (now W.Va.) to the Ohio, 1848, built Northwestern Va. R.R., 1851-52; chief engr. Pitts. and Connellsville R.R., 1871. Died Balt., Oct. 19, 1878.

LATROBE, CHARLES HAZELHURST, engr.; b. Balt., Dec. 25, 1834; s. Benjamin Henry and Maria Eleanor (Hazelhurst) L.; attended St. Mary's Coll., Balt.; m. Letitia Breckinridge (Gamble) Holliday, 1861; m. 2d, Rosa Wirt Robinson, 1869; m. 3d, Louise McKim, 1881; 3 children. Worked for B.&O. R.R.; went to Fla. as chief engr. in charge of constrn. Pensacola & Ga. R.R.; commd. lt. of engrs. Confederate Army, 1861; asso. (with father and Charles Shaler Smith) in Balt. Bridge Co., 1866-77; engr. Jones Falls Commn., Balt., 1875-89, designed and constructed several iron bridges, laid out terraced gardens along Mt. Royal Avenue; commd. by Peruvian govt. to construct bridge (highest bridge in world at that time) at Verrugas on Callao-Oroya-Huancayo R.R. Died Balt., Sept. 19, 1902; buried Greenmount Cemetery, Balt.

LATTA, ALEXANDER BONNER, inventor, mfr.; b. Chillicothe, O., June 11, 1821; s. John and Rebecca (Bonner) L.; m. Elizabeth Ann Pawson, 1847, 2 children. Worked in cotton factory in Ohio, 1831; foreman Harkness Machine Shop, Cincinnati, circa 1841; directed constrn. of locomotive for Little Miami R.R. (1st locomotive built West of Allegheny Mountains), 1845; designed and built locomotive having extra steam cylinders for Boston & Me. R.R.; patented several improvements on locomotives, steam engines and boilers; completed his 1st steam fire engine, (could be pulled by men or horses), 1852, patented self-propelled steam fire engine, 1855; formed partnership with his brother, built 30 engines by 1860; recipient gold medal for fire engine improvements at Ohio Mechanics Isnt. Fair, 1854; retired, 1862. Died Ludlow, Ky., Apr. 28, 1865.

LATTIMORE, JOHN AARON CICERO, physician; b. Selby, N.C., June 23, 1876; s. John Carpenter and Marcella (Hambrick) L.; A.B., Bennett Coll. (then co-educational), Greensboro, N.C., 1897; M.D., Meharry Med. Coll., Nashville, Tenn., 1901; post grad. work U. of Chicago; m. Naomi Anthony, Aug. 11, 1928. Engaged in private practice Louisville, Ky., since 1901. Chmn. Negro health com. in charge of venereal disease clinic Louisville Health Center; mem. staff Red Cross Hosp.; mem. Louisville Interracial Como., Louisville Area Development Assn. (mem. hosp. com.); chmn. Negro Health Com. Mem. Nat. Med. Assn. (vice pres. 1920-21; pres. 1947-48), Louisville Urban League (an organizer; mem. bd.), John Andrew Clin. Soc., Nat. Assn. Advancement Colored People (an organizer), Falls City Med. Soc., Blue Grass State Med. Assn. (past pres.; v.p.), Meharry Alumni Assn., Psi Boule, Alpha Phi Alpha (past pres.; awarded trophy for achievements in med. profession). Awarded certificate of merit by U.S. Govt. for medical work with soldiers. Democrat. Methodist. Elk. Home: 1502 W. Walnut St. Office: 1432 W. Walnut St., Louisville 3 KY*

LAUBACH, CHARLES, geologist, archaeologist; b. Durham, Pa., Aug. 29, 1836; s. Anthony L.; ed. in Durham public schools and Collegiate Inst., Easton, Pa. (grad., 1860); studied phrenology; also studied medicine with Dr. H. A. Benton, Saratoga, and obstetrics with Dr. Jacob Ludlow, Easton, Pa.; m. Jane Raub, Mar. 29, 1860. Practiced med. electricity and homoeopathy while giving phrenological lectures and delineations of character, and was also engaged in farming; began scientific investigations, 1865, and has devoted prin. attention to them, 1870—. Corr. mem. U. of Pa., archaeol. and palaeontol. dept.; mem. Anthropol. Club, Phila.; charter mem. Bucks County Hist. Soc. Wrote: History of Durham Township, 1887; Geology of Bucks County, Pa., in Warner's History of Bucks County; Prehistoric Man in the Delaware Valley, 1880. Address: Riegelsville, Pa. Died 1904.

LAUGHLIN, HARRY HAMILTON, (lawf'lin), biologist; b. Oskaloosa, Ia., Mar. 11, 1880; s. George Hamilton and Deborah Jane (Ross) L.; B.S., North Mo. State Normal Sch., 1900; M.S., Princeton, 1916, Sc.D., 1917; hon. M.D., U. of Heidelberg, Germany, 1936; m. Pansy Bowen, Sept. 13, 1902. Teacher agr., North Mo. State Normal Sch., 1907-10; supt. Eugenics Record Office (div. of Dept. of Genetics of Carnegie Instn. Washington) from its orgn., Oct. 1, 1910, until Jan. 1, 1921, in charge 1921-40; eugenics expert for Com. on Immigration and Naturalization, House of Rep., 1921-31; eugenics associate Psychopathic Lab., Municipal Court, Chicago, 1921-30; U.S. immigration agt. to Europe, Dept. of Labor, 1923-24; in charge of researches on the genetics of the thoroughbred horse since 1923; mem. Permanent Emigration Com. of Internat. Labor Office of the League of Nations, Geneva, 1925; dir. Survey of Human Resources of Conn., 1936-38. Capt. of N.Y. Home Defense Res., 1917-19. Mem. Galton Soc., Eugenics Research Assn. (sec.-treas., 1917-39); Am. Soc. Internat. Law, Am. Statis. Assn., Am. Eugenics Soc. pres., 1927-28). Mem. Internat. Commn. of Eugenics since 1921. Asso. editor Eugenical News, 1916-39; sec. 3d Internat. Congress of Eugenics, 1932; pres. Pioneer Fund, Inc., from its organization until 1941. Editor "A Decade of Progress in Eugenics," 1934. Author: Mitotic Stage Duration (Carnegie Instn.), 1918; State Institutions for the Defective, Dependent and Delinquent Classes (Bur. of Census), 1919; Eugenical Sterilization in the United States (Municipal Court, Chicago), 1922; Analysis of America's Modern Melting Pot (U.S. Govt. publ.), 1923; Europe as the Emigration-Exporting Continent and the United States as the Immigration-Receiving Nation (U.S. Govt. publ.), 1924; The General Formula of Heredity, 1933; Immigration Control, 1934; Racing Capacity in the Thoroughbred Horse, 1934; Probability Resultant, 1934; Conquest by Immigration, 1939; Current Studies on Race Conditions in the United States. Address: Kirksville, Mo. Died Jan. 26, 1943.

LAURGAARD, OLAF, (lor'gard), consulting engr.; b. Ekne, nr. Trondhjem, Norway, Feb. 21, 1880; s. Oluf Christenson and Marie Cecelia (Leinhardt) L.; brought to U.S. in infancy; B.S., in C.E., U. of Wis., 1903, M.S., in C.E., 1914; m. Goldie MaySherer, Nov. 29, 1908; children—Helen, Glenn Olaf. Asst. engr. U.S. Reclamation Service, 1903-10; chief engr. Ore., Wash. & Ida. Finance Co., 1910-13; div. engr. Pacific Power & Light Co., Jan.-June 1913; project engr. State of Ore., 1913-15; cons. engineer, Portland, Ore., 1915-17; city engr. Portland, 1917-34 (in charge of expenditure of about $55,000,000 in pub. works of Portland); engr. with U.S. Bur. of Reclamation, 1934-36, services as constrn. engr. Parker Dam on Colorado River and engr. in Denver office, 1934-36; with Tenn. Valley Authority as gen. office engr. Engring. and Constrn. Depts., 1936-37, constrn. engr. on Hiwassee Dam in N.C., 1937-40; consulting engr., Portland, Ore., 1940-42, including principal engr. War Dept., U.S. Engrs. on defense projects, Anchorage, Alaska; resident plant engr., U.S. Maritime Commission on shipbuilding, Alameda, California, since 1942. Member Oregon legislature, 1917, prepared and introduced Ore. highway and irrigation codes. Mem. Ore. State Bd. Engring. Examiners, 1919-35, pres. 1919-30; pres. Nat. Council State Bds. of Engring. Examiners, 1933. Capt. Engr. Res. Corps, U.S. Army, 1918, 23. Life mem. Am. Assn. Engrs. (ex-pres. Ore. chapter); mem. Am. Soc. C.E. (life), Am. Soc. Municipal Engrs., City Ofcls., Div. Am. Road Builders Assn., Am. Soc. Mil. Engrs., Professional Engrs. of Ore. (life mem.), N.W. Soc. Highway Engrs. (past pres.), Tau Beta Pi, Chi Epsilon. Mason (32 deg., K.T.); mem. Elks, Woodmen of the World. Member Portland Auld Lang Syne Soc., East Bay Engineers. Clubs: Alameda Forum (Calif.), Portland City. Contbr. on engring. subjects. Home: Portland, Ore. Address: 2308 Webster St., Alameda, Calif. Died June 23, 1945.

LAURIE, JAMES, civil engr.; b. Bells Quarry, Scotland, May 9, 1811; Apprentice to math. engring. instrument maker, Bells Quarry, until 1832; worked in civil engr.'s office, became asso. with James P. Kirkwood, came to U.S. with him, 1833; asso. engr. Norwich & Worcester R.R. of Mass., chief engr., supt. constrn., 1835; after completion of railroad became adviser to canal and railroad cos.; a founder Boston Soc. Civil Engrs., 1848; moved to N.Y.C., 1852, invited all engrs. in vicinity to form a civil engrs. soc.; organized Am. Soc. C.E., 1852, 1st pres., 1852-67, at 1st meeting called for elevated railway tracks in his paper "The Relief of Broadway"; examiner railroad bridges for N.Y. State, 1855-56; chief engr. N.S. R.R., 1858-60; worked for Mass. inspecting Troy & Greenfield R.R.; consultant on Hoosac Tunnel for several years, concurrently chief engr. New Haven, Hartford & Springfield R.R., designed and built bridge across Connecticut River at Warehouse Point. Died Hartford, Conn., Mar. 16, 1875.

LAURITSEN, CHARLES CHRISTIAN, educator; b. Holstebro, Denmark, Apr. 4, 1892; grad. Odense Tekniske Skole, Denmark, 1911; Ph.D., Cal. Inst. Tech., 1929; LL.D., U. Cal., 1965; m. Sigrid; 1 son, Thomas. Elec. and radio engring., 1911-26; asst. prof. physics Cal. Inst. Tech., 1930-31, asso. prof., 1931-35, prof., 1935-62, prof. emeritus, 1962-68. Mem. numerous govt. adv. groups, 1940-68, including U.S. Army Sci. Adv. Panel, Army Missile Command Missile Sci. Adv. Group, Army Combat Devel. Command Sci. Adv. Group; bd. visitors USAF Systems Command; cons. Pres.'s Sci. Adv. Com. Served with NDRC, OSRD, 1940-42. Recipient numerous honors and awards including Gold medal Am. Coll. Radiology, 1931; U.S. medal for Merit, 1948; certificates appreciation Dept. Army, 1953, USAF, 1955; Capt. R.D. Conrad award USN, 1958; T.W. Bonner prize Am. Phys. Soc., 1967. Fellow Am. Phys. Soc. (pres. 1951), Coll. Radiology, Royal Soc. Copenhagen, A.A.A.S.; mem. Nat. Acad. Scis., Am. Phil. Soc., Sigma Xi. Contbr. sci. jours. Home: Pasadena CA Died Apr. 13, 1968.

LAVENDER, HARRISON MORTON, mining engr.; b. Scotland, S.D., Oct. 31, 1890; s. Albert Webster and Mary (Edgar) L.; E.M., Colo. Sch. of Mines, 1916; m. Florence T. Brush, July 3, 1941; children by previous marriage—Harrison Morton, Caroline (Mrs. William S. Chandler). Mining engr. in Ariz., Utah, Colo. and Mexico, 1916-23; chief mining engr. Calumet and Ariz. Mining Co., Bisbee, Ariz., 1926-31; mine supt. Copper Queen Branch, Phelps Dodge Corp., Bisbee, Arizona, 1932-35, asst. to vice-pres. and gen. mgr., Douglas, Ariz., 1936-37, gen. mgr., 1937-46, vice president and gen. mgr. since 1946, dir. Phelps Dodge Corporation, since 1949; pres., director Tucson, Cornelia & Gila Bend R.R. since 1940; dir. Apache Power Co., Curtis, Ariz., since 1937. Awarded Medal for Distinguished Achievement, Colo. Sch. of Mines, 1948. Served with Engr. Corps, A.U.S., 1917-19. Mem. Am. Inst. Mining and Metall. Engrs., Am. Mining Congress. Republican. Episcopalian. Mason. Clubs: Arizona, Phoenix Country, Old Pueblo, California. Home: 910 E. Av. Office: Phelps Dodge Corp., Douglas, Ariz. Died Mar. 21, 1952.

LAVES, KURT, astronomer; b. Lyck, Germany, Aug. 24, 1866; s. Hermann Karl and Julie (Krahnefeld) L.; grad. Kgl. Human. Gymnasium, Lyck, 1886; student U. of Koenigsberg, 1886-87, U. of Berlin, 1887-91, A.M., Ph.D., 1891; asst. in Royal Obs. of Berlin, 1892-93; m. Luise Moshagen, Aug. 25, 1896. Docent, reader, asst. and asso. in astronomy, U. of Chicago, 1893-97, instr., 1897-1901, asst. prof., 1901-08, asso. prof., since 1908. Mem. Astronomische Gesellschaft (Leipzig), Astron. and Astrophys. Soc. America, Am. Math. Soc.; fellow A.A.A.S. Home: 5611 Kenwood Av., Chicago. Died March 25, 1944.

LAVINDER, CLAUDE HERVEY, physician; b. Lynchburg, Va., July 24, 1872; s. Nathan Hervey and Ella Chambers (Hamner) L.; Randolph-Mason Coll., Ashland, Va., 1891, 92; M.D., U. of Va., 1895; m. Frances Moore Fair, 1899. Entered U.S. Pub. Health Service as asst. surgeon, 1897, retired as medical dir., 1938. Engaged in hospital, quarantine, epidemic and spl. work; has devoted much time to investigating pellagra. Lecturer on public health and sanitary science, Post-Grad. Med. Sch., N.Y. City, part of sessions 1914-15, 1915-16; was in charge of Hosp. Div. of P.H.S. and supervising all of P.H.S. work in furnishing medical care and treatment to disabled veterans, World War, 1920-22. Fellow American College Surgeons; mem. A.M.A., Assn. Mil. Surgeons (pres. 1928-29), Nat. Assn. Study Pellagra (pres. 1912), Ga. Med. Soc. (hon.), Phi Beta Kappa, Beta Theta Pi. Episcopalian. Mason. Translated and edited (with Dr. J.W. Babcock), Pellagra (by Marie), 1910. Author: Epidemiologic Studies of Poliomyelitis in New York City and the Northeastern United States during the year 1916 (with A.W. Freeman and W.H. Frost), 1918. Contbr. numerous articles concerning pellagra and other med. topics. Home: 139 St. John's Pl., Brooklyn NY

LAVIS, FRED, cons. engineer; b. Torquay Devon, Eng., Jan. 8, 1871; ed. St. Luke's Sch., Torquay; m. Blanche Biddle, Dec. 22, 1902; 1 son, Fred. Came to U.S., 1887, naturalized citizen, 1904. Cons. engr., specialist in transportation, also in ry. and highway economics, location and constrn., N.Y. City, since 1903; pres. Internat. Rys. of Central America, hdqrs. N.Y. City, 1928-31; dir. Chesapeake & Potomac Telephone Cos. of Washington. Trustee Village of Scarsdale, N.Y., 1915-17, mayor, 1931-33; supervisor Town of Scarsdale, 1916-17. Cons. engr. Ministry of Pub. Works, Venezuela, 1938-44. Mem. Highway Research Bd., Am. Soc. C.E., Am. Ry. Engring. Assn.; Pan-Am. Soc. N.Y. (council), Instn. of Civil Engrs. (Great Britain), The Pilgrims. Republican. Club: Union League. Author: Railroad Location Surveys and Estimates, 1906; Building the Rapid Transit System of New York City, 1915; Instructions to Locating Engineers and Field Parties, 1916; Railroad Estimates, 1917. Contbr. papers on ry. constrn. Home: Scarsdale Lodge, Scarsdale, N.Y. Office: 30 Broad St., New York NY

LAW, JAMES, veterinarian; b. Edinburgh, Scotland, Feb. 13, 1838; ed. burgh schs., Dunbar; vet. and med. schs., Edinburgh; l'École Veterinaire, Alfort, Paris; l'École Veterinaire, Lyons, France; grad. Highland and Agrl. Soc. Vet. Bd., 1857 (V.S.); Royal Coll. of Veterinary Surgeons (M.R.C.V.S., 1863; F.R.C.V.S., 1870). Prof. anatomy and materia medica Edinburgh New Vet. Coll., 1860-65; prof. anatomy Albert Vet. Coll., London, 1865-67; prof. veterinary science, Cornell, 1868-96; dir. and dean, 1896-1908, emeritus, 1908—, N.Y. State Vet. Coll. (Cornell U.). Consulting veterinarian to the N.Y. State Agrl. Soc., 1869-96; chmn. U.S. Treasury cattle commn., 1882-83; field chief of Bur. of Animal Industry for extinction of cattle lung plague in Ill. and N.Y., 1887-88. Author: General and Descriptive Anatomy of Domestic Animals; Farmers' Veterinary Adviser; Text Book of Veterinary Medicine, 5 vols. Address: Ithaca, N.Y. Died May 10, 1921.

LAWALL, CHARLES ELMER, engineer; b. Catasauqua, Pa., Nov. 21, 1891; s. Charles Elmer and Maria (Thomas) L.; E.M., Lehigh U., 1914, M.S., 1921, LL.D., 1939; LL.D., Waynesburg Coll., 1939; Doctor of Science, Morris Harvey College, 1950; m. Marjorie Berger, April 29, 1920; 1 son, Charles Elmer. Testing engr. Pittsburgh Testing Labs., 1914; chemist N.J. Zinc Co., Palmerton, Pa., 1915-16; mining engr. Peal Peacock & Kerr, St. Benedict, Pa., 1916-17; metallurgy dept. Gen. Motors Co., Detroit, 1917; mining engineer Bethlehem Steel Co., 1917-18, research engr., 1919-21; instructor Geology Department, Lehigh University, 1921; became assistant professor West Virginia Univ., School of Mines, 1921, later prof. and dir. to 1938; acting pres. W.Va. U., 1938-39, pres., 1939-45; engr. coal properties, Chesapeake & Ohio Ry. Co., Huntington, 1945-47, asst. v.p., 1947-56, v.p., 1956-58. Chief engineer and vice president Western Pocahontas Corp., Huntington, 1956; coal consultant, 1958-73. Member executive committee Engineers Council for Professional Development, 1949; chairman mining development committee Bituminous Coal Research, Incorporated, 1948-60; regional adviser, Engineering, Science and Management War Training Program: expert cons., Army Specialized Training Program; civilian member Selection Committee of Navy V-12 College Training Program. Served in U.S.A., France, 1918-19. Recipient Bituminous Coal Research award, 1957; Mineral Industry Edn. award, Am. Inst. M.E., 1958; Percy Nicholls Award, 1962. Member Veteran Council, West Virginia Department of Vets. Affairs; trustee Waynesburg Coll. Mem. Am. Inst. Mining and Metall. Engrs. (chmn. coal div., 1940); W.Va. Coal Mining Inst. (sec.-treas. 1930-39; president 1929), Huntington Chamber of Commerce, American Legion (state historian, 1944), Vets. Foreign Wars, Newcomen Soc. (chmn. W.Va. com.), A.I.M.E. (chmn. Appalachian sect., 1948), W.Va. Soc. Profl. Engr. (pres., 1948), Am. Soc. Engring. Edn., Mining and Metal. Soc. America, W. Va. Acad. Sci., Soc. Mining Engrs. (vice president 1958-61), Scabbard and Blade, Phi Beta Kappa, Sigma Gamma Epsilon, Sigma Xi, Tau Beta Pi. Presbyn. Clubs: Mining (N.Y.C.); Engrs., Kiwanis, Guyandotte, Guyan Golf and Country (Huntington). Contbr. numerous articles on coal mining to tech. jours., bulletins, etc. Home: Huntington WV Died Apr. 1973.

LA WALL, CHARLES HERBERT, pharmacist, chemist; b. Allentown, Pa., May 7, 1871; s. John Jacob and Emma Jane (Boas) La Wall; grad. coll. prep. course, State Normal Sch., Bloomsburg, Pa., 1888; Ph.G., Phila. Coll. Pharmacy, 1893, Ph.M., 1905; hon. Phar.D., U. of Pittsburgh, 1919; Sc.D., Susquehanna U., 1920; m. Millicent Saxon Renshaw, June 5, 1907. Commercial chemist, 1894-1903; instr. pharmacy, 1900-06, asso. prof., 1906-18, prof. of theory and practice of pharmacy, and dean, 1918—, Phila. Coll. Pharmacy and Science. Chemist Pa. Dept. Agr., Bur. of Food, 1904—, Pa. State Pharm. Exam. Bd., 1905-12, 1914—, Pa. Health Dept., 1906-18; food inspection chemist, U.S. Dept. Agr., 1907-12; sec., 1910-18, chmn., 1918-20, sec., 1920—, U.S. Pharmacopoeia Revision Com. (chmn. sub-com. inorganic chemicals, 1910; chmn. sub-com. reagents, 1920; chmn. on Volatile oils, 1931); mem. revision com. Nat. Formulary, 1906-29; mem. advisory com. med. supplies, War Industries Bd., World War, 1918-19; pres. Am. Assn. Coll. Pharmacy, 1923. Mem. Internat. com. health and council League of Nations for Studying Opium Assay, 1931—. Republican. Mem. Am. Pharm. Assn. (pres. 1919), Pa. Pharm. Assn. (pres. 1911). Mason. Author: Four Thousand Years of Pharmacy, 1927. Joint Author: Leffmann and La Wall's Organic Chemistry, 1905. Collaborating editor U.S. Dispensatory, 1917—, Remington Practice Pharmacy, 1918—. Recipient of Remington medal for distinguished work in pharmacy, 1928. Home: Philadelphia, Pa. Died Dec. 7, 1937.

LAWLESS, THEODORE KENNETH, dermatologist; b. Thibodeaux, La., Dec. 6, 1893; s. Rev. Alfred and Harriet (Dunn) L.; A.B., Talladega (Ala.) Coll., 1914, D.Sc., 1945; grad. student U. Kan., 1917; M.D., Northwestern U., 1919, M.S., 1920; fellow Vanderbilt Clinic, Columbia, 1920-21, Harvard, Path. Inst. Freiburg, Germany, 1922-23; LL.D., Bethune-Cookman Coll., 1952. Fellow dermatology, syphilology Mass. Gen. Hosp., 1920-21, St. Louis Hosp., Paris, France, 1921-22, Kaiser Joseph Hosp., Vienna, Austria, also clinics Switzerland, other European med. centers; practice of medicine, Chgo., 1924-71; fellow, instr., med. sch. Northwestern U., 1924-41; cons. dermatology, syphilology Geneva Community Hosp.; sr. attending physician dept. dermatology and syphilology Provident Hosp. Chgo.; pres. Service Fed. Saving & Loan Assn., Chgo., 1951, Gentilly Garden Apts., New Orleans, 1950-71, 4213 S. Mich. Corp., 1946. Mem. Prison Welfare Com. Cook Co.; Chgo. Bd. of Health; adv. bd. Chgo. Civil Liberties Com. Chmn. bd. trustees Talladega Coll.; trustee Fisk U., Roosevelt U., Dillard U., Houston-Tillotson Coll. Rocky Mt. Coll., Ada S. McKinely Settlement House, Chgo.; chmn. budget com. Board of Home Missions of the Congregational-Christian Churches. Consultant United States Chemical Warfare Bd., adv. com. venereal diseases, World War II. Recipient Harmon award for outstanding work in medicine, 1929; Am. Mus. Festival award, 1949; award for distinguished service to community Chgo. Negro C. of C., 1952; Spingarn medal N.A.A.C.P., 1954. Diplomate Am. Bd. Dermatology and Syphilology. Mem. A.M.A., Nat., Ill., Chgo. med. socs., Chgo. Acad. Sci., Internat. Congress Dermatology, A.A.A.S., Met. Dermatol. Soc. (1st pres.), Am. Missionary Assn., Alumni Assn. U. Kan., Art Inst. Chgo., Nat. Geog. Soc. Conglist. Home: Chicago IL Died May 1, 1971; buried Mount Olivet Cemetery, New Orleans LA

LAWRANCE, CHARLES LANIER, aircraft engr.; born Lenox, Mass., Sept. 30, 1882; s. Francis Cooper and Sarah Eggleston (Lanier) L.; A.B., Yale, 1905, hon. A.M., 1927; grad. École des Beaux Arts, Paris, 3 yrs.; hon. D.Sc., Tufts, 1928; hon. A.M., Harvard, 1929; m. Emily M. G. Dix, 1910; children—Emily, Margaret, Francis Cooper. Engaged in engineering since 1915, with special interest in development of aircraft engines; founder, 1917 and pres. until 1923, Lawrance Aero Engine Corp., N.Y. City; corp. merged with Wright Aeronautical Corp., 1923, pres., 1925-28, v.p., 1928-30; organized Lawrance Engineering & Research Corp., pres. and chief engr. until 1944; chmn. bd. of dirs. and dir. of engine research, 1944-46; now chief engineer and chmn. of board, Power Industries, Inc., N.Y. City; pres. C. L. Lawrance Corp. (realty); dir. and pres. Nitralloy Corp. Ensign N.Y. Naval Militia, 1916-17; assigned by Navy Dept. to aeronautical research, World War I. Fellow Royal Aeronautical Soc., Eng.; fellow Inst. of Aeronautical Sciences (pres. 1934-35); mem. Society Automotive Engrs., Aeronautical Chamber Commerce of America (pres. 1931-32), Sons of the Revolution, Society of the Cincinnati. Decorated Chevalier Legion of Honor (France). Awarded Collier trophy, 1928. Pres. Emergency Shelter, N.Y. City. Republican. Episcopalian. Clubs: Yale, Brook. Home: 151 E. 63d St., N.Y. City 21; and East Islip, L.I., N.Y. Office: Power Industries, 22 E. 42d St., N.Y. City 17. Died June 24, 1950; buried Locust Valley Cemetery.

LAWRENCE, CHARLES KENNEDY, engineer; b. Washington, Pa., May 19, 1856; s. James Kennedy and Eleanor (Isett) L.; ed. Western U. of Pa. (now U. of Pittsburgh); m. Elizabeth Wolf, 1880; children—Frank Ellmaker, Charles Kennedy, Virginia, James Kennedy, Elizabeth. Asst. engr. and div. engr., Pa. R.R., 1880-87; engr., maintenance of way, St.P., M&M. Ry., 1887; chief engr., gen. supt. lines G.N. Ry., 1888-91; asst. chief engr., Carnegie Steel Co., 1897-99; engr. of constrn., Central of Ga. Ry., 1899-1904; engr. electric zone, N.Y. C.&H.R. R.R., 1904-05; chief engr., Central of Ga. Ry., 1906-June 1, 1926 (retired). Home: 3303 Abercorn St., Savannah, Ga. Died Sep. 12, 1942.

LAWRENCE, ERNEST ORLANDO, physicist; b. Canton, S.D., Aug. 8, 1901; s. Carl Gustavus and Gunda (Jacobson) L.; student St. Olaf Coll., Northfield, Minn., 1918-19, A.B., U. of S.D., 1922; A.M., U. of Minn., 1923; student U. of Chicago, 1923-24; Ph.D., Yale, 1925; Sc.D., U. of S.D., 1936; Princeton, Yale, Stevens Inst. Tech., 1937, Harvard, U. of Chicago, Rutgers U., 1941. McGill U., Montreal, Can., 1946; LL.D., U. of Mich., 1938, U. of Pa. 1942 Sc.D., Univ. B.C., 1947, U. So. Cal., 1949, University San Francisco, 1949; LL.D., U. Glasgow, 1951; m. Mary Kimberly Blumer, 1932; children—John Eric, Margaret Bradley, Mark Kimberly, Robert Don, Barbara Hundale, Susan. Nat. Research fellow, Yale University, 1925-27, assistant professor physics, 1927-28; associate professor physics, U. of Calif., 1928-30, prof., 1930—, dir. Radiation Lab., 1936—. Awarded Elliott Cresson medal, Franklin Inst., 1937; Research Corp. prize and plague, 1937; Comstock prize, Nat. Acad. Sciences, 1937; Hughes medal, Royal Soc. (Eng.), 1937; Nobel prize in physics, 1939; Duddell medal, The Phys. Soc., 1940; William K. Dunn award, American Legion, 1940; Holley Medal, American Society of Mechanical Engineers, 1942; Medal for Merit, 1946; Medal of Trasenster, 1947; Officier de la Legion d'Honneur, 1948; Faraday Medal, 1952; Annual award Am. Cancer Society, 1954. Board Foreign Scholarships, 1947. Mem. Solvay Conf., Brussels, 1933; mem. (hon.) U.S.S.R. Acad. Scis., 1943, Royal Swedish Acad. Scis., 1952, Royal Irish Acad., 1948. Mem. bd. of trustees, Carnegie Institution of Washington, 1944. Fellow American Physical Society, A.A.A.S., American Acad. of Arts and Sciences; Hon. Fellow Royal Soc. of Edinburgh, The Phys. Soc., Indian Acad. Sci.; mem.

Nat. Acad. Scis., Am. Philos. Soc., Phi Beta Kappa Sigma Xi, Gamma Alpha. Contbr. to Proc. Nat. Acad. Scis., Physical Review. Research in nuclear physics; invented cyclotron (using this, made researches into structure of atom, made transmutation of certain elements, produced artificial radioactivity), 1931; used radiation in study of problems in biology and medicine; made possible 1st extensive clin. use of neutron for cancer-therapy, prodn. of radio-phosphorus and other radio-isotopes for med. use, prodn. of radioiodine for 1st therapeutic use in successful treatment of hyperthyroidism; during World War II, instrumental in isolating uranium 235 (used in atomic bomb). Died Palo Alto, Calif., Aug. 27, 1958.

LAWRENCE, GEORGE NEWBOLD, ornithologist, wholesale druggist; b. N.Y.C., Oct. 20, 1806; s. John Burling and Hannah (Newbold) L; m. Mary Ann Newbold, 1834. Became interested in study of birds, circa 1820, collected some 8,000 stuffed birds over the years (collection later became property of Am. Mus. of Natural History); entered father's wholesale drug firm, N.Y.C., 1822, later became partner, then head of firm, 1835; devoted later years to complete study of ornithology; became interested in neotropical birds, circa 1858, became expert on birds of W.I. and Central Am.; a founder, hon. mem. Am. Ornithologists' Union; hon. mem. Zool. Soc. of London, Brit. Ornithologists' Union, others; a founder Coll. of Pharmacy of City of N.Y. Author: (with Spencer F. Baird, John Cassin) report of N.Am. birds published in vol. IX of Reports of Explorations to Ascertain the. . .Route for a Railroad from the Mississippi River to the Pacific Ocean, 1858. Died N.Y.C., Jan. 17, 1895.

LAWRENCE, RICHARD SMITH, inventor, mfr.; b. Chester, Va., Nov. 22, 1817; s. Richard and Susan (Smith) L.; m. Mary Ann Finney, May 22, 1842, 1 child. With N. Kendall & Co., gun-makers, Windsor, Vt., 1838, in charge of mfg. process, 1838-42; opened gunshop (with Kendall), Windsor, 1843; obtained U.S. contract for 10,000 rifles (with aid of S. E. Robbins), 1844, formed new co. Robbins, Kendall & Lawrence, Windsor, sold out to his partners, 1847; devised barrel-drilling and rifling machines, invented split pulley; introduced practice of lubricating bullets with tallow (led to eventual prodn. of repeating rifle), 1850; contracted to supply all machinery for Enfield Armory (Eng.) and for Brit. Enfield rifles, 1851; contracted to make Sharps carbines and rifles, 1852, went bankrupt before completion of contract because of unsuccessful attempt to make railroads cars in 1850; supt. Sharps Rifle Co., 1856-72; mem. water bd., bd. aldermen, fire bd. of Hartford, Conn. Died Hartford, Mar. 10, 1892.

LAWRENCE, ROBERT H., JR., astronaut; b. Chgo., 1935; s. Robert H. and Gwendolyn Lawrence; B.S. in Chemistry, Bradley U., 1956; Ph.D., Ohio State U., 1965; m. Barbara H. Cress, 1957; 1 son, Tracey. Joined USAF, 1956, advanced through grades to maj., 1967; assigned Pilot Instrn. Sch., Craig AFB, Ala., 1957, then USAF base, Furstenfeldbruck, W. Germany; grad. Aerospace Research Pilot Sch., Edwards AFB, Cal., 1967; astronaut Manned Space Program, NASA, 1967—. Home: 854 E. 52d St., Chgo. Died Dec. 8, 1967. *

LAWRENCE, WILLIAM HEREFORD, horticulturist; b. Lake City, Ia., Feb. 3, 1877; s. George Washington and Vesta (Easton) L.; B.S., S.D. State Coll. Agr. and Mechanic Arts, 1899; B.A., M.S., State Coll. of Wash., Pullman, 1902; Cornell U., 1906-7; m. Edith Florence MacDermott, of Meadville, Pa., June 8, 1908. Asst. in botany and agr., S.D. State Coll., 1897-9; asst. in botany and entomology, 1901, instr., 1902, instr. botany and asst. at Expt. Sta., 1903-6, asst. prof. plant pathology, 1906-7, supt. Western Wash. Expt. Sta. and plant pathologist State Expt. Sta., 1907-11, all State Coll. of Wash.; plant pathologist and horticulturist, Hood River Apple Growers' Assn., 1911-13; prof. horticulture and horticulturist, U. of Ariz., 1913-15; prof. horticulture, U. of Mo., 1915-18; capt., Sn. Corps U.S.A., chief ednl. officer, Reconstruction Sch. U.S.A. Gen. Hosp. 21, Denver, Colo., 1918—. Mem. Sigma Xi (Alpha Chapter, Cornell). Presbyn. Author: Apple Growing, 1911, also 22 expt. sta. bulls. Address: 1454 Williams St., Denver CO

LAWRIE, RITCHIE, JR., engr.; b. Edinburgh, Scotland, Oct. 7, 1890; s. Ritchie and Lida (McDowell) L. (parents Am. citizens); brought to U.S., 1890; B.S., Carnegie Inst. Tech., Pittsburgh, Pa., 1911; m. Helen Harriet Lowther, Mar. 7, 1914; 1 dau., Frances (Mrs. John McAllister Geisel). Asst. to gen. supt. of constrn., Thompson-Starrett Co., Chicago, 1911-17; dir. housing bur., Pa. State Chamber of Commerce, Harrisburg, 1919-21; co-partner Lawrie & Green, archtl. offices, Harrisburg, Pa., 1921—. Dir. Central Trust Co., Bowman's Dept. Store, Inc.; pres. N. Third St. Corp.; dir. Harrisburg Hotel Co., Central Trust Capital Bank. Served as 1st lt. Ordnance Dept., U.S. Army, 1917-19. Dir. Tri-County Crippled Children's Assn., State Soc. for Crippled Children; dir. United Fund of Greater Harrisburg; dir. Harrisburg Symphony Assn. (pres. 1956-57). Recipient Banjamin Rush award, Med. Society State Pa. Member of the Pa. Society Professional Engrs., A.I.A. (hon. mem. central Pa. chpt.), Nat. Soc. Profl. Engrs. (pres. 1946-47), Pa. State (treasurer, dir.) and Harrisburg Chamber Commerce, Am. Legion, Boy Scouts of Am., Y.M.C.A., Am. Soc. of Civil Engrs., Am. Soc. for Testing Materials. Republican. Presbyterian. Mason. Clubs: Rotary (dist. gov. 1933-34), Harrisburg Country. Home: 2311 N. Front St. Office: 321 N. Front St., Harrisburg, Pa. Died Dec. 29, 1962; buried Homewood Cemetery, Pitts.

LAWS, FRANK ARTHUR, elec. engr.; b. Brockton, Mass., May 28, 1867; s. Alfred and Clara Maria (Balch) L.; B.S. in E.E., Mass. Inst. Tech., 1889; Harvard, 1891-92; m. Harriet Patterson Burbank, Aug. 29, 1901. Asst. in physics, 1889-91, instr., 1891-93, instr. in elec. measurements, 1893-97, asst. prof., 1897-1902, asst. prof. elec. testing, 1902-06, asso. prof., 1906-13, prof. elec. engring., 1913-21, prof. elec. measurements, 1921—, Mass. Inst. Tech. Republican. Conglist. Author: Notes for Use in Standardizing, 1906; Electrical Measurements, 1917. Home: Brookline, Mass. Deceased.

LAWSON, ALFRED WILLIAM, pioneer aircraft editor and mfr.; b. London, Eng., Mar. 24, 1869; s. Robert Henry and Mary (Anderson) L. Interested in aeronautics since 1907; founded, edited and published Fly, first popular aeronautical mag., Phila., Nov. 1908; editor Aircraft, N.Y. City, 1910-14; aircraft mfr., Green Bay, Wis., 1917-18; elected 1st v.p. Aeronautical Mfrs. Assn. of America, 1912; designed 26-passenger airplane and built it in Milwaukee, 1919; flew with this plane carrying passengers to Chicago, Toledo, Cleveland, N.Y. City, Washington, D.C., and back to Milwaukee, Aug.-Nov. 1919 (carried a total of 400 passengers and proved commercial aviation could be profitable). Awarded first air mail contract, 1920; believed first mfr. to build airplane cabin free of truss wires, first to equip cabins with sleeping berths. After retiring from aircraft manufacture, time devoted to writing books and articles. Reg. contbr. to The Benefactor; now Supreme Head of The Humanity Benefactor Foundation, Inc., The Direct Credits Society, Inc., and the Des Moines Univ. of Lawsonomy, Inc. Organized and inc. Lawsonian Religion, 1948, apptd. First Knowlegian, Supreme Head; started construction 1000 Lawsonian churches, 1950. Author: Aircraft History (copyrighted), 1947; Lawsonian Religion, 1949. Address: care Humanity Benefactor Foundation, 600 Woodward Av., Detroit 26, Mich., and Des Moines Univ., Des Moines, Iowa. Died Nov. 29, 1954.

LAWSON, ANDREW COWPER, geologist; b. Anstruther, Scotland, July 25, 1861; s. William and Jessie (Kerr) L.; A.B., U. of Toronto, 1883, A.M., 1885; Ph.D., Johns Hopkins, 1888; D.Sc., U. of Toronto, 1923; LL.D., U. of Calif., 1935; D.Sc., Harvard, 1936; m. Ludovika von Jantsch, Nov. 30, 1889 (died Dec. 25, 1929); children—Andrew Werner, William Eric, Ludovico (dec.), James Albert (dec.); m. 2d Isabel R. Collins, Jan. 5, 1931. Geologist Geol. Survey of Can., 1882-90; prof. mineralogy and geology, 1890-1928, and dean Coll. of Mining, 1914-18, U. of Calif., retired 1928. Del. Geol. Congress, London, 1888, St. Petersburg, 1897, Toronto, 1913, Madrid, 1926; chmn. Calif. Earthquake Investigation Commn., 1906; chmn. geol. and geog., Nat. Research Council, 1923. Hayden medalist, Acad. of Natural Science, 1935. Fellow Geol. Soc. America (pres. 1926; Penrose medalist 1938), Soc. Econ. Geologists, A.A.A.S., American Acad. Arts and Sciences; pres. Seismol. Soc. America, 1909-10; mem. Nat. Acad. Sciences, Am. Philos. Soc.; hon. mem. Am. Assn. Petrol. Geologists, Sierra Club. Author of numerous geol. papers and monographs. Home: 1555 La Vereda, Berkeley, Cal. Died June 16, 1952.

LAWSON, GEORGE (MCLEAN), univ. prof.; b. Middle Haddam, Conn., May 26, 1898; s. George Newton and Ida Louise (McLean) L.; student Bates Coll., Lewiston, Me., 1915-19; M.D., Yale, 1924; D.P.H., Harvard (fellow in bacteriology, Nat. Research Council, 1924-26; Rockefeller fellow in public health, 1932), 1933; m. Gladys Holmes, May 6, 1922; 1 son, David Herbert Otis. Interne and asst. resident, pediatrics, Yale, 1923-24; mem. commn. for the Study of Whooping Cough, Boston, 1924-28; bacteriologist, Mass. Gen. Hosp., 1927-29; instr., bacteriology, Harvard Med. Sch., 1927-29; prof. of bacteriology, Univ. of Louisville Med. Sch., 1929-32, prof. of public health and bacteriology, 1932-37; epidemiologist and vital statistician, Louisville Health Dept., 1932-37; prof. of preventive medicine and bacteriology, Univ. of Va. since 1937. Chmn. bd. health, Charlottesville and Albermarle County since 1940. Served as pvt., Inf., U.S. Army, 1918-19. Fellow Am. Public Health Assn. (mem. com. on whooping cough); mem. Soc. Am. Bacteriologists (sec. Va. br.), Soc. Pediatric Research, A.A.A.S., Va. Acad. Sci. (sec. bacteriology sect.), Albermarle County Med. Soc., Albemarle T.B. Assn. (bd. dirs.), Visiting Nurses Assn. (bd. dirs.); Alpha Omega Alpha, Delta Omega, Sigma Xi. Episcopalian. Author: Sect. on whooping cough, in "Diagnostic Procedures and Reagents" (with P. Kendrick, J. Miller), 2d. ed., 1945. Contbr. articles in field of bacteriology and communicable disease control in 42 publs. Home: Box 1113, Univ. Sta. Office: U. of Va. Medical Sch., Charlottesville, Va. Died Sept. 20, 1951.

LAWSON, LEONIDAS MERION, physician; b. Nicholas County, Ky., Sept. 10, 1812; s. Rev. Jeremiah and Hannah (Chancellor) L.; M.D., Transylvania Coll., Ky., 1838; studied in London, Eng., Paris, France, 1844-45; m. Louise Cailey; m. 2d, Eliza Robinson; 7 children including Louise. Practiced medicine, Mason County, Ky., until 1841; moved to Cincinnati, 1841; founder, publisher Western Lancet, 1842-55; editor Journal of Health, 1844; taught at Transylvania Coll., 1845-47; prof. materia medica, pathology Med. Coll. of Ohio, Cincinnati, 1847-53, prof. principles and practice medicine, 1853, prof. theory and practice medicine, 1860-64; gave 2 courses at Ky. Sch. of Medicine, Louisville, 1854-56. Author: Phthisis Pulmonalis (study of tuberculosis), 1861. Died Jan. 21, 1864.

LAWTON, WILLIAM HENRY, civ. and sanitary engr.; b. Newport, R.I., Apr. 14, 1853; ed. at public schools and Rogers High School; completed special course at Mass. Inst. of Technology, 1876; engaged in practice as engr.; for several yrs. asst. U.S. engr. at Nantucket, Mass.; 4 times elected st. commr. and city engr. of Newport; m. Dec. 4, 1889, Mary Johnson Bécar. Mem. Am. Soc. Civ. Engrs. Residence: 30 Powel Av. Business Address: 24 Bellevue Av., Newport, R.I.

LAY, JOHN LOUIS, inventor, b. Buffalo, N.Y., Jan. 14, 1832; s. John and Frances (Atkins) L. Commd. 2d asst. engr. U.S. Navy, 1861, 1st asst. engr., 1863; perfected torpedo, patented, 1865; worked as naval engr. for Peruvian Govt., 1865-67; invented self-propelled torpedo (could be directed from a ship), sold many to Russia and Turkey; lived in Europe, 1870-98. Died bankrupt in Bellevue Hosp., N.Y.C., Apr. 17, 1899.

LAZEAR, JESSE WILLIAM, physician; b. Balt., May 2, 1866; s. William and Charlotte (Pettigrew) L.; A.B., Johns Hopkins, 1889; M.D., Columbia, 1892; postgrad. Pasteur Inst., Paris, France; m. Mabel Houston, 1896, 2 children. Physician, Johns Hopkins Hosp., Balt., 1895; asst. surgeon in U.S. Army at Columbia Barracks, Quemados, Cuba, 1900; mem. Yellow Fever Commn. with Maj. Walter Reed, while in charge of mosquitos was bitten. Died helping to show that mosquitos were carriers of yellow fever, Quemados, Sept. 25, 1900.

LAZENBY, WILLIAM RANE, horticulturist, forester; b. Bellona, N.Y., Dec. 5, 1850; s. of Charles and Isabella L.; B. Agr., Cornell, 1874; M.Agr., Ia. Agrl. Coll., 1887; m. Harriet E. Akin, Dec. 15, 1896. Instr. and asst. prof. botany and horticulture, Cornell, 1874-81; prof. botany and horticulture, 1881-92, horticulture and forestry, 1892-1910, prof. forestry, 1910—, Ohio State U. Dir. Ohio Agrl. Expt. Sta., 1882-87, sec. Ohio Medical Univ., 1894-1914; lecturer before farmers' institutes, 1881-1906. Mem. Soc. Promotion Agrl. Science (sec., 1886-91, pres., 1895-97), Am. Pomol. Soc. (v.p., 1905—); pres. Columbus Hort. Soc., 1895—, Ohio Acad. Science, 1902-03, Ohio State Forestry Soc., 1904—; v.p. A.A.A.S., 1896. Mason (33 deg.). Forest engr., Biltmore Forest Sch., 1912. Home: Columbus, O. Deceased.

LEA, ISAAC, malacologist, naturalist; b. Wilmington, Del., Mar. 4, 1792; s. James and Elizabeth (Gibson) L.; LL.D. (hon.), Harvard, 1852; m. Frances Carey, 1821; children—Mathew Carey, Henry Charles, 1 dau. Became mem. Acad. Natural Sciences of Phila., 1815, pres., 1858-63; partner in father-in-law's publishing firm, 1821-51; concentrated on studies of fresh-water mollusks, became recognized authority in field, described more than 1800 species mollusks, recent and fossil; A.A.A.S., 1860; v.p. Am. Philos. Soc. Died Phila., Dec. 8, 1886.

LEA, MATHEW CAREY, chemist; b. Phila., Aug. 18, 1823; s. Isaac and Frances (Carey) L.; studied chemistry under James C. Booth; m. Elizabeth Jaudon, July 14, 1852; m. 2d, Eva Lovering. Pioneered use of photography in study of chemistry in U.S.; mem. Franklin Inst., Nat. Acad. Scis. Author: A Manual of Photography, 1868. Died Phila., Mar. 15, 1897.

LEACH, ALBERT ERNEST, chemist; b. Boston, Mass., Apr. 7, 1864; s. John Brooks and Mary Pamelia (Bellows) L.; S.B., Mass. Inst. Tech., 1886; m. Martha Hughes Thompson, Sept. 2, 1890. Expert in patent causes, 1887-92; asst. analyst, Mass. State Bd. of Health, 1892-99, chief analyst, 1899-1907, having charge of analysis of food and drugs for adulteration; chief U.S. Food and Drug Inspection Lab., Denver, 1907—. Swedenborgian. Author: Food Inspection and Analysis, 1904, 2d edit., 1909. Home: Denver, Colo. Died 1910.

LEACH, RALPH WALDO EMERSON, mechanical engr.; b. Watertown, Mass., June 6, 1874; s. Charles Henry and Mary Elizabeth (Barrett) L.; M.E., U. of Pa., 1898; m. Avis Spurr Standing, of Boston, Mass., Oct. 20, 1910 (dec.). With U. of Pa. and Schuylkill Elec. Ry. Co., 1895-96; treas. and dir. Phila. Constrn. Co., and Phila. Car Equipment Co., 1897; cashier Norfolk & Ocean View Railway & Hotel Co., 1899; testing engr. Am. Stoker Co., New York, 1900-02; research in manufacture of Portland cement treatment of ores, and dissociation of hydrogen in steam at high temperatures, in cement manufacture, 1902-03; experimental engr. Eldred Process Co., 1904; mgr. stoker dept. Westinghouse Machine Co., Pittsburgh, Pa., 1905-07; mgr. Castalia Portland Cement Co., 1908-09; N.E. mgr. Am. Engring. Co., 1910-19; gen. representative same co., Phila., since 1919. Mem. 1st Pa. Vols., Spanish-Am. War, 1898; with U.S. Fuel Administration, World War.

Mem. Am. Soc. Mech. Engrs., Nat. Electric Light Assn., Am. Electric Ry. Assn., Engineers' Club (Boston), Phi Gamma Delta. Republican. Christian Scientist. Mason (32 deg., K.T., Shriner). Clubs: Blue Room, Square & Compass (Boston); Vesper Country (Lynsboro, Mass.); Commercial (Montreal, Can.). Home: 32 Fletcher St., Winchester, Mass. Office: 470 Atlantic Av., Boston MA

LEAKE, JAMES PAYTON, M.D., pub. health officer; b. Sedalia, Mo., June 4, 1881; s. James Payton and Matilda Ann (Love) L.; grad. Smith Acad., St. Louis, Mo., 1900; A.B., Harvard, 1903, M.D., 1907; m. Mary D. Ray Quinn), Alice King (Mrs. Fred S. Lawless). In U.S. Pub. Health Service, 1909-45, retired 1945; in charge serums and vaccines, Hygienic Lab., 1913-22, in charge office indsl. hygiene and sanitation, 1930-33; in charge epidemiological sect., 1933-45. First secretary Basic Science Board, District of Columbia. Mem. A.M.A (vice chmn. council on pharmacy and chemistry), Am. Epidemiol. Soc. (president 1943), Am. Pub. Health Assn. (governing council), Assn. Mil. Surgeons of U.S. (vice president), Soc. Exptl. Biology and Medicine, N.Y. Acad. Medicine, Delta Upsilon. Improved smallpox preventions, and worked toward better controls in epidemiological studies. Baptist. Club: Cosmos. Home: Washington DC Died Feb. 21, 1973.

LEAMING, JACOB SPICER, farmer; b. nr. Madisonville, O., Apr. 2, 1815; s. Christopher and Margaret Leaming; m. Lydia Middlesworth, Mar. 1, 1839, 9 children. Through selective process developed Leaming corn (an earlier maturing, more productive strand), raised productivity to over 100 bushels per acre; corn won prizes at Paris Expn., 1878; went into seed business to handle demand. Died May 12, 1885.

LEARY, TIMOTHY, pathologist; b. Waltham, Mass., May 10, 1870; s. Timothy and Catharine (Rooney) L.; prep. edn. Waltham High Sch.; M.D., Harvard, 1895; hon. A.M., Tufts Coll., 1907; m. Adelaide Olga Cushing, Sept. 17, 1901; children—Olga Cushing, Deborah, Timothy. Resident asst. pathologist Boston City Hosp., 1895-97; asst. prof. pathology and bacteriology Tufts Coll. Med. and Dental Schs., 1897-1900, prof., 1900-29, now emeritus; med. examiner Suffolk County. Acting asst. surgeon Spanish-Am. War, 1898, serving in P.R. and Cuba and as comdg. officer U.S.A. Gen. Hosp., Ponce, P.R. Mem. Assn. Am. Pathologists and Bacteriologists, Internat. Assn. Geog. Pathology, A.A.A.S., A.M.A., Mass. Med. Soc., Soc. Am. Bacteriologists, Mass. Medico-Legal Soc. (pres. 1919-21), Mass. Soc. Examining Physicians (pres. 1926), Boston Med. Library Assn., Alpha Kappa. Catholic. Home: 44 Burroughs St. Office: 784 Massachusetts Av., Boston. Died Nov. 1954.

LEATHERS, WALLER S(MITH), preventive medicine and public health; b. near Charlottesville, Va., Dec. 4, 1874; s. James Addison and Bettie Elizabeth (Pace) L.; diploma of graduation in schs. of biology, geology, mineralogy and chemistry, Univ. of Va., 1892, M.D., 1895 (Alpha Omega Alpha); LL.D., U. of Miss., 1924; grad. work, Johns Hopkins, 1896, U. of Chicago, 5 summers, also Biol. Lab., L.I., summer, 1897, Marine Biol. Lab., Woods Hole, Mass., summer 1900, Harvard Med. Sch., summer 1906; LL.D., Tulane U., 1938; m. Ola Price, Nov. 14, 1906; 1 dau., Lucy Dell. Head of dept. of chemistry, Miller Sch. of Va., 1896-97; prof. biology U. of S.C., 1897-99; prof. biology, U. of Miss., 1899, prof. physiology, 1903, prof. physiology and hygiene, 1910-24; also organized and served as dean of Med. Sch., 1903-24; prof. preventive medicine and public health, Vanderbilt Univ., since 1924, asso. dean of Med. Sch., 1927, dean since 1928. Dir. pub. health of Miss., 1910; exec. officer State Bd. of Health, mem., 1917-24; mem. Miss. State Med. Assn. (pres. 1917); mem. State and Territorial Health Officers; mem. Nat. Bd. Med. Examiners (pres., 1930-34, 1936-42); mem. Tenn. Acad. of Science (pres., 1926-27). Mem. bd. scientific dirs., Internat. Health Div. of Rockefeller Foundation; mem. advisory com. on public health of Commonwealth Fund since 1920; mem. advisory health council of U.S. Pub. Health Service, 1931-35, 1937-39; mem. health and med. advisory com., American Red Cross, 1939. Mem. Acad. Tropical Medicine, 1939; Pub. Health Council of Tenn. Mem. Raven Society, University of Virginia, 1942. Chmn. Bd. of Examiners in Basic Sciences of Tenn., 1943. Fellow A.M.A. (mem. house of delegates, A.M.A., 1918-23), (sec. sect. on preventive and indsl. medicine and pub. health, 1920-23; chmn. 1923-24; council med. service and pub. relations, 1943). Fellow A.P.H.A. (chmn. com. on professional edn. since 1932; pres. 1940-41), A.A.A.S. (vice pres., 1928), Assn. of Am. Med. Colls. (pres., 1942-43), Soc. Med. Officers of Health (Eng.), Royal Sanitary Inst. (Eng.); mem. Am. Soc. of Tropical Medicine; Southern Med. Assn. (sec. sect. on pub. health, 1913-17; pres., 1922-28); Tenn. State Med. Assn.; Pub. Health Council of Tenn.; Sigma Chi, Alpha Omega Alpha, Phi Beta Kappa, Sigma Xi (charter mem.). Democrat. Methodist. Contbr. numerous scientific articles to med. jours. Home: 2004 20th Av. S. Office: Medical School, Vanderbilt University, Nashville, Tenn. Died Jan. 26, 1946.

LEAVENWORTH, FRANCIS PRESERVED, astronomer; b. Mt. Vernon, Ind., Sept. 3, 1858; s. Seth M. and Sarah (Nettleton) L.; A.B., Ind. U., 1880, A.M., 1888; m. Jennie Campbell, Oct. 11, 1883; children—Mary Louise, Francis Maury, Richard Ormond. On staff Cincinnati Obs., 1880-82; asst. McCormick Obs., U. of Va., 1882-87; dir. Haverford Coll. Obs., 1887-92; asst. prof. astronomy, 1892-97, prof., 1897-1927, U. of Minn. Author: Double Star Observations, 1888; proc. Haverford Coll. Observatory, 1891; Parallax Lal., 1196, 1892; Photographs of Eros for Solar Parallax, 1902. Home: Minneapolis, Minn. Died Nov. 12, 1929.

LEAVITT, CHARLES WELLFORD, civil and landscape engr.; b. Riverton, N.J., Mar. 13, 1871; s. Charles Wellford and Sarah (Allibone) L.; grad. Cheltenham (Pa.) Mil. Acad., 1888; m. Clara Gordon White, Sept. 26, 1899; children—Charles (dec.), Gordon, Kent, Charlotte, Clarissa (dec.), Dundas. Began as asst. engr. E. Jersey Water Co., later in charge constrn. Caldwell Ry., and engr. Town of Essex Fells, N.J.; served as engr. Palisades Inter-State Park Commn.; designed and supervised laying out of race tracks at Saratoga, Sheepshead Bay, Belmont Park, Toronto, Winnipeg, Montreal, etc., and constrn. of estates of William C. Whitney, Foxhall Keene, Daniel S. Lamont, Charles M. Schwab, etc.; made plans for property development for Mrs. Potter Palmer, at Sarasota, Fla.; estate of W. K. Jewett, Pasadena, Calif.; development towns of Grand Marie, Manitoba, Camden, N.J., etc.; cons. engr. Bd. of Water Supply, N.Y. City, and N. Jersey Dist. Water Commn., Newark, N.J. Pres. Am. Inst. Consulting Engrs. Republican. Episcopalian. Home: Hartsdale, N.Y. Died Apr. 22, 1928.

LEAVITT, ERASMUS DARWIN, mech. engr.; b. Lowell, Mas., Oct. 27, 1836; s. Erasmus Darwin and Almira (Fay) L.; common sch. edn.; (hon. D.Engring., Stevens Inst., 1884); m. Annie Elizabeth Pettit, June 5, 1867. Served 3 yrs.' apprenticeship in shops Lowell Mfg. Co. and 1 yr. with Corliss & Nightingale, Providence, R.I.; asst. foreman City Point Works, S. Boston, 1858-59, and had charge of building the engine for flagship Hartford; chief draughtsman Thurston, Gardner & Co., Providence, 1860-61; asst. engr. U.S.N., 1861-67; resigned, and resumed practice; splty. pumping and mining machinery; consulting engr. Calumet & Hecla Mining Co., 1874-1904. Has acted as consulting engr. for cities of Boston and Louisville, Henry R. Worthington, of New York, etc. Pres. Am. Soc. Mech. Engrs.; fellow Am. Acad. Arts and Sciences. Home: Cambridge, Mass. Died Mar. 11, 1916.

LEAVITT, FRANK MCDOWELL, inventor; b. Athens, O., Mar. 3, 1856; s. Rev. John McDowell (D.D.) and Bithia (Brooks) L.; M.E., Stevens Inst., 1875, E.D., 1921; m. Gertrude Goodsell, Nov. 8, 1893. Designer steam steering-gear, 1876; head draftsman, Bliss & Williams, Brooklyn, N.Y., 1877-81; master mechanic Tex.-Mexican Ry., 1881-82; mgr. Graydon & Denton Mfg. Co., Jersey City, N.J., 1882-84; became asst. supt. E. W. Bliss Co., Brooklyn, N.Y., 1884, later chief engr.; undertook introduction of the Whitehead torpedo into U.S.N., 1890, also installed plant of U.S. Projectile Co. for manufacture shells and other projectiles used in war; invented Bliss-Leavitt torpedo, in use by U.S. Navy, and possessing a range of 12,500 yards; inventor of an automatic can-making machine which practically revolutionized the can business; inventor of a press for producing all kinds of hollow pressed ware; etc. Home: Smithtown, L.I. Died Aug. 6, 1928.

LE BARON, JOHN FRANCIS (PATCH); name changed from Patch to Le Baron, 1865, by probate court; engineer; b. Boston, Mass., Sept. 28, 1847; s. John and Margaret Ann Gurley (Poor) Patch; grad. Lawrence Acad., 1866; engring. student 3 yrs. in office of J. Herbert Shedd, Boston and Providence; m. Mary Brown Kinsman; children—Ernest Thacher, Robert Wendell P., Hattie Marie; m. 2d, Mrs. Philomena Euphemia (Brown) Manucy; 1 dau., Joan Frances; m. 3d, Carrie Louise Lakeman, Apr. 29, 1901. Asst. engr. water supply and sewerage for various cities of N.E., 1866-70; asso. engr. City of Charlestown and Middlesex Co., Mass., 1872-76; chief engr. Fitchburg R.R., 1874-77; chief engr. St. John's & Indian River R.R., Fla., 1878-79; asst. engr. U.S.A. and U.S. deputy surveyor, staff of Maj. Gen. Q. A. Gilmore, 1880-83, and Brig. Gen. J. A. Barlow, 1890; in charge Nicaragua Canal surveys and constrn., 1887-90; mem. bd. consulting engrs. Nicaragua Canal, 1888; mem. Maritime Canal Co. of Nicaragua and Nicaragua Govt. Joint Commn., 1889; consulting engr., Jacksonville, Fla., and Cleveland, O., 1891-98; raised Co. L, 10th U.S. Vol. Inf., for Spanish-Am. War, 1898; chief engr. Am. Honduras Co., 1898-1901; consulting engr. New Orleans & Gulf Ry. & Navigation Co., 1903-04; chief and consulting engr. Sumas Development & Reclamation Co., 1908-09; cons. engr. to Bd. of Trade and City of New Westminster, B.C., also to many cos. Original discoverer of immense deposits of phosphate, kaolin and fullers earth in Florida, 1881. Mason. Home: Essex, Mass. Died 1935.

LE BLANC, THOMAS JOHN, (le-blongk), prof. preventive medicine; b. Cheboygan, Mich., June 28, 1894; s. Louis John and Mary (McGurn) Le B.; A.B., U. of Mich., 1916, M.S. in pub. health, 1919; D.Sc., Johns Hopkins, 1923; m. Anna Gurklis, June 11, 1927; 1 dau., Diana. Scientist Rockefeller Inst., 1919-20; field scientist Rockefeller Foundation, 1920-21, statistician U.S. Pub. Health Service, Washington, D.C., 1924-25; head of Inst. of Human Biology, Tohoku Imperial U., Sendai, Japan, 1927-28; asso. prof., 1925-34, and prof. and head dept. of preventive medicine, Coll. of Medicine, Cincinnati, O., since 1935. Served as constrn. officer, U.S. Naval Ry. Batteries, with A.E.F., during World War. Decorated medal by Mexico for work in yellow fever; received scroll from Japanese Emperor; received citation and Silver Star (U.S.) for service at Front in World War. Mem. Am. Pub. Health Assn., Am. Soc. for Tropical Medicine. Club: Cincinnati Power Squadron of U.S. Power Squadrons. Home: 409 Warren Av., Cincinnati, O. Died Sept. 9, 1948.

LECLAIR, TITUS G., engr. exec.; b. Superior, Wis., Aug. 26, 1899; B.S., Electrical Engineering, University of Idaho, D.Sc., 1951; married; children—Richard D., Hugh G., David V., Diane B. Test engr., General Electric Co., 1922-23; various positions with Commonwealth Edison Co., 1923-32; development engr., 1932-36; supervising development engr., 1936-42; staff asst., 1943-45; chief staff engr., Commonwealth Edison Co., 1945-48, asst. chief elec. engr., 1948-50, chief electrical engr., 1950-52; mgr. engring. Commonwealth Edison Co., 1952-54, engring. assistant to v.p., 1954-56, mgr. research and development, 1956-60; nuclear cons., 1960-64, mgr. nuclear power applications gen. atomic div. Gen. Dynamics (now Gulf Gen. Atomic), San Diego, 1960-68. Fellow I.E.E.E. (dir. 1941-45, v.p. 1946-48, pres. 1950-51); mem. Am. Nuclear Soc. (dir.), Engrs. Joint Council pres. 1952), Am. Soc. Engring. Edn., Ill. Engring. Coun. (dir. and p.p.), Western Soc. Engrs. (p.p.), Ill. and Nat. socs. profl. engineers, Sigma Nu, Eta Kappa Nu. Club: Union League. Author of numerous papers pub. in technical press and given before engring. socs. Inventor pilot wire relay schemes, high current conductors, automatic multicircuit printing ammeters and other devices used in the electrical industry. Home: La Jolla CA Died Mar. 26, 1968.

LE CLERC, J(OSEPH) ARTHUR, (le-klâr), chemist; b. Ware, Mass., 1873; s. John B. and Lucy (Chicoine) L.; B.Sc., Worcester Polytechnic Institute, 1895; Ph.D., University of Halle-Wittenberg, 1903; m. Emma V. Hall, 1895; married 2d, Yona Buchanan, 1937; m. 3d, Helen G. Davis (Helen Randle), 1943. On the staff of the United States Bureau of Chemistry, 1903-19, in charge of lab. of plant chemistry; chief chemist Miner-Hillard Milling Co., Wilkes-Barre, Pa., 1919-20; spl. trade commr. to Europe; spl. agent of Dept. of Commerce, specializing on grains and grain products, 1922-28; sr. chemist Bur. of Agrl. Chem. and Engring., U.S. Dept. of Agr., 1928-43; retired Mem. Internat. Jury of Awards, Paris Expn., 1900, St. Louis, 1904, San Francisco, 1915. Decorated Chevalier du Mérite Agricole, France, 1907. Mem. Am. Chem. Soc. (pres. Washington sect. 1912), Washington Acad. Sciences, Am. Soy bean Assn., Am. Inst. Chemists, Am. Assn. Cereal Chemists, Food Technologists. Translator: L'Industrie des Cyanures (by R. Robine and M. Lenglen), 1905. Home: Friendship Pl., Kingsley Lake, Starke, Fla. Died Nov. 16, 1956; buried Magnolia Cemetery, Varnville, S.C.

LECONTE, JOHN, physicist, coll. pres.; b. Liberty County, Ga., Dec. 4, 1818; s. Louis and Ann (Quarterman) LeC.; grad. Franklin Coll. (now U. Ga.), 1838; M.D., Coll. Physicians and Surgeons, N.Y.C., 1841; m. Eleanor Graham, June 20, 1841. Prof. physics and chemistry Franklin Coll., 1846-55; prof. physics U. So. Cal., 1856-69; became prof. physics U. Cal., 1869, also pres., 1869, 75-81. Author: (papers) Experiments Illustrating the Seat of Volition in the Alligator, 1845; On the Influence of Musical Sounds on the Flame of a Jet of Coal-gas, 1858; On Sound Shadows in Water, 1882; Physical Studies of Lake Tahoe, 1883, 84. Died probably Berkeley, Cal., Apr. 29, 1891.

LECONTE, JOHN LAWRENCE, entomologist; b. N.Y.C., May 13, 1825; s. John and Mary Anne (Lawrence) LeC.; grad. Mt. St. Mary's Coll., 1842; M.D., Coll. Physicians and Surgeons, N.Y.C., 1846; m. Helen Grier, Jan. 10, 1861. Investigated and published papers on entomology and zoogeography, 1846-61; surgeon of volunteers, M.C., U.S. Army, 1861-65, later lt. col., med. insp.; studied minerology, geology and entomology, 1865-83; chief clk. U.S. Mint, Phila., 1878-83; an incorporator Nat. Acad. Scis.; pres. A.A.A.S., 1874. Contbr. papers Coleoptera of Europe and North America to Annals of Lyceum of Natural History of N.Y., 1848, The Rhynchophora of America North of Mexico to Proceedings of Am. Philos. Soc., 1876, Classification of the Coleoptera of North America to Smithsonian Miscellaneous Collections, 1883. Died Phila., Nov. 15, 1883; buried Phila.

LE CONTE, JOSEPH, prof. geology and natural history Univ. of Calif.; b. Liberty Co., Ga., Feb. 26, 1823; grad. Franklin Coll., U. of Ga., 1841; A.M., 1845; Coll. of Phys. and Surg., New York, 1845; Harvard, B.S., 1851; LL.D., U. of Ga., 1879; Princeton, 1896; m. Caroline Elizabeth Nesbit, Jan. 14, 1847. During Civil war in Confederate service, in scientific dept., as chemist of med. laboratory and chemist of the nitre and mining operations. Author: Religion and Science (a course of Sunday lectures); Elements of Geology (text-book for universities); Sight, or Principles of Monocular and Binocular Vision; A Compend of Geology for High Schools; Evolution and Its Relation to Religious Thought; etc. Home: Berkeley, Calif. Died 1901.

LE CONTE, JOSEPH NISBET, (le-kont), mechanical engr.; b. Oakland, Calif., Feb. 7, 1870; s. Joseph and Caroline Elizabeth (Nisbet) L.; B.S., Univ. of California, 1891; M.M.E., Cornell Univ., 1892; LL.D., University of California, 1945; m. Helen Marion Gompertz, June 10, 1901 (died Aug. 26, 1924); children—Helen Malcolm, Joseph; m. 2d, Adelaide Elizabeth Graham, Feb. 16, 1929. Asst. in mechanics, U. of Calif., 1892-95, instr. in mech. engring., 1895-1903, asst. prof., 1903-12, prof. engring. mechanics, 1912-30, prof. of mech. engring., 1930-37, prof. emeritus since 1937. Collaborator with Yosemite Nat. Park Adv. Bd., 1943. Mem. Am. Soc. Mech. Engrs., Zeta Psi, Sigma Xi, Tau Beta Pi, Phi Beta Kappa. Republican. Clubs: Faculty (Berkeley, Calif.); Am. Alpine, Appalachian Mountain, Sierra. Author: Elementary Treatise on Mechanics of Machinery, 1902; Hydraulics, 1926. Contbr. over 40 tech. articles to mags. Made pioneer explorations in the high Sierra of Calif. between 1890 and 1910, including first ascents of 6 peaks between 13,000 and 14,500 feet elevation. Home: Box 1312, Carmel, Calif. Died Feb. 1, 1950.

LECOUNT, EDWIN RAYMOND, pathologist; b. Fond du Lac, Wis., Apr. 1, 1868; student Carroll Coll., Waukesha, Wis., 1887-88; M.D., Rush Med. Coll., 1892; grad. study Johns Hopkins Hosp., 1893-94, Pasteur Inst., Paris, 1896, Berlin, 1905. Prof. pathology, Rush Med. Coll., 1892—; attending pathologist, Cook County, Presbyn., St. Luke's, St. Elizabeth's and St. Anthony's hosps. Pres. Am. Assn. Pathologists and Bacteriologists, Assn. Cancer Research. Home: Chicago, Ill. Died 1935.

LEDERER, ERWIN REGINALD, chem. engr.; b. Vienna, Austria, May 21, 1882; s. Josef Ignatius and Berta (Pekarek) L.; Chem. E., U. of Heidelberg, 1904; Ph.D., U. of Vienna, 1905; M.E., Technol. Inst., Vienna, 1905; spl. grad. work New York U., 1921; children—Elizabeth, Louise. Came to U.S., 1912, naturalized, 1919. Chemist and asst. supt. for Vacuum Oil Co. in Rumania and Austria-Hungary, 1906-12; chemist Standard Oil Co. of N.J., 1912-13; chief chemist Atlantic Refining Co., 1914-16; gen. supt. Galena Signal Oil Co., 1917-19; mgr. Atlantic Gulf Oil Corp., 1920-22; v.p. La. Oil Refining Co., 1922-25; v.p. Tex. Pacific Coal & Oil Co., 1925-35, dir. since 1935; pres. Bradford (Pa.) Oil Refining Co., 1936-41; cons. engr. Sun Oil Co. since 1941. Fellow Inst. of Petroleum (London, Eng.); mem. Am. Chem. Soc., Am. Inst. Chem. Engrs., Am. Society Automotive Engrs., Am. Soc. for Testing Material, Am. Petroleum Inst., Natural Gasoline Assn. of America (ex-pres.). Episcopalian. Clubs: Bradford, Bradford Country, Valley Hunt. Contbr. of papers to tech. jours. and assns., co-author books on petroleum technology. Home: 633 Overhill Rd., Ardmore, Pa. Office: 1698 Walnut St., Philadelphia, Pa. Died May 6, 1943.

LEDERER, NORBERT LEWIS, ret. chem. engr., author; b. Vienna, Austria, Dec. 28, 1888; s. James and Cecile Weller (O'Brien) L.; parents U.S. citizens; student high school and coll., Melk (Austria), 1897-1905, U. Vienna, 1905-09, Sorbonne, Paris, 1912-13; M. Elsie Zeisler, April 30, 1914 (div.); m. 2d, Lillian Day, Nov. 1, 1946, 1 stepdau., Renee (Mrs. Hugh Snelson). Chemist Scheidemandel-Motard Werke, Berlin, 1909-12; mgr. Sté. Ane. d'Industrie Chimique, Paris, 1912-14; mgr. O. Murray & Co., London, 1914-17; with C.E., U.S. Army, AEF, 1917-19 (served at Peace Conf.); mgr. chem. dept. J. Aron & Co., N.Y.C., 1919-22; U.S. rep. Scheidemandel-Motard Werke, 1922-39, export mgr. M. Golodetz & Co., N.Y.C., 1940-49; sec. Victor M. Calderon Co., Inc., 1949-52. Chmn. bd. trustees Authors Club-Carnegie Fund, N.Y.C.; tournament dir. U.S. Chess Fedn. Democrat. Episcopalian. Club: Authors (treas.). Author: Tropical Fish and Their Care, 1934; (with Lillian Day) Murder in Time, 1935; Death Comes on Friday, 1936. Contbr. articles on chess, music and criminology to mags. Home: 18 West 86th St., N.Y.C. 24. Office: 99 Hudson St., N.Y.C. Died Nov. 1955.

LEDERLE, ERNST JOSEPH, chemist, sanitarian; b. Staten Island, N.Y., 1865; s. Joseph and Clara J. (Schmidt) L.; Ph.B., Columbia Sch. of Mines, 1886, Ph.D., 1895 (Sc.D., 1904); m. Margaret C. Taylor, June 22, 1895. Chemist New York Health Dept., 1899-1902; commr. of health, 1902-04; pres. and commissioner Dept. of Health of New York, 1910-14. Home: Stamford, Conn. Died Mar. 7, 1921.

LEDOUX, ALBERT REID, mining engr.; b. at Newport, Ky., Nov. 2, 1852; s. Rev. Louis P. and Katharine C. (Reid) L.; ed. Columbia Sch. of Mines, 1870-73; U. of Berlin, 1873-75; A.M., Ph.D., U. of Göttingen, 1875; (hon. M.S., U. of N.C., 1880; m. Annie Van Vorst Powers (died 1918); m. 2d, Mrs. Alice M. Baird, Aug. 26, 1920; father of Louis Vernon L. State chemist and mem. State Board of Health, N.C., 1876-80; since 1880 in practice as consulting engineer, metallurgist, assayer and chemist, and expert in chemistry and engring. cases; for 2 yrs. expert N.Y. Elec. Subway Commn.; receiver Harney Peak Tin Mining Co. 14 yrs.; v.p. Assurance Co. of America; consulting engr. Am. Bur. of Mines; v.p. of Chapultepec Land Co. Pres. Am. Inst. Mining Engrs., 1903. Home: Cornwall-on-Hudson, N.Y. Died Oct. 25, 1923.

LEDOUX, JOHN WALTER, hydraulic engr.; b. nr. St. Croix Falls, Wis., Aug. 28, 1860; s. John and Almina (Knox) L.; C.E. (with honors), Lehigh U., 1887; m. Laura A. Ueberroth, July 8, 1888. Consulting engr. for corps. and municipalities, 1927—; designed and built more than 100 water plants in U.S. and other countries, and many special works devices. Home: Swarthmore, Pa. Died Nov. 7, 1932.

LE DUC, WILLIAM GATES, U.S. commr. of agr.; b. Wilkesville, O., Mar. 29, 1823; s. Henry Savary L.; A.B., Kenyon Coll., 1848; admitted to bar, 1849; settled at St. Paul, Minn., July 1850; m. Mary E. Bronson, 1851. Commr. to World's Fair, New York, 1853; active promoter rys. and immigration; laid out W. St. Paul; projected co. which built Wabasha St. bridge, St. Paul (first to span Miss. River); removed to, and laid out Hastings, Minn., and engaged extensively in farming. Capt. to bvt. brig. gen. U.S. vols. in Civil War. Returned to Minn.; projected and in part constructed Hastings & Dak. Ry. U.S. commr. of agr., 1877-81; established tea-farm, Summerville, S.C., and introduced from foreign countries olives, tea, Japanese persimmons and other plants now acclimated in U.S.; organized what now are the Bur. of Animal Industry and the Div. of Forestry; in service Treasury dept. in N.C., 1890-95. Home: Hastings, Minn. Died Oct. 30, 1917.

LEE, CHARLES HAMILTON, hydraulic and sanitary engr.; b. Oakland, Cal., Feb. 1, 1883; s. Rev. Hamilton and Genevieve (Littlejohn) L.; B.S., U. Cal., 1905; m. Katherine Newhall, Jan. 17, 1911; 1 son, Charles Hamilton; m. 2d, Evelyn May Grundy, Oct. 1, 1921; children—Allan Eustace, Constance Evelyn. Hydrographer U.S. Geol. Survey, 1905-06; with engring. staff Los Angeles Aqueduct, 1906-12; in charge underground water investigations of Cal. State Conservation Commn., in So. Cal., 1912; pvt. practice, 1912-17; pres. State Water Commn. of Cal., Oct. 1, 1919-June 30, 1921; chief of Div. of Water Rights, Dept. of Pub. Works, Cal., July 1921-Dec. 1921; practiced as consulting engr., San Francisco, 1921—; sr. partner Lee & Praszker, cons. engrs., 1958—; dir. Pacific Hydrologic Lab. since 1929; chief Div. Water Supply and Sanitation, Dept. of Works, Golden Gate Internat. Expn., 1936-39. Lecturer in civil engring., U. Cal., 1923. Served with A.E.F. in France as 1st lt. and capt. of engrs.; with Water Supply Service on line of communications, 9 mos.; on active front 8 mos., serving with First Army during St. Mihiel and Argonne offensives. Engring. cons. on naval and military construction, World War II. Mem. Am. Water Works Assn., Am. Geophys. Union, Am. Soc. C.E. (awarded Norman Medal for special contribution to engring. sci. 1939), Kappa Sigma. Clubs: Sierra, Commonwealth of California, Engineers (San Francisco). Author: Divine Direction or Chaos? 1952. Home: 1988 San Antonio Rd., Berkeley 7, Cal. Office: 58 Sutter St., San Francisco 4. Died May 4, 1967.

LEE, DAVID B., san. engr.; b. Douglasville, Ga., Sept. 23, 1907; s. W. A. and Mollie (Smith) L.; B.S., U. Fla., 1932, D.Sc. (hon.), 1968; M.S., Harvard U., 1937; married Billie Rawls, July 28, 1939; children—David B., and Susan Rawls. With Fla. State Bd. of Health 1932-68, field engr., 1934-35, dist. engr., 1935-37, malaria control engr., 1938-41, dir. Bur. San. Engring., 1941-68; pres. David B. Smith Engrs., Inc., Gainesville, 1968. Loaned by U.S. Army to Inst. of Inter-Am. Affairs specialist in malaria control engring; spl. consultant U.S.P.H.S. on san. engring. problems 1948-68, engring. dir. res.; vis. lectr. U. Fla., 1959-60; permanent chairman Fla. com. on water supply and sewerage edn., U. Fla.; registered prof. engr. State of Fla. Adv. to U.S. World Health Orgn.; mem. delegation 2d World Health Assembly, Rome, 1949; conferred with A.E.C. on radioactive indsl. waste disposal; served on panel of environmental sanitation of the President's Commn. on Health Needs of the Nation, 1952; mem. Nat. Research Council's Commission on san. engineering and environment. Served as maj. San. Corps, Med. Dept., U.S. Army, 1942-45. Received Kenneth Allen award Fedn. Sewage Works Assns., 1948; award Fla. Engring. Soc. for exeptional service to engring. profession State of Fla., 1949; Man of Year award, Am. Soc. San. Engring., 1954; Centennial award U. Fla., 1953; Fuller award Am. Water Works Assn., 1954; Meritorious award Fla. Pub. Health Assn., 1964. One of Ten Top Men Yr., 1961, Am. Pub. Works Assn.; Gold Merit award notable achievement state govt. service Asso. Industries Fla., 1965; Charles Alvin Emerson medal meritorious service Water Pollution Control Federation, 1966. Fellow of the Fla. Engring. Society (secretary 1946-50, president 1952-53), Am. Pub. Health Association; member Nat. Assn. Sanitation (hon.), Nat. Soc. Profl. Engrs. (dir.), Fedn. Sewage and Indsl. Waste Assns. (pres. 1954-55) Conf. State San. Engrs. (chairman 1948-49), Am. Water Works Assn. (nat. dir. 1948-51; vice chmn. Fla. sect., 1957-58, chmn. 1958-59), Newcomen Soc. N.A. (mem. Fla. com.), Acad. Sanitary Engrs. Council Cons., Nat. Sanitation Found., Harvard Pub. Health Alumni Assn., Fla. Water and Sewage Works Operators Assn. (life), Fla. Pub. Health Assn. (pres. 1950-51), Fla. Anti-Mosquito Assn. (pres. 1946-47), Am. Soc. C.E., Fla. Pollution Assn. (pres. 1941-42, hon. mem. 1956), Nat. Swimming Pool Inst., Water Pollution Control Federation (honorary), Sigma Tau. Episcopalian (sr. warden). Club: Kiwanis (pres. 1953). Home: Jacksonville FL Died Oct. 31, 1968; buried Pensacola FL

LEE, EDWARD HERVEY, civil engr.; b. Dayton, O., Jan. 29, 1863; s. John Newton and Julia (Sheldon) L.; ed. Ohio U. and U. of Wooster (O.); m. Ruth Sheldon Brooke, 1916. Asst. engr., prin. asst. engr. and chief engr. with various ry. cos., including Nickel Plate, U.P., E.,J.&E., 1880-98; served as engr., chief engr. and v.p. C.&W.I. R.R., and Belt Railway of Chicago, beginning 1898, pres., 1926-31. Home: Chicago, Ill. Died Jan. 11, 1937.

LEE, FRANCIS D., architect; b. Charleston, S.C., 1826; grad. City Coll., Charleston, circa 1846; studied architecture in office of Edward C. Jones, Charleston. Became mem. archtl. firm Jones & Lee, Charleston, 1852; designed (with Jones) buildings including St. Luke's Ch. (1859), St. James Methodist Ch., remodeling of old Unitarian Ch., Planters & Mechanics Bank (all Charleston), also Ch. of Holy Cross, Statesburg, N.C.; served to maj., as mil. engr. Gen. Beauregard's staff, Confederate Army, during Civil War; worked on planning and bldg. fortifications in Charleston harbor and improving torpedo defense system; accepted invitation from Napoleon III to visit Paris, France to explain his engring. plans and inventions, after war, later traveled throughout Europe; organized archtl. firm Lee & Annan, St. Louis, 1867; designed (with Annan) works including Mchts. Exchange (1875), Roe, Gay, C. of C. bldgs. 3d Nat. Bank, Bedford Block, Post Grad. Med. Coll., Grand Av. Presbyn. Ch. (all St. Louis). Died 1885.

LEE, FREDERIC SCHILLER, physiologist; b. Canton, N.Y., June 16, 1859; s. late Rev. John Stebbins (pres. St. Lawrence U.) and Elmina (Bennett) L.; A.B., St. Lawrence U., 1878, A.M., 1881, LL.D., 1918; Ph.D., Johns Hopkins U., 1885; U. of Leipzig, under Ludwig, 1885-86; Sc.D., Columbia U., 1929; m. Laura Billings, June 5, 1901; children—Julia, Frederick Billings. Instr. biology, St. Lawrence U., 1886-87; instr. and asso. in physiology and histology, Bryn Mawr Coll., 1887-91; demonstrator physiology, 1891-95, adj. prof., 1895-1904, Dalton prof., 1904-20, research prof., 1920-28, prof., 1928—, Jesup lecturer, 1911, mem. Univ. Council, 1913-20, Columbia U. Cutter lecturer Harvard Med. School, 1918; Parker lecturer Union Theol. Sem., 1922. Consulting physiologist, 1917-19, senior physiologist with rank of senior surgeon in reserve corps, 1919-24, U.S. Public Health Service. An editor American Jour. Physiology, 1898-1914, Columiba U. Quarterly, 1900-20. Mem. bd. mgrs. N.Y. Bot. Garden, 1903-27, v.p. 1921-23, pres. 1923-27; trustee Columbia U. Press, 1907-20. Mem. N.Y. Commn. on Ventilation. Spl. mission to Europe to investigate industrial conditions for U.S. Pub. Health Service, 1918. Fellow A.A.A.S. (chmn. sect. K); pres. Soc. for Exptl. Biology and Medicine, 1908-10, Harvey Soc., 1912-14, Am. Physiol. Soc., 1917-19; chmn. Federation Am. Socs. for Exptl. Biology, 1917. Author: Physiology—Vital Processes in Health, in "In Sickness and in Health," 1896; Reproduction, in "An American Textbook of Physiology," 1896; The School of Medicine, in "A History of Columbia University," 1904; Fatigue, in "Harvey Lectures," 1906; The Human Machine in the Factory, in same, 1919; Scientific Features of Modern Medicine, 1911; Fatigue and Occupation, in "Diseases of Occupation and Vocational Hygiene," 1916; The Human Machine and Industrial Efficiency, 1918. Joint Author: Ventilation (The Report of the N.Y. State Commn. on Ventilation), 1923. Translator and Editor: General Physiology, An Outline of the Science of Life (by Max Verworn), 1899. Reviser and Editor: Lessons in Elementary Physiology (by T. H. Huxley), 1900; Harvey's Views on the Use of the Circulation of the Blood (by John G. Curtis), 1915. Home: New York, N.Y. Died Dec. 14, 1939.

LEE, JAMES PARIS, inventor; b. Hawick, Scotland, Aug. 9, 1831; s. George and Margaret (Paris) L.; emigrated to Canada, 1836; ed. Galt, Ont., Can.; m. Caroline Chrysler, 1852 (died 1888). Invented the Lee-Metford, Lee-Enfield, Lee-Straight Pull, and other magazine rifles. Address: Hartford, Conn. Died 1904.

LEE, JOHN CLIFFORD HODGES, army officer; b. Junction City, Kan., Aug. 1, 1887; s. Charles Fenlon and John Clifford (Hodges) L. (mother given her father's name); B.S., U.S. Mil. Acad., West Point, N.Y., 1909; student Army Engring. Sch., U.S. Army Staff Coll., France, 1918, Army War Coll., Washington, D.C., 1931-32, Army Indsl. Coll., 1932-33; hon. LL.D., Bristol University; Sc.D. (hon.), Des Moines College Osteopathy and Surgery; m. Sarah Ann Row, Sept. 24, 1917 (died Aug. 25, 1939); 1 son, Colonel John Clifford Hodges, Jr.; married 2d, Eve B. Ellis, Sept. 19, 1945 (dec. 1953). Commd. 2d lt. C.E., U.S. Army, 1909, advancing through ranks to lieut. general (temp.), 1944; permanent major general, 1945; served, Panama Canal, 1909-10; 3d Battalion Engrs., 1911-13; mil. survey of Guam, 1913-14, of Luzon, 1914-15, Ohio River improvement, 1915-17; on staff Gen. Leonard Wood, 1917-18, 1919-20; with 89th Div., A.E.F. in France and

Germany, 1918-19; Gen. Staff Corps (6th Corps Area and Philippine Dept.), 1920-23; in Office Chief of Engrs., 1923-26; dist. engr., Vicksburg, 1926-31; with Civic Works Authority, and dist. engr., Washington, D.C., 1934; mem. bd. engrs. for rivers and harbors, 1934-35; dist. engr. Phila., 1934-38; div. engr. N. Pacific Div., 1938-40; temp. duty, Air Corps, May-Aug., 1939; comd. San Francisco Port of Embarkation, Ft. Mason, Calif., 1940-41; comd. 2d Inf. Div., Nov. 1941-May 1942; comdg. Services of Supply and Communication Zone, E.T.O., May 1942-Jan. 1946; dep. theatre comdr., Jan. 1944; comdg. Mediterranean Theatre Operation, Jan. 1946-Sept. 1947; ret. at lt. gen. for disability, Dec. 31, 1947. Awarded Distinguished Serv. Medal (Army and Navy), Silver Star, Croix de Guerre; Grand Officer Legion of Honor; Knight Comdr. British Empire; also Belgian, Luxembourg and Italian decorations. Mem. Soc. Am. Mil. Engineers, Society of the Cincinnati, Scabbard and Blade. Episcopalian. Clubs: Army-Navy (Washington). Author: Manual for Topographers, 1915. Home: 182 Highland Rd., Southwood Hills. Address: Brotherhood of St. Andrew, 709 W. Market St., York, Pa. Died Aug. 30, 1958; buried Arlington Nat. Cemetery.

LEE, JORDAN G., JR., dean; b. Farmersville, La., Oct. 29, 1885; s. Henry Marshall and Emma Octavia (Lee) L.; B.S., La. State U., 1906, M.S., 1929; student U. of Mo., summer 1928, Ia. State Coll., 1930-31; m. Genevieve L. Barber, Sept. 6, 1909; children—Genevieve and Jordan Grey III. In charge livestock experiments, La. Expt. Station, 1906; organized and filled position with dept. of agr., Southwestern La. Inst., Lafayette, La., 1909-18; prof. and head vocational agr. div., La. State U., 1918-31, dean of agr., in charge expt. stations, agr. extension and resident teaching, since 1931. Major on governor's staff, 1916-20. Mem. nat. advisory com. on Inter-Am. Agrl. Edn., 1940-42; bd. dirs. Farm Credit Adminstr. Recipient of plaque for distinguished service to agr. in Ia. by Epsilon Sigma Phi, 1940; recd. plaque from U.S. Treasury for sale of U.S. Savs. Bonds, named Man of the Year in Agriculture for La. by Progressive Farmer, 1943. Mem. Assn. Southern Agricultural Workers (pres. 1949-50), Phi Kappa Phi, Omicron Delta Kappa, Alpha Zeta, Alpha Tau Alpha, Kappa Delta Phi, Kappa Sigma. Mason. Co-author: Farm Crops, 1925; Southern Field Crop Enterprises, 1928. Home: 439 State St. Office: Louisiana State U. and Agr. and Mech. Coll., Baton Rouge. Died Apr. 26, 1956; buried Greenoaks Meml. Park, Baton Rouge.

LEE, OLIVER JUSTIN, astronomer; b. Montevideo, Minn., Dec. 16, 1881; s. Timan H. and Christine J. (Foss) L.; B.A., Augsburg Sem., Mpls., 1901; B.A., U. Minn., 1907; M.Sc., U. Chgo., 1911, Ph.D., 1913; m. Florence Levina Baldwin, June 10, 1912. With Yerkes Obs., U. Chgo., 1907-26; head dept. astronomy, dir. Dearborn Obs., Northwestern U., 1929-47, emeritus prof. and dir., since 1947. Lectr. astronomy and navigation U. Cal. at Berkeley, since 1948. Recipient Distinguished Alumnus citation Augsburg Coll., 1961. Fellow A.A.A.S., Royal Astron. Soc. (London); mem. Am. Astronomical Soc., Sigma Xi. Republican. Conglist. Author: Measuring Our Universe, 1950. Published research papers treating of solar physics, stellar parallaxes and proper motions, radial velocities and physics of stars, solar parallax by observations of Eros, determinations of longitude, temperature changes during solar eclipse (up to 10,000 feet). Survey for spectral classification and distbn. 44,000 faint red stars. Address: 136 Fairview Pl., Santa Cruz, Cal. 95060. Died Jan. 13, 1964; buried Elk Columbarium, Santa Cruz.

LEE, RICHARD EDWIN, chemist; b. Phila., Pa., Sept. 9, 1876; s. Matthias and Sarah Elizabeth (Cook) L.; B.S., Mt. Union Coll., Ohio, 1898; Cornell U., 1901; M.Sc., Mt. Union Coll., 1902; A.M., Harvard U., 1906; Sc.D., New York Univ., 1910; Calif. Inst. of Tech., two semesters, 1931; m. Kathleen Florence Carter, June 7, 1901. Prof. chemistry, Mt. Union Coll., 1902-07; prof. and head dept. of chemistry, Allegheny Coll., 1907—; consulting chemist Nat. Bearing Metals Co., Hookless Fastener Co., Venango Mfg. Co. Lecturer on scientific subjects before chautauquas and teachers' assns. Mem. City Planning Commn. Author: Outline of Qualitative Chemical Analysis, 1910; A Text-Book of Experimental Chemistry, 1908; The Human Body—A Chemically Regulated Organism, 1912; A New System of Qualitative Chemical Analysis (with notes), 1915; Man, the Universe Builder, 1933; Backgrounds and Foundations of Modern Science, 1935; A Technique for Testing United Concepts in Science, 1935. Home: Meadville, Pa. Died 1936.

LEE, ROGER IRVING, physician; b. Peabody, Mass., Aug. 12, 1881; s. William Thomas and Mary Emily (Farnsworth) L.; B.A., Harvard, 1902, M.D., 1905, LL.D., 1954; m. Ella Lowell Lyman, Feb. 26, 1919; children—Roger Irving, Arthur Lyman, William Thomas. Practiced in Boston, 1905-14; vis. physician Mass. Gen. Hosp., 1912-23; Henry K. Oliver prof. hygiene Harvard, 1914-24; returned to practice medicine, 1924; cons. internal medicine. Overseer, Harvard, 1930-31, fellow, 1931-54. Commd. maj. Med. Res. Corps, Apr. 5, 1917; lt. col. M.C., U.S. Army, June 6, 1918; service in France with Base Hosp. 5, and cons. in medicine to 3d Corps AEF, 1917-19; hon. discharged, Feb. 10, 1919. Mem. Pub. Health Council State of Mass., 1921-34; sec. Mass. Tb Commn., 1910. Trustee Boston Symphony Orch., 1934-50. Fellow Royal Coll. Physicians, London, Eng.; mem. Assn. Am. Physicians, Soc. Clin. Investigation, A.C.P. (pres. 1941), Am. Acad. Arts and Scis., A.M.A. (chmn. bd. trustees, pres. 1945-46), Mass. Med. Soc. (pres. 1943-44). Clubs: Somerset, Harvard (Boston). Author: Health and Disease, 1917; The Fundamentals of Good Medical Care (with Lewis W. Jones); The Happy Life of a Doctor, 1956; A Doctor Speaks His Mind, 1958; Letters From Roger I. Lee, 1962. Home: 446 Walnut St., Brookline, Mass. 02146. Died Oct. 28, 1965.

LEE, WILLIAM STATES, engineer; b. Lancaster, S.C., Jan. 28, 1872; s. W. S. and Jennie Lind (Williamson) L.; C.E., The Citadel, Mil. Coll. of S.C., 1894; m. Mary Martin, 1901; children—W. States, Martha, Martin. Pres. and chief engr. Piedmont & Northern Ry. Co.; pres. and cons. engr. W. S. Lee Engring. Corp.; v.p. and chief engr. Duke Power Co., Wateree Power Co., Western Carolina Power Co., Catawba Power Co., Catawba Mfg. & Electric Power Co., Quebec Development Co., Am. Cyanamid Co. Trustee N.C. State Coll. Agr. and Engring., Duke Endowment. Presbyn. Mason. A pioneer in high tension hydroelectric power development; inventor of the Lee pin. Home: Charlotte, N.C. Died Mar. 24, 1934.

LEE, WILLIS THOMAS, geologist; b. Brooklyn, Pa., Dec. 24, 1864; s. John C. and Louesa J. (Garland) L.; Ph.B., Wesleyan U., Conn., 1894, M.S., 1898; fellow in geology, U. of Chicago, 1898-1900, Johns Hopkins, 1902-03; Ph.D., Johns Hopkins, 1912; m. Mary Ingham, 1900; children—Elizabeth Louesa, Dana Willis. Instr. science, R.I. Coll. Agr. and Mechanic Arts, Kingston, R.I., 1894-95; prof. geology and biology, Denver U., 1895-98; prin. high sch., Trinidad, Colo., 1900-02; with U.S. Geol. Survey, 1903—; head dept. geology, U. of Okla., 1919; lecturer in geology, Yale, 1919. Conglist. Died June 16, 1926.

LEECH, PAUL NICHOLAS, chemist; b. Oxford, O., Aug. 12, 1889; s. William David and Ann Cora (Druley) L.; A.B., Miami U., Oxford, O., 1910; Sc.M., U. of Chicago, 1911, Ph.D., 1913; Pharm.M. (hon.), Philadelphia Coll. of Pharmacy and Science, 1937; m. Esther O. Birch, Mar. 10, 1916; children—Esther Doris, Paul Nicholas. Research asst., U. of Chicago, 1911-13; chemist A.M.A., 1913-24; dir. Chem. Lab. same, 1924—, also dir. of scientific exhibit, 1922-30, and editor Ann. Repts.; sec. Council on Pharmacy and Chemistry, 1932—; dir. div. of foods, drugs and physical therapy, 1936—. First lt. Sanitary Corps, Med. Dept. U.S.A., 1918. Mem. Am. Chem. Soc. (chmn.) Chicago sect. 1926-27; chmn. div. med. chemistry 1934; councillor. Home: Winnetka, Ill. Died Jan. 14, 1941.

LEEDS, CHARLES TILESTON, consulting engr.; b. Newton, Mass., May 14, 1879; s. Benjamin Ingersoll and Martha (Knapp) Huse L.; grad. (rank 2d in class) U.S. Mil. Acad., 1903; B.S., Mass. Inst. Tech., 1906; m. Amy Lee Shapleigh, Jan. 12, 1905; children—Charles Tileston, Alice Shapleigh (Mrs. E. H. Hunting), Eleanor Huse (Mrs. W. E. Fenzi), Elizabeth Chandler (Mrs. D. B. Myers, Jr.). Commd. 2d lt. A.U.S., June 11, 1903, advancing to capt. Engr. Corps, Feb. 27, 1911; exploration, rd. constrn. and port development, Mindanao, P.I., 1903-04; spl. studies at Mass. Inst. of Tech., 1905-06; post engr. ofcr. and asst. q.m., Fort Bayard, N.M., 1906-08; asst. U.S. dist. engr., Los Angeles, Calif., 1908-09, U.S. district engr., Los Angeles, Calif., 1909-12; mem. Calif. Debris Commn., 1909-12; retired (physical disability incurred in line of duty), 1912; mem. Leeds & Barnard, cons. engrs., Los Angeles, 1912-30, Quinton, Code, Hill, Leeds & Barnard, 1930-40, Leeds, Hill, Barnard & Jewett, 1940-46; Leeds, Hill & Jewett 1946—; has served as cons. engr. on harbors, water ways, sea coast protection, water supply, several govtl. agencies in Cal.; cons. engr. on seacoast protection for State of Calif., 1931—; cons. engr., Los Angeles Dept. Water & Power 1947—; tech. adv. Internat. Boundary and Water Commn., 1952—. Active duty, U.S. Army, 1917-19, maj. Engr. Corps, 1918; lt. col. Engr. R.C., 1925-30. Mem. nat. state and local profl. socs. including: Am. Soc. C.E., Soc. Am. Mil. Engrs. Republican. Presbyn. Clubs: University, Engineers, (Los Angeles); Twilight (Pasadena); Newport Harbor Yacht. Home: 640 La Loma Rd., Pasadena, Cal. Office: 609 S. Grand Av., Los Angeles 17. Died Mar. 20, 1960; buried Mountain View Cemetery, Pasadena.

LEEDS, JOHN, mathematician, astronomer; b. Bay Hundred, Talbot County, Md., May 18, 1705; s. Edward and Ruth (Ball) L.; m. Rachel Harrison, Feb. 14, 1726, 3 children. Commr. justice of peace Talbot County, 1734; clk. Talbot County Ct., 1738-77; regular mem. commn. from Md. to mark off long-disputed Md.-Pa. boundary line, 1762; observed transit of Venus, obtained results published in Royal Soc. London's Philos. Transactions. . .for the Year 1769 (pub. 1770); treas. Eastern Shore dist., Md., 1766; justice Provincial Ct., 1766; naval officer Port of Pocomoke, 1766; surveyor gen. Md., 1766-circa 1775, after 1783-90. Died Wade's Point, Md., Mar. 1790.

LEEDS, MORRIS EVANS, mfr.; b. Phila., Mar. 6, 1869; s. Barclay R. and Mary (Maule) L.; ed. Westtown Boarding Sch., 1883-86; B.S., Haverford Coll., 1888, LL.D., 1946; studied U. of Berlin, 1892-93; Dr. of Engring., Brooklyn Polytechnic Inst., 1936; m. Hadassah J. Moore, June 10, 1926; children—Esther Hallett, Mary Maule. Pres. Leeds & Northrup Co., 1903-39; chmn. of bd. since 1939. Inventor of elec. and temperature measuring instruments. Mem. corp. and bd. mgrs. Haverford Coll. since 1909, pres., 1928-45; mem. Bd. of Public Edn. of Phila., 1931-49 (pres. 1938-48). Mem. Indsl. Adv. Bd. of NRA, 1933-35; mem. bus. adv. council Dept. of Commerce, 1933-39. Fellow Am. Inst. E.E., A.A.A.S.; mem. Am. Phys. Soc., Acad. Natural Sciences, Am. Soc. Steel Treating, Franklin Inst.; Assn. Scientific Apparatus Makers of U.S. (pres. 1920-26), Metal Mfrs. Assn. of Phila. (pres. 1924-30), Am. Philosophical Soc., Am. Acad. of Arts and Sciences, Phi Beta Kappa. Awarded Edward Longstreth medal of merit, Franklin Inst., 1920, for invention of Leeds & Northrup recorder; awarded Henry Laurence Gantt medal by Inst. of Management, "for distinguished achievement in industrial management as a service to the community," 1936, A.S.M.E. Medal by Am. Soc. Mech. Engrs., 1946, Edison Medal by Am. Inst. Elec. Engrs., 1949. Mem. Soc. of Friends. Clubs: Engineers, Univ., Philadelphia Cricket (Philadelphia); Cosmos (Washington). Co-author of "Toward Full Employment." Home: 1025 Westview St., Mt. Airy, Philadelphia 19. Office: 4901 Stenton Av., Phila. 44. Died Feb. 8, 1952; buried Friends Southwestern Burial Ground, Phila.

LEFEVRE, GEORGE, zoölogist; b. Baltimore, Md., Sept. 16, 1869; s. Jacob Amos and Catharine Louise (Sauerwein) L.; A.B., Johns Hopkins, 1891, fellow, 1894-95, Bruce fellow, 1895-97, Ph.D., 1896; m. Lelia Childe Deane, Dec. 27, 1898 (died 1900); m. 2d, Julia Faris, Dec. 22, 1914. Asst. in zoölogy and embryology, Johns Hopkins, 1897-98; instr. zoölogy, Marine Biol. Lab., Woods Hole, Mass., 1898-99; prof. zoölogy, U. of Mo., Columbia, 1899—. Mem. staff of Investigation Marine Biol. Lab., 1906—, mem. bd. trustees, 1909—, sec., 1913—; temporary asst. U.S. Bur. of Fisheries, 1907-11. Editor U. of Mo. studies, 1910—. Died Jan. 24, 1923.

LEFFEL, JAMES, inventor, mfr.; b. Botetourt County, Va., Apr. 19, 1806; m. Mary Croft, July 4, 1830, 2 children. Designed, built and operated water power saw mill outside of Springfield, O. on Mad River; patented waterwheels, 1845; established and operated by waterpower 1st cotton mill and machine shop in Springfield, 1845; patented lever jack, 1850, two types of cooking stoves, 1852, double turbine wheel, 1862; organized James Leffel & Co., 1864. Died Springfield, June 11, 1866.

LEFFERTS, MARSHALL, engr.; b. Bklyn., Jan. 15, 1821; s. Leffert and Amelia (Cozine) L.; m. Mary Allen, June 4, 1845, 5 sons, 2 daus. Surveyor, engr., Bklyn., circa 1840-49; pres. N.Y. & New Eng. and N.Y. State Telegraph cos., 1849-50; owner iron factory, 1850-60; chief elec. engr. Am. Tel. & Tel. Co., 1860-61, 61-66, devised instruments for detection of elec. flaws; col. N.Y. 7th Regt. of Volunteers, 1861; head news agy. Western Union Co., 1866-71 pres. Gold & Stock Telegraph Co., N.Y., 1871-76; cons. engr. Atlantic Cable Co., 1871-76. Died nr. Phila., July 3, 1876; buried N.Y.C.

LEFFLER, WILLIAM SKILLING, cons. engr.; b. Stockton, Cal., Mar. 14, 1894; s. William H. and Mary L. (Skilling) L.; M.E., E.E., U. Cal., 1914, postgrad., 1915; m. Rita Wanamaker, Mar. 31, 1934. Asst. to gen. mgr. Great Western Power Co., San Francisco, 1915-17; sec., treas. Elec. Sales Service Corp., 1916-19; organizer Leffler, McLaughlin & Moore, 1919-22; dir. Bur. Rate Research, Bklyn. Edison Co., 1922-26; mem. Lacombe & Leffler, 1926-32; cons. engr., head firm William S. Leffler Engrs. Asso., Darien, Conn., 1932—. Served as aviator lt. AS U.S. Army, 1917-19; comdr. USCG Res. and Auxiliary, World War II. Mem. Am. Inst. E.E., Soc. Advancement Mgmt., Nat. Soc. Profl. Engrs., S.A.R. Soc. of Ark and Dove, Soc. Internat. Aeroantique (brevet 1918), Society of Colonial Wars. Presbyterian. Clubs: Darien (Conn.) Cruising; University (Hartford, Conn.); Stamford (Conn.) Yacht. Inventor elec. water header, jellified gasoline for napalm bombs videorama. Pioneered techniques utility cost analysis. Home: 17 Baywater Dr., Darien, Conn. Died July 31, 1964; buried Springrove, Darien.

LEFFMANN, HENRY, chemist; b. Phila., Sept. 9, 1847; s. Henry and Sarah Ann (Paul) L.; A.M., Central High Sch., Phila., 1865; M.D., Jefferson Med. Coll., Phila., 1869; D.D.S., Pa. Coll. Dental Surgery, 1884; m. Fannie Frank, Nov. 29, 1876. Asst. prof. chemistry, Central High Sch., 1876-80; port phys., 1884-87 and 1891-92; prof. chemistry, Wagner Free Inst. of Science, 1885—, Woman's Med. Coll. of Pa., 1888-1923. Lecturer on research, Phila. Coll. of Pharmacy and Science. Author: Analysis of Water, 1899; Analysis of Milk and Milk Products, 1888; Select Methods in Food and Analysis, 1905; About Dickens, 1908; States-Rights Fetish, 1913. Home: Philadelphia, Pa. Died Dec. 25, 1930.

LEFSCHETZ, SOLOMON, educator, mathematician; b. Moscow, Russia, Sept. 3, 1884; M.E., cole Centrale, Paris, France, 1905; Ph.D., Clark U., 1911; m. Alice Berg Hayes, July 3, 1913. With Westinghouse Electric

& Mfg. Co., Pitts., 1907-10; instr. math. U. Neb., 1911-13; instr. math. U. Kan., 1913-16, asst. prof., 1916-19, asso. prof., 1919-23, prof., 1923-25; vis. prof. Princeton, 1924-25, asso. prof., 1925-28, prof., 1928-32, H.B. Fine Research prof., 1934-53, emeritus; prof. Nat. U. Mex., 1954-72; vis. prof. Brown U.; dir. RIAS Math. Center, 1958-72. Decorated associ tranger Order Aztec Eagle; recipient Bordin prize French Acad., for work in algebraic geometry, 1919; Bocher prize Am. Math Soc., 1924; Feltrinelli prize Academia dei Lincel, 1956; Nat. Medal of Sci. for Math., 1965. Mem. Royal Soc. (fgn.), Am. Math. Soc. (pres. 1935-36), Math. Assn. Am., A.A.A.S., Nat. Acad. Scis., Am. Philos. Soc., Societe Math. de France, Sociedad Mat. Mexicana, Academie des Sciences de Paris. Author of L'Analysis Situs et la Geometrie Algebrique, 1924; Topology, 1930; Algebraic Topology, 1942; Introduction to Topology, 1949; Algebraic Geometry, 1952; Differential Equations; Geometric Theary, 1958; (with J. P. Lasalle) Stability Theory by Liepunor's Direct Method; Stability of Nonlinear Control Systems, 1962. Home: Princeton NJ Died Oct. 27, 1972.

LEHMAN, AMBROSE EDWIN, civil engr.; b. Lebanon, Pa., May 23, 1851; s. Benjamin Bringhurst and Susanna (Mustin) L.; ed. by pvt. tutors and abroad; tech. edn., Paris; m. Emilie Wyonne, d. Capt. M. Koheler, Jan. 28, 1892. Geol. engr. and topographer survey of Pa., 1874-86; was asst. chief engr. Interoceanic Ry., Mexico; chief engr. Gettysburg & Harrisburg R.R., 1882-91, Brooklyn, Bath & Coney Island R.R., 1885-89; consulting engr. Great Falls Water Power Co., N.C., 1889-93; studied European transportation systems, rys. and common roads and highways, 1894-95; mem. civ. service bd. examiners, dept. municipal engring., Phila.; consulting engr. St. Maurice Syndicate, Quebec, exploration and development of mineral deposits, Hudson's Bay region, Transcontinental Ry., Can., 1910—. Mapped the topography and geologic sections of South Mountains, Pa.; numerous expert reports on explorations for iron, coal, copper, etc., in the U.S., Can., Cuba and Mex. Author: Topographic Models and Relief Maps. Home: Philadelphia, Pa. Died Apr. 7, 1917.

LEHMAN, EDWIN PARTRIDGE, surgeon; b. Germantown, Pa., June 9, 1888; s. Benjamin N. and Emily (Partridge) L.; B.A., Williams, 1910; M.D., Harvard, 1914, John Harvard fellow, 1913-14; m. Margaret Maxwell, Oct. 1, 1921; children—Richard, Lois Ann. Surgical house officer, Peter Bent Brigham Hosp., Boston, 1914-15; asst. resident surgeon, Barnes Hosp., St. Louis, Mo., 1915-16; asst. in surgery, Washington U. Sch. of Medicine, St. Louis, 1916-20, instr. in surgery, 1920-21, instr. clin. surgery, 1921-26, asst. prof., 1926-27, asso. prof., 1927-28, also in charge of lab. of surg. pathology, 1916-17; resident surgeon, Barnes Hosp., 1919-20, asst. surgeon, 1922-28; asst. surgeon St. Louis Children's Hosp., 1924-28, St. Louis Jewish Hosp., 1927-28; cons. surgeon, St. Louis Maternity Hosp., 1927-28; surgeon, St. Louis City Hosp., 1920-27 (chief surgeon Unit No. 1, 1926-27); surgeon to out-patients, Washington U. Dispensary, 1920-28; prof. surgery and gynecology, dir. dept., U. of Virginia, 1928-50, prof. surgery, dir. dept. since 1950; chief surgeon and gynecologist U. Va. Hosp., 1928-50, chief surgeon since 1950. Maj. G. Seelig lecturer, Washington U., St. Louis, 1949; William J. Mayo lecturer Univ. Mich., 1951. First lt. M.C., B.E.F., 1917-19. Dir. Virginia Cancer Foundn., 1940-44; dir. Am. Cancer Soc. (v.p. 1944-45, pres. 1947-48). Certified mem. founders' group Am. Board Surgery. Fellow American Surgical Association (vice president 1946), Southern Surg. Assn. (v.p. 1936, pres. 1948), Internat. Surg. Soc., A.C.S. (chmn. cancer com.), Soc. Univ. Surgeons (hon.), American Association for the Surgery of Trauma; member A.M.A., Southern Medical Association (vice chairman sect. on surgery 1931, chairman, 1933; vice chmn. Section on Med. Edn., 1943, chmn. 1944), St. Louis Assn. of Surgeons, St. Louis Med. Soc. (hon.). Pres. Charlottesville and Albemarle Community and War Fund, 1943 and 1944. Phi Beta Kappa, Alpha Omega Alpha, Sigma Xi. Contbr. to med. publs., author various monographs, articles covering lab. investigation, clinical observation, etc. Address: U. of Virginia, Charlottesville, Va. Died May 27, 1954.

LEHMAN, GEORGE MUSTIN, consulting engr.; b. Lebanon, Pa., May 13, 1863; s. Benjamin Bringhurst and Susanna (Mustin) L.; ed. Episcopal Acad., Lebanon, Pa.; m. Corinne May Stockton, Nov. 12, 1891 (died Feb. 6, 1933); 1 son, George Stockton (dec.). Aid, asst. and topographer Geol. Survey of Pa., 1882-89; chief asst. engr. surveys for extension Gettysburg & Harrisburg R.R., Gettysburg, Pa., to Washington, D.C., Brooklyn, Bath & West End R.R., N.Y., topographic and geologic survey, Navassa Island, W.I., relief map of same (from this survey U.S. Navy made nautical chart), later, elec. ry. surveys, 1889-90; engr. location and constrn. Great Falls Water Power & Imp. Co.'s canal, dams and location town (now Roanoke Rapids, N.C.), 1890-93; chief asst. engr. charge surveys for ship canal from Delaware River to Raritan Bay, 1894; principal assistant engineer in charge of surveys and estimates for the Lake Erie and Ohio River Canal, from Pittsburgh to Lake Erie, 1895-96; U.S. asst. engr. on improvement Allegheny, Pa., West Fork, W.Va., Youghiogheny, Pa., rivers, etc., assisted in inspection and report for permanent U.S. Army camp sites, Conewago Valley and Somerset, Pa., 1896-1903; constructed large relief map, Pittsburgh and vicinity, for Pittsburgh Chamber of Commerce, 1903-04 (gold medal at St. Louis Expn., 1904); engr. of parks, Pittsburgh, 1905; incorporator, 1905, and since chief engr. Lake Erie and Ohio River Canal Co.; sec.-member Pittsburgh Flood Commn. and engr. in charge investigations, surveys, and plans for flood prevention and protection (suggested commission and reservoir control) since 1908; chief engr. Lake Erie and Ohio River Canal Board to 1917; investigations and report on modes and costs of transportation by canal and river, 1917, 21. Reported to Com. on Inland Waterways of U.S. Railroad Administration on various canals as a war measure; production engr., and claims adjustment, U.S. Ordnance Dept., 1918-19; engr. Dept. of Internal Affairs of Pa., 1920; chief div. of Waterways, same, 1921-23 (resigned and division abolished); cons. practice since 1923, on waterway engring., including transportation methods; engr. River Front Improvement and River-Rail Terminal Plans of Department of Public Works; chief engr. L.E.&O.R. Canal Bd. Mem. Am. Soc. C.E., Swedish Colonial Soc., Phila., Pa. Forestry Assn. (council), Engineers Soc., Western Pa., Flood Commn. of Pittsburgh, Pittsburgh Chamber Commerce, Rivers and Harbors Congress (Washington), Propeller Club, The Pa. Soc. (N.Y. City). Home: 3937 Cloverlea St., Brentwood. Office: County Office Bldg., Pittsburgh PA

LEHMANN, EMIL WILHELM, agrl. engring. consultant; born in Oldenburg, Mississippi, Apr. 19, 1887; s. Charles A. and Arminia (Volkhausen) L.; B.S. in E.E., Mississippi State University, 1910; student Cornell U., summer 1910, U. of Wis., summer 1912; E.E., Tex. Agrl. & Mech. Coll., 1913; B.S. in A.E., Ia. State U., 1914, A.E., 1919; m. Stella Spence, Aug. 5, 1915; children—Margaret Louise (Mrs. LeRoy D. Prey), Mary Bain (Mrs. Wm. B. Browder), Josephine (Mrs. Hugh J. Miser), E. Wendel, Stella Jean (Mrs. Alonzo L. Hunter). Instr. physics Tex. Agricultural & Mech. Coll., 1910-13; instr., later asst. prof. agrl. engring., Ia. State U., 1913-16; asso. prof. and head dept., later prof. agrl. engring., U. of Mo., 1916-20; agrl. engring. editor Successful Farming Mag., Des Moines, 1920-21; prof. agrl. engring. and head dept. U. of Ill., 1921-55, emeritus, 1955-72, spl. rep. v.p. farm equipment product planning Internat. Harvester Co., 1955-58, ret.; now cons.; representative Heli Coil Corp., Danbury, Conn.; collaborator Bur. Home Econs., U.S. Dept. of Agr., 1933; coop. agent Soil Erosion Service, U.S. Dept. of the Interior, 1934; collaborator Nat. Resources Bd., 1934. Mem. State Rural Electrification Com. Nat. Safety Council Occupational Advisory Com.; Subcom. on Young Workers in Wartime Agr., Children's Bur., U.S. Dept. of Labor; chmn. State Safety Com., vice chmn. Ill. Farm Electrification council. Chmn. First National Farm Safety Week; governing bd. Agrl. Research Inst. Recipient distinguished service to safety award Nat. Safety Council, 1958; John Deere medal Am. Soc. Agrl. Engrs., 1965. Life fellow Am. Soc. Agrl. Engrs.; member Ill. Soc. of Profl. Engrs. (bd. dirs., p.p. Champaign County chap.), Am. Soc. of Engring. Edn., Am. Assn. Univ. Profs., Am. Farm Bur. Fedn., Am. Forestry Assn., Ill. Fire Prevention Conf. (com. fire prevention edn.), Friends of the Land, Ill. Agrl. Assn., Nat. Fire Protection Assn. (farm fire protection com.), Nat. Soc. Professional Engrs., Nat. Farm Show Committee, Alpha Epsilon, Tau Beta Pi, also mem. Sigma Xi, Phi Kappa Phi, Alpha Zeta, Alpha Tau Alpha, Gamma Sigma Delta, Acacia. Chmn. Bd. of Dirs. U. of I. Y.M.C.A. Presbyn. (mem. session, First Ch., Urbana). Club: Rotary (Urbana). Registered professional engr. in Ill. Author numerous tech. bulls. and leaflets. Co-author: Farm Mechanics. Contbr. to farm mags. and jours. Home: Urbana IL Died 1972.

LEIDY, JOSEPH, naturalist; b. Phila., Sept. 9, 1823; s. Philip and Catherine (Mellick) L.; M.D., U. Pa., 1844; m. Anna Harden, Aug. 1864. Lectr., Franklin Med. Coll., Phila., 1846-53; prof. anatomy U. Pa., 1853-91; surgeon Satterlee Army Hosp., Phila., 1861-65; prof. natural history Swarthmore Coll., 1870-85; pioneer investigator in fields of vertebrate paleontology and parasitology; pres. Acad. Natural Scis. Phila., 1881-91; recipient Lyell medal Geol. Soc. London. Author: (articles including) On the Fossil Horse of America, pub. in Proceedings of Acad. Natural Scis. Phila., 1847; The Ancient Fauna of Nebraska, pub. in Smithsonian Contributions to Knowledge, Vol. VI, 1854; Fresh Water Rhizopods of North America, pub. as Monograph XII of Hayden Survey, 1879. Died Phila., Apr. 29, 1891; buried Phila.

LEIGH, TOWNES RANDOLPH, univ. prof., dean, v.p.; b. "Fair Oaks," Panola County, Miss., Oct. 26, 1880; s. Elbridge Gerry and Susie (Gattis) L.; B.S., Iuka (Miss.) Institute, 1901; A.B., Lebanon (O.) University, 1902; Ph.D., cum laude, U. of Chicago, 1915; D.Sc. (hon.), Stetson U., 1941; m. Blanche Baird Winfield, March 24, 1907. V.p.; later pres., Mary Connor Coll., Paris, Tex., 1903-08; pres. Tex. Mil. Acad., 1904-06; head dept. science, Ouachita (Ark.) Coll., 1907-09; head dept. chemistry. Woman's Coll. of Ala., Montgomery, Ala., 1910-14; fellow U. of Chicago, 1914-15; asst. prof. chemistry, Carleton Coll., Northfield, Minn., 1915-17; head dept. of chemistry, Georgetown (Ky.) Coll., 1917-20; head dept. of chemistry, U. of Fla., since 1920, dean Coll. of Pharmacy, 1923-33, dean Coll. Arts and Sciences including Sch. of Pharmacy, 1933-48, acting v.p. 1934-46; vice pres., 1946-48. State chemist, Fla., 1931. Inventor of Leigh fog screen for protection of vessels against submarines. Mem. orgn. com. Fla. Farm Chemurgic Council. Lieut. colonel Inactive Reserve. President local sector, Association Army of the U.S., 1923-25. Former mem. Res. Officers Assn. of Fla. (ex-pres. Gainesville chapter). Mem. Revision Com. U.S. Pharmacopeia XI, Am. Assn. of Colleges of Pharmacy (pres. 1931-32, mem. exec. com. 1932-34, chmn. com. on curriculum and teaching methods, 1928-31); fellow Am. Inst. Chemists; mem. Am. Council on Pharm. Edn. 1932-46. Am. Pharm. Assn., Fla. State Pharm. Assn. (hon.); Ala. Anthropol. Soc. (hon.), Am. Chem. Soc. (former dir. 4th dist.; former chmn. Fla. sect., also Lexington (Ky.) sect.; mem., com. reconsideration local Boundaries, 1935-37, Hertz Medalist, 1932), Ky. Acad. Sci. (corr.), Fla. Acad. Sci., Sigma Xi, Sigma Chi, Phi Kappa Phi (pres. Fla. chap. 1923-24), Gamma Sigma Epsilon (nat. pres. 1927-31), Sigma Tau, Alpha Epsilon Delta, Scabbard and Blade, Rho Chi, Herty medalist, 1942. Democrat. Baptist. Clubs: Antheneum (sec. 1924-25), Kiwanis (local pres. 1930), Propeller Club of U. S. Fellow Royal Soc. of Arts, London, Eng., 1949. Author of chem. and hist. pamphlets. Home: Gainesville, Fla. Died Feb. 15, 1949

LEIGHTON, MARSHALL ORA, engineer; b. Corinna, Me.; s. Llewellyn Morse and Annie Hinkley (Stone) L.; B.S., Mass. Inst. Tech.; m. Maud Augusta Hawkins, of Portland, Me. Resident hydrographer, 1902, chief div. hydro-economics, 1903-06, chief hydrographer, 1906-13, U.S. Geol. Survey; practiced as consulting engr. since 1913. Advisory hydrographer, U.S. Inland Waterways Commn., 1907-09, in which capacity he rendered report on flood control by reservoirs, pioneering present flood control program of U.S.; mem. Northern N.J. Flood Commn., 1903-04, Passaic River Dist. Flood Commn. (N.J.), 1905-06, Florida Everglades Engrg. Commn., 1913; chmn. Nat. Service Com. Engring. Council, 1915-20; pres. Nat. Public Work Dept. Assn., 1920-21; organized U.S. hydrographic surveys in Hawaii, 1909; explorations, Mexico and Andes of S.A., for hydro-electric power, 1923-24; v.p. and chief engr., E. Tennessee Development Co., 1925-27; dep. chief pub. works, Washington Met. Dist. Civilian Defense, 1941-43. Life mem. Am. Soc. C.E. Clubs: Metropolitan. Chevy Chase. Author: U.S. Govt. reports, treating of water supplies and water power, and numerous articles, essays and addresses. Home: Cape Elizabeth, Me. Office: 910-17th St., N.W. Washington. Died Aug. 29, 1958.

LEIGHTON, MORRIS MORGAN, geologist; b. Wellman, Ia., Aug. 4, 1887; s. Stephen Tibbetts and Jane (Wellman) L.; B.A., U. Ia., 1912, M.S., 1913 (Frank O. Lowden prize in geology), distinguished alumnus, 1947; Ph.D., U. Chgo., 1916; D.Sc. (honorary), University Southern Ill., 1954; m. Ada Harriette Beach, Aug. 12, 1913; children—Freeman Beach, Morris Wellman, Richard Tibbetts. Apprentice and printer 1901-06; supt. Weber Printing Co., Iowa City, Ia., 1908-09; instr. in geology, U. of Wash., 1915-16; instr. same, summer field course, U. of Chicago and State U. of Ia., 1916; asst. prof. geology, Ia. State Teachers Coll., Cedar Falls, Ia., 1916-17; asst. prof. geology, U. of Wash., 1917-18, also geologist Wash. Geol. Survey; acting prof. geology, Ohio State U., in absentia from U. of Wash., 1918-19; asst. prof. geology, U. of Ill., 1919-23, also geologist Ill. Geol. Survey, 1919-23; chief of Ill. Geol. Survey, 1923-54, chief emeritus, 1954-71; mem. com. on metals and minerals O.P.M., 1941-46; mem. State Mus. Bd., 1937-61, chmn., 1957-61; mem. Ill. Postwar Plan, Commn. (vice chmn. 1945-47); adv. com. U.S. Geol. Survey, 1943-59, cons. on midwest glacial geology, from 1956; dir. Am. Geol. Inst., 1950, pres., 1956; mem. delegation to XXth Internat. Geol. Congress, Mexico City, 1956; mem. coordinating com. on nat. water policy Engrs. Joint Council, N.Y., 1950-51. Instr. S.A.T.C. Ohio State U., 1918. Fellow Chgo. Geog. Soc., Geo. Soc. Am. (councillor 1937-40), A.A.A.S. (v.p. representing geology, 1941), American Ceramic Soc.; mem. American Assn. State Geologists (hon.; pres. 1931-34), Soc. Econ. Geologists (pres. 1950), Chgo. Acad. Sci., (hon.), Am. Assn. Petroleum Geologists (honorary), Am. Inst. Mining and Metall. Engrs. (chairman Indsl. Minerals Div., 1939), Ill. Soc. Engrs. (dir. 1924-27), Ill. State Academy Science (pres. 1930), American Academy of Arts and Sciences, Illinois Mining Inst. (pres. 1941), Western Soc. Engineers, Wash. award commission, 1934-1937, Sigma Xi. Methodist. Clubs: Chaos, Dial, University. Author books relating to field, from 1917, including: Atlas of Illinois Resources (a compilation), 1944; Loess Formations of the Mississippi Valley (sr. author), 1950; also numerous geol. articles. Editor State Geologists Journal, 1949-54; bus. editor Economic Geology, from 1941. Home: Urbana IL Died Jan. 7, 1971.

LEITH, CHARLES KENNETH, (leth), geologist; b. Trempealeau, Wis., Jan. 20, 1875; s. Charles A. and Martha E. (Gale) L.; B.S., U. of Wis., 1897, Ph.D., 1901. LL.D., 1956; LL.D., Kenyon Coll., 1926; D.Sc., Lawrence Coll., Appleton, Wis., 1930, Columbia U., 1940, Stevens Institute of Technology, 1943; m. Mary E. Mayers, January 6, 1898; children—Kenneth, Andrew. Asst. geologist, U.S. Geol. Survey, 1900-05; asst. prof. geology, U. of Wis., 1902-03, prof. 1903-45.

Professorial lecturer pre-Cambrian geology, U. of Chicago, 1905-17. Mineral adviser to Shipping and War Industries bds., Washington, 1918, to Am. Commn. to Negotiate Peace, Paris, 1919. Chmn. The Mineral Inquiry, 1929-38; leader of round tables on mineral resources, Institute of Politics, Williamstown, Mass., 1925 and 1926. British Institute of International Affairs, London, 1926, Inst. of Internat. Relations, Portland, Ore., 1932, Council on Foreign Relations, New York, 1933; mem. Science Advisory Bd., 1933-35; mem. Business Adv. and Planning Council for Dept. of Commerce, 1933-40; v. chmn. Planning Com. for Mineral Policy, 1934-37; chmn. Mineral Adv. Com. Army and Navy Munitions Bd., 1928-40; consultant on minerals, Nat. Def. Commn., O.P.M.; W.P.B., 1940-45. Chief Metals and Minerals Br., off. Prod. Research and Developmt. of W.P.B., 1942-45. Cons. Security Resources Bd., 1948-50, Research and Development Bd., since 1948. Atomic Energy Commn., since 1945. Hon. mem. Geol. Soc. of London. Fellow American Acad. Arts and Sciences, Geol. Soc. America (v.p. 1927; pres. 1933; Penrose medalist 1942); mem. Am. Inst. Mining and Metall. Engrs., A.A.A.S. (v.p. 1920), Wis. Acad. Sciences, Arts and Letters, Wis. Hist. Soc., Nat. Acad. of Sciences, Am. Philos. Soc., Soc. of Economic Geologists (president 1925), Mining and Metall. Soc. of America, Canadian Mining Inst., British Inst. of Mining and Metall. (hon.). Clubs: Cosmos, Chevy Chase (Washington); University (New York); University, Madison (Wis.). Author of books and articles on pre-Cambrian metamorphic, structural, economic geology, and on world minerals in their internat. relations. Latest book "World Minerals and World Peace," 1943. Asso. editor Journal of Geology and Economic Geology. Home: Sheraton Park Hotel, Washington 8. Died Sept. 13, 1956; buried Madison, Wis.

LELAND, ORA MINER, univ. dean, civil eng.; b. Grand Haven, Mich., June 28, 1876; s. George Spencer and Harriett Elizabeth (Perkins) L.; B.S. in C.E., U. of Mich., 1900, C.E., 1920; m. Mary Yoeckel, June 28, 1906 (died Oct. 2, 1913); children—Mary Louise (Mrs. Bruce L. Clark), Walter Perkins; m. 2d, Lottie Susan Potts, Aug. 5, 1914; children—Miriam Irene (Mrs. William C. Kahle), Paul Miner. Chief clerk and draftsman, office of surveyor-gen. of Fla., 1898-99; in Gen. Land Office (div. of surveys), Washington, D.C., 1900, 03; aid and computer, U.S. Coast and Geod. Survey, in U.S., Alaska and P.R., 1900-03; mem. faculty Coll. Civ. Engring., Cornell U., 1903-20, head dept. of topographic and geodetic engineering, 1911-20, prof. geodesy and astronomy, 1916-20; engring. supervisor, J.G. White Engring. Corp., 1920; dean colls. of engring., architecture, and chemistry, U. of Minn., 1920-36; dean of adminstrn., University of Minnesota, Inst. of Technology, 1936-44; dean emeritus since 1944. Surveyor and chief of party to United States commissioner for demarcation of boundary between Alaska and Canada, 1904-11; mem. Commn. of Engrs. in Costa Rica-Panama Boundary Arbitration, 1911-13, Demarcation Commn., 1921. In service U.S. Army, as capt., maj. and lt. col. engrs., Apr. 1917-June 1919; with 303d Engrs., 78th Div., A.E.F., until Nov. 1918; with 314th Engrs., 89th Div., A.E.F., Nov. 1918-June 1919; colonel commanding 313th Engr. Regt., 88th Div., 1922-40; colonel inactive since 1940. Fellow A.A.A.S.; mem. Am. Soc. C.E., Am. Assn. Engrs., American Society Engring. Edn. (ex-president). Am. Astron. Soc., Soc. Am. Mil. Engrs. (dir.), Engrs. Club of Minneapolis, Am. Legion, Sigma Xi, Tau Beta Pi, Chi Epsilon (nat. hon.), Scabbard and Blade, Phalanx, Triangle. Author: Practical Least Squares. Home: 911 Fifth St., S.E., Minneapolis 14 MN

LEMMON, JOHN GILL, botanist; b. Lima, Mich., Jan. 2, 1832; s. William and Amila (Hudson) L.; ed. pub. and private schs. and Mich. State Normal Sch.; taught village schs. 8 yrs. and was 4 yrs. school supt.; entered Univ. of Mich.; left before graduation to enter 4th Mich. cav., June 8, 1862; took part in 36 engagements in Ky., Tenn., Ala. and Ga.; captured, Aug. 24, 1864, and remained in Andersonville prison to end of war; m. Sara Allen Plummer, 1880. Moved to Calif., 1866; specialist in forestry, was botanist 4 yrs., Calif. State Bd. Forestry; has added many species of plants, including several kinds of trees, to accepted classifications. Councilman, City of Oakland, 1900-02. Author: Campaigning with Saber and Carbine, 1867; Recollections of Rebel Prisons, 1874; Reports of the Locust Scourge in California, 1878; Discovery of Potato in Arizona, 1881; Ferns of the Pacific Slope, 1884; 2d and 3d Biennial Reports, Calif. Bd. Forestry, 1888, 1890; Handbook of North American Cone-Bearers, 1895, 1900; Botanizing in Apache-land, 1901; How to Tell the Trees, 1902; Native Trees of West America, 1905. Home: Oakland, Calif. Died 1908.

LEMMON, SARA ALLEN PLUMMER, botanist, artist; b. New Gloucester, Me.; d. Micajah S. and Elizabeth (Haskell) Plummer; became a teacher in New York; m. John Gill Lemmon, botanist, 1880 (died Nov. 24, 1908). With her husband has botanically explored the Pacific coast from Mexico to British Columbia; was artist Cal. State Bd. Forestry, 1887-91; has written and illus. books and articles upon various branches of botany; apptd. chmn. on Forestry for Cal. Federation of Women's Clubs, 1900. Chmn. Nat. Floral Soc. for Cal.; mem. exec. bd. Cal. State Red Cross, Cal. Woman's Press Assn., Water and Forest Assn.; hon. mem. Cal. Floral Soc., Ebell Club, Oakland, etc. Author: Marine Algae of the West; Western Ferns; Record of Red Cross Work on the Pacific Slope, 1902; How to Tell the Trees (with J. G. Lemmon), 1902. Address: 5979 Telegraph Av., Oakland CA

LEMMON, WALTER S., radio engr.; b. NY.C., Feb. 3, 1896; s. Myron T. and Bertha (Stedecker) L.; E.E., Columbia, 1917; m. Viginia Chandler, June 18, 1932; m. 2d, Ann Handschuh, Dec. 9, 1958. Trowbridge research fellow Columbia, 1917; commd. lt. U.S. Navy, and served as signal officer; also in charge of training of radio operators and engring. officers at various naval schools, 1917-19; div. sales mgr. SKF Industries, 1919-23; pres. Malone-Lemmon Labs., Inc., 1923-28; pres. Radio Industries Corp., 1928-33; gen. mgr. radio-type div. IBM, 1933-45; founder, pres. Greenwich Broadcasting Corp. (WGCH), (Conn.), 1947—. Spl. radio officer on staff of Pres. Wilson during Peace Conf., 1919. Founded internat. Radio Sta. WRUL; founder World Wide Broadcasting Found. (engaged in internat. edn. and devel. of good will programs); pioneer in devel. and mfr. of radio typewriter for comml. purposes; invented single-dial tuning control for radio sets. Mem. Century Assn., Tau Beta Pi, Sigma Xi. Christian Scientist. Awarded Columbia U. medal of conspicuous service, 1942; Order of Cristobal Colon by Dominican Republic, 1943; civilian citation by U.S. Signal Corps., 1944; King Haakon Peace Medal (Norway), 1946; Officer, Order of Orange-Nassau (Netherlands), 1947; King Christian X Denmark Medal of Liberation, 1947; Star of Solidarity (Italy), 1949. Mem. Am. Peace Soc. (Washington) (dir.), Newcomen Soc. Eng. Clubs: University (N.Y.); Cosmos (Washington). Home: 9 Quintard Av., Old Greenwich, Conn. Office: 1 E. 57th St., N.Y.C. Died Mar. 18, 1967.

LEMON, HARVEY B., physicist; born Chicago, Apr. 23, 1885; s. Henry Martyn and Harriet Ella (Brace) L.; B.A., U of Chicago, 1906, M.S., 1910, Ph.D., 1912; m. Louise M. Birkhoff, Dec. 25, 1907; children—Harriet Birkhoff (Mrs. D. S. Moir), Doctor Henry Martyn. Began as assistant in physics, Univ. of Chicago, 1911, now prof. emeritus. Dir. sci. and edn., Mus. of Science and Industry, since 1950. Trustee, Lewis Institute and Illinois Institute Tech., 1930-42; advisor in physical science to editors Encyclopedia Britannica, 1944—. Research principles charcoal activation, 1914. Served as captain Ordnance Dept., U.S. Army, 1918. Chief physicist Ballistic Lab., Aberdeen Proving Grounds, 1942-43. Fellow Am. Physical Society; mem. A.A.A.S., Am. Assn. Physics Teachers (pres. 1939-40), Delta Upsilon, Phi Beta Kappa, Sigma Xi, Sigma Pi Sigma. Unitarian. Clubs: Quadrangle (past pres.), Chicago Literary (past pres.). Author: From Galileo to Cosmic Rays, 1934; Cosmic Rays Thus Far, 1936; Analytical Experimental Physics (with M. Ference, Jr.), 1943; What We Know and Don't Know about Magnetism, 1945; From Galileo to the Nuclear Age. 1946. Home: 5801 Dorchester Av., Chgo. 37. Died July 3, 1965; buried 1st Unitarian Ch., Chgo.

LEMON, WILLIS STORRS, physician; b. Villa Nova, Ont., Feb. 8, 1878; s. George and Jane (Honey) L.; M.B., U. Toronto Faculty of Medicine, 1905; m. Ethel M. Haines, June 29, 1909; children—Katherine Ethel (wife of Dr. George A. Lord), Janette Louise (dec.), Dr. Willis Edward. Came to U.S., 1909, naturalized, 1917. Intern Toronto Gen. Hosp., 1905-06, Parry Sound Hosp., Ont., 1906-07; demonstrator in pathology and therapy U. Toronto, 1906-07; practice of medicine, Toronto, 1907-08; asso. physician Canadian Nat. Sanatorium for Tb, Gravenhurst, Ont., 1908-09; practiced in La Grange, Ill., 1909-17; asst. in sect. in div. of medicine Mayo Clinic, Rochester, Minn., 1917-18, head of sect., 1918-46; prof. medicine Mayo Found. of U. Minn., 1934-46. Served as 1st lt. Minn. Home Guard, 1917-19. Recipient gold medal on graduation, George Brown Meml. research scholarship, Daniel Clark prize in psychiatry, all U. Toronto, 1905; gold medal (with Dr. S. W. Harrington) for exhibit at meeting of A.M.A., 1935. Mem. A.M.A., Minn., So. Minn. med. socs., Minn. Trudeau Med. Soc. (past pres.), Central Interurban Clin. Club (v.p. 1935), Minn. Soc. Internal Medicine, Assn. Am. Physicians, Am. Soc. for Clin. Investigation, Am. Assn. for Thoracic Surgery, Alpha Omega Alpha, Sigma Xi. Conglist. Contbr. chpt. The Nature of Postoperative Pulmonary Diseases, Prophylactic Measures and Treatment to (book) The Stomach and Duodenum by Eusterman and Balfour; also numerous articles to med. jours. Home: 930 7th Av. S.W., Rochester, Minn. Deceased.

LEMOND, JAMES S., civil engr.; b. Walton Co., Ga., Nov. 2, 1851; s. Robert and Mary A. (Wallace) L.; left school at age of 10 to assist in supporting family; m. Tallula Williams, of Walton Co., Dec. 26, 1877. Began as section Laborer Southern Ry., section foreman, 1883, and promoted through various positions to engr. maintenance of way, Eastern div.; asst. to gen. mgr., Lines East, 1917-20, now asst. chief engr., maintenance of way and structure, Southern Rys. Methodist. Home: 400 East Boul. Office: 326 Piedmont Bldg., Charlotte, N.C.

L'ENFANT, PIERRE CHARLES, army engr., city planner; b. Paris, France, Aug. 2, 1754; s. Pierre and Marie (Leullier) L'E. Brevetted lt. French Colonial Forces, commd. lt. engrs., 1776; came to Am. with Lafayette, 1777, joined Continental Army, commd. capt. engrs., 1778; maj. by spl. resolution of Congress, 1783; surveyor and planner new fed. city of Washington, D.C., forced to resign because his plans were so expensive, 1792 (govt. began remodeling city along his original lines, 1901); employed to lay out "Capital scene of manufacturers" for Soc. for Useful Manufactures, 1792; temporary engr. at Ft. Mifflin on Mud Island in Delaware River, 1794; engr. at Ft. Washington on Potomac River, 1812; mem. Soc. of Cincinnati. Died Prince George's County, Va., June 14, 1825; buried Arlington (Va.) Nat. Cemetery.

LENGFELD, FELIX, chemist; b. San Francisco, Calif., Feb. 18, 1863; s. Louis and Henrietta (Honisberg) L.; Ph.G., Coll. of Pharmacy, U. of Calif., 1880; spl. student U. of Calif., 1884-86; grad. student and fellow, Johns Hopkins, 1886-88, Ph.D., 1888; studied Zürich Polytechnicum, U. of Liège, U. of Munich; unmarried. Prof. chemistry and assaying, S.D. Coll. of Mines, 1890-91; instr. chemistry, U. of Calif., 1891-92; instr. chemistry and asst. prof., U. of Chicago, 1892-1901; sec., later pres. Lengfeld's Pharmacy, San Francisco. Jewish religion. Author: Inorganic Preparations. Editor Dept. of Pharmacy and Chemistry, Calif. State Med. Jour. Home: San Francisco, Calif. Died 1938.

LENHER, VICTOR, chemist; b. Belmond, Ia., July 13, 1873; s. Dr. Levi H. and Susan (Keller) L.; Dickinson Coll., 1889-90; U. of Pa., 1893, Ph.D., 1898; m. May Blood, Aug. 29, 1900; children—George, Sam. Asst. in chemistry, U. of Calif., 1893-96, Columbia, 1898-1900; instr. chemistry, Evening High Sch., New York, 1899-1900; asst. prof. gen. and theoretical chemistry, 1900-04, asso. prof. chemistry, 1904-07, prof., 1907—, U. of Wis. Mem. Bd. of Edn., Madison, Wis., 1905-19, Bd. of Health, 1921-23. Mem. com. Nat. Research Council on uses of selenium and tellurium, 1919-24, chmn., 1921-24. Maj., Chem. Service Sect. N.A.; maj., Chem. Warfare Service, U.S.A.; chief univ. relations, adj. to Maj. Gen. Sibert, chief governmental relations; hon. discharged, Dec. 5, 1918. Author: Laboratory Experiments (3 edits.), 1902; The Electric Furnace (transl. of Moissan), 2 edits., 1904, 20. Discovered the unusual solvent properties of selenium oxychloride, 1919. Home: Madison, Wis. Died June 12, 1927.

LENNOX, WILLIAM GORDON, physician; b. Colorado Springs, Colo., July 18, 1884; s. William and Annabelle (Cowgill) L.; A.B., Colo. Coll., 1909, Sc.D., 1929; M.D., Harvard, 1913; A.M., U. Denver, 1921; Sc.D. (hon.), Boston U., 1948; student Peking Union Lang. Sch., 1916-17; m. Emma Buchtel, June 18, 1910; children—Mary Belle (Mrs. Holger Jansson), Margaret Agnes (Mrs. Fritz Bucthal). In dept. medicine Peking Union Med. Coll., 1917-20; engaged in research in epilepsy and migraine Boston, 1921—; asst. prof. neurology, med. sch. Harvard, 1935-48; asso. prof. neurology, 1948-54, emeritus, 1954—; pres. Elsimore Cattle Co. Founder Am. Epilepsy League. Recipient Lasker award, 1951; science award American Pharm. Mfg. Assn., 1956—. Mem. Internat. League Against Epilepsy (pres. 1935-49), Alpha Omega Alpha, Sigma Chi. Author: The Health of Missionary Families in China, 1921; Epilepsy from the Standpoint of Physiology and Treatment, 1928; Science and Seizures: New Light on Epilepsy and Migraine, 1941; Epilepsy and Related Disorders, 1960. Home: 47 Dudley Rd., Newton Center 59, Mass. Died July 21, 1960.

LEONARD, ARTHUR GRAY, geologist; b. Clinton, N.Y., Mar. 15, 1865; s. Delavan Levant and Mary Louise (Raymond) L.; A.B., Oberlin, 1889, A.M., 1895; Ph.D., Johns Hopkins, 1898; m. Katherine Gue, Oct. 8, 1901. Spl. asst. Ia. Geol. Survey, 1893-97; prof. geology and related science, Western Coll., Toledo, Ia., 1894-96; asst. state geologist, Ia. Geol. Survey, 1896-97, 1900-03; asst. prof. geology, Mo. State U., 1899-1900; state geologist of N.D., and prof. geology, U. of N.D., 1903—. Asst., U.S. Geol. Survey, 1905-07. Home: Grand Forks, N.D. Died Dec. 17, 1932.

LEONARD, CLIFFORD MILTON, civil engr.; b. Chicago. Ill., Dec. 24, 1879; s. Arthur Gustavus and Clara C. (Yarnall) L.; B.S. in C.E., Mass. Inst. Tech., 1900; m. Flowerree K. Grey, Dec. 22, 1909; children—Fleury, Hope, Clifford. Engring. and construction business, Chicago, since 1905; chmn. board Leonard Construction Co. Was formerly dir. First Nat. Bank of Chicago, Continental Ins. Co. of N.Y., Colonial-Beacon Oil Co., Boston, War Finance Corp., Washington, D.C. Mem. Am. Soc. C.E. Clubs: Chicago, University, Onwentsia, Racquet (Chicago); Racquet and Tennis (New York). Home: Lake Forest, Ill., and Camden, S.C. Office: 37 S. Wabash Av., Chgo. Died Sept. 9, 1956.

LEONARD, FREDERICK CHARLES, (len'erd), astronomer and meteoriticist; b. Mt. Vernon, Ind., Mar. 12, 1896; s. Mark Trafton and Mary Robinson (Sullivan) L.; S.B., U. of Chicago, 1918, S.M., 1919; Ph.D., U. of Calif. (Berkeley), 1921; m. Rhoda Walton of Victoria, B.C., Can., July 4, 1942; children—Roderick Walton, Frederick David. Fellow in astronomy, U. of Chicago, 1918-19, instr. math., 1918; teaching fellow astron., U. of Calif., 1919-20, fellow Lick Obs., 1921; instr. math., U. of Calif. (Los Angeles), 1922, instr. astronomy, 1922-27; asst. prof., 1927-31, asso. prof., 1931-44, prof. since 1944, organizer dept. of astronomy, 1931, chmn. dept., 1931-39, 1940-43, 45-46, 54, 1957-59; summer faculty, U. Cal., 1930, U. of B.C., 1937, 39, 41, U. of New Mex., 1947, 52, 54; vis. astronomer Lick Observatory 1943-44; special research on visual double stars and meteorites. Fellow Royal Astron. Soc. of England, A.A.A.S., Meteoritical Soc. (organizer 1933, pres. 1933-37, editor 1933-59, councilor 1937-41); member Am. Astron. Soc. Astron Soc. Pacific (bd. dirs. 1959—), Brit. Astron. Assn., Internat. Astron. Union (commn. on meteors, etc.), Royal Astron. Soc. Can., Am. Meteor Soc., Phi Beta Kappa, Sigma Xi. Republican. Author: A Catalog of Provisional Coordinate Numbers for the Meteoritic Falls of the World, 1946; A Classificational Catalog of the Meteoritic Falls of the World, 1956; also tech. articles in field. Editor Meteoritics, 1953-56. Owner rep. collection of meteorites. Home: 10514 Rochester Av., Los Angeles 24. Died June 23, 1960.

LEONARD, JOHN CHARLES, physician; b. New Castle, Pa., Dec. 21, 1903; s. Samuel C. and Bertha May (Sickafuse) L.; B.S., Westminster Coll., 1924; M.D., Yale, 1932; m. Margaret Womer, June 10, 1931; 1 dau., Margarete (dec.). Inter Univ. Hosps., Cleve., 1932-34; asst. resident physician New Haven Hosp., 1934-35, chief resident physician, 1935-36; instr. Yale Sch. Medicine, 1935-41, asso. prof. medicine, 1947-63, clin. prof. medicine, 1963—; dir. rural hosps. div. Commonwealth Found., N.Y.C., 1941-42; dir. clinic, also dir. med. edn. Hartford Hosp., 1942-45, dir. med. edn., 1947—; asso. prof. medicine Tufts U. Med. Sch., also dir. Pratt Diagnostic Clinic, Boston, 1945-47. Chmn. postgrad. med. edn. com. A.M.A., also mem. com. continuing med. edn., 1955-64; chmn. exams com. Ednl. Council Fgn. Med. Grad., 1957—; chmn. Conn. Chronic Disease Commn., 1949-55; adv. com. U. Conn. Sch. Medicine, 1962—; edn. com. Conn. Cancer Soc., 1952—. Served as surgeon USPHS, 1942-45. Mem. A.C.P. (gov. for Conn. 1951-61, nat. 2d v.p. 1961-62, nat. bd. regents 1962—), Am. Clin. and Climatological Assn., Yale Med. Soc., Beaumont Med. Hist. Soc., Hartford Med. Soc. (pres. 1964-65), Alpha Omega Alpha. Home: 22 Foxcroft Rd., West Hartford 7, Conn. Office: 80 Seymour St., Hartford 15, Conn. Died Apr. 26, 1966.

LEONARD, WARREN H(ENRY), agronomist; b. New Sharon, Ia., July 5, 1900; s. Edward James and Zilla (Miller) L.; B.S., Colo. A. & M. Coll., 1926; M.S., U. of Neb., 1930; Ph.D., U. of Minn. 1940; m. Editha Todd, June 4, 1930; 1 dau., Kay. Asst. extension agronomist, Colo. A. & M. Coll., 1926-27, asst. editor publs., 1928; grad. asst. U. of Neb., 1928-29; asst. prof. of agronomy Colorado State Univ., 1929-34, asso. prof., 1934-42, prof., 1946-48, since 1949; asst. agronomist, asso., agronomist Colo. Agrl. Experimental Sta., 1929-42, 46-48, 49-66. Survey U. of Peshawar, Pakistan for Fgn. Operations Adminstrn. and Colorado State Univ., 1954; cons. agrl. prodn. Mission to Libya International Bank Reconstruction and Development, 1959. Member adv. bd. Am. Inst. Crop Ecology, Washington, 1952; ofcl. del. 6th Nat. Conf. UNESCO, San Francisco, 1957. Served as first lieut., captain, major C.A.C., U.S. Army, 1942-46; chief (as maj.), Agrl. Div., Natural Resources Sect., G.H.Q., Supreme Comdr. for the Allied Powers, Tokyo, Japan, 1945-46, chief (civilian) 1948-49; 1st. col. United States Army Reserve, retired. Decorated Legion of Merit by Gen. Douglas MacArthur, July 22, 1946; Department of the Army commendation for Meritorious Civilian Service, 1949; fellow Population Reference Bureau, Washington, 1956; profl. achievement award, Colo. State U., 1957. Fellow A.A.A.S., American Society of Agronomy; mem. Bot. Soc. of Am., Am. Genetics Assn., Genetics Soc. of Japan, Genetics Soc. of America, American Statis. Assn., Biometric Soc., Am. Soc. of Sugar Beet Technologists, Japanese Society of Breeding (hon. member), Sigma Xi, Phi Kappa Phi. Author: Civil Affairs Handbook: Japan: Agrl. (War Dept., Army Service Forces Manual No. 354-7A). 1945; Field Plot Technique (with Andrew Clark) 1939; Principles of Field Crop Prodn. (with John H. Martin), 1949; Field Crops in Colorado (with R. S. Whitney), 1950; (with John H. Martin) Cereal Crops, 1963; other technical works on barley genetics, applied statistics, corn breeding, gen. field crops, and Japanese agr. Home: Ft Collins CO Died Aug. 23, 1966; buried Grand View Cemetery, Ft Collins CO

LEOPOLD, ALDO, (le'o-pold), forester, game manager; b. Burlington, Ia., Jan. 11, 1886; s. Carl and Clara (Starker) L.; B.Sc., Yale, 1908, M.F., 1909; m. Estella Bergere, Oct. 9, 1914; children—Aldo Starker, Lune Bergere, Adelina, Carl Aldo, Estella. Began career as forest asst., U.S. Forest Service, 1909; dep. forest supervisor, Carson Nat. Forest, 1910-11, supervisor, 1912-14, various work, 1915-16, asst. dist. forester in charge operations, 1917-24; asso. dir. Forest Products Lab., 1925-27; game survey, Sporting Arms and Ammunition Mfrs. Inst., 1928-31; cons. forester in pvt. practice, 1932; prof. of wild life management, U. of Wis., since 1933. Awarded medal by Permanent Wild Life Protection Fund, medal by Outdoor Life. Apptd. by President Roosevelt, mem. Spl. Com. on Wild Life Restoration, 1934; member Wisconsin Conservation Commission. Fellow Soc. Am. Foresters; mem. Am. Ornithologists Union, Soc. Am. Mammalogists, Cooper Ornithol. Club, Wilson Ornithol. Club, Boone and Crockett Club, Ecol. Soc. of America (pres. 1947), Am. Wildlife Soc. (pres. 1939), Sigma Xi, Phi Kappa Phi. Mem. orgn. com. The Wilderness Soc. (council mem. since 1935, vice pres. since 1945). Club: University. Author: Game Survey of the North Central States, 1931; Game Management, 1933. Contbr. to forestry, biol. and outdoor mags. Home: 2222 Van Hise Av. Office: 424 University Farm Place, Madison, Wis. Died Apr. 21, 1948.

LEOPOLD, CHARLES S., engr.; b. Phila., Pa., May 8, 1896; s. Isaac Leopold (M.D.) and Sarah (Stein) L.; B.S. in E.E., Univ. of Pa., 1917, E.E., 1947; m. Marian Rose Bettman, Oct. 18, 1920; children—Sally Rose, Margaret Virginia, Judith Ann. Established consulting engring. office under own name, Phila., 1922; projects include: air conditioning design U.S. Capitol and (old) House Office Bldg., 1936, air conditioning and electric design Pentagon Bldg., 1942, air conditioning design, Madison Square Garden, New York Stock Exchange, Fidelity-Phila. Trust Bldg., others. Served as ensign USNR, World War I. Recipient F. Paul Anderson medal, Am. Soc. Heating and Air Conditioning Engrs., 1955, Frank P. Brown award, Franklin Inst. Fellow Am. Soc. Heating and Air Conditioning Engrs., Royal Soc. Arts, Am. Soc. Refrigerating Engrs. (pres. 1946); mem. Franklin Inst., Sigma Xi, Eta Kappa Nu. Club: Engineers. Contbr. tech. publs. Home: 7600 West Av., Elkins Park, Phila. 19117. Office: 215 S. Broad St., Phila. 7. Died Nov. 24, 1960.

LE PRINCE, JOSEPH AUGUSTIN, sanitary engr.; b. Leeds, Eng., Aug. 8, 1875; s. Louis Aime Augustin and Sarah Elizabeth (Whitley) L.; brought to U.S. at age of 6; grad. Sach's Collegiate Inst., New York, 1894; C.E., Columbia, 1898, A.M., 1899; m. Julia Mercedes Lluria, July 4, 1902; children—Julia Elizabeth, Marie Ysabel, Joseph Whitley, Alicia Ana, Aimee. Ry. surveys and constrn., W.Va., 1899-1900; engring. design and constrn., Pa., 1900; asst. to chief sanitary officer at Havana, 1901-02 inaugurating first successful campaign in the Western Hemisphere against yellow fever and malaria; res. engr. mine plant constrn., W.Va., 1903; health officer Panama Canal Zone, 1904-14, also of City of Panama, during yellow fever epidemic, 1905; determined the flight range limits of malaria conveying mosquitoes, 1912, and devised traps for making disease bearing mosquitoes trap themselves; sanitary engr. malaria investigating div. U.S.P.H.S., 1915, sr. san. engr., 1917-31; in charge anti-malaria activities at 28 extra-cantonment zones, Army and Navy camps, 1917-19, reducing malaria sick rate to one-half of one per cent of that of Southern camps in Spanish-Am. War. Dir. yellow fever control Mexican Oil Field Area, 1923; dir. Am. Red Cross malarial control activities, Miss. River flood area, 1927; consultant in malaria control to Tenn. Valley Authority since 1935. Mem. Internat. Conf. on Health Problems in Tropical America, Jamaica, British West Indies, 1924; vice chmn. and acting sec. National Malaria Com., 1929, chmn., 1930. Mem. Assn. State Sanitary Engrs., Tenn. Acad. Science, Sigma Chi.; chmn. Commn. on Engring. of Nat. Malaria Com. 12 yrs. Episcopalian. Author: Mosquito Control in Panama, 1916; also many papers before med. and engring. assns. Devised mechanical method of anopheles destruction by dusting. Home: 929 Oakmont Pl. Office: Federal Bldg., Memphis TN*

LE ROUX, CHARLES, silversmith; b. Dec. 1689; s. Bartholomew and Gertrude (Van Rollegom) Le R.; m. Catherine Beekman, 1715. Learned trade from father; ofcl. silversmith of N.Y.C., 1720-43; engraved printing plates for early paper money of N.Y. State; alderman, N.Y.C., 1734; mem. N.Y.C. Common Council, 1734-39; mayor N.Y.C. Militia, 1738; mem. grand jury during Negro Scare of 1741-42. Died Mar. 22, 1745.

LEROY, LOUIS, physician; b. Chelsea, Mass., Sept. 15, 1874; s. Charles L. A. and Lizzie F. (Somerby) L.; prep. edn., Newark (N.J.) High Sch.; A.B., U. of Nashville, Tenn., 1900; M.D., Medico-Chirurgical Coll., Phila., 1896; m. Joe Carr, Jan. 11, 1922; children—Charles Louis, Joe Carr. Asst. in pathology, Medico-Chirurg. Coll., 1896; prof. pathology and bacteriology, Harvey Med. Coll. and Ill. Med. Coll., Chicago, 1899-1900; prof. pathology and bacteriology, Vanderbilt U., 1899-1905; state bacteriologist and smallpox expert to State of Tenn. since 1897; pathologist Nashville City and St. Thomas hosps., Nashville, 1896-1904; prof. practice of medicine, Coll. Physicians and Surgeons, Memphis, since 1905; prof. theory and practice of medicine, U. of Tenn., since 1911; staff physician City and Baptist Memorial hosps.; consultant med. staff, St. Joseph Hosp.; chief of staff Memphis Gen. Hosp., 1937; ex-v.p. Tenn. State Bd. of Health. Director rescue div. Am. Red Cross, from Cairo to Rosedale, in Mississippi River flood, 1937; mem. U.S. Coast Guard Auxiliary since 1940; now boatswain's mate 1st cl., U.S. Coast Guard Temporary Reserve. Medical mem. U.S. Local Bd., Memphis, for period of war; med. mem. Memphis and Shelby County Tuberculosis Commn., 1918-28. Certificated Am. Bd. Internal Medicine, 1937. Fellow Am. Coll. Physicians, 1920. Member A.M.A., Am. Congress Tuberculosis, Tenn. State Med. Soc.; fellow Am. Coll. Physicians. Asso. editor Examiner and Practitioner, New York. Author: Essentials of Histology, 1900; Smallpox Diagnosis, Treatment, etc., 1901; Pulmonary Tuberculosis. Home: 1168 Poplar Av. Office: 1210 Madison Av., Memphis, Tenn. Died May 9, 1944.

LESLEY, J PETER, ("J" is mere signature), geologist; b. Phila., Sept. 17, 1819; grad. U. of Pa., 1838, LL.D., from same; asst. geol. survey of Pa., 1838-41; studied at Princeton Theol. Sem., 1841-44; licensed to preach by Presbytery of Phila., 1844; studied at U. of Halle following winter; employed by Am. Tract Soc., 1845-47; pastor Congl. Ch., Milton, Mass., 1848-51. His theol. views changing, left pulpit; settled in Phila. as professional expert in geology; sec. Am. Iron Assn., 1855-59; prof. geology and mining and dean scientific faculty U. of Pa., 1872-78; became emeritus prof., 1886; chief geologist in charge of complete resurvey of Pa., begun, 1874; made extensive researches in coal, oil and iron fields in U.S. and Can. Original mem. Nat. Acad. Sciences; sec. and librarian, 1858-85, Am. Philos. Soc.; pres. A.A.A.S., 1883-85; U.S. commissioner to Paris Expn., 1867; m. Susan Inches, d. Hon. Joseph Lyman, Feb. 13, 1849. Author: Man's Origin and Destiny from the Platform of Sciences; Coal and Its Topography; The Iron Manufacturer's Guide; Paul Dreifuss, His Holiday Abroad. Home: Milton, Mass. Died 1903.

L'ESPERANCE, ELISE STRANG, physician; b. Yorktown, N.Y.; daughter Albert Strang, M.D., and Kate (Depew) Strang; M.D., Woman's Medical Coll. of N.Y. Infirmary for Women and Children, 1901; D.Sc., Woman's Med. Coll., Pa.; LL.D., Lindenwood Coll.; asst., dept. of pathology, Cornell U. Med. Sch., 1910-12, instr., 1912-20, asst. prof., 1920-32, asst. prof., dept. preventive medicine, 1944-50, professor emeritus since 1950. Mary Putnam Jacobi Fellow for research in tumor pathology, Munich, Germany, 1914. Resident, Babies Hospital, New York City, 1901-02; pathologist, also dir. lab., New York Infirmary for Women and Children, 1910-44; dir. Strang Tumor Clinic since 1937; pathol., New York, Harlem, and Manhattan Maternity Hosp.; bacteriologist and asst. pathol. Memorial Hosp., also dir. Strang Cancer Prevention Clinics, 1940-50; staff, Memorial Hospital and New York Infirmary, 1937-50; attending physician in preventive medicine Memorial Hospital 1948-50. Received Lasker Award, Am. Pub. Health Assn., 1951. Fellow N.Y. Academy Medicine; member Westchester Co. N.Y. County and New York State med socs., New York Pathology Society, American Assn. Pathol. and Bacteriol., Am. Assn. Immunologists, Am. Radium Soc., Harvey Soc., Am. Cancer Soc., Woman's Am. Med. Woman's and Am. med. assns., (hon.) Am. Radiologists Soc. Cons. editor: Jour. Am. Med. Woman's Assn. Address: 535 Pelham Manor Rd., Pelham, N.Y. Died Jan. 21, 1959.

LESQUEREUX, LEO, paleobotanist; b. Fleurier, Switzerland, Nov. 18, 1806; s. V. Aimé and Marie Ann Lesquereux; m. Sophia von Reichenburg. Became specialist of peat bogs; dir. peat bogs for Swiss Govt., 1844-48; came to Boston, 1848, worked with Louis Agassiz; expert on coal formation, surveyed Ky., Ill., Ind. and Miss. for coal deposits; mem. Nat. Acad. Sci. Author: Description of the Coal Flora of the Carboniferous Formation in Pennsylvania and Throughout the United States, 2 vols., 1880-84. Died Columbus, O., Oct. 25, 1889.

LESSELLS, JOHN MOYES, (le'sels'), mechanical engineer; born Dunfermline, Scotland, February 5, 1888; s. James and Elizabeth (Moyes) L.; ed. Queen Anne Sch., 1895-1904; Lauder Tech. Sch., 1904-10; Heriot-Watt Coll., Edinburgh, 1911-12; B.S. in Engring., U. of Glasgow, 1915; m. Gladys Jackson, Apr. 5, 1917. Came to U.S., Jan. 1920; naturalized, 1930. Apprenticeship at Dunfermline, 1904-10; insp. aircraft materials, Brit. War Office, London, 1915-17; spl. engr., Rolls-Royce, Ltd., Derby, 1917-19; mgr. mech. div., Research Labs., Westinghouse Elec. & Mfg. Co., East Pittsburgh, 1920-31, mgr. engring., South Phila., 1931-35; asso. prof. mech. engring., Mass. Institute Technology, emeritus; now president Lessells & Associates, Incorporated. Fellow Acad. Arts and Scis.; hon. mem. Am. Soc. Mech. Engrs.; mem. Soc. Automotive Engrs., Am. Soc. of Testing Materials, Instn. Mech. Engrs. (London), Iron and Steel Inst. (London). Awarded Lauder (Carnegie) Scholarship, 1912; Bernard Hall prize (Inst. Mech. Engrs.), London, 1926, Levy medal (with Dr. C. W. MacGregor), Franklin Inst., Phila., 1941. Club: Braeburn Country. Co-author: Applied Elasticity, 1925. Author: Strength and Resistance of Metals, 1954. Editor: Stephen Timoshenko 60th Anniversary Volume, 1938. Hon. tech. editor: Jour. Applied Mechanics. Home: 984 Memorial Dr., Cambridge 38, Mass. Died May 17, 1961.

LESTER, OLIVER CLARENCE, physicist, educator; b. Morris County, Kan., Nov. 3, 1873; s. John Augustus and Mary Virginia (Watts) L.; A.B., Central Coll., Fayette, Mo., 1897, A.M., 1898; A.M., Yale, 1902, Ph.D., 1904; LL.D., Colo. Coll., 1941; m. Pynk Johnson, Sept. 8, 1897; children—Katherine Wheeler (Mrs. H. Laurence Humbley), Oliver Clarence, John Augustus. Prof. Latin and Greek, Hendrix Coll., Conway, Ark., 1897-98; asst. prof. Latin and Greek, Central Coll., 1898-1901; asst. in physics Yale, 1901-04, Loomis fellow in physics, 1903-04, instr. physics, 1904-07; prof. physics U. Colo., 1907—, dean Grad. Sch., 1919—, v.p., 1931—, also acting pres., 1922-23, 32-33, retired 1942, with titles of dean, prof., and v.p.

emeritus; prof. physics U. Ind., 1942-43; prof. physics, U. of Colo., 1943-49, ret. 1949; physicist Colo. State Geol. Survey, 1914-18; dir. research Carnatite Products Co. (Vanadium Products Co.), Boulder, Colo., 1919-22; cons. in geophysics Midwest Refining Co., 1925-30, Gen. Petroleum Co., 1926-28; dir. First Nat. Bank in Boulder, United Am. Life Ins. Co. Fellow A.A.A.S. (pres. S.W. div. 1933-34), Am. Phys. Soc., Am. Assn. Sci. Workers), Am. Geog. Soc.; mem. Am. Soc. Engring. Edn., Am. Geophysical Union, Colo.-Wyo. Acad. Science (pres. 1929-30), Am. Assn. Physics Tchrs., Colo. State Hist. Soc. (life), Sigma Xi, Sigma Nu, Tau Beta Pi, Alpha Chi Sigma, Sigma Pi Sigma. Club: Boulder Golf. Author: The Integrals of Mechanics, 1909; also various scientific papers. Home: 1061 11th St., Boulder, Colo. Died Sept. 28, 1951.

LESUEUR, CHARLES ALEXANDRE, artist, naturalist; b. Le Havre, France, Jan. 1, 1778; s. Jean-Baptiste Denis and Charlotte Geneviéve (Thieullent) L.; attended Royal Mil. Sch., Beaumont-En-Auge, France, 1787-96. Mem. French scientific expdn. which explored coasts of Australia, 1800-04, took many zool. specimens back to France, including 2,500 new species; in West Indies, 1815-16; came to Am., 1816; made tour (with Am. geologist William Maclure) of much of interior Am., 1816-17, painted and collected specimens on trip; engraver and tchr. of drawing, Phila., 1817-26; curator Acad. Natural Scis. of Phila., 1817-25; tchr. drawing, New Harmony, Ind. (community founded by Robert Owen), 1826-37, also continued scientific work; lived in Paris, France, 1837-45; wrote 29 monographs on Am. fishes; engraved plates for scientific publs. Author: (with others) Voyage de Découvertes aux Terres Australes, 2 vols., 1807-16. Died Dec. 12, 1846.

LETTERMAN, JONATHAN, army officer, surgeon; b. Canonsburg, Washington County, Pa., Dec. 11, 1824; s. Jonathan Letterman; grad. Jefferson Coll., 1845; M.D., Jefferson Med. Coll., 1849; m. Mary Lee, Oct. 1863. Asst. surgeon U.S. Army, serving on Western and Southwestern frontiers, 1849-61; assigned to Army of Potomac, 1861; surgeon, maj., 1862, apptd. med. dir. Army of Potomac; organizer system of field med. service featuring mobile hosps. and ambulance service which became standard for entire U.S. Army. Died Mar. 15, 1872.

LEUSCHNER, ARMIN OTTO, (loish'ner), astronomer; b. Detroit, Jan. 16, 1868; s. Otto Richard and Caroline (Humburg) L.; grad. Royal Wilhelms-Gymnasium, Cassel, Germany, 1886; A.B., U. Mich., 1888, Sc.D. (hon.), 1913; grad. student Lick Obs., U. Cal., 1888-90; Ph.D., Berlin, 1897; hon. Sc.D., U. Pitts., 1900; LL.D., U. Cal., 1938; m. Ida Louise Denicke, May 20, 1896 (died Nov. 15, 1941); children—Erida Louise, Richard Denicke, Frederick Denicke (died Dec. 8, 1941). Instr. mathematics U. Cal., 1890-92, asst. prof., 1892-94, asst. prof. astronomy and geodesy, 1894-98, asso. prof., 1898-1907, dir. Student Obs., 1898-1938, prof. astronomy and chmn. dept., 1907-38, dean Grad. Sch., 1913-18, 20-23, prof. of astronomy and dir. Students Observatory, emeritus, 1938—. Mem., sec. Cal. Earthquake Commn., 1906-10. Spl. expert U.S. Shipping Board, 1917; in charge U. Cal. Naval Tng. activities, 1917-18; chmn. scientific com. and com. on occupational selection Cal. Council of Defense, 1918; maj. C.W.S., U.S. Army, 1918-19. Awarded Watson gold medal, Nat. Acad. Sciences for researches in astronomy, 1916; Knight Order of the North Star (Sweden), 1924; Bruce gold medal, Astron. Soc. Pacific, 1936; Rittenhouse medal, 1937. Halley lectr. U. Oxford, 1938. Fellow Cal. Acad. Scis., A.A.A.S. (pres. Pacific div. 1931-32), Seismol. Soc. Am., Internat. Geophys. Union, Astron. Soc. Pacific (pres. 1908, 36, 43); mem. Nat. Acad. Sciences, NRC, Am. Philos. Soc., Am. Math. Soc., Astronomische Gesellschaft, Am. Astron. Soc., Washington Acad. Sciences, Am. Assn. U. Profs. (pres. 1923-25), Delta Tau Delta, Sigma Xi, Phi Beta Kappa; fgn. asso. Royal Astron. Soc. of London; foreign mem. Royal Physiographical Soc., Lund, Sweden. Exec. sec. Nat. Research Council and acting chmn. div. of physical sciences, 1919; chmn. com. on comets and minor planets, Internat. Astron. Union, 1919-38, hon. chmn., 1938—. Clubs: University (San Francisco); Faculty (Berkeley); Cosmos (Washington); Authors' (London). Special field of investigation, theoretical astronomy; also perturbations of the Watson asteroids; improvement in the methods of determing preliminary orbits of comets and planets; perturbations of the Hecuba group of minor planets. Author: Beitrage zür Kometenbahnestimmung, Berlin, 1897; Short Methods of Determining Orbits from Three Observations; Tables of Minor Planets Discovered by James C. Watson; Research Surveys of 1091 Minor Planets; also papers on astron. subjects. Died Apr. 22, 1953.

LEUTWILER, OSCAR ADOLPH, (lut'wi-ler), mech. engr.; b. Highland, Ill., Feb. 17, 1877; s. Adolph and Selina (Seeger) L.; B.S. in Mech. Engring., U. Ill., 1899, M.E., 1900; m. Elise Kaeser, Sept. 5, 1901; children—Lester Glen, Kathryn Elizabeth. Instr. dept. mech. engring., Lehigh U., 1901-03; asst. prof. machine design, 1903-15, prof., 1915-21, prof. mech. engring. design, U. Ill., since Sept. 1921, head dept. mech. engring. since July 1934; Prof. mech. engring. design emeritus, 1945—. Mem. Am. Soc. M.E., Soc. Automotive Engrs., Soc. Promotion Engring. Edn. Am. Gear Mfrs. Assn., Sigma Alpha Epsilon, Sigma Iota Epsilon, Tau Beta Pi, Sigma Xi, Pi Tau Sigma, Theta Tau. Author: Elementary Machine Design, 1906; Mechanics of Machinery, Part I, 1907, Part II, 1908; Notes on Power Plant Design, 1913, rewritten and enlarged, 1947; Elements of Machine Design, 1917; Problems in Machine Design, 1923. Home: 710 Pennsylvania Av., Urbana, Ill. Died May 31, 1953; buried Mount Hope Cemetery, Urbana.

LEVENE, PHOEBUS AARON (THEODORE), chemist; b. Sagor, Russia, Feb. 25, 1869; s. of Solom and Etta (Brick) L.; M.D., Imperial Military Medical Acad., St. Petersburg, Russia, 1891; special student univs. of Berne, Marburg, Berlin, Munich and Columbia; m. Anna M. Erickson, June 9, 1920. Came to U.S., 1892; asso. in chemistry, State Pathol. Inst., New York, 1896-1905; chemist Saranac Lab. for Study of Tuberculosis, Saranac Lake, N.Y., 1900-02; Herter lecturer in pathol. chemistry, New York U., 1905-06; asst. in chemistry, 1905, mem., 1907-39, member emeritus, 1939—, Rockefeller Institute. Awarded Willard Gibbs medal, Chicago sect. Am. Chem. Soc., 1931; William H. Nichols medal, N.Y. sect. Am. Chem. Soc., 1938. Author of papers on proteins, nucleins, carbohydrates, lipoids, problems of stereo-chemistry, and of monographs, "Hexosamines and Mucoproteins," 1925, "Nucleic Acids," 1931. Home: New York, N.Y. Died Sept. 6, 1940.

LEVERETT, FRANK, (lev'er-et), geologist; b. Denmark, Ia., Mar. 10, 1859; s. Ebenezer and Rowena (Houston) L.; B.Sc., Ia. Agrl. Coll., 1885; hon. Sc.D., U. of Mich., 1930; m. Frances E. Gibson, Dec. 22, 1887 (died July 10, 1892); m. 2d, Dorothy C. Park, Dec. 18, 1895. Teacher in pub. schs., 1878-79; taught natural sciences, Denmark Acad., 1880-83; entered U.S. Geol. Survey, May 1886, asst. geologist, 1890-1900, geologist, 1901-29; retired. Lecturer glacial geology, U. of Mich. Has specialized in glacial geology and water resources; glacial investigations in Europe, 1908. Fellow Geol. Soc. America, A.A.A.S., Geol. Soc. Washington; mem. Nat. Acad. Science, Am. Philos. Soc., Nat. Geog. Soc., Am. Forestry Assn., Wash., Ia., Mich. and Wis. academies of science, Sigma Xi and Phi Kappa Phi. Unitarian. Author: Water Resources of Illinois, 1896; Water Resources of Indiana and Ohio, 1897; The Illinois Glacial Lobe, 1899; Glacial Deposits of the Erie and Ohio Basins, 1901; Soils of Illinois, Report Ill. Bd. World's Fair Commrs.; Pleistocene Features and Deposits of the Chicago Area, Bull. Chicago Acad. Sciences; Flowing Wells and Municipal Water Supplies of the Southern Peninsula of Michigan, 1906; Water Supplies of the Eastern Portion of the Northern Peninsula of Michigan, 1906; Comparison of North American and European Glacial Formations, 1910; Surface Geology of Northern Peninsula of Michigan, 1911; Surface Geology of Southern Peninsula of Michigan, 1912; The Pleistocene of Indiana and Michigan and the History of the Great Lakes, 1915; Surface Formations and Agricultural Conditions of Northwestern Minnesota, 1915, Northeastern Minnesota, 1916, Southern Minnesota, 1918; Moraines and Shore Lines of the Lake Superior Region, 1929; Surface Geology of Northern Kentucky, 1929; Quaternary Geology of Minnesota and Parts of Adjacent States, 1932; Glacial Deposits in Pennsylvania, 1934; Pleistocene Beaches in the Huron, Erie and Western Ontario Basins, 1939; Stream Capture and Drainage Shiftings in the Upper Ohio Region, 1939. Home: Ann Arbor, Mich.

LEVERSON, MONTAGUE R., physician; b. at London, Eng., Mar. 2, 1830; acad. edn. in London and Germany; atty. and solicitor, London, 1852; came to America, 1865; A.M., Ph.D., U. of Göttingen, 1872; M.D., Baltimore Med. Coll., 1893. Mem. Cal. Ho. of Reps., 1882; became advocate of the doctrines of Henry George; went East, 1885; became prominent opponent of vaccination and sec., Anti-Vaccination Soc. of America. Writer on legislative science and law reform, economic science, edn., etc. Address: 927 Grant Av., New York.

LEVEY, MARTIN, educator, chemist; b. Phila., May 18, 1913; s. Joseph and Julia (Brodie) L.; A.B., Temple U., 1934; student U. Pa., 1934-37; Ph.D., Dropsie Coll., 1952; m. Mary A. McGlinchy, Jan. 8, 1944; children—Susan B., Peter A. Chemist, 1942-49; instr. chemistry Pa. State U., 1953-55; instr. math. Temple U., Phila., 1956-59; mem. Inst. Advanced Study, Princeton, 1959-60, 65-66; NSF research fellow College de France, 1960; research asso., prin. investigator Yale, 1960-64; prin. investigator Rockefeller U., 1964-65; prof. history of sci. State U. N.Y., Albany, 1966-70, chmn. dept. history and systematics of sci., 1969-70. Served with U.S. Merchant Marine, 1938-42. Fellow Medieval Acad. Am.; mem. Am. Chem. Soc. History Sci. Soc., Am. Inst. History Pharmacy (Edward Kremers award distinguished writing 1968), Soc. Study Alchemy and Ancient History, Japanese History Sci. Soc., A.A.A.S., Am. Hist. Assn., Am. Chem. Soc. (councillor 1960-64, chmn. history chem. div. 1964-65; Dexter award 1965), Am. Oriental Soc., World Future Soc., Author: Chemistry and Chemical Technology in Ancient Mesopotamia, 1959; Medieval Arabic Bookmaking and Its Relation to Early Chemistry and Pharmacology, 1962; Al-kitan al-jabr wal-muqabala of abu Kamil Shuja ibn Aslam in a Commentary by Mordecai Finzi, 1965; The Medical Formulary of Aqrabadhin of al-Kindi: The Roots of Arabic Medicine and Its Influence on Later Arabic and Latin Literature, 1965; (with M. Petruck) Kushyar ibn Labban, Principles of Hindu Reckoning, 1965; (with N. Al-Khaledy) The Medical Formulary of al-Samarqandi and the Relation of the Early Arabic Simples to Those Found in the Indigenous Medicine of the Near East and India, 1967; Medieval Arabic Toxicology; The Book on Poisons of ibn al-Wahshiya and Its Relation to Early Indian and Greek Texts, 1966; Medical Ethics of Medieval Islam with Special Reference to al-Ruhawi's Practical Ethics of the Physician, 1967; Substitute Drugs in Early Arabic Medicine with Special Reference to the Texts of Masarjawaih, al-Razi, and Pythagoras, 1969; Kitab al-Taswiyah of al-Nasawi: A Theoretical Treatise on Medicine of the Eleventh Century, 1969; Chemical Aspects of Medieval Arabic Minting in a Treatise by Mansur ibn Bara, 1969. Editor: Archeological Chemistry, 1967. Mem. bd. editors Chymia, 1964, Jour. History Chemistry, 1969; corr. editor supplements to Japanese Studies History of Sci., 1969. Contbr. articles profl. jours. Home: Albany NY Died Aug. 22, 1970.

LEVIN, ISAAC, (le-ven'), physician; b. Sagor, Russia, Nov. 1, 1866; s. Salon and Etta (Brick) L.; M.D., Mil. Med. Acad., Petrograd, 1890; m. Sophie Bloch, Feb. 25, 1890; children—Ben Fenton, Charles Emmerson, Ralph Theodore. Came to U.S., 1891, naturalized citizen, 1901. Began practice, Petrograd, 1890; asso. in pathology and cancer research, Columbia, 1909-15; clin. prof. cancer research, New York U. since 1915; chief of cancer div. Montefiore Hosp., 1912-25; chief in radiology St. Bartholomew's Hosp., 1917-22; dir. N.Y. City Cancer Inst., 1923-30; consultant in radiology Lebanon Hosp. since 1915. Fellow A.A.A.S.; mem. A.M.A., Am. Physiol. Soc., Am. Assn. Pathologists and Bacteriologists, Soc. Exptl. Biology and Medicine, Am. Assn. Cancer Research, Am. Radium Soc., Radiological Soc. N. America, Am. Genetic Assn., Am. Med. Editors' and Authors' Assn., Harvey Soc., N.Y. Acad. Medicine, Alumni Assn. New York U. Editor Archives of Clinical Cancer Research, 1925-30. Contbr. many papers and articles in exptl. and clin. medicine. Home and Office: 57 W. 57th St., New York, N.Y. Died June 19, 1945.

LEVINE, MAURICE, physician; b. Cin., June 10, 1902; s. Louis and Esther Levine; B.A., U. Cin., 1923, M.A. in Psychology, 1924; M.D., Johns Hopkins, 1928; grad. Chgo. Inst. for Psychoanalysis, 1937; m. Diana Bailen, Aug. 12, 1934; children—Ann (Mrs. Philip M. Meyers), Ellen (Mrs. Michael H. Ebert), Martha (Mrs. David M. Dunkelman). Jr. intern in surgery Twillingate, Nfld., Can., 1927; intern in medicine Johns Hopkins Hosp., Balt., 1928-29, resident in psychiatry Phipps Psychiat. Clinic, 1929-32; instr. psychiatry Johns Hopkins, 1929-32; asst. prof. psychiatry U. Cin. Coll. Medicine, 1933-44, asso. prof., 1944-46, lectr. abnormal psychology Evening Coll., 1933-46, lectr. psychiatry Sch. Pub. Adminstrn., 1934-36, prof. psychiatry, dir. dept., 1947-71; dir. psychiatry service Cin. Gen. Hosp., 1947-71, Children's Hosp., Cin., 1947-71; faculty Chgo. Inst. for Psychoanalysis, 1942-71; cons. psychiatrist, mem. dean's com. Cin. VA Hosp.; cons. psychiatrist Jewish, Drake, Dunham, Children's Convalescent hosps., Vis. prof. psychiatry U. Wash. Grad. Sch., summer 1944; dir. Central Psychiat. Clinic of Community Chest, 1947-71; Samuel D. Gross lectr. U. Louisville, 1945; Eli Moschowitz lectr. Mt. Sinai Hosp., N.Y.C., 1952; Frank L. Weil lectr. relgion and humanities Hebrew Union Coll., Cin., 1968-69; cons. to surgeon gen. USPHS, 1950-58, nat. adv. mental health council Nat. Inst. for Mental Health, 1953-57. Bd. dirs. Inst. for Intercultural Studies, N.Y.C., 1965-71. Recipient Dolly Cohen award for distinguished univ. teaching U. Cin., 1970. Diplomate Am. Bd. Psychiatry and Neurology (examiner 1945-50). Fellow Am. Psychiat. Assn. life, exec. council 1953-56), Am. Orthopsychiat, Assn. (life); mem. A.M.A., Group for Advancement Psychiatry, Am., Internat. psychoanalytic assns., Cin. Psychoanalytic Soc. (pres. 1967-68), Assn. for Research in Nervous and Mental Disease, Soc. for Applied Anthropology, Am. Psychosomatic Assn. (council 1948-51), Cin. Soc. for Neurology and Psychiatry (pres. 1946-47), Sigma Xi, Alpha Omega Alpha. Author: Psychotherapy in Medical Practice, 1942 (also Swedish, Spanish and Yugoslav edits.) Co-editor: Psychiatry and Medical Education, 1952; mem. editorial bd. Jour. Am. Psychoanalytic Assn., 1951-53; mem. editorial adv. bd. Jour. Nervous and Mental Disease, 1960-66; mem. internat. editorial bd. Mind and Medicine (monograph series), 1962-71. Contbr. articles to med. jours., chpts. to books. Home: Cincinnati OH Died May 1, 1971; buried Cincinnati OH

LEVINE, MAX, bacteriologist; b. Poland, Apr. 4, 1889; s. Julius and Rebecca (Mogelefsky) L.; brought to U.S. in infancy; prep. edn., English High Sch., Boston, Mass.; B.S. in Biology and Pub. Health, Mass. Inst. Tech., 1912; Ph.D. in Bacteriology and Preventive Medicine, State U. Ia., 1922; D.Sc. (hon.), U. Hawaii, 1960; m. Adele Dine, Nov. 30, 1911; children—Norman Dine, Boris Eugene, Saul Edgar, Melvin Lewis, Thelma Laila. Research asst., Mass. Inst. Tech., 1912-13; bacteriologist USPHS, 1914; instr. in bacteriology, Ia. State Coll. Agr. and Mech. Arts, 1913-14, asst. prof.,

1914-19; asso. prof. 1919-24, prof., 1924-47, in charge of dept., 1933-45; research prof. bacteriology, Iowa Engring. Expt. Station; dir. labs. Dept. Health, Honolulu, 1947-60, ret.; mem. Environmental Health Study Sect., Div. Research Grants and Fellowships, Insts. of Health, USPHS, 1947-50; research asso. U. Hawaii, 1948; mem. bd. trustees Blood Bank of Hawaii; now cons. bacteriology Tripler Army Hosp., Honolulu, Hawaii State Dept. Health, Leahi Hosp. Served as 1st lt. and capt., San. Corps, U.S. Army, World War I; maj. R.O.S.C.; active service as maj., lt. col., col., San. Corps. U.S. Army, World War II. Fellow Am. Pub. Health Assn., A.A.A.S., Am. Acad. Microbiology, N.Y. Acad. Sci.; mem. Soc. Am. Bacteriologists, Soc. of Exptl. Biology and Medicine, Am. Water Works Assn., Federated Sewage Works Assn., Hawaii Pub. Health Assn. (pres. 1959), Iowa Acad. of Sci., Inst. of Food Technology, Assn. Mil. Surgeon of U.S., Sigma Xi, Phi Lambda Upsilon, Phi Kappa Phi, Phi Mu Alpha. Hon. mem. Soc. Biological Chemists of India. Jewish religion. Author: Lactose Fermenting Bacteria and Their Significance in Water Analysis, 1921; Introduction to Bacteriology Laboratory Technique, 1933, 37, 54; A Compilation of Culture Media for the Cultivation of Microörganisms, 1930; also about 200 papers on intestinal bacteria, water and sewage purification and disposal, disinfectants, penicillin, food technology and other subjects. Home: 348 Hind Dr. Address: Bur. Laboratories, Territorial Dept. Health, P.O. Box 3378, Honolulu. Died July 16, 1967; buried Los Angeles.

LEVINE, SAMUEL ALBERT, physician; b. Lomza, Poland, Jan. 1, 1891; s. Abram J. and Anna (Sheinkopf) L.; came to U.S., 1894; A.B., Harvard, 1911, M.D., 1914; Sc.D., Adelphi Coll., 1959, L.H.D., Yeshiva U., 1959; m. Rosalind Weinberg, June 20, 1926; children—Carol Fay, Herbert Jerome, Joan Betsy. Asso. in medicine Peter Bent Brigham Hosp., 1914-15 and 1919-28, house officer, 1915-16; asst. in medicine Rockefeller Hosp., 1916-17; sr. asso. in medicine Peter Bent Brigham Hosp., 1928-40, physician, 1940-58, cons. cardiology, 1958—; asst. prof. medicine, Harvard Med. Sch., 1930-48, clin. prof. medicine, 1948-58, prof. emeritus, 1958—. St. Cyres lectr. Royal Acad. Med., London, July 1948; vis. physician Beth Israel Hosp., 1928-33; cons. in cardiology Newton Hosp., 1933—. Fellow Brandeis U., 1962. Served at Brit. Heart Hosp., 1917-18; AEF capt. Med. Res. Corps, 1917-19. Recipient Gold Heart award Am. Heart Assn., 1959; Am.-Israel Freedom award, 1960; Samuel Albert Levine Cardiac Center established in his honor at Peter Bent Brigham Hosp., Boston, 1965. Corr. mem. Argentine Soc. Cardiology, Soc. Francaise de Cardiologie; hon. mem. Australian Cardiac Soc., Brazilian Soc. Cardiology, Accademia Lancasiana de Roma; mem. Am. Heart Assn., Am. Coll. Cardiology, Internat. Cardiology, Internat. Cardiology Found. (council 1964), Soc. Founders Albert Einstein Coll. Medicine, Harvard Alumni Assn. (pres. 1961-62), A.M.A., Brit. Cardiac Soc., A.A.A.S., A.C.P., Acad. Arts and Scis., Am. Soc. for Clin. Investigation, Assn. Am. Physicians, N.E. Heart Assn. (pres. 1935-37), Alpha Omega Alpha, Jewish religion. Club: Harvard. Author: Coronary Thrombosis, 1929; Clinical Heart Disease (5th edit. 1959); Clinical Auscultation of the Heart (with Dr. W. Proctor Harvey), 1949 (2d edit., 1959); Current Concepts in Digitalis Therapy (with Dr. Bernard Lown), 1954; also various investigations on heart disease. Samuel A. Levine Professorship of Medicine established at Harvard by Charles E. Merrill, 1954. Home: 40 The Ledges Rd., Newton Centre 59, Mass. Office: 1180 Beacon St., Brookline, Mass. 02146. Died Mar. 31, 1966.

LEVINE, VICTOR EMANUEL, biochemist, nutritionist, explorer; b. Minsk, Russia, Aug. 4, 1892; s. Israel and Eva Leah (Meisels) L.; brought to U.S., 1898; B.A., Coll. City New York, 1909; M.A., Columbia, 1911, Ph.D., 1914; grad. study, Johns Hopkins, summers 1919, 20, 21; U. of Toronto (insulin div.), summer 1923; M.D., Creighton U., 1928; unmarried. Asst. in biol. chemistry, Coll. Phys. and Surg., Columbia, 1913-15, instr. in same, 1915-16; asst. prof. organic chemistry, Fordham, 1915-16; dir. chem. lab., Beth Israel Hosp., N.Y. City, 1916-17; dir. Chem. and Path. Labs., N.Y. City, 1917-18; asst. prof. biol. chemistry, Sch. of Medicine, Creighton U., 1918-20, prof. biol. chemistry and nutrition and head of dept. since 1920, advisory dir. Grad. Sch. of Chemistry 1928—; cons. USPHS, 1927-38 and summer 1939; vis. Fulbright prof. Univs. Madrid and Valencia, 1960-62; dir. health dept. Dwarfies Corp., Council Bluffs. Served as maj., M.C., A.U.S., 1942-45, lt. col., 1945-46; now lt. col., Med. Dept. Res. Leader sci. expdn. to Arctic for Office of Naval Research, U. S. Navy, hdqrs., Arctic Research Lab., Point Barrow, Alaska, 1948. Fellow A.A.A.S., Am. Geog. Soc., Am. Inst. Chemistry, N.Y. Acad. Scis., Am. Pub. Health Assn., Royal Soc. Arts and Scis. (Gt. Britain), Brit. Inst. Philosophic Studies, Royal Anthrop. Institute Gt. Brit. and Ireland, Internat. Dental Research Assn., Am. Med. Writers Assn., mem. nat., state and local profl. and scientific assns. and orgns. in med. and nutrition fields; has served as officer of several. Elk. Clubs: Professional Men's (dir. 1931-33), Spanish Club; Explorers. Arctic explorer primarily for biol. studies 1921—. Awarded honorary scoll by Columbia Graduate School Alumni Assn., 1937. Author and co-author several books 1929-35; (with C.P. Stewart and A. Stolman) Toxicology, 2 vols., 1916; Introducción a Toxicologia (Spanish), 1962. Contbr. articles on biology aspects of the Eskimo to Ency. Arctica. Address: School of Medicine, Creighton U., Omaha, Neb. Died Sept. 29, 1963; buried Mt. Lebanon Cemetery, Bklyn.

LEVINSON, ABRAHAM, physician; b. Aug. 25, 1888; s. Yehudah and Rebecca (Kreuger) L.; M.D., U. of Ill., 1911; postgrad. work U. of Vienna, 1914; B.S., U. of Chicago, 1917; studied Vienna and Berlin, 1923, 28, 30, 33; m. Ida Perlstein, 1912; children—Myrtle, Judith, Julian. Began practice, Chicago, 1911; child specialist; sr. attending pediatrist Michael Reese and Mt. Sinai hosps.; attending pediatrist, chief staff, children's div., Cook County Hosp.; v.p. staff Michael Reese Hosp., 1932-34; professor pediatrics Northwestern U. Med. Sch.; prof. pediatrics Cook County Grad. Sch. Medicine; dir. Dr. Julian Levinson Research Found. Pediatric Neurology. Certified Am. Bd. Pediatrics. Mem. A.M.A. (certificate honor, class 1, exhibit on cerebro-spinal fluid, 1932), Ill. Med. Soc. (certificate of merit for exhibit of original sci. research 1936, 1940; chmn. com. on mental hygiene), Chicago Med. Soc., Chicago Pediatric Soc. (v.p. 1934-35; pres. 1935-36), Am. Acad. Pediatrics, Inst. of Medicine, Am. Assn. Med. History, Sigma Xi, Phi Delta Epsilon. Recipient gold medal emblematic grand sci. award Phi Lambda Kappa for outstanding contbns. to sci. medicine, 1940, orator key of History of Medicine Soc. of Tulane U., 1942. Author: Cerebro-spinal Fluid in Health and Disease, 1919, 3d edit., 1929; Tobias and His Work, 1924; Examination of Children, 1924, 2d edit., 1927; Textbook on Pediatric Nursing, 1925, 3d edit., 1944 (Hebrew translation, 1933); Pioneers of Pediatrics, 1936, 1943; The Mentally Retarded Child, 1952; also numerous articles for med. jours. pertaining to children's diseases, chapters for various Systems of pediatrics, also translated German chapters on pediatrics. Condr. research in biochemistry and pediatrics. Home: 2933 Sheridan Rd. Office: 30 N. Michigan Av., Chgo. Died Sept. 17, 1955.

LEVY, ERNEST COLEMAN, sanitarian; b. Richmond, Va., Aug. 11, 1868; s. Abraham and Rachel Cornelia (Levy) L.; M.D., Med. Coll. of Va.; post-grad. work, Coll. Phys. and Surg. (Columbia), Mass. Inst. Tech.; m. Elisabeth Detwiler, June 19, 1912. House phys., Mt. Sinai Hosp., New York, 1890-92; prof. histology, pathology and bacteriology, Med. Coll. of Va., 1897-1900; editor Medical Register, 1897-1900; chief health officer, Richmond, 1906-17; dir. pub. welfare, Richmond, 1919-24; prof. preventive medicine, Medical Coll. of Vienna, 1925; city health officer, Tampa, Fla., 1925-28. Commd. capt. M.C., U.S.A., Aug. 1918; maj., Oct. 1918; hon. discharged, Jan. 1919. Made original investigations in origin of Southern typhoid fever, 1907-08; research in breeding and control of house fly, resulting in invention of the maggot trap, 1911; research in infantile diarrhea. Charter fellow Am. Pub. Health Assn. (pres. 1923); mem. La Société de 40 Hommes et 8 Chevaux; comdr. Richmond (Va.) Post No. 1, Am. Legion, 1925 (resigned). Democrat. Jewish religion. Died Sept. 29, 1938.

LEVY, LOUIS EDWARD, photo-chemist; b. Stenowitz, Bohemia, Oct. 12, 1846; s. Leopold and Wilhelmina (Fisher) L.; brought to U.S. in childhood; ed. pub. schs., Detroit, 1855-61; spl. studies in mathematics and physics, U. of Mich., 1866; practical studies in optics under Louis Black, Detroit, 1861-70; m. Pauline Dalsheimer, Jan. 9, 1881. Connected with meteorol. obs., U.S. Lake Survey, Detroit, 1866; made researches in microscopic photography, 1869-70. Publisher and editor The Evening Herald, Independent Dem. daily, Phila., Nov. 1887-90, The Mercury, 1887-91. Lecturer, Franklin Inst., on Techno-Graphic Arts; pres. Graphic Arts Co., Phila., 1908—. Experiments, 1873-74, resulted in his invention in photo-chem. engraving, called the "Levytype," patented, Jan. 1875 (1st patent to Am. citizen in this field); established, 1875, Levytype Co., Baltimore; removed to Phila., 1877. Mem. Com. Science and Arts, and v.p. Franklin Inst.; received 1896 (jointly with brother Max L.), John Scott legacy medal for invention of "Levy line screen," and, 1900, Elliott Cresson gold medal for invention of Levy acid blast—both from Franklin Inst.; medal and diploma, Chicago Expn., 1893, for original discoveries; decoration and diploma Imperial Photographic Soc., Moscow, Russia, 1896; gold medal, Paris, 1900, and St. Louis Expn., 1904, for invention of the acid blast; gold medal, St. Louis Expn., 1904, for invention of etch-powedring machine; Elliott Cresson gold medal for same, Franklin Inst., 1907; silver medal, San Francisco Expn., 1915. Representative of Franklin Inst. at Scientific Congresses of Paris Expn.; v.p. of Congress of Inventors' Assns., Paris, Sept. 1900. Joint founder (1884) and pres. of Assn. for Relief and Protection of Jewish Immigrants, pres. Jewish Community (Kehillah) of Phila. Author: The Jewish Year, 1895; The Russian Jewish Refugees in America, 1895; Business, Money and Credit, 1896; Cause of Business Depressions (with Hugo Bilgram), 1914. Home: Philadelphia, Pa. Died Feb. 17, 1919.

LEVY, MAX, inventor; b. Detroit, Mar. 9, 1857; s. Leopold and Wilhelmina (Fisher) L.; ed. pub. schs., Detroit; m. Diana Franklin, Sept. 22, 1885. Studied architecture, Detroit, 1875; engaged in photo engraving until 1890; introduced modern screen for half-tone process; prominent in recent advance in half-tone illustration in the development of the theory of the subject. Received from Franklin Inst., Phila., John Scott medal; Royal Cornwall Polytechnic silver medal; gold medals, Chicago, 1893, Paris, 1900, Buffalo, 1901, St. Louis, 1904; medal of honor, San Francisco Expn., 1915. Contbr. to Photographic Soc., Phila., 1896, Paper and Press, 1894-96, Royal Photog. Soc., 1906. Patented Jan. 30, 1917, counting chamber for haemocytometer, new construction, adopted in army and leading med. instns., and awarded the Edward Longstreth medal, Franklin Inst., Jan. 1918. Engaged in optical instrument program of War Dept., 1917-18. Home: New York, N.Y. Died July 31, 1926.

LEWIN, KURT, (le-ven'), univ. prof.; b. Moglino, Germany, Sept. 9, 1890; s. Leopold and Recha (Engel) L.; ed. Kaiserin Augusta Gymnasium, 1903-08, U. of Freiburg, 1908, U. of Munich, 1909, U. of Berlin, 1909-14 (Ph.D.); m. Gertrud Weiss, Oct. 1928; children—Esther Agnes, Reuven Fritz, Miriam Anna, Daniel Meier. Came to U.S., 1932. Asst., Psychol. Inst., Berlin, 1921; privatdocent of philosophy, U. of Berlin, 1921-26, prof. of philosophy and psychology, 1926-33; visiting prof. of psychology, Stanford U., 1932-33; acting prof. of psychology, Cornell U., 1933-35; prof. of child psychology, Child Welfare Research Station, U. of Ia., 1935-44; dir. Research Center for Group Dynamics, Mass. Inst. Tech., since 1944; visiting prof., Harvard, 2d semester, 1938-39, 1939-40, Univ. of California, Berkeley, summer session, 1939. Counsellor, U.S. Department of Agriculture, Washington, D.C., since 1942; Office of Strategic Services, 1944-45; chief cons., Commission on Community Interrelations, New York, since 1944. Served as private to lt., German Army, 1914-18. Member American Psychol. Assn., Midwest. Psychol. Assn., Soc. for Psychol. Study of Social Issues (chmn.), Psychometric Soc., A.A.A.S., Phi Epsilon Pi, Sigma Xi. Author: A Dynamic Theory of Personality (translated from German by D. K. Adams and K. E. Zener), 1935; Principles of Topological Psychology, 1936; The Conceptual Representation and Measurement of Psychological Forces, 1938; Studies in Topological and Vector Psychology I and II, Univ. Iowa; Studies in Child Welfare, 16. No. 3, 1940; Resolving Social Conflicts, 1947; also book pub. in Germany. Home: 57 Grove Hill Av., Newtonville, Mass. Died Feb. 12, 1947; buried in Mount Auburn Cemetery, Cambridge.

LEWIN, PHILIP, orthopedic surgeon; born Chgo., June 18, 1888; son Marks Lewin; B.S., University Chicago, 1909; M.D., Ruch Medical College, 1911; postgrad. Univ. of Paris France; married Merriel Abbott, May 26, 1921; 1 son, Frank. Intern Children's Meml. Hosp., 1911-12, St. Luke's Hosp., 1912-14; in practice, Chgo., 1914—; cons. orthopedic surgeon, Cook County Hosp.; sr. attending orthopedic surgeon and past chmn., dept. of bone and joint surgery Michael Reese Hosp.; cons. orthopaedic surgery Highland Park Found.; past chmn. dept., professor emeritus of bone and joint surg., Northwestern U. Med. Sch.; prof. orthopedic surg., Cook County Grad. Sch. of Medicine; cons. Municipal Contagious Disease Hosp., Chicago. Mem. med. adv. com. Nat. Foundn. for Infantile Paralysis; mem. Professional Adv. Com., Div. Services for Crippled Children. Internat. Soc. Orthopedic Surg. and Traumatology; mem. adv. com. Commn. for Handicapped, State of Ill.; mem. adv. com. on Infantile Paralysis, Ill. Dept. Pub. Health. Served as captain medical corps, United States Army, 1917-19; major M.O.R.C. Colonel M.C. A.U.S., chief of orthopedic surgery Mayo Gen. Hosp., Galesburg, Ill., and commdg. officer 16th Evac. Hosp., Camp Blanding, Fla., 1942-46. Diplomate Am. Bd. Orthopedic Surgery. Founder fellow, Internat. Coll. Surg., U.S. chapter. Fellow Am. Coll. Surgs.; mem. A.M.A., Ill. State and Chicago med. socs., Am. Orthopedic Assn., Clin. Orthopedic Soc., Am. Assn. for Study and Control of Rheumatic Diseases, Am. Acad. Orthopedic Surgeons (a founder—sec. 1931-36), Chicago Orthopedic Soc. (formerly pres.); mem. (hon.) Italian Orthopedic Surg. Congress, Rome, Italy, 1948. Author numerous sci. publs. in field, latest: The Back and Its Syndrome, 1953. Home: 91 Sycamore Pl., Highland Park, Ill. Office: 55 E. Washington St. Chicago 2. Died May 1960.

LEWIS, CLAUDE ISAAC, horticulturist; b. Cardiff, Wales, Apr. 12, 1880; s. Isaac and Helen (Hibbard) L.; brought to U.S. in infancy; B.S. in Agr., Mass. Agrl. Coll., Amherst, 1902; B.S., Boston U., 1902; M.S.A., Cornell U., 1906; m. Marie A. Berry, Mar. 31, 1905. Chief div. of horticulture, and vice-dir. Expt. Sta. of Ore. Agrl. Coll., 1906-19; orgn. mgr. Ore. Growers Coöperative Assn., Salem, 1919-22. V.p. Corvallis Orchard Co. Mng. editor Am. Fruit Grower (Chicago). Republican. Conglist. Writer of more than 50 bulls. on fruit, orchard economics, etc. Died Jan. 12, 1924.

LEWIS, EXUM PERCIVAL, physicist; b. Washington Co., N.C., Sept. 15, 1863; s. Henry Green and Emma (Haughton) L.; B.S., Columbian (now George Washington) U., 1888; Ph.D., Johns Hopkins, 1895; phys. research, U. of Berlin, 1898-1900; m. Louise Sheppard, July 10, 1901; children—Evelyn, John Sheppard. Asst. in physics, Johns Hopkins, 1891-95; instr. physics, 1895-96, asst. prof., 1896-1902, asso. prof., 1902-08, prof., 1908—, U. of Calif. Mem. Crocker eclipse expdn. to South Seas, Jan. 1908, and to

Goldendale, Wash., June 1918; mem. 1905-07, pres., 1907-09, Berkeley Bd. of Edn. Editor: The Effect of a Magnetic Field on Radiation, 1900. Contbr. sections on Wave Motion and Light, in Duff's Text-Book of Physics, 1908. Home: Berkeley, Calif. Died Nov. 17, 1926.

LEWIS, FRED JUSTIN, dean engring.; b. Blandford, Mass., Dec. 24, 1890; s. William Henry and Julia Freeland (Boise) L.; B.S. in C.E., U. of Me., 1914; M.S. in Hydraulic Engring., Pa. State Coll., 1923; C.E., U. of Me., 1922; m. Maude Ethel Hills, June 23, 1917; 1 dau., Alice Elizabeth (Mrs. Glenn Dixon Henderson). Instr. civ. engring., and asst. to boro engr., Pa. State Coll., 1914-16; valuation div., C.B.&Q. Ry. and M.P. R.R., 1916-17; asst. engr., City of Springfield, Mass., 1917-18, U.S. Army, 1918-19; instr. and asst. prof. civ. engring., Lehigh U., 1919-25; asso. prof., prof. civil engring., Vanderbilt University, 1925-33, dean School of Engineering since 1933; consultant in municipal and sanitary engineering. Member C. of C., Engring. Assn., Nashville (past president), American Society Civ. Engrs., Soc. Promotion Engring. Edn., Am. Pub. Health Assn., Am. Water Works Assn., Kappa Sigma, Phi Kappa Phi, Tau Beta Pi, Omicron Delta Kappa. Baptist. Club: Rotary (Nashville) (pres.). Home: Castleman Drive, Nashville, Tenn. Died Jan. 4, 1959; buried Woodlawn Cemetery, Nashville.

LEWIS, FREDERIC THOMAS, educator; b. Cambridge, Mass., Mar. 18, 1875; s. Charles Sanford and Nettie Farnum (Brown) L.; A.B., Harvard, 1897, A.M., 1898, M.D., 1901; m. Ethel May Stickney, July 30, 1904; 1 son, Thomas Lothrop. Austin fellow in histology and embryology Harvard Med. Sch., 1901-02, instr., 1902-06, asst. prof., 1906-15, asso. prof. of embryology, 1915-31, prof. of comparative anatomy, 1931-41, prof. emeritus, 1941—. Fellow American Academy Arts and Scis., Fellow of Royal Microscopical Society, A.A.A.S.; member American Assn. Anatomists (v.p. 1914-16; pres. 1936-38), Boston Soc. Natural Hist. (v.p. 1926-29), Phi Beta Kappa. Author embryol. papers and of an arrangement of Stöhr's Lehrbuch der Histologie upon an embryol. basis. Demonstrator of a 14-hedral shape of plant and animal cells. Home: 538 Chestnut St., Waban 68, Mass. Died June 2, 1951.

LEWIS, GEORGE WILLIAM, aeronautical engr.; b. Ithaca, N.Y., Mar. 10, 1882; s. William H. and Edith (Sweetland) L.; M.E., 1908, Cornell University, M.M.E., 1910; Sc.D., Norwich University; D.Eng., Ill. Inst. Tech., 1944; m. D. Myrtle Harvey, September 9, 1908; children—Alfred William, Harvey Sweetland, Myrtle Norlaine, George William, Leigh Kneeland, Armin Kessler. Instr. in engring., Cornell U., 1908-10; prof. engring., Swarthmore Coll., 1910-17; engr. in charge Clarke Thomson Research, 1917-19; sales mgr. Phila. Surface Combustion Co., 1919; exec. officer Nat. Advisory Com. for Aeronautics, 1919-24; dir. aeronaut. research Nat. Adv. Com. Aeronautics, Washington, 1924-47, research cons., 1947-48. Member Com. on Power Plants for Aircraft Nat. Adv. Com. for Aeronautics 1918; chmn. contest bd. Nat. Aeronautical Assn., 1925-38; mem. com. of judges Daniel Guggenheim Safe Aircraft Competition, 1927-29; mem. bd. judges Wright Medal Award, 1928-29, chmn. bd., 1930; mem. bd. of award Manly Memorial Medal, 1929; chmn. bd. 1931-36; mem. Guggenheim Medal Bd. of Award, 1930, chmn. 1944-45; honorary fellow, Institute of Aeronautical Sciences (vice-president, 1935-38, president, 1939), Society Automotive Engineers (v.p. 1931); mem. War Dept. Spl. Committee on Army Air Corps (Baker Bd.), 1934; American Philosophical Society, National Academy of Sciences. Awarded Daniel Guggenheim medal, 1936, Spirit St. Louis Medal 1944. Presbyn. Clubs: Cosmos, Kenwood. Home: 6502 Ridgewood Av., Chevy Chase, Md. Address: 1724 F St. N.W., Washington, D.C. Died July 12, 1948.

LEWIS, GILBERT NEWTON, chemist; b. Weymouth, Mass., Oct. 23, 1875; s. Frank W. and Mary B. (White) L.; U. of Neb., 1890-93; A.B., Harvard, 1896; A.M., 1898, Ph.D., 1899; univs. of Leipzig and Göttingen, 1900-01; hon. D.Sc., U. of Liverpool, 1923, U. of Wis., 1928, U. of Chicago, 1929, U. of Pa., 1938; Dr. Hon. Caus., U. of Madrid, Spain, 1934; m. Mary Hinckley Sheldon, June 20, 1912; children—Richard Newton, Margery, Edward Sheldon. Instr. chemistry, Harvard, 1899-1900, 1901-06 (on leave of absence, in charge weights and measures, P.I., 1904-05); asst. prof. chemistry, 1907-08, asso. prof., 1908-11, prof., 1911-12, Massachusetts Institute of Technology; professor phys. chemistry, University of Calif., since July 1, 1912; Silliman lecturer, Yale, 1925. Maj. U.S. Army, 1918; lt. col., 1919; chief of defense div. Gas Service, A.E.F. Decorated D.S.M. (U.S.); Chevalier Legion of Honor (French); awarded Nichols, Gibbs and Davy medals, 1929; Soc. Arts and Sciences medal, 1930; Richards medal, 1938; Arrhenius medal, 1939. Mem. American Philosophical Society, American Chemistry Society, American Physics Soc.; fellow Am. Acad. Arts and Sciences; hon. fellow London Chem. Soc., Royal Instn. of Great Britain, Indian Acad. Sciences; hon. mem. Swedish Acad., Danish Acad., Royal Soc., Franklin Inst. of Pa. Author: Thermodynamics and the Free Energy of Chemical Substances (with M. Randall), 1923; Valence and the Structure of Atoms and Molecules, 1923; The Anatomy of Science, 1926. Home: 948 Santa Barbara Rd., Berkeley, Calif. Died Mar. 23, 1946.

LEWIS, HOWARD BISHOP, educator; b. Southington, Conn., Nov. 8, 1887; s. Frederick A. and Charlotte R. (Parmelee) L.; B.A., Yale, 1908, Ph.D., 1913; m. Mildred L. Eaton, June 15, 1915; children—Charlotte Barber, Elizabeth Parmelee. Asst. in physiol. chemistry, Yale, 1911-13; instr. physiol. chemistry, U. of Pa., 1913-15; asso. in physiol. chemistry, U. of Ill., 1915-17, asst. prof., 1917-19, asso. prof., 1919-22; prof. and head dept. of biol. chemistry, Univ. of Mich., 1922—, also dir. College of Pharmacy, 1933-47; John Jacob Abel univ. prof. biol. chemistry, 1947—. Henry Russell lectr. U. of Mich., 1948-49. Mem. National Board of Med. Examiners, 1935-50. Mem. Council on Foods and Nutrition, A.M.A., 1936—. Elected mem. Nat. Acad. Scis., 1949. Fellow A.A.A.S.; mem. Am. Chem. Soc., American Institute Nutrition (council 1941-42; v.p. 1942-43; pres. 1943-44). Am. Pharm. Assn., A.M.A. (associate), Am. Physiol. Soc., Am. Soc. Biol. Chemists (sec. 1929-33, v.p. 1933-35; pres. 1935-37, council 1937-40, 41-42), Soc. Exptl. Biol. and Med. (ed. bd. 1927-38), Alpha Omega Alpha, Phi Beta Kappa, Alpha Chi Sigma, Phi Kappa Phi, Phi Lambda Upsilon, Phi Sigma, Sigma Xi, Rho Chi. Democrat. Episcopalian. Contbr. to scientific jours. on subjects of nutrition and physiol. chemistry. Beaumont lecturer Wayne County Med. Soc., 1932; Harvey Society lecturer, 1941. Mem. editorial bds., Physiol. Reviews, 1935-39, Jour. of Nutrition, 1935-39, 1940-45; Chem. Reviews, 1938-40, Jour. Biol. Chem., 1938—. Home: 1714 Wells St., Ann Arbor, Mich. Died Mar. 7, 1954.

LEWIS, ISAAC NEWTON, army officer; b. New Salem, Pa., Oct. 12, 1858; s. James H. and Anne (Kendall) L.; grad. U.S. Mil. Acad., 1884; m. Mary, d. Richard Wheatley, D.D., of N.Y. City, Oct. 21, 1886; children—Richard Wheatley, Laura Anne, George Fenn, Margaret Kendall. Commd. 2d lt. 2d Arty., June 15, 1884; promoted through grades to col., Aug. 27, 1913; retired on account of disability incurred in line of duty, Sept. 20, 1913. Mem. bd. on regulation of coast arty. fire, New York Harbor, 1894-98; recorder Bd. of Ordnance and Fortification, Washington, 1898-1902; instr. and dir. Coast Arty. Sch., Ft. Monroe, Va., 1904-11. Made study of methods of mfr. and supply of ordnance materials, in Europe, 1900, resulting in complete re-armament of field arty. of U.S.; orginator of plan for modern corps orgn. for artillery which was adopted by Congress, 1902. Inventor of the Lewis machine gun which was in general use by all the allies throughout the World War; also inventor of numerous mil. instruments and devices in general use, including the first successful arty. range and position finder, a replotting and relocating system for coast batteries, time interval clock and bell system of signals, quick firing field gun and mount, quick reading mech. verniers, electric car lighting and windmill electric lighting systems, etc. Republican. Methodist. Home: Montclair, N.J. Died Nov. 9, 1931.

LEWIS, IVY FOREMAN, botanist; b. Raleigh, N.C., Aug. 31, 1882; s. Richard Henry and Cornelia Viola (Battle) L.; A.B., U. N.C., 1902, M.S., 1903; Ph.D., Johns Hopkins, 1908; studied U. Bonn, Germany; m. Margaret Hunter, June 9, 1909; children—Ivey Foreman, Margaret Elliott, Penelope Battle. Prof. biology Randolph-Macon Coll., Ashland, Va., 1905-06, 1907-12; asst. prof. botany, U. Wis., 1912-14; prof. botany U. Mo., 1914-15; prof. biology U. Va. since 1915, dean since 1934. Instr. botany Marine Biol. Lab., Woods Hole, Mass., 1910-17, in charge botany, 1918-27; dir. Mt. Lake Biol. Sta., 1934-46. Chmn. div. biology and agr. NRC, 1933-36. Fellow A.A.A.S.; mem. Va. Acad. Sci., Am. Soc. Naturalists (pres. 1939), Am. Biol. Soc. (pres. 1942), Bot. Soc. Am. (pres. 1949), N.E. Bot. Sol., Phi Beta Kappa, Sigma Xi, Zeta Psi. Democrat. Episcopalian. Club: Colonnade. Home: II E. Lawn, University, Va. Died Mar. 16, 1964.

LEWIS, JAMES OGIER, petroleum engr.; b. San Jose, Calif., Jan. 21, 1886; s. Edward B. and Belle (Montgomery) L.; A.B. in Geology, Stanford U., 1917, as of 1909; m. Hazel A. McPike, July 3, 1910; children—Vesta Evadne, Beatrice May, Donald DeWitt. Geologist in Calif., Can., Tex. and Mont., 5 yrs.; with U.S. Bur. Mines 6 yrs., 1916-21, in charge petroleum div. 2 yrs.; built Bartlesville Petroleum Expt. Sta.; now cons. engr., Houston, Tex. Mem. Am. Inst. Mining and Metall. Engrs. (recipient of Anthony F. Lucas Medal, 1946), Am. Assn. Petroleum Geologists. Home: 3340 S. MacGregor. Office: 1552 Mellie Esperson Bldg., Houston. Died June 15, 1954; buried Mountain View Cemetery, Oakland, Cal.

LEWIS, J(OSEPH) VOLNEY, geologist; b. Rutherford County, N.C., Sept. 14, 1869; s. Jay Whittington and Mary Catherine (Bennett) L.; B.E., U. of N.C., 1891; S.B. in Geology, Harvard, 1893; grad. student, Harvard, Johns Hopkins, Columbia; m. Margaret Hendon, Dec. 24, 1895 (dec.); children—Eleanor (Mrs. Ellis B. Cook), Lydia (dec.); m. 2d, Mildred Leo Clemens, June 29, 1938. Asst. in biology, U. of N.C., 1889-91; prof. geology, Clemson Coll., 1896-1904; prof. geology and mineralogy, dir. geol. mus., and head of dept., Rutgers U., 1904-26; U.S. Geol. Survey, 1891, 1902, 18, 34; regional geologist, region IV, National Park Service, San Francisco, 1934-42; metals and mineral specialists Dept. of Commerce, Bur. Foreign and Domestic Commerce, Washington, June-Dec. 1942; geologist, mining engineer, section chief, Mining Div., War Production Bd., Washington, D.C., 1942-45; North Carolina Geological Survey, 1891-96, Geological Survey of N.J., 1905-25. Cons. mining and petroleum geologist in U.S., Mexico, Canada, Alaska and South America since 1906; chief staff geologist, foreign operating companies of Gulf Oil Corp. of Pa., 1925-31; in charge of design and construction of earth science exhibits, Century of Progress Exposition, Chicago, 1931-32. Special consulting editor, Engineering and Mining Journal, 1920-23. Fellow Geol. Soc. America; mem. Soc. Economic Geologists (sec. and treas. 1921, treas. 1923-26), Am. Inst. Mining and Metall. Engineers, Mining and Metallurgical Soc. America, Pan American Institute of Mining Engineering and Geology, Phi Gamma Delta, Phi Beta Kappa, Sigma Xi, Mining Club of New York (incorporator and mem. bd. govs., 1930). Author: Determinative Mineralogy (4 edits., 5th in preparation); Geologic Map of New Jersey (with Henry B. Kummel); Geology of New Jersey (with same); numerous reports, scientific papers and monographs on geology, mineralogy, and mining topics; contbr. to annual vols. of The Mineral Industry, 1914-22, to Yearbook and annual review numbers Engineering and Mining Journal, 1924-28. Address: San Francisco CA Died Jan. 1969.

LEWIS, L(EO) LOGAN, air conditioning engr.; b. Fayetete County, Ky., Apr. 16, 1887; s. William Logan and Abby Mason (Huber) L.; B.S., U. Ky., 1907, M.E., 1909; m. Agnes Wilgus Yeager, Oct. 31, 1911; children—Sarah Huber (Mrs. Craig H. Smith), Jane Yeager (Mrs. John E. Kingsbury), Mary Elizabeth (Mrs. Donald M. Lewis Jr.). Instr. U. Ky., 1908-09; engr. Carrier Air Conditioning Co., 1909-15; founder mem. Carrier Engring. Corp., 1915, organizer co. sch. for tng. engring. grads., 1921, sec., dir., 1917-36; v.p. Carrier Corp., 1936—. Mem. sub-com. on armored vehicles NRC, 1942-45. Fellow Am. Soc. Refrigerating Engrs. (past pres.); mem. Am. Soc. Heating and Air Conditioning Engrs., Sigma Alpha Epsilon. Clubs: Technology, Onondaga Golf and Country (Syracuse). Author tech. articles. Inventor bypass for air conditioning large areas. Home: 753 James St., Syracuse 3. Office: 300 S. Geddes St., Syracuse 1, N.Y. Died Mar. 8, 1965.

LEWIS, NELSON PETER, civil engr.; b. Red Hook, N.Y., Feb. 1, 1856; s. John Neher and Christina Jane (Nelson) L.; A.B., St. Stephen's Coll., Annandale, N.Y., 1875, LL.D., 1911; C.E., Rensselaer Poly. Inst., Troy, N.Y., 1879; m. Minnie Rose MacLean, Oct. 21, 1885. Ry. location and constrn., Colo., La. and Ala., 1879-84 and 1886-89; entered engring. staff, City of Brooklyn, 1884; in charge Bur. of Highways, City and Borough of Brooklyn, 1894-1902; chief engr. Bd. of Estimate and Apportionment, New York, 1902-20; dir. physical survey, Plan of New York and Environs; consultant City Planning Bd., Boston. New York rep. Internat. Road Congresses, Paris, 1908, Brussels, 1910, London, 1913, and Internat. Congress of Cities at Ghent, 1913; visited many European cities, 1910, to examine and report upon care and control of subsurface structures; mem. N.Y. City Improvement Commission and Heights of Bldgs. Commn. Mem. delegation of Am. engrs. visiting France, Dec. 1918, at request of French engrs. and ministers to advise on problems of reconstruction after war. Mem. Franco-Am. Engring. Com. Mem. Dutch Reformed Ch. Mem. visiting com. Sch. of Landscape Architects, Harvard; trustee Poly. Inst. Brooklyn. Author: The Planning of the Modern City, 1916, 22. Home: Brooklyn, N.Y. Died Mar. 30, 1924.

LEWIS, PAUL A., pathologist; b. Chicago, Ill., Apr. 14, 1879; s. Clinton H. and Caroline (Hobart) L.; studied U. of Wis., 1897-98, Wis. Coll. Phys. and Surg., Milwaukee, 1899-1901; M.D., U. of Pa., 1904; m. Louise Durbin, Aug. 6, 1906; children—Janet, Hobart. Resident in pathology, Boston City Hosp., 1904-05; asst. in Antitoxin Lab., Mass. State Bd. of Health, Boston, 1905-08; fellow in comparative pathology, Harvard, 1906-08; asso. in pathology, Rockefeller Inst., N.Y. City, 1908-10; dir. Lab. of Henry Phipps Inst., Phila., 1910-23; prof. exptl. pathology, U. of Pa., 1921-23; asso. mem. Rockefeller Inst. for Med. Research, New York, 1923—. Lt., later comdr. U.S. Naval Reserve, Aug. 1917-21; duty at Naval Hosp., League Island, and Naval Lab., Phipps Inst. (temp. establishment). Home: Princeton, N.J. Died June 30, 1929.

LEWIS, WARREN HARMON, educator; b. Suffield, Conn., June 17, 1870; s. John and Adelaide E. (Harmon) L.; student Chgo. Manual Tng. Sch., 1886-89; B.S., U. Mich., 1894; M.D., Johns Hopkins, 1900; m. Margaret Reed, May 23, 1910; children—Margaret Nast, Warren Reed, Jessica Helen. Asst. in zoölogy, U. Mich., 1894-96; asst. in anatomy, Johns Hopkins U., 1900, instr., 1901-03, asso., 1903-04, asso. prof., 1904-13, prof. physiol. anatomy, 1913-40. Research asso., dept. embryology, Carnegie Instn. of Washington, 1919-40; mem. Wistar Inst. Anatomy and Biology, 1940-58, research. Member Mount Desert Island Biological Laboratory (pres. 1933-37). Recipient Harrison Prize Internat. Soc. Cell Biology, 1960. Fellow A.A.A.S.; mem. Internat. Soc. Cell Biology (hon. pres. 1962—), Nat. Acad. Scis., Am. Assn. Anatomists (pres. 1934-36), Am. Physiol. Soc., Am. Soc. Naturalists, Am.

Philos. Soc., Internat. Soc. for Experimental Cytology (pres. 1939-47), Am. Assn. for Cancer Research; hon. mem. Tissue Culture Assn., La Société de Médecine de Gand; fgn. mem. Accademia Nazionale dei Lincei; hon. fellow Royal Micros. Soc. Author numerous important profl. papers relating to cytology and embryology. Co-author: General Cytology; The Structure of Protopalms. Editor of 20th to 24th (inclusive) edits. of Gray's Anatomy. Motion pictures of cells and eggs. Home: Hamilton Ct. Hotel, Phila. 4. Died July 1964.

LEWIS, WILFRED, mech. engr., mfr.; b. Phila., Pa., Oct. 16, 1854; s. Edward and Elizabeth I. L.; grad. Friends' Central Sch., Phila., 1871; B.S. in Mech. Engring., Mass. Inst. Tech., 1875; m. Emily Sargent, Jan. 16, 1895. Mechanic, 1875-78, draftsman, 1879-82, designer, asst. engr. and dir., 1883-1900, William Sellers & Co., Phila.; pres. The Tabor Mfg. Co., 1900—. Inventor and patentee of about 50 patents. Life mem. Am. Soc. Mech. Engrs. (v.p. 1901-03). Republican. Unitarian. Recognized as a world authority on gears, and awarded gold medal of Am. Soc. M.E., 1927, for his contributions to design and construction of gear teeth. Home: Haverford, Pa. Died Dec. 19, 1929.

LEWIS, W(INFORD) LEE, chemist; b. Gridley, Butte County, Calif., May 29, 1878; s. George Madison and Sarah Adeline (Hopper) L.; A.B., Stanford, 1902; A.M., U. of Wash., 1904; Ph.D., U. of Chicago, 1909; m. Myrtilla Mae Lewis, Sept. 1907; children—Mrs. Miriam Lee Reiss, Mrs. Winifred Lee Harwood. Asst. and instr. chemistry, U. of Washington, 1902-04; prof. chemistry, Morningside College, Sioux City, Ia., 1904-06; fellow U. of Chicago, 1907-09; instr. chemistry, Northwestern U., 1909, asst. prof., 1914, asso. prof., 1917, prof. and head of dept., 1919-24. Asst. chemist U.S. Dept. Agr., 1908-10; city chemist, Evanston, 1912-18; consulting practice; dir. dept. of scientific research Inst. Am. Meat Packers since 1924. Capt. Chem. Warfare Service, U.S. Army, 1917-18; maj. U.S.R., 1919; lt. col., 1924; col., 1933. Fellow A.A.A.S., mem. Am. Chem. Soc., Alpha Chi Sigma, Sigma Xi, Kappa Sigma, Chemists Club, Sword and Scabbard. Republican. Episcopalian. Clubs: Originalists, Chaos, Union League (Chicago); University, Rotary (Evanston). Home: 2323 Central Park Av., Evanston, Ill. Office: 59 E. Van Buren St., Chicago, Ill. Died Jan. 20, 1943.

LEWTON, FREDERICK LEWIS, technologist; b. Cleve., Mar. 17, 1874; s. George Washington and Annie Louise (Taylor) L.; student Rollins Coll., Winter Park, Fla., 1887-90; grad. Drexel Inst., Phila., 1895; A.B., George Washington U., 1922; D.Sc., Rollins Coll., 1930; m. Emilie Marie Hempel, June 29, 1899; children—Lillian Louise (Mrs. J. B. Hopkins), Myrtle Hempel (Mrs. H. I. Rothrock), Rhoda (Mrs. J. Jennings), Norma (Mrs. P. Michaelson); m. 2d, Blanche Banister Clark, July 24, 1930. Instr. chemistry Drexel Inst., Phila., 1895-1904; econ. botanist Phila. Comml. Mus., 1896-1900, curator, 1900-04; sci. asst., Bur. Plant Industry, U.S. Dept. Agr., 1904-08, asst. botanist, 1908-12; curator div. crafts and industries U.S. Nat. Mus., 1912-46, research associate in crafts and industries, 1946—. Archivist, Rollings College since 1954. Director Northwestern Fed. Savs. & Loan Assn. Mem. Washington Acad. Scis. Phila. Acad. Natural Scis. Presbyn. Author numerous papers on botany of econ. plants and history of inventions; contbr. to Century Dictionary, Bailey's Ency. Horticulture, Book of Rural Life. Home: 1911 Englewood Rd., Winer Park, Fla. Died Feb. 21, 1959.

L'HOMMEDIEU, EZRA, state senator, agriculturist; b. Southold, L.I., N.Y., Aug. 30, 1734; s. Benjamin and Martha (Borune) L'H.; grad. Yale, 1754; m. Charity Floyd, 1765; m. 2d, Mary Havens, 1803. Admitted to bar; mem. N.Y. Provincial Congresses, 1774-77, a framer Constn. of 1777; mem. N.Y. Assembly, 1777-83; del. from N.Y. to Continental Congresses, 1779-83; 87-88; mem. N.Y. State Senate, 1784-1809, Council of Appointment, 1784, 99; clk. Suffolk County, 1784-1809; noted as principal author of U. State N.Y. as reconstituted in 1787, regent, 1784-1811; mem. Interpretative Constl. Conv., 1801; wrote numerous papers on agr. for Transactions of N.Y. Soc. for Promotion Agr. Arts and Manufactures, v.p., many years. Died Southold, Sept. 27, 1811.

LI, KUO-CHING, mining engr.; b. Changsha, Hunan, China, Sept. 24, 1892; s. Chan and Queen Tan Li; M.E., Hunan Tech. Inst., Changsha, 1909; A.R.S.M., Royal Sch. Mines, London, 1915; D.Sc. (hon.), Clark University, 1958; m. Po-ku Loo, 1911; children—Lien Ming (Mrs. K.C. Koo), Lien Fung (Mrs. R. H. Ho), Lien Yen (adopted); m. 2d, Grace E. Fung, Oct. 15, 1917; children—Marjorie (Mrs. Alfred Wu), Mildred (Mrs. William Distin), Madeline (Mrs. Edward Leong Way), Kuo-ching, Jr., Marie (Mrs. Gordon Chun), and John Choi (adopted). Came to the United States, 1916, naturalized, 1948. Secretary of the Hunan Mining Bd., 1909-12; dept. commr. of Mining Bd. to Study Mining and Geol. Methods in Europe and Am., 1912-15; successively sec. of Hunan Mining Bd., pres. Kiang Wah Govt. Tin Mines; pres. Hsiao Ky San Govt. Mines, co-dir., Hunan Mining Bd., 1915-16; v.p. and N.Y. mgr. on formation Wah Chang Mining and Smelting Co., Ltd., 1915, pres. and mng. dir. of Wah Chang Trading Corp., 1916, rep. in N.Y. of the Ministry of Finance and Ministry of Agrl. and Commerce; Gov. Commodity Exchange, N.Y. City, since 1928; chmn. bd. and chief engr. Wah Chang Smelting & Refining Co. of Am., Inc., since 1940; pres. Wah Chang Corp.; dir. Central Bank of China, 1936-48; chmn. Wah Chang Mining Corp., Bishop, Cal.; dir. Howe Sound Co. Trustee China Inst. Am.; trustee, mem. finance com. China Found.; v.p. China Soc. Am. Adv. Chinese Embassy, Washington, 1943-44; mem. exec. com. UN Com. N.Y.C., 1955, Mayor's Reception Com. N.Y., 1956—. Govt. decorations: Cheaho, Peking, 1920; Order of Merit, Nanking, 1937; Order of Jade, Chungking, 1945; Order So. Cross, Brazil, 1956; Order Crown Thailand, 1960; recipient Peace and Friendship medal, Ore., 1957; Chinese Inst. Engrs. award, 1957; Chem. Engring. Achievement award, 1957. A founder the Li Found. (internal edn.), 1944, K.C. Li medal and prize at Columbia for meritorious achievement in advancing sci. of Tungsten, 1948. Discoverer 1st tungsten deposits in China, 1911; co-inventor "Li Process" for tungsten carbide mfr. Mem. Am. Inst. Mining, Metall. and Petroleum Engrs., Mining and Metall. Soc. Am., China Soc. Am., Chamber of Commerce of State of New York, Incorporated. Mason. Clubs: University, Mining, Chemists, Lawyers, Piping Rock, Creek, Downtown Athletic, Lotos. Author: Tungsten: Its History, Geology, Ore Dressing, Metallurgy, Chemistry, Analysis, Application and Economics, 1947. Editor: America Diplomacy in the Far East, ann. vols., 1938-42. Home: 22 Thompson Park, Glen Cove, N.Y. Office: 233 Broadway, N.Y.C. 7. Died Mar. 7, 1961.

LIBBY, SAMUEL HAMMONDS, engr.; b. Limerick, Me., Nov. 20, 1864; s. Hall Jackson and Mary Caroline (Hasty) L.; ed. pub. schs., Mass.; student Lowell (Mass.) Commercial Coll., 1881-82; m. Florence Emeline Price, Feb. 8, 1894; children—Eugene Herbert, Donald Price, Margaret Caroline (Mrs. Chas. P.W. Schmidt). Apprentice in iron molding, Boston, Mass., 1882-86; worker in pattern and model making, 1886-89; mech. draftsman, Thomson-Houston Electric Co., Lynn, Mass., 1889, continuing through formation of Gen. Electric Co., then filling positions in railway engring. dept., as draftsman, exptl. engr. and constrn. engr.; transferred to Schenectady (N.Y.) works, 1894; supervised equipment with electric motors Nantasket Beach branch of New Haven R.R., 1895-96; installation electric equipment South Side Elevated R.R., Chicago, Ill., 1897-98, Brooklyn Elevated R.R., 1898; engineer electric hoist department, Bloomfield (N.J.) works, 1904-23, cons. engr., 1922-26, also editor works paper 1919-26, safety engr., 1926; became supervisor personnel, continuing work with plant paper, safety work, and as mem. com. on adjustment of wages and working conditions, 1928-32; retired 1932. Fellow Am. Soc. M.E. (formerly chmn. metropolitan sect.; com. on relations with colleges; com. on admissions). Formerly active in civic, ednl. and church work in New Jersey. Mem. Kiwanis Club of East Orange since 1922; pres. 1924; lt. gov. N.J. Dist., 1925-26. Co-organizer of Retired Business and Professional Men's Association of the Oranges. Mason. Member First Baptist Church of East Orange (deacon.). Holder of 34 patents covering electrical apparatus. Home: 23 Whittlesey Av., East Orange NJ

LIBMAN, EMANUEL, physician; b. New York, N.Y., 1872; s. Fajbush and Hulda (Spivak) L.; A.B., Coll. City of N.Y., 1891; M.D., Coll. Phys. and Surg. (Columbia), 1894; house phys. Mt. Sinai Hosp., 1894-96; post-grad. work, Berlin, Vienna, Munich, 1896-97, Berlin, 1903, 09, Johns Hopkins, 1906; unmarried. Practiced, New York since 1894; asso. pathologist, 1898-1923, attending phys., 1912-25, now cons. physician, Mt. Sinai Hosp.; cons. physician, Montefiore Hosp., Harlem Hosp., Beth Israel Hosp., Hosp. for Joint Diseases, French Hosp. (New York); Methodist-Episcopal Hosp., United Israel-Zion Hosp., Beth-El Hosp. (Brooklyn), etc. Chmn. advisory bd. Selective Draft, 1918. Mem. Am. Jewish Physicians Com. (chmn. exec. com.); mem. Council Jewish Agency for Palestine; mem. bd. govs. Hebrew Univ. (Jerusalem); v.p. Am. Friends of Hebrew U.; mem. Central Com. Union des Sociétés OSE; pres. Dazian Foundation for Med. Research. Chmn. Emergency Com. in Aid of Displaced Foreign Med. Scientists. Fellow N.Y. Acad. Medicine; mem. Am. Assn. Pathologists and Bacterologists, A.A.A.S., Assn. Am. Physicians, Am. Soc. Advancement Clinical Investigation, Am. Coll. Physicians, Internat. Assn. Geographic Pathology, Internat. Med. Museums Assn., Pathol. Soc. N.Y., Harvey Soc., Am. Assn. Immunologists, Phi Beta Kappa; corr. mem. Société Française de Cardiologie. Contbr. papers appertaining to clin. medicine, pathology and bacteriology. Address: 180 E. 64th St., New York, N.Y. Died June 28, 1946. *

LICHTY, L(ESTER (CLYDE), engr., educator; b. Carleton, Neb., July 5, 1891; s. William Willis and Pauline Marie (Becker) L.; B.S. in mech. engring., Univ. of Neb., 1913; M.S., Univ. of Ill., 1916; research asst., Yale, 1923-24, M.E., 1925; M. Hazel Virginia Kelso, Aug. 5, 1919; children—Jean Lee (Mrs. Joseph K. Hill), Betty Lou (Mrs. James H. Johnson), Patricia Ann (Mrs. Thomas J. Morse). Asst. prof. mech. engring. U. Okla., 1916-21, asso. prof., 1921-24; asst. prof., Yale, 1924-30, asso. prof., 1930-45, prof., 1945-50, Robert Higgin prof. mech. engring.; 1950-72. Served as lt. with U.S. Air Service, 1917-19; contractor, A.A.F., analytical research on engine performance, 1940-43; consultant Socony-Vacuum Labs., 1945-72, U.S. Navy Underwater Ordnance Sta., 1951-72. Mem. Am. Soc. Mech. Engrs., Soc. Automotive Engrs. (v.p., diesel engine sect., 1941), Am. Chem. Soc., Am. Assn. Engring. Edn., Sigma Xi, Tau Beta Pi, Sigma Tau, Beta Theta Pi. Republican. Conglist. Clubs: Faculty, Grad., Mory's (all New Haven). Author: (Natural Gas, 1924; Thermodynamics, 1936, 1948; Internal Combustion Engines (with Streeter), 3d and 4th eds., 1929, 1933; Internal Combustion Engines, 1939; contbr. sect. on internal combustion engines to Marks' Mech. Engrs. Handbook, 1941, 51, 58. Home: New Haven CT Died Dec. 13, 1972; buried New Haven CT

LIDDELL, DONALD MACY, (lid-del'), engr.; b. Lawrenceburg, Ind., Feb. 28, 1879; s. Oliver Brown and Josephine (Major) L.; A.B. (chem. and phys. course), John Hopkins, 1900; m. Edith Stabler, Dec. 2, 1905; children—Donald M., Jr., Edith Jordan (Twiss). With Detroit Copper Mining Co., Morenci, Ariz., 1900-01, Balt. Copper Smelting & Rolling Co., 1901-05, U.S. Metals Refining Co., Chrome, N.J., and Grasselli, Ind., 1905-10; asso. editor, mng. editor Engring. and Mining Jour., N.Y.C., 1910-16; cons. engr. with Merrill, Lynch & Co., 1916-17; partner firm Weld & Liddell, cons. engrs., 1919-36; pres. Homewood Apartment Co. Balt.; dir. Nat. State Bank, Elizabeth, N.J.; dir. Compañia Minera del Sur. Cuba trustee Nat. State Corp. Capt. A.S., O.R.C., active service, Feb. 2, 1918-May 20, 1919; with Res., July 6, 1919-Sept. 22, 1924; commd. maj. Res., Sept. 22, 1924, lt. col., Nov. 20 1930; on active duty with Prodn. Engring. Br., Air Corps, July 15, 1942-Oct. 10, 1943; chief engr. War Credits Bd., Dec. 2, 1917-Apr. 25, 1918. Mem. Mining and Metall. Soc. Am., Am. Inst. M.E., Mil. Order Loyal Legion, Mil. Order Fgn. Wars, Beta Theta Pi, Phi Beta Kappa. Republican. Clubs: Army and Navy (Washington); (hon. mem.) Mining (London); Mining (pres.), Univ. (N.Y.C.). Author: Metallurgists and Chemists Handbook, 1916; Handbook of Chemical Engineering, 1922; Handbook of Non-Ferrous Metall., 1926, revised 1945; The Uncommon Metals, 1949; also numerous articles tech. jours. Co-author: International Control of Mineral Resources, 1926; The Principles of Metallurgy, 1932; Mineral Resources of the Unitd States and Its Capacity to Produce, 1934; Chessmen, 1937. Originated selenium recovery methods in use for many years in most Am. copper refineries; several waterproofing methods for stucco work; first successful commercial watermix method for magnesium-oxichloride stucco. Home: 30 E. 55th St., N.Y.C. Office: 33 Rector St., N.Y.C. Died Aug. 16, 1958.

LIDDELL, HOWARD SCOTT, prof. psychobiology; b. Cleveland, O., Nov. 9, 1895; s. Charles Skinner and Eva Antoinette (Nodine) L.; A.B., U. of Mich., 1917, A.M., 1918; Ph.D., Cornell U., 1923; m. Elzie Margerita Goodnough, 1920; children—Prescott Scott, John Skinner. Instr. of physiology, Cornell U., 1918-24, asst. prof. 1926-30, prof., 1930-39; prof. psychobiology since 1939; director of Cornell Behavior Farm Laboratory; National Research fellow in biological sciences, 1924-26. Mem. A.A.A.S., Am. Physiol. Soc., Soc. Exptl. Biology and Medicine, Am. Psychol. Assn., Am. Soc. of Naturalists, Am. Soc. for Research in Psychosomatic Problems, Soc. Applied Anthropology, Am. Psychopath. Assn., Acad. Psychoanalysis, Internat. Brain Research Organization (member panel behavioral sciences). Contributor scientific articles to jours. Field of work: comparative physiology of conditioned reflex and exptl. neurosis. Home: 116 Schuyler Place, Ithaca, N.Y. Died Oct. 24, 1962.

LIEB, CHARLES CHRISTIAN, (leb), pharmacologist; b. N.Y.C., Apr. 19, 1880; s. Charles Adam and Magdalena (Stephan) L.; student Columbia Inst., 1893-98; A.B., Columbia Coll., 1902, M.D., Coll. Phys. and Surg., 1906; post-grad. London U., 1908-09, Utrecht U., 1929; m. Henrietta Haaker, June 25, 1908. Instr., Coll. Phys. and Surg., Columbia, 1909-10, asst. prof. pharmacology, 1910-21, asso. prof., 1921-23, prof., 1923-29, Hosask prof. 1929-44, Hosack prof. emeritus, 1944—. Mem. Physiol. Soc. (London), Am. Physiol. Soc., Soc. of Pharmacology and Exptl. Therapeutics, Soc. Exptl. Biology and Medicine, A.M.A., Phi Delta Theta, Phi Beta Kappa, Sigma Xi, Alpha Omega Alpha. Presbyn. Clubs: University, Columbia University, Columbia Faculty. Home: 1 W. 72d St. Office: 630 W. 168th St., N.Y.C. Died April 1956.

LIEB, JOHN WILLIAM, mech. engineer; b. Newark, N.J., Feb. 12, 1860; s. John William and Christina (Zens) L.; ed. Newark Acad. and Stevens H.S., Hoboken, N.J.; E.D., M.E., Stevens Inst. Tech., 1880; m. Minnie F. Engler, July 29, 1886. Employed as draftsman, 1880-81; by Mr. Edison put in charge of installation of elec. equipment of old Pearl St., Edison Sta., and assisted in subsequent tests and experiments on this first elec. sta. in U.S., supplying current for incandescent lighting and power from an underground system, and on inauguration of regular service, Sept. 4, 1882, was apptd. first electrician Edison Electric illuminating Co. of New York; next installed mech. equipment, dynamos, and Edison Underground System at Milan, Italy, 1883, for Italian Edison Co.; later installed trolley system in Milan; returned to Edison

Elec. Illuminating Co., 1894; now v.p. and gen. mgr. New York Edison Co.; also pres. Elec. Testing Laboratories; dir. in a number of corps. Decorated by King of Italy, Knight Comdr. Order Crown of Italy. Trustee Stevens Institute of Technology. Home: New York, N.Y. Died Nov. 1, 1929.

LIEBER, EUGENE, educator; b. Phila., July 15, 1907; s. Samuel and Rose (Diamond) L.; B.S. in Chemistry, U. Pa., 1930; Ph.D., Poly. Inst. Bklyn., 1937; m. Gertrude Martz, June 11, 1930; 1 dau., Dorothy Sandberg. Research chemist Standard Oil Co. N.J., 1930-45; faculty Poly. Inst. Bklyn., 1937-44; asso. prof. chemistry Ill. Inst. Tech., 1948-51; asso. prof. Purdue U., 1953-55; asso. prof. DePaul U., 1955, prof. chemistry, 1957-59; prof. chemistry, chmn. dept. Roosevelt U., Chgo., 1959—, also trustee univ.; vis. prof. chemistry U. Coll., Cork, Ireland, 1964-65. Head inorganic chemistry br., research dept. U.S. Naval Ordnance Test Sta., China Lake, Cal., 1951-52, head chemistry div., 1952-53. Recipient Patriotic Civilian Service award U.S. Army, 1962. Mem. Am. Inst. Chemists (chmn. Chgo. 1961-62), Am. Chem. Soc., Am. Assn. U. Profs., Sigma Xi, Alpha Chi Sigma, Tau Beta Pi. Club: Chemists (Chgo.). Contbr. articles profl. jours. Home: White Oak Av., Hammond, Ind. Died Sept. 10, 1965.

LIFE, ANDREW CREAMOR, botanist; b. Grant Co., Ind., July 30, 1869; s. Christian and Ruth Ann (Elliott) L.; A.B., Ind. U., 1896, A.M., 1897; post grad. student Washington U., St. Louis, Mo., 1904-06, U. of Chicago, 1906-07, U. of Calif., 1923-24, also several summers; m. Cora Mae Smith, June 20, 1917. Began as instr. botany, Earlham Coll., 1904; instr. botany, Washington U., 1904-06; asst. prof. botany, U. of Southern Calif., 1907-10, asso. prof., 1910-15, prof., 1915—. Methodist. Mason. Made trip around World for ednl. purposes, 1931. Home: Los Angeles, Calif. Died Sept. 8, 1933.

LIGHT, RUDOLPH ALVIN, surgeon; b. Kalamazoo, Sept. 21, 1909; s. Stellar Rudolph and Rachel Winifred (Upjohn) L.; Ph.B., Yale, 1931; B.A. in Physiology, Oxford (Eng.) U., 1934, M.A., 1937; M.D., Vanderbilt U., 1939; m. Ann Bonner Jones, June 8, 1932 (div. 1960); one daughter, Deborah Ann (Mrs. Peter J. Perry); m. second, Helen Ann Rork, Mar. 25, 1960. Began as junior intern, then sr. intern surgery, Lakeside Hosp., Cleve., 1939-41; asst. resident, then resident surgery, Vanderbilt Hosp., 1941-43, 46-47; asst. chief surgery VA Hosp., Nashville, 1947-48, dir. research, 1947-49, acting chief surgery, 1948; asso. prof. surgery Vanderbilt U. Sch. Medicine and Hosp., 1948-57, dir. surg. research, 1949-57, dir. rehab. service, 1956-57; vis. surgeon Nuffield dent. surgery Oxford U., 1958-62. Dir. Upjohn Co., Kalamazoo. Mem. exec. bd. Middle Tenn. council Boy Scouts Am., 1949-58, later member of the National council and member of the national executive board; pres., dir. Nashville Civic Music Assn., 1951-53; pres. Nashville Ednl. Television Found., 1953-57, Light Found., Kalamazoo, from 1958; exec. com. Tenn. Heart Assn., 1955-58, dir., 1956-58, sec., 1956-57; pres., trustee Rudolph A. Light Scholarship Found., from 1966; trustee Nashville Children Mus.; dir. Middle Tenn. Heart Assn., 1950-53, 56-58. Hon. fellow St. Catherine's Coll., Oxford U., Eng.; trustee Vanderbilt U.; Senior Citizens, Inc., Nashville. Served to capt., M.C., AUS, World War II; PTO. Decorated Bronze Star medal; hon. comdr. Most Excellent Order of British Empire; recipient Silver Beaver award Boy Scouts Am. Diplomate Am. Bd. Surgery. Mem. A.C.S., Soc. Univ. Surgeons, So. Surg. Assn., Am. Fedn. Clin. Research, Southeastern Surg. Congress, A.A.A.S., N.Y. Academy Sciences, A.M.A., Tennessee State Medical Society, Sigma Xi, Alpha Chi Rho, Phi Chi. Clubs: Yale (N.Y.C.); University (Chgo.); Belle Meade Country (Nashville); Farmington Country (Charlottesville, Va.); Tryall Country, Half Moon Rose Hall Country (Jamaica, W.I.); Metropolitan (N.Y.C.); Lost Tree, Lost Tree Village (North Palm Beach, Fla.) Cumberland (Nashville). Author articles. Address: Nashville TN Died Jan. 1970.

LILIENTHAL, HOWARD, surgeon; b. Albany, N.Y., Jan. 9, 1861; s. Meyer and Jennie (Marcus) L.; A.B. cum laude, Harvard Univ., 1883, M.D., Harvard Medical School, 1887; McLean Asylum, br. Mass. Gen. Hosp., 1886; grad. Mt. Sinai Hosp., New York, 1888; m. Mary Harriss d'Antignac, Oct. 19, 1891 (died Mar. 4, 1910); children—Mary d'Antignac (Mrs. Thompson Lawrence), Howard (dec.); m. 2d, Edith Strode, Nov. 7, 1911. Lecturer on surgery, N.Y. Polyclinic, 1888; now cons. surgeon N.Y. Polyclinic; surgeon, Mt. Sinai Hosp., 1892-1940, Bellevue Hosp., 1909-40; now retired from active practice; prof. clin. surgery, Cornell U. Med. Coll. for some years from 1917. Commd. 1st lt. Med. Reserve Corps, 1911 (resigned); maj. M.R.C., Apr. 26, 1917; lt. col., M.C., U.S. Army, June 21, 1918; dir. Base Hosp. 3, at Monpont sur l'Isle; served Meuse-Argonne and St. Mihiel as head of operating team 39, at Evacuation Hosp. 8, also base hosps. 101 and 34; hon. disch. Jan. 4, 1919; cited for D.S.M., May 1, 1921. Fellow American College of Surgeons (Founders Group), and American Board of Surgery, A.A.A.S.; member American Society Control of Cancer, A.M.A., American Surg. Association, American Soc. Thoracic Surgery (ex-pres.), N.Y., Soc. for Thoracic Surgery (ex-pres.), New York Surg. Soc. (ex-pres.), Med. Soc. Co. of N.Y. (ex-pres.), New York Acad. Medicine, Société Internat. de Chirurgie, Mil. Order World Wars (ex-surg. gen.), Am. Legion, Beta Theta Pi; corr. mem. Académie de Chirurgie. Republican. Clubs: University (Winter Park, Florida); Harvard. Author: Imperative Surgery, 1900; Thoracic Surgery, 1925. Contbr. to Binnie's Treatise on Regional Surgery, 1917, and Ochsner's Surgical Diagnosis and Treatment, 1920; more than 300 contbns. to surg. literature. Advisory editor Jour. of Thoracic Surgery. Home: 20 W. 77th St., New York 24, N.Y. Died Apr. 30, 1946.

LILIENTHAL, JOSEPH LEO, JR., physician; b. N.Y. City, Nov. 1, 1911; s. Joseph Leo and Edna (Arnstein) L.; B.S., Yale, 1933; M.D., Johns Hopkins, 1937; m. Katherine Arnstein, June 25, 1937; children—Julia, Nina. Clinical Clerk, National Hospital. Queen's Square, London, England, 1937; house officer Presbyterian Hospital, New York City, 1938-40; resident physician Johns Hopkins Hospital, 1940-42, physician since 1946; asso. prof. medicine Johns Hopkins, since 1946, prof. environmental medicine since 1950; research neuromuscular and respiratory physiology. Cons. Nat. Science Found.; mem. com. aviation medicine and com. naval med. research Nat. Research Council. Mem. med. bd. Nat. Muscular Dystrophy Assn. Cons. to Sec. of Def., Research and Development Bd., 1948-53. Office of Naval Research, 1951—. Surgeon Gen. Dept. Army, 1950-53, clin. center Nat. Inst. Health. Mem. Nat. Bd. Med. Examiners, chmn. medicine test com. Physiol. Study Sect. Nat. Inst. Health USPHS, 1953—. Served as lt. comdr., U.S.N.R., 1942-46. Fellow N.Y. Academy Sci.; mem. Am. Institute Biological Sciences, American Clinical Climatological Association, Society of Medical Consultants to Armed Forces, Association of American Physicians, Am. Soc. Clin. Investigation, Am. Physiol. Society, Society Exptl. Biology and Medicine (mem. nat. council), Interurban Clinical Club, American Federation Clinical Research, Sigma Xi, Phi Beta Kappa, Alpha Omega Alpha, Phi Gamma Delta. Club: 14 W. Hamilton St. Home: 6203 Blackburn Lane, Baltimore 12. Office: Johns Hopkins Hospital, Balt. 5. Died Nov. 19, 1955.

LILJESTRAND, GORAN, educator, scientist; b. Gothenburg, Sweden, Apr. 16, 1886; s. Petter Erik and Tekla (Carlberg) L.; Candidate Medicine, Stockholm, 1909, Licentiate of Medicine, 1915, M.D., 1917, D.Sc. (honorary), 1952; M.D. (honorary), Dorpat, 1932, Ghent, 1955, Paris, 1958; was married to Elsa Margareta Wretlind, Dec. 10, 1910 (dec. 1948); children—Brita (Mrs. Sven Grape), Ake, Margit (Mrs. Kjell Halvarson); m. 2d, Maud von Koch, Oct. 24, 1949; 1 son, Nils Goran. Asst. prof. physiology Caroline Inst., Stockholm, Sweden, 1917-23; asst. prof. physiology and pharmacology, 1923-27, prof. pharmacology, 1927-51. Mem. Nobel Com., 1938-51, sec. for physiology and medicine, 1918-60; sec. 12th Internat. Physiol. Congress, Stockholm, 1926. Recipient Alvarenga prize from Swedish Med. Soc., 1918, 23, 25, Regnell prize, 1946; Bjorken prize U. Uppsala, 1930; Schmioberg Plaquette Deutsche. Pharmakol. Ges., 1962. Honorary member of the American, British, Scandinavian (secretary 1926-31, 35-51) physiological societies, British Pharmacol. Soc., Deutsche Pharmakol. Ges., Swedish Med. Soc., A.M.A., Alpha Omega Alpha; mem. Swedish, Danish, Finnish acads. sci., Akad. of Naturforscher, N.Y. Acad. Medicine, hon. mem, Acad. de Medicine Brussels Soc. Philomatique, Paris. Author: Lehrbuch der Pharmakologie (Leipzig). Contbg. author: Nobel, the Man and His Prizes; Karolinska Institutets historia 1910-60; (with B. Holmstedt) Readings in Pharmacology, 1963. Editor of Acta Physiologica Scandinavica, 1940-67, Les Prix Nobel, 1953, 64. Published over 200 papers mainly on respiration and circulation. Home: Bromma Sweden Died Jan. 16, 1968.

LILLIE, FRANK RATTRAY, zoölogist; b. Toronto, Ont., June 27, 1870; s. George W. and Emily (Rattray) L.; A.B., Univ. of Toronto, 1891; fellow Clark Univ., 1891-92, Univ. of Chicago, 1892-93, Ph.D., 1894; D.Sc., Univ. of Toronto, 1919, Yale, 1932, and Harvard University, 1938; LL.D., Johns Hopkins University, 1942; m. Frances Crane, June 29, 1895. Instr. zoölogy, U. of Mich., 1894-99; prof. biology, Vassar Coll., 1899-1900; asst. prof. zoölogy and embryology, 1900-02, asso. prof., 1902-07, prof. since 1907, chmn. dept. zoölogy, 1911-35, dean of division of biological sciences, 1931-35, U. of Chicago. Head dept. zoology, 1893-1907, assistant director, 1900-08, dir., 1908-26, pres., 1925-1942, Marine Biol. Lab., Woods Hole, Mass.; pres. Woods Hole Oceanographic Inst., 1930-39; dir. Crane Co. Mng. editor Biol. Bulletin, 1902-26; associate editor Journal Experimental Zoölogy Physiological Zoölogy. Fellow A.A.A.S. (v.p. 1914); mem. Nat. Acad. Sciences (pres. 1935-39), National Research Council (chairman 1935-36), American Philos. Soc., Acad. Nat. Sci., Phila.; Société Belge de Biologie, Société de Biologie, Paris, Am. Soc. Naturalists (v.p. 1914, pres. 1915), Am. Soc. Zoölogists (pres. Central Br. 1905-08), Assn. Am. Anatomists, Boston Soc. Natural History, Am. Philos. Soc., Royal Soc. of Edinburgh, Zoöl. Soc. of London. Clubs: Quadrangle, University (Chicago); Cosmos (Washington, D.C.); Century Assn. (New York). Contbr. to scientific jours. Home: 5801 Kenwood Av., Chicago. Died Nov. 5, 1947.

LILLIE, HOWARD RUSSELL, physicist; b. North East, Pa., May 13, 1902; s. Russell Clarence and Frances Evelyn (Middleditch) L.; B.S., Allegheny Coll., 1924; M.S., U. Wis., 1926; m. Jennie Hammond, Aug. 18, 1932; 1 dau., Alice Jane. Physicist Corning (N.Y.) Glass Works since 1927, staff manager fundamental phys. research, 1958—. Pres. exec. com. Internat. Commn. on Glass, 1959—. Mem. Am. Ceramic Soc. (chmn. upstate N.Y. sect. 1945-46, chmn. glass div. 1948-49, pres. elect 1950-51), Optical Soc. Am., Soc. Rheology (sec. 1939-40), Soc. Glass Tech., Corning C. of C.; Sigma Xi, Theta Chi. Mason. Contbr. articles to publs. Home: 191 Delevan Av. Office: Corning Glass Works, Corning, N.Y. 14830. Died Feb. 15, 1961.

LILLIE, RALPH STAYNER, biologist, educator; b. Toronto, Can., Aug. 8, 1875; s. George Waddell and Emily Ann (Rattray) L.; B.A., U. Toronto, 1896, hon. Sc.D., 1936; grad. student U. Mich., 1896; Ph.D., U. Chgo., 1901; m. Helen Eva Makepeace, June 2, 1906; children—Frank Rattray, Walter Makepeace. Asst. in physiology Harvard, 1901-02, instr. physiology, 1905-06; instr. and adj. prof. physiology U. Neb., 1902-05; research asst. Carnegie Inst. Zoöl. Sta., Naples, Italy, 1904-05; Johnston scholar Johns Hopkins, 1906-07; instr. asst. prof. physiology and exptl. zoölogy U. of Pa., 1907-13; prof. biology Clark U., 1913-20; biologist Nela Research Lab., Cleve., 1920-24; prof. gen. physiology U. Chgo., 1924-40, prof. emeritus, 1940—; instr. and investigator general physiology Marine Biol. Lab., Woods Hole, Mass., 1902—. Fellow Am. Acad. Arts and Sciences, A.A.A.S.; mem. Am. Physiol. Soc., Am. Soc. Biol. Chemists, Am. Soc. Naturalists, Soc. Exptl. Biology and Medicine, Am. Soc. Zoölogists, Am. Philos. Soc., Phi Beta Kappa, Sigma Xi. Trustee Marine Biol. Lab., Woods Hole, Mass. Spl. researches in fundamental properties of living substance and physiology of stimulation, growth, cell-division, radiation effects, philosophical aspects of biology. Home: 5545 Kenwood Av., Chgo. 37. Died Mar. 19, 1952.

LILLIE, SAMUEL MORRIS, inventor, mfr.; b. Troy, N.Y., Apr. 26, 1851; s. Lewis and Mary Converse (Morris) L.; E.M., Columbia, 1874; m. Narcissa Neff, of Phila., Pa., Jan. 31, 1894. Chemist, Kings Co. Refining Co., 1874-75, Franklin Sugar Refinery, Phila., 1876-84; introducing own inventions, 1884-88; became 1st v.p. Sugar Apparatus Mfg. Co., 1888, now pres.; inventor a multiple effect evaporator, in use in leading countries of world, also many devices applied in heat, power and mfg. problems. Member American Soc. Naval Engrs., Franklin Inst., New England Soc. of Pa., Order Founders and Patriots of America. Republican. Author: Heat in Sugar Refineries, 1889. Lillie evaporators for distilling sea water were made the standard, and projected by the U.S. Navy Dept., 1922-23, for all its vessels, 30 of the larger ships equipped (1923) at a cost of upwards of $30,000 per ship. Home: Overbrook and Lancaster Avs., Philadelphia, Pa.

LILLY, JOSIAH KIRBY, manufacturing chemist; b. Greencastle, Ind., Nov. 18, 1861; s. Eli and Emily (Lemon) L.; studied Asbury (now DePauw) U., 1874-76; Ph.G., cum laude, Philadelphia College of Pharmacy, 1882; m. Lily Marie Ridgely, November 18, 1882; m. 2d, Lila Allison, June 29, 1935. Entered manufacturing pharmacy with father, 1876; dir. laboratories of Eli Lilly & Co., 1882-98; became pres. and exec. head same on death of father, 1898, now chmn. bd. Pioneer in alkaloidal standardization of medicines. Dir. Indianapolis Y.M.C.A., 18 yrs. Episcopalian. Mem. Am. Pharm. Assn., Ind. Pharm. Assn., Am. Chem. Soc., Am. Mfrs. Assn., Loyal Legion. Clubs: University Columbia, Art, Contemporary, Country. Home: Crows Nest, Indianapolis, Inc. Died Feb. 8, 1948. *

LINCECUM, GIDEON, physician, naturalist; b. Hancock County, Ga., Apr. 22, 1793; s. Hezekiah and Sally (Hickman) L.; studied medicine privately, Ga., 1815-17; m. Sarah Bryan, Oct. 25, 1814. Commr. apptd. by Miss. Legislature to organize County of Monroe, 1821-22; Indian trader in Miss., 1823-circa 1827; practiced medicine, Cotton Gin Port, Columbus, Miss., 1830-48; owned plantation, Long Point, Tex., 1848-74, studied insects and made lengthy investigation of life of mound-building ants; corresponded with many fgn. naturalists including Charles Darwin; sent specimens to Smithsonian Instn., Acad. Natural Scis., Phila., Jardin des Plantes, Paris, France; papers on insects published in Jour. of Proc. of Linnaean Soc., Vol. 6, London, 1852, and in Proc. of Acad. Nat. Scis. of Phila., 2d series, Vol. X, 1866. Died Long Point, Nov. 28, 1874; buried Long Point.

LINCOLN, AZARIAH THOMAS, (ling'kun), chemist; b. Montfort, Wis., June 25, 1868; s. Joseph Hollis and Margaret (Laird) L.; B.S., U. Wis., 1894, M.S., 1898, fellow, 1898-99, Ph.D., 1899; m. Jennette Emeline Carpenter, June 30, 1904. Instr. chemistry, U. Cin., 1900-01; instr. chemistry U. Ill., 1901-03, asst. prof., 1903-08; asst. prof. chemistry Rensselaer Poly. Inst., 1908-12, prof. phys. chemistry, 1912-21; prof. chemistry; Carleton Coll., 1921-23, chmn. dept. chemistry, 1923-39, prof. emeritus, 1939—. Mem. Am. Chem. Soc., Am. Electro-Chemical Soc., Soc. Chem. Industry, A.A.A.S., Sigma Xi, Phi Lambda Upsilon, Alpha Chi Sigma. Republican. Conglist. Author:

Elementary Quantitative Analysis (Lincoln and Walton), 1907; Textbook of Physical Chemistry, 1918. Translator: (with David H. Carnahan) Theoretical Principles of the Methods of Analytical Chemistry, Based upon Chemical Reactions (from the French), 1910; General Chemistry, 1927. Home: 203 Maple Av., Northfield, Minn. Died Mar. 31, 1958; buried Lancaster, Minn.

LINCOLN, FRANCIS CHURCH, mining engr.; b. Boston, Mass., Sept. 8, 1877; s. Charles Thayer and Lena Simmons (Church) L.; grad. English High Sch., Boston, 1895; S.B. in mining engring., Mass. Inst. Tech., 1900; E.M., N.M. School of Mines, 1904; A.M. in geology, Columbia, 1906, Ph.D., 1911; m. Gertrude Whipple Appleton, June 19, 1901 (deceased); children—Leslie Appleton (Mrs. Jean de Berard), Francis Appleton; m. 2d, Florence May Curtis (Hill), Dec. 22, 1923; children—William Theodore, Robert Charles. Was assayer for Butterfly-Terrible Gold Mining Co., Ames, Colo., 1900-01; prof. geology and metallurgy, N.M. Sch. of Mines, 1901-04, asst. supt. Ruby Gold & Copper Co., Batamote, Mex., 1904-05; lessee, Ariz. Gold & Copper Co., Patagonia, Ariz., 1905-06; cons. mining engring. practice, New York, 1906-07, 1910-11; prof. geology, Mont. Sch. of Mines, Butte, 1907-10; asst. prof. mining, U. of Ill., 1911-13; mining engr. Bolivian Development and Exploitation Co., La Paz, Bolivia, 1913-14; state ore sampler for Nev., 1917-20; director Mackay School of Mines (University of Nevada), 1914-23; prof. mining, South Dakota State Sch. of Mines, 1923-44; cons. mining engr. United States Bureau of Mines, 1942-44; project engineer, U.S. Bureau of Mines, Platteville, Wis., 1944-45; State Inspector of Mines for S.D., 1945-46; head mining dept., acting head metall. dept., S.D. Sch. Mines and Technology, 1946-48; cons. mining engr., geologist, Chula Vista, California since 1948. Mem. Am. Inst. Mining and Metall. Engrs., Society Econ. Geologists. Republican. Unitarian. Club: Lions. Author: Coal Washing in Illinois, 1913; Mining Districts and Mineral Resources of Nevada, 1923; The Mining Industry of South Dakota, 1937; U.S. Bur. of Mines Reports of Investigations on Zinc Ore in Wis. and Ill., 1946-48. Contbr. to Economic Geology, Trans. Am. Inst. Mining Engrs., Engring. and Mining Jour., Nelson's Encyclopedia, etc. Home: 326 I St., Chula Vista CA

LINCOLN, PAUL MARTYN, elec. engr.; b. Antrim, Mich., Jan. 1, 1870; s. William E. and Louise (Marshall) L.; Western Reserve U., 1888-89; E.E., Ohio State U., 1892; Dr. of Engring. from same univ., 1933; m. Elizabeth R. Hague, June 30, 1897; children—Helen H. (Mrs. J. W. Reavis), Elizabeth H. (Mrs. H. L. Goodman). With Short Electric Co., Cleveland, 1892, Westinghouse Elec. & Mfg. Co., Pittsburgh, 1892-95; electrical supt. Niagara Falls Power Co., 1895-1902; with Westinghouse Elec. & Mfg. Co., 1902-19, as engr. of power division and gen. engr.; prof. elec. engring., U. of Pittsburgh, 1911-15; cons. engr. Lincoln Electric Co., Cleveland, 1919-22; dir. Sch. of Elec. Engring., Cornell U., since 1922; pres. Therm-Electric Meter Co. since 1938. Republican. Presbyterian. Fellow Am. Inst. E.E. (pres. 1914-15); mem. Am. Soc. Mech. Engrs. John Scott medal, 1902, for synchronism indicator from Franklin Inst. Mason (32 deg.). Club: Engineers' (New York). Address: Therm Electric Meters Co., Inc., Ithaca, N.Y. Died Dec. 20, 1944.

LINCOLN, RUFUS PRATT, physician; b. Belchertown, Mass., Apr. 27, 1840; s. Rufus and Lydia (Baggs) L.; A.B., Amherst Coll., 1862; M.D., Harvard, 1868; m. Caroline C. Tyler, 1869; 1 son, Rufus Tyler. Served to col. Mass. Volunteers, 1862-65; engaged in pvt. practice medicine, specializing in laryngology and intranasal surgery; developed technique for almost painless removal of semi-malignant retronasal growths; a founder N.Y. Laryngol. Soc.; pres. Am. Laryngol. Assn. Died N.Y.C., Nov. 27, 1900.

LIND, SAMUEL COLVILLE, chemist; b. McMinnville, Tenn., June 15, 1879; s. Thomas Christian and Ida (Colville) L.; A.B., Washington and Lee U., 1899; S.B., Mass. Inst. Tech., 1902; Ph.D., U. Leipzig, 1905; U. of Paris, 1910-11; Inst. for Radium Research, Vienna, 1911; hon. D.Sc., U. Colo., 1927; Washington and Lee, 1939, University of Michigan, 1940, Notre Dame University, 1963; m. Marie Holladay, Jan. 24, 1915. Asst. in chemistry, Mass. Inst. Tech., 1902-03; instr., later asst. prof. gen. and phys. chemistry, U. Mich. 1905-13; chemist in radioactivity, 1913-18; phys. chemist, U.S. Bur. of Mines 1918-23; chief chemist U.S. Bur. of Mines, 1923-25; asso. dir. Fixed Nitrogen Research Lab., Wash., 1925-26; dir. Sch. of Chem., U. Minn., 1926-35; dean Inst. Tech., same univ., 1935-47, emeritus. Editor Jour. Phys. Chemistry, 1933-50. Awarded Priestley medal American Chem. Soc., 1952. Fellow A.A.A.S.; mem. Am. Chem. Soc. (mem. bd. editors sci. monographs; pres. 1940), Electrochem. Soc. (pres. 1927), Minn. Acad. Sci. Nat. Acad. Sci., Am. Phys. Soc., Am. Philos. Soc. Presbyn. Author: Chemical Effects of Alpha Particles and Electrons, 1921, 28; Electro-chemistry of Gases and Other Dielectics (with G. Glockler), 1939; Radiation Chemistry of Gases, 1961; also articles on chemical and radioactive subjects. Inventor of Lind interchangeable electroscope for radium measurements; originated ionization theory of the chemical effects of radium rays. Address: 622 W. Vanderbilt Dr., Oak Ridge 37830. Died Feb. 12, 1965; buried McMinnville, Tenn.

LINDAHL, (JOHN HARALD) JOSUA, zoölogist; b. Kongsbacka, Sweden, Jan. 1, 1844; s. Rev. Johan and Mathilda (Rjoerklander) L.; A.B., Royal U. of Lund, Sweden, 1863, A.M. and Ph.D., 1874; m. Sophie, d. Maj. C. A. Pohlman, 1877 (died 1909). Accompanied Gwyn-Jeffreys and Carpenter as asst. zoölogist in British deep-sea exploring expdn. in H.M.S. Porcupine, 1870; zoölogist in charge of expdn. to Greenland, 1871, in Swedish warships Ingegerd and Gladan; docent in zoölogy, U. of Lund, 1874; sec. Royal Swedish delegation to Internat. Geog. Congress, Paris, 1875; sec. Royal Swedish commn. to Centennial Expn., Phila., 1875-77; prof. natural sciences, Augustana Coll., Rock Island, Ill., 1878-88; curator Ill. State Mus. Natural History, Springfield, 1888-93; dir. Mus. Natural History, Cincinnati, 1895-1906; mgr. Salubrin Lab., 1906—. Officier d'Academie, France, 1876; Knight Ord. of Vasa, Sweden, 1878. Home: Chicago, Ill. Died Apr. 18, 1912.

LINDBERG, DAVID OSCAR NATHANIEL, chest specialist; born at Quincy, Mass., Oct. 9, 1891; s. Olaf P. and Anna (Johnson) L.; student Adams Acad., Quincy, Mass., 1903-07; M.D., Boston U. Sch. of Medicine, 1915; married 1917; one son, David Nathaniel; married second M. Helen Gray, Sept. 19, 1941; children—Richard Oscar, Donald Everett. Began practice of med., 1915; clinical dir., U.S. Public Health Service, 1921-28; sanatorium directorships since 1928; former assistant clinical professor of medical Univ. of Utah Sch. of Med. Flight surgeon, AEF, France, 1917-19; capt. Med. Corps (regular), U.S. Army, retired 1921. Fellow American College Physicians, American College of Chest Physicians; mem. National Tuberculosis Association (past vice pres.), A.M.A., American Thoracic Society, Phi Alpha Gamma. Membro Correspondente Sociedade Brasileira de Tuberculose. Titulaire membre Internal Union Against Tuberculosis. Invitational studies Tokyo and Moscow authorities; other spl. research and study, Stockholm; Leysin and Schatzalp, Switzerland; Copenhagen; Hamburg; Paris; Oslo; Lisbon; Rio de Janeiro. Introduced fluorophotography to the U.S., 1937. Author: A Manual of Pulmonary Tuberculosis; Atlas of Thoracic Roentgenology and Contributions to med. literature. Died July 31, 1964; buried Golden Gate Nat. Cemetery, San Bruno, Cal.

LINDENTHAL, GUSTAV, civil engr.; b. Brünn, Austria, May 21, 1850; s. Dominik and Franciska (Schmutz) L.; ed. colls. Brünn and Vienna; came to America, 1874; D.Engring, h.c., Polytechnicum, Dresden, 1911, Polytechnicum, Brünn, 1921, Polytechnicum, Vienna, 1926; m. Gertrude Weil, July 10, 1902 (died 1905); m. 2d, Carrie Herndon, Feb. 10, 1910; 1 dau., Franciska. In surveys and constrn. rys. and bridges, Austria and Switzerland, 1870-74; engr. Centennial Expn., Phila., 1874-77; cons. engr. in constrn. western rys. and bridges, office at Pittsburgh, 1877-90; at New York, 1800—; commr. bridges, City of New York, 1902-03; cons. engr. for N.Y. tunnels, Pa. R.R. under Hudson and East rivers; cons. engr. and architect for the Hellgate steel arch bridge over the East River. Pres. North River Bridge Co. Chmn. music festival com. Hudson-Fulton Celebration Commn., 1909. Home: Metuchen, N.J. Died July 31, 1935.

LINDGREN, WALDEMAR, geologist; b. Kalmar, Sweden, Feb. 14, 1860; s. Johan Magnus and Emma (Bergman) L.; ed. in Sweden; M.E., Sch. of Mines, Freiberg, Germany, 1883; D.Sc., Princeton U., 1916, Harvard U., 1935; m. Ottolina Allstrin, of Gothenburg, Sweden, Mar. 8, 1886 (died 1929). Assistant geologist, 1884-95, geologist, 1895-1915, and chief geologist, 1911-12, U.S. Geological Survey; William Barton Rogers professor econ. geology, Mass. Institute of Tech., in charge dept. of geology, 1912-33 (emeritus). Author: Mineral Deposits. Home: Brighton, Mass. Died Nov. 3, 1939.

LINDHEIMER, FERDINAND JACOB, botanist; b. Frankfurt-am-Main, Germany, May 21, 1801; s. Johan H. Lindheimer; attended U. Weisbaden, U. Bonn (Germany); m. Elenore Reinarz, 1846. Came to U.S., 1834; served in Tex. Army in war for independence; travelled throughout Tex. collecting bot. specimens, 1841-52; participated in exptl. communistic colony, Bettina, Tex., 1847; editor Neu Braunfelser (Tex.) Zeitung, 1852-70; his bot. work described in Plantae Lindheimerianae published in Boston Jour. of Natural History, Vol. V, 1845, Vol. VI, 1850. Died New Braunfels, Comal County, Dec. 2, 1879.

LINDSEY, JOSEPH BRIDGEO, chemist; b. Marblehead, Mass., Dec. 26, 1862; s. Joseph W. and Emily Stuart (Blaney) L.; B.Sc., Mass. Agrl. Coll., Amherst, 1883; Ph.D., U. of Göttingen, 1891; studied Poly. Institute, Zürich, 1892; hon. D.Sc., Mass. State College, 1933; m. H. Frances Dickinson, June 20, 1888; children—Amy Blaney (Mrs. C. E. Goodhue, Jr.), Joseph B. Asst. chemist, Mass. Expt. Sta., 1883-85; chemist to L. B. Darling Fertilizer Co., Pawtucket, R.I., 1885-89; chemist, Mass. Agrl. Expt. Sta., 1892-1907, v. dir. and chemist, 1907—; Goessmann prof. agrl. chemistry, Mass. Agrl. Coll., 1911-33, head of dept. chemistry, 1911-28; retired Dec. 1932. Home: Amherst, Mass. Died Oct. 27, 1939.

LINDSEY, LOUIS, univ. prof., research scholar; b. Hartford, N.Y., Dec. 12, 1877; s. Daniel and Josephine Lindsey; student Cortland (N.Y.) State Normal Sch.; A.B., Syracuse U., 1906, M.A., 1909. Ph.D., 1911; m. Edith L. MacFarran, Aug. 2, 1922; children—Robert L., Jean Francis. Asst., U.S. Naval Observatory, Washington, 1908-12; instr. applied mathematics, Syracuse U., 1911-12; asst. prof., 1912-17, asso. prof., 1917-25, prof. applied mathematics, 1925-47, prof. emeritus since July 1947; research in applied mathematics related to engring. work since 1948. Past mem. Am. Math. Soc., Am. Math. Assn., Sigma Xi, Tau Beta Pi, Phi Beta Kappa, Pi Mu Epsilon, Phi Kappa Phi. Republican Presbyterian. Author: Definitive Orbits of Comet, 1902 and Kress comet (Astron. Jour. and Astronomische Nachrchte). Home: 854 Maryland Av., Syracuse 10 NY

LINDSTROM, ERNEST W(ALTER), (lind'strum), prof. genetics; b. Chicago, Ill., Feb. 5, 1891; s. Earnst A. and Mary (Tranell) L.; B.A., U. of Wis., 1914; Ph.D. Cornell U., 1917; m. A. Cornelia Anderson, Aug. 27, 1921; children—Eugene Shipman, Cornelia Goodrich, Rosemary Vaughn. Asst. in plant breeding and investigator, Cornell U., 1914-17; asst. prof. genetics, U. of Wis., 1919-22; prof. genetics and head of dept., Ia. State Coll. Agr. and Mech. Arts, since 1922, also vice dean of Graduate College; on leave as asst. dir. European office Internat. Edn. Bd. (Rockefeller Foundation), 1927-28; on leave, visiting prof. genetics, Universidad Nacional Facultad de Agronomia, Medellin, Colombia, S.A., 1944-45. Served as 2d lt. Air Service, U.S. Army, 1917-18. Fellow Ia. Acad. Science; mem. A.A.A.S., Am. Soc. Naturalists, Bot. Soc. America, Genetic Soc. Am. (pres. 1942), Sigma Xi, Beta Theta Pi, Gamma Alpha. Contbr. to scientific jours. Home: Ames, Ia. Died Nov. 8, 1948.

LINEBARGER, CHARLES ELIJAH, physical chemist; b. Plainfield, Ill., Feb. 21, 1867; s. Isaac and Lucy Ellen (Estes) L.; grad. Northwestern U. Sch. of Music., A.B., Northwestern U., 1888; asst. in chemistry, Chicago Med. Coll., 1888-89; student Tübingen and Paris, 1889-91; teacher of chemistry, North and South Div. high schs., Chicago, 1891-93; student Göttingen and Paris, 1893-95; fellow Clark U., 1895; m. E. Frances Diplock, Oct. 4, 1896; children—Gwendolyn (Mrs. Manfred U. Prescott), Charles Elijah. Teacher, Lake View High Sch., Chicago, 1896—. Editor of Sch. Science, 1901-06; mem. bd. of reviewers Jour. of Phys. Chemistry, 1900-04. Author: Elements of Differential and Integral Calculus (with J. W. A. Young), 1899. Home: Chicago, Ill. Died 1937.

LINEBERGER, WALTER FRANKLIN, (lin'ber-ger), ex-congressman, cons. civil and mining engr.; b. July 20, 1883; s. John Henry and Lucy (Aynesworth) L.; ed. Rensselaer Poly. Inst. of Troy, N.Y., class, 1904; m. Florence Elizabeth Hite, June 16, 1909; children—Florence Elizabeth, Walter Franklin, Janet Hite, Anne Lorraine. Engaged in mining in Mexico 9 yrs.; mem. 67th-69th Congress (1921-27), 9th Calif. Dist. co-owner and mgr. Colosseum and Majave Tungsten Mines, Jean, Nev. Enlisted in U.S. Army; served in France with engring. units of 1st, 32d combat divs.; wounded in action; returned to U.S., Apr. 1919. Awarded Croix de Guerre with palm (French); divisional citation for bravery under fire. Mem. Am. Soc. C.E., S.R. Home: 303 E. Valley Rd. (Montecito), Santa Barbara, Calif. Died Oct. 9, 1943.

LINFIELD, FREDERICK BLOOMFIELD, agriculturist; b. Twillingate, Newfoundland, July 18, 1866; s. Samuel and Rachel (Patten) L.; B.S.A., Toronto U., 1891; m. Mary A. Mahoney, Dec. 26, 1892; children—Frederick Bertil, Mrs. Rachel Azalea Sager, Mrs. Leila Mary Nye. Asst. in dairy dept. Ontario Agrl. Coll., 1891-93; prof. animal industry and dairying Utah Agrl. Coll., Logan, 1893-1902; prof. agr. Mont. State Coll., 1902-13; dean div. agr., 1913-37; dir. Mont. Agr. Expt. Sta., 1904-37, dir. emeritus, 1937-42, ret. Methodist. Home: 721 3d Av. S., Bozeman, Mont. Died Sept. 23, 1948; buried Sunset Hills, Bozeman.

LINFORD, LEON BLOOD, univ. prof.; b. Logan, Utah, July 8, 1904; s. James H. and Mary Hooper (Blood) L.; B.S., Utah State Agrl. Coll., 1923. A.M., 1925; Ph.D., U. of Calif., 1930; m. Imogene Kesler, June 20, 1936; children—Lawrence Leon, Rulon Kesler. Asso. prof. mathematics Utah State Agrl. Coll., 1932-35, head dept., 1933-36, prof. physics and head dept. 1935-41; staff mem. radiation lab. Mass. Inst. Tech., 1941-46; physicist Naval Research Lab., Boston Field Sta., 1946; prof. physics and head dept. U. Utah, 1946—, dir. Upper Air Research Project, USAF, 1947-57. Mem. U.S. Commn. III, Internat. Sci. Radio Union, 1954. Fellow Am. Phys. Soc., A.A.A.S.; mem. Am. Assn. Physics Tchrs., Am. Assn. U. Profs., Utah Acad. Scis. Arts and Letters, Sigma Xi, Sigma Pi Sigma, Phi Kappa Phi. Author of articles on moisture relations in porous media and on photoelectricity. Mem. editorial bd. Mass. Inst. Tech. Radiation Lab. Series. Home: 1584 Glen Arbor, Salt Lake City 5. Died Mar. 12, 1957; buried Salt Lake City Cemetery.

LINGLE, DAVID JUDSON, physiologist; b. Rock Island, Ill., June 6, 1863; s. David and Regina (Bowman) L.; B.S., U. of Chicago, 1885; grad. student, 1887-89, 1890-91, fellow in biology, 1891-92, Ph.D., 1892, Johns Hopkins; m. Helen Hitchcock, of Chicago, Apr. 21, 1898. Asst. in science, Beloit Coll., 1886-87; asst. prof. biology, Tulane U., New Orleans, 1889-90; reader in physiology, 1892-93, asst., 1893-94, instr., 1894-1904, asst. prof. physiology, 1904, asso. prof. since 1920, U. of Chicago. Mem. Am. Physiol. Soc., Phi Beta Kappa, Sigma Xi, Phi Kappa Psi. Baptist. Home: 1017 E. 54th Pl., Chicago, Ill.

LINING, JOHN, physician; b. Scotland, 1708; m. Sarah Hill, 1739, no children. Came to Am., 1730; practiced medicine, Charlestown (now Charleston), S.C.; made extensive studies of epidemic diseases; sent to Europe 1st scientific account of yellow fever in Am., 1748; studied effects of climate on metabolism; kept 1st published weather records in Am. Died Sept. 21, 1760.

LINTHICUM, GEORGE MILTON, surgeon; b. Anne Arundel Co., Md., Aug. 17, 1870; s. Sweetser and Laura Ellen (Smith) L.; student St. John's Coll., Annapolis, Md., 1887-89, A.M., 1893; A.B., Johns Hopkins, 1891; M.D., U. of Md., 1893; m. Lillian Noyes Howland, Apr. 12, 1898; children—Howland, Lillian (Mrs. John Scott Keech, dec.). Began practice at Baltimore, 1893; prof. of physiology and proctology, Baltimore Med. Coll., 1895-1907; v.p. med. and chirurg. faculty, 1908-09, pres., 1909-10; prof. diseases of colon and rectum, U. of Md., 1913—; proctologist Univ. of Md., Md. Gen., W. Baltimore Gen. and Baltimore City hosps.; consultant in diseases of colon and rectum, U.S. Vets. Hosp., Hosp. for Consumptives of Md. (chmn. exec. com.), U.S. Marine Hosp.; consultant Baltimore City Health Dept.; medical examiner Fidelity Life Insurance Co. of America. Served as capt. Med. Corps, Md. N.G., Mexican Border, 1916; lt. col. Med. Corps, U.S.A., 1917-19, and comdg. officer U.S. Base Hosp. 113, France; col. Med. R.C. Fellow Am. Coll. Surgeons. Democrat. Episcopalian. Mason. Home: Roland Park, Baltimore, Md. Died July 18, 1935.

LINTNER, JOSEPH ALBERT, entomologist; b. Schoharie, N.Y., Feb. 8, 1822; s. George Ames and Maria (Wagner) L.; Ph.D. (hon.), U. State of N.Y.; m. Frances C. Hutchinson, 1856. In business, N.Y.C., 1837-48, Schoharie, 1848-60; mfr. woolens, Utica, N.Y., 1860-68; began collecting insects, 1853; asst. in zoology N.Y. State Mus., 1868-74, head entomol. dept., 1874-80; N.Y. State entomologist, 1880-98; entomol. editor Country Gentleman for 25 years; pres. Assn. Econ. Entomologists, 1892. Author: (pamphlet) Entomological Contributions, 4 issues, 1872-79. Died Rome, Italy, May 5, 1898.

LINTON, RALPH, anthropologist; b. Phila., Pa., Feb. 27, 1893; s. Isaiah Waterman and Mary Elisabeth (Gillingham) L.; B.A., Swarthmore Coll., 1915; M.A., U. of Pa., 1916; Ph.D., Harvard, 1925; m. Adelin M. Hohlfeld, Aug. 31, 1934; 1 son, David Hector. Field work in archaeology, N.M., 1912, 17; Guatemala, 1913, N.J., 1915, Ill., 1916, Colo., 1919, Marquesas Islands, 1920-21, Ohio, 1924, Wis., 1932-33; in ethnology, Polynesia, 1920-22, Madagascar, 1925-27, South Africa, 1928, Okla., 1934. Asst. curator of ethnology, Field Museum of Natural History, 1922-28; prof. anthropology, U. of Wisconsin, 1928-37; prof. anthropology, Columbia, U., 1937-39; chmn. dept. of anthropology, 1939-43; Sterling prof., anthropology, Yale U. since 1946. Editor Am. Antropologist, 1939-44. Corpl. Battery D, 149th F.A., U.S. Army, Rainbow Div., 1917-19. Awarded Viking medal, 1952; Huxley Meml. medal, 1954. Mem. Am. Anthrop. Assn. (pres. 1946), A.A.A.S. (v.p. 1937), National Academy Sciences (chmn. div. anthropology 1949-51), Phi Beta Kappa, Sigma Xi, Alpha Kappa Delta; honorary member Académie Malgache. Hon. fellow Royal Anthrop. Inst. Gt. Britain. Mem. Nat. Research Council, 1931-32, 1940-45; mem. Social Science Research Council, 1932-39, American Council of Learned Societies, 1947-50. Quaker. Author: The Material Culture of the Marquesas Islands, 1924; Use of Tobacco Among North American Indians, 1924; The Archaeology of the Marquesas Islands, 1925. Guide to the Polynesian and Micronesian Collections, Field Museum, 1925; The Tanala, A Hill-Tribe of Madagascar, 1932; The Study of Man, an Introduction, 1936; Acculturation in Seven American Indian Tribes, 1940; Cultural Background of Personality, 1945; editor, The Science of Man in the World Crisis, 1945; The Tree of Culture, 1955. Editor: Most of the World, 1949. Address: Dept. of Anthropology, Yale Univ., New Haven. Died Dec. 24, 1953.

LINTON, ROBERT, engineer; b. Hudson, O., May 29, 1870; s. Robert J. and Caroline S. (Doolittle) L.; A.M., Washington and Jefferson Coll., 1902, Sc.D., 1937; post-grad. work Royal Tech. Sch., Berlin, 1892-94; m. Margaret McElveen, 1896; 1 dau., Eleanor. Mining engr. with McKinney & Smith, Pittsburgh, 1890-92; in window glass mfg., 1894-1904; asst. to chmn. Am. Window Glass Co., 1904-06, with gen. supervision operations in all factories; mining engr., 1906-23, hdqrs. first Los Angeles, later New York; pres. North Butte Mining Co., 1918-23; vice-pres. and gen. mgr. Pacific Clay Products, 1923-35; in private practice since 1935. Pres. Gen. Alumni Assn. Washington and Jefferson Coll., 1917-18; dir. and mem. exec. com. Am. Mining Congress, 1920-23, bd. of govs., western div., 1939-41; president Calif. Clay Products Inst., 1928-30; v.p. Los Angeles Chamber of Commerce, 1935; mem. Calif. State Mining Board, 1929-30 and 1937-41. Fellow A.A.A.S., Am. Ceramic Soc.; mem. Am. Inst. Mining and Metall. Engrs., Am. Soc. for Testing Materials, Mining Assn. of the Southwest (v.p.), Am. Soc. C.E., Soc. Colonial Wars, S.R., Delta Tau Delta. Republican. Episcopalian. Mason (K.T.). Club: Mining (New York). Author of numerous tech. papers and articles. Home: 517 1/2 S. Carondelet St., Los Angeles, Calif. Died Nov. 12, 1942.

LIPMAN, CHARLES BERNARD, plant physiologist; b. Moscow, Russia, Aug. 17, 1883; s. Michael Gregory and Ida (Birkhahn) L.; brought to U.S., 1889; B.Sc., Rutgers, 1904, M.S., 1909; M.S., U. of Wisconsin, 1909; Ph.D., University of Calif., 1910; Sc.D., honoris causa, Rutgers, 1934; m. Marion Amesbury Evans, May 25, 1925; 1 dau., Georgia Evans. Goewey fellow, U. of Calif., 1908-09; instr. soil bacteriology, 1909, asst. prof. soils, 1910, asso. prof., 1912, prof. soil chemistry and bacteriology, 1913-21, prof. plant nutrition, 1921-25, prof. plant physiology since 1925, U. of Calif., dean of Grad. Div. since 1923. Mem. Ednl. Advisory Bd., John Simon Guggenheim Memorial Foundation; dir. Belgian American Educational Foundation. In charge administration James D. Phelan fellowships in Literature and Art (San Francisco, Calif.), 1934-39; member board of directors International House, Berkeley. Chmn. com. 6th Pacific Science Congress, 1939; pres. Calif. Chapter American-Scandinavian Foundation, 1941, 1942; mem. State Dept. Com. on Adjustment of Foreign Students, 1941, 1942; mem. War Ration Bd., Draft Bd. No. 68, Berkeley. Fellow A.A.A.S., Soc. for Research on Meteorites; Mem. Am. Chem. Soc., Am. Soc. Plant Physiologists, Soc. American Bacteriologists, California Botanical Society, California Academy Science, Society of Experimental Biology and Medicine, Sigma Xi, Alpha Zeta, Phi Sigma, Phi Beta Kappa (senator; committee on qualifications), Golden Bear, Sigma Delta Pi. Clubs: University, Bohemian (San Francisco); Athenian-Nile (Oakland); Faculty (Berkeley); Century (New York). Author numerous papers on plant physiology, plant chemistry, and plants and soils; also with soil and marine bacteria, bacteria in ancient rocks, meteorites, etc. Asso. editor Plant Physiology, Jour. of Bacteriology, Soil Science. Home: 10 Tanglewood Rd., Berkeley, Calif. Died Oct. 22, 1944.

LIPMAN, JACOB GOODALE, prof. agr.; b. Friedrichstadt, Russia, Nov. 18, 1874; s. Michael G. and Ida (Birkhahn) L.; Baron de Hirsch Agrl. Sch., N.J., 1894; B.Sc., Rutgers Coll., 1898, hon. D.Sc., 1923; A.M., Cornell U., 1900; Ph.D., 1903; hon. Doctor, Catholic U. of Santiago, Chile, 1930; m. Cecelia Rosenthal, Nov. 26, 1902; children—Leonard Herbert, Edward Voorhees, Daniel Hilgard. Asst. chemist, 1898-99, soil chemist and bacteriologist, 1901—, N.J. Agrl. Expt. Sta.; instr. agrl. chemistry, 1902-06, asst. prof. agr., 1906-07, asso. prof., 1907-10, prof. of soil fertility and bacteriology, 1910-13, prof. agr., 1913—, and dean of agr., 1915—, Rutgers Coll.; dir. N.J. Agrl. Expt. Stas., 1911—. Lecturer U. of Ill., 1906, Cornell U., 1906, U. of Tenn., 1909, 10, Ia. Agrl. Coll., 1910, U. of Neb., 1911. Spl. investigator, U.S.A., 1918-19. Editor in chief Soil Science; asso. editor Annales des Sciences Agronomiques, Archiv für Pflanzenbau, Pennsylvania Farmer; editor John Wiley and Sons Agrl. Series. Mem. N.J. State Planning Bd., Internat. Commn. Agrl. Ecology; mem. Czechoslovakia Acad. Agriculture, French Acad. Agr., Swedish Royal Acad. Agr., Reale Academia dei Georgofill di Firenze, Am. Acad. Arts and Sciences; del. Gen. Assembly Internat. Inst. Agr., Rome, 1922, 24, 26; del. 3d Internat. Conf. of Soil Science, Prague, 1922, 4th Conf., Rome, 1924; pres. 1st Internat. Congress of Soil Science, Washington, D.C., 1927; chmn. Am. Delegation to 3d Internat. Congress of Soil Science at Oxford, England; delegate 1st Internat. Nitrogen Conf., Biarritz, 1926; del. World Dairy Congress, London, England, 1928; del. 5th Internat. Tech. and Chem. Congress of Agrl. Industries, Scheveningen, The Netherlands, 1937. Awarded Chandler medal, Columbia U., 1934. Author: Bacteria in Relation to Country Life, 1908; Laboratory Guide of Soil Bacteriology, 1912. Died Apr. 19, 1939.

LIPPINCOTT, JAMES STARR, horticulturist, meteorologist; b. Phila., Apr. 12, 1819; s. John and Sarah (Starr) L.; attended Haverford (Pa.) Coll., 1834-35; m. Susan Haworth Ecroyd, 1857; m. 2d, Anne E. Shepphard, 1861; no children. Farmer at Cole's Landing, later at Haddonfield, N.J.; del. World's Peace Congress, Frankfort, Germany, 1850; invented vapor index for measuring humidity of air; meteorol. observer for Smithsonian Instn. at Cole's Landing, 1864-66, Haddonfield, 1869-70. Author: Universal Pronouncing Dictionary of Biography and Mythology, 1870. Contbr. articles to Reports of Commrs. of Agr., including: Climatology of American Grape Vines, 1862, Geography of Plants, 1863, Market Products of West New Jersey, 1865, Observations on Atmospheric Humidity, 1865, The Fruit Regions of the Northern United States and Their Climates, 1866. Died Greenwich, Cumberland County, N.J., Mar. 17, 1885.

LIPPINCOTT, JOSEPH BARLOW, hydraulic engr.; b. Scranton, Pa., Oct. 10, 1864; s. Joshua Allen (LL.D.) and Harriet Phillips (Barlow) L.; student Dickinson Coll., 1880-82; A.B., U. of Kan., 1886, hon. C.E., 1914; m. Josephine Phillips Cook, Apr. 1890; children—Rose (dec.), Joseph Reading. With Santa Fe R.R. System, 1886-88; topographer U.S. Geol. Survey, 1888-92; asst. engr. Bear Valley Irrigation Co., 1892; in charge various irrigation investigations in Calif., 1893-94; hydrographer U.S. Geol. Survey for Calif., 1895-1902; supervising engr. for Pacific Coast dist., with U.S. Reclamation Service, 1902-06; asst. chief engr. Los Angeles Aqueduct, 1906-13; cons. engr., Los Angeles, since 1913. Consulting engr. for municipal water works in San Francisco, Fresno, Santa Barbara, Los Angeles and other Calif. towns, Denver, El Paso, Phoenix, and Los Angeles County, Hawaiian Islands, Mexico and Alaska; engr. and mgr. construction of Camp Kearney, Nat. Guard Camp, San Diego County, Calif., also Rockwell Field, San Diego, 1917-18; supervising engr. U.S. Housing Corp., Pittsburgh and Bethlehem, Pa., 1918, civil service commr. for Los Angeles; park commr. since 1910; state commr., 6th Dist. Agrl. Assn. since 1911; cons. engr., 1925, for State of Calif., Tri-County Flood Control Bd., Los Angeles County Flood Control District, 1927-28, Internat. Water Boundary Commn. between U.S. and Mex. since 1932, U.S. Army engrs. in connection with flood control work, Los Angeles County, 1939, City of Los Angeles and several cities and irrigation dists.; mem. Weather Bur. Com. of Nat. Science Advisory Bd. since 1935; architect-engineer (associated with Lippincott & Bowen) at Camp Haan and Mojave Desert Firing Center for constructing buildings and designing sewers for March Field and for Marysville Triangular Cantonment (all in Calif.), 1940-41. Awarded James R. Croes medal by American Society of Civil Engineers, 1914. Member American Society C.E. (made hon. mem. 1937). Clubs: California, Los Angeles Country (Los Angeles). Author of numerous papers and reports on water supply and irrigation topics. Home: 1256 W. Adams St. Office: 714 W. Olympic Blvd., Los Angeles, Calif. Died Nov. 4, 1942.

LITCHFIELD, ELECTUS DARWIN, (lich'feld), architect; b. New York, Apr. 25, 1872; s. William Backus and Emily (Pope) L.; grad. Brooklyn Poly. Inst., 1889; M. E. Stevens Inst. of Tech., 1892; m. Elizabeth B. Rodman, Oct. 6, 1906; children—Elizabeth Burnham, William Burnham. With Carrère & Hastings, architects, 2 yrs.; associated, and then mem. Lord & Hewlett, architects, 1901-08; mem. firm Tracy, Swartwout & Litchfield, 1908-13, alone, 1913-19, firm Electus D. Litchfield & Rogers, 1919-26; in practice under own name 1926—. Architect. U.S. Post Office and Courthouse, Denver; St. Paul Pub. Library; James J. Hill Reference Library, St. Paul; proposed Nat. Armory, Washington; Bklyn. Masonic Temple; City Club; Tuberculosis Pavilion, Riverside Hosp., N.Y.; architect, town planner Yorkship Village, a permanent industrial town of 1,700 houses built during war for Emergency Fleet Corp., N.Y. Shipbuilding Co.; 800 Park Av., other apts.; The Astoria Column, Astoria, Ore., other monuments. Cons. architect U.S. Post Office, Courthouse and Customhouse, Albany, N.Y. Mem. N.Y. Com. on City Plan, 1927; mem. Building Code Revision Commn., N.Y., 1906-07; a winner in competition for design of N.Y. City slum clearance projects and apptd. an architect for Red Hook project; in assn. with Louis Allen Abramson architect for reconstrn. of Bellevue Hosp. Fellow A.I.A. Mem. Architectural League of N.Y., Municipal Art Soc. (ex-pres.), N.Y. Fine Arts Fedn., Beaux Art Inst. Design, Citizens Housing Council (dir.), N.Y. Bldg. Congress (founder; chmn. orgn. com. 1921), Soc. Colonial Wars of N.Y. (ex-gov.), Gen. Soc. Colonial Wars (ex-deputy gov. gen. from N.Y.), The Pilgrims, Tau Beta Pi. Democrat. Episcopalian. Clubs: City, Church. Home: 171 E. 73d St. Office: 80 Fifth Av., N.Y.C. 11. Died Nov. 27, 1952.

LITCHFIELD, PAUL WEEKS, corp. official; b. Boston, Mass., July 26, 1875; s. Charles M. and Julia (Weeks) L.; B.S., Mass. Inst. Tech., 1896; m. Florence Brinton, June 23, 1904; children—Mrs. Howard L. Hyde, Mrs. A. Wallace Denny. Began with Goodyear Tire and Rubber Co., supt., 1900-15, v.p., 1915-26, pres., 1926-40, chmn. bd., 1930-58, now hon. chmn.; chmn. Goodyear Aircraft Corp., etc. Formerly mem. bd. Mass. Inst. Tech.; dir. U. Akron. Mem. Mass. Inst. Tech. Alumni Assn. (ex-pres.). Mem. Nat. Exec. Bd. of The Boy Scouts of Am., former vice chmn. Region Four, Boy Scouts of America, former chairman Region Four, Senior Scouting, Boy Scouts America, Decorated Order Cruzeiro do Sul (Brazil); Order del Sol (Peru); Royal Order of Vasa (Sweden); Order of Adolphe of Nassau (Luxemburg); Order Indsl. Merit. Mem. Soc. Automotive Engrs., Nat. Assn. Mfrs., Nat. Air Council, Navy League. Mason (33 deg.). Clubs: University, City, Portage Country, Wings, Inc., Arizona, Union (Cleve.); Automobile Old Timers, Inc. Writer of "Autumn Leaves," Indsl. Republic; Indsl. Voyage (autobiography of P. W. Litchfield); magazine articles. Leader in development work of lighter-than-air craft. Home: 1010 Merriman Rd. Office: 1144 E. Market St., Akron, O. Died Mar. 18, 1959.

LITTELL, FRANK BOWERS, astronomer; b. Scranton, Pa., Feb. 21, 1869; s. Henry Woolsey and Marie Antoinette (Bowers) L.; Ph.B., Wesleyan, 1891, Sc.D., 1919; A.M., Columbian (now George Washington) U., 1894; m. Josephine La Monte Mercereau, Apr. 9, 1902; children—Marion Mercereau, Charles Henry. Computer Naval Obs., 1891-96; teacher mathematics, Scranton High Sch., 1896-97; computer, 1897-98, asst. astronomer, 1898-1901, Naval Obs.; prof. mathematics USN, 1901-33, when retired. Mem. U.S. eclipse expdns. to Barnesville, Ga., 1900, Solok, Sumatra, 1901, Porta Coeli, Spain, 1905, Los Angeles (airship), 1925, expdn. to Sumatra, 1926; mem. U.S. party to determine Washington-Paris longitude, using radio signals, 1913-14; variation of latitude by the photographic zenith tube, 1915-33; determination of World longitudes by radio, San Diego (Cal.) sta., 1926. Made catalogue of 23,521 stars (with W. S. Eichelberger); vertical circle observations made with the 5-inch altazimuth, 1898-1907, and 1916-33 (pub. 1939); Washington-Paris longitude by radio signals (with G. A. Hill). Fellow A.A.A.S., Royal Astron. Soc. (Eng.); mem. Philos. Soc. Washington, Am. Astron. Soc. (councillor 1928-31), Washington Acad. Sciences, Sociedad Astronomica de Mex., Soc. Astron. de France, Internat. Astron. Union, Am. Geophys. Union Astron, Soc. of Pacific, Phi Beta Kappa. Spl. editor on astronomy, Webster's New Internat. Dictionary and World Book Ency. Annual. Home: 3704 Porter St., Washington 16. Died Mar. 28, 1951; buried Arlington Nat. Cemetery.

LITTLE, ARTHUR D(EHON), chemical engr.; b. Boston, Mass., Dec. 15, 1863; s. Thomas J. and Amelia (Hixon) L.; ed. pub. and high schs., Portland, Me., Berkeley Sch., New York, Mass. Inst. Tech.; hon. Ch.D., U. of Pittsburgh, 1918; hon. asso., Coll. Tech., Manchester, Eng., 1929; hon. Sc.D., Manchester U., 1929, Tufts, 1930, Columbia, 1931; Perkin medallist, 1931; m. Henrietta Rogers Anthony, Jan. 22, 1901. Chemist and supt. of first mill in U.S. making sulphite wood pulp, 1884-85; chem. engring. practice, Boston, 1886—; pres. Arthur D. Little, Inc., 1909—; dir. Arthur D. Little Industrial Corp. Mem. Corp. Mass. Inst. Tech. (life), pres. Alumni Assn., 1921-22, and founder Sch. of Chem. Engring. Practice. Chmn. Advisory Com. Nat. Expn. of Chem. Industries; chmn. subcom. on chemistry, Science Advisory Com. of Nat. Research Council, Century of Progress, Chicago 1933. Organized Natural Resources Survey of Can. for C.P. Ry., 1916-17. During war, in charge of spl. researches on airplane dopes, acetone production, smoke filters, etc., for Signal Corps and Chem. Warfare Service. Inventor processes of chrome tanning, electrolytic manufacture of chlorates, artificial silk, gas and petroleum. Fellow Am. Acad. Arts and Sciences, A.A.A.S., Chem. Soc. (Eng.), Inst. of Fuel (London). Author: Chemistry of Paper Making (with R. B. Griffin); The Handwriting on the Wall; The Fifth Estate. Home: Brookline, Mass. Died Aug. 1, 1935.

LITTLE, CHARLES NEWTON, prof. civ. engring.; b. Madura, Southern India, May 19, 1858; s. Charles and Susan (Robbins) L.; A.B., Neb. U., 1879, A.M., 1884; Ph.D., Yale, 1885; studied univs. of Göttingen and Berlin; m. Emma R. Funke, Aug. 5, 1886. Instr. mathematics and civ. engring., 1880-84, asso. prof. civ. engring., 1885-90, prof., 1890-93, U. of Neb.; prof. mathematics, Leland Stanford Jr. U., 1893-1901; prof. civ. engring., 1901—, dean Coll. Engring., 1911—, U. of Idaho, Moscow, Ida. Conglist. Died Aug. 31, 1923.

LITTLE, CLARENCE C(OOK), biologist; b. Brookline, Mass., Oct. 6, 1888; s. James Lovell and Mary Robbins (Revere) L.; grad. Noble and Greenough Sch., Boston, Mass., 1906; A.B., Harvard, 1910; S.M., Grad. Sch. of Applied Science (Harvard), 1912, Sc.D., 1914; LL.D., U. of N.H., 1924, Albion (Mich.) Coll., 1925, U. of N.M., 1929, Colby College, Waterville, Me., 1935; Litt.D., U. Maine, 1932; Sc.D., U. Chgo., 1950, Boston U., 1951; L.H.D., Dickinson Coll., 1951; Ed.D., Marietta Coll., 1952; m. Katharine Day Andrews, May 27, 1911 (div. 1929); children—Edward Revere, Louise, Robert Andrews; m. 2d, Beatrice W. Johnson, 1930; children—Richard Warren, Laura Revere. Sec. to Corp. Harvard Univ., 1910-12; research asst.in genetics, 1911-13, research fel. in genetics (cancer commn.), 1913-17, asst. dean College and acting University marshal, 1916-17, overseer, 1942-48, 1955-61, all of Harvard U.; associate in comparative pathology, Harvard Medical Sch., 1917-18; research associate, 1919-21, and 1922-25; asst. dir., 1921-22, Sta. for Exptl. Evolution, Carnegie Instn., Washington; pres. U. of Me., 1922-25; president University of Michigan, 1925-29; director Jackson Meml. Lab., 1929-56, director emeritus, 1956-71. Director Liberty National Bank, Ellsworth, Me. Dir. Am. Cancer Soc., 1929-45. Sci. dir. Tobacco Industry Research Com., from 1954; member scientific adv. bd., Gesell Inst. Child Development, from 1952. Sec. gen. and chmn. exec. com., Second Internat. Congress of Eugenics, New York, 1921; mem. Eugenics Com. of U.S. from 1922; dir. Am. Birth Control League from 1925, pres., 1936-38; president International Neo Malthusian League, 1925, American Euthanasia Society, 1938-43; mem. exec. com. First World Population Conference, Geneva, 1927; dir. council for Democracy, Euthanasia Soc. pres. 1939-43; pres. Race Betterment Congress, 1928, 29; secretary general and chmn. Council 6th Internat. Congress of Genetics, Ithaca, 1932; mem. Nat. Advisory Cancer Council, 1937-39. Trustee of Mount Desert Island Biol. Lab. (pres. 1931-33). Commissioned capt. Aviation Section R.C., 1917; maj. Adj. Gen.'s Dept., 1918; hon. disch., 1918; lt. col., Specialist Reserves, 1928-39. Vice chmn. Civilian Def. for State Me., 1941. Fellow Nat. Acad. Scis., Am. Acad. Arts and Scis., N.Y. Acad. Medicine, A.A.A.S., Nat. Inst. Social Scis.; honorary mem. St. Louis Medical Society; member American Soc. Naturalists, Am. Soc. Zoologists, Am. Assn. Cancer Research (v.p. 1929; pres. 1930, 40), Soc. Exptl. Biology and Medicine, Eugenic Research Assn., Am. Pub. Health Assn., Population Assn. America (dir.), Am. Eugenics Soc. (pres. 1928), Am. Assn. Anatomists, Am. Soc. Mammalogists, Am. Social Hygiene Assn. (v.p.), Mich. Acad., Pan-Am. Med. Soc., New Eng. Cancer Soc., Phi Beta Kappa, Phi Kappa Phi, Phi Sigma, Sigma Xi, Phi Eta Sigma, Phi Epsilon Kappa, Scabbard and Blade, Galton Soc., Harvey Soc. (hon.). Episcopalian. Mason (Shriner); Odd Fellow. Clubs: Harvard (N.Y.); Harvard (Boston); Pot and Kettle. Author: The Awakening College, 1930; Civilization Against Cancer, 1939; Genetics, Biological Individuality, and Cancer, 1954; Inheritance of Coat Color in Dogs, 1956; also articles on genetics, cancer research, edn. and social problems. Awarded Am. Cancer Soc. medal, 1950; Pioneers Hall of Fame, Utah, 1952. Address: Ellsworth ME Died Dec. 22, 1971; buried Ledgelawn Cemetery, Bar Harbor ME

LITTLE, GEORGE, geologist; b. Tuscaloosa, Ala., Feb. 11, 1838; s. John and Barbara (Kerr) L.; A.B., U. of Ala., 1855, A.M., 1856 (LL.D., 1905); Ph.D., U. of Göttingen, 1859; m. Caroline Patillo Doak, May 13, 1869. Prof. natural science, Oakland Coll., Miss., 1860-61; pvt. Lumsden's Battery, Army of Tenn., C.S.A.; capt. arty., ordnance duty on staffs of Generals Clayton, Bate, Brown, Cleburne, Cobb, Hill, Breckenridge, Cheatham, Bragg; lt. col. arty., chief ordnance officer, Hardee's corps until 1865. Prof. geology, U. of Miss., 1866-74, 1881-89; state geologist of Miss., 1870-74, of Ga., 1874-81; geol. expert, Chattanooga, Tenn., 1889-92; druggist, Tuscaloosa, Ala., 1892-1902; geol. reporter on clays, Geol. Survey of Ala., 1903, on mines and railroads, 1904-18. Trustee Pontotoc (Miss.) Presbyn. Collegiate Inst. Democrat. Home: Tuscaloosa, Ala. Died May 15, 1924.

LITTLE, HOMER PAYSON, geologist; b. Columbia, Conn., Aug. 3, 1884; s. Payson Elliot and Emma Amelia (Bascom) L.; A.B., Williams, 1906; Ph.D., Johns Hopkins, 1910; LL.D., Clark U., 1954; m. Elizabeth L. Thomson, June 24, 1911; children—Elbert Payson, John Bascom, Emma Elizabeth Thomson, Ruth Mallory. With U.S. Geol. Survey, summer 1907, Md. state Geol. Survey, summers 1908-10; fellow Johns Hopkins, 1909-10; with geol. dept. Colby Coll., Waterville, Me., 1910, prof., 1914-20; exec. sec. div. geol. geography. NRC, Washington, 1920-22; dean undergrads., prof. geology Clark U., 1922-54, dean emeritus, prof. geology emeritus; lectr. geology Bangor Theol. Sem., 1913, 16, 19, Worcester Poly. Inst., 1932-37; instr. geography John Hopkins, summer sch., 1921. Trustee Andover Theol. Sem., Monson Acad., Internat. Coll., Beirut; pres. bd. trustees Leicester Jr. Coll., 1957—. Fellow A.A.A.S., Geol. Soc. Am.; mem. Worcester Natural History Soc. (pres. 1934-41). Mem. Worcester Kiwanis Club (pres. 1938). Moderator Mass. Congl. Conf. and Missionary Soc. 1943. Bd. dirs. Worcester Free Pub. Library, 1943-48, pres. 1948. Phi Sigma Kappa, Phi Beta Kappa, Gamma Alpha. Republican. Conglist. Address: 36 Whitman Rd., Worcester, Mass. Died July 1, 1966.

LITTLEHALES, GEORGE WASHINGTON, (lit'l-halz), hydrographic engr.; b. Schuylkill County, Pa., Oct. 14, 1860; s. William Henry and Margaret (Reber) L.; grad. (B.S.), U.S. Naval Acad., 1883; C.E., Columbian (now George Washington) U., 1888; m. Helen Powers Hill, Jan. 26, 1896; children—Margaret Powers (Mrs. Philip G. Vondersmith), James Hill, George Reber. Hydrographic engr. of the U.S. Hydrographic Office, 1900-1932. A founder, 1896, and was asso. editor Internat. Jour. Terrestrial Magnetism. Cons. hydrographer, dept. terrestrial magnetism, Carnegie Inst., 1904-06; prof. nautical science, George Washington U., 1913-27. Chmn. sect. of physical oceanography, Am. Geophysical Union, 1919-22; v.p. sect. of oceanography, Internat. Union of Geodesy and Geophysics, 1921-32; v.p. Am. Geophysical Union, 1926-29, chairman section of meteorology, 1929-32. Fellow A.A.A.S.; mem. Washington Acad. Sciences (v.p. 1905, 12, 13), Philos. Soc. Washington (pres. 1905), Am. Soc. Naval Engrs.; del. to Brussels Congress, 1919, for the Establishment of the Internat. Research Council; del. to Internat. Hydrographic Conf., London, 1919, leading to establishment Internat. Hydrog. Bur.; Pan-Pacific Scientific Conf., Honolulu, 1920; to Conf. of the Internat. Geodetic and Geophysical Union, Rome, 1922, Stockholm, 1930; to Pan-Pacific Science Congress, Tokyo, 1926; to Internat. Congress Oceanography, Marine Hydrography and Continental Hydrology, Seville, 1929. Club: Cosmos. Author: Development of Great Circle Sailing; The Methods and Results of the Survey of Lower California; Submarine Cables; The Magnetic Dip or Inclination; The Meridional Parts of the Terrestrial Spheriod, 1889; The Azimuths of Celestial Bodies, 1902; The Forms of Isolated Submarine Peaks, 1891; The Azimuth and the Hour Angle from the Latitude of the Observer and the Declination and Altitude of the Observed Celestial Body, 1903; A New and Abridged Method of Finding the Locus of Geographical Position and the Compass Error; Altitude, Azimuth, and Geographical Position, 1906; Geographical Position-Line Tables, 1915; Chart for Finding Geographical Position in Aerial Navigation, 1918; Tables of the Simultaneous Altitudes and Azimuths of Celestial Bodies, 1920; The Summer Line of Position, furnished ready to lay down upon the chart by means of tables of simultaneous hour-angle and azimuth of celestial bodies, 1923; Finding Geographical Position in the Region of the North Pole, 1925; Mechanical Means for Finding Geographical Position in Navigation, 1929; Both the Latitude and the Longitude of the Ship Found in a Single Operation from the Observation of the Altitude and the Azimuth of a Celestial Body, 1937. He has made many researches in hydrography, oceanography and terristrial magnetism, results given in more than 100 papers; published about 3,000 charts used in the navigation of the vessels of the world. Edited the mathematical tables for the use of American seamen. Home: 2132 Le Roy Pl., Washington, D.C. Died Aug. 12, 1943.

LITTLEJOHN, JOHN MARTIN, president and professor of osteopathic therapeutics Am. Coll. of Osteopathic Medicine and Surgery since June, 1900; b. Glasgow, Scotland, 1867; s. Rev. James Littlejohn; grad. Univ. of Glasgow; studied theology; ordained 1886; taught theology, 1886-87; continued studies, A.M. 1889, B.D. 1890, LL.B. 1892; univ. fellow Columbia Univ., 1892-93; grad. Ph.D. (hon. D.D., LL.D.); M.D., Dunham and Hering Med. colls.; married. Was tutor Glasgow Univ.; prin. Rosemount Coll., 1890-92; pres. Amity Coll., College Springs, Ia. 1894-97; prof. of physiology, psychology and psychiatry and dean of faculty, Am. Sch. of Osteopathy, Kirksville, Mo., 1898-1900 (D.O., 1900); enrolled as lawyer, May, 1899; prof. applied physiology, Hering Med. Coll. and Nat. Med. Univ., Chicago. Fellow and gold medallist, Soc. of Science, London, 1895; fellow Royal Soc. of Literature of Great Britain, 1899; mem. Nat. Hist. and Biog. Soc. Editor-in-chief Journal of the Science of Osteopathy, 1900-07. Author: The Political Theory of the Schoolmen and Grotius (3 parts), 1894 A7; Lecture Notes on Physiology, 1898 A7; Text-book on Physiology, 1898 A7; Lectures on Psycho-Physiology, 1899 A7; Lectures on Psycho-Pathology, 1900 A7; The Science of Osteopathy, 1902; Treatise on Osteopathy, 1903; The Theory and Practice of Osteopathy, 1907; The Fee System, 1907. Contbr. to med. jours. Residence: 928 W. Adams St. Office: Masonic Temple, Chicago.

LITTLETON, J(ESSE) T(ALBOT), indsl. physicist; b. Belle Haven, Va., July 7, 1887; s. Jesse Talbot and Loulie (Rosser) L.; A.B., So. U., Greensboro, Ala., 1906; M.A., Tulane, 1908; Ph.D., U. Wis., 1911, D.Sc., 1944; m. Bessie Cook, Dec. 28, 1911; children—Martha Elizabeth, Jesse Talbot, III, Joseph Cook, Harvey Kline. Instr. physics U. Mich., 1911-13; physicist Corning Glass Works, 1913-20, chief phys. lab., 1920-40, asst. dir. research, 1940-43, v.p., asst. dir. of research, 1943-46, v.p., dir. research, 1946-51, v.p., gen. tech. adv., 1951-54, hon. v.p., 1954—. Fellow A.A.A.S.; hon. mem. Am. Ceramic Soc. (pres. 1942); mem. N.A.M. (research com.), Tulane Alumni Assn., Am. Phys. Soc., Am. Optical Soc., Am. Inst. E.E., Eng. Soc. Glass Tech., Phi Beta Kappa, Sigma Psi, Gamma Alpha. Methodist. Republican. Clubs: Lions (pres. 1929; dist. dep. gov., 1934), C. of C. (dir. 1935-38), Fish and Game (sec. 1925), Country (all Corning). Author: (with G. W. Morey) The Electrical Properties of Glass, 1933. Home: Box 738, S. Indian River Dr., Fort Pierce, Fla. Office: Corning Glass Works, Corning, N.Y. Died Feb. 25, 1966.

LITTLEWOOD, WILLIAM, aviation cons.; b. N.Y.C., Oct. 21, 1898; s. William C. and Nellie T. (Nuttall) L.; M.E., Cornell, 1920; Dr. of Engring., U. Md., 1959; m. Dorothy E. Cushman, May 6, 1922; children—William Cushman, Robert Alden. With Niles-Bement-Pond Co., Plainfield, N.J., 1920-24; Ingersoll Rand Co., Phillipsburg, N.J., 1924-27; Fairchild Engine Corp., Farmingdale, N.Y., 1927-30; with Am. Airlines, Inc., N.Y. 1930—, v.p., 1937-63, now aviation cons.; cons. and lectr. (engr.) in aviation; bd. dirs. Cornell Aero. Lab., Marquardt Corp. Tech. adv. bd. FAA. Mem. aviation adv. com. Princeton U.; trustee, exec. com. Cornell U.; permanent vice chmn. industry adr. com. Flight Safety Found. Recipient Wright Bros. medal, 1935; Flight Safety Found. award, 1956; Daniel Guggenheim metal, 1958. Monsanto Aviation Safety award Aviation Writers Assn., 1963. Fellow Canadian Aerospace Inst.; hon. fellow Am. Inst. Aeros. and Astronautics (pres. 1959), Royal Aero-Soc.; mem. Soc. Automotive Engrs. (hon.; pres. 1954), Am. Soc. M.E., Nat. Acad. Scis. Clubs: Wings (N.Y.C.); Cornell (N.Y. and Md.); Cosmos (Washington); Chesapeake Bay Yacht. Home: Martingham, St. Michaels, Md. Office: 1101 17th St. N.W., Washington 20036. Died Dec. 1967.

LITZENBERG, JENNINGS CRAWFORD, (lit'zen-berg), obstetrician; b. Waubeek, Ia., Apr. 6, 1870; s. William Denny and Lydia (Crawford) L.; B.Sc., U. of Minn., 1894, M.D., 1899; studied U. of Vienna, 1909-10, later in Berlin, London, Glasgow and Dublin;

m. Elizabeth Anna Fisher, June 3, 1902; children—Avis, Karl; m. 2d, Dr. Olga Hansen, Jan. 27, 1934. Gen. practice, 1900-10, specialized in obstetrics and gynecology since 1910; mem. The Nicollet Clinic. Instructor in obstetrics, U. of Minn., 1901-07, asst. prof., 1907-10, asso. prof. obstetrics and gynecology, 1910-14, prof. and head of dept., 1914-38, prof. emeritus since 1938; chief dept. obstetrics and gynecology, University Hosp.; obstetrician to Eitel and Northwestern hosps.; cons. obstetrician and gynecologist Fairview Hosp. Former mem. Am. Bd. Obstetrics and Gynecology; fellow Am. Gynecol. Soc. (2d v.p. and mem. council 1920, pres. 1940-41), Am. Assn. Obstetricians and Gynecologists and Abdominal Surgeons (pres. 1938), Am. Coll. Surgeons, A.M.A. (chmn. sect. obstetrics, gynecology and abdominal surgery 1928; exec. com. 1928-30), Hennepin County Med. Soc. (pres. 1919), Minn. Acad. Medicine (pres. 1932), Central Assn. Obstetricians and Gynecologists, Delta Upsilon, Nu Sigma Nu, Sigma Xi, Alpha Omega Alpha. Republican. Baptist. Club: Automobile. Frequent contbr. on professional topics. Home: 711 East River Rd. Office: 1009 Nicollet Av., Minneapolis 2, Minn. Died Aug. 15, 1948.

LITZINGER, MARIE, prof. mathematics; b. Bedford, Pa., May 14, 1899; d. Rush and Katherine (O'Connell) Litzinger; A.B., Bryn Mawr Coll., 1920, M.A., 1922; student U. of Rome, Italy, 1923-24; Ph.D., U. of Chicago, 1934. Teacher, Devon (Pa.) Manor Sch., 1920-22, Greenwich (Conn.) Academy, 1924-25; instr. Mt. Holyoke Coll., South Hadley, Mass., 1925-28, asst. prof., 1928-37, chmn. dept. mathematics since 1937, asso. prof., 1937-42, prof. since 1942, prof. mathematics John Stewart Kennedy Foundn. since 1948. Mem. Am. Math. Soc., Math. Assn. of Am., (Conn. Valley Sect. Assn. Teachers of Mathematics in New Eng. (pres. 1940-41), Sigma Xi. Democrat. Author: (article) A Basis for Residual Polynomials in N Variables (Transactions of the Am. Math. Soc., Vol. 37, No. 2, 1935). Home: Bedford, Pa. Office: Mt. Holyoke College, South Hadley, Mass. Died Apr. 7, 1952.

LIVERMORE, GEORGE ROBERTSON, urologist; b. Memphis, Sept. 20, 1878; s. Alonzo Skiles and Leila (Robertson) L.; grad. Memphis Mil. Inst., 1896; M.D., U. Va., 1899; m. Katherine Kerr Carnes, Dec. 8, 1914; 1 son, George Robertson. Asst. demonstrator histology, U. Va., 1898, asst. demonstrator anatomy, 1899-1900; began practice at Memphis, 1903; prof. genito-urinary diseases Coll. Phys. and Surg., 1905-16; prof. urology, head dept. (resigned), U. Tenn. Med. Dept., 1916—; cons. urologist John Gaston, St. Joseph's hosps.; former chief of staff, now cons. urologist Baptist Meml. Hosp. Mem. Med. Adv. Bd., Memphis, World Wars I and II. Fellow A.C.S., Internat. Urol. Soc.; mem. A.M.A., Am. Assn. Genito-Urinary Surgeons, Am. Urol. Assn. (pres.), So. Med. Assn. (chmn. urol. sect.), Mid South Post Grad. Assembly, Urol. Corr. Club, Tenn. State Med. Assn. (v.p.) Memphis and Shelby County Med. Soc. (pres.), Memphis Urol. Soc. (pres.), Am. Editors and Authors Assn., S.E. Branch Am. Urol. Assn. (pres.), Phi Chi, Phi Kappa Psi; hon. mem. Western br. Am. Urol. Assn., Okla. Clin. Soc.; corr. mem. Cuban Urol. Assn. Democrat. Episcopalian. Mason (32 deg., Shriner). Clubs: Memphis Country, Memphis Stamp. Author: Gonorrhea and Kindred Affections in the Male, 1929. Co-author: Lewis' Practice of Surgery, 1928; Oxford Loose Leaf Surgery. Contbr. articles on urol. subjects to med. jours. Mem. editorial bd. Modern Medicine; mem. adv. bd. Urol. and Cutaneous Rev. Inventor four urol. instruments and urol. operations. Home: 1720 Central Av. Office: Hickman Bldg., Memphis. Died May 1962.

LIVERMORE, NORMAN BANKS, engr.; b. Oakland, Calif., July 20, 1872; s. Horatio P. and Mattie H. (Banks) L.; student U. of Calif.; C.E., Cornell U., 1899; m. Caroline Sealy, Jan. 5, 1910; children—Norman B., George S., John S., Horatio P., Robert. Began as U.S. asst. engr., fortifications and harbors; later engr., water and power works; cons. engr., San Francisco, since 1908; dir. Calif. Packing Corp. since 1915, Pacific Gas & Electric Co. since 1916, Crocker First Nat. Bank since 1930 (also mem. exec. com.), Firemans Fund Indemnity Co. since 1930, Natomas Co. since 1920 and others. Lt. col., U.S. Army, World War I; awarded French Legion of Honor. Pres. bd. trustees Calif. Acad. Sciences. Mem. various engring. and scientific socs. Contbr. to jours. Travel and exploration (agrl. investigation and studies) in Africa and Orient. Home: Ross, Marin County, Calif. Office: 216 Pine St., San Francisco 4

LIVERMORE, WILLIAM ROSCOE, colonel U.S.A.; b. Cambridge, Mass., Jan. 11, 1843; s. George L.; freshman class Harvard; grad. U.S. Mil. Acad., 1865; m. Augusta Keen, Jan. 18, 1883. First lt. engrs., June 23, 1865; promoted through grades to col. engrs., Apr. 23, 1904. Has been connected with fortification work at Key West, Tortugas, Baltimore, Newport and New Bedford; chief engr., Dept. of Tex. and Dept. of the East, survey of N. and N.W. lakes, improvement of Missouri River, river and harbor improvement in Mass., R.I., Conn., N.Y. and N.J.; light house engr., making many improvements in the fog-signal system; mil. attaché Copenhagen and Stockholm, May 1899-June 1902; mem. bd. engrs. for fortifications, 1902-07; retired by operation of law, Jan. 11, 1907; returned to active duty, May 10, 1917, and on spl. duty with Chief of Engrs. U.S.A. With Sir Charles Bright, laid 1st Am. cable from U.S. to Havana, 1868; with Col. A. H. Russell, U.S.A., invented several mag. and automatic guns, including the method of loading by clips, patented 1880; author of "Am. Kriegspiel," a method of practicing the art of war on a map. Fellow Am. Acad. Arts and Sciences. Home: Washington, D.C. Died Sept. 26, 1919.

LIVINGSTON, BURTON EDWARD, plant physiologist; b. Grand Rapids, Mich., Feb. 9, 1875; s. Benjamin and Keziah (Lincoln) L.; B.S., U. of Mich., 1898; Ph. D., U. of Chicago, 1902; m. Grace Johnson, 1905 (divorced, 1918); m. 2d, Marguerite A. Brennan Macphilips, 1921. Asst. in plant physiology, U. of Mich., 1895-98; fellow and asst. in plant physiology, U. of Chicago, 1899-1905; soil expert U.S. Bur. Soils in charge of fertility investigations, 1905-06; staff men. dept. bot. research, Carnegie Instn., Washington, 1906-09; prof. plant physiology, Johns Hopkins U., 1909-32, prof. plant physiology and forest ecology, 1932-40, dir. lab. of plant physiology, 1913-40, emeritus prof. plant physiology since 1940. Mem. Nat. Research Council, Fellow Am. Acad. Arts and Sciences; mem. Am. Philos. Soc., Bot. Soc. America, American Soc. Naturalists (pres. 1933), Ecol. Soc. America, Am. Soc. Plant Physiologists (pres. 1934). Permanent sec. A.A.A.S., 1920-31, gen. sec., 1931-34, mem. exec. committee 1920-46, chairman exec. com., 1941-45. Author: Rôle of Diffusion and Osmotic Pressure in Plants, 1903; Distribution of Vegetation in U.S., as Related to Climatic Conditions (with F. Shreve), 1921. Editor: Physiological Researches; English edit. Palladin's Plant Physiology, 1918; Botanical Abstracts, 1918-20. Inventor: porous cup atmometer (for measuring evaporation as climatic factor); radio-atmometer (for measuring sunshine); auto-irrigator (for automatic control of soil moisture in potted plants); instruments for measuring water-supplying and water-absorbing power of soils. Writer of many tech. papers. Hales Prize Award of Am. Soc. Plant Physiologists, 1946. Home: Riderwood, Md. Died Feb. 8, 1948.

LIVINGSTON, ROBERT TEVIOT, prof. engring.; b. Indpls., July 7, 1896; s. James Duane and Mabel Channing (Wright) L.; ed. Webb Acad.; naval architecture, Rensselaer Polytech. Inst.; m. Geraldine Hull Gray, Dec. 2, 1922; children—Robert Gerald, Peter Robert. Machinist foreman, draftsman and engr. insp. for various cos.; instructor, asst. prof., asso. prof., prof., sometime executive officer, dept. indsl. and mgmt. engring., Columbia U., engr. cons., Long Island Lighting Co.; cons. research various cos.; former cons. editor McGraw Hill Book Co.; operates Utility Mgmt. Workshop and Industrial Research Conf. Sterling Forest; pres. Robert Teviot Livingston & Associates, consultants. Pres. Livingston Inst. Served as ensign USN. Recipient Freedom Foundation Award, 1950. Mem. Soc. for Advancement Mgmt., Am. Soc. Mech. Engrs., Am. Statistical Assn., Am. Soc. for Quality Control, Am. Inst. Indsl. Engrs., Nat. Planning Assn., Am. Mgmt. Assn., Am. Soc. Engring. Edn., Soc. of Applied Anthropology, Sigma Xi. Licensed profl. engr., N.Y. Clubs: Faculty (Columbia); Columbia University; Waccobuc Country. Author: The Engineering of Organization and Management, 1949. Co-author: The Human Relations of Idustrial Research, 1957; You and Management, 1958; The Job of the Manager, pub. 1960. Home: 69 High Ridge Av., Ridgefield, Conn. Office: 417 W. 118th St., N.Y.C.; and 88 Morningside Dr., N.Y.C. Died Jan. 7, 1968.

LLEWELLYN, FREDERICK BRITTON, research physicist; b. New Orleans, Sept. 16, 1897; s. Frederick Thomas and Virginia (Britton) L.; student Staunton Mil. Acad., 1917; M.E., Stevens Inst. Tech., 1922; Ph.D., Columbia, 1928; m. Beatrix Gunther, Feb. 25, 1924; 1 daughter, Barbara Elizabeth (Mrs. Joseph Matchette Walters, Jr.). Served intermittently as radio operator at sea, 1915-21; with F. K. Vreeland Laboratory, 1922-23, Western Electric Company, 1923-25; with Bell Telephone Labs., 1925-61, circuit research engr., 1935-44, cons. engr., 1945-53, systems studies engineer, 1953-55, communications cons., 1955-56, asst. to pres., 1956-61; research physicist Inst. Sci. and Tech., U. Mich., 1961-62, sci. adviser, dept. dir., 1962-65; dir. research Polytechnic Inst. Bklyn., 1965-71; expert consultant to Office Sec. of War, 1944, weapons systems evaluation group Joint Chiefs of Staff, 1951-53, exec. sec. sci. adv. com. O.D.M., 1951; member United States national com. internat. electro-tech. com. 1950-54. Alumni rep. on bd. trustees Stevens Inst. Tech., 1957-60. Licensed profl. engr. N.Y. Served in U.S. Navy, World War I. Fellow Am. Phys. Soc., Inst. of Radio Engineers (dir. 1939-45; recipient Morris Liebmann prize, 1935; chmn. papers com., 1942-45; pres. 1946). Mem. U.S. delegataion to Internat. Telecommunications Union, 1947; Internat. Cons. Com. on Radio, Stockholm, 1948. Received Stevens Honor award, 1949; Stevens Alumni award, 1962. Mem. Newcomen Society of North America, A.A.A.S., also Stevens Institute of Technology Alumni Association (pres. 1956-57), Operations Research Soc. Am., Sigma Xi, Tau Beta Pi. Clubs: University (N.Y.C.); Cosmos (Washington). Author: Electron Inertia Effects, 1941. Home: New York City NY Died Dec. 1971.

LLOYD, CURTIS GATES, botanist, mycologist; b. Florence, Ky., July 17, 1859; s. Nelson Marvin and Sophia (Webster) L.; ed. pvt. schs. Mem. Lloyd Bros., mfg. pharmacists, Cincinnati, 40 yrs. (now retired). Founder and endowed Lloyd Library, containing 52,000 volumes on botany and pharmacy; spl. student on the classification of fungi; instituted the Lloyd Museum, the largest collection of dried fungi ever brought together. Author of 6 vols. miscellaneous writings on fungi subjects, which are privately printed. Died Nov. 11, 1926.

LLOYD, E(DWIN) RUSSELL, geologist; b. Lloydsville, W.Va., Nov. 3, 1882; s. Nimrod Wesley and Mary Magdalene (Bender) L.; grad. W.Va. Conf. Sem., 1901; A.B., Ohio Wesleyan U., 1905; elected Rhodes scholar from W.Va., at Oxford U., 1905, B.A., 1908; Burdett Coutts scholar, same, 1908-09; grad. student and fellow U. of Chicago, 1909-11; m. Helen Burnett Gardner, Jan. 7, 1920 (died Jan. 11, 1934); children—Anne Gardner, Edwin Russell (dec.). Asst. and associate geologist U.S. Geol. Survey, Washington, D.C., 1911-17, in charge coal land classification, 1915-16; geologist Sinclair-Central Am. Oil Co., 1917-18; again asso. geologist U.S. Geol. Survey, 1918-19; chief geologist Sinclair-Wyo. Oil Co., Casper, Wyo., 1919-21, Mid-Kansas Oil & Gas Co., Mineral Wells, Tex., 1921-23, Argo Oil Co., Denver, Colo., 1923-24; cons. practice, also chief geologist New York Oil Co., Denver, 1924-26; dist. geologist Roxana Petroleum Corp., Roswell, N.M., 1927; cons. practice, Denver and Midland, Tex., 1928-32; dist. geologist, Superior Oil Co., Midland, Tex., 1932-36; cons. practice since 1936. Fellow Geol. Soc. America; mem. Am. Assn. Petroleum Geologists (hon. mem., asso. editor), Am. Geophysical Union, Sigma Xi, Gamma Alpha. Address: Midland, Tex. Deceased.

LLOYD, FRANCIS ERNEST, botanist; b. Manchester, Eng., Oct. 4, 1868; s. Edward and Leah (Pierce) L., both Welsh; A.B., Princeton, 1891, A.M., 1895; student at Munich, 1898, Bonn, 1901; hon. D.Sc., U. of Wales, 1933, Masaryk U., 1938; m. Mary Elizabeth Hart, May 18, 1903; children—Mary Elizabeth (dec.), Francis Ernest Llewellyn, David Pierce Caradoc. Instr. in William Coll., 1891-92; prof. biology and geology, 1892-95, biology, 1895-97, Pacific U., Ore.; adj. prof. biology, Teachers Coll. (Columbia), 1897-1906; investigator, Desert Bot. Lab., Carnegie Instn., Washington, 1906; instr. Harvard Summer Sch., 1907; cytologist, Ariz. Expt. Sta., 1907; dir. dept. of investigation, Continental-Mexican Rubber Co., 1907-08; prof. botany, Ala. Poly. Inst., 1908-12; Macdonald prof. botany, Ala. Poly. Inst., 1908-12; Macdonald prof. botany, McGill U., Montreal, 1912-34, emeritus prof. botany since 1934; consultant, U.S. Rubber Company, 1919-33. Editor The Plant World, 1905-08. Bot. explorations Lumholtz expdn. to Mexico, 1890; Columbia expdn. to Puget Sound and Alaska, 1896; N.Y. Bot. Garden to Dominica, B.W.I., 1903, Java, Sumatra, F.M.S., 1919, S. Africa, 1929, 1935; Australia, New Zealand, 1935-36. Pres. bot. sect. Brit. Assn. Advancement of Science, 1933; fellow A.A.A.S. (sec.; v.p. 1923, sect. G), Royal Soc. Can. (chmn. sect. V. 1922; pres. 1933), American Society Plant Physiology (pres. 1927; Barnes life mem.), New York Academy Sciences, California Academy of Sciences, Linnaean Soc. of London; hon. fellow, Edinburgh Bot. Soc.; hon. mem. Phila. Coll. Pharmacy; mem. Bot. Soc. America, Torrey Bot. Club (asso. editor of Bull., 1899-1902; treas., 1902-06); corr. mem. Centro de Sciencios Letras e Artees, Campinas (of Brazil), also Czechoslovakian Bot. Soc.; mem. Sigma Xi, Alpha Omega Alpha, Nu Sigma Nu, Lambda Chi Alpha. Clubs: Faculty, Pen and Pencil (Montreal, Canada). Author: The Teaching of Biology (botany) in the Secondary School (American Teachers Series), 1904; The Comparative Embryology of the Rubiaceae, 1902; The Physiology of Stomata, 1908; Guayule (a rubber plant of the Chihuahuan Desert), 1911; The Carnivorous Plants, 1942; also various other botanical papers, including studies on transpiration, stomata, tannin, rubber, cotton, growth, colloids, fluorescence, reproduction and carnivorous plants. Address: Box 842, Carmel, Calif. Died Oct. 18, 1947.

LLOYD, JAMES, physician; b. Oyster Bay, L.I., N.Y., Mar. 24, 1728; s. Henry and Rebecca (Nelson) L.; studied medicine under Dr. William Clark, Boston, 1745-50, obstetrics and surgery under William Smellie and William Cheselden, London, Eng., 1750-52; m. Sarah Corwin, at least 1 child, James. Began practice surgery, Boston, 1752; 1st physician to practice midwifery in Am.; early advocate of vaccination for smallpox; only noted physician to remain in Boston during Am. Revolution. Died Boston, Mar. 14, 1810.

LLOYD, JOHN URI, pharmacist; b. W. Bloomfield, N.Y., Apr. 19, 1849; s. Nelson Marvin and Sophia (Webster) L.; ed. pvt. schs., Florence, Burlington and Petersburg, Ky.; hon. Ph.M., Phila. Coll. of Pharmacy, 1890; Ph.D., U. of Ohio, 1897; LL.D., Wilberforce University; D.Sc., Univ. of Cincinnati, 1916; M.D., Eclectic Med. Coll., Cincinnati, 1921; m. Adeline Meader, Dec. 27, 1876; m. 2d, Emma Rouse, June 10, 1880. Prof. pharmacy, Cincinnati Coll. Pharmacy, 1883-87; prof. chemistry, 1878—, pres., 1896-1904, Eclectic Med. Inst.; asso. editor Pharmaceutical Review to 1909, Eclectic Medical Journal, Eclectic Medical

Gleaner; pres. Lloyd Bros., Pharmacists Inc. Outside of profession has investigated dialect, superstition and folk-lore of Northern Ky.; pres. Lloyd Library and Museum. Revised Cleaveland's Pronouncing Med. Dictionary, 1881. Author: Etidorhpa, The End of Earth, 1895; Stringtown on the Pike, 1900; Warwick of the Knobs, 1901; Red Head, 1903; Scroggins, 1904. Has especially investigated plant chemistry and phytochemistry as applied to medicines, alkaloids, glucosids and proximate principles, precipitates in fluid extracts, and phenomena of capilitarity. Editor: History of the Vegetable Drugs of the Pharmacopeia of the United States, 1911; A Study of Digitalis, 1912; and of Coca (with J. T. Lloyd), 1913; History of the Discovery of the Alkaloidal Affinities of Hydrous Aluminum Silicate, 1915; Continued Study in Adsorption—Kryptonine, 1916; Echinacea Angustifolia, 1917; A Study in Solvents, 1917; History of the Vegetable Drugs of the U.S. Pharmacopeia, 1920; Felix Moses, the Beloved Jew, 1930; Physics in Pharmacy (with Dr. Wolfgang Ostwald, Leipzig, Germany, 5 parts issued). Four times awarded honor medals by American Pharm. Assn., receiving Remington honor medal, 1920, for research work in colloidal chemistry. Home: Cincinnati, O. Died Apr. 9, 1936.

LLOYD, MARSHALL BURNS, inventor, mfr.; b. St. Paul, Minn., Mar. 10, 1858; s. John and Margaret (Conmee) L.; ed. pub. schs., Meaford, Can.; married. First invention was combination bagholder and scale, for farmers; founded, 1900, at Minneapolis, Minn., later at Menominee, Mich., the Lloyd Mfg. Co., mfrs. bedspring weaving machine; later invented new method and machinery for making thin seamless steel tubing; also new method for producing wicker articles and loom for weaving the wickers; now mgr. Lloyd Mfg. Co.; v.p. Automatic, Seamless Tubing Co. Mayor of Menominee, 1913-17. Republican. K. of P. Home: Menominee, Mich. Died Aug. 10, 1927.

LLOYD, MORTON GITHENS, engr.; b. Beverly, N.J., Sept. 10, 1874; s. Clement E. and Irene Emma (Githens) L.; B.S., U. of Pa., 1896, Ph.D., 1900, E.E., 1908; Harvard, 1897-98; Friedrich Wilhelms Universität, Berlin, 1898-99; m. Ethel Tucker Maurer, June 20, 1907; children—Miriam, Richard Louis. Instr. physics, U. of Pa., 1899-1902; lab. asst., asst. physicist and asso. physicist, Bur. of Standards, Washington, 1902-10; tech. editor, Electrical Review and Western Electrician, Chicago, 1910-16; electrical engr. and chief safety codes sect., Nat. Bur. of Standards, 1917—. Fellow Am. Inst. E.E.; mem. numerous societies. Member Internat. Elec. Congress, St. Louis, 1904, Turin, 1911, Internat. Engring. Congress, San Francisco, 1915; Internat. Congress on Illumination, Saranac, N.Y., 1928. Awarded Edward Longstreth medal, Franklin Inst., 1910. Home: Chevy Chase, Md. Died Apr. 26, 1941.

LLOYD, STEWART JOSEPH, prof. chemistry; b. Hamilton, Ont., Can., Sept. 12, 1881; s. Joseph and Sage (Peregrine) L.; B.A., U. of Toronto, 1904; M.Sc., McGill U., 1906; Ph.D., U. of Chicago, 1910; m. Edith Marian Dawson, Dec. 27, 1911; children—Frances Valentine, Virginia Edith, Edith Vane. Prof. chemistry and metallurgy, U. of Ala., 1909—, also dir. of lab. and dean Sch. of Chemistry, Metallurgy and Ceramics; cons. chem. engr. Ala. Power Co.; asst. state geologist, 1930—; acting State geologist of Ala., 1939-45. Mem. Am. Inst. Chem. Engrs., Am. Chem. Soc., Soc. Chem. Industry, Am. Inst. Chemists, Electrochem. Soc., Canadian Inst. Chemistry. Episcopalian. Home: University, Ala. Died Aug. 1959.

LLOYD, WILLIAM ALLISON, lawyer, agriculturist; b. Sparta, O., Sept. 9, 1870; s. James J. and Maria (Ulery) L.; B.S., Nat. Normal U., Lebanon, O., 1890 (instr. science 1891); LL.B., U. of Tex., 1893; m. Minnie Lee Rutherford, June 24, 1896; 1 dau., Leonila Marie. Admitted to Tex. bar, 1893, and practiced at Victoria, 1894-96, Georgetown, 1896-1901; editor Victoria Advocate, 1894-96; admitted to Ohio bar, 1902; admitted to bar Supreme Court of the U.S., 1940; stock raiser and farmer in Ohio, 1901-09; collaborator Ohio Expt. Sta., 1904-09, in charge extension work 23 south eastern cos., 1909-13; dist. agt. U.S. Dept. Agr., in charge county agt. work, Central States, 1913-15, in charge 33 Northern and Western states, 1915-21; in charge extension work, Western States, 1921-28; dean of agrl. extension service, U. of Hawaii (on leave from U.S. Dept. Agr.), 1928-29; in charge extension work, Western states and territories, Hawaii and Alaska, 1929-39; principal agriculturist, office of director, 1939-40; retired from Government Service Oct. 1, 1940; made agrl. survey Am. Samoa at request of gov., 1932; visited New Zealand to study agrl. orgn., 1932; advisor Joint Prep. Commn. on Philippine Affairs, apptd. by President Roosevelt and President Quezon, 1937; now dir. information, Assn. of Land Grant Colls. and Univs., Washington, D.C. Organized Extension Work in Alaska, 1930. Asst. postmaster, Georgetown, 1897-1901. Organizer and grand dir. Epsilon Sigma Phi (awarded Service Ruby for contbn. to Am. Agr. 1933). Democrat. Clubs: University, Federal, National Press. Author of numerous bulletins of U.S. Department of Agriculture and Ohio Experiment Station. Loaned to office of Indian Affairs, Dept. of Interior, to prepare spl. report land policy for Am. Indians, 1934. Author rural recreation reserve Works Progress Project for rural playgrounds, 1935; History of Extension Work, 1939. Visited South Am. Countries, Peru, Chile, Argentine, Brazil, to study adult edn., 1940. One of introducers of sweet clover as forage plant. Home: The Sedgwick, 1722 19th St. N.W. Address: 1372 National Press Bldg., Washington. Died July 10, 1946; buried in Cedar Hill Cemetery.

LOBECK, ARMIN KOHL, (lo'bek), prof. geology; b. New York City, Aug. 16, 1886; s. Adolph Christian and Elmire Celeste (Voullaire) L.; A.B., Columbia, 1911, A.M., 1913, Ph.D., 1917; m. Bertha Merrill, Dec. 25, 1917; children—Elmire, Merrill. Instructor Phila. Coll. Pharmacy, 1911-14; asst. prof. U. of Wis., 1919-24, asso. prof., 1924-29; prof. geology, Columbia, 1929-54, emeritus prof. Bd. govs. Nature Conservancy, 1954—. Founder, 1922, now pres., dir. Geographical Press. Mem. geog. sect., Am. Commn. to Negotiate Peace, Paris, World War I. Consultant War and State Depts., World War II. Neil Miner Medal, Assn. Geology Tchrs., 1956. Fellow A.A.A.S., N.Y. Acad. Science; mem. Geol. Soc. of America, Assn. of Am. Geographers, Sigma Xi. Independent. Presbyterian. Club: Men's Faculty (Columbia U.). Author: Block Diagrams, 1924; Guide to Geology of Allegany State Park, 1927; Geology of Mammoth Cave National Park, 1928; Airways of America, 1933; Geomorphology, 1939; Military Maps and Photographs (with Maj. W. Tellington, U.S. Army), 1944; physiographic descriptions of Europe, Asia, Africa, N. Am.; Geological Diorama of U.S. Trustee, Nat. Parks Assn., 1944-50; Things Maps Don't Tell Us, 1956. Contbr. maps, block diagrams, guides and articles to geol. astronomy and geog. publs. Home: 251 Sunset Av., Englewood, N.J. Died Apr. 26, 1958.

LOBERG, HARRY JOHN, educator, engr.; b. Trondheim, Norway, Oct. 28, 1905; s. John O. and Anna Marie (Olson) L.; student U.S. Naval Acad., 1923-26; M.E., Cornell, 1929, M.S., 1936; m. Aline Johnson, Nov. 8, 1932; children—Paul W., Harry J., Peter E., Eric L. Came to U.S., 1906, naturalized, 1913. Sales engr. Norton Co., Worcester, Mass., 1929-32; prodn., sales Tyler Fixture Co., Niles, Mich., 1932-34; instr. Cornell U., 1934-37, asst. prof., 1937-42, asso. prof., 1942-46, prof., head dept. indsl. and engring. administrn., 1946-50, chmn. exec. com., Housing Research Center, 1951—; prof., dir. Sibley Sch. Mech. Engring., 1950-65; dir. tng. Nat. Machine Tool Builders Assn., 1948-60. Dir. USN Steam and Diesel Engring. Tng. Program. 1943-46. Profl. engr., N.Y. Fellow Am. Soc. M.E. (chmn. materials handling div. 1954, safety div. chmn. 1956; chmn. Southern tier section 1960); mem. American Society Engineering Education, Am. Marketing Assn., Am. Statis. Assn., Tau Beta Pi, Phi Kappa Phi, Pi Tau Sigma, Phi Delta Theta. Author: Machine Tool Selling (rev. edit.), 1953. Author articles on engring., marketing. Home: 1008 Triphammer Rd., Ithaca, N.Y. Office: Cornell U., Ithaca, N.Y. 14850. Died Feb. 22, 1965; buried Mt. Pleasant Cemetery, Augusta, Me.

LOCKE, JOHN, inventor, educator; b. Lempster, N.H., Feb. 19, 1792; s. Samuel Barron and Hannah (Russell) L.; M.D., Yale, 1819; m. Mary Morris, Oct. 25, 1825, several children. Asst. surgeon U.S. Navy, 1818; curator botany Harvard, 1819-21; founded, conducted Cincinnati Female Acad., 1822-35; prof. chemistry and pharmacy Med. Coll. of Ohio, Cincinnati, 1835-53; studied geology and paleontology of Ohio, Ill., Ia. and Wis., 1835-40, later studied terrestrial magnetism and electricity; invented a surveyors' compass, level, orrery, electromagnetic chronograph (built for U.S. Coast Survey). Author: Outlines of Botany, 1819. Died Cincinnati, July 10, 1856.

LOCKETT, ANDREW M., contracting engr.; b. Marion, Ala., Sept. 4, 1865; s. Powhatan and Martha Jane (Moore) L.; student Howard Coll. (Marion), U. Tenn., Stevens Inst. Tech.; m. Anne Waddell, Jan. 29, 1895; children—Andrew M., Elizabeth W. (Mrs. J. Norton Stewart). In employ of Henry R. Worthington, contracting engr., 1887; with Comegys & Lewis, contractors, 1888; again with Henry R. Worthington, engring. dept., 1888-93, mgr. St. Louis office, 1893-95, Atlanta office, 1895-98, asst. gen. sales mgr., N.Y.C. 1898-99; pres. A. M. Lockett & Co., Ltd., New Orleans, 1899—; also agt. of Henry R. Worthington and Babcock & Wilcox Co., N.Y.; mem. indsl. adv. com. 6th Dist. Fed. Res. Bank. Chmn. for State of La., Bd. of Engrs. on Indsl. Inventory; asso. mem. Naval Cons. Bd.; pres. New Orleans C. of C., 1930-31. Mem. Am. Soc. M.E., La. Engring. Soc., Chi Psi. Democrat. Episcopalian. Clubs: Boston, Automobile, Country. Home: 322 Hillary St., New Orleans, and Pass Christian, Miss. Office: Whitney Bank Bldg., New Orleans. Deceased.

LOCKHEED, ALLAN HAINES, aircraft engring.; b. Niles, Calif., Jan. 20, 1889; s. John and Flora (Haines) Loughead; ed. elementary schs.; m. Dorothy E. Watts (died 1922); children—Flora Elizabeth, John Allan, m. 2d, Helen M. Kundert, June 5, 1938; 1 son Allan Haines, Jr. Learned to fly, 1910; exhn. flying, 1910-15; designed and built one of first successful tractor seaplanes, 1911-12; flew this seaplane and had passenger carrying concession at World's Fair, San Francisco, 1915; pres. Loughead Aircraft Co., Santa Barbara, Calif., 1916-19; with brother, Malcolm, designed first successful twin-engined 10-passenger seaplane (made sight-seeing trip in this plane with King Albert and Queen Elizabeth of Belgium, 1919); with brother designed a sport plane, first streamlined fuselage, made of plywood moulded under pressure; organized and became vice-pres. Lockheed Aircraft Co., Los Angeles, 1926; supervised design and constrn. of Lockheed Vega, a high-wing cantilever monoplane of plywood constrn. (this Vega model used by Sir Hubert Wilkins in Alaska-to-Spitzenbergen flight, by Wiley Post in 2 flights around the world, and by Amelia Earhart in flight to Ireland and flight, Honolulu to San Francisco; Col. and Mrs. Charles Lindbergh used a later model in flight to China and flight to Europe, via Greenland); resigned from Lockheed Aircraft Co. when it merged with Detroit Aircraft Co., 1929; pres. Lockheed Bros. Aircraft Co., Los Angeles, 1930-34, changed his name from Loughead to Lockheed, legally, Feb. 1934; designed and supervised constrn. Olympic high-wing cantilever, twin-engined monoplane; travel, research, consulting, 1935-36; organized and pres. Alcor Aircraft Corp., San Francisco, 1937-39; designed twin-engined, low-wing cantilever monoplane; travel, research, 1940; vice-pres. and dir. Berkey & Gay Furniture Co., Grand Rapids, Mich., as dir. aircraft engring. and mgr. aviation div., 1941. Apptd. by Jesse Jones mem. Cargo Plane Com. to approve a design for a cargo-carrying plane, Aug. 1941; com. completed its work, Jan. 1942, and planes now being built. General manager, Aircraft Div., Grand Rapids Store Equipment Co., Grand Rapids, Mich., since Nov. 1942. Mem. Early Birds. Republican. Protestant. Home: Sepulveda CA Died May 1969.

LOCKWOOD, HAROLD J(OHN), engr., educator; b. New Rochelle, N.Y., Sept. 14, 1890; s. Fred H. and Annie E. K. (Ferens) L.; E.E., Lafayette Coll., 1912, M.S., 1916; M.A., hon., Dartmouth, 1925; m. Elizabeth Van Campen, Mar. 24, 1913; children—John A., Theodore D. Instr. in physics Lafayette Coll., 1912-18, asst. prof., 1918-21; prof. power engring. Thayer Sch. of Engring., Dartmouth, 1921-31; prof. elec. engring. Manhattan Coll., 1938-42; supervisor Todd Shipyards, Bklyn., 1942-43; prof. engring. Trinity Coll., 1943—, now also head dept.; vis. lectr., Sch. of Engring., Yale, 1945-46; cons. engr., State N.H., 1931-33, Vulcan Radiator Co., Hartford, Conn., 1948-50, Industrial Sound Control, 1951-56. State director Fed. Emergency Administrn. Pub. Works for Me., N.H. and Vt., 1933-37; arbitrator, State Bd. of Mediation and Arbitration of Conn., 1947-56. Served as mem. O.T.C., 1918. Mem. Am. Inst. E.E., Am. Soc. M.E., Gamma Alpha, Tau Beta Pi, Sigma Nu. Episcopalian. Mason. Club: Hartford Engineers. Home: 632 Park Rd., West Hartford 7, Conn. Office: Trinity College, Hartford 6, Conn. Died Apr. 15, 1960.

LOCKWOOD, IRA HIRAM, physician; b. Storm Lake, Ia., Nov. 29, 1885; s. Eli and Adelia (Day) L.; B.S., Buena Vista College, Storm Lake, Iowa, 1905, Doctor of Laws, 1956; student at the Univ. of Iowa, 1905-07; M.D., General Med. Coll. of Chicago, 1909; m. Jessie King, June 8, 1915. Interne and resident, Flower Hosp., N.Y. City, 1909-11; engaged in med. parctice, Lincoln, Neb., 1911-17 and 1919-24; in practice of radiology, Kansas City, Mo., since 1924; dir. radiology Research Hosp., Kansas City; radiologist and dir. Research Clinic; cons. radiologist Kansas City Municipal hosps. 1 and 2; radiologist Children's Mercy Hosp., Fitzgibbon Memorial Hosp. (Marshall, Mo.), Olathe Community Hosp., Kan., Cushing Meml. Hosp., Leavenworth, Kan., Bothwell Meml. Hosp., Sedalia, Mo., Smithville Community Hosp., Miss., Kelling Clinic, Waverly, Mo. Served as maj. Med. Corps U.S. Army, during World War I; chief of X-ray dept. Evacuation Hosp. No. 1, A.E.F.; later head of X-ray service II army, A.E.F. Pres. Research Clinic, Blue Shield (Kansas City, Mo.); commn. mem. Dist. 9 Blue Shield Med. Care Plans; area cons. V.A. Trustee Am. Bd. Radiology (president); chairman board chancellors, Am. Coll. Radiology (gold medal award, pres.). Trustee Blue Cross-Blue Shield (Kansas City, Missouri), Frederick C. Narr Fellowship Foundation. Diplomate Am. Bd. Radiology. Fellow International College of Surgeons, American College of Radiology; mem. Am. Roentgen Ray Soc., Radiol. Soc. of N.A. (recipient award of merit for original sci. investigation or roentgenol. examination of the breast; past pres.), A.M.A., So. Med. Association American Radium Society (honorary), Am. Legion, Vets. Fgn. Wars. Clubs: Kansas City, Rotary (Kansas City, Mo.). Contbr. of numerous articles on radiol. subjects to sci. publs. Home: 4607 Jefferson. Office: Argyle Bldg., Kansas City, Mo. Died July 28, 1957; buried Forest Hill Abbey, Kansas City.

LOCKWOOD, JAMES BOOTH, army officer, explorer; b. Annapolis, Md., Oct. 9, 1852; s. Henry Hayes and Anna (Booth) L.; ed. St. John's Coll. Commd. 2d lt. 23d U.S. Inf., 1873; volunteer for duty with Lady Franklin Bay Arctic Expdn., 1881, made scientific observations, crossed Kennedy Channel to Greenland, proved that North Greenland was mountainous glacier-covered region; set out on exploratory trip, 1882, reached Cape Bryant at latitude 83° 24' 30" and longitude 40 46' 30" (most northerly point reached by any man up to that time), named island Lockwood Island; 2d in command on U.S. expdn., 1882, took over duties as naturalist of expdn., 1883. Died Cape Sabine, Arctic, Apr. 9, 1884, buried Burial Grounds, U.S. Naval Acad.

LOCKWOOD, JOHN SALEM, surgeon; b. Shanghai, China, Oct. 2, 1907; s. William Wirt and Mary Rebecca (Town) L.; A.B., De Pauw U., 1928; M.D., Harvard, 1931; Med. Sc.D., Coll. of Phys. and Surg. Columbia, 1937; m. Dorothy E. Tufts, Oct. 1, 1932; children—Elinor Towne, Marcia Robinson, Dorothy Tufts. Intern in surgery Presbyn. Hosp., N.Y.C., 1932-34, jr. and sr. fellow in surgery, 1934-37; instr. in surgery and fellow in surg. research U. Pa. Sch. of Medicine, 1937-39, asst. prof. surg. research, acting dir. dept., 1942-44; asso. in surgery and dir. tumor clinic Hosp. of U. Pa., 1940-42; prof. surgery Yale, also asso. surgeon New Haven Hosp., 1944-46; prof. surgery Columbia U. and attending surgeon Presbyn. Hosp., 1946—. Chief div. surgery, com. on med. research OSRD, Washington, 1944-46; mem. com. on surgery and com. on chemotherapy NRC, and surgery study sect. Nat. Adv. Health Council, USPHS, Washington. Civilian mem. com. on med. scis. Nat. Research and Development Bd., Nat. Mil. Establishment, 1948—. Recipient Presdl. Certificate of Merit, 1948. Mem. Am., N.Y. County med. assns., Soc. U. Surgeons (pres. 1948), Am. Soc. for Clin. Investigation, Am. Surg. Assn., Soc. of Clin. Surgery, Phila. Coll. Physicians, N.Y. Surg. Soc., A.C.S., N.Y. Acad. Medicine, Harvey Soc., Am. Assn. for Cancer Research, Phi Kappa Psi, Alpha Kappa Kappa, Sigma Xi. Contbr. articles to med. jours. Mem. editorial bd. Christopher's Textbook of Surgery, Annals of Surgery. Home: 170 Lincoln St., Englewood, N.J. Office: 630 W. 168th St., N.Y.C. Died June 16, 1950.

LOCKWOOD, THOMAS DIXON, patent lawyer, elec. expert and engr.; b. Smethwick, Staffordshire, Eng., Dec. 30, 1848; s. John F. and Mary (Dixon) L.; ed. common schs. there; tech. knowledge of elec. engring. and patent law, self acquired; m. Mary Helm, Oct. 20, 1875; children—Arthur George Frederick, Stanley Dixon (dec.). Learned and practiced machinists' trade in Eng., 1859-65, telegraphy in Can., 1866-67; made paper, Lee, Mass., 1868-69; made plate glass, Ind., 1869-71; worked on rys., Mass., Conn., N.J., telegraph operator, ticket agt., locomotive engr., 1871-75; in service Am. Tel. and Tel. Co. and predecessors, 1879—. Patent atty., expert in elec. inventions before patent office and U.S. cts.; authority on telephony and telegraphy, ret., 1919. Mem. Instn. Elec. Engrs., London; fgn. life fellow Imperial Inst., London; life fellow Am. Inst. E.E.; hon. mem. Nat. Elec. Light Assn., Old Time Telegraphers and Hist. Assn.; hon. mem. Telephone Pioneers Am. Clubs: Exchange, Algonquin, City (Boston). Author: Information for Telephonists, 1881; Electrical Measurements, 1883; Electricity, Magnetism and the Electric Telegraph, 1885. Translator, reviser of Ohm's Law, 1890. Contbr. to elec. and other jours. Home: 83 Bellevue Av., Melrose, Mass. Deceased.

LOCY, WILLIAM ALBERT, zoölogist; b. Troy, Mich., Sept. 14, 1857; s. Lorenzo D. and Sarah (Kingsbury) L.; B.Sc., U. of Mich., 1881, M.Sc., 1884; grad. student in biology, same, 1881-82; fellow in biology, Harvard, 1884-85, U. of Berlin, 1891; hon. fellow U. of Chicago, 1894-95, Ph.D., 1895; (Sc.D., U. of Mich., 1906); m. Ellen Eastman, June 26, 1883. Prof. biology, 1887-89, animal morphology, 1889-96, Lake Forest (Ill.) U.; prof. physiology, Rush Med. Coll., Chicago, 1891; prof. zoölogy, Northwestern U., 1896—. Trustee Marine Biol. Station; investigator, Zoöl. Station, Naples, Oct. 1902-Feb. 1903. Editor in charge of zoöl. articles, and author of several, in new Am. supplement to Ency. Britannica. Author: Biology and Its Makers, 1908; The Main Currents of Zoölogy, 1918. Home: Evanston, Ill. Died Oct. 9, 1924.

LODIAN, L., engr., traveler; b. Hartford Co., Conn., 1866; s. Kalos I. and Anita (Maña) L.; family removed west, 1869; edn. pvt.; professionally, self-instructed; served as teniente-general under Caceres at storming and taking of Lima; 2 yrs. on railroads of the Plata (location and shops), 1886-87; inspecting engr. of investors' coms. all over Europe, 1888-93; much professional work in Mexico, Pacific Islands, Australia, Indasia, 1894-95, visiting as engr. (at invitation of and accompanying mandarin suite) Lasá, Tibet, Sept.-Oct., 1895—believed to be 1st Am. thus traversing Himalayas; also 1st Am. to have penetrated (Apr., 1891) to ancient Republic of Andorra, east-central Pyrenees (investigating iron ore deposits). In Japan, Korea, and covering the whole of Siberia (Trans-Siberian Ry., and connecting systems), 1896-98, during which (winter, 1896-97) the cold-expansion of metals was first noted (the Lex Lodian of metallurgy); now engaged perfection own inventions (high-speed engine and accessories). Personal friend of Tolstoi, and (until his death, 1894) of Hungarian patriot, Kossuth. Prohibition-Socialist. Sec. délégué-au-pouvoir, anti-semite Convention internationale pour remédier le juif-mal, Paris, 1900. Author: Dans la terre hospitalière, 1898 P19; L'Imposture Landor, 1898 P19; Military and Strategic Aspects of the Trans-Siberian Railway, 1904 H1; Two Years Across Siberia, 1903 F14; also numerous contbns. to engring. and tech. jours. Home: San Francisco. Address: avenue de l'Opèra 21, Paris.

LOEB, JACQUES, biologist; b. Mayen, Germany, Apr. 7, 1859; s. Benedict and Barbara (Isay) L.; grad. Ascanisches Gymnasium, Berlin; studied medicine Berlin, Munich, Strassburg; M.D., Strassburg, 1884; state exam., Strassburg, 1885; asst. in physiology, U. of Würzburg, 1886-88, U. of Strassburg, 1888-90; biol. sta., Naples, 1889-91; (hon. D.Sc., Cambridge, Eng., 1909; M.D., Geneva, 1909; Ph.D., Leipzig, 1909); m. Anne L. Leonard, 1891. Asso. in biology, Bryn Mawr, 1891-92; asst. prof. physiology and exptl. biology, 1892-95, asso. prof., 1895-1900, prof., 1900-02, U. of Chicago; prof. physiology, U. of Calif., 1902-10; head div. gen. physiology, Rockefeller Inst. for Med. Research, 1910—. Fellow Am. Acad. Arts and Sciences; corr. mem. French Acad. Sci., 1914. Author: The Heliotropism of Animals and Its Identity with the Heliotropism of Plants, Würzburg, 1890; Physiological Morphology, I, 1891, II, 1892; Comparative Physiology of the Brain and Comparative Psychology, 1900; Studies in General Physiology, 1905; Dynamics of Living Matter, 1906; The Mechanistic Conception of Life, 1912; Artificial Parthenogenesis and Fertilization, 1913; The Organism as a Whole, 1916; Forced Movements, Tropisms and Animal Conduct, 1918; Proteins and the Theory of Colloidal Behavior, 1922; Regeneration, 1924. Leading mechanist in U.S.; tried to demonstrate that life phenomena can be reduced to physical chemical laws; applied theory of tropism in plants to simple animals; suggested human values might be produced by tropisms; noted for 1899 discovery of artificial fertilization of eggs and raising frogs so fertilized to maturity, 1908. Died Hamilton, Bermuda, Feb. 11, 1924.

LOEB, LEO, (lerb), pathologist; b. Germany, Sept. 21, 1869; s. Benedict and Barbara (Isay) L.; educated at Gymnasium; studied natural science and medicine, univs. of Heidelberg, Berlin, Freiburg, Zurich, 1889-96; research fellow, McGill U., 1903; Sc.D. (hon.), Washington U., 1948; m. Georgiana Sands, Jan. 3, 1922. Asst. prof. exptl. pathology, U. Pa., 1904-10; dir. dept. pathology, Bernard Skin and Cancer Hosp., St. Louis, 1910-15; prof. comparative pathology, Washington U., 1915-24, prof. pathology, 1924-37, and emeritus prof. since 1937. John Phillips memorial prize, Am. Coll. Physicians, 1935. Fellow A.A.A.S.; mem. Am. Assn. Pathologists and Bacteriologists (pres. 1914-15), Am. Physiol. Soc., Soc. of Cancer Research (pres. 1911), Internat. Assn. for Cancer Research (v.p.), Soc. Exptl. Medicine and Biology, Assn. Am. Physicians, Am. Philos. Soc., A.M.A., Washington Acad. Science; Am. Association for the study of Goitre, Nat. Acad. Sciences; hon. mem. French Soc. of Endocrinology. Author: The Venom of Heloderma (with collaborators), 1913; Edema, 1923; The Biological Basis of Individuality, 1945. Contbr. chiefly on tissue and tumor growth, tissue culture, psychiology of generative organs, pathology of circulation, venom of Heloderma, analysis of experimental ameobocyte tissue, internal secretions, biological basis of individuality, etc. Home: 40 Crestwood Drive, St. Louis 5. Died Dec. 28, 1959.

LOEB, MORRIS, chemist; b. Cincinnati, O., May 23, 1863; s. Solomon and Betty (Gallenberg) L.; bro. of James L.; A.B., Harvard, 1883; Ph.D., U. of Berlin, 1887; student U. of Heidelberg, 1887-88, U. of Leipzig, Germany, 1888; (hon. Sc.D., Union University, 1911); m. Eda Kuhn, Apr. 3, 1895. Asst. to Prof. Wolcott Gibbs, Newport, R.I., 1888-89; docent Clark U., 1889-91; prof. chemistry, 1891—, dir. chem. lab., 1895-1906, New York U. Fellow N.Y. Acad. Sciences, A.A.A.S. Jewish religion. Home: New York, N.Y. Died Oct. 8, 1912.

LOEHWING, WALTER FERDINAND, (lo'wing), prof. botany; b. Chicago, Ill., Nov. 25, 1896; s. Charles Henry and Emilie O. A. (Hildebrandt) L.; B.S., U. of Chicago, 1920, M.S., 1921, Ph.D., 1925; m. Helen Cromer, Feb. 26, 1936. Asst. professor botany, State U. of Ia., 1925-28, asso. prof., 1928-30, professor, 1930—, head of botany dept., 1940-53, dean of the graduate college, 1950—; civilian cons. biology Chemical Corps of U.S. Army, 1947-52. Served in field arty., United States Army, 1917-20, Certificat Supérieur, Alliance Française, Pasteur Institute Paris, France, 1919; fellow A.A.A.S. (vice pres. and chmn., Section G., 1947), Ia. Acad. Science (treas. 1929-32, vice president 1955-56; president 1956-57); member of the American Society Plant Physiologists (sec., treas. 1935-37, v.p. 1937-38, pres. 1938-39), Am. Soc. Grad. Schs. (v.p. 1958-59), Am. Assn. U. Profs., Bot. Soc. Am. (v.p. 1946), Am. Soc. Hort. Scis., Am. Soc. Naturalists, Am. Chem. Soc., Sigma Xi, Gamma Alpha, Acacia. Clubs: Chaos, Kiwanis (lt. governor Ia.-Neb. District, 1943). Editor-in-chief: Jour. Plant Physiology, 1945-53. U.S. del to Internat Botany Congress, Amsterdam, Holland, 1935. Home: 15 Woolf Avenue, Iowa City, Ia. Died Aug. 1, 1960.

LOEWI, OTTO, (lo'i), univ. prof.; b. Frankfort-on-Main, Germany, June 3, 1873; s. Jacob and Anna (Willstätter) L.; student Us. Strassbourg and Munich, 1891-96, M.D., Strassbourg, 1896; Sc.D. (hon.), N.Y.U., 1944, Yale, 1951; Ph.D. (hon.), Graz, 1950; M.D. (honorary), univs. Graz, Frankfurt, 1953; m. Guida Goldschmiedt, Apr. 5, 1908; children—Harold, Anna (wife of Dr. Ulrich Weiss), Victor, Geoffrey W. Asst. in pharmacology, U. of Marburg, 1897, privat-dozent in pharmacology, 1900-05; associate professor of pharmacology, University of Vienna, 1905-09; prof. pharmacology, Univ. at Graz, Austria, 1909-38; came to U.S., 1940, and since research prof. pharmacology, New York U. Coll. of Medicine; Dunham lecturer, Harvard, 1933; Harvey lecturer, New York, 1933; Ferrier lecturer, Royal Soc. London, 1935; Franqui Professor, Brussels, 1938-39; Dohme lecturer, Johns Hopkins 1941; Walker-Ames visiting prof., U. of Washington, 1942. Janeway lecturer, N.Y. 1945; Hughlings Jackson Memorial lecturer, McGill U., 1946; vis. scholar, U. of Va., 1948. Awarded Nobel prize in medicine, 1936; Cameron prize, Edinburgh, 1944; Austrian distinguished order for art and science, 1936. Honorary fellow Royal Society (Edinburgh) N.Y. Acad. Medicine; fellow Academia dei Lincei Rome; fgn. mem. Royal Soc. London; corr. mem. Bavarian, Austrian acads. sci.; hon. mem. Am., Brit. pharmacol. socs., Physiol. Soc., Societa di Biologia (Rome), Royal Soc. of Physicians (Budapest); asso. mem. Société de Biologie (Paris and Brussels). Author of papers on physiology of metabolism of kidney, heart, hormones, nervous system, etc., and on chem. transmission of nervous impulse. Home: 155 E. 93d St., N.Y.C. 28. Address: N.Y. Univ. Sch. Medicine, 550 First Av., N.Y.C. 10016. Died Dec. 25, 1961; buried Woods Hole, Mass.

LOEWY, ERWIN, hydraulic engr.; b. Becow, Sept. 18, 1897; s. Leopold and Charlotte (Sekeles) L.; student Charles U., Prague, 1914-15, Kings Coll., London, 1924; m. Margaret Zander, May 10, 1912; 1 dau., Brigitte Dolores. Came to U.S., 1940, naturalized, 1947. Banker, Eng., 1921-24; pres. indsl. enterprises, France, 1925-28; gen. sales mgr. Schloemann Engring. Co., Germany, 1928-36; v.p. Loewy Engring. Co., Ltd, London-Bournemouth-Paris, 1936-40; founder, pres. Loewy-Hydropress, Inc., N.Y.C., 1940-56, Loewy Constrn. Co., Inc., 1941—, Sintercast Corp. Am., 1947—; v.p., dir. Baldwin-Lima Hamilton Corp.; cons. USAF, 1945-51. Chmn. City Symphony Orchestra of N.Y. Served as capt. Austrian Army, 1915-18. Mem. Inst. Metals (London), Iron and Steel Inst., Naval Engrs. Soc., Iron and Steel Engrs. Home: 25 Central Park W., N.Y.C. 23. Office: 111 Fifth Av., N.Y.C.; also 19 Bradford St., Lake Placid, N.Y.; Paschall P.O., Phila. 42. Died July 13, 1959.

LOGAN, THOMAS MOLDRUP, physician; b. Charleston, S.C., July 31, 1808; s. George and Margaret (Polk) L.; grad. Med. Coll. of S.C., 1828; m. Susan Richardson; m. 2d, Mary Greely, 1864. Practiced medicine, Charleston, 1828-43, New Orleans, 1843-50, Sacramento, Cal., 1850-76; taught medicine Med. Coll. of S.C., Charleston; mem. staff Charity Hosp., New Orleans; active in fostering measures for public health protection; instrumental in founding Cal. Bd. Health, 1870, sec. until 1876; made studies of epidemiology and sch. hygiene; pres. Cal. Med. Soc. (1870), Agassiz Inst. of Sacramento, A.M.A. (1872). Author: (articles) History of Medicine in California, 1858; Report on the Medical Topography and Epidemics of California published in Transactions of A.M.A., Vol. XII, 1859. Died Sacramento, Feb. 13, 1876; buried Sacramento.

LOGAN, WILLIAM NEWTON, geologist; b. Barboursville, Ky., Nov. 5, 1869; s. Henry Elderberry and Jane Elizabeth (Points) L.; B.A., M.A., U. of Kan., 1896; Ph.D., U. of Chicago, 1900; m. Janette Cecil DeBaun, Aug. 31, 1898; children—Lois Lucene (Mrs. R. E. Esarey), Harlan DeBaun. With Kan. Geol. Survey, summers, 1893-97; supt. pub. schs., Pleasanton, Kan., 1896-98; with Wyo. Scientific expdn., 1899; prof. geology and mineralogy, St. Lawrence U., Canton, N.Y., 1900-03; with N.Y. Geol. Survey, summer 1902; prof. geology and mining engring., Miss. Agrl. and Mech. Coll., and geologist Miss. Expt. Sta., 1903-16, also geologist State Geol. Survey, 1903-16, and dean Sch. of Science, A. and M. Coll., 1913-16; asso. prof. econ. geology, Ind. U., 1916-19, prof. since 1919 and state geologist since 1919. Determined boundaries of Am. Upper Jurassic Sea ("Logan Sea"); first to suggest the biochem. theory of the origin of halloysite and other kaolin-forming minerals. Life mem. and fellow A.A.A.S.; fellow Geol. Soc. Am., Ind. Acad. Science, Royal Soc. Arts, London; mem. Am. Assn. State Geologists, Kan. Acad. Science, Miss. Acad. of Science, Sigma Xi, Phi Beta Kappa, Pi Gamma Mu; corr. mem. Soc. Geol. de France. Republican. Methodist. Kiwanian. Author: The Upper Cretaceous of Kansas, 1896; Invertebrates of Kansas Cretaceous, 1898; Brick Clays of Mississippi, 1907; Pottery Clays of Mississippi, 1909; Kaolin of Indiana, 1919; Petroleum and Natural Gas of Indiana, 1920; The Elements of Practical Conservation, 1924; Geology of the Deep Wells of Indiana, 1926; Sub-Surface Strata of Indiana; also wrote Building Stone in Indiana, Mineral Wood in Indiana, Clay Products of Indiana, Geological Map of Indiana, Rock Products of Indiana, and numerous brochures, articles, etc. General editor Handbook of Indiana Geology, Official del. 1st, 2d and 3d Internat. Conf. on Bitum. Coal. Home: Bloomington, Ind. Deceased.

LOHR, LENOX RILEY, pres., Mus. of Sci. and Industry; b. Washington, Aug. 15, 1891; s. Gustavus Peter and Margaret (Bean) L., M.E., Cornell, 1916 (honor grad.); grad. Army Gen. Staff Coll., Langres, France, 1918; Clare Coll., Cambridge U., Eng., 1919; D. Eng. (hon.), Ill. Inst. Tech. 1949; LL.D. (hon.), Knox Coll., 1950, Bradley U., 1955, Loyola U., Chgo., 1956,

De Paul U., 1958, Northwestern, 1962, C.E., Rensselaer Polytech. Inst., 1952; D.Sc. (honorary), Shurtleff College, 1954; married Florence Josephine Wimsatt (M.A., M.D.), November 18, 1924; children—Margaret Priscilla (Mrs. R.L. Brown), Patricia (Mrs. James K. Rocks), Mary Josepha, Lenox Riley, Donald. Member board directors, exec. secretary Soc. Am. Mil. Engrs. 1922-29, editor The Mil. Engr., awarded its D.S.M., 1930, pres. 1954; mem. Com. on War Memorial to Am. Engrs. at Louvain U., Belgium, 1928; gen. mgr. A Century of Progress Expn. Chicago, 1929-35; pres. N.B.C., Inc., 1935-40; president of the Museum of Science and Industry, Chicago, Illinois, 1940-58, trustee, 1935-68. Bd. mem. Met. Fair and Expn. Authority, chmn., 1952-57. Fellow Inst. Medicine of Chicago, Pres. Chicago R.R. Fair 1948-49. Dir. Civil Def. State of Ill., 1950-52; pres. Centennial of Engring., 1952, Inc.; chmn. Higher Edn. Commn. of Ill., 1954-59; hon. trustee Mary Thompson Hosp. (pres. 1952-55), Heart Assn., Chgo. La Rabida Jackson Park Sanitarium, Chgo., Thomas Alva Edison Found., N.Y.C., Air Force Mus. Found.; chmn. U. Ill. Citizens Com.; mem. U. Chicago Citizens Bd. and Northwestern U. Assos.; member citizens board Loyola University. Pres. committee Notre Dame. Mem. Sec. of Navy's Civilian Adv. Com., 1946-48. Served as 2d and 1st lt. C.A.C., U.S.A., 1916; capt. to maj. Corps Engrs., 1917-29, resigned 1929; co. comdr. and topog. officer 4th Engrs.; Brigade Adj. 57th Inf. Brigade, 29th Div.; participated in Alsace defensive sector, Meuse Argonne, returned to U.S., July 13, 1919; in Office of Chief Engrs. Decorated Silver Star medal, citation; Navy Distinguished Pub. Service award, 1954 (U.S.); Officer Order Ouissam Alaouite Cherifien of Morocco. Recipient Deutsches Museum citation, 1960; Rosenberger medal; citation U. Ill., 1964. Mem. Am. Soc. C.E., Inst. Am. Strategy (pres. 1958-62, dir.), Soc. Am. Mil. Engrs., Assn. U.S. Army, Navy League U.S., Sigma Phi Sigma (gen. pres. 1916; hon. key 1936), Phi Sigma Kappa, Chi Epsilon. Clubs: Economic, Chicago, Commercial, Antique Auto, Nat. Press. Author: Magazine Publishing, 1932; Television Broadcasting, 1940; Fair Management, 1952; Centennial of Engineering, 1953. Home: Evanston IL Died May 28, 1968.

LONG, CRAWFORD WILLIAMSON, anesthesist, surgeon; b. Danielsville, Ga., Nov. 1, 1815; s. James and Elizabeth (Ware) L.; grad. Franklin Coll. (now U. Ga.), 1835; M.D., U. Pa., 1839; m. Caroline Swain, Aug. 11, 1842. Moved to N.Y., 1839, practiced as surgeon; moved to Ga., 1841, practiced surgery; accidently discovered that sulphuric ether could be used as anesthetic in early 1840's; performed operation on neck of James Venable for removal of cystic tumor, 1842, performed 5 other operations using this procedure before 1846; published results of these expts. in So. Med. and Surg. Jour., 1849; practiced medicine and surgery, Athens, Ga., 1850-58; one of earliest users of ether in U.S. Died Athens, June 16, 1878; buried Athens.

LONG, CYRIL NORMAN HUGH, biochemist, physiologist; b. Nettleton, England, June 19, 1901; s. John Edward and Rose Fanny (Langdill) L.; came to U.S., 1932, citizen, 1942; B.Sc., U. of Manchester, Eng., 1921, M.Sc., 1923, D.Sc., 1932; M.D.C.M., McGill University, 1928; honorary M.A. degree from Yale U., 1936; M.D. (hon.), U. Venezuela, 1962; honorary D.Sc., Princeton, U., 1946, McGill U., 1961; m. Hilda Gertrude Jarman, July 28, 1928; children—Barbara (Mrs. R. P. Simons), Diana (Mrs. D. D. Hall). Demonstrator physiology, U. Coll., London, 1923-25; lectr. med. research, McGill U., 1925-29, assistant professor, 1929-32; director of George S. Cox Med. Research Inst., and asst. prof. med. U. Pa., 1932-36; professor physiol. chemistry Yale, 1936-38, Sterling prof. physiol. chemistry, 1938-52, chmn. dept., 1936-52, dean sch. Medicine 1947-52, Sterling prof. physiology, 1952-69, Sterling prof. emeritus, 1969-70. Chmn. dept. physiology, 1952-64; fellow John B. Pierce Found. Lab., 1969-70. Mem. Biochem. Society (Great Britain), Brit. Diabetic Assn. (hon. life), Physiological Society (Great Britain), Am. Soc. of Biol. Chemists, Soc. Exptl. Biology and Medicine (pres. 1953-55). Am. Physiol. Soc., Am. Assn. Physicians. Soc. for Clin. Investigation (pres. 1944-45), Nat. Acad. Sciences, The Endocrine Society, (president 1947-48), Am. Diabetes Assn., Argentine Soc. for Biology (hon. mem.), Am. Philosophical Society, Am. Acad. Arts and Scis. Sigma Xi. Alpha Omega Alpha, Nu Sigma Nu. Clubs: Yale (N.Y.C.); Faculty (New Haven). Writer numerous scientific papers reporting researches in biochemistry, physiology and experimental medicine. Home: Hamden CT Died July 6, 1970; buried Grove Street Cemetery, New Haven CT

LONG, EARL ALBERT, chemist; born Altoona, Pa., July 2, 1909; s. Arthur Russell and Grace Emma (Beattie) L.; A.B., Catawba Coll., 1930, D. Sc. (hon.), 1951; M.S., Ohio State U., 1932, Ph.D., 1934; m. Marietta Susan Moss, Feb. 8, 1947; step children George E. Shambaugh, Susan S. (dec.). Nat. Research fellow chemistry U. Calif., 1934-36, instr., 1936-37; fellow Lalor Found., 1937-38, asst. prof. U. Mo., 1938-43, asso. prof., 1943-45, prof. chemistry, 1945; with Los Alamos Lab., 1943-46, asst. dir., 1945; prof. inst. metals and dept. chemistry U. Chgo., 1946-61, dir. Inst. Study of Metals, 1957-61; asst. lab. dir. Gen. Atomic div. Gen. Dynamics Corp., 1960-66; chmn. dept. physics U. Ala., 1966-68. Fellow Am. Phys. Soc.; mem. Sigma Xi, Phi Lambda Upsilon. Home: Tuscaloosa AL Died May 15, 1968; buried Guave Pines Cemetery, Los Alamos NM

LONG, JOHN HARPER, chemist; b. nr. Steubenville, O., Dec. 1856; s. John and Elizabeth (Harper) L.; B.S., U. of Kan., 1877; studied at Tübingen, Würzburg, and Breslau, 1877-80; Sc.D., Tübingen, 1879; m. Catherine Stoneman, Aug. 24, 1885. Prof. chemistry, Northwestern U. Med. Sch., 1881—; dean Northwestern U. Sch. Pharmacy, 1913-17. Mem. referee bd. of consulting scientific experts U.S. Dept. Agr.; mem. revision com. U.S. Pharmacopoeia. Author: Elements of General Chemistry, 1898, 4th edit. 1906; Text-Book of Analytical Chemistry, 1898, 3d edit. 1906; Laboratory Manual of Physiological Chemistry, 1894; Text-Book of Physiological Chemistry, 1905, 2d edit. 1909. Home: Evanston, Ill. Died June 14, 1918.

LONG, PERRIN HAMILTON, physician; b. Bryan, O., Apr. 7, 1899; s. James Wilkinson and Wilhelmina Lillian (Kautsky) L.; B.S., U. Mich., 1924, M.D., 1924; M.D. (Hon. Caus.) U. Algers, 1944; F.R.C.P., 1946; D.Sc., Trinity Coll., 1955; m. Elizabeth D. Griswold, Sept. 6, 1922; children—Perrin Hamilton, Jr., Priscilla Griswold. Resident physician Torndike Meml. Lab., Boston City Hosp., 1924-25, interne fourth med. service, 1925-27; vol. asst., Hygienic Inst., Freiburg, Germany, 1927; asst. and asso. Rockefeller Inst. for Med. Research, 1927-29; asso. in medicine Johns Hopkins Med. Sch., 1929-37, asso. prof. 1937-40, prof., preventive med., 1940-51; physician Johns Hopkins Hosp., 1940-51; chmn. and prof., dept. medicine, coll. medicine State U. N.Y., N.Y.C., 1951-61, now emeritus; dir. u. div. med. service Kings Co. Hosp. Center, Bklyn., 1951-61, cons., 1961—, also chief dept. medicine; cons. V.A., F.D.A., P.H.S., Dept. of Army. Med. advisor O.C.D. Planning, 1948. Trustee Martha's Vineyard Hosp.; dir. Am. Field Service, 1959-64, Physician's Club, 1964—. Served Am. Field Service, 1917; pvt. AS, U.S. Army, 1917-19, with AEF, col. M.C., AUS, 1942-45, brig. gen. ret., cons. medicine N.A.T.O. and M.T.O. Awarded Croix de Guerre, Chevalier Legion of Honor, (both France); Legion of Merit, hon. officer (mil. div.) Order Brit. Empire. Fellow Royal Coll. Physicians; mem. Am. Soc. Clin. Investigation, Harvey Soc., Soc. Am. Bacteriologists, A.M.A., Assn. Am. Physicians, Zeta Psi, Alpha Omega Alpha, Sigma Xi. Presbyn. Club: 14 West Hamilton Street (Balt.). Author: Clinical and Experimental Use of Sulfanilamide, Sulfapyridine and Allied Compounds (with Eleanor A. Bliss), 1939; ABC's of Sulfonamide and Antibiotic Therapy, 1948. Contbr. many med. articles to jours. Editor-in-chief Resident Physician, Medical Times. Address: Edgartown, Mass. 02539. Died Dec. 17, 1965; buried Chappaquidick Island, Edgartown.

LONG, WILLIAM HENRY, forest pathologist; b. Navarro Co., Tex., Mar. 7, 1867; s. William Henry and Oliva (Manning) L.; A.B., Baylor U., Waco, Tex., 1888; A.M., Univ. of Texas, 1900, Ph.D., 1916; post-grad. student, Cornell U.; m. Florence B. Lumpkin, of Hubbard, Tex., June 18, 1891; children—Florence Lucile, Virgil Patton, Annie Kathleen, Evalyne Cochran, Loraine Bee, William Eugene (dec.), Malcolm Lee. Prof. natural sciences, Baylor U., 1888-93, Burleson Coll., Greenville, Tex., 1892-99; asst. in botany, U. of Tex., 1900-1901; prof. botany, N. Tex. State Normal Coll., 1901-09; editor Experiment Station Record, Washington, 1910-11; forest pathologist, Bur. Plant Industry, Aug. 1911—. Democrat. Baptist. Mem. Texas Acad. Sci., Bot. Soc. Washington, Phytopathol. Soc. America, A.A.A.S., Phi Kappa Phi, Sigma Psi. Author of various monographs and bulls. on bot. subjects. Home: 4015 N. 4th St., Albuquerque, N.M. *

LONGACRE, JAMES BARTON, engraver; b. Delaware County, Pa., Aug. 11, 1794; s. Peter Longacre. Apprenticed to engraver George Murray, Phila., 1815-19; established engraving bus., 1819; engraved portraits of George Washington, Thomas Jefferson and John Hancock on facsimile of Declaration of Independence (largest engraving of time), 1820; commd. to engrave many of portraits for Biography of the Signers of the Declaration of Independence (John Sanderson), 1820; engraved portraits on actors for Lopez and Wemyss edit. of Acting American Theatre, 1826; worked on engravings for 4 vols. of National Portrait Gallery of Distinguished Americans, 1834-39; chief engraver U.S. Mint, 1844-69, designed and engraved 1st double eagle coin, 1849; helped remodel coinage of Republic of Chile. Died Phila., Jan. 1, 1869.

LONGCOPE, WARFIELD THEOBALD, (long'kop), physician; b. Balt., Mar. 29, 1877; s. George von S. and Ruth (Theobald) L.; A.B., Johns Hopkins, 1897; M.D., Johns Hopkins, 1901; LL.D., St. John's Coll., 1934, Johns Hopkins U., 1951; D.Sc., U. Rochester, 1941; Docteur "honoris causa," U. Paris, 1945; m. Janet Percy Dana, Dec. 2, 1915; children—Barbara, Duncan, Mary Lee, Christopher. Resident pathologist of Pa. Hosp. Phila., 1901-04; dir. Ayer Clin. Lab., same, 1904-11; asst. prof. applied medicine, U. Pa., 1909-11; asso. prof. practice of medicine, 1911-14, Bard prof., 1914-21, Columbia; asso. vis. physician, 1911-14, dir. med. service Presbyn. Hosp., N.Y., 1914-21; prof. medicine Johns Hopkins Med. Sch. and physician in chief Johns Hopkins Hosp., 1922-46. Commd. maj., Med. O.R.C., 1917; on active duty med. div., Office of Surgeon Gen. U.S. Army, Washington, Aug. 1917-July 1918; col., Medical Corps, U.S. Army, A.E.F., July 1918-Jan. 1919. Fellow (hon.) Coll. Physicians (Phila.). Mem. Assn. Am. Physicians, A.M.A., Soc. Exptl. Biology and Medicine, Am. Soc. Clin. Investigation, Am. Soc. Exptl. Pathology, A.A.A.S., N.Y. Acad. Medicine, N.Y. Clin. Soc., Am. Clinic and Climatological Soc., Harvey Soc., Medico Chirurg. Faculty of Med., Balt. City Med. Soc., Nat. Acad. Scis.; fellow Am. Coll. Phys., Am. Acad. Arts and Scis.; hon. mem. Royal Soc. of Medicine, Société des Hôpital, Paris, Hon. Fellow Scandanavian Congress for Int. Med. Extensive investigations in clin. medicine and in pathology. Home: "Cornhill Farm," Lee, Mass. Died April 25, 1953.

LONGDEN, ALADINE CUMMINGS, physicist; b. Leesville, O., Feb. 19, 1857; s. Samuel and Adaline (Cummings) L.; A.B., DePauw U., 1881, A.M., 1884; postgrad. work, U. of Chicago, 1897-99; Ph.D., Columbia, 1900; m. Jean I. Humble, Dec. 24, 1884. Instr. mathematics and English, St. John's Mil. Acad., Haddonfield, N.J., 1881-82; prof. mathematics, Riverview Mil. Acad., Poughkeepsie, N.Y., 1882-83, St. James Mil. Acad., Macon, Mo., 1883-84; prof. natural sciences, same, 1884-88; prof. physics and chemistry, State Normal Sch., Westfield, Mass., 1888-97; asst. in physics, U. of Chicago, 1898-99; instr. physics, U. of Wis., 1900-01; prof. physics and astronomy, Knox Coll., 1901-26, emeritus. Comdt. St. James Cadets and capt. N.G., Mo., 1885-88. Republican. Presbyn. Home: Galesburg, Ill. Died July 12, 1941.

LONGSTREET, WILLIAM, inventor; b. Allentown, N.J., Oct. 6, 1759; s. Stoffel and Abigail (Wooley) L.; m. Hannah Randolph, 1783, at least 6 children. Interested in mech. instruments at early age; moved to Augusta, Ga., 1783, began to work seriously on steam engines; given patent on steam engine he had constructed by Ga. Legislature, 1788; invented and patented "breast-roller" of cotton gins, before 1801, also designed portable saw mill; built small steam boat which ran on Savannah River, Ga., 1806. Died Augusta, Sept. 11, 1814.

LONGWORTH, NICHOLAS, horticulturist; b. Newark, N.J., Jan. 16, 1782; s. Thomas and Apphia (Vanderpoel) L.; studied law in Judge Jacob Burnet's office, Cincinnati; m. Susan Connor, 1807, 4 children. Clk. brother's store, S.C.; moved to Cincinnati, 1803; practiced law; defended horse thief in his 1st case for which he received 2 copper stills, traded these for 33 acres which were later valued at $2,000,000; entered real estate bus., became millionaire; became interested in horticulture, 1828, producted marketable wine from grapes he had raised; also interested in cultivating strawberries, discovered that stamintate and pistillate plants had to be interplanted if crop was to be successful; waged "strawberry war" with those who doubted his findings, 1842, wrote numerous articles on subject. Author: A Letter from N. Longworth. . .On the Cultivation of the Grape and Manufacture of the Wine, Also, On the Character and Habits of the Strawberry Plant, 1846. Died Feb. 10, 1863.

LONGYEAR, EDMUND JOSEPH, mining engr.; b. Grass Lake, Mich., Nov. 6, 1864; s. Isaac and Roanna (Davis) L.; student U. Mich., 1883-86; E.M., Mich. Coll. Mines, 1888; m. Nevada Patton, Apr. 16, 1890; children—Clyde Stanley, Robert Davis, Philip Owen, Margaret (Mrs. Ralph H. Lutz), Richard Patton, Edmund Joseph. With location party, Marquette, Houghton and Ontonagan Ry., 1886-87; with J. M. Longyear, Marquette, Mich., 1887, 88-91, Mich. State Geol. Survey, 1888; pioneered in diamond drilling operations Mesabe Range, 1890, active in development of the mining area thereafter; cos. which later included mfg. cos. also, were organized under name of E. J. Longyear Co., hdqrs. Hibbing, moved to Mpls. 1911; served as pres. to 1924, v.p., dir. 1924—; operations included many areas in U.S., Can., Cuba, Mexico, numerous European, Asian and African countries; retired 1924. Sec. Hibbing sch. Bd., 1897-98; pres. Village of Hibbing, 1898-99; mem. budget and distbn. com. Community Fund, 1918-24, chmn. 1918; mem. bd. dir. YMCA, 1913-25; dir. Elliott Park Neighborhood House, 1919-24. Mem. Ulster County Hist. Soc., N.E. Hist.-Geneal. Soc., N.Y. Geneal. and Biog. Soc., Soc. Mayflower Descs., S.R. Republican. Baptist. Clubs: Minneapolis, Lafayette. Address: 454 S. Bedford Dr., Beverly Hills, Cal. Died Dec. 4, 1954; buried Forest Lawn Meml. Park, Glendale, Cal.

LONGYEAR, ROBERT DAVIS, geologist, corp. exec.; b. Petoskey, Mich., July 11, 1892; s. Edmund Joseph and Nevada (Patten) L.; A.B., Williams Coll., 1914; M.A., U. Wis., 1915; postgrad. Stanford, 1915-16, U. Minn., 1933; m. Barbara Elizabeth Lyon, Dec. 3, 1918; children—Roanne Elizabeth (Mrs. B. C. Corbus, Jr.), and Martha P. (Mrs. George R. Stevenson, Jr.) (dec.). Geologist exploration Falcombridge nickel mine, Sudbury, Ont., 1916-17; pres. E. J. Longyear Co., Mpls., 1923-58, chmn., 1958-70; dir. Cascade Corp., Kona Iron Co. Mining machinery adv. com. WPB, 1940-45; mem. Greater Mpls. Citizens League; hon. dir. Pillsbury-Waite Neighborhood Services. Second lieut., C.A.C., U.S. Army, 1918. Mem. Am. Inst. Mining, Metall. and Petroleum Engrs. (past dir. Soc. Mining Engrs.), Can. Inst. Mining and Metallurgy, Mpls. C. of

C., Diamond Core Drill Mfrs. Assn. (past president), also fraternity Beta Theta Pi. Episcopalian (past vestryman). Clubs: Minneapolis, Engineers (Mpls.). Home: Minneapolis MN Died May 20, 1970; buried Lakewood Cemetery, Minneapolis MN

LONSDALE, JOHN TIPTON, geologist; b. Dale, Ia., Nov. 8, 1895; s. John Dye and Eva Mary (Connor) L.; A.B.., U. of Ia., 1917, M.S., 1921; Ph.D., U. of Va., 1924; m. Edna Gertrude Van Arnam, Aug. 13, 1921. Asst. prof. geology U. of Va., 1921-24; asst. prof. of geology, U. of Okla., 1924-25; geologist Bur. Econ. Geology, U. of Tex., 1925-28; prof. geology and head dept., A. and M. Coll. of Tex., 1928-35; prof. and head dept. Ia. State Coll., 1935-45; dir. bur. econ. geology and prof. geology U. of Tex. since 1945. Served as 1st lt., U.S. Army, 1917-19; lt. col. and col., Gen. Staff Corps, U.S. Army, 1942-45; col. A.U.S. Res., ret. 1953. Mem. Geological Society of America, Society of Economic Geologists, Mineralogical Society of America, Assn. American State Geologists (vice pres. 1959), Am. Assn. Petroleum Geologists, Am. Inst. Mining and Metall. Engrs., A.A.A.S., Am. Geophys. Union, Sigma Xi, Gamma Alpha, Sigma Gamma Epsilon, Delta Tau Delta. Author bulls., sci. papers and articles on mineralogy, petrology, mineral resources, and ground water geology mainly of Tex. areas. Home: 2105 Meadowbrook, Austin, Tex. 78703. Died Oct. 5, 1960; buried Arlington Nat. Cemetery.

LOOFBOUROW, JOHN ROBERT, prof. biophysics; b. Cin., Nov. 1, 1902; s. John Wilson and Henrietta (Botts) L.; A.B., U. Cin., 1923; Sc.D., U. Dayton, 1936; m. Dorothea M. Gano, July 6, 1926; 1 son, John Wiltshire. Instr. physics U. Cin., 1925-29, research asso., 1929-35; prof. biophysics U. Dayton, 1935-36; research prof. Institutum Divi Thomae, 1935-40; asso. prof. Mass. Inst. Tech., 1940-45, prof. biophysics and exec. officer biol. dept., 1945—. Exec. sec. radar div., NDRC, 1942-46; pres. Cheviot Theatre Corp., 1931-40; cons. Crosley Radio Corp., 1924-34; chmn. spl. adv. bd. AEC, 1947-48. Fellow A.A.A.S., Am. Phys. Soc., Am. Acad. Scis.; mem. Chem. Soc. (London, Eng.), Physical Soc. (London), Biochem. Soc. (London), Faraday Soc., Optical Soc. Am., Beta Theta Pi. Contbr. sci. jours. Home: 68 Sparks St. Office: Mass. Inst. Tech., Cambridge, Mass. Died Jan. 22, 1951; buried Mount Auburn Cemetery, Cambridge.

LOOMIS, EBEN JENKS, astronomer; b. Oppenheim, N.Y., Nov. 11, 1828; s. Nathan and Waite Jenks (Barber) L.; ed. Lawrence Scientific Sch. (Harvard); m. Mary Alden Wilder, July 13, 1853; father of Mabel Loomis Todd. For 50 yrs. asst. in Nautical Almanac (senior asst., 1859-1900); retired; mem. U.S. eclipse expdn. to the West Coast of Africa, 1889. Author: An Eclipse Party in Africa, 1896; A Sunset Idyl, and Other Poems, 1903. Home: Amherst, Mass. Died Dec. 2, 1912.

LOOMIS, ELMER HOWARD, physicist; b. Vermillion, N.Y., May 24, 1861; s. Hiram Warren and Adaline Sabra (Sayles) L.; A.B., Madison (now Colgate) U., 1883; student Göttingen and Strassburg univs., 1890-93, Ph.D., Strassburg, 1893; hon. Sc.D., Colgate, 1910; m. Mary E. Bennett, July 23, 1885 (died 1904); 1 son, Robert B.; m. 2d, Grace Eaton Woods, Oct. 12, 1911. Teacher physics and chemistry, Colgate Acad., Hamilton, N.Y., 1883-90; instr., asst. prof. and prof. physics, Princeton U., 1894-1929. Dir. N.J. Sanitarium for Tuberculosis, McKinley Hosp., Trenton; dir. N.J. Anti-Tuberculosis Assn. Mem. Simplified Spelling Bd. (advisory council). Devised important improvement in methods of determining the freezing points of dilute solutions. Home: Princeton, N.J. Died Jan. 22, 1931.

LOOMIS, FREDERIC BREWSTER, coll. prof.; b. Brooklyn, Nov. 22, 1873; s. Nathaniel H. and Julia R. (Brewster) L.; B.A., Amherst Coll., 1896; asst. in biol. lab., Amherst, 1896-97; student U. of Munich, 1897-99, Ph.D., 1899; m. Florence C. Calhoun, Sept. 7, 1904; children—Newell Calhoun, Frederic Brewster. Instr. biology, 1891-1903, asso. prof., 1903-08, prof. comparative anatomy, 1908-17, prof. geology, 1917—, Amherst. Dir. Amherst exploring expeditions to Big Bad Lands, S.D., Wasatch Basin, Wyo., Converse Co., Wyo., Sioux Co., Neb., Maine shell heaps, Patagonia, N.E. Colo., New Mexico and Fla. Fellow Am. Acad. Arts and Sciences, Geol. Soc. America. Author: Hunting Extinct Animals in the Patagonian Pampas, 1913; The Deseado Formation of Patagonia, 1915; Common Rocks and Minerals, 1923; Evolution of the Horse, 1926. Home: Amherst, Mass. Died July 28, 1937.

LOOMIS, HENRY M(EECH), chemist; b. Yokohama, Japan, July 19, 1875; s. Henry and Jane H. (Greene) L.; B.S. in Chemistry, Mass. Inst. Tech., 1897; m. Eleanor W. Wallace, of Harrisburg, Pa., Nov. 10, 1908. Asst. chemist Mathieson Alkali Works, Niagara Falls, N.Y., 1897-1900; asst. supt. bleaching powder plant, Castner Electrolytic Alkali Works, Niagara Falls, 1900-02; chemist Internat. Acheson Graphite Co., Niagara Falls, 1902-04; with U.S. Dept. Agr. since July, 1907, as food and drug inspn. chemist, 1907-13, mem. Bd. of Food and Drug Inspn., 1913-14, chemist in charge of food control, 1914-16; now with Nat. Canners Assn. Mem. Am. Chem. Soc. Conglist. Club: Cosmos. Home: 2115 P St. N.W., Washington DC

LOOMIS, LEVERETT MILLS, ornithologist; b. Roseville, O., Oct. 13, 1857; s. Rev. Samuel and Maria Rebecca (Hamilton) L.; unmarried. Curator dept. of ornithology, 1894-1912, dir. mus., 1902-12, Calif. Acad. Sciences. Fellow Am. Ornithologists' Union. Author: A Review of the Albatrosses, Petrels, and Diving Petrels, 1918. Home: San Francisco, Calif. Died Jan. 12, 1928.

LOOMIS, MAHLON, dentist, experimenter in electricity; b. Oppenheim, N.Y., July 21, 1826; s. Prof. Nathan and Waitie (Jenks) L.; studied dentistry, Cleve., 1848; m. Achsah Ashley, May 28, 1856, no children. Practiced dentistry, Earlville, N.Y., Cambridgeport, Mass., Phila., 1848-60; began to expt. in electricity, 1860, an early expt. was to force growth of plants by buried metal plates attached to batteries; carried on 2-way "wireless" communication over distance of 18 miles, 1868; founded Loomis Aerial Telegraph Co. (inc. by Act of Congress, 1870), did not receive financial backing necessary to carry on his expts. Died Terre Alta, W.Va., Oct. 13, 1886.

LOOPER, EDWARD ANDERSON, otolaryngologist; b. Silver City, Ga., Dec. 16, 1888; s. John Anderson and Jennie (Stewart) L.; M.D., U. of Md., 1912; Emory U., 1908-10; Ophthal.D., U. of Colo., 1913; m. Lola Patenall, Jan. 15, 1920; children—Edward A., Lola Elise, Sybil Ann. Began practice as specialist in eye, ear, nose and throat, Baltimore, Md., 1913; prof. diseases of nose and throat, U. of Md., since 1921; laryngologist, Univ. Hosp. since 1921; surgeon, Baltimore Eye, Ear and Throat Hosp., since 1930; mem. exec. com. and mem. staff Woman's Hosp. since 1931; oto-laryngolist Md. State Sanatorium for Tuberculosis since 1922; otolaryngologist, Eudowood Sanatorium for Tuberculosis since 1920; laryngologist, Md. Gen., St. Agnes, Franklin Square, West Baltimore Gen., and Nurses and Child's Hosps.; mem. staff, Union Memorial and Mercy Hosps.; cons. laryngologist Kernan Hosp. for Crippled Children: bronchoscopist and esophagoscopist, University Hosp. and U.S. Marine Hosp.; cons. otolaryngologist, Provident Hosp.; otolaryngologist Baltimore City Hosps. for Tuberculosis, Edward McCready Memorial Hosp., Crisfield, Md.; and Havre de Grace Hosp., Md. Served as 1st lt. Med Reserve Corps, U.S. Army, 1918; instr. and capt., Ft. Oglethorpe; in France 2 yrs.; maj., Med. Reserve Corps. Fellow Am. College Surgeons (mem. advisory council com. for otolaryngology); mem. American Bronchoscopic Society (vice-pres.), Am. Rhinol., Laryngol. and Otol. Soc., Am. Acad. Ophthalmology and Oto-Laryngology, Am. Laryngol. Assn., Internat. Coll. of Surgeons (past state regent) Med. and Chirurg. Faculty of Md., Baltimore City Med. Soc., Southern Med. Soc. (past councillor); asso. mem. Am. Coll. Chest Physicians. Democrat. Baptist. Clubs: Baltimore Country, Gibson Island Country. Author: The Diagnosis and Treatment of Laryngeal Tuberculosis, 1937; also about 30 articles related to subjects in specialty. Home: 504 Overhill Rd., Roland Park, Baltimore. Office: 104 W. Madison St., Balt. Died Jan. 14, 1953.

LORD, FREDERIC W., constrn. engr.; b. Brooklyn, N.Y., July 3, 1871; s. Joseph and Mary (Archer) L.; ed. private schs., Brooklyn Poly. Inst., Mass. Institute Tech.; m. Mrs. Alice K. Garrison, Sept. 29, 1906; children—Anne (Mrs. Wolcott Andrews), Mrs. Mary Reed, Ellen (Mrs. Robert Pierce), (stepchildren) Lloyd K. Garrison and Mrs. Carl Binger. Founder, 1895, and chief exec., Lord Electric Co., Inc., New York, Boston, Pittsburgh, to 1948. Introduced bill in Congress, 1943, for awarding contracts on a merit basis rather than competitive. Received citation for "long and useful service and helpful suggestions for improving the procedures for letting of contracts," Nat. Elec. Contractors Assn., 1942. Author: Ethics of Contracting, 1918; Selective Method of Letting Contracts, 1938; also articles and papers same subject. Clubs: Racquet and Tennis, Engineers, Uptown, Mid-day, Mass. Inst. Tech. (New York). Democrat. Home: 238 E. 68th St. Address: 10 Rockefeller Plaza. N.Y.C. 20. Died Dec. 31, 1951.

LORD, FREDERICK TAYLOR, M.D.; b. Bangor, Me., Jan. 16, 1875; s. Samuel Veazie and Kate Eva (Taylor) L.; A.B., Harvard, 1897, M.D., 1900; m. Mabel Delano Clapp, Nov. 25, 1901; 1 dau., Mrs. Harry Butler. House officer, Mass. Gen. Hosp., 1900-1901; physician to out-patients, same, 1903, visiting phys., 1912-35, mem. bd. of consultation, 1935—; asst. in clin. medicine, 1905-09, instr., 1909-30, clinical prof. of medicine, 1930-35 (emeritus), Harvard Medical School. Mem. Am. Red Cross Commission to Serbia, 1917. Republican. Unitarian. Author: Diseases of the Bronchi, Lungs and Pleura, 1915, 25; Pneumonia, 1922, 29; Lobar Pneumonia and Serum Therapy (with Dr. Roderick Heffron), 1936, Pneumonia and Serum Therapy (with Dr. Roderick Heffron), 1938. Home: Boston, Mass. Died Nov. 4, 1941.

LORD, HENRY CURWEN, astronomer; b. Cincinnati, Apr. 17, 1866; s. Henry Clark and Eliza Burnet (Wright) L.; Ohio State U., 1884-87; B.S., U. of Wis., 1889; m. Edith L. Hudson, June 22, 1898. Asst. in mathematics and astronomy, 1891-94, asso. prof. astronomy, 1894-1900, prof., 1900—, dir. Emerson McMillin Obs., 1894—, Ohio State U. Fellow Royal Astron. Soc. Appointed instr., U.S. Army, Sch. of Mil. Aeronautics at Ohio State U., May 1917. Deceased.

LORD, NATHANIEL WRIGHT, prof. metallurgy and mineralogy Ohio State Univ.; b. Cincinnati, Dec. 26, 1854; s. Henry C. and Eliza (Wright) L.; grad. Columbia Coll. School of Mines, E.M., 1876; chemist and engr. Monte Grande Gold Mining Co., 1879; chemist, 1883-88, now cons. chemist, Ohio Geol. Survey; is chemist in charge analysis of fertilizers for Ohio State Bd. of Agriculture. Author: Notes on Metallurgical Analysis. Wrote: Iron Manufacture of Ohio, vol. 5, and Natural and Artificial Cements, vol. 6, Ohio Geol. Survey. Dir. chem. laboratory, U.S. Fuel Testing Plant, St. Louis Expn., 1904. Home: Columbus, O. Died 1911.

LORD, ROYAL BERTRAM, ret. army officer, business cons.; b. Worcester, Mass., Sept. 19, 1899; s. Edgar Harold and Elena (Lupien) L.; B.S., Brown U., 1919; B.S., U.S. Military Academy, 1923; graduate Engineering Sch., Fort Belvoir, Va., 1924; M.S. in Engring., University of California, 1927; hon. LL.D., Brown University, 1946; married Elizabeth Richardson, June 7, 1928; 1 son, Willard Richardson. Served in U.S. Navy, World War; commd. 2d lt., U.S. Army, 1923, and advanced through the grades to maj. gen., 1944; served in Philippines, later comd. 2d Batn. 3d Engrs., Hawaii, 1923-26; asst. dist. engr. San Francisco, 1926; instr. engring., grad. mgr. athletics, in charge constrn., U.S. Mil. Acad., 1927-31; comd. Co. A., 6th Engrs., Fort Lawton, Wash., 1931-33; asst. dist. engr., St. Louis, 1933-35; in charge constrn. and operations, Passamaquoddy Tidal Bay Power Project, Eastport, Me., 1935-36; coordinator of Resettlement Adminstrn. and chief engr. and coordinator of Farm Security Adminstrn., Washington, D.C. (detail from Army; in charge design constrn. of housing and farm structures, 100,000 bldgs.), 1936-38; comd. 2d Batn., 3d Engrs., Schofield Barracks, Hawaii, 1939, 9th Engrs. Squadron, Fort Riley, 1940; dep. dir., later dir., Bureau Pub. Relations, War Dept., 1941; chief of operations, Bd. Economic Warfare, Sept. 1941-Apr. 1942, asst. dir. since Apr.-Aug. 1942; assigned to E.T.O., construction work, General Staff Corps, 1942; chief of staff for Lt. Gen. Lee, Services of Supply, E.T.O., later chief of staff for communications zone European Theater Operations, France, 1943-45; deputy chief of staff for Gen. Eisenhower, Feb. 1944 to May 1945; comdg. gen. for assembly area command, France, redeployment of troops and material, 1945—; Theatre Gen. Bd., Versailles, France, 1945-46; ret.; now bus. cons. Awarded Legion of Merit, Bronze Star; officer, Legion of Honor, Croix de Guerre with Palm (France); Comdr. of the Bath (Brit.), Distinguished Service Medal. Awarded the Cross of Rhode Island as distinguished citizen of that state. Inventor of Lord portable steel emplacement and Lord portable military cableway, now in general use, U.S. Army. Originator and mem. Com. on Cargo Planes for U.S. Govt.; mem. Lighter Than Air Transportation Com. Episcopalian. Clubs: Sleepy Hollow Country; Nat. Press, Army and Navy (Washington). Contbr. articles nat. mags. Made hon. citizen Reims, France, 1945; hon. mem. French Forces of the Interior, 1945. Home: Box 375, Rancho Santa Fe, Cal. 92067. Died Oct. 21, 1963.

LORENZ, HENRY WILLIAM FREDERICK, chemist; b. Springfield, O., Apr. 27, 1871; s. Rev. Henry and Margaret L.; grad. Wittenberg Coll., Springfield, O., 1893 (A.M.); studied Univ. of Tubingen, 1893-4, Univ. of Berlin, 1894-8 (A.M., Ph.D., 1897); asst. to Prof. S. Gabriel (Univ. of Berlin), 1898. Instr. organic chemistry Univ. of Pa., 1899-1901. Mem. Deutsche Chemische Gesellschaft. Contb'r to Am. and German jours. Author: Electrolysis and Electro-synthesis of Organic Compounds, 1898 W9; Practical Urinary Analysis, 1903 W9. Address: Fernbank OH

LORENZ, ROLLAND CARL, agriculturist; b. Waseca, Minn., Aug. 19, 1907; s. Frank H. and Emma B. (Reinhardt) L.; B.S. in Forest Mgmt., U. Minn., 1930, M.S. in Forest Pathology, 1942; m. Lucile Cummings, July 3, 1942; 1 son, Blake Thomas. Instr. forest pathology U. Minn., 1930-31; research asst. Firestone Plantation Co., Liberia, 1931-33; asst. forest pathologist, div. forest pathology U.S. Dept. Agr., 1934-40, specialist rubber culture Latin Am. survey, Office Rubber Plant Investigation, 1940-41, devel. cinchona and rubber Office Fgn. Agrl. Relations, Peru, 1942-46; chief agriculturist field party Point 4 Program, Guatemala, 1947-55; chief div. agr. and natural resources, dir. coop. agr. service Point 4 Program, Paraguay, 1955-59; food and agr. officer Point 4 Program, Ethiopia, 1959—. Mem. Soc. Am. Foresters, Am. Phytopath. Soc., A.A.A.S., Sigma Xi, Alpha Zeta, Xi Sigma Pi. Home: 6855 Palomar Way, Riverside, Cal. Office: AID, Dept. State, Washington 25. Died June 24, 1965.

LORENZ, WILLIAM FREDERICK, psychiatrist; b. N.Y.C.; Feb. 15, 1882; s. Herman and Elise (Kuenzlen) L.; student N.Y.U., 1898-99; M.D., Bellevue Hosp. Coll., 1903; m. Ada Holt, May 21, 1915; children—Adrian Holt Vanderveer, William Frederick, Thomas Holt, Paul Kuenzlen, Joseph Dean. Med. interne Gen. Hosp., N.Y.C., 1903-05; med. staff Manhattan State Hosp., 1906-10; clin. dir. Wis. State Hosp., 1910-14; spl. expert, research investigation of Pellagra, USPHS, 1914-15; dir. Wis. Psychiat. Inst.,

1915—; prof. psychiatry, U. Wis., 1915—. Pres. Wis. Service Recognition Bd., 1921-24; mem. Med. Council U.S. Vets.' Bur., 1923—; pres. Wis. State Bd. Control, 1923-25; pres. Wis. Rehabilitation Bd., 1925; chmn. State Bd. Mental Hygiene, 1938—. Served in Spanish-Am. War 7 mos., 1898; maj. in comd. Field Hosp. Co. 127, with 32d Div., AEF, 1919-19. Decorated D.S.M.; citation by Gen. Pershing. Mem. A.M.A., Am. Psychiat. Assn., Assn. Research in Nervous and Mental Diseases, Central Psychiat. Soc., Milw. Neuro-psychiat. Soc., Sigma Xi, Phi Alpha Sigma, Sigma Delta Chi, Alpha Omega Alpha. Republican. Mem. Christian Ch. Contbr. new remedies for treatment of syphilis of central nervous system (with Dr. A. S. Loevenhart), 1920-25. Notable work in promoting rehabilitation of disabled ex-service men; also investigations in use of carbon dioxide gas in treatment of psychoses. Col. M.C., Wis. N.G. and U.S. Res. Home: Route 2, Madison 5, Wis. Died Feb. 18, 1958; buried Forest Hill Cemetery, Madison.

LORING, CHARLES HARDING, chief engr. U.S.N., with rank of capt.; b. Boston, Dec. 26, 1828; s. William Price and Eliza (Harding) L.; ed. Boston, 1833-41; entered U.S.N. as engr. officer, Feb. 26, 1851; m. Ruth D. Malbon (dec.). Was engr. of the fleet, N. Atlantic squadron, in early yrs. of Civil War, taking part in capture of Fts. Hatteras and Clark, and in battle between the Monitor and Merrimac, March 8 and 9, 1862. Apptd. engr.-in-chief of navy in 1884; retired for age, 1890. Died 1907.

LORING, JOHN ALDEN, naturalist; b. Cleveland, O., Mar. 6, 1871; s. Lt. Benjamin William and Nellie (Cohoon) L.; ed. Owego Free Acad., zoöl. gardens, Europe, 1 yr.; unmarried. Field naturalist U.S. Biol. Survey, 1892-97; curator of animals New York Zoöl. Park, 1897-1901; field naturalist in Europe for U.S. Nat. Mus., during which time broke all previous records for field work by collecting and preserving the skins of 913 mammals and birds in 63 days; field naturalist Smithsonian-Roosevelt scientific expdn. to Africa, 1909-10. First lt. Ordnance Dept., U.S. Army, World War. Mem. Am. Ornithologists' Union, Biol. Soc. Washington, Camp Fire Club of America. Author: Young Folks' Nature Field Book; African Adventure Stories. Also a number of articles relating chiefly to birds and mammals, in Outing Magazine, Metropolitan Magazine, Collier's Weekly, Youth's Companion. Home: Owego, N.Y. Died May 8, 1947.

LOTHROP, MARCUS THOMPSON, metallurgist, engineer; b. Buffalo, N.Y., Oct. 2, 1884; s. Benjamin L. (M.D.) and Maria (Thompson) L.; B.Sc., U. of Mich., 1906; m. Margaret Frank, June 15, 1921; children (adopted)—Margaret, John Henry. Chief metallurgist and asst. chief engr. H. H. Franklin Mfg. Co., Syracuse, N.Y., 1906-07; metallurgist and chief mech. engr. Halcomb Steel Co., Syracuse, 1907-11; with Timken Roller Bearing Co., mfrs. tapered roller anti-friction bearings, Canton, O., 1911—; pres. Timken Steel & Tube Co.; pioneer in mfr. of tapered roller bearings. Trustee Aultman Hosp., Canton. Republican. Episcopalian. Home: Hills and Dales (Canton), O. Died May 23, 1935.

LOTKA, ALFRED JAMES, (lot'ka), mathematician; b. of Am. parents at Lemberg, Austria, Mar. 2, 1880; s. Jacques and Marie (Doebely) L.; B.Sc., Birmingham (Eng.) U., 1901, D.Sc., 1912; M.A., Cornell U., 1909; grad. study, U. of Leipzig, Germany, 1901-02, Johns Hopkins, 1922-24; m. Romola Beattie, Jan. 5, 1935. Asst. chemist Gen. Chem. Co., 1902-08; asst. in physics, Cornell U., 1908-09; examiner U.S. Patent Office 1909; asst. physicist U.S. Bur. of Standards, 1909-11; editor Scientific Am. Supplement, 1911-14; chemist Gen. Chem. Co., 1914-19; supervisor math. research, Statis. Bur. Metropolitan Life Ins. Co., 1924-33, gen. supervisor, 1933-34; asst. statistician Metropolitan Life Ins. Co. since 1934. Fellow Am. Statis. Assn. (pres. 1942), A.A.A.S., Royal Econ. Soc. Population Assn. America (pres. 1938-39), Institute of Mathematical Statistics; member Internat. Union of Scientific Investigation of Population Problems, Internat. Statis. Inst., Inter-Am. Statis. Inst., Econometric Soc., Am. Mathematical Society, American Public Health Association, Swiss Actuarial Soc., Washington Acad. Science, Sigma Xi. Club: Cornell (New York). Author: Elements of Physical Biology, 1925; The Money Value of a Man (with L. I. Dublin), 1930, revised edit. 1946; Length of Life (with L. I. Dublin), 1936; Théorie Analytique des Associations Biologiques, 1934-39; Twenty Five Years of Health Progress (with L. I. Dublin), 1937; also numerous publications in scientific and tech. jours. on math. analysis of population, math. theory of evolution, actuarial mathematics applied to problems of population and of industrial replacement. Home: Beattie Park, Red Bank, N.J. Office: 1 Madison Av., New York, N.Y. Died Dec. 5, 1949.

LOUD, FRANK HERBERT, astronomer; b. Weymouth, Mass., Jan. 26, 1852; s. Francis Eliot and Mary Tolman (Capen) L.; descendant of Elder William Brewster of the Mayflower; A.B., Amherst, 1873; student Clark U.; A.M., Harvard, 1899; Ph.D., Haverford, 1900; m. Mabel Wiley, July 13, 1882 (died 1923); children—Francis Martin, Mrs. Mary Thorne, Paul D. (dec.), Harriet, Norman Wiley, William Brewster. Walker instr. mathematics, Amherst, 1873-76; prof. mathematics and astronomy, Colorado Coll., 1877-1907; retired on Carnegie foundation, 1907. In charge of sta. for stellar photography, 1885-1923. Fellow British Esperanto Assn.; sec. Western Assn. for Stellar Photography. Republican. Conglist. Author: An Elementary Geomerty on the Analytic Plan, 1878. Home: Colorado Springs, Colo. Died Mar. 2, 1927.

LOUDEN, FREDERIC ALLC, (loud'en), engr.; b. Saginaw, Mich., Oct. 7, 1897; s. Fred C. and May (Birss) L.; B.S., U. Mich., 1920; m. Emma Orr, July 5, 1921; 1 son, Frederic Orr. Marine engr. Bethlehem Shipbldg. Corp., 1920-21; aero. engr., aerodynamics lab. Washington Navy Yard, 1922-28; asst. head aerodynamics and hydrodynamics br., bur. aeros. Navy Dept., Washington, 1928-44, br. head, 1945-52; branch head and bureau of aeros. special research liaison officer, NACA Laboratories, 1952-57; member of the com. on aerodynamics NASA, 1947-58, mem. subcom. high speed aerodynamics, 1946-47, 53-56, mem. clearance panel research development investigations for mil. services, 1951-55, mem. com., procedures unitary facilities, 1953-57, mem. aircraft and missiles project allocation and priority group, 1955-57; cons., 1957—. Bur. Aeros. Weapons rep. adv. group aero. research, development NATO; mem. aerodynamics, hydrodynamics group, com. aeronautics Research and Development Bd., 1947-52; also mem. of panel on aircraft performance, Munitions Board, 1951-52. Served with United States Navy, 1918. Recipient U.S.N. meritorious civilian service award, 1945. Fellow Inst. Aerospace Sci. Presbyn. Mason (Shriner). Author or co-author numerous tech. reports on aerodynamics. Home: 6461 S.W. 27th St., Miramar, Hollywood, Fla. 33023. Died Mar. 1, 1964; buried Oak Wood Meml. Mausoleum, Saginaw, Mich.

LOUDEN, WILLIAM, inventor, mfr.; b. Cassville, Pa., Oct. 16, 1841; s. Andrew and Jane (Speer) L.; of Scotch-Irish descent; settled in Fairfield, Ia., 1842; ed. pub. schs. and Axline U. (now defunct), Fairfield, Ia.; m. Mary Jane Pattison, Jan. 2, 1868; children—Helen Craig (dec.), Agnes May, Arthur Claire, Robert Bruce. Founder Louden Machinery Co., Fairfield, with branches in various parts of U.S. and Can., and v.p. from incorporation, 1892; pres. Ia. Malleable Iron Co., Tribune Printing Co., Fairfield; v.p. Thoma & Son, Inc., Fairfield; dir. Perry-Fry Co., St. Paul, Minn.; patentee farm and factories devices; awarded 118 patents, 1866—. Pres. Fairfield Chautauqua Assn. Home: Fairfield, Ia. Died Nov. 5, 1931.

LOUDERBACK, GEORGE DAVIS, (loud'er-bak), geologist; b. San Francisco, Apr. 6, 1874; s. Davis and Frances Caroline (Smith) L.; A.B., U. Cal., 1896, Ph.D., 1899, LL.D., 1946; m. Clara Augusta Henry, Oct. 3, 1899. Asst. in mineralogy U. Cal., 1897-1900; prof. geology and mineralogy U. Nev., 1900-06; research asst. Carnegie Inst., 1903-05; asst. prof. geology, U. Cal., 1906-07, asso. prof., 1907-17, prof., 1917-44, prof. emeritus, 1944—, dean College Letters and Science, 1920-22, 30-39, faculty research lectr., 1940. In charge geol. expdn. interior of China for Standard Oil Company of N.Y., later for Chinese Govt., 1914-16. Chmn. com. on geology and mineral resources State Council Defense, 1917-19; in charge coöp. war mineral investigation in Cal., for U.S. Geol. Survey. U.S. Bur. Mines and State Council Defense, 1918-19; mem. Pacific Coast sub-com. geology of NRC, 1917-19. Mem. Cal. Commn. on St. Francis Dam Failure, 1928, other state cons. bds. on safety of dams, 1929—. Fellow A.A.A.S., Geol. Soc. Am. (ex-sec. Cordilleran sect., chmn. 1919-22; v.p. 1936); mem. Seismol. Soc. Am. (sec. 1907-10, pres. 1914, 29-35), Am. Inst. Mining and Metall. Engrs., Cal. Acad. Sciences, Washington Acad. Sciences, Am. Geog. Soc., Mineral. Soc. Am., Soc. Econ. Geologists (v.p. 1939), Am. Petroleum Geologists, Am. Geophysical union, Am. Soc. Oceanography and Limnology, Phi Kappa Sigma, Theta Tau (nat. pres. 1919-25), Phi Beta Kappa, Sigma Xi, Phi Lambda Upsilon, Tau Beta Pi. Clubs: Faculty (pres. 1939-46), City-Commons (pres. 1935-36) (Berkeley); Athenian-Nile (Oakland); Commonwealth, Engineers, Sierra, Bohemian (San Francisco). Contbr. on geol. and mineral topics, especially on basin range struc. and west coast stratigraphy, faultlines and earthquakes; discoverer of Benitoite and other minerals. Del. to Pacific Science Congress, Java, 1929, San Francisco, 1939. Editor Bulletin of Seismol. Soc. of America, 1935—. Home: 107 Ardmore Rd., Berkeley 7, Calif. Office: Bacon Hall, U. of California, Berkeley 4, Cal. Died Jan. 27, 1957.

LOUGHLIN, GERALD FRANCIS, (lok'lin), geologist; b. Hyde Park, Mass., Dec. 11, 1880; s. John Francis and Adelia (Lane) L.; S.B. in geology, Mass. Inst. Tech., 1903; Ph.D., Yale, 1906; m. Grace E. French, Aug. 22, 1906; 1 dau., Beryl Frances (Mrs. W. S. Burbank). Asst. in geology, Mass. Inst. Tech., 1903-04, Yale, 1904-06; instr. geology, Mass. Inst. Tech., 1906-12; with U.S. Geol. Survey, 1912, as chief non-metals sect., div. mineral resources, 1917-19, chief metals sect., Jan.-Dec. 1919, and chief of div. of mineral resources, 1919-23, chief of sect. of geology of metalliferous deposits, 1923-35, chief geologist, 1935-44, special scientist since 1944. Member Society of Economic Geologists, American Mineral Society, American Institute Mining and Metallurgy Engineers, Geology Society America, Geology Soc. Washington, Washington Acad. Sci., A.A.A.S. Unitarian. Club: Cosmos. Author: Clays of Conn. (Conn. Survey), 1906; Lithology of Connecticut (with J. Barrell), 1912; Gabbro and Associated Rocks Near Preston, Conn.; Geology and Ore Deposits of Tintic Utah (with W. Lindgren), 1917; Oxidized Zinc Ores of Leadville, Colo., 1919; Geology and Ore Deposits of Utah (with B. S. Butler), 1920. In charge preparation Mineral Resources of the United States (6 vols.), 1919-24; Geology and Ore Deposits of Leadville, Colo., 1926; Indiana Oolitic Limestone, Relation of Its Natural Features to Its Commercial Grading, 1929; Gold Reserves of the U.S. (with H. G. Ferguson and others), 1930; Geology and Ore Deposits of the Cripple Creek District (with A. H. Koschmann), 1935; geology and ore deposits of the Magdalena District, N.M. (with A. H. Koschmann), 1943; also papers on ore deposits, building stone and durability of concrete aggregates. Home: 3346 Runnymeade Pl., Washington. Died Oct. 22, 1946; buried in Rock Creek Cemetery.

LOVEJOY, JOHN MESTON, petroleum corp. executive; b. N.Y.C., July 1889; s. John F. and Abbie (Babson) L.; E.M., Columbia School of Mines, 1911; hon. D.Sc., Colby Coll., 1937; m. Leslie Mackintosh, Nov. 1920; children—Leslie (Mrs. John Scott Paine), John Stuart. Began business career as mining engineer; in oil business with Standard Oil Company, 1914, as geologist; v.p. and gen. mgr. Amerada Petroleum; was geologist Tex. Oil Co.; chmn. and pres. Seaboard Oil Co, of Del., 1930-54; director Drilling and Exploration Co., Inc. 1st lt., later capt. F.A., United States Army, 1917-19. Director, treasurer Nat. Multiple Sclerosis Society. Member American Inst. Mining and Metall. Engrs. (dir. and past pres.), Am. Petroleum Inst. (dir.), Am. Assn. of Petroleum Geologists, Nat. Petroleum Council. Clubs: University, Mining (New York); Round Hill, Indian Harbor Yacht (Greenwich); Petroleum (Dallas). Home: Greenwich CT Died Nov. 1968.

LOVELACE, WILLIAM RANDOLPH, II, surgeon; b. Springfield, Mo., Dec. 30, 1907; s. Edgar Blaine and Jewell (Costley) L.; A.B., Washington U., St. Louis, Mo., 1930, M.D., Harvard, 1934; student (flight surgeon), Sch. of Aviation Medicine, Randolph Field, Tex., 1937; studied surgery in Europe (J. William White Scholarship), 1939; M.S. in Surg., U. Minn., 1939; m. Mary Moulton, Sept. 15, 1933 (dec.); 3 daus., Mary C., Sharon L., Jacqueline. Interne, Bellevue Hosp., N.Y.C., 1934-36; Fellow, Mayo Foundn. for Med. Edn. and Research, 1936-39; 1st asst. Dr. Charles W. Mayo, Mayo Clinic, 1939-40, asst. surgeon, 1940-41, chief of a surg. sect., Mayo Clinic, 1941-46. Maj. then col., A.A.F.; chief Aero Med. Lab., Wright Field, 1943-45; now col. Med. Res. Surg. staff, co-chmn. bd. govs., Lovelace Clinic, since 1946; mem. staff Bataan Meml. Meth. Hospital, St. Joseph's Hosp. and Sanatorium, Presbyn. Hosp. and Sanatorium, VA Hosp., Sandia Base Hosp (all at Albuquerque, N.M.), Los Alamos (New Mexico) Medical Center. Mem. board directors The Garrett Corporation. Medical officer, United States Public Health Service. Chmn. med. panel, Internat. Air Transport Association; mem. aviation med. panel Adv. Group for Aero. Research and Development to NATO, 1952-64; mem. spl. com. space tech. NACA, 1957-59; chmn. flight medicine and biology com. Office Life Sci. Programs, 1958-61; spl. com. Life Scis. Project Mercury, 1959-63; sr. cons. NASA, 1963-64, dir. space medicine Manned Space Flight, 1964—; cons. or mem. adv. com. several airlines, univs., assns., other govt. agys. Trustee, pres. Lovelace Found. Mem. Edn. and Research; dir. Woodrow Wilson Rehabilitation Center Foundation, Incorporated, Fisherville, Virginia, 1960-64; trustee Aerospace Edn. Found., 1958—, chmn., 1961-64; trustee Air Force Academy Foundation, 1962—. Recipient Sci. award, Air Force Assn., 1959; spl. aerospace honor citation A.M.A., 1962 Boynton award Am. Astronautical Soc., 1962; Outstanding Achievement award U. of Minnesota, 1964. Diplomate Am. Bd. Surgery, Am. Bd. Aviation Medicine. Fellow Am. College Surgeons, Institute Aeronautical Sciences (1944), Aero Med. Assn. (pres. 1942-43); mem. A.M.A., Space Edn. Found., African Research Found., Air Force Assn. (past pres.), Conf. S.W. Found. (past pres.), other nat., state and spl. profl. sci. assns. and orgns. Clubs: Lotos (N.Y.C.); Univ. (Rochester, Minn.); Cosmos (Washington). Co-winner (with Dr. W. M. Boothby and Col. H. G. Armstrong) Collier Trophy Award, 1940; Jeffries Award, 1948. Awarded Distinguished Flying Cross for exptl. parachute descent from 40,200 ft. Awarded Legion of Merit, Army Commendation Ribbon; Royal Order of Sword, First Class (Sweden). Awarded Air Medal and 3 combat stars. Home: 2815 Ridgecrest Dr. S.E. Office: Lovelace Clinic, 5200 Gibson Blvd. S.E., Albuquerque 87108. Died Dec. 12, 1965.

LOVELL, EARL B., civil engr.; b. Marathon, N.Y., May 2, 1869; s. Ransom Marlow and Dorcas (Meacham) L.; grad. Marathon Acad., 1886, Cascadilla Sch., Ithaca, 1887; C.E., Cornell, 1891; m. Ida L. Peck, Oct. 4, 1899 (died Sept. 20, 1932); children—Robert Marlow, Helen Louise (dec.), Esther Hope, Gordon Peck and Ruth Caroline; m. 2d, Mrs. Helen R. Shimer, June 18, 1941; 1 stepson, Rev. H. Myron Shimer. Assistant engineer, Michigan Central Railroad, 1891-93; instr. civ. engring., Lafayette Coll., 1893-96, Cornell University, 1896-98; adj. prof. civ. engring., Columbia U., 1898-1901, asso. prof., 1901-07, prof.

since 1907, chmn. dept. civ. engring., 1916-34, retired. Advisory engr. and mgr. survey dept. Lawyers Title & Trust Co. (later Lawyers Title & Guaranty Co.), New York, 1907-33; pres. Earl B. Lovell, Inc., engineering and surveying, 1933-38, chairman board of directors since August 1938; chmn. Assn. of Dept. Heads, 1923-24; consulting engr. for Portland Cement Lumber Co., 1923-24. Owner "Lovell Farms," Marathon, N.Y. Pres. Assn. of City Surveyors, Greater New York, 1919-22; asso. mem. Am. Soc. C.E.; mem. Tau Beta Phi, Sigma Xi. Republican. Episcopalian. Has specialized in railroad engring and masonry constrn. Legal residence: Lovell Farms, Marathon, N.Y. Home: Surrey Strathmore Abby, 6D, White Plains, N.Y. Office: 141 Broadway, New York 6. Died Aug. 23, 1948.

LOVELL, JOHN HARVEY, biologist; b. Waldoboro, Me., Oct. 21, 1860; s. Harvey Hinckley and Sophronia Caroline (Bulfinch) L.; A.B., Amherst, 1882, A.M., 1899; m. Lottie Evangeline Magune, Oct. 24, 1899; children—Harvey Bulfinch, Ralph Marston. Has devoted many yrs. to original observations on floroecology of Northern plants, their manner of pollination, insect visitors, distribution of flower colors, etc.; specialist in photography of flowers, natural size. Republican. Conglist. Author: The Flower and the Bee; Plant Life and Pollination, 1918; The Honey Plants of North America, 1926. Biol. editor ABC of Bee Culture, issued triennially; contbr. daily illustrated articles on New England plants to the Boston Globe, and to other N.E. newspapers, 1926—. Home: Waldoboro, Me. Died Aug. 2, 1939.

LOVELL, MANSFIELD, army officer, civil engr.; b. Washington, D.C., Oct. 20, 1822; s. Dr. Joseph and Margaret (Mansfield) L.; grad. U.S. Mil. Acad., 1842; m. Emily Plympton, 1849. Commd. 2d lt., 4th Arty., U.S. Army, 1842, 1st lt., 1846, served in Taylor's campaign, 1846-47, aide-de-camp to Gen. John A. Quitman; brevetted capt. for gallantry at Battle of Chapultepec, 1847; resigned commn., 1854; dept. street commr. N.Y.C., 1858, later supt. street improvements; commd. maj. gen. Confederate Army, 1861, in command New Orleans, fought at Battle of Vicksburg, 2d-in-command in Battle of Corinth. Died N.Y.C., June 1, 1884.

LOVELL, RALPH L., mech. engr.; b. Millbury, Mass., Aug. 2, 1865; s. William L. and Jane E. (Harris) L.; M.E., Worcester Poly. Inst., 1888; m. Miss M. L. Brackett, June 24, 1896; 1 son, Frederick H. With Gen. Electric Co., Lynn, 1888-94; with Newport News Shipbuilding Co., 1894-1904; asst. chief engr., 1904-10, chief engr., 1910-14, Fore River Shipbuilding Co., Quincy, Mass.; consulting engr. and patent expert, 1914-16; marine engr. with Theodore E. Ferris, naval architect and engr., New York, 1916-17; chief engr. U.S. Shipping Bd. Emergency Fleet Corp., Washington and Phila., 1917-19; pres. Adams, Lovell & Burlingham, consulting marine engrs., New York, 1919-22; engr. with Bethlehem Shipbuilding Corp., Elizabeth, N.J., 1924-29; began with United Dry Docks, Inc., Staten Island, N.Y., 1929, became chief engr.; chief engr. Bethlehem Steel Co., shipbuilding dir., Staten Island Works, 1938-42 (retired); now in cons. work at home. Home: 6 Greaves Place, Cranford, N.J. Died June 3, 1945.

LOVETT, EDGAR ODELL, educator; born at Shreve, O., Apr. 14, 1871; s. Z. and M. E. (Spreng) L.; A.B., Bethany (W.Va.) Coll., 1890; M.A., Ph.D., U. of Va., 1895; Ph.D., Univ. of Leipzig, 1896; LL.D., Drake U., 1898; Tulane Univ., 1911, Baylor U., 1920. Bethany Coll., 1934; Princeton, 1954; Sc.D., Colorado College, 1927; m. Mary Ellen Hale, 1897; children—Adelaide (Mrs. W. Browne Baker), Henry Malcolm, Ellen Kennedy (dec.), Laurence Alexander. Prof. mathematics, West Ky. Coll., 1890-92; instr. astronomy, U. of Va., 1892-95; stud. Leipzig and Christiania, 1895-96; fellow by courtesy, Johns Hopkins, 1897; lecturer mathematics, univs. of Va. and Chicago, 1897; instr. mathematics, 1897, asst. prof., 1898-1900, prof., 1900-05, prof. astronomy, 1905-08, Princeton; first president Rice Institute, Houston, Texas, 1908-46, president emeritus since 1946. Decorated Officier Legion d'Honneur (France), 1938. Member American Philos. Society, Am. Astron. Soc., Belgian-Am. Ednl. Foundation; Fellow R.A.S., A.A.A.S. (v.p. sect. A, Baltimore meeting, 1908); mem. Am. (sometime mem. council and asso. editor Bulletin), France and London, math. socs., Phi Beta Kappa, Sigma Xi, Beta Theta Pi. Contbr. on geometry, mechanics and math. astronomy to various Am. and foreign jours. Address: P.O. Box 1892, Houston 1. Died Aug. 13, 1957; buried Greenwood Cemetery, Houston.

LOVEWELL, JOSEPH TAPLIN, chemist; b. Corinth, Conn., May 1, 1833; s. Nehemiah and Martha (Willis) L.; A.B., Yale, 1857, Ph.D., 1874; m. Margaret L. Bissell, Sept. 3, 1863; m. 2d, Caroline F. Barnes, of Topeka, Kan., June 30, 1885. Prin. Prairie du Chien (Wis.) Coll., 1859-63; prin. high sch. and supt. of city schs., Madison, Wis., 1863-64; prof. mathematics, Wis. State Normal Sch., Whitewater, 1870-73; prof. chem. and physics, State Coll., Pa., 1875-77, Washburn Coll., Kan., 1878-99; sec. and librarian, 1902-16, emeritus sec., 1916, Kan. Acad. Science (pres. 2 yrs., editor 5 vols. Trans.). Republican. Conglist. Home: Topeka, Kan. Died Sept. 11, 1918.

LOW, ABRAHAM ADOLPH, physician, psychiatrist; b. Baranow, Poland, Feb. 28, 1891; s. Lazar and Blossom (Wahl) L.; student U. Strasbourg, 1910-13; M.D., U. Vienna, 1919; m. Mae Willett, June 18, 1935; children—Phyllis Kay, Marilyn Carroll. Came to U.S., 1921, naturalized, 1927. Intern Allgemeines Krankenhaus, Vienna, Austria, 1919-20; practice medicine, N.Y.C., 1921-23. Chgo., 1923-25, neurology, 1925-30, psychiatry, 1931—; instr. neurology, med. sch. U. Ill., 1925-31, asst. prof. psychiatry, 1931-40 asst. dir. psychiat. inst., 1931-40, asso. prof. psychiatry, 1940, acting dir. psychiat. inst., 1940-41; asst. state alienist Ill., 1933-41; founder, med. dir. Recovery, Inc., 1937—. Served with M.C., Austrian Army, 1914-18. Fellow A.M.A., Am. Psychiat. Assn.; mem. Ill. Psychiat. Soc., Chgo. Neurol. Soc., Central Neuropsychiat. Assn., Am. Group Psychotherapy Assn. Author: Studies in Infant Speech and Thought, 1936; Techniques of Self-Help in Psychiatric After-Care (3 vols.), 1943; Mental Health Through Will-Training, 1950. Contbr. articles profl. publs. Home: 315 Davis St., Evanston, Ill. Office: 30 N. Michigan Av., Chgo. 2. Died Nov. 17, 1954; buried Memorial Park Cemetery, Evanston.

LOW, ALBERT HOWARD, chemist, educator; b. Chelsea, Mass., June 27, 1855; s. Albert Burrell and Mary Jane (Gilman) L.; B.S., Mass. Inst. Tech., 1876; D.Sc., Colo. Sch. of Mines, 1922; m. Helen A. Jones, June 12, 1888; 1 son, Albert Estabrook (dec.). Consulting practice, Denver, 1885; head chemistry dept., Colo. Sch. of Mines, 1919-26; conducting petroleum research, 1926-28. Charter mem. Colo. Scientific Society. Republican. Author: Technical Methods of Ore Analysis, 1905; Notes on Technical Ore Analysis, 1923. Home: Denver, Colo. Died 1936.

LOWE, EPHRAIM NOBLE, geologist; b. Utica, Miss., May 5, 1864; s. Edmund F. and Emily M. (Peyton) L.; Ph.B., U. of Miss., 1884; post-grad. work, in absentia, same univ., 1 yr., 1890; M.D., Tulane U., 1892; studied U. of Chicago, summers 1905, 06, 07; m. Sarah Yeager, Nov. 28, 1895 (died 1898); children—Marguerite Emily, Edmund Peyton; m. 2d, Laura Edna Haley, May 14, 1904; 1 dau., Edna May (dec.). Engaged in pvt. geol. and biol. work in Colo., 1887-89; practiced medicine in Miss., 1892-93, in Colo., 1893-1902, also geol. work; asst. in geology and biology, 1905-07, actg. prof., 1907-08, prof., 1908-09, U. of Miss.; dir. Miss. Geol. Survey, 1909—; head of Dept. of Geology, U. of Miss., 1924—. Fellow A.A.A.S., Am. Geog. Soc. Democrat. Mem. M.E. Ch., S. K.P. Author: Plants of Mississippi; Economic Geography of Mississippi. Home: University, Miss. Died Sept. 12, 1933.

LOWE, THADDEUS S.C., scientist, inventor; b. Jefferson, N.H., Aug. 20, 1832; s. Clovis and Alpha Green L. (Pilgrim ancestry); ed. common schs.; spl. studies in chemistry; m. Leontine A. Gachon, of Paris, France, 1855. Constructed balloons as an aid to study of atmospheric phenomena, 1856 and 1858-59, securing instruments from govt., invented and made other instruments for investigating upper air currents, including an Altimeter for quickly measuring latitude and longitude without a horizon; built, 1859-60, the largest aerostat that was ever made, made trip from Cincinnati to a point 900 miles distant, nr. S.C. coast, in 9 hours, Apr. 20, 1861. Entered govt. service as chief of aeronautic corps, which he organized, rendering valuable service to Army of the Potomac, from Bull Run to Gettysburg, by observations and timely warnings. In 1862 invented system of signaling to comdr. of field batteries from high altitudes—largely used in Peninsula campaign, and later by Brazilian Govt., to which he sold his outfit after Civil War. Invented compression ice machine, 1865, making first artificial ice in U.S.; built regenerative metall. furnaces for gas and petroleum fuel, 1869-72; invented and built water-gas apparatus, 1873-75, and later other machines; from 1897 inventing and putting into operation New Lowe Coke Oven system, for simultaneously producing gas and metall. coke, known as "Lowe Anthracite." Built Mt. Lowe Ry., 1891-94, and established Lowe Observatory in Sierra Madre Mountains. Home: Pasadena, Calif. Died Jan. 1913.

LOWELL, FRANCIS CABOT, mfr.; b. Newburyport, Mass., Apr. 7, 1775; s. Judge John and Susanna (Cabot) L.; grad. Harvard, 1793; m. Hannah Jackson, Oct. 31, 1798, 4 children including John. Mcht. with William Cabot, Boston, 1793-1810; went to Eng. for health, 1810, studied textile mills; formed Boston Mfg. Co. which bought land at Waltham, Mass., designed from memory or invented machines for cotton factory (1st factory in world to unite all processes of cloth under one roof); lobbied for tariff of 1816 which protected his cloth mill; Lowell (Mass.) named after him. Died Boston, Aug. 10, 1817.

LOWELL, PERCIVAL, astronomer; b. Boston, Mar. 13, 1855; s. Augustus and Katharine Bigelow (Lawrence) L.; bro. of A(bbott) Lawrence L.; A.B., Harvard, 1876; (LL.D., Amherst, 1907, Clark U., 1909); m. Constance Savage Keith, June 10, 1908. Went to Japan 1883, and lived there from time to time till 1893; counsellor and foreign sec. to Korean Spl. Mission to U.S. Established Lowell Obs., 1894; undertook eclipse expdn. to Tripoli, 1900; sent expdn. to the Andes to photograph planet Mars, 1907. Received Janssen medal of French Astron. Soc., 1904, for researches on Mars; gold medal for work on Mars from Sociedad Astronomica de Mexico, 1908; has made discoveries on the planets Mercury, Venus, Saturn, and especially Mars; apptd. non-resident prof. astronomy, Mass. Inst. Tech., 1902. Fellow Am. Acad. Arts and Sciences. Author: The Soul of the Far East, 1886; Noto, 1891; Occult Japan, 1894; Mars, 1895; The Solar System, 1903; Mars as the Abode of Life, 1908; The Evolution of Worlds, 1909. Home: Boston, Mass. Died Nov. 13, 1916.

LOWER, WILLIAM EDGAR, surgeon; b. Canton, O., May 6, 1867; s. Henry and Mary (Deeds) L.; M.D., Western Reserve U., Med. Dept., 1891; m. Mabel Freeman, Sept. 6, 1909; 1 dau., Mary. Practiced in Cleveland since 1892; asso. surgeon, Lakeside Hosp., 1910-31; attending surgeon, Lutheran Hosp. since 1896; dir. surgery, Mt. Sinai Hosp., 1916-24; asso. prof. genito-urinary surgery, Western Reserve U., 1910-1931. A founder, dir. Cleveland Clinic Foundation since 1921; surgeon Cleveland Clinic Hosp. since 1924. Acting asst. surgeon, U.S. Army, in the Philippines, 1900; maj. Med. Reserve Corps, 1917; asst. surg. dir. Lakeside Base Hosp. Unit, U.S. Army, in service with B.E.F. in France, May-Dec. 1917, comdg. officer, Dec. 1917-May 1918; lt. col., June 1918. Mem. Am. Urol. Assn. (pres. 1914-15), Am. Assn. Genito-Urinary Surgeons (pres. 1922), Ohio State Med. Soc. (pres. 1915), Acad. of Medicine, Cleveland (pres. 1909-10), Clin. Soc. of Genito-Urinary Surgeons (pres. 1922), Interuban Surg. Soc. (pres. 1926-27), Soc. of Clin. Surgery, Société Internationale de Chirurgie Urologie; fellow A.M.A., Am. Surg. Assn., Am. Coll. Surgeons, Southern Surgical Assn. Club: Union. Author: Anoci-Association (Crile and Lower), 1914; Surgical Shock and the Shockless Operation through Anoci-Association, 2d edit., 1920; Roentgenographic Studies of the Urinary System (Lower and Nichols), 1933. Home: 12546 Cedar Rd., Cleveland Heights, O. Office: Cleveland Clinic, Euclid at E. 93d St., Cleveland. Died June 17, 1948.

LOWETH, CHARLES FREDERICK, civil engr.; b. Cleveland, Mar. 3, 1857; s. Daniel and Mary A. P. (Brown) L.; student Oberlin Coll., 1877-78; hon. C.E., U. of Wis., 1915; Dr. Engring., Rose Poly. Institute, 1926; m. Carrie T. Curtis, Feb. 15, 1881; children—Mary Grace, Margaret, Frederick Curtis, Robert Charles. Began as rodman on survey for Cleveland, Loraine & Wheeling Ry., in Ohio; civil engr., 1880—, principally in ry. service; successively chief engr. Davenport, Rock Island & Northwestern Ry., and consulting engr. N.P. Ry., M.,St.P.&S.Ste.M. Ry., M.&St.L. Ry., and others; engr. and supt. bridges and bldgs., 1901-10, chief engr., 1910—, C.M.St.P&P. R.R. Republican. Presbyn. Home: Chicago, Ill. Died May 15, 1935.

LOWREY, LAWSON GENTRY, psychiatrist; b. Centralia, Mo., Dec. 23, 1890; s. Ernest (M.D.) and Eupha Orme (Sappington) L.; student Bethany Coll., Lindsborg, Kan., 1905-07; A.B., U. of Mo., 1909, A.M., 1910; M.D. cum laude, Harvard University, 1915. Pathologist at the Danvers State Hospital, 1914-17; 1st asst. physician and chief med. officer, Boston Psychopathic Hosp., 1917-20; asst. dir. Psychopathic Hosp., U. of Ia., 1920-23; dir. demonstration child guidance clinic (in Dallas, Mpls., St. Paul, Cleve.), Nat. Com. for Mental Hygiene, 1923-27; dir. Inst. for Child Guidance, N.Y., 1927-33; attending physician N.Y. Neurol. Inst., 1932-37; psychiatrist, pediatric dept. New Rochelle (N.Y.) Gen. Hosp., 1933—; cons. in psychiatry Grasslands Hosp., 1930-44; psychiatrist Clinic for Gifted Childrens, N.Y.U., 1933-35, Bklyn. Hebrew Orphan Asylum, 1937-44; dir. Mental Hygiene Research Unit, Vocational Adjustment Bur., 1937-39; psychiatrist Traveler's Aid Soc., 1938-42; dir. Bklyn. Child Guidance Centre, 1940-45; asso. attending psychiatrist Vanderbilt Clinic, 1945—; asst. in anatomy U. Mo., 1909-10, asst. prof. anatomy, 1911-12; 1909-10; prof. anatomy and histology U. Utah, 1910-11; teaching fellow in histology and embryology Harvard, 1912-14, James Jackson Cabot research fellow neuropathology, 1915-16, fellow neuropathology, 1916-18, instr. in neuropathology, 1918-20, in psychiatry, 1918-20, in psychology, 1919-20; asst. and asso. prof. U. Ia., 1920-23; lectr. So. Meth. U., 1923; lecturer in psychiatry, U. Minn. Med. Sch., 1923-24, Smith Coll. Sch. of Social Work, 1926-36, N.Y. Sch. of Social Work, 1930-36; N.Y.U. Sch. Edn., 1933-35, Hunter College, 1937; asst. clin. prof. psychiatry Columbia Coll. Phys. and Surg., 1945—. Mem. White House Conf. on Child Health and Protection, 1930; mem. program com. Internat. Congress on Mental Hygiene, 1930; exec. com. Internat. Com. Mental Hygiene, 1947—; mem. China Aid Council, 1943—; cons. many orgns.; qualified psychiatrist in the State of N.Y. Mem. Assn. of Anatomists, Assn. Pathologists and Bacteriologists, N.Y. State Med. Assn., A.M.A., Am. Psychiatric Assn. (chmn. program com. 1928-31), A.A.A.S., Boston Soc. Neurology and Psychiatry, N.E. Psychiatric Soc., N.Y. Neurol. Soc., N.Y. Acad. Medicine, N.Y. Acad. Sciences, Acad. Polit. and Social Science, Am. Orthopsychiatric Assn. (pres. 1928-30, editor, 1930-48, N.Y. City Com. for Mental Hygiene (chmn. 1930-35), Am. Psychopathol. Assn., N.Y. Psychiatric Soc., Westchester County Mental Hygiene Assn. (pres. 1946), Sigma Xi, Alpha Omega Alpha, Pi Kappa Alpha,

Phi Beta Pi (supreme officer, 1918—, moderator, 1931—). Independent Democrat. Mason (32 deg.). Author: Report of Kindergarten Project, 1937-39; Psychiatry for Social Workers, 1946. Editor: Monograph Series of American Orthopsychiatric Assn.; Institute for Child Guidance Studies. Editor of Am. Jour. Orthopsychiatry, 1930-48. Office: 25 W. 54th St., N.Y.C. 19. Died Aug. 1957.

LOWRY, H(OMER) H(IRAM), govt. ofcl.; b. Peking, China (Am. parents), Oct. 6, 1898; s. George Davis and Cora (Calhoun) L.; A.B., Ohio Wesleyan U., 1918; du Pont fellow, Princeton U., 1918-20, A.M., 1919, Ph.D., 1920; m. Helen Mary Smith, June 30, 1920 (div. 1939); children—Helen Louise, Barbara; m. Gertrude Hurney Tomlinson, Dec. 16, 1949. Chem. research Western Elec. Co., N.Y.C., 1920-25; phys. chemist Bell Telephone Labs., N.Y.C., 1925-30; dir. coal research lab., Carnegie Inst. Tech., 1930-53; cons. Army AC, 1943, Nat. Def. Research Council, 1941-43, Nat. Inventors Council, 1941-43; assistant research dir. Pitts. Coal Research Center, U.S. Bureau of Mines, Pittsburgh, Pennsylvania, 1960-64; staff research coordinator Office Dir. Coal Research, Bureau of Mines, Washington, from 1964. Chmn. committee on chem. utilization of coal, Div. of Chemistry and Chem. Tech., Nat. Research Council, 1937-45; Editor-sec., com. on chemistry of coal Nat. Academy Sciences-National Research Council, 1957-63. Mem. of tech. indsl. intelligence com. of Combined Intelligence Objectives Subcom. of SHAEF, 1945. Hon. pres. sect. on chem. in relation to fuel, power and transport, XIth Congress on Pure and Applied Chem., London, 1947. Served as pvt. C.W.S., 1918; lt. comdr. USNR, from 1936; cons. C.E. Dept. of the Army, 1948. Recipient Percy Nicholls award, Am. Inst. Mining, Metallurgy and Petroleum Engrs. and Am. Soc. M.E., 1959. Fellow A.A.A.S., Inst. Fuel (London), Royal Soc. Arts; hon. mem. Am. Coke and Coal Chems. Inst.; mem. New York Academy of Science, American Chemical Society, Am. Gas Assn., Am. Inst. Mining, Metall. and Petroleum Engineers, Geo-chemical Society of Am., Engrs. Soc. Western Pa., Eastern States Blast Furnace and Coke Oven Assn., Phi Beta Kappa, Sigma Xi, Phi Kappa Phi, Alpha Sigma Phi. Author numerous papers on gas absorption, coal, carbon, theory of dielectrics, insulating materials. Editor: Chemistry of Coal Utilization, 2 vols., 1945. Corr. editor Fuel (London, England). Home: Wilmerding PA Died May 20, 1971.

LOWSLEY, OSWALD SWINNEY, (lo'sle), urol. surgeon; b. Santa Barbara, Calif., Sept. 4, 1884; s. Vincent and Willie Ann (Swinney) L.; A.B., Stanford, 1905; M.D., Johns Hopkins, 1912; grad. Bellevue Hosp., N.Y., 1915; children—Lydia Ann, David William, Martha Winifred, Oswald Swinney; married 3d, Celeste Nocito, Aug. 29, 1949; married 4th, Winifred Atherton, Jan. 17, 1953. Practiced in N.Y. City since 1915; cons. urol. surgeon to Ruptured and Crippled Peekskill, Monmouth Memorial, Nassau County and Bloomingdale hosps., also to Stamford Hosp., St. Luke's Hosp. (Newburgh, N.Y.), Jamaica Hosp., Fitkin Memorial Hosp. (Spring Lake, N.J.), Norwalk (Conn.) Hosp., Flushing Hosp., St. Agnes Hosp. (White Plains, N.Y.) Englewood (N.J.) Hosp., Nat. Jewish Hosp. (Denver, Colo.), Kings Hosp. (Bay Shore, L.I.), St. Clare's Hosp., N.Y. Hosp. (N.Y.C.), Jersey City Med. Center; pres., dir. Oswald Swinney Lowsley Found. urology; a pioneer in surgery of genito-urinary organs under local and regional anesthesia. First director of the dept. urology, James Buchanan Brady Foundation of N.Y. Hosp. and St. Clare's Hospital. Served as private California N.G., 1905-07, 2d lt., 1907-08; lt. s.g. U.S. Navy, 1917-18; hon. consultant to Med. Corps. U.S. Navy, since 1942. Diplomate Am. Bd. Urology. Fellow A.C.S., Internat. Coll. Surgeon, New York Academy Medicine; mem. A.M.A., Am. Urological Assn. (pres. 1941-42), International Urol. Assn., Barcelona Urol. Society, New York State, New York County, Costa Rican, Mexican, Venzuelan, Uruguayan medical societies, Osler Soc. N.Y., Soc. Alumni of Bellevue Hosp. (treas. 1919-36, v.p. 1937, pres. 1938), Societa de Obstetrica, Ginecologie et Urologie (Rumania); corr. mem. Deutsche Gesellschaft für Urologie Assn. Française d'Urologie, Magyar Urolgiai Tarsasag Türk Urologi Cemiyet, Royal Soc. of Medicine of Great Britain, Societá Italiana di Urologia, Societá Piamontese di Chirurgia, Internat. Soc. of Urology, Venezuela Urol. Assn.; hon. urologist Mil. Hosp., Guatemala; Socio Honorario, La Assiación Medica Hondurana; Socio Honorario, La Juventud Medica de Guatemala; hon. prof. U. of Haiti; hon. fellow Accion Medica del Peru; hon. mem. Sociedad Peruana de Urologia y Venereologia, Pan-American Confederation Urologists, Pan-Am. Med. Assn.; life-mem. Stanford Alumni Assn. Decorated Officier l'Ordre d'Honneur et Merite (Republic d'Haiti); Al Merito (Ecudor); Commendodore Order Merit John Pablo Duorte (Dominicon Republic); Cresziere do Sul, (Brazil). Dem. Episcopalian. Mason. Clubs: Johns Hopkins, Stanford, Stanford Associates, Adventures, Physicians, University, N.Y. Athletic, Tokeneke Club, Wee Burn Country. Author: Embryology of the Prostate, 1912; A Textbook of Urology (with T. J. Kirwin), 1926; Urology for Nurses (with T. J. Kirwin), 1936; Clinical Urology (with T. J. Kirwin), 1940, 2d edit., 1943; also many articles on urol. subjects; operative treatment of the kidney and the embryology, anatomy, morphology, pathology and surgery of the prostate gland, tuberculosis of kidney, diverticulitis of bladder and urethra, and lesions of the ureter. Editor of Oxford Urological Surgery and Yearbook of Urology. Originator of Lowsley ribbon gut method of kidney operations and of operation for relief of impotence, also a new operation for hypospadias. Inventor of many operative instruments and tables. Home: 860 5th Av., N.Y.C. 21. Office: 111 E. 71st St., N.Y.C.; also 727 W. 7th St., Los Angeles. Died June 4, 1955; buried Fishkill, N.Y.

LOWY, ALEXANDER, coll. prof.; b. New York, N.Y., Mar. 31, 1889; s. David and Fanny (Weiss) L.; B.S., Columbia, 1911, A.M., 1912, Ph.D., 1915; m. Dora Landberg, Dec. 23, 1915; children—Evelyn F., Muriel A., Alexander D. Asst. in electrochemistry, Columbia U., and teaching in N.Y. City until 1918; prof. of organic chemistry, U. of Pittsburgh, 1918—; holder of numerous U.S. patents on chem. research discoveries. Vice-pres. Am. Electrochemical Soc., 1930-33 and 1938-41; chmn. of its publ. com., 1931-41. Jewish religion. Author: Introduction to Organic Chemistry, 1922; Study Questions in Organic Chemistry, 1923; Laboratory Methods in Organic Chemistry, 1926; Industrial Organic Chemicals and Dye Intermediates, 1935. Home: Pittsburgh, Pa. Died Dec. 25, 1941.

LOY, SYLVESTER K(LINE), chemist; b. Hamburg, Pa., Aug. 18, 1879; s. Walter S. and Hettie M. (Kline) L.; grad. Keystone State Normal Sch., Kutztown, Pa., 1899; A.B., Franklin and Marshall Coll., 1905; Ph.D., Johns Hopkins, 1910; m. Ella May Nash, Aug. 13, 1912. Tchr. pub. schs., 1899-1901; prof. physics and chemistry Keystone State Normal Sch., 1907-08; instr. chemistry Simmons Coll., Boston, 1910-11; asst. research chemist Colgate & Co., Jersey City, N.J., summer, 1911; research chemist U. Wyo. Agrl. Expt. Sta., 1911-13, prof. chemistry and dir. lab., 1913-18; chief chemist The Midwest Refining Co., 1918-21, Casper Plant, Standard Oil Co. (Ind.), 1921—; cons. chemist U.S. Bur. Mines (shale oil), 1920—. Mayor of Casper, Wyo., 1923. Mem. Am. Soc. Testing Materials. Home: Casper, Wyo. Deceased.

LOZIER, CLEMENCE SOPHIA HARNED, physician; b. Plainfield, N.J., Dec. 11, 1813; d. David and Hannah (Walker) Harned; grad. Syracuse Med. Coll., 1853; m. Abraham Lozier, 1830, 1 son Abraham. Moved to N.Y.C., lectured on hygiene and physiology in her home; founder N.Y. Med. Coll. and Hosp. for Women, 1863; reorganized coll., became dean and prof. gynecology and obstetrics, 1867-88; mem. Nat. Working Women's League, W.C.T.U., N.Y.C. Suffrage League (pres. 13 years), Nat. Woman's Suffrage Assn. (pres. 5 years). Died N.Y.C. Apr. 25, 1888.

LUCAS, ANTHONY FRANCIS, mining engr.; b. Trieste, Austria, Sept. 9, 1855; s. Capt. Francis Stephen and Giovanna (Giovanizio) L.; ed. Poly. Acad., Gratz, Austria, 1874-77; post-grad. course in mining engring.; m. Carolina Weed Fitzgerald, Sept. 22, 1887. Has discovered various deposits of rocksalt occurring in Domes and to great depth, 3,000 feet and over, and by drilling a discovery well on Spindle-Top near Beaumont, Tex., Jan. 10, 1901, with initial capacity of 100,000 barrels of petroleum per day, established by original work an economic precedent for the production of petroleum, sulphur and rock salt on the Coastal Plains of La., Tex. and Mex. heretofore considered barren, thus establishing his Dome theory of oil concentration about salt Domes. Home: Washington, D.C. Died Sept. 2, 1921.

LUCAS, FRANCIS FERDINAND, scientist, engr.; b. Glens Falls, N.Y., Aug. 7, 1884; s. Frank and Mary (Bateman) L.; hon. D.Sc., Lehigh University, 1931; married Rose Jennet Howe, September 19, 1905; 1 dau., Mrs. Willard H. Seaman. With Bell telephone companies, 1902-49; mem. technical staff Bell Telephone Labs., Inc., 1925-49, now cons. ret.; Watertown Arsenal, U.S. War Department, 1928-36. Awarded Henry Marion Howe medal by Am. Soc. for Steel Treating, 1924; medal by Royal Photographic Soc. of Great Britain, 1926 and 1929; John Price Wetherill medal, Franklin Inst., 1935. Del. Internat. Congress for Testing Materials, Amsterdam, Holland, 1927, Zurich, Switzerland, 1931, World Engr. Congress, Tokyo, Japan, 1929; Am. conferee 2d Worlds Metal Congress, Chgo., 1957; sci. advisory trustee Cancer Research Division of Donner Foundation, Inc., Phila. Mem. East Orange (N.J.) Fire Com., 1942-50, pres., 1947-50. Mem. Telephone Pioneers. Rep. Presbyn. Mason. Inventor, developer many items and processes used in scientific research, such as use of ultra violet rays, microscopy and micro motion pictures. The Francis F. Lucas Metallographic award created in his honor by Am. Soc. for Metals, 1957. Home: 1029 McKean Circle, Winter Park, Fla. Retired. Died June 20, 1961; buried Glens Falls (N.Y.) Cemetery.

LUCAS, JOHNATHAN, millwright; b. Cumberland, Eng., 1754; s. John and Ann (Noble) L.; m. Mary Cooke, May 22, 1774; m. 2d, Ann Ashburn, between 1783-86; 5 children including Jonathan. Moved to Charleston, S.C., 1790; 1st built pounding-mill driven by wind to remove husks from rice grain; built water mills for various plantations; also constructed tide-mills (operated automatically on movement of tides); made prodn. of rice much more profitable for South. Died Apr. 1, 1821; buried St. Paul's Churchyard, Charleston.

LUCAS, JONATHAN, millwright, inventor; b. Eng., 1775; s. Jonathan and Mary (Cooke) L.; m. Sarah Lydia Simons, July 18, 1799, some children. Came (with father) to S.C., 1790; builder and operator of rice mill, Cannonborough, S.C., 1798-1801; operated new rice mill on Middleburg Plantation on Cooper River, 1801-22; devised and patented new type of machine to remove husks from rice; took machine to Eng. because it was not widely accepted by farmers in S.C., 1822; established rice cleaning mills, London, Liverpool (Eng.), also Copenhagen (Denmark), other European cities; lived in Surrey, Eng., 1827-32. Died Surrey, Dec. 29, 1832; buried Camberwell Ch., London.

LUCAS, WILLIAM PALMER, physician; b. Lexington, Ky., Jan. 27, 1880; s. James Joseph and Eva Mary (Sly) L.; A.B., Wooster (O.) U., 1900; M.D., Western Res. U., 1905, LL.D., 1921; m. Virginia Cumming Metson, Aug. 24, 1937. Instr. dept. pediatrics Harvard Med. Sch., 1908-13; chief of staff Children's Service, U. Cal. Hosp. and prof. pediatrics U. Cal. Med. Sch., 1913-25, clin. prof. since 1925. In pvt. pediatric practice. Vis staff U. Cal., Mt. Zion, Stanford and Children's Hosps. since 1925. Made health survey of children in Belgium upon request Herbert C. Hoover, for Commn. for Relief in Belgium, May-July 1916; chief Children's Bur. of Am. Nat. Red Cross. Active duty in France, 1917-19. Decorations: Chevalier de l'Ordre de la Courronne by King Albert of Belgium; La Médaille des Epidémies, Chevalier de la Légion d'Honneur (French). Fellow Am. Acad. Pediatrics; mem. Am. Pediatric Soc., A.M.A., No. Cal. Acad. Pediatrics, Am. Genetic Assn., Cal. Acad. Medicine, Cal. Med. Assn., Am. Assn. Pub. Health (chmn. Bay Area Nutritional Council—duration of World War II), Beta Theta Pi, Nu Sigma Nu, Alpha Omega Alpha, Pi Gamma Mu, Sigma Xi, Phi Beta Kappa. Clubs: Bohemian (San Francisco), Faculty (Berkeley, Cal.); Harvard (N.Y.). Author several text books, books and monographs on various subjects relating to Pediatrics. Spl. work on problems of growth and devel., infancy through adolescence (pubertal maturation problems). Psychosomatic pediatric problems from birth to and through period of full pubertal maturation. Home: P.O. Box 495, Pebble Beach, Cal. 93953. Died Dec. 16, 1960.

LUCKE, BALDUIN, (loo ka), pathologist; b. Oedinghausen, Hesse, Germany, Nov. 3, 1889; s. Frederick and Helene (Rommel) L.; grad. Gymnasium, Kassel, 1906; M.D., U. of Pa., 1912, Dr.P.H., 1916; m. Marion Hague Rea, Mar. 2, 1917 (died Nov. 1, 1946); 1 son, Balduin; m. 2d Helen Hughes Norris, Nov. 15, 1947. Came to U.S., 1906, naturalized, 1915. Intern, Phila. Gen. Hosp., 1912-14; asst. instr. pathology, U. of Pa., 1914-17, instr., 1919-20, asst. prof., 1920-27 asso. prof. 1927-32, prof. pathology 1932—, chmn. dept., 1947—; Guiteras lectr., Buffalo, 1940. Gross lectr., Phila., 1944, Fenger lectr., Chicago, 1945, Mütter lectr., Phila., 1948. Served as lt., med. corps U.S. Army, 1917-19; mem. Med. Res., 1919-42; lt. col., med. corps active service, 1942-46, dep. dir. Armed Forces Inst. Pathology; ret. as col., 1946. Awarded Legion of Merit. Mem. bd. hon. consultants Army Med. Library; sci. adv. bd. Armed Forces Inst. Pathology (chmn. 1946); div. med. scis. Nat. Research Council, 1943—, subcom. on oncology, 1948— (chmn., 1951—); Fellow Coll. Physicians of Phila.; mem. Am. Soc. for Exptl. Pathology (pres., 1942-46), Assn. Am. Phys., Soc. Exptl. Biol. and Med., Corp. Marine Biol. Lab., Am. Assn. for Cancer Research, A.A.A.S., Sigma Xi, Alpha Omega Alpha. Clubs: Cosmos (Washington); Merion Cricket (Haverford, Pa.). Mem. editorial bd. Cancer Research. Author articles in profl. publs. Home: 623 Rose Lane, Bryn Mawr, Pa. Office: U. of Pennsylvania, Phila. 4. Died Apr. 26, 1954; buried Arlington Nat. Cemetery.

LUCKE, CHARLES EDWARD, (luk'e), cons. mech. engr.; b. N.Y.C., June 20, 1876; s. John Franklin and Sarah Frances (McGrury) L.; B.S., Coll. City N.Y., 1895; M.S., N.Y.U., 1899; Cornell U., 1899; Ph.D., Columbia, 1902, Sc.D., 1929; m. Ida M. Becker, Mar. 24, 1904. Prof. mech. engring. Columbia, 1906-41, head dept., 1908-41, Stevens prof. emeritus, 1941—; mech. engring. cons. Served in USN, World War I, comdr. USNRF. Mem. Am. Soc. M.E., Am. Soc. Refrigerating Engrs., Soc. Automotive Engrs., Am. Soc. Heating and Ventilating Engrs., Soc. Naval Architects and Marine Engrs. Clubs: Engineers', Columbia University. Author: Gas Engine Design, 1905; Power, 1911; Engineering Thermodynamics, 1912; also about 80 papers on profl. subjects. Holder more than 120 patents. Home: 88 Morningside Drive. Office: Pupin Bldg., Columbia U., N.Y.C. 27. Died Mar. 27, 1951.

LUCKEY, DAVID FRANKLIN, veterinarian; b. Brazeau, Mo., Sept. 23, 1869; s. Robert Armstrong and Margaret Jane (Wilson) L.; grad. Warrensburg (Mo.) State Normal Sch., 1891, Ontario Veterinary Coll., Toronto, Can., 1896; m. Nan Frances Doherty, June 24, 1908; children—David Franklin, Frances Louise (Mrs. James Pierce Scamman), Samuel Monroe, Supt. pub. schs., Aurora, Mo., 1891-93; engaged in tick fever quarantine work, 1896-1900; Mo. State vet., 1900-12 and 1913-22, in 1900 began campaign against contagious diseases in animals, especially cattle tuberculosis; worked successfully on tick fever eradication in Mo., also eradication of glanders in horses and mules; successful in keeping foot and mouth disease out of Mo. during violent outbreak in neighboring states, 1914-15; stamped out hog cholera in Mo. by 1918; developed intradermal method of testing cattle for tuberculosis, used in Mo. since 1911, and adopted by Fed. govt., 1921. Awarded Internat. Veterinary Congress Prize for work on the development of the Intradermal Tuberculin Test, 1944. Home: 3969 Palm St., St Louis 7 MO

LUCKHARDT, ARNO BENEDICT, (luk'härt), physiologist; b. Chgo., Aug. 26, 1885; s. Gustav Adolph and Aurelia (Weber) L.; student Conception (Mo.) Coll., 1897-1903, LL.D., 1933; B.S., U. Chgo., 1906, M.S., 1908, Ph.D., 1911; M.D., Rush Med. Coll., 1912; Sc.D., Northwestern U., 1934; m. Luella Catherine LaBolle, Apr. 24, 1912; children—Hilmar Francis, Paul Gregory, Mary Aurelia. Asst. in bacteriology U. Chgo., 1908-09, in physiology, 1909-11, asso., 1911-12, instr., 1912-14, asst. prof., 1914-20, asso. prof., 1920-23, prof., 1923-41, chmn. dept. physiology, 1941-50, Dr. William Beaumont Distinguished Service prof. in physiology, 1947-50, now Distinguished Service prof. physiology emeritus; now research cons. J. B. Roerig & Co., of the Pharm. House of Chas. Pfizer & Co., Inc., of N.Y.C. Mem. bd. dirs. Dr. William Beaumont Found., Inc., Prairie du Chien, Wis. Fellow A.M.A., Soc. for Exptl. Biology and Medicine, Internat. Coll. of Anesthetists, Internat. Soc. Dental Research, hon. fellow Am. Coll. of Dentists; hon. mem. German Med. Soc. Chgo., St. Louis Med. Soc.; mem. Internat. Anesthesia Research Soc., Order of Bookfellows, Am. Psychol. Soc. (past pres.), Inst. Traumatic Surgery Fedn. Am. Socs. for Exptl. Biology (pres. 1933-35), Gorgas Soc., Walter Reed Soc. (life), A.A.A.S., Ill. Med. Soc., Am. Dental Assn. (council on therapeutics), Kaiserlich Deutsche Akademie der Naturforscher, Phi Beta Pi, Sigma Xi, Phi Beta Kappa, Gamma Alpha, Alpha Omega Alpha, Theta Nu Epsilon, etc. Clubs: University, B.M.C. (pres. 1939-40), Chicago Literary Club (past pres.). Recipient Alpha Omega medal, 1938; Callahan Memorial Award medal, Ohio Dental Society; Phi Beta Pi "Man of the Year" citation, 1948; certificate of award Water Reed Society, 1952. Discovered, with J. Bailey Carter, of ethylene gas as an anesthetic agent with properties superior to nitrous oxide, commonly known as "laughing gas"; researches in physiology of the parathyroid glands, gastric and pancreatic secretion, and in the history of physiology, dentistry and medicine. Home: 5216 Greenwood Av., Chgo. Died Nov. 6, 1957; buried Somonauk, Ill.

LUCKIESH, MATTHEW, physicist., elec. engr.; b. Maquoketa, Ia., Sept. 14, 1889; s. John and Frances (Root) L.; B.S. in E.E., Purdue, 1909, D.E., 1935; M.S., State U. Ia., 1911; E.E., Ia. State Coll., 1912, D.Sc., 1926; m. Helen C. Pitts, Jan. 31, 1928; children—Nancy Pitts, Helen Margaret. Instr. State U. Ia., 1909-10; physicist, Nela Research Labs., 1910-20; dir. applied science Nela Research Labs., Nat. Lamp Works of Gen. Electric Co., 1920-24; dir. Lighting Research Lab., Lamp Dept. of Gen. Electric Co., 1924-50; cons. on light, lighting, color since 1950. Chmn. com. on camouflage, Nat. Research Council, World War I. Mem. Edison Electric Inst., Illuminating Engring. Soc. (pres. 1925), Am. Inst. E.E., Am. Phys. Soc., Franklin Inst., Optical Soc. Am., Am. Acad. Optometry, Sigma Alpha Epsilon, Sigma Xi, Tau Beta Pi. Awarded Longstreth medal and certificate by Franklin Inst. for work on visibility of airplanes; gold medal by Distinguished Service Foundation of Optometry for researches in seeing; medalist of Illuminating Engring. Soc. Author numerous books relating to field; latest being: Applications of Germicidal, Erythemal and Infrared Energy, 1946; also many contbns. to sci. and tech. jours. Club: The Country. Home: 21175 Shaker Blvd., Shaker Heights 22, O. Died Nov. 2, 1967.

LUDLOW, EDWIN, mining engr.; b. Oakdale, L.I., N.Y., Mar. 12, 1858; s. William Handy and Louise (Nicoll) L.; ed. Flushing (N.Y.) Inst., 1868-75; M.E., School of Mines (Columbia), 1879; m. Anna Wright, Nov. 22, 1893. Asst. engr. on river and harbor works, Phila., 1879-81; asst. supt. and supt. Mineral R.R. & Mining Co., Shamokin, Pa., 1881-89; supt. mines, Choctaw, Okla. & Gulf R.R., Hartshorne, Okla., 1889-99; gen. mgr. Mexican Coal & Coke Co., Las Esperanzas, Mex., 1899-1911; v.p. New River Collieries Co., Eccles, W.Va., 1911-12; v.p. Lehigh Coal & Navigation Co., Lansford, Pa., 1912-19; consulting mining engr., New York, July 1, 1919—. Democrat. Episcopalian. Died Feb. 10, 1924.

LUDLOW, HENRY GILBERT, inventor, mfr.; b. Nassau, N.Y., March 28, 1823; grad. Union Coll., 1843; spent some time with gas co. in Phila., in order to learn profession of gas engring.; later, with friends, engaged in constructing gas works. Invented the Ludlow straight-way slide-stop valve and engaged in its manufacture, incorporating the Ludlow Valve Mfg. Co., now the largest valve mfg. co. in the world; retired from the business, 1891, but still has an interest in it; m. Harriet M. Shattuck, 1854. Home: Troy, N.Y. Died 1904.

LUDLOW, JACOB LOTT, engineer; b. Spring Lake, N.J., Dec. 20, 1862; s. Samuel and Nancy (Johnson) L.; C.E., Lafayette Coll., Easton, Pa., 1885, later M.S.; m. Myra M. Hunt, Jan. 5, 1887. Began practice at Winston-Salem, N.C., 1890; pres. The Ludlow Engrs., Inc.; mem. and cons. engr. N.C. State Bd. of Health, 1890-1920; mem. Engring. Bd. of Review, Sanitary Dist. of Chicago, 1924, 25. Has served as cons. engr. various Southern cities, on water supply and sewerage projects, valuation of pub. utilities, etc. Col. and chief of engrs., N.C.N.G., 1908-16; supervising engr. on constrn. camp cantonments, World War, also supervising sanitary engr. U.S. Shipping Bd. for S. Atlantic and Gulf states. Democrat. Presbyn. Home: Winston-Salem, N.C. Died Aug. 18, 1930.

LUDLOW, WILLIAM, brig. gen. U.S.A., Jan. 21, 1900; b. Riverside, Islip, L.I., N.Y., Nov. 27, 1843; s. William Handy and Frances Louisa (Nicoll) L.; ed. Burlington Coll., N.J., and N.Y. Univ., 1853-60; grad. West Point, June 20, 1864; commissioned 1st lt., corps of engrs.; m. Genevieve Almira Sprigg, 1866. Chief engr. 20th army corps, under Gens. Hooker and Slocum, in Atlanta campaign, 1864; chief engr., left wing Gen. Sherman's army in Savannah, and the Carolinas campaign, 1864-65; comdg. Co. E, engr. battalion, Jefferson barracks, Mo., 1865-67; capt. engrs. U.S.A., March 7, 1867; chief engr., Dept. of Dak., in Black Hills and Yellowstone expdns.; in charge of various works of fortifications, rivers and harbors, on Atlantic coast from New York to St. Augustine, Fla.; chief engr. Phila. water dept. by election of city councils and spl. joint resolution of Congress, 1883-86; maj. engrs., June 30, 1882; engr. sec. light house bd., Washington, 1882; engr. commr. of D.C., 1886-88; charge river and harbor and light house work on Great Lakes, 1888-93; mil. attaché U.S. Embassy, London, 1893-96; lt. col. engrs., Aug. 13, 1895; pres. U.S. Nicaragua Canal Commn., 1895; brig. gen., U.S.V., May 4, 1898; chief engr. armies in the field, May, 1898; comdg. 1st brigade, 2d div., Shafter's corps, Santiago campaign; battles of Caney and San Juan and investment of Santiago June-Sept., 1898; maj. gen. U.S.V., Sept. 7, 1898; pres. bd. to organize Army Sea Transport Service, Sept.-Oct., 1898. Mil. gov. Havana, Dec. 12, 1898, to May 1, 1900; comdg. dept. Havana, Dec. 1898-May 1, 1900; pres. War Coll. Bd., May 1, 1900—. Died 1901.

LUEDDE, WILLIAM HENRY, (lüd'de), ophthalmologist; b. Warsaw, Ill.; s. Henry J. M. and Emilie M. (Naumann) L.; M.D., Washington U., St. Louis, 1900; vol. asst. eye clinic Royal U., Kiel, Germany, 1904-05; student Laboratoire d'Ophthalmologie, Sorbonne, Paris, 1906; m. Nettie B. Shyrock, Mar. 24, 1909 (died Nov. 2, 1946); children—Philip S., Fullerton W., Henry W.; m. 2d, Irene E. Garbarino, Jan. 2, 1948. Asst. to Drs. Green, Post and Ewing, 1901-04; in pvt. practice, St. Louis, 1906—; asst. surgeon, Eye Clinic, Washington U., 1908-12; ophthalmic surgeon, St. Louis Eye, Ear, Nose and Throat Infirmary, 1912-16; prof. ophthalmology St. Louis U., 1921—; ophthalmologist in chief Firmin Desloge Hosp., St. Mary's Hosp. and Infirmary; oculist Mo. Bapt. Sanitarium; attending ophthalmologist U.S. Marine Hosp.; cons. in ophthalmology St. Louis City, St. Louis County and St. Johns hosps. Recipient Gill prize (disease of children) by Washington U., 1900, Leslie Dana medal (prevention of blindness), 1933. Served from capt. to maj. M.C., U.S. Army, World War I; col. AUS, 1931-41. Dir. St. Louis Society for the Blind. Fellow A.M.A., A.A.A.S.; mem. many national, internat. and fgn. med. and ophthal. assns., S.R., Alpha Omega Alpha. Conglist. Mason (K.T.). Club: University. Home: 139 N. Tunbridge Dr., Stoneleigh Towers, St. Louis County 24. Office: 256 Hampton Village, Medical Center, St. Louis. Died Mar. 19, 1952.

LUHN, HANS PETER, inventor, author, cons.; b. Barmen, Germany, July 1, 1896; s. Johann Peter and Emma Maria (Kahle) L.; student Schweizerische Handels Hochschule, St. Gallen, Switzerland, 1914, 18-20; m. Margaret Herreshoff, Dec. 21, 1929; children—Diana (Mrs. Ted Tower), Hans Peter, Christopher Brown Herreshoff; m. 2d, Genevieve Douglass, Apr. 2, 1953. Came to U.S., 1924, naturalized, 1943. Asst. to pres. Textile Machine Works, Reading, Pa., 1926-29; engring. cons. H.P. Luhn & Assos., N.Y.C., 1930-41; sr. research engr., mgr. information retrieval research, research center and advanced systems devel. div., IMB Corp., 1941-61; cons. bus. intelligence systems and information sci., 1961—; pioneer devel. and application automatic measuring and control devices, binary arithmetic systems, swithching devices, serial binary computers, electronic information scanning, storage and retrieval devices; originator statis. methods for automatic indexing, abtracting and matching lit. information. Mem. adv. bd. Sch. Library Sci., U. So. Cal. 1959—. Mem. Inst. Elec. and Electronics Engrs., Assn. Computing Machinery, Assn. Symbolic Logic, A.A.A.S., Spl. Libraries Assn., Am. Chs., Soc., Deutsche Gesellschaft fur Dokumentation, Fedn. Internat. de Documentation, Am. Documentation Inst. (pres. 1963—). Author articles in field, also chpts. in books. Editor: Automation and Scientific Communications, 1963. Patentee in field. Home: Hadley and Creemer Rd., Armonk, N.Y. 10594. Died Aug. 19, 1964.

LULEK, RALPH NORBERT, chem. mgr.; b. Graz, Austria, Fort Lauderdale FL chem. mgr.; b. Graz, Austria, Aug. 13, 1901; s. Dr. Fery and Nelly (von Arthold) L.; Ph.D., U. Graz, 1924; m. Noronica R. Beatley, June 24, 1929. Came to U.S., 1925, naturalized, 1935. Group leader E.I. duPont de Nemours & Co., Wilmington, 1925-43; plant mgr. Publicker Industries, Phila., 1943-46; mgr. research Heyden Chem. Corp., N.Y.C., 1946, v.p., 1948-53; plant mgr. Heyden Morgantown Ordnance Works, 1946-47, v.p., dir., 1948-53; pres., dir. Heyden Pharmacal Co., Heyden Labs., Inc., 1948-53; dir. Jamieson Pharmacal Co., Detroit, Nyal Co., 1948-53, Am. Potash & Chem. Co., 1950-52; v.p., dir. St. Maurice Chem., Ltd., Can., 1952-53; v.p., dir. Grace Chem. Co., N.Y.C. 1953-55; cons. Sun Chem. Co., Johnson and Johnson, Nobel-Boyel Co., France, other, 1955-70. Recipient Modern Pioneer award, N.A.M., award for contbn. to atomic bomb War Dept., award Nat. Geographic Soc. Mem. Am. Inst. Chem. Engrs., Am. Chem. Soc., Am. Assn. Textile Chemists and Colorists, W.Va. Soc. Profl. Engrs., Assn. Research Dirs. of N.Y., Soc. Chem. Industry London, Soc. de Chemie Industrielle, N.Y. Acad. Sci. Elk. Clubs: Wall Street, Chemists; Univ. (N.Y.C.). Author tech. articles. Holder 75 patents. Address: Candlewood CT Died May 3, 1970, buried Mountain Grove Cemetery, Bridgeport CT

LULL, RICHARD SWANN, paleontologist; b. Annapolis, Md., Nov. 6, 1867; s. Capt. Edward P. (USN) and Elizabeth F. (Burton) L.; B.S., Rutgers U., 1893, M.S., 1896, hon. D.Sc., 1918; Ph.D., Columbia, 1903; hon. M.A., Yale, 1911; m. Clara Coles Boggs, July 2, 1894; 1 dau., Dorothy. With div. entomology U.S. Dept. Agr., 1893; asst. and asso. prof. zoölogy Mass. State Coll., 1894-1906; asst. prof. vertebrate paleontology Yale, 1906-11, prof., 1911-23, prof. paleontology, 1923-27, Sterling prof. paleontology, 1927-36, now emeritus. Asso. curator of vertebrate paleontology Peabody Museum, Yale, 1906-20, curator vertebrate paleontology, 1920-26, hon. curator, 1932—, dir., 1922-36, acting dir., 1937-38, now emeritus; asso. fellow Jonathan Edwards Coll., Yale; lectr. on paleontology U. Cal., summers 1925, 35, 37, Harvard, 1939. Instr. seamanship USN Tng. Unit, Yale, 1917-18. Fellow Am. Acad. Arts and Sciences, Geol. Soc. America, Paleontol. Soc. (treas. 1911-24, pres. 1925); mem. Soc. Vertebrate Paleontology, Am. Museum Natural History (hon. life), Chi Psi, Sigma Xi, Phi Beta Kappa. Recipient Elliot medal, Nat. Acad. Sciences for 1933; Society of Colonial Wars. Episcopalian. Author: Organic Evolution, and other books and memoirs. Editor Am. Jour. of Science, 1933-49. Home: 200 Livingston St., New Haven 11. Died Apr. 22, 1957; buried Evergreen Cemetery, New Haven.

LUM, DAVID WALKER, civil engr.; b. Newark, N.J., Mar. 9, 1855; s. Amos and Amanda L.; ed. Newark, (N.J.) pub. schs. and Newark Acad. until 1873; m. Carrie Williams, of Brooklyn, 1878; m. 2d, Emma S. Price, May 14, 1926. In engring. dept. of railways in Iowa, Minnesota, Pennsylvania and N.J., 1873-76; asst. engr. Hackensack River and Burgin tunnel improvements, D.,L. & W. R.R., 1876-77; in office of supervising architect, Washington, 1878-81; div. engr. Ky. Central and C. & O. Rys., 1881-85; div. engr., 1885-86, prin. asst. engr., 1886-87, chief engr., 1887-94, E.T.V.G. Ry.; also chief engr. Memphis & Charleston R.R., 1887-94; supt. maintenance of way and structures, western dist., 1894-97, asst. gen. supt. maintenance of way, 1898-1900, engr. bridges and bldgs., 1900-04, chief engr. maintenance of way and structures, 1904-11, now spl. engr. Southern Ry. Co. Mem. Am. Soc. C.E. Home: 1435 Shepherd St. N.W., Washington, D.C.

LUMSDEN, LESLIE LEON, (lums'den), U.S. Public Health Service; b. Granite Springs, Va., June 14, 1875; s. James Fife and Ann Elizabeth (Jacobs) L.; student Va. Midland and Bowling Green acads.; M.D., U. of Va., 1894; grad. student Johns Hopkins Hosp. Sch., 1894-95; m. Alfreda Blanche Healy, 1902 (died 1908); m. 2d, Flora Elizabeth Dick, Feb. 6, 1937. Commd. asst. surgeon U.S. P.H.S. (then Marine Hosp.), 1898, passed asst. surgeon, 1903, surgeon, 1912, sr. surgeon, 1928, med. dir., 1930; retired, 1939; has specialized in epidemiology of yellow fever, bubonic plague, tuberculosis, and poliomyelitis, also in rural health work; dist. dir. and research work, New Orleans, 1931-39; with Tenn. Dept. of Pub. Health, 1939-41; prof. epidemiology, Texas U. Sch. of Med. since 1943. Originated and developed full time plan of rural health service in U.S. During World War held commn. asst. surgeon gen. U.S. P.H.S. with relative rank of col. Mem. Am. Pub. Health Assn., A.M.A. Democrat. Club: Cosmos (Washington, D.C.). Author: of various U.S. P.H.S. pubIs. on typhoid fever, rural sanitation, rural health work, tuberculosis and poliomyelitis; also contbr. to med. jours. Home: 103 Park Pl., New Orleans. Died Nov. 8, 1946; buried in Garden of Memories, New Orleans.

LUND, CHARLES CARROLL, surgeon; b. Boston, Apr. 15, 1895; s. Fred Bates and Zoe M. (Griffing) L.; A.B., Harvard, 1916, M.D. cum laude, 1920; m. Alice C. Marden, May 22, 1925. Intern Mass. Gen. Hosp., Boston, 1920-22, resident in surgery, 1922-23; pvt. practice surgery, Boston, 1923-68; mem. faculty, Med. Sch., Harvard, 1923, asst. clin. prof. surgery, 1953-55, clin. prof. surgery, 1955-61, prof. emeritus, 1961-72;

asso. with Collis P. Huntington Meml. Hosp., 1924-41, Boston City Hosp., 1924-68 surgeon-in-chief 1951-60, cons. surgery, 1961-66, hon. surgeon, 1966-68; surgeon New Eng. Deaconess Hosp., 1926-68; mem. med. adv. com. Mass. Red Cross Blood Program, 1963-72. Bd. dirs., pres. Blood Research Inst., 1960-69. Fellow A.C.S.; mem. A.M.A., Am. Surg. Soc., Soc. Clin. Surgery, Am. Cancer Soc. (bd. dirs. 1947, pres. 1951-52), Nat. Research Council, N.E. Surg. Soc., N.E. Cancer Soc., Suffolk Dist., Mass. (pres. 1958-59) med. socs., Boston Surg. Soc. (pres. 1960-61), Harvard Med. Alumni Assn. (pres. 1958-59), Aesculapian, Nat. Rowing Found. (dir. 1965), Phi Beta Kappa, Alpha Omega Alpha. Clubs: Country (Brookline); St. Botolph (pres. 1946-46), Harvard (pres. 1953-55) (Boston); Friends of Harvard Rowing (chmn. 1959-69). Contbr. articles to med. jours. Home: Chestnut Hill MA Died July 27, 1972.

LUNDIE, JOHN, consulting engr.; b. Arbroath, Scotland, Dec. 14, 1857; s. James and Anne (Honeyman) L.; B.Sc., U. of Edinburgh, 1880, D.Sc., 1902; m. Iona Oakley, d. Capt. J. C. Gorham, of St. Louis, and grand-niece of Gov. Sterling Price, of Mo., July 6, 1906 (died 1925); m. 2d, Mrs. Alice Eddy Snowden (A.M., Columbia U.), July 15, 1929. Harbor work, Dundee, Scotland, 1873-77; railroad work, Ore. and Wash., 1880-84; municipal work, Chicago, 1884-90; bridge work, 1890-93; pvt. practice after 1893. Developed method for determination of yield of artesian water areas during investigation of water supply system of Memphis, Tenn.; designed the first combined electric hoist and traveler (the "telfer"); investigated and reported on electrification of I.C. R.R., Boston Elevated R.R., Brooklyn Elevated R.R., Manhattan lines, New York, Met. Underground, London, Eng., etc. Investigated costs of freight movement on U.S. Steel Corp. railroads; officer in charge of Birmingham Southern R.R. Co.; v.p. and gen. mgr. Panama-Am. Corp. in Panama; developed Lundie formula for train resistance; designed the Lundie rheostat, Lundie tie plate, Lundie duplex rail anchor, etc.; co-designer Lundie-Durham rail. Pres. The Lundie Engring. Corp. Mason. Home: New York, N.Y. Died Feb. 9, 1931.

LUNDY, AYRES DERBY, mech. and elec. engr.; b. Ft. Dodge, Ia., May 25, 1861; s. Albert D. and Jennie (Ayres) L.; A.B., Princeton University, 1884; A.M., Cornell University, 1887; m. Mary Thompson, of Topeka, Kan., Aug. 8, 1888 (deceased); 1 dau., Mrs. Esther Ayres Newcomb; m. 2d, Florence Farnsworth, of Hyde Park, Mass., June 30, 1939. Began with Sprague Electric Railway & Motor Company, Richmond, Va.; chief engineer Sprague Electric Equipment Co., Chicago, building 1st electric rys. in Ia., Ohio, Ind., Minn. and Wash., 1887-90; dist. engr. southern dist., Edison Gen. Electric Co., 1890-91; mem. firm Sargent & Lundy, mech. and elec. engrs., Chicago, 1901-19, sec. and treas. Sargent & Lundy, Inc., 1919-32; pres. Electro-Magnetic Tool Co., now retired. Fellow Am. Inst. E.E. Clubs: University, La Grange Country, Edison Pioneers. Home: 338 S. Waiola Av., La Grange, Ill.

LUNDY, WILSON THOMAS, cons. mining engr.; b. San Francisco, Oct. 6, 1884; s. David and Jemima Lundy; student U. Cal., 1907; m. Myra Lillian Burke, May 1, 1925; children—Robert Wilson, Mary Jemima. Metall. engr., Korea, 1908-12; mining engr. North Star & Empire Mines, Grass Valley, Calif., 1912-14; supt. Weedon Mining Co., Que., Can., 1914-16, mining engr. Texas Gulf Sulphur Co., Matagorda, Texas, 1917-19, Texas Co., Hoskins Mound, 1920-21; with Freeport Sulphur Co., N.Y.C., 1923-51, as v.p., gen. mgr., dir., ret. Dec. 1951; now cons. mining engr. Mem. Am. Inst. Mining and Metall. Engrs., Am. Assn. Petroleum Geologists. Republican. Clubs: Mining (N.Y.C.); Siwanoy Country, Field (Bronxville). Author, Sulphur and Pyrites, chpt. on Industrial Minerals and Rocks (Am. Inst. Mining and Metall. Engrs.); Known and Potential Sulphur Resources of the World (Indsl. and Engring. Chemistry), Nov. 1950. Home: 25 Sunny Brae Pl., Bronxville, N.Y. Office: 161 E. 42d St. N.Y.C. 17. Died Oct. 1, 1963; buried Chapel of the Chimes, Oakland, Cal

LUNKEN, EDMUND H., (surname changed to avoid business complications), inventor, mfr.; b. Cincinnati, O., June 20, 1861; s. Frederick and Louisa H. Lunkenheimer; ed. pub. schs., Cincinnati, and in tech. sch., Germany; m. Edith I. Hodgson, July 7, 1885 (divorced); 1 son, Eshelby Frederick; m. 2d, Kathryn French, Dec. 31, 1914; children—Homer Edmund, Charlotte Hope. With Lunkenheimer Co. (founded by father), mfrs. valves, etc., Cincinnati, many yrs., retiring as chief executive, 1923; inventor many standard devices in use in mechanical operations. Donor of tract of land Cincinnati, for aviation purposes, known as the Lunken Air Port. Protestant. Mason (32 deg.). Home: Compton Hills Dr., Wyoming (Cincinnati), O. Died July 19, 1944.

LUNN, ARTHUR CONSTANT, mathematician; b. Racine, Wis., Feb. 19, 1877; s. John C. and Emma R. (Martin) L.; A.B., Lawrence Coll., 1898; A.M., U. of Chicago, 1900, Ph.D., 1904; m. Anna J. Gowan, Sept. 27, 1900. Instr. mathematics and astronomy, Wesleyan U., Conn., 1901-02; asso. in applied mathematics, U. of Chicago, 1902-03, instr., 1903-10, asst. prof., 1910-17, asso. prof., 1917-23, prof. since 1923. Mem. Am. Phys. Soc., Am. Math. Soc., Am. Astron. Soc., Math. Assn. Am., A.A.A.S., Circolo Matematico di Palermo, Sigma Xi, Phi Beta Kappa, Gamma Alpha. Home: 5211 Kenwood Av., Chicago. Died Nov. 19, 1949.

LUPTON, CHARLES THOMAS, geologist; b. nr. Mt. Pleasant, O., Feb. 28, 1878; s. Benjamin C. and Anna (Thomas) L.; A.B., Oberlin, 1907; LL.B., Nat. U. Law Sch., Washington, D.C., 1915, LL.M., 1915; m. Addie White Bradshaw, Nov. 25, 1914; children—Martha, Charles T., Jr., Frantz Russell, Bradshaw Babb. With U.S. Geol. Survey, Washington, D.C., 1907-16; geologist in charge Rocky Mountain operations of Cosden Oil & Gas Co., 1916-19; chief geologist Frantz Corp., 1919-20; consulting practice, Denver, Colo., 1920—. Mem. Coal Classification Bd., U.S. Geol. Survey, 1909-11; chmn. Com. on Estimates of Oil Reserves in Rocky Mountain States, 1921. Republican. Conglist. Home: Denver, Colo. Deceased.

LUSK, GRAHAM, physiologist; b. Bridgeport, Conn., Feb. 15, 1866; s. Dr. William T. and Mary Hartwell (Chittenden) L.; Ph.B., Columbia, 1887; Ph.D., Munich, 1891; hon. A.M., Yale, 1896, Sc.D., 1908; LL.D., U. of Glasgow, 1923; hon. M.D., U. of Munich, 1929; m. May W. Tiffany, Dec. 20, 1899; children—William T., Louise (Mrs. Collier Platt), Louis T. Instr. physiology, 1891-92, asst. prof., 1892-95, prof., 1895-98, Yale; prof. physiology, Univ. and Bellevue Hosp. Med. Coll., 1898-1909; prof. physiology, Cornell U. Med. Coll., New York, 1909—; mem. Inter-Allied Scientific Food Commn., 1918; scientific director Russell Sage Inst. of Pathology. Fellow Royal Soc. of Edinburgh; corr. fellow Imperial Soc. of Physicians of Vienna. Author: Elements of the Science of Nutrition, 4th edit., 1928. Home: New York, N.Y. Died July 19, 1932.

LUSK, JAMES LORING, army officer; b. Pittsburgh, Pa., Feb. 1, 1855; s. Amos (M.D.) and Agnes Sterret (Clow) L.; grad. West Point, 1878; m. Mary E. Webster, Oct. 16, 1883. Apptd. 2d lt. June 14, 1878, 1st lt. June 14, 1881, capt. June 15, 1888, maj. July 5, 1898, corps. of engrs., U.S.A.; lt. col. and chief engr., U.S. Vols., May 9, 1898, to Dec. 7, 1898. Served in various duties of corps engrs., and as asst. instr. and instr. mil. engring. at West Point. Mem. U.S. Bd. Geographic Names, Mar. 21, 1899—; asst. to Chief of Engrs., U.S.A., Sept. 19, 1898—. Died 1906.

LUSK, WILLIAM THOMPSON, obstetrician; b. Norwich, Conn., May 23, 1838; s. Sylvester Graham and Elizabeth Freeman (Adams) L.; attended Yale, 1855, Heidelberg (Germany) U., 1858-60, U. Berlin, 1860-61; grad. Bellevue Hosp. Med. Coll., 1864; m. Mary Hartwell Chittenden, May 4, 1864; m. 2d, Matilda Myer Thorn, 1876. Served with 79th N.Y. Inf. Highlanders, 1861-63; gen. practice medicine, Bridgeport, Conn., 1865-66; practiced medicine (in partnership with Benjamin Fordyce Barker), N.Y.C., 1866-73; prof. physiology and microscopic anatomy L.I. Coll. Hosp., 1868-71; editor (with Dr. J. B. Hunter) N.Y. Med. Journal, 1871-73; prof. obstetrics Bellevue Hosp. Med. Coll., 1871-97; pres. Am. Gynecol. Soc., 1894; Known Mainly for book: The Science and Art of Midwifery, 1882. Died June 12, 1897.

LUTEN, DANIEL BENJAMIN, (lu'ten), bridge engr.; b. Grand Rapids, Mich., Dec. 26, 1869, s. Lambert and Wilhelmina (Hagens) L.; B.S. in C.E., U. of Mich., 1894; m. Edith Heath Hull, June 20, 1900; children—Granville H., Wilhelmina, Daniel B., Mary Edith. Instr. civ. engring., U. of Mich., 1894-95, Purdue U., Lafayette, Ind., 1895-1900; consulting practice, concrete bridges exclusively, 1900-32; mfr. since 1932. Home: 5024 N. Illinois St. Office: 2135 N. Illinois St., Indianapolis, Ind. Died July 3, 1946.

LUTHER, EDWIN CORNELIUS, mining engr.; b. Pottsville, Pa., Nov. 30, 1878; s. Roland Cornelius and Theresa (Yuengling) L.; grad. Hill Sch., Pottstown, Pa., 1898; C.E., Princeton, 1902, E.M., Columbia, 1904; m. Anna A. Henning, Apr. 17, 1912; children—Roland Cornelius, Edwin Cornelius, John (dec.), Isabel Therese. Mining engr. with Phila. & Reading Coal & Iron Co., 1904-08, with Estate of P. W. Sheafer, 1908-16; consulting practice, anthracite and bituminous coal mining, 1916—, also agt. for large coal estates; pres. and treas. Peerless Coal & Coke Co.; pres. Powhatan Coal & Coke Co., Pottsville Community Hotel Co., Safe Deposit Bank, Pottsville; v.p. Pottsville Water Co. Trustee Pottsville Public Library. Republican. Episcopalian. Mason. Home: Pottsville, Pa. Died Aug. 8, 1935.

LUTZ, BRENTON REID, biologist; b. Woodlawn, N.S., Can., June 2, 1890; s. Spurden Reid and Sarah Jane (Ogilvie) L.; S.B., Boston U., 1913, A.M., 1914, Ph.D., 1917; teaching fellow Harvard, 1914-16; m. Edna Baldwin, Oct. 2, 1918. Instr. biology Boston U., 1914-22, instr. exptl. physiology Sch. Medicine, 1919-21, asst. prof. physiology, 1921-30, asso. prof., 1930-40, asst. prof. biology Coll. Liberal Arts, 1922-27, prof. since 1927. Served as 1st lt. San. Corps, U.S. Army, 1918-19; capt. San. Res. Corps., 1925-30. Fellow A.A.A.S.; mem. Am. Physiol. Soc., Am. Soc. Zoologists, Am. Acad. Arts and Scis., Am. Assn. Anatomists, N.Y. Acad. Scis., Sigma Xi, Phi Beta Kappa, Beta Theta Pi. Mason. Author or co-author 48 research papers in field physiology. Co-producer sci. motion picture films on small blood vessel activity. Home: 49 Laurel St., Melrose, Mass. 02176. Office: 725 Commonwealth Av., Boston 15. Died June 22, 1960.

LUTZ, FRANK EUGENE, biologist; b. Bloomsburg, Pa., Sept. 15, 1879; s. Martin Peter and Anna Amelia (Brockway) L.; A.B., Haverford (Pa.) Coll., 1900; A.M., U. of Chicago, 1902, Ph.D., 1907; studied Univ. Coll., London, Eng., 1902; m. Martha Ellen Brobson, Dec. 30, 1904; children—Anna, Eleanor, Frank Brobson, Laura. Entomologist, Biol. Lab. of Brooklyn Inst., 1902; asst. in zool. dept., U. of Chicago, 1903; resident investigator, Sta. for Experimental Evolution (Carnegie Instn.), Cold Spring Harbor, 1904-09; asst. curator invertebrate zoology, 1909-16, asso. curator, 1916-21; curator of entomology since 1921, also editor of tech. papers, Am. Museum Natural History, and 1925-28 in charge of Station for the Study of Insects, Tuxedo, N.Y.; lecturer Columbia U., 1937. Fellow A.A.A.S., N.Y. Acad. Sciences, Entomol. Soc. America (pres., 1927); mem. Am. Soc. Zoologists, Sigma Xi, Phi Beta Kappa, etc. Baptist. Mason. Author: Field Book of Insects, 1917; A Lot of Insects, 1941. Contbr. numerous papers on variation, heredity, assortive mating, entomology, etc. Home: Ramsey, N.J. Died Nov. 27, 1943.

LYDECKER, F(REDERICK) A(CKERMAN), engring. exec.; b. Rochelle Park, N.J., Oct. 21, 1885; s. Henry Frederick and Letitia Berry (Ackerman) L.; M.E., Stevens Inst. Tech., 1907, Hon. E.D., 1947; m. Mary Catherine Carpenter, Jan. 27, 1912; children—Frederick Reimer, Robert Carpenter, Richard Ackerman, John Kent. Entered constrn. bus., N.Y.C., 1907; cadet engr., gas dept., Pub. Service Corp. of N.J., 1908, asst. supt., 1910-12, supt., 1913-17, div. engr., 1917-22, asst. gen. supt. distbn., 1922-26, gen. supt. distbn., 1926-44, asst. v.p., 1944-45, v.p. in charge gas operation Pub. Service Electric & Gas Co. since 1945; dir. Pub. Service Coordinated Transport. Sec. sectional com. on Code for Pressure Piping, A.S.M.E. sponsor for Am. Standards Assn., 1927-46. Trustee Stevens Inst. Tech., 1936-39; trustee Glen Ridge Community Chest, 1945-49 (pres. 1946-47), mem. Borough Council since 1950. Mem. Boy Scouts Am. (trustee endowment fund Eagle Rock Council; dist. sec. Glen Ridge dist. 1929, pres. 1930-32), Am. Gas Assn. (chmn. tech. coms.; dir. 1948-51), N.J. Gas Assn. (pres. 1934), Soc. Gas Lighting (pres. 1945-46), Alumni Assn. Stevens Inst. Tech. (pres. 1935), Holland Soc. N.Y. (v.p. 1943-46). P.E. Ch. Mason. Clubs: Stevens Metropolitan (pres. 1939-41) (N.Y.C.); Essex (Newark); Rock Spring (West Orange). Home: 48 Lincoln St., Glen Ridge, N.J. Office: 80 Park Pl., Newark 1. Died May 14, 1961; buried Mount Hebron Cemetery, Montclair, N.J.

LYFORD, OLIVER SMITH, exec. and cons. engr.; b. Cleve., Mar. 21, 1870; s. Oliver Smith and Lavinia A. (Norris) L.; Ph.B., Yale, 1890; post-grad. Cornell U.; m. Frances Lyman Meigs, Jan. 1896; children—Mrs. Margaret Sheldon, Olive Meigs. Chief engr. Westinghouse Electric & Mfg. Co., 1897-99, v.p., gen. mgr. Siemens & Halske Electric Co., 1899-1901; cons. engr., mng. engr. Westinghouse, Church, Kerr & Co., 1902-12; pvt. practice, 1913-16; v.p. Finance & Trading Corp., 1919-22; pvt. practice, 1923; v.p., gen. mgr. Lawrence Investing Co., and Lawrence Park Heat, Light & Power Co., 1924-26; v.p. Brooklands, Inc., 1927—; v.p. Santa Clara Lumber Co. Served from maj. to lt. col. Ordnance Dept., U.S. Army, 1917-18. Fellow Am. Inst. E.E.; mem. Berzelius soc. (Yale), Kappa Alpha (Cornell). Republican. Presbyn. Club: Yale (N.Y.C.). Home: 54 Dana Pl., Englewood, N.J. Died Mar. 5, 1952; buried Delhi, N.Y.

LYLE, HENRY HAMILTON MOORE, surgeon; b. Connor, Ulster, Ireland, Nov. 15, 1874; s. Samuel (D.D.) and Elizabeth (Orr) L.; med. prep. edn., Cornell U., 1896; M.D., Coll Physicians and Surgeons (Columbia), 1900; m. Clara Schlemmer, May 17, 1910 (died Jan. 8, 1916); m. 2d, Jessie Benson Pickens, Apr. 16, 1919. Practiced at N.Y. City since 1900; prof. clin. surgery, Coll. Phys. and Surg., 1913-19; asst. prof. surgery, Cornell University Medical Sch., 1919-31, prof. of clinical surgery since 1931; attending surgeon at St. Luke's Hosp.; dir. of cancer service, New York Skin and Cancer Hosp.; attending surgical specialist U.S. Veterans' Bureau, Dist. No. 2; cons. surgeon to Elizabeth A. Horton Memorial Hosp., Middletown, N.Y., N.Y. State Reconstruction Home, W. Haverstraw, Cornwall (N.Y.) Hospital; consultant St. Luke's Hospital, Newburgh, N.Y. Médecin chef Am. Ambulance Hosp. B, Juilly Seine et Marne, France, 1915; chirurgien chef Ambulance Longueil Annel, Oise, France, 1916; commd. maj. O.R.C., U.S. Army, Apr. 26, 1917; active duty, May 30, 1917; organized and took abroad Evacuation Hosp. No. 2; lt. col., June 6, 1918; apptd. cons. surgeon 77th div., Sept. 1918; apptd. to field staff of the chief surgeon 1st Army, in charge of western sect. of the evacuation of wounded in the St. Mihiel drive; apptd., Sept. 30, 1918, dir. of ambulances and evacuation of the wounded for the 1st Army, Meuse-Argonne offensive; chief consultant surgeon 1st Army; mem. Gas Warfare Bd., A.E.F.; col. Oct. 23, 1918. Engagements—Oise-Aisne, Aisne-Marne, St. Mihiel, Meuse-Argonne, defensive sector. Decorated D.S.M. (U.S.); British War Medal and British Victory Medal, N.Y. State Service Medal, Liberty Service Medal of Nat. Inst. Social Services; awarded hon.

testimonial for life saving by Royal Canadian Humane Assn., 1895. Fellow Am. Coll. Surgeons; mem. Am. Surg. Assn., New York Surg. Soc., Am. Soc. Clin. Surgeons, Internat. Surg. Soc. of Brussels, A.M.A., Acad. Medicine (New York), N.Y. State Soc. of Indsl. Medicine, Nat. Inst. Social Sciences, Am. Legion, Military Order of the World War, Kappa Alpha. Republican. Presbyterian. Clubs: Eclat, Charaka Club. Home: 1217 Park Av. Office: 33 E. 68th St., New York, N.Y. Died Mar. 11, 1947.

LYMAN, BENJAMIN SMITH, geologist, mining engr.; b. Northampton, Mass., Dec. 11, 1835; s. Samuel Fowler and Almira (Smith) L.; A.B., Harvard, 1855; École des Mines, Paris, 1859-61; Royal Acad. Mines, Frieberg, 1861-62; unmarried. Asst. geologist of Ia., 1858; spent yrs. in pvt. geol. work; mining engr. under public works dept., govt. of India, 1870 (surveying oil fields); chief geologist and mining engr., Japanese Govt., 1873-79; asst. geologist of Pa., 1887-95. Has traveled over U.S., British America, Europe, India, China, Japan, Philippines, etc., making geol. researches; common councilman, Northampton, Mass., 1885-86; resided in Phila., 1856-72, and since 1887. Patented a solar transit, 1871. Home: Philadelphia, Pa. Died Aug. 30, 1920.

LYMAN, CHESTER SMITH, astronomer, physicist; b. Manchester, Conn., Jan. 13, 1814; s. Chester and Mary (Smith) L.; grad. Yale, 1837; attended Union Theol. Sem., 1839-40; m. Delia Williams Wood, June 20, 1850. Pastor, 1st Ch. (Congregational), New Britain, Conn., 1843-45; traveled, pursued varied occupations including surveyor in Hawaii, gold digger in Cal., 1845-50; helped prepare definitions for Webster's Dictionary, 1850-circa 1855; prof. indsl. mechanics and physics Sheffield Scientific Sch. of Yale, 1859-71, prof. astronomy and physics, 1871-84, prof. astronomy, 1884-90; made 1st satisfactory observation of planet Venus, 1866; v.p. A.A.A.S., 1874; pres. Conn. Acad. Arts and Science, 1859-77; inventions include: 1st combined transit and zenith instrument for determining latitude; an apparatus for demonstrating wave motion; improvements in clock pendulums. Died New Haven, Conn., Jan. 29, 1890.

LYMAN, GEORGE DUNLAP, pediatrician, author; b. Virginia City, Nev., Dec. 12, 1882; s. Dean Briggs and Anna Louise (Dunlap) L.; A.B., Stanford U., 1905; M.D., Coll. Phys. and Surg. Columbia, 1909; post-grad. univs. of Munich, Vienna and Berlin, 1912-14; m. Dorothy Quincy VanSicklen, Dec. 28, 1911; children—Dorothy Quincy (Mrs. J. Wm. Beatty), Elizabeth Ann (Mrs. David Potter). Intern Bellevue Hosp., N.Y.C., 1910-11; practiced in San Francisco, 1914—; mem. faculty of medicine, Stanford, now emeritus; mem. vis. staff Stanford U. Hosp. and St. Mary's Hosp. Fellow Am. Acad. of Pediatrics; mem. Am., Cal. med. assns., Cal. Acad. Medicine, Soc. Am. Historians, Sigma Alpha Epsilon, Omega Club (Coll. Physicians and Surgeons). Republican. Clubs: Bohemian, P.E.N. (San Francisco). Author: Care and Feeding of the Infant, 1915, 2d edit., 1922; John Marsh, Pioneer, 1930; Wierzbicki—The Book and the Doctor, 1933; Saga of the Comstock Lode, 1934 (awarded Commonwealth Club gold medal, 1934); Ralston's Ring, 1937; A Friend to Man, 1938. Owner of over 6,000 vols. of Californiana; mem. Cal. adv. com. of Stanford U. Press. Home: 3673 Jackson St. Office: 384 Post St., San Francisco. Died July 26, 1949; buried Mountain View Cemetery, Oakland, Cal.

LYMAN, GEORGE RICHARD, plant pathologist; b. Lee Center, Ill., Dec. 1, 1871; s. George Alexander and Mary Eliza (Jones) L.; A.B., Beloit (Wis.) Coll., 1894; A.B., Harvard, 1897, A.M., 1899, Ph.D., 1906; m. Frances E. Badger, June 23, 1903; 1 dau., Mavis Katherine. Instr. botany, 1901-04, asst. prof., 1904-15, Dartmouth; pathologist in charge plant disease survey, U.S. Dept. Agr., 1916-23; dean W.Va. Coll. of Agr., 1923—. Mem. war emergency bd. Am. Plant Pathologists, 1918, and chmn. advisory bd. of same, 1919-21; mem. Nat. Research Council, 1919-22. Republican. Conglist. Home: Morgantown, W.Va. Died June 7, 1926.

LYMAN, HARRY WEBSTER, otolaryngolist; b. Cedar Rapids, Ia., Mar. 10, 1873; s. James Edward and Martha Elona (Day) L.; M.D., St. Louis Coll. of Physicians and Surgeons, 1895; m. Sarah Elizabeth Long, Dec. 12, 1900; children—Elizabeth Mary (Mrs. Allan E. Clark), Edward Harry. Interne St. Louis Woman's Hosp., 1895-96; gen. practice of medicine, St. Louis, Mo., 1896-1900, specialist in otolaryngology since 1900; demonstrator and prof. of anatomy, St. Louis Coll. of Phys. and Surgs., 1900-06; volunteer asst. dept. of otolaryngology, Washington Univ., Sch. of Medicine, St. Louis, 1910-14, asst. in otolaryngology, 1914-17, instr., 1917-21, asso. clin. otolaryngology, 1921-24, asso., 1924-26, asst. prof., 1926-34, asso. prof., 1934-40, prof., 1940-43, prof. emeritus since 1943. Consultant in otolaryngology U.S. Vets. Hosp., U.S. Marine Hosp. Served as capt. med. corps, U.S. Army, 1917-19. Mem. A.M.A., Am. Coll. Surgs., Am. Acad. Ophthalmology and Otolaryngology (vice pres.), Am. Laryngological, Rhinological and Otolaryngological Soc. (pres. 1946-47), Am. Laryngological Assn., Am. Otol. Soc., Southern and Mo. State Med. Assns., St. Louis Med. Soc., Phi Beta Pi. Conglist. Mason. Contbr. about 40 articles on otolaryngology to various med. jours. Home: 6224 Washington Av., St. Louis 5 MO Office: 308 N. Sixth St., St Louis 1 MO

LYMAN, JAMES, engineer; b. Middlefield, Conn., Sept. 1, 1862; s. David and Catherine (Hart) L.; Ph.B., Yale, 1883; M.E. and M.M.E., Cornell U., 1895; m. Anna J. Bridgman, June 6, 1891; 1 son, Oliver B. Engr. with The Edison Co., 1883-86, Metropolitan Mfg. Co., 1886-93, General Electric Co., Schenectady, N.Y., 1895-99; engr., western dist. Gen. Electric Co., Chicago, 1902-11; mem. Sargent & Lundy, Inc., mech. and elec. engrs., Chicago, 1911—, v.p., 1920—. Fellow Am. Inst. E.E. (life). Home: Evanston, Ill. Died Mar. 29, 1934.

LYMAN, RICHARD ROSWELL, cons. civil engr.; b. Fillmore, Utah, Nov. 23, 1870; s. Francis Marion and Clara Caroline (Callister) L.; certificate Brigham Young U., 1891; B.S. in C.E., U. Mich., 1895; M.C.E., Cornell U., 1903 (Sigma Xi, 1904), Ph.D., 1905; m. Amy Brown, Sept. 9, 1896; children—Wendell Brown (dec.), Margaret (Mrs. Alexander Schreiner). With U. Utah as prof. civ. engring., 1896-1922; city engr., Provo, 1895; has served as chief engr. Utah County Power & Light Co., Melville Irrigation Co., Deseret Irrigation Co., Delta Land & Water Co., etc.; pres. Lyman-Callister Co., Burtner Real Estate & Investment Co., Ensign Amusement Co., Giant Racer Co., Lyman Motor Co.; v.p. Utah Rd. Commn., 1909-18, Intermountain Life Ins. Co., Lyman-Oberg Motor Co.; dir. Cal.-Western States Life Ins. Co., Pleasant Green Water Co., Heber J. Grant Co., Western States Securities Corp.; cons. engr. Met. Water Dist. So. Cal. since 1929; vice chmn. Utah Water Storage Commn. 1921-37; mem. Utah-Colo. River Commn., 1929. Mem. Engr. Bd. Rev., San. Dist. Chgo., 1924-29, and Columbia Basin Bd. Engrs. for U.S. Reclamation Service, 1924-25. Pres. European Mission for Latter-day Saints Ch., hdqrs. London, 1936-38. Mem. Council of 12, 1918-43. Mem. Am. Soc. C.E., (Croes gold medal, 1915), Soc. for Promotion Engring. Edn., Utah Soc. Profl. Engrs., Am. Waterworks Assn., Am. Assn. Engrs., Utah Acad. Sci., Cornell Soc. C.E., Sons Utah Pioneers, N.E.A., Theta Tau, Phi Kappa Phi, Tau Beta Pi. Deviser house and st. numbering method which makes it easy to find any location without help. Address: 1084 3d Av., Salt Lake City 3. Died Dec. 31, 1963.

LYMAN, RUFUS ASHLEY, educator; b. Table Rock, Neb., Apr. 17, 1875; s. William Graves and Sophie Lee (Allen) L.; A.B., U. Neb., 1897, A.M., 1899, M.D., 1903; m. Carrie Day, July 1, 1899; children—Esther, Caroline (dec.), Elizabeth, Louise, Rufus Ashley, Edwin Day. Prof. pharmacology Coll. of Medicine, U. Neb., 1904-08, organizer, 1908, and dean Coll. of Pharmacy, 1908-46, also dir. dept. of student health 1919-45, became dean emeritus 1946; dir. Sch. of Pharmacy, U. Ariz., 1947, dean Coll. of Pharmacy, 1944—. Mem. com. to formulate program for Pharmacy Unit of S.A.T.C., 1918. Fellow A.A.A.S.; mem. Am., Neb. med. assns., Am., (hon. pres. 1952-53), Neb. pharm. assns., Am. Assn. Colls. of Pharmacy, Am. Assn. Sch. Physicians, Am. Pub. Health Assn., Am. Student Health Assn., United Provinces Pharm. Assn. of India (hon.), Am. Council on Edn. (vice chmn. 1929-30; also member Commonwealth Fund Com., making a study of pharm. edn. and practice for natl. application), Am. Inst. History of Pharmacy (v.p. 1941), Sigma Xi, Phi Delta Chi, Omega Beta Pi, Delta Sigma Phi, Rho Chi. Republican. Presbyn. Remington Medalist for distinguished pharmaceutical service, 1947. Founder and editor Am. Jour. Pharm. Edn., 1937—. Home: 1649 S. 21st St., Lincoln 2, Neb. Died Oct. 12, 1957.

LYMAN, THEODORE, zoologist, congressman; b. Waltham, Mass., Aug. 23, 1833; s. Theodore and Mary Elizabeth (Henderson) L.; A.B., Harvard, 1855, B.S., 1858; m. Elizabeth Russell, Nov. 28, 1856. Studied zoology under Louis Agassiz at Lawrence Scientific Sch., joined Agassiz' scientific expdn. in Fla., 1855-58; elected as original mem. Museum of Comparative Zoology at Harvard, 1859; collected scientific data on the ophiuridae in Europe, 1861-63; served under Gen. Meade in Civil War, 1863-65; chmn. Fisheries Commn. of Mass., 1866; pres. Am. Fish Cultural Assn., 1884; overseer Harvard, 1868; mem. Am. Acad. Arts and Scis., mem. U.S. Ho. of Reps. from Mass., 48th Congress, 1883-85. Died Nahant, Mass., Sept. 9, 1897; buried Mt. Auburn Cemetery, Cambridge, Mass.

LYMAN, THEODORE, physicist; b. Boston, Nov. 23, 1874; s. Theodore and Elizabeth (Russell) L.; A.B., Harvard, 1897, Ph.D., 1900. Instr. physics Harvard, 1902-07, asst. prof., 1907-17, dir. Jefferson Physical Lab., 1910-47, prof. physics, 1917-26, Hollis prof. emeritus, 1926—. Capt. Aviation Sect., Signal R.C., 1917; maj. Engr. Corps, U.S. Army, 1918; service with AEF, flash and sound ranging, 1917-19. Recipient Rumford medal Am. Acad. Arts and Scis.; Elliott Cresson medal Am. Philos. Soc.; Frederick Ives medal Optical Soc. Am. Fellow Am. Acad. Arts and Sciences (past pres.), A.A.A.S., Royal Geog. Soc.; mem. Nat. Acad. Sciences, Am. Phys. Soc. (past pres.). Unitarian. Club: Somerset (Boston). Discoverer Lyman series. Home: 105 Heath St., Brookline, Mass. Died Oct. 11, 1954.

LYNCH, FRANK W(ORTHINGTON), gynecologist; b. Cleveland, O., Nov. 5, 1871; s. Frank W. and Rebecca (Nevin) L.; A.B., Western Reserve U., 1895; M.D., Johns Hopkins, 1899; grad. study Vienna and Munich, 1910, 12; m. Rowena Tyng Higginson, Apr. 20, 1904; 1 son, Frank W. Asst. instr. and asso. in obstetrics, Johns Hopkins U. Med. Sch., 1900-04; instr. in obstetrics, Rush Med. Coll. (U. of Chicago), 1905-09, asst. prof. obstetrics and gynecology, 1909-15; prof. obstetrics and gynecology, University of California, 1915-42, professor emeritus since 1942; member of editorial board of Surgery, Gynecology and Obstetrics (abstract dept.), Am. Jour. Obstetrics and Gynecology, Western Jour. of Surgery. Mem. advisory bd. of com. on prenatal and maternal care, White House Conf.; mem. Am. Bd. Obstetrics and Gynecology. Honor guest of Pan-Pacific Surgical Congress, 1936. Fellow Am. Coll. Surgeons (bd. govs.; vice-pres. 1937-38); mem. Am. Med. Assn. (chmn. sect. on obstetrics and gynecology 1924), Am. Gynecol. Soc. (1st v.p. 1927; pres. 1933), Calif. State Med. Assn. (chmn. sect. on obstetrics and gynecology 1922), San Francisco Med. Soc., San Francisco Obstetrical and Gynecol. Soc. (pres. 1930), San Francisco Patho. Soc., Pacific Coast Surgical Soc., Pacific Coast Obstet. and Gynecol. Soc. (pres. 1931), Alpha Delta Phi, Nu Sigma Nu; mem. obstet. advisory com. Children's Bur. U.S. Dept. of Labor; mem. advisory bd. Nat. Com. on Maternal Health; hon. mem. Seattle Surg. Soc., Los Angeles Obstet. Soc., Central Assn. Obstetricians and Gynecologists; mem. exec. com. Gynecology and Obstetrics of Pan-Am. Med. Assn. Served as editor, v.p. and pres. Chicago Gynecol. Soc., 1908-14. Republican. Episcopalian. Clubs: Bohemian, San Francisco Golf. Co-Author: Pelvic Neoplasms (with A. F. Maxwell), 1922. Contbr. chapters to Am. Practice of Surgery, 1911; Oxford Surgery, 1921; Nelson's Looseleaf Surgery, 1928; Davis' Obstetrics and Gynecology, 1933; Curtis' Obstetrics and Gynecology, 1933; The Treatment of Cancer, 1937. Also contbr. on obstet. and gynecol. subjects to Am. and German med. jours. Home: 1998 Vallejo St. Office: 384 Post St., San Francisco. Died Jan. 12, 1945.

LYNCH, JEROME MORLEY, surgeon; b. Ireland; s. Daniel and Jane (Browne) L.; student Queen's Coll., Cork, Edinburgh U.; M.D., Rush Medical Coll., Chgo., 1895; m. Harriet Louise Husted; Jan. 1, 1901. Chief surgeon St. Bartholomew's Hosp., N.Y.C.; prof. proctology N.Y. Polyclinic Hosp.; cons. surgeon Doctor's Hosp., N.Y.C. Served as lt. comdr. USN, 1917; surgeon at Naval Hosp., Bklyn., and at sea, U.S.S. America. Diplomate Am. Bd. Surgery. Fellow A.C.S., Royal Society of Medicine (honorary); member A.M.A., New England Proctologic Soc., Am. Gastoenterological Assn., Am. Proctologic Soc. (pres. 1917-18), Mil. Order Fgn. Wars. Author: Diseases of Rectum and Colon, 1914; Tumors of Colon and Rectum, 1925; Know Your Patient, 1943. Contbr. to Johnson's Surgery, Woods Hand Book of the Medical Sciences, Tice's Practice of Medicine. Clubs: Union (N.Y.C.); Author's (London, Eng.). Home: Carmel, Cal. Died Apr. 22, 1951.

LYNDE, CARLETON JOHN, physics; b. Mitchell, Ont., Can., Sept. 1, 1872; s. Frederich George and Isabella (Aiken) L.; B.A., U. of Toronto, 1895; Ph.D., U. of Chicago, 1905; m. Helen Eldred Storke, June 21, 1905 (died Feb. 11, 1940); 1 son, Carleton John; m. 2d, Katharine Koon Truxell, Mar. 5, 1941. Science teacher, high sch., Auburn, N.Y., 1896-99; physics teacher, University High Sch., Chicago, 1899-1905; prof. physics, Washington and Jefferson Coll., 1906-07, Macdonald Coll., Ste. Anne de Bellevue, P.Q., Can., 1907-24; prof. physics, Teachers College (Columbia), 1924-38, prof. emeritus since 1938. Mem. Am. Phys. Soc. A.A.A.S., Am. Soc. Illuminating Engrs., Zeta Psi, Sigma Xi. Democrat. Club: Faculty. Author: Home Waterworks, 1912; Physics of the Household, 1919; Hydraulic and Pneumatic Engineering, 1920; Light Experiments, 1920; Glass Blowing, 1921; Everyday Physics, 1930; A Laboratory Course in Everyday Physics, 1931; Science Experiences with Home Equipment, 1937; Science Experience with Inexpensive Equipment, 1939; Science Experiences with Ten Cent Store Equipment, 1941. Home: 114 Morningside Drive New York NY

LYNDON, LAMAR, consulting engr.; b. Newman, Ga., Aug. 12, 1871; s. Edward Smith and Anna (Brown) L.; B.Engring., U. of Ga., 1893; spl. work, Stevens Inst. Tech.; Cornell, 1892-94; m. Sara Elizabeth Rucker, June 27, 1895; children—Elizabeth Rucker (dec.), Moselle (Mrs. Hobert Haviland); m. 2d, Grace Hudson, Apr. 1927. Engaged in engring. Installations; operated gas and electric systems, Athens, Ga.; went to Yokohama, Japan, 1896, as engr. Am. Trading Co.; then to Kobe to cover Shanghai, Korean and Japan offices of the co. and to Hongkong, Singapore, Java, Burmah, India on engring. work, and Egypt, thence to London for Am. Trading Co.; designed mech. and elec. equipment, Kobe Pier Co., steam pumping equipment of Tandjong Pagar Dock Co. (Singapore), steam power plant for Internat. Cotton Spinning Co. (Shanghai), traction system (Calcutta), equipment for Imperial Chinese Tech. Schools (Tientsin), etc.; returned from London to N.Y. City as chief engr., Am. Trading Co., 1898; joined Electric Vehicle Co., Baltimore, 1900; practiced in New York, 1902-07; mem. Duncan (Dr. Louis) & Lyndon,

1907-10; associated with Gen. Arsene Perrilliat of New Orleans, offices in New York and New Orleans, 1916-20; mem. Bd. of Spl. Problems, U.S. Naval Consulting Bd., World War; lived in Paris, 1920-22; resided in Los Angeles, 1929—. Made engring. investigations, Santo Domingo, 1903; 1st power survey, Grand Canyon of Ariz., 1908; designed and built dam and power plant on Colorado River, at Austin, Tex., 1911-15; referee for Thomas A. Edison in regard to disaster of U.S. Submarine E-2, 1916, and cons. engr. for Edison, 1916-19; made pub. utility and economic municipal investigations for Harrisburg (Pa.), Lynchburg (Va.), Atlanta (Ga.), Houston (Tex.), etc. Fellow Am. Inst. E.E. Democrat. Author: Storage Battery Engineering (transl. in French), 1903; Hydro-Electric Power (2 vols.), 1916; Rate-Making for Public Utilities, 1923. Has made about 40 inventions in electrical, hydraulic and structural arts; developed new formulae, now standard, for computing engring. problems, including backwater curve, thickness of gravity dams, windings for variable voltage dynamos, electrolyte density in storage cells, etc. Died May 4, 1940.

LYON, DORSEY ALFRED, metallurgist; b. Bureau County, Ill., July 17, 1871; s. Walter S. and Sarah S. (McKune) L.; A.B., Stanford, 1898; A.M., Harvard, 1902; D.Sc., U. of Utah, 1922; unmarried. Instr. geology and mining, 1898-99, asst. prof. mining and metallurgy, 1899-1900, prof., 1901, U. of Wash.; with U.S. Mining and Smelting Co., Midvale, Utah, 1902-03; asst. prof. metallurgy, Stanford, 1903-07; mgr. Noble Electric Steel Co., Heroult, Calif., 1907-11; cons. metallurgist, Electro-Metals Co., London, Eng., 1911-13; metallurgist, 1913-19; chief metallurgist, July 1919-July 1927, supervisor of stations, July 1917-July 1927, asst. director, Mar. 1923-July 1926, supervising engr. Intermountain Station, 1927-31, all of U.S. Bureau of Mines; dir. Utah Engineering Expt. Station, 1931-35, retired. Fellow A.A.A.S., Soc. for Promotion of Engring. Edn.; past mem. Am. Chem. Soc., Am. Mining Congress, Electrochemical Soc., Am. Inst. Mining Engrs., Delta Upsilon, Sigma Xi, Tau Beta Pi, Theta Tau, Phi Kappa Phi. Club: Rotary (Palo Alto); Commonwealth of California, Rio del Mar Country. Elk. Episcopalian. A pioneer in electric furnace work in U.S.A. Co-Author of several bulls. of U.S. Bur. Mines, dealing with use of electric furnace in metall. work; contbr. to tech. publs. on metall. subjects. Home: 540 Harvard St., Palo Alto, Calif. Died Oct. 16, 1945.

LYON, ELIAS POTTER, physiologist; b. Cambria, Mich., Oct. 20, 1867; s. Nelson J. and Mary (Hebard) L.; B.S., Hillsdale Coll., 1891, A.B., 1892; Ph.D., Univ. of Chicago, 1897; hon. M.D., St. Louis Univ., 1910, LL.D., 1920; hon. D.Sc., Hillsdale College, Mich., 1924, Univ. of Southern Calif., 1930; m. Nellie P. Eastman, Sept. 1, 1897. Instr. Hillsdale Coll., 1890-92, Harvard Sch., Chicago, 1892-96, Bradley Poly. Inst., Peoria, Ill., 1897-1900; asst. prof., Rush Med. Coll., 1900-04; asst. prof. physiology and asst. dean, U. of Chicago, 1901-04; prof. physiology, 1904-13, dean, 1907-13, St. Louis U. Med. Sch.; prof. physiology and dean, U. of Minn. Med. Sch., 1913—. Biologist, Cook Greenland expdn., 1894; investigator U.S. Bur. of Fisheries, 1908-11; investigator, Marine Biol. Laboratory various summers; trustee of same, 1921; trustee Hillsdale Coll., 1925. Lt. col., U.S.A. Reserve, Sanitary Corps, retired. Home: Minneapolis, Minn. Died May 4, 1937.

LYON, JAMES ALEXANDER, cardiologist; b. Broome County, N.Y., Feb. 28, 1882; s. Henry and Catherine (Murray) L.; student pub. schools and pvt. tutoring, Ohio U., Syracuse U.; M.D., Md. Med. Coll., Balt., 1906; grad. study Harvard Med. Sch., Univ. Coll. Hosp. and Nat. Hosp. for Disease of Heart (London), U. Vienna; m. Irene Elizabeth Moore (dec.); 1 dau., Elizabeth Moore. Intern Bay View Hosp., Balt., 1906-07; asst. physician Loomis Sanatorium, Liberty, N.Y., 1907-09; asst. supt. and sr. physician Mass State Hosp. for Tb, Rutland, Mass., 1909-16; prof. clin. cardiology Georgetown U, 1929-40; cardiologist and mem. cardiac com. The Doctors Hosp., Inc.; cons. cardiologist and mem. med. bd. Children's Hosp.; cons. cardiologist Homeopathic, and Columbia hosps.; asst. physician Out-Patient Dept. Johns Hopkins' Hospital, 1925-26; attending cardiologist and chief of cardiac clinic, Emergency Hosp., 1929-40; post grad. study, Nat. Hosp. for Diseases of Heart, London, 1923, U. of Vienna, 1924. Mass. Gen. Hosp., Boston, 1926. Mem. bd. dirs. Washington Loan and Trust Co., Inter-Am. Horse Show Assn., Inc., Community Chest of D.C.; mem. medical advisory board Civilian Defense Met. Area, D.C.; mem. nat. med. council U.S. Veterans Bureau. Served from lt. to maj. M.C., U.S. Army, 1916-25; Mexican border service, 1916-17; joined AEF, 51st brig., 26th Div., 1917; organized and commanded Camp Hosp. No. 4, Neufchateau, France, 1917, Evacuation Hosp. No. 19, Soisson Sector (French), 1918; grad. U.S. Army Sanitary Sch., Longue, France, 1918; bn. surgeon 104th U.S. Inf., 26th Div., 1918-19; asst. chief med. service U.S. Base Hosp., Camp Devens, Mass.; chief med. service Base Hosp., Camp Shelby, Miss., and Gen. Hosp. No. 8, Otisville, N.Y., 1919; asst. to attending surg. U.S.A. Dispensary, Washington, 1919-23; detached service Med. Dept., U.S. Army, London and Vienna, 1923-24; post surgeon, Fort Wayne, Detroit, Mich., 1924-25; resigned 1925, to enter pvt. practice in Washington. As bn. surgeon 104th U.S. Inf., participated in battles, Champagne-Marne, Aisne-Marne, Meuse-Argonne, St. Mihiel, Ile de France, Lorraine, defense of Toul; citations: French Army Corps, Army of the East (Verdun), and in gen. orders Nos. 28 and 74, 26th Div., U.S. Army (Aisne-Marne, Meuse-Argonne). Decorated Croix de Guerre with Gold Star, Grande Guerre, Victoire Apparaint Chateau Thiery, Verdun; Abdon Caldern (Ecuador); Purple Heart, Silver Star, Victor Medal with 5 campaign clasps, Mexican Border Service Campaign medal (U.S.); Mil. Order of Carabao (U.S.). Diplomate Am. Bd. Internal. Medicine. Fellow A.M.A., A.A.A.S., N.Y. Acad. Medicine, Am. Coll. Physicians (life mem.); mem. D.C. Med. Soc., So. Med. Soc., Am. Therapeutic Society (ex-pres.), Am., Washington (ex-pres. and sec.) heart assns., Assn. Mil. Surgeons U.S., Mil Order Fgn. Wars (surgeon gen. of Nat. Commandery; past comdr. Washington Commandery), Pan-Am. Med. Assn. (trustee; mem. regional adminstrs.; ex-pres. Washington chapter). Internat. Med. Soc. (ex-treas.; mem. bd. dirs.), Am. Inst. Banking, Washington Med. and Surg. Soc., Mil. Order of Purple Heart, Am. Assn. History Medicine, Mil. Order World War (life mem.), Mil. Order of Carabao, Nat. Sojurner's, Heroes of '76, Am. Legion, George Washington Post No. 1, Soc. Am. Legion Founders (Paris, 1918, life member nat. adv. council), 104th U.S.A. Inf. Regt. Vets. Assn.; ex-mem. Gen. Staff, Nat. Commandery, ex-comdr. D.C. Commandery), Nat. Geog. Soc., The Hippocrates-Galen Society of Washington, Ohio U. Alumni Assn., (D.C. chapter), Syracuse U. Alumni Assn. (D.C. Chapter), English-Speaking Union (dir., mem. exec. com. D.C. chapter), Phi Delta Theta (nat.; ex-pres. D.C. alumni club), Phi Chi. Clubs: Army and Navy (ex-mem. bd. govs.), Metropolitan, Chevy Chase, Woodmont (Md.) Rod and Gun (mem. bd. govs.). Home: Glenview Farm, Baltimore Blvd., Rockville, Md.; also 1028 Connecticut Av., Washington, D.C. Office: Washington Med. Bldg., 1801 I St., N.W., Washington. Died Aug. 4, 1955.

LYON, MARCUS WARD, JR., zoölogist, bacteriologist and pathologist; b. Rock Island Arsenal, Ill., Feb. 5, 1875; s. Marcus Ward and Lydia Anna (Post) L.; Ph.B., Brown U., 1897; N.C. Med. Coll., 1897-98; M.S., 1900, M.D., 1902, Ph.D., 1913, George Washington U.; m. Martha Maria Brewer (M.S., M.D.), Dec. 31, 1902; 1 dau., Charlotte. Instr. bacteriology, N.C. Med. Coll., 1897-98; aid, later asst. curator, Div. of Mammals, U.S. Nat. Museum, Washington, 1898-1912; asst. prof. physiology, 1903-04, 1907-09, prof. bacteriology, 1909-15, Howard U., Washington; prof. bacteriology and pathology, 1915-17, prof. veterinary zoölogy and parasitology, 1917-18, George Washington U. Pathologist, Walter Reed Gen. Hosp., 1917-19; maj. Med. R.C., Sept. 1919. Fellow A.M.A., A.A.A.S.; mem. St. Joseph County Med. Soc. (past pres.), Soc. Am. Bacteriologists, Washington Acad. Sciences, Biol. Soc. Washington (sec. 1915-19), Am. Chem. Soc., Am. Soc. Parasitologists, Ecol. Society America, Am. Soc. Mammalogists (pres. 1931-33), Washington Biologists' Field Club, Am. Assn. Pathologists and Bacteriologists, Ind. Acad. Science (treas. 1928-32, pres. 1933), Am. Ornithologists, Union, Am. Soc. Clin. Pathologists, Indiana Hist. Soc., Wildlife Soc., Am. Geog. Soc., N.Y. Acad. Science, Am. Soc. Tropical Medicine, Phi Beta Kappa, Sigma Xi, Delta Tau Delta. Agnostic. Clubs: University (past pres.), Round Table, Cosmos (Washington). Author: Mammals of Indiana; also 160 papers on biol. and med. subjects. Home: 214 Laporte Av., South Bend, Ind. Died May 19, 1942.

LYON, T(HOMAS) LYTTLETON, agronomist; b. Pittsburgh, Pa., Feb. 17, 1869; s. James B. and Anna M. (Lyon) L.; B.S.A., Cornell, 1891, Ph.D., 1904; studied agrl. chemistry, U. of Göttingen, 1893-94; m. Bertha L. Clark, 1899; children—John Lyttleton, George Clark. Instr. chemistry, 1891-95, prof. agr., 1895-1906, U. of Neb.; asso. dir. Nebr. Agrl. Experiment Sta., 1899-1906; prof. agronomy, Cornell U., 1906-37, prof. emeritus, 1937—. Potts medal, Franklin Inst., 1911; Chilean nitrate soda research award. Author: Soils and Fertilizers; Principles of Soil Management (with E. O. Fippin); Soils, Their Properties and Management (with E. O. Fippin and H. O. Buckman); Nature and Properties of Soils (with H. O. Buckman). Home: Ithaca, N.Y. Died Oct. 7, 1938.

LYONS, ALBERT BROWN, chemist; b. Waimea, Hawaii, Apr. 1, 1841; s. Rev. Lorenzo and Lucia Garratt (Smith) L.; desc. William Lyon, Roxbury, Mass., 1635; spent early life at a remote mission sta. in H.I.; ed. at home, and, 1857-63, at Oahu Coll.; A.B., Williams, 1865; M.D., U. of Mich., 1868; m. Edith M., d. Rev. Zachary Eddy, of Detroit, Apr. 25, 1878; children—Lucia Eddy, Albert Eddy. Prof. chemistry, Detroit Med. Coll., 1868-80; consulting chemist for Parke, Davis & Co., Detroit, 1881-86; 1st editor Pharmaceutical Era, 1887-88; head of Science Dept. Oahu Coll., also govt. chemist for Hawaii, 1888-95; chemist, 1897—, Nelson, Baker & Co., Detroit. Mem. Com. of Revision of U.S. Pharmacopoeia, 1900-20. Author: Manual of Pharmaceutical Assaying, 1887; Practical Assaying of Drugs and Galenicals, 1899; Plant Names, Scientific and Popular, 1900, enlarged edit., 1907; The Lyon Families of New England, 1905, 1907, 1908; Standardization by Chemical Assay of Organic Drugs, 1920. Home: Detroit, Mich. Died Apr. 13, 1926.

LYONS, CHAMP, surgeon; b. Lancaster, Pa., May 21, 1907; s. Joseph Henry and Margaret Olive (Houston) L.; A.B., U. Ala., 1927; M.D. cum laude, Harvard, 1931; m. Naomi Lois Currier, Oct. 3, 1934; children—Joseph Henry, Champ. Asst. in biology U. Ala., 1925-27; research fellow in physiology Harvard, 1928-30, NRC fellow in medicine, dept. bacteriology, 1933-34, Mosely traveling fellow London (Eng.) Hosp., 1936-37; surg. house officer Mass. Gen. Hosp., Boston, 1931-33, surg. resident, 1934-36, asso. surgeon, 1937-45; cons. surgeon Mass. Eye and Ear Infirmary, 1938-45, vis. surgeon Charity Hosp., New Orleans, 1945-50; mem. surg. staff Touro Infirmary, 1945-50, chief of surgery U. Hosp., Birmingham since 1950; asst. in surgery Harvard, 1934-36, instr. in surgery, 1937-39, asst. in bacteriology, also asso. in surgery, 1940-45; asso. prof. in surgery Tulane U., 1945-50; prof. of surgery U. Ala. Med. Coll. since 1950, also chmn. dept. of surgery. Sec., sub-com. on surg. infections NRC, 1940-44; responsible investigator Office of Sci. Research and Devel., 1941-43. Cons. to Sec. of War, Hemolytic Streptococcus Commn., 1941-44; nat. heart adv. council, cons. med. student research tng. program Dept. Health, Edn. and Welfare; civilian health and med. adv. council Asst. Sec. Def. Regent Nat. Library Medicine (chmn. 1958-59). Map., M.C., U.S. Army, cons. in wound mgmt., 1944-46; cons. in surgery Surg. Gen., U.S. Army, 1946-50. Responsible investigator U.S. Army (at Tulane), 1946-49, Am. Cancer Soc. (at Tulane), 1948-49. Awarded Legion of Merit and 2 citations, Diplomate Am. Bd. Thoracic Surgery, Am. Bd. Surgery. Fellow A.A.A.S., A.C.S. (bd. govs. 1960-61); mem. Soc. for Vascular Surgery, Internat. Cardiovascular Soc., Internat. Surg. Soc., A.M.A. (chmn. surg. 1959-60), NIH (study sect.), Am. Surg. Assn., Soc. Clin. Surg., Soc. U. Surgs., Am. Soc. for Surg. Trauma, Soc. U.S. Med. Consultants in World War II, Am. Assn. Bacteriologists, So. Surg. Assn., So. Society for Clin. Research, Southern Surgeons, Phi Beta Kappa, Sigma Xi, Alpha Omega Alpha, Phi Delta Theta, Phi Chi, Alpha Epsilon Delta (co-founder), Excelsior. Home: 2731 Hanover Circle, Birmingham 5. Office: 1919 7th Av. S., Birmingham 5. Died Oct. 24, 1965.

LYONS, ROBERT EDWARD, chemist; b. Bloomfield, Ind., Oct. 24, 1869; s. Mathew J. and Alice (Eveleigh) L.; A.B., Ind. U., 1889, A.M., 1890; student Fresenius' Labs., Wiesbaden, univs. of Heidelberg, Munich, and Berlin, and Joergensen's Inst. for Physiology of Fermentation, Copenhagen, 1892-95; Ph.D., U. of Heidelberg, 1894; m. Eleanor Joslyn, Mar. 23, 1898; 1 son, Robert Edward. Instr. of chemistry, Ind. U., 1889, asst. prof., 1890, asso. prof., 1891-92; pvt. asst. to Prof. Krafft, U. of Heidelberg, 1895; prof. chemistry and head dept., Ind. U., 1895-1938, prof. emeritus since 1938, dir. biol. station, 1900; chief chemist for Ind. State Dept. of Geology and Natural Resources, 1900-15; prof. chemistry, Central Coll. Physicians and Surgeons, Indianapolis, 1903-04; prof. chemistry, toxicology, and forensic medicine, and dir. chem. lab., Med. Coll. of Ind., Indianapolis, 1904-05; became chmn. dept. chemistry, Ind. U. Sch. of Medicine, Indianapolis, 1907, now retired; prof. in charge courses organic chemistry, U. of Wis., summer, 1907. Fellow A.A.A.S., Am. Inst. of Chemists, Ind. Acad. Science, Am. Chem. Soc. (mem. council, 1909, pres. Ind. Sect., 1908); mem. Deutsche Chemische Gesellschaft, Phi Delta Theta, Alpha Chi Sigma, Nu Sigma Nu, Sigma Xi. Local rep. of Com. of 100; chairman com. chemistry, State Council Defense. Republican. Author: Qualitative Analysis Inorganic Substances, 1897, 2d edit., 1900; Manual of Toxicological Analysis, 1899; also many articles on subs. in physiol., synthetic, organic and analyt. chemistry in Am. and German publs. Inventor of processes for amalgamation of platinum and of refractory gold; for recovery of used soap from laundry suds; for rapid polymerization and oxidation of drying oils; for light and weather proof coloring of oolitic limestone; for recovery of pectin from certain fruit and vegetable waste; for silver and gold mirror decoration; for reduction of nitro compounds. Club: Internat. Rotary. Home: 630 E. 3d St., Bloomington, Ind. Died Nov. 25, 1946.

LYSTER, HENRY FRANCIS LE HUNTE, physician; b. Sander's Court, Ireland, Nov. 8, 1837; s. Rev. William N. and Ellen Emily (Cooper) L.; grad. U. Mich., 1858, M.D., 1860; m. Winifred Lee Brent, Jan. 30, 1867, 5 children. Came with family to U.S., 1838; served as surgeon 5th Mich. Voluntary Inf., then with Army of Potomac, during Civil War, 1861-65; lectr. on surgery U. Mich., 1868-70, prof. theory and practice of medicine, 1888-90; a founder Mich. Coll. of Medicine; prof. practice of medicine Detroit Coll. of Medicine, 1885-93. Died Oct. 3, 1894.

MAASS, OTTO, chemist; b. N.Y.C., July 8, 1890; s. Max and Sophie (von Kolke) M.; B.A., McGill U., 1911, M.Sc., 1912, D.Sc., 1955; Ph.D., Harvard, 1919; LL.D., U. Manitoba, 1945; D.Sc., Laval U., 1944, U. Rochester, 1946, U. Toronto, 1947; m. Carol E. Robertson, June 10, 1926; 1 son, Colin. Became Canadian citizen, 1911. Dir. chem. warfare and smoke Canadian Dept. Nat. Def., 1940-46; gen. dir. Canadian Pulp and Paper Research Inst., 1940-55; Macdonald prof. phys. chemistry, chmn. chemistry dept. McGill Univ., 1934—, research scholar, 1959—; chief sci. officer div. chemistry National Research Council Can., 1955-58; special consultant Paper & Pulp Research

Institute Can., 1958—. Decorated Medal of Freedom with Bough (U.S.); Comdr. Order British Empire. Fellow Royal Soc., Royal Soc. Arts, Royal Soc. of Can. Chemistry, Canadian Inst. Chemists; hon. mem. Chemists Club, N.Y.C. Home: 32 Thornhill Av., Westmount, Que. Office: McGill U., Montreal, Que., Can. Died July 3, 1961; buried Mt. Royal Cemetery, Montreal.

MABERY, CHARLES FREDERIC, chemist; b. New Gloucester, Me.; Jan. 13, 1850; s. Henry and Elizabeth A. (Bennett) M.; S.B., Lawrence Scientific Sch., (Harvard), 1876, Sc.D., 1881; m. F. A. Lewis, Nov. 19, 1872. Asst. in chemistry, Harvard, 1874-83; prof. chemistry Case Sch. Applied Science, 1883-1911, emeritus. Researcher in organic chemistry; especially in investigations of the composition of Am. petroleum, lubricants and lubrication. Address: Cleveland, O. Died June 26, 1927.

MAC ARTHUR, ARTHUR FREDERIC, engineer, contractor; b. Oramel, N.Y., Oct. 24, 1860; s. Archibald and Keturah (Patt) M.; A.B., Harvard, 1882; Bryant & Stratton Business College, Chicago, 1882; m. Mary Seymour Barnum, June 24, 1889. Began as supt. MacArthur Bros. Co., St. Paul, 1883, became general mgr., Chicago, 1892, v.p., 1903, pres. same co., New York, 1908—; pres. U.S. Equipment Co., MacArthur Bros. Co.; Ltd., MacArthur-Hanger Co., West Coast Constrn Co.; v.p. Mason-Hanger-MacArthur Bros., Inc.; chmn. bd. W. & A. MacArthur, Ltd., Construction & Engring. Finance Co. Upon entry of U.S. into the war declined a commn. in the army, and took personal charge in the field for MacArthur Bros. Co., of entire constrn. of Camp Merritt, the Port of Newark Terminals, the constrn. and operating of Woodbury Bag Loading Plant, the construction of 1,000 houses for U. S. Shipping Bd., and reconstrn. of a double track trolley line bet. Phila. and Wilmington, Del. Address: New York, N.Y. Died Dec. 1, 1926.

MAC ARTHUR, JOHN R., contractor, engr.; b. Mt. Morris, N.Y., July 24, 1862; s. Archibald and Keturah (Pratt) M.; A.B., Harvard, 1855; student law sch.; Harvard, 1887-89; studied at École des Sciences Politiques, Sorbonne and Collège de France, Paris; m. Pauline, d. Judge William H. Arnoux, June 27, 1889. Actively identified with MacArthur Bros. Co., 1900, becoming v.p.; Construction & Engring. Finance Co., MacArthur Bros. Co., Ltd., U.S. Equipment Co., W. & A. MacArthur Co., Ltd., West Coast Constrn. Co.; treas. MacArthur-Hanger Co. In diplomatic service 4 yrs.; sec. U.S. Legation, at Madrid, Spain, 1897; apptd. spl. asst. sec. in office of Sec. of State, 1898; asst. sec. U.S. Commn. that negotiated treaty of peace with Spain, 1898, and sec. to first Philippine Commn., 1899; mem. Am. Industrial Commn. to France, Aug.-Dec. 1916. Home: 175 E. 78th St., New York, N.Y. Deceased.

MACARTHUR, ROBERT HELMER, educator, biologist; b. Toronto, Can., Apr. 7, 1930; s. John Wood and Olive (Turner) MacA.; came to U.S., 1947; B.A., Marlboro Coll., 1951; D.H.S. (hon.), 1972; M.S., Brown U., 1953; Ph.D., Yale, 1958; m. Elizabeth Bayles Whittemore, June 14, 1952; children—Duncan, Alan, Elizabeth, Donald. From asst. prof. to prof. U. Pa., 1958-65; mem. faculty Princeton, 1965-72, Henry Fairfield Osborn prof. biology, 1968-72; hon. research asso. Smithsonian Tropical Research Inst. Acad. adviser Marlboro Coll. Served with AUS, 1954-56. Recipient Mercer award Ecol. Soc. Am. Fellow Am. Acad. Arts and Scis., Nat. Acad. Scis. Research theory community structure and evolution. Home: Princeton NJ Died Nov. 1, 1972.

MACCALLUM, WILLIAM GEORGE, pathologist; b. Dunnville, Ont., Apr. 18, 1874; s. Dr. George Alexander and Florence O. (Eakins) MacC.; B.A., U. of Toronto, 1894; M.D., Johns Hopkins, 1897; unmarried. Asso. prof. pathology, 1900-08, prof. pathol. physiology, 1908-09, Johns Hopkins U.; prof. pathology, Columbia U., 1909-17; prof. pathology and bacteriology, Johns Hopkins U., since 1917. Contbr. to med. jours. on pathol. subjects. Fellow A.A.A.S.; mem. Assn. Am. Physicians, Nat. Acad. Sciences; hon. fellow Royal Soc. Medicine, London, England; hon. mem. Soc. Medicorum Sverana, Stockholm, 1918. Author: Text-book of Pathology, 1916. Contbr. to Johns Hopkins Hosp. Bull., Jour. A.M.A., Jour. Experimental Medicine, etc. Home: 701 St. Paul St. Address: Johns Hopkins Hospital, Baltimore, Md. Died Feb. 3, 1944. *

MACCARTY, WILLIAM CARPENTER, surg. pathologist; b. Louisville, June 10, 1880; s. William Orlando Butler and Rhoda Ann (Carpenter) MacC.; B.S., U. Ky., 1900, M.S., 1909, D.Sc., 1937; M.D., Johns Hopkins, 1904; studied Koenigin Hosp., Berlin, 1904-06, specializing in surg. pathology; m. Helen Maud Collin, Jan. 25, 1908; children—William Carpenter, Collin Stewart. With Mayo Clinic since 1907, as specialist in surg. pathology and biopathology; dir. labs., Mayo Clinic, emeritus prof. pathology U. Minn. Med. Dept. (Mayo Found.); emeritus cons. physician Mayo Clinic, Fellow A.C.P.; mem. Am. Assn. Pathologists and Bacteriologists, Am. Assn. Cancer Research, Minn. (asso.), So. Minn., Ky. (hon.) med. assns., Minn., Chgo. pathol. socs., Osler Med. Hist. Soc. (pres.), Chgo. Med. Hist. Soc., Charleston Med. Soc. (hon.), Am. Soc. for Control of Cancer, Pan-Am. Med. Soc., Am. Gastro-Enterological Assn., Alumni Assn. of Mayo Found., Miss. Valley Med. Soc. (hon.), Radiolo. Soc. N. Am. (hon.), Société Internationale de Gastro-Entérologie, Kappa Alpha, Alpha Kappa Kappa, Sigma Xi (pres.), Phi Beta Kappa, Pi Gamma Mu; fellow Am. Soc. Clin. Pathologists (pres.,) Internat. Coll. Surgeons (hon., trustee, rep. at large); asso. fellow A.M.A.; del. Internat. Cancer Conf., Lake Mohonk, N.Y., 1926, London, 1928, Brussels Conf. UNESCO. Mason (32 deg.). Clubs, Rochester Art, Rotary, Rochester Golf. Cons. physician, writer, investigator, lectr. on med., biol. philos. and sociol. subjects. Contbr. articles on terminology, classification and genesis of cancer; collaborator on med. books, encys. Home: 316 9th Av. S.W., Rochester, Minn. Died May 17, 1964; buried Oakwood Cemetery, Rochester.

MACCAUGHEY, VAUGHAN, (må-koi'), educator; b. Huron, S.D., July 7, 1887; s. William Franklyn and Matilda (Vaughan) MacC.; B.S.A., Cornell U., 1908; post-grad. work University of Chicago, 1916-17; B.Ed., San Francisco State College; married Janet H. Brooker, Nov. 25, 1909; children—Hamilton, Matilda, Horace, Patricia, Nancy, Phoebe-Jean. Asst. Cornel U., 1905-08; head dept. natural science and v.p. Territorial Normal Sch., Hawaii, 1908-09; prof. botany, Coll. of Hawaii, 1910-19; supt. pub. instrn. for H.T., 1919-23. Visiting prof. U. of Calif., summer, 1911, Cornell U., summer, 1912; prin. Mid-Pacific Inst. Mills Sch., 1913. Chautauqua Instn., 1906, 07, 14, 15, 16; 8 continental lecture tours; dir. Territorial Summer Sch., Kilauea Volcano, Hawaii, 1919; biol. explorations, H.I.; extension staff U. of Calif. since 1923; mem. Nat. Council Boy Scouts of America, spl. field commr. Calif., dir. edn. Region 12; dean San Francisco Training Sch. for Scout Officers; dir. Pacific Coast Survey of Race Relations, N. Calif., 1924. Mem. Hosp. Corps, 1st Inf. Nat. Guard, Hawaii, 1909-12, Co. B 1st Inf., 1913-15. Supt. Bible Sch. Central Union Ch., 1913-16. Pres. Honolulu Ad Club, 1919-21; dir. for Hawaii, N.E.A., 1916-23; mem. Nat. Editorial Council, N.E.A., 1922-23; del. World Conf. on Edn., San Francisco, 1923; chmn. exec. com. Pan-Pacific Ednl. Conf., 1921; del. Pan-Pacific Scientific Conf., 1919; joint founder and pres. Agassiz Club of Cornell. Joint founder and editor Hawaiian Educational Review, 1913-16; editor Sierra Educational News, 1923-52, ret.; dir. Audubon Camp of Cal., 1952-53; Pacific Coast rep. Nat. Audubon Soc. since 1952. Fellow A.A.A.S.; mem. S.A.R., Sigma Xi, Phi Gamma Mu. Republican. Conglist. Mason. Author: The Natural History of Chautauqua, 1917; The Schools of Hawaii; Race-Mixtures in Hawaii. Contbr. more than 200 papers to scientific and ednl. jours. Home: 726 Cragmont Av., Berkeley 8, Calif. Office: 693 Sutter St., San Francisco 2. Died Mar. 24, 1954.

MACCLINTOCK, PAUL, geologist; b. Aurora, N.Y., Feb. 2, 1891; s. William D. and Lucia (Lander) MacC.; B.S., U. of Chicago, 1912, Ph.D., 1920; m. Elizabeth S. Copeland, Sept. 5, 1925; children—Lucia, Copeland. Teacher, Indianapolis (Ind.) Manual Training High Sch., 1913-14; instr. mathematics, U. of Chicago, 1921-28, asst. prof., 1926-27, asso. prof. 1927-28; Knox Taylor prof. of geography, Princeton, 1928-59. Served with Co. A, 29th Engrs., U.S. Army, 1916-18. Mem. A.A.A.S., Geol. Soc. America, Sigma Xi, Alpha Delta Phi. Contbr. to revision of Chamberlin and Salisbury College Geology; contbr. articles on physiography and glacial geology to sci. jours. Home: Princeton NJ Died Mar. 23, 1970.

MAC COUN, TOWNSEND, cartographer; b. Troy, N.Y., 1845; s. John T. and Angelica Rachel Douw (Lane) M.; A.B., Williams, 1866, A.M., 1869; m. Annie Dean, of Quebec, Can., 1899; 1 son, Townsend Dean. Bookseller and publisher, 1869-93; since then in lit. work. Originated system of color in map work whereby successive maps contained the same colors for same nationality, and so taught history by color, now universally used in text-books; introduced this system in Labberton's Historical Atlas and General History, 1887. Mem. Chi Psi Fraternity. Author: MacCoun's Historical Geography of the United States, 1889; Historical Geography Charts of the United States, 1890; Historical Geography Charts of Europe, 1895; Holy Land in Geography and History, 1897; Map Berkshire Co., Mass., 1903; Historical Geography Charts of English History, 1903; Early New York City History Portrayed in Five Maps, 1909; France with Maps of the Battle Fields of the Western Front, 1919. Mem. Am. Geog. Soc., Société Académique d'Histoire Internationale, Paris. Address: Care American Book Co., 100 Washington Pl., New York, N.Y.

MACCUTCHEON, ALECK, (må-kuch'un), cons. elec. engr.; b. Stockport, N.Y., Dec. 31, 1881; s. Samuel J. and Janet L. (McBurney) MacC.; grad. Albany State Normal Coll., 1901; E.E., Columbia, 1908; m. Caroline S. Sheffer, Dec. 23, 1908; children—Samuel M., Richard H. Elec. engr. Crocker-Wheeler, 1909-14; elec. engr. Reliance Electric and Engring. Co., Cleve., 1914, v.p., 1922-46; ret.; dir. Engring Co. (Cleve.). Served as lt. USN, 1917-19. Received Lamme Medal awarded by Am. Inst. E.E., 1948. Mem. Am. Inst. E.E. (pres. 1936-37), Am. Standards Assn., Assn. Iron and Steel Engrs., Phi Kappa Sigma, Tau Beta Pi, Eta Kappa Nu. Conglist. Clubs: Columbia U. (N.Y.C.); Canterbury, Lost Lake Woods. Home: 3104 Woodbury Rd., Shaker Heights, Cleve. Died Mar. 3, 1954; buried Germantown, N.Y.

MACDONALD, CHARLES, civil engr.; b. Gananoque, Can., Jan. 26, 1837; s. William Stone and Isabella (Hall) M.; ed. Queen's U., Kingston, Ont. (LL.D., 1894); C.E., Rensselaer Poly. Inst., Troy, N.Y., 1857; m. Sarah L. Willard, Aug. 5, 1861. Asst. engr. on constrn. Grand Trunk Ry., in Mich., and in charge of surveys and constrn. Phila. & Reading Rd., 1863-68; removed to New York, 1868, and engaged in bridge constrn.; mem. Union Bridge Co., 1884-1900; assisted in building Hawksburg Bridge (Australia), The Leavenworth (Kan.) Bridge, Poughkeepsie Bridge, Merchants' Bridge (St. Louis), etc. Trustee Rensselaer Poly. Inst., Troy, N.Y. Pres. Am. Soc. C.E., 1908-09. Home: Brooklyn, N.Y. Died 1928.

MACDONALD, IAN (GIBBS), surgeon; b. Calgary, Can., Apr. 9, 1903; s. Alexander D. and Gertrude (Gibbs) M.; M.D., C.M., McGill U., 1928; m. Esther Case, Sept. 16, 1931; children—Alexander Case, Sharon; m. 2d, Eve March, July 14, 1946; children—Bruce, Katharine; m. 3d, Eleanor G. Clark, March 17, 1963. Came to U.S., 1932, naturalized, 1941. Intern, resident Montreal General Hosp., 1927-30; resident pathology U. Mich. Hosp., 1930-31; resident surgeon Toronto Gen. Hosp., 1931-32; pvt. practice, Los Angeles, from 1943; instr. surgery U. So. Cal., 1932-33, asso. prof., 1943-56, clin. prof. surgery, from 1956; dir. tumor clinic Cornwall Hosp., 1935-38; clin. research Am. Coll. Surgeons, 1938-40; asso. Los Angeles Tumor Inst., 1941-43; sr. attending surgeon tumor surgery Los Angeles County Hosp., Hollywood-Presbyn. Hosp., St. Vincent's Hosp.; cons. radium therapist Children's Hosp., Los Angeles, from 1943. Recipient award for distinguished service in cancer control Am. Cancer Soc., 1951. Diplomate Am. Bd. Radiology, 1938. Fellow A.C.S.; mem. Los Angeles Surg. Soc., Assn. Cancer Research, Am. Radium Soc., A.M.A., A.A.A.S., Pacific Coast Surg. Assn., Am. Coll. Radiology, Ewing Soc., Pacific Coast Roetgen Soc., Soc. Head and Neck Surgeons, Sigma Xi. Author articles on biology and treatment of cancer, contbr. textbooks. Editor bull. Los Angeles County Med. Assn. Office: Los Angeles CA Died Mar. 9, 1968.

MACDONALD, JESSE JUAN, mining engr.; b. in Iowa; s. Samuel Franklin and Amanda Catherine (Roads) M.; ed. Professor Dick's Normal Sch., Denver; spl. student Columbia, 1906, 07; m. Maty E. Gilbert, of Chicago, 1898. Began as assayer, Colo., 1893; one of the first in America to make use of cyanide process in extracting gold and silver from ores; spent many yrs. in Mexico and S.A., in remote places, working out metall. problems; was metall. engr. Utah Copper Co., and oil flotation expert Ray Consolidated Copper Co.; sales engineer Taylor Wharton Iron and Steel Co.; now mgr. Downtown Mines Co., Leadville, Colo. Republican. Baptist. Mem. Am. Inst. Mining Engrs., Am. Geog. Soc., Beta Theta Pi. Mason (32 deg.). Address: Leadville CO

MACDONALD, THOMAS HARRIS, engr.; b. Leadville, Colo., July 23, 1881; s. John and Elizabeth (Harris) MacD.; student Ia. State Tchrs. Coll., Cedar Falls, 1899-1900; B.C.E., Ia. State Coll. Agr. and Mech. Arts, Ames, 1904; D.Eng. (hon.), Ia. State Coll., 1929; m. Bess Dunham, Mar. 7, 1907 (dec. 1935); children—Thomas Harris, Margaret Elizabeth (Mrs. Charles William Weidinger); m. 2d, Caroline L. Fuller, Nov. 24, 1953. Began with engring. dept. C.G.W. Ry.; chief engr. Ia. State Hwy. Commn., 1904-19; chief U.S. Bur. Pub. Rds., Dept. of Agr., 1919-39; became commr. pub. rds., charge pub. rds. adminstrn. Fed. Works Agy., 1939. ret. from U.S. service, 1953; head hwy. research center Tex. A. and M. Coll., 1953—. Decorated Medal of Merit (U.S.); Cross Legion of Honor (France); Knight 1st class Order of St. Olav (Norway); fgn. mem. Masarykova Akademie (Czechoslovakia). Recipient Marston Medal for achievement in engring. Ia. State Coll., 1939. Mem. Am. Assn. State Hwy. Ofcls. (exec. com.), Beta Theta Pi, Tau Beta P. Presbyn. Club: Cosmos (Washington). Author papers on hwy. engring., adminstrn. and finance. Home: 1000 Puryear Dr., College Station, Tex. Died Apr. 7, 1957; buried Cedar Hill Cemetery, Washington.

MACDONALD, WILLIAM ALEXANDER, electronics engr.; b. N.Y. City, Dec. 27, 1895; s. William Fuller and Sue E. (Watson) MacD.; student U. Paris, 1918-19; m. Dorothy Belder, July 5, 1922; 1 dau., Doris Diane. Radio operator Marconi Wireless & Telegraph Co., N.Y. City, 1913-15; lab. asst. Western Elec. Corp., 1915-17; asst. radio engr. Civil Service Commn. 1919-20; engr. Radio Corp. of Am., 1920-24; chief engr. Hazeltine Corp., Little Neck, L.I., N.Y., 1934-44, dir., 1934—, v.p., 1934-52, pres., 1952-57, 59-60, chmn., 1957—; chmn., dir. Hazeltine Tech. Devel. Center, Inc., 1959—; pres. Hazeltine Electronics Corp., 1942-52, chmn., 1952-57; pres. Hazeltine Research Inc. of Cal., Los Angeles, 1946-52, dir., 1946-60; director of the Western Union Telegraph Company. Founding mem. Armstrong Meml. Research Found., Inc. Mem. electronics equipment industry adv. com. Munitions Bd.; mem. task group No. 6, Adv. Group on Reliability of Electronics Equipment. Recipient certificate of merit for outstanding contbns. to field of electronics, World War II. Profl. engr., State of N.Y. Fellow Inst. Radio

Engrs.; mem. Electronic Industries Association, Armed Forces Communications Assn., Am. Soc. Naval Engrs., Am. Ordnance Assn., Nat. Security Indsl. Assn., Def. Orientation Conf. Assn. Clubs: Chicago Athletic Assn.; Engineer, Radio of America (N.Y.C.); North Hills Golf. Patentee. Home: Bayville Rd., Locust Valley, N.Y. Office: 59-25 Little Neck Pkwy., Little Neck, L.I., N.Y. Died Aug. 1961.

MACDOUGAL, DANIEL TREMBLY, (mak-doo'gål), botanist and author; b. Liberty, Ind., Mar. 16, 1865; s. Alexander and Amanda MacD.; B.S., DePauw U., 1890, A.M., 1894, LL.D., 1912; M.S., Purdue U., 1891, Ph.D., 1897; student Tübingen and Leipzig, 1895-96; LL.D., U. Ariz., 1915; m. Louise Fisher, Jan. 24, 1893. Agt. U.S. Dept. Agr. on explorations in Ariz. and Ida., 1891-92; instr. plant physiology U. Minn., 1893-95, asst. prof., 1895-99; dir. labs. and asst. dir. N.Y. Bot. Garden, 1899-1905; dir. Dept. Bot. Research and Laboratory for Plant Physiology, Carnegie Inst. of Washington, 1905-33. Fellow Cal. Acad. Science; life mem. Bot. Soc. America, Am. Soc. Plant Physiology, A.A.A.S., Torrey Bot. Club; mem. Am. Philos. Soc., Cal. Bot. Soc.; fgn. mem. Hollandsche Maatschappe d. Wetenschappen, Societé Nationale D'Acclimatation de France; hon. mem. Bot. Soc. of Edinburgh; corr. mem. Czechoslovak Bot. Soc.; pres. Am. Soc. Naturalists, 1910; gen. sec. A.A.A.S., 1920-25. Clubs: Century (N.Y.C.); Old Pueblo (Tucson). Author: Influence of Light and Darkness Upon Growth and Development, 1903; Botanical Features of North American Deserts, 1908; The Water-Balance of Succulent Plants, 1910; Conditions of Parasitism in Plants, 1910; Alterations in Heredity Induced by Ovarial Treatment, 1911; The Salton Sea, 1913; Hydration and Growth, 1919; Growth in Trees, 1921, 1924; Hydrostatic System of Trees, 1926; The Green Leaf, 1930; Pneumatic System of Plants, Especially Trees, 1933; Studies in Tree Growth by the Dendrographic Method, 1935; Tree Growth, 1938. Editor: Species and Varieties (De Vries); contbr. Sci. Am. Hon. pres. 7th Internat. Bot. Congress, Stockholm, 1952, 8th, Paris, 1954. Home: R.F.D. No. 1, Box 185, Carmel, Cal. Died Feb. 22, 1958.

MACDOWELL, CHARLES HENRY, ex-pres. Armour Fertilizer Works; b. Lewistown, Ill., Oct. 21, 1867; s. John Ross (M.D.) and Ella (Burgett) MacD.; high school edn.; shorthand course, Wesleyan U., Bloomington, Ill.; hon. D.Sc., U. of Pittsburgh, 1921; m. Janet, d. Dr. Matthew W. Borland, Oct. 25, 1892 (died 1929); m. 2d, Claire Leavitt, Oct. 27, 1934. With Armstrong & Co. since 1887; personal stenographer and sec. to Philip D. Armour, 1888-93; organized, 1894, the fertilizer dept., now Armour Fertilizer Works, of which was pres. 1910-32; pres. Tenn. Chemical Co.; dir. Armour & Co., 1919-33; v.p., 1923-32. Unofficial adviser U.S. Dept. of State, 1910, in German potash controversy; developed, with colleague, 1915, alunite potash mine at Marysvale, Utah (first producing potash mine in America); mem. Chemicals Com., Nat. Council of Defense, summer, 1917; organized chemicals div. of War Industries Bd., 1917, and served as its dir. during war period; went to Paris, 1919, as asso. econ. advisor to Am. Commn. to Negotiate Peace and served as chmn. many meetings between Allied and German experts at Versailles. Del. and speaker Pres. Harding's Agrl. Conf., Washington, 1921; chmn. Am. sect. trade and industry group, Internat. Chamber of Commerce Conf., Rome, 1923; del. and speaker Dept. of Agr. Nat. Conf. on Utilization of Forest Products, Washington, 1924. Conf. and Round Table leader, "Fertilizer Raw Materials and Their Political Significance," at Williamstown Inst. of Politics, 1926; speaker First Congress Internat. Soc. of Soil Science, Washington, 1927; chmn. Am. Com. on Internat. Ententes, Internat. Chamber of Commerce Congress, Stockholm, 1927, del. at Amsterdam, 1929. Speaker 2d Internat. Bituminous Coal Conf., Carnegie Inst., Pittsburgh, 1928. Mem. U.S. Chamber of Commerce nat. resources prodn. com., 1928-30, and nat. water policy com., 1929-30. Pres. Chicago Better Business Bureau, 1932-33. Mem. advisory bd. Chemical Warfare Service, 4th Procurement Div., U.S. Army; apptd. mem. Nat. Research Council (div. engring. and indsl. research), 1937. Mem. bd. Davis Mus. of Natural History, Rollins College (chmn. 1944-45). Mem. industrial committee Florida State C. of C. V.p. Winter Park C. of C., 1946. Fellow A.A.A.S., Am. Geog. Soc., Ill. Acad. Science, Chicago Academy of Science, Royal Society of Arts, British Institute Philosophical Studies; honorary life mem. Nat. Fertilizer Assn. (pres. 1904-05, 1921-22); mem. Am. Forestry Assn. (vice president, 1925), American Arbitration Association, Field Museum of Natural History (life), Am. Chem. Soc., Western Soc. Engrs. (pres., 1921), Am. Mil. Engrs., Newcomen Society, Business Men's Art Club (pres. 1936-37), Am. Soc. French Legion of Honor, Belgian League of Honor in the U.S., Fla. Acad. of Science, Pi Gamma Mu; mem. exec. bd. Am. Engring. Council, 1922-23. Awarded D.S.M. (U.S.); Officer Legion of Honor (French); Comdr. Crown of Belgium; Knight Crown of Italy. Clubs: University, Glenview Golf (pres., 1928-29); University (Winter Park, Fla.). Wrote: German and Other Sources of Potash; Significance of Yorktown; The Problems of Muscle Shoals; also tech. and econ. articles. Editor: Armour's Farmers Almanac, 1898-1932. Home: 1300 College Point, Winter Park, Fla. Died Mar. 4, 1954, buried Winter Park, Fla.

MACDUFFEE, CYRUS COLTON, mathematics; b. Oneida, New York, June 29, 1895; son of Cyrus Thompson and Elizabeth Louise (Seewir) MacDuffee; B.S., Colgate University, 1917; Sc.D., 1947; S.M., University of Chicago, 1920, Ph.D., 1921; married to Mary Augusta Bean, Sept. 7, 1921; children—Robert Colton, Frederic Dearborn, Mary Elizabeth, Helen Seewir. Instr. in mathematics, S.A.T.C., Colgate U., 1917-19; instr. mathematics, Princeton, 1921-23, asst. prof., 1923-24; asst. prof. mathematics, Ohio State U., 1924-29, asso. prof., 1929-33, prof., 1933-35; prof. mathematics U. of Wis., 1935-40 and since 1943, chmn. dept., 1951-56; prof. mathematics Hunter Coll., 1940-43; vis. prof. U. of Puerto Rico, 1947, 60-61, Stanford U., summer 1959; member National Research Council, 1954. Member Institute for Advanced Study, Princeton, New Jersey, 1937-38. Member American Math. Society (editor algebra transactions 1937-43), Math. Assn. Am. (pres. 1945-46); A.A.A.S. (sec. sect. A 1957-61), Sigma Nu, Phi Beta Kappa, Pi Mu Epsilon (dir. gen. 1948-54). Author: The Theory of Matrices, Ergebnisse der Mathematik und ihrer Grenzgebiete, 1933; An Introduction to Abstract Algebra, 1940; Vectors and Matrices, 1943; Theory of Equations, 1954. Home: 506 N. Franklin Av., Madison 5. Office: North Hall, University of Wisconsin, Madison 6, Wis. Died Aug. 21, 1961.

MACELWANE, JAMES B(ERNARD), (mak'el-wan), geophysics; b. nr. Port Clinton, Ottawa County, O., Sept. 28, 1883; s. Alexander and Catherine Agnes (Carr) M.; student St. Stanislaus Coll. and John Carroll U., Cleveland, until 1907; A.B., St. Louis U., 1910, A.M., 1911, M.S., 1912; Ph.D., U. of Calif., 1923; D.Sc. (honorary), Saint Norbert College, 1949; LL.D. (honorary), Washington University, 1953; D.Sc. (honorary), John Carroll University 1954. Joined Society of Jesus (Jesuits), 1903; ordained priest R.C. Ch., 1918. Instr. in mathematics, St. John's Coll. High Sch., Toledo, 1907-08, in physics, St. Louis U., 1912-13; asst. prof. physics, same univ., 1913-15, 1918-19; asst. prof. geology, U. of Calif., 1923-25; prof. geophysics and dir. dept., St. Louis Univ., since 1925, prof. geophysical engring. since 1949, dean Graduate School, 1927-33, dean Inst. Tech. 1944—. Recipient Jackling Lecturer award, Am. Inst. Mining and Metall. Engrs. Mem. Nat. Science Board, Fellow A.A.A.S. (past v.p.), Geol. Soc. America, Am. Geog. Soc.; mem. Am. Physical Soc., Seismol. Soc. America (ex-pres.), Jesuit Seismol. Assn. (pres.), Am. Meterol. Soc. Am. Geophys. Union (president, sect. of seismology), Am. Inst. Mining and Metall. Engrs., Mo. Acad. Sciences (ex-pres.), St. Louis Acad. Sciences (ex-pres.), Optical Soc. America (asso.), Nat. Research Council, Nat. Acad. Scis., Societa Sismologica Italiana, Societa Meteorologica Italiana, Soc. Exploration Geophysicists, Am. Assn. Petroleum Geologists, Sigma Xi. Democrat. Received Bowie Medal of Am. Geophys. Union, 1948. Author: Loose Leaf Manual of Laboratory Experiments in Coll. Physics, Parts I, II, III, IV, V (with J. I. Shannon), 1914; Theoretical Seismology, Vol. I, Geodynamics, 1936, new edition, 1949; When the Earth Quakes, 1947; also more than 100 papers and articles, alone and with others, on seismology and other subjects. Editor and joint author of Bull. of Nat. Research Council on Seismology, 1933. Co-author: Internal Constitution of the Earth, 1939; Compendium of Meteorology, 1951. Home: 221 N. Grand Blvd., St. Louis 3. Office: 3621 Olive St., St. Louis 8. Died Feb. 15, 1956; buried St. Stanislaus Seminary, Florissant, Mo.

MACELWEE, ROY SAMUEL, (mak-el'we), consulting engineer; b. Parkville, Mich., Apr. 12, 1883; s. Rev. Samuel J. and Anna Belle (Mozingo) M.; prep. edn., Hudson River Mil. Acad.; B.S., Columbia, 1907; studied several European univs.; A.M., Ph.D., U. of Berlin, 1915; m. Ellen Mohlau, 1912; m. 2d, Sarah Smyrl, 1923; children—Anne Frances, Roy Samuel, Sarah Margaret. Clerk, salesman, branch manager, Eastman Kodak Company, International Harvester and Otis Elevator companies in European cities, 1899-1914; chief clerk United States Consulate Gen., Berlin, 1915; lecturer on economics and foreign trade, port and terminal engineering, Columbia, 1916-19; prof. Sch. of Foreign Service, Georgetown U., 1919, dean, 1921-22; prof. Coll. of Charleston, 1923, S.C. Mil. Coll. (Citadel), 1927. Asst. mil. instr. Columbia U. Training Corps, 1917; commd. 1st lt. R.R. Transportation Corps of U.S. Army, Feb. 12, 1918; served as aidé to Gen. Goethals; major since 1922; lt. colonel S.P.O.R.C.; agt. Fed. Bd. Voc. Edn., 1918; 2d and 1st asst. dir. and dir. U.S. Bur. Fgn. and Domestic Commerce, Jan. 1, 1919-Mar. 31, 1921; chmn. U.S. Economic Liasion Com.; chmn. U.S. Interdepartment Com. for Commercial Aviation, 1919-21; mem. Com. for Commercial Use of Army Bases; commr. of Port of Charleston, S.C., 1923-30; v.p. (for South Carolina) Great Lakes-St. Lawrence Tidewater Assn., Nat. Rivers and Harbors Congress; dir. Atlantic Deeper Waterways Assn., Am. Bur. of Shipping; del. of U.S. to 14th International Navigation Congress, Cairo, Egypt, 1926; lecturer European univs., engring. socs., and chambers of commerce, Paris and Berlin, 1926. Mem. Soc. Terminal Engrs. (v.p.), Soc. Am. Mil. Engrs., Am. Soc. Mech. Engineers, New York Society Professional Engineers, National Society Professional Engineers, Licensed Professional Engrs. of New York, Pan-Am. Soc., Mil. Order World War Am. Legion, 40 and 8, Theta Delta Chi, Delta Phi Epsilon (co-founder and 1st nat. pres.), Navy League (chmn.) for S.C., 3 European engring. socs.; fellow American Geographical Society. Episcopalian. Decorations: Officer Polonia Restituta (Poland); Comdr. Crown of Rumania; Chevalier Crown of Italy; Officer Order of Leopold II (Belgium); medals—Victory, D.C. Mil. Engineers. Club: University (Washington). Author: Bread Bullets, 1917; Vocational Education for Foreign Trade and Shipping, 1918; Ports and Terminal Facilities, 1919, 25; Training for Foreign Trade, 1920; Training for the Steamship Business, 1920; Port Development, 1925; Port Glossary, 1927; The Ports of Rumania, 1927; The Great Ship Canals, 1929. Translator of Delbrüch's Government and the Will of the People. Co-Author: Paper Work in Export Trade, 1920; Economic Aspects of the Great Lakes-St. Lawrence Ship Channel, 1921, Wharf Management, 1921. Contbr. numerous articles to mags. Drew waterfront and port development plan for Toledo, O., Cleveland, O., Canaveral, Fla., and Turiamo, Venezuela, also fixed bridge report, Chicago, port plans for Green Bay and Marinette, Wis., Sandusky, O., Rochester, N.Y.; designed and supervised constrn. Charlotte Terminal, Port of Rochester, N.Y., etc. Home: 3726 18th St. N. Office: War Dept. Ocean Traffic Branch, Water Division, Transportation Corps, Army Supply Forces, Pentagon Bldg., Arlington, Va. Died Feb. 6, 1944.

MACFARLANE, ALEXANDER, mathematician; b. Blairgowrie, Scotland, Apr. 21, 1851; of Highland ancestry; grad. Edinburgh Univ., M.A., 1875; (D.Sc., same, in math. and physical science, 1878; LL.D., Univ. of Mich., 1887); m. San Antonio, Tex., Apr., 1895, Helen Swearingen. Examiner in mathematics, Edinburgh Univ., 1881; prof. physics, Univ. of Texas, 1885; lecturer on math. physics, Lehigh Univ., 1897; gen. sec. Internat. Assn. for Promoting Space-analysis, 1899; pres. sect. of mathematics and astronomy, A.A.A.S., 1899. Fellow Royal Soc. of Edinburgh, 1878; corr. mem. Scientific Soc. of Mexico, 1894; mem. Am. Inst. Elec. Engrs., 1892, Washington Acad. Sciences, 1900. Author: Algebra of Logic, 1879 G1; Physical Arithmetic, 1885 M1; Elementary Mathematical Tables, 1889 G1; Papers on Space-Analysis, 1894 L15; also wrote Vector-Analysis and Quaternions in text book of Higher Mathematics, 1896 W9; Bibliography of Quaternions and Allied Mathematics, 1904 F5; and many papers in scientific and math. jours. Address: Chatham, Ont.

MACFARLANE, CATHARINE, gynecologist; b. Phila., Pa., Apr. 7, 1877; d. John J. and Nettie Ottinger (Huston) Macfarlane; student U. of Pa., 1893-95, M.D., Woman's Med. Coll. Pa., 1898, D.Sc., 1950; D.Sc., Ursinus Coll., 1948, Jefferson Med. College, 1958; D.M.S. (hon.), Drexel Inst. Tech., 1956; unmarried, Intern Woman's Hosp., Phila., 1898-99; pvt. practice, Phila., from 1889; instr. in obstetrics, Woman's Med. Coll., 1899-1900; prof. of gynecology, 1922-42, research prof. gynecology from 1942; gynecologist Woman's Hosp., Phila., 1908-28; gynecologist in chief Woman's Med. Coll. Hospital, 1922-42; gynecologist and obstetrician Phila. General Hosp., 1922-42; pres. bd. dirs. Phila. div., Am. Cancer Soc., 1943-53; chmn. of Commn. on Cancer, Med. Soc. Pa., 1956, Awarded grant by the Am. Med. Association for research on value of early examination for cancer, 1938, 39; awarded grants by Internat. Cancer Research Foundation for research on value of periodic examination in control of cancer 1940-43; awarded (1940) Gimbel Brothers' award for outstanding service to humanity in Philadelphia during year 1940; Strittmatter award, 1948; joint Lasker award for inspiring application of preventive medicine to cancer control, 1951. Fellow A.C.S., College Physicians of Phila. (1st woman member); president Obstetrical Society of Phila., 1943; mem. A.M.A., Pa. State Medical Society, Philadelphia County Medical Society, Am. Med. Women's Assn., Med. Women's Internat. Assn., Fellow, founder, Am. Academy Obstetrics and Gynecology, Am. Assn. Univ. Women. Republican. Presbyn. Clubs: Women's University, Cosmopolitan (Phila.). Author: Textbook of Gynecology for Nurses, 1908. Home: Philadelphia PA Died May 1969.

MACFARLANE, JOHN MUIRHEAD, botanist; b. Kirkaldy, Scotland, Sept. 28, 1855; B.S., U. of Edinburgh, 1880, D.Sc., 1883; LL.D., U. of Pa., 1920; Litt.D., LaSalle, 1929; m. Emily Warburton, Sept. 7, 1887; children—Alistair P., Ernest J. W. (dec.), Phyllis (dec.), Winifred, Norman M., Archibald H.; m. 2d, Lily Wells, June 19, 1929. With U. of Edinburgh as asst. in botany, jr. instr., lecturer and head instr. in botany, 1877-91; prof. Royal Veterinarian Coll., 1881-91; lecturer Edinburgh Coll. of Pharmacy, 1881-91; became connected with U. of Pa., 1892, prof. biology until 1893, prof. botany, 1893-98, dir. Bot. Garden, 1895-98, prof. botany and dir. dept., 1898-1920 (emeritus); bot. adviser Carnegie Inst. Trustee Woods Hole, Mass., 1894-96; editor Bot. Contribs., Pa., 1894-1920. Awarded Banksian medal, Royal Hort. Soc., 1899. Fellow Royal Soc., Edinburgh (1885), A.A.A.S.; Bot. Soc. Pa. (a founder; curator, 1897-1920; ex-pres. and hon. pres.); mem. Am. Philos. Soc., Franklin Inst., Acad. Natural Sciences, Pa. Hort. Soc. (hon.), Sigma Xi, etc. Author: Causes and Course of Organic Evolution, 1918; The Evolution and Distribution of Fishes, 1924; Fishes, the Source of Petroleum, 1924; Quantity and Sources of Our Petroleum Supplies, 1931; Evolution and Distribution of Flowering Plants—Apocynaceae and Asclepiadaceae; also numerous papers on bot. subjects. Home: 427 W. Hansberry St., Germantown, Philadelphia, Pa.

MAC GILLIVRAY, ALEXANDER DYER, entomologist; b. Inverness, O., July 15, 1868; s. John Henry and Elizabeth (Adams) M.; Ph.B., Cornell, 1900, Ph.D., 1904; m. Fanny M. Edwards, Sept. 17, 1891. Asst., 1890-1900, instr. entomology, 1900-06, asst. prof. entomology and invertebrate zoölogy, 1906-11, Cornell; asst. prof. systematic entomology, 1911-13, asso. prof., 1913-17, prof. 1917—, U. of Ill. Specialist Me. Agrl. Expt. Sta., summer, 1913. Fellow Entomol. Soc. America (2d v.p. 1911, sec.-treas. 1911-16). Wrote: The Coccidae. Address: Urbana, Ill. Died Mar. 24, 1924.

MACGILLIVRAY, WILLIAM, ornithologist; b. Scotland; assisted John James Audubon with tech. details of book Ornithological Biography; MacGillivray's warbler named in his honor (also known as Tolmie's warbler).

MAC GILVARY, PATON, engineer; b. Berkeley, Calif., June 28, 1896; s. Prof. Evander Bradley and Elizabeth Allen (Paton) M.; B.S. in E.E., U. of Wis., 1916; unmarried. Chief engr. and supt. gas. works, Waukesha (Wis.) Gas & Electric Co., 1916; power specialist, Milwaukee Electric Ry. and Light Co., 1917; pres. and gen. mgr., Curtiss Airplane Co. of New England, 1919—; dir. Curtiss Northwest Airplane Co. Joined Air Service, U.S. Army, May 1917; went abroad, July 1917, training in Italy; successively chief pilot, adjutant and comdg. officer, Camp Ovest, Foggia; engr. attached to representative in Italy of Joint Army and Navy Aircraft Bd.; on Italian Front, June 1918 till close of war, as adj. of Combat Div.; hon. discharged, Dec. 30, 1918. Decorated by King of Italy with Croce di Guerre; awarded Bronzino and two citations while at the front. Republican. Home: Boston, Mass. Died May 10, 1921.

MACINNES, DUNCAN ARTHUR, chemist; b. Salt Lake City, Mar. 31, 1885; s. Duncan and Frances Charlotte (Sayers) MacI.; B.S., U. Utah, 1907; M.S., U. Ill., 1909, Ph.D., 1911. Instr. chemistry U. Ill., 1911-14, asso., 1914-17; asst. prof. phys. chemistry research Mass. Inst. Tech., 1917-21, asso. prof., 1921-26; asso. mem. Rockefeller Inst. Med. Research, 1926-40, mem., 1940-50, now emeritus, Sigma Xi lectr., 1940; Priestley lectr. Pa. State College, 1943. Fellow Am. Phys. Soc.; mem. Nat. Acad. Scis., Am. Chem. Soc., Am. Electrochem. Soc. (pres. 1935-37), Am. Acad. Arts and Scis., Harvey Soc., Am. Philos. Soc. Author: The Principles of Electrochemistry. Contbr. to Jour. Am. Chem. Soc., others. Awarded William H. Nichols medal, 1942; President's Certificate of Merit for War Researches, 1948; Edward Goodrich Acheson Medal of Electrochem. Soc., 1948. Home: 172 W. 79th St., N.Y.C. 24. Office: Rockefeller Inst., 66th St. and York Av., N.Y.C. 21. Died Sept. 23, 1965.

MACINTYRE, ARCHIBALD JAMES, educator, mathematician; b. Sheffield, Eng., July 3, 1908; s. William Ewart Gladstone Archibald and Mary (Askew) M.; Ph.D., U. Cambridge, 1933; m. Sheila Scott, Dec. 30, 1940; children—Alister W., Douglas Scott (dec.), Susan E. Came to U.S., 1958. Asst. lectr. U. Swansea, 1930-31, U. Sheffield, 1931-36; lectr. U. Aberdeen, 1936-58; mem. faculty U. Cin., 1958-69, Charles P. Taft prof. math., 1963-69. Mem. Royal Soc. Edinburgh. Address: Cincinnati OH Died 1969.

MACK, CARL THEODORE, lawyer, elec. engr.; b. Easton, Pa., July 24, 1896; s. George Brinton and Barbara Henrietta (Kilian) M.; E.E., Lafayette Coll., 1917; LL.B., George Washington U., 1924; m. Rose B. Snyder, June 20, 1928 (dec. Apr. 1947); m. 2d, Elizabeth E. Roulette, Oct. 1, 1949. Engr., Henry L. Doherty and Co., 1917-21; asst. in patent lawyers office, 1921-28; mem. patent firm Stone, Boyden & Mack. 1928-56, Stone & Mack, 1956-67. Trustee Lafayette Coll. Research Found. Served with U.S. Army, 1917-19. Mem. Am. Patent Law Assn. (treas. 1944-46, sec. 1946-48, bd. mgrs. 1948-51). Am., D.C. bar assns., All Pa. Coll. Alumni Assn. Washington (pres. 1961-63), Phi Beta Kappa, Tau Beta Pi. Presbyterian. Mason (32, K.T., Shriner). Home: Washington DC Died Dec. 1, 1971.

MACK, JOHN GIVAN DAVIS, mech. engr.; b. Terre Haute, Ind., Sept. 5, 1867; s. William and Amanda Jane (Davis) M.; B.S., Rose Poly. Inst., Terre Haute, 1887; M.E., Cornell U., 1888; m. Laura Abby Davis, Nov. 24, 1903. In gen. engring. practice, 1888-93; instr. engring., 1893-95; asst. prof. machine design, 1895-1903, prof., 1903-15, Coll. of Engring., U. of Wis.; state chief engineer of Wis., 1915—. Chief mech. dept. R.R. Commn. of Wis., 1905-12 (except 1 yr.); made first valuations of rolling stock and other equipment of all railroads in state of Wis. Mem. Engring. Soc. of Wis. (pres. 1913-14). Vice-chmn. and engring. rep. Wis. State Council Defense, 1917-19; mem. and sec. Wis. Deep Waterways Commn.; dir. Nat. Rivers and Harbors Congress. Mem. Minn.-Wis. Boundary Commn. Mason. Home: Madison, Wis. Died Feb. 24, 1924.

MACK, JULIAN ELLIS, physicist; b. La Porte, Ind., Apr. 26, 1903; s. Charles Samuel and Laura Gordon (Test) M.; A.B., U. Mich., 1924, A.M., 1925, Ph.D., 1928; Nat. Research fellow Princeton, Mich., Minn. and Uppsala univs., 1928-30; m. Mary Brackett, on June 11, 1932; children—Newell Brackett, Cornelia. Asst., U. Mich., 1924-25, instr., 1925-28, lectr., summer 1931; summer positions Nat. Bur. Standards, 1925, 1926; faculty U. Wis. since 1930, prof. physics since 1950; vis. asst. prof. Princeton, 1941-42, physicist uranium project, 1942-43; physicist Los Alamos Lab., 1943-46; John Simon Guggenheim Meml. fellow, 1950-51; pres. Design, Inc. Mem. NRC com. on line spectra of elements; Nat. Acad. Sci. adv. panel atomic physics Nat. Bur. Standards, 1965—; cons. USAF, Project Matterhorn, Los Alamos Sci. Lab.; sci. adviser Am. Embassy, Stockholm, Sweden, 1959-61. Pres. Madison Art Assn. 1956-57. Mem. Fedn. Am. Scientists (nat. council 1954-55). Home: 3501 Sunset Dr., Shorewood Hills, Madison 5, Wis. Died Apr. 14, 1966.

MACKAY, JAMES, explorer; b. Kildonan, County Sutherland, Scotland, 1759; s. George and Elizabeth (McDonald) M.; m. Isabella Long, Feb. 24, 1800. Came to Canada, 1776, explored for British, then went to La.; dir. 3d expdn. sent by Spanish Comml. Co. to explore country on both sides of Missouri River and across continent to Pacific Ocean; constructed forts for protection of Spanish trade, resulting in peace among Indian tribes and between Indians and Spanish; took possession of Brit. fort at the Mandan village, prepared map of region explored; dep. surveyor for Spanish traders in Am., 1797; capt. St. Louis County (Mo.) Militia, comdt. of San Andres, Mo.; judge Ct. of Quarter Sessions, Mo. Territory, 1804; mem. Mo. Territorial Legislature, 1816; maj. militia; maps of his explorations later used by Lewis and Clark, 1804-06. Died Mar. 16, 1822.

MACKAY, ROLAND PARKS, neurologist; b. Atlanta, Ga., Oct. 25, 1900; s. William Robert and Alice (Farmer) M.; B.A., Emory U., Atlanta, 1920; M.D., U. Toronto (Ont., Can.), 1925; post-grad. work in neuropathology, Hamburg, Germany, 1932-33; m. Margaret Pomroy, July 31, 1929; children—Virginia Carol, Kathleen Louise, William Charles. Engaged in practice of medicine since 1925; interne Henry Ford Hosp., Detroit, Mich., 1925-26; fellow in neurology Mayo Foundation, 1926-29; asso. prof. neurology, Rush Med. Coll., U. Chgo., 1929-34; asso. prof. neurology, U. Ill., 1934-42, prof., 1942-61; prof. neurology Northwestern U., 1961—; attending neurologist St. Luke's Hosp., Chgo., 1935-59; attending neurologist, chmn. dept. neurology Presbyn.-St. Luke's Hosp., 1959-61; sr. att. neurologist Chgo. Wesley Meml. Hosp.; cons. neurologist, Hines VA Hosp., I.C., B.&O., C.R.I.&P. railroads, Ill. State Psychiatric Inst. Dir. Am. Bd. Psychiatry and Neurology, 1945-53, pres., 1953—. Mem. adv. bd. Nat. Found. (chmn. 1957), Nat. Multiple Sclerosis Soc. (chmn. 1960-62). Fellow A.C.P., Am. Acad. Neurology, A.A.A.S., Am. Psychiat. Assn.; mem. Am. Epilepsy Soc. (pres. 1958), A.M.A., Am. Neurol. Assn. (pres. 1954), Soc. Biol. Psychiatry (pres. 1952), Assn. British Neurologists (hon. fgn. mem.), Pan Am. Med. Assn., French Soc. Neurology, Assn. of Research in Nervous and Mental Disease (v.p., 1951), (past pres.), Can. Legion (hon. life mem., grand Central Neuropsychiat. Assn., Phi Beta Kappa, Alpha Omega Alpha, Sigma Xi. Presbyn. Author: The Exogenous Toxins, Tice's Practice of Medicine. Editor Year Book of Neurology, 1949—. Office: 8 S. Michigan Av., Chgo. 3. Died Feb. 21, 1968.

MACKAYE, JAMES MORRISON STEELE (STAGE NAME STEELE MACKAYE), dramatist, actor, inventor; b. Buffalo, N.Y., June 6, 1842; s. James Morrison and Emily (Steele) McKay; ed. Ecole des Beaux-Arts, Paris, 1858-59; m. Jennie Spring, June 30, 1862; m. 2d, Mary Medbery, June 6, 1865; several children, including Percy. Made 1st stage appearance as Hamlet in a regtl. performance during Civil War, 1862; inventor "photo-sculpture," launched company to commercialize it; made début in Monaldi, N.Y.C., 1872; played Hamlet, Paris, 1872, 1st Am. to play role in Eng., London, 1873; opened an acting sch., N.Y.C., 1875; wrote Won at Last, acted at Wallacks, 1877; opened Madison Square Theatre (one of the earliest small theatres), 1879; wrote Hazel Kirke (his most notable play), 1880, ran for over a year; built Lyceum Theatre, N.Y.C., established 1st dramatic sch. in Am. (later Am. Acad. Dramatic Arts); inventor mech. and elec. stage devices; 1st to light N.Y. theatre entirely by electricity, 1884; began erection of unsuccessful Spectatorium (vast auditorium) at Chgo. World's Fair, 1892. Died Timpas, Colo., Feb. 25, 1894.

MACKEE, GEORGE MILLER, dermatologist; b. Jersey City, Sept. 19, 1878; s. Horace Elber and Jennie Amanda (Updyke) MacK.; M.D., N.Y.U.-Bellevue Hospital Medical College, 1899; married Katherine M. Sullivan. Private practice, New York City, 1900- Post-grad. Med. Sch. and Hosp.; prof. emeritus dermatology Columbia U.; formerly dir. div. of dermatology and syphilology, N.Y. Skin and Cancer Unit, N.Y. Post-Grad. Med. Sch. and Hosp., Columbia; dermatologist Welfare Hosp.; cons. dermatologist N.Y. Post-Grad., St. Luke's and St. Vincent's hosps., N.Y. Skin and Cancer Unit. Fellow N.Y. Acad. Medicine, N.Y. Dermatol. Soc., Manhattan Dermatol. Soc., N.Y. Roentgen Soc., A.A.A.S.; corr. mem. British Assn. Dermatology and Syphilology; mem. A.M.A., Am. Acad. Dermatology and Syphilology (past pres.), Am. Dermatol. Assn. (past pres.), Am. Roentgen Ray Soc., Am. Radiol. Soc., Radium Soc., Am. Coll. Radiology, Radiol. Soc. N.A.; hon. mem. Cuban Dermatol. Soc., Argentine Dermatol. Soc. Author: X-Ray and Radium Treatment in Diseases of Skin, Cutaneous Cancer and Pre-Cancer; Skin Diseases in Children. Contbr. to med. jours. Address: Haviland Rd., Stamford, Conn. Died May 8, 1955.

MACKELLAR, PATRICK, mil. engr.; b. Argyllshire, Scotland, 1717. Served as engr. Brit. Army, 1742-51; accompanied Gen. Braddock to Am., 1754; considered most competent engr. in Am. as early as 1756; sub-dir., maj. in capacity of engring., in charge siege of Louisbourg under Gen. Amherst; chief engr. under Wolfe at capture of Quebec; organized tng. sch. for engrs., 1760; chief engr. under Monckton in capture of Martinique, 1762; lt. col., chief engr. under Albemarle at siege of Havana, 1763; col., dir. defenses at Minorca, Balearic Islands, West Mediterranean, 1777. Died Minorca, Oct. 22, 1778.

MACKENZIE, ARTHUR STANLEY, prof. of physics, Bryn Mawr Coll.; b. Pictou, N.S., Sept. 26, 1865; s. George Augustus M.; barrister; grad. Dalhousie Univ., Halifax, N.S., 1885 (Ph.D., Johns Hopkins, 1894); m. Indianapolis, May 29, 1895, Mary Lewis Taylor. Tutor in mathematics, Dalhousie Univ., 1887-89; scholar and fellow in physics, Johns Hopkins, 1889-91; asso., asso. prof. and prof. physics, Bryn Mawr Coll., since 1891; member American Philosophical Soc., Am. Physical Soc. Author: The Laws of Gravitation, 1900 A1. Contbr. to proc. of socs., revs., etc. Address: Bryn Mawr, Pa.

MACKENZIE, KENNETH GERARD, chem. engr.; b. N.Y.C., Feb. 4, 1887; s. Kenneth and Caroline M. (Weeks) M.; Ph.B., Yale, 1907, M.S., 1909; m. Margerie Mitchill, June 29, 1910 (div. Oct. 1960); children—Neil Mitchill, Kenneth Donald, Jean M. (Mrs. Albert T. Scully). Asst. instr. chemistry Yale, 1907-08; research chemist N.Y. Testing Lab., Maurer, N.J., 1908-10; chief chemist Nairn Linoleum Co., Kearney, N.J., 1910-11; cons. chemist The Texas Co., 1911-33, asst. to v.p., chief technologist, 1933-54; v.p., dir. research Texaco Devel. Corp., 1933-54; pres. Kenneth G. Mackenzie Assos. Cons., 1954-67. Fellow A.A.A.S., Chem. Soc., Am. Inst. Chemists, Inst. Petroleum (Gt. Britain); mem. Am. Soc. Testing Materials (past pres.), Soc. Chem. Industry Soc. Automotive Engrs., Am. Inst. Chem. Engrs., Am. Chem. Soc., Air Pollution Control Assn., Franklin Inst. (mem. com. sci. and arts), Am. Petroleum Inst., Am. Inst. Mining, Metall. and Petroleum Engrs. Republican. Episcopalian. Clubs: The Chemists' of New York (past pres.), Yale, Cloud; Chemists' of Chicago. Address: Chicago IL Died Dec. 8, 1967.

MACKEOWN, SAMUEL STUART, (mak ku'en), univ. prof., cons. engr.; b. New York, N.Y., Dec. 3, 1895; s. Joseph James and Dora (Chancellor) M.; A.B., Cornell U., 1917, Ph.D., 1923; m. Littie B. Uhrlaub, March 21, 1928 (died Oct. 8, 1948); 1 dau., Littie M. (Mrs. Littie Mackeown Hicks). Assistant physicist, United States Bureau Standards, 1919; instr. physics, Cornell U., 1920-23; Nat. Research Fellow in physics, 1923-26; asst. prof. elec. engring., Calif. Inst. Tech., Pasadena, 1926-29, asso. prof., 1929-41, prof. since 1941; cons. engr. and patent expert for Gen. Electric Co., Am. Telephone & Telegraph Co., Metro-Goldwyn-Mayer, Technicolor, Standard Oil of Calif., etc. since 1929. Served as 2d lt., S.C. (Radio Development Sect.), U.S.A., 1918-19; lt. comdr., U.S.N.R. since 1938. Fellow Inst. Radio Engrs. (mem. bd. editors), A.A.A.S.; mem. Am. Inst. Elec. Engrs., Am. Assn. Univ. Profs., Sigma Xi, Tau Beta Pi. Republican. Presbyterian. Clubs: Athenaeum, University, Valley Hunt (Pasadena); Cornell (New York). Home: California Club, 538 S. Flower St., Los Angeles 13. Died May 29, 1952.

MACKIE, THOMAS TURLAY, coll. prof., physician; b. Great Barrington, Mass., May 10, 1895; s. David Ives and Isabel (Turlay) M.; A.B., Harvard, 1918; M.D., Columbia, 1924; D.T.M. and Hygiene, London Sch. of Hygiene and Tropical Medicine, London, 1931; m. Carolyn B. Van Cortlandt, May 31, 1921 (divorced 1941); children—Mrs. Wm. H. Savage, Madame Philippe Bouriez; married second, Janet Welch, March 5, 1942 (divorced 1951); married third time Helen Holme Warnock, Dec. 19, 1951. Asst. in medicine Columbia, 1926-29; instr., 1933-33; research asso. Pub. Health and Preventive Medicine, Cornell U. Med. Coll., 1933-35, asso., 1935-46; asst. clin. prof. medicine Columbia, 1938-46; prof. preventive medicine and head of dept. Bowman Gray Sch. of Medicine, Wake Forest Coll., 1946-51; dir. Inst. of Tropical Medicine, 1947—; asst. physician. Presbyterian Hosp., N.Y. City, 1929-33; asst. attending physician Fifth Av. Hosp., 1932-35; attending physician Roosevelt Hosp. 1936-46; cons. physician Beekman St. Hosp., N.Y. Infirmary for Women and Children, Fairview Hosp., Great Barrington, Mass., 1946. Cons. in tropical medicine to U.S. sec. of war, 1940-42, Vets. adminstr. Branch 4, 1946-49; cons. in internal medicine and tropical medicine, Atlanta area, Vets. Adminstrn., 1949—; spl. cons. epidemiology div. U.S.P.H.S.; mem. subcom. on tropical diseases Nat. Research Council, 1940-42 and, 1947—; mem. health com. Office for Relief and Rehabilitation, Dept. of State, Army Bd. for Investigation of Influenza and other Epidemic Diseases 42; cons. VA Hosp., West Haven, Conn., Norwalk (Conn.) and Stamford (Conn.) hosps., Roosevelt Hosp., N.Y.C. Chmn. bd. Am. Found. for Tropical Medicine, Fellow A.C.P., Royal Soc. Tropical Medicine and Hygiene; Mem. Am. Clinical and Climatol. Assn., A.A.A.S., Am. Soc. Tropical Medicine, Am. Acad. Tropical Medicine, American Gastro Enterol. Assn., A.M.A., N.Y. Acad. Medicine, Alpha Omega Alpha. Recipient Duncan Medal, London School of Tropical Medicine, 1931; Legion of Merit, 1946. Episcopalian. Co-author: Manual of Tropical Medicine. Home: North Av., Westport, Conn. Died Oct. 5, 1955; buried Great Barrington, Mass.

MACKIN, JOSEPH HOOVER, geologist; b. Oswego, N.Y., Nov. 16, 1906; s. William David and Catherine (Hoover) M.; B.S., N.Y.U., 1930; M.A., Columbia, 1932, Ph.D., 1937; m. Esther Fisk, Sept. 16, 1930; children—Barbara Catherine, Robert Fisk. Mem. faculty U. Wash., 1934-61, prof. geology, 1946-61; Farish prof. geology, U. Tex., 1961-68; part-time geologist U.S. Geol. Survey, 1943-54. Cons. NASA, 1963; cons. engring. geology to govt., state hwy. depts., bus. firms. Chairman div. of earth scis. NRC, 1965-67. Fellow Geol. Soc. Am. (chmn. cordilleran sec. 1950, councillor 1950-53); mem. Nat. Acad. Scis., Soc. Econ. Geology, Am. Geophys. Union, Am. Assn. Petroleum Geologists (distinguished lectr. 1953), A.A.A.S., Sigma Xi (nat. lectr. 1963). Club: Cosmos (Washington). Home: Austin TX Died Aug. 12, 1968.

MACLAREN, MALCOLM, (mak-lar'en), electrical engr.; b. Annapolis, Md., June 21, 1869; s. Donald and Elizabeth Stockton (Green) MacL.; A.B., Princeton, 1890, E.E., 1892, A.M., 1893; m. Angelina Post Hodge, June 1900; children—Malcolm, Angelina Hodge, Wistar Hodge, Elizabeth Green. Engr. with Westinghouse Elec. & Mfg. Co., Pittsburgh, 1893-98 and 1905-08, London, Eng., 1898-1900; chief elec. engr., British Westinghouse Electric & Mfg. Co., Manchester, Eng., 1900-05; prof. elec. engring., Princeton, 1908-37; retired. Commd. capt., Engr. R.C., Dec. 1917; maj. N.A., Apr. 1918; lt. col., Engr. R.C., July 1919; col., 1924; on duty at Washington during service. Mem. Am. Inst. Elec. Engrs. Republican. Presbyterian. Home: Princeton, N.J. Died Sep. 24, 1945.

MACLAY, ISAAC WALKER, civil engr., real estate dealer; b. New York, May 14, 1841; s. Dr. Archibald and Julia Anne (Walker) M.; ed. Univ. Grammar Sch. and U. City of New York to 1860; grad. U.S. Mil. Acad., 1864; m. Laura Amelia Havemeyer, Nov. 1869. Commd. 2d lt., 1st U.S. Arty., 1864; served in Civil War, 1864-66; was at Ford's Theatre when President Lincoln was assassinated, assisted in carrying the President to the Peterson house, and, at request of Mrs. Lincoln, brought Dr. Stone to bedside. Promoted 1st lt. Ordnance Corps, U.S.A.; served as ordnance officer in various arsenals, 1864-73; resigned. Asst. topog. engr., Dept. Pub. Parks, New York; later chief engr. L.I. R.R.; apptd. a city surveyor engaged in practice of engring. with William E. Davies as Maclay & Davies until 1892; since then in real estate business. Pres. Maclay & Davies Real Estate Co., Yonkers Wharf & Warehouse Co.; v.p. Pelhamdale Land Co.; trustee People's Savings Bank, Yonkers. An incorporator and charter mem. New York Zoöl. Soc., Underwriters' Club, New York, Md. Soc. of N.Y. Trustee Va. Union U.; mem. bd. mgrs. Am. Bapt. Home Mission Soc.; mem. exec. com. Andrew H. Green Memorial Assn. Del. to Internat. Sunday Rest Congress and mem. Internat. Congress Arts and Science at St. Louis Expn., 1904. Author: Henry Sater (1690-1754), 1897; Life of Rev. Archibald Maclay, D.D. (1776-1860), 1902. Home: Yonkers, N.Y. Died 1909.

MACLAY, WILLIAM WALTER, civil engr.; b. N.Y.C., Mar. 27, 1846; s. Dr. Archibald and Julia Anne (Walker) M.; grad. U.S. Naval Acad., 1863; A.M., N.Y.U., 1868, C.E., 1872; m. Marian Bensel, Sept. 16, 1874. Commd. ensign, 1863; master, 1865, advanced through grades to lt. comdr., 1868; participated in both attacks on Ft. Fisher; after war made cruise of 3 yrs. around the world with Commodore John Goldsborough, as his navigating officer; apptd. by Japanese govt. to survey and designate sites for light houses, 1868; apptd. acting fleet capt. to Commodore Goldsborough, comdg. U.S. Asiatic Squadron, 1868; asst. prof. mathematics U.S. Naval Acad., 1868-69; resigned from Navy to study civil engring., 1871; asst. engr. and 1st asst. engr. N.Y. dept. of docks, 1873-93; now cons. engr.; pres., mgr. Glens Falls Portland Cement Co., 1893-1905. Mem. Inst. Civil Engrs., London, Am. Soc. C.E. (Norman gold medal, 1877), Internat. Soc. for Testing Materials; corr. mem. N.Y. Hist. Soc. Club: University (N.Y.C.). Author: Notes and Experiments on the Use and Testing of Portland Cements, 1877; Portland Cement for Engineering Works, 1892. Home: Lee, Mass. Office: 220 W. 57th St., N.Y.C. Deceased.

MACLENNAN, FRANCIS WILLIAM, mining engr.; b. Cornwall, Ont., Can., Oct. 14, 1876; s. Donald B. and Elizabeth M. (Cline) M.; E.E., McGill University, Montreal, 1898, M.E., 1900; studied Liège U., Belgium, 1898-99; LL.D., McGill University, 1931; m. Alta May Clack, Aug. 7, 1919. Engr. and assayer various mines in B.C., 1900-03, later with mines in Ore., Utah and Nev.; gen. supt. mines, Cerro de Pasco Copper Co., Peru, 1907-10; examination and reports on mines in U.S., Can. and S.A., 1910-13; with Miami (Ariz.) Copper Co. since 1913, as mine supt., 1919-38, gen. mgr., v.p. and cons. engr. since 1938. Naturalized citizen of U.S., 1920. Mem. Am. Inst. Mining and Metall. Engrs., Mining and Metall. Soc. America, Canadian Inst. of Mining and Metallurgy, Zeta Psi. Awarded William Lawrence Saunders gold medal, Am. Inst. Mining and Metall. Engrs., 1931. Clubs: California, Wilshire Country, Los Angeles Country (Los Angeles, Calif.); Arizona, Phoenix Country (Phoenix, Ariz.); Cobre Valle Country (Miami, Ariz.). Home: 406 S. June St., Los Angeles, Calif. Died June 28, 1947; buried in Forest Lawn Memorial Park.

MACLEOD, COLLN MUNRO, educator; b. Nova Scotia, Can., Jan. 28, 1909; s. John Charles and Lillian (Munro) MacL.; M.D., McGill U., 1932; m. Elizabeth Randol, July 2, 1938; 1 dau., Mary. Came to U.S., 1934, naturalized, 1941. Intern Montreal Gen. Hosp., 1932-34; resident in medicine, Rockefeller Inst. Hosp., 1937-38; asst. to asso. in medicine Rockefeller Inst. for Med. Research, 1934-41; prof. microbiology New York University College Medicine, 1941-56; professor research medicine University Pa. School Medicine, 1956-60, prof. medicine N.Y.U. Sch. Medicine, 1960-66; mem. Pres.'s Sci. Adv. Com., 1961-64; chmn. Life Scis. Panel; exec. com. div. med. scis. Nat. Research Council, 1952-56; dir. Commn. on Pneumonia Army Epidemiol. Bd., 1941-46; chief preventive medicine sect. Com. Med. Research Office Scientific Research and Development, 1944-46; pres. Armed Forces Epidemiol. Bd., 1947-55; mem. panel mil. and field medicine Com. Med. Scis. Nat. Mil. Establishment, 1948-52; adv. panel on med. scis. to Asst. Sec. Def. for research and devel., 1952-56; chmn. com. on research in influenza USPHS; member Army Sci. Adv. Panel, 1958-61; chmn. sci. adv. com. Walter Reed Army Inst. Research, 1957-61; chmn. Health Research Council N.Y.C., from 1960; deputy director Office Sci. and Tech., 1963-64; v.p. med. affairs Commonwealth Fund, from 1966; consultant President's Sci. Adv. Com., from 1964; U.S. chmn. U.S.-Japan Coop. Med. Sci. Program, 1965-72; pres., sci. dir. Okla. Med. Research Found., 1970-72; mem. sci. adv. com. Hosp. for Sick Children, Toronto; vis. com. biology Harvard; adv. bd. chemistry Princeton. Dir., Merck & Co.; trustee Merck Co. Found., Sloan-Kettering Inst. for Sci. Research. Recipient Bristol award Infectious Disease Soc., 1971. Mem. Nat. Acad. Scis., Am. Epidemiol. Soc., Am. Assn. Immunologists (pres. 1951-52), Soc. Am. Bacteriologists, Assn. Am. Physicians, Soc. Clin. Investigation, N.Y. Acad. Medicine, Am. Philos. Soc., Am. Acad. Arts and Scis., Harvey Soc. (pres. 1955-56). Club: Century Association. Contbr. articles med. jours. Home: Oklahoma City OK Died Feb. 12, 1972.

MACLEOD, JOHN JAMES RICKARD, physiologist; b. Dunkeld, Scotland, Sept. 6, 1876; s. Rev. Robert and Jane (McWalter) M.; M.B., Ch.B., U. of Aberdeen, 1898; U. of Leipzig, 1898-99; D.P.H., U. of Cambridge, Eng., 1902; m. Mary Watson McWalter, July 1903. Prof. physiology, Western Reserve Med. Coll., Cleveland, 1903—. Lt. (with captain's certificate) in Ambulance Corps of 19th Middlesex Rifles, 1900-03. Presbyn. Fellow A.A.A.S. (v.p. Sect. K). Author: Practical Physiology (jointly), 1902; Recent Advances in Physiology (jointly), 1905; Organic Chemistry (jointly), 1907; Diabetes, Its Pathological Physiology, 1913; Fundamentals of Physiology, 1917. Home: Cleveland, O. Died Mar. 16, 1935.

MACLOSKIE, GEORGE, biologist; b. Castledawson, Ireland, Sept. 14, 1834; s. Paul and Mary (McClure) M.; A.B., Queen's U., Ireland, 1857, A.M., 1858; LL.B., U. of London, 1868, LL.D., 1871; D.Sc., Queen's U., 1887; hon. A.M., Princeton U., 1896; m. Mary C. Dunn, Aug. 18, 1863 (died 1907); 2d, Mrs. Lila M. Campbell, June 19, 1909. Ordained Presbyn. ministry, 1861; pastor Ballygoney, Ireland, 1861-72; prof. biology, 1875-1906, emeritus prof., 1906, Princeton. Author: Elementary Botany, 1887; Flora of Patagonia, 1905. Address: Princeton, N.J. Died Jan. 4, 1920.

MACLURE, WILLIAM, geologist; b. Ayr, Scotland, Oct. 17, 1763; s. David and Ann (Kennedy) McC. Became partner Miller, Hast & Co., London, Eng., 1782; came to Am. 1796; apptd. a commr. to settle spoliation claims between Am. and France, 1803; made geol. map of U.S. (1st of its kind); an original mem. Acad. Natural Scis., 1812, pres., 1817-40, supr. publication of 1st vols. of Acad.'s Journal; visited West Indies, studied volcanic phases of geology, 1816-17; founder sch., New Harmony, Ind., 1824, New Harmony Working Men's Inst., 1838; pres. Am. Geol. Soc., several years. Author: Observations on the Geology of the U.S., 1817; Opinions on Various Subjects, Dedicated to the Industrious Producer, 2 vols., 1831-37. Died San Angel, Mexico, Mar. 23, 1840.

MACMILLAN, CONWAY, state botanist of Minn.; b. Hillsdale, Mich., Aug. 26, 1867; s. George and Josephine (Young) MacM.; grad. Univ. of Neb., 1885, A.M., 1886; grad. studies at Harvard and Johns Hopkins; m. Maud R. Sanborn, Aug. 8, 1891. Hon. commr. U.S. Dept. of Agr. to Eng., 1897; prof. botany, U. of Minn., since 1891. Mem. Am. Bot. Soc., Société Botanique de France. Author: Twenty-two Common Insects of Nebraska; The Metaspermae of the Minnesota Valley; Minnesota Plant Life; etc. Editor: Minnesota Botanical Studies; Postelsia—The Year Book of the Minnesota Seaside Station. Dir. Minn. Seaside Sta. in Straits of Fuca. Address: University of Minnesota, Minneapolis. Died June 5, 1929.

MACMILLAN, WILLIAM DUNCAN, mathematician, astronomer; b. LaCrosse, Wis., July 24, 1871; s. Duncan D. and Mary Jane (MacCrea) MacM.; studied Lake Forest Coll., Ill., 1888-90, Sc.D., 1930; studied U. of Va., 1895; A.B., Ft. Worth U., 1898; A.M., U. of Chicago, 1906, Ph.D., 1908; Sc.D., Lake Forest Coll., 1930; unmarried. Research asst. in geology, U. of Chicago, 1907-08, asst. in mathematics and astronomy, 1908-09, instr. astronomy, 1909-12, asst. prof., 1912-19, asso. prof., 1919-24, prof., 1924-36, prof. emeritus since 1936. Maj. Ordnance Dept., U.S. Army, 1918. Fellow A.A.A.S., Royal Astron. Soc.; mem. Am. Math. Soc., Math. Assn. America, Astron. and Astrophys. Soc. Am., Société Astronomique de France. Clubs: Quadrangle, University. Author: Statics and the Dynamics of a Particle, 1927; Theory of the Potential, 1930; Dynamics of Rigid Bodies, 1936; and many scientific memoirs. Home: Marine on St. Croix, Minn. Died Nov. 14, 1948.

MACNAUGHTON, LEWIS WINSLOW, geologist; b. Nueva Gerona, Isla de Pinas, Cuba, Apr. 23, 1902; s. David and Mabelle Asenath (Drisko) M.; brought to United States in 1908; Bachelor of Arts Cornell U., 1925; m. Ina Mantooth, Dec. 6, 1928; children—Bruce Alan, Lewis Eugene. With Humble Oil & Refining Co., 1926-28, Rycade Oil Corp., 1928-30, Amerada Petroleum Corp., 1930-36; petroleum cons., Dallas, 1936-38; partner DeGolyer & MacNaughton, 1939-49, pres., 1949-56, chmn., 1956-62, sr. chmn., 1962-67; ret.; dir. Great Plains Devel. Co. Can., Ltd., Nat. Beryllia Corp., Cities Service Co., Dresser Industries, Inc., Republic National Bank Dallas, Southwestern Public Service Co., Trunkline Gas Co. Trustee S.W. Center Advanced Studies, Ft. Burgwin Research Center, Incorporated. Pres., trustee Sci. Information Inst., Dallas; dir. Greenhill Sch. Fellow A.A.A.S., Am. Geog. Society, Geological Society of London; member Anglo-Texas Society, Asociacion Mexicana de Geologos Petroleros, Dallas Geol. Soc., Am. Assn. Petroleum Geologists, Am. Inst. Mining and Metall. Engrs., N.Y. Mineral. Soc., Tex. Acad. Sci., Alberta Soc. Petroleum Geologists, Soc. Exploration Geophysicists, also member of Dallas Council World Affairs, Am. Geophys. Union, Am. Petroleum Inst., Am. Mgmt. Assn., Am., Tex. philatelic socs., Archeol. Inst. Am., Engrs. Club Dallas, Geochem. Soc., Internat. Oil Scouts Assn., Geologische Vereinigung, Germany, Nat. Indsl. Conf. Bd., Nat. Oil Equipment Mfrs. and Dels. Soc. (hon.), Nat. Oil Scouts and Landmen's Assn. (asso.), Newcomen Soc., Paleontol. Assn., Philos. Soc. Tex., Tex. Soc. Profl. Engrs., Soc. Econ. Paleontologists and Mineralogists, Koninklijk Nederlands Geologisch Mijnbouwkundig Gerootschap, Netherlands, Dallas Hist. Soc. Sigma Gamma Epsilon. Clubs: Brook, Explorers, Cornell (N.Y.C.); University (Mex., D.F.); Petroleum (Los Angeles); Ranchmen's (Calgary); Houston; Petroleum, Dallas, Lancers, Northwood, Chaparral, Texas (Dallas). Contbr. articles profl. jours. Home: Dallas TX Died Feb. 26, 1969.

MACNAUGHTON, MORAY FRASER, quality control engr.; b. Westmount, Que., Apr. 8, 1899; s. Naughton and Mary (Anderson) M.; B.Sc., McGill U., 1922; M.S., U. Mich., 1924; m. Doris Evelyn Henry, Oct. 10, 1928; children—Edythe Margaret (Mrs. J. S. Guillon), Cara Mary. With inspection dept. Milton Hersey Co., Ltd., Montreal, Can., 1924-26, chief inspector, 1927-33, dir. inspection dept., 1934-40, v.p., 1941-54; v.p. tech. control Mt. Royal Paving Supplies Ltd., Montreal, 1955—. Mem. Assn. Asphalt Paving Tech. (pres. 1959), Engring. Inst. Can., Am. Concrete Inst., Corp. Profl. Engrs. Que., Canadian Tech. Asphalt Assn. Club: Engineers (Montreal). Home: 9 Hudson Av., Westmount, Que. Office: 3701 Jarry St. E., St. Michel, Que., Can. Died Dec. 7, 1962.

MACNEAL, WARD J., bacteriologist; b. Fenton, Mich., Feb. 17, 1881; s. Edward and Jane Elizabeth (Pratt), MacN.; A.B., U. of Mich., 1901, Ph.D., 1904, M.D., 1905, hon. Sc.D., 1939; m. Mabel Perry, Dec. 28, 1905; children—Edward Perry (dec.), Herbert Pratt, Perry Scott, Mabel Ruth. Asst. and fellow in bacteriology, U. of Mich., 1901-04, instr. histology, 1905-06; instr. in anatomy and bacteriology, W. Va. U., 1906-07; asst. chief in bacteriology, Ill. Agrl. Expt. Sta., 1907-11; asst. prof. bacteriology, U. of Ill., 1908-11; lecturer on pathology and bacteriology, 1911-12, prof. and asst. dir. labs., 1912-15, prof. and dir. of labs., 1915-22, prof. and dir. dept. pathology and bacteriology, 1922-24 and 1930-39, prof. bacteriology since 1939, prof. and dir. labs., 1924-30, mem. bd. trustees, 1921-24; v.chmn. Med. Bd., 1924-29, N.Y. Post-Grad. Med. Sch. and Hosp.; asst. to pres. Josiah Macy Jr. Foundation, 1931-36. Mem. Ill. State Pellagra Commn., 1909-12; mem. Thompson-McFadden Pellagra Commn., Am. Trench Fever Commn., France, 1918. Capt., Med. R.C., 1917; lt. col., M.R.C. U.S.

Army, 1919; col., 1925; with A.E.F. in France to Feb. 1919. Fellow A.A.A.S.; mem. Soc. Am. Bacteriologists, Am. Assn. Pathologists and Bacteriologists (council 1929-35, pres. 1932), Assn. for Cancer Research (council 1925-33; pres. 1934), Nat. Assn. Tuberculosis, A.M.A., Soc. Exptl. Biology and Medicine, N.Y. Acad. Medicine, N.Y. Pathol. Soc. (pres. 1922-23; trustee 1925-30, 1932-37 and since 1940), N.Y. State Soc. of Pathologists (v.p. 1941, pres. 1942-45), Harvey Soc., Sigma Xi. Author: Studies in Nutrition, Volumes I to V (with H. S. Grindley), 1911-29; Pathogenic Microörganisms, 1914, 2d edit., 1920. Contbr. to Marshall's Microbiology, 1917, 20, etc. Editor Third Report Thompson Pellagra Commission, 1917. Home: 301 E. 21st St., New York 10, N.Y. Office: 303 E. 20th St., New York 3, N.Y. Died Aug. 15, 1946.

MACNEVEN, WILLIAM JAMES, physician; b. County Galway, Ireland, Mar. 21, 1763; s. James and Rosa (Dolphin) MacN.; studied medicine U. Prague; M.D., U. Vienna, 1784; m. Jane Riker, 1810, 3 children. Participated in Irish Revolution, 1797-98, polit. prisoner, 1798-1802; served with Irish brigade French Army, 1804-05; came to N.Y.C., 1805; elected prof. obstetrics Coll. Physicians and Surgeons, 1808, prof. chemistry, 1812, taught materia medica, 1816-20; established 1st chem. lab. in N.Y.C.; co-editor N.Y. Med. and Philos. Jour. and Review; elected mem. Am. Philos. Soc., 1823; with colleagues founded med. sch. affiliated with Rutgers Coll., 1826-30; established employment bur. to find positions for Irish immigrants; organizer, 1st pres. Friends of Ireland, 1828-29. Author: Rambles through Switzerland in the Summer and Autumn of 1802, published 1803; Pieces of Irish History, 1807; Expositions of the Atomic Theory, 1819. Editor: Brandes Chemistry, 1821. Died N.Y.C., July 12, 1841.

MACNIDER, WILLIAM DE BERNIERE, pharmacologist; b. Chapel Hill, N.C., June 25, 1881; s. Virginius St. Clair and Sophia Beatty (Mallett) M.; U. N.C., 1898-1903, M.D., 1903; student U. Chgo.; spl. student Western Res. U.; hon. D.Sc., Med. Coll. Va., 1933; LL.D., Davidson (N.C.), Coll., 1934; m. Sarah Foard, Jan. 23, 1918; 1 dau., Sarah Foard. Kenan prof. of pharmacology U. N.C., 1905—, Kenan research prof. of pharmacology, 1920, dean med. sch., 1937-40; Harvey Soc. lectr., 1928-29; Chandler Meml. lectr. Columbia U.; Smith-Reed-Russell lecturer George Washington U. Sch. of Medicine, 1938; Brown-Sequart lectr. Med. Coll. Va., 1938; Mayo Foundation lecturer, 1939; formerly special lecturer in pharmacology, Duke U. Med. Sch.; physician in chief pro tem. Peter Bent Brigham Hosp., Apr. 1925; cons. on gerontology Nat. Inst. of Health; mem. Nat. Bd. Med. Examiners (chmn. examination com.). Mem. NRC com. on nutritional aspects of ageing; chmn. Am. div. Internat. Club for Research on Ageing. Recipient Kober medal Assn. Am. Physicians, 1941. Fellow A.A.A.S., Am. Acad. Arts and Sciences, A.C.P.; mem. Am. Soc. for Pharmacology and Exptl. Therapeutics (pres. 1932-34, mem. council), A.M.A. (chmn. sect. of pharmacology and therapeutics, 1927), Med. Soc. N.C. (pres. 1925-26), Am. Physiol. Soc., Am. Assn. Pathologists and Bacteriologists, Am. Assn. Biol. Chemists, Soc. Exptl. Biology and Medicine (pres. 1941-42), Am. Assn. U. Profs., Am. Soc. Exptl. Pathology, Assn. Am. Physicians, Am. Assn. Anesthetists, Nat. Anaesthesia Research Soc. (research com.), Internat. Anaesthesia Research Soc. (pres. 1934-35), Elisha Mitchell Sci. Soc. (pres.), Am. Assn. Hist. Medicine, N.C. Acad. Science, Nat. Research Council (mem. com. on cellular physiology; mem. exec. com. med. div.), Nat. Acad. Sciences, N.Y. Acad. Sciences, Am. Soc. Naturalists, Am. Philos. Soc., Harvey Soc. (hon.), Pathological Soc. Great Britain and Ireland, Brit. Physiol. Soc. (asso. fgn. mem.), Gerontol. Soc. (chmn. council), Sigma Xi (pres. U. chpt.), Phi Chi, Sigma Nu, Phi Beta Kappa, Alpha Omega Alpha. Democrat. Episcopalian. Club: Cosmos (Washington). Asso. editor of proceedings Soc. for Exptl. Biology and Medicine; asso. editor the Quarterly Journal of Alcohol Study, Journal of Pharmacology and Experimental Therapeutics. Contbr. many articles to medical and biological jours. setting forth results of original pharmacol. investigations; research on production of acute and chronic nephritis; toxicity of the general anaesthetics for kidney with methods for protection; stability of acid-base equilibrium of blood in nephritis and in animals of different age periods; toxaemias of pregnancy. Research papers on Toxic Action of Alcohol, Uranium and Chloroform on the Liver, Liver Regeneration, The Resistance of atypical Regenerated Liver Cells to the Above Mentioned Toxic Agents, The Influence of Liver Degeneration and Repair on the Acid Base Equilibrium of the Blood, also papers dealing with acquired resistance of fixed tissue cells. Awarded Gibbs prize for med. research, 1930-31, by New York Acad. Medicine; Research medal, Southern Med. Assn., 1933. Delivered convocation address Am. Coll. of Physicians, 1942. Home: Chapel Hill, N.C. Died May 31, 1951; buried Chapel Hill Cemetery.

MACOMBER, ALEXANDER, (ma kum'ber), cons. engr.; b. Newton, Mass., May 21, 1885; s. James and Mary Elizabeth (Simmons) M.; B.S., Mass. Inst. Tech., 1907; m. Alfrieda Terry, Aug. 15, 1929. Elec. engr. No. Cal. Power Co., 1907-10; engr. with Chas. H. Tenney & Co., mgrs. pub. utilities, 1910-17; mem. Macomber & West, cons. engrs. and mgrs. pub. utilities, 1920-50; pres. Nantucket Gas & Elec. Co., Manchester Elec. Co., Gas Service, Inc.; mng. dir. Portland Gas Light Co., Community Pub. Service Co., Northeast Gas Transmission Co. Pres. Franklin Found. Commr. Port of Boston Authority. Served as Gas Div. W.P.B., Washington, 1942-46. Served as maj. C.E., U.S. Army, 1917-19. Trustee Old South Church, Boston. Mem. Am. Gas Assn., Alpha Tau Omega (nat. treas.). Republican. Conglist. Club: Union, Algonquin, Engineers (Boston), Nashua Country, Peterbough Country (N.H.). Contbr. to tech. publs. Home: 401 Beacon St. Office: 110 State St., Boston. Died Mar. 14, 1956; buried Mount Auburn Cemetery, Cambridge.

MAC PHERSON, EARLE STEELE, engr., motor vehicle mfg. exec.; b. Highland Park, Ill., July 6, 1891; s. Arthur Grant and Emma (Eckhardt) Mac P.; B.S. in Mech. Engring., U. Ill., 1915; m. Florence Lucille Jones, Mar. 11, 1941; 1 dau., Sandra Lucille. Exptl. lab. engr. Chalmers Motor Co., 1915-17; asst. chief engr. Liberty Motor Car Corp., 1919-22; design engr., asst. chief engr. Hupp Motor Car Co., 1930-34; asst. to V.p. engring., chief engr. Chevrolet-Cleveland, chief engr. product study 6, Gen. Motors Corp., 1935-47 (all Detroit); exec. engr. Ford Motor Co., Dearborn, Mich., 1947-49, chief engr., 1949-52, v.p. engring., mem. adminstrn. com., 1952—. Served as capt., A.S., A.E.F., 1917-19; engr. Bolling Mission, France. Mem. Soc. Automotive Engrs., Inc., Engring. Soc. of Detroit, Coordinating Research Council, Inc., Phi Delta Theta, Tau Beta Pi. Mason. Clubs: Detroit Athletic; Red Run Golf (Huntington Woods, Mich.). Home: 8775 Lincoln Dr., Huntington Woods. Office: Ford Motor Co., Dearborn, Mich. Died Jan. 28, 1960.

MAC RAE, FLOYD WILLCOX, surgeon; b. Telfair Co., Ga., Dec. 6, 1861; s. Murdoch Hugh and Elizabeth (Wilcox) M.; ed. Robert Lee Inst., Atlanta Med. Coll.; M.D. (2d honor), Atlanta Coll. Phys. and Surg., 1885; continued studies in New York Polyclinic and in post-grad. schs. in New York and Europe; m. Fannie Forrest Collier, of Atlanta, Ga., 1888. Demonstrator anatomy, Atlanta Med. Coll., 1885-93; prof. clin. anatomy and gastro-intestinal and rectal diseases, Coll. Phys. and Surg., Atlanta, since 1893; surgeon to Grady Hosp. Sec. Atlanta Bd. Health; maj. and med. insp. Ga. N.G., since 1900. Mem. A.M.A.; pres. Atlanta Soc. Medicine, 1890, Med. Assn. of Ga., 1900, Southern Surg. and Gynecol. Soc., 1903. Democrat. Clubs: Piedmont Driving, Capitol City, Athletic, Automobile. Home: 1014 Peachtree St. Office: Peters Bldg., Atlanta, Ga.

MACTAVISH, WILLIAM CARUTH, educator; b. N.Y.C., June 13, 1893; s. William Caruth and Ida Gertrude (Koehler) MacT.; B.S., New York U., 1924; M.A., Columbia U., 1926; m. Josephine Munson, Sept. 14, 1928 (dec.); m. 2d, Agnes Marie Heermann, May 30, 1942. Asst. New York U. Coll. of Medicine, 1913-17, instr., 1917-26, asst. prof., 1926-30; instr. chemistry, Washington Square Coll. (New York U.), 1919-24, asst. prof. and chmn., 1924-26, asso. prof. and dir. labs., 1926-29, prof., also lab. dir., 1929-30, prof. chemistry, chmn. dept., 1930-48, prof. chemistry, 1948-58, emeritus prof. A founder N.Y. U. Bellevue Med. Center, 1950; pres. N.Y. U. Coll. of Medicine Alumni 1956-57. Visiting toxicologist Grasslands Hospital, 1932-64, hon. cons. div. pathology, 1965-68; consulting chemist, French Hospital, since 1938; mem. adv. com. on pub. health Worlds Fair, 1938-40; mem. Chandler Centenary com., Columbia U., 1938-39; academic advisor to Italian Consulate, N.Y. City, 1933-39 (passing on records of Am. students applying to Italian Med. Schs.); mem. registrants adv. bd. Selective Service, N.Y., 1941-42; mem. draft bd. No. 15, N.Y. City, 1942-68; selectman of Dennistown Plantation, Sommerset County, Maine, 1953-68, civil defense and pub. safety dir., 1963-68. Enlisted in the First F.A., N.G., 1915, served on Mexican Border, 1916, master hosp. sergt., World War, with U.S. Army Lab. No. 1, Neufchateau, 1918-19. Recipient N.Y. U. Alumni meritorious award, 1958. Fellow London Chem. Soc. (life), A.A.A.S., N.Y. Acad. Medicine; mem. Am. Chem. Soc. (nat. councillor, 1935-37; bd. dirs., 1935-37; chmn., 1937-38; mem. Nichols Medal Jury, 1937-43; chmn., 1942-43; nat. councillor, 1945-46; chmn. and mem. bd. dirs. N.Y. sect.), (asso.) A.M.A., Am. Assn. Univ. Profs., Am. Tree Farm System, Sigma Xi, Phi Lambda Upsilon, Phi Delta Theta. Episcopalian. Home: Jackman ME Died Sept. 14, 1968.

MACY, NELSON, retired engr. and exec.; b. N.Y.C., Oct. 2, 1869; s. Francis H. and Mary (Nelson) M.; student pvt. schs., Greylock Inst., S. Williamstown, Mass., Stevens Inst. Tech., Hoboken, N.J.; M.E., Cornell U., 1894; m. Katherine J. Burchell, June 6, 1899 (dec.); m. 2d, Edith Brander Mathews, Apr. 30, 1906 (dec.); children—Frances H. (dec.), Nelson, Alice, Macy Buckner. Began as machinist for Southwark Foundry & Macine Works, Phila., 1892; engring. exec. for Rathbone Sard & Co., Aurora, Ill., 1892-93, for Otto Gas Engine Works, Phila., 1894-97, for Deutz Lithographing Co., N.Y.C., 1897; pres. Corlies Macy & Co., N.Y.C., ret. as chmn. bd., 1928; past pres. Navy League of U.S. Engr. U.S. U.S. Cruiser Topeka, Spanish-Am. War, apptd. naval aide to gov. of Conn., 1941. Recipient Santiago and Spanish Campaign medals. Mem. Chi Phi. Episcopalian. Clubs: Players, N.Y. Yacht (N.Y.C.); Field (Greenwich, Conn.). Former editor: Sea Power. Home: Glenville Rd., Greenwich, Conn. Office: 441 Pearl St., N.Y.C. Died Apr. 7, 1957; buried Putnam Cemetery, Greenwich, Conn.

MADDEN, JOHN JOSEPH, physician; b. Chicago, Ill., Feb. 4, 1902; s. John Joseph and Mary B (Quinlan) M.; B.S., Loyola U., 1926, M.D., 1927; m. Hazel Rogers, June 21, 1936; 1 son, John Rogers. Interne Cook County Hosp., 1928-29; mem. med. staff specializing in neurology and psychiatry, Kankakee State Hosp., Ill., 1930-37; med. dir. Cook County Psychopathic Hosp., 1944-46; cons. physician Cook Co. Psychopathic Hosp. since 1946; engaged in pvt. practice as neurologist and psychiatrist, since 1937; chmn. dept. neurology and psychiatry, Loyola U. Med. Sch., since 1941. Sr. cons. neuropsychiatrist, Diagnostic Service, Vets. Adminstn., Hines, Ill. Mem. Ill. Gov's. Psychiatric Research Council. Decorated Knight of St. Gregory, Pope Pious XII, 1957. Mem. A.M.A., Am. Physchiat. Assn., Inst. of Medicine of Chicago, Am. Bd. of Neurology and Psychiatry, Chicago Neurol. Soc., Ill. Psychiatric Soc., Central Neuro-Psychiatric Assn. Roman Catholic. Contbr. articles to various med. jours. Home: 817 S. Brainard Av., La Grange, Ill. Office: 6 N. Michigan Av., Chgo. Died June 24, 1962.

MADDOCK, WALTER GRIERSON, surgeon; b. Toronto, Ont., Can., Nov. 26, 1901; s. Walter Richard and Jessie Helen (Liddell) M.; grad. Detroit Central, 1921; A.B., U. Mich., 1924, M.D., 1927, M.S. in surgery, 1934; children—Walter Munro, William Robert, Bruce C., Janet; m. Jeanne Turner Bowman, Oct. 1961. Instr. in surgery, 1929-32, assistant, asso. prof. surgery, dept. of surgery and post grad. med., 1932-46, U. of Mich. Med. Sch.; Elcock prof. surgery Northwestern U. Med. Sch., Ranson lectr. surgery, 1941; consultant in surgery Fifth United States Army; also surgeon Chicago Wesley Memorial Hospital, Chicago, and chmn. department, 1952—. Served as lt. col., later col., M.C., U.S. Army, July 1942-Nov. 1945; cons. in surgery, southern base sect. European theatre of operations; commanding officer 298th Gen. Hosp. (affiliated unit U. of Michigan), European theatre of operations. Awarded Legion of Merit, 1945. Fellow A.C.S.; mem. A.M.A. (chmn. sect. on surgery, gen. and abdominal, mem. conf. com. on grad. training in surgery), Am. Assn. Surgery of Trauma, Ill. state med. soc. American Surg. Assn., Soc. Clin. Surgeons, Western Surgical Assn., Central Surg. Assn. (founder group, president 1950), Am. Bd. Surgery (founder; mem. bd. 1952), Royal Soc. Medicine (London), Detroit Acad. Surgery, Chgo. Surg. Soc. (pres.), Am. Heart Assn., Am. Federation Clin. Research, Internat. Soc. Surgery, Fred A. Coller Society, Soc. Vascular Surgery (fdr. mem.), Alpha Omega Alpha, Phi Kappa Phi, Sigma Xi, Phi Chi. Republican. Author: (with Barry J. Anson) Callander's Surgical Anatomy; also of numerous papers on surg. subjects. Editorial bd. Archives of Surgery; Am. Jour. of Surgery. Home: 229 E. Lake Shore Dr. Office: 251 E. Chicago Av., Chgo. Died Oct. 26, 1962; buried Toronto.

MAGILL, WILLIAM SEAGROVE, surgeon, pathologist; b. Lynne, Conn., July 7, 1866; s. William Alexander and Mathilda Wakefield (Smith) M.; A.B., Amherst Coll., 1887, A.M., 1892; B.L., B.S., U. of Paris, 1889, M.D., 1894; studied Institut Pasteur, Paris, 1892-97, U. of Burich, 1894; m. Camille Grandclement, Princess of Graves, Russia, 1915 (died 1928); 1 son, William Camille. Prof. pathology and dean Coll. of Medicine, U. of W.Va., 1900-01; research bacteriologist Carnegie Lab., New York, 1901-03; spl. investigator, Paris, Berlin, Vienna, Munich, 1903-08; surgeon New York Nose, Throat and Lung Hosp., 1908-09; dir. labs., N.Y. State Dept. Health, 1909-14; owner and operator Wolfram (tungsten) Mines, Portugal, 1917-22. First lt. U.S. Army Med. Reserve Corps, 1909-15; chief interpreter Internat. Tuberculosis Congress, Washington, D.C., 1909, and Internat. Congress of Hygiene, Washington, 1912. Lt. gen. M.C., Russian Imperial 3d Army, 1914-15. Inventor of processes and products mostly concerning milk in dry form for which over 400 patents have been issued. Fellow Am. Acad. Medicine; mem. Internat. Univ. Com. (founder, Paris, 1896), etc. Extensive contbr. on med. subjects. Home: Amherst MA*

MAGISTAD, OSCAR CONRAD, (mag'is-tad), soil chemist; b. Forestville, Wis., Sept. 8, 1900; s. Gilbert and Marie (Hovi) M.; B.S., U. of Wis., 1922, M.S., 1923, Ph.D., 1924; m. Lila A. Simon, Aug. 4, 1926. Soil chemist, United Fruit Co., Tela, Honduras, 1924-27; asso. prof. agrl. chemistry and asso. agrl. chemist, U. of Ariz., 1927-30; chemist Pineapple Expt. Station, Honolulu, T.H., 1930-35; dir. Hawaii Agrl. Expt. Station, 1935-38; dir. U.S. Regional Salinity Lab., U.S. Dept. Agr., 1938-40, and 1942-45; asst. chief Bur. Plant Industry, 1940-41; dir. research Libby McNeill & Libby, Hawaii, since 1945. Mem. Am. Chem. Soc., A.A.A.S., Am. Soc. Plant Physiology, Am. Soc. Horticulture, Am. Soc. Agronomists, Am. Soc. Soil Scientists, Geophysiol. Union, Hawaiian Bot. Soc. (pres. 1938), Hawaiian Acad. Science (pres. 1938), Western Soc. Soil Scientists (v.p. 1942-43), Engring. Assn., Alpha Zeta, Phi Lambda Upsilon, Phi Kappa Phi, Sigma Xi. Presbyn. Mason. Club: Representatives. Contbr. to scientific jours. Home: 2721 Puuhonua St., Honolulu, Hawaii. Died May 6, 1953; buried Forestville, Wis.

MAGNUSSON, CARL EDWARD, electrical engr.; b. (Magnalpha) Harris, Minn., Sept. 29, 1872; s. Sven and Christina Maria (Stendahl) M.; B.E.E., U. of Minn., 1896, M.S., 1897, E.E., 1905, scholar in physics, 1896-97; fellow U. of Wis., 1899-1900, Ph.D., 1900; studied under Dr. Steinmetz, Schenectady, N.Y., 1911-12; m. Elva Cooper, 1913; children—Philip Cooper, Edward Fenimore. Prof. physics, U. of N.M., 1901-03, N.M. Sch. of Mines, 1903-04; asso. prof., 1904-06, prof. and head of dept. elec. engring., 1906—, dean Coll. Engring., 1917-29, U. of Wash.; dir. Engring. Expt. Sta., same, 1917—. Consulting engr. Am. Nitrogen Products Co., Seattle, 1917-18; mem. Am. com. First World Power Conference, London, 1924, 3d Conference, Washington, 1936; tech. adviser Washington State Planning Council, 1934—. Democrat. Congregationalist. Fellow and life mem. American Inst. E.E. (v.p. 1920-21). Author: Alternating Currents, 1916; Electric Transients, 1926; Direct Currents, 1929; Electric Figures Formed in Magnetic Fields, 1932; Hydro-Electric Power in Washington, 1936; International Boundary Waters, 1937; Electric Power Markets, 1938. Home: Seattle, Wash. Died July 10, 1941.

MAGOUN, HENRY A., marine engr.; b. Bath, Me., July 24, 1863; s. John W. and Harriet (Hatch) M.; student Mass. Inst. Tech., 1883; m. Amy Hawthorne, Feb. 1889; children—Katherine Hawthorne, John Warren, Priscilla, Mary Young (dec.), Harriet Hatch, Ruth Neal. Became connected with shipbuilding at Bath, Me., 1881; entered service Md. Steel Co., Sparrows Point, Md., as draftsman, 1889, and advanced to supt.; sr. v.p. New York Shipbuilding Corp., Camden, N.J., 1906-26; retired. Hon. v.p. Soc. Naval Architects and Marine Engrs. Republican. Episcopalian. Home: Bath, Me. Died Oct. 25, 1931.

MAGRUDER, WILLIAM THOMAS, mech. engr.; b. Baltimore, Apr. 22, 1861; s. William Thomas (U.S.A., C.S.A.) and Mary Clayton (Hamilton) M.; ed. Trinity Sch., New York, St. John's Sch., Sing Sing, N.Y., Peekskill Mil. Acad.; M.E., Stevens Inst. Tech., 1881 (Priestly prize, 1880), E.D., 1921; grad. student in mathematics and chemistry, Johns Hopkins, 1886-87; m. Ellen Fall Malone, June 18, 1891; children—William Thomas, Thomas Malone. Draftsman and designer, Campbell Printing Press & Mfg. Co., Taunton, Mass., 1881-86; chief chemist B.&O. R.R., Mt. Clare, Baltimore, 1887; instr., 1887-88, adj. prof. mech. engring., 1888-96, Vanderbilt U.; chief of machinery, Tenn. Centennial Expn., 1896; prof. mech. engring., Ohio State U., 1896-1933; emeritus, 1933; also consulting mech. engr. Mem. Am. Soc. Mech. Engrs. (v.p. 1925-27), A.A.A.S. (sec. Sect. D, 1899-1900 and 1902-07), Engrs. Club of Columbus (pres. 1904-05), Ohio Soc. Mech. Engrs. (pres. 1905-07); mem. Soc. Promotion Engring. Edn. (councillor 1899-1902 and 1907-11, v.p. 1905-06, sec. 1906-07, pres. 1912-13), Am. Assn. Univ. Profs. (councillor, 1915-16). In charge of dept. of engines, U.S.A. School of Mil. Aeronautics, Columbus, 1917-18. Home: Columbus O. Died June 21, 1935.

MAHAN, DENNIS HART, army officer, engr., educator; b. N.Y.C., Apr. 2, 1802; s. John and Mary (Cleary) M.; grad. U.S. Mil. Acad., 1824; A.M., Brown U., 1837, LL.D., 1852; A.M., Princeton, 1837; LL.D., Coll. William and Mary, 1852, Dartmouth, 1867. m. Mary Okill, June 25, 1839; 5 children including Alfred Thayer. Asst. prof. mathematics U.S. Mil. Acad., 1824-25, asst. prof. engring., 1825-26, asst. prof. civil and mil. engring, 1829-32, prof., 1832-71, dean faculty, 1838, sr. mem. academic bd.; sent by War Dept. to Europe to study pub. works, mil. instns., attended Sch. Application for Engrs. and Arty., Metz, France; an original incorporator Nat. Acad. Scis., 1863; commr. on bd. engrs. to find route for Wheeling & B. & O. R.R., 1850; mem. Geog. Soc. of Paris (France); overseer Thayer Sch. of Engring; Dartmouth, 1871. Died N.Y.C., Sept. 16, 1871; buried West Point, N.Y.

MAHER, ALDEA, physician; b. New Orleans, Oct. 7, 1892; dau. Thomas Francis and Joseph Anne (Rupert) Maher; B.A., Newcomb Coll., 1913, Tulane U., 1935; M.A., Tulane, 1914, student in advanced chemistry, 1915; M.D., Tulane U. Sch. Medicine, 1919. Interne Charity Hosp. New Orleans, and Mass. Gen. Hosp. (Boston) dept. biochemistry, 1920; pathol. New Orleans Dispensary for Women, 1919-20; established dept. of metabolism and chem. Hotel Dieu Hosp., 1920. asso. pathol. and biochem., 1920-39, mem. staff, 1920—, cardiol., 1933-39, acting dir. dept. pathol., Jan.-July 1934, established dept. cardiol., 1934, mem. exec. com., 1939-33, chmn. and mem. committees, 1922-45; established own clinico-pathol. lab., 1936; establ. dept. biochem. Charity Hosp., 1924, dept. biochem. Loyola U., 1929, dept. biochem. research, grad. dept. Loyola, 1929; dir. Pan-Am. Lab., 1923-40; pathol. Nix Clinic, 1930-45; supervising dir. lab. Nix Med. Bldg., 1945—. Instr. dept. clinical med. Tulane U., 1919-20, dept. pathology, 1920-23; teacher high sch. chem. Dominican Convent, 1921-23; teacher chem. Charity Hospital School of Nurses, 1921-23, Hotel Dieu Hosp. Sch. Nursing, 1931-39; prof. biochem. Loyola U., 1929-39, spl. lecturer biochem. Loyola U. Dental Sch., 1939—; dir. hosp. training and prof. med. technol. Loyola Sch. Med. Technol., 1935—. Served as sanitary insp., U.S. Pub. Health Emergency Service, 1918; jr. med. officer, U.S. Civil Service Commn., 1936, sr. med. officer, 1940-41. Accredited clin. pathol. and pathologic anatomist by Am. Bd. Pathol., 1937; accredited by Am. Assn. of Life Ins. Med. Dirs. of America, 1944. Recipient Radio Award in Radio History, U.S. Radio Commn., Washington, 1922. Special mention, med. art, La. State Med. Soc., 1928; 2d prize pastel portrait, Chgo., Am. Physicians Art Assn., 1944; medal of award oil portrait, Atlantic City, 1947. Fellow Am. Soc. Clin. Pathol., Coll. Pathol., Coll. Cardiol.; mem. La. Milk Commn., 1920—; mem. com. New Orleans Grad. Assembly, 1941-49 (chmn. pathol. committee 1941); member Louisiana division Am. Cancer Society (chmn. 1936-39, exec. com. 1937-38, bd. dirs. 1948-57); mem. Am. Med. Assn., Orleans Parish Med. Soc., La. Med. Soc., So. Med. Soc., Am. Soc. Clin. Pathol., La. Pathol. Soc., La. Heart Assn., Catholic Physicians Guild, Am. Physicians Art Assn., Pan-Am. Alliance, Nat. Women's Med. Assn., La. br. Women's Med. Assn., New Orleans Symphony and Symphony Guild, Little Theatre, Art Assn., Opera Assn., Opera Guild, Philharmonic Soc., Pop Concert (all at New Orleans); mem. Mid-Winter Sports Assn., New Orleans Soc. Stars and Bars (hon.), Am. Acad. Sciences, Beta Epsilon Upsilon (hon.), Alpha Omega Alpha, Alpha Epsilon Iota (founder and 1st pres. Tulane U. 1919-21). Roman Catholic. Clubs: Orleans, Quota. Author: numerous articles in tech. med. jours. Home: 5665 West End Blvd., New Orleans 24. Office: 1110 American Bank Bldg., New Orleans 12. Died Nov. 20, 1959.

MAHONEY, JOHN FRIEND, (må-ho'ne), retired USPHS officer; born Fond du Lac, Wisconsin, Aug. 1, 1889; s. David and Mary Ann (Hogan) M.; M.D., Marquette U., 1914; m. Leah Ruth Arnold, Sept. 29, 1926; children—Janet Ann, John Friend. Interne Milwaukee County and Chicago Lying-in Hosps., 1914-16; commd. officer in U.S.P.H.S., Sept. 1917; dir. Venereal Disease Research Lab., U.S. Marine Hosp., Staten Island, July 1929-Dec. 1949; commissioner of health of City of N.Y., 1950-53; gen. dir. Bur. Labs., N.Y.C. Dept. Health, 1954—. Fellow A.M.A., Am. Pub. Health Assn.; mem. N.Y. Acad. of Medicine, N.Y. Acad. of Sci. Club: Richmond County Country (Staten Island, N.Y.). Winner of the A.P.H.A. Lasker Award, 1946. Home: 32 Valley St., S.I. 5, N.Y. Office: Dept. of Health, 125 Worth St., N.Y.C. Died Feb. 23, 1957; buried Arlington Nat. Cemetery.

MAHONEY, JOSEPH NATHANIEL, inventor, cons. engr.; b. Boston, Mass., Aug. 25, 1878; s. Daniel J. and Anne (Leary) M.; ed. Mechanic Arts High Sch., Boston; Lowell Inst. course Mass. Inst. Tech.; m. Marie Hynes, 1897; children—Howard Joseph, Charles Francis, Daniel James. Began with Electric Storage Supply Co., Boston, 1894; successively with Electro Chem. Storage Battery Co. (New York), Electric Illuminating & Power Co. (L.I. City), N.Y. Air Brake Co. (New York), Am. Electric Brake Co. (New York) until 1906; with Westinghouse Electric & Mfg. Co., Pittsburgh, Pa., 1906-18, Westinghouse Air Brake Co., Wilmerding, Pa., 1907-14, cons. engr., Sperry Gyroscope Co., Brooklyn, N.Y., 1918-29, Condit Elec. Mfg. Co., Boston, 1920-25, also other cos.; mgr. of engring., Am. Brown Boveri Electric Corp., Camden, N.J., 1926-27; pres. 1929 and 1930, Herbert E. Bucklen Corp. (Elkhart, Ind.), and Perkins Corp. (South Bend, Ind.); cons. engr. Pacific Elec. Mfg. Corp., San Francisco, 1931-32, Sperry Corp., New York, and Wright Aeronautical Corp., Paterson, N.J., since 1933. Awarded many patents, U.S. and foreign countries. Fellow Am. Institute Elec. Engrs.; mem. Am. Soc. Mech. Engrs., Am. Soc. C.E., Am. Inst. Mining and Metall. Engrs., Am. Electrochem. Soc., Inst. Radio Engrs., Soc. Automotive Engrs. Registered professional engr. State of N.Y. Contbr. to tech. publs. Home: 615 77th St., Brooklyn 9, N.Y. Died Jan. 1, 1946.

MAIN, CHARLES THOMAS, engineer; b. Marblehead, Mass., Feb. 16, 1856; s. Thomas and Cordelia (Reed) M.; S.B., Mass. Inst. Tech., 1876; Dr. of Engring., Northeastern U.; m. Elizabeth Freeto Appleton, Nov. 14, 1883; children—Charles Reed, Alice Appleton, Theodore. Asst., Mass. Inst. Tech., 1876-79; draftsman Manchester Mills, 1880-81; engr., 1882-87, supt. and engr., 1887-92, Pacific Mills; private practice as designer industrial plants since 1893; trustee Winchester Savings Bank; chmn. Chas. T. Main, Inc. Mem. Bd. Aldermen, Lawrence, Mass., 1887-89, Water and Sewerage Bd., Winchester, Mass., 1894-1905. Mem. Corp. Mass. Inst. Tech. Republican. Congregationalist. Fellow Am. Soc. Mech. Engrs. (past pres.); mem. Am. Soc. C.E., Boston Soc. C.E. (past pres.), Nat. Assn. Cotton Mfrs., N E. Water Works Assn., Am. Acad. Arts and Sciences, Am. Inst. Consulting Engrs. (ex-pres.). Clubs: Downtown, Engineers (ex-pres.), University (Boston). Home: Winchester, Mass. Office: 201 Devonshire St., Boston, Mass. Died Mar. 6, 1943.

MAIN, HERSCHEL, chief engr., U.S.N., retired; b. in Ill., July 6, 1845; s. Prof. James Main; ed. Washington, 1851-57; Phillips Exeter Acad., N.H., 1858-61; grad. Naval Acad., 1866; spl. studies marine engring.; m. Charlotte A. Bradbury, June 1, 1875. Third asst. engr. U.S.N., Oct. 10, 1866; chief engr., U.S.N., Nov. 11, 1892; retired Sept. 10, 1895. Address: Washington, D.C. Died 1909.

MAIRS, ELWOOD DONALD, aluminum co. exec.; b. Bridgeport, Pa., Mar. 30, 1905; s. Elwood Herbert Corson and Elizabeth (Patterson) M.; student Mercersberg (Pa.) Acad.; B.S. in Metall. Engring., Pa. State U., 1926; m. Lucille E. Wallace, June 26, 1930 (dec. Sept. 1964); 1 dau., Lesly Elizabeth (Mrs. John M. Senker); m. 2d, Margaret E. Hood, Oct. 1, 1966. With Aluminum Co. Am., 1926-70, gen. mgr. personnel, 1962-63, v.p. charge personnel and indsl. relations, 1963-70. Recipient David F. McFarland award for achievement in metallurgy Pa. State U., 1957. Mem. Alpha Chi Sigma, Tau Beta Pi, Sigma Gamma Epsilon. Episcopalian. Mason. Clubs: University (Pitts.); City (Knoxville). Home: Louisville TN Died Dec. 10, 1972.

MAISCH, HENRY CHARLES CHRISTIAN, chemist; b. Brooklyn, Sept. 29, 1862; s. Prof. John M. and Charlotte J. M.; ed. private and public schools of Phila., leaving high school, 1881; grad. Phila. Coll. of Pharmacy, 1885; studied chemistry and botany, U. of Göttingen, Ph.D., 1889; m. Sarah A. P. H. C. Elwert, Dec. 31, 1889. Assisted Prof. A. Michael, 1889-90 in chem. research in Worcester, Mass.; lectured on botany and materia medica at Chicago Coll. of Pharmcy, 1890-91, and in Medico Chirurg. Coll., dept. pharmacy, Phila., 1898-1900; chemist to Stetson Laboratory of Hygiene, 1895-97; chemist of analytical dept., Hance Bros. & White, mfg. pharmacists, Phila., 1899—. Author: Maisch's Manual of Materia Medica, 1895; materia medica portion of the National Dispensatory, 1894. Address: Philadelphia, Pa. Died 1901.

MAISCH, JOHN MICHAEL, pharmacist; b. Hanau, Hesse, Germany, Jan. 30, 1831; son of Conrad Maish; m. Charlotte Justine Kuhl, 1859, 5 sons, 2 daus. Came to U.S., 1849; with pharmacies in Balt., Washington, D.C., N.Y.; employed by Robert Shoemaker's wholesale drug and pharm. mfg. co., Phila.; prof. botany and materia medica N.Y. Coll. Pharmacy, 1861-63; in charge of U.S. Army Lab., Phila., 1863-65; prof. pharmacy Phila. Coll. Pharmacy, 1866-93; sec. Am. Pharm. Assn., 1865-93; chem., bot. and pharm. editor Nat. Dispensatory, 1879-84; editor Am. Jour. of Pharmacy, 1871-93. Author: A Manual of Organic Materia Medica, 1882. Died Sept. 10, 1893.

MALCOLM, WILLIAM LINDSAY, civil engring.; b. Mitchell, Ont., Can., Feb. 2, 1884; s. George and Margaret (Milligan) M.; M.A., Queens U., Kingston, Can., 1905, B.Sc., 1907; M.C.E., Cornell U., 1934, Ph.D., 1937; m. Jessie L. Ellis, May 4, 1908; 1 son, Stewart G. W. (dec.); m. 2d, Margaret Murray, Sept. 2, 1933. City engr. Stratford, Ont., Can., 1907; asso. city engr., Guelph, 1909-10-11; asst. prof. surveying, Queens U., 1907-09, asst. prof. civil engr., 1909-14, prof. municipal engring., 1914-38; came to U.S., 1938; dir. Sch. of Civil Engring., Cornell U., since 1938. Served as capt. Canadian Engrs., C.E.F., 1914-15, major, 1915-17, lt. col., 1917-19; lt. col. Canadian Engrs. Res. since 1919. Twice mentioned in dispatches. Mem. bd. visitors Royal Mil. Coll. of Canada, 1938-41. Mem. Am. Soc. C.E., Am. Water Works Assn., Engring. Inst. of Canada, Canadian Inst. Sewage and Sanitation, Professional Engrs. of Ontario, Ontario Land Surveyors, New York State Sewage Works Assn. Presbyterian. Club: Ithaca Golf and Country. Writer of occasional articles. Home: 604 E. State St. Ithaca, N.Y. Died Jan. 18, 1948; buried Kingston, Ont., Can.

MALCOLMSON, CHARLES TOUSLEY, mech. engr.; b. St. Thomas, Ont., Can., 1874; s. Henry Chalmers and L. V. (Tousley) M.; B.S., Armour Inst. Tech., Chicago, 1897, E.E., 1901; m. Margaret Ewing Wilkinson, 1905. Engr., Anaconda Copper Mining Co., 1897-99; chief engr., U.S. Commn., Paris Expn., 1899-1901; chief engr., S.C. Inst. and West Indian Expn., 1901-02; supt. machinery, St. Louis Expn., 1902-03; gen. supt. Lanyon Zinc Co., 1903-05; engr. in charge U.S. Testing Plant, 1905-08; briquetting engr. R.I. Coal Co., 1908-09, Roberts & Schaefer Co., 1909-12; pres. Malcolmson Engineering and Machine Corp., 1912—. Home: Chicago, Ill. Died Jan. 10, 1922.

MALCOLMSON, JAMES W(ADDELL), consulting engr.; b. Dover, Kent, Eng., Oct. 9, 1866; s. James and Cherrie (Mercer) M.; student Inst. Civ. Engrs., 1886-91; grad. Royal Coll. Science, London, 1889; m. Katherine Haden Krause, Dec. 22, 1888. Asst. mining and mech. engr., Michoacan Ry. & Mining Co., Mexico, 1893; mining engr., Consolidated Kansas City Smelting & Refining Co., 1893-98; mgr. mining dept. Am. Smelting & Refining Co., 1898-1902; gen. consulting practice, 1902—. Democrat. Presbyn. Dir. Am. Mining Congress, 1906. Home: Kansas City, Mo. Died Dec. 26, 1917.

MALINOWSKI, BRONISLAW KASPER, (ma-le-nov'ski), anthropologist; b. Cracow, Poland, Apr. 7, 1884; s. Lucyan and Józefa (Lacka) M.; Ph.D., Polish U., Cracow, 1908; student U. of Leipzig, Germany, 1908-10; D.Sc., U. of London, 1916; D.Sc. (hon.), Harvard (Tercentenary), 1936; came to U.S., 1938; m. Elsie Rosaline Masson, Mar. 6, 1919 (died 1935); children—Józefa Marya, Wanda, Helena; m. 2d, Valetta Hayman-Joyce, June 6, 1940. Lecturer London Sch. of Econs., 1912-13; on anthropol. expdn. to New

Guinea, 1914-20; reader in social anthropology, U. of London, 1924-27, prof. anthropology since 1927, on leave since 1939; visiting prof. anthropology and fellow of Timothy Dwight Coll., Yale, since 1939. Hon. fellow Royal Soc. of New Zealand; mem. Royal Acad. of Science of Netherlands, Polish Acad. of Sciences and Arts, Phi Beta Kappa, Alpha Delta Kappa, Sigma Xi. Roman Catholic. Author: The Family Among the Australian Aborigines, 1913; Primitive Religion and Social Differentiation (in Polish), 1915; Argonauts of the Western Pacific, 1922; Crime and Custom in Savage Society (translated into French and Chinese), 1926; Myth in Primitive Psychology, 1926 (Chinese transl. 1935); Sex and Repression in Savage Society, 1926 (Chinese transl. 1937, also French); The Sexual Life of Savages in N.W. Melanesia (Polish, French, Spanish, Italian, German transls.), 1929; Coral Gardens and Their Magic (2 vols.), 1935; The Foundations of Faith and Morals, 1936; also author articles in Nature, Jour. of the Royal Anthropol. Inst., Man. etc. Home: 261 Canner St., New Haven, Conn. Died May 16, 1942.

MALISOFF, WILLIAM MARIAS, biochemist; b. Ekaterinoslav, Russia, Mar. 14, 1895; s. Mark and Hannah (Marias) E.; came to U.S., 1905, naturalized, 1911; B.S., Columbia, 1915, Ch.E., 1918; Ph.D., New York Univ., 1925; m. Sally Juster, May 19, 1919; children—Eda, Vera, Marias. Instr. Columbia, 1916-20, New York Univ., 1924-25; consultant, city of New York, 1925-29; dir. organic research, Atlantic Refining Co., Phila., 1929-34; research asso. and prof. Univ. of Pa., 1930, 1934-35; prof. biochemistry, Polytechnic Inst., Brooklyn, 1937-45, Essex Coll. of Medicine, Newark, N.J., 1945-46; dir. of research Longevity Research Foundation, New York, N.Y., since 1946; consultant U.S. Indsl. Alcohol Co., Air Reduction Co., American Molasses Co., Commercial Solvents, City of Phila., Robinson Foundation, Tobey Maltz Foundation. Served as chem. dir. milkweed project, U.S. Navy, 1944. Mem. Philosophy of Sci. Assn. (pres. since 1934), Am. Chem. Soc., A.A.A.S., Am. Assn. Sci. Workers, History of Sci. Soc., Phi Beta Kappa, Phi Lambda Upsilon. Author: A Calendar of Doubts and Faiths, 1930; Meet the Sciences, 1932; The Span of Life, 1937; The Dictionary of Biochemistry (also editor-in-chief), 1943. Editor-in-chief Philosophy of Science (quarterly) since 1934. Editorial bd. mem. Am. Rev. of Soviet Medicine. Contbr. numerous monographs and articles to scientific revs. Home: 360 West 55th St., New York 19. Office: 254 West 31st St., New York 1. Died Nov. 15, 1947.

MALL, FRANKLIN PAINE, anatomist; b. Belle Plaine, Ia., Sept. 28, 1862; s. Francis and Louise (Miller) M.; prep. edn. pub. and pvt. schs.; M.D., U. of Mich., 1883; student Heidelberg, Leipzig and Johns Hopkins; hon. A.M., U. of Mich., 1900; LL.D., U. of Wis., 1904; Sc.D., U. of Mich., 1908; LL.D., Washington U., St. Louis, 1915; m. Mabel Stanley Glover, Mar. 28, 1895. Fellow, 1886-88, instr. pathology, 1888-89, Johns Hopkins; adj. prof. vertebrate anatomy, Clark U., 1889-92; prof. anatomy, U. of Chicago, 1892-93; prof. anatomy, Johns Hopkins U., 1893—. Dir. dept. of embryology, Carnegie Instn. of Washington, 1915. Mem. Commn. for Neurol. Research of Internat. Assn. of Acads., 1903—; mem. Soc. Am. Naturalists (v.p. 1900, chmn. 1904); pres. Assn. Am. Anatomists, 1905-07; mem. Institute International d'Embryologie. Trustee of Marine Biol. Lab., Woods Hole, Mass. Author: Causes Underlying the Origin of Human Monsters; On the Fate of the Human Ovum in Tubal Pregnancy. Joint editor of Handbuch der Entwicklungsgeschichte des Menschen; co-editor and one of founders Am. Journal of Anatomy, and the Anatomical Record; asso. editor Journal of Morphology; editor Studies from the Anatomical Laboratory of Johns Hopkins U. Address: Baltimore, Md. Died Nov. 17, 1917.

MALLET, JOHN WILLIAM, chemist; b. Dublin, Ireland, Oct. 10, 1832; s. Robert and Cordelia (Watson) M.; A.B., Trinity Coll., Dublin, 1853; Ph.D., U. of Göttingen, 1852; M.D., U. of La., 1868; LL.D., Coll. of William and Mary, 1872, U. of Miss., 1872, Princeton, 1896, Johns Hopkins, 1902, U. of Pa., 1906; came to U.S., 1853, but is a British subject; m. Mary E., d. Judge John J. Ormond, of Ala., 1857; m. 2d, Mrs. Josephine Burthe, of La., 1888. Asst. prof. analytical chemistry, Amherst, 1854; chemist to geol. survey, Ala., 1855-56; prof. chemistry, U. of Ala., 1855-60; officer on staff Gen. Rodes, C.S.A., 1861; transferred to arty., 1862, and placed in general charge of ordnance laboratories of Confed. States; paroled as lt. col. arty., 1865; prof. chemistry, med. dept., U. of La., 1865-68; prof. analytical, industrial and agrl. chemistry, 1868-72, gen. and industrial chemistry, 1872-83 and 1885-1908, emeritus prof. chemistry, 1908, U. of Va. Lecturer, Johns Hopkins, 1877-78; prof. chemistry and physics and chmn. faculty, U. of Tex., 1883-84; prof. chemistry, Jefferson Med, Coll., Phila., 1884-85; mem. U.S. Assay Commn. 3 times. Mem. Am. Chem. Soc. (pres. 1882). Address: University, Va. Died Nov. 6, 1912.

MALLINCKRODT, EDWARD, JR., chemist; b. St. Louis, Nov. 17, 1878; s. Edward and Jennie (Anderson) M.; A.B., Harvard, 1900, A.M., 1901; LL.D. (hon.), Washington U., St. Louis, Mo., 1948; m. Elizabeth Baker Elliot, June 3, 1911. With Mallinckrodt Chem. Works, St. Louis, since 1901, now chmn. bd. Mem. Am. Chem. Soc., Franklin Inst., Overseer Harvard, 1927-33. Clubs: University, Harvard, Century Assn. (N.Y.); Boone and Crockett; St. Louis Country. Home: 16 Westmoreland Pl. Office: 3600 N. 2d St., St. Louis. Died Jan. 19, 1967.

MALLORY, FRANK BURR, (mal'lor-i), pathologist; b. Cleveland, O., Nov. 12, 1862; s. George Burr and Anna (Faragher) M.; A.B., Harvard, 1886, A.M., M.D., 1890; hon. Sc.D., Tufts, 1928, Boston Univ., 1932; m. Persis McClain Tracy, Aug. 31, 1893; children—Tracy B(urr), G(eorge) Kenneth. Asst. in histology, 1890-91, pathol. anatomy, 1891-92, instr. pathology, 1894-96, asst. prof., 1896-1901, asso. prof., 1901-19, Harvard U.; prof. pathology, Harvard U. Med. Sch., 1928-32; pathologist Boston City Hospital, 1897-1932; cons. pathologist since 1932 Member Assn. of Am. Physicians, Am. Assn. of Pathologists and Bacteriologists, Am. Assn. for Cancer Research, A.M.A., Mass. Med. Soc. Am. Social Science Assn., Internat. Assn. Med. Museums; fellow Am. Acad. Arts and Sciences. Author: The Principles of Pathologic Histology, 1914; (with James H. Wright) Pathological Technique, 1897, 8th edit., 1923. Contbr. to med. jours. Died Sept. 27, 1941.

MALLORY, TRACY BURR, pathologist; b. Boston, 1896; s. Frank Burr and Persis (Tracy) M.; M.D., Harvard, 1921; m. Edith Brandt, June 6, 1925; children—Kenneth Brandt, Jean Roberts (Mrs. William J. Childs). Moseley Travelling 1925-26, instr. bacteriology med. sch., 1923-26, instr. pathology, 1926-35, asso., 1935-37, asst. prof., 1937-48, prof. pathology since 1948; chief lab. pathology and bacteriology, Mass. Gen. Hosp., Boston since 1926; cons. pathology Regional Area I, Vets. Adminstrn. Served with Med. Corps., U.S. Army, as maj. to lt. col. 1943-45. Decorated Legion of Merit. Mem. Am. Assn. Pathologists and Bacteriologists (pres. 1950-51), Coll. Am. Pathologists (sec.-treas., 1948-51), A.M.A., Am. Soc. Exptl. Pathologists, Am. Cancer Soc. Author articles sci. jours. Asst. editor of Am. Jour. Pathology, 1941-43, mem. editorial bd. since 1943; editor case histories of Mass. Gen. Hosp. New Eng. Jour. Pathology since 1926. Contbr. to Medical History of U.S. Army in World War II. Home: 178 South St., Needham 92. Office: Mass. General Hospital, Boston. Died Nov. 11, 1951.

MALLY, FREDERICK WILLIAM, entomologist; b. Des Moines, Ia., Nov. 30, 1868; s. Frederick Henry and Anna Katherine (Stoetzel) M.; grad. Ia. State Coll., Ames, Ia., M.Sc.; m. Mattie J. Tabor, of Bryan, Tex., July 15, 1909. Asst. state entomologist, Ill., 1890; asst. entomologist, U.S. Dept. Agr., 1890-92; state entomologist of Tex. and prof. entomology, Agrl. and Mech. Coll. of Texas, 1899-1903; state entomologist, Dept. of Agr. of Tex., 1909-10; dir. farms, gardens and orchards of Cross S Farming Co., Tex., as crop and irrigation expert, 1910-15; co. agt. and farm demonstration dir., Dept. Agr., 1915-25; now co. agent Bexar Co., also sec. dept. agrl. Chamber of Commerce, San Antonio, Tex. Pres. Tex. Hort. Soc., 1900, State Truck Growers' Assn., Tex., 1900; mem. A.A.A.S., Ia. and Tex. acads. science, Entomol. Soc. Washington. Author of various bulls. U.S. Dept. Agr. and in reports state entomologist, Tex., on the Boll Weevil of Cotton, Bermuda onion culture, bee culture, Tex. soil and crop survey, etc. Address: Court House, San Antonio, Tex.

MALONE, GEORGE WILSON, consulting engineer; b. Fredonia, Kans., Aug. 7, 1890; s. J. W. and Vienna (McPherson) M.; civil engring., Univ. of Nevada, class of 1917; m. Ruth Moslander, Mar. 20, 1921; 1 dau., Molly. Cons. engr., Malone Engrs.; state engr. Nev., 1927-35, serving as mem. Pub. Service Commn., Colorado River Commn., during passage legislation Hoover Dam, advisor Sec. Interior on generation power, completed, 1934, resigned 1935; gen. cons. engring. practice including Central Valley project, Shasta and San Joaquin dams, Cal. 1935, Los Angeles Flood Control project, 1936; mng. dir., editor Indsl. West Found. until Indsl Ency. pub. 1944; spl. cons. to Sec. War on strategic and critical minerals and materials; cons. U.S. Senate Mil. Affairs Com. on strategic and critical minerals and materials, and on exam. mil. establishments including Pacific, Alaska and the South Seas, 1942-45; U.S. senator from Nev., 1946-58, mem. interior and insular affairs com., finance com. Inspected European Marshall Plan nations and Middle East countries, 1947, Asiatic countries, Malayan states and Indo China, 1948, S. American areas, 1949, Central Am. countries and Mexico, 1950. Served as pvt. and sgt., 40th Div. F.A., World War I, with A.E.F. in France; lt. line officer and Regtl. Intelligence, 1918. Former chmn. Nev. State Bd. Registered Profl. Engrs. Mem. Am. Soc. C.E., Am. Inst. of Mining & Metall. Engineers, Assn. Western State Engrs. (organizer and ex-pres.), Am. Legion past dept. comdr.; nat. vice comdr. 1929, Vets. Fgn. Wars, Sigma Alpha Epsilon. Republican. Mason (32 deg., K.T., Shriner), Elk, Eagle. Clubs: Army-Navy, National Press (Washington); San Francisco Press. Contbr. engring. and tech. jours. Winner amateur middleweight boxing championship of Pacific Coast (rep. U. of Nev.), 1920. Address: 29 E. First St., Reno. Died May 19, 1961; buried Arlington Nat. Cemetery.

MALOTT, CLYDE A(RNETT), (má'lot), geologist; b. Atlanta, Ind., Sept. 10, 1887; s. John Franklin and Alice (Fippen) M.; A.B., Ind. U., 1913, A.M., 1915, Ph.D., 1919; m. Mary Orda Clayton, July 30, 1911; children—Alice, Roland Floyd. Tchr. pub. schs., Ind., 1909-15; instrnl. staff, dept. geology, Ind. U., 1916-24, prof. geology 1924-47, acting head dept. geol. and geography, 1941-45; engaged in geol. research in Ind., 1947—; mem. staff Okla. Geol. Survey, summer 1916, Ind., 1919-21; geologist Empire Gas & Fuel Co., summers 1918, 23; geologist Pure Oil Co., 1924; acting prof. geology Williams Coll., 1st semester 1929-30; mem. staff, Ill. Geol., summer 1930; cons. Sun Oil Co., 1938-40. Mem. A.A.A.S., Geol. Soc. Am., Ind. Acad. Sci. (v.p. 1937, pres. 1944), Nat. Speleological Soc., Phi Beta Kappa, Sigma Xi. Recipient of award for distinguished publ. paper, Proc. Ind. Acad. Sci., 1948. Author: Physiography of Indiana, 1922; author of 40 or more publ. sci. papers and many pvt. reports chiefly on Indiana geology, etc.; studies in Indiana Caverns a specialty. Republican. Baptist. Home: 708 S. Woodlawn Av. Office: Indiana University, Bloomington, Ind. Died Aug. 26, 1950.

MANCE, GROVER CLEVELAND, (mans), geologist; b. Pine Bush, N.Y., Feb. 5, 1883; s. Eli Dewitt and Mabel Edith (Barroclough) M.; B.S., Colgate U., 1906; A.M., 1913, Ph.D., Ind. U., 1915; m. Martha Blanche Nelson, Sept. 1, 1906; children—Donald Roscoe, Caryl Hope. Prof. chemistry Rochester (Ind.) Coll., 1906-08; high sch. tchr. 1908-12; teaching fellow Ind. U., 1913-15; geol. investigator, Ind., 1913-16; prin. high sch., Maysville, Ky., 1916-17; prof. geology St. Lawrence U., Canton, N.Y., 1917-22; prof. geography Syracuse U. Summer Sch., 1921; prof. geography and geology Winthrop Coll. (S.C. Coll. for Women), Rock Hill, S.C., 1922-33; cons. geologist and mineralogist, Rock Hill, S.C., 1933-41; dean sch. science Oglethorpe U., 1942; dean of Oglethorpe U., 1943-44; prof. chemistry N.W. Jr. Coll., Orange City, Ia., 1943-45, also Union Coll., Barbourville, Ky., 1946-48, Lander Coll., Greenwood S.C., 1951-53. Fellow A.A.A.S., S.C. Acad. Sci. (founder, 1st pres.; sec. 1925-34); mem. Sigma Xi, Beta Theta Pi. Presbyn. Mason (K.T.). Writer and lecturer on geol. and ednl. subjects. Address: 302 Aiken Av., Rock Hill, S.C. Died May 24, 1955; buried Woodlawn Cemetery, Hamilton, N.Y.

MANDEL, JOHN ALFRED, chemist; b. Stockholm, Sweden, Oct. 18, 1865; s. Phillip H. and Agnes C. (Lundberg) M.; came to U.S., 1870; ed. Boston; Sc.D., New York U., 1901; D.Agr., U. of Berlin, 1923; m. Paula H. Heinrich, Aug. 3, 1891. Asst. in chemistry, 1884-97, adj. prof. physiol. chemistry, 1897-98, Bellevue Hosp. Med. Coll.; prof. chemistry and physiol. chemistry, Univ. and Bellevue Hosp. Med. Coll., 1898—; prof. chemistry, New York Coll. Vet. Surgeons, 1894-97; asst. prof. chemistry and physics, Coll. City of New York, 1897-98. Home: Yonkers, N.Y. Died May 5, 1929.

MANEY, GEORGE ALFRED, (ma'ne), prof. structural engring.; b. Minneapolis, Minn., Dec. 9, 1888; s. Thomas H. and Ella (Hallam) M.; C.E., U. of Minn., 1911; M.S., U. of Ill., 1914; m. Mabelle O. Draxten, Apr. 7, 1920; children—Thomas D., Elizabeth K. Draftsman Minneapolis & St. Louis R.R., 1911-12; research fellow, U. of Ill., 1913-14; instr., U. of Minn., 1914-18; served as 2d lt. C.A.C., 1918; asst. prof. structural engring., U. of Minn., until 1926; asso. prof. civ. engring., U. of Minn., 1926-27; prof. structural engring., Northwestern U., since 1928; head Dept. Civil Engring., Northwestern U. Inst. Tech., since 1939; cons. engr. on various constrn. projects, including Miss River bridge, Savanna, Ill., and Santa Fe Terminal Bldg., Dallas, Tex. Winner Wason medal of Am. Concrete Inst. for "most meritorious paper of the year 1936." Member Am. Soc. C.E., Western Soc. Engrs. Tau Beta Pi, Sigma Xi. Presbyterian. Club: University. Author: Wind Stresses in Tall Buildings (with W. M. Wilson), 1915. Made 1st gen. statement of slope deflection method, 1915, secondary stresses in steel bridges, 1922, statically indeterminate stresses (with J. I. Parcel), 1925. Home: 3751 Foster Av., Evanston, Ill. Died May 10, 1947.

MANGIN, JOSEPH FRANÇOIS, engr., architect; b. France; flourished 1794-1818; married. Asst. to chief engr. of fortifications N.Y.C., became chief engr., 1795; freeman of N.Y.C., 1795; surveyor N.Y.C., 1795, prepared map of city, published 1803; designed N.Y. State Prison, Park Theatre (1795-98), St. Patrick's Cathedral (1809-15); probably designed N.Y. City Hall.

MANION, WILLIAM CECIL, physician; b. Bethel, Conn., July 30, 1916; s. William Stephen and Anna (Flagherty) M.; B.S., Catholic U., 1939; M.D., Georgetown U., 1943; m. Billie Pappas, Aug. 7, 1944; children—William, James, Eugene, Brian. Intern, Garfield Meml. Hosp., Washington, 1943-44; resident Gallinger Municipal Hosp., Washington, 1946-48, cons. in pathology, 1963-70; pathologist Prince Georges Gen. Hosp., Cheverly, Md., 1948-52; postgrad. George Washington U., 1947; instr. pathology U. Md. Med. Sch., Balt., 1948-53; instr. pathology Georgetown U., Washington, 1950-52, asst. prof. medicine, 1960-61, asso. prof. medicine (cardiology), 1962-70; registrar cardiovascular registry Armed Forces Inst. Pathology, Washington, 1953-70, asst. chief cardiovascular pathology and geog. pathology brs., 1952-53, chief cardiovascular br., 1953-70. External examiner in medicine U. Witwatersrand (South Africa), 1963-64; cons. on research on Chagas disease in S. Am. and medicine in Europe to surgeon gen. of army; chmn. study sect. on cardiovascular diseases in animals WHO, 1961; Pauline King Meml. lectr. Vanderbilt U. Served to lt., M.C., USNR, 1944-46. Recipient citation Coll. Am. Pathologists, Am. Coll. Cardiology, Am. Coll. Chest Surgeons, Outstanding Achievement award VA, 1964, Outstanding Achievement award Catholic U., 1963, Meritorious. Civilian Service award Dept. Army, 1965. Diplomate Am. Bd. Pathology. Mem. A.M.A. (Hektoen award), Am. Soc. Clin. Pathologists, Coll. Am. Pathologists, Am. Assn. for Study Neoplastic Diseases, Assos. Clin. Pathology, A.A.A.S., Med. Soc. D.C., Washington Heart Assn., Washington Soc. Pathologists, Internat. Acad. Pathology, Am. Heart Assn., John Carroll Soc.; hon. mem. Acad. Med. Scis. (Barcelona), Nat. Heart Inst. Mexico, Pathology Soc. Venezuela. Roman Catholic. Contbr. articles to med. jours., also chpts. to books. Designed heart model of aortic arch. Home: Kensington MD Died Nov. 5, 1970; buried Gate of Heaven Cemetery Silver Spring MD

MANIS, HUBERT CLYDE, entomologist; born Bozeman, Mont., July 18, 1909; s. James Howell and Sarah C. (Clack) M.; B.S., Mont. State Coll., 1933; M.S., Kans. State Coll., 1936; Ph.D., Ia. State Coll., 1940; m. Marian Mercer, Aug. 12, 1948; children—James Morgan, Jean Marie. Began as assistant entomologist U. of Ida., 1940-42, asso., 1944-46, entomologist and head of dept. from 1946. Mem. Entomological Society of America (past chmn. Pacific br.), Ida. Acad. Sci., A.A.A.S., C. of C., Sigma Xi, Gamma Sigma Delta, Phi Sigma. Elk. Author of articles on biology and control of insects. Home: Moscow ID Died Aug. 26, 1968; buried Moscow, ID

MANLEY, F(RANK) NASON, business exec.; b. New Brunswick, N.J., June 8, 1894; s. John A. and Isabella (Askew) M.; student Rutgers U., 1915-16; m. Edna McFadden, Oct. 10, 1922; 1 son, Richard Brooks. With Interwoven Stocking Co., 1914-15; with Johnson & Johnson, 1916-17, since 1918, prodn., sales, 1929-35, engring., research, 1935-45, dir. in charge new installations since 1945. Bd. mgrs. N.J. State Prison since 1951. Served with AS, U.S. Army, World War I. Mem. C. of C., Chi Phi. Club: Bay Head Yact. Home: Hillcrest, River Rd. Office: Johnson & Johnson, New Brunswick, N.J. Died 1965.

MANLY, CHARLES MATTHEWS, mech. engr.; b. Staunton, Va., Apr. 24, 1876; s. Charles and Mary Esther Hellen (Matthews) M.; grad. Master Mathematics and Mech. Philosophy, Furman U., Greenville, S.C., 1896; M.E., Cornell, 1898; m. Grace Agnes Wishart, June 9, 1904 (died 1921); children—Charles Wishart, John Frederick. Chief asst. to Dr. Samuel P. Langley in aviation development work, Smithsonian Instn., 1898-1905; v.p. and chief engr. Manly Drive Co., New York, 1905—; mem. Manly & Veal, cons. engrs., N.Y. City; cons. engr. to British War Office, on development of large aeroplanes in America, June-Sept. 1915; cons. engr. to Curtis Aeroplane & Motor Corp., Buffalo, N.Y., 1915-19; asst. gen. mgr. same N.Y. City, 1919-20; cons. engr. various industrial corps.; mem. firm Manly & Veal. Mem. U.S. Commn. to Internat. Aircraft Standards Conference, London, Feb.-Mar. 1918; mem. automotive advisory com. to U.S. Ordnance Board. Mem. Soc. Automotive Engineers (pres. 1919, rep. on Am. Engring. Standards Com.). Baptist. Author: (with S. P. Langley) Langley Memoirs on Mechanical Flight (No. 3, Vol. 27, Contbns. to Knowledge, Smithsonian Instn.), 1911. Built and piloted the historic Langley aeroplane, in its tests, 1903, the work being stopped by lack of funds before complete tests could be made; same machine flown in 1914 by G. H. Curtiss, "demonstrating that it was the first aeroplane." Inventor some 50 patents on automotive transportation, power generation and transmission. Home: Kew Gardens, L.I., N.Y. Died Oct. 17, 1927.

MANN, ALBERT, diatomist, botanist; b. Hoboken, N.J., June 30, 1853; s. Albert and Lydia Helen (Everett) M.; A.B., A.M., Wesleyan U., Conn., 1879, Sc.D., 1924; Ph.D., Munich, 1894; m. Jennie F. Yard, Oct. 6, 1880; 1 son, Albert. Prof. botany, Ohio Wesleyan U., 1894-1900; expert U.S. Dept. Agr., 1906-19; prof. botany, George Washington U., 1907-09; with Carnegie Instn., 1919—. Republican. Presbyn. Home: Washington, D.C. Died Feb. 1, 1935.

MANN, ARTHUR ROBERT, architect, engr.; b. Eng., June 28, 1877; s. George and Eliza (Lingard) M.; student Nicker Normal Coll., 1900-01; B.S. in Engring., U. Kan., 1906; m. Ida May Smith, Aug. 24, 1904 (dec. Sept. 1971); children—Dorothy (Mrs. Ralph L. Calvert), Robert E. Came to U.S., 1879, naturalized, 1887. Partner Mann and Gerow, architects, 1909-24; owner Mann and Co., 1924-34; partner (with son) Mann & Co., architects, 1934-65, consulting architect-engineer, 1965-68 (all in Hutchinson, Kansas). Chief architect for Black & Veatch, Ski Cantonment, Camp Hale, Colo., also Hutchison Naval Air Sta. Licensed architect, Okla., Kan.; licensed engr., Kan. Fellow A.I.A.; mem. Am. Soc. Heating and Air Conditioning Engrs., Am. Concrete Inst. Home: Hutchinson KS Died July 7, 1968.

MANN, CHARLES AUGUST, chemical engineering; b. Milwaukee, Wis., June 5, 1886; s. Peter and Friedericka (Jahns) M.; B.S. in Chem. Engring., U. of Wis., 1909, M.S., 1911, Ph.D., 1915; m. Lillian E. Shorthill, Dec. 24, 1907. Asst. pharm. chemist, U. of Wis., 1906-11; instr. chem. engring., same, 1911-16; asso. prof. chem. engring., Ia. State Coll. Agr. and Mechanic Arts, 1916-17, prof. in charge of dept., 1917-19; prof. chem. engring., U. of Minn., 1919-21, chief dept. of chem. engr. and prof. since 1921; also cons. practice. Mem. Wis. Nat. Guard 7 yrs. Mem. Am. Inst. Chem. Engrs., Am. Chem. Soc. (pres. Ames sect. 1918, Minn. sect. 1939), Inst. Food Technologists, Am. Electrochemical Soc., Am. Inst. of Chemists, Society of Chem. Industry (London), Am. Soc. for Engring. Edn., Nat. Corrosion Assn., Minn. Assn. of Professional Engrs., Wis. Acad. Science, Minn. Acad. Science, A.A.A.S., Am. Assn. Univ. Profs., Minn.-Ind. Chem. Forum, Minneapolis Garden Club, Sigma Xi, Tau Beta Pi, Phi Lambda Upsilon, Alpha Chi Sigma (pres.), Scabbard and Blade. Unitarian. Mason. Clubs: Engineers', University Campus, Kiwanis, Midland Hills Country. Organized chem. engring. courses at Ia. State Coll. and U. of Minn. Contbr. chem. engring. researches and articles. Home: 35 Barton Av. S.E., Minneapolis. Died June 25, 1949.

MANN, CHARLES RIBORG, physicist; b. Orange, N.J., July 12, 1869; s. Charles Holbrook and Clausine (Borchsenius) M.; A.B., Columbia, 1890, A.M., 1891; Ph.D., U. of Berlin, 1895; Sc.D., Lafayette Coll., 1918; LL.D., Lawrence College, Temple University, 1933; m. Adrienne Amalie Graf, June 25, 1896; children—Riborg Graf, Adrienne. Research asst., 1896-97, asso. in physics, 1897-99, instr., 1899-1902, asst. prof., 1902-07, asso. prof., 1907-14, U. of Chicago; investigator for joint com. on engring. edn. of nat. engring. socs. and Carnegie Foundation Advancement of Teaching, 1914-18. Apptd. advisory mem. Com. on Edn. and Spl. Training, War Dept., Feb. 1918; permanent chmn. of civilian advisory board War Department, General Staff, 1919-25; dir. Am. Council on Education, 1922-34, pres. emeritus since 1934. Translated (from the German of P. Drude) Theory of Optics, 1902. Author: Manual of Advanced Optics, 1902; Physics (with George Ransom Twiss), 1905; The Teaching of Elementary Physics, 1912; A Study of Engineering Education, 1918; Report on the work of the Committee on Education and Special Training, 1919, D.S.M., 1919; Living and Learning, 1938. Home: 2440 Foxhall Rd. Office: 744 Jackson Pl., Washington, D.C. Died Sep. 10, 1942.

MANN, CHARLES WILLIAM, pomologist; b. Pittsburgh, Pa., Jan. 4, 1879; s. William Imrie and Sarah Melinda (Lansing) M.; student U. of Pittsburgh, 1901-02; B.S.A., Cornell U., 1906, grad. study 4 mos. 1910; m. Caroline Whalen Judd, July 24, 1912; children—Douglass Lansing, William Imrie, Robert Edward. Soil scientist with Bur. of Soils, 1906-10; asst. pomologist, Bur. Plant Industry, U.S. Dept. Agr., 1910-14, pomologist, 1914-19, pomologist in charge fruit transportation and storage investigations, 1919-22, sr. pomologist since 1922. In investigations of Dept. Agr. determined methods of modified refrigeration forming basis of present practice on western railroads; granted patents on precooling process, assigned to free use of public. Fellow A.A.A.S.; mem. Am. Pomol. Soc., Am. Soc. for Hort. Science, Federal Business Assn., Alpha Zeta. Presbyterian. Club: Cornell (Los Angeles). Writer many reports and bulls. of U.S. Dept. Agr. on fruit transportation and storage. Home: S. Walnut St., San Dimas, Calif. Office: Federal Bldg., Pomona, Calif. Died Dec. 3, 1943.

MANN, FRANK CHARLES, physician; b. Decatur, Ind., Sept. 11, 1887; s. Joseph E. and Louisa (Kiess) M.; B.S., Marion (Ind.) Normal Coll., 1907; A.B., Ind. U., 1911, M.D., 1913, A.M., 1914, LL.D., 1938; D.Sc., Georgetown Coll., 1937; m. Velma J. Daniels, July 21, 1914; children—Frank Daniel, Ruth Jacquette, Joseph Daniel. Asst. dept. physiology Ind. U., 1908-09, teaching fellow, 1909-11, teaching asso., 1911-12, asst. dept. clin. medicine, 1913, instr. exptl. surgery, 1913-14; dir. div. exptl. surgery and pathology Mayo Clinic, 1914-52, emeritus, 1952; asst. prof. exptl. surgery Mayo Found., U. Minn., 1916-18, asso. prof., 1918-20, prof., 1921-27, prof. exptl. medicine, 1927-52, emeritus, 1952. Awarded Wm. Wood Gerhard gold medal. Phila. Path. Soc., 1932; Friedenwald medal, Am. Gastroenterol. Assn., 1955. Fellow A.C.S. (hon.); mem. National Academy of Sciences, Internat. College Anesthetists, A.M.A., Am. Physiol. Soc., Am. Soc. Pharmacology and Exptl. Therapeutics, Am. Soc. Exptl. Pathology, Soc. Exptl. Biology and Medicine, Assn. Am. Physicians, Western Surg. Assn., A.A.A.S., Harvey Soc., Am. Gastro-Enterological Assn., Royal Flemish Acad. Medicine of Belgium, Soc. Argentina de Biol., Assn. Med. Argentina. Has published researches on surg. shock, physiology of the liver, gall-bladder, spleen, circulation and gastro-intestinal tract, prodn. of peptic ulcer. Address: Mayo Clinic, Rochester, Minn. Died Sept. 30, 1962.

MANN, GUSTAV, prof. physiology; b. Darjeeling, E. India, Nov. 6, 1864; s. Gustav Adolph Heinrich and Marianna (Stovel) M.; M.D., C.M., U. of Edinburgh, Scotland, 1894; B.Sc., U. of Oxford, Eng., 1898; m. Agnes Sinclair Orosz, of Edinburgh, July 11, 1890. Asst. to Prof. William Rutherford, Edinburgh, 1892-94, to Prof. Gotch, Oxford, 1894-1908; prof. physiology, Tulane U., New Orleans, 1908-16. Awarded Dobbie-Smith gold medal, Ellis, Gunning-Victoria, Goodsir and Rolleston prizes for researches in physiology, Edinburgh gold medal for M.D. thesis. Mem. Physiol. Soc. Eng., Am. Assn. Anatomists, Soc. Biol. Chemists, Am. Chem. Soc. Author: Physiological Histology, 1902; Chemistry of the Proteids, 1906; also articles on evolution of flowering plants, comparative physiology of the brain, changes in nerve and gland cells, etc. Research chemist, Houston, Tex., 1916—. Home: 1913 Hamilton St., Houston, Tex.

MANN, PAUL BLAKESLEE, biologist; b. Potsdam, N.Y., Dec. 20, 1876; s. Warren and Helen Elizabeth (Blakeslee) M.; grad. Potsdam State Normal and Tr. Sch., 1896; A.B., Cornell, 1902, A.M., 1903; m. Ruth Atherton Paul, Aug. 3, 1904 (died Jan. 27, 1939); 1 dau., Eleanor Atherton; m. H. Rosabell MacDonald, Feb. 1, 1940. Head of commercial dept. N.Y. Mil. Acad., 1896-97, science dept., high sch., Nyack, 1899-1901; asst. in zoölogy, Cornell U., 1902-03; teacher biology, etc., Hill Sch., Pottstown, Pa., 1903-04; teacher biology, Morris High Sch., N.Y. City, 1904-14; 1st asst. N.Y. City high schs., 1914; head biology dept. Evander Childs High School, N.Y. City, 1914-41; retired 1941; asst. prof. biol. methods, Cornell U., summers 1908-10, Coll. of City of N.Y., 1927-34; examiner Coll. Entrance Exam. Bd., zoölogy, 1914-35, biology, 1918-35; naturalist of Sea Pines Camp, 1920-37; associate in edn., Am. Museum Natural History, 1928-38; gave course in field natural history for teachers, 1933-38; chmn. Standing Com. of Science of N.Y. City and chmn. Science Council of N.Y. City, 1936-38; supervisor of science, sr. high schs., 1937, 38; on staff Dale Carnegie Inst., 1937; science com. and junior science projects for New York World's Fair, 1939. Official delegate from U.S. to 1st Internat. Congress on Ednl. Motion Pictures, Rome, Italy, 1934; chmn. nat. com. of Secondary Dept., N.E.A., on ednl. films, 1935-40, and chmn. biology com. to evaluate theatrical films for ednl. uses, 1937, chmn. steering com. for Conf. of Subject Assns. on Curriculum Change since 1942. Fellow A.A.A.S.; mem. Am. Inst. of N.Y. City (twice on bd. mgrs.), N.Y. Acad. of Sciences, N.Y. Assn. of Biology Teachers (twice pres.), Nat. Assn. Biology Teachers (v.p. 1942-43), Nat. Soc. for Study of Edn., Sigma Xi, Gamma Alpha, Pi Gamma Mu. Known as lecturer, contbr. and critic on zool. and biol. science, pedagogy and visual edn.; also on rifle shooting; former rifle coach and adviser to rifle clubs. Author: How to Tell Weather, and Cloud Plates, 1928; The Pursuit of the Vitamins, 1933. Co-author: (Mann and Hastings) Out-of-Doors, 1932, rev. 1937; (Moon and Mann) Biology for Beginners, 1933, rev. 1937; (Moon and Mann) Biology, 1938, rev. 1941; (Dull, Mann and Johnson) Gen. Sciences series: Modern Science in Our Environment, Modern Science in Our Daily Life, Modern Science in Man's Progress, also Teachers' Manual, 1942. Home: 441 W. 21st St., New York, N.Y. Died Oct. 22, 1943.

MANN, WILLIAM ALFRED, physician, educator; born Chicago, Mar. 21, 1898; s. William Alfred (M.D.) and Anna Damon (Cram) M.; B.S., U. Ill., 1921, M.D., 1923; grad. study, 1924-26; M.S., Northwestern, 1938; grad. study, Vienna, 1926; m. Maud L. Davison, May 30, 1931; children—William Alfred, III, Nancy Davison (Mrs. Germanetti), David Leonard. Interne, Evanston (Ill.) Hosp., 1923-24; specialist in treatment of the eye since 1926, pvt. practice Chicago since 1926; mem. faculty Northwestern U. Med. Sch., 1927-71, prof. ophthalmology, 1949-66, emeritus, 1966-71; chmn. dept. ophthalmology, Wesley Meml. Hosp., emeritus, 1966-71; consultant-in-chief in ophthalmology U.S. Veterans Hosp., Hines, Ill. Sec., treas. Ophthalmic Pub. Co., Revision Com., U.S. Pharmacopeia, 1950-60. Pres. Profl. Interfraternity Conf., 1933-35; chmn. Med. Interfrat. Conf., 1947-49. Trustee, member exec. com. Hadley School for the Blind. Mem. A.M.A., Illinois, Chicago med. socs., Chicago Ophthal. Soc. (pres., 1946-47), Am. Acad. Ophthalmology and Otolarngology, Am. Ophthal. Society, Association for Research in Ophthalmology, Pan American Association Ophthalmology, Oxford Ophthalmological Congress, Lambda Chi Alpha (organizer, pres. Mid-West Conclave, 1921-23), Alpha Kappa Kappa (grand primarius 1949-53, 63-65; past pres.; past grand v.p.; and former grand historian; also former editor in chief of the Centaur, ofcl. mag.), Omega Beta Pi (hon. nat. pres., 1932-35), Sigma Xi, Pi Kappa Epsilon, Chicago Alumni Assn. of Lambda Chi Alpha (pres. 1921). Republican. Conglist. Mason (K.T.). Associate editor, Am. Jour. Ophthalmology. Home: Chicago IL Died May 18, 1971; buried Memorial Park Cemetery, Skokie IL

MANN, WILLIAM D'ALTON, editor; b. Sandusky, O., Sept. 27, 1839; s. William R. and Eliza (Ford) M.; ed. as civ. engr.; m. Sophie Hartog, 1902. Entered Union Army at outbreak of Civil War; commd. capt. 1st Mich. Cav.; organized 1st Mounted Rifles, afterwards 5th Mich. Cav., and Daniels' Horse Battery, 1862; organized 7th Mich. Cav. and Gunther's Horse Battery (these troops composing Mich. Cav. Brigade); commd. col., 1862; devised improvements in accoutrements of troops, used in U.S. Army, and Austrian Army. Settled in Mobile, Ala., after the war; pioneer mfr. cotton-seed oil; several yrs. propr. Mobile Register; 1st Dem. candidate for Congress, under Reconstruction, from Mobile Dist. (elected to 41st Congress but not seated); invented and patented the boudoir car, 1871, and introduced it throughout Europe; founded the Compagnie Internationale des Wagons-Lits; organized Mann Boudoir Car Co., New York, 1883 (later bought out by Pullman Co.); pres. and editor Town Topics, 1891—; founder and mgr. The Smart Set. Author: The Raiders, 1876. Home: New York, N.Y. Died May 17, 1920.

MANN, WILLIAM M., zoologist; b. Helena, Mont., July 1, 1886; s. William Madison and Anna (Williams) M.; grad. Staunton (Va.) Mil. Acad., 1905; student State Coll. of Wash., 1907-09; B.A., Stanford, 1911; D.Sc., Harvard, 1915; Sheldon traveling fellowship, same univ., 1915-16; m. Lucile Quarry, Oct. 30, 1926. Entomologist, U.S. Bur. Entomology, 1916-25; asst. dir. Mulford Biol. Exploration, Amazon Basin, 1921-22; dir. Smithsonian-Chrysler Expdn., Africa, 1926; dir. Nat. Zoöl. Park Expdn. to Brit. Guiana, 1931, to Argentina, 1938, to Liberia, 1940; dir. Nat. Geog. Soc. Expdn. to East Indies, 1937; dir. Nat. Zoöl. Park, Washington, D.C., 1925-56; hon. research asso., Smithsonian Instn., 1956—. Received Franklin Burr award of Nat. Geographic Soc., 1938. Fellow American Institute Park Executives, A.A.A.S.; member Entomol. Society America, International Union of Zoo Directors, Society Ichthyologists and Herpetologists, Am. Soc. Mammalogists, Washington Biol. Soc., Entomol. Soc. Washington, Am. Soc. Naturalists, Cambridge Entomol. Club; hon. dir. Mexican Biol. Soc. Mason (32 deg., Shriner). Clubs: Cosmos, Harvard (Washington); Explorers. Author: Wild Animals In and Out of the Zoo; Ant Hill Odyssey. Has made zoöl. explorations in West Indies, tropical America, Asia, Africa, Australia, South Pacific Islands, Netherlands Indies. Home: 2801 Adams Mill Rd. Office: National Zoölogical Park, Washington. Died Oct. 10, 1960.

MANNES, LEOPOLD DAMROSCH, musician, photog. chemist; b. N.Y., Dec. 26, 1899; s. David and Clara (Damrosch) M., A.B., Harvard, 1920; m. Evelyn Sabin, July 16, 1940; 1 dau., Elena Sabin. Concert pianist, 1925—; faculty Inst. Mus. Art, N.Y.C., 1925-31; faculty Mannes Coll. of Music, 1925-31, president, 1951—; pianist Mannes-Gimpel-Silva Trio, touring U.S. and abroad; chemist Eastman Kodak Co., Rochester, N.Y., 1931-39 (inventor, with Leopold Godowsky, Jr., of Kodachrome process color photography), def. work, World War II. Pres. Walter W. Naumburg Found., Inc., 1961—. Served as pvt., U.S. Army, World War I. Recipient Longstreth Medal, Franklin Inst. Fellow Royal Photog. Soc., Photog. Soc. Am. Democrat. Composer: String quartet, suite for orchestra, for two pianos, numerous other works. Home: 120 E. 75th St., N.Y.C. 10021. Office: 157 E. 74th St., N.Y.C. Died Aug. 11, 1964.

MANNING, CHARLES HENRY, engineer; b. Baltimore, Md., June 9, 1844; s. Joseph Cogswell and Rebecca Parkman Jarvis (Livermore) M.; B.S., Lawrence Scientific Sch. (Harvard), 1862; m. Fanny Bartlett, Jan. 17, 1871. Apptd. engr. U.S. Navy, Feb. 19, 1863; served through Civil War; instr. U.S. Naval Acad., 1870-75, 1878-81; mem. 1st advisory bd. to build new navy, 1881-82; advanced to chief engr., 1906, retired, June 14, 1884; chief engr. Key West Naval Sta. during Spanish-Am. War. Gen. supt. Amoskeag Mfg. Co., 1883-1913. Designer of Manning boiler, in gen. use in textile mills. Address: Manchester, N.H. Died Apr. 1, 1919.

MANNING, HENRY PARKER, univ. prof.; b. Woodstock, Conn., Oct. 3, 1859; s. John M. and Louisa C. (Leonard) M.; A.B., Brown U., 1883, A.M., 1886; Ph.D., Johns Hopkins, 1891; m. Ida M. Forman, of Fostoria, O., June 30, 1893. Teacher since 1883; instr. mathematics, 1891-95, asst. prof. pure mathematics, 1895-1906, asso. prof., 1906-20, Brown U.; asso. editor Am. Math. Monthly, 1919-22. Author: Non-Euclidean Geometry, 1900; Irrational Numbers, 1906; Geometry of Four Dimensions, 1914; etc. Editor: (with intro.) Fourth Dimension Simply Explained, 1910. Address: 106 Carrington Av., Providence, R.I.

MANNING, ROBERT, pomologist; b. Salem, Mass., July 18, 1784; s. Richard and Miriam (Lord) M.; m. Rebecca Dodge Burnham, Dec. 20, 1824. Operated family stage coach lines; began raising fruits, 1817, developed large pomological garden with many varieties of fruit (including over 1000 varieties of pears) from European and Am.; a founder Mass. Hort. Soc. Author: Book of Fruit, 1838. Died Oct. 10, 1842.

MANNING, VAN(NOY) H(ARTROG), petroleum engr.; b. Horn Lake, Miss., Dec. 15, 1861; s. Van H. and Mary Z. (Wallace) M.; U. of Miss., 1878-81; D.Engring., U. of Pittsburgh, 1919; m. Emily S. Stevens, 1898; children—Vannoy H., Oscar Stevens. Civ. engr. with U.S. Geol. Survey, 1886-1910; with Bur. of Mines, Dept. of Interior, 1910, asst. dir., 1911-14, dir., 1914-20; dir. research, Am. Petroleum Inst., 1920-24; petroleum engr. Pan Am. Petroleum and Transportation Co., 1924-25; cons. petroleum engr., 1926-28; dir. engring. and tech. research, Petroleum Research Corp., 1928-30; cons. engr. U.S. Bur. Mines; also cons. petroleum engr., Republic of Cuba. Mem. central petroleum com., Nat. Research Council. Democrat. Episcopalian. Mason. Home: Forest Hills, N.Y. Died July 13, 1932.

MANNING, WILLIAM ALBERT, mathematician; b. Salem, Ore., Dec. 5, 1876; s. William and Catherine (Kitzmiller) M.; A.B., Willamette U., 1900; Ph.D., Stanford, 1904; studied Sorbonne, Paris, 1904-05; m. Esther Crandall, of San Francisco and Palo Alto, Calif., Sept. 18, 1908; children—Dorothy, Rhoda, Helena, Sylvia, Laurence Albert. Asst. in mathematics Stanford, 1900-02, instr. 1902-04, asst. prof., 1904-13, asso. prof., 1913-21, professor from 1921. Mem. Am. Math Soc., Am. Assn. Univ. Profs., Phi Beta Kappa, Sigma Xi. Author: Primitive Groups (Part 1), 1921. Home: Stanford CA Died Feb. 29, 1972.

MANSFIELD, GEORGE ROGERS, geologist; b. Gloucester, Mass., Aug. 30, 1875; s. Alfred and Sarah Jane (Hubbard) M.; B.S., Amherst, 1897, M.A., 1901; M.A., Harvard, 1904, Ph.D., 1906; m. Adelaide Claflin, Aug. 18, 1903; children—Harvey Claflin, James Scott, Robert Hubbard, Marion Claflin and Helen Rogers (twins). Teacher, Central High Sch., Cleveland, 1897-1903; instr. in geology, Harvard, 1906-09; asst. prof. geology, Northwestern U., 1909-13; geologist U.S. Geol. Survey since 1913, in charge sect. of non-metalliferous deposits, 1922-27; in charge sect. areal and non-metalliferous geology, 1927-43; editor of geologic maps, 1941-43, retired. Made investigations in phosphate, potash and nitrates in U.S. and dam sites in Puerto Rico, Idaho, and Wyoming, also researches in stratigraphy and structure in Rocky Mountains of Ida. Mem. Nat. Research Council, 1924-27, chmn. com. on tectonics, 1924-34. Fellow Geol. Soc. of America, A.A.A.S. (sec. sect. E. 1926-30; v.p. 1936); mem. Am. Inst. Mining and Metall Engrs., Soc. of Econ. Geologists, Am. Geophysical Union, Washington Acad. Sciences (v.p. 1931), Geol. Soc., Washington (pres. 1930), Phi Sigma Kappa, Phi Delta Theta, Phi Beta Kappa, Sigma Xi. Republican. Conglist. Club: Cosmos. Author of numerous bulls. and professional papers on phosphates in Ida., Fla., greensands in N.J., nitrates in Calif., Tex., Ida. and Ore., potash in Tex. and N.M., and physiography, stratigraphy, and geologic structure in the Rocky Mountains of Ida. Associate editor Am. Jour. Sci., 1938-45. Home: 2067 Park Road, Washington DC

MANSFIELD, JARED, U.S. surveyor gen., educator; b. New Haven, Conn., May 23, 1759; s. Stephen and Hannah (Beach) M.; grad. Yale, 1777, A.M., 1787, LL.D. (hon.), 1825; m. Elizabeth Phipps, Mar. 2, 1800, 1 son, Edward Deering. Rector, Hopkins Grammar Sch., New Haven, 1786; apptd. capt. Engrs. Corps, U.S. Army by Pres. Jefferson, 1802; acting prof. mathematics U.S. Mil. Acad., 1802-03; apptd. surveyor gen. U.S. with rank of lt. col. to survey Ohio and N.W. Territory, 1803-12; promoted maj., 1805, lt. col., 1808; prof. natural and exptl. philosophy U.S. Mil. Acad. 1812-28; Mansfield (O.) named for him. Author: Essays, Mathematical and Physical, 1801; Essays on Mathematics, 1802. Died New Haven, Conn., Feb. 3, 1830; buried Grove Cemetery, New Haven.

MANSFIELD, SAMUEL MATHER, brig. gen. U.S.A.; b. Middletown, Conn., Sept. 23, 1839; s. Maj. Gen. Joseph King Fenno and Louisa (Mather) M.; grad. U.S. Mil. Acad., 1862; m. Mrs. Anna Baldwin Wright, Apr. 16, 1874 (dec.). Promoted 2d lt., corps engrs., June 17, 1862; promoted through grades to brig. gen. U.S.A., Feb. 20, 1903. In Civil War, col. 24th Conn. Inf., Nov. 18, 1862-Sept. 30, 1863. Bvtd. capt., June 14, 1863, "for gallantry at Port Hudson, La."; maj. and lt. col., Mar. 13, 1865, "for gallant and meritorious services during the war." Has been in charge of constrn. of many fortifications; engr., 9th, 10th and 11th light house dists., and many other works; pres. commn. to run and mark the boundary lines between portion of Ind. Ty. and Texas, 1885-87; pres. Calif. debris commn. to regulate hydraulic mining, 1898-99; pres. Yosemite Nat. Park Commn., 1899; div. engr., Pacific div., Nov. 7, 1898, Northwestern div., May 3, 1901, Eastern div., July 4, 1901; retired at own request, over 40 yrs.' service, Feb. 21, 1903. Mass. harbor and land commr., July 23, 1906-July 17, 1912. Address: Boston, Mass. Died Feb. 18, 1928.

MANSON, MARSDEN, civil engr.; b. Leewood, Va., Feb. 14, 1850; s. Robert E. and Sophia A. (Smith) M.; grad. Va. Mil. Inst., Lexington, 1870, B.S. and C.E., 1877; Ph.D., U. of Calif., 1893; m. Samuella L. Chase, Sept. 12, 1883 (died 1913); m. 2d, Julia D. E. Wright, Jan. 1916; children—Julia Alexandria Wright, Marsden Wright. Asst. engr., U.S. Engr. Dept., 1873-75; asst. prof. physics and chemistry, Va. Mil. Inst., 1876-77; asst. engr., State Engring. Dept., Calif., 1879-81; asst. engr., U.S. Engr. Dept., 1881-82; chief engr., Bd. State Harbor Commn., San Francisco, 1883-92; mem. bd. engrs., San Francisco drainage, 1893-94; consulting engr., commr. pub. works, Calif., 1895-99; pres. dept. highways, Calif., 1896-99; commr. pub. works, San Francisco, 1900-03; cons. engr., 1904-07; city engr. San Francisco, 1908-12. Democrat. Episcopalian. Author: The Evolution of Climates; Geologic and Present Climates. Home: Berkeley, Calif. Died Feb. 21, 1931.

MANSON, OTIS FREDERICK, physician; b. Richmond, Va., Oct. 10, 1822; s. Otis and Sarah Dews (Ferrill) M.; attended Hampden-Sydney Coll.; m. Mary Ann Spottswood Burwell; m. 2d, Helen (Gray) Watson, 1881. Practiced medicine, Granville County, N.C.; served as maj. Confederate Army, established Vet's Hosp., Richmond, 1862; prof. pathology and physiology Med. Coll. of Va., 1869-82, prof. emeritus, 1882-88; asso. editor Va. Clin. Record. 1871-72; mem. Med. Soc. N.C.; mem. Va. Bd. Med. Examiners, 1870-88; pres. Richmond City Council. Author: Remittent Fever, 1881; Physiological and Therapeutic Action of Sulphate of Quinine, 1882. Died Richmond, Jan. 25, 1888; buried Richmond.

MANTER, HAROLD W(INFRED), univ. prof.; b. Anson, Me., June 18, 1898; s. Fred Augustus and Gusta Houghton (Tinkham) M.; A.B., Bates Coll., Lewiston, Me., 1922; A.M., Univ. Ill., 1923, Ph.D., 1925; m. Esther Ruby Welch, Aug. 16, 1927. Instr. in zoology, La. State Univ., 1925-26; asst. prof. zoology, Univ. of Neb., 1926-27, asso. prof., 1927-35, prof. of zoology from 1935; guest investigator, Biol. Lab., Carnegie Instn., Tortugas, Fla., summers, 1930, 31, 32; mem., Third Allan Hancock Expdn. to Galapagos Islands, 1934; Fulbright research scholar in New Zealand, 1951. Mem. A.A.A.S., Am. Soc. Parasit. (mem. council, 1944-46, mem. ed. bd., Jour. Parasit., 1940-43), Am. Micros. Soc., Am. Soc. Zoologists, Soc. System. Zoology, Am. Soc. Limnology and Oceanography; Phi Beta Kappa, Sigma Xi, Author: (monographs) Some North American fish trematodes, 1926; Digenetic trematodes of fishes from the Galapagos Islands and the neighboring Pacific, 1940; The digenetic trematodes of marine fishes of tortugas, Florida, 1947. Contbr. articles on parasitic worms. Home: Lincoln NB Died Apr. 15, 1971; buried Madison ME

MANWARING, WILFRED HAMILTON, pathologist; b. Ashland, Va., Sept. 14, 1871; s. Theodore Perry and Mary Frances (Griswold) M.; M.D. Johns Hopkins U., 1904; also studied at Berlin, Leipzig, Frankfort-on-the-Main, Vienna and London, 1907-10; m. Ava Mautner, June 14, 1917; children—John Hamilton, Frederick Wolcott. Fellow and asst. in pathology, U. of Chicago, 1904-05; asso. prof. pathology and bacteriology, Ind. U.; 1905-07; traveling fellow in pathology and bacteriology, Rockefeller Inst. for Med. Research, 1907-08, asst., 1910-13; prof. bacteriology and experimental pathology, Stanford U., 1913-37, emeritus since 1937. Lecturer in functional pathology, Washington U. Med. Sch., St. Louis, Mo., 1920-21, Mem. Soc. for Exptl. Pathology, Am. Assn. Pathologists and Bacteriologists, Am. Assn. Immunologists (pres. 1926), Soc. for Exptl. Biology and Medicine, Soc. Am. Bacteriologists, Sigma Xi; fellow A.M.A., A.A.A.S. Researches in theoretical immunology and experimental pathology. Address: 364 Kingsley Av., Palo Alto CA

MAPES, CHARLES VICTOR, agrl. chemist; b. New York, July 4, 1836; A.B., Harvard, 1857; m. Martha Meeker Halsted, 1863; 1 son, Victor M. Became expert in agrl. chemistry—especially in fertilizers; introduced spl. crop manures in U.S. by preparing a fertilizer adapted for growth of Irish potatoes; was associated in soil tests, with Prof. W. O. Atwater, of the Nat. Expt. Sta., at Washington; founder and pres. The Mapes Formula and Peruvian Guano Co., New York; became pres. New York Chemical and Fertilizer Exchange at its organization. Home: New York, N.Y. Died Jan. 23, 1916.

MAPES, JAMES JAY, agriculturist; b. Maspeth, L.I., May 29, 1806; s. Jonas and Elizabeth (Tylee) M.; m. Sophia Furman, 1827, 5 daus., 1 son, Charles V. Mcht., 1827-32; invented sugar refining process, 1832; became patent cons., analytical chemist; prof. chemistry and natural philosophy of colors Nat. Acad. Design, 1835-38; editor Am. Repertory of Arts, Sciences and Manufactures, 1840-42; asso. editor Jour. of Franklin Inst., 1842-43; pres. Mechanics Inst. City of N.Y., 1845; v.p. Am. Inst. City of N.Y., 1847; founder Franklin Inst. of Newark (N.J.); became farmer, 1847, purchased old N.J. farm, converted it into show-place by using advanced scientific agrl. methods; founder, editor The Working Farmer, 1849-63. Died N.Y.C., Jan. 10, 1866.

MARBLE, JOHN PUTNAM, research geochemist; b. Worcester, Mass., May 30, 1897; s. J(oseph) Russel and Emily Greene (Chase) M.; A.B., Williams Coll., 1918; student Clark U., 1919; A.M., Harvard, 1928, Ph.D., 1932; m. Adelaide Holme Maghee, May 21, 1921; children—Katharine Chase Bejnar, Richard Almy, Rosamond Weis, John Putnam, Jr. With J. Russel Marble & Co., Marble-Nye Co., drysaltery bus., Worcester, 1919-26; independent geochem. research under auspices Nat. Research Council, Washington, since 1931 (at U.S. Geol. Survey, 1931-35, U.S. Nat. Mus. since 1935, asso. in mineralogy of Mus. since 1945); tech. aide and spl. asst. Nat. Defense Research Com. of Office Sci. Research and Development, 1942-46; vice chmn., com. on measurement of geologic time, Div. Geology and Geography, Nat. Research Council, 1936-46, chmn. since 1946; part author reports of com.; sec.-treas. Am. Geol. Inst. 1950-52. Del. to 17th and 18th International Geologic Congresses, 1937, 48, 10th session Internat. Union Geodesy and Geophysics, 1954. Fellow A.A.A.S., Geological Soc.

America, Mineralogical Soc. America, Meteoritical Soc.; mem. Am. Chem. Soc., Electrochem. Soc., American Geophysical Union (general sec. 1953—), Wash. and N.Y. acads. of sci., Geol. Soc. Wash., Sons of the Revolution (Mass. soc.), Phi Beta Kappa, Alpha Chi Sigma, Gamma Alpha. Club: Petrologist, Harvard, Cosmos, Chevy Chase (Washington); Williams (N.Y. City); University (Boston); Harvard Faculty (Cambridge); Worcester, (Worcester, Mass.); Nantucket (Mass.) Yacht. Home: 3221 Macomb St., Washington 8. Office: U.S. National Museum, Washington 25. Died June 6, 1955; buried Arlington Nat. Cemetery.

MARBURG, EDGAR, civil engr.; C.E., Rensselaer Poly. Inst., Troy, N.Y., 1885; Sc.D., LL.D.; m. Fanny Dulany, Aug. 14, 1893. Prof. civil engring., U. of Pa. Mem. Engring. Com. of Nat. Research Council, 1917—. Sec. Am. Soc. for Testing Material. Author: Framed Structures and Girders. Home: Philadelphia, Pa. Died June 27, 1918.

MARBURG, OTTO, univ. prof.; b. Roemerstadt, Austria, May 25, 1874; s. Max and Adele (Berg) M.; came to United States, 1938; naturalized citizen; M.D., University of Vienna (Austria), 1899; married Malvine Knoepflmacher, September 5, 1916. Privatdozent, U. of Vienna, 1905-12, title prof., 1912-16, real prof., 1916-38, chief of the Neurological Inst., 1919-38; clinical prof. of neurology, Columbia U., since 1938. Hon. mem. Am. Neurological Assn., A.M.A. (neuropathological sect.), N.Y. and Phila. Neurological Assn. Author: Mikroskopischtopographischer Atlas des menschlichen Zentralnervensystems, 1904 (3d edit. 1927); Die sogenannte akute multiple Sklerose, 1906; Syphilis des Nervensystems (with I. A. Hirschl), 1914; Handbuch der Neurologie des Ohres (with Alexander and Brunner), 1924-26; Die Roentgenbehandlung der Nervenkrankheiten (with Sgalitzer), 1931; Unfall & Hirngeschwulst, 1934; Injuries of the Nervous System, 1939; Hydrocephalus, Its Symptomology, Pathology, Pathogenesis and Treatment, 1940. Editor "Arbeiten aus Dem Neurologischen Institut der Universitaet Wien" from 1919; author numerous med. articles. Address: 225 Central Park West, New York 24. Died June 13, 1948.

MARBUT, CURTIS FLETCHER, geologist; b. Lawrence County, Mo., July 19, 1863; s. Nathan T. and Jane (Browning) M.; B.S., U. of Mo., 1889; A.M., Harvard, 1895; studied in Europe, 1899-1900; LL.D., U. of Mo., 1916; m. Florence Martin, Dec. 17, 1891 (dec.); children—Louise, Thomas Fiske, William Martin, Helen, Frederick Browning. Inst. geology and mineralogy, 1895-97, asst. prof., 1897-99, prof. and curator Geol. Mus., 1899-1913, U. of Mo.; dir. Soil Survey of Mo., 1905-13; spl. agt. Bur. of Soils, U.S. Dept. Agr., 1909-10; in charge Soil Survey, U.S. Dept. Agr., 1910—. Democrat. Unitarian. Address: Washington, D.C. Died Aug. 25, 1935.

MARC, HENRI M(ICHEL), engineer; b. Bességes, France, Aug. 1, 1900; s. Henri G. and Pauline (Schmidt) M.; B.Sc., Carnegie Inst. Tech., 1922; fellow Mellon Inst., Pitts., 1924-31; grad. studies U. Pitts., 1925-28; m. Laura Marlier, Sept. 7, 1929; children—Lauretta M., Marilyn. Came to U.S., 1914, naturalized, 1919. Asst. dir. research Philip Carey Mfg. Co., Cin., 1932-46; asst. gen. mgr. C. J. Tagliabue Co., Bklyn., 1946-48; gen. mgr., pres. Am. Pad & Textile Co., Greenfield, 1948-59, dir., 1951—, vice chmn. bd., 1959—. Asst. exec. dir., trustee Ohio Valley Goodwill Rehabilitation Center, Cin. Vice pres. O. Safety Council, 1952-53, pres. 1945-55. Profl. engr. O. Mem. O. Soc. N.Y., Q.M. Assn. (pres. Columbus 1950-51), Am. Chem. Soc., Am. Soc. Chem. Engrs. Presbyn. Mason. Clubs: Lake Shore (Chgo.); Chemists (N.Y.C.); Cincinnati (Cin.). Home: 3536 Paxton Av., Cin. 8. Died Sept. 23, 1962.

MARCHETTI, ANDREW A., obstetrician, gynecologist; b. Richmond, Va., July 2, 1901; s. Louis and Blanca (Iaccheri) M.; student Johns Hopkins University, 1920-22, M.D., 1928; A.B., University of Richmond, 1924; m. Catherine E. Fopeano, Jan. 2, 1935; children—Marco Anthony, Peter Luigi, Michael Joseph, John Philip. Intern in obstetrics John Hopkins Hosp., 1928-29; assist. resident, later resident, obstetrics and gynecology, Strong Memorial Hospital, Rochester, New York, 1929-31; assistant resident surgery, Cincinnati (Ohio) General Hospital, 1931-32; resident obstetrics and gynecology woman's clinic N.Y. Hospital, 1932-33, attending obstetrician and gynecologist, 1943-47; instr., later asso. prof. obstetrics and gynecology med. coll. Cornell U., 1933-47; prof. obstetrics and gynecology, head dept. Georgetown University School Medicine, 1947-66, professor obstetrics and gynecology, 1947-70; director Georgetown division department of obstetrics and gynecology, D.C. General Hosp.; civilian consultant Army Med. Center, Walter Reed Hosp. Recipient Vicennial medal Georgetown Univ. Diplomate Am. Bd. Obstetrics and Gynecology (dir. 1966-70, pres. 1966-70). Fellow Am. Coll. Obstetricians and Gynecologists (1st v.p. 1958-59), Am. Assn. Obstetricians and Gynecologists, Am. (sec. 1957-61, pres. 1966-67), Washington (pres. 1952-53) gynecol. socs., A.C.S.; mem. Soc. Pelvic Surgeons, A.M.A., Med. Soc. D.C., Kappa Sigma, Alpha Omega Alpha, Alpha Kappa Kappa, Sigma Xi (honorary mem.). Republican. Roman Catholic. Co-author: The Epithelia of Woman's Reproductive Organs, 1948. Home: Silver Spring MD Died June 25, 1970; buried Gate of Heaven Cemetery, Silver Spring MD

MARCONI, (GUGLIELMO) WILLIAM, elec. engr.; b. Bologna, Italy, Apr. 25, 1874 (mother Irish-born); ed. Leghorn and U. of Bologna; LL.D., Glasgow, Aberdeen, U. of Pa.; D.Sc., Oxford; m. Hon. Beatrice O'Brien, Mar. 16, 1905. Began, 1890, on his father's estate, experiments to test the theory that the electric current is capable of passing through any substance, and, if started, in any given direction, of following an undeviating course without need for a wire or other conductor. He invented an apparatus for wireless telegraphy which attracted attention of Sir William Henry Preece, engr. and electrician-in-chief English Postal Telegraph, who tested the apparatus, with success, in England; soon afterward succeeded in sending messages from Spezia to a steamer 15 kilometers distant; also sent messages from Queen Victoria ashore to Prince of Wales on royal yacht, 1897; came to U.S., 1899; used his method in reporting election, 1900; succeeded in establishing wireless telegraphic communication across Atlantic Ocean, 1902; daily ocean news service by wireless telegraphy inaugurated by him on trans-Atlantic liners, 1904. Invented directive method of wireless telegraphy, 1905, and continuous-wave system, 1906. Awarded one-half of the Nobel Prize, for physics, 1909. Home: Bologna, Italy. Died July 19, 1937.

MARCOU, JULES, geologist; b. Salins, France, Apr. 20, 1824; attended Coll. of St. Louis 1842-44; m. Jane Belknap, 1850, 2 sons. Prof. mineralogy Sorbonne, 1846-48; traveling geologist for Jardin des Plantes, 1848-50; collected for Paris museums in North Am., especially in Lake Superior region, until 1854; prof. paleontology École Polytechnique, Zurich, 1856-60; returned to Am., 1860; geologist Mus. of Comparative Zoology, Harvard, 1862-64, made several field trips to Western U.S. Author: Lettres sur les Roches du Jura, 1857-60; Geology of North American, 1858; also produced Geological Map of the World, 1862. Died Apr. 17, 1898.

MARK, EDWARD LAURENS, anatomist; b. Hamlet, Chautauqua Co., N.Y., May 30, 1847; s. Charles L. and Julia (Peirce) M.; A.B., U. of Mich., 1871; Ph.D., U. of Leipzig, 1876; LL.D., U. of Mich., 1896, U. of Wis., 1904; m. Lucy Thorp King, Nov. 26, 1873; children—Kenneth Lamartine, Freedrica (Mrs. George H. Chase). Instr. mathematics, U. of Mich., 1871-72; astronomer U.S. Northwest Boundary Survey, 1872-73; instr. zoology, Harvard, 1877-83, asst. prof., 1883-86, Hersey prof. anatomy, 1885-1921, now emeritus, dir. Zool. Lab., 1900-21. Dir. Bermuda Biol. Sta. for Research, 1903-31; U.S. del. 4th Internat. Zool. Congress, 1898. Fellow Soc. Biol. Chemistry (London), A.A.A.S., Am. Acad. Arts and Sciences; life mem. Anat. und Zool. Gesellschaften; mem. Boston Soc. Natural History, Am. Philos. Soc., Nat. Acad. Sciences, Soc. Royale Zoologique et Malacol. Belgique; foreign mem. Koenigl, Boehmische Gesellschaft der Wissenschaften; hon. mem. Institut Internat. D'Embryologie (Holland); corr. mem. Peking Soc. Natural History. Author: Maturation, Fecundation and Segmentation of Limax, 1881; Simple Eyes in Anthropods, 1887; Studies in Lepidosteous, 1893. Translator: Text-Book of the Embryology of Man and Mammals from the German of O. Hertwig, 1892; Text-Book of the Embryology of Invertebrates, Part I (with W. M. Woodworth), from German of Korschelt und Heider, 1895. Edited contributions from the Zool. Laboratory, Museum of Comparative Zoology at Harvard Coll., 1884-1923 (334 numbers published), and contbr. Bermuda Biol. Sta., 1904— (168 numbers published). Socio honorario Sociedad Cubana de Historia Natural. "Felipe Poey." Contbr. to Bulletin of Museum Comparative Zoology, also chapter, "Zoology, 1847-1921," in Morison's History of Harvard University. Home: 109 Irving St., Cambridge 38, Mass. Died Dec. 16, 1946.

MARKEE, JOSEPH ELDRIDGE, med. educator; b. Neponset, Ill., May 22, 1903; s. Joshua W. and Josephine (Eldridge) M.; student Knox Coll., 1921-24; B.S., U. Chicago., 1924, Ph.D., 1929; m. Myrtle Clapp, July 2, 1927; children—Shirley J., Joseph Eldridge. Mem. faculty Stanford, 1929-43; prof. anatomy, 1943; prof., dept. anatomy Duke U. Med. Sch., 1943-53, James B. Duke prof., 1953-70, chmn. dept. anatomy, 1943-66, asst. dean medical admissions, 1943-66; vis. prof. anatomy U. Tennessee Med. Sch., summer 1942. Recipient Golden Apple award Student Am. Med. Assn., 1963; Council on Med. Television Roster award, posthumously. Commonwealth Fellow, 1966-67. Hon. fellow Am. Soc. Orthopedic Surgeons, Am. Orthopedic Assn.; mem. Assn. Medical Colleges (audio-visual com.), Am. Assn. Anatomist (adv. com. med. Film Inst.; executive committee, 1946-64), American Physiol. Society, American Zool. Soc., N.Y. Acad. Science, Phi Beta Kappa, Sigma Xi, Alpha Omega Alpha. Asso. editor Jour. Morphology. Producer movies on functional anatomy. Home: Durham NY Died Nov. 27, 1970; interred Duke U. Medical Center, Durham NC

MARKHAM, EDWIN C(ARLYLE), educator; b. Durham, N.C., Dec. 24, 1902; s. James William and Anna (Leigh) M.; A.B., Trinity Coll., 1923; Ph.D., U. Va., 1927; m. Anne Janet Whitlock, May 27, 1928 (dec.); children—Carlyle, Allan Whitlock. Asst. prof. chemistry U. Va., 1927-30, research asso., 1930-33; instr. chemistry U. Del., 1933-34; asst. prof. chem. U. N.C., 1934-37, asso. prof., 1937-41, prof. chem., 1941-51; Smith prof. chemistry since 1951. Mem. Am. Chem. Soc., N.C. Acad. Sci. Sigma Xi, Alpha Chi Sigma. Democrat. Baptist. Research in heterogeneous reaction rates, adsorption of gases mixtures by metals and metallic oxides, adsorption of gases at high pressures, use of organic reagents in analytical chem., indicator constants in organic media, polarography. Home: Chapel Hill, N.C. Died July 1966.

MARKHAM, JOHN RAYMOND, prof. engring.; b. Cambridge, Mass., July 23, 1895; s. John Henry and Mary (Williams) M.; M.E., Mass. Inst. Tech., 1918; m. Genevieve Triquera, June 5, 1921; 1 son, James Paul (killed in action, Mar. 8, 1945). Began as research asso. aeronaut. engring. dept., Mass. Inst. Tech., 1922, prof. aeronaut. engring. from 1946, dir. supersonic lab. from 1947; dir. Wright Bros. Wind Tunnel, Mass. Inst. Tech., cons. engr. Argentine and Brazillian govts. in design of wind tunnels and equipment, also U.S. A.A.F., Boeing Aircraft, United Aircraft Corp. and Gen. Motors Corp.; mem. sci. adv. bd. to U.S.A.A.F., from 1945; chmn. industry and ednl. adv. bd. U.S.A.F. science com. and sub-com. Nat. Adv. Council for Aeros. Chairman bd. Mithras, Inc. (Cambridge, Mass.). Served as capt. AEF, U.S. Army, 1917-19. Recipient USAF medal, 1955. Fellow Inst. Aero. Sci.; mem. Sigma Xi. Contbr. articles to engring. and sci. publs. Home: Belmont MA Died Dec. 12, 1971; buried Belmont Cemetery, Belmont MA

MARKS, LIONEL SIMEON, engr.; b. Birmingham, Eng., Sept. 8, 1871; s. Samuel Edward M.; student Mason Coll., Birmingham, 1888-92, engring. diploma, 1891; B.Sc., London U., 1892; arrived in America, 1893; M.M.E., Cornell U., 1894; m. Josephine Preston Peabody, June 21, 1906 (died Dec. 4, 1922); children—Alison Peabody, Lionel Peabody. Instr. mech. engring., Harvard U., 1894-1900, asst. prof., 1900-09, prof. 1909-40, prof. emeritus, 1940; also prof. Mass. Inst. Tech., 1914-18. Fellow Am. Acad. Arts and Sci., A.A.A.S., Am. Soc. M.E. (nat. lecturer 1944-46). Mem. Old Cambridge Shakespeare Assn. (pres.), Phi Beta Kappa, Sigma Xi (nat. lecturer 1942; pres. Harvard chapt. 1946-47), Tau Beta Pi. Consltng. engr. science and research div., Bureau of Aircraft Prodn., 1918; chmn. section on prime movers, engring. Div. Nat. Research Council, 1918. Clubs: Harvard of Boston; Faculty of Cambridge; Harvard of New York; University, Mexico City. Author: Steam Tables and Diagrams (with H. N. Davis), 1900; The Airplane Engine, 1922; Axial-Flow Fans (with C. Keller), 1937. Editor: Mechanical Engineers' Handbook. Home: 19 Garden St., Cambridge, Mass. Died Jan. 6, 1955.

MARKS, WILLIAM DENNIS, engineer; b. St. Louis, Mo., Feb. 26, 1849; s. Dennis and Elmira (Bacon) M.; Ph.B., Yale, 1870, C.E., 1871; spl. study as civ. and mech. engr.; m. Jeannette Holmes Colwell, 1874; (died 1894); father of Jeannette M. Engaged in practical engring. on various rys., gas works, iron works, etc., 1873; instr. mech. engring. Lehigh U., 1876; Whitney prof. dynamic engring., U. of Pa., 1877; supt. Internat. Elec. Exhbn., of Franklin Inst., 1884; engr. and pres. of the Edison Electric Light Co., Phila., 1887. Author: The Relative Proportions of the Steam Engine, 1880; Revised edition of Nystrom's Mechanics' Pocket Book, 1885; The Finances of Gas and Electricity Mfg. Enterprises, 1902. Home: Westport, N.Y. Died Jan. 1914.

MARKWART, ARTHUR HERMANN, engring. exec.; b. Du Quoin, Ill., Feb. 13, 1880; s. Hermann and Sarah (Beck) M.; grad. Calif. Sch. Mech. Arts, San Francisco, 1899; B.S., U. of Calif., 1904; m. Marie Louise Chesebrough, May 26, 1908; children—Arthur Hermann, Henry Chesebrough, John, Philip Gordon, Elizabeth. Employed as engr., 1904-06; chief engr., mgr. Syndicate Water Co., Oakland, Calif., 1906-07; partner Howard & Galloway, architects and engrs., San Francisco, 1907-08, Galloway & Markwart, cons. engrs., 1908-12, 1915-17 and 1919-20; chief of constrn. Panama Pacific Internat. Expn., San Francisco, 1912-15; cons. engr., 1917-19; dir. engring. Pacific Gas & Electric Co., 1920-22; v.p. in charge engineering, 1922—; member board dirs. North Am. Investment Corp., Commonwealth Investment Co., San Francisco Remedial Loan Assn., Tacoma Mill Co.; pres. Calif. Sch. Mech. Arts. Republican. Protestant. Home: Piedmont, Calif. Died Jan. 25, 1940.

MARLATT, CHARLES LESTER, (mär-lat), entomologist; b. Atchison, Kan., Sept. 26, 1863; s. Washington M. (one of founders and first prin. Blue Mont Coll., now Kan. State Coll.) and J. A. (Bailey) M.; B.S., Kan. State Coll., Manhattan, Kan., 1884, M.S., 1886, D.Sc., 1921; m. Florence L. Brown, Dec. 1, 1896 (died Oct. 28, 1903); m. 2d, Helen Stuart Mackay Smith, July 5, 1906; children—Florence, Virginia, Charles Lester (dec.), Helen, Dorothy, Constance. Asst. prof. Agricultural Coll., Manhattan, Kan., 2 yrs.; asst. entomologist, U.S. Dept. Agr., 1889-94, 1st asst. and asst. chief entomologist, 1894-1922, asso. chief,

1922-27, chief Bur. of Entomology, 1927-33; engaged in hist. and geneal. work, 1933—. Directed, 1909-12, effort to secure a national law to prevent importation of infested and diseased plants into U.S., resulting in the Plant Quarantine Act of Aug. 20, 1912; chmn. Federal Hort. Bd. to supervise enforcement of this act, 1912-28; responsible for reorganization and assembling from other bureaus of Dept. of Agr., of all plant quarantine and regulatory work, under a new office, created by the sec. of agr. of Plant Quarantine and Control Adminstrn., chief of this office, July 1, 1928-Dec. 1, 1929. Mem. editorial com. Jour. of Agrl. Research, 1919-26. Fellow A.A.A.S.; pres. Entomol. Soc. Washington, 1897-98, Assn. Econ. Entomologists, 1899; mem. Washington Acad. Sciences, Biol., Archaeol. and Geog. socs., Phi Kappa Phi. Clubs: Cosmos, Chevy Chase, Metropolitan (Washington). Author: An Entomologist's Quest, 1953; also many papers and bulletins on systematic and economic entomology and on plant quarantine; also 16 volumes of service and regulatory announcements, recording 68 foreign and domestic plant quarantines, the regulations thereunder and explanatory papers, 1914-1929. Home: (legal) 1521 16th St., Washington; also Wild Cliff, Seal Harbor, Me. Died Mar. 3, 1954.

MARMER, HARRY AARON, tidal engr.; b. Proskurof, Ukraine, June 21, 1885; s. Isaac Baer and Rechoma (Segal) M.; came to U.S., 1889; grad. Woodbine (N.J.) Agrl. Sch., 1901; B.Sc., Rutgers, 1907, M.S., 1930; m. Hazel Ellison Dakin, Nov. 16, 1916 (dec.); children—Kalmon Elias, Nancy Jane. Asst. engr. Cape May Real Estate Co., 1907; tidal computer, U.S. Coast and Geodetic Survey, Washington, D.C., 1907-20; asst. chief, Div. of Tides and Currents, same, since July 1920. Received Agassiz Medal in oceanography, 1951. Fellow A.A.A.S.; mem. Philos. Society of Washington, Assn. Am. Geographers, Am. Geophys. Union, Am. Soc. C.E. Club: Cosmos. Author: Tides and Currents in New York Harbor, 1925; The Tide, 1926; Coastal Currents Along the Pacific Coast of the U.S., 1926; Tidal Datum Planes, 1927; The Sea, 1930; Chart Datums, 1930. Contbr. to scientific and tech. publs. of articles dealing with tides, currents and gen. oceanography; contbg. editor Geog. Rev. Home: 7106 7th St. N.W., Washington. Deceased.

MARMION, KEITH ROBERT, educator, civil engr.; b. Farmington, Ia., Aug. 15, 1927; s. Robert Samuel and Clara Verne (Mills) M.; B.S. in Civil Engring., U. Denver, 1951; M.S., U. Colo., 1958; Ph.D., U. Cal. at Berkeley, 1961; m. Lois Jane Schallenberger, July 12, 1947; children—Daniel Keith, Shelly Lynn, Cynthia Jane. Constrn. engr. U.S. Corps Engrs., 1951-52; jr. civil engr. Lockwood, Andrews & Newnam, cons. engrs., Victoria, Tex., 1952-55; mem. faculty Tex. Tech. U., Lubbock, 1955-68, prof. civil engring., head dept., 1962-68. Bd. dirs. Day Care Assn. Lubbock, 1962-66, pres., 1964. Served with USNR, 1945-47. Registered profl. engr., Tex. Mem. Nat., Tex. (dir. S. Plains chpt. 1964) socs. profl. engrs., Am. Soc. C.E., Am. Soc. Engring. Edn., Am. Geophys. Union, A.A.A.S., W. Tex. Mus. Assn., Am. Water Resources Assn., Sigma Xi (pres. elect 1968), Phi Kappa Phi, Tau Beta Pi. Home: Lubbock TX Died Mar. 17, 1968; buried Resthaven Cemetery, Lubbock TX

MARMION, ROBERT AUGUSTINE, med. dir. U.S.N.; b. Harper's Ferry, Va., Sept. 6, 1844; s. Nicholas and Lydia Ingraham (Hall) M.; ed. pvt. schs. of native place, until 13 yrs. old, Mt. St. Mary's Coll., Emmitsburg, Md., A.B., 1861, A.M., 1863, Univ. of Pa., M.D., 1868; m. Beatrice Paul, Oct. 7, 1885. Apptd. from W.Va. asst. surgeon, U.S.N., Mar. 26, 1868; promoted past asst. surgeon Mar. 26, 1871, surgeon, June 3, 1879; med. insp., June 15, 1895, med. dir., Oct. 1899. Served in various depts. of sea and shore service, at hosps., navy yards, etc., trip with Juniata around the world, Jan. 1886-Mar. 1889; on spl. duty Smithsonian Instn., 1894; fleet surgeon S. Atlantic Sta., July 1894-June 1896; etc. Naval del. to Am Med. Assn., 1900, 02, 03, 04; comdg. U.S. Naval Mus of Hygiene and Med. Sch., Sept. 1902—. Mem Anatomical Bd., D.C. Catholic. Home: Washington D.C. Died 1907.

MARMON, HOWARD C., motor car designer and exec.; b. Richmond, Ind., May 24, 1876; s. Daniel W. and Elizabeth (Carpenter) M.; student Earlham Coll., 1892-94; received degree in mech. engring., U. of Calif., Berkeley, Calif.; m. Florence Myers, 1901; 1 dau., Carol Carpenter (wife of Prince Nicolas Tchkotoua); m. 2d, Martha Foster, 1911. Began as associate with father in flour mill machinery business which was absorbed by automobile industry; became vice pres. in charge engring., Marmon Motor Car Co., 1902; invented the Marmon automobile and was a pioneer in designing and producing racing cars; designed the Marmon Wasp, which won first 500-mile internat. sweepstakes on Indianapolis Speedway, May 30, 1911 (average speed of 74.61 miles per hour for the course); invented duplex downdraft manifold, widely used in building straight eights; reduced weight of 16 cylinder engine by use of aluminum parts, thus making the engine practical commercially; was a developer of Liberty airplane motor during World War I. Served as lieut. col., Army Air Corps during World War I; builder and first comdg. officer, McCook Field, Dayton, O. Mem. U.S. Commn. to Europe for selection of airplane equipment, and examination of prodn at Isotta-Fraschini Motor Car Co., Italy, 1917. Pres. Am. Soc. Automotive Engrs., 1913 and 1914 (awarded medal by Met. sect., 1931, for year's outstanding automotive design, the Marmon Sixteen). Selected as only Am. hon. mem. English Soc. Automotive Engrs., 1913. Mem. Second Presbyn. Ch., Indianapolis, Ind. Clubs: Engineers (N.Y. City); Columbia, Athletic, University (Indianapolis, Ind.). Home: Pineola, Avery County, N.C.; also Columbia Club, Indianapolis, Ind. Died April 4, 1943.

MARRIOTT, ROSS W., (mar'ri-ot), mathematician; b. Paxton, Ill., Dec. 30, 1882; s. Joshua H. and Elizabeth (Kelley) M.; B.S., Valparaiso (Ind.) U., 1904; A.B., Ind. U., 1906; A.M., Swarthmore, 1907; Ph.D., U. Pa., 1911; m. Marian Redfield Stearne, Sept. 8, 1915; 1 dau., Alice Elizabeth. Instr. mathematics Swarthmore, 1907-10, asst. prof., 1910-22, asso. prof., 1922-27, prof., 1927—. Mem. Swarthmore Coll. Eclipse Expdns., Mexico, 1923, New England, 1925, 32, Sumatra, 1926, 29; mem. U.S. Naval Obs. Eclipse Expdn., 1930. Research ballistician on spl. aircraft ammunition, E. I. du Pont de Nemours & Co., 1918. Fellow A.A.A.S., Royal Astron. Soc.; mem. Am. Astron. Soc. Am. Math. Soc., Math. Assn. Am., Sigma Xi. Republican. Quaker. Contbr. research papers on astron. subjects. Home: 213 Lafayette Av., Swarthmore, Pa. Died Oct. 19, 1955; buried North Cedar Hill Cemetery, Phila.

MARSDEN, RAYMOND ROBB, civil engring.; b. Utica, N.Y., Oct. 31, 1884; s. John and Martha (Cross) M.; B.S., Dartmouth, 1908, C.E., 1909; m. Mary Gilmour Warnock, June 25, 1913 (died Mar. 1935); m. 2d, Helen Churchill, June 30, 1939. Instr. in surveying, Thayer Sch., Dartmouth, 1909-10; engr. for H. S. Ferguson, New York, in surveys, design and field engineering of paper mill and hydro-electric developments, 1910-15; design engr. Laurentide Co. and Riordan Pulp & Paper Co., Can., 1915-17; chief of design and estimating sect. Atlas Powder Co., 1917-19; prof. civ. engring., Thayer Sch. of Civ. Engring., since 1919, dean since 1925; also cons. engr.; pres. Manchester Water Co.; leave of absence from Dartmouth, 1933-34, as engr. Pub. Works Adminstrn., Concord, N.H.; dir. Works Div., N.H. Unemployment Relief Adminstrn., 1934; dir. projects and labor management Works Progress Adminstrn. for N.H., 1935 and 36; chief statistician, Vt. Statewide Highway Planning Survey, 1938; engr. Federal Works Agency, 1939; engr. Atlas Powder Co., Wilmington, Del., since 1940. Mem. Am. Soc. Civil Engrs., Phi Kappa Psi, Gamma Alpha; ex-sec. New England Sect. Soc. for Promotion Engring. Edn. Mason. Home: Manchester Depot, Vt. Died Mar. 11, 1942.

MARSH, C(HARLES) DWIGHT, physiologist; b. Hadley, Mass., Dec. 20, 1855; s. J. Dwight and Sarah (Ingram) M.; A.B., Amherst Coll., 1877, A.M., 1880; Sc.D., 1927; Ph.D from University of Chicago, 1904; m. Florence Lee Wilder, Dec. 27, 1883; children—Hadleigh, Charles Wilder. Prof. of chemistry and biology, 1883-1889, biology, 1889-1904, dean of faculty, 1900-04, Ripon (Wis.) College; prof. biology, Earlham Coll., 1904-05; physiologist in charge field investigations of poisonous plants, Bur. of Plant Industry, Dept. Agr., 1905-15, transferred to Bur. of Animal Industry, 1915, in charge poisonous plant investigations; retired, 1931. Hon. curator fresh water copepoda, U.S. Nat. Mus. Ex-officio mem. commrs. Wis. Geol. and Natural History Survey, sec. bd., 1897-99; biologist on Geol. and Natural History Survey, Wis.; lecturer in biology, Milwaukee Med. Coll., 1903-04. Conglist. Author: Limnetic Crustacea of Green Lake; The Plankton of Lake Winnebago and Green Lake; A Revision of the North American Species of Diaptomus; A Revision of North American Species of Cyclops; The Loco Weed Disease of the Plains; Stock-Poisoning Plants of the Range; sr. joint author of Zygadenus or Death Camas; Larkspur Poisoning of Live Stock; Lupines as Poisonous Plants. Home: Washington, D.C. Died 1932.

MARSH, OTHNIEL CHARLES, paleontologist; b. Lockport, N.Y., Oct. 29, 1831; s. Caleb and Mary (Peabody) M.; grad. Phillips Andover Acad., 1856, Yale, 1860; postgrad. Heidelberg, Berlin (both Germany), 1862-65. Prof. paleontology Yale, 1866-99; made many trips to Western U.S. to collect materials, from 1866; organized 1st Yale Scientific Expdn., 1870, explored Pliocene deposits of Neb. and Miocene deposits in No. Colo.; 1st to describe fossil serpents and flying reptiles of Western U.S.; apptd. vertebrate paleontologist to U.S. Geol. Survey, 1882; pres. Nat. Acad. Scis., 1883-95. Author: Dinocerata; A Monograph on the Extinct Toothed Birds of North America, 1880; Introduction and Succession of Vertebrate Life in America, 1877. Died New Haven, Conn., Mar. 18, 1899.

MARSH, SYLVESTER, inventor; b. Compton, N.H., Sept. 30, 1803; s. John and Mehitable (Percival) M. Owner meat packing business, Ashtabula, O., 1828-33; operated beef marketing firm, Chgo., 1833-37; in grain bus., Chgo., 1837-55, invented more efficient grain dryers and mfg. process for meal; used process to produce Marsh's Caloric Dry Meal, exported product, largely to W.I.; originated plan to build railroad up Mt. Washington, N.H. (railroad completed 1869); lived in Littleton, N.H., 1865-79; patented locomotive engines designed to ascend grades, cog rail for railroads, atmospheric brake for railroad cars; lived in Concord, N.H., 1879-84. Died Concord, Dec. 30, 1884; buried Concord.

MARSHALL, ALBERT EDWARD, cons. chem. engr.; b. Liverpool, Eng., May 18, 1884; s. Edward and Marie (Sheppard) M.; student Liverpool Inst., 1896-1900; B.S., University Coll., Liverpool, 1900-04; external student South Kensington, London, 1905-06; m. Ruth Marriott Hildebrandt, Nov. 29, 1919; children—Albert Edward, Richard Sheppard. Came to U.S., 1911, naturalized citizen, 1932. Research chemist United Alkali Co., Eng., 1904-07, asst. mgr. Fleetwood Works, Eng., 1907-10; asst. mgr. Thermal Syndicate, Newcastle-on-Tyne, 1910; mgr. Thermal Syndicate, N.Y. City, 1912-16; works mgr. Davison Chem. Co., Baltimore, 1916-21; consulting chem. engr., Baltimore and New York, 1921-38; pres. Rumford (R.I.) Chem. Works, 1938-48; vice pres. Heyden Chemical Corporation, 1948-50; v.p. Gen. Aniline & Film Corp., N.Y. City, Mar.-Dec. 1942; dir. Investors Trust Co., Providence, Rhode Island Hosp. Trust Co., Providence. Pres. New England Indsl. Research Foundation, dir. New England Council; mem. corp. Northeastern U.; v.p. Coffin Sch., Nantucket, Mass.; member adv. council, Dept. of Chem. Engring., Princeton U.; mem. adv. council, R.I. State Coll. Engr. Expt. Station. Mem. Am. Inst. Chem. Engrs. (v.p. 1932-33; pres. 1934-35; dir. 1940-43), Society of Chem. Industry (chmn. 1933-34), Providence Engring. Soc. (dir. since 1941), Am. Chem. Soc., Am. Inst. Mining and Metall. Engrs., Inst. of Food Technologists, Optical Soc. of America, Royal Soc. of Arts (London). Episcopalian. Clubs: Chemists (New York); Turks Head, University (Providence); Squantum Assn. (Barrington, R.I.); Nantucket Yacht (Nantucket, Mass.). Home: 730 Elmgrove Av., Providence, R.I. Office: 603 Industrial Trust Building, Providence, R.I. Died Sept. 15, 1951; buried Providence.

MARSHALL, CHARLES EDWARD, microbiologist; b. on farm, Port Clinton, O., Oct. 6, 1866; s. Lavinas and Lurena (Crandall) M.; Ph.B., U. of Mich., 1895, Ph.D., 1902; Jorgensen's Lab., Copenhagen, Denmark, 1898; Pasteur Inst., Paris; Ostertag's Lab., Berlin, 1903; Inst. f. Infektionskrankheiten (Robert Koch), Berlin, 1913; m. Maud Alice Skidmore, July 7, 1896. Asst. in bacteriology, U. of Mich., 1893-96; asst. in bacteriology, 1896-98, bacteriologist, 1898-1912, scientific and v. dir. Expt. Sta., 1908—, prof. bacteriology and hygiene, 1902-12, Mich. Agrl. Coll.; dir. of Grad. Sch. and prof. microbiology, Mass. Agrl. Coll., 1912—. Pres. Sch. Bd. of East Lansing, Mich. Editor: Microbiology, 1911. Died Mar. 20, 1927.

MARSHALL, CHRISTOPHER, pharmacist; b. Dublin, Ireland, Nov. 6, 1709; married twice; m. 2d, Abigail, 1782. Came to Am., 1727, became pharmacist in Phila.; supported colonial cause from 1773; active in enforcement on non-importation agreements and obtaining supplies for mil. forces, 1774-75; del. Provincial Congress in Phila., 1775; mem. Com. of Safety, Lancaster, Pa., 1777-80; kept diary which is important hist. source for Revolutionary period, portions published as Extracts from the Diary of Christopher Marshall, 1877. Died Phila., May 4, 1797; buried Phila.

MARSHALL, E(LI) KENNERLY, JR., pharmacologist, physiologist; b. Charleston, S.C., May 2, 1889; s. Eli Kennerly and Julia Irene (Brown) M.; B.S., Coll. Charleston, 1908, LL.D., 1941; Ph.D., in Chemistry, Johns Hopkins, 1911, M.D., 1917; studied Halle, Germany, summer 1912; m. Alice Berry Carroll, Sept. 17, 1917; children—Katherine Berry (dec.), Julia Brown (Mrs. William Manchester), Richard Kennerly. Asst., asso. physiol. chemistry, Johns Hopkins, 1911-14, asso. and asso. prof. pharmacology, 1914-19; prof. pharmacology, Washington U., St. Louis, 1919-21; prof. physiology Johns Hopkins, 1921-32, prof. pharmacology and exptl. therapeutics, 1932-55, emeritus prof., 1955—. Editor, Jour. Pharmacology and Exptl. Therapeutics, 1932-37. Capt., M.C., U.S. Army, 1918. Fellow A.A.A.S.; mem. Am. Physiol. Soc., Am. Soc. Biol. Chemists, Am. Soc. Pharmacology and Exptl. Therapeutics, Assn. Am. Physicians, Nat. Acad. Sci., Am. Philos. Soc., Gamma Alpha, Phi Beta Pi. Conducts research work on urea determination; kidney function; urinary secretion; heart and circulation; respiratory stimulants; bacterial chemotherapy; malarial chemotherapy, alcohol metabolism. Home: Severns Apts., 701 Cathedral St., Balt. 1. Died Jan. 10, 1966.

MARSHALL, HUMPHREY, botanist; b. Chester County, Pa., Oct. 10, 1722; s. Abraham and Mary (Hunt) M.; m. Sarah Pennock, Sept. 16, 1748; m. 2d, Margaret Minshall, Jan. 10, 1788. Engaged in farming, Chester County, Pa., from 1748; built 1st conservatory for plants in area, circa 1768; constructed hot house and bot. garden with collection of fgn. and domestic plants, at his home, Marshallton, Pa.; corresponded with Dr. John Fothergill and Peter Collinson in Eng.; mem. Am. Philos. Soc. Author: Arbustrum Americanum, the American Grove (list of native forest trees and shrubs), 1785. Died Marshallton, Nov. 5, 1801.

MARSHALL, JOHN, chemist; b. Reading, Pa. Feb. 9, 1855; s. John Gloninger (M.D.) and Susan A. (Kline) M.; student Pa. Coll., Gettysburg, 1873-76; M.D., U. of Pennsylvania, 1878; studied U. of Göttingen, 1879,

Tübingen (grad. Nat. Sc.D.), 1882, Christiania, Norway; (LL.D., Pa. Coll., 1899); m. Mary W., d. Prof. Theo. G. Wormley, of Phila., Apr. 24, 1884. Asst. demonstrator of practical chemistry, 1878-79, demonstrator, 1879-89, asst. prof. chemistry, 1889-97, prof. chemistry and toxicology, 1897-1922, emeritus prof. chemistry and toxicology, 1922, med. dept. U. of Pa.; dean of faculty of Vet. Medicine, 1889-97, dean faculty of medicine, 1892-1902. U. of Pa. Author: A Course for Systematic Qualitative Testing (with G. E. Abbott), 1879; Chemical Analysis of the Urine (with Edgar F. Smith), 1881. Home: Philadelphia, Pa. Died Jan. 5, 1925.

MARSHALL, JOHN ALBERT, biochemistry, dental pathology; b. Chicago, Ill., Aug. 30, 1884; s. John Sayre (M.D.) and Isabelle M. (Carter) M.; B.S., U. of Calif., 1907, M.S., 1914, D.D.S., 1916, Ph.D., 1917; post-grad. study U. of Berlin, and Tech. U., Charlottenburg, Germany, 1909-10; m. Hazel C. Knowles, May 18, 1907; children—John A., Muriel, Shirley; m. 2d, Irene Byram Kuechler, Dec. 28, 1932. Prof. biochemistry and dental pathology, U. of Calif. Served as capt. Ordnance Dept., U.S. Army, 1917-19. Mem. A.M.A., Am. Dental Assn., Internat. Assn. Dental Research, Soc. Experimental Biology and Medicine, Pacific Coast Society of Orthodontists (hon.), American Society of Orthodontists (hon.), Sigma Xi, Phi Kappa Psi, Delta Sigma Delta, Epsilon Alpha. Republican. Baptist. Mason. Club: Faculty. Author: Military Explosives (pub. by U.S. War Dept.), 1919; Manufacturing and Testing of Military Explosives, 1919; Diseases of the Teeth, 1926; (with C. N. Johnson) Operative Dentistry, 1923; Anatomy of the Rhesus Monkey (with Hartman and Straus), 1933. Contbr. research papers to Jour. Am. Dental Assn., Jour. Am. Med. Assn., Am. Jour. Physiology, etc. Asso. editor Jour. Dental Research. Address: Univ. of California, Berkeley, Calif. Died May 7, 1941. *

MARSHALL, STEWART M., cons. engr.; b. Centralia, Pa., June 13, 1879; s. Ceylon Ward and Mary Priscilla (McCulloch) M.; B.S. in Elec. Engring., U. Pa., 1900, M.E., 1910; M.S. in Bus., Columbia, 1933; m. Ellen Eyre Morgan, June 20, 1906. Instr. mech. engring. U. Pa., 1900-02; asst. steam engr. Cambria Steel Co., Johnstown, Pa., 1902-03, asst. chief draftsman, 1903-06, engr. tests, 1906-08, asst. chief engr., 1908-12, chief engr., 1912-14; cons. engr., Johnstown, Pa., 1914-15; chief engr. and mgr. turbine dept. Southwark Foundry & Machinery Co., Phila., 1915-16; mem. firm Perin & Marshall, cons. engrs., specializing in steel plants, N.Y.C., 1916-31; cons. engr., N.Y.C., 1931-33; cons. engr., San Francisco, 1934-50, Palo Alto, Cal., since 1950. Recipient Legion of Honor award Am. Inst. Mining Metall. and Petroleum Engrs., 1957; distinguished citizenship award Palo Alto Kiwanis Club, 1957. Fellow Am. Soc. M.E., A.A.A.S.; mem. Am. Inst. Mining and Metall, Engrs. Am. Iron and Steel Inst., Brit. Iron and Steel Inst., Am. Econ. Assn., Am. Iron and Steel Engrs., Mining and Metall. Soc. Am., Kappa Sigma, Sigma Xi, Beta Gamma Sigma. Republican. Club: Engineers (San Francisco), Co-author: Elements of Steam Engineering. Home: 430 Nevada Av. Office: 748 Bryant St. Palo Alto, Cal. Died Mar. 25, 1965; buried Alto Mesa Cemetery, Palo Alto, Cal.

MARSHALL, THOMAS ALFRED, JR., mech. engr., assn. exec.; b. Savannah, Ga., Jan. 14, 1911; s. Thomas Alfred and Winefred Turner (Miller) M.; B.S. in Aero. Engring., Ga. Inst. Tech., 1932; m. Mary Lucile Bush, May 27, 1933; children—Thomas Alfred III, Susan Marie, Kathryn Penelope (Mrs. T.M. Staph), John Francis. Stationary engr., air conditioning engr.; office mgmt.; sr. analyst mgmt. engring. Met. Life Ins. Co., N.Y.C., 1932-51; exec. sec. Engring. Manpower Commn., Engrs. Joint Council, 1951-54; sec. Engrs. Joint Council, 1953-54; asst. sec. Am. Soc. M.E., 1954-57, sr. asst. sec., 1958-60, exec. sec. Am. Soc. Testing Materials, Phila., 1960-70. Mgr. Nuclear Congress, 1957-59; U.S. rep. com. on English Mgmt. terminology Comite International de l'Orgn. Sci. Served to comdr. USNR, 1940-45. Fellow A.A.A.S., Am. Soc. M.E.; mem. American Soc. Metals, Engring. Inst. Can, Am. Soc. Engring. Edn., U.S. Naval Inst., Soc. Automotive Engrs., Am. Soc. Testing Materials, Am. Water Works Assn., Standard Engrs. Soc., Instn. Mech. Engrs. (Gt. Britain), Tau Beta Pi, Phi Eta Sigma. Clubs: Army and Navy (Washington); Engineers (Phila.). Author articles on mgmt. indsl. engring. and manpower, standards, also profl. devel. engrs. Home: Radnor PA Died Apr. 9, 1970.

MARSHALL, THOMAS WORTH, civil engr.; b. Economy, Ind., Mar. 24, 1872; s. Swain and Cynthia M.; B.C.E., Purdue U., 1894; m. Kathleen C. Huff, Oct. 4, 1897. In practice as civil engr., 1895—; mem. firm of Sample & Marshall, cons. engrs., 1904—. Author: Logarithmic Tables of the Measures of Length Extending from 0 to 50 Feet at Intervals of One-sixteenth of an Inch, 1902 E 15. Home: 223 Blair Rd., Takoma Park, D.C. Died Mar. 28, 1952.

MARSHALL, WADE HAMPTON, neurophysiologist; b. Pitts., Dec. 17, 1907; s. Francis James and Ann Amos (Miller) M.; student Wooster Coll., 1924-25, U. Pitts., 1925-27; B.S., Beloit Coll., 1927-30; M.S., U. Chgo., 1931, Ph.D., 1934; m. Louise Hanson, Dec. 31, 1934; children—Thomas Hanson, Alice. Instr. physiology George Washington U. Med. Sch., 1934-36; NRC fellow physiology John Hopkins Med. Sch., 1936-38, instr., then asso. lab. physiol. optics Wilmer Opthal. Inst., 1938-43, sr. physicist Applied Physics Lab., 1946-47; engr. Bowen & Co., Bethesda, Md., 1944-46; spl. research fellow Nat. Inst. Mental Health, 1947-49, neurophysiologist, 1949-53; chief lab. neurophysiology Nat. Insts. Mental Health and Neurol. Diseases and Blindness, 1954-69; chief lab. neurophysiology Nat. Inst. Mental Health, 1969-70; research on nervous system, sensory orgn. of brain, perception, rhythmic activities of nervous system, Leao phenomenon. Mem. Joint Bd. Sci. Edn. for Greater Washington Area, 1957-59. Mem. Washington Acad. Sci., Washington Philos. Soc., Eastern Soc. Electroencephalographers, Am. Assn. Invol. Mental Hospitalization, Am. Neurol. Assn., Am. Electroencephalographic Soc., Am. Physiol. Soc., Soc. Gen. Physiologists, N.Y. Acad. Sci., Brazilian Acad. Sci. (fgn. mem.), Internat. Fedn. Med. Electronics, Biophys. Soc. Clubs: Cosmos, Potomac Appalachian Trail (Washington). Author, co-author numerous sci. and tech. papers. Home: Kensington MD Died Nov. 14, 1972.

MARSHALL, WILLIAM LOUIS, brig. gen.; b. Washington, Ky., June 11, 1846; s. Col. Charles A. and Phoebe A. (Paxton) M.; ed. Kenyon Coll., Ohio, 1859-61; pvt. Co. A, 10th Ky. Cav., Aug. 16, 1862-Sept. 17, 1863; grad. U.S. Mil. Acad., 1868; m. Elizabeth Hill Colquitt, d. late A. H. Colquitt, U.S. senator from Ga., June 2, 1886. Bvtd. 2d lt. engrs., June 15, 1868; promoted through grades to brig. gen. chief of engrs. U.S.A., July 2, 1908. Acting asst. prof. natural and exptl. philosophy, U.S. Mil. Acad., 1870-71; in charge Colo. sect. "Explorations West of 100th Meridian," 1872-76; discovered "Marshall Pass" across Rocky Mountains, 1873, also gold placers of Marshall Basin, San Miguel River, Colo., 1875; in charge constrn. of levees in Miss., La., and Ark., and improvements of Mississippi River in 3d dist., 1881-84; of harbors on Lake Michigan, 1884-1900, and also of improvement of Calumet, Chicago, Illinois and Rock rivers, Ill., and Fox and Wisconsin rivers, Wis.; in charge of construction Hennepin Canal, 1890-1900; mem. Missouri River Commn., 1898-1902; engr. in charge construction of fortifications at eastern and southern entrances to New York harbor, and improvements of main channels of New York harbor, 1900-08; constructed new 40-ft. channel (Ambrose) entrance to New York harbor; in command of the Corps of Engrs. U.S.A. and in charge of river and harbor and fortification works of the U.S. from July 2, 1908; retired, June 11, 1910. Consulting engr. to sec. of the interior, July 2, 1910—. Mem. bds. of engrs. on dam for storage reservoir in Sacramento River, Calif., at Red Bluff, for irrigation and power; on development of hydro-electric power at the Dalles, Columbia River, 1913; engr. in charge protection Imperial Valley, Calif., against overflow of Colorado River, 1914-15; mem. central bd. of review of reclamation project costs, 1915-16. Inventor automatic movable dams, lock gates and valves. Home: Washington, D.C. Died July 2, 1920.

MARSHALL, WILLIAM STANLEY, entomologist; b. Milwaukee, Wis., Dec. 16, 1866; s. Samuel and Emma (Hagar) M.; B.S., Swarthmore Coll., 1888; student biology, U. of Pa., 1888-89, U. of Berlin, U. of Leipzig, Ph.D., Leipzig, 1892; m. Clara A. Hughes, June 20, 1894; children—William Hughes, Richard Hughes, Samuel Hagar, Elizabeth, John. Instr. biology, U. of Wis., 1893-98, asst. prof., 1808-1905, asso. prof. entomology, 1905-33, prof., 1933-36, now prof. emeritus; dir. Marshall & Ilsley Bank, Milwaukee. Catholic. Mem. A.A.A.S., Am. Soc. Zoölogists, Am. Entomol. Soc., Wis. Acad. Sciences, Psi Upsilon. Clubs: University (Madison, Wis., and Chicago). Contbr. numerous papers on anatomy and embryology of insects in German and Am. zoöl. and entomol. jours. Address: 139 E. Gilman St., Madison, Wis. Died Mar. 17, 1947.

MARSTON, ANSON, (mär'stun), civil engr.; b. Seward, Ill., May 31, 1864; s. George W. and Sarah (Scott) M.; grad. West Rockford (Ill.) High Sch., 1883; studied Berea Coll., 1884; C.E., Cornell, 1889; Eng.D., U. Neb., 1925, Mich. State Coll., 1927; m. Alice Day, Dec. 14, 1892; children—Morrill Watson, Anson Day. Engr. Mo.P. Ry. on location and constrn., 1889-92; in charge constrn. Ouachita River Bridge, 1891-92; prof. civil engring. Ia. State Coll., 1892-1920, dean and dir. engring. div., 1904-32, senior dean, 1932-37, dean emeritus, 1937—. Mem. Ia. Hwy. Commn., 1904-27, chmn. 1913-15. Commd. maj. C.E., 1917, lt. col., 1918; comd. 97th Engrs. till demobilization, 1918; col. Reserves to 1944. Mem. Engring. Bd. of Review, Sanitary Dist. Chgo., 1924, 25; cons. engr. Miami, Fla., sewerage, 1925-27; mem. (Fla.) Everglades Engring. Bd. of Rev., 1927; mem. Interoceanic Canal Bd., to advise on Nicaragua Canal and enlargement Panama Canal, 1929-32; mem. Mississippi River Engring. Board Review, 1932, 33; chmn. Iowa Merit System Council, 1939—. Mem. NRC (rep. Am. Soc. C.E.), 1919. Recipient Chanute medal Western Soc. Engrs., 1903; Fuertes medal Cornell U., 1904; Lamme medal Soc. for Promotion of Engring. Edn., 1941. Mem. Am. Soc. C.E. (dir. 1920-22, v.p. 1923-24, pres. 1929), Am. Soc. for Testing Materials, Ia. Engring. Soc. (pres. 1900), Soc. Promotion Engring Edn. (treas. 1906-07, pres. 1914-15), Land Grant Coll. Engring. Assn. (pres. 1913-14), Am. Assn. of Land Grant Colls. and Univs. (pres. 1929), S.A.R. Mason (32 deg., K.T.). Club: Cosmos (Washington). Author: Sewers and Drains, 1907; Engineering Valuation (with T. R. Agg), 1936. Contbr. engring. jours. and trans. Home: Ames, Ia. Died Oct. 21, 1949; buried Ia. State Coll. Cemetery, Ames.

MARTEL, ROMEO RAOUL, educator; b. Iberville, Que., Can., Mar. 4, 1890; s. Joseph Napoleon and Aglae (Chevalier) M.; came to U.S., 1890, father naturalized, 1895; B.S., Brown U., 1912; student Harvard, 1912-13; m. Mildred Parkhurst Pray, Dec. 21, 1918; children—Nancy Chevalier, Hardy Cross. Instr. civil engr. R.I. State Coll., 1913-14, Mechanics Inst., 1914-15; with Sayles Finishing Plants, 1915-18; instr. Cal. Inst. Tech., 1918-20, asst. prof., 1920-21, asso. prof., 1921-30, prof. since 1930; cons. engr. bridge design, Pasadena, 1921-24. Del., So. Cal. Council on Earthquake Protection to 3d Pan-Pacific Sci. Congress, Tokyo, 1926 and to World Engring. Congress, Tokyo, 1929. Mem. Internat. Assn. Bridge and Structural Engrs., Seismol. Soc. Am., Am. Soc. C.E., Am. Soc. for Testing Materials, Am. Concrete Inst., Structural Engring. Assn. So. Cal. (past pres.), Sociètè Ingenieur Civil d'France, Am. Assn. U. Profs., Sigma Xi, Tau Beta Pi. Clubs: Athenaeum. Contbr. to seismology and engring. publs. Home: 809 Fairfield Circle, Pasadena, Cal. Died Feb. 28, 1965.

MARTIN, ARTEMAS, mathematician; b. Steuben Co., N.Y., Aug. 3, 1835; s. James Madison and Orenda Knight (Bradley) M.; was a short time in Franklin Select Sch., and Franklin Acad., 1852-55; (hon. A.M., Yale, 1877; Ph.D., Rutgers, 1882; LL.D., Hillsdale Coll., 1885); unmarried. As a boy worked at farming summers, chopped wood winters and later taught district sch. and drilled oil wells, devoting all spare time to math. studies and contributing problems and solutions to math. jours.; ran a market garden, 1871-85; since then employed in U.S. Coast and Geod. Survey Office. Editor and pub. Mathematical Magazine and Mathematical Visitor. Home: Washington, D.C. Died Nov. 7, 1918.

MARTIN, CHARLES CYRIL, civil engr.; b. Springfield, Pa., Aug. 30, 1831; grad. Rensselaer Poly. Inst., Troy, 1856; asst. in geodesy there 1 yr.; entered on engring. practice; held several positions; was connected with water works, bridge-building and other engring. operations in Brooklyn; engr. Prospect Park there; later 1st asst. engr. until May 1883, then chief engr. and supt. New York and Brooklyn Bridge; cons. engr. to dept. of bridges, New York, Feb. 1, 1902—. Died 1903.

MARTIN, DANIEL STROBEL, geologist; b. New York, June 30, 1842; s. Benjamin Nicholas and Louisa Caroline (Strobel) M.; A.B., New York U., 1863, A.M., 1866; grad. Union Theol. Sem., 1866; (hon. Ph.D., Regents, U. State of N.Y., 1881); unmarried. Prof. geology and related branches, Rutgers Female Coll., New York, 1868-95; regents' examiner in English studies for law students, 1882-87; asso. with geol. work at various times in Cooper Union, N.Y. Acad. Sciences, Brooklyn Inst. Arts and Sciences; prof. geology, College for Women, Columbia, s.c., 1898-1904; hon. curator geology and mineralogy, Charleston (S.C.) Mus., 1906—. Lecturer on geology, Chicora Coll., Greenville, S.C., 1908—. Pres. trustees Cuban Home Training Sch., Brooklyn. Address: Brooklyn, N.Y. Died 1925.

MARTIN, ERNEST GALE, physiologist; b. Minneapolis, Minn., Nov. 16, 1876; s. John Wesley and Mary Esther (Bullard) M.; Ph.B., Hamline U., 1897; Ph.D., Johns Hopkins Univ., 1904; m. Ruby A. Ticknor, Aug. 31, 1904; 1 daughter, Lois Ticknor. Fellow and assistant in physiology, Johns Hopkins, 1902-04; instr. physiology, Purdue U., 1904-06; instr. physiology, 1906-10, asst. prof., 1910-16, Harvard, also lecturer Sargent Sch. for Physical Edn., 1906-14; asst. prof. physiology, Radcliffe Coll., 1914-16, and physiologist, Vt. State Bd. of Health, 1915-16; prof. physiology, Stanford U., 1916—. Scientific asst. (physiologist) U.S. Pub. Health Service; mem. sub-com. on industrial fatigue, Advisory Commn. to Council Nat. Defense, 1917-18; mem. com. on physiology of Nat. Research Council, 1917-18. Capt. Sanitary Corps. U.S.A., Sept. 10, 1918-Jan. 22, 1919; div. nutrition officer 10th Div., Nov. 7, 1918-Jan. 22, 1919. Fellow Am. Acad. Arts and Sciences, A.A.A.S. (v.p. Pacific Div., 1927-31). Conglist. Author: The Measurement of Induction Shocks, 1912. Revised 9th, 10th and 11th edits. of The Human Body (by Henry N. Martin), 1910; vol. on physiology (Collier's Popular Science Library), 1921. Joint author of General Biology (with Burlingame, Heath, and Peirce); Elements of Physiology (with Weymouth), 1928. Died Oct. 17, 1934.

MARTIN, FERNANDO WOOD, chemist; b. Volga, W.Va., May 5, 1863; s. Washington and Matilda (Cool) M.; B.S., Chaddock Coll., 1886; Ph.D., Syracuse U., 1893; Univ. of Leipzig, 1897 and 1897-98; m. Emma Herron, June 26, 1889. Prof. natural science, Chaddock Coll., 1886-90; lecturer on chemistry and toxicology, Quincy (Ill.) Med. Coll., 1889-90; prof. natural science and vice president, Ft. Worth (Tex.) University, 1890-92; professor chemistry, 1893-1929, v.p., 1894-1907, Randolph-Macon Woman's Coll., prof. emeritus, 1929. Methodist. Author: Qualitative Analysis with the Blow Pipe, 1903; Text-Book on Inorganic Chemistry, 1904; Qualitative Analysis, 1907;

Introduction to Anthropology, 1913; Essentials of Organic Chemistry, 1915. Home: Lynchburg, Va. Died Mar. 22, 1933.

MARTIN, FLOYD A., physician, univ. prof.; born El Dorado Springs, Mo., Aug. 16, 1888; s. William Segal and Eula Ann (Logan) M.; A.B., U. of Mo., 1906-12, A.M., 1912; M.D., Johns Hopkins, 1914; m. Margaret Norman, Nov. 14, 1936. Instr. pathology, U. of Mo., 1914-15; bacteriol. Detroit Clinical Lab., 1916-22; gen. practice, 1923-42; asso. prof. pathol. and bacteriol., U. of Mo., 1942-45, medicine, 1945-47, prof. bacteriol. and preventive medicine, 1947. Mem. Am. Assn. Univ. Profs., Soc. Am. Bacteriol., Am. Pub. Health Assn., Mo. State Med. Soc., Sigma Xi, Phi Beta Pi. Republican. Home: 1319 Anthony, Columbia, Mo. Died June 2, 1954; buried El Dorado Cemetery, El Dorado Springs, Mo.

MARTIN, F(REDERICK O(SKAR), engr., geologist; b. Mittweida, Saxony, Germany, Aug. 20, 1871; s. Frederick August and Anna Emmeline (Heyne) M.; Realschule, Mittweida, Saxony; Columbian Univ., D.C., 1900-02; studied Harvard and Catholic U.; m. Agnes Elizabeth Riese, Aug. 13, 1908; children—Anna Elisabeth (deceased), Agnes Fritzi, Mrs. Margareth Martin Hamer. Was engaged in mining and prospecting in Alaska, California, Idaho, Washington and Montana, 1894-1900; asst. in soil survey and scientist, Bur. of Soils, U.S. Dept. of Agr., 1901-05; asst. engr. Panama Canal, div. of meteorology and river hydraulics, 1905-06; engring. work and ry. contractor, 1906-09; mineral insp., U.S. Dept. Interior, 1909-19, principally in Calif. oil fields; geologist, Union Oil Co. of Calif., 1919-30, principally in Columbia, S.A.; later in private practice; mining engineer, Division of Investigations, U.S. Department Interior, 1933-41; now in private practice. Hon. consul for Austria at Los Angeles, 1932-33. Del. to Internat. Geol. Congress, Madrid, Internat. Congress de Forage, Paris, 1929. World Engring. and Power Congress, Tokio, 1929. Fellow Royal Geog. Soc., Am. Geog. Soc., Pacific Geog. Soc.; mem. Am. Inst. Mining and Metall. Engrs., Am. Assn. Petroleum Geologists, Pi Gamma Mu. Author: Explorations in Columbia, South America. Home: 2038 Pine St., South Pasadena, Cal. Died June 30, 1951.

MARTIN, GEORGE CURTIS, geologist; b. Cheshire, Mass., July 18, 1875; s. William P. and Fannie M. (Hare) M.; B.S., Cornell U., 1898; Ph.D., Johns Hopkins, 1901; m. Estella A. Wood, of Adams, Mass., Nov. 12, 1903; children—William E., Robert T. (dec.), Louise. Field asst. U.S. Geol. Survey, 1892; asst. Phila. Acad. Natural Sciences, 1897; asst. geologist, Md. Geol. Survey, 1898-1901; instr. geology, Johns Hopkins, 1901-04; geologist Md. Geol. Survey, 1901-04; spl. asst., 1903-04, asst. geologist, 1904-06, paleontologist, 1906-09, geologist, 1909-24, and acting geologist in charge div. of Alaskan mineral resources, 1917-19, and at other times, U.S. Geological Survey. Engaged in investigation of tertiary paleontology of Atlantic Coast, 1897-1901; studied geology of coal fields of Md., Pa., W.Va. and Colo., 1900-08; govt. investigations of Alaskan coal and oil fields and of mesozoic and tertiary stratigraphy of Alaska, 1903-24; in pvt. practice as cons. oil geologist in U.S. and Mexico since 1924. In charge of Nat. Geog. Society's expdn. to Mt. Katmai (Alaska) volcanic Dist.,1912.*

MARTIN, GLENN L., airplane mfg.; b. Macksburg, Ia., Jan. 17, 1886; s. Clarence Y. and Minta (DeLong) M.; ed. Kan. Wesleyan Univ., D.Sc., 1933; hon. D.Eng., U. of Md., Case Sch. of Applied Sci., 1945; hon. D.Sc., Brown U., 1941, University of Omaha, 1945, University of Southern California, 1949; unmarried. Began in 1907 to build gliders; designed and built pusher type airplane, 1908, taught self to fly; established one of first airplane factories in U.S., 1909; constructed airplanes of various types, including monoplanes and water aircraft; held speed, altitude and endurance records, 1909-16; gave many exhibition flights in U.S. and Can., qualified for F.A.I. Aviators' Certificate, Aug. 9, 1911; holds Aviation Certificate No. 56, and Expert Aviator's Certificate No. 2, Aero Club Am.; inc. Glenn L. Martin Co., Santa Ana, Cal., 1911; moved factory to Los Angeles, 1912; built airplanes for exhbn. flying and sport use until 1913, when first order was received from War Dept. for Model TT, which was later adopted by Army for tng. purposes; produced several new models for U.S. Army, and built for the govts. of Holland and Netherlands, East Indies, 24 airplanes; factory was employing about 150 men constructing aircraft; in 1917 merged interests with Wright Co., resulting in the Wright-Martin Aircraft Corp. of New York; withdrew from Wright-Martin Co., 1917, and organized The Glenn L. Martin Co. of Cleve.; designed the first Am. designed airplane for Liberty engines and built Martin bombers; new plant completed at Cleve., 1918, co producing Martin bombers for U.S. Army, Navy and Mail planes; plant relocated at Middle River, Balt., 1929; between 1929 and 1945 built the China Clipper, Hawaiian Clipper, Philippine Clipper, B-10, British Maryland, British Baltimore, B-26 Marauder, PBM and Mars airplanes, currently producing planes for the Army and Navy and 3 types of commercial air transports; president of The Glenn L. Martin Company, 1907-49, chmn. bd., 1949-52, hon. chmn. bd., 1952—; dir. Balt. Co., 1929-33; dir. Indsl. Corp. 1933-46. Pres. East End Mfrs. Assn. of Cleve. 1924-26. Former trustee Am. Forestry Assn.; trustee N. Am. Wild Life Found., Inc.; spl. adv. bd. YMCA; former dir. Ducks Unlimited (Can.); former v.p., trustee Ducks Unlimited, Inc. Fellow Royal Aeronautic Soc. London; hon. fellow Inst. Aero. Scis., Inc. (past pres.); mem. Nat. Aero. Assn. (Ohio gov., pres. Cleve. chpt. 1924-26, life mem.), asso. mem. Soaring Soc. Am.; hon. mem. Rotary of Am., Middle River, Md., Santa Ana, Cal., and Johnstown, Pa.; mem. Soc. Automotive Engrs. (Wright Bros. Com.), Izaak Walton League Am., Md. State Game and Fish Protective Assn., Orange County Coast Assn., Am. Athletic Union (life mem.), Ak-Sar-Ben Soc., Tau Beta Pi (Md. Beta Chapt.), Delta Sigma Phi. Pres. Aircraft War Prodn. Council, 1943; pres., mem. bd. dirs. Aircraft War Prodn. Council East Coast; mem. bd. regents, U. of Md., 1945-48. Dir. Cleveland C. of C., 1924-26, Md. Commn. on Post War Planning and Development; chmn. The Alaskan Com. of Outdoor Writers Assn. of Am.; chmn. bd. dirs., All Am. Amateur Baseball Assn.; life mem. Daniel Guggenheim Medal Board of Awards; pres. League of Maryland Sportsmen. Clubs: Los Angeles Athletic, Vermejo (Los Angeles); Baltimore Country, Early Birds Maryland Flying, Annapolis Yacht, Merchants of Baltimore, The Wings, Inc., Marco Hunting and Fishing (hon.), Md. Flying, Touchdown of Washington. Recipient two medals for overocean flight from Newport to Catalina (Cal.), 1912; bars added May 10, 1927, commemorating 25th anniversary of this flight which was re-enacted in the China Clipper, designed and built by The Glenn L. Martin Co.; Collier Trophy by President Roosevelt, for greatest achievement in aeronautics in America in 1932; Civic award Advt. Club of Baltimore for business achievement in 1937; Daniel Guggenheim medal Inst. Aero. Scis. for contbn. to aero. development and prodn. of many types of aircraft of high performance, 1941; Lord and Taylor Annual Am. Design Award for 1942; Sports Afield Trophy for 1943 for America's Most Outstanding Conservationist; Forbes Mag. award as one of America's 50 foremost bus. leaders, 1947; President's Certificate of Merit for meritorious service in aiding U.S. during prosecution of World War II, 1948; Officer of French Legion of Honor, 1949. Delivered Wright Memorial Lecture before Royal Aeronautic Society, London, 1931, Van Rensselaer lecture before Drexel Inst., Phila., 1938. Founded Glenn L. Martin Coll. of Engring. and Aeronautical Sci., U. of Md., 1945. Home: 3703 Greenway. Office: Mercantile Trust Bldg., Balt. 2. Died Dec., 1955.

MARTIN, GUSTAV JULIUS, scientist; b. Hartline, Wash., Dec. 5, 1910; s. Charles and Pauline Christine (Haas) M.; B.S., U. Wash., 1932; Sc.D., Johns Hopkins, 1935; ScD. (hon.), Phila. Coll. Pharmacy and Sci., 1958; Sc.D. (hon.), Upsala Coll., 1964; m. Dorothy Patricia Rogers, July 5, 1936. Prof. chemistry Coll. St. Teresa, Winona, Minn., 1936; research asst. Sprague Inst., U. Chgo., 1937; prof. pharmacology Middlesex Med. Sch., Waltham, Mass., 1939; asso. dir. research Warner Inst., N.Y.C., 1940-44; research dir., v.p. Nat. Drug Co., Phila., 1944-60, also dir.; dir. Princeton Sci. Assos., 1956-60, treas. New York Council, 1958-61; dir. biochem. research Camden County Gen. Hosp., Camden, N.J., 1958—; dir. research Research div. William H. Rorer, Inc., Phila., 1960—; research prof. biology Gwynedd Mercy Coll., 1964—. Exec. v.p. Alcoholism Research Found., 1965—. Mem. N.Y. (treas., council 1958-62), Pa. acads. scis., Am. Chem. Soc., A.A.A.S., Am. Acad. Microbiology, Am. Inst. Chemists, Am. Pharm. Assn., Federated Biol. Socs., Soc. Exptl. Biology and Medicine, Soc. Am. Bacteriologists, Soc. Investigative Dermatology, Phila. Physiol. Soc., Endocrine Soc., Internat. Soc. Biol. Rhythms, Soc. Gen. Systems, Carl Neuberg Soc. Internat. Sci. Relations (pres.), Sigma Xi, Phi Beta Kappa. Author: Biological Antagonism, 1951; Ion Exchange and Adsorption Agents in Medicine, 1955. Editor, contbr.: Bioflavonoids and Capillary, 1955; Clinical Enzymology, 1958; also Enzymes in Mental Health, 1966. Editor Exptl. Medicine and Surgery, 1957—. Research on enzymology. Home: 372 W. Johnson St., Phila. Office: 500 Virginia Dr., Ft. Washington, Pa. Died Feb. 25, 1967.

MARTIN, HENRY AUSTIN, surgeon; b. London, Eng., July 23, 1824; s. Henry James Martin; grad. Harvard Med. Sch., 1845; m. Frances Coffin Crosby, 1848, 5 children including Stephen Crosby, Francis Coffin. Practiced medicine, Roxbury, Mass.; apptd. surgeon U.S. Army, 1861, served at Ft. Monroe, later in Mo.; became med. dir. at Norfolk, Portsmouth and Newbern, Va.; apptd. surgeon-in-chief 1st Div., II Corp., Army of Potomac, circa 1864; brevetted lt. col., 1865, ret., 1865; introduced smallpox vaccine produced from cowpox (together with innoculation method) to U.S., 1870; developed use of rubber bandage for ulcers of leg, tracheotomy operation without tube. Died Boston, Dec. 7, 1884.

MARTIN, HENRY NEWELL, physiologist; b. Newry, County Down, Ireland, July 1, 1848; B.Sc., Cambridge (Eng.) U.; M.B., U. London (Eng.); m. Hetty Pegram, 1878. Fellow, Trinity Coll., Cambridge U., 1874-76; came to U.S., 1876; prof. biology Johns Hopkins U., 1876-93, specialized in study of cardiac physiology; discovered method of studying isolated mammalian heart; founder, editor Johns Hopkins U. Studies from Biol. Lab., 1877-93; Croonian lectr. Royal Soc. London, 1883; returned permanently to Eng., 1893. Author: (with Julian Huxley) A Course of Practical Instruction in Elementary Biology, 1875; The Human Body, 1881; Physiological Papers, 1895. Died Burley-in-Wharfedale, Yorkshire, Eng., Oct. 27, 1896.

MARTIN, KINGSLEY LEVERICH, engineer; b. Brooklyn, N.Y., June 16, 1869; s. Charles Cyril and Mary Asenath (Read) M.; grad. Poly. Inst., Brooklyn, 1888; M.E., Stevens Inst. Tech., 1892; m. Elizabeth Saxe Johnson, Feb. 2, 1895. Asst. engr. Brooklyn Bridge, 1892-96; engr. in charge Williamsburgh Bridge, 1905; chief engr. Dept. of Bridges, N.Y. City, 1908-09; commr. of bridges, N.Y. City, 1910-11; v.p. The Foundation Co., 1911-13, Am. Writing Paper Co., 1913-15; pres. The Engineer Co. since 1916. Served in 2d Batt. Naval Militia, N.Y., Spanish-Am. War, comdr. of batt., 1911-13. Mem. Am. Soc. M.E. Home: 204 Highfield Lane, Nutley, N.J. Office: 75 West St., New York. Died May 28, 1947.

MARTIN, LOUIS ADOLPHE, JR., engineer, teacher; b. Hoboken, N.J., Nov. 5, 1880; s. Louis Adolphe and Pauline Justine (Feuerstein) M.; M.E., Stevens Inst. Tech., 1900; A.M., Columbia, 1903, post-grad., 1903-05; m. Alwynne Elaine Buttlar, June 30, 1904; 1 dau., Lois. Instr. mathematics, physics and chemistry, Hoboken Acad., 1900-02; instr., 1903-06, asst. prof. mathematics and mechanics, 1906-08, prof. mechanics, June 1908—, also dean, 1910-28, Stevens Inst. Tech. Author: Text-Book of Mechanics, Vol. I, Statics, 1906, Vol. II, Kinematics and Kinetics, 1907, Vol. III, Mechanics of Materials, 1911, Vol. IV, Applied Statics, 1913, Vol. V, Hydraulics, 1914, Vol. VI, Thermodynamics, 1916. Home: Hoboken, N.J. Died Aug. 16, 1938.

MARTIN, WILLIAM HOPE, college dean; b. Carlisle, Pa., June 3, 1890; s. William and Sarah Catharine (Morrison) M.; B.A., Univ. of Maine, 1915; M.S., Rutgers U., 1917, Ph.D., 1918; D.Sc., U. of Maine, 1944; m. Eugenia Mary Rodick, Sept. 11, 1918. Asst. plant pathologist, New Jersey Agricultural Experiment Sta., 1915-18, asso. plant pathologist, 1919-23, plant pathologist since 1923, dir. of research since 1935, dean and dir. since June 10, 1939, dir. extension service, 1945—; dir. of the New Brunswick Trust Co. Mem. agrl. task force Commn. on Orgn. of the Exec. Branch of the Govt. (Hoover Commn.); apptd. mem. agrl. bd. NRC, 1944. Mem. New Brunswick Bd. Edn. Served as 2d lt., AS, World War I; cons. on farm fertilizers WPB, 1942; condr. secret wartime research FSA, World War II. Fellow A.A.A.S.; member Am. Phytopathol. Soc., Potato Assn. America, Sigma Chi, Sigma Xi, Alpha Zeta. Lutheran. Clubs: Rutgers, Union (New Brunswick). Writer numerous articles on plant diseases in scientific jours. Home: 2 Delavan St., New Brunswick, N.J. Address: N.J. Agrl. Experiment Station, New Brunswick, N.J. Died Jan. 2, 1962; buried Van Liew Cemetery, North Brunswick, N.J.

MARTIN, WILLIAM JOSEPH, physician; b. Freehold, N.J., Mar. 19, 1918; s. William Redmond and Julia (Conway) M.; M.D., Georgetown U., 1943; M.Sc. in Medicine, U. Minn., 1952; m. Mary Gertrude Adams, Apr. 22, 1944; children—Mary Jo, Julia (Mrs. Thomas Vitullo), William Joseph II. Intern, Georgetown U. Hosp., Washington, 1944; fellow in medicine Georgetown U., 1944-46; postgrad. in medicine U. Minn.-Mayo Found., Rochester, 1949-53; chmn. div. internal medicine (infectious disease) Mayo Clinic, Rochester; cons. in medicine St. Mary's Hosp., Rochester, Methodist Hosp., Rochester; prof. medicine U. Minn., Mpls. Served to maj., M.C., AUS, 1943-48. Diplomate Am. Bd. Internal Medicine. Fellow A.C.P.; mem. A.M.A., Alpha Omega Alpha. Home: Rochester MN Died May 19, 1970; buried Rochester MN

MARTINDALE, EARL HENRY, elec. engr.; b. Greenwich, O., Jan. 22, 1885; s. Rev. Henry Cyrus and Mary Elizabeth (Broadwell) M.; spl. studies Ohio, No. U., Ada, 1902-03; B.S., Case Sch. Applied Sci., 1908, E.E., 1912; m. Elsie L. Marty, June 28, 1911; children—George Earl, Robert Henry. Sales engr. Nat. Carbon Co., 1909-19, except while in army; chmn. bd. Martindale Electric Co., Cleve. Capt. engrs. U.S. Army, Aug. 12, 1917-Jan. 28, 1919; served with AEF in France 1 yr., last 5 mos. as engr. officer in charge constrn. of 15,000 volt, 35-mile transmission line. Mem. Am. Inst. E.E. (former chmn. indsl. and domestic power com.; chmn. membership com., mgr. and v.p.), Assn. Iron and Steel Elec. Engrs., Elec. League, Lakewood C. of C., Council on World Affairs, Am. Legion, Smaller Businesses Am. (past dir.), Cleve. Engring. Soc., Ohio Mfrs. Assn., Tau Beta Pi. Unitarian. Contbr. tech. mags. and lectr. colls. and univs. Author: Who Really Owns My Business. Home: 1055 Erie Cliff Dr., Lakewood 7. Address: Martindale Electric Co., Cleve. Died July 1964.

MARTZ, HYMAN SCHER, dentist; b. N.Y.C., Oct. 28, 1909; s. Abraham and Sarah (Scher) M.; B.S., N.Y.U., 1929, D.D.S., 1934; M.A., Columbia, 1930; m. Evelyn Pildos, Nov. 16, 1941; 1 dau., Joan. Gen. practice dentistry, N.Y.C., 1934-69, children's dentistry, 1953-69. Participating dentist Dental Health Ins. Plan N.Y.; mem. oral hygiene com. Greater N.Y.; attending dentist N.Y.C. Health Dept., Murray & Leonie Guggenheim Clinic for Children. Served to capt. Dental Corps, AUS, 1942-46. Mem. New York Academy of Science, First District Dental Society, New

York Society for Study Orthodontics, Am. Soc. Dentistry Children, International Assn. Orthodontists, N.Y. State Academy General Dentistry. Democrat. Jewish religion. K.P.; mem. B'nai B'rith. Pioneer in use of Andresen activator therapy. Norwegian system functional orthodontics. Address: Bronx NY Died June 5, 1969.

MARVIN, CHARLES FREDERICK, meteorologist; b. Putnam, O., Oct. 7, 1858; s. George F. and Sarah A. (Speck) M.; ed. pub. schs., Columbus, O., grad. (in mech. engring.), Ohio State U., 1883, Sc.D., 1932; instr. mech. drawing and mech. and physical lab. practice, same, 1879-83; m. Nellie Limeburner, June 27, 1894 (died Feb. 27, 1905); children—Charles Frederick, Cornelia Theresa, Helen Elizabeth; m. 2d, Mabel Bartholow, Nov. 8, 1911 (died 1932); m. 3d, Sophia A. Beuter, Nov. 12, 1932. Instr. mech. drawing, Ohio State U., 1879-83; apptd. on civilian corps of signal service, 1884, and prof. meteorology, U.S. Weather Bur.; chief U.S. Weather Bur., Aug. 1913-34; retired after 50 yrs. in U.S. Weather Bur., 1934. Conducted experiments upon which are based the tables used by Weather Bureau for deducing the moisture in the air; made important investigations of anemometers for measurement of wind velocities and pressures; invented instruments for measuring and automatically recording rainfall, snowfall, sunshine, atmospheric pressure, etc.; has made extensive studies and written on use of kites for ascertaining meteorol. conditions in the free air, the registration of earthquakes, the measurement of evaporation, solar radiation, temperature with elec. resistance thermometers, etc. Mem. nat. advisory com. for aeronautics, 1915-34, and of Nat. Research Council, 1917. First sec., and dir. sect. on meteorology, Internat. Geophysical Union organized at Brussels, July 1919. Author of various tech. papers on meteorology and the simplification of the calendar, including proposal to improve Gregorian rule for leap years by omitting 4 leap years in 500 yrs. which will keep the reckoning accurate for more than 10,000 yrs. Co-author: Moses the Greatest of Calendar Reformers. Del. Internat. Conf. on Simplification of the Calendar, Geneva, Oct. 12, 1931. Home: 5746 Colorado Av. N.W., Washington, D.C. Died June 5, 1943.

MARVIN, FRANK OLIN, engineer; b. Alfred, N.Y., May 27, 1852; s. James and Armina (Lesuer) M.; A.B., with science honor, Allegheny Coll., 1871, A.M., 1874; studied engring. with practical work in the field on ry. irrigation, sanitary and city work; m. Josephine B. March, Dec. 31, 1901. Has taught in U. of Kan., 1875—, except when prin. Lawrence High Sch., 1876-77; asst. in mathematics and physics to 1883, prof. engring., 1883—, dean Sch. of Engring., 1891-1913, advisory dean, Sept. 1, 1913—, U. of Kan.; consulting engr., Kan. State Bd. of Health. Died Feb. 6, 1915.

MARVIN, HENRY HOWARD, prof. of physics; b. Grinnell, Ia., Aug. 14, 1884; s. Francis Park and Martha (Longley) M.; B.S., Grinnell Coll., 1906; Ph.D., Columbia, 1912; m. Alma Ethel Wright, Sept. 9, 1911; children—Margaret Jane (dec.), Burton Wright, James Francis, Jean Alice (Mrs. Harold T. Amrine), David Keith, Henry Howard, Ruth Janet. Teacher Grinnell (Ia.) High Sch., 1906-08; instr. in physics, Columbia, 1911, Mass. Inst. Tech., 1911-12; asst. prof. of physics, Tufts Coll., 1912-17, prof., 1917-19; prof. physics, U. of Neb., since 1919, chmn. dept. 1922-49; lecturer in physics, U. of Minn., 1941-42. Mem. A.A.A.S., Am. Physical Soc., Am. Physics Teachers Assn., Neb. Acad. of Sciences (pres. 1930), Phi Beta Kappa, Sigma Xi. Home: 5310 Colby St., Lincoln 4, Neb. Died July 24, 1954.

MARX, CHARLES DAVID, civil engr.; b. Toledo, O., Oct. 10, 1857; s. Joseph Eugen and Johanna (Pulster) M.; B.C.E., Cornell U., 1878; C.E., Karlsruhe Polytechnicum, 1881, Dr. Engring., Karlsruhe, 1925; m. Harriet Elisabeth Grotecloss, July 18, 1888; children—Roland G., Mrs. Dorothy Sherwood, Stephanie (dec.), Alberta (Mrs. Harland B. Graham). U.S. asst. engr. Mo. River improvement, 1882-84; asst. prof. civ. engring., Cornell, 1884-90; prof. civ. engring., U. of Wis., 1890-91, Stanford, 1891-1923, emeritus. Hon. mem. Am. Soc. C.E. Home: Palo Alto, Calif. Died Dec. 31, 1939.

MASON, MAX, educator; b. Madison, Wis., Oct. 26, 1877; s. Edwin Cole and Josephine (Vroman) M.; B.Litt., U. Wis., 1898, LL.D., 1926; Ph.D., U. Göttingen, 1903; D.Sc., Columbia, 1926; LL.D., Yale, 1926, Dartmouth, 1927, Pomona Coll., 1937; m. Mary Louise Freeman, June 16, 1904 (died 1928); children—William Vroman, Maxwell, Molly; m. 2d, Helen Schermerborn Young, Aug. 5, 1939 (died 1944); m. 3d, Daphine Crane Martin, Nov. 6, 1945. Instr. math. Mass. Inst. Tech., 1903-04, asst. prof. math. Yale, 1904-08; prof. math. physics U. Wis., 1908-25; pres. U. Chgo., 1925-28; dir. natural scis. Rockefeller Found., N.Y.C., 1928-29, pres., 1929-36; chmn. Obs. council and mem. exec. council Cal. Inst. Tech. since 1936. Asso. editor Trans. Am. Math. Soc., 1911-17; lectr. math. physics 2d semester, Harvard, 1911-12. Fellow A.A.A.S.; mem. Nat. Acad. Scis., Am. Math. Soc. (delivered colloquium lectrs. 1906), Am. Phys. Soc., Deutsche Mathematiker Vereinigung, Psi Upsilon, Sigma Xi, Gamma Alpha, Phi Beta Kappa, Phi Kappa Phi. Mem. staff Naval Exptl. Sta., New London, Conn.; mem. submarine com. NRC, 1917-19. Inventor submarine detection devices. Clubs: Commercial, Chicago; Annandale; Valley Hunt (Pasadena). Author: The New Haven Mathematical Colloquium, 1910. Co-author: the Electromagnetic Field. Contbr. papers on math. research to sci. jours. Home: 1035 Harvard Av., Claremont, Cal. Ret., 1949. Died Mar. 1961.

MASON, MICHAEL L(IVINGOOD), surgeon; b. Rossville, Ill., Apr. 23, 1895; s. Francis Marion and Katherine Elizabeth (Livingood) M.; B.S., Northwestern U., 1916, A.M., 1917, M.D., 1924, Ph.D., 1931; m. Alice Frances Kolb, Dec. 28, 1921. Intern, Cook Co. Hosp., Chicago, 1924-25; attending surgeon Wesley Memorial Hosp., Chicago, 1926-29, Passavant Memorial Hosp. since 1929; pvt. practice surgery, Chicago, since 1926; mem. faculty Northwestern U. since 1914, asst., later fellow in zoology, 1914-17, asst. and asso. in anatomy, 1919-27, clin. asst. in surgery, 1925-28, instr., 1929-30, asso. in surgery, 1930-32, asst. prof. surgery, 1932-36, asso. prof., 1936-52, prof. of surgery, 1952—. Mem. med. advisory com. Rehabilitation Inst., Chgo.; sub-chmn., disaster com. Chgo. chpt. A.R.C. President board directions Summer School of Painting, Saugatuck, Michigan Exhibitor: Pennsylvania Academy Fine Arts, 1938-40, Golden Gate Exhbn., 1939, Art Inst. Chicago, 1936, 38, 40, 43, Ill. Soc. Fine Arts, 1937, 38, Soc. Am. Etchers, 1949, Internat. Bienneal Color Litho. Exhibit, 1950, 52, 54, 56; Soc. Am. Graphic Arts, 1952, 56; 12th ann. exhibit Am. Color Print Soc, 1951; Print Club Phila., 1953, 56, 57; also exhibited at Brooklyn Museum, 1958. Served as sgt., A.U.S., France, 1917-19; col. Med. Corps, chief of surg., later comdg. officer 12th Gen. Hosp., M.T.O., 1942-46, col. Med. Corps, O.R.C. since 1941. Decorated Legion of Merit (U.S.); Order Nacional Do Cruzcero do Sol (Brazil). Diplomate Am. Bd. Surgery, Am. Bd. Plastic Surgery. Fellow American College of Surgeons (1st vice president 1958-59); mem. Am. Soc. for Surgery Trauma, Am. Soc. Surgery Hand (pres. 1952), Assn. Military Surgeons, A.M.A., Am. Assn. Ry. Surgeons, Am. Western (pres. 1955), Central surg. assns., Sigma Xi, Alpha Omega Alpha, Wranglers. Clubs: Literary, Cliff Dwellers, University, Surgeons (Chicago). Contbr. to Sajous-Cyclopedia of Medicine and Christopher's Text Book of Surgery; also articles in profl. jours. Asso. editor Surgery, Gynecology and Obstetrics since 1929, Quarterly Bull. of Northwestern U. Med. Sch. since 1940; editorial bd. Jour. Bone and Joint Surgery; also editor manual. Home: 443 Grove Av., Wood Dale, Ill. Office: 154 Erie St., Chgo. 11. Died Mar. 30, 1963; buried Mt. Emblem, Elmhurst, Ill.

MASON, SILAS CHEEVER, horticulturist; b. East Greensboro, Vt., Apr. 19, 1857; s. Elkanah Phillips and Adaline (Cheever) M.; B.S., Kan. State Agricultural College, 1890, M.S., 1893; hon. D.Sc. from same college, 1928; m. May V. Quinby, Jan. 1, 1884. Teacher pub. schs. 3 yrs.; asst. prof. horticulture and forestry Kan. State Agrl. Coll., 1890, prof., 1894-97; prof. horticulture and forestry, Berea (Ky.) Coll., 1897-1906; arboriculturist (under new classification horticulturist) U.S. Dept. Agr., 1907-31. Detailed by sec. of agr. to study date palm culture in Egypt and Sudan, and secure offshoots of valuable varieties, 1913-14; again in Egypt, 1920, in Algeria, 1921-22; leave of absence, 1924-25, as consulting expert on date culture, to Sudan Govt. Discovered the identity, history and geog. range of the Saidy date of the oases of the Libyan Desert, securing 7,000 offshoots for U.S. Dept. Agr., for planting in Southern Calif. Methodist. Home: Riverside, Calif. Died Oct. 19, 1935.

MASON, WILLIAM, inventor, mfr.; b. Mystic, Conn., Sept. 2, 1808; s. Amos and Mary (Holdredge) M.; m. Harriet Augusta Metcalf, June 10, 1844, at least 2 sons, 1 dau. Apprentice in cotton factory, 1822-28; patented power loom to make diaper cloth (1st in U.S.), began mfg. looms, 1832-33; developed ring frame for textile work, 1834, produced ring frames, Taunton, Mass., 1835-37; patented self-acting mule for spinning, 1840, improvement on it, 1846; engaged in textile mfg., 1842-83, expanded his firm's operations to include locomotive mfg., 1853, later made railroad wheels and arms; founder, pres. Machinists' Nat. Bank, Taunton, 1847-57. Died Mass., May 21, 1883.

MASON, WILLIAM PITT, chemist; b. New York, Oct. 12, 1853; s. James and Emma (Wheatley) M.; C.E., Rensselaer Poly. Inst., 1874, B.S., 1877; M.D., Union Univ., 1881, Sc.D., 1917; studied bacteriology, Pasteur Inst., Paris; LL.D., Lafayette Coll., Pa., 1908; m. Emilie E. Harding, 1886; children—George Harding (dec.), William Pitt; m. 2d, Margaret D. Betts, 1908. Asst. in chemistry, 1875-82, prof. analytical chemistry, 1882-93, prof. chemistry, 1893—, Rensselaer Poly. Inst. Mem. U.S. Assay Commn., 1896. Fellow A.A.A.S. (chmn. Chem. Sect., 1897). Author: Examination of Potable Water, 1890; Water Supply, 1896; Notes on Qualitative Analysis, 1896; Examination of Water, 1899. Home: Troy, N.Y. Died 1937.

MASSEY, WILBUR FISK, horticulturist; b. Accomac Co., Va., Sept. 30, 1839; s. Rev. James A. and Anne (Parker) M.; prep. edn. Washington Coll., Md., and Dickinson Coll., Pa., 1856-57; (Sc.D., N.C. State Coll. Agr. and Engring., 1917); m. Sarah E. M. Phoebus, May 4, 1861; m. 2d, Aurilla J. Phoebus, sister of first wife, Apr. 4, 1876. Engaged in railroad constrn. in the West in 1858 on N.Mo. R.R.; returned to Va. at outbreak of war. After war, in Kent Co., Md., was 1st sec., examiner and treas. of new pub. sch. system, Kent Co.; at same time, engaged in a nursery and florist business, which was later transferred to Baltimore. Engaged in agrl. and hort. edn., 1st at Miller School, Albemarle, Va., 1885—; prof. horticulture and botany, N.C. Coll. Agr. and Mechanic Arts, 1889-1905; also station investigator, Agrl. Expt. Sta., of N.C.; now agrl. and hort. expert. Asso. corr. editor of Southern Planter (Richmond, Va.), Progressive Farmer (Raleigh, N.C.), Southern Farm Gazette (Starkville, Miss.), Market Growers' Journal (Louisville, Ky.), Practical Farmer, Philadelphia, Pa. Registered Farmers' Inst. lecturer, U.S. Dept. Agr. Democrat. Author: Practical Farming for American Farmer, 1907; Massey's Garden Book for the South, 1918. Home: Salisbury, Md. Died Mar. 30, 1923.

MAST, SAMUEL OTTMAR, biologist; b. Ann Arbor Twp., Mich., October 5, 1871; s. G.F. and Beata (Staebler) M.; certificate, State Normal Coll., Ypsilanti, Michigan, 1897, M.Pd., 1912; B.S., University of Michigan, 1899, honorary Sc.D., 1941; Ph.D., Harvard University, 1906; Johnston scholar, Johns Hopkins, 1907-08; m. Grace Rebecca Tennent, 1908; children—Louise Rebecca, Elisabeth Tennent, Margaret Tennent. Prof. biology and botany Hope College, 1899-1908; asso. prof. biology and prof. botany, Goucher Coll., Baltimore, 1908-11; asso. prof. and prof. zoölogy, Johns Hopkins, since 1911, head of dept. of zoölogy and dir. zoöl. laboratory since 1938, prof. emeritus of zoölogy, 1942. Cartwright prize, Columbia, 1909. Fellow A.A.A.S.: mem. Am. Soc. Zoölogists, Am. Physiol. Soc., Am. Soc. Naturalists Society for Study of Growth and Development, Academy of Science, Philadelphia, Phi Beta Kappa, Sigma Xi; honorary member of Beta, Beta, Beta. Author: The Structure and Physiology of Flowering Plants, 1907; Light and the Behavior of Organisms, 1911; Motor Response to Light in the Invertebrate Animals, 1936; Factors Involved in the Process of Orientation of Lower Organisms in Light, 1938; Motor Response in Unicellular Animals, 1941; also papers on responses in organisms and on growth in protozoa. Home: 415 Woodlawn Rd., Roland Park, Baltimore, Md. Died Feb. 3, 1947.

MASTERS, HARRIS KENNEDY, cons. engr.; b. N.Y. City, Aug. 6, 1873; s. Hibbert B. and Clara Lovell (Everett) M.; E.M., Columbia Sch. of Mines, 1894; m. Fannie Elliott, June 20, 1908 (dec. 1948). Asst. chemist, asst. supt. Nichols Copper Co., Laurel Hill, L.I., 1895-1902; smelter supt. U.S. Smelting Co., Midvale, Utah, 1902-04; private practice, Salt Lake City, Utah, 1904-05 and 1910-11; gen. mgr. Central Chile Copper Co. (London, Eng.) at Panulcillo, Chile, 1905-10; part owner (v.p.) and operator Ohio Valley Fluorspar Co., Marion, Ky., 1912-13; metall. Griffin Wheel Co., Chicago, 1913-14; gen. foreman bayonet shop Remington Arms Co., Bridgeport, Conn., 1915-16; mgr. metal and ore dept. W.R. Grace & Co., New York, 1916-20; mgr. metal dept. Wah Chang Trading Corp., New York, 1920-24; sec. New York Metal Exchange, 1925-26; mgr. metal and ore dept. Asso. Metals & Minerals Corp., N.Y. City, 1927; v.p. Chas. Hardy, Inc., 1927-40; cons. engr. Molybdenum Corp. of America since 1942. Consultant on antimony and tungsten Advisory Commn. to Council of Nat. Defense, 1940; chief tungsten branch, Office of Prodn. Management, later War Prodn. Bd., 1941-42. Awarded medal for Alumni service, Columbia U., 1936; received Columbia U. medal, 1940. Mem. Mining and Metall. Soc. of Am., Am. Inst. Mining & Metall. Engrs., Iron and Steel Inst., Tau Beta Pi; pres. Columbia Engring. Schs. Alumni Assn., 1921-25; trustee Columbia University in N. Y. City since 1944. Republican. Protestant. Clubs: Columbia University (pres. 1937-40). Mining (N.Y. City). Contbr. to Engineering and Mining Jour. and Am. Soc. for Testing Materials Bulletin. Home: 123 E. 53d St., N.Y.C. 22 NY Office: 500 Fifth Av., NYC 36 NY

MASTERS, HOWARD RUSSELL, neuropsychiatry; b. Fredericksburg, Va., July 2, 1894; s. John William and Ada Byron (Chisholm) M.; grad. Randolph-Macon Acad., Front Royal, Va., 1912; student Randolph-Macon Coll., 1912-15, LL.D. (honorary), 1955; M.D., Medical Coll. of Virginia, 1919; m. Bealmear Dare Linthicum, Oct. 25, 1921; children—Bealmear Dare, Howard Russell; married 2d, Sarah Elizabeth Huneycutt, May 1950; children—Elizabeth Chisholm, Sarah Kathryn. Interne Johnston-Willis Hospital, Richmond, Virginia, 1919-20, N.Y. Neurol. Inst., 1920; resident physician Tucker Sanatorium, Richmond, 1921; studied endocrinology St. Louis, 1921; asst. in surg., Med. Coll. of Va., 1919-20, instr. nervous and mental diseases, 1920-25, asso. in neuropsychiatry, 1925-39, asso. prof. since 1939; lecturer in normal and abnormal psychology, Coll. of William and Mary (Richmond div. Sch. of Social Work), 1927-29; lecturer in psychiatry, same, 1927-32; lecturer Med. Coll. of Va. in normal and abnormal psychology, 1932; asso. chief of staff, Tucker Hospital, Richmond; visiting physician Hosp. Div. Med. Coll. of Va., Crippled Children's Hosp., Sheltering Arms Hosp.; attending neurologist Johnston-Willis Hosp., Richmond; mem. staff Richmond Meml. Hosp. Mem. Gov.'s Adv. Bd. on Mental Hygiene, Richmond, 1926—; mem. bd. Meml. Guidance Clinic, 1933—, v.p.,

1943-44, pres., 1945-50. Elector for N.Y.U. Hall of Fame. Mem. Med. Res. Corps, United States Army, Dec. 1917-July 1919. Diplomate Am. Bd. Psychiatry and Neurol.; mem. Am. and So. med. assns., Va. Neuropsychiatric Assn. (exec. com. 1936, 37), Neuropsychiatric Soc. of Va. (pres. 1942; executive com., 1942-43), Am. Psychiatric Assn. (mem. com. on pub. edn. since 1941), Med. Soc. of Va., Tri-State Med. Assn. (pres. 1937), Mental Hygiene Soc. of Va. (exec. com. 1936, 37; pres. 1938-40), Richmond Acad. Medicine, Assn. for Study of Internal Secretions, Soc. of Alumni Randolph-Macon Coll. (pres. 1932-34), Kappa Sigma, Phi Chi, Omicron Delta Kappa. Democrat. Methodist. Club: Commonwealth. Contbr. mags. Home: 24 Tapoan Rd. Office: 212 W. Franklin St., Richmond, Va. Died Jan. 27, 1959; buried Confederate Cemetery, Fredericksburg, Va.

MASTERSON, JOHN JOSEPH, physician; b. Brooklyn, Aug. 16, 1881; s. William Henry and Margaret Ann (Donohue) M.; student St. Patricks Acad., Brooklyn, 1887-96, Heffley Inst., 1902-04; M.D., L.I. Coll. Hosp., 1908; m. Lucille McGuire, Jan. 26, 1910; children—William F., Lucille (Mrs. Edward A. Harvey), John G. Intern Norwegian Hosp., Brooklyn, 1908-09; pvt. practice medicine, Brooklyn, since 1910, specialist in roentgenology since 1919; attending roentgenologist Coney Island, 1919-24, Victory Meml. Hospital, 1925-48, Norwegian Hosp., 1919-53; cons. roentgenologist Victory Meml., Bay Ridge and Norwegian hosps. Dir. United Med. Service N.Y., 1943-60, Asso. Hosp. Service N.Y., 1937-59. Served as mem. Medical Advisory Board, World War I and II. Member medical advisory committee New York Worlds Fair, 1939; member New York State com., 1950 White House Conf. on Children and Youth; mem. med. adv. com. on civilian defense N.Y. State Health Dept., 1950-53; director Physicians Home, Inc., N.Y.C., 1955—; med. cons. adviser on Selective Service, N.Y.C., 1948-59. Dir. Cath. Med. Mission Bd. Recipient Cath. Physician of Year, Nat. Fedn. Cath. Physicians Guilds, 1959, certificate of distinction in field of medicine State U. New York Downstate Medical Center, 1960. Diplomate of the American Board of Radiol. Fellow Am. Coll. Radiol., N.Y. Acad. Medicine; mem. A.M.A. (del. from N.Y. to House of Dels. since 1935), Radiol. Soc. N. Am., Nat. Fedn. Cath. Physician Guilds (past pres.), Pan American Medical Association, Medical Soc. State N.Y. (past pres., trustee; chmn. emergency med. preparedness com. 1950-52; chmn. publ. com. jour., 1952-58; chmn. bd. trustees), N.Y. Roentegen Ray Soc. (past pres.), Bklyn. Roentgen Ray Soc. (past pres.), Asso. Radiologists of N.Y. (p.p.), Alumni Assn. L.I. Coll. Med. (past pres.), Bay Ridge Med. Soc. (past pres.), Med. Soc. Co. of Kings, Acad. Med. of Bklyn. (past pres., trustee since 1926, chmn. bd. 1937-59), Asso. Physicians of L.I., Bklyn. Tb and Health Assn. (bd. of dirs.), Alpha Kappa Kappa, Alpha Omega Alpha. K.C. (Dongan Council). Club: 12:30 (past pres.). Home: 9425 Shore Rd. Office: 401 76th St., Bklyn. 9. Died Nov. 19, 1962.

MASTIN, CLAUDIUS HENRY, surgeon; b. Huntsville, Ala., June 4, 1826; s. Francis Turner and Ann Elizabeth Caroline (Levert) M.; attended U. Va.; M.D., U. Pa., 1849; studied medicine with Dr. J. Y. Bassett, Huntsville; attended U. Edinburgh, Royal Coll. Surgeons, U. Paris; m. Mary Eliza McDowell, Sept. 20, 1848, at least 2 sons. Practiced medicine briefly, then went to Europe for further edn.; began practice medicine specializing in genito-urinary surgery, Mobile, Ala., 1854; asso. with U.S. Marine Hosp. Service, Mobile, 1854-57; surgeon Mobile Hosp., 1855; med. dir. on staffs of Generals Polk, Bragg, G. T. Beauregard, 1861-65; a founder Congress Am. Physicians and Surgeons; fellow Am. Surg. Assn., pres., 1890-91; mem. So. Surg. and Gynecol. Assn.; founder Am. Genito-Urinary Assn., pres., 1895-96; wrote many articles published by various orgns. to which he belonged. Died Oct. 3, 1898.

MATAS, RUDOLPH, (mat'as), surgeon; b. Bonnet Carre, nr. New Orleans, La., Sept. 12, 1860; s. Dr. N. Hereu and Teresa (Jorda) M.; ed. Paris, Barcelona, Brownsville (Tex.), Soule's Coll. (New Orleans); grad. Lit. Inst. of St. John, Matamoros, Mexico, 1876; M.D., Tulane, 1880; LL.D., Washington U., 1915, U. of Ala., 1926, Tulane, 1928; Sc.D., U. of Pa., 1925, Princeton, 1928; M.D., honoris causa, Nat. U. of Guatemala, 1934; widower. Began practice at New Orleans, 1880, specializing in surgery since 1895; prof. surgery, Tulane Med. Dept., 1895-1927, emeritus since 1928; sr. surgeon Charity Hosp., 1894-1928, consultant since 1928; chief sr. surgeon Touro Infirmary, 1905-35, hon. chief surgeon, 1935—; cons. surgeon Eye, Ear, Nose and Throat Hosp.; etc. Mem. La. Council Nat. Defense, 1915-18; organizer and dir. Base Hosp. 24 (Tulane Unit) for service in France, 1916-17; maj., dir. New Orleans Sch. for Intensive Surg. War Training, M.O.R.C., 1917-18. Fellow Am. Coll. Surgeons (v.p. 1913, 20; pres. 1924-25), A.A.A.S., Havana Acad. Medical Sciences; mem. A.M.A. (chmn. sect. surg. 1908; v.p. 1920, 32-33), Am. Surg. Assn. (pres. 1909), So. Surg. Assn. (pres. 1911; hon. fellow 1927), Am. Assn. Thoracic Surgeons (pres. 1920), La. State Med. Soc. (pres. 1894-95), New Orleans Med. and Surg. Assn. (pres. 1886), Am. Soc. Clin. Surgery (v.p. 1908-10), Orleans Parish Med. Soc., Am. Assn. Cancer Research, Am. Soc. Control Cancer, Am. Assn. Exptl. Medicine, Am. Assn. Anatomists, Nat. Assn. Study and Prevention Tb, Am. Assn. Endocrinology, Assn. Mil. Surgeons U.S. Army, Nat. Inst. Social Sciences, Am. Assn. Friends of Med. Progress, Nat. Econ. League, Am. Museum Natural History, La. Hist. Soc., So. Art League, Art Assn. New Orleans, New Orleans Zoology, Soc., La. League of Civil Service Reform; hon. fellow Royal Coll. of Surgeons, Eng., 1927; pres. internat. Soc. of Surgery, 1936-38; hon. mem. New Orleans Acad. Scis., La. State Pharm. Assn., Ill. Central and Miss. Valley R.R. Surgeons, Am. Assn. Traumatic Surgery, Acad. Medicine (N.Y.), Am. Soc. Regional Anesthesia, Boston Surg. Soc., Am. Soc. History of Medicine, Phila. Acad. Surgery, Hon. pres. Pan-Am. Med. Congress, Washington, 1895, v.p. for La., 1896; mem. and rapporteur arterial surgery (surg. sect.) Internat. Med. Congress, London, 1913; mem. Assn. Française de Chirurgie (rapporteur by invitation, and hon. pres. 1922); mem. Soc. Internat. de. Chirurgie (rapporteur by invitation); hon. pres. Internat. Surgical Congress, Warsaw, 1929; hon. mem. Royal Acad. Medicine (Rome), Assn. Polish Surgeons, Soc. Ital. Physicians in America; corr. mem. Peruvian Surg. Soc., Cuban Surgical Society, Société Nationale de Chirurgie (Paris), Med. Soc. Copenhagen (Denmark), Surg. Soc. Madrid; corr. fellow Royal Acad. Medicine (Madrid); hon. fellow Royal Acad. Medicine, and Catalonian Acad. Med. Sci. (Barcelona), Royal Acad. Medicine (Belgium); hon. pres. Surgical Society (Barcelona); mem. Soc. Internat. pour l'Histoire de la Med. (Paris); hon. surgeon Eye, Ear, Nose and Throat Hosp., New Orleans; asso. mem. French Nat. Acad. Medicine; hon. mem. 12th Congress Internat. Soc. Surgery, London, 1947; hon. fellow Am. Soc. Anesthesiologists, Royal Belgian Acad. Sci.; hon. mem. Belgian Surg. Soc., Greek Nat. Soc., Surg. Soc. Lyons, La. State Acad. Sci., Am. Soc. Univ. Surgeons, American Soc. Vascular Surgeons, La. Surg. Society; hon. mem. 50 yr. Club La. State Med. Soc., Miss. State Med. Soc.; hon. pres. emeritus past pres.' adv. council La. Med. Soc. Ofcl. del. from City of New Orleans to Nat. Finlay Celebration, Havana, 1941. Honor guest, City of Havana, Municipal medal, 1941; Finlay medal Cuban Med. Fedn., 1941; Officer Order Public Instruction (Venezuela), 1925; Knight Civil Order of Alfonso XII of Spain, 1929; Chevalier Legion of Honor (France), 1932; Knight Order of Isabella the Catholic (Spanish), 1934; comdr. Nat. Cuban Order of Carlos Finlay, 1936; officer Order of Leopold, Belgium, 1939. Recipient first distinguished service medal A.M.A., 1938. Mem. Italian-Am. Soc., Stars and Bars of Tulane (pres. 1922), Nu Sigma Nu (president hon. council, 1936; merit medal, 1942), Alpha Omega Alpha, Kappa Delta Phi, hon. fellow Alpha Zeta Circle, Omicron Delta Kappa. Clubs: Boston, Round Table, Young Men's Business (honorary), Lions (hon.). Editor New Orleans Med. and Surg. Jour., 1883-85. Henry Bigelow medalist of Boston Surg. Soc., 1926; Times-Picayune award for community service, 1940. Chmn. Violet Hart Com. Award Matas Medal Vascular Surgery. Hon. 1934. Author of many treatises and monographs on surg. subjects, specially vascular surgery, and frequent contbr. to med. jours. and text books. Home: 2255 St. Charles Av., New Orleans. Died Sept., 1957.

MATHER, ALONZO CLARK, pres. Mather Stock Car Co.; b. Fairfield, N.Y.; s. William and Mary Ann (Buell) M.; ed. Fairfield Prep. Sch. After leaving sch. obtained employment at Utica, N.Y.; moved to Quincy, Ill., and in 1875 to Chicago; engaged in business; patentee of many inventions, among them the Mather Palace Stock Car for the humane transportation of horses and cattle, for which received a gold medal from Am. Humane Soc.; president Mather Stock Car Co. Was one of the first members of 1st Regiment, I.N.G. Home: Chicago, Ill. Died Jan. 25, 1941.

MATHER, COTTON, clergyman, author; b. Feb. 23, 1663; s. Increase and Maria (Cotton) M.; A.B., Harvard, 1678, M.A., 1681; D.D. (hon.), U. Glasgow (Scotland), 1710; m. Abigail Phillips, 1686; m. second, Elizabeth (Clark) Hubbard; m. third, Lydia George; fifteen children including Samuel. Ordained to ministry in the Congregational Ch., 1684; teacher at the Second Congregational Ch. of Boston, 1685-1723; wrote against govt. of Sir Edmund Andros in The Declaration of the Gentlemen, Merchants, and Inhabitants of Boston, 1689; fellow Harvard, 1690-1703; wrote statement on witch trial evidence comdemning reliance on "spectral" evidence, 1692; defended Salem witch trials in book Wonders of the Invisible World, 1693 (later attacked by Robert Calef in his book More Wonders of the Invisible World); a founder Yale Coll., refused to become its pres.; became 1st Am.-born mem. Royal Soc., 1713, contbd. many articles to its Proceedings; informed Dr. Zabdiel Boyleston of process of inoculation for smallpox, supported the radical idea financially and by his influence during smallpox epidemic of 1721; minister 2d Congregational Ch. of Boston, 1723-28; a leader in Boston charities, ednl. and social improvement plans; campaigned against imtemperance, mistreatment of slaves. Author over 450 books including: A Family Well-Ordered, 1699; Magnalia Christi Americana: or the Ecclesiastical History of New England from its First Planting (most famous work), 1702; Some Few Remarks upon a Scandalous Book. . .by one Robert Calef, 1704; The Good Education of Children, 1708; Essays to do Good, 1710; Christian Philosopher, 1721; An Account. . .of Inoculating the Small-Pox, 1722. Died Boston, Feb. 24, 1728; buried Copp's Hill Burying Grounds, Boston.

MATHER, FRED, author, fish-culturist; b. Greenbush, N.Y., Aug. 2, 1833; ed. at acad. in Albany, N.Y., 1854-57; hunter and trapper in Wis., 1857-59; was in the Kan. war, 1862; private 113th N.Y. vols.; then sergt. to capt. 7th N.Y. arty. until discharged, May 1865; lt. col. Albany Rangers, 1898; fish-culturist, 1868; asst. U.S. Fish Commn., 1873; supt. N.Y. Fish Commn., 1883-95; invented hatching cone for shad and other apparatus; had charge Am. exhibit, Fisheries Exhbn., Berlin, 1880; m. Elizabeth McDonald (died 1861), 1854; m. 2d, Adelaide Fairchild, 1877. Author: Men I Have Fished With; Fish-culture; Icthyology of the Adirondacks. Lecturer. Home: Brooklyn, N.Y. Died 1900.

MATHER, WILLIAM TYLER, univ. prof.; b. Amherst, Mass., Sept. 2, 1864; s. Richard Henry and Elizabeth (Carmichael) M.; A.B., Amherst, 1886, A.M., 1891; Ph.D., Johns Hopkins, 1897; m. Mabel Elizabeth Nevins, June 30, 1892; children—Richard Nevins, Helen Marquis, Edward Otis, Dorothy Georgia. Instr. Leicester (Mass.) Acad., 1886-87, Williston Sem., 1887-93; practicing chemist, Boston, 1893-94; univ. scholar, 1895-96, fellow in physics, 1896-97, asst., 1897, Johns Hopkins; asso. prof. physics, 1898-1907, prof., 1907—, U. of Texas. Independent Democrat. President Anti-Vice League of Austin; elder Univ. Presbyn. Ch.; mem. bd. dirs. Univ. Y.M.C.A., from 1910 (pres.); mem. State Com. Y.M.C.A. Died June 14, 1937.

MATHER, WILLIAM WILLIAMS, geologist; b. Brooklyn, Conn., May 24, 1804; s. Eleazar and Fanny (Williams) M.; grad. U.S. Mil. Acad., 1828; m. Emily Maria Baker, 6 children; m. Mary Harry, Aug. 1857, 1 son. Brevetted 2d lt. U.S. Army, 1828; professor of chemistry and mineralogy at U.S. Military Academy, West Point, N.Y., 1829-35; also prof. chemistry, mineralogy and geology Wesleyan U.; promoted 1st lt., 1834; aided G. W. Featherstonhaugh in survey of Green Bay (Wis.) region, 1835; resigned commn., 1836; prof. chemistry U. La., 1836; geologist for 1st Dist., N.Y. State, 1836-44; dir. Ohio Geologic Survey, 1837-38; state geologist Ky., 1838-39; prof. natural science Ohio U., Athens, 1842-45, acting pres. univ., 1845-47. Author: Elements of Geology for the Use of Schools, 1833. Died Columbus, O., Feb. 26, 1859.

MATHESON, ROBERT, educator; b. West River, N.S., Can., Dec. 20, 1881; s. Walter Alexander and Mary (Anderson) M.; prep. edn. Pictou Acad.; student N.S. Sch. of Science; B.S., Cornell U., 1906, M.S., 1907, Ph.D., 1911; m. Margaret Katherine Macpherson, Aug. 25, 1911; 1 son, Robert Macpherson. Prof. entomology S.D. State Coll., 1907-09; prof. zoology, N.S. Coll. Agr., 1912-13; prof. entomology (med. entomology and parasitology) Cornell U., 1914-49; cons. health sect. TVA. Fellow A.A.A.S., Entomol. Soc. Am.; mem. Am. Soc. Parasitologists (v.p. 1940; mem. editorial bd.), Am. Assn. Econ. Entomologists, N.S. Inst. Science, Am. Soc. Tropical Medicine, Washington Acad. Sciences, Phi Kappa Phi, Phi Kappa Sigma, Sigma Xi, Gamma Alpha; corr. mem. Venezuelan Soc. Natural Sciences, Acad. of Natural Sciences of Chile, Phila. Acad. Natural Sciences. Republican. Presbyn. Handbook of the Mosquitos of North America, 1929, rev. edit. 1945; Medical Entomology, 1932; Laboratory Guide in Entomology, 1939; Entomology, 1944, rev. edit. 1951; also many articles in jours. and experiment station publs. Home: 204 Parkway, Cayuga Heights, Ithaca, N.Y. Died Dec. 14, 1958.

MATHEWS, ALBERT PRESCOTT, (math'uz), physiol. chemist; b. Chicago, Ill., Nov. 26, 1871; s. William Smith Babcock and Flora E. (Swain) M.; S.B., Mass. Inst. Tech., 1892; studied biology, Cambridge, Eng., Naples, Italy, and Marburg, Germany, 1895-97; Ph.D., Columbia, 1898; hon. D.Sc. Institutum Divi Thomae, 1940; m. Jessie Glyde Macrum, Feb. 7, 1895; 1 dau., Mrs. Noreen Macrum Koller. Asst. in biology, Mass. Inst. Tech., 1892-93; fellow, 1893-95, hon. fellow, 1897-98, Columbia; asst. prof. physiology, Tufts Coll. Med. Sch., 1899-1900; instr. physiology, Harvard Med. Sch., 1900-01; asst. prof. physiol. chemistry, 1901-04, asso. prof., 1904-05, prof., 1905-18, and chmn. dept. of physiology, 1909-16, U. of Chicago; prof. biochemistry, U. of Cincinnati, 1918—, prof. emeritus, 1940—. Known for original investigations in parthenogenesis, upon the nature of nerve impulse, in pharmacology and chem. biology; trustee Marine Biol. Lab., Woods Hole, Mass. Fellow A.A.A.S.; mem. Am. Chem. Soc., Am. Physiol. Soc., Biochem. Soc., Soc. de chimie biologique, Biochemical Soc. (British), Soc. Exptl. Biology Great Britain; foreign mem. Academia Nationale dei Lincei, Rome. Commd. capt., Quartermasters Corps, Feb. 1917, and on active duty, Aug. 1917-Nov. 1918, at hdqrs. Central Dept. Author: Text Book of Physiological Chemistry (6th edit.); The Nature of Matter, Gravitation and Light; Gravitation, Space-Time and Matter, 1934; Principles of Biochemistry. Contbr. to scientific jours. Home: 1237 Glenwood Blvd., Schenectady 8. Died Sept. 21, 1957; buried Allegheny Cemetery, Pitts.

MATHEWS, EDWARD BENNETT, geologist; b. Portland, Me., Aug. 16, 1869; s. Jonathan Bennett and Sophia Lucinda (Shailer) M.; A.B., Colby Coll., 1891, D.Sc., 1927; Ph.D., Johns Hopkins Univ., 1894; m.

Helen Louise Whitman, Sept. 12, 1900; children—William Whitman (dec.), Margaret (Mrs. Richard W. Thorpe), John B. (dec.), Roger H. (dec.). Field asst. U.S. Geol. Survey, seasons of 1891-94; instr. mineralogy and petrography, 1894-95, Johns Hopkins U., asso., 1895-99, asso. prof., 1899-1904, prof. since 1904, chmn. geol. dept., 1917-39, prof. emeritus since 1939. Asst. state geologist of Md., 1898-1917, state geologist since 1917; mem. Md. State Bd. of Forestry; dir. Maryland Weather Service; chmn. div. geology and geography, Nat. Research Council, 1919-22, and mem. advisory com. since 1933; v.p. Internat. Geol. Congress, 1922, 26, and 29, treas., 1933; chmn. advisory council U.S. Bd. of Surveys and Maps, 1920-43 and since 1929; mem. Md. State Development Commn. since 1929, Md. Water Resources Commn. since 1933. Member of Maryland-Virginia Boundary commission, 1927-31. Director Department Geology, Mining and Water Resources, 1941-43. Fellow Geological Soc. America (treas. since 1917), Washington Acad. of Sciences, Am. Acad. of Arts and Sciences, A.A.A.S.; mem. Econ. Geologists, Mineralogical Soc., Am. Inst. Mining and Metall. Engrs., Am. Geog. Soc., Assn. of Am. State Geologists (pres. 1920-23), Md. Hist. Soc., Soc. Colonial Wars. Author: Bibliography and Cartography of Md.; Maps and Map-Makers of Md.; Building Stones of Md.; Limestones of Md.; History of Mason-Dixon Line; Boundary Line Between Virginia and Maryland (with W. A. Nelson); Physical Features of Md.; Water Resources of Md.; Catalogue Published Bibliographies in Geology; and other geol. and hist. papers. Home: Lombardy Apt. 10, Baltimore, Md. Died Feb. 4, 1944.

MATHEWS, JOHN ALEXANDER, metallurgist; b. Washington, Pa., May 20, 1872; s. William Johnston and Frances (Pelletreau) M.; B.S., Washington and Jefferson Coll., 1893, M.S., 1896, Sc.D., 1902; A.M., Columbia, 1895, Ph.D., 1898; Royal Sch. Mines, London, 1900-01; m. Florence Hosmer King, Jan. 29, 1903; children—Margaret King, John Alexander. Asst. in assaying, 1896-97, tutor chemistry, 1898-1900, Columbia; Barnard Fellowship for Encouragement of Scientific Research, 1900, 1901, 1902; Andrew Carnegie Research Scholarship of Iron and Steel Inst. of Great Britain, 1901; received first award of "Andrew Carnegie Gold Medal for Research" from Iron and Steel Inst., 1902; Robert W. Hunt gold medal, A.I.M. and M.E., 1928. Mem. U.S. Assay Commn., 1900, 05, 11; metallurgist and asst. mgr. Sanderson works, Crucible Steel Co. of America, 1902-08; gen. mgr. Halcomb Steel Co., Syracuse, N.Y., 1908-15, and pres., 1915-20; v.p. and director of research, Crucible Steel Company of America. Trustee Washington and Jefferson College. Served on several tech. committees during World War. Home: Scarsdale, N.Y. Died Jan. 11, 1935.

MATHEWS, JOSEPH HOWARD, chemist; b. Auroraville, Wis., Oct. 15, 1881; s. Joseph and Lydia Tibbets (Cate) M.; B.S., U. of Wis., 1903, A.M., 1905; A.M., Harvard, 1906, Ph.D., 1908; m. Ella Barbara Gilfillan, June 26, 1909; children—Marion Zoe, Jean Barbara. Assistant in chemistry, U. of Wis., 1905; instr. chemistry, Case Sch. of Applied Science, Cleveland, O., 1906-07; asst. prof. chemistry, U. of Wis., 1911, asso. prof., 1917, prof., 1919-52, also chmn. of dept. and dir. course in chemistry. Commd. capt. Ordnance Dept., U.S. Army, July 10, 1917; maj., Jan. 15, 1918; hon. disch., Dec. 16, 1918; went to France as spl. investigator of problems connected with gas warfare, Sept. 1917; returned to U.S., Jan. 1918, and placed in charge offensive gas and research br. of trench warfare sect. Engring. Div. of Ordnance Dept. Criminal identification expert. Fellow A.A.A.S.; mem. Am. Chem. Soc., Sigma Xi, Alpha Chi Sigma, Phi Lambda Upsilon, Phi Kappa Phi. Presbyterian. Clubs: University, Rotary, Professional, Scabbard and Blade (Madison); Black Hawk Country. Co-author: Experimental Physical Chemistry, 1929; author: Firearms Identification, 2 vols., 1962, reprint, with 3 vols., 1973. over 60 papers on scientific subjects. Home: Madison WI Died Apr. 15, 1970; buried Madison WI

MATHEWSON, EDWARD PAYSON, metallurgist; b. Montreal, Can., Oct. 16, 1864; s. James Adams and Amelia Seabury (Black) M.; B.S. in mining, McGill, 1885; LL.D., 1922; D.Sc., Colo. Sch. of Mines, 1920; m. Alice Barry, June 25, 1890; children—Alice Seabury (Mrs. E.V. Graybeal), Grace (Mrs. N.C. Streit), Gertrude (Mrs. A.R. Nolin), Mary Elizabeth (Mrs. E.F. Bissantz), Edward Payson. Was assayer, 1886-89, supt., 1889-97, Pueblo (Colo.) Smelting & Refining Co.; joined Guggenheim's Sons tech. staff, 1897, and supt. and mgr. at Perth Amboy, N.J., Monterey, Mex., and Antofagasta, Chile, until 1902; in employ Anaconda Copper Mining Co., 1902-16, mgr. Washoe Reduction Works of company at Anaconda, 1903-16. Mgr. until Jan. 1, 1913, of Internat. Smelting & Refining Co.'s western plants, erecting same at Internat. Utah, and E. Chicago, Ind.; gen. mgr. British Am. Nickel Corp., Ltd., Toronto, 1916-18; dir. and cons. metallurgist, Am. Smelting & Refining Co., New York, 1918-19; cons. metallurgist since 1919; became prof. adminstrn. of mineral industries, U. of Ariz., 1926, now retired. Rep. fellow McGill U., 1923-26. Awarded gold medals, Instn. of Mining and Metallurgy (London), 1911, Mining & Metall. Soc. of Am., 1917. Fellow A.A.A.S.; mem. Am. Inst. Mining and Metall. Engrs. (pres. 1923; made mem. Legion of Honor for 50 years, membership, 1939, Soc. Chem. Industry (London), Tau Beta Phi, Sigma Delta Pi, Theta Tau. Episcopalian. Clubs: Old Pueblo (Tucson); Anaconda (Mont.) Engrs. Contbr. on metallurgy to tech. press and Trans. Inst. Mining Engrs. Inventor of various improvements in blast and reverberatory furnaces for smelting copper and lead ores. Home: 1143 E. Lowell Av., Tucson AZ

MATHIAS, HENRY EDWIN, coll. dean, geologist; b. Moberly, Mo., June 8, 1901; s. John Edward and Barbara (Breusch) M.; A.B., U. Mo., 1923, A.M., 1924, grad. work, 1925; m. Lucille Florence Crews, Sept. 3, 1927; 1 son, Henry Edwin. Instr. geology U. Mo., 1924-27, U. Mo.-Utah Agr. Coll., summer 1926; geologist Marland Oil Co., summer 1927, Petroleum Information, Inc., Denver, summer 1928; con. geologist since 1929; asst. prof. geology Colo. Coll., 1927-31, asso. prof., 1931-46, dir. Lennox House (student union), 1937-42; acting dir. admission and dean of freshmen, 1942-43, dir. admission and dean of freshmen, 1943-46, laisson officer between Colo. Coll. and Navy V-12 unit, 1943-45, dean sch. arts and scis., dir. admissions, dir. summer session, 1946-50, acting dean coll., 1948-49, dean sch. arts and scis., dir. admission since 1950, dean admission, dir. summer session 1953-56, dean admission, dir. placement, 1956-58, asso. dean of coll., dir. of placement, 1958—. Dir. Colorado Springs Boys Club, 1935—; dir. local chpt., A.R.C. 1948-50. Mem. Am. Assn. Petroleum Geologists, N.E.A., Am. Assn. Sch. Adminstrs., Colo. Edn. Assn., Colo. Life Adjustment Edn. Com., Colo. Springs C. of C., Soc. Delta Epsilon (nat. sec.-treas., 1931-40), Sigma Xi, Sigma Gamma Epsilon, Gamma Alpha. Mason. Clubs: El Paso, Winter Night (sec.-treas. 1944-53, pres. 1953-54), Kiwanis (pres. 1935), Colo. Schoolmasters. Contbr. articles to sci. jours. Recipient Keystone award Boys Club of Am., 1953. Home: 1436 N. Weber St., Colorado Springs, Colo. Died Oct. 7, 1966; buried Evergreen Cemetery, Colorado Springs.

MATSON, DONALD DARROW, neurosurgeon; b. Ft. Hamilton, N.Y., Nov. 28, 1913; s. Joseph and Kathleen (Connor) M.; A.B., Cornell U., 1935; M.D., Harvard, 1939; m. Dorothy Jean Everett, Sept. 11, 1943;children—Martha Jo, Donald Everett, James Edward, Barbara Baker. Intern Children's Med. Center, Peter Bent Brigham Hosp., Boston, 1939-43, neurosurgeon, 1948-69; resident Duke U. Hosp., 1947-48; pvt. practice, Boston, 1948-69; clin. prof. surgery Harvard Med. Sch., 1961-69; cons. neurosurgery VA Hosp., West Roxbury, Mass., Mass. Hosp. Sch.; mem. spl. med. adv. bd. VA, 1963-69. Served from lt. to maj. M.C., AUS, 1943-46. Decorated Bronze Star medal. Diplomate Am. Bd. Neurol. Surgery (chmn. 1965). Fellow A.C.S.; mem. Nat. Inst. Neurol. Diseases and Blindness (neurology postgrad. tng. com.), A.M.A., Soc. Neurol. Surgeons, Harvey Cushing Soc., Acad. Neurosurgery, Soc. U. Surgeons, Halstead Soc., A.A.A.S., Am. Neurol. Soc., New Eng., Boston surg. socs., Scandinavian Neurosurg. Soc., Am. Surg. Assn. Author: Treatment of Acute Cranio Cerebral Injuries Due to Missiles, 1948; Treatment of Acute Spinal Injuries Due to Missiles, 1948; (with Franc D. Ingraham) Neurosurgery in Infancy and Childhood, 1953; also numerous articles in med. publs. Adv. bd. Medical Specialties. Home: Chestnut Hill MA Died May 1969.

MATSON, GEORGE CHARLTON, geologist, engr.; b. Strang, Neb., Feb. 4, 1873; s. Thomas and Susannah (Charlton) M.; B.S., Doane Coll., Crete, Neb., 1900; studied U. of Neb., 1900-01; A.M., Cornell U., 1903; Ph.D., U. of Chicago, 1920; m. Beulah Edwards, 1913; children—Thomas Edward, Mary Barbara, George Charlton. Asst. in geology, Cornell U., 1901-03; instr. geology, U. of Ill., 1903-04; fellow in geology, U. of Chicago, 1904-06; geologist U.S. Geol. Survey, 1906-16, Mexican Gulf Oil Co., 1916-17, Gulf Refining Co., of La., 1917; Gypsey Oil Co. and S. American Gulf Oil Co., 1917-21; consulting geologist, 1921—; vice-pres. Schermerhorn Oil Co., 1922-29; indepedent oil operator, 1929—. Writer on geol. topics. Home: Tulsa, Okla. Died Jan. 3, 1940.

MATSON, RALPH CHARLES, physician, surgeon; b. Brookville, Pa., Jan. 21, 1880; s. John and Minerva (Brady) M.; M.D., U. of Ore., 1902; grad. student, St. Mary's Hosp., London, Cambridge U., 1906, U. of Vienna, 1910, 23, 25, Acad. of Medicine, Dusseldorf, Germany, U. of Berlin, 1912, U. of Paris, 1924; m. Adeline Ferrari, Aug. 5, 1907 (divorced Oct. 1922); 1 adopted dau., Daphne; m. 2d, Chiara De Bona, Nov. 25, 1923. Physician and surgeon, Portland, Ore., since 1902; mem. firm Drs. Matson & Bisaillon; asso. clin., prof. of surgery and medicine, U of Ore. Med. Sch., since 1935, mem. exec. faculty since 1940, chief surgeon, Univ. State Tuberculosis Hosp., Portland, Ore.; dir. dept. of thoracic surgery, Portland Open Air Sanatorium, Milwaukie, Ore.; mem. visiting staff Good Samaritan Hosp.; chest consultant Multnomah County Hosp., and U.S. Pub. Health Service; attending specialist chest surg. center, Vets. Adminstrn. Hosp.; co-dir. tuberculosis clinic, med. dept., U. of Ore.; consulting thoracic surgeon Doernbecher Memorial Hosp. for Children; med. and surg. dir. Portland Open Air Sanatorium (all Portland); mem. med. advisory bd. Nat. Jewish Hosp., Denver, 1941; hon. 1st lt. Harvard U. Surg. Unit with B.E.F., 1916; served as capt. Royal Army Med. Corps, 1917; maj. Med. Corps, U.S. Army, chief med. examiner and tuberculosis specialist, Camp Lewis, 1917-19, chief of med. staff Gen. Hosp. No. 21, Denver, 1919-20; now lt. col. Med. Res. Corps. Del. to Internat. Union Against Tuberculosis, Washington, D.C., 1908, Rome, 1912, Lausanne, Switzerland, 1923; vice chmn. thoracic sect., 7th cruise congress, Pan-American Surg. Assn., 1938. Diplomate Am. Bd. Internal Medicine. Fellow Am. Coll. of Surgeons, Am. Coll. of Physicians, Le College International de Chirurgiens (Geneva), Am. Coll. Chest Physicians (pres. 1939); mem. Am. Assn. Thoracic Surgeons, Am. Med. Assn. of Vienna (life mem.) and Berlin, Am. Climatol. and Clin. Assn., Am. Trudeau Society, National Tuberculosis Association (former v.p.), Pan-Pacific Surg. Assn. (former v.p.), A.M.A., Portland City and County Med. Soc., Portland Acad. of Medicine, Ore. State Med. Soc., Pacific Interurban Clin. Club, Pacific Coast Surg. Soc., Internat. Artificial Pneumothorax Assn. (exec. com.), Ore. State Tuberculosis Assn., Alpha Kappa Kappa, Alpha Omega Alpha; hon. mem. Minneapolis Surg. Soc.; hon. mem. staff Lymanhurst Sch. for Tuberculosis Children, Minneapolis. Hollywood (Calif.) Academy Medicine, Sociedad Mexicano de Estudios Sobre Tuberculosis, Mex. Clubs: Arlington (Portland); Highlands Racquet (Oswego, Ore.). Contbr. of sects. or chapters to books: "Surgical Treatment of Pulmonary Tuberculosis" in Cyclopedia of Medicine, 1934; "Extrapleural Pneumolysis" in Surgical Diseases of the Chest by Graham, Ballon and Singer, 1935; "Artificial Pneumothorax" in Pulmonary Tuberculosis by Goldberg, 1935; "Operative Collapse Therapy in Treatment of Pulmonary Tuberculosis" in Internat. Clinics, Vol. II, 1934; etc. Contbr. of numerous articles on the med. and surg. aspects of tuberculosis, in English, French, Spanish and German. Editor in chief Diseases of the Chest; mem. editorial bd. Western Jour. Surgery, Obstetrics and Gynecology, Jour. Internat. Coll. Surgeons. Home: 2960 N.W. Cumberland Rd. Office: Stevens Bldg., Portland, Ore. Died Oct. 26, 1945.

MATSON, THEODORE MALVIN, univ. prof., traffic engr.; b. Denver, Mar. 17, 1903; s. Thomas and Alice (Swanson) M.; A.B., Stanford, 1923, E.E., 1925; m. Naomi Robinson, Aug. 14, 1926; 1 dau., Mary Jane. Electrical research asst. to Frank G. Baum, cons. engr., 1925; asst. engr. Pacific Gas and Electric Co., 1926; resident engr. San Francisco Traffic Survey Com., 1926-29; chief engr. City-wide Traffic Com. of Kansas City, Mo., 1929-30; asst. traffic engr. City of Phila., 1930-33, traffic engr., 1933-36; research asso. Bur. for Street Traffic Research. Harvard; dir. San Francisco City-wide Traffic Survey, 1935-37, research asso., 1937-38; research asst., asst. prof. Bur. for Street Traffic Research, Yale, 1938-43; dir., prof. Bur. Highway Traffic, Yale, since 1943; cons. Eno Foundn. for Traffic Control; sec. Com. on Transportation, Yale; traffic cons. to engr. bd., U.S. War Dept. Dir. Inst. Traffic Engring., 1939-41; mem. nocturnal logistics committee, Nat. Defense Research Council, 1943-45; traffic cons. for pub. and private agencies. Mem. Inst. Traffic Engrs., Highway Research Bd., Sigma Xi. Clubs: Yale (New York); Graduate (New Haven). Author: Market Street Traffic Control Plan, 1928; Street Traffic Control Plan of San Francisco, 1927; (with Miller McClintock) Report to San Francisco Traffic Survey, 1927; (with Miller McClintock) Traffic Control Plan for Kansas City, 1930; Principles of Traffic Signal Timing, National Safety Council Transactions, 1929; (with T. W. Forbes) Measurement of Overtaking and Passing Distances, 1940; (with L. Williams) Elements of Intersection Redesign, 1940; War Worker Transportation, 1943; Traffic Engineering, 1954. Home: 255 Ridgewood Av., Hamden, Conn. Died Dec. 15, 1954; buried St. Mary's Cemetery, Mount Carmel, Conn.

MATTESON, VICTOR ANDRE, architect, engr.; b. Chicago, Ill., Aug. 22, 1872; s. Andre and Ellen C. (MacNaughton) M.; grad. Chicago Manual Training Sch., 1891; U. of Ill., 1895. Studied and traveled in Europe. Early associated with various architects' offices in Chicago; now in general pvt. practice alone; architect for a large number of pub. and pvt. bldgs. scattered through U.S. and specializing in waterworks and other pub. utility bldgs. Served as asst. prin. engr., of Construction Div. of the Army, War Dept., Washington, D.C., World War I. Fellow Am. Ins. Architects; mem. Ill. Soc. Architects, S.A.R., U. of Ill. Alumni Assn., Burnham Astron. Soc., Illini Club of Chicago, Sigma Chi. Mason. Office: 20 N. Wacker Drive., Chicago 6 IL

MATTFELD, MARIE, mezzo-soprano; b. Munich, Germany; d. Herman Schmid (concert-meister Munich Royal Opera Orchestra); grad. Royal Conservatory of Music, Munich; m. William Mattfeld, of N.Y. City, July 1890. Came to U.S., 1890; with Damrosch Opera Co., 1894-98, Sembrich Opera Co., 1900-01; sang at Stadt Theatre, Bremen, Germany, 1902-03; mem. Met. Opera Co. since 1905; sings in English, Italian, French and German. Home: New York NY*

MATTHES, FRANÇOIS EMILE, (math'es), geologist; b. Amsterdam, Holland, Mar. 16, 1874; s. Willem Ernst and Johanna Suzanna (van der Does de Bije) M.; ed. in Holland, Switzerland and Germany; came to U.S., 1891; naturalized citizen U.S., 1896; B.S., Mass. Inst. Technology, 1895; LL.D., U. of Calif., 1947; m. Edith Lovell Coyle, June 7, 1911. With topographic branch of Geol. Survey, 1896-1914; with geologic branch, 1914-47. In charge of topographic surveys in Big Horn Mountains, Wyo., Glacier Nat. Park, Grand Canyon of Colo. River, Yosemite Valley, Mt. Rainier Nat. Park; geol. studies in Yosemite and Sequoia National Parks, Central Sierra, Nevada, California, central Mississippi Valley. Special studies: alpine glaciation; post-Pleistocene glaciation. Decorated Chevalier Order of Leopold II (Belgium), 1920; awarded silver beaver, Boy Scouts of Am., 1931; awarded Gold Medal of U.S. Dept. of Interior, Apr. 1948. Fellow Geol. Soc. Am., A.A.A.S.; mem. Assn. Am. Geographers (pres. 1933), Washington Acad. Sciences (vice-pres. 1933), Am. Geophys. Union (chmn. com. on glaciers), Internat. Commn. Snow and Glaciers (sec.), Internat. Assn. Sci. Hydrology (asst. sec.), Geol. Soc., Washington (pres. 1932), Am. Soc. Chemical Engineers (life), British Glaciological Society. Club Alpin Français (honorary); corr. mem. Appalacian Mountain Club; mem. Am. Alpine Club, Sierra Club (hon. v.p.); hon. mem. Mazamas. Wrote Glacial Sculpture of Bighorn Mountains, Wyo., 1900; Mt. Rainier and Its Glaciers, 1914; Geologic History of the Yosemite Valley, 1930; Geologic History of Mt. Whitney, 1937; various scientific reports and articles. Home: 858 Gelston Place, El Cerrito, Calif. Died June 21, 1948.

MATTHES, GERARD HENDRIK, civil and hydraulic engr.; b. Amsterdam, Holland, Mar. 16, 1874; s. Willem Ernst and Johanna (van der Does) M.; B.S. in Civil Engring., Mass. Inst. Tech., 1895; m. Mary M. Bewick, Mar. 3, 1904; 1 dau., Florence B. (Mrs. H. E. Stephens). Came to U.S., 1891, naturalized, 1896. Instrument man and draftsman, 1895-97; asst. hydrographer U.S. Geol. Survey, 1897-1902; engr. asst. supervising engr. U.S. Reclamation Service, 1902-07; designing engr., resident engr., and supt. constrn. Colo. Power Co., 1907-11; prin. engr. hydro-electric dept. Am. Water Works and Guaranty Co., on constrn. of power development in W.Va., 1911-13; div. engr. for State Water Supply Commn. of Pa., in charge of flood problems, 1913-15; hydraulic engr. Miami Conservancy Dist. on flood control, 1915-20; U.S. asst. engr. War Dept., Chattanooga, Tenn., charge survey of Tenn. River and tributaries which include first aerial photog. survey of rivers undertaken by war dept., 1920-23; con. engr., N.Y., specializing aerial surveys and hydro-elec. power projects, 1923-28; with War Dept. as sr. hydro-elec. engr. and later prin. engr. charge comprehensive studies relating to water power, flood control, and nav. improvements in southeastern states, 1929-32; prin. engr., head engr. and cons. to pres. Miss. River Commn. on flood control of lower Miss. River, 1932-45; also head engr. and dir. U.S. Waterways Expt. Sta., 1942-45; pvt. cons. practice specializing river, harbor and irrigation projects, N.Y.; cons. to sec. hydraulic resources, Mexico, 1948-50; cons. Associated Navigation Companies, Colombia, S.A., on improvement Magdalena River, 1952. Member astronomic expedition to Sumatra sent by Mass. Inst. Tech., 1901; cons. to Nat. Resources Bd. for lower Miss. River, 1934, for War Dept. on Conchas Dam, N.M., 1935-37; mem. spl. cons. bd. on flood control for T.V.A., 1936; charge geol. investigation of alluvial valley of Miss. River for Miss. River Commn., 1941-45. Recipient citation and award for exceptional civilian service from War Dept., 1944. Mem. Am. Soc. C.E. (chmn. com. on floods 1934-41; hon. mem. 1943; Norman medalist 1949), American Geophys. Union, Engineers Club. Inventor tetrahedral block revetments for river banks; designer of topographic slide rule for use in planetable surveying. Author and illustrator: River Engineering pub. in American Civil Engineering Practice, Vol. II, 1956; also articles and reports. Address: Broadway Central Hotel, 673 Broadway, N.Y.C. 12. Died Apr. 8, 1959; buried Oak Creek Canyon, Prescott, Ariz.

MATTHEW, WILLIAM DILLER, paleontologist; b. St. John, N.B., Can., Feb. 19, 1871; s. George Frederic and Katherine Mary (Diller) M.; A.B., U. of N.B., 1889; Ph.B., Columbia, 1893, A.M., 1894, Ph.D., 1895; m. Kate Lee, July 15, 1905; children—Elizabeth Lee, Margaret Mary, William Pomeroy. Asst., 1895-98, asst. curator, 1898-1902, asso. curator, 1902-10, curator, 1911-25, curator-in-chief, Div. I, 1922-27, Am. Mus. Natural History; prof. paleontology, U. of Calif., 1927—. Fellow N.Y. Acad. Sciences, Geol. Soc. America, Paleontol. Soc., A.A.A.S., N.Y. Zoöl. Soc., Royal Soc. (London). Home: Berkeley, Calif. Died Sept. 24, 1930.

MATTHEWS, J(OSEPH) MERRITT, chemist; b. Phila., June 9, 1874; s. Joseph Merritt and Blanche (Fowler) M.; B.Sc., U. of Pa., 1895, Ph.D., 1898; m. Augusta Spalding Gould, May 15, 1903. Head dept. chemistry and dyeing, Phila. Textile Sch., 1898-1907; mgr. of dyeing dept. of N.E. Cotton Yarn Co., 1907-10; consulting chemist, and expert in textile chemistry and dyestuffs, 1910—. Editor of Color Trade Jour., 1917—. Member National Research Council, etc. Author: Vol. III, Part I, on Dyestuffs, Allen's Commercial Organic Analysis, 1900; Textile Fibres, 1924; Laboratory Manual Dyeing and Textile Chemistry, 1909; Application of Dyestuffs, 1920; Bleaching Technology, 1921. Translator: Alexieff's General Principles of Organic Syntheses, 1906. Home: San Diego, Calif. Died 1931.

MATTHEWS, VELMA DARE, biologist; b. Burlington, N.C., Aug. 3, 1904; d. Joseph Marvin and Cora (Moore) Matthews; A.B., Woman's Coll. of Univ. of N.C., 1925; A.M., Univ. of N.C., 1927, Ph.D., 1930; research Allegany Sch. Natural History, summer 1931, Univ. of N.C., 1932-34, U. of Va., summer 1935; unmarried. Prof. of biology, Ark. Agr. and Mech. Coll., Monticello, 1930-31; prof. of biology and head dept., Coker Coll., Hartsville, S.C., since 1935; visiting prof. of mycology, Mt. Lake Biol. Sta. of U. of Va., summer 1936. Mem. S.C. Acad. Science (v.p. 1941-45, pres. 1946-47), N.C. Acad. Science, Bot. Soc. Am., A.A.A.S., Mycol. Soc., Am. Fern Soc., Torrey Bot. Club, Am. Assn. Univ. Women, Sigma Xi. Author: Studies on the Genus Pythium, 1931; Saprolegniales, North American Flora, Vol. II, 1937. Contbr. to scientific jours. Address: Coker Coll., Hartsville, S.C. Died Jan. 7, 1958.

MATTIELLO, JOSEPH J., (mat'e-el-lo), chemist; b. New York, N.Y., Feb. 28, 1900; s. Celestino and Elizabeth (Bottigliere) M.; B.S., Polytech. Inst. of Brooklyn, 1925, M.S., 1931; Ph.D., Columbia U., 1936; m. Josephine Critelli, Sept. 18, 1922; children—Margaret Anne (Mrs. Harry Kimm, Jr.), Elizabeth (Mrs. Joseph Yozzo), Rosamond, Barbara. Dir., v.p., tech. dir., mem. exec. com., Hilo Varnish Corp. Consultant on protective coatings, Q.M. gen. plastics sect., research and development br., Mil. Planning Div. Received Regimental Citation and Purple Heart, World War I, Meritorious Civilian Service award, World War II. Mem. Am. Soc. Testing Materials (Marburg lecturer 1946), Nat. Paint, Varnish and Lacquer Assn. (sci. sect.), Am. Oil Chemists, Am. Chem. Soc., Am. Inst. Chem. Engrs., Am. Inst. Chemists (v.p.), Oil and Color Chemists Assn., Soc. of Chem. Industries, Assn. Research Dirs., Oil and Color Chemists Assn. of Great Britain (hon. mem.), Fedn. of Paint and Varnish Prodn., N.Y. Printing Ink Prodn., N.Y. Paint and Varnish Prodn. (past pres.), Gallows Birds Soc., Delta Kappa Pi, Phi Lambda Upsilon, Sigma Xi. Republican. Roman Catholic. Club: Sales Execs. Editor: Protective and Decorative Coatings (5 vols.); author, pubs. dealing with paints, varnish and lacquers. Home: 536A 5th St., Brooklyn, N.Y. Office: 42 Stewart Av., Brooklyn 6, N.Y. Died May 16, 1948.

MATTILL, HENRY ALBRIGHT, (mat-til'), biochemist; b. Glasgow, Mo., Nov. 28, 1883; s. Henry and Emma (Fryhofer) M.; A.B., Adelbert Coll. (Western Reserve U.), 1906; A.M., 1907; Ph.D., U. of Ill., 1910; S.Dc. (honorary), Western Reserve Univ., 1952; m. Helen Isham, Dec. 31, 1912; 1 son, John Isham. Asst. in chemistry, U. of Ill., 1906-08, fellow in biochem., 1908-10; assistant professor physiol. and physiol. chemistry, U. of Utah, 1910-11, asso. prof., 1911-12, prof., 1912-15; asst. prof. nutrition, U. of Calif., 1915-18; prof. biochemistry, U. of Rochester, 1919-27; prof. of biochemistry and head of department. University of Iowa since 1927. Captain and maj. Sanitary Corps, Div. of Food and Nutrition, Army U.S. and A.E.F., 1918-19. Recipient Iowa medal Am. Chemical Society, 1950. Fellow A.A.A.S.; mem. Am. Soc. of Biol. Chemists (sec., 1933-38; council 1938-44; edit. com., 1944—; v p. 1951, pres. 1952), Am. Physiological Soc. (edit. bd. Physiol. Rev. since 1948), Soc. Exptl. Biology and Medicine, Am. Chem. Soc., Am. Inst. of Nutrition, A.A.U.P., Iowa Acad. Sci., Phi Beta Kappa, Sigma Xi, Gamma Alpha, Phi Lambda Upsilon, Alpha Chi Sigma, Alpha Omega Alpha. Unitarian. Home: 358 Lexington Av., Iowa City, Ia. Died Mar. 30, 1953.

MATTOON, ARTHUR MARTYN, astronomer; b. Maxtown, O., Sept. 12, 1855; s. Henry Martyn and Julia Ledyard (Hempstead) M.; A.B., Marietta (O.) Coll., 1880, A.M., 1883; U. of Cambridge, Eng., 1903-04; m. Eliza Alberta Bailey, Aug. 2, 1882. Instr. mathematics, Albany (Ore.) Coll., 1880-83, Coll. of Mont., 1883-87; prin. Bozeman (Mont.) Acad., 1887-89; prof. mathematics, Blackburn Coll., Carlinville, Ill., 1889-90; prin. Elgin (Ill.) Acad., 1890-91; prof. mathematics and astronomy and dir. Charles Smith Scott Obs. of Park Coll., Parkville, Mo., 1892-1912, prof. emeritus, 1912-17; prof. mathematics and astronomy, Albany (Ore.) Coll., 1917—. Author: Essentials of Plane and Spherical Trigonometry, 1895 (3d edit., 1907); Introduction to the Theory of Equations, 1906. Died Jan. 7, 1924.

MATZ, PHILIP BENJAMIN, pathologist; b. Baltimore, Md., Aug. 25, 1885; s. Oscar and Freda (Kaplan) M.; Litt.B., Mather Coll., Kansas City, Kan., 1911; M.D., Coll. of Medicine, L.I. Coll. Hosp., 1908; m. Eleanor Crampton, Nov. 20, 1913. Has specialized in pathology and clin. investigation; served as chief of lab. service, Base Hosp., Camp Travis, Tex., World War; commissioned as surgeon (Res.) U.S.P.H.S., 1920, and served as chief lab. service various hosps. of the U.S. Pub. Health Service; chief of Med. Research Subdivision, Veterans' Adminstrn., 1925—. Fellow Am. Soc. Clin. Pathologists, Am. Coll. Physicians. Home: Washington, D.C. Died June 25, 1938.

MATZKE, EDWIN BERNARD, botanist; b. New York City, Aug. 2, 1902; s. Conrad Joseph and Emilie (Frieling) M.; A.B., Columbia, 1924, Ph.D., 1930; student Kaiser Wilhelm Institut for Biology, Berlin-Dahlem and Univ. of Berlin (Cutting travelling fellow), 1928-29; unmarried. Asst. in botany, Columbia, 1924-28, instr. in botany, 1929-33, asst. prof., 1933-43, asso. prof., 1943-47, prof. of botany, 1947-69, chairman of department of botany, 1958-66, chairman of dept. of biological scis., 1966-67, asst. to dean Columbia Coll., 1944-60; lectr. Fordham U., 1942-44; research investigator Marine Biology Lab., summers 1949-56; bd. mgrs.; exec. com. of bd. N.Y. Bot. Garden, 1958-69. Fellow A.A.A.S., N.Y. Acad. Sciences. Member Botanical Soc. of Am., Am. Bryological Soc., Soc. for Study of Evolution, Torrey Botanical Club (treas., 1936, v.p., 1941, sec. 1942-44, pres. 1949, asso. editor 1950-59), Phi Beta Kappa, Sigma Xi. Catholic. Contributor numerous articles on cellular structure of plants, plant growth, floral morphology, coloration in plants, in numerous scientific publications. Researcher on three dimensional shapes of cells, cell division, floral anatomy and pigmentation, developmental morphology of liverworts. Home: Bronx NY Died Sept. 28, 1969.

MAUCHLY, SEBASTIAN JACOB, physicist; b. Swanton, O., July 9, 1878; s. John William and Mary Jane (Ziegler) M.; A.B., U. of Cincinnati, 1911, Ph.D., 1913; studied U. of Chicago; m. Rachel Elizabeth Scheidemantel, Dec. 27, 1905; children—John William, Helen Elizabeth. Prin. and instr. physics, Hartwell High Sch., Cincinnati, 1905-11; Hanna research fellow, dept. of physics, U. of Cincinnati, 1911-13; head dept. of physics Woodward High Sch., Cincinnati, 1913-14; apptd. asso. physicist, Dept. Terrestrial Magnetism Carnegie Instn. of Washington, Nov. 1, 1914; asst. chief obs. div. same, 1917-18, and chief of sect. terrestrial electricity same, Jan. 1, 1919—. Fellow Am. Physical Soc., A.A.A.S. Presbyn. Mason. Co-author of Vol. V, Researches Dept. of Terestrial Magnetism (Carnegie Instn., Washington), 1926. Research in earth currents and in elec. conduction in gases, including atmospheric electricity. Home: Chevy Chase, Md. Died Dec. 24, 1928.

MAUGH, LAWRENCE C(ARNAHAN), engr.; b. Wyoming, Ont., Can., Apr. 3, 1901; s. John and Ethel (Lawson) M.; B.S., U. of Mich., 1921, Ph.D., 1934; M.S., S.D. State Coll., 1923; m. Lois Amelia Rowe, June 26, 1931; children—Roger Edward, Lois Ann. Instr. in civil engring., S.D. State Coll., 1921-24; bridge designer, Ind. State High Commn., 1924-25; instr. in civil engring., U. of Mich., 1925-31, asst. prof., 1931-41, asso. prof., 1943-47, prof. civil engring. from 1948; structural cons., Goodyear Aircraft Corp., Akron, O., 1942-43. Member Am. Soc. C.E., Am. Soc. Engring. Edn., Internat. Assn. of Bridge and Structural Engring., Mich. Engring. Soc., Sigma Xi, Tau Beta Pi. Author: Statically Indeterminate Structures, 1946. Contbr. tech. articles on structural analysis in engring. publs. Home: Ann Arbor MI Died Oct. 31, 1971; buried Arborerest Cemetery.

MAURER, EDWARD ROSE, engineer; b. Fountain City, Wis., Feb. 18, 1869; s. John and Katherine (Moss) M.; B.C.E., University of Wisconsin, 1890; married May R. Dickens, September 1, 1892 (died, 1932); children—R. Edward, Mrs. Catherine Witter, Eugene D. Assistant engineer, C.&W. Railway, 1890; on U.S. Geol. Survey, 1891-92; asst. prof. and prof. mechanics in Engring. Coll. of U. of Wis., 1893-1935, prof. emeritus since 1935; dir. Soc. Promotion of Engring. Edn. Summer Sch. for Teachers of Mechanics, Madison session, 1927. Mem. Soc. Promotion Engring. Edn., A.A.A.S., Wis. Acad. Sciences, Arts and Letters, Am. Soc. Mech. Engrs., Wis. Engring. Soc., Sigma Xi, Tau Beta Pi, Chi Epsilon, Phi Kappa Phi, Phi Delta Theta. Club: University. Awarded Lamme medal by Society Promotion Engring. Edn., 1934. Author: Technical Mechanics, 1903 (rewritten as Mechanics for Engineers with R. J. Roark and G. W. Washa, 1945); Statics, 1904; Strength of Materials, 1904; Principles of Reinforced Concrete Construction (with F. E. Turneaure), 1907; Strength of Materials (with M. O. Withey), 1925. Asso. editor American Civil Engineers' Pocket Book, 1911. Home: 167 N. Prospect Av., Madison, Wis. Died May 1, 1948.

MAURY, ANTONIA CAETANA DE PAIVA PEREIRA, (maw'ri), astronomer; b. Cold Spring-on-Hudson, N.Y., Mar. 21, 1866; d. Mytton and Virginia (Draper) M.; A.B., Vassar, 1887. Asst., Harvard Obs., 1889-95, research asst., 1917-35, ret. 1935; work instr. physical sci. Gilman Sch., Cambridge, Mass., 1891-94, on classification of stellar spectra and spectroscovic binaries. Mem. Am. Astron. Soc., Audubon Soc., New Eng. Wild Flower Preservation Soc., Am. Scenic and Historic Preservation Soc. Author of Classification of Spectra of Bright Northern Stars, pub. as Harvard Annals, Vol. XXVIII, Part 1, 1897; Spectral Changes of Beta Lyrae, 1933. Home: 407 S. Broadway, Hastings on Hudson, N.Y. Deceased.

MAURY, CARLOTTA JOAQUINA, paleontologist; b. Hastings-on-Hudson, N.Y., Jan. 6, 1874; d. Mytton and Virginia (Draper) M.; studied at Radcliffe Coll., Columbia, U. of Paris; Ph.B., Cornell U., 1896, Schuyler fellow, 1898, Ph.D., 1902, Sarah Berliner fellow, 1916. Asst. in dept. of paleontology, Columbia, 1904-06, La. Geol. Survey, 1907-09; lecturer on geology, Barnard Coll. (Columbia), 1909-12; paleontologist, Venezuelan Geol. Expdn., 1910-11; prof. geology and zoölogy, Huguenot Coll. (U. of Cape of Good Hope), S. Africa, 1912-15; organized Maury expdn. to Dominican Republic, 1916; cons. paleontologist Royal Dutch Shell

Petroleum Co.; paleontologist Brazilian Govt.; has made a specialty of study of Antillean, Venezuelan and Brazilian stratigraphy and fossil faunas. Fellow Geol. Soc. America, A.A.A.S., Am. Geog. Soc. Author: Eocene of Trinidad, 1912; Dominican Type Sections and Fossils, 1917; Mollusca Gulf of Mexico, 1922; Miocene of Trinidad, 1925; Tertiary and Cretaceous of Brazil, 1925; Silurian of Santa Catharine, 1927; Silurian of Para, 1929; Puerto Rican, Dominican, and Soldado Stratigraphy and New Formational Names, 1929-31; Cretaceous of Parahyba do Norte, 1930; Bartonian and Ludian Upper Eocene in the Western Hemisphere, 1931; Cretaceous of Sergipe, Brazil; Triassic and Cretaceous of Northeastern Brazil, 1934; Lovenilampas, A New Echinoidean Genus from the Brazilian Cretaceous, 1934; New Genera and New Species of Fossil Terrestrial Mollusca from the States of Rio de Janeiro and São Paulo, Brazil, 1935. Home: Yonkers, N.Y. Died Jan. 3, 1938.

MAURY, DABNEY HERNDON, consulting engr.; b. Vicksburg, Miss., Mar. 9, 1863; s. Dabney Herndon and Nannie Rose (Mason) M.; grad. Va. Mil. Inst., 1882; M.E., Stevens Inst. Tech., 1884; m. Mary McCaw, Apr. 26, 1893; 1 son, Dabney H. Civ. and mining engr. in Colombia, S.A., 1887-92; in practice of engring., Peoria, Ill., 1893-1912; consulting engr. on hydraulic and sanitary work, Chicago, 1917-27 (retired). Adv. engr. on water supply to constrn. div. of the Army, May 1917-June 1919; commd. maj., Engr. R.C., 1917; lt. col., Q.M.C., 1918; hon. discharged, May 31, 1919. Episcopalian. Home: Chevy Chase Md. Died May 11, 1933.

MAVER, WILLIAM, JR., electrical engr.; b. Forfar, Scotland, Oct. 12, 1851; s. William and Mary McNicol (Alexander) M.; brought to Montreal, Can., by parents, 1857; ed. private school; holds veteran's medal, Fenian raid campaign, 1865-66; fifer, 5th Royals, Montreal, Can.; m. Maryannie MacTavish, Nov. 22, 1876. Came to New York, 1873; capt. of Am. Athletic Club, 1877-79; elec. expert Western Union Telegraph Co., 1880-84; elec. engr. B.&O. Telegraph Co., 1884-87; with elec. dept. Western Union Telegraph Co., 1888; elec. engr. Safety Insulated Wire & Cable Co., 1889-90; electrician Consol. Telegraph & Electrical Subway Co., New York, 1889-96; elec. expert New York Heat, Light & Power Co., 1893-97; expert in much elec. patent litigation. Propr. Maver Pub. Co. Fellow Am. Inst. E.E. Mason. Presbyn. Author: The Quadruplex and Other Articles on Telegraphy, 1884; Practical Systems of Electrical Telegraphy, 1888; American Telegraphy and Encyclopedia of the Telegraph, 1892, revised edit., 1912 (used as text book in colls. and by Signal Corps, U.S.A.); Maver's Wireless Telegraphy and Telephony, 1903, 4th edit., 1910; Progress in Wireless Telegraphy, 1905. Home: Jersey City, N.J. Died Aug 8, 1928.

MAXCY, KENNETH FULLER, M.D., educator; b. Saco, Me., July 27, 1889; s. Frederick Edward and Estelle Abbey (Gilpatric) M.; A.B., George Washington U., 1911; M.D., Johns Hopkins, 1915, D.P.H., 1921; m. Gertrud Helene McClellan, June 22, 1918; children—Kenneth Fuller, Frederic Reynolds, Selina Gilpatric. Resident house officer Johns Hopkins Hosp., 1915-16, asst. resident pediatrician, 1916-17; asst. in medicine Henry Ford Hosp., Detroit, 1917; fellow Johns Hopkins Sch. Hygiene and Pub. Health, 1919-21; asst. surgeon, passed asst. surgeon and surgeon USPHS, 1921-29; prof. bacteriology and preventive medicine U. Va., 1929-36; prof. pub. health and preventive medicine U. Minn., 1936-37; prof. bacteriology Sch. Hygiene and Pub. Health, Johns Hopkins, 1937-38, prof. epidemiology 1938-54, emeritus, 1954; cons. internat. Health Div., Rockefeller Found., 1937-40, 42-45, 48-52; cons. sec. war Army Epidemiological Bd., 1941-49; mem. Nat. Adv. Health Council, 1942-46; cons. Research and Devel. Bd. Nat. Mil. Establishment since 1946; mem. exec. com. Adv. Bd. on Health Services, A.R.C., 1945-48; mem. Med. Adv. Com., Nat. Found. for Infantile Paralysis 1940-48; trustee Internat. Polio Congress; chmn. com. on research and standards Am. Pub. Health Assn., 1939-46. Served as lt. M.C., U.S. Army, 1917, capt., 1918. Fellow Am. Pub. Health Assn. (Sedgwick Meml. medalist 1952); mem. Nat. Acad. Scis., Am. Soc. Epidemiologists, Assn. Am. Physicians, Pithotomy Club, Raven Soc., Phi Beta Kappa, Sigma Xi, Alpha Omega Alpha, Delta Omega, Theta Delta Chi, Phi Beta Pi. Epis-Rosenaus' Preventive Medicine and Hygiene, 8th warded U.S.A. Typhus Commn. medal, 1946. Editor: Papers of Wade Hampton Frost, 1941: Rosenaus' Preventive Medicine and Hygiene, 8th edit., 1956. Home: Park-Lynn Apts., 4 Upland Rd., Balt. 21210. Died Dec. 12, 1966; buried Arlington Nat. Cemetery.

MAXIM, HIRAM PERCY, inventor, mech. engr.; b. Brooklyn, N.Y., Sept. 2, 1869; s. Sir Hiram Stevens and Louisa Jane (Budden) M.; grad. Sch. of Mechanic Arts of Mass. Inst. Tech., 1886 (youngest student in class); D.Sc., Colgate; m. Josephine, d. Gov. Hamilton of Md., Dec. 21, 1898; children—Hiram Hamilton, Percy (dau.). Elec. engr. Ft. Wayne (Ind.) Jenney Electric Co., 1886-87, W. S. Hill Electric Co., Boston, 1887-88, Thomson Elec. Welding Co., Lynn, Mass., 1888-90; supt. Am. Projectible Co., Lynn, 1890-95; chief engr. Electric Vehicle Co., Hartford, Conn., 1895-1907; pres. Maxim Silencer Co. (Hartford). Inventor elec. devices and ordnance, Columbia automobiles, the Maxim silencer, etc. Pres. Am. Radio Relay League, Internat. Amateur Radio Union. Republican. Unitarian. Lt. comdr. U.S.N.R. Author: Life's Place in the Cosmos, 1933. Home: Hartford, Conn. Died Feb. 17, 1936.

MAXIM, HIRAM STEVENS, inventor; b. Sangerville, Me., Feb. 5, 1840; s. Isaac Wetson and Harriet M.; common sch. edn.; scientific knowledge obtained by study and attending lectures; 4 yrs. apprentice to coach-building; worked in various iron works; m. Louisa Jane Budden; 2d, Sarah Haynes; father of Florence and Hiram Percy M. Has patented numerous inventions in U.S.; went to England, 1881; has patented many elec. inventions, including incandescent lamps, self-regulating current machines, etc.; invented the Maxim gun, automatic system of firearms, which makes the recoil of the gun serve as the power for reloading; also other ordnance inventions, "Cordite," a smokeless powder, and more recently has devoted much time and invention to aërial navigation; consulting engr. Vicker's Ltd. Knighted by Queen Victoria, 1901. Died Nov. 24, 1916.

MAXIM, HUDSON, inventor, mech. engr.; b. Orneville Co., Me., Feb. 3, 1853; s. Isaac and Harriet Boston (Stevens) M.; ed. Me. Wesleyan Sem., Kent's Hill, Me.; D.Sc., Heidelberg, 1913; LL.D., St. Peters, 1918; m. Jane Morrow; m. 2d, Lilian Durban, Mar. 26, 1896. In printing and subscription pub. business, Pittsfield, Mass., 1883; took up bus. of ordnance and explosives, 1888; was 1st to make smokeless powder in U.S., and 1st to submit samples to U.S. Govt. for trial; built at Maxim, N.J. (named for him), 1890, dynamite factory and smokeless powder mill; in 1897 sold smokeless powder inventions to E.I. du Pont de Nemours & Co., Wilmington, Del., and is now consulting engr. and expert in development dept. of that co. U.S. Govt. adopted his smokeless powder; in 1901 sold to U.S. Government formula of "Maximite," first high explosive to be fired through heavy armor plate; has perfected "Stabillite," a smokeless powder producing much better ballistic results than any other; inventor of U.S. service detonating fuse for high explosive armor-piercing projectiles; of "motorite," a new self-combustive material for driving automobile torpedoes; of process and apparatus for mfg. multi-perforated powder grains; of improvements in smokeless powder grains, etc.; has many U.S. patents now pending. Past pres. Pan-Am. States Assn., Aeronautical Soc. of N.Y.; mem. Mil. Service Instn. Mem. Naval Consulting Bd., Sept. 1915—. Author: The Science of Poetry and the Philosophy of Language, 1910; Defenseless America, 1915; Dynamite Stories, 1916. Home: Landing P.O., N.J. Died May 6, 1927.

MAXON, WILLIAM RALPH, botanist; b. Oneida, N.Y., Feb. 27, 1877; s. Samuel Albert and Sylvia Louisa (Stringer) M.; Ph.B., Syracuse Univ., 1898, Sc.D., 1922; m. Edith Hinckley Merrill, Dorchester, Mass., June 2, 1908; 1 dau., Mary. Aid, U.S. Nat. Museum, Washington, 1899; later asst. curator, asso. curator and curator, U.S. Nat. Herbarium, 1937-46; now asso. in Botany, U.S. Nat. Museum. Has specialized in study of the Pteridophyta, mainly of tropical America. Fellow Am. Assn. for the Advancement of Science, American Acad. Arts and Sciences; member Bot. Soc. of Washington, Biol. Soc. of Washington, Washington Academy of Sciences, D.K.E., Sigma Xi. Unitarian. Club: Cosmos. Author series of papers entitled "Studies of Tropical American Ferns" in Contbns. U.S. National Herbarium; also "Ferns as a Hobby," "Pteridophyta of Porto Rico," and numerous other articles and repts. upon ferns. Home: 2333 20th St. Address: Smithsonian Institution, Washington, D.C. Died Feb. 25, 1948.

MAXWELL, JAMES HOYT, otologist; b. Paw Paw, Mich., Dec. 15, 1901; s. John Charles and Cleo Lyle (Stevens) M.; A.B., U. of Mich., 1924, M.D., 1927; m. Marjorie Arnold, Feb. 15, 1936; children—James Robert, John Charles. Intern Univ. Hospital, Ann Arbor, Mich., 1927-28; resident in otolaryngology, 1928-30, pvt. practice splty., Ann Arbor, since 1933; instr. otolaryngology U. of Mich., 1930-33, asst. prof., 1933-40, asso. prof., 1940-45, professor, 1945—, chmn. dept. Otolaryngology, 1958—; member staff Univ. and St. Joseph Mercy hosps. Chief cons. in splty., div. prof. services Central office V.A. since 1946. Diplomate Am. Bd. Otolaryngology (director). Fellow A.C.S. (past gov. and past chmn. adv. council oto-rhino-laryngology); mem. Am. Otol. Soc., Am. Laryngol. Assn., Am. Laryngol., Rhinol. and Otol. Soc., Am. Acad. Ophthal. and Otolaryn. (ex-sec. otol.), Otosclerosis Study Group (past pres.), A.M.A., Mich. and Washtenaw County med. socs., Phi Beta Kappa, Alpha Omega Alpha, Phi Kappa Phi. Clubs: Cosmos, (Washington); Ann Arbor, University (Ann Arbor). Home: 2139 Melrose Av. Office: Out Patient Bldg., University Hospital, Ann Arbor, Mich. Died June 2, 1960.

MAXWELL, SAMUEL STEEN, college prof.; b. Co. Donegal, Ireland, Aug. 4, 1860; s. John and Martha (Mitchell) M.; brought to America in infancy; B.S., Amity (Ia.) Coll., 1886 (hon. M.S., 1888); Johns Hopkins, 1889-90; Ph.D., U. of Chicago, 1896; m. Lula B. Taylor, of Lovelaceville, Ky., June 30, 1887. Instr. mathematics, 1886-87, prof. natural science, 1887-89, Amity Coll.; prof. natural science, 1890-92, prof. biology, 1892-1902, Monmouth (Ill.) Coll.; instr. physiology, Harvard Med. Sch., 1902-05; instr. physiology, 1905-07, asst. prof., 1907-10, asso. prof., 1910—, U. of Cal. Mem. Am. Physiol. Soc., A.M.A., Cal. Acad. Medicine, Soc. for Exptl. Biology; fellow A.A.A.S. Clubs: Kosmos, Faculty. Address: Berkeley, Calif.

MAYER, ALFRED MARSHALL, scientist; b. Balt., Nov. 13, 1836; s. Charles F. and Eliza (Blackwell) M.; attended St. Mary's Coll.; attended U. Paris, 1863-65; Ph.D., U. Pa., 1865; m. Katherine Duckett Goldsborough, 1865; m. 2d, Louisa Snowden, 1869, 3 children including Alfred. Asst. prof. chemistry and physics U. Md., 1856-58, Westminster Coll., Fulton, Mo., 1858-63; prof. phys. science Pa. Coll., Gettysburg, 1865-67, prof. physics and astronomy, 1867-71; prof. Stevens Inst. Tech., 1871-97; mem. Nat. Acad. Scis. Author: The Earth a Great Magnet, 1872, Sound, 1878; co-author: Light, 1877; also contbr. many articles to scientific jours. Died July 13, 1897.

MAYER, LUCIUS W., cons. mining engr.; b. New York, N.Y., Apr. 28, 1882; s. Gerson and Rosa (Wolf) M.; student Rensselaer Poly. Inst.; E.M., Columbia U., 1904; m. Mildred Mack, Apr. 19, 1910 (now dec.); 1 son, Chester Mack; married 2d, Dorothy P. Saks, September 17, 1943. With Stratton Independence Mining Co., Ltd., Cripple Creek, Colo., 1904-05; with Federal Lead Co., Flat River, Mo., 1906-07; investigating mining methods in Europe for Am. Smelters Securities Co., 1907; asso. with A. Chester Beatty in general consulting work from 1908-16; cons. engr. for Eugene Meyer Jr. & Company, 1916; partner in firm Rogers, Mayer & Ball since 1917. Dir. Air. Express International Agency, Incorporated. Mem. Am. Inst. Mining and Metall. Engrs., Mining and Metall. Soc. America. Clubs: City Midday, Mining, Columbia Yacht (N.Y. City). Author: Mining Methods in Europe, 1907; Financing of Mines, 1916. Lecturer and contbr. papers on mining. Home: 111 E. 56th St. Office: 26 Beaver St., N.Y. City. Died June 11, 1947.

MAYER, MARIA GOEPPERT, physicist; b. Kattowitz, Germany, June 28, 1906; d. Friedrich and Maria (Wolff) Goeppert; Ph.D., U. Gottingen, Germany, 1930; Dr. Science (honorary), Russel Sage College, 1960, Mount Holyoke College, 1961, Smith College, 1961; Dr. Science (honorary), Univ. of Portland, 1968; m. Joseph E. Mayer, Jan. 18, 1930; children—Maria Wentzel, Peter C. Came to U.S., 1930, naturalized, 1933. Vol. asso. Johns Hopkins, 1931-39; lectr. Columbia, 1939-46, Sarah Lawrence Coll., 1942-45; physicist SAM Labs., 1942-45; sr. physicist Argonne Nat. Lab., 1946-60; vol. prof. Enrico Fermi Inst. Nuclear Studies, U. Chgo., 1946-59, professor, 1959-60; professor at Revelle Coll. of University Cal. at La Jolla, California, from 1960. Recipient Nobel prize for physics, 1963. Fellow of American Academy of Arts and Sciences; mem. Akademie der Wissenschaften Heidelberg, Philos. Soc., Am. Phys. Soc., Nat. Acad. Scis., Sigma Xi. Author: (with Joseph E. Mayer) Statistical Mechanics, 1940; (with J.H.D. Jensen) Elementary Theory of Nuclear Shell Structure, 1951. Home: La Jolla CA Died Feb. 20, 1972; buried El Camino Meml. Park, San Diego CA

MAYNARD, CHARLES JOHNSON, naturalist; b. West Newton, Mass., May 6, 1845; s. Samuel and Emeline M.; ed. common schs.; married; 1 dau.; worked on his mother's farm, and studied nature from earliest youth. V.p., 1875, Nuttall Ornith. Club, Cambridge, Mass.; originator and editor Nuttall Bulletin (ornithological); one of original mems., and pres. 1891, Newton Natural History Soc.; made notable investigations of vocal organs of birds; discovered vocal organs of American bittern; spl. studies on the land shells of the West Indian genus Strophia (now Cerion). Instr. in econ. bird study, Mass. Agrl. Coll., Amherst, 1910-19. Author: Contributions to Science (3 vols.); Nature Studies No. 2—"Sponges"; Manual of Taxidermy; Methods in Moss Study; Field Directory to the Birds of Eastern North America; Atlas to the Directory of the Birds of Eastern North America; Records of Walks and Talks with Nature, 12 vols.; Field Ornithology; Plates to Field Ornithology; Migration of Birds and Other Animals; Vocal Organs of Talking Birds and of Other Species, 1918, 2d edit., 1922; Notes on Life History of Cerions, 1919. Home: West Newton, Mass. Died Oct. 15, 1929.

MAYNARD, EDWARD, dentist, inventor; b. Madison, N.Y., Apr. 26, 1813; s. Moses and Chloe (Butler) M.; attended U.S. Mil. Acad.; m. Ellen Sophia Doty, 1839; m. 2d, Nellie Long, 1869; 8 children including George W. Practiced dentistry, Washington, D.C., 1836-91; 1st dentist to fill teeth with gold foil, 1838; co-editor Am. Journal of Dental Science, 1843-46; patented firearm priming system, 1845; prof. theory and practice Balt. Coll. of Dental Surgery, 1857-91; developed and patented Maynard carbine (1 of 1st breech-loading rifles in Am.); court dentist to Emperor Nicholas I of Russia; named chevalier of mil. order of Red Eagle of Prussia; prof. dental theory and practice Nat. U., Washington, 1887-91; hon. mem. Am. Acad. Dental Scis. Died Washington, May 4, 1891.

MAYNARD, GEORGE WILLIAM, mining engr.; b. Brooklyn, N.Y., June 12, 1839; s. George Washington and Caroline Augusta (Eaton) M.; A.B., Columbia, 1859, A.M., 1864; U. of Göttingen and Royal Mining

Acad., Clausthal, Germany, 1860-63; m. Fannie Atkin, June 12, 1865. Had charge of metall. works in Ireland, 1863-64; engaged as mining engr. in Colo., 1864-67; prof. mining and metallurgy, Rensselaer Poly. Inst., 1868-72, also cons. engr. to various iron and steel works; cons. engr. for iron, steel and copper works in Eng. and Germany, 1873-79; cons. mining and metall. engr., 1879—. Has had charge of constrn. of various mills and reduction plants in Ireland, Colo., Russia, etc.; aided in the development of the Thomas Basic Steel Process in Eng. and introduced it in the U.S. and finally sold it to the Bessemer Assn. Home: New York, N.Y. Deceased.

MAYNARD, POOLE, cons. geologist and technologist; b. Baltimore, Feb. 15, 1883; s. Albert and Emma Dorsey (Poole) M.; A.B., Johns Hopkins Univ., 1905, Ph.D., 1909; married; children—Mary Cary, Albert. Student asst. in economic geology, Johns Hopkins, 1905-09; mem. Md. Geol. Survey and Va. Geol. Survey, 1905-09; spl. employment U.S. Geol. Survey, 1907; asst. state geologist, Ga. Geol. Survey, 1909-12; cons. geologist Central of Ga. Ry., 1912-24; industrial geologist, Atlanta, Birmingham and Coast R.R. since 1925, Atlantic Coast Line R.R. since 1938; vice pres. Maynard Furniture Co., Belton, S.C.; adviser in non-metallics to U.S. Bur. of Mines since 1939, also cons. engr.; established bus. as cons. geologist, 1912, particular reference to industrial processes in non-metallics; originated patents for manufacture heavy clay vitrified products from slag and clay. Coloring of burned clay granules by precipitation of colors; collaborator in patents and processes for concentration of bauxites, for mfr. of magnesia and other chem. products from dolomite; first to recover potash commercially from shales and to locate in Ga. bentonites, roofing slates. Some time fellow Geol. Soc. of America, A.A.A.S.; mem. Am. Inst. Mechanical Engineers, Paleontol. Soc. America, Society of Economic Geologists, mem. various mining, chem. and ceramic socs., Kappa Alpha (Southern). Democrat. Episcopalian. Author of more than 100 geol. bulls. and papers. Address: 759 Myrtle St. N.E., Atlanta, Ga. Died Aug. 22, 1952; buried West View Cemetery, Atlanta.

MAYNARD, SAMUEL TAYLOR, horticulturist; b. Hardwick, Mass., Dec. 6, 1844; s. William and Sarah (Nourse) M.; grad. Mass. Agrl. Coll., 1872, and became connected with the college and the Mass. Expt. Sta.; prof. botany and horticulture, Mass. Agrl. Coll., 1879—; botanist and pomologist Mass. State Bd. of Agr.; dir. hort. div., Mass. Expt. Sta. Sec. Mass. Fruit Growers' Assn.; mem. sch. bd. of Amherst, 8 yrs. Author: Practical Fruit Grower, 1886; Landscape Gardening as Applied to Home Decoration, 1899; Successful Fruit Culture, 1902; The Small Country Home, 1907. Asso. editor Suburban Life, Boston. Hort. specialist and landscape gardener, 1907—. Home: Northboro, Mass. Died 1923.

MAYO, CHARLES HORACE, surgeon; b. Rochester, Minn., July 19, 1865; s. William Worrall (M.D.) and Louise Abigail (Wright) M.; prep. edn., Rochester High Sch., Niles Acad.; M.D., Northwestern U., 1888, M.A., 1904; post-grad. study, N.Y. Polyclinic, N.Y. Post-Grad. Med. Sch.; LL.D., U. of Md., 1909, Kenyon Coll., 1916, Northwestern, 1921, U. of Edinburgh, 1925, Queen's U. (Belfast), 1925, U. of Manchester, 1929, Hamline U., 1930, Carleton Coll., 1932, U. of Minnesota, 1935, U. of Notre Dame, 1936, Villanova Coll., 1937; D.Sc., Princeton, 1917, U. of Pa., 1925, U. of Leeds, 1929; M.Ch., U. of Dublin, 1925; D.P.H., Detroit Coll. Medicine and Surgery, 1927; M.D., U. of Havana, 1930; B.S., Yankton Coll., 1937; F.A.C.S., 1913; F.R.C.S., England, 1920; F.R.C.S., Ireland, 1921; F.R.S.M., London, 1926; m. Edith Graham, 1893; children—Margaret (dec.), Dorothy, Charles William, Edith (Mrs. Fred W. Rankin), Joseph Graham (dec.), Louise (Mrs. George T. Trenholm), Rachel (dec.), Esther (Mrs. John B. Hartzell). Practiced surgery at Rochester, 1888—; with brother, W.J., donated $2,800,000 to establish Mayo Foundation for Med. Edn. and Research at Rochester, in affiliation with U. of Minn.; with brother, in 1919, founded the Mayo Properties Assn., to hold all the properties, endowments and funds of the Mayo Clinic and to insure permanency of the instn. for public service; now surgeon and associate chief of staff Mayo Clinic; surgeon to St. Mary's, Colonial and Worrall hosps.; professor surgery Med. Sch., U. of Minn., 1919-36, and prof. surgery Grad. Sch., U. of Minn. (Mayo Foundation), 1915-36, emeritus. Member State Bd. of Health and Vital Statistics, Minn., 1900-02; health officer, Rochester, 1912-37; v.p. Rochester School Bd., 1915-23. Apptd. 1st lt. Med. R.C., Army of U.S., 1913; served as maj., later col., 1917-19; chief consultant (alternating with brother William J.) for all surg. services, Office of Surgeon Gen., 1917-19; rec'd hon. discharge from army, Feb. 28, 1919; apptd. brig. gen. Med. O.R.C., Army of U.S., 1921; brig. gen. Med. Dept., Army of U.S., 1926, and brig. gen. Auxiliary Army of U.S., 1931. Awarded certificate Council of Nat. Defense, 1919; D.S.M. (U.S.), 1920; Officer l'Ordre Nat. de la Légion d'Honneur (France), 1925; Officer l'Instruction Publique et des Beaux Arts (France), 1925; Cross Comdr. Royal Order Crown of Italy, 1932; letter of commendation, Minn. State Med. Assn., 1934; and from Northwestern U. Alumni Assn., in recognition of worthy achievement, 1934; citation for distinguished service given by nat. orgn. Am. Legion; commemorative plaque presented by Pres. of United States in person, 1934; certificate in recognition of service to U. of Minn. and to State as prof. of surgery, 1936; bronze medal presented by Interstate Post Grad. Med. Assn. of North America for contributions to scientific medicine, 1936. Fellow or mem. numerous scientific and non-scientific organizations in U.S. and fgn. countries. Services to scientific and non-scientific periodicals—Anales de Cirugia la Habana, Cuba (fgn. collaborator), Archives of Clin. Cancer Research (editorial bd. 1924-32), Gaceta Medica Española (del. in U.S. 1926-30; internat. patron in U.S., 1931—), Internat. Clinics (collaborating editor 1907-33), Narkose Und Anaesthesie (contbr. 1928), Nosokomien (editorial bd.), The Ency. Britannica (mem. advisory bd.). Trustee Carleton Coll., Northwestern U. Ind. Democrat. Mason. Home: Rochester, Minn. Died May 26, 1939.

MAYO, FREDERICK JOSEPH, engring. exec.; b. New Haven, July 11, 1906; s. Frederick Alfred and Helen (Rochford) M.; student Georgetown U., 1924-26; C.E., Rensselaer Poly. Inst., 1930; m. Margery Jane Hart, Dec. 2, 1939; children—Susan Jane, Sandra Hart, Margery Ann. Jr. engr. N.Y. State Dept. Pub. Works, 1930-32; engring., adminstrn. teaching, 1932-34, U.S. Govt., 1934-38; cons. engr. Haller Engring. Associates, Cambridge, Mass., 1938-41; engr. F. H. McGraw & Co., Bermuda, 1941-42, project mgr., 1942-43; gen. mgr. Continental Indsl. Development Co. (subsidiary F. H. McGraw & Co.), Rio de Janeiro, Brazil, 1943-45, v.p. charge fgn. operations and N.Y. office, 1946-51, v.p., 1946-54, dir., 1949-72, exec. v.p., 1954-72; corporate officer, project mgr. Atomic Energy Plant, Paducah, Ky., 1951-54; dir., v.p. F. H. McGraw & Co. of Can., Ltd., 1947-58; pres. The Ingalls Shipbuilding Corp., Pascagoula, Miss., 1959-61, pres., 1959-66, chief exec. officer, treas., 1961-72, chairman bd., 1966-72, dir.; vice pres. Litton Industries, Inc., Beverly Hills, Cal.; exec. vice pres. Am. Export Isbrandtsen Co., 1967-72, also dir. Mem. Conn. Soc. Profl. Engrs., Assn. Iron and Steel Engrs., Navy League. Clubs: Metairie Country (New Orleans); Wykagyl Country (New Rochelle, N.Y.); Bel Air Country (Beverly Hills, Cal.); Canadian (N.Y.C.); Propeller of U.S.; Pascagoula Country. Home: Puako HI Died June 1972.

MAYO, NELSON SLATER, veterinarian; b. Calhoun County, Mich., Nov. 16, 1866; s. Perry and Mary Ann (Bryant) M.; B.S., Mich. State Agrl. Coll., 1888, M.S., 1890; D.V.S., Chicago Vet. Coll., 1889; grad. work, Cornell U., 1897-98; honorary degree University of Havana, Cuba, 1944; m. Mary Lucy Carpenter, July 30, 1890; children— Marguerite, Donald (dec.), Dorothy (dec.), Robert, Mary Louise. Asst. veterinarian Mich. Agrl. Expt. Sta., 1888-90; prof. veterinary science, Kan. State Agrl. Coll., 1890-97, Conn. Agrl. Coll., 1897-1901, Kan. State Agrl. Coll., 1901-04; vice dir. Cuban Agrl. Expt. Sta. and chief Dept. Animal Industry, Republic of Cuba, 1904-09; prof. animal husbandry and vet. science, Va. Poly. Inst., Blacksburg, 1909-13; mgr. vet. dept. Abbott Labs., Chicago, 1913-30, now retired. Mem. Am. Vet. Med. Assn. (sec. 1913-15), Phi Delta Theta. Episcopalian. Mason. Clubs: Illinois, Spanish American (Chicago). Author: Diseases of Animals, 1903. Devised and introduced an arsenical solution for destruction of cattle ticks. Home: 600 Mulberry Pl., Highland Park, Ill. Died July 5, 1958; buried Lake Orion, Mich.

MAYO, WILLIAM BENSON, mech. engr.; b. Chatham, Mass., Jan. 7, 1866; s. Andrew Benson and Amanda (Nickerson) M.; ed. pub. schs. and pvt. training; m. Susan Harratt Dana, Jan. 8, 1891. With Hooven-Owens-Reutschler Co., steam engines, mfrs., Hamilton, O., 25 yrs., chief engr. 10 yrs., gen. mgr., v.p. 10 yrs.; chief engr. Ford Motor Co. 1913-33; gen. mgr. Dept. of Street Rys., City of Detroit 2 yrs.; chmn. exec. bd. Detroit Motorbus Co.; pres. Chicago, Duluth and Georgian Bay Transit Co.; v.p. General Machinery Co. of Hamilton, O.; dir. United Aircraft Co., Hartford, Conn.; also officer or dir. other cos. Trustee Antioch College for 8 yrs. Mem. Am. Soc. Mech. Engrs., Detroit Engring. Soc., Detroit Aviation Soc. (pres.), Mich. State Board Aeronautics (pres.). Episcopalian. Mason, Elk. Clubs: Detroit, Detroit Athletic, Recess, Country; Bloomfield Hills Golf (Birmingham, Mich.); Engineers' (New York). Home: 1457 Seminole Av., Detroit, Mich. Died Jan. 31, 1944. *

MAYO, WILLIAM JAMES, surgeon; b. Le Sueur, Minn., June 29, 1861; s. William Worrall (M.D.) and Louise Abigail (Wright) M.; prep. edn. Rochester High Sch. and Niles Acad.; M.D., U. of Mich., 1883, hon. A.M., 1890; Certificated N.Y. Post Grad. Med. Sch., 1884; M.D., N.Y. Polyclinic, 1885; F.R.C.S., Edinburgh, 1905, Eng., 1913, Ireland, 1921; F.R.S.M., Eng., 1926; LL.D., U. of Toronto, 1906, U. of Md., 1907, U. of Pa., 1912, McGill U., 1923, U. of Pittsburgh, 1924, Carleton Coll., 1928, U. of Manchester 1929, Temple U., 1930, U. of Aberdeen, Scotland, 1933, U. of Minn., 1935, U. of Notre Dame, 1936, Villanova Coll., Pa., 1937; D.Sc., U. of Mich., 1908, Columbia, 1910, U. of Leeds, 1923, Harvard, 1924, Marquette and Northwestern, 1929, Yankton Coll., S.D., 1937; M.D. in Surgery, U. of Dublin and Trinity College, 1923, U. of Havana, 1929; m. Hattie M. Damon, Nov. 20, 1884; children—Carrie L. (wife of Dr. D. C. Balfour), Phoebe G. (wife of Dr. H. Waltman Walters). Engaged in practice of surgery, Rochester, Minn., 1883—; surgeon Mayo Clinic (St. Mary's Hosp.), 1889—, and asso. chief of staff. With brother donated $2,800,000 to establish Mayo Foundation for Med. Edn. and Research, at Rochester, in affiliation with U. of Minn. First lt. Med. R.C., 1912, maj. Med. O.R.C., 1917; col. M.C. U.S.A., and chief consultant for surg. service, 1917-19; col. M.R.C., 1919, brig. gen. M.O.R.C., 1921; brig. general Auxiliary Res., 1926-31. Awarded gold medal Nat. Inst. Social Sciences, 1918; D.S.M. (U.S.), 1919; certificate Council Nat. Defense, 1919; Henry Jacob Bigelow gold medal of Boston Surg. Soc., 1921; Comdr. Royal Order of Northern Star (Sweden), 1927; Finlay Congressional D.S.M. (Republic of Cuba), 1929; gold medal A.M.A., 1930; Cross of Royal Order of Knight Commander of the Crwon of Italy, 1932; special award for distinguished service to science, Sigma Xi (chapter U. of Minn.), 1933; letter of commendation, Minn. State Med. Assn., 1934; citation for distinguished service presented by Nat. Comdr. Am. Legion; commemorative plaque presented by President of U.S. in person, 1934; Scroll of Distinguished Service, Gen. Alumni Assn. U. of Minn., 1935. Regent U. of Minn., 1907—; elector, Hall of Fame, 1920—. Mem. numerous Am. and foreign scientific societies. Home: Rochester, Minn. Died July 28, 1939.

MAYOR, ALFRED GOLDSBOROUGH, zoölogist; b. Frederick, Md., Apr. 16, 1868; s. Prof. Alfred M. and Katherine Duckett (Goldsborough) M.; M.E., Stevens Inst. Tech., 1889; S.D., Harvard, 1897; m. Harriet Randolph, d. late Prof. Alpheus Hyatt, of Cambridge, Mass., Aug. 27, 1900. Asst. to Dr. Alexander Agassiz, 1892-1900; in charge radiates, Mus. Comparative Zoölogy, Harvard, 1895-1900; curator of natural sciences and curator-in-chief, 1900-04, hon. curator, 1904—, Brooklyn Inst. Museum; dir. Marine Lab., Carnegie Instn., Tortugas, Fla., 1904-05; dir. dept. of marine biology, Carnegie Instn., Washington, 1905—. On scientific expdns. as asst. to Dr. A. Agassiz, Bahamas, 1892-93, Australia, 1896, Fiji Islands, 1897; cruise of "Albatross" through tropical Pacific, 1899-1900; Dry Tortugas, Fla., 1897, 98, 99, 1902, 08; Torres Straits, and New Guinea, 1913; Samoa, 1917-20; Naples Zoöl. Sta. Lecturer biology, Princeton U., 1913. Fellow and patron New York Zoöl. Society. Author: Medusae of the World, 3 vols., 1910; Navigation illustrated by diagrams, 1918. Home: Princeton, N.J. Deceased.

MCADIE, ALEXANDER GEORGE, (mak'a-de), meteorologist; b. N.Y. City, Aug. 4, 1863; s. John and Anne (Sinclair) M.; A.B., Coll. City of New York, 1881, A.M., 1884; A.M., Harvard, 1885 hon. M.S., Santa Clara Coll.; m. Mary Randolph Browne, Oct. 7, 1893. In Physical Lab., U.S. Signal Office, 1886-87; fellow in physics and lecturer in meteorology, Clark U., Worcester, Mass., 1889-90; Weather Bur., Washington, 1891-95; local forecast official, New Orleans, 1898; forecast official, San Francisco, 1899; prof. meteorology, U.S. Weather Bur., 1903-13; A. Lawrence Rotch prof. meteorology, Harvard U., and dir. Blue Hill Obs. since 1913. Hon. lecturer U. of Calif. Lt. comdr. U.S.N.R.F. and sr. aerographic officer overseas, 1918. Mem. Astron. Society Pacific (pres. 1912), Seismol. Soc. America (pres. 1914), Am. Antiquarian Soc.; fellow Am. Acad. Arts and Sciences. Author: Principles of Aerography; Climatology of California; Rainfall of California; The Fogs and Clouds of San Francisco; The Winds of Boston; The Ephebic Oath; Wind and Weather; Cloud Atlas; Making the Weather; War Weather Vignettes; Man and Weather; Clouds, Airgraphics, Fog; also bulletins and pamphlets on meteorol. subjects, especially lightning, frost, fog and scientific units. Home: 3533 Chesapeake Av., Hampton, Va. Address: Blue Hill Observatory, Milton, Mass. Died Nov. 1, 1943.

MCALLISTER, ADDAMS STRATTON, (mak-al'is-ter), engineer; b. Covington, Va., Feb. 24, 1875; s. Abraham Addams and Julia Ellen (Stratton) M.; B.S. (1st honors), Pa. State Coll., 1898, E.E., 1900; M.M.E. (1st honors), Cornell U., 1901, Ph.D., 1905; m. Homé C. Stephens, Jan. 28, 1922; children—Julia Adeline, Homé Stephens, Lydia Addams, Addams Stratton, Sarah Billopp. Served as elec. engr. with Berwind-White Coal Mining Co., 1898, Westinghouse Electric & Mfg. Co., 1899; asst. in physics, Cornell U., 1901, instr., 1902-03, acting asst. prof. elec. engring., 1903-04; asso. editor Electrical World, 1905-12, editor, 1912-15; professorial lecturer on elec. engring., Pa. State Coll., 1909-14. Was mem. Engring. Council's War Com. of Tech. Socs. of U.S. Naval Consulting Bd.; sec. Am. Engring. Service of Engring. Council; mem. divisional com. on lighting of com. on labor of advisory commn. Council Nat. Defense; chmn. elec. engring. service com., and bd. examiners, etc. of Am. Inst. E.E. Became associated with progress sect. of control bureau, Ordnance Dept., Washington, and later head of reports branch of progress sect., Apr. 1918; sec. bd. of army ordnance officers to review the arty. program, 1918. Elec. engr. Nat. Bur. Standards, 1921; acting sec. Am. Engring. Standards Com., 1921; liaison officer Bur. of Standards and Federal Specifications Bd. with Am. Engring. Standards Com., New York, 1922-23; engr.-physicist Bur. of Standards, Washington, since 1923, chief div. of specifications, 1929, asst. dir., 1930-45; technical liaison officer, Department of Commerce and Federal Specifications Exec. Com., 1939-45; secretary Sect. Com. on Rating of Elec.

Machinery, 1921-28; mem. U.S. Nat. Com., Internat. Electrotech. Commn., 1924-27; mem. Council, Am. Standards Assn., 1930-45; pres. A. A. McAllister & Sons, Pounding Mill Water Supply Co.; pres. McAllister & Bell, Covington, Va. Fellow A.A.A.S.; member Illuminating Engineering Society (dir. 1910-11; pres. 1914-15; chmn. N.Y. Sect. 1917-18; chmn. edit. and pub. com., 1920-22); fellow Am. Inst. E.E. (mgr. 1914-17, v.p. 1917-18, chmn. pub. com., 1921-22); mem. Nat. Geneal. Soc. (pres. 1924-28), Geneal. Soc. Pa., Huguenot Soc. Pa., Hist. Soc. Pa., Baronial Order of Runnymede (a surety and mem. Court of Eligibility, 1923-28), Abracadabra Club of Washington (pres. 1932-34), N.Y. State Soc. of Washington, First Families of Va., Virginia Soc. of Washington, Southern Soc. of Washington, Huguenot Soc. of Washington (dir. 1932-35), Phi Kappa Phi, Sigma Xi, Eta Kappa Nu, Tau Beta Pi. Genealogist of Nat. Soc. Americans of Royal Descent, 1929-45. Clubs: Federal (hon.), Cleveland Park of Washington (pres. 1930). Author: Alternating Current Motors (4 editions), 1906; Standard Handbook for Electrical Engineers (3 edits.), 1907; The Descendants of John Thomson, 1917. Directed compilation of the Nat. Directory of Commodity Specifications (pub. by the U.S. Dept. of Commerce), 1925, 32, 45; Standards Year Book, 1927-33; Directory of Commercial Testing and Coll. Research Laboratories, 1927; Standards and Specifications in the Wood-Using Industries, 1927; Standards and Specifications of Non-Metallic Minerals, 1930; Standards and Specifications for Metals and Metal Products, 1933; Directory of Federal Government Testing Laboratories, 1929, 35. Contbr. about 100 original articles on engring. subjects to tech. press; inventor alternating current machinery. First to propound and formulate the law of conservation as applied to illuminating engring. calculations. Home: Rosedale, Covington, Va. Died Nov. 26, 1946.

MCALLISTER, CHARLES ALBERT, engineer; b. Dorchester, N.J., May 29, 1867; s. William and Abagail Ann (Shute) M.; M.E., Cornell U., 1887; m. Adelaide Kenyon, Mar. 6, 1907; 1 dau., Clara A. Apptd. 2d asst. engineer, U.S.R.C.S., June 30, 1892; commd. 1st asst. engineer, June 6, 1895, chief engr., Apr. 13, 1902, engineer-in-chief, Mar. 9, 1916, U.S. Coast Guard; retired, July 12, 1919. V.p. Am. Bur. of Shipping, 1919-26, president, 1926—. Passed assistant engr. U.S.N., on board U.S. Flagship Philadelphia, in Spanish-Am. War. Mem. jury awards, machinery, San Francisco Expn., 1915. Episcopalian. Author: The Professor on Shipboard, 1902; McAndrew's Floating School, 1913. Delegate to Internat. Conf. on Safety at Sea, London, 1929. Home: New York, N.Y. Died Jan. 6, 1932.

MCALPINE, KENNETH, naval officer; b. Portsmouth, Va., Aug. 16, 1860; grad. U.S. Naval Acad., 1881. Promoted asst. engr., July 1, 1883; passed asst. engr., Sept. 12, 1893; transferred to the line as lt., Mar. 3, 1899; lt. comdr., Mar. 21, 1905; comdr., June 24, 1909; capt., Mar. 4, 1911. Served on Texas, Spanish-Am. War, 1898, Monadnock, 1905-06, at Naval Sta., Cavite, P.I., 1906, on Ohio, 1906; duty at Navy Yard, Norfolk, Va., 1906-08; fleet engr., Atlantic Fleet, 1908; at Navy Yard, Norfolk, 1908-09; apptd. insp. machinery, Newport News, Va., Nov. 16, 1909. Home: Portsmouth, Va.

MCALPINE, WILLIAM H(ORATIO), cons. engr.; b. Lawrence, Mass., Aug. 22, 1874; s. William Taylor and Caroline (Lothrop) McA.; B.S., Mass. Inst. Tech., 1896; m. Mary Dudley Gray, Mar. 3, 1906 (dec.); 1 dau., Carolyn Lothrop (Mrs. Joseph Neave Field); m. 2d, Regina Walsh, Aug. 31, 1943. With U.S. Corps of Engrs., 1902-54, chief engring. div., 1934-44, spl. asst. to chief of engrs., 1944-54, ret. 1954; cons. engr. Recipient award for exceptional civilian service, U.S. War Dept., 1946. Mem. Am. Soc. C.E. (hon.), Soc. Am. Mil. Engrs., Permanent Internat. Assn. Navigation Congresses. Address: 4607 Connecticut Av., Washington 8. Died Nov. 1, 1956; buried Mount Olive Cemetery, Washington.

MCALPINE, WILLIAM JARVIS, civil engr.; b. N.Y.C., Apr. 30, 1812; s. John and Elizabeth (Jarvis) McA.; m. Sarah Learned, Feb. 24, 1841. Asso. with John B. Jervis in constrn. Carbondale R.R., 1827-36; chief engr. eastern div. Erie Canal, 1836-44; chief engr. govt. dry dock, Bklyn., 1845-49; designer and builder Albany (N.Y.) Water Works, 1850-51; state engr., ry. commr. State of N.Y., 1852-57; chief engr. Erie R.R., 1856-57, Chgo. & Galena (later Northwestern) R.R., 1857, Ohio & Miss. R.R., 1861-64; chief engr. 3d Av. drawbridge over Harlem River, N.Y.C., 1860-61; chief or cons. engr. for many gt. bridge projects including Eads Bridge over the Mississippi at St. Louis, 1865, Clifton Suspension Bridge at Niagara, 1868, Washington Bridge, N.Y.C., 1885-88; supt. constrn. N.Y. State Capitol, Albany; engr. for N.Y.C. parks, built Riverside Dr.; pres. Am. Soc. C.E., 1870, named hon. mem., 1889; 1st Am. elected mem. Instn. Civil Engrs. (Gt. Britain); recipient Telford medal for paper "The Supporting Power of Piles." Died New Brighton, R.I., Feb. 16, 1890.

MCARDLE, THOMAS EUGENE, physician; b. Washington, Apr. 12, 1852; s. Owen and Ann (Toumey) M.; A.B., U. of St. Mary, Baltimore, 1875, A.M., 1879; M.D., Georgetown U., 1879; m. Marion V. Thompson, of Washington, June 14, 1888. Asst. editor Walsh Retrospect, 1880-81; editor and pub. National Medical Review since 1898. Contbr. many articles to med. jours. Mem. Washington Acad. of Sciences, A.M.A. Address: Hotel Everett, Washington, D.C.

MCARTHUR, WILLIAM POPE, hydrographer, naval officer; b. St. Genevieve, Mo., Apr. 2, 1814; s. John and Mary (Linn) McA.; m. Mary Stone Young, May 3, 1838. Apptd. midshipman U.S. Navy, 1832; served in Seminole War of 1837-38; took part in Gulf Coast Survey, 1840; promoted lt., 1841; in command of hydrographic party that made 1st survey of Pacific Coast, 1848. Died on ship Oregon while returning from coast survey duties, Panama, Dec. 23, 1850.

MCBAIN, JAMES WILLIAM, chemistry; b. Chatham, N.B., Can., Mar. 22, 1882; s. James Afleck Fraser (D.D.) and Mary Morrison (Quin) McB.; B.A., U. of Toronto, 1903, M.A., 1904; student U. of Leipzig, 1904-05; Ph.D., U. of Heidelberg, 1906; hon. D.Sc., Brown U., 1923, U. of Bristol, England, 1928; m. Mary Evelyn Laing, Jan. 1, 1929; children—Janet Quin, John Keith. Lecturer in physical chemistry, U. of Bristol, 1906-19, Leverhulme prof. in physical chemistry, 1919-26; visiting prof., U. of California, 1926; professor of chemistry, Stanford, 1927-47, professor emeritus, 1947—. Awarded Davy medal, Royal Society, 1939. Director National Chemical Laboratory, Poona, India, 1949-52. Fellow Royal Society, Royal Institute Chemistry; member American Chem. Soc. (Counselor at large Calif. sect.), Am. Assn. Univ. Profs., Nat. Inst. Social Sciences, Chem. Soc. (British), Bunsen Gesellschaft, Faraday Soc. (hon. life mem., v.p. 26-29), Soc. of Rheology (v.p. 1946), Association of University Teachers of Great Britain (pres. 1922-23), Bristol University Alumni Assn. (pres. 1923-26), Rotary Internat (pres. Palo Alto club 1933, Poona Club 1952), Sigma Xi, Alpha Chi Sigma, Phi Lambda Upsilon (hon.), Gamma Alpha. Presbyn. Mason. Clubs: Commonwealth, Bohemian (San Francisco). Editor, Journal of Colloid Science; assisted O.S.R.D., N.A.C.A. and W.P.B. (Rubber Reserve) during World War II; invited guest from U.S.A. to 220th Anniversary celebration of the Acad. of Scis. of U.S.S.R. Author: The Sorption of Gases and Vapours by Solids, 1931; Textbook of Colloid Science, 1949. Contbns. to chem. jours. Home: Stanford University, Cal. Died Mar. 12, 1953; buried Palo Alto, Cal.

MCBEE, EARL THURSTON, chemist; b. Braymer, Mo., July 6, 1906; s. William and Lydia (Post) McB.; A.B., William Jewell Coll., 1929; M.S., Purdue U., 1931, Ph.D., 1936; m. 2d, Viola Renolds, Feb. 15, 1962; children—Beverly Ann, Robert Earl. Prof., Purdue U., 1943, alumni research counselor, 1944-73, head dept. of chemistry, 1949, Shreve prof. indsl. chemistry, 1967-73, ofcl. investigator Nat. Def. Research Com., 1942-43; research cons. U.S. Engr. Office, Madison Square Area, 1945; chmn. adv. bd. U.S. Naval Propellant Plant, 1953-73; chmn. bd., pres., chief exec. officer Great Lakes Chem. Corp.; pres. Ark. Chems., Inc., Bromet Co. Received Modern Pioneer award Nat. Assn. Mfrs., 1940; Certificate of Effective Service in Prodn. of Atomic Bomb, 1945; Certificate of Effective Service in Prosecution of 2d World War, 1945; Ann. Sigma Xi Research award, 1946. Fellow Ind. Acad. Sci., N.Y. Acad. Sci.; mem. Am. Chem. Soc. (chmn. Purdue sect. 1942-43, councilor 1944-45), Mfg. Chemists Assn. (dir.), Am. Inst. Chemists (dir.), Ind. Chem. Soc., A.A.A.S., Sigma Xi, Phi Lambda Upsilon, Alpha Kappa Lambda, Alpha Chi Sigma. Mason (32 deg.), Elk. Clubs: Chemists, Rotary Internat. Contbr. articles to profl. jours. and periodicals, also to publs. Manhattan Project Tech. Series. Home: West Lafayette IN Died Jan. 1973; buried West Lafayette IN

MCBRYDE, CHARLES NEIL, bacteriologist; b. Albemarle County, Va., Feb. 2, 1872; s. John McLaren and Cora (Bolton) M.; B.S., U. of S.C., 1891; M.S., Va. Poly. Inst., 1892; M.D., Johns Hopkins, 1897; Ph.D., George Washington U., 1911; m. Virginia Abbey Sweigard, Sept. 2, 1933. Apptd. interne Johns Hopkins Hosp., 1897 (resigned); bacteriologist, 1901, Biochemic Div., U.S. Dept. Agr., in charge bacteriol. investigations, meats and meat-food products, 1909-16. In charge Exptl. Sta., U.S. Dept. Agr., Ames, Ia., 1928-42. Apptd. chief Biochemic Div., U.S. Dept. Agr., Washington, Nov. 1, 1935 (declined); engaged in research work in the field of animal diseases; retired, 1942. Mem. Sigma Xi, Phi Kappa Phi, Sigma Nu. Club: University (Winter Park, Fla.). Author of numerous papers dealing with diseases of animals and with questions connected with the canning and preservation of meats. Address: Blacksburg VA

MCBRYDE, JAMES BOLTON, chemist; b. Buckingham Co., Va., Sept. 2, 1866; s. John McLaren and Cora (Bolton) M.; bro. of John McLaren M., Jr.; A.B., S.C. Coll., 1886; C.E., U. of S.C., 1888; m. Mary Read Comfort, Aug. 8, 1905. Asst. chemist, S.C. Agrl. Expt. Stas., 1888-91; asst. chemist, 1891-94, and chemist, 1894-1901, Tenn. Agrl. Expt. Sta.; asst. prof. chemistry, 1905-07, prof., 1907—, head of dept., 1915—, Va. Poly Inst. Author (with W.H. Beall): The Chemistry of the Cotton Plant. Home: Blacksburg, Va. Died July 2, 1925.

MCBRYDE, WARREN HORTON, engr., industrialist; Mobile, Ala., Jan. 20, 1876; s. Thomas Calvin and Julia Pierce (Horton) McB.; B.S. in Engring., Ala. Poly. Inst., 1897; LL.D., U. of Santa Clara, 1948; m. Abbie Ford White, Feb. 15, 1905; children—Lucile, Janet (Mrs. James A. Orser), Warren H., Jr. (dec.). Began with Electric Lighting Co., Mobile, Ala., 1897-98; asst. resident engr., Northern Calif., Yuba Elec. Power Co., asst. supt. Peyton Chem. Co., San Francisco and Martinez, asst. to chief engr. Calif. Gas & Elec. Co. (now Pacific Gas & Elec. Co.), 1899-1903; resident engr. E. I. duPont de Nemours & Co., Rapauno plant, Gibbstown, N.J., 1903-05, placed in charge all engring. and constrn. in Calif., 1905, asst. supt. Hercules plant (dynamite and TNT) throughout World War I; asst. to gen. mgr., sec. of the co., and handler engring. problems Calif. and Hawaiian Sugar Refining Co., 1919-27; cons. engr., San Francisco, since 1927. Served with U.S. Lighthouse Dept. and Corps of Engrs., Ft. Morgan, Ala., also chief electrician U.S. Army Transport Sheridan, Spanish-Am. War, 1898-99; served with War Dept., Washington, redesigning mech. equipment Army constrn. program, later standardizing designs and approving plans Army Ordnance and Chem. Warfare Service projects, also chief cons. mech. engr. and chief consultant munitions plants, 1941-42; chief of engring, div. U.S. Army Transportation Corps, 1942-44; subsequently cons. Transportation Corps, U.S. Army, and cons. Army-Navy Explosives Safety Bd., also mem. adv. council Indsl. Coll. Armed Forces. Mem. adv. bd. Richmond (Calif.) branch of Am. Trust Co. Mem. permanent com. Sacramento-San Joaquin Rivers Problems Conf. since 1924; mem. bldg. com. Grade Cathedral, Episcopal, San Francisco; pres. Contra Costa County C. of C.; mem. San Francisco Area Council Boy Scouts America; mem. adv. bd. Salvation Army. Trustee Mech. Inst. Library (San Francisco); mem. adv. bd. Coll. of Engring., U. of Santa Clara. Fellow Am. Soc. M.E. (pres. 1939-40); mem. Newcomen Soc. (vice chmn. Pacific Coast com.). Kappa Alpha, Tau Beta Pi. Republican. Mason. Clubs: Bohemian, Rotary, Commonwealth, Corinthian Yacht (San Francisco). Made 3 circumnavigations of globe, vis. all continents, some 80 countries, 1929-39. Office: 405 Montgomery St., San Francisco CA

MCBURNEY, JOHN WHITE, (mak-bur'ne), cons. masonry materials; b. Sumner, Wash., May 30, 1890; s. Elmer J. and Lena (McBurney) White; name changed to McBurney when adopted by maternal grandparents; ed. public schools, Cambridge, O.; A.B., Ohio State U., 1913; student George Washington University, 1916-17; D.Sc., Marietta College, 1952; m. Mary Theresa Marshall, June 6, 1913; 1 son, John Taggart. Sanitary bacteriologist U.S. Public Health Service, 1913-18; chemist Youngstown Sheet Tube Co., 1918-21; engineer tests Cleveland Board Education, 1921-24; technical service dept. Standard Paint Co., 1924-26; research asso. at Nat. Bur. Standards for Brick Mfrs. Assn., 1926-32, for Asphalt Tile Mfrs. Assn., 1932-34; rep. Am. Standards Assn. at Nat. Bureau of Standards, 1934-35; senior technologist Nat. Bur. of Standards since 1935; in charge of research in masonry materials, 1935-52, cons. on masonry and masonry materials, 1952-56; ind. cons. 1956—; liaison Nat. Bur. Standards, Nat. Inventor's Council, 1942-45; liaison Nat. Bur. Standards and Office Tech. Service also Housing and Finance Agency 1946-49, F.T.C. 1952-54. Fellow A.A.A.S., Am. Inst. Chemists, Am. Ceramic Soc.; mem. D.C. Soc. Profl. Engrs., Nat. Inst. Ceramic Engineers, British Ceramic Society, Construction Specifications Institute, Standards Engineers Society, American Concrete Inst., Soc. Chem. Industry, Washington Acad. Science, Washington Philos. Soc., Am. Soc. Testing Materials (chmn. com. on mortar 1937-44; chmn. sub-com. on building brick of com. on masonry units, 1937-49, cons. mem. 1950, award of merit, 1956), Am. Standards Assn. (secretary com. on masonry 1934-56; sec. com. on plastering 1935-53). Phi Kappa Tau, Keramos. Clubs: Cosmos, Chemists (N.Y. City). Contbr. articles to tech. jours. and reports to professional socs. Address: 4607 Connecticut Av. N.W., Washington 8. Died Oct. 6, 1961.

MCBURNEY, RALPH, bacteriologist; b. Alexandria, Va., Aug. 9, 1883; s. George and Alice (Dienelt) McB.; B.S. in Chemistry, Va. Poly. Inst., 1908; M.S., Okla. Agrl. and Mech. Coll., 1916; student U. of Ala., 1925-27; M.D., Rush Med. Coll. (U. of Chicago), 1929; M.P.H., Harvard Sch. of Pub. Health, 1931; m. Hazel Powers, Aug. 18, 1914; children—George William, Robert Powers, Charles Walker. Began as chemist Gen. Chem. Co., Baltimore, 1909; instr. chemistry, Okla. A. and M. Coll., 1910-14; instr. bacteriology, Ore. State Coll., 1914-17; asst. prof. bacteriology, U. of Mo., and asst. dir. Mo. State Health Lab., 1919-21; asso. prof. bacteriology and hygiene, U. of Ala., 1921-28, prof. since 1928; prof. and chmn. dept. of bacteriology and clin. pathology, Med. Coll. of Ala., prof. emeritus, 1954—; med. staff Ala. State Hosp. Tuscaloosa, 1954-55; Tuscaloosa (Ala.) County Health Officer, 1955-62, director of clinical laboratory Hale Meml. Tb Hosp., 1962-63, dir. laboratory services, 1963—. Vice chmn. bd. dirs. Hale Meml. Tb Hosp., Tuscaloosa, Ala. Served as lt., capt., Sanitary Corps, A.E.F., 1917-19; capt. Med. Res., U.S. Army. Recipient Distinguished Alumni award Va. Poly. Institute, 1962. Fellow Am. Public Health Assn.; mem. the A.M.A., Tuscaloosa County Medical Society (ex-sec.; ex-pres.); mem. Med.

Assn. of Ala. (former mem. com. on mental hygiene for training of physicians; chairman of the committee for post-graduate study 1936-54), Jefferson County Medical Society, Society of Am. Bacteriologists, Soc. Experimental Biology and Medicine, Ala. Acad. Science, Med. Alumni Assn. of Ala. (past pres.), Am. Legion, Mil. Order World War, Phi Beta Pi, Delta Omega, Alpha Omega Alpha, Sigma Xi, Phi Beta Kappa. Clubs: Kiwanis, Exchange of Tuscaloosa (past pres.). Mason (K.T.). Collaborator: Kracke's Textbook of Clinical Pathology, 1st and 2d edits. and Textbook of Clinical Pathology (by Parker), 4th and 5th edits. (by Miller). Author: Laboratory Manual of Bacteriology and Serology. Contbr. articles to numerous scientific and medical jours. Home: No. 9 Cherokee Hills. Office: Hale Meml. Tb Hosp., Tuscaloosa, Ala. Died June 21, 1964; buried Tuscaloosa Meml. Park.

MCCAFFERY, RICHARD STANISLAUS, (mak kaf'fer-i), mining engr.; b. New York, N.Y., June 2, 1874; s. Michael J. A. (A.M., LL.D.), and Mary (Treacy) McC.; E.M., Sch. of Mines (Columbia), 1896; m. Kathleen Kirwan, Jan. 27, 1897; children—Arthur L., Miriam, Richard S., Agatha G., Philip, John K. Supt. Copper Corp. of Chile, Chanaral, Chile, 1900; supt., 1901-02, mgr., 1905-07, Santa Fe Gold & Copper Mining Co., San Pedro, N.M.; mgr. Salt Lake Copper Co., Utah, 1905-07; general supt. Tintic Smelting Co., Silver City, Utah, 1908; prof. mining and metallurgy, U. of Ida., 1909-14; prof. mining and metallurgy, U. of Wis., 1914-41; now consulting metall. and mining engineer. Member. American Institute Mining Engrs., Canadian Mining Inst., Am. Chem. Soc., Iron and Steel Inst., Soc. Promotion Engring. Edn., Am. Foundrymens' Assn., N.Y. Acad. Sciences; Sigma Psi, Tau Beta Pi. Democrat. Catholic. Home: 235 E. 22d St. Office: 163 W. 94th St., New York, N.Y. Died June 12, 1945.

MCCAIN, DEWEY MARVEN, educator; b. Eupora, Miss., Oct. 22, 1899; s. John Milton and Eliza Missouri (Hood) McC.; B.S., Miss. State Coll., 1921; M.S., U. Tenn., 1924; research Ia. State Coll., summer 1933; m. Virginia Reynolds, June 8, 1933; children—Jane, Charles, William, Susan. Insp. levee constrn. under Maj. T. G. Dabney, 1918-19; gen. hwy. practice, 1921-23, 1925-26; asst. prof. civil engring. Miss. State Coll., 1924-25, head dept. since 1930, asst. dir. engring. and indsl. research sta., 1944-48; design structures Truscon Steel Co., 1926-27; structural engr. U. Miss. bldg. program, 1928-29; dist. engr. Concrete Steel Co., 1929-30; part-time gen. cons. practice, since 1930; engr. Engr. Bd., Ft. Belvoir, Va., summer 1942; cons. Rev. Bd., Army Ground Forces, summer 1943. Acad. Bldg. at Miss. State U. named in his honor, 1966. Fellow Gold Triangle; mem. Am. Soc. C.E., Am. Concrete Inst., Am. Soc. Engring. Edn., Miss. Soc. Profl. Engrs. (Engr. of Year 1964, pres. 1957), Tau Beta Pi, Phi Kappa Phi, Sigma Alpha Epsilon. Methodist. Rotarian. Contbr. profl. jours. Home: 104 Oktibbeha Drive, Starkville, Miss. 39759. Died June 10, 1966; buried Odd Fellows Cemetery, Starkville.

MCCAIN, PAUL PRESSLY, M.D.; b. Due West, S.C., June 26, 1884; s. John Iranaeus and Lula Jane (Todd) McC.; A.B., Erskine Coll., Due West, 1906; M.D., U. of Md., 1911; LL.D., U. of N.C., 1936; m. Sadie Lou McBrayer, Oct. 17, 1917; children—Sarah Louise, Paul Pressly, Lillian Irene, John Lewis, Jane Todd. Interne Bay View Hosp., Baltimore, Md., 1911; resident physician Gaylord Farm Sanatorium, 1912-13; chief of med. service and asst. supt. N.C. Sanatorium, 1914-23, supt., med. dir. and dir. extension dept. since 1924; supt. Western N.C. Sanatorium since 1936; supt. Eastern N.C. Sanatorium since 1941. Trustee Flora Macdonald Coll., Red Springs, N.C. Diplomate American Board Internal Medicine; fellow Am. College Physicians; member subcommittee on tuberculosis National Research Council; member Clin. and Climatol. Assn., Nat. Tuberculosis Assn. (dir., mem. exec. com., 1936-39, v.p. 1938-39, pres. 1940-41), Southern Tuberculosis Conf. (pres.), N.C. Tuberculosis Assn. (dir.; exec. com.), N.C. Med. Soc. (pres. 1935), Sigma Xi. Awarded Moore County medal, N.C. Med. Soc., 1928. Democrat. Presbyterian. Kiwanian. Member editorial bd. N.C. Med. Jour. Address: Sanatorium, N.C. Died Nov. 25, 1946; buried in Bethesda Cemetery, Aberdeen, N.C.

MCCALL, ARTHUR G(ILLETT), soil scientist; b. Buena Vista, O., Nov. 11, 1874; s. Moses D. and Elizabeth (Gillett) McC.; B.S., Ohio State U., 1900; Ph.D., Johns Hopkins, 1916; m. Harriett M. Flower, Dec. 1896; children—Herbert F., Elizabeth L., Dorothy H., Harriett A. Scientist, Bur. of Soils, U.S. Dept. Agr., 1901-04 chief, 1927, chief soil investigations, 1927-36; prof. agronomy and head dept., Ohio State U., 1904-16; prof. geology and soils, U. Md., 1916-27; in charge soil investigations, Md. Expt. Sta., 1916-27; with Soil Conservation Service, 1936—, ret. 1944, but continuing in Govt. Service in cons. capacity. Served with Army Ednl. Corps, U.S. Army, France, 1919. Exec. sec. 1st Internat. Congress Soil Sci. Fellow A.A.A.S., Am. Soc. Agronomy (ex-pres); mem. Assn. Ofcl. Agrl. Chemists, Sigma Xi, Alpha Zeta, Phi Kappa Phi, Gamma Sigma Delta, Alpha Gamma Rho; corr. mem. Czechoslovakian Acad. Soil Sci. Conglist. Club: Cosmos. Author: Physical Properties of the Soil, 1908; Broom Corn Culture, 1912; Studies of Soils, 1915; Studies of Crops, 1916. Home: College Park, Md. Address: 4707 Calvert Rd., College Park, Md. Deceased.

MCCALL, MILTON LAWRENCE, physician; b. Peru, Ind., July 10, 1911; s. Samuel Lawrence and Caroline (Haag) McC.; student U. Minn., 1930-31, 32-33, U. Chgo., summer 1933, Northwestern U., 1934-35; B.S., Ind. U., 1937, M.D., 1939; m. Jane French, Sept. 30, 1944; children—Frances French, Lawrence French. Rotating intern Phila. Gen. Hosp., 1939-41, clin. asst., asst. obstetrician and gynecologist, asso. chief obstetrics and gynecology, 1944-53; resident obstetrics and gynecology Kensington Hosp. for Women, Phila., 1941-43; asso. Dr. Edward A. Schumann, Phila., 1943-50; pvt. practice obstetrics and gynecology, Phila., 1943-53; asst. demonstrator, then instr., asso. and asst. prof. Jefferson Med. Coll., 1944-53; asso. chief obstetrics and gynecology Protestant Episcopal Hosp., Phila.; active staff Kensington Hosp. Women, Chestnut Hill Hosp., Jefferson Hosp., Germantown Hosp., Stetson Hosp., Bryn Mawr Hosp., Florence Crittenton Home, 1944-53 prof., head dept. obstetrics and gynecology La. State U. Sch. Medicine, 1953-59; obstetrician and gynecologist in chief Univ. Unit, sr. vis. surgeon Charity Hosp. of La. at New Orleans, 1953-59, also attending gynecologist Touro Infirmary and So. Bapt. Hosp., New Orleans, cons. obstetrician and gynecologist Sara Mayo Hosp., New Orleans and Lafayette Charity Hosp., Lafayette, La.; prof., chmn. dept. obstetrics and gynecology U. Pitts. Sch. Medicine, 1959—; med. dir., chief-of-staff Magee-Womens Hosp., 1959—; senior staff gynecology Presbyterian-Univ. Hosp., 1959—; cons. gynecologist John J. Kane Hosp., 1959—. Diplomate Am. Bd. Obstetrics and Gynecology. Fellow Am. Gynecol. Soc., A.C.S.; mem. Am. Assn. Obstetricians and Gynecologists, Am. Coll. Obstetricians and Gynecologists, Am. Cancer Soc. (dir. Allegheny County unit 1960-63), Pa. State Med. Soc., Internat. Corrs. Soc. Obstetricians and Gynecologists, Pitts. Obstet. and Gynecol. Soc., Soc. Gynecologic Investigation, Am. Assn. Infant and Maternal Care (dir.), Am. Soc. Study Sterility, Pan Pacific Surgical Association, Assn. Professors of Obstetrics and Gynecology, N.Y. Acad. Sciences, A.M.A., A.A.A.S. Soc. Obstetricians and Gynecologists Can. (hon.), So. (hon.), S.W. (hon.) obstet. and gynecol. socs., S.Atlantic Assn. Obstetricians and Gynecologists (hon.), Alpha Omega Alpha. Nu Sigma Nu. Home: 316 Halket St. Office: Magee-Womens Hosp., Pitts. 13. Died Oct. 8, 1963; buried Allegheny Cemetery, Pitts.

MCCALL, THOMAS MONTGOMERY, edn. exec.; b. McCallsburg, Ia., Dec. 27, 1887; s. John Newton and Olive (Quick) McC.; B.S., Ia. State Coll., 1910; M.S., 1930; m. Blanche Irene Fleetwood, June 12, 1912; children—Donald Thomas, Robert Lowell, Barbara Alice. Asst. instr. horticulture Ia. State Coll., 1910-11; instr. and field supt., horticulturist Northwest Sch. and Sta., U. Minn., 1911-37, acting supt., Crookston, Minn., 1933-34, supt. and prof. Northwest Sch. Agr., since 1937. Pres. Red River Valley Winter Shows since 1937, publicity dir. since 1937. Hon. life mem. Minn. Hort. Soc. Mem. Am. Soc. Hort. Sci. (Great Plains sect.), Minn. Acad. Sci., Red River Valley Livestock Assn. (pres. since 1937), Red River Valley Devel. Assn. (pres. since 1940), C. of C. (agrl. advisor); Alpha Zeta, Delta Sigma Rho. Republican. Mem. Christian Ch. Rotarian (past pres.). Author: Ann. reports of horticulturist Northwest Sch. and Sta.; spl. bulls. Fruit and Garden Handbook for Red River Valley, 1934, Potato Culture and Fertility Practice in Red River Valley, 1926; Root Crops for the R.R. Valley; collaborator Crops and Soils Handbook for the Red River Valley, 1931. Contbr. weekly articles to Red River Valley newspapers on agrl. edn. and results of expt. sta. work, since 1937. Home: Northwest School and Station, Crookston, Minn. Died Mar. 21, 1965.

MCCALLEY, HENRY, chief asst. State geologist of Ala., 1890—; b. Madison Co., Ala., Feb. 11, 1852; s. Thomas Sanford and Caroline Matilda McC.; grad. Univ. of Va., B.S., C.E., M.E., 1875 (A.M., causa honoris, Univ. of Ala., 1878); unmarried. Farmed, 1876; taught school, Demopolis, Ala., 1877; asst. prof. chemistry, Univ. of Ala., 1878-83; surveyed the Warrier River, above Tuscaloosa, Ala., under auspices of War Dept., 1879; chemist to Geol. Survey of Ala. and asst. State geologist, 1883-90. Treas. Ala. Industrial and Scientific Soc., 1890—; fellow Geol. Soc. of America. Home: University, Ala. Died 1904.

MCCALLIE, SAMUEL WASHINGTON, geologist; b. Sevier Co., Tenn., Aug. 2, 1856; s. Andrew Jackson and Theodosia Adeline (Cunningham) McC.; Ph.B., Wesleyan U., Athens, Tenn., 1882; grad. study Johns Hopkins, 1888-90; m. Elizabeth Macfarlane Hanleiter, Dec. 25, 1899; children—Edith Emeline, Mrs. Elizabeth Snoots. Instr. in geology, U. of Tenn., 1891-93; asst. state geologist, Ga., 1893-1908, state geologist, 1908—. Served with Signal Corps, U.S.A., 1882. Mem. advisory bd., Ga. Nat. Defense, World War. Democrat. Presbyn. Author: Mineral Resources of Georgia, 1910, 26; Handbook of Mineral Resources of Georgia, 1911, 3d edit., 1923; Drainage Investigations in Georgia, 1911; Agricultural Drainage in Georgia, 1917. Home: Atlanta, Ga. Died Oct. 26, 1933.

MCCALLUM, DANIEL CRAIG, mil. engr.; b. Johnston, Scotland, Jan. 21, 1815; m. Mary McCann, 3 children. Originator, patentee a type of bridge, 1851; gen. supt. N.Y. & Erie Ry., 1855-56; pres. McCallum Bridge Co., 1858-59; cons. engr. Atlantic & Gt. Western Ry.; apptd. mil. dir., supt. all U.S. railroads, 1862, commd. col. U.S. Army, apptd. aide-de-camp to comdr.-in-chief; brevetted brig. gen., 1864, maj. gen., 1865. Author: The Water Mill and Other Poems, 1870. Died Bklyn., Dec. 27, 1878; buried Mt. Hope Cemetery, Rochester, N.Y.

MCCANN, HAROLD GILMAN, chemist; b. Kittery, Me., Feb. 9, 1916; s. Harold G. and Cora (Hayden) McC.; B.S., Bates Coll., 1937; M.S., Poly. Inst. Bklyn., 1947; m. Virgilyn Richards Mayo, July 16, 1938;children—Harold Gilman III, Dwight Mayo, Kevin Hayden. Analytical and research chemist Gen. Chem. div. Allied Chem. Co., N.Y.C., 1937-50; prin. investigator Nat. Inst. Dental Research, NIH, Bethesda, Md., 1950-59, chief microanalytical lab. Nat. Inst. Arthritis and Metabolic Diseases, 1959-63; mem. staff Forsyth Dental Center, Boston, 1963-69. Mem. Internat. Assn. Dental Research, Am. Chem. Soc., A.A.A.S. Contbr. articles to profl. jours. Patentee in field. Home: Marblehead MA Died Jan. 18, 1969.

MCCANN, WILLIAM SHARP, physician; b. Cadiz, O., July 6, 1889; s. Dr. Charles Fremont and Carolyn (Sharp) McC.; A.B., Ohio State U., 1911, D.Sc., 1934; M.D., Cornell U., 1915; grad. Army Med. Sch., Washington, 1971; LL.D., Hobart and William Smith Colleges, 1954; m. Gertrude Guild Fisher, M.D., Dec. 29, 1916 (deceased); children—Dorothy Elizabeth, William Peter; married 2d, Ella M. Russ, 1957. Surgical house officer, Peter Bent Brigham Hosp., Boston, 1915-16; Arthur Tracy Cabot fellow in surgery, Harvard, 1916-17; instr. in medicine, Cornell U., 1919-21; research fellow, Russell Sage Inst. of Pathology, 1919-21; adj. asst. visiting physician Bellevue Hosp., 1919-21; asso. prof. of medicine, Johns Hopkins, 1921-24; asso. physician Johns Hopkins Hosp., 1921-24; Charles A. Dewey prof. of medicine, University of Rochester, 1924-57, professor emeritus, 1957-71; vis. prof. adminstrv. medicine Sloan Institute of Hospital Administration, Cornell U., Ithaca, N.Y., 1957-59; physician in chief Strong Memorial and Rochester Municipal hosps., 1924-57. Mem. tuberculosis adv. com., N.Y. State Dept. Health; mem. med. adv. com., Masonic Found. for Health and Human Welfare. Served as lt. M.C., U.S. Army, A.E.F., 1917-19; served from comdr. to capt. MC-USNR, 1942-44. Mem. Naval Research Adv. Com., from 1946; dep. chmn. com. on med. scis. Research and Development Board, Dept. of Defense; consultant in Medicine, Veterans Administration, Branch 2, from 1946. Chmn. American Board Internal Medicine, 1947-48; trustee Asso. Universities, Inc., Brookhaven Nat. Lab., 1950. Fellow A.C.P. (regent; master), N.Y. Acad. Medicine; member Assn. Am. Physicians (pres.), A.A.A.S. (v.p., chmn. section N 1952); Soc. for Clin. Investigation, Harvey Society, Society Exptl. Biology and Medicine, A.M.A., Rochester Acad. Medicine, Am. Inst. of Nutrition, American Society Biological Chemists, American Rheumatism Association, Sigma Xi, Alpha Omega Alpha, Phi Beta Kappa; associate member United States Naval Institute United Presbyterian. Mason. Clubs: Oak Hill Country, Cornell, Fortnightly, University (Rochester). Author: Calorimetry in Medicine, 1924. Contbr. many articles to med. jours. Home: Rochester NY Died June 10, 1971; buried Cadiz OH

MCCARROLL, HENRY RELTON, surgeon; b. Walnut Ridge, Ark., Aug. 6, 1905; s. Horace Rudolph and Pearl Jane (Henry) McC.; grad. Walnut Ridge High Sch., 1923; A.B. magna cum laude, Quachita Coll., Arkadelphia, Ark., 1927; M.D. cum laude, Washington U., 1931; m. Nina Elizabeth Snyder, 1934; children—Henry Relton, Sandra Beth, David Lawrence. Intern in surgery Barnes Hosp., St. Louis, 1931-32, asst. resident surgeon, 1932-33; asst. resident in surgery, Billings Hosp., Chgo., 1933-34; resident in surgery Shriners Hosp. for Crippled Children, St. Louis, 1934-37; asst. surgeon Shriners Hosp., St. Louis, 1937-50; with dept. clin. orthodpedic surgery Washington U., 1937-72, asst. prof., 1944-57, asso. prof., 1957-66, prof., 1966-70, prof. orthopedics, dept. surgery, 1970-72, orthopedic staff Barnes, St. Luke's, St. Louis Children's hosps. Served with Officers Res. Corps, Inf. and Medicine, U.S. Army, 1927-39. Received gold medal, with Dr. C. H. Crego, for exhibit on treatment congenital dislocation of hip Am. Acad. Orthopedic Surgeons, 1939; Distinguished Alumnus award Quachita Coll., 1958. Diplomate Am. Bd. Orthopaedic Surgery. Mem. A.M.A. (vice chmn. orthopedic sect. 1952, chmn. 1953, mem. ho. of dels. 1955-60), Am. Acad. Orthopaedic Surgery (pres. 1959-72), Phi Rho Sigma, Sigma Xi, Alpha Omega Alpha. Contbr. articles to Jour. Exptl. Medicine, Proc. of Soc. for Exptl. Biology and Med., Am. Jour. Physiology, Archives of Surgery, Surgery, Gynecology and Obstetrics, Annals of Surgery, Jour. Bone and Joint Surgery (asso. editor 1947-54), Jour. of A.M.A., Jour. Bone and Joint Surgery (trustee 1958-64); mem. editorial bd. Quar. Rev. of Surgery, 1950-72. Baptist. Home: St. Louis MO Died Feb. 27, 1972; buried Oak Grove Cemetery, St Louis MO

MCCARROLL, JAMES, journalist; b. Lanesboro, Ireland, Aug. 3, 1814. Went to Canada, 1831; became editor, owner Peterborough Chronicle, 1845; surveyor Port of Toronto; taught music, became music critic for Toronto Leader and Toronto Colonist; went to N.Y.C.; mem. editorial staff The People's Cyclopedia of Universal Knowledge, The American Cyclopedia; contbr. articles to Belford's Magazine; worked on fire-proof wire gauze and improved elevator. Author: The Adventures of a Night, 1865, Almost a Tragedy, a Comedy, 1874 (both plays); Terry Finnegan Letters, 1864; Madeline and Other Poems, 1889. Died N.Y.C., Apr. 10, 1892.

MCCARROLL, RUSSELL HUDSON, chem. and metall. engr.; b. Detroit, Feb. 20, 1890; s. John and Emily (Roberts) McC.; B.S. in Chem. Engring., U. of Mich., 1914, M.S. in Engring. (hon.), 1937; m. Muriel C. Channer, Sept. 30, 1916; children—Charlotte Jane (Mrs. Charles R. Vincent, Jr.), Marjorie. With Solvay Process Co., Detroit, 1914-15; connected with dept. of chem. and metall. engring., Ford Motor Co., Dearborn Mich., since 1915, in charge of dept. since 1921; became exec. engr., in charge of research, metall. engring., chem. engring. and automotive engring., Ford Motor Co., 1944, now director of chemical and metallurgical engineering and research. Mem. tech. adv. com. automotive div., O.P.M.; mem. sr. tech. adv. com. steel div., O.P.M. Mem. Am. Soc. for Metals, Am. Chem. Soc., Iron and Steel Inst. (London), Soc. of Automotive Engrs., Inc. (mem. tech. bd.; mem. exec. com.; chmn. engring. materials com.), Engring. Soc. Detroit (sec.), Am. Foundrymen's Assn. (bd. dirs.), Soc. for Promotion of Engring. Edn., Detroit Bd. of Commerce Research Com., Tau Beta Pi (trustee). Epsicopalian. Clubs: Dearborn (Mich.) Country (past sec.-treas. and pres.); Detroit Athletic; Orchard Lake Country (Birmingham, Mich.). Contbr. of articles to professional journals. Granted more than 20 metallurgical and engineering patents; has given special attention to experiments designed to widen indsl. uses of farm produced materials. Home: 205 River Lane. Office: Ford Motor Company, Engineering Laboratory, Dearborn, Mich. Died March 31, 1948.

MCCARTHY, JUSTIN HOWARD, engr., paper co. exec.; b. Portsmouth, N.H., Sept. 13, 1894; s. Thomas and Ellen (Moorhead) McC.; B.S., Dartmouth, 1915; C.E., Thayer Sch. Engring., 1916; m. Elsie Johnson, Feb. 5, 1929; children—Justin Howard, James H., Ann E. Pulp and paper industry engr., 1916-68, specializing design and constrn. prodn. units; with St. Regis Paper Co., 1946-68, v.p., chief engr., 1955-57, v.p. engring., 1957-68. Mem. Am. Soc. C.E., Am. Soc. M.E. Home: Jacksonville FL Died June 10, 1968.

MCCARTHY, KENNETH CECIL, physician; b. Niagara Falls, Ont., Can., Aug. 12, 1902; s. George Arnold and Jennie (Moffatt) McC.; student Malvern Collegiate Inst., Toronto, 1915-19; M.B., U. Toronto, 1925, M.D., 1929; m. Elizabeth Caswell, Oct. 20, 1927 (dec. 1937); children—Brian Edward, Patricia, Kathleen, Terrence; m. 2d, Shirley Caswell, Oct. 15, 1940. House surgeon Toronto Western Hosp., 1925-26; gen. med. practice, Maumee, O., 1926-29; asso. with Dr. E. I. McKesson, Toledo, 1929-35; pvt. practice limited to anesthesiology, Toledo, 1935-60; chief anesthesiology sect. U.S. Veteran Administration Hospital, Bay Pines, Florida, 1960—. Served as lt. col., M.C., AUS, 1942-46. Diplomate Am. Bd. Anesthesiology. Fellow Am. Coll. Anesthesiologists; mem. Am. (dir. 1948-53), Ohio (pres. 1940, 50) socs. anesthesiologists, Nat. Med. Vets. Soc. (pres. 1953), A.M.A. (chmn. sect. on anesthesiology). Author articles on anesthesiology in science journals. Home: 16025 Redington Dr., St. Petersburg 8, Fla. Office: U.S. VA Hosp., Bay Pines, Fla. Died Aug. 28, 1964.

MCCARTNEY, WASHINGTON, educator, mathematician, lawyer; b. Westmoreland County, Pa., Aug. 24, 1812; grad. Jefferson Coll., Canonsburg, Pa., 1834; m. Mary E. Maxwell, Apr. 18, 1839. Admitted to bar, 1838; prof. mathematics Lafayette Coll., 1835-36, prof. mathematics, modern lang., 1836-37, prof. mathematics, philosophy, astronomy, 1937-46, trustee of coll., 1847-52, prof. philosophy, 1849-52; dep. atty. gen. Northampton County, Pa., 1846-48; founded, conducted Union Law Sch., 1854-56; pres. judge 3d Pa. Jud. Dist., 1851; mem. Easton (Pa.) Sch. Bd. Author: The Principles of the Differential and Integral Calculus, 1844; Origin and Progress of the United States, 1847. Died July 15, 1856.

MCCARTY, E(DWARD) PROSPER, mining engr.; b. Clifton, Ill., Oct. 1, 1873; s. Andrew F. and Mary (Fogarty) M.; E.M., U. of Minn. Sch. of Mines, 1900; m. Ethel Keefe, of Minneapolis, Sept. 24, 1913; children—Mary Roberta, Jessie Edwarda. Prof. mining, U. of Minn. Sch. of Mines, 1900-17; chief consulting mining engr. to Minn. Tax Commn., 1909-17; consulting mining engr., Minneapolis, 1917-19; mgr. Ajax Mining Co., Biwabik, Minn., 1919-20; prof. mining engring., U. of Wyo., 1920-25; resumed practice as cons. mining engr. Capt. engrs. U.S.A., 1918. Prepared spl. reports on iron mining in Minn., and estimates of iron ore tonnages, 1910, 12, 14, 16. Various papers in trade journals and in Trans. Lake Superior Mining Inst. Mem. Am. Inst. Mining Engrs., Sigma Xi, Tau Beta Pi. Home: 2519 Humboldt Av. S. Office: Roanoke Bldg., Minneapolis MN

MCCASKEY, HIRAM DRYER, geologist; b. Fort Totten, Dak. Ty. (now N.D.), Apr. 10, 1871; s. Major General William Spencer and Eleanor Forsythe (Garrison) M.; B.S. in mining, Lehigh U., Bethlehem, Pa., 1893; M.S. in geology, same univ., 1907; m. Mary Louise Fuller, June 7, 1913. Chemist, Boston & Mont. Smelter, Great Falls, Mont., 1893-95; instr. mathematics, 1895-96, headmaster and instr. English, 1896-98, St. Thomas Hall, Miss.; instr. mathematics and English, St. Matthew's Sch., Calif., 1898-1900; mining engr., Mining Bur., Manila, P.I., 1900-03; chief of the Mining Bur. and of Div. of Mines, Bur. of Science, Manila, 1903-06; fellow in geology, Lehigh U., 1906-07; asst. geologist, 1907-10, geologist, 1911—, chief sect. of metal resources, 1912-19, geologist in charge Div. Mineral Resources, 1915-19, U.S. Geol. Survey. Del. from P.I. to 10th International Geol. Congress, Mexico City, 1906. Exploratory field work in P.I. Reorganized Mining Bur. in P.I.; asstd. in reorgn. of work of U.S. Geol. Survey in metallic mineral resources of U.S. and in charge Nov. 1912-Jan. 1919. U.S. del. Internat. Engring. Congress, San Francisco, 1915, Pan-Am. Scientific Congress, 1917. Home: Central Point, Ore. Died Apr. 26, 1936.

MCCAUSTLAND, ELMER JAMES, prof. civ. engring.; b. Quincy, Wis., Jan. 9, 1864; s. James and Luannia (Winn) M.; B.C.E., Cornell Coll., Ia., 1892; C.E., Cornell U., 1895, M.C.E., 1897; m. Annie Gwynne, Apr. 11, 1893 (died Feb. 18, 1921); children—Gwynne Gravelle, Margaret L.; m. 2d, Mrs. Elinor G. Anderson, Apr. 27, 1922. City engr., Salem, Ore., 1891-93; sec. Salem Improvement Co., 1893-96; instr. Cornell U., 1897-1900; ry. work, Chicago, Ill., 1900-02; asst. prof. civ. engring., Cornell U., 1902-07; prof. civ. engring., U. of Ala., 1907-08; prof. municipal and highway engring., U. of Wash., 1908-14; dean faculty of engring. and dir. Engring. Expt. Sta., U. of Mo., 1914-36, now emeritus, dean, prof. and dir. Pres. State Bd. of Health, Wash., 1912. Progressive. Presbyterian. Fellow A.A.A.S.; mem. Am. Soc. C.E., Pacific N.W. Soc. Engrs., Soc. for Promotion Engring. Edn., Sigma Xi, Phi Beta Kappa. Mason. Contbr. many articles to tech. jours. Club: Engineers (St. Louis). Home: 1501 E. Silver Av., Albuquerque NM*

MCCAY, CHARLES FRANCIS, educator, ins. co. exec.; b. Danville, Pa., Mar. 8, 1810; s. Robert and Sarah (Read) McC.; grad. Jefferson Coll., 1829; m. Narcissa Williams, Aug. 11, 1840. Tchr. mathematics, natural philosophy and astronomy Lafayette Coll., Easton, Pa., 1832-33, U. Ga., Athens, 1833-53; actuary, life dept. So. Mut. Ins. Co., Athens, 1848-55; agt. Mut. Life Ins. Co. of N.Y., 1846-53; became prof. mathematics S.C. Coll., 1853, pres., 1855-57; devised So. Mut. Mortality Table, proposed bill to Ga. Legislature to make it effective for valuation purposes in Ga., 1859, bill passed, (became 1st adoption of life ins. valuation table by any state); prepared 1st select and ultimate table of life ins. mortality in U.S., 1887. Died Baltimore, O., Mar. 13, 1889.

MCCAY, LEROY WILEY, chemist; b. Rome, Ga., Aug. 9, 1857; s. Robert T. and Susan L. (Wiley) M.; A.B., Princeton, 1878, A.M., 1881, D.Sc., 1883; studied at Freiberg Sch. of Mines, and U. of Heidelberg. Asst. in analytical chemistry, 1883-86, instr., 1886-89, asst. prof., 1889-92, prof. inorganic chemistry, 1892-1928, emeritus prof., 1928—, Princeton. Chief subjects of research, cobalt, nickel and iron pyrites, methods for determining arsenic, the nonexistence of sulphparsenic acid, the sulphoxyarsenic acids and their salts, the separation of the metals of the tin group, use of hydrofluoric acid in ordinary and electro-chem. analysis, use of mercury as a reducing agent. Home: Princeton, N.J. Died Apr. 13, 1937.

MCCLELLAN, CARSWELL, civil engr.; b. Phila., Dec. 3, 1835; s. Samuel and Margaret (Carswell) McC.; grad. Williams Coll., 1855. Enlisted in 32d N.Y. Regt., 1862, served in Battle of Malvern Hill; served as topog. asst. to Gen. Andrew Humphreys, Army of Potomac, served in battles of Gettysburg, Chancellorsville, Fredericksburg; taken prisoner, Aug. 1864, paroled and resigned from U.S. Army, Nov. 1864; engr. in charge of constrn. for several railroads including N.P. R.R., St. Paul & Pacific R.R., 1867-81; U.S. asst. civil engr., 1881-92. Died St. Paul, Minn., Mar. 6, 1892; buried St. Paul.

MCCLELLAN, GEORGE, anatomist, surgeon; b. Woodstock, Conn., Dec. 23, 1796; s. James and Eunice (Eldredge) McC.; grad. Yale, 1816; grad. in medicine U. Pa., 1819; m. Elizabeth Brinton, 1829, 3 children including Gen. George B., John Hill Brinton. Founder Jefferson Med. Coll. (series of pvt. lectures on anatomy and surgery resulted in charter), 1825, prof. surgery, 1825-39, prof. anatomy, 1827-30; a leading opthalmic surgeon, 1st to remove lens of an eye; obtained charter for Pa. Coll. Med. Sch., 1838, lectr., 1839-43; Author: Principles and Practice of Surgery (completed by son, John Hill Brinton), 1848; editor: Theory and Practice of Physic, (Eberle), 1840. Died Phila., May 9, 1847.

MCCLELLAN, WILLIAM, (mak-klel'lan), engring. exec.; b. Phila., Nov. 5, 1872; s. John and Margaret (Marshall) McC.; B.S., U. Pa., 1900, Ph.D., 1903, E.E., 1914; m. Caroline May Stroup. Instr. physics U. Pa., 1900-05, dean Wharton Sch., 1916-19; with Phila. Rapid Transit Co., 1900-05; engr. Westinghouse, Church, Kerr & Co., 1900-05; engr. Westinghouse, Church, Kerr & Co., 1905-07; dir. Campion McClellan Co., 1907-15; mem. Paine, McClellan & Campion, 1915-20, McClellan & Junkersfeld, 1922-29; v.p. Stone & Webster Engring. Corp., 1929-33; pres. William McClellan & Co., Ltd., 1930-33, Potomac Electric Power Co., 1933-39; pres. Washington Ry. & Electric Co., 1935-40, chmn., 1940-43; pres. Union Electric Co. of Mo., 1939-41, chmn., 1941-46; chmn. bd. Steam Motive Power, Inc.; dir. Riggs Nat. Bank, Capital Transit Co., Potomac Electric Power Co., Research Corp. N.Y.; cons. engr., Public Service Commn., 2d dist. N.Y., 1911-13; v.p. Cleveland Electric Illuminating Co., 1919-21; mem. President's Commn. on Muscle Shoals, 1925. Dir. gen. Alumni Soc. U. Pa., 1921; past trustee U. Pa.; trustee Lingnan U. Former dir. Nat. Symphony Orchestra Assn., pres., 1938-39. Fellow Am. Inst. E.E. (pres. 1921-22); mem. Am. Soc. M.E., Am. Engring Council (pres. 1938-39), Council Fgn. Relations; past pres. Asso. Pa. Clubs. Dir. Washington Board of Trade, 1939. Trustee, Com. for Economic Development. Mem. Alpha Chi Rho, Phi Beta Kappa, Sigma Xi, Beta Gamma Sigma. Republican. Episcopalian. Clubs: University, Univ. of Pa. of New York (ex-pres.); University, University of Pa. Varsity (Phila.); Cosmos, Metropolitan, Chevy Chase (Washington). Contbr. to tech. mags. and tech. socs. Home: Burgundy Farm. Alexandria, Va. Died Nov. 14, 1950; buried Ivy Hill Cemetery, Alexandria.

MCCLELLAND, JAMES FARLEY, mining engr.; b. Poughkeepsie, N.Y., Mar. 3, 1878; s. James Farley and Mary (Vincent) McC.; E.M., Columbia, 1900; A.M. (hon.), Yale, 1910; m. Jane Adams Kearney, Dec. 7, 1912; children—Jean K. (Mrs. Julian S. Barrett), James F., George K., Vincent (killed in service USN World War II). Instr. geology and mining U. Wyo., 1900-01; with Indiana Gold Dredging Co., Oroville, Cal., 1901-02; instr. in mining, Columbia, 1902-05; in gen. mining practice, Tonopah, Nev., 1905-08; prof. mining Leland Stanford Jr. U., 1908-10; prof. mining engring. Sheffield Sci. Sch. (Yale), 1910-17; editor-in-chief, specification sect. Signal Corps, 1917-18; chief prodn. engring. Bur. Aircraft Prodn., 1918-19; cons. engr. Liberty Nat. Bank, N.Y.C., 1919-20; v.p. Liberty Industrial Corp., 1921-22; asst. v.p. New York Trust Co., 1922-28, v.p., 1928-29; v.p. Chemical Nat. Bank and Trust Co. and Chemical Nat. Co., 1929-31; v.p., dir. Phelps Dodge Corp., 1931-47, ret., now dir. and mem. exec. com. Mem. Am. Inst. Mining and Metall. Engrs. Clubs: Century, Union League, India House (N.Y.C.). Home: Mead's Point, Greenwich, Conn. Office: 40 Wall St. Died May 6, 1955.

MCCLELLAND, JAMES HENDERSON, surgeon; b. Pittsburg, May 20, 1845; grad. Hahnemann Med. Coll. of Phila., 1867; returned to Pittsburg and has ever since served on surg. staff Homoe. Med. and Surg. Hosp.; organized and was several yrs. pres. and demonstrator Anatom. Soc., Allegheny Co.; became prof. surgery, Hahnemann Coll., Phila., 1876 delivered course on operative surgery, Boston Univ. School of Medicine, 1878; mem. State Bd. of Health since 1885; frequent contributor to med. journals; wrote article on "Diseases of the Kidneys" in the "System of Medicine," edited by Dr. Henry Arndt (Phila., 1886); pres. Am. Inst. of Homoepathy, 1893-94; hon. pres. Internat. Homoe. Med. Congress, Paris, 1900. Address: 5th and Wilkins Avs., Pittsburg.

MCCLELLAND, ROSS ST. JOHN, engr., banker; b. Hillsdale, Ia., Oct. 7, 1878; s. William Dunlap and Ada (Moore) McC.; ed. Highland Park Coll., Des Moines; Iowa State Coll. Agriculture and Mechanic Arts, 1903; Stanford, 1904; B.Sc., Union Coll. Schenectady, N.Y., 1905; married; 1 son, Roswell D. Constructing engr. on Pacific Coast and in Mexico, chief engr. Electric Bond & Share Co., New York, 1906-19; pres. R.J. McClelland Co., investments, 1923-31, investment banking, London, Paris, Edinburgh and Zurich. A pioneer in long-distance electric power transmission, and writer on tech. and economic topics pertaining thereto. Life mem. Union Interalliee (Paris), Lake Placid Club (N.Y.). Home: 16780 Oak View Drive, Encino, Los Angeles CA

MCCLENAHAN, HOWARD, scientist; b. Port Deposit, Md., Oct. 19, 1872; s. John Megredy and Laura Jane (Farrow) M.; E.E., Princeton U., 1895, M.S., 1897; LL.D., Washington Coll., Md., 1907, Swarthmore, 1929; Litt.D., Franklin and Marshall, 1929; Sc.D., Union Coll., Schenectady, N.Y.; D.Sc., U. of Pa., 1931; m. Bessie L. Lee, Nov., 1, 1899; children—John Megredy, Richard Lee, Elizabeth Lee. Instr. physics, 1897-1902, asst. prof., 1902-06, prof., 1906-12, dean of the Coll., 1912-25, Princeton; sec. Franklin Inst. State of Pa., May 1925—; editor Jour. of Franklin Inst., 1925—; dir. Benjamin Franklin Memorial and Franklin Inst. Mus., 1930—. Pres. Assn. Colls. and Prep. Schs. of Middle States and Md., 1919; chmn. Coll. Entrance Exam. Bd., 1919-23. Trustee Lincoln U.; asso. trustee for grad. study and research, U. of Pa. Officier de l'Ordre de la Couronne (Belgian),

1919; awarded gold medal Sesquicentennial Exhbn. for services on Internat. Jury of Awards, 1926. Author: Laboratory Directions in Experimental Physics, 1906. Died Dec. 17, 1935.

MCCLINTOCK, NORMAN, lecturer; b. Pittsburgh, Pa., June 13, 1868; s. Oliver and Clara Courtney (Childs) M.; B.A., Yale, 1891; m. Ethel M. Lockwood, Feb. 14, 1906. Mem. faculty U. of Pittsburgh, title of photo naturalist, 1925—. Has developed to a high degree the application of telephotography in securing natural history motion pictures; maker motion pictures of ecol. and zoöl. subjects. Photo-biologist to Koppers Research Corp., Pittsburgh, 1930-31; photo-naturalist ad spl. lecturer, Rutgers U., 1931—. Republican. Episcopalian. Lectures on wild birds, animal life and plant life, illustrated with motion pictures. Specialist in time-lapse motion pictures of plant movements. Home: New Brunswick, N.J. Died Feb. 26, 1938.

MCCLUNG, CLARENCE ERWIN, zoölogist; b. Clayton, Calif., Apr. 5, 1870; s. Charles Livingston and Annie Howard (Mackey) McC.; Ph.G., U. of Kan., 1892, A.B., 1896, A.M., 1898, Ph.D., 1902; grad. student, Columbia, 1897, U. of Chicago, 1899; Sc.D., U. of Pa., 1940; Franklin and Marshall College, 1941; m. Anna Adelia Drake, Aug. 31, 1899; children—Ruth, Cromwell and Delia Elizabeth. Assistant professor zoölogy, U. of Kan., 1897-1900, asso. prof., 1900-06, prof., 1906-12, head of dept., and curator vertebrate paleontol. collections, 1902-12, acting dean, School of Medicine, 1902-06; prof. zoölogy and dir. zoöl. lab., U. of Pa., 1912-40, emeritus prof. since 1940; visiting prof. Keio U., Tokyo, 1933-34, U. of Ill., 1940-41; acting head zoölogy dept., Swarthmore Coll., 1943. Mem. embryol. staff, Woods Hole Mass., 1893, and since 1914 (trustee); head of scientific expdns. to Ore., Wash., Western Kan., Japan, China, Java, Ceylon, South America and South Africa. Chmn. div. biology and agr., Nat. Research Council, Washington, 1919-21 (fellowship bd.); mem. advisory bd., Wistar Inst., Morris Arboretum. Republican. Conglist. Fellow A.A.A.S. (v.p. sect. F, 1926); mem. Am. Zoöl. Soc. (pres. 1910, 14), Am. Philos. Soc., Am. Soc. Naturalists (pres. 1927), Acad. Natural Sciences (research associate), Philadelphia, National, Washington and Kansas academies of science, American Association of Anatomists, Union of American Biol. Socs. (pres. 1922-30), Sigma Xi (pres. 1919-21), Tri Beta (pres. 1936); fgn. mem. La Sociedad de Biologia de Montevideo. Author of Microscopical Technique, Chromosome Theory of Heredity (General Cytology); also tech. papers on cytology, sex-determination, paleontology, etc. Mng. editor Journal of Morphology; mem. bd. editors Acta Zoölogica, Cytologia; pres. bd. trustees (1925-33) and seci-editor Biol. Abstracts. Clubs: Cosmos, Lenape; University (Ill.). Home: Swarthmore, Pa. Died Jan. 17, 1946.

MCCLURE, CHARLES FREEMAN WILLIAMS, anatomist; b. Cambridge, Mass., Mar. 6, 1865; s. Charles Franklin and Joan Elizabeth (Blake) McC.; A.B., Princeton University, 1888, A.M., 1892, E.M. fellow in biology, 1888-89; student College Physicians and Surgeons (Columbia), 1890-91; univs. of Berlin, 1893, Kiel, 1895, Würzburg, 1897; hon. Sc.D., Columbia, 1908; m. Grace Latimer Jones, Aug. 25, 1921. Instr. biology, Princeton U., 1891-95, asst. prof., 1895-1901, prof. comparative anatomy, 1901-34, now prof. emeritus. Mem. Peary Relief Expdn., 1899. Mem. Am. Soc. Naturalists, Am. Zoöl. Soc., Assn. Am. Anatomists (v.p., 1910-11, exec. com., 1912-16, pres., 1920-21), Am. Philos. Soc., Anatomische Gesellschaft, Phi Beta Kappa, Sigma Xi; fellow A.A.A.S. Clubs: Ivy, Nassau (Princeton). Author of numerous papers on the anatomy and development of the vascular system, oedema, etc. Formerly editor Anatomical Record. Home: Princeton, N.J. Died July 23, 1955.

MCCLURE, ROY DONALDSON, surgeon; b. Bellebrook, O., Jan. 17, 1882; s. James Albert (M.D.) and Ina Hester (Donaldson) McC.; A.B., Ohio State U., 1904, hon. D.Sc., 1936; M.D., Johns Hopkins, 1908; hon. D.Sc., Washington and Jefferson Coll., 1944; studied U. of Prague, Bohemia, 1906; m. Helen Keene Troxell, March 4, 1916; children—Mary Keene Stearns, Roy Donaldson, M.D., Douglas Templeton. Assistant to Dr. Alexis Carrel, Rockefeller Inst., 1907-08; house surgeon New York Hosp., 1909-11; resident surgeon Johns Hopkins Hosp., 1912-16, also instr. in surgery, Johns Hopkins Univ.; an organizer and surgeon in chief Henry Ford Hosp., Detroit, since 1916; dir. med. dept. Ford Rubber Plantation, Brazil, 1928-46; chief surgeon D.T.&I. R.R.; extramural lecturer in post-grad. medicine, U. of Mich.; Guest speaker Congrès Français de Chirurgie, Paris, 1937. Trustee Henry Ford Hospital since 1938. Mem. sub-com. on surg. infections, sub-com. on burns, 1940-45; committee on prosthetic devices, 1945-46, committee on artificial limbs since 1946, of National Research Council. Regional rep. coms. on admission, Johns Hopkins and Duke University Med. Schools. Chmn. Mich. Med. Advisory Bd. No. 3, World War I, 1917, same, World War II; mem. Detroit committee on Foreign Relations. Member blood procurement com., Detroit, Am. Red Cross. Maj. Med. Corps, U.S. Army, 1918-19; served as comdg. officer Evacuation Hospital No. 33, A.E.F. Member of the board of trustees of the Michigan Foundation for Medical and Health Edn. since 1946. Fellow Am. College Surgeons (gov.), Am. Surg. Assn.; member Southern Surg. Assn., Am. Med. Assn., Société Internationale de Chirurgie, Am. Coll. Surgeons (bd. govs. 1935-38), Ohio State Univ. Assn. (pres. 1925-27), Central Surg. Assn. (founder and first pres. 1940-41), Detroit Acad. of Surgery (pres. 1929), Detroit Acad. Medicine (pres. 1945-46), Johns Hopkins Med. and Surg. Assn. (act. pres. 1946), Phi Beta Kappa (Ohio State; pres. Detroit Assn. 1939-42), Sigma Xi, Delta Upsilon, Nu Sigma Nu. Republican. Presbyterian. Clubs: Detroit, Economic (bd. dirs.) Newcomen Soc., Grosse Pointe Country. Author of numerous papers giving results of studies and experiments, alone and with others. Mem. adv. bd., Annals of Surgery, also editorial bd., Am. Jour. Surgery. Home: 1490 Iroquois Av. Address: Henry Ford Hospital, Detroit 2. Died March 31, 1951.

MCCLUSKEY, EDMUND ROBERTS, physician; born Alliston, Ont., Can., Nov. 11, 1900; s. George and Elizabeth (Hand) McC.; M.B., U. of Toronto, 1923; D.Sc., Allegheny College, Meadville, Pa., 1957; m. May McDonagh, June 22, 1929. Came to U.S., 1927, naturalized, 1940. Intern Presbyn. Hosp., Chicago, 1923-24, Sick Children's Hosp., Toronto, 1924-26, Children's Hosp. of Pittsburgh, 1926-27, chief staff, med. dir., 1948-58; mem. faculty med. sch., U. Pitts., 1928—, prof. pediatrics, 1948—, chmn. dept., 1948-58, vice chancellor for health professions, 1958—; practice medicine, Pitts., 1927-48. Fellow A.C.P.; mem. Am. Acad. Pediatrics, Allegheny Co. Med. Soc., Am. Pediatrics Soc., Assn. Am. Med. Colls., Pa. Med. Soc., A.M.A. Home: 166 N. Dithridge St. Office: U. Pitts., Pitts. 13. Died June 30, 1962; buried Alliston, Ont., Can.

MCCOLL, JAY ROBERT, engineer; b. Webster, Mich., Mar. 24, 1867; s. Robert and Sophia McC.; grad. engring. dept. Mich. State Coll., 1890; post-grad. student there and at Cornell; m. Belle Gertrude Baldwin, Jan. 3, 1900; 1 dau., Jennette Baldwin. Adj. prof. mech. engring., U. of Tenn., 1890-1902; asso. prof. thermodynamics, Purdue U., 1902-03; asso. prof. steam engring. in charge dept., same univ., 1903-05; chief engr. Am. Blower Co., Detroit, 1905-10; dean engring. dept., U. of Detroit, 1910—; mem. McColl, Snyder & McLean, consulting engrs. Mem. bd. of rules, Dept. Bldg. and Safety Engring., Detroit, 1918—; mem. Mich. State College Board, 1922-34. On editorial staff Michigan Architect and Engineer. Republican. Conglist. Home: Detroit, Mich. Died Oct. 30, 1936.

MCCOLLUM, ELMER VERNER, Am. physiol. chemist; b. nr. Ft. Scott, Kan., Mar. 3, 1879; s. Cornelius Armstrong and Martha Catherine (Kidwell) M.; B.A., U. Kan., 1903; M.A., 1904; Ph.D., Yale, 1906; Sc.D., U. of Cincinnati, 1920; LL.D., U. Manitoba, 1938, Johns Hopkins, 1951, L.H.D. (hon.), Brandeis University, 1959. Instr. agricultural chemistry, 1907-08; assistant professor, 1908-11, asso. prof., 1911-13, prof., 1913-17, U. of Wis.; prof. bio-chemistry, Sch. Hygiene and Public Health, Johns Hopkins, 1917-44, Emeritus professor since 1945. Member international committee on vitamin standards of League of Nations, 1931, and international and mixed commns. on nutrition, 1935. Del. 10th Pan-Am. Sanitary Conf., Bogota, 1938; chmn. nutrition sect. Pan-Am. Sanitary Bureau, 1939; member food and nutrition bd. Nat. Research Council since 1942; cons. Lend-Lease adminstrn., 1943; cons. to Indsl. Hygienic Div., U. S. Army, 1943. Member Sci. Advisory Committee Nutrition Found.; mem. adv. com. McCollum-Pratt Inst. Johns Hopkins University. Recipient of Osborne and Mendel Award, American Institute Nutrition, 1955; Borden Fedn. Centenary award, 1958; Chas. F. Spencer award, American Chemical Society, 1958. Fellow Royal Soc., 1961, Royal Society Arts (London); member British Nutrition Society (honorary), Am. Acad. Dental Medicine (hon.), A.A.A.S., Am. Soc. Biol. Chemists (pres. 1927-29), Am. Chem. Soc., Am. Public Health Association, Am. Assn. Univ. Profs., Harvey Soc. (hon.), Am. Home Econ. Assn. (hon.), American Philosophical Society, National Academy of Sciences, Phi Beta Kappa. Des Moines Academy Medicine (hon.), Kaiserlich Deutsche Academie der Naturforscher zu Halle, Royal Acad. of Medicine (Belglum). Foreign member Swedish Academy Sciences. Received Howard N. Potts gold medal, Franklin Institute, 1921, John Scott medal from the City of Phila., 1924, Newell Sill Jenkins medal from Conn. State Dental Soc., 1927, gold medal of Am. Inst. of N.Y., 1934, Callahan medal of Ohio State Dental Society, 1935. The Borden Award in Nutrition; Award from Modern Medicine for 1960; Medal and Citation, New York Academy of Medicine, 1961. Author: Text Book of Organic Chemistry for Medical Students, 1916; The Newer Knowledge of Nutrition, 1918, 5th edit., 1939; The American Home Diet, 1919; Foods, Nutrition and Health, 1933. Authorship: History of Nutrition, 1957; From Kansas Farm Boy to Scientist (autobiography), 1964. McCollum award established by Am. Soc. Clin. Nutrition, 1965. Discovered vitamins A and D; authority on relation of nutrition and diet to disease; developed method of biol. analysis of food-stuff; synthesized several pyrimidines. Home: 2402 Talbot Rd., Balt. 16.

MCCOMB, WILLIAM RANDOLPH, engr. and govt. exec.; b. Dixon, Mo. Sept. 22, 1892; s. Charles Arthur and Betty Miller (Wilson) McC.; student Missouri Sch. of Mines, Rolla, 1914-16; B.S. in Mining Engring., Harvard, 1923; unmarried. Employed in Aztec mine, St. Louis, Rocky Mountain & Pacific Co., Raton, N.M., 1916-17; mining and metall. engr., Phelps-Dodge Co., Morencia, Ariz., 1917; engaged in mining exploration, Brazil and British Guiana, 1923; mng. dir. advertising and sales campaign of lead, zinc, oil and paint industry, New York, N.Y., 1924-27; vice pres. and dir. Craftex Co., New York, N.Y., 1927-28; vice pres. United Bldg. Materials Corp., Boston, 1928-30; vice pres. Flexwood Corp., Chicago, 1930-33; dep. adminstr. U.S. Nat. Recovery Adminstrn., Washington, D.C., 1933-36; dep. adminstr. govt. contracts and wage and hour divs. of U.S. Govt., Washington, 1937-55, adminstr. Wage and Hour and Public Contracts Division, 1947-55; labor cons., Washington, 1955—. Officer, United States Army, 1917-18. Mem. Harvard Geol. Soc. (vice pres.), Am. Inst. Mining Engrs., Harvard Engring. Soc., Harvard Business School Soc., Newcomen Soc. (England). Clubs: Harvard (New York and Washington); Chevy Chase Country (Wash.). Home: 1516 33rd St. N.W., Washington. Died Dec. 21, 1957; buried Arlington Nat. Cemetery.

MCCONNEL, ROGER HARMON, mining geologist; b. Caldwell, Ida., Dec. 8, 1908; s. Fred Homer and Ellen (Harmon) McC.; student Coll. of Ida., 1927-30; B.S. in Geology, U. Ida., 1932, M.S., 1936; m. Harriet Idell Smith, Nov. 3, 1934; children—Stephen S., Mary Alice. Jr. topographic engr. U.S. Geol. Survey, summers, 1934-35, field asst., 1936-37; geologist Bunker Hill Co., Kellog, Ida., 1938-40, chief geologist, 1940-42, 46-66, chief exploration geologist, 1967, geology cons., 1967-71. Served as capt. AUS, 1942-46; ETO. Fellow Geol. Soc. Am.; mem. Am. Inst. Mining, Metall. and Petroleum Engrs. (Engr. of Year Columbia sect. 1968); N.W. Mining Assn. (life); Mining and Metall. Soc. Am., Soc. Econ. Geologists (pres 1971); Societe de Geologique Appliquee Aux. Gites Minereaux. Contbr. articles to tech. jours. Home: Kellogg ID Died June 19, 1971; buried Greenwood Cemetery, Kellogg ID

MCCONNELL, ANDREW M., scientist and author; b. Blount Co., Ala., 1873; s. W. T. and A. M. McC.; grad. Blount Coll., Blountsville, Southern Univ., Greensboro, Ala.; m. Atlanta, Ga., Jan., 1898, Marion Delana Daniel. In 1898 purchased The Alkahest, a Southern mag.; inaugurated also the Alkahest Lyceum system, a cooperative plan for furnishing Southern towns with popular and edn'l entertainments, lectures, music, etc., of which he was pres.; also lecturer; founder McConnell Library Assn., giving pub. libraries free through lecture courses; 190 libraries established in 1st year's work; founder Consumers' Co-operative Union, a buying union for reducing the expenses of workingmen. Author: Echoes from the Heart, poems, 1896; Just Understand, 1906; Organic Electricity, 1907; Scientific Mind Healing. Address: Birmingham AL

MCCONNELL, H(AROLD) S(LOAN), entomologist; b. Anderson, S.C., Dec. 30, 1893; s. James N. S. and Frances C. (Duckworth) McC.; B.S., Clemson Agrl. Coll., 1916; M.S., U. Md., 1931; m. Pearl Anderson, Aug. 22, 1926. Asst. prof. U. Md., 1916-18; asst. research entomologist Clemson Agrl. Coll., 1919-24; research entomologist U. Md., 1925—. Served in San. Corps., U.S. Army, 1918-19, 43-46. Mem. Am. Assn. Econ. Entomologists, Entomol. Soc. Am., Entomol. Soc. Washington, Sigma Xi. Home: 6812 Pineway, College Heights, Hyattsville, Md. Died May 11, 1958.

MCCONNELL, IRA WELCH, civil engr.; b. Schell City, Mo., Oct. 17, 1871; s. James Calvin and Cecelia Elizabeth (Welch) M.; C.E., Cornell U., 1897; m. Grace Lucille Bowerman, Sept. 22, 1903; children—John Waldo, Charles Edwin. Instr. civ. engring., Cornell U., 1899-1900; contractor's supt., Chicago and New Orleans, 1901-03; prof. civ. engring., Mo. Sch. of Mines, Rolla, 1903; project engr., 1903-07, supervising engr., 1907-09, U.S. Reclamation Service; chief irrigation engr., J. G. White & Co., Inc., New York, 1909-10; v.p. and gen. mgr. Idaho Irrigation Co., Ltd., 1910-12; hydraulic engr., 1912-17, chief engr., 1917, Stone & Webster, div. of constrn. and engring.; asst. gen. mgr., Am. Internat. Shipbldg. Corp., Hog Island Shipyard, 1918; v.p. United Engineers & Constructors, Inc. (Phila.), Dwight P. Robinson & Co., Inc., New York. Conglist. Mason, Elk. Home: Hastings-on-Hudson, N.Y. Died Jan. 6, 1933.

MCCONNELL, ROBERT DARLL, b. Montrose, Colo., Mar. 30, 1889; s. Charles E. and Coie (Earll) McC.; student U. of Colorado, 1905-07; Columbia Univ., 1910 (Engineer of Mines); m. Caryll N. Esterbrook, Dec. 28, 1918; children—Mildred, Robert, Elizabeth, Richard, Caryll. Assistant engineer Chino Copper Co., 1910-11; superintendent various mines, 1911-15; examining engr. S. W. Mudd & Associates, 1915-17; mining engr., 1920-31; partner Foster McConnell & Co. (mems. New York Stock Exchange), 1922-31; pres. and dir. Centrifugal Pipe Corp., Mayflower Associates, Inc., Mayflower Consol, Inc., 1924-39; pres. and dir. Pilgrim Exploration Co., 1937-47; dir. Rhokana Corp., Cyprus Mines Corp., Hazeltine Corp., Esterbrook Steel Pen Mfg. Co., Simmons Co., Fohs Oil Co.; bus. adviser to Dept. of Commerce, Sept. 1939-Aug. 1940; consultant Office of Production Management, Mar. 1941-Mar. 1942; apptd. by Sec. of Treasury of U.S. and Alien Property

Custodian as chmn. bd. and pres. Gen. Aniline & Film Corp., Mar. 1942-July 1943; consultant, Treas. Dept., Washington, D.C., 1943-44; dep., Civil Affairs Div., War Dept., Apr.-Dec. 1945. Mayor Town of Jupiter Island, Hobe Sound, Fla., 1955-61. Member board of trustees Robert Earll McConnell Foundation. Served as lt., U.S.N.R., 1917-19. Mem. Am. Inst. Mining and Metall. Engrs., Mining and Metall. Soc. Am., Delta Tau Delta, Sigma Xi. Clubs: Links, Recess, Blind Brook, Seminole. Home: Hobe Sound FL Died Apr. 16, 1971; buried Middleburg VA

MCCORMICK, BRADLEY THOMAS, mech. engr.; b. Marietta, O., May 28, 1880; s. Frank Ross and Maria Elizabeth (Thomas) M.; M.E., Cornell U., 1903. Apprentice in shops and later in charge induction motor design Bullock Electric Mfg. Co., Cin., 1903-05; chief elec. engr. charge elec. design Allis-Chalmers-Bullock, Ltd., Montreal, 1905-13; mem. firm Forbes & McCormick, cons. engrs., Montreal, 1913-15; chief engr. Miss. Valley Metal Products Co., St. Louis, 1915-17; apptd. engr. charge small motors Wagner Electric Mfg. Co., St. Louis, 1919; now engr. with Wagner Electric Corp. Civilian, later capt. and maj. U.S. Ordnance Dept., 1917-19, serving as chief of projectile and cartridge case br. of arty. ammunition and trench warfare div. Fellow Am. Inst. E.E. Home: 847 Belt Av. Address: Wagner Electric Corp., St. Louis. Died Mar. 14, 1945.

MCCORMICK, CYRUS HALL, mfr.; b. Walnut Grove, Va., Feb. 15, 1809; s. Robert and Mary (Hall) McC.; m. Nancy Fowler, Jan. 26, 1858, 7 children. Invented and patented hillside plough, 1831; patented reaping machine, 1834, began mfg. machine commercially, 1837; erected factory in Chgo., 1847; built up nat. business for McCormick Harvesting Machine Co., by 1850; added mowing attachment to reaper, 1850's, also developed self-raking device, hand-binding harvester, wire-binder, twine-binder, 1860's; introduced reaper in Europe in London, Eng., 1851; awarded Council medal London World's Fair, 1851; won major prizes at world fairs, Paris, London, Hamburg, Lille, Vienna, Phila., Melbourne, 1855-80; named chevalier by France, later officer Legion of Honor; elected mem. French Acad. of Scis., 1879; pioneer in creation of modern business methods, among 1st to use field trials, guarantees, testimonials in advt., cash and deferred payments for merchandise; owner Presbyn. Expositor, newspaper, 1860; endowed 4 professorships in Presbyn. Theol. Sem. of N.W., 1859; The Interior (Presbyn. newspaper, later named Continent), 1872-84; became owner Chgo. Times, 1860, publisher, 1860-61; chmn. Democratic State Central Com., 1872, 76; dir. U.P. R.R.; an organizer Mississippi Valley Soc.; benefactor Union Theol. Sem., Hampden-Sydney, Va., also Washington Coll., Lexington, Va.; pres. Va. Soc. in Chgo., 1880. Died Chgo., May 13, 1884.

MCCORMICK, EDMUND BURKE, college dean; b. Normal, Ill., Nov. 24, 1870; s. Henry and Numantia B. (Kinyon) M.; grad. Ill. State Normal U., 1889; S.B. in mech. engring., Mass. Inst. Tech., 1897; m. Jeanette Maxey, Dec. 26, 1899. Machinist with C.&A. R.R., 1889-93; instr. mech. engring., 1898-99, asst. prof., 1899-1901, Mont. State Coll.; prof. mech. engring., 1901-10, dean div. of engring., 1908-13, dir. Engring. Expt. Sta., 1910-13, Kan. State Agrl. Coll.; consulting engr., 1907-13, mech. engr., 1913-15, chief div. rural engring., 1915-20, chief equipment div., July 1, 1920—, Bur. of Public Roads, U.S. Dept. Agriculture. Consulting editor Agricultural Engineering Series, McGraw-Hill Book Co. Republican. Mason. Home: Alameda, Calif. Died Jan. 15, 1926.

MCCORMICK, LEANDER HAMILTON, author; b. Chicago, Ill., May 27, 1859; s. Leander J. And Henrietta (Hamilton) McC.; B.S., Amherst, 1881; student law dept. Columbia, 1881-83, also studied architecture; m. Constance, d. Edward Plummer, of Canterbury, Eng., Feb. 15, 1887. Lived in London 17 yrs.; traveler, inventor, sculptor, art collector; author of over 100 inventions, including aeroplanes, aerial torpedo, motorcycles, a watch which records time the world over, etc.; art collection embraces early English and old Dutch schs. Presbyterian. Author: Caracterology, 1920; Students Course in Characterology, 1921. Home: Chicago, Ill. Died Feb. 2, 1934.

MCCORMICK, LEANDER J., inventor-capitalist; b. Walnut Grove, Va., Feb. 8, 1819; m. Henrietta Maria Hamilton, 1845. Became connected with the pioneer reaper mfg. industry with his father (Robert McCormick, inventor of the reaper) and his brother (Cyrus Hall McCormick) and in 1847 went to Cincinnati and engaged with his brother in the manufacture of 100 machines; moved with family to Chicago, 1848; became partner with his brother as mfrs. of reapers, 1849. Had active supervision of mfg. dept. until business was incorporated as McCormick Harvesting Machine Co., 1879, and in 1889 he retired from active business; made many valuable inventions of improvements in reapers; has large real estate and other interests in Chicago. Presented to Univ. of Va., 1871, a large 24-inch refracting telescope and the observatory now known as the McCormick Observatory. Home: Chicago, Ill. Died 1900.

MCCORMICK, ROBERT, inventor; b. Rockbridge County, Va., June 8, 1780; s. Robert and Martha (Sanderson) McC.; m. Mary Ann Hall, Feb. 11, 1808; several children including Cyrus Hall, William S., Leander James, Inventor several farm implements (none were practical or commercially valuable); inventor and patentee hempbrake, gristmill, hydraulic machine and blacksmith's bellows, 1830-31; inventor threshing machine, 1834; experimenter with grain reapers, 1809-31; built an iron furnace, 1836; mfr. reaper invented by son Cyrus, 1837-45. Died Rockbridge County, July 4, 1846.

MCCORMICK, R(OBERT) HALL, capitalist; b. Rockbridge Co., Va., Sept. 6, 1847; s. Leander J. and Henrietta M. (Hamilton) M.; g.s. Robert M., inventor, McCormick reaper; went to Chicago, 1848; ed. old Chicago U.; m. Sarah Lord Day, June 1, 1871. During 1875-76, experimented personally with the self-binder in the field from Texas to Minn., and was in charge of the field trials exhibit of the McCormick Binder at Centennial Expn., Phila., 1876, which was the introduction of the self-binder to public as the greatest labor-saving device of the age; made improvements on reaper and binder which were patented; trustee Leander J. McCormick estate. Has made a spl. study of British sch. of art; has examples of many of leading artists of that sch. in his collection; published an illustrated catalogue of the collection, which is in prin. art galleries of U.S. and Europe; interested in yachting and automobiling and was one of the first to introduce coaching in the West. Trustee Art Inst.; hon. life mem. Copley Soc. (Boston). Chmn. Rivers and Lakes Commn., 1911—. Home: Chicago, Ill. Died Mar. 14, 1917.

MCCORMICK, STEPHEN, inventor, mfr.; b. Auburn, Va., Aug. 26, 1784; s. John and Elizabeth (Morgan) McC.; m. Sarah Barnett, Feb. 1807, 3 children; m. 2d, Elizabeth M. Benson, Feb. 29, 1816, 9 children. Improved shape of nether millstone on water-power grist mill; invented, manufactured, put into use a cast-iron plow with replaceable parts and adjustable wrought-iron point, by 1816, patented 1819, 26, 37, manufactured on farm Auburn; manufactured plows in factories, Leesburg and Alexandria, Va., circa 1826-50, plows widely-used in Va., less so in other So. States; responsible (with Jethro Wood) for introducing cast-iron plows in U.S. Died Auburn, Aug. 28, 1875.

MCCOURT, WALTER EDWARD, geologist; b. Brooklyn, N.Y., Feb. 2, 1884; s. William Menzie and Elizabeth Wilson (McKeon) McC.; A.B., Cornell, 1904, A.M., 1905; m. Edna Wahlert, Aug. 4, 1910; 1 son, Andrew. Asst., fellow and instr. geology, Cornell U., 1902-06; instr. geology, asst. prof., asso. prof., 1906-15, prof. since 1915, dean Schs. of Engring, and Architecture, 1920-28, asst. chancellor since 1928, dean Coll. of Liberal Arts, 1931-32, 1937-39 and 1940-41, Washington University. Geologist New York State Agriculture Expt. Station, summer 1903; asst. geologist N.Y. State Museum, summer 1904; asst. geologist, N.J. Geol. Survey, summers 1905-06; geologist Mo. Geol. Survey, summers 1910-12; prof. geology, summer sessions U. of Colo., 1913-29, and dir. U. of Colo. Mountain Lab., 1920-29; mem. bd. mgrs. Mo. Bur. of Geology and Mines, 1930-33. Fellow A.A.A.S., Geol. Soc. America; mem. Am. Inst. Mining and Metall. Engrs. (dir. 1938-1941), Soc. Econ. Geologists, Sigma Xi. Clubs: University, Noonday, Town and Gown, Round Table. Author tech. papers and repts. Home: 6228 Pershing Av. Address: Washington University, St. Louis, Mo. Died May 30, 1943.

MCCOY, ELIJAH, inventor; b. Can., Mar. 27, 1843; s. George and Mildren (Goins) McC. Patented steamengine lubricator, 1872; obtained 6 patents for lubricators, also patent for ironing table, 1872-76; received 44 patents (36 of them for lubricating devices), 1882-1926; developed means for lubricating machinery by means of oil drops from cup, which removed need for stopping machinery for lubrication (thus increased productivity); patented steam dome for locomotives, 1885; organized Elijah McCoy Mfg. Co., Detroit, circa 1920. Died Eloise, Mich., Oct. 10, 1929; buried Detroit.

MCCOY, GEORGE WALTER, sanitarian; b. Cumberland Valley, Pa., June 4, 1876; s. Osborne George and Levanda (Walter) M.; M.D., U. of Pa., 1898; hon. D.Sc., U. of La.; m. Edith Miller, Mar. 17, 1901;children—George, Edith (Chappelear). Apptd. asst. surgeon, Pub. Health and Marine Hosp. Service, 1900; surgeon Public Health Service, 1913, and appointed medical dir. of same, July 1, 1930. In charge U.S. Plague Lab., San Francisco, 1908-11; dir. U.S. Leprosy Investigation Sta., 1911-15; sanitary adviser, Hawaiian Govt., 1911-15; dir. Nat. Inst. of Health, 1915-37; prof. preventive medicine and pub. health, Sch. of Medicine, Louisiana State University, 1938-47, professor emeritus since 1947; acting dean, 1945-46. Member A.M.A., Am. Society Tropical Medicine, Am. Assn. Pathol. and Bacteriol., Council on Pharm. and Chem. (chmn. com. on biol. products), Assn. Mil. Surgeons, Am. Pub. Health Assn., Nat. Bd. Med. Examiners, 1921-40, Pathol. Soc. of Phila., Calif. Acad. Med. U.S. Pharmacopoeia Revision (com. on biol. products), Washington Acad. of Science (pres. 1935), Assn. Am. Physicians, Am. Coll. Physicians, mem. USPHS Spl. Adv. Com. on Leprosy, Sigma Xi. Democrat. Mem. Ref. Ch. Club: Cosmos. Author numerous papers on bacteriology and pub. health subjects, particularly in regard to plague and leprosy. Home: 1532 Foucher St., New Orleans 15 LA

MCCOY, HERBERT NEWBY, chemist; b. Richmond, Ind., June 29, 1870; s. James W. and Sarah N. McC.; B.S., Purdue U., 1892; M.S., 1893, hon. D.Sc., 1938; fellow U. of Chicago, 1896-98, Ph.D., 1898; m. Ethel M. Terry, June 13, 1922. Technical chemist, Chicago, Ill., 1893-94; prof. chemistry and physics, Fargo (N.D.) Coll., 1894-96; assistant in chemistry, U. of Chicago, 1898-99; asst. prof., U. of Utah, 1899-1901; instr., 1901-03, asst. prof. chemistry, 1903-07, asso. prof., 1907-11, prof., 1911-17, U. of Chicago; sec. Carnotite Reduction Co., Chicago, 1915-17, pres., 1917-23; v.p. Lindsay Light & Chem. Co. since 1910. Mem. Am. Chem. Soc., Am. Electrochem. Soc., Am. Phys. Soc., Institute of Chem. Engrs. Awarded Willard Gibbs medal, 1937. Clubs: Quadrangle, Chemists (Chicago); Chemists (New York). Author: (with Ethel M. Terry) Introduction to General Chemistry, 1919; A Laboratory Outline of General Chemistry, 1919. Contbr. numerous papers on phys. chemistry, radioactivity and rare earths. Home: 1226 Westchester Place, Los Angeles 6, Calif. Office: care Lindsay Light & Chemical Co., West Chicago, Ill. Died May 7, 1945.

MCCREATH, ANDREW S., chemist; b. Ayr, Scotland, Mar. 8, 1849; s. William and Margaret (Crichton) M.; studied at Ayr Acad., Glasgow U., Univ. of Göttingen; came to U.S. 1870; m. Eliza Berghaus, of Harrisburg, Pa., Feb. 4, 1875. Chemist with Pa. Steel Co., 1870-74; chemist geol. survey of Pa., 1874-85; mem. Contour Topographic and Geol. Survey Commn. of Pa. since 1906; sr. mem. firm of Andrew S. McCreath & Son since 1904. Mem. Am. Philos. Soc., Am. Inst. Mining Engrs., British Iron and Steel Inst.; fellow A.A.A.S. Author: Mineral Wealth of Virginia, 1884; also (with E.V. d'Invilliers, q.v.) The New River-Cripple Creek Mineral Region (S.W. Va.), 1887; Resources of the Upper Cumberland Valley, Southeastern Kentucky and Southwestern Virginia (with same), 1887; has also published 3 vols. geol. survey reports. Address: 121 Market St., Harrisburg, Pa.

MCCREERY, CHARLES, physician; b. nr. Winchester, Ky., June 13, 1875; s. Robert and Mary (McClanahan) McC.; m. Ann Wayman Growe, 1811, 7 children. Settled in Hartford, Ky., 1810, practiced medicine, 1810-26; performed complete extirpation of clavicle (1st operation of kind performed in U.S.), 1813. Died West Point, Ky., Aug. 27, 1826; buried Hartford.

MCCRORY, SAMUEL HENRY, agrl. engr.; b. Iowa City, Ia., May 5, 1879; s. Charles Robert and Ruth Ann (Stevenson) M.; B.S. in Civil Engring., State U. Ia., 1904, C.E., 1908; A.E., Ia. State Coll., 1926; m. Blanche M. Severe, June 30, 1909 (died May 27, 1938); children—Dorothy Emogene, Ruth Roberta. In pvt. practice, Sioux City, 1904-06; drainage engr., drainage investigations Office Expt. Stas., U.S. Dept. Agr., 1907-12, engr. in charge, 1912-13, chief of drainage investigations, 1913-21, chief div. of agrl. engring., 1921-31, chief Bureau of Agrl. Engring., 1931-39, asst. chief Bureau of Agrl. Chemistry and Engring., 1939-42; dir. hemp div. CCC, 1942-46; cons. engr., 1946—; drainage adviser for the Near East, FAO of U.N., 1947-48; cons. drainage engr., Ministry of Agr., Cairo, Egypt, 1948. Mem. Am. Soc. C.E., Washington Acad. of Science, Washington Soc. Engrs., Am. Soc. Agrl. Engrs. (ex-pres.), First John Deer medalist Am. Soc. of Agrl. Engrs., 1938. Clubs: Engineers, Cosmos. Home: 6811 6th St., Washington 12. Died Feb. 18, 1949.

MCCROSKY, THEODORE TREMAIN, cons. engr.; b. Tecumseh, Neb., June 12, 1902; s. James Warren and Josephine (Tremain) McC.; grad. Barnard Sch., N.Y.C., 1919; B.S. summa cum laude, Yale, 1923; Ingenieur Constructeur, U. Catholique de Louvain, 1925; m. Agnes Herriott James, Sept. 2, 1925; children—Marion Currie (dec.), John Warren James. Instr. engring. mechanics and strength of materials Yale, 1923-24, 25-27, also engring. asso. Eno Found. for Hwy. Traffic Research, 1925-27; editorial asst. to gen. dir. Regional Plan of N.Y. and Its Environs, 1928; resident engr. for Ernest P. Goodrich, also planning engr. City of Nanking, China, 1929-30; planning dir., Yonkers, N.Y., 1931-37, also cons. Mayor's Com. on City Planning, City of N.Y., 1934-37, mem. and exec. officer Yonkers Municipal Housing Authority, 1935-37; regional project adviser U.S. Housing Authority, 1938; dir. planning N.Y.C. Dept. City Planning, 1938-40; exec. dir. Chgo. Plan Commn., 1941-42, Greater Boston Development Com., 1946-48; cons. engr., N.Y.C., 1948-68; partner McCrosky-Reuter, 1962-66, cons., 1966-68, specializing in regional and community planning, traffic engring., zoning, capital programming, and related work. Vis. lectr. various univs. Bd. dirs., mem. Belgian-Am. Ednl. Found. Served lt. comdr. to comdr., USNR, 1943-45, ret. Licensed profl. engr., N.Y., N.J., Conn. Fellow Am. Soc. C.E.; mem. American Inst. Cons. Engrs. (secretary), Inst. Traffic Engrs., Am. Inst. Planners (v.p. 1943), Yale Engring. Assn., Am. Soc. Planning Ofcls., Sigma Xi, Tau Beta Pi, Lambda Alpha, Theta Xi. Clubs: RNVR (London England); University (New York City); Yale (New York City). Author of: Surging Cities (with Chas. A. Blessing and J. Ross McKeever), 1948. Contbr.

American Civil Engineering Practice, 1956, and articles profl. jours. Home: New York City NY Died Juyly 1968.

MCCROSSIN, EDWARD FRANCIS, consulting engr.; b. Phila., Jan. 8, 1887; s. Judge William P. and Helen Theresa (Delany) McC.; student O. State University, 1906-09; married Florence Niles Rogers, Feb. 28, 1922; children—Florence Marion (Mrs. Spottswood D. Bowers), Helen Minna (Mrs. J. W. Tudisco), Edward Francis. Mining Engring. and iron ore exploration work in U.S. and Mexico, 1910-17; organized McCrossin & Co. cons. engrs., New York, 1917, since served as pres.; constructed pig iron blast furnace and chem. plant for U.S. Govt. Defense Plant Corp., McCrossin Sta., Tex., 1944; cons. engr. for numerous U.S. and fgn. indsl. and ins. cos. since 1925; lecturer U.S. Army Indsl. Coll., Wash., 1937, Polytech. Inst., Brooklyn, 1936-37, N.Y. and Conn. Ins. Socs.; dir. Seaboard F. & M. Ins. Co., Cherokee Royalty Co., Yorkshire Insurance Co., N.Y. City, Yuba Consolidated Industries; consulting engineer War Department. Served as capt. U.S. Army and asst. dir. of operations U.S. Nitrate Plants, Muscle Shoals, 1917-20, cons. engr. British Joint Insp. Bd., U.K., and Can. on ordnance matters, 1940-43; lt. col. U.S. Army Ordnance Res. Chmn. Leonia Defense Council, vice chmn. Northern Valley, N.J. Defense Council, World War II; dist. chief N.Y. ordnance dist. Army Ordnance Corps, 1953—. Licensed mining engr., W.Va., civil engr., N.J., professional engineer, New York and Pennsylvania. Recipient Citation and Certificate, Sec. Army, 1959. Mem. Am. Inst. Mining and Metall. Engrs., Am. Petroleum Inst., Newcomen Soc. of Eng., Beta Theta Pi. Clubs: Mining, Army and Navy, Downtown Association (N.Y.C.); Knickerbocker Country. Home: 100 E. Palisade Av., Englewood, N.J. Office: 120 Wall St., N.Y.C. Died Sept. 10, 1962; buried Elmwood Cemetery, Birmingham, Ala.

MCCROSSIN, WILLIAM PATRICK, JR., surgeon; b. Birmingham, Alabama, February 14, 1890; son of Judge William Patrick and Helen Theresa (Delang) McC; B.S., Univ. Alabama, 1912; M.D., Tulane U., 1916; m. Leonora Marie Hassinger, Apr. 26, 1922; 1 dau., Leonora Virginia. Interne Hillman Hosp., Birmingham, and Post Grad. Hosp., N.Y.C.; resident surgeon Woman's Hosp., N.Y.C.; served as attending surgeon Hillman Hosp., attending gynecologist St. Vincent's Hosp., and asso. surgeon Children's Hosp. (all Birmingham); moved to Colo•ado Springs, Colo.; now attending surgeon Glockner Penrose Hosp., Meml. Hosp., St. Francis Hosp., Cragmor Sanatorium; mem. staff Penrose Tumor Clinic (all Colorado Springs). Served as 1st lt., later capt., Med. Corps, U.S. Army, in charge operating room, Evacuation Hosp. No. 15, Verdun, France, 1917-19. Mem. Research Found. for Tuberculosis. Fellow A.M.A., A.C.S.; mem. El Paso County (Colo.) Med. Soc., Alpha Tau Omega, Phi Chi, Alpha Omega Alpha, Stars and Bars. Clubs: El Paso, Cheyenne Mountain Country, Cooking; Military and Naval (N.Y.C.); Birmingham (Ala.) Country; Boston (New Orleans). Address: 206 W. Del Norte Rd., Colorado Springs, Colo. Died July 7, 1960; buried Elmwood Cemetery, Birmingham.

MCCULLOUGH, CAMPBELL ROGERS, nuclear and chem. engr.; b. Washington, Apr. 12, 1900; s. Charles Edmund and Emma (Rogers) McC.; A.B., Swarthmore Coll., 1921; M.S., Mass. Inst. Tech., 1922, Ph.D. (DuPont fellow 1927-28), 1928; m. Exia Drummond, Oct. 16, 1936; children—David Rogers, Diane Exia. Chemist, Hygrade Lamp Co., 1922-26; chemist, chem. engr. prodn. and devel. organic and inorganic chemicals Monsanto Chem. Co., 1928-60; project mgr. NDRC Rocket Propellant Pilot Plant, 1944-46; dir. Power Pile div. Clinton Labs, 1946-47; v.p., dir. Nuclear Utility Services, Inc., 1960-65; consulting nuclear and chemical engr., technical director Southern Nuclear Engineering, Inc., 1965-70; Atomic Indsl. Forum; consultant CNEN of Italy. Chmn., mem. adv. com. on reactor safeguards AEC, 1951-59, vice chmn., 1960-61; sci. adviser U.S. delegation Internat. Conf. for Peaceful Uses of Atomic Energy, Geneva, 1955, 58. Recipient Presidential Certificate of Merit, 1949. Member of American Nuclear Society (president 1956-57), Am. Chemical Soc., Am. Inst. Chem. Engrs., Phi Beta Kappa, Sigma Xi. Editor: Safety Aspects of Nuclear Reactors, 1957. Contbr. to Handbook on Nuclear Engineering, Modern Nuclear Technology Mills, others. Home: Rockville MD Died Jan. 13, 1970; buried Anniston AL

MCCULLOUGH, ERNEST, civil engr.; b. Staten Island, N.Y., May 22, 1867; s. James and Caroline (McBlain) M.; grad. high sch., Wyandotte (now Kansas City), Kan., 1883; Inst. of Technology, Chicago, 1884-85; degree of C.E. from Van der Naillen Sch. of Engineering, San Francisco, 1887; m. Elizabeth Townsend Seymour, 1891 (died 1918); children—George Seymour, Caroline McBain (wife of Col. Paul C. Galleher), Elizabeth Howland (dec.), James David; m. 2d, Therese Claquin, of Tours, France, 1919. In engring. practice, San Francisco, 1887-98, Lewiston, Ida., 1898-1903, Chicago, 1903-17, Syracuse, N.Y., 1920-21, N.Y. City, 1921—. Registered architect, Illinois; registered engineer, New York and New Jersey. Editor Engineer and Contractor, San Francisco, 1893-96; asso. editor Engineering-Contracting, Chicago, 1909, Railway Age Gazette, Chicago, 1910, Am. Architect, New York, 1921-22; editor Building Age and National Builder, New York, 1925-28. Served in Ida. N.G. as capt. inf.; in Ill. N.G. as lt. engrs. and lt. F.A. In World War, maj. Engrs. O.R.C., promoted lt. col. Chem. Warfare Service; wounded near Cambrai, Nov. 1917; chief engr. Am. Red Cross, France; chief gas officer, 1st Corps; also chief gas officer, Army Arty., 1st Army; asst. chief and later chief, arty. sect. Chem. Warfare Service; constrn. engr., R.R. and C. Service, June 1917-Aug. 1919 in France; asst. comdt. Lakehurst Proving Ground, N.J., and dir. C.W.S. Officers' Sch., Aug. 1919-July 1920; lt. col. C.W.S., O.R.C., July 1920-Jan. 1926. Mason. Republican. Episcopalian. Author: Reinforced Concrete, 1908; Engineering as a Vocation, 1911; Practical Surveying, 1915, 22; Practical Structural Design, 1917, 3d edit., 1926; Everybody's Money, 1923; La Vie Chère et les Crises Monétires, 1926; Class Warfare, 1927. Home: Long Island City, N.Y. Died Oct. 1, 1931.

MCCURDY, ARTHUR WILLIAMS, scientist, inventor; b. Truro, Nova Scotia, Apr. 13, 1856; s. Hon. David (mem. legislative council) and Mary (Archibald) McC.; grad. Whitby (Ont.) Collegiate Inst.; m. 1st, Sept. 20, 1881, Lucy O'Brien; 2d, Oct. 2, 1902, Hattie M. Mace, Montreal. Student and pvt. sec. in laboratories of Prof. Alexander Graham Bell at Beinn Bhreagh, N.S., and at Washington; inventor of method of printing statistical maps by the use of interchangeable "map type." From researches in photography evolved a scientific system for automatic development of plates and films; demonstrated that salt or sea water may be used in the process; researches of 6 yrs. resulted in introduction by Eastman Kodak Co., Sept., 1902, of the "kodak" developing machine and its accessories. Awarded John Scott premium and medal by Franklin Inst., 1903. Mem. A.A.A.S., Canadian Inst. Club: Cosmos (Washington). Address: Victoria, B.C., Can.

MCCURDY, CHARLES WILLIAM, physician; b. Ossian, N.Y., Nov. 26, 1856; s. David and Lydia (Lemen) M.; B.S., Mich. Agrl. Coll., 1881, M.S., 1885; U. of Wis. and U. of Wooster (O.), Ph.D., latter, 1895; (hon. Sc.D., Milton Coll., Wis., 1892); grad. Phila. Sch. Anatomy, and D.O., Phila. Coll. of Osteopathy, 1903; m. Eva Augusta Woodruff, of Detroit, Aug. 16, 1893. Supt. city schs., Harbor Beach, Mich., 1884-88; head of science dept., Winona (Minn.) High Sch., 1888-92; prof. chemistry and chief chemist, Expt. Sta. U. of Ida., 1892-99; acting pres. and acting dir. Expt. Sta. U. of Ida., 1898; spl. agt. U.S. Govt. on sugar beet investigations for Ida., 1898-99; supt. schs., N. Yakima, Wash., 1899-1901; dean and pres. faculty, Phila. Coll. of Ostpepathy, 1902-08. Fellow A.A.A.S., Research Soc.; mem. Am. Osteopathic Assn., Delta Tau Delta; Mason. Republican. Presbyterian. Author of numerous monographs, bulls. and pub. addresses on scientific and med. subjects. Address: 838 Rosser Av., Brandon, Can.

MCDONALD, ALEXANDER RODERICK, physician; b. nr. Parkhill, Ont., Dec. 30, 1862; s. Roderick and Janet (McEachin) M.; ed. Parkhill (Ont.) High Sch.; M.D., Chicago Homoee. Med. Coll., 1897; M.D., Rush Med. Coll., 1898; m. Mary McDonald, of Sheridan, Huron Co,. Mich., Apr. 30, 1895. Taught sch. in Huron Co., Mich., 8 yrs.; settled in Chicago, 1887; in employ of Western Union Telegraph Co. until 1894; practiced in Chicago since 1897; mem. faculty Chicago Homoe. Med. Coll. and its successor, Hahnemann Med. Coll., since 1898; now prof. materia medica and lecturer on theory and practice of medicine, in same; mem. attending staff Hahnemann Hosp. Mem. Am. Inst. Homoepathy, Ill. Homoe. Med. Assn., Chicago Homoe. Med. Soc. Democrat. Home: 146 Laporte Av. Office: 22 E. Washington St., Chicago, Ill.

MCDONALD, ELLICE, bio-chemist, pathologist; b. Fort Ellice, Manitoba, Can., Oct. 27, 1876; s. Archibald and Ellen (Inkster) McD.; ed. St. John's Coll., Winnipeg, Can., McGill U. (M.D. 1901), Montreal, P.Q.; m. Ann Heebner, Oct. 15, 1907; children—Vicomtess Diane de Branges de Bourica, Ellice. Successively resident surgeon Kensington Hosp. and New York Lying-in Hosp., asst. in pathology, Albany Med. Sch., instr. Columbia U. Coll. of Pharmacy and Science, 1901-07; instr. surgery, N.Y. Post Grad. Med. Sch. and Hosp., 1907-16; asst. prof. of gynecology, Grad. Sch. of Medicine, U. of Pa., 1922-35; dir. Cancer Research Fund, 1928-35; dir. Biochemical Research Foundation of Franklin Inst. since 1935. Served with Canadian Army Med. Service, 1916-19. Awarded gold medal, Internat. Faculty of Sciences, London, 1937. Fellow Am. Coll. Surgeons; mem. Am. Inst. of City of New York, Biochem. Soc., Faraday Soc., Franklin Institute of Pa., Am. Assn. tion of Cancer Research, American Physical Soc., Am. Chem. Soc., A.A.A.S., Internat. Soc. Exptl. Cytology, N.Y. Pathol. Soc. (life), Gen. Alumni Soc. U. of Pa., Graduate Society of McGill University, Pa. Horticultural Society. Clubs: University; Wilmington Country. Author: Studies in Gynecology and Obstetrics, 1914; Ectopic Pregnancy, 1919. Editor: Reports of the Cancer Research Labratories of the University of Pa., Vol. 1, 1930-31, Vol. 2, 1932-33; Reports of the Biochemical Research Foundation of Franklin Inst., vol. 3, 1934-35, vol. 11, 1950-51, vol. 12, 1952-53; Neutron Effects on Animals, 1947. Contbr. author to biol. effects of external radiation, 1954. Home: Invercoe, Sedgely Farms, Wilmington, Del. Address: The Biochemical Research Found., Newark, Del. Died Jan. 31, 1955.

MCDONALD, FREDERICK HONOUR, cons. engr.; b. Charleston, S.C., Aug. 16, 1892; s. William Ogier and Katie (St. Clair) McD.; B.S., in Elec. and Mech. Engring., Clemson (S.C.) Coll., 1914; post grad. extension work, U. of Pittsburgh, 1915-16; m. Katharine Steed Everett, Dec. 1919; children—Mary Fay (Mrs. Lester MacLean), Katharine Everett (Mrs. John T. Jeter), Jane Honour (Mrs. William E. Craver), Anne Ewing (Mrs. James E. Bell). With Westinghouse Electric & Mfg. Co., 1914-16; field engr. Hope Engring. & Supply Co., Tulsa, 1916-17; industrial engr. Lockwood Greene & Co., Atlanta, 1921-23; dir. and chief engr. Ga. Industrial Bur., Atlanta, 1923-24, pres. McDonald & Co., engrs. and architects, 1924-32, private practice as cons. engr., Atlanta, 1932-39; founder community research Inst. and director, from 1939; president Management Research Institute; development and industrial engineer S.C. Pub. Service Authority, 1939-41; cons., industrial engr., Charleston, S.C., specializing in plant location, power developments, and mgmt., from 1941; publisher and editor of Dixie Magazine, 1947-49; dir. Ga. Geodetic Control Surveys, 1934-39. Served as 1st lt. Engr. Corps, U.S. Army, 1917-21, Chairman of the Board of Archtl. Review for Old and Historic Charleston, S.C., from 1951. Decorated Military Order of Purple Heart (U.S.). Mem. Am. Inst. Consltg. Engrs., Am. Soc. Civil Engrs. (dir. 1934-36; organized Engring. Economics Div., 1931, sec. 1931-37, chmn. 1938-39), S.C. Soc. Engrs., Huguenot Soc. of S.C., Charleston Rotary Club (pres. 1943-44), Civil Engrs. Club Charleston (co-founder, hon. life mem., recipient citation from young engrs.). Independent Democrat. Presbyterian Church. Club: Cosmos (Wash.). Author: How to Promote Community and Indsl. Development, 1938; Geodetic Survey of Georgia, 1939; Manual for the Business Aid Clinic, 1940; Manual on Manpower and Incentive Principals, 1951; The Citadel of Business, 1952; Education and Race Relations, 1954; Creative Management, 1956; The New Art of Fabrication Engineering, 1958; also tech., econ. articles in profl. and nat. mags. Home: Charleston SC Died Aug. 2, 1972.

MCDONALD, HARL, composer; b. near Boulder, Colo., July 27, 1899; s. Willis Burr and Floy (Tafflemire) McD.; student Univ. of Redlands, 1917-18; Mus.B., Univ. of Southern California, 1921; University of Leipzig, 1922, hon. Mus.D.; Litt.D., Temple University, 1953; also studied in Berlin; m. Eleanor Gosling, 1925; children—Charlotte Burr, Frances Tabor. Composer since age of 7; teacher Acad. Tournefort, Paris, 1922, Philadelphia Musical Academy, 1924-26; with U. of Pa., 1926-39, successively as lecturer, asst. prof. and prof. of music, dir. music dept., 1935-39; research work in acoustics and sound measurement (Rockefeller Foundation grant), 1930-33; mgr. Philadelphia Orchestra since 1939; European debut with Berlin Philharmonic, 1922. Served in U.S. Army, 1918. Mem. Am. Musicol. Soc., Sigma Xi. Republican. Episcopalian. Clubs: Art Alliance (Phila.); Lotos (N.Y. City). Composer: 4 symphonies, 4 symphonic suites, 3 concertos, 2 string quartets, 2 trios; also tone poems and short works for symphony orchestra, chorus, violin, piano, voice, etc.; about 110 published musical compositions. Author of monograph (with O. H. Schuck); New Methods of Measuring Sound. Home: St. David's, Pa. Office: Phila. Orchestra Assn., Phila. Died Mar. 30, 1955; buried Valley Forge Meml. Cemetery.

MCDONALD, HUNTER, civil engr.; b. Winchester, Va., June 12, 1860; s. Angus W. and Cornelia (Peake) M.; student Washington and Lee U., 1878-79; m. Mary Eloise Gordon, Feb. 8, 1893. Asst. engr. L.&N. R.R., Aug.-Dec. 1879, Nashville, Chattanooga & St. Louis Ry., 1879-89; supt. Huntsville, Fayetteville and Columbia div., same rd., 1889-91; resident engr. Western & Atlantic R.R., Atlanta, Ga., 1891-92; chief engr. Nashville, Chattanooga & St. Louis Ry., 1892-1931; consulting practice. Chief engr. N.C.&St.L. Ry., Tenn. Central R.R. and Birmingham & Northwestern R.R under federal operation, 1918-20. Episcopalian. Edited and published A Diary with Reminiscences of the War and Refugee Life in the Shenandoah Valley, 1860-1865 (by his mother), 1935. Home: Nashville, Tenn. Died Aug. 24, 1937.

MCDONALD, JAMES, engr., business exec.; b. nr. New Castle, Eng., May 15, 1875; s. James and Mary (Paterson) McD.; student Barnes Sch., 1882-88, St. John's Sci. and Art, 1888-1891 (both at So. Shields, Eng.); m. Mary Pass, Dec. 24, 1901 (died 1941). Came to U.S., 1908, naturalized, 1917. Apprentice engr. Middle Docks & Engring. Co., South Shields, 1891-96; marine engr. British-India Steam Nav. Co., R. Runciman & Co., 1896-1905; ship repair works supt. Middle Docks & Engring. Co., 1905-08; gen. mgr. Todd Combustion Equipment Corp. and predecessors, subsidiary Todd Shipyards Co., N.Y.C., 1908-19; v.p., 1919-41, pres., dir., 1946—; bd. dirs. and chmn. com. for cadet tng., Todd Shipyards Corp., N.Y.C., 1945—; dir. Thermo Products Corp. Obtained British Extra First Class Bd. of Trade Engrs. Certificate, 1901; licensed profl. engr., State N.Y., 1937. Mem. Soc. Naval Architects and Marine Engrs. Presbyn. Mason. Club: Doric 86. Home: Deeprocks, Campgaw Rd., Ramsey,

N.J. Office: Todd Shipyards Corp., Columbia and Halleck Sts., Bklyn. Died Dec. 30, 1957.

MCDOUGALL, ALEXANDER, shipbuilder; b. in Scotland, Mar. 16, 1845; s. Dougall and Ellen (MacDougall) M.; came to America, 1854, to Minn., 1870; ed. country schs.; m. Emmeline Ross, Jan. 1878. Sailed for 21 yrs. on the Great Lakes and for 35 yrs. has been closely identified with lake shipbuilding and lake transportation; pres. McDougall-Duluth Co., shipbuilders, Northern Power Co. of Wis.; dir. Great Northern Power Co. (Minn.), City Nat. Bank (Duluth), Northeastern Power Co. (Me.). Inventor of the only method devised for making merchantable the vast deposits of sand iron ores in Minn. Inventor of "whaleback" ships. Home: Duluth, Minn. Died May 23, 1923.

MCDOWELL, EPHRAIM, physician; b. Rockbridge County, Va., Nov. 11, 1771; s. Samuel and Mary (McClung) McD.; attended med. lectures Med. Sch., U. Edinburgh (Scotland), 1793-94; M.D., U. Md., 1825; m. Sarah Shelby, 1802, 6 children. Most noted surgeon West of Phila.; pioneer in abdominal surgery; performed 1st ovariotomy in U.S., 1809, had performed 12 with only one death by 1824; repeatedly performed radical operative cures for nonstrangulated hernia, at least 32 operations for stones in bladder, without a death; used lateral perineal incision; performed considerable work for charity; helped found, gave ground for Episcopal Ch., Danville, Ky.; a founder, 1st trustee Centre Coll., Danville; received diploma of membership Med. Soc. Pa., 1817. Died Danville, June 25, 1830; buried Danville.

MCDOWELL, LOUISE SHERWOOD, educator; b. Wayne, N.Y., Sept. 29, 1876; d. Francis Marion and Eva (Sherwood) McDowell; prep edn. Penn Yan Acad., N.Y.; A.B., Wellesley Coll., 1898; M.A., Cornell U., 1907; Ph.D., 1909. Tchr. sci. and English, Northfield (Mass.) Sem., 1898-1901; sci. and mathematics, Warren (O.) High Sch., 1901-06; fellow physics, Cornell U., 1908-09; instr. physics, Wellesley Coll., 1909-10, asso. prof., 1910-13, prof. head of dept., 1913-45, emeritus prof., 1945—; asst. to asso. physicist, U.S. Bur. Standards, 1918-19; research asso. Radio Research Lab., Harvard, 1945-46; research on dielectrics; asso. editor, Am. Physics Tchr. 1932-36. Fellow A.A.A.S., Am. Phys. Soc. (chmn. N.E. Sect., 1937-38); mem. Optical Soc. Am., I.R.E., Am. Assn. Physics Tchrs. (v.p. 1944), Am. Assn. Univ. Women, Phi Beta Kappa, Sigma Xi. Home: 28 Dover Rd., Wellesley, Mass. 02181. Died July 6, 1966; buried Lakeview Cemetery, Penn Yan, N.Y.

MCEACHRON, KARL BOYER, research engr. Gen. Elec. Co.; b. Hoosick Falls, N.Y., Nov. 17, 1889; s. John Henry and Dora (Peters) McE.; O. Northern U., 1912, M.E., 1913, D. Engr., 1938; M.S. in E.E., Purdue U., 1920, D.Sc., 1941; m. Leila E. Honsinger, Aug. 28, 1914; children—Karl B., William D., Gertrude Louise (Mrs. Howard Babbitt), Robert E., Alice Clare (Mrs. Richard Smith). Test engineer General Electric Company and instructor electrical engring., O. Northern University, 1914-18; research work on nitrogen fixation, 1918-20; instructor elec. engring., Purdue U., 1918-22; head research and development sect. lightning-arrester dept., Gen. Elec. Co., 1922-33, head research engr. high voltage engring. lab., 1933-45; asst. mgr. engring., 1945-49; mgr. engring., 1949-51; mgr. lab. engring. dept. 1952-53; cons. profl. employee relations, since 1953. Mem. bd. Mass. State Bd. Registration Professional Engrs. and Land Surveyors, 1941-51. Mem. panel, Research and Development Bd., Washington, 1947-49. Awarded Coffin prize for development of thyrite, 1931, Edward Longstreth medal by Franklin Inst., 1935; Edison medal of the American Institute E.E., 1949. Fellow Am. Inst. E.E. (dir. 1936-40, v.p. 1942-44); mem. Nat. Soc. Profl. Engrs., Am. Soc. Engring. Edn., Ind. Acad. Sci. Republican. Methodist. Clubs: Stanley, Rotary, Thursday Evening. Author: Magnetic Flux Distribution in Transformers, 1922; Lightning to the Empire State Building, I, 1939, II, 1941; Playing with Lightning (with K. Patrick), 1940. Author of many papers dealing with lightning and lightning protection problems. Home: 23 Waverly St. Office: General Electric Co., 100 Woodlawn Av., Pittsfield, Mass. Died Jan. 24, 1954; buried Pittsfield Cemetery.

MCELFRESH, WILLIAM EDWARD, (mak'el-fresh), physicist; b. Griggsville, Ill., Oct. 5, 1867; s. Greenbury Riggs and Elvira (Morgan) McE.; A.B., Ill. Coll., 1888; A.B., Harvard, 1895, A.M., 1896, Ph.D., 1900; m. Georgiana Frances Adams, June 25, 1903; 1 dau., Frances Adams (Mrs. William G. Perry), Asst. in physics, 1896-1901, Austin teaching fellow, 1901-02, Harvard; instr. physics, Radcliffe Coll., 1897-1901; instr. physics, Williams Coll., 1901-03, asst. prof., 1903-05, Thomas T. Read prof., 1905-36, prof. emeritus since 1936. Fellow A.A.A.S., Am. Physical Soc. Conglist. Author: Directions for Laboratory Work in Physics, 1906. Home: Williamstown, Mass. Died June 2, 1943: buried in Williams Coll. Cemetery.

MCFARLAND, DAVID FORD, chemist, metallurgist; b. Mansfield, O., Aug. 1, 1878; s. Robert S. and Mary J. (McBride) McF.; A.B., U. of Kan., 1900, A.M., 1901; fellow Yale U., 1902-03, M.S., 1903, Ph.D., 1909; m. Martha Elizabeth Pittenger, June 23, 1909; children—George Robert, Mary Louise, Elizabeth Jean, David Ford. Instr. in chemistry, U. of Kan., 1900-02, asst. prof., 1903-10; asst. in chemistry, Yale U., 1908-09; asst. prof. applied chemistry, U. of Ill., 1910-14, asso. prof., 1914-20; prof. metallurgy and head of dept., Pennsylvania State Coll., 1920-45, acting dean School of Mine and Metallurgy, 1922 and 1927-28, professor emeritus, 1945; asst. chem. Kansas Geol. Survey, summers, 1899-1907; asst. chem. and metallographist, Engring. Experiment Station, University of Illinois, summers 1910-20. Discoverer, with H. P. Cady, of helium in natural gas and methods of extracting it on laboratory scale. Mem. Am. Soc. for Metals, Phi Beta Kappa, Sigma Xi, Phi Kappa Phi, Phi Lambda Upsilon, Alpha Chi Sigma, Sigma Gamma Epsilon, Phi Eta Sigma, Alpha Tau Omega; mem. Am. Chem. Soc., 1901-28 (chmn. U. of Ill. Sect. 1919, Central Pa. Sect. 1925). Republican. Presbyterian. Writer of papers and bulletins on organic and industrial chem. and metall. subjects. Home: 121 N. Atherton St., State College, Pa. Died Feb. 5, 1955; buried Centre County Meml. Park, Centre County, Pa.

MCFARLAND, JOSEPH, pathologist; b. Phila., Pa., Feb. 9, 1868; s. Joseph and Susan E. (Grim) M.; acad. edn. Lauderbach Acad., Phila., M.D., U. of Pa., 1889, Medico-Chirurg. Coll., 1898; studied Heidelberg and Vienna, 1890, Berlin and Halle, summer of 1895, Pasteur Inst., Paris, summer of 1903; Sc.D., Ursinus Coll., Pa., 1913; m. Virginia E., d. Gen. William B. Kinsey, Sept. 14, 1892; children—Helen Josephine, Katharine A., Ruth, Joseph. Prof. pathology and bacteriology, Medico-Chirurg. Coll., 1896-1916; prof. pathology, Woman's Med. Coll. Pa., 1911-13; prof. pathology, U. of Pa., 1916-40, now emeritus; prof. gen. pathology, Temple U., Dental Sch. since 1940; visiting prof. pathology, Jefferson Med. Coll., 1943. Maj. M.C., U.S. Army; chief of lab. service, Base Hosp., Camp Beauregard, Alexandria, La., 1918, at General Hosp. 9, Lakewood, N.J., Apr.-Nov. 1918, General Hosp. 14, Ft. Oglethorpe, Ga., Nov. 1918; dir. laboratory instruction in M.O.T.C. at Camp Greenleaf, Nov. 1918. Fellow Am. Coll. of Physicians, Coll. Physicians of Phila., A.M.A., Acad. of Natural Science Phila., Acad. of Stomatology; mem. Med. Soc. State Pa., Phila. County Med. Soc., Am. Assn. Pathologists and Bacteriologists, Soc. Clin Pathologists. Author: Pathogenic Bacteria, 9 edits., 1896-1910; Text-book of Pathology, 2 edits., 1904, 09; Biology, General and Medical, 5 edits., 1910-26; The Breast (with Dr. John B. Deaver), 1917; Fighting Foes Too Small to See, 1923; Surgical Pathology, 1924; also many contbns. to med. lit. in English and German. Home: 542 W. Hortter St., Mt. Airy, Philadelphia. Died Sept. 22, 1945; buried in Arlington National Cemetery.

MCFARLAND, ROBERT WHITE, mathematician; b. Champain Co., O., June 16, 1825; s. Robert and Eunice (Dorsey) M.; A.B., Ohio Wesleyan U., 1847, A.M., 1850 (LL.D., 1884); m. Mary A. Smart, Mar. 19, 1851. Teacher of mathematics, Greenfield Sem., 1848-51; supt. pub. schs., Chillicothe, O., 1851-53; prof. mathematics, Madison Coll., Ohio, 1853-56, Miami U., 1856-73, Ohio State U., 1873-85; pres. Miami U., 1885-88; emeritus prof. civ. engring., Ohio State U., 1902—. Computed the eccentricity of the earth's orbit and the longitude of the perihelion for 4,500,000 yrs., at intervals of 10,000 yrs. (Am. Jour. Science, 1880-3, Vol. XX.) Capt. Co. A, 86th Ohio Inf., 1862; lt. col., 1863-64. Editor 6 books of Virgil, 1849. Home: Oxford, O. Died 1910.

MCFARLAND, RUSSELL S(COTT), petroleum exec.; b. Denver, Aug. 29, 1893; s. James and Helen (Russell) McF.; A.B., Park College, 1915; A.B., University of Missouri, Columbia, also graduate work, 1916; m. Jeannie L. McRuer, Oct. 25, 1917; children—Howard Russell, John Douglas, Jean Elizabeth. Petroleum geologist Empire Gas & Fuel Co., Wyo., Colo., Mont., and Tex., 1916-18; cons. geologist, Dallas, 1918-20; sec. and supt. land geol. dept. Twin States Oil Co. (subsidiary Sun Oil Co.), Tulsa, 1920-29; dir., v.p., gen. mgr. Sunray Oil Co., 1929-31; vice pres. Seaboard Oil Co., Dallas, gen. mgr. Mid-Continent operations, 1931-52, exec. v.p. in charge Seaboard operations, 1952-53, pres. from 1953, bd. dirs. from 1945. Mem. Am. Petroleum Inst. (dir.), Nat. Petroleum Council, Am. Inst. Mining and Metall. Engrs., Am. Assn. Petroleum Geologists (pres., 1928), Mid-Continent Oil and Gas Assn. (exec. com. and dir.; award 1949), Ind. Petroleum Assn. Am. (dir.), Dallas C. of C. (dir.). Clubs: Dallas Country, Athletic, Engineers, Petroleum (Dallas); University (N.Y.C.). Home: Dallas TX Died July 1968.

MCFARLAND, WALTER MARTIN, engineer; b. Washington, D.C., Aug. 5, 1859; s. John M. and Sarah J. (Slater) M.; grad. U.S. Naval Acad., 1879; unmarried. Served on various naval vessels; asst. prof. mech. engineering, Cornell, 1883-85; twice asst. (once prin. asst.) to Admiral Melville, engr.-in-chief U.S. Navy; mem. bd. to reorganize personnel of U.S.N., 1897; chief engr. U.S.N., 1898; lt. U.S.N., Mar. 3, 1899; resigned, 1899; acting v.p. Westinghouse Electric & Mfg. Co., 1899-1910; mgr. marine dept., Babcock & Wilcox Boiler Co., 1910-31. Sec. div. marine engring. Internat. Engring. Congress, 1893; pres. Soc. Naval Architects and Marine Engrs., 1922-24; v.p. Am. Soc. Mech. Engrs., 1907-08. Lecturer at Cornell, Columbia, Johns Hopkins, U.S. Naval War Coll. and Post Grad. Sch., of U.S. Navy, on engring. and econ. subjects. Pres. trustees Webb Inst. of Naval Architecture, 1926-31; pres. Naval Acad. Graduates Assn., New York, 1928, sr. mem. council, 1928—. Died 1935.

MCGANNON, MATTHEW CHARLES, physician; b. Prescott, Ont., Can., Aug. 11, 1857; s. John and Harriett M.; A.B., U. of Ottawa, 1881; M.D., McGill U., Montreal, 1885; post-grad. work, Women's Hosp., N.Y. City, 1891-93; m. Gertrude Snow, of Waterbury, Conn., Apr. 30, 1894. Practiced Brockville, Ont., 1885-91; instr. New York Post-Grad. Med. Sch. and Hosp., 1893-94; prof. diseases of women, U. of Nashville Med. Dept., since 1895; prof. surgery and clin. surgery, Vanderbilt U., since 1907; surgeon-in-chief Woman's Hospital State of Tenn., Nashville, since 1903. Fellow Am. Coll. Surgeons; mem. A.M.A., British Med. Assn., Southern Surg. and Gynecol. Assn., Tenn. State Med. Assn., Nashville Acad. Medicine. Clubs: University, Country. Maj. Med. R.C. U.S.A., 1917; brig. gen., surgeon general of Tenn. Home: 3401 West End Av. Office: Doctor's Bldg., Nashville, Tenn.

MCGAVRAN, EDWARD G(RAFTON), pub. health adminstr.; b. Pachmari, C.P., India (parents U.S. citizens), May 14, 1902; s. John Grafton and Helen (Anderson) McG.; A.B., Butler U., 1924, D.Sc., 1955; M.D., Harvard U., 1928, M.P.H., 1935; m. Mary Graydon Payne, Oct. 26, 1927; children—Edward G., Jr., Merrill P., Mary Katharine. Interne Rochester Gen. Hosp., 1928-29; teaching fellow, Harvard Medical Sch., 1926-28; med. research, Rockefeller Foundn., Egypt, 1927; gen. practice med., Sidel, Ill., 1929-33; county health officer, Hillsdale, Mich., 1934-39; dir. health, W. K. Kellogg Found., 1934-39; survey and study health conditions sugar industry in Hawaii, 1939-40; dir. W.Va. Pub. Health Training Center, Monongalia County Health Dept., Morgantown, W.Va., 1940-41; health commr., St. Louis County, Mo., 1941-46. Asso. prof. pub. health, Washington U. Med. Sch., 1941-43; Assn. Am. Medical Colls., tropical disease studies, Central Am., 1943; prof. pub. health, Washington U. Med. Sch., 1943-46; acting head dept. pub. health and preventive med., 1943-45; prof. pub. health and preventive med., head dept., U. of Kan. Sch. Med., 1946-47; prof. epidemiology, dean sch. pub. health, U. of N.C., 1947-63, professor emeritus, 1963, prof. continued edn. dept., 1969-72; consultant to the Ford Foundation and Indian government, 1963-69; national cons. to surgeon gen. USAF, 1963. Consultant, WHO Expert Com. on Edn. Med. and Auxiliary Personnel, Geneva, Switzerland, summer 1952; -Catedratico Honororio, hon. chair san. engring. National Univ. Engring., Lima, Peru, 1957. Formerly member board Civilian Defense Council for St. Louis County; chmn. med. service com. and health com., incident officer, Civilian Service Corps.; local and area War Priority Bd. Pres. N.C. Health Council, 1954-55, exec. com., 1955—; mem. cancer control com. Nat. Insts. Health. Diplomate Am. Bd. Preventive Med. and Pub. Health. Fellow Am. Pub. Health Assn.; mem. A.M.A., N.C. Public Health Assn. (pres. 1956-57), N.C. Acad. Pub. Health (pres. 1953), Elisha Mitchell Sci. Soc., Tau Kappa Alpha, Delta Omega (nat. pres. 1955). Chmn. editorial bd. Public Health Reports, 1952-59. Home: Chapel Hill NC Died Aug. 29, 1972; buried Chapel Hill NC

MCGAW, ALEX JAMES, civil engr.; b. Belfast, Ireland, Mar. 2, 1909; s. Robert and Mina (McClue) McG.; came to U.S., 1912, naturalized, 1938; A.B., U. Wyo., 1933, B.S. with honor, 1934, C.E., 1937; m. Margaret Hopkins, Dec. 20, 1931; children—Jo Ann, Michael Robert, Nancy Kathleen. Asst. combustion engr. Standard Oil Co., Ind., Aruba, N.W.I., 1929-31; structural engr. Standard Oil Co., N.J., Aruba, N.W.I., 1934; spl. engr. Wyo. State Engrs. Office, 1935; mem. faculty U. Wyo. since 1935, prof. civil engring. since 1943, head dept. civil and archtl. engring. since 1948, acting dean, grad. sch., 1949, coll. engring., 1952, dean of engineering, since 1964—; city engineer, City of Laramie, Wyo., 1940, 41; head structural design Toltz, King & Day, engrs., architects, air base, Casper, Wyo., 1942; cons. engr., 1940—. Trustee Ivinson Memorial Hospital. Fellow A.A.A.S., Am. Soc. C.E. (president Wyoming sect. 1940); Wyo. Engring. Society (pres. 1955), Wyo. Reclamation Soc., Laramie Zoning Commn. (chmn. 1941-46), Bldg. Code Com. (chmn.), Am. Soc. Testing Materials (mem. Rocky Mountain council 1958-60), Am. Soc. Engring. Edn. (chmn. archtl. engring. div. 1957, member general council 1958-60), Nat. Soc. Profl. Engrs. (dir.), Laramie Planning Bd. (sec. 1943-45), Laramie C. of C. (dir. 1941-43), Sigma Xi, Sigma Tau, Sigma Alpha Epsilon. Republican. Episcopalian. Clubs: Laramie Country (pres. 1948), Rotary. Home: Laramie WY

MCGEE, ANITA NEWCOMB, writer, M.D.; b. Washington, Nov. 4, 1864; d. Simon and Mary Caroline (Hassler) Newcomb; ed. pvt. schs., Washington, followed by spl. courses abroad, 3 yrs. being spent in Europe; M.D., Columbian (now George Washington) U., 1892; spl. post-grad. course in gynecology, Johns Hopkins Hosp.; m. W. J. McGee, geologist, anthropologist, 1888 (died Sept. 4, 1912); children—Klotho (Mrs. Willis), Donald (dec.), Eric Newcomb (dec.). In practice at Washington, 1892-96.

Dir. D.A.R. Hosp. Corps, Apr.-Sept., 1898, which selected trained nurses for army and navy service; apptd. Aug. 29, 1898, acting asst. surgeon U.S.A., being the only woman to hold such a position; assigned to duty in the surgeon-gen.'s office as superintendent army nurse corps, which she organized. When U.S. Congress approved this work by making the nurse corps of trained women a permanent part of the army, the pioneer stage was passed, and she resigned Dec. 31, 1900. In 1904, acting as pres. Soc. Spanish-Am. War Nurses and as representative of Phila. Red Cross Soc., and by agreement with Japanese Govt., took a party of trained nurses formerly in U.S. Army to Japan, for 6 mos., gratuitous service during Russo-Japanese War. Awarded Spanish war medal by U.S. Govt.; decorated Japanese Imperial Order of the Sacred Crown, spl. Japanese Red Cross decoration, also two Russo-Japanese war medals. Member United Spanish War Veterans (dept. surgeon, past camp comdr.). Lecturer in hygiene, U. of Calif., 1911; has lectured throughout the U.S. and written for various mags. Was surgeon-gen., librarian-gen., v.p.-gen. and historian-gen. Nat. Soc. D.A.R. Hon. pres. Spanish-Am. War Nurses Soc. Address: 725 15th St., Washington, D.C.

MCGEE, W.J., anthropologist, geologist, hydrologist; b. Dubuque Co., Ia., Apr. 17, 1853; s. James and Martha (Anderson) M.; self ed.; (LL.D., Cornell Coll., Ia., 1901); m. Anita, d. late Simon Newcomb, 1888. While at farm work, 1863-73, studied Latin, higher mathematics, astronomy and surveying; also read law; in land surveying and justice-court practice, 1873-75; invented, patented and mfd. agrl. implements, working at forge and bench, 1874-76; studied geology and archaeology, 1875-77; made geologic and topographic survey of Northeastern Iowa—most extensive ever executed in America without public aid, 1877-81; examined and reported upon building stones of Iowa for 10th Census, 1881-82; became attached to U.S. Geol. Survey, and in 1885 assumed charge of important div.; surveyed and mapped 300,000 sq. miles in Southeastern U.S.; compiled geologic maps of U.S. and of New York; investigated Charleston earthquake, 1886; explored, 1894-95, Tiburon Island, home of a savage tribe never before studied. Ethnologist in charge Bur. of Am. Ethnology, 1893-1903; resigned July 1903, to become chief dept. of anthropology, St. Louis Expn., 1904, bringing together an unprecedented assemblage of the world's peoples; dir. St. Louis Pub. Mus., 1905-07; U.S. commr. Inland Waterways Commn., 1907—; expert U.S. Dept. of Agr., 1907. Lecturer; U.S. commr. Am. Internat. Commn. of Archaeology and Ethnology, from 1902; chmn. organizing com. for Internat. Geographic Congress, 1904; senior speaker dept. of anthropology, World's Congress of Arts and Sciences, 1904; sec. Conf. of Governors in White House, 1908. Leading founder Columbian Hist. Soc.; pres. Am. Anthrop. Assn.; pres. Anthrop. Soc. Washington; acting pres. A.A.A.S., 1897-98; pres. Nat. Geog. Soc., 1904-05; v.p. Archaeol. Inst. America, 1902-05. Author: Pleistocene History of Northeastern Iowa, 1891; Geology of Chesapeake Bay, 1888; The Lafayette Formation, 1892; The Portable Waters of Eastern U.S., 1894; The Siouan Indians, 1897; Primitive Trephining in Peru, 1898; The Seri Indians, 1900; Primitive Numbers, 1901; Outlines of Hydrology, Bull. Geol. Soc., America, 1908; Soil Erosion, 1911; The Agricultural Duty of Water, 1911. Editor dept. anthropology, Internat. Encyclopedia. Died Sept. 4, 1912.

MCGIFFERT, JAMES, prof. mathematics; b. Stockport, N.Y., June 1, 1863; s. James D. McG.; C.E., Rensselaer Poly. Inst., 1891; student Johns Hopkins, 1891-92; A.B., Harvard, 1896, A.M., 1897; Ph.D., Columbia, 1927; m. Cora Emily Medway. Instr. mathematics, Rensselaer Poly. Inst., 1892-1900, asst. prof., 1900-10, asso. prof., 1910-20, prof. since 1920, prof. of grad. mathematics since 1930, counselor and adviser of mathematics dept. since 1935. Pres. Troy Soc. for Spoken English. Mem. Am. Math. Soc., Math. Assn. of America, A.A.A.S., Sigma Xi, Tau Beta Pi, Theta Nu Epsilon. Republican. Presbyterian. Author: Plane and Solid Analytic Geometry, 1928; College Algebra, 1934; also pamphlets, Problems in Mensuration, Mathematical Short Cuts. Contbr. to math. jours. Mem. editorial bd. National Mathematics Magazine. Lecturer. Home: 169 8th St., Troy, N.Y. Died June 18, 1943.

MCGILL, JOHN THOMAS, chemist; b. Monroe County, Tenn., Oct. 13, 1851; s. Robert and Elizabeth (Hogg) McG.; B.S., Vanderbilt U., 1879, Ph.D., 1881, Ph.G., 1882; U. of Berlin, 1885-86; m. Lizzie Allen, July 6, 1893; children—Elsa (Mrs. J. F. Daley), Allen Lenoir. Fellow, Vanderbilt U., 1879-81, instr., 1881-86, adj. prof. chemistry, 1886-1900, prof. organic chemistry and dean of the dept. of pharmacy, 1900-19, prof. organic chemistry emeritus since 1919. Fellow A.A.A.S.; mem. Am. Chem. Soc., Tenn. Hist. Soc., Phi Beta Kappa (sec. Vanderbilt Chapter since its orgn., 1901, and of the South Central District, 1925-37), president Am. Conf. Pharm. Faculties, 1907-08, Tenn. Acad. Science, 1918-19, sec.-treas., 1925-39, hon. pres. since 1939. Author: Introduction to Qualitative Chemical Analysis, 1889; Laboratory Experiments in General Chemistry, 1892; Investment in Universities (pamphlet), 1895. Report to Supreme Court U.S. in Cause State of Georgia vs. Ducktown Copper Co., 1916. Address: Vanderbilt University, Nashville, Tenn. Died Apr. 11, 1946.

MCGRAW, ROBERT BUSH, psychiatrist; b. Cortland, N.Y., Nov. 16, 1896; s. George W. and Julia (Bush) McG.; student Finsbury Tech. Coll., London, Eng., 1913-14; A.B., Cornell U., 1918, M.D., 1921; m. Catherine Ruth Ross, Jan. 2, 1924; children—Robert Bush, Ann Barbara. Intern psychiat. div. Bellevue Hosp., 1920-21, intern surgery and medicine, 1922-24; asst. physician Bloomingdale Hosp., 1924-26, Presbyn. Hosp., N.Y.C., 1925-28; cons. psychiatrist North County Community Hosp., Glen Cove, L.I., 1935—; instr. psychiatry Columbia, 1925-28, chief psychiat. div. Vanderbilt Clinic, N.Y.C., 1928-58, clin. prof. psychiatry Columbia, 1928—. Fellow Am. Psychiat. Assn., N.Y. Acad. Medicine, A.M.A.; mem. N.Y. State Med. Soc., N.Y. Psychiat. Soc. (past pres.), N.Y. Neurol. Soc., N.Y. Soc. Clin. Psychiatry (past sec., past pres.), Am. Orthopsychiat. Assn., Nat. Com. Mental Hygiene. Club: Century Assn. (N.Y.C.). Contbr. med. publs. Home: 1165 Fifth Av., N.Y.C. 29; also Newtown, Conn. Office: 2 E. 85th St., N.Y.C. 28. Died Oct. 23, 1960; buried Newtown, Conn.

MCGREGOR, ALEXANDER GRANT, (ma-greg'or), mech. engr.; b. Raymond, Kan., Mar. 1, 1880; s. Donald and Ada A. (Cole) McG.; B.S. in Mich. Engring., U. Mont., 1902; m. Beulah M. Morgan, June 15, 1905; children—Grant Morgan, Donald Thomas, John Porter, James Bennett; m. 2d, Harriet Rankin Sedman, July 11, 1935. Asst. supt. power plants and testing engr. Anaconda Copper Mining Co., 1902-08; mech. and elec. engr., design of Tooele plant, Internat. Smelting Co., 1909-10; as mem. firm Repath & McGregor, 1911-14, located and designed Ariz. Copper Co.'s smelting works, at Clifton, Ariz.; designed and directed constrn. Calumet and Ariz. Mining Co.'s smelting works, Douglas, Ariz.; located and made prelim. designs of Inspiration Consol. Copper Co.'s main hoisting shafts, etc., also its leaching plant; made general layout of United Verde Copper Co.'s smelting works. Practiced alone, 1915—, locating, designing and building many important mining and metallurgical plants, including Internat. Smelting Co.'s works, at Miami, Ariz., New Cornelia Copper Co.'s leaching plant and works at Ajo, Ariz.; United Verde Extension Mining Co.'s smelting works and mining plant, at Jerome, Ariz.; Cerro de Pasco Copper Corp.'s smelting works at Peru, S.A.; Phelps-Dodge smelting units at Douglas. Cons. engr. in connection with new plants Internat. Nickel Co., Roan Antelope Copper Mines, Ltd., Mufulira Copper Mines, Ltd., Trepea Mines, Ltd. Asso. mem. Naval Cons. Bd. during World War I; in World War II cons. engr. to Brit. Ministry of Aircraft Prodn. and to Non-Ferrous Mineral Development Control. Mem. Am. Soc. M.E., Am. Inst. Mining and Metall. Engrs., Am. Soc. (London). Club: Royal Winbledon Golf (Wimbledon, Surrey). Author: Right wages and Abundance; Collective Bargaining and Decadence; Britain's Way Out. Contbr. on econ. problems. Home: 89 Troy Court, Kensington, London W8. Address: Selection Trust Bldg., Mason's Av., Coleman St., London, E.C.2, Eng. Died Mar. 4, 1949.

MCGREGOR, JAMES HOWARD, zoölogist; b. Bellaire, O., July 23, 1872; s. Robert Alexander and Lucy (Watterson) McG.; B.S., Ohio State U., 1894; M.A., Columbia, 1896, Ph.D., 1899; Sc.D., 1954. Member zoöl. staff, Columbia U., 1897—, professor zoölogy, 1924-42, prof. emeritus since 1942; mem. staff Marine Biological Laboratory, Woods Hole, Mass., 1899-1906; asso. in human anatomy, Am. Museum Natural History, since 1916. Fellow A.A.A.S., New York Zoöl. Society; mem. Am. Soc. Zoölogists, Am. Soc. Naturalists, Am. Society of Mammalogists, Am. Association of Physical Anthropologists, Soc. Vertebrate Paleontol., Soc. for Study of Evolution, American Philosophical Society, Sigma Xi, Phi Beta Kappa. Mem. Associé Étranger, Soc. d'Anthropologie de Paris. Specializes in study of primates and fossil races of man. Club: Explorers. Contributor various zoöl. papers, especially on reptilian and primate paleontology. Address: Columbia U., N.Y.C. 27. Died Nov. 14, 1954; buried Rose Hill Cemetery, Bellaire, O.

MCGUIGAN, HUGH (ALISTER), pharmacologist; b. Lisnoe, Lisburn, County Down, Ireland, Mar. 29, 1874; s. Bernard and Susanna (Alister) McG.; B.S., N.D. Agrl. Coll., 1898; student U. Mich., 1901-02; Ph.D., U. Chgo., 1906; M.D., Rush Med. Coll., 1908; student U. Heidelberg, 1908-09; m. Mabel Leininger, June 20, 1906. Asst. prof. chemistry, N.D. Agrl. Coll., 1902-03; asst. in biologic chemistry, U. Chgo., 1903-06; asst. prof. pharmacology Washington U., St. Louis, 1906-10; prof. pharmacology Northwestern U. Med. Sch., Chgo., 1910-17; prof. pharmacology and therapeutics U. Ill. Coll. Medicine, Chgo., 1917-42, professor emeritus 1942—. Fellow A.C.P., Internat. Coll. Anesthetists; mem. Am. Biochem. Soc., Am. Physiol. Soc., Soc. Pharmacology and Exptl. Therapeutics, Inst. Medicine Chgo., Nu Sigma Nu, Sigma Xi. Mason. Episcopalian. Club: University (Chicago). Home: 2418 Park Place, Evanston, Ill. Died Mar. 1, 1964.

MCGUIRE, JAMES CLARK, civil engr.; b. nr. Ellicott City, Md., Sept. 21, 1867; s. Joseph D. and Anna (Chapman) McG.; C.E. Rensselaer Poly. Inst., 1888; unmarried. With U.S. Geol. Survey. later asst. engr. Nicaragua Canal, engr. with Phoenix Bridge Co. Phoenixville, Pa., and in Supervising Architecs Office, Washington, D.C.; settled at N.Y. City, 1894; pres. James C. McGuire & Co., engrs. and contractors, N.Y. City; pres. Porterfield Constrn. Co., Brookfield Constrn. Co.; etc. Pres. Knickerbocker Hosp., New York. Maj engrs. O.R.C., U.S.A., World War. Died Dec. 7, 1930.

MCGUIRE, LOUIS DAVID, surgeon; b. Wisner, Neb., Sept. 15, 1893; s. Richard Peter and Margaret Ellen (McMahon) McG.; M.D., Creighton U., 1917, B.S., 1919; M.S. in Surgery, U. Minn., 1924; m. Margaret Lucile Rau., Apr. 16, 1925; children—Richard George, Terence Francis, Laurence David, Michael Donald. Practiced in Omaha, 1924—; with Creighton Med. Sch., 1924—, prof. surgery, 1953—; organizer surg. group McGuire, Johnson, McCarthy & Gatewood, 1946; attending surgeon St. Joseph's, St. Catherine's hosps.; surg. staff Children's Meml. Hosp. Regent Creighton U. Served as 1st lt. M.C., U.S. Army, 1918-19. Recipient first Award of Merit, Am. Med. Edn. Found., 1953. Diplomate Am. Bd. Surgery. Fellow A.C.S., Internat. Coll. Surgeons (regent for Neb., 1950-52); mem. A.M.A., Neb., Med. Assn., Douglas Co. Med. Soc. (pres. 1952), Creighton U. Alumni Assn. (pres. 1947-48), Phi Rho Sigma, Alpha Sigma Nu. Home: 3921 Nicholas St. Office: Medical Arts Bldg., Omaha 2. Died Apr. 20, 1955; buried Calvary Cemetery, Omaha.

MCHENRY, DONALD EDWARD, naturalist; b. Great Bend, Pa., Aug. 28, 1895; s. Edward James and Elizabeth Louise (Rooker) McH.; A.B., U. Wyo., 1928; M.A. (research fellow), U. Colo., 1929; m. Bona May Ford, July 14, 1928; children—Douglas Bruce, Donald Keith (dec.). Asst. prof. botany Okla. State U., 1929-32; jr. park naturalist Grand Canyon Nat. Park, 1932-36; park naturalist Nat. Capital Parks, Washington, 1936-47; chief park naturalist, Yosemite Nat. Park, 1947-56; ret. 1956; cons. natural history Saratoga (Cal.) Sch. Dist. and Santa Clara County Cal., Boy and Girl Scouts, also Campfire Girls. Sub-dean and dir. Santa Clara County Am. Guild Organists, 1957-70; v.p., dir. Saratoga Hist. Found., 1959-70; dir. Los Gatos Community Concert Assn., 1958-70; bd. San Jose Symphony, Los Gatos-Saratoga Symphony. Served to sgt. U.S. Army, 1914-17. Mem. A.A.A.S., Audubon Naturalist Soc. (hon. v.p.). Episcopalian. Lion (past pres., dir.). Author articles profl. jours. Address: Los Gatos CA Died Dec. Dec. 28, interment Grand Canyon.

MCHENRY, EDWIN HARRISON, civil engr.; b. Cincinnati, Jan. 25, 1859; s. John and Eleanor (Harrison) M.; ed. at Pa. Military Academy, Chester, Pa., 1873-76, M.C.E., 1892; m. Blanche Handy, Apr. 14, 1892. Began with N.P.R.R., 1883, as rodman; chief engr., 1893-96, receiver, 1895-96, chief engr., 1896-1901, in charge location, constrn. and maintenance, N.P. Ry.; chief engr. Canadian Pacific Ry., 1902-04; v.p. N.Y., N.H.&H.R.R. Co., Central N.E. Ry. Co., B.&M. R.R. Co., The Conn. Co., 1904-13; now retired. Mem. Am. Soc. C.E., Engring. Inst. of Can. Home: Ardmore, Pa.

MCILHINEY, PARKER CAIRNS, chemist; b. Jersey City, N.J., Oct. 9, 1870; s. James and Martha (Cairns) M.; Ph.B., Columbia, 1892, A.M., 1893, Ph.D., 1894; m. Clarissa Ann Walker, Nov. 5, 1895. Hon. asst. in assaying, 1893-94, asst. in metallurgy, 1894-98, hon. asst. same, 1898-1900, Columbia; asso. with Louis C. Tiffany, in artistic glass, jewelry and enamel mfg., 1894—; cons. chemist, 1898—. Silver and bronze medals, Paris Expn., 1900. Home: Great Neck, L.I., N.Y. Died June 21, 1923.

MCILROY, MALCOLM STRONG, (mak'il-roi), engring. educator; b. Rochester, N.Y., Aug. 28, 1902; s. Samuel Hugh and Mary Frances (Strong) McI.; E.E., Cornell, 1923; Sc.D., Mass. Inst. Tech., 1947; m. Dorothy Wellington, Aug. 26, 1929; children—M. Douglas, Nancy W. Test engr. Gen. Elec. Co., Schenectady, N.Y., 1923-25; equipment inspector Brooklyn-Manhattan Transit Corp., Brooklyn, 1925-26; elec. engr. and dist. supt. Central Hudson Gas & Elec. Corp., Poughkeepsie, N.Y., 1926-37; instr., later asst. prof., Mass. Inst. Tech., 1937-47, also asst. dir. Radar Sch., 1942-45; asso. prof. elec. engring., Cornell, 1947-48, prof. since 1948; cons. to Standard Electric Time Co., Springfield, Mass., since 1950. Recipient of the John M. Goodell prize of the Am. Water Works Assn., 1950. Mem. Am.. Inst. E.E., Am. Water Works Assn., American Gas Association, American Society of Engineering Edn., Sigma Xi, Tau Beta Pi, Eta Kappa Nu. Mason. Inventor McIlroy pipeline-network analyzer, 1949. Home: 419 Triphammer Rd., Ithaca, N.Y. Died Mar. 4, 1956; buried Pleasant Grove Cemetery, Ithaca.

MCILVAINE, CHARLES ("TOBE HODGE"), author; b. Springton Farm (Penn Manor of Springton), Chester Co., Pa., May 31, 1840; s. Hon. Abraham Robinson McI. (congressman 7th Pa. dist., 1842-46); ed. country schools, Chester Co., Pa., until 1851; Northwest Grammar School, Phila., 1851-53; studied engring.; civ. engr. div. engr., East Brandywine & Waynesburg R.R., 1859-61; m. Sarah G. McIlvain, Oct. 20, 1864. Raised co. of vols. under war dept., which he attached to 97th regt., Pa. vols.; mustered in as capt., Oct. 1861; apptd. capt. 19th inf., U.S.A., Nov. 1861; judge advocate, dept. South, 1862; chief of ordnance, staff Maj. Gen. Alfred H. Terry, Maj. Gen. Joseph R.

Hawley; apptd. maj. 1st S.C. cav. (col.), 1863; declined; held important positions upon the staffs of several of our noted generals; resigned on account of ill health, 1863; traveled in Europe, 1873-74; chief engr. Jamesville & Washington R.R., 1888-89; inventor of copyable printing ink. Republican. Pres. Phila. Mycol. Center; prin. School of Mycology, N.Y. Chautauqua. Author: A Legend of Polecat Hollow, 1884; 1,000 American Fungi, 4to, 705 pp. (fully illustrated by the author), 1900, 02; Outdoors, Indoors and Up the Chimney, 1906. Home: Cambridge, Md. Died 1909.

MCILVAINE, HAROLD RALPH CLAIR, educator, botanist; b. Altoona, Pa., Dec. 4, 1912; s. Walter and Clair (Miller) McI.; B.A., Pa. State Coll., 1933, Ed.M., 1934, Ph.D., 1939; m. Mildred Dunkleberger, July 25, 1939. Instr. Pa. State U., 1939-43, asst. prof. botany and zoology, 1943-47; asst. prof. U. Ida., 1947-49, asso. prof. botany, 1949, now prof., department biol. scis. Served from pvt. to 1st lt. AUS, 1943-46. Mem. Sigma Xi, Psi Chi. Mason, Rotarian. Home: 404 N. Hayes St., Moscow, Ida. Died June 19, 1962.

MCINTIRE, ROSS T., (mak'in-tir), former surgeon gen., U.S.N.; b. Salem, Ore., Aug. 11, 1889; s. Charles Thaddeus and Ada (Thompson) McI.; M.D., Willamette U., Salem, Ore., 1912; student U. Ore., 1907-12; post grad. student Washington U., St. Louis, 1921, U. Pa., 1928; m. Pauline Palmer, Jan. 18, 1923. Began practice of medicine, Oregon, 1912; commd. lt. (j.g.), Med. Corps, U.S. Navy, 1917, comdr., 1934, vice admiral, 1944; surgeon gen. of the Navy and chief Bureau Medicine and Surgery, 1938-46; specialist in ophthalmology and otolaryngology; instr. Naval Hosp., Washington, 1931-38; White House physician, 1933-45; chmn. president's com. Employment of Physically Handicapped, 1947-54; exec. dir. Internat. Coll. of Surgeons, 1955—. Fellow A.C.S.; mem. Am. Surg. Assn., A.M.A., Assn. Mil. Surgeons. Methodist. Mason (Shriner). Clubs: Army and Navy, Burning Tree (Washington). Home: 825 Adella Av., Coronado, Cal. Office: 1516 Lake Shore Dr., Chgo. Died Dec. 1959.

MCINTIRE, SAMUEL, architect; b. Salem, Mass., Jan. 1757; s. Joseph and Sarah (Ruck) McI.; m. Elizabeth Field, 1778; 1 son, Samuel Field. Designer many colonial houses, chs., pub. bldgs., Old Salem, Mass., designer great house built by Jerathmeel Peirce (his 1st important archt. endeavor); designer house on Salem Common (built 1782-89), Assembly House, 1782, Washington Hall, 1785, Salem Ct. House, Nathan Read house, 1793, Theadore Lyman house, Waltham, Mass., Derby Mansion, 1795, several other houses for mem. of Derby family; remodeled great parlor of Peirce house, 1801; designed a Cook, Gardner houses (among his finest works), 1804; later works comprised hotels, bus. bldgs. of larger scale, including the Archer (now Franklin) Bldg. (his most extensive undertaking) Salem, 1809-10; pioneer in sculpture, furniture design; carved several bas-reliefs for gates of Boston Common; noted for mantelpieces, cornices; his interiors are exhibited in Met. Mus., N.Y.C., Boston Mus. Fine Arts, Essex Inst., Salem. Died Salem, Feb. 6, 1811.

MCKAY, DONALD, shipbuilder; b. Shelbourne County, N.S., Can., Sept. 14, 1810; s. Hugh and Ann (McPherson) McK.; m. Albenia Martha Boole, 1833; m. 2d, Mary Cressy Lightfield, 1849; 15 children. Came to N.Y., 1827; became apprentice ship carpenter; formed partnership as master shipbuilder with William Currier, 1841; chosen to design and build ship Joshua Bates for Boston-Liverpool Line, 1844; established shipyard, East Boston, 1844; designed, built Stag Hound (his 1st clipper ship; 1,534 tons), 1850, became greatest clipper ship builder, ships broke many speed records; converted to use of steam, steel-clad ships (realized wooden ships were obsolete), designs for some Union warships were not accepted (which caused his decline). Died Hamilton, Mass., Sept. 20, 1880.

MCKAY, FREDERICK SUMNER, dentist; b. Lawrence, Mass., Apr. 13, 1874; s. Edward and Harriet Marilla (Wells) McK.; D.D.S., U. Pa., 1900, Sc.D. (hon.), 1952; D.Sc., Western Reserve U., 1955, U. Colo., 1955, Colorado College, Colorado Springs, Colo., 1958; m. Gertrude Eleanor Ronaldson, Dec. 31, 1903; children—Helen Gertrude (Mrs. Bennett H. Horchler), Virginia Mary Neosho (dec.), Roberta Henrietta (widow of Robert Lusardi); m. 2d, Honora Bailey Fink, May 14, 1941. Practicing dentist, Colorado Springs, Colo., since 1901, N.Y.C., 1917-40; conducted research starting 1908, final determination, 1931, of fluorides in water as cause of mottling and reduction dent. decay; resulted in practice of adding fluorides to communal water systems. Awarded Sabin award, Colo. Pub. Health Assn.; Jarvie medal, N.Y. State Dental Soc.; Callahan medal, Ohio State Dental Soc., Spenadel medal, 1st Dist. Dental Soc. N.Y.; Illuminated Scroll, Am. Assn. Public Health Dentists; Lasker award, Am. Pub. Health Association; award for fifty years research on water fluoridation Colo. Dental Soc., 1958; Delta Sigma Delta award, 1959. Hon. fellow Am. Coll. Dentists; hon. mem. N.Y. Acad. Dentistry, Am. Assn. Orthodontists, Rocky Mountain Soc. Orthodontists, Colo., Colorado Springs dental socs., N.Y. chpt. Internat. Assn. Dental Research, Am. Dental Assn., Omicron Kappa Upsilon. Author treatises. Home: 17 E. Buena Ventura St. Office: Exchange Bank Bldg., Colorado Springs, Colo. Died Aug. 21, 1959; cremated.

MCKEE, ARTHUR G., cons. engr.; b. State College, Pa., Jan. 12, 1871; s. Prof. James Y. and Margaret Anne (Glenn) McK.; B.S., Pennsylvania State College, 1891, M.E. from same, 1899; D.Engring., Case School of Applied Science, Cleveland, Ohio, 1941; m. Marion Fairbanks Deane, Apr. 20, 1899; children—Mary Katherine (Mrs. Paul O. Semon, Jr.), Marion Deane (Mrs. John Latta). Engr. Edison Gen. Electric Co., Chicago, 1891-92; gen. contracting, State College, Pa., 1893-95; mining and mech. engr., H.C. Frick Coke Co., Scottdale, Pa., 1895-96; with Duquesne & Edgar Thomson Works, Carnegie Steel Co., 1896-98; asst. chief engr., Ohio Steel Co., Youngstown, O., 1898-1900; blast furnace engr., Julian Kennedy Co., Pittsburgh, 1900-01; dist. engr. Am. Steel & Wire Co., Cleveland, O., 1901-05; in practice as cons. and contracting engr., Cleveland, since 1905, operating under name of Arthur G. McKee & Co. since 1915, pres. 1915-46, chmn. of advisory com. since 1946. Mem. Cleveland Chamber of Commerce, Am. Iron and Steel Inst., Am. Inst. Mining and Metall. Engrs., Am. Inst. Mech. Engrs., Iron and Steel Engrs., Eastern States Blast Furnace and Coke Oven Assn., Blast Furnace and Coke Oven Assn. of Chicago Dist., Cleveland Engring. Soc., Iron and Steel Inst. (Eng.), Am. Hort. Council, Inc., Cleveland Orchid Soc. Presbyterian. Republican. Clubs: Union, Mayfield Country (Cleveland); Duquesne (Pittsburgh); Riomar (Vero Beach, Fla.) Country. Home: 2219 Chestnut Hills Drive. Office: 2300 Chester Av., Cleveland OH

MCKEE, RALPH HARPER, chemical engr.; b. Clinton, Mo., June 20, 1874; s. James Thomas and Mary Frances (Ricketts) McK.; A.B., U. of Wooster, 1895, A.M., 1897; Ph.D., U. of Chicago, 1901; LL.D., Carthage (Ill.) Coll., 1924, U. of Me., 1929; Sc.D., Coll. of Wooster, 1929; D.Nat.Ph., U. of Tartu, Estonia, 1932; m. Mary Coyle Noyes, June 26, 1902 (divorced); children—Margaret Harper, William Noyes; m. 2d, Marian E. Winter, Sept. 10, 1931. Prof. chemistry, Lake Forest (Ill.) U., 1901-09, U. of Me., 1909-16; prof. chem. engring., Columbia, 1917-39; retired. Chem. engr. Tenn. Copper Co.; president Swiss Borvisk Company; director Kerogen Oil Co.; pres. McKee Poplar Forestation, Inc. Dir. (United States) Ordnance School of Explosives Mfg., 1918-19. Member Perkin Medal Com., 1906, 07, 19, 20, 22, 23. Fellow A.A.A.S.; mem. Am. Chem. Soc. (councilor at large; chmn. N.Y. sect. 1920), Am. Inst. Chem. Engrs., Tech. Assn. Pulp and Paper Industry, Soc. for Promotion Engring. Edn., N.Y. Soc. Profs. Engring. Comdr. Order of Polonia Restituta. Republican. Presbyterian. Club: Chemists (New York). Contbr. about 100 scientific and technical papers in Am. and European periodicals; devised and developed to commercial success several new chem. processes. Home: 635 Riverside Drive, New York 31 NY

MCKEEN, WILLIAM RILEY, mechanical engr., inventor; b. Terre Haute, Ind., Oct. 2, 1869; s. William Riley M., Sr.; B.S., Rose Poly. Inst., Terre Haute, 1889, M.S., 1896, M.E., 1897; post-grad. work, Johns Hopkins, 2 yrs., Polytechnikum, Berlin, Germany, 1 yr. Spl. apprentice Pittsburgh, Columbus, Cincinnati & St. Louis Ry. shops, Columbus, O., 1892-3; master car builder and gen. foreman car and locomotive shops, Vandalia Line, Terre Haute, Ind., 1893-7; dist. foreman, North Platte, Neb., 1898-01, master mechanic, Wyo. div., Cheyenne, 1901-2, supt. motive power and machinery, Omaha, 1902-8, consulting engr. motor cars, 1908—. U.P. R.R.; pres. and gen. mgr. McKeen Motor Car Co., Aug. 1, 1908-21. Inventor McKeen 200 h.p. gasoline motor car for rys., and various devices for use of rys. Mem. Am. Soc. Mech. Engrs., Ry. Master Mechanics' Assn., Master Car Builders' Assn. Home: 205 Coast Highway, Santa Barbara, CA

MCKENNA, CHARLES FRANCIS, chemical engr.; b. New York, June 4, 1861; s. William and Mary E. M.; A.B., St. Francis Xavier Coll., New York, 1879, A.M., 1880; Ph.B., Columbia, 1883, Ph.D., 1894; m. Laura O'Neill, 1885 (died 1900); m. 2d, Julia Harlin, 1903. Employed as chemist, 1885-93; dir. Lab. of Phys. Testing, N.Y. City, 1893-95; chemist, Passaic Zinc Co., 1895-97; consulting chemist, 1897—, specializing in qualities of materials. Chemist member Municipal Explosives Commn., New York, 1902-04. Mem. State Bd. of Probation, N.Y. (v.p. 1907), Bd. of Parole, New York City. Chmn. sub-com. chmn. engring. Council Nat. Defense, 1918. Republican. Catholic. Home: New York, N.Y. Died Apr. 25, 1930.

MCKENNA, PHILIP M., manufacturer; b. Pitts., June 16, 1897; s. Alexander G. and Eliza DeHaven (Mowry) McK.; A.B., George Washington U., 1921; children—Philip C., Carol E. Chemist helper, analytical lab. U.S. Bur. Standards, 1913-14; chemist Chem. Products Co. of Washington, 1914-16, gen. mgr., v.p., 1916-20; chem. process cons. Vanadium Alloys Steel Co., 1916-17, research dir., v.p., 1928-38; privately engaged, 1922-25; sole propr. McKenna Metals Co., 1938-40, partner, 1940-43; pres., dir. Kennametal, Inc., chmn.; chmn. Kennametal Co. O.; director Kennametal Overseas Corp. Fellow American Association for Advancement of Science; member Gold Standard League (nat. chairman 1949-55), American Chem. Soc., Am. Institute Mining and Metall. Engring., Am. Soc. Tool Engrs., A.S.M.E. (named Towne lectr. 1953; Holley medal, 1953), Am. Acad. Polit. Scis. Clubs: University, Duquesne (Pitts.); Engineer's (N.Y.C.). Author articles tech. press. Evolved processes of extracting and refining metals, particularly tungsten; experiments instrumental in discovery intermetallic compound tungsten-titanium-carbide. Home: Greensburg PA Died Aug. 16, 1969.

MCKIBBEN, FRANK PAPE, civil engr.; b. Ft. Smith, Ark., Nov. 13, 1871; s. Frank Read and Minnie Elizabeth (Pape) McK.; student of Ark. U., 1887-90; B.S., Mass. Inst. of Tech., 1894; m. Arabelle Almy, Jan. 1899 (died 1921); 1 son, Elliot S.; m. 2d, Ariana K. Elder, Apr. 1923. Instr. civ. engring., later prof., Mass. Inst. Tech., 1894-1907; prof. civ. engring., Lehigh U., 1907-19; same, Union Coll., 1919-1926. Asst. engr. Boston Elevated Ry. Co., 1899-1901, Mass. R.R. Commn., 1901-07; consulting engr. Pa. Water Supply Commission, 1914-15; v.p. People's Trust Co., 1915-19; supervisor tech. training Emergency Fleet Corp., 1918, city engr., Schenectady, 1924-26; cons. engr. Gen. Electric Co., 1927-32, also cons. engineer City of Rochester and engineer of design and construction on two bridges; engineer examiners Pub. Works Adminstrn., 1933—. Republican. Presbyn. Part author: Taylor and Thompson's Concrete, Plain and Reinforced, 1903; American Civil Engineers' Pocket Book, 1912. Home: Fayetteville, Pa. Died Nov. 27, 1936.

MCKIBBEN, PAUL STILWELL, anatomy; b. Granville O., Mar. 14, 1886; s. George Fitch and Elizabeth Thresher (Stilwell) McK.; B.S., Denison University, Granville, O., 1906, Sc.D., 1936; Ph.D., U. of Chicago, 1911; LL.D., U. of Western Ont., Can., 1928; m. Elizabeth Kendall, Feb. 20, 1919; children—Paul Stilwell, Richard Kendall, Elizabeth Thresher, John Hansford. Fellow, asst. and instr. in anatomy, U. of Chicago, 1907-13; prof. anatomy, Faculty of Medicine, U. of Western Ont., 1913-27, also dean, 1917-27; asso. prof. and prof. anatomy, U. of Mich., 1927-29; prof. anatomy, U. of Southern Calif. Sch. of Medicine, 1929—, dean Sch. of Medicine, 1931—. Served as 1st lt. Sanitary Corps, U.S. Army, 1918-19, attached to Army Neuro-Surgical Lab., Johns Hopkins Med. School. Democrat. Episcopalian. Home: Los Angeles, Calif. Died Nov. 11, 1941.

MCKIM, ISAAC, congressman, mcht.; b. Phila., July 21, 1775; s. John and Margaret (Duncan) McK.; m. Ann Bowly, Dec. 21, 1808. Partner (with father) John McKim & Son, importers, 1796-1801, made it successful business, 1801-38; a.d.c. to Gen. Samuel Smith who commanded forces defending Balt., 1812-14; organizer, dir. B.&O. R.R., 1827-31; established free co-ednl. sch., Balt., 1821; charter mem. Protective Soc. of Md. to protect liberty of free slaves, 1816; mem. Md. Senate, 1821-23; built steam flour mill, 1822; mem. U.S. Ho. of Reps. from Md., 17th, 23d-25th congresses, Jan. 8, 1823-25, 33-Apr. 1, 1838; built copper rolling and refining works, circa 1825; originated large sailing vessel that anticipated Yankee Clipper, circa 1832. Died Washington, D.C., Apr. 1, 1838; buried St. Paul's Churchyard, Balt.

MCKINLAY, CHAUNCEY ANGUS, physician; b. Wichita, Kan., Aug. 9, 1890; s. Lincoln and Jennie (Knickerbocker) McK.; B.A., U. Kan., 1914, M.D., 1916; m. Kathryn Christine Thorbus, Sept. 5, 1921; children—Donald Thorbus (dec.), Gordon Lynn, Robert Chauncey, Eleanor Jean (dec.). Intern, Montreal (Que., Can.) Gen. Hosp., 1916-17; resident in pathology New Haven Hosp., 1917-18; resident in medicine U. Minn. Hosp., Mpls., 1919-21; practice medicine specializing in internal medicine, heart and cardiovascular disease, Mpls., 1921-58; cons. health service staff U. Minn., from 1920, clin. asso. prof. medicine, until 1958; former mem. staffs Mpls. Gen., Asbury, Methodist, Northwestern hosps. Dir., Minn. Med. Service, Inc., 1947-59, pres., 1959-60; mem. local med. adv. bd. SSS, 1942. Served to 2d lt. U.S. Army, 1918-19. Diplomate Am. Bd. Internal Medicine. Mem. A.M.A., A.C.P., Central Soc. Clin. Research, A.A.A.S., Am. Coll. Chest Physicians, Am. Heart Assn., Minn. Med. Assn., Hennepin County Med. Soc. (past 1st v.p.), Minn., Mpls. socs. internal medicine, Minn., Mpls. acads. medicine, Minn. Path. Soc. (pres. 1949-50), Minn. Tb and Health Assn. (pres 1959), Soc. Mayflower Descs., Sigma Xi, Gamma Alpha, Alpha Kappa Kappa. Republican. Presbyn. (elder). Mason, Optimist. Co-editor, contbr. to Diseases of Chest and Heart, 2 vols., 1949. Contbr. numerous articles to med. jours. Reserach on infectious mononucleosis. Home: Minneapolis MN Died Nov. 12, 1969 buried Sunset Meml. Park, Minneapolis MN

MCKINLEY, EARL BALDWIN, bacteriologist; b. Emporia, Kan., Sept. 28, 1894; s. Joseph Baldwin and Mary Elizabeth (Griffith) McK.; A.B., U. of Mich., 1916, M.D., 1922; fellow Nat. Research Council, Pasteur Inst., U. of Brussels, 1924-25; m. Leola Edna Royce, June 23, 1917; children—Elsbeth Janet, Royce Baldwin. Instr. in bacteriology and biochemistry, U. of Mich. Med. Sch., 1919-22; asst. prof. medicine, Coll. Medicine, Baylor U., 1922-23, prof. hygiene and bacteriology and chmn. dept., 1923-24; asst. prof. bacteriology, Coll. Phys. and Surgeons, Columbia, 1925-26, asso. prof., 1926-27; field dir., Manila, P.I., Rockefeller Foundation, 1927-28; mem. advisory com. to gov. gen. for control of leprosy, and lecturer, U. of

Philippines, 1927-28; prof. bacteriology, Coll. Phys. and Surgeons, Columbia, and dir. Sch. of Tropical Medicine, U. of Puerto Rico (under auspices of Columbia), 1928-31; dean Coll. of Medicine and prof. bacteriology, George Washington U., 1931—. Intelligence officer U.S.A., World War. Fellow A.M.A., Am. Coll. Physicians, Royal Soc. Tropical Medicine and Hygiene (London); mem. numerous scientific societies. Author: Filterable Virus and Rickettsia Diseases, 1929; a Geography of Disease, 1935; Agents of Disease and Host Resistance (with others), 1935. Died July 29, 1938.

MCKINLEY, J(OHN) CHARNLEY, neuropsychiatrist; b. Duluth, Minn., Nov. 8, 1891; s. John and Alice Salome (Frizzell) McK.; B.S., U. Minn., 1915. A.M., 1917, M.D., 1919, Ph.D., 1921; grad. student in psychiatry, Psychiatric Inst., N.Y.C., 1919; m. Doris I. Swedien, Apr. 29, 1944; children—(1st marriage) Marian Louise (Mrs. Leland Phelps), Helen Alice (Mrs. George W. Miners), Ruth Elizabeth (Mrs. Roy Pistore), John Charnley. Instructor pathology, U. Minn., 1917-18, teaching fellow in nervous and mental diseases, 1918-21, asst. prof. of neuro-pathology, 1921-25, asso. prof. of neurology, 1925-29, prof. of neuropsychiatry, 1929-46, acting head dept. of medicine, 1932-34, head dept. of medicine, 1934-43, head dept. of neuropsychiatry, 1943-46, prof. emeritus 1946—. Sec.-treas. Minn. State Board of Examiners in Basic Sciences, 1931-45. Guggenheim Fellow (studies at univs. Breslau and Munich, Germany), 1928-29. Mem. bd. dirs. Am. Bd. of Psychiatry and Neurology. Fellow A.A.A.S., A.M.A.; mem. Minn. Acad. Medicine, Central Neuropsychiatric Assn., Am. Neurol. Assn., Nu Sigma Nu, Sigma Xi, Alpha Omega Alpha. Contbr. to met. jours. Editor: Outline of Neuropsychiatry. Co-author: Minnesota Multiphasic Personality Inventory. Home: 3501 E. 54th St., Mpls. 6. Died Jan 3, 1950.

MCKINLEY, LLOYD, educator, chemist; b. Bridgewater, Ia., Feb. 4, 1895; s. John Bullock and Nellie (Brown) McK.; A.B., State U. of Iowa, 1919, M.S., 1924, Ph.D., 1927; m. Ruth Muriel McKeen, Sept. 12, 1926; children—Harriett Jo Ann, John McKeen, Donald Lloyd. Head sci. dept., Watertown (S.D.) High Sch., 1919-23; teaching fellow, chemistry dept., U. Ia., 1924-27; head dept. chem., U. Wichita, 1927-60, now prof. chemistry; staff mem. U. of Wichita Indsl. Research Found., 1945-47. Served with U.S. Army, 1918. Mem. Am. Chem. Soc., Electrochem. Soc., Kansas Academy of Science, Sigma Xi, Phi Lambda Upsilon, Gamma Alpha, Phi Delta Chi, Delta Epsilon. Listed in American Men of Science. Author: Bibliography of Achievements in Chemistry, 1930-41, 1942; Inorganic Chemical Nomenclature, 1947. Home: 1648 N. Holyoke St., Wichita 14, Kan. Died Feb. 4, 1961; buried White Chapel Meml. Gardens, Wichita.

MCKINNEY, THOMAS EMERY, mathematician; b. Hebron, W.Va., Apr. 26, 1864; s. Joseph Morris and Margaret (Carlin) M.; B.A., Marietta Coll., O., 1887, M.A., 1890; post-grad. work, Johns Hopkins, 1889-90, 1895-96; fellow in mathematics, U. of Chicago, 1896-97, Ph.D., 1905; m. Mary Margaret Penrose, Dec. 23, 1893; 1 dau., Margaret Jane. Instr. in mathematics, 1887-89, prof. mathematics and Lee lecturer on astronomy, 1890-1906, Marietta Coll.; asso. prof. mathematics and head of dept., Wesleyan U., Conn., 1906-08; prof. mathematics and astronomy, U. of S.D., 1908-28. Mem. Lick eclipse expdn. to Spain, 1905. Author: War-Time Talks and Essays; Life and Education, and Other Essays; Essays and Addresses. Died April 12, 1930.

MCKINSEY, J(OHN) C(HARLES) C(HENOWETH), univ. prof.; b. Frankfort, Ind., Apr. 30, 1908; s. Arthur and Alma Julia (Winks) McK.; B.S., New York U., 1933, M.S., 1934; Ph.D., U. of Calif., 1936; m. May Berger, May 30, 1940; Blumenthal Research fellow New York U., 1936-37; instr. math., N.Y. U., 1937-42; Guggenheim fellow U. of Calif., 1942-43; asst. prof. Mont. State Coll., 1943-45, U. Nev., 1945-56; prof. math. Okla. A. and M. Coll., 1946-51; prof. of philosophy, Stanford Univ., since 1951; on leave as researcher for Rand Corp., Santa Monica, Calif., 1947-49. Mem. Am. Math. Soc., Math. Assn., Assn. for Symbolic Logic. Cons. editor, Journal of Symbolic Logic since 1941. Contbr. articles to math. and philos. jours. since 1934. Researcher in algebra and math. logic. Home: 4231 Suzanne Dr., Palo Alto. Office: Philosophy Dept., Stanford Univ., Stanford. Died Oct. 26, 1953.

MCKINSTRY, CHARLES HEDGES, army officer; b. in Cal., Dec. 19, 1866; grad. U.S. Mil. Acad., 1888, Engr. Sch. of Application, 1891. Commd. add. 2d lt. engrs., June 11, 1888; 2d lt., July 22, 1888; 1st lt., Oct. 11, 1892; capt., July 5, 1898; maj., Jan. 1, 1906; lt. col., Feb. 27, 1912; brig. gen. N.A., Aug. 5, 1917. In charge works for defense of Key West, Fla., and improvements of harbor at Key West, 1898-1900; instr. civ. engring., Engr. Sch. of Application, 1901-03; instr. practical astronomy, same, 1902-03; in charge of fortification and river and harbor works of southern Cal., 1903-06; apptd. mem. Cal. Debris Commn., 1905; assigned as comdr. 158th Field Arty., Camp Sherman, Chillicothe, O., Sept. 1917. Address: War Dept., Washington, D.C.

MCKOWEN, JOHN CLAY, physician; b. Jackson, La., Mar., 1842; grad. Dartmouth Coll., A.B., A.M., 1866; Univ. of Munich, Bavaria, M.D.; served in Confederate cav. to lt.-col.; while capt., June 3, 1863, entered lines of Gen. Banks' army, 30,000 strong, with 5 scouts, and captured Gen. Neal Dow and guard (Gen. Dow was exchanged for Gen. Fitzhugh Lee). Has residences at New Orleans and Capri, Italy; at latter has noted collection of arms, curios, pictures, books, antique statues, marbles and inscriptions. Discovered new disease and remedy and published discovery under title "Aromatic Toxins." Not married. Author: Capri (historical, archaeological and ethnological study); also mag. articles. Lives in New Orleans and abroad.

MCLAUGHLIN, ALLAN JOSEPH, sanitarian; b. London, Ont., Can., June 26, 1872; s. Patrick Hugh and Katherine (MacLean) M.; grad. London Collegiate Inst., 1888; M.D., Detroit Coll. Medicine, 1896; m. Susan Mars, July 16, 1901. Appointed acting asst. surgeon, U.S. Pub. Health Service, Mar. 1900; commd. asst. surgeon, Apr. 1900; passed asst. surgeon, Apr. 1905; surgeon, Dec. 1, 1912. Served in New York, Washington, Naples, Italy, Hamburg and Berlin, Germany, Trieste, Austria, and San Francisco acting dir. of health for P.I., 1908-09; in charge federal investigation sewage pollution of Great Lakes and Missouri River, 1911-12; chief sanitary expert and director field work, Internat. Joint Commn., 1913-14; Mass. state commr. of health, 1915-17; appt. asst. surgeon gen. U.S. Pub. Health Service, 1918; served in N.Y. City, St. Louis and as dir. Dist. No. 3, hdqrs. Chicago; med. dir. U.S.P.H.S. since 1930; chief med. officer U.S. Coast Guard, 1932-36; professorial lecturer in communicable diseases and epidemiology, Div. of Hygiene and Pub. Health, U. of Michigan, 1936-40; medical administrative consultant, Ill. State Dept. of Public Health, 1942-44. Member com. making public health survey of Greece for League of Nations, 1929. Mem. Am. Med. Assn., Mass. Medical Society, American Pub. Health Assn. (pres. 1922). Author: Communicable Diseases, 1923; (with J. A. Tobey) Personal Hygiene (brochure), 1923. Contbr. many articles to med. jours. and to publs. U.S.P.H.S. Home: 107 Glenbrook Rd., Bethesda 14, Md. Address: U.S. Public Health Service, Washington DC

MCLAUGHLIN, DEAN BENJAMIN, astronomer; b. Bklyn., Oct. 25, 1901; s. Michael Leo and Celia Elizabeth (Benjamin) McL.; A.B., U. Mich., 1923, M.S., 1924, Ph.D., 1927; m. Laura Elizabeth Hill, Dec. 27, 1927; children—Elizabeth, Laura Alberta, Dean Benjamin, Sarah Jeanette, Margaret Louise. Instr. math. and astronomy Swarthmore Coll., 1924-27; asst. prof. astronomy, U. Mich., 1927-34, asso. prof., 1934-41, prof., 1941—; mem. staff Swarthmore Solar Eclipse Expdn., Sumatra, 1926, U. Mich. Solar Eclipse Expdn., Me., 1932; staff Radiation Lab. Mass. Inst. Tech., 1943-45. Fellow A.A.A.S.; mem. Am. Astron. Soc. (councilor 1936-39; sec., 1939-46), Astron. Soc. Pacific, Mich. Acad. Sci., Pa. Acad. Sci., Phi Beta Kappa, Sigma Xi, Sigma Gamma Epsilon, Scabbard and Blade. Methodist. Author: Introduction to Astronomy. Collaborating editor: Astrophys. Jour. 1942-45; Popular Astronomy 1942-51. Contbr. paper on researches on eclipsing binary stars, peculiar star spectra, spectra of novae, spectra and light curves of irregular variable stars, surface features of Mars, geology of the Triassic rocks of Eastern U.S. Home: 1214 West Washington St., Ann Arbor, Mich. 48103. Died Dec. 8, 1965; buried Washtanong Meml. Park, Ann Arbor.

MCLAUGHLIN, GEORGE DUNLAP, chemist; b. Retort, Center County, Pa., Aug. 23, 1887; s. George Edmund and Adda (Roche) McL.; grad. high sch.; hon. M.S., U. of Cincinnati, 1924; m. Emilie Sophia Gnauck, June 7, 1915. Chief chemist Leas & McVitty, Inc., Phila., Pa., 1907-11, Kullman, Salz & Co., San Francisco, 1912-19; research asso. in physiology, U. of Cincinnati, 1919-20; prof. of leather research and dir. research lab., Tanners Council of America, same univ., 1921-30; dir. B. D. Eisendrath Memorial Lab., Racine, Wis., since 1931. Awarded Fraser Muir Moffat gold medal by Research Foundation of Tanners Council for researches in tanning, 1937. Fellow A.A.A.S., Am. Inst. Chemists; mem. N.Y. Acad. Sciences, Am. Chem. Soc. (pres. Cincinnati sect. 1925), Am. Leather Chemists Assn. (pres. 1933-34), Wisconsin Acad. Science, Sigma Xi (pres. Cincinnati sect. 1929-30). Democrat. Contbr. papers concerning physical chemistry of proteins and the chemistry, bacteriology and histology of tanning. Home: 3429 N. Main St. Office: B. D. Eisendrath Memorial Lab., Racine, Wis. Died Oct. 15, 1945.

MCLEAN, FRANKLIN CHAMBERS, univ. prof.; b. Maroa, Ill., Feb. 29, 1888; s. William Thomas and Margaret Philbrook (Crocker) McL.; B.S., U. of Chicago, 1907, Ph.D., 1915; M.D., Rush Med. Coll., 1910; M.D. (hon.), University of Lund, Sweden, 1957; m. Helen Vincent, June 11, 1923; 1 son, Franklin Vincent (died May 31, 1948). Interne Cook County Hospital, 1910-11; professor pharmacology, University of Oregon, 1911-14; member staff Hosp. of Rockefeller Inst. for Med. Research, New York, 1914-16; dir. Peiping (China) Union Med. Coll., 1916-20, prof. medicine, 1916-23; prof. medicine U. Chgo., 1923-32, prof. pathol. physiology, 1933-53, emeritus, 1953-65, dir. univ. clinics, 1928-32, dir. toxicity lab., 1941-43, dir. spl. AEC project, 1948-51, dir. special project for USAF, 1951-54; visiting professor, department of histology, University of Illinois College Dentistry, 1966-68. Cons. to Santa Fe Operations office, AEC, Los Alamos, N.M., 1947-49; mem. spl. panel AEC, Washington, 1948-50; dep. chmn. Joint Panel on Med. Aspects of Atomic Warfare, 1949-53; mem. tech. adv. panel on biol. and chem. Warfare Office Asst. Sec. of Def., 1955-60; member subcommittee on Skeletal system NRC, 1952-58. Served as 1st lt. to maj. M.C., U.S. Army, World War; sr. consultant in gen. medicine, A.E.F., 1918. Served as civilian in connection with chem. warfare preparedness, Office Sci. Research and Development, 1941-43; lt. col. and col., Med. Corps A.U.S., assigned to Chem. Warfare Service, 1943-45. Mem. Research Council of Chem. Corps Adv. Bd., 1947-49. Awarded Legion of Merit, 1945, Army Commendation Ribbon, 1947; War and Navy Depts. certificate Appreciation, 1947. Trustee Easter Seal Research Found., 1960-68, past chmn.; dir., sec.-treas. Nat. Med. Fellowship, Inc., Chicago; trustee Fisk U. (chmn. bd. 1951-55). Mem. Assn. Am. Physicians, Harvey Soc., Institute of Medicine (pres. 1959) (Chgo.), Chicago Soc. Internal Medicine, American Physiol. Soc.; Am. Acad. Orthopaedic Surgeons (hon.), Assn. Bone and Joint Surgs. (hon.). Clubs: Tavern, Quadrangle (Chgo.); Cosmos (Washington). Author: (with Marshall R. Urist) Bone: An Introduction to the Physiology of Skeletal Tissue, 1955; (with Ann M. Budy) Radiation, Isotopes, and Bone, 1964). Co-editor: Radioisotopes and Bone, 1962. Home: Chicago IL Died Sept. 10, 1968.

MCLEAN, JOHN M(ILTON), physician; b. N.Y.C., Oct. 24, 1909; s. William and Ella Louise (Powel) M.; M.E., Stevens Institute Technology, 1930, Doctor of Education (honorary), 1965; M.D., Cornell U., 1934; m. Mary Lou Carlon, June 14, 1941; children—Ann Powel, Mary Margaret, John Brandon, Ellen Steele. Intern ophthalmology Johns Hopkins Hosp., 1934-35, asst. resident, 1935-38, resident, 1938-39; asst. ophthalmology Johns Hopkins Med. Sch., 1935-38, Mellon fellow, 1936-37, asso., 1939-41; asso. prof. ophthalmology Cornell U. Med. Coll., 1941-42, prof., 1942-68, prof. clin. surgery, 1942-68; dir. dept. ophthalmology N.Y. Hosp., attending surgeon ophthalmology, 1941-68; cons. ophthalmologist N.Y. Eye and Ear Infirmary, U.S. Naval Hosp., St. Albans, Hosp. Spl. Surgery, Phelps Meml. Hosp., Meml. Hosp. Center, Manhattan Eye, Ear and Throat Hospital. Member advisory bd. N.Y. State Athletic Commn. Mem. Am. Ophthal. Soc., Assn. Research Ophthalmology, A.A.A.S., N.Y. State, N.Y. County med. socs., A.M.A., N.Y. Acad. Med., Am. Acad. Ophthalmology and Otolaryngology, Internat. Congress Ophthalmology, ophthal. socs. Peru, Brazil, Mexico, Chile, Pan Am., N.Y., Miss.-La. ophthal. socs., Harvey Soc., Alpha Omega Alpha, Chi Phi, Tau Beta Pi, Nu Sigma Nu. Presbyn. Club: Univ. (N.Y.C.); Pelham Co. Author eye surgery textbooks. Contbr. sci. articles med. jours. Home: Pelham Manor NY Died May 2, 1968.

MCLENDON, SOL BROWN, psychiatrist, hosp. supt.; b. Marlboro County, S.C., Apr. 27, 1905; s. Baxter Frank and Rena (Ratliff) McL.; A.B., Presbyn. Coll. S.C., Clinton, 1925; student Coll. Charleston, 1925-26; M.D., Med. Coll. S.C., 1930; m. Verna Mae Gray, Mar. 14, 1928; children—Sol Brown, Ronald Gray, William Duane. Intern, S.C. State Hosp., 1930-31, asst. physician, 1931-32, asst. physician State Park unit, 1932-35, sr. asst. physician, 1935-52; med. dir. Palmetto State Hosp., Columbia, S.C., 1952—; asst. supt. Pineland State Tng. Sch. and Hosp., Columbia, 1965—; cons. neuropsychiatry S.C. Sanatorium, 1960—, VA regional office, Columbia, 1962—. Recipient award S.C. Mental Health Assn., 1963. Diplomate Am. Bd. Psychiatry and Neurology. Fellow Am. Psychiat. Assn.; mem. Am., So., S.C. med. assns., Columbia Med. Soc. Democrat. Lion. Spl. research malaria and chemotherapy in treatment syphillis. Home: 1426 Geiger St., Columbia 29201. Office: Palmetto State Hosp., Drawer 189, Columbia, S.C. 29202. Died Mar. 7, 1967.

MCLESTER, JAMES SOMERVILLE, physician; b. Tuscaloosa, Ala., Jan. 25, 1877; s. Joseph and Nannie (Sommerville) M.; A.B., U. Ala., 1896, LL.D.; M.D., U. Va., 1899; post-grad. Göttingen, Freiburg, 1901-02, Berlin and Munich, 1907-08; m. Ada Bowron, 1903; children—Anna, James B., Jane. Prof. meidicine U. Ala., 1919-50. Maj. Chief on Med., Base Hosp., Camp Sheridan, 1917; lt. col. AEF, comdg. officer Evacuation Hosp. 20, 1918; cons. AEF, 1918. Researches and scientific articles dealing chiefly with diseases of nutrition and metabolism; chmn. subcommittee on med. nutrition NRC. Fellow A.C.P.; mem. A.M.A. (chmn. sect. on practice of medicine, 1920; pres. 1935-36; chmn. council on foods and nutrition), Assn. Am. physicians, Am. Soc. Clin. Investigation, Am. Climatological and Clin. Assn., So., Ala. Med. Assn., (pres. 1920) med. assns. Democrat. Presbyn. Club: Mountain Brook. Author (textbooks): Nutrition and Diet in Health and Disease; The Diagnosis and Treatment of Disorder of Metabolism. Home: 3224 Country Club Rd. Office: 930 S. 20th St., Birmingham, Ala. Died Feb. 8, 1954.

MCMAHON, BERNARD, horticulturist; b. Ireland, 1775. Came to U.S., 1796; established nurseries, greenhouses, exptl. gardens nr. Germantown turnpike between Phila. and Nicetown; established seed and gen. nursery business, Phila. (one of largest in U.S. at time); published seed catalogue, 1804, Author: The American Gardener's Calendar (1st notable hort. book in Am.), 1806. Died Sept. 18, 1816.

MCMARTIN, CHARLES, urologist; b. nr. Dunlap, Ia., May 11, 1880; s. Archibald I. and Harriet Amelia (Smith) McM.; Ph.B., Grinnel (Ia.) Coll., 1902; M.D., Rush Med. Sch., 1906; m. Mary Elizabeth O'Kelly (dec. Feb. 21, 1951); children—William Joseph, Harriet Margaret (Mrs. Dale Norman). Intern Alexian Hosp., Chicago, 1906-07; pvt. practice medicine, specialist urology, Omaha, since 1908; prof. urology Creighton U. Med. Sch. since 1910, prof. dermatology, urology, 1910-45, head dept. surgery, mem. bd. adminstrn. (also St. Joseph's Hosp.), 1936-50. Diplomate Am. Bd. Urology. Fellow A.C.S.; mem. A.M.A., Am. Urol. Assn. (pres. South Central sect. 1938, nat. pres. 1947), Neb. State (pres. 1945), Douglas Co. (pres 1935), Omaha med. socs., Omaha Midwest Clin. Soc. (pres. 1941). Home: 1714 Douglas St., Omaha 2. Office: City Nat. Bank Bldg., Omaha 2, Neb. Died Sept. 14, 1954; buried Forest Lawn Cemetery, Omaha.

MCMASTER, LEROY, chemist; b. Mt. Pleasant, Md., Mar. 26, 1879; s. John Lincoln and Susan Catharine (Barrick) McM.; Ph.B., Dickinson Coll., 1901, M.A., 1902, ScD. (hon.), 1931; Ph.D., Johns Hopkins, 1906; m. Anna B. Jones, June 12, 1902; m. 2d, Ernestine T. Schafer, Feb. 7, 1923. Instr. chemistry, Dickinson Coll., 1901-04; fellow Johns Hopkins, 1905-06; instr. chemistry, Washington U., 1906, asst. prof., 1912, prof. since 1914, head of dept. since 1920, Eliot prof. since 1921. Mem. Am. Chem. Soc. Soc. Chem. Industry (London), Phi Beta Kappa, Alpha Chi Sigma, Beta Theta Pi, Sigma Xi, Tau Pi Epsilon, Tau Beta Pi. Democrat. York and Scottish Rite Mason (K.T., Shriner). Home: Gatesworth Hotel. Address: Washington Univ., St. Louis 5, Mo. Died Sept. 1, 1946; buried Valhalla Cemetery, St. Louis.

MCMASTER, PHILIP DURYEE, research physician; b. Phila., Sept. 14, 1891; s. John Bach and Gertrude (Stevenson) McM.; student pvt. schs., Phila.; B.S., Princeton, 1914; M.D., U. Pa., 1918; spl. student U. Freiburg, Germany, 1914, Columbia, 1921; m. Elizabeth Parsons Dwight, Oct. 13, 1923; children—Gail Parsons (Mrs. Charles Booth Alling, Jr.), Philip Robert Bache. Resident physician U. Pa. Hosp., 1917-19; fellow Rockefeller Inst. Med. Research, 1919-20, asst., 1920-22, asso., 1922-26, asso. mem., 1926-51, mem., prof., 1951-62, prof. emeritus, 1962-73; fellow research psychology Harvard, 1929-30. Served 1st lt. U.S. Army, 1918. Fellow A.A.A.S.; member of Nat. Acad. Scis., N.Y. Acad. Sci., N.Y. Acad. Medicine, Harvey Soc. (sec. 1927-28), Am. Assn. Immunologists, Am. Soc. Exptl. Pathology, Am. Assn. Pathologists and Bacteriologists, Am. Soc. Exptl. Biology and Medicine, Sigma Xi, Alpha Omega Alpha. Clubs: Princeton (New York); Riverside (Conn.) Yacht; Century. Home: Cos Cob CT Died Mar 1973.

MCMATH, ROBERT EMMETT, civil engr.; b. Varick, Seneca Co., N.Y., Apr. 28, 1833; grad. Williams Coll., 1857; m. Dec. 29, 1859, Frances E. Brodie, Detroit. Deputy co. surveyor, St. Louis, 1860-62; U.S. Coast Survey, 1862-65; asst. engr. U.S.A., rivers and harbors, Ill., Ark. and Miss. rivers, 1866-80; with Mississippi River Commn., 1880-83; sewer commr. St. Louis, 1883-91; private practice, 1891-93; pres. bd. public improvements, St. Louis, 1893-1901; consulting engr., 1901-03. Address: 328 Lincoln Bldg., St. Louis.

MCMATH, ROBERT R(AYNOLDS), astronomer, engr.; b. Detroit, Mich., May 11, 1891; s. Francis Charles and Josephine (Cook) M.; student Detroit U. Sch., 1903-09; B.C.E., U. of Mich., 1913, hon. A.M., 1933; hon. D.Sc., Wayne U., 1938, Penn. Mil. Coll., 1941; m. Mary Rodgers Garrison, Dec. 1, 1921, 1 dau., Madeline. Draftsman with Canadian Bridge Co., 1913-14; asst. engr. St. Lawrence Bridge Co., 1914-17; gen. mgr. Biltmore Estates Co., 1919-22; asst. mgr., later v.p. and gen. mgr., Motors Metal Mfg. Co., 1922-25, pres., 1925-38, chmn. bd. 1938-54; prof. astronomy dept. astronomy U. Mich., 1951-61, now emeritus; chmn. Abrasive & Metal Products Co., 1954—; dir. Detroit Edison Co. Pres. bd. dirs. Assn. Univs. for Research in Astronomy, 1957-58, chmn. 1958—. Codonor of the McMath-Hulbert Obs. to the U. Mich., 1931, dir. 1931-61, now emeritus. Mem. several spl. coms. or commns. and govtl. agys. Pres.'s Medal for Merit, 1948. Trustee William Beaumont Hospital, 1953—; chmn. bd. trustees Cranbrook Inst. Sci., 1946-50, 1958—; chmn. bd. trustees Rackham Engineering Foundation, 1958—. Awarded John Price Wetherill medal, Franklin Inst., 1933; Soc. Motion Picture Engrs. Jour. award, 1940; fellow A.A.A.S. (v.p. 1940), Royal Astron. Soc., Am. Phys. Soc., Am. Geog. Soc., Detroit Acad. Natural Scis., Photog. Soc. Am.; mem. Am. Astron. Soc. (pres. 1952-54), American Philosophical Society, National Academy of Sciences, other nat. and local, profl. and scientific orgns., also photographic socs. Attended Congreso Interamericano de Astrofisica, Mexico City, 1942 (invited). Republican. Episcopalian. Clubs: Detroit, Detroit Country, Turtle Lake, Bloomfield Hills Country, Cosmos; University (New York City, New York); Recess, Economic, The Hundred (Detroit). Contbr. astron. articles various publs. Died Jan. 2, 1962.

MCMEEN, SAMUEL GROENENDYKE, consulting engr.; b. Eugene, Ind., Nov. 28, 1864; s. James McEwen and Ann (Groenendyke) M.; ed. Purdue U., Ind., 1883-84; m. Myra Dale Dutton, Nov. 1, 1888; children—Maurice James, Mrs. Catherine Dale Clark; m. 2d, Auta Judith Proctor, Dec. 23, 1897. Central Union Telephone Co., 1885-1902, assistant engr., 1893-96, chief engineer, 1896-1902; with the Western Electric Co., 1902-04; mem. McMeen & Miller, 1904-18; pres. sundry public utility cos., 1912-20; pres. Columbus (O.) Ry., Power & Light Co., 1912-19; v.p. E. W. Clark & Co. Management Corp., 1913-20; chmn. bd. North Electric Mfg. Co., 1918-22. Editor of Archery mag. Fellow Am. Inst. E.E.; hon. life mem. Nat. Archery Assn. Joint Author: Telephony (with Kempster B. Miller); American Handbook for Electrical Engineers; American Archery (with Dr. R. P. Elmer). Home: Pasadena, Calif. Died June 22, 1934.

MCMURRICH, J(AMES) PLAYFAIR, educator; b. Toronto, Ont., Oct. 16, 1859; s. Hon. John and Janet (Dickson) M.; A.B., U. Toronto, 1879, A.M., 1881; Ph.D., Johns Hopkins, 1885; m. Katie Moodie, Sept. 20, 1882. Prof. biology Ont. Agrl. Coll., 1882-84; instr. mammalian anatomy Johns Hopkins, 1884-86; prof. biology Haverford Coll., 1886-89; docent, asst. prof. animal morphology Clark U., 1889-92; prof. biology U. Cin., 1892-94; prof. anatomy U. Mich., 1894-1907, dir. anat. lab., 1898-1907; prof. anatomy U. Toronto, 1907—, dean sch. grad. studies, 1922-30; instr. Woods Hole, Mass., 1887-91. Mem. adv. bd. Wistar Inst. Anatomy, Phila. Fellow Royal Micros. Soc., Royal Soc. Can. (pres. 1922), A.A.A.S. (pres. 1922); mem. Zool. Soc. London (corr.), Am. Philos. Soc., Am. Soc. Naturalists (pres. 1907), Assn. Am. Anatomists (pres. 1908-09), Am. Zool Soc. (sec. 1890-93). Author: Invertebrate Morphology, 1894; The Development of the Human Body, 1902, 7th edit. 1923; Leonardo de Vinci The Anatomist, 1930; also various papers on zool. and anat. subjects in Am. and European periodicals. Editor: Sobotta's Atlas of Anatomy, 1906; Morris' Human Anatomy, 4th edit., 1907. Home: Elgin St., Thornhill, Ont. Office: Dept. of Anatomy, U. Toronto, Toronto, Ont., Can. Died Feb. 9, 1939.

MCMURTRIE, WILLIAM, chemist; b. Belvidere, N.J., Mar. 10, 1851; s. Abram and Almira M.; E.M., Lafayette Coll., 1871, M.S., 1874, Ph.D., 1875; m. Helen M. Douglass, Apr. 5, 1876. Asst. and chief chemist, 1872-79, spl. agt. in agrl. technology, 1879-82, U.S. Dept. Agr.; prof. chemistry, U. of Ill., 1882-88; chemist New York Tartar Co., 1888—; consulting chemist Royal Baking Powder Co., 1899—; consulting prof. gen. tech. chemistry, Poly. Inst., Brooklyn, 1905—; also 2d v.p. Royal Baking Powder Co., 1908—. Chemist Ill. State Bd. Agr., 1884-88, Ill. Agrl. Expt. Sta., 1886-88. Agt. Dept. Agr. at Paris Expn., 1878; chmn. com. on wools, Bur. Awards, Chicago Expn., 1893. Chevalier du Mérite Agricole, France, 1883. Author: Culture of the Beet and Manufacture of Sugar Therefrom, 1880; The Culture of Sumac, 1880; Grape Culture in the United States, 1883; Wools and Other Animal Fibres, 1886, 1901. Home: New York, N.Y. Died May 24, 1913.

MCNAIR, JAMES BIRTLEY, chemist, botanist; b. Hazleton, Pa., Mar. 18, 1889; s. Thomas Speer and Mary (Stevens) McN.; Pomona College, Claremont, Calif., 1912-13; A.B., U. of Calif., 1916, A.M., 1917; studied U. of Pa., 1918, U. of Chicago, 1922-25, U. of Southern Calif., 1934, Chemical Warfare Sch., Edgewood, Md., 1929, 1943. Asst. in U. of Calif., 1914-16; research chemist Nev. Agrl. Expt. Sta., 1917; asst. chemist Citrus By-Product Lab., Bur. Chemistry, U.S. Dept. Agr., Los Angeles, Calif., 1919; chemist in charge Chem. Econ. Co., Los Angeles, 1920; jr. chemist Dairy Div. Bur. Animal Industry, U.S. Dept. Agr., Washington, D.C., 1920-21; asst. Fishery Food Lab., Bur. Fisheries, Washington, D.C., 1921-22; asst. chemist Bur. Internal Revenue, Treas. Dept., Chicago, Ill., May-Oct. 1922; asso. in econ. botany, 1925-26, asst. curator of econ. botany, Field Museum Natural History, Chicago, 1926-32; cons. in ethnobotany, Southwest Museum, Los Angeles, since 1929; asst. wine maker and chemist, Pacific Wines, Inc., Los Angeles, from 1945. Pvt. Med. Enlisted Reserve Corps, U.S. Army, June 1918-Apr. 1919; served in C.W.S., World War II. Awarded Certificate of Merit by Institute of Am. Genealogy, 1939. Fellow A.A.A.S., Soc. Antiquaries of Scotland; mem. profl. assns. Republican. Presbyn. Mason (32 degree, Shriner). Club: Sierra. Author: McNair, McNear, and McNeir Genealogies, 1923, supplement, 1928; Rhus Dermatitis, Its Pathology and Chemotherapy, 1923; Citrus Products, Part I, 1926, Part II, 1927; The Analysis of Fermentation Acids, 1947 (reprint 1952); Simon Cameron's Adventure in Iron, 1949; With Rod and Transit; the engineering career of Thomas S. McNair, 1951; Chemical Plant Phylogeny, 1965. Contbr. Dictionary of Am. Biography, Collier's Med. Ency.; McNair, McNear and McNeir Geneologies Supplement, 1955. Investigations in economic botany, analysis of acids, interrelation between chemical substances in plants, taxonomic and climatic distribution chemical products in plants, chem. products in relation to plant and animal evolution; also plant forms, habits and habitats, law of mass action and production of alkaloids, etc. Home: Los Angeles CA Died Dec. 31, 1967.

MCNALLY, WILLIAM DUNCAN, toxicologist, chemist; b. Saginaw, Mich., July 8, 1882; s. Edward Hilton and Elizabeth (McNally) McN. (parents not related); A.B., U. Mich., 1905; postgrad. U.Ill., 1905-06, 1914-15, U.Chgo., 1916-17; M.D., Rush Med. Coll., 1920; m. Helen Marie Pierce, Sept. 22, 1906; children—William Duncan, Jerome Pierce (dec.), George Edward. Instr. chemistry, U. Ill., 1905-06; chemist Armour & Co., 1906-10; chief chemist Health Dept., Chgo., 1910-13; asso. prof. materia medica and toxicology Rush Med. Coll., 1923—; asso. prof. U. Ill. Sch. Medicine, 1941—; chief chemist, toxicologist Cook County Coroner, 1913-29, toxicologist, 1941-48; cons. toxicologist Children's Meml. Hosp., Ill. Masonic Hosp., Chgo. Intern, St. Joseph's Hosp., Chgo., 1920-21; in practice in Chgo., 1921—, now limited to internal medicine and consultation in toxicology. Apptd. lt. col. Chem. Warfare R.C., U.S. Army, inactive 1943. Mem. Ill. State, Chgo. med. socs., Am. Chem. Soc., Chgo. Chem. Soc., Am. Assn. Ind. Phys. and Surg., Central States Soc. Ind. Medicine and Surgery, Am. Pub. Health Assn., Am. Assn. Indsl. Hygiene, Phi Beta Phi. Republican. Methodist. Mason (32 deg., Shriner). Author: Medical Jurisprudence and Toxicology, 1939. Asso. editor Indsl. Medicine. Home 3734 N. Harding Av. Office: 4753 Broadway, Chgo. Died June 1961.

MCNAUGHT, JAMES B(ERNARD), pathologist, educator; b. Girard, Kan., July 11, 1894; s. Joseph Ezra and Agnes Abbie (Johnson) McN.; A.B., U. of Kan., 1917, A.M., 1917; M.D., Stanford, 1931; unmarried. Instr. bacteriology U. Kan., 1919-21; dir. labs. Burnett Sanitarium, Fresno, Cal., 1923-27; asst. pathology Stanford, 1930-31, instr. pathol., 1931-35, asst. prof. pathol., 1935-40, asso. prof. pathol., 1940-45; exchange instr. pathol., U. Rochester, 1934-35; dir. and pathol. Palo Alto (Calif.) Hosp., 1937-45; prof. and head pathol. dept. U. Colo., 1945—. Served as 1st lt., Inf., U.S. Army, World War I. Cons. to A.E.C., Div. Biol. and Medicine, 1948—. Expert cons. to Surgeon Gen., U.S. Army, 1946—; cons. pathology to surgeon gen. U.S. Air Force, 1952—; area cons. in pathol. St. Louis Med. area, Vets. Adminstrn., 1946—; mem. sci. adv. bd. consultants to Armed Forces Inst. of Pathology, 1955—. Trustee Belle Bonfils Memorial Blood Bank, Denver, 1945—. Diplomate Am.Bd. Pathology (trustee 1944-56, pres. 1953-55). Mem. A.M.A., Am. Soc. Clin. Pathol. (pres. 1949-50), Coll. Am. Pathol. (gov. 1947), Am. Assn. Pathol. and Bacteriol. (councilor 1949—, pres. 1953-54), Internat. Assn. Med. Mus. (councilor 1949-51, v.p. 1951-52, pres. 1952-53), Am. Phys. Art Assn. (charter mem.), Am. Soc. Exptl. Pathol., A.A.A.S., Am. Soc. Tropical Med., Am. Society Parasitol., Fedn. Am. Socs. for Exptl. Biol., Soc. for Exptl. Biol. and Med., Alpha Kappa Kappa (asso. editor, The Centaur of A.K.K., 1933-46, hon. grand v.p., 1938-40), Alpha Omega Alpha, Phi Delta Kappa, Sigma Xi. Research on various phases of trichinosis, 1936—. Contbr. sci. articles on bacteriol., pathol. and med. history to profl. pubs. Office: Univ. of Colo. Med. Center, 4200 E. Ninth Av., Denver 20. Died Aug. 7, 1959; buried Girard, Kan.

MCNAUGHTON, ANDREW GEORGE LATTA, cons. engr.; b. Moosomin, Saskatchewan, Feb. 25, 1887; s. Robert D. and Christina, Mary Ann (Armour) McN.; B.Sc., McGill U., 1910, M.Sc., 1912, LL.D., 1920; D.C.L., Bishop Univ., 1937; LL.D., Queen's Univ., 1941, U. of Birmingham, 1942, University of Ottawa, 1943, U. Saskatchewan, 1944, Michigan State U., 1955, U. Toronto, 1961; Dr. Mil. Science, Royal Mil. College of Can., 1963; graduate Royal Staff Coll., Camberley, Eng., and Imperial Defense Coll., London, Eng.; m. Mabel Clara Stuart Weir, Sept. 17, 1914; children—Christina Pauline Stuart (Mrs. T. K. McDougall), Andrew Robert Leslie, Edward Murray Dalzell, Ian George Armour (killed in action 1942), Leslie Anita (Mrs. H. Calvin Sykes, Jr.). Commd. lt., Canadian Army, 1910, advancing to gen., 1944, ret.; mem. com. for reorganizing Canadian Militia, 1919; dep. chief of gen. staff Nat. Defence Hdqrs., Ottawa, 1923-26, chief, 1929-35; general officer commanding First Canadian Div., 1939, comdr. VII Corps, 1940; general officer commanding-in-chief First Canadian Army Overseas, 1942-44; mem. Privy Council of Can., minister of nat. defence, Nov. 1944-Aug. 21, 1945; pres. Canadian Atomic Energy Control Bd. to Jan. 1948; delegate of Canada to UN, 1948-50, rep. of Canada, AEC, UN, 1946-50; chmn. Internat. Joint Commn., 1950-62; chmn. Canadian sect. Can.-U.S. Joint Bd. on Def., 1945-59. Decorated Commander of Order of Bath, Comdr. Order of St. Michael and St. George, D.S.O., Companion of Honor; Order of Leopold (Belgium), 1946; also numerous medals and awards assns. and profl. orgns. Hon. mem. several assns. Mem. Anglican Ch. Clubs: Rideau (Ottawa); University, Royal St. Lawrence Yacht (Montreal). Joint inventor cathode ray direction finder, 1926. Home: Fernbank, Rockcliffe Pk., Ottawa, Can. Died July 11, 1966.

MCNEAL, ALICE, physician, anesthesiologist; born Hinsdale, Ill., Dec. 26, 1897; d. Charles Samuel and Carrie May (Johnston) McNeal; B.S., U. of Chicago, 1918, M.D., 1922. Interne Woman's Hosp., Phila.,

1921-22; mem. anesthesia staff, Presbyterian Hosp., Chicago, 1927-38, also instr., Rush Med. Coll., 1928-38; resident anesthesia, Hartford (Conn.) Hosp., 1939; anesthesia staff, Presbyterian Hosp., 1940-46; asso. prof., dept. of anesthesia, Med. Coll. of Ala., 1946-48, prof. since 1948; chief of the clinical conduct of anesthesia, University Hospital, 1946—; director school for nurse anesthetists 1946—; cons. in anesthesia, V.A. Diplomate Am. Bd. of Anesthesiology, 1941; fellow A.M.A., Internat. Coll. of Anesthesia, Am. Coll. of Anesthesiologists; mem. A.A.A.S., N.Y. Acad. Science, Internat. Anesthesia Research Soc., Am. Soc. Anesthesiologists. Contbr. articles in med. jours. Home: 3418 Pine Ridge Rd., Birmingham 9. Office: Medical Center, Birmingham 3. Died Dec. 29, 1964.

MCNEAL, DONALD HAMLIN, cons. engineer; constrn. exec.; b. Kenton, O., Apr. 28, 1901; s. Frank and Blanche (Young) McN.; B.S., U. of Colo., 1922; grad. work Mass. Inst. Tech., 1923; m. Claudia Alice Enright, Feb. 18, 1925; 1 son, John Enright. Field engr. Colo. State Highway, 1918-22; structural designer Fisher & Fisher, Denver, Colo., 1922-23; asst. engr. in charge R.R. and dam constrn. Nat. City Co. of N.Y., in Barahona, Santo Domingo, W.I., 1923-24; supt. constrn., project mgr. etc. for W. Tamanga, Denver, Colo., Hegeman Harris Co., Tampa, Fla., and for self, 1924-27; home bldg. and financing consultant, organizer home bldg. service depts. for large material cos., 1927-31; vice pres., gen. mgr. and mem. bd. Nat. Homes Finance Corp., Chicago, Ill., 1931-34; tech dir., dep. gen. mgr. U.S. Govt. Home Loan Bank, and H.O.L.C., 1934-42, in charge appraisals and reconditioning 1 million homes, land acquisition appraisals for army and navy bases; pioneered program neighborhood rehabilitation 50,000 units made available for war housing by reconditioning old properties; asst. pres. James Stewart & Co., New York City, 1942-46; vice pres. and dir. R. W. Hebard & Co., Inc., N.Y. City, 1946-47; cons. engr., N.Y.C.; supr. fgn. buildings operations for U.S. Dept. State, in United Kingdom and Italy 1948-49; asst. chief fgn. bldgs. operations 1950-51; cons. engr. U. Ill. Housing Mission to Colombia, S.A., 1955-57, now building research consultant Interamerican Housing Center, Pan American Union, Washington, 1957-59; director of programs division of the FHA since 1960. Established Constrn. Cost Index pub. in nat. bldg. mags. Assisted in drafting nat. housing act F.H.A., 1940. Commissioned to make bldgs. and finance study by govt. Paraguay, 1940. Fellow Am. Soc. C.E.; hon. mem. A.I.A.; mem. Jr. Achievement Inc. (mem. bd.), Sigma Tau, Sigma Alpha Epsilon. Roman Catholic. Mem. Knights Malta, Cross of Merit, First Class, Sovereign Military Order of Malta. Club: American (London, England). Compiler; Master Specifications for Home Repair. Author: Waverly—A Study in Neighborhood Conservation (U.S. govt.), 1940; Floor Tiles of Soil Cement, 1957. Home: 4320 Old Dominion Dr., Arlington, Va. 22207. Office: FHA, Lafayette Bldg., Washington. Died July 5, 1965.

MCNEALY, RAYMOND WILLIAM, (mak-ne'li), surgeon; b. Chambersburg, Mo., Aug. 17, 1886; s. John Willard and Georgiana (Green) McN.; M.D., U. of Ill. Med. Sch., 1910; grad. study Vienna, 1914; m. Mary Sarina Kinney, Sept. 4, 1926 (died Nov. 19, 1935); children—Raymond William, Richard Kinney, John Willard II, Thomas Warren; m. 2d, Dorothy Gallagher Frazier, Mar. 19, 1953; children—William Jay Frazier, Jr. (stepson), Douglas L., Roderick M. Intern Cook County Hosp., Chgo., 1910-12, since practice of medicine at Chicago; chief surgeon Wesley Memorial Hosp.; attending surgeon and pres. of staff Cook County Hosp.; cons. surgeon Ill. Masonic Hosp., Oak Forest Infirmary, Kenner Hosp.; associate prof. surgery Northwestern Univ. Med. Sch.; prof. of surgery, Cook Co. Grad. Sch. of Medicine. Pres. United Research Found.; mem. Bd. of Pub. Health Advisors, Dept. of Pub. Health, State of Ill.; mem. adv. bd. Chgo. Health Dept.; mem. med. adv. bd. Cancer Research Found.; counsellor staff Dyslexia Memorial Inst. Wesley Hosp. Editorial bd. Ill. State Med. Journal, Internat. Coll. of Surgeons. Sec. and treas. Hektoen Institute, Cook County Graduate School of Medicine; trustee Institute General Semantics; mem. board trustees Northwestern University (1941-42), Wesley Meml. Hosp. Served at lt. USN, World War I.; maj. Med. R.C., U.S. Army, 1931—. Decorated Comdr. Legion Merit-Juan Pablo Duarte, Dominican Republic. Fellow of International College of Surgeons, A.C.S.; mem. Western Surgical Assn., A.M.A., Ill. State Medical Soc., Chicago Med. Soc., Inst. of Medicine, U.S. Naval Inst., Chicago Surgical Soc., Alpha Omega Alpha, Alpha Kappa Kappa, Phi Kappa Epsilon. Clubs: Chicago Athletic, Bobolink Golf. Home: 2450 Lakeview Av., Chgo. 14. Office: 250 E. Superior St., Chgo. 11. Died July 29, 1958; buried Meml. Park Cemetery, Evanston, Ill.

MCNEIL, HIRAM COLVER, chemist; b. Emerald (Winchester), O., Oct. 2, 1866; s. Samuel and Elizabeth H. (Cory) M.; B.S., Denison U., 1896, M.S., 1900; student Harvard Coll. Summer Sch., 1896, U. of Chicago, 1898-99, and summer, 1901; Ph.D., George Washington U., 1905; m. Sarah M. Hooper, Sept. 4, 1901; children—Robert Hooper, Ernest Samuel, Harold Osman. Taught in pub. schs., Ohio, and N. Liberty (O.) Acad., 1889-93; instr. chemistry, Denison U., 1896-98; research chemist with Mariner & Hoskins, Chicago, 1899; prof. chemistry and head dept. of science, Shurtleff Coll., 1899-1904; research chemist on "The Constitution of the Natural Silicates," U.S. Geol. Survey, under F. W. Clarke, 1904-05; research chemist with Columbus Pharmacal Co., 1905-06; asst. chemist, Bur. of Chemistry, Washington, 1907-14; asso. chemist, Bur. of Standards, 1914-18; asst. prof. chemistry, 1910, prof., 1918—, head of dept., 1918-26, George Washington U. Baptist. Died 1937.

MCNEILL, WILLIAM GIBBS, civil engr.; b. Wilmington, N.C., Oct. 3, 1801; s. Dr. Charles Donald and Mrs. (Gibbs) McN.; grad. U.S. Mil. Acad., 1817; m. Maria Matilda Comman, 7 children. Aide-de-camp to Gen. Andrew Jackson, during Seminole War in Fla., 1819; transferred to Corps Topog. Engrs., 1823; mem. bd. of engrs. B. & O. R.R.; went to Europe to examine pub. works, especially railroads, 1828; became joint engr. (with George W. Whistler) for majority of new railroads in Eastern U.S.; brevetted maj. of engrs., 1834, resigned, 1837; became engr. State of Ga., 1837; served as maj. gen. R.I. Militia, 1842-45; helped to quell Dorr Rebellion; chief engr., prepared plans for Bklyn. dry dock; elected mem. Instn. Civil Engrs. (Gt. Britain) (1st Am. to be elected), 1857. Died Bklyn., Feb. 16, 1853.

MCNEW, JOHN THOMAS LAMAR, civil engr., educator; b. Belcherville, Tex., Jan. 20, 1895; s. Edgar Ogletree and Sarah Elizabeth (Taylor) McN.; B.S., A. and M. Coll of Tex., 1920, M.S., 1926; C.E., Ia. State Coll., 1925; m. Edna Ethel Murphy, May 27, 1920; children—Edna Elizabeth (Mrs. Don Dale Little), John Thomas Lamar. Instr., asst. prof., asso. prof. civil engring. A. & M. Coll. of Tex., 1920-25; engaged in municipal and highway engring. with various cities and counties, 1920-28; prof. highway engring., A. & M. Coll. of Tex., 1925-40, head dept. civil engring., 1940-43, vice pres. for engring. since 1944, dir. engring. extension service since 1945. Served in U.S. Army, France and Germany, as 2d lt. Corps of Engrs., 1918-19; lt. col. Corps of Engrs. as airport engr. China-Burma-India Theatre, World War II; lt. col. engrs., O.R.C. U.S. Army. Vice chmn. A. & M. Coll. of Texas. Development Fund Bd. Mem. Am. Soc. C.E. (sec.-treas. Tex. sect. 1928-37, pres. 1938, nat. dir. dist. 15 (La., Tex., Mex. and N.M.), 1942-45, vice pres. zone 4, 1946-48, chmn. com on engring. edn., 1946, Am. Soc. Engring. Edn., Am. Soc. M.E., Texas Soc. of Professional Engrs. (past dir.). Democrat. Baptist. Club: Kiwanis. Contbr. miscellaneous professional papers and discussions to pubs. of Am. Soc. C.E. Home: 100 Hereford St., College Station, Tex. Died Dec. 21, 1946.

MCNULTY, ROBERT WILKINSON, educator; b. Braidwood, Ill., June 18, 1897; s. Robert Walker and Jennie (Palmer) McN.; A.B., Hanover Coll., 1918; D.D.S., Loyola U., 1926, M.A., 1932; m. Gertrude West, June 3, 1922; children—Robert West, Carol (Mrs. Frank A. Barnes). Faculty, Hanover Coll. Prep. Sch., 1916-18; chemist U.S. Steel Co., 1918-20; asst. chief chemist Swift & Co., 1920-22; faculty Chgo. Coll. Dental Surgery, 1926-50, registrar, 1927-38, asst. dean, 1938-43, acting dean, 1943-44, dean, 1944-50; dean sch. dentistry U. So. Cal., 1950-65. Fellow Am. Coll. Dentists (v.p.); mem. Ill. (treas. 1941-44, pres. 1946), Chgo. dental socs., Am. (council on dental edn. 1946-55), So. Cal. (pres. 1960) dental assns., Am. Assn. Dental Schs. (pres. 1959), Acad. Gen. Dentistry, Am. Acad. Dental History, Fedn. Dentaire Internationale, Odontographic Soc. Chgo., Phi Gamma Delta, Delta Sigma Delta, Omicron Kappa Upsilon, Blue Key. Conglist. Mason. Editor, The Bun (Alumni Assn. Loyola U.), 1927-43. Contbr. articles to profl. jours. Home: 499A Avenida Sevilla, Laguna Hills, Cal. Office: 925 W. 34th St., Los Angeles 7. Died July 5, 1966.

MCNUTT, WILLIAM FLETCHER, surgeon; b. Truro, N.S., Mar. 29, 1839; acad. edn. Presbyn. Sem., Dalhousie U., Halifax, N.S.; student Harvard, 1861; M.D., U. of Vt., 1862; student Coll. Phys. and Surg. (Columbia), 1862-63; asst. surgeon U.S.N., 1863-65; London, Paris, Edinburgh, 1864-65; M.R.C.S. and Royal Coll. Phys., Edinburgh, 1865; m. Mary L., d. Dr. H. P. Coon, of San Francisco, 1871. Was state prison dir. of Cal.; was prof. diseases heart and kidneys, now principles and practice of medicine, U. of Cal. Mem. A.M.A., etc. Author: Diseases of Kidneys and Bladder, 1893. Address: McNutt Bldg., San Francisco.

MCPHERSON, WILLIAM, chemist; b. Xenia, O., July 2, 1864; s. William and Mary (Rader) M.; B.Sc., Ohio State U., 1887, M.Sc., 1890, D.Sc., 1895, LL.D., 1940; Ph.D., U. Chgo., 1899; LL.D., Wittenberg Coll., 1927; m. Lucretia Heston, June 21, 1893; children—William Heston, Gertrude May; m. 2d, Mary B. Henderson, Apr. 18, 1925. Instr. chemistry and physics Toledo High Sch. and Manual Tng. Sch., 1887-89, chemistry and Latin, 1889-92; asst. in chemistry Ohio State University, 1892-93, assistant professor, 1893-95, associate professor general chemistry, 1895-97, professor chemistry, 1897-1937, gen. chemistry, 1895-97, prof. chemistry, 1897-1937, dean of grad. sch., 1911-37, emeritus dean and prof., 1937—, acting pres., 1924, 38, pres. emeritus, 1938—. Fellow A.A.A.S. (v.p. Sect. C, 1908-09, 15-16); mem. Am. Chem. Soc. (pres. 1929-30), Am. Inst. Chemists (hon.), Deutsche Chemische Gesellschaft, Phi Beta Kappa, Sigma Xi, Phi Delta Theta, Alpha Chi Sigma, Phi Lambda Upsilon. Commd. maj., N.A., 1918; chem. adviser to Trench Warfare Sect., Ordnance Dept.; lt. col. C.W.S., 1918-19. Co-author (with William E. Henderson) of series of text books in chemistry; contbr. to chem. jours. Home: 198 16th Av. Address: Ohio State U., Columbus, O. Died Oct. 2, 1951.

MCQUARRIE, IRVINE, educator; b. Utah, Apr. 20, 1891; s. Robert Gray and Charlotte Anne (Macfarlane) McQ.; A.B., U. Utah, 1915; Ph.D., U. Cal., 1919; M.D., Johns Hopkins, 1921; m. Vira Perkins, June 1, 1912; children—Oane, Maris, Jeanne. Asst. in pathology, U. Cal., 1918-19; physician Henry Ford Hosp., Detroit, 1921-24, 25-26; instr. pediatrics Yale, 1924-25; asst. and asso. prof. pediatrics, U. Rochester, 1926-30; prof. pediatrics, U. Minn., 1930—; vis. prof. pediatrics, Peiping Union Med. Coll., China, 1939-40; cons. Rockefeller Found. for the survey edn. in Japan, 1947. Recipient Modern Medicine Award for distinguished achievement, 1954. Fellow A.A.A.S., Am. Coll. Dentists (hon.), A.M.A.; mem. Soc. for Exptl. Biology and Medicine, Am. Pediatric Soc., Am. Soc. for Clin. Investigation, Am. Soc. for Exptl. Pathology, Am. Inst. Nutrition, Soc. for Pediatric Research, Am. Acad. Pediatrics, Am. Heart Assn., Mexican Pediatric Soc. (hon.), Minn. Path. Soc., Minn. State Med. Assn., Endocrine Soc., Am. Physiol. Soc., Hennepin County Med. Soc., Central Interurban Clin. Club, Sigma Xi, Phi Chi, Alpha Omega Alpha; hon. mem. Cuban Pediatric Soc. Author: Experiments of Nature and Other Essays. Contbr. to scientific jours. Asso. editor Metabolism and other med. jours.; editor in chief Brennemann's Practice of Pediatrics; A Symposium on the Metabolism of Potassium. Home: 2615 Park Av., Mpls. 55407. Died 1961.

MCQUILLEN, JOHN HUGH, dentist, editor; b. Phila., Feb. 12, 1826; s. Hugh and Martha (Scattergood) Mc.Q; M.D., Jefferson Med. Coll., 1852; D.D.S., Phila. Coll. Dental Surgery, 1853; m. Amelia D. Schellenger, 1852, 5 children. Mem. Pa. Assn. Dental Surgeons, later pres.; an editor Dental Cosmos, 1859; editor-in-chief, 1865-72; prof. operative dentistry and dental pathology Pa. Coll. Dental Surgery, 1857-62; founder Phila. Dental Coll., 1863, dean and prof. anatomy, physiology and hygiene, 1863-79; an organizer Am. Dental Assn., 1859, pres., 1865; an organizer, 1st corr. sec. Odontographic Soc. of Phila., 1863, pres., 1868-70; 1st corr. sec. Assn. Colls. Dentistry, 1866; one of 1st in Am. to demonstrate importance of microscopical knowledge of human teeth in health and disease; mem. Acad. Natural Science at Phila., founder biol. and microscopical sect. Died Phila., Mar. 3, 1879; buried Phila.

MCRAE, AUSTIN LEE, educator; b. McRae, Ga., Oct. 25, 1861; s. John Colin and Elizabeth Jane (Clements) M.; B.S., U. of Ga., 1881; S.D., Harvard, 1886; m. Minnie Wood, June 15, 1893. Atmospheric electricity investigations, U.S. Signal Service, 1886-89; organized Mo. State Weather Service, 1889-91; asst. prof. Physics, U. of Mo., 1889-91; prof. physics, U. of Mo. School of Mines, Rolla, 1891-94; asso. prof. physics, U. of Texas, 1894-96; cons. engr., St. Louis, 1896-99; prof. of physics, 1899-1920, dir., 1915-20, emeritus prof., 1920—, School of Mines, Rolla. Served as capt. Co. B, U. of Ga. Cadets; chmn. Phelps Co. (Mo.) br. Am. Red Cross, also chmn. Phelps Co. br. Council Nat. Defense; mem. advisory com. for Mo. for Explosives Act. Mason. Democrat. Episcopalian. Home: Rolla, Mo. Died Mar. 18, 1922.

MCRAE, JAMES WILSON, elec. engineer; b. Vancouver, B.C., Oct. 25, 1910; s. James Hector and Isabel C. (Jamieson) McR.; B.S., U. B.C., 1933; M.S., Cal. Inst. Tech., 1934, Ph.D., 1937; D.Sc. (hon.), Hobart College, 1958. m. Marian Frances Wooldridge, July 20, 1937; children—Mary Caroline, Marion Elizabeth, James Dean, John Robert. Came to U.S., 1936, naturalized, 1940. Research transoceanic radio transmitters, microwave research Bell Telephone Labs., 1937-42, dir. radio projects, TV research, 1947, electronic, TV research, 1947-49, apparatus development, 1949-51, v.p. charge the systems orgn., 1951-53; v.p. Western Electric Co., 1953-58; pres. Sandia Corp., 1953-58; vice pres. Am. Tel. & Tel. Company 1958—. Served as col. signal corps, U.S. Army, 1942-45. Awarded Legion of Merit. Fellow Inst. Radio Engrs. (pres. 1953, dir.); mem. Am. Inst. E.E., Phi Beta Kappa. Home: 10 West Lane, Madison, N.J. Office: 195 Broadway, N.Y.C. Died Feb. 1960.

MCTAMMANY, JOHN, inventor; b. nr. Glasgow, Scotland, June 26, 1845; s. John and Agnes (McLean) McT. Came to U.S., 1862; served with 115th Ohio Volunteer Inf., 1863-65, critically wounded nr. Chattanooga; while convalescing at Nashville, repaired music box, which gave him idea for an instrument operated by depressions; developed player-piano; 1866; built 3 models of player-piano, also 2 machines to prepare perforated sheets, 1866-76; gave public exhbn. of piano, St. Louis, 1876; prevented by circumstances from getting patent on his invention within prescribed time limit; declared to be original inventor of player-piano, after long and costly litigation against competitors, 1880; received 3 patents on invention, 1881; patented 1st voting machine, which pneumatically registered votes using perforated roll (1st machine ever used in an election), 1892. Died Stamford, Conn., Mar. 26, 1915; buried Westlawn Cemetery, Canton, O.

MEAD, ALBERT DAVIS, biologist; b. Swanton, Vt., Apr. 15, 1869; s. Charles Davis and Phoebe Minerva (Harrington) M.; A.B., Middlebury Coll., 1890; A.M., Brown, 1891, LL.D., 1939; Ph.D., U of Chicago, 1895; Sc.D., U. of Pittsburgh, 1912, and Middlebury Coll., 1916, R.I. State College, 1927; m. Ada Geneva Wing, July 2, 1902. Asso. prof. comparative anatomy, 1895, prof., 1901, prof. biology, 1909, vice-pres., 1925-36, acting pres., 1931, prof. emeritus since 1936, Brown Univ. Trustee Middlebury Coll., 1933, Wellesley College, 1934-45, R.I. Sch. Design, 1923-39; trustee, 1901-34 and president, 1934-40; Rhode Island Hospital. Member American Soc. Naturalists, Am. Soc. Zoölogists, A.A.A.S., Phi Beta Kappa. Sigma Xi; fellow Am. Acad. Arts and Sciences. Address: 283 Wayland Av., Providence, R.I. Died Dec. 8, 1946.

MEAD, DANIEL WEBSTER, engr.; b. Fulton, N.Y., Mar. 6, 1862; s. Washburn and Adelia A. (Shufelt) M.; B.C.E., Cornell University, 1884; LL.D., University of Wisconsin, 1932; married Katie Ross Gould, Nov. 30, 1886 (died Apr. 25, 1944); children—Hazel Marguerite, Ruth Claudia (dec.), Harold Washburn, Ross Webster (dec.), Paul Gould (dec.), Franklin Braidwood. With U.S. Geol. Survey, 1884-85; city engr., Rockford, 1885-87; chief engr. and gen. mgr., Rockford Constrn. Co., 1888-96; cons. engr. on hydraulic works and power plants since 1896; prof. hydraulic and sanitary engring., U. of Wis., 1904-32, professor emeritus since 1932; cons. engr. Mead & Hunt (Madison); mem. Mead & Scheidenhelm (New York). Built water works at Rockford, Illinois, Fort Worth, Texas, Danville, Illinois, Moline (Ill.) filter, Kilbourn (Wis.) hydro-electric plant (10,000 h.p.), Prairie du Sac (Wis.) hydro-electric plant (20,000 h.p.), etc. Mem. Red Cross commn. to China on flood protection of Huai River, 1914; cons. engr. Miami Conservancy Dist., 1913-20 (expenditure $30,000,000); mem. Colorado River Board, apptd. by President Collidge to pass on Boulder Canyon project, 1928. Awards: Fuertes medal, Cornell U., 1911; Octave Chanute medal, Western Soc. Engrs., 1913; Norman medal, Am. Soc. C.E., 1936; Washington award, Western Soc. Engrs., 1939; awarded citation as "Pioneer Hydrologist" by the Hydrology Conference, Pa. State College, 1941. Fellow Am. Inst. Electrical Engrs., Am. Pub. Health Assn.; hon. mem. Am. Water Works Assn., Am. Soc. Civil Engrs. (pres. 1936), Ill. Soc. Engrs., Canadian Institute Engrs. (hon.), Western Soc. Engrs., member Am. Soc. Mech. Engrs., New Eng. Water Works Assn., Am. Inst. Consulting Engrs., Wis. Engring. Soc., A.A.A.S., Tau Beta Pi, Sigma Xi, Phi Kappa Phi; nat. hon. mem. Triangle, Chi Epsilon. Clubs: Union League (Chicago); University, Madison (Madison). Author: Notes on Hydrology, 1904; Water Power Engineering, 1908; Contracts, Specifications and Engineering Relations, 1916; Hydrology, 1919; Hydraulic Machinery, 1933; also numerous papers read before scientific socs. and bulls. of U. of Wisconsin. Home: 120 W. Gorham St. Office: 550 State St., Madison, Wis. Died Oct. 13, 1948; buried Forest Hill Cementery, Madison, Wis.

MEAD, ELWOOD, engineer; b. Patriot, Ind., Jan. 16, 1858; s. Daniel and Lucinda M.; B.S., Purdue, 1882, M.S., 1884, E.D., 1904; C.E., Iowa State U., 1883; LL.D., U. of Mich., 1925; m. Florence Chase; children—Tom C., Lucy F., Arthur E.; m. 2d, Mary Lewis; children—Catherine, Sue, John. Asst. engr., U.S. Engrs., 1882-83; prof. Colo. Agrl. Coll., 1883-84, 1886-88; territorial and state engr., Wyo., 1888-99; chief irrigation and drainage investigation, U.S. Dept. Agr., 1897-1907; prof. institutions and practice of irrigation, U. of Calif., 1898-1907; chmn. State Rivers and Water Supply Commn., Victoria, Australia, 1907-15; prof. rural instns., U. of Calif., 1915, and chmn. Land Settlement Bd.; commr. of reclamation, Apr. 1924—; mem. Com. Conservation and Administration of Pub. Domain. Consulting engineer for various irrigation and water works companies. Author: Irrigation Institutions; Helping Men Own Farms. Home: Washington, D.C. Died Jan. 26, 1936.

MEAD, GEORGE JACKSON, aeronautic engr.; b. Everett, Mass., Dec. 27, 1891; s. George Nathaniel Plummer and Jenny (Leman) M.; prep. edn., St. George's Sch., Newport, R.I., and Choate Sch., Wallingford, Conn.; student Mass. Inst. Tech., 1911-15; hon. D.Sc. Trinity Coll., Hartford, Conn., 1937, Williams Coll., 1940; m. E. Cary Hoge, May 18, 1921; children—George Nathaniel Jackson, Mary Randolph, Peyton H., Charles Cary, William Randolph. Experimental engr. Wright Martin Aircraft Corp., 1916-19; engr. in charge power plant labs., U.S. Air Service, Dayton, O., 1919; chief engr. Wright Aeronautical Corp., 1920-25; engring. founder and v.p. Pratt & Whitney Aircraft Co., 1925-30; v.p., mem. exec. com. and chmn. tech. advisory com. United Aircraft & Transport Corp., 1930-34; cons. engr. United Aircraft Corp., 1934-35, v.p., dir. and mem. exec. com., 1935-June 1939. Mem. and vice-chmn. Nat. Advisory Com. for Aeronautics, Oct. 1939-Feb. 1944; asst. to Sec. of Treasury, May 22-June 4, 1940; dir. Aeronautical Sect., National Defense Commn., June 4-Nov. 1, 1940; spl. asst. to William S. Knudsen, Nov. 1, 1940-Mar. 1941. Chmn. exec. com. Hartford Hosp., 1942-47. Mem. Soc. Automotive Engrs.; hon. fellow Inst. of Aeronautical Sciences; fellow Royal Aeronautical Soc., England. Republican. Conglist. Clubs: Engineers (New York); Hartford, Hartford Golf; Cosmos Club, Washington, D.C. Home: Mountain Rd., West Hartford, Conn. Office: P.O. Box 6, West Hartford, Conn. Died Jan. 20, 1949.

MEAD, STERLING V., dentist; b. Hutchinson, Kan., Oct. 16, 1888; grad. Emerson Inst., Washington, D.C., 1911; D.D.S., George Washington U., 1914; B.S. Dentistry, Georgetown U., 1929, M.S., 1930, D.Sc., 1952. Pvt. practice dentistry, Washington, 1914-69; founder Mead Dental Hosp., 1959-66; prof. oral surgery, diseases of mouth, radiography and dir. research, Georgetown Univ. for many years; past pres. Am. Dental Assn. Fellow Am. Coll. of Dentists; mem. D.C. Dental Soc. (pres. 1929), Am. Soc. Oral Surgeons, Psi Omega. Recipient award by Internat. Research Soc., 1935, Conn. Dental Assn., 1944. Author: (books) Diseases of the Mouth; Oral Surgery; Anesthesia; also numerous sci. papers. Address: Washington DC Died Dec. 9, 1972.

MEAD, WARREN JUDSON, geologist; b. Plymouth, Wis., Aug. 5, 1883; s. Major C. and Rose (Robinson) M.; B.S., U. of Wis., 1906, M.A., 1908, Ph.D., 1926; m. Bertha M. Taylor, 1909; children—Warren, Judson, Jeremiah. Mem. faculty U. of Wis., 1906-34, prof. geology, 1918-34; head dept. of geology, Mass. Inst. Tech., 1934-39, emeritus 1949; cons. practice, in econ. engring. geology. Mem. Geol. Soc. America, A.A.A.S., Soc. Econ. Geologists, Am. Acad. Arts and Sciences, Am. Soc. Civil Engrs., Am. Inst. Mining and Metall. Engrs., Nat. Acad. Sciences, Sigma Xi, Sigma Nu. Episcopalian. Author: Metamorphic Geology (with C. K. Leith), 1915; also papers in tech. mags. Home: 88 Rutledge Road, Belmont 78, Mass. Died Jan. 16, 1960; buried Madison, Wis.

MEADE, RICHARD KIDDER, chemical engr.; b. Charlottesville, Va., Nov. 28, 1874; s. Rev. Francis Alexander and Mattie (Mosby) M.; grad. U. of Virginia, 1893; hon. M.S., Lafayette Coll., 1908; m. Fannie Louise Thomas, Dec. 20, 1900; children—Martha Haskins (Mrs. George E. Baughman), Francis Alexander. City editor Independent-Herald, Hinton, W.Va., 1894; chemist Longdale Iron Co., Allegheny Co., Va., 1895-96; asst. in chemistry, Lafayette Coll., 1897-1902; chief chemist, Edison Portland Cement Co., 1902, Northampton Portland Cement Co., 1903. Dexter Portland Cement Co., 1904; founder and editor The Chemical Engineer, 1904; dir. Meade Testing Laboratories, Allentown, Pa., 1908-11, gen. mgr. Tidewater Portland Cement Co., Baltimore, 1911-12; in consulting practice, Baltimore, 1912—. Consulting chem. engr. to many Portland cement plants; inventor of numerous processes and appliances of use in the Portland cement industry. Author: The Chemists' Pocket Manual, 1900; The Chemical and Physical Examination of Portland Cement, 1901; Portland Cement, 1906; The Design and Equipment of Small Chemical Laboratories, 1907; Tables for Determination of Economic Minerals, 1907; The Technical Analysis of Brass, 1911. Home: Roland Par, Md. Died Oct. 13, 1930.

MEANS, JAMES HOWARD, physician; b. Dorchester, Mass., June 24, 1885; s. James and Helen Goodell (Farnsworth) M.; prep edn., Noble and Greenough's Sch., Boston; spl. student in biology and chemistry, Mass. Inst. Tech., 1902-03; A.B., Harvard, 1907, M.D., 1911, H.P. Walcott fellow 1913-16; m. Marian Jeffries, Jan. 11, 1915 (died Feb. 1950); 1 son, James; m. 2d Carol Lord Butler, Feb. 17, 1951. Interne, Mass. Gen. Hosp., 1911-13; teaching fellow med. Harvard Med. Sch., 1916-18, instr. in medicine, 1919-21, asst. prof. medicine, 1921-24, Jackson prof. clin. medicine, 1924-51. Jackson prof. clin-medicine emeritus since 1951, asso. in medicine. Mass. Gen. Hosp., 1917-24, chief of med. services, 1924-51; physician Mass. Inst. Tech., 1951-57; cons. social medicine Moniefiore Hosp., N.Y.C. Mem. nat. adv. health council U.S. Pub. Health Service, 1952-56; hon. mem. faculty U. Cuyo (Argentina); hon. physician Mass. Gen. Hosp.; hon. perpetual student Med. Coll. St. Bartholomew's Hosp., London. Served with Medical Corps, U.S. Army, advancing to major, 1917-19. Recipient Sidney Hillman Award, 1951, Squibb award, Endocrine Soc., 1952; George M. Kober medal Assn. Am. Physicians, 1964. Fellow Royal Soc. Medicine (London) (hon.), Am. Coll. Physicians (pres. 1937-38); fellow Am. Acad. Arts and Sciences, Mass. Med. Soc., A.A.A.S., Med. Soc. of Finland (hon.), Am. Soc. for Clin. Investigation, Assn. Am. Physicians (pres. 1942), Am. Assn. for the Study of Goiter (pres. 1947-48), Alpha Omega Alpha; hon. mem. Argentine Assn. for Endocrinology and Nutrition; corr. mem. Nat. Acad. Medicine of Buenos Aires, Gorgas Meml. Inst., Tropical and Preventive Med. Clubs: Harvard, Somerset (Boston); also Harvard (New York). Author: Dyspncea, 1924; The Diagnosis and Treatment of Diseases of the Thyroid Gland (with E.P. Richardson, M.D.), 1929; The Thyroid and Its Diseases, 1937, 2d ed. 1948; Doctors, People and Government, 1953; Lectures on Thyroid, 1954; Ward 4, 1958; The Association of American Physicians: Its First Seventy-Five Years, 1961; James Means and His Problem of Manflight, 1964. Contbr. papers to jours. Home: 60 Mount Vernon St., Boston 8. Died Sept 3, 1967; buried Boston.

MEANS, THOMAS HERBERT, consulting engr.; b. Waterford, Va., Nov. 15, 1875; s. Samuel C. and Rachael Ann (Bond) M.; B.S., Columbian (now George Washington) U., 1898, M.S., 1901; m. Constance Adams, Nov. 6, 1900; children—Alice Adams (now Mrs. Lloyd Eric Reeve), Thomas Moore. In charge Soil Survey of U.S. since 1900; engr. of soils, U.S. Reclamation Service, since 1904; project engr. U.S. Reclamation Service, 1910; consulting engr., San Francisco, since 1910, specializing in irrigation and agrl. engring. Mem. Am. Soc. C.E. Club: Engineers. Author several Dept. Agr. publs. and engineering articles. Home: 2729 Forest Av., Berkeley, CA Office: 111 Sutter St., San Francisco CA

MEARS, FREDERICK, engineer; b. Ft. Omaha, Neb., May 25, 1878; s. Frederick and Elizabeth (McFarland) M.; prep. edn. Shattuck Sch., Faribault, Minn.; distinguished grad. U.S. Inf. and Cav. Sch., 1904; U.S. Staff Coll., 1905; m. Jennie, d. late Maj. J. P. Wainwright, U.S.A., Apr. 6, 1907. With G.N. Ry., advancing to resident engr., 1897-99; enlisted U.S.A. as pvt., Oct. 1, 1899; commd. 2d lt., 5th Cav., July 1, 1901; 1st lt., 11th Cav., Sept. 20, 1906; capt., July 1, 1916; col., Jan. 1918; lt colonel engineer corps, Oct. 18, 1920. Served in Philippine Islands until July 1903; duty, Isthmian Canal Commn., 1906-14; surveyed location for new high level ry., 1906-07; res. engr. and engr. constrn. New Panama R.R., 1907-09; chief engr., same rd., 1909-14, also gen. supt., 1913-14; mem. Alaskan Engring. Commn., 1914-17; col. 31st Engrs., Jan. 16, 1918; sailed for France, June 6, 1918; asst. gen. mgr. (Aug. and Sept.) and gen. mgr. Sept. 1918-May 1919, R.R. Dept., S.O.S., France; returned to U.S., May 21, 1919; chmn. and chief engr. Alaskan Engring. Commn., 1919-23; retired as col., July 19, 1923; chief engr. St. Paul Union Depot Co., St. Paul, Minn., 1923-25; asst. chief engr., G.N. Ry., May 1925—. Awarded D.S.M. (U.S.); Officer Legion of Honor (French), 1919. Episcopalian. Home: Seattle, Wash. Died Jan. 11, 1939.

MEARS, J(AMES) EWING, surgeon; b. Indianapolis, Oct. 17, 1838; s. George Washington (M.D.) and Caroline Sidney (Ewing) M.; A.B., B.S., Trinity Coll., Conn., 1858, A.M., 1861 (LL.D., 1908); M.D., Jefferson Med. Coll., Phila., 1865; unmarried. Was lecturer on practical surgery, later clin. lecturer gynecology, Jefferson Med. Coll.; prof. anatomy and surgery, Pa. Coll. Dental Surgery, 1870-98; formerly surgeon various hosps. and surgeon-in-chief Pa. N.G. Served as capt. and q.-m. Ind. vols., med. cadet and acting exec. officer, mil. hosp., during Civil War. Trustee Hort. Hall, Phila. Episcopalian. Fellow Am. Surg. Assn. (editor Trans., 1883-92, pres., 1893), Phila. Acad. Surgery (pres. 1898), Coll. Physicians Phila. (editor Trans., 1872-88), A.A.A.S.; hon. mem. Lehigh Co. (Pa.) Med. Soc., Ga. Med. Soc., Ga. Med. Assn., Mass. Hort. Soc.; life mem. Pa. Hort. Soc., Forestry Assn. Pa., City Parks Assn., Phila., etc. One of editors Universal Medical Sciences. Author: Practical Surgery; contbr. Internat. Text-Book of Surgery; also many articles on surg. and other subjects. Address: Land Title Bldg., Philadelphia.

MEARS, LEVERETT, chemist; b. Essex, Mass., May 19, 1850; s. David and Abigail (Burnham) M.; bro. of David Otis M.; A.B., Amherst, 1874; Ph.D., U. of Gottingen, 1876; (hon. A.M., Williams, 1888); m. Mary V. Brainerd, July 9, 1878 (died 1907); m. 2d, Elizabeth Addis, June 9, 1909. Instr. chemistry, Amherst Coll., 1876-81; prof. physics and chemistry, 1881-88, chemistry, 1888—, Williams Coll. Mem. U.S. Assay Commn., 1898, 1907-08. Author: Lecture Notes on Chemistry, 1912; Qualitative Analysis, 1909. Home: Williamstown, Mass. Died June 22, 1917.

MECH, STEPHEN JOHN, agrl. engr.; b. Poland, Aug. 3, 1909; s. Pawel and Ulianna (Kondzela) M.; came to U.S., 1913, naturalized, 1921; B.S., Pa. State U., 1933; postgrad. Tex. A & M U., 1933-34; m. Eunice Samson, June 24, 1935; children—Cecile (Mrs. Thomas K. Gurney), Stephen John, William P., Mary A. Forester engr. Pa. Dept. Forest and Waters 1933; mem. staff U.S. Dept. Agr., 1934-68, engr. Soil Conservation Service, Lindale, Tex., 1934-35, engr., soil conservationist Erosion Control Research, Lindale, Pullman, Wash., Marcellus, N.Y., LaCrosse, Wis., 1935-43, research engr. irrigation div., Prosser, Wash., 1943-60, research investigation leader, Fort Collins, Colo., 1960-61, project leader, research investigation leader Agrl. Research Service, Pullman, 1961-66, research agrl. engr. Irrigation Agr. Research Center, Prosser, 1966-68. Mem. A.A.A.S., Am. Soc. Agrl. Engring., Am. Soc. Agronomy, Soil Conservation Soc. Am., Am. Geophys. Union. Episcopalian. Mason. Home: Prosser WA Died July 8, 1968.

MEDSGER, OLIVER PERRY, naturalist and educator; b. Jacob's Creek, Pa., Nov. 1, 1870; s. Henry Harrison and Elizabeth (Hough) M.; B.S., Ohio Northern U., Ada, 1898; student Columbia, 1904-05; m. Jennie A. Arnold, Aug. 24, 1905; children—Henry Otis, Thomas Arnold, Oliver Perry. Civil engr. Westmoreland County, Pa., 1898-99; prin. E. Huntington Twp. Schs., 1899-1900, and 1902-04; teacher sciences, high sch. Salem, O., 1900-01; head science dept. and vice prin., Kearny (N.J.) High Sch., 1904-09; teacher science, Dickinson High Sch., Jersey City, 1909-12; head science dept., Lincoln High Sch., Jersey City, 1912-32, asst. prin., 1932-33; prof. nature edn., in charge visual instrn., Pennsylvania State Coll., 1934-37, now emeritus; writing and lecturing since 1937. Organized and directed nature study in summer camps, 1917-27; naturalist, instr. dept. nature education, Pa. State Coll., summer sch., 1928-33; nature study courses, Rutgers U., 1929-33. Dir. Am. Nature Study Society since 1936. Member Kearny Shade Tree Commission, 1909-33, pres. or v.p., 1920-1933 and 1938-1943; chmn. biology sect. N.J. State Science Teachers Association, 1927-29, president, 1920-31; director New Jersey Federation Shade Tree Commissions since 1930, president, 1941-43; member advisory board N.J. State League of Municipalities. Fellow A.A.A.S.; mem. Torrey Bot. Club, John Burroughs Assn. (pres. 1942-44), Amateur Astronomers' Assn. of N.Y. (vice-pres.), Phi Delta Kappa Fraternity. Republican. Methodist. Club: Winter Park University (1st v.p., 1948-49). Author: Nature's Secrets (Vol. 12), 1921; Nature Rambles—Spring (1931)—Summer (1932)—Autumn 1932)—Winter (1932), and awarded John Burroughs medal for same, 1933; Edible Wild Plants, 1939. Co-author: Through Field and Woodland, 1925. Made large collections of plants for Carnegie Mus., Pittsburgh, etc.; assisted in botanical survey, San Jacinto Mtn., Calif., 1901; discovered cassia medsgeri, wild flower named in his honor. Has assembled one of best seed herbaria in U.S. Contbr. nature articles to mags.; lecturer. Mem. Winter Park (Fla.) University Club. Address: 509 Greely St., Orlando FL

MEEK, FIELDING BRADFORD, paleontologist; b. Madison, Ind., Dec. 10, 1817. Interested in geology; asst. to David Dale Owen, head of U.S. Geol. Survey of Ia., Wis. and Minn., 1848-49; asst. to James Hall, paleontologist, Albany, N.Y., 1852-58; took up residence in Smithsonian Instn., Washington, D.C., 1858-76; wrote over 100 publs.; most important publ.; Report on the Invertebrate Cretaceous and Tertiary Fossils of the Upper Missouri Country. Died Dec. 21, 1876.

MEEK, SETH EUGENE, zoölogist; b. Hicksville, O., Apr. 1, 1859; s. Hiram and Mary (Batchelor) M.; B.S., Ind. U., Bloomington, 1884, A.M., 1886, Ph.D., 1891; fellow Cornell, 1885-86; m. Ella Tourner, Dec. 25, 1886. Prof. natural science, Eureka (Ill.) Coll., 1886-87, Coe Coll., Cedar Rapids, Ia., 1887-92; asst. prof. zoölogy and geology, U. of Ark., 1892-96; asst., U.S. Fish Commn., 1896-97; asst. curator zoölogy, Field Mus. Natural History, Chicago, 1897—. Lecturer dental anatomy, Sch. Dentistry, U. of Ill., 1901—. Ichthyologist, Biol. Survey of Panama, 1911—. Explorations of streams of Central and Western U.S., Mexico, Guatemala, Nicaragua, Costa Rica and Panama. Author: Fishes of Mexico North of the Isthmus of Tehuantepec, 1904. Home: Chicago, Ill. Died July 6, 1914.

MEEKER, GEORGE HERBERT, chemist; b. Phillipsburg, N.J., Aug. 13, 1871; s. George Edward and Hannah M. (Kelly) M.; B.S. (chemistry), Lafayette Coll., Pa., 1893, M.S., 1895, Ph.D., 1898; Pharm.D., Medico-Chirurg. Coll., Phila., 1906; D.D.S., 1907; spl. chem. research in Munich, 1909-10; LL.D., Ursinus Coll., Pa., 1905, Lafayette, 1925; Sc.D., Villanova, 1913, U. of Pa., 1940; m. Annie Uhler Hunt, 1900. Chemist for various cos., 1893-95; prof. physics, chemistry, metallurgy and toxicology, Medico-Chirurg. Coll., Phila., 1897-1916; established 1907, dean Dept. Pharm. Chemistry, same to 1916; prof. chemistry, Sch. Medicine, 1916-40, est., 1918, dean Grad. Sch. Med., U. of Pa., 1918-41, now emeritus; dir. Graduate Hospital, 1924-28. Toxicologist and expert chemical witness in many prominent cases. Franklin Inst. medalist, 1906; inventor of mech., elec. and chem. devices. Fellow A.A.A.S., Am. Inst. Chemists; mem. Am. Chem. Soc., Pa. Med. Soc. (hon.), Franklin Inst., Delta Upsilon, Phi Rho Sigma, Psi Omega. Clubs: Union League, Medical, AEsculapian (hon.). Mason (K.T., Shriner). Home: 4701 Pine St., Phila., Pa. Died Sept. 4, 1945.

MEEKER, ROYAL, economist, statistician; b. Silver Lake, Pa., Feb. 23, 1873; s. William and Betsy (Hill) M.; B.Sc., Ia. State Coll., 1898; Columbia, 1899-1903, Ph.D., 1906; U. Leipzig, 1903-04; LL.D., Ursinus Coll., Collegeville, Pa., 1924; m. Dora A. Pierce, July 26, 1905. Prof. history, politics and econs. Ursinus Coll., 1904-05, preceptor Princeton, 1905-08, asst. prof. polit. economy, 1908-13; commr. of labor statistics by appmt. of President Wilson, 1913-20; chief scientific div. ILO of League of Nations, 1920-23; sec. of labor and industry Commonwealth of Pa., 1923-24; mem. Commn. on Social Research in China, 1924-25; prof. economics Carleton Coll., 1926-27; dir. of Survey of Aged Persons in Conn., 1932; pres. Index Number Inst., New Haven, 1930-36; spl. agt. Conn. Dept. of Labor, 1935, adminstrv. asst., 1941-46. Apptd. mem. meat commn., U.S. Govt., 1918. Sec.-treas. Internat. Assn. Indsl. Accident Bds. and Commns., 1916-20; mem. Fed. Electric Rys. Commn., 1919-20. Mem. Am. Econ. Assn., Am. Statis. Assn., Acad. Polit. Sci. Author: History and Theory of Shipping Subsidies, 1905; Directory of Conn. Manufacturing and Mechanical Establishments, 1939, 1942, 1943. Established the U.S. Bureau of Labor Statistics Monthly Labor Review, the Internat. Labor Review and other publs. of Internat. Labor Office. Contbr. to mags. Home: 625 Whitney Av., New Haven. Died Aug. 16, 1953.

MEES, CHARLES EDWARD KENNETH, (mez), photographic research; b. Wellingborough, Eng., May 26, 1882; s. Charles Edward and Ellen (Jordan) M.; student Kingswood Sch., Harrogate Coll. and St. Dunstan's Coll.; B.Sc. in Research, U. of London, Eng., 1903, D.Sc., 1906; hon. D.Sc., U. of Rochester, 1921, Alfred U., 1950; m. Alice Crisp, June 1, 1909 (dec.); children—Graham Charles, Doris Margaret (Mrs. Rohan Sturdy). Mng. dir. of Wratten and Wainwright, Ltd., Croydon, Eng., 1906-12; came to U.S., 1912; dir. Research Lab., Eastman Kodak Co., Rochester, N.Y., 1912-47, v.p. charge of research, 1934-55, ret., dir. Eastman Kodak Co., 1923-56; Recipient of medals from the Royal Society of Arts, 1908, 34, Royal Photog. Soc., 1913, 24, 53, City of Phila., 1921, Société Francaise d'Photographie, 1924, Soc. Motion Picture Engrs., 1936, Nat. Acad. Science, 1937. Rumford medals American Academy Arts and Sciences, 1943; Adelskold gold medal of Swedish Photo. Soc., 1948; Progress medal Photog. Soc. Am., 1948; Franklin medal, 1954; silver medal Soc. Photog. Engrs., 1954; engaged as Christmas lecturer for Royal Inst. London, 1935-36; Christmas lectures for Young People, Franklin Inst., 1941; Hitchcock lecturer, U. of Calif., 1943. Member American Chemical Soc., Am. Astron. Soc., Am. Optical Soc. (hon.), London Chem. Society, Royal Photographic Soc. (hon.), Royal Astron. Soc., Soc. Française de Photographie (hon.), Franklin Inst. (hon.), Am. Inst. Chem. Engineers, Am. Philos. Soc., Sigma Xi; fellow A.A.A.S., Am. Acad. Arts and Scis., Nat. Acad. Sci., Photog. Soc. Am., Royal Soc. London. Club: Chemists; Aahenaeum of London. Author or co-author several books, 1909—. Died Aug. 15, 1960.

MEGGERS, WILLIAM FREDERICK, physicist; b. Clintonville, Wis., July 13, 1888; s. John and Bertha (Bork) M.; B.A., Ripon (Wis.) Coll., 1910, D.Sc., 1951; M.A., U. Wis., 1916; Ph.D., Johns Hopkins, 1917; m. Edith Marie Raddant, July 13, 1920; children—Betty Jane, William Frederick, John Charles. Asst. physics Ripon Coll., 1910-11, U. Wis., 1911-12; instr. physics Carnegie Inst. Tech,. 1912-14; physicist Nat. Bur. Standards, Washington, 1914—, chief spectroscopy sect., 1920-58, contractor, 1959—; cons. AEC, 1958—; physicist Welch Sci. Co., 1960—; pres. Rydberg Centennial Conf., 1954; has specialized in measurement of wave-length standards, description and analysis of spectra, spectral line intensities, zeeman effect, investigation of spectroscopic light sources, spectochem. analysis. Chmn. com. on line spectra NRC, 1946-60; pres. Internat. Joint Commn. for Spectroscopy, 1952-58. Recipient Frederic Ives medal, 1947, gold medal Dept. Commerce, 1949, Soc. Applied Spectroscopy medal, 1952, Elliott Cresson medal Franklin Inst. Pa., 1953, Pitts. Spectroscopy award, 1963; C.E.K. Mees medal, 1964. Mem. Nat. Acad. Scis., A.A.A.S., Am. Phys. Soc., Am. Astron. Soc., Optical Soc. Am. (v.p. 1947-49, pres. 1949-51), Soc. Applied Spectroscopy, Philos. Soc. Washington, Washington Acad. Sci., Internat. Astron. Union (pres. commn. on standard wave-lengths and spectrum tables, 1935-38, 48, 52), Phi Beta Kappa, Sigma Xi, Gamma Alpha. Mason. Author numerous papers on spectroscopy, phys. optics, astrophysics and photography. Contbr. to Glazebrook's Dictionary of Applied Physics, Index to the Literature on Spectrochemical Analysis, Ency. Britannica, Tables of Wave Numbers, Tables of Spectral-Line Intensities. Home: 2904 Brandywine St., Washington 20008. Died Nov. 19, 1966; buried Ft. Lincoln Cemetery, Washington 20008.

MEGRAW, HERBERT ASHTON, (me-graw'), metallurgical engr.; b. Baltimore, Apr. 28, 1876; s. John Milton and Ellen Maria (Ryan) M.; grad. Baltimore Poly. Inst., 1894; B.S., in Chemistry, Cornell U., 1898; m. Mary Bollman French, Oct. 18, 1905. Assayer, 1899-1901, mill supt. and metallurgist, 1901-03, Guanajuato Consol. Mining & Milling Co.; staff engr. Charles Butters & Co., London, 1903; metall. engr., Iola Mining Co., 1904; mgr. Montgomery Mining Co., 1905-08; supt. Naval Milling Co., Guanajuato, Mex., 1908-12; consulting metall. engr., Mexico City, 1912; on editorial staff Engineering and Mining Journal, 1912-17, mgr. same, 1917-18; engr. Bur. of Aircraft Production, Air Service, U.S. Army, Dayton, O., and Washington, 1918-19; engr. Kennedy-Van Saun Mfg. & Engring. Corp., New York, 1919-22; v.p. and treas. Crown Oil & Wax Co. and N.C. Oil Co., Baltimore, 1922-26; v.p. and gen. mgr. Corchera Internacional, Seville, Spain, 1926-35, now practicing as cons. engr. Episcopalian. Mem. Am. Inst. Mining and Metall. Engrs., Phi Sigma Kappa. Clubs: Engineers, Tablada. Author: Practical Data for the Cyanide Plant, 1910; Details of Cyanide Practice, 1914; The Flotation Process, 1916. Extensive contbr. to leading mining and metall. jours. Home: 3902 Centerbury Road, Balt. Died Nov. 3, 1951; buried Druid Ridge Cemetery, Balt.

MEHLBERG, JOSEPHINE JANINA BEDNARSKI SPINNER (MRS. HENRY MELHBERG), mathematician, educator; b. Zurawno, Poland, May 1, 1915; s. Paul and Antonia (Morganowska-Suchodolska) Bednarski; M.S., Johannes Casimirus U., Lwow, Poland, 1936, M.A., 1937, Ph.D., 1938; postgrad. Sorbonne, 1938; m. Henry Mehlberg, Aug. 6, 1933. Came to U.S., 1956; naturalized, 1962. Lectr., Coll. of Lwow, 1939-41, mem. Inst. for Postgrad. Tng. High Sch. Tchrs., 1939-41; asso. dir. Polish Council Social Welfare, 1941-42; dir. gen., 1943-50; lectr. math. U. Toronto, Ont., Can., 1951-56; sr. mathematician, study coordinator Inst. for System Research, U. Chgo., 1957-61; asso. prof. math. Ill. Inst. Tech., 1961-66, prof., 1966-69. Mem., v.p. Coordinating Com. for Child Welfare in Poland, 1945-50; mem. exec. com. Internat. Union for Child Welfare, Geneva, Switzerland, 1948-52; v.p. gen. assembly Internat. Conf. Instns. for Child Welfare, Stockholm, Sweden, 1951; del. 9th nat. conf. UNESCO, Chgo., 1963. UN fellow, 1948-49. Mem. Am. Soc. Engring Sci. (founder), Am. Math. Soc., Am. Math. Assn., A.A.A.S., Am. Inst. Aeros. and Astronautics (treas. Chgo. sect.), Am. Soc. Engring. Edn., Canadian Math. Congress, Sigma Xi. Author: Analysis of Axiomatic Foundations of Probability, 1961. Contbr. articles profl. publs. Home: Chicago IL Died May 26, 1969; buried Chicago IL

MEIER, FRED CAMPBELL, plant pathologist; b. Riggston, Ill., Apr. 5, 1893; s. William Herman Dietrich and Lizzie B. (Campbell) M.; B.S., Harvard, 1916, M.S., 1917; m. Agnes Walton Eastman, Oct. 23, 1920. With U.S. Dept. Agr., 1915—, prin. pathologist, Bur. Plant Industry, 1930-34; sr. scientist Extension Service, 1934—. Sec. treas. Am. Phytopathol. Soc., 1929-34 and vice-pres., 1935; business mgr. of Phytopathology (internat. jour. of Am. Phytopathol. Soc.), 1930-34; fellow A.A.A.S. Research on dissemination of micro-organisms by upper air currents with govt. aviation units and commercial airlines, 1929—, Lindbergh North Atlantic flight, 1933, Century of Progress stratosphere flight, 1933, Nat. Geog. Army Air Corps stratosphere flights, 1934, 35, aerial collections over Caribbean Sea, 1935; chmn. com. on aerial dissemination of pathogens and allergens, Nat. Research Council, 1937—. Presbyterian. Home: Chevy Chase, Md. Died July 29, 1938.

MEIGS, CHARLES DELUCENA, physician; b. St. George, Bermuda, Feb. 19, 1792; s. Josiah and Clara (Benjamin) M.; grad. U. Ga., 1809, U. Pa. Sch. of Medicine, 1817; m. Mary Montgomery, Mar. 15, 1815, 10 children. Came with family to New Haven, Conn., 1796; moved to Athens, Ga., 1801; practiced medicine, Augusta, Ga., 1814-17, Phila., 1817-61; prof. obstetrics and diseases of women Jefferson Med. Coll., Pa., 1841-61; lived in retirement, Hamanassett County, Pa., 1861-69. Author: Elementary Treatise on Midwifery, 1838. Died June 22, 1869.

MEIGS, JOSIAH, lawyer, editor, educator; b. Middletown, Conn., Aug. 21, 1757; s. Return and Elizabeth (Hamlin) M.; grad. Yale, 1778; m. Clara Benjamin, Jan. 21, 1782, 2 children. Elected tutor Yale, 1781; admitted to Conn. bar, 1783; city clk. New Haven (Conn.), 1784-89; opened printing office, established New Haven Gazette, 1784; prof. mathematics and natural philosophy Yale, 1794-1800; pres., prof. U. Ga., 1800; apptd. surveyor-gen. U.S., 1812; commr. Gen. Land Office U.S., Washington, D.C., 1814; pres. Columbian Inst., 1819-22; an original corporator and trustee Columbian Coll. (now George Washington U.). Died Washington, Sept. 4, 1822.

MEIGS, MONTGOMERY, U.S. civil engr.; b. Detroit, Mich., Feb. 27, 1847; s. Gen. Montgomery Cunningham (q.m. gen. U.S.A.) and Louisa (Rodgers) M.; 2 yrs. at Lawrence Scientific Sch., Harvard; 2 yrs. Royal Poly. Sch., Stuttgart, Germany, ending in 1869; m. Grace C. Lynde, Jan. 3, 1877 (dec.); children—Mrs. Mary A. Atwater, Mrs. Louise R. Green, Mrs. Grace L. Crowder, Mrs. Alice McK. Orr, Cornelia L., Mrs. Emily F. Fales. On surveys of N.P. R.R., as resident engr., 1870-73; from 1874 employed on improvements of Miss. River from St. Paul to mouth of Mo. River; from 1882 at Keokuk, Ia., in charge U.S. Des Moines Rapids canal; at Keokuk, Ia., 1882-1926; retired under pension law, after 53 yrs.' service. Inventor of a "canvas cofferdam" for foundation work and like constructions; constructed U.S. dry dock at Keokuk. In 1898 proposed a new method of improving country roads by using oil with a sprinkler to make a watertight surface and lay dust, which attracted wide attention. Builder and designer of many steamboats and steam dredge tenders for the U.S. Local engr. for U.S. in constrn. of the great lock, dry dock and power developments in Miss. River at Keokuk, Ia., 1910-13. Home: Keokuk, Ia. Died Dec. 9, 1931.

MEIKLE, GEORGE STANLEY, research dir.; b. Milton Mills, N.H., May 30, 1886; s. George Douglas and Emma Etta (Fox) M.; B.Engring. and Master Civil Engring., Union Coll., Schenectady, N.Y., 1913; m. Louise Juliet Zimmerman (M.D.), Sept. 6, 1910. Chief safety engr., asst. dist. mech. engr. U.S. Steel Corp., 1909-11; scientific research Gen. Electric Co. Labs., Schenectady, 1912-17; pres. G. S. Meikle Co., cons. scientists and engrs., N.Y. City, 1919-24; research and engring. exec., 1924-28; mem. adminstrative staff, 1928—, dir. research relations with industry, 1928—, Purdue U.; mem. bd. dirs. and research dir. (officer) Purdue Research Foundation, 1930—; v.p. Better Homes in America, Inc.; v.p. Purdue Aeronautics Corp., Research, education and defense; W.O.C., United States Department of Commerce Coordination and Administration of Univ. and Federal War Research,

World War II. Research consultant U.S. Navy, tech. dir. and officer in charge gas mask div. U.S. Army, 1917-19; in charge development submarine dir. for U.S. Navy and model 1919 gas mask for U.S. Army (as civilian), World War I; capt. Chem. Warfare Service O.R.C. Fellow Am. Assn. for Advancement of Science, Internat. Anesthesia Research Soc.; mem. Tippecanoe County Med. Assn. (hon.), Sigma Xi, Tau Beta Pi, Scabbard and Blade. Republican. Mason (Scottish Rite). Rotarian. Research in physical chemistry, discovering hot cathode gas filled rectifers, "Tungar," and allied devices; research in heat transfer resulting in new formula and discovery of methods and devices for heating houses with liquid and gaseous fuels. Home: 606 Terry Lane, W. Lafayette, Ind. Died Mar. 30, 1960.

MEIN, WILLIAM WALLACE, (men), mining engr.; b. Nevada City, Calif., July 19, 1873; s. Thomas and Mary (Swift) M.; B.S., U. of Calif., 1900; m. Frances Williams, Apr. 4, 1907; children—Mrs. C. W. Fay, Jr., Wm. Wallace, Mrs. Charles de Bretteville, Gardner Williams. Gold and nickel mining South Africa and Can., 1892-1919; dir. Bank Am., Flintkote Co. Mem. Am. Inst. Mining and Metall. Engrs., A.A.A.S., Inst. of Mining & Metall., London; Canadian Inst. Mining and Metallurgy, S. African Inst. Engrs., Mining and Metall. Soc., Beta Theta Pi, Sigma Chi. Republican. Clubs: Pacific Union, Engineers, San Francisco Golf, Burlingame Country, Menlo Country (San Francisco); Rand (Johannesburg, South Africa). Home: Woodside, Cal. Office: 315 Montgomery St., San Francisco 94104. Died May 5, 1964; buried Mountain View Cemetery, Oakland, Cal.

MEINECKE, EMILIO PEPE MICHAEL, plant pathologist; b. Alameda, Cal., July 26, 1869; s. Charles and Angelita (Schleiden) M.; grad. high sch., Freiburg, Germany; studied univs. of Freiburg, Leipzig, Bonn and Heidelberg, Ph.D., Heidelberg, 1893; post grad. work in various European univs.; unmarried. Asst. Bot. Inst., U. Munich, 1893, U. Heidelberg, 1894; asst. Forestry Acad., U. Munich, 1898-1902; prof. botany U. La Plata, Argentine Republic, S.A., 1907-08; forest pathologist, 1910, pathologist, 1918, prin. pathologist, 1928—, U.S. Dept. Agr., in charge research planning and criticism, 1929—. Fellow A.A.A.S., Cal. Acad. Scis.; mem. Société Mycologique de France, Société de Pathologie Végétale et d'Entomologie Agricole de France, Bot. Soc. Am., Phytopathol. Soc. Am., Soc. Am. Foresters, Biol. Soc. Pacific Coast, Am. Acad. Polit. and Social Sci., Wash. Acad. Sci., Am. Mycol. Soc., Am. Soc. Naturalists, Am. Ecol. Soc., Cal. Bot. Soc., Société d'Études Océaniennes, Tahiti, Sigma Xi. Clubs: Faculty (U. Cal.); University, Commonwealth. Author: Die Hefe, 1898; Allgemeine Botanik, 1909; Forest Tree Diseases Common in California fornia and Nevada, 1914; Forest Pathology in Forest Regulation, 1916; Les Vanillières de Tahiti et Moorea, 1916 (same in Tahitian transl., 1917); also papers on tree diseases. Home: 3157 Jackson St. Office: Forest Service, 446 Phelan Bldg., San Francisco. Died Feb. 1957.

MEINHOLTZ, FREDERICK E., communications engr.; b. St. Louis, Jan. 17, 1890; s. Fred John and Anne (Bullerdieck) M.; student St. Louis pub. schs.; m. Mae M. Mackall, Nov. 22, 1922; children—Frederick Louis, Lillian Mae (Mrs. Donald Stock), Harry Becker Wheeler. Office mgr. Western Union Telegraph Co., St. Louis, 1907-17; mgr. radio dept. N.Y. Times, 1920-31, dir. communications, mgr. syndicate news dept. since 1931; installed transatlantic press receiving sta. News Traffic Bd., Ltd., Halifax, N.S., 1922, pres., dir. since 1933; handled North Pole communications, Amundsen, Byrd expdns., 1926; initiated high frequency regularly scheduled press transmissions to ships at sea, 1926; radio cons. Byrd's first Antarctic expdn., 1928-30; assisted orgn., bldg. Press Wireless, Inc., 1929, sec., 1932-43, now dir. Advisor U.S. delegation Internat. Telecommunication Conf., Cairo, Egypt, 1938, Third Inter-Am. Radio Conf., Rio de Janeiro, S.A., 1945, Brit.-Am. Telecommunication Conf., Bermuda, 1945, Internat. Telegraph and Radio Conf., Atlantic City, 1947, Internat. Administrative Telegraph Conf., Paris, France, 1949; mem. U.S. delegation Internat. Plenipotentiary Telecommunication Conf., Buenos Aires, Argentina, 1952; mem. U.S. delegation Internat. Administrative Telegraph & Telephone Conference, Geneva, 1958. Served with U.S.N., 1917-19. Mem. Am. Legion (past co. vice comdr., adjutant, post comdr.), 40 et 8, Vets. Wireless Operators Assn. (Marconi Meml. gold medal of service 1960), Am. Polar Soc. Clubs: Garden City Country, Admiral's, Stratoliner. Home: 123 Wickham Rd., Garden City, L.I., N.Y. Office: 229 W. 43d St., N.Y.C. Died Dec. 23, 1961; buried Greenfield Cemetery, Hempstead, L.I.

MEINZER, OSCAR EDWARD, geologist; b. near Davis, Ill., Nov. 28, 1876; s. William and Mary Julia (Meinzer) M.; A.B., magna cum laude, Beloit Coll., 1901 (Phi Beta Kappa), D.Sc., 1946; studied U. of Chicago, 1905-07; Ph.D., 1922; m. Alice Breckenridge Crawford, Oct. 3, 1906; children—Robert William (adopted), Roy Crawford. Prin. public schools, at Frankfort, South Dakota, 1901-03; prof. physical sciences, Lenox Coll., Hopkinton, Ia., 1903-05; instr. geology, Corr. Sch., U. of Chicago, 1906-08; with U.S. Geol. Survey, 1906 to retirement, 1946, devoting time chiefly to investigations of underground water; geologist in charge div. of ground water, 1912-46; in charge desert watering-place survey, 1917-18; del. to Edinburgh Assembly of Internat. Union Geodesy and Geophysics, 1936; U.S. rep. on Exec. Com. Internat. Assn. Hydrology since 1933; pres. Internat. Commn. on Subterranean Water since 1936. Fellow Geological Soc. Am., A.A.A.S. (mem. council since 1946); mem. Wash. Acad. Scis. (v.p. 1932-33, pres. 1936-37), Geol. Soc. Wash. (pres. 1930-31), Soc. of Econ. Geologists (councilor 1937-40, v.p. 1944, pres. 1945), National Research Council (division foreign relations 1930-33), Am. Geophysical Union (first chairman section on hydrology, 1930-33, president since 1947), Pi Gamma Mu, Sigma Xi; 30-year veteran Boy Scouts America. Presbyterian (elder, 1937-45). Club: Cosmos. Author: Outline of Ground-Water Hydrology; Occurrence of Ground-Water in the United States; Large Springs in the United States; Plants as Indicators of Ground-Water; Compressibility and Elasticity of Artesian Aquifiers; Outline of Methods for Estimating Ground-Water Supplies; History and Development of Ground-Water Hydrology; Our Water Supply; Hydrology (with others); Hydrology in Relation to Economic Geology; asso. editor Economic Geol. Commd. as capt. engrs., Oct. 23, 1918, but prevented from active duty by close of war. Awarded Bowie Medal Am. Geophys. Union. 1943; gold medal and button award for distinguished service in sci. work Dept. of Interior, 1948. Home: 2923 South Dakota Av. N.E., Washington 18. Died June 14, 1948; buried Ft. Lincoln Cemetery, Washington.

MEISSNER, K(ARL) W(ILHELM), physicist; b. Reutlingen, Germany, Dec. 15, 1891; s. Karl Emil and Ottilie (Plankenhorn) M.; student Gymnasium Reutlingen, 1898-1910; Dr. rer. nat. U. Tuebingen, 1915; student U. Munich, 1912; m. Ita B. Kohn, Sept. 27, 1919 (died July 9, 1939); m. 2d Hanna Hellinger, May 22, 1942. Came to U.S., 1938, naturalized, 1943. Privat dozent, U. Zurich, 1919-25; prof. physics, U. Frankfurt Main, 1925-37; head dept. physics, 1931-37; asst. prof. physics, Worcester Poly. Inst., 1938-41; prof. physics, Purdue U., 1941—. Mem. Am. Phys. Soc., Optical Soc. Am., Sigma Xi. Researcher in spectroscopy and atomic physics. Home: 176 E. Stadium Av., West Lafayette, Ind. Died Apr. 13, 1959.

MELANDER, A(XEL) L(EONARD), zoologist; b. Chgo., June 3, 1878; s. Silas Peter and Eda Matilda (Bjork) M.; B.S., U. Tex., 1901, M.S., 1902; U. Chgo., 1902-03; Sc.D., Harvard, 1914; m. Mabel Evans, Mar. 5, 1903; children—Charles Lewis, Ivar Evans. Lab. asst. in zoology U. Tex., 1900-01, fellow in zoology, 1901-02; fellow in zoology U. Chgo., 1902-03; investigator, Marine Biol. Lab., Woods Hole, Mass., 1900, instr. 1902; with Washington State Coll. as instr. entomology, 1904-06, prof. 1906-26, head dept. of zoology, 1907-26, also asst. entomologist, Wash. Agrl. Expt. Sta., 1904-06, entomologist, 1906-26, head div. of entomology and zoology, 1907-26; state entomologist, Wash., in charge apiary inspection, 1919-26; prof. biology and head biology dept. Coll. City N.Y., 1926-43, prof. emeritus 1943; research asso. U. Cal. Citrus Expt. Sta., Riverside, Cal., 1934-35, 43—. Fellow A.A.A.S., Entomol. Soc. Am. (pres. 1938), Am. Acad. Arts and Scis., N.Y. Acad. Sci.; mem. Am. Assn. of Univ. Profs. (emeritus), Am. Naturalists (emeritus), Am. Soc. Zoologists, Am. Assn. Econ. Entomologists, Entomol. socs. of Washington, Pacific Coast, N.Y. (hon.), Bklyn., Sigma Xi, Phi Kappa Phi. Author: (with C. T. Brues) Key to Families of North American Insects, 1915, Classification of Insects, 1932, Genera Insectorum (Belgium); Diptera, Fam. Empididae, Fasc. 185, 1927. Source Book of Biological Terms, 1937. Contbr. about 170 articles on systematic and Econ. entomology to entomol. and sci. jours. Authority on classification of Diptera; gathered one of most important pvt. collections of Diptera in Am. (now deposited with his library in U.S. Nat. Mus.); made film recordings of insect behavior; studied fossil desert and alpine insects. Home: 4670 Ladera Lane, Riverside, Cal. Died Aug. 14, 1962; buried Riverside.

MELDRUM, WILLIAM BUELL, educator; b. Hull, Que., Can., Dec. 18, 1887; B.A., McGill U., 1909, M.S., 1911; Ph.D., Harvard, 1914; m. Phillipa Ruth Coleman, Sept. 2, 1919; children—William Buell, Lestella, Thomas Wilson, Donald Nicol. Engaged in research in phys. and analytical chemistry and teaching McGill U., 1909-11, Montreal Tech. Inst., 1910-11, Harvard, 1911-12, Vassar, 1914-17; asso. Haverford Coll., 1917—, prof. chemistry, 1926—, now John Farnum prof. chemistry; research, geophys. lab., and War Industries Bd., 1919. Mem. Am. Chem. Soc. (chmn. Phila. sect. 1937-38, councillor 1938-44), Sci. Tchrs. Assn. (pres. 1926), A.A.A.S., Assn. Harvard Chemists, New Eng. Assn. Chem. Tchrs., Pa. Chem. Soc. (gov.), Franklin Inst., New Eng. Assn. Chemistry Tchrs. Author: Introduction to Theoretical Chemistry, 1936; Qualitative Analysis, 1938; Semimicro Qualitative Analysis, 1939; (with Frank T. Gucker, Jr.) Physical Chemistry, 1942; (with A. F. Daggett) A Textbook of Qualitative Analysis, 1946, Qualitative Analysis, 1955. Asso. editor Jour. Franklin Inst. Contbr. to sci. jours.; pub. many papers. Home: 747 College Av., Haverford, Pa. Died Dec. 31, 1956; buried Valley Forge (Pa.) Gardens.

MELENEY, FRANK LAMONT, (mel'en-e), surgeon; b. Somerville, Mass., Sept. 25, 1889; s. Clarence Edmund and Carolyn Ella (Coit) M.; A.B., Dartmouth Coll., 1910, D.Sc., 1955; M.D., Columbia Coll. Phys. and Surgeons, 1916; m. Helen Seelye Clark, Sept. 17, 1919; children—Frank Lamont, David Clark. Began as teacher of science and mathematics, 1910; master in Adirondack-Fla. Sch., 1910-12; surg. interne Presbyterian Hosp., N.Y. City, 1916-18; attending surgeon, since 1950; dir. of lab. for bacteriological research in Dept. of Surgery, Coll. of Physicians and Surgeons, Columbia U., 1925-46; asso. in surgery, College Physicians and Surgeons, 1925-28, asst. prof. clin. surgery, 1928-38, asso. prof., 1938-50, professor, 1950-55, prof. emeritus clinical surgery, 1955—; lectr. surgery U. Miami (Fla.), 1955—; asso. in surgery, asso. prof. Peking Union Med. Coll., Rockefeller Foundation, Peking, China, 1920-24. Served in Med. Corps, U.S. Army, during World War; with Mobile Operating Unit No. 1, Sect. 5, and Mobile Operating Team No. 103, of A.E.F., in Meuse-Argonne, St. Mihiel and Aisne-Marne offensives, 1918. Decorated by Chinese Govt., 1922, 1941. Fellow Am. Coll. Surgeons, N.Y. Acad. of Medicine; hon. mem. Western Surg. Assn.; mem. Am. Surg. Assn., Soc. of Clin. Surgery, A.M.A., So. Medical Assn., Halsted Surg. Society, N.Y. Surg. Soc., Allen O. Whipple Surg. Soc., Internat. Soc. Surgery, Southeast Surgical Congress, Chi Phi, Alpha Omega Alpha. Methodist. Clubs: Com. of 100 (Miami Beach, Florida); Coral Gables (Florida) Country; Century Association (New York, New York). Author 2 vol. Treatise on Surgical Infections, 1948; The Clinical Aspects and Treatment of Surgical Infections, 1949. Author papers in med. and surg. periodicals, articles in surg. textbooks on surg. bacteriology and surg. infections. Home: 700 Jeronimo Dr., Coral Gables, Fla. Office: Ingraham Bldg., 25 S.E. 2d Av., Miami, Fla. Died Mar. 7, 1963.

MELISH, JOHN, geographer; b. Methuen, Perthshire, Scotland, June 13, 1771; attended Glasgow U.; m. Isabella Moncrieff. Apprenticed to cotton factor, Glasgow; voyaged to W.I., 1798; sailed to Savannah, Ga., 1806, established merc. firm; in Scotland, 1808-10; settled in Phila., 1811; published and printed maps, Phila., 1812-22. Works include: Travels in the United States of America in the Years 1806, 1807, and 1809, published 1812; A Statistical Account of the United States, 1813; A Geographical Description of the United States, Showing the Boundary Proposed by the British Commissioners of Ghent, 1814; The State Map of Pennsylvania, 1822. Died Phila., Dec. 30, 1822; buried Free Quakers Cemetery.

MELLER, HARRY BERTINE, research engr.; b. Altoona, Pa., May 26, 1878; s. Charles William and Annie (Adams) M.; U. of Pa., 1906-07, 1908-09; Mich. Coll. of Mines, Houghton, 1907-08, 1909; Engr. of Mines, U. of Pittsburgh, 1910; Sc.D., U. of Toledo, 1938; m. Mary Alice Rothrock, Apr. 8, 1901. Clerk Pa. R.R. Co., Altoona, Pa., 1895-1900; clk. of faculty, dept. of medicine, U. of Pa., 1900-04; sec. same, 1904-07; instr. mining, 1910-11, asst. prof., 1911-12, prof., 1912-24, vice-dean, 1912-14, dean, 1914-23, School of Mines—all of University of Pittsburgh; head of air pollution investigation, Mellon Inst., U. of Pittsburgh, since 1923; chief Bur. of Smoke Regulation of City of Pittsburgh, 1920-38. Managing dir. Industrial Hygiene Foundation America (formerly Air Hygiene Foundation) since 1935. Enlisted Company C, 5th Regt. Nat. Guard Pa., 1897; with same company and regt. Pa. Vol. Inf., May-Oct. 1898; successively 2d lt., 1903-04, 1st lt., 1904-05, capt., 1905-07, Co. L, 3d Regt., Nat. Guard Pa.; capt. Air Service U.S. Army, 1917-19. Republican. Mem. A.A.A.S., Am. Pub. Health Assn., Phi Delta Theta, Sigma Gamma Epsilon, Alpha Omicron. Mason. Home: Schenley Apts. Office: Mellon Institute, Pittsburgh, Pa. Died June 27, 1943.

MELLIN, CARL JOHAN, mechanical engr., inventor; b. Westergotland, Sweden, Feb. 17, 1851; s. Sven and Maria Elizabeth (Bjorn) M.; coll. and tech. edn. in Sweden; apprentice in ry. offices and gen. machine works and 3 yrs.' tech. course at Gothemburg to 1873; draftsman Gothemburg, 1873-77; mech. engr. and naval architect in Sweden and with Robert Napier & Son, Scotland, the Caledonian Locomotive Works, and with Erickberg and Atlas Works, Sweden; came to America, 1887; m. Gertrude Alice Levie, Dec. 31, 1889. Mech. engr., New York, 1889-94; chief engr. Richmond (Va.) Locomotive Works, 1894-1902; cons. engr. Am. Locomotive Co., 1902—. Home: Schenectady, N.Y. Died Oct. 15, 1924.

MELLISS, DAVID ERNEST, engineer; b. New York, Mar. 11, 1848; s. David M. and Mary D. M.; ed. Columbia Univ. Sch. of Science and univs. of Göttingen and Vienna; A.M., Ph.D., Göttingen, 1870; m. Frances Pauline Botton, Sept. 4, 1890 (died 1901). Constantly engaged as consulting and constructing engr. on important works, mining and civil, in U.S., Central and S. America and Mexico. Decorated with Order Bust of Bolivar, of Venezuela. Home: San Rafael, Cal. Died Mar. 24, 1913.

MELLUISH, JAMES GEORGE, sanitary engr.; b. Bloomington, Ill., Feb. 25, 1870; s. Joseph Henry and Hannah (Bell) M.; grad. Lawrenceville (N.J.) Sch., 1891; spl. student U. of Ill., 1895; B.S., Mass. Inst. Tech., 1896; m. Ruth Kershaw, of Bloomington, Ill., Oct. 15, 1903; 1 son, James Kershaw; m. 2d, M. Teresa Galvis, Bucaramanga, S.A., May 11, 1929; 1 daughter, Gladys. Researches in sanitary biology, Massachusetts

Institute of Technology, with Prof. W. T. Sedgwick, 1897; designed sanitary engring. works of Ill. State Normal U. and Ill. Soldiers Orphans Home, 1898-1900; supt. Union Gas & Electric Co., Bloomington, Ill., 1900-01; sanitary and engring. investigations in Ia., Ill., N.Y., Fla. and La., also sewerage and sewage disposal, etc., 1901-19; project engr. U.S. Housing Corpn., Alton (Ill.) Dist., 1918; dist. dir. Div. of Industrial Hygiene and Medicine, St. Louis, 1919; capt. U.S.P.H.S., rank of asso. sanitary engr.; sanitary engr. Pearse, Greeley & Hansen, 1923-28; engr. sewerage system, Barranquilla, Colombia, 1928—. Mem. Am. Soc. C.E., Ill. Soc. Engrs., Phi Delta Theta. Republican. Unitarian. Address: 6 N. Michigan Av., Chicago IL*

MELTZER, SAMUEL JAMES, physiologist; b. in Russia, Mar. 22, 1851; gen. edn. Königsberg, Prussia; studied philosophy and medicine at U. of Berlin, 1875-82, M.D., 1882; (LL.D., U. of Md., 1906, St. Andrews U., Scotland, 1912, and Washington U., St. Louis, 1914). Came to U.S., 1883, and since in practice at New York; head dept. of physiology and pharmacology, Rockefeller Inst. for Med. Research, 1906—; cons. physician Harlem Hosp. Maj., Med. O.R.C., 1917. Fellow A.A.A.S., N.Y. Acad. Sciences, N.Y. Acad. Medicine. Home: New York, N.Y. Died Nov. 7, 1920.

MELVILLE, DAVID, pewter maker, inventor; b. Newport, R.I., Mar. 21, 1773; s. David and Elizabeth (Thurston) M.; apprenticed to a pewterer; m. Patience S. Sherman, Mar. 4, 1812, 7 children. Established as pewterer, Newport, by 1803; developed method for producing illuminating gas, succeeded in lighting his own house with coal gas, 1806, obtained 1st U.S. patent for apparatus for making coal gas, 1813; unsuccessfully attempted (with Winslow Lewis) to influence U.S. Govt. to use coal gas for light houses. Author: An Exposé of Facts Respectfully Submitted to the Government of the United States Relating to the Conduct of Winslow Lewis, 1819. Died Newport, Sept. 3, 1856.

MEMMINGER, ALLARD, M.D., author; b. Charleston, S.C., Sept. 30, 1854; s. C. G. Memminger (sec. of the treasury, C.S.A.) and Mary Withers (Wilkinson) M.; grad. U. of Va., and M.D., S.C. Med. Coll., 1880; m. Margaret Aloysius Coleman (Past Great Pocahontas of S.C., Degree of Pocahontas, I.O.R.M.), of Charleston, S.C., December 10, 1913. Dean and prof. chemistry and hygiene and clin. urinary diagnosis, S.C. Medical Coll., and dean and prof. gen. and applied chemistry, Coll. of Pharmacy of S.C.; member State Bd. Pharm. Examiners of S.C.; chairman Charleston City Bd. of Health, and made scientific examination of waters of Charleston for U.S. Govt.; co-framer with Dr. S. C. Baker, of Sumter, S.C., of laws governing practice of medicine and surgery in S.C.; state chemist of S.C.; was chemist many phosphate and fertilizer cos.; a pioneer in development of marble industry in N.C. Awarded gold medal and diploma of honor by Académie Parisienne Française des Inventeurs (hon. corr.). Delivered address, at Richmond, Va., May 13, 1905, before the Confederate Memorial Lit. Soc., presenting portraits of 3 members of the cabinet of the Confederate States—the sec. of navy, the atty. gen., and the sec. of the treasury. Mem. Vol. Med. Service Corps, World War. Author: Diagnosis by the Urine (3 edits.); Qualitative Chemical Analysis (2 edits.); Science in the Field (manual guide for the farmer); Stop and Think, or Reasons for the Decadence of Aristocrats, 1913. Home: Charleston, S.C. Died Jan. 16, 1936.

MEMMINGER, CHRISTOPHER GUSTAVUS, mining engr.; b. Charleston, S.C., Aug. 10, 1865; s. Robert Withers and Susan (Mazyck) M.; student U. of Va., 1882-86; m. Mary Lee King, Jan. 6, 1887; 1 dau., Christine Gustava. Began in mining engring., Colo., 1887; engaged in development of phosphate mining industry, Fla., 1893—; pres. State Bank of Lakeland (Fla.), 1908-12; cons. mining engr., New York, 1900—; pres. Coronet Phosphate Co., 1916—; pres. Diamond Sand Co. Pres. Bd. of Commrs., Lakeland, 1908-10; pres. Fla. State Bd. of Health, 1908; spl. trade commr. sent to Europe by U.S. Dept. Commerce, 1919. Republican. Episcopalian. Home: Asheville, N.C. Died Aug. 1930.

MENCKEN, AUGUST, engr., author; b. Balt., Feb. 18, 1889; s. August and Anna (Abhau) M.; student Balt. Polytech. Surveys, 1909-11; engr. for Stewart & Jones on r.r. constrn., N.C., 1911; constrn. div. Southern R.R., Ga., 1911-12; with B. F. Sweeten & Son, sewer construction, Balt., 1912-13; with Claiborne Johnston Co. in charge constrn. Montebello filtration plant, Balt., 1913-22; built roads, ferry dock, and charge constrn. Army camp, Fort Meade, Md., 1917-18; work on health resort, San Diego de los Banos, Cuba, 1920; v.p. T. D. Claiborne Co., bldg. roads, bridges, dams, 1922-31; with Am. Cider & Vinegar Co., designing distilleries, 1931-37; pvt. engring. practice, Balt. 1937-40; engr. supervising constrn. for Whitman, Requardt & Smith, Edgewood Arsenal, Md., 1940-45; now in pvt. practice. Asso. mem. Am. Soc. C.E. Club: 14 W. Hamilton St., Maryland (Balt.). Author: Firstclass Passenger, 1938; By the Neck, 1942; The Railroad Passenger Car. Contbr. to Scientific Am., The Balt. Engr. Home: 1524 Hollins St., Balt. Died May 19, 1967; buried Loudon Park Cemetery.

MENDEL, LAFAYETTE BENEDICT, physiological chemist; b. Delhi, N.Y., Feb. 5, 1872; s. Benedict and Pauline (Ullman) M.; A.B., Yale, 1891, Ph.D., 1893; Larned fellow, Yale, 1891-94; research student, univs. of Breslau and Freiburg, 1895-96; hon. Sc.D., U. of Mich., 1913, Rutgers Coll., 1930; LL.D., Western Reserve University, 1932; m. Alice R. Friend (A.B., U. of Wis.). Teaching at Yale, 1892, asst. prof., 1897-1903, prof. physiol. chemistry, 1903-21, Sheffield Scientific Sch. (Yale); Sterling prof. physiol. chemistry, Yale U., 1921—, also member governing bd. Sheffield Scientific Sch., Grad. Sch. of Yale and Sch. of Medicine, Yale. Hitchcock lecturer, Univ. of Calif., 1923. Dir. Russell Sage Institute of Pathology; mem. advisory board J. S. Guggenheim Memorial Foundation; research asso. Carnegie Instn. of Washington. Mem. numerous Am. and foreign scientific societies. Gold medalist Am. Institute of Chemists, 1927. Author: Nutrition—The Chemistry of Life; Changes in the Food Supply and Their Relation to Nutrition. Editor Journal of Biological Chemistry, also Journal of Nutrition, and of chem. monographs of Am. Chem. Soc. Home: New Haven, Conn. Died Dec. 9, 1935.

MENDELSOHN, ERICH, architect; b. Allenstein, East Prussia, Mar. 21, 1887; s. David and Esther (Jaruslawsky) M.; M.A., U. Munich, 1911; m. Louise Maas, Oct. 5, 1915; 1 dau., Esther (Mrs. Peter Joseph). Came to U.S., 1941, naturalized, 1946. Mem. German Expressionist movement, active in expressionist theatre; friend and asso. Kandinsky, Marc, Klee, Ball; opened archtl. office, Berlin, 1918, working largely on factory and dept. store design; visited Israel in connection with Ruthenberg electrification project, won 1st prize for Haifa bus. center designs, 1923; visited U.S., 1924; emigrated to Holland when Hitler came to power, 1933, then worked in London; lived in Israel, 1937-41; came to U.S., lectured at Columbia, Yale, Harvard, U. Mich.; cons. U.S. War Dept., Washington, 1942-44; moved to San Francisco, 1945; exhibited one-man shows Berlin, 1919, 28, N.Y.C., 1929, 41, London, 1931, Milan, 1932, Chgo., San Francisco, 1941. Served with C.E., German Army, World War I. Guggenheim fellow, N.Y.C., 1943. Fellow Royal Inst. Brit. Architects, Mexican Inst. Architects; mem. A.I.A., Acad. Arts Berlin; hon. mem. Internat. League Modern Architecture Tokyo, Arts Club London. Leading exponent of expressionism in architecture (bldgs. imaginative, yet functional); a major influence on Am. design; prin. works include: Einstein Tower (astrophysics lab.), Potsdam, 1920; Univ. Med. Center, Mt. Scopus, Israel; (with sculptor Ivan Mestrovic) meml. to 6,000,000 Jews killed in World War II, N.Y.C., 1947. Author: America—Architect's Picture Book, 1926; Russia, Europe, America—and Architectural Cross-section, 1928; The Creative Spirit of the World Crisis, 1930, New House, New World, 1931. Died Sept. 15, 1953. *

MENDENHALL, CHARLES ELWOOD, physicist; b. Columbus, O., Aug. 1, 1872; s. Thomas Corwin M. and Susan Allan (Marple) M.; B.S., Rose Poly. Inst., Terre Haute, Ind., 1894; Ph.D., Johns Hopkins, 1898; m. Dorothy M. Reed, Feb. 14, 1906; children—Thomas Corwin, John Talcott. Instr. physics, U. of Pa., 1894-95, Williams Coll., 1898-1901; asst. prof. physics, 1901-03, asso. prof., 1903-05, prof., 1905—, U. of Wis. Chmn. div. of physical sciences, Nat. Research Council. Commd. maj., Signal R.C., 1917, and in active service, 1917-19. Republican. Home: Madison, Wis. Died Aug. 18, 1935.

MENDENHALL, THOMAS CORWIN, physicist; b. Hanoverton, O., Oct. 4, 1841; s. Stephen and Mary (Thomas) M.; pub. sch. edn.; (hon. Ph.D., Ohio State U., 1878; Sc.D., Rose Poly. Inst.; LL.D., U. of Michigan, 1887, Western Reserve U., 1912); m. Susan Allen Marple, July 12, 1870; father of Charles Elwood M. Professor physics and mechanics, Ohio State U., 1873-78; prof. physics, Imperial U. of Japan, 1878-81, Ohio State U., 1881-84, emeritus prof., 1884; prof. U.S. Signal Corps, 1884-86; pres. Rose Poly. Inst., 1886-89; supt. U.S. Coast and Geod. Survey, 1889-94; pres. Worcester Poly. Institute, 1894-1901; in Europe, 1901-12. Supt. United States weights and measures, 1889-94; member U.S. Light House Board, 1889-94; mem. 1st Bering Sea Commn., 1891; U.S. and Great Britain Boundary Line Survey Commn., 1892-94; chmn. Mass. Highway Commn., 1896-1901; U.S. del. Internat. Elec. Congress, 1893; medal, Paris Expn., 1900. Hon. fellow Am. Geog. Soc. (gold medal, 1901), Nat. Geog. Soc., Franklin Institute (gold medal, 1918); fellow Am. Acad. Arts and Sciences. Decorated Order The Sacred Treasures, 2d class, Japan, 1911; gold medal, Nat. Ednl. Soc. of Japan, 1911. Trustee Ohio State U., 1919—. Author: A Century of Electricity. Home: Ravenna, O. Died Mar. 23, 1924.

MENEFEE, F(ERDINAND) N(ORTHRUP), educator, cons. engr.; b. Columbus Kan., Jan. 7, 1886; s. Harry Bostwick and Alice DiaDame (Hodgen) M.; B.S. in Civil Engring., U. Neb., 1908, C.E., 1932; C.E., Cornell, 1910; D.Eng., Lawrence Inst. Tech., Detroit, 1937; m. Lucile Cull, Sept. 17, 1909; children—Charles Cull, Ruth. Instr. civil engring., Cornell U., 1910; instr. U. Mich., 1910-13, asst. prof. drawing, 1914, asst. prof. engring. mechanics, 1915-16, prof., from, 1919, prof. emeritus, until 1973; sec. United Engring. Corp., Detroit and Ann Arbor, 1919-20, v.p., 1920-29; firm Menefee and Dodge, 1925-35; pres. Oak Park Land Co., 1925-73; ex-chmn. bd. Lus-Trus Plastics, Inc.; treas. Dana Fiduciary; dir. Am. Cement Corp. Mem. nat. council YMCA, 1927-32, state com. 1927-35, pres. Ann Arbor, 1923, dir., 1921, 22; bd. dirs. Student Christian Assn., 1929-36; mem. U. Mich. Fresh Air Camp Com., chmn. 1923-46; pres. Community Fund Assn., Ann Arbor, 1927. Mem. Ann Arbor Bd. Pub. Works, 1925-49, pres., 1935-40. Served to maj., Ordnance Dept., World War I. Mem. Am. Soc. C.E. (pres. Mich. sect. 1948, vice chmn. com. on water diversions), Am. Soc. Testing Materials, Am. Concrete Inst. (past chmn. precast floor constrn. com., dir. 1952-55), Mich. Engring. Soc. (pres. 1930), Mich. Patent Law Assn., Engring. Soc. Detroit, Am. Legion, Kappa Sigma, Sigma Xi, Sigma Tau, Sigma Rho Tau (former nat. pres.). Republican. Mem. Conglist. Ch. Clubs: Rotary (dir. 1932), Michigan Union. Author: Materials Testing Manual, 1932; St. Lawrence Seaway, 1940; Structural Members and Connections (co-reviser with R.R. Zipprodt), 1943. Editor: Michigan Engineer, 1927-37. Contbr. reports and engring. articles. Home: Ann Arbor MI Died Feb. 12, 1973.

MENNINGER, WILLIAM CLAIRE, psychiatrist, foundation exec.; b. Topeka, Oct. 15, 1899; s. Charles Fredrick and Flora (Knisely) M.; A.B., Washburn Coll. (now Washburn Municipal U.), 1919, D.Sc., 1949; M.A., Columbia, 1922; M.D., Cornell U. Med. Sch., 1924; D.Litt., Mo. Valley Coll., 1951, St. Benedict's Coll., 1963; Sc.D., Woman's Med. Coll. Pa., 1955; LL.D., Adelphi Coll., Kan State U., 1962; m. Catharine Wright, Dec. 11, 1925; children—Roy Wright, Philip Bratton, William Walter. Intern in med. and surg. Bellevue Hosp., N.Y.C., 1924-26; post-grad. training in psychiatry, St. Elizabeth's Hosp., Wash., 1927; with Menninger Clinic, Topeka, 1925—, psychiatrist, 1927—; pres. Menninger Found.; prof. psychiatry Menninger Sch. of Psychiatry; mem. courtesy staff Stormont-Vail Hosps., 1926—. Mem. nat. exec. bd. Boy Scouts Am., 1935—; mem. Group for Advancement of Psychiatry; mem. expert adv. panel WHO, 1949-50; counselor Nat. Soc. Crippled Children and Adults; adv. bd. Am. Child Guidance Found.; also mem. or chmn. of panels and coms. of various sci. orgns. many years. Bd. dirs. Nat. Com. on Alcoholism, Nat. Recreation Assn. Served as 2d lt. U.S. Army, 1918; commd. lt. col. M.C., 1942; neuropsychiat. cons. 4th Service Command, Atlanta, 1943; apptd. dir. neuropsychiatry cons. div. Surgeon Gen.'s Office, 1943, promoted col., 1944, birg. gen. M.C., 1945, separated, 1946; apptd. brig. gen. ORC, AUS, 1947; cons. in neuropsychiatry to surgeon gen. U.S. Army, 1946—. Recipient D.S.M., Army Commendation ribbon; chevalier Legion of Honor (France); Lasker award Nat. Com. Mental Health Hygiene; Great Living Americans award U.S. C. of C., 1957. Diplomate psychiatry Am. Bd. Psychiatry and Neurology. Fellow A.C.P. (regent 1958-64, 1st v.p. 1964-65), A.M.A., Am. Psychiat. Assn. (chmn. coordination com. on community aspects of psychiatry 1951-58, past pres.), Am. Orthopsychiat. Assn., Am. Psychopathic Assn., Am. Psychoanalytic Assn. (past pres.), Central Neuropsychiatric Assn. (past pres.), Central Neuropsychiatric Hosp. Assn. (past pres.), Assn. Mil. Surgeons, Assn. for Advancement Research in Nervous and Mental Disease, Am. Philatelic Soc., Alpha Omega Alpha, and other orgns. Presbyn. Mason. Clubs: University (Chgo.); Country (Topeka). Author: Juvenile Paresis (monograph), 1936; Skipper's Handbook (Official Handbook for Leaders of Sea Scouting), 1934; Psychiatry in a Troubled World, 1948; You and Psychiatry, 1948; Psychiatry: Its Evolution and Present Status, 1948; also numerous sci. papers. Mem. editorial bd. Bull. of Menninger Clinic, Nat. Parent-Teacher, Parents Mag., and others. Home: 1724 Collins Av., Topeka 66604. Office: Box 829, Topeka 66601. Died Sept. 6, 1966.

MENOCAL, ANICETO G., civil engr. U.S.N., 1872—; b. Island of Cuba, Sept. 1, 1836; ed. in schools at Havana; C.E. Rensselaer Poly. Inst., 1862; sub-chief engr. Havana water works, 1863-69; engr. dept. public works, New York, 1870-72. Has been chief engr. of all U.S. Govt. surveys for establishing practicability of a ship canal from the Atlantic to the Pacific at Nicaragua and Panama, and of the Maritime Canal Co. of Nicaragua; has made final plans and estimates of cost for a ship canal through Nicaragua. Apptd. delegate to Paris Canal Congress, 1879; decorated by President Grevy, Chevalier Legion of Honor. Has published several official reports on Nicaragua Canal, etc. Mem. commn. to select site for prin. naval station in Philippine Islands, 1900-01; mem. bd. to prepare plans and estimates of cost for naval sta. at Olongapo, Subig Bay, P.I., 1901-02; in 1902 directed by Navy Dept. to select site for coaling sta. on coast of Liberia, Africa; engaged in important drainage work in Cuba, 1906-07. Home: New York, N.Y. Died 1908.

MENVILLE, LEON, radiologist; b. Napoleonville, La., Nov. 29, 1882; s. Charles M. and Arabella (Gouaux) M.; student La. State U.; M.D., Md. Med. Coll., Baltimore, 1904; m. Marie Marmande, Jan. 25, 1905; children—Muriel, John, Lucille. Began med. practice at Houma, La., 1904; prof. emeritus radiology, Tulane U.; dir. dept. of radiology, Charity Hospital, to 1950. Ex-pres. La. State Board Med. Examiners. Lt. comdr., U.S.N.R. (retired). Mem. La. State Med. Soc. (past pres.), American Coll. of Radiology (v.p. 1937), Cuban

Radiol. Soc. (hon.), Alpha Omega Alpha, Sigma Xi. Democrat. Catholic. Club: Metairie Country. Mem. editorial staff Am. Jour. of Cancer. Awarded gold medal Radiol. Soc. of North America, 1932, for original work on the lymphatic system. Past pres. Radiol. Soc. of North America. Contbr. to Pillmore's Clinical Radiology. Home: 66 Fontainebleu Drive. Office: Maison Blanche Bldg., New Orleans. Died Jan. 24, 1955; buried Houma, La.

MENZIES, ALAN WILFRID CRANBROOK, educator; b. Edinburgh, Scotland, July 31, 1877; s. Thomas H. and Helen C. (Cranbrook) M.; M.A., U. Edinburgh, 1897, B.Sc., 1898; Ph.D., U. Chgo., 1910; student univs. Leipzig and Aberdeen, Davy-Faraday Lab., London; m. Mary I. Dickson, Mar. 20, 1908 (dec. Apr. 1960); 1 dau., Elizabeth Grant Cranbrook. Came to U.S., 1908. Asst. prof. chemistry Heriot-Watt Coll., Edinburgh, 1898-1001, prof. St. Mungo's Coll., Glasgow, Scotland, 1902-08; research asso., later instr. and asst. prof. chemistry U. Chgo., 1908-12; prof. chemistry, head dept. Oberlin Coll., 1912-14; prof. chemistry Princeton, 1914-45, Russell Moore prof., 1938-45, emeritus, 1945—. Organizer and dir. summer courses for sci. tchrs. Dept. Agr. and Tech. Instrn. for Ireland, 1905-08; asso. chemist U.S. Bur. Standards, 1918-19. Mem. Am. Chem. Soc., Chem. Soc. (London), Royal Soc. Edinburgh, Am. Assn. Univ. Profs., Sigma Xi. Author of over 80 articles in sci. jours. in U.S. and abroad. Home: 926 Princeton-Kingston Rd., Princeton, N.J. 08540. Died Sept. 8, 1966.

MERCK, GEORGE WILHELM, mfg. chemist; b. New York, N.Y., Mar. 29, 1894; s. George and Friedrike (Schenck) Merck; A.B., Harvard University, 1915; Phar.D. (honorary) Phila. Coll. of Pharmacy, 1938; D.Sc. (hon.), Temple U., 1948, Lafayette Coll., 1950, University Vt., 1952, Newark College of Engineering, 1954; LL.D., Middlebury Coll., 1951, Rutgers U., 1952; D. Eng. (hon.), Stevens Institute Tech., 1951; m. Serena Stevens, Nov. 24, 1926; children—George W., Jr., Albert W. (by prev. marr.); Serena M. (Mrs. Francis W. Hatch, Jr.), John H. C., Judith F. Associated with Merck & Co., Inc., mfg. chemists, Rahway, N.J., 1914—, pres., dir., 1925-50, chmn. bd., 1949—; chmn. bd. Merck & Co., Ltd., Merck (Pan Am.), Inc., Merck (North Am.), Inc.; dir. N.Y. & Long Branch R.R. Company, U.N.J.R.R. & Canal Co. Chmn. bd. trustees Merck Inst. for Therapeutic Research; mem. bd. Nat. Sci. Found., 1951—; mem. corp. Mass. Inst. Tech.; bd. trustees Nat. Fund for Med. Edn., Nutrition Found.; pres. and trustee Vt. Forest & Farmland Found.; member bd. Conservation Found. Mem. adv. com. Munitions Board, 1939-51, chmn. committee, 1949-51; member committee on drugs and medical supplies, National Research Council, 1942-45; director War Research Service (in charge biological warfare), 1942-44; special consultant to Secretary of War (biol. warfare), chmn. U.S. Biol. Warfare Com., 1944-45. Awarded Medal for Merit for wartime biol. services; Chem. Industry Medal by Am. sect. of Soc. of Chem. Industry, 1947. Fellow Am. Geog. Society. Mem. national executive council Am. Cancer Soc.; mem. National Conference of Christians and Jews; dir. Regional Plan Assn., New York City; Com. to Visit Dept. Biol. and Bussey Instn., Harvard U.; member exec. com. Mfg. Chemists' Assn., 1927-49, v.p., 1933-45, pres., 1949-52. Director American Forestry Assn.; past treas. N.J. State Rep. Com. Rep. Clubs: Essex County (West Orange); Metropolitan (Washington); University, Harvard, Chemists', Down Town, Railroad-Machinery, Links, Century (N.Y.); Essex (Newark); University (St. Louis); Jupiter Island (Hobe Sound, Fla.); Dorset Field (Dorset, Vt.). Home: Eagleridge Farm, Prospect Av., West Orange, N.J. Office: Lincoln Av., Rahway, N.J. Died Nov. 9, 1957.

MEREDITH, JOSEPH CARROLL, civ. engr.; b. Rushville, Ind., Mar. 23, 1856; s. William Gray and Caroline (Barrett) M.; B.M.E., Ia. State Coll., 1878; student Stevens Inst. Technology, 1879-81; m. Ella Lane, 1891. U.S. asst. engr., Mo. River improvement, 1881-87; asst. engr., 1888-93, div. engr., 1893-96, Mo. River Commn.; engr. pvt. corps., 1896-1900; asst. engr. Tampico (Mex.) harbor improvements, 1900-04; constructing engr., Florida East Coast Ry., at Miami, 1904—. Democrat. Died 1909.

MERGENTHALER, OTTMAR, inventor; b. Aachtel, Germany, May 11, 1854; s. Johann George and Rosina (Achermann) M.; m. Emma Frederica Lachenmayer, Sept. 11, 1881, at least 4 children. Watch-maker's apprentice, Bietigheim, Württemberg, Germany, 1868-72; came to Balt., 1872; with August Hahl's scientific instrument shop, Washington, D.C., 1872-76; moved to Balt., 1876, formed partnership with Hahl, Balt., 1880; patented linotype machine, 1884. Died Oct. 28, 1899.

MERICA, PAUL DYER, (mer'i-ka), metallurgist; b. Warsaw, Ind., Mar. 17, 1889; s. Charles Oliver and Alice (White) M.; student DePauw U., 1904-07; A.B., U. Wis., 1908; Ph.D., U. Berlin, 1914; D.Sc., De Pauw U., 1934, Lehigh U., 1938, Stevens Inst., 1942; m. Florence Young, Sept. 22, 1917. Research physicist U.S. Bureau of Standards, 1914-19; dir. research Internat. Nickel Co., 1919—; tech. asst. to pres. Internat. Nickel Co. of Can., 1929, successively asst. to pres., exec. v.p., pres., dir., now cons. research and development work on metals and alloys—their metallurgy and metallography; originator of the precipitation theory of hardening of alloys, developed in connection with rsch. on aluminum alloys. Fellow A.A.A.S.; mem. Am. Iron and Steel Inst., Am. Soc. for Testing Materials, Am. Phys. Soc., Am. Inst. Mining and Metall. Engrs., Am. Inst. C.E., Nat. Acad. Sciences, Inst. Metals and Iron and Steel Inst. (both Brit.), Canadian Inst. Mining and Metallurgy, Mining and Metall. Soc. Am., Am. Soc. for Metals, Beta Theta Pi, Phi Lambda Upsilon, Epsilon Chi. Republican. Presbyn. Clubs: Engineers, City Midday, University, Mining, Sleepy Hollow Country. Author articles and monographs in tech. publs. James Douglas medallist, 1929; John Fritz medalist, 1938; Institute Medals, Medallist, 1941; Franklin Institute medal, 1942; Gold medal, Am. Soc. for Metals, 1951. Home: P.O. Box 310, Ossining, N.Y. Office: 67 Wall St., N.Y.C. Died Oct. 20, 1957.

MERILH, EDMOND L(OUIS), bacteriologist; b. New Orleans, Mar. 6, 1898; s. (Jean) Edmond and Adele E. (Desmaries) M.; B.S., Spring Hill Coll., 1917; postgrad. Tulane U., Med. Sch., 1917-19; certificate of bacteriology and pathology, Loyola U., New Orleans, 1922, M.S., 1923; m. Lillian M. Stanton, Dec. 17, 1931; children—Edmond L., Jr., Lillian Marie, Jeanne-Adele, Marietta Paula. Instr. in botany, Zoology, bacteriology Loyola Univ., 1919-22, asso. prof. botany, zoology, bacteriology, histology, serology, 1922-43, prof., 1943—. Tchr. bacteriology to dental students Army Specialized Tng. Program unit, also A.R.C. instr., World War II. Mem. bd. Eye, Ear, Nose and Throat Hosp., 1925. Served in S.A.T.C., World War I. Recipient lifetime tchrs. certificate, State of La., 1938; Citation of Merit for 25 years' service. Mem. Am. Pharm. Soc., A.A.A.S., Nat. Catholic Edn. Assn., Am. Micros. Soc., Agramonte Pre-Med. Soc., B.E.U. Nat. Med. Tech. Soc., Nat. Geog. Soc., La. Acad. Scis., Cath. Round Table Soc., New Orleans Acad. Scis., New Orleans Bot. Soc., Tb Assn. New Orleans, O. L. Pothier Soc., Phi Rho Sigma, Theta Beta, Blue Key, Order of Alhambra. Democrat. Roman Catholic. K.C. (4 deg.). Author: Bacteriology Guide for Dental Students, 1941, rev. edit., 1943, 45, 49. Contbr. articles to Turtox News, A Modified Acid Fast Staining Method, 1937, A Method for Cultivating and Mounting Molds, 1939. Specialist in pathogenic bacteriology and microscopic anatomy. Home: 2219 Pine St., New Orleans 70118. Died Apr. 9, 1964.

MERKER, HARVEY MILTON, chem. engr.; b. Detroit, Feb. 24, 1888; s. Herman and Rosa (Walz) M.; B.S., U. Mich., 1909, M.S., 1940, D.Eng. (hon.), 1953; D.S., Wayne U., 1943; m. Buda Overesch Martin, June 27, 1911; children—Henry M., Marjorie (Mrs. Rudolph Sell). Chem. engr. Parke, Davis & Co., 1909-29, supt. mfg., 1929-53, dir. sci. relations, 1953-57, ret.; dir. Mich. Life Ins. Co. Pres. Detroit Pub. Library Commn., from 1953; chmn. nat. adv. com. Mich. Meml.-Phoenix Project; adv. com. Franklin Settlement. Dir. Detroit Council Churches; trustee Detroit Historical Society, Metropolitan Society for the Blind; commissioner, president Detroit Public Library; trustee, past president Detroit Institution, Cancer Research; vice pres., trustee Kresge Eye Institute, Edwin S. George Found.; trustee, sec. Cranbrook Inst. Sci.; trustee Alma Coll.; gov. Rackham Research Found. Mich. State Coll.; pres. Kresge-Hooker Scientific Library Associates; director Junior Achievement of S.E. Mich., Meth. Children's Village, Detroit chapter UN, Detroit Sci. Museum Soc., World Medical Relief, Incorporated. Member adv. bd. Detroit Dist. Nurses Assn., Nat. Fedn. of Settlements and Neighborhood Centers. Named First Citizen of Detroit, 1957; Midwest citation of honor Ind. Tech. Coll., 1958. Fellow A.A.A.S.; member Am. Chem. Soc., Am. Institute Chem. Engrs., Engring. Soc. Detroit (past pres.), Better Bus. Bur. Detroit (dir.), Sigma Rho Tau, Tau Beta Pi. Presbyn. Clubs: Torch, Orpheus, Detroit Boat, Detroit Athletic, Forest Lake Country (Detroit). Author: Book of Stainless Steels, 1933; Encyclopedia of Chemical Technology (with A.R. Whale), 1953; Centennial History of the Engineering College of the U. of Michigan, 1953. Contbr. profl. publs. Home: Detroit MI Died May 4, 1970; interred Evergreen Cemetery, Detroit MI

MERRELL, IRVIN SEWARD, mech. engr., mfr.; b. Syracuse, N.Y., Oct. 12, 1875; s. Gauis Lewis and Mary Antoinette (Seward) M.; prep. edn., Cascadilla Sch., Ithaca, N.Y.; B.S. in Mech. Engring., Mass. Inst. Tech., 1896; m. Carolyn Louise Snow, Jan. 4, 1899; children—Seward Snow, Mary Antoinette (Mrs. John Parker Welch), Harriet Powers (Mrs. Jay E. Latimer, Jr.). Began, 1896, in employ of Merrell-Soule Co., Syracuse, and specialized in research in desiccation and evaporation of food products; patent issued, 1899, for double cylinder evaporator, for desiccating vegetable pulps, now used for making dried milk; asso. with others in investigations resulting in prodn. of Spray process milk powder and original development of vacuum pack can, for which many patents have been issued; ret. Jan. 1, 1928. Chmn. Draft Bd. No. 3, Syracuse, World War. Trustee Tuskegee (Ala.) Normal and Indsl. Inst.; mem. bd. govs. St. Petersburg Jr. Coll.; mem. exec. bd. Nat. Urban League, N.Y. Republican. Unitarian. Clubs: Pass-a-Grille Yacht, St. Petersburg Yacht. Address: 345 18th Av. N.E., St. Petersburg, Fla. Died May 9, 1959; buried Meml. Park, St. Petersburg.

MERRELL, WILLIAM DAYTON, biologist; b. Bklyn., Aug. 21, 1869; s. Jonathan Dayton and Clarissa Orcelia (Justus) M.; A.B., U. Rochester, 1891; Ph.D., U. Chgo., 1899; m. Winifred Boorman, Sept. 6, 1898. Began teaching, Beaver Dam, Wis., 1891; prof. biology U. Rochester, 1905-39, prof. emeritus of botany, 1939—, was dir. univ.'s first glee club. Fellow A.A.A.S.; mem. Rochester Acad. Science. Republican. Baptist. Home: Penfield Rd., Brighton, N.Y. Died Feb. 11, 1955.

MERRIAM, C(LINTON) HART, naturalist; b. N.Y. City, Dec. 5, 1855; s. Hon. Clinton L. and Caroline (Hart) M.; student Sheffield Scientific Sch. (Yale), 1874-77; M.D., College Physicians and Surgeons (Columbia), 1879; m. Virginia Elizabeth Gosnell, Oct. 15, 1886 (died Dec. 7, 1937); children—Dorothy (Mrs. Henry Abbot), Zenaida (Mrs. M. W. Talbot). In med. practice, 1879-85; chief of U.S. Biol. Survey, 1885-1910; resigned to conduct biol. and ethnol. investigations under a spl. trust fund established by Mrs. E. H. Harriman, 1910-39. Naturalist, Hayden's survey, 1872; asst. U.S. Fish Commn., 1875; visited Arctic seal fishery from Newfoundland, 1883, as surgeon S.S. Proteus; visited Alaska, 1891, as U.S. Bering Sea Commr., and investigated the fur seal on Pribilof Islands; has conducted many biol. explorations in Far West. Chmn. U.S. Geographic Bd., 1917-25. Fellow American Ornithologists' Union (pres. 1900-02), A.A.A.S.; a founder and mem. board of trustees Nat. Geog. Soc. since 1888; mem. Nat. Acad. of Sciences, Am. Philos. Soc., Am. Soc. Naturalists (pres. 1924-25), Washington Acad. Sciences, Biol. Soc. Washington (pres. 1891, 92), Anthropol. Soc. Washington (pres. 1920, 21), Am. Soc. Mammalogists (pres. 1919-21); foreign mem. Zoöl. Soc. London. Author: The Birds of Connecticut, 1877, Mammals of the Adirondacks, 1882-84; Results of Biol. Survey of San Francisco Mountain Region and Desert of Little Colorado in Arizona, 1890; Biological Reconnaissance of Idaho, 1891; Geographic Distribution of Life in North America, 1892; Trees, Shrubs, Cactuses and Yuccas of Death Valley Expedition, 1898; Laws of Temperature Contol of Geographic Distribution of Terrestrial Animals and Plants, 1894; Monographic Revision of the Pocket Gophers (Geomyidae), 1895; Revision of the American Shrews, 1895; Synopsis of Weasels of North America, 1896; Biological Survey of Mount Shasta, Calif., 1899; Life Zones and Crop Zones of the United States, 1898; Indian Population of California, 1905; Distribution and Classification of the Mewan Indians of California, 1907; Totemism in California, 1908; The Dawn of the World, 1910; Review of the Grizzly and Big Brown Bears of America, 1917; G. K. Gilbert, Geologist, 1918; The Acorn, a Neglected Source of Food, 1918; A California Elk Drive, 1921; Earliest Crossing of the Deserts of Utah and Nevada to Southern California—Route of Jedediah H. Smith in 1826, 1923; First Crossing of the Sierra Nevada—Jedediah Smith's trip from California to Salt Lake in 1827, 1923; The Name of Mount Rainier, 1924; Baird, the Naturalist, 1924; Source of the Name Shasta, 1926; The Buffalo in Northern California, 1926; Classification and Distribution of the Pit River Indian Tribes of California, 1926; William Healey Dall, 1927; Annikadel History of the Universe as told by the Modesse Indians of Calif., 1928; also about 400 papers on zoöl., bot. and ethnol. subjects. Home: 2590 Cedar St., Berkeley, Calif. Died Mar. 19, 1942.

MERRIAM, JOHN CAMPBELL, palaeontologist, educator, administrator; b. Hopkinton, Ia., Oct. 20, 1869; s. Charles Edward and Margaret Campbell (Kirkwood) M.; B.S., Lenox Coll., Ia., 1887; Ph.D., U. of Munich, 1893; Sc.D., Columbia, 1921, Princeton, 1922, Yale, 1922, U. of Pa., 1936, U. State of N.Y., 1937; Ore. State Coll., 1939; LL.D., Wesleyan U., 1922, U. of Calif., 1924, New York U., 1926, U. of Mich., 1933, Harvard U., 1935, George Washington U., 1937, U. of Ore., 1939; m. Ada Gertrude Little, Dec. 22, 1896 (died Apr. 13, 1940); children—Lawrence Campbell, Charles Warren, Malcolm Landers; m. 2d, Margaret Louise Webb, Feb. 20, 1941. Instr. palaeontology and hist. geology, 1894-99, asst. prof., 1899-1905, asso. prof., 1905-12, prof., 1912-20, dean of faculties, 1920, U. of Calif.; chmn. Nat. Research Council, 1919; pres. Carnegie Instn., Washington, 1920-38, emeritus since 1939. Regent Smithsonian Inst. since 1928. Fellow Am. A.A.A.S. (pres. Pacific Div., 1919-20), Geol. Soc. America (pres. 1910), Am. Palaeontol. Soc. (pres. 1917); mem. Nat. Acad. Sciences (Washington), Am. Philos. Soc., Washington Acad. Sciences, Calif. Acad. Sciences, Phila. Acad. Sciences, Am. Acad. Arts and Sciences, Am. Assn. Univ. Profs., Commission du Parc National Albert; corr. mem. London Zoöl. Soc., Chr. Michelsens Institute (Bergen, Norway); hon. mem. Soc. de Geog. e Hist. de Guatemala, Acad. Nacional Cient. Antonio Alzate de Mex., La Asociacion Conservadoro de los Monumentos Arquelogicos de Yucatan, Soc. de Geog. e Hist. de Michoacán, Mexico. Pres. executive com. Pan-American Institute of Geography and History, 1935-38; chmn. research committee California State Council of Defense, 1917-20. Congregationalist. Republican. Author: Primitive Characters of the Triassic Ichthysauria, 1904; The Thalattosauria, a Group of Marine Reptiles from the Triassic of California, 1905; Cave Exploration, 1906; Triassic Ichthysauria (with special reference to the American forms), 1908; The Occurrence of Human Remains in California Caves, 1909; The Occurrence of Twisted

Horned Antelopes in the Tertiary of Northwestern Nevada, 1909; The story of the Calaveras Skull, 1910; Synopsis of Lectures in Palaeontology, 1910; The Relation of Palaeontology to the History of Man (with particular reference to the Am. problem), 1910; The Fauna of Rancho La Brea, Part I, Occurrence, 1911; Part II, Canidae, 1912; The Horses of Rancho La Brea, 1913, Discovery of Human Remains in an Asphalt Deposit at Rancho La Brea, 1914; Extinct Faunas of the Mojave Desert (their significance in a study of the origin and evolution of life in America), 1915; Relationships of Pliocene Mammalian Faunas from the Pacific Coast and Great Basin Provinces of North America, 1917; Science in Mobilization, 1917; The Beginnings of Human History Read from the Geological Record; The Emergence of Man, 1919; The Function of Educational Institutions in Development of Research, 1920; Earth Sciences as the Background of History, 1920; The Research Spirit in the Everyday Life of the Average Man, 1920; Common Aims of Culture and Research in the University, 1922; The Place of Education in a Research Institution, 1925; The Responsibility of the Federal and State Governments for Recreation, 1926; International Coöperation in Historical Research, 1926; Medicine and the Evolution of Society, 1926; Inspiration and Education in National Parks, 1927; The Place of Geology Among the Sciences, 1929; Institutes for Research in the Natural Sciences, 1929; Significance of the Border Area between Natural and Social Sciences, 1929; The Living Past, 1930; The Unity of Nature as Illustrated by the Grand Canyon, 1931; The Felidae of Rancho La Brea (with Chester Stock), 1932; Spiritual Values and the Constructive Life, 1933; Responsibility of Science to Government, 1934; Ultimate Values of Science, 1935; Science and Human Values; Time and Change in History, 1936; The Most Important Methods of Promoting Research, as Seen by Research Foundations and Institutions; Geography and History Among the Sciences, as Influencing Research in the Americas, 1937; Application of Science in Human Affairs; Influence of Science upon Appreciation of Nature; Some Aspects of Cooperative Research in History, 1938; Contribution of Geology to Shaping of Ideas on the Meaning of History; Science and Belief; The Development of Cultural and Social Values through the Relation of Science to Other Major Fields of Activity, 1939; also numerous other papers on palaeontology, hist., geology and problems of research in their relation to edn. Clubs: Cosmos (Washington); Century Association (New York); Commonwealth Club of California (San Francisco). Address: Carnegie Institution of Washington, Washington, D.C. Died Oct. 30, 1945. *

MERRICK, JOHN VAUGHAN, mech. engr.; b. Philadelphia, Aug. 30, 1828; s. Samuel Vaughan and Sarah M.; grad. Central High Sch., 1843; engring. edn. in works at Phila.; m. Oct. 23, 1855, Mary Sophia Wagner (died 1897). Senior and engring. partner Merrick & Sons, Phila., 1849-70. Mgr. from 1872 and v.p. from 1886, Zoöl. Soc. of Phila.; mem. bd. experts Phila. water supply, 1883; mem. bd. experts U.S. Navy Dept., 1867; pres. from 1873 Free and Open Church Assn., founder St. Timothy's Memorial Hosp., Roxborough, Phila.; trustee Univ. of Pa., 1870—; mem. Franklin Inst. (pres. 1867-70). Died 1906.

MERRILL, ALLYNE LITCHFIELD, engineer; b. Malden, Mass., Aug. 8, 1864; s. George S. and Myra H. (Litchfield) M.; S.B., Mass. Inst. Tech., 1885; m. Mary M. Tingey, of Cambridge, Mass., Nov. 25, 1896; children—Albenia, Elinor. Instr. mech. engring., 1885-91, asst. prof. mechanism, 1891-99, asso. prof., 1899-1905, prof. mechanism, 1905-34, prof. emeritus since 1934, sec. of faculty, 1906-34, Mass. Inst. Tech. Republican. Author: Elements of Mechanism, 1904. Home: Harrison, Me.

MERRILL, CHARLES WASHINGTON, metall. engr.; b. Concord, N.H., Dec. 21, 1869; s. Sylvester and Clara L. (French) M.; B.S., U. Cal. Coll. Mines, 1891; Met.E., U. Cal., 1922; m. Clara Scott Robinson, Feb. 9, 1898; children—Mrs. Beatrice Morse, John L., Gregor C., Bruce R.; m. 2d, Margaret Barker Cope, Sept. 14, 1938. Has designed, installed and operated many reduction works in U.S., Can., and Mex.; held over 25 patents in U.S. and fgn. countries for metall. processes and apparatus; pres., dir. The Merrill Co.; former chmn. bd., dir. Merco Centrifugal Co., San Francisco. Chief Div. Collateral Commodities, U.S. Food Administration, Washington, 1917-18; chmn. exec. com. San Francisco Community Chest, 1925-27; chmn. minerals com., Cal. State C. of C.; chmn. Cal. State Mining Bd., 1930. Regent U. Cal., 1924-25. Mem. Am. Inst. Mining and Metall. Engrs. (v.p. 1924), Alumni Assn. U. Cal. (pres. 1924-25), Sigma Xi, Mining and Metall. Soc. London, Australian Inst. Mining Engrs., Chem., Metall. and Mining Soc. S. Africa. Recipient James Douglas Internat. gold medal of Am. Inst. Mining and Metall. Engrs. for distinguished internat. metall. achievements, 1924; Nat. Modern Pioneer certificate of award N.A.M. in recognition of distinguished achievement in field sci. and invention which has advanced the Am. standard of living, 1940. Clubs: University, Engineers', Pacific Union, Commonwealth (San Francisco); Claremont (Oakland); Orinda Country (Orinda, Cal.). Home: 407 Camino Sobrante, Orinda, Cal. Office: Hobart Bldg., 582 Market St., San Francisco 4. Died Feb. 6, 1956.

MERRILL, CHARLES WHITE, mining engr.; b. La Crescenta, Cal., July 22, 1900; s. Samuel and Emilie (Scherb) M.; A.B. in Geology, Stanford, 1922, E.M., 1924; m. Lillian M. Dobbel, Aug. 15, 1925; children—Lillian D. (Mrs. Archibald C. Coolidge, Jr.), Charles White, Celine W. (Mrs. Francis B. Birkner), Henry D. With various mining cos. in U.S. and Mexico, 1924-28; with U.S. Bur. Mines, San Francisco and Washington, 1928-70, chief div. of minerals, Washington, 1955-70; asso. Behre Dolbear & Co., N.Y., 1970-72. Mem. U.S. delegations Tin Study Group Meetings, 1947-53, U.S. Tin Mission to Malaya, 1951; head U.S. delegation subcom. mineral resources Econ. Commn. Asia and Far East, Tokyo (UN), 1960. Served as pfc., Tank Corps, U.S. Army, 1918-19; capt. specialist res., 1931-42. Mem. Am. Inst. Mining Engrs. (dir. 1955-56, chmn. mineral econs. div. 1955-56; Mineral Economics award 1967), Mining and Metall. Soc. Am. Club: Cosmos (Washington). Author articles mining engring., mineral econs., strategic minerals in govt., profl. and tech. publs., jours. Home: Washington DC Died May 1, 1972.

MERRILL, ELMER DREW, botanist, educator; b. East Auburn, Me., Oct. 15, 1876; s. Daniel C. and Mary A. (Noyes) M.; B.S., U. Me., 1898, M.S., 1904, Sc.D., 1925; student dept. medicine George Washington U., 1900-01; Sc.D., Harvard, 1936; LL.D., U. Cal., 1936; m. Mary Augusta Sperry, May 21, 1907; children—Lynne, Dudley Sperry, Wilmans Noyes (dec.), Ann. Asst. in natural sci. U. Me., 1898-99; asst. agrostologist U.S. Dept. Agr., Washington, 1899-1902; botanist Bur. of Agr., Manila, P.I., 1902, Bur. of Agr. and Bur. of Forestry, 1902-03, Bur. of Govt. Labs., 1903-05, Bur. of Science from 1906; asso. prof. botany and head of dept. U. Philippines, 1912-19, prof. 1916-19; dir. Bur. of Science, Manila, 1919-23; dean Coll. of Agr. and dir. Agrl. Expt. sta. U. Cal., 1923-29; prof. botany Columbia, 1930-35; dir. N.Y. Bot. Garden, 1930-35; prof. botany, dir. Arnold Arboretum, adminstr. bot. collections Harvard, 1935-46, Arnold prof. botany, 1946-48, emeritus. Specializes in taxonomy and phytogeography of Philippine, Polynesian and Indo-Malayan plants. Mem. Am. Acad. Arts and Scis., Nat. Acad. Sciences, Am. Philos. Soc., Royal Asiatic Soc. (Malayan branch); hon. mem. Deutsche Bot. Gesellschaft, Netherlands Bot. Soc., Royal Netherlands Geol. Soc., Acad. Sci., Inst. de France, Inst. Genevoise, Swedish Acad. Science; fgn. mem. Linnean Soc., London (medalist 1939). Clubs: Century, Harvard of Boston. Author over 500 papers on botany of North America, China, Philippines, Malaya and Polynesia. Home: 960 Centre St. Office: Arnold Arboretum, Jamaica Plain 30, Mass. Died Feb. 25, 1956; buried Maplewood Cemetery, West Upton, Mass.

MERRILL, FREDERICK JAMES HAMILTON, geologist; b. New York, Apr. 30, 1861; s. Hamilton Wilcox and Louisa (Kauffman) M.; Ph.B., Columbia Sch. of Mines, 1885, Ph.D., 1890; m. Winifred Edgerton, Sept. 1, 1887. Asst. on Geol. Survey of N.J., 1885-89; asst. state geologist of N.Y., 1890-93; asst. dir., 1890-94, dir., 1894-1904, N.Y. State Mus.; state geologist of N.Y., 1899-1904; pvt. practice as mining geologist, 1904—; field asst. Calif. State Mining Bur., 1913—. Dir. scientific exhibit of N.Y. State at Chicago Expn., 1893, Buffalo Expn., 1901, St. Louis Expn., 1904. Home: Los Angeles, Calif. Died Nov. 29, 1916.

MERRILL, GEORGE PERKINS, geologist; b. Auburn, Me., May 31, 1854; s. Lucius and Anne Elizabeth (Jones) M.; B.S., U. of Me., 1879, M.S., 1883, Ph.D., 1889; student Wesleyan U., 1879-80; Johns Hopkins U., 1886-87; Sc.D., George Washington U., 1917; m. Sarah P. Farrington, Nov. 1883 (died 1894); m. 2d, Katherine L. Yancey, 1900. Asst. chemist, Wesleyan U., 1879-80; asst. in geol. dept. U.S. Nat. Mus., 1881; head curator dept. geology, U.S. Nat. Mus., 1897—; prof. geology and mineralogy, George Washington (formerly Columbian) U., 1893-1915. Expert spl. agt. of 12th Census in stonequarry statistics. Hon. corr. mem. A.I.A. J. L. Smith gold medal, Nat. Acad. Sciences, for researches in meteorites. Author: Stones for Building and Decoration, 1891, 1897, 1903; Rocks, Rockweathering and Soils, 1897, 1907; The Non-Metallic Minerals—Their Occurrence and Uses, 1904, 1910; also contributions to a History of American Geology, 1905, and History of American State Geological and Natural History Surveys, 1920; Catalogue and Handbook Meteorite Collection in the U.S. Nat. Museum, 1915; Handbook of Gems and Precious Stones (with others), 1922; The First 100 Years of American Geology, 1924. Home: Washington, D.C. Died Aug. 15, 1929.

MERRILL, JAMES ANDREW, educator, geologist; b. in Rockcastle Co., Ky., Apr. 6, 1861; s. Andrew H. and Ann Eliza (Eastin) M.; student William Jewell Coll., Liberty, Mo., 1879-80; grad. State Normal Sch., Warrensburg, Mo., 1887; S.B., Harvard U., 1893; LL.D., Mo. Valley College, 1923; m. Nellie A. Lowen, Dec. 23, 1896; children—Robt. Lowen (dec.), George Lowen, Helen Elizabeth. Teacher of natural sciences, Warrensburg (Mo.) State Normal Sch., 1887-97; same, Manual Training Sch., Kansas City, Mo., 1897-1900; prof. geology and geography, State Teachers' College, Superior, Wis., 1900-22, 1925-37, pres., 1922-25, pres. emeritus, 1936—. Assistant U.S. Geological Survey, 1890; investigated oil structures of Peace River region, Alberta, Can., summer 1921. Author: Industrial Geography of Wisconsin, 1909; Wisconsin—A Geographical Reader, 1931; Wonderland of Lake Superior, 1936. Conglist. Mason. Home: Superior, Wis. Died June 23, 1938.

MERRILL, JOHN BUXTON, electrical mfr.; b. Cumberland Center, Me., June 16, 1910; s. Wallace Lincoln and Harriet Melinda (Cutter) M.; student Northeastern U., 1 yr., B.S., Bowdoin Coll., 1933; M.S., Mass. Inst. Tech., 1936; m. Ann Killilea Tompkins, Sept. 2, 1950; children—Peter Gray, Martha Cutter. Asst. Mass. Institute of Technology, 1935-36; joined Patterson Screen Co., Towanda, Pa. as asst. of dir. of research, 1936; supt. fluorescent powder plant, 1940 until plant purchased by Sylvania Electric Co., 1941, and since asso. with latter firm, v.p. Sylvania Electric Products, Inc., also gen. mgr. Tungsten and Chem. Div., 1950, vice president operations Tungsten and Chemical, Atomic Energy and Electronics divisions, 1954—; partner Hotel David Wilmot, Towanda; dir. First Nat. Bank, Towanda. Mem. W.P.B., tungsten adv. com., 1943-45. Mem. Nat. Prodn. Authority Tungsten and Molybdenum Wire and Rod Industry Adv. Com. Trustee Robert Packer Hosp., Sayre, Pa.; dir. Salvation Army, Mills Community Hosp. Assn. Mem. Am. Soc. Metals, A.A.A.S., Am. Phys. Soc., Optical Soc. Am., Alpha Tau Omega. Presbyn. Mason. Clubs: Rotary, Towanda Country. Home: 207 Pine St. Office: Towanda, Pa. Died Oct. 6, 1955; buried Oak Grove Cemetery, Towanda.

MERRILL, JOHN LISGAR, engring., investment exec.; b. Oakland, Cal., Mar. 29, 1903; s. Charles Washington and Clara (Robinson) M.; B.S., U. Cal. at Berkeley, 1924; B.A. (Rhodes scholar), Oxford U., 1927, B.S., 1953, M.A., 1953; M. Natalie O'Maley, December 17, 1935; children—Jacqueline (Mrs. Philip E. Rollhaus), Steven, Deborah. Employed as engineer Blair & Co., 1928-31. mgr. Flintock Co., 1932-33; engr. to pres. and dir. Merco Centrifugal Co., 1933-56; pres., dir. Merrril Co., Merrill Estate Co., 1953-69; pres., dir. Merrill-Brose Co., 1949-69, J.L.M. Co., 1958-69; v.p., dir. Central Natural Gas Co., Vermillion, S.D., 1939-69; pres., dir. Metals, Inc. (war prodn. work; Army and Navy E award), 1942-45, Merrill Products Co. (war prodn. work; Navy Certificate award), 1943-45; dir. Bank of Cal. NA, Gulf Resources & Chem. Corp., Arthur D. Little, Inc., Pacific Tel. & Tel. Co., Rockwell Mfg. Co., Victor Equipment Co.; dir., mem. exec. com. U.S. Leasing Corp. Pres. San Francisco Planning and Urban Renewal Assn., 1960-61, vice chmn. exec. com. 1962-67, chmn., 1967-69; mem. Redevel. Agy. City and County San Francisco, 1957-59. Hon. chairman executive committee Golden Gate chapter American Red Cross; director Bay Area Ednl. TV Assn., San Francisco Civic Light Opera Assn., San Francisco Museum of Art; mem. bd. directors Assn. Am. Rhodes Scholars. Member Am. Inst. Mining, Metall. and Petroleum. Engrs., Am. Chem. Soc., Cal. Acad. Scis., Cal. Hist. Soc., English Speaking Union (San Francisco past pres.), Assn. Am. Rhodes Scholars (mem. bd. dirs.), Phi Delta Theta, Tau Beta Pi. Clubs: Pacific Union, Bohemian, Commonwealth, University (San Francisco); Burlingame (Cal.) Country. Home: San Francisco CA died Jan. 9, 1969.

MERRILL, LUCIUS HERBERT, chemist; b. Auburn, Me., Oct. 1, 1857; s. Lucius and Anne Elizabeth (Jones) M.; B.S., Me. State Coll., 1883; hon. Sc.D., U. of Me., 1908; m. Lydia Maria Buffum, June 24, 1893 (died 1907); 1 dau., Katharine Buffum; m. 2d, Annie Clifford Moore, June 15, 1910; children—Lucius Robert, Edward Osgood. Asst. in dept. of lithology and physical geology, U.S. Nat. Mus., 1885-86; chemist Me. Agrl. Expt. Sta., 1886-1908; instr. biol. chemistry, 1897-98, prof., 1898-1906, prof. biol. and agrl. chemistry, 1907-30, U. of Me., also served as state geologist of Maine (retired). Home: Orono, Me. Died Jan. 27, 1935.

MERRILL, OSCAR CHARLES, civil engr.; b. Manchester, Me., July 30, 1874; s. Josiah L. and Sarah Alexander (Chace) M.; B.A., Bates Coll., 1899. Sc.D., 1925; B.S., Mass. Inst. Tech., 1905; m. Elizabeth Watson, Oct. 17, 1906; 1 dau., Margaret (dec.); m. 2d, Marguerite Waters, Dec. 11, 1939. Instr. civil engring. U. Cal., 1905-06; dist. engr. U.S. Forest Service, 1909-13, chief engr., 1914-20; exec. sec. FPC, 1920-29. Chmn. Am. Com., World Power Conf., 1929-35, dir. 3d World Power Conf., 1935-38; engr.-economist U.S.-Mexico Oil Commn., 1942; prin. engr. Engr. Bd., U.S. Army, 1942; ret. 1943. Developed policy under which 85 per cent of water powers in the U.S. are under control of Fed. Govt. Life mem. Am. Soc. C.E.; mem. Washington Soc. Engrs. Universalist. Club: Cosmos (Washington). Author: Electric Power Development in the United States (Govt. Printing Office), 3 vols., 1916. Editor: Transactions Third World Power Conference; Second International Congress on Large Dams (Govt. Printing Office), 15 vols., 1938. Home: 9 W. Melrose St., Chevy Chase, Md. Died Jan. 15, 1951; buried Rock Creek Cemetery, Washington.

MERRILL, PAUL WILLARD, astronomer; b. Mpls., Aug. 15, 1887; s. Charles Wilbur and Kate Amelia (Kreis) M.; A.B., Stanford, 1908; Ph.D., U. Cal., 1913; m. Ruth L. Currier, Sept. 12, 1913. Fellow and asst. Lick Obs., Cal., 1908-13; instr astronomy U. Mich., 1913-16; asst. and asso. physicist U.S. Bur. Standards,

Washington, 1916-18; astronomer Mt. Wilson Obs., Carnegie Inst., 1919-52. Dir. City of Pasadena, 1927-31. Fellow American Academy of Arts and Sciences; mem. National Academy Scis. (Draper Medal 1946), Am. Philos. Society, American (Russell lecturer 1955, president 1956-58), Royal (fgn. asso.) astron. socs., Astron. Society of the Pacific (Bruce Medal 1946), Am. Phys. Soc. A.A.A.S., Am. Assn. Variable Star Observers, Phi Beta Kappa, Sigma Xi, Gamma Alpha. Republican. Conglist. Club: Athenaeum. Home: 1380 New York Av., Altadena, Cal. Address: Mt. Wilson and Palomar Observatories, Pasadena 4, Cal. Died July 19, 1961; buried Mt. View Mausoleum, Altadena, Cal.

MERRILL, WILLIAM EMERY, army officer; b. Ft. Howard, Wis., Oct. 11, 1837; s. Capt. Moses E. and Virginia (Slaughter) M.; grad. U.S. Mil. Acad. 1859; m. Margaret Spencer, Jan. 1873, at least 2 sons. Commd. lt. Corps Engrs., U.S. Army, 1859; captured during W.Va. campaign, 1861, held prisoner until Feb. 1862; brevetted capt. after being wounded, Yorktown, Va., 1862; promoted capt., 1863; brevetted maj., lt. col., col. for services in battles of Chickamauga, Lookout Mountain, Missionary Ridge; chief engr. Army of Cumberland, 1864-65; chief engr. Div. of Mo., under Gen. Sherman, 1867-70; originator, chief engr. of canalization of Ohio River from Pitts. to its mouth, 1879-85; U.S. del. Congress of Engrs., Paris, France, 1889. Author: Iron Truss Bridges for Railroads, 1870. Died Dec. 14, 1891.

MERRILL, WILLIAM FESSENDEN, civil engr.; b. Montague, Mass., June 14, 1842; s. James H. and Lucia (Griswold) M.; bro. of James Griswold M.; A.B., Amherst, 1863; student Lawrence Scientific Sch. (Harvard), 1865-66; m. Eliza G. Fessenden, Oct. 17, 1872. Civ. engr. on C.B.&Q. R.R., 1866-73; resident engr. Erie Ry. at Buffalo, N.Y., 1873-75; asst. engr. and supt. Toledo, Peoria & Western Ry., 1875-80; gen. supt. Chicago and Ia. div. Wabash R.R., 1880-82; gen. supt. C.&A. R.R., 1882-83; supt. Iowa lines C.,B.&Q. R.R., 1883-87; gen. mgr. Hannibal & St. Joseph, and Kansas City, St. Joseph & Council Bluffs R.R., 1887-90; gen. mgr. C.,B.&Q. R.R., 1890-96; 2d v.p. Erie R.R., 1896-1900; 1st v.p. N.Y.,N.H.&H. R.R., 1900-03; cons. engr., 1903—. Home: Plainfield, N.J. Died Feb. 3, 1922.

MERRIMAN, MANSFIELD, civil engr.; b. Southington, Conn., Mar. 27, 1848; s. Mansfield and Lucy (Hall) M.; Ph.B., Sheffield Scientific Sch. (Yale), 1871, C.E., 1872, Ph.D., 1876; Sc.D., U. of Pa., 1906; LL.D., Lehigh U., 1913. Asst. engr. U.S. Engr. Corps, 1872-73; instr. civ. engring., Sheffield Scientific Sch., 1875-78; asst. on U.S. Coast and Geod. Survey, 1880-85; prof. civ. engring., Lehigh U., 1878-1907; cons. civ. and hydraulic engr., 1907—. Author: Mechanics of Materials, 1885; Treatise on Hydraulics, 1889; Roofs and Bridges (with H. S. Jacoby), 1890; Higher Mathematics (with R.S. Woodwarth), 1896; Strength of Materials, 1897; Precise Surveying and Geodesy, 1899; Elements of Sanitary Engineering, 1906. Asso. editor Appleton's Universal Cyclopedia, 1895; editor in chief American Civil Engineers' Pocket Book, 1911. Home: New York, N.Y. Died June 7, 1925.

MERRIMAN, THADDEUS, civil engr.; b. New Haven, Conn., Apr. 6, 1876; s. Mansfield and Wanda (Kubale) M.; C.E., Lehigh U., 1897; hon. Dr. Engring., same university, 1930; m. Margaret Mather, Jan. 12, 1904; children—Margaret Mather, Mansfield. Began as asst. engr. New Britain (Conn.) Water Works, 1897; on surveys U.S. Nicaragua Canal Commn., 1897-99; chief of survey party, U.S. Isthmian Canal Commn., 1899-1900; with N.Y. Continental Jewell Filtration Co. on design Little Falls, N.J., water filtration plant, 1900-01; insp. in U.S. for Guayaquil & Quito Ry. Co., 1901-02; with Jersey City Water Supply Co. as asst. engr. constrn. Boonton Dam, later div. engr. E. Jersey, Passaic & Acquackanonk Water cos., 1902-05; with Bd. of Water Supply City of New York, surveys, plans, designs and constrn. Catskill Water Supply System, from 1905, successively asst. engr., asst. to chief engr., dept. engr., deputy chief engr., and, June 1922-Nov. 1933, chief engr. same, continuing with plans for new project for supply from Delaware River, this plan was approved by U.S. Supreme Ct. in 1913; in private practice as cons. engr., 1933-36; now cons. engr. Bd. of Water Supply on construction Delaware River Aqueduct for N.Y. City. Lecturer on hydraulics and water supply, Lehigh U. Consulting engr. to War Dept. on Ft. Peck project in Mont. and on flood control project in Los Angeles and Orange Counties, Calif.; cons. engr. to Tenn. Valley Authority. Editor in chief Am. Civil Engrs. Handbook. Home: New York, N.Y. Died Sept. 26, 1939.

MERRITT, ARTHUR HASTINGS, dentist; b. Williamsburg, Mass., May 2, 1870; s. Laroy Watson and Ida Louise (Hastings) M.; D.D.S., N.Y.U., 1895, Sc.D., 1945; M.Sc., U. Mich., 1938; Sc.D., U. Md., 1940, Columbia U., 1940; LL.D., Baylor University (Texas), 1955; married Anna T. White, October 15, 1896 (died 1912); children—Arthur H., DeVer B.; m. 2d, Ione Reynolds, June 1, 1918. Practice of dentistry since 1895. Awarded Fauchard gold medal for contributions to science, 1932; Jarvie gold medal by N.Y. State Dental Soc., "for distinguished service in the art and science of dentistry," 1940; Callahan gold medal by Ohio State Dental Assn., "in recognition of the high merit of scientific contributions made to humanity and the healing professions," 1940; Alfred C. Fones Memorial Medal by Conn. State Dental Assn., "for achievement in the art and science of dentistry," 1941; Henry Spenadel gold medal. First Dist. Dental Society, 1950; Children's Aid Soc. 100th Anniversary Award, 1953; Wm. John Gies award Am. College Dentists, 1955. President Wm. J. Gies Endowment Fund for the Advancement of Dentistry. Fellow A.A.A.S., American College Dentists (pres. 1938-39), Am. Acad. Periodontology (pres. 1925), Royal Soc. of Medicine of England; mem. First Dist. Dental Society (president 1918-19), N.Y. Second Dist. Dental Society (hon.), N.Y. Academy Dentistry (pres. 1927-29), Am. Dental Assn. (pres. 1939-40), Am. Dental Society of Europe (hon.), Am. Friends of Lafayette, N.Y. Hist. Soc. (trustee), Am. Museum Natural History. N.Y. State Hist. Assn., Soc. for Preservation of N.E. Antiquities, Omicron Kappa Upsilon, Psi Omega. Republican. Presbyterian. Author: Periodontal Diseases: Diagnosis and Treatment, 1930, 2d edit., 1939, 3rd edit., 1945; Arthur Hastings Merritt, An Autobiography, 1958; also many articles of scientific and clinical nature. Collector, writer and lecturer on Anglo-American Historical Staffordshire related to Am. history. Home: 5000 Fieldston Rd., Riverdale-on-Hudson, N.Y. 10471. Office: 580 Fifth Av., N.Y.C. 36. Died Feb. 9, 1961; buried Center Cemetery, Chesterfield, Mass.

MERRITT, ERNEST GEORGE, physicist; b. Indianapolis, Ind., Apr. 28, 1865; s. George and Paulina Tate (McClung) M.; student Purdue U., 1881-82; M.E., Cornell U., 1886; grad. student, Cornell, 1888-89, U. of Berlin, 1893-94; m. Bertha A. Sutermeister, Apr. 10, 1901; children—Louise S. (Mrs. Ralph H. Brandt), Julia S. (Mrs. J. G. Hodge), Virginia S. (Mrs. J. T. Emlen, Jr.), Grace S. (Mrs. Jürg Waser), Howard S. Instr. in physics, 1889-92, asst. prof., 1892-1903, professor, 1903-35, head of department, 1918-35, and professor emeritus since 1935, dean of Graduate School, 1909-14, Cornell Univ. Engaged in anti-submarine devices at U.S. Naval Exptl. Sta., New London, Conn., 1917-18. Mem. Nat. Acad. Sciences; fellow Am. Acad. Arts and Sciences, Am. Physical Soc. (pres. 1914-15), A.A.A.S., Sigma Xi, Tau Beta Pi, Phi Kappa Phi, Gamma Alpha, Phi Kappa Psi. Asso. editor Physical Review, 1893-1913. Contbr. to scientific jours. on investigations in physics especially on the subjects of luminescence and radio. Engaged in European relief, 1946-48. Address: 1 Grove Pl., Ithaca, N.Y. Died June 5, 1948.

MERRITT, FRANK, civil engineer; b. Scituate, Mass., June 11, 1856; C.E., Tufts Coll., 1879, M.Sc., 1929, from same college. Began, 1881, as axman on location Atchison, Topeka & Santa Fe RR., and advanced to track engr.; in city and hydraulic engring. 3 yrs.; with G.,C.&S.F. Ry. Co., successively levelman, transitman, on maintenance of way 3 yrs., construction 8 yrs., reconnaissance and location 5 yrs., resident engr., at Cleburne, Tex., until 1909, chief engr., at Galveston, Nov. 10, 1909—. Died Aug. 3, 1930.

MERRYWEATHER, GEORGE EDMUND, mechanical engr.; b. Avondale, Cincinnati, O., Aug. 28, 1872; s. George Neave and Ellen Lusanna (Beaman) M.; B.Sc., Mass. Inst. Tech., 1896; m. Laura Esselborn, Dec. 21, 1908; children—Janet, George Esselborn, Constance, Hubert Orr, Laura. Machine tool merchant, Cleveland, O., from 1904; was pres. The Motch & Merryweather Machinery Co.; dir. Central Nat. Bank. Chief of machine tool sect. War Industries Bd., 1917-19. Home: Gates Mills, O. Died June 8, 1930.

MERSHON, RALPH DAVENPORT, elec. engr., inventor; b. Zanesville, O., July 14, 1868; s. Ralph Smith and Mary J. (Jones) M.; M.E., Ohio State U., 1890; asst. in electrical engineering, same, 1890-91; D.Sc., Tufts College, 1918; Dr. of Engring., Ohio State U., 1936. With Westinghouse Electric & Mfg. Co. at Pittsburgh and New York, 1891-1900; represented same at World's Industrial Expn., 1893; consulting practice since 1900. Designed transformers for which the Westinghouse Co. received an award at Chicago Expn., 1893; in charge investigations of phenomena which occur between conductors at high voltages for Telluride (Colo.) Power Transmission, and Westinghouse cos., 1896-97; chief engr. Colo. Electric Power Co., 1897-98; reconstructed the generating, transmitting and receiving equipment of Montreal & St. Lawrence Light & Power Co.; designed various plants in U.S., S. Africa and Japan; was chief engr. during design and constrn. of Niagara, Lockport and Ontario Power Co. Invented: 6-phase rotary converter; compounded rotary converter; system of lightning protection for elec. appartus; compensating voltmeter (awarded John Scott medal by Franklin Inst.); etc. Mem. joint nat. com. on Reserve Corps of Engrs.; maj., Engr. O.R.C., 1917; maj. and lt. col., Engrs., U.S. Army; in active service, 1917-19, detailed to Naval Consulting Bd. Fellow A.A.A.S., Am. Inst. E.E. (pres. 1912-13); mem. Am. Soc. C.E., Am. Soc. Mech. Engrs., Franklin Inst., Inventors' Guild (ex-pres.), Engineering Inst. of Can., Instn. Elec. Engrs., Eng.; hon. life mem. Res. Officers Assn. of United States. Clubs: University, Engineers' (New York); Cosmos (Washington). Awarded Lamme engring. medal, by Ohio State U., 1932. For work in drafting legislation for R.O.T.C. and getting it included in Nat. Defense Act of 1916 was awarded citation by Ohio State U., 1942. Home: 2000 Tiger Tail Av., Miami, Fla. Died Feb. 14, 1952; buried Zanesville, O.

MERWIN, HERBERT EUGENE, petrologist; b. Newton, Kan., Feb. 20, 1878; s. Theodore Howard and Clarinda Anna (Mack) M.; student N.Y. State Normal and Tng. Sch., 1898-1901; B.S., Harvard, 1907, Ph.D., 1911; m. Alice Mary Denison, Dec. 29, 1910; children—Henry Denison, Ruth Minerva; m. 2d, Charlotte Emmeline Denison, Jan. 27, 1945. Began as tchr. pub. schs., N.Y., 1896; mem. faculty N.Y. State Normal and Training Sch., Oneonta, 1902-04; teaching fellow Harvard, 1907-09; asst. petrologist geophys. lab Carnegie Instn., 1909-17, petrologist, 1917-45, acting dir. part of 1940, tech. rep. on war contract, 1945, research asso. 1946-59. Chemist-at-large, ordinance dept. U.S. Army, World War I. Recipient Roebling medal, 1949. Mem. Am. Phys. Soc., Am. Geophys. Union, Geol. Soc. Am. (v.p. 1930), Mineral. Soc. Am. (pres.). Home: 2946 Newark St., Washington 20008. Died Jan. 28, 1963.

MESSINA, ANGELINA ROSE, micropalentologist; b. N.Y.C., Apr., 23, 1910; d. Michaelangelo and Josephine (Sperrazza) Messina; B.A., N.Y.U., 1932; M.A., Columbia, 1935; Ph.D., h.c., U. Basel (Switzerland), 1967. Asst. geology N.Y.U., 1932-33; instr. geology Bklyn. Coll., 1933-34; asso. dir. research project on Foraminifera, Am. Mus. Natural History, 1934-41, asso. curator dept. micropaleontology, 1941-67, chmn., curator dept. micropaleontology, 1967-68; adj. prof. geology Rutgers U.; collector, research Mediterranean and Caribbean microfaunas. Recipient Amita award, 1965. Fellow Am. Assn. Advancement Sci., Geol. Soc. Am. N.Y. Acad. Sci. (chmn. sect. geology 1953-54); mem. Am. Assn. Petroleum Geologists (sec. Eastern sect. 1952-53), Paleontological Society, Society of Economic Paleontologists and Mineralogists, Societa Paleontologica Italiana, Soc. Paleontol. Japan, Deutsche Geologische Gesellschaft, Sigma Xi. Author: (with Brooks F. Ellis) Catalogue of Ostracoda, Catalogue of Foraminifera. Editor Micropaleontology (quar.). Home: New York City NY Died Nov. 20, 1968.

MESSLER, EUGENE LAWRENCE, engr.; b. Pittsburgh, Pa., Apr. 6, 1873; s. Thomas D. and Maria R. (Varick) M.; B.Ph., Sheffield Scientific School (Yale), 1894; m. Elizabeth V. Long, Dec. 31, 1898; children—Thomas D., E. Lawrence. Began as pattern maker and moulder, Edgar Thompson Works of Carnegie Steel Co.; successively civ. engr., gen. supt. labor and transportation and asst. blast furnace supt., Duquesne Works, Carnegie Steel Co., Pa., 1895-99; supt. and gen. supt. Eliza Furnaces, Coke Works, Jones &Laughlin Steel Co., 1899-1911; asst. to pres. Riter-Conley Mfg. Co., 1912-15; v.p. and gen. mgr. Witherow Steel Co., 1916-18; also pres. Eureka Fire Brick Works; dir. Pittsburgh, Fisher Scientific Co. Commd. capt. engrs., May 20, 1918; comdg. Co. G., 21st Engrs., 1st Army A.E.F., Sept. 1918-May 1919; participated in St. Mihiel, defensive sector and Meuse-Argonne offensives; lt. col. Engr. Reserves, to 1938, now inactive due to age limit. Member American Iron and Steel Inst., Am. Inst. M.E., Am. Refractories Inst., Am. Soc. Mil. Engrs., Vets. of Foreign Wars, Engring. Soc. Western Pa., British Iron and Steel Inst., S.A.R., Am. Legion, Reserve Officers Assn. Clubs: Yale (New York); Harvard-Yale-Princeton, Cloister, Pittsburgh Golf, Rolling Rock. Home: 5423 Forbes St. Office: B. F. Jones Bldg., Pittsburgh PA

METCALF, CIELL LEE, entomologist; b. Lakeville, O., Mar. 26, 1888; s. Abel Crawford and Catherine (Fulmer) M.; A.B., Ohio State U., 1911, A.M., 1912; D.Sc., Harvard, 1919; m. Cleo Esther Fouch, Dec. 31, 1908; children—Robert Lee, James Richard. Asst., Ohio State U., 1911-12; asst. entomologist, N.C. Dept. Agr., 1912-14; asst. prof. entomology, Ohio State U., 1914-19, prof., 1920-21, prof. entomology and head of dept., U. of Ill., since 1921; chairman div. of biological sciences, 1936-38, secretary of the same since 1938; consulting entomologist, Maine Expt. Station, summers 1915-17; teacher of biology, Cornell U., summers, 1918, 19; field entomologist, New York State Museum, summer, 1929. Chairman board of directors University Y.M.C.A.; vice pres. Illini Pest Control and Service Company. Fellow Entomol. Soc. America (sec.-treas. 1921-25; v.p. 1926; pres. 1934), A.A.A.S.; mem. Am. Assn. Econ. Entomologists (v.p. 1940), Am. Assn. Univ. Professors, Illinois Academy Science, Eugene Field Society, Sigma Xi (pres. Ill. Chapter, 1937-38), Gamma Alpha. Methodist. Clubs: Rotary, Chaos, Dial, Urbana Golf and Country (bd. mgr. since 1933). Author: Destructive and Useful Insects (with W. P. Flint), 2d edition, 1939; Key to the Principal Orders and Families of Insects (with Zeno Payne Metcalf), 1928; Fundamentals of Insect Life (with W. P. Flint), 1932; Insects—Man's Chief Competitors (with W. P. Flint), Century of Progress Series, 1932. Contbr. bulls. and articles on biology and entomology. Home: 704 Pennsylvania Av., Urbana, Ill. Died Aug. 21, 1948.

METCALF, HAVEN, plant pathologist; b. Winthrop, Me., Aug. 6, 1875; s. George Shepard and Prudence (Grant) M.; A.B., Brown, 1896, A.M., 1897; studied Harvard, 1899; U. of Neb., 1901-02, Ph.D.; m. Flora May Holt, June 28, 1899 (died Apr. 26, 1935). Instr. in botany, Brown U., 1896-99; prof. of biology, Tabor

Coll., 1899-1901; instr. bacteriology, U. of Neb., 1901-02; prof. botany, Clemson Agrl. College, S.C., 1902-06; pathologist, 1906-07, in charge div. of forest pathology since 1907, U.S. Dept. Agr. Asso. editor of Phytopathology, 1910-14. Mem. Sigma Xi, Delta Upsilon; fellow A.A.A.S. Bot. Soc. America, Am. Phytopathol. Soc. (ex-pres.), Soc. Am. Bacteriologists, Soc. Am. Foresters, Bot. Soc. of Washington (ex-pres.), Am. Shade Tree Conf. (ex-pres.), Washington Acad. Sciences; U.S. del. Internat. Conf. on Phytopathology, Holland, 1923. Author of publs. on botany, plant pathology and bacteriology. Mason (K.T.). Clubs: Cosmos, Washington Country. In 1908, introduced from Italy, Colusa rice, now extensively grown in Calif. Home: 1841 Summit Pl. N.W. Office: U.S. Dept. Agr., Washington, D.C. Died May 23, 1940.

METCALF, JOEL HASTINGS, astronomer; b. Meadville, Pa., Jan. 4, 1866; s. Lewis Herbert and Anna (Hicks) M.; grad. Meadville Theol. Sch., 1890; student, Harvard Div. Sch., 1890; Ph.D., Allegheny (Pa.) Coll., 1892; Manchester Coll. (U. of Oxford), 1903; D.D., Meadville Theol. School, 1920; m. Elizabeth S. Lochman, Sept. 22, 1891. Ordained Unitarian ministry, 1890; minister, Burlington, Vt., 1893-1903, First Congl. Ch., Taunton, Mass., 1904-10, Unitarian Ch., Winchester, Mass., 1910-20, First Parish of Portland, Me., 1920—. Interested in astronomy and has discovered about 41 minor planets, several variable stars and 6 comets (2 periodic). Has made several telescopes as a recreation, his last one the largest at Harvard Obs. (16 in. double). Chmn. visiting com. Harvard Obs.; mem. visiting com. Ladd Obs. Awarded 5 medals, Astron. Soc. of the Pacific, and gold medal, Astron. Soc. Mexico. Author: World Stories, 1909. Y.M.C.A. overseas sec., 1918-19, with 3d Div., 7th Inf.; divisional citation for work at Chateau Thierry. Home: Portland, Me. Died Feb. 21, 1925.

METCALF, LEONARD, civil engr.; b. Galveston, Aug. 26, 1870; s. Joseph Houghton and Emma Augusta (Leonard) M.; B.S. in C.E., Mass. Inst. Tech., 1892; unmarried. Consulting engr., Boston, 1897; mem. firm of Metcalf & Eddy. Mem. Corp. M.I.T. Trustee Concord Free Pub. Library. Unitarian. Mem. various societies. Past chmn. Council of Affiliated Tech. Socs. of Boston. Home: Concord, Mass. Died Jan. 29, 1926.

METCALF, MAYNARD MAYO, zoölogist; b. Elyria, O., Mar. 12, 1868; s. Eliab Wight and Eliza Maria (Ely) M.; A.B., Oberlin Coll., 1889; Ph.D., Johns Hopkins, 1893; Sc.D., Oberlin, 1914; m. Ella M. Wilder, Sept. 10, 1890; children—Fern Wilder (dec.), Mildred Ella (Mrs. William P. Beetham). Asso. prof. and prof. biology, Women's Coll., Baltimore, 1893-1906; prof. zoölogy, Oberlin Coll., 1906-14 (leave of absence for zoölogical study in Germany and Naples, 1906-08); research associate and professor zoölogy, Johns Hopkins, 1925—; collaborator marine invertebrates, United States National Mus. Trustee Marine Biol. Lab., Nat. Research Council (chmn. in biology and agr., 1924-25). Mem. numerous scientific societies. Author of zoological memoirs in American and German journals, chiefly upon Protozoa, Tunicata and Mollusca and numerous papers on geog. distribution of animals since the Triassic, and of "An Outline of the Theory of Organic Evolution" also of articles upon economic theory. Home: Waban, Mass. Died Apr. 1940.

METCALF, WILLIAM, engr., steel mfr.; b. Pittsburgh, Sept. 3, 1838; grad. Rensselaer Polytechnic Inst., Troy, N.Y., 1858; in charge manufacture of heavy Rodman and Dahlgren guns at Fort Pitt Foundry, Pittsburgh, 1860-65; steel mfr., 1868—. Mem. and past pres. Am. Soc. Civ. Engrs., and Am. Inst. Mining Engrs. Home: Pittsburgh, Pa. Died 1909.

METCALF, ZENO PAYNE, zoölogist; b. Lakeville, O., May 1, 1885; s. Abel Crawford and Catherine (Fulmer) M.; A.B., Ohio State U., 1907; D.Sc., Harvard, 1925; m. Mary Luella Correll, Oct. 20, 1909; 1 dau., Katharine (Mrs. Micou F. Browne). Instr. entomology Mich. State Agrl. Coll., 1907-08; with N.C. Dept. Agr., 1908-12; prof. zoölogy N.C. State Coll. and entomologist expt. sta., 1912-50, also dir. instrn. sch. of agr., 1923-44, dir. graduate studies, 1940-50; asso. dean the graduate sch. U. N.C., 1943-50, research prof. of zoology and entomology, 1950—; instr. biol. lab. Ohio State U., 1916-18, U. Mich., 1920; vis. prof. zoölogy Duke, 1935-36. Fellow A.A.A.S., Micros. Soc. (v.p. 1922; pres. 1927), N.C. Acad. Science (v.p. 1914; pres. 1921); mem. Entomol. Soc. Am., Assn. Econ. Entomologists (chmn. Cotton States br. 1940), Ornithol. Union, Ecological Soc., Nat. Assn. Biology Tchrs., Biol. Soc. Wash., Tenn. Acad. Sci., Kan. Entomol. Soc., Soc. Systematic Zoologists, Am. Soc. Limnology and Oceanology, Am. Assn. U. Profs., Entomol. Soc. Washington, Am. Museum of Natural History, Soc. Herpetologists, Limnol. Soc. Am., Ohio Acad. Sci., Wilson Ornithol. Club, Assn. S. Eastern Biologists, Am. Biol. Assn., Chgo. Acad. Sci., N.Y. Zoöl. Soc., Soc. for Study of Evolution, Sigma Xi, Alpha Gamma Rho, Alpha Zeta, Phi Kappa Phi. Dem. Presbyterian. Kiwanian. Clubs: Raleigh Kiwanis (pres. 1932), Raleigh Torch (pres. 1940). Author: Insect Pests in Rural Efficiency Guide, 1918; Key to Insects, 1918; Key to the Family Fulgoridae, 1923; General Zoölogy, —1927; Economic Zoölogy 1927; Text Book of Economic Zoölogy, 1930; Introduction to Zoölogy, 1932; General Catalgue of Hemiptera Tettigometridae, 1932; Cixiidae, 1936; Araeopidae, 1943; Derbidae, 1945; Achilixidae, 1945; Meenoplidae, 1945; Kinnaridae, 1945; Achilixidae, 1945; Meenoplidae, 1945; Kinnaridae, 1945; Dictyopharidae, 1946; Fulgoridae, 1947; Achilidae, 1948; The Fulgorina of Barro Colorado, 1938; Bibliography of the Homoptera of the World, 1943; Cercopidae of Cuba, 1944; Homoptera of Kartabo, 1945; Homoptera of Guam, 1946, Center of Origin Theorry, 1946; Cuban Flatidae (with S. C. Bruner), 1948; Catalog of the Hemiptera, Fulgoroidea Fascicle IV, 1957, Issidae, 1958 (both posthumous). Editor Homoptera, Biol. Abstracts; mem. editorial bd. Catalog of Hemiptera of World, editorial bd. ecology, 1935-37, and editorial bd. Ecological Monographs, 1940-42. Home: 315 Forest Rd. Address: State College Station, Raleigh, N.C. Died Jan. 5, 1956; buried Oakwood Cemetery, Raleigh.

METCALFE, SAMUEL LYTLER, physician, chemist; b. Winchester, Va., Sept. 21, 1798; s. Joseph and Rebecca (Littler or Sittler) M.; M.D., Transylvania U., Lexington, Ky., 1823; studied chemistry and biology in Eng., 1831; married twice; m. 2d, Ellen Blondel, 1846. Practiced medicine in Ind., Miss., Tenn., 1823-30; contbd. scientific articles to Knickerbocker Mag., 1833-35; went to Eng. to do research in chemistry and geology, 1835. Author: The Kentucky Harmonist, 1820; A Collection of Some of the Most Interesting Narratives of the Indian Warfare in the West, 1821; A New Theory of Terrestial Magnetism, 1833; Caloric: Its Mechanical, Chemical and Vital Agencies in the Phenomena of Nature, 1843. Died Cape May, N.J., July 17, 1856.

METTEN, JOHN FARRELL, shipbuilding engr.; b. Kent County, Del., Dec. 15, 1873; s. Alexander and Elizabeth (Hoffecker) M.; student Middletown (Del.) Academy honorary; Dr. Engring., Lehigh University, 1928 and University of Delaware, 1942; unmarried. Began as draftsman, 1894; chief engineering, draftsman, William Cramp & Sons Ship & Engine Bldg. Co., Philadelphia, 1904-09, chief engr., 1909-25, v.p. in charge of engring., 1925-27; pres. Marine Engring. Corp., Phila., 1927-31; consulting engr., Phila., 1931-35; became pres. and dir. N.Y. Shipbuilding Corp., Camden, N.J., 1935, later chmn. bd. dirs. Mem. A.A.A.S., Am. Soc. Naval Engrs., Am. Soc. Naval Architects and Marine Engrs., British Inst. Naval Architects (London), Franklin Inst., Newcomen Soc., N.Y. Geog. Soc. Club: Union League (Phila.). Office: Camden NJ Died Sept 16, 1968.

METTLER, L(EE) HARRISON, M.D.; b. N.Y. City, June 1, 1863; s. Isaac Voorhees and Marcella M. (Smith) M.; A.B., Coll. City of New York, 1883, A.M., 1886; studied Coll. Phys. and Surg. (Columbia); M.D., Jefferson Med. Coll., Phila., 1886; m. Minnie Warner, of Clinton, Ill., June 12, 1900. Began practice in Phila., 1886; prosector and asst. to chair of anatomy, 1886-87, chief med. clinics, 1887-91, lecturer and clin. instr. mental and nervous diseases and electro-therapeutics, 1888-91, Medico-Chirung. Coll. of Phila.; began practice in Chicago, 1891; formerly prof. of neurology, Coll. of Medicine, U. of Ill., attending neurologist, Cook Co. Hosp., 1904-06, and Norwegian Lutheran Deaconess Home and Hosp.; retired, 1924. Mem. A.M.A., Am. Acad. Medicine, Chicago Med. Soc., Practitioners' Club, Chicago Acad. Sciences. Author: Treatise on Diseases of the Nervous System, 1905. Home: Hubbard Woods, Ill.

METZ, ABRAHAM LOUIS, chemist; b. Chicago, Apr. 22, 1864; s. Charles R. and Rosa (Baer) M.; self-ed.; Ph.G., New York Coll. Pharmacy, 1887; M.D., Tulane U., New Orleans, 1893, hon. Ph.M., 1889; m. Cecile Marx, of New Orleans, July 9, 1890; children—Waldemar Rice, Mrs. Amalie Kahn, Ruth Matas. Instr. pharmacy, Tulane U., 1887-96; prof. chemistry and med. jurisprudence, same, 1896-1920; also head dept. chemistry, 1908-18, prof. chemistry and toxicology, pharm. dept., 1908-20, and prof. chemistry and metallurgy, dental dept., 1909-20—all Tulane U.; now emeritus. Served as city chemist, New Orleans, chemist La. State Bd. Health and of New Orleans Bd. of Health, many yrs. Mem. Am. Chem. Soc., etc. Mason (33 deg.). Home: 2015 Calhoun St., New Orleans, La.

METZLER, WILLIAM HENRY, univ. prof.; b. Odessa, Ont., Can., Sept. 18, 1863; s. George F., Sr., and Anna (Shannon) M.; A.B., U. of Toronto, 1888; Ph.D., Clark University, 1892; D.Sc., Syracuse University, 1931; m. Augusta E. Philp, of Dundonald, Can., Jan. 2, 1890; children—Augusta Philp, Gerald Philp, Helen. Instr. mathematics, Mass. Inst. Tech., 1892-94; asso. prof., 1894-96, Francis H. Root prof., and head dept. of mathematics, 1896-1923, dean of Grad. Sch., 1911-17, dean of College of Liberal Arts, 1921-23, Syracuse Univ.; dean New York State Coll. for Teachers, 1923-33. Fellow Royal Soc. of Edinburgh, Royal Soc. of Canada (hon.), A.A.A.S.; mem. Am. Math. Soc., Brit. Assn. Adv. Sci., Math. Assn. of Great Britain, London Math. Soc., Deutsche Mathematiker Vereinigung, Société Mathématique de France, Circola Matematico di Palermo, Edinburgh Mathematical Soc., Archaeol. Inst. America, Phi Beta Kappa, Sigma Xi, Phi Kappa Phi, Kappa Phi Kappa; ex-pres. Association of Teachers of Mathematics for Middle States and Maryland. Methodist. Republican. Author: College-Algebra, 1906; A Treatise on the Theory of Determinants, 1929; also many articles in mathematical jours. of America and Europe. Former editor The Mathematics Teacher, Journal of Pedagogy. Address: 5003 S. Salina St., Syracuse, N.Y.

MEYER, ADOLF, (mi'er), psychiatrist, neurologist; b. Niederweningen, nr. Zürich, Switzerland, Sept. 13, 1866; s. Rudolf and Anna (Walder) M.; ed. Gymnasium, Zürich; Swiss Staatsexamen for practice of medicine, 1890; post-grad. studies at Paris, London, Edinburgh, Zürich, Vienna and Berlin, 1890-92; M.D., of Zürich, 1892; LL.D., Glasgow Univ., 1901, Clark U., 1909; Sc.D., Yale, 1934; Harvard, 1942; m. Mary Potter Brooks, Sept. 15, 1902; 1 dau., Julia Lathrop. Came to U.S., 1892. Hon. fellow, then docent in neurology, U. of Chicago, 1892-95; pathologist to Ill. Eastern Hosp. for the Insane, Kankakee, 1893-95; pathologist and later dir. of clin. and lab. work, Worcester (Mass.) Insane Hosp. and docent in psychiatry, Clark U., 1895-1902; dir. Pathol. psychiatric) Inst., N.Y. State Hosps., 1902-10; prof. psychiatry, Cornell U. Med. Coll., 1904-09; prof. psychiatry, Johns Hopkins, and dir. Henry Phipps Psychiatric Clinic, Johns Hopkins Hosp., 1910-41, prof. emeritus since 1941; Salmon memorial lecturer, 1932; Maudsley lecturer, 1933; guest lecturer Acad. of Neurology and Psychiatry, Kharkow, U.S.S.R., 1933; Thomas Salmon medal for distinguished service in psychiatry, 1942. Hon. pres. Nat. Com. for Mental Hygiene and president Internat. Com. for Mental Hygiene since 1937; hon. vice-pres. Conf. on Method in Philosophy and the Sciences; hon. mem. Boston Soc. Neurology and Psychiatry, Royal Medico-Psychological Assn., New York Psychiatric Society (pres. 1905-07); New York and Washington psychoanalytic societies, mem. Assn. Am. Physicians, Am. Neurol. Assn. (pres. 1922). Am. Psychiatric Assn. (pres. 1927), Academie der Naturforscher zu Halle, Am. Inst. Criminal Law and Criminology, A.A.A.S., N.Y. Acad. Sciences, Assn. for Research in Nervous and Mental Diseases, Am. Orthopsychiatric Assn., Am. Psychopathol. Assn. (pres. 1912, 16), American Psychological Assn., Assn. of Anatomy, Harvey Society, New England Soc. Psychiatry; corr. mem. Société de Neurologie, Société de Psychologie and Société Medico-psychologique (Paris), Sociedad Neurologia y Psiquiatria (Buenos Aires). Extensive contbr. on neurology, pathology, psychiatry, mental hygiene, etc. Zwinglian Protestant. Clubs: Century (New York); Cosmos (Washington). Address: 4305 Rugby Rd., Baltimore 10, Md. Died Mar. 17, 1950.

MEYER, ALFRED, physician; b. N.Y.C., June 18, 1854; s. Isaac and Mathilda (Langenbach) M.; A.B., Columbia, 1874; M.D., Coll. Phys. and Surg. Columbia, 1877; m. Annie Florance Nathan, Feb. 15, 1887; 1 child (dec.). Began practice in N.Y.C., 1880; clin. prof. medicine N.Y.U.-Bellevue Med. Coll., 1910—; cons. physician, Mt. Sinai Hosp., Montefiore Hosp., Washington Heights Hosp. Hon. dir. Nat. Tb Assn. Fellow A.C.P.; mem. Am. Thoracic Soc., A.M.A., N.Y. State Med. Assn., N.Y. County Med. Soc., N.Y. Acad. Medicine, N.Y. Tb. and Health Assn. (dir.), Harvey Soc., Phi Kappa Psi, etc. Received citation of N.Y. Tb. and Health Assn., 1942. Home: 1225 Park Av., N.Y.C. Died July 14, 1950.

MEYER, ARTHUR WILLIAM, anatomist; b. Cedarburg, Wis., Aug. 18, 1873; s. Henry and Louise (Wiepking) M.; B.S., U. of Wis., 1898; M.D., Johns Hopkins, 1905; m. Esther Hartshorne Robinson, Dec. 28, 1907; children—Ruth Robinson, Robert Wiepking. Asst. and asso. in anatomy Johns Hopkins Med. Sch., 1905-07; asst. prof. anatomy, U. Minn., 1907-08; prof. anatomy Northwestern U. Med. Sch., 1908-09; prof. human anatomy Stanford U., 1909-38, prof. emeritus, 1938—. Research asso. Carnegie Instn., 1917-18. Fellow A.A.A.S.; mem. Assn. Am. Anatomists, Am. Soc. Zoologists. Author: An Analysis of the De Generatione Animalium of William Harvey, 1936; Rise of Embryology, 1939; Human Generation, 1956; also publs. on investigations on embryology, growth, lymphatics, anat. variations, attrition pathology, ednl. hist. and social problems. Home: 121 Waverly St., Palo Alto, Cal. 94301. Died Jan. 18, 1966; buried Allegheny Cemetery, Pitts.

MEYER, EDWARD BARNARD, utilities engr.; b. Newark, N.J., Oct. 22, 1882; s. John H. and Katie (Schroeder) M.; grad. Newark Tech. Sch., 1901, Pratt Inst., Brooklyn, 1903; m. Anna E. Benner, May 29, 1907; children—Grace (Mrs. Erving E. Bradley, dec.), Elizabeth (Mrs. K. Price). Engring. asst. Pub. Service Corp. of N.J., 1903-06, field engr., 1906-09, asst. engr., 1909-12, asst. to chief engr., 1912-19, asst. chief engr., 1919-22; chief engr. Pub. Service Production Co., 1922-29, v.p., 1929-30; v.p. and chief engr. United Engrs. & Constructors, Inc., 1930-35; chief engr. electric engring. dept. Pub. Service Electric & Gas Co., 1935—; pres. Willow Island Assn. Republican. Presbyn. Author: Transmission and Distribution. Home: South Orange, N.J. Died Jan. 1937.

MEYER, HENRY CODDINGTON, JR., cons. engr.; b. Orange, N.J., Nov. 28, 1870; s. Henry Coddington and Charlotte English (Seaman) M.; M.E., Stevens Inst. Tech., 1892; m. Louise G. Underhill, Nov. 18, 1896; children—Henry Coddington, Emily Louise. Engring. practice, N.Y., 1893-1919; pres. Meyer, Strong & Jones, Inc., cons. mech. and elec. engrs., 1919-44; dir.

Architects Offices, Inc. Mem. Am. Soc. M.E., Am. Soc. Heating and Ventilating Engrs., Loyal Legion. Club Union League. Author: Design of Steam Power Plants, 1902. Home: Montclair, N.J. Office: 101 Park Av., N.Y.C. Died June 17, 1957.

MEYER, J(OHN) FRANKLIN, physicist; b. Spring Mills, Pa., Mar. 11, 1875; s. Jacob Sheller and Susan Catherine (Bitner) M.; A.B., Franklin and Marshall Coll., Lancaster, Pa., 1894; A.M., 1897, Sc.D., 1918; grad. study Johns Hopkins, 1897-1900; Ph.D., U. of Pa., 1904; m. Ella Jane Mather, July 12, 1909; 1 son, Theodore Franklin. Asst. prof. physics, U. of Pa., 1902-07; prof. physics, Pa. State Coll., 1907-09; research engr., Westinghouse Lamp Co., 1909-13; physicist Nat. Bur. of Standards, 1913-41; retired; lecturer in elec. engring., George Washington U., 1922-27. Mem. advisory council Franklin and Marshall College; trustee Catawba College. Mem. Optical Society of America, International Electrotech. Am. Inst. Elec. Engrs., Illuminating Engring. Soc., Optical Soc. of America, Internat. Electrotech. Commn., Phi Beta Kappa, Sigma Xi, Phi Gamma Delta, Acacia. Mem. Evang. and Ref. Ch. Mason. Club: Cosmos. Contbr. to Physical Rev., Elec. World, Jour. of Franklin Inst., pubs. of Bur. of Standards, etc. Home: 3727 Jocelyn St. N.W., Washington, D.C. Died Oct. 30, 1944.

MEYER, LOTHAR, chemist; b. Breslau, Germany (now Wroclaw), Poland, July 13, 1906; s. Gotthold and Selma (Heimann) M.; Dr.Engring., Inst. Tech., Breslau, 1930; m. Marion Meyer, Mar. 25, 1935. Came to U.S., 1946, naturalized, 1952. Asst. U. Gottingen, 1930-32; mgr. patent dept. Gesellschaft fuer Linde's Eismaschinen, Munich, Germany, 1932-39; research asso. U. Leiden (Holland), 1939-46; with U. Chgo., 1947-71, prof. chemistry, 1953-71; Gauss prof. U. Gottingen, 1961-62. Fellow Am. Phys. Soc.; mem. Faraday Soc. London, Sigma Xi. Research, numerous publs. on superfluid behavior of liquid helium, adsorption, quantum hydrodynamics, chem. reactions at hot surfaces, crystal structures at low temperatures. Home: Chicago IL Died Feb. 1, 1971; buried Chicago IL

MEYERDING, HENRY WILLIAM, surgeon; b. St. Paul, Minn., Sept. 5, 1884; s. Henry John and Adelgunda (Rosenkranz) M.; B.Sc., U. of Minn., 1907, M.D., 1909, M.Sc. in orthopedic surgery, 1918; m. Lura Abbie Stinchfield, Feb. 12, 1912 (dec. Apr. 1960); children—Augustus (dec.), Edward Henry, Anne (dec.). House surgeon Mayo Clinic, 1911-12, attending physician, 1912-14, asst. orthopedist, 1914-15, asso. orthopedic surgeon, 1915, surgeon from 1915; orthopedic surgeon St. Mary's and Colonial hosps., 1915; instr. orthopedic surgery Mayo Foundation, U. Minn. Grad. Sch., 1918-20, asst. prof., 1920-22, associate professor, 1922-37, prof. 1937-49, emeritus, 1949-69. Served in Minn. Nat. Guard, 1st lt. M.C., 1909, col. 1938. Recipient Gold medals, Am. Med. Assn., 1939; gold medal, Am. Cong. Phys. Therapy, 1939. First award, Chgo. Med. Soc., 1947; medal of honor, from the University of Bordeaux, 1952; Certificate of Merit, U. Minn., 1952. Diplomate Am. Bd. Orthopedic Surgery. Fellow A.C.S. (gov. 1946-53), Internat. Coll. Surgeons (pres. U.S. sect. 1950-51, internat. president 1958), Acad. Surgery, Spain (hon.); mem. Am. Fracture Assn. (pres. 1952-56), Internat. Soc. Orthopaedic Surgery and Traumatology (nat. chmn. U.S. sect., pres. 6th congress 1948; chmn. U.S. delegations 1946-55), hon. mem., corr. mem. fgn., internat. and nat. profl. and scientific orgns. and assns. Italian, Brazilian, Argentine and including hon. memberships in: French Socs. Orthopedic Surgery and Traumatology, Internat. Surg. Soc., World Med. Assn., Netherlands Orthopaedic Soc., Belgian, Czechoslovak, Bordeaux, Madrid, Internat. surg. socs., Brazilian Acad. Medicine, Philippine Coll. Surgeons, Turkish Assn. Surgeons. Conglist. Mason (32 deg., Shriner). Club: University. Home: Rochester MN Died Aug. 1969.

MEYERHOF, OTTO, university prof.; b. Hanover, Germany, Apr. 12, 1884; s. Felix and Bettina (May) M.; M.D., Heidelberg, 1909; LL.D. (hon.) U. of Edinburgh, Scotland, 1926; m. Hedwig Schallenberg June 4, 1914; children—George Geoffrey, Bettina Ida (Mrs. Donald E. Emerson), Walter Ernst. Came to U.S. 1940, naturalized, 1946. Research worker, U. of Heidelberg and Zoological Station, Naples, Italy, 1909-11; lecturer, U. of Kiel, Germany, 1912-18, asso. prof., 1918-24; mem. Kaiser Wilhelm Inst. of Biologie, Berlin, 1924-29; dir. Kaiser Wilhelm Inst. of Physiology, Heidelberg, 1929-38; directeur de recherche, Centre Nationale, Paris, 1938-40; research prof., U. of Pa., since 1940. Received Nobel Prize for Medicine, 1923. Mem. Harvey Soc. (hon.). Royal Soc. of London, Sigma Xi. Author: Chemical Dynamics of Life Phenomena, 1924; Chemische Vorgange im Muskel Springer, 1930, French translation, 1932. Home: Hamilton Court Apts., Chestnut and 39th St., Phila. 4. Died Oct. 6, 1951.

MEYROWITZ, EMIL B., optician; b. Danzig, Germany, Oct., 1851; s. Alexander M.; ed. High Sch., Danzig, and Optical Coll. in Moscow, Russia; m. Evelyn C. Hawley, of New York, 1881. After learning optical business at Moscow, came to New York at age of 19; started in business for self, 1875; retired. Has introduced numerous improvements in optical work. Vet. Co. D, 22d Regt. N.G.N.Y. Former sec. Bd. Edn., Ridgefield, N.J. Episcopalian. Republican. Clubs: Uptown, Old Colony. Home: Hotel Marie Antoinette. Office: 520 5th Av., New York, N.Y.

MICHAEL, ARTHUR, chemist; b. Buffalo, N.Y., Aug. 7, 1853; s. John and Clara M.; student univs. of Berlin and Heidelberg, Ecole de Médecine de Paris; A.M. (hon.) Tufts, 1882, Ph.D., 1890, LL.D., 1910; LL.D., Clark U., 1909; m. Helen C. Abbott, June 1889. Prof. chemistry, Tufts Coll., 1882-89 and 1894-1907, prof. emeritus, 1907-12; prof. organic chemistry, Harvard, 1912-36, emeritus since 1936. Mem. Nat. Acad. Sciences. Author of numerous investigations on subjects in pure chemistry. Home: Newton Center, Mass. Died Feb. 8, 1942.

MICHAEL, HELEN ABBOTT, chemist, writer; b. Phila.; d. James and Caroline Montelius Abbott; ed. by private teachers; m. Arthur Michael, 1889. Special studies in music, medicine (2 yrs. Woman's Med. Coll. Phila., passing final exams. in chemistry, anatomy, physiology); worked in chem. laboratories, Coll. of Pharmacy, 1884-88, since then Tufts Coll.; lectured winter lecture course, Franklin Inst., Phila., 1887; Nat. Museum Course, Washington, 1887; writer on chem. subjects and in gen. literature. Has published researches in plant chemistry and organic chemistry in trans. and proc. Am. Philos. Soc., Berichte, Journal Practical Chemistry, Franklin Inst. Journal, Am. Journal Chemistry. Died 1904.

MICHAELIS, LEONOR, (mi-ka'lis), med. research; b. Berlin, Germany, Jan. 16, 1875; s. Moriz and Hulda (Rosenbaum) M.; student U. of Berlin, 1893-96 (M.D.), Freiburg, 1896-97; m. Hedwig Philipsthal, Apr. 12, 1905; children—Ilse, Eva M. Became asst. to Prof. Paul Ehrlich, then at Berlin, 1898-99; asst. Municipal Hosp., Berlin, 1899-1902; oberarzt with Inst. for Cancer Research, Berlin, 1902-06; dir. lab., Berlin Municipal Hosp., 1906-22; privat-decent U. of Berlin, 1905, prof., 1908; prof. biochemistry. Med. Sch., Nagoya, Japan, 1922-26; resident lecturer Johns Hopkins U., Baltimore, 1926-29; mem. Rockefeller Inst. Med. Research, 1929-40, now mem. emeritus. Fellow A.A.A.S., N.Y. Academy of Science: member American Society Biological Chemists, American Chem. Soc., National Academy of Sciences. Author: Compendium der Entwicklungsgeschichte des Menschen mit Berücksichtigung der Wirbeltiere, 1898; Einführung in die Farbstoffchemie für Histologen, 1900; Dynamik der Oberflächen, 1909; Einführung in die Matematik für Biologen u. Chemiker, 1912; Die Wasserstoff-Ionen-Concentration, 1914; Praktikum d. Physikalischen Chemie insb. der Kolloid-Chemie, 1920; Oxydations-Reductions-Potentiale, 1929. Home: 325 E. 79th St. (21). Office: Rockefeller Institute for Medical Research, New York, 21, N.Y. Died Oct. 9, 1949.

MICHAELS, ERNEST EDWIN, engr., b. Watertown, S.D., Sept. 30, 1897; s. Herman Frederick and Bertha (Rau) M.; B.S., South Dakota State College, 1920, Dr. Engring., 1959; M.S., University of Ill., 1922; m. Emily Elizabeth Shedd, June 12, 1926; children—Elizabeth Ann, Edwin Shedd. Engr. S.D. Hwy. Commn., 1920; research grad. asst. U. Ill., 1920-22; engr., asst. chief engr. Chgo. Bridge & Iron Co., 1922-24, chief draftsman, 1924-27, asst. mgr. operations, 1927-30, mgr. Birmingham plant, 1930-47, v.p., dir., 1946, mgr. operations, 1947, exec. v.p., 1952-56, pres., 1956-70. Served as sgt. U.S. Army, 1917-19. Fellow Am. Soc. C.E.; mem. Western Soc. Engrs., Welding Research Council (chmn.), Am. Welding Soc., Sigma Xi. Republican. Home: Chicago IL Died July 1970.

MICHAL, ARISTOTLE D(EMETRIUS), (mi'käl), prof. mathematics; b. Smyrna, Asia Minor (Greek parents), May 1, 1899; s. Demetrius and Sophia (Chaousoglou) M., came to U.S., 1911, naturalized, 1924; A.B., Clark U., Worcester, Mass., 1920, A.M., 1921; Ph.D., Rice Inst., Houston, Tex., 1924; Nat. Research fellow in mathematics, univ. of Chicago, Harvard, Princeton, , 1925-27; m. Luddye Charlotte Kennerly, June 9, 1924; 1 dau., Thalia Charlotte (dec.). Instr. in mathematics, Rice Inst., 1923-25, U. of Tex., summer, 1924; asst. prof. mathematics, Ohio State U., 1927-29; asso. prof. mathematics, Calif. Inst. Tech., 1929-38, prof. since 1938, dir. of research in math. analysis, geometry and applied mathematics, also dir. Engring., Sci. Mgt. War Training program in advanced training in math. and mechanics, World War II. Lecturer, Am. Math. Soc., 1938, U. of Ill., 1940, Stanford 50th anniversary symposium, 1941. Fellow A.A.A.S.; mem. Am. Math. Soc. (council 1938-40; sec. Far West 1942-44), Math. Assn. Am. (corr.) Acad. Nacional de Ciencias Exactas, Fisicas y Naturales de Lima, Assn. of Symbolic Logic, Am. Assn. Univ. Profs., Sigma Xi. Club: Athenaeum (Pasadena). Author: Matrix and Tensor Calculus with Applications to Mechanics, Elasticity and Aeronautics, 1947; Differential Equations in Abstract Spaces with Applications to Analysis; Geometry and Mechanics. Editor Mathematics Mag. since 1947. Contbr. numerous research papers to U.S. and fgn. tech. jours. Home: 2028 Amherst Drive, South Pasadena, Cal. Died June 14, 1953; buried Mountain View Cemetery, Altadena, Cal.

MICHAUX, ANDRÉ, explorer, botanist; b. Versailles, France, Mar. 7, 1746; studied botany under Bernard de Jussieu; m. Cécile Claye, Oct. 1769; 1 son, François André. Explored Tigris and Euphrates rivers region, 1782-85; came to U.S. to study forest trees of N.Am. for French Govt., 1785; established nursery, Hackensack, N.J.; went to Charleston, S.C., 1787; explored for bot. specimens in Appalachian Mountains, 1788; went to Bahama Islands, 1789; studied bot. species, Can., 1792; explored Am. Midwest, 1793-96; returned to Paris, 1796; naturalist on Capt. Nicholas Baudin's expdn., 1800. Author: Flora Boreali-Americana, sistens caracteres Plantarum quas in America Septentrionali collegit et detexit Andreas Michaux, 1803. Died of tropical fever, Madagascar, Nov. 1802.

MICHAUX, FRANÇOIS ANDRÉ, botanist; b. Versailles, France, Aug. 16, 1770; s. André and Cécile (Claye) M.; married. Came to Am., 1785-90; agt. for French Govt. regarding tree plantations in U.S., 1801-03; returned to U.S., 1806, traveled and made bot. studies along Atlantic coast, 1806-09. Author: Voyage à l'ouest des monts Alléghanys dans les e'tats de l'Ohio, et du Kentucky, et du Tennessée, et retour à Charleston par les Hautes-Carolines, 1804; The North American Sylva, or a Description of the Forest Trees of the United States, Canada, and Nova Scotia, Considered Particularly with Respect to their Use in the Arts and their Introduction into Commerce, 3 vols., 1818-19. Died Oct. 23, 1855.

MICHEL, WILLIAM, civil engr.; b. Columbus, O., Mar. 18, 1866; ed. pub. schs. Began with Hocking Valley & Toledo Ry., 1884; transitman and asst. engr. Louisville, Cincinnati & Dayton Ry., 1886-87; again with Columbus, Hocking Valley & Toledo Ry. as asst. engr., 1887-89, continuing as asst. chief engr. and mining engr., 1889-92, engr. maintenance of way, 1892-1910, and of its successor the Hocking Valley Ry.; then chief engr. same; now chief engr. and mem. engring. advisory com., C.&O. Ry., Erie R.R., N.Y.C. & St.L. R.R., P.M. Ry. Office: Chesapeake & Ohio R.R., Cleveland, O.

MICHELSON, ALBERT ABRAHAM, physicist; b. Strelno, Germany, Dec. 19, 1852; s. Samuel and Rosalie (Przlubska) M.; grad. U.S. Naval Acad., 1873; postgrad. student at univs. of Berlin, 1880, Heidelberg, 1881, Collège de France and École Polytechnique, 1882; hon. Ph.D., Western Reserve, 1886, Stevens Inst. Tech., 1887; Sc.D., U. of Cambridge, 1899; LL.D., Yale, 1901, Franklin Bicentenary U. of Pa., 1906; Ph.D., Leipzig, 1909, Göttingen, 1911; LL.D., McGill U., 1921; m. 1st, Margaret McLean Hemingway, 1877 (div.); children—Albert Hemingway, Truman, Elsa; m. 2d, Edna Stanton, Dec. 23, 1899; children—Madeleine, Dorothy, Beatrice. Instr. U. S. Naval Acad., 1875-79; prof. of physics, Case Sch. Applied Science, Cleveland, 1883-89, Clark U., 1889-92; prof. and head of dept. of physics, U. of Chicago, 1892-1929, distinguished service prof., same, 1925-29; Lowell lecturer, 1899; exchange prof., U. of Göttingen, summer 1911, Université de Paris, 1920. Grand Prix, Paris Expn., 1900; Mattencci Medal, Soc. Italiana, Rome, 1904; awarded Nobel Prize in Physics, 1907; Elliott Cresson medal, 1912. Fellow Am. Acad. Arts and Sciences, A.A.A.S. (pres. 1910-11); Royal Society of London, 1902 (Rumford Medal, 1889, Copley Medal, 1907); mem. Am. Phys. Soc.; Nat. Acad. Scis. (Draper medal, 1916, pres. 1923-27); Am. Philos. Soc.; French Acad. Scis., 1900, others. Author: (brochure) Velocity of Light, 1902; Light Waves and Their Uses, 1903. Studies in Optics, 1927. Contbd. to found. for relativity; Michelson-Morley expt. helped destroy ether concept; designed echelon grating spectroscope, 1907; built an engine to rule diffraction gratings; contbd. important work on spectral lines; determined speed of light with extremely high degree of accuracy; measured a meter in terms of wave length of cadmium light; inventor interferometer for measuring distances by means of length of light waves; measured angular diameters of satellites of Jupiter, 1891; demonstrated that core of earth is molten, not rigid, 1916; made 1st measurement of a star's diameter (Alpha Orionis), 1920; showed that earth's viscosity is similar to that of steel. Died Pasadena, Cal. May 9, 1931.

MICHELSON, HENRY E(RNEST), dermatologist; b. Bismarck, N.D., Sept. 22, 1888; s. Herman L. and Justyna (Aurbach) M.; B.S., U. of Minn., 1910, M.D., 1912; study, London, Paris, Vienna, 1921, 29; married Dalie Lindsay, August 14, 1916; children—Robert, Margery (Mrs. Scotson Webbe). Interne, City and County Hospital, St. Paul, Minn., 1912-13; practiced at Virginia, Minn., 1913-15; assistant in dermatology, U. of Minnesota, 1915-20, associate professor dermatology, 1923-26, prof., dir. div. dermatology and syphilology, 1927-66, prof. emeritus, 1966-72. Chmn. Bd. Dermatology, Am. Med. Assn. of U.S., from 1947; hon. pres. Internat. Congress Dermatology, 1962. Recipient Gold medal award Am. Acad. Dermatology, 1962. Mem. Am. Dermatology Assn. (pres. 1951), Minn. Dermatology Soc., Chgo. Dermatology Soc., Am. Bd. of Dermatology and Syphilology from 1939, Vienna Dermatol. Soc., Beta Theta Pi, Nu Sigma Nu, Alpha Omega Alpha, Sigma Xi; corresponding member French, Danish, Italian, Swedish dermatol. socs.; hon. mem. Brit., German, Venezuelan, Austrian dermatological socs., Royal Society of Medicine

London. Clubs: Minneapolis; Tavern (Chicago, Ill.). Home: Minneapolis MN Died May 10, 1972.

MICHENER, EZRA, physician; b. Chester County, Pa., Nov. 24, 1794; s. Mordecai and Alice (Dunn) M.; M.D., U. Pa., 1818; m. Sarah Spencer, Apr. 15, 1819; m. 2d, Mary S. Walton, 1844. Practiced medicine, Chester County; hon. mem. Med. Soc. of Pa.; correspondent Acad. Natural Scis.; a founder Chester County Med. Soc.; made large natural history and herbarium collections; a founder Guardian Soc. for Preventing Drunkenness. Author: The Christian Casket, 1869; Manual of Weeds, 1872; Handbook of Eclampsia, 1883. Died Toughkenamon, Pa., June 24, 1887.

MICHIE, JAMES NEWTON, (mik'e), mathematician; b. Charlottesville, Va., July 28, 1879; s. John Augustus, M.D. and Susan (Jackson) M.; B.S., U. Va., 1908; A.M., U. Mich., 1919; m. Hazel Jacob, Dec. 29, 1909 (died Nov. 25, 1940); children—Sarah Jacob (Mrs. Victor Harris), Susan Jackson (Mrs. J. B. Johnson), Robert E. Lee, m. 2d, Johnnie McCrery, Aug. 14, 1943. Tchr., Miller's Sch., Va., 1899-1900, Eastern Coll., Front Royal, Va., 1902-93, Millersburg (Ky.) Mil. Acad. 1903-06; instr. mathematics, U. Va., 1906-09, asst. prof. summer sch., 1909-18, asso. prof., 1919-25; prof. 1925-29; asst. prof. mathematics, Tex. A. and M. Coll., 1908-18, asso. prof., 1919-20; asst. prof. mathematics Mich., 1918-19; asso. prof. U. Tex., 1920-25; prof., head dept. mathematics Tex. Tech. Coll., 1925-50, now emeritus. Fellow Tex. Acad. Sci.; mem. A.A.A.S., Am. Math. Soc., Math. Assn. Am., Inc., Kappa Mu Epsilon. Democrat. Episcopalian. Clubs: Knife and Fork, Trailers Dancing. Author: Differential and Integral Calculus, 1947; Modifications of Graeffe's Method in the Colution of Numerical Equations of Higher Degree than Six, Proceedings of Texas Acad. of Science, Vol. XX; also articles in math. jours. Specialist in math. analysis particularly differential equations, differential geometry, vector analysis. Address: 5314 Swiss Av., Dallas 14. Died Nov. 24, 1958; buried Grove Hill Cemetery, Dallas.

MICHIE, PETER SMITH, prof. natural and experimental philosophy, U.S. Mil. Acad., Feb. 14, 1871—; b. Brechin, Scotland, Mar. 24, 1839; went to Cincinnati in boyhood; grad. West Point, 1863; (Ph.D., Princeton, 1871; A.M., Dartmouth, 1873; LL.D., Union Coll., 1893); m. Maria L. Roberts, June 21, 1863. Commissioned 1st lt. engrs., June 11, 1863; capt., Nov. 23, 1865; reached bvt. rank brig. gen. vols.; participated in siege of Charleston, and in Fla. and Va. campaigns, becoming chief engr., army of the James. Author: Elements of Wave Motion Relating to Sound and Light; Life and Letters of Maj. Gen. Emory Upton; Personnel of Sea Coast Defense; Elements of Analytical Mechanics; Elements of Hydro-Mechanics; Practical Astronomy. Member bd. overseers, Thayer School Civil Engineering, Dartmouth Coll., 1871—; mem. Military Commn. to Europe, 1870. Died 1901.

MICHLER, NATHANIEL, army officer; b. Easton, Pa., Sept. 13, 1827; s. Peter S. and Miss (Hart) M.; attended Lafayette Coll., 1841-44; grad. U.S. Mil. Acad., 1848; m. Fannie Kirkland; m. 2d, Sallie Hollingsworth, Feb. 12, 1861. Brevetted 2d lt., Topog. Engrs., U.S. Army, made surveys and reconnaissances in Tex., N.M., 1848-51; commd. 2d lt., 1854, 1st lt., 1856; chief topog. engr. in charge of surveys for a canal extending from Gulf of Darien to Pacific Ocean, 1857-60; in charge of running boundary line between Md. and Va., 1858-61; became capt. with armies of Ohio and Cumberland, 1861-63; then on survey of Harpers Ferry; attached to Army of the Potomac, 1863-65, in charge of topog. dept., engaged in making various reconnaissances and bldg. of defensive works connected with battles of Wilderness, Spotsylvania, Cold Harbor, Petersburg; commd. maj. Corps. Engr., 1864, brevetted lt. col., 1864, brevetted col. for services at Battle of Petersburg, brig. gen. for services during Civil War, 1865; engaged in selecting site for presdl. mansion and public park, preparing plans for new War Dept. bldg., 1866-67; supt. public bldgs. and grounds, 1867-71, had charge of survey of Potomac River and repairing Fort Foote, Md.; lighthouse engr. on Pacific Coast, 1871-76; proposed canal connecting Coquille River with Coos Bay (Ore.); superintended river and harbor improvements on Lake Erie, 1876-78; mil. attache of U.S. legation, Vienna, Austria, 1879; engaged in river and harbor work for N.Y. and N.J., 1880-81. Died Saratoga Springs, N.Y., July 17, 1881; buried Easton.

MIDDLETON, AUSTIN RALPH, prof. zoölogy; b. Baltimore, Md., Apr. 14, 1881; s. Christopher Byrne and George Anna (Belt) M.; grad. Baltimore City Coll., 1901; grad. Baltimore Teachers' Training Sch., 1902; A.B., Johns Hopkins, 1910, Ph.D., 1915; m. Margaret Mary Loughridge, July 3, 1917. Johns Hopkins scholar, 1912-14, fellow, 1914-15, and fellow by courtesy, 1915-16; prof. zoölogy, U. of Louisville, since 1916; organized biol. labs. of the university and dir. depts. of biology, 1916-28 prof. emeritus of biology since July 1952. Member Johsn Hopkins Scientific Expedition, Jamaica, B.W.I., 1910. Capt. Sanitary Reserves, U.S. Army; colonel and comdg. ofcr., Medical Detachment, Kentucky Active Militia. Mem. committee of 100, 6th Internat. Congress Genetics. Fellow A.A.A.S. (member council and com. section F.), Conference on State Academies of Science (sec.), American Geog. Society, Royal Society Arts; member Am. Soc. Zoölogists, Ecol. Soc. America, Am. Soc. Mammalogists, Am. Soc. Parasitologists, Am. Acad. Polit. and Social Science, Am. Geneal. Soc., Kentucky Acad. Science (past pres.), Conf. of Acad. of Science (pres. 1952), Eugenics Society of America, Eugenics Research Assn., Ky. Cols. (chancellor), Pi Gamma Mu, Kappa Psi, Theta Kappa Psi, Kappa Alpha (Southern), Chi Beta Phi. Clubs: Quindecim, Torch (president 1929-31), University, Army and Navy, Kiwanis. Author College Biology, 1925-29; also numerous research articles. Editor for Ky. of The Naturalist's Guide to the Americas, biographies in American Men of Science, Index Biologorum and Menchen und Menchenwerke. Organized tropical biol. expdn. to jungles of Honduras, Central America, June-Aug. 1933 and 1934. Author (1938) of the plan for "The University of America." Home: 1329 S. Floyd St., Louisville 8. Died Apr. 11, 1956; Cave Hill Cemetery, Louisville.

MIDDLETON, PETER, physician; b. Eng.; M.D., U. St. Andrews, Scotland, 1752; m. Susannah Nicholls, Nov. 1766; 1 dau., Susannah Margaret. Made 1 of 1st recorded human dissections in Am. (with Dr. John Bard), 1752; served as surgeon gen. Crown Point expdn. in French and Indian War; a founder St. Andrew's Soc. of N.Y., pres., 1767-70; prof. physiology and pathology King's Coll. (now Columbia) Med. Sch., 1767-70, also prof. materia medica, 1770-73, gov. of coll., 1773; mem. staff N.Y. Hosp., 1774. Author: A Medical Discourse; or an Historical Inquiry Into the Ancient and Present State of Medicine. Died Jan. 9, 1781.

MIDGLEY, THOMAS, JR., research chemist; b. Beaver Falls, Pa., May 18, 1889; s. Thomas and Hattie Lena (Emerson) M.; M.E., Cornell U., 1911; D.Sc., Coll. of Wooster, 1936; m. Carrie M. Reynolds, Aug. 3, 1911; children—Thomas 3d, Jane (Mrs. Edward Z. Lewis). With Nat. Cash Register Co., 1911; research work on automobile tires, 1912-14; supt. Midgley Tire & Rubber Co., Lancaster, O., 1914-16; worked with Charles F. Kettering, Dayton, O., and later with Gen. Motors Research Corp., 1916-18; head fuel div. Gen. Motors Research Corp., 1918-23; gen. mgr. Gen. Motors Chem. Co., 1923; v.p. Ethyl Corp. since 1923 and Kinetics Chemical, Inc., since 1930; dir. Ethyl-Dow Chem. Co. since 1933. Awarded Nichols medal, Am. Chem. Soc., 1923, Perkins medal, 1937; Longstreth medal, Franklin Inst., 1925; Priestly medal, Am. Chem. Soc. 1941; Willard Gibbs Medal, 1942. Vice-pres. Ohio State U. Research Foundation since 1940; vice-chmn. Nat. Inventors Council since 1940. Pres. Am. Chemical Soc. (chmn. bd. dirs.); mem. Nat. Acad. Sciences, Sigma Xi, Phi Kappa Phi, Tau Beta Pi, Alpha Chi Sigma, Atmos. Writer many technical papers. Discovered tetraethyl lead as gasoline anti-knock compound; also certain organic fluoride compounds for refrigerants which are nontoxic and noninflammable. Holder of many patents. Home: Worthington, O. Office: Ethyl Corp., Detroit, Mich. Died Nov. 2, 1944.

MIES VAN DER ROHE, LUDWIG, architect; b. Aachen, Germany, Mar. 27, 1886; D. Engring., Inst. Tech., Karlsruhe, Germany, 1950, Tech. Inst., Braunschweig, 1950, Ill. Inst. Tech., 1966; LL.D., North Carolina State College, 1956; A.F.D., Carnegie Inst. Tech., Pitts., 1960, Northwestern U., 1963, U. Ill., 1964; H.H.D., Wayne State U., 1961. Came to United States, 1938, naturalized Am. citizen. Began as apprentice to famous deisgners and architects of Europe; with Bruno Paul, furniture designer, Berlin, 1905-07; apprentice, Peter Behrens, 1908-11; projected designs for steel and glass skyscrapers, 1919-21, for concrete office bldg., 1922-69; fgn. archtl. designs include, German bldg. Internat. Expn., Barcelona, Spain, 1929, Tugendhat house, Brno, Czechoslovakia, 1930, skyscraper on Friedrichstrasse, Berlin, Bacardi Office Bldg., Mexico City, Seagram bldg., N.Y.C., 26-story apt. bldgs., 860 Lake Shore Dr., Chgo.; dir. Bauhaus School in Germany, 1930-33; dir. Sch. Architecture, Ill. Inst. Tech., 1938-58; designer of institute's campus, Chgo.; also designer of steel furniture. Served as 1st v.p. Deutscher Werkbund (orgn. to improve quality of indsl. design), 1927. Dir. Weissenhofsiedlung Exhbn. at Stuttgart, 1927; had one-man show of work Mus. Modern Art, N.Y.C., Art Inst. Chgo. Recipient medal of honor VII Congress of Pan-Am. Architects, award of merit Ruskin Soc. of Am., Feltrinelli Internat. prize for architecture, Rome, Italy; Presidential Medal of Freedom, U.S.; numerous other medals and honors. Life mem. Order Pour le Merite (Germany). Fellow A.I.A., Am. Acad. Arts and Scis.; mem. Prussian Acad. Art, soc. Mex. Architects (hon.), Royal Inst. Brit. Architects, Internat. Congress Modern Architecture, Ill. Soc. Architects, Am. Assn. U. Profs., Am. Soc. Engring. Edn., Coll. Art Assn. of Am., Am. Inst. Arts and Letters, Nat. Inst. Arts and Letters (hon.). Home: Chicago IL Died Aug. 17, 1969; buried Graceland Cemetery, Chicago IL

MILEN, FREDERICK BLUMENTHAL, civ. and mech. engr.; b. Baltimore, Aug. 7, 1835; s. William and Sarah (Mickle) M.; ed. pvt. French sch., Baltimore, 1841-48; studied navigation, 1851; Md. Inst., 1852-56, Univ. of Glasgow, 1857-58; m. Mar., 1867, Gertrude Woodworth (died 1893). Asst. engr. Brooklyn Water-Works, 1856-59, Baltimore Water-Works, Apr.-Dec., 1859; asst. engr., 1860-63, chief engr., 1863-66, Havana (Cuba) R.R.; studied architecture, 1866-67; designer Bement & Dougherty, Phila., 1867-69, Ferris & Miles, 1869-79, alone, 1879-85, Bement, Miles & Co., 1885-1900; dir. (ex-v.p.) Niles-Bement-Pond Co., since 1900. Invented, 1870, steam hammer now in gen. use; has received 35 patents on machinery; went abroad, 1887, to study most approved foreign machinery for making armor plate, heavy steel cannon and ship-building; on return was engaged by Navy Dept. to design heavy gun lathes and other tools now in several navy yards and arsenals. Mem. Am. Soc. of Extension of Univ. Teaching (pres. since 1903). Residence: 40 W. 9th St. Office: 111 Broadway, New York.

MILES, C(HARLES) EDWIN, physician; b. at Stow, Mass., Dec. 31, 1830; s. Charles and Sophia Jewell (Brown) M.; ed. Berlin (Mass.) Acad., and Providence Conf. Sem., E. Greenwich, R.I.; M.D., Worcester Med. Coll., 1859; m. Eunice Pierce Dyer, of Boston, May 3, 1866. In practice at Roxbury since 1859; chmn. Mass. Bd. of Registration in Medicine, 1894-1908; mem. Boston Sch. Com., 1875-77; asso. editor Mass. Medical Journal, 10 yrs. Pres. Nat. Eclectic Med. Assn., 1872, 1874, Mass. Eclectic Med. Soc., 1909; ex-pres. Boston Dist. Eclectic Med. Soc., Boston Gynecol. and Obstet. Soc. Writer and speaker upon med. subjects. Republican. Methodist. Address: 126 Warren St., Rosbury, Mass.

MILHAM, WILLIS ISBISTER, astronomer; b. Kinderhook, N.Y., Feb. 11, 1874; s. Edmund and Ellen Medora (Isbister) M.; B.A., Williams Coll., 1894, M.A., 1895, L.H.D., 1946; Ph.D., U. Strassburg, 1901, m. Betsey Morgan Fairweather, June 7, 1911. Instr. mathematics and physics Williams Coll., 3 yrs., asst., prof. math. sciences, 2 yrs., absent on leave 2 yrs. and Field Meml. prof. of astronomy, 1902-42, prof. emeritus, 1942—. Fellow A.A.A.S., Am. Phys. Soc., Am. Meteorol. Soc., Royal Astron. Soc.; mem. Am. Geog. Soc., Soc. Belge d'Astronomie, Soc. Astron. de France, Nat. Assn. Watch and Clock Collectors (v.p. 1946-49), Phi Beta Kappa. Author: How to Identify the Stars, 1909; Meteorology, 1912; Time and Timekeepers, 1923; Early American Observatories, 1938; The Columbus Clock, 1945. Contbr. to sci. mags. Home: 24 Hoxsey St., Williamstown, Mass. Died Mar. 23, 1957; buried Kinderhook, N.Y.

MILLAR, PRESTON S(TRONG), electrical testing; b. Andover, New Jersey, March 9, 1880; s. George and Anna Catherine (Bowers) M.; educated in preparatory school; m. Lily Bradford Baylies, Mar. 31, 1906; children—Bradford Preston, Katherine LeBaron, Robert Visscher. Began electrical testing at Harrison, N.J., 1897; various positions in Elec. Testing Labs., including pres. and dir., 1929-42; pres. and dir. Elec. Testing Laboratories, Inc., since 1942; sec. Assn. of Edison Illuminating Cos., 1919-42; sec. and treas. Utilities Coördinated Research, Inc., 1934-43; pres. Illuminating Engineering Society, 1913, Medalist, 1945; president United States National Committee, International Commission on Illumination since 1936; president American Council of Commercial Labs., 1937-39; pres. New York Elec. Society, Inc., 1943-44; v.p. Nat. Soc. for Prevention of Blindness. Authority on electric lighting; introduced silhouette concept in street lighting. Mem. War Com. of Tech. Socs. and chmn. Com. on War Service of Illuminating Engring. Soc., World War I; also active in tech. com. work; lighting adviser Westchester County OCP, World War II. Fellow Am. Physical Soc., A.A.A.S.; mem. Am. Inst. E. E., Illuminating Engring. Soc., Am. Optical Soc., Assn. Consulting Chemists and Chem. Engrs., Am. Soc. for Testing Materials. Clubs: Engineers (New York and Boston). Contbr. Illuminating Sect. of Standard Handbook for Elec. Engrs.; also many papers in procs. of tech. socs. Home: The Buckingham, Scarsdale, N.Y. Office: 79th St. and East End Av., New York, N.Y. Died June 17, 1949.

MILLER, ALDEN HOLMES, educator, mus. dir.; b. Los Angeles, Feb. 4, 1906; s. Loye Holmes and Anne (Holmes) M.; A.B., U. Cal. at Los Angeles, 1927; M.A., U. Cal. at Berkeley, 1928, Ph.D., 1930; m. Virginia Elizabeth Dove, Aug. 1, 1928; children—Daniel Holmes, Barbara Dove, Patricia Lynn. Teaching fellow zoology U. Cal., 1927-28, asst., 1928-30, asso., 1930, instr. zoology, 1931-34, asst. prof., 1934-39, asso. prof., 1939-45, prof., 1945—, asst. dean coll. letters and sci., 1939-40, chmn. dept. paleontology, 1959-60; curator birds Mus. Vertebrate Zoology, 1939-40, dir., 1940—; curator of birds Mus. Paleontology, 1960—, vice chancellor, 1961-62. Made field investigations on vertebrates Pacific Coast states, Mexico, C.Am., Australia, Columbia. Awarded Brewster medal Am. Ornith. Union, 1943. Del., 8th Internat. Ornith. Congress, Oxford, 1934; v.p. 11th Ornith. Congress, 1954. Guggenheim fellow, 1958. Fellow A.A.A.S., Am. Ornith. Union (pres. 1953-56), Cal. Acad. Sci.; mem. Nat. Acad. Scis.; corr. mem. Zool. Soc. London; fgn. mem. British Ornith. Union; mem. Am. Soc. Naturalists, Soc. Study Evolution (v.p. 1956-57), Soc. Vertebrae Paleontology, Am. Soc. Zool., Am. Soc. Mammalogy, Am. Soc. Ichthyologists and Herpetologists, Cooper Ornithology Soc. (pres. 1948-51), Phi Beta Kappa, Sigma Xi. Author: Systematic Revision and Natural History of North American Shrikes, 1931; Adaptive modifications and Evolution of the Hawaiian Goose, 1937; Speciation in the Avian Genus Junco, 1941; Analysis of the distribution of The Birds of California, 1944-51; Fossil Birds of Pleistocene of California and Miocene of South Dakota, 1929-41; Physiology of Reproductive Cycle of Birds, 1947-60; Ecologic Factors influencing speed of Evolution, 1956; Breeding Cycles of Equatorial Birds, 1958-61; Avifauna of an American Equatorial Cloud Forest, 1962; Lives of Desert Animals, 1964. Mem. Com. on Classification and Nomenclature N.Am. Birds, 1940-57, chmn. 1960—; mem. Internat. Commn. on Zool. Nomenclature, pres. 1963—. Editorial bd. Evolution, 1950-53, Pacific Cosat Avifauna, 1939—. Editor: The Condor, 1939—; Check-list Birds of Mexico, 1950-57. Home: 81 Edgecroft Rd., Berkeley 7, Cal. Died Oct. 9, 1965; buried Lower Lake (Cal.) Cemetery.

MILLER, ALEXANDER MACOMB, lt. col. corps of engrs., U.S.A.; b. Washington; s. Gen. Morris S. M., g.s. Gen. Alexander Macomb; apptd., March 2, 1861; grad. West Point, June 23, 1865, as 1st lt. engrs.; capt., Feb. 22, 1869; maj., April 16, 1883; lt. col., 1898; has been engaged in many engring. works; now in charge office of Washington aqueduct. Home: Washington D.C. Died 1904.

MILLER, ALFRED STANLEY, mining engr.; b. Normal, Pa., Oct. 20, 1856; s. Stephen and Mary E. C. (Riddle) M.; grad. Keystone State Normal Sch., 1880, M.E., 1882; A.B., Stanford, 1895, A.M., 1895; Ph.D. (pro merito), Heidelberg U. (Ohio), 1895; E.M., The A. Van der Naillen Sch. of Engring., 1898. Prin. high sch. and supt. schs., E. Mauch Chunk, Pa., 1880-82; prof. natural science, 1889-92, pres., 1892-93, Wichita (Kan.) U.; grad. student Stanford, 1893-95; with Nev. Metall. Works, 1896; mining engr., Auburn, Calif., 1897; in research work U. of Calif., 1897; prof. mining, metallurgy, and geology, U. of Ida., 1897-1905. Author: Manual of Assaying, 1900; The Cyanide Process, 1903. Home: Moscow, Idaho. Died Aug. 23, 1928.

MILLER, A(RTHUR) K., univ. prof.; b. Kahoka, Mo., Sept. 27, 1902; s. John Henry and Margaret (Korschgen) M.; A.B., U. of Mo., 1924, A.M., 1925; Ph.D., Yale, 1930; m. Bertha Louise Kehr, Dec 21, 1927; children—Leta Louise, Margaret Bertha. Instr. geology U. of Mo., 1927-29, Yale, 1929-31; asst. prof. geology, State U. of Ia., 1931-35, asso. prof., 1935-40, prof. geology since 1940, head geology department since 1952; visiting professor paleontology, Univ. of Calif., summer 1948; research asso. Peabody Mus. Natural History, Yale, 1930-31, Am. Mus. Natural Hist. 1943-53. Conducted geol. field work in northern Mexico for Permian cephalopods, 1935, southern Mexico and Guatemala for Permian fossils, 1939, west-central shore of Hudson Bay for Ordovician cephalopods, 1945, Baffin Island for Ordovician fossils, 1947. Del. to 19th Internat Geol. Congress, Algeria, 1952. Mem. Paleontol. Soc., Geol. Soc. Am., A.A.A.S., Soc. Econ. Paleontologists and Mineralists (honorary member), American Association of Petroleum Geologists, Paleontol. Research Inst., Arctic Inst., Soc. Geol. Mexicana. Paleontol. Soc. Japan. Soc. Géol. Suisse, Societé Belgede Geol., de Paléont. et d'Hydrol. Sigma Xi. Republican. Presbyterian. Club: Kiwanis. Official del. 17th Internat. Geol. Congress, Soviet Russia, 1937. Corr. mem. Inst. Estudios Superiores, Montevideo, Am. Mus. Natural History. Mem. Princeton U. Bicentennial Conf. Genetics, Paleontol. and Evolution, 1947. Co-editor Jour. Paleontology, 1955. Research fossil cephalopods. Home: Six Melrose Circle, Iowa City, Ia. Died Jan. 31, 1963; buried Graceland Oakland Cemetery, Iowa City.

MILLER, ARTHUR MCQUISTON, geologist; b. Eaton, O., Aug. 6, 1861; s. Robert and Margaret Ann (McQuiston) M.; U. of Wooster, 1880-82; A.B., Princeton, 1884, A.M., 1887; studied U. of Munich, 1891-92; unmarried. Prin. schs., Morning Sun, O., 1884-85; prin. high sch., Eaton, O., 1885-88; fellow in biology, Princeton, 1888-89; prof. natural history, Wilson Coll., Chambersburg, Pa., 1889-91; prof. geology, U. of Kentucky, 1892—, also dean Coll. Arts and Sciences; resigned deanship, 1917, and granted leave of absence as consulting and field geologist, Federal Oil Co., June 1917-June 1918; retired as prof. emeritus of geology, June 30, 1925. Democrat. Presbyn. Wrote: The Lead and Zinc Bearing Rocks of Central Kentucky, 1905; Coals of Western Border of Eastern Coal Field in Kentucky, 1910; Geology of the Georgetown Quadrangle, 1913; Geology of Franklin County, Kentucky, 1914; Geology of Kentucky, 1919; Geology of Woodford Co., 1925 (all pub. by Ky. Geol. Survey). Home: Asheville, N.C. Died Oct. 28, 1929.

MILLER, BENJAMIN LEROY, geologist; b. Sabetha, Kan., Apr. 13, 1874; s. Jacob J. and Mary (Moorhead) M.; student Morrill (Kan.) Coll., 1889-90, Washburn Coll. (Topeka), 1891-92; A.B., U. of Kan., 1897; U. of Chicago, summer, 1898; Ph.D., Johns Hopkins University, 1903; honorary Sc.D., Moravian College, 1941; m. Mary A. Meredith, Sept. 15, 1904 (died May 30, 1930); children—Ruth Meredith (Mrs. Otto H. Spillman), Ralph LeRoy. Teacher pub. schs. of Kan., 1894-95; asst., Kan. U. Geol. Survey, summer, 1896; prof. biology and chemistry, Penn Coll., Oskaloosa, Ia., 1897-1900; spl. asst. Ia. Geol. Survey, summer, 1899; asso. in geology, Bryn Mawer Coll., 1903-07; prof. geology, Lehigh U., since 1907. Geologist, Md. Geol. Survey, 1900-11; asst., 1904-07, asst. geologist, 1907-13, U.S. Geol. Survey; asso. geologist, Pa. Geol. Survey, since 1919. Spl. consulting editor Engring. and Mining Jour., 1920-22. Fellow A.A.A.S., Mineralogical Soc. America, Geol. Soc. America, Ia. Acad. Sciences, Geol. Soc. London; mem. Am. Inst. Mining and Metall. Engrs., Soc. Econ. Geologists, Seismological Soc. America, Am. Meteorol. Soc., Am. Assn. Univ. Profs., Pa. Acad. Science (pres. 1925-26), Sigma Xi, Tau Beta Pi. Mem. Soc. of Friends. Has written numerous reports on geol. survey results, pub. by U.S. Geol. Survey and state geol. surveys of Iowa, Md., Va., N.C. and Pa.; articles on econ. geology in tech. jours., especially on limestones, cement, graphite and other non-metallic products; articles on stratigraphic geology of Eastern Pa. in geol. periodicals; reviews of Am. geog. lit. in Annuelle Bibliographie, Annales de Géographie, 1902-06; also collaborator with Dr. George B. Shattuck in "Geology and Geography of the Bahama Islands," in Bahama Islands, 1905; Geology of Mining Districts of South America and Central America; Mineral Deposits of South America (with Dr. J. T. Singewald, Jr.), 1919. Rotarian. Home: 429 N. New St., Bethlehem, Pa. Died Mar. 23, 1944.

MILLER, BLOOMFIELD JACKSON, mathematician; b. Newark, N.J., Dec. 31, 1849; s. Elias Newton and Sarah M. Coates M.; ed. Newark Acad., Rutgers Coll., scientific class of 1868; m. Jeannie Ogden Miller, Nov. 5, 1880. Entered math. dept. Mutual Benefit Life Ins. Co., 1867; apptd. actuary, 1871, mathematician, 1882, 2d v.p., 1894, v.p. and mathematician, 1902—, dir., 1894—. Charter mem. and pres. Actuarial Soc. of America. Home: Perth Amboy, N.J. Died 1905.

MILLER, DAYTON CLARENCE, physicist; b. Strongsville, O., Mar. 13, 1866; s. Charles W. D. and Vienna (Pomeroy) M.; A.B., Baldwin U., 1886, A.M., 1889; D.Sc., Princeton, 1890, Miami, 1924, Dartmouth, 1927; LL.D., Western Reserve, 1927, Baldwin-Wallace Col., 1933; D.Eng., Case, 1936; m. Edith C. Easton, June 28, 1893. Prof. natural science, Baldwin U., 1888-89; asst. in mathematics and physics, 1890-93, prof. physics, 1893—, Case Sch. Applied Science, Cleveland, O. Fellow Am. Phys. Soc. (sec. 1918-22, v.p. 1923-24, pres. 1925-26), A.A.A.S. (sec. sect. physics, 1903-07, v.p. 1908, gen. sec. 1910), Am. Acad. Arts and Sciences, Ohio Acad. Sciences; mem. numerous scientific socs. Awarded Longstreth medal, 1917; Elliott Cresson gold medal, Franklin Institute, 1926; A.A.A.S. prize, 1925; Cleveland Distinguished Service medal, 1927. Trustee Baldwin-Wallace Coll., 1899—, sec. bd., 1913-26, chmn. bd., 1936—. Lowell lecturer, 1914. Author: Laboratory Physics, 1903; Boehm on The Flute and Flute-Playing, 1908; The Science of Musical Sounds, 1916; Bibliography of the Flute, 1935; Anecdotal History of Sound, 1935; Sound Waves, Shape and Speed, 1937; Sparks, Lightning, Cosmic Rays, 1939. Died Feb. 22, 1941.

MILLER, EDGAR CALVIN LEROY, bacteriologist; b. Pelham, Mass., Aug. 24, 1867; s. Lorenzo Wallace and Helen Elizabeth (Rice) M.; grad. Neb. State Normal Sch., 1887; studied Oberlin Coll., 1888-90; M.D., U. of Mich., 1894; m. Lillian Belle Carpenter, Sept. 17, 1890; children—Leland Hubert, Pyari Frances Geraldine, Louis Charles, Gwendolyn Lucile. Instr., U. of Mich., 1894-95; med. missionary, India, 1895-1900; mem. research staff, Parke, Davis &Co., Detroit, Mich., 1900-10; prof. bacteriology, Medical College Va., 1911-29, directing librarian since 1930, ret. Mem. A.M.A., A.A.A.S., Soc. Chemical Industry (London), Am. Assn. Immunologists, Med. Soc. of Va., Richmond Acad. Medicine, Va. Acad. Science (sec.-treas. since 1923), fellow Chem. Soc. (London). Collaborator Am. Illustrated Med. Dictionary since 1922. Home: 2915 Seminary Av., Richmond VA

MILLER, EDGAR GRIM, JR., univ. dean; b. Gettysburg, Pa., Feb. 22, 1893; s. Edgar Grim and Esther Amelia (Valentine) M.; B.S., Gettysburg Coll., 1911, Sc.D., 1955; Ph.D., Columbia, 1913; student Cambridge Univ., 1928-29, London Univ., 1929; m. Margaret Motter, Sept. 7, 1921; children—Margaret Esther (Mrs. Ralph D. Junker), Edgar Grim (dec), Ledlie Sitgreaves (Mrs. L. Miller Graham). Asst. in biological chemistry, Columbia 1911-13, asso. in biochemistry, 1914-21, asst. prof. biochemistry, 1921-24, asso. prof., 1924-35, prof. of biochemistry, 1935—; dean of the grad. faculties, 1953—. Pathol. chemist, Bellevue Hospital, New York City, 1912-13; instr. in physiological chemistry, Coll. of Med., Univ. Ill., Chicago, 1913-14. Served as cadet, A.A.F., 1918. Fellow A.A.A.S., N.Y. Acad. Scis., N.Y. Acad. Med.; mem. Am. Soc. Biol. Chemists, Soc. Exptl. Biology and Medicine, Harvey Soc. (sec. 1945-47), Am. Chem. Soc., Internat. Assn. Dental Research, Phi Beta Kappa, Phi Gamma Delta, Phi Lambda Upsilon, Sigma Xi. Independent. Protestant. Club: Century Assn. Home: 4930 Goodridge Av., N.Y.C. 71. Died June 28, 1955; buried Oak Hill Cemetery, Washington.

MILLER, EDMUND HOWD, chemist, educator, author; b. Fairfield, Conn., Sept. 12, 1869; s. George M. M.; grad. Columbia, 1891; took course in chemistry School of Mines, Columbia, 1887-91 (A.M., 1892; Ph.D., 1894, Columbia); m. June 11, 1898. Engaged in teaching chemistry, 1891—; adj. prof. analytical chemistry and assaying, 1901-04, prof. analytical chemistry, 1904—, Columbia. Fellow Chem. Soc., London, A.A.A.S. Author: Notes on Assaying (with Prof. Ricketts), 1897; Calculations of Analytical Chemistry, 1900; Quantitative Analysis for Mining Engineers, 1904. Died 1906.

MILLER, EDWARD FURBER, engineer; b. Somerville, Mass., Jan. 18, 1866; s. William Gibbs and Sarah (Furber) M.; S.B., Mass. Inst. Tech., 1886; D.Sc., R.I. State Coll., 1921; m. Mary Willard Reed, Sept. 11, 1900. Teacher of mech. engring., 1886-92, prof. steam engring., 1892—, Mass. Inst. Tech., also in charge dept. mech. engring., 1911—; dean of army officers, Mass. Inst. Tech., 1922—. Col. Auxiliary Reserve; asst. dist. chief of ordnance, 1930—. Universalist. Author: Steam Boilers (with Cecil H. Peabody), 1897; Problems in Thermodynamics and Heat-Engineering (with C. W. Berry and J. C. Riley), 1911; Notes on Power Plant Design (with James Holt), 3d edit.; Notes on Heat Engineering, 1931. Home: Newton Center, Mass. Died June 12, 1933.

MILLER, EMERSON R., chemist; b. Bascom, O., June 2, 1862; s. George and Charity Ann (Hook) M.; National Normal U., Lebanon, O., 1883; Wittenberg College, Springfield, 1884-87; Ph.C., U. of Michigan, 1892, Phar.M., 1893, B.S., 1894, M.S., 1895; U. of Marburg, 1901-02; Ph.D., U. of Minn., 1918; m. Mary Adda White, June 22, 1892. Prin. high sch., Arkansas City, Kan., 1888-91; asst. in qualitative analysis, U. of Mich., 1894-95; adj. prof. pharmacy, Ala. Poly. Inst., 1895-96, prof., 1896-1905; chief chem. dept., Expt. Sta., Santiago de Las Vegas, 1905-06; prof. pharm. chemistry, Ala. Poly. Inst., 1906-13; actg. asst. prof. plant chemistry, and chemist, Pharmaceut. Expt. Sta., Wis., 1913-17; prof. of chemistry, and research chemist, Ala. Poly. Inst., 1918—. Home: Auburn, Ala. Deceased.

MILLER, EZRA, state senator, inventor; b. Pleasant Valley, N.J., May 12, 1812; s. Ezra Wilson and Hannah (Ryerson) M.; m. Amanda Miller, May 1841, 5 children. Enlisted in 2d N.Y. Militia, 1833-43, adj. gen., 1839, lt. col., 1840, col., 1842; went to Rock County, Wis., 1848; justice of peace, Magnolia, Wis., 1848; col. 8th Regt., Wis. Militia, 1851; mem. Wis. Senate from Rock County; perfected a car coupler, obtained patent, 1863, improved basic idea; granted patent for combined railroad-car platform, coupler and buffer, 1865; dep. postmaster Janesville (Wis.), 2 years; mem. N.J. Senate, 1883-85; candidate for U.S. Ho. of Reps., several times. Died Mahwah, N.J., July 9, 1885.

MILLER, FRANK EBENEZER, M.D.; b. Hartford, Conn., Apr. 12, 1859; s. Ebenezer B. and Mayette (Deming) M.; A.B., Trinity Coll., Conn., 1881; M.D., Coll. Phys. and Surg. (Columbia), 1884; m. Emily Weston, Apr. 28, 1892. Interne New York and Charity Hosps., 6 mos., St. Francis Hosp., 2 yrs., sanitary insp. Bd. of Health, N.Y. City, 1886-89; served as asst. to various specialists in treatment of nose, throat and ear; began practice, 1896; chief throat surgeon to Bellevue Hosp., 1886, Vanderbilt Clinic, 1890-93; now consulting phys. to St. Francis and St. Joseph's hosps. Tenor singer; made scientific study of the voice and originated "vocal art-science," a method of voice production. Republican. Baptist. Author: Observations in Vocal Art Science, 1909; The Voice, Its Production, Care and Preservation, 1910; Vocal Art-Science, 1917; The Banner of Universal Harmony, 1919. Home: New York, N.Y. Died Apr. 15, 1932.

MILLER, FRED J., industrial engr.; b. Yellow Springs, O., Jan. 3, 1857; s. John Z. and Elizabeth (Woodhurst) M.; ed. pub. schs.; m. Julia Kindelberger, 1876; children—Katherin C., Grace E. With Am. Machinist, 1887-1907, as editor and last 10 yrs. as editor-in-chief; gen. mgr. factories of Union Typewriter Co., 1909-18; pub. service commr. of Pa., Mar. 1924-Apr. 1925. Served as maj. Ordnance Dept., U.S.A., Jan. 4, 1918-Feb. 21, 1919. Trustee Simplified Spelling Bd. Awarded Gantt medal, by joint action of Am. Soc. M.E. and Inst. of Management, 1929. Home: New Hope, Pa. Died Nov. 26, 1939.

MILLER, FREDERIC HOWELL, educator; b. N.Y. City, June 17, 1903; s. Frederic William and Anna Margaret (Bergheim) M.; B.S., Cooper Union Inst. of Tech., 1926; M.S., Cornell, 1927; Ph.D., Columbia, 1932; m. Marie Glauser, July 30, 1927; 1 dau., Lois Ruth (Mrs. Reginald Bruce Collier). Instr. in math., Cooper Union, 1927-29, Columbia, 1929-32; asst. prof. of math., Cooper Union, 1932-42, asso. prof. of math., 1942-43, prof. and head dept. of math. since 1943. Examiner math., Coll. Entrance Exam. Bd., 1949-51. Mem. Am. Soc. Engring. Edn. (math. div. chmn., 1948-49, dir., 1949-51, council, 1951-53), Math. Assn. Am. (gov., 1948-51), Am. Math. Soc. Author: Advanced Mathematics for Engineers, 1938; Calculus, 1939, Partial Differential Equations, 1941; College Algebra and Trigonometry, 1945; Analytic Geometry and Calculus, 1949. Home: 141 W. 73rd St., N.Y.C. 23. Office: Cooper Union, N.Y.C. 3. Died Jan. 11, 1964.

MILLER, GEORGE ABRAM, mathematician; b. Lynnville, Pa., July 31, 1863; s. Nathan and Mary Miller (Sittler) M.; A.B., Muhlenberg (Pa.) Coll., 1887, A.M., 1890; Ph.D., Cumberland U., 1893; student Univs. of Leipzig and Paris, 1895-97; m. Cassandra

Boggs, Dec. 23, 1909. Prin. schs., Greeley, Kan., 1887-88; prof. mathematics, Eureka (Ill.) College, 1888-93; instr. mathematics, U. Mich., 1893-95, Cornell, 1897-1901; asst. prof. mathematics Stanford, 1901-02, asso. prof., 1902-06; asso. prof. mathematics U. Ill., 1906-07, prof., 1907-31 when retired; prof. mathematics U. Chicago summer 1912, U. Calif., summer 1913. Co-editor Am. Year Book School Science and Mathematics, and Ency. des Sciences Mathematiques. Winner internat., math. prize, 1900. Fellow Am. Acad. Arts and Sciences, A.A.A.S. (sec. Sect. A., 1907-12, chmn., 1921-22; chmn. math. sub-com. on com. of 100 on sci. research); mem. Nat. Acad. Sciences, Math. Assn. Am. (v.p., 1916, pres. 1921), Am. Math. Soc. (v.p. 1907-08), London Math. Soc., Deutsche Mathematiker Verein; corr. mem. Spanish Mathematic Soc.; hon. mem. Indian Mathematic Soc. Author: Determinants, 1892; Mathematical Monographs (co-author), 1911; Theory and Applications of Groups of Finite Order, 1916, rev. ed., 1938; Historical Introduction to the Mathematical Literature, 1916; College Teaching, 1919; Collected Works (Vol. I), 1935, (Vol. II), 1938; also articles on the theory of groups and the history of mathematics in Am. and fgn. jours. Home: 1203 W. Illinois St., Urbana IL*

MILLER, GERRIT SMITH, JR., zoologist; b. Petersboro, N.Y., Dec. 6, 1869; s. Gerrit Smith and Susan (Dixwell) M.; A.B., Harvard U., 1894; m. Elizabeth Eleanor Page, 1897; m. 2d, Anne Chapin Gates, 1921. Asst. curator mammals, U.S. Nat. Mus., 1898-1909, curator, 1909-40, asso. in biology, 1941—. Fellow A.A.A.S.; mem. Am. Acad. Arts and Scis., Am. Philos. Soc.; corr. mem. Acad. Natural Scis. (Phila.), Zool Soc. London. Clubs: Cosmos, Arts (Washington). Wrote: The Families and Genera of Bats; Catalogue of the Land Mammals of Western Europe in the British Museum; List of North American Land Mammals in the United States National Museum, 1911; List of North American Recent Mammals, 1923; about 400 monographs and contbns. to sci. jours. Address: U.S. National Museum, Washington. Died Feb. 24, 1956.

MILLER, HILLIARD EVE, gynecologist; b. Cowan, Tenn., Sept. 25, 1893; s. Charles Jewett and Elizabeth (Johnston) M.; student Sewanee Mil. Acad., 1908-10, U. of the South (both of Sewanee, Tenn.), 1910-12; M.D., Tulane U., New Orleans, 1916; m. Veva Penick, Oct. 31, 1917; children—Veva Penick, Hilliard Eve., Jr. Interne Charity Hosp., New Orleans, 1916; house surgeon New York Lying-In Hosp., New York, 1917; instr. gynecology and obstetrics Tulane U. Med. Sch., 1917-24, asst. prof. gynecology, 1924-36, prof. and head dept. of gynecology since 1936; prof. and head dept. of gynecology, Grad. Sch., Tulane U.; chief dept. of gynecology, Touro Infirmary; sr. gynecologist, Tulane Div., Charity Hosp.; cons. gynecologist, Flint-Goodridge Hosp. Served as 1st lt., Med. Corps, U.S. Army, 1917. Trustee Isaac Delgado Memorial Fund. Fellow Am. Coll. Surgeons, Southern Surg. Assn.; mem. Nat. Bd. Obstetrics and Gynecology, A.M.A., Am. Gynecol. Soc., South Eastern Surg. Congress, Southern Med. Assn., La State Med. Soc., Orleans Parish Med. Soc., New Orleans Gynecol. and Obstet. Soc., La. State Gynecol. and Obstet. Soc., Am. Gynecol. Club (pres.), Phi Delta Theta, Phi Chi. Democrat. Episcopalian. Mem. Knights of Momus; Mystic and Neptune Clubs. Clubs: Boston, Louisiana, Country. Wrote chapters for Curtis Gynecology and Obstetrics and Davis Gynecology and Obstetrics; also about 20 papers read before med. socs. and pub. in med. jours. Home: 325 Walnut St. Office: Medical Arts Bldg., New Orleans, La. Died Apr. 20, 1945.

MILLER, JOHN ANTHONY, coll. prof.; b. Greensburg, Ind., Dec. 16, 1859; s. Bruno Brunen and Katherine (Arnold) M.; A.B., Indiana U., 1890, LL.D., 1928; A.M., Stanford U., 1893; Ph.D., U. of Chicago, 1899; m. Mary Catharine Goodwine, Dec. 24, 1880; children—Max B., Harry L.; m. 2d, Frances Morgan Swain, June 23, 1932. Supt. schs., Rockville, Ind., 1890-91; instr. mathematics, 1891-93, asst. prof., 1893-94, Stanford; prof. mathematics, 1894-95, mechanics and astronomy, 1895-1906, Ind. U.; prof. astronomy, and dir. Sproul Obs., Swarthmore Coll., 1906-32, v.p. Swarthmore College, 1914-29, prof. of astronomy emeritus since 1932. Chief of expedition sent by Indiana Univ. to Spain, 1905, to observe total eclipse of the sun, and of expdn. sent by Sproul Obs. to observe total eclipse of sun, 1918, and to Mexico, 1923, by Swarthmore Coll. to observe total eclipse of sun, to New Haven, Conn., 1925, to Sumatra, 1926, 29, to Vermont, 1932; technicolor dir. expdn. by Hayden Planetarium to Peru, 1937. Fellow Am. Acad. Arts and Sciences, A.A.A.S., Indiana Academy Science, Royal Astron. Soc.; mem. Am. Math. Soc., Am. Astron. Soc., Am. Philos. Soc. (ex-sec.), Sigma Xi, Phi Beta Kappa. Republican. Friend. Author: Trigonometry for Beginners, 1896; Analytic Mechanics, 1915 (revised 1935). Contbr. to math. and astron. publs. Home: Wallingford PA*

MILLER, JULIAN CREIGHTON, horticulturist; b. Lexington, S.C., Nov. 29, 1895; s. Simeon Jeremiah and Plumie Elizabeth (Shull) M.; B.S., Clemson Coll. 1921, honorary doctor's degree, 1961; M.S., Cornell University, 1926, Ph.D., 1928; m. Caroline Stone Leichliter, Dec. 26, 1923; children—Redman B., Julian Creighton. Instr. horticulture, N.C. State Coll., 1921-23; county agrl. agt., S.C., 1923-25; asst., Cornell U., 1925-28; asso. prof. horticulture and research, Okla. Agr. and Mech. Coll., 1928-29; prof. horticulture and head dept., La. State U. 1929-71, emeritus, 1971—; developing technics for breeding vegetable crops. Agr. advisor to P.R. and Central Am.; plant exploration for Ipomea species, economic medicinal plants in West Indies in cooperation with U.S. Dept. Agr., 1953; U.S. del. to Internat. Hort. Congress, 1955. Served with U.S. Navy, 1917-19, seaman, line officer as ensign and lt. (j.g.); developed process for dehydrating sweet potatoes for Army, World War II. Named Progressive Farmer's Man of Year 1940 for La., Man of South, 1947; awarded Wilder Medal for breeding and introdn. of Klonmore strawberry, also plaques for services rendered hort. field; named Vegetable Man of the Year, Vegetable Growers Association America; recipient Presdl. commendation, 1971. La. State U. Alumni Distinguished Faculty fellow, 1967. Fellow A.A.A.S., Am. Hort. Soc. (pres. 1942, chmn. So.; mem. Am. Genetic Assn., Potato Assn. Am. (pres. 1938), Assn. So. Agr. Workers, So. Assn. Sci. and Industry, Am. Inst. Biol. Scis., La. Farm Bur. Fedn. (hon. life mem.), So. Seedsmen's Assn. (hon. life mem.). Phi Kappa Phi (provincal sec. so. sect. 1935-52; nat. regent), Sigma Xi, Omicron Delta Kappa, Alpha Gamma Rho, Alpha Gamma Delta, Alpha Zeta (Centennial hon. mem.). Democrat. Presbyn. (ruling elder). Mason. Kiwanian. Author numerous expt. sta. bulls., spl. feature articles on research; contbr. to sci. jours. Home: Baton Rouge LA Died Apr. 13, 1971; buried Roselawn Meml. Park, Baton Rouge LA

MILLER, JULIAN HOWELL, plant pathologist; b. Washington, July 16, 1890; s. Thomas Fayette and Annie Elizabeth (Wade) M.; B.S.A., U. Ga., 1911, M.S., 1924; Ph.D., Cornell U., 1928; m. Mary Douglas Morris, Sept. 1, 1921; children—Julian Howell, Anne Lewis. Tchr., 7th Dist. A. and M. Sch., Ga., 1911-12; farmer, Va., 1912-16; asso. prof. horticulture U. Ga., 1919-23, asso. prof. botany, 1924-33, asso. prof. plant pathology, 1933-35, head dept., 1933-58, prof. plant pathology, 1936-58, Regents' prof. emeritus plant pathology and plant breeding, 1958—. Collaborator, U.S. Department Agriculture in Plant Disease Survey for Ga., 1924—. Served to lt. inf. U.S. Army, 1917-19; with A.E.F., 10 months; capt. inf. Res. Corps, 1920—. Fellow A.A.A.S.; mem. Am. (v.p. 1947, pres. 1948), Brit. mycol. socs., Am. Phytopathol. Soc., N.Y., Ga. acads. sci., Ga. Naturalists, Washington Acad. Scis., Phi Beta Kappa, Sigma Xi, Phi Kappa Phi. Democrat. Mem. Christian Disciples Ch. Author: A Monograph of the World Species of Hypoxylon. Asso. editor Mycologie, 1941. Contbr. numerous articles to profl. publs. Home: 458 Dearing St., Athens, Ga. Died Mar. 25, 1961: buried Oconee Hill Cemetery.

MILLER, KEMPSTER BLANCHARD, consulting engr.; b. Boston, Aug. 14, 1870; s. Joseph K. and Eliza (Blanchard) M.; E.E., Cornell U., 1893; m. Antha Knowlton, July 3, 1897; children—Dorothea Knowlton, Antha, Ruth Blanchard. Asst. examiner, U.S. Patent Office, Washington, 1893-96; chief engr. Western Telephone Construction Co., Chicago, 1896-98; elec. engr., Scranton, Pa., 1898-99; engr. of Kellogg Switchboard & Supply Co., Chicago, 1899-1904; engaged in practice as mem. McMeen & Miller, 1904-18. Chief engr. Central Union Telephone Co. (Ill., Ohio and Ind.), 1913-18; varied practice as consulting, constructing and operating engineer, principally in telephone field in United States and Can.; has served as expert in many court suits relating to telephone and as arbitrator in controversies concerning public utility properties; designed and built several hydro-electric plants in Ore. and Calif.; designed recently completed fire-alarm telegraph system for City of N.Y. Fellow Am. Inst. E.E. Author: American Telephone Practice, 1904; Telephone Theory and Practice, 1930. Joint author: Telephony, 1912. Home: Pasadena, Calif. Died Nov. 22, 1933.

MILLER, KNOX EMERSON, U.S. Pub. Health Service; b. Norton, Kan., Nov. 26, 1886; s. Joseph Medford and Martha Washington (Whiteman) M.; A.B., William Jewell Coll., Liberty, Mo., 1908; M.D., Johns Hopkins, 1912; m. Noxie Bliss Miller, Oct. 29, 1915; children—Martha Vincent (Mrs. Pope A. Laurence), Betty Bow (Mrs. Richard O. Madson). Knox Emerson. Staff mem. Va. State Health Dept., 1912-14; commd. asst. surgeon U.S.P.H.S., 1914, passed asst. surgeon, 1918, surgeon, 1922, senior surgeon, 1934, medical director, 1940; research in rural health adminstrn., 1917-19; spl. consultant and dir. rural health adminstrn. N.C. State Dept. of Health, 1919-23; same La. State Dept. of Health, 1923-27; exec. officer Marine Hosp., N.Y., 1927-28; med. officer in charge Marine Hosp., Evansville, Ind., 1928-31; dir. rural health, Tex. State Dept. of Health, 1931-34; health consultant to states of Gulf region and Pacific Southwest, 1934-35, to states of Great Lakes region, 1935-36; asst. to asst. surgeon gen. in charge Domestic Quarantine Div., 1936-38; dir. Med. Research and Advisory Div., Federal Trade Commn., 1938-40; liason officer, 8th Service Command Headquarters, U.S. Army, Dallas, 1940-46; dist. dir. 9th Dist., U.S.P.H.S., Dallas, 1941-49, ret.; asst. state health officer of Fla. from 1949; dir. Chicago-Cook County Health Survey. Member mission to study strategic bombing in Japan. Diplomate, Am. Bd. Preventive Medicine and Pub. Health. Fellow A.M.A., Am. Pub. Health Assn.; mem. Assn. Mil. Surgeons (life), A.A.A.S., Asociacion Nacional de Venereolgia (Mexico), Tex. Acad. Sci., Sci. Soc., San Antonio, U.S.-Mexico Border Pub. Health Assn., Alpha Omega Alpha, Phi Chi, Lambda Chi Alpha, Pi Gamma Mu, Celsus Soc., Ho Din of Southwestern Medical Foundation. Clubs: Cosmos (Washington, D.C.). Contbr. professional articles to med. and pub. health mags. Home: Jacksonville FL Died May 1969.

MILLER, LOYE HOLMES, biology; b. Minden, La., Oct. 13, 1874; s. George and Cora (Holmes) M.; B.S., U. of Calif., 1898, M.S., 1903, Ph.D., 1912; m. Anne Lucia Holmes, Aug. 1, 1901; children—Alden Holmes, Holmes Odell. Instr. in natural science, Oahu Coll., Hononlulu, T.H., 1900-03; instr. biology, State Normal Sch., Los Angeles, Calif., 1904-18; asst. prof. biology, U. of Calif., 1919-20, asso. prof., 1920-23, prof., 1923-43 (emeritus). Served as expert with U.S. Bur. of Fisheries, U.S. Dept. Agr. Fellow Am. Assn. for Advancement of Science Am. Ornithol. Union; mem. Am. Soc. Naturalists, Cooper Ornithol. Club (pres. bd. govs.), Sigma Xi, Phi Beta Kappa, Thanic Shield (U. of Calif.). Conglist. Contbr. 100 papers on fossil and recent vertebrates of Pacific Coast to geol. publs. U. of Calif., publs. Carnegie Inst., Science, Jour. Mammalogy, etc. Home: Los Angeles CA Died Apr. 6, 1970.

MILLER, MALCOLM E(UGENE), vet. anatomist, educator; b. Durell, Pa., Aug. 1, 1909; s. Elliston M. and Augusta (Morey) M.; student Pa. State U., 1928-30; D.V.M., N.Y. State Vet. Coll., 1934; B.S., N.Y. State Coll. Agr., 1935; M.S., Cornell, 1936, Ph.D., 1940; m. Mary Mulford Wells, Sept. 3, 1935; children—Jesse Wells, Faith Virginia, Sharon Dawn. Mem. faculty Cornell U., 1932—, successively asst. vet. anatomy, instr. vet. anatomy, asst. prof., asso. prof., 1932-47, prof., head dept. vet. anatomy, 1947—; vet. practice summers 1934-36; state vet., N.Y., summers 1937-39; sec. N.Y. State Vet. Coll., 1948—. Mem. Am. Assn. Anatomists, Am. Vet. Med. Assn., N.Y. State Vet. Med. Soc., Am. Assn. Vet. Anatomists (pres. 1950, chmn. com. vet. anat. nomenclature 1953), Sigma Xi, Phi Kappa Phi, Alpha Zeta, Phi Zeta, Omega Tau Sigma. Republican. Conglist. Author: Guide to the Dissection of the Dog, rev. edit. 1955; Anatomy of the Dog, (posthumous), 1964. Author sci articles. Home: R.D. 4, Ithaca, N.Y. Died Apr. 18, 1960; buried French Azilum, Pa.

MILLER, NEWTON, physician, surgeon; b. Franklin County, Ind., Mar. 20, 1879; s. John and Sarah Ellen (Liming) M.) A.B., Ind. U., 1905, A.M., 1906; Ph.D., Clark U., 1908; postgrad. U. Chgo., 1920; M.D., Rush Med. Coll., 1924; m. Barbara Elizabeth Roethlein, Dec. 20, 1911; 1 son, Ralph Newton. Made zoology collections in C.Am., 1905; prof. high sch., biology, E. Waterloo, Ia., 1905-06; instr. Clark Coll., 1908-11, asst. prof., lectr. in heredity and eugenics, hon. fellow, 1911-12; prof. biology Wheaton Coll., Norton, Mass., 1912-15; asst. prof. Ind. U., summers, 1912-15; prof. zoology U. Utah, 1915-19, microscopic anatomy, Med. Sch., 1919-26; practiced medicine, Porterville, Cal., 1927—. Mem. A.A.A.S., A.M.A., Cal., Tulare County (pres. 1930) med. assns., Am. Med. Writers Assn., Sigma Xi, Phi Kappa Phi, Phi Beta Phi, Delta Upsilon. Republican. Methodist. Mason. Contbr. articles to med. and zoology jours. Address: 30 Park Dr., Porterville, Cal. 93257. Died Jan. 7, 1961; buried Fresno, Cal.

MILLER, RALPH ENGLISH, pathologist, educator; b. Tustin, Mich., Jan. 13, 1899; s. Ward Beecher and Agnes Philena (English) M.; B.S., Dartmouth, 1921-24, student medicine, 1924-25; M.D., Harvard, 1928; M.S., U. Minn., 1931; m. Elizabeth Skolfield, June 15, 1925; children—Ralph English, Elizabeth Giveen (Mrs. William Congdon), Barbara Jane (Mrs. Theodore Randell). Intern Mary Hitchcock Meml. Hosp., 1928-29; asst. instr. biology Dartmouth, 1925-26, asst. prof. pathology, 1931-41, prof., 1941—, asst. dean Med. Sch., 1936-44; pathologist Mary Hitchcock Meml. Hosp., 1931—, dir. labs., 1936—; sr. cons. VA Hosp., White River Junction, Vt., 1946—. Pres. N.H. Bd. Health, 1942-53. Recipient award Am. Cancer Soc., 1955. Mem. Am. Cancer Soc., Am. Assn. Pathologists and Bacteriologists, A.M.A., New Eng. Path. Soc., N.H. Med. Soc., New Eng. Cancer Soc., Coll. Am. Pathologists, A.A.A.S. Home: 9 Downing Rd. Hanover, N.H. Died Feb. 25, 1959.

MILLER, ROBERT TALBOTT, JR., surgeon; b. Covington, Ky., Apr. 20, 1878; s. Robert Talbott and Eliza W. (Hamilton) M.; A.B., Amherst, 1899, hon. D.Sc., 1925; M.D., Johns Hopkins, 1903; m. Mary Edes Hooper, Apr. 15, 1909; children—Robert Talbott, Mitchell Hooper, John Hamilton. Interne 4 yrs., resident surgeon 3 yrs., Johns Hopkins Hosp.; asso. prof. surgery, U. Pitts., 1910-15, prof., 1915-21; asso. prof. surgery, Johns Hopkins Med. Sch., 1922-25; became asso. prof. clin. surgery, Johns Hopkins Med. Sch., 1925; retired, 1935. Maj. M.R.C.; organized, May 1917, dir. Base Hosp. 27 (U. Pitts. Unit), with AEF, France. Fellow Am. Coll. Surgeons, Am. Surg. Assn., A.M.A., A.A.A.S., So. Surg. Assn., Am. Assn. for Thoracic Surgery, Interurban Surg. Soc. Republican, Episcopalian. Club: Eclat. Home: Mountain Lake. Lake Wales, Fla. Died June 13, 1960; buried Druid Ridge Cemetery, Balt.

MILLER, SAMUEL CHARLES, dentist; b. New

York, N.Y., Nov. 15, 1903; s. Abraham and Sarah (Miller) M.; student Coll. of City of N.Y., 1919-20; D.D.S., N.Y. Univ., 1925; m. Mae Rodgers, June 12, 1927; children—Barbara Marsak, Stphanie. Prof., chmn. Periodontia Dept.; honorary professor University Santo Domingo; cons. teacher U.S. Navy; consultant VA. Lt. USNR, ret. Chairman American Board of Oral Medicine. Fellow American College Dentists, Pierre Fanchard Acad., American Academy of Dental Medicine, A.A.A.S.; asso. fellow N.Y. Acad. Medicine; mem. Am. Dental Assn., N.Y. State Dental Society, Research Soc. Am., Am. Academy Periodontology, N.Y. Inst. Clinical Oral Pathology, Pan-Am. Odontological Soc. (v.p.), Harvey Soc., Assn. Advancement Oral Diagnosis, Omicron Kappa Upsilon (past pres.), Alumni Assn. New York U. College of Dentistry (past pres.); hon. mem. Bolivian Dental Assn. (Bolivia), El Primer Congreso Nacional de Odontologos (Colombia); president College Dental Soc. of New York U. College of Dentistry; councillor N.Y. Section, International Association for Dental Research. Author: Practical Periodontia (with Sidney Sorrin), 1928. Editor: Oral Diagnosis (with 28 contributors), 1936, 1946; Textbook of Periodontia, 1938, 43, 50. Editor: Spanish English Medical Dental Guide and Interpreter. Contbr. dental jours. Home: 101-05 72d Av., Forest Hills, N.Y. Office: 57 W. 57th St., N.Y.C. 19. Died Feb. 8, 1958; buried Mt. Hebron Cemetery.

MILLER, SPENCER, SR., engineer (retired); b. Waukegan, Ill., Apr. 25, 1859; s. Samuel Fisher and Charlotte (Howe) M.; B.S. in Mech. Engring., Worcester Poly. Inst., 1879, E.Eng. (honorary), 1928; married Harriet M. Ruggles, Jan. 1, 1885; children—Marguerite (Mrs. P. E. Grannis), Spencer, Helen (Mrs. Aurelio Giorni) (deceased); married second, Mrs. L. MacD. Sleeth, 1931 (deceased). Began with Link Belt Company, Chgo., 1881; engr., later chief engr. Lidgerwood Mfg. Co., mfrs. hoisting engines, etc., N.Y.C., 1888-1926, retired. Perfected overhead cableway system used in constrn. of Gatun locks, Panama Canal, and extensively applied on construction of the Hoover Dam, and other dams; invented an overhead log-skidding cableway now in use in lumber camps generally; a marine cableway for trans-shipping fuel under headway at sea; electric automatic tension towing engine; marine breeches buoy for transferring passengers from one ship to another at sea, used by USN. Mem. Naval Cons. Bd., 1915—. Mem. Am. Soc. M.E., Am. Soc. C.E., Am. Inst. Mining Engrs., Soc. Naval Architects and Marine Engrs., Sigma Xi. Republican. Episcopalian. Author of Joseph Miller of Newton, Mass. (a genealogy). Home: 217 Turrell Av., South Orange, N.J.; and Laguna Beach, Cal. Died June 16, 1953.

MILLER, WALTER, petroleum refining cons.; b. Canton Aargau, Switzerland, Mar. 4, 1881; s. John Rudolph and Lina (Hunziker) M.; brought to U.S., 1888, naturalized, 1893; ed. pub. schs., Flemington, Roselle and Elizabeth, N.J., also night schs. and corr. courses; Eng.D. (hon.), U. Tulsa, 1943; m. Katherine Mae McNair, Jan. 1, 1900; children—Katherine Mae (Mrs. Sherwood J. Lahman), Ruth Pitman, Walter (dec.). With Tide Water Oil Co. in refinery, Bayonne, N.J., 1909-17; gen. supt. U.S. refineries, Pierce Oil Corp., Tulsa, 1917; mfg. mgr. Cosden & Co., Tulsa, 1917-20; refinery cons., Tulsa, 1920-22; asso. with Marland Refining Co. (now Continental Oil Co.), Ponca City, Okla., 1922—, mgr., 1922-29, v.p. charge mfg., 1926-46; ret., 1946; petroleum refining cons., 1946—; dir. Gray Processes Corp. Mem. Am. Soc. M.E., Am. Inst. Mining and Metall. Engrs., Am. Soc. Testing Materials, Am. Chem. Soc., Inst. Petroleum (Brit.), Am. Petroleum Inst. Republican. Episcopalian. Clubs: Chemists (N.Y.C.); Conoco Golf (Ponca City). Hon. D. Eng. conferred by U. Tulsa, 1943. Home: 400 N. 4th St. Office: Continental Oil Co., Ponca City, Okla. Died June 8, 1949.

MILLER, WALTER MCNAB, b. Osborn, Ohio July 10, 1859; s. John Erb and Mary Jane (McNab) M.; B.Sc., Ohio State U., 1885; M.D., Cooper Med. Coll., San Francisco, 1895; post-grad. work, U. of Cal., 1896, Johns Hopkins, 1899-1900, summer course, Harvard, 1900; pathol. studies, Leipzig, 1900-01, Prague, 1901-02, 1905; m. Helen Richards Guthrie, of Zanesville, O., Jan. 10, 1889; children—Guthrie McNab, Charles Edward. Teacher science, 1882, prin., 1883-87, Portsmouth (O.) High Sch.; prof. natural science, 1887-89, prof. anatomy, physiology and geology, 1889-99, U. of Nev.; also bacteriologist and pathologist Nev. Agrl. Expt. Sta., 1896-99; prof. pathology and bacteriology, U. of Mo., 1902-10; sec. Mo. Assn. for Relief and Control of Tuberculosis, 1911-1926 (retired). Mem. Mo. State Med. Assn., Nat. Tuberculosis Assn., Phi Kappa Psi, Phi Beta Pi, Sigma Xi, Acacia (U. of Mo.). Episcopalian. Author numerous pamphlets, bulls. and articles relating to scientific and other topics. Organized state-wide edn. movement in connection with pub. schs. of Mo. for betterment of rural pub. health, particularly in respect to tuberculosis and for systematic health education of school children. Home: 1102 Rollins Av., Columbia, Mo.

MILLER, WILLIAM JASPER, educator; born at Skidmore, Bee County, Tex., Dec. 12, 1893; s. William Reed and Victoria Evelyn (Garrett) M.; E.E., U. of Tex., 1915; S.M. in E.E., Mass. Inst. Tech., 1922; m. Evelyn Christina Knipp, Mar. 14, 1932. Student engr. Gen. Electric Co., 1915-17; instr. and asst. prof. elec. engring., U. of Tex., 1917-20; instr. elec. engring., Mass. Inst. Tech., 1920-21; prof. same and head dept. Okla. A. & M. Coll., 1921-23; research engr. in charge of Engring. Expt. Station, U. of Ark. (estab. and organized Station), 1923-25; dean engring and head dept. elec. engring., Texas Tech. Coll. (organized and developed School of Engineering), 1925-32; prof. and head dept. elec. engring., Univ. of N.C., 1932-36, acting dean of engring., 1933-36; prof. and head dept. elec. engring., U. Ala., 1936-59, ret.; engr. Gen. Electric Co., Westinghouse Electric & Mfg. Co. and Tex. Power & Light Co., various summers. Fellow Am. Inst. Elec. Engrs., member Soc. Promotion Engring. Edn., Am. Assn. of University Professors, Am. Inst. of Electrical Engrs (v.p. 1955-57) Tau Beta Pi. Methodist. Mason. Clubs: Birmingham Engineers; Civitan (Tuscaloosa). Address: 609 Hillside Dr., Kerrville, Tex. 78028. Died Mar. 20, 1962; buried Garden of Memories, Kerrville.

MILLER, WILLIAM SNOW, anatomist; b. Stirling, Mass., Mar. 29, 1858; s. William and Harriet Emily (Snow) M.; M.D., Yale, 1879; fellow Clark U., 1890-92; U. of Leipzig, 1895-96; fellow Johns Hopkins, 1905-06; Sc.D., U. of Cincinnati, 1920, and from University of Wis., 1926; m. Carrie M. Bradley, Oct. 14, 1881 (died 1901); m. 2d, Alice L. Burdick, Aug. 6, 1912. Pathologist, City and Memorial hosps., Worcester, Mass., 1889-92; instr. vertebrate anatomy, 1892-95, asst. prof. anatomy, 1895-1904, prof., 1904-24, prof. emeritus, 1924—, U. of Wis. Lecturer in medicine, med. dept. Johns Hopkins, 1918-19. Mason. Conglist. Author: The Lung, 1937. Received Trudeau medeal, 1934. Home: Madison, Wis. Died Dec. 26, 1939.

MILLER, WILLIAM TODD, engr., educator; born Neponset, Ill., Sept. 14, 1888; s. James Todd and Christina (Stevenson) M.; student manual training sch., Washington U., 1906-09; B.S., Purdue, 1916; m. Leona Mabel Allen, Apr. 24, 1915; children—Todd Allen, William Stevenson, James Chapman. Supervisor of heat and power, Oklahoma State Instns., Okla., 1909-12; supt. Lafayete Boxboard and Paper Co., Lafayette, Ind., 1916-25; chief plant engr. Ft. Wayne (Ind.) Corrugated Paper Co., 1925-28; prof. mech. engring., Purdue, 1928—, emeritus prof. mechanical engring., 1959—. Recipient Sigma Delta Chi Best Teacher Award (Purdue), 1944. Fellow American Society of Heating, Refrigerating and Air Conditioning Engineers; member American Soc. for Engring. Edn., Ind. State Adminstrv. Bldg. Council; Sigma Xi, Tau Beta Pi, Pi Tau Sigma (hon.), Theta Xi. Republican. Presbyterian. Mason (York rite). Contbr. Ency. Brit., 1959. Researcher in heating, durability of insulation and heat transfer. Home: R.R. 5, Monticello, Ind. Died Nov. 15, 1962; buried Grandview Cemetery, West Lafayette, Ind.

MILLIGAN, ROBERT WILEY, naval officer; b. Phila., Apr. 8, 1843; s. James and Mary (Thornton) M.; ed. pub. and high schs., Phila.; m. Sarah Ann Du Bois, Feb. 17, 1870. Entered U.S.N., as 3d asst. engr., Aug. 3, 1863; 2d asst. engr., July 25, 1866; passed asst. engr., Mar. 25, 1874; chief engr., Feb. 20, 1892; comdr., Mar. 3, 1899; capt., Nov. 7, 1902; advanced to rank of rear adm. and retired, Apr. 8, 1905. Served on U.S.S. Mackinaw in N. Atlantic Blockading Squadron during Civil War, participating in both battles of Ft. Fisher, fall of Wilmington, N.C., and fall of Petersburg and Richmond, Va.; on duty later in N. and S. Atlantic and Pacific Squadrons and as instr. U.S. Naval Acad.; chief engr. battleship Oregon on her run from Pacific to Atlantic coast and engr. same vessel in battle of Santiago; fleet engr. N. Atlantic Fleet, on flagship New York, for 1 yr.; chief engr. Norfolk Navy Yard, 1899-1905. Episcopalian. Republican. Home: Norfolk, Va. Died 1909.

MILLIKAN, CLARK BLANCHARD, educator; b. Chgo., Aug. 23, 1903; s. Robert Andrews and Greta Irvin (Blanchard) M.; student U. Chgo., 1919-20; Ph.B., Yale, 1924; Ph.D., Cal. Inst. Tech., 1928; m. Helen Staats, June 9, 1928 (div. Feb. 1958); children—Marcia (dec.), Robert Staats (dec.), Michael; m. 2d, Mrs. Edith Nussbaum Parry, Feb. 18, 1959. Teaching fellow in physics and aero. Cal. Inst. Tech., 1926-29, asst. prof. aeronautics, 1929-34, asso. prof., 1934-40, prof., 1940—. Dir. Guggenheim Aero. Lab. 1948-61, Grad. Aero. Labs., 1961—; mem. USAF Sci. Adv. Bd. Recipient Medal for Merit, King's Medal service cause of freedom. Hon. fellow Inst. Aeronautic Sci. (pres. 1937); fellow Royal Aero. Soc., Am. Phys. Soc., Am. Acad. Arts and Scis.; mem. Nat. Acad. Engrs., A.A.A.S., Nat. Acad. Sci., Phelps Assn., Phi Beta Kappa, Sigma Xi, Tau Beta Pi, Zeta Psi. Republican. Clubs: Bohemian (San Francisco); California, Sunset (Los Angeles). Contbr. articles on aeros. to tech. jours. Home: 690 Wendover Rd., Pasadena, Cal. Died Jan. 2, 1966.

MILLIKAN, ROBERT ANDREWS, physicist; b. Morrison, Ill., Mar. 22, 1868; s. Silas Franklin and Mary Jane (Andrews) M.; A.B., Oberlin, 1891, A.M., 1893; Ph.D., Columbia, 1895; postgrad. univs. Berlin and Göttingen, 1895-96; numerous hon. degrees, including ones from Columbia, 1917, U. Dublin, 1924, Yale, 1925, Princeton, 1928, Harvard, 1932, U. Liege, 1930, U. Paris, 1939; m. Greta Irvin Blanchard, Apr. 10, 1902; children—Clark Blanchard, Glenn Allan (dec.), Max Franklin. Tutor physics, Oberlin, 1891-93; member physics staff U. Chgo., 1896-1921; dir. Norman Bridge Lab. Physics, chmn. exec. council Calif. Inst. Tech., Pasadena, 1921-45, prof. emeritus, v.p. bd. trustees, from 1945. Recipient Comstock prize Nat. Acad. Scis., 1913; Edison medal Am. Inst. E.E., 1922; Hughes medal Royal Soc. Gt. Britain, 1923; Nobel prize in physics, 1923; Faraday medal London Chem. Soc., 1924; Matteucci medal Societa Italiana della Scienze, 1925; Gold medal Am. Soc. Mech. Engrs., 1926; Messel medal Soc. Chem. Industry (British), 1928; Gold medal Holland Soc., 1928, Soc. Arts and Sciences, 1929, Radiol. Soc. N.Am., 1930; Gold medal Roosevelt Meml. Assn., 1932; Gold medal Franklin Inst., 1937; Joy Kissen Mookerjee Gold medal Indian Assn. for Cultivation Sci., 1939; Oersted medal Am. Assn. Physics Teachers, 1940; several decorations. Fellow Am. Acad. Arts and Scis., A.A.A.S. (pres. 1929); mem. Nat. Acad. Scis., Am. Philos. Soc., Am. Phys. Soc. (pres. 1916-18), many fgn. sci. socs., Sigma Xi, Phi Beta Kappa; asso. Royal Acad. Belgium. Author or co-author: A Course of College Experiments in Physics, 1898; Theory of Optics, 1900; Mechanics, Molecular Physics and Heat, 1901; A First Course in Physics, 1906; A Laboratory Course in Physics for Secondary Schools, 1906; Electricity, Sound and Light, 1908; The Electron, 1917, 25; Science and Life, 1923; Elements of Physics, 1917; Evolution of Science and Religion, 1927; A First Course in Physics for Colleges, 1928; Science and the New Civilization, 1930; Time, Matter, and Values, 1932; Electrons (and -), Protons, Photons, Neutrons, and Cosmic Rays, 1935, rev. edit., 1947; New Elementary Physics, 1936; Mechanics, Molecular Physics, Heat and Sound, 1937; Cosmic Rays, 1939; Autobiography, 1950. Contbr. to tech. jours. Carried out original research on x-rays and free expansion of gases; isolated electron and measured its electric charge, 1910; worked on verifying Einstein's photoelectric equations, also on determining Planks's constant, 1912-15, antisubmarine and meteorol. devices, World War I, hotspark spectroscopy, 1920-23, ionization chambers; his expts. in electricity led to determination of number of molecules in unit vol. of gas at a given pressure; studied cosmic rays, which he named. Died San Marino, Cal., Dec. 19, 1953. *

MILLIS, JOHN, engineer officer U.S. Army; b. Wheatland, Mich., Dec. 31, 1858; s. Walter and Jane Clark (Carlow) M.; B.S., U.S. Mil. Acad., West Point, N.Y., 1881 (No. 1 graduate Class of 1881); m. Mary Raoul, Nov. 22, 1893; children—Ralph (dec.), Walter, Janet. Commd. 2d lt. engrs., June 11, 1881; 1st lt., 1882; capt., Sept. 20, 1892; major, Apr. 2, 1900; lt. col., June 7, 1907; col., June 13, 1910. Served Willets Point, N.Y., 1881-83; on lighthouse duty, 1883-90; devised and superintended the installation of electric light plant for illuminating the Statue of Liberty, New York Harbor, October 1886; in charge improvements New Orleans harbor and levees Miss. River, 1890-94; chief engineer U.S. Lighthouse Bd., Washington, 1894-98; on duty with engrs.' batt., Willets Point, N.Y., and in Cuba, 1898-1900; U.S. del. Internat. Congress of Navigation, Internat. Congress of Electricity and Internat. Congress of Physics, Paris Expn., 1900; inspected and reported upon the canal and reservoir system of the Nile—particularly the great reservoir dam at Assouan, nr. 1st cataract, Sept.-Oct. 1900; in charge of constructing fortifications on Puget Sound, of river and harbor improvements in Wash., Ida., Mont., of first road survey and constrn. in Mt. Rainier Nat. Park, of surveys and harbor improvements in Alaska, 1900-05, of all fortification constrn., P.I., 1905-07, including defensive works on Corregidor Island; on leave of absence, returning from P.I., visiting works, etc., in China, Burma, India, Egypt and Europe; in charge harbor and river improvement works, Lake Erie and in Ohio and Ind., and mem. spl. bds. on harbor works, etc., 1908-12, in charge of river and harbor improvement works and of sea coast defense works, Mass. and R.I.; sr. mem. spl. bd. on Lake Erie, Lake Mich. inland waterway, spl. duty under Bur. of Lighthouses for N.E. coast, 1912-16; div. engr. Southeast Div. for coast defenses, harbor improvements, and inland waterways, in S.C., Ga., Fla., western portion of N.C. and eastern portion of Ala., 1916-18; chief engr. Southeastern Dept., Savannah, Ga., 1917; dept. engr. Central Dept., Chicago, Ill., 1918-22; retired 1922. Mem. Am. Soc. C.E. (mem. spl. com. to investigate Japanese earthquake), Am. Inst. E.E., A.A.A.S., Am. Astron. Soc. Clubs: University, Century (New York); Cosmos (Washington). Author: Safety of Navigation on Great American Lakes (for 12th Internat. Congress Navigation, Phila., 1912); Commercial Waterways of the United States (for Atlantic Deeper Waterways Assn.); The Constructional History of the Solar System and of Our Earth (The Dualistic Theory), 1925; Unrealities of the Visible Skies, 1931; Evidences of a Planetoid Fall in East Central Africa, 1933; The Mystery of the Star-Chains, Endogenesis of the Earth 1940; also author of numerous papers on relativity, gravitation, glacial theory, cause of drumlins, cosmogony, navigation, etc. Originated, 1918, method of observing and photographing solar eclipses from aircraft, used by U.S. Naval Observatory for total eclipse of Jan. 1925. Devised plan for emergency flood relief of Lower Mississippi which saved city of New Orleans in flood of 1927. Devised polyhedral framing system for naval and merchant vessels, airships; earthquake and wind storm resisting buildings, bridges and other shore structures. Home:

Fern Hall Hotel, 3250 Euclid Av., Cleve. Died Mar. 20, 1952; buried Wheatland, Mich.

MILLS, CHARLES WILSON, M.D.; b. South Williamstown, Mass., Sept. 1, 1879; s. Charles A. and Clara J. (Paige) M.; B.A., Williams Coll., 1902; M.D., Johns Hopkins, 1908; m. Mary Durborow, Apr. 19, 1911; children—Ruth Durborow, Margaret Abbot (Mrs. R. Y. McElroy), Charles W. Med. house officer Johns Hopkins Hosp., Baltimore, Md., 1908-09; asso. physician Loomis (N.Y.) Sanatorium, 1910-17; acting med. dir. Cragmor Sanatorium, Colorado Springs, Colo., 1917-18; in practice at Tucson, Ariz., since 1920; one of organizers Desert Sanatorium of Southern Ariz.; medical staff, Tucson Medical Center, and St. Mary's Hospital. Served in Vol. Med. Service Corps, World War I; member Examining Bd., Selective Service, Colorado Springs; chmn. med. advisory board, Selective Service, Arizona, 1940-45. Member of Committee of Expert Consultants on Dust Diseases, Arizona Industrial Commission, 1943-45. Fellow Am. Coll. Physicians; member Am. Clinical and Climatological Association, Nat. Tuberculosis Assn. (dir.-at-large 1933-36), Trudeau Soc., Am. Coll of Chest Physicians, Southwestern Medical Association, A.M.A., Arizona State and Pima County medical societies, Alpha Omega Alpha, Phi Beta Kappa, Nu Sigma Nu, Phi Gamma Delta. Episcopalian. Contbr. of many papers on tuberculosis and other subjects to med. jours. Home: El Encanto Estates, Tucson. Office: 123 S. Stone Av., Tucson, Ariz. Died Sep. 29, 1945.

MILLS, HIRAM FRANCIS, hydraulic engr.; b. Bangor, Me., Nov. 1, 1836; s. Preserved B. and Jane (Lunt) M.; ed. pub. schs., Bangor, Me.; C.E., Rensselaer Poly. Inst., 1856; (hon. A.M., Harvard, 1889); m. Elizabeth Worcester, Oct. 8, 1873. Asst. engr. Bergen Tunnel, 1858, Brooklyn Water Works, 1859; water measurements, Cohoes, N.Y., 1859; with J. B. Francis, C.E., Lowell, Mass., 1860-63; on important ry. and hydraulic work until 1867 (Hoosac tunnel, Deerfield dam, water power on Penobscot River at Bangor, etc.); hydraulic engr., Boston, 1867-9; chief engr. Essex Co., controlling water power of Merrimac River at Lawrence, 1869—; cons. engr. on hydraulic work in 10 states and Mexico, 1868—; consulting engr. of Proprs. Locks and Canals on Merrimac River at Lowell, 1893, and chief engr. same, 1894-1917. Has had charge of investigations of Mass. State Bd. Health on purification of water supplies and of sewage by filtration and otherwise, 1886-1914; designed and built Lawrence City filter, 1892-3; chmn. com. state bd. in originating and designing met. sewerage system and met. water supply; cons. engr. Wachusett dam and reservoir. Mem. Mass. State Bd. Health and chmn. com. on water supply and sewerage, 1886-1914; cons. engr. Met. Water and Sewerage Bd., 1901—. Fellow Am. Acad. Arts and Sciences. Mem. corp. Mass. Inst. Technology, 1885—. Mem. New Jerusalem Ch. Republican. Home: Hingham, Mass. Died Oct. 4, 1921.

MILLS, JAMES EDWARD, chemist; b. Winnsboro, S.C., Apr. 30, 1876; s. William Wilson and Sarah Edith Ann (Smith) M.; A.B., Davidson (N.C.) Coll., 1896, A.M., 1900; Ph.D., U. N.C., 1901; D.Sc., U. S.C., 1935; studied U. Berlin, 1904-05; m. Mary Gregory Hume, Oct. 15, 1921. Asst. in chem. N.C., 1900-01, instr., 1901-03, asso. prof., 1904-10; lectr. chemistry, 1911-13, prof., 1913-21, U. S.C.; tech. dir. research and development work, Chemical Warfare Serv., Edgewood Arsenal, 1921-24; chief chem. div., same, 1924-29; chmn. div. chemistry and chem. tech., Nat. Research Council, 1929-30; prof. chemistry U. S.C., 1930-34; chief chemist Sonoco Products Co., 1934-47, dir. chem. research, 1947-50. Recipient Herty Award, 1944. Commd. capt., Engr. O.R.C., Sept. 4, 1917; capt. Chem. Warfare Service; maj., Oct. 16, 1918; served as engr. officer, 1st Gas Regt. (30th Engrs.), A.E.F.; lt. col. C.W. Res., Mar. 14, 1925; ret. Apr. 1940. Fellow N.Y. Acad. Sci., A.A.A.S.; mem. Am. Inst. Chemists, S.C. Acad. Sci., Am. Chem. Soc., Am. Electrochem. Soc., Kappa Sigma, Phi Beta Kappa, Sigma Xi. Presbyn. Contbr. sci. jours. Address: 1212 Home Av., Hartsville, S.C. Died Aug. 12, 1950; buried Camden, S.C.

MILLS, JOHN, engineer; b. Morgan Park, Ill., Apr. 13, 1880; s. John and Sarah Elizabeth (Ten Broeke) M.; A.B., U. of Chicago, 1901; A.M., U. of Neb., 1904; B.S., Mass. Inst. of Tech., 1909; m. Emma Gardner Moore, June 1, 1909; children—John, Marion, Theodora Ten Broeke. Fellow in physics, U. of Chicago, 1901-02, U. of Neb., 1902-03; instr. physics, Western Reserve U., 1903-07, Mass. Inst. Tech., 1907-09; prof. physics, Colo. Coll., 1909-11; with engring. dept. Am. Telephone & Telegraph Co., 1911-15; with research dept. Western Electric Co., 1915-21, asst. personnel dir., 1921-23, personnel dir., 1923-24; dir. of publ., Bell Telephone Labs., Inc., 1925-45; administrative asst., Calif. Inst. Tech. since 1946. Fellow Am. Phys. Soc., Am. Inst. Elec. Engrs., Institute Radio Engineers; mem. Phi Beta Kappa, Sigma Xi, Delta Upsilon. Author: Electricity, Sound and Light, 1907; Introduction to Thermodynamics, 1909; Alternating Currents, 1911; Radio-Communication, 1917; Realities of Modern Science, 1919; Within the Atom, 1921; Letters of a Radio Engineer to His Son, 1922; Magic of Communication, 1923; Signals and Speech in Electrical Communication, 1934; A Fugue in Cycles and Bels, 1935; Electronics, Today and Tomorrow, 1944; The Engineer in Society, 1946. Inventor of several methods for wire and radio-telephony; conceived and supervised design of Bell Telephone Exhibits at the world's fairs in Chicago, 1933; San Diego, 1935; Dallas, 1936; San Francisco, 1939-40; and New York, 1939-40. Home: 300 Susquehanna Rd., Rochester 10, N.Y. Died June 14, 1948.

MILLS, ROBERT, architect, engr.; b. Charleston, S.C., Aug. 12, 1781; s. William and Anne (Taylor) M.; attended Coll. of Charleston; m. Eliza Smith, 1808, 4 children including Sarah, Mary. Studied under Thomas Jefferson; designed Congregational Ch. (the "circular ch."), 1804; supervised erection Bank of Phila.; adopted for 1st time in Am. the auditorium type of plan suited for preaching a service; designed Washington Hall, 1809; rebuilt for municipal offices some wings of Old State House (Independence Hall, Phila.), 1812; designed Brockenbrough house in Richmond, Va. which became "White House of Confederacy"; designed important pub. monument to Washington in Balt., 1814; made pres., chief engr. Balt. Waterworks Co.; returned to Charleston, 1820, became mem. Bd. Pub. Works; pub. bldgs. erected by him (on plans either made or revised by him) in Charleston include: fire-proof record bldg., begun 1822, State Hosp. for Insane at Columbia, S.C.; designed Potomac Bridge, circa 1830; apptd. by Fed. govt. as "architect of public bldgs.," 1836-51, designed Treasury, Patent Office, Post Office, Washington, D.C.; main archtl. achievement was victory in competition for design of Washington Monument, at capital, completed in 1884; mem. Soc. of Artists organized in Phila., 1810, 1st sec. Author: Treatise on Inland Navigation, 1820; Guide to the Capitol of the U.S., 1832 (appeared 1834). Died Mar. 3, 1855.

MILLSPAUGH, CHARLES FREDERICK, botanist; b. Ithaca, N.Y., June 20, 1854; s. John Hill (artist) and Marion E. (Cornell) M.; studied Cornell, 1872-73; M.D., New York Homoe. Med. Coll., 1881; m. Mary Louisa Spaulding, Sept. 19, 1877 (died 1907); m. 2d, Clara Isobel Mitchell, 1910. Practicing phys., Binghamton, N.Y., 1881-90, Waverly, N.Y., 1890-91; botanist, W.Va. Univ., 1891-93; curator dept. botany, Field Mus. of Natural History, Chicago, 1894—; prof. med. botany, Chicago Homoe. Med. Coll., 1897—; professorial lecturer econ. botany, U. of Chicago, 1895—. Mem. Pan-Am. Com. on Med. Botany; hon. mem. N.Y. Homoe. Med. Soc., Faculty of Medicine Mexico, Faculty of Medicine Brazil, Binghamton Acad. Science; fellow Am. Acad. Arts and Sciences. Explored in Mexico, 1887, 1894, 1898, 1900, West Indies, 1887, 1894, 1898, 1900, Brazil, 1888, a number of uninhabited Bahamian islets, 1904, 05, 07, 11, in interest bot. science; spl. field of botanic work, The Antillean region. Editor Homoeopathic Recorder, 1890-92. Author: American Medical Plants (illustrated), 1887; Weeds of West Virginia, 1892; Flora of West Virginia, 1892; Plantae Utowanae; Flora of St. Croix; Flora Sand Keys of Florida; Praenunciae Bahamenses; Plantae Yucatanae; Flora of West Virginia, 1891, 95, 1913; revised and enlarged MacIlvaine's "1,000 American Fungi," 1911. Home: Chicago, Ill. Died Sept. 16, 1923.

MILLSPAUGH, WILLIAM HULSE, mfr.; b. Branchport, N.Y., Dec. 12, 1868; s. Levi and Sarah (White) M.; Keuk a (N.Y.) Coll., 1887-90; m. Carrie Sliger, April 17, 1900 (died Feb. 19, 1949); 1 dau., Elizabeth (Mrs. Thomas Darlington), (died Nov. 28, 1946). Mech. engr., Salem, O., 1895; organizer Sandusky Foundry & Machine Co., mfg. large bronze tubular products, pres. until sold co., 1929, retaining fgn. bus., organized Millspaugh, Ltd., Sheffield, Eng., until co. was sold by him, April 1946; pres., dir. Centrifugal Steel, Inc.; pres., dir. The Hulse Investment Co. (both Sandusky, O.). Patented, developed suction rolls and paper-making devices, establishing, new world records for speed and prodn. paper; also patented and developed centrifugal casting of metals, which processes are licensed to large firms and to U.S. Govt. Recipient 2d Edward Langstreth Medal, Franklin Inst., outstanding contributions, art paper making, 1949. Mem. Am. Soc. M.E., Tech. Assn. Am., Pulp and Paper Assn. (gold medalist), Cleve. Engring. Soc., U.S. Mil. Engrs., Instn. Mech. Engrs. (London, Eng.), Army Ordnance Assn. Mason. Clubs: Castalia (O.) Trout; Union (Cleve.); Engineers' of N.Y. Home: 519 Wayne St. Address: P.O. Box 547, Sandusky, O. Died Apr. 1959.

MILLWARD, RUSSELL HASTINGS, explorer; b. Cincinnati, O., Apr. 5, 1877; s. Capt. Frank and Margaret Ann (Jones) M.; student Rockville (Md.) Acad., 1889-93, Emerson Inst., Washington, D.C., 1893-94, Columbia, 1901-02; m. Edna P. Boyden, Aug. 27, 1914; 1 dau., Edna Boyden. Assisted in survey of Yavapai County, Ariz., 1902-03; in charge exploring expdns. in Africa and S. America, 1903-06; Am. v-consul gen., Boma, Congo Free State, 1906-07; v-consul Durban, Natal, Jan.-Aug. 1907, Tampico, Mexico, 1907-08; in charge various exploring expdns. since 1908; holder of world's record in distance covered on foot, traveling over 20,000 miles in uncharted portions of Africa, S. and Central America and Mexico; completed charting, Dept. of Peten and Ty. of Quintana Roo, Yucatan, July 1913. Charted 1st Am. Airway, coast to coast, known as the Woodrow Wilson Airway, 1918. Dir., instr. Free Sch. Printing, Occupational Therapy; founder, Nat. Pet Therapy. Made many important contbns. in zoology, archaeology and ethnology, to museums and scientific instns. Possessor 57 decorations, hereditary and earned. Fellow Royal Geog. Soc., Royal Soc. Arts, London; mem. Am. Mus. Nat. Hist. (life), Am. Geog. Soc., N.Y. Acad. Sciences, Am. Genetic Assn., New York Zool. Soc. (life corr.), Mil. Order Loyal Legion, Army and Navy League of U.S., Sigma Chi, Lambda Epsilon, etc. Clubs: Nat. Press, Army and Navy (Washington, D.C.); Explorers, Aero of America, etc. Contbr. numerous articles to Am. and foreign mags. and newspapers. Address: 3100 Connecticut Av., Washington 8 DC

MINER, HARIAN SHERMAN, chemist; b. Chester, Vt., June 29, 1864; s. John Jay and Lurena Betsey (Hoar) M.; grad. Vt. Acad., Saxton's River, 1884; B.S., Lehigh U., Pa., 1888, Sc.D., 1922; Sc.D., U. of Pa., 1919; m. Emma Estelle Mayers, Nov. 11, 1891; children—Lurena C., Dorothy (dec.), Harlan (dec.). Asst. chemist, 1888-98, chief chemist, 1898—, Welsbach Co., Gloucester. Gold medal and diploma, St. Louis Expn., 1904. Mem. Bd. Health, Gloucester, 25 yrs. (pres. 23 yrs.); trustee Pennington Sem., N.J., 10 yrs.; hon. alumni trustee Lehigh U. 3 yrs. Asso. mem. Naval Cons. Bd. of U.S., 1917. Republican. Methodist. Home: Gloucester, N.J. Deceased.

MINER, JACK, naturalist, author; b. Dover Center, O., Apr. 10, 1865; s. John and Anne (Broadwell) M.; ed. pub. schs. 2 mos.; m. Laona Wigle, of Kingsville, Ont., Can., 1888; children—Carl (dec.), Pearl (dec.), Manly Forest, William Edward, Jasper Wilson. Owner of Jack Miner Bird Sanctuary, Kingsville, where thousands of ducks, geese and swans are fed during migration periods, spring and fall; known as "the man who made the wild geese tame"; lectures widely, the proceeds being applied in buying food for birds at his sanctuary. The first person to catch and tag wild geese. Hon. pres. several Izaak Walton leagues; founder Essex County Wild Life Assn. (now known as the Jack Miner Wild Life League); nat. dir. Izaak Walton League America; hon. pres. Hamilton Bird Protective Assn.; mem. advisory bd. of Quetico-Superior Forest Res.; mem. conservation advisory bd., Outdoor Life (mag.). Author: Jack Miner and the Birds, 1924; Jack Miner on Current Topics, 1928. Home: Kingsville, Ont., Can.

MINNAERT, MARCEL GILLES JOZEF, astrophysicist; b. Bruges, Belgium, Feb. 12, 1893; s. Jozef and Jozefina (van Overberge) M.; D.Biology, U. Ghent, 1914; D.Math. and Physics, U. Utrecht, 1925; Hon. Dr., univs. Heidelberg and Moscow; m. Marla Bourgonje Coelingh, Dec. 20, 1929; children—Koenraad, Boudewijn. Lectr., U. Ghent, 1916-18; observer U. Utrecht, 1920-37, prof. astronomy, dir. obs., 1937-63; ret. Active Flemish nat. movement, action against nuclear weapons, action against Viet Nam war. Recipient Gold medal Royal Astron. Soc. London, 1947, Bruce medal Astron. Soc. Pacific, 1951, Janssen medal Soc. Astronomique de France, 1966. Order du Merite, Societe pour a Recherche et l'Invention, 1964. Mem. Acad. Amsterdam; fgn. mem. acads. Brussels Boston, Wash., Coimbra, Uppsala, Academia Leopoldina in Halle, Academia d Lincel in Rome. Contbr. articles to Kuiper, The Solar System, Photometric Atlas of the Solar Spectrum. Author: De Natuurkunde van 't Vrije Veld, 3 vols (English trans. of 1st part; Light and Color), 1937, 39, 40; Practical Exercises in Elementary Astronomy, 1968. Research and publs. on solar physics, other astrophys. subjects, particularly Fraunhofer lines. Home: Utrecht Netherlands Died Oct. 26, 1970.

MINNICH, DWIGHT ELMER, zoologist; b. Hutchinson, Kan., Jan. 28, 1890; s. Harvey C. and Bertha Beatrice (Minnich) M.; A.B. magna cum laude, Miami U., Oxford, O., 1910, D.Sc., 1946; Ph.D., Harvard, 1917; m. Helen Benton, Dec. 30, 1922; children—Dwight Benton, Conrad Harvey. Austin teaching fellow Harvard, 1916-17, Parker traveling fellow, 1917-18; instr. in zoology Syracuse U., 1919-20; with U. Minn., 1920-58, instr. in zool., asst. and asso. prof., prof., 1929-58, chmn. dept., 1930—. Trustee Mt. Desert Island Biol. Lab., pres., 1946-50. Fellow John Simon Guggenheim Meml. Found., 1928-29. Served as 2d lt. Sanitary Corps, U.S. Army, World War I. Fellow A.A.A.S., Entomol. Soc. Am.; mem. Am. Soc. Zoologists (sec. 1924-30, v.p. 1930-31, rep. on div. biology and agr. NRC, 1941-44, pres. 1946), Am. Soc. Naturalists, Sigma Xi, Phi Beta Kappa, Gamma Alpha, Delta Upsilon. Contbr. papers, chiefly on physiology of behavior of lower animals, to zool. jours. Home: 1415 E. River Rd., Mpls. Died Sept. 4, 1965.

MINOT, CHARLES SEDGWICK, anatomist; b. W. Roxbury, Boston, Mass., Dec. 23, 1852; s. William and Katherine (Sedgwick) M.; B.S., Mass. Inst. Tech., 1872; univs. of Leipzig, Paris and Würzburg, 1873-76; S.D., Harvard, 1878; (LL.D., Yale U., 1899, U. of Toronto, 1904, St. Andrew's U., Scotland, 1911; Sc.D., Oxford U., 1902); m. Lucy Fosdick, June 1, 1889. Lecturer on embryology and instr. oral pathology and surgery, 1880-83, instr. histology and embryology, 1883-87, asst. prof., 1887-92, prof., 1892-1905, James Stillman prof. comparative anatomy, 1905, dir. of Anat. Labs., 1912, Harvard Med. School. Harvard exchange professor at univs. of Berlin and Jena, 1912-13. Invented 2 forms of automatic microtomes. Fellow A.A.A.S. (gen. sec. 1885, pres. 1900), Am. Acad. Arts and Sciences.

Author: Bibliography of Vertebrate Embryology, 1893; A Laboratory Text-Book of Embryology, 1903, 2d edit., 1910; Age, Growth and Death, 1908; Die Methode der Wissenschaft, 1913; Moderne Probleme des Biologie, 1913 (also translated into English). Died Nov. 19, 1914.

MINOT, GEORGE RICHARDS, (mi'not), physician; b. Boston, Mass., Dec. 2, 1885; s. James Jackson and Elizabeth (Whitney) M.; A.B., Harvard, 1908, M.D., 1912, S.D. (hon.), 1928; m. Marian Linzee Weld, June 29, 1915; children—Marian Linzee, Elizabeth Whitney, Charles Sedgwick. House officer Mass. Gen. Hosp., Boston, 1912-13; asst. resident physician Johns Hopkins Hosp., 1913-14; asst. in medicine and research fellow Physiol. Lab., Johns Hopkins Med. Sch., 1914-15; mem. staff, Mass. Gen. Hosp., 1915-23, now mem. bd. of consultation; asso. in medicine, Peter Bent Brigham Hosp., 1923-28, now cons. physician; chief of med. service Collis P. Huntington Memorial Hospital, 1923-28; professor medicine, Harvard, 1928-48. Visiting physician, Boston City Hosp., 1928;-dir. Thorndike Memorial Lab. (Harvard) of Boston City Hosp. to 1948, consultant physician since 1948. Served as contract surgeon several weeks, U.S. Army, 1917, 18. Hon. fellow Royal Coll. Physicians, Edinburgh, Royal Coll. Physicians (London), N.Y. Acad. Medicine, Inst. of Medicine of Chicago, Royal Soc. of Medicine, London; v.p. étranger Société Française d'Hematologie, 1938-39; fellow Am. Philos. Soc., Phila., Am. Coll. Physicians; mem. A.M.A., Assn. Am. Physicians (pres. 1937-38), Am. Soc. Clin. Investigation, Am. Acad. Arts and Sciences, American Clin. and Climatol. Assn. (pres. 1932-33), Nat. Acad. Sciences, Med. Library Assn. Am. (v.p. 1938-39), Phi Beta Kappa, Alpha Omega Alpha, Sigma Chi; hon. mem. Royal Acad. Med. (Belgium) since 1939; hon. mem. Kaiserlich Leopold Caroline Deutsche Akademie der Naturforscher (Halle), Society Biol. Chemists (India), Finland Soc. of Internal Medicine (Helsingfors). Awarded Kober gold medal, Assn. Am. Physicians, 1928; Charles Mickle fellowship, Univ. of Toronto, 1928; Cameron prize, University of Edinburgh, 1930; gold medal, Nat. Inst. Social Sciences, 1930; gold medal and award, Popular Science Monthly, 1930; Moxon medal, Royal Coll. Physicians, London, 1933; John Scott medal of City of Phila., 1933; gold medal of Humane Soc. of Mass., 1935; awarded, jointly with Wm. P. Murphy and George H. Whipple, the Nobel prize in medicine for 1934, for work on liver treatment of the anemias; scroll award of Associated Grocery Mfrs. of America, 1936. Gordon Wilson lecturer and medalist Am. Clin. and Climatol. Assn., 1939. Trustee Brookline (Mass.) Public Library since 1941. Unitarian. Author: Pathological Physiology and Clinical Description of the Anemias (with William B. Castle), 1936. Contbr. about 160 papers, chiefly on the blood. Discovered, in 1926, the curative effect of liver on pernicious anemia. Address: 311 Beacon St., Boston; or Thorndike Memorial Lab., Boston City Hosp., Boston, Mass. Died Feb. 25, 1950.

MINTO, WALTER, mathematician; b. Cowden Knowes, Merse, Scotland, Dec. 5, 1753; grad. U. Edinburgh (Scotland); LL.D. (hon.), U. Aberdeen, 1787; m. Mary Skelton. Wrote Researches into Some Parts of the Theory of the Planets, 1783; came to Am., 1786; became prin. Erasmus Hall, Flatbush, L.I., N.Y.; became prof. mathematics and natural philosophy Coll. of N.J. (now Princeton), 1787, treas. coll. Author: Inaugural Oration on the Progress and Importance of the Mathematical Sciences, 1788. Died Princeton, N.J., Oct. 21, 1796; buried Princeton Cemetery.

MISER, HUGH DINSMORE, geologist; b. Pea Ridge, Ark., Dec. 18, 1884; s. Jordan Stanford and Eliza Caroline (Webb) M.; A.B., University of Arkansas, 1908, A.M., 1912, Doctor of Laws, 1949; m. Mary Kate Goddard, Sept. 21, 1910 (dec. 1963); d., Mrs. Catherine M. Kayser. Joined U.S. Geol. Survey as field asst., 1907, jr. geologist, 1911, asst. geologist, 1912, asso. geologist, 1913-18, geologist, 1919-54, in charge sect. areal geology, 1927, regional geologist for eastern United States, 1942; chief, fuels sect., 1928-47, staff geol., 1947-54, scientific staff assistant Office of Dir., 1955-69; cons. geologist Ark. Geol. and Conservation Commission, 1959-69; geologist Ark. Geological Survey, 1907-10; geologist Tenn. Geol. Survey, 1912 and 1917; state geologist of Tennessee, 1926; acting prof. geology, U. of Ark., and state geologist of Arkansas, 1920. Made investigation of manganese deposits in U.S. during World Wars I and II; author first multicolored geologic map of Okla., 1926, 2d, 1954; geologist to engring. party that explored and mapped San Juan Canyon, Utah, 1921. Dir. Sibley Memorial Hosp., (1925-44; chmn. bd. 1936-37). Recipient Distinguished Service Medal, U.S. Dept. Interior 1955. Mem. Am. Assn. Petroleum Geologists (hon. mem. 1948), Soc. Econ., Geologists, Geol. Soc. Am., Geol. Soc. Washington (pres. 1938), Washington (v.p. 1939), Tenn. acads. scis., Mineral Soc. Am., N.M. (hon.), Tulsa (hon.), Oklahoma City (hon.) geol. socs., Okla. Mineral and Gem Soc. (hon.), Okla. Acad. Sci., Sigma Gamma Epsilon (hon.). Donated collection of 5700 rare and select Ark. quartz crystals to U. Ark. Mus., 1954. Home: Washington DC Died Aug. 1, 1969

MITCHEL, ORMSBY MACKNIGHT, astronomer, army officer; b. Morganfield, Ky., July 28, 1809; s. John and Elizabeth (MacAlister) M.; grad. U.S. Mil. Acad., 1829; LL.D. (hon.), Harvard, 1851, Washington Coll., 1853, Hamilton Coll., 1856; m. Louisa (Clark) Trask, 1831. Asst. prof. mathematics U.S. Mil. Acad., 1829; chief engr. Rittle Miami R.R., 1836-37; prof. mathematics, philosophy, astronomy Cincinnati Coll., 1836-46; published mag. Sidereal Messenger, 1846-1848; adj. gen. Ohio, 1848; inventor chronograph, 1848; chief engr. Ohio & Miss. R.R., 1848-53; dir., largely responsible for erection Cincinnati Observatory; largely responsible for erecting 2d largest telescope, and largest on Western continent under auspices of Cincinnati Astron. Soc., 1845; made approximately 50,000 observations of faint stars between 1854-59; discovered the duplicity of stars (e.g. Antares); dir. Dudley Observatory, Albany, N.Y., 1859; apptd. brig. gen. U.S. Volunteers, 1861; assigned to command Dept. of Ohio; brevetted maj. gen. volunteers, 1862; surprised and captured Huntsville, Ala. without firing a gun, thus obtained control of Memphis & Charleston R.R.; promoted maj. gen. volunteers; transferred to command Dept. of South and X Army Corps, Sept. 17, 1862. Author: Planetary and Stellar Worlds, 1848; Popular Astronomy, 1860. Died Beaufort, S.C., Oct. 30, 1862.

MITCHELL, ALLAN CHARLES GRAY, physicist; b. Houston, Tex., Oct. 1, 1902; s. Samuel Alfred and Milly Gray (Dumble) M.; B.S., U. of Va., 1923, M.S., 1924; Ph.D., California Institute of Technology, 1927; student universities of Munich and Göttingen, 1927-28; m. Georgianna Peck Fales, Sept. 8, 1926; children—Georgianna (Mrs. L. A. Rivlin), Priscilla. Asst., U. Va., 1920-24; teaching fellow, Calif. Inst. of Tech., 1924-27; fellow, Bartol Research Foundation, 1928-31; asst. prof. of physics, New York U., 1931-34, asso. prof. and chmn. dept., 1934-38; prof. of physics and head dept., Ind. U., since 1938. Research assoc., Mass. Inst. Tech., 1940, U. of Chicago, 1942; official investigator Office of Scientific Research and Development, Indiana U., 1942-44, physicist Applied Physics Lab., Johns Hopkins University, 1944-46; mem. Project Vista, Cal. Inst. Tech., 1951; bd. govs. Argonne Nat. Lab., 1949-52; now dir. Midwestern U. Research Assn., past pres. Fellow Am. Phys. Soc. (council 1943-47), A.A.A.S., Ind. Acad. Sciences; mem. Beta Theta Pi, Phi Beta Kappa, Sigma Xi, Alpha Chi Sigma. Epis. Author: Resonance Radiation and Excited Atoms (with M. W. Zemansky), 1934; chapters in Beta and Gamma Ray Spectroscopy, 1955. Asso. editor Jour. Chem. Physics, 1932-34, Phys. Review, 1941-44. Contbr. scientific articles to jours. Research in nuclear physics; chemical physics. Address: Physics Dept., Indiana Univ., Bloomington, Ind. Died Nov. 7, 1963.

MITCHELL, DAVID RAY, consulting engineer; b. Bells Landing, Pa., June 12, 1898; s. John Francis and Gertrude (Johnson) M.; B.S. in Mining Engring., Pa. State Coll., 1924, M.S., 1927; E.M., U. of Ill., 1931; m. Lois Rishell, Mar. 12, 1925; children—David Ray, Mary Patricia. Worked in coal and clay mines of Pa., 1917-27; prof. mining and metall. engring. U. of Ill., 1927-38; chmn. div. of mineral engring., Pa. State Univ., 1938-60, past associate dean college of mineral industries, dean College Mineral Industries, 1960-63; consultant mining engineer, 1963-72. Served as private, Signal Corps, U.S. Army, 1918-19. Certified fire boss and mine foreman, Pa.; professional engr., Pa. Hon. mem. Mark Twain and Eugene Field socs. Mem. Am. Inst. Mining Engrs. (sec., coal div.), Am. Mining Congress, Coal Mining Inst. Am. Ill. Mining Inst., Sigma Xi, Sigma Gamma Epsilon. Methodist. Editor and co-author: Coal Preparation, 1943, 50. Contbr. numerous tech. papers on mining and mineral preparation to professional publs. Home: State College PA Died Sept. 22, 1972.

MITCHELL, ELISHA, geologist, botanist; b. Washington, Conn., Aug. 19, 1793; s. Abner and Phoebe (Eliot) M.; grad. Yale, 1813; attended Andover Theol. Sem., 1817-18; D.D. (hon.), U. Ala., 1838; m. Maria Sybil North, Nov. 19, 1819, 7 children. Tutor, Yale, 1816-17; prof. mathematics and natural philosophy, U. N.C., 1818-25, prof. chemistry, mineralogy and geology, 1825-57; licensed to preach, 1817; ordained to ministry Presbyn. Ch., 1821; made geol. and bot. excursions throughout N.C.; contbd. articles to Am. Journal of Sci., also other publs.; 1st to measure height of highest mountain in U.S. East of Rockies, Black Mountain (now called Mitchell's Peak), N.C. Author: Elements of Geology, 1842. Killed by fall during storm while exploring Black Mountain, June 27, 1857; buried Asheville, N.C.; reinterred top of Black Mountain, 1858.

MITCHELL, GEORGE, mining engr.; b. Swansea, Wales, Sept. 28, 1864; s. George and Ann (Matthews) M.; grad. Morgan Chem. Sch., Swansea; m. Mary Woodwell, of Swansea, 1886; children—Edith (dec.), Phillipa, Alvin, George, Mazie, Harry, Consueulla. Learned practical operations of smelting and metallurgy in various works at Swansea; came to America, 1888; assisted in erection and management Helena Smelter, Trinidad, Colo., and later with Nat. Smelting & Refining Co., Allegheny, Pa., asst. supt. Boston & Mont. Copper & Silver Mining & Smelting Co., 1890-95; in charge of W.A. Clark's smelting works, Jerome, Ariz., 1895-99; organized, 1899, Cobre Grande Copper Co., later consol. with Greene Consolidated Copper Co., of which became gen. mgr. Home: Los Angeles, Calif. *

MITCHELL, HENRY, engr.; b. Nantucket, Mass., Sept. 16, 1830; s. William M. (astronomer); ed. private schools (A. M., Harvard, 1867); asst. to commrs. on harbor encroachments of New York, 1859; consulting engr. U.S. commn. on Boston harbor; later mem. of commn., now mem. advisory council, td bd. harbor commrs. of Boston. Has been prof. Am. Inst. of Technology, mem. U.S. advisory councils on harbors of Portland, Me., Providence, R.I., Norfolk and Portsmouth, Va., and Phila.; in 1874 apptd. by President Grant to represent Coast and Geodetic Survey in bd. of engrs. for improvement of mouth of Mississippi; later mem. Mississippi River commn. Mem. Nat. Acad. Sciences; fellow Am. Acad. of Sciences of Boston. Home: Nantucket, Mass. Died 1902.

MITCHELL, HUGH CHESTER, mathematician; b. Jackson County, Tex., Apr. 15, 1877; s. Isaac Newton and Callista (Stapp) M.; student St. Mary's Coll., San Antonio; C.E., U. Notre Dame, Ind., 1895, B.S., 1898; post-grad. study, Cath. U. Am.; m. Agnes V. Marr, Sept. 29, 1903 (died 1947); children—Mrs. Thomas Taylor Neill, Hugh Chester. Asso. with U.S. Coast and Geodetic Survey, 1898; duty, P.R., Chesapeake Bay, La.; astron. survey, Philippines, 1900-03; mathematician Gen. Office, Washington, 1903-11; presented Peary's North Pole data to Congress, 1911; in charge Hayford's 2d investigation of figure and size of earth, and of precise geodetic topog. survey of Cin.; pvt. engring. practice, 1913-16; ranching in Tex., 1916-20; reentered Coast and Geodetic Survey, 1921, becoming prin. mathematician; ret. from active service, Dec. 1, 1945; instr. in astronomy Cath. U. Am., 1927-35. Chmn. spl. coms. Fed. Bd. Surveys and Maps on Plane Coordinates and Definitions on Surveying and Mapping Terms. Club: Cosmos. Catholic. Author: Triangulation Along the East Coast of Florida, and on the Florida Keys, 1911; wrote (with C. R. Duvall) The Geographic Position of Camp Jesup, and the Reduction of the Observations of R. E. Peary in the Vicinity of the North Pole, X Congresso Internazionale Geografia, Rome, 1913; Topographic Survey of Cincinnati, 1914; California-Oregon Arc of Precise Triangulation, 1922; Geodetic Control for City Surveys, 1923; Triangulation in Maryland, 1925; Triangulation in Hawaii, 1929; First-order Triangulation in Texas, 1935; First and Second-order Triangulation in California, 1936; The State Coordinate Systems (a manual for surveyors), 1945; Definitions of Terms Used in Geodetic and Other Surveys, 1945; Economy of Controlled Survey, Military Engineer, 1954; Peary at the North Pole, 1959. Mem. Am. Geophys. Union, Am. Polar Soc. Mem. Nat. Geog. Soc. com. of experts which determined that Comdr. R. E. Byrd, U.S. Navy, reached the North Pole by airplane, 1926, and South Pole, 1930. Home: 3038 Newark St., Washington 8. Died Nov. 20, 1956; buried Mt. Olivet Cemetery, Washington.

MITCHELL, JAMES ALFRED, prof. geology, mineralogy and physics Mount St. Mary's Coll., Emmitsburg, Md., lecturer on natural science, St. Joseph's Acad., same place; s. M. and Jane (Petrie) M.; grad. Royal School of Mines, England; studied astronomy and meteorology at Lord Ross's Observatory, Birr Castle, Ireland; carried on further researches in geology and chemistry at Harvard, and in paleontology at Johns Hopkins; (A.M., Mt. St. Mary's Coll., 1888; Ph.D., Niagara Univ., 1894); m. Margaret J. Willson, 1889. Worked on reports for State Geol. Survey and U.S. Weather Bureau; 1st to discover fossilferous footprints in the Newark system of the Jura Trias in Maryland. Mem. of the Washington Acad. Sciences; mem. of the faculty of Mt. St. Mary's Coll. for past 13 yrs. Home: Emmitsburg, Md. Died 1902.

MITCHELL, JOHN, physician, map maker; probably born Brit. Isles; ed. U. Edinburgh (Scotland). Came to Va., 1725; justice of peace Middlesex County (Va.), 1738; practiced medicine in Va., circa 1725-46; went to Eng., 1746; elected fellow Royal Soc., 1747; made Map of the British & French Dominions in North America with the Roads, Distances, Limits, and Extent of the Settlements, published, London, Eng., 1755 (most important map in Am. history, used in various treaties, border adjustments up to 1932, basis for Webster Ashburton Treaty, 1842, Wis.-Mich. boundary dispute, 1926, others). His method of treating yellow fever thought to have saved more than 6,000 lives in Phila. during epidemic of 1793. Died, 1768.

MITCHELL, JOHN, congressman; b. nr. Newport, Pa., Mar. 8, 1781; attended common schs. Moved to Bellefonte, Pa., 1800, clk. in ironworks; elected sheriff Centre County (Pa.), 1818; engr., surveyor; laid out Centre and Kishacoquillas Turnpike, 1821; constructed numerous turnpikes in Pa.; mem. Pa. Ho. of Reps., 1822-23; mem. U.S. Ho. of Reps. (Democrat) from Pa., 19th-20th congresses, 1825-29; surveyor of proposed canal routes between Susquehanna and Potomac rivers, 1826; engr. Erie Canal extension, 1827; canal commr. Pa., 1829; Dem. presdl. elector, 1826; moved to Bridgewater, Pa., 1842, engaged in civil engring., iron mfg.; mem. Canal Survey Commn., 1845-49. Died Bridgewater, Aug. 3, 1849; buried Old Beaver Cemetery, Bridgewater.

MITCHELL, JOHN KEARSLEY, physician, chemist; b. Shepherdstown, Jefferson County, Va. (now W.Va.), May 12, 1793; s. Alexander and Elizabeth (Kearsly) M.;

grad. U. Edinburgh (Scotland); M.A., U. Pa., 1819; m. Sarah Matilda Henry, 1822, 9 children including Silas Weir. Ship's surgeon on voyages to China and East Indies, 1819-21; prof. medicine and physiology Phila. Med. Inst., 1824; lectr. chemistry Franklin Inst., 1833-38; prof. medicine Jefferson Med. Coll., Phila., 1841-58. Author: Indecision, a Tale of the Far West and Other Poems, 1839; On the Cryptogamous Origin of Malarious and Epidemical Fevers, 1849. Died Phila., Apr. 4, 1858.

MITCHELL, JOHN MCKENNEY, physician; ednl. dir.; b. Centreville, Md., Sept. 23, 1895; s. James Archibald and Eleanor Lux (McKenney) M.; A.B., Trinity Coll., 1920, Sc.D. (hon.), 1949; M.D. cum laude, Yale, 1924; LL.D. (hon.), Temple U., 1951; Sc.D., Dickinson Coll., 1953, Union U., 1958; m. Eleanor A. Janeway, Sept. 12, 1925; children—James Andrew. Eleanor Janeway (Mrs. Robert A. Huggins); m. 2d, Harriet Taylor Mauck, September 16, 1961. Intern-Resident New Haven Hosp., 1924-27; practice, specializing in pediatrics, Phila., 1927-42; faculty, sch. medicine U. Pa., 1927-62, prof. pediatrics, 1952-69, dean sch. medicine, 1948-62; dir. med. edn. Bryn Mawr Hosp., Pa., 1962-66; dir. study pediatric edn. Am. Acad. Pediatric Education, Commonwealth Fund, 1949. Served as 1st lt. Inf., U.S. Army, World War I; col. M.C., A.U.S., China-Burma-India Theatre, 1942-45; col. Medical Corps. Ret. Decorated Silver Star; recipient Abraham Jacobi award Am. Med. Assn., 1964. Exec. sec. Am. Bd. of Pediatrics since 1948. Fellow A.M.A., Am. Acad. Pediatrics (recipient Clifford Grulee award 1966); mem. Am. Pediatric Soc., Soc. for Pediatric Research, Assn. Am. Med. Colls. (pres. 1958-59), adv. bd. Med. Spltys. (pres. 1956-58), Assn. Hospital Directors of Medical Education, Sigma Xi, Alpha Omega Alpha, Delta Psi, Nu Sigma Nu. Author articles med. jours. Home: Rosemont PA Died Sept. 18, 1969.

MITCHELL, MARIA, astronomer, educator; b. Nantucket Island, Mass., Aug. 1, 1818; d. William and Lydia (Coleman) Mitchell; LL.D. (hon.), Hanover Coll., 1882, Columbia, 1887. Assisted father in his chronometer ratings during her youth; apptd. librarian Town of Atheneum, Nantucket Island, Mass., 1836; discovered new comet, Oct. 1847; recipient gold medal from King of Denmark; 1st woman elected to membership Am. Acad. Arts and Scis., hon. mem., 1848, later fellow; apptd. computer Am. Ephemeric and Nautical Almanac; 1st prof. astronomy Vassar Coll., 1865-88; elected mem. Am. Philos. Soc., 1869. Died Lynn, Mass., June 28, 1889.

MITCHELL, NATHANIEL MCDONALD, mech. engr.; b. Portland, Me., July 17, 1889; s. George W. and Sarah Nancy Belle (Small) M.; grad. Thornton Acad., 1909; student U. Me. Extension Sch., 1910-11; m. Annetta Buck, Aug. 2, 1913; children—Barbara, Robert, Dorothy, Richard; m. 2d, Edna R. Fisher, Oct. 12, 1945. Machine erector Saco Petee Shops, Biddeford, Me., 1909-12; asst. supt. Androscoggin Mills, Lewiston, Me., 1912-18; mec. engr. Palmer Mills, Three Rivers, Mass., 1918-20; supt. Hill Mfg. Co., Lewiston, Me., 1920-25; gen. supt. W. Boylston Mfg. Co., Easthampton, Mass., 1925-27; pres., treas. Barnes Textile Assos., Inc., Boston, 1927—. Staff WPB, World War II; adviser European textile missions; chmn. productivity team MSA in France; lectr., cons., Eng., Norway, Sweden, Germany, France, Greece, India, Ceylon, Australia, Columbia, Brazil, Peru, Chile, Argentina, Uruguay. Served as 1st lt. inf., U.S. Army, 1918-19. Mem. Am. Soc. M.E., Am. Assn. Textile Technologists, Am. Assn. Textile Chemists and Colorists, Nat. Assn. Cotton Mfrs., Mass. Soc. Profl. Engrs. Clubs: Wamsutta (New Bedford, Mass.); Algonquin, Downtown (Boston); Pedmont (Spartanburg, S.C.); Arkwright, Engineers (N.Y.C.). Contbr. articles tech. publs. Home: 26-A Concord St., Peterborough, N.H. 03458. Died Apr. 16, 1965.

MITCHELL, O(LIVER) W(ENDELL) H(OLMES), physician; b. Lancaster, Mo., Aug. 17, 1886; s. William Francis (M.D.) and Elizabeth (Marshall) M.; M.D., U. Mo., 1908; m. Preston Settle, May 15, 1913; 1 son, Phillip Marshall. Asso. prof. bacteriol. and path., U. Mo., 1913-14; prof. bacteriol. and pub. health, Syracuse U., 1914-40, prof. pub. health 1940—; dir. post-grad. med. edn., Med. Soc. State N.Y., 1938—. Mem. A.M.A., Assn. Am. Pathols. and Bacteriols., Exptl. Biology and Medicine, Sigma Xi, Phi Kappa Phi. Conglist. Home: 428 Greenwood Pl. Office: 428 Greenwood Pl., Syracuse, N.Y. Died Dec. 20, 1948.

MITCHELL, PHILIP HENRY, physiol. chemist; b. Southbury, Conn., Dec. 13, 1883; s. Henry Painter and Phoebe (Stoddard) M.; Ph.B., Sheffield Sci. Sch. (Yale), 1904; Ph.D., Yale, 1907; m. Alice Hinman Friend, May 30, 1910; children—Margery Fuller, Edith Stoddard. Instr. physiology, Brown, 1907-11, asst. prof., 1911-20, asso. prof., 1920-26, prof., 1926-49; dir. Woods Hole Biol. Sta., U.S. Bur. Fisheries, summers, 1914-20; cons. chemist U.S. Dept. Agr., 1913-17, investigator Conn. State Bd. Fish and Game, 1923-24. Trustee Lincoln Sch., Providence, R.I.; mem. Woods Hole Marine Biol. Lab. Corp. Mem. A.A.A.S., Am. Soc. Biol. Chemists, Sigma Xi. Unitarian. Clubs: Faculty, Art, Sphinx. Author: Textbook of General Physiology for Colleges, 1923, 4th edit., 1948; Text Book of Biochemistry, 1946; also many articles relative to purine metabolism, physiology of shellfish, especially oysters, permeability of cells and tissues, chemistry of sea water. Home: 33 Cushing St., Providence, R.I. Died Feb. 2, 1955.

MITCHELL, SAMUEL ALFRED, astronomer; b. Kingston, Can., Apr. 29, 1874; s. John C. and Sarah (Chown) M.; M.A., Queen's U., Can., 1894, LL.D., 1924; Ph.D., Johns Hopkins, 1898; LL.D., U. of Western Ontario, 1940; m. Milly Gray Dumble, Dec. 28, 1899; 1 son, Allan Charles Gray. Instructor and adj. prof., Columbia U., 1899-1913; prof. astronomy and director McCormick Observatory, U. Va., 1913-45; dir. emeritus 1945—. Astronomer, Eclipse expeditions Georgia 1900, Sumatra, 1901, Spain, 1905, Oregon, 1918, Calif., 1923, Conn., 1925, Norway, 1927, Niuafoou Island, 1930, Quebec, 1932, Canton Island, 1937; research asso. Yerkes Observatory (U. Chgo.), summers, 1907, 09, 10, 11, asst. prof. astrophysics, 1912-13. Awarded Watson Medal, 1948. Penrose lecture, Am. Philos. Soc., 1938; Arthur lecture, Smithsonian, 1937. Mem. Nat. Acad. Sciences (council mem. 1940-44), chmn. astronomical sect., 1947-50), Am. Philosophical Society, Am. Academy Arts and Sciences, A.A.A.S. (v.p. 1921); fellow and foreign asso. Royal Astron. Soc.; hon. mem. Am. Assn. Variable Star Observers; mem. Am. Astronomical Society (v.p. 1925-27); research asso. Carnegie Institution, 1934-45, Internat. Astron. Union (chmn. com. on parallaxes, 1928-35, chmn. com. on eclipses, 1935-48), Astronomisches Gesellschraft, Société Astronomique de France, Am. Asso. U. Profs. (pres. 1934, 35), Royal Astronomical Society of Canada, Beta Theta Pi, Phi Beta Kappa, Sigma Xi, Tau Beta Pi, Pi Gamma Mu. Clubs: Colonnade, Farmington. Author: Parallaxes of 260 Stars, 1920; Eclipses of the Sun, 1923, 5th edit., 1950; Parallaxes of 440 Stars, 1927; Fundamentals of Astronomy (with C. G. Abbot), 1927; Solar Eclipses, 1929, 36; Variable Stars, 1935; Parallaxes of 650 Stars (with D. Reuvl), 1940. Address: P.O. Box 3466 University Sta., Charlottesville, Va. Died Feb. 22, 1960.

MITCHELL, SAMUEL PHILLIPS, engr.; b. Richmond, Va., June 10, 1864; s. Samuel Phillips and Mary Emily M.; ed. private sch., Richmond, and Univ. of Va.; m. Feb. 4, 1888, Miss Miriam Bond. Engr. Richmond & Danville Ry., 1883, B. & O. Ry., 1884-87, Edgmoor Bridge Works, 1887-96, mgr., 1896-1900; chief engr. Am. Bridge Co. of New York since 1901. Mem. Am. Soc. Civil Engrs. Address: Philadelphia.

MITCHELL, THOMAS DACHÉ, physician; b. Phila., 1791; grad. U. Pa., 1812. Prof. animal and vegetable physiology St. John's Coll., Phila., 1812; physician Phila. Lazaretto, 1813-16; practiced medicine, Frankfort, Pa., 1822-31; prof. chemistry Miami U., Oxford, O., 1831, Med. Coll. of Ohio, 1832; co-editor Western Med. Gazette, 1832-33; prof. chemistry Med. Inst., Louisville, Ky., 1837; prof. chemistry Transylvania U., Lexington, Ky., 1837-39, prof. materia medica and therapeutics, 1839-49; prof. medicine, obstetrics, med. jurisprudence Phila. Coll. of Medicine, 1849-57; prof. materia medica Jefferson Med. Coll., 1957-65. Author: Elements of Chemical Philosophy, 1832; Hints on the Connexion of Labor with Study, as a Preventive of Diseases Peculiar to Students, 1832; Materia Medica and Therapeutics, 1850. Died May 13, 1865.

MITCHELL, THOMAS EDWARD, mining engr.; b. Nova Scotia, Can., Nov. 19, 1874; s. Robert and Elizabeth (Jackson) M.; prep. edn., pub. schs., Can.; tech. edn. U. Cal., U. So. Cal.; m. Louise Miles, Nov 9, 1909; children—Robert Arthur, Jean (Mrs. Fairman Burgess), Elizabeth (Mrs. Andrew Dithridge). Constrn. of reservoirs and flumes, and operation of placer mines nr. Breckenridge, Colo., 1895-96; asst. in operation of placer mine, Salmon City, Ida., 1897; successively miner, shift-boss, foreman and supt. mines (latter included direction of operations of 12 mines) Anaconda Copper Mining Co., Butte, Mont., 1897-1913; asst. gen. mgr., directing devel. of one of greatest silver, lead, zinc ore deposits ever discovered also driving 2 mile double track tunnel Burma Mines, Ltd., Burma, India, 1914-15, gen. mgr., 1915-18; gen. mgr. Burma Corp., Ltd., 1915-18; gen. mgr. Montizona Copper Co., 1921-25 cons. engr., 1925-30; gen. mgr. Lincoln Silver and Lead Mines Co., 1926-27; chief engr. Iron Mask Mining Co., 1928-29; also cons. engr. on numerous other mining and oil projects, 1920-29; gen. cons. practice, 1929—. Mem. various bds. dirs. Inventor, patentee several mech. devices; author many tech. and non-tech. articles. Mem. Am. Inst. Mining and Metall. Engrs. Republican. Presbyn. Home: 163 S. Lucerne Blvd. Died Apr. 17, 1959.

MITCHELL, WILLIAM, banker, astronomer; b. Nantucket, Mass., Dec. 20, 1791; s. Pelez and Lydia (Cartwright) M.; M.A. (hon.), Brown U., 1848, Harvard, 1860; m. Lydia Coleman, Dec. 10, 1812, 10 children including Maria, Henry. Del. to Mass. Constl. Conv., 1820; master 1st free school of Nantucket, 1827; sec. Phoenix Marine Ins. Co., 1830; cashier Pacific Bank, 1837-61; mem. Mass. Senate, 1845; mem. council of Gov. George Briggs, 1848-49; pursued astronomy as hobby; pres. Nantucket Atheneum for 30 years; made observations of sta. positions for U.S. Coast Survey; mem. vis. com. Harvard Coll. Observatory, 1848-65; overseer Harvard, 1857-65; fellow Am. Acad. Arts and Scis.; mem. A.A.A.S. Died Poughkeepsie, N.Y., Apr. 1, 1869.

MITCHILL, SAMUEL LATHAM, physician, senator; b. North Hempstead, L.I., Aug. 20, 1764; s. Robert and Mary (Latham) M.; M.D., U. Edinburgh (Scotland), 1786; m. Catherine Akerly, June 23, 1799. Mem. N.Y. Legislature, 1791, 98, 1810; prof. natural history, chemistry, agr. Columbia, 1792, asso. prof. botany, 1793-95; gave mineral collection to Columbia museum for use of future tchrs.; a founder Soc. for Promotion of Agr., Arts and Manufactures; made mineral exploration of banks of Hudson River, 1796; a founder Medical Repository, 1797, editor, 23 years; mem. U.S. Ho. of Reps. from N.Y. (Democrat), 7th, 9th, 12th congresses, 1801-03, 05-07, 11-13; mem. U.S. Senate (Democrat) from N.Y., 1804-09; commd. to supervise constrn. of a steam war-vessel during War of 1812; prof. chemistry Coll. Physicians and Surgeons, N.Y.C., 1807, prof. natural history, 1808-20, prof. botany and materia medica, 1820-26; an organizer Rutgers Med. Coll., v.p., 1826-30; a founder N.Y. Lit. and Philos. Soc., 1814; prin. founder Lyceum of Natural History, 1817; surgeon gen. N.Y. State Militia, 1818. Author: Explanation of the Synopsis of Chemical Nomenclature and Arrangement, 1801; A Sketch of the Mineralogical History of N.Y., 1797, 1800, 02; most notable contbns. include papers on the fishes of N.Y., the origin of Indians, Indian poetry, Indian antiquities. Died Bklyn., Sept. 7, 1831; buried Greenwood Cemetery, Bklyn.

MITKE, CHARLES A., mining engr.; b. Dorrance, Pa., Aug. 14, 1881; s. Theodore and Amelia (Zoepke) M.; ed. Stroudsburg State Normal Sch., Pa.; B.A., Yale, 1908, Ph.B., 1910; m. Jessy Grant, June 11, 1917. Mining engr. Phelps Doge Corp., 1910-16, cons. engr. 1917-70; v.p. Manila Mining Corp.; pres. Cebu Mining Corp.; cons. engr. Inspiration Consol. Copper Co., Calumet & Ariz. Copper Co., United Verde Extension Mining Co., Cia de Sta. Gertrudis. Pachuca, Mexico; Cerro de Pasco Copper Corp., Peru; Roan Antelope Copper Mines, Ltd., No. Rhodesia, S.A.; Mt. Isa Mines Ltd., Northwestern Queensland, Australia; Broken Hill Mines, South Australia; New Guinea Goldfields; Cyprus Mines Ltd.; Phila. & Reading Coal and Iron Co., Bethlehem Steel Co., Cornwall, Pa.; dir. cons. engr. Masbate Consol. Gold Mining Co., Philippines, 1938; adviser to Metals Reserve Corp., Washington (in Philippine Islands) for strategic materials, 1941; prisoner in Japanese internment camp, Santo Tomas, 1944-45; rep. of U.S. High Commr. to Philippines, in Japan, on reparations, Jan.-July 1946; developing mines in Philippines, 1946-58; examining manganese mines in India, chrome mines in Turkey, 1950; investigated copper range mine, No. Mich., for Def. Minerals Adminstrn., Washington, 1951; developing tin mines in Southwest Africa for Ventures Ltd. of Toronto, Ont., Can., 1952-54. Member Am. Inst. Mining and Metall. Engrs., N.Y. Mining and Metall. (London), Kappa Epsilon. Republican. Presbyn. Club: Bankers (N.Y.). Author: Standardization in Mining Methods, 1919, Mining Methods, 1930. Address: Tucson AZ Died Feb. 22, 1970; cremated.

MIX, ARTHUR JACKSON, educator, mycologist; b. Bolivar, N.Y., Sept. 30, 1888; s. Charles Milford and Rose (Kenyon) M.; A.B., Hamilton Coll., 1910, D.Sc. (honorary), 1955; Ph.D., Cornell Univ. 1916; student Royal College of Science London, 1929-30, Botany Institute, Hamburg, 1930, Bot. Mus., Inst. Plant Protection, Stockholm, 1939; m. Katherine Lyon, Nov. 5, 1917. Asst. botanist N.Y. Agrl. Expt. Sta., Geneva, 1915-16; instr. U. Kan., 1916-17, asso. prof., 1919-24, prof. since 1924, chmn. dept. botany, 1931-53; asst. pathologist U.S.D.A., 1918-19, pathologist, 1944-45, collaborator plant disease survey since 1946; botanist Kan. State Bd. Agr. since 1935; asst. prof. plant pathology Cornell, 1940; physiologist Pa. State Coll., 1945-46; del. 7th Internat. Bot. Congress, Stockholm, 1950. Chmn. Save The Children Fedn. Jayhawk Nursery Com., 1941-43 (nursery for bombed-out English children). Fellow A.A.A.S.; mem. Mycol. Soc. Am. (councillor 1948, v.p. 1952), Bot. Soc. Am., Am. Phytopath. Society, Soc. Linneénne de Lyon, Kan. Acad. Sci., Am. Scandinavian Found., Phi Beta Kappa, Sigma Xi (pres. Kan. 1950-52), Phi Sigma, Alpha Delta Phi. Author: Manual of Medical Mycology, 1953. Home: 1311 Engel Rd., Lawrence, Kan. Died Sept. 9, 1956.

MIXTER, WILLIAM GILBERT, chemist; b. Dixon, Ill., Sept. 23, 1846; s. George and Susan Elizabeth (Gilbert) M.; Ph.B., Sheffield Scientific Sch. (Yale), 1867, A.M., 1887; m. Ada Louise Webber, Aug. 26, 1875. Asst. in chemistry, 1868-70, instr., 1870-72, 1874-75, prof., 1875-1913, prof. emeritus, 1913, Yale U. Author: An Elementary Text-Book of Chemistry, 1889. Home: New Haven, Conn. Died Mar. 9, 1936.

MOCKMORE, CHARLES ARTHUR, civil engineer; born Platte Center, Neb., Nov. 7, 1891; s. of George Washington and Della (Proctor) M.; B. Engring., State U. of Ia., 1920, C.E., 1926; M.S., State U. of Ia., 1932, Ph.D., 1935; married Adriana Mary Margaret Corso, June 1, 1921 (died Decmeber 20, 1942); children—Charlotte A. Spring, Regina Theresa; married 2d, Buena Margason-Maris, June 27, 1946, step dau., Marjorie Maris-Peterson. Assistant superintendent of grounds and buildings, University of Ia., 1920-21; instr.

in civil engring., Ore. State Coll., 1921-31, asso. prof., 1932-34, prof. and head of dept. civil engring. since 1934; research asso., U. of Ia., 1931-32. Served in U.S. Army, 1918. Mem. City Council, Corvallis, Ore., 1935-40; mem. Ore. State Bd. of Engring. Examiners. Won Big Ten medal, U. of Ia., in dual field of scholarship and athletics, 1920; won Croes medal Am. Soc. Civil Engrs., article "Flow Characteristics in Elbow Draft Tubes," 1939. Mem. Am. Soc. Civil Engrs., Am. Soc. for Engring. Edn., Am. Legion, Theta Xi, Tau Beta Pi, Sigma Xi. Republican. Methodist. Mason. Club: Triad (Ore. State Coll.), Town Club. Author: Hydraulic Machinery, Estimating and Cost Analyses, 1935. Contbr. to professional jours. Home: R.F.D. 4, Corvallis, Ore. Died April 11, 1953.

MODJESKI, RALPH, civil engr.; b. Cracow, Poland, Jan. 27, 1861; s. Gustav and late Helena (Opid) Modrzejewski; came to U.S. with mother, 1876; name changed to Modjeski for Am. naturalization, his mother being the celebrated tragedienne, Helen Modjeska; grad. Coll. des Ponts et Chaussées, Paris, at head of class, with honors; D.Eng., U. of Ill., 1911, Pa. Mil. Coll., 1927, Polytechnic Inst. of Lwow (Poland), 1930; m. Felicie Benda, of Cracow, Poland, Dec. 28, 1885 (divorced); m. 2d, Mrs. Mary T. Giblyn, July 7, 1931. Cons. bridge engr. at Chicago, 1892-1940. Mem. firm Modjeski & Noble, chief engrs. of bridge over Mississippi River at Thebes, Ill.; designed and built new govt. bridge, Rock Island, Ill., as well as many ry. bridges; consulting engr. for city of Chicago and Sanitary District on their bascule bridges; in charge of reconstruction of Bismarck Bridge and others for N.P. Ry.; designed and built the Columbia and Willamette River bridges for Portland & Seattle Ry.; chief engr. McKinley Bridge at St. Louis; Broadway Bridge, Portland, Ore.; Columbia River Bridge, Celilo, Ore.; Cherry St. Bridge, Toledo, O. Mem. bd. engrs. Quebec Bridge (reconstruction), new Memphis (Tenn.) Bridge; chief engr. Delaware River Bridge (Phila.), Mid-Hudson Bridge, New Orleans Bridge; chief engr. Huey P. Long Bridge over Mississippi River at New Orleans, Iowa-Ill. Memorial Bridge, Davenport, Calvert St. Bridge, Washington, D.C.; chmn. bd. cons. engrs. Trans-Bay Bridge, San Francisco. Awarded John Scott medal (Phila.), 1924; John Fritz medal, 1930; Washington Award, 1931; Knight Legion of Honor (France). Died June 26, 1940.

MOENKHAUS, WILLIAM J., univ. prof.; b. Huntingburg, Ind., Jan. 6, 1871; s. William and Fredricka (Ramsbrook) M.; grad. Ind. State Normal Sch., Terre Haute, 1892; A.B., Ind. U., Bloomington, 1894, A.M., 1895; studied Harvard, 1896-99; U. of Chicago, 1899-1901, Ph.D., 1903; m. Sara Katherine Rettger, of Bloomington, Sept. 10, 1901; children—William Ernest, Charles Augustus. Asst. dir. State Museum, Sao Paulo, Brazil, 1897-98; asst. prof. zoology, 1901-04, asso. prof. physiology, 1904-05; jr. prof., 1905-08, prof., since 1908, Ind. U. Fellow A.A.A.S., Ind. Acad. Science; mem. Am. Soc. Naturalists, Am. Soc. Zoologists, Phi Gamma Delta, Phi Beta Kappa, Sigma Xi. Contbr. to scientific jours. on exptl. biology. Home: Bloomington IN

MOERK, FRANK XAVIER, chemist, educator; b. Phila., July 3, 1863; s. Ernest Gottlieb and Maria (Fehrenbach) M.; ed. German pvt. schs., Wilmington, Del., Phila. Coll. Pharmacy, Ph.G., 1884; m. Katharine Nicolai, March 22, 1888. Clerk in retail drug store, 1877-84; asst. chem. laboratory, 1884-92; asst. to chair theoretical chemistry, 1886-99, prof. analytical chemistry since 1899, Phila. Coll. Pharmacy. Mem. Am. Chem. Soc., Pa. State Pharm. Assn., Phila. Coll. Pharmacy, Am. Pharm. Assn., German Chem. Soc. Lutheran. Author: Notes on Qualitative Analysis, 1901 O1; Qualitative Chemical Analysis, 1905 X1. Residence: 646 E. Chelten Av., Germantown. Office: 145 N. 10th St., Philadelphia. Died Nov. 19, 1945.

MOFFETT, JAMES WILLIAM, fishery research biologist; b. American Fork, Utah, Aug. 3, 1908; s. Benjamin F. and Helen (Preston) M.; A.B. with honors in Zoology, U. Utah, 1933, M.A., 1935; Ph.D., U. Mich., 1939; m. Myrtle Wilde, Nov. 29, 1933; children—Mary L., James William II. Teaching asst. U. Utah, 1933-34; teaching fellow zoology U. Mich., 1935-39; aquatic biologist Mich. Conservation Dept., 1939-41, U.S. Fish and Wildlife Service, Stanford, 1941-49; lab. dir. U.S. Fish and Wildlife Service, Ann Arbor, Mich., 1950—; splty. sea lamprey control, Gt. Lakes limnology and fisheries. Mem. Am. Fisheries Soc. (pres. 1960), Am. Soc. Limnology and Oceanography (v.p. 1953), Am. Inst. Fishery Research Biologists (dist. dir. 1963—), Sigma Xi, Phi Kappa Phi. Home: 1204 Brooklyn St. Office: 1451 Green Rd., Ann Arbor, Mich. Died Feb. 20, 1967; buried American Fork Cemetery.

MOHLER, JOHN FREDERICK, physicist; b. Boiling Springs, Pa., Oct. 30, 1864; s. Samuel and Elizabeth (Williams) M.; A.B., Dickinson Coll., Pa., 1887, A.M., 1890; Ph.D., Johns Hopkins, 1897; m. Sarah Loomis, June 24, 1892; children—Frederick Loomis, Samuel Loomis, Nora May. Instr. mathematics and science, Wilmington Conf. Acad., Dover, Del., 1887-90; instr. mathematics, Wesleyan Acad., Wilbraham, Mass., 1890-94; prof. of physics, Dickinson Coll., Carlisle, Pa., 1896—. Republican. Methodist. Author: Practical Physics, 1897 (5 edits). Died Jan. 28, 1930.

MOHLER, JOHN ROBBINS, pathologist; b. Phila., Pa., May 9, 1875; s. William Casper and Harriet Robbins (Hart) M.; Central High Sch.; Phila., 1888-92; Temple U., 1892-93; V.M.D., U. of Pa., 1896, hon. D.Sc., 1925; Med. Dept., Marquette U., 1897-99; hon. D.Sc., Iowa State Coll., 1920; hon. D.Sc., U. of Md., 1928; m. Clara Moffett Clarke, Dec. 23, 1897; children—William Melvin, Miriam Clarke. Practiced as veterinarian, 1896-97; asst. insp., Bur. Animal Industry, Dept. of Agr., 1897-99; asst. pathologist, 1899-1901, zoologist, 1901-02, chief pathol. div. of the bureau, 1902-14; asst. chief of the Bur. of Animal Industry, 1914-17; chief of that bureau 1917-1943, when he retired. Baptist. Member American Veterinary Med. Assn. (pres. 1913), Soc. Am. Bacteriologists, Soc. Exptl. Biology and Medicine, Pa. State Vet. Assn., Internat. Vet. Congress (president 1934), Am. Pub. Health Assn., Washington Acad. of Sciences, U.S. Livestock Sanitary Assn. (pres. 1925), Soc. of Animal Production, D.C. Bd. of Veterinary Examiners, Washington Acad. Medicine, Royal Soc. of Medicine (Great Britain), Sigma Xi; hon. mem. Alpha Psi, Phi Kappa Phi. Hon. prof. U. of Havana, 1944. Awarded 12th Internat. Veterinary Congress prize, 1940; Dr. George Martin Kober Foundation lectureship for 1941 by the Medical Society of the D.C.; A.V.M.A. Award as Investigator and Administrator, Boston, 1946. Translator: Edelmann's Meat Hygiene, 1908 (also editor) Hutyra and Marek's Special Pathology and Therapeutics, 1912, 4th Edition, 1938; Ernst's Milk Hygiene, 1914. Author numerous articles on pathology, bacteriology and meat inspection, in govt. publs., med. jours. and encys. Home: 1620 Hobart St. N.W., Washington DC

MOHOLY-NAGY, LASZIO GEORGE, (mo-ho'li-nadj), painter, author, photographer, cinema dir.; b. Borsod, Hungary, July 20, 1895; s. Leopold Gustave and Carola Aester Moholy-Nagy; grad. in law, U. of Budapest, 1915; m. Sibyl Dorothy Peech, 1933; children—Hattula Sibylle Carola, Claudia Eve. Came to U.S., 1937, naturalized, 1946. Painter, photographer and writer since 1920; prof. teaching basic elements of art, and head of metal workshop. Bauhaus, Weimar and Dessau, Germany, 1923-28; dir. New Bauhaus, Chicago, 1937-38; pres. Inst. of Design, Chicago since 1939. Made first photograms (photographs without camera), Berlin, 1921; did experimental work with light and color in painting, photography and film, Berlin, 1928; made stage settings for Piscator's theatre and the State Opera, Berlin; produced books with photographs, films and special effects for films, London, 1935-37. Had one-man show of photographs, Royal Photographic Soc.; exhibited painting and sculpture, London and many other cities in Eng.; at Museum of Non-objective Painting and Museum of Modern Art, N.Y. City, 1942. Represented in Budapest and Berlin National Galleries and private collections in Europe and U.S. Lecturer at Cambridge and Oxford universities art societies. Served as artillery officer in Austro-Hungarian Army, World War I. Hon. mem. Cambridge and Oxford univs. art assns. and British Designer Inst.; dir. of Am. Designer's Inst., Congrès Internationale Architecture Moderne. Received Signum laudis, silver and bronze fortitude, etc., medals. Author: Horizont, 1921; (with L. Kassák) Book of New Artists, 1921; Painting, Photography, Motion Picture, 1924; From Material to Architecture, 1928; The New Vision, 1930, 2 edit., 1938, 3 edition 1946; Vision in Motion, 1946. Editor of "id" (Institute of Design) books, 1946; (with Walter Gropius) 14 Bauhaus Books, 1924-28. Book illustration in photography: 60 photographs by L. Moholy-Nagy, 1930; Telehor, 1936; (with Mary Benedetta) Street Markets of London, 1936; (with J. Ferguson) Eton Portrait, 1937; (with John Betjeman) Oxford University Chest, 1938. Films: Still Life (Berlin), 1926; Marseille Vieux Port, 1929; Light Display, Black, White and Gray, 1930; Sound ABC, 1932; Gypsies, 1932; Architecture Congress, Athens, 1933; Lobster, 1935; special effects for H. G. Wells' "Things to Come," 1935; New Architecture at the London Zoo, 1936; Design Workshops, 1942; Do Not Disturb, 1945. Portfolio of lithographs, 6 constructions, 1923. Lectured in most of the larger cities of Europe and U.S. Contbr. of articles to art, architectural and photographic magazines of Europe and U.S. Home: 2622 Lakeview Av. Address: 632 N. Dearborn St., Chicago, Ill. Died Nov. 24, 1946.

MOHR, CHARLES (CARL) THEODOR, botanist; b. in Esslingen, Würtemberg, Germany, Dec. 28, 1824; s. Louis M.; ed. Paedagogium Esslingen, Volksschule Denkendorf, private tuition; studied chemistry and natural sciences, Polytechnical School, Stuttgart, 1842-43; Ph.D., Univ. of Ala., 1890; m. Sophia Roemer, Mar. 12, 1852. Accompanied A. Kappler on exploring expdn. of Dutch Guiana, 1845; one of pioneers Calif. gold fields, 1849; pharmacist, Louisville, Ky., 1853-57, Mobile, Ala., 1857-92; explored forests of Gulf states for 10th census, 1880-81; retired from business to engage in forestry and bot. work exclusively, 1892; botanist Geol. Survey of Ala., 1884—; agt. Div. Forestry, U.S. Dept. Agr., 1889—. Author: The Timber Pines of the Southern United States, 1896, 1897; Plant Life of Alabama, 1901. (Contributions U.S. Nat. Herbarium, Vol. VI.) Wrote: The Forests of Alabama and Their Products, the Grasses and Other Forage Plants of Alabama, in Handbook of Alabama, by Saffold Berney. Died 1901.

MOISSEIFF, LEON S(OLOMON), (mo'sef), cons. engr.; b. Riga, Latvia, Nov. 10, 1872; s. Solomon and Anna (Bloch) M.: student Emperor Alexander Gymnasium, Riga, 1880-87, Baltic Poly. Inst., Riga, 1889-91; C.E., Columbia, 1895; m. Ida Assinofsky, 1893; children—Liberty (wife of Dr. Harry Weiss), Siegfried, Grace (wife of Hancel Bechtel Smith). Came to U.S., 1891, naturalized, 1896. Civil engr. pvt. engring. firm, 1895-97; asst. engr. and engr. of design Dept. of Bridges, N.Y. City, 1897-1915; engr. of design, Delaware River Bridge, Phila., 1920-26; cons. engr. George Washington and Bayonne bridges, N.Y. City, 1927-31, Ambassador Bridge, Detroit, 1928-30, Maumee River Bridge, Toledo, 1929-32, Triborough Bridge, N.Y. City, 1934-36, East River bridges, N.Y. City, 1934-37, Bronx-Whitestone Bridge, N.Y. City, 1936-39, Tacoma Narrows Bridge, 1938-40, Mackinac Straits Bridge Authority, 1938-40; mem. board of engineers, Golden Gate Bridge, 1929-37, and San Francisco-Oakland Bay Bridge, 1931-37; cons. engr. Commissariàt of Transportation, Russia, 1929-32; cons. engr. Century of Progress Expn., Chicago, 1933. Awarded gold medal, Franklin Inst., 1933; Norman medal, Am. Soc. C.E., 1934; James Laurie prize, Am. Soc. C.E., 1939; awarded Columbia U. Egleston medal for distinguished achievement in engring., 1939, Modern Pioneer award for achievement in the field of science and invention, Nat. Assn. Mfrs., 1940. Mem. Am. Soc. C.E. (life), Am. Soc. Testing Materials, Am. Ry. Engring. Assn., American Welding Society, Structural Steel Welding Com., Com. on Specifications for Welding Bridges, Joint Com. on Design of Structural Members, Alloy Steel Com., Com. on Design of Lightweight Structural Alloys (chmn.), Sigma Xi, Zeta Beta Tau. Compiler and translator, Considère's Experimental Researches on Reinforced Concrete, 1906. Author of articles "Deflection Theory for Design of Suspension Bridges," "Towers, Cables and Stiffening Trusses, Delaware River Bridge," "High Structural Steels for Bridges," "Hudson River Bridge Towers," "Investigation of Cold Drawn Bridge Wire," "Suspension Bridges Under Action of Lateral Forces," "Evolution of High Strength Steels in Structural Engineering," "Theory of Elastic Stability Applied to Structural Design," "Design Specifications for Bridges and Structures of Aluminum," 1940. Home: 530 West End Av. Office: 99 Wall St., New York, N.Y. Died Sep. 3, 1943.

MOLDENKE, RICHARD (GEORGE GOTTLOB), metallurgist; b. Watertown, Wis., Nov. 1, 1864; E.M., Columbia, 1885, Ph.D., 1887; m. Anne, d. John D. Heins of New York, Sept. 18, 1891. Specialist on metallurgy of cast iron and expert in malleable castings. Author: The Production of Malleable Castings, 1911; The Principles of Iron Founding, 1917. Extensive writer on the metallurgy of iron and steel. Address: Watchung, N.J. Died Nov. 17, 1930.

MOLÉ, HARVEY E., (mo-la'), engr.; b. Phila., Apr. 16, 1869; s. Harvey E. and Amelia (Cartwright) M.; M.E., Cornell U., 1897; m. Vena Fenno, June 24, 1904; 1 son, Harvey E. With J. G. White & Co., engrs., 1897-1901; asst. mech. engr. Manhattan Ry. Co., 1901-02; in charge power station dept. British Westinghouse Co., London, Eng., 1902-06; chief engr. in charge bldg. St. Petersburg Electric Tramways, 32 miles double track power station, substations, car barns and cars, Russian Westinghouse Co., St. Petersburg, Russia, 1906-08; cons. engring., including gen. engring., design, installment and mgmt. pub. utilities properties, in N.Y.C., 1909-34. Mem. and twice pres. Bd. of Edn., Summit, N.J., 1933-43. Fellow Am. Soc. M.E., Am. Inst. E.E. Home: 17 Essex Rd., Summit, N.J. Died Apr. 9, 1957.

MOLINEUX, ROLAND BURNHAM, chemist, author; b. Brooklyn, Aug. 12, 1866; s. Gen. Edward Leslie (q.v.) and Hattie Davis (Clark) M.; ed. Brooklyn Poly. Institute, Sedgwick Inst., Great Barrington, Mass., Cooper Union, New York; unmarried. Was employed by J. L. & D. S. Riker, chemicals, New York, 1882; 2d Brooklyn Cattle Co. in Mexico and Colo., 1883; as chemist with C. T. Raynolds & Co., 1883-93, Morris Hermann & Co., 1883-88; out of business, 1899-1902; chemist with F. W. Devoe & C. T. Raynolds Co., New York, since 1903. Author: The Room with the Little Door, 1903; Vice-Admiral of the Blue, 1903. Home: 117 Fort Greene Pl. Office: 575 Smith St., Brooklyn.

MOLITOR, DAVID ALBERT, civil engr.; b. Detroit, Aug. 16, 1866; s. Edward Philip and Catherine L. (Jung) M.; student Washington U., St. Louis, 1883-87; B.C.E., C.E., George Washington U., 1908, E.D., 1932; m. Mabel H. White. Engr. on design and constrn. strategical Ry. Weizen-Immendingen, Baden, 1887-90; asst. engr. Miss. Bridge, Memphis, in charge of erection of superstructure, 1890-92; entered Engring. Dept. U.S.A., under Gen. O.M. Poe, serving in various capacities as designing and suptg. engr., 1892-98, on works connected with Sault Ste. Marie Falls Canal and the Channels through the Great Lakes; conducted precise leveling operations for U.S. Bd. of Engrs. on deep waterways, St. Lawrence River, 1898-99; in pvt. business as cons. engr., chem. and bacteriol. lab., etc., 1899-1906; designing engr. Panama Canal, at Washington, 1906-08, visited Isthmus, May 1907; prof. civ. engring., Cornell U., 1908-11; practicing bridge and gen. engring., Kansas City, 1911-12; chief designing engr., Toronto Harbor Commrs., 1913-16; cons.

practice, Detroit, 1916-23; structural engr. with Albert Kahn, 1924-32; structural engr. U.S. supervising architect, 1932-38; structural engr. private practice since 1938. Life mem. Am. Soc. of C.E. Mason. Author: Hydraulics of Rivers, Weirs and Sluices, 1908; Kinetic Theory of Engineering Structures, 1911; Structural Engineering Problems and Practical Chimney Design, 1937; also many professional papers and monographs. Address: New Center Bldg., 1939.

MOLITOR, FREDERIC ALBERT, civil engr.; b. Detroit, Apr. 1868; s. Albert and Lucille I. (Goodell) M.; ed. Trinity Sch., New York, 1881-83, Cornell U. to 1886; m. Katherine Jefferies, 1896. Served in minor capacities on various Eastern R.R. engring. depts., 1886-89; prin. asst. engr. Ky. Central R.R., 1889; engr. maintenance of way, C.&O. R.R., 1890; asst. engr. Phila. & Reading R.R. and engr. Phila. Belt Line R.R., 1891-94; engr.-in-charge of constrn. L.I. R.R., 1895; chief engr. Choctaw, Oklahoma & Gulf R.R., and of allied cos. in charge of constrn. of 900 miles of new road, 1896-1903; gen. mgr., chief engr. and dir. Midland Valley R.R., 1903-06; also chief engr. Cherokee Constrn. Co., 1904-06; supervising ry. expert for the govt. in P.I., 1906-08; pvt. practice, New York, 1908-33, retired. Mem. spl. Panama Canal Commn., 1921; chmn. Bd. of Economics and Engring., Nat. Assn. Owners of R.R. Securities, 1922; study of terminal and post facilities of New York; rept. for receiver Brazil Ry. Co.; investigation proposed low grade line, N.Y., Pittsburgh & Chicago R.R.; mem. Arbitration Bd. St. Paul Union Depot; confidential rept. New York Rapid Transit situation; chmn. and mem. Commn. on Valuation of Damages Nat. Rys. of Mexico; cons. railroad engr. Bd. of Hudson River Regulating Dist., etc. Col. engrs. U.S.A., 1917-19; in charge of all engring. supplies at time of signing Armistice. Episcopalian. Republican. Author: Manual for Constructing Engineers, 1902. Home: New York, N.Y. Died 1938.

MOLITOR, HANS, pharmacologist; b. Maffersdorf, Czechoslovakia, Aug. 10, 1895; s. Emil and Lydia (Schmid) M.; grad. Volkesschule, Maffersdorf, 1905, Staatsgymnasium Reichenberg, Czechoslovakia, 1913; Abiturium, M.D., U. of Vienna, Austria, 1921; unmarried. Came to U.S., 1932, naturalized, 1937. Asst. prof. pharmacology U. of Vienna Med. Sch., 1922-26; Rockefeller traveling fellow Edinburgh and London, 1924; privat-dozent (lectr.) pharmacol. and toxicol., U. of Vienna Med. Sch., 1927-28, asso. prof., 1928-32; dir. Merck Inst. for Therapeutic Research, Rahway, N.J., 1932-55, chmn. bd. 1955-70; dir. sci. relations, Merck Sharp & Dohme Research Labs., div. Merck & Co., Inc., 1956-70. Fellow A.A.A.S., Internat. Coll. Anes, N.Y. Acad. Sci. (councillor 1946-48, v.p. 1948); Royal Soc. Medicine (1956); mem. Am. Physiol. Soc. Am. Soc. Pharmacol. and Exptl. Therapy, Soc. Exptl. Biol. and Med., Am. Soc. Trop. Med., Nat. Malaria Soc., Southern Med. Assn., Phila. Physiol. Soc. Club: Colonial Country (Rahway). Contbr. over 100 research articles to sci. jours. Home: Metedeconk NJ Died Sept. 1970.

MOLNAR, JULIUS PAUL, physicist; b. Detroit, Feb. 23, s. Joseph and Elizabeth (Goeney) M.; A.B., Oberlin Coll., 1937; Ph.D., Mass. Inst. Tech., 1940; Margaret Hale Andrews, July 12, 1941; 1 son, Peter Hale. Tech. aide Nat. Def. Research Com., 1940-42; physicist Gulf Research and Development Co., 1942-45; mem. tech. staff Bell Telephone Labs., 1945-49, electron tube development systems development, 1955-57, dir. mil. development engr., 1950-54, dir. electron tube development, 1955, dir. mil. development, 1957, v.p., 1957-58; v.p. Western Electric Co., 1958-60; exec. v.p. Bell Telephone Labs., Inc., 1960-73; pres. Sandia Corp., 1958-60. Mem. Am. Phys. Soc., Optical Soc. Am., Inst. Radio Engrs. Home: Summit NJ Died Jan. 11, 1973.

MOLONY, WILLIAM HAYES, clergyman, physicist; b. Crawfordsville, Ind., Dec. 4, 1884; s. James Sullivan and Mary (Hayes) M.; Litt.B., U. Notre Dame, 1907; student Cath. U. Am., Washington, 1907-10; dir. studies St. Edward's Coll., Austin, Tex., 1912-19, dir. studies and registrar, 1934-43; prof. physics and math. U. Notre Dame, 1912-32, dir. studies and registrar, 1933-34, prof. physics, 1943—. Address: Corby Hall, U. Notre Dame, Notre Dame, Ind. Deceased.

MONAELESSER, ADOLPH, M.D., surgeon; b. Laxey, Isle of Man, June 22, 1855; s. Maurice and Emilie (Schyar) M.; prep. edn., pub. sch., Manchester, Eng.; student Coelnisches Gymnasium, Berlin, Germany, 1869-73, Greifswald U., Germany, 1873-75, U. of Berlin, 1875-76, Breslau and Bonn, Germany, 1876-77, U. of Paris, 1877-79; M.D., Eclectic Med. Coll., 1882; M.D., Coll. City New York, 1886; Sc.D., Lincoln Memorial U., 1930; m. Bettina Hofker (who served as sister-in-chief of Am. Nat. Red Cross during Spanish-Am. War), Aug. 6, 1887; 1 son, Mozart. Came to U.S., 1879, naturalized citizen, 1922. Asso. curator to Dr. N. M. Miller, City Hosp., N.Y. City, 1884-87; attending surgeon St. Elizabeth's Hosp., N.Y. City, 1887—; surgeon in chief Am. Red Cross (served in Cuba, Spanish-Am. War), 1893-1903; pathologist to Commn. for Investigation of Crime, Am. Bar Assn., 1923. Fellow A.M.A., New York Acad. Medicine, New York Acad. Sciences, New York Micros. Soc., Institut Pasteur (Paris). Mem. Free Unitarian Congregation. Author: Medical Service During the Cuban Insurrection and Spanish American War, 1899; Effets du venim de cobra modifie sur les tumeurs cancereuses, 1930. Research in therapeutic value of snake venom in nerve affections and malignant growths. Died Mar. 27, 1936.

MONETTE, JOHN WESLEY, physician, historian; b. Shenandoah Valley, Va., Apr. 5, 1803; s. Samuel and Mary (Wayland) Monett; M.D., Transylvania U., Lexington, Ky., 1825; m. Cornelia Newman, Dec. 10, 1828, 10 children. Practiced medicine; 1st to suggest quarantine as means of preventing spread of yellow fever; mayor, councilman Washington (Miss.). Author: An Account of the Epidemic of Yellow Fever that Occurred in Washington, Mississippi, in the Autumn of 1825, 1827; Observations on the Epidemic of Yellow Fever of Natchez and the Southwest, 1842; Oil of Turpentine as an External Irritant, 1827; History of the Discovery and Settlement of the Valley of the Mississippi by the Three Great European Powers, Spain, France, and Great Britain, and the Subsequent Occupation, Settlement, and Extension of Civil Government by the United States until the Year 1816, 2 vols., 1846. Died Mar. 1, 1851; buried Washington.

MONKS, GEORGE HOWARD, surgeon; b. Boston, Mass., Mar. 28, 1853; s. John P. and Delia S. (Hatton) M.; A.B., Harvard, 1875, M.D., 1880; M.R.C.S., London, Eng., 1884; m. Olga E. Gardner of Boston, Mass., June 15, 1897. Interne, Mass. Gen. Hosp., Boston, 1879-80; practiced in Boston since 1884; prof. oral surgery, Harvard Dental Sch.; consulting surgeon Boston City Hosp. Fellow Am. Coll. Surgeons; mem. A.M.A., Am. Surg. Assn., Mass. Med. Soc., Boston Surg. Soc., Boston Soc. Med. Sciences, Boston Soc. for Med. Improvement. Clubs: Tavern, Somerset, Harvard, Country. Home: 51 Commonwealth Av., Boston, Mass.

MONNETT, VICTOR, geologist; b. Hale, Mo., Dec. 1, 1889; s. Ira and Ann (Todd) M.; A.B., U. of Oklahoma, 1912; student U. of Mich., 1912-13; Ph.D., Cornell, 1922; m. Kathryn Brown, Aug. 16, 1915; 1son, Victor Brown. Began as teacher of geology; asst. prof. geology, U. of Okla., 1917-22, prof., 1922-60, David Ross Boyd emeritus prof. geology, 1960-72, dir. Sch. of Geological Engring., 1922-42, Sch. of Geology 1930-55, dean of grad. sch., and dir. research inst., 1944-46. Mem. Sigma Xi, Phi Beta Kappa, Sigma Gamma Epsilon, Sigma Tan. Methodist. Club: Lions. Home: Norman OK Died Sept. 18, 1972.

MONROE, LAWRENCE ALEXANDER, chem. engr.; b. Peoria, Ill., Aug. 10, 1912; s. Edward Daniel and Sara (Weatherwax) M.; student Bradley U., 1928-30; B.S., U. Ill., 1932; S.M., Mass. Inst. Tech., 1934, Sc.D., 1936. Asst. prof. chem. engring. Mass. Inst. Tech., 1938-40; chem. engr. Allied Chem. Corp., Phila., 1940-42; chief, chem. industries br. Office Prodn. Research and Devel., WPB, Washington, 1944-45; engr. Ethyl Corp., N.Y.C., 1945-49; engr. R. R. Donnelley & Sons Co., Chgo., 1960-69. Mem. Am. Chem. Soc., T.A.P.P.I., A.A.A.S., Am. Inst. Chem. Engrs., Alpha Chi Sigma, Phi Lambda Upsilon, Delta Sigma Phi. Club: Mass. Inst. Tech., Chgo. Home: Evanston IL Died July 1969.

MONROE, WILLIAM STANTON, mech. engr.; b. Chgo., Aug. 22, 1868; s. Henry Stanton and Martha (Mitchell) M.; M.E., Cornell U., 1890; m. Anna Hamill Clarke, Oct. 31, 1898 (died May 22, 1944); children—Ernest H. (dec.), Henry S. Engaged in constrn. work for elec. power prodn., 1891—; in 1900 entered office of Sargent & Lundy (founded in 1891); pres. Sargent & Lundy, Inc., cons. engrs. for large elec. power cos., 1919-38, now ret.; ex-dir. Western Light & Telephone Co.; dir. Central Cold Storage Co. Mem. bd. trustees, Ill. Inst. Technol. In 1922 state improvement in steam power stas. for electric power involving increased steam pressures and temperatures and reheating which led to great reductions in operating costs. Mem. Am. Soc. Mech. Engrs., Western Soc. Engrs. (pres. 1929-30), Am. Soc. Civil Engrs., Franklin Inst., Acad. Polit. Sci., A.A.A.S., Chgo. Geog. Soc. (dir.). Clubs: University, Tavern (Chgo.). Home: 64 E. Elm St. Office: 105 S. LaSalle St., Chgo. Deceased.

MONTENIER, JULES BERNARD, chemist; b. Neuchatel, Switzerland, Mar. 23, 1895; s. Jules and Rose (Girard) M.; student U. Neuchatel, Geneva (Switzerland) Conservatory Music; D.Sc., U. Geneva, 1919; m. Helen Graf, Apr. 28, 1935 (dec.); 1 son, Denis Bernard. Came to U.S., 1923, naturalized, 1928. Prof. chemistry in Geneva, 1919-22; organic dye mfg. Cable Chemical Works (Wis.); 1923-25; developer hair dyes, mfr. cosmetics, creator flexi-plastic spray bottle for packaging; pres. Jules Montemier, Inc., Chgo., 1934-56; cons. Helene Curtis Industries, Inc., 1956—. Recipient Charles Welsh packaging award for toilet goods industry, 1953. Mem. Geneal. Soc. Suisse Romande. Rotarian. Patentee in field. Home: Oak Knoll Rd., Barrington, Ill. Died Aug. 20, 1962.

MONTGOMERY, EDMUND DUNCAN, biologist, philosopher; b. Edinburgh, Scotland, Mar. 19, 1835; ed. pvt. tuition in Eng., France and Germany; univs. of Heidelberg, 1852-56, Berlin, 1855, Bonn, 1856, Würzburg, 1857; M.D., Prague, 1858; Vienna, 1859; M.R.C.P., London, 1861; m. at Madeira, Elisabet Ney, sculptress, 1865 (died 1907). Resident phys. German Hosp., London, 1860-61; med. attendant Bermondsey Dispensary and Poor District, 1861-62; pathologist St. Thomas' Hosp., London, 1861-64; practiced Madeira, Mentone and Rome, 1865-70; resided in Texas, 1872—. Author: Die Kantsche Erkenntriplehre vom Standpunkt der Empirie, 1871; The Vitality and Organization of Protoplasm, 1904; Philosophical Problems in the Light of Vital Organization, 1907. Home: Hempstead, Tex. Died 1911.

MONTGOMERY, EDNA MORLEY, research chemist; b. National City, Cal., Apr. 15, 1896; d. James M. and Jessie M. (Parker) Montgomery; B.A. in Chemistry, U. Mont., 1919; M.A. in Chemistry, U. Ill., 1924. Instr. Whitworth Coll., Spokane, Wash., 1924-25; jr. chemist Nat. Bur. Standards, Washington, 1926-28; asst., asso. chemist NIH, Bethesda, Md., 1929-44; with U.S. Dept. Agr., 1945-70, Ccrn Ind. Research Found., Peoria, Ill., 1945-50, asso. chemist, then chemist No. Regional Research Lab., Peoria; chemist S. African Council Scientific and Indsl. Research, Pretoria, 1966; ret. Recipient Dunniway award in chemistry, 1919. Mem. Am. Chem. Soc., Am. Assn. Cereal Chemists, Alpha Phi. Author articles profl. jours. Patentee. Home: San Diego CA Died May 10, 1970; buried Chinook Cemetery, Chinook MT

MONTGOMERY, THOMAS HARRISON, JR., zoölogist; b. New York, Mar. 5, 1873; s. Thomas Harrison and Anna (Morton) M.; student U. of Pa., 1889-91; Ph.D., U. of Berlin, 1894; m. Priscilla Braislin, 1901. Asst. prof. zoölogy, U. of Pa., 1898-1903; prof. biology, 1898-1903, dir. mus., 1899-1903, Wagner Free Inst. of Science, Phila.; prof. zoölogy, U. of Tex., 1903-08, U. of Pa., 1908—. Trustee Marine Biol. Lab., Woods Hole, Mass. Contributed about 80 scientific monographs on biol. subjects. Author: Analysis of Racial Descent in Animals, 1906. Home: Philadelphia, Pa. Died Mar. 19, 1912.

MONTONNA, RALPH E(UGENE), (mon-ton'na), educator; b. Cape Vincent, N.Y., Oct. 13, 1894; s. William E. and Alberta (Van Vlack) M.; B.S., Syracuse U., 1916; Ph.D., Yale, 1924; m. Mary Louise Light, June 30, 1919; children—Margaret Ann (Mrs. William David Emmons), Mary Lou (Mrs. Dale Phillip Williams). Research chemist Merrell-Soule Co., 1916-17; plant chemist Solvay Process Co., 1918-19; asst. dir. organic research Semet-Solvay Co., 1920-22 (all Syracuse, N.Y.); supt. U.S. Color & Chem. Co., Ashland, Mass., 1919-20; instr. chem. engring. Yale, 1922-24; dir. Inst. Indsl. Research Syracuse U., 1946-50; asst. prof. to prof., later asst. dean grad. sch. U. Minn., 1924-46, dir. Engring. Expt. Sta., 1950—; asso. dir. Northwest Research Inst., 1935-46; dir. Minn. Inst. Research, 1943-46; lectr. chem. econ. U. Birmingham (Eng.), 1937-38; dist. service lectr. Tex. A. and M. Coll., 1940. Mem. gov's. adv. com. Com. to War Industries (Minn.), 1943-45. Mem. Am. Chem. Soc., Am. Inst. Chem. Engrs., Am. Inst. Chemists, Am. Soc. Engring. Edn., A.A.A.S., Minn. Acad. Sci., Am. Assn. U. Profs. Clubs: Skylight, Campus (Minneapolis). Home: 1499 N. Cleveland Av., St. Paul 8. Died Jan. 7, 1952.

MONTRESOR, JAMES GABRIEL, mil. engr.; b. Ft. William, Scotland, Nov. 19, 1702; s. James Gabriel and Nanon (de Hautville) Le Tresor; m. Mary Haswell, June 11, 1735; m. 2d, Henrietta Fielding, Aug. 25, 1766; m. 3d, Frances Nicholls; 1 son, John. Served as matross in Royal Arty., Minorca, 1727; commd. as practitioner engr., Gibraltar, 1731, chief engr. by 1754; commd. lt. 14th Foot Inf.; served as chief engr. under Gen. Braddock in Am., 1754; promoted maj., 1757; became dir. Corps of Engrs. and lt. col., 1758, planned and directed considerable building in No. N.Y.; in charge of rebldg. Ft. George at lower end Lake George, 1759; returned to Eng., 1760; designer, supt. constrn. of powder magazines at Purfleet; chief engr. at Chatham, Eng.; commd. col., 1772. Died Jan. 6, 1776.

MONTRESOR, JOHN, mil. engr.; b. Gibraltar, Apr. 6, 1736; s. James Gabriel and Mary (Haswell) M.; m. Frances Tucker, Mar. 1, 1764. Came to Am., 1754; served as lt. Brit. Army under Gen. Braddock, 1755; engr. in French and Indian War, 1755-63; engr. extraordinary, capt.-lt. with a commn. as barracks master for the ordnance in N. Am.; improved fortifications or repaired barracks at N.Y., Boston, Phila., the Bahamas; bought Montresor's (now Randall's) Island, N.Y.; commd. chief engr. in Am. with rank of engr. in ordinary and capt. Brit. forces, 1775; chief engr. at Battle of Brandywine; returned to Eng., 1778. Died London, Eng., June 26, 1799.

MONTZHEIMER, ARTHUR, civil engr.; b. Sharpsburg, Pa., Jan. 23, 1869; s. Julius H. G. and Isabel G. (Hillock) M.; prep. edn., high sch., Webster City, Ia.; grad. Dixon (Ill.) Coll. Civ. Engring., 1888; m. Julia McClellan Mosher, of Racine, Wis., June 28, 1893; children—Gertrude E. (dec.), Marie (Mrs. Leonard W. Gesler), Arthur M. Began with Chicago & Northwestern Railway, 1886; rodman, transitman, draftsman and asst. engr., same rd., 1889-95, and supt. bridges, hdqrs. Milwaukee, Wis., 1895-1903; chief engr. Elgin, Joliet & Eastern Ry. Co. since 1903; chief engr. Chicago, Lake Shore & Eastern Ry., 1903-09, and of Chicago, Milwaukee & Gary Ry., under U.S. R.R. Administration, Jan. 1918-Mar. 1920. Mem. engring. com. of Real Estate Advisory Commn. of Sanitary Dist. of Chicago. Mem. Am. Soc. C.E., Western Soc. Engrs.,

Am. Ry. Engring. Assn., Am. Ry. Bridge and Building Assn. (ex-pres.), Am. Ry. Signal Assn., Am. Wood Preservers' Assn., Chicago Regional Planning Assn. Republican. Presbyn. Mason (K.T., Shriner). Clubs: Engineers', Rotary, Shabbona, Shriners. Home: 602 Wilcox St. Office: Joliet Nat. Bank Bldg., Joliet IL

MOODIE, ROY LEE, anatomist, paleontologist; b. Bowling Green, Ky., July 30, 1880; s. William Lemuel and Sarah Estelle (Gregg) M.; A.B., U. of Kan., 1905; Ph.D., U. of Chicago, 1908; m. Catherine M. Wood, June 29, 1910; children—William Ross, Catherine Ann, Sarah Lee. Prof. biology, Warrensburg (Mo.) Normal Sch., 1908; instr. zoölogy, U. of Kan., 1908-09, asst. prof., 1909-13; prof. anatomy, Baylor U., Dallas, Tex., 1913-14; instr. in anatomy, 1914-15, associate, 1915-16, asst. prof., 1916-18, asso. prof., 1918-23, U. of Ill. Coll. of Medicine; sabbatical yr. in Southern Calif., in research work, 1923-24; asso. prof. anatomy and research librarian, U. of Ill., at Chicago, 1924-28; prof. paleodontology, Coll. of Dentistry, U. of Southern Calif., 1928; paleopathologist Wellcome Hist. Med. Mus., London, 1929—. Democrat. Baptist. Author: Coal Measures Amphibia of North America (Carnegie Instn.), 1916; The Antiquity of Disease, 1923; Paleopathology—an Introduction to the Study of Ancient Evidences of Disease, 1923. Editor: Studies in the Paleopathology of Egypt (by Ruffer), 1921; also author Studies in Paleopathology (Annals of Med. History); Studies in Paleodontology, I-XXV. Home: Los Angeles, Calif. Died Feb. 16, 1934.

MOODY, HERBERT RAYMOND, chemist; b. Chelsea, Mass., Nov. 19, 1869; s. Luther Richmond and Mary Emily (Sherman) M.; S.B., Mass. Inst. Tech., 1892; A.M., Columbia, 1900, Ph.D., 1901; m. Edna Wadsworth, Aug. 20, 1895. Asst. labs. of Chelsea High Sch., 1887-88; asst. gen. chemistry, Mass. Inst. Tech., 1892-94, instr. analyt. chemistry, 1894-95; instr. science, Gilbert Sch., Winsted, Conn., 1895-99; prof. chemistry, Hobart Coll., 1901-05; prof. chemistry, Coll. City of N.Y., 1905-20, prof. chem. engring., 1921, prof. chemistry and dir. of dept. 1922-38, now prof. emeritus. Chief of tech. br., chem. div. of War Industries Bd., Washington, 1917-18; asst. in dept. of adminstrn. NRA, part of 1934. Mem. Div. Chemistry and Chem. Tech. of Nat. Research Council, 1936-41. Mem. Am. Chem Soc., London Soc. Chem. Industry, London Chem. Soc., Societe de Chimie Industrielle,, Phi Beta Kappa; fellow Am. Inst. of Chemistry. Club: Cosmos (Washington). Author: Reactions at the Temperature of the Electric Arc, 1901; College Text-book of Quantitative Analysis, 1914; Chemistry of the Metals, 1923. Home: Vienna, Va. Office: Nat. Research Council, Washington, D.C. Died Oct. 20, 1947.

MOODY, H(OWARD) W(ILSON), prof. civil engring.; b. Garrison, Ia., Oct. 24, 1877; s. James S. and Mary E. (Utley) M.; A.B., Cornell Coll., Mt. Vernon, Ia., 1902; Ph.D., U. Chgo., 1912; m. Lida Auld, Dec. 30, 1902; children—Hope Louise, Roger Lyle. Tchr. high sch., Ludington, Mich., 1902-05, Ft. Dodge, Ia., 1905-07; instr., Northwestern U. Acad., 1907-08; instr. physics Lafayette Coll., Easton, Pa., 1912-13; instr. physics, acting head, dept., Williams Coll., Williamstown, Mass., 1913-14; prof. physics head dept., Miss. A. and M. Coll., 1914-30, dean Sch. Engring., 1925-30; prof. C.E., Valparaiso (Ind.) U., 1930—, dean Coll. engring., 1930-40. Mem. Am. Phys. Soc., A.A.A.S., Soc. Promotion Engring. Edn., Am. Ry. Engring. Assn., Phi Beta Kappa, Sigma Xi. Republican. Methodist. Club: Rotary of Valparaiso; gov. Dist. 154, Rotary Internat., 1943-44. Home: 414 Elmhurst Av., Valparaiso, Ind. Died Mar. 25, 1949; buried Graceland Cemetery, Valparaiso, Ind.

MOODY, LEWIS FERRY, hydraulic engr.; b. Philadelphia, Pa., Jan. 5, 1880; s. Carlton Montague and Elizabeth Eddy (Lewis) M.; B.S., Towne Scientific School (U. of Pa.), 1901, M.S., 1902; m. Eleanor Carman Greene, June 22, 1909 (died 1937); children—Mary Elizabeth (dec.), Lewis Ferry, Arthur Maurice Greene, Eleanor Lowry (Mrs. Edw. M. Broadhurst). Instructor mechanical engineering Univ. of Pa., 1902-04; engineering staff hydraulic dept. of I. P. Morris Co., Phila., 1904-08; asst. prof. mech. engring., later prof. hydraulic engring., Rensselaer Poly. Inst., 1908-16, also independent practice; consulting engr. I. P. Morris Company (now Baldwin Lima Hamilton), 1911-46; consulting engr. Worthington Pump & Mchy. Corp. 1938-49; prof. emeritus hydraulic engring., Princeton. Fellow A.A.A.S.; Am. Soc. Mech. Engrs. (dir. at large, 1947-48; past chmn. Phila. sect.; past chmn. exec. com. hydraulic div.). Mem. Franklin Inst., Am. Soc. for Engring. Edn., Sigma Xi, Tau Beta Pi. Republican. Swedenborgian. Clubs: Nassau (Princeton). Inventor numerous improvements in hydraulic turbines, pumps and accessories; has been awarded many patents for inventions, including spiral draft tube, Moody spreading draft tube, Moody spiral pump, new high speed turbine, etc. Awarded Elliott Cresson medal by Franklin Inst., 1945. Author: Lectures on Machine Design, 1942; section on hydraulic machinery in Handbook of Applied Hydraulics, 1942— and various tech. papers read before engring. socs. and articles in tech. periodicals. Home: 930 Woodland Av., Plainfield, N.J. Died Apr. 18, 1953; buried Princeton (N.J.) Cemetery.

MOODY, PAUL, inventor; b. Byfield Parish, Newbury, Mass., May 21, 1779; s. Capt. Paul and Mary Moody; m. Susannah Morill, July 13, 1800, 3 children. Established (with Francis C. Lowell) cotton mill and other machinery plant, Waltham, Mass.; secured patent for mechanism to wind yarn from bobbins or spools, 1816; perfected soapstone rollers, doubled efficiency of Horrock's dressing machine, 1818; granted patents for machines to make cotton roping, also to rope and spin cotton, 1821; supt. cotton mills, East Chelmsford (now Lowell), Mass., 1823; under his direction the manufacture of cotton machinery was continued and improved designs of machinery were perfected at Lowell Machine Works, 1825. Died Lowell, July 8, 1831.

MOODY, WALTER SHERMAN, electrical engr.; b. Chelsea, Mass., Sept. 20, 1864; s. Luther R. and Emily Sherman M.; B.S. in E.E., Mass. Inst. Tech., 1887; m. Florence C. Gilmore, 1891; 1 dau., Jean (Mrs. Guglilmo Camilli). Instr. physics and electricity, Mass. Inst. Tech., 1887-88; asst. engr., Thomson Electric Welding Co., 1889-92; in engring. dept. Thomson-Houston Co. (now Gen. Electric Co., of Schenectady, N.Y.), 1892-1932; was chief engr. transformer dept. of the co., later cons. engr. for the entire dept., including works at Pittsfield and Lynn, Mass., Erie, Pa., Ft. Wayne, Ind., and Oakland, Calif.; now cons. engr. Identified specially with design and mfr. of transformers, developing the "H" and air blast types of transformers. Conglist. Republican. Fellow Am. Inst. E.E. Home: Pittsfield, Mass. Died Nov. 7, 1938.

MOONEY, ROBERT LEE, physicist; b. Chadbourn, N.C., Nov. 10, 1911; s. Emery Aubert and Elina (Thompson) M.; B.S., Furman U., 1933; M.S. Syracuse U., 1936; Ph.D., Brown U., 1938; m. Dora Lide, Aug. 29, 1938; 1 dau., Marguerite Dora. Instr. to asso. prof. physics Georgetown U., 1938-44, prof., head dept., 1955—; theoretical physicist Naval Ordnance Lab., 1944-45; prof., head dept. physics Coll. William and Mary, 1947-55. Mem. Am. Assn. Physics Tchrs. (exec. com. Chesapeake sect.), Am. Phys. Soc., Sigma Xi. Unitarian. Contbr. articles profl. jours. Office: Georgetown University, Washington 7. Died Mar. 21, 1960.

MOORE, ANDREW CHARLES, biologist; b. Spartanburg County, S.C., Dec. 27, 1866; s. Thomas John and Mary Elizabeth (Anderson) M.; A.B., S.C. Coll. (now U. of S.C.), 1887; grad. student, U. of Chicago, 1898-99, fellow, 1899-1900; studied, Marine Biol. Lab., Woods Hole, Mass., summers, 1901-03; m. Vivian May, Sept. 20, 1900. Supt. city schs., Spartanburg, S.C., 1888, Camden, S.C., 1888-90; prin. City High Sch., Birmingham, Ala., 1890-98; asso. prof. biology, geology and mineralogy, 1900-03, prof. biology, 1903—, chmn. faculty, 1907-08, acting pres., 1908-09, and 1913-14, dean, 1909-13, U. of S.C. Mem. Bd. of Sch. Commrs., Columbia, S.C., 1902— (chmn. 1906—). Democrat. Presbyn. (elder). Home: Columbia, S.C. Deceased.

MOORE, AUSTIN TALLEY, orthopedic surgeon; b. Ridgeway, S.C., June 21, 1899; s. Augustus Talley and Florence (Pooser) M.; student Carlisle Prep. Sch., 1916; A.B., Wofford Coll., 1920; M.D., Med. Coll. State S.C., 1924; postgrad. course in orthopedic surgery, U. Pa., 1925-27; LL.D. (hon.), University of South Carolina, 1958; Sc.D. (hon.), Wofford College, 1963; m. Mary Frances Walker, Nov. 9, 1927; 1 son, Austin Talley. Began pvt. practice orthopedic surgery, Columbia, S.C., 1927; a founder The Moore Clinic, Sept. 1939, orthopedic surgeon Columbia, Baptist, Waverly, S.C. State and Timmons hosps. since 1927; consulting orthopedic surgeon Toumey's Hosp., Sumter, S.C., Tri-County Hosp., Orangeburg, S.C., Urol. Inst., Orangeburg, Oliver Gen. Hosp., Augusta, Ga., 1948—; orthopedic lectr. Post-Grad. Seminar, New Orleans, 1950; owner and operator Glencoe Farm; lectr. U. London, 1960; lecture tour Europe 1900; lectr. U. Chgo., Am. College Surgeons, 1961. Mem. adv. council S.C. Vocational Rehabilitation Service, orthopedic adviser, 1958. Recipient key to Sitka, Alaska, for work with crippled children in Alaska; award of Merit certificate, Wofford Coll., 1956. Served as 2d lt., M.C., U.S. Army, World War I; capt., S.C.N.G. Admiral in Great Navy, Nebraska, 1958. Diplomate Am. Bd. Orthopedic Surgeons, 1938. Fellow A.C.S. (district examiner and adviser 1947), Internat. Coll. Surgeons (founder fellow and regent State S.C. 1945), Am. Acad. Orthopedic Surgeons. (mem. of teaching faculty instructional course program annual meeting, 1953, 59; member A.M.A., Southern Med. Assn., Tri-State, South Carolina, 5th District, Richland Co. med. socs., Am. Orthopaedic Assn., Soc. Internat. Surgery Orthopedica and Traumatology, Latin American Society of Orthopedics and Traumatology, American Orthopedic Academy (chmn. sci. investigation com. 1951), Editor's and Author's Assn., Med. Coll. Alumni Assn. S.C. (sec., 1937-38, pres., 1938-39); S.A.R., Blue Key, Kappa Sigma, Kappa Psi, Phi Beta Kappa. Democrat. Episcopalian. Clubs: Rotary, Forest Lake, Tarantella, Cotillion, Pine Tree Hunt, Centurion, Medical (pres. 1936-37) (Columbia); Springdale Hall (Camden, S.C.). Editor orthopedic sect. Tri-State Med. Jour., 1951. Contbr. articles relating to field in profl. jours. Home: 303 Saluda Av. Office: The Moore Clinic, 1528 Gervais St., Columbia, S.C. Died 1963.

MOORE, BURTON EVANS, physicist; b. Westerville, O., Apr. 8, 1866; s. Royal and Rachel (Evans) M.; A.B., Otterbein U., Westerville, 1888; A.M., Cornell, 1890; student, univs. of Strassburg and Berlin, 1893-94; Ph.D., U. of Göttingen, 1907; m. Harriette Clemens, Sept. 1, 1897 (died 1909); m. 2d, Hanna Eberle, Dec. 16, 1911. Instr. physics, Lehigh U., Pa., 1891-92, U. of Ill., 1895-96; instr. physics, 1896-1902, asst. prof., 1902-06, prof., 1906—, U. of Neb. Made research in excitation stages in Open Arc Spectra. Home: Lincoln, Neb. Died July 15, 1925.

MOORE, CARL RICHARD, prof. zoölogy; b. Green County, Mo., Dec. 5, 1892; s. Johnathan Newton and Sarah Francis (Harris) M.; A.B., Drury Coll., Springfield, Missouri, 1913, M.S., 1914; Sc.D., 1948; Ph.D., University of Chicago, 1916; graduate study Marine Biological Laboratory, Woods Hole, Massachusetts, summers, 1914, 15, 16; m. Edith Naomi Abernethy, July 2, 1920; children—Howard Frederick (dec.), Harris Mason, Ellen Abernethy. Lab. instr., Drury Coll., 1911-14; asst., later asso. in zoölogy, U. of Chicago, 1914-18, instr. in zoölogy, 1918-22, asst. prof., 1922-25, asso. prof., 1925-28, prof. since 1928; mem. editorial bd. Biol. Bull. since 1926, mng. editor, 1926-29; mem. editorial bd. Physiological Zoölogy. Received First Francis Amory Award, 1941, medal from the Endocrine Society, 1955. Member American Society Zoölogists (vice pres. 1926), Am. Soc. Naturalists, A.A.A.S. (v.p. sect. F, 1943), Inst. Medicine, Marine Biol. Lab. Corp., Sigma Xi, Gamma Alpha, Assn. for Study Internal Secretions (pres. 1944-46), Soc. Exptl. Biology and Medicine, National Academy of Sciences. Republican. Club: Quadrangle. Home: 5702 Blackstone Av., Chgo. Died Oct. 16, 1955.

MOORE, CARL VERNON, physician, educator; b. St. Louis, Aug. 21, 1908; s. Carl V. and Mary (Kamp) M.; student Elmhurst Coll., 1924-27, LL.D., 1955; A.B., Washington U., 1928, M.D., 1932; m. Dorothy Adams, May 25, 1935; 1 dau., Judith. NRC fellow in medicine Ohio State U., 1934-35, asst. prof. medicine, 1935-38, asst. prof. medicine Washington U., 1938-41, asso. prof., 1941-46, prof., 1946-72, dean Sch. Medicine, 1954-55, head dept. medicine, 1955-72, vice chancellor for medical affairs, 1964-65. Chmn. hematology study sect. USPHS, 1952-56; chmn. com. blood and blood derivatives NRC, 1953-60; mem. adv. com. on biology and medicine AEC, 1960-66; mem. sci. adv. bd. Nat. Cancer Inst., 1957-59; mem. council Nat. Arthritis and Metabolic Diseases Inst., Nat. Insts. Health, 1958-62, 68-72; drug research bd. NRC, 1962-66. Jacobeus lectr. Sweden, Malthe Lectr., Norway, 1955; George Minot lectr. A.M.A. 1958; McIlrath vis. prof. U. Sydney, Australia, 1962; Stratton lectr., medal Internat. Soc. Hematology, 1964. Recipient Joseph Goldberger award, A.M.A., 1959. Fellow A.C.P. (gov. 1958-60, v.p. 1962-62, regent 1962-72; John Phillips Meml. award 1970); mem. Nat. Acad. Scis., Am. Acad. Arts and Scis., Assn. Am. Physicians (pres. 1963-64), Am. Soc. Clin. Investigation (pres. 1954), Central Soc. Clin. Research (pres. 1947), Am. Soc. Exptl. Pathology, Soc. Exptl. Biology and Medicine, Inst. Nutrition, Internat. (councillor 1953-58, pres. 1966-68), Am. (pres. 1959) socs. hematology, Am. Assn. Med. Colls. (Abraham Flexner award 1971), Alpha Omega Alpha, Sigma Xi. Editor Jour. Lab. and Clin. Medicine, 1944-49; asso. editor Blood, The Jour. of Hematology, 1946-72, Am. Jour. Medicine, 1955-72; co-editor Progress in Hematology. Home: University City MO Died Aug. 13, 1972.

MOORE, CHARLES CADWELL, engineer; b. Alpine, N.Y., July 12, 1868; s. Lewis William and Mary Beaks (Harding) M.; grad. St. Augustine Coll. (now defunct), Benicia, Calif., 1884; m. Lillian M. Breed, Nov. 15, 1893. In employ San Francisco Tool Co., 1885-95; succeeded to the business as Charles C. Moore & Co., engineers, which was inc. 1902 as Charles C. Moore & Co., Engineers, Inc., specializing in motive power and hydraulic work, of which pres.; chmn. board C. C. Moore & Co., Engineers, Inc.; pres. Sylmar Packing Corp.; dir. Anglo & London Paris Nat. Bank, Anglo Calif. Trust Co., Anglo-National Corp., North American Investment Co., Occidental Insurance Co., West Coast Life Ins. Co., Ocean Shore Ry. Co. Commr. to Europe to secure foreign warships for Portola Celebration, San Francisco, 1906 (secured 7 ships); pres. Chamber of Commerce, San Francisco, 1908-09 (elected hon. mem. 1909); chmn. exec. com. Citizens' Health Com. for eradication of bubonic plague through extermination of rats, 1908; chmn. financial com. P.P.I. Expn., 1910-11; elected pres. P.P.I. Expn., 1911; dir. foreign land div. Liberty Loan Com. 12th Federal Reserve Dist., 1918; dir. State Council of Defense, May-Nov. 1918. Decorated 2d Class Order of Chia Ho (China), 1st Class, Order of Sacred Treasure (Japan), Knight of Order of Crown (Italy), Order of St. Olaf (Norway); Grand Commander Order of George I (Greece); Commander of the Legion of Honor (France). V.p. Boy Scouts America; pres. Soc. of Calif. Pioneers. Republican. Home: San Francisco, Calif. Died Apr. 17, 1932.

MOORE, CHARLES J(AMES), prof. of chemistry; b. Flint Hill, Va., Aug. 9, 1875; s. John Randolph and Elizabeth Jane (Green) M.; B.S., Va. Mil. Inst., 1895; Ph.D., U. of Va., 1901; A.M. Harvard, 1909; m. Sophie Schwartz, June 25, 1919; children—Elizabeth Jane,

Charles James. Instr. mathematics, Horner Sch., N.C., 1896-98; prof. chemistry and geology, Western Md. Coll., 1901-02; instr., U. of Ga., 1902-04, adjunct prof., 1904-07; Austin teaching fellow, Harvard, 1908-12; instr. chem., New York U., 1912-14; asst. prof. chem., Hunter Coll., 1914-17, asso. prof., 1917-20, prof., 1921-45, emeritus since 1945; chief. chem. Bur. Soils, U.S. Dept. Agr., 1920-21. Awarded Jackson-Hope medal. Fellow A.A.A.S.; mem. Am. Chem. Soc., Alpha Chi Sigma. Episcopalian. Republican. Researches: aliphatic metal amines, colloidal materials in soils, purification of mercury, atomic weight of phosphorus. Author: Logarithmic reduction tables for analytical chemists, 1913. Exercises in organic chemistry. Lecture table demonstrations of common gases. Home: York Harbor, Me. Died Jan. 25, 1950.

MOORE, CLARENCE LEMUEL ELISHA, mathematician; b. nr. Bainbridge, O., May 12, 1876; s. George Taylor and Lydia Ann (Bradshaw) M.; B.Sc., Ohio State U., 1901; A.M., Cornell U., 1902, Ph.D., 1904; studied univs. of Göttingen, Turin and Bonn; m. Belle Pease Fuller, June 11, 1913; 1 dau., Hazel Fuller. Asst. in mathematics, Ohio State U., 1900-01, scholar in mathematics, 1901-02, fellow, 1902-03, asst., 1903-04, Cornell U.; instr. mathematics, 1904, asst. prof., 1909, asso. prof., 1916, prof., 1920—, Mass. Inst. Tech. Fellow Am. Acad. Arts and Sciences. Democrat. Contbr. to Am. Jour Mathematics, Annals of Mathematics, Proc. Am. Acad. Home: Newton, Mass. Died Dec. 5, 1931.

MOORE, D(ANIEL) MCFARLAN, electrical engr.; b. Northumberland, Pa., Feb. 27, 1869; s. Rev. Alexander Davis and Maria Louisa (Douglas) M.; Lehigh U., 1886-89; m. Mary Alice Elliott, June 5, 1895. With Edison Co., 1890-94; organizer and v.p. Moore Light Co., and Moore Elec. Co. and gen. mgr. both cos. for 18 yrs.; a pioneer in commercializing luminous and non-luminous gaseous conduction; sold Moore Light interests to Gen. Electric Co., 1912. Granted over 100 U.S. patents on elec. and other inventions, many of them among the earliest in radio, X-ray and tube-lighting fields. Fellow Am. Inst. Elec. Engrs. Republican. Presbyterian. Invented gaseous conduction lamps, 1924, that made facsimile photographs by radio reception; and produced lamps, 1925, that were the first to receive motion by radio; made greatly improved television, 1929, and facsimile lamps that were used exclusively for the most advanced demonstrations at expositions in large cities. Author of many published scientific papers read before univs., colls. and scientific socs. Formerly mgr. Moore Light Dept., Gen. Electric Co.; retired, but was active in writing, speaking, inventing the Pianochord, etc. Died June 15, 1936.

MOORE, DEWITT VAN DEUSEN, civil engr.; b. Perry, Lake Co., O., Apr. 6, 1874; s. Webster Oliver and Anna Electa (Van Deusen) M.; ed. Hiram (O.) Coll.; m. Flora Mable Berg, June 14, 1898, 2d, Dorothy Daisy Comer, of Indianapolis, Nov. 19, 1902. Asst. engr. Indianapolis Union Ry., 1895-02; same Pa. Lines West, at Indianapolis, 1897-02; v.-p., sec. Moore-Mansfield Constn. Co., Indianapolis, 1902-11; consulting engr., Indianapolis, 1911-13; dist. engr., central dist., div. of valuation, Interstate Commerce Commn., since Sept. 1, 1913. Dir., charter mem. Am. Soc. Engring. Contractors; mem. Ind. Engring. Soc. (ex-pres.). Republican. Mem. Disciples of Christ. Wrote: Forty-one Concrete Reasons; Contracting Practice; Cost Analysis Engineering; also many papers on cost keeping, analysis and related topics. Home: 5310 Cornell Av. Office: Karpen Bldg., Chicago

MOORE, EDWARD JAMES, physicist; b. Chili, N.Y., June 13, 1873; s. Thomas and Margaret (Hill) M.; A.B., Oberlin, 1903, A.M., 1906; grad. student in physics, U. of Chicago, 1908-10, fellow, 1909-10, Ph.D., 1913; m. Amelia May Eade, July 12, 1905; children—Margaret Carolyn, Edward James. Began as tutor mathematics, Oberlin, 1903, and advanced to asso. prof. physics, 1910; prof. physics, U. of Buffalo, since Sept. 1919, dean Grad. Sch. Arts and Sciences, 1939-46; dean emeritus since 1946. Fellow Am. Assn. for Advancement of Science; member Am. Physical Soc., Am. Assn. Univ. Profs., Sigma Xi. Conglist. Has specialized in molecular physics and the electron theory. Contbr. on tech. topics. Perfected, with J. A. Demuth, an autographic system for recording employees' time, known as the "Symbol System." Home: Getzville, N.Y. Died March 11, 1948.

MOORE, FORRIS JEWETT, chemist; b. Pittsfield, Mass., June 9, 1867; s. Forris Jewett and Ellen S. (Wightman) M.; B.A., Amherst, 1889; Ph.D., U. of Heidelberg, Germany, 1893; m. Emma B. Tod, of Edinburgh, Scotland, Aug. 9, 1892. Lab. asst., Amherst Coll., 1889-90; instr. in chemistry, Cornell U., 1893-94; asst. in chemistry, 1894-95, instr., 1895-1902, asst. prof., 1902-10, asso. prof., 1910-12, prof. organic chemistry, 1912—, Mass. Inst. Tech. Lecturer organic chemistry, Harvard, 1910-11, 1917-18, 1918-19. Fellow Am. Acad. Arts and Sciences. Author: Outlines of Organic Chemistry, 1910; Experiments in Organic Chemistry, 1911; A History of Chemistry, 1918. Home: Cambridge, Mass. Died Nov. 20, 1926.

MOORE, GEORGE THOMAS, botanist; b. Indianapolis, Ind., Feb. 23, 1871; s. George T. and Margaret (Marshall) M.; B.S., Wabash Coll., 1894; A.B., Harvard Univ., 1895, A.M., 1896, Ph.D., 1900; m. Emma L. Hall, Dec. 30, 1896 (died Jan. 1934); children—Harriet Hall, Thomas Gaunt; m. 2d, Katherine H. Leigh, Feb. 20, 1937 (died Oct. 1945). Asst. in cryptogamic botany, Harvard; teacher Radcliffe Coll.; in charge botany, Dartmouth Coll., 1899-1901; became physiologist and algologist, Bur. Plant Industry, Dept. Agr., 1901; in charge Lab. of Plant Physiology, Dept. Agr., 1903-05; in charge of botany, Marine Biol. Lab., Mass., 1909-19; prof. applied botany and plant physiology, Shaw Sch. of Botany (Washington U.) and physiologist to Mo. Bot. Garden, Sept. 1909-May 1912; dir. Mo. Bot. Garden since May 1, 1912; pres. board of trustees Tower Grove Park. Pres. bd. trustees St. Louis Country Day School. Discoverer of a method for preventing pollution of water supplies by algae and certain pathogenic bacteria; perfected method for inoculating the soil with bacteria which enable certain crops to use atmospheric nitrogen. Reviser for "algae," Century Dictionary; contbr. to scientific jours. and Dept. Agr. bulls. upon Pollution of Water Supplies by Algae, with recommendations for preventing these growths, and upon Fixation of Nitrogen by Bacteria, etc. Fellow A.A.A.S.; mem. Am. Philos. Soc., Washington Acad. Sciences, St. Louis Acad. Science, Botanical Society America, Bot. Soc. Washington, Soc. Am. Bacteriologists, English-Speaking Union (v.p.), Phi Gamma Delta, Sigma Xi, Phi Beta Kappa. Overseer, Harvard University. Clubs: University, Noonday, Round Table, Town and Gown, St. Louis Country; Cosmos (Washington); Harvard (St. Louis, New York and Boston). Address: Missouri Botanical Garden, St. Louis. Died Nov. 27, 1956; buried Bellefontaine Cemetery, St. Louis.

MOORE, HENRY FRANK, biologist; b. Phila., June 4, 1867; s. John P. and Emma C. (Frank) M.; A.B., Central High Sch., Phila., 1885; Ph.D., U. of Pa., 1895; m. Annie Florence Dennis, Apr. 13, 1903. Naturalist, Internat. Fishery Commn., 1893-95; chief naturalist, Steamer Albatross, 1896-1903; sci. asst., 1903-11, in charge of sci. inquiry, 1911-15, and dep. commr., 1915-23, U.S. Bureau of Fisheries. Recipient of various awards for investigations; U.S. del. and v.p. 5th Internat. Fishery Congress, Rome, 1911. Fellow A.A.A.S.; hon. mem. Société Internationale Protectrice des Pêcheurs d'Éponges; mem. Am. Geophys. Union, N.C. Forestry Assn., Acad. Natural Science (Phila.), Psi Upsilon. Writer on zoölogy and fisheries. Mem. Inter-departmental Bd. on Internat. Ice Patrol, 1915-23; mem. Nat. Research Council, 1917-25, Internat. Com. on Marine Fishery Investigations (chmn.), 1919-23. Home: Linville Falls, N.C. Died Jan. 8, 1948.

MOORE, HUGH KELSEA, chemical engr.; b. Andover, Mass., Jan. 3, 1872; s. Albert Weston and Sarah Frances (Norton) M.; grad. high sch., Lynn, Mass., 1891; student Mass. Inst. Tech., 1893-96; hon. D.Sc., Univ. of Me., 1924; m. Mary Esther Tebbetts, Jan. 1, 1902; children—Mrs. Katherine Burgess Durell, Hugh Kelsea, Jr., Dorothy Esther. Began with Electro-Chem. Co. at Rumford Falls, Me., 1897; with Moore Electro-Chem. Co. and Am. Electro-Chem. Co. until 1903; with Burgess Sulphite Fibre Co. (later Brown Co.) as chief chemist and chem. engr., 1903-34. Served as mem. Chem. Engring. Com., Council of Nat. Defense, 1917-18, also mem. Div. of Chemistry Nat. Research Council, and mem. and treas. Naval Consulting Bd. of New Hampshire; mem. N.H. legislature, 1923-24; candidate at primaries for gov. of N.H., 1930. Pres. Am. Inst. Chem. Engrs., 1925-26. Congregationalist. Mason, Elk. Author: Incomplete Hydrogenation of Cotton Seed Oil, 1917; Testing of Lubricating Oils, 1917; Chemical Engineering Aspect of Renovating a Sulphite Mill, 1918; Analysis of the Explosion Process of Recovering Soda Salts from Black Liquor, 1919; Accident Prevention in the Mill, 1919; Fundamentals of Electrolytic Diaphragm Cells, 1920; The Use and Value of Physical and Chemical Constants, 1920; Scientific Facts about Pure and Impure Milk, 1921; The Production of Hydrochloride Acid by Direct Union of Hydrogen and Chlorine, 1922; Development of Taxation, 1923; Fundamental Principles of Multiple Effect Evaporative Separation, 1923. Made investigation in evaporation and separation, and in 1929, designed, built and operated a ten-effect multiple effect evaporator; made investigations in refrigeration; investigations in electrolysis, inventing and patenting the unsubmerged diaphragm cell, 1897, which revolutionized that industry; invented and patented, 1925-27, new method of making calcium arsenate; invented and patented, 1913-15, stationary furnace for recovery of soda content from black liquor; invented and patented, 1926-27, a new acid resisting hydraulic cement; invented and patented, 1932-34, a new process of converting sodium sulphate into caustic soda and other chemicals; invented and patented, 1934, new metal filter cloth and method of making same; took out about 45 other patents in U.S. with the corresponding foreign patents, relating to pulp making, pulp bleaching, evaporation, continuous process of hydrogenating oil, mfg. of sodium sulphide, refrigeration, etc. Awarded gold medal, Am. Inst. Chem. Engrs., 1920, "for best contributions to applied science since 1913"; Perkin medalist, 1925. Retired from active business 1934. Home: New Port Ritchie, Fla. Died Dec. 18, 1939.

MOORE, JAMES W., physicist, educator; b. Easton, Pa., June 14, 1844; s. Samuel and Elizabeth Barnes (Wamsley) M.; grad. Lafayette, 1864, A.M., 1867; M.D., Univ. of Pa., 1869; m. Rachel Phillips, d. Rev. James Flannery, Phila., July 30, 1874. Prof. mechanics and experimental philosophy, Lafayette Coll. Conferee Internat. Congress of Electricians, Phila., 1884; Chicago, 1893. Author: The Elements of Natural Philosophy; and numerous works, lectures, addresses and papers on physics; also on med. subjects, Dean Pardee Sch. of Science. Home: Easton, Pa. Died 1909.

MOORE, J(OHN) PERCY, zoologist; b. Williamsport, Pa., May 17, 1869; s. John P. and Emma (Frank) M.; A.B., Central High Sch., Phila., 1886; B.S., U. of Pa., 1892, Ph.D., 1896; m. Kathleen Carter, May 16, 1892 (dec.); children—Warren (dec.), Kathleen (dec.), Elinor (Mrs. J. Logan Irvin), Caroline (dec.). Scientific asst. U.S. Fish Commn., periodically, since 1890; asst. instrm. zoölogy, U. of Pa., 1890-92, instr., 1892-1907, asst. prof., 1907-12, prof., 1912-39, prof. emeritus since 1939; also asst. curator and corr. sec. Acad. Natural Sciences, Philadelphia, 1902-39, member board trustees, 1938-57, hon. life trustee, 1957—; instructor biology, Hahnemann Med. Coll., Phila., 1896-98; instr. Marine Biol. Lab., Wood's Hole, Mass., 1901-02; Ludwick Inst. lecturer, 1902-20, mgr. since 1920, pres., 1941-57. Research asso. Smithsonian Instn. Fellow A.A.A.S.; mem. Soc. Systematic Zoology, Soc. Study Evolution, American Soc. Naturalists, Am. Soc. Zoölogists, Ecol. Soc. America, Am. Philos. Soc., Phila. Acad. Science, Soc. Zoöl. de France, Sigma Xi. Contbr. to scientific jours. and books. Home: 361 Highland Av., Media, Pa. Died Mar. 1, 1965.

MOORE, JOHN WALKER, educator; b. McConnellsville, S.C., Jan. 29, 1884; s. James Oscar and Hattie (Walker) M.; B.S., Davidson (N.C.) Coll., 1906, hon. D.Sc., 1940; med. student Univ. of N.C., 1908-10; M.D., U. of Pa., 1912; m. Anna Stockett Kent, Aug. 19, 1920; children—Marjorie Kent, William Kent, John Walker. Interne Episcopal Hosp., Philadelphia, Pa., 1913-15; instr. in pathology and bacteriology, U. of Louisville, 1915-17, instr. in medicine, 1919-20, prof. research medicine, 1920-23, prof. medicine, 1923-49, dean of Sch. of Medicine, 1929-49, Alben W. Barkley prof. of medicine, since 1949; director division medicine and staff exec. Louisville City Hosp. 1923-49. Served as capt., Med. Corps, U.S. Army, later maj., lab. officer to hosp. center, Nantes, France, 1917-19. Received faculty award of merit, University of Louisville, 1936. Technical supervisor, American Red Cross Blood Donor Service, since 1942; consultant for Army Specialized Training Program. Member Association American Physicians, American Coll. Physicians, A.M.A., Central Soc. Clin. Research (pres. 1942-43), Am. Clin. and Clinatol. Assn., Southern Med. Assn. (chmn. sect. on med. edn. 1933), Assn. Am. Med. Colleges (v.p. 1942-43, pres. 1945-46), Alpha Omega Alpha, Kappa Sigma, Phi Chi, Phi Beta Kappa, Phi Kappa Phi, Gorgon's Head (U. of N.C.). Democrat. Presbyterian. Clubs: Pendennis, Pierian. Home: 623 Cochran Hill Rd. Office: Louisville General Hosp., Louisville. Died Nov. 10, 1952.

MOORE, JOHN WHITE, chief engr. U.S.N.; b. Plattsburg, N.Y., May 24, 1832; s. Amasa C. and Charlotte E. (Mooers) M.; ed. Plattsburgh Acad. and Williston Sem. and pvt. instrn., New York; m. Emily, d. Capt. Horace B. Sawyer, U.S.N., Nov. 19, 1863. Apptd. 3d asst. engr. U.S.N., May 21, 1853; promoted 2d asst. engr., June 27, 1855; 1st asst. engr., July 21, 1858; chief engr., Aug. 5, 1861; retired with rank of commodore, May 24, 1894; advanced to rank of rear admiral retired, June 29, 1906, for services during Civil War. Served in Navy Dept., 1853; on Saranac, Mediterranean Sta., 1853-56; Niagara, first Atlantic cable expdn., 1857-58, flagships Colorado and Roanoke, Home Squadron, 1858-60; flagship Richmond, Mediterranean Squadron, 1860-61; Richmond in West Indies, West Gulf Blockading Squadron and Lower Miss. River, 1861-63; engagements with rebel batteries and ram Manassas at head of passes and with rebel defenses at Pensacola, 1861; passage and capture of Fts. Jackson and St. Philip; capture of New Orleans; passage of Vicksburg batteries; Vicksburg batteries and ram Arkansas, 1862; batteries at Port Hudson; capture of Port Hudson, 1863; originator of chain cable protection on sides of wooden ships; also of "war paint" for making ships less visible in action and at night, and of fighting-tops, later universally used in war vessels; supt. of ironclads at New York and Boston, 1863-67; fleet engr. on staff of Admiral Farragut, European Squadron, 1867-68; Navy Yard, Portsmouth, N.H., 1868-72; fleet engr. of Asiatic sta., 1872-75; Navy Yard, Washington, 1876-79; Bd. of Inspection, 1879-82; fleet engr. Pacific sta., 1882-84; Navy Yard, New York, 1886-88; Navy Yard, Mare Island, 1888-93; insp. machinery at Union Iron Works, San Francisco, 1893-94; Navy Yard, New York, during the Spanish War, 1898. Home: Brooklyn, N.Y. Died Mar. 30, 1913.

MOORE, JOSEPH EARLE, physician; b. Phila., July 9, 1892; s. Joseph Howard and Adelaide Marie (Lovett) M.; A.B., U. of Kan., 1914; M.D., Johns Hopkins, 1916; m. Grace Douglas Barclay, May 24, 1917 (dec.); m. 2d Irene Mason Gieske, Dec. 23, 1954. Asst., instr., asso., asso. prof. medicine and adjunct prof. of pub. health adminstrn., Johns Hopkins, 1916-45, visiting physician Johns Hopkins Hospital 1923-45, physician in charge chronic disease div. Medical Clinic, Johns Hopkins Medical Sch. and Hosp., 1929—, prof. medicine, 1957—; spl. cons. USPHS; cons. Md. State Dept. of Health. Served as first lieutenant and as captain Marine Corps, U.S. Army, A.E.F., 1917-19; maj. M.C. Res., 1920-28. Awarded Medal for Merit. Mem. A.M.A., Assn. of Am. Phys., Am. Soc. for Clin. Investigation, Am. Clin. and Climatol. Soc., Med. and Chirurg. Faculty of Md., Phi Beta Kappa, Sigma Xi, Phi Chi. Author: The Modern Treatment of Syphilis, 1933, 2d edit., 1941; Penicillin in Syphilis, 1947. Co-editor, Jour. Chronic Diseases. Contbr. articles to med. jours. Home: Warrington Apts., 3908 N. Charles St., Balt. Office: Johns Hopkins Hosp., Balt. 5. Died Dec. 6, 1957; buried Greenmount Cemetery.

MOORE, JOSEPH HAINES, astronomer; b. Wilmington, O., Sept. 7, 1878; s. John Haines and Mary A. (Haines) M.; A.B., Wilmington Coll., 1897; Ph.D., Johns Hopkins U., 1903; m. Fredrica Chase (B.A., Vassar, 1904), June 12, 1907; children—Mary Kathryn, Margaret Elizabeth. Asst., 1903-06, asst. astronomer, 1906-09, Lick Obs.; acting astronomer in charge of the D. O. Mills Expdn. to Chile, 1909-13; asst. astronomer, 1913, asso. astronomer, 1918-23, astronomer since 1923, asst. dir., 1936-42, dir., 1942-46, Lick Observatory; mem. five Lick Observatory Eclipse Expeditions, 1918-32. Republican. Mem. Soc. of Friends (Quaker). Fellow A.A.A.S. (v.p and chmn. sect. D, 1931), Royal Astron. Soc., Calif. Acad. Science; mem. Nat. Acad. Science, Am. Astron. Soc. (v.p. 1942), Astron. Soc. Pacific (pres. 1920 and 28); mem. com. 30, Internat. Astron. Union. Author of various astron. papers. Address: 6138 Swainland Rd., Oakland 11, Calif. Died March 15, 1949.

MOORE, JOSIAH JOHN, pathologist; b. Anaconda, Mont., Aug. 26, 1886; s. William and Jane (Peters) M.; B.S., U. Mont., 1907; M.D., M.S., U. Chgo. and Rush Med. Coll., 1912; LL.D. (hon.), U. Mont., 1945; m. Florence M. Johnson, June 19, 1909; children—Franklin Johnson, William Aubrey. Fellow, asst. pathology, U. Chgo., 1909-12; fellow Sprague Meml. Inst., 1912-13; instr. and asst. prof. pathology, bacteriology and exptl. medicine, U. Ill. Coll. Medicine, 1913-21; sec. sect. pathology and physiology A.M.A., 1919-43, vice chmn., 1943-44, chmn., 1944-45; dir. Nat. Pathol. Lab., Chgo., 1921-36, dir. Moore Clin. Lab., Chgo., 1936—, now partner; pathologist Ravenswood Hosp., Chgo., 1912-49; pathologist Little Co. of Mary Hosp., Evergreen Park, Ill., 1932—; pathologist Jackson Park Hosp., 1928—. Vice pres. bd. dirs. Municipal Tb Sanitarium. Mem. Bd. Health Chgo. Spl. instr. USN, 1918; mem. med. adv. bd., Selective Service, 1941-43; Procurement and Assignment Bd., 1943—; asso. editor Ill. Med. Jour., 1941. Diplomate Internat. Bd. Surgery, Am. Bd. Pathology. Founding fellow, Coll. Am. Pathologists (bd. govs. 1946); fellow Internat. Coll. Surgeons, A.C.P.; mem. Ill. Soc. Clin. Path. (past pres. 1911), Med. Com., 1943-55, Bd. Registration and Edn. of Ill., Chgo. Med. Soc. (pres. 1944-45), Inst. Medicine Chgo. (pres. 1958), Chgo. Pathol. Soc. (pres. 1921-22), Chgo. Soc. Internal Medicine, Ill. Med. Soc,. Soc. Ill. Bacteriologists (past pres., 1942-43), A.M.A. (treas. 1943-58), Am. Soc. of Clin. Pathologists (v.p.), Am. Assn. Pathologists and Bacteriologists, The Tuberculosis Inst. (dir.), Am. Cancer Soc. Ill. Div., Inc. (dir., mem. exec. com.), Am. Assn. Coll. Honor Socs. (pres. 1940-45), Alpha Omega Alpha (sec. treas. 1932—), Sigma Xi, Sigma Nu, Phi Chi, Acacia. Mason (Shriner). Clubs: Quadrangle (U. Chgo.), Rotary (v.p.) (Chgo.); University, Chiseler's. Asso. editor Ill. Med. Jour., 1941—. Home: 6937 Bennett Av. Address: 55 E. Washington St., Chgo. Died May 5, 1964.

MOORE, MERRILL, (mor), psychiatrist; b. Columbia, Tenn., Sept. 11, 1903; s. John Trotwood and Mary Brown (Daniel) M.; student Montgomery Bell Acad., Nashville, 1916-20; B.A., Vanderbilt U., Nashville, 1924, M.D., Vanderbilt Med. Sch., 1928; married Ann Leslie Nichol, Aug. 14, 1930; children—Adam G. N. Moore, John Trotwood, Leslie and Hester. Interne, St. Thomas Hospital, Nashville, Tenn., 1928-29; teaching fellow neurology, Harvard Med. Sch., 1930-31, asst. in neuropathology, 1931-32, research fellow psychiatry, 1936-42; neurological house officer, Boston City Hosp., 1930-31, res. neurological physician, 1930-31; asst. physician, Boston Psychopathic Hosp., 1932-35; grad. asst., Psychiatric Clinic, Mass. General Hospital, 1933-34. Military service, S.W. Pacific, 1942-45; col. M.C., A.U.S.; surgeon, Nanking Hdqrs. Command, 1946. Vis. psychiat., Boston City Hosp.; clin. asso. psychiatry, Harvard Med. Sch.; research asso., Boston Psychopathic Hosp. Awarded Bronze Star (Bougainville), 1944; Army Commendation Ribbon (China), 1946. Fellow American Psychiat. Assn., Am. Neurol. Assn., Mass. Med. Soc., Am. Psychopathol. Assn., A.A.A.S.; mem. Am. Med. Assn., Sigma Chi, Phi Beta Kappa (hon. 1941). Author: The Noise That Time Makes, 1929; Six Sides to a Man, 1935; M: one thousand autobiog. sonnets; Clinical Sonnets, 1949; Illegitimate Sonnets, 1950; Case Record From a Sonnetorium, 1952; More Clinical Sonnets, 1952; A Doctor's Book of Hours, 1954; Dance of Death, 1957; The Phoenix & The Bees (poems), 1958; also other vols. of poetry, prose essays; contbr. articles on alcoholism, syphillis, suicide, psychiatry and conchology. Home: 10 Crabtree Rd., Squantum, Quincy 71, Mass. Died Sept. 20, 1957.

MOORE, RANSOM ASA, agronomist; b. Kewaunee, Wis., June 5, 1861; s. Seth and Johanna (Werner) M.; ed. State Normal Sch., Oshkosh, Wis.; M.A., U. of Wis., 1932; m. Nettie M. Rogers, July 17, 1889. Lived on farm until 1882; teacher common and graded schs., 8 yrs.; county supt. schs., 6 yrs., resigned, 1895, to become asst. to Dean Henry, of Coll. of Agr., U. of Wis.; was given gen. charge of short course in agr., later took up breeding of grains and forage plants; emeritus agronomy. Congregationalist. Author of many bulls. and editor ann. reports Wis. Experiment Assn., 1902-29; also of agronomy sect. "Plant Production" (text-book). Home: Madison, Wis. Died Feb. 26, 1941.

MOORE, RICHARD BISHOP, chemist; b. Cincinnati, May 6, 1871; s. William Thomas and Mary A. (Bishop) M.; went to Eng. with parents, 1878; student Argyle Coll., London, Eng., 1881-83, St. Edmund's Coll., London, 1883-85, Institut Keller, Paris, 1885-86, Univ. Coll., London, 1886-90, U. of Chicago, 1896-97, B.S., 1896; D.Sc., U. of Colo., 1916; m. Callie Pemberton, June 11, 1902; m. 2d, Georgie Elizabeth Dowell, June 18, 1924. Lived in Southport and London, Eng., 1878-95; instr. chemistry, Oswestry High Sch., Eng., 1890-91, Birkbeck Inst., London, 1891-93; asst. in chemistry, U. of Chicago, 1896; instr. chemistry, U. of Mo., 1897-1905; prof. chemistry, Butler Coll., Indianapolis, 1905-11; soil scientist, Lab. of Phys. and Chem. Investigations, Bur. of Soils, Washington, Aug. 20, 1911-Oct. 1912; phys. chemist in charge of the chemistry and metallurgy of rare metals, 1912-19, chief chemist and chief div. mineral technology, U.S. Bur. Mines, 1919-23; gen. mgr. The Door Co., engrs., New York, 1923-26; dean of science, head chem. dept., Purdue, 1926—. Made survey for U.S. Geol. Survey, of the thermal waters of the Yellowstone Nat. Park for radio-active properties, 1906; with Sir William Ramsey, London, Eng., 1907-08; in charge all helium work for U.S. Bur. Mines, 1918-23. Mem. U.S. Helium Bd., 1920-23. Author: A Laboratory Chemistry, 1904; also papers on radio-activity, inorganic physical chemistry, and rare gases. Died Jan. 20, 1931.

MOORE, ROBERT, civil engr.; b. New Castle, Pa., June 19, 1838; s. Henry C. and Amelia (Whippo) M.; A.B., Miami U., 1858, A.M., 1866; m. Alice Filley, Oct. 3, 1878. Engaged in civ. engring., 1863—, chiefly in location and constrn. of rys.; built lines which are now parts of larger ry. systems, such as I.C., Ill. Southern, C.&A. and B.&O. Southwestern rys.; was sewer commr. and mem. Bd. Pub. Improvements, St. Louis, 1877-81; acted as consulting engr. for numerous rys. and reorganization coms.; was apptd. mem. Brazos River Bd., and Southwest Pass Bd. of Engrs.; mem. Bd. of Edn. of St. Louis, 1897-1913 (pres. bd. 1905-06, 1909-10). Past pres. Am. Soc. C.E., St. Louis Engrs. Club. Republican. Home: St. Louis, Mo. Died July 24, 1922.

MOORE, ROBERT ALLAN, physician, educator; b. Chgo., Ill., July 12, 1901; s. Ellis Philip and Nelly (Clymer) M.; A.B., Ohio State U., 1921, M.D., 1928, M.Sc., 1927, D.Sc., 1956; Ph.D., Western Res. U., 1930; D.Sc. (hon.), Ohio State U., 1954, Union Coll., 1954, Waynesburg, 1957; L.H.D., U. Miami, 1956; LL.D. (honorary), Long Island University, 1959; m. Ruth Miller, June 15, 1922; children—Richard Allan, Calvin Cooper. Instr. pathology, O. State U., 1924-28; research fellow, pathology, Western Res. U., 1928-30, instr., 1930-33; asst. prof. pathology, Cornell U., 1933-37, asso. prof., 1937-39; prof. of pathology, Washington U., St. Louis, Mo., 1939-54; dean, Washington U. Sch. Medicine, 1946-54; vice chancellor schs. of health professions, Univ. Pitts., 1954-57, prof. pathology 1954-57; pres. Downstate Med. Center, dean Coll. Medicine State U. N.Y., 1957-66; Guiteras lectr., Am. Urol. Assn., 1950; Poynter lecturer University Nebraska, 1951; Melon lecturer, University Pittsburgh, 1951; Luis Guerrero lecturer, U. Santo Tomas, 1952; Macgregor lectr. U. Western Ontario, 1952; Ballenger lectr., Southeastern Sec., Am. Urol. Assn., 1956; sr. cons. path. surgeon gen., AUS; mem. com. pathol., 1942-58, Nat. Research Council; civilian adviser on epidemic diseases to secretary of war, 1942-46; spl. consultant to surgeon gen., U.S. Army; scientific adv. bd. Army Inst. Pathol. (chmn. 1953); mem. adv. com. VA; adv. com. med. pub. health Rockefeller Found.; mem. Am. Bd. Pathology (pres. 1951-53); advisory committee Cancer Control USPHS (chmn. 1952-55); hon. cons. surgeon gen. USN, 1956-59; Nat. adv. council Health Research Facilities, USPHS, 1956-60. Coordinating dir. U. Pitts. Health Center, 1954-57; mem. bd. trustees Nat. bd. Medical Examiners, 1948-60, pres. 1954-57, China Med. bd. N.Y., 1955-71; adv. council Med. Edn., 1950-56; adv. com. Nat. Com. Resettlement Fgn. Physicians, 1956-63; adv. bd. Med. Specialties, pres. 1953-57; Mem. Am. Assn. Pathol. and Bacteriol. (president 1952), Federation Biol. Societies, Club for Rsrch. on Aging, Soc. Exptl. Pathol., Am. Soc. Clin. Pathol., Am. Soc. Cancer Research. Gerontological Soc. (pres. 1951), Internat. Soc. Geographic Pathology (pres. 1952-54), Coll. Am. Pathol., Am. Soc. Clin. Pathologists, Mexican Association of Pathologists (hon.), Alpha Omega Alpha, Sigma Xi. Republican. Episcopalian. Author: Textbook of Pathology, 1944, 1951. Contbr. sci. jours. Christian Fenger lectr. Chgo. Inst. Medicine, 1947. Home: Pittsburgh PA Died Sept. 24, 1971; buried Woodland Cemetery, Van Wert OH

MOORE, ROBERT MARTIN, physician; b. Somerville, Ind., Nov. 18, 1884; s. Robert (M.D.) and Laura (Martin) M.; A.B., Ind. U., 1911, M.D., 1913; postgrad. work, Harvard Med. Sch., summers 1920-21, 22; m. Eva Belle Van Dyke, Nov. 12, 1919; children—Robert (dec.), Philippe Van Dyke. Began practice, 1913; prof. clin. cardiology, Indiana University Sch. of Medicine, since 1931, and member of the board of councilors; chief of Cardiac Clinic, Indianapolis City Hospital; past pres. Ind. Heart Found.; chmn. bd. trustees, Ind. Heart Foundn.; member staff Indiana University Hosp.; mem. visiting staff St. Vincent's Hosp.; mem. staff and mem. adv. bd. Methodist Hosp. Capt. Med. Corps, U.S. Army, with A.E.F., World War I. Certified by American Board Internal Medicine and Cardiovascular Disease Fellow American Coll. Physicians (Ind. gov. 16 yrs.); mem. Am., Ind. State and Marion County med. assns., Indianapolis Med. Soc. (pres. 1938), Am. Heart Assn. (councilor), Indianapolis Acad. of Medicine and Surgery, Central Soc. for Clinical Research, Am. Assn. for Study of Goitre, Delta Tau Delta, Nu Sigma Nu, Sigma Xi. Republican. Presbyterian. Mason. Contbr. to med. jours. Home: 5617 N. Meridian St. Office: Home Mansur Bldg., Indpls. Died June 23, 1952; buried Crown Hill Cemetery, Indpls.

MOORE, ROBERT THOMAS, zoölogist; b. Haddonfield, N.J., June 24, 1882; s. Henry Dyer and Mary J. (Smith) M.; A.B., U. Pa., 1903; A.M., Harvard, 1904; grad. study U. Munich; D.S. (hon.), Occiental Coll., Los Angeles, 1949; m. Selma Helena Muller, Dec. 22, 1903; children—Terris, Karlene; m. 2d, Margaret Forbes Cleaves, June 17, 1922; 1 dau., Marilynn; step-children—Waddell Austin, Paul Austin. Editor Cassinia, ofcl. publ. Del. Valley Ornithol. Club, 1911-16; breeder of silver black foxes; owner Borestone Mountain Fox Ranch, Onawa, Me., 1915-30, Western bus. inc., 1923, as Big Bear Fox Ranch of Cal.; asso. dept. vertebrate zoölogy Cal. Inst. Tech., 1929-50; asso. in vertebrate zoölogy and dir. zoölog. lab. Occidental Coll., Los Angeles 1950-55; formerly v.p. Moore Securities Co. (Phila.); pres. Big Bear Fox Ranching Co. until 1928; dir. Guanajuato Reduction & Mines Co., Empire Lumber Co., Cowichan Lake Lumber Co. Founder of World's 1st National Silver Fox Show, Boston, 1919. Leader of ornithol. expedition to Ecuador, 1927, zoölogical expedition to South Ecuador, 1929 (made first successful ascent of Mt. Sangai, active volcano, large zool. collection from hitherto unexplored regions; zoöl. species new to science), to Mexico for Calif. Inst. Tech., 1933, 34, 36, 37, 38, 42, 43, 45; (secured many birds new to science); lectured in Cultural Relations Mexico, i942-45; chmn. Galapagos Com., 1934-38; instrumental in having a large part of Galapagos Archipelago set aside by Ecuador as sanctuary for zoölogical life. Trustee the Poetry Soc. Am. Fellow Royal Geog. Soc. (London), Am. Geog. Soc., Am. Ornithol. Union (mem. council); mem. Am. Com. for Internat. Wild Life Protection, Acad. Natural Sciences, Am. Nat. Fox Breeders Assn. (bd. govs. and first hon. pres.), Am. Fox Breeders Assn. (bd. govs.), Soc. Mayflower Descs., John Howland Descs., Phi Beta Kappa. Presbyn. (elder). Clubs: Twilight, Valley Hunt, (hon. mem.; gov.; past pres.) (Los Angeles); Orpheus (Phila.); Explorers (N.Y.C.); Cosmos (Washington). Author: Eileen, a Sonnet Sequence, 1946; chairman of authors: Check List of Mexican Birds, 1950; co-author: Biotic Provinces of Mexico (with A. E. Goldman). Editor in chief Poetry Awards, an annual anthology of mag. poetry. Contbr. more than 60 articles on zoology, breeding and exploration. Contbr. many poems to mags. Home: Zephyr Cove, Lake Tahoe, Nev.; (winter) Sunny Gables, Meadow Grove Place, Pasadena 3, Cal. Died Oct. 30, 1958.

MOORE, SHERWOOD, physician; b. Lynchburg, Va., Oct. 28, 1880; s. Israel Sneed and Nellie Hayward (Wise) M.; student U. of Va., 1900-01; M.D., Washington U., St. Louis, Mo., 1905; m. Veronica Mollison, September 1, 1917; children—Andrew, Peter. Interne, St. Louis (Mo.) City Hosp., 1905-06; sr. resident in obstetrics. Washington U. Hosp., 1906-07; surgeon in pvt. practice, 1907-12; asst. in surgery, St. Louis Children's Hosp., 1910-13; resident radiologist, Mass. Gen. Hosp., 1916-17; asst. in surgery and radiology, Washington U. Sch. of Medicine, 1917-20, asso. in surgery, 1920-27, prof. radiology, 1927-49, emeritus; dir. Edward Mallinckrodt Inst. of Radiology since 1930; roentgenologist, Barnes Hosp., St. Louis Children's Hosp., St. Louis Maternity Hosp., Shriners' Hosp. and McMillan Hosp. Recipient (with Dr. Evarts A. Graham, Dr. Warren H. Cole and Glover H. Copher) of gold medal St. Louis Med. Soc., 1927; hon. mention A.M.A. and Canadian Med. Assn., 1935; Silver medal Am. Acad. Orthopedic Surgeons, 1936; hon. mention Southern Med. Assn., 1937; hon. mention 5th Internat. Congress of Radiology, 1937; bronze medal Miss. Valley Med. Soc., 1938; 1st award Radiol. Soc. of N.A., 1939; certificate of merit Am. Roentgen Ray Soc., 1936, Am. Med. Assn., 1936 and 1939. Served as lt., M.C., U.S.N.R.F., 1917-22; major and lt. col., M.C., Army of U.S., 1922-42. Diplomate Am. Bd. of Radiology, 1935. Director-at-large, American Cancer Society, 1947. Fellow A.M.A., Am. Coll. of Radiology; mem. Am. Roentgen Ray Soc. (past pres.; chmn. exec. council,

1935-36), Nat. Advisory Cancer Council, Radiol. Soc. of N.A., Southern and Mo. State med. assns., St. Louis Med. Soc.; former corr. mem. Deutsche Röntgen Gesellschaft. Author or co-author of books relating to field; recipient many awards for sci. and med. exhibits. Home: 425 Hazelgreen Dr., St. Louis 19. Died July 9, 1963; buried Lynchburg, Va.

MOORE, THOMAS MORRELL, inventor, designer; b. New York, Nov. 13, 1856; s. John and Cornelia (Morrell) M.; ed. Pingree Inst., Elizabeth, N.J., and partial course, Rutgers Coll., class 1876. Has been mfr. agrl. implements; invented many implements and improVements; traveled in Europe and S. America, 1894-95, and 1907-14; was chief machinery, transportation and agrl. implements, Pan-Am. Expn.; chief dept. of machinery, St. Louis Expn., 1904; commr. gen. Panama-Pacific Internat. Expn., 1915. Contbr. to Am. and foreign jours. Clubs: Engineers, Nat. Republican, New York Athletic Address: 54 W. 40th St., New York, N.Y.

MOORE, WILLIAM STURTEVANT, commodore U.S.N.; b. Duxbury, Mass., Feb. 23, 1846; s. Josiah and Maria Foster (Doane) M.; B.S., Lawrence Scientific Sch. (Harvard), 1867; grad. U.S. Naval Acad., 1868; m. Caro Garland Burwell, Feb. 6, 1901. Apptd. from Mass., acting 3d asst. engr. vol. navy, Oct. 10, 1866; 3d asst. engr. in regular service, June 2, 1868; promoted 2d asst. engr., June 2, 1869; passed asst. engr., June 11, 1876; chief engr., Aug. 10, 1893; comdr., Mar. 3, 1899; capt., Mar. 21, 1903; retired as commodore, June 30, 1906. At U.S. Naval Acad., 1866-67; Navy Yard, Boston, 1867; Naval Acad., 1867-68; on board Yantic, 1868-69; Bur. of Steam Engring., 1870-72; Frolic, 1872-73; Navy Yard, Washington, 1873; Bur. Steam Engring., 1873; Brooklyn, 1873-74; Bur. Steam Engring., 1875-76; coast survey steamer Blake, 1876-78; Minnesota, 1878-79; Bur. Steam Engring., 1879-82; Tallapoosa, 1882-84; Ossipee, 1884-87; Bureau of Steam Engineering, 1887-91; Vesuvius, 1891-94; Naval Examining Board, Phila., 1894-95; Dolphin, 1895-96; Texas, 1896-97; Columbia, 1897-98; receiving-ship Vermont, 1898-99; insp. machinery for the navy at Cramps' shipyard, 1899-1903; insp. of machinery for Mass. dist., 1903-05; Navy Yard, Boston, 1905-06. Mem. Mass. Ho. of Rep., 1909, 1910. Died July 12, 1914.

MOORE, WILLIS LUTHER, meteorologist; b. Scranton, Pa., Jan. 18, 1856; s. Luther T. and Lucy E. (Babcock) M.; ed. Binghamton pub. schs.; student of natural sciences under scientific staff of Weather Bur., 15 yrs.; LL.D., Norwich, 1896; D.Sc., St. Lawrence, 1906. Entered signal corps (now weather bur.), rose through successive grades to local forecast official, Milwaukee, 1891-94; won professorship meteorology, open competitive exam. against 23 contestants, 1894; chief U.S. Weather Bureau, 1895-1913; one of U.S. representatives in First Internat. Radio Congress, London, 1912; prof. applied meteorology, George Washington U. Owner and manager, 1907-19, large fruit, grain and stock farm, at Rockville, Md. Lecturer for the Royal Inst., London, 1912; lecturer in lyceum and chautauqua circuits. Author: Moore's Descriptive Meteorology, 1901; The New Air World, 1922; Spiritual Gravity of the Cosmist. Home: Pasadena, Calif. Died Dec. 18, 1927.

MOORHEAD, LOUIS DAVID, (moor'hed), surgeon; b. Chicago, Ill., Nov. 22, 1892; s. Edward Louis (M.D.) and Jeannette (Snell) M.; A.B., St. Ignatius Coll., Chicago, 1913; S.B., U. of Chicago, 1914, S.M., 1915; A.M., Loyola U., 1916; M.D., Rush Med. Coll., 1917; LL.D., Creighton U., 1931; m. Ann Patricia Dorsey, Aug. 25, 1932; children—Louis David, Edward Louis II, Patrick Henry. Practiced in Chicago since 1917; sr. house surgeon Cook County Hosp., 1917-19; became dean and asso. prof. surgery, Loyola U. Sch. of Medicine, 1918, dean, prof. and head of dept. of surgery, 1928-40; formerly chief of staff; sr. attending surgeon Mercy Hosp. since 1920; cons. surg. Rock Island R.R. System, C.&E.I. R.R., Belt R.R. of Chicago, Chief of med. bd. archdiocese of Chgo., Chgo. Bd. of Health, Chicago Fire Dept. Chmn. bd. trustees Lewis Memorial Maternity Hosp., Loretto Hosp., St. Georges Hosp., Holy Cross Hosp. Mem. bd. govs., Cath. Ch. Extension Soc. of U.S. and Can., since 1948; mem. bd. dirs. Cath. Charities, Chicago; adv. com., Institutem Divi Thomae. Fellow Am. Coll. Surgeons; mem. Founders Group, Am. Bd. of Surgery; mem. Internat. Coll. of Surgeons, A.M.A., Ill. State and Chicago med. socs., Phi Beta Pi, Kappa Pi Epsilon, Sigma Xi. Catholic. Decorated Knight of St. Gregory by the Pope, 1931; Knight of Order of Crown of Italy, 1932; Knight of Cap and Sword by Pope Pius XI, 1938, reknighted by Pope Pius XII, 1939; Knight Comdr. Order of Crown of Italy, 1946. Club: University. Home: 1101 N. Elmwood Av., Oak Park, Ill. Office: 31 N. State St., Chicago. Died Sept. 14, 1951; buried family mausoleum, Calvary Cemetery.

MOOSER, WILLIAM, architect; b. Switzerland, 1834; at least 2 sons including William. Came to U.S., 1852; pioneer architect, San Francisco; designed and built Met. Hall, Cosmos Club (San Francisco), French Hosp. (Richmond, Cal.), McDonough Theatre (Oakland, Cal.), Woolen Mills (North Beach, Cal.); became partner (with his 2 sons) firm William Mooser & Sons. Died Nov. 17, 1896.

MORAN, DANIEL EDWARD, consulting engr.; b. Orange, N.J., April 12, 1864; s. Daniel E. and Annie A. (Blake) M.; C.E., Sch. of Mines, Columbia U., 1884, M.Sc., 1911; m. Sarah V. Kelly, of Glasgow, Scotland, 1896; children—Sarah Sylvester (Mrs. George C. Fraser), Daniel E., Dorothy A. (Mrs. Carl Bricken), Archibald A., Hugh B. Became mem. Moran, Maurice & Proctor, 1917, title now Moran & Proctor; cons. engr. Phila. and Camden Bridge, Mid-Hudson Bridge (Poughkeepsie, N.Y.), Federal Reserve Bank Bldg., Port of New York Authority, Hudson River Bridge and Detroit Internat. Bridge, San Francisco-Oakland Bay Bridge, Triborough Bridge. Democrat. Home: Mendham, N.J. Died July 3, 1937.

MORAN, ROBERT, shipbuilder, mech. engr.; b. N.Y. City, Jan. 26, 1857; s. Edward and Jean Dear (Boyack) M.; ed. pub. schs.; m. Miss M. E. Paul, of Victoria, B.C., 1882; children—John M., Frank G., Malcolm E., Nellie M., Mary R. (Wood). Went to Seattle at 18, and became steamboat fireman, later engr.; established Moran Bros., steamboat and sawmill machy., 1889; organized Moran Bros. Co., Ship & Engine Bldg. Co., 1890; built in 4 mos., fleet of 12 steamers and 10 barges, delivered on the Yukon River to carry food to the miners, 1898; built many large steel and wood vessels, including the 15,000 ton U.S. Battleship Nebraska; sold out business, 1905, and retired, at Rosario, on Orcas Island, Wash. Mayor of Seattle 2 terms, 1888-90; state director Public Service Reserve during the World War. Donated 4,000 acres to the State of Wash., now Moran State Park. Mem. Soc. Naval Architects and Marine Engrs., Soc. of U.S. Mil. Engrs., Am. Shipmasters' Assn., Marine Engrs. Assn., Franklin Inst., Inst. Naval Architects (London), Washington Pioneers' Assn. Clubs: Rainer, Seattle Yacht, Seattle Athletic, Home: Orcas, San Juan Co., Wash.

MORDECAI, ALFRED, army officer, engr.; b. Warrenton, N.C., Jan. 3, 1804; s. Jacob and Rebecca (Myers) M.; grad. U.S. Mil. Acad., 1823; m. Sara Hays, 6 children including Alfred. Commd. 2d lt. Corps Engrs., U.S. Army, 1823; asst. prof. engring. U.S. Mil. Acad., 1823-25; asst. engr. in charge of constructing Ft. Monroe, Va., 1825-28; commd. capt. Ordnance Dept., U.S. Army, 1832; commanded 1st Washington (D.C.) Arsenal, then Frankford (Pa.) Arsenal, 1833-38; asst. to chief of ordnance, 1838-42; commanded Washington Arsenal during Mexican War, brevetted maj.; commd. maj. Ordnance Dept., 1854; mem. U.S. Mil. Commn. to Crimea War, 1855-57; resigned from Army at outbreak of Civil War; tchr. mathematics, Phila., 1861-63; asst. engr. Mexico & Pacific R.R., 1863-66; sec., treas. Pa. R.R., 1867-87. Author: A Digest of Laws Relating to the Military Establishment of the United States, 1833; Artillery for the United States Land Service, 1849. Died Phila., Oct. 23, 1887.

MORE, CHARLES CHURCH, engr., educator; b. Rock Island, Ill., Jan. 21, 1875; s. David Fellows and Sara Jane (Hubbell) M.; C.E., Lafayette Coll., 1898, M.S., 1901; M.C.E., Cornell, 1899; m. Myra Hadlock Ober, Aug. 24, 1904. Began with Pencoyd Iron Works, Phila., 1899; acting prof. civ. engring., U. Wash., 1900, asst. prof., 1904, asso. prof., 1907, prof., 1912, prof. and head dept., 1917-25, prof. structural engring., 1925-47, emeritus, 1947—; with Am. Bridge Co. (Phila.), D. H. Burnham & Co. (Chgo.), U.S. Engr. Dept. (Ft. Worden, Wash.), 1901-04; with C.,M.&St.P. Ry. Co., Seattle, 1906-07, Turner Constrn. Co., N.Y.C., 1911-12. Commd. capt. Engr. R.C., June 19, 1917; in training at Engr. O.T.C., Vancouver Barracks, Wash., Sept.-Oct. 1917; capt. O.R.C., Oct. 18, 1917; maj. ordnance, U.S. Army, July 25, 1918. On duty at Ordnance Office, Washington, Nov. 1917-Nov. 1918; instr. at Engr. Sch., Camp Humphreys, Va., Dec. 1918-Sept. 1919; hon. discharged Oct. 1, 1919. Mem. Soc. for Promotion Engring. Edn. (council, 1919-22), Am. Assn. Univ. Profs., Am. Soc. C.E., Am. Legion, Phi Beta Kappa, Sigma Xi, Tau Beta Pi, Phi Kappa Psi. Sec. John More Assn., 1900-25, asso. sec., 1925—. Conglist. Compiler: Genealogy of Descendants of John More, 1893. Home: 4545 Fifth Av. N.E., Seattle, Wash. Died Nov. 19, 1949.

MOREHEAD, FRENCH HUGH, cons. engr.; b. Paris, Mo., Nov. 23, 1883; s. John Quarles and Mary Martha (Glascock) M.; B.S. in M.E., U. Mo., 1904; m. Clo Searcy, July 8, 1907 (died 1914); 1 son, T. Searcy (dec.); m. 2d, Frances Thornton, Aug. 10, 1925. Began as draftsman and surveyor, U.S. Geol. Survey, 1904; machine designer Am. Steel Wire Co., 1904-06; sales and office mgr. Kewanee Pvt. Utilities Co., 1906-18; successively works engr., chief engr. Walworth Co., 1918-29, v.p., cons. engr., 1929-46. Mem. Am. Soc. M.E., Am. Soc. Testing Materials. Republican. Contbr. tech. jours. Home: Sierre Madre, Cal. Died Nov. 27, 1949.

MOREHOUSE, DANIEL WALTER, astronomer, coll. pres.; b. Mankato, Minn., Feb. 22, 1876; s. Aaron and Sabra Ann (Burleson) M.; N.W. Christian Coll., Excelsior, Minn., 1895-97; S.B., Drake University, 1900; S.B., U. of Chicago, 1902; S.M., Drake U., 1902; Ph.D., U. of Calif., 1914; LL.D., Butler U., 1932; m. Myrtle Slayton, June 9, 1903; children—Charles Aaron, Vega Lorraine, Frances Roberta. Prof. physics and astronomy, Drake U., 1900—. Vol. research asst., Yerkes Obs., summer 1909; instr. astronomy, U. of Calif., 1911-12; dean of men, Drake U., 1919-22, acting pres. and dean Coll. of Liberal Arts, 1922-23, pres. and dean Coll. of Liberal Arts, 1923-1930, again president, 1930—. Fellow Ia. State Acad. of Science (pres. 1921-22). Discovered Comet (c), 1908 (Morehouse), Sept. 1, 1908; awarded Donahue Comet Medal, 1908; also community award to citizen rendering most distinguished service to the city of Des Moines in 1928. Mem. Christian (Disciples) Church; pres. Internat. Conv. of Disciples of Christ, 1934-35. Home: Des Moines, Ia. Died Jan. 21, 1941.

MOREHOUSE, JULIUS STANLEY, coll. dean; b. Amenia, N.Y., Nov. 19, 1894; s. Henry Stebins and Bertha (Humphreyville) M.; M.E., Stevens Inst. Tech., 1921; Dr. of Sci., Villanova University, 1956; married Justine Rose Kumhera, June 1930; 1 son, Julius Stanley. Instr. mech. engring. Villanova Coll., 1921-23, asst. prof., 1923-24, asso. prof., 1924-26, prof. since 1926, dean engring. since 1938. Fellow Am. Soc. M.E. (past chmn. Phila. sect.); mem. Soc. Engring. Edn. (past chmn. Middle Atlantic sect.), National Society of Professional Engineers, American Society Engineering Education, Newcomen Soc. Eng., Tau Beta Pi, Sigma Nu, Pi Tau Sigma. Club: Engrs. Author: Text on Mechanisms, 1930; Heating, Ventilating and Air Conditioning, 1932. Died July 12, 1961; buried Valley Forge Gardens, King of Prussia, Pa.

MOREHOUSE, LYMAN FOOTE, telephone engr.; b. Big Rapids, Mich., Oct. 21, 1874; s. Amos Robert and Lucy P. (Foote) M.; B.S. in E.E., U. of Mich., 1897, A.M., 1904; Dr. Engring. (hon.), 1934; grad. student in analyt. chemistry, U. of Chicago, and in mathematics, physics, and elec. engring., U. of Mich.; m. May Cornelia Wyman, June 25, 1904 (died Feb. 12, 1921); children—Dorothy May, Marjorie Lucellen; m. 2d, Mary Spencer Schuessler, Sept. 30, 1922. Instr. in physics, Washington U., 1901; instr. in physics, U. of Mich., 1902-04, instr. and later asst. prof., elec. engring., 1904-06; transmission engr. Western Electric Co., London, Eng., 1906-09; equipment engr. Am. Telephone & Telegraph Co., New York, 1909-19; equipment development engr. same co., 1919-33; asst. dir. of systems development, Bell Telephone Labs., 1933-35; tech. rep. Am. Telephone & Telegraph Co. and Bell Telephone Labs. in Europe since 1935. Mem. N.J. State Board of Education, 1928-35. Fellow Am. Inst. E.E. (mgr. 1919-23; v.p. 1925, 26); fellow A.A.A.S.; mem. British Instn. of Elec. Engrs., Sigma Xi, Tau Beta Pi. Republican. Methodist. Home: 30 Draper Terrace, Montclair, N.J.; 40 Landsdowne House, Mayfair, London, England. Office: Bush House, London Eng*

MORELAND, EDWARD LEYBURN, cons. engr.; b. Lexington, Va., July 1, 1885; s. Sidney T. and Sally Preston (Leyburn) M.; A.B., Johns Hopkins U., 1905; M.S., Mass. Inst. Tech., 1908; m. Francina H. Campbell, Sept. 18, 1913. Asst. engr. D. C. and William B. Jackson, engrs., Boston, 1908-12, mgr. Boston office, 1912-16, mem. firm, 1916-18; mem. firm Jackson & Moreland, 1919—; head dept. elec. engring., Mass. Inst. Tech., 1935-38, dean engring., 1938-46, exec. v.p., 1946—. Regional adviser to the U.S. Office Edn. of Engring. Defense Training in Region I, 1940-42; mem. adv. com. for Coordinating Available Facilities for Def. Prodn., OPM, in Region I, 1941-42; also member Labor Supply Committee 1941-42; executive officer Nat. Def. Research Com., 1942-45; expert cons. to Sec. War, assigned G.H.Q.-Armed Forces in Pacific; chief, scientific survey in Japan, 1945. Served capt. and maj., E.C., U.S. Army Tech. Board and War Damage Bd., A.E.F., 1918-19. Fellow Am. Inst. E.E.; mem. Am. Soc. M.E., Am. Soc. C.E., Am. Acad. Arts and Sci., Am. Soc. for Engring. Edn., Engring. Socs. of N.E., Boston Soc. C.E., Phi Gamma Delta. Republican. Conglist. Clubs: Engineers (N.Y.C.); Engineers, Merchants, St. Botolph (Boston); Algonquin, Cosmos (Washington); Wellesley Country. Home: 4 Berkeley Court, Wellesley Hills 82, Mass. Office: Mass. Institute of Technology, Cambridge, Mass. Died June 17, 1951, buried Druid Ridge Cemetery, Pikesville, Balt.

MOREY, SAMUEL, inventor; b. Hebron, Conn., Oct. 23, 1762; s. Israel and Martha (Palmer) M.; m. Hannah Avery, 1 child. Participated in constrn. Conn. River locks between Windsor (Conn.) and Okott Falls, engr. in charge, Bellows Falls, Vt.; obtained 1st patent for steam-operated spit, 1793; patented rotary steam engine, 1795; patented windmill, water wheel, steam pump; built stern wheel steamboat, ran from Hartford, Conn. to N.Y.C., 1794; attempted to persuade Robert Fulton to adopt his steamboat model, claimed his ideas were stolen by Fulton; patented internal combustion engine, 1826; propelled boat Aunt Sally by a vapor engine on Fairlee (Vt.) Pond (now known as Lake Morey), 1820. Died Fairlee, Apr. 17, 1843.

MORFIT, CAMPBELL, chemist; b. Herculaneum, Mo., Nov. 19, 1820; s. Henry Mason and Catherine (Campbell) M.; attended Columbian Coll. (now George Washington U.); m. Maria Clapier Chancellor, Apr. 13, 1854, 1 dau. Left sch. to go to pvt. chemistry lab. of James Curtis Booth, Phila.; became indsl. chemist, owner of business in Phila.; prof. applied chemistry U. Md., 1854-58, offered to set up chemistry dept. in conjunction with med. sch. (offer rejected); published his research in various scientific journals; prepared (with Booth) Encyclopedia of Chemistry, 1850; went to Eng.,

1861. Author: A Treatise on Chemistry Applied, 1856; Chemical and Pharmaceutical Manipulations, 1857. Died South Hampstead, Eng., Dec. 8, 1897.

MORGAN, ALFRED POWELL, electrical engr.; b. Brooklyn, N.Y., Apr. 15, 1889; s. Frederick Powell and Margaret (Pattison) M.; grad. Montclair (N.J.) High Sch., 1908; student Mass. Inst. Tech.; m. 2d, Ruth Whigham Shackleford, Nov. 19, 1927; children—by 1st marriage, William; by 2d marriage, Alfred Powell, Charles Shackleford, Thomas Burris. Formerly president Adams-Morgan Co., Inc., Cole & Morgan, Inc., Morgan-Kline, Inc., A.P. Morgan, Inc., R.H. McMann, Inc.; formerly editor mechanical and electrical department Boys' Magazine. Author books on elementary sci. handcraft and engring.; latest: Home Electrical Repairs, 1950; 1st Chemistry Book for Boys and Girls, 1950; A Boy's First Book of Radio and Electronics, 1954; A Boy's Second Book of Radio and Electronics, 1956; A Boy's Third Book of Radio and Electronics, 1962; A Boy's Fourth Book of Radio and Electronics, 1969. Contributed to devel. of radio telegraphy; developed and produced the first short wave regenerative receivers, with Paul Godley; holder of U.S. patents covering radio and mech. devices. Home: Upper Montclair NJ Died Mar. 16, 1972; buried Mt. Hebron Cemetery, Upper Montclair NJ

MORGAN, ANN HAVEN, educator; b. Waterford, Conn., May 6, 1882; d. Stanley Griswold and Julia Alice (Douglas) Morgan; student Wellesley Coll., 1902-04; A.B., Cornell U., 1906, Ph.D., 1912; postgrad. U. Chgo., summer 1916, Harvard, 1920, Yale, 1921, Tropical Lab., British Guiana, 1926. Asst., Mt. Holyoke Coll., 1906-07, instr. in zoology, 1907-09, 1912-14, asso. prof., 1914-18, prof., 1918—, chmn. dept., 1916-47; instr. summers, Cornell U., 1910, 1911, Marine Biol. Lab., Woods Hole, Mass., 1918, 19, 21, 23; mem. staff Mass. State Biol. Survey, summer 1944-46. Received research grants Sigma Xi, 1926, 1930, A.A.A.S., 1926, 1930. Fellow A.A.A.S.; mem. Am. Soc. Zoologists, Am. Soc. Naturalists, Am. Assn. Museums, Entomol. Soc. Am., Am. Limnol. Soc., Ecol. Soc., N.Y. Herpetol. Soc., Assn. Social Hygiene, Com. on Bd. of Eugenics, Nat. Com. on Policies in Conservation. Conglist. Author: Fieldbook of Ponds and Streams, 1930; Animals in Winter, 1939; Kinship of Animals and Men, 1955. Contbr. articles to professional jours. and reference books. Lectr. on biology and conservation of fresh waters. Home: South Hadley, Mass. Died June 5, 1966.

MORGAN, CHARLES HILL, mechanical engr., mfr.; b. Rochester, N.Y., Jan. 8, 1831; s. Hiram and Clarissa Lucina (Rich) M.; ed. Lancaster and Clinton acads. and evening schs., Clinton, Mass.; m. Harriet C. Plympton, 1852 (died 1862); m. 2d, Rebecca A. Beagary, Aug. 4, 1863. Draftsman, 1855-60; in business at Phila., 1860-64; gen. supt., 1864-87, dir., 1876-87, Washburn & Moen Co., Worcester, Mass.; consulting engr. Am. Wire Co., Cleveland, 1887—; pres. Morgan Spring Co., 1881—, Morgan Constrn. Co., 1891—; 1st v.p. and dir. Am. Wire Co. of Cleveland. Trustee Worcester Poly. Institute. Conglist. Republican. Home: Worcester, Mass. Died 1911.

MORGAN, CLIFFORD VERYL, army medical officer; b. Elmwood, Neb., Dec. 18, 1901; s. Butler Garibaldi and Margaret Elizabeth (Murray) M.; A.B., Neb. Wesleyan U., 1922; B.S., U. Neb., 1925, M.D., 1927; grad. Army Med. Sch., 1929, Army Indsl. Coll., 1940, Command and Gen. Staff Sch., 1943, Indsl. Coll. Armed Forces and Nat. War Coll., E-1946; m. Anna Marie Herrmann, July 20, 1927; children—Monte Herrmann, Marvin Leon, Walter Albert. Commd. 1st lt. M.C., U.S. Army, 1927, advanced through grades to col., 1942; intern Walter Reed Gen. Hosp., Washington, 1927-28; internist William Beaumont Gen. Hosp., El Paso, Tex., 1929-30, Tripler Gen. Hosp., Honolulu, T.H., 1930-33, U.S. Army Hosp., Ft. Sill, Okla., 1933-36; specialist med. supply and adminstrn. N.Y. Gen. Depot and S.G.O., War Dept., 1936-39; army chief, commodities div. Army-Navy Munitions Bd., 1940-43; cheif commodities div., planning br. Office Under Sec. War, 1940-42; chief, raw materials br., resources div. Army Service Forces, 1942-43; dep. chief for materiel, supply div. S.G.O., 1943; dep. gen. purchasing agt., E.T.O., 1943-45; exec. officer Crile Gen. Hosp., 1945-46; dep. post comdr. Walter Reed Army Med. Center, Washington, 1946-48; dep. chief surgeon Hdqrs., European Command, 1948-52; insp. gen. Office Surgeon Gen., Washington, 1952-54; chairman Army Physical Review Council, 1954—. Decorated Legion of Merit with oak leaf cluster, Bronze Star Medal, Army Commendation with oak leaf cluster; Croix de Guerre with palm (France); Officer, Order of Oaken Wreath (Luxembourg). Fellow A.M.A., Assn. Mil. Surgeons, A.A.A.S.; mem. Am. Coll. Hosp. Adminstrs., Phi Kappa Tau, Phi Kappa Phi, Phi Chi, Alpha Omega Alpha. Editor of EUCOM Medical Bull., 1948-52. Home: 2945 Macomb St. N.W., Washington 8. Office: Army Physical Review Council, Pentagon Bldg., Washington 25. Died Oct. 3, 1954; buried Arlington Nat. Cemetery.

MORGAN, FRED BOGARDUS, physician, med. researcher; b. Belvidere, Ill., Apr. 17, 1874; s. Russell Williams and Sarah Amelia (Bogardus) M.; M.D., Chgo. Homeopathic Med. Coll., 1898; M.D. (hon.), Hahnemann Med. Coll., Chgo., 1904; numerous postgrad. courses; m. Louie Margaret Bucey, May 18, 1898; children—Russell Paul, Ruth Irene (Mrs. Arnold Rapp); m. 2d, Minnie Violet Smith, Sept. 18, 1926. In practice of internal medicine, Clinton, Ia., 1898—; mem. bd. med. examiners, State of Ia., 1942-44. Mem. Hahnemann Med. Assn. Ia. (pres. 1936, 1940), Am. Inst. Homeopathy (pres.-elect. 1943-44, 44-45, pres. 1945-47), Pan.-Am. Med. Congress, Internat. Homeopathic Med. Assn. Republican. Methodist. Contbr. many articles med. jours. Address: 716 S. 4th St., Clinton, Ia. Died Nov. 28, 1950.

MORGAN, HERBERT ROLLO, astronomer; b. Medford, Minn., Mar. 21, 1875; s. Henry D. and Olive Sabre (Smith) M.; B.A., U. Va., 1899, Ph.D., 1901; m. Fannie Evelyn Wallis, May 25, 1904; 1 dau., Amy Eleanor (Mrs. George Hoffman). Fellow in astronomy Leander McCormick Obs., 1896-1901; prof. mathematics Pantops Acad., Charlottesville, Va., 1900-01; computer Naval Obs., Washington, 1901-05; prof. astronomy and mathematics Pritchett Coll., also dir. Morrison Obs., 1905-07; asst. astronomer U.S. Naval Obs., 1907-24, astronomer, 1925-28, sr. astronomer, 1928-29, prin. astronomer, 1929-44; research asso., Yale, 1947—. Mem. Am. Astron. Soc. (v.p. 1940-42), Am. Geophys. Union, Internat. Astron. Union (pres. Com. Meridian Astronomy 1938-48), A.A.A.S. (v.p. 1935-36), Washington Acad. Sci. Methodist. Author publ. U.S. Naval Obs., Vol. XIII, and co-author of Vols. IX, XIV, XV. Contbr. to various sci. jours. Home: 2252 Hall Pl. N.W. Office: U.S. Naval Obs., Washington. Died June 11, 1957; buried Glenwood, Washington.

MORGAN, HUGH JACKSON, physician; b. Nashville, Jan. 25, 1893; s. Joseph Bedinger and Jean (Gibson) M.; B.S., Vanderbilt U., 1914; M.D., Johns Hopkins, 1918; D.Sc., U. N.C., 1946, U. So. Cal., 1953; m. Robert Ray Porter, July 22, 1924; children—Caroline Lee (Mrs. Saxon Graham), Hugh Jackson, Jean (Mrs. J. Alexander Cortner), Robert Porter. Resident house officer Johns Hopkins Hosp., 1919-20, asst. resident physician, 1920-21; instr. medicine Johns Hopkins, 1920-21; asst. and resident physician Rockefeller Inst. for Med. Research, 1922-24, traveling fellow (Europe), 1924-25; asso. prof. medicine Vanderbilt U., 1924-28, prof. clin. medicine, 1928-35, prof. medicine also physician-in-chief Vanderbilt U. Hosp., 1935-58, prof. emeritus, 1958—, trustee Vanderbilt U., 1958—, Hugh Jackson Morgan visiting professorships in medicine established in his honor, 1958. Served as pvt. and 1st lt. M.C., U.S. Army, AEF, 1917-18; lt. col. Med. Res. Corps, U.S. Army, 1940; active duty since 1942, as col., 1942, brig. gen., 1943; chief cons. in medicine, Office of Surgeon Gen, Washington, 1942-46; chmn. com. on medicine N.R.C., 1946-48; mem. med. adv com to sec. of war, 1946-48; sci. dir. Internat. Health Div. Rockefeller Found., 1946-48, sci. cons., 1950, Div. of Medicine and Pub. Health, 1952; mem. Nat. Adv. Arthritis and Metabolic Diseases Council, 1954-56; cons., mem. adv. com. Howard Hughes Med. Inst., 1955—; mem. Nat. Adv. Heart Council 1950-52; mem adv. health council USPHS, 1948-50; Fed. Med. Service Com. Commn. Orgn. of Exec. Br. of Govt. Trustee Meharry Med. Coll., 1946—, chmn. of bd., 1955-57. Decorated D.S.M., 1945., Master A.c.P. (regent 1936—, pres. 1947, Alfred Stengel Meml. award, 1959); mem. A.M.A. (cons Counci Nat Emergency Med. Services, 1948—, Vets. Adminstrn. cons. to Central adv. com. on radioisotopes to dept. medicine and surgery, 1947-58), Am. Bd. Internal Medicine (vice chmn., 1947, chmn., 1948,) Assn. Am. Physicians (pres. 1950), Assn. Hon. Consultants to Army Med. Library, Soc. U.S. Med. Consultants in World War II, Johns Hopkins Med. and Surg. Assn. (pres. 1948). Am. Soc. for Clin. Investigation, Am. Clin. and Climatol. Assn. (pres. 1953), Am. Heart Assn., A.A.A.S, Phi Beta Kappa, Alpha Omega Alpha, Phi Delta Theta. Sigma Xi, Methodist. Club: Belle Meade Country (Nashville). Contbr. med. articles to profl. jours. Home: 15 White Bridge Rd., Nashville 5. Died Dec. 24, 1961.

MORGAN, JEROME J(OHN), chem. engr.; b. Russell, Pa., Apr. 22, 1880; s. Martin and Christine (Hinkle) M.; B.S., Pa. State Coll., 1905, M.S., 1910; Ph.D., Columbia, 1919; m. Elizabeth Ella Perry, Aug. 21, 1907; children—Florence Alice (Mrs. William L. F. Hardham), Jerome Perry Morgan. N.Y. state engring. license, 1923. Asst. and asst. prof. chemistry Md. Agrl. Coll., 1905-08; asst. chemist U.S. Bur. Chemistry, 1908; prof. chemistry Coll. Hawaii, 1908-09; instr. chemistry Stevens Inst. Tech., 1909-11, asst. prof., 1911-19; asst. prof. chem. engring. Columbia, 1919-26, asso. prof., 1926-37, prof. 1937-48, prof. emeritus, 1949—; cons. chem. engr., 1919—; cons. Babcock & Wilcox, 1926-31, Bklyn. Union Gas Co., Consol. Gas Co. of N.Y. and other pub. utilities; cons. chem. engr U.S. Treasury Dept., 1942-43. Mem. Am. Gas Assn. (chmn. chem. com. 1937-38), A.A.A.S., Am. Chem. Soc., Am. Inst. Chem. Engrs., Tau Beta Pi, Sigma Xi, Phi Lambda Upsilon, Phi Kappa Phi. Republican. Methodist. Mason. Club: Faculty. Author: Chemical Laboratory Manual for Engineering Students (with F. J. Pond), 1911; American Gas Practice, 2 vols.; Production of Manufactured Gas, 1926-31; Distribution and Utilization of City Gas, 1928-35; Gasification of Hydrocarbon for Production of Gases to Supplement Natural Gas in City Supplies, 1953. Prepared and directed home study course in gas engring., approved by Am. Gas Assn. Contbr. chapter on Water Gas in Chemistry of Coal Utilization, 1945; also many articles on fuel to tech. jours. Home: 67 Salter Pl., Maplewood, N.J. Died Apr. 19, 1967; buried Fairview Cemetery, Westfield, N.J.

MORGAN, JOHN, physician; b. Phila., June 10, 1735; s. Evan and Joanna (Biles) M.; grad. Coll. of Phila. (now U. Pa.), 1757; M.D., U. Edinburgh (Scotland), 1763; m. Mary Hopkinson, Sept. 4, 1765. Admitted to Academie Royal de Chirurgie de Paris (France), 1764, mem. Royal Soc. London (Eng.) Belles-Lettres Soc. of Rome (Italy); licentiate Royal Coll. Physicians, London and Edinburgh; established med. sch. in connection with U. Pa., 1765, apptd. prof. theory and practice of physic; author oration A Discourse upon the Institution of Medical Schools in America, 1765; published Four Dissertations on The Reciprocal Advantages of a Perpetual Union between Great Britain and her American Colonies (won a gold medal), 1766; dir. gen. hosps. Continental Army, 1775, physician in chief, 1775, dir. hosps. East of Hudson River, 1776-77; physician Pa. Hosp.; mem. Am. Philos. Soc.; Phila. Coll. Physicians was an outgrowth of his suggestion (organized 1787). Author: A Recommendation of Inoculation, According to Baron Pimsdale's Method, 1776. Died Phila., Oct. 15, 1789.

MORGAN, (JOHN) HARCOURT ALEXANDER, entomologist; b. Strathroy, Ont., Can., Aug. 31, 1867; s. John and Rebecca (Truman) M.; B.S.A., U. Toronto, 1889; grad. work, Cornell U., 1891-98, Marine Biol. Lab., Woods Hole, 1895; LL.D., Emory and Henry U., Southwestern U., 1920, U. Western Ont., 1939; Sc.D., Clemson Agrl. Coll., 1937; m. Sara Elizabeth Fay, June 25, 1895. Entomologist, horticulturist, La. State U. and Agrl. Expt. Stas., 1889-94; zoölogist, entomologist, same, 1894-1904; entomologist La. Expt. Sta. and crop pest commr., Feb. 1904-Jan. 1905; dir. U. Tenn. Agrl. Expt. Sta. and prof. zoölogy and entomology, 1905-19, dean Coll. Agr., 1913-19, pres., July 1, 1919-33, U. Tenn.; mem. TVA, 1933-48, chmn., 1938-41. Conductor farmers' insts. in La., 1895-1904; spl. field agt. Bur. Entomology, U.S. Dept. Agr., 1904. Food adminstr. Tenn., 1917. Asst. commr. La., Atlanta Expn., 1895; dir. Gulf Biol. Sta., 1900-05; Tenn. State entomologist, 1905-19; mem. Am. Commn. for Study of Rural Credits and Cooperation, 1913; chmn. Sec. of Agr.'s com. of scientists to investigate Mediterranean fruit fly situation in Fla. and advise concerning its control, 1929; mem. adv. council of Agr. Com. of Am. Bankers Assn., 1930-31; mem. com. on Capper Award for outstanding service to agr., 1930-31; mem. Nat. Land-Use Planning Com. Received Am. Farm Bur. Fed. award for distinguished service to agr., 1937, man of the year award, The Progressive Farmer, 1940. Trustee The Berry Schs.; mem. bd. advs., (V.P.I.) Inst. Rural Affairs. Mem. A.A.A.S., Soc. Promotion Agrl. Sci.; ex-pres. La. Soc. Naturalists; pres. Entomol. Sect. A.A.A.S., 1905; mem. Am. Fisheries Soc., Am. Assn. Econ. Entomologists (pres. 1907), Entomol. Soc. of Washington, Entomol. Soc. Am., Tenn. Acad. Sci., Assn. Land Grant Colls. and Univs (pres. 1927), Am. Country Life Assn., Phi Kappa Phi, Gamma Alpha, Alpha Zeta. Mason. Rotarian. Home: Belfast, Tenn. Died Aug. 25, 1950; buried Knoxville, Tenn.

MORGAN, JOHN LIVINGSTON RUTGERS, chemist; b. New Brunswick, N.J., June 27, 1872; s. Brockholst (D.D.) and Mary (Rutgers) M.; B.S., Rutgers Coll., 1892, Sc.D., 1916; A.M., Ph.D., U. of Leipzig, 1895; m. Luna M. Rutgers, June 2, 1914. Asst. in chemistry, Stevens Inst., 1895-96, instr. quantitative analysis, Brooklyn Poly. Inst., 1896-97; tutor chem. physics and chem. philosophy, 1897-1901, adj. prof. physical chemistry, 1901-05, prof., 1905—, Columbia. Fellow Chem. Soc. London, A.A.A.S. Author: The Principles of Mathematical Chemistry (from the German of G. Helm), 1897; The Theory of Solution and Its Results, 1897; The Elements of Physical Chemistry, 5th edit., 1914; Physical Chemistry for Electrical Engineers, 2d edit., 1909. Home: New York, N.Y. Died Apr. 13, 1935.

MORGAN, LEWIS HENRY, anthropologist; b. Aurora, N.Y., Nov. 21, 1818; s. Jedediah and Harriet (Steele) M.; grad. Union Coll., 1840, LL.D. (hon.), 1873; m. Mary Elizabeth Steele, Aug. 13, 1851. Admitted to N.Y. bar; legal adviser of a railroad under constrn. between Marquette, Mich. and Lake Superior iron region, 1855; mem. N.Y. State Assembly, 1861-68, N.Y. State Senate, 1868-69; known as "father of Am. anthropology"; leading mem. The Grand Order of the Iroquois (chief purposes were to study and perpetuate Indian lore, to educate Indians, reconcile them to conditions imposed on them by civilization); succeeded in defeating ratification of a fraudulent treaty by which the Seneca would have given up their lands to Ogden Land Co.; adopted by Hawk clan of Seneca, 1847, given name Tayadawahkugh; entrusted by Univ. State N.Y. with executing the enlargement of its Indian collection, for which an appropriation had been made, 1849; author League of the Ho-de-no-sau-nee, or Iroquois (1st sci. account of an Indian tribe), 1851; published Laws of Consanguinity and Descent of the Iroquois, 1859; Systems of Consanguinity and Affinity of the Human Family; Ancient Society or Researches in the Lines of Human Progress, 1877; studied various ruins, visited some of existing pueblos, 1878; wrote On the Ruins of a Stone Pueblo on the Animas River in New Mexico, 1880; Houses and House-Life of the American Aborigines, 1881; The American Beaver and His Works, 1868; instrumental in organizing anthropology sect. A.A.A.S., 1875, 1st chmn.; mem. Nat. acad. Scis.; pres. A.A.A.S., 1879. Died Rochester, N.Y., Dec. 17, 1881.

MORGAN, SISTER M(ARY) SYLVIA, sci. educator; b. Glynneath, Glamorganshire, South Wales; d. William J. and Mary (Williams) Morgan; B.S., Coll. New Rochelle, 1916, A.B., 1917; M.S., Fordham U., 1920; D.Sc., U. Cal., 1925; grad. study, U. Notre Dame, Columbia U., 1915. Tchr.; Marywood Coll, Scranton, Pa, 1915-43, pres., 1943-49. Fellow A.A.A.S.; mem. Am. Chem. Soc., Nat. Geog. Soc., Audubon Soc. Am Assn. Univ. Profs., N.Y., Pa. acads. sci. Author: Analysis of Various Types of Oranges; Surface Tension in Detoxication Products Home: Marywood Coll., Scranton, Pa. 18509. Died July 24, 1964.

MORGAN, ORA SHERMAN, agriculturist; b. Hampshire, Ill., Aug. 11, 1877; s. Lyman Delos and Elizabeth Ann (Helmer) M.; grad. State Normal U., Normal, Ill., 1899; A.B., U. of Ill., 1905; M.S.A., Cornell U., 1907, Ph.D., 1909; m. Rose LeVille Huff, Oct. 4, 1908 (died Apr. 19, 1939); m. 2d, Lucy P. Berry, Dec. 15, 1950; 1 stepson, Walter L. Substitute principal Training Sch. of No. Ill. State Normal Coll., 1905-06; dir. N.Y. State Sch. Agr., Alfred, N.Y., 1908-11; prof. agrl. economics and head dept., Columbia U., 1911-43, professor emeritus since July 1, 1943; agrl. economics specialist, Fgn. Econ. Adminstrn., 1944-Oct. 1945; agriculturist and officer in charge U.N.R.R.A., Chekiang Province, China, 1946-48. Agrl. adviser for N.Y. City Draft Bd., by appmt. U.S. Dept. Agr., 1918-19; made agrl. surveys for Near East Relief, in southern U.S.S.R. and Greece, 1926, 1927; dir. of edn. for Near East Relief in Armenia, summer 1926; trustee Michael Anasgnos Schs., Greece, since 1929; a dir. Near East Foundation since 1930; made agrl. studies in Japan, China and India, 1934, Argentina and Brazil, 1936. Caribbean area, 1938. Editor, Agrl. Systems of Middle Europe, 1933. On leave from Columbia Univ. first half 1942-43 academic year to make agrl. survey of Near Eastern countries as collaborator of Bd. of Econ. warfare and surveyor Near East Found. Mem. Patrons of Husbandry, Gamma Alpha, Sigma Xi. Mason. Died Aug. 14, 1961; buried Chico, Cal.

MORGAN, RAYMOND A., engr., educator; b. Lutesville, Mo., Oct. 12, 1903; s. Ura A. and Minnie (Lusk) M.; E.M., Colo. Sch. Mines, 1929, M.Sc., 1933; m. Marjorie S. Kelly, Dec. 23, 1948. With safety div. U.S. Bur. Mines, 1930-32, petroleum engring. oil and gas div., 1944-46; dep. county surveyor Jefferson County, Colo., 1933-35; engr. Stanolind Oil & Gas Co., 1935-41; instr. U. Wyo., 1941-44, prof., head dept. gen. engring., 1946—, asst. dean engring. coll., 1960—; asst. materials engr. Toltz, King & Day, Casper Air Base, summer 1942; engr. charge civic improvements Flora Engring. Co., Anchorage, Alaska, summer 1949; engr. cons. U. Kabul, summer 1958. Registered profl. engr., Colo. Mem. Am. Soc. Engring. Edn., Wyo. Soc. Engrs., Nat. Soc. Profl. Engrs., Soc. Petroleum Engrs., Young Republican Club of Jefferson County (Colo.), Blue Key, Acacia, Sigma Tau, Sigma Gamma Epsilon. Republican. Mason (Shriner). Home: 1819 Garfield Av., Laramie, Wyo. Died Nov. 10, 1964; buried Grand Junction, Colo.

MORGAN, THOMAS HUNT, zoölogist; b. Lexington, Ky., Sept. 25, 1866; s. Charlton H. and Ellen Key (Howard) M.; B.S., State Coll. of Ky., 1886, M.S., 1888; Ph.D., Johns Hopkins, 1890; LL.D., Johns Hopkins, 1915, U. of Ky., 1916, McGill U., 1921, U. of Edinburgh, 1922, U. of Calif., 1930; hon. Sc.D., U. of Mich., 1924; Ph.D., Heidelberg U., 1931; hon. M.D., U. of Zurich, 1933; Docteur Honoris Causa, U. of Paris, 1935; m. Lilian V. Sampson, 1904; children—Howard Key, Edith Sampson, Lilian Vaughn, Isabel Merrick. Prof. biology, Bryn Mawr, 1891-1904; prof. exptl. zoölogy, Columbia, 1904-28; dir. William G. Kerckhoff Labs. Biol. Sciences, Calif. Inst. Tech., since 1928. Fellow A.A.A.S. (pres. 1929-30); mem. Nat. Acad. Science (pres. 1927-31), Am. Soc. Naturalists, Am. Soc. Zoölogists, Soc. Exptl. Biology and Medicine, N.Y. Acad. Sciences, Royal Soc. London; corr. mem. or fgn. asso. numerous European socs. Author: Regeneration, 1901; Evolution and Adaptation, 1903; Experimental Zoölogy, 1907; Heredity and Sex, 1913; Mechanism of Mendelian Heredity, 1915; Critique of the Theory of Evolution, 1916; The Physical Bases of Heredity, 1919; The Theory of the Gene, 1926; Experimental Embryology, 1927; The Scientific Basis of Evolution, 1932; Embryology and Genetics, 1933; also monographs and papers on biol. and embryol. subjects. Awarded Nobel prize, 1933, for discoveries concerning the laws and mechanism of heredity. Address: 1149 San Pasqual St., Pasadena, Calif. Died Dec. 4, 1945.

MORGAN, WILLIAM CONGER, chemist; b. at Albany, N.Y., June 21, 1874; s. William and Josephine Amelia (Conger) M.; B.A., Yale, 1896, Silliman fellow in chemistry, Ph.D., 1899; m. Charlotte Elizabeth Lansing, of Albany, June 21, 1900. Instr. chemistry, 1899, prof., 1900-1, Washburn College, Topeka, Kan.; instr. chemistry, 1901-6, asst. prof. since 1906, U. of Cal. Fellow A.A.A.S.; mem. Am. Chem. Soc., Deutsche Chemische Gesellschaft. Sigma Xi, Phi Beta Kappa. Congregationalist. Clubs: Outlook (Oakland), Faculty (Berkeley). Author: Qualitative Analysis as a Laboratory Method for the Study of General Inorganic Chemistry, 1906; also numerous papers on chemistry and edn. Address: 2440 Hillside Av., Berkeley CA

MORGULIS, SERGIUS, biochemist; b. Russia, Aug. 6, 1885; s. Samuel and Hannah (Spigel) M.; Ananieff Gymnasium; A.M., Columbia, 1907; Ph.D., Harvard, 1910; studied in Vienna, Berlin, Naples, Woods Hole, etc.; m. Fannie Bashkirtzeva, 1911. Came to U.S., 1904, naturalized citizen, 1910. Austin teaching fellow, Harvard, 1909; traveling fellow from Harvard, 1910-12; asso. in animal metabolish, Carnegie Instn., 1912-13; asso. in biochemistry, Coll. Physicians and Surgeons (Columbia), 1913-16; spl. research asso., U.S. Bur. Fisheries, 1914-16; prof. physiology and biochemistry, Creighton U., Omaha, Neb., 1916-21; prof. biochemistry, U. of Neb. Coll. of Medicine, from 1921. Fellow A.A.A.S.; mem. Soc. Biol. Chemistry, Am. Physiol. Soc., Am. Soc. Zoologists, Biochem. Assn., Societe Chimie Biologique, Paris, 1934, Biochem. Soc. (Great Britain), Sigma Xi. Author: Fasting and Undernutrition, 1923; Experiments in Physical and Physiological Chemistry, 1929; Nutritional Muscular Dystrophy, 1938; (with Oparin) The Origin of Life, 1938; Biochemical Evolution (with Florkin), 1949; also numerous exptl. and general articles in mags. Address: Omaha NB Died Dec. 20, 1971; cremated.

MORISON, GEORGE SHATTUCK, civil engineer; b. New Bedford, Mass., Dec. 19, 1842; s. Rev. Dr. John Hopkins and Emily (Rogers) M.; grad. Harvard, 1863 (A.M., LL.B., 1866); admitted to bar New York, 1866; engaged as engineer at Kansas City, 1867-71; in Mich. and Ind., 1871-73; at New York, 1873-87; first on Erie Ry., later in gen. practice; lived at Chicago, 1887-98, retaining New York office; returned to New York, 1898. Apptd. by President Cleveland, 1894, mem. bd. engrs. to determine greatest practical length of span for bridge across the North river at New York; mem. bd. to locate deep water harbor in Southern Calif., 1896-97; mem. bd. cons. engrs. dept. of docks, New York, 1895-97. Mem. Isthmian Canal Commn., 1899-1901. Was chief engr. bridge across the Ohio at Cairo, Ill., and across the Mississippi at Memphis, Tenn.; also 4 others across the Mississippi, 10 across the Missouri, etc. Died 1903.

MORLEY, EDWARD WILLIAMS, chemist; b. Newark, 1838; s. Sardis Brewster and Anna C. (Treat) M.; A.B., Williams Coll., 1860, A.M., 1863, LL.D., 1901; Ph.D. (hon.), U. Wooster, 1878; LL.D., Adelbert Coll., 1891, Lafayette Coll., 1907, U. Pitts., 1915; ScD., Yale, 1909; m. Isabella E. Birdsall, Dec. 24, 1868. Prof. chemistry Western Res. Coll., Hudson, O. (afterward removed to Cleve. and named Adelbert Coll.), 1869-1906; prof. chemistry, Cleve. Med. Coll., 1873-88. Recipient Davy medal Royal Soc., 1907. Fellow A.A.A.S. (pres. 1895-96), Am. Acad. Arts and Scis. (asso.); mem. Royal Inst. (London) (hon.). Author: On the Densities of Oxygen and Hydrogen, and on the Ratio of Their Atomic Weights, 1895. Has devised improved apparatus for gas analysis; asso. with Michelson in expt. on ether drift and velocity of light (negative result led to theory of relativity); invented a measuring instrument, interferometer; made accurate determination of ratio of combining weights of oxygen and hydrogen; density of oxygen and hydrogen. Died Feb. 24, 1923.

MORREY, CHARLES BRADFIELD, educator, bacteriologist; b. Chesterhill, O., Nov. 5, 1869; s. John Cheetham and Mary Jenkinson (Wright) M.; B.A., Ohio State U., 1890; M.D., Starling Med. Coll., Columbus, O., 1896; studied in Europe; m. Grace Hamilton Jones, 1898; children—Marion (Mrs. O. C. Richter), Jessie (Mrs. Michael Condoide), Charles Bradfield. Joined Faculty Ohio State U., 1899, founded dept. bacteriology, 1903, became prof. bacteriology, head dept., 1904, emeritus prof., 1935—; cons. in fields of medicine, agriculture, industry; pioneered in use of vaccine therapy. Mem. Soc. Am. Bacteriologists, Am. Chem. Soc., A.A.A.S., Ohio Acad. Sci., Sigma Xi. Club: University. Author: Laboratory Exercises in General Bacteriology, 1906, 10th edit. 1929; Fundamentals of Bacteriology, 4th edit. 1929; also various brochures. Home: 188 W. Tenth Av., Columbus 1, O. Died Apr. 21, 1954; buried Columbus, O.

MORRILL, ALBRO DAVID, biologist; b. Tilton, N.H., Aug. 29, 1854; s. Smith and Mary (Clark) M.; B.S., Dartmouth, 1876, M.S., 1879; U. of Mich., 1876-77; A.M. (hon.) Belmont Coll., College Hill, O., 1886; m. Lena E. Carver, Dec. 23, 1879. Science teacher, Lewistown, Pa., 1878-83; prof. chemistry, physics and higher mathematics, Belmont Coll., 1883-88; prof. biology and geology, Ohio U., Athens, 1888-92; prof. chemistry and biology, 1892-96, biology, since 1896, Hamilton Coll. Fellow A.A.A.S.; mem. Am. Soc. Naturalists, Am. Soc. Zoölogists, Boston Soc. Natural History. Republican. Presbyterian. Home: Clinton, N.Y. Died June 8, 1943.

MORRIS, CASPAR, physician; b. Phila., May 2, 1805; s. Israel Westar and Mary (Hollingsworth) M.; M.D., U. Pa., 1826; m. Anne Cheston, Nov. 11, 1829. Apptd. physician Phila. Dispensary, 1828; founder House of Refuge, physician, 1830-34; helped establish Pa. Instn. for Instrn. of Blind, mgr., physician, 1833-84; published an article which resulted in movement to establish Episcopal Hosp., became mgr. hosp.; wrote Appeal on Behalf of the Sick, 1851; "Five Essays Relating to the Construction, Organization and Management of Hospitals" published in Hospital Plans, 1875; mem. Nat. Acad. Scis., 1829-38, Am. Philos. Soc., 1851-60; fellow Coll. of Physicians; aided in founding Phila. Med. Inst., 1838; one of 5 selected to submit ideas for bldg. of Johns Hopkins Hosp. in Balt. Died May 17, 1884.

MORRIS, CLYDE TUCKER, prof. civil engring.; b. Morrow County, O., Apr. 19, 1877; s. Byrant Washington and Adelade (Ashley) M.; C.E., Ohio State U., 1898; m. Mabel Taylor, Oct. 18, 1899; children—Ruth Elizabeth (Mrs. F. D. Young), Wilametta Esther (Mrs. Warren R. Sisson), Eugene Bryant. Began as draftsman with Columbus Bridge Co., Columbus, O., 1898-99, Youngstown (O.) Bridge Co., 1899-1901, King Bridge Co., Cleveland, O., 1901-02; asst. engr. Puget Sound Bridge & Dredging Co., Seattle, Wash., 1902-04, King Bridge Co., 1904-06; asso. prof. structural engring., Ohio State U., 1906-08, prof. civil engring. since 1908, chmn. dept. civil engring., 1938-47; emeritus prof. of civil engring., since 1947. Mem. American Soc. C.E., American Concrete Inst., Am. Society for Engring. Edn., Sigma Xi, Tau Beta Pi. Acacia, Triangle. Republican. Mason (32 deg.). Clubs: Faculty, Engineers. Author: Steel Structures, 1909; Stresses in Structures (with A. H. Heller), 1916; Structural Frameworks (with S. T. Carpenter), 1943. Contbr. on engring. Home: 2442 Northwest Blvd., Columbus 12 OH

MORRIS, FREDERICK KUHNE, geologist; b. Salt Lake City, Feb. 11, 1885; B.S. Coll. City N.Y., 1904; M.A., Columbia U., 1910, Ph.D., 1936; m. Florence E. Eddowes, Dec. 30, 1922. Asst. geologist, Canadian Geol. Survey, summer, 1912; asst. lectr., instr. in geology, Columbia, 1914-20, research work, 1917-18; advisor in geography to Dept. State, Washington, 1920; vis. prof. geology, Pei Yang U., Tientsin, China, 1920-21; geologist Central Asiatic Expdns., Am. Mus. Natural History, 1922-25, research asso. in geology, 1925—; asst. prof., 1931-50, prof. emeritus, 1950—; chief prof. structural geology Mass. Inst. Tech., 1927-31, Tropic sect. Arctic-Desert-Tropic Information Center, Maxwell AFB, Ala., 1950-57; field studies, Asia, Europe and Egypt, 1937-38, N. Africa, 1952. Fellow A.A.A.S., Geol. Soc. Am., Geol. Soc. China, Mineral. Soc. Am., Am. Geophys. Union, Am. Acad. Arts and Scis.; mem. Mass. Forest and Park Assn., Am. Inst. Mining and Metall. Engrs., Geol. Soc. Boston (past pres.), Children's Mus. Boston (v.p.), Sigma Xi, Chi Epsilon, Phi Beta Kappa, Tau Beta Pi. Protestant. Clubs: Faculty of Mass. Institute Technology (pres. 1934), Explorers, Ends of the Earth, Harvard Travellers. Author: (with Prof. J. E. Kemp) sect. on Engring. Geology in Blanchards Handbook for Highway Engineers, 1915; (with H. E. Gregory) Military Geology, 1918; (with Prof. C. P. Berkey) Geology of Mongolia, 1927; (with A. W. Grabau) Permian of Mongolia; The Making of the Valley, 1936; also many papers. Home: 3334 Southmont Dr., Montgomery 5, Ala. Died Oct. 2, 1962.

MORRIS, J(AMES) CHESTON, physician; b. Philadelphia, Pa., May 28, 1831; s. Dr. Caspar and Anne (Cheston) M.; A.B., U. of Pa., 1851, A.M. and M.D., 1854; m. Hannah A., d. Isaac Tyson, Jr., of Baltimore, 1854 (died 1867); m. 2d, Mary E., d. Lawrence Johnson, Jan. 11, 1870 (died 1912). Specialty nervous diseases, Phila.; holds important hosp. appmts.; contract surgeon U.S.A., Oct. 1862-Aug. 1863; examiner and lecturer U. of Pa., 1855-63. Has invented and patented several devices. Curator Am. Philos. Soc., 1889-1901; dir. biol. and micros. dept. Phila. Acad. Natural Sciences, 1897-1917. Pres. Va. Mining & Improvement Co., 1874-1903, and forester, 1903-1909. Translator: (with notes and additions) Lehmann's Chemical Physiology, 1856; Ethics of Solomon, 1894; Kosmos of Solomon, 1909. Author: Milk Supply of Large Cities; Water Supply of Philadelphia. Fellow Coll. of Physicians, Phila., 1857—. Home: West Chester, Pa. Died 1923.

MORRIS, ROBERT NELSON, physician; b. Hillsdale Co., Mich., July 14, 1860; s. Robert and Ellen (Whan) M.; prep. edn., Reading (Mich.) High Sch.; M.D., Hahnemann Med. Coll., Chicago, 1889; M.D., ad eundem, Hering Med. Coll.; m. Rosa Woodward, of Brooklyn, Mich., July 25, 1886. Practiced at Constantine, Mich., 1889-95, since in Chicago; prof. diseases of the chest, Hering Med. Coll., 1895—, registrar of the coll., and dean, Jan., 1909—. Mem. Am. Inst. Homoeopathy, Chicago Homoe. Med. Soc., Internat. Hahnemannian Soc. Socialist. Mason (K.T., Shriner). Home: 4517 N. Ashland Av. Office: 7 W. Madison St., Chicago.

MORRIS, ROBERT TUTTLE, surgeon; b. Seymour, Conn., May 14, 1857; s. Gov. Luzon Burritt and Eugenia Laura (Tuttle) M.; student Cornell U., 1876-79; M.D., Coll. Phys. and Surg. (Columbia), 1882; (hon. A.M., Centre Coll., Ky., 1891); m. Mrs. Aimée Reynaud Mazergue, June 4, 1898; 1 dau., Eugenia Reynaud; m. 2d, Mary Hannah Best, May 1, 1922; 1 dau., Mary. Prof. surgery, New York Post-Grad. Med. Coll., 1898-1917 (emeritus). Pres. Am. Assn. Obstetricians and Gynecologists, 1907; pres. Am. Therapeutic Assn.,

1916; fellow Am. Coll. Surgeons. Clubs: Cornell, Alpha Delta Phi, Campfire. Author: How We Treat Wounds Today, 1886; Lectures on Appendicitis, 1895; Hopkins's Pond, 1896; Dawn of the Fourth Era in Surgery, 1910; To-morrow's Topics Series 1915; Microbes and Men; A Surgeon's Philosophy; Doctors versus Folks; The Way Out of War, 1918; Nut Growing, 1921; Editorial Silence, 1927; Fifty Years a Surgeon, 1934; also various monographic repts. on original investigations. Home: Stamford, Conn. Died Jan. 9, 1945.

MORRIS, SAMUEL BROOKS, engr., utility exec.; b. Los Angeles, Aug. 24, 1890; s. Brooks Samuel and Elizabeth Price (Shoemaker) M.; student Throop Poly. Inst. (now Cal. Inst. Tech.), 1903-07; A.B. in civil engring., Stanford, 1911; LL.D. U. Cal., 1953; m. Annabel Millar Johnson, Aug. 31, 1912 (dec. July 1960); children—Brooks Theron, Robert Field. Engr., North Pasadena Land & Water Co., 1911-12; with Water Dept., City of Pasadena, 1912-35, as asst. engr., 1912-13, chief engr., 1913-35, supt., 1921-25, gen. mgr., 1925-35; prof. civil engring., head dept. Stanford, 1935-44, also dean Sch. Engring. 1936-44; gen. mgr., chief engr. Dept. Water and Power, City of Los Angeles, 1944-55; mem. Colorado River Bd. Cal.; cons. civil and hydraulic engr., 1935—; cons. engr. Water Dept., City of Pasadena, 1935-44; cons. engr. Zone Constructing Q.M., War Dept., 1941; cons. engr. Bonneville Power Adminstrn., 1941-44; Nat. Resources Planning Bd. and predecessor, 1936-43; cons. engr. City of San Diego, 1943-44; regional adviser Engring. Sci. Mgmt. War Tng. and predecessor programs, U.S. Office Edn., 1940-44, also regional rep. War Manpower Commn. on this program, 1943-44; mem. Pres.'s Water Resources Policy Commn., 1950 Mem. Bd. Pub. Works, City of Palo Alto, 1936-44, chmn. 1937-44; dir. Los Angeles County Conservation Assn., 1930-35. Awarded John M. Diven medal Am. Water Works Assn., 1933. Designed and built Morris Dam, 328 feet high, San Gabriel Canyon, for City of Pasadena, 1932-34; dam named in his honor and dedicated by Herbert Hoover, 1934. Mem. committee on geophysical sciences, commission on geophysics and geography Research and Devel. Bd., 1947-48; mem. Am. exec. com. commn. on high dams World Power Conf.; mem. Panel Impact of Peaceful Uses Atomic Energy, 1955-56; mem. Am. delegations Internat. Conf. on Peaceful Uses of Atomic Energy, Geneva, Switzerland, 1955. Bd. dirs. Engrs. Joint Council. Mem. A.A.A.S., Am. Inst. E.E., Am. Pub. Power Assn. (pres. 1949-50, dir. 1947-51), Nat. Reclamation Assn., Earthquake Engring. Research Assn. (v.p. 1949-50), Am. Geophys. Union, Am. Pub. Health Assn., Am. Soc. C.E. (pres. Los Angeles 1925, pres. San Francisco, 1943, nat. dir., 1953-56, nat. v.p. 1957-59, hon. mem.) Am. Water Works Assn. (dir. 1931-33; v.p. 1942-43, pres. 1943-44; pres. Cal. Sect., 1927-28), Seismol. Soc. Am. (dir., 1936-41; v.p., 1938-40), Am. Soc. Engring. Edn., Newcomen Soc. Eng., Los Angeles C. of C., Cal. Municipal Utilities Assn. (adv. council), Sigma XI, Tau Beta Pi. Episcopalian. Clubs: Engineer's (San Francisco); University (Pasadena); Cosmos (Washington); University, Town Hall (Los Angeles), Electric, Contbr. to tech. jours. Home: 3716 Amesbury Rd., Los Angeles 27. Office: Dept. Water and Power, 207 So. Broadway, Los Angeles. Died Mar. 6, 1962.

MORRISON, A. CRESSY; b. Wrentham, Mass., Dec. 6, 1884; s. Abram Batchelder and Mary Elizabeth (Pond) M.; ed. pub. schs.; m. Emma Webster Conway, June 18, 1900 (died Mar 15, 1904); m. 2d, Marguerite Snow, May 14, 1908 (died May 6, 1946); 1 daughter, Valeria Elizabeth (Mrs. Dwight T. Bond); m. 3d, Mrs. Marion C. Jacobus, May 1947 (dec. June 30, 1949). Executive, Union Carbide & Carbon Corp., New York, and affiliated cos., 1906-30. Pres. of Am. Inst. City of New York, 1930-31; hon. mem., 1944 (Am. Inst., City of N.Y.); mem. exec. bd. Nat. Research Council, 1931-32; chmn. chemical advisory com. U.S. Dept. Commerce, 1925-32. Mem. council Amateur Astronomers' Assn.; fellow and chmn. Com. on Astronomy and Planetarium Am. Mus. Natural History; mem. vis. bd. dept. of astronomy, Harvard, since 1949. First v.p. League of Am. Wheelmen, 1896-98; fellow N.Y. Acad. Sciences (pres. 1938, 39); mem. A.A.A.S., Am. Chem. Soc., Electro-Chemical Soc., Am. Inst. Mining and Metall. Engrs., Internat. Fixed Calendar League (treas.), Nat. Assn. Mfrs. (tariff com.), Merchants Assn. of New York, Am. Mining Congress, Internat. Acetylene Assn. (sec.-treas. 1906-31; awarded Morehead medal for 1930; hon. mem.), Compressed Gas Mfrs.' Assn. (ex-pres.; hon. mem.), Am. Tariff League (chmn. exec. com. 1927-37), Synthetic Organic Chem. Assn. (bd. of govs., 1927-30), Mfg. Chemists Assn. of U.S., N.Y. Elec. Soc. (v.p. 1931), Royal Instn. of Great Britain, Am. Inst. of Chemists (hon.), U.S. Chamber Commerce, Home Market Club of Boston (dir.). Prepared for Ways and Means Com. of U.S. Ho. of Rep., exhaustive report on European wages and standards of living, 1921; unofficial observer for Am. Chem. Industry, World Econ. Conf., League of Nations, 1926; spokesman del. Internat. Chamber Commerce, League of Nations, 1931; chmn. finance com. Tercentenary Am. Chem. Industry, 1935, and of Unemployed Chemists, 1933-37; pres. R.O.T.C. Assn. of United States, 1937. Organized American Valuation Assn. (improved tariff adminstration for American Chemical Industry). Republican. Unitarian. Mason, K.P. Clubs: Union League, Chemists (N.Y. City); Cosmos, National Press, Congressional Country (Washington); The Authors' (London, Eng.). Author: Damon and Pythias—Lay Version, 1894; The Story of the Man Who Resembled Christ, 1897; The Baking Powder Controversy (2 vols.), 1902; Man in a Chemical World, 1937; Man Does not Stand Alone, 1944. Compiler: Encyclopedia of Superstition (3 volumes). Discovered method of separating oxygen and nitrogen in magnetic field; active in promotion of American policy of protection. Home: Spruce Harbor, Stonington, Me. Office: 30 E. 42d St., N.Y. City. Died Jan. 9, 1951; buried Wrentham, Mass.

MORRISON, CHARLES SAMUEL, agrl. engr.; b. Black Lick, O., Sept. 10, 1919; s. Samuel Melville and Mary (Palmer) M.; B.S. in Agr., Ohio State U., 1941, B.Agrl. Engring., 1942; M.S. in Agrl. Engring., Ia. State U., 1946; m. Nina B. Smith, Sept. 21, 1944; children—James Robert, Charles Richard, Janet Ann, Sandra June. With Huber Mfg. Co., Marion, O., 1941; farmer, Black Lick, 1942; with Deere & Co., Moline, Ill., from 1947, mgr. product research and devel., 1960-63, mgr. agrl. engring. research, from 1963. Patron Tri City Symphony Orch. Served to lt. USNR, 1942-46. Registered profl. engr., Ill. Mem. Am. Soc. Agrl. Engrs. (chmn. power and machinery div. 1957-58, chmn. quad city sect. 1956-57, v.p. 1962-64, pres. elect 1964-65, pres. 1965-66), Chemurgic Council (bd.), Farm and Indsl. Equipment Inst. (adv. engring. com.), Soc. Automotive Engrs., Am. Soc. Metals, Ill. Soc. Profl. Engrs., Agrl. Research Inst., Tau Beta Pi, Gamma Sigma Delta, Phi Eta Sigma, Alpha Gamma Sigma. Meth. Club: Short Hills Country (E. Moline, Ill.). Home: Moline IL Died July 8, 1967.

MORRISON, FRANK BARRON, univ. prof.; b. Ft. Atkinson, Wis., May 19, 1887; s. Charles Irving and Harriet (Barron) M.; B.S., U. of Wis., 1911, postgrad. work, D.Sc., 1950; D.Sc., University of Vermont, 1947; married Elsie Rea Bullard, November 24, 1910; children—Roger Barron, Spencer Horton. Asst. agrl. chemistry, U. of Wis., 1911-12, instr., 1912-14, asst. prof. animal husbandry, 1914-17, asso. prof., 1917-19, prof., 1919-27; also asst. dir. Wis. Agrl. Expt. Sta., 1915-27, acting dean Wis. Coll. of Agr., 1925-26; dir. N.Y. State Agrl. Expt. Sta. and Cornell U. Agrl. Expt. Sta., 1927-28; professor animal husbandry and animal nutrition, Cornell Univ., 1928-55, emeritus, 1955—. Member Am. Commn. to Study Live Stock Industry in Germany, 1928. Conducted survey of live stock industry of Philippine Islands for Philippine Gov., 1937; conducted survey of livestock prodn. in Argentina for Arlentina Livestock Producers Association, 1949, also for Venezuelan Ministry of Agr., 1953-54. Fellow A.A.A.S.; mem. Am. Chem. Soc., Am. Soc. Animal Production (ex-pres.), Am. Dairy Science Assn., Sigma Xi, Alpha Zeta, Phi Kappa Phi, Phi Lambda Upsilon, Phi Sigma Kappa. Republican. Presbyterian. Author: Feeds and Feeding (with W. A. Henry), 1915, 20th edit. (sole author), 1936, 22d edit. 1956; Feeds and Feeding Manual, 1915; Feeds and Feeding, Abridged (with W. A. Henry), 1917, 7th edit. (sole author), 1937, 8th edit., 1949, 9th edit., 1958. Home: 7769 Westmoreland Dr., Sarasota, Fla.; also Elsimore, Saranac Inn P.O., N.Y. Died Apr. 7, 1958.

MORRISON, JAMES FRANK, electrical engr.; b. St. Johns, N.B., Apr. 18, 1841; ed. by pvt. tutor; m. Irene C. Sifford, of Frederick City, Md., Sept., 1872. Learned telegraphy; operator for B. & O. R.R., 1862-68; night mgr. for Western Union Telegraph Co., at Baltimore, 1868-70; became supt. fire-alarm system, Baltimore, 1870, entirely reorganizing it; in 1878 constructed, for Chesapeake & Ohio Canal Co., the first long distance telephone line in the world, 210 miles, from Georgetown, D.C., to Cumberland, Md.; also the pioneer in electric lighting business, having built 1st complete lighting sta., Baltimore, Clerk Md. Senate, 1876; fire commr. for Baltimore, 1874-87; warden city jail, Baltimore, 1879-87. Since 1880 connected with elec. construction and mfg.; mgr. Edison Electric Illuminating Co. and Fort Wayne Electric Corp.; organized, Oct., 1897, Northern Electric Co., consolidated, Jan., 1899, with Edison, Brush and others in United Electric Light & Power Co., of Baltimore. Pres. Nat. Electric Light Assn. of U.S., 1885-88. Home: 2017 Eutaw Pl. Office: 317 N. Paca St., Baltimore, Md.

MORRISON, JOSEPH, physician, astronomer, mathematician; b. Oxford, Ont., 1848; ed. University Coll., Toronto; graduated A.M., Middlebury Coll., Vt., 1869; mem. Coll. Phys. and Surg., Ont., 1869; M.B. (M.D.), 1872, Univ. of Toronto; (M.A., ad eundem, Acadia Univ., N.S., 1872; Ph.D., Univ. of Syracuse, 1884); m. July 4, 1871, Charlotte Sophia, d. late John Greene, Toronto. Mem. med. council and examiner chemistry and botany, Coll. Phys. & Surg., Ont., 1872-79; asst. astronomer Am. Ephemeris and Nautical Almanac, 1881-93; prof. chemistry, toxicology and metallurgy, med. dept. Nat. Univ., 1885-89; civil service examiner for Scientific Bureaus of U.S., 1885-89. Fellow Royal Astron. Soc., England, 1884-90. Author: Treatise on Trigonometry, 1880 C10; The Transits of Mercury and Venus, 1874 and 1882, 1883 C10; also numerous scientific papers in Monthly Notices of the Royal Astron. Soc. of England; in Popular Astronomy, and other scientific journals; and in Trans. Astron. and Phys. Soc., Toronto. Address: 1757 P St. N.W., Washington.

MORRISON, ROGER LEROY, educator; b. Winnetka, Ill., Aug. 28, 1883; s. George H. (M.D.) and Della (Baker) M.; A.B., U. Ill., 1911, B.S., 1912, C.E., 1917; A.M., Columbia, 1914; m. Clare Weadock, Dec. 26, 1914; 1 dau., Isabel (Mrs. William P. Byrne). Engr. S.P. Co. and W.P. R.R. Co., 1905-09; instr. civil engring., U. Tenn., 1911-12; jr. engr. Ill. Hwy. Dept., 1912; supt. road constrn., then sales engr., United Gas Imp. Co., 1913-14; prof. hwy. engring., A. and M. Coll., Tex., 1914-19; engr. of tests, Pitts. Testing Lab., 1919-21; treas., gen. mgr. Concrete Products Co., Birmingham, Ala., 1921-24; dir. Mich. State Hwy. Lab., 1924-27; asso. prof., later prof. hhwy. engring., hwy. transport, U. Mich., 1924—, also curator Transportation Library, 1945—; cons. engr., 1916—; mem. adv. bd. Mich. State Hwy. Dept.; mem. adv. com. Mich. State Safety Commn. Mem. Ann Arbor City Council, 1935-37. Capt. engrs. U.S. Reserves, 1918. Mem. Am. Soc. C.E. (p. chmn. hwy. div.), Army Transportation Assn., Assn. Asphalt Paving Technologists (past pres.), Inst. Traffic Engrs. (past pres.), Internat. Assn. Road Congresses, Am. Soc. Engring. Edn., Hwy. Research Bd. Nat. Research Council (past chmn.), Nat. Safety Council (past gen. chmn. traffic sect.), Eno Foundn. for Hwy. Traffic Control (mem. bd. cons.), Ann Arbor Engrs. Clubs, Engring. Soc. Detroit, S.A.R. (past pres. Washtenaw chapter), Sigma Xi, Sigma Rho Tau. Club: University (Ann Arbor). Author: (with A. H. Blanchard) Elements of Highway Engineering, 1928. Contbr. to tech. mags. and bulletins. Home: 1424 Kensington Dr., Ann Arbor, Mich. Died Mar. 23, 1952.

MORRISON, WILLARD LANGDON, engr., inventor; b. Lynn, Mass., Aug. 27, 1892; s. Willard N. and Amy Leland (Holder) M.; student Chandler Bus. Coll., 1909-10, Boston U., 1911-14, Babson Sch. Bus. Adminstrn., 1915-17; m. Ruth Barker Ansell, Jan. 1, 1917 (dec.); children—Willard L., Edwin Ansell; m. 2d, Lois Mae Weidman, Aug. 29, 1928; children—Maxine Mae, Harold Marshall, Lois M., Donald Carter. With White Motor Truck, Boston, 1915-17, Butte, Mont., Manganese Ore for U.S. Army, 1917-21; Chgo. with Dole Valve Co., Chgo., 1921-33, Clark Equipment Co., Buchanan, Mich., 1933-35, Pines Winterfront, Chgo., 1935-36; with Deepfreeze div. Motor Products Corp., North Chicago, Detroit, 1936-46; with Gen. Am. Transp. Corp., 1946-47; cons. research for Equipment Steel Products div. Union Asbestos, 1947-50; research project (with W. W. Prince) Union Stock Yards, Chgo., 1950-57; asso. Isbrandtsen Co., Inc. Mem. Constock and Thames Gas Bd. Mem. Am. Soc. Refrigeration Engrs., Am. Gas Assn., Am. Petroleum Inst., Soc. Naval Architects and Marine Engrs. Club: Chemists (N.Y.C.). Patentee, inventor pivoted glass window wing, home freezer system for liquefying natural gas for transp.; pioneered prodn. low temperature equipment. Address: 470 King Muir Rd., Lake Forest, Ill. Died July 19, 1965.

MORROW, ALBERT SYDNEY, surgeon; b. Madison, N.J., Apr. 2, 1878; s. Prince A. (M.D.) and Lucy B. (Slaughter) M.; A.B., Columbia, 1898; M.D., Univ. and Bellevue Hosp. Med. Coll., N.Y. U., 1901; m. Marjorie Wyld, Oct. 23, 1909; children—Albert S. Alison. Intern, Bellevue Hosp., 1901-03; asst. attending surgeon Lying-In Hosp., 1903-05; attending surgeon Workhouse Hosp., 1904-17; attending physician Almshouse Hosp., 1905-06; attending surgeon Central and Neurol. Hosp., 1907-19; prof. surgery, vis. surgeon, N.Y. Polyclinic Med. Sch., 1906-24; vis. surgeon City Hosp., 1919-36, St. Bartholomew's Hosp., 1920-26; attending surgeon Stuyvesant Sq. Hosp., 1929-34, skin and cancer unit Post Grad. Hosp., 1934-39; cons. surgeon City Hosp., also Cornwall (N.Y.) Hosp. Commd. capt. M.R.C., U.S. Army, 1917, lt. col. M.C., 1918. Fellow A.C.S., Acad. Medicine; mem. A.M.A., Med. Soc. State of N.Y., N.Y. County Med. Soc. Home: 108 E. 91st St., N.Y.C. 10028. Died Feb. 27, 1960.

MORROW, JAY JOHNSON, army officer; b. Fairview, W.Va., Feb. 20, 1870; grad. U.S. Mil. Acad., 1891, Engr. Sch. of Application, 1894; m. Harriet M. Butler, Oct. 15, 1895. Commd. add. 2d lt. engrs., June 12, 1891; promoted through grades to lt. col., Mar. 11, 1915; col. (temp.), Aug. 5, 1917; brig. gen. N.A., June 26, 1918; returned to rank of col., May 20, 1919; retired at own request, Aug. 5, 1922. Instr. dept. practical mil. engring., U.S. Mil. Acad., 1895-96, 1898-1901; in Philippines, 1901-03; mil. gov. Province of Zamboanga, 1901-02; engr. Commr. Dist. of Columbia, 1907-09; engr. of maintenance and at times acting gov. Panama Canal, 1916-17; arrived in France, May 12, 1918; chief engr. 1st Army, and dep. chief engr. A.E.F., 1918; assigned to comd. Camp A. A. Humphreys, Va., Dec. 30, 1918; again engr. of maintenance, Panama Canal, June 1919-Mar. 1921; gov. same, Mar. 1921-Oct. 1924; Am. mem. and chmn. Spl. Commn. on Boundaries, Tacna-Arica Arbitration, Mar. 1925-June 1929. Decorated Officer Legion of Honor (France), 1918. Presbyn. Home: Englewood, N.J. Died Apr. 16, 1937.

MORROW, THOMAS VAUGHAN, pioneer in eclectic medicine; b. Fairview, Ky., Apr. 14, 1804; s. Thomas and Elizabeth (Vaughan) M.; attended Transylvania U., Reformed Med. Coll. of N.Y.; m. Isabel Greer. Pres., dean, prof. materia medica, obstetrics, theory and practice of medicine Reformed Med. Coll. of Ohio, 1830-39; organized Reformed Med.

Sch. of Cincinnati, 1842, became Cincinnati Eclectic Med. Inst., 1845, dean, treas., prof. physiology, pathology and theory and practice, 1845-50; advocated the eclectic system of medicine, founder of 1st schs. of that cult in West; pres. Nat. Eclectic Med. Assn., 1848; wrote articles, editorials for Western Med. Reformer and Eclectic Med. Jour. Died Cincinnati, July 16, 1850; buried Wesleyan Cemetery, Cincinnati.

MORSE, CHARLES ADELBERT, engineer; b. Bangor, Me., Jan. 1, 1859; s. Charles B. and Elsie (Emery) M.; C.E., U. of Me., 1879. Instrumentman, office man and div. engr., C.,B. & Q. R.R., 1880-81; div. engr. Mex. Central Ry., 1881-84; again C.,B. & Q. R.R., 1884-85; with A.,T. & S.F. Ry. as transitman, div. engr., and resident engr., Ft. Madison, Ia., and Pueblo, Colo., 1886-1901, asst. to chief engr., Topeka, 1901-02, prin. asst. engr., La Junta, 1902-03, engr. eastern grand div., Topeka, Mar.-July, 1903, acting chief engr., Topeka, 1903-04, asst. chief engr., Topeka, 1904-05, acting chief engr., A.,T. & S.F. Ry. Coast Lines, Los Angeles, 1905-06, chief engr. A.,T. & S.F. Ry., Topeka, 1906-09, chief engr. A.,T. & S.F. System, Topeka, 1909-13; chief engr. Rock Island Lines, Chicago, Apr. 1, 1913-Sept. 1, 1918, and 1919-29. Assistant director engring. and maintenance, U.S.R.R. Administration, Washington, Sept. 1, 1918-June 1, ern Soc. Engrs. (pres. 1923-24), Washington Soc. 1919. Apptd. mem. Board of Review, Construction Dept. U.S.A., 1918. Mem. Am. Soc. C.E. (ex-pres. Ill. sect.), Am. Ry. Engring. Assn. (ex-pres.), West-Engrs. Clubs: Engineers (ex-pres.), University. Home: Windermere Hotel. Chicago, Ill.

MORSE, EDWARD SYLVESTER, zoölogist; b. Portland, Me., June 18, 1838; s. Jonathan K. and Jane Seymour (Beckett) M.; ed. at Bethel, Me., Acad.; later 3 yrs. with Louis Agassiz at Lawrence Scientific Sch. (Harvard); (hon. Ph.D., Bowdoin College, 1871; A.M., Harvard Univ., 1892; D.Sc., Yale Univ., 1918; Doctor of Human Letters, Tufts Coll., 1922). Professor of comparative anatomy and zoölogy, Bowdoin, 1871-74; prof. zoölogy, Imperial U., Tokio, Japan, 1877-80; dir. Peabody Museum, Salem, Mass., 1880—. Lecturer, Harvard U., 1872-73; keeper Japanese pottery, Mus. Fine Arts, Boston, 1892—; authority on Japanese ceramics. Mem. jury of awards, Chicago Expn., 1893, Buffalo Expn., 1901, St. Louis Expn., 1904. Fellow Am. Acad. Arts and Sciences; mem. numerous scientific societies. Decorated with Order of the Rising Sun (Japan), 1898; 2d degree Order of Sacred Treasure (Japan), 1922. Author: First Book of Zoölogy, 1875; Japanese Homes and Their Surroundings, 1886; Catalogue of the Morse Collection of Japanese Pottery (Mus. of Fine Arts, Boston), 1901; Glimpses of China and Chinese Homes, 1902; Mars and Its Mystery, 1906; Japan Day by Day, 1917. Home: Salem, Mass. Died Dec. 20, 1925.

MORSE, EDWIN KIRTLAND, engr.; b. Poland, Mahoning County, Ohio, July 3, 1856; s. Henry Kirtland and Mary A. (Lynn) M.; A.B., Yale, 1881; m. Caroline U. Shields, Sept. 25, 1884; m. 2d, Elizabeth Wood, Apr. 12, 1914. In various depts. of brother's bridge works at Youngstown, O., and gen. agt. for the co. at Chicago, to 1887; went to Sydney, Australia, 1887, and contracted for erection of superstructure, under firm head of Ryland & Morse, Hawkesbury Bridge, at Dangar Island (7 spans, 415 ft. each, the largest bridge in the southern hemisphere); returned to Pittsburgh, 1889; cons. engr. since 1892. Built substructures for Buffalo, Rochester & Pittsburgh R.R. Bridge, and Carnegie's Railroad, both across Allegheny River; foundations or hot metal bridges at Port Perry and Homestead, across Monongahela River for Carnegie Steel Co., substructures for Jones & Laughlin Steel Co.'s bridge across Monongahela River; 3 suspension bridges across Ohio River with channel spans 700 to 800 ft. each; consulting engr., chmn. engr. com. of Flood Commn. Transit commr. for city of Pittsburgh, 1916-20; cons. engr. City of Pittsburgh for study of flood control, wharf apptd. mem. Water and Power Resources Bd., by Gov. John S. Fisher, Nov. 9, 1927, reapptd., 1931, by Gov. Gifford Pinchot. Mem. Am. Inst. Cons. Engrs., Inc., Am. Soc. C.E. (dir.); ex-pres. Engrs. Soc. of Western Pa. Cons. engr. Allegheny County Authority. Club: Duquesne. Home and Office: 401 S. Graham St., Pittsburgh, Pa. Died May 28, 1942.

MORSE, HARMON NORTHROP, chemist; b. Cambridge, Vt., Oct. 15, 1848; s. Harmon and Elizabeth Murray (Buck) M.; A.B., Amherst (Mass.) College, 1873 (LL.D., 1915); Ph.D., U. of Göttingen, 1875; m. Caroline Augusta Brooks, Dec. 13, 1876 (died 1887); m. 2d, Elizabeth Dennis Clarke, Dec. 24, 1890. Asst. in chemistry, Amherst, 1875-76; asso. prof. chemistry, Johns Hopkins U., 1876-91, and prof. analytical chemistry and adj. dir. of the chem. lab., 1891, prof. inorganic and analytical chemistry, and dir. of chem. laboratory. Fellow Am. Acad. Arts and Sciences. Avogadro medalist. Research asso. Carnegie Instn. of Washington; prin. investigations, osmotic pressure. Author: Exercises in Quantitative Chemistry, 1905. Home: Baltimore, Md. Died Sept. 8, 1920.

MORSE, HARRY WHEELER, physicist; b. San Diego, Calif., Feb. 25, 1873; s. Philip and Sarah (McDonald) M.; A.B., Leland Stanford Jr. U., 1897; Ph.D., U. of Leipzig, 1901; m. Isabel Grace Gray, Aug. 8, 1904; children—Philip Gray, Cecily, Constance, Anthony John. Instr. physics, 1902-10, asst. prof., 1910-12, Harvard; prof. chemistry, U. of Calif., 1912-13; in charge of scientific work, Western Precipitation Co., Los Angeles, 1913-18; tech. mgr. Am. Trona Corp., 1918-19; consulting chemist and matallurgist, 1920—. Fellow Am. Acad. Arts and Sciences. Translator: Ostwald, Letters to a Painter on the Theory and Practice of Painting, 1906; Ostwald, Fundamental Principles of Chemistry, 1907. Joint Author: Ostwald and Morse's Elementary Modern Chemistry, 1907. Author: Chemistry and Physics of the Lead Accumulator, 1912. Home: Stanford University, Calif. Died Mar. 12, 1936.

MORSE, HENRY DUTTON, diamond cutter; b. Boston, Apr. 20, 1826; s. Hazen and Lucy (Cary) M.; m. Ann Hayden, May 22, 1849; 4 children. Partner in retail firm Crosby, Hunnewell & Morse, Boston, until 1875; organized Morse Diamond Cutting Co., 1877; 1st Am. to learn technique of diamond-cutting, made improvements which revolutionized the art; invented labor-saving machinery for sawing and polishing stones; cut 1st modern brilliants with 56 facets and powers of refraction; cut Dewey diamond, 1859; cut Tiffany No. 2 diamond, 125 carats, reduced to 77 carats in cutting (largest diamond ever handled in U.S.). Died Jamaica Plains, Mass., Jan. 2, 1888.

MORSE, IRVING HASKELL, sugar chemist; b. Emporia, Kan., Mar. 24, 1868; s. Grosvenor C. and Abby Prentis (Barber) M.; student Emporia Coll., 1885-87; B.S., U. of Kan., 1891; 3 months' spl. work in U. of Chicago, 1894; m. Caroline Johnston, July 31, 1902; 1 son, James Johnston. Factory chemist for Miles Planting & Mfg. Co., New Orleans, 1891-1901; for Cuban-Am. Sugar Co., Tinguaro, Cuba, 1901-03; chief chemist for Longmont (Colo.) Sugar Co. and supt. of cane sugar factory "Mercedita," in Cuba, 1903-10; supervising chemist for La. Sugar Co., New Orleans, 1910-13; pres. Morse Lab. Co., Inc., since 1917. Inventor apparatus for separating impurities from cane juice or other liquors. Author: Calculations Used in Cane-Sugar Factories, 1904; Laboratory Record, 1911. Developed "open kettle" system of mfg. pure sugar direct from cane. Home: 2806 State St., New Orleans LA

MORSE, SAMUEL FINLEY BREESE, inventor, artist; b. Charlestown, Mass., Apr. 27, 1791; s. Rev. Jedidiah and Elizabeth (Breese) M.; grad. Yale, 1810, LL.D. (hon.); attended Royal Acad., London, Eng., 1811-15; m. Lucretia Walker, Sept. 29, 1818; m. 2d, Sarah Griswold, Aug. 9, 1848; 8 children. Painter in Eng.; noteworthy works include: Hercules, 1812 (recipient gold medal), The Dying Hercules, 1813, The Judgment of Jupiter, 1815; engaged in portrait painting in U.S., 1815-29, best-known were two portraits of Lafayette, 1821, 22, also The Old House of Representatives; a founder N.A.D., 1st pres., 1826-42, also pres., 1861; made trip to Europe for artistic study, 1829-31; prof. painting, sculpture N.Y.U., 1832; invented electro-magnetic recording telegraph; invented sending and receiving apparatus, code (Morse Code), by 1832; worked out system of electro-magnetic relays to be placed in the telegraph line weak points, 1836; Congress voted $30,000 for an exptl. line from Washington, D.C. to Balt., 1843, line completed, May 24, 1844; Morse's rights to profits from his invention were upheld in the courts; electrician for Cyrus W. Field's Co., engaged in laying Transatlantic Cable, 1857-58; a founder Vassar Coll., 1861. Died N.Y.C., Apr. 2, 1872; buried Greenwood Cemetery, Bklyn.

MORSE, SIDNEY EDWARDS, editor, inventor; b. Charlestown, Mass., Feb. 7, 1794; s. Jedidiah and Elizabeth (Breese) M.; A.B., Yale, 1811; attended Litchfield (Conn.), Law Sch., then Andover Theol. Sem., 1817-20; m. Catharine Livingston, Apr. 1, 1841, 2 children. A founder, Recorder (1st religious newspaper in Boston), 1816; a founder N.Y. Observer, 1823, sr. editor, propr., 1823-58; editor (with father) A New System of Modern Geography . . . Accompanied by an Atlas, 1822; patentee (with brother Samuel) flexible piston pump; inventor process "cerography" (map of Conn. was first example), 1839; patentee (with son) bathometer, 1866. Author: The New States, or a Comparison of the . . . Northern and Southern States: With a View to Expose the Injustice of Erecting New States at the South (collection of reprinted articles), 1813; An Atlas of the United States, 1823; Cerographic Atlas of the United States, 1842-45; A System of Geography for the Use of Schools, 1844. Died Dec. 23, 1871.

MORSE, WARNER JACKSON, plant pathologist; b. Waterbury Center, Vt., Oct. 30, 1872; s. Daniel Jackson and Jane (McKee) M.; grad. Johnson (Vt.) Normal Sch., 1893; B.S., U. of Vt., 1898, M.S., 1903, Sc.D., 1923; Ph.D., U. of Wis., 1912; m. Mary A. Leland, July 6, 1898; 1 dau., Ruth Esther. Teacher natural sciences, Montpelier (Vt.) Sem., 1899-1901; asst. botanist, Vt. Expt. Sta., 1901-06; instr. botany, 1901-05, asst. prof. bacteriology, 1905-06, U. of Vt.; plant pathologist, 1906-23, dir., 1921—, Me. Agrl. Expt. Sta. Mason. Home: Orono, Me. Died Mar. 25, 1931.

MORSE, WITHROW, biochemist; b. at Dayton, O., May 7, 1880; s. David Appleton (M.D.) and Amanda (Withrow) M.; B.Sc., Ohio State U., 1903, A.M., 1904; Ph.D., Columbia, 1910; m. Winning Allan, 1934; children—John, Priscilla. Prof. biochemistry successively med. depts., U. of Neb., W.Va. Sch. of Medicine and Jefferson Med. Coll., 1916-29; served on staffs of U. of Wis., Cornell U. and Trinity Coll.; biochemist, N.Y. State Psychiatric Inst., Columbia U. Med. Center; also consultant to Lederle Labs., New York, Rohm & Haas Co., Inc., Phila., The Kalak Co., New York; vice pres. Vogelbach Associates, Ind. Mem. Am. Soc. Biol., Chemists (life mem.), British Biochemistry Soc., Sigma Xi, Phi Beta Kappa, Delta Upsilon. Author: Applied Biochemistry (2 edits.); Organizer of Biochemistry (a British-Am. coöperative treatise); Development of Biochemistry; Mineral Physiology; Flugel (blood transfusion substitute), 1940. Home: 32 Manchester Rd., Tuckahoe 7, N.Y. Offices: 30 Rockefeller Plaza, N.Y.C. 20. Died Feb. 10, 1951; buried London, O.

MORTENSON, ERNEST DAWSON, civil engr.; b. Boston, Oct. 31, 1895; s. Nils and Mary (Wyke) M.; B.S., Tufts U., 1917; m. Gladys Fullerton Hill, July 27, 1922; children—Olive (Mrs. Kenneth Ernest Blackwell), Leonard Earl, Judith (Mrs. Robert Twarog). Spl. agt. engr. New Eng. dist. PWA, 1935-37; contract, specification engr. Met. Water Supply Commn., Boston, 1938-40; supervising engr. U.S. Navy Quonset Air Sta., R.I., 1940-46; asst. city plan engr. New Haven, 1946-47; chief and asso. engr. Lyons & Mather Architects, Bridgeport, Conn., 1947-66, exec. engr., 1966-68. Cons. engr. various firms New Eng., 1935; lectr. Franklin Tech. Inst., Boston, 1933-40, Bridgeport Engring. Inst., 1950-52. Mem. Melrose (Mass.) City Plan Commn., 1934-40; advancement chmn. Boy Scouts Am., Melrose, 1938-40. Registered profl. engr. Mass., Conn., R.I. Fellow Am. Soc. C.E.s; mem. Greater Bridgeport Engring. Socs. Council, Nat. Soc. Profl. Engrs. (pres. Conn. 1938-39), Am. Concrete Inst., Boston Tufts Club. Mason (32 deg.). Home: Stratford CT Died May 1968.

MORTON, CONRAD VERNON, botanist; b. Fresno, Cal., Oct. 24, 1905; s. Walter Crow and Noma (Bartholomew) M.; B.A., U. Cal. at Berkeley, 1928. Aide div. plants' U.S. Nat. Museum, Smithsonian Instn., 1928-38, asst. curator, then asso. curator, 1938-48, curator div. ferns, 1948-70, sr. botanist, 1970-72; asso. editor Am. Fern Jour., 1940-47, editor-in-chief, 1948-61, asso. editor, 1962-72; editor for pteridophyta Biol. Abstracts, 1946-72. Guggenheim fellow, 1954. Mem. Phi Beta Kappa, Sigma Xi, Phi Sigma. Author numerous articles in field. Home: Washington DC Died July 29, 1972.

MORTON, HENRY, pres. Stevens Inst. of Technology, 1870—; b. New York, Dec. 11, 1837; s. Rev. Dr. Henry Jackson and Helen (McFarlan) M.; ed. Episcopal Acad., Phila.; grad. Univ. of Pa., A.M., 1857 (Sc.D., Univ. of Pa.; Ph.D., LL.D., Princeton); m. Clara Whiting Dodge, 1863. Published translation of hieroglyphic text of the Rosetta Stone, 1859; conducted expdn. to observe and make photographs of total solar eclipse in Iowa, 1868; was prof. chemistry Univ. of Pa., 1868-70; resident sec. Franklin Inst. and editor of its journal, 1864-70. Mem. U.S. Light House Bd., 1878-86; mem. Nat. Acad. of Sciences, 1873—. Has given over $80,000 toward endowment of the Stevens Inst. of Technology. Home: Hoboken, N.J. Died 1902.

MORTON, JACK A., engineer; b. St. Louis, Sept. 4, 1913; s. Mack Ray and Minette (Hirsfeld) M.; B.Sc., Wayne University, 1935, D.Sc. (honorary), 1956; M.Sc., University Michigan, 1936; graduate study Columbia, 1937-41; Ph.D. (hon.), Ohio State U., 1954; m. Helen Read, May 27, 1938; children—Kim, Mack. Asst. dir. electronic apparatus development Bell Telephone Labs., Inc., Murray Hill, N.J., 1952-53, dir. transistor development, 1953-54, dir. development solid state devices, 1954-55, dir. device development, 1955-58, v.p., 1958-71. Mem. planning bd. Hillsborough (N.J.) Twp. Recipient Univ. Alumni award Wayne U., 1951, Certificate of Merit, 1958. Distinguished Alumnus citation U. Mich., 1953; David Sarnoff award, 1965. Fellow Inst. Elec. and Electronics Engrs. (chmn. electron tube conf. 1949); mem. MacKenzie Honor Soc., National Academy Engineering, Phi Beta Kappa, Sigma Xi, Eta Kappa Nu, Alpha Delta Psi, Phi Kappa Phi, Tau Beta Pi. Home: South Branch NJ Died Dec. 11, 1971.

MORTON, JAMES ST. CLAIR, army officer, engr., author; b. Phila., Sept. 24, 1829; s. Dr. Samuel George and Rebecca Grellet (Pearsall) M.; grad. U.S. Mil. Acad., 1851. Asst. engr. in constrn. defenses of Charleston harbor, S.C., 1851-52; commd. 2d lt., 1854, asst. prof. engring. U.S. Mil. Acad.; promoted 1st lt., 1856; charge Potomac Water Works, 1859-60; engr. in charge Chiriqui Expdn. to C.Am. of Washington Aqueduct, 1860-61; capt. engrs., 1861; chief engr. Army of the Ohio, 1862; brig. gen. U.S. Volunteers, 1862; chief engr. Army of the Cumberland, 1862-63; brevetted lt. col. engrs. in regular army, 1863; maj. Corps Engrs., 1863; brevetted col., 1863; supt. defenses of Nashville, Murfreesboro, Clarksville, Ft. Donelson, 1863-64; asst. to chief engr., Washington, D.C., 1864; brevetted brig. gen., 1864. Author: Memoir on the Dangers and Defenses of New York City, 1858;

Memoir on American Fortification, 1859. Died Petersburg, Va., June 17, 1864; buried Laurel Hill Cemetery, Phila.

MORTON, ROSALIE SLAUGHTER, surgeon; b. Lynchburg, Va., Oct. 28, 1876; d. John Flavel and Mary Haines (Harker) Slaughter; student pvt. schs., Va. and Md.; M.D., with honors, Woman's Med. Coll. of Pa., 1897; interne City Hosp., Phila., 1897; resident physician Alumni Hosp. and Dispensary Woman's Med. Coll. of Pa., 1897-98; post-grad. study in nervous diseases, gynecology and surgery, Berlin, Vienna, Paris and London, 1899-1901; tropical diseases, Ceylon and India, 1901; hon. Dr. Humanities, Rollins Coll., 1929; D.Sc., Rutgers, 1939; m. George B. Morton, Jr., Sept. 1905 (died 1912). Practiced at Washington, 1902-05, New York, 1906-29; at Winter Park, Florida, since 1930, specializing in endocrinology and arthritis; clin. asst. and instr. gynecology, 1912-14, lecturer on surgery, 1914-16, adj. prof. gynecology, 1916-18, N.Y. Poly. Med. Sch. and Hosp.; attdg. surgeon, Vanderbilt Clinic of Coll. Physicians and Surgeons (Columbia), 1916-18; founded social service dept. N.Y. Polyclinic Hosp., 1917; visiting surgeon and consultant Volunteer Hosp., 1919-23; mem. visiting staff Orange Gen. Hosp. since 1930. Specialist in treatment of arthritis since 1929. Active service in France and on Salonica front, 1916; was first chmn. war service com. of Am. Women's Nat. Assn.; founder and first chmn. of Am. Women's Hosps.; under apptmt. of U.S. Govt. represented 6,000 women physicians on U.S. Council Nat. Defense, Washington, 1917-18, World War; provided hosp. equipment for 2 Yugoslav hosps., and tuberculosis camp for children under Serbian Red Cross, 1919; founder and chmn. Internat. Serbian Ednl. Com., under which 60 Yugoslav students were educated in Am. univs., 1919-28. Lectured widely in U.S., also in Serbia, Australia and S. Africa. Commr. on Internat. Education to Eng., France, Germany and Italy, 1921-26; from League of Am. Pen Women and Women's Med. Soc. of N.Y. State to S. Africa, 1926, to Iraq and Iran, 1935; del. Pan Pacific Scientific Congress, Australia, 1923; to Congress of Socs. to Promote League of Nations, France, 1924; ambassador of good will from various organizations to Mexico, Hayti and Porto Rico, 1928, 29; hon. pres. and ambassador of good will to med. women in Near and Middle East, summer 1935; business and professional commr. of nat. and internat. assns. to Greece, Turkey and Syria, summer 1935. For distinguished services on Salonica front, on Mediterranean, in Serbia, Yugoslavia and France, was decorated 9 times by France, Serbia and State of N.Y., 1916-23; tree in Honor Grove, Central Park, New York, planted in her honor "for distinguished patriotic service," 1926; awarded Palm of Officer French Acad., 1927; presented with loving cup by a group of members of Am. Med. Assn., 1934. Fellow A.M.A.; mem. Fla. Med. Assn., Orange County Med. Soc. (Fla.) Women's Med. Assn. N.Y. City (pres. 1917-18), Woman's Med. Soc. State of N.Y. (pres. 1927-28), Nat. Inst. Social Sciences, Colonial Dames, D.A.R., U.D.C., Nat. Soc. Patriotic Women of America, Soc. of Va. Women in New York, Vets. of Foreign Wars, Am. Assn. Univ. Women, League of Am. Pen Women, Inst. of Internat. Edn., N.Y. Acad. Sciences, Am. Red Cross (life mem.), Assn. of Mil. Surgeons of the U.S., Am. Inst. for Iranian Art and Archaeology, Sociedad Medica Yucateca (hon. since 1928), Zeta Phi (pres. 1926-28), etc. Episcopalian. Club: Zonta (twice pres.). Has studied sociological and economic problems in Sweden, Finland, Estonia, Latvia and Lithuania. Author: A Woman Surgeon (autobiography; pub. U.S., Eng. and Sweden), 1937; A Doctor's Holiday in Iran, 1940. Invented 9 surg. instruments and appliances; author of numerous articles on gynecol., arthritis and other scientific subjects. Home: 667 Osceola Av., Winter Park FL

MORTON, SAMUEL GEORGE, physician, naturalist; b. Phila., Jan. 26, 1799; s. George and Jane (Cummings) M.; M.D., U. Pa., 1820; M.D., U. Edinburgh, 1823; m. Rebecca Pearsall, Oct. 23, 1827, 7 children including James St. Clair. Became mem. Acad. Natural Scis. Phila. circa 1820, recording sec., 1825-29, corr. sec., 1831, v.p., 1840, pres., 1849-51; prof. anatomy Pa. Med. Coll., 1839-43; collected large number human skulls for comparative study, concluded that races of man were of diverse origin; credited with describing new species of hippopotamus. Author: Synopsis of the Organic Remains of the Cretaceous Group of the U.S., 1834; Illustrations of Pulmonary Consumption, 1834; Crania Americana, 1839; Crania Egyptiaca, 1839; Human Anatomy, Special, General and Microscopic, 1849. Died Phila., May 15, 1851.

MORTON, THOMAS GEORGE, M.D.; b. Philadelphia, Aug. 8, 1835; grad. med. dept. Univ. of Pa., 1856; general surgical practice; served in Union army, Civil war, in field in Va. and in Washington hospitals; was surgeon Satterlee Hosp.; consulting surgeon Mower Army Hosp., Chestnut Hill, Pa. Founded Philadelphia Orthopaedic Hospital, 1867; now surgeon to Jewish Hospital; emeritus surgeon Wills' Eye Hospital; consulting surgeon Women's Hosp.; senior surgeon and pres. med. staff Pennsylvania Hosp.; prof. orthopaedic surgery Polyclinic Hosp. and Coll. for Graduates. Became, 1880, pres. Pa. Soc. for Restriction of Vivisection and v.p. Soc. for Prevention of Cruelty to Children. Pres. Acad. of Surgery, Philadelphia; fellow Coll. Physicians; corr. member British Orthopaedic Soc.; chairman of committee High School for Girls; was commr. State Public Charities, 1883. Invented hospital ward carriage, ward bed elevator, etc., receiving Centennial medal, 1876. Author: Surgery in the Pennsylvania Hospital; Transfusion of Blood and Its Practical Application; History of the Pennsylvania Hospital; etc. Address: 1617 Chestnut St., Philadelphia.

MORTON, WILLIAM THOMAS GREEN, dentist; b. Charlton, Mass., Aug. 9, 1819; s. James and Rebecca (Needham) M.; studied dentistry Coll. Dental Surgery, Balt., 1840-42; also studied dentistry Harvard Med. Sch.; M.D. (hon.), Washington U. of Medicine, Balt.; m. Elizabeth Whitman, May 1844, 4 children including William James. While experimenting with mesmerism and nostrums became involved with sulfur ether which he later connected and linked to use in dental anaesthesia; used ether in drops as local anaesthetic during filling of a tooth, 1844, extracted a tooth with this method, 1846; etherized a patient from whom Dr. John Warren removed vascular tumor from left side of neck, 1846; applied for patent to protect his rights, received patent for 14 years, 1846; issued weekly circular Morton's Letheon, 5 editions, under his direction, 1846; awarded Montyon prize of 5,000 francs from French Acad. Medicine, 1847; although he was not only discoverer of anaesthesia he convinced surg. world of value of discovery of a surg. anaesthetic; during Civil War worked in various hosps.; made many improvements on crude methods of attaching false teeth. Author: Remarks on the Proper Mode of Administering Sulphuric Ether by Inhalation, 1847; On the Loss of the Teeth and the Modern Way of Restoring Them, 1848; On the Physiological Effects of Sulphuric Ether, and Its Superiority to Chloroform, 1850. Died N.Y.C., July Mass.

MOSENTHAL, HERMAN (OTTO), (mo'zen-thäl), physician; b. N.Y. City, July 8, 1878; s. Joseph and Augusta Ernestine (Andreae) M.; student Williams Coll., 1895; A.B., Columbia, 1899; M.D., Coll. Phys. and Surg. (Columbia), 1903; m. Johanna Kroeber, Sept. 3, 1908; children—Barbara Andreae (Mrs. Winston T. Kellogg), Joseph, Joan Elizabeth (Mrs. Adrian William De Wind), Edward Kroeber. Served as interne at New York Hospital, 1904-06, N.Y. Foundling Hosp., 1906-07; asst. instr. and asso. in biol. chemistry and medicine, Columbia, 1908-14; attending physician in diseases of metabolism, Vanderbilt Clinic, 1910-14; asst. visiting physician Presbyn. Hosp., 1911-14; asst. prof. medicine and asst. physician, Johns Hopkins Med. Sch. and Hosp., Baltimore, Md., 1914-18; prof. of clinical medicine, New York Post-Grad. Med. Sch., Columbia U., and attending physician N.Y. Post-Grad. Hosp., 1922-48; consulting physician Bellevue Hosp., N.Y. City, Sea View Hosp., Staten Island; consultant in medicine N.Y.U.-Bellevue Medical Center; consultant St. Luke's Hospital, Newburgh, N.Y.; N.Y. Infirmary for Women and Children; Goshen Hosp., Goshen, N.Y.; dir. Dept. of Medicine N.Y. Post-Grad. Med. Sch. and Hosp., 1925-35. Associate clinic professor medical and assoc. attending physician, New York Medical College. Chairman New York Diabetes Association, 1935 (member board directors since 1936); president American Diabetes Association, 1941-42 (mem. Council since 1942). Served as captain Medical Officers Reserve Corps, 1918-19. Fellow American College Physicians; member A.M.A., Assn. Am. Physicians, N.Y. Acad. of Medicine, Internat. Soc. of Gastroenterology, Am. Soc. of Advancement Clin. Investigation, Soc. Exptl. Biology and Medicine, Nu Sigma Nu. Club: Century. Contributor on internal medicine to med. publs. Home: 210 E. 68th St. Office: 889 Lexington Av., N.Y.C. Died Apr. 24, 1954; buried Gaylordsville, Conn.

MOSER, JEFFERSON FRANKLIN, naval officer; b. Allentown, Pa., May 3, 1848; s. John B. and Henrietta (Beidelman) M.; grad. U.S. Naval Acad., 1868; m. Nancy C. McDowell, Oct. 20, 1874; children—Robert McD. (dec.), Samuel B. (dec.), Jefferson F. (dec.), Helen C. Commd., midshipman, June 2, 1868; promoted through grades to rank of rear adm. and retired after 40 yrs.' service, Sept. 29, 1904. Mem. expdns., 1869-70, 72, 73, 75, exploring and surveying ship canal routes across Nicaragua and Panama; coast survey service, 1875-80, 1884-90, 1893-96; comd. U.S. Steamer Albatross in exploring salmon streams of Alaska and on Agassiz expdn. to South Seas, etc.; comd. gunboats Albatross and Bennington during Spanish-Am. War; gen. supt. and v.p. Alaska Packers Assn., San Francisco, 1904-18. Ordered to active service in U.S.N., Apr. 6, 1917, on special duty 12th Naval Dist. until June 15, 1919. Author: Alaska Salmon and Salmon Fisheries, 1899; Alaska Salmon Investigations, 1902. Home: Alameda, Calif. Died Oct. 11, 1934.

MOSER, WILLIAM, physician; b. New York, Aug. 2, 1868; s. John M. and Teresa (Foertsch) M.; ed. pub. sch. and Packard's Bus. Coll.; M.D., Univ. Med. Coll. (New York U.), 1888; also studied at U. of Berlin; m. Josephine Bossert, of Far Rockaway, L.I., Sept. 19, 1900. Engaged in med. practice at Brooklyn since 1892; phys. to German Hosp., Brooklyn; formerly pathologist to St. Catherine's, St. Mary's, German, and Brooklyn Throat (now Williamsburg) hosps.; now pathologist Deaconess Hosp.; attending phys. St. Catharine's Hosp. Dispensary. Mem. German Soc. of Brooklyn; former mem. Pathol. Soc. and Kings Co. Med. Soc. Contbr. to New York Medical Record on physiology and anatomy of the blood, etc., and on the pathol. topics in New York and Philadelphia Medical Journal and Brooklyn Medical Journal. Address: 573 Decatur St., Brooklyn, L.I., N.Y.

MOSES, ALFRED JOSEPH, mineralogist; b. Brooklyn, July 25, 1859; s. Thomas P. and Margaret M.; acad. edn., Woburn, Mass.; E.M., Columbia, 1882, Ph.D., 1890; U. of Munich, 1895-96; m. Elizabeth B. Gilbert, June 23, 1887; 2d, Margaret C. Magrath, Aug. 18, 1906. Asst. in mineralogy, 1882-85, instr. mineralogy and metallurgy, 1885-90, adj. prof. mineralogy, 1890-97, prof., 1897—, Columbia U. Fellow N.Y. Acad. Sciences, A.A.A.S. Author: Mineralogy, Crystallography and Blowpipe Analysis, 1895; Characters of Crystals, 1899. Home: New York, N.Y. Died Feb. 27, 1920.

MOSHER, WILLIAM ALLISON, chemist; b. Salem, Ore., Dec. 26, 1912; s. Daniel Harrison and Maud (Stone) M.; B.A., Willamette U., 1935, D.Sc., 1961; M.S., Ore. State U., 1936; student U. Mich., 1937; Ph.D., Pa. State U., 1940; m. DeLaurice E. Yarnes, Oct. 3, 1936; children—Allison Jean, Carol Anne. Food chemist, Reid, Murdock & Co., Salem, Ore., 1932-36; research fellow, asst., Ore. State Coll., 1935-37; asst. prof. chemistry, Willamette U., 1937-38; asst. fellow, Pa. State U., 1938-40; research chemist Hercules Powder Co., Wilmington, Del., 1940-41; asst. to dir. research Hercules Powder Co., 1941-45; prof. chemistry, head dept. chemistry, U. Del., 1945-72, Willis F. Harrington Prof. and chmn., 1962—; Lank lectr. U. Montreal, 1960; Zinn lectr., Gettysburg, 1962; Baugher lectr., Elizabethtown, 1962; mem. adv. council Biochemical Research Found., Franklin Inst. since 1946; chem. advisor Biochem. Research Found. since 1948; gas cons. Del., 1942-45; Fulbright lectureship in Austria, 1952-53; cultural del. to Rumania, 1958; cons. to Army Chem. Corps. Served with Chem. Corps. Res. as 1st lt. Member Am. Chem. Soc., Chem. Soc. (London), Nat. Com. Professional Relations, A.A.A.S., N.Y. Acad. Sci., Franklin Inst., Sigma Xi, Phi Kappa Phi, Alpha Chi Sigma, Phi Lambda Upsilon, Alpha Tau Omega. Theta Alpha Phi, Tau Kappa Alpha, Blue Key. Republican. Methodist. Contbr. scientific articles profl. jours. Home: Newark DE Died July 23, 1972; interred Gracelawn Meml. Park, New Castle DE

MOSIER, JEREMIAH GEORGE, prof. soil physics; b. Pike Co., O., Jan. 8, 1862; s. David and Amanda Rachel (Brill) M.; student Nat. Normal U., Lebanon, O., 1883-85; B.S., U. of Ill., 1893; m. Lydia C. Miller, June 22, 1892. Teacher in rural schs., Champaign Co., Ill., 1885-88, and village sch., Sadorus, Ill., 1893-94; asst. in geology, U. of Ill., 1894-97; engaged in farming, 1897-98; instr. in high sch., Urbana, 1899-1900, Champaign, 1900-02; instr. soil physics, 1902-05, asst. prof., 1905-11, prof., 1911—, U. of Ill., also chief of soil physics, Agrl. Expt. Sta.; in charge of detailed soil survey of State of Ill. Pres. Bd. of Edn., Urbana, 1907-09. Methodist. Author: Laboratory Manual of Soil Physics, 1911; Soil Physics and Management; Climate of Illinois; Soils and Crops. Home: Urbana, Ill. Died 1922.

MOSS, FRED AUGUST, psychologist; b. Hayesville, N.C., Aug. 31, 1893; s. James Madison and Ora (Russell) M.; A.B., Mercer U., 1913; M.A., Columbia, 1920; Ph.D., George Washington U., 1922, M.D., 1927; m. Rosa Mercer, Apr. 15, 1914; children—Claudine, James, Gordon (dec.); m. 2d, Catharine Summers, May 25, 1943; 1 dau., Fredricka Catharine. Supt. pub. sch., Alma, Ga., 1913-17; dir. standards and tests, 1st Div. U.S. Army, 1919-21; prof. psychology George Washington U., 1921-36; prof. psychology Columbia, summer 1931; vis. prof. psychology Grad. Sch., U.S. Naval Acad., Annapolis, summers 1932-37, staff psychologist, Bur. Pub. Personnel, 1924-25; asst. alienist D.C., 1929-35. Sec., Hoover Com. on Causes of Automobile Accidents, 1925-26; dir. physiol. studies for Soc. of Automotive Engrs., 1929—; dir. aptitude test, Assn. Am. Med. Colls., 1929-47; dir. Doctors Hosp., Washington Med. Bldg. Corp., Columbia Med. Bldg. Corp., Empire & Bay State Telegraph Co.; director Riggs Nat. Bank. Fellow A.A.A.S., mem. A.M.A., Am. Psychol. Assn., Med. Soc. D.C., Am. Med. Editors' and Authors' Assn., Nat. Soc. Promotion Biol. and Physiol. Psychiatry, So. Assn. Philosophy and Psychology, Phi Delta Kappa, Alpha Kappa Kappa. Awarded Baylock sci. medal Mercer U., 1913. Baptist. Club: University. Author: Applications of Psychology, 1929; Psychology for Nurses, 1931; Foundations of Abnormal Psychology (with Thelma Hunt), 1932; Comparative Psychology, 1934; Quest of Happiness, 1965. Editor, Prentice-Hall Psychology Series, 1931—. Devised first objective method for measuring strength of emotional drives, 1922. Home: Seminary Hill, Alexandria, Va. Office: 1835 I St. N.W., Washington. Died July 27, 1966; buried Fairview Ch., Lawrenceville, Ga.

MOSS, JOHN CALVIN, photoengraver; b. Bentleyville, Pa., Jan. 5, 1838; s. Alexander J. and Mary (Calvin) M.; m. Mary Bryant, 1856. Publisher, Colleague, Washington, Pa., 1859; a founder Actinic Engraving Co., N.Y.C., 1871; founder Photoengraving Co., N.Y.C., 1872, Moss Engraving Co., N.Y.C., 1881; 1st to establish photoengraving as comml. bus. in U.S.; developed Moss Process. Died N.Y.C., Apr. 8, 1892.

MOSS, WILLIAM LORENZO, physician; b. Athens, Ga., Aug. 23, 1876; s. Rufus LaFayette and Elizabeth (Luckie) M.; B.S., U. Ga., 1901, D.Sc., 1928; M.D., Johns Hopkins, 1905; grad. student Berlin, 1907-08; m. Marguerite Eleanor Widle, June 1, 1925; children—Marguerite Eleanor, Elizabeth, William Lorenzo, II. Resident house officer Johns Hopkins Hosp., 1905-06, asst. resident physician, 1910-i4; asst. physician Johns Hopkins Med. Sch., 1906-07, instr. medicine, 1908-10, asso., 1910-14; internist State Inst. Study Malignant Diseases, Buffalo, 1914-15; asst. prof. health dept. Yale, 1917; asst. prof., dept. preventive medicine and hygiene Harvard, 1919-21, bacteriology and immunology, 1924-29, acting dean, sch. pub. health, 1926; prof. preventive medicine and dean U. Ga. Sch. Medicine, 1931-34. Expeditions: Tropical Medicine, Central America, 1914; Harvard, Peru, 1916, Santo Domingo, 1920, 1925; Crane Pacific, Field Museum, 1928-29; Crane-Peabody Museum, New Guinea, 1937-38. Served from capt. to lt. col. M.C., AEF, 1917-19, col. Med. Res., 1924—. Decorated Officer d'Acad., France, Order University Palms. Mem. A.A.A.S., Am. Assn. Pathologists and Bacteriologists, A.M.A., Am. Acad. Arts and Sciences, Med. Assn. Ga., Ga. Acad. Science, Am. Soc. Clin. Investigation, Assn. Am. Physicians, Am. Soc. Topical Medicine, Tb Assn., Phi Beta Kappa. Club: Cosmos. Contbr. sci. jours. on immunity, anaphylaxis, tuberculosis, hemorrhagic diseases, blood groups, transfusion, diptheria, influenza, etc. Home: 2815 Jefferson Rd. Address: P.O. Box 231, Athens, Ga. Died Aug. 12, 1957; buried Athens.

MOTT, VALENTINE, surgeon; b. Glen Cove, L.I., N.Y., Aug. 20, 1785; s. Henry and Jane (Way) M.; M.D., Columbia, 1806; M.D. (hon.), U. Edinburgh (Scotland); LL.D. (hon.), Univ. State N.Y., 1851; m. Louisa Mums, 1819, 9 children. Prof. surgery Columbia, 1811-13; prof. surgery Coll. Physicians and Surgeons, 1813-26, 30-35, mem. staff during 1850's; a founder Rutgers Med. Coll.; a founder med. dept. Univ. State N.Y., 1840, prof. surgery and anatomy until 1850; 1st to tie innominate artery with aim of preventing death from subclavian aneurism, 1818; successfully tied common iliac artery for an aneurism of external iliac, to perform successful amputation of hip joint, 1824; a pioneer in vein surgery; hon. fellow Imperial Acad. Medicine of Paris (France); mem. Paris Clin. Soc. Author: Pain and Anaesthetics, 1862. Co-editor Medical Mag., 1814-15, Medical and Surgical Reporter, 1818-20. Died N.Y.C., Apr. 26, 1865.

MOTT, WILLIAM ELTON, civil engr.; b. Burlington, N.J., Jan. 24, 1868; s. Richard Field and Susan (Thomas) M.; U. of Pa., 1884-85; S.B. in C.E., Mass. Inst. Tech., 1889; m. Amy Coughlin, Aug. 20, 1891 (died Dec. 11, 1905); children—Margaret Burling, Katharine; married 2d, Oli Coughlin, Dec. 26, 1911 (died Aug. 12, 1945). Instructor civil engineering, Massachusetts Institute Tech., 1889-90; instr. and asst. prof. civ. engring. Cornell U., 1892-1905; asso. prof. hydraulic engring., Mass. Inst. Tech., 1905-09; prof. civ. engring., 1909-17, dean and dir. Coll. of Engring., 1917-32, Carnegie Inst. Tech., Pittsburgh, Pa.; retired Jan. 1933. Pres. Library Co. of Burlington, Asso. Charities; dir. Bur. Savings Inst., Burlington, Asso. mem. Am. Soc. C.E.; mem. A.A.A.S., Soc. Promotion Engring. Edn., Am. Forestry Assn., Theta Xi, Sigma Xi, Tau Beta Pi. Republican. Episcopalian (vestryman, St. Mary's Ch.). Home: 315 Wood St., Burlington, N.J. Died Oct. 5, 1945.

MOTTIER, DAVID MYERS, botanist; b. Patriot, Ind., Sept. 4, 1864; s. John David and Lydia (Myers) M.; A.B., Ind. U., 1891, A.M., 1892; Ph.D., U. of Bonn, 1897; U. of Leipzig, 1898; Biol. Sta., Naples, 1898; m. Antoinette J. Snyder, Aug. 31, 1893. Instr. botany, 1891-93, asso. prof., 1893-98, prof., 1898-1937 (emeritus), Indiana University. Life mem. Bot. Soc. America; fellow A.A.A.S. Author: Practical Laboratory Guide, for First Year in Botany, 1902; Fecundation in Plants, 1904; College Textbook of Botany, 1932. Home: Bloomington, Ind. Died Mar. 25, 1940.

MOTZKIN, THEODORE S., educator, mathematician; b. Berlin, Germany, 1908; s. Leo and Pauline M.; student University of Berlin, 1924-27, U. Goettingen (Germany), 1928, U. Paris (France), 1930; Ph.D., U. Basel (Switzerland), 1934; m. Naomi Orenstein; children—Aryeh Leo, Joseph J. Elbanan, Gabriel G. H. Naturalized U.S. citizen, 1958; mem. faculty U. Jerusalem, 1936-48, Boston Coll., 1950; mem. faculty U. Cal. at Los Angeles, 1950-70, prof. math.; vis. prof. U. Jerusalem, 1968, Rockefeller U., 1966; cons. U. Chgo., 1953. Harvard Research fellow, 1948; NSF sr. postdoctoral fellow, U. Copenhagen (Denmark), 1963. Mem. Am., Danish, France, Israel (pres. 1936-48), London, Switzerland math. socs. Editorial bd. Jour. Approximation Theory, Jour. Combinatories, Jour. Lin. Algebra and Applications. Author articles abstract structures, polynomial alegebra and geometry, convexity and approximations theory. Died Dec. 15, 1970.

MOULTON, CHARLES ROBERT, chemist; b. Clifton, Pa., Sept. 16, 1884; s. Charles Lewis and Maria Ross (Harper) M.; academic certificate, Lewis Inst., Chicago, 1903; B.S. in Chem. Engring., U. of Ill., 1907; M.S. in Agr., U. of Mo., 1909, Ph.D., 1911; m. Edith Ione Lehnen, June 24, 1911; children—Ruth Elizabeth, Marjorie. Asst. agrl. chemistry, 1907-10, instr. in agrl. chemistry, 1910-11, asst. prof., 1912-18, asst. in animal nutrition, Inst. of Animal Nutrition, 1917-18, prof., 1918-22, U. of Mo.; dir. Dept. of Nutrition, Inst. of Am. Meat Packers, 1923-33; lecturer Inst. of Meat Packing, Univ. of Chicago, 1926-32; lecturer Schs. of Speech and Edn., Northwestern Univ., 1933-37; cons. chemist since 1935; curator dept. of chemistry, Museum of Science and Industry, Chicago, 1937-40; lecturer Ill. Inst. of Tech., 1941-42; personnel dir., Metallurgical lab., U. of Chicago, 1942-43, research asso., 1942-43; technical adviser, Chicago O.S.R.D. Patent Group, 1943-46; asst. dir., Chicago Patent Group, Argonne Natl. Lab., since 1946; tech. editor Meat Mag., 1934-35, mng. ed., 1935-37, ed., 1937-40; consulting ed., The National Provisioner, 1941-42. Fellow A.A.A.S., American Public Health Association; member American Chem. Soc., Am. Inst. Nutrition, Inst. Food Technologists, Am. Soc. Animal Production, Research Council, Sigma Xi, Phi Lambda Upsilon, Alpha Chi Sigma, Gamma Sigma Delta. Author: Meat Through the Microscope; also sect. on meat, meat products, poultry, eggs, fish in Vol. IX of Allen's Commercial Organic Analysis, Editor and joint author "The Service of Science in the Packing Industry"; also jt. author (with H. P. Armsby) of "The Animal as a Converter of Matter and Energy." Home: 5602 Dorchester Av. Office: Argonne National Laboratory, Chicago, Ill. Died Dec. 4, 1949.

MOULTON, CHARLES WILLIAM, chemist; b. Elmira, N.Y., May 6, 1859; s. William J. and Alice (Lyon) M.; A.B., U. of Minn., 1885; Ph.D., Johns Hopkins, 1889; m. Emma Selden, Sept. 20, 1887. Instr. physics and chemistry, Shattuck School, Faribault, Minn., 1885-87, 1889-92; asso. prof. chemistry, 1892-94, prof., 1894—, Vassar College. Home: Poughkeepsie, N.Y. Died Sept. 13, 1924.

MOULTON, FOREST RAY, astronomer; b. Le Roy, Mich., Apr. 29, 1872; s. Belah G. and Mary C. (Smith) M.; A.B., Albion Coll., 1894; Ph.D. summa cum laude, U. Chgo., 1899; Sc.D., Albion (Mich.) Coll., 1922; LL.D., Drake U., 1939; Sc.D., Case Sch. Applied Sci., 1940; m. Estelle Gillette, Mar. 25, 1897; 2 sons, 2 daus. Asso. in astronomy U. Chgo., 1898-1900, instr., 1900-03, asst. prof., 1903-08, asso. prof., 1908-12, prof., 1912-26; asso. editor Transactions Am. Math. Soc., 1907-12; adminstrv. sec. A.A.A.S., 1937-48. Research asso. Carnegie Instn., 1908-23; dir. Utilities Power & Light Corporation, 1920-38. Maj., Ordnance Dept. U.S. Army, in charge of ballistics of Am. arty., 1918-19; lt. col. Ordnance U.S.R. Fellow Royal Astron. Soc., A.A.A.S., Am. Philos. Soc., Am. Acad. Arts and Sciences; mem. Nat. Acad. Sciences, Am. Math. Soc., Am. Astron. Soc.; hon. fgn. asso. Brit. Assn. Adv. Science. Author: Celestial Mechanics, 1902, 14; Introduction to Astronomy, 1905, 16; Descriptive Astronomy, 1911; Periodic Orbits, 1920; New Methods in Exterior Ballistics, 1926; Differential Equations, 1929; Astronomy, 1931; Consider the Heavens, 1935; Autobiography of Science (with J. J. Schifferes), 1945. Contbr. and editor of The World and Man, 1937. Editor of 25 A.A.A.S. sci. symposium vols. Contbr. to math. and astron. jours. Trustee and dir. of Concessions World's Fair, Chicago, 1933. Home: 1637 Orrington St., Evanston, Ill. Died Dec. 8, 1952.

MOULTROP, IRVING EDWIN, mech. engr.; b. Marlboro, Mass., July 24, 1865; s. Edwin and Lucy (Rice) M.; ed. pub. schs. and by pvt. study; hon. M.E. Stevens Inst. Technology, 1931; m. Zaidee Abbie Hopkins, of Melrose, Mass., Apr. 24, 1888; children—Norman I. (dec.), Mabel E. (Mrs. Russell J. Neagle), Walter J. (dec.). With Edison Electric Illuminating Co. of Boston since 1892, now chief engr. and supt. construction bureau. Mem. Am. Soc. M.E. (ex-vice pres.), Am. Inst. E.E. (ex-v.p.), Assn. Edison Illuminating Cos., Am. Engring. Council (ex-v.p.), U.S. Nat. Com. of Internat. Electrotech. Commn., Am. Standards Assn. Conglist. Odd Fellow. Clubs: Engineers of Boston (a founder; now pres.); Engineers (New York); Woodland Golf of Auburndale, Mass. (ex-pres.); Mohawk (Schenectady, N.Y.). Home: 28 Adams St., Belmont, Mass. Office: 39 Boylston St., Boston, Mass.

MOWAT, MAGNUS, cons. engr.; b. Bombay, India, Nov. 10, 1875; s. Hon. Magnus and Jane (Stodart) M.; ed. Aberdeen Grammar Sch. and Kings Coll., London; unmarried. Apprentice in locomotive work, North British Ry., Glasgow, Scotland; asst. engr. on construction Great Central Ry. (Leicester sect.), Indian Midland Ry., Jhansi, India; resident engr. G.I.P. Ry., Agra, India; chief engr. Millwall Dock Co., London; dir. engring. firm Southern Counties. Comd. Royal Engrs. of A Div., 2 yrs. during World War I, later dir. of roads at War Office, 1919-20. Mem. council and fellow King's Coll., London. Vice pres. The Roads Improvement Assn. Fellow Royal Soc. Engrs. (hon. life mem.), Am. Soc. Mech. Engrs.; mem. Inst. Civil Engrs., Inst. Mech. Engrs. (sec. emeritus), Inst. Engrs. and Shipbuilders (Scotland). Decorated Comdr. Order of British Empire, Territorial Decoration. Address: Ebor House, Sheen Gate Gardens, East Sheen, London SW 14 Eng*

MOWBRAY, GEORGE MORDEY, oil refiner, inventor; b. Brighton, Eng., May 5, 1814; m. Annie Fade. Came to U.S., 1854; producer 1st refined oil in Tutsville, Pa. (after Edwin L. Drake had drilled 1st successful well); 1st oilman to use nitroglycerin (which he called tri-nitro-glycerin) in shooting dormant wells; only Am. mfr. producing nitroglycerin in quantity; supplier explosives for Hoosac Tunnel, 1868, also for building of C.P. Ry.; developer method of diluting nitroglycerin with finely divided scales of mica; a developer of zylonite; tech. mgr. Am. Zylonite Co., 1881-91; contracted with Maxim-Nordenfeldt Guns and Ammunition Co. to turn over all patents for smokeless powder that might result from his researches. Died North Adams, Mass., June 21, 1891.

MOWRY, HAROLD, (mou'ri), agrl. research adminstr.; b. Valley Falls, Kan., Mar. 26, 1894; s. Lyman and Margaret Olive (Wilson) M.; B.S.A., University of Florida, 1929, M.S.A., 1934, Doctor of Science, 1950; married to Anne Stutz, September 11, 1915; 1 son, Ross Elbert. With Fla. State Plant Bd. engaged in citrus canker eradication, nursery inspection and plant quarantine work, 1916-22; asst. horticulturist Fla. Agrl. Expt. Sta., 1922-30, asso. horticulturist, 1930-32, horticulturist, 1932-33, asst. dir., 1933-42, asso. dir., 1942-43, dir. 1943-50; ret., emeritus; agriculturist, cons. dir. Office of Fgn. Agr. Relations, U.S. Dept. of Agriculture, 1950-54; cons. dir. U.S. Foreign Operations Adminstrn., 1954, cons. dir. Internat. Cooperation Adminstrn. also supr. U. Fla. Agrl. Mission to Costa Rica, 1954-58; mem. agr. survey missions to Surinam, British Guiana, area development mission Bolivia, 1954. Chmn. adv. com., agrl. div. Fla. State Defense Council, 1942-45. Received Distinguished Service award, Fla. Vegetable Com., 1947; Alpha Zeta Agricultural Fla. Entomological Society, Fla. State Florists Assn. award, 1950; Medal of Merit and scroll Govt. of Costa Rica, 1958. Fellow A.A.A.S.; mem. Bot. Soc. Am., Am. Soc. Hort. Sci., Fla. Acad. Sciences, (hon. life mem.), Fla. State Hort. Soc. (hon. life member) Phi Kappa Phi, Sigma Xi, Alpha Zeta, Phi Sigma, Pi Gamma Mu, Alpha Gamma Rho, Gamma Sigma Delta. Democrat. Conglist. Mason, Kiwanian (pres. Gainesville, 1942). Author numerous expt. sta. bulls., also tech. and popular articles on agrl. subjects. Home: 203 NW 15th Terrace, Gainesville, Fla. Died Nov. 12, 1958; buried Fort Lauderdale, Fla.

MOYER, ANDREW JACKSON, microbiologist; b. Star City, Ind., Nov. 30, 1899; s. Edward R. and Minnie (McCloud) M.; A.B., Wabash Coll., 1922; student U. Wis., 1922-23; M.S., N.D. Agrl. Coll., 1925; Ph.D., U. Md., 1929; m. Dorothy Randall Phillips, Apr. 4, 1931. With Dept. Agr. 1929—, last assignment No. Utilization Research, and Development Div., Fermentation Sec., U.S. Dept. Agr., Peoria, Ill., research physiology of fungi; mold fermentations; gluconic, lactic, kojic, glauconic, citric and itaconic acids from glucose; penicillin. Devised methods for producing substantial increase in yields of penicillin, making large scale prodn. possible; discovered menthanol process for submerged mold fermentation of crude carbohydrates to citric acid; improved fermentation of glucose and Molasses to fumanic acid. Lasker group award, 1946. Contbr. sci. jours. Mem. Bot. Soc. of Am., Ill. Acad. Sci Phi Kappa Phi, Sigma Xi. Presbyn. Patentee in field. Address: Montgomery County, Md. Died Feb. 17, 1959.

MOYER, BURTON JONES, coll. dean, physicist; b. Greenville, Ill., Feb. 24, s. Jacob and Mabel(Jones) M.; A.B., Seattle Pacific Coll., 1933, Sc.D. (hon.), 1955; Ph.D., U. Wash., 1939; m. Lela Brushwood, June 22, 1937; children—Burton Jones, John Howard, Robert Philip, Lela Virginia. Tchr. physics and math. Greenville Coll., 1939-42; physicist Lawrence Radiation Lab., 1942-70; with Manhattan Dist., Berkeley and Oak Ridge, 1942-45 mem. faculty U. Cal. at Berkeley, 1947-70, prof. physics, 1954-70, chmn. dept., 1962-68, prof. emeritus, 1971-73; dean Coll. Liberal Arts, U. Ore., 1971-73; cons. nucleonics and radiation Shielding. Staff mem. Kanpur Indo-Am. programs, 1965-66. Fellow Am. Phys. Soc. Presbyn. (elder). Author articles on meson physics, high energy nuclear physics. Home: Eugene OR Died Apr. 21, 1973.

MOYER, JAMES AMBROSE, (moi'er), educator, engineer; b. Norristown, Pa., Sept. 13, 1877; s. Isaac Kulp and Jane Hunsicker (Grater) M.; E.B., State Teachers College at Westchester, Pa., 1893; S.B., Lawrence Scientific Sch., Harvard, 1899; A.M., Harvard, 1904; m. Dorothy Tremble, May 18, 1922; 1 dau., Jane Modella. Draftsman, 1899-1900; instr. in Harvard, 1901-04, in Harvard Engring. Camp, 1902-04; mech. engr. and chief computer, Gen. Electric Co., 1905-07; gen. engr. Westinghouse, Church, Kerr & Co., New York, 1907-08; asst. prof. mech. engring. in charge mech. and hydraulic labs., U. of Mich., 1908-11; jr. prof. mech. engring., U. of Mich., 1911-12; prof. mech. engring. in charge of dept., Pa. State Coll., 1912-15; dir. Pa. Engring. Expt. Sta. and of univ. extension dept. of Pa., 1913-15; dir. Univ. Extension Mass. Dept. of Edn. since 1915. Pres. Nat. Commn. on Enrichment of Adult Life (N.E.A.); New Eng. rep. U.S. Dept. of Interior, 1917-20; chmn. U.S. com. of scientists on war inventions, 1918-19. Pa. del. First Nat. Conf. on Univ. Extension; past pres. Nat. Assn. Univ. Extension; mem. advisory com. on edn., U.S. Navy; mem. commn. of U.S. Dept. of Interior on edn. by radio broadcasting; advisory bd. Nat. Home Library Foundation; edn. advisory com. World Wide Broadcasting Corp.; v.p. Nat. Acad. Visual Instrn., Am. Assn. for Adult Edn.;

sec. Internat. Elec. Congress; mem. visiting com. Univ. Extension, Harvard; mem. state advisory com. on Higher Edn. in Conn.; mem. Survey Commn. on Noncollegiate Tech. Edn., 1928-31; mem. Mass. Com. Pub. Safety (recreation chmn.). Fellow Royal Acad. (London), A.A.A.S., Am. Inst. Genealogy; mem. Am. Acad. Polit. and Social Science, Verein deutscher Ingenieure, Franklin Inst., Am. Soc. M.E., Assn. Internationale du Froid (Paris), Nat. Council of Safety, Engrs. Soc. Pa. Soc. Automotive Engrs. (chmn. New Eng. sect. and mem. nat. council). League of Nations Assn. (dir.), Am. Assn. Refrigerating Engrs., Am. Inst. E.E., Soc. Promotion Engring. Edn., Boston Adult Edn. Council (dir.), Mass. Youth Council, Assn. Harvard Engrs., Lawrence Scientific Assn., Nat. Edn. Assn., Pi Gamma Mu (pres. Boston chapter), Phi Sigma Kappa, etc. Presbyterian. Clubs: City, Harvard, Schoolmasters (Boston); Union (Ann Arbor); Authors' (London). Author: Elements of Descriptive Geometry, 1904; Descriptive Geometry for Engineers, 1905; Internal Combustion Motors, 1905; Steam Turbines, 1905; Power Plant Testing, 1911; Engineering Thermodynamics (with J. P. Calderwood and A. A. Potter), 1915; Gasoline Automobiles, 1921; Marine Steam Turbines, 1922; Oil-burning Boilers, 1923; Practical Radio (with J. F. Wostrel), 1924; Radio Construction and Repairing, 1926; Refrigeration, 1928; Radio Receiving Tubes, 1929; Industrial Electricity, 1930; Radio Handbook, 1931; Air Conditioning, 1933; Oil Fuels and Burners, 1937; Welding, 1942. Editor Bull. of Dept. of Edn.; Enrichment of Adult Life; contbr. to ednl. and engring. jours. Home: 382 Kenrick St., Newton 58, Mass. Address: State House, Boston: and Pa. Bldg., Philadelphia, Pa. Died Nov. 29, 1945.

MUCKENFUSS, ANTHONY MOULTRIE, chemistry; b. Charleston, S.C., Aug. 5, 1869; s. Benjamin Anthony and Martha Louisa (Stewart) M.; A.B., Wofford (S.C.) Coll., 1889, A.M., 1890; Ph.D., Johns Hopkins, 1895; studied univs. of Berlin, Va., Columbia, Karlsruhe and Chicago; m. Margaret Katherine Galloway, 1897; children—Ralph Stewart, Elizabeth Willis, Charles Galloway (dec.). Prof. chemistry and physics, Millsaps Coll., Miss., 1893-1902; prof. chemistry, U. of Ark., and state chemist, 1902-05; prof. chemistry, U. of Miss., 1905-15; prof. chemistry, Emory U., Atlanta, Ga., 1915-20; research chemist, Roessler and Hasslacher Chemical Co., Perth Amboy, N.J., 1920-32; acting prof. chemistry, U. of Fla., 1932-35. Methodist. Home: Melrose, Fla. Died Apr. 17, 1941.

MUCKLE, JOHN SEISER, engineer; b. Phila., Pa., Dec. 12, 1862; s. Mark Richards and Caroline (Seiser) M.; ed. pvt. schs.; m. Katharine Craig Wright, Dec. 28, 1901; 1 son, Craig Wright. Mem. engring. firm Muckle & Co., Phila., 22 yrs.; now retired. Inventor of high pressure fire pumping system, also of elevator door safety lock. Was 3d Comdr. Pa. Naval Force (Naval Militia); lt. U.S.N., Spanish-Am. War, 1898; naval aide staffs of Govs. Stone and Stuart of Pa., rank of capt. (naval); hon. mem. Canadian Soc. of Phila.; mem. Brit. and Canadian Recruiting Mission, World War. Pres. Pa. Seamen's Home: v.p. (br.) English-Speaking Union. Cavalier Order of the Crown (Italian), 1920, cavalier officer, 1925. Chmn. Citizens' Reception Com., Phila., Jan.-Oct. 1924. Republican. Episcopalian. Mason. Home: Haverford, Pa. Died Mar. 20, 1929.

MUDD, HARVEY SEELEY, mining engr.; b. Leadville, Colo., Aug. 30, 1888; s. Seeley Wintersmith and Della (Mulock) M.; student Stanford, 1906-08; E.M., Columbia, 1912, Sc.D., 1947; LL.D., U. of Calif., 1941, Loyola U., 1943; m. Mildred Hardy Esterbrook, Mar. 12, 1913; children—Henry Thomas, Caryll Esterbrook. Began as mining engineer, Bisbee, Ariz., 1912; chairman of the board dirs. Cyprus Mines Corporation; dir. So. Pacific Co., Texas Gulf Sulphur Co.; dir. Founders Inc., Co., Mesabi Iron Company, Marcona Mining Company; voting trustee Pacific Mutual Life Ins. Co. Trustee, Rand Corp. Engineer U.S. Bureau of Mines and asst. sec. War Minerals Committee, World War I. Awarded Egleston Medal. Trustee Southwest Museum, California Inst. Tech.; v. chmn. bd. of fellows Claremont College; mem. advisory com., Henry E. Huntington Library and Art Gallery. Mem. American Institute Mining and Metall. Engineers (mem., p.p.); mem. Mining and Metall. Soc. Am., Soc. Colonial Wars, S.R., Soc. Civil Engrs. (hon.), Sigma Xi, Delta Tau Delta, Tau Beta Pi. Republican. Conglist. Clubs: University, California, Bohemian, Los Angeles Country, Knickerbocker, Recess (N.Y.C.). Home: 1240 Benedict Canyon Drive, Beverly Hills, Cal. Office: Pacific Mutual Bldg., Los Angeles, Cal. Died Apr. 12, 1955.

MUDD, SEELEY WINTERSMITH, mining engr.; b. Kirkwood, Mo., Aug. 16, 1861; s. Henry Thomas and Sarah Eliz. (Hodgen) M.; E.M., Washington U., St. Louis, 1883; m. Della Mulock, Feb. 24, 1887; children—Harvey S., Elizabeth (dec.), Seeley G., Henry T. (dec.). Assayer and supt. copper dept., St. Louis Smelting & Refining Co., 1883-85; went to Leadville, Colo., 1885; mgr. Small Hopes Consolidated Mining Co. and Borel Mining Co., 1887-1912; mgr. Ibex Mining Co. (Little Johnnie Mine), 1899-1902; consulting engr. in the West for N.J. Zinc Co., 1902-04; moved to Los Angeles, Calif., 1903; consulting engr. on Pacific Coast for Guggenheim Exploration Co. and Am. Smelting & Refining Co., 1904-05; pres. and mgr. Queen Esther Mining and Milling Co., Kern Co., Calif., 1904-09; pres. Cyprus Mines Corp., Coeur d'Alene Syndicate Mining Co. Commd. maj., Engr. O.R.C., Feb. 12, 1917; active duty, Jan. 14, 1918; asst. dir. U.S. explosives plants, Washington; promoted col. U.S.A., May 24, 1918; hon. disch., Jan. 20, 1919. V.p. Y.M.C.A., Los Angeles; trustee Pomona Coll., Southwest Museum. Republican. Conglist. Home: Los Angeles, Calif. Died May 24, 1926.

MUEHLBERGER, CLARENCE WEINERT, toxicologist; b. Chgo., July 16, 1896; s. Otto and Rose (Weinert) M.; B.S. in Chem. Engring., Armour Inst. Tech., 1920; M.S., U. Wis., 1922, Ph.D., 1923; m. Mary Ellen Finn, Sept. 15, 1923; 1 son, Robert Mortelle. Asst. instr. in chemistry U. Wis., 1920-21, research asst. in chemistry, 1921-23; state toxicologist, Wis., 1923-30; also asst. prof. pharmacology and toxicology U. Wis. Med. Sch., 1924-30; toxicologist and asst. dir. Sci. Crime Detection Lab., Northwestern U., 1930-35; asst. prof. toxicology and pharmacology Northwestern U. Med. Sch., 1930-35, asso. prof., 1935-39; professorial lectr. toxicology U. Ill. Med. Sch., 1934-41; lectr. toxicology Loyola U. Med. Sch., 1940-41; professorial lectr. toxicology U. Chgo. Med. Sch., 1935-39, asso. prof. toxicology, 1939-41; coroner's toxicologist, Cook County, Ill., 1930-41; staff toxicologist Cook County Hosp., 1930-41; cons. expert to Chgo. Police Dept. on bombs and explosions; lectr. toxicology U. Mich., since 1941; Mich. State toxicologist and dir. Mich. Crime Detection Lab., since 1941. Asso. editor Am. Jour. Police Sci. since 1939. Pvt. Chem. Warfare Service, U.S. Army, 1918-19. Fellow A.M.A.; mem. Am. Chem. Soc., Soc. for Pharmacology and Exptl. Therapeutics, Soc. Exptl. Biology and Medicine, A.A.A.S., Am. Acad. Forensic Scis., Inst. Medicine Chgo., Am. Pub. Health Assn., Phi Beta Pi, Alpha Chi Sigma, Gamma Alpha, Tau Beta Pi, Phi Lambda Upsilon, Sigma Xi frats. Club: Chicago Literary. Contbr. studies in forensic chemistry and toxicology, alcohol intoxication. Office: Mich. Dept. of Health Labs., Lansing, Mich. Died Sept. 2, 1966.

MUELLER, EDWARD, chemist; b. South Bend, Ind., Oct. 16, 1883; s. Frederick William and Anna Margaret (Sack) M.; B.S., Purdue, 1902; A.M., Harvard, 1905, Ph.D., 1907; studied Heidelberg U., Germany, 1908; m. Georgiana Crane, Aug. 21, 1913. Chemist Norfolk & Western Ry. Co., Roanoke, Va., 1902-04; asst. in chemistry, Harvard, 1905-07; instr. chemistry, Washington U. Med. Sch., 1907-10, Tufts Coll., 1910-11; instr. chemistry, Mass. Inst. Tech., 1911-13, asst. prof., 1913-20, asso. prof., 1920-29; chemical consultant since 1929; in charge of chemistry Franklin Tech. Inst., 1942-46. Fellow A.A.A.S., Am. Acad. Arts and Sciences; mem. Am. Chem. Soc., Tau Beta Pi. Translator: Holde's Hydro-carbon Oils and Saponifiable Fats and Waxes, 1915, 2d edit., 1922. Contbr. to publs. Carnegie Instn. Washington, also to Jour. Am. Chem. Soc., Chem. News, etc. Redetermined the atomic weights of potassium and chromium. Home: Burton Halls, 10 Dana St., Cambridge 38, Mass. Died Aug. 9, 1954.

MUELLER, JOHN HOWARD, bacteriologist; b. Sheffield, Mass., June 13, 1891; s. John Henry and Sarah Eva (Pease) M.; B.S., Ill. Wesleyan U., 1912; M.S., U. of Louisville, 1914; Ph.D., Columbia U., 1916; m. Mary R. Gilbert, July 6, 1916. Instr. biol. chemistry, U. of Louisville, 1912-14; Alonzo Clark fellow, Columbia U., 1914-16; asst. in pathology, Columbia U., 1916-17, asst. in bacteriology, 1919-20, asst. prof. bacteriology, 1920-22, asso. prof., 1922-23; asst. prof. bacteriology and immunology, Harvard Med. Sch., 1923-30, asso. prof., 1930-42, prof. and head of dept. since 1942. Successively private, sergeant and 1st lt. Sanitary Corps, U.S. Army, May 1917-Mar. 1919. Consultant to Sec'y of War, 1941-45. Consultant to Fed. Sec. Agency, 1942-44, and to C.W.S., 1944-46. Mem. Nat. Acad. Sciences, Am. Acad. Arts and Sciences, N.Y. Acad. Sciences, Soc. Am. Bacteriologists, Soc. Biol. Chemistry, Assn. Pathology and Bacteriology, Soc. Immunology, Soc. Exptl. Biology and Medicine, Harvey Society. Fellow A.P.H.A. Author various articles on bacteriology and immunology. Club: Harvard of Boston. Home: 2176 Centre St., West Roxbury, Mass. Died Feb. 16, 1954.

MUELLER, PAUL, chemist; b. Olten, Switzerland, Jan. 12, 1899; s. Gottlieb and Fanny (Leypoldt) M.; Ph.D., U. Basle, 1925; Dr. honoris causa, U. Eva Peron (Argentina), 1954; also Dr. honoris causa, Thessolonia, Greece; m. Friedel Ruegsegger, Oct. 6, 1927; children—Henry, Niklaus, Margaret. Chemist J.R. Geigy A. G., Basle, since 1925, sci. partner since 1930, vice dir. since 1947. Awarded Nobel prize for devel. DDT, 1948; hon. prof. Dept. of Ministry Pub. Health Argentina. Mem. Soc. Industrielle de Chimie (Paris), Schweizerische Naturforschende Gesellschaft. Home: 78. Glaserbergstrasse. Office: Schwarzwaldalle, Basle, Switzerland. Died Oct. 1965; buried Basle.

MUENSCHER, WALTER C(ONRAD), botanist; b. Fischbach, Germany, May 30, 1891; s. Heinrich Franz and Anna (Hilgenberg) M.; came to U.S., 1894; A.B., State Coll. Wash., 1914; A.M., U. Neb., 1915; Ph.D., Cornell U., 1921; m. Minnie Worthen, May 20, 1918; children—Elizabeth (Mrs. Robert DeVelbiss), Frank (dec.), Helen (Mrs. John Tryon), Joanne (Mrs. Garrett Droppers). Instr. Sioux Falls (S.D.) High Sch., 1915-16; instr. botany Cornell U., 1916-23, asst. prof., 1923-37, prof., 1937-54, emeritus, 1954—; instr. Puget Sound Marine Sta., summers 1915-16; field asst. Bur. Plant Industry, U.S. Dept. Agr., 1917, botanist, 1923, asso. botanist, 1924; botanist N.Y. Biol. Survey, 1926-38. Served with U.S. Army, 1918-19. Fellow A.A.A.S.; mem. Am. Assn. U. Profs., Am. Fern Soc., Am. Soc. Limnology and Oceanography, Am. Soc. Plant Taxonomists, Bot. Soc. Am., Phycol. Soc. Am., Wild Flower Preservation Soc. (trustee), DeWitt Hist. Soc., Am. Automobile Assn., Cal., Torrey bot. socs., New Eng. Bot. Club, Rochester (N.Y.) Acad. Sci. (hon.), Sigma Xi, Lambda Chi Alpha, Phi Kappa Phi. Unitarian. Author: Keys to Woody Plants, rev. edit., 1950; Keys to Spring Plants (with L. C. Petry), rev. edit. 1949; Aquatic Plants of the United States, 1948; Poisonous Plants of the United States, rev. edit. 1951; Weeds, rev. edit. 1955; The Flora of Whatcom County, State of Washington, 1941; Garden Spice and Wild Potherbs (with Myron A. Rice), 1954. Contbr. tech. and popular periodicals. Home: 1001 Highland Rd., Ithaca, N.Y. 14850. Died Mar. 20, 1963.

MUHLEMAN, GEORGE WASHINGTON, chemistry; b. Hannibal, O., Apr. 26, 1871; s. John Godfrey and Margaret Magdalena (Anshutz) M.; B.S., Northwestern U., 1899; M.S., State U. of Ia., 1912; D.Sc., U. of Geneva, Switzerland, 1927; m. Pamelia Florence Woods, Sept. 7, 1898. Teacher of Science, prin. and supt. pub. schs., Wis. and Ill., 1899-1910; instr. chemistry, Ia. State Teachers Coll., 1910-11; prof. chemistry, Meth. U. of Okla., 1913-15; business adminstr., Davenport, Ia., 1915-16; prof. chemistry, Mount Union Coll., Alliance, O., 1916-18, Hamline Univ. St. Paul, 1918-41, retired by bd. of trustees, June 1941; visiting prof. Alma (Mich.) Coll., 1941-42; head of dept. of inorganic chemistry, N.D. Agrl. College, 1942-43; instr. chemistry University of Florida, 1943-47; acting assistant Prof. of Chem., 1944-47; president Prairie-Garfield Co.; research Minn. Mining & Mfg. Co., summer 1944; delegate to 6th Congress of Industrial Chemists, Brussels, 1926; rep. of St. Paul Pioneer Press-Dispatch at Council of League of Nations, Mar.-June 1927; mem. Com. One Hundred for Law Enforcement, pres. Hamline Branch Library Council, St. Paul, since 1937, made life mem., 1940. Author of the nine papers read before sections of the Am. Chem. Society at different meetings. Received Merit Award of Northwestern Univ. Alumni Assn., 1941. Fellow A.A.A.S.; mem. Am. Chem. Soc., Swiss Chem. Soc., Am. Assn. Univ. Profs. (pres. 1932), Am. Men of Science, Leaders in Education, Twin City Northwestern University Alumni Assn. (pres.), Phi Beta Kappa, Sigma Xi. Republican. Presbyn. Mason; mem. Eastern Star. Author: Qualitative Analysis, 1926; Teaching of Chemistry in Colleges and Universities, 1921; Lecture Demonstrations in General Chemistry, 1934; Chemical Elements and their Discoverers (chart), revised, 1946; Must Life End at Sixty-Five (bulletin). Joint author: General Chemistry, 1926. Editor and joint author of General Chemistry, 1937, 38, 39. Contbr. to scientific publs. Lecturer on chemistry. Studied and traveled in Europe and British Isles, 1926-27. Inventor of fume hood for chem. labs. Home: 1450 Englewood Av., St Paul E 4 MN

MUIR, DOWNIE DAVIDSON, JR., mining engr.; b. Lincoln, Neb., Jan. 1, 1884; s. Downie Davidson and Armista (Wilson) M.; E.M., Columbia, 1906; m. Jewel Balfour, Sept. 24, 1908; children—Milene Balfour, Downie Davidson 3d. Began as mucker, 1906; supt. Combination Fraction Mine, Goldfield, Nev., 1908-09; with U.S. Smelting, Refining & Mining Co., Salt Lake City, Utah, 1910—, in exploration dept., 1910-16, mgr. zinc smelters and mines, Mo., 1917-18, mgr. mines, Salt Lake City, 1919-22, gen. mgr. Utah dist., 1922-24, v.p. and gen. mgr. in charge western operations, 1924—; v.p. in charge of western operations U.S. Smelting, Refining and Mining Co., Mar. 1934—; v.p. and gen. mgr. U.S. Fuel Co., 1924-35, pres., 1935—. Mem. President's Economic Com., 1932. Home: Boston, Mass. Died Oct. 23, 1937.

MUIR, E(DWIN) STANTON, veterinarian; b. at Danville, Pa., May 1, 1863; s. Christian and Grace H. M.; ed. at Lock Haven, Pa., until 1875; Ph.G., Phila. Coll. Pharmacy, 1881; V.M.D., U. of Pa., 1890; m. Annie Taite, of Phila., Sept. 5, 1883. Was in retail drug business, 1875-89; apptd. to chair of pharmacy, 1890, instr. pharmacy and materia medica, dept. vet. medicine, U. of Pa., since 1892. Also veterinary practitioner; mem. staff meat and cattle inspectors, Phila. Bd. of Health. Address: 2145 N. 2d St., Philadelphia.

MUIR, JOHN, geologist, explorer, naturalist; b. Dunbar, Scotland, Apr. 21, 1838; s. Daniel and Anne (Gilrye) M.; ed. in Scotland and at U. of Wisconsin; (hon. A.M., Harvard U., 1896; LL.D., U. of Wis., 1897, U. of California, 1913; Litt.D., Yale U., 1911); m. Louise Strentzel, 1880. Discoverer of the Muir Glacier, Alaska; visited the Arctic regions on the U.S. steamer Corwin in search of the DeLong expdn.; has labored many yrs. in cause of forest preservation and establishment of nat. reservations and parks. Mem. Am. Acad. Arts and Letters; fellow A.A.A.S. Author: The Mountains of California, 1894; Our National Parks,

1901; Stickeen, the Story of a Dog, 1909; My First Summer in the Sierra, 1911; The Yosemite, 1912; Story of My Boyhood and Youth, 1913. Editor: Picturesque California. Traveled and studied in Russia, Siberia, Manchuria, India, Australia and New Zealand, 1903-04, in S. America, 1911, in Africa, 1911-12. Home: Martinez, Calif. Died Dec. 24, 1914.

MULHOLLAND, HENRY BEARDEN, physician, educator; b. Knoxville, Tenn., Jan. 9, 1892; s. John Henry and Martha (Bearden) M.; high sch. edn. by tutors; student U. Toronto, 1917; M.D., U. Va., 1920; m. Elizabeth Caldwell Brown, Oct. 19, 1925; children—Elizabeth Brown, John Henry. Interne, resident U. Va. Hosp., 1920-22, Mass. Gen. Hosp. summer 1923; faculty U. Va. Med. Sch., 1922, became prof. internal medicine, 1937, now prof. emeritus, acting head dept. internal medicine, 1942-49, asst. dean, 1942-58, cons. medicine U. Va. Hosp.; active practice internal medicine; research diseases of metabolism, Wurzburg, Germany, and Copenhagen, Denmark, also visited various clinics in Europe, 1927-28. Mem. U.S. del. to WHO, Geneva, Switzerland, 1951; mem. sub-com. Hoover Task Force, 1954. Recipient Algeron Sullivan award, 1962; Thomas Jefferson award U. Va., 1962. Master A.C.P.; mem. A.M.A. Am. Clin. and Climatol. Assn., Am. Diabetes Assn. (past pres.), Medicine Soc. Va., (past pres.), Va. Council Health and Med. Care (hon. chmn.), Alpha Omega Alpha, Phi Delta Theta, Phi Rho Sigma, Phi Beta Kappa (hon.). Democrat. Episcopalian. Contbr. papers on Diabetes Mellitus, clin. problems to med. jours. Home: 1817 Fendall Av. Office: 1400 Jefferson Park Av., Charlottesville, Va. Died Oct. 1966.

MULHOLLAND, WILLIAM, hydraulic engr.; b. Belfast, Ireland, Sept. 11, 1855; s. Hugh and Ellen (Deakers) M.; ed. Christian Bros. Sch., Dublin; LL.D., U. of Calif., 1914; m. Lillie Ferguson, July 3, 1890. Supt. and chief engr. water works of Los Angeles, 1886—; devised plans and estimated and superintended the construction of Los Angeles aqueduct for conveying a supplementary water supply from Sierra Nevada Mts., 250 miles distant, at a cost of $24,500,000; consulting engineer numerous irrigation and water supply projects. Chief engr. Dept. of Pub. Service, Los Angeles. Died July 22, 1935.

MULLENIX, ROLLIN CLARKE, zoölogist; b. Ironton, Wis., Nov. 26, 1869; s. William Cox and Cynthia Ann (Bates) M.; A.B., Wheaton (Ill.) Coll., 1895, A.M., 1897; Ph.D., Harvard, 1908; m. Mary Walker, June 25, 1895; children—Carlos Walker, Ralph Bernard. Prof. biology and chemistry, Wheaton Coll., 1895-1905; scholar of Harvard Club of Chicago, at Harvard U., 1905-07; research student, Harvard, 1907-08; prof. biology, Yankton (S.D.) Coll., 1908-11; prof. zoölogy, 1911-35, prof. emeritus, since 1935, Lawrence Coll., Wis. Fellow A.A.A.S.; mem. Am. Soc. Zoölogists, Am. Genetic Assn., Ethical Soc. of Chicago. Conglist. Awarded Bowdoin prize and bronze medal by Harvard U. in 1909 for essay, The History and Present Status of the Neurone Theory; author of Peripheral Terminations of Eighth Cranial Nerve in Vertebrates. Home: Oracle, Ariz. Died June 8, 1949.

MULLER, HERMANN JOSEPH, biologist; b. N.Y.C., Dec. 21, 1890; s. Hermann J. and Frances L. (Lyons) M.; B.A., Columbia, 1910, M.A., 1911, Ph.D., 1916, D.Sc., 1949; D.Sc., U. Edinburgh, 1940, U. Chgo., 1959, Swarthmore, 1964; M.D., Jefferson, 1963; m. Jessie M. Jacobs, June 11, 1923; 1 son, David Eugene; m. 2d, Dorothea Kantorowicz, May 20, 1939; 1 dau., Helen Juliette. Instr. biology, Rice Inst., Houston, 1915-18, in charge dept., 1916-18; instr. zoology Columbia, 1918-20; asso. prof. zoölogy, U. Tex., 1920-25, prof., 1925-36; sr. geneticist Inst. Genetics, Moscow, 1933-37; research assoc., lectr. Inst. Animal Genetics, U. Edinburgh, 1937-40; research assoc. in biology, Amherst Coll., 1940-42, vis. prof., 1942-45; prof. zoology Ind. U., 1945—, Distinguished Service prof., 1953-64, emeritus, 1964—, vis. prof. 1966-67; vis. prof., U. Wis., 1965-66; mem. Inst. Advanced Learning, City of Hope Med. Center, Duarte, Cal., 1964-65. Engaged in genetics research, 1911—, conducted by breeding experiments on fruit fly Drosophila; analysis of arrangement and method of recombination of hereditary units; explanation of so-called mutations in evening primrose; studies on mutation and evolution; theory of gene; artificial transmutation of gene by X-rays; prodn. of chromosome changes; heredity in man. Recipient Kimber Genetics award, 1955; Darwin Medal, Linnean Soc., 1959; Alexander Hamilton award, Columbia U., 1960; named Humanist of Year, Am. Humanist Assn., 1963. Nobel laureate in physiology, med., 1946; fgn. mem. Royal Swedish Acad. Sci., Royal Danish Acad. Sci., Royal Soc. London, Genetical Soc. Japan, Nat. Inst. Sci. India, others; mem. A.A.A.S., Am. Humanist Assn. (pres. 1955-59), Nat. Acad. Sci., Am. Soc. Naturalists, Soc. for Study of Evolution, Am. Soc. Zoologists, Soc. Exptl. Biology and Medicine, Am. Genetic Assn., Genetics Soc. Am., Am. Soc. Human Genetics, Am. Assn. U. Profs. (hon.), Genetical Soc. (Brit.), Am. Acad. Arts and Sci., Am. Philos. Soc., (hon.) Mendelian Soc. Lund, (fgn.) Accademia Nazionale dei Lincei, Sigma Xi, Phi Beta Kappa; Eighth International Congress Genetics (pres.), 1948. Author: The Mechanism of Mendelian Heredity (with others), 1915, 22; Out of the Night, 1935; Genetics, Medicine and Man (with others), 1947; Studies in Genetics, 1962; also papers and lectures on biol. and genetic subjects. Home: 916 S. Mitchell, Bloomington, Ind. 47401. Died Apr. 5, 1967.

MULLGARDT, LOUIS CHRISTIAN, architect; b. Washington, Mo., Jan. 18, 1866; s. John Christian and Wilhelmina (Hausgen) M.; ed. pub. and pvt. schs.; architects' offices, St. Louis, Boston and Brookline, Mass.; Dept. Fine Arts, Washington U.; spl. student Harvard, 1889-90; m. Laura R. Steffens, of Chicago, June 9, 1897. Practiced in St. Louis, 1893-1902, in Eng., 1902-05, San Francisco, Calif. 1905—, Honolulu, Hawaii, 1920-21. Designed Davies Bldg., Honolulu; Commercial Center, Honolulu; University Club Bldg., St. Louis; Arlington Hotel, Hot Springs, Ark.; president's residence, Stanford U., Calif.; Memorial Museum, Golden Gate Park, San Francisco, Calif.; also many private residences on Pacific Coast and elsewhere. Advisory architect for Territorial War Memorial, Honolulu. Mem. Architectural Commn. and architect for "court of Ages," Panama-Pacific Internat. Expn. and mem. Internat. Jury, Department Fine Arts, same; dir. San Francisco Art Inst.; archtl. adviser nat. parks on Pacific Coast. Fellow A.I.A.; ex-pres. San Francisco Soc. Architects, Calif. Soc. Etchers; ex-v.p. San Francisco Soc. Artists; life mem. Harvard Engineers' Club; hon. mem. San Francisco Book Club, Gamut Club, Los Angeles. Clubs: Bohemian, Commonwealth (San Francisco), Press (hon.). Contbr. on architectural subjects. *

MULLIKEN, SAMUEL PARSONS, chemist; b. Newburyport, Mass., Dec. 19, 1864; s. Moses J. and Sarah D. (Gibbs) M.; S.B., Mass. Inst. Tech., 1887; Ph.D., U. of Leipzig, 1890; post-grad. study Clark U., Mass., 1891; m. Katherine W. Mulliken, June 27, 1893; children—Robert S., Samuel G. P., Katherine F. Asst. in chemistry, U. of Cincinnati, 1887-88; asso. in chemistry, Bryn Mawr Coll., 1892; instr. and acting head of chem. dept., Clark U., 1892-94; instr. organic chemistry and organic analysis, 1895-1904, asst. prof., 1905-13, asso. prof. organic chem. research, 1913-26, professor of organic chemistry, 1926—, Mass. Inst. Technology. Major Chemical Warfare Service, U.S.A., 1918. Author: Laboratory Experiments on the Class Reactions and Identification of Organic Substances, 1896; The Compounds of Carbon with Hydrogen and Oxygen, 1904; The Commerical Dye-stuffs, 1909; The Compounds of Carbon with Nitrogen, Hydrogen, and Oxygen, 1916; The Compounds of the Higher Orders, 1922. Home: Newburyport, Mass. Died Oct. 24, 1934.

MULLOWNEY, JOHN JAMES, (mul-lo-ne), med. educator; b. Seacombe, Eng., July 20, 1878; s. Michael and Hannah (Craven) M.; came to U.S. 1887, naturalized, 1902; student Phillips Exeter Acad., 1899-1902, Harvard, 1902-03; M.D., U. Pa., 1908; m. Emily Evans, June 30, 1908; children—John Evans, Penn Evans, William Thomas; m. 2d, Esther Garriss Thomas, Nov. 1, 1938 (died Apr. 19, 1942); m. Mrs. Mabel Mize, June 18, 1944 (died Oct. 11, 1952). Began as principal of high school, Bath, N.H., 1903-04; prof. nervous and mental diseases North China Union Medical Coll., Peking, 1908-12; insp. tenement and lodging houses, Phila., 1912-13; asst. chief Pa. Dept. Health, 1913-17; head dept. science and prof. chemistry and hygiene Girard Coll., Phila., 1917-21; prof. pub. health and pres. Meharry Medical Coll., Nashville, 1921-38, ret. Mem. Friends of Hist. Soc., Acacia, Kappa Delta, Pi Pi. Mem. Soc. of Friends. Author: Chinese Hospitals for Chinese; Revelation of Chinese Revolution; Epidemic of Pneumonic Type of Bubonic Plague; Hygiene of the Home; The Power of Thought; Effects of Depression on Internships; Development of Medical Education, Is State Medicine Coming?; The Crisis in Dentistry—What Can be Done About It? Medical History in Brief; A Doctor's Faith; America Gives a Chance; Asthma Is Not a Disease; Shall America Depend on the Way of Force or on Spiritual Power?; The Christ Religion as a Positive Dynamic Religion. I Believe, 1944, 2d edit. 1944 called a Gift Book on Christian Healing. Home: 630 E. Seminary St., Gainesville, Fla. Died Oct. 17, 1952.

MUMPER, WILLIAM NORRIS, physicist; b. at Dillsburg, Pa., Aug. 16, 1858; s. John and Elizabeth Ann (McAllister) M.; A.B., Dickinson Coll., 1879, A.M., 1882; Johns Hopkins, 1881-82, 1884-85; Ph.D., Syracuse U., 1886; m. Amelia Cooper Hewitt, of Trenton, N.J., June, 1898. Teacher physics and chemistry, Pennington Sem., N.J., 1880-81, Md. Agrl. Coll., 1883-84, State Normal Sch., Oshkosh, Wis., 1885-89, Hughes High Sch., Cincinnati, 1889-93; prof. physics, State Normal Sch., Trenton, N.J., since 1893. Mem. N.E.A., N.J. State Council Edn., N.J. State Science Teachers' Assn. (pres., 1911), Phi Kappa Psi, Phi Beta Kappa; charter mem. Cincinnati Branch Am. Chem. Soc. Independent Republican. Episcopalian. Clubs: Schoolmasters', Engineers (charter mem.). Author: A Text-Book in Physics, 1907. Address: 823 W. State St., Trenton, N.J.

MUNCIE, CURTIS HAMILTON, (mun'si), otologist, aurist; b. Bklyn., Jan. 5, 1887; s. Edward Henry (M.D.) and Elizabeth Hamilton (M.D.) M.; student chem. engring. Bklyn. Poly. Inst., 1902-06; student Phila. Coll. and Infirmary of Osteopathy, 1906-08; grad. Kirksville Coll. of Osteopathy and Surgery, 1910; D.Sc. (hon.), Fla. So. Coll., 1938; m. Louise Jennings, 1914; children—Douglas (D.O., M.D.), Louise (Mrs. B. L. Thompson). Gen. practice osteopathy, Bklyn., 1910-12; ear, nose and throat surgeon Muncie Sanatorium, 1912-30; prof. surgery Phila. Coll. Osteopathy and Surgery, 1920-22; practicing otologist. Mem. American, Eastern osteopathic associations, Osteopathic Society City of New York, New York, Fla., New Eng. osteopathic socs., Phi Sigma Gamma. Conglist. Club: Atlas (New York City). Author numerous articles relating to field. Contbr. to profl. jours. Conducted research on isolated types of deformity of Eustachian tube, also developed non-surg. treatments for various allied conditions. Home: Horse Shoe Cove, Nassau Point, Cutchogue, L.I., N.Y. Office: 521 Park Av., N.Y.C. Died Feb. 12, 1963; buried Methodist Cemetery, Cutchogue, L.I., N.Y.

MUNCIE, J(ESSE) H(OWARD), plant pathologist; b. Middlebury, Ind., July 3, 1890; s. William Rasnic and Sarah (Varley) M.; A.B., Wabash Coll. Crawfordsville, Ind., 1912; M.A., Cornell U., 1916; Ph.D., Ia. State Coll., 1925; m. Helen Marie Baber, Sept. 20, 1913. Asst. botanist Ohio Agrl. Expt. Sta., 1913; asst. and research asst. in plant pathology Mich. Agrl. Expt. Sta., 1913-17; plant disease survey U.S. Dept. Agr., 1917-18; asst. prof. botany Pa. State Coll., 1918-21; agent U.S. Dept. Agr., 1922-29; research asso., research prof. Mich. State Coll., 1929—. Mem. Am. Phytopathol. Soc., Potato Assn. Am., Sigma Chi, Sigma Xi, Gamma Sigma Delta, Epsilon Sigma Phi. Author tech. bulls. and research papers in plant pathology. Research in diseases of potatoes, field crops, bacterial plant diseases. Home: 656 Sunset Lane, East Lansing, Mich. Died July 4, 1954.

MUNDT, G. HENRY, ophthalmologist; born Mason City, Ill., Jan. 30, 1886; s. Peter N. and Kate (Knobbe) M.; Ph.G., Valparaiso (Ind.) U., 1903; M.D., University of Illinois, College of Medicine, 1911; m. Grace Wood, June 8, 1906; children—Joyce Wood (Mrs. William C. MacLean), G. Henry, Jr. (M.D.). Practiced in Chicago since 1906; chief ophthalmologist, rhinologist, and otolarynagologist Evangelical Hosp.; chief oculist, New York Central System, C.&E.I. Railway. Past president, Chicago Medical School, Diplomate Am. Bd. of Ophthalmology, Am. Board of Otolaryngology. Fellow Am. Coll. of Surgeons, Am. Med. Assn. (member House of Delegates since 1924), Am. Acad. Ophthalmology and Otolaryngology; mem. Am. Laryngol., Rhinolo. and Otolo. Soc.; Miss. Valley Med. Soc. (mem. advisory com.), Chicago Ophthal. Soc. (ex-pres.), Chicago Laryngol. and Otol. Soc. (ex-pres.), Ill. State Med. Soc. (ex-pres.), Inst. of Medicine, Chicago Med. Soc. Mason (K.T., 32 deg., Shriner). Clubs: Chicago Athletic Assn., South Shore Country. Home: 5805 S. Dorchester Av., Chgo. Office: 6306 S. Halsted St., Chgo. 21. Died Apr. 2, 1962.

MUNRO, DONALD, neurological surgeon; b. Boston, Mass., Aug. 10, 1889; s. John Cummings and Mary (Squibb) M.; A.B., Harvard, 1911, M.D., 1914; m. Margaret Harbison, May 1, 1928, 1 dau., Mary Frances. Formerly asst. prof. neurol. surgery Harvard Med. Sch., asso. prof. neurosurgery, Boston U. Sch. Med. surgeon in chief and dir. dept. neurosurgery Boston City Hosp. then consultant. Diplomate Am. bds. surgery and neurosurgery; mem. N.E. Surg. Soc., Am. Neurol. Soc., Soc. Neurol. Surgeons, Boston Surg. Soc., Boston Soc. Neurology and Psychiatry, Harvey Cushing Society, A.C.S., A.M.A., Societe de Neuro-Chirurgei de langue Francaise (honorary). Author: Craniocerebral Injuries, 1938; Injuries to the Nervous System, 1952. Contbr. articles on neurosurgery to med. jours. Home: Milton MA Died Mar. 10, 1973.

MUNROE, CHARLES EDWARD, chemist; b. Cambridge, Mass., May 24, 1849; s. Enoch and Emeline Elizabeth (Russell) M.; S.B., summa cum laude, Harvard U., 1871; Ph.D., George Washington U., 1894, LL.D., from same univ., 1912; m. Mary Louise, d. Prof. George Frederick Barker, June 20, 1883; children—Mrs. Winifred M. Mathews, Russell Barker, (George) Treadway Barker, Mrs. Dorothy Rouzer, Mrs. Charlotte Dolph. Assistant in chemistry, Harvard, 1871-74; professor chemistry, U.S. Naval Acad., 1874-86; chemist to torpedo corps, U.S. Naval Torpedo Sta. and War College, 1886-92; head prof. chemistry, 1892-1918, dean Corcoran Scientific School, 1892-98, and dean faculty of graduate studies, 1893-1918 (emeritus), George Washington U. Mem. U.S. Assay Commn. 1885, 90, 93; visitor U.S. Naval Acad., 1898; organized and directed on Analostan Island a vol. torpedo corps, 1898; consulting expert of Engr. Bd. on defense of Washington, 1898; expert spl. agt. in charge chem. industries of the U.S. for censuses of 1900, 05, 10; consulting expert U.S. Geol. Survey, U.S. Bur. of Mines and Civil Service Commn.; chmn. advisory com. Am. Ry. Assn. for drafting of regulations governing transportation of explosives, 1905; supt. denatured alcohol exhibit, Jamestown Expn., 1907, and mem. jury on chemicals. Apptd. by Swedish Acad. Sciences, 1900, to nominate candidate for Nobel prizes in chemistry. Inventor of smokeless powder and authority on explosives; author of over 100 books and papers on chemistry and explosives. Chmn. com. on explosives investigations, Nat. Research Council, 1918-28; chief explosives chemist, U.S. Bur. Mines, 1919-33. Cons. specialist on explosives, U.S. Forest Service, 1934—. Comdt. Order of Medjidieh, Turkey, 1901; Officer

Order of Leopold of Belgium, 1920. Hon. fellow Am. Inst. Chemists; fellow Chem. Soc., London, Am. Acad. Arts and Sciences, Soc. Chem. Industry, Eng., A.A.A.S.; pres. Am. Chem. Soc., 1898-99, Washington Chem., Soc., 1895-96; chmn. com. on explosives Am. Soc. Testing Materials. Fellow Am. Inst. Chemistry. Home: Forest Glen, Md. Died Dec. 7, 1938.

MUNROE, HENRY SMITH, mining engr.; b. Brooklyn, Mar. 25, 1850; E.M., Columbia, 1869, Ph.D., 1877 (hon. Sc.D., 1904); m. Alice M. Brown, Sept. 12, 1882; children—Mrs. Eleanor M. Green, Robert K. Munroe. Asst. geologist Ohio State Geol. Survey, 1870-71; asst. chemist U.S. Dept. Agr., 1870-72; asst. geologist and mining engr. Geol. Survey of Yesso, Japan, 1872-75; prof. geology and mining, U. of Tokio, 1875-76; adj. prof. surveying and practical mining, 1877-91, prof. mining, 1891-1915 (emeritus), dean faculty applied sciences, 1897-99, mem. univ. council, 1895-1915. Columbia U. Consulting engr. U.S. Bureau Mines, 1917. Home: Litchfield, Conn. Died Mar. 4, 1933.

MUNROE, HERSEY, topographic engr.; b. Lake City, Fla., Jan. 30, 1868; s. Benjamin Hersey and Jennie Lucy (Bowen) M.; ed. common schs. and Corcoran Scientific Sch., Washington; received certificate from Columbian U. for topog. drafting, 1889; m. Alice Lindsay Brandon, Dec. 3, 1890; 1 son, Thomas Brandon; m. 2d, Daisy W. Cushman, Dec. 21, 1912. Appointed topographer U.S. Geol. Survey, 1894; surveyed and mapped large areas of phosphate land in Fla., iron in N.C. and Ohio, and coal in W. Va.; in charge topographic work on Colorado River, Ariz. and Calif., for irrigation of arid lands, 1902-03; in charge of topographic field work in Me., N.H., Vt., N.J., 1903-05; made surveys vicinity of Lewiston, Me., 1906, topographic surveys in Me., 1907, Pa., 1908, Me. and N.H., 1909; in charge topographic surveys in Me., 1910-11, in Me. and Pa., 1912-13, Me. and Vt., 1914-15, Me. and N.H., 1916-17; apptd. geographer, U.S. Geol. Survey, July 1, 1917. Mil. mapping for War Dept., Hampton Roads and vicinity, Va., 1918; topographic work in Vt., 1919; in charge topographic work in Miss., 1920-21; topographic survey in Vt., 1922-23, Vt. and N.H., 1924-25; in charge topographic mapping in N.E. states, 1925-26; instr. topographic mapping, Atlantic Div., U.S. Geol. Survey, 1927; in charge mapping Shenandoah Nat. Park, Va., 1928-30; mapping vicinity of Healing Springs, Va., 1931, vicinity of Catskill, N.Y., 1931-32. Served 2d and 1st lt. Co. A, 2d Battalion, D.C.N.G., 1889-94 (resigned). Home: Washington, D.C. Died Feb. 17, 1935.

MUNSELL, CHARLES EDWARD, chemist; b. New York, N.Y., Apr. 22, 1858; s. Jabez E. M.; Ph.B., Columbia Sch. of Mines, 1878, Ph.D., 1884. Employed as chemist, 1878-79; milk insp., New York City Health Dept., 1880-85; state milk insp., N.Y. State Bd. of Health, 1881-83; analyst and asst. chemist, Devoe & Raynolds Co., 1886-1917; chemist Standard Oil Co., Nov. 1917—. Home: Portchester, New York. Died Mar. 16, 1918.

MUNSON, JAMES EUGENE, stenographer, inventor; b. Paris, N.Y., May 12, 1835; studied at Amherst, but was not grad.; studied shorthand and became an expert stenographer. Settled in New York, 1857, and was court stenographer over 30 yrs.; reported Beecher-Tilton case for New York Sun. Expended much labor in simplifying existing systems of shorthand, the result being the "Munson System." Invented process of setting and justifying type automatically, and machines for doing same; also assisted in inventing a machine for operating typewriting machines by telegraph. Author: The Complete Phonographer, 1866; Dictionary of Practical Phonography, 1875, 1906; Phrase Book of Practical Phonography; The Art of Phonography, 1898; A Shorter Course in Munson Phonography, 1900; First Phonographic Reader, 1904; Phonographic Dictation Book, 1904; Munson's Pocket Dictionary of Phonography, 1906. Home: New York, N.Y. Deceased.

MUNSON, JOHN P., biologist; b. Jolster Sunfjord, Norway, Feb. 21, 1860; s. Peter and Elizabeth (Dvergsdal) M.; came to U.S., 1864; B.S., U. of Wis., 1887, M.S., 1892; Ph.B., Yale, 1891; Ph.D., U. of Chicago, 1897; m. Sophie Josephine, d. Rev. A. Mikkelsen, of Chicago, Dec. 30, 1897; 1 dau., Esther Ingeborg (dec.). Master in English, Augustana Coll., Sioux Falls, S.D., 1889-91; fellow in zoölogy, U. of Chicago, 1893-97; investigator in biology, Woods Hole, Mass., 1894; hon. fellow in biology, Clark U., 1897; head Dept. of Biology, Wash. State Teachers' Coll., 1899—; dir. zoölogy, Seaside Lab., Port Renfrew, B.C., 1903. Lecturer 7th Internat. Zoöl. Congress, Boston, 1907, 8th Internat. Zoöl. Congress, Graz, Austria, 1910; research Christiana, Berlin, Naples, 1910. Awarded Walker 1st prize, Boston Soc. Natural History, 1911. Fellow A.A.A.S., Western Soc. Naturalists, Royal Soc. (London). Author: Education through Nature, 1903; Supermatogenesis of the Butterfly, 1906. Collaborator on Am. Jour. Anatomy, etc. Spent many yrs. in comparative cell studies, 25 plates completed. Home: Ellensburg, Wash. Died Feb. 27, 1928.

MUNSON, THOMAS VOLNEY, nurseryman, viticulturist; b. Astoria, Ill., Sept. 26, 1843; s. William and Maria (Linley) M.; bro. of William Benjamin M.; B.S., Ky. U., Lexington, 1870; M.Sc., State Agrl. and Mech. Coll., Ky., 1883, on thesis "Forests and Trees of Texas"; (D.Sc., Ky. State U., 1906); m. Ellen Scott Bell, 1870. Taught common sch. 3 yrs. in Ill.; prof. science, Ky. U., 1870-71; 3 yrs. at Lexington, Ky., in nursery business with wife's father; 3 yrs. at Lincoln, Neb.; then in business at Denison, Tex., as nurseryman and originator of new fruits. Mem. Texas World's Fair Commn., 1903-04; chmn. exec. com. Texas Farmers' Insts., 1902-03; mem. Internat. Jury Awards, St. Louis Expn., 1904. Chevalier du Mérite Agricole, 1888, for aid to France in viticultural matters. Author: Foundations of American Grape Culture, 1909. Home: Denison, Texas. Died Jan. 21, 1913.

MURALT, CARL LEONARD DE, cons. engr.; b. Brooklyn, N.Y., Jan. 29, 1873; s. Carl and Lily (Wegmann) de M.; M.E. and E.E., Polytechnic of Zurich, Switzerland, 1895; post-grad. work, U. of Munich; m. Jeanette Lathrop, Dec. 10, 1898. Entered employ of Gen. Electric Co., 1895, first in shops, then in engring. dept., Schenectady; detailed to German branch of the co., 1897, as engr. of lighting and power dept. and built some of the most important electric plants in Europe; entered employ of Brown, Boveri & Co., Swiss engrs., 1900; original work in high tension power transmissions and electrification of mountain rys.; returned to U.S., 1902, and established firm of Muralt & Co., engrs., in N.Y. City; prof. elec. engring. U. of Mich., 1907-13; cons. engr. since 1913. Mem. Am. Inst. E.E., Am. Soc. C.E., Verein Deutscher Ingenieure, Elektrotechnischer Verein, Gesellschaft Ehemaliger Polytechniker. Clubs: University (Ann Arbor, Mich.); Players (New York); Herrenclub (Munich). Contbr. to Trans. of Am. Inst. Elec. Engrs. Portrait painter. Address: 23 Fuersten St., Munich Germany

MURDOCK, GEORGE JOHN, inventor; b. New Berlin, N.Y., Apr. 17, 1958; s. Chester and Elizabeth (Armstrong) M.; acad. and engring. edn.; m. Jeanette P., d. Thomas W. Waterman (law author), April 23, 1883; 2 children living. Studied mech. and elec. science and engring.; discovering in 1879 that electric lamp carbons when isolated from atmospheric air were of much longer life, he took out in 1883 the first patent in the U.S. on the enclosed form of arc lamp which is now commonly used throughout the civilized world; prior to 1885 had developed a complete system of electric lighting, including dynamo, regulator for arc lamps, arc lamps, and other accessories; other patented inventions have followed including bolt machines, files, and holder button, and button fastener (with A. L. Lesher), an exhaust turbine, an electric surface gage, magnetic drill holder, electric ry. signal indicator, and many other tools, and instruments that have come into common use; constructed, 1903, first gasoline tank with a rubber composite cover; inventor of self-sealing fuel tanks for war airplanes of the type used by the U.S. and foreign govts. in World War; since war chiefly engaged in research and development. Elected to membership in many Am. and foreign socs. Contbr. to tech. press on subjects relating to electricity and mechanics. Address: 213 W. Market St., Newark, N.J. Died July 25, 1942.

MURIE, OLAUS JOHAN, biologist; b. Moorhead, Minn., Mar. 1, 1889; s. Joachim D. and Marie (Frimanslund) M.; A.B., Pacific U., 1912, D.Sc. (hon.), 1949; M.S., U. Mich., 1927; m. Margaret E. Thomas, Aug. 19, 1924; children—Martin L., Joanne E., Donald O. Natural history work, Ore., 1912-13; exploration Hudson Bay for Carnegie Mus., 1914-15, natural history work across Labrador Peninsula, 1917; field biologist U.S. Biol. Survey (now Fish and Wildlife Service, Dept. Interior), 1920-46; 2 expdns. to Aleutian Islands, field trips on waterfowl studies, B.C., field studies in western U.S.; life history N. Am. elk, bears of Yellowstone region. Dir. Wilderness Soc. since 1946, pres., 1950-57. Served with Balloon service, World War I. Recipient Pugsley bronze medal Am. Scenic and Historic Preservation Soc., 1954; Am. Forestry Assn. conservation award, 1954; Audubon medal Nat. Audubon Soc., 1959. Mem. A.A.A.S., Ecol. Soc. Am., Am. Soc. Mammalogists, Am. Ornithologists Union, Wilson and Cooper Ornithol. Clubs, Izaak Walton League, Friends of the Land, Wildlife Soc. (Aldo Leopold Meml. award 1952). Author: The Elk of North America, 1951; Field Guide to Tracks, North American Animals, 1954; (with Margaret E. Murie) Wapiti Wilderness. Contbr. articles on natural history to profl. publs. Home: Moose, Wyo. 83012. Died Oct. 21, 1963.

MURPHREE, EGER V(AUGHAN), petroleum corp. exec.; b. Bayonne, N.J., Nov. 3, 1898; s. John Burford and Sarah Elizabeth (Vaughan) M.; B.S. in chemistry U. Ky., 1920, M.S., 1921, D.Sc. (hon.), 1949; m. Georgie C. Rabelais, Sept. 7, 1934; 1 dau., Sarah Vaughan. Physics and mathematics instr. Paris (Ill.) High Sch., 1921-22; staff asst. Mass. Inst. Tech., 1922-23, research asso., 1923-24; chem. engr. Solvay Process Co., Syracuse, N.Y., 1924-26, dir., chem. engring. div., 1926-30; dir., Jasco Inc., Standard Oil Co. of La., Baton Rouge, 1930-34, mgr., development and research dept., 1932-34; v.p. and dir., Hydro Engring. and Chem. Co., 1934-45; mgr. development and research Standard Oil Development Co., N.Y. City, 1934-37, v.p., 1937-46, exec. v.p., 1946-47, pres. 1947—, co. name now Esso Research and Engineering Company; dir. Jasco, Standard Catalytic Co. Spl. asst. to Sec. Defense for Guided Missiles, 1956. Chairman planning bd., mem. Office of Sci. Research and Development S-I Exec. Com., World War II; general adv. com. A.E.C. since 1950; pres. permanent council World Petroleum Congress, 1951-59. Awarded the Perkin medal 1950 for work in applied chemistry by Am. sect., Soc. Chem. Industry. Mem. Am. Chem. Soc., Am. Petroleum Inst., Am. Inst. Chem. Engrs., Am. Phys. Soc., Soc. Chem. Industry, Am. Inst. Physics. Contbr. articles to trade and technical jours., Inst. Petroleum, Indsl. Research Inst., Nat. Acad. Scis. Patentee in field. Home: 60 Edgewood Rd., Summit, N.J. Office: P.O. Box 111, Linden, N.J. Died Oct. 29, 1962; buried Fairview Cemetery, Westfield, N.J.

MURPHY, FRANCIS DANIEL, physician; b. New Diggings, Wis., Nov. 7, 1895; s. Michael J. and Mary (Driscoll) M.; B.S., Marquette U., 1918, M.D., 1920, LL.D., 1961; M.S., U. Pa., 1924; m. Madaline McNamara, June 27, 1925; children—Joan Ellen, Francis Daniel. Began practice in Milwaukee, 1920; specializes in internal medicine; clin. dir. Milwaukee Co. Hosp., 1924-58, emeritus; prof. medicine, Marquette U., 1928-58, emeritus; chief staff emeritus St. Joseph's Hosp. Certificate of Honor, A.M.A., 1933, for special work on Bright's Disease; special research on nephritis at Milwaukee County Hosp. Named Marquette U. Alumnus of year, 1956, Francis D. Murphy Chair Medicine established Marquette U., 1957. Fellow Am. Coll. Physicians, A.M.A., Am. Coll. Dentists (hon.); mem. Central Soc. for Clin. Research, Wis. State and Milwaukee County med. socs., Milwaukee Acad. Medicine, Chicago Soc. of Internal Medicine, Milwaukee Surg. Soc., Am. Therapeutic Soc., Am. Heart Assn., Soc. Internal Medicine (Am. bd.), Wis. Hist. Soc., A.A.A.S., American Soc. for Study of Arteriosclerosis, Am. Found for High Blood Pressure, American Geriatric Society, Alpha Sigma Nu, Alpha Omega Alpha, Phi Beta Pi. Catholic. Clubs: University, Wisconsin. Author: Dr. Murphy's Bedside Clinics (8 vols.), 1934-39; Medical Emergencies, 1955. Wrote section on Bright's Disease, Tice's Practice of Medicine, 1937; Lipoid Nephrosis; Acute Diffuse Glomerular Nephritis; Phases of Renal Edema. Contbr. numerous articles to med. pubs. and yearly review on Bright's Disease for Cyclopedia of Medicine. Home: Milwaukee WI Died June 15, 1968.

MURPHY, JAMES B(UMGARDNER), pathologist; b. Morganton, N.C., Aug. 4, 1884; s. Patrick Livingston and Bettie (Bumgardner) M.; B.S., U. N.C., 1905, D.Sc., 1927; M.D., Johns Hopkins, 1909; hon. Dr. U. Louvain, Belgium, 1927; D.Sc., Oglethorpe U., 1938; m. Ray Slater, 1919; children—James Slater, Ray Livingston. Med. intern. Pathol. Inst., N.Y.C., 1909-10; asst. in pathology and bacteriology Rockefeller Inst., 1910-13, asso., 1913-15, asso. mem., 1915-23, life mem., 1923—, in charge Lab. of Cancer Research; mem. Nat. Adv. Cancer Council 1938-44; mem. bd. visitors N.Y. State Institute for the Study of Malignant Diseases; bd. Sloan-Kettering Inst. for Cancer Research; com. on growth NRC. Thayer lecturer, 1934; Hatfield lecturer, 1936; Tufts College Harvey lecturer, 1937; Cancer ednl. lectr. U. Chgo., 1939; Cutter lecturer, Harvard, 1940; Phi Beta Pi lecturer, U. Va., 1940; Barnard Hosp. lectr., St. Louis, 1941. Commr. N.Y. Bd. Charities, 1922-30. Maj. M.C., staff of surgeon gen., 1917-19. Mem. bd. mgrs. Memorial Hosp. (New York), Mt. Desert Hosp. (pres. 1928, v.p. 1929—). Decorated Officer, Order of Leopold, 1939; Chinese medal of Honored Merit, 1940. Mem. Fedn. Am. Societies for Exptl. Biology, Am. Soc. for Exptl. Pathology, N.Y. Acad. of Medicine, A.A.A.S., Am. Soc. for Clinic Investigation, Assn. Assn. Am. Physicians, Am. Assn. for Cancer Research (council, v.p. 1921, pres. 1922), Assn. Française pur L'Étude du Cancer, Leewenhoek-Vereeniging, Am. Cancer Soc., Roscoe Jackson Meml. Lab. of Bar Harbor (mem. bd.), Nat. Acad. Sciences, Sigma Xi, Sigma Nu, Nu Sigma Nu. Clubs: Knickerbocker (gov.), Coffee House Club, Century (N.Y.C.); Seal Harbor Yacht (gov.), Pot and Kettle of Bar Harbor. Author of numerous articles in medical and sci. jours., dealing with tissue grafting, cancer immunity, also role of the lymphocyte in tuberculosis, and studies in X-ray effects, nature of malignant tumors of fowls, cancer inhibitor from normal tissues. Mem. advisory bd. and chmn. editorial com. of Cancer Research. Home: 177 E. 64th St., N.Y.C. Office: Rockefeller Inst., 66th St. and York Av., N.Y.C. 21. Died Aug. 24, 1950; buried Bethel Ch., Staunton, Va.

MURPHY, JOHN BENJAMIN, Am. surgeon; b. Appleton, Wis., Dec. 21, 1857; s. Michael and Ann (Grimes) M.; M.D., Rush Med. Coll., 1879; postgrad., Germany, 1882-84; LL.D., U. Ill., 1905, Catholic U. Am., 1915; M.Sc., U. Sheffield (Eng.), 1908; m. Jeanette C. Plamondon, Nov. 25, 1885. Practiced medicine, Chgo., 1879-82, 84—; with Rush Med. Coll., Chgo., 1884—, prof. surgery, 1905-08; with Northwestern U., 1884—, prof. surgery, 1901-05, 08-16, also head dept. surgery and clin. surgery Med. Sch.; chief surgeon Mercy Hosp. Recipient Laetare medal Notre Dame U., 1902. Fellow A.C.S., Am. Surg. Assn., Royal Coll. Surgeons Eng.; pres. A.M.A. Pub. notes on clin. consultations; pioneer in work on gall bladder; developed method of repairing injured blood vessels; revolutionized intestinal surgery with device for linking severed ends of intestine; adapted Italian method of relaxing tubercular lungs; studied joint diseases. Died Mackinack Island, Mich., Aug. 11, 1916.

MURPHY, JOHN W., bridge engr.; b. New Scotland, N.Y., Jan. 20, 1828; grad. Rensselaer Poly. Inst., 1847; married twice, 2 children. Builder of the levees on Alabama River, 1851-52; chief engr. Montgomery (Ala.), 1860-61; builder Union Hall, Phila., 1864; initiator use of pin connections, metal bridge constrn., 1859; designer (for Lehigh Valley R.R.) pin connected bridge with all wrought iron members (1st bridge of kind in U.S.), 1863; builder Broad Street Bridge, Phila. Died Phila., Sept. 27, 1874.

MURPHY, ROBERT CUSHMAN, naturalist; b. Brooklyn, N.Y. Apr. 29, 1887; s. Thomas D. and Augusta (Cushman) M.; Ph.B., Brown U., 1911; A.M., Columbia, 1918; D.Sc., honoris causa, Univ. of San Marcos, Lima, Peru, 1925, Brown, 1941; D. Sc. (hon.), Long Island U., 1964; m. Grace E. Barstow, Feb. 17, 1912; children—Alison M. Conner, Robert Cushman, Amos Chafee Barstow. Curator of mammals and birds, Brooklyn Mus., 1911-17, curator of the dept. natural sci., 1917-20; asso. curator of birds, Am. Mus. Natural History, 1921-26, asst. dir., 1924-36, curator of oceanic birds, 1927-42, chmn. dept. of birds 1942-54, Lamont curator of birds, 1948-55, emeritus 1955-73, research asso., 1955-73. Leader expedition for Am. Mus. Natural History and Brooklyn Mus. into tropical and sub-antarctic Atlantic Ocean, 1912-13; into Lower Calif., Mexico, for Brooklyn Mus., 1915; to coast and islands of Peru for Brooklyn Mus., Am. Mus. Natural History and Am. Geog. Soc., 1919-20; to Peru and Ecuador for Am. Mus. Natural History, 1924-25; to western Mediterranean, 1926; to Pacific Coast of Colombia, 1937, and 1941; to Pearl Islands, 1945; to New Zealand and Islands to the South, 1947-49. Bermuda, 1951, 71, Venezuela and Caribbean Islands, 1952; Peru, 1953-54; Bahama Islands, 1953-54; Antarctica, 1960; del. 3d PanAm. Sci. Cong., Lima, 1924; to 6th Internat. Ornithol. Cong., Copenhagen, 1926; to Brit. Assn. Advancement of Sci., Oxford, 1926; to 7th Pacific Sci. Congress, New Zealand, 1949, Internat. Ornithol. Congress, Upsala, 1950; U.S. delegate 8th Pacific Sci. Congress, P.I. 1953, 9th Pacific Sci. Congress Bangkok, 1957, 12th Pacific Sci. Congress, Canberra, Australia, 1971; pres. Cold Spring Harbor Lab., 1940-52. Mem. Antarctic programs com. NSF, 1963-67; adv. commn. Fire Island Nat. Seashore, 1965-73; exec. council L.I. Univ. at Brookhaven, 1964-73. Recipient Congl. medal for Antarctic Service, also numerous other awards and medals. Fellow Am. Geog. Soc. (councilor), N.Y. Acad. Sci. (v.p. 1924), Am. Ornithologists' Union, A.A.A.S., N.Y. Zool. Soc., Zool. Soc. London; mem. L.I. Biol. Assn., Assn. Am. Geographers, Am. Geophys. Union, Am. Philos. Soc., Nat. Audubon Soc. (past, and hon. pres.), Cal. Acad. of Scis., Linnaean Soc. of N.Y., Royal Soc. of N.Z. corr. mem. Deutsche Ornithologische Gesellschaft, Sociedad Ornitologica del Plata (Argentina); Royal Australasian Ornithologists Union; hon. mem. Royal Hungarian Inst., Sigma Xi, Phi Beta Kappa. Unitarian. Clubs: Explorers, Century Assn. Author 12 books. Contbg. editor Geog. Rev. Home: Stony Brook NY Died Mar. 1973.

MURPHY, TIMOTHY FRANCIS, physician, statistician; b. Lewiston, Me., Dec. 5, 1875; s. Thomas and Mary (Downey) M.; student Bowdoin Coll., 1894-98, Me. Med. Sch., 1899-1902; M.D., George Washington U., 1906; m. Juliana Randall Elliott, Apr. 26, 1910; 1 son, Elliott Munroe. Chief statistician Div. Information, Publication and Records, Bur. of Census. Mem. Nat. Conf. on Nomenclature of Disease. Fellow Am. Pub. Health Assn., A.M.A., Southern Medical Assn. Mem. Society for Prevention of Asphyxial Deaths, American Statistical Assn., Zeta Psi, Phi Chi. Club: University. Author and compiler of statistical articles and reports. Home: 1673 Columbia Rd. N.W. Address: Bureau of the Census, Washington DC*

MURRAY, A(LBERT) N(ELSON), geologist; b. Madison, Conn., Sept. 25, 1894; s. Frederick P. and Jennie Maude (Robson) M.; student Worcester Poly. Inst., 1916-17; A.B., U. of Colo., 1922, M.S., 1924; Ph.D., U. of Ill., 1928; m. Esther Utzig, July 27, 1928; children—Ann, Frederick. Instr. geol., U. of Colo., 1923-25; jr. geol., Colo. Geol. Survey, 1924-25; asst. geol., U. of Ill., 1925-26; research fellow, Am. Petroleum Inst., 1926-28; prof. geol. head of dept., U. of Tulsa, since 1928; jr. geol. Mid-West Refining Co., summer 1923; geol., Ga. Geol. Survery, summer 1926, Okla. Geol. Survey, summer 1936; sr. geol., Stanolind Oil and Gas Co., summer 1945, 46, Carter Oil Co., summer 1948. Trustee of the Rocky Mountain Biological Lab. Served as corpl., radio operator, Air Serv., 31st Balloon Co., U.S. Army, 1917-19, 18 months. Fellow A.A.A.S., Okla. Acad. Sci. (pres. 1954), Geol. Soc. Am.; mem. Soc. Economic Geologists, Mineralogical Soc. Am., Am. Geophys. Union, Am. Assn. Petroleum Geols., Tulsa Geol. Soc., Am. Inst. Mining Engrs., Sigma Xi, Gamma Alpha, Sigma Gamma Epsilon. Republican. Presbyn. Contbr. articles to geol. publs. Home: 1211 S. College, Tulsa 74104. Died June 18, 1961; buried Meml. Park, Tulsa.

MURRAY, CHARLES BERNARD, chemist, metallurgist; b. Worcester, Mass., Apr. 6, 1866; s. Peleg Freeman and Mary (Prince) M.; grad. Worcester High School, 1883; B.S., Worcester Poly. Inst., 1887, Dr. Engring., 1937; m. Ellen Lincoln Robinson, Jan. 29, 1890; children—Philip Freeman, Mildred Alice (Mrs. Grover C. Burrows). Employed by Joliet (Ill.) Steel Works, 1887; chemist Buena Vista Furnace Co., at Buena Vista, Va., 1891-92, Minn. Iron Co., Two Harbors, Minn., 1892; chemist and metallurgist Carnegie Steel Co., Pittsburgh, 1892-1905; partner Crowell & Murray, 1907—, pres., 1927—. Registered professional engr., state of Ohio. Republican. Episcopalian. Mason. Author: Iron Ores of Lake Superior (with Benedict Crowell), 1911 (7 edits.). Home: Cleveland, O. Died Mar. 25, 1939.

MURRAY, GRACE PECKHAM, (MRS. CHARLES H. MURRAY), physician; b. Killingly, Conn., Oct. 16, 1848; d. Fenner Harris (M.D.) and Catharine Davis (Torrey) Peckham; grad. Mt. Holyoke Coll., 1867 (A.B., 1906); M.D., Woman's Med. Coll. of New York Infirmary for Women and Children, 1882; m. Charles H. Murray, of N.Y. City, Feb. 11, 1893. Interne Woman's Med. Coll., 1882-84; practiced in New York since 1884; instr. Med. Coll. N.Y. Infirmary, and phys. Infirmary Hosp., 1884; adj. prof. women's diseases, New York Post-Grad. Sch. and Hosp., 1902-11. Mem. A.M.A., Med. Soc. State of N.Y., N.Y. Co. Med. Soc., New York Acad. Medicine, New York Neurol. Soc., Women's Med. Assn., Women's Med. Soc. of N.Y. State (hon. pres.). Collaborator of Jour. of Nervous and Mental Diseases; mem. editorial staff New York Med. Record, Women's Med. Jour., etc. Inventor the aethesiometer. Address: 50 W. 45th St., New York, N.Y.

MURRAY, LEO TILDON, biologist; b. Eastland County, Tex., May 4, 1902; s. Adrian Albert and Olivia May (Jones) M.; A.B., Sul Ross State Tchrs. Coll., Alpine, Tex., 1927; M.S., Cornell U., 1931; Ph.D., 1935; m. Zoe Ellen Jenne, June 18, 1921; children—Ellen, Leo Tildon, Jr. Tchr. Tex. pub. schs., 1922-30, night sch., Itaca, 1930-31, Doyle Academy, Ithaca, 1931-32; N.Y. State Biol. Survey, summers, 1932-35; asst. prof. biology Ball State Tchrs. Coll., Muncie, Ind., 1935-36; asso. prof. biology, and dir. of Museum, Baylor U., 1936-44; asso. prof. biology, A. and M. Coll. Tex., 1944-46; aquatic biologist U.S. Fish and Wild Life Service, 1946—; leader, project investigations Mo. River Basin Studies; asso. prof. zoology U. So. Cal., summer, 1947. Mem. A.A.A.S., Tex. Acad. Sci., Ecol. Soc. Am., Am. Soc. Ichthyologists and Herpetologists, Am. Soc. Mammalogy, Am. Fisheries Soc., Am. Ornithol. Union, Wilson Soc., Herpetologists Union, Ind. Acad. Sci., Tex. Herpetological Soc., Alpha Chi, Sigma Xi. Baptist. Home: 1227 Princeton, Billings, Mont. Died Mar. 2, 1958; buried Billings.

MURRAY, NATHANIEL CARLETON, crop statistician; b. Cincinnati, O., Nov. 29, 1872; s. Charles Burleigh and Sallie (Powell) M.; B.Litt., U. of Cincinnati, 1898; m. Elsie Johnson, June 7, 1900; children—Donald P., Janet, Natalie. Market and financial reporter, 1892-94; asst. editor Cincinnati Price Current, 1898-1904; spl. agt. U.S. Dept. Agr., 1904-07; asst. statisitican, 1907-10; statistician and asst. chief, 1910-21, chief statistician, 1921-23, Bur. of Crop Estimates; also permanent mem. crop reporting bd. same; initiated govt. monthly estimates of crop prodn., monthly farm prices, farm labor supply, demand and wages, and other agrl. investigations; crop statistician with Clement Curtis & Co., Chicago, 1923-38, making frequent trips to Argentina to investigate wheat crop; same with Jackson & Curtis, 1939-42. Am. del. to Internat. Inst. of Agr., Rome, 1922. Writer upon agrl. economics and statistics. Home: 4th and Chapman, Waynesville, O. Died Aug. 26, 1952; buried Waynesville.

MURRAY, WILLIAM SPENCER, cons. engr.; b. Annapolis, Md., Aug. 4, 1873; s. of James Daniel and Elizabeth (Spencer) M.; E.E., Lehigh U., South Bethlehem, Pa., 1895, Dr. Engr., 1923; m. Ella Day Rush, Sept. 23, 1907; children—Richard Rush, John Maynadier, William Spencer. In charge of electrification New York div. of N.Y.,N.H.&H. R.R., 1905-17; mem. McHenry & Murray, gen. ry. engring. and electrification, 1913-17; pres. Housatonic Power Co., 1917-19; chmn. U.S. Superpower Survey, 1912-21; chmn. bd. dirs. Murray & Flood, Inc. Fellow Am. Inst. Elec. Engrs. (v.p. 1913-14); mem. Chi Phi. Clubs: Engineers, Bankers (N.Y. City); Graduate (New Haven); Cosmos (Washington, D.C.). Home: Catskill, N.Y. Office: 7 Dey St., New York, N.Y. Died Jan. 9, 1942.

MURRAY-AARON, EUGENE, editor, geographer; b. Norristown, Pa., Aug. 4, 1852; s. Prof. Charles E. and Anna Griffiths (Murray) Aaron; ed. pvt. tutors, in boarding sch., and under father, who was noted educator; collegiate studies, postgrad., etc.; m. Germany, 1892, Anna Louisa Stauder. Engaged as author, journalist and editor for most of active life; has explored Am. tropics as representative of British Mus., Nat. Mus., Hof-Museum, Vienna, etc. Was hurricane observer, U.S. Signal Service, in W. Indies, 1890-91; vice-consul of U.S., Kingston, Jamaica, 1890, etc. Prohibition candidate for Congress, 6th Pa. dist. (W. Phila.), 1886; now Republican, Agnostic. V.p., Am. Liberals. Formerly editor "Papilo," jour. Entomol. Soc., New York, Entomol. News, Phila.; now editor for George F. Cram, geog. publisher. Pres. Am. Geog. Inst., Chicago; fellow A.A.A.S.; life mem. Brooklyn Entomol. Soc.; hon. asso. mem. Brooklyn Inst.; pres. Am. Cartographic Assn.; formerly curator Am. Entomol. Soc.; entomol. custodian Acad. Natural Sciences, Phila.; fellow Nat. Geog. Soc., Chicago Geog. and other geog. socs.; mem. Entomol. socs. of Ontario, London, Belgium, etc. Was 1st sec. and editor of League of Am. Wheelmen; twice chief-consul Pa. Div. same; rode 1st wheel ridden by American on Am. soil. Author: The New Jamaica, 1891 01; Caribbean Trade, 1891 01; The Butterfly Hunters in the Caribbees, 1894 S3; Ancient and Modern Atlas, C39; Success Atlas, 1902 (Success Co., New York); Imperial Atlas of Canada, 1905 C10; Unabridged Atlas, 1905 C39; Army and Navy Atlas (with Rear-Admiral Clifford H. West, U.S.N.), 1907 C39. Residence: Wilmette, Ill. Office: Occidental Bldg., Chicago.

MURRILL, WILLIAM ALPHONSO, botanist; b. Campbell County, Va., Oct. 13, 1869; s. Samuel Leroy and Virginia Daniel (Woodroof) M.; B.S., Va. Poly. Inst., 1887; B.S., Randolph-Macon Coll., Va., 1889, A.B., 1890, A.M., 1891; Ph.D., Cornell U., 1900; research student N.Y. Bot. Garden, 1900-04; m. Edna Lee Luttrell, Sept. 1, 1897. Prof. natural sci. Bowling Green Sem., Va., 1891-93, Wesleyan Female Inst., Va., 1893-97; scholar in botany Cornell U., 1897-98, asst. in botany, 1898-99, asst. cryptogamic botanist, 1899-1900; tchr. biology DeWitt Clinton High Sch., N.Y.C., 1900-04; asst. curator N.Y. Bot. Garden, 1904-05, 1st asst., 1906-07, asst. dir., 1908-22. Mem. Torrey Bot. Club, Bot. Soc. Am., N.Y. Acad. Sciences, Am. Phytopathol. Soc., Sigma Xi. Author: North American Flora, Vol. IX, parts 1-7, 1907, 08, 10, 15, 16, Vol. X, parts 1-3, 1914, 17; Northern Polypores, 1914; American Boletes, 1914; Southern Polypores, 1915; Western Polypores, 1915; Tropical Polypores, 1915; Edible and Poisonous Mushrooms, 1916; Billy, the Boy Naturalist, 1918; Three Young Crusoes, 1918; The Naturalist in a Boarding-school, 1919; The Natural History of Staunton, Virginia, 1919; also (pocket guides), Stars, Rocks, Trees, Reptiles, Autobiography, Florida Plants, Florida Animals, Historic Foundations of Botany in Florida (and America) and illustrated guides), Ferns, Flowers, Pore Fungi, Familiar Trees; also many botany pamphlets and articles in scientific journals. Editor Mycologia, 1909-24; asso. editor North American Flora. Has named and described 1,700 species of fungi new to science. Has made extensive bot. explorations in Europe, tropical Am., S.A., and on the Pacific Coast, securing over 70,000 specimens and recently completed important studies of Florida fungi, Florida hawthorns and a botanic survey of Alachua County, Fla. Gold medal from Holland Soc. of New York, for mycological work, 1923. Address: Gainesville, Fla. Died Dec. 25, 1957.

MUSSELMAN, J(OHN) ROGERS, univ. prof.; born Gettysburg, Pa., Dec. 1, 1890; s. John Elmer and Euphemia Duncan (Rogers) M.; student Gettysburg Acad., 1906; A.B., Gettysburg Coll., 1910, A.M., 1913; Ph.D., Johns Hopkins U., 1916; m. Paula Wilson, May 23, 1925; 1 son, Peter Rogers. Instr. math., U. of Ill., 1916-18; statistician, U.S. Food Adminstrn., Feb.-May 1918; instr. math., Washington U., 1919-20; asso. math., Johns Hopkins, 1920-25, asso. prof., 1925-28; prof. math. Western Reserve, 1928-61, chmn. div. math., 1935-59. University scholar, Johns Hopkins Univ., 1913-14, univ. fellow, 1914-16. Served as 1st lt., statistics br., Gen. Staff, U.S. Army, 1918-19. Fellow A.A.A.S.; mem. Am. Math. Soc., Math, Assn. Am., Phi Delta Theta, Gamma Alpha, Phi Beta Kappa, Sigma Xi. Republican. Asso. editor: Am. Mathematical Monthly, 1928-43. Contbr. tech. articles to Am. and fgn. jours. Home: Cleveland OH Died Aug. 1968.

MUSSEY, REUBEN DIMOND, surgeon, educator; b. Pelham, N.H., June 23, 1780; s. John and Beulah (Butler) M.; A.B., Dartmouth, 1803, M.B., Med. Dept., 1805, LL.D. (hon.), 1854; M.D., U. Pa., 1809; m. Mary Sewell, before 1807; m. 2d, Mehitable Osgood, 1813; 9 children including William Hand Francis. Taught theory and practice of medicine, materia medica, obstetrics Dartmouth, 1814-20, prof. anatomy and surgery, 1822-38; proved union was possible in cases of intra-capsular fracture, 1830; 1st to tie both carotid arteries successfully; lectr. on anatomy and surgery Coll. Physicians and Surgeons, Fairfield, N.Y., 1836-38; prof. surgery Med. Coll. Ohio, 1838; founder Miami Med. Coll., prof. surgery, 1852-57; fellow Med. Coll., Phila.; mem. A.M.A. (pres. 1850), N.H. Med. Soc. (pres.), Mass. Med. Soc., Am. Acad. Arts and Scis. Died Boston, June 21, 1866.

MUSTARD, HARRY STOLL, physician, pub. health; b. Charleston, S.C., Oct. 10, 1888; s. Allan Calvitte and Mary Elizabeth (Stoll) M.; student Porter Mil. Acad., 1899-1904; B.S., Coll. Charleston, 1914, LL.D., 1938; M.D., Medical College of S.C., 1911, also Doctor of Public Health, 1955; m. Sarah Hopkins Haile, Aug. 1, 1912; children—Harry Stoll, Mary Boykin (Mrs. Moylan Lansdale DuVal), Elizabeth Haile (Mrs. Thomas Jones Wooten). Intern Roper Hosp., Charleston, 1911; asst. in clin. pathology, Med. Coll. S.C., 1912-16, instr. medicine, 1920; sci. asst. to asst. surgeon USPHS, 1916-20; health officer Preston

County, W.Va., 1923; dir. Child Health Demonstration, Rutherford County, Tenn., 1924-28; asst. to commr. of health, Tenn., 1929-30, asst. commr., 1930-32; asso. prof. pub. health adminstrn. Johns Hopkins U., 1932-37, lectr. on preventive medicine, 1936; prof. preventive medicine N.Y. U. Coll. Medicine, 1937-40; dir. Columbia U. Sch. Pub. Health, 1940-50, prof. pub. health practice since 1950. Health commr. City N.Y., 1947-49; exec. dir. State Charities Aid Assn., N.Y. Mem. Bd. Health and Bd. Hosps., N.Y.C. Mem. bd. sci. dirs. Rockefeller Found., 1939-41, 43-45. Fellow Am. Pub. Health Assn. (pres. 1946-47); mem. Assn. Pub. Health Sch. (pres.) since 1945; nat. adv. health council USPHS, 1944-49. Mem. tech. bd. Milbank Meml. Fund since 1947. Fellow N.Y. Acad. Medicine, mem. Delta Omega, Alpha Kappa Kappa, Alpha Omega Alpha. Episcopalian. Author: Cross Sections of Rural Health Progress, 1930; An Introduction to Public Health, 1935, 2d edit., 1944; Rural Health Practice, 1936, Government in Public Health, 1945. Editor Am. Jour. Pub. Health, 1941-43. Died Aug. 1966.

MUYBRIDGE, EADWEARD, photographer; b. Kingston-on-Thames, Eng., Apr. 9, 1830; s. John and Susannah Muggeridge; never married. Photographer on U.S. Coast and Geodetic Survey, Pacific coast, 1872; engaged by Leland Stanford to ascertain whether at any point a running horse has all 4 feet off ground, May 1872, used camera operated by string stretched across horse's path, definitely proved that all 4 feet are off the ground at certain times; performed series of experiments designed to make more detailed study of moving horse, 1872-78; continued experiments, using men, dogs and birds, 1878-81; developed zoopraxiscope (machine which reproduced moving figures on screen), 1879; worked on animal motion studies with Dr. E. J. Marey, Paris, France, 1881-82; did series of electro-photographic experiments in animal movement under sponsorship of U. Pa., 1884-86; lectured at World's Columbian Expn. Chgo., 1893. Author: The Horse in Motion, 1878; Animal Locomotion; An Electro-Photographic Investigation of Consecutive Phases of Animal Movements, 1872-85, 11 vols., published 1887; Descriptive Zoopraxography, 1893; The Human Figure in Motion, 1901. Died May 8, 1904.

MYERS, BURTON DORR, anatomist; b. Attica, O., Mar. 30, 1870; s. John T. and Eliza E. (Meyers) M.; Ph.B., Buchtel Coll., 1893; A.M., Cornell U., 1900; M.D., U. of Leipzig, 1902; m. Maud A. Showers, Mar. 4, 1904; children—James Showers (dec.), Mary Isabel, Rudolf Burton, Margaret Ann. Supt. high sch., Greenwich, O., 1893-97; asst. in physiology, Cornell U., 1898-1900; asst. in anatomy, Johns Hopkins, 1902-03; prof. anatomy, Ind. U., 1903-40; also dean of the Indiana U. School of Medicine, at Bloomington, emeritus prof. and dean since July 1940. Mem. Am. Assn. Anatomists A.M.A., Assn. Am. Med. Colleges (pres. 1928-29), Sigma Xi, Phi Beta Kappa, Alpha Omega Alpha. Methodist. Dist. gov. Ind. Kiwanis Dist., 1923; trustee Kiwanis Internat. Contbr. to med. mags. and revs. Vice chmn. Ind. State Planning Bd. Author: History of Medical Education in Indiana, History of Ind. Univ., 1902-37; Trustees and Officers of Indiana University, 1820 to 1950, 1951. Home: Bloomington, Ind. Died Feb. 28, 1951; buried Bloomington.

MYERS, CHARLES AUGUSTUS, mfr.; b. New York, N.Y., Jan. 26, 1889; s. Charles Augustus and Ella (Hays) M.; desc. (9th generation) Adolph Myer, who came from Westphalia, Germany, and settled in Harlem (New York), 1661; desc. (on mother's side) David Hays, one of soldiers serving under George Washington in Braddock's Defeat; student of spl. course in perfumes, extracts, and allied products, Columbia U. Coll. of Pharmacy, 1926-27; m. Harriet Horn, Apr. 5, 1913 (dec.); m. 2d, Ruth Glenn, June 17, 1933; children—Charles Augustus, Edith Hays. With Dodge and Olcott Company, manufacturer essential oils, aromatic chemicals, New York City and Bayonne, N.J., 1907-48, asst. to sec., 1911-19, asst. to vice pres., 1919-23, prodn. mgr. factory, 1923-26, gen. mgr. factory, 1926-38, became 1st v.p., 1938, member bd. dirs. 1928; vice pres. Dodge & Olcott, Inc., mem. bd. dir., 1945, exec. vice pres., 1946, pres. 1947-48. Served with U.S.N.R.F., 1917-19, chief petty ofcr. chem. service; in U.S.N.R.F., 1919-21. Contbd. a number of new devices to science of fuel analysis; holds navigator's license for vessels up to 15 gross tons. Awarded Victory Medal by U.S. and N.Y. State. Fellow Am. Geog. Soc.; mem. N.Y. Acad. Scis. (life), Am. Legion; Marine Mus. City N.Y. (life), Bayonne, N.J. C. of C. (dir.), Mus. of City of N.Y. Republican. Clubs: Railroad and Machinery (life). Chemists. Home: 99 Glenwood Rd., Englewood, N.J. Died July 29, 1955; buried Woodlawn Hays Mausoleum.

MYERS, CURTIS CLARK, mech. engr.; b. South Livonia, N.Y., July 9, 1879; s. James E. and Jennie (Eaton) M.; M.E., Cornell U., 1903, M.M.E., 1905; m. Florence MacClelland, July 22, 1908; 1 son, Curtis MacClelland (dec.). Instr. Cornell U., 1903; constrn. engr. Lackawanna Steel Co., 1906-07; mech. engr. Diamond Chain Co., Indpls., 1907-09; asst. prof. in charge coop. engring. courses, U. Cin., 1909-13, prof. indsl. engring., 1913-18; mech. engr. Aluminum Co. of America, 1919, chief mech. engr. Pitts., 1919-24; supt. Aluminum Co. of Can., Toronto, 1924-29; in charge fgn. bldg. program Aluminum, Ltd., Montreal, Can., 1929-32; chief prodn. engr. Ford Instrument Co., Long Island City, N.Y., 1934-35, factory mgr., 1935-37; N.Y. sales rep. Doyle Machine Tool Co., 1937-39, factory mgr., Syracuse, N.Y., 1930-40; asst. mgr. W.P.B., Syracuse, N.Y., 1940-41, spl. research engr., aluminum and magnesium br. Washington, 1941-43; resident dir. Daniel Guggenheim Airship Inst., Akron, O., 1943-49, ret. Served as capt. ordnance, U.S. Army, 1918-19. Life mem. Am. Soc. M.E. Clubs: Torch, Rotary (Akron); Engineers (N.Y.C.). Home: 211 Aurora St., Hudson, O. Died Dec. 3, 1954.

MYERS, DAVID MOFFAT, cons. engr., specialist on indsl. power supply; b. Owasco, N.Y., Jan. 8, 1879; s. Rev. Alfred E. and Mary (Moffat) M.; M.E., Columbia, 1901; m. Emily N. Huyck, 1911 (dec.); m. 2d, Jennette Kennedy. Mech. engr. U.S. Leather Co., 1901-06; cons. engr. in pvt. practice, 1906-15; partner firm of Griggs & Myers, 1915-25; cons. engr., alone and later as mem. of firm Orrok, Myers & Shoudy, N.Y.C., later Myers & Addington; now cons. engr. with Seelye, Stevenson, Value & Knecht; consulting engr. Bur. of Yards and Docks, U.S. Navy, last 7 yrs. cons. engr. N.Y. Board of Water Supply. Served with U.S. Fuel Adminstrn. as volunteer during World War I, apptd. advisory engr. and chief of fuel engring. sect. which he organized. Dir. Gramercy Boys Club (N.Y. City), Larchmont (N.Y.) Civic Assn. Fellow Am. Soc. M.E., A.A.A.S.; mem. Am. Inst. C.E., Soc. Older Grads. of Columbia, Westchester Shore Humane Soc. (dir.). Mem. Dutch Reformed Ch. Clubs: Horseshoe Harbor Yacht (commodore 1939-40), Columbia U., Univ. (Larchmont); former mem. Cosmos (Wash., D.C.). Author: Factory Power Plants: The Power Plant; Cost Cutting for Industrial Power Plants Reducing Industrial Power Costs, 1935. Contbr. numerous articles and papers to tech. publs. and orgns. Inventor of furnaces for spl. fuels, sail slide guide and speed indicator for boats. Home: 3 Cliff Way, Larchmont, N.Y. Office: 101 Park Av., N.Y.C. 17. Died Jan. 20, 1954.

MYERS, DEAN WENTWORTH, surgeon; b. Ionia County, Mich., Apr. 27, 1874; s. David Wallace and Rebecca Jane (Macomber) M.; grad. high sch., Muir, Mich., 1893; M.D., U. of Mich. Homeo. Med. Sch., 1899; post-grad. study same, 1899-1903; m. Cora Louise Owen, Aug. 29, 1900 (died May 4, 1904); 1 dau., Dorothy Louise; m. 2d, Eleanor Sheldon, Aug. 19, 1922. Asst. dept. ophthalmology and oto-laryngology, U. of Mich. Homeo. Med. Sch., 1899-1903; practiced in Grand Rapids, Mich., 1903-07; prof. oto-laryngology, 1907-08, prof. ophthalmology and oto-laryngology, 1908-22, U. of Mich. Homeo. Med. Sch. First lt. Med. Reserve Corps, U.S. Army, 1915. Fellow Am. College of Surgeons (gov. 1920-26); mem. Am. Med. Assn. Pan-American Assn. Ophthalmology, Am. Inst. Homeopathy, Am. Homeo. Ophthal., Otol. and Laryngol. Soc. (sec. 1910-14; pres. 1914-15), Mich. State Homeopathic Med. Soc. (pres. 1910-11), Michigan State Medical Society (house of delegates 1933-1943; councilor 14th District 1943-49), Washtenaw County Medical Society (president 1942), Alpha Sigma, Theta Kappa Psi, Ann Arbor Chamber of Commerce (pres. 1938), U.S. Chamber of Commerce (nat. councilor 1939). Pres. Ann Arbor City Council, 1929-31; mem. Ann Arbor School Bd., 1928-31. Pres. U. of Mich. Alumni Club of Ann Arbor, 1935-36. Mem. Internat. Rotary Clubs: pres. Ann Arbor Rotary Club, 1936-37. Democrat. Chmn. Washtenaw Co. Dem. Com., 1942-46. Presbyterian; elder since 1938. K.T. Contbr. numerous articles to med. jours.; widely recognized for successful surgery of the eye, and one of first surgeons in America to remove cataractous lens in its closed capsule; first to establish the exact center of rotation of the eye by a series of X-Ray photographs of a needle passed directly through eyeball. Home: 2220 Washtenaw Av., Ann Arbor, Mich. Died July 2, 1955; buried Forest Hill Cemetery, Ann Arbor.

MYERS, GEORGE WILLIAM, b. Champaign Co., Ill., Apr. 30, 1864; s. Robert Henry and Mary Helen (Shawhan) M.; B.L., Univ. of Ill., 1888, M.L., 1891; studied engring., Univ. of Ill., and science, U. of Munich, Ph.D., 1896; m. Mary Eva Sin, June 27, 1889; children—Sarah Helen, Joseph William, Margaret Elizabeth, Eleanor (dec.). Instr., asst. prof. and asso. prof. mathematics, 1888-96, asso. prof. astronomy and mathematics and dir. of obs., 1896-97, prof. astronomy and applied mathematics and dir. of obs., 1897-1900, U. of Ill.; head of astronomy and mathematics, Chicago Inst., 1900-01; prof. teaching of mathematics and astronomy, College of Education, Univ. of Chicago, 1901-29. Author: Rational Elementary and Grammar School Arithmetics; Myers-Brooks Elementary and Grammar School Arithmetics, 1907; Myers Arithmetics (three). Joint author: First Year Mathematics for Secondary Schools, 1907; Geometric Exercises for Algebraic Solution, 1907; Second-Year Mathematics for Secondary Schools, 1909; Teachers' Manual for First-Year Mathematics, 1911; Myers and Atwood, Algebra; Myers' Elementary Algebraic Geometry, 1921; editor and joint author of Standard Mathematical service; etc. Home: Chicago, Ill. Died Nov. 23, 1931.

MYERS, JOHN QUINCY, physician; b. Wilkes County, N.C., Sept. 25, 1877; s. Trelius C. and Julia Ann (Brown) M.; 18th generation in descent from Joseph Myers (English); student Davidson Coll. and N.C. Med. Coll., 1901-04, M.D., 1904; post-grad. work N.Y. Polyclinic, Johns Hopkins, Mayo Clinic, Rochester, Minn., etc.; m. Elizabeth Crosland, 1906 (died Jan. 21, 1929); children—John Quincy, Wm. Turrelius, Elizabeth. Practiced at Charlotte since 1909; founder and propr. Tranquil Park Sanitarium. Mem. Draft Bd., Charlotte, World War; pres. State Bd. Med. Examiners, 1914-20; pres. N.C. Bd. U.S. Pension Examiners; apptd. to Board of Med. Examiners for State of N.C. by Nat. Board of Examiners of The Life Extension Inst., N.Y., 1933; Organizer and 1st sec. N.C. Hosp. Assn.; med. referee Life Extension Inst., Met. Life Ins. Co., North Western Life Ins. Co. Capt. Med. O.R.C. Mem. A.M.A. (N.C. del., 1919-39; com. on rules since 1939), Med. Soc. State of N.C. (pres. 1926-27), Mecklenburg Med. Assn., Wilkes County Med. Soc., Pi Gamma Mu; elected med. mem. Nat. Council Traveling Salesmen's Assn., for Charlotte, Dec. 17, 1923; fellow Hotel Physicians Assn. of America. Republican. Deacon 1st Bapt. Ch. Mason (32 deg., Shriner). Clubs: Charlotte Executive, Myers Park Country. Chmn. Charlotte Med. Com., Procurement and Assignment Service, U.S. Manpower Commn., since 1942. Home: Selwyn Hotel, Charlotte, N.C. Died Dec. 3, 1944.

MYERS, SUMNER B(YRON), mathematician; b. Boston, Feb. 19, 1910; s. Solomon and Nettie (Cohen) M.; student Boston Latin Sch., 1921-25; A.B., Harvard, 1929, Ph.D., 1932; m. Alison Tennant, June 10, 1942; children—David, Alison. Instr. math. Harvard, 1933-34; Nat. Research fellow, 1934-36; faculty U. Mich. since 1936, prof. math. since 1948, dir. Air Force Pre-Meteorology Program, 1943; mem. research staff, Radiation Lab., Mass. Inst. Tech., 1944. Mem. Am. Math. Soc. (mem. exec. council), Math. Assn. Am., A.A.A.S., Phi Beta Kappa, Sigma Xi. Contbr. articles in math. jours. Home: 904 Forest Av., Ann Arbor, Mich. Died Oct. 8, 1955.

MYERS, VICTOR CARYL, biochemist; b. Buskirk Bridge, N.Y., Apr. 13, 1883; s. Dr. Adam Young and Mary Evelyn (Defandorf) M.; B.A., Wesleyan U., 1905, M.A., 1907, D.Sc., 1930; Ph.D., Yale Univ., 1909; m. Marion Christine Smith, Sept. 7, 1910. Adj. prof. physiol. chemistry, and exptl. physiology and dir. of these labs., Albany Med. Coll. (Union U.), 1909-11; with New York Post-Grad. Med. Sch. and Hosp. as lecturer on chem. pathology, 1911-12, prof. pathol. chemistry, 1912-22, acting dir. labs., 1917-19, prof. biochemistry and dir. dept., 1922-24; prof. and head biochemistry, State U. of Ia., and pathol. chemist to Univ. hosps., 1924-27; prof. biochemistry and director of department, School of Medicine, Western Reserve University, since 1927; visiting biochemist, Cleveland City Hospital, since 1927; secretary Medical Faculty, 1929-44; asso. editor Jour. of Lab. and Clin. Medicine and Gastroenterology; associate editor, Cyclopedia of Medicine; sectional editor Biology Abstracts. Mem. council on dental therapeutics American Dental Association. Maj. Sanitary Corps, O.R.C., U.S. Army, 1924-34. Fellow A.A.A.S.; associate fellow A.M.A., New York Academy Medicine; mem. American Society Biology Chemists (sec. 1919-23; councilor 1924), Fedn. Am. Socs. Exptl. Biology (exec. sec. 1922), Soc. Exptl. Biol. Medicine (councilor, 1921-23; sec.-treas., mng. editor, 1923-24, chmn. Ia. br. and v.p., 1927), Am. Physiol. Society, American Institute of Nutrition, American Gastroenterol. Association, Harvey Society, Am. Chem. Soc., Cleveland Acad. Medicine (chmn. sect. experimental medicine, 1929), Soc. de Chim. Biologie, Internat. Assn. of Dental Research, S.R. of State of N.Y., Delta Kappa Epsilon, Phi Beta Kappa, Sigma Xi; hon. mem. Des Moines Acad. of Medicine, St. Louis Medical Society. Methodist. Club: University (Cleveland). Author: Essentials of Pathological Chemistry, 1913; Practical Chemical Analysis of Blood, 1921, 24; Laboratory Directions in Biochemistry, 1942. Home: 21059 Claythorne Rd., Shaker Heights, O. Summer Residence: 329 Washington Terrace, Middletown, Conn. Address: School of Medicine, Western Reserve U., Cleveland, O. Died Oct. 7, 1948.

MYERS, WILL MARTIN, scientist, educator; b. Bancroft, Kan., June 11, 1911; s. Samuel Edwin and Amelia Askew (Woodall) M.; B.S., Kan. State Coll., 1932; M.S., U. Minn., 1934, Ph.D., 1936; m. Emma Louise Manchester, June 1, 1935; children—Susan Louise, Mary Jane, James Martin. Instr. U. Minn., 1932-37, prof., head dept. agronomy and plant genetics, 1952-63, dean of Office of Internat. Programs, 1963-65; associate geneticist, later geneticist U.S. Regional Pasture Research Lab., Dept. of Agr., 1937-46, sr. geneticist, 1947-49, head agronomist charge div. forage crops and diseases Bur. Plant Industry. Soils and Agr. Engring., 1949-51, dir. field crops research, 1951-52; head agrl. research br., agr. div. Natural Resources Sect., G-Hdqrs., Supreme Comdr. Allied Powers, Tokyo, Japan, 1946-47; prof. cytogenetics Pa. State U., 1947-49; asso. dir. agrl. sciences Rockefeller Found., 1965-67, vice president, 1967-70. Vice chmn. organizing com., chmn. exec. com., chmn. program com., sec. gen. 6th Internat. Grassland Congress; spl. consultant Rockefeller Found., 1959-60. Recipient Stevenson award Am. Soc. Agronomy, 1949; Outstanding Achievement award U. Minn., 1951; Distinguished Service award Kan. State U., 1970. Fellow Am. Soc. Agronomy (chmn. crops div. 1947, pres. 1958); mem. Bot. Soc. Am., Am. Soc. Naturalists, Am. Genetic Assn., Genetics Soc. Am., Am. Soc. Range

Mgmt., Sigma Xi, Alpha Zeta, Phi Kappa Phi. Home: Port Chester NY Died July 26, 1970; buried Sunset Meml. Park, Minneapolis MN

MYERS, WILLIAM KURTZ, engr.; b. Millville, N.J. Dec. 17, 1883; s. Christian and Louisa (Kurtz) M.; B.S., Pa. State Coll., 1905; m. Margaret Steinbach, June 23, 1909; draftsman Pa. Steel Co., 1905-07; engr. Chicago Traction Co., 1908-19; valuation mgr. and engr. Phila. Rapid Transit Co., and Internat. Ry. Co. of Buffalo, 1919-23, v.p. Phila. Rapid Transit Co., 1923-26, pres. 1926-27; exec. v.p. Mitten Bank Securities Corp., 1927-29, pres., 1929-38; v.p. Mitten Management, Inc., 1927-43; chmn. exec. com. and vice chmn. bd. of dirs. Phila. Rapid Transit Co., 1928-31; mem. exec. com. Internat. Ry. Co., 1928-43; president Mitten Bank & Trust Co., 1928-40; chmn. bd. of dirs. Penn. Steel Castings Co., Chester, Pa., since 1933. Mem. Am. Soc. of M.E., Am. Soc. C.E. Club: Engrs. Home: Merion, Pa. Office: Penn Steel Castings Co., Chester, Pa. Died Sept. 7, 1953.

MYERS, WILLIAM SHIELDS, chemist; b. Albany, N.Y., Dec. 15, 1866; s. Benjamin F. and Elizabeth (Shields) M.; desc. of Christian Myers, who came to N.Y. from Huguenot France, 1710; educated Albany Acad., 1881-85; B.Sc., Rutgers University, 1889, M.Sc., 1894, D.Sc., 1908; studied at Munich, Berlin, under von Hofmann, and at London, under Sir William Ramsay, 1890-92; m. Annie Tayler Lambert, September 11, 1889; 1 son, W. Lambert, Assistant chemist, N.J. Experiment Station, 1888-89; chemist, Lister Chemical Works, 1892-93; instr. and later asso. prof. chemistry, Rutgers Coll., 1893-1901; dir. Chilean Nitrate Com. for U.S. and Colonies, 1901-26, agr. consumption of Chilean nitrate in U.S. increasing nearly forty fold under his adminstrn., compared to increase of threefold in gen. fertilizer consumption in U.S. during same period; first to use motion pictures in presenting qualities and character of Chilean nitrate to North Am. farmers (leading woman was Claudette Colbert, in this, her first picture work). Chmn. Com. on Survey of Coll. of Agr., Rutgers U.; Pres. Rutgers League of N.J.; author of bill which organized dept. ceramics in Rutgers Coll., which passed N.J. Legislature, 1902, securing first annual income from the state for the coll.; trustee Rutgers Coll., 1902-07 and since 1912; mayor New Brunswick, N.J., 1904-06 (cut down number of saloons by 20 per cent and cut city tax rate by 10 per cent). Mem. jury award, Jamestown Expn., 1907. Trustee Okolona (Miss.) Sch. Bd., 1913-18; member mng. com. N.J. State Coll. Agr. since 1920; spl. consul of Chile in U.S. since 1918; trustee Central High Sch., Banbridge, N.Y. Life fellow Chem. Soc., London, 1891; life mem. Soc. Chem. Industry of Great Britain; mem. Am. Chem. Soc., A.A.A.S., Chi Phi. Ind. Republican. Clubs: University, Chemists (charter mem.), Canadian, British Schools and Universities (New York); Authors' (London). Contbr. papers to Chem. Soc. of London, Am. Chem. Soc., tech. jours. on water, soils and clays of N.J. Editor and pub. of monographs on scientific fertilization, water transportation and freights. Joint author, with late Prof. E. B. Voorhees, of plan for systematic development of agrl. edn. in Mexico, accepted by govt. Spent 6 months in Europe in a study of crop production and soils, Britain, France, Germany, Italy and Denmark, 1926. Delivered anniversary address, Aug. 1929, at unveiling of Clinton-Sullivan monument on the Old Frontier of New York Colony and Indian Territory, at junction of the Susquehanna and Unadilla Rivers, first point of invasion of Indian Territory by Am. troops. Leader in centralization movement of rural schs. of southern tier of counties of N.Y., Jan.-June 1931; made survey of orgn. and procedure of 10 northeastern colls., 1931; asso. of late Myron T. Herrick in promoting agrl. co-operative socs. Wrote "Some Causes of the Depression and Some Aids to Convalescence" for Sunday Times, New Brunswick, N.J.; author of Bureaucrats Song In Washington and Out; The Cult of Incompetence; Philosophies of Governments, Christian and Barbarian, 1939. Founder (with L. F. Loree) Jour. of Soil Science. Home: "Stonehenge," Bainbridge, N.Y. Died Jan. 10, 1945.

MYERSON, ABRAHAM, (mi'er-sun), neurologist, psychiatrist; b. Yanova, Russia, Nov. 23, 1881; s. Morris Joseph and Sophie (Segal) M.; grad. English High Sch., Boston, 1898; M.D., Tufts, 1908; m. Dorothy Marion Loman, Mar. 9, 1913; children—Paul Graves, David John, Anne. Began practice at Boston, 1908; resident neurologist Alexian Bros. Hosp., St. Louis, 1912-13; also instr. in neuropathology, St. Louis U. Sch. of Medicine; asst. physician Boston Psychopathic Hosp., 1913-14; pathologist and clin. dir. State Hosp., Taunton, Mass., 1914-18; chief med. officer, out patient dept., Boston Psychopathic Hosp., 1918-20; cons. neurologist Boston City Hosp.; former chief of neuropsychiatry, Beth Israel Hosp.; cons. neuropsychiatrist Washingtonian Hosp.; cons. physchiatrist McLean Hosp.; cons neurologist Boston Psychopathic Hosp.; prof. neurology emeritus Tufts Coll. Med. Sch.; former clinical prof. of psychiatry, Harvard; director research Boston State Hospital; member Com. on Research in Mental Health, Commonwealth of Mass.; trustee Assoc. Jewish Philanthropies Diplomate Am. Bd. Psychiatry and Neurology. Member A.M.A., Am. Neurol. Assn., Am. Psychiatric Assn., Am. Psychopathol. Assn., Phi Delta Epsilon. Author: The Nervous Housewife, 1920; Foundations of Personality, 1921; Inheritance of Mental Diseases, 1925; When Life Loses Its Zest, 1926; Psychology of Mental Disorders, 1927; The German Jew—His Share in Modern Culture (with Isaac Goldberg), 1933; Social Psychology, 1934; Eugenical Sterilization, 1936; book published posthumously, 1950; also many papers and articles on mental and nervous diseases. Home: 33 Taylor Crossway, Brookline, Mass. Office: 171 Bay State Rd., Boston, Mass. Died Sept. 3, 1948.

NABOURS, ROBERT KIRKLAND, zoologist; b. Many, La., Nov. 5, 1875; s. George Maston and Mary Elizabeth (Gibson) N.; diploma La. State Normal Sch., 1900; B.Ed., U. of Chicago, 1905, Ph.D., 1911; m. Mayme T. Davis (B.S., Ohio State U.), June 3, 1916; children—Elizabeth Frances, Robert Kirkland, Catherine Ann, Richard Davis. Asst. in museum and teacher natural history, Sch. of Edn., U. of Chicago, 1906-09, asst. in zoology, 1909-10; instr. zoology, 1910-12, prof. and head of dept. 1912-44, Kan. Agrl. Coll.; zoologist and experimenter in genetics, Expt. Sta. same since 1944; zoologist Kan. State Bd. Agr.; asso. in genetics Carnegie Instn., 1929-30. Made expdn. to Russia and Bokhara., Central Asia, 1914, to study Karakul sheep; trip around world for further study of sheep, 1916; also trip, 1920, to reopen trade in furs with Bokhara. Fellow A.A.A.S., Am. Soc. Zoologists; mem. Am. Soc. Naturalists, Kan. Acad. Science (ex-pres.), Sigma Xi, Alpha Zeta, Phi Kappa Phi, Phi Sigma Kappa. Conglist. Home: Manhattan KS

NACHTRIEB, HENRY FRANCIS, animal biologist; b. near Galion, O., May 11, 1857; s. Christian and Friedericka (Diether) N.; German Wallace Coll., Berea, O., 1874-77; B.S., U. of Minn., 1882; Johns Hopkins, 1882-85; m. Anna Eisele, June 21, 1886. With U. of Minn., 1886, prof. animal biology and head of dept., 1887; state zoölogist, Minn., 1889-1912. Edited Reports of the Geological and Natural History Survey of Minnesota, Zoölogical Series, 1892-12; published papers on Echinoderms and Polyoden Spathula. Fellow A.A.A.S.; mem. Am. Soc. Naturalists, Am. Soc. Zoölogists, Am. Assn. Anatomists, Am. Genetic Assn., Phi Beta Kappa, Sigma Xi, Psi Upsilon. Home: 2317 Pleasant Av., Minneapolis. Died July 25, 1942.

NAFFZIGER, HOWARD CHRISTIAN, (naf'zig-er), surgeon; b. Nevada City, Cal., May 6, 1884; s. Christian Jacob and Lizzie (Scott) N.; B.S., U. of Calif., 1907; M.S., 1908, M.D., 1909; m. Louise McNear, 1919; children—Marion, Jean Louise, Elizabeth. Began practice at San Francisco, 1912; prof. surgery, chmn. dept. U. of Calif., 1929-47, prof. neurological surgery, chmn. dept. 1947-51, prof. emeritus U. of Cal., 1951-61; regent U. of Cal., 1952-61. Served at lt. col. M.C., United States Army, in United States and with A.E.F., 2 years; colonel Medical Reserve; commanding officer U.S. Gen. Hosp. No. 30. Spl. consultant Office Scientific Research and Development; hon. consultant surgeon generals' library; chmn. UNRRA Med. Mission to Poland, 1946, WHO Med. Mission to P.I., 1948; cons. Far Eastern Comd., Korea and Japan, 1951. Fellow Phillipine Coll. Surgeons (hon.); fellow Am. Coll. Surgeons (regent; pres. 1939); fellow Royal Coll. Surgeons (hon.) Eng., 1943; founder, chmn. Am. Bd. Neurol. Surgery, 1939-49; founder, mem. American Bd. of Surgery; mem. A.M.A., Soc. Neurol. Surgeons (pres. 1929), Internat. Neurol. Assn., Internat. Surg. Assn., German Neurosurg. Soc. (hon.), Am. Neurol. Assn., Am. Surg. Assn. (pres. 1953-54), Assn. Research Nervous and Mental Diseases, Pacific Coast Surg. Assn., San Francisco County Med. Soc. (pres.), San Francisco County Neurol. Soc. (pres.), Western Surg. Assn., Cal. Acad. Medicine (pres.), mem. com. on surgery and chmn. subcommittee on neurol. surgery Nat. Research Council, 1940-46; mem. Royal Soc. of Medicine (hon.) England, Phila. Academy of Surgery, Southern Surgical Assn., Australasian Society of Neurological Surgeons, Howard C. Naffziger Surg. Soc. (hon.); mem. Psi Upsilon, Alpha Omega Alpha, Nu Sigma Nu. Republican. Episcopalian. Clubs: University, Pacific Union, San Francisco Golf and Country. Contbr. on surgery and the nervous system and exptl. research in anatomy and surgery of same; mem. editorial bd. Western Jour. of Surgery, Am. Jour. of Surgery, Annals of Surgery, Jour. Neurol. Surg. Home: 2565 Larkin St., San Francisco 94109. Died Mar. 21, 1961.

NAGLE, JAMES C., civil engr.; b. Richmond, Va., Oct. 9, 1865; s. John and Ellen Mary (Smith) N.; B.Sc., U. of Tex. (engring. course), 1889, M.A., 1892; C.E., Western U. of Pa. (now U. of Pittsburgh), 1892; M.C.E., Cornell U., 1893; m. Emily St. P. Davis, July 1, 1903. Asst. engr. Austin & Northwestern Ry., 1888; topographer Tex. Geol. Survey, 1889-90; prof. civ. engring., 1890-1913, dean engring. faculty, 1911-13, Agrl. and Mech. Coll. of Tex.; chmn. Bd. of Water Engrs., State of Tex., Sept. 1, 1913-Aug. 31, 1917; prof. civ. engring., dean of engring. and dir. Tex. Engring. Experiment Station, Agrl. and Mech. Coll. of Tex., 1917-22. Was chief engineer Brazos & Burleson Ry., 1894; asst. chief engr. Houston, East & West Tex. Ry., 1899; agt. and expert in irrigation investigation, U.S. Dept. Agr., 1899-1902, and spl. agt., 1908; engr. Burleson Co. Improvement Dist. No. 1, 1908-10, 1914-16; consulting engineer, gen. practice; mem. Nagle, Witt, Rollins Engineering Co., Dallas, Tex., 1919—; also mem. Nagle & Thompson, hydraulic engrs., 1923—. Author: Field Manual for Railroad Engineers, 1897. Home: Dallas, Tex. Died Apr. 6, 1927.

NAGLER, FLOYD AUGUST, hydraulic engring.; b. Howard City, Mich., Jan. 11, 1892; s. August Frederick and Carrie (Fox) N.; B.S., Mich. State Coll., 1914; M.S., U. of Mich., 1915, Ph.D., 1917; m. Marion Dell Truax, Sept. 1, 1921; children—Robert Carlton, Phyllis Jane, Donald Floyd. Asst. engr. Fargo Engring. Co., 1914-17; same with Robert E. Horton, 1917-20; with State U. of Ia., 1920—; asst. prof. mechanics and hydraulics until 1922, asso. prof., 1922-26, prof. hydraulic engring., 1926—; dir. Ia. Inst. Hydraulic Research, 1931—; part time sr. engr. in charge hydraulic investigations, U.S. Engr. Dept., Rock Island Dist., 1927-29; cons. practice. Was 2d lt. science and research div., meteorol. sect. U.S. Signal Corps, 1918-19. Awarded Collingwood prize, Am. Soc. C.E., 1919, 20; Norman medal, same soc., 1930. Republican. Methodist. Home: Iowa City, Ia. Deceased.

NAGLER, FORREST, (nâgler), mech. engr.; b. Freeport, Mich., Apr. 21, 1885; s. John G. and Helen (Moore) N.; B.S., U. Mich., 1906; m. Aletta Seefeld, Dec. 1911; children—John W., Mary (Mrs. Maynard Meyer). Hydro-electric power engring, hydraulic dept. Allis-Chalmers Mfg. Co., Milwaukee, 1908-30, chief mech. engr. engring. development div., 1942-48, mgr. chief engr. atomic power sect. since 1948; research engr. A. O. Smith Corp., Milwaukee, 1930-32; chief engr. Canadian Allis-Chalmers, Lt., Toronto, Ont., 1933-42; cons. mech. engr. since 1952; author, inventor. Served with 1st Wis. Cav. 1907-11. Mem. A.S.M.E. (life mem., past v.p.), Am. Soc. C.E., Wis. Soc. Profl. Engrs. Canadian amateur champion archer, 1935-39; Internat. Archery title since 1940; Wis. Archery champion, 1942. Home: 7428 Oakhill Ave., Wauwatosa 13, Wis. Office: Allis-Chalmers Mfg. Co., P.O. Box 512, Milw. 1. Died Apr. 1, 1952.

NAIR, JOHN HENRY, JR., cons. indsl. chemist; b. Chgo., Feb. 20, 1893; s. John H. and Isabel Bratton (Painter) N.; B.S. cum laude, Beloit Coll., 1915; D.Sc., 1958; student Syracuse U. 1916-17; m. Claire Louise Cook, Mar. 22, 1920; children—John, Janet Cook (Mrs. Clarence L. Adams). Chemistry instr. Wausau (Wis.) High Sch., 1915-16, Syracuse U., 1916-17; research chemist Merrell-Soule Co., Syracuse, N.Y., 1919-28; asst. dir. research Borden Co., Syracuse, 1928-38; tech. sales Borden Co., N.Y.C., 1938-42; asst. dir. research T. J. Lipton, Inc., Hoboken, N.J., 1942-57; v.p., dir. L & N Corp., Raleigh, N.C.; secretary-treas. Elmenair Corporation, Raleigh, N.C. Member advisory board Jour. Agrl. and Food Chemists, 1953-57; dir. Avi Pub. Co.; vis. prof. N.C. State Coll., U.N.C., 1963-64. Trustee Beloit Coll., 1961-64. Served as capt. Signal Corps C.W.S., AEF, 1917-19. Mem. Am. Chem. Soc. (nat. councillor, 1929-35, 1945-63, dir. 1964-71), Inst. Food Technologists (chmn. N.Y. sect. 1946-47, nat. council 1947, 51-53, 57-59, pres. elect 1965-66), Am. Inst. Chemists (nat. councilor 1957-61, pres. 1956-57, hon. mem. 1962-71), N.A.M. (research com.), Assn. Research Dirs. (pres. 1956-57), American Dairy Science Assn., Sci. Research Soc. of Am., Society Chimie Industrielle, also Sigma Xi, Phi Tau Sigma, Delta Sigma Rho, Alpha Chi Sigma, Tau Kappa Epsilon. Mason. Clubs: Chemists (N.Y.C.); Raleigh (N.C.) Country; North Carolina State Faculty. Contributing author: Handbook of Food and Agriculture, 1955; Food Dehydration, volume 2, 1964. Contributing editor Food Engring. Author numerous articles on chem. research. Home: Raleigh NC Died July 25, 1971.

NALLY, EDWARD JULIAN, communication exec.; b. Phila., Apr. 11, 1859; s. Patrick and Mary (Cullen) N.; common school edn.; m. Lee Warren Redd, June 10, 1897; children—Marylee (Mrs. Frederic H. Hahn), Edward Julian. Started as messenger boy in St. Louis, with Western Union Telegraph Co., Sept. 1, 1875, filling various positions in St. Louis and Mpls. until Oct. 1890; asst. gen. supt. and gen. supt. Western div. Postal Telegraph-Cable Co., hdqrs. at Chicago, 1890-1906, becoming v.p. and dir. at New York, Sept. 1906, and 1st v.p. and gen. mgr., Apr. 11, 1907-Oct. 1, 1913; v.p., gen mgr., dir. Marconi Wireless Telegraph Co. of America, 1913-19; pres. RCA, which took over Marconi Co., 1919-23; mng. dir. internat. relations RCA, 1923-25; mng. dir. Commercial Radio Internat. Consortium (Paris), 1923-25; dir. RCA, RCA Communications, Inc., RCA Mfg. Co., Inc., NBC. Asso. with 1st Edison telephone exchange at St. Louis, 1878; supervised the accounting and prepared estimates for 1st telegraph lines to follow all Northwestern trans-continental ry. lines constructed during 1880-89; opened first commercial wireless circuit between U.S. and Hawaii, 1914, extended to Japan, 1916, and between U.S. and Great Britain, Norway, Germany and France, 1920, Italy, Sweden, Poland, Argentine, Brazil and Colombia, 1924-25. Retired Jan. 1, 1925, after 50 years' service; was a pioneer in telegraph, telephone and radio. Decorated Officer Polonia Restituta (Poland). Hon. mem. Wireless Veterans Assn., Nat. Geog. Soc., NBC 20-year Club, RCAC 25-year Club; mem. Friendly Sons of St. Patrick, Am. Irish Hist. Soc., Japan Soc., N.Y., Soc. for Japanese Studies. Roman Catholic. Clubs: Ends of the Earth, Century Assn. (N.Y.C.); Overseas Press (hon.). Home: 11 Northway, Bronxville, N.Y. Office: 30 Rockefeller Plaza, N.Y.C. Died Sept. 22, 1953; buried Sleepy Hollow Cemetery, Tarrytown, N.Y.

NASH, LUTHER ROBERTS, engineer; b. Ridgefield, Conn., Jan. 22, 1871; s. John D. and Sarah J. (Holmes) N.; S.B., Mass. Inst. Tech., 1894; S.M., Harvard, as of 1898; m. Bonnibel Remington, of Boston, Mass., Oct. 15, 1896; 1 son, Frank Remington (dec.). With Stone & Webster, Inc., Boston, since 1895; designing and constg. engr., 1895-1904, mgr. pub. utilities, 1904-08; appraisal engr. and rate expert, 1908-19; consultant on regulation, rates, taxation, depreciation and pub. relations, 1919-32; v.p. Stone & Webster Engring. Corpn., in charge appraisals and rate investigations, 1933-37, cons. engr. since 1937; pres. Acorn Press, Inc., since 1938. Lecturer at Mass. Inst. Tech., Harvard and Mass. Dept. of Edn. Mem. Am. Inst. Elec. Engrs., Edison Electric Inst., Am. Gas Assn., Chi Phi. Republican. Conglist. Clubs: Silver Spring Country, Lions. Author: Economics of Public Utilities, 1931, Public Utility Rate Structures, 1933; also monographs and papers on utility and economic subjects. Home: 155 Main Street, Ridgefield, Conn. Office: Stone and Webster Building, 90 Broad Street, New York NY

NASON, FRANK LEWIS, mining engr.; b. New London, Wis., May 12, 1856; s. Lewis Clark and Maria Julia (Stickles) N.; A.B., Amherst, 1882, A.M., 1885; one term Yale Div. Sch.; m. Thalia Abigail Painter, July 26, 1885 (died 1906); children—Stanley Lewis, Alexis Painter (dec.); m. 2d, Madeleine Reynolds, December 1909. Instr. mathematics, Rensselaer Polytec. Inst., 1882-88, taking special course in chemistry and metallurgy; asst. state geologist of N.J., 1888-90, of Mo., 1890-92; mining engr. and consulting engr. for the Ringwood Co., Ringwood, N.J., Basic Iron Ore Co., Oxford, N.J., 1892—, mining geologist, N.J. Zinc Co., 1903-15, Standard Oil Co., Witherbee, Sherman & Co.; mining engineer U.S. Steel Corp., Va.-Carolina Chem. Co. Author: Iron Ores of Missouri, 1892; To the End of the Trail, 1902; The Blue Goose, 1903; The Vision of Elijah Berl, 1905. Home: W. Haven, Conn. Died Sept. 12, 1928.

NASON, HENRY BRADFORD, educator, chemist; b. Foxboro, Mass., June 22, 1831; s. Elias and Susanna (Keith) N.; grad. Amherst, 1855; Ph.D., U. Gottingen, 1855-57; M.D., Union Coll., 1880; LL.D., Beloit Coll.; m. Frances Townsend; 2 children. Prof. natural history Rensselaer Poly. Inst., 1858-66, prof. chemistry and natural sci., 1866-95; prof. natural history Beloit (Wis.) Coll., 1858-66; chem. adviser Standard Oil Co., 1880-90; insp. petroleum oils N.Y. State Bd. of Health, 1881; rep. U.S. at Paris Exposition of 1878; prominent in orgn. Geol. Soc. Am., Am. Chem. Soc. (pres. 1889-90). Fellow A.A.A.S., London Chem. Soc., Soc. Chem. Industry; mem. Gen. Alumni Assn. Rensselaer Poly Inst. (sec. 1872-86) Am. Chem. Soc. Died Jan. 18, 1895.

NASSAU, JASON JOHN, (nas'saw), astronomy; b. Smyrna, Asia Minor, Mar. 29, 1892; s. John and Maria (Christie) N.; C.E. and M.S., Syracuse U., 1915, Ph.D., 1920; hon. D.Sc., 1940; Columbia, summers, 1913, 14; U. of Edinburgh, Jan.-July 1919; Cambridge U., 1927-28; LL.D. (honorary), Lake Erie College, 1956; married to Laura Alice Johnson, June 27, 1920; children—James, Sherwood. Came to U.S., 1910, naturalized citizen, 1917. Instr. in mathematics and astronomy, Syracuse U., 1919-21; asst. prof. astronomy, Case Institute of Technology, 1921-24, asso. prof., 1924-29, dir. Warner and Swasey Obs., 1924-59, now prof. emeritus; in charge Case Eclipse Expdn., 1932; chmn. Grad. Division of Case Institute Technology, 1936-40; active in War Research at Case since May 1942. Chmn. U.S. Nat. Committee I.A.U. since 1949; mem. div. phys. scis. Nat. Research Council 1949-52. Mem. bd. Cleve. Mus. Natural History, Karamu House. In World War I, served with the A.E.F. in France; commd. comdr., U.S. Coast Guard Reserve, 1946. Recipient Distinguished Citizen award, Denison University 1956. Fellow Am. Assn. Arts and Sciences (v.p. 1945), Royal Astron. Soc., Am. Acad. Arts, Scis.; mem. Nat. Acad. Greece (corr.), Am. (treas. 1946-54), Cleve. (past pres.) astron. socs., Phi Beta Kappa, Sigma Xi, Tau Beta Pi, Phi Kappa Phi, Pi Mu Epsilon. Author: Practical Astronomy, 1932, 36, 48. Contbr. chapter to Theory of Determinants, 1930; also contbr. to scientific jours. Home: 2019 Taylor Road, East Cleveland 12, O. Died May 11, 1965.

NATHAN, ALFRED, engineer; b. N.Y. City, Nov. 21, 1866; s. Max and Rosalie (Hettheimer) N.; M.E., Stevens Inst. Tech., 1890; m. Mabel Lauer, of N.Y. City, Oct. 26, 1892. Began practice in N.Y. City, 1891; now pres. Nathan Mfg. Co.; treas. Ludlow Valve Mfg. Co., Troy, N.Y. Mem. Am. Soc. Mech. Engrs., Beta Theta Pi, Theta Nu Epsilon. Clubs: Criterion, Lambs. Home: 910 Fifth Av. Office: 250 Park Av., New York, N.Y.

NEAL, HERBERT VINCENT, biologist; b. Lewiston, Me., Apr. 3, 1869; s. John and Caroline (Noyes) N.; A.B., Bates Coll., 1890, also Sc.D.; A.B., Harvard, 1893, A.M., 1894, Ph.D., 1896; U. of Munich, 1896-97; m. Helen Phillips Howell, June 8, 1899; children—Margaret, Helen, John Howell. Prof. biology, Knox Coll., Galesburg, Ill., 1897-1913; prof. zoölogy, Tufts Coll., 1913—, also dean Grad. Sch. Researches on the morphology of the vertebrate head; associate director Harpswell Lab., South Harpswell, Me., 1908-15; director Mt. Desert Island Biol. Laboratory, 1926-32. Trustee of Bradford and Bates Colleges. Alderman, 6th Ward, Galesburg, 1906-09. Republican. Episcopalian. Fellow A.A.A.S. (sec. sect. F, 1910-20), Am. Acad. Arts and Sciences; member American Society Zoölogists (sec., treas. Central br., 1910-11, pres. 1930). Author: Comparative Anatomy of Vertebrates, 1936; Chordate Anatomy, 1939. Home: Salisbury Cove, Me. Died Feb. 21, 1940.

NEAL, JOSEPHINE BICKNELL, physician; b. Belmont, Me., Oct. 10, 1880; d. Alton J. and Mary (Alexander) Neal; A.B. (1st honor, physics), Bates Coll., 1901, hon. D.Sc., 1926; M.D. (2d honor), Cornell U. Med. Coll., 1910; hon. D.Sc., Russell Sage Coll., 1937. Licensed to practice medicine, N.Y. State, 1913, practice limited to consultation in neurology, 1918—; asst. in meningitis div., research lab., Dept. of Health, N.Y. City, 1910-14, in charge of div., 1914—; instr. in medicine, Cornell U. Med. Coll., 1914-20; instr. in medicine, Coll. of Physicians and Surgeons, Columbia U., 1922-27, clin. prof. of neurology, 1929-44; attending physician Children's Tuberculosis Clinic and Vanderbilt Clinic, 1922-27; consultant in acute infections of central nervous system, N.Y. Infirmary for Women and Children, 1925—, Neurol. Inst. of N.Y., 1936-44, Vanderbilt Clinic, 1936-44; dir. dept. of infectious diseases, Neurol. Inst., 1937-39; visiting physician on neurol. service, Willard Parker Hosp., 1937—; asst. attending neurologist, Neurol. Inst. and Vanderbilt Clinic, 1939—; consultant in pediatrics, St. Vincent's Hosp. Asso. dir. research lab., N.Y. Dept. of Health, 1937-44; dir. William J. Matheson Survey of Epidemic Encephalitis, 1927-29; exec. sec. Matheson Commn. for Encephalitis Research, 1929—; sec. Internat. Com. for Study of Infantile Paralysis, 1929-32; Certified in neurology by Am. Bd. of Psychiatry and Neurology, 1936. Awarded John Metcalfe Polk Prize, Cornell U. Fellow Am. Coll. Physicians; mem. N.Y. State, N.Y. County med. socs., A.M.A., Am. Pub. Health Assn., Assn. for Research in Nervous and Mental Diseases, N.Y. Acad. of Medicine, Phi Beta Kappa, Alpha Epsilon Iota, Alpha Omega Alpha. Author of chapters in Abt's System of Pediatrics; Tice's Practice of Medicine; Barr's Modern Medical Therapy in General Practice; 1st, 2d, and 3d Reports on Epidemic Encephalitis (Matheson commn.); Poliomyelitis (Internat. Commn. for Study of Infantile Paralysis); The Human Cerebral Spinal Fluid; Infections of the Central Nervous System; chapter on Viral Diseases of the Central Nervous System in Cyclopedia of Medicine, 1940; Encephalitis, A Clinical Study, 1942; also about 75 articles on acute infections of the central nervous system for med. jours. Home: 60 Gramercy Park. Office: William H. Park Laboratory, Foot of E. 15th St., N.Y.C. Died Mar. 19, 1955; buried Lewiston, Me.

NEEDHAM, CLAUDE ERVIN, (ned'am), mineral economist, geologist; b. near Newton, Ill., Sept. 10, 1894; s. John Newton and Alice Amanda (Gibson) N.; ed. Central Normal Coll., Danville, Ind., 1915-16, Ia. State Coll., 1916-17, Miss. State Coll., 1922-25 (B.S., 1924, M.S., 1925), Northwestern U., 1927-31 (Ph.D.); m. Pauline Hyde Wesch, June 1927; children—John Wesch, Darrell Ervin. Chem. work, St. Louis, 1917-20; asst. in geol., Miss. State Coll., 1923-25; supt. of schools, Cortez, Colo., 1925-26; asst. prof. of geology, Miss. State Coll., 1926-27; instr. geology, Northwestern U., 1927-30, fellow, 1930-31; asst. prof. geology, N.M. Sch. of Mines, 1931-35, asso. prof., 1935-38, prof., 1938-39, pres., 1939-42; also dir. N.M. Bur. of Mines and Mineral Resources, 1939-42; economic analyst, editor Minerals Yearbook, U.S. Bur. of Mines, 1942-45; supervising engr., Salt Lake sect. Metal econ. div., U.S. Bur. Mines, since 1945; with Ill. Geol. Survey summers 1929, 30; visiting prof., U. of Miss., summers 1935, 36. Mem. Am. Assn. Petroleum Geologists, Am. Inst. Mining and Metall. Engrs., Geol. Soc. America, Utah Geol. Soc., Utah Acad. Sci., N.M. Miners and Prospectors Assn., Sigma Xi. Contbr. to professional jours. and Bur. of Mines publs. Home: 3303 Plains Blvd., Amarillo, Tex. Died Oct. 15, 1950; buried Cortez, Colo.

NEEDLES, ENOCH RAY, cons. engr.; b. Brookfield, Mo., Oct. 29, 1888; s. Sim Gesmer and Elma (Bray) N.; B.S., Mo. Sch. Mines, 1914, C.E., 1920, D.Eng. (hon.), 1937; m. Ethel Schuman, Sept. 12, 1916; children—Elma (Mrs. J.W. Wight), Margaret (Mrs. H.P. Williams), Mary (Mrs. H.P. McJunkin), Thomas E., Carolyn (Mrs. C.E. Homer), Sally Jane (Mrs. H.J. Toffey). Various engring. positions, 1914-28; partner Howard, Needles, Tammen & Bergendoff, cons. engrs., N.Y.C., also Kansas City, Mo., from 1928; prin. projects include: Del. Meml. Bridge, Pulaski Skyway, Harlem River Lift Bridge, Me. Turnpike, N.J. Turnpike, W.Va. Turnpike, Ohio Turnpike, 5 other state turnpikes, numerous other state and fed. projects, various Miss. River bridges. Served as col., Corps. Engrs., AUS, 1942-45. Decorated Legion of Merit; recipient UMR Silver Centennial medal honor, 1971. Mem. Am. Road Builders Assn. (pres. 1949-50), Am. Soc. C.E. (pres. 1955-56), Am. Inst. Cons. Engrs. (pres. 1946), Soc. Am. Mil. Engrs., Nat. Soc. Profl. Engrs., Am. Association for Advancement of Science, Engineers Joint Council (president 1958-59), Newcomen Soc., Tau Beta Pi, Phi Kappa Phi, Chi Epsilon, Pi Kappa Alpha. Clubs: Bankers, Engineers (N.Y.C.); Canoe Brook (N.J.) Country; Morris County (N.J.) Golf. Webhannet (Me.) Golf; Army and Navy (Washington). Home: New Vernon NJ Died Jan. 5, 1972; buried New Vernon NJ

NEEF, FREDERICK EMIL, surgeon; b. Springfield, Ill., July 11, 1872; s. Emil and Caroline (Armbruster) N.; B.S., Notre Dame U., 1892, B.L., 1893, M.L., 1895; M.D., Columbia, 1904; m. Kathryn M.E. Brandt, Oct. 11, 1912; children—Kathryn Marie Caroline, Frederick Emil, Dorothy Eileen, Alice Hopeful. Began practice at New York, 1907; served as jr. surgeon, Lincoln Hosp., attending surgeon, St. Elizabeth's Hosp. and N.Y. City Cancer Inst.; taught at Fordham U., 13 years, dean, dept. of gynecology and obstetrics, 1919-21; post grad. teacher, N.Y. City Cancer Inst., dir. gynecology, Misericordia Hosp. since 1935; cons. in gynecology, Lenox Hill, Rockaway Beach and St. Francis hosps. Fellow Am. Coll. Surgeons; mem. Clin. Soc., German Med. Soc. Republican. Author: Practical Points in Anesthesia, 1908; Guiding Principles in Surgical Practice, 1914; Surgical Nursing, 1933, Contbr. to med. jours. Home: Smithridge Rd., Lewisboro, N.Y. Office: 1070 Park Av., NYC 28

NEEL, WILLIAM D., physician; b. Union Co., Ky., Aug. 25, 1851; s. Solomon K. and Mary Isabelle (Bell) N.; ed. high sch., Corydon, Ky.; grad. med. dept. Univ. of Louisville, 1879; m. Mary K. Willett. Pathologist and specialist on diseases of the lungs; writer on consumption, demonstrating that lack of oxygen in the blood creates necessary conditions for attack by the tubercle bacilli and other disease germs. Invented electrical method of oxydizing the blood and creating an inhalent of turpene, camphoric peroxide, by the action of ozone upon volatile oils. Residence: Hotel Vendome. Office: Baltimore Bldg., Chicago.

NEF, JOHN ULRIC, chemist; b. Herisau, Canton Appenzell, Switzerland, June 14, 1862; s. John Ulric and Anna Katharine (Mock) N.; A.B., Harvard, 1884; Kirkland fellow, Harvard, 1884-87; Ph.D., U. of Munich, 1886; m. Louise Bates Comstock, May 17, 1898 (died 1909). Prof. chemistry and dir. chem. lab., Purdue, 1887-89; asst. prof. chemistry and acting head chem. lab., Clark U., 1889-92; prof. chemistry, 1892-96; head of dept., 1896—, U. of Chicago. Fellow Am. Acad. Arts and Sciences. Home: Chicago, Ill. Died Aug. 13, 1915.

NEFF, ELMER HARTSHORN, mech. engr.; b. Clio, Mich., Mar. 6, 1866; s. Henry Clinton and Emily (Hartshorn) Neff; B.S. in Mechanical Engring., University of Michigan, 1890, M.E., 1901, awarded citation, 1941; m. Isabella Cottrell, June 28, 1894; 1 dau., Dorothy Isabel (wife of Prof. Walter Andrew Curry). Erecting engr., Edw. F. Allis Co., Milwaukee, Wis., 1890-91; designer, Gisholt Machine Co., Madison, Wis., 1891-92; with Westinghouse interests, Pittsburgh, Pa., 1893; instr. in mech. engring., Purdue U.; with Brown & Sharpe Mfg. Co., Providence, R.I., since 1896, mgr. N.Y. Co., 1897-1937. Served as mem. first N.J. State Park, Commn.; mem. Montclair (N.J.) Bd. Edn., 5 yrs. Mem. Essex Co. (N.J.) Republican Com. over 30 yrs.; mem. Upper Montclair Rep. Club. An organizer of Machinery Club (N.Y. City) and of Montclair (N.J.) Soc. Engrs. Mem. S.A.R. Conglist. Mason. Clubs: Commonwealth (Upper Montclair); University of Michigan, Railroad-Machinery (New York). Home: 69 Oakwood Av., Montclair, N.J. Died Jan. 26, 1946.

NEFTEL, WILLIAM B., physician; b. Riga, Russia, Sept. 22, 1830; thorough classical and math. edn.; grad. from coll. with honors, 1847; studied in med. dept. Univ. of St. Petersburg, 1847-52; received degree M.D., and one of the 3 medals awarded for spl. proficiency; m. Nadine, Princess of Georgia, g.d. of late King George XIII. Apptd. surgeon Mil. Hosp., St. Petersburg, and asst. to chair of surgery; surgeon to Imperial Guards in Crimean Campaign; scientific mem. of an expdn. to Central Asia, 1857; promoted to rank of Hofrath and sent by govt., 1859, for further studies and researches to France, Germany and England; settled in U.S., 1865. Fellow and corr. mem. of various med. and scientific socs. Author of original contributions to neuro-pathology, electro-therapy and electro-surgery, published in America and Europe, among others: On American Nervousness; Periodical Melancholia; Nervous Diseases of Women; Electrolytic Treatment of Malignant and Non-Malignant Tumors. Address: 16 E. 48th St., New York.

NEGUS, SIDNEY STEVENS, (ne'gus), univ. prof.; b. Dudley, Mass., Jan. 31, 1892; s. Joseph William and Mary M. (Ring) Negus; Study in Germany, 1911; A.B., Clark University, 1913; M.A., Harvard, 1917; Ph.D., Johns Hopkins University 1923; m. Dorothy May Watson, March 21, 1925; children—Dorothy Ann (Mrs. Kenneth Gray Gentil), Sidney Stevens. Instructor in science, The Mercersbury (Pa.) Acad., 1913-15; assistant in organic chemistry, Harvard, 1915-17; head department chemistry, The Mercersburg Academy 1917-21; assistant in analytical chemistry, Johns Hopkins, 1922-23; associate professor, organic chemistry, U. of Richmond (Va.), 1923-26, prof., 1926-27; head dept. of chemistry, Med. Coll. of Va., since 1927, administrator Richmond Area Univ. Center 1947-48. Consultant U.S. Atomic Energy Commission. President Dairy Council of Richmond, Inc.; past pres. Robert E. Lee-Virginia Council, Boy Scouts of America. Received Silver Beaver award, Boy Scouts of Am., 1938. Fellow A.A.A.S. (dir. pub. information); mem. Am. Chem. Soc. (distinguished service award, 1949),

So. Assn. Sci. and Industry, Nat. Assn. Sci. Writers (hon.), Am. Inst. Nutrition, Fedn. Am. Socs. Exptl. Biol., Va. Acad. Sci. (past pres.), Va. State Water Control Bd. (cons.), Virginia State Chamber Commerce (science consultant), Gamma Alpha, Alpha Chi. Sigma, Kappa Sigma, Chi Beta Phi (hon.), Phi Beta Pi, Phi Delta Chi. Presbyn. (elder). Club: Harvard Club of Virginia (past pres.). Contbr., scientific and lay jours. Home: 4102 Wythe Av., Richmond, Va. Died May 17, 1963.

NEHER, FRED, chemist; b. Troy, N.Y., Apr. 30, 1867; s. John Henry and Harriet Vandenberg (Price) N.; A.B., Princeton, 1889, A.M., 1891; fellow U. of Chicago, 1896-98; m. Harriet Hutchins, Sept. 7, 1898; children—John Hutchins, Sara Wadsworth. Chemist, U.S. Fish Commn., 1890; asst. in chemistry, 1891-92, instr., 1892-98, asst. prof. organic chemistry, 1898-1903, prof., 1903—, head of dept., 1903-14, Princeton U. Coöperating with Bur. of Mines in war gases investigation, 1817-18. Home: Princeton, N.J. Died Dec. 10, 1929.

NEHRLING, HENRY, ornithologist, botanist; b. Howard's Grove, Sheboygan County, Wis., May 9, 1853; s. Carl and Elizabeth (Ruge) N.; grad. Teachers' Sem., Addison, Ill., 1873; m. Sophia Schoff, July 20, 1874 (died 1911); children—Lydia, Walter, Bruno, Hildegard (dec.), Hulda, Arno, Werner, Hedwig Else (dec.), Berthold; m. 2d, Mrs. Betty P. Mitchell, June 7, 1916. Deputy collector and insp. customs, Milwaukee, 1887-90; sec. and custodian Pub. Mus., Milwaukee, 1890-1901. Investigator in ornithology, botany, horticulture; specialist in ecology of N.Am. birds; collaborator Bur. Plant Industry, U.S. Dept. Agr.; specialist in ecology of N.Am. birds, also in palms, tropical shade trees, etc. Fellow Am. Ornithologists' Union; mem. Am. Forestry Assn. Author: Die Nordamerikanische Vogelwelt, 1891; Our Native Birds of Song and Beauty (2 vols.), 1893, 1896; Die Amaryllis, 1908. Home: Gotha, Fla. Died Nov. 22, 1929.

NEIFERT, IRA EDWARD, (ni'fert), educator; b. Galesburg, Ill., June 21, 1891; s. Edward and Caroline Catherine (Hechler) N.; B.S., Knox Coll., Galesburg, 1915, M.S., 1916; Ph.D., U. Ia., 1939; student U. Chgo., summers 1917, 31, Cornell, 1928, U. Colo., summers 1923, 25; m. Martha Gordon Campbell, June 15, 1917. Asst. in chemistry Knox Coll., 1916-17, prof. chemistry, 1920—, chmn. dept. chemistry, 1934—, Griffith prof. chemistry on Abbott Found., 1934—; chemistry and gas expert U.S. Dept. Agrl. Bur. Chem., Washington, 1919-20. Served as sgt. C.W.S., Am. U. Expt. Sta., U.S. Army, 1918-19. Fellow A.A.A.S.; mem. Am. Chem. Soc., Am. Assn. U. Profs., Ill. Acad. Sci., Sigma Xi, Alpha Chi Sigma, Omega Beta Pi, Phi Lambda Upsilon, Phi Gamma Delta. Conglist. Mason (32 deg.). Club: Galesburg. Home: 755 N. Kellogg, Galesburg, Ill. Deceased.

NEILER, SAMUEL GRAHAM, (na'ler), elec. and mech. engr.; b. Erie, Pa., Nov. 14, 1866; s. Samuel E. and Lovina (Jackson) N.; spl. student, Mass. Inst. Tech., 1884-86; mech. engring. course, U. of Minn., 1888-89; m. Mary A. Gowdy, May 14, 1901; 1 son, Richard. Asst. mech. engr., M., St.P.&S.S.M. Ry., 1889-90; engr. at Boston office of Thomson-Houston Electric Co., 1891-92; asst. elec. engr., World's Fair, Chicago, 1892-94. Mem. Pierce, Richardson & Neiler, cons. and designing engrs., 1895-1911, pres., 1911-13; mem. Neiler, Rich & Co. since 1913; also mem. firm Fugard, Olsen Urbain & Neiler. Mem. of Internat. Jury of Awards St. Louis Expn., 1904; mem. com. on elect. generation, Century of Progress, Chicago, 1933. Life mem. Am. Inst. of E.E., Am. Soc. M.E., Am. Soc. Heating and Ventilating Engrs.; mem. Franklin Inst., A.A.A.S., Inst. of E.E. of Gt. Britain, Nat. Dist. Heating Assn., Am. Soc. Civil Engrs., The Electric Assn. of Chicago (v.p. and dir.). Republican. Episcopalian. Club: Union League. Home: 737 N. Oak Park Av., Oak Park, Ill. Office: 431 S. Dearborn St., Chicago, Ill.; and 520 N. Michigan Av., Chicago, Ill. Deceased.

NEILL, JAMES MAFFETT, bacteriologist, immunologist; b. Clarion, Pa., July 6, 1894; s. William Alexander and Sarah Dales (Moorhead) N.; B.S., Allegheny Coll., Meadville, Pa., 1917, D.Sc., 1940; Ph.D., Mass. Agrl. Coll., 1920; m. Jessie Stratton, Apr. 4, 1917; children—Ilah Dales (Mrs. Bruno DePaoli), William Alexander Neill. Graduate assistant and instructor in microbiology, Massachusetts Agriculture Coll., 1917-20; asst. Hosp. of Rockefeller Inst. for Med. Research, 1920-24; traveling fellow, Gen. Edn. Bd., 1924-25; asso. prof. bacteriology and immunology, Vanderbilt U. Med. Sch., 1925-26, prof., 1926-31; prof. bacteriology and immunology Cornell Med. Coll., 1931-62, emeritus professor, 1962—. Fellow Am. Assn. Advancement Science, New York Academy Medicine; member Am. Assn. Immunologists, Am. Assn. Pathologists and Bacteriologists, Soc. Am. Bacteriologists, Am. Pub. Health Assn., Soc. Exptl. Biology and Medicine, Harvey Society, New York Academy Science, Sigma Xi, Phi Delta Theta. Republican. Presbyn. Contbr. articles in sci. periodicals. Conductor research in oxidation and reduction of blood pigments and of bacterial hemotoxins; hypersensitiveness and anaphylaxis to diphtheria toxin and bacterial products; serologically reactive substances in sugars and other foods; serol. properties of dextrans and levans of microbiol. origin; immunological relationships between bacteria and fungi; general microbiology. Home: 170 E. Hartsdale Av., Hartsdale, N.Y. Office: 1300 York Av., N.Y.C. 21. Died Sept. 16, 1964; buried Whitehaven Park Meml. Gardens, Cleve.

NEILL, JOHN, surgeon; b. Phila., July 9, 1819; s. Dr. Henry and Martha R. (Duffield) N.; B.A., U. Pa., 1837, M.D., 1840; m. Anna Maria Hollingsworth, Sept. 24, 1844. Demonstrator anatomy Med. Dept., U. Pa., 1845, prof. surgery 1854-59, prof. clin. surgery, 1874-75; surgeon Pa. Hosp., 1852-59; med. dir. 1st U.S. Mil. Hosp., Phila., 1861; med. dir. 1st U.S. Mil. Hosp., Phila., 1861; med. dir. Pa. Militia, 1863; inventor apparatus for the treatment of leg fractures; co-compiler An Analytical Compendium of the Various Branches of Medical Science, 1848. Died Phila., Feb. 11, 1880.

NEILSON, CHARLES HUGH, (nel'sun), univ. dean; b. Berkshire, O., July 19, 1871; s. Arthur Wright and Nellie Alice (Schanck) N.; A.B., Ohio Wesleyan U., 1894; A.M., 1897; Ph.D., Chicago U., 1903; M.D., Rush Med. Coll., 1905; post-grad. work in Germany, 1911; m. Ebba Amelia Anderson, June 11, 1903; children—Arthur Wright, Reka. Asso. prof. physiol. chemistry, St. Louis U., 1904-07, prof., 1907-11, dir. dept. medicine, 1911-24, asso. dean, sch. of medicine, 1928-49; asst. city pathol., 1906; staff, St. Mary's Infirmary, 1907-08, 1912, sec. exec. council, 1939—; chief of staff, Alexian Brothers Hosp., 1909-21; physician St. Louis City Hosp., 1912-35; dir. University staff, 1935—; physician in chief, St. John's Hospital, 1924-50, member council, 1924—; staff St. Mary's Group of Hosps., 1933—; pres. Mo. State Bd. of Health. Certified by Bd. of Internal Medicine. Mem. St. Louis Med. Soc. (past pres.), St. Louis Soc. for Internal Medicine (past pres.), Mo. State Med. Soc., A.M.A., Am. Coll. Physicians, Am. Soc. Biol. Chemists, Am. Therapeutics Soc., Southern Med. Assn., Assn. Am. Med. Colls., Nat. Bd. Med. Examiners, A.A.A.S., Alpha Tau Omega, Phi Rho Sigma, Phi Beta Kappa, Sigma Xi, Alpha Omega Alpha. Presbyterian. Mason. Club: University. Home: 6319 Alexander Dr., Clayton 5, Mo. Office: Humboldt Bldg., St. Louis. Died Aug. 13, 1958.

NEILSON, WILLIAM GEORGE, metallurgical engr.; b. Phila., Aug. 12, 1842; grad. Polytechnic Coll. of Pa., 1862; connected with Elizabethtown forges, 1869-70; Pa. Steel Co., 1870-71; gen. mgr. Logan Iron & Steel Co., 1871-76; mgr. Standard Steel Works, 1877-90; v.p. Wellman Iron and Steel Co., 1890-92; mgr. Taylor Iron and Steel Co., 1893-95; pres. Republic M. and M. Co., 1892-1905, Adirondack Mountain Reserve, 1887-1904; treas. Keystone Drop Forge Wks., 1899-1905. Mem., 1872— (sec. centennial com., 1876, and mem. bd. mgrs., 1886-88), Am. Inst. Mining Engrs. Address: Philadelphia, Pa. Died 1907.

NEL, LOUIS TAYLOR, geologist; b. Wolmaransstad, South Africa, Feb. 24, 1895; s. Paul and Mabel (Taylor) N.; M.Sc. cum laude, U. Stellenbosch, South Africa, 1920, D.Sc., 1927; postgrad. U. Feiburg U. Bonn, 1930; m. Muriel Isabelle Malherbe, Mar. 15, 1932; children—Paul Malherbe, Muriel Mabel (Mrs. J.G.M. Antelme), Louis Hubert Alvin. With Geol. Survey of South Africa, 1920-55, dir., 1948-55, ret., 1955; geol. adviser Atomic Energy Bd. South Africa, 1955-68. Bd. curators Transvaal Mus., 1944-63; mem. mgmt. com. Govt. Metall. Lab., 1948-60; mem. Nat. Com. for Advancement Sci., 1955-62. Recipient Prix Spendiaroff, Internat. Geol. Congress, 1929. Fellow Geol. Soc. London; mem. Geol. Soc. S. Africa (Draper Meml. medal 1943, council 1937-64, pres. 1942), S. African Assn. Advancement Sci. (life), S. African Acad. Sci. and Arts (Havenga prize 1955). Author: The Geology of the Country Around Vredefort, 1927; Geology of the Postmasburg Manganese Deposits, 1929; Geology of the Kierksdorp and Ventersdorp District, 1935; also articles, ofcl. publs. Research on Witwatersrand System, Dredefort Dome, genesis of gold and uranium deposits, resources of nuclear raw materials in S. Africa. Home: Pretoria Republic of South Africa Died June 1968.

NELL, LOUIS, civil engr.; b. Altenkirchen, Germany, Jan. 3, 1842; ed. at Coblenz; grad. Berlin as civ. engr. and surveyor, 1863; m. Elise Pezel, Dec. 27, 1875. Publisher of state maps, New York, 1865; chief topographer, explorations W. of 100th meridian, corps of engrs. U.S.A., 1870; in charge of topog. party, U.S. Geol. Survey, 1884; made Nell's Topog. Map of Colo., 1880, with various revised editions; examiner of surveys, U.S. surveyor-gen.'s office, Denver, since 1893. Home: 2558 W. 32d Av., Denver, Colo.

NELSON, CHARLES DONALD, educator; b. Stratford, Ont., Can., Sept. 16, 1927; s. Albert Ernest and Grace (Mitchell) N.; student Ont. Normal Sch., 1946; B.A. with honours, Queen's U. at Kingston, 1951, M.A., 1952, Ph.D., 1955; m. Frances McEwen, Aug. 22, 1953; children—Nancy, Barbara, Elizabeth, Donald. Tchr. elementary schs., Ottawa, Can., 1946-48; tchr. secondary schs., Ottawa, 1949; research asso. Atomic Energy of Canada, Ltd., Chalk River, Can., 1952; instr. U. Pa., 1953; research officer NRC, Ottawa, 1955-59; asst. prof. Queen's U., Kingston, 1959-60, asso. prof., 1960-65, chmn. dept. biology, 1964-65; prof., head dept. biol. scis. Simon Fraser U., Burnaby, B.C., 1964-68, dean sci., 1965-68. Mem. com. plant sci. NRC, 1966-68. Mem. Acad. Bd. of B.C. Gov., Vancouver Aquarium Assn. Fellow Royal Soc. Can., N.Y. Acad. Sci.; mem. Canadian Soc. Plant Physiologists, Am. Soc. Plant Physiologists. Research in translocation of organic compounds in plants; photosynthesis, primary productivity, and photorespiration; patentee herbicides. Home: Burnaby BC Canada Died June 22, 1968; interred Fife Cemetery Keene Ontario Canada

NELSON, DANIEL THURBER, physician; b. Milford, Mass., Sept. 16, 1839; s. Drake and Lydia Thurber (Pond) N.; A.B., Amherst, 1861, A.M., 1864; M.D., Harvard, 1865; m. Sarah Helen Travis, Nov. 24, 1862. Med. cadet Mason U.S. Gen. Hosp., 1862-65; acting asst. surgeon in armies of James and Potomac, 1865; surgeon Flying Hosp. of 24th Army Corps at surrender of Gen. Lee; practiced, Chicago, 1865—; prof. physiology and histology, Chicago Med. Coll., 1866-79; prof. clin. gynecology, Rush Med. Coll., 1880-98; inventor of several surgical instruments. Del. Internat. Med. Congress, London, 1881, Washington, 1887, Berlin, 1890. Address: Chicago, Ill. Died July 19, 1923.

NELSON, EDWARD WILLIAM, naturalist; b. Manchester, N.H., May 8, 1855; s. William and Nancy M. (Wells) N.; grad. Cook County Normal School, Chicago, 1875; hon. A.M., Yale, 1920; hon. Sc.D., George Washington U., 1920; unmarried. Scientific explorations in Alaska, 1877-81; naturalist of the U.S. revenue steamer Corwin during her cruise on the Arctic search expdn. for the Jeannette in 1881; with Bur. Biol. Survey, Dept. of Agr., 1890-1929, chief field naturalist, 1907-12, in charge of biol. investigations, 1913-14, asst. chief, 1914-16, chief, 1916-27, prin. biologist, 1927-29; engaged in research, 1929-31; research asso., Smithsonian Institution, 1930—. Mem. Death Valley expdn. (Dept. of Agriculture), 1890-91; a large part of time from 1892-1906 was passed in zoöl. and bot. explorations in Mexico. Fellow Am. Ornithologists' Union (pres. 1908-09); pres. Biol. Soc. Washington, 1912-13; mem. Washington Acad. Sciences; corr. mem. Soc. Natural History of Mex.; v.p. Am. Soc. Mammalogy, 1918-19, pres. 1920-23; hon. mem. Calif. Acad. Sciences, Cooper Ornithological Club. Author: Report on Natural History Collections Made in Alaska, 1887. Also numerous monographs. Home: Orosi, Calif. Died May 19, 1934.

NELSON, ELMER MARTIN, biochemist, govt. ofcl.; b. Clark, S.D., July 5, 1892; s. Eric and Adelina (Hanson) N.; B.S., U. Wis., 1918, M.S., 1919, Ph.D., 1923; m. Mariana Theresa Sell, June 19, 1923; children—Donald Sell, Edith Adeline (Mrs. Milton D. Clark). Faculty mem. dept. biochemistry U. Wis., 1920-25; dir. chemistry and nutrition Soft Wheat Millers Assn., Nashville, 1925-26; research nutrition Bur. Chemistry and Soils, Dept. Agr., 1928-35; chief vitamin div. Food and Drug Adminstrn., 1935-49, dir. div. nutrition since 1949. Del. Internat. Vitamin Conf. under League of Nations, 1934; mem. expert com. vitamin standardization WHO, 1949; mem. sci. adv. com. Nutrition Found., Inc.; mem. Nat. Research Council adv. com. on food for Q.M. Army. Served as pvt. M.C., U.S. Army, 1918. Recipient Am. Grocery Mfrs. award, 1949; Babcock-Hart award, 1957. Mem. Am. Chem. Soc., A.A.A.S., Am. Inst. Nutrition, Am. Soc. Biol. Chemists, Food and Nutrition Bd. NRC, A.M.A. (council on drugs), Vitamin Adv. Bd. U.S. Pharmacopeia, Sigma Xi, Alpha Zeta, Phi Lambda Upsilon, Sigma Phi Epsilon. Home: 300 N. Fillmore St., Arlington 1, Va. Office: Food and Drug Administration, Washington 25. Died Dec. 24, 1958; buried Fort Lincoln Cemetery, Washington.

NELSON, ELNATHAN KEMPER, chemist; b. Cincinnati. Nov. 25, 1870; s. Henry Francis and Maria Louisa (Davis) N.; B.S. in chemistry, U. of Illinois, 1894; m. Tuley C. Wetzel, Apr. 29, 1903; children—Elnathan Kemper, Berkeley Everett; m. 2d, Blanche Kennon Parker, Nov. 17, 1931. Served as chief chemist, Swift & Co., Chicago, 1895-1902; with Joslin, Schmidt & Co., chem. engrs., Cincinnati, 1902-03; chemist, Nelson Morris & Co., Chicago, 1903-04; in business on own account, 1904-07; asst. chemist, 1908-12, chief essential oils lab., drug div., 1912-27, sr. chemist div. of food research, 1927—, United States Bureau of Chemistry and Soils. Researches on composition of essential oils and chem. constitution of their constituents, also analytical work on oils and pharm. preparations containing them, and their derivatives, etc. Presbyn. Home: Silver Spring, Md. Died Nov. 9, 1940.

NELSON, JULIUS, biologist; b. Copenhagen, Denmark, Mar. 6, 1858; s. Christian and Julie Marie Pauline (Jorgensen) N.; B.S., U. of Wis., 1881, M.S., 1883; Ph.D., Johns Hopkins, 1888; m. Nellie Cynthia Chase, Aug. 9, 1888. Prof. biology, Rutgers Coll., and biologist, N.J. Agr. Coll. Expt. Sta., 1888—. Biologist, N.J. Expt. Sta., investigating oyster culture, 1888-92, bovine tuberculosis, 1893-1901; biologist, N.J. State Tuberculosis Commn., 1894-95; biologist under spl. act of N.J. Legislature, 1901, renewed 1907; coöperating with chief, Bur. of Shell Fisheries, N.J., 1911—; v.p. and consulting adviser, Lederle Labs., New York, 1910-11. Mem. Highland Park (N.J.) Bd. Edn. 3 terms (resigned). Pres. N.J. State Micros. Soc. Contbr. to Chandler's Cyclo., Bailey's Encyclo. of Agr. Address: New Brunswick, N.J. Died Feb. 16, 1916.

NELSON, MARTIN, agronomist; b. Crawford County, Wis., Dec. 12, 1871; s. Erik and Christene (Oleson) N.; grad. State Normal Sch., Stevens Point, Wis., 1900; B.S., University of Wisconsin, 1905, M.S., 1906; LL.D., (hon.) U. of Arkansas, 1945; m. Maude Agnes Farnham, Jan. 22, 1910; children—Helen Christine, Isabel May. Teacher pub. schs., Vernon County, Wis., 1896-97; prin. Star Lake (Wis.) High Sch., 1900-02; adj. prof. agronomy, 1906-07, asso. prof., 1907-08, Coll. of Agr. and Expt. Sta., Univ. of Neb.; prof. agronomy, 1908-13, dean and dir., 1913-20, vice dean and dir. Coll. of Agr. and Agrl. Expt. Sta., vice dean and head dept. agronomy, 1920-41; prof. emeritus since 1941, U. of Arkansas. Presbyterian. Mem. Am. Soc. Agronomy, Am. Genetic Assn., A.A.A.S., Alpha Zeta, Pi Gamma Mu. Home: Fayetteville AR

NELSON, THURLOW C(HRISTIAN), prof. zoology; b. Highland Park, N.J., Sept. 22, 1890; s. Julius and Nellie Cynthia (Chase) N.; ed. Rutgers Prep. Sch., 1897-1909; B.S., Rutgers U., 1913, hon. D.Sc., 1939; Ph.D., U. of Wis., 1917; student London Sch. of Tropical Medicine, 1931; m. Dorothy Lewis, April 5, 1921; children—Thurlow Christian, Edwin Lewis, John Eric, Marjory. Grad. asst. and fellow in zoology, U. of Wis., 1913-17; asst. biologist, N.J. Oyster Research Lab., 1916-17; biologist Oyster Research Lab. of N.J. Agrl. Expt. Sta., since 1919; asst. prof. zoology, Rutgers U., 1919-22, asso. prof., 1923-25, chmn. dept. 1925-54, prof., 1926-56, on permanent leave as Julius Nelson, professor zoology; research specialist N.J. Division Shell Fisheries; biologist N.J. State Bd. of Shell-fisheries, Trenton, since 1920; in charge N.J. Oyster Research Lab. (started by his father, 1888), 1916-50, research prof. since 1950. Served as private to sergeant 1st class, Medical Dept., A.U.S., 1917-18; 1st lt., San. Corps., 1918-19. Chmn. Water Policy and Supply Council N.J., 1945—, commr., 1929—. Received Rutgers award, medal "Distinguished Scientist and Gifted Teacher," Rutgers Alumni Federation award, 1958. Trustee Bermuda Biol. Lab. Asso. Trustee U. of Pa. Mem. Am. Soc. Zoologists (treas. 1939-41), Am. Micros. Soc., Soc. Parasitologists, Ecol. Soc. of Am., Am. Soc. Limnology & Oceanography, (pres. 1953-54). Am. Soc. Naturalists, Soc. Exptl. Biology and Medicine, Nat. Shellfisheries Assn., (pres. 1931-33), Phi Beta Kappa, Gamma Alpha, Sigma Xi, Phi Sigma. Club: Rutgers University Outing (New Brunswick, N.J.). Contbr. articles on oyster and marine biology, water supply, erosion, etc. Home: 8 N. Main St., Cape May Court House, N.J. Died Sept. 12, 1960.

NELSON, WARREN OTTO, med. dir.; b. Moline, Ill., Apr. 16, 1906; s. Otto G. and Clara F. (Krone) N.; A.B., Augustana Coll., Rock Island, Ill., 1928; M.S., U. Ia., 1929; Ph.D., N.Y.U., 1931; NRC fellow U. Chgo., 1931-33; M.D. (hon.), Giessen U. (Germany), 1957; m. Caroline L. Kramer, July 23, 1931; 1 d., Jeannine. Lab. asst. Augustana Coll., 1925-28, U. Ia., 1928-29; instr. N.Y.U., 1929-31; asst. prof. anatomy U. Mo., 1933-34, Yale, 1934-36; prof. anatomy and chmn. div. basic med. scis., Wayne U., Detroit, 1936-44; prof. anatomy U. Ia., 1944-54; med. dir. Population Council, Inc., Rockfeller Inst., N.Y.C., 1954—; prof. anatomy, endocrinology Inst. Exptl. Pathology, Albany (N.Y.) Med. Sch., 1964. Cons. USPHS, 1951—; spl. research work Parke, Davis & Co., Detroit, summers 1933, 34; guest investigator Cold Spring Harbor Biol. Lab. summers 1937, 38; Baconian lectr. U. Ia. Centennial, 1947. Examiner in anatomy and pathology Basic Sci. Bd., State Mich., 1938-44. Am. rep. Internat. Congress on Lactation, Strasburg, France, 1950; conferee CIBA Found. Conf. on Pituitary Gland, London, 1951; European lect. tour, 1953; U.S. rep. Pan Am. Congress on Endocrinology, 1954; conferee Internat. Planned Parenthood Congress, 1955. Recipient Am. Urol. Assn. prize award, 1952, Amory award, 1955, Lasker award, 1956. Hon. mem. Royal Soc. Medicine, Argentinian Endocrine Soc., Endocrine Soc. Haiti; mem. Endocrine Soc. (chmn. com. on awards, 1947-49, chmn. publs. bd., 1948-54, pres. 1955-56), Am. Soc. Study Sterility (dir. 1955—), Am. Assn. Anatomists, Am. Soc. Physiologists, Histochem. Soc., Am. Cancer Soc., Am. Soc. for Cancer Research, Soc. for Exptl. Biology and Medicine, A.A.A.S., Johnson County Med. Soc., Sigma Xi, Triangle Club. Lectr. numerous postgrad. courses. Contbr. articles on endocrinology and physiology of reproduction. Specialist in physiology of endocrine glands. Died Oct. 19, 1964.

NELSON, WOLFRED, physician, author; b. Montreal, P.Q., Can., Apr. 9, 1846; s. Dr. Horace and Cornelia B. (MacNeil) N.; g.s. late Dr. Wolfred N., the Canadian rebel of 1837; ed. McGill U. in faculties of science, arts, and medicine, M.D., 1872; C.M., M.D., Bishop's Coll., Lennoxville, Que., 1872; mem. Coll. Phys. and Surg. P.Q., 1876; m. Frederika W., d. James de Long, Apr. 27, 1875. Practiced at Panama, Colombia, 1880-85; traveled in Central and S. America, Mexico and W.I., collecting data in climatology and tropical diseases, 1885-88; in practice at New York, 1890—; sanitary commr. to Cuba for New York Herald, 1904, 05. Non-resident representative fellow McGill U. for U.S.; a founder of Canadian Soc. of New York, 1897, an incorporator, 1910, 2d pres., 1898-99; dir. Calvary Chapter No. 283, Brotherhood of St. Andrew, New York; a founder and pres. New York Graduates' Soc. of McGill U., 1895. Apptd. by Queen Regent of Spain, a commr. in ordinary Royal Order of Isabella the Catholic. Author: Apercu de Quelques Difficultés à vaincre dans le Construction du Canal de Panama, 1887; Five Years at Panama, 1888, 1891; Cinq Ans. à Panama, Paris, 1890. Address: New York, N.Y. Died Jan. 1913.

NESMITH, JOHN, realtor, mfr., inventor; b. Londonderry, N.H., Aug. 3, 1793; s. John and Lucy (Martin) N.; m. Mary Ann Bell, June 1825; m. 2d, Eliza Thorn Bell, 1831; m. 3d, Harriet Rebecca Mansur, Oct. 1840; 9 children. Real estate dealer, Lowell, Mass., 1831; inventor machines for shawl fringing, weaving wire fences; a founder Lawrence, Mass.; mem. N.H. Legislature, 1 term; lt. gov. Mass., 1862; presdl. elector Republican party, 1860, 64; collector internal revenue Mass., 1863-69; v.p. Mass. State Temperance Soc. Died Lowell, Mass., Oct. 15, 1869.

NETTLETON, EDWIN S., civil and irrigation engr.; b. Medina, O., Oct. 22, 1831; s. Lewis Baldwin and Julia (Baldwin) N.; attended Oberlin (O.) Coll., 1853-54; m. Lucy F. Grosvenor, Oct. 17, 1861, 4 children. Engr. of Union or Greeley colony on its way to Colo., 1870; surveyed present site of Greeley (Colo.), laid out irrigation ditches (46 miles along) used by farmers; built for Larimer and Weld Canal between Ft. Collins and Greeley Colo. Mortgage and Investment Co. (also known as English co.); surveyed sites of Colorado Springs, 1871, Manitou, 1872, South Pueblo (now Pueblo), 1873; engr. State of Colo., 1883-87; chief engr. in project diverting Yaqui River (Mexico) for irrigation purposes; U.S. cons. engr., 1889-93; a founder, one of 1st trustees Colo. Coll., Colorado Springs; established weather bur. on Pike's Peak, Colo. Died Denver, Apr. 22, 1901; buried Forest Hill Cemetery, Kansas City, Mo.

NEUBERG, CARL ALEXANDER, research prof.; b. Hanover, Germany, July 29, 1877; s. Julius Alexander and Alma (Niemann) N.; Ph.D., U. Berlin, 1900; student U. of Wurzburg, 1897-98; Dr. Medicine, U. Breslau, 1922; Dr. of Biology, U. Petersburg, 1925; Dr. of Engring., Danzig, 1929; Dr. Med. Chem., U. of Palermo, 1933; LL.D., St. Andrews U., Eng., 1934; Dr. Agr., U. of Milano, Italy, 1949; m. Hela Franzisca Lewinski, May 21, 1907; children—Irene Stephanie, Alma Marian. Began as asst. Path. Inst., U. Berlin, 1898, teacher, 1903-06, prof.-by-name 1906-16, prof., 1916-19, full prof., 1919-38; also full prof. Agrl. Acad. of Berlin, 1920; dir. Kaiser Wilhelm Inst. of Biochemistry and Exptl. Therapy, 1913-38; research prof. N.Y.U., 1941-50; vis. prof. Poly. Inst. Bklyn.; also research asso. prof. New York Med. College since 1951. Awarded Emil Fischer medal Assn. German Chemists; Scheele medal Soc. Swedish Chemists; Berzelius medal Swedish Med. Soc., Delbrück medal Agrl. Acad. of Berlin; Leblanc medal Société Chimique de France; Pasteur medal Société de Biochimie de France. Rep. of Germany at Institut International d'Agriculture à Rome, 1927-35; Neuberg Medal; v.p. or dept. pres. Internat. Congress for Bacteriology, Microbiology and Biochemistry, London, New York, Paris and Washington, 1937, 38, 39. Fellow N.Y. Acad. Sci.; mem. or hon. mem. acads. of sciences in Göttingen, Halle, Helsingfors, Copenhagen, Lisbon, Lund, Petersburg, Amsterdam, and Uppsala; Agrl. Acad. in Prague; mem. acads. in Barcelona and Rome; socs. of physicians in Budapest, Charkow, Moscow and Vienna. Home: 536 W. 113th St., N.Y.C. 25. Died June 1956.

NEUMANN, FRANK, seismologist; b. Balt., Feb. 11, 1892; s. Conrad Otto and Sophia (Ackerman) N.; student Balt. Poly. Inst., 1910; m. Pearl Mary Power, July 25, 1925; 1 dau., Pearl Marie. Geomagnetic field and office work U.S. Coast and Geodetic Survey, 1911-25, chief seismologist on ofcl. transfer of seismol. function, Washington, 1925-48, chief seismology br. 1948-53. Dir. seismograph sta. U. Wash. 1953—. Mem. Internat. Seismol. Assn., Earthquake Engring. Research Inst., Seismol. Soc. Am., Am. Geophys. Union, Geol. Soc. Am., Washington Acad., Sigma Xi. Author U.S. Coast and Geodetic Survey publs. in seismology and monographs on seismol. investigations; U. Wash. monographs on Wash. earthquakes and engring. seismol. research. Home: 4546 45th Av. N.E. Office: Geology Dept. U. Wash. Seattle 5. Died May 22, 1964.

NEUTRA, RICHARD JOSEPH, architect; b. Vienna, Austria, Apr. 8, 1892; s. Samuel and Elizabeth (Glaser) N.; grad. Poly Coll., U. of Vienna; diploma with distinction, U. of Zurich, Switzerland, 1918; honorary Doctor's Degree univs. of Graz and Berlin; D.F.A. (hon.), Adelphi University, 1963; hon. doctorate U. of Rome, 1965, U. Cal., Los Angeles, 1969; m. Dione Niedermann, December 22, 1923; children—Frank Lucian, Dion, Raymond Richard. Came to U.S., 1923, naturalized, 1929. Began as architect, city planner, Switzerland, 1919-23; asso. with Holabird & Root, Frank Lloyd Wright, 1923-25; own practice, Los Angeles, 1926-66; mem. Richard and Dion Neutra, Architects and Assos., 1966-70; cons. Richard J. Neutra Insts., Cal., Switzerland. Designed and built large and small dwellings, many office bldgs., open air schs.; universities in U.S.A., East and West Pakistan; architect for resident centers for National Youth Administration, 1940-41; 5 pub. housing projects, 1939-41. Channel Heights, 160 acres postwar housing project with full traffic segregation, 1943; housing project in Spain, Germany, Italy. Lectr. Harvard, Princeton, Columbia, other colls. U.S., Mexico, Japan, Switzerland, Belgium, and many other countries; recent work includes: Mathematics Park, Princeton, Benmore Gardens Housing Project, Johannesburg, S. Africa, U. Pa. Grad. Student Housing, Orange County Courthouse, Santa Ana, Cal., Roberson Meml. Cultural Center, Binghamton, N.Y.; consultant, National Youth Adminstrn., U.S. Housing Authority, Fed. Works Agy., Fed. Pub. Housing Authority, 10 year devel. plan for Guam; redevel. plans for Sacramento and Tulsa; chmn. Cal. Planning Bd. Mem. Calif. Bd. Examiners, Architect and consultant for hosps., schs., Govt. of Puerto Rico. Recipient over 50 1st and 2d prizes in competitions for projects and executed comml. and residential designs. Awards from World Expn., Paris 1938, Hall of Fame, N.Y. World's Fair, 1940; German Great Cross of Merit; God medal Ethiopia; hon. ring City of Vienna; award of excellence Am. Institute Steel Construction, 1962. Member advisory board for schoolhouse planning U.S. Dept. of Edn. American International Congress for Modern Architecture; special consultant to government of Austria, 1969; mem. adv. bd. Los Angeles Internat. Design Center; mem. Joint A.I.A.-A.M.A. Com. on Environmental Health; mem. archtl. rev. and adv. panel U.S. Navy. Benjamin Franklin fellow Royal Soc. Arts, London. Fellow A.I.A. (residential honor award 1954), Sociedad Central de Arquitectos Argentina (hon.); hon. mem. Academia de Belle Arti de Venzia, Academia Lucca, Assn. Mexican Architects. Assn. of Cuban and of Bolivian architects, Royal Inst. British Architects, Society of German Architects (hon. pres. 1969); member of French Acad. of Architecture, N.A.D., Nat. Inst. Arts and Letters, Assn. Argentinian (hon.), Assn. Peruvian Architects (hon. mem.). Author: How America Builds, 1926; America New Building in the World, 1929; Mystery and Realities of the Site, 1951; Buildings &Projects, 1952, vol. 2, 1959, vol. 3, 1961-66; Therapy by Design, published 1965; Naturnahes Bauen, 1970; co-author Preface to a Master Plan, 1941; New Architecture and City Planning; Architecture of Social Concern (Portuguese and English), 1949; Survival through Design, 1954; World and Dwelling, 1962; Life and Shape, 1962; Life and Human Habitat, Spl. Neutra edition of French mag. L'Architecture d'Aujourd'hui. Principal several feature mag. stories. Home: Los Angeles CA Died Apr. 16, 1970.

NEVILLE, DONALD WESTON, civil engr.; b. Lawrence, Mass., Mar. 11, 1912; s. George Duncan and Alice (Weston) N.; student Clark Sch., Hanover, N.H., 1932, Colgate U., 1936; m. Dorothy Price, July 13, 1935; children—Patrick Richard, Susan Alice. Constrn. engr. United Engrs. & Constructors, Phila., 1934-35, TVA, 1935-38. Stone & Webster, 1938; engring. in field, advancing to dist. mgr., vice president director F. H. McGraw & Co., Chgo., 1939-59, sr. v.p., dir. 1959; pres., dir. McGraw Terminals, Inc., Burnside, La., 1957-59; pres. D. W. Neville & Assos., Chgo., 1960-62, Edward Gray Corp., Chgo., 1962—; chmn. bd. Great Lakes Supply Corp., Chgo. Clubs: Union League, Chicago Athletic Assn. (Chgo.); Evanston (Ill.) Golf; Alta (Salt Lake City); Bull Valley Hunt (Woodstock, Ill.). Home: Skokie IL Died Mar. 26, 1971.

NEWBERRY, JOHN STRONG, geologist; b. Windsor, Conn., Dec. 22, 1822; s. Henry and Elizabeth (Strong) N.; grad. Western Res. Coll., 1846, LL.D. (hon.), 1867; grad. Cleve. Med. Sch., 1848; m. Sarah Brownell Gaylord, Oct. 22, 1848, 6 children. Asst. surgeon, geologist on expdn. from San Francisco Bay to Columbia River, May 1855; prof. geology Columbian U. (now George Washington U.), 1856-57; physician, naturalist on mil. exploration expdn. of Colorado River, 1857-58; an organizer, prof. geology and paleontology Sch. of Mines, Columbia, 1866, pres. A.A.A.S., 1862; geologist State of Ohio, 1869-74; incorporator, mem. Nat. Acad. Scis.; recipient Murchison medal Geol. Soc. of London, 1888; v.p. Internat. Geol. Congress, 1891. Author: Report on the Colorado River of the West, Explored (1857-58), 1861; Report of the Exploring Expedition from Santa Fe to the Junction of the Grand and Green Rivers, 1876. Died New Haven, Conn., Dec. 7, 1892.

NEWBERRY, WILLIAM BELKNAP, chemist; b. Cleveland, O., Jan. 15, 1867; Ph.B., Sheffield Scientific School, Yale, 1889. Instr. chemistry Cornell, 1889-93; chemist Sandusky (O.) Portland Cement Co., 1893-96; chemist Alpha Portland Cement Co., Easton, Pa., 1896-97, and mgr. since 1897. Author: (with his brother, S. B. Newberry) Chemical Constitution of Portland Cement. Address: Easton, Pa.

NEWCOMB, JOHN LLOYD, univ. pres.; b. Sassafras, Va., Dec. 18, 1881; s. Benjamin Carey and Martha Jane (Coleman) N.; A.B., Coll. of William and Mary, 1900, LL.D., 1935; C.E., U. Va., 1903; D.Sc., Washington and Lee U., 1933; LL.D., George Washington U., 1934, Duke, 1935; m. Mrs. Grace Shields Russell, Oct. 24, 1924 (dec. Oct. 10, 1941). Began as computer in engineer's office Rapid Transit Subway Construction Co., N.Y.C., summer 1902; asst. engr. on location and constrn. Norfolk & Southern R.R. Co., 1903-04, div. engr. maintenance of way, 1904-05; adj. prof. civil engring. U. Va., 1905, asso. prof., 1907, prof., 1910-33, dean dept. of engring., 1925-33, asst. to pres., 1926-31, acting pres., 1931-33, pres., 1933-47, ret. Pres. Nat. Assn. State Univs., 1943-44. Mem. Spl. Com. on

Aeronaut. Research in Ednl. instns.; mem. bd. trustees Carnegie Foundation for Advancement of Teaching; mem. bd. of visitors U.S. Naval Acad.; mem. wartime commn. Office of Edn.; mem. divisonal com. on state and local sch. administrn., Office of Edn.; mem. bd. trustees Va. War Fund; pres. Nat. Assn. State Univs., 1934-44. Am. Asso. for United Nations, Inc., 1945-46. Supervisor Sect. B, S.A.T.C., U. Va., May-Dec. 1918. Mem. Soc. for Promotion Engrng. Edn., Am. Assn. U. Profs., N.Y. Southern Soc., Soc. of Virginians, Newcomen Soc., Pi Kappa Alpha, Sigma Beta Pi, Phi Beta Kappa, Tau Beta Pi. Democrat. Episcopalian. Club: Colonnade. Home: 132 Bollingwood Rd., Charlottesville, Va. Died Feb. 22, 1954; buried U. Va. Cemetery, Charlottesville.

NEWCOMB, SIMON, astronomer; b. Wallace, N.S., Mar. 12, 1835; s. John Burton and Emily (Prince) N.; ed. by his father; came to U.S., 1853; teacher in Md., 1854-56; computor on Nautical Almanac, 1857; grad. Lawrence Scientific Sch., Harvard, B.S., 1858; hon. LL.D., Columbian, 1874, Yale, 1875, Harvard, 1884, Columbia, 1887, Edinburgh, 1891, Glasgow, 1896, Princeton, 1896, Cracow, 1900, Johns Hopkins, 1902, Toronto, 1904; Sc.D., Heidelberg, 1886, Padua, 1892, Dublin, 1892, Cambridge, 1896; Doctor of Mathematics, Christiania, 1902; D.C.L., Oxford, 1899; Master of Mathematics and Doctor of Natural Philosophy, Leyden, 1875; m. Mary Caroline, d. Dr. Charles A. Hassler, U.S.N., and g.d. of the founder of the Coast Survey, Aug. 4, 1863. Apptd., 1861, prof. mathematics, U.S.N.; assigned to duty as U.S. Naval Observatory; negotiated contract for and supervised construction of 26-inch equatorial telescope; sec. U.S. Transit of Venus Commn., 1871-74; observed transit of Venus at Cape of Good Hope, 1882. Dir. Nautical Almanac Office, 1877-97; retired 1897. Made many astron. researches, given to the world in over 300 papers; prof. mathematics and astronomy, Johns Hopkins, 1884-94, and editor Am. Jour. Mathematics, 1874—, correspondent, and 1893—, one of the 8 foreign associates, Institute of France (first native American since Franklin to be so honored); made Officer of Legion of Honor of France, 1893, Comdr., 1907; Knight of the Prussain Order of Merit for Science and Art, 1906 (receiving spl. authority from U.S. Congress to accept these honors); mem., 1869—, v.p., 1883-89, later foreign sec. Nat. Acad. Sciences; pres. Soc. for Psychical Research, 1885-86; pres. A.A.A.S., 1877, of Am. Math. Soc., 1897-98, of Astron. and Astrophys. Soc. of America, 1899, 1905; pres. Internat. Congress of Arts and Sciences at La. Purchase Expn., 1904; honorary or corr. mem. of every scientific, astron. or math. soc. of 1st rank in the world. Received Royal Astron. Soc. gold medal, 1874, Huygens gold medal, Dutch Soc. of Sciences, 1878, Royal Soc. gold medal, 1890; Bruce medal, Astron. Soc. of Pacific, 1898, Schubert prize (Russia), and Sylvester prize (Johns Hopkins Univ.). Author: The Stars, 1901; Astronomy for Everybody, 1903; Reminiscences of an Astronomer, 1903; Spherical Astronomy, 1906; Side Lights on Astronomy, 1906; also various other books on astron. and econ. topics, mag. articles, etc. Published the tables of the motions of the stars, the planets and the moon now used by astronomers in their computations and as the basis of the navigation of the vessels of the world. Address: Washington, D.C. Died 1909.

NEWCOMBE, FREDERICK CHARLES, botanist; b. Flint, Mich., May 11, 1858; s. Thomas and Eliza (Gayton) N.; B.S., U. of Mich., 1890; Ph.D., U. of Leipzig, 1893; m. Susan Eastman, June 25, 1884. Teacher Mich. Sch. for Deaf, 1880-87; instr. botany, 1890-92, asst. prof., 1893-97, jr. prof., 1897-1905, prof., 1905-23, U. of Mich., later emeritus. Fellow A.A.A.S. (v.p. Sect. G, 1910); mem. Bot. Soc. America (pres. 1917), Botanists of Central States (pres.), Mich. Acad. Science (pres.), Hawaiian Bot. Soc. (pres. 1924), Hawaiian Acad. Science (pres. 1925). Del. Internat. Congress Arts and Sciences, St. Louis, 1904 (sec. sect. plant physiology). Author of many articles describing original researches on plants. Editor-in-chief Am. Jour. of Botany, 1914-18. Home: Honolulu, T.H. Died Oct. 4, 1927.

NEWELL, FREDERICK HAYNES, engineer; b. Bradford, Pa., Mar. 5, 1862; s. Augustus William and Anna M. (Haynes) N.; grad. Mass. Inst. Tech. (mining engr.), 1885; m. Effie Josephine Mackintosh, Apr. 3, 1890; children—Josephine (wife of Prof. James M. O'Gorman), Constance, Roger Sherman (dec.), John Mackintosh. Mining in Colo.; asst. Ohio Geol. Survey; miscellaneous engrng. in Pa., Va., etc.; asst. hydraulic engr. U.S. Geol. Survey, 1888-90, hydrographer, 1890-1902; chief engr., 1902-07, dir., 1907-14, consulting engr., U.S. Reclamation Service, 1914; prof. civil engineering, U. of Ill., 1915-19; pres. Research Service, 1919. Member of U.S. Land Commission, U.S. Inland Waterways Commn., Nat. Advisory Bd. for Fuels and Structural Materials, Giant Power Survey of State of Pa.; engr. mem. Pa. Water and Power Resources Bd. Sec. Nat. Geog. Soc., 1903; mem. Am. Engineers (pres. 1919), Washington Soc. Engrs. (pres. 1907), Washington Acad. Sciences (v.p. 1907). Awarded Cullum gold medal by Am. Geog. Soc. Author: Agriculture by Irrigation, 1894; Hydrography of the Arid Regions, 1891; The Public Lands of the United States, 1895; Irrigation in the United States, 1902; Hawaii, Its Natural Resources, 1909; Principles of Irrigation Engineering, 1913; Irrigation Management, 1916; Engineering as a Career, 1916; Water Resources, Present and Future Uses, 1919; Water Powers of Virginia; Natural Resources of Puerto Rico. Home: Washington, D.C. Died 1932.

NEWELL, JOSEPH SHIPLEY, aero-structural engrng.; b. Springfield, Mass., Aug. 10, 1897; s. Frederick William and Emma Freeman (Shipley) N.; B.S. in Civil Engrng., Mass. Inst. Tech., 1918; m. Lena M. Dwelley, Aug. 29, 1922; children—Joseph Shipley, Naomi, Frederick Dwelley, Charles William. Employed as draftsman Frigorifico Armour, La Plata, Argentina, 1919-20; asst. dept. of civil engrng., Mass. Inst. Tech., 1920-21; asst. engr. structures branch McCook Field, Dayton, O., 1922-26; instr. aero-structural engrng., asst. prof., prof., exec. officer aero-engrng. dept. and sec. of faculty, Mass. Inst. of Tech. since 1927. Mem. exec. com. Column Research Council. Fellow Inst. of Aeronautical Scis.; mem. Sigma Xi. Republican. Author: Airplane Structures (with A. S. Niles); papers in field of aeronautical structures. Home: Trapelo Rd., Lincoln, Mass. Died May 5, 1952; buried Lincoln, Mass.

NEWELL, ROBERT REID, physician; b. Stockton, Cal., Jan. 21, 1892; s. Allan Hovey and Lucy Annette (Reid) N.; M.D., U. Cal., 1916; m. Jeannette Le Valley, Nov. 11, 1922; children—Ann, Allen. Interne U. Cal. Hosp., San Francisco, 1916-17, resident in medicine, 1917-18; asst. Meml. Metabolic Clinic, Santa Barbara, 1919; instr. radiology Stanford, 1920-31, prof. radiology, 1931-57, biophysics, 1948-57, ret.; cons. U.S. Naval Radiol. Def. Lab., 1957-63; mem. Nat. Com. Radiol. Units and Protection, 1930—, Internat. Com. on Radiol. Units and Protection, 1950-53; cons. NRC (visual problems 1942-45, glossary of nuclear energy, 1947-53), Dept. Def. Research and Devel. Bd., 1950-52, USPHS, 1947-52; Am. Standard Assn., VA Hosp. Mem. Unitarian Service Com. Med. Edn. Team for Japan, 1951. Mem. Am. Gerontological Soc., Fedn. Am. Scientists, World Med. Soc., Am. Com. for UN and WHO, Am. Soc. Nuclear Medicine, A.M.A., Radiol. Soc. N.Am., Am. Roentgen Ray Soc., Am. Coll. Radiol. (chmn. com. units and protection, 1947-51, pres., 1951), A.A.A.S., Optical Soc. Am., California Academy of Medicine (president 1939), Institute of Radio Engineers, Radiation Research Soc., Phi Beta Kappa, Alpha Omega Alpha, Sigma Xi. Club: Commonwealth of California (San Francisco). Contbr. chpts. Glasser's Medical Physics, Yearbook, 1944, 50, 60; McLaren's Diagnostic Radiology, 1948, Pillmore's Clinical Radiology, 1946, Buschke's Progress in Radiation Therapy in 1958. Home: 50 Yerba Buena Av., San Francisco 27. Office: U.S. Naval Radiation Defense Lab., Hunters Point, San Francisco. Died Aug. 27, 1965.

NEWELL, WILMON, entomologist; b. Hull, Ia., Mar. 4, 1878; s. William J. and Elizabeth A. (Anderson) N.; B.S., Iowa State Coll., 1897, M.S., same 1899; D.Sc., 1920; D.Sc., Clemson Coll., 1937; m. Helen M., d. Dr. and Mrs. O. P. Mabee, of Galesburg, Ill., Feb. 12, 1907. Asst. entomologist, Ia. Agricultural Expt. Sta., 1897-99, Ohio Agrl. Expt. Sta., 1899-1902; asst. entomologist and apiarist, Tex. Agrl. Expt. Sta., 1902-03; state entomologist of Ga., 1903-04; entomologist, La. Agrl. Expt. Sta. and sec. and entomologist State Crop Pest Commn. of La., 1904-10; entomologist, Tex. Agrl. Expt. Sta. and state entomologist, 1910-15; plant commr. Fla. State Plant Bd. since 1915; dean Coll. of Agr., 1921-38, dir. Expt. Sta. and Agrl. Extension Div., U. of Fla. since 1921, provost for agriculture since 1938; administrator of Florida State Soil Conservation; chmn. Fla. State Land-Use Planning Com. since 1940; chmn. advisory com. on agr., Fla. State Defense Council since 1941. Fellow A.A.A.S.; mem. Entomol. Society of America, Assn. Econ. Entomologists (pres. 1920), Assn. of Southern Agrl. Workers (pres. 1929-30), Soil Science Soc. America, Kappa Sigma, Alpha Zeta, Phi Kappa Phi, Gamma Sigma Delta. Mason (Shriner). Pres. Gainesville Rotary Club, 1920-21. Home: 504 E. Church St., Gainesville, Fla. Died Oct. 25, 1943.

NEWHART, HORACE, otolaryngologist; b. New Ulm, Minn., Dec. 9, 1872; s. Jude and Sarah (Parker) N.; student Carleton Coll., Northfield, Minn., 1891-93; A.B., Dartmouth, 1895; M.D., U. of Mich., 1898; post-grad. work Vienna, 1898-99, 1905, 08, 12; certificate of Am. Board of Otolaryngology, 1925; m. Anne Hendrick, Sept. 4, 1904; 1 son, Ellwood Hendrick. Practiced at Minneapolis, Minn., since 1901; became asso. with U. of Minn., 1912; prof. emeritus, otolaryngology, U. of Minn. Med. Sch.; also same U. of Minn. Graduate School; staff member University, Northwestern, Abbott and St. Barnabas hospitals and Glen Lake Sanatorium; consulting otologist Minneapolis pub. schs., since 1925. Fellow Am. Coll. Surg., Am. Acoustical Soc.; mem. A.M.A., Hennepin County Med. Soc., Am. Otol. Soc. (pres. 1939-40), Am. Laryngol. Assn., Am. Lary- ngol., Rhinol. and Otol. Assn., Am. Acad. Ophthalmology and Otolaryngology (pres. 1924-25), Am. Soc. for the Hard of Hearing (pres. 1927-28), Minneapolis Society for Hard of Hearing (pres. 1925-29), Minn. Acad. Ophthalmology and Otolaryngology, Minn. Acad. Medicine, Phi Beta Kappa, Sigma Chi, Phi Rho Sigma. Clubs: Minneapolis, Minikahda, Lafayette, Campus. Contbr. numerous articles on med. topics, especially on diseases of the ear and the conservation of hearing. Home: 212 W. 22d St. Office: Medical Arts Bldg., Minneapolis 2, Minn. Died July 9, 1945.

NEWHOUSE, WALTER HARRY, geologist; b. Fisher, Pa., Dec. 13, 1897; s. Edward Winfield and Hattie May (Elder) N.; B.S., Pa. State Coll., 1921; M.S., Mass. Inst. Tech., 1923, Ph.D., 1926; m. Grace Edna Brown, June 30, 1923; 1 child, Jan. Mem. staff Mass. Inst. Technology, 1923-46, prof. of econ. geology, 1944-46; chmn. dept. of geology U. Chicago, 1946-57; consulting work various mining companies. Mem. Geol. Soc. of America, Soc. Econ. Geology, Am. Inst. M.E., Can. Inst. Mining Engrs., Am. Acad. Arts and Scis., Ill. State Bd. Natural Resources and Conservation. Soc. Geology de Belgigue, Sigma Xi. Editor: Ore Deposits as Related to Structural Features, 1942. Mem. editorial bd. Jour. Geology. Contbr. articles to sci. jours. Home: Chicago IL Died Sept. 21, 1969.

NEWMAN, ALBERT BROADUS, chem. engr.; b. Toronto, Canada, May 3, 1888 (parents U.S. citizens); son of Albert Henry and Mary (Ware) Newman; A.B., University of Michigan, 1910, B.Ch.E., 1911, M.S., 1926, Ph.D., 1928; grad. student U. of Mich., 1926-27; m. Esther Edwards, Sept. 2, 1911; children—Albert Henry II, Philip Edwards. Asst. chemist Corn Products Refining Co., Edgewater, N.J., 1911-12; instr. chemistry, Pa. State Coll., 1912-13; foreman charge production, Nat. Zinc Co., Kansas City, Mo., 1913-15; supt. chem. mfr., Am. Metal Co., Ltd. (Langeloth, Pa. plant), 1915-17; works mgr., Monsanto Chem. Co., East St. Louis plant, 1918-19; gen. mgr. Thermo Chem. Co., St. Louis, Mo., 1920-25; chem. engr. research div., Gen. Chem. Co., N.Y. City, 1927-28; prof. chem. engr., and in charge dept., Cooper Union, N.Y. City, 1928-38; prof. chem. engrng. and chmn. of dept., Coll. of City New York since 1938; dean of Sch. of Tech., Coll. of City New York, 1941-47; lecturer, chem. engrng., New York U. Grad. Div., 1941-45; consultant in chem. engrng., Northwestern Univ., 1939-41; consultant War Research, Columbia Univ., 1944; chmn. sect. on heat exchange, Chem. Engrng. Congress of World Power Conf., London, June 1936; chmn. bd. dirs. Defense Training Inst. of Engrng. Colls. of Greater New York, 1941-43; mem. com. on engrng. schs. of Engrs. Council for Professional Development, and chmn. Region IV, com. on accrediting, 1938-41; dir. American Inst. of Chem. Engrs., 1936-38 and 1939-41, also chmn. com. chem. engrng. edn., 1937-42; v.p., 1945, 47, pres. 1948; regional adv. Engrng. War Training Program, U.S. Office of Edn. since 1941; regional representative Engrg. War Training Program to War Manpower Commission, 1943-45; chmn. advisory commn. to N.Y. City Hdqrs. Selective Service System, 1943; mem. Labor Supply Com., Office Production Management, for N.Y. State, 1941-42; heading chem. industries under Gen. Lucius D. Clay, U.S. Mil. Govt., Germany, 1945-46; U.S. rep. on quadripartite com. on liquidation of German war potential, Berlin, Mar.-June 1946; member Regional Loyalty Board (N.Y. and N.J.), U.S. Civil Service Commission since 1949. Member of Am. Soc. of Engrng. Edn., Am. Inst. of Chem. Engrs., Am. Chem. Soc., Engrs. Council for Professional Development, Sigma Xi, Phi Lambda Upsilon, Iota Alpha, Tau Beta Pi, Sigma Chi. Club: Chemists (trustee 1940-43). Author numerous publs. on engrng.; contbr. to engrng. jours.; editor papers on engrng. Home: 120 Cabrini Blvd., N.Y.C. 33. Died May 1952.

NEWMAN, HORATIO HACKETT, zoölogist; b. nr. Seale, Ala., Mar. 19, 1875; s. Albert Henry N. and Mary Augusta (Ware) N.; B.A., McMaster U., Toronto, 1896, D.Sc., 1933; spl. student, U. of Toronto, 1896-97; fellow in zoölogy U. Chgo., 1898-1900, 1904-05, Ph.D., 1905; m. Isobel Currie Marshall, 1907; children—Elizabeth Ware, Marshall Thornton; m. 2d, Marie E. Heald, June 5, 1954. Instr. biology and Latin, Des Moines (Ia.) Coll., 1897-98; instr. biology and chemistry Culver (Ind.) Mil. Acad., 1900-04; instr. zoölogy, 1905-08, asst. prof. elect, 1908, U. of Mich., prof. and head dept. zoölogy, U. of Tex., 1908-11; asso. prof. zoölogy and embryology U. Chgo., 1911-17, prof. zoölogy, 1917-40, emeritus since 1940, dean in the Colleges of Science, 1915-22. Head of instrn. force in physiology, Marine Biol. Lab., Woods Hole, Mass., 1909-12. Fellow A.A.A.S.; mem. Am. Soc. Zoölogists, Am. Soc. Naturalists, Sigma Xi, Sigma Chi, Phi Chi. Author: The Biology of Twins, 1917; Vertebrate Zoölogy, 1919; Readings in Evolution, Genetics, and Eugenics, 1921; The Physiology of Twinning, 1923; Outlines of General Zoölogy, 1924; The Gist of Evolution, 1926. Editor, contbr. to The Nature of the World and of Man, 1926; Evolution Yesterday and Today, 1932; Twins—A Study of Heredity and Environment (with F. N. Freeman and K. J. Holzinger), 1937; The Phylum Chordata, 1939; Multiple Human Births, 1940. Home: 173 Devon Dr., Clearwater, Fla. Died Aug. 29, 1957; buried Sylvan Abbey Meml. Park, Clearwater.

NEWMAN, ROBERT, physician; b. Königsberg, Prussia; s. Gustav Lebrecht and Rosalie Jacobine (Molkentin) N.; ed. at gymnasium; engaged in war for liberty, 1849, fighting in barricades; later adj. Batallion Homburg, in the Palatinate. After Liberalists were defeated went to Switzerland; later came to U.S.; grad. Long Island Coll. Hosp., 1863; Bellevue Hosp. Med. Coll., 1869; m. Ada B.K. Blackwell, Oct. 1877. Commissioned 1863, State's vol. surgeon, going to front several times on gov.'s order; has held many dispensary and hosp. apptmts. Mem. Am. Electro-Therapeutic Assn. (pres., 1896, later chmn. exec. council); pres. faculty and prof. N.Y. School of Physical Therapeutics; one of the founders, 1878, and first v.p. Medico-Legal Society. Author: Electricity in Genito-Urinary Diseases; also monographs and papers on electrolysis and electro-therapeutics. Inventor of electrodes for treatment of stricture by electrolysis, and of devices for use in electrotherapy. Address: New York, N.Y. Deceased.

NEWSOM, JOHN FLESHER, mining geologist; b. Elizabethtown, Ind., Sept. 6, 1869; s. Nathan and Mary (Flesher) N.; A.B., Ind. U., 1891; A.M., Leland Stanford Jr. U., 1892; post-grad. student and teacher, Stanford U., 1899-1901, Ph.D., 1901; m. Adelaide Frances Perry, Mar. 17, 1896; 1 son, John Branner. Asst. geologist, Geol. Survey of Ark., 1891-93; structural and stratigraphic work on carboniferous strata of Northern Arkansas, 1891-93; instructor geology, 1895-96, assistant professor 1896-98, Indiana Univ.; in charge geol. field work in Southern Ind., 1896-97; examined phosphate deposits of Ark., 1897-99; studied prin. mining regions of central and western U.S., 1898; asst. prof., 1898, asso. prof. mining, 1901-09, prof., 1909, Leland Stanford Junior U. Engaged in work on geology of Santa Cruz Mountains, Calif., during summers 1901-04; also various professional exams. of mining properties, 1900-09; professional exams. of mining properties in South America, North America and the Orient, 1910-24. Republican. Author: Syllabus of Lectures on Economic Geology, 1895. Home: Palo Alto, Calif. Died Oct. 24, 1928.

NEWTON, HENRY JOTHAM, inventor, mfr.; b. Hartleton, Pa., Feb. 9, 1823; s. Sr. Jotham and Harriet (Wood) N.; m. Mary Gates, 1850, 3 children. Partner piano firm Lights, Newton & Bradbury, 1853; pres. Henry Bonnard Bronze Co., 1884; interested in photography, improved the dryplate process, pioneered in preparation of ready-sensitized paper credited with paraffin paper process; treas. photog. sect. Am. Inst. City N.Y., chmn., after 1873; effected 1st scientific cremation of human body in Am.; pres. 1st Soc. Spiritualists, N.Y.; founder, treas. Theosophical Soc., 1875. Died Dec. 23, 1895.

NEWTON, HUBERT ANSON, mathematician; b. Sherburne, N.Y., Mar. 19, 1830; s. William and Lois (Butler) N.; grad. Yale, 1850; LL.D. (hon.), U. Mich., 1868; m. Anna C. Stiles, Apr. 14, 1859. Tutor, Yale, July 1852, became head mathematics dept., 1853, prof. mathematics, 1955-90; mem. Nat. Acad. Scis.; mem., recipient Lawrence-Smith medal for meteoric studies Am. Philos. Soc.; elected to Royal Astron. Soc., London, 1872; v.p. A.A.A.S., 1875, pres., 1885; pres. Conn. Acad. Arts and Scis.; a founder Am. Metrol. Soc.; asso. editor Am. Jour. of Sci. Author: Investigatigations on the Construction of Certain Curves by Points; Certain Transcendental Curves . . . ; The Metric System of Weights and Measures (advocating adoption of metric system), 1868. Died New Haven, Conn., Aug. 12, 1896.

NEWTON, ISAAC, naval architect; b. Schodack, N.Y., Jan. 10, 1794; s. Abner and Alice (Baker) N.; m. Hannah Humphreys Cauldwell, 10 children including Henry, Isaac. Founder, People's Line Assn., steamboat line between Albany, N.Y. and N.Y.C., built approximately 80 steamboats; designer boats North America, 1840, South America, 1841; introduced burning of anthracite coal; designer boats Hendrick Hudson, 1845, Isaac Newton, 1846, New World, 1847; introduced grand saloon; president Mohawk & Hudson R.R., 1846; designer boats Western World, Plymouth Rock, 1854; a projector N.Y. Central, Lake Shore and Mich. So. rys. Died N.Y.C., Nov. 23, 1858.

NEWTON, JOHN, army officer, engr.; b. Norfolk, Va., Aug. 24, 1823; s. Thomas and Margaret (Jordan) Pool N.; grad. U.S. Mil. Acad., 1842; LL.D., St. Francis Xavier Coll., 1886; m. Anna M. Starr, 1848, 6 children. Commd. 2d lt. Corps Engrs., 1842; asst. to Bd. of Engrs.; asst. prof. engring. U.S. Mil. Acad.; 1st lt., 1852, capt., 1856; chief engr. Utah Expdn., 1858; chief engr. Dept. of Pa. and Dept. of Shenandoah; commd. brig. gen. U.S. Volunteers, 1861; constructed Ft. Lyon; commanded brigade at West Point, Va., also at battles of Gaines' Mill, Glendale, South Mountain, and Antietam, 1862; maj. gen.; brevetted lt. col., col., brig. gen., maj. gen. of volunteers, 1863-64; maj. gen. U.S. Army; lt. col. engrs., 1865, col., 1879, brig. gen. and chief engrs., 1884; commr. public works of N.Y.C., 1886; pres. Panama R.R. Co., 1888-95; mem. Nat. Acad. Scis.; hon. mem. Am. Soc. C.E. Died N.Y.C., May 1, 1895; buried Post Cemetery, N.Y.

NEWTON, ROBERT SAFFORD, physician, editor; b. Gallipolis, O., Dec. 12, 1818; s. John Newton; grad. Louisville Med. Coll., 1841; m. Mary M. Hoy, Sept. 14, 1843, 1 son, Robert Safford, Jr. Prof. surgery Memphis Inst., 1849; prof. surgery Eclectic Med. Inst. of Cincinnati, 1851, prof. med. practice and pathology, 1853-62; condr. Newton's Clin. Inst.; founder Eclectic Med. Jour., 1852, editor, 1852-62; co-editor Western Med. News of Cincinnati, 1851-59, Am. Eclectic Med. Rev., N.Y., 1866-72, Am. Eclectic Register, N.Y. 1868; founder Eclectic Med. Soc. of State N.Y., pres., 1863-66; a founder Eclectic Med. Coll. of City N.Y., 1665, also prof. surgery, Died N.Y.C., Oct. 9, 1881.

NEYLAND, ROBERT REESE, JR., football coach, army officer; b. Greenville, Tex., Feb. 17, 1892; s. Robert Reese and Pauline (Lewis) N.; student Burleson Coll., Greenville, 1909-10, Tex. A. and M. Coll., 1910-11; grad. U.S. Mil. Acad., 1916; B.S. in Civil Engring., Mass. Inst. Tech., 1921; m. Ada Fitch, July 16, 1923; children—Robert Reese, Lewis Fitch. Commd. 2d lt. C.E., U.S. Army, June 13, 1916; advanced through grades to brig. gen. Nov. 11, 1944; prof. mil. sci., tactics U. Tenn., 1926-31; also head football coach, 1926-34 (only 7 games lost by teams in this period), became head coach U. Tenn. Feb. 1936; detailed by War Dept. as dist. engr. on river and harbor work, Nashville Dist., Tennessee and Cumberland rivers and their tributaries. Served as capt. and adj. 1st Bn., 1st Engrs., later instr. 1st C.E. Sch., Gondrecourt, France; in charge pioneer sect. 1st Army Sch., Langres, France, Dec. 1917-Aug. 1918; comdg. 8th Engrs., Mounted, El Paso, Tex., Oct. 1918-May 1920, 1st Bn., 11th Engrs., 1935-36; ret. as maj. U.S. Army, voluntarily, Feb. 29, 1936, after 24 yrs. service. Recalled to active duty U.S. Engrs., assigned as dist. engr. Norfolk (Va.) Dist., May 1941; assigned as div. engr. Southwestern Div., Dallas, Oct. 1942; served overseas; comdg. Advance Sect. 1, S.O.S., C.B.I., June-Nov. 1944; comdg. gen. Base Sect., I.B. Theater Nov. 1944; ret. brig. gen. 1946. Awarded Legion of Merit with oak leaf cluster, D.S.M. (U.S.), Order of Brit. Empire; Chinese Order of Cloud and Banner. Mem. Am. Mil. Engrs. Episcopalian. Club: Army and Navy. Address: U. Tenn., Knoxville, Tenn. Died Mar. 28, 1962; buried Nat. Cemetery, Knoxville.

NEYMANN, CLARENCE ADOLPH, (na'man), psychiatrist, neurologist; b. Chicago, Ill., Nov. 7, 1887; s. Adolph M. and Emma H. (Huscher) N.; A.B., Harvard, 1909, M.D., Heidelberg U., Germany, 1915; degree in medicine, honoris causa, U. of Ghent, 1946; m. Virginia Hall, May 7, 1927. Instr. psychiatry, Phipps Clinic, Johns Hopkins Hosp., 1915-18, also dir. lab. of Internal Med.; supt. of Cook County (Ill.) Psychopathic Hosp., 1919-22; asst. prof. psychiatry, Rush Med. Coll., 1919-21; asso. prof. psychiatry Northwestern U. Med. Sch., 1921-48, prof. since 1948, mem. University Senate, 1948; apptd. hon. prof. Med. Nat. U. of Mexico, 1933; exchange prof. Belgian-Am. Ednl. Foundation to univs. of Ghent, Louvain, Liege and Brussels, 1935; chief of staff Cook County Psychopathic Hospital; consultant in neuropsychiatry, Illinois Charitable Eye, Ear, Nose and Throat Infirmary, Veterans Rehabilitation Center, Chicago and Wesley Memorial Hospital, Chicago. Decorated officer Belgian Order de la Couronne; member Belgian League of Honor. Fellow A.M.A., Royal Society of Medicine, American Academy of Phys. Medicine, American Psychiatric Assn.; member Am. Psychopathol. Soc., Ill. Psychiatric Soc. (pres. 1943-44), Central Neuro-Psychiatric Soc., Chicago Neurol. Soc. (pres. 1946-47), Soc. de Medicine Mentale de Belgique (hon.), Indian Psychiatric Society (honorary), Chicago Inst. Med., Chicago Med. Soc., Chgo. Soc. of Med. Hist., Chicago Soc. for Personality Study, Chicago Acad. Criminology, Chicago Pathol. Soc., Ill. State Med. Soc., Soc. of Harvard Chemists, Johns Hopkins Med. Soc., Yucatan Med. Soc. (hon.), Phi Chi, Phi Kappa Epsilon. Contbr. to Rosanoff's text Book of Psychiatry, Pemberton, Mock and Coulter's Principles and Practice of Physical Therapy; Goldberg's Clinical Tuberculosis. Author: Artificial Fever Produced by Physical Means, Its Development and Application, 1937. Contbr. articles to Journal A.M.A., Jour. of Nervous and Mental Disease, British Jour. of Physical Medicine, Proceedings of Royal Soc. of Medicine, Am. Jour. of Psychiatry, etc. Author under the pseudonyms of Clarence Sheraton and Jan Van Hoff, of a series of magazine stories. Home: 52 E. Elm St. Office: 104 S. Michigan Blvd., Chicago. Died Jan. 11, 1951.

NICHOLAS, JOHN SPANGLER, (nik'o-las), biologist; b. Pittsburgh, Pa., Mar. 10, 1895; s. Samuel Trauger and Elisabeth Ellen (Spangler) N.; B.S., Pa. Coll., 1916, M.S., 1917; Ph.D., Yale, 1921; m. Helen Benton Brown, Dec. 17, 1921. Instr. in biology, Pa. Coll., 1915-17; master Gettysburg Acad., 1916-17; instr. in anatomy, U. of Pittsburgh, 1921-22, asst. prof., 1922-26; asst. prof. biology, Yale U., 1926-32, asso. prof. comparative anatomy, 1932-35, Bronson prof. of comparative anatomy, 1935-39, Sterling prof. of biology, 1939-63, Sterling prof. biology emeritus, 1963—, chairman dept. zoology, 1946-56; fellow Trumbull College, 1933-45, master, 1945-63; hon. fellow St. Catherine's Coll., Cambridge, Eng.; dir. Osborn Zoological Lab., 1946-56; Mellon lectr. U. Pitts., 1948; Woods Hall lectr., 1953; Rockefeller Inst. lectr., 1956; visiting professor, 1956—; speaker Humanities Seminar, University of Massachusetts, 1958; member planning commission. Internat. Congress Developmental Biology; mem. Brookhaven Biol. vis. commn. Chmn. Div. Biology and Agr., Nat. Research Council, 1948, vice chmn., 1949; sec. Seventh Internat. Congress for Cell Biology; adviser National Selective Service, 1948-53. Served as pvt. Med. Corps, U.S. Army, 1918-19; lt. San. O.R.C., 1923-34. Mem. bd. of trustees, Sheffield Scientific Sch. of Yale U., sec., 1941-56; mem. scientific advisory bd. Wistar Inst. of Anatomy and Biology, N.Y. Zoöl. Soc.; Nat. Research Council rep. on Nat. Roster of Scientific and Specialized Personnel, 1940-47; mem. at large Nat. Research Council; consultant Nat. Resources Planning Bd., 1940-43, War Manpower Commn., 1943-48, Sci. Manpower Commn., vice president 1953-54 mem. exec. com., 1954-58, pres., 1955-58; mem. vis. com. Brookhaven Nat. Labs., 1955-58, chairman, 1958. Seminar moderator Gettysburg College, 1961. Mem. research subcom. Nat. Manpower Adv. Com., 1963. Fellow A.A.A.S., Conn. Acad. Arts and Scis., Am. Inst. Biol. Scis. (governing bd.); member Nat. Sci. Found. (member div. biol. sci., 1951-53), Am. Acad. of Arts and Scis., Nat. Acad. of Scis. (chmn. Anatomy and Zoology sect. 1955-58). Soc. for Cell Biology, Growth Soc., l'Institute International d'Embryologic, American Soc. Physiology, Am. Soc. Zoology, Am. Biol. Soc. (pres. 1945), Am. Philos. Soc. (councilor 1954-57), Am. Soc. Anatomy, Am. Cancer Assn., Soc. for Exptl. Biology and Medi., Phi Beta Kappa, Sigma Xi (mem. nat. exec. committee 1954-57), Phi Kappa Psi, Phi Beta Pi, Gamma Alpha, Torch. Rep. Conglist. Mason. Clubs: Yale (N.Y.); Graduate (gov.), Faculty (New Haven); Beaumont. Assn. editor Jour. of Morphology, 1933-36; editor Biological Abstracts, Vertebrate Embryology since 1938; co-editor Anatomical Memoirs since 1940; mem. editorial bd. Jour. Exptl. Zoology, 1946, mng. editor, 1947; pres. Yale Jour. Biology and Medicine, 1954-62; adv. editor Exerpta Medica, Yale Sci. Mag.; other numerous papers on exptl. embryology. Home: 170 Cold Spring St., New Haven 06511. Address: Yale U., New Haven. Died Sept. 11, 1963; buried Grove Street Cemetery, New Haven.

NICHOLS, CHARLES HENRY, civil engineer; b. Braintree, Vt., July 12, 1864; s. Norman and Hannah Tracy (Brigham) N.; B.S., Norwich U., Vt., 1886, M.C.E., 1893; C.E., Thayer Sch. Civ. Engring. (Dartmouth), 1888; m. Isa Dyer, Feb. 9, 1889. Draftsman Boston Bridge Works, 1888-89; asst. bridge engr., N.Y., Providence & Boston R.R., 1889-91; asst. engr. Keystone Bridge Works, Pittsburgh, 1891-93; engr. for Milliken Bros., New York, 1893-94; asst. engr. for Post & McCord, 1894-1902; engr. for Snare & Triest, 1902-03, Kirby, Petit & Green, architects, 1903-08, McKim, Mead & White, 1908-10; chief engr. Trowbridge & Livingston, architects, 1910-12; entered in pvt. practice, Feb. 1912; mem. firm Bigelow & Nichols, 1913—. Trustee Norwich U. Republican. Home: Bogota, N.J. Died Oct. 30, 1927.

NICHOLS, EDWARD LEAMINGTON, physicist; b. of American parentage, at Leamington, Eng., Sept. 14, 1854; s. Edward Willard and Maria (Watkinson) N.; B.S., Cornell, 1875; univs. of Leipzig, Berlin, 1875-78; Ph.D., U. of Göttingen, 1879; fellow Johns Hopkins U., 1879-80; LL.D., U. of Pa., 1906; D.Sc., Dartmouth Coll., 1910; m. Ida Preston, May 25, 1881 (died 1928); children—Elizabeth (Mrs. Montgomery Hunt Throop), Robert Preston. With Edison at Menlo Park, N.J., 1880-81; prof. physics and chemistry, Central U. of Ky., 1881-83; prof. physics and astronomy, U. of Kan., 1883-87; prof. physics, Cornell, 1887-1919, prof. emeritus, 1919—. Founder of the Physical Review and editor, 1893-1912. Fellow Am. Acad. Arts and Sciences. Pres. A.A.A.S., 1907, Am. Physical Soc., 1908-09, Kan. Acad. Science, 1884-86. Author: The Galvanometer, 1894; A Laboratory Manual of Physics and Applied Electricity, 2 vols. (with Profs. Merritt, Bedell and others), 1895; The Elements of Physics, 3 vols. (with Prof. W.S. Franklin), 1896; Outlines of Physics, 1897; Studies in Luminescence (with Prof. Merritt), 1910; Fluorescence of the Uranyl Salts (with Prof. Howes), 1919; Cathodo-Luminescence and the Luminescence of Incandescent Solids (with Howes and Wilber), 1928; and numerous papers in scientific jours. on experimental physics. Home: Ithaca, N.Y. Died Nov. 10, 1937.

NICHOLS, ERNEST FOX, physicist; b. Leavenworth, Kan., June 1, 1869; s. Alonzo Curtis and Sophronia (Fox) N.; B.Sc., Kan. Agrl. Coll., 1888; M.Sc., Cornell U., 1893, D.Sc., 1897; student physics, Cornell, 1889-92, U. of Berlin, 1894-96, Cambridge U., 1904-05; hon. D.Sc., Dartmouth, 1903; LL.D., Colgate, Clark, Wesleyan, 1909, Vt., 1911, Pittsburgh, 1912, Dennison, 1914, Dartmouth, 1916; m. Katharine Williams West, June 16, 1894. Prof. physics, Colgate U., 1892-98, Dartmouth Coll., 1898-1903; prof. exptl. physics, Columbia, 1903-09; pres. Dartmouth Coll., 1909-16; professor physics, Yale, 1916-20; dir. pure science, Nela Research Labs., Nat. Lamp Works, Cleveland, O., 1920-21; pres. Mass. Inst. of Technology, June-Nov. 1921 (resigned because of poor health); dir. Nela Research Lab., 1929—. Research associate Carnegie Institution Washington, 1907-09, Bur. of Ordnance, Navy Dept., 1917-19. Rumford medal of Am. Acad. Arts and Sciences, 1905. Mem. Nat. Acad. Sciences (chmn. physics and engring. sect. 1917-20); fellow Am. Acad. Arts and Sciences, A.A.A.S. (v.p. 1903). Collaborator Astrophysical Journal; contbr. of many papers to scientific jours. in U.S. and abroad, on radiation and other physical subjects. Address: Cleveland, O. Died Apr. 29, 1924.

NICHOLS, GEORGE ELWOOD, botanist; b. Southington, Conn., Apr. 12, 1882; s. George Edward and Mary Sampson (Smith) N.; grad. Hillhouse High Sch., New Haven, 1900; B.A., Yale, 1904, Ph.D., 1909; studied U. of Chicago, 1910; m. Grace Elizabeth

Walker, June 23, 1909; children—Marion Louise, Grace Evelyn, George Emory, Mary Martha. Asst. in botany, Yale, 1904-09, instr. same, 1909-15, asst. prof., 1915-23, asso. prof., 1923-26, prof., 1926—; asso. prof. University of Michigan Biol. Sta., 1920-26, professor, 1926—; director Yale Botanical Gardens. Bot. adviser on sphagnum (for surg. dressings) to A.R.C. during World War. Mem. Botanical Society America (treas. 1925-32; vice pres. 1933), Ecological Soc. America (pres. 1932). Republican. Baptist. Home: New Haven, Conn. Died June 20, 1939.

NICHOLS, HENRY WINDSOR, economic geologist; b. Cohasset, Mass., Dec. 7, 1866; s. Levi L. and Ellen H. N.; grad. Mass. Inst. Technology, S.B., 1893; m. Apr. 30, 1895, Anna L. Giles, of Troy, N.Y. Asst. in geology there, 1894; curator economic geology, 1895-97, and since 1897 asst. curator of geology Field Columbian Museum, Chicago. Author: The Ores of Colombia, 1899. Residence: 6011 Kimbark Av. Office: Field Columbian Museum, Chicago.

NICHOLS, JAMES ROBINSON, chemist; b. West Amesbury, Mass., July 18, 1819; s. Stephen and Ruth (Sargent) N.; M.D., Yale, 1867, M.A. (hon.); m. Harriet Porter, 1844; m. 2d, Margaret Gale, 1851; 1 child. Founder J.R. Nichols & Co., 1857; inventor soda-water apparatus, carbonic-acid fire extinguisher, improved hot-air furnace; founder Boston Jour. of Chemistry and Pharmacy (1st U.S. publ. devoted to chemistry in popular manner), 1866, merged into Popular Science News and Boston Jour. of Chemistry, 1881, editor-in-chief, 1881-88; founder Merrimac Pub. Library, 1877; mem. Mass. Bd. Agr., 1878; pres. Vt. & Can. R.R., 1873-78; dir. Boston & Me. R.R., 1873-88; trustee George Peabody Fund. Author: Chemistry of the Farm and Sea, 1867; From Whence, What, Where?, 1882. Died Haverhill, Mass., Jan. 2, 1888.

NICHOLS, JESSE CLYDE, b. Olathe, Kan., Aug. 23, 1880; s. Jesse Thomas and Josie (Jackson) N.; A.B., U. of Kan., 1902; A.B., Harvard, 1903 (Beta Theta Pi, Phi Beta Kappa); m. Jessie Eleanor Miller, June 28, 1905; children—Eleanor, Miller, Clyde. Engaged in development of Country Club Dist. (5,000 acres), Kansas City; dir. Commerce Trust Company, Kansas City Title Insurance Company, Business Men's Assurance Co., Kansas City Fire & Marine Ins. Company, Plaza Bank of Commerce. Member Kansas City Board of Education 8 years. Chairman or vice chairman all local money-raising campaigns, World War I. Head Miscellaneous Equipment Div. of National Defense Council, O.P.M., 13 mos., 1940-41; cons. Pub. Bldgs. Adminstrn., Washington, D.C., 6 mos. Mem. Nat. Conf. on City Planning (dir.), Am. City Planning Inst. (hon.), Am. Inst. Architects (hon.), Am. Soc. Landscape Architects, Nat. Conf. for State Parks, Am. Civic Planning Assn.; pres. Nat. Conf. of Subdividers of High Class Residential Property; mem. bd. govs. Kansas City Art Inst.; vice pres. Mo. River Navigation Assn. Apptd. by Presidents Hoover, Coolidge and Roosevelt to membership in Nat. Capital Park and Planning Com., has served 22 years. Chmn. board of trustees Midwest Research Institute. Mem. Harvard Commn. on Univ. Resources; chm. trustees of William R. Nelson fund of $12,000,000 for purchase of objects of art. Mem. business advisory council, Dept. of Commerce of U.S. Democrat. Clubs: University, Kansas City, Mission Hills Country, Kansas City Country, Indian Hills Golf. Author numerous pamphlets on city planning; developing residential properties and outlying shopping centers; river navigation; fgn. trade possibilities; indsl. research; also speaker on same subjects. Leader in work for good roads and appropriate highway development throughout Middle West. Elected "Kansas City's Man of the Year" by Metro Club of Kansas City, 1940. Home: 1214 W. 55th St. Office: 310 Ward Parkway, Kansas City, Mo. Died Feb. 16, 1950.

NICHOLS, JOHN FRANCIS, mech. engr.; b. Bay City, Mich., June 19, 1873; s. Frederick A. and Emma (Luxton) N.; B.S., U. of Mich., 1895; m. Florence Maude Evans, Oct. 12, 1897 (died Feb. 17, 1937); children—Marian Maude (Mrs. Michele A. Fiore), Elizabeth (dec.), Norman Montgomery (dec.), John Evan; m. 2d, Elinor L'Amoureux Hayes, Sept. 1, 1938. Began as draftsman, Newport News Ship-building and Dry Dock Co., 1898, chargeman, 1900-08, chief draftsman, 1908-13, asst. chief engr., 1913-18, chief engr., 1918-41, dir. engring., 1941-47, now retired; dir. Newport News Bldg. & Loan Assn. Trustee county schs., Elizabeth City Co., 1918-20. Council mem. Soc. Naval Architects and Marine Engrs.; mem. Am. Soc. Naval Engrs., North-East Coast Inst. of Engineers and Shipbuilders, Am. Bureau Shipping (special sub-committee on marine engineering). Republican. Episcopalian. Club: James River Country. Home: 108 Holly St., Hampton VA

NICHOLS, OTHNIEL FOSTER, civ. engr.; b. Newport, R.I., July 29, 1845; s. Thomas Pitman and Lydia Foster N.; C.E., Rensselaer Poly. Inst., 1868; m. Jennie Swasey, Nov. 21, 1876. Chief engr., 1888-95, gen. mgr., 1892-95, Brooklyn Elevated R.R.; 1896-1903, prin. asst. engr. in charge Williamsburg (East River) bridge; chief engr., 1904-06, now consulting engr. Dept. of Bridges, New York; pres. dept. engring., Brooklyn Inst. Arts and Sciences. Residence: Brooklyn, N.Y. Died 1908.

NICHOLS, RUTH ROWLAND, aviator; b. N.Y.C., Feb. 23, 1901; d. Erickson Norman and Edith Corlis (Haines) Nichols; B.A., Wellesley Coll., 1924; D.Sc. (hon.), Beaver Coll., 1939; postgrad. Columbia, 1944-47. Began flying with Rogers Airline, Inc., 1922; established women's world altitude record at 28,743 ft., Mar. 1931; women's world speed record of 210.754 miles per hour, Apr. 1931; world's long distance record for women, Oakland, Cal. to Louisville, 1,977 miles, Oct. 1931; trans-continental record Los Angeles to N.Y.C., 13 hours, 21 min.; holder Diesel altitude record for both men and women, Feb. 17, 1932 (1st American woman recipient); also awarded U.S. women's championship for flying by Ligue Internationale des Aviateures, 1931; 1st woman to pilot a passenger airline (N.Y. and N.E. Airlines), Dec. 1932, acting as traffic mgr. and resident pilot; received 1st woman's internat. seaplane license, 1924, 2d transport license for women, 1927, and 2d airplane and engine mechanic's license; 1st woman to pilot in Am. a twin engine, exec. jet. aircraft, Moraine Saulnier, 1955; co-pilot supersonic jet reaching altitude higher than any woman in world, 1958; a founder of Aviation Country Clubs and Sportsman Pilot mag.; has held exec. positions with Nat. City Bank, Fairchild Aviation Corp.; cons. dir. Dayton Sch. Aviation, spring 1943, flight instr., 1943-57; floor supr. Pack Med. Group, N.Y.C., 1951-52; dir. women's activities Save the Children Fedn., N.Y.C., 1952-54; dir. women's div. United Hosp. Fund, Bklyn., 1954-56; field dir., pilot 21 state tour for Nat. Nephrosis Found., 1958; lectr. Mem. Nat. staff Emergency Peace Campaign, 1936-37; dir. Relief Wings, Inc., 1940-44, Inst. Internat. Relations for Am. Friends Service Com., 1944; dir. pub. relations White Plains Hosp., 1945-47; dir. air missions People's World Congress, 1947-48; pioneer world pilot, serving as courtesy pilot and spl. corr. for U.S. com. for UNICEF, 1949, pioneer woman pilot to experience various space tests at Wright Air Development Center, 1959. Trustee Beaver Coll., 1939. Hon. mem. Chgo. council Girl Scouts. Lt. col. Civil Air Patrol, adviser to nat. com. matters related to aeromed. adminstrn.; med. adminstr. N.Y. Wing, 1954-58. Recipient citation Gen. Fedn. Women's Clubs, 1941; Lady Drummond Hay trophy ann. award N.Y. br. Women's Internat. Assn. Aero., 1958; citation for distinguished citizenship Bates Coll. Mem. Shakespeare Soc. Wellesley Coll., Sirosis (hon.). Club: The Ninety-Niners. Author: Wings for Life (autobiography), 1957. Died Sept. 1960.

NICHOLS, THOMAS FLINT, educator, eng'r; b. Pownal, Me., Nov. 10, 1870; s. Charles Lewis and Anna (Flint) N.; grad. Bowdoin Coll., A.B., 1892. Clark Univ., Ph. D., 1895; m. Clinton, N. Y., Dec. 20, 1900, Alice Gordon Root. Asst. mathematics, Univ. of Wis., 1895-6; asst. prof. mathematics, 1896-1904, prof. applied mathematics since 1904, Hamilton Coll. Eng'r for Franklin Iron Mfg. Co. since 1899. Member eng'r corps Glenfield & Western R. R., N. Y. Central & Hudson River R. R., and now mem. N. Y. State Eng'rs Corps. Mem. Am. Math. Soc. Congregationalist. Republican. Address: Clinton NY

NICHOLS, WILLIAM HENRY, mfg. chemist; b. Brooklyn, N.Y., Jan. 9, 1852; s. George Henry and Sarah Elizabeth (Harris) N.; student, Poly. Inst., Brooklyn, 1865-68; B.S., New York U., 1870, M.S., 1873; LL.D., Lafayette, 1904, New York U., 1920; Sc.D., Columbia, 1904, U. of Pittsburgh, 1920, Tufts, 1921; m. Hannah W. Bensel, Feb. 14, 1873. Engaged as mfg. chemist, copper refiner and smelter, 1870—; pres. Nichols Copper Co., 1890-1918, later dir.; chmn. bd. Allied Chem. & Dye Corp.; pres. Gen. Chem. Co., 1899-1907, chmn. bd., 1907-20, later dir.; dir. Corn Exchange Bank, Title Guarantee & Trust Co. Vice chmn. bd. of Poly. Inst. of Brooklyn. Apptd. chmn. com. on chemicals, Council Nat. Defense, Apr. 1917. Incorporator Am. Chem. Soc. (pres. 1918-19); mem. Soc. Chem. Industry (pres. 1904-05); past pres. Soc. Chem. Industry, 8th International Congress Applied Chemistry, 1912. Commendatore of Crown of Italy, 1912; Knight Order of SS. Maurizio e Lazzaro, 1920. Conglist. Republican. Home: New York, N.Y. Died Feb. 21, 1930.

NICHOLS, WILLIAM WALLACE, engineer, mfr.; b. N.Y. City, Nov. 17, 1860; s. Edward Erastus and Anna Maria (MacAuley) N.; student Colorado Coll.; Ph.B., Yale, 1884, M.E., 1886; m. 2d, Mary Emily Miller, June 26, 1912; 1 dau., Marian (by 1st marriage). With motive power dept. C.,C.,C.&St.L. Ry., 1885-86; with C.,B.&Q. Ry. as engr. of tests, asst. master mechanic and supt. telegraph, 1886-90; supt. Chicago Telephone Co., 1890-93; instr., mech. engring., Yale, 1894-1900; works mgr. Baltimore Copper Works, 1900-04; with Allis-Chalmers Co. as vice president, 1904-13, became assistant to president, 1913. Served as chmn. American Industrial Commn. to France, 1916; chmn. Am. Industrial Commn. to Mexico, 1924. Trustee Arbitration Foundation, Inc.; dir. Am. Arbitration Assn. Member Inter-Am. High Commission, Nat. Industrial Conf. Board, Am. Engineering Standards Com., Am. Iron & Steel Inst., Am. Soc. Mech. Engrs., Acad. Polit. Science, Am. Mfrs. Export Assn. (ex-pres.), Mexican Chamber of Commerce in U.S. (hon. v.p., dir.), Elec. Mfrs.' Club (ex-pres.), Edgemont Assn. (ex-pres.), Berzelius Soc., Mexico Soc. (dir.), Machinery Builders Soc. (ex-pres.), Acad. Polit. Science, Seniors' Golf Assn., Sigma Xi. Republican. Episcopalian. Clubs: Machinery, Engineers', Scarsdale Golf. Contbr. many articles on engring. edn., foreign trade and business conduct. Home: Scarsdale, N.Y. Office: 50 Church St., New York, N.Y. Died Aug. 14, 1948.

NICHOLSON, FRANK LEE, civil engr.; b. Portsmouth, Va., Aug. 12, 1868; s. Francis James and Catharine Olevia (Culpepper) N.; ed. pub. and high schs. and Suffolk Mil. Acad. (2 yrs. civ. and railroad engring.); corr. courses in bridge engring., architecture, and elec. engring.; m. Ada Starr Parker, Dec. 4, 1890; children—Ethel (widow of Dr. Richard H. Peake), Clyde Parker. Rodman, chainman, levelman and office asst. to chief engr. on location surveys of Atlantic & Danvill R.R. (now Danville div. of Southern Ry.), 1887-89; levelman, later resident engr. on construction, Wilmington, N.C., Terminal, and First Residency, Wilmington, Newbern & Norfolk R.R. (now Newbern branch of Atlantic Coast Line R.R.), 1889-90; private practice, Jan.-June, 1890; asst. engineer maintenance of way, Norfolk Southern R.R., 1890-92, acting engr. m. of w., 1892-98, engr. m. of w., 1898-1909, chief engr., 1909-47, ret. in charge of valuation of same ry. and allied properties, 1914-47; chief engineer Raleigh, Charlotte and Southern R.R. from 1912 until rd. was purchased by Norfolk Southern R.R.; cons. engr. Virginia Ry., July-Dec. 1918, and chief engr., 1918-19; served in Washington, D.C., as a representative of the Southern Region on a com. for drafting rules and working conditions for maintenance of way employees and shop labor during Federal administration of rys. Chmn. Com. XX on Uniform General Contract Forms of Am. Ry. Engring. Assn., 1932-37; chmn. City Planning Commission, Norfolk, Va. Mem. Am. Ry. Engring. Assn. (dir. 1937-40; chmn. com. Outline of Work, 1938-40; chmn. com. on standardization, 1939-42); member American Society Civil Engineers (director 1929-31; chairman com. on professional conduct 1931; pres. Va. sect. 1926-27; chairman Section Com. of Va. for Civilian Protection in War Time, chairman Transportation Div. of the Section Com. of Va.; chmn. local membership com. for Va., (1943-46), Assn. Am. Railroads (engring. sect.), Engrs. Club of Hampton Roads (pres. 1925-26), Norfolk Yacht and Country Club. Democrat. Baptist. Mason (K.T., Shriner), Odd Fellow. Home: 512 Graydon Park, Norfolk 7, Va. Died May 24, 1954; buried Elmwood Cemetery, Norfolk.

NICHOLSON, HENRY HUDSON, engr.; b. Rushford, Wis., May 25, 1850; s. Henry Williams and Sarah D. (Howe) N.; ed. Antioch Coll., O., Harvard, and Heidelberg, Germany; A.M., hon. causa, Lawrence U., Wis., 1872; m. Jennie S. Higgins, Mar. 1872; children—Edward Everett, Winifred Christine, Rachel Lloyd. Served pvt. 49th Wis. Inf., 1864-65; prof. science, State Normal Sch., Peru, Neb., 1874-82; prof. chemistry and dir. chem. labs., U. of Neb., 1882-1905; consulting engr. Hamilton Mines Co., 1898-1903, Ingold Placer Mining Co., Black Jack Gold Mines Co., Ore.; mgr. and engr. Standard Consolidated Mines Co.; directing engr. Killen-Warner-Stewart Co., Chicago; consulting engr. Killen-McLaughlin-Reese Co., Cuba, 1907; also for Alpine Gold Mining Co., Red Cliff, Colo., Plumas-Lincoln Copper Co., Doyle, Calif. Author several papers on scientific subjects. Home: Lincoln, Neb. Died Aug. 17, 1940.

NICHOLSON, SETH BARNES, astronomer; b. Springfield, Ill., Nov. 12, 1891; s. William Franklin and Martha (Ames) N.; B.S., Drake U., LL.D., 1949; Ph.D., U. Cal., 1915; m. Alma M. Stotts, May 29, 1913; children—Margaret Ruth, Donald Seth, Jean Cary. Instr. physics, Drake U., 1911-12; fellow in astronomy, U. Cal., 1912-13; instr., 1913-15; astronomer Mount Wilson Obs. (Carnegie Instn., Washington), Pasadena, 1915-57, ret.; lectr. astronomy, U. Cal., summers, 1915, 23, 28, 44; lectr., vis. profs. program, 1957-62. Discovered 9th, 10th, 11th and 12th satellites of Jupiter; specialized in solar astronomy and stellar radiation. Mem. Nat. Acad. Scis., A.A.A.S., Am. Astron. Soc., Astron. Soc. of Pacific (pres. 1935-36, editor publs.). Internat. Astron. Union, Sigma Xi, Phi Beta Kappa. Home: 1785 Pepper Dr., Altadena, Cal. 91001. Died July 2, 1963.

NICHOLSON, WILLIAM THOMAS, inventor, mfr.; b. Pawtucket, R.I., Mar. 22, 1834; s. William and Eliza (Forrestell) N.; m. Elizabeth Gardiner, 1857, at least 5 children. Machinist apprentice at 14, later worked in various machine shops; patented spirit level, egg beater, 1860, manufactured both in his Providence (R.I.) shop; demand for war materials during Civil War gave him opportunity to manufacture spl. machinery for prodn. of small arms; obtained 2 patents for file-cutting machine, 1864; organized Nicholson File Co., Providence, 1864, devised over 400 different kinds of files, pres., gen. mgr.; city alderman Providence; trustee Providence Pub. Library; dir. several pub. utilities, banks, R.I.; mem. Am. Soc. M.E. Died Providence, Oct. 17, 1893.

NICOLL, MATTHIAS, JR., state health commr., N.Y.; b. N.Y. City, Feb. 12, 1868; s. Matthias and Alice Mary (Large) N.; B.A., Williams Coll., 1889; M.D., Coll. Phys. and Surg. (Columbia), 1892; m. Alice Maude Wing, Dec. 14, 1899; children—Alice Mary, Lilian Wing, Nancy Fay. Resident phys. Chambers Street Hosp., New York, 1893-95, New York Foundling Hosp., 1896-97; pathologist and attending phys. New York Foundling Hosp. 10 yrs., New York Infant

Asylum 3 yrs.; attending phys. Seton Hosp. (for tuberculosis) 3 yrs., Willard Parker Hosp. 13 yrs. (for some time cons. phys.); asst. dir. and chief div. of diagnosis, N.Y. City Dept. of Health, 6 yrs., 1908-14; clin. prof. infectious diseases Univ. and Bellevue Hosp. Med. Sch.; dir. pub. health edn. and sec. N.Y. State Dept. Health, 1915-17; dep. commr. of health, N.Y., 1917-23, commr. of health, 1923-30; county commr. health, Westchester County, N.Y., 1930-38. Mem. bd. visitors State Hosp. for Incipient Tuberculosis; pres. State and Provincial Health Authorities of North America. Fellow Am. Pub. Health Assn. (Governing council, exec. board), Acad. of Medicine. Episcopalian. First demonstrated (with Dr. William H. Park) the value of intraspinal use of tetanus antitdxin in treatment of lockjaw, 1914-15. Author of many articles on med. and other subjects. Retired from public service, Apr. 1938. Home: Rye, N.Y. Died May 13, 1941.

NICOLLET, JOSEPH NICOLAS, explorer, mathematician; b. Cluses, Savoy France, July 24, 1786; ed. Coll. of Cluses. Discovered comet in constellation Pegasus, 1821; apptd. astron. asst. French Bur. of Longitude, 1822; prof. mathematics Coll. Louis-le-Grand; came to U.S., 1832; made 1st expdn. (an ascent up Mississippi River to find its source), 1836; head ofcl. expdn. for survey of upper Missouri River, 1838, head 2d expdn., 1839. Author: Report Intended to Illustrate A Map of the Hydrographical Basin of the Upper Mississippi (a map of region N.W. of the Mississippi), 1843. Died Sept. 11, 1843, Washington, D.C.,

NICOLLS, WILLIAM JASPER, civil and mining engr.; b. Camden, N.J., Apr. 23, 1854; grandnephew Lt. Gen. Sir Jasper Nicolls, K.C.B. (English comdr.-in-chief in India, 1839), g.s. Lt. Col. William Dann Nicolls, Royal Arty., Jamaica; s. Jasper William N. (C.E.) and Ellen Baillie, d. of Rev. William Baillie; ed. Hill Sch., Pottstown, Pa.; m. Clara Valentine Lyon, 1882. Asst. engr. Reading Ry., 1873; chief engr. Pa. Steel Co., 1875; chief engr. L.I. Ry., 1880; mining engr., 1882—. Author: The Railway Builder; Story of American Coals, 1898; Coal Catechism, 1900; Greystone, 1901; A Dreamer in Paris, 1904; Brunhilda of Orrs Island, 1908; Daughters of Suffolk, 1910; Wild Mustard, 1914. Home: Malvern, Pa. Died Feb. 14, 1916.

NIELSEN, JOHANNES MAAGAARD, psychiatrist, neurologist; b. Denmark, Oct. 17, 1890; s. Soren Peter and Elise (Maagaard) N.; brought to U.S., 1896, naturalized, 1913; B.S., U. Ill., 1921, M.D., 1923; m. Celia Evelyn Owens, July 20, 1922 (dec.); children—Robert Johannes, Theodore Milton, Lois Evelyn, Paul Vernon; married second, Dorothy Cadwell, April 1, 1947 (died 1958); one daughter, Dorothy. Intern Los Angeles County Hospital, 1923-24; asst. in neurology and psychiatry, sanitarium, Battle Creek, Mich., 1924-26, asso., 1926-30; asso. prof. neurology Coll. Med. Evangelists, Los Angeles, 1930-31; asso. clin. prof. neurology and psychiatry U. So. Cal., 1931, clin. prof., 1948-52; now clin. prof. neurology U. Cal. at Los Angeles; pvt. practice neurology and psychiatry, Los Angeles, 1930-69. Chief cons. in aphasia VA, Washington; sr. cons. neurology Long Beach VA Hosp. Fellow A.C.P., Am. Acad. Neurology, Am. Psychiatric Assn.; hon. mem. Phila., N.Y. neurol. socs., Northwest Soc. Neurology and Psychology, Am. Paraplegic Soc.; member A.M.A., American Neurological Association (president 1955-56), Assn. for Research Nervous and Mental Diseases, Harvey Cushing Soc., Soc. Biol. Psychology (past pres.), A.A.A.S., Alpha Omega Alpha, Phi Chi. Author: Agnosia, Apraxia, Alphasia, 1936; Clinical Neurology, 1941; Engrammes of Psychiatry (sr. author); Memory and Amnesia. Contbr. sci. jours. Home: Los Angeles CA Died Dec. 12, 1969.

NIEMANN, CARL (GEORGE), educator; b. St. Louis, July 6, 1908; s. Julius Henry and Ella Louise (Danner) N.; B.S., U. Wis., 1931, Ph.D., 1934; Gen. Edn. Bd. fellow Rockefeller Inst., for Med. Research, 1935-36, fellow Rockefeller Found., 1937-38; m. Mary Grant Parkhurst, Aug. 15, 1934; children—Dorothy Louise, Linda Grant. With U. Coll. Hosp. Med. Sch., London, Eng., 1937-38; asst. prof. organic chemistry Cal. Inst. Tech., Pasadena, 1938-43, asso. prof., 1943-45, prof. since 1945. Served as official investigator NDRC, 1942-45, div. mem. and sect. chmn., 1943-46; Com. Med. Research, 1945; expert cons. Gen. Hdqrs., S.W. Pacific Area, 1944. Recipient Presdl. certificate of Merit. Mem. Nat. Acad. Scis. (chmn. chemistry sect. 1962-64), Am. Chem. Soc. Am. Soc. Biol. Chemists, A.A.A.S., Chem. Soc. (London), Sigma Xi, Gamma Alpha, Phi Lambda Upsilon, Alpha Chi Sigma. Author sci. papers. Died Apr. 29, 1964.

NIERMAN, JOHN L., chemist and coll. pres.; b. Howell, Mo., Feb. 11, 1887; s. John A. and Maria (Schierbaum) N.; B.Pd., Mo. State Tchrs. Coll., Kirksville, 1910; B.S., U. Mo., 1918, A.B., 1919, A.M., 1920, Ph.D., 1924; m. Augusta L. Mueller, Dec. 28, 1910; children—Florence, Anna May (Mrs. R. J. Tozer), Virginia (Mrs. William P. Stewart). Tchr. rural sch., St. Charles County, Mo., 1906-08; prin. village sch., Augusta, Mo., 1908-10, high sch., Wentzville, Mo., 1910-14; supt. schs., Hopkins, Mo., 1914-17; head dept. of chemistry Sweet Briar (Va.) Coll., 1919-22; head dept. chemistry Tex. Coll. Arts and Industries, Kingsville, since 1925, coll. dean, 1929-34, acting pres., 1932-33, 34-35, 41-42, dir. grad. studies since 1947. Mem. Tex. Acad. Sci., Am. Chem. Soc., Sigma Xi. Democrat. Presbyn. Home: 716 W. Richard Av., Kingsville, Tex. Died Oct. 9, 1950.

NIGHTINGALE, WILLIAM THOMAS, geologist; b. Carbonado, Wash., July 6, 1897; s. Charles S. and Sarah A. (Roberts) N.; B.S., U. Wash., 1919, M.S., 1924; LL.D., U. Wyo., 1955. Geologist Wash. Geol. Survey, 1919, Whitehall Petroleum Corp., Ltd., London, Eng., 1920-23; cons. geologist, 1924; geologist N.Y. Oil Co., Wash., Ore., Cal., 1924-26, Ohio Oil Co., Mont., Wyo., Colo., Neb., Utah, N.M., Wash., Ore., 1926-29; chief geologist Mountain Fuel Supply Co., Rock Springs, Wyo., 1929-45, v.p., 1941-51, dir. exploration, prodn., transmission, 1945-51, pres., 1951—, chmn. bd., 1963—; dir., mem. adv. com. First Security Bank Utah; dir. First Security Corp., Ideal National Insurance Co., Salt Lake City. Dir. Intermountain Hosp. Service, Indsl. Relations Council of Utah; vice chmn. Utah Natural Resources Com.; chmn. for Utah Gen. Gas Com.; mem. Utah Conf. Edn.; chmn. Utah Payrolls Savs. and Bond Com. Gen. chmn. Community Chest of Salt Lake County, 1952, dir., 1954—; dir. Salt Lake City United Fund; pres. Salt Lake City YMCA; member executive committee Utah Safety Council; chmn. citizens adv. board Salt Lake County Hosp.; trustee Sweetwater County Meml. Hosp. Columbia scholar, 1919. Fellow A.A.A.S., Am. Geog. Soc., Geol. Soc. Am., Am. Geophys. Union; mem. Am. Assn. Petroleum Geologists, Am. Petroleum Inst., Rocky Mountain Gas & Oil Assn. (dir., v.p.), National Association Manufacturers (director), Pacific Coast Gas Assn. (dir., v.p.), Am. Inst. Mining & Metall. Engineers, Am. Gas Assn., Salt Lake City C. of C. (past pres.; gov.), Newcomen Soc., Am. Legion (past Wyo. comdr.), 40 and 8 (past grand chef de guerre Wyo.), Phi Kappa Psi. Mason (33 deg., Shriner, Jester), Elk. Clubs: Jonathan (Los Angeles); Alta, Salt Lake City Country, Rotary (Salt Lake City). Author tech. papers profl. bull. Home: 1235 E. 2d S. Office: 180 E. First South, Salt Lake City 10. Died May 4, 1964; buried City Cemetery, Salt Lake City.

NIKOLSKY, ALEXANDER A., aeronautical engr., educator; b. Russia, Oct. 23, 1902; s. Alexander Modest and Elizabeth (Pletheff) N.; certificate math. and phys. mechanics, U. Paris, 1926; E.E., Sch. Elec. and Mech. Engring., 1926; M.S., Mass. Inst. Tech., 1929; m. Marion Mosher Hubbell, Feb. 3, 1933; 1 son, Alexander Hubbell. Came to U.S., 1928, naturalized, 1937. Stress engr. Sikorsky Aircraft, Stratford, Conn., 1929-34, chief structures, 1934-42, asst. chief design, 1940-42, consultant helicopters, 1942-47; asso. prof. Princeton, 1942-45, prof. aeronautical engring., 1945-53, Robert P. Patterson prof. aero. engineering, 1953—; cons. to Office of Secretary of Defense, sci. advisory bd. U.S. Army, Office Naval Research; mem. sci. adv. com. to President Kennedy; research helicopters, blade analysis U.S.A.F., Nat. Adv. Com. for Aeronautics, 1949, U.S.N. Fellow Inst. Aeronautical Scis. (asso.); mem. Sigma Xi. Club: Princeton (N.Y. City). Author: Helicopter Design Theory, 1944; Helicopter Blade Analysis, 1947; Technical Reports, 1949; Helicopter Analysis, 1951. Home: 234 Western Way, Princeton, N.J. Died Feb. 15, 1963.

NILES, EDWARD HULBERT, univ. dean; b. Oriskany, N.Y., Aug. 24, 1882; s. Andrew Julius and Susan (Owens) N.; Ph.C., Indpls. Coll. Pharmacy, 1912, Pharm. D., 1914, B.S., 1929; A.B., Butler U., 1936; student U. Chgo., 1923, Ind. U., 1937-38; m. Pearl Marguerite Coffin, Nov. 30, 1916; 1 son, Richard Hulbert. Instr. Indpls. Coll. Pharmacy, 1915-16, prof., 1917-20, dean, 1921-45; lectr. pharmacy Ind. Vet. Coll., 1920-23; lectr. in materia medica and pham. Ind. U. Sch. Medicine, 1920—; dean Butler U., Coll. of Pharmacy, 1945—. Licensed chem. engr., Ind.; registered pharmacist, Ind.; cons. Mem. Am. Pharm. Assn., Am. Chem. Soc. (chmn. Ind. sect. 1939-40, councillor, 1940), Ind. Acad. Sci., Ind. Interprofessional Health Council, Ind. Pharm. Assn. (chmn. edn. and vets. program coms.), Phi Kappa Phi, Kappa Psi. Republican. Episcopalian. Mason (Shriner). Contbr. profl. jours. Home: 4071 College Av., Indpls. 5. Died Sept. 23, 1958; buried Washington Park.

NILES, WILLIAM HARMON, geologist; b. Northampton, Mass., May 18 1838; s. Rev. Asa and Mary A. (Marcy) N.; student in comparative anatomy with Prof. Louis Agassiz, 1862-66; S.B., Lawrence Scientific Sch. (Harvard), 1866; Ph.B., Sheffield Scientific Sch. (Yale), 1867; hon. A.M., Wesleyan U., 1870; LL.D., Temple U., Phila., 1903; m. Helen M. Plympton, 1869. Prof. geology and geography, 1871-1902, emeritus prof. geology, 1902, head dept. geology, 1878-1902, Mass. Inst. Tech.; stated lecturer, 1882-88, prof. and head dept. geology, 1888—, Wellesley Coll. Lecturer on Natural Science, Mass. State Teachers' Inst., 10 yrs.; gave pub. lectures upon geol. and geog. subjects, speaking from 50 to 100 times each session, 1867-90. Pres. Boston Soc. Natural History, 1892-97 (councillor, 1870); pres. Appalachian Mountain Club three terms; fellow Am. Acad. Arts and Sciences. Address: Boston, Mass. Died 1910.

NIPHER, FRANCIS EUGENE, physicist; b. Port Byron, N.Y., Dec. 10, 1847; s. Peter and Roxalana P. (Tilden) N.; Ph.B., State U. of Ia., 1870, A.M., 1873; LL.D., Washington U., 1905; m. Matilda Aikins, July 1, 1873; children—Mary E. (Mrs. E.N. Birge), Edith C. (Mrs. H.M. Pollord), Elma F. (Mrs. J.C. Dawson), Clara Ellen, Edwin Tilden. Instr. in phys. lab., State U. of Ia., 1870-74; prof. physics, 1874-1914, and prof. emeritus, 1914—, Washington U., St. Louis. In 1889 showed that positive or reversed photographic pictures could be best produced by development in the light instead of in the dark-room; developed perfect pictures on the most sensitive plates with the developing bath fully exposed to direct sunlight. Made an extensive study of the nature of elec. discharge. Mem. and addressed Internat. Congress Arts and Sciences, St. Louis, 1904, also chmn. sect. cosmical physics. Research asso. Carnegie Instn., Washington. Author: Theory of Magnetic Measurements, 1886; Electricity and Magnetism, 1895; Introduction to Graphical Algebra, 1898; Experimental Studies in Electricity and Magnetism, 1914. Home: St. Louis, Mo. Died Oct. 6, 1927.

NISSEN, HARRY ARCHIBALD, (nis'sun), physician; b. Omaha, Neb., Mar. 6, 1891; s. George Christian and Louise Clare (Strenzke) N.; A.B., U. of S.D., 1911; M.D., Harvard, 1916; married Lillian Bruce, 1947. Interned at the Boston City Hospital, 1916-18, assistant and instr. in medicine Harvard Med. Sch., 1918-27; mem. staff New England Deaconess Hosp., 1932—. Mem. A.M.A., Mass. Med. Soc., Am. Rheumatism Assn., etc., Phi Beta Pi. Episcopalian. Mason (32 deg.). Contbr. med. articles to jours. Developed continuous study life course of arthritics. Home: Leach-Holt, Sherborn, Mass. Died Dec. 14, 1956.

NISSEN, HENRY W., psychologist; b. Chicago, Feb. 5, 1901; s. Adolf J. and Marie (Mendius) N.; B.A., U. Ill., 1923; M.A., Columbia, 1927, Ph.D., 1929; m. June 11, 1927; children—Dora Jane, Joanna Marie. Asst. in psychology Barnard Coll., Columbia, 1927-28; univ. fellow Columbia, 1928-29; research asso. Yale, 1929-33, asso. prof. psychobiology, 1933-39, asso. prof., 1939-44, research asso., 1944-56; asst. dir. Yerkes Labs. of Primate Biology, 1939-52, asso. dir., 1952-55, dir., 1955—; prof. psychobiology, Emory U., 1956—; research associate Psychiatric Inst. and Hosp., N.Y. City, 1944, research cons., 1946-47. Mem. Am. (div. exptl. psychol.), Fla. (pres. 1954-55) psychol. assn., National Academy Sciences, Society Exptl. Psychologists, A.A.A.S., Am. Soc. Naturalists. Contbr. articles on primate psychology to profl. pubs. Home: Orange Park, Fla. Office: Yerkes Labs. of Primate Biology, Orange Park, Fla. Died Apr. 27, 1958.

NIVEN, WILLIAM, mineralogist; b. Bellshill, Lanarkshire, Scotland, Oct. 6, 1850; s. William and Sarah (Brown) N.; ed. common schs.; came to U.S. 1879; m. Nellie Blanch Purcell, Jan. 26, 1886 (dec.); children—William Albert, David Sumner (dec.), Norman Sumner, Kingsley Burns, Harold Andrew, Mrs. Elna Blanche Harrison, Francis Joseph, Malcolm, Robert Nelson. Engaged in mineral investigations. Discovered 3 new minerals, yttrialite, thorogummite and nivenite, in Llano Co., Tex., 1889, and the new mineral aguilarite, at Guanajuato, Mex., 1891; discovered remains of prehistoric city or nation, hundreds of square miles in extent, in State of Guerrero, Mgx., 1891; also discovered buried prehistoric cities beneath the Valley of Mexico, 1911. Was asst. commr. of Arizona to New Orleans Expn. Hon. life mem. Am. Mus. Natural History; titled mem. Scientific Society Antonio Alzate, Mexico; fellow Am. Geog. Soc. (New York), Royal Soc. of Arts (London). Address: Houston, Tex. Died June 2, 1937.

NOBACK, GUSTAVE J(OSEPH), (nō'bak), prof. anatomy; b. New York, N.Y., May 29, 1890; s. Alfred and Marie (Mirejovsky) N.; prep. edn. Dwight Sch.; B.S., Cornell U., 1916; A.M., U. of Minn., 1920, Ph.D., 1923; m. Hazel Ogden Kilborn, June 17, 1917; 1 son, Richardson Kilborn. Asst. in histology and embryology, Cornell U., 1914-16; mgr. med. dept. Macmillan Co., Chicago, 1917-18; instr. in anatomy, U. of Minn., 1918-21; asso. prof. of anatomy. Med. Coll. of Va., 1921-22, prof., 1922-24; with New York U., 1924, asst. prof. anatomy, 1924-26, asso. prof., 1926-30, prof., 1930-45; chmn. biol. and geol. sciences, Grad. Sch.; dean, Essex Coll. Med., Newark, N.J., April 2, 1945; resigned July 21, 1945; asso. prof. Cornell Univ. Coll. Med., 1946-50; prof. of anatomy and head dept. U. of Puerto Rico Sch. Medicine, 1950-53, also chmn. board of anatomy; retired 1953. Fellow A.A.A.S., Am. Geo. Soc.; asso. fellow N.Y. Acad. Medicine; member American Assn. Anatomists, Am. Assn. Phys. Anthropologists, Harvey Soc., Soc. Med. Jurisprudence (pres.; sec. 1936-41), Gerontological Soc. Am. Artists Profl. League (national exec. com., pres.), Biol. Photographers Association, Society for Study of Arterio-Sclerosis, National Arts Club, Sigma Xi (v.p. Cornell U. Chapter, pres. New York Chapter 1938-39), Phi Alpha Sigma. Contbr. to scientific and professional jours. Research work in human growth and physical development; morphological and physiological changes incident to birth, especially respiratory and vascular systems; age changes in tissues and organs. Sculptor; exhibited 51st annual, 1st nat. exhbn., Archtl. League, N.Y. City, 1938; 135th annual, Pa. Acad. Fine Arts,

Phila., 1940, 137th annual, 1942; 141st annual, 1946; 8th annual Metropolitan States (hon. mention), Washington, D.C., 1940; 28th annual, Allied Am. Artists, N.Y. City, 1941, 30th annual, 1943, 31st annual, 1944, 32d annual, 1945; 118th annual, Nat. Acad. Design, 1944, 120th annual, 1945. Home: 70-05 Groton St., Forest Hills 75, N.Y. Died Sept. 8, 1955; buried Quinnepiac Cemetery, Plantsville, Conn.

NOBLE, ALFRED, civil engr.; b. Livonia, Mich., Aug. 7, 1844; s. Charles and Lovina D. N.; served in Army of the Potomac, 3 yrs.; C.E., U. of Mich., 1870, LL.D., 1895, U. of Wis., 1904; m. Georgia Speechly, May 31, 1871. In charge improvements of St. Mary's Falls Canal and St. Mary's River, 1870-82; gen. asst. engr. N.P. R.R., 1883-86; supervised constrn. of various important ry. and other bridges across the Miss. River and elsewhere, 1886-1904; mem. Nicaragua Canal Bd., 1895, U.S. Bd. Engrs. on Deep Waterways, 1897-1900, Isthmian Canal Commn., 1899-1903; mem. bd. consulting engrs. Panama Canal, 1905; chief engr. East River div., P.,N.Y.&L.I. R.R. Co., 1902-09. Awarded John Fritz medal, for "notable achievements as a civil engr.," 1910; Elliott Cresson medal, Franklin Inst. for "distinguished achievement in field of civ. engring." 1912. Home: New York, N.Y. Died Apr. 19, 1914.

NOBLE, G. KINGSLEY, curator, explorer; b. Yonkers, N.Y., Sept. 20, 1894; s. G. Clifford and Elizabeth (Adams) N.; high sch., Yonkers, 1913; A.B., Harvard, 1917, A.M., 1918; Ph.D., Columbia, 1922; m. Ruth Crosby, Aug. 13, 1921; children—G. Kingsley, Alan Crosby. Leader of Harvard expdn. to Guadeloupe, 1914, to Newfoundland, 1915; zoölogist Harvard expdn. to Peru, 1916; leader Am. Mus. expdn. to Santo Domingo, 1922; lecturer on vertebrate palaeontology, Columbia; curator of herpetology, Am. Mus. Natural History, 1919—, also curator exptl. biology, 1928—. Visiting prof. zoölogy, U. of Chicago, 1931; visiting prof. in biology, New York U., 1939. Member Advisory Bd. New York Aquarium. Ensign U.S.N.R.F. Republican. Unitarian. Author: The Biology of the Amphibia, 1931. Asso. editor Jour. of Morphology. Home: Englewood, N.J. Died Dec. 9, 1940.

NOE, ADOLF CARL, paleobotanist; b. Gratz, Austria, Oct. 28, 1873; s. Adolf Gustav and Marie (Krauss) von N oé; student U. of Gratz, 1894-97, U. of Göttingen, 1897-99; A.B., U. of Chicago, 1900, Ph.D., 1905; hon. mem. University of Innsbruck, 1922; hon. Ph.D., Gratz, 1923; Golden Medal from University of Vienna, 1923; m. Mary Evelyn Cullaton, July 3, 1901; children—Mary Helen, Valerie. Demonstrator in paleobotany, U. of Gratz, 1895-97; came to U.S., 1899, naturalized citizen, 1904; instr. science and modern langs., Burlington Inst., 1901-02; instr. German, Stanford, 1901-03; instr., asst. prof. German lit., U. of Chicago, 1903-23; asst. prof. paleobotany, same, 1923-24, asso. prof., 1924—. Geologist Ill. State Geol. Survey, 1921—, Ia. Geol. Survey, 1923-25, Ky. Geol. Survey, 1922; mem. Allen & Garcia Coal Commn. to Soviet Russia, 1927. Treas. Am. Com. for Vienna Relief, 1921. Author: Fossil Flora of Northern Illinois, 1926; Golden Days of Soviet Russia, 1931; Ferns, Fossils and Fuels, 1931. Home: Chicago, Ill. Died Apr. 10, 1939.

NOEGGERATH, EMIL OSCAR JACOB BRUNO, physician; b. Bonn, Germany, Oct. 5, 1827; s. Jacob John Noeggerath, attended U. Bonn; M.D., U. Berlin (German), 1853; m. Rolanda Noeggerath, 4 children. Came to Am., 1857; a founder Am. Gynecol. Soc., N.Y. Obstet. Soc.; prof. obstetrics and gynecology N.Y. Med. Coll.; considered one of most talented physicians of his time, believed in conservative treatment of disease, one of earliest to be interested in bacteriology; developed a surg. aseptic technique which was better than Joseph Lister's. Author: Die Latente Gonorrhae in Weiblichen Geschlecht (greatest work), 1872. Died Germany, May 3, 1895.

NOGUCHI, HIDEYO, medical research; b. Inawashiro, Yama, Fukushima, Japan, Nov. 24, 1876; s. Sayoske Kobiyama and Shika N.; pub. schs., Japan, and spl. instrn. under pvt. tutors in German, French and English, and in Chinese lit.; M.D., Tokyo Med. Coll., 1897; U. of Pa., 1901-03; Statens Serum Institut, Copenhagen, 1903-04; hon. M.Sc., U. of Pa., 1906; titular professorship, Imperial Govt. of Japan, 1911; Ph.D., Japanese Govt., 1914; hon. M.D., Sch. of Med. and Pharm. of Yucatan; D.Sc., Brown, 1921, Yale, 1921; M.D., honoris causa, U. of Paris, 1925. Asst. Gen. Hosp., Tokyo, 1897-98; asst. Govt. Inst. for Infectious Diseases, 1898-1900; quarantine officer, Yokohama Harbor Sta., 1899; phys. in charge of Central Hosp. under Internat. Sanitary Bd. of New Chwang, China, 1899-1900; lecturer on pathol. anatomy, Tokyo Dental Coll., 1898-99; asst. in pathology, U. of Pa., 1901-03; research asst., Carnegie Instn., 1903-04; asst., asso., asso. mem., 1903-14, mem., 1914—, Rockefeller Inst. for Med. Research. Contributions: Pure cultivation of syphilitic organism (Treponema pallidum); demonstration of presence of Treponema pallidum in the brain of general paresis and in the spinal cord of locomotor ataxia (connection between syphilis and general paresis and tabes dorsalis); cultivation of causative micro-organisms of infantile paralysis and rabies (hydrophobia); introduction of skin test for syphilis (luetin reaction); introduction of a method for obtaining a bacteria-free vaccine for smallpox; isolation and cultivation of the micro-organisms causing yellow fever (Leptospira icteroides), and development of preventive vaccine and curative serum for yellow fever, 1918-21. Awarded Order of Merit by Emperor of Japan, 1915; John Scott Medal, City of Phila., 1921; etc. Author: Snake Venoms, 1909; Serum Diagnosis of Syphilis and Luetin Reaction, 1910; Laboratory Diagnosis of Syphilis, 1923. Home: New York, N.Y. Died May 21, 1928.

NOONAN, EDWARD J., cons. civil engr.; b. La Salle, Ill., Apr. 24, 1874; s. Edward and Catherine (Golden) N.; ed. St. Patrick's Acad., La Salle; m. Josephine Hayden, June 8, 1897; children—Helen Marie, Eddy Jo. Engaged in municipal work, 1891-1901, interurban ry. constrn., Ill., 1901-05; chief engr. railroad constrn. in the South and Southwest until 1910; cons. practice on railroad and other projects since 1910; asso. with John F. Wallace (now dec.), offices in New York and Chicago, 1910-21; chief engr. Chicago Ry. Terminal Commn., 1914-21; mem. Chicago Ry. Terminal Commn., 1921-23; consultant to City of Chicago and other cities on ry. terminals since 1923. Mem. Am. Soc. C.E., Western Soc. Engrs., Am. Ry. Engring. Assn., Structural Engrs'. Assn. of Ill., Soc. Terminal Engrs.; fellow Am. Geog. Soc. Clubs: City, Engineers' (Chicago); Transportation (New York). Home: 1400 Lake Shore Drive. Office: 309 W. Jackson Blvd., Chicago IL*

NORCROSS, ORLANDO WHITNEY, builder and contractor; b. Clinton, Me., Oct. 25, 1839; s. Jesse S. and Margaret Ann (Whitney) N.; moved to Salem, Mass., 1843; ed. pub. schs.; m. Ellen P. Sibley, May 17, 1870. Worked in leather business; served in Union Army, 1861-64; associated with his brother, James A., in firm of Norcross Bros., Salem, 1866; moved to Worcester, 1868; bought brother's interest, 1897; sole owner, 1897-1902; later pres. The Norcross Brothers Co. Firm built important structures in all leading Am. cities. Was mem. of commn. to investigate and report on the condition of Chicago Custom House and Postoffice, apptd. by Sec. of Treasury Bristow, 1875; remodeled White House, 1902-03; built New York Pub. Library, Astor, Lenox and Tilden Foundations, 1903-07, Harvard Med. Schs., Boston, 1903-06; removed by submarine excavation Henderson's Point at Kittery Navy Yard, providing 45 feet of water in channel where there was 10 feet of ledge above water; constructed pneumatic caisson foundations of new Boston Custom House, 1910-11. Furnished 500,000 cubic ft. of granite for Pa. Sta., N.Y. City. Dir. State Mut. Life Assurance Co. Trustee Clark Coll. Address: Worcester, Mass. Died Feb. 27, 1920.

NORDBERG, BRUNO VICTOR, mechanical engr., inventor; b. Helsingfors, Finland, Apr. 11, 1857; s. Carl Victor and Dores (Hinze) N.; grad. Poly. Institute, Helsingfors, 1878; Dr. Engring., U. of Mich., 1923; m. Helena Hinze, Sept. 24, 1882. Came to U.S., 1879; naturalized citizen, 1897; mfr. steam engine regulators, Milwaukee, 1891; later built motive power engines and machinery for mines, complete power plants, etc.; pres. and chief engr. Nordberg Mfg. Co. Inventor of many machines and devices used throughout the world; built complete system of air compressors and hoists, operated with compressed air, covering the principal shafts in the Butte, Mont., mining camp; built the first modern steam engines with equilibrium poppet valves in America. Republican. Lutheran. Home: Milwaukee, Wis. Died Oct. 30, 1925.

NORDHOFF, HEINRICH, engr.; b. Hildesheim, Germany, Jan. 6, 1899; s. Johannes and Ottlie (Lauenstein) N.; Diplom-Ingenieur, Technische Hochschule, Berlin-Charlottenburg, 1927; Eng.D. (hon.), Technische Hochschule, Braunschweig, 1950; Dr. rer. pol. h.c., Gottingen U., 1964; hon. doctorate natural sci. Hamburg U., 1964; hon. doctorate commercial science Boston (Mass.) Univ., 1964; m. Charlotte Fassunge, Aug. 12, 1930; children—Barbara, Elisabeth. Bayerische Motoren-Werke A.G. (BMW), Munich; mem. mgmt. A. Opel AG., automobile factory, Ruesselsheim 1936-46; cons. engr., Hamburg, 1946-48; chmn. bd. mgmt. Volkswagenwerk AG, Wolfsburg; prof. Technische Hochschule, Braunschweig, 1955; v.p. Verband der Automobil industrie, Frankfurt; mem. executive com. Prasidium des BDI, Dusseldorf; mem. adv. bd. Allianz-Versicherungs-AG, Munich, Braunschweigische Staatsbank, Braunschweig; mem. bd. August Thyssen-Hutte AG, Duisburg Erste Allgemeine Unfall-und Schadens-Versicherungs-Gesellschaft, Vienna, Berlinsche Feuer-Versicherungs-Anstalt, Munich, Frankfurter Versicherungs-AG, Frankfurt, Dresdner Bank AG, Hamburg, Salzgitter AG., Salzgitter-Drutte, Deutsche Continental Gas-Gesellschaft, Dusseldorf, Frederich Krupp Gmblt, Essen. Mem. governing body German Soc. for Indsl. Mgmt. Hon. freeman Town of Wolfsburg, 1955, Sao Bernardo do Campo, 1960; honorary senator Technische Universitat, Berlin, 1951. Decorated Landesmedaille un Grosses Verdeinstkreuz des Niedersachs Verdienstordens, Knight Order of Holy Sepulchre; also the Southern Cross (Brazil); Comdr. Cross 1st class of Order of Vasa (Sweden); Grand Cross Fed. Order of Merit with Sash and Star, 1964; recipient Elmer A. Sperry award, U.S.A., 1958; Grosskreuzdes Bundesverdienstkreuzes mit Stern, completion millionth Volkswagen, 1955; Daidalos medal, 1967, Wakefield Gold medal, 1967, Amico del Populo Italiano medal, 1967. Mem. World Brotherhood N.Y. Club: Rotary (Braunschweig). Home: Wolfsburg Germany Federal Republic of Germany. Died Apr. 12, 1968.

NORDSTROM, SVEN JOHAN, engr.; b. Stockholm, Sweden, May 26, 1881; s. Martin Svenson and Hanna Gertrud (Askemstrom) N.; student tech. schs. of Stockholm, 1896-1901; Internat. Corr. Sch., 1901-04; manual training as machinist and carpenter, 1891-96; m. Lela Vandervort, Nov. 23, 1924. Came to U.S., 1901, naturalized, 1930. Mechanic and draftsman, Dr. De Laval, Stockholm, 1896-1901; draftsman and tool designer, 1901-10; designer and builder cyanide plants, 1910-18; invented Nordstrom valve, 1915, manufactured by Merrill Metall. Co., San Francisco, pres. mfg. since 1926; dir. Rockwell Mfg. Co. Clubs: Athens, Athletic (Oakland, Calif.); Tulsa (Okla.). Office: care of the Merrill Co., 582 Market St., S.F. 4. Died Dec. 11, 1951; buried Tulsa.

NORGREN, CARL AUGUST, mfr., engr.; b. Riverside, S.D., Nov. 21, 1890; s. Gustavus and Caroline (Anderson) N.; B.S. in Mech. Engring., U. S.D., 1912; m. Juliet E. Lien, Aug. 24, 1922; children—Carl Neil, Gene Ellen, Leigh Hyatt, Donald Kent, Vanda Caroline. Gen. engring. practice, Yankton, S.D., 1912-13; charge engring. Fairbanks Morse Co., Omaha, Neb., 1913-17; mgr. machinery dept. Salt Lake Hardware Co., Salt Lake City, 1917-18; mgr. N.W. ty. Chgo. Pneumatic Tool Co., Seattle, 1918-19; designer, inventor mech., hydraulic, pneumatic devices; owner, operator ranch at Rifle Colorado 1920-25; organized C. A. Norgren Co., engineers and mfrs., Denver, 1926, pres., 1926-62, chmn. bd., 1962-68; Norgen Farms; with Carl E. Lien organized the Uniited American Life Insurance Company in 1938, president, 1939-43, chairman, from 1943; director First National Bank Englewood, Empire Savings Building and Loan, First Colorado Bankshares, Inc., Denver Realty Assos., Presbyterian Hospital. Member of nat. council Boy Scouts of Am., from 1942, exec. com. Denver, from 1946, past pres. Denver area council. Recipient Silver Beaver, Silver Antelope awards. Licensed mech. engr., Colo. Mem. Am. Soc. Tool Engrs., Am. Soc. M.E., Soc. Automotive Engrs., Am. Soc. Lubrication Engrs., Am. Ordnance Assn., N.A.M. (dir. 1947-49), Izaak Walton League (nat. bd. 1943, 44, 48), Nat. Farm Chemurgic Council, Nat. Western Live Stock Assn., Am., and Colo., Hereford assns., Colo., Denver (dir. 1948-51) C.'s of C., Colo. Com. Indsl. Research and Development, Denver Mus. Natural History (trustee, v.p. 1944-55, pres. 1955-63), Mfrs. Assn. Colo. (v.p. 1944, also dir.), Colo. Engring. Soc., Engring. Soc. Detroit, Denver Civic Symphony Soc. (bd., pres. 1952-53), Nat. Westrn Polled Hereford Assn., (pres. 1955), Mountain State Employers Council, Game and Fish Commn. Colo. (pres. 1945-48), Colo. Farm Bur. Fedn., Denver Zool. Soc., Beta Theta Pi, Sigma Tau, Beta Gamma Sigma. Mason. Clubs: Denver, Athletic, Cherry Hills Country, Kiwanis (v.p. 1943), Saddle and Sirloin, Pinehurst Country, Mile High, Press (Denver). Home: Denver CO Died Aug. 7, 1968; buried Fairmount Cemetery, Denver CO

NORMAN, JOHN, engraver, publisher; b. Eng., 1748. Came to Am., circa 1774; very few facts known about his life; in 1789 engraved portrait of Gen. Washington which appeared in Phila. Alamnack for the Year of Our Lord 1780; printed at intervals Geographical Gazetteer of Mass.; made plates for An Impartial History of the War in America between Great Britain and the United States, 2 vols., 1781-82; published Wetherwise's Federal Almanack for the Year of Our Lord 1790. began publishing The American Pilot, 1791; published A Map of the Present Seat of the War, 1776; 1st Boston Directory, 1789. Died Boston, June 8, 1817; buried Copp's Hill, Boston.

NORRIS, CHARLES CAMBLOS, physician; b. Phila., Pa., June 1, 1876; s. William Pepper and Laura (Camblos) N.; M.D., U. of Pa. Med. Sch., 1898; m. Helen E. Farr, Jan. 12, 1928. Interne, Pa. Hosp., 1898, U. of Pa. Hosp., 1899, Johns Hopkins Hosp., 1900; gynecologic anesthetist, U. of Pa. Hosp., 1900-03; instr. clin. gynecology, U. of Pa. Med. Sch., 1902-11, asst. in gynecologic pathology, 1907-21, instr. gynecology, 1911-22, asst. prof., 1922-27, prof. obstetrics and gynecology and dir. dept., 1927-41; dir. Gynecean Hosp. Inst. Gynecol. Research of U. of Pa., 1926-41; prof. gynecology, U. of Pa. Grad. Sch. Medicine, 1927-41; emeritus prof. obstetrics and gynecology since 1941; attending obstetrician and gynecologist, U. of Pa. Hosp., 1927-41; asso. obstetrician and gynecologist in chief, Pa. Hosp., 1935-41; hon. cons. gynecologist, Phila. Gen. Hosp., 1930-41; formerly cons. obstetrician and gynecologist, Henry Phipps Inst. and Children's Hosp., Phila., retired from active practice, 1941. Served as lt., U.S. Navy, 1916-18. Fellow Am. Coll. Surgs., Phila. Coll. Phys. Mem. Am. Gynecol. Soc. (pres. 1930), Am. Neisserian Med. Soc. (pres. 1937), Am. Bd. Obstetrics and Gynecology, Am. Radium Soc., Am. Gynecol. Club, Am. Soc. for Control of Cancer (dir. 1929-38), A.M.A., Pa. State and Phila. County med. socs., Phila. Obstet. Soc. (pres. 1929-30), Pathol. Soc. of Phila., Delta Psi. Republican. Episcopalian. Club: Philadelphia. Author: Gonorrhea in Women, 1913; Gynecological and Obstetrical Tuberculosis, 1921, rev.,

1931; Uterine Tumors, 1930. Co-author (with Dr. John G. Clark). Radium in Gynecology, 1927. Contbr. about 100 articles and papers on obstetrics and gynecology. Home: Bryn Mawr PA

NORRIS, EARLE BERTRAM, dean emeritus; born Jamestown, N.Y., Sept. 17, 1882; s. Harry E. and Belle (Barker) N.; B.S. in M.E., Pa. State Coll., 1904, M.E., 1908; M. Faye Hurd, 1905. Designer of spl. machinery, E. Bement's Sons, Lansing, Mich., 1904, cost clk., 1905; asst. supt. Central Implement Co., Standish, Mich., 1905; instr. in mech. engring., Pa. State Coll., 1906-08; asst. prof. mech. engring., U. of Wis., 1908-12, asso. prof., 1912-16; industrial commr. St. Paul (Minn.) Assn. of Commerce, 1916-17; dean of engring, U. of Mont., 1919-28; dean of engring., Va. Poly. Inst., Blacksburg, 1928-52, dean emeritus, 1952, also dir. Engring. Expt. Sta., 1931-52; pres. Va. Poly. Inst. Research Foundation, 1935-53; consulting mechanical engineer. Capt. and maj. Ordnance Dept. U.S. Army, 1917-19; chief engr. Rock Island Arsenal, 1919; lt. col. Ordance Reserve, 1925-40. Cited by General Pershing for eminently meritorious and conspicious services in the A.E.F., 1919; awarded Purple Heart medal. Profl. mech. engr. Va. Mem. So. Assn. Sci. and Industry (trustee), A.S.M.E., Virginia Acad. Science (pres. 1939), Am. Soc. Engring. Education (v.p. 1946-47), Newcomen Soc., Phi Gamma Delta, Tau Beta Pi, Phi Kappa Phi, Sigma Xi, Pi Tau Sigma, Omicron Delta Kappa, Alpha Pi Mu, Scabbard and Blade. Mason. (32 degree). Co-author: Shop Arthmetic (with K.G. Smith), 1912; Advanced Shop Mathematics (with R.T. Craigo), 1913; Gas Engine Ignition (with W.C. Weaver and R.K. Winning), 1916; Heat Power (with Eric Therkelsen), 1931; The Plastic Flow of Metals, 1936; Applied Thermodynamics (with C.E. Trent), 1955. Home: Blacksburg VA Died Oct. 15, 1966.

NORRIS, EDGAR HUGHES, educator; born La Grange, Ind., Oct. 19, 1893; s. Joseph Irving and Anna (Hughes) N.; student U. of Wooster (O.), 1911-12; B.S., U. of Minn., 1914, M.S., 1916, B.M., 1918, M.D., 1919; m. Loana M. Miller, 1919; children—Edgar Robert, Marguerite Loana, Helen Catherine; m. 2d, Lillian E. Elliott, 1932; children—Paul Elliott Hughes, Charles Irving, James Philip. Doctor of medicine, Oct. 1919—; asso. Dr. Arnold Schwyzer, St. Paul, Minn., 1919-22; partner of Dr. F. H. Neher, St. Paul, 1922-24; independent practice of surgery, 1924-31; inactive due to illness, 1931-35; retraining in pathology, 1935-38; prof. of pathology, Wayne U. Coll. of Med., 1938-46; dean, 1939-45; dir. med. sciences for Wayne Univ., 1943-45; visiting prof. anatomy, Washington University, 1945-46; research fellow, Massachusetts General Hospital, 1946-47; dir. edn. and research Lynn Clinic, Detroit. Member R.O.T.C., 1917-19. Founder of Am. Fedn. of Medical Centers, 1951. Fellow Am. Coll. of Surgeons; mem. A.M.A., Mich. State Med. Soc., Wayne County Med. Soc., Assn. Am. Med. Colls., Delta Tau Delta, Alpha Kappa Kappa, Sigma Psi, Alpha Omega Alpha. Presbyterian. Mason. Author: Medicine Rededicated, 1951. Home: 8106 E. Jefferson Av., Detroit 14. Office: 2900 S. Fort St., Detroit 17. Died Oct. 6, 1955; buried Mpls.

NORRIS, HARRY WALDO, zoölogist; b. Pittsfield, N.H., Sept. 11, 1862; s. Moses Leavitt and Lydia Ann (Joy) N.; A.B., Iowa (now Grinnell) Coll., 1886, A.M., 1889, Sc.D., 1924; Cornell U., 1888-90; U. of Neb., 1890-91; U. of Freiburg, 1901-02; m. Harriet Victoria Ruliffson, June 14, 1893; children—Waldo Willard, Genevieve Eugenia, Selden Harmon. Inst. natural history, Grinnell Coll., 1888, prof. biology, 1891-1903, prof. zoölogy, 1903-31, research prof. zoölogy, 1931-41, emeritus prof. zoölogy since 1941; exchange lecturer, Harvard University, 1913-14. Congregationalist. Fellow A.A.A.S., Iowa Academy Since; mem. Am. Micros. Soc., Am. Soc. Naturalists, Am. Assn. Anatomists. Author: (with M. L. Macy) Physiology for High School, 1899; The Plagiostone Hypophysis, General Morphology and Types of Structure, 1941. Engaged in research on comparative anatomy of nervous system; contbr. scientific jours. and procs. of socs. Home: Grinnell, Ia. Died Jan. 15, 1946. *

NORRIS, HENRY HUTCHINSON, electrical engr.; b. Phila., Apr. 26, 1873; s. Samuel Wilson and Mary Rachel N.; ed. Phila. Manual Training High Sch.; took course in applied electricity, Johns Hopkins, 1894; M.E., Cornell, 1896; B.Engring., Johns Hopkins, 1927; m. Annie T. Reese, Dec. 23, 1899 (died 1922); children—Elinor Rachel (Mrs. P.C. Roundy), Rachel Hutchinson (Mrs. H.C. Haydn II); m. 2d, Helena R. Walley, June 5, 1926. Was designer and draughtsman for elec. firms; assistant instr. Johns Hopkins, 1892-94; asst. prof., 1900-05, prof. elec. engring., 1905-13, head dept., 1909-13, Cornell; asso. editor, 1913-21, mng. editor, 1921-22, engring. editor, 1922-23, Electric Railway Journal; supervisor of personnel and special instruction, Boston Elevated Railway. Supt. tests, Electric Ry. Test Commn., and mem. Internat. Jury of Awards, sec. group on elec. machinery, St. Louis Expn., 1904; spl. expert in connection with reorganization of Am. St. Ry. Assn., 1905. Sec. Soc. Promotion of Engring. Edn., 1909-14; fellow American Institute Electrical Engrs. (manager 1909-12). Author: Electrical Machinery (with H.J. Ryan and George L. Hoxie); Introduction to the Study of Electrical Engineering. Editor: (with B.V. Swenson) Report of Electric Railway Test Commission; editor for Am. Electric Ry. Assn., of annual vol. entitled "Electric Railway Practices," 1923-28. Home: Winchester Mass. Died Apr. 14, 1940.

NORRIS, HENRY MCCOY, mech. engr.; b. Trenton, N.J., Jan. 21, 1868; s. John Hurd and Cora McCoy (Bunnell) N.; State Normal and Model schs., Trenton; Trenton Acad.; Lawrenceville (N.J.) Sch.; Sibley Coll. (Cornell U.), 1890-91; m. Sarah Boyd Nixon, Nov. 24, 1892. Served apprenticeship, Bement, Miles & Co., Phila.; designer Ferracute Machine Co., Bridgeton, N.J., Brown & Sharpe Mfg. Co., Providence, R.I., Pond Machine Tool Co., Plainville, N.J., to 1892; insp. Garvin Machine Co., New York, 1893; supt. Appleton Mfg. Co., Phila., 1894, Riehle Bros. Testing Machine Co., 1895; gen. mgr. Campbell & Zell Co., Baltimore, 1896; supt., engr. and works mgr., Bickford Drill & Tool Co., Cincinnati, 1897-09; sec., dir. Cincinnati Bickford Tool Co., 1909—. Republican. Presbyterian. Mem. Am. Soc. M.E. (chmn. Cincinnati Sect., 1919, mgr. nat. society, 1920-23), Ohio Soc. S.R. (pres. 1919), Ohio Soc. Colonial Wars (gov. 1916). Editor: Digest of Physical Tests. Author: Fifty-six Points of Vantage; Ancestry and Descendants of Lieutenant Jonathan and Tamesin (Barker) Norris, 1906; History of the Drilling Machine. Inventor first speed-box used on a machine tool; designed 1st high-speed lathe and high-speed, high-power radial drill; devised current formula for ascertaining the power required to drive drills in metals at various speeds and feeds. One of 8 efficiency engrs. selected for service in ordnance dept., Watertown Arsenal, 1917; mech. expert, Council Nat. Defense, 1917; mech. engr., Ordnance Dept. at-large, 1918. Mem. U.S. War Industries Board. Address: Cincinnati, O. Died Dec. 27, 1925.

NORRIS, JAMES FLACK, chemist; b. Baltimore, Jan. 20, 1871; s. Rev. Richard and Sarah Amanda (Baker) N.; A.B., Johns Hopkins, 1892, fellow in chemistry, 1894-95, Ph.D., 1895; honorary Sc.D., Bowdoin Coll., 1929; m. Anne Bent Chamberlin, Feb. 4, 1902. Asst., 1895-96, instr., 1896-1900, asst. prof. organic chemistry, 1900-04, Mass. Inst. Tech.; prof. chemistry, Simmons Coll., Boston, 1904-15, Vanderbilt U., 1915-16; prof. organic chemistry, in charge grad. students in chemistry, dir. research lab. organic chemistry, Mass. Inst. Tech., 1916—. In charge offense chem. research, war gas investigations, U.S. Bur. Mines, 1917-18; asso. mem. Naval Consulting Bd., 1916; lt. col., U.S.A., in charge U.S. Chem. Warfare Service, Eng., 1918; in charge investigation mfr. war gases in German chem. plants, 1919. Chmn. div. chemistry and chem. tech. Nat. Research Council, 1924-25, mem. exec. bd., 1925-33. Lecturer on organic chemistry, Harvard, 1912-14, Clark U., 1913-14, Bowdoin, 1929. Medalist American Institute of Chemists, 1937; Secretary Soc. of Arts of Boston, Mass., 1902-04; president Am. Chem. Soc., 1925-26 (pres. Northeastern sect., 1905-06); pres. Chem. Teachers' Assn. of N.E., 1906-08, Technology Club, 1906-09; v.p. Internat. Union of Pure and Applied Chemistry, 1925-28. Fellow Am. Acad. Arts and Sciences (v.p., 1934—), A.A.A.S. (chmn. Sect. C, 1930). Author: The Principles of Organic Chemistry; Experimental Organic Chemistry; Text-book of Inorganic Chemistry for Colleges (with R.C. Young); Laboratory Exercises in Inorganic Chemistry (with K.L. Mark). Home: Boston, Mass. Died Aug. 4, 1940.

NORRIS, WILLIAM, locomotive builder; b. July 2, 1802; s. William and Mary (Schaefer) N.; grad. St. Mary's Coll.; m. May Ann Heide, 1825, 1 child. Built and demonstrated steam carriage with upright boiler in Phila.; organized (with Col. Stephen Long) Am. Steam Carriage Co., 1832; constructed engine "Black Hawk," 1833, used on Phila. & Columbia R.R., later on Phila. & Germantown R.R.; attained fame through constrn. of another engine "George Washington," sold it to various countries, including England, France, Austria, Germany; chief engr. Eastern div. Panama R.R., 1846. Died Jan. 5, 1867.

NORTH, CHARLES EDWARD, sanitarian; b. Scarborough, N.Y., July 28, 1869; s. Charles Randolph and Anna Mary (Haight) N.; A.B., Wesleyan U., Conn., 1893; M.D., Coll. Physicians and Surgeons (Columbia), 1900; post-grad. work in bacteriology, Columbia, 1905, in pub. health, Harvard, 1909-10; m. Amelia Potter Palmer, 1903; children—Anna P., Jean P., Amelia P., Charlotte T., Charles E. Manager Purity Milk Company, 1900-04; bacteriologist Lederle Laboratories, 1905-08; appointed 1908, by Department of Health, N.Y. City, director of research on value of bacterial vaccines and Opsonic Index; consulting bacteriologist Jersey City Water Dept., 1908-10; established clean milk supply for infant milk stas. of N.Y. Milk Com., 1908-10; cons. expert on part of N.Y. State in litigation with State of N.J. of pollution of New York Harbor by Passaic Valley Sewer, 1913; apptd. chmn. Mayor Mitchel Com. on Milk, 1917; drew plans for municipal milk plant, Jamestown, N.Y., 1918; survey milk supply City of Rochester, N.Y., 1919; expert for Montclair, N.J., in water supply litigation, 1919; survey of milk supply of Kansas City, 1921. Ex-sec. Nat. Commn. on Milk Standards; sec. Grade A Milk Assn., 1938. Chmn. Com. on Longevity, Class of 1900, Coll. Phys. and Surgeons (Columbia) N.Y., 1940. Recipient citation Phila. Dairy Tech. Soc., 1955. Mem. A.M.A., N.Y. County Med. Soc., N.Y. Acad. Medicine. Inventor numerous processes and machines for dehydration and reconstitution of milk products. Author numerous reports and papers on bacteriology, pub. health, and sanitation. Home: 147 Park St., Montclair, N.J. Office: 23 E. 26th St., New York, N.Y. Died July 1961.

NORTH, ELISHA, physician; b. Goshen, Conn., Jan. 8, 1771; s. Joseph and Lucy (Cowles) N.; M.D. conferred by Conn. Med. Soc., 1813; m. Hannah Beach, 1797, 8 children. Instigated 1st use of Kine-pox for vaccination purposes in N.Y.C.; established 1st eye dispensary, New London, Conn., 1812. Author: A Treatise on a Malignant Epidemic Commonly Called Spotted Fever, 1811. Died Dec. 29, 1843.

NORTH, SIMEON, mfr.; b. Berlin, Conn., July 13, 1763; s. Jedediah and Sarah (Wilcox) N.; m. Lucy Savage, 1786; m. 2d, Lydia Huntington, Mar. 2, 1812; 9 children including Simeon, Reuben. Opened scythe mill, 1795; received U.S. Govt. contract for 500 pistos, 1799, one of 1st to use interchangeable parts in mfg., manufactured pistols, carbines, rifles for U.S. govt. until 1852; lt. col. 6th Conn. Regt., 1811-13; a founder Berlin Acad. Died Aug. 25, 1852.

NORTHCOTT, JOHN A(NDREW), JR., univ. prof.; b. Winton, N.C., Oct. 9, 1897; s. John A. and Maime (Lassiter) N., Sr.; B.S., N.C. State Coll., 1918; m. Virginia A. Williams, Jan. 5, 1924; 1 d., Virginia Wrenn. Mem. staff, dept. elec. engring., Notre Dame Univ., S. Bend, Ind., since 1922, prof. elec. engring. since 1932, head dept. since 1939. Mem. Am. Inst. E.E., Am. Soc. Engring. Edn.; Sigma Phi Epsilon. Home: 435 Parkovash Av., S. Bend, Ind. Died Apr. 4, 1956.

NORTHCOTT, WILLIAM NEWTON, coll. adminstr.; b. Sugar Branch, Ind., Mar. 5, 1874; s. Thomas William and Mary L. (Newton) N.; grad. Moores Hill (Ind.) Coll., 1892; m. Lora Delle Gerkin, June 10, 1896; children—Mary Mildred (dec.), Roger Loraine. On internat. YMCA staff, r.r. dept., N.Y.C., 1911-13; metropolitan r.r. sec., YMCA, Chgo., 1912-19 (asst. exec., transportation dept., internat. YMCA, 1916-18); Ia. gen. state sec. YMCA, 1919-23; gen. sec. YMCA, Bridgeport, Conn., 1923-26; asst. to pres. Cornell Coll., Mt. Vernon, Ia., 1927-28; partner Howard T. Beaver and Asso., fund raising consultants, 1938-47; v.p. and dir. of expansion program and centennial Austin Coll., Sherman, Tex., 1947—. Originated plan for using stereopticon slides for daylight pictures to be used in safety program in r.r. shops and other indsl. centers, 1912, adapted same plan to teach English to immigrants, 1913. Pres., Chicago Parent-Teacher Orgn. for oral deaf, 1912-15, Ia. Parent-Teacher Orgn. for oral deaf, 1919-20. Presbyn. Mason. Home: Grayson Hotel, Sherman, Tex. Died June 21, 1950; buried Meml. Park Cemetery, Sherman.

NORTHRUP, EDWIN FITCH, electrothermic engr.; b. Syracuse, N.Y., Feb. 23, 1866; s. Ansel Judd and Eliza Sophia (Fitch) N.; A.B., Amherst, 1891; Cornell U. last half of 1891; fellow and Ph.D. in physics, Johns Hopkins, 1895; hon. D.Sc., Lehigh U., 1932; m. Margaret Jane Stewart, Oct. 9, 1900. In practical elec. work in the West, 1895-96; prof. physics, U. of Tex., 1896-97; became asst. to Prof. H.A. Rowland, Baltimore, 1898, in development of his multiplex printing telegraph system, and later chief constructing engr. Rowland Printing Telegraph Co. until 1902; sec. Leeds & Northrup Co., mfrs. of elec. instruments, Phila., 1903-10; mem. physics faculty, Princeton U., 1910-20; v.p. and tech. adviser Ajax Electrothermic Corp., Trenton, N.J. Has been granted a number of U.S. patents for new instruments and methods of producing and measuring high temperatures. Author: Methods of Measuring Electrical Resistance, 1912; Laws of Physical Science, 1917; Zero to Eighty, 1937. Extended research upon elec. conductivity and properties of matter at elevated temperatures. Inventor of Ajax-Northrup high frequency induction furnace; patentee of methods and numerous devices for inductive heating used throughout the world; developed means for producing high speed linear motions with polyphase currents. Médaille de bronze, Paris Expn., 1900; Edward Longstreth medal, 1912; Elliott Cresson medal, 1916; Edward Goodrich Acheson gold medal and $1,000, 1931. Home: Princeton, N.J. Died Apr. 29, 1940.

NORTHRUP, WILLIAM PERRY, M.D.; b. Peterboro, N.Y., Jan. 11, 1851; s. Rensselaer and Clarissa (Judd) N.; A.B., Hamilton Coll., 1872, A.M., 1875; M.D., Coll. Physicians and Surgeons (Columbia), 1878; LL.D., Knox Coll., Galesburg, Ill., 1920; m. Antoinette Stebbins, Sept. 1, 1886 (dec.); m. 2d, Julia Radcliffe Cowing, Feb. 1914 (died 1922). Instr. Greek, Knox Coll., 1872-76; adj. prof. pediatrics, 1893-96, prof., 1896-1919, emeritus prof., 1919—; Univ. and Bellevue Hosp. Med. Coll. (New York U.). Attending phys. to Presbyn. Hosp., cons. prof. pediatric service, 1919—; cons. phys. New York Foundling Hosp.; cons. phys. to Willard Parker Hosp. and the hospitals of Health Dept. of New York, N.Y. Infant Asylum, Washington Heights Hosp., Open Air Hosp. for tuberculosis in children, Seabreeze, Coney Island, N.Y. (under care of Assn. for Improvement Condition of the Poor), Babies' Hosp., Newark, N.J., State Orthopedic Hosp., Haverstraw, N.Y. American editor: Ashley and

Wright's Diseases of Children, 1900; Nothnagel's Encyclopaedia of Practical Medicine, Am. edit., vol. 4, 1902; wrote original article on diphtheria in latter. Contbr. to med. jours. on open air treatment of pneumonia, open air roof gardens on city houses, open air roof wards, city hosp., etc. Address: New York, N.Y. Died Nov. 20, 1935.

NORTON, CHARLES HOTCHKISS, cons. engr.; b. Plainville, Conn., Nov. 23, 1851; s. John C. and Harriet (Hotchkiss) N.; student pub. schs.; m. Julia E. Bishop, Jan. 1873; children—Ida (Mrs. William H. Munson), Fannie Norton; m. 2d, Mary E. Tomlinson, 1895 (died 1915); m. 3d, Mrs. Grace Harding, 1917 (died 1923). Began in employ of Seth Thomas Clock Co., Thomaston, and continued for 20 yrs., advancing to supt. machinery; asst. engr. Brown & Sharpe Mfg. Co., Providence, 1886-90; partner Leland, Faulconer & Norton Co. (now Cadillac Automobile Co.), Detroit, 1890-95; engr. Brown & Sharpe Co., 1895-1900; founder, 1900, Norton Grinding Co., Worcester, Mass., was originator of the modern methods of machine grinding; company merged, 1919, into the Norton Co., of which was chief engr. machinery div.; now retired. Recipient John Scott medal by Corp. of Phila. for invention of accurate grinding devices of high power, 1925. Mem. Am. Soc. M.E., Nat. Machine Tool Builders' Assn., Nat. Soc. for Constl. Govt., others. Republican. Conglist. Author: Principles of Cylindrical Grinding, 1917. Patentee in field. Home: Plainbille, Conn. Deceased.

NORTON, CHARLES LADD, engr.; b. Springfield, Mass., Dec. 11, 1870; s. Francis and Jennie Maria (Atwater) N.; B.S., Mass. Inst. Tech., 1893; m. Frances Torrey, Sept. 24, 1895. Prof. Industrial physics and dir. Div. Industrial Coöperation and Research, Mass. Inst. Tech.; officer and dir. of a number of indusl. corps., interested in the manufacture of asbestos products; cons. engr. on matters relating to heat and fire protection. Fellow Am. Acad. Arts and Sciences. Episcopalian. Home: Boston, Mass. Died Sept. 8, 1939.

NORTON, EDWIN, manufacturer, inventor; b. Rockton, Ill., Mar. 27, 1845; s. Oliver W. and Henrietta W. N.; ed. common schs.; served in Union Army in Civil War; m. Lucy E. Akin, Oct. 9, 1876. Inventor and mfr. sheet metal working machinery, rolling mills; v.p. Norton Bros., Chicago, many yrs.; 1st pres. Am. Can Co. Among his notable inventions are: Automatic furnace and rolling mill for making tin plate and thin sheet steel; machine for automatic manufacture of hermetically sealed cans; machines and processes for preserving food products in vacuum. Address: New York, N.Y. Died Jan. 1, 1916.

NORTON, J(OHN) PEASE, financial writer; b. Suffield, Conn., July 28, 1877; s. John Hughes and Annie Lord (Lombard) N.; A.B., Yale, 1899, Ph.D., 1901; m. Nancy Jane Burwell Harris, July 29, 1940. Instr. economics and statistics, 1891-1904, asst. prof. ry. and trade statistics, 1905-10; Yale actuary and report writer for New York banking houses, 1905-14; ry. credit expert for 16 western states and western farmers' assns. in western rate advance case, 1915; editorial writer Wall Street Journal, 1916; railway credit expert for Western States, shippers' orgns. and Nat. Assn. Ry. Commrs., 1917. Oil statis. expert Fuel Adminstrn., 1918. Past mem. Acad. Polit. Science, Am. Mus. of Natural History, A.A.A.S. (sec. Sect. I, 1906-10, v.p. 1911-12), Econometric Society, Royal Economic Society of London, Sigma Chi, Phi Beta Kappa. Author: Statistical Studies in the New York Money Market, 1902; Theory of Loan Credit in Relation to Corporation Economics, 1904; Proposal for an Electric Dollar; Econometric Society; also Exhibits on Railway Credit in western rate advance case of 1915, and in fifteen per cent case of 1917. Home: 463 Ocean Av., West Haven, Conn.; also 140 Main St., Suffield, Conn., and 123 Arlington Way, Ormond Beach, Fla. Died July 16, 1952; buried Suffield, Conn.

NORTON, JOHN PITKIN, educator, agrl. chemist; b. Albany, N.Y., July 19, 1822; s. John Treadwell and Mary (Pitkin) N.; m. Elizabeth Marvin, Dec. 15, 1847, 2 sons. Studied chemistry with various tchrs., various places; apptd. prof. agrl. chemistry Yale, 1846, helped to found dept. scientific edn. which later became Sheffield Scientific Sch. Author: Elements of Scientific Agriculture, 1850; also numerous papers, particularly in field of chemistry of corps. Died Farmington, Conn., Sept. 5, 1852.

NORTON, SIDNEY AUGUSTUS, chemist; b. Bloomfield, Trumbull County, O., Jan. 11, 1835; s. Charles H. and Caroline Brayton (Cornell) N.; A.B., Union Coll., N.Y., 1856, A.M., 1859; M.D., Miami Med. Coll., Cincinnati, 1869; univs. of Bonn, Leipzig and Heidelberg, 1870-71; hon. M.D., Western Reserve, 1869; Ph.D., Kenyon, 1878; LL.D., U. of Wooster, 1881, Union U., 1899; m. Sarah J. Chamberlain, June 20, 1864 (died 1868); m. 2d, Jessie Carter, June 20, 1876 (died 1911). Instr. natural science, Cleveland High Sch., 1858-66; prof. chemistry, Miami Med. Coll., 1867-72; acting prof. physics, Union Coll., 1873; prof. chemistry, Starling Med. Coll., 1878-79; prof. chemistry, 1873-95, prof. emeritus, 1899, Ohio State U. Author: Elements of Natural Philosophy, 1870; Essays and Notes, 1874; Elements of Physics, 1875; Elements of Inorganic Chemistry, 1878; Organic Chemistry, 1884. Editor revised edition of Weld's English Grammar, 1863. Address: Columbus, O. Died Aug. 30, 1918.

NORTON, THOMAS HERBERT, chemist, editor; b. Rushford, N.Y., June 30, 1851; s. Rev. Robert and Julia Ann Granger (Horsford) N.; desc. Thos. Norton, a founder of Guilford, Conn., 1639; A.B., Hamilton (valedictorian), 1873, Sc.D., 1895; Ph.D., University of Heidelberg, 1875, Dr. Natural Science, 1936; grad. student Univs. of Berlin and Paris, 1876-78; m. Edith Eliza Ames, Dec. 27, 1883 (died Oct. 30, 1929), 1 son, Robert Ames. Was manager of large chem. works, Paris, France, 1878-83; prof. chemistry, U. of Cincinnati, 1883-1900; traveled 12,000 miles on foot through Europe and Asia, the first to traverse Greece and Syria in this manner. Apptd. by President McKinley, May 1900, to establish the U.S. consulate at Harput, Turkey; sent by U.S. Govt. to investigate conditions in Armenia, 1904, to Persia, 1904-05; Am. consul at Smyrna, Turkey, 1905-06; at Chemnitz, Saxony, 1906-14. Detailed under Dept. of Commerce to report on chem. industries of Europe, 1911-12; to further development of Am. chem. industries, especially dyestuffs, 1915-17; editor of The Chemical Engineer, 1917-18. Chemist with E. I. du Pont de Nemours & Co., 1917-20; editor Chemicals, 1920-29; research chemist Am. Cyanamid Co. since 1930. Awarded Lavoisier medal by La Société Chimique de France, 1937. Fellow A.A.A.S. (sec. council, 1892; gen. sec., 1893; v.p., 1894), Chemical Society (London); mem. Washington Acad. Sciences, New York Acad. Sciences, Am. Chem. Soc. (councilor 1897-99), Nat. Inst. Social Sciences, Internat. Inst. of China (sec. of council), Soc. Chem. Industry, Soc. Chimique de France, Deutsche Chem. Gesellschaft, Russian Chem. Society, Delta Kappa Epsilon, Phi Beta Kappa, Sigma Xi, S.A.R., S.R., Soc. War of 1812, Soc. Colonial Wars, English-Speaking Union, Hamilton Coll. Alumni Soc. (pres. New England Assn., 1917-20). Republican. Presbyterian. Author: Report on Chemical Industry, Paris Exposition, 1878; Utilization of Atmospheric Nitrogen, 1912; Chemical Industries of Belgium, Holland, Norway and Sweden, 1913; Dyestuffs for American Textile Industry, 1915; Cottonseed Industry in Foreign Countries, 1915; The Dyestuff Census, 1916; Training Materials of Latin America, 1917; Reflections at the 70th Milestone, 1921; also many papers on chem. tech. and econ. subjects in Am. and European jours. As genealogist, compiler of Ancestry of Gov. Wm. Leete (2,000), 1934, and personal ancestry (6,390), 1935. Died Dec. 2, 1941.

NORTON, WILLIAM HARMON, geologist; b. Willoughby, O., Apr. 3, 1856; s. Rev. Roderic and Caroline (Pardee) N.; A.B., Cornell Coll., Iowa, 1875, A.M., 1878; LL.D., State U. of Ia., 1911; m. Mary Florence Burr, (prof. mathematics Cornell Coll., 1886-1919), Aug. 27, 1883. Tutor Latin and Greek langs., 1875-77, adj. prof., 1877-81, prof. Greek lang. and lit, and geology, 1881-90, curator museum, 1882-1923, prof. geology, 1890-1923, Cornell Coll. Spl. asst. Ia. Geol. Survey, 1892-1932; asst. U.S. Geol. Survey, 1903-13. Mem. board trustees Cornell College, 1917-40, also mem. exec. com., 1934-40. Fellow Geol. Society America; pres. Iowa Acad. Sciences, 1900; pres. science sect. N.E.A., 1902; mem. Sigma Xi Fraternity, Phi Beta Kappa. Methodist. Republican. Author: Artesian Wells of Iowa (Vol. VI, Iowa Geol. Survey, 1897); Norton's Elements of Geology, 1905; Underground Water Resouces of Iowa (U.S. Geol. Survey), 1913; Deep Wells of Iowa (Vol. XXXIII, Ia. Geol. Survey), 1927, and (Vol. XXXVI, Ia. Geol. Survey), 1935; The Church and Social Action, 1936; also various geol. and ednl. papers. Address: Mt. Vernon, Ia. Died May 3, 1944.

NORWOOD, CHARLES JOSEPH, geologist, mining engr.; b. New Harmony, Ind., Sept. 17, 1853; s. Joseph Granville and Mary Frances (Pugh) N.; ed. U. of Mo. and under pvt. teachers, M.S., Ky. Agrl. and Mech. Coll., 1906; m. Sarah E. White, Oct. 5, 1876. Asst. geologist, Mo. Geol. Survey, 1872-74, Ky. Geol. Survey, 1874-80; prof. natural science, Bethel Coll., Russellville, Ky., 1877-81; editorial writer Russellville Herald-Enterprise, 1879-82; mining engr., gold, silver and coal companies, 7 yrs.; chief insp. mines, Ky., 1884-97; curator Ky. State Geol. Dept., 1893-97; dean and prof. mining and metallurgy, Coll. Mines and Metallurgy of State U. of Ky., Jan. 1902-June 1918; chief State Dept. of Mines, 1902-20; dir. State Geol. Survey, 1904-12; prof. mining and head dept. mines and metallurgy, Coll. of Engring., U. of Ky., Jan. 1920—. Supt. and designer Ky. mineral exhibit, St. Louis Expn., 1904; represented Ky. at Nat. Conf. Weights and Measures, 1906-07; mem. Ky. Commn., Jamestown Expn., 1907. Episcopalian. Mason (32 deg.). Home: Lexington, Ky. Died Jan. 20, 1927.

NOSTRAND, PETER ELBERT, civil engr.; b. at Brooklyn, N.Y., Jan. 15, 1856; s. John Lott and Ellen (De Bevoise) N.; grad. Brooklyn Poly. Inst., 1875; m. Ella Frances, d. Benjamin F. Arcularius, of Brooklyn, Dec. 27, 1881. As asst. chief engr. in part designed and constructed first elevated railway in Brooklyn; expert on water works, foundations for large bldgs. and dams; etc.; chief engr. Ramapo Water Co.; also city surveyor of New York. Trustee Bushwick Savings Bank, Brooklyn. Mem. Am. Soc. C.E. Country House: Shelter Island Heights, N.Y. Home: 235 Stuyvesant Av., Brooklyn. Office: 7 Beekman St., New York.

NOTMAN, ARTHUR, mining engr.; b. Brooklyn, N.Y., Apr. 28, 1883; s. George and Katherine Parker (Howard) N.; ed. Brooklyn Poly. Inst., 1897-99; B.S., Harvard, 1903, E.M., 1908; grad. study, Columbia, 1905-07; married Florence Hancock, Apr. 22, 1913; children—John Hancock, Arthur (dec.). Began career as mining engineer and geologist with Phelps Dodge Corp., Ariz., 1908-17, asst. gen. supt. and gen. supt., Bisbee, Ariz., 1917-22; consulting engr. in New York, 1923—; president and director Verde Exploration, Ltd.; dir. New Jersey Zinc Co., San Manuel Copper Company, Campbell Chibougamau Mines, Limited, Magma Copper Co. Member Harriman Mission and Mission for Econ. Affairs in London, representing War Shipping Adminstrn. and Combined Prodn. and Resources Bd., 1942-44. Mem. Am. Inst. Mining and Metall. Engrs. (past pres.), Mining and Metall. Soc. America, Soc. Econ. Geologists, Acad. Polit. Sci., N.Y., Am. Acad. Polit. Science, A.A.A.S., Canadian Inst. Mining and Metallurgy. Democrat. Presbyterian. Mason (32 deg.). Clubs: Harvard, University, Down Town Assn., Mining, Richmond County. Editor: (chmn. editorial com.) Copper Resources of the World, 1935. Contbr. numerous articles to mining and metall. jours. Home: 93 Circle Rd., Dongan Hills, Staten Is. 4. Office: 55 Liberty St., N.Y.C. 5. Died July 19, 1961; buried Keene, N.Y.

NOTT, JOSIAH CLARK, physician, author; b. Columbia, S.C., Mar. 31, 1804; s. Abraham and Angelica (Mitchell) N.; grad. S.C. Coll. (now U.S.C.), 1824; studied medicine under Dr. James Davis, Columbia; attended Coll. Physicians and Surgeons, N.Y.C., 1825; M.D., U. Pa., 1827; m. Sarah Deas, 1832, 8 children. Demonstrator anatomy U. Pa., 1827-29; practiced medicine, Columbia, 1829-35; an organizer Mobile (Ala.) Med. Soc., 1841; prof. anatomy U. La., 1857-58; a founder Med. Coll. of Ala., 1858, prof. surgery, 1858-61; served in Confederate Army during Civil War; mem. N.Y. Obstet. Soc., 1868; best known for his conclusions on yellow fever (believed it was living organism and had nothing to do with atmospheric conditions). Author: (with George R. Gliddon) Types of Mankind, 1854, Indigenous Races of the Earth, 1857; Contributions to Bone and Nerve Surgery, 1866; contbr. paper on anatomy to New Orleans Med. Jour., 1844. Died Mobile, Mar. 31, 1873.

NOTT, OTIS FESSENDEN, physician; b. Ballston Springs, Saratoga County, N.Y., Mar. 6, 1825; s. Oran Gray and Lucy (Kingman) O.; A.M. (hon.), Union Coll., 1851; grad. N.Y. Med. Coll., 1852; m. Frances Helen Cooke, 1867. Took up landscape painting, 1843, also taught landscaping; ship surgeon in Panama and Pacific service; practiced medicine, N.Y.C., 1860; police surgeon for N.Y.C., 1861-71; pres. med. bd. N.Y. Police Dept., 1868-71; lectr. Coll. Physicians and Surgeons, N.Y.C., 1871-90; 1st man to cure stricture in male urethra. Author: Essays Lessons in Landscape, 1856; Stricture of the Male Urethra: Its Radical Cure, 1878; Classroom Lectures on Syphilis and the Genito-Urinary Disease, 1878; Clinical Lectures on the Physiological Pathology of Syphilis and Treatment of Syphilis, 1881. Died New Orleans, May 24, 1900.

NOTTINGHAM, WAYNE B(UCKLES), coll. prof., cons. physical electronics; b. Tipton, Ind., Apr. 17, 1899; s. Otis W. and Gertrude (McCrea) N.; B.S., Purdue, 1920, E.E., 1929; A.M., Princeton, 1926, Ph.D., 1929; Benjamin Franklin fellow, Am.-Scandinavian Foundn., Upsala (Sweden) Univ., 1920-21; Bartol research fellow of Franklin Inst., 1926-31; m. Vivian Keplinger, June 21, 1922; 1 son, Marsh W.; married Eveline van Berkum, November 26, 1953. Engineer Western Electric and Bell Telephone Labs., 1921-25; asst. prof. Mass. Inst. Tech., 1931-36, asso. prof., 1936-42, prof. physics, 1942—; consultant Nat. Research Corporation, 1958-62; v.p. research Electronics Corp. Am., 1954-55; dir. Aero Vac Corp.; cons. NASA, 1960—, Thermo-Electron Engring. Corp., 1958—, Gen. Telephone & Electronics Corp., 1960—, Electronics Corporation Am., 1962—; cons., mem. of scientific adv. com. Allison division Gen. Motors, Indpls., 1963—. Served as spl. rep. Mass. Inst. Tech. radiation lab. to O.S.R.D., 1944; cons. chem. warfare development lab., 1942-50. Awarded Louis E. Levy medal of Franklin Inst., 1932. Fellow Am. Acad. Arts and Scis., Am. Phys. Soc. (chmn. div. electron physics, 1948), Inst. Radio Engrs.; mem. Am. Optical Soc., Franklin Inst., Eta Kappa Nu, Sigma Xi. Contbr. articles to sci. jours. Home: The Tokfarm, Rindge, N.H. 03461. Office: Mass. Inst. Tech., Cambridge 39, Mass. Died Dec. 4, 1964.

NOURSE, HENRY STEDMAN, civil engr.; b. Lancaster, Mass., April 9, 1831; s. Stedman N.; grad. Harvard, 1853, A.M.; m. Mary B. Thurston, Sept. 12, 1870. Prof. ancient languages, Phillips Exeter Acad., 1853-55; adj. and capt. 55th Ill. vol. inf. and commissary of musters, 17th army corps, 1861-65; constructional engr. and supt. Bessemer Steel Works, Steelton, Pa., 1866-74; mem. Mass. Ho. Reps., 1883; mem. Massachusetts senate, 1885-86; trustee Worcester Insane Hosp., 1888-98; mem. Mass. Free Public Library Commn., 1890-1903, Mass. Bd. Charity, 1898-1903. Republican. Author: Early Records of Lancaster,

1643-1725, 1884; The Story of the 55th Regiment of Illinois Infantry, 1887; The Military Annals of Lancaster, 1740-1865, 1889; The Birth, Marriage and Death Register, etc., of Lancaster, Mass., 1643-1850, 1890; History of the Town of Harvard, Mass., 1891; The Ninth Report of the Free Public Library Commission, 1899; Narrative of the Captivity and Restoration of Mrs. Mary Rowlandson, 1903. Address: South Lancaster, Mass. Died 1903.

NOVY, FREDERICK GEORGE, (nō'vi), bacteriologist; b. Chicago, Ill., Dec. 9, 1864; B.S., U. of Mich., 1886, M.S., 1887, Sc.D., 1890, M.D., 1891; studied in Koch's lab., Berlin, 1888, Pasteur Inst., Paris, 1897, at Prague, 1894; LL.D. U. of Cincinnati, 1920, U. of Mich., 1936; m.; children—Robert L., Frank O., Marguerite F., Frederick G., Frances L. Asst., organic chemistry, 1886; instr. hygiene and physiol. chemistry, 1887-91, asst. prof., 1891-93, jr. prof., 1893-1902, prof. of bacteriology, 1902-35, and dir. Hygienic Lab., U. of Mich.; chmn. exec. com. and faculty of Med. Sch., U. of Mich., 1930-35, also dean Med. Sch.; dean emeritus and prof. emeritus since 1935. Russell lectr., 1927, Kober lecturer, 1931. Mem. U.S. Commn. to investigate plague 1901; mem. State Bd. of Health, 1897-99. Awarded gold medal, Am. Med. Assn., 1930; testimonial of Mich. Legislature, 1931; Bausch and Lomb's 250,000th microscope by A.A.A.S., 1936. Hon. pres 3d. Internat Congress for Microbiology, 1939. Hon. fellow N.Y. Acad. Medicine, Internat. Coll. of Surgeons; mem. Nat. Acad. Scis., Am. Philos. Soc., A.M.A. (mem. council on pharmacy and chemistry, 1905-30), hon. mem. Assn. Am. Immunologists, Harvey Soc. (New York), Pathol. Soc. (Phila.), Am. Soc. Tropical Med., Soc. Am. Bacteriol. (Mich. branch), Am. Trudeau Soc., Wayne Co. Med. Soc., Detroit Acad. Med., Assn. Am. Physicians (emeritus), Am. Acad. Tropical Med. (emeritus), Am. Soc. Biological Chemists (emeritus), Société de pathologie exotique, Paris, Sociéte royale des scis. médicales et naturelles, Bruxelles (asso. mem.); corr. mem. Société de Biologie Paris. Chevalier Legion of Honor (France); Order of White Lion (Czechoslovakia). Author: Cocaine and Its Derivatives, 1887; Laboratory Work in Bacteriology, 1899; Laboratory Work in Physiological Chemistry, 1898; Cellular Toxins (with Dr. V. C. Vaughan), 1902. Home: 721 Forest Av., Ann Arbor, Mich. Died Aug. 8, 1957; buried Forest Hill Cemetery, Ann Arbor.

NOYES, ARTHUR AMOS, chemist; b. Newburyport, Mass., Sept. 13, 1866; s. Amos and Anna Page (Andrews) N.; S.B., Mass. Inst. Tech., 1886, S.M., 1887; Ph.D., U. of Leipzig, 1890; LL.D., U. of Me., 1908, Clark U., 1909, U. of Pittsburgh, 1915; Sc.D., Harvard, 1909, Yale, 1913; unmarried. Assistant in analytical chemistry, 1887-88, instr., 1890-92, instr. organic chemistry, 1892-94, asst. and asso. prof., 1894-99, prof. theoretical chemistry, 1899-1919, dir. Research Lab. Physical Chemistry, 1903-07 and 1909-19, acting pres., 1907-09, Mass. Inst. Tech.; dir. Gates Chem. Lab., Calif. Inst. Tech., 1915—. Editor Review of Am. Chem. Research, 1895-1901. Mem. Nat. Acad. Sciences (editor of its Proc., 1915-16), National Research Council (chmn. 1918), American Chemical Society (pres. 1904); fellow American Academy of Arts and Sciences, A.A.A.S. (pres. 1927). Awarded Willard Gibbs medal of Am. Chem. Society, 1915; Davy medal of Royal Society of London 1927; Richards medal of American Chemical Soc., 1932. Author: Qualitative Chemical Analysis of Inorganic Substances, 1895; Laboratory Experiments on the Class Reactions and Identification of Organic Substances (with S.P. Mulliken), 1899; The General Principles of Physical Science, 1902; Electrical Conductivity of Aqueous Solutions, 1907; Chemical Principles (with M.S. Sherrill), 1921; Qualitative Analysis for the Rare Elements (with W.C. Bray), 1927; Chemistry of Solutions, 1932. Home: Pasadena, Calif. Died June 3, 1936.

NOYES, HARRY ALFRED, research chemist; b. Marlboro, Mass., July 7, 1890; s. Lambert Alfred and Bertha (Keirstead) N.; B.S., Mass. Agrl. Coll., Amherst, Mass., 1912, M.S., 1914; m. Florence Fisherdick, June 25, 1913; children—Mrs. Lorraine Fisherdick Nicholson, Arthur A. (dec.), Carol W. (Mrs. Joseph Graff). Research asst. in chemistry and bacteriology, Purdue U. Exptl. Station, 1913-16; research asso., same, 1916-18; research work with Mellon Inst. Industrial Research and Sch. of Specific Industries, Pittsburgh, Oct. 1918-Mar. 1922; in charge research dept. Welch Grape Juice Co., 1919-22; research chemist Mich. State Dept. Agr., 1922; cereal chemist Mich. Agrl. Expt. Sta., 1922-23; research chemist and food technologist with Dr. Raymond F. Bacon, 1923-32; research chemist for Tex. Gulf Sulphur Co., 1923-32; food technologist having research and production for Foods, Inc., 1933; mng. dir. Applied Sugar Laboratories, Inc., 1934-35; consultant and food technologist with Arthur D. Little, Inc., Dec. 1935 to July 1939. Consultant for food enterprises from 1939; ednl. and training work on nat. defense for Kingsbury Ordnance plant, La Porte, Ind., 1941. Serving as an industrial engr. for Ordnance Dept., U.S. Army, 1942-43. Technologist with Nat. Fireworks, Inc., and asso. companies, 1944; technologist for Noyes Products, Inc. Fellow A.A.A.S., Am. Chem. Soc. (chmn. agrl. and food div. 1922-23); mem. of scientific socs., American Society of Refrigeration Engineers, Beta Kappa Phi, Sigma Xi, Pi Gamma Mu. Lecturer and contbr. to professional jours. on scientific problems, giving emphasis to laboratory orgn. and the "problem method" of making industrial research economically practical. Developed processes and procedures for freezing foodstuffs by sugar and sugar-salt solutions based upon taste disired. Inventor of processes using frozen state to produce "food conditioning" and producing concentrates from mixtures in the frozen state. Author: Frozen Foods, 1947. Home: Lake Wales FL Died Dec. 22, 1970; buried Wildwood Cemetery Amherst MA

NOYES, IRVING GEORGE, botanist; b. Trenton, Me., Sept. 12, 1859; s. George Jewett and Mary Jarvis (Osgood) N.; ed. pub. schs. and by pvt. study; m. Carrie Louise Dalton, of Cambridge, Mass., June 5, 1884; children—Walter Irving, Ethel Ann, Alice Louise, Herbert Miokell, Grace Evelyn, George Wendell, Gladys Ruth. After learning printer's trade removed to Boston, 1887; machinist Eagle Shade Roller Co., 1882-86, Sun Electric Co., Woburn, Mass., 1886-88; foreman with P. Forg, since 1888. Republican. Baptist. Has made a spl. study of Cacti Stapelias, and the Crassulaceae. Contbr. Cactus Journal (Baltimore); Sharon Cactus Guide, Cactus Journal (London); Portland Transcript, Boston Globe, etc. Address: Somerville, Mass.

NOYES, JOHN RUTHERFORD, army officer; b. Oneida, N.Y., Apr. 5, 1902; s. Charles Rutherford and Gertrude Hayes (Noyes) N.; B.S., U.S. Mil. Acad., 1923; C.E., Cornell, 1926; grad. Army Indsl. Coll., 1939; m. Eunice Gertrude Zimmerman, Mar. 6, 1928 (dec. 1952); children—John Zabriskie, Daniel Hayes; m. 2d, Lily Florence Ericson, Mar. 4, 1955; 1 son, Eric Rutherford. Commd. 2d lt., U.S. Army, 1923, advanced to col., 1942; served in C.E., 1923-50, in Alaska, 1926-28, 1931-32, 1948-51; asst. district engineer Juneau, 1926-28, Seattle, 1932-34, Conchas, 1935-37, Mobile Engr. Dist., 1939-42; instr. engrs., N.M.N.G., 1934-38; served as transportation officer, Services of Supply and Transportation Officer, Sixth Army Group, North Africa, Italy, France, and Germany, World War II; asst. to dir. gen. railways in Germany, 1945; transferred to Transportation Corps, 1950; commr. roads for Alaska, hdqrs. Juneau, 1948-51; transferred Corps Engineers, 1952, management officer, The Engr. Sch. U.S. Army, 1952, ret. 1953, brig. gen., N.G. U.S., adj. gen. Alaska, 1953. Lectr. hist. 1947, 48, 49. Awarded Bronze Star medal with Oak Leaf Cluster, Legion of Honor (French), Croix de Guerre (French). Fellow Am. Geog. Soc., Royal Geog. Soc. (British); mem. Am. Soc. C.E., Soc. Am. Mil. Engrs., Nat. Defense Transportation Assn., Permanent Internat. Assn. Navigation Congresses, A.A.A.S., N.G. Assn. U.S., Arctic Institute N. America (asso.), West Point Soc. N.Y. Elk. Author: Transportation in Alaska; the Influence of Geographical Environment Thereon (with Gen. James G. Steese), 1934; Transportation in Undeveloped Regions (with Gen. James G. Steese), 1938; Transportation in Alaska, 1952. Club: Army and Navy (Washington). Geographer-historian. Address: Kenwood Station, Oneida, N.Y. Died Jan. 30, 1956; buried Oneida.

NOYES, WILLIAM ALBERT, chemist; b. nr. Independence, Ia., Nov. 6, 1857; s. Spencer W. and Mary (Packard) N.; A.B. and S.B., Ia. (now Grinnell) Coll., 1879; Ph.D., Johns Hopkins, 1882; LL.D., Clark U., 1909; Chem.D., U. of Pittsburgh, 1920; hon. D.Sc., Grinnell Coll., 1929; m. Flora E. Collier, Dec. 24, 1884 (dec.); children—Helen Mary (dec.), Ethel (dec.), William Albert, Jr.; m. 2d, Mattie L. Elwell, June 18, 1902 (dec.); 1 son, Charles Edmund; m. 3d, Katharine Haworth Macy, Nov. 25, 1915; children—Richard Macy, Henry Pierre. Prof. chemistry U. of Tenn., 1883-86; Rose Poly. Inst., 1886-1903; chief chemist Nat. Bureau of Standards, 1903-07; prof. chemistry and dir. Chemical Lab., U. of Ill., 1907-26 (emeritus). Editor Journal Am. Chemical Soc., 1902-17, Chemical Abstracts, 1907-09, Scientific Monographs, Am. Chem. Soc., since 1919, Chemical Reviews, 1924-26; sec. State Bd. of Nat. Resources and Conservation since 1917. Awarded Nichols medal, 1908, Willard Gibbs medal, 1919, Priestley medal, 1935. Fellow Am. Acad. of Arts and Sciences; mem. Nat. Acad. of Sciences, Am. Philos. Soc., Am. Chem. Soc. (sec. 1903-07, pres. 1920); chmn. chem. sect. A.A.A.S., 1896 and 1918. Author: Organic Chemistry for the Laboratory, 1897; Elements of Qualitative Analysis, 1888; Organic Elements of Qualitative Analysis, 1888; Organic Chemistry, 1903; Kurzes Lehrbuch der organischen Chemie (translation), 1907; Text-book of Chemistry, 1913; Laboratory Exercises in Chemistry, 1917; College Textbook of Chemistry, 1919; Building for Peace, 1923; Building for Peace, II; Pour la Paix (translation), 1924; Organic Chemistry, 1926; Modern Alchemy (with W. Albert Noyes, Jr.), 1932; also many scientific, economic, internat. and religious papers. Died Oct. 24, 1941.

NUGENT, PAUL COOK, civil engr., educator; b. New Orleans, La., Jan. 4, 1871; s. Perry and Amanda (Cook) N.; A.B., Roanoke Coll., 1889; A.M., 1894; C.E., Rensselaer Poly. Inst., 1892; m. Mary Louise Logan, Sept. 12, 1899. Teacher of civ. engring., 1896—; prof. civ. engring., Syracuse U., 1902-19; prof. civ. engring., U. of Ariz., 1920—. Methodist. Author: Plane Surveying. Address: Tucson Ariz. Died July 15, 1924.

NUNN, PAUL N., engr.; b. Medina, O., July 31, 1860; s. Charles Robert and Miriam (Kendall) N.; ed. science, pedagogy and engring.; m. Agnes Aird Geddes, June 24, 1886. Prin. high sch., 1885-88; chief engr. Telluride (Colo.) Power Co., 1890-1911, builder and operator of first hydro-electric power industry in U.S. and later (in Utah) of the highest-voltage and longest-distance transmission, including experimental research and educational work; chief engr. Ontario Power Co., Niagara Falls, 1902-10, during design and constrn. of that plant; pres. Telluride Power Co. Mason. Home: San Diego, Calif. Died Oct. 27, 1939.

NUTHEAD, WILLIAM, printer; b. England, 1654; m. Dinah Nuthead. Set up printing press Jamestown, Va. (1st press South of Mass.); forbidden to continue printing by Va. Council because he had printed account of Va. Assembly of 1682 without license, 1863; operated press, St. Mary's, Md., 1686-95, printed documents for Md. Assembly. Died 1695.

NUTTALL, GEORGE HENRY FALKINER, biologist; b. San Francisco, July 5, 1862; s. Robert Kennedy (M.D.) and Magdalena (Parrott) N.; ed. U.S., Germany, England, France, Switzerland; M.D., U. of Calif., 1884; Ph.D., U. of Göttingen, 1890; hon. M.A., Cambridge, 1900, Sc.D., 1906; m. Paula von Oertzen, Apr. 26, 1894. Asst. and later asso. in hygiene, Johns Hopkins, 1891-94; hon. asst. Hygienic Inst., Berlin, 1894-99; univ. lecturer in bacteriology and preventive medicine, later reader in hygiene, 1900-06, Quick prof. of biology, 1906—, U. of Cambridge. Fellow Christ's College, later fellow Magdalene Coll., Cambridge; hon. sec. British Nat. Com. for Internat. Hygienic Congresses, 1906—; Harben lecturer, Royal Institute Public Health, 1908; Herter lecturer, Johns Hopkins, 1912; Harvey lecturer, New York Acad. Medicine, 1912; Weir Mitchell lecturer, Coll. Phys. and Surg., Phila., 1912; examiner for diplomas in pub. health and tropical medicine and hygiene, Cambridge; same for diplomas in tropical medicine, U. of Liverpool, and for Royal Army Med. Corps; dir. Molteno Inst., U. of Cambridge; founder and editor jours. of Hygiene and Parasitology. Mem. Advisroy Com. for Plague Investigations in India (Indian Govt.), Imperial Bur. Entomology (Colonial Office, London); Fish Preserv. Com. (Dept. Agr. and Fish, London); Pathol. Advisory Com. (War Office); Tropical Diseases Com. Royal Soc.; fgn. hon. mem. Am. Acad. Arts and Sciences. Author: Hygienic Measures in Relation to Infectious Diseases (published in both English and German), 1893; Blood Immunity and Blood Relationship, 1904; The Bacteriology of Diphtheria (with Graham Smith and others), 1908, 1913; Ticks (with C. Warburton and others). Address: Cambridge, Eng. Died Dec. 16, 1937.

NUTTALL, THOMAS, naturalist; b. Settle, Eng., Jan. 5, 1786; s. Jonas Nuttall. Came to U.S. (Phila.), 1808; investigated flora up Missouri River, 1809-11; went along Arkansas and Red rivers in Ark., La., Indian territories, 1818-20; with Wyeth Expdn. to mouth of Columbia River, 1834-35; fellow Linnaean Soc. of London, 1813; mem. Am. Philos. Soc.; contributed many articles to Jour. of Acad. of Natural Scis., Transactions of Am. Philos. Soc., and others; curator Bot. Garden of Harvard, 1822-33; delivered paper to Phila. Acad. Natural Scis. entitled "Observations on the Geological Structure of the Valley of the Mississippi" (1st attempt in America to correlate by means of fossils geog. formations widely separated geographically; mem. Phila. Acad. Natural Sciences, Phila. Author: The Genera of North American Plants, and a Catalogue of the Species, to the Year 1817, 1818; A Journal of Travels into the Arkansas Territory during the Year 1819, 1821; A Manual of the Ornithology of the United States and Canada, 1832; An Introduction to Systematic and Physiological Botany; wrote supplement to Michaux's North American Sylva, 3 vols., 1846. Died Liverpool, Eng., Sept. 10, 1859.

NUTTER, EDWARD HOIT, mining engr.; b. Healdsburg, Calif., May 24, 1876; s. Rev. David and Hannah Van Wyck (Hoit) N.; A.B., Stanford, 1902; m. Gertrude Monier Allen, Mar. 7, 1905; children—Edward Allen, Katherine Louise (Mrs. John Prey Tynes), Sheldon Hoit. Mining foremanships, Calif., 1902-03; editor Mineral Wealth, Redding Calif., 1903-04; asst. supt. and supt. Standard Consol. Mining Co., Bodie, Calif., 1904-06; asst. gen. supt. and supt. Liberty Bell Gold Mining Co., Telluride, Colo., 1906-09; engr. Minerals Separation, Ltd., London, 1910; chief engr. Minerals Separation, North Am. Corp. and its predecessor companies in N. America since 1911. Mem. Am. Inst. of Mining and Metall. Engrs., Sigma Xi, Tau Beta Pi, Swedenborgian. Clubs: Commonwealth, Commercial (San Francisco). Known for development and application of flotation process for metalliferous ores in connection with most of the important lead, zinc, copper, silver and molybdenum mines of N. America and many mines abroad; inventor of a number of patented improvements in the process. Orange grower, Redlands dist., Calif. Home: 2834 Hillegass Av., Berkeley, Calif. Office: 220 Battery St., San Francisco CA

NUTTING, CHARLES CLEVELAND, zoölogist; b. Jacksonville, Ill., May 25, 1858; s. Rev. Rufus and Margaretta Leib (Hunt) N.; A.B., Blackburn U., Ill., 1880, A.M., 1882; m. Lizzie B. Hersman, Aug. 10, 1886;

1 dau., Elizabeth H.; m. 2d, M. Eloise Willis, June 16, 1897; children—Willis D., Carl B. Engaged in explorations for Smithsonian Instn. in Central America, 1881-82; prof. zoölogy and curator Mus. of Natural History, 1886—, prof. and head dept. of zoölogy, 1890—, State U. of Ia. Engaged in spl. scientific researches in Costa Rica, 1882; Nicaragua, 1883; Florida, 1885; Saskatchewan River, 1891, West Indies, 1888, 1893, Plymouth, Eng., and Naples, Italy, 1895; Calif., 1905 and 1909; Barbados, 1917-18; member of civilian scientific staff of U.S.S. "Albatross" during Hawaiian cruise, 1902; collaborator, Reports of the Siboga Expdn., 1909-11; dir. Barbados-Antiqua Expdn. from State Univ. of Ia., 1918, and Fiji-New Zealand Expdn., 1922. Author: Narrative of Bahama Expedition from University of Iowa, 1893; American Hydroids, Parts 1, 2, 3, 1900, 1904; Report on Gorgoniacea of the Siboga Expedition, 1910; Narrative Barbados-Antigua Expedition, 1918; Narrative of the Fiji-New Zealand Expedition, 1924. Home: Iowa City, Iowa. Died Jan. 23, 1927.

NUTTING, PERLEY GILMAN, physicist; b. at Randolph, Wis., Aug. 22, 1873; s. Charles and Cordelia (Gilman) N.; Carleton College, Northfield, Minn., 1891-92; A.B., Stanford, 1897; M.S., U. of Calif., 1899; studied U. of Göttingen, 1901-02; Ph.D., Cornell U., 1903; m. Edith Eva Lightfoot, Oct. 12, 1906; m. 2d, Julia E. Stouffer, Apr. 7, 1928. Asst. physicist, 1903-09, asso. 1909-12, Bureau of Standards, Washington; physicist and asst. dir. research lab., Eastman Kodak Co., Rochester, N.Y., 1913-16; dir. Westinghouse Research Lab., East Pittsburgh, Pa., 1916-21, cons. engr., 1921-24; geophysicist U.S. Geol. Survey since 1924. Asst. professor physics, George Washington University, 1907-09. Author: Outlines of Applied Optics, 1911; Visibility of Radiation, 1911; New Precision Colorimeter, 1912; Organized Knowledge and National Welfare, 1917; Factors in Achievement, 1919. Author 173 papers in the fields of optics and geophysics. Address: 3216 Oliver St., Washington. Died Aug. 8, 1949; buried Rock Creek Cemetery, Washington.

NYSWANDER, REUBEN EDSON, JR., prof. physics; b. Antwerp, O., Jan. 4, 1878; s. Reuben Edson and Henrietta W. (Youche) N.; A.B., Indiana U., 1901, A.M., 1904; Ph.D., Cornell U., 1908; m. Ada M. DeBell, Aug. 17, 1909; children—Virginia Ruth, Reuben Edson. Asst. in physics, Ind. U., 1899-1902, Purdue U., 1903; magnetic observer, U.S. Coast and Geodetic Survey, 1903-06; instr. in physics, Ind. U., 1908-09; prof. physics, 1909, prof. physics and electrical engring., 1919-20, prof. physics, dir. Sch. Elec. Engring., 1919-30, asso. dean Sch. of Science and Engineering, 1931-37, dean Sch. of Elec. Engineering, 1929-31, dean School of Science and Engineering, 1937—, U. of Denver, Prof. physics, Ind. U. Summer Sch., 1915. Methodist. Inventor polarization photometer. Home: Denver, Colo. Died Apr, 8, 1941.

OBER, FRANK ROBERTS, physician, educator; b. Mt. Desert, Me., June 1, 1881; s. Otis Merriam and Josephine (Roberts) O.; M.D., Tufts U., 1905, D.Sc. (hon.), 1943; D.Sc. (hon.), U. Vt., 1948; m. Ina Spurling, Nov. 15, 1907. Intern Carney Hosp., Boston, 1905-06; intern Children's Hosp., Boston, 1913-14, chief orthopedic resident, 1914-15, jr. asst. orthopedic surgeon, 1915-19, asst. orthopedic surgeon, 1919-23, asso. orthopedic surgeon, 1923-31, chief orthopedic surgeon, 1931-46; asst. orthopedic surgeon New Eng. Peabody Home for Crippled Children, 1922-29, surgeon in chief, 1929-46, emeritus, trustee, 1946—; cons. orthopedic surgeon Peter Bent Brigham Hosp., Boston, 1936—; gen. practice of medicine, Northeast Harbor, Me., 1906-13; partner Obrebar Corp., 1948—; with Harvard Med. Sch., 1914—, beginning as alumni asst., successively asst. orthopedic surgeon, instr. orthopedic surgery, asst. prof., clin. prof., John B. and Buckminster Brown clin. prof., asst. dean grad. courses, emeritus, 1946—. Mem. adv. com. Nat. Found. Infantile Paralysis, 1938—. Served with U.S. Army, 1917-19; lt. col. M.C. Res. Diplomate Am. Bd. Orthopedic Surgery. Fellow Boston Med. Library, New York Academy of Sciences; member of the American Academy of Orthopedic Surgeons, A.A.A.S., Am. Orthopedic Assn. (pres. 1943), Am. Rheumatism Soc., Boston Orthopedic Club (pres. 1925), Internat. Soc. Orthopedic Surgeons, Mass. (pres. 1940), Suffolk Dist. med. socs., A.M.A., Nat. Inst. Social Scis., Nat. Tb. Soc., New Eng. Surg. Society, The New York Academy of Medicine, International Poliomyelitis Congress (trustee), Sigma Xi, Alpha Omega Alpha. Mason (32). Clubs: Saint Botolph, Harvard (Boston). Editor: Orthopedic Surgery (by Sir Robert Jones and Dr. Robert W. Lovett) (with Dr. Nathaniel Allison and Harry Platt), 2d edit. 1929; Lateral Curvature of the Spine and Round Shoulders (by Dr. Robert W. Lovett) (with Dr. A. H. Brewster), 1931. Contbr. profl. jours. Home: 195 St. Paul St., Brookline, Mass. Office: 234 Marlborough St., Boston 16. Died, Dec. 26, 1960.

OBERHOLSER, HARRY CHURCH, ornithologist; b. Bklyn., June 25, 1870; s. Jacob and Lavera S. O.; Columbia U., 1888; B.A., M.S., George Washington U., 1914, Ph.D., 1916; m. Mary Forrest Smith, June 30, 1914. Ornithologist U.S. Biol. Survey, 1895-1914, asst. biologist, 1915-23, biologist, 1924-28, sr. biologist, 1928-41, asst. editor, 1942; curator ornithology Cleve. Mus. Natural History, 1941-47, mem. bd. mgrs., 1942-46, ret. Explorations in U.S. and Canadian provinces; prof. zoology Biltmore Forest Sch., 1904-10; prof. ornithology Pa. Summer Sch. for Tchrs., 1914; prof. zoology Am. U. Grad. Sch., 1920-35; lectr. Am. Sch. of Wild Life Protection, 1919-39; delivered many series of lectures on conservation and birds in many states before many sportsmen's conservation and ornithol. orgns. Fellow A.A.A.S., Am. Ornithologists Union, Ohio Acad. Sci.; mem. Schweizerische Gesellschaft für Vogelkunde und Vogelschutz, Süddeutsche Vogelwarte, Bombay Nat. Hist. Soc., Ornithol. Soc. New Zealand, Va. Ornithol. Soc., Cooper Ornithol. Club, Wilson Ornithol. Club (v.p. 1920-21), Cleve. Bird Club, Wash. Acad. Scis., Biol. Soc. Washington (v.p. 1920-25; pres. 1925-27), Ornithol. Soc. Japan, Royal Australian Ornithologists Union, Am. Nature Assn., Kirtland Bird Club, Schenectady Bird Club, Sigma Xi; hon. member Royal Hungarian Inst. Orinthology, Brit. Ornithologists Union; Neb. Ornithologists Union; hon. corr. mem. Md. Acad. Scis.; corr. mem. Deutsche Ornithologische Gesellschaft, Deutscher Verein zum Schutze der Vogelwelt, Sociedad Ornithológica del Plata, Ornithologische Gesellschaft in Bayern. Club: Professional Men's (Cleve.). Author: Birds of Mt. Kilimanjaro, 1905; Birds of Anamba Islands (S. China Sea), 1917; The Bird Life of Louisiana, 1938. Co-author: Measurements of Birds, 1931. Contbr. faunas, monographs, revisions and synopses of various families and genera to Proc. U.S. Nat. Mus., The Auk, others. Home: 2933 Berkshire Rd., Cleveland Hts., Cleve. 18. Died Dec. 25, 1963.

OBERNDORF, CLARENCE PAUL, (o'bern-dôrf), psychiatrist; b. N.Y. City, Feb. 16, 1882; s. Joseph and Augusta (Hammerstein) O.; A.B., Cornell, 1904, M.D., 1906; grad. Bellevue Hosp., 1908; unmarried. Began practice at N.Y. City, 1908; instr. in neurology, Cornell U. Med. Sch., 1914-20; adj. neurologist, Bellevue Hosp., 1915-20; asso. psychiatrist, Mt. Sinai Hosp., 1925-39; editor Internat. Jour. Psycho-analysis since 1922; associate editor American Journal of Psychiatry, 1948; contbg. editor Psychoanalytic Review since 1937; clin. prof. psychiatry, Columbia U., 1936-49. Dir. Jewish Child Care Assn. of N.Y., Hillside Hosp. Recipient Samuel W. Hamilton Award, 1951. Mem. Am. Neurol. Assn., Am. Psycho-analytic Assn. (ex-pres.), N.Y. Psychoanalytic Soc. (ex-pres.), N.Y. Society Psychotherapy (ex-president), American Psychiatric Assn., Am. Psychopath. Assn. (president) New York Neurol. Society (ex-pres.), N.Y. Acad. of Med., N.Y. Psychiatric Soc., N.Y. Soc. for Clin. Psychiatry (ex-pres.), Bellevue Alumni Soc., Phi Kappa Tau. Club: Cornell. Author: The Psychiatric Novels of Oliver Wendell Holmes; Which Way Out; A History of Psychoanalysis in America. Contbr. on psychoanalytic and psychiatric subjects to technical jours. Address: 40 W. 59th St., N.Y.C. 19. Died May 30, 1954.

O'BRIEN, EDWARD JAMES, thoracic surgeon; b. Hatley, Wis., Apr. 28, 1887; s. James and Elizabeth (Hayes) O'B.; M.D., Detroit Coll. Medicine, 1909; m. Marion Robb, Nov. 11, 1911 (died 1946) m. 2d Marie Rasmussen, Aug. 18, 1958. Interne Harper Hosp., Detroit, and practiced medicine Detroit, 1911—, chief surgeon Herman Kiefer Hosp., 1922—, head div., chest surgery Harper Hosp., thoracic surgeon Detroit & Northville T.B. Sanitarium; thoracic surgeon Am. Legion Hosp. (Battle Creek), Saginaw Co. Contagious Tuberculosis Hosp., 1926—, prof. surg. Wayne U., 1934—, cons. surgeon Mich. State T.B. Sanitarium 1938—, thoracic surgeon Lima Dist. T.B. Hosp., 1940—. Developed collapse therapy and other surg. methods for treatment t.b., also instigated Detroit program for early t.b. diagnosis and hospitalization; instrumental in obtaining state subsidies for tuberculosis patients. Pres. Mich. State Sanatorium Commn., 1930—. Mem. council Am. Assn. for Thoracic Surgery (pres.); fellow A.C.S., A.M.A.; mem. Am. Acad. Tuberculosis Phys. (pres.), Central Surg. Soc., Mich. and Am. Trudeau Soc., Detroit Acad. Surgeons, Wayne County Med. Assn., Mich. State Med. Assn. Contbr. U.S. Marine Hosp., Ellis Island, N.Y., 1919-20, Manhattan Maternity Hosp. and Dispensary, 1920; staff mem. Bur. Mines, USPHS, 1920-21; mem. internat. health bd. Rockefeller Found., Thailand, 1921-25; asst. resident in surgery Cin. Gen. Hosp., 1925-26; asso. physician McCormick Hosp., Chiengmai, Thailand, 1926-31; commr. health Lorain County, O., 1931-34, Chattaraugus County, N.Y., 1935-41; asst. dist. state health officer N.Y. State Dept. Health, 1934-35; dir. local health adminstrn. Conn. Dept. Health, 1941-43; commd. lt. col. USPHS, 1943, advanced through grades to col.; assigned to Cairo, Sydney, Manila, Shanghai, Washington, Addis Ababa, 1943-55; dir. profl. edn. Pa. Dept. Health, 1955-64. Guest lectr. Western Res. U., Cornell U., U. Minn. Diplomate Am. Bd. Preventive Medicine. Fellow Am. Pub. Health Assn., A.C.S., Royal Soc. Tropical Medicine and Health, Am. Coll. Preventive Medicine; mem. A.M.A., Am. Soc. Tropical Medicine and Health, Sigma Xi, Alpha Omega Alpha. Home: Camp Hill PA Died Aug. 16, 1970; buried Camp Hill PA

O'BRIEN, FREDERICK WILLIAM, radiologist; b. Boston, Sept. 27, 1881; s. Jeremiah and Margaret (Quinlan) O'B.; A.B., Boston Coll., 1903, LL.D., 1948; M.D., Tufts Coll., 1911; postgrad. Sch. Arts and Sci., Harvard, 1920-23; m. Sara Green, Oct. 10, 1921; children—Frederick William, Richard Green, Marie Therese. Instr. radiology Tufts Coll. Med. Sch., 1916-19, asst. prof., 1919-24, asso. prof., 1924-30, prof., 1930-41, emeritus prof. since 1941; chief tumor clinic Boston City Hosp. since 1939; radiologist Cambridge City Hosp. since 1916; radiologist Mattapan Tb Sanatorium since 1917. Served as 1st lt. Ambulance Co. No. 1, Mass. N.G., during World War I; lt. comdr. USNR, 1935-41. Recipient Janeway Medal, 1946. Mem. Am. Bd. Radiology (examiner since 1940). Mem. Brit. Inst. Radiology, Am. Radium Soc. (pres. 1940); Am. Roentgen Ray Soc. (1st v.p. 1941), Radiol. Soc. N.Am. (pres. 1947). Clubs: Harvard, Algonquin (Boston). Author numerous brochures on med. subjects. Home: 465 Beacon St., Boston 15. Died Dec. 20, 1965.

O'BRIEN, HENRY RUST, physician; b. Oberlin, O., July 14, 1891; s. James Putnam and Lizzie (Coffin) O'B.; M.D., U. Mich., 1919; M.P.H., Johns Hopkins U., 1931; m. Mary L. Phillips Carr, Mar. 24, 1926; children—Martha Jane (Mrs. Giles C. Fenn), Susan (Mrs. Susan Bowman), James Putnam. Intern, Bklyn. Hosp., 1919, numerous research papers to med. jours. Address: David Whitney Bldg., Detroit 26. Died Oct. 19, 1959.

O'BRIEN, WILLIAM JAMES, bus. exec.; b. Rosendale, N.Y., Mar. 21, 1888; s. James and Elizabeth (King) O'B.; grad. Cornell U.; m. Helen M. Scott, Feb. 9, 1924: 1 dau., Shirley. Chemist, Geneva Expt. Sta., 1911-12; instr. Cornell U., 1912-14; scientist U.S. Dept. Agr., 1914-18; research dir. Grasselli Chem. Co. (N.J.), 1918-20; gen. mgr. chem. and pigment div. Glidden Co., 1920-29; dir., v.p. in charge tech. mfg., 1929-50, v.p., dir., 1950-52; v.p., chmn. research and mfg. com., adminstrv. charge chem. and pigment, metals refining Euston Lead & Naval Stores Div., 1945-46; v.p., dir. Gen. Biochems., Inc., Chagrin Falls, O., since 1952. Mem. Am. Chem. Soc., Shell Com. Am. Ordnance Assn., Sigma Xi. Clubs: Union, Mayfield, Chagrin Valley Hunt (Cleve.); Union League (Chgo.). Contbr. numerous articles to profl. jours. Home: Gates Mills, O. Office: Union Commerce Bldg., Cleve.; also Chagrin Falls, O. Died 1960.

O'CALLAGHAN, EDMUND BALLEY, physician, historian; b. Mallow, Ireland, Feb. 28, 1797; m. Charlotte Crampe; m. 2d, Ellen Hawe, May 9, 1841; 2 children. Admitted to med. practice in Can., 1823; editor Vindicator, Montreal, 1834; mem. Canadian Parliament, 1836; participated in Louis Joseph Papineau's Revolution, 1837; moved to Albany, N.Y., 1837; treas. Albany County Med. Soc.; contbr. poetry to The Northern Light, 1842-44; editor The Documentary History of the State of New York, 1849-51; Documents Relative to the Colonial History of the State of New vols. 1-11, 1853-61; Laws and Ordinances of New Netherland, 1638-74, 1868. Author: History of New Netherland, 2 vols., 1846-48; Jesuit Relations, 1847; Remonstrances of New Netherland, 1856; "Orderly Books" of Commissary Wilson, 1857. Died N.Y.C., May 29, 1880.

OCHSNER, EDWARD H., surgeon; b. Honey Creek, Sauk County, Wis., Jan. 12, 1868; s. Henry and Judith (Hottiger) O.; B.S., U. of Wis., 1891; M.D., Rush Med. Coll., 1894; post-grad. study, Vienna, Leipzig, Hamburg, 1896-97; m. Julia I. Andersen, Sept. 2, 1899; children—Marion Louise (Mrs. Marion Pease), Herbert Edward, Alice Constance (Mrs. Homer Kieweg), Raymond Bertram. Intern Cook County Hosp., Chicago, 1894-95; attending surgeon St. Mary's of Nazareth Hosp., 1899-1903; attending surgeon Augustana Hosp., 1904-32, cons. surgeon since 1932. Adjunct prof. clin. surgery, Coll. of Physicians and Surgeons, Univ. of Illinois, 1900-16. Mem. Med. Advisory Bd. No. 3B, Selective Service, 1917-18. Pres. Ill. State Charities Commn., 1912-16. Fellow Am. Coll. Surgeons; mem. Chicago Med., Surg. and Pathol. socs., Ill. State Med. Soc. (pres. 1923-24), A.M.A., Southern Surg. Assn. Club: City. Author: Physical Exercises for Invalids and Convalescents; Chronic Fatigue Intoxication; Social Insurance and Economic Security; Social Security; Fundamentals of Personal Hygiene. Contbr. articles to med. and quasi-med. jours. Address: 172 Sheridan Rd., Chgo. Died Jan. 22, 1956.

OCKERSON, JOHN AUGUSTUS, civil engr.; b. Skane, Sweden, Mar. 4, 1848; s. Jons and Boel Jons (Dotler) Akerson; came to U.S., 1851; B.S., C.E., Univ. of Ill., 1873 (D.Eng., 1903); m. Helen M. Chapin, of Detroit, Nov. 8, 1875 (died 1886); 2d, Clara W. Shackelford, of St. Louis, June 4, 1890. Served in Civil War in 132d Ill. Inf. and 1st Minn. Heavy Arty.; in milling business in Minn., 1865-68; recorder and later asst. in field and office on survey Great Lakes, 1871-79; asst. engr. location and constrn. A.,T. & S.F. R.R., 1872; U.S. asst. engr. Eads jetties, 1876, survey Miss. River, 1879-87; mgr. and engr. gold and silver mine in Colo., 1888-89; chief asst. engr., 1889-98, and since Aug. 4, 1898, mem. Miss. River Commn.; also consulting engr. Chief Dept. Liberal Arts, St. Louis Expn., 1904; mem. Internat. Jury of Awards, Paris Expn.; del. Internat. Congress of Navigation, 1900, Milan, 1905, St. Petersburg, 1908, Phila., 1912, Congress of Merchant Marine, Paris. Decorated Officer Public Instruction Meritede Agricole (France); Knight Crown of Italy; Knight Order of Vasa (Sweden); comdr. Order of the Vasa (Sweden), Knight Crown of Germany; Knight Crown of Belgium; Order of Double Dragon (China).

Author numerous papers on topog. and engring. subjects. Mem. Am. Soc. C.E. (pres., 1912), St. Louis Engrs. Club (twice pres.), Nat. Geog. Soc. Clubs: Noonday, Bellerive. Home: 5305 Delmar Av. Office: International Life Bldg., St. Louis, Mo. Died Mar. 22, 1924.

ODELL, FRANK GLENN, statistician; b. Bushnell, Ill., July 20, 1864; s. John J. and Jennie (Goodrich) O.; studied law, U. of Neb., 1893; m. Elizabeth McMillen, of Lincoln, Neb., Aug. 12, 1894; children—Jay Geddes, Mrs. Dorothy Schneider, Maurice Glenn, Mrs. Katherine Schanuel, Robert McMillen. Sec. Neb. Rural Life Commn., 1910-12; chief of bur. agrl. statistics, Neb., 1912; editor Neb. Farm Mag., 1913-14; sec. Federal Land Bank of Omaha, 1917-19; exec. sec. Nat. Conservation Congress; dir. of research, The Capper Farm Press, Topeka, Kan., 1919-20. Mem. Am. Statis. Assn. Democrat. Presbyn. Clubs: Elks, Kiwanis, Commercial, Advertising. Home: 725 W. Lockwood Av., Kirkwood, Mo. Office: 2206 Pine St., St. Louis, Mo.

ODEN, (AXEL) ROBERT, physician; b. Göteborg, Sweden, Oct. 29, 1882; s. Adolph and Anna (Johanson) O.; B.S., Gymnasium, Göetborg, 1901; M.D., Ph.D., George Washington U., 1919; grad. study Johns Hopkins, 1919-22; post grad. study Guys Hosp. (London); 6 months Petit Hosp. (Paris), 6 months, Allgemeines Krankenhaus, Vienna, 1924; post grad. study, Berlin, 1926; m. Lilly Hermine Tingstrom, Feb. 8, 1909 (dec. 1943); married 2d, Helga Bosser, January 8, 1956. Came to U.S. 1907, naturalized 1919. Phys. Johns Hopkins Hosp., gastrointestinal clinic, 1919-23; in practice of internal med., Washington, D.C., 1923, and since 1927; instructor Johns Hopkins, 1926; specialist in arthritis and diagnosis. Commander Naval Reserve Corps, 1927-36. Life mem. A.M.A. of Vienna; mem. A.M.A., Washington Med. and Surg. Soc. (pres. 1938-39), George Washington U. Med. Soc., George Washington Univ. Alumni (life mem.), Internat. Med. Club, Am. Assn. for Study and Control Rheumatic Diseases, Internationale Contre le Rhumatisme, Amsterdam (Holland), Science Club of America, Pan-American Medical Asns., Am. Geriatric Soc., Med. Soc. of D.C., A.M.A., American Association Advancement Science, Alpha Kappa Kappa. Lutheran. Mason (32 deg., K.T., Shriner). Clubs: Sulgrave, Cosmos, Burning Tree Golf, Army and Navy (Washington, D.C.); Old Pueblo (Tucson). Original research work on Macacus rhesus monkeys in cerebral motor control. Decorated Order of North Star (Swedish), Comdr. Order of Vasa (Swedish), Comdr. of St. Olaf (Norway), Comdr. Scanderberg, Austrian Red Cross, Legion of Honor, Palms Academic. Author of med. articles and monographs. Address: Catalina Foothills Estates, R.R. 4, Box 92, Tucson, Ariz. Died June 6, 1964.

ODENBACH, FREDERICK LOUIS, meteorologist; b. Rochester, N.Y., Oct. 21, 1857; s. John and Elizabeth (Minges) O.; A.B., Canisius Coll., Buffalo, N.Y., 1881; studied in univs. of Europe. Joined Soc. of Jesus, 1881; prof. physics and chemistry, 1893-1903, then prof. astronomy and meteorology, St. Ignatius Coll., Cleveland, also founder, 1895, and dir. Meteorol. Obs.; now prof. astronomy, John Carroll U., Cleveland. Inventor of ceraunograph and an elec. seismograph; the 6th observer of the Helvetian halo, Dec. 6, 1901. Died Mar. 15, 1933.

O'DWYER, JOSEPH, physician; b. Cleve., Oct. 12, 1841; grad. Coll. physicians and Surgeons, N.Y.C., 1866; m. Catherine Begg, 8 children. First physician to successfully employ intubation for asphyxia in diptheria, and to use diptheria serum; apptd. to staff N.Y. Foundling Asylum, 1872. Died N.Y.C., Jan. 7, 1898.

OEFELE, FELIX VON, medical chemistry; b. Wildberghof, Mittelfranken, Germany, Dec. 24, 1861; s. Edgar von and Emile (Hoermann) O.; ed. Switzerland and Germany; Biol. Sta., Naples; univs. of Erlangen and München; M.D., U. of Bonn, 1894; m. Ida Roll, of Edenkoben, Mar. 6, 1897. Early made extensive bot. collections; presented Alpine plants to U. of Giessen, 1883, and large collection of herbs, in sects and petrifactions to Pub. Mus., Milwaukee, 1887; extensive researches in bot. pharmacology and its history; practiced medicine German health resorts, 17 yrs., in meantime studied 30 langs. and became an authority in old Egyptian and Babylonian med. texts (hieroglyphic and cuneiform medicine); specialized in chemistry of faeces in diabetes, gallstones, incomplete mastication; preliminary publications concerning the atoms of the chemical elements as crystals of a continuous crystallographical series; located in New York, 1909—. Proprietor Oefele Lab., Oefele Chemiatry (preparation of rare elements, etc.). Author: Mediaeval Low German, Bartholomeus Salernitanus, 1892; Vergleichstabellen zur praktischen Koprologie, 1903; Technik der chemischen Untersuchung, 1908; Geschichte der Kekidologie, "history of the gallnuts" (with Konrad Böhner), 1933. Also contbr. various European publs. on history of medicine, Egyptian and Babylonian medicine, astrology in medicine, superstition in medicine, chem. constitution of saliva, duodenal contents, faeces and urine, etc. Address: 1431 Madison Av., New York, N.Y.

OEMLER, ARMINUS, agriculturist; b. Savannah, Ga., Sept. 12, 1827; s. Augustus Gottlieb and Mary Ann (Shad) O.; grad. with honors Dresden Technische Bildungsanstalt, 1848; M.D., U. City N.Y., 1856; m. Elizabeth P. Heyward, Apr. 10, 1856, 6 children. Joined Confederate Army, commd. capt. 2d Company, deKalb Riflemen; made 1st map of Chatham County (Ga.); founder 1st comml. oyster packing plant in South, Wilmington Island, Ga.; discoverer presence of nitrogen-fixing bacteria in nodules of leguminous plants, 1886, discouraged from further research by U.S. Dept. of agr. (actual discovery made in Germany 2 years later). Died Savannah, Aug. 8, 1897; buried Wilmington Island.

OENSLAGER, GEORGE, research chemist; b. Harrisburg, Pa., Sept. 25, 1873; s. John and Harriet (Freaner) O.; grad. Phillips Exeter Acad., 1890; A.B., Harvard, 1894; A.M., 1896; m. Ruth Alderfer, July 15, 1939. Chemist S. D. Warren & Co., Cumberland Mills., Me., 1896-1906; research chemist Diamond Rubber Co., 1906-12, B. F. Goodrich Co., 1912-20, 22-40; tech. adviser Yokohama Rubber Co., Japan, 1922. Trustee Akron Art Inst. Awarded Perkin medal for development in vulcanization, 1933; also Charles Goodyear Medal, 1948. Fellow Inst. Rubber Chemistry; mem. Am. Chem. Soc., Inst. Chem. Engrs., Instn. of Rubber Industry. Republican. Episcopalian. Clubs: Portage Country, University (Akron). Conducted experimental lab. 1940-56. Oenslager award, Japan, established, 1958. Home: 85 N. Wheaton Rd., Akron 13, O. Died Feb. 5, 1956; buried Glendale Cemetery, Akron, O.

OGDEN, FRANCIS BARBER, engr., diplomat; b. Boonton, N.J., Mar. 3, 1783; s. Gen. Matthias and Hannah (Dayton) O.; m. Louisa Pawnall, 1837. Aide-de-camp under Gen. Andrew Jackson in Battle of New Orleans, 1815; built 1st low pressure condensing engine with 2 cylinders, Leeds, Yorkshire, Eng., 1817; apptd. U.S. consul, Liverpool, Eng., 1830; consul, Bristol, Eng., 1840-57; helped make John Ericssen (inventor of Monitor) known in U.S. Died Bristol, July 4, 1857.

OGDEN, HENRY NEELY, civil engr.; b. Dexter, Me., Apr. 30, 1868; s. Charles Talcott and Anna (Bennett) O.; ed. Episcopal and Cheltenham acads., Phila.; C.E., Cornell, 1889; m. Mary G. Smith, Dec. 26, 1895; children—Katharine, Priscilla Campbell, John Bennett, William Hall, Robert Neely (dec.), Ruth Patterson. Made study of sewerage in Europe, 1897; engr. in charge of the sewer system of Ithaca, New York; was the designer of the plans for the stone arch 64 ft. span and retaining wall 30 ft. high, Cornell U.; prof. civ. engineering, 1896-1906, prof. sanitary engring. since 1906, professor emeritus since 1938, Cornell University. Engineer to New York State Board of Health, 1906-13. Member Public Health Council State of N.Y. since 1913. Mem. Am. Soc. C.E., Sigma Xi. Author: Sewer Design, 1899; Sewer Construction, 1908; Rural Hygiene, 1910. Consulting engr. Home: 416 Hanshaw Rd., Ithaca, N.Y. Died Sep. 29, 1947.

OGDEN, HERBERT GOUVERNEUR, asst. U.S. Coast and Geodetic Survey, 1869—; and insp. of hydrography and topography, 1898; b. New York, April 4, 1846; s. Morgan Lewis and Eliza Glendy (McLaughlin) O.; ed. private schools and tutors; apptd. aid, April 22, 1863, promoted to asst., 1869, U.S. Coast and Geodetic Survey; m. Mary A. Greene, May 28, 1872. Served, 1863, with army on defenses of Washington; 1864, with navy in sounds of N.C.; 1865, with Nicaragua expdn.; 1870, as topographer with 1st naval exploring expdn. to Isthmus of Darien; 1893, in charge of party locating internat. boundary between British Columbia and Alaska; etc. Mem. U.S. Bd. on Geographic Names; expert in topography and chartography. Deceased.

OGDEN, JAY BERGEN, physician, chemist; b. West Sparta, N.Y., Aug., 1868; s. of Charles W. O.; prep. edn. Nunda Acad., 1875-80, Geneseo State Normal School, 1881-85; grad. Harvard Med. School, 1893; m. Buffalo, N.Y., Sept. 11, 1895, Alice Lewellyn Parry. Instr. in chemistry, Harvard Med. Sch., 1894-1901; asst. in clinical pathology, Boston City Hosp., 1893-1901; visiting med. chemist, Long Island Hosp., 1896-1901; med. chemist, Carney Hosp., 1897-1901; Children's Hosp., 1900-01; sec. Suffolk dist. branch, Mass. Med. Soc., 1899-1901. Author: Clinical Examinations of the Urine and Urinary Diagnosis, 1900 S15. Contbr. to med. jours. Address: 262 5th Av., New York.

OGLE, KENNETH NEIL, educator; b. Lake City, Colo., Nov. 27, 1902; s. Wesley Harlan and Luella (Moore) O.; A.B., Colo. Coll., 1925; A.M., Dartmouth, 1927, Ph.D., 1930; Dr. Medicine honoris causa, U. Uppsala, 1962; D.Sc. honoris causa, Colo. Coll., 1963; m. Elizabeth Bartlett, Sept. 18, 1934; children—Betsy (Mrs. Jordan), Nancy (Mrs. Richard F. Brubaker). Teaching fellow U. Minn., 1927-28; research fellow physiol. optics Dartmouth, 1930-34; asst. prof. physiol. optics Dartmouth Eye Inst., 1934-46, prof., 1946-47; staff sect. biophysics Mayo Clinic, Rochester, Minn., 1947-68, research cons. sect. ophthalmology, 1947-68, chmn. sect. biophysics, 1958-68; professor physiol. optics Mayo Grad. Sch. Medicine U. Minn., 1952-68; prof. ophthalmology U. Minn. Med. Sch., 1968; dir. initial phase survey U.S. eye care needs Nat. Inst. Neurol. Diseases and Blindness-Med. Sch. U. Minn., 1968. Member of Am. com. optics and visual physiology A.M.A.; mem. Armed Forces Nat. Research Council vision com.; spl. consultant, U.S. Public Health Service; mem. edn. adv. com. Ednl. Found. in Ophthalmic Optics, Am. Bd. Opticianry; mem. optical aids adv. com. Am. Found. for Blind. Mem. of bd. of directors Rochester Art Center. Recipient Tillyer medal Optical Soc. Am., 1967; Beverly Myers Nelson Achievement award Am. Bd. Opticianry, 1957. Member Biophys. Society, Psychonomic Society, Am. Academy of Ophthalmology and Otolaryngology, Nat. Society Prevention Blindness (mem. com. basic and clin. research), Internat. Acad. of Opticianry (mem. council), A.A.A.S., Am. Assn. for History Medicine, Optical Soc. Am. (asso. editor jour.). Am. Minn. psychol. assns., American Physiological Society, Association for Research Ophthalmology (Proctor medal 1962), Minn. Acad. Sci., Sigma Xi, Pi Kappa Alpha, Gamma Alpha. Rotarian. Author: Researches in Binocular Vision, 1950; Optics-An Introduction for Ophthalmologists, 1961; Oculomoter Imbalance in Binocular Vision and Fixation Disparity, 1967. Asso. editor: Investigative Ophthalmology; hon. editor: Vision Research. Contbr. profl. jours. Home: Rochester MN Died Feb. 22, 1968; buried Rochester MN

OGLESBY, NICHOLAS EWING, (o'g'lz-bi), chemical engineer, registered patent agent; b. in Wythe County, Va., May 25, 1892; s. John Thompson and Emma Montgomery (Painter) O.; student Emory and Henry Coll., Emory, Va., 1909-11; A.B., U. of Va., 1913; A.M., 1917, Ph.D., 1929; m. Mary Louise Sandidge, Nov. 4, 1920; children—Nicholas Ewing, John Thompson, 2d. High Sch. teacher sci. and mathematics, 1913-15; asst. in chemistry, U. of Va., 1915-17; jr. chem. engr., Aluminum Co. of America, 1917; teaching fellow U. of Va., 1919-20; research chemist Glamorgan Pipe and Foundry Co., 1920; chief munitions dept., chem. div., Chem. Warfare Service, 1920-24, asst. chief chem. div., 1924-29; tech. dir. Behr-Manning Corp., mfrs. coated abrasives and spl. products, 1929-45; technical consultant, mgr. of Patent Dept. 1945—, bd. dirs., 1954—. Served Ordnance Dept., 2d lt. Chem. War Service, U.S. Army, 1918. Fellow A.A.A.S.; mem. Am. Chem. Soc., Am. Inst. Chem. Engrs. Mem. New York Acad. of Sciences, Eastern New York Section of Am. Chemical Soc. (Chmn.), 1943-45, S.R. in N.Y. State, Alpha Chi Sigma, Raven Soc. (U. Va.). Republican. Presbyn. Mason (32 deg., Shriner). Club: Country (Troy). Joint inventor of tear gas grenades used by police and airplane smoke curtain used by Army and Navy; inventor abrasive processes and products. Home: 181 Pinewoods Av., Troy, N.Y. Office: Behr-Manning Corp., Troy, N.Y. Died Mar. 8, 1957; buried Spring Hill Cemetery, Lynchburg, Va.

O'HANRAHAN, INKA IRENE (MRS. SEAMUS O'HANRAHAN), clin. bioanalyst; b. Warsaw, Poland; d. Hermann and Ala (Eiznerowicz) Winter; student U. Freiburg, Berlin, Germany, 1931-32, U. Berne (Switzerland), 1932; B.A., U. Cal., Berkeley, 1945; m. Seamus O'Hanrahan, 1933; children—Janina (Mrs. Charles Paul), Brigid, Tighe. Came to U.S., 1932, naturalized, 1938. Owner, dir. O'Hanrahan Clin. Lab., San Francisco, 1936-70; lectr. on status of women, 1960-70; vice chmn. bd. dirs. Lab. Services, Inc. Vice chmn. Adv. Commn. on Status of Women, 1965-67. Pres., bd. dirs. Pacific Mus. Soc. Mem. A.A.A.S., U.S. Pub. Health Assn., Soroptimist Fedn. of Americas (pub. affairs chmn.), Nat. Orgn. For Women (nat. sec.-treas.), Bus. and Profl. Women, Am. Assn. U. Women (pres. S.W. chpt.), Guild Psychol. Studies, Cal. Assn. Clin. Labs. (past pres.), Am. Assn. Bionalysts (past nat. bd.), Analytical Psychology Club (past pres.). Club: Soroptimist (past pres. San Francisco). Contbr. articles to profl. jours. Home: San Francisco CA Died Jan. 15, 1970.

O'HARRA, CLEOPHAS CISNEY, geologist; b. Bentley, Ill., Nov. 4, 1866; s. Jefferson Wood and Paulina (Robertson) O.; A.B., Carthage (Ill.) Coll., 1891, LL.D., 1920; Ph.D., Johns Hopkins, 1898 (Phi Beta Kappa); m. Mary Phebe Marvel, June 15, 1893; children—Berry Marvel, Paul Wyatt, Wayne Gilder, Mariam. Instr. Latin and physics, 1891-92, prof. natural and phys. sciences, 1892-95, v.p., 1894-95, Carthage Coll.; prof. mineralogy and geology, 1898-1911, pres. and prof. geology, July 1, 1911—, S.D. State Sch. of Mines, Chmn. S.Dak. State Coal Commn., 1917-18; mem. State Advisory Bd. Federal Fuel Administration, 1917-19; ednl. dir. Soldier Training, S.Dak. State Sch. of Mines, World War. Fellow Geol. Soc. America, A.A.A.S. Conglist. Author: The White River Badlands; The Mineral Wealth of the Black Hills, 1929; joint author The Geology, Mineralogy, and Scenic Features of Custer State Park, S.D. Editor in chief, Black Hills Engineer. Home: Rapid City, S.D. Died Feb. 21, 1935.

OHLMACHER, JOSEPH CHRISTIAN, pathologist; b. Sycamore, Ill., Oct. 27, 1874; s. Christian John and Gertrude Anna (Sherer) O.; M.D., Rush Med. Coll., Chicago, 1901; m. Florence E. Jayne, Oct. 24, 1910; children—Joseph Philip, William Arthur, Jayne Elizabeth, Gertrude Ann, Albert Edgar. Research student in pathology, Rush Med. Coll., 1899-1901; instr. pathology, Northwestern U. Med. Sch., 1901-02;

pathologist and clin. dir. Independence (Ia.) State Hosp., 1902-10; pathologist and asst. supt. Clarinda (Ia.) State Hosp., 1913-18; prof. and head of dept. pathology, Med. Sch., Univ. of S.D. since 1918, dean of Sch. of Med., 1934-46; emeritus prof. since 1948; dir. State Health Lab. of South Dakota since 1918; pathologist Sacred Heart Hosp., Yankton, S.D., since 1923, dir. training med. technologists, since 1948. Member Am. Medical Assn., Am. Public Health Assn., S.D. State Med. Assn., Sioux Valley Med. Soc., S.D. Acad. Science; hon. mem. Woodbury County Med. Assn. Past pres. Sioux Valley Medical Soc., Southwest Iowa Med. Society, Yankton Dist. S.D. State Med. Assn. Republican. Universalist. Mason. Rotarian. Phi Chi. Contbr. on original researches in pathology, bacteriology and serology. Home: 309 Lewis St., Vermilion SD

O'KANE, WALTER COLLINS, entomologist, author; b. Columbus, O., Nov. 10, 1877; s. Henry and Catherine (Van de Water) O'K.; A.B., Ohio State Univ., 1897, A.M., 1909; hon. D.Sc., Ohio State University, 1932; m. Clifford Hetherington, Dec. 30, 1902; children—Elizabeth Wells, Catherine Van de Water, William Henry, Richard Hetherington. In newspaper and mag. work, 1897-1909; circulation mgr. Woman's Home Companion, and Farm and Fireside, Springfield, O., 1900; same, Twentieth Century Farmer, Omaha, Neb., 1901; asst. entomologist, 1909, asso., 1910, entomologist since Sept. 1911, N.H. Exptl. Sta.; prof. of econ. entomology, U. of N.H., 1911-47, prof. emeritus, since 1947. State moth agt., N.H., 1911-13; dep. commr. agr., N.H., 1913-47. Sergt. major, 10th Ohio Regt., Spanish-Am. War. Chairman govs. Crop Protection Inst.; fellow A.A.A.S., Entomol. Soc. America; mem. Am. Assn. Econ. Entomologists (pres. 1919), N.H. Acad. Science (pres. 1924-25), Beta Theta Pi, Sigma Xi, Phi Kappa Phi. Clubs: Authors (New York); Appalachian Mountain; Green Mountain; Authors' (London). Author: Injurious Insects, 1913; Jim and Peggy at Meadowbrook Farm, 1917; Jim and Peggy at Apple-Top Farm, 1923; Trails and Summits of the White Mountains, 1925; Trails and Summits of the Green Mountains, 1926; Trails and Summits of the Adirondacks, 1928. Home: Durham NH

OLCOTT, EBEN ERSKINE, mining and metall. engr., transportation official; b. N.Y. City, Mar. 11, 1854; s. John N. and Euphemia Helen (Knox) O.; student Coll. City of New York; E.M., Columbia, 1874; m. Kate, d. Commodore Alfred Van Santvoord, of New York, 1884. Mining and metall. engr. formerly in practice in Western States, Mexico and S. America; pres. Hudson River Day Line; v.p. Lincoln Safe Deposit Co. Inaugurated movement for Tri-centennial celebration, 1909, of entrance of Hendrick Hudson into Harbor of New York, Sept. 11, 1609. Pres. Am. Inst. Mining Engrs., 1901-02. Home: New York, N.Y. Died June 5, 1929.

OLCOTT, WILLIAM JAMES, mining engr.; b. Detroit, Feb. 22, 1862; s. Harlow and Elizabeth (Fifield) O.; Ph.B., U. of Mich., 1883, M.S., 1884; m. Fannie Bailey, of Ann Arbor, Mich., Dec. 26, 1887. Asst. engr. and engr. various mines in Lake Superior regions until 1894; supt. Lake Superior Consolidated Iron Mines, 1894; general supt. U.S. Steel Corp. mines, April 1, 1901-July 25, 1902; since then gen. mgr., same, pres. Duluth, Missabe & Northern R.R.; also pres. Oliver Iron Mining Co. since 1909. Pres. Lake Superior Soc. of Mining Engrs., 1902; mem. Am. Inst. Mining Engrs. Address: Duluth, Minn.

OLD, HOWARD NORMAN, sanitary engr.; b. Phila., Pa., Aug. 17, 1890; s. Abner Howard and Kathryn Jeffries (Hunsicker) O.; grad. Germantown Acad., Phila., Pa., 1908; m. Mary Bennett, Apr. 11, 1918. Civil engr. with cons. firms, Phila., 1910-12; mining engr., Nevada, 1912-13; sanitary engr. Phila. City Health Dept., 1914-17; U.S. Pub. Health Service, Fort Riley-Camp Funston Zone, Kan., 1918-19; assigned to malaria control operations in various southern states, U.S.P.H.S., hdqrs. Memphis, Tenn., 1919-25; sanitary engr. in charge of shellfish sanitation activities in Middle Atlantic States, Baltimore, Md., 1925-28; dist. engr. of P.H.S. dist. No. 4, Memphis, Tenn., 1928-29, hdqrs. New Orleans, 1929-39; charge engring. activities incident to interstate travel, nation-wide, U.S.P.H.S., Washington, District of Columbia, 1939-48; liaison officer U.S.P.H.S. with various other federal agencies, 1948-50; sanitary engr. cons. branch of health, U.S. Indian Service since 1950; through grades from jr. asst. sanitary engr. (2d lt.), 1918, to sanitary engr. dir. (col.), 1944; commd. corps. of P.H.S. br. of Armed Forces since 1945. Mem. Am. Soc. of C.E., Fed. Sewage Works Assn., Am. Pub. Health Assn., Conf. of State Sanitary Engrs. (sec.-treas. 1940-48), Nat. Geog. Soc., Commd. Officers Assn. of U.S.P.H.S. Presbyterian. Author numerous papers prepared and presented before techn. groups engaged in sanitary engring. and pub. health work. Widely known for improvements effected in living conditions of Am. Indians. Home: 6629 32d St. N.W., Washington 15. Office: 4130 Dept. of Interior, Washington 25. Died May 7, 1953; buried Germantown Ivy Hill Cemetery, Phila.

OLDBERG, OSCAR, pharmacist; b. Alfta, Sweden, Jan. 22, 1846; s. Anders and Frederika Katrina (Ohrstromer) O.; ed. Swedish pub. schs., pvt. teachers and, 1857-60, at Gymnasium, Gefle, Sweden; (Pharm. D. honoris causa, Nat. Coll. Pharmacy, Washington, 1881; LL.D., Northwestern U., 1911); came to U.S., 1864; m. Emma Parritt, May 19, 1873; father of Arne O. Engaged in ednl. and lit. work; vice-consul of Sweden and Norway at Memphis, Tenn., 1872; chief clerk and acting med. purveyor, U.S. Marine Hosp. Service 7 yrs., and at same time mem. faculty of Nat. Coll. Pharmacy; dean Sch. of Pharmacy, Northwestern U., 1886-1911. Mem. Com. Revision U.S. Pharmacopoeia, 1880—. Author: Companion to the United States Pharmacopoeia (Oldberg and Wall), 1884; Weights and Measures, 1885; Laboratory Manual of Chemistry (with John H. Long), 1894; Home Study in Pharmacy, 1890; Fifteen Hundred Examples of Prescriptions and Formulas, 1892; Inorganic Chemistry, General, Medical and Pharmaceutical, 1900; Pharmaceutical Problems and Exercises. Home: Chicago, Ill. Died Feb. 27, 1913.

OLDER, CLIFFORD, cons. engr.; b. Lincoln, Adams County, Wis., Nov. 17, 1876; s. Milton DeWitt and Elizabeth Ann (Clark) O.; B.S. in C.E., Univ. of Wis., 1900; m. Kitty May Drake, May 28, 1903; children—Fern Elizabeth, Kitty Beatrice, Clifford Dewilton, David Drake, Grenfell. Asst. engr. with Pa. R.R., 1900-01, Wabash Pittsburgh Terminal R.R., 1901-02; div. engr. C.&A. R.R., 1902-06; bridge engr. Ill. State Highway Dept., 1906-17; chief state highway engr. of Ill., 1917-24 (handling road constrn. involving outlay of over $100,000,000); conducted Bates test road research; now cons. engr. Mem. design com. U.S. Research Council. Mem. Am. Soc. C.E., Western Soc. Engrs. Republican. Methodist. Mason. Home: 1026 Elmwood Av., Wilmette, Ill. Died Nov. 28, 1943; buried in Silver Lake Cemetery, Portage, Wis.

OLDS, EDWIN GLENN, statistician; b. Buffalo, Apr. 20, 1898; s. Edwin Nelson and Effie Ruth (Wells) O.; A.B., Cornell U., 1918; A.M., U. Pitts., 1925, Ph.D., 1931; m. Marion McNeil Knowles, Mar. 30, 1918; children—David McNeil, Marcia Elisabeth (Mrs. Wilbur J. Singley Jr.). Instr. Carnegie Inst. Tech., 1922-25, asst. prof., 1925-31, asso. prof., 1931-51, prof., 1951—; statis. cons. indsl. and research orgns., 1938—; lectr. statis. quality control, 1943—. Chief statis. cons. Office Prodn. Research and Development, WPB, 1943-45. Recipient Brumbaugh award, 1954, Shewhart medal, 1955. Fellow Inst. Math. Statistics (v.p. 1946, pres. 1954), Am. Statis. Assn., Am. Soc. Quality Control; mem. Math. Assn. Am., Res. Sect. Royal Statis. Soc., Am. Mathematical Soc., Sigma Xi, Phi Kappa Phi. Presbyn. (ruling elder 1939—). Mason. Author: Vocational Mathematics, 1930. Contbr. sci. articles profl. publs. Home: 222 Gladstone Rd., Pitts. 15217. Died Oct. 9, 1961; buried Cold Springs Cemetery, Lockport, N.Y.

OLDS, GEORGE DANIEL, mathematician; b. Middleport, N.Y., Oct. 14, 1853; s. Eli D. and Mary (Shurtleff) O.; A.B., U. of Rochester, 1873, A.M., 1876; grad. work Heidelberg and Berlin, 1879-83; LL.D., Rochester, 1907, Amherst College, 1921, Wesleyan U., Conn., 1927; m. Marion E. Leland, June 16, 1886; children—Leland, George Daniel, Clara Leland (Mrs. I.J. Bissell), Marion (Mrs. Geoge E. Keeler). Teacher Albany (N.Y.) Acad., 1873-79; prof. mathematics, U. of Rochester, 1884-91, Amherst Coll., 1891-1927, dean, 1909-22, acting pres. and pres.-elect, 1923-24, pres. 1924-27, pres. emeritus. Home: Amherst, Mass. Died May 10, 1931.

OLDS, RANSOM ELL, automobile mfr.; b. Geneva, O., June 3, 1864; s. Pliny Fisk and Sarah (Whipple) O.; student high sch., Lansing; D.Eng. (hon.), Mich State Coll., Mich. Coll. Mining and Tech.; D.Sc., Kalamazoo Coll.; m. Metta U. Woodward, June 5, 1889; children—Gladys Marguerite (Mrs. Gladys O. Anderson), Bernice E. (Mrs. C. S. Roe). A pioneer in automobile business; built the first 3-wheeled horseless carriage, 1886; brought out a practical 4-wheeled automobile, 1893, pres. Reo Motor Car Co., 1904-24, chmn. bd., 1924-36. Dir. Kalamazoo College, Hillsdale Coll. Donor Science Hall to Kalamazoo Coll., engring. bldg. to Mich. State Coll., club house to the affiliated women's clubs, civic social welfare house to City of Lansing, etc. Mason (33 deg., K.T., Shriner), Knight of Holy Sepulchre. Baptist. Clubs: Detroit, Detroit Athletic, Detroit Yacht, Detroit Boat; Congressional (Washington); City, Country (Lansing). Home: Lansing, Mich.; (winter) Daytona Beach, Fla. Died Aug. 26, 1950.

O'LEARY, PAUL ARTHUR, dermatologist, syphilologist; b. Brooklyn, N.Y., Nov. 11, 1891; s. Jeremiah J. and Anna Belle (Coy) O'L; student Dartmouth Coll., 1910-11; M.D., Long Island Coll., 1915; m. Ruth Youmans, June 18, 1921; children—Paul Arthur, Patricia. Interne Long Island Coll. Hosp., 1915-16; associate sect. on dermatology, Mayo Clinic, Rochester, Minn., 1917-24, head sect. on dermatology and syphilology since 1924; prof. of dermatology, Mayo Foundation Grad. Sch., U. of Minn., since 1924. Diplomate Am. Bd. Dermatology and Syphilology. Fellow Am. Coll. of Physicians; mem. Southern Minn. Med. Assn., Minn. Dermatol. Soc., Chicago Dermatol. Soc., Am. Dermatol. Assn. (pres. 1946), A.M.A. (chmn. sect. on dermatology, 1936-37), Pan-Am. Medical Association, A.A.A.S., Minnesota Academy Medicine, Minnesota Academy of Science, Minnesota State Medical Society, Soc. for Investigative Dermatology, Dermatol. Conf. Miss. Valley; former mem. National Advisory Health Council; mem. Cooperative Clin. Group, Am. Acad. of Dermatology and Syphilogy (pres. 1938-39), Am. Assn. Univ. Profs., Sigma Xi, Alpha Kappa Kappa, Beta Theta Pi; hon. mem. several foreign socs. Sec. gen., 10th Internat. Congress of Dermatology and Syphilology. Editor in Chief: Archives of Dermatol., 1947—. Home: 225 7th Av. S.W. Office: Mayo Clinic, Rochester, Minn. Died July 20, 1955; buried Oakwood Cemetery.

OLIN, HUBERT LEONARD, chem. engring.; b. Marcus, Ia., May 10, 1880; s. Frank William and Christine (Johnson) O.; B.A., U. of Ia., 1908; student U. of Chicago, 1910; M.S., U. of Ill., 1911, Ph.D., 1914; studied Columbia, 1914-15; m. Helen Leigh Hanes, June 2, 1917; 1 dau., Ida Helen. Instr. in chemistry, Vassar, 1913-14, U. of Ill., 1914-16; asst. prof. chemistry Ohio State U., 1916-18; research chemist Barrett Co., 1919; asso. prof. chem. engring. U. of Ia., 1919-29, prof., 1929-50, emeritus, 1950—; chairman of Iowa State Mining Board, 1962—; tech. adviser to Mexican govt., 1949. Made numerous researches in utilization of coal and its by-products, colloidal clays and activated carbons. Served as capt. 3d Chem. Batt., Edgewood Arsenal, 1918. Mem. Governor's Coal Com. Dir. Ia. Coal Institute; tech. adviser Iowa State Planning Bd. Fellow Royal Soc. Arts; mem. Society of Chemical Industry, American Institute Chemical Engineers, American Chem. Soc. Am. Gas Assn.; mem. Am. Water Works Assn., Soc. for Promotion of Engring. Edn., Am. Legion, Tau Beta Pi, Gamma Alpha, Phi Lambda Upsilon, Sigma Xi. Republican. Presbyterian. Clubs: Triangle, Research, Kiwanis, Engineers (Iowa City); Executives (Cedar Rapids). Writer numerous papers on tech. and scientific subjects in field of chem. engring. and fuel technology. Home: 321 Blackhawk St., Iowa City, Ia. Died Mar. 6, 1964; buried Oakland Cemetery, Iowa City.

OLIN, WALTER HERBERT, scientific agriculturist; b. Walnut Grove, Calif., Aug. 7, 1862; s. Nelson and Harriet M. (Holly) O.; grad. Kan. Agrl. Coll., Manhattan, 1889, M.Sc., 1893; spl. history student, U. of Chicago, 1898; m. Winnifred Estella Cotton, Nov. 27, 1890 (died 1910); children—Winnifred Helen (Mrs. W.H. Roberts), Estella G. (dec.), Walter Eugene; m. 2d, Eleanor Lee, June 7, 1915. Teacher of rural schs., 1880-86; prin. and supt. schs., Waverly, Osborne and Ottawa, Kan., 1890-1901; instr. farm crops, Ia. State Coll., 1902-04; prof. agronomy, 1904-06, vice dean of agr., 1906-08, Colo. Agrl. Coll.; dir. agrl. extension, U. of Ida., 1911-14; organized agrl. dept. and commr. of agr., D.&R.G.W. R.R., Denver, 1914-16; supervisor farm marketing, Frisco Lines, St. Louis, Mar. 1, 1916-Oct. 1918; supervisor of agr., D.&R.G. R.R., Oct. 15, 1918—. Baptist. Mason. Author: Olin's Commercial Geography, 1900; American Irrigation Farming, 1913. Home: Denver, Colo. Died June 21, 1933.

OLITSKY, PETER KOSCIUSKO, (o-lit'ski), pathologist; b. N.Y. City, N.Y., Aug. 20, 1886; s. Davis and Elizabeth G. (Lianski) O.; ed. N.Y. City pub. schs.; M.D., Cornell U., 1909; m. Frances R. Kidder, Sept. 4, 1920; 1 dau., Ruth Kidder. Successively asst., asso., asso mem. and mem. Rockefeller Inst., 1917-52, member emeritus since 1952; member of expert advisory panel on zoonoses WHOFAO of United Nations, 1952-62. Collaborator U.S. Bureau of Animal Industry, 1925-27; cons. Greenwich Hosp. First lt. Med. Corps, U.S. Army, 1918-19. Mem. N.Y. Acad. Med., Am. Assn. Immunologists, Harvey Soc., Soc. Exptl. Biology and Medicine. Contbr. to microbiology subjects, especially viruses and central nervous system. Home: 151 Milbank Av., Greenwich, Conn. Address: Rockefeller Institute, 66th St. and York Av., N.Y.C. 21. Died July 20, 1964; buried Putnam Cemetery, Greenwich, Conn.

OLIVE, EDGAR WILLIAM, botanist; b. Lebanon, Ind., Apr. 1, 1870; s. David Henry and Caroline Elizabeth (Lawrence) O.; B.S., Wabash Coll., Crawfordsville, Ind., 1893, M.S., 1895; A.M., Harvard, 1897, Ph.D., 1902; U. of Bonn, Germany, 1903; m. Elizabeth Williams Ristine, of Crawfordsville, Sept. 6, 1898; children—Theodore Ristine, Marian Lawrence. Asst. in botany, Harvard, 1897-98; instr. botany, Harvard and Radcliffe colls., 1898-1903; research asst. of the Carnegie Instn. of Washington at Bonn, 1903-04, U. of Wis., 1904-06; lecturer in botany, U. of Wis., 1905-07; prof. botany, State Coll. of Agr. and Mech. Arts, Brookings, S.D., and state botanist, 1907-12; curator, Brooklyn Botanic Garden, 1912-20. Fellow A.A.A.S., Bot. Soc. America; mem. Sigma Xi, Phi Beta Kappa, Phi Delta Theta, Am. Phytopathol. Soc. Contbr. chiefly on fungi and fungous diseases of plants. Home: 721 E. 46th St. Office: Chamber of Commerce Bldg., Indianapolis, IN

OLIVER, EDWIN LETTS, mining engr.; b. San Francisco, Nov. 9, 1878; s. William Letts and Carrie (Brown) O.; student coll. of mines U. Cal., 1900, LL.D., 1945; m. Minnie Giffin Walker, Sept. 23, 1905; children—Roberta (Mrs. F. L. Greenlee), William, Mary (Mrs. A. F. Shannon), Edwin Letts. Various surveying jobs in several mines, 1900-03; surveyor, engr. North Star Mines Co., Grass Valley, Cal., 1903-06, research, designer builder two cyanide plants,

1906-10; operator Union Hill Mines, Grass Valley, 1914-17; pres. Idaho Maryland Mines Group, 1925-50; established Oliver Continuous Filter Co., San Francisco, 1910; pres. Oliver United Filters, Inc., 1928-54; merged with The Dorr Co. in 1954 to form Dorr-Oliver Inc., founder-chmn., 1954. Recipient James Douglas (gold) Medal for distinguished achievement in nonferrous metallurgy. Mem. Am. Inst. Mining and Metall. and Petroleum Engrs., Mining and Metall. Soc. Am., Chem. Metall. and Mining Co. of S. Africa, Soc. of Golden Bear, Sigma Xi, Delta Upsilon, Sigma Gamma Epsilon. Republican. Episcopalian. Clubs: Engineers, Bohemian (San Francisco); Claremont Country (Oakland); Tahoe Yacht. Home: 60 King Av., Piedmont, Cal. Office: 260 California St., San Francisco 11. Died 1955.

OLIVER, FITCH EDWARD, physician; b. Cambridge, Mass., Nov. 25, 1819; s. Daniel and Mary Robinson (Pulling) O.; grad. Dartmouth, 1839; studied medicine Dartmouth, Med. Coll. Ohio, also under Oliver Wendell Holmes; M.D., Harvard, 1843; m. Susan Lawrence Mason, July 17, 1866, at least 6 children. Mem. staff Boston City Hosp.; instr. materia medica Harvard Med. Sch., 1860-70; editor Boston Med. and Surg. Jour., 1860-64; cabinet keeper Mass. Hist. Soc., 1880-92; published A Selection of Ancient Psalm Melodies, Adapted to the Canticles of the Church in the United States of America, 1852, also an arrangement of De Profundis. Translator: (with W.W. Marland) Elements of General Pathology, (A.F. Chomel), 1848. Author: (paper) The Health of Boston, 1875; (paper) The Use and Abuse of Opium; A Sketch of the History of the Parish of the Advent in the City of Boston 1844-94, published 1894. Editor The Diaries of Benjamin Lynde and of Benjamin Lynde, Jr., 1880; (with P.O. Hutchinson). The Diary and Letters of His Excellency Thomas Hutchinson, Esq. Died Dec. 8, 1892.

OLIVER, JAMES, inventor; b. Whitehaugh, Roxburghshire, Scotland, Aug. 28, 1823; came with family to U.S., 1835; lived on farm, nr. Geneva, N.Y., 1835-36; at Mishawaka, Ind., 1836-55. Learned foundry trade; began to manufacture plows, 1855; invented the "chilled plow" and acquired wealth. Home: South Bend, Ind. Died 1908.

OLMSTEAD, FRANK ROBERT, highway research engr.; b. Uniontown, Pa., Oct. 28, 1904; s. Harry R. and Bertha N. (Bowser) O.; B.S., Waynesburg Coll., 1928; M.S., U. Mich., 1930; m. Sarah Jenkins, Dec. 17, 1934. Research engr. Mich. State Highway Dept., 1929-34, engr. field testing in charge soil research, design and inspection secondary rds., design ednl. exhibits for engring. convs. and expns., spl. tng. programs field and lab. insps., 1934-43; sr. soils specialist, engr. soils U.S. Bur. Pub. Rds., 1943-51; supervising highway phys. research engr., asst. chief soil sect., 1951-54, chief soils branch, 1954-57, supervisory highway research engineer, 1957—; chmn. dept. of Soils, Geology and Found., Nat. Research Council, 1954—. Mem. sub-committee Standards for Basic Data of President's Water Resource Commn., 1950. Recipient Meritorious Service award Dept. Commerce, 1958. Registered profl. civil engr., Mich., Dist. Columbia. Mem. American Society of Photogrammetry, Assn. Asphalt Paving Technologists (past dir., pres., 1953), Nat. Research Council (chmn. com. surveying and mapping soils inplace for engring. purposes 1943-54), Am. Soc. C.E., Am. Soc. Testing Materials, Am. Assn. State Hwy. Ofcls., Sigma Xi, Sigma Gamma Epsilon. Mason. Contbr. tech. jours. Home: 3503 S. Wakefield St., Arlington 6, Va. Office: Bureau of Public Roads, Washington 25. Died Apr. 2, 1958; buried Uniontown, Pa.

OLMSTED, DENISON, scientist, educator; b. nr. East Hartford, Conn., June 18, 1791; s. Nathaniel and Eunice (Kingsbury) O.; A.B., Yale, 1813, M.A., 1816; m. Eliza Allyn, 1818; m. 2d, Julia Mason, 1831; 7 children. Tchr. Union Sch., New London, Conn., 1813-15; apptd. tutor Yale, 1815; prof. chemistry U. N.C., 1817; apptd. state geologist and mineralogist N.C., 1822, made 1st survey of and reports on state's natural resources; prof. mathematics, natural philosophy Yale, 1825, prof. natural philosophy and astronomy, 1836-59. Author: Introduction to Natural Philosophy, 2 vols., 1831-32; Compendium of Natural Philosophy, 1833 (100 edit.); Introduction to Astronomy, 1839; A Compendium of Astronomy (for schs.), 1839; Letters on Astronomy Addressed to A Lady, 1840; Rudiments of Natural Philosophy and Astronomy, 1844 (also pub. in raised letters for the blind); also papers dealing with meteoric showers of Nov. 13, 1833, study of hailstorms; invented a gas process called gas light from cotton seed, patented, 1827, also a lubricant for machinery made from lard and rosin. Died New Haven, Conn., May 13, 1859.

OLMSTED, JAMES MONTROSE DUNCAN, educator; b. Lake City, Ia., May 21, 1886; s. Jeptha Montrose and Ada Maria (Duncan) O.; A.B., Middlebury (Vt.) Coll., 1907, D.Sc., 1942; B.A., Oxford U., Eng. (Rhodes Scholar, 1908-11), 1911, M.A., 1914; A.M., Harvard, 1917, Ph.D., 1920; m. Evangeline Harris, June 30, 1927. Vice-prin. Spring Valley (N.Y.) High Sch., 1907-08; prof. natural sci. Shorter Coll., Rome, Ga., 1911-12; asst., later asso., prof. of biology Richmond (Va.) Coll., 1912-15; Austin teaching fellow Harvard, 1916-17, asst., 1919-20; asst. prof., later asso. prof. physiology U. Toronto, 1920-27; prof. physiology U. Cal., 1927-53, prof. emeritus, 1954-56. Served as pvt. Base Hosp. No. 7, U.S. Army, 1917-18; 2d lt. San Corps, 1918-19. Senior fellow Com. for Relief in Belgium, 1931. Fgn. corr. mem. Société Philomathique (Paris). Fellow A.A.A.S.; mem. Am. Physiol. Soc., Am. Assn. History Medicine, Soc. Exptl. Biology and Medicine, Delta Kappa Epsilon, Phi Beta Kappa, Sigma Xi. Author: Cluade Bernard, Physiologist, 1938; Francois Magendię. Physician and Physiologist, 1945; Charles-Edouard Brown-Sequard, Nineteenth Century Neurologist and Endocrinologist, 1947; (with E. H. Olmsted) Claude Bernard and the Experimental Method in Medicine, 1952; (with others) Macleod's Physiology in Modern Medicine, 1924-47, Macleod's Laboratory Manual, 1924, Bard: Medical Physiology, 1956. Contbr. to sci. jours. Elected active artist mem. San Francisco Art Assn. (water-colors), 1939. Recipient French Acad. Scis. prix Binoux, 1949; French Acad. Medicine prix de Martignoni, 1953. Home: 2853 Buena Vista Way, Berkeley 8, Cal. Died May 26, 1956; buried Sunset View Cemetery, Berkeley.

OLMSTED, VICTOR HUGO, statistician; b. at Marion, O., March 3, 1853; s. Edwin B. and Adelia J. O.; student Columbian (now George Washington) U.; m. Nancy Elizabeth Patton, of N.C., Apr. 13, 1873; father of E. Stanley O. (q.v.) Admitted to the bar, 1884; chief div. of results, 10th Census; employed deciding contested land cases in Gen. Land Office, 1883-89; statis. expert U.S. Dept. Labor, 1889-1901; detailed 1899, asst. dir. Cuban Census; investigated labor conditions, H.I., 1900-01; especially employed by U.S. Labor Commn., 1900; commr. Nat. Metal Trades Assn., Dec., 1901-June, 1902; apptd. asst. statistician and spl. field investigator, U.S. Dept. Agr., 1901; detailed, 1903, asst. dir. of census of P.I.; chief div. of domestic crop reports, 1904; asso. statistician, 1905; chief Bur. of Statistics, 1906, 14; detailed as dir. of Cuban Census of 1907; field agt. Bur. of Crop Estimates U.S. Dept. Agr., 1913—. Del. Gen. Assembly Internat. Inst. of Agr., Rome, 1911. Clubs: Cosmos. Home: Clarendon, Va.

OLNEY, ALBERT J(ACKSON), horticulturist; b. Fremont, Mich., Apr. 15, 1888; s. Bert John and Alice Maude (Beem) O.; B.S., Mich. State Coll., 1913, M.H., 1920; S.M., U. of Chicago, 1925; m. Lydia Marie Branstrom, July 8, 1914; children—Charles Bert, Robert Branstrom. Sci. and agrl. teacher, Greenville (Mich.) High Sch., 1913-14; horticulturist, Theodore N. Vail Agrl. Sch., Lyndon, Vt., 1914-16; horticulturist, U. of Ky., since 1916, asst. prof., 1916-26, asso. prof. 1926-28, prof. horticulture since 1928, head dept. horticulture since 1930. Fellow A.A.A.S.; mem. Am. Soc. for Hort. Sci., Am. Pomol. Soc., Ky. Acad. Sci., Sigma Xi. Presbyterian. Home: 240 Tahoma Rd., Lexington 1, Ky. Died June 29, 1958.

OLNEY, LOUIS ATWELL, (ol'ne), chemistry; b. Providence, R.I., Apr. 21, 1874; s. Albert H. and Frances E. (Olney) O.; high sch. and business coll., Providence; B.S., Lehigh U., 1896, M.S., 1908, Sc.D., 1926; m. Bertha Haynes Holden, June 24, 1903; children—Margaret Lucia (Mrs. Edward Alan Larter), Edna Elizabeth (Mrs. Dexter Nichols Shaw), Richard Holden. Instr. in chemistry, Brown U., 1896-97; prof. chemistry and dyeing, and director department chemistry and textile coloring, Lowell (Mass.) Textile Institute, 1897-1944 professor emeritus since 1944. Chemist Lowell Machine Shop, 1902-03, Lowell Gas Light Company, 1904-05, Lowell Board of Health, 1904; pres. of Stirling Mills, 1912-42, treas., 1936-42; pres., director, Wannalancit Textile Co.; pres., dir., Lowell Lingerie Co.; trustee Lowell Instn. for Savings (president, chairman bd. of investment); dir. Lowell Morris Plan Co.; dir. Howes Publishing Co., N.Y. City. Asst. editor Chem. Abstracts since 1907; editor Am. Dyestuff Reporter since 1920. Mem. Draft Board No. 87, Lowell, Mass. Treas. Northfield Conf. of Religious Edn.; v.p. Lowell Ministry at Large; dir. Lowell Y.M.C.A. since 1914, pres., 1916-21, trustee since 1940. Dir. Isle of Shoals Congregational Corp. since 1944. Fellow A.A.A.S., Am. Inst. Chemists; mem. Am. Chem. Soc. (ex-chmn. N.E. Sect.), Am. Inst. Chem. Engrs., Am. Assn. Textile Chemists and Colorists (pres. 1921-27, now emeritus; chmn. research com. since 1921, dir. of research 1940-46, U.S. Inst. for Textile Research (v.p., mem. research com.; acting pres. 1941, dir. since 1930). Dir. Textile Research Institute since 1944. National Association Wool Mfrs., Soc. Philatelic Americans, Boston Philatelic Society, Lowell Philatelic Society, Lowell Histology Society, British Society Dyers and Colourists, British Society Chemical Industry, Sigma Xi (Lehigh chapter). Republican. Congregationalist. Mason (K.T., 32 deg.). Clubs: Temple, Lowell Congregational (ex-pres.), Lehigh (ex-pres.); Engineers (Boston); Chemists (New York); Yorick (Lowell, Mass.), Vesper Country. Olney Medal est. 1943 by Am. Assn. of Textile Chemists awarded for achievement in textile chemistry; first medal awarded (1944) to L. A. Olney, for whom it was named. Author: Textile Chemistry and Dyeing, 1903; Chemical Technology of Fibers, 1921, 47; Elementary Organic Chemistry, 1941; Roger's Industrial Chemistry (with others), 1942; also chapters and sects in Colloidal Chemistry, Chemistry in Industry, Municipal Chemistry, Textile Research, Acetate Silk and its Dyes, Review American Chemical Research, Casein. Asso. editor Century Dictionary, 1904-05. Home: 118 Riverside St., Lowell, Mass.; (summer) Lake Penacook, Concord, N.H. Died Feb. 11, 1949.

OLSEN, JOHN CHARLES, chemist; b. Galesburg, Ill., July 22, 1869; s. Michael Cecelia (Johnson) O.; A.B., Knox Coll., Galesburg, 1890, A.M., 1893; U. of Chicago, summers, 1897, 98; Ph.D., Johns Hopkins, 1900; Sc.D., Knox, 1925; m. Ella Walker, Aug. 31, 1898; children—Julian W., Eugene U., Elizabeth. Prin. schs., Ipava, Ill., 1891-94; teacher physics and chemistry, Austin (Ill.) High Sch., 1895-98; prof. analytical chemistry, Poly. Inst. of Brooklyn, 1900-14, Pratt Inst., Brooklyn, 1900-06, Adelphi Coll., 1913-14; prof. chemistry and head dept., Cooper Union, N.Y., 1914-19; prof. chem. engring., Poly. Inst. of Brooklyn, 1918-44, head department, 1918-37; professor emeritus of chem. engring. since 1944. Lecturer analytical chemistry and foods, Brooklyn Institute Arts and Sciences and for Bd. Edn. City of New York since 1900; editor Van Nostrand's Chemical Annual since 1907, and Trans. Am. Inst. Chem. Engrs., 1909-26; sec. Am. Inst. Chem. Engrs., 1908-26, dir. 1926-27, v.p., 1928-29, pres., 1931; mem. Am. Chem. Soc., Brooklyn Chamber of Commerce. Republican. Methodist. Mason. Author: Quantitative Chemical Analysis, 1904; Pure Foods, 1911; Qualitative Chemical Analysis, 1916; Unit Processes and Principles of Chemical Engineering, 1932. Clubs: Chemists (New York). Home: 316 Argyle Rd., Brooklyn 18, N.Y. Died June 8, 1948.

OLSON, AXEL RAGNAR, prof. chemistry; b. Halsingborg, Sweden, Feb. 6, 1889; s. Nels and Ingrid Sophia (Nordfeldt) O.; B.S., U. of Chicago, 1915; Ph.D., U. of Calif., 1917; m. Hanna Kinell, Aug. 22, 1919; children—William John, Peter Andrew; came to U.S., 1891, naturalized citizen, 1896. Fellow Nat. Research Council, 1919-22; asst. prof. of chemistry, U. of Calif., 1922-26, asso. prof., 1926-30, prof., 1930—. Served as lt., C.W.S., U.S. Army, A.E.F., 1918-19. Guggenheim fellow, 1929-30; mem. A.A.A.S., Am. Chem. Soc., Phi Beta Kappa, Sigma Xi, Alpha Chi Sigma, Alpha Sigma Phi. Club: Faculty (Berkeley). Home: 2696 Cedar St., Berkeley 8, Cal. Died Dec. 22, 1954; buried Sunset View Cemetery, Berkeley.

ONDERDONK, GILBERT, horticulturist; b. at Sharon, Schoharie Co., N.Y., Sept. 30, 1829; s. John and Margaret (Ward) O.; grad. State Normal College, Albany, N.Y., 1849; began teaching in Niagara Co., N.Y., but health failed and went to southwest Tex., and became a cowboy on Indian frontier; m. Martha Jane Benham, Oct. 23, 1855; father of Frank Scovill O. (q.v.). Began experiments in horticulture at 12 yrs. of age by gathering a hat full of potato balls in field in Homer, Central N.Y.; from these finally obtained 22 varieties of potatoes and won premium at New York State Fair; continued investigations in Tex. and established and conducted an expt. sta. and nursery for 40 yrs. Explored for U.S. Dept. of Agr. in Central Mex., 1902. '03, '06. Ex-pres. Tex. State Hort. Society. Democrat. Methodist. Author of pamphlets, etc.; contbr. to press and speaker on hort. subjects. Address: Nursery, Victoria Co. Tex.

O'NEILL, EDMOND, chemist; b. Nashville, Tenn., Dec. 13, 1859; s. Eugene and Bertha (Strachauer) O'N.; Ph.B., U. of Calif., 1879; post-grad. studies Coll. of Chemistry, U. of Calif. and univs. of Berlin and Strassburg; m. Edith Vernon Ward, June 1904. Instr. chemistry, 1879-86, asst. prof., 1888-90, asso. prof., 1890-1906, prof., 1906—, and dir. labs., U. of Calif. Consulting chemist Union Oil Co., Calif. Del. from Calif., and v.p. Congress Applied Chemistry, Berlin, 1903, Rome, 1906. Chmn. chemists com. Calif. State Council Defense, 1917-18; mem. exec. com. engring. div., Nat. Research Council. Mem. Am. Chem. Soc. (organizer and 1st pres. Calif. sect.). Home: Berkeley, Calif. Died Oct. 4, 1933.

O'NEILL, JOHN J(OSEPH), editor; b. New York, N.Y., June 21, 1889; s. James and Catherine (Kelleher) O'N.; ed. public schools and night school, New York, N.Y., and Internat. Corr. Schools; m. Marie Bock, July 7, 1912; children—Kenneth Horace, Peggy Theresa (Mrs. Clyde T. Grayson). Began as printer, 1903-04; electrician, 1905-06; with N.Y. (Astor) Public Library, 1906-07; with New York Herald library, 1907-08; reporter, 1908-15; reporter, Brooklyn (N.Y.) Daily Eagle, 1915-17, feature editor, 1918-22, radio editor, 1922-25, automobile and aviation editor, 1925-26, science editor, 1926-32, supervisor construction of new building and plant, 1929-30; science editor New York Herald Tribune since 1933. Organizer Suffolk County Home Defense Regt., 1917, Newspapermen's Officers Training Corps, 1917. Served as pvt., Machine Gun Co., 7th Regt., N.Y. Nat. Guard, 1917-19. Recipient of Pulitzer Award in Journalism, Columbia U., 1937; Best Science Story of Year, U. of Kan., 1938; Clement Cleveland Award (shared), N.Y. Cancer Soc., 1938; Westinghouse Distinguished Science Writing Medal from A.A.A.S., 1946. Revealed that atomic energy had been released, Mar. 1940. Mem. Arts and Science Conf., 1937. Fellow Am. Geog. Soc., Arctic Institute of North America; mem. Amateur Astronomers Association, A.A.A.S., Am. Genetic Assn., Am. Inst. City of N.Y. (chmn. bd. mgrs., 1933-37), Am. Soc. Psychical Research (chmn. research com. and trustee, 1933-37), Am. Polar Soc., India-Am. Science Assn.

(founding mem.), Am. Acad. Polit. and Social Science, Acad. Polit. Sci., Am.-Irish Hist. Soc., Am. Newspaper Guild (founding mem.), Am. Rocket Soc., Am. Oriental Soc., Am. Meteorol. Soc., Am. Geophys. Union, Nat. Assn. Science Writers (charter mem.; v.p., 1939, pres., 1940); Royal Astron. Soc. (Canada), Assn. Lunar and Obs., Astron. Society of Pacific, Am. Assn. Physics Teacher. Author: Enter Atomic Energy, 1940; Prodigal Genius, The Life of Nikola Tesla, 1944; Almighty Atom, The Real Story of Atomic Energy, 1945; You and the Universe, 1945; Engineering The New Age, 1949. Contbr. tech. articles to sci. publs. Home: 209 N. Long Beach Av., Freeport, L.I., N.Y. Office: 230 W. 41st St., New York, N.Y. Died Aug. 30, 1953.

O'NEILL, LEWIS PATRICK, oil co. exec.; b. McAlister, Okla., July 28, 1905; s. Joseph Patrick and Catherine (Maire) O'N.; B.S. in Chem. Engring., Okla. A. and M. Coll., 1927; M.S. in Petroleum Engring., Okla. U., 1928; m. Georgiana Trask, Nov. 11, 1932; children—Patrick Shane, Michael Jerome, Sharon (Mrs. Ronald J. Peebles). Ind. oil and gas chemist, Okmulgee, Okla., 1928; chem. plant operator, Tulsa, 1929-34; engaged in spl. refining projects Phillips Refining Co., Borger, Tex., 1934, Lion Refining Co., Eldorado, Ark., 1935; with Gen. Am. Oil Co. Tex., 1936, v.p. engring. and Prodn., 1957-61, sr. v.p. engring. and prodn., 1961-66, exec. v.p. operations, 1966-69, exec. v.p., 1969-70, cons., 1971, dir., mem. exec. com., 1961-70; v.p. dir. Gen. Am. Oil Ltd.; pres. Gen. Am. Pipeline Co., 1968-70; pres. Premier Petrochem. Co., 1967-70; dir. Gen. Am. Bldg. Corp., Pipeliner Co. Registered professional engrs., Am. Inst. Mining, Metall. and Petroleum Engrs., Ind. Producers Assn., Mid Continent Oil and Gas Assn., Royalty Assn. Clubs: Texas, Engineers (dir.), Petroleum, Petroleum Engrs. Home: Dallas TX Died Dec. 17, 1972; buried Calvary Hill Cemetery, Dallas TX

OOSTING, HENRY J., educator; b. Holland, Mich., Mar. 12, 1903; s. John H. and Minnie (Bouwman) O.; A.B., Hope Coll., 1925; M.A., Mich. State U., 1927; Ph.D., U. Minn., 1931; m. Cornelia Ossewaarde, Aug. 17, 1927; children—Jan Kurt, Marta Joy. Instr. botany U. Minn., 1927-32; faculty Duke, from 1932, prof. botany, from 1949, chmn. dept., 1953-63. Mem. A.A.A.S., Am. Inst. Biol. Scis., Bot. Soc. Am. Ecological Soc. Am. (past pres., bus. mgr. from 1950), Assn. Southeastern Biologists, N.C. Acad. Scis. Author: The Study of Plant Communities, 2d edit., 1956. Bot. editor: Ecological Monographs, from 1950. Home: Durham NC Died Oct. 30, 1968; cremated.

OPHÜLS, WILLIAM, pathologist; b. Brooklyn, Oct. 23, 1871; s. Carl Julius and Clara (Wilhelms) O.; grad. gymnasium, Crefeld, Germany, 1890; U. of Würzburg, 1890-93; U. of Berlin, 1894; med. staatsexamen, Göttingen, 1895; M.D., U. of Göttingen, 1895; m. Emmy Feldmann, May 6, 1903; children—Clara Louise, Ernst Carl, Elinor Helen, Gertrud. Asst. at Pathol. Inst., Göttingen, 1896-97; prof. pathology and bacteriology, U. of Mo., 1897-98, Cooper Med. Coll., San Francisco, 1898-1912; prof. pathology, Stanford, 1919—; pathologist, Lane Hosp., San Francisco, 1898—. Pres. Bd. Health, San Francisco, 1907-10. Republican. Writer on tuberculosis, coccidioidal granloma, arteriosclerosis, nephritis, etc. Home: San Francisco Calif. Died Apr. 27, 1933.

OPIE, EUGENE LINDSAY, pathologist; b. Staunton, Va., July 5, 1873; s. Thomas and Sallie (Harman) O.; A.B., Johns Hopkins, 1893, M.D., 1897, LL.D., 1947; Sc.D., Yale, 1930; LL.D., Washington U., 1940; D.Sc. (hon.), Rockefeller University, 1966; m. Gertrude Lovat Simpson, Aug. 6, 1902; children—Thomas Lindsay, Anne Lovat, Helen Lovat, Gertrude Eugenie; m. 2d, Margaret Lovat Simpson, Sept. 16, 1916. Medical house officer Johns Hopkins Hosp., 1897-98; asst. instr., asso. in pathology Johns Hopkins, 1898-1904; mem. Rockefeller Inst. for Med. Research, 1904-10. bd. sci. dirs., 1928-32; vis. pathologist Presbyn. Hosp., N.Y.C., 1907-10; prof. pathology Washington U., St. Louis, 1910-23. dean med. sch., 1912-15; prof. pathology, dir. dept. U. Pa., dir. labs. Henry Phipps Inst., 1923-32, acting dir., 1942-46; prof. pathology Cornell Med. Coll. and pathologist to N.Y. Hosp., 1932-41; sci. dir. Internat. Health Div., Rockefeller Found., 1935-38; vis. prof. Peiping Union Med. Coll., 1939; research Rockefeller Inst. Med. Research, 1941-70. President Nat. Tb. Assn., 1929; research Council Pub. Health Research Inst., N.Y.C. Served from capt. to col. Med. R.C., A.E.F., 1917-19. Awarded Gerhard, Trudeau medals, 1929; medal. Soc. Puertorriquena de Tisologos. 1938; Weber-Parkes Medal and Award of Royal Coll. of Physicians. 1945: Banting Medal, 1946; Jessie Stevenson Kovalenko medal Nat. Acad. Scis., 1959; medal of New York Academy of Medicine, 1960; T. Duckett Jones Memorial award Helen Hays Whitney Found., 1965. Fellow Am. Assn. Advancement Sci.; mem. Nat. Acad. Scis., Assn. Am. Physicians, Am. Assn. of Pathologists and Bacteriologists (pres. 1917). American Association Immunologists (president 1929) Harvey Society (president 1936-38). A.M.A. Episcopalian. Author: Diseases of the Pancreas, 1902; Epidemic Respiratory Disease, 1921. Co-editor of The Jour. Exptl. Medicine, 1904-10. Home: New York City NY Died Mar. 12, 1971; buried Baltimore MD

OPIE, THOMAS, one of founders, 1872, and since dean Coll. of Phys. & Surg., Baltimore; b. Martinsburg, Va., May 14, 1842; s. Hierome Lindsay and Anne Stephenson (Locke) O.; academic edn. and Univ. of Va., Staunton, Va.; studied medicine, Univ. of Va.; grad. Univ. of Pa., 1861; served in 25th Va. regt., C.S.A., as pvt. and later surgeon, 1861-65. Has practiced, Baltimore, since 1865; prof. obstetrics, Coll. of Phys. & Surg., 1872-92; since then prof. gynecology. Gynecologist and abdominal surgeon, Baltimore City and Bayview hosps.; consulting gynecologist to Hebrew Hosp. Mem. Am. Med. Assn.; founder and mem. Am. Assn. Obstetricians and Gynecologists; etc. Address: 14 W. Franklin St., Baltimore.

OPPENHEIMER, J. ROBERT, Am. physicist; b. New York, N.Y., Apr. 22, 1904; s. Julius and Ella (Freedman) O.; A.B., Harvard U., 1925, student Cambridge U., Eng., 1925-26; Ph.D., Göttingen U., Germany, 1927; m. Katherine Harrison, Nov., 1940; children—Peter, Katherine. National Research fellow, 1927-28; Internat. Edn. Bd. fellow, U. of Leyden and Zurich, 1928-29; asst. prof. physics, U. Cal. and Cal. Inst. Tech., 1929-31, asso. prof., 1931-36, prof., 1936-47. Dir. Los Alamos Sci. Lab., Los Alamos, N.M., 1943-45; director and professor of physics, Institute for Advanced Study, Princeton, 1947—. Chmn. gen. adv. com. AEC, 1946-52. Recipient Fermi award AEC, 1963. Fellow Phys. Soc. (pres. 1948), Philos. Soc., Am. Acad.; mem. Royal Danish (fgn.), Brazilian (fgn.), Japanese (hon.) acads. Important in devel. of quantum theory, understanding of cosmic rays, fundamental particles and relativity; introduced use of symmetrical and antisymmetrical functions in scattering problems; worked out theory of neutron stars; instrumental in devel. of atomic bomb. Died Princeton, N.J., Feb. 20, 1967.

ORD, GEORGE, naturalist, philologist; b. Phila., Mar. 4, 1781; s. George and Rebecca (Lindemeyer) O.; m. 1815, 2 children including Joseph Benjamin. Employed in father's ship chandler and rope making business, 1806-29; completed book by friend Alexander Wilson, American Ornithology or, the Natural History of Birds of the United States, 9 vols., 1808-14, edited vol. 8, wrote entire text vol. 9, pusblished another edit. of work with much additional material, 1824-25; attempted (with Charles Waterton) to discredit Audubon, circa 1824; accompanied Thomas Say, Titian Peale and William Maclure on extensive field trip to Ga. and Fla., 1818; prepared memoirs of Say and C.A. Lesueur; prepared anonymous account of zoology of N. Am. for 2d Am. edit. New Geographical and Commercial Grammar (William Guthrie), 1815; disposed of manuscripts on philology to Latham of London who used them in compilation new edit. Johnson's Dictionary, circa 1860; mem. Am. Philos. Soc.; pres. Phila. Acad. Scis., 1851-58; contbd. personal library to Coll. Physicians Phila., $16,000 to Pa. Hosp. Died Phila., Jan. 24, 1866.

ORDONEZ, CASTOR, biologist; b. Palencia, Spain, Mar. 28, 1880; s. Nicanor and Rufina (Cabiedes) O.; A.B., Central House of Padres Paules, Madrid, 1901, A.M., 1902; Ph.D., St. Mary's Sem., Perryville, Mo., 1915; Sc.D., De Paul U., 1917. Mem. faculty St. Vincent's Sem., Philippine Islands, 1904-10; editor weekly mag., "Eco de Leyte y Samar," 1911-12. Sec. Spanish section Eucharistic Congress, Chicago. Teacher, De Paul U., 1914—, dir. dept. of biology and mem. bd. of trustees. Known for experimental work in crossing turkey and hen, experiments on cancer in rats, and discoveries in uses of electricity. Naturalized citizen, 1926. Catholic; mem. Congregation of the Mission. Author: Primer Sinodo Diocesano (Culbayog, Samar, P.I.), 1911; Educational Biology, Genetics and Eugenics, 1932; also various laboratory manuals. Compiler: Abridged Calculus, 1908; Compendium of Universal History, 1908. Home: Chicago, Ill. Died June 28, 1938.

ORDWAY, JOHN MORSE, educator, chemist; b. Amesbury, Mass., Apr. 23, 1823; s. Samuel and Sally (Morse) O.; A.M., Dartmouth, 1844; m. Virginia C. Moore, 1854 (died, 1860); m. 2d, Mrs. Charlotte H. Manross, 1864 (died, 1874); m. 3d, Evelyn M. Walton, 1882. Worked in apothecary shop, Lowell, Mass., 1836-38; mgr. chem. works, Lowell, 1 yr.; supt. Roxbury Color and Chem. Co., Roxbury, Mass., 6 yrs.; chemist Drybrook Chem. Works, Johnston, R.I., 2 yrs.; chemist, then mgr., then supt., Manchester Print Works, Manchester, N.H., 5 yrs.; supt. Bayside Alkali Works, Boston, 9 yrs.; prof. industrial chemistry and metallurgy, Mass. Inst. of Tech., 15 yrs., and part of same time instr. in Boston U.; 13 yrs. prof. Tulane U., and prof. biology in H. Sophie Newcomb Coll. (dept. of Tulane U.). Address: New Orleans, La. Died 1909.

ORDWAY, THOMAS, physician; b. Dorchester (Boston), Mass., May 7, 1877; s. George Frank and Julia Maria (Gilbert) O.; A.B., Harvard, 1900, A.M., 1901, and M.D., 1905; hon. Sc.D., Union Coll., 1919; m. Mary Olive Baker, Apr. 6, 1906; 1 son, Thomas. Assistant in zoölogy, Harvard, and Radcliffe Coll., 1900-01; asst. in physiology, Harvard Med. Sch., 1902-03; asst. in pathol. dept. Boston City Hosp., 1905; house officer Boston City Hosp., 1905-07; asst. in pathology, Harvard Med. Sch., 1907-08; 1st asst. in pathology, Boston City Hosp., 1908-09; director Bender Hygienic Laboratory, Albany, N.Y., 1909-11, also Professor Pathology Albany Medical Coll.; physician in charge Huntington Hosp. Harvard Med. Sch., 1911-15 (resigned); was also lecturer in pathology, grad. dept. Harvard Med. Sch., instr. in medicine, Harvard Med. Sch. and asst. visiting physician, Boston City Hosp., 1911-15; prof. medicine, dean Albany Med. Coll., 1915-37; physician-in-chief, Albany Hosp., 1915-37; cons. physician Albany Hospital Member A.M.A., Assn. Am. Physicians, Am. Assn. Pathologists and Bacteriologists, Am. Assn. for Cancer Research, Soc. for Advancement Clin. Research, Mass. Med. Soc., Boston Soc. Med. Sciences (ex-sec.), etc. Club: Harvard (Boston and Eastern N.Y.). Contbr. to med. jours. Home: 297 S. Manning Blvd. Office: 161 S. Lake Av., Albany, N.Y. Died May 12, 1952; buried Rensselaerville Cemetery, Rensselaerville, Albany County, N.Y.

ORE, OYSTEIN, prof. mathematics; b. Oslo, Norway, Oct. 7, 1899; s. Michal Beer and Christiane Benedicte (Samuelsen) O.; Ph.D., Oslo U., 1924; grad. study, Gottingen (Germany) U.; 1922, Sorbonne, Paris, 1924; fellow Math. Inst. Stockholm, 1923, Rockefeller Internat. Edn., Bd., 1924-25; naturalized citizen, 1934; m. Gudrun Lundevall, Aug. 25, 1930; children—Elisabeth, Berit. Asst. prof. of mathematics, Oslo U., 1925-28; asst. prof. mathematics, Yale, 1927, asso. prof., 1928, prof., 1929-31, Sterling prof. math., 1931-68, chmn. dept., 1936-45; fellow Branford College since 1933. Mem. Nat. Search Council, 1939-42. Mem. bd. dirs. Norwegian Relief, Inc. (chmn. for Conn. since 1940); Am. Relief for Norway, 1942-47; chairman Relief Mission to Norway, 1945. Decorated Knight, Order of St. Olav (Norwegian), 1947; Guggenheim fellow for hist. studies, Italy, 1954. Member American Mathematics Society (council, 1934-36; colloquium lecturer 1941), American Acad. of Arts and Sciences, also mem. Oslo Academy Science, Sigma Xi; honorary member Gamma Alpha, 1941. Co-editor: Gesammelte Werke of R. Dedekind (with E. Noether), 3 vols., 1930. Author: Les Corps Algebriques et la Theorie des Ideaux, 1934; L'algebre abstraite, 1936; Number Theory and Its History, 1948; Cardano the Gambling Scholar, pub. 1953; Niels Henrik Abel, 1954; Theory of Graphs, 1962; Graphs and Their Uses, 1963; The Four Color Problem, published in 1967. Contributor math. articles to Am., French, German, Norwegian publs. Mem. editorial bd. Annals of Mathematics, 1939-40, Duke Math. Jour., 1935-41, Transactions (Am. Math. Soc.), 1937-44. Am. Jour. Math., 1938-41, Jour. Combinational Math., 1965-68. Home: Hamden CT Died Aug. 13, 1968; buried New Haven CT

O'REILLY, ANDREW JOHN GOLDSMITH, elec. and civ. engr.; b. Montgomery County, Mo., Jan. 13, 1863; s. Thomas (M.D.) and Helen Barbour (Dunlop) O'R.; B.E., Washington U., St. Louis, 1888; m. Mary E. Howard, Sept. 3, 1883 (dec.); children—Thomas (dec.), Helen (Mrs. Thomas Caldwell), Elizabeth (Mrs. Charles H. Lewis), Jeannette (Mrs. August J. Johnson), Margarette (dec.); m. 2d, Clara Witte, Feb. 23, 1924 (died Aug. 8, 1934). Began as pattern maker and draftsman, St. Louis, 1878; electrician and operator in Fire Alarm Office, 1884-86; engr. Municipal Electric Light & Power Co., 1889-90; supervisor of city lighting, 1890-1903; pres. Bd. of Pub. Improvements, 1905-09; consultants Laclede Gas Light Co., Union Electric Light & Power Co.; supt. plant construction Miss. River Power Distributing Co. since 1913; safety engr. Nat. Bd. Fire Prevention; mem. Pub. Service Commn. of Mo., 1921-25; chief elec. engr. Dept. Pub. Safety, 1925-32; consultant on public safety. Served as asst. supervisor of gauges, U.S. Ordnance Dept., 1917-19. Mem. A.A.A.S., Am. Inst. E.E., St. Louis Engrs. Club, St. Louis Acad. Science, Am. Geog. Soc., Mo. Acad. Science. Republican. Mason (33 deg.; pres. Masonic Relief Bd.). Address: 2207 S. Grand Blvd., St. Louis, Mo. Died Jan. 27, 1943.

ORMSBY, WATERMAN LILLY, engraver; b. Hampton, Conn., 1809; studied Nat. Acad. Design, N.Y.C., 1829. Settled in N.Y., became propr. N.Y. Note Co.; a founder Continental Bank Note Co.; inventor engraving machinery including ruling machines, transfer presses and grammagraph; designer bank notes which were widely used by govt. by 1861. Author several pamphlets including Cycloidal Configurations, or the Harvest of Counterfeiters; A Description of the Present System of Bank Note Engraving, 1852. Died Bklyn., Nov. 1, 1883.

ORNDOFF, BENJAMIN HARRY, physician; b. Graysville, Pa., Feb. 3, 1881; s. John and Minerva (Roseberry) O.; Ph.G., Valparaiso U., 1905, M.A., 1916; M.D., Loyola U., 1906; Dr. Med. Radiology and Electrology, Cambridge U., Eng., 1926; m. Bernice Harvey, June 29, 1907; children—John Roseberry, Ruth, Jane, Sarah, Harvey Hawkins. Intern Frances Willard Hosp., Chicago, 15 months, 1906-07; pathologist and roentgenologist, same, 1907-21; prof. pathology and roentgenology, Chicago Coll. of Medicine and Surgery, 1910-16; surgeon div. of electrosurgery, Grant Hosp.; med. staff Swedish Covenant Hosp.; sr. staff mem. dept. radiology, Luth. Gen. Hosp., Park Ridge, Ill. prof. and chmn. dept. of radiology, Loyola U. School of Medicine, Chgo. U.S. Navy, 1937-39 (lt. comdr. MC-V), USNR (ret.). Awarded Silver Medal, Western Roentgen Soc., 1916; Gold Medal Radiol. Soc. of N.A., 1927; Gold Medal

Am. Coll. of Radiology, 1954; Silver Medal, Swedish delegation, 5th Internat. Congress of Radiology, 1937; Gold Medal, English delegation, 5th Internat. Congress of Radiology, 1950; Citation and Scroll, Radiol. Soc. of N.A., 1954; Stritch gold medal Stritch Sch., Loyola U., 1960; gold medal Centre Antoine Beclere, Paris, 1965. Fellow Am. Coll. of Surgeons, Am. Med. Assn., Am. Coll. of Radiology (treas. 1925-31, exec. sec., 1931-36), Inter Am. Coll. of Radiology, A.C.P.; hon. mem. Italian Soc. of Radiol. Medicine, Columbian Soc. of Radiology, Argentina Assn. of Radiology, Argentina Radiol. Soc., Soc. of Radiology and Physiotherapy of Cuba, Cuban Radiol. Soc.; mem. Radiol. Soc. of N.A. (pres. 1917-18), Am. Roentgen Ray Soc. Soc., Ill. State and Chgo. Med. Socs., British Inst. of Radiology, Rocky Mountain Radiological Soc., (hon. member), Inst. of Medicine of Chgo., Am. Phys. Soc., Am. and Chgo. Heart Assn., Am. Geriatrics Soc., Egon Fischman Meml., S.A.R., Chgo. Art Inst., Chgo. Museum Nat. History, Century of Progress Assn., Chgo. Roentgen Soc. (pres. 1921-23, sec. 1919-21), Physics Club of Chgo., Ill. Acad. of Sci., Chgo. Hist. Soc., A.A.A.S., Sigma Xi, Lambda Rho, Theta Kappa Psi. Del. Internat. Congress of Radiology, Stockholm, 1928, Paris, 1931, pres. of delegates, 4th Congress, Zurich, Switzerland, 1934; del. 2d Inter Am. Congress Radiology, Havana, 1946; chmn. exec. council First Am. Congress of Radiology, 1933; gen. sec. 5th Internat. Congress of Radiology, Chicago, 1937; mem. internat. executive committee 6th International Congress of Radiology, London, 1950; mem. 6th International Congress on Cancer, Paris, 1950. Mason (32 deg., K.T., Shriner). Engaged in research in radiology and electrosurgery. Author of articles in exptl. research and clin. medicine. Address: Park Ridge IL Died Mar. 6, 1971; buried Rogersville PA

ORNDORFF, WILLIAM RIDGELY, chemist; b. Baltimore, Sept. 9, 1862; s. William Wellmore and Mary J. (Ridgely) O.; student Baltimore City Coll., 1876-81; A.B., Johns Hopkins, 1884, Ph.D., 1887; studied at univs. of Greifswald, Berlin, Heidelberg, 1897-98, U. of Munich, 1906-07; m. Charlotte Heinrich, 1912; children—Mary Ridgely, William Ridgely. Instr. chemistry, 1887-90, asst. prof. organic chemistry, 1890-1908, organic and physiol. chemistry, 1898, Cornell U.; prof. organic and physiol. chemistry, 1902—, and mem. faculty Arts and Sciences, the faculty of the Grad. Sch. and Univ. faculty, and of med. faculty (at Ithaca), Cornell. Mem. Internat. Jury of Awards, Paris Expn., 1889, St. Louis Expn., 1904 (sec. Group Jury No. 23, Dept. of Liberal Arts), Panama P.I. Exposition, San Francisco, 1915; special agent U.S. Census, 1890. Contbr. of results of original chem. research to Am. Chem. Jour., Berichte der Deutschen Chemischen Gesellschaft, Jour. Am. Chem. Soc. and Jour. of Physical Chemistry. Author: Laboratory Manual of Organic Chemistry, 1922. Translator: Dr. E. Salkowski's Laboratory Manual of Physiological and Pathological Chemistry, 1904. Co-author in revision of Remsen's Organic Chemistry, 1922. Home: Ithaca, N.Y. Died Nov. 1, 1927.

O'ROURKE, CHARLES EDWARD, (o-rork') professor and consulting eng.; b. New York, N.Y., June 4, 1896; s. John Aloysius and Lillie Helen (Bailey) O'R.; C.E., Cornell U., 1917; m. Hilda Julia Mullen, Oct. 19, 1917; children—Patricia Ann, Robert Edward. Asst. to city engr., Ithaca, N.Y., 1916; with Wright-Martin Aircraft Co., New Brunswick, N.J., 1919; engr. Tenn. Inspection Bur., 1919; instr. structural engring., Cornell Univ., 1919-23, asst. prof. 1923-34, prof. since 1934; prof. concrete design, Carnegie Inst. Tech., 1921; prof. structural engring., Imperial Peiyang Univ., Tientsin, China (on leave from Cornell), 1926-27; vis. prof. structural engring., U. of Hawaii, 1941; designer Concrete Steel Co., N.Y. City, summers 1921-28; private cons. practice structural engring. 1924-45; consultant Internat. Corr. Schs. Scranton, Pa., 1933-35, cons. editor, same, since 1934; engr. Finger Lakes State Parks Commn., 1936-37; cons. engr., Cooperative Grange League Fed. Exchange, Inc., Ithaca, N.Y., since 1937; engineering consultant American LaFrance-Foamite Corporation, Elmira, New York, since 1943. Served as 2d lieutenant A.S., U.S. Army, Aug. 1917-Dec. 1918, World War. Pres. bd. trustees Union Free Sch., Ithaca; mem. exec. bd. local council, Boy Scouts of America. Mem. Am. Concrete Inst., Cornell Soc. Engrs., Gargoyle, Pyramid (Cornell), Tau Beta Pi, Chi Epsilon, Sigma Phi Sigma. Republican. Episcopalian. Author: Design of Concrete Structures, 1923; Stresses in Simple Structures, 1926; Design of Steel Structures, 1930; Elementary Structural Engineering, 1940 (all with L. C. Urquhart); Handbook of Formulas and Tables for Engineers (with C. A. Peirce and W. B. Carver), 1929. Editor-in-chief: General Engineering Handbook, 1932. Author of following textbooks for Internat. Corr. Schs.: Design of Flat Slab Floors, 1935; Elements of Masonry Design, 1936; Design of Culverts, 1938; Foundations and Piling, 1941. Cons. editor Internat. Textbook Co., Civil Engring. Series. Contbr. tech. articles to mags. Home: 424 Hanshaw Rd., Ithaca, N.Y. Died Jan. 10, 1947.

ORR, GUSTAVUS JOHN, educator; b. Orrville, Anderson County, S.C., Aug. 9, 1819; s. James and Anne (Anderson) O.; grad. Emory Coll., Oxford, Ga., 1844; m. Eliza Caroline Anderson, 1847, 10 children. Prof. mathematics Emory Coll., 1848-58; apptd. Ga. commr. to settle boundary dispute with Fla., 1859; pres. So. Masonic Female Coll., Covington, Ga., 1867-70; prof. mathematics Oglethorpe Coll., Atlanta, Ga., 1870; Ga. sch. commr., 1872-87; v.p. N.E.A., 1881, pres., 1882; agt. Peabody Fund in Ga. Died Atlanta, Dec. 11, 1887.

ORR, H(IRAM) WINNETT, surgeon; b. West Newton, Pa., Mar. 17, 1877; s. Andrew Wilson and Frances J. (Winnett) O.; U. of Neb., 1892-95; M.D., U. of Mich., 1899; m. Grace Douglass, Sept. 7, 1904; children—Douglass, Willard, Josephine, Dorothy, Gwenith. In practice at Lincoln, Neb., since 1899. Editor Western Medical Review, 1899-1906; lecturer on history of medicine, Coll. of Medicine, U. of Neb., since 1903; chief med. insp., Lincoln pub. schs., 1908; supt. Neb. Orthopedic Hosp., 1911-17, chief surgeon, 1919-47, cons. surgeon since 1947; cons. surgeon dept. orthopedic surgery, Lincoln Gen. Hosp. Editor Jour. Orthopedic Surgery, 1919-21. Commd. capt., Med. R.C., May 18, 1917; on duty Welsh Met. War Hosp., Whitchurch, Cardiff, Wales, June 1917-Aug. 1918; with A.E.F., France, Aug. 1, 1918-Feb. 24, 1919; maj. M.C., Oct. 1, 1918; lt. col., Feb. 17, 1919; relieved, June 1, 1919; was col. M.C., U.S. Army Reserve, with spl. assignment as consultant orthopedic surgery. Librarian, Neb. State Med. Assn., 1900-12, sec., 1907, pres., 1919-20; sec. Am. Orthopedic Assn., 1915-17, editor, 1919-21, pres., 1936; sec. Central States Orthopedic Club, 1913-17. Recipient Distinguished Service award (posthumously) from the American College of Surgeons. Member A.M.A. (chmn. orthopedic sect., 1921-22), Miss. Valley and Mo. Valley med. assns., Elkhorn Valley Med. Soc., Lancaster County Med. Soc., Soc. Internat. de Chirurg Orthopedique (U.S.), Am. Med. Library Assn. (hon. mem.); Assoc. Bone and Joint Surgeons (hon.); member Chi Phi, Phi Rho Sigma, Sigma Xi, Alpha Omega Alpha (Nebraska). Clubs: Commercial, Country, Lincoln University; University (Chgo.). Author numerous books, 1903—; latest publ. Selected Pages from the History of Medicine in Nebraska, 1952; contbr. to Sajous Cyclo., 1931; speaker on osteomyelitis Brit. Med. Assn., Dublin, 1933, on surgery Ill. State Med. Soc., 1939, on compound fractures So. Med. Assn., 1940; lectr. Am. Acad. Orthopedic Surgeons, 1952. Home: 1601 Smith St., Lincoln 2. Office: 2300 S. 13th St., Lincoln, Neb. Died Oct. 11, 1956; buried Arlington Nat. Cemetery.

ORR, HUGH, inventor, firearms mfr.; b. Lochwinnoch, Renfrewshire, Scotland, Jan. 2, 1715; s. Robert Orr; m. Mary Bass, Aug. 4, 1742, 10 children including Robert. Came to America, 1740; employed by a scythe-maker, East Bridgewater, Mass., 1741, became owner of shop, circa 1745; inventor trip-hammer (said to have been 1st in colonies); became mfr. firearms, made 500 muskets (believed to be 1st made in colonies), 1748; inventor machine to clean flaxseed, 1753; began producing muskets again, 1775, built foundry for casting cannon, Bridgewater, Mass.; built machines for carding and roping wool in own shop with mechanic from Scotland, 1785-87; mem. Mass. Senate, 1786, obtained state grants for encouragement of textile industry; brought various European mechanics to U.S., also introduced new types of machinery. Died Bridgewater, Dec. 6, 1798.

ORR, LOUIS MCDONALD, physician; b. Cumming, Ga., Sept. 27, 1899; s. Louis McDonald and Etta (Wise) O.; B.S., Emory U., 1922, M.D., 1924; D.S., Stetson U., 1960; Univ. of Fla., 1960; Emory University 1960; m. Dorothy Brown, December 16, 1927; children—Louis McDonald, Doris Brown. Intern Peter Bent Brigham Hosp., Boston, 1924-25, also preceptee tng. urology with Dr. Arthur Chute, Boston; resident Lakeside Hosp., Cleve., 1926; practice of medicine, Orlando, Fla., 1927—; dir. postgrad. edn. Orange Meml. Hosp. Trustee Rollins Coll. Served from maj. to col., M.C., AUS, 1942-45; comdg. officer 15th Hosp. Center. Decorated Bronze Star; recipient S. Sullivan award Rollins Coll., 1946. Mem. Am. Urological Assn. (pres. Southeastern sect. 1943), Civic Music Assn. (pres. 1939-52), A.M.A. (chmn. fed. med. services com.; pres. 1959-60), Am. Assn. Genito-Urinary Surgeons, So. Med. Assn., A.C.S., Southeastern Surg. Congress, Internat. Soc. Urology, World Med. Assn., Soc. Nuclear Medicine, Phi Delta Theta, Alpha Omega Alpha, Omicron Delta Kappa, Phi Rho Sigma. Episcopalian. Author med. articles. Home: 750 Gatlin Av. Office: 1300 S. Orange Av., Orlando, Fla. Died May 23, 1961.

ORR, THOMAS E., engr.; b. Wheeling W.Va., Apr. 9, 1894; s. Joseph Reid and Mary St. Clair (Hamilton) O.; B.S., in C.E., Carnegie Inst. Tech., 1917, C.E., 1947; m. Kathryn Donald, Oct. 5, 1940; children—Thomas E., Janet B., Duncan H. Constrn. work Am. Bridge Co., Panama Canal, Latin Am., 1911-12, U.S., 1912-13; civil engring. bus., Pittsburgh, 1929-40, Cleveland since 1940. Pres. Plastray Corp., Detroit, since 1948; v.p., sec. Plastic Engring., Inc., Cleveland, since 1941; owner Lighthouse Service Co., Highway Lighthouse Service Co., Keystone Plastics Co. (all at Pittsburgh); pres. Plastray Ltd. (Canada), Port Credit, Ontario. Served in U.S. Army, 79th div., 2d French Colonials, 1917-19; maj. A.C., 1942-44. Awarded: Purple Heart with palm, service medals for combat. Mem. Engrs. Soc. Western Pa., Soc. Plastic Engrs. (hon. life, past pres.), Ohio Professional Engrs., Cleveland C. of C., Disabled Emergency Officers of the World Wars, Am. Legion, Vets. Fgn. Wars, 316th Inf. Assn. (past nat. pres.), Beta Theta Pi, Tau Beta Pi. Republican. Presbyterian. Mason. Club: Cleveland Athletic. Home: 12506 Edgewater Dr., Cleve. 7. Died Jan. 29, 1952; buried Knollwood Mausoleum, Cleve.

ORROK, GEORGE ALEXANDER, (or'rok), consulting engr.; b. Dorchester, Mass., July 3, 1867; s. James L. P. and Laura (Davenport) O.; ed. Mass. Inst. Tech., 1885-88; M.E. honora causa, Stevens Inst. of Tech., 1929; m. Jessie Waldo, Dec. 24, 1898; m. 2d, Elene E. Geer, Oct. 20, 1923; With late Dr. F. S. Pearson, engr., 1891-98; with New York Edison Co., 1898-1928, cons. engr. since 1928; mem. Orrok & Myers Associates; lecturer on steam engring., Sheffield Scientific Sch., Yale, 1921-39, on power plant engring., Harvard, 1927-39; cons. engr. Board Water Supply, New York City, and Bureau of Yards and Docks, Navy Department. Honorary member American Society M.E.; mem. Am. Soc. C.E., Am. Inst. Mining Engrs., Inst. of Consulting Engrs., Franklin Inst., Instn. Mech. Engrs. (London). Republican. Unitarian. Club: Engineers (New York). Author: (with Professor R. H. Fernald) Engineering of Power Plants. Contbr. on tech. subjects to periodicals, Proc. Am. Soc. Mech. Engrs., etc. Home: Riverside, Conn. Office: 21 E. 40th St., New York, N.Y. Died Apr. 6, 1944.

ORTH, O(SWALD) SIDNEY, anesthesiologist; b. Cin., June 29, 1906; s. Charles Lorenz and Grace Irene (Gibson) O.; B.S. in Physical Edn., U. Ill., 1929, M.S. in Physiology, 1932; Ph.D., U. Wis., 1939, M.D., 1942; m. Ottilia Caroline E. Blodau, June 29, 1931. Sci. tchr. and coach Malden (Ill.) High Sch., 1929-30; asst. physiology U. Ill., 1930-36; instr. med. physiology U. Wis., 1936-42; intern Wis. Gen. Hosp., 1943; asst. prof. pharmacology U. Wis., 1942-45, asso. prof., 1945-48, prof., 1948-52, chmn. dept. anesthesiology, 1952—. Diplomat American Board Anesthesiology, 1950. Mem. Am. Physiol. Soc., Am. Soc. Pharmacology and Exptl. Therapeutics, Inc., A.A.A.S., Soc. Exptl. Biology and Medicine, Am. Soc. Anesthesiology, A.M.A., Am. Therapeutics Soc. Assn. U. Anesthetists. Home: 6309 Mound Dr., Middleton, Wis. Office: 1300 University Av., Madison, Wis. Died Feb. 2, 1964; buried Madison.

ORTMANN, ARNOLD EDWARD, naturalist; b. Magdeburg, Prussia, Apr. 8, 1863; s. Prof. Edward Franz and Bertha (Lorenz) O.; gymnasium edn., Magdeburg and (grad.) Schleusingen (Thuringia); studied at univs. of Jena, Kiel and Strassburg; Ph.D., Jena, 1885; Sc.D., U. of Pittsburgh, 1911; m. Anna Zaiss, Dec. 5, 1894. Served as 1-yr. vol. in 5th Thuringia Inf., German Army, 1882-83; qualified as lt. reserves, Mar. 1883; zoölogist and palaeontologist; on collecting expdn. to Zanzibar, Africa, 1890-91; came to U.S., 1894; curator invertebrate palaeontology, Princeton, 1894-1903; curator invertebrate zoölogy, Carnegie Mus., Pittsburgh, 1903—; instr. geol. geography, 1909-10, prof. phys. geography, 1910-25, prof. zoölogy, 1925—, U. of Pittsburgh. Mem. Princeton Arctic (Peary relief) expdn., 1899. Author: Flora Hennebergica, 1887; Grundzüge der Marinen Tiergeographie, 1896; Continuation of Die Decapodon in Bronn's Klassen und Ordnungen des Tierreiches, 1898-1900; Tertiary Intertebrates of the Princeton Expdn. to Patagonia, 1902. Home: Pittsburgh, Pa. Died Jan. 3, 1927.

ORTON, CLAYTON ROBERTS, plant pathologist; b. East Hardwick, Vt., Apr. 1, 1885; s. Lyman Squire and Ellen Mandana (Stevens) O.; prep. edn., Essex Classical Inst., 1901-03, Hardwick Acad., 1904-05; B.S., U. Vt., 1909, Sc.D., 1942; M.S., Purdue, 1915; Ph.D., Columbia, 1924; m. Ethel M. Chapman, Sept. 22, 1911; children—Jan, Gardner Chapman, Patricia. Spl. agt. U.S. Dept. Agr. June 1909-Jan. 1910; asst. plant pathologist, U. of Wis., Feb.-Sept. 1910; asst. botanist, Ind. Agrl. Expt. Sta., 1910-12; asst. prof. botany, Pa. State Coll., 1913-16, asso. prof., 1916-19, also asso. prof. plant pathology, 1917-19, prof., 1919-27; plant pathologist, Pa. Agrl. Expt. Sta., 1913-27; also collaborator, Bureau Plant Industry of the U.S. Dept. of Agriculture, 1913-25 and 1930—; plant pathologist, in charge research and extension, agrl. dept. The Bayer Co., Inc., 1925-28, Bayer-Semesan Co., Inc., 1928-29; prof. plant pathology and head dept., W.Va. Univ., 1929-33; plant pathologist W.Va. Agrl. Expt. Sta. 1928-38; head dept. of biology, W.Va. Univ., 1933-36, head dept. plant pathology and forestry, 1936-38; dean, Coll. Agrl. Forestry and Home Economics, 1938—; dir. Agrl. Exptl. Sta., 1938—; on leave, 1950-53, spl. appointment as agrl. consultant to Liberia for OFAR, U.S. Dept. Agriculture. Sec. Advisory Bd. Am. Plant Pathologists, 1918-21; chmn., 1922-23; mem. Nat. Research Council (div. biology and agr., 1922-24; liaison mem. div. states relations, 1923-24); mem. bd. govs. Crop Protection Inst., 1920-25, 1935—; mem. W.Va. Planning Bd., 1935—, chmn., 1941—; chmn. Land-Use Com. of W.Va., 1934-38. Fellow American Assn. Advancement of Science (pres. State Coll. br., 1923); mem. Am. Phytopathological Soc. (pres. 1939), Mycological Soc. America, S. Appalachian Bot. Club, W.Va. Acad. Science, N.Y. Acad. Sci., Soil Conservation Soc. America. Sigma Xi, Kappa Sigma, Alpha Zeta, Gamma Sigma Delta. Episcopalian. Home: 369 Mulberry St., Morgantown, W.Va. Died June 16, 1955; buried East Grove Cemetery Morgantown.

ORTON, EDWARD, geologist; b. Deposit, Delaware County, N.Y., Mar. 9, 1829; A.M., Hamilton Coll., 1848, Ph.D., LL.D., Ohio State U.; m. Mary M. Jennings, 1855; m. 2d, Anna D. Torrey, 1875. State geologist of Ohio, 1869—; pres. Antioch Coll., O., 1872-73; pres. Ohio State U., 1873-81, prof. of geology, 1873—. Author of "Petroleum," etc., in U.S. Geol. reports, Kentucky geol. survey. Joint author Vols. 1, 2 and 3 and author Vols. 5, 6 and 7, "Geology of Ohio;" also many geological papers. Pres. Geol. Soc. of America in 1897; pres. Am. Assn. Adv. Science, 1898-99. Address: Columbus, O. Died 1899.

ORTON, EDWARD, JR., engineer, mfr.; b. Chester, N.Y., Oct. 8, 1863; s. Dr. Edward and Mary (Jennings) O.; E.M., Ohio State U., 1884; D.Sc. from Rutgers Coll., N.J., 1922; m. Mary Princess Anderson, Oct. 30, 1888 (died 1927); m. 2d, Mina Althea Orton, Oct. 6, 1928. Chemist and supt. blast furnaces, 1884-88; 1st to regularly mfr. "ferro-silicon," or high silicon alloy of iron in U.S., Bessie Furnace New Straitsville, O., 1887-88; entered clay industries, 1888; managed several plants, 1888-93. Began agitation, 1893, which resulted in establishing, 1894, of 1st school in U.S. for instr. in tech. of clay, glass and cement industries, of which was dir. until 1916; dean Coll. Engring. Ohio State U., 1902-06 and 1910-16; retired from univ. work, 1917. State geologist of Ohio, 1899-1906. Commd. maj., O.R.C., Jan. 5, 1917; called into active service in motors div. Q.M. Corps, May 9, 1917; lt. col. Motor Transport Corps, Sept. 6, 1918. Awarded D.S.M., June 2, 1919. Col. Q.M., O.R.C., Sept. 25, 1919; brig. gen. Q.M., O.R.C., Sept. 27, 1923. Pres. Reserve Officers' Assn. of Ohio, 1922-23. Began manufacture, 1896, of pyrometric cones, for regulating firing process of ceramic products and other wares burned in kilns; developed lab. and testing sta. for study of clay and ceramic products, 1900. Wrote: Clays of Ohio and the Industries Established Upon Them, Rep. Ohio Geol. Survey, Vol. V, 1884; The Clay-Working Industries of Ohio, Vol. VII, same, 1893. Also numerous tech. articles and reports. Home: Columbus, O. Died Feb. 10, 1932.

ORTON, SAMUEL TORREY, neuropsychiatrist; b. Columbus, O., Oct. 15, 1879; s. Edward and Anna Davenport (Torrey) Orton; A.B., Ohio State University, 1901; M.D., University of Pennsylvania, 1905, D.Sc., 1945; A.M., Harvard Univ., 1906; m. Mary Pelton Follett, Oct. 15, 1908 (died Sept. 7, 1926); children—Samuel Torrey, Sarah Patterson, Mary Follett; m. 2d, June Frances Lyday, July 16, 1928. Pathologist and clin. dir. Worcester (Mass.) State Hosp., 1910-14; instr. neuropathology, Harvard, 1913; scientific dir. Pa. Hosp., Phila., 1914-19; prof. psychiatry, State U. of Ia., 1919-27, also dir. State Psychopathic Hosp. Neuropathologist, N.Y. Neurol. Inst., 1929-36; prof. neurology and neuropathology, Coll. Physicians and Surgeons (Columbia), 1930-36; Consultant in lang. disabilities, Inst. of Pa. Hosp., Phila., 1943; lecturer in neurology, Clark U., 1913-15. Mem. A.A.A.S., Am. Psychiatric Assn., A.M.A., Am. Assn. Research in Nervous and Mental Diseases, Am. Neurol. Assn., N.Y. State Med. Soc., New York Academy of Medicine. Home: 12 E. 86th St., New York 28, N.Y. Died Nov. 17, 1948.

ORTON, WILLIAM ALLEN, plant pathologist; b. N. Fairfax, Vt., Feb. 28, 1877; s. Gardner Gregory and Electa Wilcox (Allen) O.; B.S., U. of Vt., 1897. M.S., 1898, Sc.D., 1915; m. Helen A. Davis, Apr. 20, 1903; children—Helen Alberta, Alice Louise, William Allen (dec.). Asst. botanist, Vt. Agrl. Expt. Sta. and instr., U. of Vt., 1897-99; plant pathologist, U.S. Dept. of Agr., June 1, 1899-Oct. 31, 1924, in charge investigation cotton, truck and forage crop diseases, Bureau Plant Industry, and v. chmn. Federal Hort. Bd., 1912-24; sci. dir. and gen. mgr. Tropical Plant Research Foundation, 1924—. Conglist. Writer bulletins U.S. Dept. Agr. on sea island cotton, cotton and potato diseases, plant breeding and related subjects, and tropical agr. Home: Takoma Park, D.C. Died Jan. 7, 1930.

ORVILLE, HOWARD T(HOMAS), naval officer retired, meteorological consultant, corp. executive; born Saratoga, Wyo., June 16, 1901; s. William and Lucy D. (Wiant) O.; student Army and Navy Prep. Sch., 1918-19; B.S., U.S. Naval Acad., Annapolis, 1925; student Navy Post Grad. Sch., 1928-29; S.M. in meteorology, Mass. Inst. Tech., 1930; m. Lillian L. Duvall, June 5, 1926; children—Howard Thomas, Harold Duvall, Richard Edmonds. Bank clk. Stockgrowers State Bank, Saratoga, Wyo., 1917-18, Rawlins Nat. Bank, 1919-21; commd. ensign U.S. Navy, 1925, and advanced through grades to capt., 1944, ret. 1950; assigned to battleships and destroyers, 1925-28; officer in charge aerographer's sch. Naval Air Sta., Lakehurst, N.J., 1930-31, 1934-35; co-pilot nat. and internat. free balloon races, 1934-35; aerolog. officer U.S.S. Langley, 1931-32; force aerolog. officer on staff comdr. battleships, Battle Force, 1932; fleet aerologist on staff comdr. in chief, U.S. Fleet, 1936-38; lighter-than-air pilot, head aerolog. dept. and sch., Lakehurst, N.J., 1938-40; head naval aerology, flight div. Bur. Aeronautics, 1940-43, transferred to dept. chief Naval Operations (Air), 1943-50; during these yrs. served on numerous commns. and coms. working on meteorol. field; served as del. or mem. delegations several internat. confs.; ordered to North Atlantic Treaty Orgn., 1950; mem. vis. com. Blue Hill Obs., Harvard; cons. to gen. mgr. Friez Instrument Div., Bendix Aviation Corporation, 1950-58; vice president of Beckman & Whitley, Incorporated, 1958—. Awarded the Legion of Merit; Commendation Ribbon; Officer Military Order of British Empire; Cravate Blue of Yun Hwei (cloud and banner) (China). Mem. several profl. and scientific orgns. and assns. Kiwanian (dir.). Author instrn. manuals and numerous articles on meteorology. Home: Long Green, Md. Office: care Beckman & Whitley, Inc., Long Green, Md. Died May 24, 1960; buried Arlington Nat. Cemetery.

OSBORN, CYRUS RICHARD, executive; b. Dayton, O., Aug. 27, 1897; s. Cyrus and Stella (Hopkins) O.; M.E., U. of Cincinnati, 1921, D.Sc. (hon.), 1948; m. Jeannette Powell, Feb. 20, 1926; children—Sarah Ann, Cyrus William. Tech. engr. Overseas Motor Serv. Corp., 1923-26, gen. mgr., 1926-29; v.p. in charge mfg. Gen. Motors Export Co., 1929-32; mng. dir. Gen. Motors Nordiska, Stockholm, Sweden, 1932-34; asst. to gen. mgr., Gen. Motors Export Div., 1934-36; gen. mgr., Adam Opel, Russelsheim, Germany, 1936-40; asst. to vice pres., Gen. Motors Corp., 1940-41, asst. group exec., 1941-43, vice pres. Gen. Motors Corp., gen. mgr. Electro-Motive div., 1943-50, v.p. in charge engine group Gen. Motors Corp., 1950-59, dir., 1951-63, exec. v.p. engine divs., 1959-63. Served as pvt., U.S. Army, 1918-19. Mem. Soc. Automotive Engrs., Phi Delta Theta, Tau Beta Pi. Republican. Presbyterian. Clubs: Detroit, Bloomfield Hills Country, Economic. Home: Bloomfield Hills MI Died Nov. 15, 1968; buried Dayton OH

OSBORN, FREDERICK ARTHUR, prof. physics; b. Tecumseh, Mich., Mar. 3, 1871; s. Benjamin A. and Sarah (Whittemore) O.; Ph.B., U. of Mich., 1896, Ph.D., 1907; m. Mary L. Osborn, Aug. 16, 1898; 1 dau., Margaret Anna. Asst. in physics, high sch., Saginaw, Mich., 1890-91; lab. instr. physics, high sch., Ann Arbor, 1893-96; prof. physics, Olivet (Mich.) Coll., 1896-1902; prof. physics and dir. physics labs. U. of Wash., since 1902. Mem. Am. Phys. Soc., Am. Assn. Univ. Profs., A.A.A.S., Illuminating Engring. Soc., Central Assn. Physics and Math. Teachers, Acoustical Soc. of America. Republican. Conglist. Mason. Author: Physics Manual, 1906; College Physics, 1920-24; Physics of the Home, 1925. Home: 17763 15th N.E., Seattle, Wash. Died Dec. 28, 1942.

OSBORN, H(ENRY) FAIRFIELD, paleontologist; b. Fairfield, Conn., Aug. 8, 1857; s. William Henry and Virginia Reed (Sturges) O.; A.B., Princeton, 1877, Sc.D., 1880; LL.D., Trinity, 1901, Princeton, 1902, Columbia, 1907, Union Univ., Schenectady, N.Y., 1928; D.Sc., Cambridge U., 1904, Yale, 1923, Oxford, 1926, New York, 1927, Ph.D. from Christiana, 1911; honorary Doctorate from U. of Paris, 1931; m. Lucretia Thatcher, d. Gen. Alexander J. and Josephine Adams Perry (died 1930); children—Virginia Sturges (Mrs. Robt. Gordon McKay), Alexander Perry, Henry Fairfield, Josephine Adams (Mrs. Jay Coogan), Gurdon Saltonstall (dec.). Asst. prof. natural science, 1881-83, prof. comparative anatomy, 1883-90, Princeton Da Costa professor biology, 1891-96, zoölogy, 1896-1910, research professor zoölogy, 1910—, dean faculty of pure science, 1892-95, Columbia; curator department vertebrate paleontology, 1891-1910, hon. curator, 1910—, asst. to pres., 1899-1901, v.p. and trustee, 1901-08, pres. trustees, 1908-33, honorary president, 1933—, American Museum Natural History; vertebrate paleontologist, 1900-24, sr. geologist, 1924—, U.S. Geol. Survey; with Canadian Geol. Survey, 1900-04; as chmn. exec. com. N.Y. Zoöl. Soc., 1896-1903, was active in founding N.Y. Zoöl. Park; chmn. zoöl. and paleontol. advisory coms. Carnegie Instn., Washington, 1902; elected sec. Smithsonian Instn., Dec. 4, 1906, but declined. Pres. Am. Soc. Naturalists, 1892, Am. Morphol. Soc., 1898, N.Y. Acad. Sciences, 1898-1900, Marine Biol. Assn., 1896-1901, New York Zoöl. Soc., 1909-23 (later hon. life pres.), Am. Soc. Paleontologists, 1903, Audubon Soc. N.Y. State, 1910, Am. Bison Soc., 1914-15, Second Internat. Congress of Eugenics, 1921, A.A.A.S., 1928; v.p., N.Y. Zoöl. Soc., 1897-98, Washington Acad. Sci., 1911, Am. Philos. Soc., 1922-28, Hispanic Soc. America, 1919-24 (later hon. v.p.); trustee Brearley School for Girls, 1894-1919 (president 1901-16), Marine Biological Lab., 1890-1901, Hispanic Society America, 1909-24, Kahn Foundation for Foreign Travel of Am. Teachers, 1911-26, N.Y. Pub. Library, 1911-19. Councilor, Nat. Acad. Sciences, 1906-13, Am. Philos. Soc., 1907-19, Institut de Paléontologie Humaine, 1919—. Mem. award com., Hayden Geol. Memorial medal of Phila. Acad. Natural Sciences, Nat. Inst. Social Sciences, Daniel Giraud Elliot fund of Nat. Acad. Sciences and Popular Science Inst. Elector N.Y. U. Hall of Fame, 1910—. Chmn. N.Y. State Roosevelt Memorial Commn., 1920—. Fellow New York Acad. Sciences, American Geog. Soc. (life), American Acad. Arts and Sciences. Medals: Nat. Inst. Soc. Sciences, 1913; Hayden Memorial Geol. Award, 1914; Gaudry (Geol. Soc. of France), 1918; Darwin (Royal Soc.), 1918; Cullom (Am. Geog. Soc.), 1919; Pasteur Inst., 1921; Société Nationale d'Acclimatation de France, 1923; Roosevelt Memorial Association, 1923; Holland Scoeity, 1925; Wollaston (Geol. Soc. of London), 1926; Daniel Giraud Elliot Medal, 1929. Comdr. de l'Ordre de la Couronne de Belgique, 1919. Author: From the Greeks to Darwin, 1894; Evolution of Mammalian Molar Teeth, 1907; The Age of Mammals, 1910; Huxley and Education, 1910; Men of the Old Stone Age, 1915; Origin and Evolution of Life, 1917; Impressions of Great Naturalists, 1924; The Earth Speaks to Bryan, 1925; Evolution and Religion in Education, 1926; Creative Education, 1927; Man Rises to Parnassus, 1927; Fifty-Two Years of Research, 1939; Cope, Master Naturalist, 1931; also 8 memoirs; over 860 scientific and educational papers. Editor: A Naturalist in the Bahamas (John L. Northrup Memorial) 1910; Fifty Years of Princeton '77, 1927. Home: Garrison, N.Y. Died Nov. 6, 1935.

OSBORN, HENRY LESLIE, zoölogist; b. Newark, N.J., July 5, 1857; s. Moses Morris and Susan Amelia (Hedenberg) O.; student prep. dept. Drew Theol. Sem., 1872-75; A.B., Wesleyan U., Conn., 1878; Ph.D., Johns Hopkins, 1884; traveled and studied in Europe, 1889, 1926, studied at Zoöl. Sta., Naples, 1907, 10; LL.D., Hamline U., St. Paul, Minn., 1927; m. Effie Miller Loag, July 7, 1887. Assistant in zoölogy, Wesleyan U., 1878-81; fellow Johns Hopkins, 1881-84; agt. U.S. Fish Commn., 1879-80; prof. zoölogy, Purdue U., Lafayette, Ind., 1884-87; prof. biology, 1887—, dean of faculty, 1918-31, acting president, 1923 and 1923-35, Hamline U., dean emeritus, 1931—. In charge of summer school courses in zoölogy, Cold Spring Harbor, New York, 1891-92, Chautauqua, N.Y., 1895-1904, Dept. Animal Biology, U. of Minn., 1913, 14. Wrote: Report on Newfoundland Cod-fishing Industry (U.S. Census), 1880; Hamline University in the World War, 1920; Alumni Record of Hamline University, 1924; articles on morphology of Trematodes in scientific publs. Home: St. Paul, Minn. Died Jan. 3, 1940.

OSBORN, HERBERT, biologist; b. Lafayette, Wis., Mar. 19, 1856; s. Charles Paine and Harriet Newell (Marsh) O.; B.S., Iowa State College, 1879, M.S., 1880, also D.Sc., 1916; LL.D. from U. of Pittsburgh, 1930; L.L.D. from Ohio State Univ., 1936; m. Alice Isadore Sayles, Jan. 19, 1883; children—Morse Foster, Herbert Tirrill, Evelyn, Dorothy, Margaret Stanton. Asst. 1879-83, asst. prof., 1883-85, prof. zoology and entomology, 1885-98, Ia. State Coll.; entomologist, of expt. sta., 1890-98; state entomologist of Ia., 1898; prof. zoölogy and entomology, 1898-1916, research prof., 1916-33, emeritus prof. since 1933, Ohio State U.; also dir. of Lake Laboratory, 1898-1918. Dir. Ohio Biol. Survey since 1912. Spl. agt. div. entomology, U.S. Dept. Agr., 1885-94; cons. entomologist, Maine Experiment Sta. since 1913; cons. entomologist Tropical Plant Research Foundation, 1925, trustee of same, 1926-43; collaborator U.S. Bureau Entomology since 1930. Fellow A.A.A.S. (v.p. Sect. F. 1917); pres. Ia. Acad. Sciences, 1887 (sec. and editor Proc., 1890-98), Assn. Econ. Entomologists, 1898, Ohio Acad. Sciences, 1904-05, Am. Micros. Soc., 1907-09, Entomol. Soc. America, 1911 (mng. editor Annals, 1908-28), Soc. Promotion Agrl. Science, 1917-18; trustee Biological Abstracts, 1927-37; trustee Research Fund Ohio Acad. Science since 1917; fellow Calif. Acad. of Science, 1937; mem. Internat. Entomol. Congress, Am. Soc. Naturalists, Am. Entomol. Soc., Am. Soc. Zoölogists, Biol. Soc. Washington, Société Entomologique de France, Entomol. Soc. Washington, Sigma Xi (rec. sec. 1907-08), Phi Kappa Phi (hon.), Alpha Zeta (hon.), Gamma Alpha (hon.). Clubs: University, Faculty. Author: Pedicull and Mallophaga of Man and Lower Animals, 1891; Insects Affecting Domestic Animals, 1896; The Hessian Fly in the United States, 1898; The Genus Scaphoideus, 1900; Economic Zoölogy, 1908; Agrl. Entomology, 1916; Leafhopper of Ohio, 1928; Fragments of Entomol. History, 1937, part II, 1946; Meadow and Pasture Insects, 1939. Wrote articles Insects, Parasitic, and Insects, Poisonous, in Wood's Reference Handbook of the Med. Sciences (new edit.), 1903 and 1915; Neotropic Homoptera in the Carnegie Museum, 7 parts, 1923-39; also many papers in jours., proc., etc. Address: Ohio State U., Columbus, O. Died Sept. 20, 1954.

OSBORNE, LOYALL ALLEN, mech. engr.; b. Newark, N.J., June 22, 1870; s. Frederick Allen and Eliza J. (Rathbone) O.; M.E., Cornell U., 1891; m. Emma Louise Hines, Nov. 27, 1895; children—Loyall A., Nancy B., John S., Louise. Engr., 1891-95, asst. supt., 1895-97, asst. to v.p., 1897-99, mgr. of works, 1899-1902, 4th v.p. in charge of mfg. and engring., 1902-04, 3d v.p., same duties, 1904-06, v.p. in charge of commercial and engring. dept., 1906-17, chmn. Gen. Commercial Com. Westinghouse Electric & Mfg. Co., 1917-29; v.p. New Eng. Westinghouse Co., 1915-19; mem. Nat. War Labor Bd., 1917-19; pres. Westinghouse Electric Internat. Co., 1920-34; now retired. Pres. Stockbridge Library Assn.; mem. Stockbridge Planning Bd.; chmn. Stockbridge Traffic Com. Fellow Am. Inst. Elec. Engrs.; mem. Franklin Inst., Am. Soc. M.E., Nat. Industrial Conf. Bd. (councillor; ex-chmn.), Kappa Alpha. Republican. Club: University (New York). Home: Stockbridge, Mass. Died Aug 18, 1944.

OSBORNE, REGINALD STANLEY, elec. exec.; b. nr. Foxton, N.Z., Feb. 2, 1892; s. Edmund John and Harriet (Nye) B.; student Tech. Coll., Palmerston North, N.Z., 1910; extension courses Columbia, N.Y., William and Mary, Va. univs.; m. Olga Wood, Mar. 25, 1923; children—Jacquelyn Wood (Mrs. William Ross), Geraldyn Frances (Mrs. Robert K. Molloy). Came to the United States, 1912, naturalized, 1924. Gen.

superintendent, consulting engineer Acme Bldg. Corp., N.Y. City, 1914-18; orgn. Virginia-Carolina Elec. Works, Inc., Norfolk, Va., 1918, served as pres., 1922-45, director, from 1918, chairman of the board, from 1956; president of Virginia-Carolina Electric Sales, Inc., from 1945, Petroleum Shipping Company, Incorporated, from 1946, Stanart Corporation, from 1954, Electrical Suppliers, Inc., 1936-44, Virginia-Caroline Engineering, Inc., 1930-42. Orgn. received Certificate of Achievement (Navy) for services rendered during World War II. Mem. Am. Orchid Soc., Norfolk Portsmouth Real Estate Board, Y.M.C.A. (director), Society Naval Architects and Marine Engrs., Maritime Assn., Isaac Walton League, C. of C., Nat. Defense Transportation Association (1st v.p.). Presbyn. (deacon). Clubs: Cedar Island Gunning (pres.); Lions; Propeller of U.S. (nat. v.p., mem. bd. govs., Port of Norfolk, com. sponsoring sea scout activities, Norfolk); The Cavalier Yacht and Country, Norfolk Yacht and Country, Virginia (Norfolk). The Osborne Family portrait hangs in the Nat. Archives Gallery, Wellington, N.Z., in recognition of family contribution toward World War I effort. Home: Virginia Beach VA Died Feb. 8, 1967; buried Forest Lawn, Norfolk VA

OSBORNE, THOMAS BURR, chemist; b. New Haven, Conn., Aug. 5, 1859; s. Arthur D. and Frances Louisa (Blake) O.; A.B., Yale, 1881, spl. studies chemistry, Ph.D., 1885, hon. Sc.D., 1910; m. Elizabeth Annah Johnson, 1886; children—Arthur Dimon, Francis Blake (dec.). Research chemist, Conn. Agrl. Expt. Sta., 1886—; also research asso. Carnegie Instn., Washington, and Yale. Asso. editor Journal of Biological Chemistry. Dir. Second Nat. Bank of New Haven. Fellow Am. Acad. Arts and Sciences; mem. Am. Soc. Biol. Chemists (pres. 1910). Gold medal, Paris, 1900; John Scott medal, 1922. Author: Proteins of the Wheat Kernel, 1907; The Vegetable Proteins, 1909, rev. edit., 1924; also numerous papers on the chemistry and nutritive value of the vegetable proteins. Home: New Haven, Conn. Died Jan. 29, 1929.

OSGOOD, EDWIN EUGENE, medical educator; b. Fall River, Mass., Jan. 25, 1899; s. William Pleasants and Lydia Lee (Smith) O.; McMinnville (now Linfield) Coll., 1916-18; B.A., U. of Ore., 1923, M.A., M.D., 1924; grad. study, Mayo Clinic, Rochester, Minn., 1923, 26, U. of Vienna, 1927-28. Basel, Freiburg, London, 1928; m. Mable Maru Wilhelm, May 30, 1934; children—Barbara Delight, Beverly Maru, Edwin Boyd, Brenda Gay, Beatrice Joy. Asst. in biochemistry, U. of Ore., 1919-21, instr. in biochemistry, 1921-25, asso. in same, 1925-28, asso. in medicine, 1925-29, asst. prof. biochemistry, 1928-33, asst. prof. medicine, 1929-39, asso. prof., 1939-47, prof. since 1947; director of laboratories, University of Oregon Medical School, 1928-1936; member of staff of Multnomah County and Doernbecher hosps. from 1928, head div. experimental medicine, 1936-64, associate head, 1964-69. Recipient bronze metal sci. exhibit American Medical Association, 1929, hon. mention, 1934, certificate merit, 1938. Distinguished Achievement award, Modern Medicine mag., 1957; U. Ore. Med. School Alumni Assn. meritorious achievement award, 1962; Gov.'s Northwest Scientist award for research in leukemia and Osgood growth prediction charts, 1962; N.W. Sci. award for unraveling human chromosome Ore. Mus. Sci. and Industry, 1963; Robert Roesler de Villiers award for research in leukemia, 1963. Master Am. Coll. Physicians; fellow International Soc. Hematology (councilor U.S. 1950-52), N.Y. Acad. Sci.; mem. Am. Med. Assn., Am. Heart Assn., Pacific Interurban Clin. Club, Ore. State and Portland City and Co. med. socs., Soc. Exptl. Biology and Medicine, N. Pacific Soc. of Internists (pres. 1950-51), Portland Acad. of Medicine (pres. 1952), Society Clinical Investigation, Western Association of Physicians (v.p., 1958-59), American Society of Hematology (vice president, 1958-59), Alpha Kappa Kappa, Alpha Omega Alpha, Sigma Xi. Republican. Club: University. Author: Textbook of Laboratory Diagnosis, 1931 (3d edit. 1940). Co-author of Atlas of Hematology, 1937. Contbr. to Jour. A.M.A., Jour. Lab. and Clin. Medicine, Archives of Internal Medicine, etc. Originator of method of culture of human marrow; developed method to keep human blood cells living over 10 yrs. in culture; Alpha-N concept cell div., cancer and aging. Home: Portland OR Died Oct. 22, 1969; buried Skyline Meml. Gardens, Portland OR

OSGOOD, FARLEY, electrical engr.; b. Boston, Mass., Apr. 5, 1874; s. George Laurie and Jeannette Callotte (Farley) O.; student Mass. Inst. Tech., class of 1897; m. Clare Stratford Hoe, Nov. 12, 1902; 1 son, Richard Hoe. Began with Am. Telephone & Telegraph Co., 1897, advancing to tech. div. mgr.; gen. mgr. and chief engr., New Milford (Conn.) Power Co., 1903-07; with Pub. Service Electric Co., Newark, N.J., 1907—, v.p. and gen. mgr., Apr. 1, 1917-Oct. 1, 1924, later cons. engr. Fellow Am. Inst. Elec. Engrs. (pres. 1924-25); Episcopalian. Home: South Orange, N.J. Died Oct. 6, 1933.

OSGOOD, SAMUEL WALTER, mining engr.; b. Chicago, Sept. 20, 1876; s. Samuel and Elizabeth (Olds) O.; B.Sc. and M.E., Mich. Coll. of Mines, 1900; m. Mary Isalene Kenner, Sept. 1, 1909. Served as consulting engr., superintendent or mgr. for many well known mining men or cos.; mgr. old Clark mine, Keweenaw Co., Mich.; discoverer, 1907, of Tenn. zinc fields and mgr. Am. Zinc, Lead & Smelting Co.'s mines, mills and exploration work, also mgr. for American Metal Co., same dist.; pres. Samuel W. Osgood & Co., and successor, Osgood, Carter and Co., consulting mine and mill engrs.; pres. Am. Graphite Co., Chemical Carbon Refining Co. Mem. Joint Com. on Mil. Engring., Chicago, 1917. Home: Chicago, Ill. Died Oct. 4, 1921.

OSGOOD, WILFRED HUDSON, naturalist; b. Rochester, N.H., Dec. 8, 1875; s. Marion Hudson and Harriet Amanda O.; A.B., Stanford U., 1899; Ph.D., U. of Chicago, 1918; unmarried. Biologist in U.S. Dept. Agr., 1897-1909; in charge U.S. biol. investigation in Alaska, 1899-1909; asst. curator of mammalogy and ornithology, Field Museum of Natural History, Chicago, 1909-21, curator of zoölogy, 1921-40, retired. Conducted biol. explorations in Alaska, Canada, many parts U.S., Venezuela, Peru, Chile, Argentine, Brazil, Ethiopia, Indo-China; studied in European museums, 1906, 10, 30; spl. U.S. investigator fur-seal question, 1914; leader of Field Museum Abyssinian Expedition, 1926-27, and of Magellanic Expedition, 1939-40. Fellow A.A.A.S., American Ornithologists Union; founder and 1st pres. Cooper Ornithol. Club of Calif.; sec. Biol. Soc. Washington, 1900-09; corr. mem. London Zoöl. Soc., British Ornithol. Union; mem. Am. Soc. Mammalogists (pres. 1924-26), Chicago Zoöl. Soc. (trustee); associate mem. Boone and Crocket Club; Geog. Society, Chicago. Member div. biology, Nat. Research Council, 1919-20. Author of Revision of Pocket Mice, 1900; revision of Mice of Genus Peromyscus, 1909; Biological Investigations Alaska and Yukon, 1909; Fur Seals of Pribilof Islands, 1915 (joint author); Monographic Study of Caenolestes, 1921; Mammals of Asiatic Expeditions, 1932; Artist and Naturalist in Ehtiopia, 1936 (joint author); Mammals of Chile, 1943; and about 180 shorter papers on classification, anatomy, and habits of mammals and birds. Contbr. zoöl. definitions to Webster's New Internat. Dictionary. Clubs: University, Quadrangle (Chicago); Explorers (New York). Home: 1155 E. 57th St., Chicago, Ill. Died June 20, 1947.

OSGOOD, WILLIAM FOGG, mathematician; b. Boston, Mass., Mar. 10, 1864; s. William and Mary Rogers (Gannett) O.; A.B., Harvard, 1886, A.M., 1887; U. of Göttingen, 1887-89; Ph.D., U. of Erlangen, 1890; LL.D., Clark U., 1909; m. Therese Ruprecht, July 17, 1890; children—William Ruprecht, Frieda Bertha (Mrs. Walter Silz; now dec.), Rudolf Ruprecht; m. 2d, Mrs. Céleste Phelps Morse, Aug. 19, 1932. Instr. Harvard, 1890-93, asst. prof. mathematics, 1893-1903, prof., 1903-33, prof. emeritus; prof. mathematics, Nat. U. Peking, China, 1934-36. Mem. Internat. Commn. on the Teaching of Mathematics; editor Annals of Mathematics, 1899-1902, Transactions Am. Math. Soc., 1909-10. Mem. Nat. Acad. of Sciences, Am. Philos. Soc., Am. Math. Soc. (pres., 1904-05), Deutsche Mathematiker-Vereinigung, Leopoldinisch-Carolinisch Deutsche Akademie der Naturforscher, Circolo Matematico de Palermo; corr. mem. Math. Soc. of Charkow, Göttinger Gesellschaft der Wissenschaften; hon. mem. Calcutta Math. Soc.; mem. Phi Beta Kappa. Author: Introduction to Infinite Series, 3d edit., 1906; Lehrbuch der Funktionentheorie, 1905-07; First Course in Differential and Integral Calculus, 1907; Madison Colloquium Lectures, 1914; Analytic Geometry (with W. C. Graustein), 1921; Advanced Calculus, 1925; Functions of Real Variables, 1936; Functions of a Complex Variable, 1936; Mechanics, 1937; also monographs in math. jours. Home: 10 Dorset Rd., Belmont, Mass. Died July 22, 1943.

O'SHAUGHNESSY, M.M., hydraulic engr.; b. Limerick, Ireland, May 28, 1864; s. Patrick and Margaret (O'Donnell) O'S.; Queen's Coll., Cork; Queen's Coll., Galway; B.Engring., with honors, Royal U., Dublin, 1884; m. Mary Spottiswood, Oct. 21, 1890. Came to America, 1885; asst. engr. S.P. Co., 1886-87; civ. engr., townsites and water, 1890, 1892-93; chief engr. Calif. Midwinter Internat. Expn., San Francisco, 1893-94; chief engr. Mountain Copper Co., etc., 1895-96; practiced at San Francisco, 1897-98; consulting and constrn. hydraulic engr., 20 sugar plantations, Hawaii, 1899-1906; in practice in Calif., 1907; chief engr. Southern Calif. Mountain Water Co.; city engr. of San Francisco, 1912-32; consulting engr. Public Utilities Commission, 1932—; builder Hetch Hetchy Water and Power Supply, Eleanor Dam, O'Shaughnessy Dam, Priest Dam and Aqueduct, Twin Peaks Tunnel, Stockton St. Tunnel, Sunset Tunnel, San Francisco Municipal Rys.; cons. engr. for Detroit, Seattle, Portland, San Diego. Republican. Roman Catholic. Author of articles on irrigation in Hawaii and other tech. subjects. Awarded James Laurie prize, An. Soc. C.E., 1913. Home: San Francisco, Calif. Died Oct. 12, 1934.

OSMOND, I(SAAC) THORNTON, physicist; b. nr. Phila., Pa.; s. William Ramsey and Ann (Samms) O.; A.B., Mt. Union Coll., 1871, A.M., 1874; M.S., Cornell, 1881; married. Asst. prof. Mt. Union Coll., 3 yrs.; adj. prof. Poly. Coll., Phila., 2 yrs., Clinton (N.Y.) Liberal Inst., 2 yrs.; prof. physics, Pa. State Coll., 1879—. Mem. bd. examiners Internat. Elec. Exhbn., Phila., 1884; meteorologist State Bd. of Agr., Pa., several yrs. physicist for construction of respiration calorimeter for U.S. Bur. of Animal Industry and Pa. Agrl. Expt. Sta. Died Sept. 7, 1939.

OSMUN, A(LBERT) VINCENT, botanist, educator; b. Danbury, Conn., Jan. 20, 1880; s. John Wilbur and Emma (Cook) O.; B. Agr., U. Conn., 1900; B.S., U. Mass., 1903, M.S., 1905; B.S., Boston U., 1903; m. Lena Latimer, June 27, 1907; children—Kenneth Latimer, John Vincent. Asst. Conn. Expt. Sta., 1900-02; mem. faculty U. Mass. and Mass. Expt. Sta., 1903-50, emeritus prof. botany, 1950—; botanist Mass. Dept. Agr., 1914-21. Mem. nat. com. on Dutch elm disease, 1934-50, chmn. Mass. com. Fellow A.A.A.S.; mem. Am. Fern Soc., Bot. Soc. Am., Phytopath. Soc., New Eng. Bot. Club, Sigma Xi, Phi Kappa Phi. Mason. Home: 78 Northampton Rd. Office: Shade Tree Labs., U. Mass., Amherst, Mass. Died Jan. 10, 1955.

OSTERBERG, MAX, consulting engr.; b. Frankfort-on-Main, Germany, June 12, 1869; s. Henry and Toni O.; ed. realschule, Germany, 1876-85; E.E., Columbia Coll. Sch. of Mines, 1894; A.M., Columbia Coll. Sch. of Pure Science, 1896; apptd. hon. univ. fellow, 1895, in mathematical physics; unmarried. Past v.p. New York Elec. Soc. Editor Electric Power, 1894-96. Editor Proceedings of the International Electrical Congress, Chicago, 1894 (Am. Inst. Elec. Engrs.). Author: Thermo-dynamics of Reversible Cycles in Gases and Saturated Vapors, 1894; Synopsis of Current Electrical Literature, 1896. Home: Staten Island, N.Y. Died 1904.

OSTERHOUT, WINTHROP JOHN VANLEUVEN, physiologist; b. Bklyn., Aug. 2, 1871; s. John Vanleuven and Annie Loranthe (Beman) O.; A.B., Brown U., 1893, A.M., 1894, Ph.D., 1926; student U. Bonn, 1895-96; Ph.D., U. Cal., 1899; ScD. (hon.), Harvard, 1925; m. Anna Marie Landstrom, June 17, 1899; children—Anna Maria (Mrs. Theodore M. Edison), Olga (Mrs. Harold B. Sears); m. 2d, Marian Irwin, Feb. 27, 1933. Instr. botany Brown U., 1893-95, Woods Hole, Mass., 1894-95; instr. botany U. Cal., 1896-1901, asst. prof., 1901-08, asso. prof., 1908-09; asst. prof. botany Harvard, 1909-13, prof., 1913-25; mem. Rockefeller Inst. Med. Research, 1925-39, mem. emeritus, 1939—. Trustee Marine Biol. Lab., Woods Hole. Fellow A.A.A.S.; mem. Nat. Acad. Sci., Am. Philos. Soc., Bot. Soc. Am., Am. Physiol. Soc., Soc. Exptl. Biology and Medicine, Am. Chem. Soc., Am. Soc. Naturalists, Am. Acad. Arts and Scis., Washington, N.Y. acads. scis., Bot. Soc. Edinburgh, Kungliga Fysiog. Sallskapet Lund, Leopold-Carolin Deutsche Akad. d. Naturforscher (Halle). Club: Century (N.Y.C.). Author: Experiments with Plants, 1905; Nature of Life, 1924; others. Co-editor Jour. Gen. Physiology, 1919—. Died Apr. 1964.

OSTRANDER, JOHN EDWIN, mathematician; b. Slingerlands, N.Y., Mar. 20, 1865; s. John and Catharine (Van Den Bergh) O.; A.B. and C.E., Union Coll., N.Y., 1886, A.M., 1889; m. Sarah C. Cowan, Sept. 26, 1888; children—Katharine, John Edwin. Engr. sewer constrn., West Troy, N.Y., 1886; asst. engr. C.G.W. Ry., 1887; engr. in state engring. dept. of N.Y., 1888-91; instr. civ. engring., Lehigh U. 1891-92; prof. civ. engring. and mechanic arts and irrigation engr., Expt. Sta., U. of Ida., 1892-97; prof. mathematics and civ. engring. Mass. State Coll., 1897-1935, prof. emeritus, 1935—; meteorologist, Mass. Agrl. Expt. Sta., 1897-1928; acting prof. astronomy, Amherst, 1900, 01, 07. Mem. Com. No. 6 on Mathematics in Tech. Secondary Schs. of U.S. for Internat. Commn. on Teaching of Mathematics; mem. Pub. Safety Com., 1917. Democrat. Episcopalian. Mason. Contbr. Johnson's Ency., 1893, Webster's New Internat. Dictionary, 1907. Home: Amherst, Mass. Died Oct. 19, 1938.

OSTROMISLENSKY, IWAN IWANOWICH, chemist; b. Moscow, Russia, Sept. 8, 1880; s. Iwan and Olga (Iowanowa) O.; attended U. Moscow, 1896-99; Ph.D., U. Zurich (Switzerland), 1902, M.D., 1906; grad. Karlsruhe Polytechnicum, Germany, 1907; m. Olga; children—Tatiana, George. Asst. prof. chemistry Polytechnicum of Moscow, Moscow U., Sch. Dentistry of Moscow, 1907-12; researcher, pvt. chem. lab., Moscow, 1911-16; dir. chemotherapeutic dept. Scientific Inst., Moscow, 1916; prof. chemistry U. Nizhni-Novgorod, 1917; went to Riga, Latvia; mem. research staff United Rubber Co., N.Y.C., 1922-25; developed many improvements in synthetic rubber mfg.; established Ostro Research Labs. (became Hopkinson Labs.), N.Y.C., 1925; became U.S. citizen, circa 1930. Died N.Y.C., Jan. 16, 1939; cremated Mt. Olivet Cemetery, Fresh Pond, L.I., N.Y.

OSWALD, FELIX LEOPOLD, author, naturalist; b. Namur, Belgium, Dec. 6, 1845; grad. Brussels U., 1865; also studied at Göttingen and Heidelberg, A.M., M.D. Went to Mexico with the corps of Belgian vols., 1866; corr. of various French and English periodicals, 1878-97. Author: Physical Education, 1882; Household Remedies, 1885; Summerland Sketches, 1880; The Poison Problem, 1886; Zoölogical Sketches, 1883; Days and Nights in the Tropics, 1888; The Bible of Nature: Body and Mind, 1901; also many essays and papers in mags. and reviews. Address: Grand Rapids, Mich. Died 1906.

OTIS, ARTHUR SINTON, psychologist, author; b. Denver, July 28, 1886; s. George Frank and Margaretta Jane (Sinton) O.; A.B., Stanford, 1910, A.M., 1915, Ph.D., 1920; m. Jennie Theresa Minnick, June 15, 1919; m. 2d, Edna (Farmer) Jackson; one stepson, Marvin F. Jackson. Commd. 1st lt. San. Corps, U.S. Army, Sept. 1917; duty as dir. research Div. of Psychology, Office of Surgeon Gen., Washington; trans. to Camp Lee, Va., July 1918, as psychol. examiner draftees; hon. disch., Jan. 1919. Instr. statis. method Stanford, 1919; devel. specialist, attached to adv. bd. Gen. Staff, U.S. War Dept., 1920; editor tests and math. World Book Co., 1921, later cons., div. research and test service. Fellow A.A.A.S.; mem. Am. Psychol. Assn., N.Y. Acad. Sci., Am. Ednl. Research Assn., Nat. Acad. Econs. and Polit. Sci., Acad. Polit. Sci., Acad. World Econs., Am. Econ. Assn., Sigma Xi, Phi Delta Kappa (honor key), Pi Gamma Mu; tech. mem. Inst. Aero Scis.; mem. Soaring Soc. Am. Author: Otis Group Intelligence Scale, 1918; Otis Self-Administering Tests of Mental Ability, 1922; Otis Classification Test, 1923; Statistical Method in Educational Measurement, 1925; (with J. R. Clark) Modern Plane Geometry, 1926; Modern Solid Geometry, 1928, (with A. J. McAllister) Child Accounting Practice, 1927; (with J. R. Clark and Caroline Hatton) First Steps in Teaching Number, 1929; Modern School Arithmetics, 1929; Primary Arithmetic Through Experience, 1939; First Number Book, 1939; Second Number Book, 1940; (with Francis Pope) Elements of Aeronautics, 1941; The Airplane Power Plant, 1944; Reducing Traffic Congestion, 1954; Financing Highway Improvement, 1954; also script for Bray-Otis Aviation Series ednl. motion pictures, 1943; The Conceptional Interpretation of the Einstein Theory of Relativity, Is It Valid, 1957; Added Revenue Without Burden, A New Plan of Taxation, 1958. Author and composer: (mus. comedy) Love Among the Stars, 1954. Psychol. cons. USN Bur. Aeros., 1944. Ret. from Navy Feb. 1945; as psychol. and aerodynamical cons. for CAA, Washington, 1945-48. Devised group intelligence test which served as basis for testing 1,700,000 men drafted into U.S. Army. Pvt. pilot. Home: 401 22d Av. S.E., St. Petersburg, Fla. 33705. Died Jan. 1, 1964.

OTIS, ELISHA GRAVES, mfr., inventor; b. Halifax, Vt., Aug. 3, 1811; s. Stephen and Phoebe (Glynn) O.; m. Susan Houghton, June 2, 1834; m. 2d, Mrs. Elizabeth Boyd; at least 2 children including Charles R., Norton P. Mfr. wagons and carriages in Vt., 1838-45; constructed and invented a turbine water-wheel, Albany, N.Y.; with bedstead factory, Bergen, N.J., master mechanic, 1851; in charge of erection and installation of machinery in new factory, Yonkers, N.Y.; devised, incorporated unique features into the elevator (1st one with safety features); established own shop, Yonkers (thought to be the beginning of elevator bus.); demonstrated his safety elevator at Am. Jnst. Fair, N.Y., 1854; patented railroad car trucks and brakes, 1852; patented steam plow, 1857, bake oven, 1858; established The Otis Elevator Co., after invention, patenting of steam elevator, 1861. Died Yonkers, Apr. 8, 1861.

OTT, EMIL, chemist; b. Zurich, Switzerland, May 19, 1902; s. Emil and Anna (Goldinger) O.; diploma physics and chemistry Swiss Inst. Tech., 1925, D.Sc., Ph.D., 1927; m. Dorothy Aiken Wright, Oct. 2, 1933; children—John Wright, Joan Nancy (Mrs. John Guyton), Dorothy Ann (Mrs. George E. Darmstatter, Jr.), David Emil. Came to United States, 1927, naturalized, 1937. American Inst. Petroleum fellow Johns Hopkins U., 1928-29, asso. chemistry, 1929-33; research chemist Hercules Powder Co., 1933-37, head research div. Hercules Expt. Sta., 1937-39, dir. research Hercules Powder Co., 1939-55; v.p., dir. charge central chem. research Food Machinery & Chem. Corp., Princeton, N.J., 1955-58, vice president of Research & Development, Chemical Division, New York City, 1958-60; research specialist Rutgers University, 1960-62; research prof. Stevens Institute Technology, 1962—. Fellow Am. Phys. Soc., Am. Inst. Chemists, A.A.A.S., N.Y. Acad. Sci.; mem. Am. Chem. Soc., Indsl. Research Inst., Assn. Research Dirs., Dirs. Indsl. Research, Soc. Chem. Industry, NRC, Internat. Union Chemistry, Sigma Xi, Phi Lambda Upsilon; hon. mem. Societe de Chimie Industrielle. Editor: Cellulose and Cellulose Derivatives, 1943. Contbr. articles profl. publs. Home: 99 Braeburn Dr., Princeton, N.J. Died Sept. 29, 1963.

OTT, HARVEY NEWTON, designer and mfr. of microscopes and scientific apparatus; b. Walker, Mo., Sept. 18, 1868; s. James Harvey and Mary Sofia (White) O.; grad. high sch., Albion, Mich., 1844; Ph.B., Albion Coll., 1889, hon. D.Sc., 1940; Ph.M., U. of Mich.., 1891; m. Zua Warren Thomas, July 16, 1890; children—Helen Marie (dec.), Harry Glenn; m. 2d, Elizabeth Louise Smith, Oct. 12, 1915. Teacher of biology, Puget Sound Coll., Tacoma, Wash., 1891-93; professor zoology and comparative anatomy, S.D. State Coll., 1893-95; salesman Bausch & Lomb Optical Co., 1896-1903; salesman Spencer Lens Co., mfrs. microscopes and scientific optical instruments, Buffalo, N.Y., 1903-07, gen. mgr., 1907-37, pres. 1919-39, chmn. bd. of dirs., 1939-42, retired Jan. 1, 1942. Trustee Albion Coll. since 1941. Mem. Bd., Buffalo Goodwill Industries. Mem. A.A.A.S., Am. Assn. Scientific Apparatus Makers (ex-pres.), Delta Tau Delta. Republican. Methodist. Clubs: Buffalo Athletic, Buffalo Automobile. Home: 103 Woodbridge Av., Buffalo 14 NY

OTTO, BODO, surgeon; b. Hanover, Germany, 1711; s. Christopher and Maria (Nienecken) O.; m. Elizabeth Sanchen, 1736; m. 2d, Catharina Dahncken, 1742; m. 3d, Maria Paris, 1766; at least 3 children, including John Conrad. Mem. Coll. of Surgeons, Luneburg; chief surgeon for dist. of Schartzfels, Germany, 1749; came to Am., 1755; del. Pa. Provincial Congress, 1776; apptd. sr. surgeon middle div. Continental Hosps., 1776; ordered by Continental Congress to establish mil. hosp. for treatment of smallpox, Trenton, N.J., 1777; in charge hosps., Yellow Springs, Pa., spring 1778; selected for hosp. dept., 1780; mem. Am. Philos. Soc. Died Reading, Pa., June 12, 1787; buried Trinity Luth. Churchyard, Reading.

OTTO, JOHN CONRAD, physician; b. nr. Woodbury, N.J., Mar. 15, 1774; s. Dr. Bodo and Catherine (Schweighauser) O.; grad. Coll. of N.J. (now Princeton), 1792, U. Pa., 1796; m. Eliza Tod, 1802; 9 children including William Tod. Physician, Phila. Dispensary, 1798-1803; physician Orphan Asylum, Magdalen Asylum, many years; most important contbn. to med. sci. was description of hemophilia in paper An Account of an Hemorrhagic Disposition Existing in Certain Families, (pub. in Med. Repository, vol. VI, 1803, reprinted in London Med. and Phys. Jour., 1808); physician Pa. Hosp., 1813-34; mem. com. of 12 leading physicians appt. to deal with cholera epidemic in Phila., 1832; mem. Phila. Coll. of Physicians, 1819, censor, many years, v.p., 1840-44. Died Phila., June 26, 1844; buried Woodlands Cemetery, West Phila.

OTTOFY, LOUIS, dental lexicographer, educator; b. Budapest, Oct. 22, 1860; s. Leopold and Louise (Lauffer) O.; came to U.S., 1874; D.D.S., Western Coll. Dental Surgeons, St. Louis, Mo., 1879; hon. M.D., St. Louis Coll. Phys. and Surgs., 1915; LL.D., McKendree Coll., Lebanon, Ill., 1928; m. Nellie Freeman, Dec. 27, 1887; children—Gloria Columbia (dec.), Frederic Freeman. Practiced at Chicago, Yokohama and Manila; prof. physiology, 1890-93, prof. clin. dental therapeutics, 1896-98, Chicago Coll. Dental Surgery; dean and prof. dental pathology, Am. Coll. Dental Surgery, Chicago, 1893-96; resided Japan, 1898-99 and 1920-21, Manila, 1899-1920; dir. Sch. of Dentistry, U. of Philippines, 1915-19; maj. and supervising dental surgeon, Dental Corps, U.S. Army, 1918; ednl. dir. McCarrie Schs. of Mechanical Dentistry, 1926-28, ednl. counselor same since 1928; dean and prof. dental technology, Institute of Dental Science, Oakland, Calif., 1929-30. Made first survey and tabulation of condition of human teeth in the history of dentistry of a group of children in pub. sch., Lebanon, Ill., 1882; made similar surveys in Japan and Philippines, of Chinese, Igorots, Negritos, lepers, etc. Mem. Am. and Ill. (life) dental socs., Chicago Dental Soc. (pres. 1896), Am. Soc. Stomatologists (pres. 1927), Alameda County (Calif.) Dist. Dental Soc., Assn. Mil. Dental Surgeons of U.S.; Mil. Order World War, Delta Sigma Delta, Pi Gamma Mu; founder, fellow and registrar Internat. Coll. of Dentists, 1928; sec. Bd. of Dental Examiners of Philippine Islands, 1914-15. Mason (K.T., Shriner). Club: University (Manila). Author: Outlines of Dental Pathology, 1895; Plantation of Teeth (in Am. Textbook of Operative Dentistry), 1897-1911; All About Your Teeth, Gums and Dentist, 1938; compiler and editor Standard Dental Dictionary, 1923; editor Polk's Dental Register of U.S. and Can., 1925-27 and 1928-30, Internat. Dental Review since 1931. Contbr. over 200 articles on dentistry to jours. Hon. mention and cash prize for essay on "Rootfilling and Focal Infection," Internat. Bur. for Protection of Animals, Geneva, 1933. Address: 175 Vernon Terrace, Oakland CA*

OUGHTERSON, ASHLEY W., surgeon; b. Geneva, N.Y., Sept. 28, 1895; s. Nathan and Mary Ann (Hatch) O.; student Syracuse U., 1918-20; M.D., Harvard Med. Sch., 1924; m. Dr. Marion Howard, March 21, 1942. Intern Peter Bent Brigham Hosp., Boston, Mass., 1924-25, New York Hosp., 1925-27, Bellevue Hosp., 1927-28, Peter Bent Brigham Hosp., 1928-29, William Harvey Cushing fellow in surgery, Yale Sch. of Medicine, 1929-30; postgrad. study, Europe, 1930. Surgeon, New Haven, Conn., 1930; asst. prof. surgery, Yale, 1930-34, asso. prof., 1934-42, now clinical prof. surgery. Served as cons. surgeon, Pacific Ocean areas; col. Med. Corps, World War II, 1942-46. Awarded Legion of Merit with oak leaf cluster. Chmn. Joint Commn. for Investigating Med. Effects of Atomic Bomb in Japan. Exec. v.p., med. and scientific dir. Am. Cancer Soc., Inc.; mem. Am. Med. Assn. A.C.S. (gov.), Am. Surg. Assn., Am. Cancer Soc., Am. Assn. Cancer Research, Am. Heart Assn., N.E. Surg. Soc. (pres.), New England Cancer Soc., Am. Radium Soc., Soc. Exptl. Biology and Medicine, Sigma Xi. Clubs: Lawn, Grad. (New Haven); Yale (New York). Contbr. numerous papers on Surgery and Cancer. Address: Rockefeller Found., 49 W. 49th St., N.Y.C. Died Nov. 17, 1956; buried Bellona Cemetery, Yates County, N.Y.

OUTERBRIDGE, ALEXANDER EWING, JR., metallurgist; b. Phila., July 31, 1850; s. Alexander Ewing and Laura C. (Harvey) O.; ed. Episcopal Acad., Phila., and pvt. tutor in analyt. chemistry; attended lectures on physics and chemistry as asst. to Prof. Henry Morton, U. of Pa.; m. Mary Ely Whitney, 1880 (died 1881); 1 son, George Whitney; m. 2d, Margaret Hall Dunn, Jan. 29, 1905. Apptd. asst. in assay lab. U.S. Mint., Phila., 1868; sent to New Orleans to establish assay dept. of branch mint, 1879-80; metallurgist for A. Whitney & Sons Car Wheel Works, Phila., 1880-88; metallurgist William Sellers & Co., Inc., Phila., 1888—. Lecturer on indsl. economics, Wharton Sch. of Finance, U. of Pa.; apptd. prof. metallurgy, Franklin Inst., 1901. Republican. Episcopalian. Mem. Franklin Inst. of Phila. Awarded Elliott Cresson gold medal and John Scott legacy medal and premium from Franklin Inst. and City of Phila. for original discoveries in "molecular physics of iron." Extensive contbr. to newspapers and tech. mags. Home: Philadelphia, Pa. Died Jan. 15, 1928.

OVERBECK, REYNOLDS COVEL, chemist; b. Hallton, Pa., July 17, 1918; s. Malcolm Thomas and Bessie (Covel) O.; B.A., Wooster Coll., 1940. Chemist, Ohio Agrl. Expt. Sta., Wooster, O., 1938-44; critic prof. edn. Wooster (O.) Coll., 1940-47; chemist Battelle Meml. Inst., Columbus, 1948-51, cons., 1951-71. Fellow Am. Inst. Chemists; mem. Am. Chem. Soc. A.A.A.S., N.Y. Acad. Scis., Ohio Acad. Sci., Nat. Inst. Food Tech. Inventor mercury cathode for chem. analysis, high speed copper analysis apparatus; research trace element analyses, odor and perfume chemistry, nutrition, flavor. Home: Columbus OH Died Nov. 1971.

OVERHOLSER, EARLE LONG, horticulturist; b. Kansas City, Mo., Dec. 19, 1888; s. Milton Plean and Fannie Elizabeth (Long) O.; grad. N.M. Mil. Inst., Roswell, N.M., 1909; B.S., U. of Mo., 1913, M.A., 1914; Ph.D., Cornell U., 1926; m. Grace Elizabeth McClary, Oct. 18, 1917; children—Earle Long, Grace Anne. Student asst. in botany U. of Mo., 1911-13, research fellow in botany, 1913-14; instr. pomology Cornell U., 1914-17, asst. prof., 1917-18, exchange prof. at U. of Calif., 1918-19; asst. prof. pomology U. of Calif., 1919-25, sabbatical leave prof. at Cornell U., 1925-26, asst. prof. pomology U. of Calif., 1926-29, asso. prof., 1929-30; prof. horticulture, head dept., and chmn. div. of horticulture State Coll. Wash., and Wash. Agrl. Expt. Sta., 1930-45; head dept. horticulture Va. Poly. Inst., Blacksburg, Va., since 1945. Del. of U. of Calif. and Pacific States Cold Storage Assn. to 4th Internat. Refrigeration Congress, London, Eng., 1924; conducted investigation marine refrigeration fruits enroute to Far East countries, 1929. Pres. Northwest Fertilizer Conf. Horticulturists, 1931-45. Mem. U. of Wash. Arboretum Council, 1940-45; mem. bd. dirs. Va. State Hort. Soc. since 1946; collaborator from Va. Agrl. Expt. Sta., Eastern Region Research Lab., 1947. Fellow A.A.A.S.; mem. Am. Soc. Hort. Science, Am. Soc. Plant Physiology, Am. Bot. Soc., Am. Pomol. Soc., Nat. Assn. Refrigerated Warehouses (hon.), Sigma Xi, Gamma Sigma Delta, Alpha Gamma Rho, Phi Sigma, Epsilon Sigma Phi. Editor V.P.I. sect. in Virginia Fruit. Contbr. to State Expt. Sta. agrl. publs. and other sci. pubs. Home: 801 Draper Rd., Blacksburg, Va. Died Apr. 18, 1949; buried in Orient Cemetery, Harrisonville, Mo.

OVERMAN, FREDERICK, metallurgist; b. Elberfeld, Germany, circa 1803; s. Johann and Maria Catherina (Ruhl) Overmann; studied metallurgy Royal Poly. Inst., Berlin, Germany. Apprenticed to cabinet maker in Germany; became authority in iron metallurgy before age of 40; came to U.S., 1842, engaged in writing technol. works; died after inhaling arsenic gas in laboratory. Author: The Manufacture of Iron 1850; The Manufacture of Steel, 1851; Practical Mineralogy, Assaying and Mining, 1851; A Treatise on Metallurgy, 1851. Died Phila., Jan. 7, 1852.

OVERTON, JAMES BERTRAM, plant physiologist; b. Richmond, Mich., Dec. 23, 1868; s. John M. and Charlotte Stuart (Mills) O.; Ph.B., U. of Mich., 1894; Ph.D., U. of Chicago, 1901; honorary Sc.D., Illinois Coll., 1930; m. Mary E. Cochran, December 26, 1901; children—James Bertram, Mary Katherine, Jane Cochran (Mrs. T. W. Vieaux). Assistant principal, high school, Black River Falls, Wisconsin, 1894-95; sr. master in mathematics, St. John's Mil. Acad., Delafield, Wis., 1895-98; asst. in botany, U. of Chicago, 1901; research asst. Carnegie Instn., Washington (at Bonn, Germany), 1903-04; prof. biology, Ill. Coll., Jacksonville, 1901-04; instr. botany, 1904-07, asst. prof., 1907-12, asso. prof. plant physiology, 1912-15, prof., 1915—, U. of Wis. Research asso., part time, Carnegie Instn., 1925-29. Republican. Episcopalian. Author: A Textbook of General Botany (with G. M. Smith and others), 1924. Contbr. to scientific jours. of Europe and America. Address: Madison, Wis. Died Mar. 18, 1937.

OVINGTON, EARLE, aeronautical engr.; b. Chicago, Ill., Dec. 20, 1879; s. Edward J. and Mary Wickes (Barnes) O.; E.E., Mass. Inst. Tech., 1904; grad. Bleriot Sch. of Aeronautics, Pau, France, 1911; m. Adelaide Alexander, Apr. 19, 1911; children—Audrey, Kester. Began as asst. in X-ray lab. of Thomas A. Edison, 1898, later with expt. lab. Edison Electric Illuminating Co.; with New York Telephone Co., 1899-1900; founder, 1905, pres., 1905-08, Ovington Mfg. Co.; founder, 1908, pres., 1908-10, Ovington Motor Co.; pres. Vitalait Lab., Inc., Vitalait Lab. of N.E., and Vitalait Lab. of Pacific Coast, preparing bacteriol. cultures for med. use, 1912-19; founder, 1918, pres. 1918-20, Sandy Point (Me.) Shipbuilding Co.; pres. Curtiss Flying Sta., Atlantic City, N.J., 1918-20; cons. elec. and aeronautical engr., Santa Barbara, Calif., 1920—; Pacific Coast factory rep. Curtiss Aerocars. Lieutenant comdr. U.S.N. Res. Winner Boston Globe Tri-State Air Race and $10,000 prize, also John R. McLean trophy ($2,500), 1911. First U.S. Air Mail pilot, 1911. Founder, mem. and pres., Early Birds (aviation assn.). Republican. Presbyn. Inventor Ovington High Frequency Apparatus and other elec. appliances; owner Ovington Air Terminal, Santa Barbara. Address: Santa Barbara, Calif. Died July 21, 1936.

OWEN, DAVID DALE, geologist; b. New Lanark, Scotland, June 24, 1807; s. Robert and Ann (Dale) O.; attended ednl. inst. of Phillip Emanuel von Fellenberg, Berne, Switzerland, 1824-27; M.D., Ohio Med. Coll., Cincinnati, 1836; m. Caroline Neef, Mar. 23, 1837; 4 children. Came to Am., 1827; state geologist Ind., 1837-38; made survey of Dubuque (Ia.) and Mineral Point (Wis.) dists. under U.S. appointment, 1838 (report published as House Document 239, 1840); U.S. geologist to survey Chippewa Land Dist., 1847-52; published Report of a Geological Exploration of a Part of Iowa, Wisconsin and Minnesota and, Incidentally, a Portion of Nebraska Territory, 1852; state geologist Ky., 1854-59, Ark., 1857-60; apptd. state geologist Ind., 1860, died before taking office; 1st to point out rich mineral nature of Ia., Wis. lands, also that lead and zinc ores were limited to the magnesian limestone; 1st to give name sucarboniferous to beds underlying Ind. coal; published Geological Survey of Kentucky, 4 vols., 1856-61; The Report of a Geological Reconnaissance of Indiana Made During the Years 1859 and 1860 Under the Direction of the Late D.D. Owen, published by Richard Owen, 1862. Died New Harmony, Ind., Nov. 13, 1860.

OWENS, MICHAEL JOSEPH, inventor, mfr.; b. in Mason County Va. (now W.Va.), Jan. 1, 1859; s. John and Mary (Chapman) O.; ed. pub. schs.; m. Mary E. McKelvey, 1889. Learned glass blower's trade at Wheeling, Va.; founder Union Flint Glass Co., Martins Ferry, O., 1882; entered employ of Libbey Glass Co., Toledo, O., 1888, made mgr. of works same yr.; in charge of model glass factory of the company, at Chicago Expn., 1893; an organizer, 1895, of Toledo Glass Co., for mfr. of glass tumblers by means of a machine, which he invented, which gathers from furnace the glass required for each bottle, revolutionizing the bottle-making industry; inventor machine for mfr. cut glass; perfected sheetglass drawing appartus, by means of which a sheet of glass 6 feet wide is continuously drawn from molten glass at a speed of 108 feet per hour; v.p. and gen. mgr. Owens Bottle Co., Libbey-Owens Sheet Glass Co. Awarded Elliott Cresson medal, by Franklin Inst., for bottle-making machine, 1916. Home: Toledo, O. Died Dec. 27, 1923.

OWENS, ROBERT BOWIE, electrical engr.; b. Anne Arundel County, Md., Oct. 29, 1870; s. James and Maria Louise (Bowie) O.; grad. Charlotte Hall Mil. Sch., Md., 1886; Johns Hopkins, 1887-89; E.E., Columbia, 1891, A.M., 1899; B.Sc., ad eundem, McGill U., Montreal, 1900, McSc., 1900, D.Sc., 1903; research student Cambridge U., Eng., 1899; unmarried. Supt. Greenwich Gas & Elec. Co., 1889-91; prof. elec. and steam engring., U. of Neb., 1891-98; Tyndall fellow in physics, Columbia, 1898-1901; Macdonald prof. elec. engring., McGill U., 1898-1909; elec. engr. Southern Power Co., 1909-10; sec. Franklin Inst., Phila., 1910-24, also editor Jour. Franklin Inst., and dir. Bartol Research Foundation, 1921-24; pres. Fox Hall Farm, Harwood, Md., 1927—; dir. Md. Acad. Scis., 1930-31, and editor its jour. Commd. capt. Signal Corps, U.S.A., May 1917, and served in office of chief signal officer, Washington, D.C.; liaison officer French and British scientific commns., and with Personnel Div. of Aviation Sect. Signal Corps; capt. and maj. Signal Corps, A.E.F.; chief of Signal Corps Intelligence Div. in charge of organization; chief signal officer A.E.F., H.Q., London; in charge of and operated all telephone and telegraph communications between A.E.F., France and Eng., and all Am. owned cables (Western Union and Commercial) between Eng. and U.S., June-Dec. 1918. Mem. Internat. Elec. Congress and Internat. Jury of Awards, World's Fair, Chicago, 1893; dir. Electricity and Machinery Bldg., Trans-Miss. Expn., 1898 (gold medal); mem. Internat. Elec. Congress and Internat. Jury Awards, La. Purchase Expn., 1904 (commemorative medal). Mem. Am. Inst. E.E. (v.p.), Canadian Soc. of Civil Engineers (pres. elec. sect.). Hon. Companion D.S.O. (British); fellow Royal Soc. Can. Discoverer of the Alpha ray; inventor of radio direction finding, electromagnetic system for guiding ships and aeroplanes, differentiating machine, electric accelerometer. Address: Washington, D.C. Died Nov. 1, 1940.

PABST, CHARLES FREDERICK, physician, dermatologist; b. N.Y.C., Dec. 3, 1887; s. Charles and Margaret (Connorton) P.; M.D., L.I. Coll. Hosp., 1909; intern Brooklyn Hosp., 1910-12; unmarried. Student skin diseases in Puerto Rico and Venezuela; conducted clinic for skin diseases at Brooklyn and Greenpoint hosps., 1914-28; attending dermatologist and chief of clinic for skin diseases at Greenpoint Hosp., 1915-57, consultant dermatologist, 1957-71. Commissioned lieutenant (jr. grade), U.S. Navy R.F., Feb. 20, 1918; lt., grade of passed asst. surgeon, Sept. 18, 1918, in charge treatment of skin diseases at U.S. Naval Hosp., Norfolk, Va., until May 1, 1919. Recipient award from Med. Soc. of State N.Y. Fellow A.M.A., Am. Acad. of Dermatology and Syphilology; mem. N.Y. State Med. Soc., Kings County Med. Soc., Alumnus Club L.I. Hosp., Brooklyn Hosp. Presbyn. Mason (32 deg., K.T.). Contbr. numerous articles on skin diseases and regarded as an authority on the subject. An expert swimmer, and saved several persons from drowning, at different times, on L.I. beaches. Gave U.S. Govt., 1934, nonpatented inexpensive formula for fireprofing ships, clothing and other fabrics; called attention to widespread prevalence of ringworm infection of feet, and started health campaign against bare feet; originated term "athlete's foot"; secured almost universal adoption of distinctive shape and color for bichloride of mercury tablets; pointed out dangers of overexposure to summer sun and gave the term "heliophobe" to individual whose skin will not tan. Address: Brooklyn NY Died Apr. 15, 1971; buried Long Island Cemetery, Farmingdale NY

PACENT, LOUIS GERARD, electric and radio engr.; b. N.Y. City, June 23, 1893; s. Louis and Mary (Tomasino) P.; ed. Mt. Carmel Acad., spl. schs. abroad; grad. Pratt Inst.; m. Antoinette Marie Andriola, Sept. 10, 1917; children—Louis Gerard, Homer Cosmos. Employee Manhattan Electric Co., 1909-19; organizer, dir., Pacent Electric Co., 1919, Pacent Reproducer Corp., 1929, Pacent Engring. Corp. since 1933; engaged in development work on new throat microphone; cons. engr. Sonotone Corp., Elmsford, N.Y. Served as civilian engr., World War I. Recipient Engring. Key of Inst. Radio Engrs., 1946. Fellow Am. Inst. E.E., Inst. Radio Engrs., Soc. Motion Picture Engrs., Radio Club of Am., mem. Motion Picture Acad. (found. mem.), V.W.O.A. (life mem.), A.S.A. Republican. Roman Catholic. Clubs: Norway Country, Pratt, North Hills, Engrs. (N.Y. City); Cosmos (Washington). Author: The Complete Radio Book; numerous tech. papers. Home: Little Neck, L.I.; (summer) Norway, Me. Office: 79 Madison Av., N.Y.C. Died Apr. 7, 1952. *

PACK, FREDERICK JAMES, geologist; b. Bountiful, Utah, Feb. 2, 1875; s. John and Mary Jane (Walker) P.; B.S. in M.E., U. of Utah, 1904; M.A., Columbia, 1905, Ph.D., 1906; m. Sadie Grant, Nov. 25, 1896; children—Eugene Grant, Alvin Grabau, Marion, Eleanor. Deseret prof. geology, U. of Utah, 1907—; pres. and mgr. Utah-Wyo. Consolidated Oil Co. Acquired title to large tracts of land in Wyo., 1908, and developed region into one of most important oil and natural gas dists. of Wyoming. Mormon. Author: New Discoveries Relating to the Wasatch Fault, 1926; Structure of Thermal Springs on the Wasatch Fault, 1927; Dinosaurs in Western America, Ten Lessons in Geology, 1931; Breadth of Mormonism, 1932; Origin and Meaning of Six Hundred Place Names in Utah, 1935; Origin and Nature of the Barmeville Salt Flats, 1937; Lake Barmeville, 1938. Home: Salt Lake City, Utah. Died Dec. 2, 1938.

PACK, ROBERT WALLACE, petroleum exec.; b. Berkeley, Cal., June 15, 1885; s. John Wallace and Grace (Van Name) P.; B.S., U. Cal., 1908; s. Evelyn Lockhart, Dec. 14, 1921; children—Sarah Evelyn (Mrs. H. J. Thomas III), Mary Margaret (Mrs. F. E. Buchanan), Robert Wallace. Asst. minerology and petrography U. Cal., 1908-09; asst., asso. geologist U.S. Geol. Survey, 1910-13, paleontologist, 1914-15, geologist, 1916-17; geologist Sun Oil Co., 1917-19, chief geologist, 1920, gen. mgr. Gulf Coast div., 1920-48, v.p., gen. mgr. Sun Pipe Line, 1920-48, dir. prodn. Sun Oil Co., 1948-56, also co. dir. Mem. Am. Assn. Petroleum Geologists, Geol. Soc. Am. Paleontol. Soc., Am. Inst. Mining and Metall. Engrs., Sigma Xi. Clubs: Racquet, Philadelphia Country. Home: 804 River Rd., Beaver, Pa. 15009; also Montreat, N.C. Died July 4, 1965; buried Beaver (Pa.) Cemetery.

PACKARD, ALPHEUS SPRING, prof. zoölogy and geology, Brown Univ., 1878—; b. Brunswick, Me., Feb. 19, 1839; s. Prof. Alpheus Spring and Frances Elizabeth (Appleton) P.; (mother a sister of Mrs. President Pierce); grad. Bowdoin, 1861; LL.D., 1901; Me. Med. School, 1864; studied under Agassiz, Lawrence Scientific School, 3 yrs.; S.B., Harvard Univ. (out of course), 1864; m. Elizabeth Derby, d. Samuel Baker Walcott, Oct. 1867. Asst. surgeon Me. Vet. Vols., 1864-65; librarian and custodian Boston Soc. Natural History, 1865-66; curator Essex Inst., 1866; curator, afterward dir., Peabody Acad. Science, 1867-78; State entomologist Mass., 1871-73; mem. U.S. Entom. Commn., 1877-82; an honorary pres. Zoöl. Congress, Paris, 1889; a founder and 20 yrs. editor-in-chief, Am. Naturalist. Author: Observations on the Glacial Phenomena of Labrador and Maine, 1891; A Text Book of Entomology, 1898; Lamarck, the Founder of Evolution, His Life and Work, 1901, also (in French), 1903; A Naturalist on the Labrador Coast, 1891. Home: Providence, R.I. Died 1905.

PACKARD, GEORGE ARTHUR, mining engr.; b. Wakefield, Mass., Apr. 17, 1869; s. George and Marietta Fulton (Swain) P.; desc. Samuel Packard, Hingham, 1638, John Alden and other Mayflower pilgrims, 1620; S.B., Mass. Inst. Tech., 1890; m. Edythe R. Morrill, Apr. 12, 1899 (died Dec. 16, 1929); m. 2d, Myrtle S. Foster, Aug. 27, 1931. Chemist and supt. copper smelting and leaching in Vt. and Ariz., 1890-92; supt. Desloges Consol. Lead Co., Mo., 1893-94; installing cyanide process and supt. gold and silver mines in Mont., Ariz., Utah and Colo., 1895-1900; consulting mining engr. and metallurgist since 1900 (work covering N. and S. America); mgr. Raven Copper Co., Butte, Mont., 1910-13. Acting prof. metallurgy, U. of Mo. Sch. of Mines, 1907. Mem. Alumni Council Mass. Inst. Tech. Mem. Mining and Metall. Soc. America, Am. Inst. Mining Engrs. (chmn. mining methods com. on precious and rare metals, 1923-29; chmn. advisory board 1930; chmn. Boston sect. 1932), Canadian Inst. of Mining and Metallurgy, Geol. Soc. of Boston; Engring. Socs. of New Eng.; former asso. mem. South African Chem., Metall. and Mining Soc. Clubs: Technology Faculty; Mining Club (New York, N.Y.). Contbr. to tech. press and jours. of tech. socs. Contbr. to tech. press and jours. of tech. socs. Home: Wakefield, Mass.; (summer) Westport Point, Massachusetts. Office: 53 State St., Boston 9 MA

PACKARD, RALPH GOODING, civil engr.; b. Niagara Falls, N.Y., 1840; grad. Rensselaer Polytechnic Inst., 1864; civ. engr. in U.S. navy yards, 1864-69; later engr. in removal of Hell Gate reefs, construction of Raritan River and Poughkeepsie bridges, and other important undertakings. Pres. R. G. Packard Co. Residence: 84 Columbia Heights, Brooklyn. Office: 130 Pearl St., New York.

PACKARD, WALTER E., cons. agrl. engr.; b. Oak Park, Ill., Feb. 22, 1884; s. Samuel W. and Clara A. (Fish) P.; B.S.A., Ia. State Coll., 1907; M.S., U. Cal., 1909; grad. Harvard, 1920; m. Emma Leonard, Dec. 20, 1909; children—Clara (Mrs. Joel Coffield), Emmy Lou (Mrs. Byron Randall). Spl. agt. Packard & Niece, attys., London, 1905; field agt. U.S. Irrigations Investigations, 1909; supt. Imperial Valley Agrl. Expt. Sta., U. Cal., 1910-17, asst. state leader farm advisers, 1917-18; lectr. Army Ednl. Corps, AEF, France, 1919; tutor econs. Harvard, and instr. econs. Mass. Inst. Tech., 1919-20; supt. Cal. State Land Settlement, 1920-24; chief, agrl. div. Nat. Irrigation Commn., Mexico, 1925-29; spl. cons. U.S. Army Engr., Pacific Gas & Electric Co. Water and Power Div., City of Los Angeles, Cowell Portland Cement Co., U.S. Bur. Reclamation, State Engr. Office, Cal., 1930-33; with A.A.A., 1933-34; regional and nat. dir. Rural Resettlement Adminstrn., 1935-38; spl. cons. Farm Security Adminstrn. Bur. Agrl. Econs., Youth Adminstrn., Haynes Found., Cal. Planning and Housing Assn., 1939-44; cons. to gov. P.R., 1945-47, to minister of agr., Venezuela, 1947; irrigation specialist AMAG, Athens, 1948; chief, land reclamation unit E.C.A., Greece, 1948-54; rep. E.C.A.G. on internat. com. directing Evros River project between Greece and Turkey; agrl. cons. Kaiser Aluminum & Chem. Corp., Jamaica, 1955; research work and lecturing. Recipient award for preeminent service advancing human welfare Chgo. Alumni, Ia. State Coll. Hon. citizen 4 Greek villages, 1954; bust erected Anthili, Greece, 1954. Mem. Am. Soc. Agrl. Engrs., Am. Farm Econ. Assn., Cal. Power Users Assn., Beta Theta Pi. Alpha Zeta. Club: Commonwealth (San Francisco). Author: While There is Yet Time, 1961. Address: 773 Cragmont Av., Berkeley 8, Cal. Died Oct. 31, 1966.

PACKARD, WINTHROP, naturalist; b. Boston, Mass., Mar. 7, 1862; s. Hiram Shepard and Maria (Blake) P.; Mass. Inst. Tech., class of 1885; m. Alice Harrington Petrie, 1905; children—John Winthrop, Theodore, David. Chemist with Henry A. Gould & Co., Boston, 1885; with A. W. Folsom & Co., Boston, 1889; editor Canton (Mass.) Journal, 1894; associated with National Magazine, Boston, 1896; editorial staff, Youth's Companion, 1899; mem. Corwin exploring expdn. to Alaska, Siberia and the Arctic, 1900, as corr. for Boston Transcript, New York Evening Post and St. Paul Dispatch. Then special article writer on Boston Transcript, and in general journalism; editor The New England Magazine, 1905-08. Served 3 yrs. in Mass. Naval Brigade; landsman, ordinary seaman and able seaman U.S. Navy, in Spanish-Am. War, 1898; 1st lit. Co. D, 13th Regt., Mass. State Guard, 1917. Field sec., Nat. Assn. Audubon Socs., 1914-18; field sec., then sec.-treas. and exec. officer Mass. Audubon Soc., 1913-36, an incorporator, 1915, established and financed society's nat. known Moose Hill Bird Sanctuary at Sharon, Mass., and established its ednl. and protective work there. Founder and editor Bull. of Mass. Audubon Soc., 1914-36. Established "Everything for Wild Birds," a nat. service in bird study and protection, 1936. Author: The Young Ice Whalers, 1908; Wild Pastures, 1909; Wildwood Ways, 1909; Woodland Paths, 1910; Wood Wanderings, 1910; Florida Trails, 1910; Literary Pilgrimages of a Naturalist, 1911; White Mountain Trails, 1912; Old Plymouth Trails, 1920; He Dropped Into Poetry, 1940. Home: Canton, Mass. Died Apr. 1, 1943.

PADDOCK, R(ICHARD) B(OLLES), mech. and elec. engr.; b. Ft. McKinney, Buffalo, Wyo., Apr. 16, 1891; s. Capt. Richard Bolles and Grace (Pershing) P.; student U. Neb., 1907-10; B.S., U.S. Mil. Acad., 1914; grad. Army War Coll. (war course), 1918; grad. U.S. F.A. Sch., Ft. Sill, Okla., 1921 and 1925; grad. U.S. Command and Gen. Staff Sch., 1926; m. 2d Kathryn Fowler Wilson, June 4, 1949; children by previous marriage—Richard Bolles, John Pershing. Commd. 2d lt., C.A.C., 1914; mil. instr., N.Y. City Police Dept., 1916; transferred to Signal Corps, 1916; promoted through grades to lt. col., 1918; transferred to Field

Arty., 1920; chief engring. and research div., Signal Corps, 1919; instr. Signal Sch., 1919, 1920, Field Arty. Sch., 1921-25; served as maj. Gen. Staff Corps and chief of staff, Philippine Div., 1927-29; dep. adminstr. NRA, 1933-34; exec. dir. Cotton Garment Code Authority, 1934-36; v.p. Wilson-Jones Co., 1937-40; chief tech. service, engr. and gen. sales mgr., Western Plastics, Inc., 1943-45; pres. Bone Engring. Corp., 1945-46; internat. rep. Tech. Oil Tool Corp., 1949-50; mem. engring. staff Gilfillan Bros., Inc. since 1950. Mem., Gen. Pershing's original staff; tech. officer staff of chief signal officer, A.E.F.; signal officer 1st Div., A.E.F., World War I. Awarded Silver Star, Order of the Purple Heart, Oak Leaf Cluster (U.S.), Croix de Guerre (France) Fourragère, Croix de Guerre (France) as personal decoration (2d Field Signal Batn.). Mem. Inst. Radio Engrs., Phi Gamma Delta. Democrat. Episcopalian. Mason (32 deg., K.T., Shriner). Clubs: University (Washington); Baltic Society, University, Army and Navy (Manila); Jefferson Islands (Tilghman, Md.). Home: 156 S. Canyon View Dr., Brentwood, Los Angeles 49. Office: 1815 Venice Bldg., Los Angeles. Deceased.

PAGE, CHARLES GRAFTON, inventor; b. Salem, Mass., Jan. 25, 1812; s. Jeremiah Lee and Lucy (Lang) P.; grad. Harvard, 1832; m. Priscilla Webster, Sept. 23, 1844, at least 5 children. Devised self-acting circuit breaker, (probably 1st to apply it to produce extreme alterations necessary in induction machines), circa 1837; his inventions incorporated in a coil machine by Daniel Davis, Jr., 1838; an examiner in U.S. Patent Office, 1841-52; prof. chemistry med. dept. Columbian Coll. (now George Washington U.), 1844-49; completed small reciprocating electro-magnetic engine by 1846; developed induction apparatus (which in principle is modern induction coil); granted spl. Congressional appropriation to continue work on larger scale, 1849; built several large stationary reciprocating electro-magnetic engines of both vertical and horizontal type; established (with J.J. Greenough and Charles L. Fleischmann) Am. Poly. Journal of Science, Washington, D.C., 1852; patented design of reciprocating electro-magnetic engine, 1854; examiner of patents U.S. Patent Office, 1861-68. Author: Psychomancy, Spirit-Rappings and Table-Tippings Exposed, 1853; History of Induction: The American Claim to the Induction Coil and its Electrostatic Developments, 1867. Died Washington D.C., May 5, 1868.

PAGE, JAMES, engineer; b. Baltimore, Oct. 31, 1864; s. Arthur and Mary J. (Campbell) P.; A.B., Johns Hopkins, 1882; also studied at Mass. Inst. Tech.; m. Clara Wood Merriman, of Lawrence Park, N.Y., June 10, 1903. Asst. in Allgheny (Pa.) Astron. Obs., 1887-89; in service of U.S. Coast and Geod. Survey, Internat. Boundary Commn. U.S. and Mexico, and Internat. Boundary Commn. U.S. and Brit. America, 1889-95; writer and editor of publs., U.S. Hydrographic Office, Washington, 1895-1905; chief of Div. of Ocean Meteorology, U.S. Weather Bur., 1905-07; asst. engr. Dept. of Pub. Works of Cuba, 1907-08; chief engr., water supply and sewer system of Cienfuegos, Cuba, 1908-12; since consulting engr., New York. Author of numerous pamphlets and articles upon commerce, navigation and allied subjects. Mem. Nat. Geog. Soc., Philos. Soc. Washington; asst. sec. 7th Internat. Geog. Congress. Clubs: Cosmos, Chevy Chase (Washington), Reform (New York). Address: Bronxville, N.Y.

PAGE, JOHN CHATFIELD, cons. engr.; b. Syracuse, Neb., Oct. 12, 1887; s. Walter Ernest and Emma Jerusha (Chatfield) P.; B.S., U. Neb., 1908; grad. work Cornell U., 1910-11; m. Mildred Rebecca Sloan, May 29, 1914; children—Jean Rebecca (Mrs. C. L. Killgore), Mildred (Mrs. P. Danielson). Topographer U.S. Bur. Reclamation, 1909; asst. city engr. Grand Junction, Colo., 1909-10; jr. engr. Bur. of Reclamation, 1911-15, supt. Grand Valley (Colo.) project, 1925-30, office engr. on constrn. of Boulder Dam, 1930-35, acting commr., 1936-37, commr. of reclamation, 1937-43; resigned as commr. Aug. 3, 1943, designated cons. engr. Mem. Am. Soc. C.E., Sigma Tau. Mason (32 deg., Shriner). Home: 5335 Montview Blvd. Office: Bureau of Reclamation, Dept. of the Interior, Denver. Died Mar. 23, 1955; buried Crown Hill Cemetery, Jefferson County, Colo.

PAGE, JOHN RANDOLPH, otologist; b. U. Va., Nov. 15, 1876; s. Dr. John Randolph and Delia (Bryan) P.; ed. pvt. prep. schs.; M.D., U. Va., 1899; m. Dorothy Dawson, Oct. 21, 1908; children—Dorothy Dawson (Mrs. Andrew Gibson Curry), Mary Elizabeth (Mrs. Joseph Hurd Hodgson). Interne Hudson St. Hosp., July-Oct. 1899, N.Y. Lying-In Hosp., 1899-1900; interne, house surgeon and house physician Hudson St. Hosp., 1900-02; resident N.Y. Eye and Ear Infirmary, 1902-04; asst. surgeon Manhattan Eye, Ear and Throat Hosp. since 1905; otologist to Babies Hosp., N.Y.C.; cons. otologist St. Lukes Hosp., Newburgh, Bronx Eye and Ear Infirmary; dir., v.p., chmn. bd. surgeons Manhattan Eye, Ear and Throat Hosp.; cons. surgeon, formerly chmn. bd. surgeons, Manhattan Eye, Ear and Throat Hosp. Fellow A.C.S.; mem. Am. Otol. Soc. (past pres.), Am. Laryngol., Rhinol., and Otol. Soc., N.Y. Acad. Medicine, A.M.A., Phi Beta Kappa, Delta Psi. Clubs: Union, St. Anthony (N.Y.). Author: Diseases of the Internal Ear, 1929; The Surgery of Suppuration Labyrinthitis (Nelson Loose-Leaf Surgery of Ear), 1945. Home: 127 E. 62d St., N.Y.C. 21. Died July 1960.

PAGE, LEIGH, physicist; b. South Orange, N.J., Oct. 13, 1884; s. Edward D. and Cornelia (Lee) P.; Ph.B., Sheffield Scientific Sch. (Yale), 1904; Ph.D., Yale, 1913; m. Mary Cholmondeley Thornton, June 27, 1910; children—Thornton Leigh, Barbara Helen, Marjory. Instr. physics, 1912-16, asst. prof., 1916-22, prof. math. physics since 1922, Yale. Apptd. judge Einstein contest by Scientific American, 1921; developed a new theory of electromagnetism. Fellow Am. Acad. of Arts and Sciences, Am. Phys. Soc., A.A.A.S.; mem. Am. Math. Soc., Nat. Research Council (1923), Sigma Xi, Phi Gamma Delta, Gamma Alpha. Republican. Conglist. Author: An Introduction to Electrodynamics, 1922; An Introduction to Theoretical Physics, 1928; Principles of Electricity, 1931; Electrodynamics, 1940; also numerous professional papers. Home: 244 Livingston St., New Haven, Conn. Died Sept. 14, 1952.

PAGE, LOGAN WALLER, engineer; b. Richmond, Va., Jan. 10, 1870; s. Legh R. and Page (Waller) P.; ed. Powder Point Sch., Bear Island Acad., Va. Poly. Inst. and Harvard; m. Anne P. Shaler, Oct. 17, 1903. Geologist Mass. Highway Commn. and dir. testing lab., Lawrence Scientific Sch. (Harvard), 1893-1900; chief Div. of Tests, Dept. Agr., 1900-05; dir. U.S. Office of Pub. Roads, 1905—. Author: The Testing of Road Materials, 1901; Roads, Paths and Bridges. Home: Washington, D.C. Died Dec. 9, 1918.

PAGE, ROBERT M., educator, biologist; b. Pasadena, Cal., Feb. 5, 1919; s. Benjamin Edwin and Marie (Markham) P.; A.B., Harvard, 1941, M.A., 1946, Ph.D., 1948; m. Virginia Michaud, Sept. 7, 1944. Mem. faculty Stanford, 1948-68, prof. biology, 1963-68. Served with AUS, 1942-45. Mem. Bot. Soc. Am., Mycological Soc. Am., Western Soc. Naturalists, Cal. Acad. Scis., Sigma Pi. Home: Palo Alto CA Died May 17, 1968.

PAGE, WILLIAM NELSON, civil and mining engr.; b. Campbell Co., Va., Jan. 6, 1854; s. Edwin Randolph and Olivia (Alexander) P.; prep. edn., Leesburg (Va.) Acad.; spl. course in engring., U. of Va.; m. Emma Hayden Gilham, Feb. 9, 1882; children—Delia Hayden, Edwin Randolph, Mary Josephine, Randolph Gilham. Rodman on location and constrn. C.&O. Ry., New River Cañon, 1871-72; located and built Mill Creek Cañon br. ry., 1874; in charge of party locating double track ry., ordered by Congress, from the Ohio River to Hampton Roads, Va., 1875-76; gen. manager Hawk's Nest Coal Co., 1877-80; built and operated Victoria Blast Furnace, Goshen, Va., 1880-85; located and built Powellton br. of C.&O. Ry., 1885-89, and developed Mt. Carbon Collieries; organized and developed the Gauley Mountain Coal Co., 1889-1917, and now consulting engr. same; built the Deepwater, Tidewater, and Virginian rys.; was consulting coal engr. for Amalgamated Copper Co. and many other cos. Mem. W.Va. N.G. 20 yrs., advancing to brig. insp. gen. Mayor of Ansted, W.Va., 10 yrs. An incorporator and dir. Sheltering Arms Hosp. Chief of Internat. Jury of Awards, Mines and Metallurgy, St. Louis Expn., 1904. Episcopalian. Mason. Home: Washington, D.C. Died Mar. 7, 1932.

PAINE, ELLERY BURTON, electrical engr.; b. Willington, Conn., Oct. 9, 1875; s. Albert Aplin and Ellen (Smith) P.; B.S., Worcester Poly. Inst., 1897, M.S., 1898, E.E., 1904; m. Mabel Harriet Hyde, June 6, 1908; 1 dau., Sylvia. With testing dept. Gen. Electric Co., Schenectady, N.Y., 1898-99; elec. engr., Lehigh Valley Coal Co., Wilkes-Barre, Pa., 1899-1902; prof. elec. engring., Stetson U., De Land, Fla., 1902-04, N.C. Coll. Agr. and Engring., Raleigh, N.C., 1904-07, U. of Ill. since 1907, and in charge dept. elec. engring., 1913-44; retired Sept. 1944. Mem. Am. Inst. Elec. Engrs., Soc. for Promotion Engring. Edn., Western Soc. of Engrs., Sigma Xi, Tau Beta Pi, Eta Kappa Nu. Home: 606 Pennsylvania Av., Urbana IL

PAINE, FRANCIS BRINLEY HEBARD, electrical engr.; b. Chicago, Apr. 12, 1869; s. Charles and Olivia B. (Hebard) P.; m. Julia Wood Miller, May 2, 1900. Labs. of Westinghouse Electric & Mfg. Co., Pittsburgh, 1889-91; mem. Charles Paine & Sons, cons. engrs., New York, 1891-93; mgr. and engr. Westinghouse Electric & Mfg. Co., Boston, New York, and for 2 yrs. in the Orient, 1893-1906; gen. mgr. constrn. Ontario Power Co., 1906-13, Niagara, Lockport & Ontario Power Co., 1906-13; cons. engr., 1913—. Episcopalian. Fellow Am. Inst. E.E. Home: New York, N.Y. Died Sept. 16, 1917.

PAINE, FRANCIS WARD, mining engr.; b. Boston, Mass., Aug. 1, 1888; s. William Alfred and Ruth Felton (Ward) P.; grad. Hill Sch., Pottstown, Pa., 1906; B.A., Yale, 1910; M.A., U. of Wis., 1911; m. Frances Joyce Hatch, Jan. 5, 1929. Prof. mining geology, Mich. Coll. of Mines, 1911-12; mem. Paine, Webber & Co., brokers and investment bankers, Boston, 1919—; treas. Copper Range Co.; dir. New River Co., Midland Steel Products Co., Maine Gas Co. President Free Hosp. for Women. Conglist. Home: Chestnut Hill, Mass. Died Aug. 22, 1940.

PAINE, HARLAN LLOYD, physician; b. Rockland, Mass., Nov. 3, 1884; s. Ernest M. and Etta J. (Hunt) P.; M.D., Tufts U., 1908; m. Amy M. Yeo, June 10, 1914 (dec.); children—Harlan Lloyd, Dorothy (Mrs. Norton G. Chaucer), Marion (Mrs. Soli Morris), Louis H.; m. 2d, Lucie G. Ratte, May 21, 1949. Intern, Cambridge (Mass.) Hosp., 1908-09; asst. commr. Mass. Dept. Mental Health, 1918-20; chief exec. officer Boston Psychopathic Hosp., 1920-21; supt. Grafton (Mass.) State Hosp., 1921-48, Channing Sanitorium, 1948-51; psychiat. cons. Westborough (Mass.) State Hosp., 1966-71, Westborough and Marlborough Dist. Cts., 1951-71. Trustee, Westborough Savs. Bank, 1934-66, trustee emeritus, 1966-71, mem. investment bd., 1953-66. Mem. Minn. Gov.'s Commn. for Mental Health Survey, 1954; cons. R.I. Devel. Council, 1952-53. Bd. dirs. United Fund Westborough, 1963-71; trustee Grafton Pub. Library, 1929-48; trustee Westborough Pub. Library, 1952-69, treas., 1955-69. Recipient award of merit Tufts U. Sch. Med., 1958. Diplomate Am. Bd. Psychiatry and Neurology. Mem. A.M.A., Am. Psychiat. Assn., New Eng. Soc. Psychiatry, Mass., Worcester Dist. med. socs. Conglist. (trustee until 1948, deacon 1953-56). Mason. Home: Westborough MA Died July 7, 1971; buried RiversideCemetery, Grafton MA

PAINE, MARTYN, physician, educator; b. Williamstown, Vt., July 8, 1794; s. Elijah and Sarah (Porter) P.; A.B., Harvard, 1813, M.D., 1816; LL.D., U. Vt., 1854; m. Mary Ann Weeks, 1825, 1 dau., 2 sons. A promoter of med. coll. U. City N.Y., 1841-67, prof. insts. of medicine, 1841-50, prof. therapeutics and materia medica, after 1850; leading prof. of therapeutics in nation sent by faculty colleagues to Albany to use influence for passage of legislation permitting dissections in N.Y. (act passed, 1854); mem. Royal Soc. Prussia, Med. Soc. Sweden, Soc. Naturalists and Physicians of Dresden, Med. Soc. Leipzig. Author: On the Cholera Asphyxia as It Appeared in the City of N.Y. in 1832; Medical and Physiological Commentaries, 1840-44; Essays on the Philosophy of Vitality and on the Modus Operandi of Remedial Agents, 1842; Institutes of Medicine, 1847; Materia Medica and Therapeutics, 1848. Died N.Y.C., Nov. 10, 1877.

PAINTER, THEOPHILUS SHICKEL, zoologist; b. Salem, Va., Aug. 22, 1889; s. Franklin Verzelius Newton and Laura Trimble (Shickel) P.; B.A., Roanoke Coll., Salem. Va., 1908; M.A., Yale, 1909, Ph.D., 1913, hon. Sc.D., 1936; studied U. of Wurtzburg, 1913-14; LL.D., Roanoke Coll., 1942; m. Anna Mary Thomas, Dec. 29, 1917; children—Elizabeth Tyler (Mrs. S.P.R. Hutchins), Anne Trimble (Mrs. Thornton C. Greer), Theophilus S., Joseph Thomas. Instr. in zoology, Yale, 1914-16; adj. prof. zoology, U. Texas, 1916-21, prof., 1922-44, acting pres., 1944-46, pres., 1946-52, distinguished prof., 1952-66, prof. emeritus, 1966-69, also dir. U. Tex. Radiobiol. Lab. Adviser on research Am. Cancer Soc.; bd. dirs. Oak Ridge Inst. Nuclear Studies. Recipient Daniel Giraud medal for sci. research, 1934; 1st Anderson award M.D. Anderson Hosp. and Tumor Inst., 1969. Mem. 10th F.A., Conn. N.G., 1916; 1st lt. S.C., U.S. Army, later capt. A.S., till 1919. Mem. Am. Soc. Zoologists, Nat. Acad. Sci., English Speaking Union, Sigma Xi, Phi Eta Sigma, Alpha Omega Alpha, Phi Kappa Phi, also numerous other sci. socs. Presbyn. Clubs: University, Town and Gown. Am. editor 10th edit. Vade-Mecum. Contbr. numerous sci. articles on cytology, cytogenetics and exptl. zoology. Home: Austin TX Died Oct. 5, 1969; buried Austin Meml. Park, Austin TX

PAINTER, WILLIAM, engr., inventor; b. Montgomery County, Md., Nov. 20, 1838; s. Dr. Edward and Louisa (Gilpin) P.; m. Harriet Deacon, Sept. 9, 1861, 3 children. Apprentice, patent leather factory, Wilmington, Del., 1855-59; patented a fare box, 1858, railroad car seat and couch, 1858, kerosene lamp, 1863, wire-retaining rubber stopper which could be removed with 1 hand, 1885; founder Triumph Bottle Stopper Co., Balt., 1885; patented bottle seal, 1885, organized Bottle Seal Co. for its manufacture; patented a metal bottle cap (of type still used), 1892; sec., gen. mgr. Crown Cork and Seal Co., 1892-1903. Died July 15, 1906.

PALACHE, CHARLES, mineralogist; b. San Francisco, July 18, 1869; s. James and Helen M. (Whitney) P.; B.S., U. Cal., 1891, fellow, 1892-94, Ph.D., 1894, LL.D., 1941; m. Helen Harrington Markham, Aug. 15, 1899; children—Eliza Jeanette, Mary, Alice Helen. Instr. in mineralogy Harvard, 1896-1901, asst. prof., 1902-10, prof., 1910-40, prof. emeritus, 1940—. Pres. Mineral Soc. Am., 1921. Fellow A.A.A.S.; mem. Geol. Soc. America (pres. 1937), Nat. Acad. Sciences. Protestant. Home: 106 Appleton St., Cambridge, Mass. Died Dec. 5, 1954.

PALMER, ALBERT DE FOREST, physicist; b. Tewksbury, Mass., July 26, 1869; s. Albert deForest and Mary Jane (Spear) P.; Ph.B., Brown U., 1891, Ph.D., 1895; grad. study Johns Hopkins, 1891-93; m. Charlotte Morrill, July 5, 1899; children—Edward Standish, Albert deForest. Instr. in physics, Brown U., 1893-96, asso. prof. physics, 1896-1934, asso. prof. emeritus, 1934—, chmn. of dept. of physics, 1926-34; works in his private laboratory, Pasadena, 1935—; visiting research fellow, Calif. Inst. Tech., 1927-28. Fellow Am. Physical Soc., Optical Soc. of Am., A.A.A.S. Baptist. Author: Theory of Measurements, 1912. Home: Pasadena, Calif. Died Jan. 12, 1940.

PALMER, ALONZO BENJAMIN, physician, educator; b. Richfield, N.Y., Oct. 6, 1815; s. Benjamin and Anna (Layton) P.; grad. Coll. Physicians and Surgeons, Fairfield, N.Y., 1839; LL.D. (hon.), U. Mich., 1881; m. Caroline Wright, July 29, 1843; m. 2d, Love Root, 1867. City physician Chgo., 1852-55, became ofcl. med. adviser to city health officer; prof. materia medica, therapeutics and diseases of women and children U. Mich., 1854, prof. pathology and practice of medicine, 1860-87, dean med. dept., 1875-87; prof. pathology and practice medicine Berkshire Med. Instn., Pittsfield, Mass., 1864-67; prof. practice medicine Bowdoin Coll., 1869-79; served as surgeon 2d Mich. Inf., 1861; editor Peninsular Jour. of Medicine and the Collateral Scis., also Peninsular and Independent Med. Jodur., 1853-60; pres. Mich. State Med. Soc., 1872-73. Author: Observations on the Cause, Nature, and Treatment of Epidemic Cholera, 1854; Treatise on the Science and Practice of Medicine, or the Pathology and Treatment of Internal Diseases, 2 vols., 1882; A Treatise on Epidemic Cholera, 1885; The Temperance Teachings of Science, 1886. Died Ann Arbor, Mich., Dec. 23, 1887.

PALMER, ANDREW HENRY, meteorologist, climatologist; b. Dubuque, Ia., May 1, 1886; s. John and Mary (Gorius) P.; A.B. ("with distinction"), U. of Minn., 1908; univ. scholar, Harvard, 1908-09, A.M., 1909; Ph.D., U. of Santa Clara, Calif., 1923; unmarried. Research asst., Blue Hill Meteorol. Obs. of Harvard U., 1908-12; instr. geography, Mass. State Normal Sch., Salem, 1912; magnetic observer, Carnegie Instn. of Washington, 1913; asst. observer, 1914-15, observer, 1915-18, and meteorologist, 1918-24, U.S. Weather Bureau, San Francisco; supt. Crop and Weather Dept., Automobile Insurance Co., San Francisco, since 1924. Fellow Am. Geog. Soc., Am. Meteorol. Soc.; mem. A.A.A.S., Seismol. Soc. Am., Calif. Acad. Sciences, Phi Beta Kappa. Co-author (with the late A. Lawrence Rotch): Charts of the Atmosphere for Aeronatus and Aviators, 1911. Editor of Notes on Meteorology and Climatology, in "Science," 1910-12; has written many papers on meteorol. and climatol. subjects. Home: 37 Columbus Av. Office: 37 Columbus Av., San Francisco. Died Dec. 26, 1942.

PALMER, BARTLETT JOSHUA, chiropractor; b. What Cheer, Ia., Sept. 10, 1881; s. Daniel David and Olivia P.; student pub. schs., Davenport, Ia.; m. Mabel Heath, Apr. 30, 1904 (dec. Mar. 30, 1949); 1 son, Daniel David. Chiropractic practitioner since 1898; acting head Chiropractic Sch., Davenport, since 1903; lectr., instr. chiropractic sci. and philosophy since 1906; pioneer in use x-ray equipment, application x-ray to chiropractic sci.; pres. radio sta. WHO, Des Moines, 1919—, WOC, Davenport, 1919—, Stereocolor, Inc., B. J. Palmer Assos., Inc., Palmer Sch. Chiropractic, Inc.; owner Clear View Mental Sanitarium; dir. B. J. Palmer Chiropractic Research Clinic, Ia.; lectr., instr. radio salesmanship, 1942-48. Member board Circus Hall of Fame, Inc.; dir. Circus Hall of Fame, Sarasota, Florida. Licensed chiropractor, Ia. Mem. Radio Pioneers, Radio and TV Execs. Soc., Showmen's League Am., Greater Tampa Showman's Assn., Circus Hist. Soc., Circus Model Builders Assn., Show Folks Am., Tri-City Musical Soc. Union, Ia. State Sheriffs Assn., Am. Soc. Mil. Chiropractors, Chiropractic Soc. Ia., Internat. Chiropractic Assn. (pres. since 1926), Davenport C. of C. Elk, Mason (Shriner, Jester). Clubs: Knife and Fork; Trowel Radio Executives (New York City); Royal American Shrine (Tampa, Florida); also Kiwanis; Outrigger Canoe (Honolulu); 25-Year, Davenport, Gotham (Des Moines). Author: Around the World with B. J.; The Greatest Mystery of History; Upside Town and Right Side Up; Palmers Law of Life (vol. 36). Home: 800 Brady St., Davenport, Ia. Died May 27, 1961.

PALMER, CARROLL (EDWARDS), med. research; born Fairmont, Minn., Nov. 3, 1903; s. Roy W. and Grace (Edwards) P.; B.S. Hamline U., 1925, D.Sc., 1959; M.A., U. Minn., 1927, M.D., 1928, Ph.D., 1929; M.D. honoris causa, U. Oslo, Norway, 1956; m. Margaret Michaelson, June 30, 1928; children—Gaela, Richard. Teaching fellow U. Minn., 1926-27, research fellow Inst. of Child Development, 1927-29; asso. in biostatistics Johns Hopkins Sch. of Hygiene and Pub. Health, 1929-36; consultant in child hygiene U.S. P.H.S., 1932-36; statistician and supervisor of med. records Johns Hopkins Hosp., 1935-36; commd. passed asst. surgeon U.S.P.H.S., 1936, medical dir. 1950, dir. of research Child Hygiene Office, 1936-42. Tb research, 1942-67; prof. biostatistics Sch. Pub. Health, U. Cal., Berkeley, 1967-71; spl. projects cons. Mayo Clinic, Rochester, Minn., 1971-72; dir. tuberculosis research office WHO, 1949-55. Recipient Weber-Parkes prize Royal College of Physicians, London, England, 1957; Trudeau medal National Tb Association, 1964. Diplomate of the American Board of Preventive Medicine amd Pub. Health (Founder). Fellow Soc. for Growth and Development; mem. Am. Assn. Anatomists, Soc. Research in Child Development (sec.-treas. 1936-48, chmn. publ. com. 1936-48). Am. Trudeau Soc. Am. Pub. Health Assn., Am. Epidemiol. Soc. Internat. Epidemiol. Assn., Alpha Omega Alpha, Sigma Xi. Club: Cosmos (Washington). Editor: Child Development Abstracts and Bibliography 1933-48. Died Jan. 8, 1972.

PALMER, CHARLES SKEELE, chemist; b. Danville, Ill., Aug. 4, 1858; s. Rev. William Randall and Clara E. (Skeele) P.; A.B., Amherst, 1879, A.M., 1882; Ph.D., Johns Hopkins Univ., 1886; University of Leipzig, Germany, 1892-93; m. Harriet B. Warner, Sept. 30, 1886 (died 1932); children—Mrs. Helen W. P. Bissell, Leigh W., Mrs. Winifred W. P. Bennett. Prof. chemistry, U. of Colo., 1887-1902; pres. Colo. Sch. of Mines, 1902-03; chief chemist Washoe Smelter, Anaconda, Mont., 1903-04; asso. editor Engineering and Mining Journal, 1904-06; chem. engr. for large textile mills; fellow, Mellon Inst. of Industrial Research, U. of Pittsburgh, Nov. 1915-17. Consulting chemist United Fuel Gas Co., Charleston, W.Va., 1920. Episcopalian. Mason. Defined chemical terms in Webster's Internat. Dictionary, 1890 edition. Translated 1st edition Nernst's "Theoretical Chemistry," 1895. Invented, 1900, and patented, 1907, basic process for cracking oils to gasoline, sold to Standard Oil Co. of Ind., 1916. Author: Chemical Oxidation Tables, 1897; A Possible Approach to the Shakespeare Question (paper in Johns Hopkins Alumni Mag.), June 1937. Home: Pittsburgh, Pa. Died Nov. 30, 1939.

PALMER, CHASE, chemist; b. Saco, Me., Sept. 19, 1856; s. Bartlett and Elizabeth (Chase) P.; student Princeton, 1874-76; A.B., Johns Hopkins, 1879, grad. prize scholar, fellow, 1879-82, Ph.D., 1882; m. Olive Edwards, Nov. 26, 1895. Instr. Mass. Inst. Tech., State Normal Sch. (Salem, Mass.), and Tufts Coll., 1882-88; state assayer, Mass., 1885-88; prof. chemistry, Wabash Coll., 1888-90; mgr. lead and zinc mines, Joplin, Mo., 1890-94; prof. chemistry, Du Pont Manual Training High Sch., Central U., and Ky. State Coll., 1895-1906; spl. chemist for water, 1906-07, chemist, 1907-19, U.S. Geol. Survey; chief chemist for Southern Pacific Co., 1919-21; consulting chemist, San Francisco. Episcopalian. Home: San Francisco, Calif. Died Nov. 18, 1927.

PALMER, DANIEL DAVID, founder chiropractic; b. nr. Toronto, Can., Mar. 7, 1845; 1 son, Bartlett Joshua. Practiced magnetic healing, Burlington, Ia., 1883-95; made 1st attempt at spinal adjustment, Davenport, Ia., 1895; founded Palmer Sch. of Chiropractic, 1898; opened Portland Coll. of Chiropractic, Portland, Ore., 1903; arrested and imprisoned for practicing medicine without license, 1906. Author: The Science of Chiropractic, 1906; Textbook of the Science, Art and Philosophy of Chiropractic, 1910; The Chiropractor, 1914. Died Los Angeles, Oct. 20, 1913.

PALMER, FREDERIC, JR., educator; b. Brookline, Mass., Oct. 17, 1878; s. Frederic and Mary (Towle) P.; A.B., Harvard, 1900, A.M., 1904, Ph.D., 1913; m. Helen Wallace, June 19, 1907; children—Frederic, Helen Wallace. Tchr., Asheville (N.C.) Sch., 1900-01, Worcester (Mass.) Acad., 1901-03; instr., Haverford Coll., 1904-08. dean, 1908-29, asso. prof. physics, 1909-16, prof. physics 1916-45, emeritus. Mem. Div. 1, NDRC, 1944-45. Mem. exec. com. Am. Inst. Physics, 1931; v.p. Am. Assn. Physics Tchrs., 1932, pres., 1933, 34; mem. commn. on sci. Coll. Entrance Exam. Bd., 1935, mem. com. on physics, 1936—. Fellow A.A.A.S., Am. phys. Soc.; mem. Physics Club Phila. (past pres.), Franklin Inst. (past chmn. com. sci. and arts), Phi Beta Kappa, Sigma Xi, Delta Upsilon. Democrat. Presbyn. Ednl. sec. YMCA, Newport, R.I., 1918; lectr. physics Harvard, 1918-19. Home: Haverford, Pa. Died Apr. 1967.

PALMER, HOWARD, author, explorer; b. Norwich, Conn., Nov. 28, 1883; s. George S. and Ida Amelia (Cooke) P.; B.A., Yale, 1905; LL.B., Harvard, 1908; unmarried. Admitted to Mass. bar, 1908; sec. dir. Palmer Bros. Co., mfrs. bed comfortables, New London, 1918-28. A pioneer explorer, Selkirk Mts., B.C., 1907-15, ascending 50 new or little-visited peaks; made 1st conquest of Mt. Sir Sandford, 1912; Canadian Govt., confirmed his names for fifty new mountains, glaciers, etc. and named in his honor a peak, glacier and river; visited remote sections Canadian Rockies, 1916-27, ascending a score of new peaks; assisted in organizing Mt. Logan expdn. to Alaska, 1925; lecturer in mountaineering; made studies and measurements of movements of glaciers pub. by Royal Geog. Soc. (London) and Smithsonian Instn. Trustee Pub. Library, New London. Mem. exec. com. for celebration of Sesquicentennial of Battle of Groton Heights, 1931. Fellow Royal Geog. Soc.; mem. New London County Hist. Soc. (v.p.), Am. Inst. of Mining Engrs.; corr. mem. Geographic Soc. Phila. Republican. Clubs: Am. Alpine (pres. term 1926-29), British Alpine, Explorers', Harvard Travelers, Appalachian Mountain; Fresh Air, Century (N.Y. City); etc. Author: Mountaineering and Exploration in the Selkirks, 1914; A Pioneer of the Canadian Alps, 1931. Joint Author: A Climber's Guide to the Rocky Mountains of Canada, 1921, 40. Editor: Life on a Whaler, for New London County Hist. Soc., 1929; also editor of American Alpine Journal, 1930-33. Contbr. to Harvard Handbook of Travel, 1917, 35, Ency. Britannica, 1929, and periodicals on history and exploration of Canadian Cordillera. Home: Pawcatuck, Conn. (P.O. Westerly, R.I.). Died Oct. 24, 1944.

PALMER, IRVING ALLSTON, metallurgist; b. New Waverly, Ind., May 20, 1866; s. Lawson and Margaret (Sottlemeyer) P.; B.S. in chemistry, Lafayette Coll., 1887, M.S., 1890; m. Mary A. Maxwell, Sept. 12, 1895. Assayer, chemist, asst. supt., supt. and consulting metallurgist, various smelting and refining companies in U.S. and Mexico, 1887-1916; prof. metallurgy Colo. Sch. of Mines, 1917—. Republican. Joint author: (with A. J. Weinig) The Trend of Flotation. Home: Golden, Colo. Died Apr. 29, 1936.

PALMER, LEROY SHELDON, univ. prof.; b. Rushville, Ill., Mar. 23, 1887; s. Samuel C. and Annie Jane (Geodman) P.; B.S. in Chem. Engring.; U. of Mo., 1909, A.M., 1911, Ph.D., 1913; m. Nina Gay Wilcox, Sept. 14, 1911; children—Bess Wilcox (Mrs. Andrew Justus), Leroy Sheldon, James Samuel. Chemist, dairy division U.S. Dept. Agr., 1909-11; chemist charge coop. lab. of dairy div., U.S. Dept. Agr., at U. of Mo., 1911-13; asst. prof. dairy chemistry, U. of Mo., 1913-19; asso. prof. agrl. biochemistry, U. of Minn., 1919-22, prof. since 1922, chief, div. of agrl. bio-chemistry, U. of Minn., since 1942; also dairy chemist Minn. Agrl. Expt. Station. Fellow A.A.A.S.; mem. Am. Chem. Soc. (councillor 1925, 31, 37), Am. Soc. Biol. Chemists, Soc. Exptl. Biology and Medicine, Am. Dairy Science Assn., Am. Inst. of Nutrition, Am. Genetic Assn., Inst. Food Technologists, Am. Acad. Polit. and Social Science; Minn. United Nations Com., Phi Lambda Upsilon, Sigma Xi, Alpha Chi Sigma, Gamma Sigma Delta, Tau Beta Pi, Alpha Zeta, Phi Mu Alpha; v.p. World's Dairy Congress, 1923. Borden medal and award, Am. Chem. Soc., 1939. Republican. Conglist. Clubs: Eckles (permanent sec.), Campus. Author: Carotinoids and Related Pigments, 1922; Laboratory Experiments in Dairy Chemistry, 1926; also more than 175 papers and bulls. giving results of researches. Joint author: Fundamentals of Dairy Science, 1928, 1935; Outlines of Biochemistry (Gortner), 1929, 1938; asso. editor Journal of Dairy Science. Revised Eckles' Dairy Cattle and Milk Production (with E. L. Anthony), 1939. Home: 2262 Carter Av., St. Paul, Minn. Died Mar. 8, 1944.

PALMER, MARTIN FRANKLIN, logopedist; b. Adrian, Mich., Oct. 25, 1905; s. Orren Leander and Elizabeth (Gibbs) P.; student Highland Park (Mich.) Jr. Coll., 1923-24; A.B., Olivet Coll., Olivet, Mich., 1927; A.M., Univ. of Mich., 1931; Sc.D. magna cum laude, 1937; m. Mary Campbell, Dec. 30, 1932; 1 dau., Susan Christine. Teacher of speech Port Huron (Mich.) pub. schs., 1927-30; chmn. dept. of speech, Kan. Wesleyan Univ., Salina, Kan., 1931-32; prof. of speech pathology Marymount Coll., Salina, Kan., 1933-34; prof. of logopedics and head dept. of logopedics, Wichita (Kan.) State University, 1934—; dir. Inst. of Logopedics, Wichita, Kan., 1934—; cons. dept. phys. medicine and rehab. Ohila. Gen. Hosp.; WHO cons., Govt. Japan, 1960—; Recipient Distinguished Alumni citation Olivet (Mich.) Coll., 1958. Mem. Am. Bd. Examiners Speech Pathology and Audiology, dir., 1961—, v.p., 1963—. Fellow Am. Speech and Hearing Assn. (exec. counc., chmn. com. on edn. 1940-50, pres. 1948); mem. Internat. Assn. Logopedics and Phoniatrics, Internat. Counc. Exceptional Children, Internat. Soc. Rehab. Disabled (chmn. U.S. internat. com. deafness, speech and hearing 1962—), Japanese Voice and Speech Therapy Soc. (hon.), A.A.A.S., Kan. Council for Children and Youth, Am. Hearing Soc., Kan. Speech and Hearing Assn., Central Speech Assn., United Cerebral Palsy Assn. (clinical adv. bd.), Am. Acad. for Cerebral Palsy (hon.), Acoustical Soc. Am., Am. Dialect Soc., Central States Speech Assn., Am. Assn. U. Profs., American Assn. Promote Teaching of Speech to the Deaf, Am. Council Exceptional Children, Nat. Rehabilitation Assn., Speech Assn. of Am., Kan. Acad. of Sci. Presbyterian. Club: Kiwanis International. Abstracting editor of all articles dealing with speech, hearing, and related topics for Biol. Abstracts and other profl. jours. Mem. editorial bd. Jour. Speech and Hearing Disorders; Jour. Speech and Hearing Research. Contbr. articles to profl. jours. Office: Inst. of Logopedics, 2400 Jardine Dr., Wichita, Kan. 67219. Died Aug. 13, 1965.

PALMER, ROBERT (CONRAD), chemist; born Rushville, Ill., Mar. 23, 1887; s. Samuel Cornelius and Annie Jane (Goodman) P.; B.S., U. of Mo., 1909, Chem. E., 1910; m. Myrtle L. Ogle, Feb. 23, 1911 (died 1921); 1 dau., Jane C. (Mrs. Alfred F. Wicke, Jr.); m. 2d, Florence V. Glass, June 5, 1923; children—Emma Glass, Robert C. Chemist, Forest Products Lab., U.S. Dept. Agr., Madison, Wis., 1910-16, Newport Turpentine & Rosin Co., Pensacola, Fla., 1916-21; chief chemist The Newport Co., Pensacola, 1921-31; chief chemist and dir. research Newport Industries, Inc., Pensacola, 1931-38, chem. dir., 1939—, v.p. and chem. dir. since 1944. Mem. Am. Chem. Soc., Am. Soc. Testing Materials, Fla. Soc. Colonial Wars, S.A.R. (p. state v.p.), Am. Camellia Soc., Order Founders and Patriots of America, General Society of Mayflower Descendants, also Sigma Xi, Alpha Chi Sigma. Democrat. Presbyn. Clubs: Kiwanis, Pensacola Country. Inventor. Home: 1380 N. Spring St. Office: Newport Industries, Inc., P.O. Drawer, 911, Pensacola, Fla. Died June 11, 1957; buried Bayview Meml. Cemetery, Pensacola, Fla.

PALMER, SILAS H., engr.; b. Oakland, Calif., July 7, 1874; s. Charles Edgar and Mary Louise (Grigsby) P.; student U. Calif.; m. Olive Holbrook, June 3, 1903 (died March 28, 1958). Served as member of Palmer & McBryde Engring. Co., 1903-33; dir. Pacific Cement &

Aggregates, Inc., Bank of Cal., N.A., Pacific Gas & Electric Co., Fibreboard Paper Products Corporation; trustee Cypress Lawn Cemetery Assn., Union Square Garage Corp. Clubs: Menlo Country, San Francisco Golf, The Pacific-Union, Olympic. Home: 1201 California St., San Francisco 9. Office: 58 Sutter St., San Francisco 4. Died Feb. 8, 1963; buried Mountain View Cemetery, Oakland, Cal.

PALMER, THEODORE SHERMAN, naturalist; b. Oakland, Cal., Jan. 26, 1868; s. Herny A. and Jane (Day) P.; A.B., U. Cal., 1888, M.D., Georgetown U., 1895; m. Bertha M. Ellis, Nov. 21, 1911. First asst. ornithologist U.S. Biol. Survey, 1890-96, in charge Death Valley Expdn., 5 months in 1891, asst. chief, 1896-1902 and 1910-14, asst. in charge game preservation, 1902-10, 1914-16, expert in game conservation, 1916-24, biologist, 1924-28, sr. biologist, 1928-33; asso. in zoölogy, U.S. Nat. Museum from 1933; retired. Fellow A.A.A.S., Am. Ornithologists Union (sec. 1917-37), Cal. Acad. Sciences; mem. Am. Soc. Naturalists, Am. Bison Soc., Am. Fisheries Soc., Am. Forestry Assn., Am. Genetic Assn., Baird Ornithol. Club, Nat. Parks Assn., Save Redwoods League, Am. Game Protective Assn., Internat. Com. Bird Protection, Washington Acad. Sciences, Wilson Ornithol. Club, Sigma Xi; asso. mem. Soc. Am. Foresters, Am. Mus. Natural History, Boone and Crockett Soc.; corr. mem. Ornithol. Gesellschaft in Bayern, Royal Hungarian Inst. Ornithol.; hon. mem. Cooper Ornithol. Club, Internat. Assn. Game Commrs., Soc. Preservation Fauna Empire (London); pres. Biol. Soc. Washington, 1909-10, Audubon Soc. D.C., 1924-41 (pres. emeritus, 1941—); v.p. Nat. Assn. Audubon Socs., 1905-35; v.p. Am. Soc. Mammalogists, 1928-34. Author: Jack Rabbits of United States (2d edit.), 1897; List of Generic and Family Names of Rodents, 1897; Legislation for the Protection of Birds Other than Game Birds (2d edit.), 1902; Review of Economic Ornithology in the United States, 1900; Index Generum Mammalium, 1904; Hunting Licenses, 1904; Chronology and Index American Game Protection, 1912; Game as a National Resource, 1922; Place Names of the Death Valley Region, 1948; Chronology of the Death Valley Region, 1951; Biographies of members of the American Ornithologists Union, 1884-1954, 1954; also numerous shorter papers on game protection; (with Henry Oldys and others) Laws Regulating the Transportation and Sale of Game, 1900; Digest of Game Laws for 1901; Game Birds and Eggs for Propagation, 1904. Chmn. com. which prepared regulations under federal migratory bird law, 1913; prepared preliminary draft of treaty for protection of migratory birds in U.S. and Can., 1916, whaling treaty act, 1936. Club: Cosmos. Contbr. to ornithol. journals. Home: 1939 Biltmore St. N.W., Washington. Died July 23, 1955; buried Mountain View Cemetery, Oakland, Cal.

PALMER, TRUMAN GARRETT, statistician; b. West Walworth, N.Y., Mar. 27, 1858; s. Nathaniel L. and Margaret Lavinia (De Nise) P.; ed. pub. and high schs., Rochester, N.Y.; m. Virginia Elizabeth Lincoln, June 13, 1884. Western mgr. for a number of yrs. of Frank Leslie's Illustrated Weekly, New York Daily Graphic, and other eastern illustrated papers; became interested in Calif. land operations and began study of agrl. economics, especially in its relation to culture of sugar beets; exec. sec. Am. Beet Sugar Assn., U.S. Beet Sugar Industry, U.S. Sugar Mfrs.' Assn., 1902—. Republican. Methodist. Author: Sugar at a Glance; Beet Sugar Industry of the U.S.; Concerning Sugar; Sugar Beet Seed; Production of Sugar from Beet Roots. Home: Washington, D.C. Died May 29, 1925.

PALMER, WALTER WALKER, physician, educator; b. Southfield, Mass., Feb. 27, 1882; s. Henry Wellington and Almira Roxana (Walker) P.; B.S., Amherst, 1905, Sc.D., 1922; M.D., Harvard, 1910; Sc. D., Columbia, 1929; m. Francesca Gilder, Oct. 12, 1922; children—Helena Francesca Gilder, Gilder, Walter de Kay. H. P. Walcott fellow in medicine and instr. in physiol. chemistry Harvard, 1913, asst. in medicine, also resident physician Mass. Gen. Hosp., 1913-15; asst. in medicine Rockefeller Inst., N.Y.C., 1915-17; asso. prof. medicine Columbia, 1917-19, also acting dir. med. service Presbyn. Hosp.; asso. prof. medicine Johns Hopkins Med. Sch., 1919-21, also asso. vis. physician Johns Hopkins Hosp.; Bard prof. medicine Columbia, 1921-47; cons. Presbyn. Hosp., 1947—; dir. Pub. Health Research Inst. of N.Y., 1947—. Commd. 1st lt. Med. R.C., U.S. Army, 1917-19, maj., 1926-31. Mem. Nat. Bd. of Med. Examiners, 1921-43. Mem. A.M.A. (council pharmacy and chemistry), Soc. for Clin. Investigation, Assn. Am. Physicians, N.Y. Acad. Medicine, Harvey Society of N.Y.C. (pres. 1926-27), Theta Delta Chi, Phi Beta Kappa, Alpha Omega Alpha. Republican. Club: Century Assn. Specializes in research work in metabolic fields—diabetes, nephritis, etc. Contbr. to profl. jours. Home: 24 Gramercy Park. Address: Foot of E. 15th St., N.Y.C. 9. Died Oct. 28, 1950; buried Tyringham, Mass.

PALMER, WILLIAM BEACH, civil engr.; b. Bridgeport, Conn., Sept. 22, 1854; s. Theophilus Middlebrook and Comfort Anna (Middlebrook) P.; Ph.B., Sheffield Scientific Sch. (Yale), 1876; m. Sarah Louise Clark, of Bridgeport, Jan. 12, 1909. In archtl. work, 1876-78; asst. engr. with B. H. Hull, Bridgeport, 1878-80; div. engr. Lehigh & Hudson River R.R., 1880-84; prin. asst. engr. Cincinnati, Van Wert & Michigan R.R., Citizens Water Co., Bridgeport, and other water cos. in Conn., since 1884; location engr. Conn. Western R.R., N.Y., Bridgeport & Eastern R.R., Shore Line Electric R.R.; acted as chief engr. Fitchburg R.R. resurvey, Winsted Water Power Improvement Co., Housatonic Power Co., at Zoar Bridge, Rockingham Park & Track (Salem, N.H.); civ. engring. and surveying work on various projects since 1900; chief engr. W. B. Palmer Engring. Co. since 1930; lay-out and town planning of "Rivercliffe," Devon, Conn., and "Middlebury Shores" and "Long-Lake-Park," Middlebury, Conn.; survey and engring. of New U.S. Post Office Bldg., Bridgeport. Mem. Conn. Soc. of C.E. (exec. com. 1891-1896, past pres.). Republican. Episcopalian. Clubs: Bridgeport, University. Home: 953 Broad St., Stratford, Conn. Office: Court Exchange Bldg., Bridgeport, Conn.

PAMMEL, LOUIS HERMANN, botanist; b. La Crosse, Wis., Apr. 19, 1862; s. Louis and Sophie (Freise) P.; B.Agr., U. of Wis., 1885, M.S., 1889; Ph.D., Washington U., 1898; D.Sc., U. of Wis., 1925; m. Augusta Emmel, June 29, 1888; children—Edna Caroline (Mrs. R. A. Needham), Harriet Mathilda (Mrs. J. L. Seal), Doris Marie, Lois Hermina (Mrs. L. L. Blundell), Violet Emmeline, Harold Emmel. Pvt. sec. Dr. W. G. Farlow, of Harvard, 1885-86; asst. to Dr. Trelease, Shaw Sch. of Botany, St. Louis, 1886-89; spl. work U.S. Dept. Agr., and Div. Forestry, 1889; prof. botany, Ia. State Coll. Agr. and Mechanic Arts, 1889—, and botanist of the Expt. Station. Pres. Ia. Acad. Sciences, 1893 and 1923, Ia. Park and Forestry Assn., 1905-07. V.p. Sect. G, A.A.A.S., 1919. Author: Weeds of the Farm and Garden, 1910; Manual of Poisonous Plants, 1910. Home: Ames, Ia. Deceased.

PANCOAST, JOSEPH, anatomist, surgeon; b. nr. Burlington, N.J., Nov. 23, 1805; s. John and Ann (Abbott) P.; M.D., U. Pa., 1828; m. Rebecca Abbott, June 2, 1829, 1 son, William Henry. Conducted Phila. Sch. Anatomy, 1831-38; elected physician to Phila. Hosp., 1835; vis. surgeon, 1838-45; prof. surgery Jefferson Med. Coll., 1838, prof. anatomy, 1841-74; mem. staff Pa. Hosp., 1854-64; prin. achievements in surgery include operation for remediation of exstrophy of bladder by plastic abdominal flaps, for soft and mixed cataracts, for correction of occlusion of nasal duct; originated an abdominal tourniquet; mem. Am. Philos. Soc., Phila. County Med. Soc., Med. Soc. Pa. Author: Treatise on Operative Surgery, 1st edit., 1844, 3d edit., 1852. Died Phila., Mar. 7, 1882.

PANCOAST, SETH, physician, cabalist; b. Darby, Pa., July 28, 1823; s. Stephen and Anna (Stroud) P.; M.D., U. Pa., 1852; m. Sarah Osborn; m. 2d, Susan Osborn; m. 3d, Carrie Fernald; some children. Prof. anatomy Female Med. Coll. Pa., 1853; prof. anatomy Pa. Med. Coll., 1854-59, prof. emeritus, 1859; built what was probably largest library dealing with occult scis. ever assembled in U.S. Author: Ladies Medical Guide, 1858; Boyhold's Perils, 1860; The Kabbala; or the True Science of Light; an Introduction to the Philosophy and Theosophy of the Ancient Sages (1st book written in English to explain the "Ten Sepheroth," and gave mystical interpretation of Holy Scriptures as contained therein), 1877; Blue and Red Light. . ., 1877; Bright's Disease, 1882. Died Phila., Dec. 16, 1889.

PANETH, F.A., scientist; b. Vienna, Austria, Aug. 31, 1887; s. Dr. Joseph and Sophie (Schwab) P.; student U. Munich, U. Glasgow; Ph.D., U. Vienna, 1910; m. Else Hartmann, Dec. 6, 1913; children—Eva, Heinrich Rudolph. Asst., Inst. for Radium Research, Vienna, 1912-18; prof. Prague Inst. Tech., 1918, Hamburg U., 1919-22, U. Berlin, 1922-29; George Fisher Baker lectr. Cornell U., 1926-27; prof., dir. chem. labs. U. Koenigsberg, 1929-33; guest Imperial Coll. of Sci. and Tech., London, 1933-38; reader in atomic chemistry U. London, 1938; prof. chemistry Durham U., 1939-53; head chemistry div. Joint British-Canadian Atomic Energy Team, Montreal, 1943-45; dir. Max Planck Inst. for Chemistry, 1953—. Pres. Joint Commn. on Radioactivity, Internat. Council of Sci. Unions, 1949-55. Fellow Royal Soc. London; mem. Am. Acad. Arts and Scis. (hon.), Soc. Austrian Chemists (hon.), Austrian Acad. Scis. (corr.). Author: Radioelements as Indicators and Other Selected Topics in Inorganic Chemistry, 1928; Manual of Radioactivity (with G. Hevesy), 1938; The Origin of Meteorites, 1940; also articles in field. Home: Brentanostrasse 13, Wiesbaden, Germany. Office: Max-Planck-Institut für Chemie, Mainz/Rhein, Germany. Died Sept. 17, 1958; buried Vienna, Austria.

PANNILL, CHARLES JACKSON, (pan' nil), radio electronic cons.; b. Petersburg, Va., May 13, 1879; s. Capt. Thomas and Virginia Knox (Walthall) P.; m. Ethel M. Worrell, Dec. 10, 1910. Asso. with Prof. Reginald A. Fessenden, Old Point Comfort, Va., and elsewhere, in research and dev. wireless communication, 1902-07; transmitted pioneer wireless message across Atlantic Ocean, received at Machrehanish Bay (Scotland) Fessenden Wireless sta., 1906; sent and received pioneer wireless messages between Fessenden Wireless stas., Washington-Collinswood, N.J., and Jersey City, 1904; v.p., gen. mgr. pioneer wireless ship-shore communication co., Massie Wireless Telegraph Co., Providence, 1907-09; supt. So. Div., United Wireless Telegraph Co., Balt., 1909-12, Marconi Wireless Telegraph Co. of Am., 1912-14; v.p. Liberty Electric Co., Portchester, New York, 1919; organized Independent Wireless Telegraph Co., 1919; elected v.p., gen. mgr., dir., pres., 1927; merged radio div. RCA with Ind. Wireless Tel. Co. radio services, forming Radiomarine Corp. of Am., 1928, became v.p., gen. mgr., dir., 1928, exec. v.p., 1931, pres., 1935, also elected pres., dir. RCA Insts., Inc., 1932, retired from both corps., 1947; RCA cons. until 1950. Chmn. bd. editors RCA Rev., 1938-46; mem. Adv. com. RCA Lab., Princeton, 1941-45; mem. RCA President's Adv. Com. 1945-47; member RCA Internat. Committee, 1945-46; chmn. radiomarine adv. com. RCA Pension Bd., 1943-46. U.S. del. to internat. confs. on radio and telecommunications, Washington, 1927, Madrid, 1932, The Hague, 1937, Cairo, 1938, Atlantic City, N.J., 1947. Vice pres. Comité Internat. Radio-Maritime, Brussels, Belgium, 1928-39. Dir. bd. mgrs. Seamen's House, 1939-42. Served with U.S.N., 1898-1902, Spanish-Am. War; became expert radio aide Arlington Wireless Sta., 1914, later asst. to dir. naval communications Navy Dept., Washington. Recipient letter of commendation from sec. of navy for outstanding services to Navy, 1918, gold medal Vets. Wireless Operators Assn., 1942, for achievements during World War II. Decorated Chevalier Order King Leopold of Belgium, 1937. Fellow Inst. Radio Engrs. (hon. life mem. with fellowship); life mem. Vets. Wireless Operators Assn., Navy League of U.S.; mem. Soc. Naval Architects and Marine Engrs., Maritime Exchange of N.Y., Radio Pioneers Club (awarded scroll for outstanding pioneer work from 1902). Republican. Episcopalian. Gov. Propeller Club of U.S. (Port of N.Y.), 1943-55, mem. Pres's. adv. com., 1945-49, chmn. ways and means com., 1947-49. Clubs: Cosmos (Washington); Rockefeller Luncheon, Whitehall, India House (N.Y.C.); Lake Placid; Sleepy Hollow Country. Author: U.S. Naval Commercial Traffic Regulations, 1915. Received certificate of skill from U.S. Govt., 1911, No. 1 comml. wireless operators government license, 1912. Radiomarine Corp. received, during World War II, Army-Navy "E" with 4 gold stars, Victory Fleet Flag and Maritime "M" with four gold stars; RCA Inst. received letter of commendation from sec. of navy for training of naval personnel (under his direction). Home: Lawrence Park W., Bronxville, N.Y. Office: 30 Rockefeller Plaza, N.Y.C. 20. Died Feb. 7, 1955; buried Norfolk, Va.

PAPANICOLAOU, GEORGE NICHOLAS, (pä-päne'kä-lau), scientist; b. Comi (Euboea), Greece, May 13, 1883; s. Nicholas and Mary (Critsutas) P.; M.D., U. Athens, 1904; Ph.D., U. Munich, 1910; hon. degrees U. Athens, U. Turin, Hahnemann Med. Coll. Phila.; m. Mary Mavroyeni, Sept. 15, 1910. Came to U.S., 1913, naturalized 1927. Physiologist in expdn. organized by Prince of Monaco, 1911; with dept. pathology, New York Hosp., 1913; successively instr., asst. prof., asso. prof. anatomy, prof. clinical anatomy, Cornell Univ. Medical Coll., 1924—, now emeritus, director Papanicolaou Research Laboratory, also consultant to Papanicolaou Cytology Lab. of Cornell; research on problems relating to sex, reproduction, endocrine glands, sex hormones; now conducting research chiefly on early diagnosis of cancer through recovery and identification of exfoliated cancer cells; consultant to the Kate Depew Strang Cancer Prevention Clinic; permanent hon. cons. Soc. Pelvic Surgs.; hon. cons. St. Luke's Hosp.; mem. med. adv. bd. Medico, Inc., mem. N.Y.C. Dept Health Cancer Adv. Com.; med. advisor N.Y. State Selective Service. Served as 2nd lieutenant, Medical Corps, Greek Army during Balkan War, 1912-13. Decorated Cross of Grand Comdr. of Royal Order of Phoenix (Greece); Royal Order of George The First (Greece). Received Borden Award, Assn. Am. Medical Colleges, 1948 Amory Award Am. Assn. Arts and Scis., 1948; Lasker award, American Pub. Health Assn., 1950; Honor Award, Am. Cancer Soc., 1952; Modern Medicine Award, 1954; Bertner Award, 1955; Clement Cleveland award 1960. Fellow Am. Gynecological Soc. (hon.), Am. Assn. Obstetricians and Gynecologists (hon.), Internat. Coll. Surgeons (hon.), Coll. Am. Pathologists (hon.), Am. Coll. Clin. Pathologists (hon.), mem. Am. Association of Anatomists, Am. Assn. of Cancer Research, N.Y. Acad. of Medicine, Soc. for Exptl. Biology and Medicine, A.A.A.S., Assn. for Study of Internal Secretions, Gerontological Society, New York Academy Sciences, Harvey Soc., Inter-Society Cytology Council (past pres.), Am. Academy of Athens (corr.). Member Greek Orthodox Ch. Author: The Sexual Cycle in Human Females as Revealed by Vaginal Smears, 1933; Diagnosis of Uterine Cancer by the Vaginal Smear, 1943; Epithelial of Woman's Reproductive Organs, 1948; Atlas of Exfoliative Cytology, 1954. Author over 100 articles, 2 monographs published in Am. Journal Anatomy and by Commonwealth Fund. Home: 617 E. De Lido Dr., Di Lido Island, Miami Beach, Fla. Died Feb. 19, 1962; buried Clinton, N.J.

PAQUET, ANTHONY C., engraver; b. Hamburg, Germany, 1814. Came to Am., 1848; worked in Phila., 1850-55, N.Y.C., 1856-58; asst. engraver U.S. Mint, Phila., 1857-64; engraved 1st Congressional Medal of Honor; exhibited medals at Pa. Acad. during Civil War. Died Phila., 1882.

PAQUETTE, CHARLES ALFRED, civil engr.; b. Detroit, Mich., Apr. 2, 1872; s. Gervais Paquette de la Vallee and Josephine (L'Etourneau) P.; B.S., U. of Notre Dame, Ind., 1890, C.E., 1891, Litt.B., 1891, M.S., 1896; m. Bertha Mathias, of Elkhart, Ind., Oct. 9, 1894; 1 son, Charles Alfred. Joined engr. corps L.S. & M.S. Ry., 1891; with C.,C.,C. & St.L. Ry. since 1892, as engr. maintenance of way, 1894-99, supt. 1899-1906, asst. chief engr., 1906-12, chief engr. maintenance of way, 1912-15, chief engr., Mar. 1915-Apr. 1, 1924; was also chief engr. Cincinnati Northern R.R., and Evansville, Indianapolis & Terre Haute Ry.; formerly pres. White Construction Co.; pres. Paquette Engring. Corpn.; dir. M.E. White Co. Mem. Am. Soc. Civil Engrs., Am. Ry. Engring. Assn., Western Soc. of Civil Engrs. Republican. Catholic. Home: White Pigeon, Mich. Office: 35 E. Wacker Drive, Chicago IL*

PARDEE, HAROLD ENSIGN BENNETT, physician; b. N.Y. City, Dec. 11, 1886; s. Ensign Bennett and Clara (Burton) P.; A.B., Columbia, 1906; M.D., Coll. Physicians and Surgeons (Columbia), 1909; m. Dorothy Dwight Porter, Apr. 15, 1918; children—Althea, Hobart Porter, Pamela. Interne, New York Hosp., 1909-11; in practice in N.Y. City, specializing on diseases of heart and circulation, since 1911; instr. in physiology, Coll. Physicians and Surgeons, 1912-15; instr. in clin. medicine, Cornell U. Med. Sch., 1916-22, asso. in medicine, 1923-27, asso. prof. clin. medicine since 1927; asso. attending physician New York Hospital; attending phys. (cardiac diseases) Polyclinic Hosp.; cons. physician for cardiac disease, Woman's Hosp., M.E. Hosp., N.Y. City. Served as 1st lt. Med. Corps, U.S. Army, July 1917-Jan. 1918; capt. Jan. 1918-Apr. 1919. Mem. A.M.A., Am. Soc. Clin. Investigation, Assn. Am. Physicians, Am. Heart Assn., N.Y. State Med. Soc., New York County Med. Soc. Republican. Conglist. Clubs: Rockaway Hunting (Lawrence, L.I.); Union Club (N.Y. City). Author: Clinical Aspects of the Electrocardiogram, 1924, 4th edit., 1941; What You Should Know About Heart Disease, 1928. Chmn. com. which wrote Criteria for Diagnosis of Heart Disease, 1928, 4th edit., 1939. Many articles on diagnosis and treatment of heart disease in various medical journals. Home: New York City NY Died Feb. 28, 1972.

PARDUE, LOUIS A(RTHUR), physicist; b. Scottsville, Ky., July 21, 1900; s. William Francis and Lucy Ann (Dunn) P.; A.B., U. of Ky., 1925, M.S., 1927; Ph.D., Yale, 1931; m. Mary Allie Marshall, Sept. 3, 1927; children—Mary Lou, William Marshall. Instr. physics U. of Ky., 1926-27; prof. physics and mathematics Lincoln Memorial U., summer 1927; instr. physics Lehigh U., 1927-28, Yale, 1928-31; asst. prof. U. of Ky., 1931-35, asso. prof., 1935-43, prof., 1943-50, dean Grad. Sch., 1948-50; v.p., dir. grad. studies Va. Poly. Inst. since 1950; research in nuclear physics Cal. Inst. Tech., 1938-39. With Manhattan project U. Chgo. and Oak Ridge, Tenn., 1943-45; v.p. Oak Ridge Inst. Nuclear Studies, 1959—. Mem. Conf. Deans So. Grad. Schs. (pres. 1959-60), Am. Assn. Land Grant Colls. and State Universities, American Physical Society, Am. Assn. Physics Tchrs., Am. Assn. U. Profs., Phi Kappa Phi, Phi Beta Kappa, Sigma Xi, Pi Mu Epsilon, Sigma Pi Sigma, Omicron Delta Kappa. Mem. Disciples of Christ. Rotarian (dist. gov. 1957-58). Home: 1005 Airport Rd., Blacksburg, Va. Died Apr. 26, 1963.

PARET, THOMAS DUNKIN, inventor; b. New York, Dec. 20, 1837; ed. there and, 1860-65, at Univ. of Edinburgh, Scotland; devoted attention to chem. and mech. expts.; invented process for treating waste leather so as to fit it for lining petroleum barrels, fire-proof safes, etc., and, under name of "tanite," for use as substitute for jet and ebonite for various purposes, and as a base for solid emery wheels. Pres. Tanite Co., mfrs. emery wheels. Brother of Bishop William Paret. Address: Stroudsburg, Pa.

PARIS, AUGUSTE JEAN, JR., engr., inventor; b. N.Y.C., Jan. 31, 1874; s. Auguste Jean and Anne (Mercer) P. de Bourgogne; ed. under pvt. tutors; hon. Sc.D., St. John's Coll., Annapolis, 1921; m. Gertrude Eugenie van Ness deMore, 1900. Began as research chem. engr., at Bradford, Pa., 1900; has served as dir. and consulting engr. of many chem. and mfg. cos.; inventor of many processes, covered by patents. Upon entry of U.S. into the World War, offered his entire pvt. income and his services to War Dept., also the use of his inventions for the period of the war, to U.S., Great Britain, France and Italy; associated with brother, Capt. W. Francklyn Paris, in erection of plant at Charleston, W.Va., without govt. subsidy; work carried on under general direction of Nat. Advisory Com. for Aeronautics; assigned to War Dept. free use of invention relating to gaoline engines, contributed to govt. his services as research chem. engr. developing new methods of operating internal combustion engines; now operating research laboratories at Bradford and Charleston, mainly on processes relating to petroleum and chem. industries. Appt. by gov. of W.Va. del. to Yorktown (Va.) Sesquicentennial Expn., 1931. Mem. Soc. Am. Mil. Engrs.; hon. mem. Federation Ancien Combatants (French War Veterans), France. Office French Acad., 1930. Club: University (Washington). Home: Bradford, Pa. Died Mar. 1955.

PARK, CHARLES FRANCIS, prof. mechanism; b. Boston, Mass., Apr. 11, 1869; s. William Robert and Ann E. (Eldredge) P.; B.S. in Mech. Engring., Mass. Inst. Tech., 1892; m. Maud W. White, Oct. 31, 1894. Instr. mechanism, 1894-1900, asst. prof., 1900-06, asso. prof., 1906-12, prof., 1912-35, prof. emeritus since 1935, Mass. Inst. Tech., also dir. mechanical laboratories. Planned and organized, 1903, now emeritus; dir. Lowell Inst. Sch., Massachusetts Inst. Tech. Fellow Am. Acad. Arts and Sciences, A.A.A.S.; mem. Am. Assn. Univ. Prof., Am. Soc. Mech. Engrs., Soc. Promotion Engring. Edn., Alpha Tau Omega. Lt. col. Ord. O.R.C. Republican. Club: Harvard Segregansett Country (Taunton). Home: 21 Propsect St., Taunton, Mass. Died Sep. 26, 1944.

PARK, EDWARDS ALBERT, pediatrician; b. Gloversville, N.Y., Dec. 30, 1877; s. William Edwards and Sara Billings (Edwards) P.; grad. Phillips Acad., Andover, Mass., 1896; A.B., Yale, 1900, hon. A.M., 1922; M.D., Coll. Physicians and Surgeons (Columbia), N.Y. City, 1905; hon. D.Sc., U. of Rochester, 1936; m. Agnes Bevan, Aug. 2, 1913; children—Sara Bevan, Charles Rawlinson, David Chapman. Interne, Roosevelt Hosp., N.Y. City, 1906-08, New York Foundling Hosp., 1908-09; Proudfit fellow in medicine and instr. in medicine, Coll. Physicians and Surgeons, 1909-12; instr. in pediatrics, Johns Hopkins, 1912-15, asso. prof., 1915-21; Sterling prof. pediatrics, Yale Sch. Medicine, 1921-27; prof. pediatrics, Johns Hopkins Sch. of Medicine and pediatrician Johns Hopkins Hosp., 1927-46; prof. pediatrics emeritus, Johns Hopkins School of Medicine, since 1946. Editor Excerpta Medica, Revue Francaise de Pediatrie. Jahrbuch fur Kinderheilkunde. Major Am. Red Cross, World War. Mem. Assn. of Am. Physicians, Am. Pediatric Soc., Acad. of Pediatrics, Soc. Clin. Investigation, A.A.A.S., Am. Soc. Exptl. Pathology, Soc. Exptl. Biology and Medicine, Interurban Clin. Club, Brit. Pediatric Assn., Alpha Delta Phi. Decorated Order of Leopold (Belgium), 1919; Reconnaissance Francaise (France), 1919. Contbr. on rickets, deformities of the skull, physiology of the thymus gland. Home: Birdwood, Garrison, Md. Office: Johns Hopkins Hosp., Baltimore 5, MD

PARK, JAMES, iron and steel mfr.; b. Pitts., Jan. 11, 1820; s. James and Margaret (McCurdy) P.; m. Sarah Gray, 7 children. Partner (with brother David E.) firm Park, Brother & Co., 1840, became James Park, Jr. and Co., 1843; founded Lake Superior Copper Works for manufacture of sheathing copper, 1857, had partial control his whole life; encouraged introduction new indsl. processes; instrumental in increasing tariff schedule which entrenched steel in position of special privilege; established Black Diamond Steel Works, 1862; incorporated (with others) Kelly Pneumatic Process Co., 1863, made 1st steel in U.S. by complete Bessemer process, 1864; 1st to introduce Siemens gas furnace into U.S. for metal conversion (1st Siemens furnace completed by Park, McCurdy & Co., 1863); v.p. Am. Iron and Steel Assn., 1873-83; had great influence in securing final result as embodied in tariff bill approved 1883. Died Allegheny, Pa., Apr. 21, 1883.

PARK, WILLIAM HALLOCK, M.D.; b. New York, Dec. 30, 1863; s. Rufus and Harriet (Hallock) P.; A.B., Coll. City of New York, 1883; M.D., Coll. Phys. and Surg. (Columbia), 1886; U. of Vienna, 1 yr., 1889-90; LL.D., Queen's U., 1910; D.Sc., New York U., 1926, Yale U., 1929, Columbia U., 1929; unmarried. Prof. bacteriology and hygiene, Univ. and Bellevue Hosp. Med. Coll. (New York U.), 1897-1937, and dir. New York Health Dept. Bur. of Labs., 1894-1937 (emeritus); consulting bacteriologist, State Dept. of Health, 1914—, and med. examiner in bacteriology, 1917—; cons. bacteriologist, U.S. Quarantine Service, 1921—. Pres. Am. Public Health Assn., 1923. Author: Pathogenic Microörganisms, 10th edit., 1933; Public Health and Hygiene, 2d edit., 1927; Who's Who Among the Microbes, 1929. Home: New York, N.Y. Died Apr. 6, 1939.

PARKE, JOHN GRUBB, engineer-soldier; b. Chester Co., Pa., Sept. 22, 1827; grad. West Point, 1849; assigned to topographical engrs.; engaged in boundary surveys for Govt. until 1861. Promoted capt. topographical engrs., Sept. 9, 1861; apptd. brig. gen. vols., Nov. 23, 1861; served in Burnside's expedition to N.C.; bvtd. lt. col. U.S. army; promoted maj. gen. vols.; chief of staff under Burnside; reached bvt. rank maj. gen., U.S. army; commd. maj. engrs., June 17, 1864; lt. col., Mar. 4, 1879; col., Mar. 7, 1884; retired, 1889; supt. Mil. Acad., West Point, 1887-89. Author: Explorations and Surveys for a Railroad Route from the Mississippi River to the Pacific Ocean. Died 1900.

PARKER, EDWARD WHEELER, statistician; b. Pt. Deposit, Md., June 16, 1860; s. William Price and Henrietta Hyde (Donnell) P.; ed. schs. there and at Baltimore, and in City Coll., Baltimore; m. Laura Harrison Bryan, of Galveston, Tex., Apr. 29, 1891. Apptd. statistician U.S. Geol. Survey, 1891; in charge Div. of Mineral Resources, 1907-15, dir. Anthracite Bur. of Information, Phila., 1915-37. Expert special agent 12th U.S. Census; mem. Anthracite Coal Strike Commn., 1902. Mem. Am. Inst. Mining and Metall. Engrs., Washington Acad. Sciences, Geol. Soc. Washington, Washington Soc. Engrs., Coal Mining Inst. America, Acad. Polit. Science. Clubs: Cosmos (Washington); Engineers (New York); Westmoreland (Wilkes-Barre); Engineers (Phila.). Author: Annual Reports of Production of Coal in United States; Production of Coke in United States, and other chapters in annual vols. U.S. Geol. Survey; also reports on coal mining, coke mfr. and petroleum refining for U.S. Census. Home: 136 W. Upsla St., Mount Airy, Philadelphia, Pa.

PARKER, GEORGE HOWARD, zoölogist; b. Phila., Dec. 23, 1864; s. George Washington and Martha (Taylor) P.; S.B., Harvard, 1887, S.D., 1891, Colby Coll., 1935; spl. student at univs. Leipzig, Berlin, Freiburg, 1891-93; m. Louise Merritt Stabler, June 15, 1894. Asst. and instr. zoölogy Harvard, 1888-91, Parker fellow in Europe, 1891-93, instr., 1893-99, asst. prof., 1899-1906, prof. zoölogy, 1906-35, prof. emeritus since 1935. William B. Clark lectr. Amherst Coll., 1914; sent by U.S. Govt. to investigate Pribilof seal herd, 1914. Exchange prof. to western colleges, 1921. Awarded Elliot medal Nat. Acad. Sciences, 1937, Lewis prize, Am. Philos. Soc., 1941. Fellow A.A.A.S. (v.p. 1916), Am. Acad. Arts and Sciences (pres. 1933); mem. Nat. Acad. Sciences, Am. Philos. Soc., Washington Acad. Sciences, Boston Soc. Natural History, Am. Zoöl. Soc. (pres. 1903), Mass. Med. Soc., Am. Soc. Naturalists (pres. 1929), Am. Physiol. Soc., Assn. Am. Anatomists, Soc. Exptl. Biology and Medicine, Ecol. Soc. America, Marine Biol. Lab., Soc. Vert. Paleontology, Phi Beta Kappa, Sigma Xi (nat. pres. 1934-35); hon. mem. Am. Otol. Soc., Cal. Acad. Sciences, Cambridge Philos. Soc., Buffalo Soc. Natural History; corr. mem. London Zoöl. Soc., Acad. Natural Sciences Phila., N.Y. Acad. Sciences, Soc. Biol. (Paris), Peking Soc. Nat. History; asso. mem. Soc. Belge de Biol.; foreign mem. Linnaean Soc., London. Club: Harvard (Boston). Author: Biology and Social Problems, 1914; The Elementary Nervous System, 1919; Smell, Taste and Allied Senses, 1922; The Evolution of Man (co-author), 1922; What Evolution Is, 1925; Creation by Evolution (co-author), 1928; Human Biology and Racial Welfare (co-author), 1930; Humoral Agents in Nervous Activity, 1932; The Problem of Mental Disorder (co-author), 1934; Color Changes in Animals in Relation to Nervous Activity, 1936; The World Expands, 1946; Animal Colour Changes and Their Neurohumours, 1948. Contbr. articles to zoöl. journals, dealing chiefly with anatomy and physiology of nervous organs and animal reactions. Home: 16 Berkeley St., Cambridge 38, Mass. Died Mar. 26, 1955.

PARKER, GLENN LANE, hydraulic engr.; b. Butte, Mont.; s. Claude F. and Margaret (Lane) P.; B.S., C.E. University of Kansas, 1906; post-grad. work, 1908; m. Grace I. Guy, December 16, 1914; Chainman and topographer Western Pacific R.R., Calif., 1904-05; concrete insp., instrument man. and asst. div. engr. C.B.&Q. R.R., Lincoln, Neb., 1906-07; deck officer, U.S. Coast and Geodetic Survey, Washington, 1908; jr. engr., U.S. Geol. Survey, Washington, D.C., Nome and Fairbanks, Alaska, 1909-11; jr. and asst. engr., U.S. Geol. Survey, Portland, Ore., 1911-13, dist. engr. Tacoma, Wash., 1913-39, chief hydraulic engr., Washington, since 1939. Mem. Am. Soc. Civil Engrs. (past dir.), Am. Geophysical Union, Washington Acad. of Science, A.A.A.S., Washington Irrigation Inst. (life), Tau Beta Pi, Phi Kappa Psi. Republican. Presbyn. Club: Cosmos (Washington, D.C.). Joint author: Placer Mining in the Yukon-Tanana Region, Alaska, 1911; Water Powers of the Cascade Range, parts 2-3-4, 1913-15-22; Surface Water Supply of Seward Peninsula, Alaska, 1913; Summary of Hydrometric Data in Washington, 1923; Summary of Records of Surface Waters of Washington, 1940. Home: 2706 44th St. N.W. Address: U.S. Geol. Survey, 2223 Federal Works Bldg., Washington. Died Feb. 12, 1946; buried in Rock Creek Cemetery, Washington.

PARKER, HERSCHEL CLIFFORD, consulting and mining engr.; b. Brooklyn, N.Y., July 9, 1867; s. Herschel and Hannah (Walker) P.; Ph.B., Columbia Sch. of Mines, 1890; m. Evelyn Naegele, May 20, 1911; children—Evelyn, Cynthia. Adj. prof., 1903, and prof. physics until 1911, Columbia. Exploration and first ascents in Canadian "Alps," 1897, 99, 1903; first ascents, Mts. Goodsir and Dawson, Hungabee, Deltaform, Biddle, Lefroy (Alberta); exploration of the Mt. McKinley region, Alaska, 1906, 10, 12; 1st ascent highest peak Mt. McKinley, 1912; Mt. Olympus, Wash., 1907. Fellow American Geographical Soc., A.A.A.S., and of the Royal Society (London); mem. Am. Inst. Mining and Metall. Engrs., Am. Physical Soc., Nat. Inst. Social Science, Appalachian Mountain Club, Am. Alpine Club, Explorers' Club, Arctic Club, Canadian Alpine Club, English Alpine, Camp Fire Club America, Arctic Brotherhood Alaska, Sigma Xi. Clubs: Salmagundi (New York); Crescent Athletic (Brooklyn). Author: A Systematic Treatise on Electrical Measurements, 1897; also various scientific and mountaineering articles. One of the discoverers of helion; inventor of the helioscope and motor torpedo. Home: Hotel Chapman, 5th and Wall Sts., Los Angeles, Calif.

PARKER, HILON ADELBERT, engineer; b. Plessis, N.Y., Dec. 30, 1841; s. Alpheus and Lucinda P., of Revolutionary stock; acad. edn.; m. Mary E. Cunningham, May 25, 1871 (dec.); 2d, Grace Rowley,

Nov. 1894. Served pvt. to 1st lt., 1861-65; fought at Cold Harbor, Petersburg, Shenandoah Valley, Richmond, etc. Entered ry. service, 1866; held various positions, 1866-85; v.p. and chief engr. Chicago, Kansas & Neb. Ry., 1885-89, also gen. mgr., 1888; asst. to the pres. C.R.I.&P. Ry., 1889-90, and 1893-98, 3d v.p. 1890-93, 2d v.p. 1898-99, 1st v.p. and gen. mgr. Mar. 1899-Apr. 1903; resigned; cons. engr. Grand Trunk Pacific Ry., 1909. Home: Chicago, Ill. Died 1911.

PARKER, HORATIO NEWTON, bacteriologist; b. Cambridge, Mass., Feb. 3, 1871; s. Horatio G. and Harriet (Newton) P.; student Mass. Inst. Tech., 1890-95; m. Margaret L. Irwin (A.B., U. of Kan.), Feb. 25, 1922; children—Jeannette Harriet, Horatio Newton, Margaret Irwin. Asst. biologist Boston Water Works, 1896-99; asst. and chief biologist, Metropolitan Water Works, 1900-01; health officer, Montclair, N.J., 1901-04; asst. hydrographer and asst. engr. U.S. Geol. Survey, 1904-10; dairy bacteriologist, U. of Ill., and asst. at Expt. Sta., 1910-17; lecturer on municipal sanitation, Ind. U., 1917; bacteriologist and program editor Delineator 7th baby campaign, 1917-18; city bacteriologist and chemist, Jacksonville, Fla., 1918-45; dir. food and lab. div., Health Dept., 1923-45. Fellow American Pub. Health Assn., A.A.A.S., Fla. Acad. Sciences; mem. Soc. Am. Bacteriologists, Am. Chem. Soc., Am. Dairy Science Assn., Internat. Assn. Milk Sanitarians (pres. 1932-33), Association Food and Drug Officials of U. S., Association Food and Drug Officials of S.E. States (pres. 1924), New England Water Works Assn., Fla. Pub. Health Assn. (pres. 1931-32), etc. Episcopalian. Mason (K.T.). Clubs: Torch, Civitan (pres. 1939-40). Author: City Milk Supply, 1917; also many repts. and tech. articles. Home: 3603 Hedrick St., Jacksonville 5. Office: Engineer Bldg., Jacksonville, Fla. Died Dec. 22, 1946.

PARKER, JAMES, printer, journalist; b. Woodbridge, N.J., circa 1714; s. Samuel and Janet (Ford) P.; m. Mary Ballareau; children—Samuel Franklin, Jane. In printing business (with Benjamin Franklin as silent partner), N.Y.C., 1742-48; financial auditor Franklin & Hall of Phila.; public printer of N.Y., 1743-circa 1760; founder, publisher N.Y. Weekly Post-Boy), (later called N.Y. Gazette or Weekly Post-Boy), 1743-73; librarian Library of Corp. of City of N.Y., 1746; established (with John Holt as mgr. and silent partner) Conn. Gazette, New Haven, 1755; comptroller, sec. gen. of post offices of Brit. Colonies, 1756; judge Ct. of Common Pleas, Middlesex County, N.J., 1764; compiled and printed Conductor Generalis (designated duties and powers of justices), 1764; public printer N.J.; printer to Yale; set up 1st permanent printing office of N.J. at Woodbridge, issued Constl. Courant (1st newspaper in N.J.), 1765; published periodicals including Independent Reflector (1752-53), Occasional Reverberator (Sept. Oct. 1753), John Englishman (Apr.-July 1755), Instructor (1755), New Am. Mag. (1758-60). Died Burlington, N.J., July 2, 1770; buried Woodbridge.

PARKER, JAMES W., cons. engr.; b. Auburn, New York, Nov. 28, 1886; s. Charles A. and Sara (Cole) P.; M.E., Cornell U., 1908; M.S. in mech. engring. (hon.), Detroit Inst. Tech., 1935; E.D., Stevens Inst. Tech., 1942, Poly. Inst. Bklyn., 1948, Rensalaer Poly. Inst., 1950; LL.D., Wayne U., 1953; Dr. Engring., U. Mich., 1953; m. Dorothy Dow, 1913; children—Ann Cole (Mrs. R. E. Valk), Alan Breck; m. 2d, Verna Elmslie Dow, 1948; 1 stepson, Paul H. Dow. Plant operating engr. DeKalb (Ill.) Power & Light Co., 1908-09; chief plant engr. Vincennes (Ind.) Street Ry. Co., 1909; boiler room engr. The Detroit Edison Co., 1910-13, chief asst. engr. of power plants, 1913-14, supt. central heating, 1914-17, assistant to v.p., 1917-35, chief engr., 1924-43, v.p. and chief engr., 1935-42, v.p. and gen. mgr. 1943-44; pres., dir., gen. mgr., 1944-51, cons., dir., 1952; dir. Air Preheater Corp. of N.Y., Liberty Life & Accident Insurance Company, Standard Accident Ins. Co., Mfrs. National Bank, Detroit Edison Co. President, trustee Rackham Engring. Found.; past pres. Assn. Edison Illuminating Cos., The Engring. Soc. of Detroit, Am. Soc. M.E.; mem. Tau Beta Pi, Sigma Xi. Clubs: Detroit, Detroit Athletic, Detroit Prismatic, University of Ann Arbor; Engineers (N.Y.C.). Address: 1125 Country Club Rd., Ann Arbor, Mich. Died Dec. 30, 1957; buried Moravia, N.Y.

PARKER, LOVELL HALLET, tax consultant; b. Osterville, Mass., Dec. 13, 1882; s. Charles Francis and Emma (Mathews) P.; student Tabor Acad., Marion, Mass., 1899-1901; B.S., Mass. Inst. Tech., 1905; LL.B., Nat. U., Washington, 1931; m. Mary Frances Murphy, Aug. 11, 1909; children—Margaret Frances (Mrs. Armistead Williams Gilliam), Helen Matthews (dec.), Marion Elizabeth (Mrs. W. C. H. Needham), Jean (Mrs. Paul N. Gardner). Assistant engring. corps, Pa. R.R., lines west of Pittsburgh, 1905-06; asst. engr. Pa. R.R. tunnels, N.Y. City, 1906-08; asst. engr. state engr's. office, Albany, N.Y., 1908-09; dep. div. engr. highway dept., N.Y. state, 1909-12; contractor on pub. works, 1912-17; constrn. engr. Camp Upton, L.I., N.Y., 1917-18; material engr. Hog Island, Pa., 1918-19; field supervisor, head of inventory and appraisal sect. U.S. Shipping Bd., 1919-23; practicing appraisal engr., 1923; chief engr. for U.S. Senate com. investigating Bur. of Internal Revenue, 1924-26; chief of staff of joint Congressional Com. on Internal Revenue Taxation, 1926-38; tax consultant since 1938. Clubs: Burning Tree Golf, Montgomery County, Md. Author or co-author of various govt. reports on taxes. Died Jan. 17, 1961.

PARKER, MOSES GREELEY, physician; b. Dracut, Mass., Oct. 12, 1842; s. Theodore and Hannah (Greeley) P.; desc. through father from Deacon Thomas P., and through mother from Andrew Greeley; prep. edn. Phillips Acad., Andover, Mass., to 18; studied, L.I. Coll. Hosp. Med. Sch., Brooklyn; M.D., Harvard Med. Sch., 1864; U. of Vienna, 1873-74, Paris, 1874-75; unmarried. Asst. surgeon 2d U.S.C. Cav., 1864-65; located in Lowell, Mass., 1866; specializes as oculist and aurist; phys. to St. John's Hosp., Lowell, 30 yrs., Lowell Gen. Hosp. (trustee, 1898—), Dispensary and Ministry at Large, 10 yrs. Dir. and mem. exec. com. since orgn., 1883, N.E. Telephone and Telegraph Co. (also interested in Bell Telephone Co. since its orgn.). Pres. Ayer Home, Lowell Day Nursery Assn.; trustee Howe Sch., Billerica, Mass., 1877—. Del. Nat. Arbitration and Peace Congress, New York, 1907. Republican. Unitarian. Mem. various med. societies. Mason. Has made a spl. study of electricity and was the first to photograph the elec. current and show that it takes the form of spirals. Home: Lowell, Mass. Died Oct. 1, 1917.

PARKER, RALPH ROBINSON, pub. health entomologist; b. Malden, Mass., Feb. 23, 1888; s. Frank Howard and Marion Ellen (King) P.; B.S., Massachusetts State Coll., 1912, M.Sc., 1914, Ph.D., 1915, LL.D., 1943; D.Sc., Montana St. U., 1937; married Adah L. Nicolet, 1916 (died 1931); children—Jane Louise, Robert Adams; m. 2d, Vivan Kaa, June 22, 1932. Asst. entomologist Mont. State Bd. of Entomology, 1915-21; spl. expert, U.S. Pub. Health Service, 1921-47, dir. since 1947; dir. Rocky Mountain Lab., U.S. Pub. Health Service, Hamilton, Mont., since 1928. Pres. Internat. Northwestern Conf. on Diseases of Nature Communicable to Man, 1947-48. Mem. Alpha Sigma Phi, Phi Kappa Phi, Phi Sigma. Author of over 100 papers on Rocky Mountain spotted fever and other diseases. Home: Hamilton, Mont. Died Sep. 4, 1949.

PARKER, THEODORE BISSELL, civil engr.; b. Roxbury, Mass., Aug. 20, 1889; s. Franklin Wells and Sarah (Bissell) P.; B.S. in C.E., Mass. Inst. Tech., 1911, grad. study, 1912; grad. U.S. Army Engr. Sch., 1922, U.S. Command and Gen. Staff Sch., 1933; m. Estelle Peabody, May 10, 1913; children—Franklin Peabody, Nancy. Asst. instr. in civil engring., Mass. Inst. Tech., 1911-12; engr. with H. C. Keith, N.Y. City, 1912; engr. Utah Power & Light Co., Salt Lake City, 1912-17; with Elec. Bond & Share Co., N.Y. City, 1919-20; engr. with Stone & Webster, Inc., 1922-33; state engr. and acting state dir. Pub. Works Adminstrn. for Mass., 1933-35; chief constrn. engr. Tenn. Valley Authority, 1935-38, chief engr., 1938-43; prof. civil engring., Mass. Inst. Tech. and head dept. civil and sanitary engring. since 1943. Served as 1st lt. and capt. U.S. Army Engrs., 1917-19; capt. Corps of Engrs., 1920-22. Mem: American Soc. Civil Engrs., Soc. Am. Mil. Engrs., Boston Soc. Civil Engrs., Sigma Chi. Home: 115 Woodlawn Av., Wellesley Hills, Mass. Office: Mass. Institute of Technology, Cambridge, Mass. Died Apr. 27, 1944.

PARKER, WILLARD, surgeon, educator; b. Lyndeborough, N.H., Sept. 2, 1800; s. Jonathan and Hannah (Clark) P.; A.B., Harvard, 1826, M.D., 1830; M.D., Berkshire Med. Instn.; LL.D. (hon.), Princeton, 1870; m. Caroline Stirling, June 21, 1831; m. 2d, Mary Bissell, May 25, 1844; 5 children. Prof. anatomy and surgery Clin. Sch. Medicine, Woodstock, Vt., 1830-33; prof. surgery Berkshire Med. Instn., 1833-36; prof. anatomy, Geneva, N.Y., 1834-36; prof. surgery, Cincinnati, 1836-37; prof. principles and practice of surgery Coll. of Physicians and Surgeons, N.Y.C., 1839-70, emeritus prof. surgery, 1870; performed cystotomy for irritable bladder, 1850; tied subclavian artery for aneurism on 5 occasions, 1864; 1st American to operate successfully on abscessed appendix; pres. N.Y. Acad. Medicine, 1856; Willard Parker Hosp. (N.Y.C.) named in his honor. Author (med. monograms) Cystotomy, 1850; spontaneous Fractures, 1852; Concussion of Nerves, 1856; Ligature of the Subclavian Artery, 1864; Cancer, 1873. Died N.Y.C., Apr. 25, 1884.

PARKER, WILLIAM EDWARD, civil engr.; b. Newton, Mass., Mar. 21, 1876; s. William Chipman and Emily A. (Goodwin) P.; B.S. in C.E., Mass. Inst. of Tech., 1899; m. Annie Marie Knowles, June 5, 1905; 1 dau., Emily Louise. With Boston & Albany R.R., 1899; asst. engr. Newport News (Va.) Shipbuilding & Dry Dock Co., 1900-01; successively aid, asst. hydrographic and geodetic engr., U.S. Coast and Geodetic Survey, since 1901; transferred to Naval R.F., Sept. 24, 1917, with rank of lt. comdr. for duration of war; in charge compass office, Naval Obs., to Mar. 1919; chief of div. of hydrography and topography, U.S. Coast and Geod. Survey, 1919-31; retired from active duty with relative rank of capt., U.S.N., Nov. 1934. Mem. Am. Soc. C.E., Am. Geophys. Union, Washington Acad. Sciences, Assn. Mil. Engrs., Am. Legion. Club: Federal (Washington). Home: Fort Lauderdale, Fla. Died Sept. 30, 1942.

PARKHURST, FREDERIC AUGUSTUS, organizing engr.; b. Woburn, Mass., Aug. 11, 1877; s. George Ezekiel and Sarah Frances (Turner) P.; ed. Woburn High Sch., by pvt. study and 2 yrs.' course of lectures on advanced steam engring., Mass. Inst. Tech.; m. Abby Joanna Glidden, Feb. 3, 1904; children—Anna Glidden, Walter Glidden. Began as spl. apprentice, Vaughn Machine Co., Peabody, Mass., 1895, advancing to asst. supt., organization work, same place, 1902; with Portland Co. 2 yrs., associated with Harrington Emerson as chief of staff; gen. mgr. Pacific Iron Works, Bridgeport, Conn., 1905-07; organizing engr. with Ferracute Machine Co., Bridgeton, N.J., 1907-12; organizing engr. Aluminum Castings Co. plants in Detroit, Cleveland, Buffalo, etc., 1912-18; became organizing engr., New York, since 1919; cons. expert in orgn. management and process development; with tank sect., Ordnance Dept., 1918. Republican. Conglist. Author: Applied Methods of Scientific Management, 1912; Scientific Management in the Foundry, 1914; The Predetermination of True Costs and Relatively True Selling Prices, 1916; Symbols, 1917; Lectures, The Science of Management, 1917; also booklets, lectures and articles in mags., etc. Home: Russell Av., Suffield, Conn. Office: Suffield CT

PARKHURST, JOHN ADELBERT, astronomer; b. Dixon, Ill., Sept. 24, 1861; s. Sanford Britton and Clarissa (Hubbard) P.; A.B., Wheaton (Ill.) Coll., 1897; S.B., Rose Poly. Inst., Terre Haute, Ind., 1886, S.M., 1897; m. Anna Greenleaf, Nov. 21, 1888. With pvt. astron. obs., Marengo, Ill., 1892-97; with Yerkes Obs., 1898—, successively as vol. research asst., asst. Carnegie investigator in stellar photometry, instr., asst. prof. and as asso. prof. astronomy, 1919—. Conglist. Author: Spectra of Stars of Secchi's Fourth Type (with Hale and Ellerman), 1903, Researches in Stellar Photometry, 1906. Home: Williams Bay, Wis. Died Mar. 1, 1925.

PARKINS, ALMON ERNEST, geographer; b. Marysville, Mich., Jan. 10, 1879; s. John H. and Mariah (Cooley) P.; B.Pd., Mich. State Normal Coll., Ypsilanti, 1906, A.B., 1911, hon. M.Edn., 1922; B.S., U. of Chicago, 1912, Ph.D., 1914; m. Eleanor Grace Stone, June 29, 1905. Instr. agrl. geology and geography, U. of Mo., 1914-16; prof. geography, George Peabody Coll., 1916—. Field rep. division of cotton, Agrl. Adjustment Administration, 1935. Distinguished service award, Nat. Council of Geography Teachers, 1934. Unitarian. Mason. Author: Historical Geography of Detroit; Development of Transportation in Pennsylvania; The South, Its Economic-Geographic Development, 1937; author of the department of "Junior High School Geography" in the Class Room Teacher. Co-author: McMurry and Parkins Geographies, 1921; Maddox and Parkins, Forestry and Forest Industries; Miller and Parkins, Geography of North America. Co-editor and co-author: Our Natural Resources and Their Conservation, 1937. Editor: Annals of Assn. Am. Geographies; of series of sch. and coll. maps. Mem. publn. bd. Peabody Jour. of Edn.; chmn. com. 1933 Yearbook, Nat. Soc. Study of Edn. Home: Nashville, Tenn. Died Jan. 3, 1940.

PARKS, FRANK THOMAS, civil engr., utility exec.; b. Smith Center, Kan., May 18, 1890; s. James B. and Fannie O. (Glen) P.; B.S. in Civil Engring., Kan. State Coll., 1910, C.E., 1930; m. Minnie L. Forceman, Sept. 6, 1911; children—Preston, Pauline (Mrs. Richard H. Cooper). High sch. coach, tchr., Albia, Ia., 1911; head engring. dept., coach Ark. State Coll., 1912-13; engr. U.S. Reclamation Dept., 1914-16; oil and gas engrs. Cities Service Co., 1916-20, mgr. various natural gas cos., 1920-28; in charge change-over from manufactured to natural gas, City of Denver, 1928; in charge natural gas operations Pub. Service Co. of Colo., Denver, since 1928, v.p. since 1943, dir. since 1947; v.p., dir. Western Slope Gas Co.; dir. Natural Gas Producers, Inc., Colo. Interstate Gas Co., Colo. Oil & Gas Corp. Mem. Am., Pacific Coast, Rocky Mountain gas assns., Rocky Mountain Oil and Gas Assn., C. of C. Clubs: Wigwam (Deckers, Colo.); Broadmoor (Colorado Springs); Rotary, Cherry Hills Country, Athletic, Petroleum (Denver). Home: 25 Ivy St., Denver 80220. Office: Pub. Service Co. of Colo., Denver. Died Oct. 22, 1959.

PARKS, HENRY MARTIN, cons. geologist; b. Peoria, Ill., Nov. 29, 1872; s. Steen B. and Amanda (Yates) P.; B.S. in M.E., Ia. State Coll., 1902, E.M., 1909; studied Colo. Sch. of Mines 1 yr.; m. Alice Merritt, Dec. 31, 1903; children—Ruth Gwendolyn, Merritt Yates. Instr., mining engring. dept., Ia. State Coll., 1903-04; mining in Butte, Mont., Cripple Creek, Colo., and Tonopah, Nev., 1904-08; asst. prof. mining and metallurgy, Northwestern U., 1906-07; prof. mining engring., 1907-12, dean Ore. State Sch. of Mines, 1912-17; dir. Ore. Bur. of Mines and Geology, 1912-23; geologist and mining engr., 1923—; pres., mgr. Fort Rock Development Co. Capt., engr. O.R.C., 1917. Mem. Am. Inst. Mining Engrs., Am. Mining Congress, Am. Assn. State Geologists, Ore. Acad. Sci. Republican. Presbyn. Home: Fort Rock, Ore. Office: Spalding Bldg., Portland, Ore. Died Feb. 26, 1945.

PARKS, JOHN LOUIS, univ. dean, physician; b. Muskogee, Okla., Jan. 4, 1908; s. John S. and Della N. (Northcutt) P.; B.A., U. Wis., 1930, M.S., 1932, M.D., 1934, tng. obstetrics, gynecology, 1935-37; m. Mary Dean Scott, Aug. 31, 1930; 1 son, John Scott. Intern U. Cin., 1934-35; instr. U. Cin., 1934-35; instr. pathology

U. Wis., 1937-38; chief med. officer obstetrics and gynecology Gallinger Municipal Hosp., 1938-44; prof. obstetrics and gynecology George Washington University, from 1944, dean Sch. Medicine, 1957-67, dean University Medical Center, from 1967, v.p. for med. affairs, 1972; medical dir. hosp., 1957-65; cons. D.C. Gen. Hosp., Walter Reed Med. Center, Nat. Insts. Health. Exec. com. Gorgas Meml. Inst. Trustee Greater Washington Ednl. TV, Inc. Decorated Eloy Alfaro Fundacion Internacional (Panama). Diplomate Am. Bd. Obstetrics, Gynecology (past dir.). Fellow A.C.S. (bd. govs. 1956-59). Royal College of Obstetricians and Gynaecologists; hon. fellow Bklyn. Gynecol. Soc., Central, S. Atlantic assns. obstetricians and gynecologists, S.W., Fla., Wash., Miami, Panama obstet. and gynecol. soc., Obstet. Soc. Phila., Soc. Obstetricians and Gynaecologists Can., La Societa Triventa di Ostetricia e Ginecologia; mem. American College of Obstetrics and Gynecology (v.p. 1957), Assn. Am. Med. Colls. (pres. 1967-68, mem. exec. council), Nat. Bd. Med. Examiners (exec. com., pres.), Interstate Postgrad. Med. Association (president 1966), Med. Soc. D.C., Washington Gynecol. Soc., Smith-Reed-Russell Soc., Am. Gyneocology Soc. (treas. 1955-59, pres. elect 1972-73), American Assn. Obstetrics and Gynecology (pres. 1961), So. Medical Association, Am. Medical Assn., Sigma Xi, Osler Soc., Alpha Omega Alpha, Nu Sigma Nu, Alpha Delta Phi. Contbr. med. jours. Home: Annapolis MD Died July 5, 1972.

PARMELE, HARRIS BARNUM, (par'mel-e), chemist; b. Rockford, Ill., Oct. 18, 1901; s. Arthur Gilbert and Blanche (Barnum) P.; B.S., U. Wis., 1923, M.S., 1924, Ph.D., 1927; m. Louise Turner, June 22, 1929; children—Sallie Virginia, Harris Barnum. Asst. biochemistry research U. Wis., 1923-27; bacteriologist Gen. Labs., Madison, Wis., 1928-29; dir. research P. Lorillard Co., 1929—, co. dir., 1950—, now vice president and director of research. Member of the American Chem. Society, A.A.A.S., Sigma Xi, Phi Lambda Upsilon, Alpha Zeta. Home: 120 Stonehouse Rd., Glen Ridge, N.J. Office: 200 E. 42d St., N.Y.C. Died Sept. 27, 1965.

PARMELEE, CULLEN WARNER, prof. ceramic engring.; b. Bklyn., June 27, 1874; s. Lauren Sylvester Everett and Mary Alida (Payne) P.; B.Sc., Rutgers Coll., New Brunswick, N.J., 1896, M.Sc., 1926, D.Sc., 1936; m. Julia Russell Davis, Oct. 3, 1901; children—Cullen Everett, Eleanor Paulding, Theodore Davis, Mary Payne (dec.). Chemist N.Y. & Boston Dyewood Co., 1896-1901; instr., asso. prof. chemistry, Rutgers Coll., 1901-08, organizer, dir. dept. ceramics; prof. ceramic engring., U. of Ill., 1916-42, head of dept., 1923-42, emeritus. Life mem. Am. Ceramic Soc. (pres. 1914-15; dean fellows, 1934-35). Fellow Soc. Glass Technology (Eng.), Mem. British Ceramic Soc., Deutsche Keramische Gesellschaft (hon.), Keramos, Inst. of Ceramic Engrs., Beta Theta Pi, Phi Beta Kappa, Sigma Xi, Gamma Pi Upsilon, Alpha Chi Sigma, Phi Kappa Phi. Episcopalian. Author: Clays and Some Other Ceramic Materials; Essentials of Glaze Composition. Home: 802 W. Florida St., Urbana, Ill. Died Aug. 1947.

PARMENTER, GEORGE FREEMAN, chemist; b. Dover, Mass., Mar. 26, 1877; s. Freeman Artemus and Lucy (Goulding) P.; B.Sc., Mass. State Agrl. Coll., Boston U., 1900; M.A. and Ph.D., Brown, 1903; D.Sc., Colby Coll., 1916; m. Martha Elizabeth Ellis, Nov. 26, 1903 (dec. July 17, 1938); 1 son, Ellis Freeman; m. 2d, Lillian Esther Evans, Apr. 2, 1942. Instr. chemistry Mass. State Coll., 1900; asst. chemist R.I. Exptl. Sta., 1901; instr. chemistry Brown U., 1901-03; asso. prof. chemistry Colby Coll., 1903-04, prof., head of dept., 1904-47; emeritus prof., 1947—. Fellow A.A.A.S.; mem. Am. Chem. Soc., Phi Sigma Kappa, Sigma Xi. Republican. Baptist. Author: Laboratory Experiments for Colby College. Home: No. 7 Sheldon Pl., Waterville, Me. Died Oct. 22, 1955; buried Pine Grove Cemetery, Waterville.

PARMENTIER, ANDREW, horticulturist, landscape gardener; b. Enghien, Belgium, July 3, 1780; s. Andre Joseph P.; m. Sylvia Marie Parmentier, before 1814, 5 children including Adele Bayer. Came to Am., 1824; purchased 24 acre triangular tract of land to establish bot. gardens and nursery, Bklyn., 1825, enclosed area with high stone wall, collected fgn. and domestic plants; introduced black beech tree, several species vegetables, shrubs and vines to U.S.; contbd. to New Eng. Farmer and N.Y. Farmer; earliest profl. landscape gardener in U.S., laid out grounds and gardens for clients from Can. to the Carolinas. Died Nov. 26, 1830.

PARMLEY, WALTER CAMP, civil engr.; b. Rock Co., Wis., Dec. 8, 1862; s. Russell and Lucy Esther (Dean) P.; B.Met. Engring., U. of Wis., 1887, M.S., 1893; m. Rose Webster, Mar. 13, 1889; children—Marjorie (Mrs. Wm. Lentz), Florence (Mrs. Roy W. Chesnut). Mem. Parmley & Finkle, engrs., San Bernardino, Calif., 1887-89; engr. on Bear River Canal, Ogden City Water Works, and city engr., Ogden, 1889-93; asst. city engr., Peoria, Ill., 1893-96, also pvt. practice; engr. spl. sanitation, Cleveland, O., 1896-1903; cons. practice, N.Y. City, 1904—; has specialized in reinforced concrete constrn. for sewers and pipe lines; inventor of reinforced concrete designs widely in use. Pres. Essex County Mosquito Extermination Commn. Republican. Congregationalist. Home: Upper Montclair, N.J. Died Feb. 19, 1934.

PARPART, ARTHUR KEMBLE, educator; b. Bklyn., Dec. 28, 1903; s. Edward George and Grace Kemble (Dear) P.; B.A., Amherst Coll., 1925, M.A., 1927; Ph.D., U. Pa., 1931; m. Ethel Roberta Bennett, Aug. 29, 1925; children—Joan Corlette (Mrs. Raymond C. Zoeter), Arthur Kemble. Instr., Amherst (Mass.) Coll., 1925-28, U. Pa., 1928-31, Princeton, 1931-33, asst. prof., 1933-40, asso. prof., 1940-48, prof., chmn. dept. biology since 1948; chmn. panel on cellular physiology of com. on growth NRC since 1947; mem. adv. council biology Brookhaven Nat. Lab. since 1951. Trustee, mem. exec. com. Marine Biol. Lab., 1946-52, v.p., 1952-63, pres., 1963—; mem. panel NIH, 1954. Mem. Am. Zool. Soc., Am. Physiol. Soc., Am. Soc. Naturalists, N.Y. Acad. Scis., Soc. Gen. Physiologists (pres. 1954). Author sci. articles in profl. jours. Editor: The Chemistry and Physiology of Growth, 1949. Mng. editor Jour. Cellular and Comparative Physiology, 1955—; asso. editor Am. Scientist, 1955—. Home: 23 S. Stanworth Dr., Princeton, N.J. 08540. Died Sept. 17, 1965; buried Ch. of Messiah, Woods Hole, Mass.

PARR, HARRY L., engr.; b. Yonkers, N.Y., Mar. 20, 1880; s. Benjamin and Susie (Lillienthal) P.; A.B., Columbia, 1902, M.E., 1904; m. Clare Van Dyke Lambert, Apr. 4, 1908. Asst., mech. engring., Columbia, 1905-06; in engring. dept. Power Specialty Co., N.Y. City, 1906-07; instr. mech. engring., Columbia U., 1907-12, asst. prof., 1912-21, asso. prof., 1921-28, prof., 1928-41, Stevens prof., 1941-46, Stevens prof. emeritus since 1946; consultant mechanical engineer since 1907. Served as lieutenant, U.S.N.R.F., during World War I. Fellow A.A.A.S.; mem. A.S.M.E. Club: University (N.Y.C.). Contbr. technical handbooks, also articles to tech. mags. Died 1964.

PARR, SAMUEL WILSON, univ. prof.; b. Granville, Ill., Jan. 21, 1857; s. James and Elizabeth Fidelia (Moore) P.; B.S., U. of Ill., 1884; M.S., Cornell U., 1885; studied U. of Berlin, 1900, Polytechnikum, Zürich, 1901; hon. Sc.D., Lehigh U., 1925, Illinois Coll., Jacksonville, Ill., 1929; m. Lucie A. Hall, Dec. 27, 1887; children—Elisabeth, Harold Lucien. Instr. gen. science, 1885-86, prof., 1886-91, Ill. Coll; prof. applied chemistry, U. of Ill., Jan. 1891—; dir. 1904-05, Ill. State Water Survey; consulting chemist on coal investigation, Ill. State Geol. Survey, 1905—. Devised the Parr calorimeter for determining the heat value of coal and other hydrocarbons, widely used in America and Europe; also a new type of calorimeter for determining and recording the heat value of combustible gases; alloys with acid resisting properties, and a new calorimeter bomb with effective platinum substitution in its construction. Author: The Chemical Examination of Water, Fuel, Flue-gases and Lubricants. Wrote reports on Composition and Analysis of Ill. Coals, also bulls. of U. of Ill. Engring. Expt. Sta., Ill. Geol. Survey, etc. Awarded Chandler medal, 1926. Home: Urbana, Ill. Died May 16, 1931.

PARRAN, THOMAS, physician, found. exec.; b. St. Leonard, Md., Sept. 28, 1892; s. Benjamin and Mary (Latimer) P.; A.B., St. John's Coll., 1911, A.M., 1915; M.D., Georgetown U., 1915; LL.D., St. Johns Coll., Syracuse U., St. Bonaventure Coll., Toronto U., U., Cal.; Sc.D., Georgetown U., Duquesne U., Colgate U., Columbia, Wesleyan U., Tufts Coll., U. Md., Rutgers U., U. Utah, Marietta Coll., Washington and Jefferson Coll., Marquette U., Duke, U. Pa., N.Y. U.; Dr.P.H., N.Y. U.; Pharm. D., Phila. Coll. Pharmacy and Sci.; Doctor of Science, U., Pitts.; m. Angela Bentley Vandoren, June 26, 1918 (dec.); children—Thomas, Benjamin, Theodore Vandoren, Richard Bentley; m. 2d, Buda Carroll Keller, Aug. 30, 1930 (dec.). Commd. officer, USPHS, 1917; surgeon gen., 1936-48; dean grad. sch. pub. health U. Pitts., 1948-58; pres. Avalon Found., N.Y.C., 1958-61, trustee, 1955—; cons. Avalon Found. and Pan-Am. Health Orgn., 1961—; med. mission to Liberia, 1962. Mem. N.Y. State Regents Com. on Medical Edn., 1961—; health commr., New York State, 1930-36; U.S. rep.; Interim Commr., W.H.O., dir. council, Pan-Am. San. Bur., 1938-49; fellowship, Soc. Med. Officers of Health (Eng.). Mem. adv. bd. Point Four Program, 1950. Recipient Leon Bernard award, WHO, 1958. Life mem. Am. Pub. Health Assn. (treas., 1931-32, chmn. exec. com., 1932-35, pres., 1936), life mem. Assn. Mil. Surgeons of U.S. (pres. 1938-39). Hon. fellow Royal San Inst., Royal Inst. of Pub. Health and Hygiene (Eng.); fellow, Royal Coll. Medicine, Am. Med. Assn., N.Y. Acad. Medicine, Washington Acad. Medicine, A.C.S., Nat. Vitamin Found. (pres. 1960), A.C.P. (bd. govs.); Am. Neisserian Med. Soc. (pres. 1936), Assn. Am. Phys., Nat. Tuberculosis Assn. (v.p., 1937). Author: Shadow on the Land, 1937; Plain Words About Venereal Diseases, 1941. Awarded Mendel medal, Villanova, Coll.; Sedgwick medal, Am. Public Health Assn.; Wm. Freeman Snow award, Am. Social Hygiene Assn.; Doctor Eduardo Liceaga Medal of Mexico; Kober (Georgetown U.) Lectureship; Grand Officer Order of Carlos Finlay of Cuba, Order of Aesculapius (Med. Soc. Colombia), Comdr. Order Public Health of France; U.S. Typhus Commn. Medal; A.P.H.A. Lasker Award, 1947; D.S.M., U.S. Army, 1948; Cutter Lectureship, Harvard, 1954. Home: 631 St. James St., Pitts. 32. Died Feb. 1968.

PARRETT, ARTHUR N., chemist; b. Marshalltown, Ia., July 7, 1896; s. Arthur N. and Margaret (Trotter) P.; B.S., Chem.E., U. Minn., 1922; Ph.D., U. Pittsburgh, 1924; m. Doreen Aldwell, Apr. 4, 1940. Research chemist E. I. duPont de Nemours & Co., 1925-30; asst. dir. chem. research A. O. Smith Corp., 1930-32; chem. dir. Rayonier, Inc. since 1932, v.p. since 1952. Mem. Am. Chem. Soc., Am. Inst. Chem. Engring., Tau Beta Pi, Alpha Chi Sigma, Phi Lambda Upsilon. Club: Rainier (Seattle). Holds U.S. and fgn. patents relating to cellulose mfg. and use. Home: 45 E. 62d St., N.Y.C. 21. Office: 122 E. 42d St., N.Y.C. 17. Died Dec. 27, 1956.

PARRISH, ISAAC, physician, reformer; b. Phila., Mar. 19, 1811; s. Isaac Parrish; grad. U. Pa., 1832; m. Sarah Redwood Longstreth, 1834. Practiced medicine, Phila.; surgeon Wills Hosp., Phila., 1834-52, gave 1st instrn. in opthalmic surgery, 1839; mem. Phila. Soc. for Relieving Miseries of Prisons; toured prisons of Md., R.I., N.Y., 1846-47, advocated equal treatment for all prisoners, regardless of race. Died July 31, 1852.

PARRISH, JOSEPH, physician; b. Phila., Sept. 2, 1779; s. Isaac and Sarah (Mitchell) P.; M.D., U. Pa., 1805; m. Susanna Cox, Oct. 20, 1808, 11 children including Isaac, Joseph, Edward. Resident physician to emergency hosp. established by Bd. Health during yellow fever epidemic, Phila., 1805; gave course of popular lectures on chemistry, 1808; mem. staff, mgr. Phila. Dispensary, physician Phila. Almshouse, 1807-11, mem. surg. staff, 1811-21; mem. staff Pa. Hosp., 1816-29; pres. bd. mgrs. Wills Eye Hosp., 1833-40; v.p. Coll. Physicians of Phila., Phila. Med. Soc.; in charge of cholera hosp. during epidemic, Phila., 1832; pres. Pa. Abolition Soc. Author: Practical Observations on Strangulated Hernia, and Some of the Diseases of the Urinary Organs, 1836. Died Phila., Mar. 18, 1840.

PARRISH, KARL CALVIN, mining engr.; b. Leon, Ia., Dec. 12, 1877; s. Robert Leal and Himena (Hoffman) P.; Parsons Coll., Fairfield. Ia.; M.E., Colo. Sch. of Mines, 1901; m. Blanche Emmons, Nov. 5, 1908; children—Karl Calvin, Jane Emmons. Assayer, Blue Grass Mining Co., Nederland, Colo., 1901; mining expert for Western Venture Co., examining properties in N.M., Ariz. and Calif., 1903-04; supt. Andes Mining Co., Guamoco, Colombia, S.A., 1904-09; prospecting for mines in Colombia, 1909-10; discovered and located Chicago and Las Ramas group of mines in Guamoco Dist., Colombia, and general mgr. same; in charge Bar Principal Mining Co., Guamoco, 1913-19; consulting engr., Barranquilla, Colombia; mgr. Parrish & Co., Compañia Urbanizadora de "El Prado," Parrish Investment Co., Compañia Minera de los Valles, Barranquilla, 1919—, Cia. Minera del Nare; built residential addition to Barranquilla and modern water works system; also various municipal elec. power plants in Colombia; with others, building railroad over Andes Mountains, to cost approximately $10,000,000; etc. Home: Des Moines, Ia. Died Nov. 3, 1933.

PARROTT, PERCIVAL JOHN, entomologist; b. Croydon, Eng., May 28, 1874; s. Joseph and Emma (Belgrove) P.; brought to America, 1882; A.B., Kan. State U., 1897, A.M., 1898; D.Sc., Kansas State College, 1943; m. Florence Mildred Hubbard, Sept. 5, 1906; children—Florence Margaret, John Percival. Asst. entomologist Kan. State Agrl. Coll., 1898-99. N.Y. Agrl. Expt. Sta., 1900-02; entomologist Ohio Agrl. Exptl. Sta., 1902-04; entomologist N.Y. Agr. Exptl. Sta., 1904—, dir. 1938-42. Entomologist Kansas Agrl. Soc., 1898-99, Western N.Y. Hort. Soc., 1904—. Mem. exec. com. Div. of Biology and Agr., NRC, 1920-21. Fellow A.A.A.S., Entomol. Soc. America; pres. Am. Assn. Econ. Entomologists, 1913-14 (v.p. 1909-10); mem. Sigma Xi, Phi Beta Kappa. Republican. Presbyn. Mason. Contbr. articles on injurious insects, and systematic studies on Coccidae and Eriophyidae. Address: 386 Castle St., Geneva, N.Y. Died Aug. 10, 1953; buried Geneva, N.Y.

PARROTT, ROBERT PARKER, ordnance inventor, manufacturer; b. Lee, N.H., Oct. 5, 1804; s. John Fabyan and Hannah (Parker) P.; grad. U.S. Mil. Acad., 1824; m. Mary Kemble, 1839, 1 adopted son. Asst. prof. natural and experimental philosophy U.S. Mil. Acad., 1824-29; commd. 1st lt., 1831; promoted capt. of ordnance, 1836, went to Washington (D.C.) as asst. to bur. of ordnance; resigned from army to become supt. West Point Foundry, Cold Spring, N.Y., 1836, became lessee of foundry, 1839, directed bus. until 1877; bought 7,000 acre tract of land, built Greenwood Iron Furnace (ran with his brother), 1839-77; patented design for strengthening cast-iron cannon with a wrought-iron hoop shrunken on the breech, also an improved expanding projectile for rifled ordnance, 1861; received large orders for guns and projectiles in Civil War; began (with brother) 1st comml. prodn. of slag wool in U.S., 1875; 1st judge Ct. of Common Pleas for Putnam County, N.Y., 1844-47. Died Cold Spring, Dec. 24, 1877.

PARRY, CHARLES CHRISTOPHER, botanist; b. Admington, Eng., Aug. 28, 1823; s. Joseph and Eliza (Elliott) P.; A.B., Union Coll., 1842; M.D., Columbia Coll., 1846; m. Sarah M. Dalzell, 1853; m. 2d, Emily R. Preston, 1859. Came to U.S., 1832; botanist under David Dale Owen in geol. survey of Wis., Ia. and Minn.,

1848; apptd. botanist to U.S. and Mexican boundary survey, 1849; author intro. "Botany of the Boundary" for Report on the U.S. and Mexican Boundary Survey, 2 vols. in 3, 1857-59; botanical explorer of western states and territories, 1850-79; 1st botanist in U.S. Dept. Agr.; organized plant collections brought back by govt. scientists and surveying expdns. at Smithsonian Instn., 1869-71; discoverer Picea Engeimannii spruce, new species Cal. manzanitas, lilium Parryi of So. Cal. mountains, lote bush of Colorado Desert, Ensenada Buckeye, many others; 1st investigator of these groups to study living plants in the field in connection with specimens in herbarium. Died Davenport, Ia., Feb. 20, 1890.

PARRY, JOHN STUBBS, physician; b. Drumore Twp., Pa., Jan. 4, 1843; s. Seneca and Priscilla P. M.D., U. Pa., 1865; m. Rachel Sharpless, Apr. 5, 1866. Apptd. dist. physician to Phila. Dispensary; became vis. obstetrician to Phila. Hosp., 1867, reorganized obstet., gynecol. depts.; physician for diseases peculiar to women Phila. Presbyn. Hosp., 1872; a founder State Hosp. for Women and Infants, 1872; mem. council Phila. Coll. Physicians; pres. Phila. Obstet. Soc.; v.p. Path. Soc. of Phila. Author: Extra-Uterine Pregnancy, 1876; contbr. 28 articles to med. jours., primarily on obstetrics and children's diseases; wrote on rachitis (proved prevalence of this "disease" in Phila.), 1870. Died Jacksonville, Fla., Mar. 11, 1876.

PARSHLEY, HOWARD MADISON, (pärsh'le), prof. zoölogy; b. Hallowell, Me., Aug. 7, 1884; s. John Howard and Julia Maria (Tuck) P.; student Boston Latin Sch., 1901-05; A.B., Harvard, 1909, A.M., 1910, Sc.D., 1917; student N.E. Conservatory of Music, 1906-09; m. Nancy Fredricson, June 28, 1910; children—Thomas Fredricson, Elsa Madison. Instr. zoölogy, U. of Me., 1911-14; research in zoölogy, Bussey Inst. (Harvard), 1914-17; asst. prof. zoölogy Smith Coll., Northampton, Mass., 1917-19, asso. prof., 1919-25, prof., 1925-52, emeritus since 1952; teacher summers Biol. Lab., Cold Springs Harbor, N.Y., and U. of Chicago. Mem. A.A.A.S., American Society Zoölogists, Entomological Society of America, Genetics Soc. of Am., Am. Soc. Naturalists, Sigma Xi. Author: Bibliography of North American Hemiptera Heteroptera, 1925; Science and Good Behavior, 1928; Science of Human Reproduction, 1933; Survey of Biology, 1940. Translator The Second Sex (Simone de Beauvoir's), Life and Habits of the Mammals (F. Bourliere's), 1953. Contbr. to books and jours. Home: 250 Elm St., Northampton, Mass. Died May 19, 1953.

PARSONS, ARTHUR BARRETTE, mining engr.; b. Salt Lake City, Utah, Nov. 22, 1887; s. Arthur Huntington and Katherine Maybanks (Barrette) P.; B.S. in Mining Engring., Utah Sch. of Mines, 1909; hon. Dr. Engring., S.D. State Sch. of Mines; m. Mary Snell, July 31, 1915; children—Richard, Arthur B. Assayer and mining engr. in Nev., 1910; supt. Candor (N.C.) Mines, 1911-15; constrn. engr., Utah, 1916; smelter foreman, Burma Mines, Ltd., India, 1917-18; mining engr. with Butte & Superior Mining Co., Butte, Mont., 1918-19; asso. editor, Mining and Scientific Press, San Francisco, 1919-22; asst. editor, Engineering and Mining Journal, New York, 1922-26, asso. editor, 1926-29; pres. Mineral Research Corp., 1929-30; asst. sec. Am. Inst. Mining and Metall. Engrs., 1930-31, sec., 1931-49; editor Mining and Metallurgy, Mining Technology, Petroleum Technology, Metals Technology; sec. Engrs. Council Professional Development and Engineers Defense Board; engr. Def. Minerals Adminstn., 1950; dir. program development div. Def. Materials Procurement Agy., 1951-52. Consultant on tariff, taxation to various fed. agys., domestic corps. Registered profl. engineer, N.Y. State. Mem. Soc. Engring. Edn., Mining and Metall. Soc. America, Am. Inst. Mining and Metall. Engrs., Inst. of Mining and Metallurgy (London); A.A.A.S., Acad. Polit. Sci., Tau Beta Pi, Beta Theta Pi. Episcopalian. Mason. Clubs: Engineers, Commonwealth (San Francisco); Engineers, Mining (N.Y.C.); Cosmos (Washington). Author 125 spl. articles on tech., econ. and polit. phases of the mineral industries. Author: The Porphyry Coppers, 1933; Taxation of Mining Enterprise, 1950; The Porphyry Coppers in 1956, published, 1957. Editor 75 Years of Progress in Mineral Industry, 1947. Contbr. Ency. Britannica, 1961. Home: 4444 W. Point Loma Blvd., San Diego 92107. Died Apr. 14, 1966.

PARSONS, CHARLES LATHROP, chemist; b. New Marlboro, Mass., Mar. 23, 1867; s. Benjamin Franklin and Leonora (Bartlett) P.; B.S., Cornell U., 1888; D.Sc., U. Me., 1911; D.Chem., U. Pitts., 1914; D.Sc., U.N.H., 1944; m. Alice Douglas Robertson, Dec. 29, 1887 (dec.); children—Leonora Elizabeth, Charles Lathrop, Anna Guerard, Enith Alice, Priscilla Bartlett (dec.). Prof. chemistry N.H. Coll., 1890-1911; chief chemist Bur. of Mines, Washington, 1911; cons. practice since 1919. Mem. Nitrate Commn.; mem. Adv. Bd. on Gas Warfare. Vice pres. for America of Internat. Union Pure and Applied Chemistry, 1919-22. Awarded Nichol's medal for research on atomic weight of beryllium, 1904; Priestly medal for distinguished service, 1932, A.C.S. special gold medal of honor, 1946. Fellow A.A.A.S. (sec. Sect. C. 1904-08); mem. Am. Chem. Soc. (sec. 1907, sec. and bus. mgr. 1930), Am. Inst. Chemists (life), Sigma Xi, Kappa Sigma, Alpha Chi Sigma, Phi Lambda Upsilon, Soc. Colonial Wars, Mayflower Descendants, Colonial Govs.; hon. mem. Chem. Soc. of Rumania, Soc. of Chem. Industry; life mem. Soc. Chimique de France. Officer Legion of Honor (France), 1922; Officer Crown of Italy, 1926. Author: (with Prof. A.J. Moses) Mineralogy, Crystallography and Blow-pipe Analysis, 1895, 1901, 04, 09, 11, 16; Beryllium, Its Chemistry and Literature, 1908; also many sci. papers in chem. jours. and govt. bulletins. Address: Cosmos Club, Washington. Died Feb. 14, 1954.

PARSONS, FLOYD WILLIAM, editor, engr.; b. Keyser, W.Va., Jan. 23, 1880; s. Marshall J. and Mary C. (Long) P.; ed. U. of W.Va.; E.M., Lehigh U., 1902; m. Maud A. Freystedt, Oct. 28, 1903; children—Doris L., Jean M. Chief engr. Stonewall (W.Va.) Coal & Coke Co., 1902; dist. engr. Lehigh Valley Coal Co., Wilkes-Barre, Pa., 1903; res. engr. Consolidation Coal Co., Frostburg, Md., 1904; chief engr. New River Consolidated Coal & Coke Co., Rush Run, W.Va., 1905; asst. prof. mining, Mich. Coll. of Mines, Houghton, Mich., 1905-06; chief engr. Victor Am. Fuel Co., and C.&S.E. Ry. Co., Denver, Colo., 1906; asso. editor Engineering and Mining Journal, 1907-10; founder, and editor Coal Age, 1910-18; regular contbr. to World's Work, 1918-22; mem. board of dirs., editorial dir. and vice-pres. Robbins Publishing Co.; editor Gas Age-Record, and Industrial Gas (both of New York); contbg. editor Advertising and Selling; dir. Richmond Radiator Co., Dresser Mfg. Co., Vitaglass Corp. of America. Asst. to Harry A. Garfield, U.S. Fuel Administrator, World War; mem. commn. of journalists invited by British and French govts. to visit England and France, 1918. Presbyn. Author: American Business Methods, 1921; Everybody's Business, 1923. Home: New York, N.Y. Died Aug. 7, 1941.

PARSONS, HARRY DEBERKELEY, engineer; b. N.Y. City, Jan. 6, 1862; s. William Barclay and Eliza Glass (Livingston) P.; B.S., Columbia, 1882; M.E., Stevens Inst. Tech., 1884; hon. D.E. from same institution in 1926; m. Frances Walker, Dec. 16, 1890. Consulting engr. in New York, 1885—; prof. steam engring., 1891-1907, emeritus prof. practical engring., 1907—, Rensselaer Poly. Inst.; cons. engineer Nicaragua Canal constrn., 1893. Mem. N.Y. State Voting Machine Commn., 1898-1915, and Met. Sewerage Commn., 1908-14; consulting engr. for New York Zoöl. Soc., reports and appraisals Cramp Ship & Engine Building Co., Pressed Steel Car Co., Consol. Gas Co.'s plants, numerous paper cos., Seaboard Air Line, New Hampshire Traction Co., and many water powers, etc. Designed dams at Spier Falls, and Sherman Island, and cons. engr. for Palmer Falls and Glens Falls dams; chmn. Commn. on Street Cleaning and Waste Disposal, N.Y. City, 1906-07, and cons. engr. Bd. of Estimate, City of N.Y., for work connected with Catskill water supply, 1909-11; dist. appraisal officer, Detroit, Bur. Aircraft Production, U.S.A., 1918-19. Awarded Rowland prize, 1925, Croes medal, 1930, Am. Soc. Civil Engineers. Episcopalian. Author: Steam Boilers, Their Theory and Design, 5th edit., 1917; Disposal of Municipal Refuse, 1906; Tidal Phenomena of the Harbor of New York. Home: New York, N.Y. Died Jan. 26, 1935.

PARSONS, JOHN FREDERICK, aero. research sci.; b. Joliet, Ill., May 10, 1908; s. John Francis and Cora Belle (Lingle) P.; student San Diego State Coll., 1924-26; A.B., Stanford, 1928, Engr. in Mech. Engring. Aero., 1930; m. Evalyn Katharine Hughes, June 19, 1937; children—Patricia Jean (Mrs. Dennis I. Winsten), John Fredrick, Richard Alan. Aeronautical research engineer for the Langley Aero. Lab., NACA, 1931-40; aero. research sci. Ames Aero. Lab., NACA, 1940-48, asst. to dir., 1948-50, asso. dir. (became Ames Research Center NASA, 1958), 1952-69, chief unitary plan wind tunnel program NACA, 1950-56. Fellow Am. Inst. Aeros. and Astronautics; mem. Sigma Xi. Home: Palo Alto CA Died Mar. 2, 1969.

PARSONS, LLEWELLYN B(RADLEY), chemist; b. Saginaw, Mich., Feb. 28, 1897; s. Edward L. and Maude Winifred (Morey) P.; B.S., Syracuse U., 1919; M.S., U. Wis., 1921, Ph.D., 1923; m. Edna Marcia Claflin, June 15, 1921. Research chemist Cudahy Packing Co., Omaha, 1923-24, supervising chemist, 1924-33, research dir., 1933-39; research supervisor Lever Bros. Co., Cambridge, Mass., 1939-41, chief chemist, 1941-48, mgr. basic research labs., 1948-50, asst. dir. research and devel., 1950-51, dir. research and development, 1951-54, v.p. research development, 1954-60, v.p., 1960-62, dir. Mem. Am. Chem. Soc., Am. Oil Chemists Soc., A.A.A.S., Am. Soc. for Testing Materials, Sigma Xi, Sigma Chi, Alpha Chi Sigma, Phi Lambda Upsilon, Phi Kappa Alpha. Home: 138 Monte Vista Av., Ridgewood. Office: Lever Bros. Co., Edgewater, N.J. Died Feb. 28, 1968; buried Ridgewood, N.J.

PARSONS, PAYN BIGELOW, sanitary expert; b. Baldwinsville, N.Y., Feb. 12, 1872; s. Eben Burt and Clara (Bigelow) P.; A.B., Williams Coll., 1892; M.D., Albany Med. Coll., 1897; Cornell Med. Coll., 1904-05; m. Ella Mae Emerson, June 30, 1900. Bacteriologist, New York Subway air investigations, 1905, New York Bay investigation, 1906, Pollution Commn. and Met. Sewerage Commn., 1907, Lederle labs., 1908; dir. labs. of Met. Sewerage Commn., New York, 1909-13; chief bacteriologist, New York lab. of U.S. Bur. Chemistry, Nov. 1, 1913-25; bacteriologist N.Y. State Conservation Commn., 1925—. Home: New York, N.Y. Died Sept. 1931.

PARSONS, ROBERT STEVENS, civil engr.; b. Hohokus, N.J., May 26, 1873; s. Solomon and Louise (Towt) P.; B.S., Rutgers Coll., 1895, C.E., 1900; m. Eleanor Howse, 1897; children—Eleanor, Roberta. Connected with various depts. of engring., Erie R.R., leading to gen. supt., 1912-15; chief engr. same rd., 1915-20, gen. mgr., 1920-22, v.p., 1922—. Mem. N.J. Highway Commn., 1917-20. Trustee Rutgers Coll. Republican. Methodist. Mason. Rotarian. Home: Youngstown, Ohio. Died May 18, 1928.

PARSONS, THOMAS SMITH, agronomist; b. Ivinghoe, Eng., Aug. 5, 1873; s. Henry and Emily (Williams) P.; brought to America, 1880; B.S., S.Dak. Agrl. Coll., Brookings, S.D., 1897, M.S., 1899; post-grad. work Mich. Agrl. Coll.; m. Mabel Doughty, June 25, 1902. Science teacher and prin. high schs., S.D., and Durango, Colo., to 1909; prof. agronomy, U. of Wyo., and agronomist U.S. Expt. Sta., Laramie, Wyo., 1910—. Crops and soils specialist for Wyo., 1918—; editor Wyoming Stockman-Farmer, Cheyenne; state seed analyst. Republican. Methodist. Author: Manual of Agriculture and Nature Study, 1908. Home: Laramie, Wyo. Died Feb. 27, 1923.

PARSONS, WILLIAM BARCLAY, surgeon; born N.Y. City, May 22, 1888; s. William Barclay and Anna DeWitt (Reed) P.; grad. St. Mark's Sch., 1906; A.B., Harvard, 1910; M.D., Coll. Physicians and Surgs., Columbia U., 1914; m. Rose Saltonstall Peabody, Mar. 22, 1919; children—William Barclay, Jr., Rose Peabody (Mrs. Russell Vincent Lynch), Anne Barclay (now Mrs. Harold A. Priest, Jr.). Member of the faculty of medicine, Coll. Phys. and Surgs, Columbia U., 1935-39, and 1945-53, attending surg. Presbyn. Hosp., Vanderbilt Clinic, 1939-52, mem. med. bd., from 1945; prof. clin. surgery, Coll. of Phys. and Surg., 1949-53, professor emeritus clinical surgery, 1953-73; director of surgery, first surg. div. Welfare Hosp.; cons. in surg., N.Y. Orthopedic Hosp., from 1946. Served as lt., later capt., Am. Ambulance Field Service, France, 1916. Presbyn. Hosp. Unit, France, Mobile Hosp., Champagne, Aisne-Marne, St. Mihiel, Meuse Argonne offensives, Army Occupation, 1916-19; served as lt. col. to col., chief surg. service and unit dir. 2d Gen. Hosp., chief surg. cons. Southwest Pacific area; chief surg. cons., 6th Service Command. Awarded Legion of Merit, 1945. Trustee N.Y. Inst. for Edn. of the Blind, and St. Mark's School. Fellow Am. Coll. Surgeons; fellow Sect. Surgery, N.Y. Acad. Medicine; mem. Am. Surg. Assn. Am. Bd. Surg. (founders' group), Soc. clin. Surg. (sec. 1934-35), Med. and Surg. Soc., New York Surg. Soc., New York Acad. Med. (chmn. com. on professional standards, 1932-42, com. on med. information, pres. 1951-52), A.M.A. (vice-chmn. sect. on surg., gen. and abdominal, 1940), Soc. Clin. Research, Harvey Society, Nat. Bd. Med. Examiners (2d term of 6 yrs. 1947), Soc. Med. Consultant to the Armed Forces (councilor, 1946), Societe Internationale de Chirurgie (sec. Am. br. 1947-49), Century Assn., Soc. of The Cincinnati, New Hampshire Br. Chmn. coms. on radioactive research and blood bank, Presbyn. Hosp. Republican. Episcopalian. Clubs: Harvard (New York and Boston). Author: Sections in Surgical Clinics of North America, vol. 16, 1936, vol. 19, 1939, 1947; sect. in Operative Surgery, 1941; sect. in Surgical Treatment, 1947; also numerous papers on surg. Home: Darien CT Died Jan. 2, 1973; buried Wilton CT

PARSONS, WILLIAM BARCLAY, civil engr.; b. N.Y. City, Apr. 15, 1859; s. William Barclay and Eliza Glass (Livingston) P.; A.B., Columbia, 1879, C.E., 1882; LL.D., St. John's, Md., 1909; Sc.D., Princeton, 1920, Trinity, 1921; D.Eng., Stevens, 1921; m. Anna DeWitt Reed, May 20, 1884; children—Mrs. Sylvia Weld, Wm. Barclay. Consulting engr., N.Y. City, 1885; dep. chief engr., 1891-94, chief engr., Rapid Transit Commn. New York, 1894-1904; survey Chinese railways, 1898-99; mem. Isthmian Canal Commn., 1904; bd. of consulting engrs., Panama Canal, 1905; advisory engr. Royal Commn. London Traffic, 1904; chief engr. Cape Cod Canal, 1905-14; chmn. Chicago Transit Com., 1916; also many other engring. wks. Lecturer Cambridge U., 1929. Chief of engrs. (brig. gen. N.G.N.Y.), Spanish-Am. War; maj., lt. col., col. 11th U.S. Engrs., World War; now brig. gen. engr. R.C., U.S.A. Awarded D.S.M. (U.S.), also citation for conspicuous distinguished service and victory medal and 5 clasps; D.S.O. (British); Officer Legion of Honor (French); Order of Crown (Belgian). Fellow Am. Acad. Arts and Sciences; etc. Trustee Columbia U., 1897—(chmn. bd. from 1917), N.Y. Pub. Library, Carnegie Instn. (Washington). Vestryman Trinity Ch., New York. Author: Turnouts, 1883; Track, 1885; Rapid Transit in Foreign Cities, 1895; American Engineer in China, 1900; The American Engineers in France, 1920; Robert Fulton and the Submarine, 1923; etc. Home: New York, N.Y. Died May 9, 1932.

PARTRIDGE, ALDEN, educator; b. Norwich, Vt., Feb. 12, 1785; s. Samuel and Elizabeth (Wright) P.; attended Dartmouth, 1802-05, U.S. Mil. Acad., 1805-06; m. Ann Swasey, 1837, 2 sons. Commd. 1st lt. Corps Engrs., U.S. Army, 1806, promoted capt., 1810;

assigned to duty as instr. U.S. Mil. Acad., became prof. mathematics, 1813, prof. engring., 1813, acting supt., 2 years, tried by court martial on numerous charges of neglect of duty and insubordination, sentenced to be cashiered, 1817, punishment remitted; resigned 1818; established Am. Lit., Scientific and Mil. Acad., Norwich, 1819, (chartered as Norwich U., 1834), pres. until 1843; opened and ran mil. prep. sch., Norwich, 1827-29; established young ladies sem., Norwich, 1835; founded mil. prep. schs. in Va., Pa., Del., N.H., 1839-53; founder system of mil. acads. of elementary and secondary grades; surveyor gen. Vt., 1822-23; mem. Vt. Legislature, 1833, 34, 37, 39. Died Norwich, Jan. 17, 1854.

PARTRIDGE, EVERETT P(ERCY), chem. engr.; b. Edinburg, N.Y., Dec. 15, 1902; s. Edward Everett and Minnie Amelia (Wood) P.; B.S., Syracuse University, Syracuse, New York, 1925; M.S., University of Michigan, 1926, Ph.D., 1928; m. Jane Harris Hazard, June 20, 1925; 1 son, Everett George. Asso. editor Indsl. and Engring. Chemistry, 1928-31; supervising engr. Nonmetallic Minerals Expt. Sta., U.S. Bur. Mines, 1931-35; dir. research Hall Labs. div. Calgon Corp., 1935-60, dir. labs., 1960-66, corporate v.p., 1966-67, dir., 1950-67, cons., 1967-69. Mem. exec. com. div. engring. and indsl. research NRC, chmn. Internat. Water Conf.; mem. Nat. Tech. Adv. Com. on Water Quality Requirements. Pres. Beaver area Community Chest; chmn. local unit Am. Cancer Soc.; dist. chmn. Boy Scouts Am. Named Engr. of Year, Beaver County chpt. Pa. Soc. Profl. Engrs., 1967. Fellow A.A.A.S., Am. Soc. M.E., mem. Am. Chem. Soc., Am. Inst. Chem. Engrs., Am. Soc. Testing and Materials, Newcomen Soc., Delta Upsilon. Clubs: University (Pitts.); Beaver Valley Country. Home: Beaver PA Died Apr. 1969.

PARVIN, THEOPHILUS, obstetrician, gynecologist; b. Buenos Aires, Argentina, Jan. 9, 1829; s. Theophilus and Mary (Rodney) P.; grad. Ind. U., 1847; studied Hebrew at Princeton Theol. Sem.; doctorate in medicine U. Pa., 1852; m. Rachel Butler, 1853, 3 children. Elected pres. Ind. Med. Soc., 1861; prof. materia medica Med. Coll. of Ohio, 1864-69; prof. obstetrics Louisville (Ky.) U., 1869; transferred to Ind. Med. Coll., 1872; pres. A.M.A., 1879; prof. obstetrics and gynecology Jefferson Med. Coll., Phila., 1883-98; co-editor Cincinnati Jour. of Medicine, 1866-67; editor Western Jour. Medicine, 1867-69; co-editor Am. Practitioners, 1869-83; pres. Am. Med. Journalists Assn., Am. Acad. Medicine, Am. Gynecol. Soc., Phila. Obstet. Soc.; hon. pres. obstet. sect. Internat. Med. Congress, Berlin, Germany, 1890; pres. Periodic Internat. Congress of Gynecology and Obstetrics, Brussels, Belgium, 1892; mem. Am. Philos. Soc.; hon. mem. Washington (D.C.) Obstet. and Gynecol. Soc.; hon. fellow Edinburgh (Scotland) Obstet. Soc. Author: Science and Art of Obstetrics, 1886. Died Phila., Jan. 29, 1898.

PASCALIS-OUVRIERE, FELIX, (known as Felix Pascalis after 1801), physician; b. in Southern France, circa 1750; M.D., Montpellier U. Came to Am., 1793, settled in Phila.; v.p. Chem. Soc. of Phila., 1801; mem. editorial staff Medical Repository, N.Y.C., 1813-20; a founder, pres. N.Y. br. Linnaean Soc., of Paris, 1 term. Author: The Medico-Chymical Dissertations on the Causes of the Epidemic Called Yellow Fever, and on the Best Antimonial Preparations for the Use of Medicine, by a Physician, Practitioner in Philadelphia, 1796; An Account of the Contagious Epidemic Yellow Fever, Which Prevailed in Philadelphia in the Summer and Autumn of 1797, 1798; An Exposition of the Dangers of Internment in Cities, 1823. Died N.Y.C., July 29, 1833.

PATCH, EDITH MARION, author, entomologist; b. Worcester, Mass., July 27, 1876; d. William Whipple and Salome (Jenks) Patch; B.S., U. of Minn., 1901; specializing in entomology, M.S., U. of Me., 1910; Ph.D., Cornell U., 1911; Sc.D., 1937. Teacher English and zoölogy Hastings (Minn.) High Sch., 1901-02; tchr., dept. English, Crookston (Minn.) High Sch., 1902-03; organized dept. entomology Me. Agrl. Exptl. Station, and entomologist, same, 1903-37, entomologist emeritus, 1937—. Research in entomology with problems concerning ecology and economic entomology; research guest Rothamsted Exptl. Sta, Harpenden, Eng., 1927. Fellow Entomol. Soc. America (pres. 1930), A.A.A.S.; mem. Am. Soc. Zoölogists, Assn. Econ. Entomologists, Am. Soc. Naturalists, Am. Nature Study Soc. (pres. 1937), Nat. Audubon Soc. (life), Fla. Audubon Soc. (life), Nat. Council on Elementary Science, Fla. Entomol. Soc. (hon.), Am. Sci. Tchrs. Assn., Sigma Xi, Phi Kappa Phi, Delta Delta Delta, Delta Kappa Gamma (hon.), Phi Sigma, Phi Beta Kappa, Pi Gamma Mu, Sigma Delta Epsilon (hon.). Club: Woman's. Author: Hexapod Stories (Little Gateways to Science Series), 1920; Bird Stories (same series), 1921; First Lessons in Nature Study, 1926; Holiday Pond, 1929; Holiday Meadow, 1930; Holiday Hill, 1931; Hunting; Outdoor Visits, 1932; Surprises; Through Four Seasons, 1933; Science at Home, 1934; The Work of Scientists, 1935 (last six in Nature and Science Readers series); Holiday Shore, 1935; Mountain Neighbors, 1936; Desert Neighbors, 1937; Forest Neighbors, 1938; Prairie Neighbors, 1940; also more than 80 entomol. publs. in bulls. and tech. periodicals. Address: P.O. Box 150, Orono, Me. Died Sept. 28, 1954; buried Mt. Hope Cemetery, Worcester, Mass.

PATON, STEWART, physician; b. New York, N.Y., 1865; s. William and Anne Stavely (Agnew) P., A.B., Princeton, 1886, A.M., 1889; M.D., Coll. Phys. and Surg. (Columbia), 1889; post-grad. study Germany and Italy; m. F. Margaret Halsey, 1892; children—F. Evelyn, William, R. Townley. Formerly asso. in psychiatry, Johns Hopkins, and dir. of lab., Sheppard and Enoch Pratt Hosp., Baltimore; lecturer in neurobiology, Princeton U., in psychiatry, Columbia; consultant in mental hygiene and lecturer in psychiatry, Yale, 1926-28. Trustee Carnegie Instn., Washington, D.C. Fellow A.A.A.S.; mem. Am. Philos. Soc., Am. Neurol. Assn., N.Y. Acad. Medicine, Eugenics Research Assn. (pres. 1919). Club: Century (New York). Author: Text-Book of Psychiatry for Use of Students and Practitioners of Medicine; Education in Peace and War, 1919; Human Behavior, 1921; Signs of Sanity and the Principles of Mental Hygiene, 1922; Prohibiting Minds, 1932. Died Jan. 7, 1942.

PATRICK, GEORGE EDWARD, chemist; b. Hopedale, Mass., Oct. 22, 1851; s. Delano and Mary (Maynard) P.; B.S., Cornell, 1873, M.S., 1874; m. Hattie E. Lewis, June 19, 1879. Instr. chemistry, Cornell, 1873-74; asst. prof. and prof. chemistry, U. of Kan., 1874-83; chemist Ia. Agrl. Expt. Sta., 1888-95; prof. agrl. chemistry, Ia. State Coll., 1890-95; asst. chemist U.S. Dept. Agr., 1896—; in charge dairy lab. Bureau Chemistry, 1901—. Died Mar. 22, 1916.

PATRICK, JOSEPH CECIL, research chemist; b. Jefferson City, Mo., Aug. 28, 1892; s. James C. and Mary (Ryan) P.; student Kansas City (Mo.) Hahnemann Med. Coll., 1914-17; M.D., Kansas City (Mo.) Coll. Medicine, 1922; m. Leah Burns, July 11, 1922 (dec. Dec. 1935); 1 son, James Burns; m. 2d, Olive Hudson, Sept. 13, 1937; children—Eileen, Kathryn. Established chem. control packing plants of Armour & Co., Buenos Aires, Argentina, 1920-22; founder, pres. Indsl. Testing Lab., Kansas City, Mo., 1924-28; founder, pres., chmn. bd. Thiokol Corp., Kansas City, Mo. and Trenton, N.J., 1928-47; dir. research which led to 1st comml. synthetic rubber, solid rocket fuel. Mem. Am. Chem. Soc. (Goodyear medal 1958), A.A.A.S., Franklin Inst. Phila. (Elliott Cresson medal 1958), Am. Museum Natural History. Address: 11 Williams Lane, Yardley, Pa. Died Apr. 6, 1965.

PATTEE, ERNEST NOBLE, (pat'te'), chemist; b. Ottawa, Can., July 21, 1864; s. James Albert and Harriet (Inglee) P.; brought to U.S., 1870; B.S., U. of Rochester, 1886, M.S., 1888; D.Sc., Syracuse U., 1922; m. Mary Norton Peck, Apr. 30, 1891. Prof. chemistry, also organizer and head of dept., Syracuse University, 1890-1942, prof. emeritus since February 1942; consulting chemist; specialist in sanitary and agricultural chemistry; city chemist, Syracuse, 1920-31. Member Am. Chem. Soc., Delta Upsilon, Phi Beta Kappa, Sigma Xi. Republican. Methodist. Home: 408 Euclid Av., Syracuse 10, N.Y. Died Jan 17, 1946.

PATTEN, BRADLEY MERRILL, embryologist; b. Milwaukee, Wis., June 14 1889; s. William and Mary Elizabeth (Merrill) P.; A.B., Dartmouth Coll., 1911, Chamberlin fellow 1911-12; A.M., Harvard, 1912. Ph.D., 1914; m. Barbara Standish, June 13, 1914; 1 daughter, Elizabeth (Mrs. Walter E. Garrey). Assistant in zoology Harvard University, 1912-14; instructor in histology and embryology, Western Reserve U. Med. Sch., Cleveland, O., 1914-16, sr. instr., 1916-18, asst. prof., 1918-21, asso. prof., 1921-34; asst. dir. for med. sciences. Rockfeller Found., 1934-36; prof., head dept. anatomy, med. sch. U. Mich., 1936-59, emeritus, 1959-71; U.S. hydrographer Internat. Ice Patrol, 1914; visiting investigator, Carnegie Embryological Inst., Baltimore, Md., 1925, Pathol. Inst., Vienna, 1927. Nat. Sigma Xi lecturer, 1949-50; vis. prof. U. P.R., 1952, U. Otago Medical School, New Zealand., 1954, Medical School, Univ. Buenos Aires, 1958. U. Miami, 1959; U. Adelaide, Australia, 1961. Contributing mem. White House Conf. on Child Health and Protection, 1930. Fellow A.A.A.S., Ohio Acad. Science; mem. Am. Naturalists, Am. Soc. Zoologists, Am. Assn. Anatomists (2d v.p. 1934-36), Marine Biological Lab., Woods Hole, Massachusetts, Michigan Medical Society (honorary life), Phi Beta Kappa, Phi Sigma Kappa, Sigma Xi, Alpha Omega Alpha. Author: The Early Embryology of the Chick, 1920; The Embryology of the Pig. 1927; The Cardiovascular System, in Morris' Anatomy, 1942; Human Embryology, 1946; Heart Development, in Gould's Pathology of the Heart, 1953; Foundations of Embryology, 1958. Micro-moving picture methods of recording activities of living embryos. Asso., editor Am. Jour. Anatomy, 1941-58. Contbr. to zool., med. jours. Home: Ann Arbor MI Died Nov. 8, 1971; buried Woods Hole MA

PATTEN, WILLIAM zoölogist; b. Watertown, Mass., Mar. 15, 1861; s. Thomas and Mary Low (Bradley) P.; B.S., Lawrence Scientific Sch. (Harvard), 1883; A.M., Ph.D., Leipzig, Germany, 1884; m. Mary Elizabeth Merrill, June 28, 1883; 1 son, Bradley Merrill. Asst. in Lake Lab., Milwaukee, Wis., 1886-89; prof. biology, U. of N.D., 1889-93; prof. zoölogy, Dartmouth, 1893—. Trustee Marine Biol. Lab., Woods Hole, Mem. Nat. Research Council for Biology and Agr. Author: The Evolution of the Vertebrates and Their Kin, 1912; The Grand Strategy of Evolution, 1920. Pres. Sect. F (zoölogy) A.A.A.S., 1918. Home: Hanover, N.H. Died Oct. 27, 1932.

PATTERSON, A(RTHUR) L(INDO), physicist; b. Nelson, N.Z., July 23, 1902; s. Arthur Henry and Nellie Tweeddale (Slack) P.; B.Sc. (hons.), McGill U., 1923, M.Sc., 1924, Ph.D., 1928; m. Elizabeth Lincoln Knight, Sept. 14, 1935. Came to U.S., 1929, naturalized, 1945. Research worker Royal Instn., London, Eng., 1924-26, Kaiser Wilhelm Institut für Faserstoffchemie, Berlin-Dahlem, Germany, 1926-27; lectr. physics McGill U., 1928-29; asso. Rockefeller Inst. for Med. Research, 1929-31; lectr. Johnson Foundn. for Med. Physics, Phila., Pa., 1931-33; research worker Mass. Inst. Tech., 1933-36; asst. prof. physics Bryn Mawr Coll., 1936-40, asso. prof., 1940-49; research physicist Naval Ordnance Lab., Washington, 1944-45; sr. mem. and head dept. molecular structure Inst. for Cancer Research, Phila. Mem. U.S.A. Nat. Com. on Crystallography 1948-55, 57—, chmn. com., 1948-50; mem. exec. com. Internat. Union Crystallography, 1948-54; mem. div. phys. scis. NRC, 1957-62. Fellow Am. Phys. Soc., Phys. Soc. London, Mineral. Soc. Am., N.Y. Acad. Sci.; mem. Am. Soc. for X-ray and Electron Diffraction (v.p. 1948, pres. 1949), Am. Crystallographic Assn. Author: (with W. C. Michels) Elements of Modern Physics; also papers on x-ray analysis of crystal structures; devised Patterson Synthesis for applying x-ray diffraction to analysis of crystal structure, 1934. Office: The Inst. for Cancer Research, Fox Chase, Phila. 19111. Died Nov. 6, 1966.

PATTERSON, AUSTIN MCDOWELL, chemist; born Damascus, Syria, May 31, 1876, of American parents; s. John Fulton Hutchison (M.D.) and Charlotte Isabella (McDowell) P.; A.B., Princeton, 1897; Ph.D., Johns Hopkins, 1900; honorary D.Sc., Antioch, 1944; m. Anne Elizabeth Bailey, May 31, 1911; children—John Fulton (dec.), Elizabeth (dec.), James Fulton, Nancy Elder. Instructor in chemistry, Centre College, Danville, Ky., 1900-01, Rose Poly. Inst., 1901-03; chemistry editor Webster's New Internat. Dictionary, 1903-53; associate editor Chemical Abstracts, 1908-09, editor, 1909-14; prof. chemistry, Antioch Coll., 1921-41, prof. emeritus, 1941—, also v.p., 1930-41, trustee 1941-45; principal specialist in chemical edn., Engineering, Science, and Management War Training, U.S. Office of Education, 1941-43. Chemist, United States Chemical Warfare Service, 1918-19. Received award in Documentation of Chemistry, sponsored by Dayton sect., Am. Chemical Soc., 1949 Mem. Internat. Com. organic chem. nomenclature, 1924-53; councillor Internat. Union Chemistry, 1925-31, 36-38; mem. National Research Council, 1932-41. Fellow American Association Advancement Science; member Am. Chemical Soc., Phi Beta Kappa, Sigma Xi and Phi Lambda Upsilon fraternities. United Presbyn. Clubs: Cosmos (Washington); Kiwanis. Author: A German-English Dictionary for Chemists, 1917; A French-English Dictionary for Chemists, 1921; A Guide to the Literature of Chemistry (with E. J. Crane), 1927; The Ring Index (with L. T. Capell), 1940. Home: Xenia, Ohio. Address: 221 N. King St., Xenia, O. Died Feb. 26, 1956.

PATTERSON, HARRY JACOB, chemist; b. Yellow Springs, Pa., Dec. 17, 1866; s. William Calvin and Adaline (Mattern) P.; B.S., Pa. State Coll., 1886; post-grad. work in chemistry, same; D.Sc., Md. State Coll., 1912; m. Elizabeth Hayward Hutchinson, Oct. 25, 1895; children—Blanche Seely (Mrs. Francis T. Mack), William Calvin. Asst. chemist, Pa. State Agrl. Expt. Station, 1886-88; chemist and vice-dir., Md. Agrl. Expt. Sta., 1888-98, dir., chemist, 1898; pres. Md. Agr. Coll., 1913-17; dean Coll. of Agr., U. of Md., 1925; emeritus, 1937—. Specialist in food, fertilizer and dairy chemistry and corn fodder products; author bulls. and articles on these subjects. Fellow A.A.A.S.; mem. Assn. Official Agrl. Chemists, Am. Chem. Soc., Soc. Chem. Industry, London, Master Md. State Grange, 1905-13; sec. Md. State Bd. of Agr., 1907-17. Home: College Park, Prince Georges County, Md. Died Sept. 11, 1948; buried St. Johns Beltsville, Md.

PATTERSON, JOHN THOMAS, zoölogist; b. Piqua, O., Nov. 3, 1878; s. James and Anna M. (Linn) P.; student Ohio Northern U., Ada, O., 1897-98; B.S., U. of Wooster, 1903, D.Sc., 1938; Ph.D., U. of Chicago, 1908; m. Alice Jane Tozer, Sept. 12, 1906; children—Edith Ruth (Mrs. E. F. Simpson), John Thomas (deceased), Robert Maitland. Professor of biology Buena Vista College, Storm Lake, Iowa, 1903-05; asst. in zoölogy, U. of Chicago, 1905-08; instr. zoology, U. of Tex., 1908, in physiology, 1909, adj. prof. zoölogy, 1911, prof. since 1913 and dir. of research in zoology since 1928, distinguished prof. since 1937. Research fellowship U. of Tex., 1926-27. Fellow A.A.A.S. (vice pres. 1941), Nat. Acad. Sci. (Daneil Giroud Elliot Medal 1951); mem. Am. Soc. Zoölogists (pres. 1939), Am. Assn. Anatomists, Am. Soc. Naturalists, Genetics Soc. (pres. 1954), Evolution Soc. (pres. 1947), Phi Beta Kappa, Sigma Xi. Democrat. Presbyn. Club: Town and Gown. Contbr. articles in field. Home: 1908 Cliff St., Austin, Tex. Died Dec. 4, 1960.

PATTERSON, LAMAR GRAY, chemist; b. in Prince George Co., Md., Sept. 19, 1865; s. Thomas Leiper and Louisa (Sprigg) P.; grad. U. of Va., 1885; spl. studies in chemistry; m. Mary T. Humphreys, of Columbus, Miss., Sept. 14, 1892. In practice as chemist since 1885, first in pvt. lab., Cumberland, Md.; chemist Miss. Expt. Sta., 1888, Washington Carbon Co., Pa., 1894; metallurgist Aetna Standard Iron and Steel Co., 1898; chemist Ala. Steel and Ship Building Co., 1899, Va. State Fertilizing Co., 1900—; formerly supt. Lynchburg (Va.) branch, supt. Montgomery (Ala.) branch, Dec. 1, 1911—, Va.-Carolina Chem. Co. Fellow London Chem. Soc. Mem. Am. Philos. Soc. Author of various bulls. Miss. Expt. Sta.; also contbns. to chem. jours. Home: 1401 S. Perry St., Montgomery, Alabama.

PATTISON, GRANVILLE SHARP, anatomist; b. nr. Glasgow, Scotland, 1791; s. John Pattison; attended U. Glasgow. Prof. anatomy, physiology, surgery in Andersonian Instn. (U. Glasgow); came to U.S., 1819; became mem. Medico-Chirurg. Soc. of London also fellow Royal Coll. Surgeons, 1819; gave a series pvt. lessons in anatomy in Phila., 1819-20; prof. anatomy, physiology, surgery U. Md., Balt., 1820-26; editor: Observations on the Surgical Anatomy of the Head and Neck (Allen Burn), 1824; prof. anatomy U. London, 1828-31; prof. anatomy Jefferson Med. Coll., Phila., 1832-41; prof. anatomy U. City of N.Y., 1841-51; editor of Register and Library of Medicine and Surgical Science, Washington, 1833-36; co-editor American Medical Library and Intelligencer, Phila., 1836. Author: Experimental Observations on the Operation of Lithotomy, 1820; "A Refutation of Certain Calumnies" in pamphlet Correspondence Between Mr. Granville Sharp Pattison and Dr. Nathaniel Chapman, 1821. Died N.Y.C., Nov. 12, 1851.

PATTON, HORACE BUSHNELL, geologist; b. Chicago, Sept. 18, 1858; s. William Weston (D.D., LL.D.) and Mary Boardman (Smith) P.; bro. of Normand Smith and Cornelius Howard P.; A.B., Amherst, 1881; studied geology, mineralogy and petrography, U. of Leipzig, 1883-85, U. of Heidelberg, 1885-87, Ph.D., 1887; m. Louise Alice Torrey, June 10, 1904. Instr. natural science and mathematics, Howard U., 1881-83; instr. petrography and mineralogy, U. of Heidelberg, 1887-88; prof. geology, Rutgers, 1888-90; mem. Mich. State Geol. Survey and instr. mineralogy, Mich. Sch. Mines, 1891-92; prof. geology and mineralogy, Colo. Sch. Mines, Golden, Sept. 1893—. Author: Lecture Notes on Crystallography, 1896. Died 1929.

PATTON, LEROY THOMPSON, prof. geology; b. Fairpoint, O., Dec. 5, 1880; s. John and Lauretta Close (Thompson) P.; A.B., Muskingum Coll., New Concord, O., 1905; B.S., U. Chgo., 1913; M.S., State U. Ia., 1916, Ph.D., 1923; m. Bertha Eubank, Aug. 20, 1927; children—Joseph Thompson, Bruce Bransford. Prin. high sch. and supt. schs., 1905-12; prof. chemistry and geology, Geneva Coll., Beaver Falls, Pa., 1912-18; prof., head dept. chemistry and geology, Muskingum Coll., New Concord, O., 1918-21, prof. geology, head dept., 1921-22; asso. geologist, Bur. Econ. Geology, U. Tex., 1922-25; tech. adviser Tex. State Bd. of Water Engrs., 1923; prof. geology 1925—, head dept. geology, petroleum engring., Tex. Tech. Coll., Lubbock, 1925-48. Mem. water resources com. Tex. State Planning Bd., 1935-39; mem. council Ohio Athletic Conf., 1920-22. Fellow A.A.A.S., Geological Soc. Am., mem. Am. Assn. Petroleum Geologists, Soc. of Econ. Paleontologists and Mineralogists, Sigma Xi, Gamma Alpha. Presbyn. Author: Geology of Potter County, Texas, 1923; Geology of Stonewall County, Texas, 1930; also various papers on geol. topics. Home: 2415 19th St., Lubbock Tex. Died June 22, 1957; buried Lubbock (Tex.) Meml. Park.

PATTON, RAYMOND STANTON, hydrographic engr.; b. Degraff, O., Dec. 29, 1882; s. Oliver and Ida M. (Cloninger) P.; Ph.B., Western Reserve U., 1904; m. Virginia Mitchell, Nov. 7, 1912; children—Raymond Stanton, Virginia Mitchell, Helen Mitchell. With Coast and Geodetic Survey, 1904—; engaged in field surveys, Atlantic and Pacific coasts of U.S., Alaska and Philippine Islands, and was made chief of party and comdg. officer survey vessles, in charge surveys in Western Alaska, among them, of appraoches to Kuskokwim River, 1912-13, 1914-15; chief of Coast Pilot Sect., 1915-17; lt. and lt. comdr. U.S. Navy, 1917-19; in charge chart production and correction to 1929; dir. Coast and Geodetic Survey, Apr. 29, 1929—. Life trustee Nat. Geog. Soc. Mem. engineering advisory com. on coast erosion, N.J. State Bd. of Commerce and Navigation; mem. National Research Council. Dir. Am. Shore and Beach Preservation Assn.; trustee Woods Hole Oceanographic Institute. Author: U.S. Coast Pilot, Alaska—Yakutat Bay to Arctic Ocean (Govt. Printing Office), 1916; U.S. Coast Pilot, Pacific Coast—California, Oregon and Washington (same), 1917; Report of Engring. Advisory Com. of N.J. Bd. of Commerce and Navigation on Coast Erosion, 1922-24. Died Nov. 25, 1937.

PATTON, WILLIAM MACFARLAND, civ. engr.; b. Richmond, Va., Aug. 22, 1845; s. John M. and Margaret F. P.; ed. pvt. schs.; grad. E. M., and C. E., Va. Mil. Inst., 1869; m. Annie G. Jordan. Was chief engr. Mobile & Birmingham R.R. and of Louisville, St. Louis & Texas R.R.; engr. in charge of bridges across Susquehanna, Schuylkill, Ohio, Warrior, Tombigbee and Mobile rivers; engr. sewers for cities and other important works. Was prof. engring., Va. Mil. Instl; later prof. civ. engring., Va. Poly. Inst. Author: Practical Treatise on Foundations, 1893 W9; General Treatise on Civil Engineering, 1894. Home: Blacksburg, Va. Died 1905.

PAUL, CHARLES EDWARD, mech. engr., educator; b. Belfast, Me., Dec. 6, 1876; s. Jesse Granville and Annie Julia (Leach) P.; grad. Chauncy Hall Sch., Boston, 1895-96; S.B. in Mech. Engring., Mass. Inst. of Tech., 1900; m. Mary E. Yenawine, June 14, 1905. Began as designer and sales engr. James W. Tufts Co., Boston, 1900; asst. prof. mech. engring., Kan. State Coll., 1903-05; prof. mech. engring., N.M. Coll. Agr. and Mech. Arts, 1905-07; prof. mechanics Pa. State College, 1907-08; with Armour Institute of Technology (now Ill. Inst. Tech.) since 1908, successively asso. prof. mechanics until 1914, professor mechanics in charge dept., 1914-41; dir. dept. engring. science, 1933-41, chairman department mathematics, 1934-37, retired as prof. emeritus of mechanics, 1941; consulting practice, specializing in industrial construction and materials since 1908; asso. editor Am. Builder and of Cement World, 1910-15; constrn. engr. Nat. Lumber Mfrs. Assn., 1915-21. Mem. Am. Soc. for Testing Materials (member sub-com. on timber specifications), American Soc. for Engring. Education, Western Soc. Engrs., Tau Beta Pi, Theta Xi, Sphinx. Republican. Club: University of Chicago. Author of booklets and tech. articles relating to building constrn., concrete, lumber, estimating and contracting. Home: 1528 Farwell Av., Chicago IL

PAUL, CHARLES HOWARD, civil engr.; b. Rockport, Mass., Mar. 10, 1875; s. Howard H. and Lucy D. (Dousett) P.; High Sch., Malden, Mass.; Mass. Inst. Tech., 1892-95; m. Camilla M. Wheeler, June 19, 1907. With Mass. State Bd. of Health, 1895; Met. Water Works, Boston, 1896-1900; Bur. of Filtration, Phila., 1901-04; engr. U.S. Reclamation Service, 1904-15. Was constrn. engr. Lower Yellowstone project engr. Minidoka project, irrigation investigations eastern Ore.; in charge of constrn. Arrowrock Dam, Boise, Ida., Jan. 1911-Dec. 1915 (then world's highest dam); with Miami Conservancy Dist., Dayton, O., Dec. 1915—, on design and constrn. of flood control works for Miami Valley, including five large hydraulic fill dams, constrn. engr., 1915-16, later asst. chief engr., chief engr., also cons. engr. and in gen. cons. practice; consultant to various govt. depts. on dams, river control, etc. Mgr. Internat. Air Races, 1924; mng. dir. Dalton Industrial Assn., 1925-31; member Dayton City Commission, 1926-29; dir. Dayton Community Chest. Trustee Y.M.C.A. (pres. 1933-34). Home: Dayton, O. Died Oct. 6, 1941.

PAUL, HENRY MARTYN, astronomer; b. Dedham, Mass., June 25, 1851; s. Ebenezer and Susan (Dresser) P.; A.B., Dartmouth, 1873, C.E., 1875, A.M., 1876; m. Augusta Anna Gray, Aug. 27, 1878. Asst. astronomer, U.S. Naval Obs., 1875-80; prof. astronomy, Imperial U. Tokyo, Japan, 1880-83; again asst. astronomer, Naval Obs., 1883-97; prof. mathematics, U.S.N., 1897—; astronomer Naval Obs., 1897-99; engr. Bur. Yards and Docks, Navy Dept., 1899-1905; teaching mathematics, U.S. Naval Acad., 1905-12; on retired list of Navy, 1913. Choir-singer and precentor in Washington chs.; pres. 1896-98, financial sec. 1898-1903, Choral Soc. of Washington. Home: Washington, D.C. Died Mar. 15, 1931.

PAUL, JOHN R., physician; b. Phila., Pa., Apr. 18, 1893; s. Henry Neill and Margaret Crosby (Butler) P.; A.B., Princeton, 1915; M.D., Johns Hopkins Med. Sch., 1919; honorary Master of Arts, Yale University, 1940; D.Sc. (honorary), University of Chicago, 1956; married Mary Leita Harlan, Sept. 30, 1922. Asst. pathologist, Johns Hopkins Med. Sch., 1919-20; intern, Pa. Hosp., Phila., 1920-22; dir., Ayer Clinical Lab., Phila., 1922-28; asst. asso. prof. internal med., Yale U. Med. Sch., 1928-40; prof. preventive medicine, 1940-61, emeritus prof. epidemiology and preventive medicine, 1961-71; dir. regional serum bank World Health Orgn., 1961-66; mem. coms. virus research, Nat. Found. Infantile Paralysis, 1940-48; cons. sec. of War, 1941-46; dir. neurotropic Virus Disease Com., Army Epidemiol. Bd., 1941-46, dir. com., virus, rickettsial diseases, 1946-56; chmn. virus and rickettsial study sect. research grants div. USPHS, 1946-51; govt. service in Middle East, 1943-44, Japan, 1946, Korea, 1953, Med. Mission to Soviet Union, 1956; mem. live poliovirus vaccine com. Nat. Insts. Health, 1958-71, sr. cons. internat. fellowship program, 1957-62; mem. com. investigate U.S. Food and Drug Adminstrn., Nat. Research Council, 1960. Recipient Alvarenga prize, Coll. Physicians, Phila., 1928; John Phillips Meml., A.C.P., 1942; Medal of Freedom U.S.A., 1946; Howard T. Ricketts award, U. Chgo., 1954; Charles V. Chapin award, R.I. Med. Society, 1959; Kober medal Association American Physicians, 1963. Mem. subcom. cardiovascular disease NRC, 1946-53. Fellow A.C.P., Royal College Physicians, Royal Soc. Health (Eng.); mem. Assn. Am. physicians (pres. 1956), Am. Soc. Clin. Investigation (pres. 1938), Nat. Acad. Sci., Am. Acad. Arts and Scis., Royal Soc. Medicine London (hon.), World Health Organization (past member of the expert committee on viruses 1952-66). Clubs: Graduate (New Haven); Ivy (Princeton); Century, Yale (N.Y.); Authors (London). Author: The Epidemiology of Rheumatic Fever, 1942; Clinical Epidemiology, 1958, 2d edit., 1966; A History of Poliomyelitis, 1971; also sci. papers. Home: Guilford CT Died May 6, 1971; buried Grove Street Cemetery, New Haven CT

PAULEY, SCOTT SAMUEL, forest geneticist; b. Sault Ste. Marie, Mich., Dec. 21, 1910; s. John Livingood and Flossa Viola (Scott) P.; B.S., U. Minn., 1939; M.S., Mich. State Coll., 1942; Ph. D., Harvard, 1947; m. Fritzi Klawans, Dec. 28, 1937; 1 dau., Nan Fritzi. Forest ranger Wis. Conservation Dept., 1939-40; instr. forestry Mich. State Coll., 1942-43; asst. prof. Harvard, 1947-52; lectr. forest genetics, geneticist Maria Moors Cabot Found. Bot. Research, Harvard, 1952-55; asso. prof. University Minn., 1955-57, prof., 1957-70. Vice pres., dir. Forest Genetics Research Found. Served as lt. USNR, 1943-45. Mem. Soc. Am. Foresters, A.A.A.S., Am. Inst. Biol. Sci., Genetics Soc. Am., Soc. Study Evolution, Sigma Xi, Alpha Zeta, Gamma Sigma Delta, Xi Sigma Pi. Author articles in field. Home: Mahtomedi MN Died Apr. 18, 1970; cremated.

PAULI, WOLFGANG, (pou'le), physicist; b. Vienna, April 25, 1900; s. Wolfgang Joseph and Bertha (Schutz) P.; Ph.D., U. of Munich, 1921; m. Franciska Bertram, Apr. 4, 1934. Asst. at U. of Göttingen, 1921-22, U. of Copenhagan, 1922-23; dozent, U. of Hamburg, 1923-28; became prof. theoretical physics, Eidgenössische Technische Hochschule, Zürich, Switzerland, 1928—; visiting prof. theoretical physics, Inst. for Advanced Study, Princeton, N.J., 1935-36, 1940-45, 49-50, 54; lectr., U. Mich., summers 1931, 41, Purdue U., May-June, 1942. Awarded Lorentz Medaille, 1930; Nobel Physics Prize, 1945; also Franklin Medal, 1952; Max Planck medal, 1958. Member Royal Soc., London (foreign), Swiss Physics Society, American Physics Society, A.A.A.S. Contbr. to technical encyclopedias and other reference works in many countries. Address: care Physikal Institut E.T.H., Gloriastr. 35, Switzerland. Died Dec. 15, 1958.

PAULLIN, JAMES EDGAR, physician; b. Fort Gaines, Ga., Nov. 3, 1881; s. James Edgar and Leola Elizabeth (Wiggins) P.; A.B., Mercer U., 1900, grad. study, same univ., 1901, LL.D., 1929; M.D., Johns Hopkins University, 1905; LL.D., Emory University, 1943; married Edna Frederick, December 17, 1908; children—Caroline, James Edgar (dec.). Resident pathologist R.I. Hosp., Providence, 1905-06; pathologist, Ga. State Bd. Health, 1906-11; asso. prof. pathology, Atlanta Coll. Phys. and Surg., 1907-11; asso. visiting physician Grady Hosp., 1909-13, now visiting physician; adj. prof. medicine Atlanta Med. Coll., 1913-15; prof. clin. medicine Emory U. and chief of medicine, Emory U. div., Grady Hospital, 1915-30; consultant internal medicine, central of Georgia Railway; consultant, Greenbrier Clinic. Served as maj. Med. Corps, U.S. Army, 1918-19. Member A.M.A. (chmn. med. sect. 1927; president 1943-44), Southern Medical Assn. (chmn. med. sect. 1920), Am. Clin. and Climatol. Soc. (pres. 1937), Assn. Am. Physicians, Am. Coll. Physicians (pres. 1942-43, master, 1947), Med. Assn. Ga. (ex-pres.), Fulton Co. Med. Soc. (ex-pres.), Med. Com. Nat. Research Council, Med. Bd. of Nat. Foundn. of Infantile Paralysis, Directing Bd. of Procurement and Assignment Agency for Physicians, Dentists and Veterinarians; mem. bd. trustees Nat. Foundation for Education; hon. consultant to the Surgeon General of U.S. Navy. Regent Am. Coll. Physicians, 1944; Corr. Mem. Soc. Internal Medicine, Buenos Aires, since Mar. 3, 1944; pres. Interstate Postgrad. Med. Assn., 1946-47. Mem. Order of Carlos Finley (Cuba), Sigma Nu, Phi Chi, Alpha Omega Alpha, Phi Beta Kappa. Presbyn. Clubs: Capital City, Piedmont Driving. Contbr. to Trans. Med. Assn. of Ga., So. Med. Jours., Jour. of A.M.A., etc. Home: 2834 Andrews Dr. Northwest. Office: Medical Arts Bldg., Atlanta, Ga. Died Aug. 13, 1951; buried Westview Cemetery, Atlanta.

PAULSON, FREDERICK HOLROYD, cons. engr.; b. Cranston, R.I., Jan. 26, 1898; s. Harry Charles and Fanny (Holroyd) P.; B.S., Brown U., 1920; m. Doris Kerfoot, Oct. 16, 1922; 1 son, John Frederick. Structural engr. F. P. Sheldon & Son, Providence, 1920-35; chief structural engr. Oresto D. Saia, Providence, 1935-39; chief structural engr., mgr. Charles A. Maguire & Asso., Newport, R. I., 1940-43, Providence, 1943-53, partner, mgr., 1953—. Served with U.S. Army, 1918. Fellow A.A.A.S.; mem. Am. Inst. Cons. Engrs., Internat. Assn. Bridge and Structural Engineers, American Society C.E. (national director 1954-57), Am. Soc. Engring. Edn., Engring. Inst. Can., Boston Soc. Civil Engrs., Nat. Soc. Profl. Engrs., Tau Beta Pi, Alpha Tau Omega. Episcopalian (sr. warden). Clubs: Turks Head, British Empire. Home: 286 Spring Green Road, Warwick 5, R.I. Died Sept. 29, 1959; buried Acote Hill Cemetery, Chepachet, R.I.

PAWLOWSKI, FELIX WLADYSLAW, prof. aeronautical engring.; b. nr. Warsaw, Poland, July 23, 1876; s. Joseph Korwin and Joanna (Wojciechowska) P.; M.E. and E.E., Tech. Coll., Mittweida, Saxony, 1896; Certificat d'Etude, U. of Paris, 1910; M.S., U. of Mich., 1914; married to Wladyslawa Buchwald (now dec.); children—George, Halina; married second to Emma Louise Minier, July 18, 1918. Came to the United States, 1910, naturalized, 1916. Designer, engr. and chief engr. with machine industries in Poland, 1896-1908; designer engines and cars with Am. automobile industries, 1910-12; teaching asst. to prof. aeronautical engring. in charge courses, U. of Mich., 1912-29, Guggenheim Prof. aeronautical engring., 1929-46; prof. emeritus since July 1946. Consultant Douglas Aircraft Co., Santa Monica, Calif., 1946-47. Aeronaut. engr., War Dept., World War I; chief div. aeronautics, Tech. Mil. Inst., Warsaw, Poland, 1919-20; lecturer Sch. Aeronautical Engring., U.S.A.A.F., Dayton, O., summer 1925. Fellow Royal Aeronautical Soc., Inst. Aeronautical Sciences. Hon. mem. Assn. Polish Engrs. in Am.; mem. Early Birds, Polish Inst. Arts and Sciences in Am., Union des Ingenieurs de France; hon. mem. Internat. Inst. Psychic Investigation; mem. Sigma Xi. Roman Catholic. Democrat. Author paper and articles in Am. and fgn. profl. jours. and tech. reports for various govts. and industries. Address: 3 rue de l'Ecole Normale Pau, Bassés-Pyrénees, France. Died Feb. 17, 1951.

PAYNE, GEORGE FREDERICK, pharmacist; b. Macon, Ga., Apr. 7, 1853; s. George and Emily Hebsibah (Sims) P.; prep. edn. pvt. schs., Ga.; Ph.G., New York Coll. Pharmacy, 1876; student Columbia Sch. Mines, 1873-74; M.D., Atlanta Coll. Phys. and Surgeons, 1892; Phar. D., Atlanta Coll. of Pharmacy, 1910; m. Anna Ruby Nichols, Nov. 11, 1884. State chemist of Ga., 1890-98; chemist Ga. State Bd. of Pharmacy, 1891-1906 (sec. and treas. 1899-1906); one of founders, 1891, prof. pharmacy, 1891—, pres., 1910—, Atlanta Coll. Pharmacy; prof. chem. analysis, Southern Dental Coll., 1899-1910. Chmn. com. of Am. Pharm. Assn. on advancement of status of pharmacists in U.S. Army, Navy and Pub. Health Service, 1894-1905 and 1909-10; mem. com. of revision of U.S. Pharmacopoeia, 1900-10; pres. Am. Pharm. Assn., 1902-03; 1st v.p. Nat. Assn. Bds. of Pharmacy, 1904-05. Mason. Author: Payne's Dictionary of Pharmacy. Home: Atlanta, Ga. Died Apr. 19, 1923.

PAYNE, WILLIAM WALLACE, astronomer; b. Somerset, Mich., May 19, 1837; s. Jesse D. and Rebecca Ann (Palmer) P.; A.B., Hillsdale (Mich.) Coll., 1863, M.A., 1864; LL.B., Chicago Law Sch., 1866; hon. Ph.D., Hillsdale, 1894; D.Sc., Carleton Coll., 1916; m. Josephine Vinecore, June 8, 1870; 1 dau., Jessie Vinecore. Prof. mathematics and astronomy and dir. Goodsell Obs., 1871-1908, acting dean, 1896-99, Carleton Coll.; dir. of obs. of Nat. Watch Co., Elgin, Ill., May 15, 1909—. Editor Sidereal Messenger, 1882-92, Astronomy and Astro-Physics, 1892-95, Popular Astronomy, 1893-1909. Home: Elgin, Ill. Died Jan. 29, 1928.

PEABODY, CECIL HOBART, engineer; b. Burlington, Vt., Aug. 9, 1855; s. Selim H. and Mary Elizabeth (Pangborn) P.; S.B., Mass. Inst. Tech., 1877; m. Sarah Angeline Knight, 1885. Prof. mathematics, Imperial Agrl. Coll., Sapporo, Japan, 1878; asst. prof. mech. engring., U. of Ill., 1881; asst. prof. steam engring., 1883, prof. naval architecture and marine engring., 1893-1920 (emeritus), Mass. Inst. Tech. Author: Thermodynamics of the Steam Engine, 1889; Tables of the Properties of Saturated Steam, 1888; Valve Gear for Steam Engines, 1892; Steam Boilers (with Prof. E. F. Miller), 1897; Manual of Steam Engine Indicator, 1900; Naval Architecture, 1904; Thermodynamics of the Steam Turbine; Propellers, 1912; Computations for Marine Engines, 1913. Imperial Order of the Rising Sun (Japanese), 3d class. Died 1934.

PEABODY, ERNEST H., mech. engr.; b. Knoxville, Tenn., June 30, 1869; s. Daniel Webster and Mary Hillary (Saltmarsh) P.; student Gramercy (N.Y.) Park Sch. and Tool House, 1885-87; M.E., Stevens Inst. Tech., 1890, D.Eng. (hon.), 1948; m. Martha Cobb Sanford, 1925. Rodman on constrn. Norfolk & Western R.R., 1890; draftsman, Babcock & Wilcox Co., 1891, later in erection depts., engr. tests (all types of fuel), 1893, research in burning oil fuel, 1902-04 (gained internat. reputation); formed Peabody Engring. Corp., 1920; pres. Peabody Engring. Corp., N.Y.; chmn. bd. dirs. Peabody, Ltd., London. Attended tng. camp at Plattsburg; disch. as sharpshooter, 1916. Trustee Stevens Inst. Tech., 1951. Pres., founder League for Less Noise, Inc. Mem. Stevens Alumni, Am. Soc. M.E., Soc. Naval Architects and Marine Engrs., Am. Naval Engrs., Am. Inst. Newcomen Soc. Clubs: University, Engineers. Author tech. pamphlet Fuel Oil, 1915, and Newcomen address entitled "Oil Fuel—A World-wide Adventure," treating the subject historically, 1942. Home: Wilson Point, South Norwalk, Conn. Office: 580 Fifth Av., N.Y.C. 19. Died Mar. 6, 1965.

PEACOCK, M(ARTIN) A(LFRED), univ. prof., scientist; b. Edinburgh, Scotland, Jan. 15, 1898; s. Alfred Norman and Antonie Ida (Fuller) P.; B.Sc., Glasgow U., Scotland, 1922, Ph.D., 1925, D.Sc., 1932; A.M., Harvard, 1927; research asso. in crystallography, U. of Heidelberg, summers 1929, 33; m. Katharine Louisa West, Apr. 2, 1937; children—Barbara Clendon, Nancy Bligh. Lecturer geology and geography U. of B.C., Can., 1929-30, asst. prof., 1930-31; research asso. mineralogy Harvard, 1932-37; asso. prof. mineralogy and petrography U. of Toronto, Can., 1937-42, prof. mineralogy, 1942-46, prof. crystallography and mineralogy since 1946. Mem. Canadian Nat. Com. on Crystallography. Mem. Royal Soc. Canada, Walker Mineral. Club, Geol. Soc. Am. (v.p. 1948), Mineral. Soc. Am. (pres. 1948), Mineral. Soc. of Gt. Britain (abstractor since 1941), Crystallographic Soc. of Am. Author and editor of sci. papers on crystallography, mineralogy; study and recognition of minerals by X-ray diffraction. Home: 33 Fairlawn Av., Toronto 12, Ont., Can. Died Oct. 30, 1950; buried Toronto.

PEALE, ALBERT CHARLES, geologist, paleobotanist; b. Heckscherville, Pa., Apr. 1, 1849; s. Charles W. and Harriet (Friel) P.; A.B., Central High Sch., Phila., 1968, A.M., 1873; M.D., U. of Pa., 1871; m. Emily W., d. Rev. George F. Wiswell, Dec. 23, 1875. Mineralogist and geologist, U.S. Geol. and Geog. Survey of the Territories, 1871-79; geologist U.S. Geol. Survey, 1883-98; aid, sect. paleobotany, U.S. Nat. Mus., 1898—. Author: Yellowstone National Park and Thermal Springs, 1882; The Classification of American Mineral Waters, 1887; Mineral Springs of the United States, 1886; The Natural Mineral Waters of the United States, 1895; Classification of Mineral Waters, 1902; Biographical Sketches of Charles Willson Peale and of Titian R. Peale, 1905; The Stratigraphic Position and Age of the Judith River Formation. Home: Washington, D.C. Died 1913.

PEALE, TITIAN RAMSAY, naturalist, artist; b. Phila., Nov. 17, 1799; s. Charles Willson and Elizabeth (De Peyster) P.; studied anatomy U. Pa.; m. Eliza Cecilia La Forgue, 1822; m. 2d, Lucy Mullen; 6 children. Apprenticed to spinning machine mfr., 1814; worked with his brother Rubens (curator of mus., Phila.), 1816-18; joined William MacLure and Thomas Say in expdn. to coasts of Ga. and Fla. to study and collect fauna specimens, 1818-19; asst. naturalist under Stephen H. Long on U.S. Army expdn. to Upper Missouri, 1819-20; asst. mgr. Phila. Mus., 1821-24; exhibited 4 water color paintings Pa. Acad. Fine Arts, 1822; sent to Fla. by Charles Lucien Bonaparte to collect specimens and make drawings for book American Ornithology, 1824; mem. civil staff U.S. exploring expdn. to South Seas under Charles Wilkes, 1838-42, made drawings which appeared in published accounts of expdn.; examiner U.S. Patent Office, Washington, D.C., 1849-72. Died Mar. 13, 1885.

PEARCE, CLINTON ELLICOTT, educator, engr.; b. Jersey City Heights, N.J., May 6, 1891; s. Frederick William and Margaret Atchison (McKenzie) P.; B.S., Mass. Inst. Tech., 1913; M.S., Cornell, 1937; m. Marion Margaret Thomas, Mar. 15, 1917; 1 dau., Mrs. Raymond C. Schneider. Faculty mem. dept. mech. engring. Lafayette Coll., Easton, Pa., 1913-17; joined faculty Kan. State Coll., 1917, prof., head dept. machine design, 1924-56; on leave from Kan. State Coll. to subsurface ordnance Naval Ordnance Lab., White Oak, Md., 1944-45, summers, 1948-52, 54; now with U. Ill. program in India. Registered profl. engr., Kan. Mem. Am. Soc. M.E., Am. Soc. Engring. Edn., Kan. Engring. Soc., Naval Ordnance Lab. Tech. Res., Delta Sigma Phi, Phi Kappa Phi, Sigma Tau, Pi Tau Sigma. Author: Rail Steel Reinforcement Bars (with F. Burgraf), 1931; Principles of Mechanism, 1934. Home: 316 Denison Av., Manhattan, Kan. 66502. Office: India Inst. Tech., Kharagpur, India. Died Mar. 11, 1967.

PEARCE, J(AMES) NEWTON, chemist; b. Oswego, Ill., Dec. 21, 1873; s. James Titsworth and Mary Catherine (Gannon) P.; Ph.B., Northwestern U., 1896, Ph.M., 1897; studied U. of Chicago, 1900-02; Ph.D., Johns Hopkins, 1907; m. Martha Anne Slater (Ph.B., U. of Mich., 1899), Aug. 25, 1904. Chemist with James S. Kirk & Co., soap mfrs., Chicago, 1897-99; instr. chemistry, Township High Sch., La Salle, Ill., 1900-02; instr. chemistry, Northwestern U., 1902-05; asst. prof. chemistry, 1907-19, asso. prof. phys. chemistry, 1919-20, prof., 1920—, State U. of Iowa. Methodist. Mason. Mem. com. on contact catalysis of colloid div., Nat. Research Council, 1927—. Mem. bd. editors Jour. Physical Chemistry, 1932. Home: Iowa City, Ia. Died Nov. 14, 1936.

PEARCE, LANGDON, engr.; b. Boston, Mass., Nov. 12, 1877; s. John Barnard and Mary Langdon (Williams) P.; A.B., Harvard, 1899; B.S., Mass. Inst. Tech., 1901, M.S., 1902; m. Eleanor Howard Dean, June 1, 1910. With Charles River Dam Commn., Boston, 1902; commn. on additional water supply, N.Y. City, 1903; Augusta Water Dist.; also at Cleveland, O., and Jersey City, N.J., 1904; engr. for Columbus, O., 1904-07; engr. Peoples Water Co., Oakland, Calif., 1907-08; div. engr. San Dist. of Chicago, 1909-17, and san. engr. same 1918—; also cons. hydraulic and san. engr. Mem. Am. Soc. Civ. Engrs., Am. Inst. of Cons. Engrs., Inst. of Civ. Engrs., Inst. of San. Engrs., Western Soc. Engrs., Am. Pub. Health Assn., New Eng. Water Works Assn., Boston Soc. Civ. Engrs., Am. Chem. Soc., A.A.A.S., Engring. Inst. of Can., Phi Beta Kappa, etc. Clubs: University, Indian Hill. Contbr. various articles and papers on water and sewage purification, etc. Home: Winnetka, Ill. Office: 100 E. Erie St. Chgo.. Died July 20, 1956.

PEARCE, LOUISE, med. research; b. Winchester, Mass., Mar. 5, 1885; d. Charles Ellis and Susan Elizabeth (Hoyt) Pearce; prep. edn., Girls' Collegiate Sch., Los Angeles, Calif., 1900-03; A.B., Stanford, 1907; M.D., Johns Hopkins, 1912; Sc.D. (hon.) Wilson College, 1947, Bucknell U., 1950; LL.D. (hon.) Skidmore Coll., 1950; Litt.D. (honorary) Beaver College, 1948; D.M.S. (hon.), Women's Medical College, 1952. Medical house officer, Johns Hopkins, 1912-13; with Rockefeller Institute of Medical Research, 1913—, successively as fellow, assistant, associate, asso. mem., 1923-51; retired conducted African Sleeping Sickness Mission, Belgian Congo, 1920-21; visiting prof. medicine, Peiping Union Med. Coll., China, 1931-32; mem. bd. corporators Women's Med. Coll., Phila., 1941—, (pres. 1946-51); Gen. Advisory Council of Am. Social Hygiene Assn., 1925-44; Nat. Research Council, 1931-33; trustee New York Infirmary for Women and Children, 1921-28, Princeton Hosp. 1940-46. Awarded Order of the Lion; Elizabeth Blackwell Citation, 1951, Woman's Medical College Citation, 1952, Leopold II Award, 1953. Member of the executive board of Am. Med. Women's Assn., 1935-36. Mem. A.A.A.S., N.Y. Acad. Medicine, Harvey Soc., Am. Soc. Exptl. Pathology, Am. Assn. U. Women (dir. 1945-51), Am. Soc. Pharmacol. and Exptl. Therapeutics, Am. Assn. Pathologists and Bacteriologists, Soc. for Exptl. Biology and Medicine, Am. Assn. for Cancer Research, New York Soc. Tropical Medicine, Johns Hopkins Surgical and Medical Assn., American Society Tropical Medicine, College of Physicians of Philadelphia, Pathol. Soc. Gt. Britain and Ireland, Royal Soc. Tropical Medicine and Hygiene, British Soc. for Study of Venereal Disease (hon.), Société belge de Médicine tropicale, Peiping Soc. Natural History, Pi Beta Phi, Phi Beta Kappa, Sigma Xi, Alpha Omega Alpha. Awarded Order of the Crown (Belgium). Club: Cosmopolitan. Author: Treatment of Human Trypanosamiasis with Tryparsamide (monograph of Rockefeller Inst.), 1930; also author or co-author of many papers in med. jours. and procs. Home: Trevenna Farm, Orchard Rd., Belle Mead, N.J. Address: Rockefeller Institute for Medical Research, N.Y. City. Died Aug. 10, 1959.

PEARCE, RICHARD MILLS, JR., pathologist; b. Montreal, Can., Mar. 3, 1874; s. Richard Mills and Sarah (Smith) P.; ed. Boston Latin Sch.; M.D., Harvard, 1897; spl. study at U. of Leipzig, Germany, 1902, D.Sc., Lafayette Coll., Pa., 1915; m. May Harper Musser, Nov. 6, 1902; children—Agnes M., John M. Resident pathologist, Boston City Hosp., 1896-99; instr. pathology, Harvard, 1899-1900; demonstrator and later asst. prof. pathology, U. of Pa., 1900-03; dir. Bender Hygienic Lab., Albany, N.Y., 1903-08; prof. pathology and bacteriology, Albany Med. Sch., 1903-08; dir. Bur. of Pathology and Bacteriology, N.Y. State Dept. of Health, 1903-08; prof. pathology, Univ. and Bellevue Hosp. Med. Coll. (New York U.), 1908-10; prof. pathology, 1910-11, prof. research medicine, 1910-20, U. of Pa.; gen. dir. Div. of Med. Edn., Rockefeller Foundation, 1920—. Chmn. med. div. Nat. Research Council, 1918; maj., M.C. U.S.A., 1918. Author: Medical Research and Education, 1913; The Spleen and Anemia, 1917. Home: New York, N.Y. Died Feb. 16, 1930.

PEARL, RAYMOND, biologist; b. Farmington, N.H., June 3, 1879; s. Frank and Ida May (McDuffee) P.; A.B., Dartmouth, 1899, Sc.D., 1919; Ph.D., U. of Mich., 1902; U. of Leipzig, 1905, Univ. Coll., London, 1905-06, Carnegie Instn. Table, Naples Zoöl. Station, 1906; LL.D., University of Maine, 1919; Litt.D., from St. John's College, 1935; m. Maud M. DeWitt, June 29, 1903; children—Ruth DeWitt, Penelope Mackey. Asst. in zoölogy, 1899-1902, instr. 1902-06, U. of Mich.; instr. U. of Pa., 1906-07; biologist and head of dept. biology, Maine Agrl. Expt. Sta., 1907-18; prof. biometry and vital statistics, Sch. of Hygiene and Pub. Health, Johns Hopkins, 1918-25, research professor, 1925-30, prof. biology, Medical School, Johns Hopkins, 1923—; statistician, Johns Hopkins Hospital, 1919-35; director Inst. for Biol. Research, Johns Hopkins, 1925-30, professor of biology, School of Hygiene, 1930—. Engaged in biol. researches on variation in fishes, with Biol. Survey Great Lakes (U.S. Fish Commn.), 1901-02; awarded grants for research on variation in organisms from Carnegie Inst., 1904, 05, 06; expert, poultry breeding, U.S. Dept. Agr.; non-resident lecturer Grad. Sch. of Agr., Ames, Iowa, 1910, Lansing, Mich., 1912, Washington, 1939; Lowell lecturer, Boston, Mass., 1920; special lecturer, U. of London, 1927; Harrington lecturer U. of Buffalo, 1928; Heath Clark lecturer U. of London, 1937; Patten Foundation lecturer, Indiana University, 1938. Member exec. com. and chmn. agrl. com. Nat. Research Council, 1916-18, and mem. exec. board, 1919-35; chief of statis. division U.S. Food Administration, 1917-19; pres. Internat. Union for Scientific Investigation of Population Problems, 1928-30. Mem. bd. visitors and govs. St. John's Coll., 1928-34; trustee Science Service, 1929-35. Editor Quarterly Review of Biology, Human Biology; asso. editor Biometrika, 1906-10, Journal Agrl. Research, 1914-18, Genetics, 1915—, Journal Exptl. Zoölogy, 1915—, Metron, 1920—, Biologia Generalis, 1923-27, Acta Biotheoretica, 1937—. Decorated Knight of the Crown of Italy, 1920, Officer, 1929. Author: Variation and Differentiation in Ceratophyllum, 1907; Variation and Correlation in the Crayfish (with A. B. Clawson), 1907; Poultry Diseases and Their Treatment (with F. M. Surface and M. R. Curtis), 1911; Modes of Research in Genetics, 1915; Diseases of Poultry (with F. M. Surface and M. R. Curtis), 1915; The Nation's Food, 1919; The Biology of Death, 1922; Introduction to Medical Biometry and Statistics, 1923; Studies in Human

Biology, 1924; The Biology of Population Growth, 1925; Alcohol and Longevity, 1926; To Begin With, 1927; The Rate of Living, 1928; Constitution and Health, 1933; The Ancestry of the Long-lived (with Ruth D. Pearl), 1934; The Natural History of Population, 1939. Home: Roland Park, Baltimore, Md. Died Nov. 17, 1940.

PEARSE, ARTHUR SPERRY, (pers), zoölogist; b. Crete, Neb., Mar. 15, 1877; s. Sherman L. and Sarah Louise (Gardner) P.; B.S., U. Neb., 1900, A.M., 1904, LL.D., 1941; Ph.D., Harvard, 1908; m. Mary Oliver Lehmer, Dec. 22, 1902; children—Frederick Deweese (dec.), Richard Lehmer, Frank (dec.), Elizabeth (Mrs. William Henry Caufman). Tchr. Omaha High Sch., 1900-04; asst. in zoölogy Harvard, 1904-07, teaching fellow in zoölogy, 1908; tchr. Lake High Sch., Chgo., 1907; instr. in zoölogy U. Mich., 1909-10, asst. prof., 1911; asst. prof. zoölogy U. Philippines, 3 mos., 1911; asso. prof. zoölogy St. Louis U. Sch. Medicine, 1911; asso. prof. zoölogy U. Wis., 1912; prof., 1919-26; mem. faculty grad. dept. Duke U., beginning 1927, now ret., dir. Marine Lab., 1938-45; editor of Ecology Monographs, 1931-51. Vis. prof. Keio U., Tokyo, Japan, 1929-30. Spl. investigator U.S. Bur. of Fisheries, 1913-25, 35-36. Internat. Health Bd., 1925-26, Carnegie Inst., 1928, 31, 32, 36. Cpl. 2d Neb. Vol. Inf., Spanish-Am. War. Fellow A.A.A.S. (v.p. sect. F, 1933); mem. Am. Soc. Zoölogists (pres. 1945), Am. Soc. Parasitologists, Am. Soc. Naturalists, Ecol. Soc. Am. (pres. 1925), S.E. Biol. Assn. (pres. 1942), N.C. Acad. Sci., Arts and Letters, Phi Kappa Psi, Phi Beta Pi, Phi Sigma, Phi Kappa Phi, Sigma Xi, Phi Beta Kappa. Contbr. books and papers on parasites, animal behavior, ecology, fisheries and crustacea; also articles on animals of U.S., P.I., Africa, Japan, Yucatan and S.A. Author: General Zoölogy; Animal Ecology; Homoiothermism; Environment and Life; Migration of Animals from Sea to Land; Cenotes of Yucatan; Fauna of Caves of Yucatan; Hell's Bells; Introduction to Parasitology; Fauna in Encyclopedia Yucateca. Home: 803 2d St., Durham, N.C. Died Dec. 11, 1956.

PEARSE, JOHN BARNARD, consulting engineer and metallurgist since 1881; b. in Phila., Apr. 19, 1842; grad. Yale, 1861; studied chemistry, Phila., 1861-64; in charge chem. div. U.S.A. laboratory there, 1863-65; studied Freiberg (Saxony) School of Mines, etc.; connected with Pa. Steel Co., 1868; its gen. mgr., 1870; improved Bessemer processes; in charge engring. dept., S. Boston Iron Co., Boston, 1876-81. Author: A Concise History of the Iron Manufacture of the American Colonies up to the Revolution and of Pennsylvania till the Present Time. Address: 317 Walnut Av., Boston.

PEARSON, FRED STARK, engineer; b. Lowell, Mass., July 3, 1861; s. Ambrose and Hannah P.; A.M.B., Tufts Coll., 1883, A.M.M., 1884 (Sc.D., 1900, LL.D., 1905); m. Mabel Ward, Jan. 5, 1887. Instr. chemistry, Mass. Inst. Tech., 1879-80; instr. mathematics and applied mechanics, Tufts, 1883-86; mining engr. U.S. and Brazil, 1886-88; mgr. Somerville (Mass.) Electric Light Co., 1888-89; chief engr. West End St. Ry., Boston, 1889-93, Dominion Coal Co., 1893-94, Met. St. Ry. Co., New York, 1894-99; consulting engr., 1899—. Pres., dir. Barcelona Traction, Light & Power Co., Limited, Mexico Tramways Co., Rio de Janeiro Tramway, Light & Power Co., Mexican Light & Power Co., Ltd., Mexico North Western Ry. Co. Home: Great Barrington, Mass. Died May 7, 1915.

PEARSON, GUSTAF ADOLPH, silviculturist, forestry; b. Holdredge, Neb., Nov. 14, 1880; s. Anders Peter and Anna Christina (Arvidson) P.; A.B., U. of Neb., 1906, B.S., 1906, A.M., 1907; m. May Perkins, June 14, 1910; children—Arthur Adolph, Margaret Angeline. In charge Ft. Valley Forest Expt. Sta., U.S. Forest Service, Flagstaff, 1909-29; dir. Southwestern Forest and Range Expt. Sta., 1930-35, senior silviculturist in charge Fort Valley Exptl. Forest, 1935-44; collaborator U.S. Forest Service, 1945. Pioneer research in reforestation, forest meteorology, forest ecology and silviculture; developed new method of improving forest stands. Trustee Northern Ariz. Soc. of Science and Art. Fellow A.A.A.S., Soc. Am. Foresters; mem. Ecol. Soc. Am., Sigma Xi (honorary scientific). Presbyterian. Mason. Author: Natural Reproduction of Western Yellow Pine, 1923; Forest Types in the Southwest as Determined by Climate and Soil, 1931; Timber Growing and Logging Practice (with R. E. Marsh), 1935; Forest Land Use, 1940. Author of govt. bulletins and contbr. to tech. jours. Received 1944 award of Soc. Am. Foresters for best article on forestry. Home: 1828 E. 5th St. Office: P.O. Box 951, Tucson, Ariz. Died Jan. 31, 1949.

PEARSON, JAMES JOHN, engineer; b. Thornhill, Dumfriesshire, Scotland, Sept. 22, 1858; s. Rev. James and Frances P., of Newcastle-on-Tyne, Eng.; prep. edn. Elmfield Coll., St. Peter's, York, Eng.; grad. Elswick Sch. Tech., Newcastle, 1878; studied engring. under Lord (then Sir W. G.) Armstrong; medallist with honors in all physics; m. Mabel Hattersley, of Harrowgate, Eng., July 22, 1912. Tech. and traveling corr. for Textile Manufacturing, Mechanical World, Sanitary Engineering; Chemical News, 1879-81; chief engr. for Palmer's Ship & Iron Co., Jarrow-on-Tyne, 1881-84; asst. mgr. afloat and guarantee engr. for Hawthorne, Leslie & Co., St. Peter's-on-Tyne, 1884-86; charge of machinery construction in Austrian torpedo chasers, Leopard and Panther; the fighting equipment of the Chilean cruisers, Blanco Encalada and Almirante Cochrane; the steam trials of the Italian cruiser, Giovanni Bausan; the machinery constrn., at Yokosuka Sta. (Japan), of the Japanese cruisers, Naniwa and Takachiho-Kan, 1886-88; cons. and contracting engr., Yokohama, Japan; constructing and installing textile mills, ice plants, bridges, steam vessels, arsenal equipment, etc., 1888-91; mgr. Nassau Elec. Co., New York, 1892-95; cons. engr. at New York, 1895—. Volunteered for war service to Brit. Govt. and served in Eng. through 1916-17, as examining and investigating engr. for Ministry of Munitions, War Office and Naval Bd.; also chief dilution officer for Bedford Area, and acting chief for London. Made inspection and report of the principal shipyards throughout all Europe for clients, 1918-19. Home: New York; Bridgewater, Conn.; and San Francisco, Calif. Died Sept. 25, 1926.

PEARSON, SAMUEL, mining engr.; b. in S. Africa, Jan. 2, 1862; s. William T. and Charlotte (Ogle) P.; ed. S. Africa pub. schs. and Hilton Coll.; m. in Transvaal, S. Africa, M. J. Stoptorth, 1885. Entered Boer service as pvt., 1899, serving through Boer War; q.-m.-gen. Boer Army, 1900; spl. agt. of Boers in U.S., 1900-01; is an exile, having been refused passport to S. Africa by British Govt. Pres. Am. S. African Commerce Co. since Jan. 1, 1909. Contbr. to mags. Address: 1321 Monsey Av., Scranton, Pa.

PEARSON, T(HOMAS) GILBERT, ornithologist, wildlife conservationist; b. Tuscola, Ill., Nov. 10, 1873; s. Thomas Barnard and Mary (Eliott) P.; B.S., Guilford (N.C.) Coll., 1897; B.S., U. of N.C., 1899, LL.D., 1924; spl. study Harvard; m. Elsie Weatherly, June 17, 1902; children—Elizabeth (Mrs. C. T. Jackson), T. Gilbert, William. Prof. biology, Guilford Coll., 1899-1901, State Normal and Industrial Coll. for Women, 1901-04; state game commr. of N.C., under title of sec. state Audubon Soc., 1903-10; sec. and exec. officer Nat. Audubon Soc., 1910-20, pres., 1920-35, now pres. emeritus. Founder, 1922, and pres., 1922-38, Internat. Com. for Bird Preservation (organized in 30 countries), now chmn. Pan-Am. Sect. of Com.; founder and chmn. Nat. Com. on Wildlife Legislation; mem. Conseil Internat. de la Chasse, advisory bd. Migratory Bird Treaty Act; mem. Pres. Hoover's Yellowstone Park Boundary Commn.; official collaborator Nat. Park and Federal Fish and Wildlife Services; nat. dir. Izaak Walton League of America. Decorated Nat. Order of Oaken Crown, Luxembourg, 1925; Société Nationale d'Acclimatation medal (France), 1937; John Burroughs Memorial Assn. medal, 1939. Clubs: Camp Fire (hon.), Boone and Crockett Club (New York City); Explorers Club of America. Author: Stories of Bird Life, 1901; The Bird Study Book, 1917; Adventures in Bird Protection—An Autobiography, 1937. Editor-in-chief: Birds of America, 3 vols., 1917; Tales from Birdland, 1918. Sr. author: Birds of North Carolina, 1919; Co-editor: The Book of Birds, 1937. Contbr. to scientific and popular mags. on ornithol. and wildlife conservation subjects. Lectured in Europe, North, Central and South America and West Indies. Home: 2257 Loring Pl. Office: 1006 5th Av., New York, N.Y. Died Sep. 3, 1943.

PEARY, ROBERT EDWIN, arctic explorer, discoverer of North Pole; rear admiral U.S.N. (retired); b. Cresson, Pa., May 6, 1856; s. Charles N. and Mary (Wiley) P.; C.E., Bowdoin Coll., 1877 (Sc.D., 1894, LL.D.; LL.D., Edinburgh and Tufts); m. Josephine Diebitsch, 1888. Entered U.S. Navy as civil engr., Oct. 26, 1881; asst. engr. Nicaragua Ship Canal under Govt. orders, 1884-85; engr. in charge of Nicaragua Canal Surveys, 1887-88; invented rolling-lock gates for canal. Made reconnaissance, 1886, of the Greenland inland ice-cap, east of Disco Bay, 70 deg. N. lat.; chief of Arctic expdn. of Acad. National Sciences of Phila., June 1891-Sept. 1892, to N.E. angle of Greenland (Independence Bay, 81 deg. 37' N. lat.); discovered and named Melville Land and Heilprin Land, lying beyond Greenland; determined insularity of Greenland, for which he received the Cullom medal of Am. Geog. Soc., Patron's medal of Royal Geog. Soc., London, and medal of Royal Scottish Geog. Soc., Edinburgh. Made another arctic voyage, 1893-95; made thorough study of little tribe of Arctic Highlanders; discovered, 1894, famous Iron Mountain (first heard of by Ross, 1818), which proved to be meteorites, one of them weighing 90 tons (the largest known to exist); made summer voyages, 1896-1897, bringing the Cape York meteorites to U.S.; comdr. Arctic expdn. under auspices of Peary Arctic Club of New York, 1898-1902; rounded northern extremity of Greenland Archipelago, the last of the great Arctic land groups; named the northern cape, the most northerly land in the world (83 deg. 39' N. lat.), Cape Morris K. Jesup; attained highest north in Western Hemisphere (84 deg. 17' N. lat.). Sailed north again, July 1905, in S.S. Roosevelt, specially built by Peary Arctic Club; returned Oct. 1906, having reached "highest north" (87 deg. 6' N. lat.). Started on 8th Arctic expdn., July 1908, on the Roosevelt, proceeding northward to Kane Basin, through Robeson channel, establishing winter base at Cape Sheridan, Sept. 5, 1908; left Cape Sheridan for Cape Columbia, Feb. 15, 1909, in 5 detachments; the detachments were sent back one after another, the 4th, in command of Capt. Bartlett, leaving Peary nr. the 88th Parallel; from here, with 1 member of his crew and 4 Eskimos, made final dash of 130 miles to the pole in 5 days, which they reached Apr. 6, 1909; spent 30 hours at and beyond the pole; the journey from Cape Columbia to the pole was made in 27 marches, the return trip to Cape Columbia was made in 16 marches. Promoted to rank of rear admiral, and given thanks of Congress by special act of Congress, Mar. 3, 1911. Spl. gold medals of Nat. Geog. Soc. (Washington); Royal Geog. Soc. (London); Phila. Geog. Soc., Peary Arctic Club and Explorers Club; awarded the Hubbard gold medal by the Nat. Geog. Society, Culver gold medal, Chicago Geog. Soc.; Kane gold medal, Phila. Geog. Soc.; Daly and Cullom gold medals, Am. Geog. Soc.; gold medal of Imperial German, Austrian, and Hungarian socs.; Royal, Royal Scottish, Italian, and Belgian socs.; Swiss, Paris, Marseilles, Normandy, and City of Paris. Pres. Am. Geog. Soc., 1903; pres. 8th Internat. Geog. Congress, Washington, 1904; hon. v.p. 9th Internat. Geog. Congress, Geneva, 1908, and 10th, at Rome, 1913; pres. Explorers Club, and Aerial League America. U.S. Govt. del. Internat. Polar Commn., Rome, 1913; sec. Internat. Polar Commn.; chmn. Nat. Aerial Coast Patrol Commn. Made Grand Officier d'Honneur, France, 1913; hon. mem. Philadelphia Geog. Soc., Am. Alpine Club, Nat. Geog. Soc., Am. Mus. Natural Hist., N.Y. Chamber of Commerce, and all prin. home and foreign goeg. socs. Author: Northward Over the Great Ice, 1898; Nearest the Pole, 1907; The North Pole, 1910; Secrets of Polar Travel, 1917. Died Feb. 20, 1920.

PEASE, FRANCIS GLADHEIM, astronomer; b. Cambridge, Mass., Jan. 14, 1881; s. Daniel and Katharine Bangs (James) P.; high sch., Highland Park, Ill.; B.S., Armour Inst. Tech., 1901, M.S. 1924, D.Sc., 1927; D.Sc., Oglethorpe U., Atlanta, Ga., 1934; m. Caroline T. Furness, Apr. 20, 1905. Optician and observer, Yerkes Obs., Williams Bay, Wis., 1901-04; instrument designer, Mt. Wilson Obs., Pasadena, Calif., 1904-07, 1908-13, astronomer, 1911—; supt. "Scientific Shop" Works, Evanston, Ill., 1907-08. Chief draftsman for the Nat. Research Council, Washington, D.C., World War, 1918. Protestant. Has made direct photographs and spectograms of nebulae and star clusters and of the moon and planets; also interferometer measures of star diameters, measurement of the velocity of light. In charge of the design of 100-inch telescope, 50-foot interferometer telescope; asso. in optics and instrument design, 200-inch reflector, Calif. Inst. Tech., etc. Home: Pasadena, Calif. Died Feb. 7, 1938.

PEASE, ROBERT NORTON, chemist; b. Burlington, Vt., Apr. 12, 1895; s. Frederick S. and Mary M. (Henry) P.; B.S. in chemistry, U. of Vt., 1916; Ph.D., Princeton, 1921; m. Margaret S. Perkins, Dec. 21, 1929; children—Margaret Jane, Clement Flick. Asst. and associate professor chemistry U. Va., 1922-26; National Research Fellow, 1921-22; research asso., Princeton, 1926-31, asso. prof. chem., 1931-47, prof., 1947—, chairman dept., 1954-58; ofcl. investigator, Nat. Defense Research Committee, Washington, 1941-45; project research, Princeton, for Bur. Ordnance and Office Naval Research Navy Dept., Washington, 1945-57; mem. sub-com. on combustion Nat. Adv. Com. Aeronautics, 1946-53; cons. on hydrocarbon and combustion chemistry, catalysis. Awarded Army-Navy Certificate of Appreciation, 1947. Served as 2d lt., Chemical Warfare Service, 1918-19. Fellow, A.A.A.S., N.Y. Acad. Sci.; mem. Am. Chem. Society, International Combustion Institute (Director), Phi Beta Kappa, Sigma Xi, Sigma Phi. Conglist. Author: Equilibrium and Kinetics of Gas Reactions, 1942; articles chem. jours. Home: 35 Cedar Lane, Princeton, N.J. Office: Frick Chemical Laboratory, Princeton, N.J. Died June 15, 1964.

PEASLEE, EDMUND RANDOLPH, physician; b. Newton, N.H., Jan. 22, 1814; s. James and Abigail (Chase) P.; grad. Dartmouth, 1836; attended Dartmouth Med. Sch., 1837-39; M.D., Yale, 1840; m. Martha Kendrick, 1841, 2 children. Prof. anatomy and physiology Dartmouth, 1842-69, lectr. on diseases of women, 1868-70, prof. obstetrics and diseases of women, 1870-73, prof. gynecology, 1873-78, trustee, 1860-78; prof. surgery and anatomy Med. Sch. of Me., 1843-60; prof. pathology and physiology N.Y. Med. Coll., 1852-56; prof. obstetrics, 1856-60; lectr. obstetrics Albany Med. Coll., 1872-74, prof. gynecology, 1874-78; prof. gynecology Bellevue Hosp. Med. Coll., 1874-78; attending physician Demilt Dispensary, N.Y.C., 1858-65; pvt. practice medicine, N.Y.C., 1858-78. Author: Necroscopic Tables for Postmortem Examinations, 1851; Human Histology in Its Relations to Descriptive Anatomy, Physiology, and Pathology, 1857; Ovarian Tumors; Their Pathology, Diagnosis, and Treatment, Especially by Ovariotomy, 1872. Died N.Y.C., Jan. 21, 1878.

PEATTIE, DONALD CULROSS, (pet'ti), author, botanist; b. Chicago, Ill., June 21, 1898; s. Robert Burns and Elia (Wilkinson) P.; grad. Univ. High Sch., 1916; student U. of Chicago, 1916-18, A.B., cum laude, Harvard, 1922, A.M., 1946; m. Louise Redfield, May 23, 1923; children—Celia Louise (dec.), Malcolm Redfield, Mark Robert, Noel Roderick. Botanist Office of Fgn. Seed and Plant Introduction, U.S. Dept. Agr., 1922-25; John Guggenheim fellow, 1936-38. Fellow A.A.A.S.; mem. Nat. Inst. Arts and Letters; Society of American Historians, California Historical Society,

California Academy of Sciences; Phi Gamma Delta. Author: Cargoes and Harvests, 1926; Bounty of Earth (with wife), 1926; Up Country (with wife), 1927; Down Wind (with same) 1929; Flora of the Sand Dunes and the Calumet District of Indiana, 1930; Vence, the Story of a Provencal Town, 1930; Port of Call, 1932; Flora of the Tryon Region of North and South Carolina (six parts), 1928-32; Sons of the Martian, 1932; Natural History of Pearson's Falls, 1933; The Bright Lexicon, 1934; An Almanac for Moderns (awarded Limited Editions Club's gold medal), 1935; Singing in the Wilderness, 1935; The Happy Kingdom (with wife), 1935; Green Laurels, 1936; A Book of Hours, 1937; A Child's Story of The World, 1937; A Prairie Grove, 1938; This Is Living (with Gordon Aymar), 1938; A Gathering of Birds, 1939; Flowering Earth, 1939; Audubon's America, 1940; The Road of a Naturalist, 1941; Forward the Nation, 1942; Journey into America, 1943; Immortal Village, 1945; American Heartwood, 1949. A Cup of Sky (with Noel Peattie), 1950; A Natural History of Trees of Eastern and Central America, 1950; Sportsman's Country, 1952; A Natural History of Western Trees, 1953; Lives of Destiny, 1954; Parade with Banners, 1957; The Rainbow Book of Nature, 1957. Roving editor Reader's Digest. Address: 2784 Glendessary Lane, Santa Barbara, Cal. Died Nov. 16, 1964.

PEAVEY, LEROY DEERING, pres. Babson's Reports, Inc.; b. Exeter, N.H., Mar. 11, 1876; s. Sam Roswell and Mary Augusta (Smith) P.; grad. Phillips Exeter Acad., 1894; B.S., Mass. Inst. Tech., 1898; m. Fannie R. Nottage, Oct. 31, 1901; children—Ethelyn Bartlett, Dorothy Nottage, Marion Frances, Grace Augusta, Roswell Charles, Edith Gilman. Engaged in structural steel work, N.Y. City and Boston, 1898-1900; asst. engr. Am. Bridge Co. and Boston Bridge Works, 1900-03; chief engr. H. P. Converse Co., bridge and building contractors, Boston, 1903-10; with Babson's Statis. Orgn., 1910—, dir. and v.p., 1912-25, pres., 1925-34. Mem. Ch. of the Nazarene. Lecturer. Home: Watertown, Mass. Died Mar. 25, 1937.

PECK, CHARLES HORTON, botanist; b. Sand Lake, N.Y., Mar. 30, 1833; s. Joel B. and Pamelia (Horton) P.; A.B., Union Coll., N.Y., 1959, later A.M. (D.Sc., 1908); m. Mary C. Sliter, Apr. 10, 1861. Taught in Sand Lake Collegiate Inst. and Albany Classical Inst., 1959-67; in charge bot. dept., N.Y. State Mus., and state botanist, 1883-1915. Republican. Presbyn. Author of annual reports giving results of bot. investigations, including Edible and Poisonous Fungi of N.Y.; Boleti of the United States. Fellow A.A.A.S.; mem. Bot. Soc. Am., N.E. Bot. Club, Am. Forestry Assn., Albany Inst., Hist. and Art Soc.; hon. mem. Dana Natural History Soc., Buffalo Soc. Natural Scis., and several mycol. clubs. Home: Menands. Office: Education Bldg., Albany, N.Y. Died July 11, 1917; buried Sand Lake, N.Y.

PECK, FREDERICK BURRITT, geologist; b. Seneca Castle, N.Y., Aug. 19, 1860; s. Henry Jones and Mary Diantha (Gray) P.; A.B., Amherst, 1886; Ph.D., U. of Munich, Germany, 1896; m. Cora Burr Horton, June 12, 1901. Teacher mathematics and natural sciences, Trinidad, Colo., 1886-91; asst. in geology, Amherst and Smith colls., 1891-94; asso. prof. geology, 1897-1901, prof. mineralogy and geology, 1901—, Lafayette Coll., Easton, Pa. Asst. geologist U.S. Geol. Survey, 1898-1909. Presbyn. Died Nov. 2, 1925.

PECK, HENRY ALLEN, astronomer; b. Mexico, N.Y., May 4, 1863; s. Henry Carter and Margaret Augusta (Allen) P.; A.B., Syracuse U., 1885, A.M., 1888; Ph.D., U. of Strassburg, 1896; m. Kittie V. Becker, Aug. 3, 1887; 2d, Jessie Rankin Tyler, Dec. 22, 1898. Teacher common schs., 1879-81; teacher mathematics, Williamsport-Dickinson Sem., Williamsport, Pa., 1885-87; instr. astronomy, 1887-93, prof., 1893—, dean Coll. Liberal Arts, 1917—, Syracuse U. Methodist. Republican. Home: Syracuse, N.Y. Died Nov. 17, 1921.

PECK, JOHN SEDGWICK, electrical engr.; b. New Haven, Conn., Nov. 20, 1871; s. Henry Dwight and Jennie M. (Tucker) P.; prep. edn. Staunton Mil. Acad., Va.; M.E., Cornell, 1892; m. Josephine H. Arnold, of Boston, 1900. Began work in shops of Eddy Electric Co., Hartford, 1892; entered students' course, 1893, Westinghouse Electric & Mfg. Co., finally being placed in charge of the designing and constrn. of transformers; appointed acting chief elec. engr. British Westinghouse Elec. & Mfg. Co., Oct. 1, 1904, chief elec. engr., Oct. 1, 1905, consulting elec. engr., July 1906; chief elec. engr., Metropolitan-Vickers Elec. Co., Ltd., 1919—. Fellow Am. Inst. E.E.; mem. Inst. Elec. Engrs. Gt. Britain, Manchester Assn. Engrs., A.A.A.S. Clubs: Engineers (London and Manchester). Address: Schenley, Bentinck Rd., Altrincham England

PECK, MORTON EATON, prof. botany; b. La Porte City, Ia., Mar. 12, 1871; s. Geo. D. and Clara (Eaton) P.; A.B., Cornell Coll., Mt. Vernon, Ia., 1895, A.M., 1911, hon. Sc.D., 1940; m. Jessie Grant, May 15, 1905. Instr. biology, Marionville, Mo., 1896-97; prof. biology, Ellsworth (Ia.) Coll., 1897-1905; professor botany, Ia. Wesleyan Coll., 1907-08, Willamette U., since 1908. Made bot. collection in Brit. Honduras, 1905-07. Mem. Bot. Soc. America, Phi Beta Kappa, Sigma Xi. Republican. Methodist. Author: The Book of the Bardons and Other Poems, 1925; also A Manual of the Higher Plants of Oregon. Contbr. on distribution of seed plants and many taxonomic papers. Home: Salem OR

PECK, STAUNTON BLOODGOOD, civil and mech. engr.; b. N.Y. City, Oct. 20, 1864; s. Thomas Bloodgood and Mary Frances (Staunton) P.; student Columbia, 1882-86, fellow in engring., 1886-87, M.E., 1886, C.E., 1887; m. Clarabelle Moberly, 1893 (died 1910); m. 2d, Lola Maurene Downin, 1914. Mech. engr. with Burr & Dodge, Phila., 1887-88; asst. chief engr., Link-Belt Engring. Co., Phila., 1881-91; chief engr., Link-Belt Machinery Co., 1891-1906; v.p. Link-Belt Company, 1906-28, served as president during World War; retired 1928. Member Alpha Delta Phi. Republican. Episcopalian. Clubs: Union League, Rittenhouse, Sunnybrook Golf (Phila.); University (New York). Home: Montgomery Av., Chestnut Hill, Philadelphia PA

PECK, WILLIAM BUCKLEY, surgeon; b. Freeport, Ill., Oct. 11, 1872; s. William Ford and Natalie (Price) P.; student, Willamette U., Portland, Ore., 1888-93; M.D., Rush Med. Coll., Chicago, 1897; postgrad. work, Univs. of Vienna and Berlin, 1907-08; m. Alvina Weber, Sept. 26, 1912. Intern, London (Eng.) Hosp., Whitechapel, 1909; in practice surgery at Freeport, Ill., since 1897; mng. dir. Inter-State Postgraduate Med. Assn. of North America since 1916, in charge of post-graduate div. arranging scientific and clin. post-graduate studies in cooperation with the leading univs. of U.S., Canada, Europe and South America since 1923, now also editor of proceedings of same; district surgeon Chicago & Northwestern R.R. Co. Fellow A.M.A., Am. Coll. Surgeons; mem. Ill. State and Stephenson County med. socs., Am. Assn. Ry. Surgeons, Assn. Pour le Developpement des Relations Medicales (Paris, France). Republican. Presbyterian. Mason. Clubs: Country, Rotary. Home: 1556 W. Lincoln Blvd. Office: State Bank Bldg., Freeport, Ill. Died Aug. 20, 1941.

PECK, WILLIAM DANDRIDGE, naturalist; b. Boston, May 8, 1763; s. John and Hannah (Jackson) P.; B.A., Harvard, 1782; never married. Lived with father on farm at Kittery, Me., 1785-1805, engaged in botanical and zoological studies; 1st prof. natural history Harvard, 1805-22; established Botanic Garden, Cambridge, Mass.; 1st tchr. of entymology in U.S.; a founder Am. Antiquarian Soc., 1812; recipient Gold medals from Mass. Agrl. Soc. for article The Description and History of the Canker-Worm, 1795, also for book Natural History of the Slug Worm, 1799; 1st to discover and describe an egg parasite in U.S. Died Oct. 3, 1822.

PECK, WILLIAM GUY, educator, mathematician; b. Litchfield, Conn., Oct. 16, 1820; grad. U.S. Mil. Acad., 1844; A.M., Trinity Coll., 1853, LL.D., 1863; Ph.D., Columbia Coll., 1877; m. Miss Davis. Mem. survey of mil. fortifications of Portsmouth, N.H.; brevetted 2d lt. Topog. Engrs., U.S. Army; mem. John C. Fremont's 3d expdn. to Rocky Mountains; promoted lt. Topog. Engrs.; asst. prof. philosophy and mathematics U.S. Mil. Acad., 1846-55; prof. physics and civil engring. U. Mich., 1855-57; prof. mathematics Columbia, 1857-61; mem. bd. visitors U.S. Mil. Acad., 1868. Author: Elementary Mechanics, 1859; Manual of Arithmetic, 1874; Popular Astronomy, 1883. Died Greenwich, Conn., Feb. 7, 1892.

PECKHAM, STEPHEN FARNUM, chemist; b. Fruit Hill, Providence, R.I., Mar. 26, 1839; s. Charles and Hannah Lapham (Farnum) P.; student chemistry, Brown U., 1859-61 (hon. A.M., 1870); m. Mary Chace Peck, June 13, 1865 (died 1892); m. 2d, Dr. Hattie C. W. Van Buren, Aug. 1, 1902. Hosp. steward U.S.A., 1862-65; chemist to Calif. Petroleum Co., 1866, Calif. Geol. Survey, 1867; instr. chemistry, Brown, 1867-68; prof. chemistry, Washington and Jefferson Coll., 1868-69, Me. Agrl. Coll., 1869-71, Buchtel Coll., 1871-72, U. of Minn., 1872-80; spl. agt. U.S. Census, 1880-85; chemist, Union Oil Co. of Calif., 1893-94; chemist to Commrs. of Accts., New York, 1898-1908, Dept. of Finance, New York, 1908-11; cons. chemist, New York, 1911—. State assayer, Me., 1869-71, Minn., 1873-80, R.I., 1887. Author: Elementary Chemistry, 1873; Report on Production, Technology and Uses of Petroleum, 1885; Solid Bitumens, 1909. Home: Brooklyn, N.Y. Died July 12, 1916.

PECKHAM, WILLIAM CLARK, physicist; b. S. Royalston, Mass., Aug. 13, 1841; s. Rev. Samuel Howland and Sarah (Clark) P.; pvt. 23d Mass. Vols., 1861-62; A.B., Amherst, 1867, A.M., 1873; student Union Theol. Sem., 1871-72; m. Katalena Whittier, Jan. 1, 1868. Prof. mathematics and physics, Adelphi Acad., 1875-96; prof. physics, Adelphi Coll., 1896—. On editorial staff of Scientific American, 1897—, contributing editor, 1921—; science lecturer in Free Lectures for the People, Bd. of Edn., New York. Fellow Am. Physical Soc., Am. Acad. Arts and Sciences, Brooklyn Inst. Arts and Sciences. Home: Brooklyn, N.Y. Died Oct. 3, 1922.

PEDDER, JAMES, agriculturist; b. Newport, Isle of Wight, Eng., July 29, 1775; m. Eliza. Asst. to chemist Dr. Samuel Parks, London, Eng., 1809-19; in charge of various large estates, Eng., 1819-32; came to U.S., 1832; employed by Phila. Beet Sugar Soc. to study French methods of mfg. beet sugar, 1832-33; editor Farmers' Cabinet, Phila., 1840-43; mem. Phila. Soc. for Promoting Agr., librarian, 1842; corr. editor Boston Cultivator, 1844-48, resident editor, 1848-59. Author: The Yellow Shoestrings, or The Good Effects of Obedience to Parents, 1814; Report Made to the Best Sugar Society on the Culture in France of the Beet Root, 1836; The Farmer's Land Measurer, or Pocket Companion, 1842. Died Roxbury (now part of Boston), Aug. 27, 1859; buried Forest Hills Cemetery, Jamaica Plain, Mass.

PEEBLES, FLORENCE, biologist; b. Pewee Valley, Ky., June 3, 1874; d. Thomas Chalmers and Elizabeth Southgate (Cummins) P.; A.B., Goucher Coll., Baltimore, Md., 1895; Mary E. Garrett scholar in biology, Bryn Mawr Coll., 1895-96; Mary E. Garrett fellow, student U. of Munich and U. of Halle, 1899; Ph.D., Bryn Mawr Coll., 1900; grad. study univs. of Bonn, 1905, Wurzburg, 1911, Freiburg, 1913; unmarried. Demonstrator in biology, Bryn Mawr Coll., 1897-98; instr. in biology, Goucher Coll., 1899-1902, asso. prof., 1902-06; instr. in science, Miss Wright's Sch., Bryn Mawr, Pa., 1906-12; European fellow Assn. Coll. Alumni, 1912-13; acting head of dept. biology, Bryn Mawr Coll., 1913; head of dept. biology, Sophie Newcomb Coll., Tulane U., 1915-17; asso. prof. biology, Bryn Mawr, 1917-19; prof. biol. sciences, Calif. Christian (now Chapman) Coll., since 1928; extension lecturer, U. of Calif., since 1927. Research worker, Marine Biol. Lab., Woods Hole, Mass., 10 times between 1895 and 1924; holder Am. Woman's Table at Naples Zool. Station, Italy, 5 times between 1898 and 1927. Fellow A.A.A.S.; mem. Am. Soc. Naturalists, Corpn. Marine Biol. Lab., Phi Beta Kappa. Episcopalian. Contbr. to Biol. Bull., Jour. Exptl. Zoology, etc. Home: Altadena CA

PEEK, FRANK WILLIAM, JR., electrical engr.; b. Mokelumne Hill, Calif., Aug. 20, 1881; s. Frank W. and May (Stedman) P.; A.B., Stanford, 1905; M.E.E., Union U., Schenectady, N.Y., 1911; m. Merle Bell, Aug. 9, 1913. With Gen. Electric Co., 1905, cons. and research engr., 1910—; engr. in charge gen. transformer engring. dept., 1927-31, chief engr. Gen. Electric Co., Pittsfield, 1931—. Specialized in development laws of corona, research in high voltage phenomena, in lightning, high voltage transmission, measurements of natural lightning and production of 5,000,000 volts artificial lightning. Rep. of Am. Inst. E.E. on Nat. Research Council. Fellow Am. Inst. E.E. (dir.), Am. Physical Soc., Franklin Inst. Awarded Thomas Fitch Rowland prize, Am. Soc. C.E., 1924; Levy medal, Franklin Inst., 1926. Episcopalian. Author: Dielectric Phenomena in High Voltage Engineering, 1915, 29 (in French, 1924). Home: Pittsfield, Mass. Died July 26, 1933.

PEELE, ROBERT, (pel), mining engr.; b. N.Y. City, July 15, 1858; s. Robert and Anne (Westervelt) P.; E.M., Sch. of Mines (Columbia), 1883; unmarried. In the field as mining engr., 1883-92; mem. firm of Olcott, Fearn & Peele, mining engrs., 1896-1901, Olcott, Corning & Peele, 1901-07; adj. prof. mining, Columbia, 1892-1904, prof. 1904-25, prof. emeritus. Presbyterian. Mem. Am. Inst. Mining and Metall. Engrs. (hon. 1937), Instn. Mining and Metallurgy of London (hon. 1921), Mining and Metall. Soc. Am. (gold medal for contbns. to lit. of mining engring., 1923), Tau Beta Pi. Clubs: Century, Columbia U. Author: Compressed Air Plant, 1908, 5th edit., 1930; Mining Engineers Handbook, 1918, 3d edit., 1941. Translator (from German of J. Riemer) Shaftsinking Under Difficult Conditions, 1907. Contbr. on mining subjects. Traveled professionally in Peru, Bolivia, Chile, Colombia and Dutch Guiana, 1888-92; made trip around the world, 1903-04, to S. Africa and S. America, 1910. Home: 490 West End Av., New York, N.Y. Died Dec. 8, 1942.

PEET, MAX MINOR, surgeon; b. Iosco, Mich., Oct. 20, 1885; s. LaFayette and Eunice Ann (Minor) P.; A.B., U. of Mich., 1908, A.M., 1910, M.D., 1910; hon. M. Ed., Mich. State Normal Coll., Ypsilanti, Mich., 1934; m. Grace Stewart Tait, Oct. 5, 1915; children—Max Minor, Stewart Tait, Martha Eunice Ann. Intern, R.I. Hosp., Providence, 1910-12; Robert Robinson Porter fellow in research medicine, U. of Pa., 1912-13; asst. instr. surgery, U. of Pa., 1913-15; asst. chief surgeon, Phila. Gen. Hosp., 1914-16; instr. in surgery, U. of Mich., 1916-17, asst. prof., 1918-27, asso. prof. of neuro-surgery, 1927-30, prof. of surgery since 1930; chief of neurosurgical div., Univ. Hosp., University of Michigan, since 1918. Member general advisory committee, virus research, medical publications and chmn. ed. comm. Nat. Foundation for Infantile Paralysis. Mem. Internat. Neurol. Congress, Berne, 1931, London, 1935; Internat. Surg. Congress, Brussels, 1938. Fellow A.M.A., Am. Coll. of Surgeons; mem. Soc. of Neurol. Surgeons, Am. Surg. Assn., Am. Bd. of Surgery, Am. Neurological Assn., vice chmn. Am. Board Neurological Surg.; mem. Central Surgical Assn., Internat. Soc. of Surgery, Mich. State Med. Soc., Washtenaw Co. Med. Soc., Harvey Cushing Soc.; honorary mem. Sociedad Argentina de Cirujanos, Los Angeles Surgical Society, Detroit Academy of Surgery; member Alpha Omega Alpha, Sigma Xi, Alpha Kappa Kappa. Mason. Clubs: Cooper Ornithol., Wilson Ornithol., American Ornithologists Union, Barton Hills Country. Ornithologist, U. of Mich. Museums expdns., 1904, 05, 32. Contbr. numerous articles on neurosurgical problems to med. jours, and chapters on neuro-surgery in various surgical works. Home: 2030 Hill St. Office: University Hospital, 1313 E. Ann St., Ann Arbor, Mich. Died Mar. 25, 1949; buried Forest Hill Cemetery, Ann Arbor, Mich.

PEFFER, HARRY CREIGHTON, chemistry; b. Enon Valley, Pa., Aug. 15, 1873; s. Christian Gottloeb Luther and Fannie Jane (Creighton) P.; B.S., Pa. State Coll., 1895, M.S., 1908; m. Mary Carolyne Rebhun, Dec. 29, 1897; children—Ella Louise, Jane Creighton (Mrs. Charles Wheeler Shook), Harry Creighton, David McNair. Chemist, Carnegie Steel Co., Homestead, Pa., 1895; control chemist Pa. Salt Mfg. Co., 1896-1900; supt. expt. plant and lab. dir. Pittsburgh Reduction Co., 1900-03; gen. supt. and dir. research, Aluminum Co. of America, E. St. Louis, Ill., 1903-08; consultant same as Pittsburgh, 1908-13; dir. Sch. of Chem. Engring., Purdue, 1911—; mem. bd. management Purdue Engring. Expt. Sta.; v.p. Rostone, Inc. Orgn. mgr. U.S. Explosives Plant C, World War. Mem. Ind. Gas Standards Commn., 1917-18. Republican. Episcopalian. Mason. Kiwanian. Holder patents on chem. and industrial processes, bldg. materials, mech. devices, welding. Home: West Lafayette, Ind. Died July 17, 1934.

PEGRAM, GEORGE BRAXTON, (pe'gram), physicist; b. Trinity, N.C., Oct. 24, 1876; s. William Howell and Emma Lenore (Craven) P.; A.B., Trinity Coll., Durham, N.C., 1895, Ph.D., Columbia, 1903; studied U. of Berlin, 1907, Cambridge U., 1908; D.Sc., Trinity (Duke), 1918, Columbia, 1929, George Washington, 1937, U. of N.C., 1946, Northwestern U., 1946, Case Inst. Tech., 1951; LL.D., U. of Denver, 1950; married Florence Bement, June 3, 1909; children—William Braxton, John Bement. With Columbia U. since 1901 as asst. in physics, 1901-03, tutor, 1903-05, instr., 1905-07, Tyndall fellow, 1907, asst. prof. physics, 1909-12, asso. prof., 1912-18, prof. since 1918, acting dean Sch. of Mines, Engring. and Chemistry, 1917-18, dean, 1918-30, dean, Grad. Faculties, 1937-49, v.p., 1949-50, spl. adviser to the pres. since 1950; chmn. Columbia com. on War Research, 1941-45; sci., also ednl. consultant Oak Ridge Institute Nuclear Studies. Fellow A.A.A.S., Am. Phys. Soc. (treas. 1917-57), Am. Soc. M.E., Inst. Aero. Scis.; mem. Am. Inst. Physics (treas., 1939-55), Nat. Acad. Scis., Am. Philos. Soc., Inst. Radio Engrs., Sigma Xi (pres. 1949-51). Contbr. research papers in physics. Clubs: Columbia University, Century. Home: 220 Kings Rd., Madison, N.J. Office: Columbia U., N.Y.C. 27. Died Aug. 12, 1958.

PEGRAM, GEORGE HERNDON, civil engr.; b. Council Bluffs, Ia., Dec. 29, 1855; s. Capt. Benjamin Rush and Mercy Adelaide (Robbins) P.; C.E., Washington U., 1877, M.A., 1905, LL.D. from the same university in 1928; m. Jessie Mirrielees Crawford, Sept. 8, 1897; children—Jean Forsyth, Mercy Robbins, Geo. H. (dec.). Engr. on construction Utah & Northern Ry. of Ida., 1877-78; prin. asst. to C. Shaler Smith, bridge engr., 1878-80; chief engr. Edge Moor Iron Co., Wilmington, Del., 1880-86; cons. engr., New York, 1886-89; cons. engr., Mo.P. R.R., 1889-93; chief engr. U.P. System, 1893-98; was also cons. engr. Pioneer Electric Power Co. during constrn. of its plants at Ogden and Salt Lake City; chief engr. Manhattan Elevated R.R., 1898-1905, Interborough Rapid Transit Co., 1905—, also Rapid Transit Subway Constrn. Co., 1905—, and New York Rys. Co., 1912—. Was designer Kansas City Elevated R.R. and St. Louis Union Sta.; invented and patented Pegram truss for bridges, 1889; designed and built combined highway and ry. bridge across Arkansas River at Ft. Smith, Ark., 1890. Home: South Orange, N.J. Died Dec. 23, 1937.

PEGUES, BOYKIN WITHERSPOON, prof. civil engring.; b. Stonewall, La., Oct. 1, 1874; s. Thomas Godfrey and Rebecca (Witherspoon) P.; B.S. in Civil Engring., La. State U., 1895; grad. work, Cornell U., summers, 1905-22; M.S. in Civil Engring., U. of Wis., 1928; m. Mable Chapman, June 17, 1923. Chainman, transitman, U.S. govt. Engrs., 1895-99; with La. State U. since 1899, as asst. prof. civil engring., 1899-1901, prof., 1901-26, acting dean coll. of engring., 1926-31, head dept. of civil engring. since 1931. Mem. La. State Bd. Engring. Examiners. Life mem. La. Engring. Soc.; mem. Am. Soc. Civil Engrs., Phi Kappa Phi, Tau Beta Pi. Home: 3804 Perkins Road, Baton Rouge LA*

PEIRCE, BENJAMIN, mathematician, astronomer; b. Salem, Mass., Apr. 4, 1809; s. Benjamin and Lydia (Nichols) P.; grad. Harvard, 1829; m. Sarah Hunt Mills, July 23, 1833, 5 children including Charles S., James Mills, Herbert Henry Davis. Instr., Round Hill Sch., Northampton, Mass., 1829-31; tutor mathematics Harvard, 1831-33, prof. astronomy and mathematics, 1833-42, Perkins prof. mathematics and astronomy, 1842-80, largely responsible for establishment of Harvard Observatory, 1843; founder, editor Cambridge Miscellany of Mathematics, Physics, and Astronomy, 1842-43; cons. astronomer for Am. Nautical Almanac, 1849-67, renamed Astronomical Almanac for the Use of Navigators, 1860; mem. Am. Philos. Soc., 1842-80; asso. mem. Royal Astron. Soc., 1850-80; pres. A.A.A.S., 1853; fellow Am. Acad. Arts and Scis., 1858-80; hon. fellow U. St. Vladimir, Kiev, Russia, 1860-80; corr. mem. Brit. Assn. for Advancement Science, 1861-80, Royal Soc. Sciences, Göttingen, Germany, 1867-80; hon. fellow Royal Soc. Edinburgh, 1867-80; an organizer Smithsonian Instn., 1847; dir. longitude determinations of U.S. Coast Survey, 1852-67, supt., 1867-74, cons. geometer, 1874-80, directed Am. expdn. to Sicily to observe eclipse of sun, 1870; a founder Nat. Acad. Scis., 1863, chmn. mathematics and physics class; asso. editor Am. Jour. of Mathematics, 1878; proved there is no odd perfect number having fewer than 4 prime factors, 1832; computed gen. perturbations of Uranus and Neptune; formulated "Peirce's criterion," object of which was to solve practically important problem of probabilities in connection with series of observations. Author: An Elementary Treatise on Sound, 1836; An Elementary Treatise on Algebra, 1837; An Elementary Treatise on Plane and Solid Geometry, 1837; An Elementary Treatise on Plane and Spherical Trigonometry, 1840; An Elementary Treatise on Curves, Functions, and Forces, vol. I, 1841, vo. II, 1846; Tables of the Moon, 1853; A System on Analytic Mechanics, 18550 Tables of the Moon's Parallax, 1856; Linear Associative Algebra, 1870. Died Oct. 6, 1880.

PEIRCE, BENJAMIN MILLS, mining engr.; b. Cambridge, Mass., Mar. 19, 1844; s. Benjamin and Sarah Hunt (Mills) P.; grad. Harvard, 1865; postgrad. Sch. of Mines, Paris, France, 1865-67, U. Freiburg (Germany), 1867. Worked in Iceland and Greenland, 1867-68, wrote U.S. Govt. report on mineral resources and conditions there (his most noted work); mining engr. in Mich., 1868-70. Died Ishpeming, Mich., Apr. 22, 1870.

PEIRCE, BENJAMIN OSGOOD, physicist; b. Beverly, Mass., Feb. 11, 1854; s. Benjamin Osgood and M. (Seccomb) P.; A.B., Harvard, 1876; Ph.D., U. of Leipzig, 1879; student Berlin, 1879-80; m. Isabella Turnbull Landreth, July 27, 1882. Taught in Boston Latin Sch., 1880-81; instr. mathematics, 1881-84, asst. prof. mathematics and physics, 1884-88, Hollis Prof. mathematics and natural philosophy, 1888—, Harvard. Fellow Am. Acad. Arts and Sciences, Am. Philos. Soc., A.A.A.S., etc. Author: Theory of the Newtonian Potential Function; Table of Integrals, Boston, 1899; Experiments in Magnetism. Home: Cambridge, Mass. Died Jan. 14, 1914.

PEIRCE, CHARLES SANTIAGO SANDERS, Am. logician, phychologist; b. Cambridge, Mass., Sept. 10, 1839; s. Benjamin Peirce; mother was d. U.S. Senator Mills, of Mass.; A.B., Harvard, 1859, Sc.B. in Chemistry summa cum laude, 1863; m. (Harriett) Melusina Fay, 1862; m. 2d, Juliette Froissy. Mem. staff U.S. Coast Survey, 1861-91; lectr. Johns Hopkins, 1897-84, Harvard, 1903, Lowell Inst., 1903-04; pvt. research in logic, Pike County, Pa., from 1887. Fellow Am. Acad. Arts and Scis. Author: Photometric Researches, 1878; Collected papers, 8 vols., 1931-58. Editor (with extensive additions); Studies in Logic (mems. of Johns Hopkins U.), 1883; Linear Associative Algebra (Benjamin Peirce), 1882. Founder pragmatism, 1878 (later developed by William James), also of pragmaticism; laid founds. of logic of relations, instrument for logical analysis of math., 1867-85; contbd. to theory of probability and to logic of sci. methodology; modified Booleian algebra to accomodate De Morgan's logic; distinguished 3-fold div. of predicates; elaborated triadic theory of meaning; demonstrated his father's algebra to be operational and matricular; represented Brassmann's system in logical notation; proved that bodies in 4-fold space must rotate about 2 axes at once or lose a dimension; made studies of pendulum; research in meteorology, psychophysics, philology. Died Milford, Pa., Apr. 14, 1914.

PEIRCE, GEORGE JAMES, (pûrs), botanist; b. Manila, P.I., Mar. 13, 1868; s. George Henry and Lydia Ellen (Eaton) P.; S.B., Lawrence Scientific Sch. (Harvard), 1890, fellow, 1892-94; univs. of Bonn, Leipzig, Munich, 1892-94; A.M., Ph.D., Leipzig, 1894; m. Anna Hobart, June 14, 1897; children—Elizabeth, Carolyn, Rosamond Hobart. Asst. prof. botany, Ind. U., 1895-97; asst. prof. botany, Stanford, 1897-1900, asso. prof., 1900-10, prof., 1910-33, now emeritus. Collaborator U.S. Forest Service, 1909-10; spl. agt. Dept. of Justice, studying effect of smoke on vegetation, 1910-11; studied effect of cement dust on vegetation, 1911. Mem. later chmn. Palo Alto Cal. Bd. Health; chmn. Palo Alto Chpt. Red Cross, 1914-41; mem. wood fuel adv. com., Fuel Adminstrn. for Cal., 1917-18. Fellow Am. Acad. Arts and Scis., A.A.A.S., Bot. Soc. Am. (pres. 1932); mem. Brit. Assn. for Advancement of Sc., Deutsche Botanische Gesellschaft; charter mem. Am. Assn. Univ. Profs. Clubs: Commonwealth, Harvard (San Francisco). Author: Textbook of Plant Physiology, 1903; The Physiology of Plants—The Principles of Food-Production, 1925; Experimental Plant Physiology, 1931. Joint Author: General Biology. Contbr. articles to Dictionary of Am. Biographies, Sci. Monthly, Botanical Gazette, etc. Home: 281 Embarcadero Rd., Palo Alto, Cal. Died Oct. 15, 1954.

PEIRCE, JAMES MILLS, prof. mathematics, Harvard, 1869—; b. Cambridge, Mass., May 1, 1834; grad. Harvard, 1853 (A.M.). Tutor there, 1854-58 and 1860-61; asst. prof. mathematics, 1861-69, univ. prof., 1869-85, Perkins professor, 1885—, sec. academic council, 1872-90, dean of grad. school, 1890-95, dean of faculty of arts and sciences, 1895-98; unmarried. Author: Text-Book of Analytic Geometry, 1857; Three and Four-Place Tables, 1871; Elements of Logarithms, 1874; Mathematical Tables Chiefly to Four Figures, 1879. Home: Cambridge, Mass. Died 1906.

PEIRCE, WILLIAM HENRY, retired engr.; b. Baltimore, Aug. 22, 1865; s. William Henry and Georgia V. (Browne) P.; M.E. Stevens Inst. Tech., 1884, D.Engring., 1935; m. Esther Royston Belt, Aug. 23, 1933. Apprentice with Pa. R.R., Wilmington, Del., 1884-87; draftsman, etc., Aurora, Ill., 1887-88; asst. master mechanic, C.,B.&Q. Ry., Galesburg, 1888-89; supt. constrn. United Edison Co., New York, 1889-90; apptd. spl. investigator electrolytic copper refining Baltimore Copper Smelting & Rolling Co., 1890; asst. mgr., mgr., v.p. and pres. B.C.S.&R. Co., 1891-1933; ex-pres. Peirce-Smith Converter Co.; ex-v.p. Am. Smelting & Refining Co.; past dir. and 1st v.p. Revere Copper and Brass Inc. Mem. Am. Soc. M.E.; Am. Inst. Mining Engrs., Am. Electrochem. Soc., Sigma Chi. Republican. Episcopalian. Clubs: Merchants, Baltimore Country, Elkridge (Baltimore); Bankers (New York). Inventor of methods of smelting and refining of copper, particularly in basic converting of copper matte to blister copper and electrolytic refining of resulting blister copper. James Douglas medalist, Am. Inst. of Mining and Metal. Engrs., 1931. Home: 100 W. University Parkway, Baltimore, Md.; and Western Run Farm, Cockeysville, Maryland. Died May 25, 1944.

PELHAM, PETER, engraver; b. England, 1695; s. Peter Pelham; m. Martha Pelham; m. 2d, Margaret Lowrey, Oct. 15, 1734; m. 3d, Mary (Singleton) Copley, May 22, 1748; several children including George, Henry. Came to Am., circa 1728; one of 1st to use mezzotint technique of engraving; besides engraving portraits conducted small sch. and tobacco shop, Boston; portrait subjects included Queen Anne, King George I, Gov. Samuel Shute of Mass., Rev. Cotton Mather, John Smibert. Died Boston, Dec. 1751.

PELLETT, FRANK CHAPMAN, naturalist; b. Atlantic, Ia., July 12, 1879; s. Ambrose and Ellen (Chapman) P.; student pub. schs.; m. Ada E. Neff, Apr. 8, 1902; children—Kent Louis, Frank Melvin, Fred Gustin, Ruth Mona. Admitted to Mo. bar, 1905, practiced at Salem 2 yrs.; returned to farm, 1907; state apiarist of Ia., by apptmt. of gov., 1912-17. Fellow A.A.A.S., Am. Assn. Econ. Entomologists, Ia. Acad. Sci. (life), Royal Hort. Soc. (London); mem. Beta Beta Beta (hon.). Republican. Methodist. Odd Fellow. Author: Productive Bee-keeping, 1915; Practical Queen Rearing, 1917; Our Backdoor Neighbors, 1916; Beginner's Bee Book, 1919; American Honey Plants, 1920; Birds of the Wild, 1928; Practical Tomato Culture (with Melvin Pellett), 1930; Romance of the Hive, 1931; Flowers of the Wild, 1931; History of American Beekeeping, 1938; A Living from Bees, 1943; How to Attract Birds, 1947; Success with Wild Flowers, 1947. Field editor Am. Bee Jour. Home: Hamilton, Ill.; (summer) Pellett Gardens, Atlantic, Ia. Died Apr. 28, 1951; buried Atlantic, Ia.

PEMBERTON, HENRY, chemist; b. Phila., Feb. 11, 1826; s. John and Rebecca (Clifford) P.; brother of the late Confederate lt. gen., John C. P.; ed. in Phila. and under Daniel Murray, nr. Baltimore; m. Caroline Hollingsworth, 1841; m. 2d, Agnes, d. Hon. Thomas Williams, 1867. For 17 yrs. chief chemist, mng. dir. and v.p. Pa. Salt Mfg. Co. (chemicals); retired from business. In 1865 contracted in Denmark for monopoly of kryolite for N. and S. America. Author: The Path of Evolution Through Ancient Thought and Modern Science, 1903. Address: Philadelphia, Pa. Died 1911.

PEMBERTON, JOHN DE JARNETTE, surgeon; b. Wadesboro, N.C., May 3, 1887; s. John de Jarnette and Emma Marshall (Lilly) P.; A.B., U. N.C., 1907, LL.D., 1932; M.D., U. Pa., 1911; M.S. in surgery, U. Minn., 1918; m. Anna T. Hogeland, June 4, 1918; children—John de Jarnette, Albert Hogeland, Henry Walter, Robert Gray, Elizabeth Anne. Intern, Episcopal Hosp., Phila., 1911-13; intern Mayo Clinic, Rochester, Minn., 1913-14, asst. in surgery, 1914-18, surgeon, 1918—; also prof. surgery Mayo Found. Grad. Sch., U. Minn., 1936—. First lt. Med. R.C., World War. Fellow A.C.S.; mem. A.M.A., Am. Surg. Assn., Soc. Clin. Surgery, So. Surg. Assn., Minn. State Med. Assn., Am. Assn. for Study Goiter (pres. 1941-42), So. Minn. Med. Assn., Internat. Soc. Surgery, Am. Bd. Surgery, Alpha Tau Omega, Nu Sigma Nu, Alpha Omega Alpha, Sigma Xi. Democrat. Episcopalian. Clubs: University, Country. Contbr. on gen. surgery and surgery of thyroid gland. Home: 930 8th St. S.W. Office: Mayo Clinic, Rochester, Minn. Died May 18, 1967; buried Oakland Cemetery.

PEMBERTON, RALPH, M.D.; b. Phila., Pa., Sept. 14, 1877; s. Henry and Agnes (Williams) P.; B.S., U. of Pa., 1898, M.S., 1899, M.D., 1903, Woodward fellow physiol. chemistry, Pepper Lab., 1908-10; grad. study Berlin, 1911, U. of Strassburg, 1912; m. Virginia Breckenridge Miller, May 23, 1911. Began practice, Phila., 1905; instr. in medicine, U. of Pa., 1907-10, asso. prof. medicine, Grad. Sch., 1928-31, prof. since 1931; asst. visiting physician, U. of Pa. Hosp., 1908-10; asst. visiting neurologist, Phila. Gen. Hosp., 1905-08; visiting physician and dir. dept. clin. chemistry, Presbyterian

Hosp., 1913-33; visiting physician to Abington Memorial Hosp.; consulting physician to Chester County Hosp. Nat. consultant in rheumatism and arthritis under Program of War-Time Grad. Med. Meetings since 1943; chmn. com. on rheumatic diseases of Advisory Health Bd., Dept. of Health, Phila., since 1944. Served as major Medical Corps, U.S. Army, in charge intensive study and treatment of arthritis. Awarded meritorious service medal, Commonwealth of Pa., 1939. Dr. Ralph Pemberton, Prof. of Medicine, Grad. School, Univ. of Pa., was awarded the gold key of the American Congress of Physical Medicine at its 24th annual meeting New York City, Sept. 4 to 7, 1946. Dr. Pemberton was given the reward in recognition of his research on Arthritis and in the advance of Physical Medicine. Mem. standing com. on preventive medicine, Dept. of Health, Phila., 1921-22; chmn. American Committee for Control of Rheumatism, 1927-35; president American Rheumatism Association, 1938-39; president Ligue Internationale contre le Rhumatisme; president, Pan-American League for the Study and Control of Rheumatic Diseases since 1944. Fellow American College Physicians, Coll. Physicians Phila.; mem. A.M.A. (member standing council on physical therapy, 1928-42), Academy of Physical Medicine, American Soc. for Clin. Investigation, American Institute Nutrition, Phila. County Med. Soc. (med. advisory com. on pub. welfare, 1939), Acad. Natural Sciences, Franklin Inst., Internat. Soc. of Med. Hydrology, Mil. Order of the Loyal Legion of U.S., Sigma Xi, Delta Psi; hon. fellow Royal Soc. of Medicine, London; hon. mem., Societatea Anatomo Clinica, Bucharest, Liga Argentina contre el Reumatismo; hon. mem. Liga Uruguaya contre el Reumatismo; hon. member Liga Brasileira contra o Reumatismo. Unitarian. Clubs: Philadelphia, Racquet, University Barge. Author: Arthritis and Rheumatoid Conditions, 1929, translated into French, 1933, second edition, 1935; (with R. B. Osgood) Medical and Orthopedic Management of Chronic Arthritis, 1934. Contbr. to Nelson Loose Leaf System of Medicine, 1922, Bedside Diagnosis (by American authors), 1927, Text book of Medicine (by same), 1928, internat. Ency. of Medicine since 1931, Tice System of Medicine since 1934; also articles to professional journals. Editor of vol. on Medicine in Principles and Practice of Physical Therapy, 1932. Home: Paoli, Pa. Office: 2031 Locust St., Philadelphia, Pa. Died June 17, 1949.

PENBERTHY, GROVER CLEVELAND, surgeon; b. Houghton, Mich., Mar. 1, 1886; s. Edward Rawlings and Ellen Martha (McKernan) P.; M.D., U. Mich., 1910, M.S. (hon.), 1942; U. Pa., 1918 (Army assignment); m. Elizabeth Wardner, July 16, 1921 (div. 1939); children—Philip Edward, Grover Wardner, John McKernan. House Officer, N.Y.C. Hosp., 1910-12, dep. med. supt., 1912-13; began genl. practice, Detroit, 1913; instr. anatomy, Detroit Coll. Medicine (now Med. Coll., Wayne U.), 1913-14; asst. to Harry N. Torrey, surgeon, 1915-17; in gen. practice of surgery, 1919-42; in military service, 1942-46; surgeon, out-patient clinic, Harper Hosp., Detroit, 1915, junior surgeon Harper Hospital, 1919, surgeon, 1934-48, chief, general surgery, 1948-49, and sr. surgeon, cons. staff since 1950; asso. surgeon Childrens Hospital of Mich., 1919, dir. dept. of surgery, 1920, cons., 1953; asso. surgeon Herman Kiefer Hosp., 1926, also chief of staff; non-resident lecturer, dept. surgery U. Mich., 1920-55, prof. emeritus, 1955—, prof. clin. surgery, Wayne U., 1935; now clin. surgeon at Wayne State U.; extramural lecturer, Post Graduate School, U. Mich. cons. surgeon, Detroit Receiving Hospital, Jennings Memorial Hospital, Detroit Orthopedic Clinic, Sinai Hosp., Detroit Meml. Hosp. and Blain Hospital, surg. dir., Mich. Mutual Liability Co., 1946, Cons. Surgeon, Herman Kiefer Hospital, 1946; cons. surgeon Vets. Adminstrn. Hosp., 1946. Mem. adv. bd. to Surgeon Gen. AUS, 1951-52. Member Detroit City Plan commn., 1957—. Served as seaman Michigan Naval Brigade, 1908, hospital steward, 1909; lieut., Med. Corps, U.S. Army, 1917, advancing through grades to maj. 1918; lt. colonel, Med. Reserve Corps, 1919, col., 1925; called to active duty as col., Med. Corps, U.S. Army, 1942; serving as surg. cons., 7th S.C. Hdqrs., Omaha, Neb., discharged as col. June 1946. Hon. Reserve Med. Corps, U.S. Army, 1948. Dir. Cranbrook Sch., 1950-55, chmn. bd. dirs., 1954-55. Legion of Merit, Res., 1946. Diplomate Am. Bd. of Surgery, 1928. Fellow A.C.S. (gov., regent); mem. Soc. Med. Consultants to Armed Forces (pres. 1951-52), Wayne Co. Med. Soc., Mich. State (pres. 1935-36), Medical Society, Detroit Academy Surgery (past pres.), Detroit Academy of Medicine (past pres.) Mich. Soc. Mental Hygiene (past pres.), Detroit Med. Club (hon.), Flint (Michigan) Academy Surgery (hon.), Terre Haute (Ind.) Acad. Med. (hon.), A.M.A. (rep. surg. sect., sci. exhibit 1938-44; del. sect. abdominal and gen. surgery 1942-45), Royal Soc. Medicine (London), Am., So., Western surg. assns., Am. Assn. Surgery Trauma (pres. 1944-45), Central Surg. Assn. (pres. 1941-42), Am., Mich. (past pres.) indsl. med. assns., Detroit Bd. Commerce, Assn. Mil. Surgeons, Société Internationale de Chirurgie, Detroit Bd. of Commerce, A.A.A.S., Phi Rho Sigma, Alpha Omega Alpha. Republican. Episcopalian. Mason (Shriner). Clubs: Detroit, University, Athletic, University Mich. (gov. 1957), Economic, Torch (Detroit). Home: 1130 Parker Av. Office: 1553 Woodward Av., Detroit 26. Died Sept. 2, 1959.

PENCE, WILLIAM DAVID, civil engr.; b. at Columbus, Ind., Nov. 26, 1865; s. David and Nancy (Hart) P.; student U. of Ill., 1883-86, C.E., 1895; m. Charlotte Gaston, Dec. 31, 1888 (died May 6, 1938); children—Ada (Mrs. S. H. Slichter), Helen Charlotte (Mrs. A. J. B. Wace), Esther Nancy (Mrs. A. F. Britton). Asst. and resident engr., A.T.&S.F. Ry., 1886-92; instr., asst. prof. and asso. prof. civ. engring., U. of Ill., 1892-99; prof. civ. engring., Purdue U., 1899-1906; prof. ry. engring., U. of Wis., 1906-15; editor publs. Am. Ry. Engring. Assn., 1903-15; mem. U.S. Commn. Investigation Drainage Kankakee Marsh Region, 1904-06; chief engr. Wis. Ry. Commn., and Wis. Tax Commn., 1906-13; mem. engring. bd. Interstate Commerce Commn., in charge of Central Dist., federal valuation of rys., May 1913-Nov. 1921; consulting practice. Awarded Octave Chanute medal, Western Soc. Engrs. (thermal expansion of concrete), 1901. Pres, Ind. Engring Soc., 1903-05; mem. Am. Soc. C.E., Am. Ry. Engring. Assn. (editor publications, 1903-15; dir. 1915-18), Western Soc. Engrs., Soc. Promotion Engring. Edn., Alpha Tau Omega, Sigma Xi, Tau Beta Pi. Author: Stand Pipe Accidents and Failures in the United States, 1895; Surveying Manual (with Milo S. Ketchum), 1900, 1904, 1915, 1932; also technical papers dealing with structural analysis, public regulation, railways, terminal air rights, etc. Home: 1201 Michigan Av., Evanston, Ill. Office: 120 S. La Salle St., Chicago, Ill. Died June 16, 1946.

PENDER, HAROLD, elec. engr.; b. Tarboro, N.C., Jan. 13, 1879; s. Robert H. and Martha Wallace (Hanks) P.; A.B., Johns Hopkins, 1898, Ph.D., 1901; Sc.D., U. of Pa., 1923; m. Alice Matthews, June 28, 1905; m. 2d, Ailsa Craig MacColl, December 22, 1934; 1 son, Peter Alexander. Teacher McDonogh School, Maryland, 1901-02; instr. Syracuse U., 1902-03; spent winter of 1903 La Sorbonne, Paris, France, upon special invitation of univ. authorities where established beyond question the existence of a magnetic field around a moving electrically charged body; elec. engr. Westinghouse Electric & Mfg. Co., 1903-04, N.Y.C. R.R., 1904-05; associated with Cary T. Hutchinson, elec. engr., New York, 1905-09; sec.-treas. McCall Ferry Power Co., 1905-09; prof. elec. engring., Mass. Inst. Tech., 1909-13; dir. research div., dept. of elec. engring., Mass. Inst. Tech., 1913-14; dir. dept. elec. engring., U. of Pa., 1914-23, dean Moore Sch. Elec. Engring., 1923-49; cons., July 1949—. Mem. Internat. Electrotechnical Com. Fellow Am. Academy Arts and Sciences, Am. Inst. E.E.; mem. Am. Philos. Soc., Franklin Inst. Author: Principles of Electrical Engineering, 1911; Electricity and Magnetism for Engineers, 1918; Direct-current Machinery, 1921; Electric Circuits and Fields (with S. R. Warren, Jr.), 1943. Editor-in-chief Electrical Engineering Handbook (new edit.). Has written numerous scientific and technical papers. Unitarian. Clubs: Merion Golf, Merion Cricket. Home: 313 Hathaway Lane, Wynnewood, Pa. Office: 200 S. 33d St., Philadelphia 4. Died Sept. 5, 1959.

PENDLETON, EDMUND MONROE, physician, chemist; b. Eatonton, Ga., Mar. 19, 1815; s. Coleman and Martha (Gilbert) P.; grad. Med. Coll. of S.C., Charleston, 1837; m. Sara Jane Thomas, Nov. 27, 1838, 11 children. Practiced medicine, Warrenton, Ga., 1837-38, Sparta, Ga., 1838-67; owned large plantation nr. Sparta; organized fertilizer mfg. firm Pendleton & Dozier, Augusta, Ga., 1867; 1st to use cotton seed in manufacture of fertilizer; taught agr. U. Ga., 1872-76. Author: Text Book of Scientific Agriculture, 1875. Died Jan. 26, 1884.

PENDLETON, JOHN B., lithographer; b. N.Y.C., 1798; s. William Pendleton; m. Eliza Matilda Blydenburgh, 1830; m. 2d, Hester Travis, 1846. Copper plate engraver, Pitts., 1820-23, Boston, 1824-25; brought one of 1st lithographic machines to U.S., 1825; partner brother in firm W. S. & J. B. Pendleton, lithographers, Boston, 1825-30; head firm Pendleton, Kearny & Childs, lithographers, Phila., 1830; established own firm, N.Y.C., 1832-66. Died N.Y.C., Mar. 10, 1866.

PENDLETON, ROBERT L(ARIMORE), soil scientist; b. Minneapolis, June 15, 1890; s. John Louis and Jessie (Larimore) P.; B.S., U. of Calif., 1914, Ph.D., 1917; student N. India Hindustani Lang. Sch., 1918, N. China Lang. Sch., 1931-33; m. Anne Laurel Miltimore, June 10, 1917. Asst. in soil survey, Calif. Soil Survey, 1914-15; asst. dir. Dept. Agrl., Gwalior State, India, 1918-20, dir., 1920-23; prof. soil technology Coll. Agr. U. of Philippines, Los Baños, Laguna, 1923-35, head, dept. soils, 1930-35; chief soil technologists Nat. Geol. Survey of China, 1931-33; soil scientist and agriculturist, dept. agr. Siamese Govt., Bangkok, 1935-42; soil scientist Office Fgn. Agrl. Relations, United States Department Agriculture, 1942-52; soil scientist S.T.E.M. to Siam, Mut. Security Agency, 1952-53; and prof. topical soils and agrl. Isaiah Bowman Sch. Geography, John Hopkins University, 1946-55, emeritus, 1955; soil technologist to Ministry Agriculture, Thailand Government, 1956—; field work in soils and land use in Central and S. Am., Philippines, Siam, China, India, Central and Brit. W. Africa. Mem. Mindanao Exploration Commn., Philippines, 1939. Adviser FAO Mission to Siam, 1948. Fellow Belgian Am. Ednl. Found., Belgian Congo, 1948-49. Cons. War Dept., 1942-44, E.C.A., 1949-50. Decorated Knight Comdr., Order Crown Thailand, 1946; The David Livingstone Centenary medal, Am. Geog. Soc., 1950. Hon. mem. Am. Geog. Soc.; mem. Assn. Am. Geographers, Am. Chem. Soc., Am. Soc. Agronomy, Soil Sci. Society Am., Am. Geophys. Union, A.A.A.S.; Siam Society, Bangkok, Sigma Xi, Alpha Zeta. Clubs: Cosmos (Washington), Army and Navy (Manila); Royal Bangkok Sports (Bangkok). Author: Lateritte and Lateritic Soils (with J. A. Prescott), 1952. Translator (from Dutch); Soils of Equatorial Regions, 1944. Editor of Natural History Bull. of the Siam Soc., Bangkok. Address: Kasetsart University, Bangkhen, Bangkok, Thailand; also Box 3519 Terminal Annex, Los Angeles 54. Died June 23, 1957.

PENDLETON, THOMAS P., ret. chief topographic engr. U.S. Geol. Survey; b. Nicolaus, Cal., Sept. 25, 1885; s. Samuel Alvah and Carrie (Arens) P.; U. Cal., 1911; m. Florence H. Beel, Apr. 14, 1925; 1 son, Thomas Arens. Topographic mapping U.S. Geol. Survey western U.S., 1905-17, Alaska, 1919, Palestine and Balkan states, 1920-22, chief sect. photo-mapping, 1923-26; chief engr. Brock & Weymouth, Inc., Phila., 1926-30; chief engr. Aerotopograph Corp., Washington, 1931; chief photo compiler U.S. Coast & Geodetic Survey, 1932-33; asst. sect. chief in charge Chattanooga, Tenn. office U.S. Geol. Survey, 1934-41, chief sect. photo-mapping, Washington, 1942, chief topographic engr., Washington, 1943-47. Del. second Consultative Pan-Am. Conf. on Geography and Cartography, Rio de Janeiro, 1944. Received Award for Distinguished Service, Dept. of Interior. Past pres. Am. Soc. Photogrammetry (hon. mem.). Served as 2d lt., E.O.R.C., U.S. Army, 1918. Mem. Tau Beta Pi. Club: Cosmos. Author: Map Compilation from Aerial Photographs, U.S.G.S. Bulletin 788. Contbr. numerous articles on photogrammetry to tech. jours. Home: 6005 Dellwood Pl., Bethesda, Md. Died May 28, 1954.

PENHALLOW, DAVID PEARCE, botanist; b. Kittery Point, Me., May 25, 1854; s. Andrew Jackson and Ann Josepha (Pickering) P.; B.S., Mass. State Coll., 1873, Boston U., 1888; M.S., McGill U., 1896, D.Sc., 1904; m. Sarah A. Dunlap, May 4, 1876. Prof. botany and chemistry, 1876-80, acting pres., 1879-80, Imperial Coll. of Agr., Sapporo, Japan; botanist to Houghton Farm Expt. Sta., 1882-83; prof. botany, McGill U., 1883—. Editor Canadian Record of Science, 1888-90; asso. editor American Naturalist, 1897-1907; editor for paleobotany Botanisches Centralblatt, 1902-07. Mem. Brit. Assn. com. on Canadian ethnology, 1897-1904 (chmn., 1902-04); chmn. Royal Soc. of Can. com. on ethnology, 1902-04; spl. commr. World's Indstl. and Cotton Centennial Expn., 1884. Trustee Marine Biol. Lab., Woods Hole, Mass.; dir. and sec. Biol. Stas. of Can.; dir. Atlantic Coast Biol. Sta., St. Andrews, N.B., 1907—; chmn. Assn. Am. Biol. Research Stas., 1908-09; Brit. Assn. com. on pleistocene fauna and flora of Can., 1897-1901; Governors Fellow on corp. of McGill U. Pres. Montreal Hort. Soc., 1888-92, Dominion Pomol. Soc., 1890, Soc. Plant Morphology and Physiology, 1899, Am. Soc. Naturalists, 1908-09, Natural History Soc. Montreal, 1904—; fellow Royal Soc. Canada (pres. Sect. IV, 1896-97), A.A.A.S. (v.p. Sect. G, 1908-09), Bot. Soc. America, Geol. Soc. America. Publications on bot. subjects, chiefly on paleobotany, about 150 titles. Address: Montreal, Quebec. Died 1910.

PENNELL, WALTER OTIS, electrical engr.; b. Exeter, N.H., Jan. 13, 1875; s. Robert Franklin and Martha Morgan (Otis) P.; B.S., Mass. Inst. Tech., 1896; m. Sarah M. Corson, of Phila., June 8, 1903; children—Dorothy, Ford; m. 2d, Elizabeth H. Kimball, of Exeter, N.H., July 11, 1936; 1 daughter, Martha. Teacher electrical engineering Lafayette College, Pennsylvania, 1896-98; asst. engr. Bell Telephone Co. of Phila., 1898-1902; engr. Am. Telephone & Telegraph Co., Boston, 1902-03; chief engr. Mo. & Kan. Telephone Co., Kansas City, Mo., 1903-12; bldg. and equipment engr., 1912-16, acting chief engr., 1916-17, chief engr., 1918-36, Southwestern Bell Telephone System, St. Louis; retired, 1936. Planned and supervised erection of telephone plants in many states of the Union; originator of several patents of widely-used telephone devices. Mem. N.H. Ho. of Reps., 1939-40; v.p. Exeter Hosp. Corporation; director Exeter News Letter; director New England Council. Past president St. Louis Electrical Board of Trade, Engineers Club of St. Louis. Fellow Am. Inst. E.E.; mem. Math. Assn. America, Order Founders and Patriots of America, N.H. Seacoast Regional Development Assn. (dir.). Republican. Conglist. Club: Exeter Country. Author of papers on engineering and mathematics. Home: Exeter NH

PENNEY, JAMES THEOPHILUS, educator; b. Charlotte, N.C., July 1, 1900; s. James Theophilus and Nerah (Grimes) P.; A.B., U. N.C., 1921, M.A., 1925, Ph.D., 1929; m. Martha Thigpen, Aug. 25, 1925; 1 dau., Patricia Ann (Mrs. C. M. Lide). Instr. biology Charlotte (N.C.) High Sch., 1921-23; teaching fellow U. N.C., 1923-25, research asst., 1927-29; instr. histology U. Tenn. Med. Sch., 1925-27; asso. prof. biology U. S.C., 1929-42, prof., 1942—, head dept., 1959—, dean of men, 1956-59. Served with S.A.T.C., 1918. Mem. Am. Soc. Zoologists, Southeastern Assn. Biologists (past pres.), S.C. Acad. Sci. (past pres.), Sigma Xi, Delta Sigma Phi. Episcopalian. Home: 1 Gibbes Ct.,

Columbia, S.C. Died Mar. 29, 1964; buried Elmwood Cemetery, Columbia.

PENNINGTON, LEIGH H., botanist; b. Macon, Mich., Oct. 26, 1877; s. Baron H. and Claribel (Pratt) P.; high sch., Tecumseh, Mich., 1897; A.B., U. of Mich., 1907, Ph.D., 1909; m. Mary Blanche Van Fleet, Aug. 27, 1902; 1 dau., Edna Phyllis (Mrs. Walter Clement Percival). Instr. in botany, Northwestern U., 1909-10; asst. prof. botany, Syracuse U., 1910-12, asso. prof., 1912-14; prof. forest pathology, N.Y. State Coll. Forestry, 1914—; expert in forest pathology, U.S. Dept. Agr., summers 1911, 12; collaborator, New York Bot. Garden, summers, 1913, 14; pathologist or collaborator U.S. Dept. Agr., 1917—. Republican. Methodist. Mason. Research in white pine blister rust. Home: Syracuse, N.Y. Deceased.

PENNINGTON, MARY ENGLE, chemist; b. Nashville, Oct. 8, 1872; d. Henry and Sarah B. (Molony) Pennington; Ph.D., U. Pa., 1895, U. fellow in botany, 1895-97; fellow physiol. chemistry Yale, 1897-98. Research worker dept. hygiene U. Pa., 1898-1901; pres. Phila. Clin. Lab., 1900-08; bacteriologist Municipal Lab., Phila., 1904-07; bacteriol. chemistry, bur. of chemistry U.S. Dept. Agr., 1905-08, chief of food research lab., 1908-19; in charge of dept. of research and development Am. Balsa Co., N.Y., 1919-22; consultation and research, 1922—; mem. adv. bd. Subsistence Research and Development Br., Mil. Planning Div. Office Q.M. Gen.; cons. Food Control Div., War Shipping Administrn. Fellow A.A.A.S., Am. Soc. Refrigerating Engrs. (dir.); mem. Am. Chem. Soc., Soc. Biol. Chemists, Am. Inst. Refrigeration, Inst. Food Technol., Inst. Am. Poultry Industries, Poultry Sci. Assn., Sigma Xi, Kappa Kappa Gamma, Iota Sigma Pi. Awarded Francis P. Garvan gold medal by the Am. Chem. Soc., 1940. Home: 100 Riverside Drive. Address: 233 Broadway, N.Y.C. 7. Died Dec. 27, 1952.

PENNOYER, FREDERICK WILLIAM, JR., naval officer; b. East Orange, N.J.; s. Frederick William and Huldah (Palmer) P.; student Stevens Inst. Tech., 1910-11; B.S., U.S. Naval Acad., 1915; M.S., Mass. Inst. Tech., 1920; naval aviator, Flight Training Naval Air Station, Pensacola, Fla., 1923; m. Margarette W. Bispham, Apr. 6, 1918; 1 son, Frederick William III (capt. USN ret.). Commd. ensign, U.S. Navy, 1915, and advanced through the grades to vice adm., 1950; specialized in aeronautical engineering since 1921; Bureau of Aeronautics general representative, Wright Field, Dayton, Ohio; ret. comdr. Naval Air Material Center, U.S. Naval Base, Phila. Decorated Legion of Merit (Gold Star), Air Medal, Commendation ribbon. Fellow Inst. Aeronautical Sciences. Address: Coronado CA Died Jan. 21, 1971; buried Mt. Rosecrans Cemetery, San Diego CA

PENROSE, CHARLES, cons. engineer; b. Philadelphia, Pa., Jan. 24, 1886; s. Walter Elliot and Emily (Thompson) P.; student Prep. Sch., Dresden, Germany, 1896-97; grad. Episcopal Acad., Phila., 1903; B.S., Princeton, 1907, E.E., 1910; LL.D., Cumberland University, Lebanon, Tenn., 1940; D.Eng., South Dakota School Mines and Technology, 1944; Litt.D., Ursinus Coll., Pa., 1951; L.H.D., Whitman Coll., Walla Walla, Washington, 1951; m. Beatrice de'Este, June 4, 1910 (deceased); children—Beatrice (Mrs. John Cadwalader, Jr.) (deceased), John Rowan, Julian d'Este, Charles; m. 2d, Virginia Carlisle, June 11, 1930; a daughter, Barbara (Mrs. Edmund Charles Tarbell, III). Began as assistant to elec. engr. of Phila. Electric Co., 1910; engr. in charge erection Schuykill No. 2 Sta. for same co., 1914-15, later other power constrn. work; with Day & Zimmermann, Inc., cons. engr., Philadelphia, New York and Chicago, 1917—, asst. gen. mgr., 1920-32, v.p., 1932-56, cons., 1956—; pres. Newcomen Publs. in N.A., Kittery, Me., 1947—. Progress engr. A.U.S. Supply Base, Phila., 1918-19. Special consultant to U.S. Govt. in Federal Housing Adminstrn., 1934. Cyrus Fogg Brackett lecturer Princeton Univ.; Henry J. Fuller lecturer, Worcester Poly. Institute; served as mem. Bartol Research Foundation Com. (administering Henry R. Bartol Found., Phila. Fellow Royal Soc. Arts (London). Mem. Am. Soc. Mech. Engrs., Am. Inst. Elec. Engrs., Franklin Inst. (bd. mgrs.), Pa. Electric Assn., Nat. Assn. Cotton Mfrs. (Boston), Am. Cotton Mfrs.' Assn. (Charlotte, N.C.), Pa. State Chamber of Commerce (industrial relations Com.), Princeton Engring. Assn. of N.Y. (past pres.), Md. Acad. of Sciences, Hist. Soc. of Pa., N.H. Hist. Soc., Hist. Soc. of N.M., R.I. Hist. Soc.; Old Dartmouth Hist. Soc. (Mass.); English Speaking Union, St. George Soc. of N.Y., Engrs. Soc. Winston-Salem, N.C. (hon.); Constrn. Div. Assn. (U.S. Army), Newcomen Soc. of England (council, London; Am. sr. v.p.); The Guild of Brackett Lecturers of Princeton Univ. (exec. com.); The Pilgrims of the U.S.; Pa. Soc. of New York; assoc. mem. Am. Soc. Civil Engrs., Econ. Hist. Assn., Portsmouth Athenaeum (Proprietership), Piscataqua Pioneers, Pi Tau Sigma (hon.). Mem. administrative bd., Am. Engring. Council. Republican. Episcopalian. Clubs: Princeton, Midday (Phila.); Princeton (New York); Hope (Providence, R.I.); Charter (Princeton, N.J.). Author: New England's Power Resources, 1922; Power in Pennsylvania, 1925; American Colonial Transportation (1629-1783), (1933); Industrial Surveys, 1935; New England—Today! (Boston), 1937; Industry and The State (Alabama), 1937; 1838 April Fourth 1938, (Atlantic Centenary Address, New York), 1938; Initiative for Americans, 1938:. . .That This Nation 1940; Retrospect of Mountain Pilgrimage, 1940; They Faced to the East: 1784, 1941; To The Sea for Whales: 1846;. . .Whether in New Hampshire or South Dakota, 1944; Brackett of Maine: A Fragment of Northern New England in the 1850's, 1945; Look Towards the Sea—There is England (1946); Samuel Vaughan Merrick (1801-1870)—Merchant, Engineer, Industrialist, First President of The Pennsylvania Railroad (1946); Old Kittery, 1647—Land of Adventure, 1947; British Royalty in North America, 1860; vice Admiral James Pine, U.S.C.G., 1947; John P. Benson; American Artist (1865-1947), 1948; William Carter Dickerman, (1874-1946), Locomotive Builder, Scholar, Good Citizen, 1951; William C. Dickerman (1874-1946) Never his Courage Faltered!, 1951; Two Men—and their Contributions in Two Countries, 1951; The Sands of Times, 1953; George B. Cortelyou (1862-1940), 1954; L. F. Loree, 1955; Newcomb Carlton, 1956. First Newcomen lecturer before U.S. Coast Guard Acad., New London, Conn. Home: Hilltop Cottage, R.F.D. 2, West Chester, Pa. and Bayberry House, Kittery Point, Me. Office: 500 Fifth Av., N.Y.C. 36; 1700 Samsom St., Phila. 3; P.O. Box 113, Downington, Pa. Died May 16, 1958; buried West Chester, Pa.

PENROSE, RICHARD ALEXANDER FULLERTON, JR., geologist; b. Phila., Pa., Dec. 17, 1863; s. Richard Alexander Fullerton and Sarah Hannah (Boies) P.; A.B., Harvard, 1884, A.M., Ph.D., 1886; unmarried. Geologist in charge survey of Eastern Tex., for Tex. Geol. Survey, 1888; apptd., 1889, by Geol. Survey of Ark. to make detailed reports on the manganese and iron ore regions of Ark.; asso. prof. economic geology, 1892-95, prof., 1895-1911, U. of Chicago. Lecturer on economic geology at Stanford, 1893; spl. geologist U.S. Geol. Survey, 1894, to examine and report on gold dists. of Cripple Creek, Colo. Mem. bd. mgrs. Phila. Germantown & Norristown Ry. Co.; dir. various mining corps., also Ridge Avenue Passenger Ry. Co. of Phila. Trustee U. of Pa., 1911-27; pres. Acad. Natural Sciences of Phila., 1922-26. Asso. editor Journal of Geology. Mem. Soc. Economic Geologists (pres. 1920-21); mem. Nat. Research Council (geology com., 1917-18, div. of geology and geography, 1919-23); del. Internat. Geol. Congress, Stockholm, 1910, Toronto, 1913, Brussels, 1922, Madrid, 1927; mem. Fairmount Park Commn. (Phila.). Republican. Author: The Nature and Origin of Deposits of Phosphate of Lime; Geology of the Gulf Tertiary of Texas; Manganese: Its Uses, Ores, Deposits; The Iron Deposits of Arkansas; What a Geologist Can Do in War; The Last Stand of the Old Siberia. Home: Philadelphia, Pa. Died July 31, 1931.

PENROSE, SPENCER, mining engr.; b. Phila., Nov. 2, 1865; s. Richard Alexander Fullerton and Sarah Hannah (Boise) P.; A.B., Harvard, 1886; m. Mrs. Julie Villiers (Lewis) McMillan, Apr. 26, 1906. A founder, dir. Utah Copper Co.; a pioneer in Cripple Creek (Colo.) Mining Dist. and identified with several of its mines; pres. Broadmoor Hotel Co., Cheyenne Mountain Co., Garden City Co. Manitou & Pikes Peak By., Pikes Peak Auto Highway Co., Pikes Peak Automobile Co., Mt. Manitou Park & Incline Ry. Co., Broadmoor Hotel Water & Power Co., The Manitou Mineral Water Co.; dir. Kennecott Copper Corp., Beaver Park Co., Braden Copper Co. Col. on staff of Gov. Peabody of Colo., 1903-04. Home: Colorado Springs, Colo. Died Dec. 7, 1939.

PEO, RALPH FREDERICK, inventor, mfr. constrn. materials; b. Rochester, N.Y., May 3, 1897; s. Julian F. and Flora (Van Schaick) P.; M.E., Rochester Inst. Tech., 1917; m. Magdalene Heath, Jan. 1, 1918 (dec.); children—Jack H.; m. 2d, Ethelmay Brent, Dec. 4, 1943; children—Elizabeth Forbes, Barbara Brent. Engring. dept. various automobile mfrs.; asst. chief engr. Am. Radiator Co., 1923-24, chief engr., 1925-27; v.p., Houdaille-Hershey Corp., 1935-45; v.p., gen. mgr. Houde Engring. Co., 1927-45; pres., chmn. Frontier Industries, Inc., 1946-55; chmn., chief exec. officer, dir. Houdaille Industries Inc. (merger Frontier Industries, Inc., Houdaille-Hershey), 1955—; pres., chmn. bd. Hobam, Inc., Buffalo, 1964-66; dir. Marine Trust Co. Western N.Y., DuBois Chems., Inc., Am. Bosch Arma Corp. Dir. Buffalo br. Fed. Res. Corp. Trustee YMCA. Named outstanding businessman Niagara Frontier, U. Buffalo, 1955, Sylvania, 1955. Mem. Am. Ordnance Assn. C. of C. (past v.p., dir.), Soc. Automotive Engrs., Newcomen Soc. N.A. Mason. Clubs: Country of Buffalo, Automobile, Canoe, Buffalo Yacht, Buffalo (Buffalo), Cherry Hill Country (Ridgeway, Ontario). Patentee. Home: 925 Delaware Av., Buffalo 14209. Office: 1280 Main St., Buffalo 9. Died Nov. 28, 1966; buried Forest Lawn Cemetery, Buffalo.

PEPPER, BAILEY B(REAZEALE), entomologist; b. Easley, S.C., Mar. 20, 1906; s. Bailey B. and Eugenia (Sheriff) O.; B.S., Clemson Coll., 1929; M.S., Ohio State U., 1931; Ph.D., Rutgers, 1934; m. Margaret M. Forgham, Oct. 9, 1937; children—James Bailey, Carl Forgham. Mem. faculty Rutgers U., from 1935, prof. entomology, from 1945; staff N.J. Agrl. Expt. Sta. since 1935, research specialist, chmn., from 1945. Mem. Middlesex Co. Mosquito Extermination Commn., 1946-70; sec. State Mosquito Control Commn. Mgr. Marlboro State Hosp. Mem. Am. Assn. Econ. Entomologists, Entomological Society of Am. (chmn. Eastern br. 1963-64; pres. 1968), A.A.A.S., New Jersey State Hort. Soc., N.J. Health and San. Assn., Am. Mosquito Control Assn., N.J. Mosquito Extermination Assn. (sec.), Sigma Xi. Contbr. articles sci. jours. Home: Edison NJ Died Dec. 22, 1970.

PEPPER, O(LIVER) H(AZARD) PERRY, physician; b. Phila., Apr. 28, 1884; s. William and Frances S. (Perry) P.; B.S., U. Pa., 1905, M.D., 1908; ScD., Lafayette Coll., 1938; m. Eulalie Willcox, Dec. 2, 1916; children—Eulalie, Oliver H.P. Interne U. Hosp., Phila., 1908-10, asst. physician, 1913-37, physician since 1937; asst. instr. U. Pa., 1911-12, asso. in medicine, 1912-19, asso. in research medicine, 1913-19, asst. prof. medicine, 1922-28, prof. clin. medicine, 1928-34, prof. medicine, 1934-51, Com. on Fed. Med. Services, Hoover Commn. on Orgn. Exec. Br. of Govt. Served as lt. col. M.C., U.S. Army; chief med. service Base Hosp. 69, Savenay, France, World War. Mem. A.M.A., Assn., Am. Physicians (past pres.), Am. Soc. for Clin. Investigation, Am. Climatol. and Clin. Assn., A.C.P., Coll. Physicians of Phila. (ex-pres.), Am. Philos. Soc.; Com. on Vets Med. Problems, N.R.C. (chmn.). Republican. Episcopalian. Club: Philadelphia. Author: (with Dr. David L. Farley) Practical Hematological Diagnosis, 1933; Medical Etymology, 1949. Contbr. to med. jours. Home: Ithan, Pa. Office: 36th and Spruce St., Phila. Died Jan. 28, 1962.

PEPPER, WILLIAM, physician; b. Phila., Aug. 21, 1843; s. William and Sarah (Platt) P.; grad. U. Pa., 1862, Med. Dept., 1864; m. Frances Sargeant Perry, June 25, 1873, 4 children. Resident physician Pa. Hosp., Phila., 1864-65; pathologist, vis. physician Pa. Hosp., Phila. Hosp., 1865-68; lectr. morbid anatomy U. Pa., 1868-70, prof. clin. medicine, 1876-84, provost, 1880-94, prof. theory and practice of medicine, 1884-98, founder Univ. Hosp. (1st hosp. in U.S. directly associated with and staffed by faculty of univ. med. sch.), 1874, founded nurses' tng. sch., 1887, as provost founded Wharton Sch. Finance, vet., hygiene, biol. and archtl. schs., univ. extension lectures, Bennett Sch. (for grad. instrn. of women); med. dir. Phila. Centennial Exhbn., 1875-76; founder Am. Climatol. Soc., 1884, pres., 1886; pres. Am. Clin. Assn., 1886, Assn. Am. Physicians, 1891; founded Coll. Assn. of Pa., 1886; mem. exec. com. A.M.A.; pres. 1st Pan-Am. Med. Congress, 1893; founded, endowed William Pepper Lab. of Clin. Medicine, U. Pa. (1st lab. in U.S. devoted to advanced clin. studies of causes of disease), 1894; directed establishment of 1st Phila. Free Library (endowed by his uncle George S. Pepper), 1890; founded Archaeol. Assn. of U. Pa., 1892, founded Univ. Museum. Author: The Morphological Changes of the Blood in Malarial Fever, 1867; A Practical Treatise on the Diseases of Children, 1870; Higher Medical Education, the True Interest of the Public and the Profession, 1877, 94; A System of Practical Medicine, 5 vols., 1885-86; Textbook of the Theory and Practice of Medicine, 2 vols., 1893-94. Died Pleasanton, Cal., July 28, 1898.

PERCIVAL, JAMES GATES, poet, geologist; b. Kensington, Conn., Sept. 15, 1795; s. James and Elizabeth (Hart) P.; grad. Yale, 1815, Med. Instn., 1820; attended U. Pa. Med. Sch., 1818-19; never married. Apptd. asst. surgeon U.S. Army and prof. chemistry U.S. Mil. Acad., 1824; surgeon recruiting offices, Boston, 1824-25; editor Am. Atheneum, N.Y.C., 1825; Phi Beta Kappa poet Harvard, 1824; Phi Beta Kappa orator Yale, 1825; assisted Noah Webster in editing An American Dictionary of the English Language, 1827-28; state geologist of Conn., 1835-42; surveyor Am. Mining Co., Ill. and Wis., 1853; state geologist of Wis., 1854-56. Author: Zamor, 1815, Prometheus, 1821 (both single poems); Poems, 1821; Clio I and II, 1822; Prometheus Part II with Other Poems, 1822; Poems, 1823; Clio Number III, 1827; The Dream of a Day, and Other Poems, 1843; Report on the Geology of the State of Connecticut, 1842; editor: Elegant Extracts (Vicesimus Knox), 6 vols., 1825; System of Universal Geography (Malte-brun), 3 vols., 1827-34. Died Hazel Green, Wis., May 2, 1856.

PERCY, JAMES FULTON, surgeon; b. Bloomfield, N.J., Mar. 26, 1864; s. James and Sarah Ann (Fulton) P.; M.D., Bellevue Hosp. Med. Coll. (now Med. Dept. New York U.), 1886; postgrad. student on experimental problems in abdominal surgery, Chicago Vet. Coll., 1895; postgrad. student pathology and surgery, in Germany, Switzerland, Belgium, 1897-98; visited clinics in England, France, Germany, Austria, 1914; hon. A.M., Knox Coll., Galesburg, Ill., 1914; m. Mrs. Edna B. Post, 1925. Med. practice, Mazeppa, Minn., 1886-88, Galesburg, Ill., 1888-1917; developed surgical instruments, 1904, known as Percy actual cauteries for treatment of accessible cancers; practice limited treatment of cancer since 1917; surgical practice, San Diego, Calif., 1920-22, in Los Angeles, since 1922; attending sr. surgeon, cancer service, and founder member (1922) Malignancy Board and Tumor Clinic, Los Angeles County Hospital (vice chairman and chairman 8 years); clinical professor of surgery (neoplasms), College of Medical Evangelists Medical School (emeritus); attending surgeon French Hospital, 12 years; consulting surgeon, Orthopedic Hospital and

School for Crippled Children (all in Los Angeles). Member 1st draft board, Knox County, Ill., 1916; student training courses for officers, Fort Riley, Kan., 1917; chief of surgical staff, U.S. Army Base Hosp., Camp Kearny, Calif., 1917-19; retired with rank of major; apptd. lt. col., Med. Reserves, U.S. Army, 1925, reapptd. for term, 1940-45, called first meeting, Galesburg, Ill., out of which grew Galesburg Cottage Hosp., 1888. Was honor guest at Clinical Congress of Surgeons, North America, at meeting held in London, 1914. Fellow Am. Coll. Surgeons (founder mem.); mem. A.M.A., Calif. Med. Assn., Los Angeles Med. Assn. (v.p. 1931), Los Angeles Surg. Soc. (pres. 1929), Los Angeles Cancer Soc. (pres. 1939), American Board of Surgery (founder member), Western Surgical Association (president 1918), Illinois State Medical Soc. (pres. 1907; sec. Jud. Council 17 years), Southern Calif. Med. Assn. (hon. 1914), Am. Soc. for Control of Cancer, Am. Assn. Obstet., Gynecol. and Abdominal Surgeons, Hollywood Acad. of Med. (hon. 1926), Reserve Officers Assn., U.S. Army, U.S. Mil. Surgeons Assn. Mason (32 deg.). Bahai religion. Contbr. about 40 articles to med. jours., principally on actual cautery in treatment of cancer. Home: 1030 S. Alvarado St., Los Angeles 6. Died Apr. 26, 1946; buried in Forest Lawn Memorial Park, Glendale, Calif.

PERIN, CHARLES PAGE, consulting engr.; b. West Point, N.Y., Aug. 23, 1861; s. Col. Glover (asst. surgeon gen. U.S.A.) and Elizabeth (Page) P.; A.B., Harvard, 1883; studied École des Mines, Paris; m. Keokee Munroe Henderson, July 7, 1887 (died 1913); m. 2d, Katharine Sharp Hoyt, Nov. 5, 1925. Served in various capacities with Carnegie Steel Company, later gen. mgr. and pres. blast furnaces collieries, Va. and Ky.; made study of fuel supply for Trans-Siberian Ry., for Russian Govt.; conducted surveys for iron and coal across India and developed iron resources of that country, resulting in Tata Iron & Steel Co. and Mysore Iron Works; consulting engr. Lung Yen Mining Corp., China; chief engr. appraisal commn. attached to Peace Commn., 1919; mem. firm Perin & Marshall, New York City; also dir. Stonega Coke & Coal Co. Mem. Am. Iron and Steel Inst. (past pres.), China Soc. (v.p.). Episcopalian. Author: Mission en Sibérie (pub. in France), 1901. A pioneer in development of manufacture of pure iron by electrolysis. Home: New York, N.Y. Died Feb. 16, 1937.

PERISHO, ELWOOD CHAPPELL, geologist; b. Westfield, Ind.; s. Joshua M. and Lydia Anna (Champell) P.; B.S., Earlham Coll., Ind., 1887, M.A., 1891, LL.D., 1913; M.S., U. of Chicago, 1895; hon. D.Sc. from State Coll. of S.Dak., 1928; m. Inez Beebe, Aug. 30, 1916. Prof. mathematics, Guilford Coll., 1887-93; fellow, U. of Chicago, 1894-95; prof. geology, State Normal Sch., Platteville, Wis., 1895-1903; prof. geology and dean Coll. Arts and Sciences, U. of S.D., and state geologist of S.D., 1903-14; pres. S.D. State Coll. Agr. and Mech. Arts, 1914-19; lecturer and prof. geology, Guilford Coll., N.C., 1921—. Mem. S.D. State Council Defense, 1917-19; lecturer patriotic work, 1917-18; work in Am. army camps, 1918-19; ednl. adminstr. and lecturer, faculty of Am. Army U., Beaune, France, 1919—, mem. U.S.A. Ednl. Corps in Europe, 1919. Pres. S.D. Ednl. Assn., 1913, S.D. Conservation Congress, 1911-13; chmn. coll. work and adminstrn. sect. Assn. Am. Agrl. Colls., 1916-17. Chautauqua lecturer, 1920. Republican. Mem. Soc. Friends. Editor The Friends Messenger, 1926-32. Author: The Erosion History of Southwest Wisconsin; The Ores of Southwestern Wisconsin; South Dakota's Artesian Basin and Its Wells; Stage College and the Tenth Generation. Died Aug. 14, 1935.

PERKINS, CHARLES ALBERT, physicist; b. Ware, Mass., Oct. 31, 1858; s. Rev. Ariel Ebenezer Parish and Susan Osborn (Poor) P.; A.B., Willimas Coll., 1879; Ph.D., Johns Hopkins, 1884; m. Angie Villette Warren, Sept. 19, 1883 (died 1921); children—Marcia Villette, Margaret Duggan, Alice Warren, Warren A. Prof. mathematics, Lawrence, 1880-81; fellow in physics, 1883-84, asst. in physics, 1884-87, Johns Hopkins; prof. physics, Bryn Mawr Coll., 1887-91; prof. science, Hampden-Sidney Coll., 1891-92; prof. physics and elec. engring., 1892-1906, elec. engring., 1906-41, prof. elec. engring. emeritus since 1941; dir. Engineering Experimental Station, University of Tennessee, 1921-41, consultant since 1941. Fellow American Inst. Electric Engineers; mem. Nat. Conf. Electricians, 1884. Author: Outlines of Electricity and Magnetism, 1896. Contbr. to scientific jours. Address: 1715 W. Clinch Av., Knoxville, Tenn. Died Nov. 26, 1945.

PERKINS, EDMUND TAYLOR, civil engr.; b. Scottsville, Va., Sept. 8, 1864; s. Edmund Taylor and Mary Sydnor (Addison) P.; C.E., A.B., Union Coll., N.Y., 1885, A.M., 1888; m. Jean Waters, June 3, 1903 (dec.); m. 2d, Louise Lamson-Scribner, Aug. 17, 1918. Topographer U.S. Geol. Survey, 1885-1902; engr. U.S. Reclamation Service, 1902-10; pres. Edmund T. Perkins Engring. Co., Chicago, Nov. 1, 1910—. Pres. Am. Reclamation Federation; pres. Nat. Drainage Congress; mem. State of Fla. Everglades Engring. Commn. Mem. Am. Assn. Engrs. (pres. 1917-18). Democrat. Episcopalian. Home: Chicago, Ill. Died May 21, 1921.

PERKINS, ELISHA, physician; b. Norwich, Conn., Jan. 27, 1742; s. Joseph and Mary (Bushnell) P.; attended Yale; m. Sarah Douglass, Sept. 23, 1762, 10 children including Benjamin Douglas. Practiced medicine, Plainfield, Conn.; incorporator Conn. Med. Soc., 1792; chmn. Windham County (Conn.) Med. Soc.; invented "tractor" (U-shaped piece of metal which when applied to affected parts of body eased pain and cured disorders), patented, 1796, popular in U.S., England, parts of Europe, until 1800; expelled from Conn. Med. Soc., 1798; devised remedy composed of vinegar and muriate of soda; went to N.Y.C. during yellow fever outbreak to test remedy, 1799. Died of yellow fever, N.Y.C. Sept. 6, 1799.

PERKINS, HENRY AUGUSTUS, physicist; b. Hartford, Connecticut, November 14, 1873; s. Edward H. and Mary E. (Dwight) P.; A.B., Yale, 1896; M.A., E.E., Columbia, 1899; graduate student Yale, 1900-02; University of Paris, 1908-09; College de France, 1921-22; Sc.D., Trinity, 1920; L.H.D., Gallaudet, 1944; m. Olga Flinch, April 8, 1903; children—Henry Augustus, Evelyn Ingeborg (Mrs. Amyas Ames). Prof. physics, Trinity Coll., Hartford, 1902-42, ret. 1942, recalled 1943, ret. 1946; acting pres. 1915-16 and 1919-20. Dir. Phoenix Mutual Life Ins. Co. Pres. bd. Am. School for Deaf, 1913—; president Hartford Park Board, 1919-20; president Hartford Public Library, 1945—. Chmn. of Bd. of Avon Old Farms Sch., 1946—. Mem. Am. Inst. Elec. Engrs., Am. Physical Soc., Société Française de Physique, Am. Alpine Club, Explorers' Club, Alpha Delta Phi (pres., 1949—), Phi Beta Kappa, Sigma Xi, Elihu (Yale). Clubs: Hartford, Hartford Golf, Century (N.Y.); Graduate (New Haven). Contbr. to Am. Jour. of Science, Le Radium, Science, Am. Journal of Physics, Physical Review, Journal de Physique. Author: Thermodynamics, 1912; College Physics, 1938; College Physics, Abridged, 1941; Basic College Physics, 1949; also articles in Educational Review, Yale Review, North American Review, Am. Mercury, Physical Review. Research in velocity of magnetism, discontinuous discharges, metallic conductivity, residual magnetism, etc. Address: 55 Forest St., Hartford, Conn. Died July, 1959.

PERKINS, HENRY FARNHAM, zoologist; b. Burlington, Vt., May 10, 1877; s. George H. and Mary Judd (Farnham) P.; A.B., U. of Vt., 1898; Ph.D., Johns Hopkins, 1902; m. Mary Keyser Edmunds, June 11, 1903. Instr. biology, 1902-06, asst. prof. zoology, 1906-11, prof. zoology, 1911-45; emeritus since 1945, University of Vermont; curator University Museum, 1926-31, director Robert Hull Fleming Museum, U. of Vermont, 1931-45; research assistant Carnegie Institution, 1903-05; assistant in fish investigation, Bur. of Fisheries, 1906, 08, 13. Fellow Johns Hopkins, 1916-17. Dir. Eugenics Survey of Vt., 1925-37; sec. Vt. Commission on Country Life, 1928-31, exec. v.p., 1932-44; chmn. Interstate Commn. on Lake Champlain Fishing since 1936. Republican. Conglist. Fellow A.A.A.S.; mem. American Society Zoologists, American Eugenics Society (president 1931-34, director, 1934-47), Champlain Valley Archaeol. Society (v.p. since 1937), Life Extension Inst., Delta Psi, Phi Beta Kappa. Clubs: Ethan Allen, Vt. Bird (pres. 1922-23), Chittenden County Fish and Game (dir.). Contbr. numerous papers on invertebrates, birds, heredity and eugenics. Lecturer on zoology, museum adminstrn., archaeology and eugenics. Address: 205 S. Prospect St., Burlington VT

PERKINS, JACOB, inventor; b. Newburyport, Mass., July 9, 1766; s. Matthew and Jane (Noyes) Dole P.; m. Hannah Greenleaf, Nov. 11, 1790, 6 children. Apprenticed to goldsmith, Ipswich, Mass., 1779-81; Operated own goldsmith shop, Ipswich, 1781-87; employed by State of Mass. in manufacture of dies for copper coins, 1787-90; owned mfg. company making nails and tacks using machine he had invented, 1790-95; published series of school books (in partnership with Gideon Fairman) entitled Perkins and Fairman's Running Hand (using 1st steel plates in Am.), 1809-10; worked in bank-note improvements, 1814-17; began firm Perkins, Fairman & Heath, printers, 1819-40; began work in expts. in steam boilers, 1823; patented steam-pressure boiler for steam vessel. Died July 30, 1849.

PERKINS, JANET RUSSELL, botanist; b. Lafayette, Ind., May 20, 1853; d. Cyrus Grosvenor and Jane Rose (Houghteling) P.; U. of Wis., 1867-72, A.B., 1901; studying France and Germany, 1872-75; teacher in Chicago, 1875-95, except 3 yrs.' study and travel Sandwich Islands, Europe, Azores and Calif.; U. of Berlin, 1895-98; U. of Heidelberg, 1898-99, Ph.D. Apptd. by Carnegie Instn. of Washington to prepare material for flora of Philippines, 1902; collected plants in Jamaica, B.W.I., three winters, 1914-17. Wrote 3 monographs on Monimiaceae and other higher tropical plants, in Engler's Botanische Jahrbücher; also Part IV, "Monimiaceae," for Das Pflanzenreich, 1901; Fragmenta Florae Philippinae, Contributions to the Flora of the Philippine Islands, 3 Fascicles, 1904; "Styracaceae" for Das Pflanzenreich, 1907, published by Royal Prussian Academy; "Monimiaceae" for Das Pflanzenreich, 1911; Beiträge zur Kenntnis der Monimiaceen Papuasiens, Engler's Botanische Jahrbücher, 1915; Uebersicht ueber die Gattungen der Monimiaceae sowie Zusammenstellung der Abbildungen und der Literatur ueber die Arten dieser Familie bis zum Jahre, 1925; Uebersicht über die Gattungen der Styracaceae sowie Zusammenstellung der Abbildungen und der Literatur über die Arten dieser Familie bis zum Jahre, 1928. Unitarian. Address: Chicago, Ill. Died July 7, 1933.

PERLSTEIN, MEYER AARON, pediatrician; b. Chgo., Apr. 6 1902; s. Moses Aaron and Rose (Silverman) P. B.S., U. Chgo., 1924, M.D., 1928; m. Minnie Oboler, May 7, 1928; children—Lee R. (wife of Dr. Bernard J. Axelrad), Ruth N. (wife of Dr. Michel Stein), Paul. Intern Cook County Hosp., Chgo., 1927-28, chief children's neurology service, attending staff; pvt. practice pediatrics, Chgo., 1929-69, San Jose, Cal., 1969; attending staff pediatrics Michael Reese Hosp., Chgo.; chief med. staff Ill. Children's Hosp. Sch.; prof. pediatrics Cook County Postgrad. Sch. Medicine; asso. prof. pediatrics Northwestern U. Med. Sch.; cons. neuropediatrics dept. phys. medicine U. P.R. Mem. adv. panel Cerebral Palsy project Nat. Inst. Neurologic Diseases and Blindness; adv. com. cerebral palsy Am. Pub. Health Assn.; adv. com. neuropediatrics U. P.R.; research adv. bd. United Cerebral Palsy, 1955; sci. council Brain Research Found.; bd. govs. Ill. Assn. Crippled; mem. Acad. Dentistry for Handicapped; med. adviser Ill. Epilepsy League, Chgo. Club Crippled Children, Spastic Children's Center, United Cerebral Palsy Chgo., Julian D. Levinson Research Foundation, Chicago; professional advisory council National Soc. Crippled Children and Adults, 1957; neuropediatric cons. Jewish Children's Bur., Chgo. cerebral palsy cons. Nat., Mich., socs. crippled children and adults, Crippled Children's Sch., Jamestown, N.D. Recipient citation Illinois Council Exceptional Children, 1964; U.S. Com. award distinguished internat. service rehab. disabled, 1965. Diplomate American Bd. Pediatrics. Mem. A.M.A., Ill., Chgo. med. socs., Chgo. Pediatric Soc., Chgo. Diabetes Assn., Inst. Medicine Chgo., Am. Acad. Neurology, Am. Acad. Pediatrics. Am. Acad. Cerebral Palsy (past pres.), Internat. Council Exceptional Children, Am. League Against Epilepsy, A.A.A.S., Ill. Epilepsy League, Am. Assn. Mental Deficiency, Am., Ill. pub. health assns., Israel Med. Assn. (Am. physicians fellowship com.), Nat. Geographic Soc., Phi Beta Delta, Alpha Omega Alpha. Mem. B'nai B'rith. Author numerous articles, papers in field. Asso. editor Cerebral Palsy Rev., Digest of Pediatrics. Address: San Jose CA Died Oct. 29, 1969; interred San Jose CA

PERLZWEIG, WILLIAM A., (perl'svig), biochemist; b. Ostrog, Russia, Apr. 23, 1891; s. Isaac Boris and Miriam (Schreyer) P.; B.S., Columbia, 1913, M.A., 1914, Ph.D., 1915; m. Olga Marx, Apr. 26, 1919; 1 dau., Judith Margaret. Came to U.S., 1906, naturalized, 1909. Asst. biochemistry Columbia, 1913-16; asst. chemist Rockefeller Inst., New York, 1916-17; research biochemist U.S. Pub. Health Service, 1919-21; instr. and asso. in medicine. Med. Clinic Johns Hopkins U., 1921-30; prof. biochemistry Duke Med. Sch., biochemist, Duke Hosp. since 1930; consultant to surgeon gen., U.S. P.H.S. since 1946. Served as 1st lt., Sanitary Corps., U.S. Army, 1917-19. Fellow A.A.A.S.; mem. Am. Soc. Biol. Chemists, Inst. of Nutrition, Am. Chem. Soc., Soc. Exptl. Biol. and Medicine, Am. Assn. Univ. Profs., Phi Beta Kappa, Sigma Xi. Home: 3918 Dover Rd. Office: Duke Hospital, Durham, N.C. Died Dec. 10, 1949.

PERRET, FRANK ALVORD, volcanologist; b. Hartford, Conn., Aug. 2, 1867; s. Charles and Mary Elizabeth (Alvord) P.; ed. Brooklyn Poly. (non-grad.); unmarried. Began as asst. in Edison's East Side Lab., 1886; invented Perret electric motor and assisted in organizing Elektron Mfg. Co., Brooklyn; later engaged in manufacture Perret electric motors, Springfield, Mass. Took up volcanology, 1904, and became hon. asst. to Prof. Matteucci in Royal Observatory, Mt. Vesuvius, Italy, representing Volcanic Research Soc., Springfield, Mass., etc.; investigated by direct research Mt. Vesuvius eruption of 1906; Stomboli, 1907, 12, 15; Messina, 1908; Teneriffe, 1909; Sakurashima, 1914; Etna, 1910; dir. Hawaiian expdn. Mass. Inst. Tech. and lived at crater of Kilauea through summer of 1911; later volcanologist to Carnegie Geophysical Lab., Washington; founder and now dir. Volcanological Mus., St. Pierre, Martinique. A founder and mem. dept. electricity, Brooklyn Inst. Arts and Sciences. Decorated Knight of Italian Crown; Legion of Honor (France). Republican. Episcopalian. Address: St. Pierre, Martinique. *

PERRINE, CHARLES DILLON, astronomer; b. Steubenville, O., July 28, 1867; s. Peter and Elizabeth Dillon (McCauley) P.; grad. Steubenville High Sch., 1884; tech. edn. by pvt. exertion and at Lick Obs.; Sc.D., Santa Clara Coll., 1905; m. Bell Smith, 1905; children—Charles Dillon, Mary Lyford, Dillon Ball, Isabel Clara, Charlotte Elizabeth. Resided in Calif., 1886-1909; astronomer in Lick Observatory to 1909; dir. Argentine Nat. Observatory since 1909. Observed total solar eclipse of May 28, 1900, in Ga., 1905 in Spain; 1908 in Flint Island; in charge expdn. from Lick Obs. to Sumatra to observe total solar eclipse of May 18, 1901. Fellow A.A.A.S.; hon. mem. Astron. Soc. Mex.; mem. Astron. Soc. of the Pacific, Astron. and Astrophys. Soc. America, Astronomische Gesellschaft; foreign asso. Royal Astron. Soc. Awarded medals for discovery of comets by Astron. Soc. of the Pacific;

Lalande prize and gold medal by Paris Acad. of Sciences, 1897; gold medal from Aston. Soc. of Mexico, 1905, for discovery of Jupiter's 6th and 7th satellites. Besides discovery and observation of 13 comets, his chief contbns. to scientific work have been the discovery of the remarkable motion in the nebulosity about the New Star in Perseus, in 1901, the discovery of the 6th and 7th satellites of Jupiter, the investigation of solar eclipse problems; determination of the solar parallax from observations of Eros; observations of nebulae and star clusters; computation of orbits and ephemerides of comets; investigations of photographic problems in astronomy, etc. Has contributed many articles to astron. and other scientific journals of U.S. and Europe. Address: Córdoba, Argentine Republic.

PERRINE, FREDERIC AUTEN COMBS, elec. engr.; b. Manalapan, N.J., Aug. 25, 1862; s. James A. and Rebecca A. (Combs) P.; ed. Freehold, N.J., Inst., 1870-79; grad. Princeton, 1883, A.M., 1886, D.Sc., 1885; spl. studies in elec. engring.; post-graduate student Princeton, 1883-85; m. Margaret J. Roebling, June 28, 1893. Asst. electrician U. S. Electric Light Co., 1885-89; mgr. insulated wire dept., John A. Roebling's Sons Co., 1889-92; treas. Germania Electric Co., 1892-93; prof. elec. engring., Leland Stanford Jr. U., 1893-1900; chief engr., Standard Electric Co., of Calif., 1898-1900, pres. Stanley Electric Mfg. Co., Pittsfield, Mass., 1900-04; later consulting engr. Editor Journal of Electricity, San Francisco, 1894-96; Elec. Engring., Chicago, 1896-98. Author: Conductors for Distribution, 1903. Residence: Plainfield, N.J. Died 1908.

PERRINE, HENRY, botanist; b. Cranburg, N.J., Apr. 5, 1797; s. Peter and Sarah (Rozengrant) P.; m. Ann Fuller Townsend, Jan. 8, 1822, 3 children. Practiced medicine, Ripley, Ill., 1819-24, Natchez, Miss., 1824-27; U.S. consul at Campeche, Mexico, 1827-37; made bot. collections in Mexico; introduced useful tropical plants to Fla. including henequen and sisal; built nursery, Indian Key, Fla., 1833; received grant of land in Fla. from Congress, 1838. Killed by Seminole Indians, Aug. 7, 1840.

PERRINE, IRVING, geologist, oil operator; b. Wallkill, N.Y., Aug. 5, 1884; s. Alfred and Agnes Estella (Van Kleeck) P.; grad. New Paltz State Normal Sch., 1903; A.B., Cornell, 1907, A.M., 1911, Ph.D., 1912; m. Hilda Aurelia Sweet, Aug. 25, 1910; 1 dau., Phyllis Sweet (Mrs. Turner Whitworth). Asst. state geologist, La., 1908-09, also field asst. geologist, U.S. Geol. Survey; instr. geology, Cornell U., 1907-12; prof. geology summer sessions Cornell, 1912-14; prof. geology and paleontology U. Okla., 1912-15; chief geologist Marland Oil Co., Okla., 1913-15, Pierce Oil Corp. and Pierce Fordyce Oil Assn., 1915-16; cons. geologist, oil operator, 1917—; pres. Belle Isle Royalty Co., Unidos Royalty Co.; v.p. Kilpatrick Bros. Lumber Co.; prof. geology, Oklahoma City U., 1948—. Spl. cons. SEC, Washington, on sale of oil and gas interests, 1934-35; cons. geologist War Dept., also U.S. Dept. Justice, 1940—. Fellow A.A.A.S.; mem. Am. Inst. of Mining and Metall. Engrs.; Am. Assn. Petroleum Geologists (v.p. 1919), Okla. Soc. Profl. Engrs., Oklahoma City Geol. Soc. (pres. 1922-23), Kan. Acad. Scis., Okla. Acad. Scis., N.Y. Acad. Scis., Sigma Xi, Phi Gamma Delta, Sigma Gamma Epsilon. Republican. Unitarian. Mason (32 deg., K.T., Shriner), Elk. Clubs: Cornell of Okla., Men's Dinner, Beacon Club. Home: 506 N.W. 14th St., Oklahoma City. Died Apr. 25, 1955.

PERRY, CLAY LAMONT, mathematician, educator; b. San Francisco, Feb. 26, 1920; s. Clay Lamont and Matie V. (Bishofberger) P.; A.B. (La Verne Noyes scholar), U. Cal. at Los Angeles, 1942; Ph.D. (NRC fellow), U. Mich., 1949; m. Kathleen Kelly, Sept. 6, 1946; children—Virginia, Carol. Sr. mathematician Oak Ridge Nat. Lab., 1950-53; dir. Computer Center, prof. U.S. Naval Postgrad. Sch., Monterey, Cal., 1953-55; mgr. math. scis. dept. Stanford Research Inst., Menlo Park, Cal., 1955-60, cons., from 1960; dir. Computer Center, prof. math. U. Cal. at San Diego, La Jolla, from 1960. Served to 1st lt. USAAF, 1942-46. Mem. Assn. for Computing Machinery, Am. Math. Soc., Math. Assn. Am., Soc. Indsl. and Applied Math., Sigma Xi. Author: Programming and Coding for Digital Computers, 1961. Office: San Diego CA Deceased.

PERRY, JAMES CLIFFORD, sanitarian; b. Pasquotank County, N.C., Jan. 5, 1864; s. James Decatur and Margaret Caroline (Morgan) P.; student U. of N.C., 1881-83; M.D., U. of Md., 1885; m. Nancy Nash Elliott, 1916. Apptd. asst. surgeon U.S.P.H.S., Mar. 21, 1889; passed asst. surgeon, Apr. 19, 1893; surgeon, Mar. 1, 1904; sr. surgeon, Mar. 4, 1915; asst. surgeon gen., Feb. 1, 1918; med. dir., July 10, 1930, U.S. Pub. Health Service. Organized protective quarantine at Hongkong, China, governing vessels for U.S. ports, 1899; organized quarantine service Philippine Islands and chief quarantine officer, 1900-03; on sanitary staff Isthmian Canal Commn. as chief quarantine officer, 1905-14, also health officer City of Panama, 1909-14; spl. investigations Chicago Health Dept.; spl. investigations at Richmond, Ind., to determine incidence of tuberculosis, and Health Dept., Columbia, S.C., 1915; served as chief med. officer Ellis Island, N.Y.; experience in control of cholera plague, yellow fever, also other communicable diseases and pub. health adminstrn. Democrat. Methodist. Address: San Francisco, Calif. Died Oct. 19, 1936.

PERRY, OSCAR BUTLER, mining engr.; b. Bloomington, Ind., Sept. 1876; s. Maj. H. F. P.; A.B., Ind. U., 1897, LL.D., 1931; E.M., Columbia U., 1900; m. Anlo Marquee Cramer, Apr. 1923; children—Anlo Louise, Yvonne Chauvigny. Manager Ind. Gold Dredging Co., 1900, 02, Western Engring. & Construction Co., San Francisco, 1902-04; engr., 1904-06, gen. mgr. placer mining properties since 1906, Guggenheim Exploration Co.; gen. mgr. Yukon Gold Co., operating gold mines in U.S. and Yukon Territory, and tin mines in Malay, 1920-26; mng. dir. Bolivian Internat. Mining Corp. since 1930. Entered U.S. Army, May 1917; discharged, Apr. 1919, with rank of col. of engrs.; comd. 27th Engrs., A.E.F.; asst. engr. light rys. and roads, and engr. in charge of bridge sect., 1st Army. Mem. Beta Theta Pi, Tau Beta Pi. Clubs: Family (San Francisco); Engineers', Columbia University, Bankers (New York). Author of Gold Dredging in the Yukon and other professional papers. Home: 444 El Arroyo Rd., Hillsborough, Calif. Address: 315 Montgomery St., San Francisco 4, Calif. Died July 24, 1945.

PERRY STUART, inventor; b. Newport, N.Y., Nov. 2, 1814; grad. Union Coll., 1837; m. Amy Jane Carter, 1837; m. 2d, Jane W. Maxson, 1873; 1 child. In partnership with brother in wholesale dairy products business, Newport, 1840-60; invented internal combustion gas engine, patented, 1844; patented lock, key, and safe bolt, 1857, combination lock, 1858; also invented milk cooler, stereopticon, velocipede, hay tender and improved sawmill machinery. Died Feb. 9, 1890.

PERSONS, AUGUSTUS ARCHILUS, chemist; b. Enon, Ala., Nov. 15, 1866; s. J. W. and E. P. P.; B.S., Ala. Poly. Inst., 1886, M.S., 1888; U. of Chicago, summer sessions, 1899, 1900; m. Mabel Knox, Sept. 27, 1893. Prof. natural science, Ala. Normal Coll., Troy, 1889-92; prof. chemistry and chemist, Fla. Agrl. Coll. Expt. Sta., and consulting chemist, F.C.&P. and Plant Ry. systems, 1892-98; prof. chemistry, U. of Ala., 1898-1908; supt. city schs., Bessemer, Ala., 1908-09. Consulting chemist M.&O. Ry., 1898—; agrl. editor Fla. Citizen, Jacksonville, Fla., 1894-96. Mem. bd. of visitors U.S. Mil. Acad., 1905. Pres. dept. superintendence Ala. Ednl. Assn., 1911-12. Address: Bessemer, Ala. Died Feb. 25, 1917.

PETER, ALFRED MEREDITH, chemist; b. Lexington, Ky., May 25, 1857; s. Dr. Robert and Frances (Dallam) P.; ed. Acad. and Coll. of Arts, Ky. U.; B.S., State Agrl. and Mech. Coll. of Ky., 1880, M.S., 1885; Sc.D., Ky. State Coll., 1913; m. Mary B. McCauley, of Lexington, Ky., Sept. 27, 1887 (died Nov. 2, 1925). Instr. Ky. U., 1876-78; adj. prof. chemistry and natural history, State Agrl. and Mech. Coll., 1880-81; asst. chemist Ky. Geol. Survey, 1881-86; chemist Ky. Agrl. Expt. Sta., 1886-1909, chief chemist, 1909-27, emeritus since 1927 (acting dir., Sept. 24, 1916-Jan. 3, 1918); mem. State Bd. of Agr., 1917; supervising chemist Ky. Geol. Survey, 1904-12; prof. soil technology, State U. of Ky., 1910-18, emeritus since 1929; head chemistry dept., Kentucky Agrl. Expt. Sta., 1912-27; chmn. Publications Com., 1929. Reporter on soils and ash for Association Official Agricultural Chemists, 1894-95. Member 8th Internat. Congress Applied Chemistry, 1912. Mason. Fellow A.A.A.S., Am. Inst. of Chemists; mem. Am. Chem. Soc., Ky. State Hist. Soc., Ky. Acad. Science (sec.), Soc. Chem. Industry, Am. Assn. Univ. Profs., Alpha Chi Sigma Xi, Phi Beta Kappa, Phi Gamma Mu. Home: Lexington, Ky.

PETER, ROBERT, physician, chemist; b. Launceston, Cornwall, Eng., Jan. 21, 1805; s. Robert and Johanna (Dawe) P.; attended Rensselaer Sch. (now Rensselaer Poly. Inst.), Troy, N.Y.; M.D., Transylvania U., 1834; m. Frances Paca Dellam, Oct. 6, 1835, 11 children including Alfred M. Came to U.S., 1817, naturalized, 1826; lectr. chemistry Western U. of Pa., 1830-31; mem. Hesperian Soc., Pitts. Philos. Soc.; prof. chemistry Morrison Coll., Lexington, Ky., 1833-38; editor Transylvania Jour. of Medicine and Asso. Scis., 1837; prof. chemistry and pharmacy med. dept. Transylvania U., Lexington, 1838-57, dean med. faculty, 1847-57; prof. chemistry and toxicology Ky. Sch. Medicine, Louisville, 1850-53; chemist to geol. surveys of Ky., 1854, Ark., Ind.; 1st to note that richness of bluegrass soils of Ky. is caused by high phosphorous content; acting asst. surgeon in charge of U.S. mil. hosps., Lexington, 1861-65; prof. chemistry and exptl. philosophy Agrl. and Mech. Coll. of Ky. U., 1865-78; asst. editor Farmer's Home Jour., 1867-68; prof. chemistry Ky. Agrl. and Mech. Coll. (now separate instns.), 1878-87, prof. emeritus, 1887-94. Author: Chemical Examination of the Urinary Calcali in the Museum of the Medical Department of Transylvania University, 1846. Died Winton, Ky., Apr. 26, 1894.

PETERMAN, MYNIE GUSTAV, pediatrist; b. Merrill, Wis., Mar. 5, 1896; s. Albert Frederick and Ida (Braatz) P.; Sc.B., U. of Wis., 1918; A.M., Washington U., St. Louis, 1920; M.D., Washington U. Sch. of Medicine, 1921 (fellowship, scholarship, 1920-21); m. Mildred Mackenzie, Sept. 29, 1924; children—Albert Frederick, Mary Jean. Practiced as physician in Milwaukee since 1925; introduced new treatment for epilepsy in childhood, 1924, new test for syphilis, 1927, classification for convulsions, 1933; chief resident physician City and County Hosp., St. Paul, 1921-22; fellow, 1st asst. and asso. in pediatrics, Mayo Foundation and Clinic, 1922-25; dir. laboratories and research, Milwaukee Children's Hosp., 1925-33; former chief staff Milwaukee County Hospital; med. dir. Nat. Children's Rehab. Center, 1967-68; cons. USPHS Bur. Indian Affairs; cons. Bur. Medicine, FDA, med. staff drug surveillance br., 1964-67; cons. staff Columbia Hosp., Milw. In Chem. Warfare Div. U. Wis., 1917-18; 1st sgt. S.A.T.C., 1918, World War; 1st lt. Med. R.C., 1924, col., 1950. Diplomate Am. Bd. Pediatrics. Fellow Am. Acad. Neurology; mem. A.M.A., Internat. Congress Pediatrics, Am. Academy of Pediatrics, Central Soc. Clin. Research, American Association for research Nervous and Mental Diseases, Wis. State and Milwaukee Co. med. soc., Am. Epilepsy Soc., Milw. Pediatric Soc., Osler Soc., Madrid Pediatric Society, Sigma Xi, Phi Sigma. Clubs: Army and Navy, Torch (Washington). Author chpts. in med. works and research articles in med. publs. Editor English transl. Diseases of Children (5 vols.), 1935. Home: Milwaukee WI Died Oct. 14, 1971.

PETERS, ALBERT THEODORE, veterinarian; b. Chicago, Feb. 10, 1868; s. Joachim and Frederica P.; ed. Chicago pub. schs. and Royal Vet. Coll., Stuttgart, Germany, 1893; m. Emma B. Rickert, of Chicago. Veterinarian, U.S. Agrl. Expt. Sta. at U. of Neb., 1893-1909; with Ill. State Bd. Live Stock Commn. and dir. State Biol. Lab., since Jan. 1, 1910. Translator: Guide to Practical Meat Inspection, including Examination for Trichinae, from German of Dr. F. Fischoeder; The Methods of Milk Inspection for Physicians, Chemists, Hygienists and Veterinarians, from German of Dr. P. Somerfield; Leisering's Atlas of the Anatomy of the Horse and of Other Domestic Animals. Author of bulls. U.S. Agrl. Expt. Sta., Neb.; conducted spl. investigations of cornstalk disease among horses and cattle. Mem. Am. Medical Assn. Address: Capitol, Springfield, Ill.

PETERS, CHRISTIAN HENRY FREDERICK, astronomer; b. Coldenbüttel, Schleswig, Germany, Sept. 19, 1813; Ph.D., U. Berlin (Germany), 1836. With expdn. surveying Mt. Etna, 1838-43; dir. trigonometrical survey in Sicily, 1843-48; came to U.S., 1854; with U.S. Coast Survey, 1854-58; dir. observatory Hamilton Coll., 1858-67, Litchfield prof. astronomy, dir. Litchfield Observatory, 1867-90; led expdn. to observe solar eclipse, Des Moines, Ia., 1869; led U.S. expdn. to New Zealand to observe transit of Venus, 1874; described apparent division of sun spots by bridges of luminous gas; discovered 48 new asteroids, 2 comets, 1846, 57; revised Ptolemy's Almagest, catalogue stars' positions; mem. Nat. Acad. Scis.; fgn. asso. Royal Astron. Soc. Author: Celestial Charts, 1882; Heliographic Positions of Sun Spots, Observed at Hamilton College form 1860 to 1870 (edited by E.B. Frost), published 1907; articles "Contributions to the Atmospherology of the Sun" in Proceedings of A.A.A.S., Vol. IX, 1856, "Corrigenda in Various Star Catalogues" in Memoirs of Nat. Acad. Sciences, Vol. III, part 2, 1886. Died July 19, 1890.

PETERS, EDWARD DYER, mining engr.; b. Dorchester, Mass., June 1, 1849; s. Henry Hunter and Susan Barker (Thaxter) P.; Sch. of Mines, Freiberg, 1869; M.D., Harvard, 1877; m. Anna Quincy, d. Benjamin Cushing, Sept. 28, 1881. Territorial assayer of Colo., 1872; lecturer, 1903-04, prof. metallurgy, Harvard, 1904—. Mem. Am. Inst. Mining Engrs. Author: Modern Copper Smelting, 1887; Principles of Copper Smelting, 1907; also many tech. and scientific monographs. Address: Dorchester, Mass. Died Feb. 17, 1917.

PETERS, JAMES ARTHUR, biologist; b. Durant, Ia., July 13, 1922; s. Arthur J. and Jane Terrell (Pascoe) P.; student U. Ill., 1941-42; B.S., U. Mich., 1948, M.A., 1950, Ph.D., 1952; postgrad. student U. Tex., 1950; m. Beatriz Moisset de Espanes, June 18, 1964; 1 son, Steven; children by previous marriage—Jane, Arthur James, Jennifer Laura, Druscilla Anne, Jeffrey Edward. Mem. faculty Brown U., 1952-58, asst. prof. biology, 1955-58; Fulbright prof., Quito, Ecuador, 1958-59; asso. prof., then prof. biology San Fernando Valley State Coll., Northridge, Cal., 1959-64; asso. curator Smithsonian Instn., Washington, 1964-66, curator and supr., 1966-72. Served with USAAF, 1942-45. Fellow Herpetologists League; mem. Am. Soc. Ichtyologists and Herpetologists (pres. 1970), Soc. Study Evolution, Soc. Systematic Zoology, Brit. Herpetological Soc. Herpetological Assn. Africa, Assn. Tropical Biology (asso. editor 1969-70), Biol. Soc. Washington, S. Cal. Acad. Scis. Author: Snakes of the Subfamily Dipsadinae, 1960; (with others) Catalogue of Neotropical Squamata, 1970. Editor: Classic Papers in Genetics, 1959. Compiler: Dictionary of Herpetology, 1964. Cons. Am. Heritage Dictionary, Ency. Brit. Home: Rockville MD Died Dec. 18, 1972; buried Greenup IL

PETERS, JAMES L(EE), ornithologist; b. Boston, Mass., Aug. 13, 1889; s. Austin and Frances Howie (Lee) P.; student Roxbury Latin Sch., 1902-08; A.B., Harvard, 1912; m. Eleanor K. Sweet, May 28, 1932.

Expeditions to Mexico, West Indies, Central and South America, 1911-30; asst. curator of birds, Museum of Comparative Zoölogy, Harvard Coll., 1927-32, curator since 1932. Served as 2d lt. U.S. Army, in France and Germany, World War I, 1917-19. Fellow Am. Ornithologists Union, Am. Acad. of Arts and Sciences; mem. Washington Acad. of Sciences, Am. Soc. of Mammologists, Internat. Commn. Zoölogical Nomenclature, Deutsche Ornithologische Gesellschaft (corr.), Ornithologische Gesellschaft Bayern (corr.), Sociedad Ornithologica del Plata (corr.), Nuttall Ornithological, Cooper Ornithological, Biol. Soc. of Wash. Clubs: Harvard of Boston, Faculty. Author: Check-List of Birds of the World. Vols. I-VII, 1931-48; contbr. numerous articles to professional jours. Home: Harvard, Mass. Office: Museum Comparative Zoölogy, Cambridge 38, Mass. Died Apr. 19, 1952.

PETERS, WALTER HARVEST, animal husbandryman; b. Keokuk, Ia., July 9, 1885; s. Henry C. and Katherine (Wende) P.; B.S.A., Ia. State Coll., 1908, hon. M.Agr., 1920; m. Millie Gillette, Aug. 7, 1912; children—Robert Gillette, Eunice Margaret. Instr. animal husbandry Ia. State Coll., 1908-09; prof. animal husbandry Manitoba Agrl. Coll., Winnipeg, Can., 1909-14; head of animal husbandry sect. N.D. Expt. Sta., 1914-18, U. Minn., 1918—. Mem. Am. Soc. Animal Prodn. (pres.). Methodist. Author: Livestock Production (coll. textbook), 1942; (with Geo. P. Deyoe) Raising Livestock, 1946. Contbr. to The Farmer, Farm Stock and Home. Peters Hall, St. Paul campus U. Minn. named in his honor. Home: 1452 Hythe St., St. Paul. Died Aug. 8, 1949; buried Keokuk, Ia.

PETERSEN, CARL EDWARD, naval architect, marine engr.; b. Brooklyn, N.Y., Jan. 21, 1897; s. Christian Edward (Thinggaard) and Magdalene (Hoy) P.; ed. Pratt Inst., Tri-State Coll. of Engring., Brooklyn Poly. Inst.; grad. U.S. Navy Steam Engring. Sch., Stevens Inst. Tech., 1918; m. 2d, Ann Suber, Oct. 28, 1937; children—Carl Thinggaard (by 1st marriage), Dianne Mary. With Morse Dry Dock & Repair Co., 1910-18, successively as marine machinist, draftsman, estimator and outside superintendent; engr. officer, transport duty, U.S. Navy, 1918; supt. engr. U.S. Army Transport Service, during period of conversion of merchants vessels to troop ships, 1919; estimator in charge cost of ship repairs at Port of New York, U.S. Shipping Bd., 1919-20; naval architect U.S. Mail Steamship Co., 1920; naval architect U.S. Lines in charge reconditioning the George Washington, America, President Harding, President Roosevelt, etc., 1921-27; asst. to v.p. Newport News Shipbuilding Dry Dock Co., 1928-37; asst. mgr. const. and repair dept. Matson Navigation Co., 1938-41; had charge gen. design steamships President Hoover and President Coolidge. Lt. comdr. U.S. Naval Res. Called to active duty as comdr. Vol. Naval Res., engr. spl. service duties, Dec. 17, 1941; coordinator ship repairs and asst. material officer, Honolulu, T.H., on spl. orders from sec. of navy, Dec. 21, 1941-Apr. 1942; exec. and repair officer, U.S. Naval Sect. Base, New Orleans (Algiers), La., to July 1943; stationed Tampa, Fla., sr. asst. supervisor of shipbuilding U.S.N., 1943-44. Mem. Am. Soc. Mech. Engrs., Am. Bur. of Shipping (also Pacific Coast Com.); life mem., hon. corr. mem. Institution of Naval Architects, London; life mem. N. E. Coast Institution of Engrs. and Shipbuilders (Newcastle-on-Tyne, Eng.); life mem., v.p. Inst. Marine Engrs. (London), life mem. Soc. Naval Architects and Marine Engrs. (council mem.); naval mem. Am. Soc. Naval Engrs.; tech. mem. Tech. Com. of Engring. Am. Bur. Shipping. Fellow Am. Geographic Soc. Licensed engr. State of N.Y., chief engr. ocean steam vessels (any tonnage). Address: care Supervisor of Shipbuilding, U.S. Navy, Tampa, Fla. Died in active service, July 23, 1944.

PETERSEN, WILLIAM EARL, educator; b. Pine City, Minn., Feb. 3, 1892; s. Matz and Mary Kathryn (Sorensen) P.; B.S., U. Minn., 1916, M.S., 1917, Ph.D., 1928; D.Sc. (honorary), University of Vermont, 1956; married Alma Agnes Lindstrom, Aug. 24, 1917; children—Dorothy May (Mrs. John F. Grimmel), William Earl, Allan Donald, Raymond George, Joanne Marlene. Dairy extension specialist Kan. State Coll., 1917-20; field sec. Holstein Frierian Assn., Minn., 1920-21; mem. faculty U. Minn. from 1921, prof. dairy husbandry, from 1943; hon. prof. Peru Agricultural Coll., LaMolina, Peru. Decorated Knight Cross Order of Danneborg (Denmark); recipient Borden award, 1942; Morrison award, Am. Soc. Animal Prodn., 1956; listed One Hundred Living Great in Minnesota, 1949. Foreign honorary member Royal Academy Agr., Sweden, 1945. Member New York Academy Science, Society Exptl. Biology and Medicino, Am. Chem. Soc., A.A.A.S., Am. Genetic Assn., Am. Soc. Animal Prodn., Am. Physiol. Soc., Am. Dairy Sci. Assn. (pres. 1949-50), Sigma Xi (state pres. 1951), Gamma Alpha (nat. treas. 1932-40), Alpha Zeta, Alpha Gamma Rho. Unitarian. Producer tech. motion picture in color, The Science of Milk Production, 1945, No Hand Stripping (in 7 langs.), 1947. Author: Dairy Science, 1939 (1950); American Agriculture (with A. Boss, H. K. Wilson), 4 vols., 1939-46. Contbr. articles sci. jours. Home: St Paul MN Died Mar. 15, 1971.

PETERSEN, WILLIAM FERDINAND, physician; b. Chicago, Mar. 25, 1887; s. Eduard and Wilhelmina Joanna (Klockziem) P.; student Armour Inst., 1904-06; B.S., U. of Chicago, 1910; M.D., Rush Med. Coll. (U. of Chicago), 1912; m. Alma Catherine Schmidt, Sept. 16, 1919; children—Eduard Schmidt, Conrad William, William Otto. Instr. pathology, Vanderbilt U., 1913, asst. prof. exptl. medicine and pathology, 1914-17; asso. in pathology and bacteriology, U. of Ill. Coll. of Medicine, 1919-24, prof., 1924-42; pres. Petersen Oven Co. Served as pvt. and 1st lt. with M.C., U.S. Army, 1917-19. Mem. A.M.A., Inst. of Medicine, Soc. Exptl. Pathology, Am. Soc. Pathology and Bacteriology, Chicago Pathol. Soc., Chicago Soc. Internal Medicine, Am. Assn. Physical Anthropology. Clubs: University, Chicago Literary (Chicago). Author: Protein Therapy and Non-Specific Reactions, 1922; Skin Reactions, Blood Chemistry and Physical Status of Normal Men and Clinical Patients (with S. A. Levinson), 1930; The Patient and the Weather (monographs with Margaret E. Milliken), 1934-38; Destiny—Lincoln-Douglas, 1943; Hippocratic Wisdom, 1945; Man-Weather-Sun, 1947. Home: 1322 Astor St., Chicago. Died Aug. 20, 1950.

PETERSON, LAWRENCE EUGENE, cons. engr.; b. Sheboygan, Wis., Nov. 5, 1897; s. Peter John and Anna Elizabeth (Pedersen) P.; B.S., U. Ill., 1920, C.E., 1927; m. Margery M. Hansen, Feb. 19, 1920; children—Lawrence Eugene, Betty Jean; m. 2d, Eleanore S. Blakely, Feb. 14, 1949; 1 dau., Pepper E. Structural engr. Kalman Co., Chgo. & Milw. Corrugating Co., 1920-25; cons. engr. since 1925, maj. partner Lawrence Peterson & Assos., N.Y.C., Milw. since 1946. Led expdn. to study sun's total eclipse, God's Lake, Man., Can., 1945. Registered profl. engr., N.Y., Ohio, Ill., Ind., Ariz., Ia., Wis., Minn., Fla., and Mich. and nat. council. Represented Nat. Soc. Profl. Engrs. and Am. Inst. Cons. Engrs. at 1st Internat. Congress Civil Engring., Mexico, 1949; retained as indsl. cons. to govt., Union of Burma. Mem. bldg. code coms. State of Wis. and Milw., Am. Inst. Cons. Engrs. (past mem. council), Am. Soc. C.E., Am. Astron. Soc., Am. Auto. Assn.; Nat. Soc. Profl. Engrs. (v.p. 1948), Soc. Am. Mil. Engrs., Am. Concrete Inst., Am. Shore and Beach Preservation Assn., Milw. Met. Plan Assn. (pres.), Greater Milw. Com., Tau Beta Pi, Sigma Tau, Lambda Chi Alpha. Baptist. Club: University (N.Y.). Address: 1060 Park Av., N.Y.C. 28. Died Apr. 1963.

PETERSON, OLOF AUGUST, paleontologist; b. Hellgum och Radom, Westernorrlands, Län, Sweden, Jan. 2, 1865; s. Pher Isaacson and Christina Brita Christopherson; ed. pub. sch. near birthplace; came with parents to U.S., 1882; m. Eda Louise Hermann, Oct. 15, 1901. Employed, 1888-91, with Prof. O. C. Marsh, then U.S. paleontologist; after that with Prof. H. F. Osborn in Am. Mus. Natural History, New York, 1891-96; with Princeton scientific expdn. to Patagonia, 1896, and continued in Princeton U. Mus. until Jan. 1, 1900; curator mammalian paleontology, Carnegie Mus., Pittsburgh. Writer of numerous papers on research topics in paleontology. Address: Pittsburgh, Pa. Died Nov. 13, 1933.

PETERSON, WILLIAM H(AROLD), educator; b. Libertyville, N.Y., Nov. 14, 1880; s. Per John and Clara (Säterlöv) P.; B.S., Wesleyan U., 1907; M.A., Columbia, 1909; Ph.D., U. Wis., 1913; m. Mary Katherine White, Aug. 7, 1913 (died 1923); m. 2d Mary Lambert Shine, Jan. 30, 1926. Asst. in chemistry Columbia, summers 1909-11; asst. in bio-chemistry U. Wis., 1909-10, instr., 1910-14; asst. prof., 1914-18, asso. prof., 1918-25, prof. since 1925. Served with Chem. Warfare Service, U.S. Army, 1918; served as $1-a-year man, WPB, 1944-45. Fellow Kaiser Wilhelm Inst., Berlin, 1914. Mem. A.A.A.S., Am. Chem. Soc., Am. Soc. Biol. Chemists, Biochem. Soc. (Brit.), Inst. Nutrition, Soc. Am. Bacteriologists, Soc. Exptl. Biology and Medicine, Harvey Soc. (hon.), Phi Beta Kappa, Gamma Alpha, Sigma Xi. Author: Elements of Food Biochemistry (with J. T. Skinner and F. M. Strong), 1943; Laboratory Manual of Food Biochemistry (with F. M. Strong), 1948. Contbr. more than 300 research papers to sci. jours. of U.S., Gt. Britain, Germany. Specialist in prodn. penicillin, other antibiotics, nutrition of bacteria, biochemistry of microorganism. Home: 304 Princeton Av., Madison 5, Wis. Died July 1960.

PETROFF, STRASHIMER ALBURTUS, (pet'rof), dir. med. research; b. Varna, Bulgaria, Aug. 20, 1883; s. Attanas and Dobra Ivanova (Pinchot) P.; Ph.D., Columbia, 1923; hon. Sc.D., Colgate, 1932; m. Mary Fears Gilmer, Jan. 18, 1912; 1 son, Gilmer. Came to U.S., 1900, naturalized citizen, 1907. Asst. in lab., Trudeau (N.Y.) Sanitarium, 1909-21, dir. med. research, 1921-35; now bacteriologist Sea View Hosp., S.I., N.Y. Mem. Am. Soc. Bacteriologist, Soc. Immunologists, Soc. Exptl. Biology and Medicine, Am. Med. Editors and Authors Assn. Republican. Presbyterian. Author: Tuberculosis Bacteriology, Pathology and Laboratory Diagnosis (with E. R. Baldwin and L. U. Gardner), 1927. Contbr. many papers and articles on bacteriology and immunity to tuberculosis. Died Nov. 26, 1948.

PETRUNKEVITCH, ALEXANDER, zoologist; b. Pliski, Russia, Dec. 22, 1875; s. Ivan Ilitch and Anna Petrovna (Kandiba) P.; ed. gymnasiums, Kiev, Tuver and Moscow, Russia, and U. Moscow; Ph.D., U. Freiburg, 1901; D.Sc., U. P.R., 1926, U. Ind., 1951; m. Wanda Hartshorn, Apr. 8, 1903 (died 1926); m. 2d, Myrtle Hallworth, 1927 (div. 1930). Privat-docent, Freiburg, 1902-04; lectr. Harvard, 1904-05; acting prof. zoology Ind. U., 1906; asst. prof. zoology, 1910-17, prof., 1917-44, Yale emeritus, 1944—. Pres. Russian Collegiate Inst. N.Y., 1919-26; asso. editor Current Hist. Mag., 1923. Hon. curator arachnida, Am. Mus. Natural Hist., N.Y.C., 1909-12. Chmn. sect. comparative physiology Internat. Congress Zoology, Boston, 1907. Recipient Addison Emery Verrill medal Yale, 1959. Fellow A.A.A.S., Paleontol. Soc.; mem. Am. Soc. Zoologists, Entomol. Soc. Am., Am. Mus. Nat. History (corr.), N.Y. Entomol. Soc., Nat. Acad. Sci., Sigma Xi. Translator: (in Russian) Byron's Manfred, 1898; (in English) Lay of the Warride of Igor, Poet Lore, 1920; Selected Poems of Pushkin, 1938. Author: Gedanken über Verebung, 1903; Free Will, 1905; Index Catalogue of Spiders of North Central and South America, 1911; Terrestrial Palaeozoic Arachnida of North America, 1913; Morphology of Invertebrate Types, 1916; Systema Aranearum, 1928; The Spiders of Porto Rico, 1930; An Inquiry into the Natural Classification of Spiders, 1933; A Study of Amber Spiders, 1942; Palaeozoic Arachnida of Illinois, 1945; Choice and Responsibility, 1947; A Study of Palaeozoic Arachnida, 1949; Baltic Amber Spiders in the Museum of Comparative Zoology, 1950; Principles of Classification, 1952; Macroevolution and the Fossil Record of Arachnida, 1952; Paleozoic and Mesozoic Arachnida of Europe, 1953; Archnida in Treatise on Invertebrate Paleontology, 1955; Amber Spiders in European Collections, 1958; Chiapas Amber Spiders, 1963, 2d study, 1964. Home: 97 Pool Rd., North Haven. Died Mar. 9, 1964.

PETRY, EDWARD JACOB, biologist, chemist; b. nr. Gnadenhutten, O., June 24, 1880; s. Jacob and Anna Catherine (Schmitt) P.; B.S. in Agr., Ohio State U., 1907; grad. study Cornell U., 1907-11; M.S., Purdue U., 1914; grad. study U. of Mich., 1918-20; Ph.D., Mich. State Coll., 1925; m. Dora Margaret Plueddemann, Sept. 16, 1909; 1 son, Ralph Aurelius. Teacher pub. schs., Tuscarawas County, O., 1899-1901; asst. in chemistry and botany, Ohio State U., 1906-07; asst. in botany, Cornell U., 1907-10; instr. in agronomy, Purdue, 1911-16, asst. prof. agrl. botany, 1916-18, field asst. U.S. Dept. Agr., 1918; instr. in botany, U. of Mich., 1918-20; prof. botany and head of dept. of botany and plant pathology, S.D. State Coll., 1920-23; cons. botanist, 1923-24; collaborator, U.S. Dept. Agr., 1920-29; survey botanist S.D. Geol. and Biol. Survey, 1924-25; prof. biology and head of dept., Hendrix Coll., 1926-29; same, Central Coll., Fayette, Mo., 1929-31; prof. botany and asso. in physiology, Coe Coll., Cedar Rapids, Ia., 1931-33; cons. biologist Cedar Rapids Water Works, 1933-35; pres. Iowa Memorial Arboretum Assn., 1933—; consulting biochemist, 1933—; chief chemist Consumers Cooperative Assn.; chemist Ebony Paint Company, Kansas City, Mo., 1937—. Temporary agent U.S. Department of Agriculture, 1926; bot. curator, Ark. Mus. of Natural History, Little Rock, 1928-29. Moravian. Mason. Author of Experiment Sta. Bulls. Original research furnishing proof of symbiotic nitrogen fixation in non-legume flowering plants. Home: Cedar Rapids, Ia. Died Oct. 8, 1939.

PETTERSON, LEROY DAVID, mining exec., pharm. chemist; b. Lee, Nev., June 28, 1885; s. Niles Fredrick and Elizabeth B. (Ogilvie) P.; Pharm. Chemist, U. Cal. Coll. Pharmacy, 1910; m. Lillian L. Abbee, Dec. 8, 1913 (div. 1924); children—Carmon E. (Mrs. Russel Clardy), Le Roy Hampton; m. Laura Powers, Apr. 8, 1928; 1 dau., Georgia Lou (Mrs. Grant W. Trimlett). Pharmacist, Palace Hotel Pharmacy, San Francisco, 1909-11; asst. adv. mgr. Owl Drug Co., San Francisco, 1912-13; mgr. ranch, 1913-15; druggist Kimberlin Drug Co., Kingsburg, Cal., 1915-16; raisin farmer, nr. Selma, Cal., 1916; wheat farmer, nr. Lincoln, Cal., 1916-19; druggist J. A. Riley Co., Chico, Cal., 1919-20; pharm. chemist Napa (Cal.) State Hosp., 1922-25, Patton State Hosp., 1925-32; mgr. Petterson Titus Labs., 1932-38; druggist Thrifty Drug Co., San Bernardino, Cal., 1939-40, Arcade Drug Co., Colton, Cal., 1940-45, Sav on Drugs, San Bernardino, 1945-59. Gen. mgr. Shiffer Mining Syndicate, Los Angeles, 1958-70; pres. LeRoy D. Petterson & Assos., San Bernardino, 1958-70. Bd. dirs. Shiffer Assos. Sci. Found., 1960-70, pres., 1963-70; bd. dirs. mem. exec. council Thinking Unlimited, Inc. Recipient certificate of appreciation Cal. Bd. Pharmacy, 1965. Mem. Cal. Pharm. Assn., Cal. Alumni Assn. (life), Pharmacy Alumni Assn. (life), Nev. Mining Assn. (asso.), Retail Clks. Internat. Assn. (life), Phi Delta Chi. Presbyn. (deacon). Mason (K.T.); member Order Eastern Star. Research in earth metals. Home: San Bernardino CA Died Apr. 9, 1970.

PETTET, ZELLMER ROSWELL, statistician; b. Cleve., Nov. 16, 1880; s. Jonathan and Delia M. (Wolke) P.; Ph.B., U. Chgo., 1902; m. Nettie Harris, Nov. 20, 1912. Agrl. statistician, Ga., 1914-19; regional cotton statistician, U.S. Dept. Agr., 1921-25; mgr. crop ins. dept. Hartford Fire Ins. Co., So. div., 1919-20; agrl. statistician Garside & Am. Cotton Services, 1928-29; agrl. economist U.S. Census Bur., 1930-33; chief statistician for agr. Census Bur., 1933-45; ret., 1945. Author: The Farm Horse: Ga. statis. publs. Originator many methods of estimating crops and numbers of livestock and forecasting agrl. changes. Home: 322 E. Oregon Av., Phoenix. Died Aug. 23, 1962; buried Greenwood Meml. Park, Phoenix.

PETTIS, CHARLES EMERSON, cons. civil engr.; b. Salem, O., July 16, 1901; s. Charles Willis and Cora (Norris) P.; student Mt. Union Coll., 1918-20; B.C.E., Ohio State U., 1923, C.E., 1933; m. Genevieve Marie Kenyon, Dec. 11, 1923; 1 dau., Marilyn Joyce (Mrs. Lisle E. Nied). Instrumentman, N.Y.C. R.R., Toledo, 1923-27, asst. supr. bldgs., 1927-31, asst. engr., 1931-32; asst. engr. Champe, Finkbeiner & Assos., Toledo, 1932-40; partner Finkbeiner, Pettis & Strout, Toledo, 1940-64, mng. partner, 1965-70, cons.; cons. civil engring. Named Toledo Area Engr. of the Year, 1969. Registered profl. engr., Ohio, Mich., Ind., Ill., Ga., Ky., Tenn., S.C., Va., W.Va.; certified Am. San. Engring. Intersoc. Bd. Mem. Tech. Soc. Toledo, Nat., Ohio, Toledo socs. profl. engrs., Am. Soc. C.E., Cons. Engrs. of Ohio (recipient Distinguished Cons. award 1970), Mich. Engring. Soc., Ohio Water Pollution Control Conf., Water Pollution Control Fedn., Am. Waterworks Assn., Am. Acad. San. Engrs., Ohio State U. Assn., Sigma Nu. Presbyn. Kiwanian. Club: Toledo. Address: Toledo OH Died May 22, 1972.

PETTIT, HENRY, civ. engr. and architect; b. Phila., Dec. 23, 1842; s. Robert (U.S.N.) and Laura (Ellmaker) P.; great g.s. Col. Charles P., mem. Continental Congress, also of Chief Justice Thomas McKean, signer Declaration of Independence; ed. U. of Pa. to jr. yr.; hon. M.S., U. of Pa., 1877; studied civil engring., architecture, music; unmarried. In engring. dept. Pa. R.R. Co., bridges and buildings constrn. dept., 1862-74; sent by U.S. Centennial Commn. as spl. agt. to Vienna Expn., 1873; engr. and architect U.S. Centennial Exposition, Phila., 1873-77, main bldg., machinery hall, etc.; chief Bur. of Installation, U.S. Centennial Expn., 1876; architect U.S. Commn., Paris Expn., 1878; mem. Advisory Art Com. for Pa. at Chicago Expn., 1893. Traveled extensively; made 2 tours round the world. Republican. Presbyn. Mem. Am. Philos. Soc. (curator 1897-1900); mem. Legion of Honor of France; Order of St. Olaf, Norway; Isabella of Spain; Iftakar of Tunis; Loyal Legion U.S. Dir. Union League, Phila., 1877-78. Author: A Twentieth Century Idealist, 1905; Symbolism in Christianity (pamphlet), 1906. Also system of "peace flags"—nat. ensigns with white border; being the evolution of ordinary flags of truce in war times, into higher significance, indicative of peaceful methods in lieu of war—originally published, Oct. 1891, and adopted, Oct. 12, 1891, at Independence Hall, Phila., by the Human Freedom League; since then used extensively in many countries, notably in The Hague Peace Temple, in connection with jud. arbitration confs.; the U.S. ensign with a white order as peace flag planted by Capt. Peary at the North Pole, 1909. Home: Philadelphia, Pa. Died Aug. 11, 1921.

PEYTON, GARLAND, geologist; b. Mt. Airy, Ga., Oct. 2, 1892; s. John Thomas and Emma Jane (Ayers) P.; B.S., E.M., Sch. Mines N. Ga. Agrl. Coll., 1914; student, Ohio State U., 1926, U. Minn., 1930; m. Martha Gara Griswold, Aug. 28, 1918; children—Garland, Martha Ann, Barbara Jane. Mining engr. U.S. Smelting, Refining & Mining Co., 1914-17; dir. Sch. Mines N. Ga. Agrl. Coll., 1919-29; research engr. Tenn. Copper Co., 1929-31; state mining engr. Ga. Dept. Mines and Geology, 1937-38; dir., state geologist Ga. Dept. Mines, Mining and Geology, from 1938. Served as 1st lt., inf., U.S. Army, 1917-19, as capt., 1933-37. Mem. Geol. Soc. Am., Am. Assn. Petroleum Geologist, Am. Inst. Mining and Metall. Engrs., Soc. Econ. Geologists, Assn. Am. State Geologist (pres. 1948), Pi Kappa Alpha, Sigma Gamma Epsilon. Democrat. Baptist. Mason, Elk. Home: Decatur GA Died Oct. 18, 1964.

PFAHLER, GEORGE EDWARD, (fa'ler), radiologist; b. Numidia, Pa., Jan. 29, 1874; s. William H. and Sarah A. (Stine) P.; B.E., Bloomsburg State Normal Sch. (now Tchrs. Coll.), 1894; M.D., Medico Chirurg. Coll., Phila., 1898; Sc.D., Ursinus Coll., also LL.D., 1942; D.M. R.E., Cambridge U., Eng., 1926; m. Frances Simpson, Nov. 8, 1908 (died Mar. 15, 1910); m. 2d, Muriel Bennett July 10, 1918. Intern Phila. Gen. Hosp., 1898-99, asst. chief resident physician, 1899-1902; clin. prof. roentgenology Medico-Chirurg. Coll., 1909-12, prof., 1912-16; prof. radiology U. Pa., 1916—; dir. radiological dept. Misericordia Hosp., Phila. Trustee Ursinus Coll. Hon. fellowship Faculty Radiologists, London, 1950. Mem. Am. Roentgen Ray Soc. (pres. 1910), Am. Electrotherapeutic Assn. (pres. 1912), Am. Radium Soc. (pres. 1922), Am. Coll. Radiology (pres. 1923), A.M.A., Pa. Med. Soc., Phila. Dermathol. Soc. (pres. 1956-57), Phila. County Med. Soc. (pres. aid assn. 1953—); hon. mem. Brit., French, German, Austrian, Scandinavian and Russian, Panama, Cuba, Peru radiol socs., Radiol. sect. Royal Soc. Medicine London, England, and Mexico. Episcopalian. Clubs: Medical, Medical Literature (Phila.). Pioneered in radium and X-ray treatment of cancer. Contbr. to med. jours. Home: 6463 Drexel Rd. Office: 1930 Chestnut St., Phila. Died Jan. 29, 1957; buried Valley Force Cemetery.

PFANSTIEHL, CARL, (fan'stel), b. Columbia, Mo., Sept. 17, 1887; s. Albertus A. (Rev.) and Julia (Barnes) P.; spl. work Armour Inst. Tech., Chicago; m. Caryl Cody, June 24, 1915; children—Cody, Alfred, Rose-Caryl, Grace. Organized (1907) Pfanstiehl Electrical Lab. (now Fansteel Metall. Corp.), pres. and dir. research until 1919; pres. and dir. res. Pfanstiehl Radio Co., 1922-28; v.p. and dir. res. Pfanstiehl Chemical Co. (chem. and metal Divs.) since 1918; special research work for War and Medical Depts. of the Government during World War; spl. interest in research in applied physics, metallurgy, radio, and consultant in these fields; has been granted 135 patents in elec., chem. and metall. fields; work largely concerned with prodn. of metals such as metallic tungsten, molybdenum, tantalum, rhenium, osmium, ruthenium and their alloys, special anti-friction and hard tipping alloys, and with cold lighting, fluorescent powders, and rare biol. chemicals. Mem. Am. Chem. Soc., Electrochem. Soc., A.A.A.S., N.Y. Acad. of Science, Am. Phys. Soc., Optical Soc. of America, Am. Inst. Mining and Metall. Engrs., Am. Soc. for Metals. Club: University (Chicago). Recipient of Modern Pioneer Award, 1940. Author: Ignition, 1912; also articles on radio theories and biochemical subjects. Home: 614 Wood Path, Highland Park, Ill. Died Mar. 1, 1942.

PFISTERER, HENRY ALBERT, educator, cons. engr.; b. Hyde Park, N.Y., June 11, 1908; s. Albert G. and Louise (Beck) P.; C.E., Cornell U., 1929; M.A. (hon.), Yale, 1957; m. Hortense Marchessault, Aug. 26, 1939; children—Carole E., Charles H. A. Engr., H. G. Balcom, 1929-30; instr. engring. Cornell U., 1930-33; engr. Nat. Park Service, 1934-38, Wilcox & Erickson, 1939-41; asst. prof. architecture Yale, 1941-46, asso. prof., 1946-56, prof., 1956-72; cons. engr., New Haven, 1941-72; partner Wilcox, Erickson & Pfisterer, 1941-50; owner Henry A. Pfisterer, cons. engr., 1951-72; dir. New Haven Trap Rock Co. Mem. Hamden Zoning and Planning Commn.; pres. Conn. Bldg. Congress, 1955-56, Conn. Fedn. Planning and Zoning Agencies, 1958. Mem. Conn. (past dir.), Nat. socs. profl. engrs., Am. Soc. C.E., Am. Concrete Inst., Conn. Soc. Civil Engrs. Clubs: Quinnipiack; Faculty (Yale); Cornell (N.Y.C.). Author: (with Harold Dana Hauf) Design of Steel Buildings, 1949. Home: Hamden CT Died May 26, 1972.

PFUND, A. HERMAN, (foont), physicist; b. Madison, Wis., Dec. 28, 1879; s. Herman and Anna (Scheibel) P.; B.S., U. of Wis., 1901; Ph.D., Johns Hopkins U., 1906; m. Nelle Fuller, Aug. 30, 1910; 1 dau., Alice Elizabeth. Carnegie research asst., 1903-05, asst. in physics, 1906-07, Johnston scholar, 1907-09, asso. in physics, 1909-10, asso. prof., 1910-27, professor since 1927, Johns Hopkins University. Member Am. Physical Society, Optical Society of America (pres. 1943), Gamma Alpha, Phi Beta Kappa. Awarded Science Club medal, U. of Wis., 1901; Longstreth medal, Franklin Inst., Phila., 1922; Dudley medal, Am. Soc. for Testing Materials, 1931; Frederic E. Ives medal of the Optical Society of America, 1939. Home: 4404 Bedford Place, Baltimore, Md. Died Jan. 5, 1948.

PHALEN, HAROLD ROMAINE, (fa'len), mathematics; b. Acton, Mass., Apr. 21, 1889; s. Edwin Anthony and Harriet Davis (Reed) P.; B.S., Tufts, 1912; M.S., U. Chgo., 1923, Ph.D., 1926; m. Lucie Hortense Snyder, Dec. 20, 1914 (died Aug. 1933); children—Carolyn Annette, Edward Snyder (dec.); m. 2d, Elizabeth Nagle Kinder, July 2, 1938. Draftsman with Improved Paper Machine Co., Nashua, N.H., 1912, Am. Locomotive Co., Providence, R.I., 1913; instr. in mathematics, James Millikin U., 1913-15, Berea Coll., 1915-18, Armour Inst. Tech., 1918-26; prof. mathematics, St. Stephen's Coll. (now Bard Coll.), Columbia, 1926—, provost, 1929-33; (on leave) prof., Brown U., 1939-40; asso. prof. mathematics, Coll. William and Mary, 1941-46, prof. 1946-54, head dept., 1954—. Mem. Am. Math. Soc., Math. Assn. Am., A.A.A.S., Sigma Xi, Sigma Tau Alpha, Triangle. Episcopalian. Mason, Club: Exchange of Red Hook, N.Y. (ex-pres.). Author: History of Action, 1954. Translator: Lezioni de Geometria Proviettiva (by Enriques). Home: 130 Chandler Court, Williamsburg, Va. Died May 30, 1955; buried Action, Mass.

PHANEUF, LOUIS EUSÉBE, physician; b. St. Helaire, P.Q., Can., Feb. 27, 1884; s. Wilbrod E. and Laura (L'Heureux) P.; Pharm.D., Mass. Coll. Pharmacy, 1905, Ph.C., 1905; M.D. summa cum laude, Tufts Coll., 1913, D.Sc., 1933; M.D. (hon.), Laval University, 1952; married Florence Alles, September 24, 1921. In practice as gynecologist and obstetrician 1915—; prof. gynecology, Tufts Coll. Med. Sch., 1927; surgeon-in-chief, dept. obstetrics and gynecology, Carney Hospital, South Boston, Massachusetts; consultant, department of gynecology, New England Medical Center and Malden (Mass.) Hospital; surgeon-in-chief dept. of gynecology, Boston Dispensary (unit of N.E. Med. Center); consulting gynecologist. Beth Israel, Leonard Morse, Henrietta D. Goodall, Noble and Attleboro hosps.; cons. gynecol. and obstetrician, Fall River Gen. and St. Anne's hosps. (both Fall River), Burbank Hosp. (Fitchburg, Mass.); cons. specialist in gynecology, U.S. Marine Hosp., Boston. Served as 1st lt., Med. Corps, U.S. Army, World War I. Decorated Office of Order of Crown (Belgium). Fellow Am. Coll. Surgns.; mem. A.M.A., Am. Gynecol. Soc., Am. Assn. Obstet., Gynecol. and Abdominal Surgeons, Mass. Med. Soc., Am. Bd. Obstetrics and Gynecology (dir. 1938-47), Internat. Soc. of Surgery, Am. Radium Soc., Boston Surg. Soc., Boston Obstet. Soc., New Eng. Obstet. and Gynecol. Soc., Am. Assn. History of Medicine; hon. mem. Société Royale de Gynécologie et d'Obstétrique (Belgium), Gynecol., Obstet. Soc. of Bucharest (Roumania), Los Angeles Surg. Soc., Los Angeles Obstet. Soc.; corr. mem. Société d'Obstétrique et de Gynécologie de Paris, Assn. des Gynécologues et Obstétriciens de Langue Francaise (both France); mem. Alpha Omega Alpha, Sigura K. Club: Algonquin (Boston). Author of over 120 monographs, also numerous articles in French and Belgian med. jours. Home: 84 Hammondswood Rd., Chestnut Hill, Mass. Office: 270 Commonwealth Av., Boston 16. Died Sept. 20, 1953.

PHELPS, CHARLES EDWARD, JR., engineer; b. Baltimore, Jan 31, 1871; s. Charles Edward and Martha (Woodward) P.; ed. through primary and grammar schs. of Baltimore; grad. manual training sch., 1889, tech. course, Johns Hopkins, 1891-94, receiving certificate of proficiency; m. Maude Griswold Thelin, Nov. 29, 1899. Engaged with elec. st. ry., and engring. cos., 1888-96; in pvt. practice as consulting engr. Retained, 1902, by City of Cleveland to report and estimate upon cost of elec. st. and commercial lighting project adopted by city council; retained by cities of Johnstown and Rochester, N.Y., 1903, in litigation over construction and operation of underground elec. conduit systems; and by City of Montreal, to report and estimate upon an underground conduit system, project adopted by bd. of aldermen; retained by Comptroller Grout of New York, 1905, to assist in investigation of prices charged for electric st. lighting; chief engineer of Electric Commn. of Baltimore, 1898, in charge constrn. of underground conduit; sec. Municipal Lighting Commn. of Baltimore, 1900—; chief engr. Pub. Service Commn. of Md., 1910—; engr. mem. Md. State Bd. of Health, 1915—. From 1898 devoted efforts to questions affecting relations of public service corps. to public; retained, 1906, by Nat. Civic Fedn. in investigation and appraisal of municipal electric lighting plants and their operation; and, 1907, by Cambridge, Mass., in connection with constrn. of underground conduits by the city. Episcopalian. Home: Baltimore, Md. Died Dec. 23, 1918.

PHELPS, EARLE BERNARD, sanitarian; b. Galesburg, Ill., July 10, 1876; s. Lucius Joshua and Ida May (Taylor) P.; desc. of William Phelps, the immigrant, Dorchester, Mass., 1630; B.S. in Chemistry, Mass. Inst. of Tech., 1899; m. Helen May Ellis, Oct. 29, 1902; children—Ellis K., Eleanor Frances, Winston, Barbara Ruth, Natalee Helen. Asst. bacteriologist, Mass. St. Bd. of Health, Lawrence Expt. Sta., 1899-1903; chemist and bacteriologist, Sanitary Research Lab., Mass. Inst. Tech., 1903-13; asst. prof. chem. biology, Mass. Inst. Tech., 1908-13; asst. hydrographer, U.S. Geol. Survey, 1906-11; consulting sanitary expert, 1906-13; prof. chemistry and chief div. of chemistry, Hygienic Lab., U.S. Pub. Health Service, 1913-19; prof. sanitary science, Coll. Physicians and Surgeons (Columbia), 1925-43; prof. emeritus since 1943; prof. sanitary sci., University of Fla., since 1944. Recipient Lasker award Am. Public Health Assn., 1953. Mem. Am. Public Health Association A.A.A.S., Member medical section. Advisory Commission of Council National Defense, 1917. Author: Principles of Public Health Engineering, 1925; Stream Sanitation, 1944; Public Health Engineering, 1948, Vol. II, 1949; also papers on sewage disposal and pub. health subjects in proceedings of socs. and tech. journals. Address: University of Florida, Gainesville, Fla.; (summer) South Harwich, Mass. Died May 29, 1953; buried Gainesville, Fla.

PHELPS, ISAAC KING, chemist; b. Enfield, Conn., Feb. 16, 1872; s. John and Corintha Jane (King) P.; B.A., Yale, 1894, Ph.D., 1897; A.M., Harvard U., 1898; studied U. of Heidelberg; m. Martha Austin, June 27, 1904 (died Mar. 15, 1933). Asst. in chemistry, Yale, 1894-97, also Silliman fellow same period; Thayer scholar Harvard, 1897-98; instr. in chemistry, Yale, 1899-1908; asst. prof. physiol. chemistry, George Washington U., 1909-10; jr. organic chemist Bur. Chemistry, Washington, D.C., 1910-12; organic chemist Bur. of Mines, 1912-13, chemist, Bur. of Chemistry, 1913-23; chem. dir. Wamesit Chem. Co., Lowell, Mass., 1923-25; consultant in chemistry and in food production and distribution; biochemical work, staff of the Connecticut State Hosp., retired 1942; teaching and chem. research, Wesleyan U., 1942-44. Professor of Chemistry, Rollins College, 1944-48, Bethune-Cookman Coll. since 1948. Mem. Joint Com. of Definitions and Standards of foods and drugs, U.S. Dept. Agr., 1914-21; collaborator in preparation of U.S. Pharmacopaea X. Mem. A.A.A.S. Club: University (Winter Park). Republican. Conglist. Contbr. research papers in chem. jours. Address: Bethune-Cookman College, Daytona Beach FL

PHILBRICK, HERBERT SHAW, educator; b. Waterville, Me., Apr. 13, 1875; s. Frank B. and Addie F. (Shaw) P.; A.B., Colby Coll., 1897, Sc.D., 1929; S.B., Mass. Inst. Tech., 1906; m. Grace E. Mathews, June 23, 1904; children—Benjamin Mathews, Shailer Shaw, Herbert Shaw, Frances Elisabeth. Submaster and master Calais (Me.) High Sch., 1897-1902; draftsman Waterville Iron Works, Keyes Fiber Co., summers, 1905-06; engr. Lombard Log Hauler Co., 1906-07; asst. prof. mech. engring. U. Mo., 1907-12; prof. mech. engring. Northwestern U., since 1912, acting dean men, 1923-25; chmn. dept. mech. engring. Northwestern Tech. Inst., 1939-42, emeritus since Sept. 1942. Cons. in hydraulics and mech. engring.; on leave of absence from Northwestern U., 1919-20, with Phipps Estate, Chgo.; cons. Northwestern U. in constrn. bldgs. McKinlock Campus, Chgo., 1924-27; pres. Waterville Iron Works, 1927-50. Trustee Colby Coll., 1927-30; bd. dirs. Family Welfare Assn., 1933-53, pres. 1935-40; pres. Family Service Assn., Evanston, 1947-50. Mem. Am. Soc. M.E., Delta Kappa Epsilon, Sigma Xi, Tau Beta Pi (hon.). Baptist. Club: University of Evanston (pres. 1927-28). Home: 2130 Sherman Av., Evanston, Ill. 60201. Died June 21, 1963; buried Pine Grove Cemetery, Waterville.

PHILIPPE, ROBERT RENE, engr.; b. Boston, Mar. 17, 1906; s. Rene Edward and Anna F. (Robert) P.; S.B., Mass. Inst. Tech., 1929; student Carnegie Inst. Tech., 1938-39; m. Mary Alice Allen, June 15, 1935; children—Allen R., Catherine R., Sharon Y. Constrn. worker Compressed Air Tunnel, N.Y.C., 1929-32; asst. soils mechanics lab. Mass. Inst. Tech., 1932-34; chief soils mechanics lab. Muskingum Dams, O., 1934-37; chief soils mechanics lab. Corps. Engrs., Pitts., 1937-41, dir. Ohio River div. labs., 1941-51, chief spl. engring. br. research and development Office Chief Engrs., from 1951; cons. engr. dams, airfields, foundations; lectr. soil mechanics Carnegie Inst. Tech., 1938-39; guest lectr. U. Ill., from 1949; lectr. prof. George Washington U., 1955. Mem. Am. Soc. C.E., Internat. Soc. Soil Mechanics and Found. Engring., Soc. Am. Mil. Engrs. Home: Alexandria VA Died June 29, 1968; buried Ivy Hill Cemetery Alexandria VA

PHILLIPS, ALFRED EDWARD, civil engr.; b. Rouses Point, N.Y., June 18, 1863; s. John and Jane Annie (Irwin) P.; A.B. and C.E., Union U., Schenectady, N.Y., 1887, A.M., 1890, Ph.D., 1894; m. Lizzie Langdon, June 19, 1895; children—Jane Ann Langdon, Laura Langdon. Prof. civil engring., Purdue U., Lafayette, 1887-94; pvt. practice, Indianapolis, 1894-99; also acting prof. bridge and hydraulic engring., U. of Wis., 1895-96; prof. civil engring., Armour Inst. Tech., 1899—. Republican. Episcopalian. Author: Stresses in Bridges and Roof Trusses, 1901; Plane Surveying, 1904; Highway Construction (with A. H. Byrne), 1904; Masonry Construction (with same), 1904; Irrigation, 1907. Home: Evanston, Ill. Died Apr. 19, 1931.

PHILLIPS, ASA EMORY, consulting engr.; b. Sept. 8, 1869; s. Robert A. and Anne (d'Boyer) P.; C.E., Lehigh U., 1890; m. Myra Estelle Randall, Mar. 7, 1891; children—Donald Boyer, Mrs. Dorothy Randall Moyer, Mrs. Ruth Sutherland Martinez, Charles Emory; m. 2d, Virginia Boyd, Nov. 6, 1909; children—Asa Emory, James Boyd. Began practice at New York, 1890; engr. on flood prevention and sewer disposal, Dist. of Columbia, 1899—; designed and built largest pump station (at that time) in the world, 1907. Episcopalian. Home: Washington, D.C. Died Jan. 1, 1936.

PHILLIPS, EVERETT FRANKLIN, apiculturist; b. Hannibal, O., Nov. 14, 1878; s. Taylor Franklin and Belle (Hofer) P.; A.B., Allegheny Coll., Pa., 1899, D.Sc., 1929; Ph.D., U. of Pa., 1904; m. Mary Hibbs Geisler, Oct. 27, 1906; children—Everett Franklin, William Taylor, Howard Geisler. Acting in charge of apiculture, U.S. Bur. of Entomology, 1905-07, and in charge same, 1907-24; prof. apiculture, Cornell U., 1924-46, emeritus since 1946. Fellow A.A.A.S.; pres. (1925-26) and fellow Apis Club (internat.); fellow Entomol. Soc. America; mem. Ithaca Council of Social Agencies since 1941; mem. bd. Tompkins Co. Memorial Hosp. and other local agencies; mem. Academy of Natural Sciences (Phila.), American Society Zoologists, American Assn. Econ. Entomologists (pres. 1933-34), Phi Delta Theta, Phi Eta, Phi Beta Kappa, Sigma Xi, Pi Gamma Mu, Ecologists' Soc. Author: Bee-keeping, 1915, revised edit., 1928; also various Govt. publs. on bee-keeping and the diseases of bees. Gov. 28th dist., Rotary Internat., 1935-36, chmn. Internat. Service Com. and mem. Aims and Objects Com., 1936-37, 3d, v.p., 1939-40; nominating com. for pres. 1939-42 (chmn. 1941-42). Home: 508 Stewart Av., Ithaca NY

PHILLIPS, JOHN CHARLES, naturalist; b. Boston, Mass., Nov. 5, 1876; s. John Charles and Anna (Tucker) P.; S.B., Lawrence Scientific Sch. (Harvard), 1899; M.D., Harvard, 1904; grad. Boston City Hosp., 1906; m. Eleanor Hyde, Jan. 11, 1908; children—John C., Jr., Madelyn, Eleanor, Arthur. Not in practice. Trustee Peabody Mus., Cambridge; pres. bd. trustees Peabody Mus., Salem. Joined second Harvard Surgical Unit, November 1915, and assigned to British Gen. Hosp. No. 22, in France; served with Med. Corps, Sept. 20, 1917-July 22, 1919; maj. in comd. Field Hosp. No. 33, 4th Div. regular army. Asso. curator of birds, Mus. Comparative Zoölogy, Harvard. Trustee Boston Soc. Natural History; chmn. Mass. Conservation Council. Author of papers on birds, genetics, experimental animal breeding, sport, travel and conservation. Home: Wenham, Mass. Died Nov. 14, 1938.

PHILLIPS, NORMAN ETHELBERT, physiologist; b. Cleve., May 31, 1894; s. Taylor Franklin and Belle (Hofer) P.; B.S., Allegheny Coll., 1916; Ph.D., Cornell, 1931; m. Rachel Virginia Cleveland, Oct. 18, 1919; children—Nancy Jean (Mrs. Barton Marshall), Norman Frederick. Asst. prof. entomology Mass. Agr. Coll., 1921-22; extension specialist entomology Pa. State Coll., 1922-25; instr. zoology Syracuse U., 1925-30; faculty U. Md., 1931—, head dept. zoology, 1936-53; prof. zoology, 1953—; research dir. on contract with Office Naval Research since 1946, research on respiration and metabolism since 1946. Mem. A.A.A.S., Sigma Xi, Phi Eta, Phi Delta Theta. Methodist. Contbr. articles sci. jours. Home: 4326 Van Buren St., Hyattsville, Md. 20782. Office: Dept. Zoology, U. Md., College Park, Md. Died Aug. 1, 1961; buried Ft. Lincoln Cemetery, Washington.

PHILLIPS, RICHARD HARVEY, civil engr.; b. Boone Co., Mo., Feb. 17, 1866; s. Hiram Cave and Frances (Pemberton) P.; ed. Boone Co. pub. schs.; T.E., U. of Mo., 1885, C.E., 1890; m. Nellie Catherine Shults, Mar. 10, 1897. Has been engaged in design and construction of water works, sewer systems, bridges and viaducts and steam and interurban rys., 1885—. Chief civ. engr. and sec. Internat. Jury of Awards, Transportation Dept., St. Louis Expn., 1904. Mem. Am. Soc. C.E. Clubs: St. Louis, Engineers', Railway. Home: 5467 Delmar Boul. Office: 810 Olive St., St. Louis.

PHILLIPS, T(HOMAS) D(AVID), physicist; born Chardon, O., Apr. 1, 1891; s. Thomas Davis and Martha (Thomas) P.; student Rollins Coll., Winter Park, Fla., 1910-11, A.B., Oberlin Coll., 1916; Sc.M., U. of Mich., 1923; Ph.D., Boston Univ., 1934; D.Sc. (honorary), Marietta College, 1956; married Josephine Elvira Frye, Dec. 25, 1916; children—Gwyneth J(osephine) (Mrs. F(rancis) Howard Rexroad), Mary, Marcia (Mrs. James L. Thornton). Instr. physics, Marietta (O.) Coll., 1920-23, asst. prof., 1923-24, 1927-32, professor, 1933-42, 45-55, professor emeritus, 1955—; technical writer United States Navy, 1955-57, physicist, 1957—; instructor, N.Y. University, 1924-27; research in physics, U.S. Nat. Bur. Standards, Washington, D.C., Sept. 1937-Sept. 1938, summer 1939; civilian pilot training specialist on textbook writing project, Civil Aeronautics Adminstrn., Washington, D.C., summer 1940. Served as pvt., U.S. Army, 1918; entered active service, U.S. Naval Reserve as lt., 1942; assigned air stations, adminstr.; disch. Oct., 1945, comdr. U.S.N.R., inactive. Mem. A.A.A.S., Am. Physical Soc., Acoustical Soc. Am., Optical Soc. Am., Am. Assn. Physics Teachers, Ohio Acad. Sci., Phi Beta Kappa. Democrat. Unitarian. Researcher in heat transfer. Collector books and manuscripts on Old Northwest Terr. Died Mar. 21, 1960.

PHILLIPS, WILLIAM BATTLE, mining engr.; b. Chapel Hill, N.C., July 4, 1857; s. Charles and Laura Caroline (Battle) P.; A.B., U. of N.C., 1877, Ph.D., 1883; studied Sch. of Mines, Freiberg, Germany; m. Minerva Ruffin McNeil, Oct. 8, 1879; m. 2d, Angie Isabel Miller, Jan. 21, 1908. Chemist, N.C. Expt. Sta., 1877-82, Navassa Guano Co., 1882-85; prof. agrl. chemistry and mineralogy, U. of N.C., 1886-88; mining engr., Birmingham, Ala., 1888-92; prof. chemistry and metallurgy, U. of Ala., 1891-93; chemist, Tenn. Coal, Iron & Ry. Co., Birmingham, 1894-98; with Engineering and Mining Journal, and American Manufacturer, and Iron World, 1893 and 1897-98; dir. U. of Tex. Mining Survey, 1901-05, Bur. Economic Geology and Technology, U. of Tex., 1909-14; pres. Colo. Sch. of Mines, 1914-16; removed to Houston, Tex. Democrat. Presbyn. Mason. Contbr. nearly 300 articles to scientific and tech. publs. Died June 8, 1918.

PHOENIX, CHARLES E., mining engr.; b. in Wisconsin, Mar. 26, 1871; s. Ludger and Eliza Ann (Lutz) P.; student U. of Wis., 1893; Law Dept., U. of Wis., 1894, and 1902; m. Olla May Johnson, June 19, 1909. Began engring. work with C. & N.W. Ry., 1897; with W. G. Kirchoffer, Baraboo, Wis., 1898-01; removed to Whatcom (now Bellingham), Wash., 1903; with Alaska Central Ry., summer, 1904; U.S. deputy mineral surveyor since 1907; surveyed the Skagit Queen Group Wash., embracing 36 locations and 4 millsites; Republican. Mem. Am. Inst. Mining Engrs. Mason. Address: Bellingham Washington DC

PICCARD, JEAN FELIX, aeronaut. engr.; b. Basle, Switzerland, Jan. 28, 1884; s. Jules and Helene (Haltenhoff) P.; ed. U. Basle, Switzerland, 1902-03, Swiss Inst. Tech., Zurich, 1903-09 (degrees Chem. Engring., 1907, Dr. Nat. Sci., 1909); D.Sc., Jamestown Coll., 1957, So. Ill. U., 1959; m. Jeanette Ridlon, Aug. 19, 1919; children—John Auguste, Paul Jules, Donald Louis. Came to U.S., 1916, naturalized, 1931. Pvt. asst. to Adolph von Baeyer, 1910; faculty U. Munich, 1910-14, privatdocent, 1914, U. of Lausanne, 1914-16; asst. prof. chemistry U. Chgo., 1916-18, asso. prof., 1918-19; prof. chem., U. Lausanne, 1919-26; research instr. Mass. Inst. Tech., 1926-29; research Hercules Powder Co., 1929-32; research asso. Bartol Research Found., 1933-36; made stratosphere flight, 1934; lectr. U. Minn., 1936-37, prof. aero. engring., 1937-52, prof. emeritus since 1952. Served with U.S. Army Air Document Research Center, London, 1945, with Swiss mblzn. in lighter-than-air service, 1915. Awarded Certificate of Performance of Nat. Aero. Assn., 1935, license free balloon pilot, 1944. Mem. Am. Inst. Aeros. and Astronautics, Minn. Acad. Sci., Franklin Inst., Am. Chem. Soc., Am. Meteorol. Soc., Am. Assn. U. Profs., Nat. Aero. Assn., A.A.A.S., Tau Omega, Pi Delta Phi, Sigma Xi. Episcopalian. Contbr. to professional jours. Named one of Minn. 100 Living Great, Minn. Centennial, 1950. Co-designer (with A. Picard) Bathyscaph, 1905; inventor plastic film balloon, 1935; developed, constructed, launched 1st plastic film balloon, 1936; developed theory of multiple balloon aerostat, 1936. Home: 1445 E. River Rd., Mpls. 14. Died Jan. 28, 1963.

PICKARD, GREENLEAF WHITTIER, electrical engr., inventor; b. Portland, Me., Feb. 14, 1877; s. Samuel Thomas and Elizabeth Hussey (Whittier) P.; grandnephew John Greenleaf Whittier; ed. Westbrook Sem., Lawrence Scientific Sch., Harvard, and Mass. Inst. Tech.; m. Miriam Watson Oliver, Apr. 5, 1902 (died Dec. 17, 1912); m. 2d, Helen Liston, Apr. 27, 1914; children—Helen Liston, Elizabeth Whittier, Geraldine, Greenleaf Whittier, Mary Katharine, John. Specialized in radio communication, receiving many U.S. and foreign patents for inventions. One of the first to obtain successful transmission of speech by electrical waves; inventor of the crystal detector, the radio compass and the static eleminator. Engr. Am. Telephone & Telegraph Co., 1902-06; consulting engineer Wireless Specialty Apparatus Co., 1907-30, R.C.A. Victor Co. of Mass., 1930-31; consultant, 1932-42; dir. of Research Am. Jewels Corp., Attleboro, Mass., 1942-45; president Pickard & Burns, Inc., 1945-52, chairman of board, 1952—. Past president and fellow Institution Radio Engineers (medal of honor 1926); fellow Radio Club of America (Armstrong medal 1941); Am. Inst. E.E., A.A.A.S., Am. Acad. Arts and Sciences; mem. Am. Meteorol. Soc. Home: 59 Dalton Rd., Newton Centre 59, Mass. Office: 240 Highland Av., Needham, Mass. Died Jan. 8, 1956; buried Newton Cemetery.

PICKEL, FRANK WELBORN, biologist; b. Williamston, S.C., Jan. 17, 1864; s. James Elbert and Mary (Welborn) P.; A.B., Furman U., Greenville, S.C., 1886; M.S., U. of S.C., 1890; studied Johns Hopkins, 1891-94; M.Sc., U. of Chicago, 1899; m. Allie Bush Deupree, Aug. 8, 1901. Prin. high sch., Williamston, S.C., 1886-88; instr. bacteriology and hygiene, U. of S.C., 1889-91; prof. natural science, Agrl. and Mech. Coll. of Fla., 1891-92; prof. Greek and German, Mississippi Coll., Clinton, Miss., 1895-97; prof. biology, U. of Ark., 1899—. Democrat. Baptist. K.P. Home: Fayetteville, Ark. Died Oct. 18, 1922.

PICKERING, EDWARD CHARLES, astronomer; b. Boston, July 19, 1846; s. Edward and Charlotte (Hammond) P.; ed. Boston Latin School, S.B., Lawrence Scientific Sch. (Harvard), 1865, hon. A.M., 1880; LL.D., univs. of Calif., 1886, Mich., 1887, Chicago, 1901, Harvard, 1903, Pa., 1906; Ph.D., Heidelberg Univ., 1903; D.Sc., Victoria Univ., England, 1900; L.H.D., Allegheny Coll., 1912; m. Lizzie Wadsworth, d. Jared Sparks, Mar. 9, 1874. Instr. mathematics, Lawrence Scientific Sch., 1865-67; Thayer prof. physics, Mass. Inst. Tech., 1867-76; prof. astronomy and dir. Harvard Coll. Obs., 1876—. Established 1st physical lab. in U.S.; under his direction, invested capital and income of the observatory increased four-fold. Study of light and spectra of the stars spl. features of his work; devised meridian photometer and made 1,400,000 measures of the light of the stars with it. By establishing an auxilliary sta. in Arequipa, Peru, Southern stars also observed, extending the work from pole to pole, in which 240,000 photographs included. Accompanied Nautical Almanac expdn. to observe total eclipse of sun, Aug. 7, 1869; mem. U.S. Coast Survey expdn. to Xeres, Spain, Dec. 22, 1870. Awarded Henry Draper medal for work on astron. physics; gold medals, Rumford, 1891, Bruce, 1908, Royal Astron. Soc., 1886, 1901. Knight German Order pour le Mérite, 1911. Mem. Nat. Acad. Sciences; hon. mem. socs. at Mexico, Cherbourg, Liverpool, Toronto, Cristiania, Upsala, Lund and mem. numerous Am. and European socs.; fellow Am. Acad. Arts and Sciences; founder and 1st pres. Appalachian Mountain Club. Author: Elements of Physical Manipulation, and edited 70 vols. of annals and other publs. of Harvard Coll. Observatory. Died Feb. 3, 1919.

PICKERING, WILLIAM HENRY, astronomer; b. Boston, Feb. 15, 1858; s. Edward and Charlotte (Hammond) P.; grad. Mass. Institute Tech., 1879; instr. there, and asst. prof. Harvard Observatory; m. Anne Atwood, d. Isaac Butts, of Boston, June 11, 1884; children—William T., Esther. Led expedition to observe total solar eclipses in Colo., 1878, Grenada, West Indies, 1886, Calif., 1889, Chile, 1893, Ga., 1900, New Hampshire, 1932; expdn. to Southern California to make observations of the moon, 1904; in 1899 discovered Phoebe, the ninth satellite of Saturn, and showed later why it revolved in a direction opposite to others; predicted existence and gave location, 1919, of 9th planet, Pluto; visited Hawaii, 1905, the Azores in 1907, in order to compare their crater formations with those in the moon. Established temporary observatory in Southern Calif., 1889, and Arequipa Sta. of Harvard Obs., 1891. Also erected obs. and telescope for Dr. Lowell at Flagstaff, Ariz., 1894; established an astron. station for Harvard Obs., in Mandeville, Jamaica, W.I., 1900, reestablished it in 1911 and converted it into a private obs., 1925, with the substitution of a new telescope for the older one, which was returned to Harvard. Interested in mountain climbing. Ascended Half Dome in Yosemite Valley, 1878, and El Misti in Peru (altitude, 19,400 feet), besides over 100 other peaks. Mem. Internat. Astronomical Union and other astron. socs.; fellow American Acad. Arts and Sciences. Author: Walking Guide to Mt. Washington Range, 1882; Investigations in Astronomical Photography (Vol. XXXII, Part I, Annals), 1895; Visual Observations of the Moon and Planets (Vol. XXXII, Part II, Annals), 1900; An Atlas of the Moon (Vol. LI, Annals), 1903; The Moon, 1903; Miscellaneous papers (Vol. LIII, Annals), 1905; Lunar and Hawiian Physical Features Compared, 1906; Researches of the Boyden Department (Vol. LXI, Part I, Annals), 1908; A Search for a Planet Beyond Neptune (Vol LXI, Part II, Annals), 1909; A Statistical Investigation of Cometary Orbits (Vol LXI, Part III, Annals), 1911; Mars, 1921. Began a series of "Reports on Mars," in Popular Astronomy, 1914 (Rept. No. 44 issued in 1930). Home: Jamaica, West Indies. Died Jan. 16, 1938.

PIERCE, CLAUDE CONNOR, sanitarian; b. Chattanooga, Tenn., June 15, 1878; s. David James and Annie (Flora) P.; Chattanooga High School, 1895; M.D., Chattanooga Med. Coll., 1898; m. Miss Reeves, May 17, 1905; children—John Reeves (killed in naval action Jan. 1943), George Ellis (U.S. Navy), Claude Connor, Jr. (U.S. Army). Served in Spanish-American War; appointed assistant surgeon U.S. P.H.S., June 20, 1900; passed assistant surgeon, July 26, 1905; surgeon, December 1912; senior surgeon, Act of Congress, March 4, 1915; assistant surgeon general, July 13, 1918. Quarantine officer, Panama, 1904-12; superintendent Colon Hospital, 1913; established disinfection plants along Texas-Mexico border to prevent introduction of typhus fever, 1916; in charge of extra cantonment sanitation, Little Rock, Ark., 1917; in charge div. of veneral diseases, U.S.P.H.S., Washington, 1918-22; director of District 3, Chicago, 1922-26; med. dir. in supervisory charge of U.S.P.H.S., activities in Europe, 1934-37; dir. Dist. 1, U.S.P.H.S., 1937-42; retired July 1942; now med. dir. Planned Parenthood Fedn. Member American Med. Assn., tel, Brooklyn, N.Y. Office: 501 Madison Av., New York, N.Y. Died Mar. 19, 1944.

PIERCE, FREDERICK ERNEST, analytical psychologist; b. Farmington, Conn., Mar. 6, 1878; s. Edwin Bruce and Elizabeth (Deming) P.; student Dartmouth. Rousseau Inst. (Geneva, Switzerland) and Psychol. Seminar, Vienna; m. Elizabeth Brown (div. 1924); children—Florence Utley, Beatrice Brown; m. 2d, Jeannie Emmet French, Oct. 23, 1925; children—Donald, Laurence. Spl. researches for 4 yrs., in phys. responses to spl. brain images; comparative research 6 yrs., in relation of mental states to action of glands of internal secretion. Served as mng. dir. (1907-09) Lincoln Birthplace Meml. Assn. which created Lincoln Farm Meml. Ky. (now nat. park); organized nat. vol. div. (100,000 men) Progressive Party, 1912. Republican since 1915. Past trustee Clark Sch. Mem. Dartmouth Sci. Assn., Phi Kappa Psi. Conglist. Clubs: New York Athletic, Dartmouth of New York. Author: Our Unconscious Mind, 1922; Psychology of Selling, 1923; Mobilizing the Mid-Brain, 1924; Understanding Our Children, 1926; Dreams and Personality, 1931. Home: Box 198, Castine, Me. 04421. Died Dec. 24, 1963.

PIERCE, GEORGE WASHINGTON, educator; b. Webberville, Tex., Jan. 11, 1872; s. George W. and Mary Elizabeth (Gill) P.; B.Sc., U. Tex., 1893, M.A., 1894; Harvard, 1898-1900, A.M., 1899, Ph.D., 1900; U. Leipzig, 1900-01; m. Florence H. Goodwin, Aug. 12, 1904 (died 1945); m. 2d, Helen Russell, Nov. 2, 1946. Asst. prof. physics Harvard, 1907-17, prof., 1917-21, Rumford prof., 1921-40, emeritus since 1940, Gordon McKay prof. communication engring., 1935-40, chmn. div. phys. sciences, 1927-40, emeritus since 1940; dir. Cruft High Tension Elec. Lab., 1914-40. Fellow Am. Acad. Arts and Sciences; mem. Nat. Acad. Sciences, Am. Physical Soc., Am. Inst. E.E., Inventors Guild, Philos. Soc. of Texas. Pres. Radio Inst., 1918. Awarded medal of Inst. of Radio Engrs. for distinguished services in radio communication, 1928; Franklin medal of Franklin Inst. for inventions, theoretical and experimental. Contbr. in field of electric communication, and teaching, 1943. Clubs: Harvard (Boston); Faculty (Harvard U.). Author: The Principles of Wireless Telegraphy, 1910; Electric Oscillations and Electric Waves, 1920; The Songs of Insects, 1948. Home: 7 Berkeley Pl. Office: Cruft High Tension Elec. Lab., Harvard Univ., Cambridge, Mass. Died Aug. 25, 1956.

PIERCE, JOSIAH, JR., engr., maj. and engr. officer, U.S.V.; b. Alexandrofsky, Russia, Jan. 30, 1861; ed. in Russia, England and U.S.; asso. King's Coll., London, 1879; grad. Emmanuel Coll., Cambridge, Eng., B.A., 1882 (M.A., 1886); student Mass. Inst. Tech., 1883; later at Johns Hopkins, Baltimore. Lecturer and prof. Columbian Univ.; instr. and asst. prof. Catholic Univ., Washington; asso. mem. (Telford medal and premium) Instn. Civil Engrs., London; topographer and engr., Northern Transcontinental Survey, 1883; U.S. Coast and Geodetic Survey, 1885; U.S. Geol. Survey, 1886; Ordnance Survey of Great Britain, 1888; U.S. Irrigation Surveys, 1888-91; Sinipuxent Beach Co., 1893; C.,B.&Q. R.R. and B.&O. R.R. Prin. asst. engr., topog. survey city of Baltimore, 1893; chief engr., Va. Electric Co., 1897; chief engr., 1st div., 2d army corps, Camp Alger, 1898; chief engr., San Juan dist., Puerto Rico, 1898-99. Consulting engr. Great Falls Power Co., Washington, D.C. Home: Boonsboro, Md. Died 1902.

PIERCE, NEWTON BARRIS, vegetable pathologist; b. Brockport, N.Y., Sept. 26, 1856; s. Franklin B. and Melissa (Hinman) P.; ed. common and high schs. of N.Y., Wis. and Mich., Mus. of Comparative Zoölogy, Cambridge, Mass., 1882-83; U. of Mich., 1887-89; pvt. biol. lab., 1876-89; study of plant diseases, France, Italy, and Algeria, 1890; m. Maude B. Lacy, Mar. 11, 1897. Lumber insp., 1874, chief insp., 1876, and established office of Pierce Bros., lumber inspectors, 1876-95; established pvt. lab. for biol. study, 1876-89; conducted geol. work in connection with early sinking of salt wells in Western Mich.; apptd., 1889, from U. of Mich., to take charge of vegetable pathol. investigations in Calif.; established, 1889, in charge until 1906, Pacific Coast Lab. of Vegetable Pathology for U.S. Dept. Agr.; established Wild Plant Improvement Gardens for U.S. Dept. Agr., 1902; propr. same, July 1, 1906—. Life fellow A.A.A.S. Author: California Vine Disease, 1892; Peach Leaf Curl, etc. Home: Santa Ana, Calif. Died 1917.

PIERON, HENRI, psychophysiologist; b. Paris, France, July 18, 1881; s. Dominique and Madeleine (Wendling) P.; M.A., U. Paris, 1899, M.S., 1904, D.Sc., 1912; Dr. Honoris Causa, U. Montreal, 1954, Wittenberg Coll., 1928; m. Mathilde Angenout, Oct. 25, 1902. Dir. Sorbonne Psychology Lab., 1912-51; professor Psychology Institute, University Paris, 1921-51, director, 1940-51; professor emeritus sensation physiology College de France, 1923-64; director National Inst. for Study of Work and Profl. Orientation, 1928-60; pres. sect. Natural Scis. School of High Studies, 1927-51. Mem. Superior Council Sci. Research, 1934-40; dir. Inst. Marey, 1941-50. Fellow American Association for Advancement of Science; mem. French Assn. Advancement Scis. (pres. 1940-49), Fed. Natural Sci. Orgns. (pres. 1945-49), Internat. Congress Psychology (pres. Paris 1937), Internat. Union Sci. Psychology (pres. 1948-54), Am. Acad. Arts and Scis. (hon.), Nat. Acad. Scis. Decorated Comdr. Legion of Honor. Author: Thought and the Brain, 1927; Principles of Experimental Psychology, 1929; The Sensations, 1952. Home: 52 Route de la Plaine, Le Vesinet. Seine et Oise, France. Died Nov. 6, 1964; buried Cimetiere Montparnasse, Paris.

PIETERS, ADRIAN JOHN, agronomist; b. Alto, Wis., Nov. 18, 1866; s. Roelof and Hendrika (Van Zwaluwenburg) P.; B.S., U. of Mich., 1894, Ph.D., 1915; traveled and studied in Germany, 1910-12; m. Hattie May Bailey, June 30, 1896 (died 1935); m. 2d, Mary R. Burr, 1936. Botanist in charge of seed and plant introduction and distribution, U.S. Dept. Agr., 1900-06; seed grower, 1906-10; instr. botany, U. of Mich., 1912-15; agronomist with U.S. Dept. Agr., 1915-38, principal agronomist to 1938, retired. Fellow Am. Soc. Agronomy, A.A.A.S. Home: Takoma Park, D.C. Died Apr. 25, 1940.

PIEZ, CHARLES, engineer; b. (of naturalized Am. parents) Mayence, Germany, Sept. 24, 1866; s. P. Jacob and Catherine (Liebig) P.; E.M., School of Mines (Columbia), 1889; hon. Dr. Commercial Science, U. of New York, 1920; m. Mrs. Laura Sadler Cocke, 1922. Entered engring. dept. of Link Belt Co., mfrs. elevating and conveying machinery, at Phila., 1889, and became successively chief engr., gen. supt., gen. mgr., and pres., chmn. bd.; dir. Drexel State Bank. V.p. and gen. mgr. Emergency Fleet Corp., 1917-18, dir. gen., Dec. 1918-May 1919. Chmn. Ill. Workmen's Compensation Commn., 1911; pres. Ill. Mfrs.' Assn., 1911-13, 1924-25. Republican. Home: Chicago, Ill. Died Oct. 2, 1933.

PIFER, DRURY AUGUSTUS, engr., educator; born Charleston, S.C., Mar. 18, 1905; s. Drury Fair and Elizabeth Chalmers (Tarrant) P.; B.S., U. of Washington, 1930, M.S., 1931; m. Patricia Martincevic, Sept. 21, 1929 (dec.); children—Drury Louis, Patricia Elizabeth (Mrs. Dimitri Papahadjopoulos); m. 2d Virginia Senner nee Davis, July 7, 1951; children—David Senner, Barbara Senner (Mrs. Thomas Corson), John Senner. Mine ofcl. Sub Nigel Ltd., Nigel, Transvaal, S. Africa, 1932-37; mine ofcl. DeBeers Consolidated Mines Ltd., Kimberley, S. Africa, 1937-45; mgr. seconded to Cape Coast Exploration Ltd., 1937-39; mgr. seconded to Consol. Diamond Mines S.W. Africa, 1939-42; mgr. Dutoitspan and Bultfontein Mining Cos. 1942-45; prof. mining engring. U. Washington, 1947-71, emeritus, 1971, director of School of Mineral Engineering, 1947-69; director of the McGregor Mus., Kimberley, 1942-45. Mem. Wash. State Indsl. Com., Mining Sect., 1950-52, Wash. State Bd. Registration Profl. Engrs., 1951-56, South African Govt. Mining Engrs. Commn. Examiners, Diamond Mines, 1943-45; mem. Wash. State Govs. Forest Area Use Council, 1963-65. Awarded Union S. Africa Mine Mgr's. Certificate of Competency, 1935. Mem. Am. Inst. Mining and Metall Engrs. (vice chmn. indsl. minerals div. 1948, chmn. North Pacific sect. 1950-51), Assn. Mine Mgrs. South Am. Mining Congress, Northwest Mining Assn. (trustee 1958-61), W. Coast Mineral Assn., Loyal Knights Round Table (pres. Seattle table 1955-56), Sigma Xi. Home: Seattle WA Died Oct. 18, 1971; buried Seattle WA

PIGUET, LEON A., chem. engr., farmer; b. S. Hannibal, N.Y., July 2, 1894; s. Frank A. and Anna E. (Upcraft) P.; B.S. in Chemistry, Syracuse U., 1915; m. Grace A. Hess, July 15, 1916; children—Leon R., Doris (Mrs. Jerry S. Nickerson), Frank L.; m. 2d, Grace U. Smith, Feb. 3, 1951. Chem. engr. Nat. Aniline div. Allied Chem. Co., 1915-60, mgr. Buffalo plant 1942-46, cons., 1960—; engaged in farming, E. Aurora, N.Y., 1935—. Mem. Holstein Friesian Assn. Am., 1936—, bd. dirs., 1949-57, v.p., 1957-58, pres., 1959-60. Mem. Am. Chem. Soc., N.Y. Holstein Friesian Assn. (pres. 1949-50), Western N.Y. Holstein Club, Phi Beta Kappa, Alpha Chi Sigma. Methodist. Home: Jamison Rd. Office: 408 North St., East Aurora, N.Y. Died Aug. 31, 1962; buried East Aurora.

PIKE, CLAYTON WARREN, consulting elec. engr.; b. Fryeburg, Me., July 11, 1866; s. Cassius W. and Abbie J. (Barker) P.; ed. Fryeburg Acad.; Mass. Inst. Tech., 1886-89; m. Margaret E. Rattoo, June 30, 1909; children—Helen Margaret, John Clayton (dec.). Elec. engr., Merrimack Mfg. Co., Lowell, Mass., 1889-90; instr. elec. engring., U. of Pa., 1890-92; elec. engr., Queen Co., Inc., Phila., 1893-94, Falkenau Engring. Co., 1894-1900; v.p. and gen. mgr. Keller-Pike Co., Phila., 1900-11; chief of Elec. Bur., Phila., 1912—; cons. engr. City of Pittsburgh, 1919, Pub. Improvement Commn., Baltimore, 1922, Phila. Rapid Transit Co., 1923—, Ambassador Bridge (Detroit to Can.), 1929, Public Service Commission of New Hampshire, 1930, State Tax Commn. of N.H., 1931, Power Authority of State of N.Y., 1931. Mem. Park Commn., Fryeburg, Me., 1933. Trustee Fryeburg Acad. Republican. Author: Roper's Engineers' Handbook (joint author), 1899; Questions and Answers for Engineers, 1901. Commd. maj. Ordnance Dept. U.S.A., 1918; chief statis. sect., 1919. Home: Fryeburg, Me. Died Dec. 30, 1938.

PILAT, CARL FRANCIS, landscape architect; b. Ossining, N.Y., Aug. 19, 1876; s. Carl Francis and Anna (Enzinger) P.; grad. Ossining High Sch., 1893; Mt. Pleasant Mil. Acad., 1894; New York U., 1894-96; B.S. in Agr., Cornell U., 1900; travel and study in Eng., Germany, France and Italy, 10 months; m. Aloysia A. Cavanagh; 1 dau., Mary Olive. Asst. landscape architect to Charles W. Leavitt, Jr., New York, 1901-06; mem. firm of Hinchman, Pilat & Tooker, 1906-10, Hinchman & Pilat, architects and landscape engrs., 1910—. Landscape architect, Dept. of Parks of Greater New York. Asso. Technical Advisory Corpn. Mem. Nat. City Planning Conf., Am. City Planning Inst., Architectural League of New York, Am. Soc. Landscape Architects, Am. Civic Assn., Phi Gamma Delta. Clubs: City, Phi Gamma Delta. Home: 106 W. 56th St. Office: 15 Park Row, New York NY*

PILLEMER, LOUIS, (pill' em-er), biochemist; b. Johannesburg, South Africa, July 4, 1908; s. Jacob and Rebecca Alice (Faivus) P.; came to U.S., 1909, naturalized, 1916; B.S., Duke, 1932; Ph.D. in Biochemistry, Western Res. U., 1938; m. Jean Burrell, June 30, 1948; children—Stephen Jacob, David Burrell, Eric Anthony, Karl Andrew. Demonstrator immunology Western Res. U., 1938-39, instr. immunology, 1939-41, sr. instr. immunology, 1941-44, asst. prof. immunochemistry, 1945-46, asso. prof. immunochemistry, 1946-50, prof. biochemistry, 1950—. Asso. commn. immunization Armed Forces Epidemiological Bd., 1954. Recipient R. E. Dyer lectureship award, 1956. Fellow N.Y. Academy Science, A.A.A.S., Internat. Soc. Hematology; mem. Am. Chem. Soc., Soc. Exptl. Biology and Medicine, Am. Assn. Immunologists, Am. Soc. Biol. Chemists, Inc., Sigma Xi. Contbr. profl. jours. Home: 2634 Dartmoor Rd., Cleveland Heights 18, O. Office: 2085 Adelbert Rd., Cleve. 6. Died Aug. 31, 1957.

PILLSBURY, EDWIN S., elec. engr.; b. Manhattan, Kan., 1867; s. Leonard Hobart and Evelyn (Sanborn) P.; prep. edn., Pinkerton Acad., Derry, N.H.; student Mass. Inst. Tech., 1886; m. Harriette Brown, 1907; children—Fred H., Joyce S., William E. Settled in St. Louis, 1894; invented an alternating current single phase motor, abt. 1895; later engaged in mfr. same and now pres. the Century Electric Co., mfrs. electric motors and fans, St. Louis. Trustee William Jewell Coll., Mo. Bapt. Hosp. Republican. Baptist. Home: 680 McKnight Rd., St. Louis 5. Office: 1806 Pine St., St. Louis. Died Sept. 29, 1955; buried Valhalla Cemetery, St. Louis.

PILLSBURY, GEORGE BIGELOW, army engr.; b. Lowell, Mass., Dec. 19, 1876; s. George Harlin and Mary Augusta (Boyden) P.; student Mass. Inst. Tech., 1894-96; grad. U.S. Mil. Acad., 1900; m. Bertha Eldredge Smith, June 22, 1909; children—George Harlin, Elizabeth Eldredge (Mrs. William B. Pringle, Jr.), Philip Lansdale, Thomas Sidney. Commd. 2d lt. Engr. Corps, U.S. Army, June 13, 1900, and advanced through grades to col., Nov. 30, 1928; engr. Alaska Rd. Commn., 1904-08; asso. prof. mathematics, U.S. Mil. Acad., 1908-12; dist. engr., New London (Conn.) Dist., 1912-16, Los Angeles (Calif.) Dist., 1916-17; comdr. 115th Engrs., 1917-18, 102d Engrs., 1918; corps engr., 2d Corps, A.E.F., 1918-19; mem. joint bd. of engrs., St. Lawrence Waterway, 1923-26; dist. engr., Phila. Dist., 1928-30; asst. to chief of engrs. U.S. Army, with rank of brig. gen., June 27, 1930, to Dec. 31, 1937; retired from active service, on own request. Awarded Distinguished

Service Medal (U.S.). Clubs: Rittenhouse (Philadelphia); Bohemian (San Francisco). Home: Ross CA

PILLSBURY, JOHN ELLIOTT, rear admiral U.S.N.; b. Lowell, Mass., Dec. 15, 1846; s. John Gilman and Elizabeth (Wimble) P.; grad. U.S. Naval Acad., 1867; m. Florence Greenwood Aitchison, 1873. Promoted through grades to rear admiral, July 4, 1908. Served on various duties and stas., including 1 yr. in Hydrographic Office and 10 yrs. in coast survey service; comd. Coast Survey Steamer Blake, 1884-91, investigating Gulf Stream currents by anchoring the Blake in the Stream and observing the current (by means of an instrument of his invention) at various depths below surface; established position of axis of the stream in Straits of Florida and off Cape Hatteras and determined many of the laws by which its flow is governed; comd. dynamite cruiser Vesuvius off Santiago during Spanish-Am. War; afterward stationed at Boston Navy Yard, in charge of the equipment dept.; comd. U.S.S. Prairie, 1901-02; afterward on duty in Washington as mem. Gen. Bd. and asst. to chief of Bur. of Navigation, and in 1905 chief of staff North Atlantic Fleet; chief Bur. Navigation, 1908-09; retired, Dec. 15, 1908; relieved from active duty, July 1909. Died Dec. 30, 1919.

PILSBRY, HENRY AUGUSTUS, (pilz'bri), zoologist; b. Iowa City, Ia., Dec. 7, 1862; s. Dexter Robert and Elizabeth (Anderson) P.; student State U. Ia., Sc.D. (hon.), 1899; Sc.D., U. Pa., 1940, Temple U., 1941; m. Adeline Bullock Avery, 1890 (died 1924); children—Elizabeth, Grace P. Barcroft. Leading authority on mollusks, especially land shells; curator of molluske and other invertebrates Acad. Natural Scis., Phila., 1888-1957. Author: The Manual of Conchology, 31 vols. 1888-31; Marine Mollusks of Japan, 1895; Guide to the Study of Helices; Barnacles of the United States, 1916; Mollusks of the Belgian Congo, 1927; Land Mollusca of North America, 2 vols. 1939-47; other books and articles on conchology, paleontology, zoology. His. sci. contbns. pub. by Am. Malacological Union, lists 986 titles, 1882-39, The Nautilus, lists 154 titles, 1940-57. Pub. and editor The Nautilus, 1889-1957. Recipient Leidy Medal, 1928. Fellow Am. Acad. Arts and Scis. (Boston); mem. Malacological Soc. London, Am. Soc. Naturalists, A.A.A.S., Am. Conchological Soc. (1st pres. 1907), Am. Malacological Union (1st pres. 1931), Phila. Shell Club (hon. life pres.), Sigma Xi; corr. mem. Academia De Ciencias de Madrid, Zool. Soc. London; hon. fgn. corr. Zoöl. Survey of India; hon. mem. Conchological Soc. Gt. Britain and Ireland, Birmingham Natural History and Philos. Soc., Société Royale zoologique de Belgique, Senckenbergische naturforschende Gesellschaft, Cal. Acad. Scis., Sociedad de historia natural Felipe Poey, Sociedad Malacológica Carlos de la Torre, Sociedad Geológica del Peru. Address: Acad. Natural Scis., Phila. 3. Died Oct. 26, 1957; buried St. Asahp's Church Yard, Bala, Pa.

PINCHOT, GIFFORD, ex-gov., forester; b. Simsbury, Conn., Aug. 11, 1865; s. James W. and Mary (Eno) P.; A.B., Yale, 1889; studied forestry France, Germany, Switzerland and Austria; hon. A.M., Yale, 1901, Princeton, 1904; Sc.D., Mich. Agrl. Coll., 1907; LL.D., McGill, 1909, Pa. Mil. Coll., 1923, Yale, 1925, Temple, 1931; m. Cornelia Elizabeth Bryce, 1914; 1 son, Gifford Bryce. First Am. professional forester; began first systematic forest work in U.S. at Biltmore, N.C., Jan. 1892; mem. Nat. Forest Commn., 1896; forester and chief of div. afterward Bur. of Forestry, and now the Forest Service, U.S. Dept. Agr., 1898-1910; pres. Nat. Conservation Assn., 1910-25. Prof. forestry, Yale, 1903-36, professor emeritus since 1936. Commr. of forestry of Pa., 1920-22; gov. of Pa., 1923-27 and and 1931-35. Inspected forests of P.I., 1902, and recommended forest policy for same; mem. com. on orgn. govt. scientific work, apptd. Mar. 13, 1903, commn. on pub. lands, apptd. Oct. 22, 1903, commn. on dept. methods, apptd. June 2, 1905, Inland Waterways Commn., apptd. Mar. 14, 1907, commn. on country life, appted. Aug. 10, 1908; chmn. Nat. Conservation Commn., apptd. June 1908; chmn. Joint Com. on Conservation, apptd. by the conf. of govs. and nat. orgns. at Washington, Dec. 1908. Member Society American Foresters, Royal English Arboricultural Soc., American Mus. Natural History, Washington Academy Sciences, Pennsylvania Academy of Sciences, American Academy Political and Social Science. Member of Commn. for Relief in Belgium, 1914-15. Mem. U.S. Food Administration, Aug. 1917-Nov. 1918. Negotiated settlement of anthracite coal strike in 1923. Clubs: Century, Explorers (New York); Cosmos of Washington (pres. 1908). Author: Biltmore Forest, 1893; The White Pine (with H. S. Graves), 1896; Timber Trees and Forests of North Carolina (with W. W. Ashe), 1897; The Adirondack Spruce, 1898; Report to the Secretary of the Interior on Examination of the Forest Reserves, 1898; A Study of Forest Fires and Wood Production in Southern New Jersey, 1899; A Primer of Forestry, Part I, Bull. 24, Div. of Forestry, 1899, Part 2, 1905; Recommendations on Policy, Organization and Procedure for the Bureau of Forestry of the Philippine Islands, 1903; The Fight for Conservation, 1909; The Country Church (with C. O. Gill), 1913; The Training of a Forester, 1914, 4th edit. (rewritten), 1937; Six Thousand Country Churches (with C. O. Gill), 1919; To the South Seas, 1930; Just Fishing Talk, 1936; Breaking New Ground, 1946. Home: Milford, Pike County, Pa. Died Oct. 4, 1946.

PINCUS, GREGORY, biologist; b. Woodbine, N.J., Apr. 9, 1903; s. Joseph William and Elizabeth Florence (Lipman) P.; B.S., Cornell U., 1924; D.Sc., Harvard, 1927, Sc.D., 1927; student Kaiser Wilhelm Inst., Berlin, 1930, Cambridge U., England, 1929-30; m. Elizabeth Notkin, Dec. 2, 1924; children—Alexis John, Laura Jane (Mrs. Michael M. Bernard). Fellow NRC, 1927-30; instr. biology Harvard, 1930-31, asst. prof., 1931-38; vis. investigator, Cambridge U., 1937-38; vis. prof. exptl. zoology, Clark U., 1938-45; prof. physiology Tufts Med. Sch., 1944-51; research prof. biology Boston U., 1951—; hon. prof. San Marcos U., Lima, Peru. Dir. labs. Worcester Found. for Exptl. Biology, 1944-56, research dir., 1956—; chmn. endocrine panel Nat. Cancer Chemotherapy Service Center, 1956-60; chmn. USPHS study sect. on endocrinology, 1953-58; mem. Fulbright fellowship com., 1958-60. Hon. pres. Internat. Conf. Hormonal Steroids, Milan, 1962. Trustee S.W. Found. for research and Edn. Recipient Lasker award in planned parenthood, 1960, Oliver Bird Prize, London, 1960. Fellow Nat. Acad. Scis., Am. Acad. Arts and Scis., A.A.A.S. (chmn. hormone conf.); mem. Am. Soc. Naturalists, Am. Soc. Zoologists, Fedn. Atomic Scientists, Am. Assn. Anatomists, Am. Genetic Soc., Am. Physiol. Soc., Japan (hon.), Mexican (hon.), Swedish (hon.), endocrine socs., The Endocrine Soc., N.Y. Acad. Sci., Am. Soc. Human Genetics, Societe de'Endocrinologie, Am. Assn. Cancer Research; chmn. U.S. Pharm. Gonadotrophin Com.; mem. Soc. Study Growth and Devel.; corr. mem. Soc. Biologie de France; mem. Sigma Xi. Clubs: Boston University Faculty, Cosmos. Author: The Eggs of Mammals, 1936; Hormones, Chemistry Physiology etc.; The Control of Fertility, 1965; also articles in profl. mags. Editor: Experimental Biology Monograph Series; Recent Progress in Hormone Research; Hormones and the Aging Process; Hormones and Atherosclerosis, Developed contraceptive pill. Home: 30 Main St., Northboro, Mass. Office: 222 Maple Av., Shrewsbury, Mass. Died Aug. 1967.

PINNER, MAX, physician; b. Berlin, Germany, Nov. 28, 1891; s. Emil and Ida (Rothe) P.; Abiturium, Ober-Real Sch., Constance, Germany, 1911; med. student U. of Berlin, 1911-15; M.D., U. of Tübingen, 1919; m. Berna Rudovic, Mar. 1, 1924. Came to U.S., 1921, naturalized, 1928. Became asst. Eppendorf Hosp., Hamburg, 1920; lab. asst. Municipal Tuberculosis Sanitarium, Chicago, Ill., 1924-26; instr. pathology and bacteriology, U. of Ill., 1924-26; pathologist, Maybury Sanitorium and Herman Kiefer Hosp., Detroit, 1926-30; asso. dir. in charge labs. and research Desert Sanatorium, Tucson, Ariz., also cons. pathologist South Pacific Hosp., Tucson, 1931-35; pathologist tuberculosis hosps., N.Y. State Dept. Health, 1935-38; chief, div. pulmonary diseases, Montefiore Hosp., New York, 1938-45; clin. prof. medicine, Columbia, 1939-46; asst. editor Am. Rev. of Tuberculosis, 1937-40, editor since 1940. Fellow Am. Coll. Physicians; mem. Am. Assn. Thoracic Surgery, Am. Trudeau Soc., Soc. Exptl. Biology and Medicine, Am. Assn. Pathologists and Bacteriologists, Sigma Xi; hon. mem. Soc. Chiliena de Tisiologia and Sociedade Brasileira de Tuberculose. Author: Pulmonary Tuberculosis in the Adult, 1945. Contbr. to med. jours. of about 100 papers on tuberculosis and related subjects. Recipient of Trudeau Medal of Nat. Tuberculosis Assn., June, 1946. Home: 463 Vermont Av., Berkeley 7, Calif. Office: 384 14th St. Oakland 12, Calif. Died Jan. 7, 1948.

PIPER, CHARLES VANCOUVER, botanist; b. Victoria, B.C., June 16, 1867; s. Andrew William and Minna (Hausman) P.; B.S., U. of Wash., 1885, M.S., 1892; M.S., Harvard, 1900; (D.Sc., Kan. State U.); m. Laura Maude Hungate, Sept. 15, 1897. Prof. botany and zoölogy, Wash. Agrl. Coll., 1892-1903; agrostologist in charge of forage crop investigation, U.S. Dept. of Agr., 1903—. Fellow Am. Acad. Arts and Sciences. Author: Flora of the Palouse Region, 1901; Flora of Washington, 1906; Flora of Southeast Washington, 1914; Forage Plants and Their Culture, 1914; Flora of Northwest Coast, 1915; Turf for Golf Courses, 1917 (sr. author); The Soybean (sr. author), 1923. Home: Washington, D.C. Died Feb. 11, 1926.

PIPES, LOUIS A(LBERT), scientist; b. Mexico City, Mexico, Oct. 22, 1910; s. David F. and Nela (de la Garza) P.; B.S., Cal. Inst. Tech., 1933, M.S., 1934, Ph.D., 1936; m. Johanna Woelfl. Teaching fellow Cal. Inst. Tech., 1934-36; instr. Rice Inst., 1936-37; postdoctoral fellow U. Wis., 1937-38; asst. prof. Harvard, 1938-46; prof. U. Cal. at Los Angeles, 1947-71, also research engr.; cons. Aerospace Corp., El Segundo, Cal., U.S. Naval Ordnance Test Sta., China Lake, Cal. Fellow I.E.E.E.; asso. fellow Inst. Aero. and Space Sics.; mem. Am. Math. Soc., Operations Research Soc. Author: Applied Mathematics for Engineers, 1946; Matrix Methods for Engineering, 1963; Operational Methods in Non Linear Mechanics, 1965; Computational Methods in Engineering; Marix-Computer Methods in Engineering, 1969; Digital Computer Methods in Engineering, 1969. Mem. bd. editors Jour. Applied Physics, 1952-71; asso. editor Jour. of Franklin Inst., Transp. Sci. Home: Playa del Rey CA Died Jan. 17, 1971; buried Westwood Memorial Chapel, Los Angeles CA

PIRQUET, CLEMENS FREIHERR VON, university prof.; b. Vienna, Austria, May 12, 1874; s. Peter Freiherr and Flora Frelin (von Pereira) von P.; Ph.B., U. of Louvain, 1894; univs. of Vienna, Konigsberg and Graz; N.D., Graz U., 1900; m. Maria van Husen, of Borbeck, Germany, Sept. 1, 1904. Asst. to Prof. Escherich, Vienna, 1901-9; privat docent, Vienna, 1908; prof. pediatrics, Johns Hopkins U., and dir. Harriet Lane Home for Children since Feb. 1, 1909. Roman Catholic. Author: Die Serumkrankheit, 1905; Klinische Studien uber Vakzination und vakzinale Allergie, 1907. Studied the symptomatical effects of injection of horse serum in man, as it is used in diphtheria antitoxin, and wrote, with Dr. Schick, a monograph on this morbid entity under the name of "Serumdisease"; in exact studies of the symptoms of cowpox vaccination, he formed a new theory as to the incubation time of infectious diseases, and the immunity in same, attributing it to the accelerated reaction at a second infection. Gave the name "allergy" to the changed kind of reaction of the organism, which had been in touch with a disease; on the basis of these theoretical and clin. studies, devised a new means of cutaneous diagnosis, which proved practical in tuberculosis, and is applied especially to children ("cutaneous tuberculin test" of "von Pirquet test"). Address: 118 W. Franklin St., Baltimore

PIRSSON, LOUIS VALENTINE, geologist; b. New York, N.Y., Nov. 3, 1860; s. Francis M. and Louise (Butt) P.; Ph.B., Sheffield Scientific Sch. (Yale), 1882, A.M., 1902; also studied at Heidelberg and Paris; m. Eliza Trumbull, d. late George Jarvis Brush, May 17, 1902. Asst. in analyt. chemistry, 1882-83, 1884-88, instr. geology and lithology, 1892-94, asst. prof. inorganic geology, 1894-97, prof. physical geology, 1897—, Sheffield Scientific Sch. Asso. editor Am. Jour. of Science, 1897—; asst. and spl. expert, 1893-1904, and geologist U.S. Geol. Survey, 1904—. Fellow Am. Acad. Arts and Sciences. Home: New Haven, Conn. Died Dec. 8, 1919.

PITCHER, ZINA, physician, naturalist, mayor Detroit; b. Washington County, N.Y., Apr. 12, 1797; s. Nathaniel and Margaret (Stevenson) P.; M.D., Middlebury (Vt.) Coll., 1822; m. Anne Sheldon, 1824; m. 2d, Emily L. (Montgomery) Backus, 1867. Apptd. asst. surgeon U.S. Army, 1822; served on posts in Mich., 1822-30; in Indian Territory, 1830-36; resigned, 1836; made extensive studies of natural history of regions in which he served; practiced medicine; mem. staff St. Mary's Hosp., Detroit, 1836-71; mem. 1st Mich. Bd. Regents, 1837-52; mayor of Detroit, 1840-42, 43-44; founder med. dept. U. Mich., 1850; served as city physician, county physician, mem. city bd. health, surgeon to Govt. Marine Hosp.; pres. Mich. Territorial Med. Soc., 1838-51, Mich. Med. Soc., 1855-56, A.M.A., 1856; a founder Detroit Sydenham Soc.; a founder Mich. Hist. Soc., 1822; librarian, 1836; a founder Peninsular Jour. Medicine, 1853, co-editor, 1855-58; asso. editor Richmond and Louisville Med. Jour. Died Detroit, Apr. 5, 1872.

PITTS, HIRAM AVERY, inventor; b. 1800; s. Abial and Abiah Pitts; m. Leonora Hosley, 4 children. Blacksmith, Winthrop, Me., 1825-27; developed improved chain type of hand pump; invented chain band for horse-power treadmill, patented, 1834, manufactured this invention in partnership with brother John; built portable combined threshing and fanning mill, 1834, patented, 1837; carried on business alone, 1840-47; manufactured threshers, Alton, Ill., 1847-52, Chgo., 1852-60; invented machine for breaking hemp and separating stalk from fiber, also several corn and cob mills. Died Chgo., Sept. 19, 1860.

PITTS, LLEWELLYN WILLIAM, architect; b. Uniontown, Ala., Sept. 10, 1906; s. William Llewellyn and Mattie (Harwood) P.; B.S., Ga. Inst. Tech., 1927; m. Garnette Northcott, June 5, 1935; 1 dau., Sally (Mrs. James M. Stokes). With Robert & Co. and Felch & Southwell, architects, Atlanta, 1927-30; mem. firm Stone & Pitts, architects and engrs., Beaumont, Tex., 1930-57; sr. partner Pitts, Mebane & Phelps, architects and engrs., Beaumont, 1957-64, Pitts, Mebane, Phelps and White, 1964—; prin. works include 19 Coca-Cola bottling plants (first honor award indsl. architecture Houston plant, A.I.A. 1951), 1940-60, master plan and 35 bldgs. Lamar State Coll. Tech., Beaumont (medal of honor S.E. Tex. chpt. A.I.A. 1955), numerous bldgs. for Gulf Oil Co., Port Arthur, Tex., 1952-60, Socony Mobil Oil Co. bldgs., Beaumont, 1952, Shell Oil Lab., New Orleans, 1958, library bldg. Tex. Tech. Coll., Lubbock, 1960, Texaco Research Center, Port Arthur, 1960, also u. bldgs., schs. and hosps. in Tex.; co-designer State Office Bldg., 1957, Tex. Employment Commn. Bldg. (both Austin), 1958, U.S. Embassy Office Bldg., Mexico City, 1959; cons. Beaumont Planning Commn., 1953; chmn. archtl. adv. com. Tex. Bldg. Commn., 1958-61. Dir. First Security Nat. Bank (Beaumont, Tex.). A.I.A. del. to Union Internat. Architects, 1963. Gen. chmn. Beaumont United Appeals fund campaign, 1954. Served to lt. comdr. USNR, 1942-45. Fellow A.I.A. (nominating com. 1961; nat. dir. 1963—); mem. Texas Soc. Architects (pres. 1961), Sociedad de Arquitectos Mexicanos (hon.), Alpha Tau Omega, Phi Kappa Phi, Tau Beta Pi, Pi Delta Epsilon. Episcopalian. Clubs: Beaumont Country (pres. 1953), Rotary (pres. 1956), Round Table (pres. 1952) (Beaumont). Home: 1080

Thomas Rd. Office: Beaumont Savs. Bldg., 470 Orleans, Beaumont, Tex. 77701. Died June 1967.

PLANK, WILLIAM BERTOLETTE, mining engr.; b. Morgantown, Pa., June 24, 1886; s. David Heber (M.D.) and Ida Eugenie (Bertolet) P.; prep. edn., Keystone State Normal Sch.; B.S. in Mining Engring., Pa. State Coll., 1908, E.M., 1909; m. Helen Josephine Beck, Apr. 8, 1912; 1 dau., Adaline Jane. Instr. Sch. of Mines, Pa. State Coll., 1908-09; mining engr. with Phila. & Reading Coal & Iron Co., Shamokin, Pa., 1909-12, Pitts. Coal Co., 1912-16; with U.S. Bur. Mines, 1916-20, successively as jr. mining engr. (Pitts.), asst. mining engr. (Pitts.), mining engr. (Urbana, Ill.), dist. mining engr. (Birmingham, Ala.); head dept. mining and metall. engring. and John Markle prof., Lafayette Coll., 1920-52, emeritus prof., 1952—; now cons. mining engr., dir. Boys Engring. Conf. of Coll., 1934-36; dir. A.S.T.P. engring. studies, 1943-44; coordinator, U.S. Army Ordnance Research Project, Lafayette Coll., 1944-45. Mem. mine safety com. U.S. Coal Commn., 1923, pres. Civil Service Bd. of Easton, 1926-52; chmn. Emergency Fuel Commn. of Easton during anthracite strike, 1925-26; chmn. Smoke Abatement Commn. of Easton, 1929; mem. engr. div., Pres'. Com. on Civil Service Improvement, 1939. Pres. Northampton County Pa. Hist. Soc., 1941-42; London rep., Metals and Minerals Sect. Tech. Indsl. Intelligence Com. of F.E.A., summer 1945. Mem. Am. Inst. Mining and Metall. Engrs. (mgr. Lehigh Valley sect.; chmn. div. of mineral industries edn., 1936-38; sec. 1938-47), director 1945-48, mem. Mining and Metall. Soc. of Am. Coal Mining Inst. Am., Engrs. Council for Profl. Development (one of 3 reps. of Am. Inst. Mining and Metall. Engrs.), Am. Soc. for Testing Materials (chmn. com. D-16 on slate, 1928), Am. Soc. for Engring. Edn. (chmn. mining and metall. com., 1936; Council, 1938-46; chmn. Lafayette Chpt., 1940-41), Am. Mine Rescue Assn., Am. Soc. for Metals, Pa. Acad. Sci., Am. Coll. Personnel Assn., Am. Assn. U. Profs., Civic Assn. (pres.), Engrs. Club of Lehigh Valley, Newcomen Soc. of England, Phi Kappa Phi, Tau Beta Pi, Delta Tau Delta, Sigma Gamma Epsilon. Episcopalian. Mason. Clubs: Faculty of Lafayette Coll. (pres. 1926-27, 1939-40), Rotary (pres., 1926-27, 1953-54). Contbr. articles on mineral technology field pub. principally by Am. Inst. Mining and Metall. Engrs. Address: Morgantown, Pa. Died June 19, 1956; buried Coernarvon Cemetery, Morgantown, Pa.

PLATOU, RALPH VICTOR, physician; b. Valley City, N.D., Jan. 20, 1909; s. Ludwig Stoud and Martha (Schoyen) P.; B.S., U. Minn., 1932, M.B., 1935, M.D., 1936, M.S. in Pediatrics, 1941; m. Joanne Pierson, Jan. 23, 1942; children—Peter, Thomas, Mary Kirk. Intern and resident physician Babies' Hosp., N.Y.C., 1936-38; resident physician and instr., dept. pediatrics U. Minn., 1938-41; asso. prof., acting head dept. pediatrics Tulane U. Med. Sch., 1942-43, prof., chmn. dept. pediatrics., 1944-67; prof. pediatrics, chmn. dept. pediatrics U. Hawaii, 1967-68; medical director Kaui-Keolani Children's Hospital, Honolulu, Hawaii; cons. USAF; cons. to surgeon-gen. U.S. Army (Europe), 1962; chmn. Fulbright Com. in med. and biol. scis., 1964-68. Diplomate Am. Bd. Pediatrics (dir.; exec. sec. 1968). Mem. Am. Acad. Pediatrics (cons. com. med. edn.), Am. (v.p. 1962-63), La. pediatric socs., Soc. Pediatric Research, Am., La. med. assns., Soc. Clin. Investigation, Alpha Omega Alpha, Phi Gamma Delta, Nu Sigma Nu, Delta Omega. Contbr. profl. jours. and texts. Former editor Pediatrics. Office: Honolulu HI Died Sept. 15, 1968.

PLATT, FRANKLIN, geologist; b. Philadelphia, Pa., Nov. 19, 1844; ed. Univ. of Pa.; left before graduation; served in 32d Pa. Gray Reserve Regt., 1863. In 1864 on U.S. Coast Survey, doing surveying work with North Atlantic squadron; then on staff Gen. Orlando M. Poe, chief engr. Mil. Div. of the Mississippi until April 1865. Asst. geologist of Pa., 1874-81; then pres. Rochester & Pittsburgh Coal and Iron Co. Author: Waste in Mining Anthracite; Coke Manufacturing. Home: Philadelphia, Pa. Died 1900.

PLATT, JOHN, engineer; b. Gloucester, Eng., June 1, 1864; s. James and Elizabeth (Waddington) P.; engring. student Univ. Coll., London, 1886-87; m. Mary Bourne Bartlett, 1891; children—Hilda (Mrs. Wilfred H. Wolfs), John, Robert, Hugh. Came to U.S., 1888; introduced marine steam turbine into U.S. Navy and Merchant Marine. Mem. Am. Soc. M.E., Soc. Naval Architects and Marine Engrs., Instn. Civ. Engrs. (Eng.). Clubs: Engineers (New York); Army and Navy (Washington, D.C.); St. Stephen's (London). Collector early Chinese and Korean pottery. Home: 532 Woodland Av., Westfield, N.J. Died Apr. 27, 1942.

PLATT, ROBERT SWANTON, geographer; b. Columbus, O., Dec. 4, 1891; s. Rutherford H. and Maryette A. (Smith) P.; student St. George's Sch., Newport, R.I., 1906-09, Hotchkiss Sch., Lakeville, Conn., 1909-10; A.B., Yale, 1914; Ph.D., U. Chgo., 1920; m. Harriet Shanks, Dec. 30, 1922; children—Robert Swanton, Nancy Field (Mrs. R. C. Rayfield). Instr., Yale-in-China, 1914-15; instr. geog. U. Chgo., 1919-22, asst. prof., 1922-28, asso. prof. 1928-39, prof. since 1939, chmn. dept. geography since 1949; adviser Office of Geographer, U.S. Dept. State, 1943. Chief, Div. of Maps, Library Congress, 1944-45. Adviser, Conselho Nacional de Geographia, 1947. Served as capt. 82d Inf., U.S. Army, W.W. I. Mem. NRC, 1936-39; mem. Assn. Am. Geographers (treas. 1929-34, v.p. 1943, pres. 1945), Sigma Xi, Phi Beta Kappa, Gamma Alpha, Zeta Psi. Episcopalian. Clubs: University (Chgo.); Explorers (N.Y.C.); Cosmos (Washington). Author: Latin America, Countrysides and United Regions, 1942. Home: 10820 Drew St., Chgo. 60643. Died Mar. 1964.

PLUMMER, JAMES KEMP, chemist; b. Middleburg, N.C., Sept. 20, 1886; s. James Kemp and Mary Boyd (Henderson) P.; B.S., N.C. State Agrl. and Engring. Coll., 1907, M.S., 1909; M.A., Cornell, 1911, Ph.D., 1915; m. Lucy Williams Haywood, June 12, 1912; 1 dau., Emily Haywood (Mrs. Baker). Chemist Rockdale Iron Co., Rockdale, Tenn., 1907; asst. chemist, N.C. Expt. Station, 1909, soil chemist, 1911; explosive chemist Hercules Powder Co., Kenvil, N.J., 1917; cons. chemist Tenn. Copper and Chem. Corp., N.Y. City, 1918; state chemist of N.C., 1919-20; gen. mgr. Tenn. Corp., Atlanta (bd. dirs.); chmn. research com., dir. Products Div. Mem. A.A.A.S., American Institute of Chemical Engineers, American Society Agronomy, Am. Chem. Soc., Civil Legion, Sigma Xi, Pi Gamma Mu. Episcopalian. Club: Capitol City. Author various research articles in professional jours. and bulletins. Home: 2492 Habersham Road. Office: Grant Bldg., Atlanta, Ga. Deceased.

PLYMPTON, GEORGE WASHINGTON, engr., educator; b. Waltham, Mass., Nov. 18, 1827; s. Thomas R. and Elizabeth (Holden) P.; grad. Rensselaer Poly. Inst., C.E., 1847 (A.M., Hamilton Coll.; M.D., Long Island Coll. Hosp.); m. Delia M., d. Col. Thomas Bussey of Troy, N.Y., 1855 (died 1858); m. 2d, 1861, Helen M. Bussey, sister of 1st wife. Learned machinist trade, 1844-47; practiced engring., 1847-52; prof. architecture and engring., Cleveland Univ., 1852-53; prof. mathematics, N.Y. State Normal School, Albany, 1853-56; prof. physics and engring., State Normal School, Trenton, N.J., 1857-63; prof. physics and engring., Cooper Union, New York, 1869— (dir. 1879—); same chair, Brooklyn Polytechnic Inst., 1863—; prof. chemistry and toxicology, Long Island Coll. Hosp., 1864-86; editor Van Nostrand's Engring. Mag., 1870-86; commr. elec. subways, Brooklyn, 1885-89 and 1892-96. Author: The Blowpipe; How to Become an Engineer, 1892; The Starfinder; The Aneroid. Home: Brooklyn, N.Y. Died 1907.

POETKER, ALBERT H(ENRY), educator; b. Cin., Jan. 4, 1887; s. Henry and Catherine (Steinkamp) P.; A.B., St. Xavier Coll., Cin., 1907; Jesuit novitiate, Florissant, Mo., 1907-11; A.M., St. Louis U., 1914; Colegio San Ignacio, Barcelona, Spain, 1919-22; Ignatiuskolleg, Valkenburg, Holland, 1922-23; Ph.D., Johns Hopkins, 1927; LL.D., Wayne U., 1950. Joined Soc. of Jesus, 1907; ordained priest R.C. Ch., 1921; instr. in physics and mathematics, Campion Coll., Prairie du Chien, Wis., 1914; instr. in physics, St. Louis U., 1915-17, asst. prof. physics, 1917-19; research fellow, Johns Hopkins, 1926-27; prof. physics, head of dept. and regent Coll. of Engring., Marquette U., 1927-31; same, U. of Detroit, 1931-32, made acting pres., Feb. 1932, pres., 1932-39, exec. dean, 1939-50; prof. physics Xavier U. since 1950. Mem. spl. State Mediation Commn. in Ford strike, 1941; arbitrator Ford Labor Bd. cases, 1942. Mem. Am. Phys. Soc., Optical Soc. Am., N.E.A., A.A.A.S., Cath. Edn. Assn., Detroit Com. on Fgn. Relations. Research in infra-red spectroscopy, molecular structure. Contbr. to Physical Review. Address: Xavier U., Cin. 7. Died May 6, 1960.

POHLMAN, AUGUSTUS GROTE, (pol'man), anatomist, otologist; b. Buffalo, Feb. 21, 1879; s. Julius and Louise (Grosser) P.; M.D., U. Buffalo, 1900; U. Freiburg, 1901-03; m. Kathleen Black, Sept. 12, 1904 (died Feb. 10, 1933); children—Kathleen (dec.), Dorothea, David, Max, Margaret; m. 2d, Heln Bridge Shartle, Nov. 21, 1933. Asst. in anatomy Cornell U., 1900-01, instr., 1901-03; asst. in anatomy Johns Hopkins, 1903-04; asst. prof. Ind. U., 1904-06, asso. prof., 1906-07, jr. prof., 1907-08, prof., 1908-13; prof. anatomy St. Louis U., 1913-32; dean and prof. anatomy U. S.D., 1932-33; prof. anatomy Creighton U., 1933-38; asso. prof. dept. otolaryngology U. So. Cal. Asso. Riverbank Labs., Geneva, Ill., 1922-28. Fellow A.A.A.S., Acoustical Soc. Am.; mem. Am. Physiol. Soc., Assn. Am. Anatomists. Collegium oto-rhino-laryngologicum, Sigma Xi, Nu Sigma Nu, Alpha Omega Alpha. Contbr. to med. lit. on embryology of urolonital system, circulatory system, hearing mechanisms in vertebrates, middle ear prostheses, etc. Address: 1306 Seal Way, Seal Beach, Cal. Died Apr. 31, 1950.

POILLON, HOWARD ANDREWS, (poi-lon), former mining engr., ret. research corp. exec.; b. N.Y.C., July 22, 1879; s. Cornelius and Clara Louise (Andrews) P.; student Columbia Sch. Mines; m. Frances Hanford Wright, Sept. 22, 1914; children—Cornelius III, Jeanne, Peter. Engaged in mining in Alaska, B.C., Western U.S. and Mexico, 1900-12; pres. Research Corp., 1927-45; Thatcher Furnace Co., Concrete Plank Co. Vice chmn. div. engring. and indsl. research NRC. Mem. Am. Inst. Mining and Metall. Engrs., Mining and Metall. Soc. Am., Met. Mus. Art. Episcopalian. Mason. Clubs: Union, Columbia University. Home: 20 E. 74th St., N.Y.C.; also Westhampton Beach, L.I. Office: 405 Lexington Av., N.Y.C. Died Jan. 20, 1954. *

POLIVKA, JAROSLAV JOSEPH, cons. engr., educator; b. Prague, Bohemia, Apr. 20, 1886; s. Joseph and Francisca (Urbanova) P.; Master deg., Tech. U., Prague, 1909, Dr. Tech. Sci., 1917; grad. study Conf. Tech. U., Zurich; m. Maria I. Polakova, Sept. 16, 1913; children—Belca, Jan, Milos. Came to U.S., 1938, naturalized 1945. Asst. constrn. navigation locks, Bohemia, 1907-09, concrete arch bridge over Ohre River, 1910; chief engr. Sander & Co., Soc. Cemento Armato, Zurich, Florence, 1911-13; cons. engr., Zurich, research asst. Inst. Testing Materials, Zurich, 1914-15; chief engr., partner Dr. E. von Emperger, Vienna, 1916-17; chief engr. design and constrn., Ruse, Austria, 1918; Czechoslovak govt. expert change study pub. works program, France 1919; research with Prof. Mesnager, Ecole des Ponts de Chaussées, 1920, cons. engr., architect, Prague, research engr. Material Lab., 1921-38; research photoelelastic stress analysis, Podolsko Bridge, Bohemia, 1937; research asso. civil engring. U. Cal., 1939-45; research Bethlehem Alameda (Cal.) Shipyard, Kaiser Shipyards on various heavy constrn. projects, 1943-45; cons. engr., Berkeley, San Francisco, 1946—; pres. Soil Solidification Engrs., Inc., San Francisco, Los Angeles; structural design of bridges, factories, dams, theaters, apartment houses, hotels, industrial buildings, churches, using special types and materials; cons. engr. F. L. Wright, on Guggenheim's Modern Gallery, N.Y.C., Johnson's Research Tower, Racine, Wis., Toiga Bldg., Berkeley, Cal., and other structures in precast and prestressed concrete; lecturer on contemporary structures Stanford U., 1951—; organized Internat. Assos.-Engrs. and Architects, 1958. Winter internat. competition Belvedere Tunnel, Prague, 1909; Colombet award, French Soc. Civil Engrs., for best structural achievements in past 4 yrs., 1936; gold medal and two diplomas of honor, Paris Internat. Expn., 1937; Officer Legion of Honor French Etoile Noire de Benin, 1951. Mem. Masaryk Acad., Com. Research and Testing Structural Material, Am. Soc. C.E., Am. Concrete Inst., Am. Soc. Profl. Engrs., Soc. Am. Mil. Engrs., Inst. Aero. Scis., A.S.M.E., Welding Soc., Soc. Seismology, Am. Soc. Ceramics, Am., Swiss socs. testing materials, Mexican Soc. Engrs. and Architects, French Soc. Civil Engrs., Sigma Xi. Author books and articles in the field. Inventor hyperbolic-paraboloid-structures (with Victor di Suvero). Patentee in field. Home: 1150 Arch St., Berkeley 8, Cal. Died Feb. 9, 1960.

POLLARD, CASH BLAIR, (pol'ärd), chemist, toxicologist; b. Hannibal, Mo., Feb. 22, 1900; s. William Braxton and Nannie Elizabeth (Robinson) P.; A.B., William Jewell Coll., 1921; M.S., Purdue U., 1923, Ph.D., 1930; D.Sc., Purdue U., 1954; student U. Wis., 1924; m. Ailene Atherton; 1 son, Thomas David. Grad. asst. chemistry, Purdue U., 1921-23; with Graver Corp., 1923; instr. chemistry, Purdue U., 1923-30; asst. prof. chemistry, U. of Fla., 1930-35, asso. prof., 1935-37, prof., 1937—, chmn. organic div.; cons. chemist, toxicologist, 1927—; cons. chemist Fla. states attys. sci. crime detection, 1930—; expert witness Fla. and Fed. cts., on toxicology, blood stains and powder marks. Research engr., Office of Production Research and Development, W.P.B., 1944; mem. faculty Alachua Gen. Hosp. Nurses Tng. Sch.; lectr. physiol. and pathol. chemistry 1945—. Cons. toxicologist Alachua Gen. Hosp., Morton Plant Hosp., Clearwater, Fla., Munroe, Meml. Hosp., Ocala, Fla. Served as pvt., W.W.I. Recipient Fla. Acad. Scis. Achievement Award (with John H. Pomeroy), 1945, for a study of the Sensitivity of Aldehyde Reagents; recipient U.S. Pub. Health Service Research Grant, 1948, 49, research grants, Navy Department, Office Naval Research 1948, 49, 50, Parke, Davis and Co., 1950—; Fla. award of Am. Chem. Soc., 1954; research grant from Dow Chem. Co., 1956. Fellow A.A.A.S., Am. Inst. Chemists (chmn. S.E. Regional com. on membership, 1942); mem. Am. Chem. Soc. (chmn. Fla. sect., 1935), Fla. Acad. Sci.; life mem. (hon.) Fla. Peace Officers Assn., Eugene Field Soc., Am. Legion, Am. Assn. Clin. Chemists, Nat. Rifle Assn., Sigma Xi, Phi Lambda Upsilon, Gamma Sigma Epsilon, Phi Kappa Phi, Alpha Epsilon Delta, Kappa Sigma. Democrat. Baptist. Mason. Clubs: Kiwanis, Fla. West Coast Pistol League, Gainesville Pistol, Alachua County Riding Horse Assn. Author: Laboratory Manual and Study Outline of General Chemistry (with L. A. Test), 1928, rev. 1937; Bibliography of Animal Venoms (with Ralph W. Harmon), 1947; Problems in Organic Chemistry (with E. G. Rietz), 1951; asst. editor: Outline of Organic Chemistry, 1937; asso. editor: Quadri-Service Manual of Organic Chemistry, 1938. Collaborator on Fundamental Organic Chemistry, 1940; The Work Book on Fundamental Organic Chemistry, 1941. Contbr. research articles to sci. jours. Home: "Holly Brook," Newberry Rd. Address: Leigh Hall, University Station, Gainesville, Fla. Died May 31, 1959.

POLLARD, CHARLES LOUIS, (pol'ärd), botanist, entomologist; b. New York, N.Y., Mar. 29, 1872; s. Charles William and Sarah Ann (Lyman) P.; A.B., Columbia, 1893, A.M., 1894; unmarried. Asst. curator div. of botany, U.S. Dept. Agr., 1894-95, U.S. Nat. Museum, 1895-1903; consulting botanist G. & C. Merriam Co., Springfield, Mass., 1903-06; curator in chief and patron, Pub. Museum of Staten Island Assn.

of Arts and Sciences, 1907-13; editor Plant World, 1897-1913. Founder and 1st pres. Washington Biologists Field Club; hon. mem. Phila. Bot. Soc. Spl. nat. field commr. Boy Scouts of America, 1917-20; scout executive, 1920; specialist in museum installation since 1926; librarian Martha Canfield Free Library, Arlington, Vt., since 1937. Contbr. many bot. terms to Supplement of Webster's Internat. Dictionary, also to Century Dictionary, 1898-1900; editor for botany and horticulture, Webster's New Internat. Dictionary. Has written many short articles. Address: Arlington, Vt. Died Aug. 16, 1945.

POLLARD, ISAAC, pomologist; b. Plymouth, Vt., July 11, 1830; s. Isaac and Sallie (Conant) P.; ed. Black River Acad., Ludlow, Vt.; m. Viola Welch, Mar. 11, 1861 (died 1914). Went to Calif. gold fields by way of Panama, 1849; settled in Neb., 1856, and has spent many yrs. in selecting apples that can be made productive in Central Mo. Valley; owns bearing orchard of 165 acres—the largest in Neb.; imported seedless apples from Hawaiian Islands and experimenting in growing same; also extensive experiments in growing shrubs and trees adapted for prairie country. County clk., Cass Co., Neb., 1 term; county commr. 3 years. Republican. Home: Nehawka, Neb. Died Nov. 25, 1916.

POLLOCK, HORATIO MILO, statistician, editor; b. Patria, N.Y., Sept. 2, 1868; s. Jesse W. and Mary Malvina (Daggett) P.; B.S., Union Coll., N.Y., 1895, M.S., 1897, LL.D., 1946; M.A., Ph.D., U. Leipzig, 1897; m. Georgiana Shafer, Sept. 18, 1895; children—Katherine Esther (dec.), Robert Shafer (dec.), Dorothy Affiah, Carolyn Mary; m. 2d, Mary Culver, Feb. 1, 1939. Tchr. sci. and German, Albany High Sch., 1897-1900; sr. examiner N.Y. State Civil Service Commn., 1900-07; sec. Civic League of Albany, 1907-11; tchr. econs. State Normal Coll., Albany, 1907-08; tchr. sociology and econs. Union Coll., 1908-10; dir. statis. bur. N.Y. Dept. Mental Hygiene, 1911-44, ret. Asso. editor Am. Education (monthly), 1905-25; editor Psychiatric Quarterly and predecessor The State Hospital Quarterly, 1915-35, Mental Hygiene News, 1935-43. Pres. N.Y. Edn. Co., pub. Am. Edn., 1912-23; organizer, 1908, and pres. N.Y. State Tchrs.' Bur. Fellow Am. Statis. Assn. (v.p. 1933); mgr. Am. Occupational Therapy Assn., 1927-36; mem. Nat. Com. for Mental Hygiene, Internat. Com. on Mental Hygiene, Am. Assn. on Mental Deficiency (pres. 1942-43), Medical Council U.S. Vet. Bur., Philos. Soc. of Albany, Phi Gamma Delta, A.A.A.S., Am. Acad. of Social and Polit. Sci., Sigma Xi.; hon. mem. Am. Psychiatric Assn. Cons. statistician with rank of 1st lt. Office Surgeon Gen. of the Army, 1917. Adv. statistician Nat. Com. for Mental Hygiene, 1916—; organized statistical work in instns. of Ill., 1920; spl. adviser Federal Census Bureau, 1921-26; statis. adviser Joint Com. on Methods of Preventing Delinquency, 1924-25; chmn. com. on statistics, Internat. Congress on Mental Hygiene, 1930. Del. of U.S. to Pan-Am. Neuropsychiatric Conf., Lima, Peru, 1939. Unitarian. Author: Modern Cities (with W. S. Morgan); U.S. Census Report on Patients in Instns. for Mental Disease, 1923; Expectation of Mental Disease; Family Care of Mental Patients; Hereditary and Environmental Factors in the Causation of Manic-Depressive Psychoses and Dementia Praecox (with Benjamin Malzberg); Mental Disease and Social Welfare; The Story of Old Bill Marshall, 1948; also numerous educational and statistical monographs. Edited 4-vol. History of Care of the Mentally Ill in the State of New York, 1946. Clubs: Torch, University. Home: 447 Manning Blvd., Albany, N.Y.; summer home: Middleburgh, N.Y. Died May 8, 1950; buried Schenectady.

POLYAK, STEPHEN, scientist; b. Gjurgjevac, Yugoslavia, Dec. 13, 1889; Emilian and Anna (Shostarets) P.; student Classical Gymnasium at Zagreb, Croatia, 1901-09, med. sch. at Graz, Austria, 1909-14, Zagreb, Yugoslavia, 1920; spl. studies London, Madrid, Chicago; m. Donna Irene Bibler, Apr. 11, 1931; 1 son, Stephen Francis. Came to U.S., 1928, naturalized, 1936. Asst. prof. neuroanatomy U. Calif., 1928-30; asst. prof. neurol. U. of Chicago, 1930-32, asso. prof., 1932-42, prof. anatomy since 1942. Mem. Am. Assn. Anatomists, Am. Neurol. Assn. Investigator nervous system, especially of visual organs and centers, including their structure and function; history of optics and of the investigations of brain, and of the sense organs, particularly the eye. Interested in natural history, history of civilization, and allied subjects. Home: 5801 Harper Av., Chgo. Died Mar. 9, 1955; buried Oakwood Cemetery, Mt. Morris, Ill.

POMERAT, CHARLES MARC, zoologist; b. Southbridge, Mass., July 23, 1905; s. Charles Marius and Maria Edna (Demers) P.; A.B., Clark U., 1932; A.M., Harvard, 1934, Ph.D., 1937. Asst. in biology Clark U., 1927-28, instr., 1932-36, asst., 1937-39; asso. prof. biology U. Ala., 1939-40, prof., 1940-43, chmn. dept., 1939-43; prof. anatomy U. Tex. Med. Sch., since 1943; on leave of absence from U. Ala., July 1942-43, to do research work for Woods Hole Oceanographic Inst. on an anti-fouling project for Bur. Ships, USN; adj. prof. anatomy U. Cal. Sch. Medicine; clin. prof. pathology Coll. Med. Evangelists Sch. Medicine, 1960—; prof. and cons. cytology, dir. Tissue Culture Lab. of John Sealy and Allied Hosps., 1945—; dir. tissue culture course, 1954-56; dir. cellular biology Pasadena Found. Med. Research; cons. air and indsl. hygiene lab. Cal. Bd. Pub. Health; vis. lectr. U. Cal., San Francisco, 1957. Apptd. mem. of corp. Bermuda Biol. Sta., 1943. Rockefeller Found. fellow U. Buenos Aires, Argentina, and Cambridge U., Eng., 1937-38. Fellow A.A.A.S., Internat. Oceanographic Found., N.Y. Acad. Scis., Royal Micros. Soc. (London) (hon.); mem. Tissue Culture Assn. (pres. 1952-53), Am. Soc. Zoölogists, Soc. for Exptl. Biology and Medicine, Hist. of Sci. Soc., Assn. Anatomists, Physiol. Soc., Am. Assn. U. Profs., Tex. Acad. Sci.; corr. mem. Soc. Mexicana de Hist. Nat., Sociedad Argentina de Biologia, Societa Italiana di Biologia Spermentale; mem. Phi Beta Kappa, Sigma Xi. Contbr. to sci. jours. Office: 99 N. El Molino Av., Pasadena, Cal. Died June 17, 1964.

POND, FRANCIS JONES, prof. chemistry; b. Holliston, Mass., Apr. 8, 1871; s. Abel and Lucy A. (Jones) P.; B.S., Pa. State Coll., 1892; M.A., Ph.D., U. of Gottingen, Germany, 1896; m. Nellie Olds, of Circleville, O., June 10, 1902; children—Catherine Olds (dec.), Elizabeth Olds, Nathan Jones. Instr. chemistry and assaying Pa. State Coll., 1896-1901, asst. prof. chemistry and metallurgy, 1901-03; asst. prof. engring. chemistry Stevens Inst. Tech., 1903-06; asso. prof. chemistry, 1906-09, prof. chemistry since 1909, dean freshmen since 1907. Mem. Sigma Chi, Tau Beta Pi, Phi Kappa Phi; fellow A.A.A.S., Am. Chem. Soc. Conglist. Club: Commonwealth (Upper Montclair). Author: The Chemistry of the Terpenes, 1902. Contbr. to chem. jours. Home: 167 Summit Av., Upper Montclair NJ*

POND, GEORGE GILBERT, chemist; b. Holliston, Mass., Mar. 29, 1861; s. Abel and Amelia H. (Robinson) P.; A.B., Amherst, 1881, A.M., 1884, Ph.D., 1889; U. of Göttingen, 1881-82, 85; univs. of Berlin and Munich, 1894-95; m. Helen Palmer, Aug. 1, 1888. Instr. chemistry, Amherst, 1883-88; prof. chemistry, 1888—, dean Sch. of Natural Science, 1896—, Pa. State Coll. Mem. Jury of Awards, Buffalo Expn., 1901. Episcopalian. Died May 20, 1920.

POOLE, CECIL PERCY, engineer; b. Elizabeth City, N.C., Oct. 16, 1865; s. James Madison and Matilda (Bamford) P.; ed. pvt. schs., Elizabeth City; m. Florence D. Bockover, June 16, 1886. Asso. editor Electrical World, 1895-97, Power, 1897-99; editor Am. Electrician, 1900-05, Power and the Engineer, 1905-12; mech. engr., City of Atlanta, 1913—. Fellow Am. Inst. Elec. Engrs. Episcopalian. Author: Wiring Handbook, 1900; Designs for Small Dynamos and Motors, 1903; Diagrams of Electrical Connections, 1907; The Gas Engine, 1908. Edited dynamo and motor sect. and part of electromagnet sect. of Foster's Electrical Engineer's Pocket Book, 1909. Died Feb. 23, 1921.

POOLE, HERMAN, chemist, metallurgist; b. Boston, Mar. 9, 1849; s. Lott H. and Anna G. P.; ed. Boston pub. schs., Mass. Inst. of Technology, Cornell Univ., Univ. of Buffalo; m. Cleveland, 1889, Elizabeth Barrett. Mem. Am. Chem. Soc., Soc. of Chem. Industry, Am. Soc. Mech. Engrs., Am. Inst. Mining Engrs. Author: Geometry in Ten Lessons, 1876 XI; Calorific Power of Fuels, 1898 W9. Contbr. to tech. jours. on chemistry, petroleum, fuel, and gas manufacturer and purification. Address: 395 Broadway, New York.

POOLE, SIDMAN PARMELEE, geographer; b. Syracuse, N.Y., Oct. 19, 1893; s. Theodore Lewis and Carrie (Law) P.; B.S., Syracuse Univ., 1921, M.S., 1925; Ph.D., Univ. of Chicago, 1932; student Cambridge (Eng.) Univ., 1925; m. Rachel Sumner, August 31, 1922. Instr. Syracuse Univ., 1921-25, asst. prof. of geography, 1925-32, asso. prof., 1932-39, prof., 1939-40; summer lecturer Cornell Univ., 1932; prof. and chmn. Dept. of Geography, Univ. of Va., since Sept., 1946; dir. Virginia Geographical Institute since 1947. Geographer to Syracuse Andean Expdn., 1930-31, Syracuse Gaspe Expdn., 1933, dir. and geographer to Syracuse Yucatan Expdn., 1937-38; detailed field work in New York State, Vermont (with Vt. geol. survey), upper Great Lakes region, Chicago area, England, Brittany, Venezuela, Gaspe and Yucatan. Geographic advisor Air Command and Staff Sch., Air Univ., Maxwell Field, Ala. since Oct. 1946. Served as 1st lt., F.A., A.E.F., World War I; capt. and maj. F.A., O.R.C., 1920-40; col. chief topographic br., War Dept., Washington, D.C., U.K., N. Africa, 1940-46. Decorated Hon. Comdr. Order British Empire, Am. Legion of Merit. Mem. U.S. Bd. on Geog. Names, 1943-46. Fellow Am. Geog. Soc., Royal Geog. Soc.; mem. Nat. Council Geography Teachers (contbg. mem. and chmn. com. on geographic edn. for world understanding), Assn. Am. Geographers (mem. com. on Atlas of U.S., inter-soc. com. on sci. foundation legislation), Am. Soc. for Profl. Geographers (v.p. 1947), Am. Unitarian Assn. (nat. dir.), Phi Beta Kappa, Sigma Xi, Phi Gamma Delta. Clubs: Cosmos (Washington); Farmington Country (Charlottesville, Va.); Colonnade; Rotary International; Explorers (New York). Author: Manual for College Geography, 1933; chapter on Geography of Central New York (An Inland Empire by W. Freeman Galpin), 1941; chapter on Geography in America's Life (Twentieth Century America), 1947-51; History of Virginia (junior author). Contbg. editor: Econ. Geography. Contbr. articles to geog. pubs., mags. and newspapers. Consultant editor Bobbs-Merrill Co. series of geog. texts and readers 1945—. Home: Rio Rd., Box 83, R. 5, Charlottesville, Va. Died Oct. 28, 1955; buried U. Va. Cemetery, Charlottesville.

POOR, CHARLES LANE, astronomer; b. Hackensack, N.J., Jan. 18, 1866; s. Edward Eri and Mary Wellington (Lane) P.; B.S., Coll. City N.Y., 1886, M.S., 1890; Ph.D., Johns Hopkins, 1892; m. Anna Louise Easton, Apr. 19, 1892; children—Charles Lane, Alfred Easton, Edmund Ward. Asso. in astronomy Johns Hopkins, 1892-96, asso. prof., 1895-99; prof. astronomy Columbia, 1903-10, prof. celestial mechanics, 1910-44, prof. emeritus, 1944—. Inventor of various navigational devices. Fellow Am. Acad. Arts and Sciences (asso.), Royal Astron. Soc. Club: New York Yacht. Author: Simplified Navigation, 1918; Gravitation versus Relativity, 1922; Relativity and the Motion of Mercury, 1925; The Relativity Deflection of Light, 1926; Rules and Regulations for the Construction of Racing Yachts, 1928; Men Against the Rule, 1937. Home: Dering Harbor, N.Y. Address: 35 E. 69th St., N.Y.C. Died Sept. 27, 1951.

POOR, JOHN MERRILL, astronomer; b. West Newbury, Mass., Jan. 28, 1871; s. John Merrill and Mary Alice (Merrill) P.; A.B., 1897, Dartmouth; post-grad. work, Princeton U., 1900-03; Thaw fellow in astronomy, same, 1900-02, grad. student in astronomy, 1902-03, Ph.D., 1904; spl. study, U. of Chicago, summer of 1902; Lund (Sweden) U., 1911; m. Sarah Helen Noyes, Dec. 26, 1905; children—Dorothy Noyes, Elizabeth Merrill. Prin. Hanover High Sch., 1897-98; instr. in astronomy and mathematics, 1898-1900, instr. in astronomy, 1903-06, asst. prof., 1906-15, asso. prof., 1915-17, prof., 1917—, Dartmouth. Died Dec. 11, 1933.

POOR, RUSSELL SPURGEON, govt. ofcl.; b. Cowgill, Mo., Mar. 10, 1899; s. Alvin Eustace and Mollie (Petty) P.; student Mo. Wesleyan, Cameron, Mo., 1917-19; B.S., U. of Ill., 1923, M.S., 1925, Ph.D., 1927; D.Sc., Birmingham-Southern College, 1955; married Cleta Viola Price, June 17, 1927 (dec.); children—William Russell, Robert Clair; m. 2d, Edna G. Ketchum, Nov. 18, 1967. Asst. chemistry Mo. Weslyan Coll., 1918; asst. city chemist, Kansas City, Mo., 1919; prin. Brookfield (Mo.) High Sch., 1920; asst. geology, U. of Ill., 1923-27, fellow in geology, 1927; jr. geol. Ill. Geol. Survey, summers 1923-24, 26, Ky. Geol. Survey, summer 1925; asso. prof. geol. Birmingham-Southern Coll., Birmingham, Ala., 1927-28, prof. geol. and head geol. dept., 1928-43, dir. extension dept., 1936-39, chmn. div. of natural scis., 1937-43, adminstrative asst. to the pres., 1943-44; dean grad. Sch. and dir. Auburn Research Foundation, Ala. Polytech. Inst., Auburn, 1944-49; chmn. Univ. Relations Div. Oak Ridge Inst. of Nuclear Studies, 1949-53; administrator for 32 Southern univs. in making research facilities of Oak Ridge Nat. Lab. available to scientists of the country; Nat. Sci. Found., Washington, 1952; dir. med. center study, U. Fla., 1952-53; became provost Univ. Fla., 1953; then dir. div. nuclear edn. and tng. U.S. AEC. Mem. Pres.'s Com. on Employment of the Handicapped, 1956-62; asso. chmn. com. on dental health Commn. on the Survey of Dentistry in the U.S., American Council on education, 1958-60. Fellow Society of Economic Geologists, Geological Society of Am., American College of Dentists (hon.); mem. Am. Inst. Mining, Metall. and Petroleum Engineers (chmn., southeast sect. 1943), Ala. Acad. Sci. (pres. 1935); mem. adv. council So. Research Inst.: mem. Conf. Deans So. Grad. Schs. (sec.-treas., 1940-49), Nat. Insts. Health (nat. adv. council dental research), Newcomen Soc., Sigma Xi, Phi Beta Kappa, Phi Kappa Phi, Omicron Delta Kappa. Clubs: Engineers (Birmingham); Kiwanis (Gainsville); Cosmos (Washington). Contbr. sci. publs. Home: Bethesda MD Died Feb. 17, 1972.

POORMAN, ALFRED PETER, prof. engring. mechanics; b. Altamont, Ill., Feb. 13, 1877; s. George Warner and Eliza Jane (Watson) P.; B.S. in C.E., U. of Ill., 1907; A.B. and C.E., U. of Colo., 1909; m. Sarah Elizabeth Ellmaker, June 22, 1910 (died Jan. 30, 1935); children—Mary Esther, George Ellmaker; married 2d, Genevieve Louise Lippoldt, June 29, 1936. Engineer, Weber Concrete Chimney Company, June-Aug. 1907; instructor in civil engineering, Univ. of Colo., 1907-09; hydrographer, Wind River Indian Reservation, July-Nov. 1909; asst. prof. applied mechanics, Purdue, 1909-17, 1919-20, asso. prof., 1920-22, prof. since 1922, head dept. applied mechanics, 1942-44, professor emeritus, 1947. Capt. Engr. Corps U.S. Army, 1917-18; supply officer, Gen. Hdqrs., A.E.F., June 1918-June 1919. Mem. Am. Soc. Civil Engrs., Am. Soc. for Testing Materials, American Soc. of Engring. Edn., Am. Concrete Inst., A.A.S.S., Am. Assn. Univ. Profs., Tau Beta Pi, Sigma Xi, Chi Epsilon. Scabbard and Blade. Methodist. Club: University. Author: Applied Mechanics, 1917 (5 edits.); Strength of Materials, 1925 (4 edits.); Sect. on theoretical mechanics O'Rourke's Engineering Handbook, 1940. Home: 329 Russell St., West Lafayette, Ind. Died Feb. 12, 1952; buried Grand View Cemetery, West Lafayette.

POPE, FRANKLIN LEONARD, electrician, inventor; b. Great Barrington, Mass., Dec. 2, 1840; s. Ebenezer and Electa (Wainwright) P.; attended Amherst Acad.; m. Sarah Amelia Dickinson, Aug. 6, 1873, 5 children. Edited and published small newspaper, Great

Barrington; operator for Am. Telegraph Co., Great Barrington, 1857-59; asst. engr. Am. Telegraph Co., serving as circuit mgr. Boston & Albany R.R. telegraph lines, Springfield, Mass., 1826; reestablished communication between N.Y.C. and Boston during draft riots, 1863; asst. to the chief engr. Russo-Am. Telegraph Co., 1864-66, made preliminary exploration and survey of Brit. Columbia and Alaska; N.Y. editor The Telegrapher, 1867-68; made valuable improvements in stock ticker, 1869; partner firm Pope, Edison & Co., 1869-70; devised system which made practicable the automatic electric block signal for railways (invented by Thomas S. Hall); in charge all patent interests of Western Union Telegraph Co., 1875-81; editor Electrician and Elec. Engineer and Engring. Mag., 1884-93; cons. engr. Great Barrington Electric Light Co., converted plant from steam to water power, 1893-95; charter mem. Am. Inst. E.E., an original v.p., pres., 1886-87. Author: Modern Practice of the Electric Telegraph, 1869; The Telegraphic Instructor, 1871; Life and Work of Joseph Henry, 1879; Evolution of the Electric Incandescent Lamp, 1889, 94. Died Great Barrington, Oct. 13, 1895.

PORCHER, FRANCIS PEYRE, physician, botanist; b. St. John, S.C., Dec. 14, 1825; s. Dr. William and Isabella (Peyre) P.; A.B., S.C. Coll., 1844; grad. Med. Coll. S.C., 1847; m. Virginia Leigh; m. 2d, Margaret Ward. Established Charleston (S.C.) Prep. Med. Sch.; mem. Charleston Bd. of Health; surgeon, physician marine and city hosps.; prof. clin. medicine, materia medica, therapeutics Med. Coll. State S.C.; opened hosp. for Negroes, 1855; surgeon Holcombe Legion, also naval hosp., Norfolk, Va., S.C. Hosp., Petersburg, Va., during Civil War; asso. fellow Coll. of Physicians of Phila.; mem. S.C. Med. Assn. (pres. 1872), Elliot Soc. Natural History, A.M.A. (v.p. 1879), 105h Internat. Med. Congress, Berlin, 1890, Pan. Am. Congress (pres. sect. on gen. medicine 1892); editor Charleston Med. Jour. and Review, 1853-58, 73-76; authority on diseases of the heart and chest. Author: A Medico-Botanical Catalogue of the Plants and Ferns of St. John's Berkely, S.C., 1847; A Sketch of the Medical Botany of South Carolina, 1849; The Medicinal, Poisonous and Dietetic Properties of the Cryptogamic Plants of the United States, 1854; Illustrations of Disease with the Microscope, and Clinical Investigations aided by the Microscope and by Chemical Reagents, 1861; The Resources of the Southern Fields and Forests, 1863. Died Nov. 19, 1895.

PORRO, THOMAS J(OSEPH), pharmacist; b. Lead, S.D., Nov. 19, 1891; s. Felix and Margaret (Peradotte) P.; m. Ann E. Morman, June 29, 1922; 1 son, Thomas Joseph. Established Porro Biol. Labs., Tacoma, 1921. Mem. bd. trustees Coll. Puget Sound; former mem. Tacoma Library Trustees, State Library Commn. Served with M.C., United States Navy, 1917-20. Member American Chemical Soc., A.A.A.S., Tacoma C. of C., N.Y. Acad. Sci., Royal Soc. Arts, Am. Inst. Graphic Arts. Rotarian. Contbr. sci. jours. Member exec. board Am. Library Assn., 1950-54. Home: 2918 N. Alder St., Tacoma. Office: Medical Arts Bldg., Tacoma 2. Died Dec. 3, 1959.

PORTER, HOLBROOK FITZ-JOHN, engineer; b. New York, Feb. 28, 1858; s. Gen. Fitz-John and Harriet Pierson (Cook) P.; M.E., Lehigh U., Pa., 1878; m. Rose Smith, Aug. 27, 1888; children—Fitz John, Holbrook Smith (dec.). Apprentice and draftsman, Delamater Iron Works, New York, 1878-82; asst. engr. N.J. Steel & Iron Co. (Cooper, Hewitt & Co.), Trenton, N.J., 1882-84; college engineer, 1884-86, supt. buildings and grounds, Columbia College, 1886-90; supt. Cary & Moen Steel Spring & Wire Mills, New York, 1890; supt. Braddock Wire Co., Pittsburgh, Pa., 1891; asst. mech. engr., 1891-93, asst. chief machinery dept., 1893-94, Chicago Expn.; Western representative Bethlehem Steel Co., Chicago, 1894-1901, Eastern representative, New York, 1901; v.p. and gen. mgr. Westinghouse, Nernst Lamp Co., Pittsburgh, 1902-05; cons. industrial engr., New York, 1905-12. Founder and 1st sec. Efficiency Soc., 1911; sec. Organizing Com. for Congress of Internat. Assn. for Testing Materials, 1912; expert on industrial hygiene, Pittsburgh Survey, Russell Sage Foundation, 1912; expert on "fire hazard to life," N.Y. State Factory Investigating Commn., 1912-14; installed first means of escape from fire, for bedridden hospital patients in city hospitals, N.Y. City, 1912-14; cons. engineer on employment management, Hercules Powder Co., Wilmington, Del., 1915-18; sec. Nat. Mus. of Engring. and Industry, 1918—; dir. Nat. Com. for Prevention of Blindness. Episcopalian. Home: New York, N.Y. Died Jan. 25, 1933.

PORTER, JAMES MADISON, III, consulting engr., educator; b. Easton, Pa., May 10, 1864; s. James Madison, II., and Ruth Pierson (Cook) P.; ed. Easton schs. and Hackettstown and Blairstown acads.; grad. Lafayette Coll., 1886; m. Easton, 1888, Mary V. Drake. Prof. civ. engring. Lafayette Coll. Mem. Internat. Assn. Testing Materials, A.A.A.S., Am. Inst. Mining Engrs., Am. Soc. Civ. Engrs., Engrs. Club, Phila., Automobile Club of America. Clubs: University, Pomfret, Markham, Engineers. Address: Easton, Pa.

PORTER, JERMAIN GILDERSLEEVE, astronomer; b. Buffalo, N.Y., Jan. 8, 1852; s. John Jermain and Mary (Hall) P.; A.B., Hamilton Coll., 1873, A.M., 1876, Ph.D., 1888; U. of Berlin and Royal Obs., 1873-74; Sc.D. from the U. of Cincinnati, 1930; m. Emily Snowden, July 3, 1879; children—John Jermain, Ruth May (dec.), Harold Mitchel. Asst. prof. astronomy, Hamilton Coll., 1875-78; mem. U.S. Coast and Geod. Survey, 1878-84; dir. Cincinnati Obs. and prof. astronomy, U. of Cincinnati, 1884-1931. Observer Internat. Latitude Service, 1899-1905. Received Astron. Journal Comet prize, 1894. Author: The Stars in Song and Legend, 1901; Catalogue of 4,280 Stars, 1905; Variation of Latitude, 1908; Catalogue of Nebulae, 1910; Catalogue of 3,164 Proper Motion Stars, 1918; All-American Time, 1918; How to Find the Stars and Planets, 1920; Catalogue of 5,000 Stars, 1925; Catalogue of Proper Motion Stars, 1930. Died Apr. 14, 1933.

PORTER, JOHN ADDISON, chemist; b. Catskill, N.Y., Mar. 15, 1822; s. Addison and Ann (Hogeboom) P.; grad. Yale, 1842, M.D. (hon.), 1854; m. Josephine Sheffield, July 16, 1855, 2 sons. Prof. rhetoric Delaware Coll., Newark, N.J., 1844-47; studied agrl. chemistry, Germany, 1847-50; prof. chemistry applied to the arts Brown U., 1850-52; prof. analytical, agrl. chemistry Yale (later Sheffield) Scientific Sch., 1852-56, prof. organic chemistry, 1856-64, 1st dean Sheffield Sci. Sch., Yale, consolidated depts. of instrn., established and extended courses of study which emphasized science, made available reliable, useful information about agr. and nutrition; a founder Scroll and Key of Yale, 1842. Author: Plan of an Agricultural School, 1856; Principles of Chemistry, 1856; First Book of Chemistry and Allied Sciences, 1857; Outlines of the First Course of Yale Agaricultural Lectures, 1860. Died New Haven, Conn., Aug. 25, 1866.

PORTER, JOSEPH YATES, physician; b. Key West, Fla., Oct. 21, 1847; s. Joseph Yates and Mary (Randolph) P.; ed. in N.J.; M.D., Jefferson Med. Coll., Phila., 1870; m. Louisa Curry, 1870. Entered army, July 1870, as acting asst. surgeon; asst. surgeon U.S.A., June 26, 1875; capt. asst. surgeon, June 26, 1880; apptd. deputy surgeon-gen. with rank of lt. col., and placed on retired list, Mar. 8, 1907, by Act of Congress, Mar. 2, 1907. Went through yellow fever epidemic at Dry Tortugas, 1873, Key West and Tampa, Fla., 1887, Key West, 1899, Miami, 1899, Pensacola, 1905; in charge govt. relief measures at Jacksonville, Fla., during epidemic in 1888; made 1st demonstrations of mosquito law of yellow fever transmission in U.S. in Tampa, 1905, in an imported case of yellow fever from New Orleans. State health officer of Fla., 1889-1917; recalled to active duty as lt. col., Med. Corps U.S.A., June 6, 1917; camp surgeon, Camp Joseph E. Johnston, Jacksonville, Fla., Oct. 1, 1917-Jan. 31, 1919; now quarantine insp. U.S. Pub. Health Service. Home: Jacksonville, Fla. Died Mar. 16, 1927.

PORTER, ROLAND GUYER, electrical engr.; b. South Norwalk, Conn., June 9, 1894; s. William Lovett and Ella Cook (Guyer) P.; B.E.E., Northeastern Univ., 1918; M.S., Harvard Grad. Sch. of Engring., 1932; m. Mildred Claire Plummer, June 18, 1921; 1 son, Robert Guyer, Comml. radio operator Marconi Co. of Am. at Sea, 1913-14; student apprentice standardizing and testing dept., Boston Edison Co., 1914-16; instr. mathematics and physics, Northeastern Univ., 1919-20, instr. elec. engring., 1920-23, asst. prof., 1923-29, asso. prof., 1929-37; prof. and head elec. engring. dept., 1937—. Mem. sch. com., Beverly, Mass., 1937-41. Served as ensign U.S.N.R.F., 1st class radio electrician, chief radio electrician, radio gunner, June 1917-Apr. 1919. Registered professional engr. (elec.), Mass., 1942—. Fellow Am. Inst. Elec. Engrs. (past chmn. Boston sect., mem. nat. sect. com. and nat. ednl. com., 1943-48; member national student branch committee, 1948—; national summer convention committee 1948-49); mem. Inst. Radio Engrs. (past sec.-treas. Boston sect., member national educational committee 1947-49), Illuminating Engr. Soc. (past mem. bd. mgrs., Boston), Am. Soc. Engring. Edn., Harvard Engring. Soc., Engring. Soc. of New England, Tau Beta Phi, Eta Kappa Nu. Republican. Episcopalian. Club: North Shore Harvard. Home: 19 Woodbury St., Beverly, Mass. Office: 360 Huntington Av., Boston 15. Died Sept. 2, 1953; buried North Beverly (Mass.) Cemetery.

PORTER, ROYAL A(RTHUR), physicist; born Adair, Ill., Feb. 8, 1877; s. George E. and Mary (Ritter) P.; B.S., Northwestern, 1901, M.S., 1902; Ph.D., Gottingen Univ., 1912; m. Eleanore Lukens, June 22, 1914. Fellow in physics, Northwestern, 1901-02; instr. Syracuse U., 1902-05, asst. prof., 1905-06, asso. prof., 1906-12, prof. physics, 1912-47, chmn. dept., 1919-39, prof. emeritus since 1947. Fellow Am. Physical Soc., A.A.A.S.; mem. Am. Inst. E.E., Soc. Engring. Edn., Am. Assn. Univ. Profs., Phi Beta Kappa, Sigma Xi, Acacia. Republican. Methodist. Mason. Home: 861 Ostrom Av., Syracuse 10 NY

PORTER, RUFUS, inventor, editor; b. Boxford, Mass., May 1, 1792; s. Tyler and Abigail (Johnson) P.; at least 1 child. Servgd as pvt. Me. Militia, War of 1812; invented cameraobscura (produced portraits in 15 minutes), 1820, cord-making machine, 1825; founder, editor Am. Mechanic (1st scientific mag. of its kind), circa 1840; established publ. Scientific American, 1845; published Aerial Navigation, 1849; other inventions include: horse-drawn flat boat, clock carriage, washing machine, fire alarm, portable house, revolving rifle, rotary plow, reaction wind wheel. Died New Haven, Conn., Aug. 13, 1884.

PORTER, RUSSELL WILLIAMS, explorer; b. Springfield, Vt., Dec. 13, 1871; s. Frederick W. and Caroline (Sillsbie) P.; studied architecture, Mass. Inst. Tech.; M.S. (hon.), Norwich U., 1917; m. Alice Belle Marshall, 1907; children—Marshall (dec.), Caroline. Made 8 trips to Arctic regions with Peary, Fiala-Ziegler, Baldwin-Ziegler, as artist, astronomer, topographer, surveyor or collector for natural history; made 3 trips into interior of Alaska, British Columbia and Labrador. Instr. architecture, Mass. Inst. Tech., 1916-17; optical work, Bur. of Standards, Washington, D.C., 1917-18; now asso. in optics and instrumental design, Calif. Inst. Tech. Contbr. to astron. jours. Home: Pasadena, Calif. Died Feb. 22, 1949.

PORTER, WILLIAM TOWNSEND, physiologist; b. Plymouth, O., Sept. 24, 1862; s. Dr. Frank Gibson and Martha (Townsend) P.; M.D., St. Louis Med. Coll. (Washington U.), 1885, D.Sc., 1915; post-grad. studies univs. of Kiel, Breslau and Berlin, Germany; LL.D., U. of Md., 1908. Resident physician St. Louis City Hosp., 1886-87; for some time in charge of med. and surg. work in same; prof. physiology, St. Louis Med. Coll., 1887-93; asst. prof. physiology, Harvard, 1893-98, asso. prof., 1898-1906, prof. comparative physiology, 1906-28, now emeritus. Author: Introduction to Physiology, 1900; Shock at the Front, 1918; also various monographs and papers on physiol. subjects. Home: Dover, Mass. Died Feb. 16, 1949. *

PORTEVIN, ALBERT MARCEL GERMAIN RENE, educator, engr.; b. Paris, France, Nov. 1, 1880; s. Paul Albert and Marie Felicie (Ollivier) P.; Dr. Honoris Causa univs. Brussels, Cracovie, Genes, Liege, Louvain, Pribram, Quebec, Zurich; m. Madeleine Castillon, 1929; children—Philippe, Jean-Paul. Decorated Grand Officer Legion of Honor, Order of Alphonse X; Comdr. o'Ordre de Leopold, de l'Ordre de la Couronne de Chêne de l'Ordre de l'Etoile Polaire; Officier du Lion Blanc et de la Couronne d'Italie, Croix d'or du Merite de Pologne, Commander of the Order of the British Empire. Recipient award Acad. Sciences, Iron and Steel Inst., Inst. Metals. Mem. Acad. Sci., Royal Soc. London, Acad. Sciences of U.S. Address: Boulevard Beausejour 21, Paris 16, France. Died Apr. 12, 1962.

PORTMANN, URSUS VICTOR, radiologist; b. Jackson, Minn., Jan. 20, 1887; s. William C. and Emma Elizabeth (Ball) P.; A.B., Western Res. U., 1909, M.D., 1913, hon. Sc.d., 1960; m. Ina Fuller, June 14, 1914; m. 2d, Jessie Harriet Raine, Jan. 14, 1934; 1 son, Ralph Fuller. Interne St. Vincents' Charity Hosp., Cleve., 1913-14; practiced med., Jackson, 1913-17, Grand Rapids, Mich., 1919-22; head, dept. therapeutic radiology Cleve. Clinic, 1922-52, ret.; mem. staff St. Mary's Hosp., Tucson Med. Center, Pima Co. Hosp.; practicing therapeutic radiologist, Tucson; cons. radiology VA, 1942-52. Diplomate Am. Bd. Radiology, 1934, trustee and examiner since 1939. Mem. A.M.A., (sec., sect. on radiology, 1945-49, chmn. sect., 1949-50, del. for sect. to Sixth Internat. Congress of Radiology, London, July 1950; mem. phys. medicine Com. on Roentgen Rays, Radium and Med. Aspects of Atomic Energy), Am. Roentgen Ray Soc. (exec. council, 1939-44, chmn. exec. council, 1945, pres. 1949-50), Radiol. Soc. N. Am. (mem. com. on standardization since 1926, subchmn. since 1930), Am. Coll. Radiology (fellow, mem. com. on mil. affairs 1941-46), Ohio State Radiol. Soc. (charter mem., pres. 1941, 42), Ohio State Med. Assn., Cleve. Acad. Medicine (mem. subcom. on cancer since 1947), Cleve. Med. Library Assn., Cleve. Radiol. Soc. (charter mem., pres. 1941-42, hon. pres. 1948-49), Western Res. U. Alumni (mem. council since 1949); hon. mem. Sociedad Columbiana de Radiologia, Republic of Columbia, S.A., Tenn., Tex., Rocky Mountain radiol. socs., Detroit Roentgen Ray and Radium Soc., St. Louis County Med. Soc., St. Louis Soc. Radiologists, Delta Tau Delta, Nu Sigma Nu. Club: Cleveland Country. Editor Clin. Therapeutic Radiology; cons. editorial bd. Am. Jour. Roentgenol. Radiol. Therapy and Nuclear Medicine. Contbr. articles in med. jours. Invented (with O. Glasser and V. Seitz) condenser dosimeter. Home: 331 S. Alvernon, Tucson 85711. Office: Tucson Tumor Clinic, 721 N. 4th Av., Tucson. Died May 21, 1966.

POST, CHARLES WILLIAM, manufacturer; b. Springfield, Ill., Oct. 26, 1854; s. Charles Rollin and Caroline (Lathrop) P.; student U. of Illinois but was not grad.; m. Leila D. Young. Partner hardware business, commercial traveler, mgr. plow factory, Springfield, Ill.; broke down from overwork, 1884; invalid and traveled for health until 1891; studied medicine, hygiene, dietetics, psychology, experiment and practice in America and Europe; led into food business; originator of prepared food industry, and Postum Coffee. Now chmn. Postum Cereal Co., Ltd., Battle Creek Paper Co., Home and Fireside Co., Ltd.; pres. Double U Co., Post Land Co. Republican. Home: Washington, D.C. Died May 9, 1914.

POST, CHESTER LEROY, consulting engr.; b. Gordon, O., Aug. 2, 1880; s. Ezra and Mary Frances (Berry) P.; B.S., Rose Poly. Inst., 1903, M.S., 1905,

C.E., 1934; m. Jennie Marie Jensen, May 6, 1908. Asst. engr. C.,C., C.&St.L. Ry., 1902; assistant engineer and masonry insp. same rd., 1903-04; supt. with A. J. Yawger Co., 1905-06, and R. M. Shankland, 1907-08; with Unit Constrn. Co. and Chicago Unit Constrn. Co. in charge of all work in Chicago territory, 1908-10; with T. L. Condron, and v.p. and mgr. Condron Co., 1910-18, v.p. and sec., 1919-24, designing and superintending constrn. large number bldgs for Sears, Roebuck Co., Ford Motor Co., Wagner Electric Corp., etc.; mem. Condron & Post, 1924-42, engaged in the design and construction of South Park Boulevard Viaduct, Western Electric Co., American Colortype Co., etc. Supervising designing engr. Q.M. Corps, U.S. Army, Army Supply Base Brooklyn, N.Y., etc., 1918-19. Cons. engr. and chmn. engring. advisory com. Federal Works Agency. Pub. Bldgs. Adminstrn., Washington, D.C., 1935—. Cons. to Division 2, National Defense Research Com., Washington, D.C., 1943. Mem. Am. Concrete Inst. (chmn. bldg. code com.; mem. award com.). Mem. Am. Soc. Civ. Engrs., Western Soc. Engrs., Republican. Methodist. Mason (K.T.), Shriner. Club: Chicago Engineers. Author: Building Superintendence for Reinforced Concrete, 1916. Home: 1 Scott Circle, Washington 6, D.C. Office: 19th & F, Washington 25. Died Aug. 21, 1950; buried Chgo.

POST, WILEY, aviator; b. Grand Plain, Tex., 1900; s. William Frank and May P.; m. May Lane, 1927. Farmer in Tex., later oil driller in Okla.; lost one eye in an accident, and was awarded $2,000; invested the award in a 2d hand airplane and began as flyer, 1924; made nearly 100 parachute jumps; winner of Chicago-Los Angeles Air Derby, in 9 hrs., 9 minutes and 4 seconds, 1930; made trip around the world with Harold Gatty, in 8 days, 15 hrs. and 51 minutes, in 1931; 2d round-the-world trip alone (the 1st to fly alone around the world), in 7 days, 18 hrs. and 49 minutes, 1933. Served as aerial navigation instr. and adviser, U.S. Army. Home: Oklahoma City, Okla. Died Aug. 15, 1935.

POSTLETHWAITE, ROBERT HODGSHON, engineer; b. Cumberland, England, Jan. 16, 1862; s. William and Annie Camilla (Brisco) P.; ed. Christ's Coll., New Zealand; m. Edith Mary Radford, of Hillam Hall, Yorkshire, England, May, 1883. Contracting engr. and owner New Zealand Engring. Works until 1895; engaged in mining in Cal., 1896, and later introduced first successful gold dredge into Cal.; dredge designer and chief of construction for Risdon Iron Works, San Francisco, 1905-11; mgr. mining dept. Union Iron Works, 1911-13. Home: Coachella, Riverside County, Cal.

POSTNIKOV, FEDOR ALEXIS (F. A. POST), engineer, aeronaut; b. Kovno, Russia, Feb. 29, 1872; s. Alexis Semen and Mary Fedor (Radchenko) P.; grad. 1st Imperial Mil. Sch. (Petrograd), 1891, with rank 2d lt. of Ussuri Cossack Army; Officers' Aeronautical Sch., St. Petersburg, 1897; grad. as mil. engr., St. Petersburg, 1899; capt., mil. engr., 1901; lt. col. Russian Admiralty (Navy Dept.), 1905; M.S. in C.E., U. of Calif., 1907; m. Mary Nicolas Smirnov, of St. Petersburg, Aug. 9, 1895. Cossacks scout comdr., 1892-4; sr. engr. Yards and Docks Dept., under Russian Govt., 1899-1906; officer-aeronaut in Russian Army, 1898; as head Navy Aero Detachment took part in defense of Vladivostok, and in raids with cruisers during Russo-Japanese War, in capacity as organizer and comdr. Navy Aero Detachment, 1904-5; commd. 1st lt. Aviation Sect. Signal Corps, U.S.A., Mar. 27, 1917; capt. jr. mil. aviator, July 24, 1917, at Ft. Omaha, Neb.; asst. aero engr., experimental work and designing dirigibles, with Good year Co., Akron, O., Jan.-May 1918; designing engr., with dock and terminal sect. Constrn. Corps, U.S. Army, Washington, D.C., until June 1919. Has designed and built numerous buildings, dams, harbors, etc. Internat. balloon pilot certificate No. 77. Mem. Russian Tech. Soc. (life), Aero Club of America, Internat. Esperanto Assn., etc. Author: Siberian Cossack Cousin, 1916. Writer on tech. subjects in English, Russian and Esperanto langs. Home: 1633 Dwight Way, Berkeley CA

POTTENGER, FRANCIS MARION, physician; b. Sater, O., Sept. 27, 1869; s. Thomas and Hannah Ellen (Sater) P.; Ph.B., Otterbein U., 1892, Ph.M., 1897, A.M., 1905, LL.D., 1909; Med. Coll. of Ohio, 1892-93; M.D., Cin. Coll. of Medicine and Surgery, 1894 (highest honors); post-grad., N.Y., 1900, and went abroad for study four times; m. Carrie Burtner, 1894 (died 1898); m. 2d, Adalaide Gertrude Babbitt, Aug. 29, 1900; children—Francis Marion, Robert Thomas, Adelaide M.; m. 3d, Caroline Lacy, Sept. 15, 1917; 1 dau., Caroline L. Practiced gen. medicine at Norwood, O., 1894-95, Monrovia, Cal., 1895-1901; specialized in diseases of chest, Monrovia and Los Angeles, since 1901. Established Pottenger Sanatorium for diseases of lungs and throat, 1903, of which is owner and med. dir. Asst. chair of surgery Cin. Coll. of Medicine and Surgery, 1894; lectr. on diseases of chest, and climatology U. So. Cal., 1903-04, prof. clin. medicine and diseases of chest, 1905-09, 1914-20 and 1931-42; prof. emeritus since 1942. Cons., Los Angeles County, Collis P. and Howard Huntington Meml. hosps.; v.p. Cal. Bd. Pub. Health, 1940-43, cons. tb control Cal. Bd. Health since 1943; chmn. tb adv. com. Dept. of Charities, Los Angeles Co. Founder, pres. So. Cal. Anti-Tb League, 1902-06, chief helping sta., 1906-08. Distinguished Alumnus award Otterbein Coll., 1952. Fellow Am. Geog. Soc., A.A.A.S., A.M.A., A.C.P. (councillor 1916-23, regent 1917-40, v.p. 1929-31, pres. 1932); founding fellow Internat. Psychosomatic Soc.; mem. Los Angeles County Med. Assn. (pres. 1906-07), Los Angeles Acad. Medicine, Los Angeles Clin. and Path. Soc. (pres. 1923-24), So. Cal. Med. Soc. (pres. 1912-13), Am. Therapeutic Soc. (pres. 1914-15), Miss. Valley Med. Assn. (pres. 1917-19), Cal. Med. Assn., A.M.A., Am. Climatol. and Clin. Assn., Pacific Interurban Clin. Club (chmn. 1931-32), Assn. for Study Internal Secretions (sec. 1917-1935, pres. 1935-37), Pacific Geog. Soc. (regent), Am. Pub. Health Assn., Am. Trudeau Soc., Cal. Tb Assn. (pres. 1931, dir. 1930-40), Nat. Tb Assn., Los Angeles County Tb and Health Assn. (pres. 1939-41, dir. since 1924, pres. emeritus since 1946), Trudeau Soc. Los Angeles (pres. 1935), Eugenics Soc. U.S.A., Am. Acad. Polit. and Social Sci., Sci. League Am., Am. Acad. Tb Physicians, Am. Coll. Chest Physicians, Am. Acad. Applied Nutrition (life), Am. Soc. for Research in Psychosomatic Problems, Gerontol. Soc., Inst. Am. Genealogy, Soc. Colonial Wars, S.R.; corr. mem. Tb. Soc. Scotland, First Internat. Central Com. to Combat Tb., Internat. Union Against Tb. Club: Calif. Author: Pulmonary Tuberculosis, 1908; Muscle Spasm and Degeneration in Intrathoracic Inflammation and Light Touch Palpation, 1912; Tuberculin in Diagnosis and Treatment, 1913; Clinical Tuberculosis (2 vols.), 1917, 2d edit, 1922; Symptoms of Visceral Disease, 1919, 6th edit., 1944; Tuberculosis and How to Combat It, 1921, 2d edit., 1928; Tuberculosis in the Child and Adult, 1934; Tuberculosis, 1948; The Fight Against Tuberculosis. An Autobiography, 1952. Author about 300 papers on medical subjects. Home: 195 S. Hill Av., Pasadena, Cal. Address: Pottenger Sanatorium, Monrovia, Cal. Died June 10, 1961; buried Mountain View Cemetery, Altadena, Cal.

POTTER, CHARLES LEWIS, army engr.; b. Lisbon Falls, Me., Jan. 24, 1864; s. Benjamin R. and Susan E. (Smullen) P.; grad. U.S. Mil. Acad., 1886; grad. Engr. Sch. of Application, 1889; m. Mrs. Sophie H. Nichols, Feb. 15, 1905. Commd. 2d lt. 5th Cav., July 1, 1886; transferred to engrs., Feb. 2, 1887; promoted through grades to col., Nov. 27, 1916. Spanish War and Philippine Insurrection, 1898-1900; with river and harbor works, Memphis, 1900-03, Duluth, 1903-06, Puerto Rico, 1907-10, St. Louis, 1910-12, St. Paul, 1912-15, Portland, Ore., 1915-16, Boston, 1916-17; dir. gas service, Washington, 1917-18; in charge 2d San Francisco Engr. Dist., 1918-20; pres. Miss. River Commn., Mar. 19, 1920—. Mason. Died Aug. 6, 1928.

POTTER, HENRY NOEL, research engr.; b. at Rochester, N.Y., Jan. 20, 1869; s. Charles Barton and Sarah Jane (Weaver) P.; B.S., Amherst, 1891; student course of Westinghouse Electric Co., 1892-3; Berlin and Gottingen, Germany, 1894-8; (Sc.D., honoris causa, Amherst, 1905); m. Lilian Heron, of Allegheny, Pa., Oct. 15, 1894. With Westinghouse Electric & Mfg. Co., Pittsburgh, 1891-4; asst. to Prof. Walter Nernst, Gottingen, 1898; with George Westinghouse as spl. engr., 1898-07 (in charge pvt. research lab., 1903-7); engring. expert Sawyer-Mann Electric Co., 1904-7; pvt. work, and gold mining, Raw hide, Nev., 1908; development of electrolytic amalgamation machinery, 1909—; president of Potter Engineering Company, Los Angeles. Brought Nernst Lamp to America; discovered silicon monoxide; has taken out over 100 patents for processes and devices, in U.S. and Europe. Mem. Am. Chem. Soc., Delta Kappa Epsilon (Ahmerst). Club: Chemists (New York). Republican. Address: 7032 Hawthorn Av., Hollywood, Los Angeles CA

POTTER, NATHANIEL, physician; b. Easton, Md., 1770; s. Dr. Zabdiel and Lucy (Bruff) P.; M.D. U. Pa., 1796; m. Miss Ford, 2 children. Physician, Balt. Gen. Dispensary, 1803; prof. theory and practice of medicine Med. Coll. of Md. (now U. Md. Sch. of Medicine), 1807-43; sec. Med. and Chirurgical Faculty of Md., 1801-09; dean faculty physic U. Md., 1812-14; pres. Balt. Med. Soc., 1812. Med. Soc. of Md., 1817; established non-contagiousness of yellow fever. Author: An Essay on the Medicinal and Deleterious Qualities of Arsenic, 1796; Memoir on Contagion, 1818; Some Account of the Rise and Progress of the University of Maryland, 1838; editor Balt. Med. and Philos. Lycaeum, 1811; co-editor Md. Med. and Surg. Jour., 1840-43. Died Balt. Jan. 2, 1843; buried Greenmount Cemetery, Balt.

POTTER, NATHANIEL BOWDITCH, physician; b. Keeseville, N.Y., Dec. 25, 1869; s. George Sabine and Mary Gill (Powell) P.; brother of Mary Knight P. (q.v.); A.B., Coll. City of New York, 1888; A.B., Harvard, 1890, M.D., 1896; m. Mary Sargent, of Brookline, Mass., Jan. 25, 1908. Med. interne Mass. Gen. Hosp., 1896-8; visiting phys. New York City, Ruptured and Crippled, and French hosps.; consulting phys. Manhattan State Hosp. for the Insane at Central Islip; assso. in medicine, Columbia Univ. Mem. N.Y. Co. Med. Soc., New York Pathol. Soc., N.Y. Acad. Sciences, Harvard Med. Soc. Editor of English transl., Sahli's Clinical Diagnosis (with Francis P. Kennicutt, q.v.), 1905; Ortner's Therapeutics, 1908. Address: 48 W. 35th St., New York

POTTER, WILLIAM BANCROFT, engineer; b. at Thomaston, Conn., Feb. 19, 1863; s. of Horace A. and Charlotte S. P.; ed. Thomaston High Sch.; m. Loretta Harward, July 3, 1890; m. 2d, Rose Hubbard, Sept. 23, 1912. Training for engr. in machine shop at Hartford, which included gen. steam engring.; with Thomson-Houston Co., Lynn, Mass., on arc lighting, afterward specializing on apparatus for electric rys.; with this co. when consolidated into the Gen. Electric Co., and has resided at Schenectady. 1894—; became chief engr. ry. engring. dept., Gen. Electric Co., 1895; cons. engr. transportation dept. same co., 1929; retired 1930. Home: Schenectady, N.Y. Died Jan. 15, 1934.

POTTER, WILLIAM BLEECKER, mining engr.; b. Schenectady, N.Y., Mar. 23, 1846; s. Bishop Horatio and Mary Jane (Tomlinson) P.; A.B., Columbia, 1866, A.M., E.M., 1869 (Sc.D., 1904); m. Agnes Kennett Farrar, Nov. 14, 1888. Asst. in geology, Columbia, 1869-71; prof. mining and metallurgy, Washington U., 1871-93; founder, manager St. Louis Sampling & Testing Works. Asst. Mo. Geol. Survey, 1872-74; engr. Pilot Knob Iron Co., 1874-78; metallurgist Vulcan Iron & Steel Works, 1876-78; engr. Iron Mountain Co., 1882-93; mem. bd. mgrs. Mo. Geol. Survey, 1889-93. Home: St. Louis, Mo. Died July 14, 1914.

POTTS, WILLIS JOHN, surgeon; b. Sheboygan, Wis., Mar. 22, 1895; s. Horace and Hannah (Boeyink) P.; A.B., Hope Coll., Holland, Mich., 1918; S.B., U. of Chicago, 1920; M.D., Rush Med. Coll., 1924; interne Presbyn. Hosp., Chicago; Logan fellowship in surg. Rush Med. Coll., 1925-26; post grad. work, Frankfort, Germany, 1930-31; m. Henrietta Neerken, July 7, 1922; children—Willis John, Edward Eugene, Judith Eleanor. Began gen. practice, Oak Park, Ill., 1925; specialized in surgery, 1931-65, ret.; author syndicated newspaper column, 1965-68; professor of emeritus surgery Northwestern U. Med. sch., 1960-68; cons. surgery, Children's Memorial Hospital, Chicago. Sergt. Chem. Warfare Service, 1917-18; 1 year in U.S. and 1 year in France; lt. col. &colonel A.U.S., serving in Southwest Pacific with 25th Evacuation Hosp., 1942-45. Fellow Am. Coll. Surgeons; certified by Am. Bd. of Surgery; mem. Am. Med. Assn., Ill. and Chicago Med. Socs., Chicago Surg. Soc., Western Surg. Soc., Inst. Med. of Chicago, Am. Assn. Thoracic Surgery, Am. Surg. Assn., Central Surg. Assn. Am. Heart Assn. (pres. Chgo. 1960-61). Unitarian. Author: The Surgeon and The Child, 1959; Your Wonderful Baby, 1966. Contbr. to med. jours. Home: Sarasota FL Died May 5, 1968.

POTZGER, JOHN E., educator; b. Presque Isle County, Mich., July 31, 1886; s. Bruno and Augusta (Glaess) P.; certificate Concordia Tchrs. Coll., River Forest, Ill., 1906; student Ithaca Conservatory Music, summer, 1914-15; A.B., Butler U., 1927, M.A., 1931; Ph.D., Ind. U., 1932; m. Margaret Esther Whitney, June 9, 1947. Tchr. Luth. Day Schs., 1906-30; instr. botany Butler U., 1932-37, asst. prof., 1937-40, asso. prof., 1940-48, prof., 1948—, head dept. botany, also editor Butler Botanical Studies, 1953—; field botanist biol. survey group U. Wis., summer 1940; vis. lectr. ecology Purdue Conservation Camp, 1946-52; guest mem. sci. team, dir. research, Mont Tremblant Biol. Sta., P.Q., summers 1952-54. Recipient Eli Lilly Research Labs. grant, 1954, 55. Fellow A.A.A.S. (mem. council, 1955), Ind. Acad. Sci. (research grants, 1945, 46, 54); mem. Am. Philos. Soc. (research grants, 1941, 48, 53), Wis. Acad. Sci., Arts and Letters, Ohio Acad. Sci., Ecol. Soc. Am. (pres. 1953-54), Bot. Soc. Am., Nature Conservancy, Central Assn. Sci. and Mathematics Tchrs. (pres. 1948), Am. Soc. Limnology and Oceanography, Am. Bryological Soc. Lutheran. Editor biology sect. School Science and Mathematics, 1952-54. Conducted pioneer research in palynology (pollen analysis) dealing with post-Pleistocene forest history and climatic changes in eastern N.A., plant sociology studies, forest surveys; research and spl. bull. for President's Com. on Quetico-Superior Internat. Peace Meml. Forest, 1950-53; studies of primeval forests in Ind., based on records of witness trees in original U.S. land survey, 1949-55; bog expdns. by plane to wilderness areas about James Bay and into tundra of No. Quebec, summers 1953-55 (sponsored by Service de Biographie of U. Montreal, Dept. of Fish and Game, Biol. Bur. of P.Q.). Author numerous contbns. to Am. and Canadian sci. and ednl. jours. Home: 2814 N. Park Av., Indpls. 5. Died Sept. 18, 1955; buried Concordia Cemetery, Indpls.

POWELL, CHARLES FRANCIS, officer of engr. corps, U.S.A.; b. Jacksonville, Ill., Aug. 13, 1843; ed. pub. high schs., Milwaukee; m. Margaret, d. James H. Foster, Albany, Ore., May 17, 1883. Served pvt. to sergt. maj. 5th Wis. vols., May 1861, to Sept. 1863; apptd. cadet at West Point by President Lincoln for gallantry on the field of battle; grad., 1867, as 2d lt., corps engr.; promoted successively, 1st lt., capt., maj., lt. col. Has served with U.S. battalion of engrs.; on geodetic and topographic surveys, etc.; engr. in charge Cascades Canal, Ore., and at commencement of great jetty, mouth of Columbia River; sec. Mississippi River Commn.; engr. in charge Missouri River survey and improvement; engr. commr. D.C.; engr. Monongahela River Slack-Water System; engr. defenses and certain harbors. Long Island Sound. Home: New London, Conn. Died 1907.

POWELL, CHARLES UNDERHILL, civil engr., city planner; b. Glen Head, L.I., July 16, 1896; s. George S. and Hannah (Jackson) P.; desc. Thomas Powell, of Bethpage, 1641; C.E., Cornell University, 1898; m. Harriet L. Van Nostrand, October 15, 1902; children—Fred Jackson, Eleanor Frost (Mrs. Paul E. Case), Louise Underhill (Mrs. John F. Burke). Engineer Brooklyn Bridge and Jersey Central Railroad, 1898-99; engineer subway construction, N.Y. City, 1901-02, and for City of New York, 1902-42; planned Borough of Queens, 75,000 acres, 2,500 miles of streets; as chief engr. of Topog. Bureau, 1915-42; introduced Phila. system of house-numbers and street names for the Borough; was in charge of title surveys for acquiring property for streets costing $180,000,000; planned and laid out public ocean beach at Rockaway, 6 miles long, and 1,100 acres of Queens Parks; promoted 30 public improvement laws including Rockaway boardwalk, Conduit Boulevard, Cross-Bay Rd. and street-closing laws; cons. engr. Queen's Planning Commn., 1929-42, planning layout of State Parkway System through Borough of Queens costing over $18,000,000; a founder, 1910, Flushing Nat. Bank, dir., 1910-28. Chmn. New York World's Fair Zoning Com.; mem. com. on basis improvements, New York World's Fair 1939, planned and mapped land acquisitions for improvements costing 80 million dollars in and leading to the Fair. Mem. Com. of 5, 1909-20, promoting N.Y. State licensing of civil engrs. and surveyors. Chmn. Highway and Traffic Com. of Queens until 1942. Trustee Queens Company Savings Bank; vice president Flushing Cemetery Assn. Mem. Board of Examiners for City Surveyors, New York. Mem. Flushing Hist. Soc.; former pres. Upper Flushing Assn., Municipal Engineers City of N.Y.; mem. Am. Soc. C.E., Farmers' and Taxpayers' Assn. of Boro of Queens (secretary); member Municipal Engineers of New York City. Trustee Flushing Meeting Society of Friends. Club: Fireside (Flushing, N.Y.). Wrote: Private and Family Cemeteries of Borough of Queens, Paving Primer, Erosion of Rockaway, Graphic History of Queens Borough, City N.Y., The Quakers in Flushing, 1657-1937. American and Canadian high jump champion, 1896, and Intercollegiate champion, 1898. Home: 43-23 165th St., Flushing, N.Y.; Stony Creek, Warren Co., N.Y. and Delray Beach, Fla. Died May 26, 1956; buried Flushing (N.Y.) Cemetery.

POWELL, FREDERICK, mining engr.; b. Coxsackie, N.Y., Jan. 4, 1859; s. Wheeler and Emeline (Mosher) P.; A.B., Coll. City of New York, 1880; E.M., Sch. of Mines (Columbia), 1883; m. Julia Reed, of South Carolina, 1888. Draftsman and assayer until 1885; mgr. Denbigh Mining Co., Colo., 1886-87; engring. work, 1888-93; consulting engr. Charlotte Mineral & Mining Co., Wash., 1894; mgr. Yorkville Mining Co., 1895; mgr. Morton Island Dredging Co., Ida., 1896-97; consulting engr., Hammond Mfg. Co., Portland, Ore., 1898-1903, Ladd Metals Co., 1904-05; now consulting engr. Seattle Constrn. & Dry Dock Co. and in gen. mining practice. Episcopalian. Mem. Am. Inst. Mining Engrs., Oregon Soc. Engrs., Pacific Northwest Soc. Engrs., Delta Beta Phi. Address: Seattle, Wash.

POWELL, JOHN WESLEY, naturalist; b. Mt. Morris, N.Y., Mar. 24, 1834; s. of Methodist minister; attended schools in Ohio, Wis., and Ill., 2 yrs. each at Oberlin and Wheaton (Ill.) colls.; grad. Ill. Wesleyan, A.M., Ph.D. (LL.D. Columbian, 1882, Harvard, 1886, Ill. Coll., 1889; Ph.D., Heidelberg, 1886); m. Emma Dean, 1861. Served through Civil war in 2d Ill. arty., reaching rank of maj., losing right arm at Shiloh. Explored Grand Cañon of the Colorado River, 1869. Apptd. dir. U.S. Bureau of Ethnology, 1879, and of U.S. Geol. Survey, 1880; resigned latter, 1894, retaining former. Author: Explorations of the Colorado River; Report on Geology of the Uinta Mountains; Report on Arid Regions of United States; Introduction to the Study of Indian Languages; Studies in Sociology; Cañons of the Colorado; etc. Home: Washington, D.C. Died 1902.

POWELL, WILLIAM M., medical author; b. Phila., Feb. 14, 1862; s. G. Washington and Annie E. P.; grad. P.E. Acad., Phila., 1880; M.D., U. of Pa., 1884; m. Florence K. Stokes, Apr. 15, 1886. Formerly instr. physical diagnosis and sr. phys. to clinic for diseases of children, U. of Pa.; chief med. clinic, Phila. Polyclinic; attending phys. Mercer Memorial House for Invalid Women, and Children's Seashore House for Invalid Children, Atlantic City, N.J. Mem. Phila. Path. Soc., Am. Acad. Medicine, Atlan-Phila. Med. Club. Author: Physiological Action of Drugs, 1889; Essential of Diseases of Children, 1890; Medical Pocket Formulary, 1891. Asso. editor Sajous Annual of the Medical Sciences. Address: 122 W. Miner St., West Chester, Pa.

POWER, FREDERICK BELDING, chemist; b. Hudson, N.Y., Mar. 4, 1853; s. Thomas and Caroline P. (Belding) P.; grad. Phila. Coll. Pharmacy, 1874; Ph.D., U. of Strassburg, 1880; asst. to prof. of materia medica there, 1879-80; LL.D., U. of Wis., 1908; m. Mary Van Loan Meigs, Dec. 27, 1883 (died 1894); children—Mrs. Annie Louise Heimké, Donald Meigs. Prof. analytical chemistry, Phila. Coll. Pharmacy, 1881-83; prof. pharmacy and materia medica, U. of Wis., 1883-92; dir. labs. of Fritsche Bros., 1892-96, Wellcome Chem. Research Laboratories, London, Eng., 1896-1914; in charge Phytochem. Lab., Bur. of Chemistry, Washington, 1916—. Awarded Ebert prize, Am. Pharm. Assn., 1877, 1902, 06; gold medal, St. Louis Expn., 1904; silver medal, Liège, 1905; gold medal and diploma of honor, Milan, 1906; gold medal, Franco-British Exhbn., 1908; grand prize, Brussels, 1910; gold medal and diploma of honor, Turin, 1911; Hanbury gold medal, 1913. Gold medal presented by Henry S. Wellcome, London, in 1914, for chemical research; awarded the Flueckiger gold medal, 1922. Member com. of revision U.S. Pharmacopoeia, 1890; U.S. del. Internat. Congress for Unification of the Formulae of Potent Medicaments, Brussels, 1902. Editor: (with Dr. Fred Hoffman) Manual of Chemical Analysis, 1883. Died Mar. 26, 1927.

POWERS, EDWIN B(OOTH), zoologist; b. Ellis Co., Tex., Aug. 6, 1880; s. William Wilson and Evaline Crocia (Woods) P.; A.B., Trinity U., Waxahachie, Tex., 1906; M.S., U. of Chicago, 1913; Ph.D., U. of Ill., 1918; student, Cambridge U., Eng., 1922; m. Pauline Watkins, June 9, 1918; children—Edwine Watkins, Wilson Watkins, M.D. Instr. and prof. in biology, Trinity U., 1908-15; research asst. Puget Sound Biol. Sta., U. of Wash., summer, 1914, asst. in zoology, summer, 1918, prof. zoology, summers, 1919, 21, 22, 24, 27; asst. prof. zoology, Colo. Coll., 1918-19; traveled and studied Imperial Inst. (London), Danish Biol. Sta., Naples Biol. Sta., 1919-20; instr. in zoology, U. of Neb., 1920-22; asso. prof. anatomy and embryology, U. of Tenn. Med. Coll., Memphis, Tenn., 1922-23; prof. zoology and acting head of dept., U. of Tenn., Knoxville, Tenn., 1923-24, head of dept. zoology and entomology since 1941; at Marine Biol. Lab., Woods Hole, Mass., summer 1920; prof. limnology, Mt. Lake Biol. Sta., U. of Va., summer 1934; prof. physiology Franz Theodore Stone Lab., Put-in-Bay, Ohio State U., summers 1935 and 1936; stream pollution adv. to N.C. Pulp Co., 1940-41; at Solomon Island, Md. State Lab., 1945-46. Mem. A.A.A.S., Zool. Soc. America, Ecol. Soc. America (pres. 1933-34), Limnol. Soc. America, Am. Fish Soc., Entomol. Soc. America, Tenn. Acad. Science, Sigma Xi. Democrat. Presbyterian. Asso. editor of Ecology, 1925-32, Ecological Monographs, 1935-39. Contbr. of more than 65 sci. papers and monographs on salmon migration, toxicities, physiology of respiration of fishes, etc. Home: 133 E. Hillvale Drive. Office: University of Tennessee, Knoxville, Tenn. Died Aug. 25, 1949; buried Highland Memorial Cemetary, Knoxville, Tenn.

POWERS, GROVER FRANCIS, pediatrician; b. Colfax, Ind., Aug. 12, 1887; s. Francis William and Elizabeth Catherine (Shobe) P.; B.S., Purdue U., 1908, Sc.D., 1935; M.D., Johns Hopkins U., 1913; M.A., Yale U., 1927; honorary Sc.D., Indiana University, 1949; married Beatrice Farnsworth, Aug. 21, 1916; 1 son, Ross Farnsworth. Laboratory assistant in biology, Purdue University, 1908-09; interne and assistant resident in pediatric Johns Hopkins Hospital, Baltimore, 1913-16, physician in charge pediatrics, out-patient department, 1916-21; instructor and asso. in clin. pediatrics, Johns Hopkins U., 1916-21; med. dir. Babies Milk Fund Assn., Baltimore, 1916-21; asst. later asso. prof. pediatrics, Yale U., 1921-27, prof. pediatrics, 1927-52, prof. emeritus, 1952-68; cons. pediatrician Grace-New Haven Community Hosp., pediatrician in chief Henry Ford Hosp., Detroit, 1927; New Haven Hosp. from 1927; former consultant Mental Hygiene Division, USPHS; hon. chmn. sci. research adv. bd. Nat. Assn. of Retarded Children. Trustee of the Southbury Training School; mem. of editorial board. Pediatrics. Recipient Borden Award, Am. Acad. Pediatrics, 1947, John Howland award Am. Pediatric Soc., 1953; Jos. P. Kennedy Jr. award; 2d International award. Certified by Am. Bd. Pediatrics. Fellow A.M.A., Am. Acad. Pediatrics; mem. Am. Pediatric Soc. (p. pres.), Soc. for Pediatric Rsrch., Am. Soc. for Clin. Investigation, Inter-urban Clin. Club, National Association for Retarded Children (chmn. sci. research adv. bd.), Brit. Pediatric Soc. (corr.), Sigma Xi, Alpha Omega Alpha. Episcopalian. Club. Faculty (new Haven). Home: New Haven CT Died Apr. 18, 1968.

POWERS, LEGRAND, statistician; b. Preston, N.Y., 1847; s. Wesley and Electa (Clark) P.; student Tufts Coll., 1868-70, Litt.D., 1900; A.B., State U. Ia., 1872; m. Amanda Kinney, 1873; children—Mrs. Irma Louise Koch, Florence (dec.), Lorin Charles, Mrs. Hazel Lewis. Engaged in ministry, 1874-90; commr. labor, Minn., 1891-99; chief statistician of census in charge of agr., 1899-1914. Republican. Lectr. statistics U. Wis., 1917. Author; Minnesota Bureau of Labor Biennial Reports, 1890-99; Farmer Hayseed (a reply to Coin's Financial School); vols. V and VI, Twelfth Census of the United States; census report on wealth, debt. and taxation and on official statistics cities, 1902 17. Contbr. to newspapers and to Am. and English revs. and financial and statis. jours. Home: 3331 18th St. N.W., Washington. Died 1933.

POWERS, SAMUEL RALPH, univ. prof.; b. Petersburg, Ill., May 16, 1887; s. John William and Nancy Temperance (Erwin) P.; grad. Ill. Normal U., 1910; B.A., Illinois U., 1912; M.A., Minn. U., 1919, Ph.D., 1923; m. Eda May Olds, Oct. 10, 1910 (dec. Feb. 1972); children—Philip Nathan, Merrill E., Samuel Ralph, Karol R. (dec.). Teacher rural schs. Menard County, Ill., 1905-08; Garfield High, Terre Haute, Ind., 1912-16; Univ. High Sch., U. of Minn., 1916-20; prof. edn., U. of Ark., 1920-21; instr. edn., U. of Minn., 1921-23; asso. prof. natural sciences, Teachers College, Columbia U., 1923, prof., 1927-52, emeritus, 1952-70, head dept. teaching of natural scis., 1928-52; edn. cons. Bur. of Medicine, U.S.N., 1952-53; visiting prof. Abbassia Men's Tchr. College, 1954-55, St. Paul's Coll., Lawrenceville, Va., 1959-62; specialist sci. adult edn. sect. Office of Edn., 1960. U.S. Educational Foundation in Egypt., 1954-55; adminstr. ofcr. Tchrs. Coll. Bur. Ednl. Rsrch. in Science (supported by Gen. Education Board), 1935-43. Expert Industrial Personnel Division, Army Service Forces, War Dept., 1942-44. Presented with Outstanding Achievement Award, U. of Minn., 1951; Fulbright Award, visiting prof., Cairo, Egypt 1954-55. Mem. Assn. for Edn. Sci. Teachers (hon. member), National Sci. Tchrs. Assn. (commn. edn. basic scis., 1957-58), Nat. Soc. Study Edn. (chmn. com. sci. teaching, 1932), Am. Ednl. Research Assn. (chmn. com. research teaching sci. and math., 1941-42, 1947-48), Nat. Assn. Research in Science Teaching (pres. 1938), Nat. Council Sci. Teachers (chmn. com. teacher edn., 1938-42), N.E.A., A.A.A.S. (fellow), Phi Delta Kappa, Tau Kappa Epsilon. Author of research papers in the teaching of natural sciences, and numerous articles in educational jours. Co-author of textbooks for high schs. and colleges. Editor: Science in Modern Living Series, 1935-42; mem. editorial bd. World Book Ency., 1936-52; editor: Science Education mag., 1944-45. Home: Haworth NJ Died Aug. 26, 1970; buried Rosehill Cemetery, Petersburg IL

POWERS, SIDNEY, geologist; b. Troy, N.Y., Sept. 10, 1890; s. Albert W. and Tillie (Page) P.; A.B., Williams Coll., 1911; M.S., Mass. Inst. Tech., 1913; Sheldon traveling fellow to Hawaiian Island, Harvard, 1915, A.M., Ph.D., 1915, research fellow, 1915-16; m. Dorothy Edwards Powers, Sept. 8, 1917; children—Deborah, Eleanor. Div. geologist Tex. Co., 1916-17; asst. geologist U.S. Geol. Survey, 1917-18; geol. officer, A.E.F., U.S.A., 1918-19; chief goelogist Amerada Petroleum Corp., 1919-26, consulting geologist, 1926—. Fellow Geol. Soc. America (councilor 1931-33). Home: Tulsa, Okla. Died 1932.

POYNTER, CHARLES WILLIAM MCCORKLE, (point'er), anatomist, anthropologist; b. Eureka, Ill., July 16, 1875; s. William Amos and Maria Josephine (McCorkle) P.; B.S., U. Neb., 1898, M.D., 1902; grad. study Vienna, Austria, 1907-08, Harvard, 1912, 14; m. Clara Eliza Axtell, Sept. 3, 1907; 1 dau., Helen Josephine. Instr. in anatomy U. Neb., 1903-10, prof., 1910—, charge dept., 1912-14, head prof., 1914—, apptd. acting dean Coll. of Medicine, 1929, dean, 1930-46, dean emeritus, 1946—. Trustee Omaha Child Savings Inst.; mem. exec. com., bd. Trustees Children's Meml. Hosp., Omaha. Fellow A.A.A.S. (sec. med. sect. 1930-33); mem. Am. Assn. Med. Colls. (v.p. 1934, exec. com. 1935, pres. 1941-44, Am. Assn. Anatomists, Am. Assn. Anthropologists, British Assn. Anatomists, Sigma Xi, Alpha Omega Alpha, Phi Rho Sigma. Republican. Episcopalian. Mason. Writer of papers on growth phenomenon, blood vessels and lymphatics. Home: 625 S. 37th St., Omaha, Neb. Died Oct. 25, 1950.

PRATT, FREDERICK HAVEN, physiologist; b. Worcester, Mass., July 19, 1873; s. Frederick Sumner and Sarah M. (Hillard) P.; student Fish and Dalzell Prep. schools, 1887-92; A.B., Harvard, 1896, A.M., 1898, M.D., 1906; student U. of Göttingen, 1899; m. Margery Wilerd Davis, June 12, 1912; children—Frederick Sumner, Margery Willard (Mrs. James C. Koren), Rogert Conant, Elisabeth Haven (Mrs. George Cheely), Stephen Davis. Instructor in physiology, Wellesley Coll., 1909-12; prof. of physiology, Univ. of Buffalo, 1912-19; hon. fellow in biology, Clark U., 1919-20; teaching fellow in physiology, Harvard, 1920-21; prof. of physiology, Boston U., 1921-42, emeritus prof. since 1942. Hon. mem. Mass. Med. Soc. Fellow Am. Acad. Arts and Sciences (librarian 1941-48); mem. Am. Physiol. Soc., Soc. Exptl. Biology and Medicine, Am. Antiquarian Soc., Marine Biol. Lab., Woods Hole, Bermuda Biol. Sta. Author technical papers on muscle and heart physiology; biographical studies. Home: 105 Hundreds Rd., Wellesley Hills, Mass. Died July 11, 1958; buried Worcester, Mass.

PRATT, GEORGE K., psychiatrist; b. Detroit, Mich., Dec. 17, 1891; s. George Oscar (M.D.) and Alice Elizabeth (Beedzler) P.; M.D., Detroit Coll. Medicine and Surgery, 1915; grad. study, State Psychopathic Hosp., U. of Mich., 1917; m. Neva Emma MacArthur, Dec. 30, 1916; children—Shirley Jane (Mrs. Carleton W. Clark), Rodney George, Douglas MacArthur. Asst. physician Oak Grove Hosp., Flint, Mich., 1915-20; capt. U.S. Army Medical Corps, Neuro-Psychiatric Div., 1917-19; in private practice and asst. health officer, Flint, 1920-21; med. dir. Mass. Soc. for Mental Hygiene, 1921-25; also in out-patient dept. Boston Psychopathic Hosp., 1921-25; lecturer in mental hygiene, Smith Coll., 1923-25; asst. med. dir. Nat. Com. for Mental Hygiene, New York, 1925-33; med. dir. Mental Hygiene Com. N.Y., State Charities Aid Assn., 1930-35, and Conn. Society for Mental Hygiene, 1936-42; consultant mental hygiene, U. of Vt., 1925-29; grad. study psychoanalytic therapy, Europe, 1926; mem. faculty New Sch. for Social Research, N.Y. City, 1930-33, and Brooklyn Inst. Arts and Sciences; consultant in psychiatry, St. Christopher's School, Dobbs Ferry, N.Y., 1932-36 and since 1942; assistant clinical professor of psychiatry and mental hygiene,

School of Medicine, Yale, 1936-43; psychiatric director Stamford Child Guidance Service, also Bridgeport Mental Hygiene Clinic, 1936-47; instr. Mental Hygiene, New Haven State Teachers Coll., 1939-42. Nat. chmn. mental hygiene, Congress of Parents and Teachers, 1926-34; chmn. tech. advisory com. Emergency Work Bur., N.Y. City, 1933. Consultant in psychiatry Med. Adv. Bd. No. 5, Fairfield County, Selective Service System; psychiatric examiner, Induction Center, New Haven, 1943-46; associate neuro-psychiatrist, Bridgeport Hospital; medical director Hall-Brooke Sanitarium, 1948-54. Diplomate Am. Board of Psychiatry and Neurology. Fellow American Psychiatric Association, also Royal Medico-Psychological Assn. Great Britain, Connecticut State and Fairfield County med. socs. Nu Sigma Nu. Author: Your Mind and You, 1924; Why Men Fail (with others), 1928; Our Neurotic Age (with others), 1932; Morale; the Mental Hygiene of Unemployment, 1933; Three Family Narratives, 1935; Soldier to Civilian, 1944. Contbr. tech. articles. Home: Woods Grove, Westport, Conn. Office: 881 Lafayette St., Bridgeport 4, Conn. Died Dec. 11, 1957; buried Westport, Conn.

PRATT, HENRY SHERRING, zoölogist; b. Toledo, O., Aug. 18, 1859; s. Charles and Catherine (Sherring) P.; A.B., U. of Mich., 1882; admitted to Ohio bar, 1885; Ph.D., Leipzig, 1892; univs. of Freiburg, Geneva, and Harvard, 1888-93; Innsbruck, 1902-03; Graz, 1910-11; m. Agnes Woodbury Gray, Sept. 1, 1894; 1 dau., Anna. Instr. biology, Haverford Coll., 1893-98, asso. prof. 1898-1901, prof., 1901-29, (emeritus). Instr. comparative anatomy, Cold Spring Harbor Biol. Lab., 1896-1926. Mem. Commn. for Relief in Belgium, 1916-17. Pres. Cambridge Entomol. Club, 1896; mem. Am. Soc. Naturalists, Am. Soc. Zoologists (sec. and treas. Eastern br., 1905-06); fellow A.A.A.S. Knight Order of the Crown (Belgium). Author: Invertebrate Zoölogy, 1902; Vertebrate Zoölogy, 1906, 2d edit., 1925, 3d edit., 1937; Manual of Common Invertebrates, 1916, revised edit., 1935; Manual of Vertebrates of the U.S., 1923, 2d edit., 1935; A Course in General Zoölogy, 1927; A Course in General Biology, 1927; General Biology—an Introductory Study, 1931; also various zoöl. papers. Home: Haverford, Pa. Died Oct. 6, 1946.

PRATT, JAMES ALFRED, mechanical engr.; b. Chelsea, Mass., Apr. 6, 1873; s. James Woodman and Clara (Noble) P.; ed. pub. schs., Providence, R.I.; studied mech. engring. as cadet engr. under G. W. Bartlett, in shops, Providence; pedagogy, New York U., 1908; m. Edith I. Harris, of Providence, Aug. 4, 1902. Instr. Sockanosset Sch. and asst. to consulting engr., 1901-6; instr. Pratt Inst., Brooklyn, and acting head, machine dept., 1907-8; instr., now dir. Williamson Free Sch. Mech. Trades. Methodist. Mem. Soc. Promotion Engring. Edn., Am. Soc. Mech. Engrs., etc. Author: Materials and Construction, 1912. Address: Williamson School P.O., PA

PRATT, JOSEPH HYDE, geologist, engr.; b. Hartford, Conn., Feb. 3, 1870; s. James C. and Jennie A. (Peck) P.; Ph.B., Sheffield Scientific Sch. (Yale), 1893, Ph.D., 1896; hon. M.A., 1923; m. Mary Discus Bayley, Apr. 5, 1899; 1 son, Joseph Hyde; m. 2d, Harriet White Peters, Aug. 29, 1930. Instr. mineralogy, Yale, 1895-97; summer, Harvard, 1895; lecturer mineralogy, U. of N.C., 1898-1901; state mineralogist of N.C., 1897-1906; state geologist, 1906-24; asst. field geologist, U.S. Geol. Survey, from 1899; prof. econ. geology, U. of N.C., 1904-25; chief Dept. Mines and Metallurgy, Jamestown Exposition, 1907. Member Internat. Jury of Awards, St. Louis Expn., 1904; spl. expert 12th U.S. Census on asbestos, etc.; dir. briquetting expts., U.S. Geol. Coal Testing Plant, St. Louis, 1904-05. Awarded diploma and gold medal, Pan-Am. Expn., 1901, for exhibit N.C. gems and gem minerals, etc.; diplomas, gold medal, and silver medals for same, Charleston Expn., 1902. Lt.-col. N.C.N.G. (engr. dept.). Pres. Am. Peat Soc., 1907-09, Southern Appalachian Good Roads Assn., 1909-15; sec. N.C. Drainage Assn., 1908-11 and 1912-23 (pres. 1911); sec. N.C. Fisheries Assn., 1911-19, N.C. Good Roads Assn., 1908-20, N.C. State Highway Commn., 1915-19, N.C. Lit. and Hist. Soc., N.C. Forestry Assn. (pres. 1925-27; chmn. exec. com., 1927-40), Am. Assn. State Highway Officials, 1914-20; pres. Nat. Assn. Shell Fish Commrs., 1912-13; dir. Am. Assn. Highway Improvement, Nat. Drainage Cong.; fellow Geol. Soc. America, Am. Chem. Soc., A.A.A.S., Nat. Geog. Soc., Mineralogical Soc. of America, Am. Geog. Soc.; mem. Am. Soc. Civil Engrs., Am. Inst. Mining Engrs., Mining and Metall. Soc. America, Sigma Xi, N.Y. Acad. Sciences, N.C. Acad. Science, Am. Forestry Assn. (dir. 1922-29 and since 1934), Nat. Parks Assn. (dir. since 1936), Wilderness Soc., Am. Road Builders Assn., Am. Fisheries Soc., Mil. Engineers Soc. (dir. since 1926); v.p. N.C. Agrl. Soc., 1921-28; pres. Western North Carolina, Inc., 1924-25; pres. Southern Forestry Congress, 1916-19 (chmn. exec. com., 1919-25; exec. sec., 1928-40); pres. Southern Appalachian Power Conf., 1922 (chmn. exec. com., 1923-40); pres. N.C. Conf. for Social Service, 1924, dir. since 1925; pres. N.C. Soc. for Preservation of Antiquities since 1940; hon. mem. Appalachian Engring. Soc.; apptd. by sec. of agr. mem. Appalachian Forest Research Council (chmn. exec. com. since 1925); chmn. Chapel Hill Chapter Am. Red Cross; pres. N.C. Symphony Soc. since 1932; pres. Battle Park Assn.; mem. advisory com. President Hoover's Timber Conservation Board; chmn. Central Welfare Com., Orange County; chmn. Chapel Hill Health and Welfare Com. since 1940; pres. Chapel Hill Pub. Recreation Commn. since 1940; chmn. Chapel Hill Negro Community Center Assn. since 1940; mem. Chapel Hill City Planning Board since 1941. Received annual award as Chapel Hill's most valuable citizen, 1940. Clubs: Cosmos (Washington, D.C.); Washington Philatelic Soc., Chapel Hill (North Carolina) Country. Contbr. many articles to scientific mags., domestic and foreign, on mineral., geol. and chem. subjects, since 1895. Publisher War Diary of Col. Joseph Hyde Pratt, 1928. Member State Council Defense. Major, Engr. R.C., 1917, and assigned to 105th Regt. Engr.; lt. col., Nov. 11, 1917; col., Oct. 9, 1918; with regt. at Camp Sevier, Greenville, S.C.; ordered to France, May 1918; comdr. of regt. and div. engr., 30th Div., A.E.F., July 1918-May 1919; served 6 mos. at the front in Ypres sector, Flanders and Belgium, and in Somme offensive in breaking the Hindenburg line; former col. Engr. R.C., U.S. Army. Awarded D.S.M. State engr. C.W.A. for N.C., Nov. 1933-Feb. 1934; senior regional engr. C.W.A. and F.E.R.A., 1934-35; senior regional engr. Resettlement Adminstrn., 1935; research engr. Works Progress Adminstrn., 1936, 37; engr. consultant, U.S. Geol. Survey, 1938, senior engr., consultant, 1939, 40. Home: Chapel Hill, N.C. Died June 2, 1942.

PRATT, THOMAS WILLIS, civil engr., inventor; b. Boston, July 4, 1812; s. Caleb and Sally (Willes or Willis) P.; attended Rensselaer Poly. Inst.; m. Sarah Bradford, 1835, 2 children. Engring. asst. with U.S. Govt. on constrn. dry docks, Charleston, S.C., also Norfolk, Va., 1830; division engr. on constrn. of Norwich & Worcester Ry. and supt. of road, 1835; engr. and supt. Providence & Worcester Ry., 1845-47, Hartford & New Haven Ry., 1847-50; chief engr. Middletown Branch R.R.; chief engr., supt. N.Y. & Boston R.R.; chief engr., supt. Conway & Great Falls br. Eastern Ry., 1871-75; built number of important bridges, largest over Merrimac River at Newburyport, Mass.; invented Pratt Truss (bridge and roof truss), patented 1844; patented improved type of combined timber and steel truss, 1873; invented new method of hull constrn. and proplusion for ships, 1875. Died Boston, July 10, 1875.

PREBLE, EDWARD A., naturalist; b. Somerville, Mass., June 11, 1871; s. Edward Perkins and Marcia (Alexander) P.; ed. high sch., Woburn, Mass., 1886-89; m. Eva A. Lynham, Dec. 29, 1896; children—Dorothy Marcia (dec.), Marjorie Elizabeth, Evelyn Morgan. With Biol. Survey, U.S. Dept. Agr., 1892-1935. Has specialized in geog. distbn., life habits, and ecology of birds, mammals and plants. Established wild life sanctuary and library, Ossipee, N.H. Member Am. Ornithologists Union, Biological Soc. Washington, Am. Soc. Mammalogist, Am. Soc. Ichthyologists and Herpetologists, etc. Associate editor Nature Mag., Washington. Republican. Author: A Biological Investigation of the Hudson Bay Region (U.S. Govt. publ.), 1902, A Biological Investigation of the Athabaska-Mackenzie Region, 1908; The Fur Seals and other life of the Pribilof Islands, Alaska, in 1914 (in collaboration), 1915. Birds and Mammals of the Pribilof Islands, Alaska (in collaboration), 1923. Contbr. many sci. and popular articles. Home: 3027 Newark St., Washington. Died Oct. 4, 1957; buried Ossipee, N.H.

PRENTICE, GEORGE GORDON, mfr.; b. Oberlin, O., Oct. 23, 1865; s. Harvey Monroe and Jennie Elizabeth (Hillyer) P.; ed. pub. and night schs., N.Y. City; m. Janet Eleanor Stirling, Dec. 3, 1890; children—George Gordon, Stirling Garvin (dec.), Helen Sheldon (wife of Capt. John C. Glithero), Janet Elizabeth (wife of Rev. Heinrich W. Falk), Hillyer. With Francis H. Richards Engring. Co., Cleveland, O. (assisted in bldg. 1st automatic machine for gumming, printing and folding envelopes, 1883; with Pratt & Whitney Co., Hartford, Conn., 1884-85; supt. and mgr. Yost Writing Machine Co., Bridgeport, Conn., 1886-90; with Garvin Machine Co., N.Y. City, 1891-95; organizer, 1896, owner and pres. until retirement, 1911, George G. Prentice & Co., automatic turret machinery; mem. reorgn. com. C.,R.I.&P. R.R., 1915; owner 2000-acre Prentice Ranch. Mem. Sch. Bd., New Haven, Conn., 1912-15. Rep. State of Conn. at Panama Pacific Expn., San Francisco, Calif., 1915. Inventor and patentee typewriter improvements, 1886-90; designed and built typewriter for printing on bound ledgers, 1892; improved and built Doremus automatic stamp cancelling machines, 1893; designed, built Prentice automatic multiple spindle turret (toolroom machine), 1898; designed and built steam turbine engine, 1899. Awarded gold medal by Belgium, 1905. Republican. Episcopalian. Mason. Home: San Diego, Calif. Died Dec. 5, 1941.

PRENTISS, HENRY JAMES, anatomist; b. Flushing, N.Y., July 22, 1867; s. Andrew Morgan and Henrietta (Driggs) P.; M.E., Stevens Inst. Tech., 1889; M.D., Bellevue Hosp. Med. Coll., 1898; m. Lué Bradley, Apr. 18, 1895. Prosector, demonstrator and prof. of practical anatomy, Univ. and Bellevue Hosp. Med. Coll., 1898-1904; prof. anatomy, histology and embryology, State U. of Iowa, 1904—, also head of dept. and dir. labs. histology and embryology. Warden of Trinity Ch. Republican. Episcopalian. Mason. Home: Iowa City, Ia. Died May 17, 1931.

PRESCOTT, ALBERT BENJAMIN, chemist; b. Hastings, N.Y., Dec. 12, 1832; s. Benjamin and Experience (Huntley) P.; ed. Univ. of Mich.; grad., M.D., 1864 (Ph.D., 1886, LL.D., 1896, Univ. of Mich.; LL.D., Northwestern, 1903); m. Abigail Freeburn, Dec. 25, 1866. Asst. surgeon, U.S.V., 1864-65; in Univ. of Mich., asst. prof. chemistry, 1865; prof. organic and applied chemistry, 1870; dean school of pharmacy, 1876—; dir. chem. laboratory, 1884—. Pres. A.A.A.S., 1891; fellow Chem. Soc., London, 1876. Author: Qualitative Chemical Analysis, 1874; First Book of Qualitative Chemistry, 1879. Home: Ann Arbor, Mich. Died 1905.

PRESCOTT, GEORGE BARTLETT, telegraph engr.; b. Kingston, N.H., Sept. 16, 1830; s. Mark Hollis and Priscilla (Bartlett) P.; m. Eliza Curtis Parsons, Dec. 9, 1857, 1 dau., Mrs. Philip V.R. Van Wyck, Jr. Joined N.Y. & New Eng. Telegraph Co., 1850, in Boston, 1850-52; mgr. N.Y. & Boston (or Comml.) Telegraph Co., Springfield, Mass., 1852; mgr. submarine telegraph cos. along Eastern coast; gen. mgr. Am. Telegraph Co., 1859, supt. all lines in Eastern N.Y., Conn., Vt., 1861; apptd. electrician Western Union Telegraph Co., 1866; an original mem. bd. dirs. Am. Speaking Telephone Co.; v.p., dir. Gold & Stock Telegraph Co., 1878-81. Author: History, Theory, and the Practice of the Electric Telegraph, 1860; Electricity and the Electric Telegraph, 1877; The Speaking Telephone, 1878; Dynamo-Electricity, 1884; Bell's Electric Speaking Telephone: Its Invention, Construction, Application, Modification, and History, 1884; The Electric Telephone, 1890. Died N.Y.C., Jan. 18, 1894.

PRESCOTT, OLIVER, physician; b. Groton, Mass., Apr. 27, 1731; s. Benjamin and Abigail (Oliver) P.; grad. Harvard, 1750, M.D. (hon.), 1791; studied medicine under Dr. Ebenezer Robie; m. Lydia Baldwin, Feb. 19, 1756. Commd. brig. gen. Middlesex County (Mass.) Militia, 1775, maj. gen. Mass. Militia, 1778; mem. Mass. Com. of Correspondence, mem. supreme exec. council, 1777-80; judge of probate Middlesex, 1799-1804; trustee, 1st pres. bd. Groton Acad.; an original incorporator Mass. Med. Soc.; mem. N.H. Med. Soc.; pres. Middlesex Med. Soc., also Western Soc. of Middlesex Husbandmen; fellow Am. Acad. Arts and Scis., 1780. Died Groton, Nov. 17, 1804.

PRESCOTT, SAMUEL CATE, bacteriologist; b. South Hampton, N.H., Apr. 5, 1872; s. Samuel M. and Mary E. (Cate) P.; S.B., Mass. Inst. Tech., 1894; postgrad. study Europe; Sc.D. (hon.), Bates Coll., 1923, Lehigh U., 1947; m. Alice Durgin Chase, June 30, 1910; children—Robert Sedgwick, Samuel Chase, Eleanor. With Mass. Inst. Tech., 1895—, successively asst. in biology, instr., asst. prof. indsl. biology and bacteriology, asso. prof., prof. indsl. microbiology, 1914-42, head dept. biology and pub. health, 1922-42, dean sch. sci., 1932-42, prof. emeritus, 1942—, hon. lectr., 1942-43; instr. bacteriology Simmons Coll., 1902-09; dir. Boston Bio-Chem. Lab., 1904-21, research lab. United Fruit Co., Port Limon, Costa Rica, 1914-17; chief div. dehydration Bur. Chemistry, Washington, 1918-19; chmn. bd. Refrigeration Research Found., 1943—; pres. Benjamin Chase Co., DerryVille, N.H. Served as maj. San. Corps, U.S. Army, 1919, lt. col. to col. O.R.C., 1920-25, ret. 1936. Recipient Appert Medal, 1943. Fellow A.A.A.S., Am. Acad. Arts and Scis.; mem. Am. Chem. Soc., Soc. Am. Bacteriologists (pres. 1919), Am. Pub. Health Assn., Mass. Inst. Tech. Alumni Assn. (pres. 1927-28), Inst. Food Technologists (pres. 1939-41). Clubs: Harvard Travellers, Brookline Thursday. Joint author: Science and Experiment in Canning Industry, 1903; Elements of Water Bacteriology, 1904, Sanitary Science and Public Health, 1935; Food Technology, 1937; Industrial Microbiology, 1940. Translator: Enzymes and Their Application (from French of Jean Effront), 1902; Biochemical Catalysts (from Effront), 1917. Contbr. Am. Cyclopaedia of Agr.; also tech. jours., on bacteriology, food tech. and indsl. biology. Editor Food Research, 1936—. Died Mar. 1962.

PRESSEY, HENRY ALBERT, engineer; b. Lewiston, Me., Sept. 24, 1873; s. Warren E. and Annie R. (Irish) P.; B.S., Columbian (now George Washington) U., 1893, Ph.D., 1906; B.S., Mass. Inst. Tech., 1896; m. Perley Fitch, of Washingtonville, Orange Co., N.Y., Oct. 18, 1899; children—Henry Albert, Warren Fitch. Engr. on Met. Water Works, Boston, 1897; engr. with U.S. War Dept., 1898; hydrographer U.S. Geol. Survey and prof. civil engring., Columbian U., from 1899; in pvt. practice since 1903; v.p. Spencer Water Company; also director of the Southern Pub. Service Corpn., Oxford Water & Electric Co., Graham Water & Electric Co., Morgantown Water Co. Consulting engr. N.Y. State Water Supply Commn., 1909. Dir. Am. Forestry Assn.; mem. Am. Soc. C.E., American Institute of Electrical Engineers, Washington Society Engineers. Comd. Engr. Co. D.C. N.G. Presbyterian. Clubs: University, Washington Country. Author: Hydrography of Southern Appalacian Region, Parts I and II, 1902; Water Powers of the State of Maine, 1902; Flow of Rivers in the Vicinity of the City of New York, 1903; Hydrography of Cecil County, Md., 1903. Home: Mt. Vernon, N.Y. Office: 350 Madison Av., New York NY

PRESTON, ANN, physician; b. Westgrove, Pa., Dec. 1, 1813; d. Amos and Margaret (Smith) Preston; grad. Female Med. Coll. of Pa., Phila., 1852 (one of 1st grads.). Sec., Clarkson Anti-Slavery Soc.; sec. temperance conv. of women, Chester County, Pa., 1848; published Cousin Ann's Stories for Children, 1848; prof. physiology and hygiene Female Med. Coll. of Pa., 1853; prin. founder Woman's Hosp. of Phila., 1861, mem. bd. mgrs., cons. physician, corr. sec., 1st dean, 1866; wrote article in reply to resolution of Philadelphia County Med. Soc. expressing its disapproval of women in med. profession, 1867. Died Phila., Apr. 18, 1872.

PRESTON, CECIL ANTHONY, valuation engr.; b. Phila., Sept. 16, 1852; s. Edward Hall and Margaret (McIntyre) P.; C.E., Poly. College, Phila., 1872; m. Leila Coffin Rogers, Nov. 6, 1883. Engaged in ry. survey and constrn., 1872-77; with Madeira and Mamore Ry. in Brazil, 1877-79; in service Pa. R.R., 1879-80, Nat. Rys. of Mexico, 1880-82; returned to U.S., 1882, and from then in employ Pa. R.R., successively as asst. supervisor, supervisor, asst. engr., prin. asst. engr., supt. Elmira Div., Williamsport Div., Middle Div.; valuation engr. same road, June 1, 1913—. Mason. Episcopalian. Home: Philadelphia, Pa. Died Oct. 9, 1922.

PREVOST, FRANCOIS MARIE, surgeon; b. Pont-de-Ce, France, circa 1764; s. Jean Pierre and Maria Anne (Kenotaire) P.; grad. in medicine U. Paris; m. Marie Therese Burrychon, Dec. 13, 1799; m. 2d, Victorine Castellain, May 29, 1838; at least 2 children, Jean Louis and adopted son, John Robertson. Came to U.S., 1800; practiced medicine, Donaldsonville, La., 1800-42; saved 7 out of 8 lives in 4 operations by Caesarian section on Negro slave mothers, 1822-31; thought to be 2d U.S. physician to perform Caesarian section. Died Donaldsonville, May 18, 1842.

PRICE, DAVID JAMES, research engr.; b. Ashland, Pa., Mar. 27, 1884; s. James and Anna Jane (Vaughan) P.; B.S. in mining engr., Pa. State Coll., 1925, E.M., 1927; M.S. in engring., George Washington U., 1927; Ph.D., Am. U., 1931; m. Esther Bevan Leib, Sept. 30, 1908; children—David George, Frank Leib. Chainman engring. corps, Lehigh Valley Coal Co., Lost Creek, Pa., 1900-02; mining engr. with H. J. Hinterleitner, Spangler, Pa., 1902-05; resident mining engr. Clearfield Bituminous Coal Corp., Clymer, Pa., 1905-12; asst. mining engr. U.S. Bureau of Mines, Pittsburgh, 1912-14; engr. in charge of dust explosion investigations and development work, Bureau of Chemistry, U.S. Dept. of Agr., Washington, 1914-27; principal engr. in charge chem. engring. research div. Bureau of Chemistry and Soils, 1927-39, and principal chemical engineer in Bureau of Agricultural Chemistry and Engineering and Bureau of Agricultural and Industrial Chemistry since 1939. Dept. Agr. Superior Service Award from Sec. of Agr. Brannan, 1949; hon. life mem. National Fire Waste Council, 1951. Mem. Nat. Fire Protection Assn. (pres. 1942-44; hon. life mem., 1950; mem. dust explosion hazards com., chmn. 1922-42; chmn. farm fire protection com. 1927-45), U.S. Chamber of Commerce (mem. nat. fire waste council), Am. Standards Assn. (as rep. of U.S. Dept. Agr.), Tau Beta Pi, Sigma Gamma Epsilon, Sigma Phi Sigma; hon. mem. Internat. Assn. Fire Chiefs, Internat. Assn. Fire Fighters, Grain Elevator Supts. Assn. of N. America, also firemen's orgns. of several states. Methodist. Mason (32 deg., Shriner). Author: Dust Explosions, Theory and Nature of Phenomena, Causes and Methods of Prevention (with H. H. Brown and others), 1922; also many bulletins on dust explosions in industrial plants and on farm fires. Contbr. to Nat. Fire Protection Assn. Quarterly and other jours. Nat. authority on dust explosion prevention, farm and rural community fire prevention and indsl. utilization of agrl. products. Home: 701 Whittier St. N.W. Office: U.S. Dept. of Agriculture, Washington. Died May 28, 1951; buried Cedar Hill Cemetery, Suitland, Md.

PRICE, FRANK, structural engr.; b. Dos Oris, Glen Cove, L.I., N.Y., May 4, 1852; s. George James and Susan Louise (Thompson) P.; ed. pub. and pvt. schs. and under tutors; mech. training in iron works of Bailey & Debevoise, New York. Apptd. supt. of building of U.S. Lighthouses, at Phoenix Iron Works, Trenton, N.J., 1879; designed and supervised machinery and apparatus for moving 220-ton obelisk, accompanied ship to Egypt and directed erection of obelisk in Central Park, New York, 1881; in charge structural dept. Phoenix Iron Co., 1881-83; asst. supt. Am. Shipbuilding Co., Phila., 1883-85; supt. reconstruction of New York Stock Exchange Bldg. without interrupting business, 1885; supt. composite Iron Works, New York, 1888; Pres. Price & Co., 1889-94; chief mill and shop inspr., L.I. R.R. Co., 1902-08; chief shop inspr. N.Y. State Barge Canal, 1909-10; chief shop inspr. for U.S. Govt. of 60-ton steel lock gates for Panama Canal, 1911-12, of Panama Canal fender chains, 1913-14; retained by Govt. in Panama Canal lock gate litigation, 1915. Home: Dos Oris, L.I., N.Y. Died Feb. 5, 1927.

PRICE, GEORGE CLINTON, zoologist; b. Sugar Grove, Ind., May 30, 1860; s. George Culp and Sarah Jane (Watson) P.; B.S., De Pauw U., 1890; studied biology, Johns Hopkins, 1890-92, U. of Munich, 1895-96; Ph.D., Stanford, 1897; m. Edith Basye, of Rockport, Ind., Dec. 27, 1899; 1 son, John Basye. Connected with Stanford since 1892, now prof. zoology. Home: Stanford University, Calif.

PRICE, GEORGE MCCREADY, author; b. Havelock, N.B., Can., Aug. 26, 1870; s. George Marshall and Susan (McCready) P.; student Battle Creek (Mich.) Coll., 1891-93; grad. Provincial Normal Sch., Fredericton, N.B., 1897; B.A., Loma Linda Coll., 1912; M.A., Pacific Union Coll., 1918; m. Amelia A. Nason, Dec. 15, 1887; children—Ernest Edward, Portia Harmon, Beatrice Heloise. Tchr., N.B., 1897-1902; prin. Williamsdale (N.S.) Acad., 1903-04; research work N.Y.C., Washington, 1904-05; tchr. Loma Linda Med. Coll., 1906-12; prof. English lit. Fernando Acad., 1912-13; prof. chemistry and physics Lodi (Cal.) Acad., 1914-20; prof. geology Pac. Union Coll. (Cal.), 1920-22; prof. geology, Union Coll., Neb., 1922-24; leave of absence, spent in teaching and research work in Europe, 1924-28; prof. geology and philosophy Emmanuel Missionary Coll., Berrien, Mich., 1929-33; prof. geology and philosophy Walla Walla Coll., Wash., 1933-38. Author: Outlines of Modern Christianity and Modern Science, 1902; God's Two Books, 1911; The Fundamentals of Geology, 1913; Back to the Bible, 1916; A Textbook of General Science, 1917; O.E.D., Or New Light on the Doctrine of Creation, 1917; Socialism in the Test Tube (joint author), 1921; Poisoning Democracy, 1921; The New Geology, a Textbook for Colleges, 1923; The Phantom of Organic Evolution, 1924; The Predicament of Evolution, 1925; Evolutionary Geology and the New Catastrophism, 1926; A History of Some Scientific Blunders, 1930; The Geological-Ages Hoax, 1931; Modern Discoveries Which Help Us to Believe, 1934; The Modern Flood Theory of Geology, 1935; Some Scientific Stories and Allegories, 1936; If You Were the Creator, 1942; Genesis Vindicated, 1941; How Did the World Begin?, 1942; Common-Sense Geology, 1946; The Man from Mars, 1950, The Greatest of the Prophets: A New Commentary on the Book of Daniel, 1955. Contbr. to many mags. Awarded Langhorn-Orchard prize Victoria Inst., 1925. Home: 24998 East Prospect St., Loma Linda, Cal. 92354. Died Jan. 24, 1963.

PRICE, HARVEY LEE, horticulturist; b. Price's Fork, Va., Mar. 18, 1874; s. William Taylor and Margaret Ellen (Hawley) P.; B.S., Va. Poly. Inst., 1898, M.S., 1900; m. Daisy Conway, Sept. 21, 1904; children—Wm. Conway, Harvey L., Margaret Hawley (dec.), Mary Luster, Jule. Instr. horticulture, Va. Poly. Inst., 1900-03, prof., 1903-45, also dean of agr. Fellow A.A.A.S.; mem. Soc. for Horticultural Science, Am. Pomol. Soc., Am. Genetic Assn. Mem. Ch. of the Disciples. Mason (K.T., Shriner). Home: Blacksburg, Va. Died Feb. 18, 1951; buried Blacksburg.

PRICE, HICKMAN, agriculturist; b. Jefferson City, Mo., June 9, 1886; s. John Ewing and Mary D. (Hickman) P.; B.S., Columbia, 1909; m. Mary Washington Frazer, Nov. 16, 1910; 1 son, Hickman. Reporter New York Sun, 1909-10; pub. Nashville Democrat, 1911-12; editor-pub. El Commercio, 1912-15; v.p. Am. Press Assn., 1915-20; exec. staff Motion Picture Producers and Distributors, Inc., 1920-25, Fox Film Corp., 1925-29. Grain producer in Tex., 30,000 acres; developed engineering and agronomy practices in industrialized growing of wheat which established new low cost production methods; perfected equipment to plow, plant and harvest 1,000 acres a day for each operation. In charge activities of U.S. Com. on Pub. Information in several fgn. countries. World War. Lecturer and writer on agro-industrial exploration and development. Anglo-Saxon relations and the fulfilling of Am. destiny. Home: Southport, Conn. Died Dec. 14, 1939.

PRICE, JOSEPH LINDON, physician; b. Davenport, Okla., Mar. 22, 1911; s. Thomas E. and Florence (Elliott) P.; M.D., U. Ia., 1937; m. Edna Henrie, June 1, 1940, (div.); children—Michael, Patrick, Sally. Intern, Salt Lake County Gen. Hosp., Salt Lake City, 1937-39; asst. to Dr. E.R. Dumke, Ogden, Utah, 1940-41; gen. practice medicine and surgery, Redding, Cal., 1946-68; mem. staff Meml. Hosp., Redding, 1946-68, bd. dirs., 1963-68, pres. bd., 1963-68. Cattle rancher, 1951-68; almond rancher, 1953-68. Mem. Shasta County, Cal. Republican Central Com., 1951-59, chmn., 1957-59; mem. Cal. Rep. Central Com. Served to capt., M.C., AUS, 1941-46. Mem. Am., Cal. med. assns., Shasta County Med. Soc., Am. Hereford Assn. Republican. Elk. Developer almond tree; inventor vet. instrument. Home: Cottonwood CA Died Sept. 17, 1968.

PRICE, MARSHALL LANGTON, sanitarian; b. Fort Gaston, Calif.; Apr. 28, 1878; s. Maj. Curtis Ethelbert (U.S.A.) and Frances (Shaw) P.; ed. mainly by pvt. tutelage; S.I. Acad., N.Y., 1891-93; M.D., U. of Md., 1902; m. Henrietta Cowman George, June 14, 1907. Sr. resident phys., Univ. Hosp., Baltimore, 1902-03; med. officer Tuberculosis Commn. of Md., 1903-05; sec. State Bd. of Health, Md., 1907-13; mem. Md.-D.C. Sewerage Commn., 1912; commd. 1st lt. Med. Reserve Corps U.S.A., Apr. 26, 1911. Independent Democrat. Episcopalian. Delegate 6th Internat. Congress on Tuberculosis, 1908 (v.p. Sect. 6), 15th Internat. Congress on Hygiene and Demography, 1912 (sec. Sect. 6). Author of first law for state control of tuberculosis, now in effect in over 11 states in U.S. and known as the "Maryland System." Home: Baltimore, Md. Died Apr. 16, 1915.

PRICE, ROBERT HENDERSON, prof. horticulture and mycology in Agrl. and Mech. Coll. of Texas since June 9, 1892; b. Blacksburg, Va., Jan. 16, 1864; s. A. R. and S. E. Price; ed. Blacksburg, Va., 1883-91; grad. Agrl. and Mech. Coll. of Va., B.S.; grad. in agr.; m. Newport, Va., Aug. 16, 1893; Texie Williams. Mem. Am. Forestry Assn., Am. Pomol. Soc., Texas Acad. Science, A.A.A.S. Has written several bulls. pertaining to results of his original expts. in horticulture and mycology, published by Texas Agrl. Expt. Station. Address: Blacksburg, Va.

PRICE, SADIE F., botanist; b. Bowling Green, Ky.; grad. St. Agnes Hall; unmarried. Received award medal and diploma, World's Columbian Expn., 1893, for bot. work; teacher of botany; from 1887 has been engaged in studying the flora of southern Ky., traveling through counties that are without railroads, by stage, farm-wagon, skiff, etc. Has discovered many rare plants; has made an herbarium, also sketches in water colors of the plants (1,000 or more in the higher orders alone); also water color sketches of Ky. birds. Author: Fern-Collector's Handbook and Herbarium, illustrated, 1897; Flora of Warren County, Ky., 1893; Trees and Shrubs of Kentucky, 1898. Home: Bowling Green, Ky. Died 1903.

PRICE, WILLIAM WIGHTMAN, educator, naturalist, author; b. Milwaukee, Jan. 20, 1871; s. Robert Martin and Harriet (Wightman) P.; removed to Calif., 1880; ed. pub. schs. of Riverside and Oakland, Calif.; grad. Stanford Univ., 1897, M.A., 1899; teacher in Thacher Sch., Nordhoff, Calif., 1899-1900; m. June 6, 1900, Bertha de Laguna. At age of 16 explored the deserts and mountains of Ariz., discovering new and little-known birds, mammals and reptiles. Author of scientific papers; contb'r to Overland Monthly and Sunset mags. Mem. Beta Theta Pi, Calif. Acad. Sciences, Am. Ornithologists' Union, Am. Hist. Assn., Sierra Club, Cooper Club. Founder of Agassiz Hall, school for boys, and Camp Agassiz, a summer school of nature study in the Sierras. Address: Alta Placer Co CA

PRIEST, IRWIN G., physicist; b. nr. Londonville, Ohio, Jan. 27, 1886; s. Morgan A. and Julia A. (Schauweker) P.; B.A. from Ohio State U., 1907; m. Edna Ryan, June 26, 1917. With Bur. of Standards, Washington, D.C., 1907—, successively as lab. asst. until 1908, asst. physicist, 1908-15, asso. physicist, 1915-19, physicist, 1919—; also chief of colorimetry sect., Bur. of Standards, 1913—; research asso. of Munsell Color Co. and Munsell Research Lab., at Bur. of Standards for several periods, 1922-25, while on leave from bureau duty. Fellow A.A.A.S., Am. Phys. Society. Home: Washington, D.C. Died 1932.

PRIESTLEY, JOSEPH, scientist, educator, writer; b. Fieldhead Leeds, Yorkshire, Eng., Mar. 13, 1733; s. Jonas and Mary (Swift) P.; attended Daventry Acad., Eng., 1751-54; LL.D. (hon.), U. Edinburgh (Scotland), 1765; m. Mary Wilkinson, June 23, 1762; children—Joseph, Sarah, William, Henry. Pastor, Needham Market, Surrey, Eng., 1755; ordained to ministry Congregational Ch., 1762; tutor belles-lettres Warrington Acad. until 1767; preached, wrote, taught history, anatomy, botany, astronomy; pastor Mill Hill Ch., Leeds, Eng., 1767-72; librarian to Lord Shelburne, 1772-80; minister New Meeting, Birmingham, Eng., 1780-91; made citizen of France for Revolutionary sympathies, 1792; pastor, Hackney, Eng., 1792-94; came to U.S., 1794; settled in Northumberland, Pa.; made many notable experiments in chemistry; 1st to isolate and describe oxygen, nitrous oxide, nitric oxide, nitrogen peroxide, ammonia, silicon flouride, sulphur dioxide, hydrogen sulphide and carbon monoxide; chief early proponent of Unitarianism in U.S. Author: History and Present State of Electricity, 1767; Essay on the First Principles of Government, 1768; The History and Present State of Discoveries Relating to Vision, Light and Colours, 1772; Experiments and Observations on Different Kinds of Air, 3 vols., 1774, 75, 77; An History of the Corruptions of Christianity, 1782; A General History of the Christian Church, 4 vols., 1790-1802; Unitarianism Explained and Defended, 1796; The Doctrine of Phlogiston Established, 1803. Died Northumberland, Feb. 6, 1804.

PRINCE, LEON NATHANIEL, physician; b. Phila., Dec. 8, 1906; s. Nathaniel and Elizabeth N. Prince; B.S., William and Mary Coll.; M.D., Jefferson Med. Coll., 1933; m. Marie J. De Prisco, Nov. 12, 1931; children—Robert Leon, Patricia Marie, Barbara Elizabeth (Mrs. Paul Cirilis). Asso. prof. obstetrics and gynecology Jefferson Med. Coll., Phila.; chief obstet. ward St. Vincent's Hosp. Mem. med. com. Southeastern Pa. Planned Parenthood Assn. Served with USCGR, World War II. Diplomate Am. Bd. Obstetrics and Gynecology. Fellow A.C.S., Am. Coll. Obstetricians and Gynecologists (founder); mem. A.M.A. Contbr. numerous articles on perinatal mortality and morbidity to med. jours. Home: Philadelphia PA Died Jan. 27, 1970; buried Laurel Hill Cemetery.

PRINCE, WILLIAM, horticulturist; b. Flushing, L.I., N.Y., circa 1725; s. Robert and Mary (Burgess) P.; m. Anne Thorne, 13 children including William, Benjamin. Pioneer Am. horticulturist, 1 of 1st to sell budded or grafted stock and to attempt to breed new varieties; established Prince's Nursery, developed Prince's Gage plum, raised fruits, trees and shrubs; thousands of his cherry trees made into barrel hoops during Revolutionary War. Died Flushing, 1802.

PRINCE, WILLIAM, horticulturist; b. Flushing, L.I., N.Y., Nov. 10, 1766; s. William and Ann (Thorne) P.; m. Mary Statton, 4 children including William Robert. Founder Linnaean Botanic Garden and Nurseries, 1793, imported and introduced many varieties of fruits and plants, also exported Am. plants and trees to Europe; introduced Isabella grape (which he renamed), 1816; standardized name of Bartlett pear, others; mem. N.Y. Hort. Soc., Mass. Hort. Soc., Linnaean Soc. of Paris, Hort. Soc. of London and Paris, Imperial Soc. of the Georgofili, Florence, Italy. Author: A Short Treatise on Horticulture, 1828; (with son William Robert) A Treatise on the Vine, 1830, The Pomological Manual, 1831. Died Flushing, Apr. 9, 1842.

PRINCE, WILLIAM ROBERT, horticulturist; b. Flushing, L.I., N.Y., Nov. 6, 1795; s. William and Mary (Stratton) P.; m. Charlotte Goodwin Collins, Oct. 2, 1826, 4 children including LeBaron Bradford. Botanized entire range of Atlantic states; importer 1st merino sheep to U.S., 1816; became mgr. (with brother) Linnaean Botanic Garden and Nurseries, circa 1835; pioneer (with father) in introducing silk culture, 1837; importer mulberry Morus multicaulis (became very popular.); from Tarascon, France; introduced culture of osiers and sorghum, 1854-55; importer Chinese yam, 1854; corr. mem. Mass. Hort. Soc., 1829; mem. Am. Pomological Soc.; greatest contbn. to Am. horticulture: advancement of grape-growing. Author: Prince's Manual of Roses, 1846; (with father) Treatise on the Vine, 1830; The Pomological Manual, 1831. Contbr. many short articles and arguments to Gardeners' Monthly and Rural New Yorker. Died Flushing, Mar. 28, 1869.

PRINGLE, CYRUS GUERNSEY, botanist; b. Charlotte, Vt., May 6, 1838; s. George and Louisa (Harris) P.; classical edn. in various schs. of Vt. and Canada; (hon. A.M., Middlebury Coll., 1876; Sc.D., U. of Vt., 1906). Collected extensively in forestry and gen. botany in Ariz., Sonora, Calif., Ore., and Wash., as collector for Am. Mus. Natural History, New York, 1881-84; bot. collector to Harvard U., 1885—; also keeper herbarium to U. of Vt. Has been engaged upon the thorough exploration of the flora of Old Mexico, placing large collections (about one in five of the plants new species) in 50 or more of the most important herbaria of the world. From 1888-94 contributed to Garden and Forest, Notes on the Forest Vegetation of Mexico, and Notes on Botanical Travel in Mexico. Asso. fellow Am. Acad. Arts and Sciences. Home: Burlington, Vt. Died 1911.

PRITCHARD, JOHN F(RANKLIN), cons. engr.; b. Manitowoc, Wis., Jan. 6, 1891; s. John F. and Emily (Hill) P.; A.B., Cornell U., 1911, M.E., 1913; m. Lucile Martin, Feb. 10, 1913; children—Mary Lucile (Mrs. Philip Eckels), John Franklin, Dorothy Hazel (Mrs. Chas. Williams). Pres. J. F. Pritchard & Co., Kansas City, 1920—; dir. First Nat. Bank, Kansas City. Trustee Park Coll., Kansas City Art Inst., Midwest Research Inst., Kansas City Philharmonic Assn.; pres. dir. Kansas City Starlight Theater Assn.; dir., v.p. Kansas City Mus. Mem. Am. Soc. M.E., Kansas City C. of C. (dir., v.p.), Nat. Constructors Assn. (pres.). Presbyn. (trustee). Clubs: Engineers, Kansas City, Mission Hills Country, Rotary, Mercury (Kansas City). Home: 2353 Guilford Lane, Shawnee Mission, Kan. Office: 4625 Roanoke Pkwy., Kansas City 12, Mo. Deceased.

PROBERT, FRANK HOLMAN, mining engr.; b. London, Eng., June 13, 1876; s. Isaac and Mary J. (Holman) P.; nat. biol. scholar, Royal Coll. Science, London, 1893; associate Royal Sch. of Mines, London, 1897; m. Jessie Agnes McGaw, May 25, 1907; 1 son, Aylwin. Engaged in investigation of mineral resources N.W. Ont., Can., 1897-98; gen. mgr. of Llanfair lead mines, N. Wales, 1898-99; mgr. Anhaltische Blei und Silberwerke, Anhalt, Germany, 1899-1900; engring. research in Ariz., for Phelps, Dodge & Co., New York, 1901-02; consulting engr., Los Angeles, Calif., 1902-09. Weed & Probert, Los Angeles and New York, 1910-12, etc.; prof. mining, 1916, dean Coll. of Mining, 1917—, U. of Calif.; consulting engr. U.S. Bur. Mines, 1918—. Mem. spl. com. on war minerals investigation, U.S. Bur. of Mines, 1917-18; mem. Am. mining mission to Europe for investigation of mineral industry, and reparation in Northern France, 1919. Episcopalian. Died May 7, 1940.

PROCTER, WILLIAM, scientist; b. Cincinnati, O., Sept. 8, 1872; s. Harley Thomas and Mary Elizabeth (Sanford) P.; grad. Phillips Exeter Acad., 1891; Ph.B., Yale, 1894; grad. student Sorbonne (Paris), 1896-97, Columbia, 1917-20; D.Sc., U. of Montreal, 1936; m. Emily Pearson Bodstein, Feb. 3, 1910. During early career specialized in railroad organization and securities; organized firm of Proctor & Borden, 1902, retired, 1929; established lab. on Mt. Desert Island (Me.), 1921; established Biol. Survey of Mt. Desert Region, 1936; has contributed to curricula of univs. and state biol. depts. Trustee Am. Mus. Natural History, N.Y. City. Mem. bd. of mgrs. Wistar Inst. of Anatomy and Biology (Phila.), 1928-40. Director Procter & Gamble Co. Mem. advisory bd., dept. of zoölogy, Columbia U. Fellow Entomol. Soc. America, A.A.A.S.; mem. Acad. Natural Sciences, Boston Soc. of Natural History, Entomological Soc. of Am. (mem. edit. bd., 1940-47), Am. Microscopical Soc., Acad. Natural Sciences of Phila., Ornithologists Union, Santa Barbara Natural History Soc., Brooklyn Entomol. Soc., Genetic Soc., Ray Soc. of London (England), Plymouth Marine Assn. (England), Southern Calif. Acad. Sciences, New York Entomol. Soc., Entomol. Soc. of Washington, Ecologists Union, Ecol. Soc. of America, Royal Canadian Institute, Am., Pacific Coast and Cambridge entomol. socs., Sci. Research Soc. Am. (co-founder and a gov.), Sigma Xi. Episcopalian (warden). Clubs: Century, University (New York); Graduate (New Haven, Conn.). Author of publs. on the marine life and the insect life of the Mount Desert Region. Home: Bar Harbor, Me. Died Apr. 19, 1951.

PROCTOR, BERNARD EMERSON, educator, food technologist; b. Malden, Mass., May 5, 1901; s. Arthur L. and Vina (Dolloff) P.; B.S., Mass. Inst. Tech., 1923, Ph.D., 1927; m. Miriam H. Patten, Oct. 18, 1924. Instr. biochemistry sch. medicine, Boston U., 1923-27; instr., later prof. food tech., Mass. Inst. Technology, 1926; head dept. food tech., 1952—; cons. to U.S. Pub. Health service, 1951—; cons. food development research and prof. dir. food research Office Q.M., Gen. U.S. Army. Recipient of the Nicholas Appert medal, 1957. Fellow American Public Health Assn.; mem. A.A.A.S., Am. Chem. Soc., Soc. Am. Bacteriologists, Inst. Food Technologist (pres. 1952-53), Am. Soc. Refrigeration Engrs., Sigma Xi. Club: Cosmos (Washington, D.C.) Baptist. Author: Food Technology (with S. C. Prescott), 1937; over 100 papers on food tech. in science periodicals. Home: 100 Memorial Drive, Cambridge 42, Mass. Died Sept. 24, 1959.

PROSSER, CHARLES SMITH, educator, geologist; b. Columbus, N.Y., Mar. 24, 1860; s. Smith and Emeline A. (Tuttle) P.; B.S., Cornell, 1883, M.S., 1886; (D.Sc., Union U., 1906); Ph.D., Cornell, 1907; m. Mary F. Wilson, Aug. 28, 1893. Instr. paleontology, Cornell, 1885-88; asst. paleontologist U.S. Geol. Survey, 1888-92; prof. natural history, Washburn Coll., Topeka, Kan., 1892-94; prof. geology, Union Coll., 1894-99; asso. prof. hist. geology, 1899-1901, prof. geology and head of dept., 1901—, Ohio State U. Asst. geologist U.S. Geol. Survey and on state geol. surveys of Kan., N.Y., and Ohio; geologist Md. Geol. Survey. Fellow Geol. Soc. of America, A.A.A.S. (v.p. Section E, 1915—), Am. Paleontological Society. Author: The Devonian System of Eastern Pennsylvania and New York, 1895; The Classification of the Upper Palaeozoic Rocks of Central Kansas, 1895, 1902; The Upper Permian and Lower Cretaceous of Kansas, 1897; The Classification of the Hamilton and Chemung Series of New York, Part I, 1898, II, 1900; Cottonwood Falls (Kansas) Folio (with J. W. Beede), 1904; Revised Nomenclature of the Ohio Geological Formations, 1905; Anthracolithic or Upper Paleozoic Rocks of Kansas, 1910; Devonian and Mississippian Formations of Northeastern Ohio, 1912; Middle Devonian Deposits and Paleontology of Maryland (with Edward M. Kindle), 1913; Upper Devonian Deposits of Maryland (with Charles K. Swartz), 1913. Home: Columbus, O. Deceased.

PROUT, HENRY GOSLEE, engineer; b. Fairfax Co., Va.; s. William and Amanda (Goslee) P.; served in Army of the Potomac, 1863-5; C.E., University of Mich., 1871; (hon. A.M., Yale, 1902; LL.D, University of Mich., 1911); m. Gabriella Perin, Dec. 19, 1877. Maj. of engrs., and later col. of gen. staff, army of the Khedive of Egypt, 1873-8; comd. expdn. in the Soudan and was gov. of the Provinces of the Equator; editor Railroad Gazette, 16 yrs.; v.-p. and gen. mgr. Union Switch & Signal Co., 1903-14; retired. Mem. Am. Soc. C.E., Am. Geog. Soc. Clubs: Century, Railroad (New York); University (Pittsburgh); Yountakah (Nutley). Home: Nutley NJ

PROWSE, ROBERT JOHN, bridge engr.; b. Concord, N.H., Sept. 4, 1906; s. John Thomas and Ruth (Potter) P.; B.S.C.E., Northeastern U., 1928; postgrad. Carnegie Inst. Tech., 1942; m. Mildred Katherine Veino, June 1, 1934; children—John James, Joan Mary (Mrs. Irving Richard Gourley), Kathryn (Mrs. Hugh Goodwin Butterfield). Draftsman, Hamilton (Ont., Can.) Bridge Co. Ltd., 1929-34; designer N.H. Hwy. Dept., Concord, 1934-41; designer Koppers Co., Pitts., 1942-43; chief bridge designer N.H. dept. of pub. works and hwys., Concord, 1947-56, asst. bridge engr., 1957-68, bridge engr., 1968-69; cons. engr. David B. Steinman, Concord, 1956-57. Spl. lectr. Northeastern U. grad. sch., Boston, 1956-57; instr. New Eng. Coll., Henniker, N.H., 1957-59. Served to lt. with USNR, 1943-46. Recipient Bridge Design Award, Lincoln Arc Welding Found., 1958, 61, 64. Registered profl. engr., N.H. Fellow Am. Soc. C.E.; mem. Am. Legion (comdr. 1948). Home: Concord NH Died Dec. 20, 1969.

PRUDDEN, T(HEOPHIL) MITCHELL, pathologist; b. Middlebury, Conn., July 7, 1849; s. Rev. George P. and Eliza A. Johnson (Prudden) P.; B.S., Sheffield Scientific Sch. (Yale), 1872, M.D., 1875 (LL.D., 1896); unmarried. Instr. chemistry, Yale, 1872-74; hosp. interne and studies in Heidelberg, Vienna, Berlin, 1875-78; asst. in pathology and histology, 1878-82, dir. pathol. and bacteriol. lab., 1882-91, prof. pathology, 1892-1909, emeritus prof., 1909, Coll. Phys. and Surgeons (Columbia U.). Lecturer normal histology, Yale, 1880-86. Dir. Rockefeller Inst. for Med. Research, 1901—. Fellow Am. Acad. Arts and Sciences. Author: Manual of Normal Histology; Textbook of Pathology, 1885, 11th edit., 1919; Story of the Bacteria; Dust and Its Dangers; Water and Ice Supplies; On the Great American Plateau, 1907. Home: New York, N.Y. Died Apr. 10, 1924.

PRUD'HOMME, JOHN FRANCIS EUGENE, engraver; b. St. Thomas, W.I., Oct. 4, 1800. Came to U.S., 1807; engraved number of plates for Nat. Portrait Gallery of Distinguished Americans, 1831, important portraits were of Henry Clay, DeWitt Clinton, Oliver Cromwell, Stephen Decatur, Alexander Hamilton, John Paul Jones, Dolly Madison, George Washington; curator Nat. Acad. of Design, 1834-53; designer-engraver of decorative work for banknote engraving firm. N.Y., 1852-69; with Bur. Engraving and Printing, Washington, D.C., 1869-85; designer of the ornamentation of bank notes and securities. Died Georgetown, D.C., June 27, 1892.

PRUTTON, CARL FREDERICK, chem. engr.; b. Cleve., July 30, 1898; s. Daniel J. and Julia (Seelbach) P.; B.S., Case Inst. Tech., 1920, M.S., 1923, D.Eng. (hon.), 1955; Ph.D., from Western Res. U., 1928, D.Sc., 1963; D.Eng. (hon.), Clarkson Coll. Tech., 1960, Manhattan Coll., 1960, Marietta Coll., 1962; m. to Marie A. Saunders, June 2, 1919; children—Carl F., Dorothy E. (Mrs. Jose Castillo), Carolyn A. (Mrs. J.R. Small), Mary L. (Mrs. R.L. Sutherland), John R., Helen M. (Mrs. G.L. Conrad). Instr. Case Inst. Tech., 1920-26, asst. prof., 1926-28, asso. prof., 1928-35, prof., 1935-36, head dept. chemistry and chem. engring., 1936-48; v.p. Mathieson Chem. Corp., 1948-53; v.p. and tech. director Food Machinery and Chemical Corporation, N.Y.C., 1954-56, executive vice pres., 1956-60, dir., 1960-70; mem. bd. dirs. Commercial Solvents Corp. Head process development br. Rubber Dir.'s Office, U.S. Government, 1942-44. Trustee Clarkson Institute of Technology, 1960-70. Received Nat. Assn. Mfrs. Modern Pioneer Award, 1938, Perkin Medal, 1961. Member of the American Institute of Chemical Engrs., Am. Chem. Soc., Soc. Automotive Engrs., Am. Petroleum Inst., Petroleum Inst. Britain, Sigma Xi, Tau Beta Pi. Author: Physical Chemistry (with Dr. S. H. Maron), 1944. Author articles tech. jours. Issued about 100 patents chem. field. Home: Oklawaha FL Died July 1970.

PUCKETT, WILLIAM OLIN, educator; b. Cornelius, N.C., May 3, 1906; s. William Lawrence and Mary (Washam) P.; A.B.,, Davidson Coll., 1927; M.A., U. N.C., 1931; Ph.D., Princeton, 1934; m. Virginia Lewis House, June 18, 1942; children—Virginia Northington, John Lawrence, James Butler. Asst. prof. biology Southwestern Coll., Memphis, 1935; instr. biology Princeton, 1935-38, asst. prof., 1939-46; research investigator OSRD, 1943-45; prof. biology Davidson Coll., from 1946, chmn. pre-med. studies, chmn. biology dept., 1946-70. Recipient Thomas Jefferson award. Mem. N.C. Acad. Sci. (pres. 1954), Am. Soc. Zoologists, Am. Assn. Anatomists, Sigma Xi, Gamma Sigma Epsilon, Omicron Delta Kappa, Sigma Chi. Presbyn. (ruling elder 1958-72). Mason. Home: Davidson NC Died June 3, 1972; buried Mimosa Cemetery, Davidson NC

PUCKNER, WILLIAM AUGUST, chemist; b. New Holstein, Wis., Feb. 24, 1864; s. Rudolph and Marie (Heins) P.; Ph.G., Chicago Coll. Pharmacy (now U. of Ill. Sch. of Pharmacy), 1885; attended summer course in chemistry, Harvard, and took lectures and lab. work in chemistry at U. of Heidelberg; (hon. Phar.D., U. of Pittsburgh, 1912; hon. Phar.M., Phila. Coll. Pharmacy, 1919); unmarried. In retail drug business, at Chicago, 1880-90; prof. chemistry, U. of Ill. Sch. of Pharmacy, 1890-1910; chemist for Searle & Hereth Co., mfg. pharmacists, Chicago, 1896-1907; sec. council on pharmacy and chemistry, A.M.A., 1906—; mem. Com. on Revision of U.S. Pharmacopoeia IX and X; mem. com. on synthetic drugs, Nat. Research Council. Home: Chicago, Ill. Died Oct. 1, 1932.

PUGH, EVAN, chemist, coll. pres.; b. Jordan Bank, E. Nottingham Twp., Pa., Feb. 29, 1828; s. Lewis and Mary (Hutton) P.; studied U. Leipzig (Germany), 1853-54; Ph.D. in Chemistry, U. Gottingen (Germany), 1856; m. Rebecca Valentine, Feb. 4, 1864. Researcher at labs. Sir John Bennett Lawes and Sir Joseph Henry Gilbert, Rothamsted, Eng.; laid down principles of plant growth, 1859; pres. Agrl. Coll. Pa., 1856-64, (now Pa. State Coll.); helped push Land-Grant Coll. Act through Congress, 1862. Authdr: On a New Method for the Quantative Estimation of Nitric Acid., 1860; On the Sources of the Nitrogen of Vegetation, 1862; A Report Upon a Plan for the Organization of Colleges for Agriculture and the Mechanic Arts, with Especial Reference to the . . . Agricultural College of Pennsylvania . . . in View of the Endowment of this Institution by the Land Script Fund 1864. Died Bellefonte, Pa., Apr. 19, 1864.

PUGH, WILLIAM SAMUEL, mining engr.; b. Pottsville, Pa., June 27, 1871; s. John and Rosanna (Beidelman) P.; grad. high sch., Pottsville, 1888; grad.

corr. course Internat. Corr. Schs., Scranton, Pa., 1896; m. Jennie June Edwards, Oct. 27, 1896. Pvt. practice as civil and mining engr., 1892—; now cons. mining engr. for Schuylkill County, Pa.; frequently called to testify before cts. of anthracite region and Pub. Service Commn. of Pa.; employers' rep. Fed. Labor Bd., Schuylkill County, Pa., 1917-18. Mem. Pa. Engrs. Soc. Am. Inst. of Mining and Metall. Engrs. Republican. Presbyn. Mason (33 deg., K.T. Shriner). Home: 1816 Mahantango St., Pottsville, Pa. Office: Mortimer Bldg., Pottsville, Pa. Died Jan. 19, 1954; buried Chas-Barber Cemetery, Pottsville, Pa.

PULLMAN, GEORGE MORTIMER, inventor, railroad car mfr.; b. Brocton Chautauqua County, N.Y., Mar. 3, 1831; s. James Lewis and Emily Caroline (Minton) P.; m. Harriet Sanger, June 13, 1867, 4 children. Contractor in Chgo., 1855-59, successful in raising the level of some bldgs. and streets; store-keeper in mining town, Colo., 1859-63; contracted with Chgo & Alton R.R. to remodel 2 day coaches into sleeping cars (incorporating his basic idea of upper berth hinged to side of car), 1858, constructed a 3d car, 1859; patentee (with friend Ben Field) folding berth, 1864, lower berth, 1865; completed 1st car The Pioneer, 1865, constructed number of other cars modeled after The Pioneer; organized Pullman Palace Car Co., 1867 (grew to be greatest car bldg. orgn. in world); established 1st mfg. plant at Palmyra, N.Y., then moved to Detroit; built Town of Pullman (Ill.) for accomodation of employees, completed 1881; responsible for combined sleeping and restaurant car, 1867, dining car, 1868, chair car, 1875, vestibule car, 1887; owner Eagleton Wire Works, N.Y.; pres. Met. Elevated R.R., N.Y.; contbd. bequest of $1,200,000 for establishment free manual tng. sch. at Pullman. Died Chgo., Oct. 19, 1897.

PULSIFER, HARRY BRIDGMAN, metallurgist; b. Lebanon, N.H., December 23, 1879; s. Charles Edward and Ellen Diantha (Bridgman) P.; B.S., Mass. Inst. Tech., 1903; post-grad. work, U. of Munich, 1906-07; Chem. E., Armour Inst. Tech., Chicago, 1915; M.S., U. of Chicago, 1918; m. Sarah Cecelie Cantlion, Sept. 9, 1909; children—Carmen, Phyllis, Verne, Harrison. Instr. chemistry, N.H. State Coll., 1903-04; chemist, Henry Souther Engring. Co., Hartford, Conn., 1904; assayer and mining engr., Sonora, Mex., 1905; supt. placer mine, Ore., 1907; wrote consular reports, "Zinc in Mexico," 1908; foreman, A.S.&R. Co., Murray, Utah, 1909-11, U.S. Co., Midvale, Utah, 1911; instr. metallurgy, 1911-15, asst. prof., 1915-17, Armour Inst. Tech., Chicago; prof. metallurgy, Mont. State Sch. of Mines, Butte, 1917-20; asst. prof. metallurgy, Lehigh U., 1920-24; metallurgist with Am. Steel & Wire Co., Cleveland, 1935-41; asst. to pres. Am. Metal Treating Co., Cleveland, since 1941. Mem. Am. Inst. Mining Engrs., Am. Soc. Metals, A.A.A.S., Inst. Metals (London). Contbr. on topics relating to mining, milling and metallurgy. Home: 9907 Lamont Av., Cleveland, O. Died Sep. 1, 1947.

PULTZ, LEON M(ERLE), horticulturist; born Lake Preston, S.D., July 6, 1904; s. Andrew Miller and Caroline (Hintz) P.; B.S., S.D. State Coll., 1925, M.S., 1927; Ph.D., U. of Chicago, 1929; m. Mary Ora Halfhill, June 4, 1926; children—Patricia Ann (Mrs. John H. Bolinger, Jr.), Mary Caroline (Mrs. Charles A. Magee). Agricultural research on sugar beets Department of Agriculture, Salt Lake City, 1929-36, agrl. research on weed control, Ames, Ia., 1938-40, prin. horticulturist Beltsville, Md., 1949-57, chief oilseeds and indsl. corps br., 1957-70; asst. prof. botany U. of Ariz., 1936-38, head dept. botany and range ecology, 1940-47, head dept. horticulture, 1947-49. Fellow A.A.A.S., mem. Am. Soc. Agronomy, Botanical Soc. of Washington, Sigma Xi, Phi Kappa Phi. Mason. Home: Hyattsville MD Died Feb. 7, 1970; buried San Diego CA

PUMPELLY, RAPHAEL, author, geologist; b. Owego, N.Y., Sept. 8, 1837; s. William and Mary H. (Welles) P.; ed. Owego Acad. and pvt. schs.; studied sciences and mining engring., 1854-60, in Paris, France, and at Freiberg, Saxony; LL.D., Princeton U., 1920; m. Eliza Frances Shepard, Oct. 20, 1869. Made geol. explorations in Corsica; had charge of mines in Ariz., 1860-61; made scientific explorations for Japanese Govt., 1861-63; pvt. geol. expdn. through Central, Western, and Northern China and Mongolia, 1863-64; explored Northern coal field for Imperial Chinese Govt., 1864; journey of exploration across the Gobi desert, returned to Europe through Siberia, 1864-65; prof. mining, Harvard, 1866-73; state geologist, Mich., 1869-71; dir. Mo. Geol. Survey, 1871-73; chief of div., U.S. Geol. Survey, and in charge of mineral industries the Tenth Census, 1879-81; organized and directed Northern Transcontinental Survey, 1881-84; made the explorations of discovery inaugurating the development of the iron-ore industry of most of the iron-ore ranges of Mich. and Western Ont., 1867-1901; initiated and directed a physical-geographical and archeol. exploration of Central Asia, 1903-04, under auspices of Carnegie Instn. of Washington. Author: Exploratioons in Turkestan, Expedition of 1903; Explorations in Turkestan, Prehistoric Civilizations of Anau, 1908; Reminiscences, 1918; Adventures of Raphael Pumpelly, 1920. Homes: Newport, R.I., and Dublin, N.H. Died Aug. 10, 1923.

PUPIN, MICHAEL IDVORSKY, physicist, inventor; b. Idvor, Banat, Yugoslavia, Oct. 4, 1858; s. Constantine and Olympiada P.; A.B., Columbia, 1883; Sc.D., 1904; Ph.D., U. of Berlin, 1889; LL.D., Johns Hopkins U.; m. Sarah Katharine Jackson, 1888 (dec.). Asst. teacher elec. engring., 1889-90, instr. math. physics, 1890-92, adj. prof. mechanics, 1892-1901, prof. electro-mechanics, 1901-31, Columbia, prof. emeritus. Mem. various societies. Awarded Washington medal (engring.), 1928; Pulitzer Prize, 1924. Author: Die Wirkung der Vakuumentladungen aufeinander, 1892; Elektrische Entladungen durch verdünnte Gase und koronaartige Entladungen, 1892; Über elektrische Oszillationen von geringer Frequenz und ihre Resonanz, 1893; Thermodynamics of Reversible Cycles in Gases and Saturated Vapors, 1894; Resonanz-Analyse automatische Quecksilberpumpe, 1895; Das Gesetz des elektromagnetischen Inductionsflusses, 1895; Versuche mit Kathodenstrahlen, 1896; From Immigrant to Inventor, 1924; The New Reformation, 1927; The Romance of the Machine, 1930. Applied automatic induction coils to decreasing capacity of telegraph for use in shallow depths; invented Pupin bobbins for use in telephone lines; studied electric phenomena in rarified gases and electric resonators; devised X-ray sensitive flourescent screen; improved radio transmitters; worked on gaseous discharge; devel. higher efficiency transmission lines by distbd. inductance. Died New York, N.Y., Mar. 12, 1935.

PURCELL, CHARLES HENRY, (pûr-sel'), civil engr.; b. North Bend, Neb., Jan. 27, 1883; s. John and Mary (Gillis) P.; student Stanford U., 1903; C.E., U. of Neb., 1906; E.D., 1936; LL.D., U. of Calif., 1937; m. Minnie Pullen, Feb. 24, 1914. Resident engr. on railroad constrn. in Wyo., 1906-07; asst. chief engr. smelting and power development, Peru, 1909-10; highway and bridge engr. in Northwest on state and pvt. projects, 1910-17; bridge engr. for U.S. Bur. Pub. Roads, Ore., 1917-27; highway engr. State of Calif., Division Highways, 1928-42; appointed dir. public works, Calif.; ex-officio chmn. Calif. Highway commn.; ex-officio chmn. State Reconstruction and Reemployment Commn., 1943; apptd. sec. Hoover-Young San Francisco-Oakland Bay Bridge Commn., 1929; made traffic survey and design for San Francisco-Oakland Bay Bridge in 1931; apptd. chief engr. San Francisco-Oakland Bay Bridge. Rep. of U.S. on the Permanent Internat. Commn. of the Permanent Internat. Assn. of Road Congresses; mem. Interregional Highway Committee since 1941. Mem. Am. Soc. Civil Engineers (hon.), Am. Assn. of State Highway Officials (past president; mem. executive committee), Chi Phi. Clubs: Family, Press, Commonwealth (San Francisco); Sutter and Del Paso Country Club (Sacramento). Home: 2231 N. St. Office: P.O. Box 1079, Sacramento. Died Sept. 7, 1951.

PURDON, CHARLES DE LA CHEROIS, civil engr.; b. Belfast, Ireland, Oct. 6, 1850; s. Charles de la Cherois (M.D.) and Jane Maria (Calvert) P.; univ. course under pvt. tutor; m. Jennie Theo Arthur, of Arthur City, Tex., May 11, 1887; children—Arthur, Eleanor de la Cherois. Began as axman Intercolonial Ry., Can., 1876, and advanced to asst. engr.; asst. engr. pub. works dept., Canadian Govt., on St. Lawrence River, 1872-75; surveyor, in Tex., 1876-80; asst. engr. Tex. & St. Louis Ry., 1880-84; resident engr. Little Rock Jct. Ry., 1884-85; asst. engr. St. L.&S.F. Ry., 1886-87; asst. chief engr. St. Louis, Ark. & Tex. Ry., 1887-88; res. and div. engineer L.&N. R.R., 1888-90; assistant on canal bridge, Duluth, Minn., June-Aug. 1890; bridge engr., A.T.&S.F. 1890-93; res. engineer Chicago div. same rd., 1893-95; prin. asst. engr., 1895-97, asst. chief engr., 1897-1901, same rd., also chief engr. Kansas City Belt Ry., Jan.-May 1901; chief engr. St.L.&S.F. R.R., 1901-04; engr. maintenance of way, 1904-06, consulting engr., 1906-09, same rd.; chief engr. Memphis Rd. Terminal, Apr.-Sept. 1909; asst. engr. Mo.P. Ry. on valuation of Neb. lines and grade separation in St. Louis, 1909-10; chief engr. St. L. Southwestern Ry., 1910-18, and since consulting engr. same. Mem. Am. Soc. C.E., Am. Ry. Engring. Assn., Am. Soc. Testing Materials. Democrat. Episcopalian. Mason. Clubs: Engineers, Railway. Home: 6157 Kingsbury Boul. Office: Buder Bldg., St. Louis, Mo.

PURDUE, ALBERT HOMER, geologist; b. Warrick Co., Ind., Mar. 29, 1861; s. Samuel Leroy and Phoebe (Priest) P.; grad. Indiana State Normal Sch., 1886; A.B., Leland Stanford Jr. U., 1893; grad. work there, 1894; senior fellow, dept. of geology, U. of Chicago, 1895-96; (LL.D., U. of Arkansas, 1912); m. Bertha Lee Burdick, Sept. 1, 1887 (died 1888); m. 2d, Ida Pace, Dec. 22, 1898. Supt. pub. schs., West Plains, Mo., 1887-88; asst. supt. U.S. Indian Sch., Albuquerque, N.M., 1889-91; asst. geologist, Ark., 1892-93; prof. geology, 1896-1902, head prof. geology and mining, 1902-12, U. of Ark.; state geologist of Tenn., 1912—. Field asst., U.S. Geol. Survey, 1895, 1901-03, spl. field asst., 1903—; supt. mines and metallurgy for Ark., St. Louis Exposition; ex-officio state geologist of Ark., 1907-12. Editor: Resources of Tennessee. Home: Nashville, Tenn. Died Dec. 12, 1917.

PURDY, CORYDON TYLER, civil engr.; b. Grand Rapids, Wis., May 17, 1859; s. Samuel J. and Emma J. (Tyler) P.; A.B., U. of Wis., 1885, C.E., 1886; m. Rose E. Morse, Mar. 19, 1892. Pres. and chmn. bd. Purdy & Henderson Co., engrs. and contractors, New York, many years, now retired. Chiefly known for activity in promoting development of modern building construction by use of steel and iron. Contributor to technical mags. Mem. Am. Soc. C.E., Western Soc. Engrs., Instn. C.E. Great Britain. Republican. Conglist. Clubs: Engineers' (New York); Commonwealth (Montclair, N.J.). Home: Melbourne, Fla. Died Dec. 26, 1944.

PURDY, ROSS COFFIN, ceramic engr.; b. Jasper, N.Y., Mar. 3, 1875; s. Andrew and Mary Elizabeth (Coffin) P.; student Syracuse U., 1894-96; Ceramic Engr., Ohio State U., 1908; D.Sc., Alfred U., 1936; m. Myra J. Watts, June 17, 1901; children—Reliance S., Constance H., Lois B. Chemist and asst. supt., Mosaic Tile Co., Zanesville, 1899-1901; chemist Roseville Pottery Co., Zanesville, 1901-02; asst. in ceramics, Ohio State U., 1902-04; 1st instr. in ceramics, U. of Ill., 1904-06; asst. prof. ceramics Ohio State U., 1906-08, prof., 1908-12; dir. research, Norton Co., Worcester, Mass., 1912-18. Gen. sec. and editor Jour. Am. Ceramic Soc., 1921-46; author forty tech. papers. Formerly mem. Ohio Nat. Guard; four-minute man, World War, also chmn. N.E. Fuel Conservation and active in Liberty Loan drives. Fellow A.A.A.S., Am. Soc. for Testing Materials; hon. fellow Am. Ceramic Soc., Soc. of Glass Technology (Eng.); hon. life mem. Ohio Ceramic Industries Assn., Canadian Ceramic Soc., Czechoslovak Ceramic Soc., Indian Ceramic Soc.; mem. Psi Upsilon, Sigma Xi, Keramos. Republican. Presbyterian. Mason (Shriner). Club: Internat. Rotary. Home: 59 E. Longview Av., Columbus 2, O. Died Jan. 6, 1949.

PURVES, CLIFFORD BURROUGH, educator; b. Cupar-Fife, Scotland, Feb. 6, 1902; s. Alexander Murray and Elizabeth (Burrough) P.; ed. Bell-Baxter Sch., Cupar-Fife, 1906-19; B.S., St. Andrews U., 1923, Ph.D., 1929; D.Sc. (hon.), Laurence Coll., Wis.; m. Doris Elizabeth Ferry, Sept. 29, 1934; children—Elizabeth Burrough, John Montague, James Grant, Anne Alexandra, Alan, Patricia. Research asso. carbohydrate chemistry, dept. physiology Marischal Coll., Aberdeen, Scotland, 1929-31; came to U.S. as Commonwealth Fund fellow attached to Polarimetric Sect., U.S. Bur. Standards, 1926-29; research asso. carbohydrate chem. NIH, Bethesda, Md., 1931-36; asso. prof. cellulose chemistry Mass. Inst. Tech., 1936-43; E. B. Eddy prof. indsl. and cellulose chemistry McGill U., 1943—, also head wood chemistry div. Pulp and Paper Research Inst. Can. Mem. Am. Chem. Soc., T.A.P.P.I., Chem. Soc. (London), Can. Pulp and Paper Assn., Chem. Inst. Can. (pres. 1956-57), Sigma Xi. Contbr. tech. articles. Home: 2 Hudson Av., Westmount 28, Que. Office: McGill U., Montreal, Can. Died Sept. 30, 1965.

PUTNAM, FREDERIC WARD, anthropologist, zoölogist; b. Salem, Mass., Apr. 16, 1839; s. Eben and Elizabeth (Appleton) P.; B.S., Harvard, 1862; (hon. A.M., Williams, 1868; Sc.D., U. of Pa., 1894); m. Adelaide Martha Edmands, 1864 (died 1879); 2d, Esther Orne Clarke, 1882. Curator ornithology, 1856-64, curator vertebrata, 1864-66, supt. of mus., 1866-73, v.p., 1871-94, Essex Inst., and of East India Marine Soc., 1867-69, dir. of mus. Peabody Acad. Sciences, Salem, 1869-73; asst. in ichthyology, Mus. of Comparative Zoölogy, 1857-64 and 1876-78; asst. Geol. Survey of Ky., 1874, survey West of 100th meridian, U.S. engrs., 1876-79; prof. Am. archaeology and ethnology, Harvard, 1886-1909, prof. emeritus, 1910; curator Peabody Museum of Harvard Univ., 1874-1909, honorary curator, 1909-13, hon. director in charge, 1913; prof. anthropology and dir. Anthrop. Mus. U. of Calif., 1903-09, prof. emeritus, 1909; state commr. inland fisheries, 1882-89; chief dept. ethnology, Chicago Expn., 1891-94; curator anthropology, Am. Mus. Natural History, 1894-1903. Decorated by French Govt. with Cross of Legion of Honor; awarded Drexel gold medal for archeol. research. Fellow Am. Acad. Arts and Sciences; mem. numerous Am. and foreign Societies. Was originator and editor of Naturalists' Directory, 1865. One of the founders of The American Naturalist, 1868. Has published over 400 papers on zoölogy and anthropology; from 1870 engaged in researches and explorations in Am. archeology. Died Aug. 14, 1915.

PUTNAM, GEORGE ROCKWELL, engr., author; born Davenport, Ia., May 24, 1865; s. Charles E. and Mary L. (Duncan) P.; B.S., Rose Poly. Inst., 1890, M.S., 1895, Dr.Engring., 1933; D.Sc., Stevens Inst. of Technology, 1922; married Marta, d. Thomas P. Wick, September 11, 1913; children—Elizabeth Duncan (Mrs. C. L. Barber), Kristi Aresvik (Mrs. John Hay). Entered field service, United States Coast and Geodetic Survey, 1890; was on Mexican and Alaskan boundary surveys; in 1895 made series of gravity measurements, and developed reduction, results of which were the first consistent confirmation of isostatic condition of earth's crust; accompanied scientific expedition to Greenland, 1896; engaged on survey of Pribilof Islands, 1897, and of the delta of the Yukon River, 1898-99; made observations connecting Am. and European gravity stas., 1900; 1st dir. coast surveys in the P.I., 1900-06; developed plan of Philippine coast surveys; prepared plan for revision of charts of coasts of U.S.; commr. of lighthouses, 1910-35; carried out reorganization of U.S. Lighthouse Service; del. Internat. Lighthouse

Conference, London, 1929. Mem. Am. Soc. C.E., Washington Soc. Engrs. (pres. 1915), Washington Acad. Sciences. Author: Sentinel of the Coasts; Lighthouses and Lightships of the United States; Nautical Charts; Radiobeacons and Radiobeacon Navigation; also tech. papers and reports. Clubs: Cosmos (pres. 1920), Chevy Chase. Home: 2126 Bancroft Pl., Washington D.C.; also Dorset, Vt. Died July 2, 1953; buried Dorset.

PUTNAM, H(ENRY) ST. CLAIR, consulting engr.; b. Davenport, Ia., July 8, 1861; s. Charles Edwin and Mary Louisa (Duncan) P.; grad. Davenport High Sch., 1880; LL.B., State U. of Ia., 1882; B.S., Rose Poly. Inst., Terre Haute, Ind., 1886, M.S., 1905, E.E., 1907; m. Dorothy van Patten Torrey, Feb. 19, 1918. In practice of law, 1882-84; in engineering dept. Thomson-Houston Electric Co., 1886-87; in mfr. of arc light carbons, 1887-96, Thomson-Houston Carbon Co., Brush Carbon Co., Am. Carbon Co.; consulting elec. engr., Chicago, 1896-1900. Phila., 1900-02, New York, 1902—; dir. Continuous Transit Co. Fellow Am. Inst. Elec. Engrs. Republican. Presbyn. Home: New York, N.Y. Died Jan. 30, 1924.

PYKE, W(ESLEY) E(MERSON), chemist, educator; b. Richmond, Kan., Mar. 30, 1896; s. John William Hull and Minnie Agusta (Fuhlhage) P.; A.B., Baker U., Baldwin, Kan., 1918; Gregory scholar, U. Mo., 1928-29; Ph.D., U. Calif., 1940; m. Lela B. Buchheister, June 30, 1923; children—Betty Jane (Mrs. L. C. Wilson), Lela (Mrs. C.L. Faller), and Ruth Emily (Mrs. J. A. Randall). High sch. tchr. Plainville, Kan., 1922-23, Gallup, N.W., 1923-24; instr. chemistry Colorado State U., 1924-26, asst. prof. chem., 1926-35, associate prof., 1935-38, head chem. dept. and head chem. sect. Colo. Agrl. Expt. Sta. since 1945; rsrch. asso. in foods, Colo. Agrl. Expt. Sta., rsrch. prof. in foods, 1942-45. Chmn. trustees Colo. State U., Rsrch. Found., 1941-45; sec. since 1951, treasurer since 1952, trustee since 1941; trustee Colorado-Wyoming Academy Science Research Found. since 1949. Academic representative Colo. Development Council since 1950. Served as 2d lt., Q.M.C., U.S. Army, 1917-19. Mem. Nat. Food Industries award com., 1949; mem. Hoblitzelle Nat. award, regional com. for Colo. and Wyo., 1950-51. Mem. Am. Chem. Soc., Swiss Chem. Soc., A.A.A.S., Am. Assn. U. Profs., Inst. of Food Technologists, Am. Soc. Exptl. Biology and Medicine, Sigma Xi, Gamma Sigma Delta, Sigma Kappa Delta, Delta Tau Delta. Author expt. sta. bulls.; contbr. to agrl. jours. Home: 708 Smith St., Fort Collins, Colo. Died Dec. 21, 1959; buried Ft. Collins.

PYLE, JOHN SHERMAN, surgeon; b. at Dennison, O., Feb. 22, 1865; s. John and Catherine (Walker) P.; M.D., Bellevue Hosp. Med. Coll. (New York U.), 1886; LL.B., New York U., 1897; m. Lenore, d. Gen. Isaac R. Sherwood, of Toledo, O., July 16, 1897; 2d, Mary, d. Judge D. R. Austin, of Toledo, Oct. 8, 1913. Prof. anatomy and clin. surgery, Toledo Medical Coll., 1900-07; prof. physiology, Toledo U., 1909—. Inventor of numerous surgical instruments; has performed many original surg. operations of note along advanced lines. In 1893 advocated appropriation of capital criminals for advancement of science, and had bill introduced in Ohio legislature for that purpose. Contbr. to med. jours. Mem. bd. dirs. Toledo U., 1904—. Address: 209 Wayne Bldg., Toledo, O.

QUADE, MAURICE NORTHROP, civil engr.; b. Kewanee, Ill., Sept. 30, 1900; s. John Conrad and Florence A. (Northrop) Q.; B.S. with honors, U. Ill., 1925, M.S., 1926; m. Helen Louise Hamilton, Sept. 24, 1927; children—Robert Northrop, Susan McKinley (Mrs. William Brown Bahrenburg). Designer large bridge projects Waddell & Hardesty, 1926-36; engr. Parsons, Klapp, Brinckerhoff & Douglas, 1932-41; asso. engr. charge structural and hwy. projects Parsons, Brinckeroff Hogan & Macdonald, 1942-47; partner charge structural and hwy. projects Parsons, Brinckerhoff, Quade & Douglas, N.Y.C., 1947—; projects include George P. Coleman Meml. Bridge, Yorktown, Va., Susquehanna River Bridge on Pa. Turnpike, Sunshine Skyway, St. Petersburg, Fla., Hampton Roads Bridge-Tunnel, Norfolk, Va., Richmond-Petersburg Turnpike, Va., others. Chief structural engr., Caribbean architect and engr. U.S. Army bases, 1941-42. Recipient Thomas Fitch Rowland prize Am. Soc. C.E., 1955. Mem. Nat. Soc. Profl. Engrs., Am. Soc. C.E. (past pres. Met. sect.), Soc. Am. Mil. Engrs., Am. Concrete Inst., Am. Ry. Engring. Assn., Am. Soc. Testing Materials, Am. Inst. Cons. Engrs., Moles, Sigma Xi, Tau Beta Pi, Chi Epsilon, Theta Tau. Clubs: Commonwealth (Va.); N.Y. Downtown Athletic; Rock Spring (N.J.). Home: 12 Elliott Pl., West Orange, N.J. 07052. Office: 165 Broadway, N.Y.C. 6. Died June 12, 1966; buried Rosedale Cemetery, Orange, N.J.

QUAINTANCE, ALTUS LACY, entomologist; b. New Sharon, Ia., Dec. 19, 1870; s. Greenberry Plumley and Sarah Jane Q.; B.S.A., Fla. Agrl. Coll. (U. of Fla.), 1893; M.S., Ala. Poly. Inst., 1894, Sc.D., 1915; m. Nellie M. Yocum, of Lake City, Fla., Dec. 12, 1895;children—Leeland Charles, Howard Wilbur. Entomologist with Ala. Poly. Inst., 1894, Fla. Agrl. Coll. and Expt. Sta., 1895-98, Ga. Agrl. Expt. Sta., 1899-1901; with Md. Agrl. Coll. and Expt. Sta, and state entomologist of Md., 1901-03; spl. agt. Bur. Entomology, U.S. Dept. Agr., 1903—; entomologist in charge deciduous fruit insect investigations, 1905—; asso. chief of bur. in charge research work, 1923-31. Fellow Entomol. Soc. America, A.A.A.S.; pres. Assn. Econ. Entomologists, 1904, Entom. Soc. Washington, 1912; sec. Md. State Hort. Soc., 1902-03; chmn. sect. entomology Assn. Agrl. Colls. and Expt. Stas., 1903. Has written numerous expt. sta. bulls. and contributed to publs. U.S. Dept. Agr.; joint author Coccidae Americanae. Home: Silver Spring MD

QUAYLE, HENRY JOSEPH, entomologist; b. Isle of Man, Eng., Apr. 29, 1876; s. John and Jane (Skinner) Q.; A.B., U. of Ill., 1903; M.S., U. of Calif., 1911; m. Mary Elizabeth Reed, July 7, 1915. Came to U.S., 1880. Nursery insp., Ill., 1903; asst. in entomology, U. of Calif., 1903-05; instr. zoology, Ia. State Coll., 1905-06; asst. prof. entomology and asst. entomologist, Agr. Expt. Sta., U. of Calif., 1906-12, asso. prof. and asso. entomologist, 1912-15; now prof. entomology, U. of Calif. Citrus Expt. Sta.; conducted 1st large scale mosquito campaign in west, 1904-06; collaborator Federal Hort. Bd. on Mediterranean fruit fly study, Spain, Italy, Egypt, Palestine, and general citrus insects in India, Japan, and Hawaii; studied citrus insects in Australia, Spain, and Italy, 1923; introduced cyanide fumigation methods, particularly calcium cyanide, in Australia; introduced liquid hydrocyanic acid and dust method of fumigation in Spain, dust cyanide method of controlling rabbits in Australia. Del. Pan-Pacific Scientific Congress, Sidney and Melbourne, Australia; del. 4th Internat. Entomol. Congress, Ithaca, N.Y., 1928; in charge federal govt. fruit fly survey, Bermuda, Azores, Mediterranean region and S.Africa, 1929-30; mem. com. to advise on fruit fly campaign in Fla., 1930. Twice pres. Am. Assn. Econ. Entomologists (Pacific slope br.); 1st pres. Entomol. Club of Southern Calif.; fellow A.A.A.S.; mem. Sigma Xi, Alpha Zeta. Author: Citrus and Other Subtropical Fruit Insects, 1938; also numerous bulls., report and papers, chiefly on subtropical fruit insects. Address: U. of Calif. Citrus Experiment Station, Riverside CA

QUINBY, WILLIAM CARTER, physician; b. Worcester, Mass., May 26, 1877; s. Hosea Mason and Sarah Rumford Pierce (Carter) Q.; A.B., Harvard U., 1899; M.D., Harvard Med. Sch., 1902; m. Marguerite E. Thayer, Jan. 29, 1910; children—John Thayer, William Carter, Jr. House pupil Mass. Gen. Hosp., 1902-03; asst. genito-urinary surgeon Boston Dispensary, 1907-09; asst. surgeon New England Baptist Hospital, Boston, 1908-14; in charge experimental surgery Brady Clinic, Johns Hopkins Hospital; asso. in urology same, 1915-16; asst. in surgery, Harvard, 1916, instr., 1917, asst. prof. genito-urinary surgery, 1921-27, clin. prof., 1927-41, emeritus 1941, emeritus, active service, 1942-45; urologist Peter Bent Brigham Hosp., 1916-45, urol. surg. emeritus, 1946, Brigham Hosp., 1916-45, urol. surg. emeritus, 1946; acting surg.-in-chief, Peter Bent Brigham Hospital, 1947-48. Fellow Am. Coll. Surgeons, A.A.A.S.; mem. Am Assn. Genito-Urinary Surg., A.M.A., Am. Urol. Assn., Am. Physiol. Soc., Am. Soc. Clin. Investigation, Clin. Soc. Genito-Urinary Surgeons, Surgical Research Soc., New England Surg. Soc., Boston Surg. Soc., Am. Acad. Arts and Sciences, Brit. Assn. Urol. Surgeons (hon.). Clubs: Harvard, The Country. Home: 83 Penniman Rd., Brookline, Mass. Office: 1101 Beacon St., Brookline MA

QUINN, CHARLES HENRY, elec. engr.; b. Sacramento, Calif., Oct. 7, 1876; s. John and Harriet H. (Owner) Q.; grad. West Tex. Mil. Acad., San Antonio, 1896; B.S., Purdue U., 1899; m. Florence M. Letts, Dec. 11, 1944 (dec.). Chief elec. engr. Norfolk & Western Ry. Co., 1901-23; vice pres. and dir. Basin Oil Co., Los Angeles, since 1942; chmn. bd. Elec. Products Corp. since 1946; mem. adv. com. to bd. dirs. Bank of America Nat. Trust & Savings Assn. since 1942; dir. Blue Diamond Corp., Pacific Finance Corp., So. Calif. Edison Co. Mem. Franklin Inst., Phila. Republican. Home: 727 S. Beverly Glen Blvd., Los Angeles 24. Office: Pacific Mutual Bldg., 523 W. 6th St., Los Angeles

QUINTON, JOHN HENRY, civil engr.; b. Enniskillen, Ireland, Oct. 19, 1850; s. William and Anne (Thompson) Q.; B.A., Queens U., Ireland, 1871, B.E., 1872; m. Sophia Inglis Donnell, May 22, 1888. Came to U.S., 1873; leveler and transitman, S.P. Ry., until 1876; asst. engr. in charge location and constrn. South Pacific Coast Ry., Calif., 1878-80; in charge construction 80 miles Oregonian Ry., 1880; asst. engr. and acting chief engr., Pacific Br. Mex. Central Ry., 1881-84; pvt. practice, Southern Calif., 1884-88; asst. engr. War Dept., at Portland, Ore., 1888-89; successively field engr. for Hoffman & Bates (bridge builders), asst. engr. in charge location and constrn. Santa Ana Canal, Calif., San Gabriel Power Canal, 3d St. and Broadway tunnels, Los Angeles, and in pvt. practice until 1903; consulting or supervising engr., U.S. Reclamation Service, 1903-15, also consulting engr. U.S. Indian Service. Identified with many important irrigation projects, among them the Truckee Carson Project (Nev.), Uncompahgre Project (Colo.), Strawberry Project (Utah), Minidoka Project (Ida.), Milk River Project (Mont.), Shoshone Project (Wyo.), etc., involving reclamation of 3,000,000 acres of land; mem. Quinton, Code, Hill, Leeds & Barnard, consulting engrs. (retired). Republican. Protestant. Mason. Home: Los Angeles, Calif. Died May 1939.

QUIRKE, TERENCE THOMAS, (kwerk), prof. geology; b. Brighton, Eng., July 23, 1886; s. William Michael and Ellen Maude (Grace) Q.; E.M., U. of N.D., 1912, M.Sc., 1913; Ph.D., U. of Chicago, 1915; m. Anne Laura McIlraith, Sept. 23, 1916; children—Frances Grace, Dorothy Geneva, Terence Thomas. Came to U.S., 1904. Field asst. State Geol. Survey of N.D. and Geol. Survey of Can. 4 summers each, and chief of survey party in Can., summers 1919-31; instr. in geology, U. of Minn., 1915-17, asst. prof., 1917-19; asso. prof. geology, 1919-25, U. of Ill., chmn. dept., 1919-28, prof. since 1925. Fellow Am. Mineral. Soc., Soc. of Economic Geologists, Geol. Soc. of America, Am. Inst. of Mining and Metall. Engineers; member Am. Acad. Advancement of Science, Sigma Xi, Sigma Nu. Del. Internat. Geol. Congress, Brussels, 1922, Madrid, 1926. Episcopalian. Author: Española District, Ontario, 1917; Michipicoten Iron Ranges (with others), 1926; Elements of Geology, 1925; Disappearance of the Huronian (with W. H. Collins), 1930; also numerous articles and repts. Consultant in ore deposits; specialized on deposits of Cuba and Pre-cambrian deposits of N.A.; research on optical mineralogy and problems of the Precambrian. Home: 705 W. Oregon St., Urbana, Ill. Died Aug. 9, 1947.

RAAB, JULIUS, statesman, cons. engr.; b. St. Poelten, Lower Austria, Nov. 29, 1891; s. Julius and Franziska (Wohlmayr) R.; Tech. Engr., Inst. Tech., Vienna; m. Hermine Haumer, Jan. 14, 1922. Former bldg. contractor. Mem. Lower House of Parliament, Austria, 1927-34; Fed. Minister of Commerce and Transportation, 1938; Sec. of State for Pub. Works, Econ. Readjustment and Reconstrn., 1945; mem. Lower House of Parliament, 1945—; Fed. Chancellor of Austria 1953-61; founder Austrian People's Party, 1945, chairman, 1952-60; chmn. Austrian Federal Economic Chamber. Home: 8 Sauerburggasse, Vienna XIX. Office: Austrian Fed. Economic Chamber, Stubenring, Vienna 1, Austria. Died Jan. 8, 1964.

RAAB, WILHELM, physician and univ. prof.; b. Vienna, Austria, Jan. 14, 1895; s. Dr. Richard and Rosa (Gerenyi) R.; grad. cum laude, Schotten-Gymnasium, Vienna, 1913; M.D., Med. Faculty, U. of Vienna, 1920; 'M.d., German U. of Prague (Czechoslovakia), 1926; research fellow, Harvard Med. Sch., 1920-30; m. Olga Elizabeth Palmborg, June 17, 1930; children—Karl-Herbert, Fredrik-Holger; m. 2d, Helen Hubaczek, May 26, 1970; came to U.S. to reside, 1939. Began as med. house officer, Vienna, 1920; first asst. to Clin. Prof. Biedl, German U., Prague, 1921-26, privat-dozent in pathol. physiology, 1926-35; asst. and first asst., First Med. Clinic, U. of Vienna, 1926-36, privat-dozent in internal medicine, 1935-39; ofcl. examiner in internal medicine, U. of Vienna, 1936; physician in chief, Krankenhaus d. Kaufmannschaft, Vienna, 1936-39; asst. prof. clin. medicine, U. of Vt., 1939-45; prof. experimental medicine, since 1945; cons. specialist Mary Fletcher Hosp., Placid Meml. Hosp.; attending physician and head cardiovascular research unit, DeGoesbriand Meml. Hops., Burlington, Vt.; founder Preventive Heart Reconditioning Found., 1963. Cons. High Commrs. Office, Germany, 1950; Fulbright research prof. U. of Innsbruck, Austria, 1957-58. Mem. Pres.' Citizens' Com. on Fitness of Am. Youth, 1959. Served as lt. Med. Corps., Austro-Hungarian Army and German Army, 1916-18, 1938. Awarded 2 Austrian war medals for bravery (silver 1st class and bronze), other Austrian and Hungarian war decorations. Diplomate Am. Bd. Internal Medicine. Fellow Am. Coll. Physicians, Am. Coll. Cardiology, Am. Coll. Chest Physicians, Am. Coll. Sports Medicine, Life mem. Austro-Am. Inst. of Edn.; mem. A.M.A., New York Acad. Sciences, Soc. Exptl. Biology and Medicine, Vt. State Med. Soc., Chittenden Co. Med. Soc., Am. Physiol. Soc., Endocrine Soc., Soc. Internal Medicine, American Heart Association, Society of Gerontology, Society Study Arteriosclerosis, N.E. Cardiovascular Soc.; corr. mem. Gesellschaft d. Aerzte, Vienna; mem. Sigma Xi. Unitarian. Clubs: Research, Faculty, Layman's League. Author: Hormone und Stoffwechsel, 1926; Innersekretorische Storungen und Organotherapie, 1932; Hormonal and Neurogenic Cardiovascular Disorders, 1952; (with Hans Kraus) Hypokinetic Disease, 1961; Preventive Myocardiology, 1970; also numerous sci. articles and monographs. Editor: Prevention of Ischemic Heart Disease, 1966. Home: Burlington VT Died Sept. 21, 1970.

RABER, ORAN LEE, botanist; b. Wolcottville, Ind., Jan. 14, 1893; s. Levi L. and Lida (Cowley) R.; A.B., magna cum laude, Ind. U., 1912; student Purdue U., 1913; A.M., Harvard, 1915, Ph.D., 1920; U. of Montpelier, France, 1921, U. of Paris, 1922; unmarried. Austin teacher, Harvard, 1915-17; instr. botany, U. of Wis., 1920-21; asst. prof. botany, U. of Mich., 1923-24; asst. prof. botany, U. of Ariz., 1924-26; prof. same, First Univ. Cruise Around World, 1926-27; prof. of botany, Immaculata Coll., 1929-31; editorial staff Biological Abstracts, 1927-33; asso. ecologist of the U.S. Dept. of Agriculture, 1933-34, plant physiologist, Forest Service, 1935-37; editor Southern Forest Expt. Sta., 1937—. Lt. A.S. (balloon branch), 1918-19; licensed observer and pilot spherical balloons, A.S., O.R.C.; translator with

French High Commn., Washington, D.C., 1918-19; traveling fellow Am. Field Service Soc., to France, 1921-22. Unitarian. Mason. Author: Biographical Sketches of the Samuel Olin Family, 1921. Translator: The Elongated Captive Balloon (from the French), 1919; Principles of Plant Physiology, 1928; Water Utilization by Tress, 1937. Home: Wolcottville, Ind. Died Feb. 29, 1940.

RADEMACHER, HANS, mathematician; b. Hamburg, Germany, Apr. 3, 1892; s. Henry Adolph and Emma Friderike (Weinhover) R.; Ph.D., U. Gottingen, 1917; Doctor of Science, University of Pa., 1962; m. Susanne Gaspary, Apr. 1921; m. 3d, Irma Schoenberg Wolpe, Sept. 10, 1949. Privatdocent U. Berlin, 1919-22; prof. extraordinarius U. Hamburg, 1922-25; prof. ordinarius U. Breslau, 1925-34, dismissed by Nazis, 1934; with U. Pa., 1934-69, successively vis. prof., asst. prof., prof. mathematics, 1939-62, prof. emeritus, 1962-69; mem. Inst. for Advanced Study, Princeton, 1953, 60-61; vis. prof., Guggenheim fellow Tata Inst. Fundamental Research, Bombay, India, 1954-55; vis. prof. N.Y.U., 1962-64; visiting professor Rockefeller Inst., N.Y.C., 1964-66; affiliate Rockefeller University, 1966-69. Mem. Am., London math. socs., Math. Assn. Am., Soc. Indsl. and Applied Mathematics, Societe Mathematique de France, Sigma Xi. Author articles math. jours. Home: Philadelphia PA Died Feb. 7, 1969.

RADFORD, WILLIAM H(ENRY), educator; b. Phila., May 20, 1909; s. William Atkin and Evelyn (Felton) R.; B.S., Drexel Inst., Tech., 1931, D. Engring. (hon.), 1957; M.S., Mass. Inst. Tech., 1932; m. Pauline Newington, Dec. 22, 1941. Faculty, Mass. Inst. Tech., 1932—, successively researcher phys. properties of natural fog, faculty and research electronic computers, in charge elec. communications theory and lab., asso. dir. radar sch., in charge classified war projects, group leader def. research electronics lab., 1950-52, prof. elec. communications, 1951—, div., head Lincoln Lab., 1952-57, asso. dir. Lincoln Lab., 1957-64, dir., 1964—. Mem. USAF Sci. Adv. Bd., 1957—; U.S. Army Signal Corps Research and Devel. Adv. Council 1957-62. Profl. engr., Mass. Fellow I.E.E.E., A.A.A.S.; mem. Am. Soc. Engring. Edn., Sigma Xi, Tau Beta Pi, Eta Kappa Nu. Club: New Bedford (Mass.) Yacht. Home: 121 Poplar St., Watertown 72, Mass. Office: 77 Massachusetts Av., Cambridge 39, Mass. Died May 9, 1966.

RADO, TIBOR, educator; b. Budapest, Hungary, June 2, 1895; s. Alexander and Gizella (Knappe) R.; student Poly. Inst., Budapest, 1913-15; Ph.D., U. Szeged, Hungary, 1923; D.Sc. (hon.), Kenyon Coll., 1960; m. Ida Barabas de Albis, Oct. 30, 1924; children—Judith Viola (Mrs. W. Santasiere), Theodore Alexander. Came to U.S., 1929, naturalized, 1935. Privat-docent U. Szeged, 1927; Internat. Research fellow Rockefeller Found., Germany, 1928, 29; vis. lectr. Harvard, Rice Inst., 1929-30; prof. math. Ohio State U., 1930-48, chmn. dept., 1946-48, research prof. math., 1949—; vis. prof. math. U. Chgo., 1942, U. P.R., 1947; cons. Battelle Meml. Inst., Columbus, O., 1961—. Served as 1st lt. Royal Hungarian Army, World War I; sci. cons. to USAAF, ETO, World War II. Mem. Am. Math. Soc. (Colloquim lectr. 1945), Assn. for Computing Machinery, Math. Assn. Am. (Hedrick Meml. lectr. 1952), A.A.A.S. (v.p. 1953). Presbyn. Mason. Author: On the Problem of Plateau, 1933; Subharmonic Functions, 1937; Length and Area, 1948; Continuous Transformations in Analysis (with P.V. Reichelderfer), 1955; also research papers. Home: 2299 Tremont Rd., Columbus 21, O. Died Dec. 29, 1965; buried Bellview Meml. Park, Daytona Beach, Fla.

RAE, CHARLES WHITESIDE, naval engr.; b. Hartford, Conn., June 30, 1847; s. Rev. Luzern and Martha (Whiteside) R.; prep. edn. Champlain (N.Y.) Acad.; C.E., Rensselaer Poly. Inst., 1866; grad. U.S. Naval Acad., 1868; D.Sc., U. of Pa., 1906; m. Rebecca Gilman Dodge, Jan. 9, 1890. Promoted through grades, becoming capt., Jan. 3, 1903; served at bombardment of San Juan, P.R., also in several minor actions on S. coast of Cuba and at naval battle of Santiago, July 3, 1898; advanced "for eminent and conspicuous conduct in battle" (medal). Apptd. engr.-in-chief U.S.N., with rank of rear admiral, and chief bureau of steam engring., Navy Dept., Aug. 9, 1903. Residence: Washington, D.C. Died 1908.

RAFINESQUE, CONSTANTINE SAMUEL, naturalist; b. Galata, Constantinople, Turkey, Oct. 22, 1783; s. G.F. Rafinesque; m. Josephine Vaccaro, 1809, 2 children including Emily. Came to U.S., 1802; collected bot. specimens, So. N.J. and Dismal Swamp of Va., 1804; went to Palermo, Sicily, 1805; sec., chancellor to Am. consul, Palermo, for a while; exporter squills, medicinal plants, Palermo, 1808; returned to U.S., 1815; explored Hudson Valley, Lake George, L.I. and other regions, 1815-18; prof. botany, natural history, modern langs. Transylvania U., 1818-26; advocated Jussieu's method of classification. Wrote and published books and articles on botany, ichthyology, banking, econs. and other topics, including: Icthyologia Ohioensis, 1820; Medical Flora of the United States, 1828-30; (autobiography) A Life of Travels and Researches in North America and South Europe, 1836. Died Phila., Sept. 18, 1840.

RAHN, OTTO, (rän), prof. bacteriology; b. Tiegenhof, West Prussia, Apr. 9, 1881; s. Isbrand and Marie (Claassen) R.; Real-Gymnasium, Elbing, Germany, 1891-99; Ph.D., Göttingen U., 1902; m. Bell S. Farrand, Sept. 4, 1911; children—Hermann, Marie, Margarete, Otto. Asst. in dairy science, Göttingen U., 1902-06; asst. in soil bacteriology, Halle Expt. Sta., 1906-07; asst. prof. bacteriology, Mich. State Coll. Agr. and Applied Science, East Lansing, 1907-12; asst. prof. bacteriology, U. of Ill., 1912-14; served in Germany army, 1916-18; asst. in soil bacteriology, Agrl. Coll., Berlin, 1919; prof. dairy physics, Research Inst., Kiel, Germany, 1920-26; prof. bacteriology, Cornell U., 1927-49, Ida. State Coll., 1949-54; retired 1949. Dir. Physikalischen Institut (Prusz-Versuchs) and Forschungsanstalt für Milchwirtschaft (Kiel), 1922; first to establish lab. for colloidal and physical chemistry of milk. Co-Author: Physik der Milchwirtschaft (with P. F. Sharp), 1928; Handbuch der Milchwirtschaft (with others), 1931; Physiology of Bacteria, 1932; Invisible Radiation of Organisms, 1935; Mathematics in Bacteriology, 1939, Microbes of Merit, 1945; Injury and Death of Bacteria by Chemical Agents, 1945. Contbr. to Jour. of Bacteriology, Jour. of Gen. Physiology, Centralblatt für Bakteriologie, etc. Home: Millsboro, Del. Died Sept. 26, 1957.

RAKE, GEOFFREY WILLIAM, med. scientist; b. Fordingbridge, Eng., Oct. 18, 1904; s. Herbert Vaughan and Rosemary (Satchell) R.; student Cliff House, Bournemouth, Eng., 1910-11, Christ Ch., Choir Sch., Oxford, Eng., 1911-19, King's Sch., Canterbury, Eng., 1919-21; Guy's Hosp. Medical School, London, Eng., 1922-28, M.B., B.S., 1928; came to U.S., 1928; became naturalized U.S. citizen, Dec. 14, 1942; m. Orpha May McNutt, July 1, 1932; 1 son, Adrian Vaughan; m. 2d, Helen Jones, March 23, 1946; children—Geoffrey, Juliet, James, Jane, Neave. House officer Guy's Hosp., London, 1926-28; asst., pathol., Johns Hopkins U., 1928-29, instr., 1929-30; asst. pathol., and bacteriol., Rockefeller Inst., New York, 1930-32, asso., 1932-36; research asso. Connaught Labs., U. of Toronto, Canada, 1936-37; head division of microbiology, member of the Squibb Inst. for Med. Research, New Brunswick, N.J., 1937-49; med. director E. R. Squibb & Sons, 1949-53; Consultant to pres., 1953-56; scientific director Internat. div. Olin Mathieson Chem. Corp., 1956—; director Squibb Institute of Medical Research, 1949-53; research prof. Sch. Medicine, U. Pa.; member Wistar Inst. Anatomy and Biology, Phila., 1953—. Fellow Royal Society Medicine (London), New York Academy of Medicine, American College of Physicians; licentiate Royal College Physicians (London); mem. Royal Coll. Surg. (Eng.), Harvey Soc., Am. Epidemiol. Soc. Awarded Hiltonprize in anatomy, 1923, Stokes prize in pathology, 1924, Beaney prize in pathology, 1927, gold medal in medicine, 1927—all Guy's Hosp.; Rettlinger prize, London, 1928, Stokes traveling scholarship in pathology, London, 1930. Episcopalian. Clubs: New York Bacteriological; Guy's '28 (London, Eng.); Charaka, University (N.Y.). Home: Great Rd., Princeton, N.J. Office: 745 5th Av., N.Y.C. Died Apr. 20, 1958.

RALSTON, JOHN CHESTER, consulting engr.; b. Ontario, Can., May 1867; s. James G. and Mary A. (Johnston) R.; came to U.S., 1881; studied engring. under pvt. tutors; student Art Students' League, New York; m. Mary Kean Buckner, Apr. 1897; children—J. W. B., Mary Elizabeth. City engr., Spokane, Wash., 1907-09; served as chief engr. Grand Canal Irrigation Works; engr. in development of power in Sacramento Valley; asst. and dir. engr., location and constrn. 800 miles of rys.; hydraulic engr. various enterprises; supt. constrn. 5 miles of sea wall, reclaiming Potomac Flats, Potomac Park, D.C.; v.p. Pacific Coast Pipe Co. Trustee St. Luke's Hosp. Republican. Episcopalian. Mason. Home: Spokane, Wash. Died July 15, 1928.

RALSTON, OLIVER CALDWELL, metallurgist; b. Colorado Springs, Colo., Sept. 6, 1887; s. Orlandus Frank and Martha Jane (Caldwell) R.; B.S., Colorado Coll., 1910, LL.D.; m. Lala Chrisman Bartleson, Mar. 28, 1912. Assayer, chemist, techr. chemistry, Leadville, Colo., 1910-12; chemist U.S. Bur. Mines, Pitts., 1912-14, metallurgist, Salt Lake City, 1914-17; metallurgist Hooker Electro-chem. Co., Niagara Falls, N.Y., 1917-20; asst. chief metallurgist U.S. Bur. Mines, 1920-28; dir. research United Verde Copper Co., 1928-35; prin. chem. engr. U.S. Bur. Mines, New Brunswick, N.J., 1935-37; chief metallurgy div. U.S. Bur. of Mines, College Park, Md., Washington, 1937-1944, chief metall. br., 1946—, chief metallurgist U.S. Bur. Mines since 1950; v.p. Sharp Lead Co.; tech. dir. Ariz. Minerals Corp. Sec. research and inventions State Council Def., Utah, 1917. Recipient D.S.M., Army Citation. Mem. Am. Inst. M.E., Am. Chem. Soc., Am. Electrochem. Soc., Faraday Soc., Am. Ceramic Soc. Author: Flotation, 1917; Electro-deposition and Hydrometallurgy of Zinc, 1921; Zink Elektrolyse and Nassverfahrung, 1928; Iron Oxide Reduction Equilibria, 1929; also numerous bulls. U.S. Bur. Mines, 1942-57. Home: 4333 Claggett Rd., University Park, Hyattsville, Md. 20782. Office: Interior Bldg., Washington 25. Died June 21, 1965; buried Evergreen Cemetery, Colorado Springs.

RAMALEY, FRANCIS (r'ma'le), botanist; b. St. Paul, Minn., Nov. 16, 1870; s. David and Louisa Mary (DeGraw) R.; B.S., U. of Minn., 1895, Ph.D., 1899; m. Ethel Jackson, June 14, 1906; children—Edward Jackson, David, John DeGraw, Francis. Instr. botany, U. of Minn., 1894-98; asst. prof. biology, 1898-99, prof., 1899-1939, editor of University Studies since 1939, U. of Colo. Dir. Mountain Lab., Tolland, Colo., 1909-19; pres. Bd. Edn., Boulder, 1911-12. Republican. Fellow A.A.A.S. (pres. Southwestern div. 1930); mem. Am. Soc. Naturalists, Bot. Soc. America, Ecol. Soc. America (v.p. 1931, pres. 1940), Soc. Exptl. Biology and Medicine, Theta Delta Chi, Phi Beta Kappa, Sigma Xi. Author: Wild Flowers and Trees of Colorado, 1909; Prevention and Control of Disease, 1913; Outlines of Economic Botany, 1926; Colorado Plant Life, 1927; Plants Useful to Man, 1937; Plant Science Manual, 1937; Survey of Plant Kingdom, 1940; also articles in tech. jours. on botany and pub. health. Botanical editor of Ecology since 1940. Home: Boulder, Colo. Died June 10, 1942.

RAMSAY, ALEXANDER, anatomist; b. Edinburgh, Scotland, circa 1754; studied anatomy under Cruikshank, Baille and Munroe; M.D. (hon.), U. St. Andrews, 1805. Began teaching anatomy, Edinburgh, 1790, founded in anat. soc.; came to U.S., circa 1801, settled in Fryeburg, Me., founded unsuccessful sch. of anatomy; practiced medicine and lectured on anatomy in region, 1801-08; lectr. Dartmouth Med. Sch., 1808; lectured in Europe, 1810-16; lectured on natural philosophy in U.S., 1816-24. Author: Anatomy of the Heart, Cranium, and Brain, 1812. Died Parsonfield, Me., Nov. 24, 1824; buried Fryeburg.

RAMSAY, ERSKINE, (ram'zi), corp, ofcl.; b. Pitts., Sept. 24, 1864; s. Robert and Janet (Erskine) R.; grad. commercial tech. course, St. Vincent's Coll., Westmoreland County, Pa., 1883. Trained in mining under father; made supt. H. C. Frick Coke Co.'s Monastery Mines at age of 19; supt. Morewood Coke Co. and South West Coal & Coke Co. at 20, later asst. engr. H. C. Frick Coke Co.; in 1887 went with the Tenn. Coal, Iron & R.R. Co. as supt. and engr. Pratt Mines, later became chief engr. and asst. gen. mgr. same co., 1894-1901; in 1901 became v.p. and chief engr. Pratt Consol. Coal Co. (now part of Ala. By-Products Corp.); chmn. bd. and gen. cons. engr. Ala. By-Products Corp.; pres. Ramsay-McCormack Land Co.; v.p. Goodall-Brown Dry Goods Co., Avondale Mills; dir. and cons. engr. Newcastle Coal Co.; chmn. bd. Ala. Mineral Land Co.; dir. Protective Life Ins. Co.; Birmingham Fire Ins. Co., First Nat. Bank of Birmingham (exec. com.), Buffalo Rock Co. (chmn. bd.). Dollar-a-year man and mem. Peabody Com., World War. Pres. bd. edn., Birmingham, 1922-41; mem. bd. dirs. Boys' Club (all of Birmingham). Awarded the William Lawrence Saunders gold medal by Am. Inst. Mining and Metall. Engrs., 1937, for bituminous coal mining inventions; for improvement in coke making that resulted in the establishment of the steel industry in Ala.; for administering large enterprises and for benefactions to ednl. instns. Mem. Am. Soc. Mech. Engrs., Am. Soc. C.E., Am. Inst. Mining and Metall. Engrs., Coal Mining Inst. of Am., Mine Inspectors' Inst. of Am. Republican. Presbyn. Mason. Clubs: Birmingham, Country (ex-pres.), Mountain Brook Club (ex-pres.). Kiwanis (ex-pres., dist. gov. of Ala.). Patented about 40 inventions in coal mining. Home: 3720 Redmont Rd. Office: First Nat. Bldg., Birmingham, Ala. Died 1953. *

RAMSER, CHARLES ERNEST, (ram'zer), agrl. and hydraulic engr.; b. Montezuma, Ia., Nov. 1, 1885; s. Paul and Mary Angeline (Retz) R.; B.S. in Civil Engring., U. of Ill., 1909; m. Anne Lillian Larkin, July 27, 1925; children—Anne Ernestine, Charles Ernest. Instr. highway engring. and asst. to prof. of municipal, hydraulic and sanitary engring., Polytechnic Inst. of Brooklyn (N.Y.), 1909-11; asst. engr., N.Y. Bd. of Water Supply, summer 1910; chief hydrographer, Knoxville Power Co., Alcoa, Tenn., 1911-12; asst. drainage engr., bureau pub. roads, U.S. Dept. Agr., 1913-15, drainage engr., 1915-17, sr. drainage engr., bureau pub. roads and bureau agrl. engring., 1917-35, sr. soil conservationist, head of div. of watershed studies, soil conservation service, 1935-37, prin. soil conservationist, chief hydrologic div., 1937-42, prin. soil conservationist, research specialist in hydraulics and hydrology, 1942-47; consulting engineer Bureau Reclamation, Department of Interior, 1948-49; consultant in drainage, flood control, soil and water conservation since 1947; work includes devising and developing pioneer scientific methods of terracing farm lands to prevent soil erosion; also experiments on flow of water through wooded floodways, results used in Miss. River flood-control plans; supt. of first Federal soil erosion experiment station located at Guthrie, Okla.; planned and directed engineering experiments on first ten Federal erosion stations; inaugurated publication of a special government series of large hydrologic bulletins relating to soil and water conservation. Recipient John Deere gold medal Am. Soc. Agrl. Engrs., 1944. Life mem. Am. Soc. C.E., Am. Soc. Agrl. Engrs. (Council 1937-40); mem. A.A.A.S., Soil Conservation Soc. Am. (hon.), Friends of Land Soc., Am. Soc. Agrl. Sciences, Am. Geophys. Union, Tau Beta Pi, Sigma Xi. Mason (32 deg.). Club: Cosmos (Washington). Mem. Rotary Club of Guthrie, Okla., 1929-35. Author of more than

100 govt. bulls., articles and reports relating to soil and water conservation, terracing, drainage and flood control, including: Prevention of Erosion of Farm Lands by Terracing, 1917; Gullies—How to Control and Prevent Them, 1935; Flow of Water in Drainage Channels, 1929; Erosion and Silting of Drainage Ditches, 1930; Farm Terracing, 1935. Address: 4615 Kenmore Dr., Washington 20007. Died Apr. 29, 1962; buried Mt. Olive Cemetery, St. Joseph, Ill.

RAMSEY, ROLLA ROY, prof. physics; b. Morning Sun, O., Apr. 11, 1872; s. Joseph Steele and Sarah (McQuiston) R.; grad. high sch., Oxford, O., 1891; student Miami U., 1891-92; A.B., Ind. U., 1895, A.M., 1898; studied Clark U., 1898-99; Ph.D., Cornell U., 1901; studied in Europe, 1912-13; m. Clara Ethel Smith, of Bloomington, Ind., Dec. 29, 1897; 1 son, Hugh Smith. Teacher high sch., Decatur, Ind., 1895-96; lab. asst. Ind. U., 1896-97; prof. physics, Westminster Coll., New Wilmington, Pa., 1897-98; asst. in physics, Cornell U., 1899; instr. in physics, Ind. U., 1900; instr. physics, U. of Mo., 1901-03; asst. prof. physics Indiana University, 1903-05, asso. prof., 1905-19, became professor, 1919, now retired; acting head of physics department Indiana University, 1937-38; radioactivity specialist for Bur. of Standards, Washington, D.C. Chief instr. U.S. Radio Sch., Ind. U., 1918. Fellow A.A.A.S., Ind. Acad. Science, Am. Physical Soc.; mem. Inst. Radio Engrs., Phi Beta Kappa, Sigma Xi. Republican. United Presbyn. Kiwanian. Author: Experimental Radio, 1923, 4th edit., 1937; The Fundamentals of Radio, 1929, 2d edit., 1935; also about 98 papers in scientific mags. Inventor of model of the atom. Home: 420 E. 1st St., Bloomington, Ind. Died June 11, 1955; buried Covenanter Cemetery.

RAND, GERTRUDE, psychologist; b. New York, N.Y., Oct. 29, 1886; d. Lyman Fiske and Mary Catherine (Moench) Rand; B.A., Cornell U., 1908; M.A., and Ph.D., Bryn Mawr, 1911; Sc.D., Wilson College, Pa., 1943; m. Clarence Errol Ferree, Sept. 28, 1918 (died 1942). Research fellow Bryn Mawr, 1911-12, Sarah Berliner research fellow, 1912-13; demonstrator and reader in experimental and ednl. psychology, same Coll., 1913-14, and asso. in exptl. and applied psychology, 1914-25; demonstrator in exptl. psychology and research asst., Nat. research Council's Com. on Industrial Lighting, 1925-27; asso. prof. of research ophthalmology, Johns Hopkins U. Sch. Medicine, 1928-32, asso. prof. physiol. optics, 1932-36; asso. dir. Research Lab. of Physiol. Optics, Baltimore, Md., 1936-43; research asso. in ophthalmology on Knapp Foundation, Coll. Phys. and Surg., Columbia U., 1943-57; cons. Knapp Memorial Laboratory, College of Physcians and Surgeons, Columbia University, 1957-70. Mem. Armed Forces NRC Vision Com., subcom. on Color Vision and Illumination Standards. Recipient Edgar D. Tillyer Medal, Optical Soc. Am., 1959. Fellow A.A.A.S., Am. Psychol. Assn., Illuminating Engineering Society (Gold medal 1963), Optical Soc. of Am., American Acad. of Ophthalmology and Otolaryngology (hon.); mem. N.Y. State Psychol. Assn., Am. Inst. Physics, University Profs., American Assn. University Women, Inter Society Color Council (color blindness com.), Internat. Council Women Psychologists; mem. adv. com. and com. on Vision Testing Procedures, Nat. Society for Prevention Blindness. Republican. Presbyterian. Clubs: Cosmopolitan (N.Y.) Oldfield (L.I.), Women's Faculty (Columbia); Cornell Women's (New York). Author: the Factors Which Influence the Sesitivity of the Retina to Color, 1913; Radiometric Apparatus for Use in Psychological and Physiological Optics, 1917, Studies in Physiological Optics, 2 vols., 1934 (with C. E. Ferree). Co-inventor Ferree-Rand perimeter, light-sense tester, acuity projecter, multiple-exposure tachistoscope, variable illuminator, and other optical and ophthalmol. instruments. Inventor Rand Anomalscope; co-inventor Hardy-Rand-Rittler Pseudoisochromatic Plates. Contbr. mags. Home: Stony Brook LI NY Died June 30, 1970; buried Baltimore MD

RAND, HERBERT WILBUR, biologist; b. Oil City, Pa., July 2, 1872; s. Henry Howard and Ella Augusta (Davis) R.; A.B., Allegheny Coll., 1892, C.E., 1893; A.B., Harvard, 1897; A.M., 1898; Ph.D., 1900; m. Claire Forbes Hammond, Dec. 27, 1900 (dec.); children—Henry Forbes, Dorothy Garrison; m. 2d, Marion Josephine MacCallum, July 2, 1928. Draftsman Westinghouse Electric & Mfg. Co., Pitts., 1892-94; asst. prin. Oil City (Pa.) High Sch., 1894-96; instr. zoology, Harvard, 1900-09, asst. prof., 1909-19, asso. prof. 1919-38, emeritus, 1938—; an incorporator Bermuda Biol. Sta., 1926, trustee, 1926-43, sec., 1926-37; lectr. zoology Wellesley Coll., 3 periods between 1908-19; Harvard exchange prof. to Grinnell, Beloit and Colorado colls., 1928-29 (2d semester). Fellow Am. Acad. Arts and Scis., A.A.A.S., Am. Inst. Biol. Scis., Am. Soc. Zoologists (v.p. 1934), Am. Soc. Naturalists, Philos. Sci. Assn. Author books on comparative anatomy of vertebrates and various papers on regeneration of animals: exptl. morphology. Asso. editor Jour. Morphology, 1938-44. Home: 7 Siders Pond Rd., Falmouth, Mass. Died Dec. 23, 1960.

RAND, JAMES HENRY, mfr. office supplies and equipment; b. North Tonawanda, N.Y., Nov. 18, 1886; s. James Henry and Mary (Scribner) R.; Class of 1908, Harvard; m. Evelyn Greely, May 3, 1929; children by previous marriage—Miriam R. Boxwell, James Henry III and Marcell N. (twins). Founder Remington Rank Inc., mfrs. office supplies and equipment, 1926, president, 1926-55, vice chairman of Sperry Rand Corp. (merger of Remington Rand Inc., and Sperry Corporation), 1955-68. Clubs: Fishers Island (N.Y.) Country; Harvard (New Canaan, Conn.); Norwalk (Conn.) Yacht; Saturn (Buffalo); Metropolitan, Union League, University (N.Y. City); Tokeneke, Wee Burn Country (Darien, Conn.); Turf & Field (N.Y.); Everglades (Palm Beach, Fla.). Home: Darien CT Died June, 1968.

RAND, THEODORE DEHON, retired lawyer; b. Phila., Sept. 16, 1836; s. Benjamin H. and Eleanor S. R.; ed. Episcopal Acad.; attended Polytechnic Coll.; admitted to bar, 1858; practiced law; m. Elizabeth Belrose, March 10, 1864. Engaged as amateur in scientific work, chiefly in mineralogy and geology; published a number of papers on these branches, and lectured before scientific bodies. Fellow A.A.A.S.; dir. mineralogical and geol. sect. Acad. Nat. Sciences; v.p. Franklin Inst.; treas. Am. Inst. of Mining Engrs. for 30 yrs. Address: Radnor, Delaware County, Pa. Died 1903.

RANDALL, ALEXANDER, urologist; b. Annapolis, Md., Apr. 18, 1883; s. John Wirt and Hannah Parker (Parrott) R.; B.A., St. Johns Coll., Annapolis, 1902, M.A., 1907; studied Johns Hopkins, 1902-03, Johns Hopkins Med. Sch., 1903-07, M.D., 1907; m. Edith T. Kneedler, June 2, 1915; children—Alexander, Peter, Virginia. Resident German Hosp., Phila., 1907-09; pvt. asst. to Dr. H. H. Young, Balt., 1910; resident urologist Johns Hopkins Hosp., 1911; asst. prof. surgery U. Pa., 1923-26, asso. prof., 1926-29, prof. urology, 1929-46; retired. Served from lt. to maj. M.C., U.S. Army, 1917-19; with AEF, 1918-19. Fellow A.C.S.; mem. A.M.A., Phila. Acad. Surgery, Coll. Physicians Phila., Am. Surg. Assn., Am. Urol Assn (pres. 1932), Am. Assn. Genito-Urinary Surgeons (pres. 1938), Société Internationale d'Urologie. Republican. Episcopalian. Clubs: Rittenhouse, Corinthian Yacht (Phila.). Author: Surgical Pathology of Prostatic Obstructions, 1931; also articles giving results of med. research. Home: 20 Laughlin Lane, Phila. Office: Medical Arts Bldg., Phila. Died Nov. 18, 1951; buried St. Thomas Cemetery, White Marsh, Pa.

RANDALL, FRANK ALFRED, structural engr.; b. Cambridge, Ill., Nov. 1, 1883; s. Samuel Benjamin and Anna Louise (Carlson) R.; B.S. in Civil Engring., U. Ill., 1905, C.E., 1909; m. Mabel Madeline Morris, Feb. 1, 1908; children—Ruth Louise, Helen Anna, Frank Alfred, John Deacon. Draftsman Am. Bridge Co., 1905; bridge designer and insp. C., M.&St.P. Ry., 1906; cons. engr. Morey, Newgard & Co., Chgo., 1907, 11-14; bridge designer Sanitary Dist. Chgo., 1908-11; structural engr. Randall & Warner, 1914-17; N.Y. rep. for Seattle, North Pacific Shipbuilding Co. and Patterson MacDonald Shipbuilding Co., 1918; mem. Berlin, Swern & Randall, Chgo., 1919-23; practicing alone, 1923-47, partner Frank A. Randall & Sons, 1947—; cons. bridge engr. Chgo. Park Dist., 1935—; cons. structural engr. Dept. of Subways and Superhighways, City of Chgo., 1938—; structural engr. for 1400 Lake Shore Drive, Chgo. (21 stories, concrete) Medinah Athletic Club bldg. (42 stories), Foshay Tower, Mpls. Ramsey Tower, Oklahoma City, Victor Lawson YMCA, Dearborn Homes, 27th to 30th sts. on S. State St.; building commr. Century of Progress Expn., 1933-34; charge constrn. Outer Drive Improvement, 1936-37. Mem. bd. edn., Wilmette, Ill., 1940-45, Wilmette Planning Bd., 1945—. Mem. Am. Soc. C.E., Western Soc. Engrs., Chgo. Bldg. Congress (dir.), Am. Concrete Inst., Am. Soc. for Testing Materials, Soc. Naval Architects and Marine Engrs., N.E. Historic Geneal. Society, Order of the Founders and Patriots Am., S.A.R., Newcomen Soc. Alpha Delta Phi, Tau Beta Pi, Sigma Xi, Phi Kappa Phi. Republican. Mason (K.T., Shriner). Clubs: Union League, Chicago Engineers', Illini. Author and pub.: William Randall of Scituate and his descendants with ancestral families of Frank A. Randall; History of Building Construction in Chicago, 1949. Home: 912 12th St., Wilmette, Ill. Office: 205 W. Wacker Dr., Chgo. 6. Died Dec. 2, 1950; buried Meml. Park, Evanston, Ill.

RANDALL, HENRY STEPHENS, agriculturist, educator; b. Brookfield, Madison County, N.Y., May 3, 1811; s. Roswell and Harriet (Stephens) R.; grad. Union Coll., 1830; m. Jane Rebecca Polhemus, Oct. 4, 1834, 3 children. Admitted to bar, 1834; youngest regular del. to Democratic Nat. Conv., 1835; supt. schs. Madison County (N.Y.), 1843-47; sec. state N.Y., also ex officio supt. public instrn., 1851-53; responsible for creation of a separate dept. public instrn. State of N.Y.; mem. Nat. Dem. Com. at Charleston, 1860; mem. N.Y. Legislature, 1871; corr. sec. N.Y. State Agrl. Soc.; Proposed the N.Y. State Fair; editor sheep husbandry dept. Moore's Rural New Yorker, 1864-67. Author: The Life of Thomas Jefferson (the most detailed biography of Jefferson), 3 vols., 1858; The Practical Shepherd, 1863 (orginially written as "Fine Wool Sheep Husbandry"). Died Cortland, N.Y., Aug. 14, 1876.

RANDALL, LAWRENCE MERRILL, physician; b. LaMoille, Ia., Aug. 12, 1895; s. Addison J. and Edith (Cox) R.; M.D., U. Ia., 1921; M.S., U. Minn., 1931; m. Faith Meek, Mar. 29, 1923; children-Robert Lawrence, Mary Virginia (Mrs. Douglas Fulton), David Addison. Intern U. Ia., 1921-22, resident obstetrics and gynecology, 1922-24; 1st asst. obstetrics and gynecology U. Minn., Mayo Found., 1925, asst. prof., 1932-35, asso. prof., 1936-46, prof., 1946-60, emeritus prof., 1960-69; head sect. obstetrics and gynecology Mayo Clinic, 1937, chmn. sections, 1949, mem. bd. govs., 1948-55. Diplomate Am. Bd. Obstetrics and Gynecology (chmn.). Mem. A.M.A., Am. Coll. Obstetricians, Am. Assn. Obstetricians and Gynecologists, Central Assn. Obstetricians and Gynecologists, Minn. Soc. Obstetricians and Gynecologists, Alumni Assn. Mayo Found. Med. Edn. and Research, Societe Royale Belge de Gynecologie et d'Obstetrique (fgn. corr.) Am., Chgo. gynecol. socs., Sigma Xi, Phi Kappa Sigma, Nu Sigma Nu. Republican. Episcopalian. Contbr. med. articles profl. jours. Home: Rochester MN Died Jan. 11, 1969.

RANDALL, MERLE, chem. and chem. engring. cons.; b. Poplar Bluff, Mo., Jan. 29, 1888; s. Warren Smith and Anna Elizabeth (Marks) R.; A.B., University of Missouri, 1907, A.M., 1909; fellow Mass. Institute Technology, 1909-12, Ph.D., 1912; m. Lillian Frances Denham, June 14, 1916; children—Merle Denham, Robert Warren. Began as clk. in postoffice, Poplar Bluff, 1902-04; research asst. U. of Calif., 1912-13, research asso., 1914-17, asst. prof. chemistry, 1917-22, asso. prof., 1922-27, prof. 1927-44, prof. emeritus since 1944. Chmn. sub. com. on chemistry, Termite Investigations Com., 1929, mem. editorial bd., 1931; dir. research, Stuart Oxygen Co., 1944-48, Randall and Sons, since 1942. Fellow A.A.A.S.; member Society Promotion Engineering Education, American Inst. Chem. Engring., Am. Chem. Soc., Am. Soc. Testing Materials, Am. Soc. Refrig. Engrs., Am. Soc. Metals, Am. Welding Soc.,Sigma Xi, Alpha Chi Sigma. Republican. Presbyterian. Mason. (K.T., Shriner). Club: Faculty. Author: Thermodynamics and the Free Energy of Chemical Substances, 1923; Termites and Termite Control, 1934; Elementary Physical Chemistry, 1942. Home: 2512 Etna St., Berkeley 4, Calif. Died Mar. 19, 1950.

RANDALL, OTIS EVERETT, univ. prof.; b. N. Stonington, Conn., Feb. 28, 1860; s. Darius Hewitt and Abby Palmer (Frink) R.; A.B., Brown U., 1884, A.M., 1887, Ph.D., 1896; student at Technische Hochschule, Charlottenburg, Germany, and U. of Berlin, 1899-1900; m. Mabel Herbert Goffe, June 19, 1899; children—Wallace Everett, Mabel Maye (dec.). Served as teacher Providence High School, 1884-85; instr. mathematics and civil engineering, 1885-91, asst. prof., 1891-92, asso. prof. mech. drawing, 1892-96, prof., 1896-1905, prof. mechanics and mech. drawing, 1905-31, dean of the university, 1912-31, Brown University. Chmn. advisory bd. The Delphian Society. Mem. Sigma Chapter Psi Upsilon, Phi Beta Kappa, and Sigma Xi fraternities. Republican. Conglist. Author: Directions in Regard to the Construction of Plates in Mechanical Drawing, 1895; Directions in Regard to the Construction of Plates in Mechnical Drawing and in Descriptive Geometry, 1902; Shades and Shadows and Perspective, 1902; Elements of Descriptive Geometry; The Dean's Window, 1934. Retired, 1931. Home: 236 Butler Av., Providence, R.I. Died Aug. 11, 1946.

RANDALL, ROBERT HENRY, cons. engr.; b. Waynesville, O., Dec. 22, 1890; s. George Eddy and Jennie Williams (Bail) R.; student Ohio Wesleyan U., 1911-12; D.Sc., U. Santo Domingo, 1952; m. Maree Gard, Feb. 11, 1915; children—Robert Henry, William Eddy, Richard Rainier; m. 2d, Marguerita Dinsmore Gard, Feb. 11, 1964. Asst. city engr., Dayton, O., 1914; city surveys various cities, 1914-18; pres. R.H. Randall & Co., geodetic and topographic engrs. (city surveys in Conn., Fla., Ind., Mich., N.Y., Ohio, Pa., Tex., W.Va.), 1918-35; pres. Randall Press, map publs., 1927-35; cons. Nat. Resources Planning Bd. (state and regional planning and pub. works), 1935-40; cons. TVA, 1938-39; cons., asst. on cartography Bur. of Budget, 1940-60; v.p. Aero Service Corp. of Litton Industries, Phila., 1960-64; cons. on Latin Am. program AID, 1964—. U.S. mem. internat. pub. works com. ILO, Geneva, 1938; U.S. mem. commn. on cartography Pan Am. Inst. Geography and History, 1942-62, pres. inst., 1950-55, hon. pres., 1955—. Chmn. U.S. delegation Pan Am. Consultations on Cartography, Washington, 1943, Rio de Janeiro, 1944, Caracas, 1946, Buenos Aires, 1948, 61, Santiago, 1950, Ciudad Trujillo, 1952, Mexico City, 1955, Havana, 1958. Chmn. com. experts on cartography, UN, 1949. Cons. Cuban govt. symposium on natural resources, 1957-58; vice chmn. U.S. delegation to UN 2d Regional Conf. Cartography, Tokyo, 1958; cons. OAS Mission to Chile, 1960. Recipient Order of Duarte (Dominican Rep.); cons. OAS Mission to Chile, 1960. Order Cruzeiro do Sul (Brazil). Registered profl. engr., Ohio, N.Y. Fellow A.A.A.S.; mem. Assn. Am. Geographers, Am. Geog. Soc. (hon. mem.), Geog. Soc. Chile (patron), Am. Soc. C.E. (life), Chileen Soc. Geog., Am. Inst. Planners, Am. Planning and Civic Assn., Am. Congress on Surveying and Mapping (1st pres., hon. mem.), Am. Geophys. Union, Am. Soc. Photogrammetry (hon. mem.), Mexican Soc. Geography and Statistics, Nat. Inst. Geog. Investigations of Uruguay, Phi Gamma Delta. Presbyn. Club: Cosmos (Washington). Co-author, Manual 10, Technical Procedure for City Surveys, Am. Soc. C.E., Modern Cartography—Base Maps for World Needs, UN; prin. author: AID Manual Number

1—National Resources Inventory, Procedures and Descriptive Specifications. Contbr. papers to engring., sci. jours. Pub. reports on geodetic and topog. surveys. Home: 4009 East-West Hwy., Chevy Chase 15, Md. Died Sept. 1966.

RANDALL, WYATT WILLIAM, chemist; b. Annapolis, Md., Jan. 10, 1867; s. Alexander and Elizabeth Philpot (Blanchard) R.; B.A., St. John's Coll., Md., 1884; Ph.D., Johns Hopkins, 1890; research work, Univ. Coll., London, 1895; m. Eliza P. Colston, June 23, 1898. Asst. and asso. in chemistry, 1889-98, Johns Hopkins; science master, Lawrenceville (N.J.) Sch., 1898-1900; prof. chemistry, Jacob Tome Inst., Port Deposit, Md., 1900-01; head master, Mackenzie Sch., Dobbs Ferry, N.Y., 1901-10; chemist to Md. State Dept. Health, 1911—; asso. in biochemistry, Johns Hopkins Sch. of Hygiene and Pub. Health, 1921—. Mem. Joint Com. on Definitions and Standards, 1918-26; mem. Assn. Official Agrl. Chemists (pres. 1925-26). Episcopalian. Author: Chemical Experiments (with Prof. Remsen), 1895; The Expansion of Gases by Heat, 1901; also monographs on chem. subjects and contbns. to chem. pubis. Home: Guilford, Md. Deceased.

RANDOLPH, ISHAM, civil engr.; b. on farm, New Market, Clarke County, Va., Mar. 25, 1848; s. Robert C. (M.D.) and Lucy Nelson (Wellford) R.; ed. chiefly by mother and 21 months in pvt. day schs. in Va.; engring. acquired by study and actual work, beginning as axman in employ of B.&O. R.R.; D.Eng., U. of Ill., 1910; D.Com.Sc., Washington and Lee U., 1917; m. Mary Henry Taylor, June 15, 1882. Chief engr. Chicago & Western Ind. R.R., and Belt Ry. of Chicago, 1880, Chicago, Madison & Northern Ry., 1886, Sanitary Dist. of Chicago, 1893-1907, consulting engr. until 1912; designed and built for the Queen Victoria Niagara Falls Park Commn. the "obelisk" dam above Horse Shoe Falls, which was built upright, on end, and tipped over into the stream, accomplishing the desired purpose; mem. Internat. Bd. of Consulting Engrs. for Panama Canal, 1905-06; mem. Advisory Bd. of Engrs. for Panama Canal, 1909; engr. Milwaukee Outer Harbor, 1909; mem. Rivers and Harbors Commn. State of Ill., 1911; chmn. Fla. Everglades Engring. Commn., 1913; chmn. Internal Improvement Commn. of Ill., Chicago Harbor Commn., etc. Was consulting engr. on track elevation, City of Baltimore, and Toronto, Can.; reviewed plans for Lake Erie and Ohio River Canal Bd., for barge canal, 1916. Awarded gold medal, Paris Expn., 1900, for work on Chicago Drainage Canal; Elliott Cresson medal, Franklin Inst., 1913, "for distinguished achievement in the field of civil engineering"; gold medal, St. Louis Expn., 1904, for useful invention (moving platform). Home: Chicago, Ill. Died Aug. 2, 1920.

RANDOLPH, JACOB, physician; b. Phila., Nov. 25, 1796; s. Edward Fitz and Anna Julianna (Steel) R.; M.D., U. Pa., 1817; m. Sarah Emlen Physick, 1822. Practiced as surgeon, circa 1820-35; asst. in Almshouse Infirmary, Phila.; introduced new operation for removing stones from the bladder (lithotripsy), 1831; surgeon Pa. Hosp., 1835-48; prof. clin. surgery U. Pa., 1847-48; performed early radical operations, including amputation of the lower jar for osteosarcoma, ligation of an external iliac aneurism. Author: A Memoir of the Life and Character of Philip Syng Physick, 1839; contbr. articles to Am. Jour. Med. Sci., N. Am. Med. and Surg. Jour., Med. Examiner. Died Phila., Feb. 29, 1848.

RANDOLPH, JOHN COOPER FITZ, consulting mining engr.; b. Trenton, N.J., Dec. 1846; s. Judge Joseph Fitz and Sarah Ann (Cooper) R.; brother of Joseph Fitz R.; A.B., Princeton, 1866, A.M., 1869; E.M., Columbia Sch. Mines, 1869; univs. of Göttingen, Tübingen, and Vienna, 1869-72; unmarried. In service of U.S. Govt., 1872; Japanese Govt., 1874; Chinese Govt., 1885; govt. of Republic of Colombia, S.A., 1888; took expdn. into Borneo for mining purposes, 1890; in Peru and Chile, 1899; in Nizam's State, India, 1900-01. Author of numerous tech. papers and reports. Home: Morristown, N.J. Died 1911.

RANDOLPH, LINGAN STROTHER, mech. engr.; b. Martinsburg, W.Va., May 13, 1859; s. James L. (chief engr. B.&O. R.R.) and Emily (Strother) R.; ed. Shenandoah Valley Acad., 1873-76, and Va. Mil. Inst., Lexington, 1876; M.E., Stevens Inst. Tech., 1883, D.Eng., 1921; m. Fanny Robbins, Oct. 15, 1890. Engr. of tests N.Y.,L.E.&W. R.R., 1883-85; supt. motive power F.R.&N. Co., Fernandina, Fla., 1885-87, Cumberland & Pa. R.R., Mt. Savage, Md., 1887-90; engr. of tests B.&O. R.R., 1890-92; elec. engr. Baltimore Electric Refinery, 1892-93; prof. mech. engring., 1893-1918, dean Sch. Engring., Va. Poly. Inst. Research sect. U.S. Shipping Bd. Emergency Fleet Corp., Phila., Pa. Address: Govanstown, Baltimore, Md. Died Mar. 7, 1922.

RANDOLPH, ROBERT ISHAM, cons. engr.; b. Chicago, Ill., Apr. 14, 1883; s. Isham and Mary Henry (Taylor) R.; student Cornell U., 1903-04; m. Martha A. Maclean, Oct. 17, 1912. Asst. engr. Sanitary Dist. of Chicago, 1904-07, sec. Internal Improvement Commn. of Ill., 1908-11, Rivers and Lakes Commn. of Ill., 1911-13; sec. Isham Randolph & Co., 1913-21, Randolph-Perkins Co. since 1921; dir. of operations, Century of Progress Exposition, Chicago, 1932-34; chief engr. Construction Div., Office of Quartermaster General, Zone 6, Chicago, 1941. Served on Mexican border with Battery C, 1st Ill. F.A., 1916; maj. comdg. 535th Engrs., A.E.F., 1918; lt. col. comdg. 381st Engrs., O.R.C., 1923-24; colonel Gen. Staff Corps, Asst. Chief of Staff, G-4, Seattle Port of Embarkation, 1942-43. Deputy chief Chicago ordnance district, 1943-46; associate director War Assets Adminstrn., Chicago, 1946-47. Mem. Am. Soc. C.E., Western Soc. Engrs., Psi Upsilon, Citizens' Assn. (dir.), Mississippi Valley Assn. (pres., 1932-35), Chicago Assn. Commerce (pres. 1930-31). Republican. Episcopalian. Clubs: University, Engineers'. Home: 1731 Santa Barbara St., Santa Barbara, Cal. Died Oct. 18, 1951.

RANDOLPH, ROBERT LEE, ophthalmologist; b. Fredericksburg, Va., Dec. 1, 1860; s. Alfred Magill and Sallie Griffith (Hoxton) R.; ed. Episcopal High Sch. of Va., 1875-80; M.D., U. of Md., 1884; studied in Vienna, 1885-86; hon. A.M., Johns Hopkins, 1902; m. Phoebe W. Elliott, Apr. 15, 1891. Asst., 1892-99, asso., 1899, asso. prof. ophthalmology and otology, 1901—, Johns Hopkins; asso. ophthalmic and aural surgeon, Johns Hopkins Hosp. and Dispensary; ophthalmic and aural surgeon-in-chief to B.&O. R.R. Winner Alvarenga prize of Coll. of Physicians, Phila., 1901; Boylston prize of Harvard U., 1902. Address: Baltimore, Md. Died Dec. 9, 1919.

RANDOLPH, WILLIAM MANN, M.D.; b. Albemarle County, Va., Jan. 14, 1870; s. William L. and Agnes (Dillon) R.; M.D., U. of Va., 1890; grad. study N.Y. Post Grad. Hosp., 1890-92, Vanderbilt Clinic, New York, 1890; m. Mary Walker, Oct. 20, 1894; children—Carolina R., Sarah Nicholas, Agnes Dillon, Thomas J., Mary Walker, Hollins N., Francis M. Practiced Charlottesville, Va., 1892-1913, and since 1930; prof. gynecology and surgery, U. of Va., 1905; surgeon Phelps-Dodge Corp., Douglas, Ariz., 1913-18, Central Copper Co., Mascot, Ariz., 1924-28; clinician and specialist in tuberculosis, Va. State Dept. of Health, since 1930, holding "traveling clinics" to reach effectively country dists. Capt. Troop K, Albemarle Light Horse, 1892-97; maj. Med. Service, 17th Inf., Va. Vols., 1898-1904, commd. capt. M.C., 1917; chief of med. service and comdg. officer hospital, Camp Harry J. Jones, Douglas, Ariz., 1918; maj. M.C., 1918, surgeon Ariz. dist. Mem. bd. visitors U. of Va., 1912; mem. sch. bd., Tombstone, Ariz., 1918, Dem. County Com., 1924. Democrat. Episcopalian. Address: State Dept. of Health, Richmond, Va. Died Jan. 25, 1944. *

RANE, FRANK WILLIAM, forester; b. Whitmore Lake, Mich., Dec. 11, 1868; s. William Benjamin and Ellen (Connelly) R.; B.Agr., Ohio State U., 1891; M.S., Cornell, 1892; m. Elizabeth Bailey, Sept. 6, 1893. Prof. horticulture and microscopy, W.Va. U., 1892-95; prof. agr. and horticulture, 1895-98, horticulture, 1898-1900, forestry and horticulture, 1900-06, N.H. Coll.; Mass. state forester, 1906—; lecturer on forestry Mass. Agr. Coll.; chmn. Mass. Conservation Commn., Mass. Taxation Commn., Mass. State Forest Commn. and Mass. Soldiers' Land Commn. Home: Waban, Mass. Died May 3, 1933.

RANGER, RICHARD H(OWLAND), electronic mfr.; b. Indianapolis, Ind., June 13, 1889; s. Rev. John Hilliard and Emily Anthen (Gillet) R.; B.S., Mass. Inst. Tech., 1911; post war course Ecole Superievre de l'Electricite, Paris, 1919; m. Laura Anne Lewis, Nov. 27, 1923; children—Mary Wheatley (Mrs. John L. Scripp). Prop. Ranger Co., printers, Boston, 1911-17; design engr. Radio Corp. of Am., New York, N.Y., 1920-30; pres. Rangertone, Inc., Newark, N.J., since 1930. Served as 2d lt., F.A., U.S. Army, World War I; as capt. signal corps in France, 1918-19, in charge signal corps labs., Fort Monmouth, 1919-20; in signal corps in charge radar and communication field lab. for Air Corps, Orlando, Fla., 1942, tech. exec. signal corps Standards Agency, Red Bank, 1943; on tech. intelligence missions to Europe, 1944-46; disch. as col. Fellow Inst. Radio Engrs., Royal Soc. (London), Am. Institute Elec. Engrs., Audio Engring. Soc., Sco. Motion Picture Engineers; mem. Am. Guild of Organists, Acoustical Society, Optical Society, Franklin Institute, Phi Beta Epsilon. Republican. Episcopalian. Clubs: M.I.T., Downtown, Sapphire (New York); M.I.T. of Northern New Jersey, Downtown, Forest Hill Literary (Newark). Inventor: transoceanic radio facsimile, 1924; electronic organ, 1932; electronic chimes, 1933; radar developments, 1938-44; airbourne radio relay, 1942; magnetic recording, 1947; synchronized tape and motion pictures (received Oscar award, 1956, Samuel L. Warner award, 1957, in recognition of this invention), stereo-dimensional sound for legitimate theatres, 1958. Author: Artillery Lines of Information, 1918; Radio Pathfinder, 1922; Fighter Control Communications, 1943. Established transoceanic radio pictures transmission, 1925. Home: 574 Parker St., Newark 4. Office: 73 Winthrop St., Newark 4. Died Jan. 10, 1962.

RANKIN, FRED WHARTON, surgeon; b. Mooresville, N.C., Dec. 20, 1886; s. Watson Wharton and Margaret (Houston) R.; A.B., Davidson Coll., 1905; M.D., U. of Md., 1909; A.M., St. John's Coll., 1913; hon. Sc.D., Davidson Coll., 1937, U. of Md., 1939, U. of Ky., 1942; LL.D., Temple U., 1943, Northwestern U., 1943; Sc.D., U. of Louisville, 1947; m. Edith Mayo, June 12, 1923; children—Fred Wharton, Edith Graham, Charles Mayo, Thomas Alexander. Resident surgeon Univ. Hosp., Baltimore, 1909-12; asst. demonstrator anatomy and asso. in surgery, Univ. of Md. Med. Sch., 1913-16; asst. surgeon St. Mary's Hosp., Mayo Clinic, Rochester, 1916-22; prof. surgery, U. of Louisville, 1922-23; served as asso. prof. surgery, U. of Minn. Med. Sch., Mayo Foundation; surgeon to Mayo Clinic, 1926-33; surgeon to St. Joseph Hospital, Lexington, Ky., since Jan. 1, 1934; clinical prof. of surg., U. of Louisville, since 1941. Pres. Interstate Postgrad. Assembly, 1943. Served as maj. Medical Corps, U.S. Army, 17 mos., World War; attached to 1st A.C., 4th and 26th divisions, in France; commanding officer Base Hospital No. 26; col. Med. Reserve, U.S. Army; chief cons. surg. U.S. Army, rank brig. gen. Awarded Victory Ribbon, World War I; Distinguished Service Medal, Victory Ribbon, E.T.O. Ribbon, Asiatic-Pacific Ribbon, Am. Defense and Am. Theatre Ribbons; Cross, Chevalier Legion of Honor, World War II. Fellow Am. Coll. Surgeons, Am. Surg. Assn. (pres. 1948-49), A.M.A. (pres. 1942), Am. Proctologic Soc. (hon.), Southern Surg. Assn. (past pres.); fellow Internat. Société Chirurgie; mem. Eastern Surg. Assn., Western Surg. Assn., Southern Med. Assn., Southeastern Surg. Congress (past pres.), Minn. and Ky. medical societies, Southern Minnesota Medical Society, Society of Clinical Surgery, Visiting Surgeons Club, Beta Theta Pi, Phi Chi, Phi Beta Kappa, Sigma Xi, Alpha Omega Alpha; founder mem. Am. Bd. Surgery. Democrat. Episcopalian. Clubs: Army-Navy, Idle Hour Country, Filson. Author: (monograph) Surgery of the Colon. Co-Author: (with J. A. Bargen and L. A. Buie) The Colon, Rectum and Anus, 1932; (with A. S. Graham) Cancer of the Colon and Rectum, 1939. Contbr. chapter in Lewis' Surgery entitled "Malformations of the Colon"; chapter Sajous Med. Cyclo. "Surgery of the Colon"; chapters "Carcinoma of the Rectum," "Carcinoma of the Colon" in Christopher's A Textbook of Surgery; also numerous papers on operative and clin. surgery. Home: Cave Hill Farm. Office: Security Trust Bldg., Lexington, Ky. Died May 22, 1954.

RANKIN, WALTER MEAD, biologist; b. Newark, N.J., Dec. 1, 1857; s. William and Ellen Hope (Stevens) R.; A.B., Williams, 1879; M.S., Princeton, 1884; Ph.D., U. of Munich, 1889; unmarried. Instr. biology, Princeton U., 1889-95, asst. prof., 1895-1901, prof., 1901-23, emeritus since 1923. Fellow A.A.A.S.; mem. Am. Soc. Naturalists. Presbyterian. Club: Nassau (Princeton). Home: 5 Evelyn Pl., Princeton, N.J. Died May 25, 1947; buried Mount Pleasant Cemetery, Newark, N.J.

RANKIN, WILLIAM DURHAM, farmer, stockman; b. Onarga, Ill., Feb. 12, 1876; s. William A. and Mary (Durham) R.; ed. Grand Prairie Sem.; student Rush Med. Coll., Chicago, 1896-97; m. Nellie May Atwood, Feb. 21, 1914. Clerk Onarga Bank, 1899-1910; organized drainage dist., Iroquois County, Ill., 1910; pres. Iroquois Canning Co., 1912-16; succeeded father in live stock business at Tarkio, Mo., 1916; widely known for demonstration of sweet clover as a medium for increasing fertility of soil and for fattening cattle; also known for extensive use in tiling of a system of checks by which workmen may verify surveyor's figures and for erosion control in hilly country through certain types of dams. Republican. Mason. Home: 1800 S.W. 13th St., Miami, Fla. Died Mar. 5, 1943.

RANNEY, HENRY JOSEPH, civil engr.; b. Middletown, Conn., circa 1800; s. Moses and Elizabeth (Gilchrist) R.; grad. Norwich U., 1828. Asst. engr. B&O. R.R., 1831; chief engr. Lexington & Ohio R.R., Ky., 1832-35; chief engr. New Orleans & Nashville R.R., 1835-42; cons. engr., New Orleans, from circa 1842; pres. New Canal & Shell Rd. Co., New Orleans, circa 1850; Whig, became active in local politics, 1850's; mem. La. Legislature from New Orleans, 1850's; a promoter New Orleans, Jackson & Gt. Northern R.R., 1858-62. Died Lewisburg, La., May 1, 1865.

RANNEY, LEO, engineer; b. New Hartford, Ia., Aug. 26, 1884; s. Wallace Austin and Adelaide (Clayton) R.; B.Di., Iowa State Teachers Coll., 1905; B.S., Northwestern Univ., 1911; m. Claire Sussex Fairbank, July 2, 1927; stepsons—Charles O., Henry, Robert Fairbank. Began as consulting engineer, 1914, in Texas and Okla., 1920-25; pres. Ranney Oil Mining Co. (subsidiary of Standard Oil Co. N.J.), 1926-30; vice chmn. Industrial Water Commn. of Ohio, 1940; appointed director of oil production by Australian government, 1941; in charge Ranneywells oil installations for Australian govt. and prodn. natural gas from coal seams; dir. Seerley Foundation. Spl. asst. to chief of ordnance, U.S. Army, 1918-19; mem. O.R.C. Designer and builder of largest water well; driller of first horizontal oil well. Inventor of Ranney processes of mining water, oil from exhausted fields, charging flood and waste water into the ground; protecting city water supplies against atom bombs; converting coal to gas without mining; of forming underground gas storage reservoirs; of degasification of unmined coal; of excavating and earth moving processes and machinery. Mem. A.A.A.S., Am. Petroleum Inst., Am. Inst. Mining and Metallic Engrs., Am. Soc. Mech. Engrs., Phi Beta Kappa, Sigma Chi, Deru, Sigma Gamma Epsilon. Contbr. to Am. and European tech. jours. Club: Santa

Barbara. Home: Petrolia, Ont., Can.; Morro Bay, Calif. Died Sept. 15, 1950; buried Morro Cayucos Cemetery.

RANSOM, BRAYTON HOWARD, zoölogist; b. Mo. Valley, Ia., Mar. 24, 1879; s. George Howard and Martha (Roach) R.; B.Sc., U. of Neb., 1899, A.M., 1900, Ph.D., 1908; fellow in zoölogy, U. of Mo., 1900-01, U. of Neb., 1901-02; student George Washington U. Med. Sch., 1902-04; m. Virginia Smith, May 4, 1904. Asst., div. of zoölogy, hygienic lab., U.S. Pub. Health and Marine Hosp. Service, 1902-03; scientific asst. in zoölogy, 1903, in charge zoölogical lab., 1904—; chief div. of zoölogy, 1906—, Bur. Animal Industry, Dept. Agr. Asst. custodian (hon.) U.S. Nat. Mus., 1905—. Author of govt. publications and articles in scientific jours. on parasitology and medical zoölogy. Mem. edit. bd. Jour. of Parasitology, Am. Jour. Tropical Medicine. Address: Washington, D.C. Died Sept. 17, 1925.

RANSOME, FREDERICK LESLIE, geologist; b. Greenwich, Eng., Dec. 2, 1868; s. Ernest Leslie and Mary Jane (Dawson) R.; B.S., U. of Calif., 1893, Ph.D., 1896; fellow in geology, U. of Calif. (teaching mineralogy), 1893-95; m. Amy Cordova Rock, May 25, 1899; children—Janet (Mrs. H. M. Baxter), Susan Clarkson (Mrs. E. D. Fry), Violet Jane (Mrs. H. Rodney Gale, dec.), Alfred Leslie. Asst. in mineralogy and petrography, Harvard, 1896-97; asst. geologist, 1897-1900, geologist, 1900-23, United States Geol. Survey; in charge sections of western areal geology, 1912-16, and of metalliferous deposits, 1912-23; prof. econ. geology, U. of Ariz., 1923-27, and dean of Grad. College, 1926-27; prof. econ. geology, Calif. Inst. Tech., 1927—; cons. geologist U.S. Bur. Reclamation and Metropolitan Water Dist. of Southern Calif., 1928—. Lecturer on ore deposits, U. of Chicago, 1907; Silliman lecturer, Yale, 1913. Mem. Nat. Acad. Sciences (treas. 1919-24), Nat. Research Council (treas. 1919-24), Soc. Economic Geologists (pres. 1926-27), Washington Acad. Sciences (pres. 1918), Geol. Soc. Washington (pres. 1913). Author of numerous official monographs on the geology of western mining dists. and papers in scientific jours. Asso. editor Economic Geology. Address: Pasadena, Calif. Died Oct. 6, 1935.

RANSON, S(TEPHEN) WALTER, anatomist; b. Dodge Center, Minn., Aug. 28, 1880; s. Stephen William and Mary Elizabeth (Foster) R.; B.A., U. of Minn., 1902; M.S., U. of Chicago, 1903, Ph.D., 1905; M.D., Rush Med. Coll., 1907; m. Tessie Grier Rowland, Aug. 18, 1909; children—Stephen William, Margaret Jane, Mary Elizabeth. Fellow in neurology, U. of Chicago, 1904-06; intern Cook County Hosp., 1907-08; instr. anatomy, 1909-10, asst. prof., 1910-12, prof. and head of dept., 1912-24, Northwestern U. Med. Sch.; prof. neuroanatomy and head of Dept. of Neuroanatomy and Histology, Washington U. Med. Sch., 1924-27; prof. neurology and dir. Neurological Research Inst., Northwestern U. Med. Sch., since 1928. Fellow A.A.A.S.; mem. Am. Neurological Assn., Am. Assn. Anatomists (pres. 1938-40), Am. Physiol. Soc., Phi Beta Pi, Sigma Xi, Alpha Omega Alpha. Protestant. Author: The Anatomy of the Nervous System, 6th edition, 1939. Contbr. results of investigations on structure of the peripheral nervous system of mammals, etc. Mem. editorial bd. Archives of Neurology and Psychiatry. Address: 180 E. Delaware Pl., Chicago, Ill. Died Aug. 30, 1942.

RANTZ, LOWELL ADDISON, physician; b. Placerville, Cal., June 1, 1912; s. William Addison and Besse Lowell (Miller) R.; A.B., Stanford, 1932, M.D., 1936; m. Helen Heilbronner, Sept. 10, 1939; 1 dau., Elizabeth Russell. Research fellow medicine Thorndike Meml. Lab., Harvard, 1937-39; from instr. to asso. prof. medicine Stanford, 1939-55, prof. medicine, 1955—, asso. dean Med. Sch., 1958—. Mem. med. adv. panel Bank of Am.-Giannini Found., 1951—; mem. med. bd. Lowell M. Palmer Found., N.Y., 1953-56; member bacteriology and mycology study section NIH, 1962—. Diplomate of the American Board of Internal Medicine. Fellow A.C.P., New York Academy Sci., Am. Society of Internal Medicine, A.A.A.S.; mem. Am. (sec. sci. council 1948-53), Cal., San Francisco (pres. 1950-51) heart assns., Council on Rheumatic Fever and Congenital Heart Disease (exec. com. 1959-62), Am. Assn. U. professors, Association American Physicians, A.M.A., Am., No. Cal. (pres. 1952) rheumatism assns., Am. Soc. Clin. Investigation (mem. council 1955-58), Am. Fedn. Clin. Research, Santa Clara Med. Soc., Cal. Med. Assn., Cal. Acad. Medicine, Western Soc. Clin. Research (pres. 1950), Soc. Exptl. Biology and Medicine, Soc. Pharmacology and Exptl. Therapeutics, Cal. Soc. Internal Medicine, Western Assn. Physicians, Alpha Omega Alpha. Author numerous publs. on infectious disease. Home: 574 Foothill Rd., Stanford, Cal. 94305. Office: 300 Pasteur Dr., Palo Alto, Cal. Died June 6, 1964; buried Placerville, Cal.

RANUM, ARTHUR, mathematician; b. La Crosse, Wis., Dec. 13, 1870; s. Ingebrigt and Elise (Myhren) R.; A.B., U. of Minn., 1892; grad. student and fellow Cornell U., 1893-96; grad. student and fellow, U. of Chicago, 1896-97, Ph.D., 1906; unmarried. Prof. mathematics and astronomy, U. of Wash., 1897-1904; instr. mathematics, U. of Wis., 1904-05; asst. in mathematics, Stanford, 1905-06; instr. mathematics, 1906-10, asst. prof., 1910-23, prof., 1923—, Cornell U. Contbr. articles in math. jours. of U.S. and Europe; specialist in non-Euclidean geometry and in differential geometry. Home: Ithaca, N.Y. Deceased.

RAPPORT, DAVID, physiologist; b. Pitts., Aug. 29, 1891; s. John and Fannie (Binder) R.; A.B., Harvard, 1912, M.D., 1916; m. Jean DeWilde Simpson, June 18, 1931; children—Elizabeth, Nancy. Austin teaching fellow in physiology, Harvard, 1919, instr., 1920-21; research fellow, Cornell Med. Sch., 1921-24; instr. and sr. instr., Western Res. Med. Sch., 1925-29; prof. physiology, Tufts U. Med. Sch., 1929-70. Served as 1st lt. med. corps, A.E.F., 1917-19. Fellow Am. Acad. Arts and Sciences, A.A.A.S.; mem. Am. Physiol. Soc., Soc. Exptl. Biology and Medicine, Radiation Research Soc., Alpha Omega Alpha, Sigma Xi. Clubs: Harvard (Boston), Faculty (Cambridge). Contbr. articles on circulation, metabolism, endocrines, cellular respiration. Home: Cambridge MA Died Oct. 1970.

RASMUSSEN, FREDERIK, agriculturalist; b. Hals, Denmark, July 18, 1876; s. Neils and Kirstine (Jensen) R.; came to U.S., 1899, naturalized citizen, 1912; B.S. in Agr., Ia. State Coll., 1905; m. Faith Winifred Elliott, Oct. 2, 1919; children—Frederick, John Elliott, Holger and Howard (twins), Norman, David. Assistant in dairying, Purdue U., 1905-06; asst. prof. dairying, Ia. State Coll., 1906-07; prof. dairying New Hampshire State Coll., 1907-16; prof. dairy husbandry, Pa. State Coll., 1916-19; sec. of agr. of Pa., term 1919-23. Pres. Pa.-Md. Joint Stock Land Bank, Harrisburg, Pa.; exec. sec. Nat. Assn. Ice Cream Mfrs., Mar. 1, 1925—. Mem. State Council of Edn. Mem. U.S. Food Administration, World War I. Trustee Pa. State Coll. Republican. Lutheran. Mason. Traveled extensively in northern and middle Europe studying agrl. conditions. Author of various bulletins and articles relating to agr. and dairying. Home: Harrisburg, Pa. Died Feb. 21, 1932.

RATHBUN, JOHN CHARLES, educator, civil engr.; b. Mondovi, Wis., Mar. 14, 1882; s. John Chauncey and Elizabeth (Goldenberger) R.; A.B., U. Wash., 1903, A.M., 1904, B.S., 1908, C.E., 1909; Ph.D., Columbia, 1934; m. Dora Frances Breece, June 29, 1910; children—Elizabeth (dec.), John Charles (dec.), Mary Charlotte. Asst. prin. Tung Wen Inst., Amoy, China, 1904-06; engr. Seattle (Wash.) Park Bd., 1908-09; chief draftsman Wash. State Highway Commn., 1909-11; designing engr. City Water Dept., Tacoma, Wash., 1911-12; engr. Bur. Pub. Works, Philippine Govt., Manila, 1912-15; engr. Weymouth Constrn. Co., Seattle, Wash., 1915; supt. bridge constrn. City of Seattle, 1915-18; supervising draftsman, bridge and bldg. dept., C.,M. & St.P. Ry., Seattle, 1918; asst. prof. civ. engring., U. Wash., 1919-25; hydraulic investigator City of Seattle, 1920; Peters fellow research lab., Columbia, 1923-24; head dept., prof. civ. engring. S.D. Sch. Mines, Rapid City, 1925-29; also consultant Westchester County (N.Y.) Park Commn., 1926; State Highway Dept., Conn., 1927-28; prof., chmn. dept. engring., Antioch Coll., 1929-30; asso. prof. civ. engring., College City of N.Y., 1930-41, prof., 1941-49, prof. emeritus, 1949—. Investigated wind stresses in tall buildings for Am. Inst. Steel Constrn. Mem. Am. Soc. C.E., Soc. Promotion Engring. Edn., Internat. Assn. for Bridge & Structural Engring. Circumnavigators Club, Kappa Sigma, Acacia, Phi Beta Kappa, Sigma Xi, Tau Beta Pi. Republican. Methodist. Mason (Shriner). Originator and developer of the elastic skew arch theory. Contbr. tech. articles, etc., trans. and proc. Am. Soc. C.E. Home: 706 Riverside Dr. N.Y.C. 31. Office: College of City of N.Y., N.Y.C. Died Nov. 12, 1958; buried Kensico Cemetery, Valhalla, N.Y.

RATHBUN, MARY JANE, carcinologist; b. Buffalo, N.Y., June 11, 1860; d. Charles Howland and Jane (Furey) R.; ed. common and high schs.; A.M., U. of Pittsburgh, 1916; Ph.D., George Washington U., 1917; clk. U.S. Fish Commn., 1884-87; copyist, later aid and asst. curator, div. marine invertebrates U.S. Nat. Mus., 1887-1914; hon. asso. in zoology same, since 1915. Fellow A.A.A.S.; mem. Biol. Soc. Washington, Washington Acad. Sciences, Am. Soc. Naturalists, Audubon Soc., Wild Flower Preservation Soc., Soc. Chilena Hist. Nat.; corr. mem. Peiping Soc. Natural History; hon. mem. Acad. Chilena Ciencies Nat., Panama Canal Natural History Soc. Republican. Unitarian. Home: Hammond Court, Washington, D.C.

RATHBUN, RICHARD, naturalist; b. Buffalo, N.Y., Jan. 25, 1852; s. Charles Howland R.; student Cornell, class of '75; M.S., Ind. U., 1883; hon. D.Sc., Bowdoin, 1894; m. Lena Augusta Hume, Oct. 6, 1880. Asst. in zoölogy, Boston Soc. Natural History, 1874-75; asst. geologist, Geol. Commn. of Brazil, 1875-78; asst. in zoölogy, Yale, 1879-80; curator, U.S. Nat. Mus., 1880—. Scientific asst. on U.S. Fish Commn., 1878-96, having charge of the scientific inquiry subsequent to 1887; U.S. rep. on joint commn. with Great Britain relative to preservation fisheries in waters contiguous to U.S. and Can., 1892-96; asst. sec. Smithsonian Instn., 1897—; in charge U.S. Nat. Mus., 1899—. Writer on paleontology, marine invertebrate zoölogy, fisheries and mus. adminstrn. in govt. and other publs. Address: Washington, D.C. Died July 16, 1918.

RATNER, BRET, physician; b. Brooklyn, N.Y., Apr. 28, 1893; s. Dr. Leo and Sonia (Maazel) R.; student New York U.; M.D., New York U. Sch. of Medicine, 1918; m. Jeanne Schulman, June 5, 1917; 1 dau., Barbara (Mrs. Murray Dworetzky). Served internships in pathology, N.Y. City Hosp., in pediatrics, N.Y. Nursery and Child's Hosp., for 3 yrs.; pediatric research, Cornell Med. Coll., 1920-22; immunology research (under Prof. Zinsser), Physicians and Surgeons Coll., 1922-23, dept. of physiology and immunology, New York U., Coll. of Medicine, 1923-36; asst. visiting pediatrician Manhattan Maternity Hosp., Harlem Hosp., City Hosp., 1922-27; lecturer in immunology, N.Y. Coll. of Medicine, 1928-36; clin. prof. of pediatrics, N.Y. U., 1928-49; professor clinical pediatrics (allergy) and associate prof. immunology N.Y. Med. Coll.; attending pediatrician, Flower and Fifth Avenue Hosp. and director Pediatric Allergy; director of pediatrics and visiting pediatrician Sea View Hospital for Tuberculosis; associate attending physician children's medical div. Bellevue 1928-49; cons. pediatrician French Hosp. Mem. bd. govs. Playtex Park Research Institute; mem. Child Welfare Com. County Med. Soc. of N.Y.; chmn. sect. of allergy, Am. Acad. of Pediatrics; member board of allergy, Board of Pediatrics; member board of trustees Am. Found. Allergic Diseases; Cons. on med. information, N.Y. Acad. of Medicine. Served in Med. Reserve Corps, World War I. Invited to address 3d Internat. Congress of Pediatrics, London, Eng., 1933; appointed Nobel Prize com. on medicine, 1935; pres. Metropolitan Med. Soc., 1943. Fellow Am. Acad. Pediatrics, Am. Acad. Allergy, Internat. Assn. Allergists (hon.), A.A.A.S., N.Y. Acad. of Medicine, N.Y. Acad. of Sci.; mem. Am. Immunologists, Am. Soc. for Exptl. Pathologists, Am. Pathologists and Bacteriologists, Am. Coll. Chest Physicians, Am. Coll. of Allergists (board of regents), Society of Exptl. Biology and Medicine, American Public Health Assn., Harvey Soc., N.Y. County Med. Soc., N.Y. Acad. of Science, Am. Tuberculosis Assn., Alpha Omega Alpha, Sigma Xi, Phi Delta Epsilon. Licentiate, Am. Board of Pediatrics, Pediatric Board of Allergy. Democrat. Clubs: N.Y. Andiron; The Bohemians. Author: Allergy, Anaphylaxis and Immunotherapy, 1943; Allergy in Relation to Pediatrics, 1950. Contbr. articles to med. jours. on problems of allergy in childhood; asso. editor, Annals of Allergy. Laid basis for placental permeability in various animal species, reproducted experimental asthma in the guinea pig, etc. Home: 22 E. 88th St. Office: 50 E. 78th St., N.Y.C. Died Oct. 11, 1957.

RAU, CHARLES, archaeologist, mus. curator; b. Verviers, Belgium, 1826; attended U. Heidelberg (Germany); Ph.D. (hon.), U. Freiburg (Baden, Germany), 1882. Came to Am., 1848; resident collaborator in ethnology U.S. Nat. Mus., 1875, curator dept. archeology, 1881-87; assisted in preparation for Centennial Exposition of 1876; made contbns. to process of classification; 1st Am. to recognize importance of study of aboriginal technology. Author: The Archeological Collection of the United States National Museum; Early Man in Europe, 1876; Prehistoric Fishing in Europe and North America, 1885. Translator: Account of the Aboriginal Inhabitants of the California Peninsula (Jacob Buegert), 1863. Died Phila., July 25, 1887.

RAUCH, JOHN HENRY, physician; b. Lebanon, Pa., Sept. 4, 1828; s. Bernard and Jane (Brown) R.; grad. Med. Sch., U. Pa., 1849. Joined Ia. Med. Soc., 1850, 1st del. to A.M.A., 1852, published article in Proceedings "Report on the Medical and Economical Botany of Iowa," 1851; effected establishment of marine hosps., Galena, Ill., and Burlingame, Ia.; mem. Ia. Hort. Soc., Ia. Hist. Soc., Ia. Geol. Soc.; made a natural history collection from the upper Mississippi and Missouri rivers, 1855-56; aided in effecting passage of a bill providing for a geol. survey of Ia., 1856; prof. materia medica Rush Med. Coll., Chgo., 1857-58; founder Chgo. Coll. Pharmacy, 1859, 1st prof. materia medica; served as surgeon during Civil War; helped reorganize Chgo. Bd. Health, 1867; made collections in Venezuela, 1870; a founder Am. Public Health Assn., treas., 1872, pres., 1876; 1st pres. Ill. Bd. Health, 1877-91, superintended adminstrn. of Med. Practice Act; assisted in establishing a quarantine sta. for cholera cases and suspects, 1892; editor public health dept. Jour. of A.M.A., 1894, made nation-wide study of prevalence and control of smallpox published as "The Smallpox Situation in the United States"; mem. bd. trustees A.M.A. Died Lebanon, Mar. 24, 1894.

RAUTENSTRAUCH, WALTER, (rou'ten-strouk), indsl. engr., educator; b. Sedalia, Mo., Sept. 7, 1880; s. Julius and Anna (Nichter) R.; B.S., U. of Mo., 1902; LL.D., 1932; M.S., U. Me., 1903; studied Cornell, 1903-04; m. Minerva Babb, Sept. 7, 1904. Instr. U. Me., 1902-03; asst. prof. Cornell, 1904-06; prof. endsl. engring., Columbia, 1906-46, emeritus prof., 1946—; cons. indsl. econs. Bank of Mex., Mexico City. Cons. engr. to mfg. industry. Mem. NRC. Fellow N.Y. Acad. Sciences, A.A.A.S.; mem. Am. Soc. Refrigerating Engrs., Am. Soc. M.E., Franklin Inst., Am. Acad. Polit. and Social Science, Tau Beta Pi, Sigma Xi. Author: Syllabus of Lectures on Machine Design, 1906; Machine Drafting, 1908. The Economics of Business Enterprise, 1939; Who Gets the Money?, 1939. Co-Author: Mechanical Engineers Handbook, 1916; The Successful Control of Profits, 1930; Tomorrow in the Making, 1939; Industrial Surveys and Reports, 1940; The Design of Manufacturing Enterprises, 1941; Principals of Modern Industrial Organization, 1944;

Economics of Industrial Management, 1949. Contbr. mags. Home: 235 Dorin Court Rd., Palisade, N.J. Died Jan. 3, 1951.

RAVDIN, ISIDOR SCHWANER, phys. and surg.; b. Evansville, Ind., Oct. 10, 1894; s. Marcus and Wilhelmina (Jacobson) R.; B.S., Ind. U., 1916; M.D., U. Pa., 1918; L.H.D. (hon.); LL.D., Sc.D.; m. Elizabeth Glenn, June 2, 1921; children—Robert Glenn (dec. 1972), Elizabeth, William Dickie. Intern U. Pa. Hosp., 1918-19, chief resident phys., 1919-20; instr. surgery U. Pa., 1920, asso. in surgery, 1922-27, asst. prof. surg. research, 1927, prof., 1928-35, Harrison prof. surgery, 1935-45, John Rhea Barton prof. surgery, 1944-59, dir. Harrison Dept. Surg. Research, 1944-59, prof. surgery, v.p. for med. affairs University Pennsylvania, 1959-65, vice chmn. medical devel., from 1965; surgeon in chief U. Pa. Hosp., 1945-59. Dir. Mead Johnson & Co., 1962-68. Pres. American Cancer Society, 1962-63; mem. Nat. Adv. Health Council; alternate mem. Civilian Advisory Council to Sec. of Def.; sr. civilian cons. surgeon Surgeon Gen. of the Army. Chmn. clin. studies panel Cancer Chemotherapy Nat. Service Center, Nat. Insts. Health. Member board of trustees Phila. Mus. Art, Rosenbach Mus. Phila. Served as brig. gen. M.C., AUS, 1942-45; maj. gen. ret. Decorated Legion of Merit with oak leaf cluster; Olaf of Acrel medal (Sweden); recipient Phila. award. Diplomate of American Board of Surgery. Hon. fellow England, Scotland, Canada royal colls. surgeons; mem. Internat. Fedn. Surg. Colleges and Societies (vice president), Am. Surgical Association (pres. 1958-59), A.C.S. (pres. 1960), International Blood Transfusion Soc. (past president), Pan-Pacific Surg. Assn. (ex-pres.), Phila. Acad. Surgery (ex-pres.), Am. Assn. Surgery Trauma, A.M.A., Am. Soc. Exptl. Pathology, Societe Internat. de Chirurgie, Internat. Soc. Surgery, Am. Physiol. Soc. Editor: Kirschner Surgery (3 vols.), 1932-36. Home: Philadelphia PA Died Aug. 27, 1972; buried West Laurel Hill Cemetery

RAVENEL, EDMUND, physician, naturalist; b. Charleston, S.C., Dec. 8, 1797; s. Daniel and Catherine (Prioleau) R.; M.D., U. Pa., 1819; m. Charlotte Ford; m. 2d, Louisa Ford; at least 1 son. Prof. chemistry 1st faculty Med. Coll. of S.C., 1824-35; corr. mem. Acad. Natural Scis. of Phila., 1832; published a catalogue of shells, 1834; bought The Grove (plantation on Cooper River, S.C.), 1835; v.p. Elliot Soc. of Natural History, 1853; purchased patent rights in Sawyer's brick-making machine for S.C., 1836, similar rights in Brown's machine, 1838; in charge of hosp. at Ft. Moultrie; chmn. polit. meeting in St. Thomas's Parish which endorsed secession, 1860; remains of his collection now in Charleston Mus. Author: Echinidae, Recent and Fossil of South Carolina, 1848. Died Summerton Plantation, Berkley County, S.C., July 27, 1871.

RAVENEL, HENRY WILLIAM, botanist, agrl. writer; b. "Pooshee", Berkely, S.C., May 19, 1814; s. Henry and Catherine (Stevens) R.; grad. S.C. Coll., 1832; LL.D., U. N.C., 1886; m. Elizabeth Gaillard Snowden, 1835; m. 2d, Mary Huger Dawon, 1858; 10 children. Given plantation and slaves by his father, became planter, circa 1832-65; elected correspondent Acad. Natural Science, Phila., 1849; published best known of his botanical works The Fungi Cardiniani Exsiccati, 5 vols., 1853-60 (1st published series of named specimans of Am. fungi); published (with English botanist Prof. M. C. Cooke) 2d series Fungi Americani Exsiccati, 8 parts, 1878-82; sent by U.S. Govt. to Tex. to aid in investigation of a cattle disease, 1869 (investigation proved disease not due to eating of poisonous fungus); agrl. editor Weekly News and Courier, 1882-87; collected and classified herbarium and fungi, mosses and lichens, later sold to Brit. Mus. and Converse Coll., Spartanburg, S.C.; became mem. Zoölogische Botanische Gesellschaft, Vienna, 1884. Died Aiken, S.C., July 17, 1887.

RAVENEL, MAZYCK PORCHER, bacteriologist; born Pendleton, S.C.; s. Henry Edmund and Selina E.R.; grad. Univ. of the South; studied medicine, Med. Coll. State of S.C.; m. Jennie Carlile Boyd, Oct. 1898. Bacteriologist State Live Stock Sanitary Bd. of Pa., 1896-1904; asst. med. dir. Henry Phipps Inst. for Study, Treatment and Prevention of Tuberculosis; chief of laboratory, Henry Phipps Inst., 1904-07; prof. bacteriology, Univ. of Wis., since 1907. Mem. Nat. Assn. for Study and Prevention of Tuberculosis (1st v.p., 1907-08), Coll. Physicians, Phila., Am. Philos. Soc., Am. Pub. Health Assn., Am. Med. Assn., Am. Assn. Pathologists and Bacteriologists, Phila. Pathol. Soc., S.C. Huguenot Soc. Author numerous published papers on med. and bacteriol. subjects, especially on tuberculosis and rabies. Residence: Madison, Wis. Died Jan. 14, 1946.

RAVENEL, ST. JULIEN, physician, agrl. chemist; b. Charleston, S.C., Dec. 19, 1819; s. John and Anna Elizabeth (Ford) R.; grad. Charleston Med. Coll., 1840; studied medicine in Phila. and Paris, France; m. Harriet Horry Rutledge, Mar. 20, 1851, 9 children. Established 1st stone lime works in S.C. at Stoney Landing on Cooper River, 1857; surgeon in charge Confederate hosp., Columbia, S.C., also in charge Confederate lab. (where much of medicine used for Confederate Army was made) during Civil War; designer torpedo cigarboat Little David; orginated a process which rendered phosphate rocks readily soluble, produced an ammoniated fertilizer, produced phosphate fertilizer without the use of ammonia (acid fertilizer), developed process of adding marl to acid fertilizers to counteract free acid; chemist Charleston Agrl. Lime Co.; discovered that lanting and plowing of leguminous plants restored to the worn out soil properties which made it produce larger crops; proposed artesian well system for Charleston. Died Charleston, Mar. 17, 1882.

RAVENEL, WILLIAM DE CHASTIGNIER, naturalist; b. Pineville, S.C., Aug. 25, 1859; s. William F. and Ellen (DuBose) R.; A.B., Union College, N.Y., 1878, hon. M.A. from same, 1925; m. Elizabeth FitzSimons, Feb. 15, 1883; children—DuBose (dec.), Julia FitzSimons (Mrs. Stanton C. Peelle), Gaillard FitzSimons, Ellen DuBose (dec.), William de Chastignier (killed in World War, 1918), Henry. Entered U.S. Fish Commn., 1883; chief spl. agt. Chicago Expn., 1893; rep. Fish Commn. on govt. bd. of management at expns. at Atlanta, 1895, Nashville, 1896, Omaha, 1898, Buffalo, 1901 (mem. superior jury awards), and St. Louis, 1904; represented Smithsonian Inst. in charge govt. exhibits, Internat. Marine Expn., Bordeaux, France, 1907; mem. U.S. Govt. Bd., Seattle, Sept., 1909; asst. in charge fish culture, U.S. Fish Commn., 1895-1902; acting commissioner Fish and Fisheries under Commrs. Brice and Bowers, 1897-1902; administrative asst., 1902-18, administrative asst. to the sec. Smithsonian Instn., in charge Nat. Mus., 1918-25; administrative asst. to the sec. and dir. of arts and industries, U.S. N. Mus., since Apr. 1925. Mem. Nat. Geog. Soc., Huguenot Soc. of S.C. Clubs: Cosmos, Chevy Chase. Home: Ontario Apts., Washington, D.C.

RAY, ARTHUR BENNING, chemist; b. Leaksville, N.C., Sept. 12, 1889; s. Bryant Wesley and Helen (Betts) R.; A.B., Wake Forest (N.C.) Coll., 1910, M.A., 1911; Ph.D., Cornell U., 1916; m. Deolice Hickman, June 21, 1919; children—Margaret Benning, Joan Rutledge. Asso. prof. Industrial Chemistry, Texas A. & M. Coll., 1916-17; chemist, Nat. Carbon Co., Inc., New York, N.Y., 1919-34; sales engr. and exec., Carbide and Carbon Chem. Corp., New York, N.Y., since 1934. Capt., C.W.S., U.S. Army, 1917-19; member National Technol. Advisory Com. Mem. Am. Chem. Soc., Am. Inst. Chem. Engrs. Club: Chemists. Author technol. monographs. Home: 104 Summit Rd., Port Washington, N.Y. Office: 30 E. 42d St., N.Y.C. Died Dec. 24, 1951.

RAY, DAVID HEYDORN, engr.; b. N.Y.C., July 14, 1878; s. Martin Hasset and Caroline (Heydorn) R.; A.B., Coll. City N.Y., 1897; B.S., Columbia, 1901, A.M., 1902; C.E., N.Y. U., 1902, Sc.D., 1908; studied abroad, 1898, 1905, 1908; m. Sara Beecher, June 25, 1908 (died Apr. 17, 1940); 1 son, S. David Tryon; m. 2d, Florence A. Grasmuk, Aug. 20, 1941. Engr., N.Y. Instn. Blind and N.Y. Rapid Transit Subway, 1902; examining engr. Municipal Civil Service Commission N.Y. City 1902-04; instr. physics and engring., Coll. City N.Y., 1905-10; chief engr. Bur. Bldgs., N.Y.C., 1910-12; U.S. appraisal officer N.Y. Dist., 1918-19; prof. mechanics Cal. Inst. Tech., 1919-20; structural engr. Bur. Bldgs., Los Angeles, 1923-27; examing engr. Civil Service Commn., Los Angeles, 1927, also spl. examiner in engring. Civil Serv. Commn. Los Angeles, 1933; asst. mech. engr. Bur. Power and Light, Los Angeles, 1936; sr. structural engr. State Dept. Pub. Works, 1933. Dir. lab. U.S. Signal Corps Sch., N.Y., 1917-18; capt. insp. gen. Res.; served in N.Y.N.G. 7 yrs. capt. engr. corps. Sec. Planning Commn., High Sch. Bd. (both Arcadia, Cal.). Mem. Dist. Sch. Bd., Queens and Manhattan, N.Y.C. Fellow A.A.A.S., Am. Geog. Soc.; mem. Am. Soc. M.E. Author: Articles on engring. topics Home: 214 Harwood Av., Philipse Manor, N. Tarrytown, N.Y. Died Apr. 2, 1960; buried Woodlawn Cemetery, Bronx, N.Y.

RAY, FRANKLIN ARNOLD, engr.; b. Rome, Ashtabula County, O., Apr. 13, 1862; s. Samuel and Fidelia (Hulburt) R.; E.M., Ohio State U., 1887; studied mining engring.; m. Pauline W. Hollenbeck, June 24, 1896; children—Helen Drury (Mrs. Thomas Hornsby Ferril), Frances Hurlbert (Mrs. Stuart E. Price). Chief engr. Columbus-Hocking Coal & Iron Co., 1889-92, Congo Coal Mining Co., 1892-94; asst. prof. mining engring., 1894-97, asso. prof., 1897-1900, prof., 1900-27, later prof. emeritus, dean Engring. Coll., 1904-06, Ohio State U., also consulting dir. Sch. of Mines; chief engr. Sunday Creek Coal Co., 1932, later consulting engr. in Russia, investigating coal deposits, mining conditions, coal reserves, etc., 1916—. Author of repts. and bulls. on mining investigations. Home: Granville, O. Died Aug. 9, 1938.

RAY, G(EORGE) J(OSEPH), cons. engr.; b. Metamora, Ill., Mar. 25, 1876; s. Jerry and Harriett (Swallow) R.; A.B., U. Ill., 1898, C.E., 1910; D.Sc., Lafayette Coll., Easton, Pa., 1916; m. Edna Rose Hammers, June 23, 1903 (died Jan. 1942); m. 2d, Ethel Pearce, Apr. 25, 1943. Rodman, transitman, asst. engr., track supr. and roadmaster I.C. R.R., 1898-1903; div. engr., 1903-09, chief engr., 1909-19, D., L.&W. R.R. As chief engr., had charge constrn. Hopatcong Slateford cut-off, one of heaviest pieces of constrn. work yet accomplished on any r.r.; in charge design and building Tunkhannock viaduct, Nicholson, Pa., largest concrete bridge ever built (2,375 ft. long, 243 ft. high). Engring. asst. to regional dir. Eastern Region, U.S. R.R. Adminstrn., N.Y., Feb. 1, 1919-Feb. 1920; later chief engr. D., L.&W. R.R., v.p. and gen. mgr. same since Jan. 1, 1934-Apr. 1946, ret.; now cons. engr. Republican. Baptist. Home: 114 Woodland Av., Summit, N.J. 07901. Died Mar. 5, 1962; buried Restland, Hanover, N.J.

RAY, MILTON S., industrialist, ornithologist, poet; b. San Francisco, Feb. 26, 1881; s. William S. Ray (mfr., ship-owner) and Julia Henrietta (Ruth) R.; ed. Crocker High Sch.; Univ. of Calif.; m. Rose Carolyn Etzel, Oct. 7, 1915; children—Cecily, Virginia, Rosalyn. Secretary, treas. and dir. W. S. Ray Mfg. Co., San Francisco, 1907, elected v.p., 1915; sec., treas. Ray Burner Co. of Calif., 1929, Ray Burner Co. of Delaware, 1930; pres., treas., dir. Ray Burner Co. of Del., San Francisco, and New York, 1933, and same, Ray Oil Burner Co. and subsidiaries since 1935; curator and director Pacific Museum of Ornithology since 1904; has made exploration trips to over 35 countries, obtaining specimens for the Museum. Owner, Ray Park Subdivision, Burlingame, Calif., and Raycliff Terrace Subdivision, San Francisco. Member San Francisco Contract Bd., War Dept., San Francisco Dist. Ordnance Office since 1934. Received Honor Flag from U.S. Government as dir. of an auxiliary War Plant, 1918. Academician Acad. of Coimbra, Portugal. Fellow Am. Geog. Soc.; asso. Am. Ornithologists Union; research asso. in ornithology, Calif. Acad. Sciences; mem. P.E.N., Am. Ornithologists Union, Cooper Ornithol. Club, Nat. Geog. Soc. Brit. Oologists Club. Republican. Protestant. Club: Burlingame Country. Awarded prize for peom, "San Francisco," used for Sesquicentennial Celebration in San Francisco, 1926. Author: The Farallones, The Painted World and Other Poems (2 vols.), 1934; Poems (1 vol.), 1936; The Poet and The Messenger; Dune-Glade and Other Poems, 1945, also over 100 mag. articles. Home: 2901 Broadway; (summer) Snow Line Villa (Vade P.O.), Lake Tahoe, Calif. Office: 401-499 Bernal Av., San Francisco 12, Calif. Died May 5, 1946.

RAYMOND, CHARLES WALKER, brig. gen. U.S.A.; b. Hartford, Conn., Jan. 14, 1842; s. Prof. Robert R. R.; grad. Brooklyn Poly. Inst., 1861; Ph.D., Lafayette Coll., 1875; grad. U.S. Mil. Acad., 1865; spl. studies civ. and mil. engring.; M. Clara Wise, Nov. 8, 1866. Apptd. 1st lt. engrs., June 23, 1865; capt., Mar. 21, 1867; maj., Feb. 20, 1883; lt. col., May 18, 1898; col., Jan. 23, 1904; brig. gen. and retired at own request after 40 yrs. service, June 11, 1904. Engaged on exploration of Yukon River, Alaska, 1869; prin. asst. prof. natural and experimental philosophy, U.S. Mil. Acad., 1872-74; comd. U.S. expdn. to Northern Tasmania to observe transit of Venus, 1874; instr. mil. engring., mil. signaling and telegraphing, U.S. Mil. Acad., 1878; engr. commr., D.C., 1888-89; on engr. duty at New York and Phila.; chmn. bd. engrs. in charge of constrn. of tunnels at New York for Pa. R.R. Address: Philadelphia, Pa. Died May 3, 1913.

RAYMOND, ROSSITER WORTHINGTON, mining engr.; b. Cincinnati, Apr. 27, 1840; s. Prof. Robert R. and Mary Ann (Pratt) R.; grad. Brooklyn Poly. Inst., 1858; studied univs. Munich and Heidelberg and Mining Acad., Freiberg; hon. Ph.D., Lafayette, 1869; LL.D., Lehigh U., 1906, and U. of Pittsburgh, 1915; m. Sarah M. Dwight, 1863. Capt. a.d.c. in Union Army, 1861-64; consulting engr., New York, 1864-68; U.S. commr. of mining statistics, 1868-76; lecturer on econ. geology, Lafayette Coll., 1870-82; editor Am. Jour. of Mining, 1867-68; an editor and spl. contbr. Engineering and Mining Journal, 1868—. U.S. commr. to Vienna Expn., 1873; N.Y. State commr. of electric subways for Brooklyn, 1885-88; lecturer on mining law, Columbia, 1903. One of origianl mems., v.p., 1871, 1876-77, pres., 1872-74, sec., 1884-1911, sec. emeritus, 1911—, Am. Inst. Mining Engrs.; Japanese Imperial Order of Rising Sun, 4th class, 1911. Author: Die Leibgarde (German), 1863; Mineral Resources of the United States in and West of the Rocky Mountains (8 vols.), 1868-75; Brave Hearts, 1873; The Man in the Moon, 1874; The Book of Job, 1878; Camp and Cabin, 1879; Glossary of Mining and Metallurgical Terms, 1881; Two Ghosts, 1879; Life of Alex L. Holley, 1883; Life of Peter Cooper, 1901; also tech. works and papers, especially on mining law. Home: Brooklyn. Died Dec. 3, 1918.

RAYMOND, WILLIAM GALT, engr.; b. Princeton, Ia., Mar. 2, 1859; s. W. H. V. and Laura Guernsey (Peet) R.; ed. pub. and high schs. and U. of Kan.; C.E., Washington U., 1884, LL.D., 1905; Eng.D., U. of Mich., 1919; m. Helen Williams Bay, July 1, 1885; children—Mrs. Margaret Leonard Hammond, William Yale, Edwin Bay, Laurence Guerney (dec.). Asst. engr. in location and constrn. of rys. in Miss. Valley before graduation; instr. civ. engring., U. of Calif., 1884-90; pvt. practice (Raymond & Bay), 1890-92; town engr. Berkeley, Calif., 1892; prof. geodesy, road engring. and topog. drawing, Rensselaer Poly. Inst., 1892-1904; prof. civ. engring., 1904-22, prof. engring., 1922—, dean Coll. Applied Science, 1905—, State U. of Ia. Mem. Soc. Promotion Engring. Edn. (pres. 1911-12). Author: Plane Surveying, 1896; Elements of Railroad Engineering, 1908; Railroad Field Geometry, 1910; Railroad Field Manual for Civil Engineers, 1915; What Is Fair?, 1917; Public and Its Utilities, 1925. Mem. Ia. State Bd. of Conciliation, 1918-19, adjusting pub. utility rates during war. Address: Iowa City, Iowa. Died June 17, 1926.

REA, PAUL MARSHALL (ra), museum consultant; b. Cotuit, Mass., Feb. 13, 1878; s. John T. and S. Helen R.; A.B., Williams Coll., Williamstown, Mass., 1899, A.M., 1901; student Marine Biol. Lab., Woods Hole, Mass., 1898-99, Columbia Grad. Sch., 1899-1900, 1902-03; m. Carolyn Morse, June 28, 1904 (died May 11, 1913); 1 son, John Morse; m. 2d, Marian Goddard Hussey, June 25, 1919; 1 dau., Dorothy Helen. Asst. in biology, Williams Coll., 1900-02; prof. biology, Coll. of Charleston, 1903-14; dir. Charleston Museum, 1903-20; instr. Marine Biol. Lab., 1906-11; prof. embryology and physiology, Med. Coll. of S.C., 1911-19, prof. embryology, 1919-20; dir. Cleveland Museum Natural History, 1920-28; exec. officer, Pa. Museum Art, 1929; consultant to advisory group on museum edn., Carnegie Corp., 1930-32; dir. Santa Barbara Museum Natural History, 1933-36. Vice dir. war savings for S.C., 1917-19. Fellow A.A.A.S., Ohio Acad. Science (pres. 1925-26); member Am. Assn. Museums (sec. and editor Proceedings, 1907-17, pres. 1919-21). Formerly editor Bulletin Charleston Museum and Contributions from the Charleston Museum. Author: Directory of Am. Museums, 1910; The Museum and the Community, 1932. Also author annual reports on ednl. work Am. museums, in Ann. Rept. U.S. Commr. of Edn.; also papers on museum administration and ednl. work and on fungi of Southern Calif. Address: 436 E. Padre St., Santa Barbara, Calif. Died Jan. 15, 1948.

READ, NATHAN, iron mfr., inventor; b. Warren, Mass., July 2, 1759; s. Rueben and Tamsin (Meacham) R.; grad. Harvard, 1781; m. Elizabeth Jeffrey, Oct. 20, 1790. Tchr., Beverly and Salem, Mass., 1781-83; tutor Harvard, 1783-87; devised double-acting steam engine, 1788; invented manually-operated paddle-wheel propelled boat, 1789; granted patents, on portable multitubular boiler, improved double-acting steam engine, chain wheel method of propelling boats 1791; organized Salem Iron Factory, 1796-1807; patented rail cutting and heading machine, 1798; mem. U.S. Ho. of Reps. (Federalist) from Mass., 6th-7th congresses, 1800-03; apptd. spl. justice Ct. of Common Pleas for Essex County (Mass.), 1803; chief justice Hancock County (Me.) Ct. of Common Pleas, 1807; mem. Am. Acad. Arts and Scis., 1791; hon. mem. Linnaean Soc. New Eng., 1815. Died Belfast, Me., Jan. 20, 1849.

READ, THOMAS ALBERT, physicist, educator; b. Montclair, N.J., Oct. 21, 1913; s. Thomas Thornton and Mary Carleton (Peck) R.; A.B., Columbia, 1934, Ph.D., 1940; student Technische Hochschule, Munich, Germany, 1932-33; m. Doris Pascal, Nov. 4, 1935; 1 son, Thomas Thornton II. Westinghouse research fellow Westinghouse Research Lab., East Pittsburgh, Pa., 1939-41; prin. physicist Frankford Arsenal, Phila., 1941-47, Oak Ridge Nat. Lab., 1947-48; asso. prof. metallurgy Columbia, 1948-54; prof., head dept. mining, metall., petroleum engring. U. Ill., 1954—. Fellow Am. Phys. Soc.; mem. Am. Inst. Mining and Metall. Engrs., Am. Soc. for Engring. Edn., Am. Soc. Metals, Inst. Metals (London), Phi Beta Kappa, Sigma Xi, Tau Beta Pi. Home: 507 E. Harding Dr., Urbana, Ill. Died Sept. 11, 1966.

READ, THOMAS T(HORNTON), mining engr.; b. Monmouth County, N.J., Feb. 10, 1880; s. Thomas H. and Hannah C. (Thornton) R.; E.M., Columbia, 1902, fellow, 1904-05, Ph.D., 1906; m. Mary C. Peck, July 26, 1910; children—Mary Celia, Thomas Albert, Myron. Asso. prof. mining, U. of Wyo., 1902-04; asst. in mineralogy, Columbia U., 1905-06; prof. mining and metallurgy, Colorado Coll., 1906-07; prof. metallurgy, Pei Yang U., Tientsin, 1907-10; associate editor Mining and Scientific Press, 1910-15; metall. engr. N.J. Zinc Co.; New York, 1916-18; metallurgist, Army Ordnance, 1918-19; chief of information service, U.S. Bur. of Mines, 1919-23, supervising mining engr., 1923-24, safety service, dir., 1924-26; asst. sec. Am. Inst. Mining and Metallurgical Engineers, 1926-29; Vinton prof. of mining engring., Columbia, since 1929. Editor of Mining and Metallurgy, 1926-32. Mem. A.A.A.S., Am. Inst. Mining Engrs., Council on Foreign Relations, Am. Acad. Polit. Science. Author: Our Mineral Civilization; Recent Copper Smelting; Ores and Industry of South America; Careers in the Mineral Industries; Mineral Industry Education in the U.S.; also numerous contbns. to scientific socs. and tech. jours. Home: 9 Windmill Lane, Scarsdale, N.Y. Address: Columbia University, New York. Died May 29, 1947; interred Ferncliff Mausoleum, Hartsdale, N.Y.

READE, JOHN MOORE, prof. botany; b. Toronto, Can., Dec. 17, 1876; s. John Moore and Janet Drysdale (Bain) R.; B.S. in Agr., U. of Toronto, 1900; studied U. of Munich, 1905; Ph.D., Cornell U., 1908; m. Julia MacArthur, June 17, 1914; children—John Moore III, William Woodthorp, Janet Drysdale. Teacher and div. supt. Dept. of Pub. Instrn., Philippines, 1901-04; with U. of Ga., 1907—, prof. botany, 1908—, dir. biol. labs., 1917—. Episcopalian. Home: Athens, Ga. Died May 9, 1937.

READY, LESTER SEWARD (red'i), cons. engr.; b. Ventura, Calif., Dec. 9, 1888; s. William Edward and Martha Hind (Seward) R.; grad. Union High Sch., Ventura, 1907; B.S., U. of Calif., 1912; m. Eileen Ana Ong, Oct. 9, 1916; children—Lester Seward, Ralph William, Robert Allen, Richard Thomas. Asst. engr. Pacific Gas & Electric Co., Oakland, Calif., 1912-13; asst. gas and elc. engr. Calif. R.R. Commn., 1913-17, gas and elec. engr. 1918-23, chief engr., 1923-26; pres. Key System Transit Co., Oakland, Jan.-July 1927; cons. engr. since 1927; chief cons. engr. Nat. Power Survey, Electric Rate Survey, Federal Power Commn., 1934-36. Mem. bd. dirs. Oakland Forum, 1937-42; Registered civil engr. State of Calif.; registered professional engr., State of Ore. Fellow Am. Inst. E.E.; mem. Order of Golden Bear (U. of Calif.), Big "C" Soc., Sigma Xi, Eta Kappa Nu, Tau Beta Pi, Phi Beta Kappa. Republican. Presbyterian. Mason. Clubs: Engineers, Kiwanis (San Francisco); University (Los Angeles); Commonwealth Club of Calif. (bd. govs. 1932-35; chmn. exec. com.). Home: 1050 Mariposa St., Berkeley, Calif. Office: 116 New Montgomery St., San Francisco, Calif. Died April 9, 1947.

REAVES, SAMUEL WATSON, (revz), mathematician; b. Dillon County, S.C., July 27, 1875; s. James Robert and Sarah Frances (McMillan) R.; grad. S.C. Mil. Acad., 1895; B.S., U. N.C., 1899; A.B., Cornell U., 1900; A.M., U. Chgo., 1912, Ph.D, 1915; m. Ella Betha, Aug. 28, 1901 (died Apr. 8, 1945); 1 son, Henry Wilson (adopted); m. 2d, Ima James, June 6, 1946. Tchr. high sch., Marion, 1895-98; tchr. mathematics Mich. Mil. Acad., Orchard Lake, 1900-01; asst. prof. mathematics Clemson (S.C.) Coll., 1901-05; prof. mathematics U. Okla., 1905-48, prof. emeritus, 1948—, head dept., 1905-40, acting dean Coll. Arts and Sciences, 1923-25, dean, 1925-40, dean emeritus, 1949—. Mem. Exec. com. Okla. State Bldg. and Loan Assn.; dir. Norman Building & Loan Assn., 1908—. Studied arty. at Ft. Sill, Okla., summer 1918, and later gave instrn. in same to 150 univ. students. Chmn. Cleveland County (Okla.) chpt. A.R.C., 1918-19. Mem. Am. Math. Soc., Math. Assn. Am., Sigma Xi, Phi Beta Kappa, Delta Chi. Democrat. Episcopalian. Mason. Club: Lions (pres. 1924). Home: 527 Chautauqua Av., Norman, Okla. Died Aug. 2, 1950.

REBER, LOUIS EHRHART (re'ber), engineer; b. Nitany, Pa., Feb. 27, 1858; s. Jacob and Elizabeth R.; B.S., Pa. State Coll., 1880, M.S., 1887; grad. student Mass. Inst. Tech., 1883; D.Sc., Pa. State Coll., 1908; m. Helen Jackson, June 1888; children—Louis E., Hugh Jackson. Prof. mech. engring., 1887-95, dean Sch. of Engring., 1895-1907, Pa. State Coll.; dean extension div., U. of Wis., 1907-26, now emeritus. Pa. commr. Paris Expn., 1889; Pa. asst. exec. commr. in charge mines, mining and machinery; mem. Jury of Awards, Chicago Expn., 1893; in charge dept. mines and metall., Pa. Commn., St. Louis Expn., 1904. Fellow Am. Soc. of Mech. Engrs.; mem. Franklin Inst., Phila. Soc. Promotion Engring. Edn., Nat. Soc. Promotion Industrial Edn., Nat. Univ. Extension Assn. (pres. 1914-15), Sigma Xi, Phi Kappa Phi. Asso. dir. public service reserve, labor dept., U.S. Army, Washington, Aug. 1917-Mar. 1918; dir. edn. and training, Emergency Fleet Corp., Mar.-Dec. 1918; dir. engring. and trade education, Army Ednl. Corps, A.E.F., France, Jan.-July 1919. Mem. Wis. State Bd. for Vocational Edn., 1911-17. Clubs: Madison, Maple Bluff (Madison); University (Madison and Milwaukee). Home: 242 Lakeland Drive, West Palm Beach, Fla. Address: care Fiduciary Trust Co., 1 Wall St., New York Died May 12, 1948.

RECTOR, THOMAS M., chemist; b. Warrenton, Va., Feb. 26, 1894; s. Jacquelin and Elizabeth Frances (Rector) R.; grad. Western High Sch., Washington, 1911; m. Elizabeth Hall Schoenly, Feb. 22, 1919; children—Jacqueline Lee (Mrs. Robert A. Stringer), Virginia Phoebe (Mrs. Norbert Osterland). Lab. asst., later asst. chemist Inst. of Indsl. Research, Washington, 1911-15, chief chemist, founder div. food technology, 1919-20; chief chemist Pompeian Olive Oil Co., Balt., 1915-17, 19; mgr. mfg. dept. Franklin Baker Co., N.Y.C. and Phila., 1922-27; dir. chem. dept. Pease Labs., 1920-22; dir. engring. research v.p. in charge research and development Gen. Foods Corp., 1927—. Served as 1st lt. C.W.S., U.S. Army, 1917-19. Mem. Am. Chem. Soc., Inst. Food Technologists, Franklin Inst., Indsl. Adv. Com. of Nutrition Found., Sci. Council of Refrigeration Found. Recipient Nicholas Appert Medal for contbns. field food technology (posthumously), 1950. Author; Scientific Preservation of Food, 1925; also numerous articles in scientific jours. on lab. management food preservation and processing. Holder approximately 30 U.S. and fgn. patents covering mech., phys. and chem. processes, principally in the food industry. Introduced cashew nuts into U.S. from India. Home: 100 Burnham Parkway, Morristown, N.J. Office: 250 Park Av., Died Mar. 31, 1950.

REDDICK, DONALD, plant pathologist; b. Sheridan, Mo., Mar. 1, 1883; s. Elias Albert and Ruth Anna (Boone) R.; A.B., Wabash Coll., 1905; Ph.D., Cornell, 1909; m. Emma Brill, Oct. 19, 1909; children—Robert Brill, Emma Louise, Anna Elizabeth; m. 2d, Adeline Newman, Oct. 30, 1946. Asst. in botany, Cornell U., 1905-07, instr. plant pathology, 1907-09, asst. prof., 1909-11, prof., 1911—; botanist N.Y. Agrl. Expt. Sta., 1920-24; bus. mgr., later editor, "Phytopathology," 1911-17; editor for pathology of Bot. Abstracts, 1918-19, chmn. bd. control, 1918-20, bus. mgr., 1922-24. Fellow A.A.A.S.; Soc. Am. Naturalists, Am. Phytopathol. Soc. (pres. 1921), Am. Assn. Univ. Profs., Gamma Alpha, Sigma Xi.; corr. mem. Nederlandsche Botanische Vereeniging; lime mem. Société Linnéenne de Lyon; v.p. Internat. Union of Biol. Scis., pres. sect. for pathology, 1935-47. Researches in grape diseases and methods of control; mosaic diseases of plants; breeding for disease resistance, potato blight. Home: 18 N.W. 27th St., Gainsville, Fla. Died Apr. 2, 1955; buried East Lawn Cemetery, Ithaca, N.Y.

REDDISH, GEORGE FULTS, bacteriologist; b. Somerset, Ky., June 30, 1894; s. George Marshall and Margaret Anne (Shaw) R.; B.S., U. Ky., 1919; Ph.D., Yale, 1922; D.Sc., St. Louis College Pharmacy and Allied Scis., 1950; m. Ruth Bathurst Edmondson, Aug. 9, 1922; children—Ruth Lee, Virginia Anne. Asst., Ky. Food and Drug Dept., 1915-19, dept. bacteriology, Yale, 1919-22; asso. prof., dept. bacteriology, Med. Coll. of Va., 1922-24; asso. bacteriologist, bur. chemistry, U.S. Food and Drug Adminstrn., Dept. Agr., 1924-27, sr. bacteriologist, 1928-29; dir. bacteriol. research, Hynson, Westcott & Dunning, 1927, Lambert Pharmacal Co., St. Louis, since 1929; prof. bacteriology, St. Louis Coll. Pharmacy and Allied Sciences, since 1932. Mem. A.A.A.S., Soc. Am. Bacteriologists, Am. Pub. Health Assn., Propietary Assn. Am., Asso. Drug and Chem. Industries of Mo. Author approximately 60 papers on bacteriol. subjects pub. in professioanl jours. or presented before sci. socs. Editor: Antiseptics, Disinfectants, Fungicides, and Sterilization, 1954. Specialist in pub. health and indsl. bacteriology. Home: 3 Clayton Terrace, Clayton 31, Mo. Office: 14588 Parkview Pl., St. Louis 10. Died Arp. 16, 1962; buried Oak Hill Cemetery, St. Louis County, Mo.

REDFIELD, CASPER LAVATER, patent atty., evolutionist; b. Closter, N.J., Nov. 22, 1853; s. James W. (M.D.) and Sarah H. (Bowen) R.; student Worcester (Mass.) Poly. Inst., 1873-74; m. Lillian A. Phillips, June 4, 1880; children—Howard A., Mabel G., Walter H., James C., Hazel L. and Harold P. Machinist, later draftsman, mech. engr., inventor. Consulting engr., Minneapolis, 1886-89; editor Wood and Iron, 1887-88; settled in Chicago, 1889; solicitor of patents and expert in patent causes since 1892. Designed many power plants and about 100 successful machines; partly originated, and developed new forms of machine design; designed 3 machines (bolt-cutting, engraving and brickmaking) receiving awards at Chicago Expn., 1893; received more than 50 patents for inventions. Original investigations in mathematics, mechanics and physics; first to solve problem of unbalanced rotating body on a yielding support; investigated effects of inertia in steam engines, ball-bearings, cam-operated machines; wrote first description of modern automatic telephone exchange, and successfully defended inventor's rights. Was first to make scientific investigation of inheritance of powers developed by exercise; devised math. formula to represent energy changes occurring from generation to generation in animals, and applied it to explain evolution of intelligence in man, etc. Author: Control of Heredity, 1903; Dynamic Evolution, 1914; (brochure) Great Men, 1915; Human Heredity, 1921. Contbr. about 400 articles to scientific jours. Home: 1842 N. Tripp Av. Office: Monadnock Block, Chicago, Ill. Died Dec. 15, 1943.

REDFIELD, WILLIAM C., saddle and harness maker, meteorologist; b. Middletown, Conn., Mar. 26, 1789; s. Peleg and Elizabeth (Pratt) R.; m. Abigail Wilcox, Oct. 15, 1814; m. 2d, Lucy Wilcox, Nov. 23, 1820; m. 3d, Jane Wallace, Dec. 9, 1828; 4 children, including Charles Bailey. Apprenticed to saddle and harness maker, Upper Middletown, Conn., 1804; introduced correct and fundamental concept. of hurricanes in article "Remarks on the Prevailing Storms of the Atlantic Coast of the North American States", published in Am. Jour. Sci. and Arts, Apr. 1831, published meterol. classic "Observations on the Hurricanes and Storms of the West Indies and the Coast of the United States", Oct. 1833; devised set of practical rules by which mariners could know their position during hurricanes; published pamphlet on proposed railroad to connect the Hudson and Mississippi rivers; a founder A.A.A.S., pres. 1848. Died N.Y.C., Feb. 12, 1857.

REDIGER, MICHEL JON, physicist; b. Humbolt, Neb., Nov. 13, 1939; s. Lavern Chester and Dorothy (Swanson) R.; B.S., U. Neb., 1961, M.S., 1964; postgrad. U. Minn., 1964-66; m. Leila Beverly Ammon, Sept. 10, 1966. Grad. teaching asst. physics dept. U. Neb., 1961-64; grad. teaching asst. physics dept. U. Minn., 1964-65, research asst., 1966, research asso., 1966; physicist Los Alamos Sci. Lab., 1965; physicist Goodyear Atomic Corp., Piketon, O., 1966-69; predoctoral fellow Summer Inst. Theoretical Physics, Physics Dept. U. Colo., 1964. Nat. Defense Edn. Act fellow, 1965-66. Mem. Am. Phys. Soc., Waverly Jr. C. of C. Republican. Methodist. Home: Waverly OH Died May 29, 1969; buried Milford NB

REDINGTON, PAUL GOODWIN, chief Bur. of Biol. Survey; b. Chicago, Ill., Jan. 25, 1878; s. Edward Dana and Mary Ann (Chamberlin) R.; A.B., Dartmouth, 1900; M.F., Yale, 1904; m. Ermina Elizabeth Weaver, Sept. 21, 1910; children—Edward Dana, Mary Ann, Paul Goodwin. Field work, U.S. Forest Service, 1904-Jan. 1, 1918, July 1, 1918-26, district forester,

1926-27; chief of Bur. of Biol. Survey, U.S. Dept. Agr., 1927—. City mgr. Albuquerque, N.M., Jan.-July 1918. Mem. Soc. Am. Foresters (pres. 1929). Republican. Conglist. Contbr. to Jour. of Forestry, Am. Forests and Forest Life. Home: Falls Church, Va. Died Jan. 12, 1942.

REDWAY, JACQUES WARDLAW, geographer; b. near Murfreesboro, Tenn., May, 1849; s. John W. and Lady Alexandrina (Wardlaw) R.; spl. studies at univs. of Calif. and at Munich; m. Lilian Burnham von Ebert, an American, residing in Dresden. Became instr. chemistry, U. of Calif., and prof. phys. geography and chemistry State Normal Sch. of Calif.; engaged in mining engring. and exploration in Calif. and Ariz., 1870-80; visited S. America, Europe and Asia for geog. study. Fellow Royal Geog Soc.; hon. fellow Universidad Nacional La Plata. Author: Manual of Geography, 1887. Joint Author: New Basis of Geography, 1901; Commercial and Industrial Geography, 1923, revised edition of same, 1929; Making the Empire State; Inquiry Concerning the First Landfall of Columbus; The Treeless Plains of North America; Elementary Physical Geography, 1907; All Around Asia, 1909; Redway School History, 1910. Editor: Sir John Mandeville's Travels, 1899; Kinglake's Eothen, 1899; Observer's Handbook of Meteorology, 1920; Story of the Weather, 1931; The Case of Anne Hutchinson. Contbr. articles on atmospheric dust; editorial contributions to various newspapers. Home: 20 E. 4th St., Mt. Vernon, N.Y. Died Nov. 6, 1942.

REED, CHARLES DANA, meteorologist; b. near Coon Rapids, Ia., Feb. 27, 1875; s. Dana and Alice Celesta (Webber) R.; B.Agr., Ia. State Coll., 1894, M.Sc. in Agr., 1896; m. Elmeta C. McGuire, Sept. 12, 1897 (died Mar. 3, 1941); children—Noama (dec.), Charles Dana, Charlotte Elmeta. Began as asst. in bacteriol. lab., Ia. State Coll., 1894; in charge Ia. State Coll. farm, 1895-96, of field experiments, Ia. Exptl. Sta., 1897; farmed, 1898; entered U.S. Weather Bur., at Vicksburg, Miss., 1899; served in Weather Bur., at Columbus, O., 1900, Omaha, Neb. 1900-05, in charge at Sioux City, Ia., 1905-10, 1st asst. at N.Y. City, 1910-16, in charge at Des Moines, Ia., 1918-44; exec. head weather and crop reporting and forecast service in Ia.; mem. faculty, School of Philosophy, U.S. Dept. Agr., Amarillo, Tex., Oct. 1940; nonresident lecturer in climatology, Ia. State Coll., 1944, research prof. since 1945. Served as coll. cadet capt. Member Weather Bureau Committee of Science Advisory Board, 1933; technical advisor of Iowa Planning Commn.; chmn. supervisory com. Federal Employees Credit Union. Fellow A.A.A.S.; mem. S.A.R. (Ia. Pres., 1934-35; v.p. gen. Upper Miss. Valley states 1941-43, Am. Meteorol. Soc. (Minneapolis chmn. 1935; councilor 1936-41), Iowa Acad. Science. Republican. Mem. Church of Christ (treas. Ia. Student Centers Foundation). Mason (32 deg.). Club: Des Moines Economic (1st pres.). Contbr. tech. articles. Office: U.S. Court House, Des Moines, Ia. Died Oct. 26, 1945.

REED, CHARLES JOHN, consulting engr.; b. Jasper Co., Ia., June 29, 1858; s. Thomas M. and Julia Ann R.; A.B., U. of Mich., 1881; m. Mary J. Crawford, of Burlington, Ia., Sept. 8, 1886. Has practiced as elec. engr. since 1886. Mem. Am. Inst. Elec. Engrs., Engrs. Club, Phila., Franklin Inst., Phila.; sec. Am. Electrochem. Soc., 1902-03. Contbr. of papers on electro-chemistry to Journal Franklin Institute, Electrical World, Electrical Engineer, Transactions of American Institute of Electrical Engineers, St. Louis Acad. Science. Address: 507 Brannan St., San Francisco.

REED, FRANK HYNES, chemist; b. Carroll County, Ind., Jan. 12, 1890; s. Jacob A. and Effie Alice (Hynes) R.; A.B., Wabash Coll., Crawfordsville, Ind., 1911; Ph.D., U. of Chicago, 1917; m. Helen Louise Kennedy, Oct. 27, 1917 (died Apr. 22, 1945); children—Sherman Kennedy, Mary-Alice (Mrs. Robert L. Sutherland); m. 2d, Frances Elizabeth Brown, August 24, 1946. Instr. in chemistry, Wabash Coll., 1913-14, Mich. State Coll., 1914-15, chemist Sherwin-Williams Co., Chicago, 1917-19, Butterworth-Judson Corp., Newark, N.J., 1919-22; supt. chem. plant Tower Mfg. Co., Newark, N.J., 1922-27; chemist Chem. Dye & Mfg. Co., Springfield, N.J., 1927-28; plant supervisor Nat. Aniline & Chem. Co., Buffalo, N.Y., 1928-30; chemist Roessler & Hoslacher Chem. Co., Niagara Falls, N.Y., 1930-31; chief chemist in mineral industries research, coal chemistry, etc., Ill. Geol. Survey, Urbana, Ill., since 1931; consultant, National Defense Research Com., 1942-43, War Production Board, 1943-45, sci. cons., Fed. Econ. Adminstrn., Northwest Europe, 1945; vis. expert to Gen. MacArthur's hdqrs., Tokyo, Dec. 1948-Feb. 1949. Fellow A.A.A.S.; mem. Am. Chem. Soc. (chmn. gas and fuel div. 1939, chmn. U. of Ill. sect. 1946-47), Am. Inst. Mining and Metall. Engineers (sec.-treas. industrial minerals div. 1939-40; chmn. chem. raw materials com. 1937-38; mem. sectional com. on classification of N. Am. Coals since 1933), Nat. Research Council (mem. com. on chem. utilization of coal since 1938), Sigma Xi, Phi Lambda Upsilon, Alpha Chi Sigma, Kappa Sigma. Club: Urbana Golf and Country. Home: 1207 S. Busey. Office: Natural Resources Bldg., Urbana, Ill. Died Apr. 27, 1957; buried Roselawn Cemetery, Urbana, Ill.

REED, HOWARD SPRAGUE, plant physiologist; b. North East, Pa., Aug. 6, 1876; s. Joseph Harlan and Emma Gertrude (Sprague) R.; A.B., U. Mich., 1903; Ph.D., U. Mo., 1907; m. Mary Hannah Dewey, Aug. 17, 1904 (died July 5, 1939). Asst. in plant physiology U. Mich., 1899-1903; instr. botany U. Mo., 1903-06; soil expert Bur. of Soils, U.S. Dept. Agr., 1906-08; prof. mycology and bacteriology Va. Poly. Inst., and plant pathologist Va. Agrl. Expt. Sta., 1908-15; prof. plant physiology U. Cal. Citrus Expt. Sta., Riverside, 1915-35; prof. plant physiology U. Cal., 1935-46, emeritus, 1946—; guest prof. Inst. de Botanique, Geneva, 1930. Fellow A.A.A.S. (exec. com. Pacific div. 1938-45); mem. Am. Soc. Biol. Chemists, Bot. Soc. Am. (chmn. physiol. section 1938), Cal. Bot. Soc. (pres. 1943), Western Society Naturalists (pres. 1923), Phytopathol. Soc. (pres. Pacific div. 1921-22), Western Soc. Soil Science (sec. 1926-28), Am. Soc. Naturalists, Washington Acad. Sci., Cal. Hist. Soc., Soc. Linnéenne de Lyon, Inst. Sieroterapico Milanese, Sigma Xi; mem. 9th Internat. Hort. Congress, London, 1930, 3d Internat. Congress of Comparative Pathology. Athens, 1936; Bronze medal Société Nationale d'Acclimation de France, 1935; corr. Museum National d'Histoire Naturelle de France. Presbyn. Club: Faculty (Berkely). Asso. editor U. Cal. Publs. in Agrl. Science, 1922-35; mem. council of editorial bd. of Growth, 1936—. Author: Manual of Bacteriology, 1914 What Can Biology Contribute to the World of Today?, 1923; La Nature de la Croissance, 1933; A Short History of the Plant Sciences, 1942; Ingenhausz' Experiment upon Vegetables, 1948, also about 180 papers on plant physiology and pathology. Home: 3044 1/2 Telegraph Av., Berkeley 5, Cal. Died May 12, 1950.

REED, HUGH DANIEL, zoölogist; b. Hartsville, N.Y., Mar. 4, 1875; s. Charles Hart and Sarah (Acker) R.; B.S., Cornell, 1899, Ph.D., 1903; student Freiburg, 1909-10; m. Madeline Kingsley Church, Aug. 20, 1919; 1 daughter, Sarah Acker. Fellow in zoölogy, Cornell U., 1899-1900; with same univ., 1900—, as instr., asst. prof., prof., head dept. zoölogy, 1910-24. Republican. Congregationalist. Writer on sound transmitting organs in Amphibia, the poison organs and skin of fishes, the dermal rays of fishes, the fauna of Cayuga Lake Basin, melanosis in fishes, biological significance of the family, etc. Home: Ithaca, N.Y. Died Aug. 23, 1937.

REED, RALPH JOHN, civil engr.; b. Port Huron, Mich., Apr. 30, 1833; s. Arthur Lucius and Anna Virginia (Kelly) R.; B.A., Pomona Coll., Claremont, Calif., 1905; B.S. in C.E., U. of Mich., 1908; m. June E. Miller, June 9, 1909 (dec.); children—John Miller, Robert Pearson; m. 2d, Alberta Mann, Sept. 23, 1929. Began with Union Oil Co. of Calif., 1908, and continued as engr. in transportation dept. until 1911, in charge engring. div., Los Angeles, 1911-14, engr. transp. dept., 1915, acting chief engr., 1916-17, chief engr., 1918-29; cons. practice, 1929—; dir. Whittier (Calif.) Nat. Trust & Savings Bank. Trustee Pomona Coll. Mem. State Bd. of Registration for Civil Engrs., Calif. Republican. Conglist. Scottish Rite Mason. Home: Los Angeles, Calif. Died July 27, 1939.

REED, SYLVANUS ALBERT, engineer; b. Albany, N.Y., Apr. 8, 1854; s. Rev. Sylvanus and Caroline (Gallup) R.; A.B., Columbia, 1874, A.M., E.M., 1877, Ph.D., 1879; univs. Würzburg and Berlin, 1878-79; m. Ella Wilshire Pomeroy, May 1895 (died 1897). Sec. to asst. commr. gen., Paris Expn., 1878; mining engr. in West till 1885; expert physical hazards, fire ins., 1886; with Commonwealth Ins. Co., 1886-93, Official Ins. Rating, Boston, 1893; mgr. at Chicago, Western Factory Ins. Assn., 1893; with Continental Ins. Co., Chicago, 1894; mgr. Fire Ins. Tariff Assn., New York, 1895-96; consulting engr. Nat. Bd. Fire Underwriters, 1905-06; made report on San Francisco fire; sec., mgr. Suburban Fire Ins. Exchange, New York, 1908. Mem. New York Naval Battalion, 1890-92. Home: New York, N.Y. Died Oct. 1, 1935.

REED, WALTER, physician; b. Belroi, Gloucester County, Va., Sept. 13, 1851; s. Lemuel Sutton and Pharaba (White) R.; M.D., U. Va., 1869, Bellevue Hosp. Med. Coll., N.Y.C., 1870; A.M. (Hon.), Harvard, 1902; LL.D. (hon.), U. Mich., 1902; m. Amelia Laurence, 1876, 2 children. Commd. asst. surgeon with rank of lt., M.C., U.S. Army, 1875; stationed at Ft. Lowell, Ariz., 1876-87; attending surgeon and examiner of recruits, Balt., 1890-93; promoted maj., 1893; curator Army Med. Museum, prof. bacteriology and clin. microscopy Army Med. Sch., Washington, D.C., 1893-1902; made extensive studies of bacteriology of erysipelas and diptheria; apptd. chmn. com. to study typhoid fever among U.S. soldiers in Cuba, 1898, proved that disease transmitted by dust and flies; head commn. to study yellow fever, Cuba, 1900, discovered disease transmitted to mosquito Aëdesoegypti; prof. pathology and bacteriology Columbia U., Washington, 1901-02; died of appendicitis, 1902. Author: The Contagiousness of Erysipelas, 1892. Died Washington, Nov. 22, 1902; buried Arlington Nat. Cemetery.

REEDER, CHARLES LEONARD, consulting eng'r; b. Baltimore, Oct., 1876; s. Andrew J. and Anna E. R.; prep. ed'n Baltimore City Coll.; grad. Johns Hopkins, 1896; sp'l studies in elec. and mech. engineering; married. In eng'ring Gen. Elec. Co., 1896-7; City Passenger Ry. System, Baltimore, 1897-8; began individual practice, Apr., 1897. Residence: Arundel Apartments. Office: Equitable Bldg., Baltimore

REES, JAMES, steamboat builder, inventor; b. Wales, Dec. 25, 1821; s. Thomas and Mary (Bowen) R.; m. Mary Morris, 10 children. Came to Am., 1828; foreman Snowden & Co., Brownsville, Pa., also Stackhouse & Thompson; supervised constrn. engines for revenue cutter Lake Michigan, 1843; in charge shop Rowe & Davis, which he subsequently leased and operated; bought establishment of Robert Whiteman; in early 1850's, started passenger and freight steamer line on Allegheny River (his vessels being important factors in oil-carrying trade); popularized "sternwheeler" in U.S.; had orders from South Am. countries, also built boats for carrying trade on Volga and Dneiper rivers; inventor hot die press for making nuts and bolts; improved steamboat constrn., especially protection of working parts; introduced 10-hour day in his shops; mem. Pitts. City Council. Died Sept. 12, 1889.

REES, JOHN KROM, prof. astronomy, Columbia, 1892—; b. New York, Oct. 27, 1851; grad. Columbia, 1872; Columbia School of Mines, E.M., 1875, A.M., 1875; Ph.D., 1895, Columbia; m. Louise E. Sands, Sept. 7, 1876. Asst. in mathematics, School of Mines, 1873-76; prof. mathematics and astronomy, Washington U., St. Louis, 1876-81. At Columbia as dir. of observatory, 1881—; instr. geodesy and practical astronomy, 1881-82; chmn. bd. of editors, School of Mines Quarterly, 1883-90; frequent contributor to astron. jours. V.p. Am. Math. Soc., 1890-91; pres. New York Acad. Sciences, 1894-96; sec. Am. Metrol. Soc., 1882-96; v.p., 1896—; sec. Univ. Council of Columbia, 1892-98. Received from French govt. decoration of Chevalier de la Legion d'Honneur, Jan. 1901. Address: New York, N.Y. Died 1907.

REESE, ALBERT MOORE, zoologist; b. Lake Roland, Md., Apr. 1, 1872; s. Henry and Mary Anna (Miller) R.; A.B., Johns Hopkins, 1892, Ph.D., 1900; m. Nelle Summers, June 29, 1927; 1 son, Albert Moore, Jr. Lectr. chemistry So. Homeo. Med. Coll., Balt., 1893-97; lectr. histology and embryology Pa. Coll., 1897, prof. biology and geology Allegheny Coll., 1901-02; asso. prof. histology and embryology Syracuse U., 1902-07; prof. zoology W.Va. State U., 1907-46, prof. emeritus since 1946. Recipient Vandalia award for distinguished service W.Va. U., 1964. Fellow A.A.A.S.; mem. Am. Soc. Zoologists, Am. Soc. Naturalists, Am. Micros. Soc., Beta Theta Pi, Phi Beta Kappa, Sigma Xi. Quaker. Author: Introduction to Vertebrate Embryology, 1904, 2d edit., 1910; The Alligator and Its Allies, 1915; Outlines of Economic Zoology, 1919, 4th edit., 1942; Wanderings in the Orient 1919. Home: Morgantown, W.Va. Died Dec. 30, 1965; buried East Oak Grove Cemetery, Morgantown.

REESE, CHARLES LEE, chemist; b. Baltimore, Md., Nov. 4, 1862; s. John S. and Arnoldina O. (Focke) R.; grad. U. of Va., 1884; Ph.D., Heidelberg, 1886; hon. Sc.D., U. of Pa., 1919, Colgate U., 1919, U. of Delaware, 1928; hon. Sc.D., Wake Forest (N.C.) Coll., 1934, Heidelberg, 1936; m. Harriet S. Bent, April 10, 1901; children—Charles Lee, John Smith, David Meredith, Eben Bent, William Fessenden (dec.). Asst. in chemistry, Johns Hopkins. 1886-88; prof. chemistry, Wake Forest Coll., 1888, S.C. Mil. Acad., 1888-96; instr. Johns Hopkins, 1896-1900; chief chemist New Jersey Zinc Co., 1901-02, and of Eastern Dynamite Co., and dir. Eastern Lab., 1902-06; in charge chem. div. high explosive operating dept. of E. I. du Pont de Nemours Powder Co., 1902-11, chem. dir., 1911-June 1, 1924, consultant, until 1931 (retired); dir. E. I. du Pont de Nemours & Co. Member American Chem. Soc. (chmn. bd. 1930—; also pres. 1934), Am. Inst. Chem. Engrs. (pres. 1923-25), Mfg. Chemists' Assn. (pres. 1920-23). Asso. mem. Naval Consulting Bd., also chairman Delaware sect.; mem. Nat. Industrial Conf. Bd.; mem. advisory bd. to prohibition commr.; mem. visiting com. Bur. of Standards, 1930—. V.p. Internat. Union of Pure and Applied Chemistry, 1929-34; founder and chemn. Bd. Industrial Research, chmn. emeritus, 1931. Episcopalian. Contbr. to chem. jours. Home: Wilmington, Del. Died Apr. 12, 1940.

REESE, HERBERT MEREDITH, prof. physics; b. Balt., Dec. 1, 1873; s. John Evan and Alice Virginia (Gibbs) R.; A.B., Johns Hopkins, 1897, Ph.D., 1900; studied U. of Berlin, U. of Leyden; m. Anna Willis Pape, June 4, 1921; children—Jane Willis (Mrs. Alfred Walter Schultz), Ann Meredith (dec.). Fellow and asst., Lick Observatory, 1900-03; asst. Yerkes Obs., 1903-04; successively instr., asst. prof., asso. prof., prof. physics, U. Mo., 1904-43, prof. emeritus, 1944—. Fellow Am. Physical Soc.; mem. Optical Soc. Am., Phi Beta Kappa, Sigma Xi, Gamma Alpha, Sinfonia. Methodist. Author: Laboratory Instruction in General Physics, 1914; Light, 1921. Contbr. to Bull. of Lick Obs., Sci., Astrophys. Jour., Physical Rev., etc. Home: Georgetown, Colo. Died May 10, 1954; buried Columbia, Mo.

REESE, JOHN JAMES, physician, toxicologist; b. Phila., June 16, 1818; s. Jacob and Leah (James) R.; A.B., U. Pa., 1836, A.M., M.D., 1839; m. Sallie Gibson, several children. Lectr. on materia medica and therapeutics Phila. Med. Inst.; prof. med. chemistry med. dept. Pa. Coll., 1852-59; prof. med. jurisprudence and toxicology U. Pa., 1865-91; mem. firm Booth, Reese

& Camac, analytic chemists, Phila.; commd. asst. surgeon U.S. Army during Civil War, head Christian Street Hosp., Phila.; treas. Phila. County Med. Soc.; pres. Med. Jurisprudence Soc. of Phila., 1886-87; gave expert testimony on toxicology in ct., expecially in trial of Mrs. Warton (J.T. Morse, Jr. in Am. Law Rev. July 1872). Author: The American Medical Formulary, 1850; Syllabus of a Course of Lectures on Medical Chemistry, 1857; Manual of Toxicology, 1874. Died Atlantic City, N.J., Sept. 4, 1892.

REESIDE, JOHN BERNARD, JR., (re'sid), geologist; b. Baltimore, Md., June 24, 1889; s. John Bernard and Florence May (Feathers) R.; A.B., Johns Hopkins U., 1911, Ph.D., 1915; m. Adelaide C. Quisenberry, May 3, 1918; children—John Bernard III, Corinna. Geologist U.S. Geol. Survey since 1915, charge Sect. of Paleontology and Stratigraphy, 1932-49. Served as 1st lt. field arty., United States Army, 1918. Awarded Mary Clark Thompson Medal, 1946. Fellow A.A.A.S.; Geol. Soc. of America, Nat. Acad. of Sciences, Paleontological Soc. (pres. 1943); mem. Am. Assn. Petroleum Geologists, Washington Acad. Science, Washington Geol. Soc. (pres. 1941), Biol. Soc., Soc. Geol. Perú, Phi Beta Kappa, Sigma Xi. Episcopalian. Club: Cosmos (Washington, D.C.). Contributor to geol. jours. Home: 5104 41st Av., Hyattsville, Md. Office: U.S. Nat. Museum, Washington, Died July 2, 1958.

REEVE, SIDNEY ARMOR, mech. engr.; b. Dayton, O., Mar. 27, 1866; s. John Charles (M.D.) and Emma Griswold (Barlow) R.; Ph.B., Sheffield Scientific Sch. (Yale), 1885, M.E., 1887; m. Lella A. Wellington, Dec. 7, 1892. Engaged in commercial engring. with Westinghouse, Church, Kerr & Co., 1887-94; editor Progressive Age, 1895; prof. steam and hydraulic engring., Worcester Poly. Inst., 1896-1906; lecturer on steam engring., Harvard, 1907. Lecturer, Graduate Naval Sch., Annapolis, 1911; consulting mech. engr., New York, 1908—. Author: The Entropy-temperature Analysis of Steam-engine Efficiencies, 1898; The Thermodynamics of Heatengines, 1901; The Cost of Competition, 1906; Energy, 1909; Modern Economic Tendencies, 1921. Home: New Brighton, S.I., N.Y. Died June 12, 1941.

REEVE, WILLIAM DAVID, mathematician; b. Edwardsport, Ind., Sept. 11, 1883; s. Charles Hamilton and Martha Ellen (McLin) R.; B.S., U. Chgo., 1909; Ph.D., U. Minn., 1924; grad. student Columbia, 1923-24; m. Isabel Jaensch, June 16, 1911; 1 dau., Katherine Ellen. Tchr. pub. schs., Ind., 1903-05; prin. high sch., 1905-08; tchr. math. U. High Sch., Chgo., 1910-14; head dept. math. U. High Sch., Minn. 1915-21, prin. 1921-23; prof. math. Tchr. Coll., Columbia, 1924-49. Mem. Joint Com. on Place of Math. in Secondary Schs. Mem. Math. Assn. Gt. Britain (hon.), Nat. Council Tchrs. Math., Math. Assn. Am., Tau Kappa Epsilon (nat. pres. 1918-21). Awarded Honor Key from Phi Delta Kappa. Democrat. Clubs: Men's Faculty (Columbia), Gypsy Trail (Carmel, N.Y.). Author: Gen. Mathematics, 1919; Essentials of Algebra, 1926; Essentials of Trigonometry, 1927; Texts and Tests in Plane Geometry, 1933; also many other text and test books. Editor: Yearbooks 2-20 of Nat. Council Tchrs. Math. Editor of Math. Tchr., 1928-50. Home: 460 Riverside Dr., N.Y.C. 27. Died Feb. 16, 1961.

REEVES, ALEC HARLEY, scientist; b. Redhill, Eng., Mar. 10, 1902; s. Edward Ayearst and Grace (Harley) R.; B.S. in Engring., Imperial Coll. Sci., London, 1923. Research engr. Internat. Western Electric Co., London, 1923; project leader Paris (Eng. and France) lab. Internat. Tel. & Tel. Co., 1924-40; prin. sci. officer Royal Aircraft Establishment, 1940-45; divisional head Standard Telecommunications Labs., Ltd., Harlow, Eng., 1945-60, senior scientist, 1964-70, sr. prin. research engr.; head Reeves Telecommunications Labs., London, 1970-71. Boy Scout leader, 1918-29, 35-40; vol. probation officer, Surrey and London, 1950-71. Mem. Outward Bound Trust of Eng., 1950-71; bd. govs. Royal Hosp. Incurables, London, 1952-71. Served to wing comdr. RAF, World War II. Decorated officer British Empire, 1965, also Commander Order of British Empire, 1969; recipient Ballantine Gold medal Franklin Inst., Phila., 1965; City of Columbus award Internat. Communications Inst., Genoa, Italy, 1966. Fellow Radar and Electronics Assn., Instn. Elec. Engrs. Club: Ski of Great Britain. Inventor pulse code modulation, 1937; co-inventor, oboe system bombing through overcast, 1941. Home: Harlow Essex England Died Oct. 13, 1971.

REEVES; ROBERT JAMES, radiologist; b. Matador Tex., Dec. 28, 1898; s. Walter Eugene and Henrietta (Bryant) R.; A.B., Baylor U., 1920, M.D., 1924; m. Gipsie Proctor, Aug. 30, 1936; children—Elizabeth James, Judith Bryant. Resident physician radiology Mass. Gen. Hosp., Boston, 1926; asst. radiologist Columbia U. Med. Center, 1926-30; radiologist, dir. and chmn. dept. radiology Duke Hosp., Durham, N.C. 1930—; cons. AEC. Pvt. med. corps S.A.T.C., World War I. Fellow Am. Coll. Radiology; mem. Nat. Research Council, A.M.A., Am. Roentgen Ray Soc., So. Med. Soc., Radiol. Soc. N.A., Soc. Nuclear Med., Sigma Xi. Author papers on cancer, radiol. Home: 920 Anderson St. Office: Duke Hospital, Durham, N.C. Died Feb. 1968.

REGER, DAVID BRIGHT, (re'ger), cons. geologist; b. Rural Dale, W.Va., Apr. 11, 1882; s. Joseph Socrates and Sirene (Bunten) R.; prep. edn., W.Va. Conf. Sem. (now W.Va. Wesleyan Coll.; A.B., West Virginia University, 1909, B.S. in Civil Engring., 1911; m. Ella Gertrude Mattingly, Nov. 24, 1914; children—Helen E. (Mrs. M. K. Armentrout), Jane (Mrs. D. Cruise), Joseph E. Field asst. U.S. Geol. Survey, 1903-06; hydrographic surveyor U.S. Naval Sta., Guantanamo Bay, Cuba, 1906-07; with W.Va. Geol. Survey, 1909-30, as field asst., 1909-13, asst. geologist, 1913-27, acting state geologist, 1927-29, asso. geologist, 1929-30; cons. geologist for oil, gas and coal, water supply, etc., 1919—, office in Morgantown, W.Va., 1930—; pres. Pringle Run Coal Co., 1918-38; v.p. Columbia Coal & Coke Co., 1918-22; sec.-treas., mgr. Reger Oil Co., 1920-29. Member Am. Assn. of Petroleum Geologists, Am. Inst. Mining and Metall. Engrs., Geol. Soc. America, Soc. Econ. Geologists, A.A.A.S., W.Va. Acad. Science (v.p. 1932-33; pres. 1933-34), W.Va. Coal Mining Inst., Appalachian Geol. Soc., Phi Kappa Psi (dir. James Cochran House Assn.), Phi Beta Kappa, Sigma Xi. Rep. Methodist. Author: (Geologic Reports of the W.Va. Geol. Survey) Preston County (with R. V. Hennen), 1914; Logan and Mingo Counties (with R. V. Hennen), 1914; Lewis and Gilmer Counties, 1916; Barbour and Upshur Counties and Western Portion of Randolph County, 1918; Webster County, 1920; Nicholas County, 1921; Tucker County, 1923; Mineral and Grant Counties, 1924; Mercer, Monroe and Summers Counties, 1926; Randolph County, 1931; also contbg. author to other reports. Contbr. numerous articles to scientific jours. Home: 112 Wilson Av. Office: 68 High St., Morgantown, W.Va. Died Sept. 10, 1958; buried Beverly Hills Meml. Gardens, Morgantown.

REHDER, ALFRED (ra'der), botanist; b. Waldenburg, Sachs., Germany, Sept. 4, 1863; s. Paul Julius and Thekla (Schmidt) R.; ed. gymnasium and at univs. of Berlin and Göttingen; hon. A.M., Harvard, 1913; m. Anneliese Hedwig Schrefeld, Mar. 31, 1906; children—Harald Alfred, Gerhard Oskar and Sylvia Sophia (Mrs. Warren F. Witherell, II). Came to Ameica, 1898; assistant, 1898-1918, curator Herbarium of Arnold Arboretum (Harvard), 1918; asso. prof. dendrology, Harvard, 1934-40, emeritus since 1940. Awarded gold medal by Mass. Horticultural Soc., 1937. Foreign member Linnean Soc. of London; hon. fellow Bot. Soc. of Edinburgh, Royal Hort. Soc. (London); fellow Am. Acad. of Arts and Sciences, A.A.A.S.; mem. Soc. Hort. Science, Deutsche Botanische Gesellschaft, Boston Natural History Soc., N.E. Bot. Club, Bot. Soc. America; hon. mem. Duetsche Dendrol. Gesellschaft, Denrol. Soc. of Czechoslovakia, Rhododendron Soc., Pa. Hort Soc.; corr. mem. Peking Soc. Nat. History, Bot. Soc. Japan. Author: Synopsis of the Genus Lonicera, 1903; Bradley Bibliography (5 vols.), 1911-18; Mongraph of Azaleas (with E. H. Wilson), 1921; Manual of Cultivated Trees and Shrubs, 1927; 2d edit., 1940; Bibliography of Cultivated Trees and Shrubs, 1949. Editor: Journal of Arnold Arboretum, 1926-40. Collaborator of Standard Cyclopedia of Horticulture, and of Cultivated Evergreens by L. H. Bailey; of Plantae Wilsonianae, and of Trees and Shrubs by C. S. Sargent; of Species of Rhododendron. Has published many papers on woody plants in bot. and hort. jours. Home: 62 Orchard St., Jamaica Plain 30, Mass. Died July 21, 1949.

REICHARD, JOHN DAVIS, pub. health officer (ret.); b. Fairplay, Md., Feb. 19, 1889; s. Valentine Milton and Fanny (Line) R.; grad. St. James Sch., 1907; A.B., Trinity Coll., 1910; M.D., Johns Hopkins, 1914; m. Pansy Guyther Mitchell, Nov. 2, 1916 (dec.); married second, Mrs. Bernice C. Hires, 1955. Commd. asst. surgeon USPHS, 1916, passed asst. surgeon, 1920, surgeon, 1924, sr. surgeon, 1936, med. dir., 1941, positions included field duty in pellagra investigations, hosps., quarantines and immigration duty; immigration duty in Germany and Poland, 1926-29; charge neuro-psychiatric service, Ellis Island, 1930-39; med. officer USPHS, Hosp., Lexington, Ky., 1939-46; retired; spl. cons. Diplomate Am. Bd. Psychiatry and Neurology. Fellow Am. Psychiatric Assn., A.M.A.; mem. Soc. Biol. Psychiatry, A.A.A.S., N.Y. Acad. Scis., N.Y. Neurol. Soc., Assn. Mil. Surgeons, Phi Chi. Author bulls. USPHS, also articles profl. jours. Produced med. motion pictures: An Introduction to Clinical Neurology; The Nature and Treatment of Narcotic Drug Addiction; Disturbances in Human Behavior. Clubs: Army & Navy (Coral Gables); Propeller (Port of Miami). Home: 1541 Palancia Av., Coral Gables 34, Fla. Died Aug. 18, 1961; buried Arlington Nat. Cemetery.

REICHERT, EDWARD TYSON, univ. prof.; b. Phila., Feb. 5, 1855; s. Gabriel Adam (Jr.) and Emma Rebecca (Horn) R.; ed. pub. and pvt. schs., Phila., and U. of Pa.; post-grad. work in univs. of Berlin, Leipzig and Geneva; M.D., U. of Pa., 1879, Sc.D., 1913; m. Marion C. Welsh, June 7, 1883 (dec.); m. 2d, Jessie Adéle Ward, Nov. 11, 1919. Demonstration exptl. therapy, 1879-84, asst. in Nervous Dispensary, 1879-80, demonstrator in physiology, 1884-86, prof. 1886-1920, U. of Pa. (later emeritus prof.). Contbr. med. and other scientific articles, the results of original research, especially researches on respiration, circulation, animal heat mechanism and hemoglobins; the toxic principles of serpent venoms; on the differentiation and specificity of corresponding vital substances in relation to genera and organic evolution; and on biochemic basis for the study of problems of taxonomy, heredity, sex, species, organic evolution, etc. Assisted Edweard Muybridge in his pioneer work on animal motion and moving pictures; among the first inventors of storage battery plates; devised many forms of scientific apparatus. Research asso., Carnegie Instn., Washington. Address: Mt. Airy, Philadelphia, Pa. Deceased.

REID, DAVID BOSWELL, chemist, educator, engr.; b. Edinburgh, Scotland, June 1805; s. Peter and Christian (Arnot) R.; M.D., U. Edinburgh, 1830; m. Elizabeth Brown, 1834; at least 5 children. Pvt. lectr. on chemistry and sanitation in his own pvt. sch. (contained lab. larger than any in Eng.); circa 1833; tested principles of ventilation and acoustics in "1st systematic plan of ventilation ever carried out in any public building," in Temporary Ho. of Parliament Bldg., 1835; arranged and superintended ventilation and lighting of new Houses of Parliament, London, Eng., 1840; came to U.S., 1855; prof. physiology and hygiene, dir. Museum Practical Scis., U. Wis., 1859-60; inspector mil. hosps. throughout U.S., 1863. Author: Introduction to the Study of Chemistry, 1832; Rudiments of the Chemistry of Daily Life, 1836; Outlines for the Ventilation of the House of Commons, 1837; Illustrations of the Theory and Practice of Ventilation, 1844. Died Washington, D.C., Apr. 5, 1863.

REID, ELLIOTT GRAY, aero. engr.; b. Sycamore, O., May 29, 1900; s. J. Nelson and Etta A. (Bennington) R.; B.S., U. Mich., 1922, M.S., 1923, Aero. Engr., 1938; m. Charlotte Katherine Jenkins, May 15, 1926; 1 dau., Margaret Anne (Mrs. T. j. Fogel). Jr. aero. engr., NACA Langley Field, Va., 1922, asst., 1924, associate, 1927, exptl. and theoretical aerodynamics; prof. aerodynamics, Stanford; cons. engrs., 1927-68; currently aerodynamic cons. Hdqrs. USAF. Private S.A.T.C., U. Mich. Oct.-Dec. 1918. Recipient citation Distinguished Alumnus, Engring. Centennial, U. Mich., 1953. Fellow Royal Aero. Soc. (Gt. Britain), Am. Inst. Aero. and Astronautics; member of Sigma Xi, Tau Beta Pi. Author: Applied Wing Theory, 1932; also tech. reports and notes NACA. Contbr. to tech. journals. Home: Menlo Park CA Died Sept. 24, 1968.

REID, ERNEST W., chemist; b. Chase, Kan., Dec. 17, 1891; s. James William and Ella (Kelly) R.; A.B., Southwestern Coll., 1916; M.S. and Ph.D., U. Pitts., 1929; m. Leila E. English, Sept. 21, 1921. Research chemist Mellon Inst., 1916-21; supt. chem. plant Carbide & Carbon Chem. Corp., 1921-25, dir. sales devel., 1926-36, European rep., 1936-40; sr. indsl. fellow Mellon Inst., 1925-36; mem. adv. commn. Council Nat. Defense, 1940-41; asst. chief chem. sect. Office Prodn. Mgmt., 1941-42; chief chem. br. WPB, 1942, dep. dir. gen., 1942-43; dir., chmn. bd. Corn Products Refining Co.; dir. Comml. Solvents Corp., Alco Products, Inc. Recipient Chem. Industry medal, Soc. Chem. Industry. Mem. Am. Chem. Soc. (Chem. in Industry Award, 1951), Am. Inst. Chemists. Clubs: University (Pitts.); Chemist, Whitehall (N.Y.). Contbr. to sci. jours. Holds several patents on chem. processes. Home: New Weston Hotel. Office: 17 Battery Pl., N.Y. Died July 1966.

REID, HARRY FIELDING, geologist; b. Baltimore, Md., May 18, 1859; s. Andrew and Fanny Brooke (Gwathmey) R.; A.B., Johns Hopkins, 1835; studied in Germany and England, 1884-86; m. Edith Gittings, Nov. 22, 1883; children—Francis Fielding, Doris Fielding. Prof. mathematics, 1886-89, physics, 1889-94, Case School of Applied Science, Cleveland; lecturer Johns Hopkins, 1894-96; asso. prof. physical geology, U. of Chicago, 1895-96; asso. prof., Johns Hopkins U., 1896-1901, prof. geol. physics, 1901-11, prof. dynamical geology and geography, 1911-30, prof. emeritus since 1930. Chief of highway div., Md. Geol. Survey, 1898-1905; spl. expert in charge of earthquake records, U.S. Geol. Survey, 1902-14. Mem. Commn. Internationale des Glaciers; rep. of U.S. in the Internat. Seismol. Assn. since 1906; hon. mem. Société Helvétique des Sciences Naturelles; corr. mem. Phila. Acad. of Natural Sciences; fellow Geol. Soc. America, Am. Phys. Soc., Washington Acad. Sciences; mem. Nat. Acad. Sciences, Am. Philos. Soc., Seismol. Soc. America (pres. 1913), Am. Geophys. Union (chmn. 1924-26). Author: Parts vi, vii, viii of Highways of Maryland, 1899. Joint author: (with A. N. Johnson) Second Report on the Highways of Maryland, 1902; Vol II of Report of Calif. State Earthquake Investigation Commn., 1910; also several reports and articles on glaciers, earthquakes, etc. Mem. com. Nat. Acad. Sciences apptd. at request of the President to report on the possibility of controlling the Panama slides, 1915. Home: 608 Cathedral St., Baltimore, Md. Died June 18, 1944. *

REID, HENRY JOHN EDWARD, aeronautical engr.; b. Springfield, Mass., Aug. 20, 1895; s. Henry and Sophia (Mowle) R.; B.S. in E.E., Worcester Poly. Inst., 1919, Dr. Engring. (hon.), 1946; married Mildred J. Woods, June 26, 1920; children—Phyllis Virginia, Henry J. E. Began as student research engineer, Westinghouse Company (East Pittsburgh), 1919; in charge of maintenance and millwrighting Noiseless Typewriter Company, Middletown, Conn., 1920-21; jr. mech. engr. Nat. Advisory Com. for Aeronautics,

Langley Field, Va., 1921-26, engr. in charge laboratories and director, 1926-60. Served as private, Engineers Reserve, United States Army, 1918; member ALSOS mission to Europe, 1944-45. Member board of directors, Hampton-Elizabeth City County Community Chest, 1943-45, pres. 1946. Fellow Inst. of Aeronautical Sciences; mem. Soc. Automotive Engrs., Nat. Rifle Assn. (life), A.A.A.S., Tau Beta Pi, Sigma Alpha Epsilon. Conglist. Mason. Clubs: Rotary (Hampton); Engineers Club of Va., Peninsula. Author of Tech. Notes, Nat. Adv. Com. on Aeronautics. Office: Landley Field VA Died July 30, 1968.

REID, JAMES L., corn breeder; b. Red Oak, O., Dec. 26, 1844; s. Robert Drake and Anne (Moore) R.; m. Marietta Jenks, Apr. 1870. Corn farmer, Boynton Center, Ill., 1865-80, developed new type of corn (Reid's Yellow Dent) by crossing a late maturing Ohio variety with type known as Little Yellow; unsuccessfully farmed (according to Ill. methods) in Osage County, Kan., 1880-88; farmed at Boynton Center, 1888-1910; his breed of corn introduced at World's Columbian Expn., 1892; established mail-order firm to handle seed-corn orders, East Lynn, Vermillion County, Ill., 1902; attended Nat. Corn Expn., Omaha, Neb., 1908. Died June 1, 1910.

REID, JOHN SIMPSON, mech. engr., educator; b. Kilmarnock, Ayrshire, Scotland, Mar. 25, 1856; s. David and Sarah Crichton (Simpson) R.; studied acad. Irvine, Scotland, in British Govt. science and art schs., and in engring. shops in Kilmarnock and Glasgow, Scotland, and in Boston, Schenectady, N.Y., and Rome, N.Y.; m. Rome, N.Y., Dec. 18, 1884, Elvire Lee Vandermark. Instr. in machine design, Cornell Univ., since 1891. Mem. Am. Soc. Mech. Engrs., N.Y. R.R. Club. Pres. YMCA, Ithaca; active in Sunday School work as supt. Sunday School Home Dept. Union, Ithaca, supt. Presbyn. Sunday School Home Dept., supt. Eastlawn Sunday School. Author: A Course in Mechanical Drawing, 1897 W9; Mechanical Drawing and Elementary Machine Design (with D. Reid), 1899 W9. Address: Ithaca, N.Y.

REID, LOUDON CORSAN, physician; b. North Bay, Ont., Can., Oct. 13, 1893; s. Herbert Gates and Mary Fisher (Ferguson) R.; M.D., McGill U., 1916, C.M., 1916; m. Grace A. Lodge, Feb. 12, 1925; children—H. G., Martha. Came to U.S., 1924, naturalized, 1944. Intern Royal Victoria Hosp., 1920-25; pvt. practice surgery, Detroit, 1925-30; asso. prof. pathology N.Y. Med. Coll., 1930-39; prof. physiology N.Y.U. Sch. Medicine, 1939-69, Rush H. Kress prof. research surgery, 1950-69. Served with Canadian Army, 1915-19, with AUS, 1942-46. Home: Bronxville NY Died July 15, 1969.

REID, THORBURN, electrical engr.; b. London, Eng., May 1, 1864; s. Charles Henry and Mary Helen (Cochran) R.; A.B., Hampden-Sidney Coll., 1882; U. of Va., 1882-85; M.E., Stevens Inst. Tech., 1888; m. Bertha Van Kleeck, Jan. 9, 1900; children—Thorburn, Graeme. Instr. mech. engring., U. of S.C., 1888-89; head of testing dept. U.S. Elec. Illuminating Co., Newark, N.J., 1889-90; in charge alternating current design, Edison Gen. Electric Co., N.Y.C. and Schenectady, N.Y., 1890-91; with Gen. Elec. Co., Schenectady, and Lynn, Mass., 1891-97; consulting engr. N.Y.C., 1897-1912; head of cost dept. Simms Magneto Co., East Orange, N.J., 1912-25. Retired. Mem. Am. Inst. E.E., Phi Gamma Delta. Presbyn. Discovered cause and effect of sparking, at the commutators, of direct current dynamos and motors. Home: Essex Fells, N.J. Died Nov. 22, 1933.

REIDY, PETER J., cons. engr.; b. Long Island City, Mar. 15, 1900; s. Maurice Alphonse and Mary Agnes (Hession) R.; student Bklyn. Polytech. Inst., 1922; m. Alby Eugenia Cobb, July 22, 1947. Engr., Purdy & Henderson Co., N.Y.C., 1922-32; mem. firm Purdy & Henderson Assos., Inc., cons. engrs., N.Y.C., 1933-42, pres., chmn. bd., 1943-58; v.p., dir. Purdy & Henderson Co., N.Y.C. and Havana, Cuba, 1942-52; commnr. dept. bldgs., N.Y.C., 1958-62, comdr. dept. pub. works, 1962-63; exec. dir. Triborough Bridge and Tunnel Authority, 1963-71; dir. General Analine & Film Corp., Ninth Federal Savings and Loan Association. Bd. govs. N.Y. Bldg. Congress, Inc. Mem. Mayor N.Y.C. Slum Clearance Com.; mem. Grand Jury Assn. N.Y. County; chmn. constrn. div. Greater N.Y. council Boy Scouts Am. Fellow Am. Soc. Cons. Engrs.; mem. N.Y. Assn. Cons. Engrs. (pres. 1957-58). Home: New York City NY Died June 4, 1971; buried Gate of Heaven, Mt. Pleasant NY

REIGHARD, JACOB (ELLSWORTH), (ri'kard), zoölogist; b. LaPorte, Ind., July 2, 1861; s. Dr. John Davison and Mary (Hulbert) R.; Ph.B., U. of Mich., 1882, hon. Sc.D., 1936; studied Harvard U., 1883-85, Univ. of Michigan Medical School, 1885-86, also Freiburg-in-Breisgau; married Katharine E. Farrand, July 1, 1887 (now deceased); children—Paul Roby (dec.), John Jacob, Catherine Farrand, Farrand Kitchel (dec.). Teacher of sciences, High Sch., LaPorte, Ind., 1882-83; pvt. tutor North Attleboro, Mass., 1883-85; instr. zoölogy, 1886-87 and 1888-89, acting asst. prof. zoölogy, 1887-88, asst. prof., 1889-91, prof. animal morphology, 1891-95, prof. zoölogy, 1895-1927, prof. emeritus in zoölogy since 1927, dir. zoölogy laboratory, 1895-1925, and dir. Biol. Sta., U. of Mich.; dir. Univ. Museum, 1895-1913. In charge of scientific work of Mich. Fish Commn., 1890-95; dir. biological survey of Great Lakes for U.S. Fish Commn., 1898-1901; formerly trustee Marine Biol. Lab., Woods Hole, Mass., and mem. bd. advisers Mich. State Geol. Survey. Fellow A.A.A.S.; mem. Am. Soc. Naturalists, Am. Soc. Zoölogists, Am. Fisheries Soc. (pres. 1916), Mich. Acad. Science. Clubs: University, Ann Arbor Golf and Outing, Pleasant Lakes, Research of Univ. of Mich., Delta Upsilon. Author: (with Dr. H. S. Jennings) Anatomy of the Cat, 1901, rev., 1937 also articles on lip reading for the adult deafened, and numerous scientific papers on fresh water biology, evolution, development, behavior and habits of fishes, sub-aquatic photography. Address: Natural Science Bldg., Ann Arbor, Mich. Died Feb. 13, 1942.

REIK, THEODOR, psychologist, author; b. Vienna, Austria, May 12, 1888; s. Max and Caroline (Trebitsch) R.; Ph.D., U. Vienna, 1912; m. Marla Cubelic, 1932; children—Arthur, Theodora, Miriam. Came to U.S., 1938, naturalized, 1944. Asso. Sigmund Freud, U. Vienna, 1910-38; lectr. Psychoanalytic Inst., Vienna, Berlin, Germany, The Hague, Netherlands, N.Y.C., 1912-44; dir. Soc. for Psychoanalytic Psychology, N.Y.C., 1941-70; also professor of psychology Adelphi University. Recipient 1st prize for psychoanalytic paper, 1915. Diplomate Am. Psychol. Assn. Author: Ritual (preface by Sigmund Freud), 1931; The Unknown Murder, 1936; Surprise and the Psychoanalyst, 1937; From Thirty Years With Freud, 1940; Masochism in Modern Man, 1941; A Psychologist Looks at Love, 1944; Psychology of Sex Relations, 1945; Listening With the Third Ear, 1948; Fragment of a Great Confession, 1948; The Secret Self, 1952; The Haunting Melody, 1953; The Search Within, 1956; Myth and Guilt, 1957; On Love and Lust, 1957; A Mystery on the Mountain, 1959; The Compulsion to Confess, 1959; The Creation of Woman, 1960; Sex in Man and Woman, 1960; The Temptation, 1961; Jewish Wit, 1961; The Need to be Loved, 1963; Curiosities of the Self, 1965; The Many Faces of Sex, 1966; 17 psychol. books in German. Contbr. to English, German, Dutch, Spanish psychol. publs. Address: New York City NY Died Dec. 31, 1969.

REIMER, MARIE, chemist; b. Sunbury, Pa.; d. David and Cornelia (Collins) R.; A.B., Vassar, 1897; Ph.D., Bryn Mawr, 1904; Univ. of Berlin, 1902-3. Asso. prof. chemistry, Barnard Coll. (Columbia), 1903—. Protestant. Member Am. Chem. Soc., Deutsche Chemische Gesellschaft. Contbr. articles to Am. Chem. Journal, etc. Address: 604 W. 112th St., New York NY

REINHARDT, RALPH HOMER, indsl. engr.; b. Chgo., Dec. 1, 1907; s. Homer Lewis and Grace (Gibbs) R.; student Northwestern U., 1931-33; m. Virginia Ruth Benz, Mar. 30, 1934; children—Arden Georgiana (Mrs. Daniel H. Thompson), John Allen. Bonus clk. R. R. Donnelley & Sons, Chgo., 1926-28, time study man, 1928-32, efficiency man, 1932-42; mgmt. engr. Stevenson, Jordan & Harrison, Inc., N.Y.C., 1942-43, mgmt. engring. supr., 1943-47; plant mgr. Richardson Co., Melrose Park, Ill., 1947-52, indsl. engring. mgr., 1952-68. Mem. Soc. Packaging and Handling Engrs., Industrial Management Soc., Indsl. Engring. Group, Rubber Mfrs. Assn., Tau Delta Kappa. Episcopalian. Home: Lombard IL Died Apr. 29, 1968.

REINKE, EDWIN EUSTACE, (rin'ke), biologist; b. of Am. parents, Jamacia, W.I., June 27, 1887; s. Rev. Jonathan (D.D.) and Mary Virginia (Caffrey) R.; Moravian Preparatory Sch., Bethlehem, Pa.; B.A., Lehigh U., 1908, M.A., 1909; Ph.D., Princeton, 1913; m. Emily Feuring, Aug. 14, 1915; children—Mary Louise, Dorothy Virginia, Caroline Emily. Grad. asst. Lehigh U., 1908-09; fellow in biology, Princeton, 1909-13, Procter fellow, 1913-14; instr. in biology, Rice Inst., Houston, Tex., 1914-15; research asso. Dept. Marine Biology of Carnegie Instn., Washington, 1912-15; with Vanderbilt U. since 1915, successively asst. prof. biology until 1917, asso. prof., 1917-22, prof. since 1922, sec. of faculty, Coll. of Arts and Science, 1929-41, chmn. div. natural sciences and math. since 1941; dir. Highlands Museum and Biol. Lab., Inc., 1929-35 (resigned). Fellow A.A.A.S.; mem. Am. Soc. Zoölogists, Assn. of Southeastern Biologists (pres. 1938-39), Am. Assn. Anatomists, Ala. Acad. Science (hon.), Phi Beta Kappa, Sigma Xi. Democrat. Episcopalian. Home: 1702 Beechwood Av., Nashville, Tenn. Died Jan. 25, 1945.

REINKING, OTTO AUGUST, educator; b. Madison, Wis., Feb. 11, 1890; s. John Juergin and Lydia (Bierbach) R.; B.S.A., U. Wis., 1912, M.S., 1915, Ph.D., 1922; m. Addie E. Piehl, July 22, 1940. In charge dept. agr. Mid-Pacific Inst., Mills Sch., Honolulu, Hawaii, 1912-13; instr. Colo. Agrl. Coll. and asst. botanist, expt. sta., 1915-16; asst. prof. and prof. plant pathology and plant pathologist Agrl. Expt. Sta., Coll. Agr., U. Philippines, 1916-21; pathologist United Fruit Co., Central Am. and research dept., Boston, 1922-27, dir. tropical research, 1927-32; pvt. research and study, Europe, and guest scientist, Biologische Reichsanstalt für Land und Forst-wirt-schaft, Berlin, Germany, 1932-35; consultant plant pathology United Fruit Co., Central Am., 1935-36; prof. plant pathology and head div. plant pathology N.Y. State Agrl. Expt. Sta., Cornell U., Geneva, N.Y., 1936-50, prof. emeritus, 1950—; agriculturist, fgn. agrl. adviser, research adminstrn. Office of Fgn. Agrl. Relations, U.S. Dept. Agr., Manila, P.I., 1950-54, Fgn. Operations Adminstrn., Washington, 1954-55; consultant United Fruit Company, Boston, 1956-59. Mem. tropical com. Nat. Research Council, 1921, plant pathology bd. Tropical Plant Research Found., 1922; chmn. Fusarium Conf., Madison, Wis., 1924. Recipient U.S. Dept. Agr. Superior Service Award, 1952. Fellow A.A.A.S.; mem. Am. Phytopathol. Soc., Bot. Soc. Am., Sigma Xi, Phi Sigma, Alpha Zeta. Republican. Presbyn. Clubs: Explorers' Cosmos. Home: 5213 Worthington Dr., Westgate, Washington 20016. Died May 31, 1962.

REISSNER, ALBERT, psychoanalyst and research in organo-therapy; born in Chemnitz, Germany, Mar. 5, 1883; s. Falk and Helen (Fuchs) R.; student psychiatry, psychology, medicine, biology, oral surgery, univs. of Berlin, Munich, Tuebingen, Phila., Cairo, Naples, Florence, London, Paris, New York; Dr. Med. Faculty summa cum laude, Tuebingen; B.A. (hon.), Oriental U., Alexandria; married Johanna Krafft; children—Dr. Fritz A., Helga Karker. Came to the United States, 1940, naturalized, 1946. Research worker Polyclinic Royal University Munich, 1905-22; certified specialist to royal family; served as head various hosps. during World War I; formerly prof. materia medica, comparative medicine; affiliated with Columbia, N.Y.U., L.I. Coll. Medicine, New Sch. Social Research, Alfred Adler Inst. for Individual Psychology, Mental Hygiene Service at Community Ch., N.Y.; mem. of staff Alfred Adler Consultation Center, New York; consultant and lecturer at Pastors' Clinic, Methodist Hospital, Brooklyn; mem. psychiat. forum Bklyn. State Hosp. First v.p. Community Mental Health Council. Recipient 7 honors and medals. Fellow Assn. Advancement Psychotherapy; mem. Rudolph Virchow Med. Soc., Am. Soc. Sci. Study of Religion, American Academy Psychotherapists, Order St. Luke the Physician, Institute Individual Psychology, New York State, Brooklyn psychol. assns., Association for Scientific Study Sex, American Assn. Religious Psychotherapy, American Assn. Alfred Adler Psychology, New York Acad. Sci., A.A.A.S. Episcopalian. Author many publs. Discoverer Reissner-Rhodan-Reaction (new method for diagnostic purposes), Vaduril Organo-therapeutic, and other discoveries relating to field. Address: Brooklyn NY Died Jan. 23, 1970.

REIST, HENRY GERBER, (rist), engineer; b. Mount Joy, Pa., May 27, 1862; s. Henry B. and Catharine (Gerber) R.; ed. country, high and state normal schs.; M.E., Lehigh U., 1886, Eng.D., 1922; m. Margaret E. Breed, Aug. 1907. Early life on farm; engr. for Harrisburg Car Co., 1886-88; accompanied Am. Engring. Soc. on trip to England and Paris Expn., 1899. Connected with the Thomson-Houston Elec. Co., 1889, and in 1894, took charge of designs of alternating current machinery for General Electric Co.; designed much of the most important elec. machinery in this country and abroad; now retired. Fellow Am. Soc. Mech. Engrs., Am. Inst. E.E., A.A.A.S.; mem. Tau Beta Pi, Sigma Xi. Author: Peter Reist of Lancaster County, Pa., and Some of His Descendants, 1933. Contbr. to proc. engring. socs. and tech. press. Home: 1166 Avon Rd., Schenectady, N.Y. Died July 5, 1942; buried in Kraybill Mennonite Cemetery, Twp. East Donegal, Pa.

REMINGTON, ELIPHALET, mfr.; b. Suffield, Conn., Oct. 27, 1793; s. Eliphalet and Elizabeth (Kilbourn) R.; m. Abigail Paddock, May 12, 1814, at least 5 children, including Philo, Samuel, Eliphalet. Made gun out of scrap metals, subsequently received orders for gun barrels; was forging barrels and rifling, stocking, lock fitting for guns, by 1828; erected new gunshop, 1828; purchased entire gun-finishing machinery of Ames & Co., Springfield, Mass., 1845, assumed unfinished contract for several thousand carbines for U.S. Govt.; procured contract in own right for 5,000 Harper's Ferry rifles; marketed Remington pistol, 1847; began mfg. agrl. implements, beginning with cultivator tooth, later plows, moving machines, wheeled rakes, horse hoes; received large contract from U.S. Govt. for rifles, carbines, pistols during the Civil War; 1st pres., one of 1st dirs. Ilion Bank (N.Y.). Died Ilion, Aug. 12, 1861.

REMINGTON, JOSEPH PRICE, pharmacist; b. Phila., Mar. 26, 1847; s. Dr. Isaac and Lydia (Hart) R.; ed. Central High Sch.; Ph.G., Phila. Coll. Pharmacy, 1866, later Ph.M.; hon. Pharm.D., Northwestern U., 1899; F.C.S., F.L.S., and F.R.M.S., London; m. Elizabeth Baily Collins, June 3, 1874. Prof. pharmacy, 1874—, dir. Pharm. Lab., 1877-1915, dean, 1893—, Phila. Coll. Pharmacy. Mem. revision com. U.S. Pharmacopoeia, 1880— (chmn., 1901—); pres. 1st Internat. Pharm. Congress, 1893; del. Pan-Am. Med. Congress, Washington, 1893, Mexico, 1896, 8th Internat. Pharm. Congress, Brussels, 1896; chmn. sect. 8b, 7th Internat. Congress Applied Chemistry, London, 1909, New York, 1912; del. Internat. Congress, The Hague, 1913. Author: Remington's Practice of Pharmacy, 1886. Editor: United States Dispensatory, 1883; Lippincott's Medical Dictionary, 1897; U.S. Pharmacopoeia, 1890, 1906, 1913. Address: Philadelphia, Pa. Died Jan. 1, 1918.

REMINGTON, PHILO, mfr.; b. Litchfield, N.Y., Oct. 21, 1816; s. Eliphalet and (probably) Abigail (Paddock) R.; ed. Cazenovia Sem.; m. Caroline Lathrop, Dec. 28, 1841; at least 2 children. Took charge of father's factory, 1861, reorganized firm, separating agrl. implements from armory; manufactured and aided in developing over 50 types of pistols; then manufactured Remington Breechloader rifle; organized armory as E. Remington & Sons, pres. until 1889; manufactured sewing machines (1st marketed), 1870; sole owner Sholes & Glidden typewriter after 1873; began manufacturing Remington typewriter, 1873 (introduced to public at Centennial Exhbn., Phila., 1876). Died Silver Springs, Fla., Apr. 4, 1889; buried Ilion, N.Y.

REMSEN, IRA, educator, chemist; b. N.Y. City, Feb. 10, 1846; A.B., Coll. City of New York, 1865; M.D., Coll. Phys. and Surg. (Columbia), 1867; Ph.D., University of Göttingen, 1870; LL.D., Columbia, 1893, Princeton, 1896, Yale, 1901, Toronto, 1902, Harvard, 1909, Pa. Coll., 1910, U. of Pittsburgh, 1915; D.C.L., U. of the South, 1907; m. Elisabeth H. Mallory, Apr. 5, 1875; children—Ira Mallory, Charles Mallory. Prof. chemistry, Williams College, 1872-76; prof. chemistry, 1876-1913, dir. Chem. Lab., 1876-1908, sec. Academy Council, 1887-1901, president 1901-Apr. 1912, pres. and prof. emeritus, 1913, Johns Hopkins U. Founded, 1879, and became editor, Am. Chem. Jour. Medalist, 1904, pres., 1910-11, Soc. Chem. Industry; mem. Nat. Acad. Sciences (pres., 1907-13); Priestley medal, Am. Chem. Soc., 1923. Author: The Principles of Theoretical Chemistry, 1876; An Introduction to the Study of the Compounds of Carbon, or Organic Chemistry, 1885; Introduction to the Study of Chemistry, 1887; The Elements of Chemistry, 1888; Inorganic Chemistry, 1889; A Laboratory Manual, 1889; Chemical Experiments, 1895; also many scientific articles and addresses. Address: Baltimore, Md. Died Mar. 5, 1927.

RENNER, GEORGE THOMAS, JR., geographer; b. Winfield, Kan., July 11, 1900; s. Rev. George Thomas and Mildred May (Dodd) R.; B.A., Cornell College, Mount Vernon, Ia., 1922, LL.D., 1943; M.A. Columbia Univ., 1924, Ph.D., 1927; grad. study, U. of Chicago, summers, 12922, 23, 24, 25; m. Mayme Margaret Pratt, June 12, 1924; 1 son, George Thomas, 3d. Athletic dir. high sch., Anita, Ia., 1920-21; lecturer in econ. geography, Columbia, 1922-26, instr. in geography, 1926-27, visiting asso. prof., summer 1929; asso. prof. geography and chmn. dept., U. of Wash., 1927-33; visiting asso. prof. geography, U. of Minn., summer 1932; geographer Ia. Forest Survey, 1933-34; professorial lecturer in economics, George Washington U., 1934-35; asst. agrl. economist, land policy sect., U.S. Nat. Resources Bd., 1934-36; senior economist and mem. tech. com. regional planning, U.S. Nat. Resources Com., 1935-36; geographic consultant, U.S. National Resources Planning Bd. 1936-43; visiting asso. prof. of edn. Teachers College, Columbia, 1936-37, asso. prof. geography, 1937-39, prof., 1939—; vis. prof. geography Stanford U., 1947-48, Fresno State Coll., 1948, 49, San Jose State College, 1951, U. So. Cal., summer, 1952; geographical editor T. V. Crowell, N.Y., 1944—. Spl. educational consultant to the Air Force, 1951; edn. consultant on Air Force Academy affairs, to U.S. Air Force, 1952. Mem. aviation edn. research com. U.S. Civil Aeronautics Adminstrn., 1942. Am. Geographers, Am. Geophys. Union (meteorology, oceanography), Nat. Council of Geography Teachers, Am. Inst. of Planners, American Legion, Sigma Xi, Pi Gamma Mu, Beta Gamma Sigma, Phi Delta Kappa, Alpha Kappa Psi. Unitarian. Mason. Author: Primitive Religion in the Tropical Forests, 1927; Geography of Washington (with A. L. Seeman), 1928; World Climatic Regions, 1930; Regional Factors in National Planning and Development (with J. Crane, M. Dimock and J. Gaus), 1935; Maladjustments in Land Use (with C. P. Barnes and C. I. Hendrickson), 1936; Geography—An Introduction to Human Ecology (with C. L. White), 1936; Conservation and Citizenship (with W. H. Hartley), 1940; Conservation of National Resources—An Educational Approach to the Problem, 1942; Human Geography in the Air Age, 1942; The Air We Live In, 1942; Geographical Education for the Air Age, 1942; World Map for the Air Age, 1942; Global Geography (with others), 1944; Home Geography (with E. H. Reeder), 1944; Human Geography (with C. L. White), 1948; World Economic Geography (with Durand, White, Gibson), 1951. Contbr. to Econ. Geography, Geog. Review, Jour. of Geog. (asso. ed.), Annals of Assn. Am. Geographers, Social Forces, Frontiers of Democracy, Social Edn., Collier's, The Saturday Evening Post, Harpers, American Magazine, Aero Digest, geographical editor The Kings English Dictionary, 1930; edn. map editor Denoyer-Geppert Co., 1933—. Home: 128 Lakeview Av., Leonia, N.J. Address: Teachers College. Columbia University, N.Y.C. 27. Died Oct. 14, 1955; buried Anita, Ia.

RENNER, OTTO, botanist; b. Neu-Ulm, Germany, Apr. 25, 1883; s. Ludwig and Marie (Kopf) R.; Dr.Phil., U. München, 1906; Dr.Phil. Nat. honoris causa, U. Jena, 1953; Dr. Rer. Nat. honoris causa, U. Erlangen, 1953; Gov. Rer. Nat. honoris causa, U. Frieburg, 1957; m. Johanna Unterbirker 1920; children—Hildegard, Erwin (dec.). Privatdozent U. München, 1911-13, prof. extraordinarius, 1913-20; prof. ordinarius U. Jena, 1920-48; prof. ordinarius U. München, 1948-52, prof. emeritus, 1952—; prof. botany, dir. bot. gardens, Jena and Munich, 1920-52. Fgn. hon. mem. Am. Acad. Arts and Scis.; fgn. asso. Nat. Acad. Scis.; corr. mem. Bot. Soc. Am.; hon. mem. Genetical Soc. Gt. Britain, Genetics Soc. Japan; fgn. mem. Royal Soc. London, Am. Philos. Soc. Phila. Editor: Planta, Archiv für wissenschaftliche Botanik, 1948-56, Fortschritte der Botanik, 1949-55. Home: 63 Menzinger St., Munich, Germany. Died July 8, 1960.

RENNIE, THOMAS A. C., physician, psychiatrist; b. Motherwell, Scotland, Feb. 28, 1904; s. David and Elizabeth (Cumming) R.; brought to U.S., 1911, naturalized, 1916; B.S., U. of Pittsburgh, 1924; M.D., Harvard, 1928. Interne Peter Bent Brigham Hospital, Boston, 1928-29; resident in medicine and instr., U. of Mich., 1929-30; house officer in psychiatry, Henry Phipps Psychiatric Clinic, Johns Hopkins, 1930-31, asst. resident in psychiatry, 1931-32, resident psychiatrist, 1932-36, instr. in psychiatry, 1933-36; asso. psychiatrist, 1936-41; visiting psychiatrist, Baltimore City Hosp., 1937-41; asso. prof. psychiatry, Cornell Med. Sch., 1941-50; prof. psychiatry (social psychiatry) since 1950; attending psychiatrist N.Y. Hosp.; cons. in psychiatry F.D.R. VA Hosp., Montrose, N.Y. Dir. Nat. Assn. for Mental Health; chmn. N.Y.C. Community Mental Health Bd.; mem. tech. adv. com. on research N.Y.C. Youth Bd.; mem. Army advisory com. of Greater N.Y.; trustee American Found. Mental Hygiene. Fellow Am. Psychiat. Assn., N.Y. Acad. Medicine; mem. New York Soc. for Clinical Psychiatry, A.M.A., Med. Soc. of State N.Y., Am. Psychopathol. Assn., A.A.A.S. Clubs: Century (N.Y.C.); Hamilton Street (Balt.). Author: (with L. E. Woodward) Jobs and the Man, 1945; (with L. E. Woodward) Mental Health in Mod. Society, 1945; (with others) Tchng. Psychotherapeutic Med., 1948; Vocational Rehabilitation of Psychiatric Patients: A Study of Post-Hospital Vocational Work (with others); Vocational Services for Psychiatric Clinic Patients (with Bozeman). Co-editor Internat. Jour. of Social Psychiatry. Contbr. articles to profl. jours. Home: 34 Gramercy Park. Office: 525 E. 68th St., N.Y.C. 21. Died May 21, 1956; buried Washington, Conn.

RENO, JESSE WILFORD, engineer; b. Ft. Leavenworth, Kan., Aug. 4, 1861; s. Maj.-Gen. Jesse Lee and Mary Bradley Beanes (Cross) R.; E.M., Lehigh U., 1883, later Bachelor of Metallurgy; m. Marie H. Snowman, of New York, Jan. 15, 1901. Engaged in mining and metallurgy in Colo., 1885-90; electric ry. expert for Thomson-Houston Co. and Edison Co., 1890-91; invented inclined elevator or moving stairway, 1892. Home: 1158 5th Av. Office: 261 Broadway, New York, N.Y.

RENOUF, EDWARD, chemist; b. Lowville, N.Y., Sept. 4, 1846; s. E. A. (D.D.) and Harriet L. R.; ed. Boston grammar and Latin schs., Heidelberg, Jena and Munich; Ph.D., U. of Freiburg, 1880; m. Annie V. Whelpley, Feb. 1871. Asst. in chemistry, U. of Munich, 1880-85; collegiate prof. chemistry, Johns Hopkins, 1885-1911. Author: Volhard's Experiments in General Chemistry (translation), 1887; Inorganic Preparations, 1894. Address: Monkton, Md. Deceased.

RENTSCHLER, HARVEY CLAYTON, physics; b. Hamburg, Pa., Mar. 26, 1881; s. Joseph F. and Rebecca (Ritzman) R.; B.A., Princeton, 1903, M.A., 1904; Ph.D., Johns Hopkins, 1908, hon. D.Sc., Princeton University, 1941; LL.D., honorary, Ursinus College, 1942; m. Margaret Bender, 1904; 1 son, Lawrence Bender. Instr. physics, U. of Mo., 1908-10, asst. prof., 1910-13, asso. prof., 1913-17; dir. of research lamp div. Westinghouse Electric & Mfg. Co., 1917-47. Fellow A.A.A.S.; mem. Am. Optical Soc., Am. Physical Soc., Am. Inst. Elec. Engrs., New York Elec. Soc. (past pres.), Am. Inst. of Science (New York), Sigma Xi, Epsilon Chi, Sigma Pi Sigma. Presbyterian. Democrat. Mason. Contbr. to tech. publs. Home: 15 Monroe Av., East Orange, N.J. Died March 23, 1949.

RENWICK, EDWARD SABINE, patent expert; b. New York, Jan. 3, 1823; s. James and Margaret Anne (Brevoort) R.; A.B., Columbia, 1839, A.M., 1842; widower. Became civ. and mech. engr. and supt. large iron works at Wilkes-Barre, Pa.; 1849—, in practice as expert in patent cases. In 1862, with his brother, Henry B. Renwick, repaired the Great Eastern while afloat, replating a fracture in the bilge, 82 feet long and 10 feet in greatest width, which other experts had declared an impossible feat. Invented many machines and mech. devices. Author: Practical Invention, 1893. Home: Short Hills, N.J. Died Mar. 19, 1912.

RENWICK, HENRY BREVOORT, engr., patent expert; b. N.Y.C., Sept. 4, 1817; s. James and Margaret Anne (Brevoort) R.; grad. Columbia, 1833; m. Margaret Janney, June 22, 1852, at least 2 children. Studied engring., 1835-37; entered U.S. Govt. service as asst. engr., 1837, took part in bldg. breakwaters at Sandy Hook and Egg Harbor, N.J.; asso. with U.S. Boundary Commn., 1840-47; became examiner U.S. Patent Office in charge of divisions of metallurgy, steam engines, navigation, civil engring., ordnance, 1847; 1st U.S. insp. steam vessels Port of N.Y., 1853; took part in great patent litigations, 1870-95, including cases involving the sewing machines, McCormick reaper, Bell telephone; sr. warden St. Mark's Protestant Episcopal Ch., N.Y.C. Author: (with father) The Lives of John Jay and Alexander Hamilton, 1840. Died N.Y.C., Jan. 27, 1895.

RENWICK, JAMES, engr., educator; b. Liverpool, Eng., May 30, 1792; s. William and Jane (Jeffery) R.; grad. Columbia, 1807, A.M., 1810, LL.D. (hon.), 1829; m. Margaret Anne Brevoort, 1816; 4 children—Henry Brevoort, Edward Sabine, James, Laura K. Brought to U.S. as child; lectured on natural philosophy Columbia, 1812, trustee, 1817-20, prof. natural philosophy and exptl. chemistry, 1820-53, 1st emeritus prof., 1853-63; topog. engr. with rank of maj. U.S. Army, 1814; commd. col. of engrs. N.Y. Militia, 1817; authority in every branch of engring. of his day; his suggestions for uniting Hudson and Delaware rivers resulted in Morris Canal, a system of inclined planes or railways for transporting canal boat in cradle up or down the incline (awarded medal from Franklin Inst. for cradle innovation, 1826); commd. to test "the usefulness of inventions to improve and render safe the boilers of steam-engines against explosions," 1838; a commr. to survey Northeastern boundary of disputed territory between U.S. and New Brunswick, 1840; Author: Outlines of Natural Philosophy (1st extensive treatise on subject from Am. writer), 2 vols., 1822-23; Treatise on the Steam Engine, 1830; Applications of the Science of Mechanics to Practical Purposes, 1840. Editor: (Am. editions with notes) Rudiments of Chemistry (Parke), 1824, Chemical Philosophy (Daniell), 2 vols., 1840. Translator: (from French) Treatise on Artillery (Tallemand), 2 vold., 1820. Contbd. biographies including David Rittenhouse (1839), Robert Fulton (1845), Count Rumford (1848) to Sparke's Library of American Biography. Died N.Y.C., Jan. 12, 1863.

RENWICK, JAMES, architect; b. Bloomingdale, N.Y., Nov. 1, 1818; s. James and Margaret Anne (Brevoort) R.; grad. Columbia Coll., 1836; m. Anna Lloyd Aspinwall, Dec. 16, 1861. Joined engineering staff Erie R.R., 1836; mem. engring. staff Croton Aqueduct, supt. for building of distbg. reservoir that stood between 40th and 42d sts. on Fifth Av.; architect of New Grace Ch., 1843, Cavalry Ch., Ch. of the Puritans on Union Square, both 1846, St. Stephen's and St. Bartholomew's, 1872, St. Patrick's Cathedral, opened 1879 (all N.Y.C.); designed fountain for Bowling Green, 1843; architect for New Smithsonian Instn., Washington, D.C., 1846; designed hotels including Clarendon, Albemarle and St. Denis; designed Fulton Bank, Bank of State of N.Y., N.Y.C., new facade for N.Y. Stock Exchange; residences in N.Y. for Charles Morgan and Courtlandt Palmer; architect on Bd. Govs. Charities and Correction of N.Y.C.; designed Work House, Smallpox Hosp. on Blackwell's Island, Inebriate and Lunatic asylums on Ward's Island, Children's Hosp. on Randall's Island; designed Vassar Coll., Poughkeepsie, N.Y., 1865, Booth's Theatre, N.Y.C., Corcoran Gallery (example of French Renaissance), Washington, D.C., tchr. of apprentices and draftsmen; favored Gothic and Romanesque styles. Died N.Y.C., June 23, 1895; buried Greenwood Cemetery, Bklyn.

RENWICK, WILLIAM WHETTEN, architect; b. Lenox, Mass., Oct. 30, 1864; s. Edward Sabine and Alice (Brevoort) R.; M.E., Stevens Inst. Tech., 1885; studied architecture under uncle, James Renwick, New York; sculpture, under Magnalier, of the École des Beaux Arts, Paris; painting in New York, Paris and Rome; m. Ilka Howells, Apr. 26, 1902. Entered office of the late James Renwick, 1885, jr. partner firm, 1890; engaged on many well known bldgs. in New York, among them St. Patrick's Cathedral, St. Bartholomew's Ch., All Saints' Ch., Grace Ch., etc.; later practiced alone, devoting time exclusively to ecclesiastical architecture and decoration. Architect of the Cathedral of St. Peter and St. Paul, Indianapolis; St. Aloysius' Church, New York; All Saints' Parish buildings; the chantry, south porch and open air pulpit of Grace Ch., Broadway and 10th St., New York, and many altars, monuments and decorations. Inventor of a kind of mural decoration known as "Fresco-Relief." Republican. Episcopalian. Home: Short Hills, N.J. Died Mar. 15, 1933.

REQUA, MARK LAWRENCE, mining engr.; b. Virginia City, Nev., Dec. 25, 1866; s. Isaac Lawrence Requa and Sarah J. (Mower) R.; ed. pvt. schs.; studied at Yale, 3 years; m. Florence Herrick, 1895. Developed Nev. Consol. Copper Co.; cons. engr. Bur. of Mines (resigned); built Nev. Northern Ry. Asst. to Herbert C. Hoover, U.S. food adminstr., June 1917-Jan. 1918; gen. dir. oil div., U.S. Fuel Adminstrn., Jan. 10, 1918-June 30, 1919; chmn. com. on standardization petroleum specifications, U.S. Govt., 1918-19. Mem. Am. Inst. Mining and Metall. Engrs. (v.p. 1917-20), Am. Petroleum Inst. (hon.). Chmn. valuation com. Independent Oil Producers Agency of Calif., 1915. Chmn. Calif. delegation Rep. Nat. Conv., Kansas City, Mo., 1928; mem. Rep. Nat. Com. for Calif., 1931—. Author: Relation of Government to Industry; (novel) Gurbstake. Home: Santa Barbara, Calif. Died Mar. 6, 1937.

RETTGER, LEO FREDERICK, bacteriologist; b. Huntingburg, Ind., Mar. 17, 1874; s. John Henry and Mary Catherine (Woellner), R.; grad. Ind. State Teachers Coll., 1894; B.A., U. of Ind., 1896, M.A., 1897, LL.D., 1931; Ph.D., Yale, 1902; student U. of

Strassburg; m. Clara V. Snyder, June 9, 1903; 1 son, James Frederick. Asst. in bacteriology and chem. U. of Ind., 1897-1900; instr. bacteriology, Yale, 1902-06, assistant professor, 1906-19, professor, 1910-42, professor emeritus since June 1942. Research fellow Rockefeller Institute for Med. Research, 1903-06; part time bacteriologist in charge, department of animal diseases, Storrs Agrl. Expt. Sta., 1908-46; lecturer in bacteriology, Wesleyan Univ., 1916-17. Mem. Soc. Am. Bacteriologists (pres. 1916), A.A.A.S., North-Am. Conf. of Research Workers in Animal Diseases (pres. 1932), Sigma Xi, Delta Omega, Phi Gamma Delta. Republican. Conglist. Author: Intestinal Flora; Animal Diseases; contbr. to various scientific and med. jours. Home: 340 Ogden St., New Haven CT

REULING, GEORGE, ophthalmologist; b. Romrod, Germany, Nov. 11, 1839; s. Dr. Robert and Amalie (Vogler) R.; M.D., Giessen, 1865; studied ophthalmology at Berlin and Vienna; m. Elisa, d. Capt. F. Külp, Sept. 21, 1871. Surgeon Prussian Army during war with Austria; asst., Eye Hosp., Wiesbaden, 1866-67; studied, Paris, 1867-68; phys.-in-chief Md. Eye and Ear Infirmary Baltimore, 1869—; prof. eye and ear surgery, Washington U., Baltimore, 1870—; prof. ophthalmology, U. of Baltimore, 1881—; prof. eye and ear diseases, Baltimore Med. Coll., 1886-1910, emeritus prof., 1910—; eye and ear surgeon Md. Gen. Hosp., to Med. Home of the Aged, to B.&O. R.R. Wrote papers on and invented apparatus for eye and ear surgery. Fellow Am. Acad. Arts and Sciences. Address: Baltimore, Md., Died Nov. 25, 1915.

REUTER, IRVING JACOB, b. Indianapolis, Ind., Feb. 26, 1885; s. Jacob and Wilhelmina (Mottery) R.; grad. Emmerich Manual Training High Sch., Indianapolis, 1903; B.S., Purdue, 1907; m. Jeanette M. Graham, Feb. 24, 1909; 1 dau., Wilma Pearl (dec.). Asst. engr. Overland Motor Co., 1909; chief engr., factory mgr. and gen. mgr. Remy Electric Co., 1909-25; pres. and gen. mgr. Olds Motor Works, 1925-29; pres. and gen. mgr. Oakland Motor Car Co., 1930-31; pres. and gen. mgr. Olds Motor Works and Buick Motor Co., 1931-33; also mng. dir. Opel Motor Works, Germany, 1930. Mem. Delta Tau Delta. Presbyterian. Mason. Clubs: Biltmore Country (Biltmore, N.C.); Asheville Country, Everglades; Bath and Tennis (Palm Beach, Fla.). Home: Asheville NC Died Apr. 21, 1972.

REVERE, PAUL, silversmith, patroit; b. Boston, Jan. 1, 1735; s. Paul and Deborah (Hichborn) R.; m. Sarah Orne, Aug. 17, 1757; m. 2d, Rachel Walker, Oct. 10, 1773; 16 children. Applied silverwork techniques to copper plate, 1765; did engravings for Royal Am. Magazine; manufactured artifical dental devices; participaed in Boston Tea Party; ofcl. courier for Mass. Provincial Assembly to Continental Congress, 1774; rode to Concord, Mass., to warn patriots to move mil. stores, Apr. 16, 1775; made ride to warn countryside that Brit. troops were marching, also to warn John Hancock and Samuel Adams that they were in danger of being captured, Apr. 18, 1775; completed mission to Lexington, Mass., but was stopped by Brit. en route to Concord; designed, printed 1st Continental money; made 1st ofcl. seal for colonies; designed Mass. State Seal; directed manufacture of gunpowder, Canton, Mass.; mem. Com. of Correspondence, 1776; discovered process for rolling sheet copper. Died Boston, May 10, 1818.

REYBOLD, EUGENE, cons. engr.; b. Delaware City, Del., Feb. 13, 1884; s. John Franklin and Lydia Maxwell (Tybout) R.; B.C.E., Del. Coll., 1903; grad. Coast Arty. Sch., Fort Monroe, Va., 1916, Coast Arty. Field Officers Sch., Monroe Va., 1922, Command and Gen. Staff Sch., Fort LeaVenworth, Kan., 1923, Army War Coll., Washington, D.C., 1927; hon. D.Eng., U. Del., 1941; D.Sc., U. Ark., 1942, Drexel Inst. Tech., 1943; m. Margaret Eyre Moore, Jan. 6, 1906 (dec.); children—Elizabeth Tybout (Mrs. Paul F. Yount), Franklin Bell; m. 3d, Marie Stanley Elder, Aug. 1, 1949. Engr. with U.S. Engr. Dept., 1903-08; commd. 2d lt. CAC, U.S. Army, 1908, advanced through grades to brig. gen., 1940, lt. gen., Apr. 1945; duty at Fort Mott, N.J., 1908; in P.I., 1910-13; coast defs. Boston Harbor, 1913-15; instr., dir., comdt. Coast Arty. Sch., Fort Monroe, Va., 1916-22; instr. Command and Gen. Staff Sch., Fort Leavenworth, 1923-26; transferred to C.E., 1926; asst. to dist. engr. in Buffalo Engr. Dist., 1927, later dist. engr.; then assigned to Bd. Engrs. for Rivers and Harbors, Washington; dist. engr., Wilmington, N.C., to 1935; dist. engr., Memphis (flood control work on Miss.), 1935-37; div. engr. S.W. Div., Little Rock, 1937-40; asst. chief of Staff for Supply, War Dept. Gen. Staff, Aug. 1940-Sept. 1941; chief engrs., 1941-45; ret. Apptd. exec. v.p. Am. Road Builders Assn. Awarded D.S.M. with oak leaf cluster; hon. comdr. Order Brit. Empire; Officer Legion of Honor (French). Mem. Am. Soc. Mil. Engrs., Am. Soc. C.E. Clubs: Army and Navy, Columbia Country (Washington). Address: Washington. Died Nov. 1961.

REYERSON, LLOYD HILTON, univ. prof.; b. Dawson, Minn., May 1, 1893; s. John Emil and Lydia (Hilton) R.; Bachelor of Arts, Carleton College, 1915, D.Sc., 1956; Master of Arts degree, U. of Ill., 1917; Ph.D., Johns Hopkins U., 1920; m. Nelle Nickell, Mar. 7, 1918; children—Jean Elizabeth (Mrs. A. H. Moseman), James Hilton (killed in action March 5, 1945). Instr. in chemistry, U. of Minn., 1919-21, assistant prof., 1921-26, asso. prof., 1926-30, prof. since 1930; dir. Northwest Research Inst., U. of Minn., 1934-60, administrative asst. in charge of chemistry, 1937; assistant dean, 1945-54, prof. phys. chemistry emeritus, 1961-69; mem. New Eng. Inst. for Med. Research, 1962-69. Welsh Foundation lectr. in chemistry, 1962. Chmn. sci. adv. com. Minn. War Industries, 1942-45. Apptd. chmn., canvassing com. for Am. Chem. Soc. Award in Pure Chemistry, 1944-45. Served as 2d lt., Chemical Warfare Service, 1918-19. Fellow John Simon Guggenheim Found., 1927-28, 58. U.S. del. to Internat. Union of Pure and Applied Chemistry, Warsaw, Poland, 1927, The Hague, The Netherlands, 1928, Stockholm, Sweden, 1953. Scientific consultant to the Royal Norwegian government, summer, 1946. Chmn. fgn. research scientists program, Nat. Acad. Scis. Knight 1st class Royal Order St. Olav (Norway), 1950; Distinguished Alumni Award, Carleton Coll., 1955. Fellow A.A.A.S., Am. Inst. Chemists (councillor at large 1958-60, president 1965-66), Faraday Society, member of American Chem. Soc. (sec. colloid div., 1937, chmn., 1939, counselor, 1943-44, 50-51, 55-57, mem. council policy com., 1952-54, 1956-61, chmn. nat. meeting, Mpls., 1955, councillor from Colloid Div., 1952-53, chmn. Minn. Sect., 1952, apptd. to Manpower Commn., 1952), Am. Phys. Soc. (chmn. bd. 1966-67), Minnesota Academy Science, American Association University Professors, American Inst. of Chemists (honorary, councillor at large 1958-63), Sigma Xi (president of the Minn. chapter 1956-57, Distinguished Service award Minn. chpt. 1962), Phi Beta Kappa (pres. Minn. Alpha. 1943-44), Phi Lambda Upsilon, Alpha Chi Sigma. Rep. Conglist. Mason. Clubs: Tonskeklubben (Minneapolis); Chemists (N.Y.C.); Cosmos (Washington). Author articles professional jours. Asso. editor Jour. of Phys. Chemistry, 1937-38. Home: Ridgefield CT Died Sept. 7, 1969.

REYNDERS, JOHN V.W., (rin'derz), steel maker; son of John and Louise (Sellers) R.; C.E., Rensselaer Poly. Inst., 1886, Dr. Engring., 1925; m. Clare Charlton, Oct. 4, 1894; children—John Van Wicheren (dec.), Charlton, Clare Charlton (Mrs. Byam K. Stevens). Began in mfr. of steel, at Pittsburgh, Pa., 1886; managing head Pa. Steel Co., 1892-1906; actively engaged for many yrs. in bridge building enterprises of this company, in the course of which built the steel ry. arch across the Niagara River; Gokteik Viaduct, 2,000 feet long, 320 feet high, Burma India; Queensboro Bridge, N.Y.; Memphis Bridge, Miss. River; Williamsburg Bridge, N.Y.; rebuilt the steel-making facilities of Pa. Steel Co. and managed its affairs as v.p., 1906-16; had charge of construction Bear Mountain Bridge across Hudson River, north of Peekskill, N.Y.; receiver Central Iron & Steel Co., Harrisburg, Pa., 1912-17; pres. Am. Tube & Stamping Company. 1917-19; director Vt. Copper Company, Lone Star Steel Co., Russian Finance & Constrn. Corp., Brewing Corp. of America; tech. advisor and sponsor of initial manufacture of steel using native ores State of Texas, professional adviser steel works and banking institutions. Adviser to U.S. Govt. in formulation of code of fair practice for steel industry, 1933. Originated "Harrisburg Plan" of civic improvement, 1904, resulting in park system water filtration, sewage systems, and paving; pres. Town Council, Steelton, Pa., 1906-16, and completed many public improvements there; del. Rep. Nat. Conv., 1908. Trustee Bard Coll. (Columbia U.). Episcopalian. Mem. Am. Inst. Mining and Metall. Engrs. (past pres.), United Engring. Soc., Engineers Soc., Central Pa. (ex-pres.), American Inst. Mining and Metall. Engrs. (hon.). Alternate mem. representing Dept. of Commerce Temporary Nat. Econ. Com. during steel hearings, 1939-40. Clubs: University, City Midday, Bankers, Union, Greenwich Country. Home: Greenwich, Conn. Office: 120 Broadway, New York, N.Y. Died July 10, 1944.

REYNIERS, JAMES A., scientist; b. Mishawaka, Ind., Apr. 16, 1908; s. Leo A. and Alice Ann (Bath) R.; B.S., U. Notre Dame, 1930; M.S. (magna cum laude), 1931; LL.D., St. Thomas University, 1952; m. Carolyn M. Shelton, June 15, 1930; children—James A., Carol Lee, Leon Francis, Jon Philip, Yvonne Ann. Mem. faculty, U. Notre Dame, 1931-59, research prof. bacteriology since 1945, Head Lobund (labs. of bacteriology, U. Notre Dame), 1937, dir. 1937-50, dir. Lobund Inst. for Research in Life Scis. 1950-59; director Germ-free Life Research Center, 1950—. Recipient faculty prize for Distinguished Service, U. Notre Dame, 1934-35, faculty award, Notre Dame Club of Chgo., 1948; Pasteur award, Soc. Am. Bacteriologists of Ill., 1954; Centennial award, Mich. State Coll., 1955. Mem. sci. adv. bd. Damon Runyon Fund Cancer Research 1949—. Lt. comdr. USNR, 1950—. Mem. A.A.A.S., Am. Assn. U. Professors, Am. Pub. Health Assn., Soc. of Bacteriologists, Hist. of Sci. Soc., Philosophy of Sci. Assn., N.E.A., Catholic Round Table of Sci., Catholic Commn. on Intellectual and Cultural Affairs, Am. Assn. for Cancer Research, also Sigma Xi. Roman Catholic. Club: Cosmos (Washington). Holder patents on germ-free apparatus, biological equipment, surgical operating devices, etc. Home: 72 Ladoga Av. Office: One Davis Blvd., Tampa 6. Fla. Died Nov. 1967.

REYNOLDS, CARL VERNON, physician; b. Asheville, N.C., June 13, 1872; s. John Daniel and Theresa Elmire (Shepherd) R.; student Asheville Mil. Acad., Wofford Coll., Spartansburg, S.C., 1889-91; M.D., U. City of New York, 1895; post grad. course Bromnton Hosp., London; m. Nellie Alyne Cocke, Apr. 1, 1896; 1 child, Alyne Johnston; m. 2d, Edith Holland Randolph. Practiced medicine, specializing in tuberculosis, Asheville, N.C., 1895-1934; altruistic city health officer, Asheville, part-time, 1898-1910, 1914-23; mem. med. staff of Mission, Biltmore and French Broad Hosps.; chief med. examiner Prudential Life Ins. Co. (uninterrupted service for 30 yrs. receiving bronze, silver, gold and locket medal for service); examiner New Eng. Mutual Security Life Ins. Cos.; State Health Officer, 1934-47, re-elected for 4 yr. term, 1947; retired July 1948. Mem. teaching staff Sch. of Pub. Health, Chapel Hill, N.C., 1936; Officer and dir. Blue Ridge Nat. Bank; dir. Am. Nat. Bank of Commerce, Asheville. Pres. Certified Milk Commn. Consultant in War Manpower Comm., Procurement and Assignment Service for Physicians, July 1942; chmn. subcom. on Pub. Health, Procurement and Assignment Service, Office of Defense Health and Welfare Services, Nov., 1941; mem. Nat. Com. of Malaria Prevention Activities, 1942, 43, 44, 45; mem. nat. com. for Celebration of Pres. birthday for Nat. Foundation for Infantile Paralysis; chmn. State Nutrition com.; mem. com. on Health and Pub. Welfare Planning Bd.; mem. and sec. N.C. Hosp. and Med. Care Commn., 1944; mem. State Stream Sanitation and Conservation com., 1945-46; mem. N.C. Resource-Use Edn. Commn. of the State Planning Bd.; mem. exec. com. of N.C. State Planning Bd. com. on Services for Children and Youth, 1946; Fellow Am. Pub. Health Assn. (1st vice pres. southern br. 1939). Mem. Buncombe County Med. Soc. (pres.-sec. 1904), Tri-State Med. Soc. (exec. council, 1911, vice pres. council, 1916), N.C. Med. Soc. (pres. 1920, mem. med. preparedness com. 1944-45), Miss. Valley Med. Assn., Southern Med. Assn., A.M.A., Nat. Assn. for Prevention of Tuberculosis, Bd. of Trade, Good Rd. Assn. (past pres.), N.C. State Bd. of Health (pres. 1933), Raleigh Acad. of Medicine, 1935, Health Officers Qualifying Bd. of U.S. Conf. of Mayors, 1937, State and Terr. Health Officers' Assn. (chmn. subcom. of Fed. Relations com. for securing seriologic tests among registered men in U.S.), State, Terr. and Provincial Health Authorities of N.Am. (vice pres., 1941-42, pres. 1942-43), Internat. Soc. of Med. Health Officers (vice pres. 1942), N.C. Mental Hygiene Soc. (mem. exec. com. 1943-46), Calhoun Literary Soc., Kappa Alpha. Methodist. Clubs: Asheville Country (pres.), Biltmore Forest Country (mem. bd.), Rotary. Home: 1100 New York Drive, Altadena CA

REYNOLDS, EDWIN, inventor; b. Mansfield, Conn., Mar. 23, 1831; ed. in schools there; entered machine shop, 1847; as apprentice. After 3 yrs. worked in various other shops; supt. shops Stedman & Co., Aurora, Ind., 1857-61; went to Corliss Steam Engine Co., Providence, R.I., 1861, gen. supt., 1871-77; gen. supt. E. P. Allis & Co. (Reliance Works), Milwaukee, 1877—; one of trustees estate of E. P. Allis after death of latter; 2d v.p. and dir. The Allis Company; pres. Milwaukee Boiler Co., the Daisy Roller Mills Co., and German-Am. Bank. Inventor of the Reynolds-Corliss engine; introduced the 1st triple-expansion pumping engine; cross-compound hoisting engines for mining work; etc. Address: Milwaukee, Wis. Died 1909.

REYNOLDS, ELMER ROBERT, ethnologist, botanist; b. Dansville, N.Y., July 30, 1846; s. Dr. Allen B. and Sarah W. (Van Amburg) R.; ed. New Lisbon, Wis., 1852-60; Columbian U., 1874-80; (hon. Sc.D., Albertus Magnus Univ., Wichita, Kan., 1901); in 10th Wis. vol. light arty., 1861-65; teacher U.S.N., 1866-76; in U.S. civ. service as examiner of pensions, 1877—; engaged in exploring aboriginal antiquities of Md. and Va.; knighted by King Humbert of Italy, 1887; medal from King of Portugal; bronze medal from Royal Portuguese Soc. Archaeology, Lisbon, 1899. Writer of numerous monographs on the archaeology of D.C., Md. and Va., scientific papers, newspaper serials, stories, etc. Address: Washington, D.C. Died 1907.

REYNOLDS, ERNEST SHAW, botanist; b. Glendale, Mont., Dec. 7, 1884; s. Henry Sheldon and Frances Adelia (Potter) R.; Ph.B., A.M., Brown U., 1907; Ph.D., U. Ill., 1909; m. Ruth Evelyn Caverly, 1912; children—Eleanor Frances, Ernest Shaw, Robert Caverly. Instr., asst. prof. botany U. Tenn., 1909-12; asso. prof., prof. botany, head dept. botany and plant physiology Agrl. Coll., N.D., 1912-27; plant physiologist Mo. Bot. Garden, 1927-39, asso. prof. plant physiology Henry Shaw Sch. Botany, Washington U., St. Louis, 1927-40; plant physiologist N.D. Agrl. Expt. Sta., 1920-22; spl. agt. Dept. Agr., summers. Fellow Boyce Thompson Inst. Plant Research, Yonkers, N.Y., 1926-27. Liaison officer Keystone Ordnance Works, Meadville, Pa., 1942-44; dir. Fla. Field Sta., Centro Research Labs., Coral Gables, Fla., 1944-46; research asso. prof. Marine Lab., U. Miami, 1946—, charge deterioration research, later prin. investigator Office Naval Research project. Recipient Naval Ordnance Development award for exceptional service, World War II. Fellow A.A.S.; mem. New Eng. Bot. Club, Am. Soc. Limnology and Oceanography, Bot. Soc. Am., Mycol. Soc. Am., Soc. Indsl. Microbiology, Sigma Xi, Phi

Kappa Phi, Gamma Alpha. Protestant. Home: 903 Pizarro St., Coral Gables, Fla. Died May 31, 1961; buried Newington (N.H.) Cemetery.

REYNOLDS, FRANK WILLIAM, plastics engr.; b. Scotia, N.Y., Nov. 11, 1901; s. Herbert Caleb and Lizzie (Betts) R.; grad. tech. course, Gen. Electric Co., 1922; m. Anne Winkler, Aug. 9, 1931; children—Patricia (Mrs. Alexander Wilson II), Shirley (Mrs. Robert C. Beaty), Mark, Nancy (Mrs. David A. Davenport), Phyllis (Mrs. Bradford G. Weekes III). With Internat. Bus. Machines Corporation, from 1931, mgr. plastics research lab., Endicott, N.Y., from 1951. Mem. Soc. Plastics Industry (founder, 1st pres. Binghamton sect. 1957, nat. council from 1957), Internat. Soc. Plastics Engrs. (pres. 1961-62, exec. com. 1961-63). Home: Binghamton NY Died Nov. 17, 1971; buried Vestal Hills Meml. Park Vestal NY

REYNOLDS, HERBERT BYRON, mech. engr.; b. Baltimore, Md., Apr. 8, 1888; s. Byron and Ulyssa Irene (Williamson) R.; grad. Baltimore Poly. Inst., 1908; M.E., Cornell U., 1911, M.M.E., 1915; m. Sarah Genet Haswell, June 22, 1914 (died Oct. 6, 1918); m. 2d, Ruth Herlong, Jan. 21, 1922. Apprentice, Westinghouse Electric & Mfg. Co., 1911-12, inspector, 1912; turbine tester, Gen. Electric Co., 1913; asst. engr. Interborough Rapid Transit Co., N.Y. City, 1913-17; mech. asst. to supt. of motive power, United Railways & Electric Co., Baltimore, Md., 1917-18; fuel engr., U.S. Govt. Bureau of Mines, 1918; mech. research engr., Interborough Rapid Transit Co., N.Y. City, 1919, mech. engr. 1919-41 (Interborough Rapid Transit Co. became part of N.Y. City Transit System, 1940), supt. of motive power, IRT div. 1941-44, supt. of power generation, the entire system, 1944-49; engr. J. G. White Engring. Corp., 1949-53; cons. engr., 1953-68. Member trustees Garden School. Fellow A.S.M.E., Am. Inst. Elec. and Electronic Engrs.; mem. Sigma Xi. Club: Engineers (N.Y.C.). Contbr. articles to mags.; also papers delivered before A.S.M.E. Home: Jackson Heights NY Died Oct. 10, 1968.

REYNOLDS, LAWRENCE, physician; b. Skipperville, Ala., Feb. 11, 1889; s. Dr. Robert Davis and Mary Frances Reynolds; A.B., U. Ala., 1912, LL.D., 1950; M.D., Johns Hopkins, 1916; Doctor of Laws, Wayne State University, 1956. Interne Johns Hopkins, 1916-17, instr., roentgenology, Johns Hopkins, 1919, roentgenol., Peter Bent Brigham Hosp., Boston, 1919-22; instr. roentgenol., Harvard, 1920-22, private practice, 1922—; chief dept. radiology, Harper Hosp.; pres. Am. Coll. Radiology; adv. com. Hist. Med. Library, Yale; exec. com. William L. Clements Library, University of Mich.; pres. Detroit Pub. Library Com. Began medical career as vol. with Am. Ambulance Hosp., Neuilly-sur-Seine (France), 1917; 1st lt., in chg. X-Ray dept., Red Cross Mil. Hosp., Neuilly, 1917-19, capt., 1918. Recipient Gold Medal award, Radiological Society N.A., 1956, American College of Radiology, 1960; award from Michigan State Med. Soc. for distinguished service rendered to medicine and teaching, 1959. Editor: Am. Jour. Roentgenol. and Radium Therapy, since 1930; diplomate, Am. Bd. Radiol. Mem. Am. Roentgen Ray Soc., A.M.A., Radiol. Soc. of N.Am., Am. Coll. of Radiology, A.C.P., Detroit Acad. Medicine, Detroit Roentgen Ray and Radium Soc., Mich. State Med. Soc., A.A.A.S., Deutsche Roentgen-Geselschaft, Societas Radiologiae Medicar Italiana, Detroit Med. Club, Harvey Cushing Soc., Sigma Psi, Sigma Alpha Epsilon, Corinthians. Mason (K.T.). Club: Grolier (New York). Home: 2100 Seminole Av. Office: Professional Bldg., Detroit. Died Aug. 17, 1961; buried Ozark, Ala.

REYNOLDS, SAMUEL GODFREY, inventor; b. Bristol, R.I., Mar. 9, 1801; s. Greenwood and Mary (Caldwell) R.; m. Elizabeth Anthony, 1823; m. 2d, Catherine Ann Hamlin, Nov. 18, 1845; 5 children. Invented machine for making wrought-iron nails and rivets, patented 1829, improvements to original machine patented, 1835; patented, a spike-making machine, went directly to Eng., secured financial backing for manufacture of machines from Coates & Co., bankers, also obtained patents in Eng., Holland, Belgium, France; patented machinery for heading and pointing pins, 1845; returned to U.S. in 1850; invented horse-nail machinery, patented 1852, patented improvements, 1866, 67; perfected steam plow, invented a rotary plow. Died Bristol, R.I., Mar. 1, 1881.

REYNOLDS, WALTER FORD, mathematician; b. Baltimore, Md., May 25, 1880; s. Robert Fuller and Catherine (Myers) R.; Baltimore City Coll., 1899; A.B., Johns Hopkins, 1902; grad. work, same univ., 1902-05; m. Ada C. Williams, June 26, 1907; children—Catherine A. Mummert, Robert W., Walter F. Instr. Baltimore City Coll., 1905-06; computer U.S. Naval Obs., Washington, D.C., Jan.-Feb. 1907; with U.S. Coast and Geodetic Survey since 1907; computer U.S. and Can. boundary survey, 1908-11; chief mathematician, 1912-24; chief sect. triangulation, div. of geodesy, since 1924. Mem. Washington Philos. Soc., Math. Assn. of America, Am. Geophysical Union, Nat. Geog. Society, Washington Acad. Sciences, National Congress on Surveying and Mapping. Methodist. Author: Triangulation in Alabama and Mississippi, 1915; Triangulation in Maine, 1918; Relation between Plane Rectangular Co-ordinates and Geographic Positions, 1921; Manual of Triangulation Computation and Adjustment, 1927; First-Order Triangulation in Southeast Alaska, 1929; Triangulation in Missouri, 1934; Triangulation in Minnesota, 1935. Home: 848 W. 37th St., Baltimore, Md. Died May 1, 1942.

RHOAD, ALBERT OLIVER, agrl. scientist; b. Mt. Airy, Phila., Sept. 26, 1902; s. Robert Daniel and Carrie Virginia (Nickum) R.; B.S., Pa. State U., 1926; M.S., Cornell, 1929; m. Juanita Jane Harris, Dec. 20, 1930; 1 son, Richard Harris; m. 2d, Hendrika Wilhelmina van Egmond, Nov. 3, 1950; 1 son, Albert Dirk. Prof. catherdractico and head dept. Escola Superior de Agricultura de Minas Gerais, Brazil, 1929-36; officer charge Iberia Livestock Expt. Farm, U.S. Dept. Agr., Jeannette, La., 1936-45; head dept. animal industry Inter-Am. Inst. Agrl. Scis., Turrialba, Costa Rica, 1945-51; research adviser, geneticist King Ranch, Kingsville, Tex., 1951—. Mem. governing bd. Agrl. Research Inst., Washington; agrl. bd. Nat. Acad. Sci.-NRC; exec. dir. Santa Gertrudis Breeders Internat., Kingsville, Tex. Recipient Outstanding Alumni award in animal scis. Pa. State U., 1961. Fellow A.A.A.S.; mem. Am. Soc. Animal Prodn., Am. Genetic Assn., Tex. Acad. Sci., Sigma Xi, Delta Upsilon, Gamma Alpha. Republican. Episcopalian. Author: Breeding Beef Cattle for Unfavorable Environments, 1955. Home: King Ranch, P.O. Box 1267, Kingsville, Tex. Died June 23, 1962; buried Chamberlain Cemetery, Kingsville.

RHOADES, NELSON OSGOOD, consulting engr., capitalist; b. Madison, Wis., June 2, 1869; s. Nelson Carrier and Lucy Eunice (Osgood) R.; ed. pub. schs. and under pvt. instructors. Cons. engr. in U.S., Alaska, Mexico, India and Egypt; actively interested in Mexico, 1890—, and retained by Mexican Govt. to build railroads, survey pub. lands, make municipal improvements; owner large tracts of land in Mexico; pres. Oso Sugar Co., Navito Sugar Co.; gen. mgr. Chapultepec Heights Co., mem. firm Garfield & Rhoades, Mexican counsellors and fiscal agts. Editor Colonial Families of the U.S. Mason. Died Dec. 4, 1928.

RHOADS, CORNELIUS PACKARD, dir. hosp. research; b. Springfield, Mass., June 20, 1898; s. George Holmes and Harriet (Barney) R.; A.B., Bowdoin Coll., 1920, D.Sc. (hon.), 1944; M.D. cum laude, Harvard, 1924; D.Sc. (honorary), Williams College, 1952; married Katherine S. Bolman, Sept. 9, 1936. Interne, dept. of surgery, Peter Bent Brigham Hosp., Boston, 1924-25, Trudeau fellow, Trudeau Sanatorium, N.Y.C., 1925-26; instr. in pathology Harvard Med. Sch., and asst. pathologist Boston City Hosp., 1926-28; asso. Rockefeller Inst. for Med. Research, 1928-33; asso. mem. in charge service for study hematologic disorders, 1933-39; pathologist Hosp. of Rockefeller Inst. for Med. Research, 1931-39, dir. Memorial Center for Cancer and Allied Diseases, N.Y.C., 1940-52, scientific dir., 1953—; dir. of The Sloan-Kettering Inst. for Cancer Research, 1945—, James Ewing Hosp., N.Y.C., 1950—; prof. pathology, dept. pathology, Cornell U. Med. Coll. 1940-52; prof. pathology, dept. biology and growth, Sloan Kettering Div., Cornell U. Med. Coll., 1952—. spl. cons. U.S. Public Health Service, Nat. Adv. Cancer Council, 1947—; cons., med. div., Chem. Corps, Army Chem. Center, Md., 1948-50. Col., M.C., A.U.S.; chief med. div., Chem. Warfare Service, 1943-45. Awarded Legion of Merit. Mem. com. to visit dept. of chemistry, Harvard. Trustee Kettering Foundation. Member National Research Council (member sub. com. on blood substitutes 1940-42; chmn. blood procurement 1941-42; mem. com. for treatment of war gas casualties 1941-43; mem. com. on veterans med. problems 1945-47; chmn. com. on growth 1945-48; mem. com. on atomic bomb casualties, 1946; chmn. exec. com. of com. on growth, 1946-47; mem. adv. com. of chem.-biol. coordinator center 1946-47; mem. at large, div. of med. sciences 1946-49), Office of Sci. Research and Dev. (mem. com. on insect and rodent control 1945-46). Fellow A.C.P., N.Y. Acad. Medicine (mem. com. on public health relations 1943-43; v.p. 1943-45), A.A.A.S. (v.p. 1953, chmn. sect. med. sci. 1953), Am. Geriatrics Soc.; mem. Am. Pub. Health Assn., Am. Soc. Control Cancer, Am. Cancer Soc. (bd. dirs. 1941-46; exec. com. 1944-46; mem. N.Y.C. cancer com. 1943-51) Blood Transfusion Assn. (bd. 1940-51), Harvey Soc., Soc. Exptl. Biology and Medicine, Soc. of Med. Jurisprudence, Am. Assn. Pathologists and Bacteriologists, Am. Assn. for Cancer Research, Am. Indsl. Hygiene Assn., A.M.A., Am. Radium Soc., Am. Soc. for Clin. Investigation, Am. Soc. Exptl. Pathology, Am. Soc. Tropical Med., Armed Forces Chem. Assn., Assn. Am. Physicians, Med. Soc. of State of N.Y., Med. Soc. of County of N.Y. (mem. spl. com. on cancer control, spl. com. on illegal practice of medicine), N.Y. Soc. Tropical Medicine, N.Y. Acad. Scis., N.Y. Zool. Soc., N.Y. City Welfare Council (mem. com. on chronic illness), Harvard Med. Alumni Assn., Interurban Pathol. Club, Interurban Clin. Club, Halsted Club. Clubs: University, Century Assn. (N.Y.C.); Harvard (Boston). Contbr. med. articles in profl. jours. Address: Sloan-Kettering Institute for Cancer Research, 410 E. 68th St., N.Y.C. 21. Died Aug. 13, 1959.

RHOADS, SAMUEL NICHOLSON;, b. Philadelphia, Pa., Apr. 30, 1862; s. Charles and Anna (Nicholson) R.; ed. Friends' Sch.; spl. course in journalism, Harvard; studies in natural science, Acad. Natural Sciences and Museum Science and Art, Phila., and Carnegie Museum, Pittsburgh; m. Mary A. Cawley, Apr. 5, 1898; 1 son, Evan L. Since 1893 has collected museum specimens of natural history in nearly every state in the Union, Can., B.C., Cuba, Mex., Central and S. America. Life mem. Acad. Natural Sciences, Phila.; mem. Am. Philos. Soc., Am. Ornithologists' Union. Mem. of Society of Friends, Orthodox branch. Edited reprint of Ord's Zoology, 1894; Facsimile Reprint of Young's Catalogue of American Plants of Paris (1783). Author: The Mammals of Pennsylvania and New Jersey, 1903. Contbr. many papers on Am. and African mammals and on Am. birds, reptiles and molluscs to zool. jours. describing about 100 new species and races of mammals and birds. Home: Haddonfield NJ

RHODES, FREDERICK LELAND, elec. engr.; b. Boston, Mass., Oct. 25, 1870; s. John Brewer and Annie Williams (Leland) R.; S.B. in E.E., Mass. Inst. Tech., 1892; m. Effie Chandler, 1895; children—Leland Chandler, Eleanor Ann. Began with Am. Bell Telephone Co., 1892, continuing with Am. Telegraph and Telephone Co.; outside plant development engr., 1919-32; known for important work in connection with standardization of materials, apparatus and practices in underground and overhead wire systems. Fellow Am. Inst. E.E. (past chmn. bd. examiners, etc.). Republican. Unitarian. Author: Beginnings of Telephony, 1929. Contbr. to Nelson's Loose Leaf Ency., Ency. Americana and Supplement to Britannica. Home: Short Hills, N.J. Died Mar. 28, 1933.

RHODES, ROBERT CLINTON, biology; b. Magnolia, Ark., Oct. 12, 1887; s. James Clinton and Virginia Isabella (Scott) R.; A.B., Henderson-Brown Coll., Arkadelphia, Ark., 1906; A.B., Vanderbilt, 1907, A.M., 1908; Ph.D., U. of Calif., 1917; grad. study, U. of Chicago and Marine Biol. Lab.; m. Lou Clark, Nov. 27, 1912; children—Marguerite, Robert Clark, James Scott, Martha. Instr. in biology, U. of Miss., 1908-10, asst. prof. biology, 1910-12; v.p. and prof. science, Henderson-Brown Coll., 1912-15; asst. in zoölogy, U. of Calif., 1915-17; prof. biology, Emory U., Atlanta, Ga., and chmn. dept., 1918-48. Ordained ministry Meth. Ch., 1905. Treas. bd. trustees, Emory Sch., 1922-27; chmn. adv. board Juvenile Ct. of DeKalb County, Ga., 1935. Fellow A.A.A.S.; mem. Am. Soc. Zoölogists, Ga. Acad. Sciences (pres. 1933-34), Am. Eugenics Soc., Ga. Ornithological Soc. (life mem.), Am. Soc. of Parasitologists, Am. Genetics Soc., Ga. and Atlanta Soc. Biologists, Southeastern Soc. of Biologists (pres. 1940-41), Southern Assn. for Advancement of Science, Sigma Xi, Phi Sigma, Pi Gamma Mu, Sigma Upsilon, Kappa Alpha, Omicron Delta Kappa, Alpha Epsilon Upsilon. Democrat. Author: Binary Fission in Collodictyon triciliatum Carter, 1918; Some Biological Factors Involved in Democracy, 1941. Home: 1126 Clifton Road N.E., Atlanta, Ga. Address: Emory University, Ga. Died Nov. 7, 1948.

RICARD, JEROME SIXTUS, astronomer; b. Plaisians, Drome, France, Jan. 21, 1850; s. Leger and Marianne (Eyssartel) R.; ed. high sch., Turin, Italy; came to America, 1873; student Woodstock Coll., Md.; joined Soc. of Jesus, 1872; Ph.D., U. of Santa Clara, Calif., 1887. Steadily observed and studied sunspots and faculae, 1900 23, and discovered a method of using them in forecasting the weather long in advance. Published a daily forecast for Santa Clara County; a monthly long range weather forecast for the U.S., "The Sunspot"; also occasional seismographic record. Trustee U. of Santa Clara. Democrat. Contbr. to Popular Astronomy (mag). Home: Santa Clara, Calif. Died Dec. 8, 1930.

RICE, ALEXANDER HAMILTON, geographer, explorer; b. Boston, Aug. 29, 1875; s. John Hamilton and Cora Lee (Clark) R.; A.B., Harvard, 1898, M.D., 1904, A.M. (hon.), 1915; D.Sc., (hon.), Hamilton, 1951; surgical intern Mass. Gen. Hosp., 1903-05; certificate Royal Geog. Soc. Sch. of Geog. Surveying and Field Astronomy, 1908-10; m. Mrs. Eleanor Elkins Widener, Oct. 6, 1915 (died July, 1937); m. 2d, Mrs. Dorothy Farrington Upham, Nov. 5, 1949. Surgeon, dir. Hosp. No. 72, Société de Secours aux Blessés Militaires, Paris, France, 1914-15; surgeon Am. Ambulance, Neuilly, 1914-15; commd. lt. U.S.N.R., 1917; instr. navigation and nautical astronomy, 2d Naval Dist. Training Sch., Newport, R.I., 1917; dir. same sch., 1917-19; lectr. Lowell Inst., 1922; instrumental in establishing Indian Sch., hosp. and créche at São Gabriel, Brazil; established Inst. of Geog. Exploration, Harvard, dir., prof. same; hon. curator S.A. sect. Peabody Mus. Archaeology and Ethnology; lectr. diseases of tropical S. America, Dept. Tropical Medicine, Harvard Med. Sch. Has devoted much time to exploration, research and sci. investigations of tropical S.A.; organized and conducted 7 expdns. into the Colombian Caqueta, Brazilian Amazonas and Venezuelan Guayana, exploring, surveying and mapping an area of 500,000 sq. miles, carrying out at the same time investigations of geol., biol., anthropol., ethnol., character; expdn., 1924-25, to Rio Branco-Uraricuera-Parima, hydroplane successfully employed in reconnaissance and air photography, efficiency of short wave, low power wireless in such work first conclusively demonstrated. Fellow Royal Astron., Soc., Royal Meteorol. Soc., Royal Anthrop. Inst., Geol. Soc., Am. Assn. Advancement of Sci. N.Y. Acad. Medicine; mem. Royal Geog. Society, London (hon. corr. fellow, former v.p.), Am. Geog. Soc., Reale

Società Georgrafica Italiana, Société des Américanistes (Paris), La Sociedad Geogràfica (Madrid) (hon. fellow all three), Instituto Hispano Americano de Relaciones Culturales, Madrid (hon. councillor), Hispanic Soc. of America (corr. mem.), Newport County Med. Soc., Am. Museum of Health (dir.); Socio Honorario Touring Club do Brasil, Rio de Janeiro; chmn. Spanish National Relief Committee; mem. Geol. Soc. Am., Société de Geographie de Paris, Société de Geographie d'Anvers, Phila. Geog. Soc., Royal Institution of Great Britain, Am. Anthrop. Soc., Council on Fgn. Relations, Nat. Inst. Social Scis., Soc. of Cin., Mass. Soc. Mayflower Descendants, Soc. Colonial Gov's., Soc. Colonial Wars, The Pilgrims, Mass. Hist. and Geneal. Soc., N.Y. Hist. Soc., N.Y. Geneal. and Biog. Soc., Soc. N.Y. Hosp., Soc. Descs. of Knights of Most Noble Order of the Garter, Hereditary Order Descs. Colonial Gov's. (hon. v. gov. gen.); Newport Hist. Soc., R.I. Hist. Soc.; patron Phila. Mus. of Art; trustee Am. Mus. Natural History, Lycée Français de N.Y., Mus. of City, N.Y., Am. Soc. French Legion of Honor, Cathedral St. John the Divine, N.Y. Dispensary; Institut Français aux Etats-Unis, N.Y. Awarded Patron's gold medal, Royal Geog. Soc., 1914; David Livingstone centenary medal, Am. Geog. Soc., 1920; Elisha Kent Kane medal, Phila. Geog. Soc., 1920; gold medal Harvard Travellers Club, 1914; Resolution and Testimonial for geog. exploration and sci. research carried out in S.A. tendered by the City of Newport, 1925; gold medal Société Royale de Geographie d'Anvers, 1931; gold medal Soc. Mayflower Descs. State of N.Y.; Chevalier de la Legion d'Honneur, 1934; Cross of Commander, 1938; gold medal, Soc. de Geog., Paris, 1939; Gran Cruz Ordem de Isabel la Catolica by decree of Gen. Franco, 1940. Republican. Episcopalian (vestryman Emmanuel Ch., Boston). Clubs: Tavern, Tennis and Racquet, Harvard, Harvard Travelers of Cambridge (ex-pres.), Somerset (Boston); Knickerbocker, Union, Brook, River, Turf and Field, Harvard, Explorers, New York Yacht, Racquet and Tennis, Ends of the Earth, Boone and Crockett, Automobile (New York); Philadelphia (Phila.); Hope (Providence); Geographical, Hurlingham, Internat. Sportmen's, Boodle's, Royal Automobile (London); Travellers, Union Interalliée (Paris). Contbr. numerous articles to Geog. Jour. Quito to Iquitos via River Napo, Apr. 1903; The River Uaúpes, with Map, June 1910; Further Explorations in Northwestern Amazon Valley, Map, Aug. 1914; Notes on the Rio Negro (Amazonas), Map, Oct. 1912; The Rio Negro, the Casiquiare Canal and the Upper Orinoco (map), Nov. 1921; Rio Branco-Uraricuera-Parima (maps), 1928; El rio Negro (Amazonas) y sus grandes afluentes de la Guayana Brasileña, 1934; Exploration en Guyane Brésilienne, Paris, 1937. Address: Miramar, Newport, R.I. Died July 23, 1956; buried St. Columbia's Berkeley Meml. Cemetery, Middletown, Newport, R.I.

RICE, ARTHUR LOUIS, publisher, mechanical engr.; b. Barre, Mass., May 14, 1870; s. Henry Edward and Elizabeth Fitch (Rawson) R.; B.S., Worcester (Mass.) Poly. Inst., 1891, E.E., 1893; M.M.E., Cornell U., 1896; m. Anne E. Cook, June 29, 1893; children—Kingsley Loring, Elisabeth Beals, Arthur Louis; m. 2d, Madge Waters, Jan. 21, 1928; 1 son, Reginald Waters. Was in charge of steam engring. lab., Worcester Poly. Inst., 1892-95; in charge dept. applied electricity, Pratt Inst., Brooklyn, 1896-1901; cons. engr. and asst. sec. Am. Soc. Mech. Engrs., New York, 1901-03; editor The Engineer, Cleveland and Chicago, 1903-08; mng. editor Practical Engineer, Chicago, 1908-11; consulting engr. on power plant constrn. and operation, and cons. engr. and mem. advisory bd. La Salle Extension U., 1909-10; treas. Tech. Pub. Co. since 1910; editor Power Plant Engineering since 1917. Trustee Wilmette Pub. Library; mem. Bd. Edn. Republican. Conglist. Mem. Am. Soc. M.E., Nat. Soc. Power Engrs., Western Soc. Engrs. Mason. Home: Wilmette, Ill. Office: 53 W. Jackson Blvd., Chicago. Died Nov. 10, 1946; buried in Memorial Park Cemetery, Evanston, Ill.

RICE, CALVIN WINSOR, engr.; b. Winchester, Mass., Nov. 4, 1868; s. Edward Hyde and Lucy J. (Staples) R.; S.B., Mass. Inst. Tech., 1890; Dr. Engineering, Tech. Hochschule, Darmstadt; m. Ellen M. Weibezahn, Aug. 6, 1904; children—Edward Winslow, Marjorie C. With Thomson-Houston Electric Co., 1889-93, and with its successor, General Electric Co., working up to the position of asst. engr. of the power and mining dept., until 1895 when he was apptd. local engr. at Cincinnati for same co.; elec. supt. Silver Lake Mines, Colo., 1895-96; later cons. engr. Anaconda Copper Mining Co.; elec. engr. Kings Co. Electric Light & Power Co., Brooklyn, 1898, and soon after elec. engr. Consolidated Telegraph & Elec. Subway Co., owning and operating the high-tension subways of New York; also chief of meter and testing dept. New York Edison Co.; 2d v.p. and sales mgr. Nernst Lamp Co., 1903; consulting engr. Gen. Electric Co., 1904-06. Mem. Jury of Awards, San Francisco Expn., 1915. Sec. Am. Soc. M.E., 1906; sec. and mem. bd. trustees New York Mus. of Science and Industry; mem. Corp. of Mass. Inst. of Tech.; mem. Am. Com., World Power Conf.; nat. counselor Purdue Research Foundation. Lt. col. O.R.C. Knight Cross Order of the White Lion (Czechoslovakia). Awarded medal of honor from Verein deutscher Ingenieure, presented at its 50th anniversary, Cologne, 1931, "in appreciation of services to technical-scientific achievement, particularly in promoting mutual internat. interests of engrs. of entire world." Home: Montclair, N.J. Died Oct. 2, 1934.

RICE, CHARLES, chemist, philologist; b. Munich, Bavaria, Germany, Oct. 4, 1841; never married. Came to U.S., 1862; served as surgeon's steward U.S. Navy, 1862-65; chief chemist dept. of public charities and correction City of N.Y., 1865; supt. gen. drug dept. Bellevue Hosp., N.Y.C. until 1901; trustee, librarian Coll. of Pharmacy of City of N.Y., 1870-1901; chmn. com. of revision of U.S. Pharmacopoeia, 1880-1901; a leading Sanskrit scholar in U.S., also spoke or read 12 other langs. including Greek, Arabic, Chinese. Died May 13, 1901.

RICE, EDWARD LORANUS, zoölogist; b. Middletown, Conn., Mar. 18, 1871; s. William North and Elizabeth Wing (Crowell) R.; A.B., Wesleyan U., Conn., 1892; U. Berlin, 1892-93; U. Munich, 1893-95, Ph.D., 1895; U. of Chicago, summer 1898; Columbia, 1st semester, 1906-07; U. Freiburg, 2d semester, 1906-07; Harvard, 2d semester, 1916-17; Sc.D., Wesleyan U., 1927; Johns Hopkins, 2d semester, 1927-28; m. Sarah Langdon Abbott, Mar. 20, 1901; children Charlotte, William Abbott. Asst. in zoölogy, Wesleyan U., 1896; prof. biology and geology, Allegheny (Pa.) Coll., 1896-98; prof. zoölogy, Ohio Wesleyan U., 1898-1941, emeritus since 1941, acting pres., 1938-39, prof. zoölogy, (war emergency), 1942-45. Inst. zoölogy, Lake Lab. (Ohio State U.), Sandusky, O., summers, 1905, 06, 08, 09, 12; instr. biology, Bay View (Mich.) Summer College, 1943. Fellow A.A.A.S. (v.p. and chmn. Sect. F, 1923), Ohio Acad. Science (pres. 1906-07; sec. 1912-23); mem. Am. Soc. Naturalists, Assn. Am. Anatomists, Am. Soc. Zoölogists, Am. Genetic Assn., Phi Beta Kappa, Sigma Xi, Phi Nu Theta. Methodist. Author: An Introduction to Biology, 1935. Home: 2241 S. Seneca Av., Alliance, O. Died Feb. 4, 1960.

RICE, EDWIN WILBUR, JR., engineer; b. La Crosse, Wis., May 6, 1862; s. Edwin Wilbur and Margaret Eliza (Williams) R.; A.B., Central High School, Phila., 1880, A.M., 1885; hon. A.M., Harvard, 1903; Sc.D., Union U., 1906; U. of Pa., 1924; Dr.Engring., Rensselaer Poly. Inst., 1917; began practice as elec. engr., 1880; m. Helen K. Doen, May 28, 1884; m. 2d, Alice M. Doen, Aug. 28, 1897. Supt. Thomson-Houston Electric Co., 1883-88, and tech. dir., 1884-94; v.p., 1894-1913, pres., 1913-22, hon. chmn. of board, 1922—, General Electric Co. Awarded Edison medal, 1928. Decorated Chevalier Légion d'Honneur, France; Order of Rising, Sun, 3d Class with Cordon, Japan. Fellow Am. Inst. E.E. (pres. 1917). Home: Schenectady, N.Y. Died Nov. 25, 1935.

RICE, GEORGE SAMUEL, mining engr.; b. Claremont, N.H., Sept. 8, 1866; s. George Samuel and Abby Parker (Rice) R.; student Coll. City of New York, 2 yrs.; E.M., Sch. of Mines (Columbia), 1887; D.Sc., Lafayette, 1936; m. Julia Sessions, Dec. 23, 1891 (died Aug. 13, 1934); children—Abby (dec.), Katharine Peabody, Julian Brewster; m. 2d, Sarah M. Benson, Dec. 21, 1935. Was asst. engr., Colo.&Utah Railroad, 1887; mining engr. with Colo. Fuel Co., Denver, 1888-90; mining engr., Whitebreast Fuel Co., Ottumwa, Ia., 1890; chief mining engr., same co. and allied cos., Chicago, 1897, also gen. supt. Cardiff Coal Co., 1899, Shoal Creek Coal Co., 1902; consulting mining work for A.,T.&S.F. Ry., C.,M.&St.P. Ry., and other corps., 1900-08, also for Armour Fertilizer Works in phosphate fields, Tenn. and Fla., also reported on zinc and lead mines in Mo. and Wis., etc. Apptd. mining engr. in charge of field investigations, technologic br. of U.S. Geol. Survey, 1908; chief mining engr. U.S. Bureau of Mines from establishment, 1910, to his retirement, Sept. 1937; in charge government rescue and recovery work in mine fire and explosion disasters, 1908-26; sent on investigative trips to European mines and testing stations, 1908, to report on safety and conservation methods; in charge of unique series of investigations in govt. exptl. mine in which large coal dust explosions are produced; first in U.S. to advocate (1913) rock dusting for prevention such explosions; developed use in mines of gunite for fire protection and preventing weathering of roof; initiated, 1918, testing of liquid oxygen explosives; reported on oil sand and potash mining methods in Europe; investigated outbursts of gas, bumps, rockbursts in mines of U.S., Canada and Europe; chmn. Am. Inst. Mining and Metall. Engrs. Com. on ground movement and subsidence; reported on losses of coal in mining for U.S. Coal Commn., 1924; prepared regulations for coal mine leasing in Alaska, 1917, and Public Domain, 1920, covering conservation and safety; planned testing in exptl. mine of novel method of vehicular tunnel ventilation for Holland Tunnel, N.Y.-N.J., 1922. On committee to investigate post-war mining conditions in Europe, especially in devastated coal and iron regions of France; adviser on mining matters to Am. Economic Mission at Cologne Conf. with Germans, Mar. 1919. Episcopalian. Del. of Bur. Mines and Am. Inst. Mining & Metall. Engrs. to 6th Internat. Mining Exhbn. and Conf., London, 1923. Planned coöperation in research between British Mines Dept. and Bur. Mines. Chmn. Mine Safety Bd. since 1924. Hon. mem. British Instn. Mining Engrs., Am. Inst. Mining and Metall. Engrs., Mining Soc. Nova Scotia; member (hon.) Coal Mining Institute of America; fellow A.A.A.S.; mem. Washington Acad. Scis., Washington Geol. Soc., etc. Medalist British Instn. of Mining Engrs., 1929; awarded Columbia University medal, 1931. U.S. rep. to 7th Internat. Congress Mining, Metallurgy and Applied Geology, Paris, France, 1935. Club: Cosmos. Author of numerous papers for tech. socs. and jours. and bulls. of U.S. Bureau Mines. Home: Wellington Villa on Mt. Vernon Highway. Address: R.F.D. 1, Box 135, Alexandria, Va. Died Jan. 4, 1950.

RICE GEORGE STAPLES, engineer; b. Boston, Feb. 28, 1849; s. Reuben and Harriet Tyler (Kettell) R.; S.B., Harvard, 1870; m. Rose Breuchaud Porter, Oct. 10, 1889. Asst. engr. Lowell (Mass.) Water Works and Boston Water Works, 1869-72; div. engr. additional water supply, Boston, 1872-77; asst. engr. in direct charge main drainage works, 1877-80; mining engr. in Ariz. and Colo., 1880-87; prin. asst. engr. main drainage works, Boston, 1887, deputy chief engr. New Croton Aqueduct, New York, 1887-91; chief engr. Boston Rapid Transit Co., 1891-92; in pvt. practice and instr. in water supply and sanitary engring., Harvard, 1892-1900; deputy chief engr., 1900-04, chief engr., 1905-07, Rapid Transit Commrs., New York; div. engr. Pub. Service Commn., 1st Dist., New York, 1907-19. Home: New York, N.Y. Died Dec. 7, 1920.

RICE, JAMES EDWARD, farmer, educator; b. Aurora, Ill., Mar. 12, 1865; s. James R. and Emeline (Wing) R.; grad. Granville Mil. Acad., N. Granville, N.Y., 1885; B.S. in agr., Cornell, 1890; m. Elsie Van Buren, Sept. 14, 1898 (dec.); m. 2d, Louise E. Dawley, Oct. 31, 1936. Asst. in Coll. of Agr., Cornell, 1891-92; farmer in Bucks County, Pa., 1892-93; partner firm White & Rice, operating Fernwood Fruit & Poultry Farm, at Yorktown, N.Y., 1893-1903. Lecturer in farmers' insts. in states of N.Y., N.J., Md. and Minn., 1893-1903 (winters); prof. poultry husbandry, Cornell, 1903-34, prof. emeritus since July 1, 1934; member of Egg and Apple Farm; Trumansburg, New York, and Appledale Orchards, Mexico, New York. President Yorktown Telephone Co., 1901-03; pres. Tompkins County Improvement Assn. Chmn. Nat. Breeder and Hatchery Fair Trade Practice Com.; pres. N. Eastern Poultry Producers Council; chmn. 1st and 7th U.S. World's Poultry Congress Com. Fellow Poultry Science Assn.; life mem. N.Y. State Fruit Growers Assn., New York State Agricultural Society, Ithaca Automobile Association (v.p.), American Poultry Assn. (chmn. committee on protection of poultry industry), World's Poultry Science Assn. (president), Poultry Science Assn. (pres.), N.Y. State Grange, Sigma Xi; hon. mem. Alpha Zeta, Helios Soc., Ho-Nun-De-Ka Soc. Mem. council Nat. Boy Scouts of America. Chmn. U.S. Com. of 1st World's Poultry Congress, 1921; president of 8th World's Poultry Congress, 1939-48; pres. Trumansburg Rotary Club, 1927, 28. Co-Author: Practical Poultry Management (textbook); Judging Poultry for Production. Editor Poultry Science series of textbooks. Presbyterian. Progressive Republican. Home: 536 N. E. 62d St., Miami 38 FL

RICE, JAMES HENRY, JR., naturalist; b. "Riverlands Plantation," Abbeville County, S.C., July 2, 1868; s. James Henry and Anna (Lawton) R.; ed. high sch. and S.C. Coll.; m. Jennie Maner, Apr. 30, 1892; children—James Henry, Edward Carew, Margaret (Mrs. J. L. Patterson), Samuel Maner (dec.), William Lawton, Frederic, Robert Ridgway. Various occupations, principally teaching, until 1895; editor Colonial Records of South Carolina, 1895; editor The Columbia Evening News, 1895; editorial writer on The State (Columbia, S.C.), 1896-98; editor The Field (weekly industrial), 1903-04, The Carolina Field (Georgetown, S.C.), 1905-06; sec. Audubon Soc. of S.C., 1907-10; chief game warden of S.C., 1911-13; also field agt. Nat. Assn. of Audubon Socs., 1910-13; insp. U.S. Biol. Survey, 1913-17. Democrat. Presbyn. Author: Glories of the Carolina Coast. Contbr. numerous articles and book reviews, pertaining to birds, plants, etc. Home: Wiggins, S.C. Died Mar. 23, 1935.

RICE, JOHN WINTER, bacteriologist; b. Williamsport, Pa., July 4, 1891; s. William and Margaret Christiana (Winter) R.; B.S., Bucknell U., 1914, M.S., 1915; A.M., Columbia, 1918, Ph.D., 1922; m. Edna Amelia Miller, Aug. 21, 1918 (died 1921); children—John Miller, Martha Jane; m. 2d, Ruth Miriam (Hoffa) Frantz Aug. 6, 1922;children—Jasper Hoffa Frantz (stepson), Andrew Cyrus, William Floyd, Ruth Eleanor. Teacher of biology, high sch., Hazleton, Pa., 1915-16; instr. of biology, Bucknell U., 1916-18, asst. prof., 1918-23, asso. prof., 1923-24, prof. of bacteriology 1924-59, professor emeritus 1959-71; chmn. dept. biology, 1939-42, 44-58; dir. Health Service, from 1950; instr. bacteriology, Yale Army Laboratory Sch., 1918, Columbia, summer 1922; special investigator on bacteriology of paper milk containers, N.Y. State Agrl. Exp. Station, Geneva, N.Y., summers 1938 and 39. Consultant bacteriologist, Geisinger Memorial Hosp. Pres. Lewisburg, Bd. of Health, 1924-47; pres. Milk Control Dist. 4 of Pa. since 1927; pres. Pa. Assn. of Dairy and Milk Inspectors, 1927-28. Chmn. com. of Pa. Dept. of Health to study York plate pasteurizer, 1931, Union County (Pa.) Nutrition Council, 1942-43. Served as 2d lieutenant Sanitary Corps, U.S. Army, during World War. Mem. Am. Pub. Health Assn., Am. Social Hygiene Assn., A.A.A.S., Soc. Am. Bacteriologists (pres. Central Pa. br. 1935-36), Inst. Food Technologists, Am. Forestry Assn., Am. Soc.

Quality Control, Delta Upsilon, Omicron Delta Kappa. Republican. Methodist. Mason. Home: Lewisburg PA Died Jan. 29, 1971; buried Lewisburg Cemetery.

RICE, LEWIS FREDERICK, architect, civil engr.; b. Boston, Mass., May 17, 1839; s. Lewis and Susan Augusta (Brigham) R.; ed. public schools, 1845-52; West Point, 1853-54; grad. Rensselaer Poly. Inst., C.E., 1858; engr. on construction, Brooklyn water works, 1858-59; div. engr. Troy & Greenfield (Hoosac Tunnel) R.R., 1860-61; in U.S. army as lt., capt. and maj. 31st Mass. vols., 1862-65; gen. practice civ. engr., Boston, 1865-66; asst. engr. Reading & Columbia R.R., Pa., 1867; asst. engr. St. Louis, Mo., water works, 1867-71; in gen. practice architect and civ. engr., Boston, 1872-90; asst. engr. and architect Am. Bell Telephone Co., 1890—. Home: Brookline, Mass. Died 1909.

RICE, THURMAN BROOKS, bacteriology, public health; b. Landess, Ind., Aug. 17, 1888; s. Robert Tilton and Ruth (Porter) R.; B.S., Marion (Ind.) Normal Coll., 1909; B.Pd., Valparaiso U., 1912; A.B., Muncie (Ind.) Normal Inst., 1913; A.B., Ind. U., 1914, A.M., 1917, M.D., 1921; m. Ada Charles, Sept. 1, 1910 (died Feb. 13, 1922); 1 dau., Aïda Louise; m. 2d, Ruby Orene Caster, Mar. 29, 1923; children—Robert Caster, Thurman Brooks, James Abel, Reed Porter. Teacher pub. schs., Huntington County, Ind., 1906-08; teacher high sch., Wheeler, Ind., 1910-12; instr. in biology, Winona Coll., 1914-16; instr. in pathology, Ind. U., 1921-24; dir. lab., Ind. State Bd. of Health, 1924-26; prof. bacteriology and pub. health, Ind. U., 1926-46, prof. public health, chmn. Dept. Pub. Health, since 1946; asst. dir. Ind. Div. of Pub. Health, 1933-36; chief div. of health and phys. edn., Ind. State Bd. of Health and Ind. State Bd. of Edn., 1936-42; State Health Commn. and sec. Indiana State Bd. of Health, 1942-45; cons. on Pub. Health, Ind. State Bd. Health, since 1945. Served as pvt., S.A.T.C., World War I. Recipient of Gold Medal award, Am. Cancer Soc., 1949. Fellow Am. Med. Assn.; mem. Am. Public Health Assn., Ind. Assn. Clin. Pathologists, Ind. State Med. Assn., Ind. Assn. of the History of Medicine, Ind. Hist. Soc., Ind. Cancer Soc. (pres.), Phi Beta Kappa, Nu Sigma Nu, Alpha Omega Alpha, Sigma Xi. Awarded Ravdin medal, Ind. University Sch. of Medicine, 1921; member White House Conf. on Rural Edn., Oct. 1944. Democrat. Presbyn. Clubs: Professional Men's Forum, Ind. University Club, Indianapolis Literary, Schoolmasters. Author: The Conquest of Disease, 1927; Racial Hygiene, 1929; Applied Bacteriology, 1932; Sex Education, 1933; Textbook of Bacteriology (medical), 1935, 4th edit., 1947; The Human Body, 1936; The Hoosier Health Officer (a biography of John N. Hurty; Serial), 1939-46; Living, 1940. Co-author: Adventures in Health Series for Common Schools, 1936; Public Safety, 1937; Microbiology and Pathology, 1942; Sex, Marriage and Family, 1946; March Against Cancer, 1946; Effects of Alcohol, Tobacco and Habitforming Drugs, 1949; "The Salt Free" or Low Sodium Diet, 1951; The Story of the Medical Campus, Ind. Univ. Sch. of Med., 1949. Editor, Indiana State Bd. of Health Bulletin. Contributor to Hygeia, Jour. Outdoor Life, etc. Lecturer on sex edn. preparation for marriage and public and personal health. Research on vital statistics, therapeutic bacteriology, etc. Home: 3167 N. Delaware St., Indianapolis, Ind. Died Dec. 27, 1952; buried Crown Hill Cemetery, Indpls.

RICE, W(ILLIA)M NORTH, geologist; b. Marblehead, Mass., Nov. 21, 1845; s. William and Caroline Laura (North) R.; A.B., Wesleyan U., Conn., 1865; Ph.D., Sheffield Scientific Sch. (Yale), 1867; LL.D., Syracuse U., 1886, Wesleyan U., 1915; m. Elizabeth W. Crowell, Apr. 12, 1870 (died 1916); children—Edward Loranus, Charles William (dec.). Prof. geology and natural history, 1867-84, geology, 1884-1918, emeritus, 1918—, acting pres., 1907, 1908-09, 1918, Wesleyan U. Absent for study and travel in Europe, 1867-68, 1892-93, and 1911-12; asst. U.S. Fish Commn., 1873-74; asst. geologist U.S. Geol. Survey, 1891-92; supt. Conn. State Geol. and Natural History Survey, 1903-16. Mem. Geol. Soc. America (v.p., 1911), A.A.A.S. (v.p. and chmn. sect. E, 1905-06), Am. Acad. Arts and Sciences, Am. Soc. Naturalists (pres. 1891), Conn. Council Edn., 1902-08 (pres. 1902-05); became mem. N.Y. East Conference M.E. Ch., 1869 (chmn. board of examiners, 1896-1925); mem. Council of Conn. Federation of Churches, 1908—(pres. 1910-11); sec. 1913-19; pres. 1919-20; hon. pres. 1920—). Author: Geology of Bermuda, 1884; Science Teaching in the Schools, 1889; Twenty-five Years of Scientific Progress, and Other Essays, 1894; Christian Faith in an Age of Science, 1903; (with H. E. Gregory) Manual of the Geology of Connecticut, 1906 (Conn. Geol. and Natural History Survey); Return to Faith, and other Addresses, 1916; Through Darkness to Dawn, 1917; Poet of Science, and other addresses, 1919; Science and Religion—Five Supposed Conflicts, 1925. Editor 5th edit. Dana's Text-book of Geology, 1897. Address: Middletown, Conn. Died Nov. 13, 1928.

RICH, ARNOLD RICE, pathologist; b. Birmingham, Ala., Mar. 28, 1893; s. Samuel and Hattie (Rice) R.; A.B., U. of Va., 1914, M.A., 1915; M.D., Johns Hopkins University, 1919; M.D. (honorary) University Zurich; married Helen Elizabeth Jones, June 3, 1925; children—Adrienne Cecile, Cynthia Marshall Asst. in pathology, Johns Hopkins U., 1919-20, instr., 1920-21, asso., 1921-23, asso. prof., 1923-44, prof., 1944-47, Baxley prof., dir. dept., 1947-58, Baxley professor emeritus, 1958-68; resident pathologist, Johns Hopkins Hosp., 1920-26, asso. pathologist, 1929-44, pathol.-in-chief, 1947-58, now hon. cons.; expert cons. to the Surg. Gen., U.S. Army; mem. sci. adv. bd. Armed Forces Inst. of Pathology (chmn. 1951); special cons. USPHS; consultant in pathology Veterans Administration; consultant in med. research, Chem. Warfare Service, since 1943; adv. consultant Tuberculosis Control Div., U.S.P.H.S.; Nat. Research Council (com. on pathol., 1947-52). U.S. State Dept. del., 1st Internat. Allergy Congress, 1951; mem. Comite d'Honneur, 50th anniversary celebration of discovery of anaphylaxis, Paris, 1952. Served with U.S. Army, 1917-18; lt. commander USNR, ret. Decorated Chevalier Legion of Honor (France); awarded Charles Mickle hon. fellowship, U. Toronto Faculty of Medicine, 1956; Kober medal, Assn. of Am. Physicians, 1958; Gordon Wilson medal, Am. Clin. and Climatol. Assn., 1960; Trudeau medal, Nat. Tb Assn., 1960; Gairdner Found. (Can.) Internat. award, 1960; honorary Plaque, Japanese Soc. for Tb, 1960; medal A.C.P., 1963; Seaman award Assn. Mil. Surgeons U.S., 1963. Trustee Roland Park Co. Sch., 1944-51. Fellow A.A.A.S., Internat. Assn. Allergists, Royal Soc. Medicine London (hon.); honorary member Pathological Society of Great Britain and Ireland, Am. Clin. and Climatol. Assn., Harvey Soc., Soc. Francaise d'Allergie; fgn. corr. mem. Soc. Med. des Hopitaux de Paris; fgn. mem. Soc. Aregentina de Anat. Norm. y Patol.; corr. mem. Soc. Brasileria de Tuberc., Tb Soc. of Scotland; asso. mem. Soc. Anat. de Paris. Dir. Md. Tb Assn., 1947-51. Mem. Nat. Acad. Scis., Assn. Am. Physicians, Soc. Exptl. Biology and Medicine (editorial bd. Proc. 1943-47), Soc. Exptl. Pathology, Am. Assn. Pathologists and Bacteriologists, Phi Beta Kappa, Sigma Xi, Alpha Omega Alpha. Club: 14 W. Hamilton St. Author: The Pathogenesis of Tuberculosis 1944, rev. 1951, Spanish edit., 1946, Japanese edit., 1954. Mem. editorial bd. Bull. of the Johns Hopkins Hosp., 1925-63, Internat. Archives Allergy and Immunology, Internat. Review Experimental Pathology. Contributor articles in field. Home: Baltimore MD Died Apr. 17, 1968; buried Baltimore Nat. Cemetery, Baltimore MD

RICH, EDWARD P., consulting engr.; b. Chicago, Ill., July 16, 1879; s. Marshall Byron and Mary E. (Prickett) R.; ed. Manual Training Sch., Chicago; student U. of Chicago, 1898-1900; B.S. in M.E., U. of Mich., 1903; m. Lilabel Griffiths, 1911; children—Marshall G., Kenneth G. Practiced in Chicago, 1903—; mem. firm Neiler, Rich & Co., cons. engrs. and indsl. architects, 1908—. Republican. Episcopalian. Home: Chicago, Ill. Died Apr. 19, 1937.

RICHARDS, ALFRED NEWTON, pharmacologist, b. Stamford, N.Y., Mar. 22, 1876; s. Rev. Leonard E. and Mary E. (Burbank) R.; B.A., Yale, 1897, M.A., 1899; Ph.D., Columbia, 1901; hon. Sc.D., U. Pa., 1925, Western Res. U., 1931, Yale, 1933, Harvard, 1940, Columbia, 1942. Williams Coll., 1943, Princeton, 1940. N.Y. U., 1955, Rockefeller Inst., 1960, Oxford U., 1960; hon. M.D., U. Pa., 1932, U. Louvain, 1949; LL.D., U. Edinburgh (Scotland), 1925; Johns Hopkins, 1949; m. Lillian L. Woody, Dec. 26, 1908. Instr., physiol. chemistry Columbia, 1898-1904, pharmacology, 1904-08; prof. pharmacology Northwestern U., 1908-10; prof. pharmacology U. Pa., 1910-46, emeritus prof., 1946—, v.p. charge med. affairs, 1939-48; Herter lectr. N.Y. U., Bellevue Hosp. Med. Coll., 1926; Beaumont lectr., 1929; Croonian lectr. Royal Soc. London, 1938. Chmn. Com. on Med. Research, Office Sci. Research and Devel., U.S. Govt., 1941-46. Mem. Com. on Fed. Med. services Hoover Commn. on Orgn. Exec. Br. Govt., May-Dec. 1948. Mem. sci. staff Brit. Med. Research Com., London, 1917-18; maj. San. Corps, U.S. Army, attached to Chem. Warfare Service. Chaumont, France, July-Dec. 1918. Mem. Nat. Acad. Scis. (pres. 1947-50), Assn. Am. Physicians, Am. Philos. Soc., (v.p. 1944-47), Am. Physiol. Soc., Wistar Assn., Brit. Physiol. Soc. (hon.), Am. Soc. Biol. Chemists, Am. Pharmacol. Soc., Soc. Exptl. Biology and Medicine, Harvey Soc., Physiol. Soc. Phila., Phila. County Med. Soc. (hon.). Interurban Clin. Club (hon.), Sigma Xi, Alpha Omega Alpha, Phi Beta Kappa (hon.), corr. mem. Gesellsch. der Aertze in Wien; hon. mem. Am. Urol. Soc., Royal Soc. Medicine (London); fgn. mem. Royal Soc., London, Royal Danish, Acad. Sci., Royal Soc. Edinburgh; fellow Am. Acad. Arts and Scis., A.A.A.S., Coll. of Physicians Phila. (hon.); fgn. corr. mem. Brit. Med. Assn. Awarded Gerhard medal, 1932; Kober medal, 1933; Keyes medal, 1933; John Scott medal, 1934; N.Y. Acad. Med. medal, 1936; Phila. award, 1937; Procter medal; Guggenheim Cup Award; Lasker award, 1946; Kovalenko medal Nat. Acad. Sci., 1953; Abraham Flexner award Assn. Am. Med. Colls., 1959. Decorated Medal for Merit, 1946; hon. comdr. Order Brit. Empire, 1948. Trustee Rockefeller Found., 1937-41. Clubs: Century (N.Y.); Rittenhouse, Republican. Presbyn. Author papers on action chloroform, histamine, function of kidneys. Successively asst., assoc. and mng. editor Jour. Biol. Chem., 1905-14. Home: 737 Rugby Rd., Bryn Mawr, Pa. 19010. Died Mar. 24, 1966.

RICHARDS, CHARLES BRINCKERHOFF, mech. engr.; b. Brooklyn, Dec. 23, 1833; s. Thomas Fanning and Harriet Howland (Brinckerhoff) R.; ed. pvt. schs., 1838-49; hon. A.M., Yale, 1884; m. Agnes Edwards Goodwin, Sept. 16, 1858. Was many yrs. engr. supt. Colt's Arms Co., Hartford, and, 1880-84, supt. Southwark Foundry and Machine Co., Phila.; Higgin prof. mech. engring., Yale, 1884-1909, emeritus prof., 1909. Consulting engr. for many pub. bldgs.; U.S. expert commr. to Paris Expn., 1889; inventor, 1861, of Richards' indicator for steam engine. Chevalier Legion of Honor, France. Editor Vol. III and part Vol. IV (1400 pp.) Report of U.S. Commrs. to Paris Expn. Editor engring. and tech. words and terms in Webster's International Dictionary. Home: New Haven, Conn. Died Apr. 20, 1919.

RICHARDS, DICKINSON W., physician; b. Orange, N.J., Oct. 30, 1895; s. Dickinson W. and Sally (Lambert) W.; A.B., Yale, 1917, D.Sc., 1957; A.M., Columbia, 1922, M.D., 1923, D.Sc., 1966; m. Constance B. Riley, Sept. 19, 1931; children—Ida E., Gertrude W., Ann H., Constance L. Research fellow Nat. Inst. for Med. Research, London, Eng., 1927-28; research on problems of pulmonary and cardiac physiology Coll. Phys. and Surg., Columbia, 1928-73, Lambert prof. medicine, 1947-61, emeritus, 1961-73, dir. 1st med. div. Bellevue Hosp., N.Y.C., 1945-61. Served as 1st lt. U.S. Army, 1917-18, A.E.F., 1918. Decorated chevalier Legion of Honor (France); recipient Nobel Prize in medicine and physiology (with others), 1956. Fellow Am. Acad. Arts and Scis.; mem. Assn. Am. Physicians (pres. 1962), Nat. Acad. Scis. Presbyn. Club: Century Assn. (N.Y.C.). Editor: (with A. P. Fishman) Circulation of the Blood: Men and Ideas, 1964. Home: Lakeville CT Died Feb. 23, 1973.

RICHARDS, EDGAR, analytical chemist; b. New York, Feb. 23, 1858; s. Edgar Henry and Mary (King) R.; ed. St. Paul's School, Concord, N.H., 1870-75; course in chemistry, School of Mines, Columbia, 1876-81; asst. chemist U.S. Dept. Agr., July, 1882, to June, 1887; chemist Internal Revenue Bureau, U.S. Treasury Dept., Washington, June, 1887, to Jan., 1892. Pres. Washington Chem. Soc., 1889; mem. Am. Inst. Mining Engrs., also Am., London and Paris chem. socs., Soc. of Chem. Industry, Soc. of Public Analysts, Am. Public Health Assn., etc. Author: Principles and Methods of Soil Analysis, 1886 W8; Some Food Substitutes and Adulterants (president's address, Washington Chem. Soc.); various papers in scientific periodicals, govt. reports, etc. Address: 341 W. 88th St., New York.

RICHARDS, ELLEN HENRIETTA, sanitary chemist; b. Dunstable, Mass., Dec. 3, 1842; d. Peter and Fanny Gould (Taylor) Swallow; A.B., Vassar, 1870, A.M., 1873; S.B., Mass. Inst. Tech., 1873; m. Robert Hallowell Richards, June 6, 1875. Instr. in Woman's Lab., 1876-84, sanitary chemistry, 1884—, Mass. Inst. Tech. As chemist of Mfrs.' Mutual Fire Ins. Co. had much to do with oils, in reference to safety from spontaneous combustion, explosion, etc.; also specialist in water analysis. Author: Air, Water and Food, 1900; First Lessons in Minerals; The Cost of Food, 1900; Cost of Shelter, 1905; First Lessons in Food and Diet; The Art of Right Living, 1905; Sanitation in Daily Life, 1907; Cost of Cleanness, 1908; Industrial Water Analysis, 1909. Home: Jamaica Plain, Mass. Died 1911.

RICHARDS, HERBERT MAULE, botanist; b. Germantown, Pa., Oct. 6, 1871; s. William T. (artist) and Anna (Matlack) R. (author); S.B., Harvard, 1891, S.D., 1895; studied at Leipzig, 1895-96; visited bot. garden, Buitenzorg, Java, 1899-1900, and traveled in Japan, China, Straits Settlements and Malay Archipelago; m. Marion Elizabeth Latham, July 17, 1915. Asst. in Harvard and instr. Radcliffe Coll., 1892-95; tutor Barnard Coll. (Columbia), 1896-97; instr. Harvard U. and Radcliffe Coll., 1897-98; instr. 1898-1902; adj. prof. botany 1902-06, prof. botany, 1906—, Barnard Coll. Scientific dir. N.Y. Bot. Garden. Fellow A.A.A.S. (v.p. sect. G, 1908). Home: New York, N.Y. Died Jan. 9, 1928.

RICHARDS, JOSEPH WILLIAM, metallurgist; b. Oldbury, Eng., July 28, 1864; s. Joseph and Bridgett (Harvey) R.; A.B., Central High Sch., Phila., 1882, A.M., 1887; A.C., Lehigh U., 1886, M.S., 1891, Ph.D., 1893; Univ. of Heidelberg and Mining Acad., Freiberg, 1897-98; m. Arnamarie Gadd, of Gloucestershire, Eng., Mar. 12, 1887. Instr. metallurgy and mineralogy, 1887-97, asst. prof., 1897-1902, acting prof. metallurgy, 1902-03, prof., 1903—, Lehigh U.; prof. electro-chemistry, Franklin Inst. of Phila., 1907-10. Legal expert in chemical and metall. cases; mem. U.S. Assay Commn., 1897; rep. of Franklin Inst. to Internat. Geol. Congress, Russia, 1897; mem. jury of awards, dept. chemistry, Nat. Export Exhbn., Phila., 1899; mem. jury of awards (and chairman metall. sub-jury) Panama P.I. Expn., 1915; mem. U.S. Navy Consulting Board, 1915-18. Mem. numerous professional societies. Author: Aluminum (only treatise on that metal in English), 1887; 3d edit., 1895; Metallurgical Calculations, Part I, General Metallurgy, 1906, Part II, Iron and Steel, 1907, Part III, Non-ferrous Metals, 1908. Died Oct. 12, 1921.

RICHARDS, ROBERT HALLOWELL, metallurgist; b. Gardiner, Me., Aug. 26, 1844; s. Francis and Anne Hallowell (Gardiner) R.; B.S., Mass. Inst. Tech., 1868; LL.D., U. of Mo., 1908; m. Ellen Henrietta Swallow,

June 6, 1875; m. 2d, Lillian Jameson, June 8, 1912. Asst. in chemistry, Mass. Inst. Tech., 1868-69, instr. assaying and qualitative analysis, 1869-70, asst. prof. analytical chemistry, 1870-71, prof. mineralogy and assaying and developed mining and metall. labs., 1871-72, prof. mining engring., 1873-84, head dept. mining, 1873-1914, prof. mining engring. and metallurgy, 1884-1914, emeritus prof. mining engring. since July 1, 1914, sec. faculty, 1878-83. Invented a jet aspirator for chem. and physical labs., 1873; a prism for stadia surveying in 1890; an ore separator for the Lake Superior copper mills, 1881, one for Va. iron ores in 1900, 3 for western U.S., 1906, 07, 08; designed and installed apparatus for Mass. Cremation Soc. Fellow Am. Acad. Arts and Sciences, A.A.A.S.; hon. mem. Am. Inst. Mining Engrs. (pres. 1886); mem. Mining and Metall. Soc. America, Am. Forestry Assn., Soc. of Arts, Am. Inst. Mining Engrs. Mem. Legion of Honor. Clubs: Economic Engineers', University, Technology. Holder of gold medal from Mining and Metall. Soc. America. Author: Ore Dressing, Vols. I and II, 1903, Vols. III and IV, 1909; Ore Dressing (text-book), 1909, revised (with Charles E. Locke), 1925. Home: 32 Eliot St., Jamaica Plain, Mass. Died Mar. 27, 1945.

RICHARDS, THEODORE WILLIAM, chemist; b. Germantown, Pa., Jan. 31, 1868; s. William T. (artist) and Anna (Matlack) R. (authpr); S.B. Haverford Coll., 1885; A.B., Harvard, 1886, A.M., Ph.D., 1888; chem. student, univs. of Göttingen, Leipzig and Tech. Sch., Dresden; S.D., Yale, 1905; LL.D., Haverford, 1908; Chem.D., Clark U., 1909; Ph.D., Royal Bohemian U., Prague, 1909; Sc.D., Harvard, 1910; M.D., Berlin U., 1910; D.Sc., Cambridge (Eng.), Oxford, Manchester, 1911; Ph.D., Christiania, Norway, 1911; LL.D., U. of Pittsburgh, 1915, U. of Pa., 1920; Sc.D., Princeton U., 1923; m. Miriam Stuart, d. of Prof. J. H. Thayer, of Cambridge, Mass., May 28, 1896; children—Grace Thayer (wife of Prof. James Bryant Conant), William Theodore, Greenough Thayer. Asst. prof., 1894-1901, prof. chemistry, 1901—, chmn. chem. dept., 1903-11, dir. Gibbs Memorial Lab., 1912—, Harvard. Exchange prof. from Harvard to Berlin U., 1907; Lowell lecturer, 1908; mem. Internat. Com. on Elements and Atomic Weights; adviser Carnegie Instn., 1902, research asso., 1902—, Davy medalist, Royal Soc., 1910; Faraday lecturer and medalist, Chem. Soc., 1911; Willard Gibbs medalist, Am. Chem. Soc., 1912; Nobel laureate in chemistry, 1914 (awarded 1915); Franklin medal, Franklin Inst., 1916; Lavoisier and Le Blanc medalist (Paris), 1922. Member Nat. Research Council and allied coms., 1916; consulting chemist, War Department and Bur. of Mines, 1918. With help of assistants has revised atomic weights of oxygen, copper, barium, strontium, calcium, zinc, magnesium, iron, nickel, cobalt, uranium, caesium, sodium, chlorine, potassium, nitrogen, silver, sulphur, carbon, lithium, radioactive lead, gallium, aluminum. Investigator in physical and inorganic chemistry; recent papers concern the significance of changing atomic volume, and other effects of internal cohesive and chemical pressure; also thermochemistry and electrochemistry, etc. Fellow Am. Acad. Arts and Sciences (pres. 1919-21), A.A.A.S. (pres. 1917). Officier de la Legion d'Honneur, 1925. Home: Cambridge, Mass. Died Apr. 2, 1928.

RICHARDS, WILLIAM JOSEPH, mining engr.; b. Minersville, Pa., Apr. 14, 1863; s. Joseph H. and Mary Elizabeth (Weaver) R.; m. Katherine Johnson Carty, of Ashland, Pa., May 9, 1889. Mining engr. with Phila. & Reading Coal & Iron Corp., 1883-87, with Mineral Railroad & Mining Co., 1888, again with P.&R.C.&I. Co., 1889; chief engr. Lehigh & Wilkes-Barre Coal Co., 1889-97; gen. supt. same, 1897-1902; gen. mgr. P.&R.C.&I. Co., 1903-07, v.p., 1907-14, pres., 1914-27, also pres. P.&R.C.&I. Corp., 1924-27; chmn. bd. Sovereign-Pocahontas Co., Ashland Coal and Coke Co., Majestic Collieries Co., Pemberton Coal Co. President Patriotic League of Schuylkill Co., World War; chmn. Mine Cave Commn., State of Pa.; mem. Anthracite Conciliation Board, 1904-27. Mem. Am. Inst. Mining and Metall. Engrs. Republican. Presbyn. Clubs: Pottsville, Schuylkill Country; Union League (Phila.); Railroad (New York); Westmoreland (Wilkes-Barre). Home: 1311 Howard Av., Pottsville, Pa. Office: Whitehall Bldg., New York, N.Y.

RICHARDSON, GEORGE BURR, geologist; b. New York, Aug. 21, 1872; s. George Wentworth and Emma (Breck) R.; grad. Harvard, S.B., 1895, S.M., 1898; Ph.D., Johns Hopkins, 1901; unmarried. Has done geol. work for U.S. Geol. Survey in different parts of the U.S. since 1896; asst. geologist same since 1900. Author: Reconnaissance in the Cape Nome Region, Alaska (assisting Alfred H. Brooks), 1901 U6; Indiana Folio, Geologic Atlas of the United States, 1903 U6. Address: U.S. Geol. Survey, Washington

RICHARDSON, HENRY SMITH, mfg. chemist; b. Greensboro, N.C., July 19, 1885; s. Lunsford and Mary Lynn (Smith) R.; Davidson (N.C.) Coll., 1906; student U.S. Naval Acad.; m. Grace Stuart Jones, Dec. 16, 1914; children—Grace Stuart, Mary Keene, Henry Smith, Robert Randolph, John Page. Salesman, Vick Chem. Co., 1907-15, gen. mgr., 1915-19, pres., 1919-29, chmn. bd., 1929-38, chmn. exec. com., 1938-53, chmn. bd., 1953-57, hon. chmn., 1957-72 (name changed to Richardson-Merrell, Inc. 1962). Founder L. Richardson Meml. Hosp. for Negroes, Greensboro, and donor (with L. Richardson, Jr.) Richardson Field at Davidson Coll.; founder, trustee, chmn. bd. Smith Richardson Found.; exec. bd. Boy Scouts Am., 1942-72; a leader in effecting passage of legislation for state commn. for conservation of wild life in N.C. Mem. Kappa Sigma, Omicron Delta Kappa. Democrat. Presbyn. Home: Greens Farms CT Died Feb. 11, 1972; buried Green Hill Cemetery Greensboro NC

RICHARDSON, MARK WYMAN, M.D.; b. Fitchburg, Mass., Dec. 27, 1867; s. Nathan Henry and Martha Ann (Barber) R.; brother of Maurice Howe Richardson; A.B., Harvard, 1889, M.D., 1894; med. study in Europe, 1895; m. Josephine Lord, of Boston, Feb. 6, 1895. Practicing medicine at Boston since 1894; asst. in pathology, Harvard, 1898-1900; sec. State Bd. of Health of Mass., Jan. 1909-14; examiner for life ins., 1914—. Mem. Assn. Am. Physicians, A.M.A., Mass. Med. Soc., A.A.A.S. Republican. Contbr. to med. jours. of articles relating to bacteriology and immunity in typhoid fever, and concerning epidemiology of poliomyelitis. Investigating phenomena connected with psychic research since 1923, more especially the "Margery" mediumship, Boston. Home: Newton Center, Mass. Office: 100 Milk St., Boston, Mass.

RICHARDSON, ROLAND GEORGE DWIGHT, mathematician; b. Dartmouth, N.S., May 14, 1878; s. George Josiah and Rebecca (Newcomb) R.; B.A., Acadia College, N.S., 1898, D.C.L., 1931; B.A., Yale 1903, M.A., 1904, Ph.D., 1906; Univ. of Göttingen, 1908-09; honorary LL.D. from Lehigh University, 1941; m. Louise J. MacHattie, June 4, 1908; 1 son, George Wendell. Teacher Margaretsville (N.S.) Sch., 1895-96, 1898-99; prin. Westport (N.S.) High Sch., 1899-1902; instr. in mathematics, Yale, 1904-07; asst. prof. mathematics, Brown U., 1907-12, asso. prof., 1912-15, prof. since 1915, head of department, 1915-42, dean of Graduate School since 1926, director of advanced instruction and research in mechanics, 1941-46. Fellow American Academy Arts and Sciences; member A.A.A.S., American Math. Soc. (v.p. 1920); sec. 1921-40; mem. bd. of trustees since 1923), Math. Assn. America (v.p. 1919), Deutsche Mathematiker Vereinigung, Phi Beta Kappa, Sigma Xi. Baptist. Contbr. to Trans. and Bull. Am. Math. Soc., Am. Jour. Mathematics, Mathematische Annalen, etc. Address: Brown University, Providence 12. Died July 17, 1949; buried in Camp Hill Cemetery, Halifax, N.S., Can.

RICHARDSON, SIR OWEN WILLANS, physicist; b. Dewsbury, Eng., Apr. 26, 1879; s. Joshua and Charlotte Maria (Willans) R.; B.A., U. of Cambridge, Eng., 1900, M.A., 1904; B.Sc., U. of London, 1900, D.Sc., 1903. Fellow of Trinity Coll., Cambridge, 1902-8; m. Lillian Maud Wilson, June 12, 1906. Prof. physics, Princeton, 1906-13; dir. research physics Kings Coll., 1924-44. Has made exptl. discoveries fundamental to electronic and kinetic theories of matter. Created Knight, 1939. Recipient of Nobel Prize, 1928. Author of numerous papers in Philos. Mag., Trans. Royal Soc., London, Phys. Review, etc. Fellow Royal Soc. London, Cambridge Philos. Soc., Phys. Soc. London; mem. Am. Philos. Soc., Am. Phys. Soc., Soc. Francaise de Physique (council). Author: The Electron Theory of Matter, 1914. Died Feb. 15, 1959.

RICHARDSON, TOBIAS GIBSON, surgeon, educator; b. Lexington, Ky., Jan. 3, 1827; M.D., U. Louisville (Ky.), 1848; m. Ida Ann Slocum, Nov. 12, 1868; 3 children including Sarah Short. Demonstrator of anatomy U. Louisville, 1848-56; published Elements of Human Anatomy, 1854; co-editor Louisville Med. Review, 1856; prof. anatomy Med. Dept. of Pa. Coll., Phila., 1856-58; prof. anatomy U. La. (now Tulane), New Orleans, 1858-62, 65-72, prof. surgery, 1872-89, dean of coll., 1865-85; asst. med. dir. Army of Tenn., 1862-63, med. insp., 1862, med. dir. to Gen. Braxton Bragg, 1865; volunteer visiting surgeon to Charity Hosp. of New Orleans, 28 years; pres. A.M.A., 1877; urged appointment of nat. sec. of health, pleaded for appropriations from fed. govt. to promote research for investigation and prevention of disease, 1878; a founder Orleans Parish Med. Soc., 1877, La. State Med. Assn., 1878, Am. Surg. Assn., 1880; an original mem. New Orleans Auxiliary Sanitary Assn., 1878; mem. Am. Pub. Health Assn.; fellow Coll. of Pharmacy and Acad. Phys. Scis. of Phila.; adminstr. of fund established by Paul Tulane for benefit of U. La., 1884; ruling elder First Presbyn. Ch. of New Orleans, 1860-92; gave $150,000 to Tulane Med. Sch. Died New Orleans, May 26, 1892.

RICHARDSON, WILLIAM D., chemist; b. Jackson, Mich., Nov. 24, 1876; s. William L. and Elna (Dyer) R.; ed. high sch. and U. of Chicago, 1894-99. Chemist, 1899-1901, chief chemist, 1901—, Swift & Co., packers, Chicago. Editor, 1908-11, mem. bd. editors, 1911-16, Jour. Industrial and Engineering Chemistry. Fellow A.A.A.S. Home: Chicago, Ill. Died 1936.

RICHE, CHARLES SWIFT, civil engr.; b. Philadelphia, Pa., July 19, 1864; s. George Inman and Elizabeth Ramsay (Wetherill) R.; grad. Friends' Central Sch., Phila., 1881; grad. U.S. Mil. Acad., 1886; grad. Engr. Sch. of Application, Willet Point, N.Y., 1889; m. Annie Weir, June 6, 1889 (died 1897); children—Swift, Weir (killed in France Dec. 19, 1918). Commd. addt. 2d lt. Corps of Engrs., July 1, 1886; promoted through grades to col., July 1, 1916; served as col. 1st U.S. Vol. Inf., May 20, 1898-Oct. 28, 1898; retired Jan. 18, 1921. Engaged extensively in river and harbor work; Great Lakes harbors and connecting channels; U.S. lake survey; upper Miss. River improvement; completion Hennepin Canal, Tex. harbors, Coast Canal, Houston Ship Channel and Texas City Dike; fortifications of New Orleans, Galveston and Panama Canal; consulting engr. on grade raising of City of Galveston, Tex., 1903-04. Mem. Engring. Bd. of Rev., Sanitary Dist. of Chicago, 1924-25. Democrat. Episcopalian. Mason. Elk. Died Mar. 20, 1936.

RICHEY, ALBERT SUTTON, electrical engr.; b. Muncie, Ind., Apr. 10, 1874; s. Webster Scott and Julia M. (Thomas) R.; B.M.E., Purdue U., 1894, E.E., 1908; m. Edith Holman Kendrick, June 14, 1907; children—Frances, Janet. Elec. engr., Union Traction Co. of Ind., until 1905; prof. electrical engring., Worcester Poly. Inst., 1905—; consulting engr., 1905—. Republican. Presbyn. Fellow Am. Inst. Elec. Engrs. Mason. Author: Electric Railway Handbook. Home: Worcester, Mass. Died June 24, 1936.

RICHEY, FREDERICK DAVID, (rich'e), geneticist; b. St. Louis, Mo., Sept. 3, 1884; s. Frank Evans and Fannie (Lippman) R.; B.S.A., U. of Mo., 1909; D.Sc. (honorary), University of Missiouri, 1949; married Hazel Grace Clough, Dec. 11, 1912; children—Frances, Guida. Began as mgr. of farm, 1909; with Food and Drug Commn. of Mo., 1910-11; with U.S. Dept. Agr., engaged in corn investigations, 1911-33, in charge, 1922-33, collected maize in S.A., 1923, asso. chief Bur. of Plant Industry, Dept. of Agr., Washington, D.C., 1934, chief, 1934-38, professional corn breeding, 1938-42, prin. agronomist in charge Southern corn breeding, U.S. Department Agriculture 1943-54; pvt. cons. & corn breeder, 1954(—). Dept. Agrl. Award. Fellow A.A.A.S. Am. Soc. Agronomy (v.p. 1936, pres. 1937); mem. Am. Genetic Assn., Genetics Soc. of America (v.p. 1932), Am. Soc. of Naturalists, Am. Soc. of Plant Physiologists, Gamma Sigma Delta, Sigma Xi. Club: Cosmos. Writer numerous publs. on corn growing, breeding and statis. methods. Address: 11 Century Ct., Knoxville, Tenn. Died Sept. 11, 1955.

RICHEY, THOMAS B., engring. cons.; b. Capon Rd., Va., Nov. 24, 1887; s. John Sinnard and Ellen Marshall (Locke) R.; student Augusta Mil. Acad., Ft. Defiance, Va., 1901-05, U.S. Naval Acad., 1905-09; M.S., Mass. Inst. Tech., 1914; m. Katherine M. Fowler, Nov. 6, 1914; children—Thomas Beall, Katherine Elizabeth. Passed midshipman, 1909, and advanced through the ranks to rear adm., 1942; indsl. dept., Boston Navy Yard, 1914-20, Naval Station, New Orleans (indsl. mgr.), 1920-21, San Diego, 1921-23, Norfolk Navy Yard (planning officer), 1923-27; production supt., Phila. Navy Yard, 1927-31, Mare Island Navy Yard, 1931-34, Brooklyn Navy Yard, 1934-41; mgr. Norfolk Navy Yard 1941 to 1943, attached to Joint Chiefs of Staff, Washington, D.C., 1943-45; retired from Navy Nov. 6, 1945. Consultant, Cargoaire Engring. Corp., N.Y. City, since 1945. Awarded Victory medal. Mem. Soc. Naval Architects and Marine Engrs., Soc. Naval Engrs., Naval Inst. Home: 405 W. 118th St., New York 27. Office: 15 Park Row, New York 7. Died March 30, 1949; buried Arlington National Cemetery, Washington.

RICHMOND, CHARLES WALLACE, ornithologist; b. Kenosha, Wis., Dec. 31, 1868; s. Edward Leslie and Josephine E. (Henry) R.; ed. Kenosha, Wis., 1874-80, Washington, 1881-83; M.D., Georgetown (D.C.) U., 1897; student Corcoran Scientific Sch., 1886-87; m. Louise H. Seville, Aug. 31, 1897. Made natural history explorations in Central America, 1892; asst. curator div. birds, U.S. Nat. Mus., 1894-1918, asso. curator, 1918—. Fellow Am. Ornithologists' Union; mem. numerous societies. Author many papers on ornithology in Proceedings U.S. Nat. Mus., Biol. Soc. Washington, The Auk, etc. Home: Washington, D.C. Died May 19, 1932.

RICHMOND, HAROLD BOURS, mfr.; b. Medford, Mass., Mar. 22, 1892; s. Benjamin and Effie Louise (Libby) R.; S.B., Mass. Institute Tech., 1914; D.Eng. (hon.), Norwich U., 1947; m. Florence Hoefler, Oct. 5, 1921; children—Robert Bours, Priscilla (Mrs. Raymond V. Randall). Elec. engr. with Stone & Webster Management Assn., 1914-15, Gen. Vehicle Co., 1915-16; instr. in elec. engring., Mass. Inst. Tech., 1916-19; with Gen. Radio Co., mfrs. elec. and radio laboratory apparatus, since 1919, director, 1922, treasurer 1926-44, chairman board and management committee, 1914-70; dir., member investment com. Liberty Mutual Ins. Co., Liberty Mutual Fire Insurance Company. Corporator Home Savings Bank, Boston, 1941-70, trustee 1945. Chief Guided Missiles Division of Nat. Defense Research Com., Wash., D.C., 1942-45. Chmn. Nat. Acad. of Science Adv. Com. to Army Ord. Dept. on Guided Missiles 1945-48. Commissioned first lieutenant Coast Artillery Res. Corps, May 15, 1917; served Coast Defenses, Chesapeake Bay and Coast Defenses, Boston, May 1917-July 1918; comdr. supply co., 45th Arty., C.A.C., service in U.S. and France, July 1918-Feb. 1919. Awarded Presidential Medal for Merit for defense work; recipient award Scientific Apparatus Makers, 1956. Town Meeting rep., Arlington, Mass., 1925-29; mem. aviation com. N.E. Regional Planning Commn., 1935-45; mem. corp., Mass. Inst. Tech., 1932-44, since 1952; pres. Alumni Assn., 1938-39;

mem. Corp. Northeastern U., 1943-70, trustee, 1944-70; trustee Norwich U., 1946-70; trustee, American Child Guidance Foundation, 1953-70. Member adv. com. James Jackson Cabot Foundation (Norwich U.). Fellow Inst. Radio Engrs., Am. Inst. Elec. Engrs.; mem. Radio Mfrs. Assn. of Washington, D.C. (dir. 1926-32; pres. 1929-30). Dir., pres., chmn. Scientific Apparatus Makers Assn., 1938-52; treas. and trustee New England Industrial Research Found., Incorporated, 1938-51. Vestryman Church of Epiphany, Winchester, Massachusetts, 1933-36. Clubs: Winchester Country (Winchester); Arlington Rifle (Woburn, Mass.); Technology (New York); Commercial (Boston); Kennebunk Beach (Maine) Chowder and Marching. Home: Winchester MA Died May 1970.

RICHTER, RICHARD BIDDLE, physician; b. La Porte, Ind., May 9, 1901; s. Harry Walter and Elizabeth (Biddle) R.; S.B., U. Chicago, 1922; M.D., Rush Medical Coll., 1925; m. Gudrun Anderson, Jan. 27, 1926;children—Tor, Anders. Interne Presbyn. Hosp., Chicago, 1924-25; grad. work in neurology, Rush Med. Coll., 1925-30, asst. clin. prof. neurology, 1932-39; asst. prof. medicine, U. of Chicago, 1936-45, asso. prof. of medicine, 1945-46, prof. of neurology, 1946-71; attending neurologist, Albert Merritt Billings Hosp., 1936-71, Cook County Hosp., 1934-38. Mem. American Neurological Assn. (pres. 1963), Am. Association of Neuropathologists (president 1960-61), Assn. for Research Nervous and Mental Diseases, Am. Acad. Neurology, American Association for Advancement of Sci., A.M.A., Chicago Neurol. Soc. (past pres.), Chicago Med. Soc., Phi Beta Kappa, Alpha Omega Alpha, Sigma Xi. Clubs: Quadrangle, Chicago Literary (Chicago). Mem. editorial adv. bd., Jour. of Neuropathology and Experimental Neurology since 1950, and Neurology, 1950-71. Home: Chesterton IN Died Apr. 6, 1971.

RICHTMYER, F(LOYD) K(ARKER), physicist; b. Cobleskill, N.Y., Oct. 12, 1881; s. Robert and Elmina (Karker) R.; A.B., Cornell U., 1904, Ph.D., 1910; m. Bernice Davis, Aug. 3, 1904; children—Robert Lawson (dec.), Robert Davis, Sarah Elizabeth, Lawson Edward. Instr. physics, Drexel Inst., Phila., 1904-06; instr. physics, 1906-11, asst. prof., 1911-18, prof., 1918—, dean Grad. Sch., 1931—, Cornell U. Physicist Bur. of Standards, summer 1915; investigator Gen. Elec. Research Lab., 1919-20; lecturer Summer School, U. of California, 1923, summer quarter, Stanford, 1925, 31, summer school, Columbia U., 1929. Radio engr. Signal Corps, U.S.A., 1918; major of the Ordnance Reserve Corps, U.S.A., 1925—. Mem. Nat. Research Council (chmn. div. physical sciences 1930-35); mem. Am. Acad. Arts and Sciences, Am. Assn. Physics Teachers (v.p., 1935-36; pres., 1937—). Awarded Levy medal, Franklin Inst., 1929. Unitarian. Editor: Jour. Optical Soc. of America; Review of Scientific Instruments, International Series in Physics. Home: Ithaca, N.Y. Died Nov. 7, 1939.

RICKARD, BRENT NEVILLE, (ri-kärd'), metallurgist; b. Anaconda, Mont., June 28, 1885; s. Stephen and Constance (Neville) R.; ed. Manual Training High Sch., Denver, Colo., and University of Michigan; m. Edith Cutter, Apr. 7, 1916; children—Constance Neville (Mrs. Wyndham Kemp White), Brent Neville. Began as chemist for Am. Smelting & Refining Co., Monterey, N.L., Mexico, 1905; chief chemist Cia. Minera de Peñoles, Mapimi, Durango, Mexico, 1907-10; with Am. Smelting & Refining Co. since 1910, successively as metallurgist and asst. supt. Murray, Utah, 1910-14, Monterey and Chihuahua, Mexico, and Garfield, Utah, 1915-16, Tacoma, Wash., 1916-18, Murray, Utah, 1919-21, asst. mgr. Utah Dept., Salt Lake City, 1922-25, mgr. E. Helena, Mont., 1926-27, mgr. El Paso, Tex., 1928-39, mgr. Southwestern Ore. Purchasing Dept., Tucson, Ariz., 1939-50, ret. Mem. Am. Inst. Mining and Metall. Engrs. (past dir.), Sigma Chi. Republican. Episcopalian. Address: 2211 East Speedway, Tucson, Ariz. Died Mar. 8, 1951; buried Evergreen Cemetery, El Paso, Tex.

RICKARD, THOMAS ARTHUR, mining engr.; b. Pertusola, Italy, Aug. 29, 1864; s. Thomas and Octavia Rachel (Forbes) R. (both English); early edn. in Russia and at Queen's Coll., Taunton, Eng.; U. of London, 1881; asso., Royal Sch. of Mines, London, 1885; Sc.D., Colo. Sch. Mines, 1927; came to U.S., 1885; m. Marguerite Lydia Rickard, Dec. 20, 1898. Assayer and surveyor, Colo., 1885-87; mine mgr., Calif., 1887-89; travel and examination of mines in Australia and New Zealand, 1889-91; mine mgr., France, 1891-91; state geologist of Colo., 1895-1901; examining mines in Can. and W. Australia, 1896-98; consulting mining engr. at Denver, during intervals. Editor Engineering and Mining Journal, 1903-05; editor Mining and Scientific Press. San Francisco, 1906-09, The Mining Magazine, London, 1909-15, Mining and Scientific Press, San Francisco, 1915-22; contbg. editor Engring. and Mining Jour.-Press, 1922-29. Lecturer, mining geology, Harvard, 1912-15. Fellow Royal Anthrop. Inst.; mem. Am. Inst. Mining and Metall. Engrs. (hon.), Instn. Mining and Metallurgy, London (gold medalist 1932). Pres. Calif. branch English-Speaking Union, 1926-32. Club: Union (Victoria, B.C.). Author: Stamp-Milling of Gold Ores, 1897; Across the San Juan Mountains, 1903; The Sampling and Estimation of Ore in a Mine, 1904; The Copper Mines of Lake Superior, 1905; Journeys of Observation, 1908; Through the Yukon and Alaska, 1909; Flotation Process, 1916; Technical Writing, 1919; Man and Metals, 1932; A History of American Mining, 1932, Retrospect, 1937; The Romance of Mining, 1944. Home: 33 Sylvan Lane, Victoria BC

RICKENBACKER, EDWARD VERNON ("EDDIE"), aviator; b. Columbus, O., Oct. 8, 1890; s. William and Elizabeth R.; Dr. Aeronautical Sci., Pa. Mil. Coll., 1938, Brown U., Siloam Springs, 1940 U. of Miami, 1941; D.Sc., U. of Tampa (Fla.), 1942; L.H.D., U. Founds. and Am. Theol. Sem., Wilmington, Del., 1943; Sc. D., Westminster Coll., New Wilmington, Pa., 1944; LL.D., Okla. City U., 1944, Capital U., Columbus, O., 1945, Coll. of South Jersey, 1948, Hamilton Coll., 1956, William Jewell Coll., 1962; Dr. Eng., Lehigh U., 1948; Sc.D. (hon.), Lafayette Coll., Easton, Pa., 1952; Sc. D., The Citadel, Charleston, S.C., 1954, Ohio State U., 1957; graduate Internat. Correspondence Sch.; m. Mrs. Adelaide F. Durant, Sept. 16, 1922; children—David E., William F. Became widely known as auto-racer and won championships at nat. and internat. meets; accompanied Gen. Pershing to France as mem. Motor Car Staff, June 1917; trans. to Air Service at own request, Aug. 25, 1917, and assigned as engr. officer to Issoudon Tng. Field; became comdg. officer 94th Aero Pursuit Squadron, the first Am. aero unit to participate actively on the Western front (this unit was credited with 69 victories-the largest number of victories of any Am. unit-Rickenbacker heading the list with 26 victories to his credit); was the first comdg. officer to conduct his own squadron into Coblenz; retired at close of war with rank of capt. World War II activities included; spl. mission for sec. of War to England, So. Pacific, N. Africa, Iran, India, China, Russia, Iceland, Greenland and Aleutians. Awarded Medal of Merit, 1947; awarded D.S.C. with 9 oak leaves, Congressional Medal of Honor (U.S.); Legion of Honor, Croix de Guerre with 4 palms (French). Silver Buffalo Boy Scouts Am., 1944, Big Brother of the Year, 1953. V.p. Am. Airways, Inc., asst. to pres. Aviation Corp., 1932-33; v.O. North Am. Aviation, Inc., 1933-34; gen. mgr. Eastern Air Lines, Inc., 1935; pres., gen. mgr., director, 1938-53, chairman bd., 1954-63; director Wackenhut Corp., Fla. Press. Air Force Aid Soc. Mem. exec. bd. Boy Scouts Am.; dir. Boys' Clubs of Am. Forced down while on a Pacific flight, 1942, rescued after 24 days at sea on a life raft. Author: Fighting the Flying Circus, 1919; Seven Came Through, 1943; Rickenbacker An Autobiography, 1967. Home: New York City NY Died July 23, 1973.

RICKER, GEORGE ALFRED JOY, civ. engr.; b. Portsmouth, N.H., June 30, 1863; s. Charles Clement and Sarah Mehitabel (Joy) R.; prep. edn. under father at sea, and pvt. tutor, 1881-82; spl. student in civ. engring., Mass. Inst. Tech. 1882-85; m. Bessie Turner, Nov. 24, 1887. Transit man, Erie R.R., 1881-82, asst. engr. Buffalo div., 1885-86; topographer and locating engr. N.P. Ry., 1886-87; pvt. practice civ. engring., Buffalo, 1887-1913; resident engr. Buffalo Creek R.R., 1887-97; as chief engr. built Niagara Gorge R.R., 1890-1908; chief engr. Buffalo Traction Co., 1895-99, Buffalo & Depew Electric Ry., 1900-03, Niagara Gorge Power Co., 1901-08; cons. engr. Twin Lakes (Colo.) Land & Water Co., 1898; dep. commr. highways, N.Y., 1913-15; cons. engr., Albany, N.Y., 1915-16; highway engr., Portland Cement Assn., Chicago, 1916-17; dist. engr. of same, Washington, D.C., 1918-29, and mgr. of its Gen. Educational Bur. at Chicago, 1929-30; practicing as cons. engr. Editor Motordom (official mag. N.Y. State Automobile Assn.), 1915-16. Mem. Buffalo City Civ. Service Commn., 1900-12, pres., 1910-12; mem. coördinating com. of Nat. Capital Park and Planning Commn. Democrat. Unitarian. Home: Washington, D.C. Died Nov. 2, 1933.

RICKETTS, LOUIS DAVIDSON, mining engr.; b. Elkton, Md., Dec. 19, 1859; s. Palmer C. and Elizabeth (Getty) R.; B.S., in Economic Geology, Princeton, 1881; W.S. Ward fellowship same univ., 1881-83, Sc.D. (in course), D.Eng., 1925; LL.D. U. of Ariz., 1918; m. Kate Bruce Greenway, Apr. 26, 1916. Surveyor and supt. Colo. mines, 1883-85; geologist for Wyo., 1887-90; cons. engineer Phelps, Dodge & Co., 1890-1906; chmn. bd. and dir. Valley National Bank, Phoenix, Ariz.; cons. engineer of Inspiration Consol. Copper Co., Greene Cananea Copper Co. Anaconda Copper Mining Co., etc.; dir. Phelps Dodge Corp. Trustee Calif. Inst. Technology. Author: The Ores of Leadville and Their Mode of Occurrence, 1883; Geological Reports of Wyoming, 1888-90. Home: Pasadena, Calif. Died Mar. 4, 1940.

RICKETTS, PALMER CHAMBERLAINE, engineer, educator; b. Elkton, Md., Jan. 17, 1856; s. Palmer C. and Elizabeth (Getty) R.; C.E., Rensselaer Poly. Inst., 1875; E.D., Stevens Inst., 1905; LL.D., New York U., 1911; m. Miss Viera Conine Renshaw, Nov. 12, 1902. Instr., 1875-82, asst. prof., 1882-84, prof. tech. mechanics, 1884, dir., 1892-1901, pres. and dir., Feb. 1901—, Rensselaer Poly. Inst. Served as bridge engr., Rome, Watertown & Ogdensburg R.R. Co., 1887-91; engr. Pub. Improvement Commn., Troy, 1891-92; engr. River Commn., Corning, N.Y., 1897-98; expert in patent cases, 1886-97; dir. Nat. City Bank. Trustee and v.p. Troy Pub. Library; trustee Dudley Observatory (Albany), Albany Acad., Albany Med. Coll., N.Y. State College for Teachers; dir. Samaritan Hosp. Comdr. Order of the Crown of Italy; Comdr. Legion of Honor (France). Author: History of Rensselaer Polytechnic Institute, 2d edit., 1914. Home: Troy, N.Y. Died Dec. 10, 1934.

RICKETTS, PIERRE DE PEYSTER, chemist; E.M., Columbia, 1871, Ph.D., 1876. Asst. in mineralogy, 1871-72, assaying, 1872-77, instr., 1877-85, prof., 1885-93, prof. analytical chemistry and assaying, 1893-1900, Columbia U.; consulting chem. engr., New York, 1900—. Fellow A.A.A.S., N.Y. Acad. Sciences. Home: New York, N.Y. Died Nov. 20, 1918.

RICKEY, JAMES WALTER, hydraulic engr.; b. Dayton, O., Nov. 10, 1871; s. James and Rosaltha Jane (Jones) R.; C.E., Rensselaer Poly. Inst., 1894; m. Lucy Amelia Mitchell, Jan. 24, 1899. Began as accountant, N.P. Ry., Minneapolis, 1894; prin. asst. engr. Lake Superior Power Corp., Sault Ste. Marie, Mich., 1896-97, St. Anthony Falls Water Power Co., and Minneapolis Mill Co., 1897-1907; chief hydraulic engr. Aluminum Co. of America, Pittsburgh, Pa., 1907-38, now cons. engr.; has designed and constructed large dams in the states of N.C., N.Y., Tenn., also Chute a Caron Dam, 200 ft. high, and 260,000 h.p. power-house, on Saguenay River, near Kenogami, Que. (the first stage of one of the largest hydro-electric developments in the world), 1927-30. Dir. Pittsburgh Branch, Pa. Assn. for Blind; mem. Engrs. Soc. of Western Pa. (dir.), Am. Soc. Civ. Engrs., Engring. Inst. of Can., Internat. Commn. on Large Dams (Am. Tech. Com.), Rensselaer Soc. of Engrs., Sigma Xi, Theta Nu Epsilon. Republican. Presbyterian. Contbr. tech. articles to mags. Home: 2101 Connecticut Av., Washington, D.C. Office: 801 Gulf Bldg., Pittsburgh, Pa. Died Apr. 19, 1943.

RICORD, PHILIPPE, physician; b. Balt., Dec. 10, 1800; M.D. from med. sch. Paris, France, 1826. Became surgeon to Central Bur., Paris, 1828; surgeon-in-chief for syphilis Hopital du Midi, 1831-61; established a rational therapy of syphilis and gave laws of transmission of disease in precise terms, 1834; demonstrated that gonorrhea is entirely distinct from syphilis; recieved Monthyon prize for devising a new method of curing varicocele and a spl. technique in urethroplasty; became mem. Acad. Medicine in Paris, 1850, pres., 1868; became ofcl. surgeon to Prince Napoleon, 1852, later to Emperor Napoleon III; of cons. surgeon to imperial troops; dir. Lazaretto (instn. for care of needy and ailing poor) during Siege of Paris; decorated officer Legion d'Honeur by Thiers (1st pres. 3d Republic of France). Author: De la Blennorrhagie de la Femme, 1834; Monographic du Chancre, 1837; Traite pratique maladies veneriennes (treatise on venereal disease) 1838; Lettress sur la Syphillis, 1851; Lecons sur le Chancre, 1857. Died Paris, Oct. 22, 1889.

RIDDELL, GUY CROSBY, mining, metall. engr.; b. Charlestown, Mass., 1882; s. Robert Hugh and Anne Otis (Daggett) R.; B.Sc., Mass. Inst. Tech.; m. Isabel Anderson Southgate; children—Robert Southgate, Virginia Gay. With Am. Smelting & Refining Co., supt. lead smelting plant, Mont., 1910-16; cons. mining, metall. and petroleum Engr., 1916-53, in Eng., Can., Germany, Poland, Australia, Russia, China, Japan, Alaska, Mexico, Central and S.Am., Korea, and U.S.A. Cons. engr., Broken Hill Asso. Smelters, Australia, 1916-17, directing reorgn., modernization world's largest lead smeltery, Port Pirie; cons. U.S. Tariff Commn., 1918-20; dir. and Am. mgr. Wah Chang Trading Corp., 1920-23; chief minerals and petroleum div. U.S. Dept. Commerce, 1924-25; Dept. Commerce rep. on Fed. Oil Conservation Bd., 1925; mining and petroleum trips to Panama and Venezuela, financial mission to Eng., 1926-29; cons. engr. to Soviet govt. (depts. of NKRKI, Rare Metals, Natural Gas Trust), for rationalization of existing mining, oil, and rare metal industries throughout U.S.S.R., 1930-33; cons. for creation Russian helium industry, 1933-35; surveys of Russian potash, sulphur, nickel and petroleum industries for Am. corps., 1935. Cons., gen. supt. gold placer and lode mines, Sinaloa and Chihuahua, Mex., Cal., Ariz., Colo., Mont., Can., 1936-42. Cons. to U.S. govt. depts., 1943-46; Washington (Bd. Econ. Warfare, Fgn. Econ. Adminstr.). Advisor to F.E.A. and Chinese Govt on Five Year Plan for mining and metallurgical industries, 1945; research adminstr., Dept. Commerce, 1946-47; mining advisor U.S. Mil. Govt., Korea, 1947-48; cons. U.S. Bur. Mines, 1950-51. Mem. Sr. Cons., Inc., N.Y.C. Mem. Inst Mining and Metallurgy (Gt. Britain), Mining and Metall. Soc. Am., Am. Inst. Mining and Metall. Engrs., Pan-Am. Inst. Mining and Geology. Editor and author publs. relating to field. Home: 527 S. Washington St., Easton, Md. Died July 19, 1959.

RIDDELL, JOHN LEONARD, physician, scientist; b. Leyden, Mass., Feb. 20, 1807; s. John and Lephe (Gates) R.; grad. Rensselaer Sch., Troy, N.Y., 1829; M.D., Cincinnati Med. Coll., 1836; Adjunct prof. chemistry and botany Cincinnati Med. Coll., 1835-36; published Synopsis of the Flora of the Western States, 1835; prof. chemistry Med. Coll. of La., 1836-65; published Catalogus Florae Ludovicianae (catalogue of La. plants), 1852; apptd. by Pres. Van Buren as melter and refiner in branch of U.S. Mint, 1838/39-49; mem. commn. to devise means of protection for New Orleans against Mississippi River, 1844; later discovered microscopial characteristics of blood and black vomit in yellow fever; devised binocular microscope, 1851, instrument finished and sent to him, 1854; active mem. 1st La. State Med. Soc. (founded 1849), New Orleans Physico-Medico Soc. Died New Orleans, Oct. 7, 1865.

RIDDLE, LINCOLN WARE, botanist; b. Boston, Mass., Oct. 17, 1880; s. Charles W. and Mary (Ware) R.; A.B., Harvard, 1902, A.M., 1905, Ph.D., 1906; m. Gertrude Hollister Paine, June 7, 1906. Asst. in botany, 1902, Austin teaching fellow, 1905-06, Harvard; instr. in botany, 1906-09, asso. prof., 1909-18, prof., 1918-19, Wellesley; asst. prof. cryptogamic botany, and asso. curator Cryptogamic Herbarium, Harvard, 1919—. Fellow Am. Acad. Arts and Sciences, A.A.A.S. Home: Cambridge, Mass. Died Jan. 16, 1921.

RIDDLE, OSCAR, biologist; b. Cincinnati, Ind., Sept. 27, 1877; s. Jonathan and Amanda Emiline (Carmichael) R.; A.B., Ind. U., 1902, LL.D., 1933; Ph.D., U. Chgo., 1907; D.H.C., Cath. U. of Chile, 1946; m. Leona Lewis, June 3, 1937. Tchr. biology Model and Tng. Sch., San Juan, P.R., 1899-1901; mem. natural history expdn. to Orinoco River, 1901, Cuba, 1902; tchr. physiology Central High Sch., St. Louis, 1903-05; asst. in zoology U. Chgo., 1904-07, asso. in zoology and exptl. therapeutics, 1908, instr., 1908-11; travel and study in Europe, 1910-11; research asso. at Chicago and Cold Spring Harbor, Carnegie Instn., 1912-14; research staff Carnegie Sta. for Exptl. Evolution, 1914-45; lectr. S.A. and Mexico, 1945-47. Chmn. Am. delegations 2d Internat. Congress for Sex Research, London, 1930; del. Carnegie Instn. to 2d Pan-Am. Congress of Endocrinology, Montevideo, 1941. Capt. with U.S. Army, 1918-19. Recipient humanist of yr. award Am. Humanist Assn., 1958, distinguished service certificate award National Association of Biology Teachers, 1958. Fellow of the A.A.A.S. (vice pres. 1935), American Acad. Arts and Scis., fgn. corr. Academia Nacional de Medicina, Buenos Aires, Soc. de Patologia Clinica, Brazil, Soc. de Biologia, Montevideo and Santiago, Physiological Soc. of India, Facultad de Ciencias Biologicas y Medicas, Santiago; hon. mem. Societa Italiana di Endocrinologia, Royal Soc. Arts London; mem. Soc. Linneenne de Lyon, Am. Philos. Soc., Nat. Acad. Scis., Am. Soc. Zoologists, Am. Physiol. Soc., Genetics Soc. Am., Am. Soc. Naturalists, Washington Acad. Scis., Soc. for Study of Evolution, Assn. for Study of Internal Secretions (pres. 1928-29), Soc. Exptl. Biology and Medicine, Harvey Soc., Nat. Inst. Social Scis., American Rationalist Fedn. (president 1959-60), Am. Inst. City N.Y. (trustee, v.p.; gold medal 1934), Sigma Xi, Pi Gamma Mu, Phi Delta Theta, Gamma Alpha. Author: The Unleashing of Evolutionary Thought (awarded 2 first prizes), 1955. Contbr. papers on physiology of development and reproduction, physiol. and chem. basis of sex, heredity, endocrinology. Sect. editor Biol. Abstracts, 1926-46; Excerpta Medica, 1946-68; mem. publ. bd. Endocrinology, 1931-34, 39-42. Home: Plant City FL Died Nov. 29, 1968; buried Grandview Cemetery, Bloomfield IN

RIDENOUR, LOUIS N(ICOT), JR., physicist; b. Montclair, N.J., Nov. 1, 1911; s. Louis Nicot and Clare (Wintersteen) R.; B.S., U. of Chicago, 1932; Ph.D., Calif. Inst. Tech., 1936; m. Gretchen Hickley Kraemer, June 18, 1934; 2 daus., Eleanor, Nancy Page. With Inst. for Advanced Study, Princeton, N.J., 1935-36; instr. Princeton U., 1936-38; asst. prof., U. of Pa., 1938-41, asso. prof., 1941-46, prof. 1946-47; prof. physics, dean Grad. Coll., U. of Ill., 1947-51, on leave as spl. asst. to Sec. of Air Force, 1950-51; dir. of research for Missile Systems div. Lockheed Aircraft Corp., 1956-59, v.p. in charge electronics and avionics div., 1959—; v.p. Internat. Telemeter Corp. Cons., Sec. of War, 1942-46, radar adviser U.S. Strategic War Forces in Europe, 1944, member radar committee, Combined Chiefs Staff, 1943-45; mem. div. 5, div. 15, Nat. Defense Research Com. Awarded Bronze Star; President's Medal for Merit. Fellow Am. Phys. Soc., A.A.A.S. (councillor), Institute of Radio Engrs.; mem. Phi Beta Kappa, Sigma Xi. Clubs: Cosmos (Washington); University (Chgo.). Contbr. articles on mil. and sci. subjects to various publs. Editor-in-chief Radiation Lab. Series of 27 tech. vols. Editor Radar System Engineering, 1947, Modern Physics for the Engineer, 1954. Home: 1425 University Av., Palo Alto, Cal. Office: Missile Systems div. Lockheed Aircraft Corp., Sunnyvale, Cal. Died May 21, 1959.

RIDGWAY, ARTHUR OSBOURNE, (rij'wa), engineer; b. Lawrence, Kan., Feb. 23, 1870; s. Robert M. and Sarah (Schimmel) R.; B.Sc., U. of Kan., 1892; m. Mary Rayhawk, May 18, 1905; children—Louise, Dorothy. Draftsman D.&R.G. R.R. Co., 1892-93; with Bellefontaine (O.) Bridge & Iron Co., 1893-94; again with D.&R.G. Ry. Co. successively as instrumentman, 1895, asst. div. engr., 1895-98, acting div. engr. and div. engr., 1898-1902, in charge design and constrn. steel bridges; locating engr. in charge constrn. R.G.&Southwestern R.R., 1903-04; gen. supt. maintenance and operation Silverton Ry. and Silverton Northern Ry. (branches of D.&R.G.), 1904-05; office engr. and acting engr. bridges and buildings, D.&R.G. R.R. Co., 1905-08, asst. chief engr., 1909-23, also chmn. valuation com., 1913-23, and safety officer, 1918-23, D.&R.G. and associate cos.; chief engr. D.&R.G. Western Ry. System, 1923-1941, also Denver Union Terminal Railway Co., Salt Lake Union Depot & Railway Co. and Denver & Salt Lake Western R.R. Co., engring. consultant same companies, 1941-48. Awarded Colo. Engring. Councils' gold medal, 1940. Mem. Am. Soc. C.E. (life), Am. Ry. Bridge and Bldg. Assn. (ex-pres.), Colo. Engring. Council (ex-pres.), Am. Ry. Engring. Assn. (life), Colo. Sci. Soc. (hon. life), Sigma Xi, Tau Beta Pi, Chi Epsilon; fellow A.A.A.S. Republican. Presbyterian. Author of History of Transportation in Colorado, Effects of Route Characteristics on Cost of Rail Transportation; The Figure of the Earth; Arkansas River Flood of 1921; The Mission of Colorado Toll Roads; Engineering in Colorado (inc. in History of Colorado), 1947. Home: Olin Hotel, Denver 3. Died Jan. 18, 1953.

RIDGWAY, ROBERT, ornithologist; b. Mt. Carmel, Ill., July 2, 1850; s. David and Henrietta James (Reed) R.; common schs.; hon. M.S., Ind. U., 1884; m. Julia E. Perkins, Oct. 12, 1875; 1 son, Audubon Wheelock (dec.). Zoölogist, U.S. Geol. Exploration of 40th Parallel (under Clarence King), in Calif., Nev., Southern Idaho, and Utah, 1867-69; curator, div. of birds, U.S. Nat. Museum, July 1, 1880—. Mem. permanent ornithol. com. First Internat. Congress, Vienna, 1885; hon. mem. 2d Congress Ornithologique Internat., Budapest, 1891; mem. com. of patronage Internat. Congress of Zoölogy, London, 1897. Mem. various societies. Author: A History of North American Birds (5 vols., with Prof. Spencer F. Baird and Dr. Thomas M. Brewer); A Manual of North American Birds; A Nomenclature of Colors for Naturalists and Compendium of Useful Information for Ornithologists; Color Standards and Color Nomenclature; The Ornithology of Illinois (2 vols.); The Birds of North and Middle America (8 vols. published). Home: Olney, Ill. Died Mar. 25, 1929.

RIDGWAY, ROBERT, civil engr.; b. Brooklyn, N.Y., Oct. 19, 1862; s. Joseph Skidmore and Margaret (Stephens) R.; ed. pub. schs. and at home; hon. A.M., Harvard, 1925; hon. M.S. in C.E., New York U., 1915, and C.E., same, 1919; D.Eng., Lehigh U., 1929; D.Eng., Brooklyn Poly. Institute, 1933; m. Lillie A. Littell, May 10, 1888 (died 1927); m. 2d, Isabel L. Law, Sept. 15, 1928. Chainman, rodman and leveler, Northern Pacific Railroad, in Montana and Wisconsin, 1882-84; entered employ Aqueduct Commn., N.Y. City, 1884; asst. engr. constrn. aqueduct and various reservoirs and dams, 1886-1900; with Rapid Transit Commn., 1900-05, as asst. engr., later div. engr. in charge constrn. South Ferry Loop, tunnels under East River, from South Ferry to Joralemon St., Brooklyn, and various subways in Brooklyn; with Bd. of Water Supply for N.Y. City, 1905-12, as div. engr., later dept. engr. in charge location and constrn. of Catskill Aqueduct work including upper 60 miles of the aqueduct and Hudson River crossing at Storm King, approximate cost $30,000,000 (aqueduct drops vertically 1200 feet down shaft, crosses, under Hudson River and rises in shaft on opposite side); engr. of subway constrn. for Pub. Service Commn., 1st Dist., New York, and its successors, Transit Constrn. Commn. and Transit Commission, 1912-21; in charge of rapid transit constrn. in N.Y. City, estimated cost of work more than $300,000,000; apptd. chief engr. Transit Commn., May 1921; in charge of all engring. work of commn. in connection with new constrn. and maintenance of rapid transit lines in dual system of rapid transit for N.Y. City; apptd., July 1924, chief engr. Bd. Transportation, City of New York, in charge of all rapid transit design and construction in the city; apptd. consulting engr. same bd., 1932, retired, Dec. 16, 1933; cons. engr. Port of N.Y. Authority, Dec. 1933—; mem. Chicago Traction and Subway Commn., by apptmt. of City Council of Chicago, 1916-17, commn. reported upon and made recommendations for improvement of local transit conditions; chmn. bd. engrs. Trans-Bay Bridge, San Francisco, 1927; mem. Colorado River Bd. for Boulder Canyon Dam, 1928-32; cons. engr. Rapid Transit Subways, City of Chicago, 1930-31; cons. engr. rapid transit studies City of San Francisco, 1935. Decorated Order of the Rising Sun, 3d class (Japan), 1929. Home: New York, N.Y. Died Dec. 19, 1938.

RIES, ELIAS ELKAN, inventor; b. Baden, Germany, Jan. 16, 1862; s. Elkan Elias and Bertha (Weil) R.; brought to U.S. at age of 3; ed. pub. schs., New York and Baltimore; tech. instrn. at Md. Inst., Baltimore; physical sciences, Johns Hopkins; m. Helen Hirshberg, Apr. 21, 1895. Elec., mech. and tech. engr.; has taken out over 250 patents. Principal pioneer inventions: The underground electric ry. conduit or "sub-trolley" system; the modern urban and long-distance alternating-current system of generation, transmission and conversion of electricity for operating electric railways, by which the earlier restrictions of the 500-volt trolley systems were successfully overcome, and which has made possible the operation of rapid-transit elevated, subway and tunnel systems now operating in N.Y. City and elsewhere, and the electrification of suburban and long distance steam rys.; also the original automatic electric motor-starters; the Ries regulating socket, the first practical device for "turning down" the light of incandescent lamps without wasteful resistance; the controller system used on electric elevators; original methods and apparatus for electric welding, riveting, soldering, metal working, etc.; methods and appliances for electric heating and cooking; telephone, phonograph and tele-phonograph systems; original processes and apparatus for mfg. iron and steel tubes from the hot billets in one continuous operation; the first practical self-starting electric motors adapted to operate on single-phase alternating current circuits; original methods and apparatus for producing talking motion pictures directly from the film; new methods and appliances for detecting the presence of unseen vessels, icebergs, etc., in fog, as well as locating and following position of hostile aircraft and submarines and also for the precise location and salvage of sunken vessels directly from the surface, by means of a novel electro-acoustic range-finder, indicating and signalling apparatus, which effectively accomplishes for the ears, in the domain of sound, what the binocular telescope has done for the eyes. Submarine detector and other inventions offered to U.S. Govt., 1917. Fellow A.A.A.S. Mason. Pres. Am. Audioscope Co. Home: New York, N.Y. Died Apr. 20, 1928.

RIES, HEINRICH, (res), geologist; b. Bklyn., Apr. 30, 1871; s. Heinrich and Caroline Bowman (Atkins) R.; Ph.B., Columbia, 1892, A.M., 1894, Ph.D., 1896; Sc.D. (hon.) Alfred U., 1945; m. Millie Timmerman, July 1, 1893; (dec.); children—Victor H., Donald T.; m. 2d, Adelyn Halsey Gregg, June 7, 1948. On N.Y. geol. survey, 1891-92; asst. geologist summer of 1895; lectr. pub. schs. N.Y., 1895-97; asst. in mineralogy, Columbia, 1896-97; instr. econ. geology, Cornell U., 1898-1902, asst. prof., 1902-05, prof., 1905-39, head dept., 1914-37, emeritus prof. 1939—. Asst. dir. N.Y. sci. exhibits, Chgo. Expn., 1893; mem. jury of awards, Cotton States and Internat. Expn., 1896, Buffalo Expn., 1901, St. Louis Expn. 1904. Del. Geol. Congress, St. Petersburg, 1897, Internat. Geol. Congress, Paris, 1900, Mexico, 1906, Toronto, 1913, Washington, 1933; Fellow. Am. Geog. Soc., Am. Mineral. Soc., A.A.A.S., Seismol. Soc., British Ceramic Soc., Soc. Econ. Geologists; mem. Am. Ceramic Soc. (hon., pres. 1910-11); Am. Foundrymens Assn., (tech. dir., hon.), Rochester Acad. Sci.; Ky. Acad. Sci.; Geol. Soc. Am. (1st v.p. 1925-26, pres. 1928-29); Am. Inst. Mining Engrs. (life mem.); Can. Mining Inst. (life mem.). Author: Economic Geology; Clay, Occurrence, Properties and Uses; History of Clay Working Industry of United States (with H. Leighton); Building Stones and Clay Products; Engineering Geology (with T. L. Watson); Elements of Engineering Geology (with same); Elementary Economic Geology; Conservation in United States (with others). Has published reports on clays of N.Y., Ala., La., Fla., N.C., Mich., Md., Colo., N.J., Va., Tex., Wis., Can., in state geologists' and govt. reports. Contbr. articles on geology and mining, Internat. Year-book, 1898-1901, articles on geology, New International Encyclopaedia. Address: 401 Thurston Av., Ithaca, N.Y. Died Apr. 11, 1951.

RIESENBERG, FELIX, author, engineer; b. Milwaukee, Wis., Apr. 9, 1879; s. William and Emily (Schorb) R.; ed. pub. schs. and at sea; master mariner, sail and steam; C.E., Columbia, 1911; m. Maud Conroy of Queenstown, Ireland, June 29, 1912; children—Felix Jr., William, Margaret, John. At sea, sail and steam, 1896-1907, on voyages to many parts of the world; officer U.S. Coast and Geodetic Survey, 1901-02, Wellman Polar Expdn., 1906-07; wintered at Dane's Island, Spitzbergen, in charge of camp; navigator Airship America in first attempt to reach North Pole by dirigible balloon, Sept. 1907; lt. comdr. U.S.N.R.; comdr. U.S.S. Newport, barkentime, schoolship service, 1917, 18, 19; 2d tour of duty, 1923-24. Made record passage, sail, Santa Cruze de Tenerife to New London, 26 days, Sept. 1923. Asst. dept. of buildings and grounds, Columbia U., 1911; asst. engr. Catskill Aqueduct constrn., 1912-13; chief engr. Dept. of Parks, Queens, N.Y., 1914-15; asst. engr. Bur. of Bldgs., Manhattan, 1916-17; resident engr. Columbia-Presbyn. Med. Center (constrn. work), N.Y. City, 1925-27; v.p., consulting engineer Martin Motors, Inc. Author: Under Sail, 1915; The Men on Deck, 1918; Standard Seamanship, 1922; Bob Graham at Sea, 1925; P.A.L. (novel), 1925; Vignettes of the Sea, 1926; East Side, West Side (novel), 1927; Red Horses (novel), 1928; Shipmates, 1928; Endless River, 1931; Passing Strangers, 1932; Clipper Ships, 1932; Log of the Sea, 1933; Early Steamships, 1933; Mother Sea (novel), 1933; The Left Handed Passenger (novel), 1935; Living Again (autobiography), 1936; Portrait of New York, 1938. Home: New York, N.Y. Died Nov. 19, 1939.

RIETHMULLER, RICHARD HENRI, (ret'mul-er), oral surgeon; b. Erzingen, Germany, Apr. 20, 1881; s. Carl L. and Minna (Oeffinger) R.; grad. Royal Carls-Gymnasium, Heilbronn, 1895; Royal Theol. sems., Maulbronn and Blaubeuren, 1899; U. of Grenoble, 1900; Royal Eberhard fellowship, U. of Tübingen, 1901; U. of Berlin, 1904; Harrison research fellow, U. of Pa., 1905-06, Ph.D., 1905; Medico-Chirurg. Coll., 1911; D.D.S., 1913; m. Eleanor Brunswick, Feb. 11, 1911; 1 dau., Thea Angelica; m. 2d, Lucy Doraine, Nov. 30, 1928. Instr. in German, 1905-07, lecturer in German lit., 1907-09, Univ. of Pa.; asso. editor Dental Cosmos, 1908-16; demonstrator, dental dept., Medico-Chirurg. Coll., Phila., 1913-16; instr. local anesthesia, Post-Grad. Sch. of Dentistry of Phila., 1914-16; attending oral surgeon, Lenox Hill Hosp., and oral surgeon, N.Y. Throat, Nose and Lung Hosp., 1916-17; instr. Post-Grad. Sch. Dentistry (Columbia), 1916-18; lecturer on oral hygiene, L.I. Hosp. Coll., 1916-18; prof. of anaesthesia, U. of Southern Calif. Coll. of Dentistry, since 1920; prof.

stomatology, Coll. of Med. Evangelists, since 1923. Fellow A.M.A.; mem. Am. Dental Assn., Southern Calif. dental assns., Los Angeles County Dental Soc., Psi Omega; honorary mem. Eastern Dental Soc., Los Angeles County Dental Soc., Southwestern Dental Soc. Author: (articles) Walt Whitman and the Germans, 1904; Gleim's Imitations of the Middle High German Minnesong, 1905; The All-Porcelain Jacket Crown, 1905; Local Anesthesia in Dentistry, 1914; The Kinematograph, A Future Adjunct in Teaching Dentistry, 1914; Further Studies on Novocain-Suprarenin Anesthesia, 1915; Anoci-Association in Dentistry, 1915; Pyorrhea Alveolaris and Its Cure, 1915; Causes of Failures in Conduction Anesthesia, 1918; Oral Tumors, 1919; Anesthesia in Children's Work, 1924; The Reality of Focal Infections, 1925; Specific Treatment of Infectious Mouth Lesions, 1926; Removal of Impacted Third Molars as a Prophylactic Measure, 1926; Novocain-Cobefrin Solution in Local Anesthesia, 1936; George Washington and His Dentist, John Greenwood, 1937; The Dental Centenary Celebration, 1939; War Oral Surgery, 1940; Novocain-Pontocain-Cobefrin, 1941. Translator: Fischer's Dental Anesthesia, 1911. Contbr. to Am. Year Book. Home: 627 S. St. Andrews Pl. Office: 122 E. 16th St., Los Angeles, Calif. Deceased.

RIGGE, WILLIAM FRANCIS, astronomer; b. Cincinnati, Sept. 9, 1857; s. Frederick and Elizabeth (Zeppenfeld) R.; ed. St. Xavier Coll., Cincinnati, 1870-75; St. Louis U., 1881-82; Woodstock (Md.) Coll., 1882-84, and 1887-91; Ph.D., Georgetown U., D.C., 1896. Joined Soc. of Jesus, 1875; ordained priest R.C. Ch., 1890; held professorships various colleges; dir. Creighton U. Obs. and prof. astronomy and physics, 1896—. Fellow Royal Astron. Soc. A.A.A.S. Author: The Graphic Construction of Eclipses and Occultations, 1924. Specialty occultation and eclipse maps; in a notable criminal case, designated the time a photograph was taken, from a shadow in the picture. Died Mar. 31, 1927.

RIGGINS, H. MCLEOD, physician; b. Charlotte, N.C., Nov. 30, 1900; s. Charles Robert and Eleanor (De Armond) R.; B.S., U. of N.C., 1922; M.D., Jefferson Med. Coll., 1924; m. Mildred Kimberly, November 16, 1929; children—Robert C.K., Anne Kimberly. Intern. Phila. Gen. Hosp., 1924; asst. physician Loomis Sanatorium, Loomis, N.Y., 1926-29; resident physician Bellevue Hosp., Chest Service, N.Y. City, 1929; chief resident physician Bellevue Hosp. Chest Service, 1931, 1932; vis. physician Columbia U. Div. Bellevue Hosp.; attending physician N.Y. Eye and Ear Infirmary; formerly asso. clin. prof. medicine Coll. Physicians and Surgeons, Columbia U.; med. dir. N.Y. Cancer Research Inst., 1959-68. Head U.S. delegation XVI Conf. Internat. Union Against Tb, Istanbul, Turkey, 1959; del. Nat. Health Council. Fellow N.Y. Acad. Medicine (chmn. hist. and cultural sect. 1959-61); mem. Am. Thoracic Soc. (past v.p. and pres.), New York Soc. for Thoracic Surgery (past sec.-treas., v.p. and pres.), New York Tb. and Health Assn. (mem. bd. dirs.), Nat. Tb. Assn. (pres. 1959-60), Am. Assn. for Thoracic Surgery, N.Y. County Med. Soc., N.Y. State Med. Soc., Am. Med. Assn., Am. Coll. Physicians, Am. Clin. and Climatol. Assn., N.Y. Acad. Medicine, Bellevue Alumni Assn., Kappa Psi. Presbyterian. Club: University, River (New York City). Co-editor of Streptomycin and Dihydrostreptomycin in Tb., 1949. Author numerous papers and articles in various med. and sci. jours. Home: Mercer Island WA Died Apr. 1973.

RIGGS, HENRY EARLE, civil engr.; b. Lawrence, Kan., May 8, 1865; s. Judge Samuel Agnew and Catharine (Earle) R.; A.B., U. of Kan., 1886; C.E., U. of Mich., 1910; Dr. Engring., 1937; m. Emma King, d. late S. B. Hynes, Oct. 1, 1890; children—Ellen (Mrs. Stratford B. Douglas), Genevieve (Mrs. William B. Thom, dec.), Samuel H., Emma (Mrs. George L. Ohrstrom), Joseph A., Catherine (Mrs. James Mann Miller), Finley B. With engring. dept. Burlington and A.T.&S.F. rys., 1886-90; chief engr. Toledo, Ann Arbor—& N. Mich. Ry., 1890-96; in pvt. practice as consulting and designing engr. as mem. Riggs & Sherman, 1896-1912; prof. and head dept. of civ. engring., U. of Mich., May 1, 1912-June 30, 1930, hon. prof. civ. engring. since 1930; retired; acted as cons. engr. in various cases for railroad commissions of several states and for cities in a number of states, 1916-21; cons. engr. on railroad grade separation for city of Detroit, 1915-20. Has devoted much time since 1920 to the subject of depreciation in connection with railroads, electric and gas utilities. In connection with valuation and recapture proceedings has represented a number of carriers, including Ill. Central System, N.Y. Central System, Union Pacific System, Frisco, Norfolk & Western, Virginian and Chesapeake & Ohio. Has also been retained in cases involving Detroit Edison Company, Alabama Power Company, Georgia Power Company, Carolina Power and Light Co., South Carolina Power Co. Mem. Bd. of Edn., Maumee, O., 1900-11, Ann Arbor, 1916-25. Mem. John Fritz Medal Board of Award, 1939-42, chmn., 1941. Mem. Am. Soc. C.E. (dir. 1932-34, v.p. 1935-36, president 1938; made honorary member 1941), Engineering Institute of Canada, American Inst. Cons. Engrs., Am. Ry. Engring. Assn., Engring. Soc. of Detroit, Am. Soc. for Engring. Edn.; hon. mem. Mich. Engring. Soc. (past pres.), Sigma Xi, Tau Beta Pi, Phi Kappa Phi, Phi Gamma Delta. Republican. Congregationalist. Club: Detroit (Detroit). Author: Depreciation, 1922; Principles of Railway Engineering (with W. G. Raymond and W. C. Sadler), 1937; Our Pioneer Ancestors. Vol. I, 1942, Vol. II, 1943; American Ancestors of Margaret Thom, 1945; The Troublesome Problem of Depreciation, 1947; also papers on different phases of regulation of public service property. Address: care Dept. Engring., Univ. of Mich., Ann Arbor, Mich. Died July 5, 1949.

RIGGS, JOHN MANKEY, dentist; b. Seymour, Conn., Oct. 25, 1810; s. John and Mary (Beecher) R.; A.B., Trinity Coll., Hartford, Conn., 1837; attended Jefferson Med. Coll., Phila. Prin., Brown Sch. (now 1st Dist. Sch. of Hartford), circa 1837-39; studied dentistry with Dr. Horace Wells, began practice circa 1840; extracted a tooth from a patient who was under influence of nitrous oxide gas (laughing gas) (becoming one of pioneers in use of modern anesthesia), 1844; interested in scientific agr., spoke at agrl. soc. meetings; strong advocate of hygienic care of mouth; specialist in treatment of pyorrhea alreolaris which he first demonstrated at conv. Am. Dental Assn., 1865; joined Conn. Valley Dental Assn., 1865, pres. 1871-72; pres. Conn. State Dental Assn., 1867, mem. com. of Conn. State Dental Assn. that succeeded in having statue of Horace Wells erected at Hartford, 1874; mem. Am. Dental Assn.; attended 7th Internat. Med. Congress, London, Eng., 1881. Died Nov. 11, 1885.

RIGGS, LOUIS WARNER, chemist; b. Georgetown, Me., Apr. 13, 1862; s. John Alexander and Sarah Ann Maria (White) R.; B.M.E., U. of Me., 1885; Ph.B., Ill. Wesleyan U., 1887, A.M., Ph.D., 1894; m. Alice Jane Merrill, of Cumberland, Me., June 27, 1889. Instr. sciences, Greely Inst., Cumberland, Me., 1885-86, chemistry and physics, Mt. Hermon (Mass.) Sch., 1887-89, sciences, Englewood (N.J.). Sch. for Boys, 1890-93, chemistry, Med. Dept., New York U., 1893-98, chemistry, Med. Dept., Cornell U., New York, since 1899. Mem. Am. Chem. Soc., Maine Soc. of New York. Unitarian. Author: Elementary Manual for the Chemical Laboratory, 1904. Home: Flushing, N.Y. Address: 414 E. 26th St., New York, N.Y.

RIGGS, NORMAN COLMAN, mathematician; b. Bowling Green, Mo., Nov. 1, 1870; s. James William and Lucretia Smith (Jones) R.; La Grange (Mo.) Coll., 1889-90; B.S. and M.S., U. of Mo., 1895; M.S., Harvard, 1898; m. Jean Augusta Shaefer, Aug. 15, 1905; children—Philip Shaefer, Paul Flood, William Horace. Inst. mathematics, Pa. State Coll., 1899-1902; asst. and asso. prof. mathematics, Armour Inst. Tech., Chicago, 1902-08; asst. prof. mathematics, Carnegie Inst. Tech., 1908-10, asst. prof. and prof. mechanics, 1910-40, prof. emeritus since 1940. Mem. Am. Math. Soc., Math. Assn. America. Am. Assn. Advancement of Science, Phi Beta Kappa, Tau Beta Pi. Author: Analytic Geometry, 1910. Reviser of Hancock's Applied Mechanics for Engineers, 1915; Applied Mechanics, 1930; Strength of Materials (with M. M. Frocht), 1938. Home: R.D. 9, So. Hills, Pittsburgh, Pa. Died July 18, 1943.

RIGGS, ROBERT BAIRD, chemist; b. Hazelwood, Minn., May 22, 1855; s. Stephen Return and Mary A. (Longley) R.; A.B., Beloit Coll., 1876; Ph.D., Göttingen, 1883; Sc.D., Trinity, 1920; m. Maida L. Sisson, June 26, 1895. Chemist U.S. Geol. Survey, 1884-87; prof. chemistry, Nat. Coll. of Pharmacy, 1885-87, Trinity Coll., 1887-1920, retired. Home: Hartford, Conn. Died May 11, 1929.

RIKER, ANDREW LAWRENCE, engineer, inventor; b. N.Y. City, Oct. 22, 1868; s. William J. and Charlotte L. R.; student Columbia U.; m. Edith Whiting, Apr. 9, 1890; children—Edith Whiting, Charlotte Lawrence, Andrew Lawrence. Began as elec. and mech. engr.; was pres. Riker Electric Motor Co.; was designer the Locomobile; designed and built an elec. tricycle, 1884, 4-wheeled elec. motor car, 1895, gasoline car, 1902, car which won Vanderbilt Cup race, 1908; established world's speed record on Long Island for electric cars, 1899, which was held for 10 yrs.; pres. Ventilouvre Co.; apptd. mem. Naval consulting bd., 1915 (chmn. com. on internal combustion motors). Died June 1, 1930.

RIKER, CARROLL LIVINGSTON, mech. engineer; b. Staten Island, N.Y., July 31, 1854; s. Andrew Jackson and Caroline Elizabeth (Tysen) R.; ed. Sheck's Inst., New Brighton, S.I., N.Y., Leonard Inst., Coytesville, N.J., and under pvt. tutors; m. Elizabeth Chipman Carman, of St. Johns, N.B., May 10, 1877. Began in boyhood to study current and wave action in the ocean and rivers; has been granted more than 20 patents for mech. inventions; designed hull of steamboat Castleton at age of 17; designed and built refrigerating warehouses in N.Y. City, 1874 (the first ever built); designed and built, 1887, the most powerful pumping dredge constructed to that time, which was employed in filling Potomac Flats, below Long Bridge, at Washington, D.C.; established, 1882, on the Hudson River, the first factory in the U.S. for mfr. of unfermented grape juice; designed during Spanish-Am. War, 1898, and presented to U.S. Govt. a new type of torpedo that would float at any desired depth, and submitted plan by which a string of these torpedoes could be floated down upon enemy vessels or drawn around them; originator of project to control the Gulf Stream by inducing compulsory deposits of sand on the Grand Banks, by the Labrador Current (bill for appmt. of Govt. Commn. introduced in Congress, 1912); originator of plan for control of the Miss. River, so as to yield a net ann. income of $100,000,000; originator of plan for neutral control of the seas, outlined in joint resolution introduced in Congress, Feb. 1915; a founder, 1914, of Volunteers for Peace, advocating a preliminary continuous conference looking towards peace between belligerent nations in Europe. Home: New York, N.Y. Died May 7, 1931.

RILEY, CHARLES VALENTINE, entomologist; b. Chelsea, London, Eng., Sept. 18, 1843; s. Charles and Mary (Valentine) R.; took incompleted course U. Bonn (Germany); Ph.D. (hon.), Washington U., St. Louis, Mo. State U.; A.M. (hon.), Kan. State Agrl. Coll.; m. Emilie Conzelman. Reporter, artist, editor entomological dept. of Prairie Farmer, Chgo., 1864; served with U.S. Army during latter part of Civil War; founder (with B.D. Walsh) journal Am. Entomologist, 1868; entomologist state of Mo., 1868-77, published 9 annual reports (considered the beginning of science of econ. entomology); influential in securing passage of bill creating U.S. Entomol. Commn., 1877, 1st chief, 1877-78; entomologist to U.S. Dept. Agr. (post grew in size and importance in his adminstrn.), 1878-79, 81-94, began publishing Insect Life, 1889-94; decorated by French Govt. for work on grapevine Phylloxera; hon. mem. Entomol. Soc. of London; 1st pres. Entomol. Soc. of Washington; held honorary position in Nat. Museum. Compiler: bibliography of 1657 individual titles; co-compiler (with Walsh) 479 titles, (with L.O. Howard) 364 titles. Died Sept. 14, 1895.

RILEY, HENRY ALSOP, physician; b. New York, N.Y., July 23, 1887; s. Henry Augustus and Marianna (Littlefield) R.; ed. Collegiate Sch., N.Y., 1904; B.A., Yale, 1908; A.M., Columbia, 1912, M.D., 1912; Sc.D. (honorary), Columbia University, 1959; m. Mary Chapman Edgar, Oct. 6, 1917 (dec.); children—Edgar Alsop, Mary (Mrs. Herbert McCoy Patton, Jr.); m. 2d, Mrs. Sidney P. Henshaw, July 8, 1954. Interne, Presbyterian Hospital, 1913; hosp. appts. at Presbyterian, N.Y. Nursery and Child's, Volunteer, Vanderbilt Clinic, Neurol. Inst., N.Y. Orthopaedic, Post-Graduate, Englewood, Greenwich; pvt. practice in neurology and psychiatry, N.Y. City, 1916-63. Consulting neurologist, Neurol. Inst. of N.Y.; prof. emeritus clin. neurology Coll. of Phys. & Surg., Columbia U.; cons. neurologist, Presbyterian Hospital, N.Y.C. Served with the 105th Machine Gun Bn., Med. Corps. 1917-18; adjutant, N.Y. Neurosurg. Sch., War Dept., 1918. Mem. Med. Adv. Bd., Selective Service System, 1941-45. Decorated Chevalier, Legion of Honor (France), 1949. Honorary mem. Spanish Neurological Society, Italian Neurol. Soc.; corr. mem. Paris Neurol. Soc.; hon. mem. Soc. Neurology and Psychiatry of Rosario, Argentina; corr. mem. Acad. Medicine, Paris; mem. American Neurological Association, Am. Psychiatric Association, Am. Assn. Anatomists, Association Research in Nervous and Mental Disease, N.Y. Acad. of Medicine, Alpha Delta Phi, Sigma Xi, Alpha Omega Alpha. Clubs: University, Union (N.Y.C.). Author of books, including: (with F. Tilney) Form and Functions of the Central Nervous System, 1938; Atlas of the Basal Ganglia, Brain Stem and Spinal Cord, 1943. Home: New York City NY Died Nov. 1, 1966.

RINEHART, JAMES FLEECE, pathologist; b. Oakland, Cal., May 7, 1901; s. James Fleece and Malvina (Raybourne) R.; student Centre Coll., 1920; A.B., U. Cal., 1923, M.D., 1927; m. Marie McCord, Jan. 20, 1930; children—James Fleece, Robert McCord. Intern Alameda Co. Hosp., 1926-27; asst. dept. pathology U. Cal. Med. Sch., 1927-28, instr. pathology, 1929-30, asst. prof., 1931-36, asso. prof. 1936-39 asso. prof. pathology and medicine, 1939-42, prof. pathology, chmn. dept., 1942—; research fellow Thorndike Meml. Lab., Boston, 1930-31. Vice pres. Cal. State Bd. Pub. Health, 1945—. Diplomate Am. Bd. Pathology. Mem. Am. Soc. Exptl. Pathology (pres. 1950), A.A.A.S., A.M.A., Am. Rheumatism Assn., Am. Soc. Clin. Investigation, Am. Assn. Pathologists and Bacteriologists, Soc. Exptl. Biology and Medicine, Alpha Tau Omega, Phi Beta Pi, Alpha Omega Alpha. Club: Bohemian. Home: 259 Bridge Rd., San Mateo, Cal. Office: University of California School of Medicine, San Francisco. Died Nov. 30, 1955.

RINKENBACH, WILLIAM HENRY, chemist; b. Carbon County, Pa., Mar. 17, 1894; s. Leopold and Ellamanda (Oplinger) R.; grad. Perkiomen Sch., Pennsburg, Pa., 1911; A.B., Cornell U., 1915; M.S., U. Pitts., 1922; m. Ruth M. Allender, Feb. 22, 1933. Chemist E. I. du Pont de Nemours & Co., 1915-18; asst. explosives chemist U.S. Bur. Mines, 1919-27; lectr. indsl. chemistry U. Pitts., 1921-23; lectr. popular sci., and travel, 1925-27; asst. chief chemist Picatinny Arsenal, U.S. Dept. Army, Dover, N.J., 1927-29; chief chemist, 1929-43, head chemist 1943-48; holder patents on explosives and chem. processes; leader Carnegie Mus. (Pitts.) Ichthyological Expdn. to Can., 1924-25. Instr. George Sch. Soc. Scis., 1940-48; cons. chemist, 1950—. Fellow A.A.A.S., Am. Inst. Chemists; mem. Am. Chem. Soc., S.A.R., Am. Ordnance Assn., Pa. German Soc., Phi Lambda Upsilon, Sigma Xi. Contbr. sci. articles on explosives to jours. and govt. bulls., also papers on ichtyology and geneal. research, article on explosives in Ency. Chem. Tech., Ency. Chemistry. Recipient Exceptional Civilian Service award. Home: 2010 Cypress Av., R.D. 60, Allentown, Pa. 18103. Died June 29, 1965; buried Indianland Cemetery, Northampton County, Pa.

RIPLEY, CHARLES TRESCOTT, mech. engr.; b. Oak Park, Ill., Apr. 20, 1886; s. Joseph Perce and Harriet (Konantz) R.; B.S. in E.E., U. of Ill., 1909, hon. M.E., 1912; m. Mabel Thomson, Apr. 20, 1918; children—Charles Purcell, Barbara Ann, Trescott. Began with A.,T.&S.F. Ry., Chicago, 1902, chief mech. engr., 1922-38; chief engr. Tech. Bd. Wrought Steel Wheel Industry, 1938-46; now cons. mech. engr. Fellow Am. Soc. M.E.; mem. Sigma Xi, Tau Beta Pi, Eta Kappa Nu, Beta Theta Pi. Republican. Presbyterian. Clubs: Union League, Edgewater. Inventor ry. devices and mfg. machinery. Home: South Laguna, Calif. Died Feb. 6, 1949.

RIPLEY, GILES EMMETT, physicist; b. Adams County, Ind., June 18, 1874; s. John Frazer and Mary Elizabeth (Edwards) R.; B.S., Purdue U., 1899, M.S., 1902; studied U. of Chicago, summers 1907, 08; m. Harriet Louise Marsh, Oct. 18, 1900; children—Vincent Marsh, Kenneth Clay, Mary Pauline. Prof. science, Eastern Ind. Normal Sch., Muncie, Ind., 1899-1900; teacher physics and chemistry, high sch., Racine, Wis., 1900-02, Marquette, Mich., 1904-05; prof. phys. sciences, State Normal Sch., Valley City, N.D., 1905-08; prof. physics and head of dept., U. of Ark., 1908-40, dean of men since 1923, professor of physics, emeritus, since 1940. Pres. and mem. board directors, Vickers Cleaning and Laundry, Inc. Mem. A.A.A.S., Am. Inst. Elec. Engrs., Ark. Science Assn., Central Assn. Science and Mathematics Teachers. Progressive Rep. Methodist. Invented and patented with W. N. Gladson, improved motion picture apparatus; also inventor of new self-closing faucet without packing and springs and other devices, granted patent, 1937. Contbr. on tech. subjects. Home: 7 S. Duncan. Office: 323 W. Dickson, Fayetteville, Ark. Died Jan. 28, 1943.

RIPLEY, JOSEPH, civil engr.; b. St. Clair, Mich., Jan. 3, 1854; s. Volney Abner and Maria (Klein) R.; C.E., U. of Mich., 1876, M.E., 1911; m. Rebecca McNaughton, Feb. 5, 1881 (died 1907); children—Eva, Florence, Alice Maynard; m. 2d, Mary J. Roper, June 23, 1909; 1 son, Joseph (dec.). United States asst. engr., improvement of St. Mary's River, Mich., and St. Mary's Falls Ship Canal, Sault Ste. Marie, 1877-1906, which included building of Weitzel lock, finished 1881, Poe lock, finished in 1896; U.S. asst. engr. in charge survey and preparation of plans and estimates for canal 64 miles long, connecting Birmingham, Ala., with the Black Warrior River, 1897; general supt. St. Mary's Falls Ship Canal, Mich., 1898-1906; mem. consulting bd. internat. engrs., Panama Canal, 1905; prin. asst. engr. Panama Canal, in charge of designing the locks, dams and regulating works, and asst. chief engr. Panama Canal, 1906-07; advisory engr. N.Y. State Dept. Pub. Works, 1907-09; mem. advisory bd. of consulting engrs. N.Y. State Canals, 1909-18; chief engr. Grand Canal Improvement, China, 1918-20; consulting engr., 1920-27. Republican. Methodist. Home: Albany, N.Y. Died Sept. 28, 1940.

RISING, WILLARD BRADLEY, prof. chemistry, Univ. of Calif., 1872—; b. Mechlenburg, N.Y., Sept. 26, 1839; grad. Hamilton Coll., N.Y., 1864; M.E., Univ. of Mich., 1867; Ph.D., Heidelberg, Germany, 1871; instr. in chemistry, 1866-67, and prof. natural sciences, 1867-69, Coll. of Calif. State analyst of Calif., 1885—, also adviser and chemist State bd. of viticulture and State bd. of health. His splty. is thermal chemistry, and he has made a number of important discoveries. During the past 15 yrs. has been the consulting chemist of a large powder co. and has rendered important service in the field of chemistry of explosives. Mem. of jury of award, World's Columbian Expn., 1893, and at Paris Expn., 1900; mem. Assay Commn., Phila., 1903. Home: Berkeley, Calif. Died 1910.

RISLEY, PAUL L(EMUEL), zoologist; b. Elk Rapids, Mich., May 28, 1906; s. Carl Shugart (Rev.) and Laura Maude (Gray) R.; A.B., Albion (Mich.) Coll., 1927; M.S., U. of Mich., 1929, Ph.D., 1931; m. Louise Evelyn Clark, Dec. 31, 1931; children—Barbara Gray, Carolyn Clark. Instr. zoology, U. of Mich., 1930-31; asso., zoology, State U. of Ia., 1931-37, asst. prof., 1937-42, asso. prof., 1942-45; prof. biology, University of Oregon from 1945, chmn. dept. biology, 1945-53. Spl. research fellow Karolinska Inst., Sweden, 1965-66; participant 5th World Congress Fertility and Sterility, Stockholm, 1966, 9th World Congress of Anatomists, Leningrad, USSR, 1970. Mem. Am. Assn. Advancement of Science, Soc. of Reprodn., American Soc. Zoologists, Am. Assn. Anatomists, Am. Soc. Naturalists, Am. Assn. U. Profs., Ore. Acad. Sci., Sigma Xi, Sigma Nu, Phi Sigma, Gamma Alpha. Contbr. articles on embryology, cytology, histology, endocrinology, sex and reproduction in animals in scientific publs. Home: Eugene OR Died May 10, 1971.

RITCHEY, GEORGE WILLIS, astronomer; b. Tuppers Plains, O., Dec. 31, 1864; s. James and Eliza (Gould) R.; U. of Cincinnati, 1883-84, 1886-87; m. Lillie M. Gray, of Cincinnati, Apr. 8, 1886. Instr. manual training, Chicago Manual Training Sch., 1888-96, optician, 1896-99, supt. instrument constrn., Yerkes Obs., 1899-1904; instr. practical astronomy, 1901-94, asst. prof. astonomy, 1904-05, U. of Chicago; astronomer and supt. instrument constrn., Solar Obs., Carnegie Inst., 1905-09; astronomer and engr. in charge of design and constrn. of 60-inch and 100-inch reflecting telescopes, Mt. Wilson Obs. Dir. astrophotographic lab., Observatoire d'Paris, 1924-30. Chevalier Legion d'Honneur, 1928. Co-inventor Ritchey-Chrétien aplanatic type of reflecting telescope; inventor of fixed vertical universal type of reflecting telescope and of cellular type of optical mirrors; designer, 1931, and constructor of 40-inch Ritchey-Chrétien reflecting telescope, U.S. Naval Obs. Address: U.S. Naval Observatory, Washington, D.C.

RITCHIE, JOHN, scientist; b. Boston, Mass., 1853; s. John and Mary (White) R.; grad. English High Sch., Boston, 1869: m. Hattie M. Malcombe, 1885. Was engaged in business with father as builder; retired, 1885; pres. Alvan Clark Corp. (makers telescopes). Asst. at Harvard Coll. Obs., 1882-90. Collector of shells; largest pvt. library of conchology, and one of largest collections of shells in U.S. For 23 yrs. official in charge of collection and distribution of astron. news for U.S. Health commr. City of Boston, 1908-10. Fellow Boston Scientific Soc. (pres. 1908—), Am. Meteorol. Society, Am. Pub. Health Assn. Has done much translating of technical work of scientific and med. investigators into terms understood by the people, and has written hundreds of such articles for Boston, New York and Phila. papers. Asso. editor Am. Journal of Public Health, 1918-21. Author: (with Dr. S. C. Chandler) Science Observer Code, 1888. Home: Malden, Mass. Died July 22, 1939.

RITT, JOSEPH FELS, mathematician; b. New York, N.Y., Aug. 23, 1893; son of Morris and Eva (Steinberg) R.; student Coll. of City of N.Y., 1908-10; A.B., George Washington U., 1913. D.Sc., 1932; Ph.D., Columbia, 1917; m. Estelle Fine, June 29, 1928. Instr. in mathematics, Columbia, 1910-21, asst. prof., 1921-27, asso, prof., 1927-31, prof. since 1931, executive officer, department of mathematics, 1942-45, Davies Prof. Mathematics since July 1, 1945. Master computer ordnance dept., 1918-19. Mem. Nat. Acad. Sciences, Nat. Research Council, 1938-41, Am. Math. Soc. (v.p. 1938-40). Author; Differential Equations from the Algebraic Standpoint, 1932; Theory of Functions, 1947; Integration in Finite Terms, 1948; Differential Algebra, 1950. Contbr. to math. jours. Address: Columbia U., N.Y. City. Died Jan. 5, 1951; buried Mt. Zion Cemetery, Maspeth, L.I., N.Y.

RITTENHOUSE, DAVID, inventor, astronomer, mathematician; b. Paper Mill Run, nr. Germantown, Pa., Apr. 8, 1732; s. Matthias and Elizabeth (Williams) R.; m. Eleanor Colston, Feb. 20, 1766; m. 2d, Hannah Jacobs, 1772; 3 children. Conducted boundary survey for William Penn to settle dispute with Lord Baltimore, 1763-64; designed his orrery (represents motions of bodies of the solar system and illustrates solar and lunar eclipses and other phenomena for a period of 5000 years either forward or back), 1767; experimented on compressibility of water; invented metallic thermometer; published article Easy Method of Deducing The True Time of the Sun's Passing the Meridian, 1770; presented calculations on the transit of Venus that was to occur (1769) to Am. Philos. Soc., 1768; said to have made 1st telescope in Am.; invented collimating telescope (introduced spider threads in eyepiece), 1785; measured grating intervals, deviations of several orders of spectra; experimented on magnetism and electricity; measured barometric effect on a pendulum clock rate and expansion of wood by heat; constructed compensating pendulum, wooden hygrometer; solved math. problem of finding the sum of the several powers of the sines, 1792; published papers Method of Raising the Common Logorithm of any Number, 1795, To Determine the True Place of a Planet, in an Elliptical Orbit, 1796; engaged in boundary surveys and commns. involving Pa., Del., Md., Va., N.Y., N.J., Mass.; conducted canal and river surveys; served on coms. to test specimens of flint glass, to inspect the 1st steam-engine in U.S.; supervised casting of cannon, manufacturer of saltpeter; engr. Council of Safety, 1775, v.p., 1776, pres., 1777; mem. Pa. Gen. Assembly, Pa. Constl. Conv., 1776; trustee loan fund (Pa. loan to Continental Congress); mem. Bd. of War created by Continental Congress; treas. State of Pa.; prof. astronomy, trustee U. Pa.; mem. commn. to organize U.S. Bank; 1st dir. U.S. Mint (apptd. by George Washington), 1792-95; curator, librarian, sec., v.p., pres. (1791-96) Am. Philos. Soc.; fgn. mem. Royal Soc. of London (Eng.). Died Phila., June 26, 1796.

RITTER, LOUIS E., civil engr.; b. Cleveland, O., Mar. 14, 1864; s. Louis and Harriet (Lambert) R.; ed. pub. schs. of Cleveland; B.S., Case Sch. of Applied Science, 1886; m. Mary Stair, 1889; children—Louis Stair, Francis Hamilton. Engaged in surveys and constrn. of Cleveland & Mahoning Valley Ry., 1886-89; U.S. asst. engr. on improvement of Miss. River, 1889-92; engr. with Jenney & Ritter & Mott, cons. civil engrs., 1899-1917; operating as L. E. Ritter, Consulting Engineer, 1917—. Identified with development of steel and reinforced concrete building design and constrn., 1892—. Died July 3, 1934.

RITTER, WILLIAM EMERSON, zoölogist; b. Hampden, Wis., Nov. 19, 1856; s. Horatio and Leonora (Eason) R.; grad. State Normal Sch., Oshkosh, Wis., 1884; B.S., U. of Calif., 1888; A.M., Harvard, 1891, Ph.D., 1893; student Stazione Zoölogica, Naples, Italy, and U. of Berlin, 1894-95; LL.D., U. of Calif., 1932; m. Mary E. Bennett, June 23, 1891. Was teacher in pub. schs., Wis. and Calif.; instr. biology, Univ. of Calif., 1891-93, asst. prof. biology, 1893-98, asso. prof. zoölogy, 1898-1902, apptd. prof., 1902, now emeritus. Ex-dir. Scripps Inst. for Biol. Research (now Scripps Instn. of Oceanography). Pres. Calif. Acad. Sciences, 1898-1900; fellow A.A.A.S. (v.p. sect. F, 1909-10, pres. Pacific div., 1920-21), Am. Acad. Arts and Sciences; mem. Am. Soc. Naturalists, Am. Soc. Zoölogists, Am. Ecol. Soc.; corr. Phila. Acad. Science; hon. pres. Science Service; honorary mem. Phi Beta Kappa (Berkeley chapter). Unitarian. Clubs: Commonwealth (San Francisco); Cosmos (Washington). Author: War, Science and Civilization; The Higher Usefulness of Science and Other Essays; The Probable Infinity of Nature and Life; The Unity of the Organism or the Organismal Conception of Life; and An Organismal Theory of Consciousness; The Scientific Method of Reaching Truth; The Natural History of Our Conduct (with Edna W. Bailey); The Organismal Conception (with same); Why Aristotle Invented the Word Entelecheia; Naturalism vs. Supernaturalism or Man as a Unified Whole and Part of Nature as a Unified Whole; the California Woodpecker and I (sub-title, A Study in Comparative Zoölogy); also of many contbns. to zoöl. and other journals. Home: Hotel Claremont. Address: University of California, Berkeley, Calif. Died Jan. 10, 1944.

RITTMAN, WALTER FRANK, consulting engineer; born at Sandusky, Ohio, December 2, 1883; s. Christian A. and Louisa A. (Scheel) R.; C.E., Ohio Northern U., 1905; A.B., Swarthmore Coll., 1908, M.A., 1909, M.E., 1911, Chem. E. 1917; Ph.D. Columbia, 1914; m. Anna Frances Campbell, Sept. 11, 1913; children—Frank Sears, William Campbell, Eleanor Anne. Chemist with United Gas Improvement Co., Phila., 1908-09; consulting engr., Phila., 1909-12; chem. engr. U.S. Bur. of Mines, 1914-21; prof., head engring. dept., Carnegie Inst. Tech., 1921-33; cons. engr. to State of Pa., 1923-24; cons. engr. U.S. Dept. Agr., 1925-37; lecturer on industrial chemistry, Swarthmore Coll., 1909-12, at Columbia U. 1913. Trustee Ohio Northern Univ., 1928-41. Fellow A.A.A.S.; mem. Am. Chem. Soc., Am. Inst. Chemical Engrs., Franklin Inst., Am. Soc. M.E., Am. Inst. Mining and Metall. Engrs., Soc. Industrial Engrs. (nat. pres. 1925-30), Administrative Bd. Am. Engring. Council, 1925-30, Sigma Psi, Phi Lambda Upsilon, Tau Beta Pi, Sigma Phi Epsilon, etc. Clubs: Chemists, University (New York); Union League (Chicago); Duquesne (Pittsburgh). Contbr. numerous articles dealing with application of physical chemistry to industrial processes, especially those dealing with fuel, oil and gas. Address: 6112 Alder St., Pitts. 6. Died Sept. 26, 1954; buried Chautauqua, N.Y.

RITZMAN, ERNEST GEORGE, animal nutrition; b. Switzerland, May 20, 1875; s. John George and Maria Ursula (Gisel) R.; brought to U.S., 1883; B.S., Ia. State Coll. Agr. and Mech. Arts, 1903; M.S. (hon.), New Hampshire U., 1928; m. Lois Alexander, Nov. 25, 1909; children—Thomas Alexander, Barbara Bicknell Asst. animal husbandman Bur. Animal Industry, Washington, 1903-08; animal husbandman, Expt. Sta., Puerto Rico (Fed. sta.), 1908-13; prof. animal husbandry, U. of Puerto Rico, 1913-15; research prof. in animal nutrition and genetics, U. New Hampshire, 1915-47, now emeritus; research asso. Carnegie Instn. Washington, 1934-40. Served as vol. in Spanish-Am. War, 1898-99; vol. Plattsburg Camp, 1918. Pres. Central Wool Marketing Corp. (eastern br. Nat. Wool Marketing Corp.); mem. com. animal nutrition Nat. Research Council. Mem. Am. Soc. Animal Prodn., Genetic Soc. Am., Am. Inst. of Nutrition, Am. Dairy Sci. Assn., Phi Kappa Phi. Co-author of monographs 324, 377 and 494 (Carnegie Instn.) issued 1923, 1927 and 1937. Contbr. 50 tech. articles, ann. reports or bulls. and popular articles. Home: Durham, N.H. Died May 15, 1955; buried Durham (N.H.) Cemetery.

RIVAS, DAMASO DE, pathologist, parasitologist; b. Diria, Granada, Nicaragua, Dec. 11, 1874; s. Mauricio and Carmen (Aleman) R.; B.S., U. of Pa., 1908, M.S., 1909, M.D., and Ph.D., 1910; m. Rosa Reinish, Jan. 23, 1904; children—Carlos Theodore, Ana Rosa, Maria Luisa. Bacteriologist to filtration bur. of Phila., 1904-06, state health dept., Pa., 1907-10, pathologist since 1917; research fellow in biology, U. of Pa., 1910, asst. dir. dept. of comparative pathology and Sch. of Tropical Medicine since 1910, asst. prof. parasitology, 1917-22, prof. since 1922; pathologist to Friend's Hosp., Frankford, Pa., since 1916; also pathologist Skin and Cancer Hosp., Phila.; dir. and pathologist Pan-Am. Hosp., New York, 1927. Formerly co-worker at Pasteur Inst.; asst. Koch Inst., Berlin, and student at univs. of Paris, Lille, and Heidelberg; has been mem. of scientific excursions for study of tropical diseases of Africa. Awarded medal of Inst. Pasteur, Paris. Mem. Internat. Council of World Court League and rep. to the Peace Conf. in Paris. Pa. del. to 2d Internat. Congress of Tuberculosis, Washington, D.C., 1908; pres. Nicaraguan delegation of 2d Scientific Pan-Am. Congress, Washington, D.C., 1916-17; delegate from

Nicaragua to Sexto Mexico Latino-Americo, Havana, 1922; mem. A.M.A., Am. Soc. of Tropical Medicine; Coll. of Physicians (Phila.), Pan-Am. Med. Assn., Societe de Pathologie Exotique of Paris (corr.), Alpha Kappa Kappa. Roman Catholic. Author: Human Parasitology, 1920; Clinical Parasitology and Tropical Medicine, 1935. Contbr. to med. journals. Home: Villa Rosa, Lansdowne PA

RIVERS, THOMAS MILTON, med. research; b. Jonesboro, Ga., Sept. 3, 1888; s. Alonzo Burrel and Mary Martha (Coleman) R.; A.B., Emory Coll., Oxford, Ga., 1909; M.D., Johns Hopkins, 1915; hon. Sc.D., Emory University, 1936, Rochester University, 1938, University of Chicago, 1941; m. Teresa Jacobina Riefle, August 5, 1922. Intern Johns Hopkins Hospital, 1915-16, assistant resident physician, pediatrics, 1916-17, resident pediatrician and instr. in pediatrics, 1917-18; instr. in bacteriology, Johns Hopkins, 1919-21, asso. in bacteriology, 1921-22; pathologist St. Joseph's Hosp., Baltimore, 1920-22; asso. Rockefeller Inst., N.Y. City, 1922-25, asso. mem., 1925-27, mem. since 1927; dir. of Hosp. of Rockefeller Inst., 1937-55; dir. 1953, member emeritus, 1955; med. dir. Nat. Found. Infantile Paralysis, 1956-58; vice president med. affairs Nat. Found., 1958—. Served as 1st lt. Med. Corps, U.S. Army, February 1918-Jan. 1919; captain Medical Corps, U.S. Naval Reserve; rear admiral, retired reserves, 1955. Was president of the 3d International Congress for Microbiology, New York, 1939. Mem. A.A.A.S., Am. Soc. Clin. Investigation (pres. 1932), Assn. Am. Physicians, Interurban Clin. Club (pres. 1942-43), American Pediatric Society, American Epidemiological Soc., Am. Soc. Exptl. Pathology, Soc. Am. Bacteriologists (pres. 1936), Soc. Am. Immunologists (pres. 1934), Harvey Society, Am. Assn. Pathologists and Bacteriologists, Am. Clin. and Climatological Assn., Nat. Acad. Sciences, Am. Philos. Soc., Phi Beta Kappa, Alpha Omega Alpha, Sigma Nu, Pi Mu, Century Assn. Democrat. Contbr. to E.L. Opie's Epidemic Respiratory Disease, 1921; editor and contbr. to Filterable Viruses, 1928, to Viral and Rickettsial Infections of Man, 1948, 52, 58. Discover Bacillus Parainfluenzae, and Virus III infections in rabbits; cultivated vaccine virus for human use. Home: 163 Greenway S., Forest Hills, L.I., N.Y. Address: York Av. and 66th St., N.Y.C. 21; also 800 2d Av., N.Y.C. 17. Died May 12, 1962; buried Arlington Nat. Cemetery.

RIVES, ALFRED LANDON, engr.; b. Paris, France, March 25, 1830; s. William Cabell R. (then U.S. minister to France); studied at Va. Mil. Inst. and Univ. of Va.; grad. École des Ponts et Chaussées, Paris, 1854; asst. engr. in completing U.S. Capitol Bldg., Washington; later engr. on aqueduct, Washington; then in charge U.S. Survey in improving Potomac River; later col. engrs. Confederate army; after was engr. on Chesapeake & Ohio R.R., chief engr. South & North Ala. R.R. Offered charge of civ. engring. works of Egypt; v.p. and gen. mgr. Mobile & Ohio R.R.; v.p. and gen. mgr. Richmond & Danville R.R.; gen. supt. Panama R.R. Now chief engr. Cape Cod Canal, and gen. consulting engr. Is father of Amélie Rives (Princess Troubetzkoy) authoress. Home: Cobham, Va. Died 1903.

ROACH, DAVID JAMES, business exec.; b. Sedalia, Colo., Apr. 12, 1887; s. Phillip and Louisa (Cook) R.; B.S., Colo. State Coll., 1908; m. Katherine B. Higgins, June 14, 1911; children—Mary Louise (Mrs. John D. Edmiston), Elizabeth Ann (Mrs. Robert F. Hemphill). Chief chemist and traveling chem. Great Western Sugar Co., 1908-17, asst. to gen. supt., 1917-20, plant mgr., Ft. Collins and Windsor, 1920-29, Scottsbluff and Gering, 1929-35; dist. mgr., Neb. Dist., 1935-39, asst. gen. mgr., Denver, 1939, v.p., 1940-47, exec. v.p., 1947—. Republican. Presbyn. Mason. Clubs: Denver Rotary, Denver. Writer on economics, agr. and technol. of beet sugar industry. Home: 2222 E. Seventh Av. Office: 1530 Sixteenth St., Denver. Died Oct. 1953.

ROACH, JOHN, ironmaster, shipbuilder; b. Mitchlestown, County Cork, Ireland, Dec. 25, 1813; s. Patrick and Abigail (Meany) Roche; m. Emeline Johnson, 1836, 9 children. Came to U.S., 1829; naturalized, 1842; purchased (with others) small iron works, circa 1841, became sole owner, obtained contract for constructing iron drawbridge over Harlem River, N.Y.C., 1860, had one of best-equipped foundries in U.S. by end of Civil War; carried out plans for devel. iron shipbldg. industry in U.S., 1868, purchased small marine-engine plants in nr. N.Y.C., consolidated then with Morgan Iron Works; tranferred hdqtrs. to Chester, Pa., 1871; produced City of Peking, City of Tokio (iron vessels for fgn. service), Pacific Mail S.S. Co., 1874; authorized by Dept. of Navy to install compound engine in ram Tennessee; built sloops of war Alert and Huron for U.S. Govt., launched, 1874; built sectional dry dock, Pensacola, Fla.; obtained contracts for monitors Miantonomoh, and Puritan; built Dolphin, cruisers Atlanta, Boston, Chicago; launched 126 iron vessels 1872-86. Died N.Y.C., Jan. 10, 1887.

ROADHOUSE, CHESTER LINWOOD, univ. prof.; b. Watsonville, Calif., Jan. 5, 1881; s. John James and Imogene (Kimberlin) R.; student, U. of Calif., 1902-03; D.V.M., Cornell U., 1906; student, U. of Bern, Bern, Switzerland, 1927-28; m. Christine Judah, Dec. 2, 1910; children—Katharine (Mrs. Robert F. Black), Frances (dec.), Donald (dec.). Vet. insp., U.S. Dept. Agr., 1906-09; chief dairy insp., Dept. of Health, San Francisco, 1909-10; chief veterinarian, Dept. of Health, Berkeley, 1910-11; asso. prof., vet. science, U. of Calif., 1911-17; veterinarian and bacteriologist, San Francisco and Alameda Counties Med. Milk Commns., 1911-17; prof. Dairy Industry, Univ. of Calif., 1917-69; inaugurated supervision city milk, San Francisco, city dairy and milk, Berkeley; director California Dairy Council; U.S. del. to World's Dairy Congress, Berlin, Germany, 1937. Mem. Internat. Assn. Milk Sanatarians (pres. 1921), Am. Dairy Science Assn. (pres., 1934-35); Pacific Slope Dairy Assn. (pres. and dir., 1922-47), A.A.A.S., Theta Delta Chi, Sigma Xi, Alpha Zeta. Republican. Mason. Clubs: Davis Rotary (pres. 1931). Author: (textbook) The Market Milk Industry (with Dr. J. Lloyd Henderson), 1941; Lab. Manual for Market Milk, 1947. Contbr. circulars and bulletins on dairy science. Home: Santa Rosa CA Died Sept. 23, 1969; buried Santa Clara (Cal.) City Cemetery.

ROBB, RUSSELL, engineer; b. Dubuque, Ia., Dec. 6, 1864; s. Patrick and Catharine Sedgwick (Newbury) R.; S.B., Mass. Inst. Tech., 1888; m. Edith Owen Morse, Mar. 1, 1898; children—Russell, Catharine. Engr. Thomson Electric Welding Co., 1888-91; with Stone & Webster, mgrs. pub. service corporation, 1891—, mem. firm 1905-20; sr. v.p. and treas. Stone and Webster, Inc., 1920—; dir. numerous traction, light, power and other cos. Trustee Concord Free Pub. Library. Author: Electric Wiring, 1896; Lectures on Organization, 1909. Home: Concord, Mass. Died Feb. 15, 1927.

ROBB, WILLIAM LISPENARD, electrical engr.; b. Saratoga, N.Y., May 9, 1861; s. Alexander J. and Esther (Lispenard) R.; B.A., Columbia, 1880; univs. of Würzburg and Berlin, 1880-83; Ph.D., U. of Berlin, 1883; Federal Poly., Zürich, Switzerland; LL.D., Trinity Coll., Conn., 1902; m. Winifred Matthews, 1893; children—Winifred Lispenard (Mrs. Wm. L. Powers), Leonard Lispenard. Submarine Mine Service, Spanish-Am. War, 1898; cons. engr., Hartford Electric Light Co., Gen. Ry. Signal Co.; head, dept. elec. engring., Rensselaer Poly. Inst., Troy, N.Y., 1902—. Democrat. Episcopalian. Home: Troy, N.Y. Died Jan. 26, 1933.

ROBBINS, ARTHUR GRAHAM, prof. topog. engring.; b. Carlisle, Mass., July 11, 1862; s. George Heald and Mary Heald (Melvin) R.; B.S., Mass. Inst. Tech., 1886; m. Sara A. Andrews, of Bridgewater, Mass., Jan. 19, 1899 (died May 8, 1926); children—Helen C., James M.; m. 2d, Stella R. Root, of Wichester, Mass., June 10, 1927. Teacher of surveying, highway and civ. engring., Mass. Inst. Tech., since 1886, prof. topog. engring. since 1909. Mem. Boston Soc. C.E.; Affiliate of Am. Soc. C.E. Republican. Unitarian. Clubs: City, Appalachian Mountain. Home: 12 Grove St., Winchester, Mass.

ROBBINS, BENJAMIN H(OWARD), anesthesiologist; b. Byrdstown, Tenn., Dec. 18, 1904; s. Lansdon Breckinridge and Viola Ann (Groce) R.; B.A., Berea Coll., 1925; M.S., Vanderbilt U., 1926, M.D., 1933; m. Berenice Gay Baker, Aug. 26, 1932; children—Ruth Gay, Benjamin Howard, Ann Berenice. With Vanderbilt U. Sch. Medicine, 1926—, asst. pharmacology, 1926-33, asst. prof., 1933-35, asso. prof., 1935—, prof. anesthesiology, 1946—; fellow anesthesiology Mayo Clinci, 1946; anesthesiologist in chief Vanderbilt Hosp., 1946—; cons. anesthesiology VA, Nashville and Memphis. Mem. Unitarian Service Med. Mission to Germany, 1948. Diplomate Am. Bd. Anesthesiology. Mem. Am. Soc. Pharmacology and Exptl. Therapy, Am. Soc. Anesthesiology, Assn. U. Anesthesiologists, So. Soc. Clin. Research, S.E. Soc. Anesthesiology (pres. 1959-60), Sigma Xi, Phi Chi, Alpha Omega Alpha. Author: Cyclopropane Anesthesia, 1958. Home: 2429 Bear Rd., Nashville 37215. Died Jan. 10, 1960; buried Woodlawn Meml. Park, Nashville.

ROBBINS, SAMUEL DOWSE, speech pathologist; b. Belmont, Mass., Dec. 28, 1887; s. Chandler and Maria Wellington (Mead) R.; A.B., Harvard, 1911, A.M., 1919; L.H.D. (honorary), Emerson College, 1955; married Rosa Margaret Seymour, July 10, 1917; children—Chandler Seymour, Roger Wellington, Samuel Dowse, Jr. Established sch. for correction of stammering, 1914-15; conducted research in speech pathology, Harvard, 1918-19, resulting in discovery of some changes in cerebral circulation in stammering and fright; instituted plan for systematic classification of speech disorders, adopted by Am. Speech Correction Assn., 1930; dir. of Boston Stammerers' Inst., 1916-40; in charge speech correction Mass. Gen. Hosp., 1920-43; speech therapist, Mass. Div. Mental Hygiene, 1927-57; later prof. emeritus speech therapy Emerson Coll. and mng. trustee of Inst. of Speech Correction, Inc., lecturer Tufts Coll. Dental Sch., 1948-52; awarded research grant under Pub. Health Service Act, 1961. Mem. Belmont Town Meeting since 1926. Trustee Belmont Savings Bank. Fellow A.A.A.S., Am. Speech and Hearing Assn. (permanent sec. 1931-40, pres. 1941-42, chmn. Terminology Committee 1929-54), American Psychol. Assn. Republican. Conglist. Author: Stammering and Its Treatment, 1926; A Dictionary of Terms Dealing with Disorders of Speech (with Sara M. Stinchfield), 1931; Correction of Speech Defects of Early Childhood (with Rosa S. Robbins), 1937; A Dictionary of Speech Pathology and Therapy, 1951. Contbr. to scientific jours. Home: Belmont MA Died Jan. 28, 1968; buried Mt. Auburn Cemetery Cambridge MA

ROBERDEAU, ISAAC, civil and mil. engr.; b. Phila., Sept. 11, 1763; s. Daniel and Mary (Bostwick) R.; studied engring. London, Eng., 1785-87; m. Nov. 7, 1792, 3 children. Employed with U.S. Topog. Engrs. to lay out new City of Washington (D.C.), 1791-92; most important work was canal to connect Schuylkill and Susquehanna rivers; mem. Topog. Engrs. U.S. Army in war with Great Britain, 1813-15, commd. maj. 1813; assigned to duty at Ft. Mifflin; employed on fortification work; charged with survey of No. boundary which he carried westward to Sault St. Marie; reinstated as maj., 1816; stationed at U.S. Mil. Acad., until 1818; became chief Topog. Bur., Washington, 1818; brevetted lt. col., 1823. Author: Observations of the Survey of the Seacost of the U.S., 1827; Mathematics and Treatise on Canals; An Oration upon the Death of Gen. George Washington (delivered at Trenton, N.J. Feb. 22, 1800), published 1800. Died Georgetown, D.C., Jan. 15, 1829.

ROBERT, JAMES MARSHALL, univ. dean; b. St. Paul, June 20, 1885; s. Alonzo Beauregard and Alice (Fonseca) R.; B.Engring., Tulane U., 1906; m. Gladys Roberta Kearny, Apr. 21, 1909; children—James Marshall (dec.), Kearny Quinn, William Douglas, Gladys Kearny (dec.). Instr. mech. engring. Tulane U., 1906-12, asst. prof. exptl. engring., 1912-16, asso. prof. machine design, 1916-20, prof., 1920-34, prof. mech. engring., 1934-50, acting dean coll. engring., 1935-36, dean, 1936-50; cons. and testing engr. since 1906; in charge motor mechanics div., Camp Martin, during World War; in charge U.S. Shipping Bd. Marine Engr. Sch., Tulane U., 1917-21. Mem. Bd. Examiners for Operating Engrs., New Orleans, 1934-1940. Mem. Am. Soc. M.E. (chmn. New Orleans sect. 1923-24), La. Engring. Soc. (sec. 11 yrs., v.p. 1923, pres. 1924), Soc. for Promotion Engring. Edn. (vice chmn. S.E. sect. 1937-38, chmn. 1938-39), Newcomen Soc., Sigma Phi Delta, Omicron Delta Kappa, Tau Beta Pi, Pi Kappa Alpha. Clubs: Rotary, Boston (New Orleans). Editor Proc. La. Engrs. Soc., 1931-41. Home: 2141 State St., New Orleans. Died June 8, 1964; buried Metairie Cemetery, New Orleans.

ROBERTS, BENJAMIN STONE, army officer, engr.; b. Manchester, Vt., Nov. 18, 1810; s. Gen. Martin and Betsey (Stone) R.; grad. U.S. Mil. Acad., 1835; m. Elizabeth Sperry, Sept. 18, 1835, 3 children. Chief engr. Champlain & Ogdensburg R.R., 1839; geologist N.Y. State, 1841; assisted in constrn. of ry. in Russia from St. Petersburg to Moscow, 1842-43; began practice of law, Des Moines, Ia., 1843; lt. col. Ia. Militia, 1844-46; commd. lt. U.S. Army, 1846, capt., 1847; brevetted maj. for gallantry at Battle of Chapultepec, 1847, lt. col. for gallantry nr. Matamoras, 1847; received sword of honor from State of Ia.; maj. 3d Cavalry, 1861, commanded Southern mil. dist. of N.M.; active in battles at Ft. Craig, Albuquerque, Valverde, Peralta; brevetted col., 1862; promoted brig. gen. U.S. Volunteers, 1862, brig. gen., maj. gen., 1865; in command 1st Div., XIX Army Corps in La., 1864; chief cavalry Dept. of Gulf, until 1865; lt. col. 3d Cavalry, 1866; served in N.M., 1867-68; prof. tactics in mil. science Yale, 1868-70; ret. from active service, 1870; practiced law and prosecution of claims before govt., Washington, D.C. Author: Description of Newly Patented Solid Shot and Shells for Use in Rifled Ordnance, 1864; Lt. Gen. U.S. Grant, an address delivered at Yale, 1864. Died Washington, Jan. 29, 1875.

ROBERTS, CHARLOTTE FITCH, chemist; b. New York, Feb. 13, 1859; d. Horace and Mary (Hart) R.; A.B., Wellesley Coll., 1880; U. of Cambridge, Eng., 1886-87; Ph.D., Yale, 1894; U. of Berlin, Germany, 1899-1900. Instr. chemistry, 1881-87, asst. prof., 1887-92, prof., 1892—, Wellesley Coll. Fellow A.A.A.S. Author: Stereochemistry, 1894. Home: Wellesley, Mass. Died Dec. 5, 1917.

ROBERTS, EDWARD ALEXANDER, cons. engr.; b. Cambridge, Mass., June 14, 1893; s. John W. and Isabel (Alexander) R.; B.S. cum laude, Harvard, 1914; research fellow U. Ill., 1916-17; m. Dorothy Murdock, June 26, 1919; children—Edward, Elizabeth (Mrs. M.L. Linscott). With Beeler Orgn., cons. engrs., 1917-21; cons. traffic expert N.Y. Transit Commn., 1921-22, chief transit bur., 1923; gen. mgr. N.Y. & Queens Co. Ry. Co., 1923-32; gen. mgr. N.Y. & L.I. Traction Co., 1924-26, L.I. Electric Ry. Co., 1924-26; mem. Fisk & Roberts, 1925-41; pres. N.Y. & Queens Transit Corp., 1932-40, Queens-Nassau Transit Lines, Inc., 1933-42, Briarwood Bus. Co., 1934-38; transit consultant to transit corporation counsel N.Y.C., 1958—; cons. engr. for numerous concerns, cities, specializing in passenger transp. Asso. dir., div. local transport Office Def. Transp., 1942-44, dir. hwy. passenger operations, 1944-45. Vice chmn. YMCA, Flushing Profl. engr. N.Y. and Pa. Fellow I.E.E.E.; mem. Harvard Engring. Soc. (past pres.), Am. Transit Assn. Clubs: Harvard (N.Y.C.); Rotary (past pres. Queensboro). Home: 145-21 29th Rd. Office: Chase Manhattan Bank Bldg., Flushing 54, N.Y. Died Apr. 9, 1965.

ROBERTS, FRANK HAROLD HANNA, anthropologist, archeologist; b. Centerburg, O., Aug. 11, 1897; s. Frank Hunt Hurd and Lou Ella (Hanna) R.; A.B., U. Denver, 1919, A.M., 1921, LL.D., 1962; A.M., Harvard, 1926, Ph.D., 1927; LL.D., U. N.M., 1957, U. Colo., 1959; m. Linda Butchart May 6, 1927. Instr. U. Denver, 1921-24; asst. curator archeology Colo. State Mus., Denver, 1923-24; asst. anthropology Harvard, 1925-26; archeologist Bur. Am. Ethnology, Smithsonian Instn., 1926-44, asst. chief 1944-46, asso. chief, 1946, asso. dir., 1947-58, dir., 1958-64, research asso., 1964—; collaborator Nat. Park Service, 1962—; dir. River Basin Archeol. Surveys, 1946-64. Conducted field work in archeology, U.S., Can., Mexico. Served with U.S. Army, World War I. Awarded Viking Fund medal, 1951. U.S. rep. Internat. Congress Archeologists, Cairo, 1937, Internat. Commn. Historic Monuments, 1939. Mem. Am. Anthropol. Assn. (v.p. 1944), Soc. for Am. Archeology (pres. 1950), A.A.A.S. (v.p. 1952), Anthropol. Soc. Wash. (pres. 1936-37), Wash. Acad. Scis. (pres. 1949), Am. Geog. Soc., Phi Beta Kappa, Sigma Xi, Beta Theta Pi. Club: Cosmos. City editor Las Vegas (N.M.) Daily Optic, 1919-20. Author (under name Frank H. H. Roberts, Jr.) some 50 monographs, papers and articles on N.Am. archeology and ethnology, southwestern and Mex. archeology, early man in the New World, and Egypt. Home: 3535 Chevy Chase Lake Dr., Chevy Chase, Md. 20015. Office: Smithsonian Instn., Washington. Died Feb. 23, 1966; buried Arlington Nat. Cemetery.

ROBERTS, JAMES COLE, mining engr.; b. Warren Co., N.C., Dec. 14, 1863; s. Frederick Cox and Lavinia Ellis (Cole) R.; Bingham Sch. (military) N.C.; Ph.B., U. of N.C.; studied Columbia; m. Alice Mary Pomeroy, 1897; 1 dau., Alice Pomeroy. Chemist and mill engr. in N.C., 1885-87; chemist and metallurgist, Woodstock Iron Works, Anniston, Ala., 1887-89; examination phosphate lands in Fla., 1889-91; mgr. Enterprise Mine, Rico, Colo., 1892-95; chemist and asst. metallurgist, Globe Smelting Works, Denver, 1895-97; metallurgist, Anaconda (Mont.) Copper Co., 1897-99; prof. metallurgy, Colo. Sch. of Mines, 1899-1902; cons. engr. for Detroit Capitalists, 1902-04; engr. and metallurgist, Ampere Electro-Chem. Co. and Atmospheric Products Co., Niagara Falls, 1904-08; with U.S. Bureau Mines, in charge installations, investigations, etc., 1908-15; prof. coal mining and safety and efficiency engring., Colo. Sch. of Mines, 1915-23; now mgr. Safety Council, Denver. Democrat. Episcopalian. Mason. Home: Golden, Colo. Deceased.

ROBERTS, JOB, agriculturist; b. Whitpain, Pa., Mar. 23, 1756; s. John and Jane (Hunk) R.; m. Mary Naylor, May 22, 1781; m. 2d, Sarah (Williams) Thomas, Oct. 12, 1820; at least 2 children. Began experimenting in better farming methods, 1785; published results of experiments as The Pennsylvania Farmer, 1804; experimented with fertilizers, use of lime, plaster, various barnyard manures, deep ploughing of land; built improved harrow, devised new roller, 1792; attached water wheel to dairy churn making it possible to churn 150 pounds of butter a week, 1797; invented machine for planting corn, 1815; advanced growing season of corn by soaking before planting; introduced Merino sheep into Pa.; interested in cultivation of mulberry for silk culture; substituted green fodder for his cattle for grazing; apptd. justice of peace, 1791; called Squire Job Roberts. Died Whitpain, Aug. 20, 1851.

ROBERTS, NATHAN SMITH, civil engr.; b. Piles Grove, N.J., July 28, 1776; s. Abraham Roberts; m. Lavinia White, Nov. 4, 1816, at least 1 son, Nathan Smith. Tchr., Oriskany, N.Y., 1804-06; prin. acad. Whitesboro, N.Y., 1806-16; bought farm nr. Lenox (N.Y.) 1816; asst. engr. in constrn. of middle sect. of Erie Canal, 1816-22, in charge of constrn. Western sect., 1822-25; cons. engr. for Chesapeake and Del. Canal, 1825-26; made survey for ship canal around Niagara Falls, 1826; chief engr. for Western end Pa. State Canal, 1826-28; mem. bd. engrs. Chesapeake & Ohio Canal Co., 1828-30; made survey for ship canal around Muscle Shoals in Ala., circa 1830; made surveys to estimate expenses of enlarging Erie Canal, 1835, chief engr. for enlargement, 1839-41. Died nr. Lenox, Nov. 24, 1852.

ROBERTS, SHELBY SAUFLEY, civil engr.; b. Louisville, Ky., Apr. 13, 1874; s. Bolin Emery and Margaret K. (Pickens) R.; A.B., Louisville Male High Sch., 1894; B.S., Rose Poly. Inst., Terre Haute, Ind., 1898, C.E., 1907; LL.B., Washington Coll. of Law, 1925; m. Nell Ackley Richardson, Nov. 26, 1901; children—Nell Richardson, Shelby Chilton, Sarah Pickens. Track apprentice, maintenance dept., I.C. R.R., 1898; location surveys and constrn., St. L.,P.&N. R.R., 1898-99; with L.&N. R.R., 1899, successively as asst. to engr. in charge of constrn. of terminals at Nashville; engr. in charge of improvements at Henderson, Ky., Evansville, Ind., and East St. Louis, Ill.; engr. in charge maintenance of way, Henderson and St. Louis divs.; roadmaster main stem, 1st div.; roadmaster and engr., Louisville terminals, until 1905; supt. building constrn. for F.C. Brent, Pensacola, Fla., 1905-06; asst. engr. constrn., I.C. R.R., Chicago, 1906-08; prof. ry. civ. engring., Coll. of Engring., U. of Ill., 1908-10; div. engr. on constrn., I.C. R.R., Chicago, 1911-13; pvt. practice, gen. and ry. civ. engring., 1913-18; staff officer engring. and sr. asst. engr., U.S. R.R. Administration, Southern Region, Atlanta, Ga., 1918-20; asst. dir. Bur. of Finance, Interstate Commerce Commn., in charge of the forces handling matters before the bur. in which engring. principles are involved, 1920-35, chief sect. of securities, 1935—. Admitted to bar of D.C., 1925, Supreme Court U.S., 1930. Democrat. Episcopalian. Author: Track Formulae and Tables, 1910. Home: Washington, D.C. Died May 6, 1936.

ROBERTS, SOLOMON WHITE, civil engr., transp. exec.; b. Phila., Aug. 3, 1811; s. Charles and Hannah (White) R.; m. Anna Smith Rickey. Asst. engr. for State of Pa. in constrn. of canal on Conemaugh River, 1829-31; prin. asst. engr. Allegheny Portage R.R., resident engr., supt. transp. until 1836; designed, supervised constrn. masonry railroad viaduct over Conemaugh River; went to Eng. to procure and superintend manufacture of iron rails for several railroads, 1836-38; chief engr. Catowissa R.R., 1838-41; pres. Phila., Germantown & Norristown R.R. Co., 1842, Shuylkill Navigation Co., 1843-45; mem. Pa. Ho. of Reps., 1848; chief engr. Ohio & Pa. R.R., 1848, gen. supt. chief engr., gen. supt. North Pa. R.R., 1856-79; mem. Am. Philos. Soc. Author: Reminiscenses of the First Railroad over the Allegheny Mountain; The Destiny of Pittsburgh and the Duty of Her Young Men, 1850. Died Atlantic City, N.J., Mar. 22, 1882.

ROBERTS, THOMAS PASCHALL, engineer; b. Carlisle, Pa., Apr. 21, 1843; s. W. Milnor and Annie (Gibson) R.; g.s. Chief Justice John Bannister Gibson; ed. Dickinson Coll., Pa.; m. Juliet E., d. James M. Christy, of Pittsburgh bar, June 8, 1870. Engaged, 1863-65, under his father on Dom Pedro R.R. in Brazil; later on Northern Pacific R.R., Baltimore & Cumberland Valley and other railroads. Executed surveys for railroad, Pittsburgh to Harrisburg, Pa., near Md. state line; for many yrs. identified with river improvement; late chief engr. Monongahela Navigation Co.; executed surveys for ship canal to connect Ohio River with Lake Erie. Author: Memoir of the Late Chief Justice Gibson of Pennsylvania, 1890. Home: 519 Aiken Av., Pittsburgh, Pa.

ROBERTS, THOMAS REASER, physicist; b. Mpls., Mar. 13, 1923; s. Thomas Cleveland and Dorothy (Reaser) R.; A.B. cum laude, Harvard, 1943; M.A., U. Minn., 1949, Ph.D., 1950; m. Carol Naus, May 2, 1942; children—Thomas Naus, Margaret Elizabeth, Shelley. Research chemist Shell Oil Co., Wood River, Ill., 1943; tchr., research asst. U. Minn., 1946-50; research physicist aero. research div. Mpls. Honeywell Regulator Co., 1950-51; staff mem. Los Alamos Sci. Lab., 1951-68. Chmn. Republican Party, Los Alamos County, 1956, mem. N.M. Central Com., 1957-68; mem. N.M. Ho. of Reps., 1957-60. Pres., bd. dirs. Mesa Pub. Library; mem. bd. of regents U. of New Mexico, 1961-68 pres., 1967-68. Served to lt. (j.g.) USNR, 1944-46. Mem. Am. Phys. Soc., Sigma Xi. Unitarian. Home: Los Alamos NM Died Feb. 24, 1968.

ROBERTS, THOMAS SADLER, physician, ornithologist; b. Phila., Pa., Feb. 16, 1858; s. John and Elizabeth Jane (Sadler) R.; moved to Minn., June 1867; U. of Minn., 1877-79; M.D., U. of Pa., 1885; D.Sc., U. of Minn., 1940; interne, Phila. Children's Hosp. and Phila. City Hosp.; m. Jane Cleveland, Oct. 19, 1887; children—Thomas Cleveland, Catherine Lyon, John Carroll; m. 2d, Mrs. Agnes Williams Harley, Oct. 9, 1937. Prof. pediatrics, 1901-06, clinical prof., 1906-13, emeritus prof. pediatrics since 1913, medical dept. U. of Minn.; prof. ornithology, Museum Natural History, U. of Minn. since 1915, also dir. Was 12 yrs. on staff St. Barnabas Hosp. and 6 yrs. chief of staff. Awarded Brewster gold medal for The Birds of Minnesota, by Am. Ornithologists Union, 1938. Fellow Am. Ornithologists' Union (past mem. council), A.A.A.S.; mem. Cooper Ornithol. Olub, Wilson Ornithol. Club, Minn. Acad. Science (ex-pres.); corr. mem. Biol. Soc. Washington; mem. Minn. Acad. Medicine, County and State med. socs., A.M.A.; mem. Sigma Xi, Nu Sigma Nu, Alpha Omega Alpha. Clubs: Minneapolis, Automobile. Author: Birds of Minnesota (2 vols.); Bird Portraits in Color, 1936; Log-book of Minnesota Bird Life, 1938; Annals of Museum of Natural History (1872-1939), 1940. Home: 2303 Pleasant Av. Address: Minnesota Museum of Natural History, Univ. of Minn., Minneapolis, Minn. Died Apr. 19, 1946.

ROBERTS, WARREN RUSSELL, civil and mining engr.; b. Sadorus, Champaign Co., Ill., Oct. 20, 1863; s. Samuel Martin and Celestia Wood (Brayton) R.; B.S. in C.E., U. of Ill., 1888; m. Lucy C. Stewart, Oct. 7, 1891; children—Jerome G., Mary Brayton, Kathryn Stewart, Elizabeth Evans; m. 2d, Jennie May Dean, 1907. Gen. engring. practice, 1888-92; engr. of bridges, Chicago, 1893-94; gen. engring., contracting, 1895-1903; pres. Roberts & Schaefer Co., engrs., contractors, 1904-39, chmn. bd. since 1939. Mem. Am. Soc. C.E., Am. Inst. Mining and Metall. Engrs., Am. Mining Congress, Western Soc. Engrs., Am. Forestry Assn., Am. Geog. Soc., Am. Legion (past post comdr.). Col. O.R.C., staff of Q.M. Gen. Democrat. Clubs: Chicago Illini; Army and Navy (Washington, D.C.). Home: Whitehall Hotel, 105 E. Delaware Pl. Office: 400 N. Michigan Av., Chicago, Died June 22, 1944.

ROBERTS, WILLIAM MILNOR, civil engr.; b. Phila., Feb. 12, 1810; s. Thomas Pascal and Mary Louise (Baker) R.; m. Annie Gibson, June 1837; m. 2d, Adeline Beelen, Nov. 1868; at least 9 children. Assistant in survey and constrn. Lehigh Canal between Mauch Chunk and Phila., 1826; sr. asst. engr. for proposed Allegheny Portage R.R., 1831-34, gen. mgr., 1834-35; chief engr. Lancaster & Harrisburg R.R., 1836-37; greatest engring. accomplishments include constrn. of two-level lattice-truss bridge across Susquehanna River at Harrisburg, 1837; in charge of extensions of Pa. state canals, 1838-40; built Bellefontaine & Ind., Allegheny Valley, The Atlantic & Miss., Iron Mountain railroads; chmn. commn. to consider reconstrn. of Allegheny Portage R.R.; constructed railroads in Mid-West, 1855-57; contracted to build Dom Pedro Segundo R.R., Brazil, 1865; proposed improvements of Mississippi River at Keokuk, Ia., 1866; U.S. engr. in charge of improvement of navigation of Ohio River; asso. chief engr. in constrn. Eads Bridge across Mississippi River at St. Louis, 1868; chief engr. No. Pacific R.R., 1869-79; mem. Mississippi River Jetty Commn.; chief engr. all pub. works in Brazil, 1879-81; v.p. Am. Soc. C.E. 1873-78, pres., 1878. Died Soledade, Brazil, July 14, 1881.

ROBERTSON, A. JAMES, astronomer; b. Rockford, Ill., May 1, 1867; s. Charles A. and Henriette G. (Ward) R.; B.S., U. of Mich., 1891; D.Sc., U. of Georgetown, 1933; m. Carolina Ancona, Oct. 8, 1903;children—Armand J., Marie Ancona, John Ancona; m. 2d, Martha P. Worthington, Sept. 21, 1911; children—Arabella Piatt, Charles Worthington. Asst. Nautical Almanac Office of U.S. Naval Observatory, 1893-1908, prin. asst., 1908-24, astronomer, 1924-27, sr. astronomer, 1927-30, head astronomer since 1930, asst. dir., 1927-29, and dir., 1929-39; professional consultant of Navy Dept. Math. Astonomy, and allied subjects since 1930. Derived the elements of the orbit of the fifth satellite of Jupiter now in use by internat. agreement in all important almanac offices; derived method for computing eclipses now in general use; also new method for computing occulations. Mem. Am. Astron. Union, Internat. Astron. Union, Astronomischer Gesellschaft, Societe Astronomique de France. Contbr. to astron. jours. and monthly notices of R.A.S. Pub., 1940, a zodiacal catalogue of 3539 stars for equinox 1950, under auspices of Nautical Almanac Office. Home: Box 3642, Georgetown Station, Washington DC

ROBERTSON, ALICE, zoölogist; b. Phila., Pa.; d. James and Janet (Greaves) R.; B.S., U. of Calif., 1898, M.S., 1899, Ph.D., 1902. Asst. in hygiene for women, 1902-04, in zoölogy, 1904-06, U. of Calif.; instr. physiology and zoölogy, 1906-09, asso. prof. zoölogy, 1909-12, prof. zoölogy, 1912-19, Wellesley Coll. Fellow A.A.A.S. Home: Seattle, Wash. Died Sept. 22, 1922.

ROBERTSON, CHARLES, botanist, entomologist; b. Carlinville, Ill., June 12, 1858; s. William Addison and Nanette Hill (Halliday) R.; ed. Carlinville pub. schs. and Blackburn Coll.; m. Indianapolis, Nov. 12, 1879, Alice McDonald Venable. Instr. botany and Greek, Blackburn Coll., 1880-86; prof. biology, same, since 1898. Mem. A.A.A.S., St. Louis Acad. of Sciences. Contbr. to scientific jours. on relations of flowers and insects and on bees. Address: Carlinville, Ill.

ROBERTSON, GEORGE, geographic sculptor; b. Glasgow, Scotland, 1878; s. William and Sarah (Johnston) R.; came to U.S., 1883; ed. Brimmer Sch. and Sch. of Art, Mus. Fine Arts, Boston; grad. in architecture Drexel Inst., Phila., 1908; m. Mary T. Reynolds, Apr. 17, 1915. With art dept. Boston Herald, 1895-98; with George Carrol Curtis, relief map maker, Boston, 1898-1901; mgr. Howell's Natural Sci. Establishment, Washington, 1911. Mem. Battery D, 1st Regt. Mass. Heavy Arty., U.S.V., Spanish-Am. War. Prepared ofcl. relief map of Panama Canal, as a part of govt. exhibit San Francisco (awarded gold medal); also topographic map N.Y. State, largest relief map of any state ever prepared from instrumental survey (30X40 feet, awarded grand prize); prepared large relief model European war zone for Chgo. Daily News, 1917. Div. mineral tech. Nat. Mus. Models showing prodn. and conservation natural gas, sulphur, oil, soda and copper, 1918-19; relief model D.C., showing the permanent system parks and hwys., 1921; archtl. model showing details Wilson Dam, at Muscle Shoals (War Dept.), 1926; model showing successive steps in lock design of Am. Locks at Sault Ste. Marie, Mich. (War Dept.), 1927; large relief of N.Am. Continent, installed in lobby Tribune Tower, Chgo., 1927; relief map Great Smoky Mountain Nat. Park, Tenn. (1st relief map to be prepared from aerotopographic survey), 1930; developed for War Dept. new method of preparing topographic relief-maps by use of unvulcanized rubber. Commd. capt. C.E., O.R.C.; spl. topographic engring. duties, Army Map Service, Corps of Engineers, U.S. Army, Washington, D.C. since 1922. Mem. Soc. Am. Mil. Engrs., Washington Soc. Engrs., Sojourners Club. Mason. Odd Fellow. Home: 5925 16th St. North, Arlington, Va. Died Oct. 19, 1960.

ROBERTSON, H(AROLD) E(UGENE), pathologist; b. Waseca, Minn., Oct. 8, 1878; s. James M. and Kate (Deuel) R.; A.B., Carleton Coll., Minn., 1899; M.D., U. of Pa., 1905; studied Columbia, 1900-01, U. of Berlin,

1914, U. of Freiburg, 1915; m. Edith Ellam, July 31, 1907. Instr. pathology, Albany Med. Coll., 1905-06; asst. pathologist Boston City Hosp., 1906-07, instr. pathology, Harvard, 1907 (resigned); instr. in pathology, U. of Minn., 1907, asst. prof. pathology and bacteriology, 1909, asso. prof., 1910, prof. pathology, 1914-21, also dir. dept. pathology, bacteriology and pub. health until 1921; prof. pathology, University of Minnesota Graduate School and head section pathologic anatomy, Mayo Clinic, 1921-43. Consultant, sect. pathologic anatomy, Mayo Clinc, since 1943 (Oct.) Commissioned maj. Med. O.R.C., June 20, 1917; sailed for France, July 26, 1917; served in laboratory div., A.E.F., 18 mos.; hon. discharged Jan. 28, 1919. Member American Association Pathologists and Bacteriologists, A.M.A., Am. Soc. of Clinical Pathologists, Assn. Military Surgeons of the U.S., Phi Beta Kappa, Sigma Xi, Alpha Omega Alpha, Nu Sigma Nu. Republican. Presbyterian. Club: University. Contributor of numerous articles on pathology of tetanus, pathology of poliomyelitis, etc. Col. Med. O.R.C. Home: Rochester, Minn. Died Mar. 8, 1946.

ROBERTSON, HOWARD PERCY, scientist; b. Hoquiam, Wash., Jan. 27, 1903; s. George Duncan and Anna (McLeod) R.; B.S., U. of Wash., 1922, M.S., 1923; Ph.D., Calif. Inst. of Tech., 1925; m. Angela Turinsky, Jan. 27, 1923; children—George Duncan, Mariette. Nat. research fellow, Göttingen, Munich, Princeton U., 1925-28; asst. prof. mathematics, Calif. Inst. Tech., 1927-29; asst. prof. math. physics, Princeton U., 1928-31, asso. prof., 1931-38, prof., 1938-47; prof. math. physics, Calif. Inst. Tech., 1947—; sci. adviser Supreme Allied Comdr. Europe, 1954-56; dir. Northrop Corp. Chmn. sci. bd. Dept. of Defense; member div. I, sect. B, Nat. Defense Research Com., 1940-43; sci. liaison officer, London Mission, Office Sci. Research and Development, 1943-46; expert cons. Office sec. of War, 1944-47; director of research Weapons Systems Evaluation Group, Office Sec. Def., 1950-52. Trustee Carnegie Endowment International Peace. Awarded Medal for Merit, 1946. Fellow Am. Phys. Soc., Royal Astron. Soc.; mem. Am. Math. Soc., Am. Philos. Soc., Nat. Acad. Scis. (fgn. secretary 1958—), Am. Astronomical Society Edinburgh Math. Soc., Sigma Xi, Phi Beta Kappa. Clubs: Athenaeum, Cosmos. Author: researches on differential geometry, theory of relativity, quantum theory, cosmology and applied mechanics. Home: 590 Auburn Av., Sierra Madre, Cal. Office: Cal. Inst. Tech., Pasadena, Cal. Died Aug. 29, 1961.

ROBERTSON, ROBERT CRAWFORD, orthopedic surgeon; b. Coulterville, Ill., July 29, 1899; s. John Wylie and Mary Elizabeth (Crawford) R.; A.B., U. Ill., 1921, B.S., 1922, M.S., 1924, M.D., 1925; m. Frankie Marion Condray, Sept. 7, 1925; children—Elizabeth Eugenia (Mrs. Stephen Tripp Smith), Mary Louise (Mrs. Thomas Burke Hodgson). Intern, resident St. Luke's Hosp., Chgo., 1924-26; fellow Willis C. Campbell Clinic, Memphis, 1926-27; practice medicine, specializing in orthopedic surgery, Chattanooga, 1927-69; founder, chief orthopedic services Baroness Erlanger Hosp., T.C. Thompson's Childrens Hosp.; mem. staff Meml. Hosp., Tenn. State Tb. Hosp., past chief of staff Pine Breeze Sanitorium; cons. Hamilton Meml. Hosp., Dalton, Ga., Copper Basin Gen. Hosp., Copper Hill, Tenn., Emerald-Hodgson Hosp., Sewanee, Tenn.; designated orthopedic surgeon U.S. Employees Compensation Commn., Tenn. Crippled Children's Service Bd. dirs. Little Theater, Meml. Hosp., Chattanooga. Served to 2d lt. with inf., U.S. Army, 1918-19, to col. with M.C., AUS, 1942-45, 51-55. Decorated Legion of Merit, Bronze Star medal, Purple Heart; recipient Arrowhead award. Diplomate Am. Bd. Orthopedic Surgery. Fellow A.C.S., Am. Acad. Orthopedic Surgeons, Internat. Acad. Medicine, Am. Geriatric Soc.; mem. A.M.A., So. Tenn. med. assns., Hamilton County (past pres.), Chattanooga med. socs., Chattanooga Acad. Surgery (past pres.), Clin. Orthopedic Soc. (past v.p.), Internat. Soc. Orthopedic Surgery and Traumatology, Soc. Med. Cons. to Armed Forces, Sigma Xi, Alpha Omega Alpha, Zeta Psi, Phi Beta Pi. Rotarian. Clubs: Chattanooga Golf and Country, Lookout Mountain Fairyland. Contbr. articles to profl. jours. Home: Chattanooga TN Died Jan. 15, 1969; buried National Cemetery Chattanooga TN

ROBERTSON, WILLIAM BRYAN, aviation exec.; b. Nashville, Tenn., Oct. 8, 1893; s. John Joseph and Myrtle (Harmon) R.; ed. pub. schs.; m. Marjorie Livingston, May 3, 1924; 1 son, James Livingston. Pres. Robertson Aircraft Corp., 1919-28; pres. and chmn. bd. Curtiss-Robertson Airplane Mfg. Co., 1928-30; v.p. Curtiss-Wright Airplane Co. and St. Louis Aviation Corp., 1930-33; now pres. Robertson Aircraft Corp. Was maj. Mo. N.G. A.S. and capt. Air Service, U.S. Army. Mem. Soc. Automotive Engrs., Quiet Birdmen of America, Inst. Aeronautical Sciences. Club: Bellerive Country. Was employer and backer of Charles A. Lindbergh. Home: Bridgeton, Mo. Office: Lambert Field, Robertson, Mo. Died Aug. 1, 1943.

ROBIE, EDWARD DUNHAM, rear admiral U.S.N.; b. Burlington, Vt., Sept. 11, 1831; s. Jacob Carter and Louisa Willes (Dunham) R.; ed. pvt. schs. and Binghamton, (N.Y.) Acad.; m. Helen Adams, June 3, 1858. Asst. engr. U.S.N., Feb. 16, 1852; promoted through various grades and retired on account of age, with rank of commodore, Sept. 11, 1893; advanced to rank of rear admiral retired, by Congress for creditable record in Civil War, May 29, 1906. Circumnavigated the globe in U.S. flagship Mississippi, of Commodore M. C. Perry's Japan expdn., 1852-55; erected and operated the first line of electric telegraph ever seen in Japan and instructed Japanese in building and operating the first steam railroad and in taking the first daguerreotypes ever seen there; on bd. U.S.S. flagship Susquehanna in expdn. to capture filibusters in Nicaragua and in laying the first ocean electric cable, Ireland to America, 1857, when cable broke; on bd. U.S. steam frigate Niagara when that vessel left Charleston, S.C., 1858, with 271 captured slaves and landed 200 of them in Monrovia, Liberia; chief engr. U.S.S. Mohican at capture of fts. at Port Royal, S.C., 1861; mem. bd. which designed the first iron floating dry dock for the U.S.N.; fleet engr. of the combined fleets at Key West, Fla., during the trouble with Spain over the Virginius, 1874, and selected and fitted out many vessels for the auxiliary naval force during Spanish-Am. War, 1898. Sr. engr. mem. of "Goldsborough Bd." to decide condition of naval vessels on Atlantic coast after Civil War; fleet engr. N. Pacific sta., 1866-69, European sta., 1871-74, Pacific Fleet, 1879-81; chief engr. Norfolk Navy Yard, 1874-77 and 1887-91, Boston Navy Yard, 1881-84, New York Navy Yard, 1884-87. Was mem. guard of honor over body of Gen. W. S. Hancock, Norristown, Pa., and body of Abraham Lincoln, City Hall, New York, Apr. 25, 1865. (Of 191 officers serving on Perry's Japan Expdn., 3 were alive Oct. 7, 1909.) Home: Washington, D.C. Died 1911.

ROBINS, THOMAS, inventor, mfr.; b. Highland Falls, N.Y., Sept. 1, 1868; s. Thomas and Emma (Davis) R.; student Princeton Prep. Sch., N.J., 1886-87; Princeton, 1887-89; m. Winifred Howard Tucker, Apr. 26, 1894; children—Thomas, Samuel Davis. Began series of inventions, 1892, leading to the "belt conveyor," now largely used for carrying ores, coal, etc.; awarded Grand Prize, Paris Expn., 1900, and highest in its class at Buffalo and St. Louis expositions; chmn. bd. Hewitt-Robins, Inc., ret., 1955. Mem., sec. Naval Cons. Bd., U.S., 1915—. Mem. Princeton Engring. Assn. (ex-pres.), Inventors' Guild (sec.), Am. Inst. Mining and Metall. Engrs., Nat. Research Council. Episcopalian. Mason. Clubs: Century, Down Town, Pilgrims (N.Y.C.); Royal Thames Yacht. Home: Saybrook Point and 40 E. 66th St. Office: 370 Lexington Av., N.Y.C. Died Nov. 4, 1957.

ROBINSON, BENJAMIN LINCOLN, botanist; b. Bloomington, Ill., Nov. 8, 1864; s. James Harvey and Latricia Maria (Drake) R.; A.B., Harvard, 1887; Ph.D., Strasburg, 1889; m. Margaret Louise Casson, June 29, 1887; 1 dau., Chriemhild (dec.). Asst. in herbarium, 1890-92, curator Gray Herbarium, 1892—, instr. German, 1891-94, Asa Gray prof. systematic botany, 1899—, Harvard. Fellow Am. Acad. Arts and Sciences; associate Acad. Natural Sciences of Phila.; hon. mem. Chilean Soc. Natural History; mem. numerous societies. Awarded bronze medal, St. Louis Expn., 1904; Centennial gold medal, Mass. Hort. Soc., "for eminent service to botany," 1929. Editor: Synoptical Flora of North America (by Gray, Watson, Robinson and others), 1892-97. Editor Rhodora, jour. of N.E. Bot. Club, 1899-1928; editor 7th edit. Gray's New Manual of Botany. Home: Cambridge, Mass. Died July 27, 1935.

ROBINSON, B(RITTAIN) B(RAGUNLER), agronomist; b. Topeka, Kan., Dec. 4, 1899; s. Harold and Nettie Maude (Bragunier) R.; B.S., Tex. A. and M. Coll., 1922; M.S., Mich. Agr. Coll., 1924; Ph.D., Mich. State Coll., 1932; m. Lois Chamberlin, 1923; children—Nancy June, Thomas Wood; m. 2d, Clara Mildred Green, Dec. 28, 1932; 1 dau., Alice Roxana. Asst., Mich. State Coll., 1922-24; jr. and asst. plant breeder U.S. Dept. Agr., East Lansing, Mich., 1924-31, asst. and asso. plant breeder, Corvallis, Ore., 1932-35, agronomist, sr. agronomist, Washington, 1936-50, charge fiber plants other than cotton, ARA, 1946-50, prin. agronomist charge abaca prodn. Central Am., Inter-Am. Inst. Agrl. Scis., Turrialba, Costa Rica, 1950-52; research agronomist RFC, then U.S. Gen. Services Administrn. charge abaca prodn. C.A., 1953-57; research adviser crops ICA, Beirut, Lebanon, 1958, Dacca, East Pakistan, from 1959. Field exploratory survey fiber plants, Haiti, 1941, 55; fiber cons., Peru, Chile, Ecuador, 1941; textile cons. Tech. Indsl. Intelligence Com., U.S. Army, Germany and Italy, 1945; fiber cons. Pan Am. Union, 1947, 49; del. Seed Conf., Ankara, Turkey, 1959. Mem. Sigma Xi, Gamma Sigma Delta, Phi Sigma. Episcopalian. Mason. Club: Dacca (East Pakistan). Author: The Braqunier Family in America, 1969; also numerous tech. articles. Home: Lake Worth FL Died Dec. 10, 1969; buried Oakwood IL

ROBINSON, CYRUS, mining engr.; b. Cullingworth, Yorks, Eng., Mar. 4, 1870; s. William J. and Leah (Ainsworth) R.; ed. Bradford Technical School, England; m. Harriet Newell Brooks, 1890 (she died Feb. 2, 1931); children—Leah Brooks, Eva Adelaide (dec.), Rachel Ainsworth, Richard Holt (dec.). Came to U.S., 1890; draftsman for Am. Ship Windlass Co., Providence, R.I., 1890; draftsman, later engr., Thomson-Houston Co., later General Electric Co., Lynn, Mass., 1891-93; chief engr. Jeffery Mfg. Co., Columbus, O., 1893-96; engr. and asst. to v.p. E. P. Allis Co., Milwaukee, Wis., 1896-99; chief engr. Westinghouse Machine Co., Pittsburgh, 1899; chief engr. M. Guggenheim's Sons, later Am. Smelting & Refining Co., 1900-04; consulting engr., N.Y., 1904-14 (retired). Active in design, constrn. and operation of trench digging machinery and tractors for British, French and Russian governments during World War. Home: Mt. Vernon, N.Y., and West Harwich, Mass. Died June 30, 1930.

ROBINSON, DWIGHT PARKER, engineer; b. Boston, Mass., May 1, 1869; s. Edgar and Susannah (Powell) Robinson; A.B., Harvard, 1890; S.B., Mass. Inst. Tech., 1892; m. Mary Elizabeth Stearns, May 20, 1897 (died Nov. 20, 1907); m. 2d, Mary Elizabeth Dahlgren, July 25, 1912 (deceased). With Stone & Webster, constrn. engrs., etc., Boston, 1893, admitted to partnership, 1911, and served as pres. Stone & Webster Engring. Corp., Stone & Webster Constrn. Co., etc.; organized Dwight P. Robinson & Co., Inc., 1919, with headquarters in New York, and engaged in engineering and construction work in U.S. and abroad; merged, Jan. 1, 1928, with three other orgns. to form the United Engrs. & Constructors, Inc.; now retired. Fellow Am. Inst. E.E. Home: Pocasset, Cape Cod, Mass. Died Mar. 17, 1955.

ROBINSON, FRANKLIN CLEMENT, chemist; b. E. Orrington, Me., Apr. 24, 1852; s. Harrison and Mary (Clement) R.; A.B., Bowdoin Coll., 1873, A.M., 1876; studied chemistry during parts of 2 yrs. in Harvard; (LL.D., Bowdoin, 1903); m. Ella M. Tucker, Aug. 29, 1877. Instr. chemistry, 1874-78, prof. and Josiah Little prof. natural science, 1878-85, prof. chemistry and mineralogy, 1885—, Bowdoin, Supt. schs., Brunswick, 1877-1900; chmn. sch. com., 1901—; state assayor, 1877-1909; mem. State Bd. of Health, 1894-99. Republican. Author: The Metals (text-books), 1878; Qualitative Analysis (text-books), 1897. Home: Brunswick, Me. Died 1910.

ROBINSON, G(EORGE) CANBY, med. educator; b. Balt., Nov. 4, 1878; s. Edward Ayrault and Alice (Canby) R.; A.B., Johns Hopkins, 1899, M.D., 1903; studied U. Munich, 1908-09; LL.D., Washington U., 1928; Sc.D., George Washington U., 1932; m. Marion B. Boise, Dec. 7, 1912; children—Margaret R. Angell, Otis Boise. Asst. demonstrator anatomy Cornell U., 1903-04; resident pathologist, resident physician Pa. Hosp., Phila., 1904-08; dir. Pathol. Lab. Presbyn. Hosp., Phila., 1909-10; resident physician Rockefeller Inst. Hosp., N.Y., asso. in medicine Rockefeller Inst., 1910-13; asso. prof. medicine Washington U., St. Louis, 1913-20, dean med. sch., 1917-20; prof. medicine and dean Vanderbilt Med. Sch., 1920-28; acting prof. medicine Johns Hopkins Med. Sch., 1921-22; dir. N.Y. Hosp. and Cornell Med. Coll. Assn., 1928-35; prof. medicine Cornwell U. Med. Coll., 1928-35; vis. prof. medicine Peiping (China) Union Med. Coll., 1935; lectr. medicine and preventive medicine Johns Hopkins, 1936-46. Nat. dir. A.R.C. Blood Donor Service, 1941-45. Md. Tb Assn. (exec. sec. since 1946). Mem. A.M.A., Assn. Am. Phys. (pres.), Am. Soc. Clin. Investigation, Harvey Soc. (pres.), Am. Physiol. Soc., Am. Pharmacological Soc., Alpha Delta Phi, Nu Sigma Nu, Alpha Omega Alpha; Fellow A.A.A.S. Mem. Soc. of Friends. Author: Therapeutic Use of Digitalis, 1923; Patient as a Person, 1939; Adventures in Medical Education, 1957; also numerous papers on physiology and pathology of human circulation, med. edn., social aspects of medicine. Home: 4712 Keswick Rd., Balt. Died Aug. 1960.

ROBINSON, JESSE MATHEWS, entomologist; b. Higginsport, O., Jan. 30, 1889; s. George Foster and Mary Etta (Mathews) R.; A.B., Miami U., Oxford, O., 1911; A.M., Ohio State U., 1916; student Ia. State Coll., summer 1923; m. Lena May Shinkle, Aug. 21, 1919. Asst. prof. of zoology-entomology, Coll. of Agr., and asst. entomologist, Ala. Agr. Expt. Sta., Ala. Poly. Inst., Auburn, 1919-21, asso. prof. and asso. entomologist, 1921-24, acting entomologist and head prof., 1924-29, chief entomologist and head prof. since 1929. Fellow A.A.A.S.; mem. Assn. Econ. Entomology, Entomol. Soc. America, Am. Genetics Assn., Eugenics Research Assn., Ala. Acad. Science, Ohio Acad., Phi Kappa Phi, Gamma Sigma Delta, Alpha Epsilon Delta, Alpha Gamma Rho, Phi Kappa Tau. Democrat. Presbyterian (elder). Mason. Club: Rotary. Home: 337 Armstrong St., Auburn, Ala. Died Aug. 27, 1949; buried Felicity, O.

ROBINSON, JOHN, botanist; b. Salem, Mass., July 13, 1846; s. John and Lucy Pickering (Stone) R.; ed. in schools at Salem under pvt. instr., supplemented by courses in botany at Harvard; m. Elizabeth Rollins Kremble, Oct. 17, 1869. Trustee Peabody Mus., Salem, and sec. museum com.; also trustee of Ropes Memorial (mansion house and garden), Salem Hospital, Salem Athenaeum, Salem East India Marine Soc. Author: Ferns in Their Homes and Ours, 1878; Flora of Essex County, Mass. (catalogue and notes), Essex Inst., Salem, 1880; Our Trees (street trees in Salem and vicinity), Essex Inst., 1891; Bibliog. catalogue oriental coins, Essex Inst., 1913; The Marine Room of Peabody Museum, 1921. Home: Salem, Mass. Died Apr. 9, 1925.

ROBINSON LYDIA GILLINGHAM, translator; b. Geneva, Ill., Nov. 12, 1875; d. James C. and Emma J. (Gillingham) R.; A.B., Rockford (Ill.) Coll., 1896. Asst., Chicago Pub. Library, 1898-1905; asst. editor The Monist and The Open Court, 1907-17; editor of publs., Chicago Pub. Library, since 1919. Translator: Babel Bible, Third Lecture (Delitzsch), 1906; Music in the Old Testament (Cornill), 1909; Akbar, Emperior of India (Garbe), 1909; Geometrical Solutions Derived from Mechanics (from Heiberg's German translation of Archimedes), 1909; Has the Psychological Laboratory Proved Helpful? (Billia), 1909; Spinoza's Short Treatise on God, Man and Human Welfare (from Dutch), 1909; The Algebra of Logic (Couturat), 1914; What is Dogma? (Le Roy), 1918; also numerous scientific and philos. articles from the French and German. Trustee Rockford Coll. Mem. A.L.A., Ill. Library Assn. Clubs: Library, College. Home: Versailles Hotel. Address: Public Library, Chicago IL‡

ROBINSON, MONCURE, civil engr.; b. Richmond, Va., Feb. 2, 1802; s. John and Agnes (Moncure) R.; m. Charlotte Taylor, Feb. 2, 1835, 10 children. Accompanied topograhic survey from Richmond (Va.) to Ohio River, 1818; attended lectures in mathematics and science in France, studied public works in France, England, Wales, The Low Countries, 1825-28; made surveys for Pottsville & Danville Ry. (Pa.), 1828 (1st railroad constructed in U.S.); apptd. to make surveys for Allegheny Portage R.R.; built Petersburg & Roanoke, Richmond and Petersburgh, Winchester and Potomac railroads; began building Phila. & Reading R.R., 1834; locomotive Gowan and Mary built in Phila. from his plans; mem. commn. which recommended Wallabout Bay as site for drydock to be constructed in N.Y. Harbor; ret. from profl. activity, 1847; mem. Am. Philos. Soc., 1833; hon. mem. Am. Soc. C.E. Died Phila., Nov. 10, 1891.

ROBINSON, REMUS GRANT, surgeon; b. Birmingham, Ala., Dec. 15, 1904; s. Remus G. and Lily (Hill) R.; B.S., U. Mich., 1927, M.D., 1930; M. Marybodine Busey, Dec. 28, 1933; children—Carole Y., Ilene E., Frederick E. Intern Homer G. Phillips Hosp., St. Louis, 1930-31, resident, 1931-34; practice medicine specializing in gen. surgery, Detroit, 1934-70; mem. staff Providence Hosp., 1953-70, sr. attending surgeon, 1957-70; mem. staff Sinai Hosp., 1955-70. Mem. med. hosp. study com. Detroit Commn. Community Relations, 1957-70; mem. Boys Com. Detroit, 1960-70; co-chmn. United Negro Coll. Fund, 1952; mem. Detroit Met. Regional Planning Commn., 1955-70; mem. diocesan com. on Christian social relations Episcopal Ch., 1961-62. Mem. Detroit Bd. Edn., 1955-70, pres., 1958-59, and 1965-66. Trustee Citizens Redevel. Corp. Detroit; chmn. bd. govs. Wayne State U., 1958-59. Named hon. alumnus Wayne State U., 1959; recipient numerous awards for public service, including those from Urban League, 1952, Booker T. Washington Trade Assn., 1950, N.A.A.C.P., 1956, Wayne State U., 1956; Lamp of Learning award Mich. Fedn. Tchrs., 1965. Diplomate Am. Bd. Surgery, Internat. Bd. Surgeons. F. A.C.S., Internat. Coll. Surgeons; mem. Wayne County, Nat., Mich., Detroit (Physician of Year 1961) med. socs., A.M.A., Am. Fracture Soc., Internat. Soc. Proctology, Greater Detroit Bd. Commerce, Alpha Phi Alpha, Sigma Pi Phi. Episcopalian. Club: Detroit Economic. Home: Detroit MI Died June 14, 1970.

ROBINSON, SAMUEL MURRAY, naval officer; b. Eulogy, Tex., Aug. 13, 1882; s. Michael and Susan Sinai (Linebarger) R.; grad. U.S. Naval Acad., 1903; post grad. in elec. engring.; hon. Dr. Science, Union Coll., Schenectady, N.Y.; Dr. of Engring., Stevens Inst., Hoboken, N.J.; m. Emma Mary Burnham, Mar. 1, 1909; children—James Burnham (comdr. U.S.N.), Murray. Served 11 years at sea; manager Puget Sound Navy Yard, 1925; promoted through grades to rear admiral, 1931, and apptd. chief of Bureau of Engring. and engr. in chief of Navy; inspector of machinery, Schenectady, N.Y., 1935; head of Compensation Bd., 1938; chief of Bureau of Engring. and Coordinator of Shipbuilding, 1939; chief of Bureau of Ships and coordinator of shipbuilding, 1940; promoted to vice admiral, 1942, and apptd. chief of Office of Procurement and Material; promoted to admiral 1945; adminstr. Webb Inst. Naval Architecture, 1949-52; ret., 1952. Decorated D.S.M.; Order British Empire; Officer de l'Ordre de la Couroune (Belgium); Order Southern Cross (Brazil). Mem. Am. Soc. Naval Engrs., U.S. Naval Inst.; hon. mem. Soc. of Mech. Engrs. Clubs: University (Washington, D.C.); New York Yacht, Nassau (New York). Author: Electric Ship Propulsion. Home: Houston TX Died Nov. 11, 1972; buried Houston TX

ROBINSON, SOLON, agriculturist, writer; b. Toland, Conn., Oct. 21, 1803; s. Jacob and Salinda (Ladd) R.; m. Mariah Evans, Oct., 1828; m. 2d Mary Johnson, June 30, 1872, 5 children. Formed Squatter's Union, Ind., 1836; known as "king of the squatters"; county clk., justice of peace, register of claims, postmaster (all Lake County, Ind.); pub. intermittently a small news sheet, Crown Point, Ind.; began contbg. articles on aspects of frontier to Albany Cultivator, 1837; prominent participant Log Cabin Conv., Lafayette, Ind., 1840; delivered address, later published as "History of Lake County," 1847; a founder U.S. Agrl. Soc., 1852; contbd. travel sketches and observations to Cultivator, Am. Agriculturist, Prairie Farmer (articles from a valuable hist. record of rural soc. of time); agrl. editor N.Y. Tribune, 1853; conducted exptl. farm, Westchester, N.Y.; played influential role in establishment Dept. of Agr., 1862; pub. Florida Republican, Jacksonville, Fla. Author: The Will: A Tale of the Lake of Red Cedars & Shabbona, 1841; Hot Corn (novel), 1853; Life Scenes in N.Y., Tales of Slum Life, 1854; How to Live; or Domestic Economy Illustrated, 1860; Facts for Farmers: Also for the Family Circle, 1864; A Tale of Frontier Life and Indian Character, 1867; Mewonitac, 1867. Died Jacksonville, Fla., Nov. 3, 1880.

ROBINSON, STILLMAN WILLIAMS, engineering expert; b. Reading, Vt., Mar. 6, 1838; s. Ebenezer, Jr. and Adeline (Williams) R.; brother of Albert Alonzo R.; C.E., U. of Mich., 1863; (Sc.D., Ohio State U., 1896); m. Mary E. Holden, Dec. 29, 1863 (died 1885); m. 2d, Mary Haines, Apr. 12, 1888. Served 4 yrs. apprenticeship in machine shop; has taken out about 40 patents; first invention was thermometer graduating machine; invented various machines afterward, notably for shoe mfg. Asst. engr. U.S. Lake Survey, 1863-66; asst. in engineering, geodesy and mining, U. of Mich., 1866-70; prof. mech. engring. and physics, 1870-82, dean Coll. Engring., 1878, U. of Ill.; prof. mech. engring. and physics, 1882-95, prof. emeritus, 1899—, Ohio State U.; resigned to care for inventions; pres. S. W. Robinson & Son. Inspr. rys. of Ohio, 1880-84; cons. engr. Santa Fé Ry., 1888-90; also Lick telescope mountings, 1887. Received several awards and medals at expns., 1876 and 1903. Author: Teeth of Gear Wheels and the Robinson Templet Odontograph, 1876; Railroad Economics, 1882; Strength of Wrought Iron Bridge Members, 1882; Compound Steam Pumping Engines (part 2, analytical and graphical treatment), 1884; Principles of Mechanism (coll. text-book), 1896. Home: Columbus, O. Died 1910.

ROBINSON, WILLIAM, inventor, engr.; b. Coal Island, County Tyrone, Ulster, Ireland, Nov. 22, 1840; grad. Wesleyan U., 1865; Ph.D., Boston U. Brought to U.S., 1844; prin. high sch., Ansonia, Conn., 1865-66; worked in Pa. oil fields, 1866-67; prin. Spring Valley Acad., N.Y., 1867-69; in oil bus., Pa., 1869-72; exhibited model of automatic railroad signal system, 1870; patented closed track circuit system of automatic electric signalling for railroads in U.S. and France, 1872; organized Robinson Electric Ry. Signal Co., St. Petersburg, Pa., 1872; organized firm in Boston area, 1875-82; other inventions include bond wire system of connecting adjacent rails electrically, wireless electric ry. signal system; developed use of fiber for insulated rail-joints. Author: History of Automatic Electric and Electrically Controlled Fluid Pressure Signal Systems for Railroads, 1906. Died Bklyn., Jan. 2, 1921; buried Bklyn.

ROCKWELL, ALFRED PERKINS, mining engr., soldier; b. Norwich, Conn., Oct. 16, 1834; s. John Arnold and Mary Watkinson (Perkins) R.; grad. Yale, 1855; studied mining engring. 2 yrs. in scientific dept., Yale; 1 yr. in Mus. of Practical Geology, London, and 1 yr. at Sch. of Mines, Freiberg, Saxony (Ph.B., 1857, A.M., 1858, Yale); m. Katharine Virginia, d. Samuel E. Foote, New Haven, Conn., June 20, 1865 (died 1902). Pulled an oar in the Atlanta boat, 1852, in 1st regatta ever rowed bet. Yale and Harvard. Served 3 yrs. in army during Civil war, as capt., 1st Conn. Light Battery, Jan. 21, 1862, to June 18, 1864; col. 6th Conn. vol. inf., June 18, 1864, to Feb. 9, 1865; took part in many active engagements; bvtd. brig. gen. U.S.V., 1865, for "gallant and distinguished services in the field during campaign of 1864." On bd. of visitors U.S. Mil. Acad., 1865; prof. mining, Sheffield Scientific Sch., 1865-68, same Mass. Inst. Tech., 1868-73; chmn. bd. fire commrs., Boston, 1873-76; pres. Eastern R.R. Co., 1876-79; treas. Great Falls Mfg. Co., 1879-86; retired from active business, 1886. Represented Yale Univ. at Millenary celebration of King Alfred the Great, Winchester, Eng., Sept. 1901. Author: Roads and Pavements in France, 1896. Died 1903.

ROCKWELL, ALPHONSO DAVID, physician; b. New Canaan, Conn., May 18, 1840; s. David S. and Betty R.; A.M., Kenyon Coll., 1868; M.D., Bellevue Hosp. Med. Coll. (New York U.), 1864; m. Susie Landon, Oct. 7, 1868. Asst. surgeon 6th Ohio Cav. and brigade surgeon with rank of maj., 1864-65; prof. electro-therapeutics, New York Post-Grad. Sch. Medicine, 1888-92; neurologist and electro-therapeutist, Flushing Hosp., 1904-12; retired. Member commn. to aid in establishing the method of executions by electricity. Author: Relation of Electricity to Medicine and Surgery; Treatise on the Medical and Surgical Uses of Electricity (with G. M. Beard), 9 3dits.; Nervous Exhaustion, 1901; Rambling Recollections (autobiography), 1920. Home: Flushing, L.I. Died Apr. 12, 1933.

ROCKWELL, EDWARD HENRY, civ. engr.; b. Worcester, Mass., Apr. 20, 1869; s. Edward Munson and Martha Josephine (Smith) R.; B.S., Worcester Poly. Inst., 1890, C.E., 1920; hon. D.Eng. from same inst., 1933; m. Lena Hortense Warfield, Oct. 29, 1891; children—Grace Margaret (Mrs. Stanley R. Kingman), Dorothy (Mrs. Mark A. Burns), Doris, Donald Edward, Rosamond (Mrs. W. W. Cheney); m. 2d, Nellie May Owens, June 4, 1941; with George S. Morrison, cons. engr., Chicago, 1890-92; submaster high sch., Leominster, Mass., 1893-95; with Norcross Bros., bldg. steel work, Worcester, Mass., 1895-97; in charge installation of machinery, and supt. Holliston (Mass.) Yarn Co., 1897-99; draftsman Boston Bridge Works, 1899-1900, Boston Navy Yard, 1900-01; asst. engr. Boston Bridge Works, 1901-02; instr. in civ. engring., Tufts Coll., 1902-03, asst. prof., 1903-06, prof. structural engring., 1906-18, prof. civ. and structural engring., 1918-22; dean of engring. and prof. civ. engring., Rutgers U., 1922-28; Simon Cameron Long prof. civ. engring., Lafayette Coll., since 1928. With Boston Bridge Works, summer, 1906; asst. engr. Boston Transit Commn., summer, 1907; designing engr. Suffolk County Court House extension, Sept. 1907-June 1908, cons. engr. on constrn. same, June 1908-Jan. 1910; cons. engr. commn. on Galveston causeway reconstruction, Oct. 1916-Jan. 1917; engr. and architect in charge design, contract and constrn. of chem. lab., Tufts Coll., July 1921-Sept. 1922; cons. engr. Gen. Crushed Stone Co., Easton, Pa., City of Perth Amboy, N.J., Oliver Iron Mining Co., Duluth, Minn., etc. Mem. Am. Soc. Civil Engrs. (ex-pres. Lehigh Valley section), Soc. for Promotion Engring. Edn., Am. Assn. Univ. Profs., N.J. Soc. Professional Engrs. (ex-pres.), Phi Beta Kappa, Sigma Xi, Lambda Chi Alpha, Tau Beta Pi. Republican. Conglist. Club: Northampton County Country. Author: Vibrations Caused by Blasting and their Effect on Structures. Contbr. to Am. Highway Engrs. Handbook and bulls. Soc. for Promotion Engring. Edn. Home: 712 Cattell St., Easton, Pa. Died May 26, 1943.

ROCKWELL, SAMUEL, civil engr.; b. Brooklyn, Feb. 20, 1847; s. William and Susan Lawrence (Prince) R.; Ph.B., Sheffield Scientific Sch. (Yale), 1873; m. Cordelia A. Geiger, of St. Joseph, Mo., June 7, 1881. Resident engr., D., L. & W. R.R., Hobeken, N.J., 1873-77; built tunnel through Bergen Hill, N.J., and contractor, 1877-81; asst. city engr., Kansas City, 1881-82; prin. asst. engr. St. Paul Water Works, 1882-84; locating and constructing engr., St.P.M.&M. Ry., 1884-90; chief engr. Santa Fe Cal. extension, 1890; chief engr. Duluth & Winnipeg R.R., 1891; engr. Michigan Southern div. L.S.&M.S. Ry., 1891-99, prin. asst. engr., 1899-1904, asst. chief engineer, 1904-05, chief engr., 1905-12, consulting engr., 1912-18, retired on pension, May 1, 1918; consulting engr. in pvt. practice, 1918—. Mem. Am. Society C.E., Am. Ry. Engring. Assn. Mason. Club: Cleveland Athletic. Home: 6712 Carnegie Av. Office: Citizens Bldg., Cleveland, Ohio.

ROCKWOOD, ELBERT WILLIAM, chemist; b. Franklin, Mass., July 4, 1860; s. William and Laura Matilda (Blake) R.; B.S., Amherst, 1884, A.M., 1901; student U. of Göttingen, 1889, U. of Strassburg, 1890-91, U. of Leipzig, 1892 and 1894, U. of Chicago, 1893; M.D., State U. of Ia., 1895; Ph.D., Yale, 1904; m. Laura Clarke, Mar. 21, 1894; children—Paul Reed, Alan Clarke; m. 2d, Lillian Gertrude Smith, of Somerville, Mass., Jan. 1, 1925. Asst. in chemistry, Wesleyan, 1884-86; instr. chemistry, Cornell, 1886-87; chemist Hatch Expt. Sta. (Conn.), 1888; made prof. chemistry and toxicology, 1888, head dept. chemistry, 1904-20, prof. chemistry, 1920—, State U. of Iowa. Author: A Laboratory Manual of Physiological Chemistry, 1899, 5th edit., 1924. Introduction to Chemical Analysis for Medical Students, 1901. Home: Iowa City, Iowa. Died July 17, 1935.

ROCKWOOD, GEORGE GARDNER, photographer, inventor; b. Troy, N.Y., Apr. 12, 1832; acad. edn.; Ph.D., U. of Chicago; m. Araminta Bouton, 1853. Took up photography in 1855 and produced 1st carte-de-visite made in U.S.; inventor of many improvements in the art; famed for his art studies of children. Author of the scientific hoax, "Brain Pictures." Lecturer in Free Lecture Course, N.Y. Dept. Edn. Home: New York, N.Y. Died 1911.

ROCKWOOD, GEORGE I., engr., mfr.; b. Boston, Mass., Jan. 13, 1868; s. Edward Otis and Caroline (Washburn) R.; descendant of Gov. William Bradford, of Plymouth, Mass., 1620; ed. Phillips Acad. and Worcester Poly. Inst.; Dr.Engring. from the latter in 1929; m. Ellen T. Cheever, Nov. 13, 1890 (died Apr. 6, 1933); m. 2d, Anna V. Outhouse, May 12, 1933; children—George I., Ellen V. With Wheelcock Engine Co., Worcester, 1888-1892; consulting engr., Worcester, 1893-1905; pres. and treas. Rockwood Sprinkler Co., 25 yrs.; dir. Worcester Bank & Trust Co. Prof. thermodynamics, 1907, 08; life trustee Worcester Poly. Inst., pres. ad interim since 1939; pres. bd. trustees Rural Cemetery, Worcester. Hon. mem. Am. Soc. M.E. (v.p.); mem. Am. Antiquarian Soc. Founder the Alexander Lyman Holley Gold Medal for Great Achievement, administered by The Am. Soc. of Mechanical Engineers, New York. Pres. bd. trustees, Home Aged Females, Worcester. Republican. Conglist. Clubs: Worcester, Tatnuck. Author: Cheever, Lincoln and the Causes of the Civil War. Home: 2Military Rd., Worcester MA

RODD, THOMAS, engineer; b. London, Eng., June 13, 1849; s. Horatio and Anne (Theobald) R.; came to U.S., 1856; ed. pvt. and pub. schs. and U.S. Naval Acad., 4 yrs.; served in U.S.N., 1862-65; m. Mary Watson Herron, of Allegheny, Pa., Oct. 23, 1879. In city engrs.' office, Phila., 1869-72; began ry. service, Pa. Co., as rodman, 1872; asst. engr., 1872-77, prin. asst. engr., 1877-89, chief engr. since 1889, Pa. Lines west of

Pittsburgh; also engaged in extensive pvt. practice, 1890-1905, building many large mfg. and other plants. Dir. Commonwealth Trust Co., People's Natural Gas & Pipeage Co., and many ry. cos. Mem. Am. Soc. C.E., Am. Ry. Engring. and Maintenance of Way Assn., Engrs. Soc. of Western Pa. Clubs: Pittsburgh, Duquesne, Allegheny Country, University, Pittsburgh Golf (Pittsburgh), Metropolitan (New York), Chicago (Chicago). Home: 5407 Ellsworth Av. Office: Union Sta., Pittsburgh.

RODDY, HARRY JUSTIN, b. Landisburg, Pa., May 25, 1856; s. William Henry and Susan Catherine (Waggoner) F.; B.S., First Pa. State Normal Sch., Millersville, 1881; M.S., 1891; Ph.D., Kansas City (Mo.) U., 1906; m. Anna Houck Graver, Dec. 21, 1891; children—Anna Mary (Mrs. Clair G. Kinter), Henry Justin. Teacher pub. schs., 1877-87; teacher, First Pa. State Normal Sch., 1887-1904, dir. geography and geology work, 1906-08, head of science work, 1908-26; curator of museum and prof. geology, Franklin and Marshall Coll., since 1926. Sec. Lancaster City Tree Commn. Dir. Nature Study Club, Lancaster. Author: Common School Geography (two books), 1913, 15; Industrial and Commercial Geography of Lancaster County, Pa., 1916; Origin of Concretions in Streams, 1917; The Reptiles of Lancaster County and the State of Pennsylvania, 1926; The Geology and Geography of Lancaster Co., Pa., 1920. Contbr. chapters on natural history to several books, also contbr. to newspapers; lecturer on natural history subjects. Home: Conestoga, Pa. Address: Franklin and Marshall Coll., Lancaster, Pa. Died Sept. 4, 1943.

RODENBAUGH, HENRY NATHAN, ry. exec., cons. engr.; b. Norristown, Pa., Nov. 20, 1879; s. William Henry and Teresa Jane (Shanks) R.; B.Sc. in Mech. Engring., U. Pa., 1901, M.E., 1931; Wagner Inst. Sci., Phila., 1908-09; m. Caroline Pickett Bransford, Nov. 17, 1904; children—Thomas Bransford, Jean Crawford (Mrs. Henry A. Soleliac, Jr.), Caroline Carrington. Draftsman, N.&W. Ry., 1902-03; yard supt. Alan Wood, Iron & Steel Co., Conshocken, Pa., 1903-04; asst. engr. So. Ry., Washington, 1904-05; with Carolina Clinchfield & Ohio Ry., Bristol, Va., 1905-06; prin. asst. engr. Va.&S.W. Ry., 1906-08; structural engr. on track elevation, Phila., Germantown & Norristown Ry. (P.&R. Ry.), 1908-09; with So. Ry. as asst. engr. bridges, 1909-11, engr. in charge terminal improvements, hdqrs. Atlanta, 1911-14, supervising engr., Washington, Jan.-May 1914, prin. asst. engr. valuation dept., 1914-18; engring. asst. to regional dir. So. Region, U.S. R.R. Adminstrn. at Atlanta, 1918-20, regional engr. So. and Pocahontas regions, Mar.-July 1920; chief engr. Fla. East Coast Ry., 1920-23, gen. mgr., 1923-25, dir. and v.p. in charge operation, traffic, constrn. and valuation, Mar. 1925-June 1932; also for same period, v.p. and dir. Fla. East Coast Car Ferry, Jacksonville Terminal Co. (mem. exec. com.); dir. and mem. exec. com. Fruit Growers Express Co., 1925-32; dir. North Am. Aviation, Inc., 1928-32; cons. engr. and adv. counsel on transp. co. problems, 1 Wall St., N.Y.C., 1832-37; v.p. in charge ry. work Day & Zimmermann, Inc., 1937-44; chmn. bd. Rodenbaugh, Miller & Assos., cons. engrs., 1949; cons. engr. since 1949. Pres. Haverford Civic Assn. since 1947; dir. research inst. Temple U. since 1947. Mem. Price Adjustment Bd., Phila. Ordnance Dist., U.S. Army, Apr. 1944-47. Trustee Fla. Normal and Indsl. Inst., Flagler Meml. Hosp., Temple U.; chmn. St. John's County (Fla.) trustees Free Dental Clinic for Children. Mem. Am. Soc. C.E. (ex-pres. Fla. sect.), Am. Soc. M.E., Ry. Guild, Soc. Am. Mil. Engrs., Naval Inst., Soc. Naval Engrs., Am. Ry. Engring. Assn., Scotch-Irish Soc. of Pa., Newcomen Soc. Eng., Am. Acad. Polit. and Social Sci., Montgomery County Hist. Soc., St. Augustine (Fla.) Hist. Soc., Sigma Alpha Epsilon. Republican. Episcopalian. Clubs: St. Augustine Yacht, Ancient City Yacht, St. Augustine Country, Boca Ratan (Fla.); Merion Cricket, Home: Seven Pines, Elbow Lane, Haverford, Pa. Died Jan. 15, 1966.

RODGERS, JOHN, naval officer; b. Sion Hill, Md., Aug. 8, 1812; s. Capt. John and Minerva (Denison) R.; attended U. Va. one year; m. Ann Hodge, Nov. 27, 1857, 3 children. Apptd. midshipman U.S. Navy, 1828, passed midshipman, 1834; comdr. in Wave, then Jefferson in Seminole War; commd. lt., 1840; commanded ship Boxer of Home Squadron, 1842-44; ordered to duty with North Pacific Surveying Expdn., 1852, 2d in rank commanding ship John Hancock; surveyed Liu-Kius, Ladrones and other islands, Hawaiian and Society Islands; promoted comdr., 1855; in charge of office in Washington (D.C.) preparing results of expdn. for publication, 1856; commanded ship Flag, 1861; aide to Rear Adm. Samuel Du Pont at Battle of Point Royal (S.C.); commanded ship Galena, 1862; commd. capt., 1862; served in attack on Ft. Sumter, 1863; promoted to commodore by Congress, 1863; served in ships Dictator, 1864, Monadnock, 1866-67; comdt. Boston Navy Yard, 1866-69; commd. rear adm., 1869; commanded Asiatic Squadron as rear adm., 1870-72; pres. Naval Examining and Retiring bds., 1872-73; comdt. Mare Island (Cal.) Navy Yard, 1873-77; supt. Naval Observatory, 1877-82; chmn. Light House Board, 1878-82; pres. U.S. Naval Inst., Transit of Venus Commn., 1st Naval Adv. Bd., Jeannette Relief Bd.; charter mem. Nat. Acad. Scis. Died Washington, May 5, 1882.

RODMAN, THOMAS JACKSON, inventor, army officer; b. Salem, Ind., July 30, 1815; s. James and Elizabeth (Burton) R.; grad. U.S. Mil. Acad., 1841; m. Martha Black, 1843, 7 children. Commd. capt. U.S. Army, 1855, lt. col., 1867; had original idea of casting guns upon hollow core, cooling inner surface by flow of waters; did experiments resulting in successful manufacture of so-called mammoth and perforated-cake, or prismatic gun powder; inventions approved and adopted by govt., 1859; methods utilized by Russia, Gt. Britain, Prussia; commanded arsenal at Watertown, Mass.; supervised casting of smooth bores and rifled guns during Civil War; brevetted lt. col., col., brig. gen., 1865; comd. Rock Island (Ill.) Arsenal, 1865. Died Rock Island Arsenal, June 7, 1871.

RODMAN, WALTER SHELDON, elec. engring.; b. Wakefield, R.I., Sept. 1, 1883; s. Charles Lewis and Imogene Ethel (Sheldon) R.; B.S., R.I. State Coll., Kingston, 1904, M.S., 1907; Saltonstall fellow, Mass. Inst. Tech., 1909-10, M.S., 1909; m. Sarah Wilcox Palmer, Sept. 6, 1904. Instr. in physics, mathematics and elec. engring., R.I. State Coll., 1904-08; adj. prof. elec. engring., U. of Va., 1910-13, asso. prof., 1913-17, prof. since 1917 and apptd. acting dean of engineering, May 1931, dean since 1933, sec. engring. faculty, 1910-33. Asso. mem. Naval Cons. Bd. (dir. for Va., World War); asso. dir. in charge road work, Motor Truck Drivers' Training Detachment, U. of Va., 1918. Fellow A.A.A.S., Am. Inst. E.E. (v.p. Dist. 4, 1929-31); mem. Illuminating Engring. Soc., Soc. for Promotion Engring. Edn. (2d v.p. 1926-27), Am. Association Univ. Profs. asso. mem. Tau Beta Pi; hon. mem. Phi Beta Kappa (sec. 1922-40), Phi Sigma Kappa, Theta Tau, Phi Kappa Phi, Sigma Xi, Pi Gamma Mu; rep. of Am. Inst. E.E. on engineering research com. of Engineering Foundation, 1930-35, and in Assembly of Am. Engineering Council, 1931 and 1932. Republican. Episcopalian. Club: Colonnade. Contbr. to Engring. End., U. of Va., Jour. of Engring., Trans. Illuminating Engring. Soc. Home: Lyndhall Apartments, University, Va. Address: Thornton Hall, University of Va., Charlottesville, Va. Died Dec. 31, 1946.

ROE, EDWARD DRAKE, JR., mathematician; b. Elmira, N.Y., Jan. 4, 1859; s. Edward Drake and Eleanor Jane (Frost) R.; A.B., Syracuse U., 1880; student Harvard Med. Sch., 1882; A.B., Harvard, 1885; Harvard Grad. Sch., 1885-86, 1888-92, A.M., 1886; scholarship in the Med. Sch., Thayer scholarship in the Grad. Sch.; a founder and charter sec. Graduate Club of Harvard; studied U. of Erlangen, 1897-98, Ph.D., magna cum laude, 1898; m. Harriet Adelaide Bridge (Gourley), Mar. 15, 1890 (died 1898); children—Eva Gourley (Mrs. Edwin H. Gaggin), Edward Drake (dec.); m. 2d, Josephine Alberta Robinson, A.M., Feb. 1, 1911. Instr. mathematics, acad., Media, Pa., 1886-88; instr. same, pro tem., Harvard, 1890, Boston Univ., 1890-92; asso. prof. mathematics, Oberlin Coll., 1892-99, Syracuse U., 1900-01; John Raymond French prof. mathematics, Syracuse U., 1901—, and dir. of the observatory, 1919—, research prof., 1925—. Traveled in Germany, Austria and Switzerland, 1897-98, 1903, 04; tour of German univs. and 3d Internat. Congress of Mathematicians at Heidelberg, 1904. Research asso. Yerkes Obs., summer of 1915. Erected pvt. astron. obs., 1906, equipped with 61/2 in. equatorial telescope, as part of residence in Syracuse. Author of some 64 publs. in math. and scientific jours., etc. Nephew of late Rear Adm. Francis Asbury Roe. Home: Syracuse, N.Y. Died Dec. 11, 1929.

ROE, JOSEPH HYRAM, biochemist, educator; b. Winchester, Va., Dec. 27, 1892 s. Joseph Ashby and Julia Abbott (Winkfield) A.B., Roanoke Coll., 1916; A.M., Princeton, 1917; Ph.D., George Washington Univ., 1923; Ph.D., Yale, 1934; m. Clara Grace Lauck, Aug. 19, 1922; 1 son, Joseph Hyram. Instr. biochemistry, George Washington Univ. Sch. of Medicine, Washington, D.C., 1919, asso. prof., 1919-22, prof., 1922-67, head of department, 1922-32, 1938-59, sabbatical leave, 1932-33; visiting prof. U. So. Cal., summer 1951. Served as pvt. F.A., World War I; 2d lt. F.A. Res., 1918-23; capt. to maj. San. Corps Res., 1925-42; cons. War Dept. selection med. trainees, 1944-45; cons., com. on food composition, Nat. Research Council, on vitamin C assay of foods, 1943-46; regional gas officer Office Civil Def., Washington Region, 1943-45; mem. Sci. Manpower Commn., 1952-54; biochemistry com. Nat. Bd. Med. Examiners, 1958-62, Am. Bd. Clin. Chemistry, 1959-67; cons. med. research VA Center at Martinsburg, W.Va., 1956-60, 64-67. Recipient award of merit George Washington U. Med. Soc., 1954; Alumni achievement award George Washington U., 1955; Ernest Bischoff award Am. Assn. Clin. Chemists, 1956, Eloy Alfaro award, 1961. Fellow A.A.A.S. (council 1953-56, 61-63); mem. Cosmotographers (pres. 1962-63), Am. Soc. Biol. Chem., Am. Chem. Soc., Am. Inst. Nutrition (sec. 1948-51, mem. council 1958-61), Am. Assn. Clin. Chemists (chmn. of the Capital section 1963-64), Soc. Exptl. Biology and Medicine (chmn. D.C. sect. 1944-45), A.M.A. (affiliate), Am. Assn. U. Professors, Washington Academy Medicine (pres. 1960-62), George Washington Univ. Alumni Assn. (v.p. 1940-44, 54-56), Smith-Reed-Russell Soc., Alpha Omega Alpha, Alpha Chi Sigma, Sigma Xi. Lutheran. Club: Cosmos (Washington). Author: Principles of Chemistry, 9th edition, 1963; A Laboratory Guide in Chemistry, 4th edition, 1963; A Laboratory Manual of Biochemistry (with C. R. Treadwell), 6th edition, 1959; sect. Chemical Determination of Vitamin C in Methods of Biochemical Analysis, 1953. Contbr. articles to biochem. and med. jours., sects. of books. Home: Washington DC Died May 18, 1967.

ROEBLING, JOHN AUGUSTUS, civil engr., bridge builder, mfr.; b. Mühlhausen, Thuringia, Germany, June 12, 1806; s. Christoph Polycarpus and Friederike (Mueller) R.; studied architecture, engring., bridge constrn., hydraulics, langs., also philosophy (under Hegel) Royal Poly. Inst., Berlin, Germany, civil engr. degree, 1826; m. Johanna Herting, May 1836; m. 2d, Lucia Cooper; 9 children including Washington Augustus, Ferdinand W., Josephine. Roadbuilder for Prussian govt. in Westphalia, 1826-29; made spl. study of chain suspension bridge, Bamberg, Bavaria; came to U.S., 1831, naturalized, 1837; engr. working on constrn. dams and locks on Beaver River, Pa., 1837; conceived idea of twisted wire rope (to replace hempen cables), devised equipment to manufacture wire rope, produced 1st wire rope made in U.S. in his factory, Saxonburg, Pa., 1841; built wooden aqueduct for Pa. Canal, 1844-45; completed hwy. bridge over Monongahela River at Pitts. (his 1st suspension bridge), 1846; constructed 4 suspension aqueducts for Del. and Hudson Canal; built pioneer railroad suspension bridge at Niagara Falls, 1851-55; built suspension bridge over Ohio River between Cincinnati and Covington, Ky. (completed 1867), bridge over Allegheny River at Pitts., 1858-60; apptd. chief engr. for bridge over East River between Lower Manhattan and Bklyn., drew up plans (approved 1869), died before constrn. started on Bklyn. Bridge (completed by his son Washington Augustus, 1883); an early advocate of railroad transp., trans-Atlantic telegraph. Author: Diary of My Journey from Mühlhausen in Thuringia via Bremen to the United States of North America in the Year 1831, Written for My Friends, published 1931; Long and Short Span Railway Bridges, 1869. Died Bklyn., July 22, 1869.

ROEBLING, WASHINGTON AUGUSTUS, engineer; b. Saxonburg, Pa., May 26, 1837; s. late John A. and Johanna (Herting) R.; bro. of Ferdinand W. R.; C.E., Rensselaer Poly. Inst., 1857; m. Emily Warren, Jan. 18, 1865. Joined father in constrn. of Pittsburgh suspension bridge across Allegheny River; served in Union Army, pvt. to bvtd. col., 1861-65; resigned Jan. 1865, to assist his father in building Cincinnati and Covington suspension bridge. The Brooklyn bridge was undertaken by his father, but his death, July 22, 1869, before the work had been begun, left the entire construction in his hands, and he directed it to completion. Pres. and dir. John A. Roebling's Sons Co., mfrs. iron and steel wire and wire rope, Trenton, N.J. Author: Military Suspension Bridge; etc. Home: Trenton, N.J. Died July 21, 1926.

ROEBUCK, JOHN RANSOM, physicist; b. London, Ont., Can., Sept. 23, 1876; s. Henry Simpson and Lydia Abigail (Macklem) R.; A.B., Toronto U., 1902, Ph.D., 1906; m. Maegaret Hilda Kittson, Sept. 29, 1906. Demonstrator in physics McGill U., 1902-05, lectr., 1905-07; instr. physics, 1907, asst. prof., 1913, asso. prof. since June 1919, U. Wis. Mem. Am. Chem. Soc., Am. Phys. Soc., A.A.A.S. Author: The Science and Practice of Photography, 1917. Home: 2210 Hollister Av., Madison, Wis. Died Oct. 9, 1965; buried Chapel Lawn Meml. Cemetery, Schererville, Ind.

ROEMER, (KARL) FERDINAND, geologist; b. Hildesheim Hanover, Germany, Jan. 5, 1818; s. Friedrich and Charlotte (Lüntzel) R.; student law at U. Göttingen, Germany, 1836-39; doctor's degree in science, U. Berlin (Germany), May 10, 1842; m. Katharina Schäfer, spring 1869. Contbr. to Neues Jahrbuch fur Mineralogie Geologie und Palaeontologie, until circa 1887; sailed for Am. on funds provided by Soc. for the Protection of German Emigrants in Tex. and Berlin Acad. Science, 1845, undertook mission to study conditions of colonists in Tex. and to report on natural resources of country; became privat-docent in mineralogy and paleontology at U. Bonn (Germany), 1848; became dir. mineral cabinet at U. Breslau (Germany), 1855, also prof. geology and paleontology; recipient Murchison medal Geol. Soc. London, 1855. Author: Texas—Mit besonderes Rücksicht auf deutsche Auswandesung und die physischen Verhältnisse des Lands nach eigener Beobachtung geschildert, 1849, Die Kreidbildungen von Texas and ihre organischen Einschulüsse, 1852, Die Silurische fauna des Westlichen Tennessee, 1860; Geologie von Oberschlesien, 3 vols. with maps and plates, 1870. Died Breslau, Dec. 14, 1891.

ROEVER, WILLIAM HENRY, (ro'ver), mathematician; b. St. Louis, Mo., May 26, 1874; s. William and Sophie (Deppe) R.; grad. St. Louis Manual Training Sch., 1893; B.S., Washington U., 1897; A.M., Harvard U., 1904, Ph.D., 1906; m. Minnie D. Hamilton, June 23, 1906; children—William Alexander, Frederick Hamilton. Instr. astronomy, Washington Univ., 1899-1901; instr. mathematics, Mass. Inst. Tech., 1905-08; asst. prof. mathematics, 1908-16, asso. prof., 1916-17, prof. since 1917, Washington U., head dept. mathematics and astronomy since 1932; leave of absence for study and travel in Europe, 1931-32;

professor emeritus teaching veterans since 1947. Taught nautical astronomy, U.S. Naval Auxiliary Reserve Sch., Municipal Pier, Chicago, and mathematics, U. of Chicago, summer, 1918; master computer Aberdeen (Md.) Proving Ground, fall of 1918; taught mathematics, U. of Tex., summer 1920. Fellow A.A.A.S. (sec. sect. A, 1921-25, chmn. 1926); mem. Am. Math. Soc., Math. Assn. America, Am. Forestry Assn.; v.p. and trustee Acad. of Science of St. Louis. Represents Am. Math. Soc. on Sectional Com. on Standards for Graphical Presentation sponsored by Am. Soc. M.E. Episcopalian. Contbr. book and papers in fields of geometry and mechanics. Home: 6802 Waterman Av., St. Louis. Died Jan. 31, 1951; buried St. Louis.

ROGERS, ALLEN, chem. engineer; b. Hampden, Me., May 22, 1876; s. Franklin G. and Georgianna (Higgins) R.; B.S. in Chemistry, U. of Maine, 1897, M.S., 1900; Ph.D., U. of Pa., 1902; m. Maude F. Couillard, Dec. 25, 1897; 1 son, Allen Ellington. Instr. chemistry, U. of Me., 1897-1900; sr. fellow U. of Pa., 1902-03; instr. organic chemistry, same, 1903-04; research chemist Oakes Mfg. Co., L.I. City, N.Y., 1904-05; in charge industrial chemistry, Pratt Inst., Brooklyn, 1905—, also supervisor course in industrial chem. engring.; consulting practice. Maj. Chem. Warfare Service, U.S.A., in charge industrial relations, May 1917-Jan. 1918. Awarded Grasselli medal, 1920, for work done in connection with fish skins for leather. Democrat. Universalist. Mason. Author: Manual of Industrial Chemistry, 1912, 15, 20, 25. Laboratory Guide of Industrial Chemistry, 1908, 17; Elements of Industrial Chemistry, 1916, 26 (spl. overseas edition, 1919); Practical Tanning, 1922. Home: Brooklyn, N.Y. Died Nov. 4, 1938.

ROGERS, ALLEN HASTINGS, mining engr.; b. Marshfield, Mass., Feb. 19, 1871; s. Alfred and Grace Hastings (Phillips) R.; B.S. in Mining Engring., Mass. Inst. Tech., 1890; m. Sara James Damon, Sept. 14, 1897; children—Phillips Damon (dec.), Priscilla (Mrs. Maurice A. Hall), John Phillips, Elizabeth (Mrs. Jason C. Balsbaugh), Barbara Damon (Mrs. Trask H. Wilkinson). With Am. Smelting & Refining Co. and allied cos., also with other concerns, in Western States and Mexico, until 1906; independent practice, 1906—; mem. Rogers, Mayer & Ball. "Dollar a year" man with U.S. Bur. Mines, Washington, D.C., 1917-19. Republican. Unitarian. Home: Brookline, Mass. Died Feb. 14, 1938.

ROGERS, AUSTIN LEONARD, seedsman; b. Cape Vincent, N.Y., Oct. 29, 1855; s. Charles and Harriet (Wilson) R.; high sch., Watertown, N.Y.; grad. Eastman Business Coll., Poughkeepsie, N.Y., 1885; m. Della M. Guile, Aug. 1882 (died 1904); children—Mabel H. (Mrs. K. D. Rose, dec.), Inez A. (Mrs. A. H. Shearer); m. 2d, Elizabeth Mulvena, July 1911. Founder, 1876, with bro. Everett E., of Rogers Bros. Seed Co.; continued business under same title after death of brother, 1890, and pres. from incorporation, 1902; has specialized as breeder and grower of garden varieties of peas and beans. Originated 2 new peas, Rogers Green Seeded Admiral and Rogers Winner; also 2 new beans, Rogers Improved Kidney Wax and Rogers Stringless Refugee. Hon. mem. Am. Seed Assn. Republican. Presbyn. Mason. Home: Alpena, Mich. Died Oct. 19, 1937.

ROGERS, CHARLES EDWIN, prof. civil engring.; b. Saratoga County, N.Y., June 5, 1874; s. Charles and Catherine (Schoonmaker) R.; C.E., Rensselaer Poly. Inst., 1896; M.C.E., Harvard, 1915; m. Sarah Elizabeth Chase, Sept. 7, 1898. Began teaching at Lehigh U., 1901; prof. civ. engring., Trinity Coll., Hartford, since 1905. Mem. Soc. for Promotion Engring. Edn., Am. Assn. Univ. Profs., Rensselaer Soc. Engrs., Harvard Engring. Soc., Conn. Society Civ. Engrs., Am. Astron. Soc., Sigma Xi, Pi Gamma Mu. Mem. Dutch Ref. Ch. Home: 33 Concord St., W. Hartford, Conn. Died June 30, 1942.

ROGERS, CHARLES GARDNER, zoölogist, physiologist; b. Perry, N.Y., Mar. 4, 1875; s. James Harvey and Cornelia M. (Gardner) R.; A.B., Syracuse U., 1897, A.M., 1899, hon. Sc.D., 1920; studied U. Chgo., Ph.D., U. Cal., 1904; m. Rose Humann, July 3, 1906; children—Mary Cornelia, Martin Humann. Instructor physiology Syracuse U., 1899-1902, asst. prof., 1905-07, asso. prof., 1907-10, prof., 1910-13; asst. in physiology U. Chgo., autumn quarter, 1902, U. Cal., 1903-04, U. Kan., 1904; prof. zoölogy Oberlin Coll., 1913-15, prof. comparative physiology, 1915-41, acting dean, Coll. Arts and Sciences, 1924-25, head zool. dept., 1936-41, prof. emeritus, 1941—; vis. prof. zoology Duke, prof. 1942-43. Mem. embryological staff Marine Biol. Lab., Woods Hole, Mass., 1914-30. Fellow A.A.A.S., Ohio Acad. Science; mem. Am. Physiol. Soc., Am. Soc. Zoölogists, Soc. Naturalists, Sigma Xi, Phi Beta Kappa, Phi Kappa Phi, Delta Upsilon. Conglist. Author: Textbook of Comparative Physiology, 1927, 2d edition, 1938; Laboratory Outlines in Comparative Physiology, 1929, 2d edition, 1938; also numerous papers on physiological subjects. Home: 378 Reamer Pl., Oberlin, O. Died Oct. 12, 1950; buried Oberlin.

ROGERS, DAVID BANKS, archaeologist, paleontologist; b. Paw Paw, Lee Co., Ill., Sept. 13, 1868; s. Joze W. and Lura Lestina (Wilson) R.; grad. Marysville (Kan.) High Sch., 1887; special studies U. of Kan. and other univs. (non-grad.); m. Emma Hinshaw, Apr. 16, 1891 (died Dec. 24, 1935); m. 2d, Lucile Derbyshire, June 1939. Began as teacher pub. schs., 1888; specialized in various edn. instns. and in field research; mem. staff Santa Barbara Mus. Nat. Hist., 1925; curator, 1930-39; retired. Discoverer (1931) of specifically new Pliocen Age bird Phalacrocorax rogersi (Howard). Fellow American Geographical Society. Mem. A.A.A.S., Southwest Federation Archaeologists. Ind. Republican. Unitarian. Author: Prehistoric Man of the Santa Barbara Coast, 1929. Contbr. on scientific subjects. Home: 2936 Hermosa Road, Santa Barbara, Cal.

ROGERS, EDWARD STANDIFORD, horticulturist; b. Salem, Mass., June 28, 1826; s. Nathaniel Leverett and Harriet (Wait) R.; never married. Worked in counting room of his father's firm until 1858; devoted himself to horticulture, expecially experiments in grape hybridization, Salem, 1858-99; succeeded in crossing Am. grape Vitis labrusca with European wine grape Vitis vinifera; produced 45 varieties of grapes, of which Agawam is the only one still grown. Died Peabody, Mass., Mar. 29, 1899.

ROGERS, ERNEST ALBERT, univ. prof.; b. Vinton, Ia., Aug. 10, 1866; s. Richard and Ann (Cannon) R.; grad. Tilford Acad., 1889; student Ia. State Teachers Coll., 1889-90; D.D.S., State U. of Ia., 1892, M.D., 1904, post-grad. work in bacteriology; m. Adelaide F. Joy, January 4, 1901. With State University of Iowa since 1892, as assistant demonstrator in laboratory, 1892-95, lecturer on dental anatomy, and demonstrator dental technology, 1895-98, lecturer regional anatomy and clin. dentistry, 1899-1904, prof. and head of dept. of clin. dentistry, supt. of clinics, 1904-16, asst. chair of oral surgery, lecturer dental jurisprudence, 1910-15, lecturer gen. hygiene, 1913-43, prof. and head dental econ. and roentgenology, and dir. dental infirmary, 1916-40, prof. roentgenology and dental econs., 1940-43, prof. of dentistry (emeritus) since 1943. Has done pioneer work in arousing interest in oral hygiene, lecturing and conducting examinations in schools throughout Iowa. Major, Dental Reserve, (inactive). Fellow Am. College Dentists; member American Dental Assn., Iowa State Dental Soc., Radiol. Soc. of N.A., Omicron Kappa Upsilon Xi, Psi Phi. Republican. Presbyterian. Contbr. on dental subjects. Club: Triangle. Home: Fort Collins CO

ROGERS, FAIRMAN, civil engr.; b. Philadelphia, Nov. 15, 1833; grad. Univ. of Pa., 1853; prof. civil engring. there, 1855-70; also lecturer on mechanics Franklin Inst., Philadelphia, 1853-65; in Union cavalry service, 1861, and later volunteer officer U.S. engrs.; completed survey of Potomac River northward from Blakiston Island, 1862. One of original members Nat. Acad. Sciences. Author: The Magnetism of Iron Vessels. Died 1900.

ROGERS, FRAZIER, engr.; b. Ora, Miss., Feb. 7, 1893; s. Joel Cooper and Mary (Duckworth) R.; B.S.A., Miss. State Coll., 1915; student Kan. State Coll., 1929; M.S.A., U. of Fla., 1930; m. Gladys Tanner, May 26, 1917; children—Frazier Vernon, Mildred R. Brown, Marion R. Kennard, Thomas, Betty Ann. Insp. Fla. State Plant Bd., 1916-17; county agt. Perquimans Co., N.C., 1917-18; asst. prof. agrl. engring U. of Fla., 1918-22, prof. since 1923; head agrl. engr. Fla. Agr. Extension Service, since 1946, head research agr. engr., Fla. Agr. Expt. Sta., since 1947. Mem. Fla engring. com., Soil Conservation Service; mem. state adv. com., Nat. Defense Training; mem. bd. dirs. Univ. Athletic Assn., Inc. Mem. Kiwanis, Phi Kappa Phi, Alpha Zeta, Sigma Delta Psi, Alpha Gamma Rho. Democrat. Batpist. Mason. Home: 211 NE 6th St., Gainesville, Fla. Died July 22, 1959.

ROGERS, HENRY DARWIN, geologist, educator; b. Phila., Aug. 1, 1808; s. Patrick Kerr and Hannah (Blythe) R.; LL.D. (hon.), U. Dublin, 1857; m. Elza Lincoln, Mar. 1854, 1 child. Lectr. in chemistry Md. Inst., Balt., 1828; prof. chemistry and natural philosophy Dickinson Coll., 1830-31; accompanied socialist Robert Dale Owen to London, Eng., 1832; became asso. Geol. Soc. of London; lectr. geology Franklin Inst., Phila., circa 1833-35; prof. geology and mineralogy U. Pa., 1835-46; dir. N.J. Geol. Survey, 1835-38, Pa. Geol. Survey, 1836-42; Regius prof. natural history U. Glasgow (Scotland), circa 1855-66; published Geology of Pennsylvania, 2 vols., 1858 (a report on the Pa. Geol. Survey which was one of the most important geol. documents of its time in Am.); advanced noteworthy ideas regarding structures of Appalachian Mountains. Author: Description of the Geology of New Jersey, 1840. Died Glasgow, May 29, 1866.

ROGERS, HENRY J., telegraph pioneer, inventor; b. Balt., Mar. 10, 1811; s. John H. Rogers; attended St. Mary's Coll., Balt; m. Miss McGlennan, 4 children. Employed by Samuel F. B. Moorse in constrn. of demonstration telegraph line between Balt. and Washington, D.C., 1843, apptd. telegraph operation when Balt, office opened for pub. business; an incorporator Magnetic Telegraph Co., 1845; joined N. Am. Telegraph Co., 1846, supt., 1848-52; supt. House Printing Telegraph Co. (organized 1852), 1852-55; patented marine signaling system using flags, 1844, system adopted by U.S. Navy, 1846; at outbreak of Civil War established field telegraph lines for Army of Potomac; sec. Potomac flotilla; navigation officer Washington (D.C.) Navy Yard; patented semaphore telegraph system at Washington, 1864; supt. Bankers' & Brokers' Telegraph Line, 1865-67; with So. & Atlantic Telegraph Line, 1867-73; devised flare signal code for use at night; patented insulation system for telegraph lines, 1872. Died Balt., Aug. 20, 1879.

ROGERS, JAMES BLYTHE, chemist, educator; b. Phila., Feb. 11, 1802; s. Patrick Kerr and Hannah (Blythe) R.; attended Coll. William and Mary, 1820-21; M.D., U. Md., 1822; m. Rachel Smith, 1830, 3 children. Supt. chemical works of Tyson and Ellicott, 1827; prof. chemistry Washington Med. Coll., Balt., circa 1827; lectured at Md. Inst.; wrote with George W. Andrews and William R. Fisher) "Minutes of an Analysis of Soup Containing Arsenic" for Jour. of Phila. Coll. of Pharmacy, 1834; wrote (with James Green) "Experiments with the Elementary Voltaic Battery" published in Am. Jour. Science and Arts, 1835; prof. chemistry med. dept. Cincinnati Coll., 1835-39; worked on Va. survey with his brother William, 1837; helped brother Henry who was conducting Pa. Geol. Survey; prof. chemistry Med. Inst. of Phila., 1841, Franklin Inst., Phila., 1844; mem. Am. Philos. Soc., 1846; became prof. chemistry U. Pa., 1847; published (with brother Robert) A Text Book on Chemistry, 1846, article "On the Alleged Insolubility of Copper in Hydrochloric Acid . . ." in Am. Jour. Science and Arts, 1848. Died Phila., June 15, 1852.

ROGERS, JAMES FREDERICK, hygienist; b. Malta, O., May 31, 1870; s. James M. and Margaret (Sprague) R.; grad. New Haven Normal Sch. Gymnastics, 1898; M.D., Yale, 1905, C.P.H., 1919, Dr. P.H., 1920; m. Harriet Betts Comstock, 1907; 1 son, Percival Comstock. Med. insp. pub. schs., New Haven, 1910-11; tchr. physiology, hygiene, phys. diagnosis, 1910-20; with U.S.P.H.S., 1920-23; chief Div. Sch. Hygiene and Phys. Edn., U.S. Bur. Edn. (now Office Edn.), 1923-30; expert cons. in hygiene, Office Edn., 1930-41. Hon. mem. Am. Sch. Health Assn.; hon. fellow Am. Acad. Phys. Edn. Hon. award Am. Phys. Edn. Assn. U.S. del. 5th Internat. Conf. on Pub. Instrn., Geneva, 1st Internat. Congress on Student Health Services, Athens, 1936. Author: Life and Health, 1910; also The Health of the Teacher, The Physique of School Children, other govt. publs. Prepared survey of med. inspection in U.S. for League of Nations. Editorial contbr. N.Y. Med. Jour., 1914-23; contbr. on hygiene to sci., other mags., studies of phys. characteristics of gt. men and many essays on music. Home: 2041 Rosemont Av. N.W., Washington 20010. Died July 31, 1965.

ROGERS, J(AMES) HARRIS, inventor; b. Franklyn, Tenn., July 13, 1850; s. James Webb and Cornelia (Harris) R.; ed. under pvt. tutors and at St. Charles Coll., London, Eng.; D.Sc., Georgetown U., 1919, U. of Md., 1919; unmarried. Settled at Hyattsville, Md., 1895; devoted life to scientific work, especially elec. research; awarded many patents relating to multiplex and rapid printing telegraphy; electric lights; the telephone and radio telegraphy. Discoverer of visual synchronism; the secret telephone and underground and underwater radio communication, the latter enabling the U.S. Govt. to carry on uninterruptedly during the World War I, communication with the allied govts., also with submarines when submerged, and with battleships, aeroplanes, etc. Hon. fellow, Med. Acad. Sciences, 1919, also Inventor's Medal; extended thanks by Md. Legislature, 1919, "for distinguished contribution to science," also by Md. Legion of Honor. Democrat. Catholic. Home: Hyattsville, Md. Died Dec. 12, 1929.

ROGERS, J(AMES) SPEED, biologist; b. Dayton, Ind., Nov. 4, 1891; s. Henry Martin and Alma Goodloe (Smith) R.; A.B., U. of Mich., 1915, A.M., 1916, Ph.D., 1930; m. Irene Russell, Apr. 18, 1918; children—James Speed, Irene Russell (Mrs. J. N. Howard). Asst. prof. zoology, Grinnell (Ia.) Coll., 1920-22; prof. biology, U. of Fla., 1922-46; prof. zoology and dir. Mus. of Zoology, U. of Mich., since 1947. Served with A.E.F., 1918-19. Mem. Am. Soc. Naturalists, Am. Entomol. Soc. (fellow), Soc. for Study Evolution, Soc. for Study of Systematics. Home: 240 Oakway, Ann Arbor, Mich. Died 17, 1955; buried Hanover, Ind.

ROGERS, JOHN RAPHAEL, inventor; b. Roseville, Ill., Dec. 11, 1856; s. Rev. John A. and Elizabeth Lewis (Embree) R.; A.B., Oberlin Coll., 1875, A.M., 1898, D.Sc., 1930; LL.D., Berea (Ky.) Coll., 1919; m. Clara A. Saxton, Dec. 25, 1878. Teacher and supt. pub. schs., 1875-86; civ. engr., 1886-88; patented machine for setting type (the Rogers Typograph), 1888, and later granted between 400 and 500 patents on typesetting machines, in U.S. and foreign countries. Pres. Internat. Typograph. Co.; chief inventor in charge experimental dept., Mergenthaler Linotype Co. Trustee Berea Coll. (Ky.), Oberlin Coll. Independent Republican. Conglist. Home: Brooklyn, N.Y. Died Feb. 18, 1934.

ROGERS, LORE ALFORD, bacteriologist; b. Patten, Me., Feb. 7, 1875; s. Luther B. and Mary E. (Barker) R.; B.S., U. of Me., 1896; U. of Wis. 1 yr.; D.Sc., U. of Md. 1923, U. of Me., 1925; m. Beatrice C. Oberly Oct. 3, 1906; 1 son, John Oberly. Asst. bacteriologist, N.Y.

Expt. Sta., Geneva, N.Y., 1899-1902; dairy bacteriologist, U.S. Dept. Agr. since 1902, in charge research laboratories, Bureau Dairy Industry (retired 1942); chairman program committee World's Dairy Congress, 1923; Borden Award, 1937. Member Society American Bacteriologists (president 1923), Dairy Science Association, Washington Acad. Sciences, Washington Acad. Medicine, Kappa Sigma. Home: 3635 S. St. N.W., Washington DC; also from May to Oct., Patten ME

ROGERS, MARVIN CARSON, chem. engr.; b. North St. Paul, Minn., May 13, 1904; s. Charles Wesley and Marie (Rufenacht) R.; B.S., U. Minn., 1926; M.S., U. Mich., 1927, Ph.D. 1929; m. Evelyn Beatrice Zehner, June 11, 1932; children—John William, Marvin Carson. Engr., Whiting-Swenson Co., Ann Arbor, Mich., 1929-32; group leader research Standard Oil Co. (Ind.), Whiting, 1932-37; asst. prof. chem. engring. U. Minn., 1938-40; dir. research R. R. Donnelley &Sons Co., Chgo., 1940-57; exec. dir. Photoengravers Research Inst., Chgo. and Park Forest, Ill., 1957-68; cons., dir. Chgo. Paper Testing Lab., 1957-68; corp. dir. Printing Plate Supply Co., Chgo.; mem. adv. bd. ABC Industries, Inc., Paterson, N.J. Mem. exec. bd. Calumet Council, Boy Scouts of Am., 1952-68, Silver Beaver award, 1954, nat. council rep., Cal. Council, 1959-64. Mem. graphic arts adv. com. Carnegie Inst. Tech., 1959-68. Served to lt. col. Chem. Corps, AUS, 1943-45. Fellow Inst. of Printing; mem. T.A.P.P.I., Am. Chem. Soc. (dir., chmn. 1946-60), A.A.A.S., Am. Inst. Chem. Engrs., Tech. Assn. for Graphic Arts (pres. 1950-51). Mason. Home: Flossmoor IL Died Mar. 13, 1968.

ROGERS, ROBERT EMPIE, chemist, educator; b. Balt., Mar. 29, 1813; s. Patrick Kerr and Hannah (Blythe) R.; M.D., U. Pa., 1836; m. Fanny Montgomery, Mar. 13, 1843; m. 2d, Delia Saunders, Apr. 30, 1866. Connected with ry. surveying parties in New Eng., 1831-32; chemist 1st Pa. Geol. Survey; made independent analysis of limestones (with Martin H. Boye); prof. gen. and applied chemistry U. Va., 1842; devised (with brother William) new process for preparing chlorine; improved processes for making formic acid, and aldehyde, perfected method of determining carbon in graphite, studied volatility of potassium and sodium carbonates, decomposition of rocks by meteoric water, absorption of carbon dioxide by liquids; studied (with brother James) alleged insolubility of copper in hydrochloric acid; published Textbook on Chemistry, 1846; prof. chemistry Med. Sch., U. Pa., 1852, dean, 1856; asst. surgeon West Phila. Mil. Hosp.; made study of petroleum, circa 1864; investigated waste silver in Phila. mint, made suggestions about refining, 1872; prepared plans for equipment of refinery of mint, San Francisco, 1875; prof. med. chemistry and toxicology Jefferson Med. Coll., Phila., 1877-circa 1884; an original mem. Nat. Acad. Scis.; an organizer Assn. Am. Geologists and Naturalists (now A.A.A.S.). Died Phila., Sept. 6, 1884.

ROGERS, THOMAS, locomotive mfr.; inventor; b. Groton, Conn., Mar. 16, 1792; s. John and Mary (Larrabee) R.; m. Marie Small, 5 children. Organizer (with John Clark) firm Clark & Rogers, 1819, began mfg. new loom, spinning of cotton; completed textile machine mfg. plant, Patterson, N.J., known as Jefferson Works, 1832; organizer, pres. Rogers, Ketchum & Grosvenor Machine Works, began mfg. railroad car wheels, boxes, other railroad castings, 1832, constructed locomotives, 1836, sold 1st locomotive to (given name Sandusky; 1st locomotive West of Allegheny Mountains); to Mad River & Lake Erie R.R.; credited with shifting link valve motion on locomotives in U.S.; 1st to apply wagon top boiler; initiated use of two pairs of coupled driving wheels. Died N.Y.C., Apr. 19, 1856.

ROGERS, WALTER ALEXANDER, civil engr., contractor; b. Milwaukee, Wis., Jan. 19, 1868; s. Alexander H. and Martha M. (Ross) R.; C.E., U. of Wis., 1888; m. Julia Cushing, July 1, 1891; children—Lester, Margaret, Ross, Carl, Walter, John. In engring. dept. Wis. Central R.R. and N.P. R.R., 1889-92, C.,M.&St.P. Ry., 1892-1901; pres. Bates & Rogers Constrn. Co., contractors, 1901-38, chmn. since 1938. Mem. Am. Soc. C.E., Western Soc. Engrs., Assn. Gen. Contractors of America. Republican. Clubs: Union League, Engineers, Chicago Golf. Home: Glen Ellyn, Ill. Office: 111 W. Washington St., Chicago, Ill. Died Jan. 3, 1944.

ROGERS, WILLIAM AUGUSTUS, mathematician, astronomer, physicist; b. Waterford, Conn., Nov. 13, 1832; s. David Potter and Mary (Rogers) R.; M.A., Brown U., 1857; m. Rebecca Titsworth, 1857, 3 children. Instr. and tutor in mathematics Alfred Acad., 1857; prof. mathematics Alfred U., 1859, prof. indsl. mechanics, 1860-circa 1870, built and equipped astron. observatory, 1865; pursued advanced mechanics Yale; studied practical astronomy under Prof. Bond at Harvard Observatory; served with U.S. Navy 14 months at close of Civil War; asst. Harvard Observatory, 1870, asst. prof. astronomy, 1877-86; prof. physics and astronomy Colby U., 1886-98; sent to Europe by Am. Acad. Arts and Scis. to obtain copies of imperial yard and French meter; organized physical lab. with model for accurate measurements Colby U.; contbr. scientific papers to 10 vols. of Harvard Annals; did research on value of yard and meter, his changes therein among most important ever made; hon. fellow Royal Soc. of London; fellow Royal Micros. Soc., A.A.A.S.; mem. Am. Micros. Soc., pres., 1887; mem. Am. Acad. Arts and Scis., Nat. Acad. Scis. Died Waterville, Me., Mar. 1, 1898.

ROGERS, WILLIAM BARTON, geologist, coll. pres.; b. Phila., Dec. 7, 1804; s. Patrick Kerr and Hannah (Blythe) R.; grad. Coll. William and Mary, 1822; LL.D. (hon.), Harvard, 1866; m. Emma Savage, June 20, 1849. Conducted sch. (with brother Henry), Windsor, Md.; lectr. Md. Inst., 1827; prof. natural philosophy and chemistry Coll. William and Mary, 1828-35; prof. natural philosophy U. Va., 1835; state geologist Va., 1835-48; state insp. gas meters Mass., 1861; responsible for act incorporating Mass. Inst. Tech., 1861, 1st pres., 1862-70, pres., 1878-81; prof. emeritus of geology and physics, 1878-82; noted for work (with brother Henry) on structure of Appalachian Mountain chain. Chmn. Assn. Am. Geologists and Naturalists, 1845, 47; corr. sec. Am. Acad. Arts and Scis., 1863-69; an original mem. Nat. Acad. Scis., pres., 1878-82. Author: A Reprint of Annual Reports and Other Papers on the Geology of the Virginias. Died Boston, May 30, 1882.

ROHN, OSCAR, mining engr.; b. Jackson, Wis., June 27, 1870; s. Frederick O. and Janette (Wilke) R.; B.S., U. of Wis., 1895; m. Mary E. Couse, May 19, 1896; m. 2d, Lou Foster Lauzier, Dec. 23, 1919. In govt. work on Alaskan exploration, 1898-99; examination of iron lands in Minn., 1900-01; mgr. Donora Mining Co., Duluth, Minn., 1902-03; cons. mining engr., 1903-06; mgr. Pittsburgh & Mont. Copper Co., 1906-09, E. Butte Copper Mining Co., 1909—. Mem. Am. Inst. Mining and Metall. Engrs., Lake Superior Mining Inst. Wrote: Report on Chittina River and Mt. Wrangell Dist., Alaska, 22d Ann. Report U.S. Geol. Survey; also articles in tech. jours. Address: Denver, Colo. Died Sept. 19, 1923.

ROHRER, ALBERT LAWRENCE, (ror'er), eng.; b. Farmersville, O., Feb. 29, 1856; s. Aaron and Elizabeth (Ozias) R.; ed. common schs., followed by spl. course in physics and mechanics, Ohio State University; m. Carrie L. Gould, Apr. 8, 1891; 1 dau., Miriam (Mrs. Joseph Bryan Shelby). Entered employ of the Thomson-Houston Electric Co., June 1884; has been with that Co. and its successor, The Gen. Electric Co., since; recruited the engineering personnel and supervised training, 1894-1914. Had 70 U.S. colls. and univs. on the visiting list and maintained corrs. in England, France, Germany, Sweden, China, Japan and South American countries. In that period 3,000 coll. graduates were brought to the General Electric Co.; elec. supt. Schenectady works, Gen. Elec. Co., 1892-93, advisory engr., 1923-26, retired. Ex-pres. Bd. Edn.; ex-treas. Free Pub. Library, Schenectady. Mem. Am. Inst. E.E., Am. Soc. M.E., Ohio Soc. New York, Phi Gamma Delta. Unitarian. Fifth class Order of Chia Ho (China). Author: History and Genealogy of the Ozias Family. Home: 307 Wyoming Av., Maplewood, N.J. Died Oct. 18, 1951.

ROHWER, HENRY, engineer; b. nr. Rendsburg, Holstein, Germany, Oct. 17, 1847; s. Henry and Margarete (Rohwer) R.; grad. Dr. Jessen's Poly. Inst., Hamburg, 1865; student Royal Poly. Sch., Hanover, 1865-69; came to U.S., 1869; m. Anna Sievers, Oct. 8, 1873. Topographer, chief draftsman, engr. in charge constrn., and chief engr. Burlington & Mo. River R.R., 1869-74, in Neb., and 1872, also resident engr. at Omaha of Omaha & S.W. Ry.; city engr. of Omaha, Neb., 1876-81; div. engr. locating and constructing Oregon Short Line (then branch of U.P. Ry.); engr. in charge of tunnel and later resident engr. and engr. maintenance of way, same line, 1881-85; engr. in charge location and constrn. Omaha Belt Ry. and Mo.P. extension to Omaha and Lincoln, Neb., 1885-87; assistant engineer in charge of maintenance of way M.P. Ry., Sedalia, Mo., 1887-1901; chief engr., 1901-05, cons. engr., 1905-06, same system; pvt. consulting civ. engr., 1906— Chmn. bd. engrs. Miss. River Bridge at Thebes; mem. bd. chief engrs. for new Union Depot and terminals, Kansas City; chmn. com. engrs. for City of St. Louis, 1908, to locate municipal bridge across Miss. River. Republican. Evang. Lutheran. Home: St. Louis, Mo. Died May 4, 1916.

ROLFE, CHARLES WESLEY, geologist; b. Arlington Heights, Ill., Apr. 17, 1850; s. Charles Wesley and Melissa Deete (Haven) R.; B.S., U. of Ill., 1872, M.S., 1878; m. Martha Kinsman Farley, Dec. 26, 1877; children—Deette, Mary A., Susan F. (Mrs. H. G. Butler), Amy L. (Mrs. A. E. Emerson). Instr. in science, U. of Ill., 1872-73; prin. schs., Sidney, Ill., 1873-74; teacher sciences, Jennings Sem., Aurora, Ill., 1874-76; prin. schs., Waterman, Ill., 1876-77; supt. schs., Kankakee, Ill., 1877-81; prep. dept., U. of Ill., 1881-85, prof. geology, 1885-1917, prof. emeritus, 1917—, U. of Ill., dir. ceramics, 1904-10. Home: Champaign, Ill. Died Apr. 5, 1934.

ROLFE, DANIEL THOMAS, physician, coll. dean; b. Tampa, Fla., Mar. 1, 1902; s. Everett R. and Carrie Lee (Thomas) R.; B.S., Fla. A. and M. Coll., 1922; M.D. with honors, Meharry Med. Coll., 1927; grad. study U. Chgo., 1928-30; m. Birdie Lucile Scott, Aug. 9, 1952. Intern George W. Hubbard Hosp., Nashville, 1927-28, now mem. adv. com.; instr. Meharry Med. Coll., 1927-28, prof. physiology, 1930-38, chmn. dept. physiology and pharmacology, 1938-52, acting chairman dept. anatomy, 1950-52, chmn. dept. physiology, dean Sch. Medicine, 1952-66, dean student affairs, 1966-68; guest dept. physiology Cornell U. Med. Coll., 1943-44; mem. med. adv. com. VA Hosp., Tuskegee, Ala. Diplomate Nat. Bd. Med. Examiners, 1935. Recipient Tolbert Anatomy prize Meharry Med. College, 1927; Distinguished Service plaque Fla. A. and M. Coll., 1953; Distinguished Service medal Nat. Med. Assn., 1956. Fellow A.A.A.S.; member World, Am., Nat., Tenn., Nashville, Volunteer State med. assns., Am. Physiol. Soc., Assn. Am. Med. Colls., Nat. Soc. Med. Research, Tenn. Acad. Sci., Nashville Acad. Medicine, Tenn. Council Human Relations, Nashville Symphony Assn., Nashville Community Relations Council, Homer G. Phillips Interns Alumni Assn., Meharry Alumni Assn. (exec. sec. 1939-59), Nashville Arts Council, Assn. UN, Alpha Omega Alpha (chpt. counselor), Kappa Alpha Psi. Mason. Author profl. articles. Home: Nashville TN Died May 26, 1968; buried Greenwood Cemetery, Nashville TN

ROLFE, GEORGE WILLIAM, chemist; b. Cambridge, Mass., Feb. 10, 1864; s. William James and Eliza Jane (Carew) R.; A.B., Harvard, 1885, A.M., 1886; spl. grad. course, Mass. Inst. Tech., 1895; m. Mabel Stuart, Feb. 28, 1888 (died 1913); 1 dau., Dorothy Stuart; m. 2d, Mary Eager Gifford, Sept. 1914. Chemist, Charles Pope Glucose Co., Geneva, Ill., 1886-89, 1892-93; sub-master, Brookline High Sch., 1889-90; chemist, Parque Alto, Cuba, 1891, Central Soledad, Cuba, 1892; chemist sewer purification expert, George E. Waring, Newport, R.I., 1894; instr. analyt. chemistry and sugar analysis, Mass. Inst. Tech., 1895-1915; instr. chemistry, Franklin Union, Boston, 1913-19. Chemist and factory supt., Central Aguirre, Puerto Rico, Boston and Puerto Rico, 1900-02 and 1907-09. The Cuba Co., Jatibonico, Cuba, 1913-14, Constancia, Puerto Rico, 1906, Cortada, Puerto Rico, 1907, Central Manopla, Cuba, 1921-22, expert in U.S. and Canadian cts. on starch products. Mem. Am. Chem. Soc., Nat. Geog. Soc. Clubs: Pi Eta, Delta Upsilon (Harvard), Authors. Author: The Polariscope, 1905; also numerous scientific papers. Translator (with Wm. T. Hall): Claasen's Beet Sugar Manufacture, 1906. Contbr. to Rogers Industrial Chemistry, 1st to 5th edits. Unitarian. Home: Eastville, Oak Bluffs, Mass. Died June 21, 1942.

ROLFS, PETER HENRY, plant pathologist; b. LeClaire, Ia., Apr. 17, 1865; s. Maas Peter and Maria Christina (Neimeier) R.; B.S., Iowa State Coll., Ames, 1889, M.S., 1891, asst. in botany, 1891; D.Sc., U. of Fla., 1920; m. Effie Stone, Aug. 25, 1892 (died Mar. 31, 1920); children—Mrs. Effie Hargrave, Clarissa. Entomologist and botanist, 1891-92, botanist and horticulturist, 1892-98, Fla. Expt. Sta.; prof. botany and horticulture, Fla. Agrl. Coll., 1895-99; botanist and bacteriologist, Clemson Coll. (S.C.) and Agrl. Expt. Sta., 1899-1901; plant pathologist, Subtropical Lab., U.S. Dept. Agr., Miami, Fla., 1901-06; dir. Fla. Agrl. Expt. Sta., 1906-21; dir. extension div., 1913-21; dean Coll. of Agr., U. of Fla., 1915-21; commd. to locate, organize and conduct agrl. coll. for State of Minas Geraes, Brazil, 1921-29; consultor Technico de Agricultura do Estado de Minas Geraes, 1929-33; state supt. of Farmers' Inst., 1907-19; agrl. dir. Fla. State Fair, 1917. Chmn. State Food Commn. and State Council of Defense, 1917-18. Fellow A.A.A.S.; mem. Bot. Soc. America (hon. life mem. since 1938), Assn. Am. Agrl. Colls. and Expt. Stations, Fla. State Hort. Soc. (pres., 1907, 08), Internat. Assn. Botanists, St. Louis Acad. Science, Sociedade Mineira de Agricultura, Sociedade Nacional (Brazil) de Agricultura, Club de Engenharia (Nacional). Democrat. Methodist. Author: Vegetable Growing in the South for Northern Markets, 1896; Subtropical Vegetable Gardening, 1915; also numerous pamphlets on plant diseases, hort. and agrl. subjects. Address: 1422 W. Arlington St., Gainesville, Fla. Died Feb. 23, 1944.

ROLLEFSON, GERHARD KROHN, chemist; b. Grand Forks, N.D., Jan. 12, 1900; s. Carl Jacob and Marie (Krohn) R.; A.B., U. of Wis., 1920, A.M., 1921; Ph.D., U. of Calif. (DuPont fellow, 1922-23), 1923; fellow John Simon Guggenheim Foundation, Gottingen, Germany, 1925-26; m. Nellie Marie Fogerty, Aug. 10, 1928; 1 son, Gerhard Carl. Prin. Minong (Wis.) High Sch., 1917-18; teaching asst. U. of Wis., 1919-21; teaching fellow, U. of Calif., 1921-22, instr. in chem., 1923-27, asst. prof., 1927-31, asso. prof., 1931-40, prof., 1940—, dir. of labs., 1945-47; cons. Los Alamos Scientific Lab., 1947—. Member Am. Chem. Soc., A.A.A.S.; Phi Beta Kappa, Sigma Xi, Phi Lambda Upsilon, Alpha Chi Sigma. Club: Faculty. Author: Photochemistry of the Halogens, 1938; (with M. Burton) Photochemistry and the Mechanism of Chemical Reactions, 1939; (with E. D. Eastman) Physical Chemistry, 1947. Editor of Annual Review of Physical Chemistry, 1948—. Contbr. articles in various sci. jours. Home: 920 Regal Rd., Berkeley 8, Cal. Died Nov. 15, 1955.

ROLLINS, JAMES WINGATE, civil engr.; b. Boston, Mass., Oct. 17, 1858; s. James W. and Sophia Webb (Atwill) R., S.B. in Civ. Engring., Mass. Inst. Tech., 1878; m. Clara Boyden Clark, June 17, 1892; children—Elizabeth Sargent, Wingate. Mem. Holbrook,

Cabot & Daly, gen. contractors, Boston; pres. Holbrook, Cabot & Rollins Corp., 1906—; v.p., treas. Blakeslee Rollins Corporation, Boston, 1924—. Republican. Congregationalist. Home: Milton, Mass. Died Nov. 19, 1935.

ROLLINSON, WILLIAM, engraver; b. Dudley, Worcester, Eng., Apr. 15, 1762; s. Robert and Mary (Hill) R.; m. Mary Johnson, May 10, 1782, 1 child. Came to Am., 1789; became engraver, N.Y.C., made silver ornaments, engraved portraits, bookplates, maps, certificates; made portraits of George Washington (1790) and Alexander Hamilton (1804); became banknote engraver, developed method of ruling lines by machine to prevent counterfeiting; Mason; mem. Soc. Mechanics and Tradesmen; served as lt. arty. N.Y. Militia. Died Sept. 21, 1842.

ROMANS, BERNARD, civil engr., naturalist; b. Netherlands, 1720; m. Elizabeth Whiting, Jan. 28, 1779, at least 1 child, Hubertus. Sent to N. Am. by Brit. Govt. for engring. work, 1757; apptd. dep. surveyor Ga., 1766; went to East Fla. to survey Lord Edgmont's estates on Amelia Island and St. John's River; apptd. prin. dep. surveyor Fordham dist.; explored Fla. and Bahama banks, and West Coast as far as Pensacola, Fla.; assisted in survey of West Fla., also in map preparation, circa 1771; made bot. discoveries, became king's botanist in Fla.; elected mem. N.Y.C. Marine Soc., 1773, Am. Philos. Soc., 1774; contbd. article on Indigo to Royal American Magazine, 1774; mem. Conn. com. to take possession of Ticonderoga and its outposts, 1775; with N.Y. Com. of Safety to construct fortifications on the Hudson nr. West Point, N.Y., 1775; gave allegiance to N.Y. Provincial Congress, 1775; commd. capt. of a co. of Pa. arty., 1776; ordered to join So. Army at S.C., circa July 1780, captured and taken to Montigo Bay, Jamaica, B.W.I. Author: A Concise Natural History of East and West Florida, vol. I, 1775; The New American Military Pocket Atlas, 1776; Annals of the Troubles in the Netherlands, vol. 1, 1778, vol. 2, 1782; also author printed maps, including plans of Pensacola Harbor, Mobile Bay, Tampa Bay. Died at sea, 1784.

ROMINGER, CARL LUDWIG, geologist; b. Schnaitheim, Würtemberg, Dec. 31, 1820; s. Ludwig and Johanna Dorothea (Hoecklin) P.; ed. in Latin sch., then became apprentice in drug store and prepared for U. of Tübingen, where studied 1839-44, and was grad. M.D.; asst. in chem. laboratory of univ., 1844-47, and received from State annual gift of money to prosecute geol. studies, traveling over large portions of Germany, France, Austria, Switzerland, etc.; m. Frederica Mayer, Nov. 30, 1854. Came to U.S., 1848, to continue geol. studies; practiced medicine over 25 yrs., but afterward devoted attention exclusively to geology and palaeontology; State geologist of Mich., 1870-84. Received medal of merit from Royal Acad., Munich, 1892. Extensive contbr. to geol. reports (wrote entire 3d and 4th vols. Mich. Reports and parts of others), 1869-83. Address: Ann Arbor, Mich. Died 1907.

ROMMEL, GEORGE MCCULLOUGH, (rom'el), agrl. consultant; b. Mt. Pleasant, Ia., Feb. 26, 1876; s. Alexander and Rachel Penn (McCullough) R.; B.S., Ia. Wesleyan Coll., 1897; B.S. Agr., Iowa State Coll., 1899; m. Sallie Russell Reeves, Sept. 19, 1906; children—Anna Margaret (Mrs. W. S. Tallman), Sarah Elizabeth (Mrs. J. M. Boze, Jr.), George McCullough (dec.), Alexander Ross. Asst. in animal husbandry, Iowa State Coll., 1899-1901; mgr. Ore. R.R. & Nav. Experimental Farm, Walla Walla, Wash., Mar.-June, 1901; expert in animal husbandry, U.S. Dept. Agr., 1901-05; animal husbandman, U.S. Dept. Agr., Jan. 1905-21, and chief of animal husbandry div., 1910-21; editor in chief, Am. Internat. Pubs., Inc., 1921-22; Morse Agrl. Service, 1923-28. Lecturer, Columbia U., 1923-26; technical consultant U.S. Dept. of Agr., 1927-28, U.S. Bur. Standards, 1928; became ind. commr. of Industrial Com. of Savannah, 1928; with Tennessee Valley Authority, Aug. 1, 1933-July 31, 1945; retired at own request, Aug. 1, 1945. Member United States Agricultural Commission to Europe, 1918; chairman Department of Agriculture committee on live stock drouth relief, 1919; U.S. del. 1st Pan-Am. Scientific Congress, Santiago, Chile; mem. executive com. 2d Congress, Washington, 1915; U.S. del. Inter-American Conf., Washington, 1930. Fellow A.A.A.S. Author: Farm Products in Industry, 1928. Contbr. to mags. Has written various bulletins and monographs on animal husbandry. Address: P. O. Box 1085, Bradenton, Fla. Died Nov. 26, 1945.

RONGY, ABRAHAM JACOB, (ron'ji), gynecologist, obstetrician; b. Russia, Sept. 27, 1878; s. Pincus and Lena (Bakst) R.; M.D., Long Island Coll. Hosp., 1899; m. Fanny F. Fields, Jan. 1, 1914. One of the founders of Jewish Maternity Hospital; attending gynecologist Lebanon Hosp. and Hosp. for Joint Diseases; consulting gynecologist Rockaway Beach Hospital and Royal Hospital; consulting gynecologist and obstetician, Bronx Maternity and Women's Hospital. Chmn., Greater New York Committee on Periodic Health Examination, 1928-33; chmn., Nat. Council, Zionist Orgn. of America, 1935-36; v.p., Am. Jewish Congress, 1925-26; del. World Relief Conf., Karistad, 1924; mem. editorial bd. Preventive Medicine, 1929-40. Mem. bd. of dirs. Conf. on Jewish Relations; mem. American Jewish Com.; mem. of Nat. Council and dir., mem. exec. com. of Am. Joint Distribution Committee; chairman American Section Jewish Health Committee; honorary president Zionist Organization, 7th District; trustee at large Fedn. of Jewish Philanthropies. Honorable fellow, American Association of Obstetricians and Gynecologists, and Abdominal Surgeons. Fellow American College of Surgeons, N.Y. Academy of Medicine; mem. A.M.A., Medical Society State of New York, Medical Society County of New York, A.A.A.S., American Genetic Assn., Acad. of Polit. Science, Am. Med. Editors and Authors Assn., Phi Delta Epsilon, Judeans. Author: Abortion—Legal or Illegal?, 1933; Childbirth Yesterday and Today, 1937; Safely Through Childbirth, 1937; The Contribution of the German Jew to Medicine, 1933; Half a Century of Jewish Medical Activities in New York City, 1937; Collation Chats; The Palatal Arch and the Pelvis, 1940; Unusual Consultations, 1941; Radium Therapy in Benign Uterine Bleeding, 1942; Jews in American Medicine, 1949; also numerous articles on gynecology. Home: 40 Central Park South, New York 24. Address: 2 W. 71st St., New York, N.Y. Died Oct. 10, 1949.

RONNEBERG, EARL FRIDTHJOV, architect, structural engr.; b. Chgo., May 15, 1905; s. Nathal T. and Hedvig (Jensen) R.; B.S., U. Ill., 1929; m. Bertha J. Cohn, Oct. 7, 1929; children—Jenny L. (Mrs. Laude E. Hartrum), Earl Fridthjov, Ronnie N., Peter L. Supt., Ronneberg Engring. Co., Chgo., 1929-31; spl. field agt. U.S. Govt., 1931-39; propr. N. Ronneberg Co., Chgo., 1939-72. Dist. chmn. Chgo. Area council Boy Scouts Am., 1952-54, cubmaster, 1940-57. Recipient Silver Beaver, Boy Scouts Am., 1954. Mem. Ill. Soc. Architects, Am. Assn. Engrs., Structural Engrs. Soc. Ill., Am. Soc. C.E. Home: Chicago IL Died Feb. 12, 1972.

ROOD, JAMES THERON, elec. engr.; b. Worcester, Mass., Mar. 26, 1876; s. James Timothy (M.D.) and Ellen Louise (Miles) R.; B.S., in E.E., Worcester Poly. Inst., 1898; Ph.D., Clark U., 1906; m. Myrtle Merrill, July 29, 1908. Prof. mathematics and physics, Ursinus Coll., Collegeville, Pa., 1906-07; prof. physics and elec. engring., U. of Ala., 1907-09; prof. elec. engring., Lafayette Coll., 1909-18; prof. ry. elec. engring., U. of Ill., 1918-20; prof. elec. engring., U. of Wis., 1920-29; later prof. elec. engring., dean of engring., dir. engring. expt. sta. and radio sta. KOB, N.M. Coll. Agr. and Mechanic Arts; consulting practice, 1907—. Republican. Episcopalian. Contbr. articles on original investigations. Died May 23, 1934.

ROOD, OGDEN NICHOLAS, prof. physics Columbia, 1863—; b. Danbury, Conn., Feb. 3, 1831; s. Rev. Anson and Aleida Gouverneur (Ogden) R.; grad. Princeton, 1852; studied at Univs. of Munich and Berlin, 1854-58; prof. chemistry and physics Troy U., 1858-63; m. Matilde Prunner, 1858. Was first to apply stereoscopic photography to the microscope and first to make quantitative experiments on color-contrast, to measure the duration of flashes of lightning and to make a photometer that is independent of color. Author: Modern Chromatics, 1879; also about 70 scientific papers. Mem. Nat. Acad. of Science. Address: New York, N.Y. Died 1902.

ROOS, DELMAR GERLE, mech. and elec. engr.; b. N.Y.C., Oct. 11, 1887; s. Christian Philip and Alexandra A. (Gerle) R.; grad. Cornell U., 1911, degree in mech. and elec. engring.; m. Christine H. Flagler, June 11, 1914 (div.); children—Katherine Harloe, Robert Barnard; m. 2d, Frances Homer; 1 dau., Delmar Alexandria. Engr. turbine research, Gen. Elec. Co., 1911-12; with Locomobile Co. of Am., 1912-20, as research engr. and chief engr., then v.p. in charge of engring. and production; chief engr. Pierce-Arrow Motor Car Co., 1920-21; v.p. Locomobile Co. Am., 1921-25; chief engr. Marmon Motor Car Co., 1925-26; chief engr. and then v.p. in charge of engring. Studebaker Corp., South Bend, Ind., 1926-37; then tech. adviser to Studebaker Corp. of America and cons. engr. to Humber, Hillman, Talbot and Sunbeam motor cos., hdqrs. Coventry, Eng.; now dir.; cons. engr. Willys-Overland Co.; dir. Gear Grinding Co., Form Spray Co., Baker Bros. Machine Tool Co. Councilor St. Joseph Co., 1935. Fellow Nat. Geog. Soc.; mem. Soc. of Automotive Engrs. (past pres.), Army Ordnance Assn., British Inst. Mech. Engrs., French Societé des Ingeneurs Automobile. Mason (32 deg., K.T.). Clubs: Country, Answer, Toledo. Home: 2234 Meadowood Av. Office: Willys-Overland Co., Toledo. Died Feb. 13, 1960.

ROOSEVELT, HILBORNE LEWIS, organ builder, inventor; b. N.Y.C., Dec. 21, 1849; s. Silas Weir and Mary (West) R.; m. Kate Watson, Feb. 1, 1833. Pioneer in devel. of electric organ and in application of new elec. devices to organ mfg.; took out 1st patent for electric organ action, 1869; operated own factory, N.Y.C., 1872, added factories in Phila. and Balt., constructed some of largest church organs then known in U.S., including those at Grace Ch. and Trinity Ch., N.Y.C.; constructed organ for main bldg. of Phila. Centennial Exhbn., 1876 (1st electric action organ built in Am.); interested in Bell Telephone Co., invented several telephone devices including automatic switch-hook. Died N.Y.C., Dec. 30, 1886.

ROOSEVELT, NICHOLAS J., inventor, engr.; b. N.Y.C., Dec. 27, 1767; s. Jacobus and Annetje (Bogard) R.; m. Lydia Latrobe, Nov. 15, 1808, 9 children. Dir., N.J. (Schuyler) Copper Mine Assn., 1793; interested in steam engines and their manufacture, succeeded in inducing his assos. to purchase land in Belleville (N.J.) and erect metal foundry and shop; entered into agreement with Robert R. Livingston and John Stevens to build steamboat, engines for which were to be constructed at his foundry, circa 1797, exptl. boat Polacca attained speed equivalent to 3 miles an hour in still water; became associated with Robert Fulton in introduction of steamboats in Western Rivers, 1809, built steamboat New Orleans at Pitts., 1811; granted patent for use of vertical paddle wheels, Dec. 1, 1814. Died Skaneateles, N.Y., July 30, 1854.

ROOSEVELT, THEODORE, twenty-sixth president of the U.S.; b. New York, Oct. 27, 1858, s. Theodore (1831-78) and Martha (Bulloch) R.; A.B., Harvard, 1880; LL.D., Columbia, 1899, Hope Coll., 1901, Yale, 1901, Harvard, 1902, Northwestern, 1893, U. of Chicago, 1903, U. of Calif., 1903, U. of Pa., 1905, Clark U., 1905, George Washington U., 1909, Cambridge U., 1910; D.C.L., Oxford U., 1910; Ph.D., U. of Berlin, 1910; m. Alice Hathaway, d. George Cabot Lee, Oct. 27, 1880 (died 1884); m. 2d, Edith Kermit, d. Charles Carow, Dec. 2, 1886. Mem. N.Y. Legislature, 1882-84; del. Rep. Nat. Conv., 1884; resided on ranch in N.D., 1884-86; candidate for mayor of New York, 1886; U.S. civil service commr., 1889-95; pres. New York Police Bd., 1895-97; asst. sec. of the navy, 1897-98; resigned to organize, with Surgeon (later Maj.-Gen.) Leonard Wood, 1st U.S. Cav. (popularly known as Roosevelt's Rough Riders); was lt. col. of regt., which distinguished itself in Cuba; promoted col. for gallantry at battle of Las Guasimas; mustered out Sept. 1898. Gov. N.Y., Jan. 1, 1899, to Dec. 31, 1900; elected Vice-President of the United States, Nov. 4, 1900, for term, 1901-05; succeeded to the presidency on death of William McKinley, Sept. 14, 1901; elected President of the U.S., Nov. 8, 1904, for term 1905-09, by largest popular majority ever accorded a candidate; Progressive Party candidate for president of U.S., 1912. Awarded the Nobel Peace Prize ($40,000), 1906. Spl. ambassador of U.S. at funeral of King Edward VII, 1910. Long a contbr. to leading mags. and reviews; known for yrs. as advocate of civil service and other reforms, nat. and municipal; contbg. editor The Outlook, 1909-14. Did much shooting of big game in the West; hunting trip in Africa, 1909-10; plaintiff in suit for libel against G. H. Newett, who had, in a newspaper article, during presdl. campaign of 1912, charged him with intoxication, but after submission of the evidence of defendant's witnesses, the charge was withdrawn in open court (Marquette, Mich., May 31, 1913) and judgment was immediately rendered in favor of plaintiff; visited S. America, 1913, and delivered addresses before univs. and learned socs.; went to Brazil, 1914, and at head of exploring party discovered and explored (Feb. 27-Apr. 26, 1914) for a distance of about 600 miles, a tributary of the Madeira River, subsequently named in his honor by Brazilian govt. "Reo Teodoro"; visited Madrid, Spain, June 1914, and lectured same month before Royal Geog. Soc., London. Defendant in suit brought by William Barnes, Jr., of Albany, N.Y., for alleged libelous utterances contained in a statement made on July 22, 1914, charging, among other things, that the "rottenness" of the N.Y. State government was due directly to the dominance in politics of Charles F. Murphy, Tammany Hall leader, and his sub-bosses aided and abetted by Mr. Barnes and the sub-bosses of Mr. Barnes; and that there was an invisible government of party bosses working through alliance between crooked business and crooked politics; the verdict of the jury, rendered at Syracuse, N.Y., May 22, 1915, was in favor of defendant. Nominated for President by Progressive Party Conv., Chicago, 1916; about 1 month later declined the nomination and supported Charles Evans Hughes, the Republican nominee. Offered to raise an army division, after declaration of war, and to go to France with same, 1917, but offer was declined by Pres. Wilson. Hon. fellow Am. Mus. Natural History, 1917. Author: Winning of the West, 1889-96; History of the Naval War of 1812, 1882; Hunting Trips of a Ranchman, 1885; Life of Thomas Hart Benton, 1886; Life of Gouverneur Morris, 1887; Ranch Life and Hunting Trail, 1888; History of New York, 1890; The Wilderness Hunter, 1893; American Ideals and Other Essays, 1897; The Rough Riders, 1899; Life of Oliver Cromwell, 1900; The Strenuous Life, 1900; Works (8 vols.), 1902; The Deer Family, 1902; Outdoor Pastimes of an American Hunter, 1906; American Ideals and Other Essays; Good Hunting, 1907; True Americanism; African and European Addresses, 1910; African Game Trails, 1910; The New Nationalism, 1910; Realizable Ideals (the Earl lectures), 1912; Conservation of Womanhood and Childhood, 1912; History as Literature, and Other Essays, 1913; Theodore Roosevelt, an Autobiography, 1913; Life Histories of African Game Animals (2 vols.), 1914; Through the Brazilian Wilderness, 1914; America and the World War, 1915; A Booklover's Holidays in the Open, 1916; Fear God, and Take Your Own Part, 1916; Foes of Our Own Household, 1917; National Strength and International Duty (Stafford Little lectures, Princeton Univ.), 1917. Home: Oyster Bay, L.I., N.Y. Died Jan. 6, 1919.

ROOT, ELISHA KING, mechanic, inventor; b. Ludlow, Mass., May 10, 1808; s. Darius and Dorkas (Sikes) R.; m. Charlotte Chapin, Oct. 16, 1832; m. 2d, Matilda Colt, Oct. 7, 1845, 4 children. Employed by Collins Co., mfg. axes, 1832-49, supt., 1845-49, his inventions and improvements in axe mfg. machinery and methods converted co. into a modern factory; supt. Colt Armory, Hartford, Conn., 1849, designed, built factory, most of machinery, 1849-54; pres., 1862-65; adopted principle of interchangeable parts, automatic machinery was widely used; patented a drop hammer, 1853; invented machines for boring and rifling gunbarrels, for stock-turning, for splinting; patented a cam pump to raise water from Connecticut River to a reservoir in the workmen's village, 1856; trained many of Am.'s tool builders. Died Hartford, Aug. 31, 1865.

ROOT, HOWARD FRANK, physician; b. Ottumwa, Ia., Aug. 28, 1890; s. Frank Lane and Clara B. (Squire) R.; A.B., Harvard, 1913, M.D., 1919; H.H.D., Suffolk U., 1953; m. Hester King, Oct. 8, 1921 (dec. Feb. 9, 1954); m. 2d, Kathleen Berger. House officer Peter Bent Brigham Hosp., Boston, 1919-20; May fellow Johns Hopkins Med. Center; practice of medicine, Boston, 1921—; medical director of Joslin Clinic, 1962—; physician-in-chief New Eng. Deaconess Hosp.; lectr. medicine Harvard Med. Sch. Served as lt. comdr. USNR, surgeon USPHS. Mem. Am. Coll. Physicians, Am. Soc. Clin. Investigation, Am. Coll. Chest Physicians, Mass. Med. Soc. (past pres.), Am. Diabetes Assn. (past pres.), Internat. Diabetes Fedn. (pres. 1961—), Am. Therapeutic Soc., Am. Endocrine Soc., Am. Clin. and Climatol. Assn., Am. Soc. Nutrition, Diabetes Found., Inc. (pres.) Mass. Soc. Internal Medicine (past pres.), Phi Beta Kappa, also Sigma Xi. Author: (with others) Treatment of Diabetes, 1958; (with L.S. McKittrick) Surgery and Diabetes, 1928; (with P. White) Diabetes Mellitus, 1956. Home: 195 St. Paul St., Brookline 46, Mass. Office: 15 Joslin Rd., Boston. Died Nov. 1967.

ROOT, JOSEPH POMEROY, physician, diplomat; b. Greenwich, Mass., Apr. 23, 1826; s. John and Lucy (Reynolds) R.; grad. Berkshire Med. Coll., Pittsfield, Mass., 1850; m. Frances Evaline Alden, Sept. 1851, 5 children. Elected as Whig to Conn. Legislature, 1855; moved to Kan., 1856; chmn. Free-State Exec. Com.; elected to Kan. Senate under Topeka constn., 1857; one of pioneer corps who located public road from Topeka to Nebraska City; editorial contbr. to Wyandotte (Kan.) papers, Register, 1857, Gazette, 1858; elected Republican lt. gov. Kan., 1859; chosen an officer of 1st annual meeting of Kan. Temperance Soc., 1861; surgeon 2d Kan. Cavalry during Civil War, med. dir. Army of Frontier; presided over Kan. Rep. Conv., 1866; by Pres. Grant apptd. as minister to Chile, 1870-73, undertook on his own account to have Chile establish system of towboats in Straits of Magellan, helped during smallpox epidemic, 1872, served on Santiago (Chile) Bd. of Health, contributed his services to hosps. and private patients, laboring to improve sanitary treatment of the disease; Calle de Root (street in Santiago) named for him; elected v.p. Temperance conv., 1874; published Catechism of Money (advocating greenbackism), 1876; mem. Chilean Centennial Commn., 1876; del. Rep. Nat. Conv., 1884; mem. staff sanitarium at Clifton Springs, N.Y., 1877-79; interested in Kan. Hist. Soc., contbd. several manuscript writings to its archives, among them a memoir of his experiences in Kan. in 1856; surgeon gen. of Kan., 1874; Mason; mem. Grand Army of Republic. Died Wyandotte, Kan., July 20, 1885.

ROOT, WALTER STANTON, educator; b. Buffalo, Sept. 18, 1902; s. William Francis Stanton and Leontine Margaret (Root) R.; student Rutgers Coll., 1920-21; B.Sc. cum. laude, Wesleyan U., 1922-24; postgrad. Univ. and Bellevue Hosp. Med. Sch., 1925-27; Ph.D., U. Pa. 1930; m. Elizabeth Wigfall, Jan. 26, 1928 (dec.); 1 son, Richard Wigfall; m. 2d, Pauline Elizabeth Warner, Nov. 4, 1961. Asst. in biology Wesleyan U., 1924-25; asst. physiologist U.S. Army Sch. Aviation Medicine, summer 1925; asst. instr. physiology U. Pa. Med. Sch., 1927-29; asst. prof. physiology Syracuse Med. Sch., 1929-31, asso. prof., 1931-36; asso. prof. U. Md. Med. Sch., 1936-37; asso. prof. Coll. Physicians and Surgeons Columbia, 1937-48, prof. physiology, 1948-68, emeritus, 1968-72. Spl. field staffs, cons. Rockefeller Found., Mahidol U., Bangkok, Thailand, 1968-69; Woods Hole scholar (Wesleyan U.), Marine Biol. Lab., summer 1924; investigator Marine Biol. Lab., summers 1928-36, mem. corp.; group research program Am. Bur. Med. Aid to China, Nanking, summer 1948; dir. Am. Bur. for Med. Aid to China, 1949-61, v.p., 1951-61; mem. 18th Internat. Physiol. Congress, Copenhagen, 1950. Research asso. med. physics. U. Cal., fall 1952; mem. physiology test com. Nat. Bd. Med. Examiners, 1957-61; mem. med. scis. screening com. Conf. Bd. Asso. Research Councils (Fulbright awards), 1957-62, chmn., 1962-64; com. nomenclature for randombred animals Inst. Lab. Animal Resources Nat. Acad. Scis.-NRC, 1964-70. Decorated Armed Forces medal (China). Fellow N.Y. Acad. Scis. (council 1949-50, v.p. 1951, pres. 1956), N.Y. Acad. Medicine (asso.); mem. Assn. Research Nervous and Mental Disease (asso.), Research Def. Soc. Eng. (life), S.A.R., Nat. Resuscitation Soc. (adv. bd.), Am. Physiol. Soc., Soc. Exptl. Biology and Medicine (sec.-treas. 1958-67), Order of Founders and Patriots, N.Y. State Soc. Med. Research (pres. 1954-55), Am. Heart Assn. (sci. council), A.A.A.S. (council 1964), Harvey Soc., Sigma Xi (chpt. pres. 1962-63), Nu Sigma Nu. Republican. Episcopalian. Cons. editor Hematopoietic Mechanisms, N.Y. Acad. Scis., 1959; mng. editor: Proc. Soc. Exptl. Biol. and Med., 1958-67; editor Life History of the Erythrouyte in Methods in Medical Research. Vol. 8, 1960; co-editor Physiol. Pharmacology, Vol. I, 1962, II, 1965, III, IV, 1967; hon. mem. editorial adv. board Jour. Photochemistry and Photobiology, 1962-66. Contbr. Am. Jour. Physiol., Macleod's Physiol. in Modern Medicine, 1941; Jour. Applied Physiology, Jour. Biological Chemistry. Bard's Med. Physiology, 1956, 61, Handbook of Physiology, 1963, 65, Mountcastle, Med. Physiology, 1968. Home: Woods Hole MA Died Mar. 30, 1972; buried Kensington CT

ROPER, DENNEY WARREN, ret. elec. engr.; b. Grafton, Ill., Oct. 18, 1869; s. John Sylvester and Adelaide Thompson (Benner) R.; M.E., Cornell U., 1893; m. Anne Bartlett Newell, Apr. 15, 1903; children—Helen Jessie (Mrs. V. M. Marquis), John Newell; m. 2d, Sarah M. Farley, Sept. 16, 1924. With Gen. Electric Co., Schenectady, 1894, Niagara Falls Power Co., 1894-95, Mo. Edison Electric Co., 1897-1901; cons. engring. work, 1901-03; with Chgo. Edison Co., and its successor Commonwealth Edison Co., 1903—, as asst. to chief operating engr., 1905-15, supt. street dept., 1915-33, asst. elec. engr., 1933-35; retired. Past chmn. com. Nat. Elec. Light Assn. and Assn. Edison Illuminating Cos.; supervising cable insulation research at Harvard, Mass. Inst. Tech., Johns Hopkins, U. Ill.; mem. U.S. Nat. Com. of Internat. Electrotech. Commn., 1924-30; mem. conf. on elec. insulation NRC. Mem. Am. Inst. E.E. (past chmn. Chgo. sect.), Western Soc. engrs. (ex-v.p.). Unitarian. Recipient Chanute medal by Western Soc. Engrs., 1907; best paper prize by Am. Inst. E.E., 1927. Home: Carmel-by-the-Sea, Cal. Died Oct. 5, 1949.

RORER, JAMES BIRCH, plant pathologist; b. Ogontz, Pa., Dec. 29, 1876; s. William A. and Sarah Tyson (Heston) R.; B.A., Harvard, 1899, M.A., 1902; m. Ethel Stuart Wimer, of Washington, D.C., Feb. 10, 1909. Asst. in botany, Harvard, 1899-1902; scientific asst. U.S. Dept. Agr., 1902-05; asst. pathologist same, 1906-08; mycologist Bd. of Agr., Trinidad, B.W.I., 1909-18; dir. Dept. of Agr., Associacion de Agricultores del Ecuador, and plant pathologist, 1919-22; agr. adviser and mgr. of Hacienda Panigon. Fellow A.A.A.S.; mem. Bot. Soc. America, Am. Phytopathol. Soc. Contbr. papers dealing with diseases of peaches and apples, sugar cane, cocoanuts, cacao and other tropical crops. Has specialized in tropical agr. Address: Casilla de correo "X", Guayaquil Ecuador

RORTY, MALCOLM CHURCHILL, engineer; b. Paterson, N.J., May 1, 1875; s. Richard Mackay and Octa (Churchill) R.; grad. Walkill Acad., Middletown, N.Y., 1892; M.E. in E.E., Cornell U., 1896; m. Margaret McNaughten, Mar. 23, 1904; children—Margaret McNaughten, Malcolm McNaughten, James McNaughten (dec.). With J. G. White Co. and New York Telephone Co. until 1899; engr. and traffic engr. with Am. Bell Telephone Co., 1899-1903; gen. supt. traffic, etc., Central Dist. Telephone Co., Pittsburgh, Pa., 1903-10; comml. engr. Am. Telephone & Telegraph Co., 1910-13; asst. v.p. Western Union Telegraph Co., New York, 1913-14; spl. agt. Am. Tel. & Tel. Co., 1914-17, chief statistician, 1919-21; v.p. Bell Telephone Securities Co., 1921-22; asst. v.p. Am. Tel. & Tel. Co., 1922-23; pres. Internat. Telephone Securities Corp., 1923-27; v.p. Internat. Telephone & Telegraph Corp., 1923-30; v.p. American Founders Corp., 1930-31. President Am. Management Assn., 1934—. Served as lt. col. U.S.A., 1917-18; with Ordnance Dept. and Gen. Staff; attached to Interallied Munitions Council; participated in Meuse-Argonne offensive. Fellow Am. Statistical Assn. (pres. 1930-31); mem. Nat. Bur. Economic Research (pres. 1922-23, chmn. bd. 1924-25); corr. mem. faculty Univ. of Buenos Aires. Republican. Author: Some Problems in Current Economics, 1922; Bolshevism, Fascism, and Capitalism (with others), 1932. Home: Lusby, Md. Died Jan. 18, 1936.

ROSA, EDWARD BENNETT, physicist; b. Rogersville, N.Y., Oct. 4, 1861; s. Rev. Edward David and Sarah G. (Rowland) R.; B.S., Wesleyan U., 1886, Sc.D., 1906; Ph.D., Johns Hopkins, 1891; m. Mary Evans, Mar. 22, 1894. Prof. physics, Wesleyan U., 1891-1902; physicist, 1901-10, chief physicist, 1910—, Nat. Bur. of Standards. Contbr. to Am. and European jours. of physics and electricity and the papers of the Nat. Bur. of Standards, making a specialty of theoretical and applied electricity and elec. measurements. In charge elec. div. of Bur. of Standards, including investigations on standards of service and safety for public utilities; sec. Internat. Com. on Elec. Units and Standards. Mem. Nat. Acad. Sciences. Died May 17, 1921.

ROSANOFF, MARTIN ANDRÉ, (ro'sa-nof), chemist; b. Nicolaeff, Russia, Dec. 28, 1874; s. Abraham H. and Clara (Bertinskaya) R.; Imperial Classical Gymnasium, Nicolaeff, 1883-91; Ph.B., New York U., 1895; studied U. of Berlin, 1895-96, U. of Paris, 1896-98; research fellow, New York U., 1899-1900, Sc.D., 1908; m. Louise Place, Feb. 2, 1901 (died Aug. 30, 1918); children—Boris Place, Elizabeth Place, Marian Place (dec.), James Keyes Place; m. 2d, Charlotte Adèle Walker, Nov. 17, 1932. Editor for exact sciences, New Internat. Ency., 1900-03; research asst. to Thomas A. Edison, Orange, N.J., 1903-04; instr. theoretical chemistry, 1904-05, asst. prof., 1905-07, New York U.; head dept. of chemistry, and dir. chem. labs., Clark U., 1907-14; also prof. organic chemistry, Clark Coll., 1910-12; prof. chem. research, Mellon Inst., U. of Pittsburgh, 1914-15, head dept. of research in pure chemistry, 1915-19; prof. chem. research, Duquesne U., 1933-40, dean of the grad. school, 1934-40; local research adminstr. office of edn., U.S. Dept. of Interior, 1936-37; Public Panel Chmn. War Labor Bd., 1943-46. Received United States Certificate of Merit, 1943. Fellow Am. Acad. Arts and Sciences, A.A.A.S.; mem. Am. Chem. Soc. (Nichols medalist), Royal Soc. of Arts, Nat. Inst. Social Sciences, Am. Arbitration Assn. Hon. Mem. Internat. Mark Twain Soc. Phi Beta Kappa. Clubs: Chemists (New York); Royal Societies (London). Contbr. to Jour. Am. Chem. Soc., Chem. News (London), Zeitschrift für physikalische Chemie (Leipzig). Administrative dir. of "Guide to the School Laws of Pennsylvania," 1938; Supplement, 1940; Edison in his Laboratory, 1932, repub. 1942; Select Topics of Plane Analytic Geometry, 1944. Home: 124 Longuevue Drive, Mt. Lebanon, Pa. Died July 30, 1951; buried Homewood Mausoleum, Pitts.

ROSE, ALBERT CHATELLIER, hwy. engring.; b. Washington, Oct. 14, 1887; s. Albert Jones and Caroline Agnes (McCormick) R.; grad. Germantown Acad., Phila., 1905; B.S. in Civil Engring., U. Wash., 1924, C.E., 1935; m. Ella Potts Lancaster, July 3, 1913; children—Elinor Katherine (Mrs. Joseph Hale Darby), Samuel Lancaster, Caroline Anne. Resident and locating engr. Wash. State Hwy. Dept., 1910-11; roadmaster Clatsop County, Ore., 1914-19; hwy. engr. dist. office U.S. Bur. Pub. Rds., Portland, Ore., 1919-24; chief sec. visual edn. in div. information U.S. Bur. Pub. Rds., now Bur. Pub. Rds. Dept. Commerce, Washington, 1925-43, chief Visual Edn. br. engaged in preparation exhibits, motion pictures, models, dioramas, etc., for rd. congresses, convs. and expns., 1943-51; historian Bur. Pub. Rds. since 1952. Designed model Appian Way now on display Nat. Mus., Washington, also series of dioramas depicting 400 yrs. hwy. devel. in U.S. Mem. Tau Beta Pi (1913), Phi Kappa (local, now Psi Upsilon). Republican. Presbyn. Author govt. bulls., reports: Via Appia in the Days When All Roads Led to Rome, 1935; Smithsonian Report, Historic American Highways, 1940; Smithsonian Report, The Old Roadbuilder, American Highways, 1944-49; Public Roads of The Past—3500 B.C.—1800 A.D., 1952; Public Roads of the Past—Historic American Highways, 1953. Home: Starfish Rd., Anna Maria, Fla. Office: Gen. Services Adminstrn. Bldg., Washington 25. Died June 24, 1966.

ROSE, CARLTON RAYMOND, chemist, metallurgist; b. Ann Arbor, Mich., June 16, 1873; s. Preston B. and Cornelia (Robinson) R.; Ph.B., U. of Mich., 1894, A.M., 1896; Mass. Inst. Tech., 1900-1; m. Winifred Higbee, of Buchanan, Mich., Aug. 12, 1897. Instr. chemistry, U. of Ill., 1896-1900; prof. metallurgy, Colo. Sch. of Mines, 1901-03; supt. smelters, U.S. Zinc Co., Pueblo, Colo., 1903—. Mem. Am. Inst. Mining Engrs., Colo. Scientific Soc., Delta Upsilon. Mason (K.T.). Clubs: Pueblo Commerce, Minnequa Country. Address: Box 860 Pueblo CO

ROSE, CHARLES BEDELL, indsl. cons.; b. Burton, Mich., Octl 28, 1879; s. John Woodman and Eva Grace (Bedell) R.; Mich. State Coll., 1899-1903; m. Lillian Love, Dec. 19, 1905; children—Charles B., Mary Love, Elizabeth G., Capt. Robert W. (USMC, killed at Tarawa, Nov. 20, 1943). Chief draftsman Olds Motor Works, 1903-06; chief engr., v.p. and gen. mgr. Velie Motors Corp., 1908-17; v.p. Moline Plow Co., 1919-24; v.p. and gen. mgr. Fageol Motors Co., 1924-26; pres. Am.-La France & Foamite Corp., 1927-36; also pres. Am.-La France and Foamite Industries, Inc., La France-Republic Corp.; chmn. bd. Linn Mfg. Corp.; later v.p. Baldwin Locomotive Works; v.p. Am. Oerlikon Gazda Corp., Providence; v.p. Elec. Fault Anticipator Corp., N.Y.C. Dairy farmer. Served as capt. and lt. col. Army AS, 1917-19. Mem. Am. Soc. M.E., Soc. Automotive Engrs. Presbyn. Mason. Address: R.F.D. 1, Ovid, Mich. 48866. Died May 27, 1962.

ROSE, E(RNEST) H(ERBERT), metall. engr.; b. Kinsley, Kan., July 6, 1897; s. George Alonzo and Bertha (Ginn) R.; B.S. in Chem. Engring., U. Kan., 1920; m. Lucile Collins, Sept. 25, 1919; children—Miriam (Mrs. M. MacAskill), George H. Mill supt. Patino Mines, Bolivia, 1925-27; mill supt. Moctezuma Copper Co., Mexico, 1928-30; asst. mill supt. Internat. Nickel Co. of Can., 1930-36, mill supt., 1936-45; cons. metallurgist Copper Range Co., Mich. 1946-47; research engr. Tenn. Coal and Iron div. U.S. Steel Corp., 1947-54; project dir. metallurgy, materials adv. bd. Nat. Acad. Scis., 1954-56; chief beneficiation engr. Koppers Co., Pitts., from 1957. Mem. raw materials adv. com. AEC, 1949-59. Mem. Am. Inst. Mining, Metall. and Petroleum Engrs. (dir.), Mining and Metall. Soc. Am., A.A.A.S., Tau Beta Pi. Author articles, holder patents on utilization low grade minerals and ores. Home: Pittsburgh PA Died May 27, 1968, buried Mt. Hope Cemetery Penn Hills PA

ROSE, JOSEPH NELSON, botanist; b. nr. Liberty, Ind., Jan. 11, 1862; s. George W. and Rebecca (Corrington) R.; A.B., Wabash Coll., 1885, A.M., 1887, Ph.D., 1889, LL.D., 1925; m. Lou B. Sims, 1888; children—Joseph Sims, Rebecca, Martha, Walter Deane (dec.), George. Asst. in botany, Wabash Coll., 1888-89; asst. and 1st asst., div. of botany, Dept. Agr., 1888-94; asst. curator, Dept. Botany, U.S. Nat. Mus., 1894-1905; asso. curator, U.S. Nat. Mus., Jan. 16, 1905-Jan. 16, 1912, and directly in charge of Nat. Herbarium; asso. in botany, U.S. Nat. Mus., 1912—, and research asso., Carnegie Instn. of Washington, 1912-23. Traveled extensively Mex. and S.A. Spl. study of cacti. In 1888 (with Dr. John M. Coulter) published a Revision of the Umbelliferae of the U.S.; in 1905 (with Dr. N. L. Britton) published Revision N.A. Crassulaceae; published numerous papers in tech. jours. on the order Umbelliferae, Cactaceae and Mexican plants; in 1899, Useful Plants of Mexico; in 1901, Monograph of North American Umbelliferae; (with Dr. Britton) The Cactaceae, 4 vols., 1919-23. In honor of his services in his spl. line of research Dr. Sereno Watson named the genus Rhodosciadium in 1890; Prof. Cogniaux the genus Roseanthus in 1896; Dr. Small the genus Roseanthus, 1910; Prof. Speggasini the genus Brittonrosea, 1923; Mr. Alwin Berger, Roseocactus, 1925. Presbyn. Home: Washington, D.C. Died May 4, 1928.

ROSE, RUFUS EDWARDS, agrl. chemist; b. New Orleans, La., Mar. 19, 1847; s. Alfred James (M.E.) and Albina Stanhope (Johnston) R.; student Dolbear Tech. and Commercial Coll., New Orleans, 1862-64; m. Emeline Sahl, Mar. 20, 1871; children—Alfred Henry (dec.), Ruby Edwards; m. 2d, Mary Anna Morgan, July 18, 1894; children—Muriel Mary, Rufus Edwards. Supt. La. Reclamation Co., 1876-81, Disston Everglade Drainage Co., 1881-86, Disston-St. Cloud Sugar Company, 1886-89; state chemist of Fla., 1901—. Presbyn. Mason, K.P., Elk. Author: (brochures) The Sugar Industry of Florida; Everglades of Florida; Drainage of Farm Lands. Home: Tallahassee, Fla. Died Apr. 23, 1931.

ROSE, S. BRANDT, physician, pathologist; b. London, Eng., June 22, 1901; s. A. and Y. (Brandt) Rose; M.D., McGill U., 1925, M.S., 1926; D.Sc., U. Pa., 1930; m. Florence DeBring, Oct. 9, 1937;children—John, Robert. Intern Univ. Hosp., Ann Arbor, Mich., 1926-27; asso. immunology U. Pa., 1930-32; prof. bacteriology and immunology Woman's Med. Coll. of Pa., Phila., 1929-36; dir. Coll. Hospital Laboratory, 1930-32; chief division of bacteriology Philadelphia General Hospital, 1936-48, chief div. med. microbiology, 1967-71; dir. lab. Chestnut Hill Hosp., 1948-66. Diplomate Am. Bd. Pathology in clinic pathology (trustee). Fellow Coll. Am. Pathologists; mem. A.M.A., Am. Soc. Clin. Pathologists, Soc. Am. Bacteriologists. Editorial bd. biol. abstracts Am. Jour. Clin. Pathology. Home: Cynwyd PA Died Aug. 25, 1971; buried West Laurel Hill Cemetery, Bala-Cynwyd PA

ROSECRANS, WILLIAM STARKE, army officer, diplomate; b. Kingston Twp., Delaware County, O., Sept. 6, 1819; s. Crandall and Jemima (Hopkins) R.; grad. U.S. Mil. Acad., 1842; m. Ann Eliza Hegeman, Aug. 24, 1843, 8 children. Brevetted 2d lt. of engrs., 1842; served as 2d lt. on the fortifications of Hampton Roads, Va., 1843-47; asst. prof. natural and exptl. philosophy dept. engring. U.S. Mil. Acad.; supt. repairs at Ft. Adams, Mass., also in charge of various govt. surveys and improvements, 1847-53; promoted 1st lt., 1853, resigned commn., 1854; architect and civil engr., Cincinnati; pres. Coal River Navigation Co., Kanawha County, Va. (now W. Va.), 1856; organizer Preston Coal Oil Co., mfrs. kerosene, 1857; became volunteer a.d.c. to Gen. George B. McClellan in Ohio, 1861; made col., chief engr. Dept. of Ohio, U.S. Army, 1861; apptd. col. 23d Ohio Volunteer Inf., 1861; commd. brig. gen. U.S. Army, 1861; commanded brigade, won Battle of Rich Mountain, 1861; succeeded McClellan as comdg. gen. Dept. of Ohio, 1861; chief new dept. of western Va., 1861, expelled Confederates, making formation of W.Va. possible; promoted maj. gen. U.S. Volunteers, 1862; succeeded Gen. John Pope in command Miss. Army, involved in successful engagements at Iuka and Corinth, 1862; commanded Army of the Cumberland; defeated at Battle of Chickamauga, 1863, relieved of command; commanded Dept. of Mo., 1864; brevetted maj: gen. for services at Murfreesboro, 1865; resigned from U.S. Army, 1867; U.S. minister to Mexico, 1868, 69; engaged in mining operations, Mexico, later Cal.; pres. Safety Powder Co., Los Angeles, Cal., 1875; mem. U.S. Ho. of Reps. from Cal., 47th-48th congresses, 1881-85, chmn. com. on mil. affairs; commd. brig. gen. on ret. list U.S. Army, 1889; register of the treasury, 1885-93. Died Mar. 11, 1898; buried Arlington (Va.) Nat. Cemetary.

ROSENAU, MILTON JOSEPH, (roz'n-now), sanitarian; b. Phila., Pa., Jan. 1, 1869; s. Nathan and Matilda (Blitz) R.; pub. and high schs., Phila.; M.D., U. of Pa., 1889; post-grad. studies in Hygienische Institut, Berlin, 1892-93; L'Institut Pasteur, Paris, 1900; Pathologisches Institut, Vienna, Austria, 1900; hon. A.M., Harvard U., 1914; m. Myra F. Frank, July 16, 1900 (dec.); children—William Frank (dec.) Milton J., Bertha (Mrs. Max L. Ilfeld); m. 2d, Maud H. Tenner, Jan. 13, 1934; 1 stepson, Leonard P. Tenner. Surgeon U.S. Pub. Health and Marine Hosp. Service, 1890-1909, dir. Hygienic Lab. same, 1899-1909, resigned; prof. preventive medicine and hygiene, Harvard Med. Sch., 1909-35, prof. emeritus since 1935; prof. epidemiology, Harvard School Public Health, 1922-35; dir. Div. Pub. Health, U. of N.C., since 1936; dean, Sch. of Pub. Health, U. of N.C., 1940-41; dir., same, 1941-43; dean, same since 1943; mem. of the adv. bd., National Health Council, U.S. Public Health Service, since 1929; mem. science adv. board National Research Council since 1934. Dir. School of Public Health of Harvard Univ. and Mass. Inst. Tech., 1913-22; mem. Mass. Bd. of Health, 1912-14; dir. Antitoxin and Vaccine Laboratory and chief division of biologic laboratories, same, 1914-21. Quarantine officer, San Francisco, 1895-98; del. of U.S. to 10th Internat. Conf. Hygiene and Demography, and 13th Internat. Congress Medicine and Surgery, Paris, 1900; mem. Internat. Com. Revision of Nomenclature of the Causes of Deaths, Paris, 1900; sanitary expert to 2d Pan-Am. Conf., Mexico, 1901; special lecturer on tropical diseases, Georgetown U. Awarded gold medal of Am. medicine for service to humanity, 1912-13; awarded the Sedgwick memorial medal for achievements in pub. health, 1934; awarded Gold Medal of Annual Forum on Allergy for outstanding contribution to allergy, 1945; mem. Association of Am. Physicians, A.M.A., Soc. of Am. Bacteriologists (pres. 1934) Am. Assn. Pathologists and Bacteriologists and others. Organized quarantine at Santiago and other Cuban ports, 1898-99. Author: Disinfection and Disinfectants, 1902; Experimental Studies in Yellow Fever and Malaria, 1904; The Immunity Unit for Diphtheria Antitoxin, 1905; A Method of Inoculating Animals with Precise Amounts, 1905; The Cause of Sudden Death Following the Injection of Horse Serum, 1906; Experimental Gastric Ulcer, 1906; The Origin and Spread of Typhoid Fever, 1907; The Standardization of Tetanus Antitoxin, 1908; The Milk Question, 1912; Preventive Medicine and Hygiene, 6th edition, 1935; also writer of many papers and articles on anaphylaxis, foot and mouth disease, pasteurization, milk and its relation to the public health, viability of the tubercle bacillus, infantile paralysis, organic matter in the expired breath, influenza, etc., and reports on sanitary and bacteriol. subjects. Mem. med. advisory bd. Am. Red Cross. Med. insp. (comdr.), U.S. bd. Am. Red Cross. Med. insp. (comdr.), U.S. N.R.F., 1917-19; capt. (ret.); asst. surgeon-gen., U.S. P.H. Service (ret.). Home: Laurel Hill Road, Chapel Hill, N.C. Died Apr. 9, 1946.

ROSENBLUETH, ARTURO STEARNS, physiologist; b. Chihuahua, Mexico, Oct. 2, 1900; s. Julio G. and Maria (Stearns) R.; student Nat. Sch. Medicine, Mexico City, Mexico, 1918-21, Sch. Medizin, Berlin, Germany, 1923; M.D., Ecole de Medecine, Paris, France, 1924-27; m. Virginia Thompson, Sept. 5, 1931. Faculty, U. Mexico, 1928-30, prof., 1929-30; J.S. Guggenheim Found. fellow Harvard, 1930-32, fellow in physiology, 1932-33, asst. prof., 1934-44; head dept. physiology Nat. Inst. Cardiology, Mexico City, 1944-60; head dept. physiology, dir. Center for Research and Advanced Studies, Nat. Poly. Inst., Mexico City, 1960-70. Mem. El Colegio Nacional, Instituto Nacional de La Investigacion Cientifica. Author: (with W. B. Cannon) Autonomic Neuroeffector Systems, 1937, The Supersensitivity of Denervated Structures, A Law of Denervation, 1949; Transmission of Nerve Impulses at Neuroeffector Junctions and Peripheral Synapses, 1950; Mind and Brain, A Philosophy of Science, 1970; also numerous articles. Research on transmission nervous impulses in autonomic and synaptic junctions, physiology central nervous system and of heart. Home: Mexico City Mexico Died Sept. 20, 1970.

ROSENGARTEN, GEORGE DAVID, chemist; b. Phila., Pa., Feb. 12, 1869; s. Harry B. and Clara J. (Knorr) R.; B.S., U. of Pa., 1890; Ph.D., U. of Jena, 1892; hon. Sc.D., U. of Pa., 1927; m. Susan E. Wright, Apr. 23, 1895. V.p. Rosengarten & Sons, Inc., 1901-05; v.p. Powers, Weightman-Rosengarten Co., 1905-27, later dir. successors Merck & Co., Inc.; retired. Mem. Com. of Revision of United States Pharmacopoeia, 1910-30. Mem. Am. Chem. Soc. (pres. 1927), Am. Inst. Chem. Engrs. (pres.). Republican. Episcopalian. Home: Malvern, Pa. Died Feb. 24, 1936.

ROSENHOLTZ, JOSEPH LEON, educator; b. Kingston, N.Y., July 31, 1899; s. Morris and Sadie (Safran) R.; Ch.E., Rensselaer Polytech. Inst., 1920, M.S., 1921, Ph.D., 1924; student Columbia, 1921, U. of Wis., 1922, U. of Mich., 1922; m. Blanche Frances Goldowsky, July 3, 1927; children—Claire Irene (Mrs. Robert K. Ruslander), Ann Rita (Mrs. Edward J. Segel). Instr., Rensselaer Polytech. Inst., Troy, N.Y., 1920-22, asst. prof., 1922-24, prof. of geology and mineralogy, since 1924, head, dept. of geology and mineralogy since 1945; lecturer, Samaritan Hosp., Troy, 1922-28. Fellow: A.A.A.S., Am. Mineral Soc., Geol. Soc. Am.; mem. Nat. Assn. Geology Tchrs. (pres. eastern sect. 1960-61), N.Y. State Geol. Assn. (president 1960-61), Geochem. Soc., American Geophysical Union, American Crystallographic Association, Am. Soc. Engring. Edn., Sigma Xi, Phi Sigma Delta. Mason. Author: Applied Chemistry for Nurses, 1924; Elements of Ferrous Metallurgy, 1930. Contbr. numerous papers on geology and mineralogy in tech. jours. Home: 101 Oakwood Av., Troy, N.Y. Died Mar. 21, 1963; buried Berith Sholom Cemetery, Troy.

ROSEWATER, ANDREW, civil and sanitary engr.; b. in Bohemia, Oct. 31, 1848; ed. in common and high schools, Cleveland, O.; m. Frances Meinrath, Oct. 18, 1883. Flagman engr. corps, Union Pacific Ry. explorations and surveys, 1864; later in other engring. position same road; asst. city engr., Omaha, 1868-70; city engr., 1870-75; mgr. and ad interim editor Omaha Bee, 1876-77; engr. in charge construction Omaha & Northwestern Ry., 1878-80; resident engr. Omaha Water Works Co., 1880-81; city engr., Omaha, 1881-87; 1887-91 cons. and designing engr. of sewerage for 25 cities; pres. elec. subway commn. of Washington, 1891-92; consulting engr. for cities in Colo., S.D., etc. City engr. Omaha, and pres. Bd. Public Works, 1897—. Wrote Report Elec. Commn. of D.C. to the President, 1891. Address: Omaha, Neb. Died 1909.

ROSS, BENNETT BATTLE, chemist; b. Tuskegee, Ala., Dec. 25, 1864; s. Bennett Battle and Charlotte Augusta (Walker) R.; B.Sc., Ala. Poly. Inst., 1881, M.Sc., 1886; univs. Göttingen and Berlin, 1 semester each; LL.D., Southern U., 1917, Emory U., 1918; m. Letitia Roane Dowdell, Aug. 18, 1897. Asst. chemist, Ala. Poly. Inst., 1884-87; prof. chemistry, La. State U., 1887-93; prof. chemistry, 1893—, dean College of Agricultural Sciences, 1908-21; dean dept. of science, 1921—, Ala. Poly. Inst. (acting pres. during greater part of 1919-20). State chemist of Alabama, 1893—. Mem. State Bd. Industrial Preparedness, Ala., 1916; asso. mem. Naval Consulting Bd. of U.S. Democrat. Methodist. Co-author: Chemistry in Agriculture, 1926. Home: Auburn, Ala. Died Apr. 4, 1930.

ROSS, DAVID E., b. Brookston, Ind., Aug. 25, 1871; E.E., Purdue U., 1893. Inventor of Ross gears; v.p. and gen. mgr. for many yrs. of Ross Gear & Tool Co., La Fayette, Ind.; was actively identified with many industrial projects; retired, 1927, to devote attention to promotion of Purdue U.; now chmn. bd. Ross Gear & Tool Co., Rostone Corp. One of donors Ross-Ade Stadium to the univ., also donor, to the univ. of various tracts of land as well as money, patents and inventions. Pres. bd. trustees Purdue U. Fellow Am. Soc. Mech. Engrs.; hon. mem. Sigma Xi, Sigma Pi Sigma. Home: La Fayette, Ind. Died June 28, 1943.

ROSS, FRANK ELMORE, astronomer; b. San Francisco, Calif., Apr. 2, 1874; s. Daniel Walter and Katherine (Harris) R.; B.S., U. of Calif., 1896, fellow, 1897-98; at Lick Obs., 1898-99; Ph.D., U. of Calif., 1901; m. Margaret J. Benton, May 5, 1904; 1 son, Robert D.; m. 2d, Elizabeth Bischoff, June 10, 1913; children—Alan K., Barbara H.; m. 3d, Anna Lee, Aug. 21, 1939. Teacher mathematics and physics, Mt. Tamalpais Mil. Acad., Calif., 1896-97; asst. prof. mathematics, U. of Nev., 1900; asst. Nautical Almanac Office, 1902-03; research asst. Carnegie Inst., 1903-05; dir. Internat. Latitude Obs., 1905-15; physicist Eastman Kodak Co., 1915-24; prof. atronomy, Yerkes Observatory, 1924-39, prof. emeritus, 1939—. Mem. National Academy, American Astronomical society. Republican. Presbyterian. Has specialized in math. astronomy, variation of latitude, physics of the photographic plate, planetary and stellar photography, development of wide-angle high-speed lenses, corrector lenses for mirrors. Home: 1100 Mt. Lowe Dr., Altadena, Cal. Died Sept. 21, 1966; buried Mt. View Cemetery, Altadena.

ROSS, JAMES DELMAGE, elec. engr.; b. Chatham, Ont., Can., Nov. 9, 1871. Supt. municipal power system, Seattle, Wash., 1903—, on leave absence, 1933—; advisory engr. on power, Pub. Works Adminstrn., 1933-35; mem. Securities and Exchange Commn., Washington, D.C., 1935-37; adminstr. Bonneville Project, Columbia River, 1937—. Home: Seattle, Wash. Died Mar. 14, 1939.

ROSS, JOHN O., engr.; b. Aberdeen, Scotland, Sept. 17, 1885; s. John and Anna (Ogg) R.; came to U.S., 1895, naturalized, 1918; student Mass. Inst. Tech., 1904-05, Lowell Inst., 1905-06; m. Anne K. Dingee, Sept. 1, 1910. Engr. B.F. Sturtevant Co., 1904-08, div. mgr., 1913-20; dept. mgr. Green Fuel Economizer Co., 1908-12; pres., chmn. bd., dir. J. O. Ross Engring. Corp., N.Y.C., since 1921; dir. Ross Engring. of Can., Ltd., John Waldron Corp. Profl. engr., N.Y. Mem. Am. Soc. M.E., Am. Soc. Heating and Air-Conditioning Engrs., Am. Ordnance Assn., T.A.P.P.I., Newcomen Soc. Mason. Clubs: N.Y. Athletic; Tuxedo. Author articles on engring. subjects. Home: E. Lake Rd., Tuxedo Park, N.Y.; also 39 E. 79th St., N.Y.C. Office: 444 Madison Av., N.Y.C. Died June 1966.

ROSS, LUTHER SHERMAN, zoologist; b. Reno, Bond Co., Ill., Sept. 6, 1864; s. John Milton and Ruth Naomi (Jones) R.; B.S., U. of Ill., 1889, M.S., 1890; post-grad. work same; Ph.D., U. Chicago, 1919; m. Ellen Maria Bardwell, Champaign, Ill., June 22, 1892; children—Ruth Lovilla, Helen Bardwell, Mary Kellogg. Prof. natural sciences, Winona (Minn.) State Normal Sch., 1890-91; prin. schs., Oswego, Ill., 1891-92; prof. biology, and chemistry, 1892-96, biology and geology, 1896-1907, zoology since 1914, Drake U. Fellow A.A.A.S., Am. Micros. Soc., Ia. Acad. Science (sec. 1906-12, pres. 1917-18); mem. Am. Assn. Univ. Profs.,

Phi Beta Kappa, Sigma Xi. Republican. Conglist. Clubs: Frontier, University, Professional Men's Club. Home: 1308 27th St., Des Moines, Ia.

ROSS, PERLEY ASON, prof. physics; b. Panacea, Mo., Apr. 6, 1883; s. William McKay and Zaida (Gittings) R.; A.B., Stanford, 1908, A.M., 1909, Ph.D., 1911; grad. study U. of Chicago, 1920; m. Olive Durbin, June 7, 1911; children-Ruth Eleanor, Betsy. Instr. in physics, Stanford, 1910-16, asst. prof. physics, 1916-24, asso. prof., 1924-26, prof., 1927—; acting asso. prof. physics, Cornell, 1926-27. Contributing scientist, Internat. Critical Tables. Fellow Am. Physical Society. Republican. Unitarian. Home: Palo Alto, Calif. Died Mar. 20, 1938.

ROSS, WILLIAM HORACE, chemist; b. N.S., Can., Dec. 27, 1875; s. Daniel and Mary (Murray) R.; B.Sc., Dalhousie U., Halifax, N.S., 1903, M.Sc., 1904, 1851 sci. research scholar, 1905-07; Johns Hopkins, 1904-05; Ph.D., U. of Chicago, 1907; m. Catherine Allen, June 10, 1908; children—Allen Murray, William Horace. Asst. chemist, Agrl. Expt. Sta., U. of Ariz., 1907-12; scientist Bur. of Soils, 1912-27; sr. chemist, Bur. of Chemistry and Soils, 1927-40; senior chemist Bureau of Plant Industry, 1940-44; principal chemist 1944-45. Capt., C.W.S., United States Army, 1918-19. Abstracter Chemical Abstracts since 1907. Mem. Am. Chem. Soc., A.A.A.S., Am. Soc. Agronomy, Am. Inst. Chemists, Assn. of Official Agricultural Chemists (pres. 1945-46), Sigma Xi. Presbyterian. Co-author: Fixed Nitrogen; Principles and Practice of Agricultural Analysis. Contbr. to chem. and other scientific jours. Home: 2811 Woodley Rd., Washington, D.C. Died May 16, 1947.

ROSSBY, CARL-GUSTAF ARVID, (ros'bi), meteorologist; b. Stockholm, Sweden, Dec. 28, 1898; s. Arvid and Alma Charlotta (Marelius) R.; studied U. of Stockholm, 1917-18, 1922-25; student Geophysical Inst., Bergen, Norway, 1918-19, U. of Leipzig, 1920; hon. D.Sc., Kenyon Coll., 1939; m. Harriet Marshall Alexander, Sept. 2, 1929; children—Stig Arvid, Hans Thomas, Carin. Came to U.S., as fellow Swedish-Am. Found., 1926. Research asso. in meteorology Daniel Guggenheim Fund for Promotion of Aeronautics, and chmn. com. on aero meteorology, 1927-28; prof. meteorology Mass. Inst. Tech., 1931-39; research asso. Woods Hole Oceanographic Inst. since 1931; asst. chief for research and edn. U.S. Weather Bureau, 1931-41; distinguished service prof. meteorology U. of Chicago since 1943, on leave to serve as prof. meteorology U. of Stockholm, 1947-48. Expert cons. to Office of Sec. of War, and cons. on weather problems to comdg. gen. of A.A.F., during World War II. Hon. fellow Royal Meteorol. Soc., London; mem. Inst. Aero. Sciences, Am. Meteorol. Soc. (pres. 1944-45), Am. Philos. Soc., Nat. Acad. Sciences, Det Noske Videnokaps-Akademi (Oslo). Received (with H. C. Willett) the Sylvanus Albert Reed award from Inst. Aero. Scis., 1934; received the Robert Losey award, 1947. Club: Quadrangle (Chicago). Organizer model aero-weather service for Guggenheim Fund, 1928. Contbr. articles to sci. jours. in U.S. and abroad. Home: Stockholm, Sweden. Died Aug. 19, 1957.

ROSSER, THOMAS LAFAYETTE, soldier, civ. engr.; b. Campbell Co., Va., Oct. 15, 1836; s. John and Martha M. (Johnson) R.; family removed to Tex., 1849; entered West Point, 1856, in class of 1861; class being ordered into army when Fort Sumter was fired upon, he resigned; went to Montgomery, Ala.; apptd. 1st lt. arty., C.S.A.; soon after capt. Co. D, Washington arty., New Orleans; severely wounded, Mechanicsville, Va., 1862; promoted lt. col. arty., and a few days later col. 5th Va. cav., in brigade of J. E. B. Stuart; brig. gen. cav. fall of 1863; maj. gen. cav. fall 1864; served in Army of Northern Va.; refused to surrender at Appomattox with Lee, but charged through lines and escaped; while endeavoring to reorganize scattered troops of the army was captured and made prisoner of war; was seriously wounded 4 times in battle; m. Betty B. Winston, 1863. Studied law after the war, but did not enter profession; was one of supts. Nat. Express Co. under Gen. Joe Johnston; later engr. in ry. service, including chief engr. Northern and Canadian Pacific railroads from 1870 until 1886, when he retired to an estate in Va.; apptd. brig. gen. U.S.V., June 10, 1898, and comd. 3d brigade, 2d div., 1st army corps, composed of 14th Minn., 2d Ohio and 1st Pa. regts., vol. inf., in war with Spain. Home: Charlottesville, Va. Died 1910.

ROTCH, A(BBOTT) LAWRENCE, meteorologist; b. Boston, Mass., Jan. 6, 1861; s. Benjamin Smith and Annie Bigelow (Lawrence) R.; pvt. schs. and tutor, Paris, Florence, Berlin, Boston, 1875-80; S.B., Mass. Inst. Tech., 1884; (hon. A.M., Harvard, 1891); m. Margaret Randolph Anderson, Nov. 22, 1893. In 1885 established and has since maintained the Blue Hill Meteorological Obs., nr. Boston, famous for its investigations of clouds, and for 1st use of kites to record meteorol. data; prof. meteorology, Harvard, 1906—. Mem. Internat. Jury Awards, Paris Expn., 1889, and then made Chevalier Legion of Honor; received Prussian Orders of the Crown, 1902, and Red Eagle, 1905, in recognition of efforts to advance knowledge of atmosphere; mem. various Am. and foreign scientific socs. and coms. Obtained 1st observations high above Atlantic Ocean with kites, 1901, 1st observations 5 to 10 miles above Am. Continent with registration balloons, 1904; 1st trigonometrical measurements of pilot balloons in U.S., 1909; collaborated with Teisserenc de Bort in sending a steam yacht to explore the tropical atmosphere, 1905-06; has taken part in scientific expdns. in U.S., S. America, Europe and Africa. Asso. editor of Am. Meteorological Journal, 1886-96; lectured before Lowell Inst. of Boston, 1891, 98; librarian Am. Acad. Arts and Sciences; trustee several ednl. instns., Boston. Editor: Observations and Investigations at Blue Hill, pub. in Annals Harvard Coll. Observatory. Author: Sounding the Ocean of Air, 1900; The Conquest of the Air, 1909; Charts of the Atmosphere for Aeronauts and Aviators (with A. H. Palmer), 1911. Home: Boston, Mass. Died Apr. 7, 1912.

ROTCH, ARTHUR, architect; b. Boston, May 13, 1850; s. Benjamin Smith and Annie Bigelow (Lawrence) R.; grad. Harvard, 1871; attended Sch. Architecture, Mass. Inst. Tech., 1871-73; attended Ecole des Beaux Arts, Paris, France, 1873; m. Lissette de Wolf Colt, Nov. 16, 1892. In charge of part of restoration and redecoration Chateau of Chenonceaux, late 1870's; formed partnership with George J. Tilden, 1880, built large houses in Boston, Washington, D.C., Bar Harbor, Me., churches of Messiah and Ascension, Boston, Ch. of Holy Spirit, Mattapan, Mass., art museum at Wellesley Coll., public libraries, Bridgewater and Groton, Mass., Eastport, Me.; trustee Boston Museum of Fine Arts; a founder Rotch Traveling Scholarship (endowed by his father, 1884) to enable draftsmen or architects to study abroad; furnished archtl. library of Mass. Inst. Tech.; financed entire 1st of Harvard Sch. Architecture (founded 1893); he left $25,000 Boston Mus. Fine Arts, $40,000 to Sch. Architecture, Mass. Inst. Tech. Died Beverly, Mass., Aug. 15, 1894.

ROTCH, WILLIAM, engineer; b. New Bedford, Mass., July 22, 1844; s. William J, and Emily (Morgan) R.; A.B., Harvard, 1865; C.E. École Centrale des Arts et Manufactures, Paris, 1869; m. Mary Rotch Eliot, Sept. 6, 1873. Asst. engr., 1871-74, chief engr., 1875-80, Fall River Water Works; consulting engr. and purchasing agt. Mexican Central R.R. Co., Sonora R.R. Co., Atlantic & Pacific R.R. Co., and Southern Cal. R.R. Co., 1880-82; apptd., 1881, by Gov. John D. Long, one of commrs. who established boundary between Mass. and R.I.; consulting engr. several railway companies, 1882-90. President Fed. Wharf & Storage Co., Railroad Wharf & Storage Co., and Denbigh Mining Corp.; v.p. State Wharf & Storage Co.; treas. Broadway Storage Co. Dir. Adams Nervine Asylum, Infants' Hosp.; trustee Rotch Traveling Scholarship for Architects, etc. Home: Boston, Mass. Died Aug. 15, 1925.

ROTH, FILIBERT, forestry expert; b. Würtemberg, Germany, Apr. 20, 1858; s. Paul Raphael and Amalie (Volz) R.; early edn. in Würtemberg; came to U.S., 1871; on Western frontier, 1874-82; teacher, 1883-85; studied U. of Mich., 1885-93, B.S., 1890; m. Clara Hoffman, Oct. 7, 1888; 1 dau., Stella Rosa (wife of Prof. Orlan William Boston). Spl. expert on timber U.S. Dept. Agr., 1893-98; asst. prof. forestry, Cornell, 1898-1901; expert asst. Bur. Forestry, Dept. Agr., July-Nov. 1901; chief Div. Forest Reserves, Gen. Land Office, U.S. Dept. Interior, 1901; prof. forestry, U. of Mich., 1903-23, emeritus; LL.D., Marquette U., 1923. Author: Timber, 1895; Forest Conditions of Wisconsin, 1898; Cypress; The Annual Ring; Timber Physics, 1899; Uses of Wood, 1896; Grazing in Forest Reserves, 1902; First Book of Forestry, 1902; Forest Reserves Manual, 1902; Forest Regulation, 1914; Forest Valuation, 1915. Died Dec. 4, 1925.

ROTHBERG, SIDNEY, pharmacologist; b. Bklyn., Apr. 17, 1914; s. Harry and Sarah (Horowitz) R.; B.S., Bklyn. Coll., 1939; postgrad N.Y.U., 1947-48, U. Md., 1956-60; m. Dorothy Schaffel, Oct. 15, 1939 (dec. Apr. 1959); children—David Michael, Frances B., Eric Joseph, Cathy Ann. Research asso. Jewish Hosp., Bklyn., 1930-33; biochemist Cumberland Hosp., Bklyn., 1933-43; research pharmacologist, directorate med. research Med. Research Lab., Edgewood Arsenal, Md., 1954-70. Served with AUS, 1943-54, now lt. col. Res. Mem. Armed Forces Chem. Assn., Soc. Exptl. Biology and Medicine, Soc. Am. Microbiologists, Sci. Research Soc. Am., A.A.A.S. Contbr. articles in field to sci. jours. Patentee in field. Home: Edgewood MD Died July 26, 1970.

ROTHMAN, STEPHEN, physician, educator; b. Budapest, Hungary, Sept. 10, 1894; M.D., U. Budapest, 1917. Came to U.S., 1938, naturalized, 1944. Mem. staff dept. physiology U. Budapest, 1918-20; in hosp. and clinics U. Giessen, Germany, 1921-28; with clinic for skin and veneral diseases Social Health Inst., State Hungary, Budapest, 1929-38; mem. staff dept. medicine, sect. dermatology U. Chgo., 1938-41, head sect. dermatology, 1942-60, prof. dermatology, 1945-60; prof. emeritus, 1960—. Mem. A.M.A., Chgo. Dermatol. Soc., Am. Dermatol. Assn. Author: Physiology and Biochemistry of the Skin. Contbr. profl. jours. Home: 5801 S. Dorchester Av. Office: 950 E. 59th St., Chgo. 37. Died Aug. 31, 1963.

ROTHROCK, ADDISON M(AY), physicist; b. West Chester, Pa., May 12, 1908; s. Henry Abraham and Eleanor (Cleves) R.; B.S., Pa. State Coll., 1925; D.Sc., Ashland College, 1964; married to Elizabeth Thomas Bland, Jan. 5, 1929; 1 son, Richard Cleves. Grad. asst. Pa. State Coll., 1925-26; head fuel injection section, Langley Lab., Nat. Adv. Com. for Aeronautics, 1926, chief fuels and lubricants div., Lewis Lab., 1942, chief research, 1945, assistant director NACA, 1947-58; assistant director of NASA, 1958, scientist for propulsion NASA, 1959-61, asso. dir. Office of Plans, 1961-63, dir., 1963; prof. applied sci. George Washington U., 1964-68. Mem. AEC Lexingon Project, 1948. Served on various coms. Co-ordinating Research Council, NASA, Dept. Def. Fellow Inst. Aero. Sci., Am. Inst. Aeros. and Astronautics; mem. Am. Rocket Soc. (sr. mem.), Sigma Xi, Sigma Pi Sigma. Club: Cosmos. Home: Alexandria VA Died June 21, 1971.

ROTHROCK, JOSEPH TRIMBLE, botanist; b. McVeytown, Pa., Apr. 9, 1839; s. Dr. Abraham and Phoebe B. R.; B.S., Harvard, 1864; M.D., U. of Pa., 1867; m. Martha E., d. Addison and Elizabeth Shafer May, May 27, 1869. Corpl. Co. D, 131st Pa. Inf. and capt. Co. E, 20th Pa. Cav., in Civil War; wounded at Fredericksburg. Prof. botany, U. of Pa., 1877-93; commr. of forestry for Pa., 1893-1905. Founded, 1903, and supt. until 1908, South Mountain Camp Sanatorium for Consumptives (state instn.). Author: Vacation Cruisings, 1884; Botany of the Wheeler Expedition, 1878, Vol. VIII; Flora of Alaska, 1867; Revision of North American Guarineae, Proceedings of American Academy; Pennsylvania Forestry Reports, 1895, 1896, 1897. Home: West Chester, Pa. Died June 2, 1922.

ROTZELL, WILLETT ENOS, physician, naturalist; b. Philadelphia, June 19, 1871; s. Dr. Joseph M. and Elizabeth (Whitehead) R.; ed. Eastburn Acad., Phila., also spl. studies in botany and zoölogy, especially ornithology; M.D., Hahnemann Med. Coll., Phila., 1892; (hon. B.S., Hiwassee Coll., Tenn., 1904); m. Amanda W. Lever, 1895. Lecturer on botany and zoölogy, 1895-1905, prof. med. botany, 1905-08, Hahnemann Med. Coll. Founder, 1903, and editor Atlantic Slope Naturalist. Author: Man—An Introduction to Anthropology, 2d edit., 1905. Home: Philadelphia, Pa. Died July 1913.

ROUS, (FRANCIS) PEYTON, pathologist; b. Baltimore, Md., Oct. 5, 1879; s. Charles and Frances Anderson (Wood) R.; B.A., Johns Hopkins, 1900, M.D., 1905; (hon.) Sc.D., Cambridge Univ., U. of Mich., 1938. Yale, U. of Birmingham, McGill U., 1949, U. Chgo., 1954, Rockefeller Inst., 1959, Jefferson Univ., 1966, U. of Hartford, 1967; M.D. (hon.), U. Zurich, 1946, Jefferson Med. Coll., 1966; LL.D., St. Lawrence Univ., 1963; m. Marion Eckford de Kay, June 15, 1915; children—Marion (Mrs. Alan Hodgkin), Ellen deKay, Phoebe (Mrs. Thomas J. Wilson). Resident house officer, Johns Hopkins Hosp., 1904-06; instr. in pathology, U. of Mich., 1906-08; asst., asso., asso. mem., Rockefeller Inst. for Med. Research, 1909-20, mem. in pathology and bacteriology, 1920-45, mem. emeritus 1945; mem. bd. scientific consultants Sloan-Kettering Inst. Cancer Research, New York City, 1957-70; Linacre Lecturer Cambridge U., 1929, honorary fellow Trinity Hall, same. Fellow A.A.A.S.; mem. Nat. Acad. Sciences, Am. Philos. Soc., Assn. Am. Physicians, Am. Assn. Pathologists and Bacteriologists, Am. Soc. for Exptl. Pathology, Soc. for Experimental Biology and Medicine, Harvey Soc., N.Y. Pathological Soc., N.Y. Acad. Medicine, Am. Assn. for Cancer Research, Phi Beta Kappa, Alpha Omega Alpha, Sigma Xi. Foreign mem. Royal Society; hon. fellow Royal Soc. Medicine and Coll. Pathologists, London, Weizmann Inst. Science, Israel; hon. mem. British Physiol. Soc., Pathol. Soc. of Great Britain and Ireland, American Society for Microbiology, New York Path. Soc., Conn. Med. Soc., fgn. corr. mem. British Med. Association, Academie de Medecine, Paris; mem. Royal Acad. Sciences of Denmark, Norwegian Academy of Science and Letters. Awarded John Scott medal and award, 1927; Walker prize, Royal Coll. Surgeons, England, 1941; Anna Fuller Award, 1952; Kober Medal, Assn. Am. Physicians, 1953; Bertner medal and award, U. Tex. 1954; Kovalenko Medal, Nat. Acad. Scis., 1956 distinguished service award Am. Cancer Soc., 1957 Lasker award Am. Pub. Health Assn., 1958 Landsteiner award, Am. Assn. Blood Banks, 1958; N.Y Acad. Medicine medal, 1959; Judd award, Memorial Center for Cancer, 1959; Gold Medal, Royal Soc. of Medicine (London), 1962, United Nations Prize for cancer research, 1962; Gold-headed Cane award American Assn. of Pathologists and Bacteriologists 1964; Cleveland medal Am. Cancer Soc., 1966; Nat Medal of Sci., 1966; Paul Ehrlich award, Germany 1966; Nobel prize in medicine, 1966. Co-editor Jour Exptl. Medicine. Contbr. researches on cancer and viruses. Club: Century. Home: New York City NY Died Feb. 16, 1970.

ROUSH, GAR A., (roush), mineral economist; b Harrisburg (now Gas City), Ind., Oct. 21, 1883; s. Isaac N. and Clementine H. (McCarty) R.; A.B., Ind. U. 1905; M.S., U. Wis., 1910; m. Lillian Belle Coleman July 16, 1911. Asst. prof. metallurgy, 1912-20, asso prof., 1920-26, Lehigh U.; acting prof. metallurgy Mont. Sch. Mines, 1926-27; spl. adviser Mus. Peaceful Arts, N.Y., 1927-30; editor, 1913-43, Mineral Industry ann. devoted to world mineral interests; mineral technologist, U.S. Bur. of Mines, 1943-46; became metals engr., Strategic and Critical Materials Div., bur Fed. Supply (formerly U.S. Treasury Dept.) 1946, with planning br. procurement div., Gen. Service Adminstrn. until 1955, ret. 1955. Appointed supr. tng. of inspection div. Ordnance Dept., AUS, 1918; commd. capt. Ordnance Dept., 1918, and appointed head of ednl. br., inspection div., and later chief of tests, metall. br.; hon. discharged, 1919, commd. maj., Staff Specialist Reserve, U.S. Army, 1924, and for several years served as spl. lectr. on strategic mineral supplies, Army Industrial Coll.; later assigned to Commodities Div., Planning Branch Office of Asst. Sec. of War; mem. Inactive Reserve, 1941—. Mem. Electrochem. Soc. (asst. sec. 1912-18), Am. Inst. Mining and Metall. Engrs. (mng. editor 1917), Soc. of Am. Mil. Engrs. (Toulmin medalist, 1939). Presbyn. Contbr. numerous articles on electrochem. and metall. and mineral econs. in the tech. press, various standard encyclos. and other works of reference. Author of the sect. on Mineral Industries in rev. edit. Van Hise's Conservation of Natural Resources; sect. on Electrochemistry and Electrometallurgy in 6th edit. and on Electrochemistry in 7th edit. Standard Handbook for Electrical Engineers; Strategic Mineral Supplies; articles on strategic mineral supplies in foreign countries in Mil. Engr. Home: 4416 Seventeenth St. North, Arlington, Va. Address: Planning Branch, Procurement Div., General Service Administration, Washington 25. Died Aug. 17, 1955.

ROVENSTINE, E(MERY) A(NDREW), physician; b. Atwood, Ind., July 20, 1895; s. Cassius Andrew and Lulu (Massena) R.; A.B., Wabash Coll., Crawfordsville, Ind., 1917, D.Sc., 1948; M.D., Ind. U., 1928; student Grad. Sch., U. of Wis., 1930-34; m. Jewel Sonya Gould, 1939. Asst. prof. of anesthesia, U. of Wis., 1934; asst. prof. surgery, Coll. of Medicine, New York U., 1935-36, prof. of anesthesia since 1937, prof. of anesthesia Coll. of Dentistry since 1938; dir. of div. of anesthesia, Bellevue Hosp. since 1935; guest dir. anesthesia, Oxford (Eng.) U., 1938; guest prof. anesthesia, U. Rosario (Argentina), 1939; mem. med. teaching mission to Czechoslovakia, 1946. Cons. anesthetist—Beth Israel Hosp., Hosp. for Spl. Surgery, Goldwater Meml. Hosp., Knickerbocker Hosp., Horace Harding Hosp., Gouverneur Hospital (N.Y.C.). Sr. cons. in anesthesia Veterans Hosp. (Bronx, N.Y.); director of anesthesia, University Hospital, 1949—. Served as 1st lt. Engrs., A.U.S., 1917-19. Fel. A.M.A., N.Y. Acad. Med., N.Y. Acad. Science; mem. Am. Bd. Anesthesiology (pres. 1948), Am. Soc. Anesthetists (past pres.), Am. Soc. Regional Anesthesia (past pres.), Nat. Research Council (med. sci. div., 1941-46), Soc. Exptl. Biology and Medicine, Soc. Pharmaceutical and Experimental Therapy, International Anesthesia Research Society, Alpha Omega Alpha, Sigma Xi; honorary member French and Mexican socs. of anesthesia, honorary member South African Society Anesthesia. Recipient Internat. Anesthesia Research Award, 1938. Decorated Order of the White Lion (Czechoslovakia). Asso. editor: Anesthesiology, Geriatrics. Contbr. to numerous med. and dental publs. Conducted original research in cyclopropane anesthesia and spinal anesthesia, devising endotracheal airway and laryngoscope; prepared system for collecting statis. data of anesthesia and surgery. Home: 320 E. 57th St. Office: 550 First Av., New York 16. Died Nov. 9, 1960.

ROWE, ALBERT HOLMES, physician; b. Oakland, Cal., Sept. 15, 1889; s. Albert and Susan Abbie (Holmes) R.; B.S., U. Cal. at San Francisco, 1911, M.S., 1912, M.D., 1914; m. Mildred E. Porter, 1915; children—Albert Porter, Charles Adams, Edward Holmes, Robert Nelson. Intern, U. Cal. at San Francisco Hosp., 1914-15, allergist, until 1970; asst. in medicine Mass. Gen. Hosp., Boston, 1915-16; practice medicine specializing in internal medicine and allergy, Oakland, San Francisco, 1916-70; allergist Cowell Infirmary, U. Cal. at Berkeley; cons. in allergy and metabolic diseases Highland Alameda County Hosp., Oakland; lectr. medicine U. Cal. Med. Sch., San Francisco, 30 years, lectr. meritus, until 1970; founder allergy clinic Children's Hosp. of East Bay, Oakland; cons. in allergy Merritt Hosp., Oakland. Diplomate Am. Bd. Internal Medicine. Mem. Am. Assn. for Study Allergy (pres. 1928), Allergy Found. Am. (past chmn. No. Cal. sect.). Republican. Conglist. Mason (Shriner). Author: Handbook for Diabetics, 1928; Food Allergy, 1931; Clinical Allergy, 1937; Elimination Diets and the Patient's Allergies, 1941, 43; Food Allergy and the Elimination Diet, 1971. Mem. editorial staff Jour. Allergy. Founder 1st allergy soc. in Am. Home: Oakland CA Died Oct. 29, 1970; buried Oakland CA

ROWE, HARTLEY, bus. exec., engr.; b. Goodland, Ind., Nov. 8, 1882; s. Winfield S. and Florence (Mann) R.; B.S., Purdue U., 1904, Eng. Dr., 1947; m. Inez M. Oswald, June 24, 1908; 1 dau., Margaret F. (Mrs. Angelo W. Ghirardini). Elec. engr. Isthmian Canal Commn., Panama, 1904-17; resident engr. charge constrn. div. Panama Canal Commn., 1917-19; mgr. Detroit office Lockwood, Green & Co., engrs., 1919-21, mgr. Boston office, 1921-26; chief engr. United Fruit Co. since 1926, v.p. since 1928, dir., 1951—; dir. Scott & Williams, Inc., Nat. Research Corp. Chief div. transp. and naval architecture, Nat. Def. Research com. OSRD, World War II; tech. adv. to supreme comdr. AEF, Eng., France, 6 mos., 1944; cons. Manhattan dist., Los Alamos, 1944-45; mem. gen. adv. com. AEC, 1946-50. Awarded Bronze Star medal, Medal for Merit. Fellow Am. Soc. M.E., Am. Inst. E.E. Home: 17 Vineyard Rd., Newton Centre, Mass. 02159. Office: 80 Federal St., Boston 10. Died Nov. 5, 1966.

ROWE, HENRY CLARKE, oyster culturist; b. New Haven, Conn., Apr. 23, 1851; s. Ruel and Abbie (Gordon) R.; ed. Fair Haven Sem.; Gen. Russell's Mil. Inst., New Haven; Conn. Lit. Instn., Suffield. Engaged in oyster culture since 1868; head of firm of H. C. Rowe & Co., oyster growers. Pres. Conn. Oyster Growers' Assn. of N. America, 2 terms (resigned 1913); mem. Conn. Acad. Science. Author papers and articles on oyster culture for various mags. and for Am. and Internat. Fisheries assns.; also much legislation relation to the oyster industry. Home: (summer) Bath, Me.; (winter) Daytona Beach, Florida.

ROWE, JESSE PERRY, geologist; b. Salem Centre, Mich., May 5, 1871; s. Perry and Lydia Louise (Weed) R.; student U. of Ore., 1893; B.S., U. of Neb., 1897; fellow in dept. of geology, U. of Neb., 1897-98, M.A., 1903, Ph.D., 1906, hon. Sc.D., 1935; student U. of Calif., summer, 1901, U. of Chicago, summer, 1905; m. Anna Elizabeth Richards, June 11, 1901 (died Oct. 5, 1939);children—Helen Elizabeth, John Philip, Thomas Dudley. Asst. prin. and head science dept., Butte High Sch., 1898-99; prin. Lincoln Sch., Butte, 1899-1900; instr. physics and geology, U. of Mont., 1900-01, prof. since 1901. Asst. U.S. Geol. Survey, 1906-07; dir. 5 summer sessions, U. of Mont.; prof. geology, U. of Mich., 1921-22; prof. geology, Columbia, summer 1922; in charge geology dept., U. of Mich., summer 1923; prof. geology, Columbia, summers 1925, 26; prof. geology, Cornell U., Ithaca, summer 1927, 28; visiting prof. geology, Princeton, 1928; prof. geology and geography, "The Floating Univ.," 1928-29; prof. geology, U. of Mich., summer 1929. U. of Southern Calif., summer 1930, U. of Calif., Berkeley, summer 1936; visiting prof. geology U. of North Carolina, 1942-45. Fellow A.A.A.S., Geol. Soc. America; mem. Am. Forestry Assn., Am. Inst. Mining and Metall. Engrs., Am. Assn. Petroleum Geologists, Mont. Acad. Science, Arts and Letters, Pan Hellenic Soc. Mont. (pres. 1907), Mont. State Teachers Assn. (pres. 1908), State Assn. of School Trustees (pres. 1915), Mont. Geog. Soc. (pres. 1915-16), Elisha Mitchell Scientific Soc. (U. of N.C.). Mem. State Text Book Commn. Exec. and community organizer War Camp Community Service, in charge of work in Los Angeles and surrounding cities, 1918-19. Mem. Phi Kappa Psi, Sigma Xi. Clubs: Missoula, Missoula Country (sec.-treas.), Elks. Author of bulletins and books on "Some Volcanic Ash Beds of Montana," "Montana Coal and Lignite Deposits," "Some Economic Geology of Montana," "Practical Mineralogy Simplified," "Essentials of Miner-alogy," "Geography of Montana," and many articles on econ. geology, in leading geol., scientific, and mining publs. Home: Missoula MT; Carolina Inn, Chapel Hill NC

ROWE, JOSEPH EUGENE, educator, mathematician; b. Emmitsburg, Md., Mar. 21, 1883; s. Charles Jacob and Cora (Hoke) R.; of Scotch-Irish and Huguenot ancestry; A.B., first honor, Gettysburg (Pa.) Coll., 1904, LL.D., 1930; student U. of Va., 1904-05; fellow in mathematics, Johns Hopkins, 1909-10, Ph.D., 1910; m. Nina King, Sept. 6, 1911; children—Joseph Eugene, Richard King. Instructor in mathematics, Goucher Coll., 1910-11, Haverford, 1911-12, Dartmouth, 1912-14; asst. prof., asso. prof., and prof. mathematics, Pa. State Coll., 1914-20; prof. and head dept. of mathematics, Coll. of William and Mary, 1921-28, dir. extension, 1924-28; pres. Clarkson Memorial Coll. of Technology, Potsdam, N.Y., 1928-32 (resigned); engaged in research in social sciences, Johns Hopkins U., 1932-33; apptd. mem. Bd. Veterans Appeals, Feb. 23, 1934. Asst. physicist Nat. Advisory Com., Aero, May 1917-Feb. 1918. Chief ballistician, Aberdeen Proving Ground, Ordnance Dept., U.S.A., 1920-21. Democrat. Episcopalian. Author: Introductory Mathematics. Co-author: History of Gettysburg College, 1931. Inventor mathematical instruments. Home: Baltimore, Md. Died Oct. 2, 1939.

ROWE, WALTER ELLSWORTH, civil engr.; b. Bristol, Ind., Sept. 18, 1875; s. Perry and Lydia Louisa (Weed) R.; student U. of Ore., 1891-92; B.S. in C.E., U. of Neb., 1896; post-grad. work, U. of Chicago, summers, 1899, 1900; m. Adaline Meech Hume, Aug. 27, 1903; children—Gilbert Hume, Gertrude Hume, Helen Hume, Ann Ellsworth (dec.). County supt. schs., Greeley County, Neb., 1897-98; prof. mathematics and comdt. Cadets, Trinity Hall Sch., Louisville, Ky., 1898; supt. schs., White Sulphur Springs, Mont., 1898-1901; prof. science, high schs., Butte, Mont., 1902-03; prin. high sch., Anaconda, Mont., 1903-04; prof. mathematics and physics, U. of N.M., 1904-05; prof. civ. engring., Okla. Agrl. and Mech. Coll., 1905-06; dean Coll. Civ. Engring., U. of Ky., 1906-17; dean of engring., U. of S.C., 1917-18; head prof. civil engring., Drexel Inst., Phila., 1918-19; exec. evening sch. Drexel Inst., 1919-20; engr., and mgr. John E. Hand & Sons Co., New Orleans and Baltimore, 1920-22; dean Sch. of Engring. and dir. engring. expt. sta., U. of S.C., 1922; now dean emeritus; partner Rowe & Chapman, design & cons. engrs., 1950—; consulting engineer S.C. Pub. Service Authority; mem. Archtl. Exam. Bd. for S.C. Organizer, and pres. Ky. Civ. and Sanitary Engring. Assn., 1916-17; mem. Am. Soc. C.E., Am. Assn. Engrs., Soc. Promotion Engring. Edn., Le Conte Scientific Soc. (pres.), Tau Beta Pi. Promoter state highway laws for Ky.; chief of Road Material Survey of S.C. Appointed May 16, 1931, by S.C. Supreme Court, a member of Bd. of Rehabilitation Engrs. for Columbia St. Ry. System. Episcopalian. Home: Williston, S.C. Died Sept. 5, 1952; buried Williston, S.C.

ROWLAND, ARTHUR JOHN, engring. educator; b. Cincinnati, O., Feb. 19, 1867; s. Adoniram Judson and Harriet E. (Frick) R.; ed. pvt. schs., Phila.; freshman yr., U. of Pa.; partial course langs. and elec. engring., Johns Hopkins; m. Flora B. Dobler, May 16, 1895. Organized course in elec. engring., 1893, dir. Sch. of Engring., 1896-1913, dean, July 1913—, Drexel Inst., Phila. Author: Texts in Applied Electricity. Home: Philadelphia, Pa. Died 1934.

ROWLAND, CHARLES LEONARD, engineer; b. Brooklyn, N.Y., Nov. 28, 1852; s. James and Mary E. R.; ed. common schs., Fairfield, Conn.; m. Alice Lucille Ackerly, Oct. 24, 1883; m. 2d, Kathryn Ethel Schweizer, July 20, 1917. Pres. Am. Welding Co., Dec. 1907—. Home: Carbondale, Pa. Died Apr. 18, 1926.

ROWLAND, HENRY AUGUSTUS, prof. physics Johns Hopkins, 1876—; b. Honesdale, Pa., Nov. 27, 1848; C.E., Rensselaer Poly. Inst., 1870 (Ph.D., Johns Hopkins, 1880); LL.D., Yale, 1895; LL.D., Princeton, 1896; engaged in railroad surveys, 1871; taught in Wooster Univ., 1871-72; instr., 1872-74, and asst. prof. physics, 1874-75, Rensselaer Poly. Inst.; studied abroad a year, then took present chair. Was member Electrical Congress at Paris, 1881; served on jury of electrical exhibition there, 1881; made chevalier, 1881, and in 1896 Officer Legion of Honor; m. Henrietta Harrison, June 4, 1890. Principal scientific work has been the discovery of magnetic action due to electric convection; the exact determination of the mechanical equivalent of heat; the discovery of concave grating and the machine for ruling gratings by which spectrum analysis has been revolutionized; also other papers on physical questions. Received Rumford, Draper and Mattenci medals for his discoveries. Home: Baltimore, Md. Died 1901.

ROWLEE, WILLARD WINFIELD, botanist; b. Fulton, N.Y., Dec. 15, 1861; s. George W. and Sarah C. (Distin) R.; B.L., Cornell, 1888, D.Sc., 1893; m. May Howard, Dec. 22, 1887. Instr. botany, 1888-93, asst. prof., 1893-1905, prof., 1905—, Cornell Univ. Author: Lieut. Heman Rowlee (1746-1818) and His Descendants, 1907. Home: Ithaca, N.Y. Died Aug. 8, 1923.

ROY, ARTHUR J(AY), astronomer; b. Clyde, New York, Nov. 7, 1869; s. Lyman and Ann Eliza (Bishop) R.; descendant on mother's side of Richard Warren and John Howland of the Mayflower; C.E., Union College, Schenectady, N.Y., 1893, A.M. from same school, 1897; m. 2d, Carolyn E. Eyre, Oct. 16, 1912; children—(by first marriage) Earl Bishop (dec.), Olive Elizabeth (Roy) Armstrong. First asst. Dudley Obs. (astronomy dept. Union U.) since 1893; chief astronomer Dept. of Meridian Astronomy of Carnegie Institution, Washington, D.C., 1907-36, research asso., 1936-39. Has specialized in meridian astronomy for many years; associated with Dr. Lewis Boss (in charge of Dudley Obs.) on positions and motions of the stars, until his death, 1912; in charge of tech. operations, at San Luis, Argentina, 1909-11, making over 80,000 observations; discovered that the personal equation of the observer and the atmospheric refraction are different north and south. Supervised formation of the General Catalog. Au organizer Albany Civic League, 1905; dir. Albany City Mission. Mem. Am. Astron. Soc., A.A.A.S., Albany Philos. Soc., Sigma Xi. Democrat. Baptist. Club: Aurania. Author: Albany Zone Catalogs for 1900 (with Lewis Boss), 1918; San Luis Catalog of Stars for 1910, 1918; Albany Catalog of Stars for 1910, 1932; Madison Catalog of Stars for 1910, 1939. Contbr. to Astron. Jour. Home: 369 Morris St., Albany, N.Y. Died Sept. 11, 1948.

ROY, SHARAT KUMAR, geologist; b. Shamnagar, India, Aug. 27, 1897; s. Nabin Krishma and (Devi) Govinda Mohini R.; student St. Columbus Coll., Hazaribagh, India, and Bangabashi Coll., Calcutta; spl. student, London, 1919; I.Sc., U. of Calcutta, 1915; A.B., U. of Ill., 1922, M.S., 1924, Ph.D., 1941; m. Elsa Barandun. Research in geology and paleontology, U. Chgo., 1925-37. Naturalized Am. citizen. Assistant paleontologist New York State Museum, Albany, 1924-25; asst. curator paleontology Chicago Natural History Museum, 1925-34, asst. curator geology, 1934-37, curator, 1937-42, acting chief curator geology, 1946-47; chief curator geology since 1947; geologist Rawson-MacMillan Arctic Expdn. of Chicago Natural History Museum, 1927-28; leader Capt. Marshall Field Geol. and Paleontol. Expdn. to Newfoundland, 1928; Geol. Expdn. to the Salt Range, Punjab, India, 1945; conducted expdns. in many parts of United States, Mexico and Central America, 1950—. Nat. Sci. Found. Grant for Europe, India, 1957-58. Private Calcutta U. Inv., 1917-18; capt., U.S. Air Corps, 1942-46, Am., European and Pacific theatres, World War II; maj., O.R.C., mem. A.F.A. Fellow Royal Geog. Soc., Geol. Soc. America, Artic Inst. N. America, Geol. Soc. London; mem. A.A.A.S., Paleontol. Soc., Polar Soc., Mineral Soc., Soc. Research in Meteorites, Royal Soc. Arts, N.Y. Acad. Sci., Sigma Xi, Theta Delta Phi, Theta

Epsilon Pi. Clubs: Cosmopolitan, Quadrangle. Author of numerous papers in geology and paleontology, arctic stratigraphy, meteorites, volcanology. Contbr. to Science, Popular Astronomy, Outdoor America, Esquire, Gemological Mag., Delphian. Home: 5523 Everett Av., Chicago, Ill.; Beach Point, Provincetown, Mass. Home: 5523 S. Everett Av., Chgo. 60637. Office: Chicago Natural History Museum, Chicago, Ill. Died Apr. 17, 1962.

ROYSTER, HUBERT ASHLEY, surgeon; b. Raleigh, N.C., Nov. 19, 1871; s. Dr. W. I. and Mary (Finch) R.; A.B., Wake Forest Coll., 1891, hon. Sc.D., 1931; M.D., U. of Pa., 1894; m. Louise Page, Nov. 6, 1901; children —Mrs. Virginia Page Oxnard. Dr. Hubert Ashley, Jr., Dr. Henry Page. Intern Mercy Hosp., Pittsburgh, 1894-95; surgeon in chief (emeritus) St. Agnes Hosp.; hon. chief surg. service Rex Hosp.; Southern Surg. Assn. (sec. 1916-25; pres. 1926), fellow Am. Surg. Assn., Am. Bd. Surgery; pres. N.C. Lit. and Hist. Assn., 1941-42. Author: Appendicitis, 1927; Medical Morals and Manners, 1937. Home: 2318 Beechridge Rd., Raleigh NC‡

ROYSTER, LAWRENCE THOMAS, physician; b. Norfolk, Va., Aug. 18, 1874; s. Lawrence and Alice Josephine (Ridley) R.; Norfolk Acad., 1884-92; student U. of Va., 1892-97, M.D., 1897; post-grad work in hosps. and clinics of New York, Boston, Baltimore, etc.; m. Ola Park, Dec. 9, 1903 (dec.). Practiced at Norfolk, 1900-23; prof. and head dept. pediatrics, U. of Va., 1923-42. Mem. State Bd. of Health, Va.; mem. Sch. Bd. of Norfolk, 11 yrs.; mem. Children's Code Commn. of Va.; founder and ex-pres. Norfolk Soc. for Prevention of Cruelty to Children; ex-pres. Norfolk Assn. Philanthropics, Bonney Home for Girls; was founder and chief of staff, King's Daughters Clinic; active in promoting med. exam. of school children in the South. Mem. A.M.A. (ex-chmn. pediatric sect.), Southern Med. Assn. (ex-chmn. pediatric sect.), Am. Pediatric Soc., Am. Anthropol. Soc., Am. Assn. of Physical Anthropologists, Va. Soc. of the Cincinnati, Phi Beta Kappa, Alpha Omega Alpha, Sigma Chi, Sigma Xi; fellow Am. Acad. Pediatrics, A.A.A.S. Democrat. Baptist. Author: Nutrition and Development. Part Author: (Chapin and Royster) Diseases of Children. Speaker and writer on med. and sociol. topics, especially pertaining to children. Retired. Home: University Station, Charlottesville VA

RUCKER, WILLIAM COLBY, sanitarian; b. Kenney, Ill., Sept. 28, 1875; s. Hamline P. and Lydia Marie (Colby) R.; ed. U. of N.D.; U. of Minn., 1890-94; M.D., Rush Med. Coll., Chicago, 1897; M.S., Univ. of Calif., 1912, Dr.P.H., 1915; m. Annette Guequierre, July 19, 1902 (died 1910); m. 2d, Elizabeth Harwood Neff, Nov. 11, 1912. Asst. surgeon, 1902, passed asst. surgeon, 1907, surgeon, 1914, asst. surgeon gen., Apr. 1, 1912-Mar. 1, 1918, surgeon, Mar. 1, 1918-July 1, 1919, asst. surgeon gen., Reserve Corps, July 1, 1919-Sept. 15, 1920, surgeon, Sept. 15, 1920—, U.S., Public Health Service. Served at San Francisco, Boston, Vineyard Haven, Mass.; yellow fever campaign, New Orleans, 1905; Jamestown Expn., 1907; exec. officer plague campaign, San Francisco, 1907-10, and in command 1912; Rocky Mt. spotted fever campaign, Victor, Mont., 1911; comd. plague eradicative campaign, New Orleans, 1914. Fellow Am. Coll. Surgeons, Am. Coll. Physicians, A.M.A.; charter mem. Nat. Bd. Medical Examiners; member National Bd. on First Aid Standardization; life mem. Assn. Mil. Surgeons (Enno Sander gold medal, 1908; treas. 1917). Episcopalian. Has traveled extensively in Central and South America, making sanitary surveys and promoting public health work. Sec. com. on Hygiene and Sanitation Gen. Med. Bd. of Council Nat. Defense, 1917; detailed to army, and with A.E.F., Jan.-July 1918; port of embarkation, Newport News, Va., July 1918-June 1919; chief med. adviser, Bur. War Risk Ins., Washington, 1919-20; chief quarantine officer, the Panama Canal, Oct. 1920-Feb. 1924; med. officer in charge U.S. Marine Hosp. No. 14, New Orleans, La., June 7, 1925—. Died May 1930.

RUCKMICK, CHRISTIAN ALBAN, psychologist; b. N.Y.C., Sept. 4, 1886; s. Alban Victor and Pauline (Schroeder) R.; A.B., Amherst Coll., 1909, A.M., 1912; Ph.D., Cornell U., 1913; m. Katherine Theilen, June 7, 1915; children—Helen, John. Instr. psychology Cornell U., 1911-13; instr. psychology U. Ill., 1913-15, asso., 1915-17, asst. prof., 1917-19, acting head dept., 1918-19, asso. prof., 1919-21; asso. prof. psychology Wellesley, 1921-24; prof. psychology State U. Ia., 1924-38; gen. sales mgr., sec. C.H. Stoelting Co., 1939-42; chief civilian psychologist U.S. Armed Forces Induction Sta., Peoria, Ill., 1942-43; panel chmn. in labor disputes Regional War Labor Bd. Region VI, 1943-44, panel cons. Tng. Within Industry Sect., War Manpower Commn., 1943-45; supr. tng. C.&N.-W. Ry., 1943-45; dir. employe tng. Chgo. Park Dist., 1945-46; supt. edn. Ministry of Edn. and Fine Arts, Imperial Ethiopian Govt. 1946-52; cons. on pub. relations Ethiopian Air Lines, Inc. (TWA), 1946-52; lectr. psychology U. Miami, 1952-55. Editor Psychol. Index, 1917, 18, U. Ia. Studies in Psychology, 1928-37; coop. editor Am. Jour. Psychology, 1926-28; apptd. mem. sci. com. Century of Progress Expn., Chgo., 1931; mem. adv. bd. editors Dictionary of Psychology and Cognate Sciences, 1931-34. Mem. NRC, 1938-41. Fellow A.A.A.S.; mem. Am. Psychol. Assn. (com. on terminology 1916-23), Midwestern Psychol. Assn. (pres. 1935-36, hon. life mem. 1952—), Psychol. Corp., Phi Beta Kappa, Sigma Xi, Theta Xi. Republican. Episcopalian. Author: Brevity Book on Psychology, 1920; German-English Dictionary of Psychological Terms, 1928; The Mental Life, 1928; (with Dr. Wendell S. Dysinger) The Emotional Responses of Children to the Motion Picture Situation, 1933; Psychology of Feeling and Emotion, 1936. Contbr. to psychol. publs. and Internat. Year Book, inventor affectometer and other sci. instruments. Home: 4019 El Prado Blvd., Coconut Grove, Miami 33, Fla. Died 1961.

RUDDIMAN, EDSEL ALEXANDER, (rud'di-man), chemist; b. Dearborn, Mich., Dec. 27, 1864; s. William and Catherine (Noble) R.; grad. Detroit High Sch., 1884; Pharm. Chemist, U. Mich., 1886; M.Pharm., 1887; M.D., Vanderbilt U., 1893; m. Jennie Evelyn Perry, July 29, 1889; children—Stanley Perry, Edith Helen. Chemist in charge mfg. lab. of Milburn & Williamson, 1887-90; chemist to Tenn. Bd. Pharmacy, 1897-1920; food and drug inspection chemist, 1907-14; prof. pharmacy and materia medica, in dept. of pharmacy, 1890-1920, dean Sch. of Pharmacy, 1919-20, Vanderbilt U.; chief chemist John T. Milliken & Co., pharm. chemists, 1921-26; research chemist with Ford Motor Co., 1926-42. Author: Incompatibilities in Prescriptions, 1897; Whys in Pharmacy, 1906; Manual of Materia Medica, 1907; Theoretical and Practical Pharmacy, 1917. Home: 22179 Long Blvd., Dearborn, Mich. Died Mar. 21, 1954; buried Evergreen Cemetery, Dearborn, Mich.

RUDENBERG, REINHOLD, educator; b. Hannover, Germany, Feb. 4, 1883; s. Georg and Elsbeth (Herzfeld) R.; ed. Leibnitz Sch., 1889-1901; diploma engring. Inst. Tech., Hannover, 1906; D.Engring., Hannover Tech., 1906; hon. D.Engring. Inst. Tech., Karlsruhe, 1921; hon. prof. Inst. Tech., Berlin, 1927; hon. A.M., Harvard, 1942; m. Lily Minkowski, Sept. 7, 1919; children—Gunther Angelika, Hermann. Came to U.S., 1938, naturalized, 1944. Instr. mech. engring. Göttingen U., 1906; elec. engr., Siemens-Schuckertwerke, Berlin, 1908, chief elec. engr., 1923-36; lectr., professor Inst. Tech., Berlin, 1913-36; vis. lectr. Mass. Inst. Tech., 1929; cons. engr. Gen. Elec. Co., Ltd., London, 1936-38; prof. elec. engring. Harvard, 1939-52; vis. prof., univs. Montevideo, Uruguay, Rio de Janeiro, São Paulo, Brazil, 1952, Univs. Cal., Los Angeles, Berkeley, 1955. Awarded Montefiore prize, Liége Univ. (Belgium), 1912, honor award medallion Stevens Inst. Tech., 1946; Gold Cedergren medal U. Tech., Sweden, 1950; Elliott Cresson medal Franklin Inst., 1961. Fellow American Assn. Advancement Sci.; mem. Sigma Xi, Am. Inst. E.E. (fellow), Am. Phys. Soc. (fellow), Am. Soc. Engring. Edn. (fellow), Am. Acad. Arts and Scis. (fellow). Club: Harvard, Harvard Faculty. Author: Energie der Wirbelströme, 1906; Theorie der Kommutation, 1907; Machines a Collecteur a Champ Tournant, 1913; Aussendung u. Empfang Elektrische Wanderwellen, 1962; Elektrische Schaltvoränge, 4th edit., 1953; many tech. papers; inventions include brush adjustable three-phase shunt motor, 1910; self-starting eddy current induction motor, 1916; smooth, hollow conductors for high voltage transmission lines, 1919; electron microscope, 1931; Transient Performance of Electric Power Systems, 1950. Home: 32 Ross Rd., Belmont, Mass. 02178. Died Dec. 25, 1961.

RUDER, WILLIAM ERNST, metallurgist; b. Stockdale, Pa., Dec. 22, 1886; s. Ernst and Mary (Sidonia) R.; tchrs. certificate Southwestern State Normal (Pa.); B.S., Pa. State Coll., 1907; m. Nellie Veenschoten, July 20, 1911; children—William E., Jr. (dec.), Frances (Mrs. R.D. Zentmire), Richard Collison. Research lab. Gen. Electric Co. since 1907; dir., Allegheny-Ludlum Steel Corp. since 1933; consultant, W.P.B., since 1942; splty. magnetics and magnetic materials, ferrous metals. Dir. metall. res. Gen. Elec. Co. Mem. A.A.A.S., Theta Xi, Am. Iron and Steel Inst., Am. Soc. Metals. Republican. Presbyn. Home: 1674 Rugby Rd., Schenectady 12309. Died Feb. 10, 1963; buried Vale Cemetery, Schenectady.

RUEHE, HARRISON AUGUST, (roo'he), dairy husbandman; b. Gilman, Ill, June 26, 1888; s. August Henry and Sarah (Williams) R.; B.S., Univ. of Ill., 1911, M.S., 1916; Ph.D., Cornell U., 1921; m. Phoebe Olive Barnicoat, Sept. 7, 1918; children—Harrison Barnicoat, Richard Williams. Instr. in dairy manufactures, U. of Calif., 1911-12, U. of Ill., 1912-14; asso., dairy mfrs. U. of Ill., 1914-18, asst. prof., 1918-21, actg. head dept. dairy husbandry, 1919-20 (leave of absence, 1920-21), prof. dairy mfrs. and head of dept. dairy husbandry, 1921-45 (leave of absence 1943-45); sec. Am. Butter Inst., Chicago, 1943-45; prof. dairy sci., Coll. of Agr. and Chief Dairy Sci. Ill. Agrl. Experimental Station, 1945—. Member American Dairy Science Assn. (pres. 1935-36), Sigma Pi, Alpha Zeta, Phi Kappa Phi, Gamma Sigma Delta, Sigma Xi, Alpha Tau Alpha, Phi Sigma. Episcopalian. Author of many bulletins on dairying and articles in trade papers; devised method of inverting sugar for ice-cream making widely used during the war. Developed method for standardizing intensity of flavor in butter. Apptd. official state del. to World's Dairy Congress, Washington, 1923; official state del. to Internat. Dairy Congress, Copenhagen, 1931; chmn. Commn. to Study Milk Markets, 1939. Republican. Mason. Contbr. to dairy journals, World Book Ency. and Ency. Britannica. Home: 908 S. Lincoln Av., Urbana, Ill. Died Oct. 8, 1953; buried Roselawn Cemetery, Urbana.

RUFFIN, EDMUND, agriculturist, publisher; b. Prince George County, Va., Jan. 5, 1794; s. George and Jane (Lucas) R.; attended Coll. William and Mary, 1810; m. Susan Travis, 1813, 11 children. Assumed charge of Coggin's Point farm, 1813; mem. Va. Senate (1st as Whig, then Democrat), 1824-27; published essay "Calcareous Manures," 1832; published and edited Farmers Register (an agrl. jour. which helped arouse interest in farming), 1833-43; early advocate of fertilizing and crop rotation; a founder Prince Goerge Soc. in Va., a leader in move to form local socs. to oppose protective tariffs; apptd. mem., 1st corr. sec., 1st Va. State Bd. Agr., 1841, agrl. surveyor of S.C., 1842; published Report of the Commencement and Progress of the Agricultural Survey of South Carolina, 1843; pres. Va. State Agrl. Soc., 1852-54, commr., 1854; wrote and spoke much on agrl. improvement for newspapers, farm jours., agrl. socs., including Address on the Opposite Results of Exhausting and Fertilizing Systems of Agriculture, 1853, Premium Essay on Agricultural Education, 1853; one of 1st secessionists in Va.; wrote pamphlet The Political Economy of Slavery, probably 1858; advocate of direct trade with Europe, attended 3 So. comml. convs., served as chmn. Va. delegation at conv. held in Montgomery, Ala., 1858; originated League of United Southerners; served as volunteer with Palmetto Guard of Charleston, 1861-65, fired 1st shot from Morris Island against Ft. Sumter. Committed suicide after fall of Confederacy, Redmoor, Amelia County, Va., June 18, 1865; buried Marlbourne, Hanover County, Va.

RUFFNER, CHARLES SHUMWAY, elec. engineer; b. Chicago, June 22, 1880; s. Vivion Whaley and Nellie (Shumway) R.; Centenary Coll., Palmyra, Mo., 1894-96; B.S. in E.E., U. of Mo., 1900; m. Hazel R. Wesson, June 5, 1911. With Telluride Power Co., until 1909; supt. operation Central Colo. Power Co., 1909-11; at St. Louis, Mo., 1911-19; pres. and gen. mgr. Miss. River Power Distributing Co.; v.p. and gen. mgr. Elec. Co. of Mo., St. Louis County Gas Co., Arrow Engring. Co., Union Electric Light & Power Co., Union Colliery Co.; at New York, 1919-21, as v.p. North Am. Co. and subsidiaries; served as dir., v.p. and pres. Adirondack Power & Light Corp., 1921-26; pres. Mohawk Hudson Power Co., 1925-30, N.Y. Power and Light Corp., 1927-29; chmn. bd. Schenectady (N.Y.) Trust Co. Dir. N.Y. State Econ. Council, Boy Scout Council, Y.M.C.A., Bur. Municipal Research (treas.), Schenectady County Clearing House Assn. (pres.); chmn. group V, N.Y. State Bankers Assn., 1935-36. Fellow Am. Inst. E.E. (v.p. and mgr. 1919-20). Republican. Mason. Died Jan. 21, 1939.

RUFFNER, ERNEST HOWARD, colonel U.S.A.; b. Louisville, Ky., June 24, 1845; s. Lewis and Viola (Knapp) R.; ed. pub. and pvt. schs.; grad. 1st in class U.S. Mil. Acad., 1867; A.B. and A.M., Kenyon Coll., Gambier, O., 1877; m. Mary Hungerford Watson, of Detroit, Dec. 7, 1869. Second lt. and 1st lt. engr. corps, June 17, 1867; capt., Oct. 31, 1879; maj., July 2, 1889; lt.-col., Apr. 13, 1903; col., Sept. 9, 1906; retired, June 24, 1909. Engaged on river and harbor work at Detroit, Ft. Leavenworth, Leavenworth, Charleston, W.Va., Willets Point, N.Y. Harbor, Rock Island and Quincy, Ill., Buffalo, Baltimore, Charleston, S.C., New York, Cincinnati, New Orleans. Address: 2038 Auburn Av., Cincinnati.

RUFFNER, WILLIAM HENRY, educator, geologist; b. Lexington, Va., Feb. 11, 1824; s. Henry R., D.D., LL.D., pres. Washington Coll.; grad. Washington Coll. (now Washington and Lee Univ.), 1842, A.M., LL.D., same; m. Harriet A. Gray (dec.), 1850. Chaplain Univ. of Va., 1849-51; pastor 7th Presbyn. Ch., Phila., 1851-53; author of school law of Va. and 1st supt. public instruction, Va., 1870-82; founder State Female Normal School and prin. same, 1884-87. Was for yrs. editor official dept. Educational Jour. of Va. Author: School Reports of Virginia, 11 vols., 1871-82; Geological Report on Washington Territory; History of Washington and Lee Univ., 1893; Charity and the Clergy. Home: Lexington, Va. Died 1908.

RUFUS, WILL CARL, astronomer; b. of Am. parents, at Chatham, Can., July 1, 1876; s. William James and Eliza Ann (Comer) R.; A.B., Albion (Mich.) Coll., 1902, A.M., 1908; Ph.D., U. of Mich., 1915; m. Maude Squire, Sept. 29, 1902; children—Merlin Quinton (dec.), Clinton Howard, Herman Douglas. Asst. mathematics, Albion Coll., 1901-02; teacher high sch., Flint, 1902-04, Lansing, 1904-05; pastor M.E. Ch., Dryden, Mich., 1905-06, Owosso, 1906-07; instr. in mathematics and astronomy, Union Coll., Pyeng Yang, Korea, 1907-11; supt. edn., M.E. Mission, Seoul, Korea, 1911-13; fellow U. of Mich., 1913-15; prof. mathematics and astronomy, Chosen Christian Coll., Seoul, 1915-17; instr. in astronomy, U. of Mich., 1917-20, asst. prof.,

1920-1934, asso. prof., 1934-41, professor since 1941; acting director Observatory, 1930-31; acting chmn. dept. astronomy, 1930-31, 1938-39, and since 1942; sec. of com. in charge Barbor Scholarships for Oriental Women, since 1920; prof. math. and astronomy, U. World Cruise, 1926-27. Del. of History of Sci. Soc. to Rittenhouse Bicentenary, 1932. Fellow A.A.A.S. (v.p. sect. L, 1926-27), Am. Geog. Soc., Soc. for Research on Meteorites; mem. Am. Astron. Soc., History of Science Soc. of America (mem. council), Rittenhouse Astron. Soc., Mich. Acad. Science, Am. Council Inst. of Pacific Relations, Korea Br. Royal Asiatic Soc., Sigma Nu. Hon. member Detroit Astronomical Society, Astronomical Society of the Philippines, Samfundet for Astronomisk Historieforskning I Lund. Republican. Clubs: Junior Research (pres. 1925-26), Research, University. Research in stellar spectroscopy, atmospheric motion in Cepheid variables; established place of class R stars in evolutionary sequence; contbr. on astron. and Asiatic subjects. Home: 1334 Arlington Blvd., Ann Arbor, Mich. Died Sep. 21, 1946.

RUGGLES, WILLIAM BURROUGHS, engineer; b. Eaton, N.Y., Dec. 31, 1853; s. Henry E. and Julia A. (Bierce) R.; grad. high school, Springfield, Ill., 1872; m. Cynthia B. Walker, of Omaha, Neb., Jan. 9, 1883. Has been chief engr. of several rys. in Ohio Valley region. Went with Army of Occupation to Cuba, acting as asst. engr. Dept. of Cuba; was chief engr. Sandy Valley & Elkhorn Ry. and later of Sinaloa Ry. Co. of Mex. and later resident engr. for Isthmian Canal Commn.; chief engr. Alaska Northern Ry. since Apr., 1909. Mem. Am. Soc. C.E. Clubs: Engineers' (Cincinnati), University (Panama). Home: Cambridge, Mass. Address: Seward, Alaska.

RUMSEY, JAMES, inventor; b. Bohemia Manor, Cecil County, Md., Mar. 1743; s. Edward and Anna (Cowman) R.; 1st wife unknown; m. 2d, Mary Morrow; 3 children. Began operating grist mill, Sleepy Creek, Md., 1782; opened (with a friend) gen. store, engaged in bldg. trade, Bath (now Berkley Springs), W. Va., 1783-84; accepted position as supt. constrn. of canals Potomac Navigation Co., 1785; began to experiment with steam engine, 1785, experimented in bldg. steamboat, 1783; exhibited boat propelled by streams of water forced out through stern, steam engine being employed to operate the force pump on Potomac River, nr. Sherpherdstown, W. Va., 1787; Rumseian Soc. formed to promote Rumsey's projects which included improved saw mill, improved grist mill, improved steam boiler, 1781; sent by Rumseian Soc. to Eng. to patent his improvements and to interest English capital; secured English patents on boiler and steamboat, 1788, secured U.S. patents 1791. Died (shortly before his 2d steamboat was completed) London, Eng., Dec. 20, 1792; buried St. Margaret's Churchyard, nr. Westminster, Eng.

RUNKLE, JOHN DANIEL, Walker prof. of mathematics, Mass. Inst. Tech., 1865—; b. Root, N.Y., Oct. 11, 1822; s. Daniel and Sarah (Gordon) R.; ed. public schools, acads. at Canajoharie, Ames and Cortland, N.Y.; grad. Lawrence Scientific School, Harvard, 1851 (A.M., Harvard; Ph.D., Hamilton; LL.D., Wesleyan); m. Catharine Robbins Bird, 1862. Apptd. asst. on Am. Ephemeris and Nautical Almanac, 1849; resigned, 1884; originated, 1858, Mathematical Monthly, and edited it until outbreak of Civil war; acting pres. Mass. Inst. Technology, 1868; pres. same, 1870-78; introduced manual training into U.S. from Russia, 1876. Author: Analytic Geometry. Wrote: New Tables for Determining the Values of the Coefficients in the Perturbative Function of Planetary Motion, Smithsonian Contributions, 1856; The Manual Element in Education; Report on Industrial Education. Home: Cambridge, Mass. Died 1902.

RUNNING, THEODORE RUDOLPH, prof. mathematics; b. Colfax, Wis., Dec. 14, 1866; s. Ole Aslaksen and Birgit (Sletveit) R.; B.S., U. of Wis., 1892, M.S., 1896; Ph.D., 1899; m. Clara Bertine Anderson, Sept. 21, 1898 (died February 7, 1942). Professor mathematics, chemistry and physics, St. Olaf College, Northfield, Minnesota, 1893-95, 1900-03; fellow in mathematics, Univ. of Wisconsin, 1895-97; instr. in mathematics, U. of Wis., 1897-1900; instr. mathematics, U. of Mich., 1903-07, asst. prof., 1907-13, junior prof., 1913-15, asso. prof., 1915-20, prof., 1920-37, prof. emeritus since 1937; acting asst. dean Coll. Engring. and Architecture, U. of Mich., 1924-25. Fellow A.A.A.S.; mem. Am. Math. Soc., Math. Assn. of America, Soc. for Promotion Engring. Edn., Am. Soc. Univ. Profs., Mich. Acad. Science, Arts and Letters, Sigma Xi. Democrat. Presbyterian. Author: Empirical Formulas (translated into French and Japanese), 1917; Graphical Mathematics (translated into Japanese), 1927; Graphical Calculus, 1937; First Year College Mathematics (with L. C. Plant), 1939. Co-editor of chapter on mathematics in Chemical Engineering Handbook. Home: 1019 Michigan Av., Ann Arbor MI

RUNYAN, ELMER GARDNER, asst. chemist U.S. Dept. of Agr.; b. Utica, Mich., Aug. 11, 1862; s. S. Cordelia and Hiram S. R.; grad. Univ. of Mich. as pharm. chemist, 1886; (B.S. in chemistry, Columbian Univ., 1889). Has been engaged in agrl. chemistry and chem. problems of sugar manufacture since 1890. Not married. Residence: Disco, Macomb Co., Mich. Business Address: U.S. Dept. Agriculture, Washington.

RUSBY, HENRY HURD, M.D., botanist; b. Franklin, N.J., Apr. 26, 1855; s. John and Abigail (Holmes) R.; Mass. State Normal Sch., 1872-74; M.D., Univ. Med. Col. (New York U.), 1884; hon. Pharm.M., Phila. Coll. Pharmacy and Science, 1923; Sc.D., Columbia, 1930; m. Margaretta Saunier Hanna, 1887. Awarded medal at Centennial Exhibition, 1876, for herbarium of plants of Essex Co., N.J.; made bot. explorations, N.M. and Ariz., 1880-81, and 1883, as agt. Smithsonian Instn., and S. America, 1885-87, interest of med. botany, crossing the continent; also on lower Orinoco River, 1896, and the Republic of Colombia, 1917; Bolivia and Brazil, 1921-22. Prof. of botany, physiology and materia medica, Dept. Pharmacy, Columbia, 1888-1930, and dean of faculty; prof. materia medica, U. and Bellevue Hosp. Med. Coll., 1897-1902. Hon. curator Economic Mus., New York Bot. Garden (chmn. bd. scientific directors, 1908-17, and mem. board of managers); Revision Com. 7th, 8th and 9th revisions, U.S. Pharmacopoeia; mem. Revision Com. of Nat. Formulary; chmn. Commn. Pan-Am. Med. Congress for study of Am. medicinal flora; hon. mem. Pharm. Soc. of Great Britain; hon. mem. Instituto Medico Nacional of Mexico; pres. Torrey Bot. Club, 1905-12; pres. Am. Pharm. Assn., 1909-10. Expert in drug products in Bur. Chemistry, U.S. Dept. Agr., 1907-09; then pharmacognosist in same bur., 1912-17. Secured the vindication of Dr. Wiley and associates from charges, 1911. Fought successfully to stop the common use of decomposed ergot in those medicinal preparations for use in childbirth, from 1929 to 1935. Author: Essentials of Pharmacognosy, 1895; Morphology and Histology of Plants, 1899; Materia Medica of Buck's Reference Handbook of the Medical Sciences (8 volumes), 1899; National Standard Dispensatory, 1905; Wild Vegetable Foods of United States, 1906; Fifty Years of Materia Medica, 1907; Manual of Botany, 1911; Three Hundred New Species of South American Plants; A Guide to the Economic Collections of the New York Botanical Garden; Properties and Uses of Drugs, 1930; Jungle Memories, 1933. Introduced important drugs to Am. Materia Medica, among them pichi, cocillana, miré and caäpi. Awarded Hanbury medal, Brit. Pharm. Assn., 1929; Flueckiger medal, German Apothecaries Assn.; hon. mem. Brit. Pharm. Assn., 1930. Home: Sarasota, Fla. Died Nov. 18, 1940.

RUSH, BENJAMIN, physician, Continental congressman, humanitarian; b. Phila., Jan. 4, 1746; s. John Harvey and Susanna (Hall) R.; A.B., Coll. of N.J. (now Princeton), 1760; studied medicine under Dr. John Redman, 1761-66; attended 1st lectures of Dr. William Shippen and Dr. John Morgan in Coll. of Phila.; M.D., U. Edinburgh (Scotland), 1768; m. Julia Stockton, Jan. 11, 1776, 13 children including James, Richard. Returned to Phila., 1769, began practice of medicine; prof. chemistry Coll. of Phila., 1769-91, also prof. theory and practice, 1789; published A Syllabus of A Course of Lectures on Chemistry (1st Am. text on chemistry), 1770, reissued 1773; published anonymously Sermons to Gentlemen upon Temperance and Exercise (one of 1st Am. works on personal hygiene) 1772; mem. Am. Philos. Soc.; published An Address to the Inhabitants of the British Settlements in America, upon Slave-Keeping, 1773; an organizer Pa. Soc. for Promoting the Abolition of Slavery, 1774, pres. 1803; elected to Pa. Provincial Conv., 1776; mem. Continental Congress, 1776-77, signer Declaration of Independence; apptd. surgeon gen. Armies of the Middle Dept. Contintental Army, 1777; became lectr. U. State of Pa., 1780; mem. staff Pa. Hosp., 1783-1813; established 1st free dispensary in Am., 1786; recognized as the "instaurator" of the Am. temperance movement; persuaded the Presbyns. to found Dickinson Coll., 1783, served as trustee; mem. Pa. Conv. which ratified U.S. Constn. 1787, with James Wilson led successful fight for adoption; with James Wilson inaugurated a campaign which secured a more liberal and effective constn. for Pa., 1789; apptd. treas. U.S. Mint by Pres. John Adams, 1797-1813; became prof. the Institutes Medicine and Clin. Practice, U. Pa., 1792, prof. theory and practice, 1796; a founder Phila. Coll. Physicians, 1787; thought to be pioneer worker in exptl. physiology in U.S.; 1st Am. to write on cholera infantum, 1st to recognize focal infection of the teeth; greatly contributed to the establishment of Phila. as the leading Am. center of med. tng. during 1st half of 19th century. Author: Medical Inquiries and Observations, initial vol., 1789; An Account of the Bilious Remitting Yellow Fever, As It Appeared in the Essays, Literary, Moral and Philosophical, 1798; Medical Inquiries and Observations upon the Diseases of the Mind, 1812. Died Phila., Apr. 19, 1813; buried Christ's Church Graveyard, Phila.

RUSHMORE, DAVID BARKER, electrical engr.; b. Old Westbury, N.Y., Aug. 21, 1873; s. John Howard and Julia Anna (Barker) R.; B.S. in engring., Swarthmore Coll., 1894, C.E., 1897, Sc.D., 1923; M.E., Cornell U., 1895; unmarried. During vacations with Pond Machine Tool Co. and Westinghouse Electric & Mfg. Co., Newark, N.J.; with Westinghouse Electric & Mfg. Co., E. Pittsburgh, Pa., 1895, Royal Electric Co., Montreal, Can., 1897-99, Stanley Electric Mfg. Co., Pittsfield, Mass., 1899-1905; entered service Gen. Electric Co., 1905; chief engr. power and mining dept., 1907-22, and consulting engr., 1922-25 (resigned); pres. Español-Americano Co.; v.p. Spanish American Fruit Co. Dir. Northeastern Dispensary. Fellow American Inst. E.E. (v.p. 1911-13); mem. exec. com. Am. Sect. World Power Conf.; rep. of U.S. Govt. at World Power Conf., Barcelona, 1929; mem. bd. govs. Manhattan Council Boy Scouts America. Republican. Mem. Soc. of Friends. Mason. Home: New York, N.Y. Died May 5, 1940.

RUSS, JOHN MEGGINSON, educator; b. Mitchell, S.D., Oct. 18, 1891; s. William Cyrus and Lila Elnora (Megginson) R.; grad. Ohio Mil. Inst., Cin., 1912; student Ohio Mechanics Inst., Cin., 1913-15; B.S. in Indsl. Engring., Ohio State U., 1929, M.S., 1930; m. Virginia Grace Smith, Sept. 2, 1934. Instr. English and mathematics Ohio Mil. Inst., 1912-13; instr. engring. drawing, machine design, mathematics Ohio Mechanics Inst., 1915-23; various engring. positions Lodge & Shipley Machine Tool Co., Toledo Electric Welder Co., Cincinnati Milling Machine Co. (all Cin.), 1915-23; asst. to cons. engr., 1923; asst. prof. engring. drawing Ohio State U., 1923-30, asso. prof., 1930-35; exchange prof. Purdue U., 1932-33; guest prof. Carnegie Inst. Tech., 1933-34; vis. instr. engring. drawing U. Ia., 1935-36, asso. prof., 1936-45, prof., 1945-51, prof., head dept., from 1952. Profl. engr., Ia. Mem. Am. Soc. M.E., Am. Soc. Engring. Edn., Iowa City Engrs. Club, Am. Inst. Indsl. Engrs., Nat. Soc. Profl. Engrs., Sigma Xi, Tau Beta Pi, Pi Tau Sigma, Theta Xi. Presbyn. Mason. Author: (with F. G. Higbee) Engineering Drawing Problems, 1940. Contbr. profl. publs. Home: Iowa City IA Died July 4, 1969; buried Bellevue OH

RUSSELL, BERTRAND, EARL RUSSELL, author; b. Eng., May 18, 1872; s. John (Viscount Amberley) and Katherine (Stanley) R.; M.A., Trinity Coll., Cambridge University; m. Alys W. Smith, 1894 (div.); m. 2d, Dora Winifred Black, 1921 (div.); children—John Conrad, Katharine Jane; m. 3d, Patricia Helen Spence, 1936 (div.); 1 son, Conrad Sebastian Robert; m. 4th, Edith Finch, 1952. Began as fellow and lecturer Trinity College, Cambridge; temporary professor Harvard University, Lowell lecturer, 1914; professor philosophy, National Univ. of Peking, 1920-21; lecturer, U. of Chicago, 1938; professor philosophy, University of California at Los Angeles, 1939. Awarded Nicholas Murray Butler medal, 1915; Sylvester medal of Royal Society, England, 1934; received Order of Merit, 1949; recipient of the Nobel Prize for literature, 1950. Fellow Royal Society; fellow Trinity College. Author Proposed Roads to Freedom, 1918; Introduction to Mathematical Philosophy, 1919; The Analysis of Mind, 1921; The ABC of Atoms, 1923; The ABC of Relativity, 1925; Philosophy, 1927; Sceptical Essays, 1928; Marriage and Morals, 1929; Mysticism and Logic, 1918; Our Knowledge of the External World as a Field for Scientific Method in Philosophy, 1915; Principia Mathematica (with Dr. A. N. Whitehead), 1910-13; The Conquest of Happiness, 1930; The Scientific Outlook, 1931; Education and the Good Life, 1926; Education and the Social Order, 1932; In Praise of Idleness, 1935; Which Way to Peace?, 1936; The Amberley Papers (with Patricia Russell), 1937; Power, 1938; An Inquiry Into Meaning and Truth, 1940; A History of Western Philosophy, 1946; Human Knowledge, its Scope and Limits, 1948; Authority and the Individual, 1949; Unpopular Essays, 1950; New Hopes for a Changing World, 1951; The Impact of Science on Society, 1952; Satan in the Suburbs, 1953; Nightmares on Eminent Persons, 1954; Human Society in Ethics and Politics, 1954; Portraits from Memory, 1956; Why I Am Not A Christian, 1957; Common Sense and Nuclear Warfare, 1958; Wisdom of the West, 1959; My Philosophical Development, 1959; Fact and Fiction, 1961; Has Man a Future?, 1961; Unarmed Victory, 1963; Autobiography, Vol. I, 1967; Vol. II, 1968; War Crimes in Vietnam, 1967. Home: Merioneth Wales Died Feb. 2, 1970.

RUSSELL, FREDERICK FULLER, physician; b. Auburn, N.Y., Aug. 17, 1870; s. George Daniel and Anna Cecelia (Fuller) R.; M.D., Coll. Phys. and Surg. (Columbia), 1893; U. Berlin, 1897-98; Sc.D., George Washington U., 1917; m. Mathilde J. W. Busse, Nov. 2, 1899. Commd. 1st lt. asst. surgeon, U.S. Army, Dec. 12, 1898; capt. asst. surgeon, Dec. 1903; maj., Jan. 1909, col., May 1917, resigned July 11, 1920. Brig. gen. M.O.R.C., U.S. Army, Nov. 4, 1921. Curator, Army Med. Mus., Washington, 1907-13; instr. bacteriology and clin. microscopy Army Med. Sch., 1907-13; pathologist Columbia Hosp., 1908-13; prof. pathology and bacteriology George Washington U., 1909-13; lectr. tropical medicine N.Y. Post-Grad. Med. Sch., 1913-14; chief Bd. of Health Lab., Ancon, C.Z., 1915-17; in charge Div. Infectious Diseases and Lab. Service of Surgeon Gen.'s Office, U.S. Army, during World War; dir. Pub. Health Lab. Service of Internat. Health Bd., 1920-23; gen. dir. Internat. Health Bd., div. Rockefeller Found., 1923-35; lectr. preventive medicine and hygiene Harvard Med. Sch., Harvard Sch. Pub. Health, 1935, prof. preventive medicine and epidemiology, 1936-38, prof. emeritus since 1938. Mem. Pub. Health Council, State N.Y., 1924-36. Decorated D.S.M.; recipient Marcellus Hartley medal Nat. Acad. Scis., Washington, 1936; Buchanan medal Royal Soc. London, 1837; Gorgas medal, 1942. Fellow A.S.C., Am. Pub. Health Assn., N.Y. Acad. Medicine; mem. A.M.A., Assn. Am. Physicians, Royal Med. Soc.

Budapest, Hungary, Zeta Psi, Theta Chi; corr. mem. Gesellschaft der Aerzte, Vienna, Austria. Club: Harvard (Boston). Address: Rural Route 6, Box 39, Louisville. Died Dec. 1960.

RUSSELL, HARRY LUMAN, research; b. Poynette, Wis., Mar. 12, 1866; s. E. Fred (M.D.) and Lucinda Estella (Waldron) R.; B.S., U. of Wis., 1888, M.S., 1890; post-grad. studies U. of Berlin, Pasteur Inst., Paris, Zool. Sta., Naples; Ph.D., Johns Hopkins U., 1892; hon. Sc.D., U. of Wis., 1934; m. H. May Delany, Dec. 20, 1893 (dec.); children—Gertrude E. (dec.), Eldon Babcock; m. 2d, Susanna Cocroft Headington, July 27, 1932 (dec.). Assistant prof. bacteriology, 1893-97, prof., 1897-1907, dean College Agriculture, director Experimental Station, 1907-31, U. of Wisconsin; dir. Wis. Alumni Research Foundation since 1931. Dir. Wis. State Hygiene Lab., 1903-08; pres. advisory board Wis. Tuberculosis Sanatorium; mem. Wis. com. U.S. War Finance Corp.; apptd. mem. staff U.S. Food Adminstrn., Jan. 1918; mem. agrl. advisory com. Am. Bankers Assn., 1922-40; rep. Internat. Edn. Bd. in making survey of ednl. instns. of Far East, 1925-26 (leave of absence from coll.). Republican. Author: Outlines of Dairy Bacteriology, 1894-1905; Agricultural Bacteriology, 1898; Public Water Supplies (with Prof. F. E. Turneaure), 1939; Experimental Dairy Bacteriology (with Prof. E. G. Hastings), 1909; Agricultural Bacteriology (with same), 1921; Dairy Bacteriology (with same), 1919; also reports and bulls. Wis. Expt. Sta., 1893-1930. Home: 1 Langdon St., Madison WI

RUSSELL, HENRY NORRIS, astronomer; b. Oyster Bay, N.Y., Oct. 25, 1877; s. Alexander Gatherer and Eliza Hoxie (Norris) R.; A.B., Princeton, 1897, A.M., 1898, Ph.D., 1899; research student, King's Coll., Cambridge U., Eng., 1902-03; Docteur, Lauvain, 1927; D.Sc. (hon.), Dartmouth, 1923, Harvard, 1929, U. Chgo., 1941, Michoacau, Mexico, 1942, Yale, 1951, Princeton, 1954; married Lucy May Cole, Nov. 24, 1908; children—Lucy May, Elizabeth Hoxie, Henry Norris, Emma Margaret. Research asst. Carnegie Instn., Washington, stationed at Cambridge, Eng., 1903-05; instr. astronomy Princeton, 1905-08, asst. prof., 1908-11, prof. 1911-27, dir. of obs. 1912-47, research prof. 1927-47, emeritus 1947; research associate Harvard College Observatory, 1947-52, Mt. Wilson Observatory, 1922-42. Engineer Aircraft Service U.S. Army, 1918. Fellow A.A.A.S. (pres. 1933); mem. Nat. Acad. Sciences, Am. Philos. Soc. (pres. 1931-32), Am. Acad. Arts and Sciences, Am. Astron. Soc. (pres. 1934-37), Am. Phys. Soc.; fgn. asso. Royal Astron. Soc., London (gold medalist 1921); fgn. mem. Royal Soc., 1937; hon. fellow Royal Soc. of Edinburgh; asso. Belgian Royal Acad.; corr. French Acad. of Sciences; fgn. asso. Academia dei Lincei, Rome, 1948. Awarded Henry Draper medal Nat. Acad. Sciences, 1922; Lalande medal, French Acad., 1922; Bruce medal Astron. Soc. Pacific, 1925; Rumford medal, Am. Acad. Arts and Sciences, 1925; Franklin medal, 1934; Janssen medal French Acad., 1936. Presbyn. Author: Determinations of Stellar Parallax, 1911; Astronomy, 1926; Fate and Freedom, 1927; The Solar System and Its Origin, 1935; The Masses of the Stars, 1940. Contbr. on astron. topics to sci. jours. Address: 79 Alexander St., Princeton, N.J. Died Feb. 18, 1957; buried Princeton (N.J.) Cemetery.

RUSSELL, ISRAEL COOK, prof. geology, U. of Mich., 1892—; b. Garrattsville, N.Y., Dec. 10, 1852; s. Barnabas and Louisa (Cook) R.; grad. New York U., 1872; post-grad. studies School of Mines, Columbia Coll.; M.S., C.E., LL.D., New York U.; m. J. Augusta Olmsted, Nov. 27, 1886. Mem. U.S. Transit of Venus expdn. to New Zealand, 1874-75; asst. prof. of geology, School of Mines, Columbia, 1875-77; asst. geologist U.S. Geog. and Geol. Survey West of 100th Meridian, 1878; traveled in Europe; geologist U.S. Geol. Survey, 1880—. Author: Lake Lahontan, 1885; The Newark System, 1892; Lakes of North America, 1895; Glaciers of North America, 1897; Volcanoes of North America, 1897; Rivers of North America, 1898; A View of the World in 1900—North America. Died 1906.

RUSSELL, RICHARD JOEL, educator; b. Hayward, Cal., Nov. 16, 1895; s. Frederick James and Nellie Potter (Brennan) R.; A.B., U. Cal., 1920, Ph.D., 1926; m. Dorothy King, 1924 (dec. 1936); 1 son, Benjamin James; m. 2d, Josephine Burke, 1940; children—Robert Burke, Charles Douglas, John Walter, Thomas William. Teaching fellow U. Cal., 192-22, asso. in geography, 1923-25, Hitchcock prof., 1965; asso. prof. geology Tex. Technol. Coll., 1926-27; asso. prof. geography La. State U., Baton Rouge, 1928-29, prof. phys. geography, 1930-71, head dept., 1936-49, asst. dir. Sch. Geology, 1944-49, dean grad. sch., 1949-51, dir. Coastal Studies Inst., 1953-66; lectr. geography, summers, U. Cal., Harvard, Clark U.; collaborator Soil Conservation Service, 1935-71; geologist La. Geol. Survey, 1935-40. NSF cons. adv. govt. Indonesia, 1959-60; mem. panel of scientists adv. Ho. Reps. Com. on Sci. Astronautics, 1960-71; U.S. del. Internat. Geog. Congress, Amsterdam, 1938, Stockholm, 1960, U. Cal.; La. State U. del. to Internat. Geog. Congress, Paris, 1931, Rio de Janeiro, 1956, to Internat. Geol. Congress, Moscow, 1937, to Internat. Geol. Congress, London, 1948, Algiers, 1952; mem. coastal geomorphology commn. Internat. Geog. Union, 1952-69; council Internat. Assn. Sedimentologists, 1952-58; pres. conf. deans So. Grad. Schs., 1952; mem. U.S. Mil. Establishment Research and Devel. Bd., Com. Geophys. and Geog., 1948-56, panel on Gen. Scis., 1956-61. Served to ensign, USNRF, 1918-19. Recipient 1st W.W. atwood award for studies in phys. geography Assn. Am. Geographers, 1937. Vega medalist Royal Swedish Soc. Anthropology and Geography, 1961; USN Distinguished Pub. Service award, 1967. Fellow A.A.A.S., Am. Geog. Soc. (Cullum Geog. medal 1962), Geol. Soc. Am. (pres. 1957; chmn. S.E. div. 1970); mem. Assn. Am. Geog. (council 1937-39, pres. 1948, Outstanding Achievement award 1960), NRC (rep. 1941-41; mem. exec. com. div. geol. and geog., 1942-44, com. on high level waste disposal 1954-62, chmn. earth scis. div. 1954-55), So. Assn. Land Grant Colls and Univs. (sec. 1954-59), Am. Assn. Petroleum Geologists (Distinguished lectr. 1943), Am. Geophys. Union, Nat. Acad. Scis., Acad. Scis. Gottingen (corr.), Royal Danish Acad. Sci. and Letters (corr.), Geol. and Mineral Soc. Am. Univs. (hon.), So Belge Geol. Paleo et Hydrologie, 1948; Royal Geography Soc. Netherlands (hon.), Sigma Xi, Phi Sigma Kappa, Theta Tau (nat. pres. 1928-32), Gamma Alpha, Phi Sigma, Phi Kappa Phi. Democrat. Mason. Clubs: Faculty (La. State U., pres. 1946); Cosmos (Washington). Author: River Plains and Sea Coasts, 1967; co-author Culture Worlds. Asso. editor Geologie der. Meere and Binnengewasser (Berlin), 1939-41; Zeitschrift fur Geomorphologie, 1957-71. Contbr. numerous articles to sci. jours. Home: Baton Rouge LA Died Sept. 17, 1971.

RUSSELL, WALTER, artist, scientist; b. Boston, May 19, 1871; s. Jacob and Melinda R.; ed. Mass. Normal Art Sch., Boston, Mass., Museum of Fine Arts, Drexel Inst., Phila., Acad. Julian, Paris, pupil of Albert Munsell, Ernest Major, Howard Pyle, and Jean Paul Laurens; D.Sc. (hon.), American Acad. Sciences, 1941; married Helen Andrews, Jan. 10, 1894; married 2d, Lao Stebbing, July 29, 1948. Illustrator for New York mags., 1890-97; artist and corr. during Spanish-Am. War for Century Mag. and Collier's Weekly; formerly devoted attention to specialty of painting children's portraits and child subjects; painted portraits of children of President Theodore Roosevelt, Ex-Gov. Ames of Mass., and other prominent people of the U.S. and many in Europe; also one allegory, "The Might of Ages," exhibited at Turin Expedition; sculptor, 1927—; appointed sculptor Mark Twain Memorial, Hannibal, Mo.; executed Memorial to Charles Goodyear for Akron, Ohio; Jean d'Arc memorial for presentation to France; colossal bust of Mark Twain to be erected in Victoria Embankment Garden, London; colossal bust of Frank-D. Roosevelt for Fed. Bldg., N.Y. World's Fair; also a colossal bust called "The War President," for Roosevelt Memorial Library at Hyde Park, N.Y.; Colin Kelly Meml., Madison, Fla.; The Four Freedoms, Washington, tribute to Am. soldier, 1950; statue The Christ of Blue Ridge (with Lao Russell), Va., 1950; among other sculpture works: Busts of Thomas Edison, Mark Twain, Ossip Gabrilowitsch, Thomas J. Watson, Sir Thomas Lipton, Victor Herbert, John Phillip Sousa, etc. Originator, in 1899, of tenant ownership, or coöperative plan of home ownership and built the Artists' Colony, 67th St., N.Y., on this plan, 1899-1914, also "Pierres," 290 Park Av., N.Y., 1920. Maintains lab. for scientific research, mainly elec. and chem. Founder N.Y. Skating Club, pres., 1916; introduced figure skating in U.S. Founded Walter Russell Found. (with Lao Russell), 1948, name changed to U. Sci. and Philosophy, 1957, v.p. Recipient medal Acad. Fine Arts and Letters, Toledo, Spain, 1923. Mem. Society Arts and Sciences (president emeritus), Numismatic Soc., Acad. Fine Arts and Lit. (Spain). Club: Authors. Author: The Sea Children, 1901; The Bending of the Twig, 1903; The Age of Innocence, 1904; The Universal One, 1927; Salutation to the Day, 1927; Russell Genero Radiative Concept, 1930; "The Secret of Light," 1946; "Your Day and Night," 1946; "Great Men I Have Known," 1946; Message of The Divine Iliad, Vol. I and Vol. II, 1948-49; The Book of Early Whisperings, 1950; Scientific Answer to Sex Promiscuity, 1949; Natural Law and Living Philosophy (with Lao Russell), 1950; Scientific Answer to Human Relations (with Lao Russell), 1951; The Russell Cosmogony—A New Concept of the Universe, 1953; Atomic Suicide (with Lao Russell), 1958; The World Crisis (with Lao Russell), 1958; The One World Purpose (with Lao Russell), 1960. Compiled the Russell Chart of the Elements. Address: U. of Sci. and Philosophy, Swannanoa, Waynesboro, Va. Died May 19, 1963; buried Swannanoa.

RUSSELL, WALTER C(HARLES), biochemist; b. Bellaire, O., Oct. 1, 1892; s. Charles C. and Eliza Jane (Kneff) R.; B.S., Ohio Wesleyan, 19, Sc.D. (hon.), 1947; student Sorbonne, 1919, Harvard (grad. fellow in biochem.), 1919-20; M.S., Syracuse U., 1923; Ph.D., U. of Chicago (Swift fellow in chem., 1923-25), 1927; m. Mildred Irene Stephens, Aug. 25, 1923; 1 dau., Ruth Elizabeth. Teacher Chillicothe (O.) high sch., 1914-15; instr. chem., Ohio Wesleyan, 1915-17, Syracuse U., 1920-23; asst. prof. agrl. biochem., Rutgers, 1925-29, asso. prof. agrl. biochem., 1929-31; prof. and chemn. dept. agrl. biochem.; research splist. In agrl. biochem., N.J. Agrl. Expt. Sta., Rutgers, since 1925; exec. sec. grad. faculty, Rutgers U., 1935-52, dean of the graduate school since July 1952. Member adv. scientific council Com. on Foods of Am. Vet. Med. Assn. and Am. Animal Hosp. Assn. since 1937; mem. Nat. Research Council since 1943. Served as pvt. to capt., San. Corps, U.S. Army, 1917-19; overseas. Mem. Am. Chem. Soc., Am. Soc. Biol. Chemists, Am. Inst. Nutrition (mem. council 1950-53), Assn. Land-Grant Colls. and Univs. (chairman council on instrn. 1952), A.A.A.S., Society Exptl. Biol. and Medicine, Delta Tau Delta, Sigma Xi, Phi Lambda Upsilon, Alpha Chi Sigma, Phi Kappa Phi, Phi Beta Kappa (hon.). Presbyn. Author: Grass Silage and Dairying (with Ray Ingham, Willis A. King and Carl B. Bender), 1949. Mem. editorial bd. Journal of Nutrition, 1945-49. Contbr. articles on nutrition and biochemistry to various professional jours. Home: 27 Oak Hills Rd., Metuchen. Office: Rutgers Univ., New Brunswick, N.J. Died Mar. 10, 1954.

RUST, JOHN DANIEL, inventor, executive, cons. engr., student of world affairs; b. Stephens County, Tex., Sept. 6, 1892; son of Benjamin Daniel and Susan Minerva (Burnett) R.; ed. public schools of Texas and private study; married Thelma Ford, December 1, 1933. Assisted in development of better farm machinery 1922-27; inventor of Rust cotton picker, discovered its basic principles, 1927, and since engaged in perfecting and promoting it; also inventor of Rust cotton cleaner, 1940, attachment for lawn mowers, 1945; cons. engr. Allis-Chalmers Mfg. Co., 1944-47; cons. engr. Ben Pearson, Inc.; founder and pres. John Rust Found., Inc., and The John Rust Co., 1951. Mem. Internat. Auxiliary Lang. Assn., World Calendar Assn., Am. Acad. Polit. and Social Science, Nat. Geographic Soc., West Tenn. Hist. Soc. Home: 3520 Cherry St. Office: 1416 Poplar St., Pine Bluff, Ark. Died Jan. 20, 1954.

RUST, MACK DONALD, engr., inventor; b. nr. Breckenridge, Tex., Jan. 12, 1900; s. Benjamin Daniel and Susan Minerva (Burnett) R.; B.S. in Mech. Engring., U. Tex., 1925, grad. student, 1925-26; student Gen. Electric Co. Tng. Sch., Schenectady, 1926-28; m. Alma Wood, July 7, 1934. Co-inventor Rust cotton picker, and designing engr. since 1928; engaged in operation, promotion, devel. cotton harvesting, cleaning, and handling equipment. Trustee Rust Found. Mem. A.S.M.E., A.A.A.S., Tau Beta Pi. Address: P.O. Box 777, Coalinga, Cal Died Jan. 11, 1966.

RUSTIN, HENRY, elec. engr.; b. Omaha, Neb., Sept. 4, 1865; s. C.B. and Mary (Wilkins) R.; grad. Phillips Acad., Andover, Mass., 1883; Sheffield Scientific Sch., Yale, 1886; spl. studies in elec. and mech. engring., chemistry; m. Vancouver Barracks, Wash., June 2, 1894, Lola Goodwin. Installed elec. plant and street ry. and in charge of lighting and electrical work of Omaha Espn., 1898; in charge of elec. work Pan-Am. Expn., Buffalo, 1901; chief Mech. and Elec. Dept., La Purchase Expn. from Nov. 20, 1901. Mem. Am. Inst. Elec. Engrs., Engineers Club, St. Louis. Club: St. Louis. Residence: 5431 Cabanne Pl. Office: World's Fair Station, St. Louis.

RUTH, HENRY SWARTLEY, physician, anesthesiologist; b. Phila., Pa., Aug. 12, 1899; s. Henry Laban Swartley and Carrie Anders (Kindig) R.; student Swarthmore Coll., 1917-18; student Hahnemann Sch. of Science, 1918-19, B.S., 1921; M.D., Hahnemann Med. 1923; m. Lola Althouse Zendt, July 16, 1924; children—Patricia Anne (Mrs. James C. Straus, 3d), Henry Swartley, Jr. Anesthetist Hahnemann Hosp., 1924—St Luke's and Children's Hosp., Phila., 1927-41; clin. prof. anesthesia, Hahnemann Med. Coll. and Hosp., 1933-40, prof. and head dept. Anesthesiology since 1942; chief, div. of anesthesia Phila. Gen. Hospital, 1933-40, consulting anesthetist since 1940; chief, anesthetic service, West Jersey Homeo. Hosp., Camden, 1941-42. Civilian cons. U.S. Naval Hospital, Phila., 1948-52. Served in S.A.T.C., 1918. Director courses in anesthesiology, U.S. Army and Navy, World War II. On Am. Bd. of Anesthesiology, 1937-52 (pres. 1943-44). Fellow Internat. College of Surgeons, Am. Med. Writers Assn.; mem. Soc. of Anesthetists, Inc. (pres. 1938); Phila. County Med. Soc. (chmn. anesthesia study commn.), A.M.A., (rep. sect. on anesthesiology in Ho. Dels., 1941-54), Internat. Anesthesia Research Soc., Homeo. Med. Soc. of Pa., Germantown Homeo. Med. Soc. of Phila. (pres. 1936), Am. Inst. Homeop., Montgomery Co. Med. Society, Phila. Soc. Anesthesiol. (pres. 1947-48), Pa. Soc. Anesthesiol. (pres. 1943-49), World Med. Assn. Episcopalian. Mason. Clubs: Union League, Rotary, Penn, Merion Golf, Bachelor's Barge, Merion Cricket (Phila.). Author: Sect. on "Anesthetics," Revision Service Vol. of Cyclopedia of Medicine, 1944; sect. on "Regional Anesthesia," Bancroft's Operative Surgery, 1941. Asso. editor: Anesthesia Subjects in Cyclopedia of Medicine, Surgery and Specialties, 1939-52; articles on anesthesia, scientific and medical subjects in med. jours. Editor: Anesthesiology (organ of Am. Soc. Anesthetists, Inc.) since 1940. Mem. editorial bd., Am. Journal of Surgery. Home: 225 Cheswold Lane, Haverford, Pa. Office: Hahnemann Med. Coll. and Hosp., 230 N. Broad St., Phila. 2. Died 1956.

RUTHERFURD, LEWIS MORRIS, astrophysicist; b. Morrisania, N.Y. Nov. 25, 1816; s. Robert Walter and Sabina (Morris) R.; grad. Williams Coll., 1835; m. Margaret Stuyvesant Chamler, July 22, 1841, 7 children. Admitted to N.Y. bar, 1837; practiced law N.Y.C., 1837-49; began work in astronomical photography and spectroscopy, 1856; invented a photographic telescope, 1858; made his 1st attempt at classification of stellar spectra, 1862; made many photographs of sun and moon and various star fields; trustee Columbia, 1858-84, responsible for establishing dept. of geodesy and astronomy, 1881, donated all his equipment to Columbia. Died N.Y.C., May 30, 1892.

RUTHVEN, ALEXANDER G(RANT), univ. pres.; b. Hull, Ia., Apr. 1, 1882; s. John and Katherine (Rombough) R.; B.S., Morningside Coll., 1903; U. of Chicago, summer quarter, 1902; Ph.D., U. of Mich., 1906; Sc.D., Kalamazoo Coll., 1931, Mich. Coll. of Mining and Technology, 1937; LL.D., Albion Coll., 1930, Northwestern U., 1930, Morningside Coll., 1931, Denison U., 1933, Tulane U., 1938, U. of Calif., 1938, U. of N.M., 1944, Wayne U., 1950; Dr. Honoris Causa, Catholic University of Chile, 1944; m. Florence Hagle, September, 1907; children—Katherine Lenora, Alexander Peter, Bryant Walker. With Univ. of Michigan since 1906; successively instr. zoology and curator Museum of Zoology, 1906-11, asst. prof. and curator Museum of Zoology, 1911-13, asst. prof. and dir. Museum of Zoology, 1913-15, prof. and dir. Museum of Zoology, 1915-29, dir. univ. museums, 1922-36, chmn. dept. of zoology and dir. Zool. Labs., 1927-29, dean adminstrn., 1928-29, pres., 1929-51, emeritus since 1951. Chief field naturalist, Mich. Geol., Biol. Survey, 1908-12. Dir. various sci. expeditions, in North, South and Central America. Awarded Blue Grand Cordon of the Order of the Brilliant Jade, 1938. Fellow A.A.A.S., Am. Acad. Arts and Sciences; mem. Am. Soc. Zoologists, Am. Soc. Naturalists, Mich. Acad. Science, Arts and Letters (pres. 1913-15), Am. Philos. Soc., Am. Soc. Ichthyologists and Herpetologists, Assn. Am. Geographers, Phi Sigma, Gamma Alpha, Sigma Xi, Phi Beta Kappa, Phi Kappa Phi; corr. mem. London Zool. Soc. Author of numerous papers on zool. subjects. Home: Ann Arbor MI Died Jan. 18, 1971; buried Ann Arbor MI

RUTTER, HENLEY CHAPMAN, physician; b. Pearisburg, Va., Feb. 6, 1849; s. John Harrison and Lovinia (McDonald) R.; ed. high sch., Bellefontaine, O.; pvt. Co. B, 132d Ohio Inf., enlisting at age of 14; M.D., Med. Coll. of Ohio, Cincinnati, 1869; m. Margaret M. Cretcher, July 6, 1892. Interne, Good Samaritan Hosp., Cincinnati, 1869-70; asst. phys., Dayton Hosp. for Insane, 1871-72, supt. same, 1872-74; supt. Athens (O.) Hosp. for Insane, 1875-78, 1879-81; supt. Columbus Hosp. for Insane, 1882-84; mgr. Hosp. for Epileptics, 1893-1901; med. dir. Park View Sanatorium; in intervals engaged in gen. practice of Medicine at Bellefontaine, Cincinnati, and Columbus, O. Republican. Author: Criminal Responsibility of the Insane; also many essays and papers upon care and treatment of epileptics. Home: Columbus, O. Died 1910.

RUYLE, JOHN BRYAN, (rool), archeologist, dentist; b. Athensville, Ill., Oct. 5, 1896; s. John and Celia Pricilla (Biggs) R.; ed. U.S. Mil. Acad., 1915-16; Varparaiso (Ind.) U., 1916; Chicago Coll. of Dental Surgery, 1916-18; St. Louis (Mo.) Dental Coll., 1918-19; U. of Ill., 1934-36; m. Mary Esther Gaul, Aug. 7, 1918; children—Jo Ann Virginia, John Bryan, Joyce Elaine. Served in U.S. Army, 1918. Mem. American Dental Society, Champaign-Danville District Dental Society, Illinois State Dental Society, Miss. Valley Fedn. Archeol. Socs. (pres.), Ill. State Archeol. Soc. (pres. emeritus and dir.), Champaign County Archeol. Soc. (pres.), Soc. Am. Archeology, Mo. and Wis. archeol. socs., Ill. State Acad. Science, Ill. State Hist. Soc., McLean Co. Hist. Soc., Sons of the Revolution (Ill. chap.), S. Ill. Historical Soc., Psi Omega, Sigma Xi, Phi Sigma. Awarded gold medal and citation from Ill. State Archeol. Soc., Northwestern University, 1941, for outstanding research in the field of Am. archeology and notable contributions to the advancement of archaeology. Merit badge, counselor Indian lore, Arrowhead Council (Champaign). Democrat. Mem. Christian Ch. Clubs: Exchange, Audubon, Champaign Country. Contbr. to archeol. and sci. publs. Dir. Animal Ecology, Inc., Vivarium Bldg., U. of Ill. Home: 1411 W. Church St. Office: 133 W. Park St., Champaign, Ill. Died May 7, 1952.

RYAN, EDWARD WILLIAM, sanitarian; b. Scranton, Pa., Dec. 14, 1884; s. Jerimiah E. and Bridget Ellen (Loftus) R.; M.D., Fordham U., 1912; unmarried. Spl. agt. Dept. of State, U.S., in Mexico, 1913-14, also surgeon Am. Embassy, Mexico City; with Am. Red Cross in evacuating Americans from troubled zone in Mexico; dir. Red Cross unit to Serbia, 1914; assigned to Salonika, 1917, instituting clean-up pub. health measures behind army as it advanced; dept. Red Cross commr. Germany after Armistice; also operating for Inter-Allied Commn., Berlin; assigned to Baltic States and continued there 1919-July 1922; stamped out epidemic in Esthonia, 1920. Mem. Legion of Honor. Awarded Croix de Guerre, Medaille des Epidemie (French); Comdr. White Eagle, Comdr. Order St. Sava, Charity Cross, Red Cross (Serbian); Comdr. St. Danilo (Montenegrin); Officer Order Savior (Grecian); Comdr. Order White Rose (Finnish); Comdr. Order St. Ann, Order St. Stanislaw (Russian); Officer 1st Class, Order of Liberty (Esthonian); Knight Order of Lithuania, etc. Home: Scranton, Pa. Died Sept. 1923.

RYAN, FRANCIS JOSEPH, biologist; b. Bklyn., Feb. 1, 1916; s. Joseph Louis and Marie (Frisse) R.; A.B., Columbia, 1937, M.A., 1939, Ph.D., 1941; m. Elizabeth Wilkinson, May 28, 1940. Nat. Research Council fellow Stanford, 1941-42; instr. dept. zoology Columbia, 1942, prof., 1953—; visiting professor Hebrew University, Jerusalem, 1960. Fellow American Academy of Arts and Sciences. Fulbright and Guggenheim fellow Pasteur Inst., Paris, 1950-51, Fulbright fellow U. Tokyo, 1955-56. Recipient Newberry prize Columbia, 1941. Mem. numerous profl. orgns. Home: 80 LaSalle St., N.Y.C. 27. Died July 14, 1963.

RYAN, HARRIS JOSEPH, electrical engr.; b. Powell's Valley, Pa., Jan. 8, 1866; s. Charles W. and Louisa (Collier) R.; Baltimore City Coll., 1880-81; Lebanon Valley Coll., Annville, Pa., 1881-83; M.E., Sibley Coll. (Cornell U.), 1887; m. Katharine E. Fortenbaugh, Sept. 12, 1888. Instr. physics, 1888-89, prof. elec. engring., 1889-1905, Cornell; prof. elec. engring., Leland Stanford Jr. U. (now Stanford U.), 1905-31, prof. emeritus, 1931—, also hon. dir. Harris J. Ryan High Voltage Lab., Stanford U. Cons. engr. Los Angeles Aqueduct Power Bur., 1909-24. Mem. Jury of Awards, dept. electricity, Chicago Expn., 1893; del. Internat. Elec. Congress, St. Louis Expn., 1904; mem. jury, Panama-P.I. Expn., 1915. Fellow Am. Inst. E.E. (v.p., 1896-98; hon. v.p. representing Inst. at P.-P.I. Expn., 1915; pres. 1923-24). Author: (with H.H. Norris and G. L. Hoxie) Text-Book of Electrical Machinery, Vol. I, 1903. Contbr. to Trans. Am. Inst. Elec. Engrs.; numerous monographs on elec. subjects. Dir. Anti-submarine Supersonics Lab., of Nat. Research Council, Pasadena, Calif., 1918-19. Died July 3, 1924.

RYAN, PATRICK JOHN, chem. co. exec.; b. Cleve., Oct. 28, 1908; s. Patrick and Florence (Mara) R.; m. Theresa Eileen Karvana, June 24, 1933; children—Patricia Anne (Mrs. Edmund M. Hurley), Beverly June (Mrs. George W. Finkbohner, Jr.). Analytical chemist Nat. Carbon Co., 1926-29; chief chemist Continental Products and Gibson Homans Co., Cleve., 1929-32; research dir., plant mgr. Donohue Varnish Co., Detroit, 1932-36; with Reichhold Chems., Inc., 1936—, v.p. prodn., Detroit, 1936-46, v.p. So. div., Tuscaloosa, Ala., 1946—, also dir.; lectr. in field. Mem. exec. bd. Black Warrior council Boy Scouts Am., 1948-53. Bd. dirs. Tuscaloosa United Fund, 1956-59. Mem. Am. Chem. Soc., Photog. Soc. Am., I.E.E.E. Roman Cath. K.C. (4 deg.). Clubs: Tuscaloosa Country. Catholic. Men's (pres. 1948-49), Lake Wildwood (bd. dirs. 1963-64) (Tuscaloosa). Contbr. profl. jours. Home: 7 Druid Ct., Tuscaloosa 35401. Office: Reichhold Chemicals, Inc., Tuscaloosa, Ala. 35403. Deceased.

RYAN, WILLIAM PATRICK, chem. engring.; b. West Medway, Mass., Mar. 11, 1895; s. John Henry and Catherine Maria (Hilferty) R.; grad. high sch., Medway, 1912, Phillips Acad., Andover, Mass., 1914; B.S., Mass. Inst. Tech., 1920 as of 1918; m. Pauline LaVerne Collins, Sept. 16, 1922; children—Mary Louise, Patricia Anne, Kathleen. Chem. engr. Nat. Lamp Co., Cleveland, O., Mar.-Sept. 1919; instr. in chem. engring., Mass. Inst. Tech., 1920-22, asst. prof., 1922-27, asso. prof., 1927-29, dir. Sch. of Chem. Engring. Practice, 1927—, prof. and head of dept., 1929—. Enlisted as pvt. Ordnance Dept., U.S.A., advancing to 2d lt. Chem. Warfare Service, World War. Catholic. Contbr. tech. articles to Jour. Industrial and Engring. Chemistry, Trans. Am. Inst. Chem. Engrs. Home: Wollaston, Mass. Deceased.

RYAN, WILLIAM THOMAS, electric power engring.; b. Bristol (now Joice), Ia., Feb. 28, 1882; s. Edward Thomas and Sarah (Slater) R.; E.E., U. of Minn., 1905; m. Ella I. Ryan, June 18, 1908. Connected with U. of Minn., 1906—, prof. electric power engring., 1922—. Mem. Am. Inst. Elec. Engineers (chmn. Minn. sect. 1912, 22; v.p. 1929-30) and other engring. socs. Mem. Minn. N.G., 1904. Catholic. Author: Design of Electrical Machinery (Vol. I), 1912 (Vol. II), 1912 (Vol. III), 1913; Electrical Problems, 1915. Contbr. over 40 papers pub. in tech. mags. Home: Minneapolis, Minn. Died Feb. 5, 1939.

RYDBERG, PER AXEL, botanist; b. Odh, Sweden, July 6, 1860; s. Adolf Fredrik and Elfrida (Otterstrom) R.; grad. Royal Gymnasium, Skara, Sweden, 1881; B.S., U. of Neb., 1891, M.A., 1895; Ph.D., Columbia U., 1898; m. Alfrida Amanda Rydberg, Nov. 11, 1903; children—Arthur Alfred, Elsa Margreta (dec.), Lilly Irene, Linnea Astrid. Prof. natural sciences and mathematics, Luther Acad., Wahoo, Neb., 1884-90, 1891-93; at Upsala Inst., Brooklyn, 1895-96 and 1897-98; Upsala Coll., New Orange, N.J., 1898-99; fellow in botany, Columbia, 1896-97; asst. Bot. Lab., U. of Neb., 1894-95; field agt. dept. agr., divs. of botany and agrostology, summers of 1891-96; curator New York Botanic Garden, Bronx Park, 1899—. Author of monographs on Potentilleae, Physalis, Saxifragaceae, Rosaceae, Carduaceae and Fabaceae; Catalogue of the Flora of Montana and the Yellowstone Park, 1900; Flora of Colorado, 1906; Flora of the Rocky Mountains and Adjacent Plains, 1917; Key to the Rocky Mountain Flora, 1919. Home: New York, N.Y. Died July 25, 1931.

RYERSON, WILLIAM NEWTON, engineer; b. in New York, Dec. 7, 1874; s. William Tunis and Julia H. (Newton) R.; E.E., Sch. of Mines (Columbia), 1896; m. Martha Taft, of Brooklyn, Oct. 31, 1900. With operating dept., Met. St. Ry. Co., New York, 4 yrs., Manhattan Ry. Co., 4 yrs., Interborough Rapid Transit Co., 1 yr.; supt. Ont. Power Co., Niagara Falls, Ont., 1905-9; gen. mgr., and chief engineer, Great Northern Power Co., Duluth, 1909-22; pub. utilities management dept. Day & Zimmermann, Inc., Phila., Aug. 1, 1922—. Fellow Am. Inst. E.E.; mem. Am. Soc. M.E., Engring. Institute of Can., Nat. Elec. Light Assn., Delta Kappa Epsilon. Episcopalian. Club: Engineers. Contbr. to engring. socs. Home: 255 W. Tulpehocken St. Office: 1600 Walnut St., Philadelphia PA

RYS, C(ARL) F(RIEDRICH) W(ILHELM), (res), metall. engr.; b. Essen, Germany, Mar. 23, 1877; s. Francis and Louise (Hausmann) R.; grad. high sch., Essen; studied mech. engring., tech. schs., Hagen, Germany, 2 yrs.; grad. Sch. of Mines, Freiberg, 1902, grad. study England, 6 mos.; Dr. Engineering, U. of Freiberg, 1930; m. Helen M. Witt, June 24, 1908; children—Louise, Frederick. Came to U.S., 1903, naturalized, 1911. Began with Krupp Works, Essen; with LaBelle Iron Works, Steubenville, O., 1903-04; in metall. dept., Homestead Steel Works (Carnegie Steel Co.), 1904-08; in inspection dept., Pittsburgh office, Carnegie Steel Co., 1908-10, asst. metall. engr., 1910-11, metall. engr., in charge metall. dept., since 1911, apptd. asst. to pres., May 7, 1928, also continuing as metall. engr.; apptd. chief metall. engr. of Carnegie-Ill. Steel Corp., Oct. 1, 1935, chief consulting metallurgist, June 1, 1942. Member American Iron and Steel Inst., Engrs. Soc. Western Pa., Am. Soc. for Metals, Soc. Automotive Engrs., Am. Inst. Mining and Metall. Engrs., Am. Ry. Engring. Assn., Am. Soc. for Testing Materials, Brit. Iron and Steel Inst., Army Ordnance Assn. Republican. Protestant. Mason (Shriner). Clubs: Duquesne, Railway, Pittsburgh Athletic Assn. (Pittsburgh). Home: 5463 Aylesboro Av. Office: Carnegie Bldg., Pittsburgh, Pa. Died Oct. 11, 1946.

SABIN, ALVAH HORTON, chemist; b. Norfolk, N.Y., Apr. 9, 1851; s. Henry S. and Zaida (Vernal) S.; S.B., Bowdoin College, 1876, M.S., 1879; hon. D.Sc. from same college, 1917; m. Mary E. Barden, Oct. 29, 1880 (died 1934); children—Raymond E., Warren D. Prof. chemistry, U. of Vermont, 1880-86; state chemist Vt., 1882-86; varnish mfr. at New York, 1888-1905; consulting chemist, Nat. Lead Co., New York, 1910-37. Invented and patented, 1883, modern process for making sugar of milk. Lecturer New York Univ., 1896-1925; sect. editor, Chem. Abstracts Jour. of Am. Chem. Soc., 1907—. Republican. Author: Industrial and Artistic Technology of Paint and Varnish, 1904, 3d edit., 1927; House-painting, 1908, 4th edit., 1928; German and American Varnish-Making, 1911; Red Lead as Paint Material, 1917, 2d edit., 1933; White Lead, 1919; Painting Structural Steel, 1929. Home: Flushing, L.I., N.Y. Died July 11, 1940.

SABIN, FLORENCE RENA, anatomist; b. Central City, Colo., Nov. 9, 1871; d. George Kimball and Rena (Miner) Sabin; B.S., Smith Coll., 1893, Sc.D., 1910; M.D., Johns Hopkins, 1900; Sc.D., U. of Mich., 1926, Mt. Holyoke, 1929, New York U., 1933, Wilson Coll., 1933, Syracuse U., 1934, Oglethorpe, 1935, U. of Colo., 1935, U. of Pa., 1937, Oberlin Coll., 1937, Russell Sage College, 1938, U. of Denver, 1939, Woman's Medical Coll. of Pa., Phila., 1950; LL.D., Goucher Coll., 1931. Teacher mathematics, Wolfe Hall, Denver, Colo., 1893-94; asst. in zoölogy, Smith Coll., 1895; interne, Johns Hopkins, 1900-01; fellow Baltimore Assn. for Advancement of Univ. Edn. of Women, 1901; asst. in anatomy, Johns Hopkins, 1902, asso., 1903-05, asso. prof., 1905-17, prof. histology, 1917-25; mem. Rockefeller Inst. for Med. Research, 1925-38; mem. emeritus since 1938. Pres. board Finney-Howell Res. Foundn. Mem. Am. Assn. Anatomist (v.p. 1908-09; president 1924-26), Am. Assn. Physiologists, Soc. Exptl. Biology and Medicine (councilor 1932), Nat. Tb Assn., Nat. Acad. Scis.; hon. life member N.Y. Acad. Scis., Harvey Society, A.A.A.S., Am. Assn. Univ. Women, Nat. Achievement award, 1932; M. Carey Thomas prize, 1935; Lasker award, 1951. Clubs: Cosmopolitan, Am. Woman's Assn., Soc. Colonial Dames. Author: An Atlas of the Medulla and Mid-Brain, 1901; Biography of Franklin Paine Mall, 1934; also articles on the lymphatic system in Am. Jour. of Anatomy and Anatomical Record; on the blood vessels and origin of blood cells in the Contributions to Embryology pub. by the Carnegie Inst. of Washington and Johns Hopkins Hosp. Bull.; on blood and bone marrow in Physiol. Rev. and Proc. Soc. Exptl. Biology and Medicine; and on tuberculosis in the Jour. of Exptl. Medicine, Trans. of Nat. Tuberculosis Assn. and Am. Rev. of Tuberculosis. Bronze statue of her placed in Statuary Hall, Washington. Address: 1333 E. 10th Av., Denver. 18. Died Oct. 3, 1953; buried Fairmount Mausoleum, Denver.

SABIN, LOUIS CARLTON, civil engr.; b. Memphis, Mich., June 25, 1867; s. Carlton and Cordelia (Bristol) S.; B.S., U. of Mich., 1890; C.E., 1894, hon. M.E., 1916; m. Nellie Blanchard, June 22, 1890 (dec.); children—Hope (Mrs. F. E. Bagger), Carlton Richard; m. 2d, Ruth E. Doucette, Sept. 1945. Insp. with Morison & Corthell, engrs., 1887-88; insp., engr. U.S. Engring. Dept., 1890-1905; sec. Am. sect. Internat. Waterways Commn., 1905-06, study regulation of Lake Erie and other waterway problems of Great Lakes; asso. engr. U.S. Engr. Dept. and gen. supt. St. Marys Falls Canal, 1906-25, design and constrn. Davis and Sabin locks, channel improvements, emergency dams, etc.; v.p. Lake Carriers' Assn., 1925-48; ret. Hon. mem. Am. Soc. C.E., Cleve. Engring. Soc.; mem. Ohio C. of C. (hon. mem. bd. dirs.), Mich. Engring. Soc., Internat. Assn. Navigation Congresses, Tau Beta Pi. Clubs: University of Michigan, Mid-day. Author: Cement and Concrete, 1894. Home: 2160 St. James Pkwy., Cleveland Heights 6, O. Died Dec. 30, 1950; buried Lakeview Cemetery, Cleve.

SABINE, WALLACE CLEMENT, physicist; b. Richwood, O., June 13, 1868; s. Hylas and Anna (Ware) S.; A.B., Ohio State U., 1886; A.M., Harvard, 1888; (D.Sc., Brown U., 1907; D.S., Harvard, 1914); m. Jane Downs Kelly, Aug. 22, 1900. Asst. physics, 1889-90, instr., 1890-95, asst. prof., 1895-1905, prof., 1905—, and dean of Scientific Sch., Harvard. Prof. Agrée a l'Université de Paris, 1916-17. Mem. Nat. Acad. Sciences; corr. mem. A.I.A.; fellow Am. Acad. Arts and Sciences, A.A.A.S. Author: Architectural Acoustics. Home: Boston, Mass. Died Jan. 10, 1919.

SACHS, BERNARD, (säks), neurologist; b. Baltimore, Md., Jan. 2, 1858; s. Joseph and Sophia (Baer) S.; A.B., Harvard, 1878; M.D., U. of Strassburg, 1882; m. Bettina R. Stein, Dec. 18, 1887; children—Alice (Mrs. J. M. Plaut), Helen (Mrs. Nathan Straus); married 2d, Rosetta Kaskel, 1940. Formerly alienist and neurologist, Bellevue Hospital; neurologist, Mt. Sinai Hospital; consulting physician Manhattan State Hospital, Montefiore Home; director emeritus Division Child Neurology, Neurol. Institute; dir. Child Neurology Research (Friedsam Foundation); prof. clin. neurology, Coll. of Physicians and Surgeons. Pres. of First Internat. Neurol. Congress; ex-pres. N.Y. Acad. Medicine; mem. Assn. Am. Physicians; hon. mem. Royal Soc. of Medicine, Sect. of Neurology (London); corr. mem. Paris and Moscow neurol. socs., etc. Author: Mental and Nervous Diseases of Children, 1895; Nervous Disorders from Birth Through Adolescence (with Dr. L. Hausman), 1926; Keeping Your Child Normal, 1936; also many med. monographs. Address: 2 W. 59th St., New York, N.Y. Died Oct. 26, 1943.

SACHS, JOSEPH, engr., inventor; b. N.Y. City, Aug. 17, 1870; s. Louis Von and Bertha (Sanger) S.; student Coll. City of N.Y. (non grad.) spl. tutoring and study; m. Caroline Norman, June 5, 1895; children—Kelvin N., Margaret N. (Mrs. J. J. Bissell). Began with Sprague Elec. Motor Co. prior to 1890, later with Edison Machine Works (now Gen. Electric Co.), Schenectady, N.Y.; developed trolleyless elec. ry., nonarcing enclosed fuse, elec. ry. appliances, 1892-94; cons. patent expert, also engaged in constrn. and operation engring. work and pioneer magnetic ore separating plant, 1892-98; developed electric fire alarm signalling system, elec. fire engine system, canal boat haulage, cable and elec. ry. signals, elec. type-setting machinery, electric metal heating and melting, 1893-98, elec. drive and control for motor vehicles, electrically controlled carburetor, elec. primer and other automobile accessories, 1900-15; cons. and chief engr. Johns-Pratt Co. (later elec. div. Colts Patent Fire Arms Mfg. Co.), mfrs. elec. devices, Hartford, Conn.; pres. and mgr. The Sachs Co., and v.p. and mgr. Sachs Laboratories, Inc.; identified with development, mfr. and sale of Sachs inventions, including elec. protective devices, enclosed fuses, cutouts, switches, circuit breakers, enclosed safety switches, meter service switches, meter testing devices, standardized service installations, etc., 1898-1937; research and invention, also engring. and evelopment consultant for several mfg. cos. since 1939; awarded over 250 U.S. patents. Awarded John Scott Legacy Medal by Franklin Institute for pioneer invention electric fuse protective devises, 1903. Fellow Am. Inst. E.E.; mem. Am. Soc. M.E., Nat. Elec. Mfrs. Assn. Republican. Episcopalian. Mason (32 deg.). Clubs: Engineers, Hartford, Get-Together, Hartford Golf, Wampanoag Country, Automobile, Church Club (of Conn.). Author: (with T. C. Martin) Electrical Boats and Navigation, 1894. Contbr. articles to technical publs.; lecturer before technical socs. Home: 1900 Albany Av., West Hartford 5. Office: 1900 Albany Av., West Hartford 5, Conn. Died Nov. 15, 1946.

SACK, HENRI S(AMUEL), educator; b. Davos, Switzerland, Nov. 25, 1903; s. Hermann and Isabelle (Pohli) S.; diploma math. and physics Tech. Hochschule (Zurich, Switzerland), 1925, D.Sc. in Math., 1927; m. Charlotte Fein, Aug. 30, 1933; children—Renee A., Claudia M. Came to U.S., 1940, naturalized, 1946. Asst., Eidg. Tech. Hochschule, Zurich, 1925-27; asst. U. Leipzig, 1927-33; asst. U. Brussels, 1933-37, chef de travaux, 1937-40; research asso. Cornell U., 1940-44, asso. prof. engring. physics, 1944-49, prof., 1949-64, Walter S. Carpenter Jr. prof., 1964-72, dir. Materials Sci. Center, 1963-68; asst. editor Physikal Zeitscr, 1929-33; indsl. cons. Mem. Am. Phys. Soc., Swiss Phys. Soc., Sigma Xi, Gamma Alpha (hon.). Author: (with P. Debye) Theorie der elektr. Molecular Eigenschaften, 1934; also publs. field dielectric properties, electrolytes, supersonics. Home: Ithaca NY Died Mar. 16, 1972.

SACKETT, ROBERT LEMUEL, cons. engr.; b. Mt. Clemens, Mich., Dec. 2, 1867; s. Lemuel Miller and Emily Lucinda (Cole) S.; B.S. in C.E., U. of Mich., 1891, C.E., 1896, Dr.Engring., 1937; m. Mary Lyon Coggeshall, July 22, 1896; children—Ralph L., Mrs. Frances L. Kramer (dec.). Prof. applied mathematics, Earlham Coll., 1891-1907; prof. sanitary and hydraulic engring., Purdue U., 1907-15; dean Sch. of Engring., Pa. State Coll., Sept. 1, 1915-June 30, 1937; dean emeritus; also dir. Engring. Expt. Sta., and of engring. extension, Fellow A.A.A.S. (v.p. 1928 and 1940), Am. Soc., mech. engrs.; mem. Am. Soc. Civil Engrs., Soc. for Promotion Engineering, Education, (president 1927-28), Engineer's Council for Professional Development, 1944-45; member Sigma Xi, Tau Beta Pi, Phi Kappa Phi, Phi Gamma Delta. Republican. Mem. Friends Ch. Consulting engr. to Ind. State Bd. of Health, 1910-15, and to other state comns. Author: The Engineer, His Work and His Education; also numerous technical articles. Home: 303 Lexington Av. Office: Secretary Am. Soc. Mech. Engrs., 29 W. 39th St., New York, N.Y. Died Oct. 6, 1946.

SADTLER, SAMUEL PHILIP, chemist; b. Pine Grove, Pa., July 18, 1847; s. Rev. Benjamin and Caroline (Schmucker) S.; A.B., Pa. Coll., 1867; Lehigh U., 1867-68; S.B., Harvard U., 1870; Ph.D., U. of Göttingen, 1871; (LL.D., Pa. Coll., 1902; Phi Beta Kappa); m. M. Julia Bridges, Dec. 17, 1872. Prof. natural science, Pa. Coll., 1871-74; prof. chemistry, Univ. of Pa., 1874-91, Phila. Coll. of Pharmacy, 1878-1916; consulting chem. expert. Fellow A.A.A.S. Author: Handbook of Chemical Experimentation for Lecturers, 1877; Handbook of Industrial Organic Chemistry, 5th edit., 1923 (also of German and Russian translations); Text-book of Pharmaceutical Chemistry (with Virgil Coblentz), 5th edit., 1917. Chem. editor 15th to 20th edits. of U.S. Dispensatory and mem. Com. of Revision of the U.S. Pharmacopoeia, 1900-10, 1910-20. Home: Philadelphia, Pa. Died Dec. 20, 1923.

SAFFORD, WILLIAM EDWIN, botanist; b. Chillicothe, O., Dec. 14, 1859; s. Judge William Harrison and Pocahontas (Creel) S.; grad. U.S. Naval Acad., 1880; post-grad. studies, botany and zoölogy, Yale, 1883-85; marine zoölogy, Harvard, 1885; Ph.D., George Washington U., 1920; m. Clare, d. late Chief Justice Decius S. Wade, of Mont., Sept. 14, 1904; children—Decius Wade, Bernice Galpin. Served in U.S.N., 1880-1902; served in Spanish-Am. War, collecting for U.S. Nat. Mus. in the depts. of ethnology and ethnobotany, resigned Aug. 1, 1902, while on active duty in the Library and Naval War Records Office, Navy Dept.; asst. botanist, 1902-15, economic botanist, Apr. 1915—, Dept. Agriculture. Commr. to Peru and Bolivia, 1891-92, for Chicago Expn. (medal, 1893); v.gov. Island of Guam, 1899-1900; exec. officer U.S. receiving ship Independence, 1900-01; Smithsonian Instn., 1901-02. Author: A Year on the Island of Guam, 1902-04; Useful Plants of the Island of Guam, 1905; The Chamorro Language of the Island of Guam, 1905; Cactaceae of Northeastern and Central Mexico, 1909; the classification of the genus Annona with descriptions of new and imperfectly known species, 1913; An Aztec Narcotic, 1915; Lignum nephriticum, 1916; Narcotics and Stimulants of the Ancient Americans; Chenopodium nuttaliae, a food-plant of the Aztecs, 1918; Cosmos sulphureus, the Xochipalli, or Flower-paint of the Aztecs, 1918; Notes on the genus Dahlia, with descriptions of two new species from Guatemala, 1919; Natural History of Paradise Key and the nearby Everglades of Florida, 1919; Synopsis of the Genus Datura; Datura, an Inviting Genus for the Study of Heredity, 1921; Peyote, the narcotic Mescal Button of the Indians, 1921; Daturas of the Old World and New, 1922; Ant Acacias and Acacia Ants of Mexico and Central America, 1923; The Potato of Romance and of Reality, 1925. Home: Washington, D.C. Died Jan. 10, 1926.

SAGUE, JAMES E., mech. engr.; b. Poughkeepsie, N.Y., July 20, 1862; s. Horace and Harriet Jane (Kelsey) S.; M.E., Stevens Inst. Tech., Hoboken, N.J., 1883; m. Jeannette Kenyon, of Brooklyn, N.Y., Oct. 30, 1890. Asst. engr. of tests, C.,B.&Q. R.R., Aurora, Ill., 1883-85; engr. of tests, gen. foreman machine shops, Jersey City, N.J., and div. master mechanic, Erie R.R., 1885-90; mech. engr. West India Improvement Co. and supt. motive power, Jamaica R.R., Jamaica, W.I., 1890-92; mech. engr. Schenectady (N.Y.) Locomotive Works, 1892-1901; chief mech. engr. and 1st v.p., Am. Locomotive Co., New York, 1901-07; pub. service commr., 2d Dist. N.Y., 1907-14; now chief consulting engr. Worthington Pump Machinery Corpn. Mem. Am. Soc. M.E. Clubs: University, Engineers, Nat. Arts. Home: Poughkeepsie, N.Y. Office: 115 Broadway, New York, N.Y.

ST. JOHN, CHARLES EDWARD, solar physicist; b. Allen, Mich., Mar. 15, 1857; s. Hiram A. and Lois A. (Bacon) S.; grad. classical course, Mich. Normal Coll., 1876; B.S., Mich. Agrl. Coll., 1887; studied U. of Mich., 1890-92; A.M., Harvard, 1893, Ph.D., 1896; U. of Berlin, 1894-95; hon. Pd.M., Mich. Normal Coll., 1906; hon. Sc.D., Oberlin College, 1931; unmarried. Teacher of physics, Michigan Normal College, 1885-92; instructor in physics, U. of Mich., 1896-97; asso. prof. physics and astronomy, 1897-99, prof., 1899-1908, dean Coll. of Arts and Sciences, 1907-08, Oberlin Coll.; astronomer, Mt. Wilson Observatory of Carnegie Instn., 1908—. Mem. internat. commns. on solar rotation and on standards of wavelength; pres. Internat. Commn. on Solar Physics. Author of Revision of Rowland's Preliminary Table of Solar Spectrum Wave-lengths. Home: Pasadena, Calif. Died Apr. 26, 1935.

ST. JOHN, ISAAC MUNROE, army officer, engr.; b. Augusta, Ga., Nov. 19, 1827; s. Isaac Richards and Abigail Richardson (Munroe) St.J.; grad. Yale, 1845; m. Ella J. Carrington, Feb. 28, 1865, 6 children. Asst. editor Balt. Patriot, circa 1847; mem. engring. staff B. & O. R.R., 1848-55; in charge of constrn. divs. Blue Ridge R.R. in Ga., 1855-60; enlisted for engring. duty in U.S. Army, 1861, transferred to Magruder's Army of Peninsula, became chief engr.; commd. capt. engrs., 1862, promoted to maj. 1862, chief of the nitre and mining bur., Richmond, Va.; lt. col. and col.; apptd. commissary gen. with rank brig. gen. Confederate States Army, 1865, organized an efficient system for collecting and storing supplies and for forwarding them to the armies; chief engr. Louisville, Cincinnati & Lexington R.R., 1866-69; city engr. Louisville (Ky.), 1869-71; made 1st topog. map of Louisville and planned city's 1st complete sewerage system; became cons. engr. C. & O. R.R., 1871; chief engr. Elizabeth, Lexington & Big Sandy R.R., 1873. Died "Greenbrier," White Sulphur Springs, W.Va., Apr. 7, 1880.

SALANT, WILLIAM, pharmacologist; b. Courland, Russia, Feb. 2, 1870; s. Solomon and Theresa (Geffen) S.; came to America, 1884; B.S., Cornell U., 1894; grad. student in biology, Columbia, 1894-5; M.D., Coll. Phys. and Surg. (Columbia), 1899; studied Sch. of Biology and Sch. of Mines, Columbia; m. Annie Oser, of Waterbury, Conn., 1899. Fellow Rockefeller Inst., 1899-07; asst. Cornell Med. Sch., 1902-3, Coll. Phys. and Surg., 1905-7; adj. prof. pharmacology and physiol. chemistry, U. of Ala., 1907-8; chief Pharmacol. Lab., Bur. of Chemistry, U.S. Dept. Agr., since June, 1908. Mem. Am. Soc. Pharmacology and Exptl. Therapeutics, Am. Physiol. Soc., Am. Soc. Biol. Chemists, Soc. Exptl. Biology and Medicine, Am. Chem. Soc., A.M.A., Sigma Xi. Author of numerous publs. in pharmacology, physiology and pathology, in various scientific jours.; also monographs pub. by Bur. of Chemistry, U.S. Dept. Agr. Home: 3429 34th St., Washington DC

SALERNO, VITO LORENZO, cons. engr.; b. N.Y.C., May 16, 1915; s. Vincenzo and Vincenzo (Gatti) S.; B. Civil Engring. cum laude, Coll. City N.Y., 1939, M. Civil Engring. (Grad. Study award 1939), 1939; D. Aero. Engring., Poly. Inst. Bklyn., 1947; m. Carmela Gravina, July 18, 1942; children—Vivian, Valerie. Naval architect Bur. Ships, Navy Dept., 1939-46; mem. faculty Poly. Inst. Bklyn., 1946-51, asso. prof. aero. engring., asso. dir. aero. and submarine structures, 1948-51; prof. aero. engring. Rensselaer Poly. Inst., 1951-52; from cons. to tech. dir. nuclear components div. Combustion Engring., Inc., 1953-57; cons. research Grumman Aircraft Engring. Corp., 1957-58; dean Coll. Sci. and Engring. Fairleigh Dickinson U., 1958-62; cons. engr. aero-space and nuclear power companies, 1958-62; dir. Applied Technology Assos., Incorporated, Ramsey, N.J., 1962-66, president, tech. dir., 1966-71. Recipient Community Service award Bergen County (N.J.) Soc. Profl. Engrs., 1961, Alumni Achievement award Stuyvesant High Sch., N.Y.C., 1961. Registered prof. engr., N.Y., N.J. Asso. fellow Inst. Aero-Space Scis.; mem. Am. Soc. M. E., Pressure Vessel Research Council. (chmn. design div.), N.Y. State Soc. Profl. Engrs. (president New York City chapter 1968-69), Sigma Xi, Tau Beta Pi, Sigma Gamma Tau. Home: Bronx NY Died July 24, 1971; buried Woodlawn Cemetery, Bronx NJ

SALISBURY, JAMES HENRY, physician; b. Scott, N.Y., Oct. 13, 1823; s. Nathan and Lucretia (Babcock) S.; grad. (B.N.S.) Polytechnic Inst., Troy, N.Y., 1846; grad. Albany Med. Coll., 1850 (A.M., 1852; LL.D., 1887, Union Coll.; LL.D., Amity Coll., Ind.); m. Clara Brasee. Asst. chemist, 1846-48; prin. chemist, 1849-52, N.Y. State Geol. Survey; lecturer on elementary and applied chemistry, N.Y. State Normal School, Albany, 1851-52. Conducted micros. investigations, which were published in Trans. A.A.A.S.; later devoted himself as specialist to the causes and treatment of chronic diseases, publishing his therapeutical discoveries in New York Jour. of Medicine. Practiced in Cleveland some yrs., later in New York. Author: Anatomy and Histology of Plants, 1848 (gold medal, essay Young Men's Assn., Albany); The Chemical and Physiological Examination of the Maize Plant, 1849 (prize essay, N.Y. Agrl. Soc.); Alimentation and Disease, 1886. Home: Dobbs' Ferry, N.Y. Died 1905.

SALISBURY, ROLLIN D., university dean; b. Spring Prairie, Wis., Aug. 17, 1858; s. Daniel and Lucinda (Bryant) S.; Ph.B., Beloit Coll., 1881, A.M., 1884 (LL.D., 1904). Instr. geology and biology, 1883-84, prof. geology, 1884-91, Beloit Coll.; student in Europe (chiefly at Heidelberg), 1887-88; prof. general and geographic geology, U. of Wis., 1891-92; prof. geographic geology, 1892—, dean of Univ. Colls., 1894-96, dean of Ogden (grad.) Sch. of Science, 1899—, head of dept. of geography, 1903-19, head dept. of geology, 1919—, U. of Chicago. U.S. geologist, glacial div., 1882-94, geologist, 1894—, geologist in charge of Pleistocene geology of N.J., 1891-1915. Fellow Geol. Soc. America, Assn. Am. Geographers, A.A.A.S., Ill. Acad. Sciences. Died Aug. 15, 1922.

SALMON, UDALL J., gynecologist and obstetrician, born in Montreal, Can., October 5, 1904; s. Solomon and Rebecca (Mazur) S.; student Faculty of Arts, McGill U., 1921-23, Faculty of Med., 1924-29 (B.S.,

M.D., C.M., 1929); student Sorbonne, Paris, France, 1923-24. Came to the United States, 1927, naturalized, 1940. Intern Michael Reese Hosp., Chgo., 1930-32; resident gynecologist Mt. Sinai Hosp., N.Y.C., 1932-34, staff gynecologist 1934-44; research fellow in gynecology and endocrinology, Mount Sinai Hosp., 1934-38; pres., exec. dir. Salmon Found., Incorporated, New York City, 1949—. Diplomate Am. Bd. Obstetrics and Gynecology. Fellow Am. Coll. Obstetrics & Gynecology, Am. Soc. Study of Sterility; mem. Soc. Exptl. Biology and Medicine, N.Y. Acad. Scis., A.M.A., N.Y. State Med. Soc., Internat. Fertility Assn., Endocrine Soc., A.A.A.S., Am. Fedn. Clin. Research, Alpha Omega Alpha. Contbr. Am. Jour. Obstetrics, and Gynecology, Science, Endocrinology, Progress in Gynecology. Address: 875 Fifth Av., N.Y.C. Died July 10, 1963; buried Westchester Hills Cemetery.

SALSBURG, ZEVI WALTER, educator, phys. chemist; b. Wilkes-Barre, Pa., Aug. 9, 1928; s. Theodore and Frances (Shinkman) S.; B.S. in Chemistry, U. Rochester, 1950; student Cal. Inst. Tech., 1950-51; Ph.D. in Chemistry, Yale, 1953; m. Bertha Rosen, Dec. 21, 1958;children—Alan Israel, Linda Sydel. Mem. faculty Rice U., 1954-70, prof. chemistry, 1962-70; cons. Los Alamos Sci. Lab., 1955-70, Lawrence Radiation Lab., Livermore, Cal., 1957-70, Bell Telephone Labs, 1964; FMC lectr. Princeton, 1964. Chmn. panel chemistry for evaluating nat. NSF grad-fellowship application, NRC., 1965-67, Grantee NSF, 1952-53; NRC fellow, 1953-54; Guggenheim fellow, 1961-62; recipient Teaching Excellence award Brown Coll., Rice U., 1968. Mem. Am. Chem. Soc. (tour lectr. 1961), Am. Math. Soc., Phi Beta Kappa, Sigma Xi. Distinguished guest prof. La. State U., 1967. Editor: Solution Theory Section of the Collected Works of J.G. Kirkwood; (with J. Poirer) Simple Dense Fluids: Data and Theory, 1968. Home: Houston TX Died June 20, 1970.

SALSICH, LEROY, mining engr.; b. Hartland, Wis., Dec. 20, 1879; s. Hamilton Enos and Jane Withington (Atwater) S.; B.S.C.E., Univ. of Wis., 1901; m. Elizabeth Frazer, Aug. 15, 1904 (dec. Dec. 28, 1943); m. 2d, Margaret Culkin Banning, Nov. 15, 1944. With Oliver Mining Co., Duluth, Minn., 1901-46, pres., 1930-46, ret.; cons. engr., 1946—. Recipient William Lawrence Saunders Gold Medal awarded by Am. Inst. Mining and Metall. Engrs. for achievement in mining and for significant contbn., as operating head of World's largest mining enterprise, to nation's prodn. of steel during World War II. Mem. Am. Inst. Mining and Metall. Engrs. (vice pres., 1941-44, dir., 1938-44). Republican. Episcopalian. Clubs: Kitchi Gammi, Northland Country (Duluth); Minneapolis (Minneapolis); Chicago (Chicago). Home: 60 E. Kent Rd., Duluth 5, Minn. and Tryon, N.C. Office: Alworth Bldg., Duluth 2, Minn. Died Oct. 26, 1957; buried Polk Meml. Gardens, Tryon, N.C.

SALTER, WILLIAM THOMAS, pharmacologist; b. Boston, Mass., Dec. 19, 1901; s. William Thomas Hall and Frances B. F. (Patten) S.; student Roxbury Latin Sch. grad. 1918, A.B., Harvard Univ., 1922, M.D., Harvard U. Med. Sch., 1925; m. Eleanor Vallandigham, June 27, 1935; children—Frances V., Eleanor C., Katharine C. Medical interne, Mass. Gen Hospital, 1925-27, resident, 1927-28; Moseley traveling fellow, Harvard Univ., 1928-29, research fellow in medicine, 1929-32; instr. biochem. sciences, Medical Sch., 1928-39; asst. prof., 1934-41; asso. physician Huntington Memorial Hosp., 1929-39; jr. asso. in medicine, Peter Bent Brigham Hosp., 1937-39; research fellow in biochemistry, Harvard Univ. Cancer Commn., 1929-39; faculty instr. medicine, Harvard U., 1932-34; prof. pharmacology, Yale U. Sch. of Medicine, since 1941; asso. physician, Thorndike Memorial Laboratoy, 1939-41. Received Iodine Ednl. Bur. Inc. award for research in pharmaceutical chemistry of iodine. Mem. American College Physicians, Am. Assn. for the History of Medicine, Am. Assn. for Cancer Research, Am. Inst. of Nutrition, Am. Soc. Clin. Investigation, Assn. for Study of Internal Secretions, Biochem. Soc. (Eng.), Am. Chem. Soc., Alpha Chi Sigma Xi, Phi Beta Kappa, Alpha Omega Alpha. Episcopalian. Home: 178 Cold Spring St. Office: 333 Cedar St., New Haven 11. Died July 30, 1952.

SAMPEY, JOHN RICHARD, JR., educator; b. Louisville, Aug. 5, 1896; s. John Richard and Annie (Renfroe) S.; student U. Louisville, 1919; S.B., U. Chgo., 1920, S.M., 1921, Ph.D., 1923; post doctorate research, Johns Hopkins, 1923-24, 30-31; m. Jewell Cheatham, Sept. 4, 1925; children—John Richard III, Jane Renfroe. Grafflin scholar Johns Hopkins, 1923-24; asso. prof. chemistry Howard Coll., 1924-26, prof., 1926-34; prof. chemistry Furman U., 1934-67. Served from pvt. to 2d lt., inf., U.S. Army, 1918-19; AEF in France; as lt. col., inf., AUS, 1941-45; ETO, PTO. Decorated various service medals. Recipient coll. chemistry teacher award, Manufacturing Chemists Association, 1961. Fellow A.A.A.S.; member American Chemical Society (chmn. Ala. and S.C. sects; Charles H. Herty medal 1954), Ala. (past pres.), S.C. (pres. 1940) acads. scis., So. Assn. Sci. and Industry (trustee). Res. Officers Assn., Am. Legion. Baptist (deacon, Sunday sch. tchr.). Contbr. numerous articles profl. jours. Home: Greenville SC Died 1967.

SAMUELS, EDWARD AUGUSTUS, zoölogist; b. Boston, July 4, 1836; s. Emanuel and Abigail S.; common school edn.; has been engaged in literary work for about 50 yrs.; asst. sec. Mass. State Bd. of Agr., 1860-80; was 7 yrs. pres. Mass. Fish and Game Protective Assn. Author: Ornithology and Oölogy of New England; Among the Birds; With Fly-Rod and Camera; With Rod and Gun in New England and the Maritime Provinces; Mammalogy of New England; The Living World (2 vols., with Augustus C. L. Arnold). Home: Fitchburg, Mass. Died 1908.

SANBORN, JOHN ALBERT, assn. exec., mech. engr.; b. Norway, Maine, Feb. 25, 1901; s. Albert Lincoln and Annie B. (Keene) S.; B.S., U. Me., 1926; Certificate of Proficiency in elec. engring., Westinghouse Elec. and Mfg. Co., 1927; student George Washington U. Law Sch., 1928-29; LL.B., N.Y.U., 1932, J.S.D., 1933; student Sch. Accounting and Bus. Adminstrn., 1934-35; m. Helen M. Clayton, Oct. 31, 1928; children—John Clayton, Joanne Helen. With Central Maine Power Co., Augusta, 1922-25; apprentice, dept. gen. engring., later grad. student Sci. Research Lab., Westinghouse Elec. & Mfg. Co., E. Pittsburgh, 1926-27; asst. examiner U.S. Patent Office, 1928; Office of Judge Adv. Gen., War Dept., also tech. advisor relative to aircraft and radio, German-Austrian Patent Claims Commn. (Berlin, Vienna, Prague, Budapest, Amsterdam, London, Paris), 1928-29; dir. patent research Mfrs. Aircraft Assn., Inc., N.Y. City, 1929-37, gen. mgr. since 1937, v.p. since 1948. Arbitrator for aircraft industry in proceedings under Patent Cross-License Agreement since 1931; consultant on patents and related subjects to Fed. Aviation Commn., 1935, Internat. Conf. on Civil Aviation, Chicago, 1944-45; pres. Air Policy Commn., 1947, Congl. Aviation Policy Bd., 1948. Asso. fellow Inst. Aeronautical Scis.; mem. Soc. Automotive Engrs., Nat. Aeronautics Assn., N.Y. Patent Law Assn., Soc. Colonial Wars for State of N.Y., Beta Theta Pi, Tau Beta Pi. Clubs: University (N.Y. City); Larchmont (N.Y.). Yacht; Yonkers (N.Y.) Yacht. Home: 40 Edgewood Av., Larchmont, N.Y. Office: 45 Rockefeller Plaza, N.Y.C. 20. Died Oct. 25, 1966; buried Norway, Me.

SANDERS, LEE STANLEY, lawyer, engr.; b. Chgo., Sept. 25, 1913; s. Walter and Valentine (Zolock) S.; B.S., Northwestern U., 1935; J.D., Loyola U., 1938; m. Rosemary T. Shea, July 13, 1940; children—Lee S., Melissa R. Admitted to Ill. bar, 1938, Cal. bar, 1948; dir. endowment funds, Real estate Northwestern U., 1935-43; v.p., sec. Roadmaster Products Co., Los Angeles, 1946-51; sec., dir. Dist. Bond Co., 1946-51; sec. Indsl. Mgmt. Corp., 1946-51, Gross, Rogers & Co., 1946-51, Tetco Co., 1946-51; exec. v.p. Los Angeles Orthopaedic Found. and Orthopaedic Hosp., 1951-70. Served as officer USNR, 1943-46. Home: Pasadena CA Died Apr. 14, 1970.

SANDERS, W(ILLIAM) BURTON, univ. prof., engr.; b. Wellington, Ill., Dec. 2, 1893; s. Robert Hayes and Minnie Amelia (Ferry) S.; B.S. in M.E., Purdue U., 1919, M.S. in M.E., 1922; m. Emma Christina Nehrig, Oct. 14, 1915; children—William Burton, Elizabeth Louise (Mrs. Donald S. Payne). Tchr. mathematics and physics, Mecca (Ind.) pub. schs., 1914-15; engr. Ind. Ry. and Light Co., Kokomo, 1915-17, Studebaker Corp., South Bend, Ind., 1917-18; Instr. physics, Purdue U., 1919-20, instr. applied mechanics, 1920-25, asst. prof., 1925-31, asso. prof., 1931-44, prof. engring. mechanics, since 1944, mem. spl. univ. schedule com., since 1925, coordinator, research projects in engring. mechanics, Purdue U., since 1945; cons. engr. Registered professional engr., Ind. Mem. Am. Soc. M.E., Am. Assn. Univ. Profs., Am. Soc. Engring. Edn., Theta Tau, Sigma Delta Psi, Tau Beta Pi. Republican. Methodist. Elk, Odd Fellow, O.E.S., Mason (32 deg., K.T., Grand Master of the Grand Council Royal and Select Masters of Ind., 1945). Club: Reamers. Home: 610 Evergreen St., West Lafayette, Ind. Died Jan. 9, 1961; buried Grand View Cemetery, West Lafayette.

SANDERSON, EDWIN NASH, engineer; b. Brooklyn, N.Y., Dec. 2, 1862; s. Elnathan Lawrence and Mary Elizabeth (Nash) S.; C.E., Rensselaer Poly. Inst., 1886; M.E., Cornell, 1887; m. Sarah E. Rogers, Apr. 19, 1889 (died 1905); children—Mrs. Helen Rogers Chamberlin, Mrs. Sibyl Edwina Sloane, Mrs. Katharine Mary McCaddon; m. 2d, Mildred Hays, Feb. 7, 1907. Mem. engring. firm Sanderson & Porter, New York; pres. Federal Light & Traction Co. and officer or dir. numerous pub. utility corps. Trustee Cornell U. Republican. Conglist. Home: New York, N.Y. Died Nov. 9, 1932.

SANDERSON, (EZRA) DWIGHT, sociologist, entomologist; b. Clio, Mich., Sept. 25, 1878; s. John P. and Alice G. (Wright) S.; B.S., Mich. Agrl. Coll., 1897; B.S. Agr., Coll. of Agr. Cornell U., 1898; Ph.D., U. of Chicago, 1921; m. Anna Cecilia Blandford, Sept. 19, 1899; 1 dau., Alice Cecilia. Asst. state entomologist of Md., 1898-99; asst. Div. Entomology, U.S. Dept. Agr., summer 1899; entomologist Del. Agrl. Expt. Sta. and asso. prof. zoölogy, Del. Coll., 1899-1902; State entomologist of Tex. and prof. entomology, Tex. Agrl. and Mech. Coll., 1902-04; prof. zoölogy, N.H. Coll., and entomologist, N.H. Agrl. Expt. Sta., 1904-07; dir. N.H. Agrl. Expt. Sta., 1907-10; dean, Coll. of Agr., W.Va. U., 1910-15; and dir. W.Va. Agrl. Expt. Sta., 1912-15; fellow in sociology, U. of Chicago, 1916-17; prof. rural sociology, Cornell University, 1918-43, professor emeritus since 1943. Fellow A.A.A.S.; member American Sociological Society, Sigma Xi, Phi Kappa Phi past pres. Association Economic Entomologists, Rural Sociol. Society, Am. Country Life Assn. Author: Insects Injurious to Staple Crops, 1902; Insect Pests of Farm, Garden and Orchard, 1911; Elementary Entomology (with C. F. Jackson), 1911; School Entomology (with L. M. Peairs), 1916; The Farmer and His Community, 1922; The Rural Community, 1932. Rural Community Organization (with R. A. Polson), 1939; Leadership for Rural Life, 1940; Rural Sociology and Rural Social Organization, 1942; reports and bulls. of Del., Tex., N.H., W.Va. and Cornell agrl. expt. stas., and U.S. Bur. of Entomology. Editor Proc. 1st Nat. Country Life Conference; Farm Income and Farm Life, 1927. Home: Ithaca, N.Y. Died Sep. 27, 1944.

SANDERSON, HENRY, banker; b. Titusville, Pa., Dec. 20, 1868; s. Edward Patterson and Elisa (Crassous) S.; ed. pub. and prep. schs.; m. Beatrice Walter (died 1921); children—James Reed, Henry G. Sec., later v.p. and pres. Mt. Morris Electric Light Co., 1890-98; pres. Union Trust Co., Newark, N.J., 1899-1900; pres. New York Transportation Co., Fifth Av. Stage Co., Met. Express Co., 1900-05; sr. partner Sanderson & Brown, members New York Stock Exchange, until 1911; sr. partner Charles D. Barney & Co., bankers, until 1920; dir. various corps. Installed first mechanically operated stage on Fifth Av.; instituted first trolley express in N.Y. State. Financial adviser to Am. Relief Assn. (Herbert Hoover), Paris, France, Jan.-June 1919. Republican. Episcopalian. Home: New York, N.Y. Died Mar. 24, 1934.

SANDERSON, ROBERT, silversmith; b. Eng., 1608; m. Lydia, m. 2d, Mrs. Mary Cross, 1642; m. 3d, Elizabeth; 5 children. Learned, practiced trade of silversmith in Eng.; came to Am., circa 1635; among 1st settlers, Hampton, N.H., 1638; landholder, freeman, Watertown, Mass., 1639; probably 1st tchr. of John Hull; did much to establish New Eng. tradition of silverworks as examplified in works of Jeremiah Dummer, John Coney, and the two Reveres; established (with John Hull) a mint in the colonies, 1652; became deacon First Ch., Boston, 1668. Died Boston, Oct. 7, 1693.

SANDS, HERBERT STEAD, elec. engr.; b. Stamford, Conn., July 27, 1874; s. James Stopford and Elizabeth Victoria (French) S.; prep. edn., St. Austin Sch., Staten Island, N.Y.; completed course of the Edison General Electric Co., 1893; E.E. from U. of Colorado, 1926; m. Elizabeth Westcott Clarke, Sept. 10, 1919. Supt. Baltic (Conn.) Power Co., 1893-98, Colorado Springs and Cripple Creek Dist. Ry., 1898-99, La Bella Mill, Water & Power Co., Goldfield, Colo., 1899-1901, Seaton Mountain Electric Light & Power Co., Idaho Springs, Colo., 1901-05; mgr. indsl. div. Westinghouse Electric & Mfg. Co., Denver, Colo., 1905-27; private practice since April 1, 1927. Mem. bd. of dirs. Home Loan Bank, Topeka, Kan. Pres. Colo. Engring. Council, 1925-27; mem. Am. Inst. E.E. (v.p. from dist. 6, 1923-27), Colo. Scientific Soc. (pres. 1923-25); mem. State Bd. Engr. Examiners of Colo. since 1919, pres. since 1922; dir. Denver C. of C., 1928-30, pres., 1929-31; mem. Denver Bd. Water Commissioners since 1933, pres. 1943. Mem. Tau Beta Pi (University of Colo.), Eta Kappa Nu (asso.). Episcopalian (mem. Vestry St. John's Cathedral). Mason (33 deg.; grand comdr. K.T. 1931). Clubs: Cactus, Rotary, Denver Athletic. Home: 2515 Ash St. Office: First National Bank Bldg., Denver, Colo. Died Dec. 13, 1944.

SANDSTEN, EMIL PETER, horticulturist; b. Nybro, Sweden, Sept. 15, 1868; s. Joel and Charlotte (Gustafson) S.; came to U.S., 1888, naturalized, 1894; grad. Sch. Agr. U. of Minn., 1891, B.S., 1895, M.S., 1898; Ph.D., Cornell, 1903; m. Pearl Dew, of Norfolk, Va., Sept. 24, 1903; 1 dau., Emilie Dew (Mrs. Edmundo Lassalle). Prof. horticulture and head dept., U. of Wis., 1903-11; in commercial horticulture, Mont., 1911-13; prof. horticulture, state horticulturist, Colo. State Coll., 1913-33; dean agr. and dir. Colo. Agricultural Experimental Station, 1933-39, emeritus professor since July 1, 1939. Mem. State and Federal Soil Conservation bds., Colo. State Planning Bd., Fort Collins, Zoning Bd. Fellow A.A.A.S.; mem. Royal Hort. Soc. of Eng., Soc. Am. Foresters, Colo. Wyo. Acad. of Sci. N.Y. Acad. of Sci., Colo-Ednl. Assn., Sigma Xi, Alpha Zeta, Phi Kappa Phi. Democrat. Unitarian. Author of 28 Agrl. Expt. Sta. bulletins on hort. subjects and studies in crop production in altitudes from 7500 to 9000 ft. Home: 1419 Walnut St., Berkeley, Calif.

SANDWEISS, DAVID JACOB, physician; b. Stolin, Russia, Dec. 27, 1898; s. Samuel and Eva (Goberman) S.; brought to U.S., 1909, naturalized, 1911; B.S., U. Mich., 1921, M.D., 1923; m. Freda Levin, Dec. 16, 1934; children—Samuel Herbert, Flora Irene, Donald Arthur, Sandra Gail. Physician, St. Joseph Mercy Hosp., Detroit, 1923-24, Michael Reese Hosp., Chgo., 1924-25; pvt. practice medicine, Detroit, 1925—; asst. physician, then physician div. internal medicine and mem. active staff Harper Hosp., Detroit; from instr. to clin. asso. prof. medicine Wayne State U. Coll. Medicine, 1937—; chief sect. gastroenterology, attending physician div. internal medicine Sinai Hosp., Detroit; asso. physician div. internal medicine Receiving Hosp. of Detroit; exam. physician Selective Service, Detroit, 1939-45; spl. cons. mem. ad hoc com. gastroenterology USPHS; mem. Old Age Bur., Detroit. Bd. dirs. Hebrew Benevolent Soc., Detroit; bd. trustees Jewish Social Service Bur., Detroit. Recipient certificate of merit for sci. exhibit Relation of Sex Hormones to Peptic Ulcer, A.M.A., 1938. Fellow A.C.P., A.M.A., Am. Coll. Gastroenterology; mem. Am. Gastroenterol. Assn., Internat., Am., Mich. socs. internal medicine, Am. Assn. Study Liver Disease, Am. Gastroscopic Soc., Am., Detroit physiol. socs., Fedn. Am. Soc. Exptl. Biology and Medicine, Am. Fedn. Clin. Research, N.Y. Acad. Medicine, Am. Med. Writers Assn., Detroit Gastroenterol. Soc., Mich., Wayne County, Maimonides med. socs., A.A.A.S., Phi Lambda Kappa. Jewish religion. Mason. Editorial bd. Rev. Gastroenterology. Contbr. chpts., articles to profl. publs., also profl. papers. Home: 20687 Kensington Ct., Southfield, Mich. 48075. Office: 15201 W. McNichols Rd., Detroit 35. Died Aug. 15, 1962.

SANDYS, GEORGE, colonist, poet; b. Bishopsthorpe, nr. York, Eng., Mar. 13, 1578; s. Edwin and Cicely (Wilford) S. Toured Middle East, 1610; shareholder in Va. Co. under its 3rd charter, also of Bermudas Co., 1611; came to Va. from Eng., 1621; treas. Va. Colony, 1621-28; commanded punitive force against Tappahannock Indians; built 1st water-mill in Am.; sponsored iron manufacture; engaged in making glass; introduced shipbldg. into the colony; apptd. mem. Va. Gov's. Council, 1624, reapptd., 1626, 28; mem. commn. for better plantation of Va., 1631; made a gentleman of the privy chamber to King Charles, circa 1632; acted as an unofcl. London rep. of colonial liberal party, 1630's; apptd. agt. Va. Colony in Eng., 1640, presented the Assembly's petition to Parliament (which renewed original charter). Author: A Relation of a Journey Begun Anno Domingo 1610, published 1615; Ovid's Metamorphosis Englished by G.S., 1626; A Paraphrase upon the Psalmes of David and upon the Hymnes Dispersed Throughout the Old and New Testaments, 1636; Christ's Pasion (translated from Latin of Grotius), 1640; A Paraphrase upon the Song of Solomon, 1641. Died Boxley Abbey, Eng., Mar. 15, 1644; buried Boxley Church.

SANFORD, FERNANDO, physicist; b. Taylor, Ill., Feb. 12, 1854; s. Faxton and Mariah (Bly) S.; B.S., Carthage (Ill.) Coll., 1879, M.S., 1882, Sc.D., 1920; studied with Helmholtz in Berlin, 1886-88; m. Alice E. Crawford, Aug. 12, 1880; children—Burnett, Alice. Prof. physical science, Mt. Morris Coll., 1879-82; county supt. schs., Ogle County, Ill., 1882-86; instr. in physics and chemistry, Englewood High Sch., Chicago, 1888-90; prof. physical science, Lake Forest U., 1890-91; prof. physics, Leland Stanford jr. University, 1891-1919, since prof. emeritus. Fellow A.A.A.S., Am. Phys. Soc. Author: Elements of Physics, 1902; A Physical Theory of Electrification Charges of Atoms and Ions, 1919; A Diurnal Variation in the Electrical Potential of the Earth, 1920; Terrestrial Electricity, 1931; also numerous monographs pertaining to original investigations in physics. Engaged in investigations in the terrestrial electric observatory which he established at Palo Alto, 1920. Address: Palo Alto, Calif. Died May 21, 1948.

SANFORD, ROSCOE FRANK, astronomer; b. Faribault, Minn., Oct. 6, 1883; s. Frank William and Alberta Arilla (Nichols) S.; B.A., U. Minn., 1905; Ph.D., U. Cal., 1917; m. Mabel Aline Dyer, Dec. 12, 1917; children—Jane Dyer, Eleanor Nichols, Wallace Gordon, Allan Robert, Marguerite Anne. Tchr. mathematics, Marshall (Minn.) High Sch., 1905-06; Carnegie asst., Lick Obs., Mt. Hamilton, Cal., 1906-08, So. Obs. of Carnegie Inst., San Luis, Argentina, 1908-11; with D. O. Mills Expdn., Lick Obs., Santiago, Chile, 1911-15; on staff Dudley Obs., Albany, N.Y., 1917-18, Mt. Wilson Obs., Pasadena, Cal., 1918-50, Naval Ordnance Test Sta., Pasadena br., 1950—. Mem. Am. Astron. Soc., Astron. Soc. of Pacific, Internat. Astron. Union (Commn. No. 30), A.A.A.S. Presbyn. Contbr. to pubs. of astron. socs. Home: 1521 E. Mountain St. Office: Mt. Wilson Observatory, 813 Santa Barbara St., Pasadena, Cal. Died Apr. 7, 1958.

SANGER, CHARLES ROBERT, chemist; b. Boston, Aug. 31, 1860; s. George Partridge and Elizabeth Sherburne (Thompson) S.; A.B., Harvard, 1881, A.M., cum laude, 1882, A.M., and Ph.D., 1884; m. Almira Starkweather Horswell, Dec. 21, 1886 (died 1905); m. 2d, Eleanor Whitney Davis, May 2, 1910. Asst. in chemistry, Harvard Univ., 1881-82, 1884-86; prof. chemistry, U.S. Naval Acad., 1886-92, Washington U., St. Louis, 1892-99; asst. prof. chemistry, 1899-1903, prof. and dir. chem. lab., Sept. 1, 1903—, Harvard Univ. Fellow Am. Acad. Arts and Sciences. Home: Cambridge, Mass. Died Feb. 25, 1912.

SANGER, RALPH G(RAFTON), mathematician, educator; b. Cin., Apr. 10, 1905; s. Andrew Lewis and Louise (Pomeroy) S.; S.B., U. Chgo., 1925, S.M., 1926, Ph.D., 1931, student U. Wis., 1926-28. Instr. mathematics U. Wis., 1926-28; asst. U. Chgo., 1928-30, instr., 1930-40, asst. prof. 1940-46, asst. dean of students div. phys. scis., 1943-44, dean, 1944-46; prof. mathematics, head dept. Kan. State Coll., 1946—, acting dean sch. arts and scis., summer 1955, acting asso. dean sch. arts and sciences; 1955-56. Mem. Am. Math. Soc., Math. Assn. Am. (asso. editor Monthly 1931-40, gov. 1944-46, 49-51). Nat. Council Tchrs. Mathematics, Phi Beta Kappa, Sigma Xi. Author: Synthetic Projective Geometry, 1939. Home: 1400 Houston St., Manhattan, Kan. Died Mar. 1968.

SANTE, LE ROY, (sän'te), radiologist; b. St. Louis, Mo., Mar. 31, 1890; s. August Henry and Laura (Woodrow) S.; M.D., Washington U., St. Louis, Mo., 1913; grad. U.S. Army Sch. of Roentgenology, Fort Oglethorpe, Ga., 1918; m. Jewel Hartt, July 2, 1914; children—Elsie Eleanor (Mrs. Carl Edward Weaver), Le Roy (dec.), Henry. Interne and dispensary physician, St. Louis City Hosp., 1913-15; physician to St. Louis pub. schs., 1915-16; in gen. med. practice, Ellendale, N.D., 1916-18; chief radiologist St. Louis City Hospital, 1919-45, consulting radiologist, 1945-60; radiologist St. Louis University hospital group; St. Mary's Hosp., Firmin Desloge Hosp., Mount St. Rose Sanitorium, since 1920; consultant radiologist Koch Hosp. for Tuberculosis, St. Louis Training Sch., and Mo. State Sanitorium, since 1919; prof. radiology and dir. of dept., St. Louis U. Sch. of Medicine, 1919-60. Served with Med. Corps, U.S. Army, 1918-19. Diplomate and charter mem. Am. Bd. Radiology. Fellow Am. Coll. Physicians, Am. (recipient of the gold medal 1959), Inter American colleges radiology, American Trudeau Society; member Radiol. Soc. North Am., American Radium Soc. (past 1st v.p.), A.M.A., Mo. State and St. Louis (past president) med. socs., St. Louis Soc. Radiol. (past pres.), Am. Roentgen Ray Soc. (past 1st v.p., rep. on Am. Bd. Radiol. 10 yrs.), Am. Registry X-ray Technicians (past pres.), Denver, Panamanian (both hon.) radiol. socs., Tex. Society (hon.), Brit. Inst. Radiology (hon.), Mexican Radiol. and Physiotherapy Society (hon.), Alpha Omega Alpha and Sigma Xi fraternities. Republican. Presbyterian. Mason. Author: Lobar Pneumonia, a Roentgenological Study, 1928; The Chest Roentgenically Considered, 1929 (4 eds.); Manual of Roentgenological Technique, 1934 (20th rev. edit., 1962); Principles of Roentgenological Interpretation, 1937 (12th edit. 1961); Radiology For Nurses, 1936 (4th edit., 1945); Atlas of Miniature Roentgenograms, 1952. Contributor numerous articles on radiolog. subjects to professional jours. Home: 308 Orchard Av., Webster Groves, Mo. 63119. Office: Missouri Theatre Bldg., St. Louis, Mo. Died Oct. 27, 1964; buried Valhalla Cemetery, St. Louis.

SANTEE, HARRIS ELLETT, anatomist, neurologist; b. Snodes, O., Oct. 15, 1864; s. William B. and Catherine (Ellett) S.; A.B., Northeastern Ohio Normal Coll., 1889, hon. A.M., 1907; M.D., U. of Pa., 1892; A.M., Taylor U., 1900, Ph.D., 1901; m. Grace M. Brown, Aug. 28, 1895 (died 1903); children—Martha Boyle (Mrs. William Scott Walker), Mary Elizabeth (Mrs. George A. Langeler); m. 2d, Martha J. Pitt, Mar. 30, 1905. In practice at Chicago, 1892—; prof. anatomy, Harvey Med. Coll., 1896-1906, Jenner Med. Coll., 1906-18; prof. anatomy, Coll. of Phys. and Surg. (Univ. of Ill.), 1900-10; prof. nervous anatomy, Chicago Coll. Medicine and Surgery (med. dept., Valparaiso (Ind.) U.), 1910-17; dean and prof. diseases nervous system, Chicago Medical School, 1919-24. Republican. Conglist. Author: Anatomy of Brain and Spinal Cord (5th edit., 1915); Neurones and the Neurone Concept; The Brain of a Black Monkey; Important Anatomic and Physiologic Factors in Subarachnoid Medication; etc. Home: West Chicago, Ill. Died Feb. 28, 1936.

SAPIR, EDWARD, anthropologist, linguist; b. Lauenburg, Pomerania, Jan. 26, 1884; s. Jacob David and Eva (Sigel) S.; came with parents to U.S., 1889; A.B., Columbia, 1904, A.M., 1905, Ph.D., 1909, Sc.D., 1929; m. Florence Delson, 1911 (died 1924); children—Herbert Michael, Helen, Philip; m. 2d, Jean V. McClenaghan, 1926; children—Paul Edward, James David. Research assistant in anthropology, U. of California, 1907-08; instr. in anthropology, U. of Pa., 1908-10; chief of division of anthropology, Can. Nat. Museum, 1910-25, asso. prof. anthropology, U. of Chicago, 1925-27, prof. same and gen. linguistics, 1927-31; Sterling prof. anthology and linguistics, Yale, 1931. Mem. Am. Acad. Arts and Sciences; mem. Am. Anthropol. Assn. (pres.). Author: Wishram Texts, 1909; Takelma Texts, 1909; Yana Texts, 1910; The Takelma Language of S.W. Oregon, 1912; Time Perspective in Aboriginal American Culture, 1916; Language, an Introduction to the Study of Speech, 1921 (with Marius Barbeau) Folk-Songs of French Canada, 1925; The Southern Paiute Language, 1931. Home: Hamden, Conn. Died Feb. 4, 1939.

SAPPINGTON, CLARENCE OLDS, cons. industrial hygienist; b. Kansas City, Mo., Sept. 29, 1889; s. Lewis James and Cecelia May (Thompson) S.; A.B., Whitman Coll., 1911; M.D., Stanford, 1918; Dr.P.H., Harvard, 1924; m. Bertha Radovich, Feb. 3, 1920; 1 son, John Harvard (killed in action, Germany, Dec. 17, 1944). Assistant resident physician, Sacramento County Hosp., Calif., 1918-19, San Quentin Prison, Calif., 1919; alternating chief of Women's clinic Stanford U. Med. Sch., San Francisco, 1919-20; chief surgeon Pacific Coast Shipbuilding Co., Bay Point, Calif., 1919; asst. surgeon U.S.P.H.S., since 1920 (inactive list); fellow and teaching fellow in industrial hygiene, Harvard Sch. of Pub. Health, Boston, 1922-24; spl. lecturer in indsl. Hygiene, Stanford U., 1924-28; med. dir. Montgomery Ward & Co., Oakland, Calif., 1924-28, also served as spl. lecturer Stanford U., U. of Calif. and spl. editor on industrial medicine for "California and Western Medicine"; dir. Div. of Industrial Health of Nat. Safety Council (advisory service to industry on problems of health and safety), 1928-32; consultant, Indsl. Vision Inst., Purdue Univ. Pres. Central States Society Industrial Medicine and Surgery, 1942-43. Fellow Am. Med. Assn., Am. Public Health Assn., A.A.A.S., Am. Assn. Industrial Phys. and Surg.; fellow Am. Acad. Occupational Medicine; diplomate Am. Bd. Preventive Medicine and Public Health; mem. Am. Industrial Hygiene Assn., Indsl. Hygiene Foundation of Am.; chairman sect. on Preventive and Indsl. Medicine and Public Health, A.M.A., 1946-47; pres. Harvard Pub. Health Alumni Assn., 1945-47. Member Am. Chem. Soc., Nat. Safety Council, Indsl. Management Soc., Ill. Mfrs. Assn., Ill., State and Chicago Med. Socs., Ill. State Acad. Science, Delta Omega, Alpha Kappa Kappa, Pi Gamma Mu. Del. Internat. Hygiene Congresses, Dresden, 1930; mem. 6th Internat. Congress Industrial Accidents and Diseases, Geneva, 1931 and 7th Congress, Brussels, 1935. Republican. Congregationalist. Mason. Clubs: South Shore Country, Executives (Chicago). Contbr. on industrial hygiene, industrial medicine and occupational diseases. An authority on medico-legal aspects of occupational diseases and indsl. health adminstrn. First American to receive degree of Dr.P.H. in the field of industrial hygiene. Mem. bd. editors Sight Saving Review. Editor of "Industrial Medicine." Author: Medico-legal Phases of Occupational Diseases, 1939, (received the first Wm. S. Knudsen award for the most outstanding contribution to industrial medicine, 1938-39); Industrial Health—Asset or Liability, 1939; Essentials of Industrial Health, 1943. Recently lecturer on indsl. health, univ. nursing schs., Loyola U. and U. of Chicago, U. of Ill., Med. Sch., and Purdue U. Engring. Schs. Home: 1949 E. 73d Pl. Office: 330 S. Wells St., Chicago 6. Died Nov. 6, 1949.

SAPPINGTON, JOHN, physician; b. Md., May 15, 1776; s. Mark Brown and Rebecca (Boyce) S.; attended course med. lectures U. Pa., 1814-15; m. Jane Breathitt, Nov. 22, 1804. Settled in Saline County, Mo. (Kan.), 1817; strong advocate use of quinine for malaria without recourse to treatment by bleeding, vomiting, purging; began wholesale distbn. Dr. John Sappington's Anti-Fever Pills, 1832. Author: Theory and Treatment of Fevers (perhaps 1st med. treatise written West of Mississippi River), 1844. Died Sept. 7, 1856.

SARDESON, FREDERICK WILLIAM, (sar'de-sun), geologist, paleontologist; b. Owego Mills, town of Wiota, Wis., Feb. 22, 1866; s. Joseph and Petra (Rossing) S.; B.L., U. of Minn., 1891, M.S., 1892; Ph.D., U. of Freiburg, 1895; m. Edna A. Mitchell, June 16, 1903; 1 dau., Marion Petra. Instr. of palaeontology, 1892-94, 1898-1905, asst. prof., 1905-14, Univ. of Minn. Geologist, U.S. Geol. Survey, 1911-24; geologist examiner for Minn. State Securities Commn., 1917-34, now cons. geologist. Mem. Internat. Geol. Congress, 1894. Fellow A.A.A.S., Geol. Soc. America, Phi Beta Kappa, Sigma Xi, etc. Writer geology reports and contbr. on geol., paleontol., philos. and ednl. subjects. Address: 2434 S. 158 St., Seattle 88. Died Aug. 28, 1958; buried Forest Lawn Mausoleum, Seattle.

SARGENT, CHARLES SPRAGUE, dentrologist; b. Boston, Mass., Apr. 24, 1841; s. Ignatius and Henrietta (Gray) S.; A.B., Harvard, 1862, LL.D., 1901; m. Mary Allen, d. Andrew Robeson, of Boston, Nov. 28, 1873. First lt. 2d La. Inf., June 25, 1863; capt. a.d.c. vols., Mar. 15, 1865; bvtd. maj. vols., Mar. 26, 1865, "for faithful and meritorious services" during campaign against Mobile; hon. mustered out, Aug. 26, 1865. Prof. horticulture, 1872-73, dir. Botanic Garden, 1873-79, dir. Arnold Arboretum, 1872—, prof. aboriculture, 1879—, Harvard. Editor Garden and Forest, 1887-97. Planned Jesup collection of N. Am. woods for Am. Mus. Natural History, New York; was chmn. commn. for preservation of Adirondack forests, 1885; chmn. commn. apptd. by Nat. Acad. Sciences upon a forest policy for the forestry lands of the U.S., 1896-97; trustee Mus. Fine Arts, Boston; mem. Park Commn., Town of Brookline. Fellow Am. Acad. Arts and Sciences; pres. Mass. Soc. Promotion Agriculture, 1890—; trustee Mass. Hort. Soc. Author: Catalogue of the Forest Trees of North America; The Woods of the United States; The Forest Flora of Japan; Silva of North America; Report of the Forests of North America; Manual of the Trees of North America, 1905, 1922; Trees and Shrubs. Home: Brookline, Mass. Died Mar. 22, 1927.

SARGENT, FREDERICK, engineer; b. Liskeard, Cornwall, Eng., Nov. 11, 1859; s. Daniel and Jane (Yates) S.; ed. Anderson U., Glasgow; came to U.S., 1883; m. Laura S. Sleep, 1885. Consulting engr., Chicago, 1890—; mgr. mech. and elec. depts., World's Fair, Chicago, 1893 (awarded artists' medal); sr. mem. Sargent & Lundy, engrs. Home: Glencoe, Ill. Died July 26, 1919.

SARGENT, FREDERICK LE ROY, botanist, artist; b. Boston, Dec. 25, 1863; s. George Frederick and Mary Motley (Gavett) S.; Coll. City of New York, 1879-81; spl. course botany, Lawrence Scientific Sch. (Harvard), 1883-86; m. Helen M. C. Child, July 9, 1902; m. 2d,

Bertha Taylor Parker, June 15, 1905. Teacher summer sch. of botany, Harvard, 1886; head dept. botany, U. of Wis., 1886-87; instr. botany, Med. Sch., Boston U., 1894-95; pres. Columbine Assn.; pres. Nat. Flower Conv., Asheville, N.C., 1896. Author: Guide to Cryptogams, 1886; Through a Microscope (joint author), 1886; A Key to North American Species of Cladonia, Cambridge, 1893; How to Describe a Flowering Plant, 1894; Corn Plants—Their Uses and Ways of Life, 1899; Omar and the Rabbi, 1919; Plants and Their Uses, 1913. Fellow A.A.A.S. Home: Cambridge, Mass. Died Jan. 16, 1928.

SARGENT, HENRY WINTHROP, horticulturist; b. Boston, Nov. 26, 1810; s. Henry and Hannah (Welles) S.; grad. Harvard, 1830; m. Caroline Olmsted, Jan. 10, 1839, 3 children. Partner banking house of Gracie & Sargent, N.Y.C., 1831-41; ret. to estate nr. Fishkill-on-the-Hudson (now Beacon), N.Y., 1841, engaged in horticulture and landscape gardening; travelled in Europe to gather plants and study parks, 1847-49, Author: Skeleton Tours, 1870; also supplements for 2 books by Andrew Downing: A Treatise on the Theory and Practise of Landscape Gardening, 1841; Cottage Residences, 1842. Died Fishkill-on-the-Hudson, Nov. 11, 1882.

SARGENT, JAMES, inventor; b. Chester, Vt., Dec. 5, 1824; s. William and Hannah S.; ed. dist. schs.; worked on farm and later foreman in woolen mill; m. Angeline M., d. Job and Hannah Foster, Apr. 29, 1847. Was traveling daguerreotyper, 1848-52; mfd. and sold an automatic apple-parer, 1852-57; partner Yale & Greenleaf Lock Co., 1857-65; invented burglar-proof locks and established in business in Rochester, 1865; invented Sargent timelocks, 1873; later added many styles of patented locks; pres. Sargent & Greenleaf Co., mfrs.; pres. Pfaudler Vacuum Fermentation Co., and inventor their glass enameled steel tanks and vacuum pump; inventor, automatic electric "semaphore" ry. signals, and pres. Gordon Railway Signal Co.; inventor automatic smoke consumer; pres. Waterloo Gold Mining Co., Calif. Home: Rochester, N.Y. Died 1910.

SARGENT, PAUL DUDLEY, civil engr.; b. Machias, Me., May 8, 1873; s. Ignatius Manlius and Helen Maria (Campbell) S.; B.C.E., U. of Me., 1896; m. Sarah Sawyer McAllister, of Calais, Me., June 6, 1900. Asst. engr., Washington Co. R.R., Me., during construction, 1897-98, and same position, maintenance of way dept., 1899-1903; register of deeds, Washington Co., 1903-05; state highway commr., Me., 1905-11; asst. dir. Office of Pub. Rds., U.S. Dept. Agr., Feb. 15, 1911-Sept. 1, 1913; chief engr. State Highway Commn. Me., since Sept. 1, 1913. Mem. Me. N.G., 1896-99. Mem. Am. Soc. C.E., Am. Soc. for Testing Materials, Me. Soc. C.E., S.A.R., Mass. Highway Assn., Am. Rd. Builders' Assn., Phi Gamma Delta. Mem. exec. com. Federal Highway Council; mem. Am. Assn. State Highway Officials (pres. 1920). Republican. Universalist. Mason (K.T., Shriner). Clubs: Abnaki, Augusta Rotary (pres. 1923-24), Augusta Country. Home: 83 Western Av., Augusta ME

SARNOFF, DAVID, chmn. RCA; b. Uzlian, Minsk, Russia, Feb. 27, 1891; s. Abraham and Lena (Privin) S.; brought to U.S., 1900; ed. pub. schs. and spl. course in elec. engring. Pratt Inst., Brooklyn, N.Y.; D.Sc., St. Lawrence U., 1927; D.Sc., Marietta College, 1935, Suffolk Univ., 1939, Suffolk Univ., 1939, Pa. Mil. College, 1952; D.Litt., Norwich U., 1935; D.C.S., Oglethorpe U., 1938, Boston U., 1948; LL.D., Jewish Theol. Sem. of Am., 1946, Bethany Coll., 1946, John Carroll U., 1950, University Pa., 1952, Fairleigh Dickinson Coll., 1953, U. So. Cal. Pratt Inst., 1954; L.H.D., U. Louisville, 1950; D.Eng., Drexel Inst. Tech., 1953; D.Sc., U. Notre Dame, 1955, Temple U., 1958; LL.D., Fordham U., 1955, Dropsie Coll., 1957, U.R.I., 1957; m. Lizette Hermant, July 4, 1917; children—Robert William, Edward, Thomas Warren. Messenger boy with Comml. Cable Co., 1906; same yr. became office boy Marconi Wireless Telegraph Co.; promoted to mgr. Marconi Sta., Sea Gate, N.Y., 1909; wireless operator on S.S. Beothic, Newfoundland, and equipped vessel and made trip as operator to Arctic ice fields on sealfishing expdn., 1911; wireless operator on S.S. Harvard, 1910, later at John Wanamaker's, N.Y., 1911-12; radio insp. Marconi Co. and instr. Marconi Inst., 1912; chief radio insp. and asst. chief engr., Marconi Co., 1913; successively contract mgr., asst. traffic mgr. and commercial mgr. same co., until 1919, and upon absorption of Marconi Co., by Radio Corp. of America, 1919, was taken over as commercial mgr. of latter, then elected gen. mgr., 1921, v.p. and gen. mgr., 1922, exec. v.p., 1929, pres., 1930, chmn. bd., 1947-69, hon. chmn., 1970-71; chmn. bd. dir. RCA Communications Inc.; dir. NBC, Chatham Square Music School. Trustee American Heritage Found., Ednl. Alliance, Thomas A. Edison Found., Nat. Found. Infantile Paralysis, United Seamen's Service, Inc., U.S. Council Internat. C. of C., Pratt Inst., N.Y. U. Dir. Armed Forces Communications Assn.; councillor N.Y.U. Nat. chmn. A.R.C. Fund Campaign, 1954. Chmn. Nat. Security Training Commission, 1955. Commd. lieut. col., S.C. Res., U.S. Army, 1924, col., 1931, brig. gen., 1944, brig. gen. Army of the U.S. Hon. Reserve. Decorated Officer Polonia Restituta (Poland), Chevalier Legion of Honor, Officer Legion of Honor, Comdr. Legion of Honor (France), Officer Order Oaken Crown (Luxembourg), Legion of Merit, Medal for Merit, U.S. Treasury's Silver Medal, Richard J. H. Gettheil Medal; recipient Horatio Alger award, 1951; Gold Citizenship Medal and Citation of Vets. Fgn. Wars, 1950; Pub. Service Award of Merit presented by Civil Service Leader, 1951; Annual award from Radio-Television Mfrs. Assn., 1952; founder award Inst. Radio Engrs., 1953; first ann. Keynoter award Nat. Assn. Radio and Television Broadcasters, 1953; Engring and Science award Drexel Institute of Technology, 1953, numerous others. Fellow I.E.E.E., Royal Soc. Arts (London); hon. fellow Weizmann Inst. Sci.; hon. mem. Brit. Instn. Radio Engrs.; mem. Academy of Political Science, Armed Forces Advisory Com., N.Y. State C. of C., Council Fgn. Relations, Mil. Govt. Assn., Mil. Order World Wars, Nat. Aero Assn., Nat. Inst. Social Scis., N.Y. Soc. Mil. and Naval Officers World Wars, Grant Monument Assn. (trustee), Naval Order U.S. (life mem.), U.S. Naval Inst., Am. Shakespeare Festival Found., Crusade for Freedom (chmn. Greater N.Y. com. 1951). Newcomen Soc. Eng., Res Officers Assn., Radio Pioneers, Vet. Wireless Operators Association, honorary mem. Brit. Instn. Radio Engrs., Radio Club America, Beta Gamma Sigma, Tau Delta Phi. Clubs: India House, Century Country, Lotos, Rockefeller Center Luncheon (New York City); Army-Navy, Metropolitan, Federal City (Washington). Author: Looking Ahead, 1968. Office: New York City NY Died Dec. 12, 1971; buried Valhalla Cemetery Valhalla NY

SATTERTHWAITE, THOMAS EDWARD, M.D.; b. New York, Mar. 26, 1843; s. Thomas Wilkinson and Ann Fisher (Sheafe) S.; A.B., Yale, 1864; Harvard Med. Sch., 1864-65; M.D., Coll. Phys. and Surg. (Columbia), New York, 1867; interne New York Hosp., 1867-69 (for 20 months), receiving diploma for surgery; LL.D., U. of Md., 1908; Sc.D., St. John's Coll., Md., 1912; m. Isabella, d. Dr. James Lenox Banks, of New York, 1884. Studied in Vienna, 1869-70; served in Franco-German War as asst. surgeon and surgeon Prussian Army. Microscopist and later pathologist at St. Luke's Hosp., N.Y. City, 1872-82; pathologist Presbyn. Hosp., 1873-88; one of the founders, sec. 2 yrs., prof. pathol. anatomy, 1 yr., and of gen. medicine, 7 yrs., v.p., 1890, prof. medicine, 1904-08, Post-Grad. Med. School; lecturer comparative pathology, Columbia Vet. Coll., 1881-82; organized med. and surg. staff, Chambers St. House of Relief (now Hudson St. Hosp.), 1875; a founder, and pres., 1894-99, Babies' Hosp.; now consulting physician to Post-Graduate, Orthopedic and Manhattan State hosps., New York. First lt., U.S.A.M.R.C., 1911-17. Pres. New York Pathol. Soc., 1880-81; one of founders and pres., 1902-03, Am. Therapeutic Soc.; a founder Am. Coll. Physicians; fellow N.Y. Acad. Medicine. Author: Manual of Histology, 1881; Practical Bacteriology, 1887; Diseases of the Heart and Aorta, 1905; Cardiovascular Diseases, 1912; Diseases of the Heart and Blood Vessels, 1918. Retired from practice, 1923. Died Sept. 19, 1934.

SAUGRAIN DE VIGNI, ANTOINE FRANCOIS, physician; b. Paris, France, Feb. 17, 1763; s. Antoine and Marie (Brunet) Saugrain; m. Genevieve Rosalie Michau, Mar. 20, 1793, 6 children. Went to Mexico to examine mines and mineral prodn., 1785-86; sailed for U.S., 1787; taken captive by Indians in attack, escaped, 1788; apptd. post surgeon by Spanish lt. gov. Delassus, St. Louis, 1800; army surgeon (apptd. by Jefferson), 1805-11; only practicing physician in St. Louis when Upper Louisiana was transferred to U.S.; made and sold ink, thermometers, phosphoric lights for hunters, barometers; conducted experiments in electricity and had electric battery; introduced 1st smallpox vaccine virus brought to St. Louis and publicly offered to vaccinate free of charge all indigent persons, paupers and Indians, 1809. Died circa May 19, 1820.

SAUNDERS, DEALTON, botanist, S. Dak. Agr'l Coll. Expt. Sta. since 1897; b. Alfred, N.Y., 1869; grad. Univ. of Neb., 1893 (A.M., 1894); m. Dec. 29, 1897, Eva Merritt, Wellsville, N.Y. Instr. in biology, Lincoln High School, 1895-6; specialist on the algae (phycology). Address: Brookings SD

SAUNDERS, FREDERICK A(LBERT), physicist; b. London, Ont., Can., Aug. 18, 1875; s. William and Sarah Agnes (Robinson) S.; B.A., Toronto U., 1895; Ph.D., Johns Hopkins, 1899; m. Grace A. Elder, June 2, 1900; children—Anthony Elder (dec. 1943), Margery (Mrs. John B. Middleton); m. 2d, Margaret Tucker, Oct. 21, 1925. Instr. physics, Haverford (Pa.) Coll., 1899-1901: instr. physics, Syracuse. 1901-02, asso. prof., 1902-05, prof., 1905-14; prof. physics, Vassar College, 1914-19; asst. prof. physics, Harvard, 1919-20, asso. prof., 1920-23, prof., 1923-41, prof. emeritus, 1941—; vis. lectr. in physics, Mt. Holyoke, 1942-48. Fellow Nat. Acad. Scis., A.A.A.S., Am. Physical Soc., Acoustical Soc. Am. (pres. 1937-39); mem. Phi Beta Kappa, Sigma Xi. Home: South Hadley, Mass. Died June 9, 1963.

SAUNDERS, LOWELL WALTER, oil geologist; b. Red Bluff, Cal., Sept. 30, 1901; s. Edgar Waller and Frances Elvira (Swain) S.; A.B., Stanford, 1922, grad. student, 1923; m. Edna Mae Sells, Dec. 5, 1923; children—Edward William, Diane (Mrs. Don C. Lake), Doska, Susan Gene. Surveyor, draftsman Nat. Coal Co., Price, Utah, 1920; drilling dept. Ethel D. Oil Co., Maricopa, Cal., 1923; insp. Cal. State Mining Bur., Taft, Cal., 1924, Los Angeles, 1925, engr. Long Beach and Huntington Beach, 1926; resident geologist Hugh B. Evans, Inc., Taft, 1927; geologist Cal. Petroleum Corp. and The Texas Co., 1927-28; geologist The Ohio Oil Co., Bakersfield, Cal., 1929-35; cons. geologist KCL Bldg., Bakersfield, 1935-39; with Intex Oil Co. since 1939, v.p., 1939-48, pres., 1948-52, chmn. bd. since 1953. Councilman, Bakersfield. Mem. Am. Assn. Petroleum Geologists, Soc. Econ. Geologists, Am. Soc. Mil. Engrs. Clubs: Stockdale; Los Angeles Petroleum. Home: 2731 18th St. Office: 531 California Av., Bakersfield, Cal. Died June 20, 1954.

SAUNDERS, WALTER MILLS, chemist; b. Johnston, R.I., July 28, 1866; s. Joseph Henry and Sophronia (Waterman) S.; ed. pub. schs. Johnston and Providence; studied Mass. Inst. Technology and Brown Univ., 1884-88; m. Providence, Feb. 11, 1896, Florence M. Sutcliffe. In practice as analytical and consulting chemist since 1894; v.p. Am. Chem. Soc., 1900-02. Mem. Soc. Chem. Industry, Franklin Inst. and other scientific socs. Residence: 20 Dewey St. Office: 184 Whittier Av., Providence.

SAUNDERS, WILLIAM, horticulturist; b. St. Andrews, Scotland, Dec. 7, 1822; attended U. Edinburgh (Scotland); m. Martha Mildwaters, 1848. Came to U.S., 1848; in partnership with Thomas Meehan in landscape gardening, Phila., 1854-62; designed several parks and cemeteries including Rose Hill Cemetary, Chgo.; supt. exptl. gardens of U.S. Dept. Agr., 1862-1900; designed grounds of Dept. Agr. at Washington, D.C., nat. cemetary at Gettysburg, grounds for Lincoln monument in Springfield, Ill., and U.S. Dept. Agr. exhibits for Centennial Exhbn., Phila., 1876, New Orleans Expn., 1884, Paris Exhbn., 1889; established conservatories and greenhouses for study of economically important plants; mem. Parking Commn. of Washington, 1871; introduced Washington Navel orange from Brazil, 1871, several hundred varieties of Russian apples, 1870, eucaylptus globulus from Australia, 1866; co-founder Patrons of Husbandry, 1867, pres., 1867-73. Died. Sept. 11, 1900.

SAUNDERS, WILLIAM LAWRENCE, engineer; b. Columbus, Ga., Nov. 1, 1856; s. W. T. (D.D.) and Eliza (Morton) S.; B.S., U. of Pa., 1876 (Sc.D., same, 1911); m. Bertha Louise Gaston, Aug. 4, 1886 (died 1906). In charge of hydrographic work, 1878, and sub-aqueous rock excavation, 1878-82, Nat. Storage Co., of Communipaw, N.J.; chmn. bd. Ingersoll-Rand Co.; pres. Stayley-Saunders Corp.; dir. A. S. Cameron Steam Pump Works, N.Y. & Honduras Rosario Mining Co. Gov., dir., dep. chmn. Fed. Res. Bank of N.Y., also mem. dist. com. on capital issues, Federal Reserve Bd., World War. Invented apparatus for sub-aqueous drilling, using tube and water jet system in gen. use in Baku oil fields, Russia; system of pumping liquids by compressed air; radialaxe system of coal mining; invented apparatus for Ingersoll track and bar channelers and gadders for quarrying stone. Aptd. mem. N.J. Harbor Commn.; mem. N.J. Bd. Commerce and Navigation; chmn. Permanent Group Com. for Nicaragua; mem. Naval Consulting Bd. of U.S., 1915—(chmn.). Was mem. N.J. State Dem. Com.; twice elected mayor of N. Plainfield, N.J.; mem. Dem. Nat. Campaign Com., 1916. Fellow Am. Geog. Soc., Acad. Polit. Science, Am. Acad. Polit. and Social Science; mem. numerous societies, civic orgns., etc. Del. as representative of A.I.M.E. at 1st Empire Mining and Metall. Congress, Wembly Expn., London, Eng., 1924. An organizer, and mem. during World War, of Mil. Engring. Com. which, at its own expense, equipped a regt. and sent it to France—the 1st regt. of engrs. to pass through London, and the 1st in action at the front. Episcopalian. Editor, now pres. Compressed Air Magazine. Author: Compressed Air Information; Compressed Air Production. Co-author: The Subways and Tunnels of New York; Rock Drilling. Founder, 1926, of Mining Medal, to recognize achievement in mining, by A.I.M.E. Home: Plainfield, N.J. Died June 25, 1931.

SAUVEUR, ALBERT, univ. prof., b. Louvain, Belgium, June 21, 1863; s. Lambert and Hortense (Franquin) Sauveur (French parentage); ed. Athénée Royal (Brussels, Belgium), and in School of Mines (Liège), 1881-86; S.B., in mining and metallurgy, Mass. Inst. Tech., 1889; Sc.D., Case Sch. of Applied Science, 1921; Sc.D., U. of Grenoble, France, 1924, U. of San Marcos, Peru, 1925, Harvard, 1935, Dr. of Engring. Lehigh U., 1926; m. Mary Prince Jones, June 4, 1891; children—Hortense (Mrs. Romeyn Taylor), Mary Isabella (Mrs. George C. Eaton), Albert (dec.). Chemist and metallurgist various steel cos., 1889-97; instr. metallurgy, 1889-1900, asst. prof. metallurgy and metallography, 1900-05, prof. metallurgy, 1905, Gordon McKay professor, 1924-35, emeritus, 1935—, all of Harvard University. Editor The Metallographist, 1898-1903; editor Iron and Steel Magazine, 1903-06. Officier d'Académie; Officier Légion d'Honneur; Officier Order of Leopold (Belgium); awarded Elliott Cresson gold medal, Franklin Inst., Phila., 1913; Bessemer medalist, Brit. Iron and Steel Inst., 1924; first recipient of the Albert Sauveur Achievement medal, from the Am. Society for Metals. Fellow Am. Acad. Arts and Sciences, A.A.A.S.; pres. John Fritz Medal Bd. of Awards, 1916-17; hon. mem. Am. Inst. Mining and Metall. Engineers (v.p. 1910-12), Am. Society for

Metals, Society Engineers Liège Sch. of Mines, Soc. Ingénieurs Civils ce France, Society de l'Industrie Nationale; corr. mem. Society Encouragement Nat. Industry (France); pres. Salon Français (Boston), 1920-24. Metallurgist, Am. Aviation Commn. in France, 1917-19; metallurgical expert to the French Ministry of Munitions, 1917-19. Henry Marion Howe lecturer for 1924 (Am. Inst. Mining and Metall. Engrs.); Henry de Mille Campbell lecturer for 1929 (Am. Soc. for Steel Treating); Marburgh lecturer for 1938 (Am. Soc. for Testing Materials). U.S. del. 3d Pan.-Am. Scientific Congress, Lima, Peru, 1924. Author: The Metallography of Iron and Steel; Metallurgical Dialogues. Home: Cambridge, Mass. Died Jan. 26, 1939.

SAVAGE, ELMER SETH, prof. animal husbandry; b. Lancaster, N.H., June 15, 1884; s. John and Catherine M. (Daley) S.; B.S.A., N.H. Coll., Durham, 1905; M.S.A., Cornell, 1909, Ph.D., 1911; hon. D.Sc., U. of New Hampshire, 1933; m. Clara Blandford, Sept. 9, 1908; children—Ruth Cecelia, Clara Catherine Margaret; m. 2d, Genevieve Boyle, June 29, 1916; children—Mary Gene, Joan. Asst. in animal husbandry, 1907-08, instr., 1908-10, asst. prof., 1910-13, prof. since 1913, Cornell U. Fellow A.A.A.S.; mem. Am. Soc. Animal Production, Sigma Xi, Gamma Alpha, Kappa Sigma, Alpha Zeta. Republican. K.C. Author: Feeds and Feeding Manual, 1913; Feeding Dairy Cattle, 1917; (with L. A. Maynard) Better Dairy Farming, 1923. Home: 106 Harvard Pl., Ithaca, N.Y. Died Nov. 22, 1943.

SAVAGE, HIRAM NEWTON, civil engr.; b. Lancaster, N.H., Oct. 6, 1861; s. Hazen Nelson and Laura Ann (Newton) S.; B.S., New Hampshire Coll. Agr. and Mechanic Arts, 1887; C.E., Thayer Sch. of Civil Engring. (Dartmouth), 1891; D.Sc., Univ. of N.H., 1913; m. Linna Belle Clough, Dec. 1891 (died 1897); children—Lucy Eunice (Mrs. Robert L. Colthart), Laura Ada (Mrs. Laurence W. Hope); m. 3d, Eugenia Hurlock, 1927. Assistant engineer, East Tennessee, Virginia & Georgia R.R., Nashville & Tellico R.R. and Athens (Tenn.) Improvement Co., 1888; chief engr. Hydraulic Mining & Irrigation Co., N.M., 1889-90; engr. and supt. constrn. Billings Park and race track, White River Junction, Vt., and designed and located sewerage system for W. Randolph, Vt., 1890; chief engr. San Diego (Calif.) Land & Town Co., Sweetwater dam system, San Diego, 1891-1903; chief engr. Sweetwater Park and Race Track, 1893-94; cons. engr. San Diego & Cuyamaca R.R., San Diego & La Jolla R.R., Coronado Beach R.R., 1893-1903, Cuyamaca (Calif.) Water Co., 1896; chief engr. to contractor for U.S. Govt. San Diego Bay-Zuninga Shoals Jetty, 1894-98; cons. engr. Southern Calif. Mountain Water Co., Lower Otay Dam, Upper Otay Dam. Barrett Dam, Morena Dam & Carrying System to San Diego, 1893-1903; cons. engr. U.S. Govt. Reclamation Service, Aug. 12, 1903—; also supervising engr. Northern Div. in charge investigation, designs, construction, operation 12 irrigation projects and storage features, including Shoshone Dam (highest in the world), Corbett Tunnel, etc., total expenditures about $3,000,000 annually, 1904-15; cons. and constrn. engr. Sweetwater Water Co., enlargement extension Sweetwater Dam and Water Carrying System, 1916-17; hydraulic engr. City of San Diego (Calif.) Municipal Water System impounding and carrying features; designed and constructed with city forces, Lower Otay Dam, Barrett Dam, Morena Dam and Spillway enlargement, Rapid High Pressure Filtration Plant; directed investigation of all additional Water Supply resources in San Diego Co. and vicinity; field location and design all impounding and carrying features for fifty years future water requirements, estimated cost over $100,000,000, 1917-23. Toured world 3 times for engring. and architectural research; reported on tech. administrative matters and requirements to the President of U.S., 1925-26; cons. engr. The Research Service (internat.), Washington, also of Newell, Corse & McDaniel, Washington, D.C.; recalled to San Diego, 1928, to take charge of Municipal Bur. of Water Development. Mason. Home: San Diego, Calif. Deceased.

SAVAGE, JOHN LUCIAN, civil engr.; b. Cooksville, Wis., Dec. 25, 1879; s. Edwin Parker and Mary Therese (Stebbins) S.; B.S. in C.E., U. Wis., 1903, D.Sc., 1934; D.Sc., U. Denver, 1946; D.Eng., U. Colo., 1947; m. Jessie Burdick Sexsmith, June 1, 1918 (died July 1940); m. Olga Lacher Miner, Jan. 14, 1950. Asst. engr. and engr., U.S. Reclamation Service, Idaho Div., 1903-08; asso. with A.J. Wiley, cons. engr., on gen. cons. practice in irrigation and hydro-electric fields, projects in western states, 1908-16 designing engr. for U.S. Reclamation Service in charge of civ. engring. design, 1916-24 chief designing engr. in charge of all designing including civ., elec. and mech. work, 1924-45; maj. projects include dams and power plants throughout western U.S. Cons. engr. on hydro projects, power and irrigation projects for fgn. govts. in Australia, Asia, Near East, Africa and Latin Am.; cons. engr. Bur. of Reclamation and T.V.A., 1945—. Received Engring. Council gold medal, 1937, John Fritz medal. 1945, Henry C. Turner gold medal, 1946, Nat. Resources Commn. of China gold medal, 1944, Washington award, 1949; Gold Medal award, Dept. Interior, elected Reclamation Hall Fame, 1950; Popular Mechanics Hall Fame award, 1952; Order of Ching Hsin (Nationalist Govt. China), 1952. Hon. life mem. Reclamation Tech. Club. Fellow A.A.A.S.; mem. Nat. Acad. Scis., Am. Soc. C.E. (hon.), Am. Soc. Testing Materials, Colo. Soc. Engrs., Am. Concrete Inst., Instn. Civil Engrs. (London), Tau Beta Pi, Sigma Xi, Chi Epsilon. Home: 1651 Dahlia St., Denver 7. Died Dec. 1967.

SAVAGE, LEONARD JIMMIE, educator, statistician; b. Detroit, Nov. 20, 1917; s. Louis and Mae (Rugawitz) S.; B.S., U. Mich., 1938, Ph.D. in Math., 1941; D.Sc. (hon.), U. Rochester; m. Jean Strickland, July 10, 1964; children by previous marriage—Sam Linton, Frank Albert. Rackham fellow Inst. Advanced Study, Princeton, 1941-42; instr. math. Cornell U., 1942-43; research mathematician Brown U., 1943; research asso. Columbia, 1944-45, N.Y.U., 1945-46; Rockefeller fellow Marine Biol. Lab., Woods Hole, Mass. and U. Chgo., 1946-47; research asso. U. Chgo., 1947-49, mem. faculty, 1949-50, prof., 1954-60, chmn. dept., 1956-59; prof. U. Mich., 1960-64; Eugene Higgins prof. statistics Yale, 1964-71. Guggenheim fellow Paris, France and Cambridge, Eng., 1951-52, Rome, Italy, 1968; Fulbright grantee, France, 1951-52; fellow Center Advanced Study Behavioral Sci., 1963-64. Fellow Inst. Math. Statistics (pres. 1957-58), Am. Statis. Assn., A.A.A.S.; mem. Internat. Statis. Inst., Am. Math. Soc. Author: Foundations of Statistics, 1954; (with L. E. Dubins) How to Gamble If You Must, 1965. Home: New Haven CT Died Nov. 2, 1971.

SAVAGE, MARION ALEXANDER, designing engr.; b. Walterboro, S.C., Sept. 3, 1885; s. Charles Alexander and Ina (Dunwody) S.; B.S., Clemson Coll., 1906, hon. E.E., 1927; m. Jessie Rivers, June 20, 1911; children—Jessie Rivers, Evelyn Henderson. With Gen. Electric Co. since 1909, in alternating current engring. sect., 1909-23, in charge turbine generator dept., 1923-31, designing engr. turbine generator dept., Schenectady, N.Y., since 1931; has worked on transformer tests, built tech. foundation in marine equipment, induction motors, generators, turbines, etc. Received Coffin award, 1932; Lamme medal, 1938. Mem. Am. Inst. E.E. Contbr. numerous scientific articles to Am. Inst. E.E. publs.; presented paper on "Economic Development in Turbin Generators in the U.S." before Second World Conf. of Am. Inst. E.E., Berlin, Germany, 1930. As result of numerous inventions he has made possible use of high speed steam driven generators of large capacity. Home: 17 Sunnyside Rd., Scotia 2, N.Y. Office: General Electric Co., Schenectady, N.Y. Died Apr. 9, 1946.

SAVAGE, THOMAS EDMUND, geologist; b. Salem, Ia., Jan. 8, 1866; s. of John and Tacy (Crew) S.; B.A., Iowa Wesleyan U., 1895; B.S., U. of Iowa, 1897, M.S., 1899; Johns Hopkins, 1906-07; Ph.D., Yale, 1909; m. Elinor Dubal, of Iowa City, Ia., July 21, 1900. Prin. high sch., Mt. Pleasant, 1895-96; prof. geology and biology, Western College, Toledo, Ia., 1899-1903; asst. geologist, Ia. Geol. Survey, 1899-1903; assistant state geologist, Ia., 1903-06; now prof. geology, U. of Ill., and geologist, Ill. Geol. Survey, 1906—. Fellow Geol. Soc. America, A.A.A.S., Ill. State Acad. Science; mem. Paleontol. Soc. America, Beta Theta Pi, Sigma Xi. Republican. Conglist. Contbr. numerous scientific papers on geology and paleontology. Geologist Navy Alaskan Coal Commn., 1920-21. Address: 613 W. Nevada St., Urbana, Ill.

SAVILLE, CALEB MILLS, hydraulic engr.; b. Melrose, Mass., May 27, 1865; s. George W. W. and Helen (Mills) S.; A.B., Harvard, 1889; post-grad. work Lawrence Scientific Sch. 1 yr.; m. Elizabeth Thorndike, Oct. 1891; 1 son, Thorndike. Div. engr. Met. Water Bd., Boston, 1895-1905; hydraulic specialist with French & Bryant, Brookline, 1905-07; engr. in charge 3d div., Isthmian Canal, 1907-12, conducting investigations on foundations, etc., of Gatun Dam, resulting in construction of the dam at that locality; also investigations in hydrology and meteorology of Panama Canal, triangulation survey of Canal Zone, etc.; mgr. and chief engr. Bureau of Water, Metropolitan Dist., Hartford, Conn., for installation and operation of new water supply for Hartford costing about $40,000,000; consulting engineer The Water Bureau since 1948; mem. Com. on Regional Planning, Metropolitan Dist. Awarded Norman medal, Am. Soc. C.E., 1914, Brackett Memorial medal, N.E. Water Works Assn., 1917, 27 and 34; President's Premium, Inst. of Water Engrs. (Eng.), 1931; prize of Conn. Soc. Civil Engrs., 1945. Honorary mem. New England Water Works Assn. (past pres.), Connecticut Soc. Civil Engrs.; mem. Institute of Water Engrs. (England), Am. Water Works Assn., Am. Soc. C.E.; Boston Soc. C.E., Harvard Engring. Soc., Am. Meteorol. Soc., Royal Meteorol. Soc. (Eng.), Am. Geophysical Union, Soc. Mayflower Descendants, Soc. Colonial Wars. Club: Harvard (Boston). Writer on water supply subjects. Cons. editor Water Works Engineering. Home: 53 N. Beacon St. Office:

SAVILLE, THORNDIKE, cons. engr.; b. Malden, Mass., Oct. 3, 1892; s. Caleb Mills and Elizabeth (Thorndike) S.; A.B., Harvard, 1914, M.S., 1917; B.S., Dartmouth, 1914, C.E., 1915; M.S., Mass. Inst. Tech., 1917; E.D. (hon.), Clarkson Coll., 1944, Syracuse University, 1951; D.Sc., New York University, 1957; m. Edith Stedman Wilson, Sept. 10, 1921; 1 son, Thorndike. Sheldon traveling fellow, Harvard, 1919; asso. prof., later prof. hydraulic and sanitary engring., U. of N.C., 1919-32, also chief engr. N.C. Dept. of Conservation and Development, 1920-32; prof. hydraulic and sanitary engring., New York U., 1932-57, emeritus, 1957-69, asso. dean Coll. of Engring., 1935, dean, 1936-57, now emeritus; vis. prof. in hydraulics, U. Cal. at Berkeley, 1956; director Science and Engring. Center Study, University of Florida, 1958-60, consultant, 1960-66; chmn. Cons. Panel on Water Supply, N.Y.C., 1950-51; engr. mem. N.Y. State Pub. Health Council, 1947-58; rep. N.Y. State to Del. River Adv. Com., 1956-58; cons. Water Resources, N.Y. State Commn. Revision Constrn., 1957-58; cons. engr. Rockefeller Found. to govt. of Venezuela on water supply for Caracas, leave of absence, 1926-27. Student O.T.C., Plattsburg and Ft. Monroe, Aug.-Nov. 1917; commd. 2d lt. C.A.C., 8th Co.; transferred to Signal Corps, Dec. 12, 1917; promoted 1st lt. and detailed to Langley Field, Va., as sanitary engr.; mem. Beach Erosion Bd., Office of Chief Engr. U.S. Army, 1930-63, Coastal Engineering Research Board, 1963-69; exec. engr. water resources sect. of Nat. Resources Bd., 1934-35; mem. water resources com. of Nat. Resources Planning Bd., 1935-43, chairman project review com., 1940-43; cons. engr. on water resources and coastal engring. Mem. adv. council USPHS, 1949-52. Recipient jubilee medal Am. Soc. Mech. Engineers. Del. engring. socs. U.S. to Conf. Engring. Edn., London, 1953, Zurich, 1954; chmn. U.S. delegation, Paris, 1957, London, 1962; pres-gen. 5th Internat. Congress Coastal Engring., 5th, 1954, 6th, Fla., 1957. Fellow Am. Pub. Health Assn., A.A.A.S., Am. Soc. C.E. (hon. mem.; pres. met. sect. 1942-43, dir. 1945-48); mem. Water Pollution Control Fedn., Engrs. Joint Council (pres. 1954-55), Engrs. Council for Profl. Devel. (pres. 1955-56), Am. Soc. Engring. Edn. (hon.), Am. Water Works Assn., N.E. Water Works Assn., N.Y. Sewage Works Assn., Boston Soc. C.E., Am. Soc. Engring. Edn. (v.p. 1948-49, pres. 1949-50; Lamme award 1954), Harvard Engring. Soc. (pres. 1948), Mayflower Descs., Am. Inst. Cons. Engrs., Am. Meteorol. Soc., Am. Geophys. Union, Am. Acad. San. Engrs., Nat. Soc. Professional Engineers, International Association Hydraulic Research, Phi Beta Kappa, Sigma Xi, Tau Beta Pi. Clubs: Harvard (New York City). Author reports and articles on hydrology, water power, water supply, sewage and coastal engring. Home: Gainesville FL Died Gainesville FA Died Feb. 21, 1969; buried Chapel Hill NC

SAWDERS, JAMES CALEB, chem. engr., lecturer; b. Pitts., Sept. 21, 1894; s. Francis Patrick and Mary (Reddy) S.; B.S., Carnegie Inst. Tech., 1916; m. Eunice Yasinski, June 7, 1932. Began as chem. engr. Goodyear Tire & Rubber Co., 1916; mem. Sawders & Fulton, chemists, Pitts., 1919-23; has made 19 expdns. to various parts of Latin America, visited many sections of Mexico, Central America, the West Indies and S.A. Has lectured on Latin Am. travel and on both N. and S. Am. archaeology. Travels and studies in Italy, 1937, Scandinavian countries, 1938, Hawaii, 1941. Served as maj. O.R.C., 1917-19; from lt. col. to col., asst. chief indsl. div. C.W.S., U.S. Army, 1942-46. Fellow Am. Geog. Soc.; mem. Soc. for Am. Archaeology, Am. Chem. Soc., Alpha Tau Omega. Democrat. Catholic. Clubs: University (Pitts.); Town Hall, Chemists (N.Y.C.); Army-Navy (Washington); Rotary (hon.). Author articles on Latin Am. travel and history, Pre-Columbian history, gen. Am. archaeology, and Latin Am. economics. Address: Briarcliffe Acres, Myrtle Beach, S.C. 29577. Died Aug. 7, 1960; buried Ocean Woods Meml. Park, Myrtle Beach.

SAWYER, CHARLES BALDWIN, metall. engr.; b. Cleve., July 15, 1894; s. John Pascal and Mary Candee (Baldwin) S.; B.A., Yale, 1915; Ph.D., Mass. Inst. Tech., 1921; m. Caroline Fisher, 1921; children—Baldwin, Margaret Hazard; m. 2d, Katherine Beaumont Hirsh, Aug. 19, 1933; children—Samuel Prentiss, Charles Brush, William Beaumont. Instr. naval aviation inspection and heat treatment of metals Mass. Inst. Tech., 1917-19, mem. vis. com. of corporation, dept. metallurgy, 1954-58; co-founder Brush Laboratories Co., 1921, pres., 1927-36, 52-55, chmn., 1936-52; co-founder Brush Development Co. (now Brush Electronics Co.), 1930, treas., 1930-47, chmn. bd., 1935-38, v.p., 1938-52; founder Brush Beryllium Co., 1931, pres., 1931-46, chmn. bd., 1936-60, dir., chmn. exec. com., 1960-62, vice chmn. bd., 1962—; founder Sawyer Research Products, Inc., 1956, pres., 1956—, also dir.; dir. Clevite Corp., United Improvement Co. Mem. U.S. tech. indsl. intelligence com. mission to Germany and Italy, 1945. Mem. A.A.A.S., Am. Chem. Soc., Am. Inst. Mining and Metall. Engrs., Am. Phys. Soc., Am. Soc. Metals, Inst. of Metals (Brit.). Clubs: Kirtland Country, Union (Cleve.); Yale (N.Y.C.); Mentor (O.) Harbor Yacht. Home: 17485 Shelburne Rd., Cleveland Heights 18, O. Office: 35400 Lakeland Blvd., Eastlake, Ohio. Died Mar. 24, 1964.

SAWYER, DONALD HUBBARD, civil engr.; b. Mt. Pulaski, Ill., Aug. 26, 1879; s. George Silas and Phoebe Content (Hubbard) S.; grad. Oak Park (Ill.) High School, 1897; B.S., U. of Ill., 1902; m. Elizabeth Osborn Merriam, Sept. 25, 1929; 1 son, George Osborn Sawyer (dec.). Began practice as civ. engr., 1902; city engr. Paris, Ill., 1903; chief engr. Ill. Traction System, 1904-09; mem. Sawyer Bros., Seattle and Spokane, Wash., 1910-17; with James Stewart & Co., N.Y. City,

1920-22; sec. Asso. Gen. Contractors of America, 1923-29; sec. Heating Bd. of Trade, New York, 1930; dir. Federal Employment Stabilization Bd. 1931-36; spl. asst. to Dir. of Procurement Div., Treasury Dept., 1936-39, since chief Real Estate Sect., Pub. Bldgs. Adminstrn.; chmn. Federal Real Estate Bd.; pres. U.S. Housing Corp. Served as maj., lt. col. Construction Div., U.S.A., 1917-20; charge constrn. Camp Grant, Rockford, Ill., nitrate plant, Cincinnati, and Camp Bragg, Fayetteville, N.C.; col. Q.M. Res. Baptist; chmn. bd. trustees Calvary Ch., Washington. Home: Alexandria, Va. Died June 21, 1941.

SAWYER, SYLVANUS, inventor; b. Templeton, Mass., Apr. 15, 1822; s. John Sawyer. Sent to work in gunsmith shop, Augusta, Me., 1839; invented several things, including a small railroad car operated by foot; employed in coppersmith's shop, Boston, 1844; employed by mfr. locks and house trimmings, 1845; patentee machinery for splitting and dressing rattan, 1849, for cutting rattan, 1851, additional rattan machinery, 1854, 55; supt. Am. Rattan Co., Fitchburg, Mass., circa 1852-55; patented improvements in rifled cannon and projectiles, 1855, dividers and calipers, 1867, steam generator, 1868, shoe-sole machine, 1876, centering lathe, 1882. Died Fitchburg, Oct. 13, 1895.

SAXTON, JOSEPH, inventor; b. Huntington, Pa., Mar. 22, 1799; s. James and Hannah (Ashbaugh) S.; m. Mary Abercrombie, 1850, 1 child. Watchmaker, Phila., 1817-28; made clock for Belfry of Independence Hall; in England, 1828-37; invented magneto-electric machine, 1833, also invented a fountain pen, locomotive differential pulley; constructor and curator of standard weighing appratus of U.S. Mint, Phila., 1837-43; designed standard balance used in govt. assay and coining offices; supt. weights and measures for U.S. Coast Survey, Washington, D.C., 1843-73; invented hydrometer, fusible metal seal, eversharp pencil; mem. Nat. Acad. Scis., Am. Philos. Soc. Died Oct. 26, 1873.

SAY, THOMAS, entomologist, conchologist; b. Phila., June 27, 1787; s. Benjamin and Ann (Bonsall) S.; m. Lucy Way Sistaire, Jan. 4, 1827. Called father of descriptive entomology in Am.; an original mem. Phila. Acad. Natural Scis., 1812; apptd. zoologist to accompany expdn. to Rocky Mountains under Maj. Stephen H. Long, 1819; accompainied Long's 2d expdn. which explored sources of the Minnesota River, 1823; curator Am. Philos. Soc., 1821-27; prof. natural history U. Pa., 1822-28; went to Ind. (with others) to Robert Owen's village, New Harmony (an attempt to establish an ideal community), 1825; fgn. mem. Linnaean Soc. of London; his collections and library went to the Phila. Acad. Natural Scis. after his death. Author: American Entomology; or Descriptions of the Insects of North America, 3 vols., 1824, 25, 28; American Conchology, 6 vols., 1830-34; prepared for publ. American Ornithology; or the Natural History of Birds Inhabiting the United States (Charles Bonaparte), 1825; works collected in The complete Writings of Thomas Say on the Conchology of the United States (W. G. Binney), 1858; The Complete Writings of Thomas Say on the Entomology of North America with a biographical memoir by George Ord (edited and published by J.L. LeConte), 2 vols., 1859. Died New Harmony, Oct. 10, 1834.

SAYLES, ROBERT WILCOX, geologist; b. Pawtucket, R.I., Jan. 29, 1878; s. Frederick Clark and Deborah Cook (Wilcox) S.; A.B., Harvard, 1901; m. Adelaide K. Burton, June 1, 1904; children—Deborah W., Robert W. Began geol. work in Montana, 1899; curator Harvard Geol. Museum, 1907-28; research asso. Division of Geology, Harvard, since 1928. President Baltic Mills Co., Baltic Ct. Fellow Geol. Soc. Am., A.A.A.S., Am. Acad. Arts and Sciences, Am. Geog. Soc.; mem. Seismol. Soc. America, Am. Meteorol. Soc., Boston Soc. Natural History, Geol. Soc. Boston (pres. 1928-29), Washington Acad. Sciences, Conf. Geophys. Union. Trustee of the Boston, Mass., Children's Museum. Author of monographs and papers on glacial geology and seismology. Research work on origin of Bermuda Islands, on seasonal banding in rocks and on glacial geology of Southern Maine and Cape Cod. Home: 263 Hammond St., Chestnut Hill, Mass. Died Oct. 23, 1942; buried in Swan Point Cemetery, Providence, R.I.

SAYRE, A(LBERT) NELSON, geologist; b. Granville, O., Jan. 28, 1901; s. Albert Thomas and Ida (Clouse) S.; B.S., Denison U., 1923, D.Sc., 1949; postgrad. U. Kan., 1923-24; Ph.D., U. Chgo., 1928; m. May Harriet Ludenslager, June 25, 1927 (dec. 1955); 1 dau., Elizabeth May (Mrs. Frank U. Naughton III); m. 2d, Elizabeth Dyer Gregg, Feb. 8, 1958. Geologist, Indian Terr. Oil & Illuminating Gas Co., Bartlesville, Okla., 1924; instr. U. Pa., 1926-29; geologist Ground Water div. U.S. Geol. Survey, Washington, 1929-46, chief of div., 1946-59, staff scientist, 1959-62; cons. ground water geologist, Washington, 1962-67; asso. Behre, Dolbear & Co. N.Y.C.; geologic adviser Office Inter-Am. Affairs, 1943; adviser U.S. Army, S.W. Pacific Area, 1944-45; rep. Dept. Interior on panels of Research and Devel. Bd., Munitions Bd. Dept. Def., 1946-52; del. Nat. Acad. Sci. to assemblies of Internat. Union Geodesy and Geophysics, 1948-67; cons. State N.C., Southampton Assn. (N.Y.). Recipient Medal of Freedom, 1946, Erasmus Haworth Distinguished Alumnus award, 1952, Distinguished Service award Dept. Interior, 1959. Fellow Geol. Soc. Am., A.A.A.S., Am. Geophys. Union (gen. sec.), Internat. Commn. on Subterranean Waters (past pres.); mem. Washington Acad. Sci. (past pres.), Am. Assn. Petroleum Geologists, Soc. Econ. Geologists, Am. Water Works Assn. Episcopalian. Club: Cosmos. Contbr. sci. jours. Home: Washington DC Died Oct. 12, 1967.

SAYRE, DANIEL CLEMENS, aeronautical engr.; b. Columbus, O., Feb. 1, 1903; s. Joel Grover and Nora (Clemens) S.; grad. Columbus Acad., 1919; B.S., M.S., Mass. Inst. Tech.; m. Ann Hamilton, Sept. 10, 1925; m. 2d Rosamond Foster, Sept. 5, 1931. Organizer, dir. Boston Airport Corp., 1925-28; instr., later asst. prof. aeronautical engring. Mass. Inst. Tech., 1928-32; asst., later asso. editor Aviation Mag., 1933-39; aviation editor Newsweek mag., 1934-39; dir. statistics and information, later chief safety regulations U.S. Civil Aeronautics Authority, 1939-41; organizer, chmn. dept. aeronautical engring. Princeton, 1941-51, apptd. dir. James Forrestal Research Center, 1951; asso. clean engring., 1955—. Fellow Inst. Aeronautical Scis.; mem. Am. Rocket Soc. Author articles profl. and popular mags. Home: Forrestal Rd., Princeton, N.J. Died Oct. 19, 1957.

SAYRE, ROBERT H(AROLD), mining engr.; b. Denver, Dec. 18, 1885; s. Hal and Elizabeth (Dart) S.; A.B., Harvard, 1908; m. Gertrude Bart Berger, July 9, 1912; children—Robert, Hal, William, Damaris, Phyllis, Constance. Engaged in mining and leasing Colo., 1908-12; cons. engr., mine operator, 1913-16; field engr. Ludlum Steel Co., 1919-21; operating mines nr. Breckenridge, Colo., 1922; cons. engr. Chipman Chem. Co., 1923-24, U.S. Dept. Justice, 1927-28; operating Lake Mine, nr. Idaho Springs, Colo., 1925; cons. engr. Western Exploration Co., 1926; gen. mgr. Quartz Hill Holding Co., 1928-29; cons. mining engr. Ludlum Steel Co., 1929; then in gen. cons. work; mine mgr. Pardners Mines Corp., operating in N.M., 1933-34; pres. and gen. mgr. Veta Mines, Inc., 1935-40; v.p. in charge prodn. Rustless Mining Corp. (subsidiary Rustless Iron & Steel Co. of Baltimore) producing chrome on Pacific Coast, 1941-42; chief Strategic Mineral Mission to Guatemala and other Central Am. countries for Bd. Econ. Warfare, 1942-44. Pres., Compañia Minera de Guatemala, S.A., 1944-46; Cons. engr., Central Am. since 1946. Aviator, U.S. Army advancing to 1st lt., 1917-18. Pres. bd. Colo. Sch. of Mines, 1934-35, trustee 12 yrs.; dir. Colo. Metal Min. Fund, 8 yrs. Mem. Am. Inst. Mining and Metall. Engrs. (chmn. Colo. sect.), Mining and Metall. Soc. Am., Colo. Sci. Soc., Colo. Mining Assn. (formerly a dir.), Denver C. of C. (formerly a dir.). Republican. Episcopalian. Clubs: University, Mile High (Denver); Harvard (N.Y.C.): American (Guatemala). Home: 2400 E. Iliff Av., Denver 80210. Office: Boston Bldg., Denver. Died May 8, 1960.

SAYRE, ROBERT HEYSHAM, civil engr., ry. official; b. Columbia County, Pa., Oct. 13, 1824; s. William H. S.; ed. common schs. and under James Nowlin, mathematician. Entered, 1840, engr. corps engaged in enlargement of Morris Canal, N.J.; on repairs of Lehigh Canal, 1841-43; on surveys and construction Back Track R.R., between Mauch Chunk and Summit Hill, 1844-45; later built the Switchback R.R. and inclined planes into Panther Creek Valley; development of coal mines, etc.; after 11 yrs. service with Lehigh Coal and Navigation Co. was elected chief engr. Delaware, Lehigh, Schuylkill & Susquehanna R.R. (later Lehigh Valley), serving 1852-82, and supervising extensions of system north and east; pres. and chief engr. S. Pa. R.R.; then 2d v.p. Lehigh Valley R.R. with oversight of traffic and engring. depts. and of extensions to Buffalo, and building branch roads. Pioneer in introduction of iron bridges, steel fire boxes, and the 1st to introduce the fish-bar track joint; began use of steel rails, 1864. One of promoters Bethlehem Iron Co.; dir., 1862 (gen. mgr., 1886; v.p., 1891); other large interests in corporations; chmn. bd. trustees Lehigh U.; chmn. exec. com., same, St. Luke's Hosp. Address: S. Bethlehem, Pa. Died 1907.

SCARR, JAMES HENRY, meteorologist; b. nr. South Boston, Ionia County, Mich., Jan. 10, 1867; s. Francis O. and Joanna Eastman (Wilmarth) S.; student State Normal Sch., Emporia, Kan., 1887-89; studied law in office of Hon. John W. Sheafor, Concordia, Kan.; m. Laura E. Brown, Dec. 21, 1890; children—James Bernard (dec.), Francis Joseph. Teacher in pub. schs., Kan. and Okla., 1889-95; admitted to bar, 1892; practiced law, also newspaper and real estate business until 1898; entered service U.S. Weather Bur., 1898; stationed at St. Louis, Mo., and Cairo, Ill., 1898-1900, Helena and Havre, Mont., 1900-01; local forecaster, Sacramento, Calif., 1901-08, Tampa, Fla., 1908-09; dist. forecaster, New York, 1909-24; sr. meteorologist, New York, 1924-26, prin. meteorologist, 1926—. Fellow Am. Meteorol. Soc.; scientific mem. Inst. Aeronautical Sciences. Presbyn. Home: Hasbrouck Heights, N.J. Died Feb. 14, 1936.

SCARSETH, GEORGE DEWEY, (skär'set), agronomist; b. Galesville, Wis., Oct. 7, 1898; s. Idius Barnard and Sena (Semb) S.; B.S., U. of Wis., 1924; grad. student, Yale, 1925-26; Ph.D., Ohio State U., 1935; D.Sc. (honorary), Purdue University, 1952; married Ida H. Bierke, August 6, 1926; children—Mary Sena, Dwight (dec.). Dairy tester, Wis. Herd Improvement Assn., 1917-18; with Wis. Soil Survey, 1923-24; asst. soil chemist, Conn. Agrl. Expt. Sta., 1924-26, United Fruit Co., Honduras, Central America, 1926-28; asso. prof. soil science, Ala. Poly. Inst., 1928-38; prof. soil science, Purdue U., 1938-43, chief in agronomy, 1943-44; dir. research Am. Farm Research Assn., Lafayette, Ind., since 1944; consultant soil scientist Standard Fruit and Steamship Co., 1935—, (agonomy) Central Farmers Fertilizer Co. (Chgo.), 1957—; agrl. consultant Univ. of Alaska, 1954-57. Collaborator, soil conservation service, U.S. Dept. Agr., 1935-44, tropical agr., Office Fgn. Relations, 1942-47; mem. adv. com. U.S. Dept. Agr., 1954; del. Internat. Congress Soil Science, Belgian Congo, 1954; lecturer Alaskan Farm Forum, 1955. Served with the United States Navy during World War I. Recipient Freedom Found. award, 1951, 52. Fellow Am. Soc. Agronomy; A.A.A.S.; mem. Am. Chem. Soc., Soil Sci. Soc. of Am. (pres. 1936), Internat. Soc. Soil Sci., Sigma Xi (pres. Purdue chpt. 1943-44), Alpha Chi Sigma, Gamma Sigma Delta, Alpha Zeta (hon.), Ceres, Scabbard and Blade. Presbyn. Club: Kiwanis (pres. Auburn, Ala., 1936). Elk. Author: Development, Classification and Characteristics of Soils, 1936; (reference book) Hunger Signs in Crops (chapter I, with R.M. Salter), 1941; 2d edit. (with N.J. Volk); also Man and His Earth, 1962. Contributor to about 40 scientific papers and bulls. on soil science to tech. publs. Home: 1414 Ravinia Rd., West Lafayette, Ind. Office: American Farm Research Assn., 100 Willayne Plaza, West Lafayette, Ind. Died Mar. 20, 1962.

SCATTERGOOD, EZRA FREDERICK, elec. and hydr. engr.; b. Burlington County, N.J., Apr. 9, 1871; s. Ezra and Lucy Ann (Engle) S.; B.S., Rutgers, 1893, M.S., 1896, Sc.D., 1931; fellow Cornell University, 1898-99, M.M.E., 1899; LL.D., University of California, 1944; m. Lulie Chilton, April 17, 1901; 1 dau., Elisabeth Harding. Instr. in mathematics and elec. science, Rutgers Coll., 1894-98; prof. physics and elec. engring., later elec. and experimental engring., Ga. Sch. Tech., 1899-1901; spl. engr. Huntington Light Power and Elec. Ry. Cos., Los Angeles, Calif., 1902-06; cons. elec. and hydr. engr., Los Angeles, 1906-09; chief Electrical Engr., General Mgr. Bureau of Power & Light, Dept. of Water and Power, Los Angeles, 1909-40; adv. engr. to dept. water and power, City of Los Angeles, 1938-47; pres. Am. Public Power Assn. 1947-48; non-resident lecturer, electrical engineering, Stanford, since 1926. Apptd. mem. Pub. Works Adv. Com. for Calif. under NRA, 1933; advisory engr. Nat. Power Policy com., 1939-40; mem. Colo. River Bd. of Calif.; chairman of the Committee on Electric Power of Calif. State War Council, 1942-43. Fellow American Institute Electric Engineers; mem. Seismological Society of America, Los Angeles Art Assn., Southern Calif. Symphony Assn., Pacific Geographic Soc., Sigma Xi, Phi Beta Kappa, Tau Beta Pi. Quaker. Clubs: California, Los Angeles Athletic, Engineers. Contbr. papers to tech. jours. and engring. socs. Home: 524 Muirfield Rd., Los Angeles 5. Office: 207 S. Broadway, Los Angeles 54, Calif. Died Nov. 15, 1947; buried in Forest Lawn Memorial Park, Glendale, Calif.

SCHAAF, ROYAL ALBERT, surgeon; b. Boone, Ia., Mar. 28, 1892; s. Rudolph George and Susan Maria (Doud) S.; M.D., New York University, 1913; D.Sc., Rutgers University, 1956; LL.D. (hon.), Bloomfield College and Seminary, 1957; married Helen Devore Thomas, Jan. 1, 1917; children—Royal Sommer (M.D.), Kate Coleman (Mrs. Perry J. Culver). Intern, resident Bellevue Hosp., N.Y.C., 1913-15; practice medicine, 1916, specializing surgery, Newark, 1919—; trustee, chmn. bd. United Hosps. Newark; consulting surgeon St. Barnabas Hospital Women and Children, Newark, St. Mary's Hospital, Orange, N.J.; mem. sr. staff Harrison S. Martland Med. Center, Babies Hosp., Coit Meml., Presbyn. Hosp.; (all Newark); chmn. bd. Medical-Surgical Plan of N.J.; pres. Med. Service Adminstrn. of N.J.; pub. dir. Prudential Ins. Co. Am., 1953-62; mem. of state board of med. examiners N.J., 1940-60. Trustee N.Y. University. Trustee N.J. division American Cancer Soc. Served as capt. M.C., U.S. Army, World War I. Recipient Edward J. Ill. award Acad. Medicine of N.J., 1948, Am. Cancer Soc. award, 1951, also N.J. div. award, 1952. Fellow A.C.S., Acad. Medicine of N.J. (past pres.), Med. Soc. of N.J. (past pres.); mem. Soc. Surgeons of N.J. (past pres.), Essex County Med. Soc. (past pres.), A.M.A., Bellevue Hosp. Alumni Assn. Home: Stillpond, Califon, N.J. 07830. Died Apr. 14, 1964.

SCHAEBERLE, JOHN MARTIN, astronomer; b. in Germany, 1853; s. Anton and C. Catherine (Voegele) S.; removed to Ann Arbor, Mich., 1854; apprentice in Chicago machine shop, 1868-71; became interested in astronomy; studied at Ann Arbor High Sch.; constructed a number of telescopes; C.E., U. of Mich., 1876; LL.D., U. of Calif., 1898; unmarried. Pvt. asst. to Prof. Watson, 1876-78; asst. Ann Arbor Obs., instr. in astronomy and acting prof. of astronomy, U. of Mich., 1878-88; astronomer Lick Obs., Mt. Hamilton, Calif., 1888-97, acting dir., 1897-98; had charge of eclipse expdns. of Lick Obs., 1889, 1893, Cayenne and Chile, and in 1896 to Japan; discovered 3 comets, and did much original work; extensive contbr. to astron. jours. Address: Ann Arbor, Mich. Died Sept. 17, 1924.

SCHAEFER, FREDERIC, engr., mfr., inventor; born Stavanger, Norway, Sept. 8, 1877; s. Capt. Thomas Michelsen and Rachel Johanna (Clausen) S.; student Stavanger Tech. Sch.; M.S., hon., U. Pittsburgh, 1929; m. Sarah Beatrice Bubb, Sept. 5, 1912; children—Jane (Mrs. A. L. Whittemore, Jr.), Frederic Michelsen, Katharine (Mrs. Louis A. Foy). Came to U.S., 1894, naturalized, 1902. Mech. engr., Boston; design engr., Westinghouse Elec. Co., Pitts. and Le Havre France, 1902-06; mech. engr. Summers Steel Car Co., Pittsburgh, 1906-14; organized, pres. Schaefer Equipment Co., since 1914. Exec. asst. Chief Dist. Ordinance Officer. Trustee Carnegie Inst. since 1935; trustee, vice pres. Am. Scandinavian Found. Republican. Episcopalian. Clubs: Duquesne, Rolling Rock, Pittsburgh Golf, Wianno, H.Y.P., Fox Chapel. Decorated Knight of St. Olaf, Comdr. of St. Olaf (Norway). Home: Park Mansions, Pitts. 13. Office: Koppers Bldg., Pitts. 19. Died Feb. 20, 1955.

SCHAEFER, HUGO H(ERMAN), chemist, educator; b. Bklyn., July 3, 1891; s. George Ludwig and Marie Hedwig (Mueller) S.; Ph.G., Ph.C., Columbia, 1912, Pharm.D., 1913; Ph.D. cum laude, U. Berne, Switzerland, 1925; m. Elizabeth Louise Kish, July 7, 1921; children—George Theodore, Betty Marie. Chemist, N.Y. Quinine & Chem. Works, 1914-16; instr. chemistry, physics N.Y. Coll. Pharmacy, Columbia U., 1916-21, asst. prof., 1921 to 1937; chemist N.Y. State Bd. Pharmacy since 1930; dean, prof. chemistry Bklyn. Coll. Pharmacy, L.I. U., 1937-56; pres. Schaefer Labs., Inc., 1931—; dir. American Druggist Fire Ins. Co. Mem., sec. pharmacopoeial revision com. U.S.; v. chmn. Nat. Formulary Com. Sec., Remington honor medal award com.; dir. Am. Found. Pharm. Ed. Reg. pharmacist, N.Y., N.J. Fellow N.Y. Acad. Science; mem. Am. Pharm. Assn. (treas.; chmn. legislative com.; Remington medallist 1951), Am. Coun. Pharm. Edn., Am. Assn. Colls. Pharmacy (past pres.), Am. Chem. Soc., N.Y., N.J. pharm. assns., Nat. Assn. Retail Druggists, Am. Inst. History of Pharmacy (dir.), N.Y. Acad. Pharmacy. Clubs: Chemical Square (N.Y.C.); Rotary (Bklyn.). Author: Qualitative Analysis (with A.R. Bliss), 1928. Home: 144 Buckingham Rd., Yonkers 2, N.Y. Office: 600 Lafayette Av., Bklyn. 16. Died Sept. 1967.

SCHAEFER, MILNER BAILY, oceanographer; b. Cheyenne, Wyo., Dec. 14, 1912; s. Heinrich Gottlieb and Kate Rosse (Baily) S.; B.S. magna cum laude, U. Wash., 1935; Ph.D., 1950; m. Isabella Long, May 4, 1949; children—Kate Baily, Kurt Milner, Patrick Joseph. Sci. asst. Internat. Fisheries Commn., 1934-35; asst. biologist, then biologist Wash. Dept. Fisheries, 1935-39; scientist Internat. Pacific Salmon Fisheries Commn., 1939-42; instr. Sch. Fisheries, U. Wash., 1946; with U.S. Fish and Wildlife Service, 1946-50, chief research and devel. Pacific Oceanic fishery investigation, Honolulu, 1948-50; dir. investigations Inter-Am. Tropical Tuna Commn., La Jolla, Cal., 1951-63, sci. cons., 1963-70; mem. staff Scripps Instn. Oceanography, La Jolla, 1951-70, prof. oceanography, dir. Inst. Marine Resources, 1962-70. Mem. com. effects atomic radiation oceanography and fisheries, Nat. Acad. Scis.-NRC, 1956-63, com. oceanography, 1957-68, chmn., 1964-67, mem. Latin Am. sci. bd., 1963-68; sci. adv. com. marine protein resources devel., 1963-70; expert fisheries, secretariat Internat. Conf. Law of Sea, Geneva, Switzerland, 1958; cons. spl. fund UN, 1960-65; chmn. standing com. marine sci. Pacific Sci. Assn., 1962-66; mem. expert panel tuna research FAO, 1964-69, chmn. 1964-66, mem. IWP working group marine resources appraisal, 1966-70; mem. Gov. Cal. Adv. Council Marine Resources, 1965-70, chmn., 1965-66; adv. com. fisheries and oceanography State Dept., 1965-65; adv. com. marine resources devel. Dept. Interior, 1967, science adviser, since 1967-69, consultant National Council Marine Resources and Engring. Devel., 1967-70. Served as officer USNR, 1942-46. Recipient Diploma de Reconocimienta (Costa Rica), 1967. Founding fellow Am. Inst. Fishery Research Biologists; fellow of the California Academy of Sciences, mem. Am. Soc. Icthyologists and Herpetologists, Nat. Oceanography Assn. (bd. dirs. 1966-67), Pacific Fishery Biologists (pres. 1939-40), Am. Fisheries Soc., Am. Geophys. Union, Am. Statis. Assn., Biometrics Soc., Am. Soc. Limnology and Oceanography (pres. Western div. 1956-57), Marine Tech. Soc., Phi Beta Kappa, Sigma Xi. Home: San Diego CA Died July 27, 1970.

SCHAFFNER, JOHN HENRY, botanist; b. Agosta Marion County, O., July 8, 1866; s. Daniel S., Jr. and Anna (Miller) S.; A.B., Baker U., Baldwin, Kan., 1893, M.S., 1896; A.M., U. of Mich., 1894; U. of Chicago, 1896-97; U. of Zürich, 1907-08; m. Cordelia Garber, 1916; children—Grace Odile, John Garber, James Daniel. Assistant in botany, U. of Mich., 1894-95; prof. natural science, S.D. U., 1895-96; asst. in botany, 1897-90, asst. prof. 1899-1902, asso. prof., 1902-11, prof., 1911-28, head of dept., 1908-18, research prof. of botany, 1928—, Ohio State U. Editor-in-chief Ohio Naturalist, 1900-15, of Ohio Jour. of Science, 1915-17. Presbyn. Author: Laboratory Outlines for General Botany, 1905; Trees of Ohio and Surrounding Territory, 1909; The Pteridophytes of Ohio, 1910; Field Manual of Trees, 1914; Catalog of Ohio Vascular Plants, 1914; The Grasses of Ohio, 1917; Field Manual of the Flora of Ohio and Adjacent Territory, 1928; Manual of Ohio Weeds (with H. A. Runnels), 1931; also numerous articles on cytology, morphology, the classification and evolution of plants, nature of sex, etc. Home: Columbus, Ohio. Died Jan. 27, 1939.

SCHAIRER, JOHN FRANK, research scientist; b. Rochester, N.Y., Apr. 13, 1904; s. John George and Josephine Marie (Frank) S.; B.S. in Chemistry, Yale, 1925, M.S. in Geology, 1926, Ph.D. in Chemistry, 1928; m. Ruth Naylor, July 20, 1940; children—John Everett and Jeanne Evelyn (twins). Physical chemist, geophysical lab. Carnegie Instn. of Washington, 1927-69, research asso., 1969-70; spl. asst. div. one Nat. Def. Research Com., 1942-45. Recipient Hillebrand award, Chem. Soc. Washington, 1942; President's Certificate of Merit, 1948; Medal of Honor (Eng.), 1948, Arthur L. Day medal, Geol. Soc. Am., 1953. Mem. Nat. Acad. Scis., Mineral. Soc. Am. (pres. 1943, recipient Roebling medal 1963), Geological Soc. Am. (v.p. 1944), Am. Chem. Society, Am. Geophys. Union, Nat. Capital Orchid Soc. (pres. 1949-50, 63-64, editor bull. 1951-70), Geochem. Soc. (p.p.), Internat. Assn. Volcanology (v.p. 1957-60), Sigma Xi, Gamma Alpha, Alpha Chi Sigma. Clubs: Cosmos (Washington); Men's Garden of Montgomery County. The mineral Schairerite named in his honor, 1931; The Schairer Vol. of Am. Jour. Sci., 1969. Home: Chevy Chase MD Died Sept. 26, 1970; buried Rock Creek Cemetery, Washington DC

SCHALLER, WALDEMAR THEODORE, mineralogist; b. Oakland, Cal., Aug. 3, 1882; s. Theodore P. and Eliza (Borneman) S.; B.S., U. Cal., 1903, fellow, 1903; Ph.D., U. Munich, 1912; m. Mary E. Boyland, Aug. 20, 1908. Chemist, mineralogist and geologist, U.S. Geol. Survey, since Oct. 1, 1903; geochemist in charge (chief chem.), sec. chem. and physics, 1944-47, research mineralogist, 1947-52, ret. Aug. 1952, reapptd. Sept. 1952. Awarded D.S.M., U.S. Dept. of Interior, 1952. Fellow Am., Acad. Arts and Sciences, Geol. Soc. Am., Mineral. Soc. Am. (v.p. 1921; pres. 1926; treas. 1931-41); mem. Washington Acad. Scis. (v.p. 1936, 37), Geol. Soc. Washington (v.p. 1934; pres. 1935), Am. Chem. Soc., Am. Inst. Mining and Metall. Engrs. (chmn., Washington, D.C., sect., 1937), N.Y. Mineralogical Club (hon.), Sigma Xi, Société Francaise de Minéralogie, Deutsche Mineralogische Gesellschaft, Wiener Mineralogische Gesellschaft, Mineral. Soc. Gt. Britain (hon.). Author or co-author bulls. U.S. Geological Survey, also over 100 papers on mineralogy in various scientific jours. Club: Cosmos. Awarded Roebling medal for meritorious achievement from Mineral. Soc. of America, Dec. 1938. Author of more than 200 papers on minerals, geology and chemistry. Home: 1661 Crescent Pl., Washington 9. Office: U.S. Geological Survey, Washington 25. Died Oct. 5, 1967.

SCHARFF, MAURICE ROOS, cons. engr.; b. Natchez, Miss., Apr. 14, 1888; s. Monroe and Rosa (Roos) S.; prep. edn., Phillips Exeter Acad., Exeter, N.H.; B.S., Mass. Inst. Tech., 1909, M.S., 1911; m. Jeanne Adler, Apr. 30, 1919; 1 son, Samuel Adler. Asst. engr., Morris Knowles, cons. engr., Pittsburgh, Pa., 1911-14, prin. engr., 1914-16, asst. chief engr. and v.p., 1916-21; valuation engr., Phila. Co. and affiliated corps, 1921-25, chief engr., 1925-27; chief engr., Pittsburgh br. Byllesby Engring. and Management Corp., 1927-28; cons. engr., Pittsburgh, 1928-32, N.Y.C., 1932-42, 1946-67; director Duquesne Light Company (Pittsburgh). Consultant to Task Force on Water Resources, Commn. on Orgn. Exec. Branch of Govt., 1954-55; cons. ICA and govts. Viet Nam, Laos, 1956-58. 1st lt. to capt. C.E., U.S. Army, 1918-19. Maj. to col., Corps of Engrs., U.S. Army, 1942-46. Mem. Am. Inst. Cons. Engrs., Am. Soc. C.E.; asso. mem. Am. Inst. E.E., Soc. Am. Military Engrs., Military Order World War. Republican. Clubs: City, Technology (New York); Cosmos (Washington, D.C.). Author: Electrical Utilities (with W. E. Mosher and others), 1929; Depreciation of Public Utility Property, 1940. Home: New York City NY Died Apr. 6, 1967; buried Arlington Nat. Cemetery Arlington VA

SCHEIDENHELM, FREDERICK WILLIAM, (shi'denhelm), hydraulic engr.; b. Mendota, Ill., June 16, 1884; s. Jacob and Katherine (Faber) S.; A.B., Cornell U., 1905, C.E. 1906; m. Clare Louise Espenschied, Jan. 22, 1912; children—Faber (dec.), Mrs. Jean S. Wolff. Structural and hydraulic engr. West Penn Rys. Co., 1906-09; organized 1909, Pittsburgh Hydro-Electric Co., of which was v.p. and chief engr. until 1914; organizer, sec.-treas. Mt. Pk. Land Co.; chief engineer Georgia-Carolina Power Company, 1910; v.p. and chief engr. Hydro-Electric Co. of W.Va., 1911-14, etc.; consulting engr., Pittsburgh, 1914-15; consulting engr., reconstruction of Stony River, W.Va., dam; associated with Daniel W. Mead in cons. hydraulic and hydroelectric practice, New York, 1916-17, and 1919-48; cons. engring. practice in own name since 1948; sec.-treas., Scheidenhelm Construction Corp., gen. contractors, N.Y., 1916-17; supervising consultant, Claytor dam and hydro-electric development, New River, Va., 1937-39. Mem. Engring. Coll. Council Cornell U., 1939-57. Served from captain to lieutenant colonel U.S. Army Engrs., 1917-19, comdr. 26th Engrs., water supply regt. AEF; col. Engrs. Res. 1919. Decorated D.S.M.; recipient Fuertes gold medal Cornell, 1917; Thomas Fitch Rowland prize Am. Soc. C.E., 1918. Fellow A.A.A.S.; mem. Am. Soc. C.E. (chmn. com. on cost allocation for multiple water projects, 1945—), Cornell Soc. Engrs., American Arbitration Association, American Institute of Cons. Engrs., Soc. American Mil. Engrs. (pres. N.Y. 1926). Tau Beta Pi. Clubs: Cornell, Downtown Athletic, R.R.-Machinery (N.Y.C.); Ocean (Atlantic Beach). Contbr. Trans. Am. Soc. C.E., other tech. publs. Invented anchoring wall for dams. Home: 82-28 Abingdon Rd., Kew Gardens 15, N.Y. Office: 50 Church St., New York 7, N.Y. Died Oct. 17, 1959; buried Arlington Nat. Cemetery.

SCHEIN, MARCEL, (shin), physicist, educator; b. Trstena, Czecho-Slovakia, June 9, 1902; s. Henry and Hermina (Messinger) S.; student U. Wurzburg, Germany, 1921-23; Ph.D., U. Zurich, Switzerland, 1927; m. Hilde Schoenbeck, June 2, 1927; 1 son, Edgar H. Came to U.S., 1938, naturalized, 1943. Asst. physics dept., U. Zurich, 1926-29, dozent, 1931-35; prof. exptl. physics, U. Odessa, 1935-37; fellow Rockefeller Found., U. Chgo. 1929-30, research in cosmic rays, 1938-42, asst. prof., 1942-45, prof. physics 1946—; cons. Research Lab., Gen. Elec. Co., 1945-46, Fermi Inst. Nuclear Studies, 1946; vis. prof. Princeton U., spring 1946, Stanford, summer 1948; cons. Manhattan Dist., 1945-46; dir. Task Order 18, Office of Naval Research project, U. Chgo., 1947—; charge cosmic ray research dept. of physics; vis. prof. Brazilian Center Phys. Research, 1951. Numerous expedns. on cosmic rays to Colo. (Mt. Evans, Climax); research on Mt. McKinley, Alaska, 1947, in B-29 planes, Aircraft Carrier (balloon flights); Balloon ascensions from Chgo. to study cosmic-rays close to the top of our atmosphere, 1940—; expdn. to Guam, 1957; worked with Berkeley Bevatron on K-mesons and hyperons, 1956—. Awarded prize, Schnyder von Wartensee Stiftung, Zurich, 1928. Fellow Am. Phys. Soc., N.Y. Acad. Sci., A.A.A.S.; mem. Ill. Acad. Sci., Swiss Phys. Soc, Brazilian Acad. Sci. Club: Quadrangle (Chgo.). Author: Problems in Cosmic Ray Physics, 1946. Home: 5650 Dorchester Av., Chgo. 37. Died Feb. 20, 1960.

SCHENCK, HUBERT GREGORY, geologist; b. Memphis, Sept. 24, 1897; s. William Johnson and Lida (Egbert) S.; A.B., Ore. U., 1922, A.M., 1923; Ph.D., U. Calif., 1926; m. Inga Bergström, Nov. 5, 1924; 1 dau., Ingrid (Mrs. Edward L. Beach). Geologist, div. mines, Bur. Science, Manila, P.I., 1920-21; instr. U. Calif., 1923-24; asst., asso. and prof. geology, Stanford, 1924-43; advance fellow, Belgium-Am. Ednl. Found., 1934, 1935, paleontologist Amiranian Oil Co. (Iran and Afghanistan), 1937-38; cons. geologist at intervals, 1926—. Served with U.S. Army, 1916-19, maj. to col., 1943-51, col. USAR retired, 1953; chief of Natural Resources Section, General Hdqrs., Supreme Comdr. Allied Powers, Tokyo, 1945-51; chief Mut. Security Mission to China, 1951-54; cons. Fgn. Operations Adminstrn., 1954-55; prof. geol. Stanford U., 1954—; cons. Pacific Sci. Bd., 1955—; mem. adv. council, Inst. Marine Resources, U. of Cal., 1956-59; research asso. Hoover Institution, Stanford, 1945—. Awarded Bronze Star, Bronze Star with oak leaf cluster, Legion of Merit, Distinguished Service Medal, Philippine Legion of Honor medal; Order of Brilliant Star (China). Member Geological Society Am., Am. Assn. Petroleum Geologists, Geol. Society France, Paleontological Society Japan, Geol. Society Belgium (corr. mem.), Malacol. Soc. London, Paleontol. Soc., Soc. Econ. Paleontologists and Mineralogists, Geol. Soc. Philippines, A.A.A.S., Cal. Acad. Sci., Am. Malacological Union, Am. Acad. Polit. Social Sci., Phi Beta Kappa, Sigma Xi, Theta Tau. Mason (32 deg., Shriner). Club: Explorers. Contbr. U.S. and fgn. publs. Home: 585 Washington, Palo Alto, Cal. Office: School of Mineral Sciences Stanford, Cal. Died June 19, 1960.

SCHEPPEGRELL, WILLIAM, laryngologist; b. (of American parents) Hanover, Germany, Sept. 22, 1860; high sch. and coll. edn.; A.M., 1884; M.D., Med. Coll. State of S.C.; spl. course, 1887-89; m. Jessie A., d. Prof. Allessandro Gambati, 1882. In practice at Charleston, S.C., until 1890, at New Orleans, 1890—; asst. surgeon, Eye, Ear, Nose and Throat Hosp.; chief of hay fever clinic, Charity Hospital. Inventor of many appliances in ear, nose and throat specialty. Pres. Audubon Park Commn. Asso. editor The Laryngoscope; co-editor Annals of Otology, Rhinology and Laryngology. Author: Hay Fever and Asthma, Cause, Treatment and Cure; Electricity in Diseases of the Nose, Throat and Ear; Non-Malignant Tumors of the Throat; and other works. Home: New Orleans, La. Deceased.

SCHERER, ROBERT PAULI, engineer; b. Detroit, Oct. 10, 1906; s. Dr. Otto and Josephine L. (Hesselbacher) S.; A.B., U. Mich., 1928, B.S., 1930; M.S. (hon.), Phila. Coll. Pharmacy and Sci.; m. Margaret Lindsey, Mar. 15, 1930; children—Josephine L., Robert Pauli, Karla, John S. Invention, development, rotary die capsulation process, 1930-33; founder Gelatin Products Co., 1933, since pres., co. name became R.P. Scherer Corp., 1947, now also chmn.; established fgn. affiliates, Can., 1935, Eng., 1937, Germany, 1950, Argentina, 1951, Italy, 1958, also chmn.; invention, devel. needleless hypodermic injection. Home: 665 Lake Shore Rd., Grosse Pointe Shores 36, Mich. Office: 9425 Grinnell Av., Detroit 13, Mich. Died July 27, 1960; buried Woodlawn Cemetery, Detroit.

SCHERZER, ALBERT H., engr.; b. Peru, Ill., July 22, 1865, s. William and Wilhelmina S.; ed. Peru (Ill.) High Sch. and Tech. Sch., Zürich, Switzerland; LL.B., Union Coll. of Law, Chicago, 1892; m. Donna G. Adair, May 8, 1902. Engaged in law practice, Chicago, until death of his brother, William, inventor of the Scherzer rolling lift bridge, becoming pres. and chief engr. of The Scherzer Rolling Lift Bridge Co.; designed and built many large and important ry., electric ry. and highway bridges in U.S. and abroad; also invented improvements in bridges. Office: Chicago, Ill. Died Jan. 28, 1916.

SCHICK, BELA, pediatrician; b. Bolgar, Hungary, July 16, 1877; s. Jacob and Johanna (Pichler) S.; grad. 2d Staats Gymnasium, Gray, Austria, 1894; M.D., Karl Franz U., Graz, 1900; m. Catharine C. Fries, Dec. 3, 1925. Began practice in Vienna, 1902; with U. Vienna, 1902-23, prof. pediatrics, 1918-23; came to U.S., 1923, naturalized citizen, 1929; cons. pediatrician, Mt. Sinai Hosp.; cons. pediatrician, Sea View Hosp.; cons. pediatrician Willard Parker Hosp., N.Y. Infirmary for Women and Children; cons. pediatrician Beth Israel Hosp.; clin. prof. and lectr. diseases children, Columbia U., 1936-43; dir. pediatric dept. Beth-El Hosp., Bklyn; vis. prof. pediatrics, Albert Einstein Coll. Medicine. Mem. Finnish Pediatric Soc. Am. Hungarian Med. Soc., Acad. Medicine, Am. Pediatric Soc., Acad. of Pediatrics (a founder), Soc. for Exptl. Biology and Medicine, Am. Assn. Immunologists, Nat. Inst. for Social Scis., Acad. Sci.; hon. mem. Deutsche Gesellschaft für Kinderhelkunde, Harvey Soc., Assn. for Study of Allergy, Bronx Pediatric Soc., Virchow Soc., N.Y., Southwest Cal. Pediatric Soc., Pediatric Research Soc., Mississippi Valley Soc., Sociedad Boliviana de Pediatria; corr. mem. Gesellschaft der Aerzte in Vienna. Author: Serum Krankhett (with Clemens Pirquet), 1905; Scarlet Fever (with Theodore Escherich), 1912; Pirquetsche System der Ernährung, 1918; Child Care Today (with William Rosenson), 1933; also articles on tuberculosis, diphtheria, scarlet fever, nutrition of new born children, and concentrated feeding in childhood. Discoverer of "Schick test" for determining susceptibility to diptheria, 1913. Awarded gold medal of N.Y. Acad. of Medicine, 1938; Addingham gold medal, Apr. 12, 1938, at Leeds, England, in absentia, presented by the Lord Mayor of Leeds; gold medal of Midwest Forum on Allergy, Indpls., 1941, Semelweis medal Am. Hungarian Med. Soc. 1954; John Howland award Am. Pediatric Soc., 1954; John Brandeis gold medal, 1956, award Am. Jewish Congress, 1957, and others. Home: 1045 Park Av., N.Y.C. 28. Died Dec. 1967.

SCHIEDT, RICHARD CONRAD FRANCIS, coll. prof.; b. Weissenfels, Prussia, Sept. 21, 1859; s. Francis and Julia (Jansen) S.; grad. Gymnasium, Zeitz, Prussia, 1878; student in mathematics, zoology, chemistry, univs. of Erlangen and Berlin, 1878-81; theology at Lancaster, Pa., 1885-87; post-grad. work, U. of Pa. and Harvard; Ph.D., U. of Pa., 1899, hon. Sc.D., 1910; m. Sophie E. Gantenbein, Aug. 23, 1888; children—Mary Madeleine Julia, Norma Ruth (Mrs. Persifor H. Smith), Richard Conrad Francis. Prof. biology and geology, Franklin and Marshall Coll., Pa., 1887-1918; prof. anatomy and embryology, U. of Tenn. 1919; professor biology emeritus, Franklin and Marshall Coll., since 1927; retired, 1919. Research chemist for Armstrong Cork Company (linoleum division), 1924-28; entomologist Pa. State Board Agr., 1893-1900. Mem. academic council Carl Schurz Memorial Foundation. One of first members Woods Hole (Mass.) Marine Biol. Orgn. Fellow A.A.A.S.; mem. Am. Chem. Soc., Soc. Am. Zoologists, Soc. Old German Students in American, Societe Jean Jacques Rousseau, Geneva, Deutsche Philos. Gesellschaft, Euckenbund, Steuben Society, Concord Soc. of America, Phi Beta Kappa, Phi Kappa Sigma. Min. of Reformed Ch. in U.S. Author: Principles of Zoology, 1893; Laboratory Guide in Zoology, 1898; Plant Morphology, 1900; On the Threshold of a New Century, 1900; Glimpses into the Growth of America's Art Life, 1909; American Art in the Making, 1926; The Verdict of History-a Plea for Peace, 1940. Contbr. on scientific and ednl. subjects. Address: 1043 Wheatland Av., Lancaster PA*

SCHIEFFELIN, WILLIAM JAY, (shef'lin), chemist; b. New York, N.Y., Apr. 14, 1866; s. William Henry and Mary (Jay) S.; Ph.B., Columbia Sch. Mines, 1887; Ph.D., Munich, 1889; m. Louise Shepard, Feb. 5, 1891; children—William Jay, Margaret, Mary, John Jay, Louise, Bayard, Elliott, Barbara, Henry. Civ. service commr., 1896; adj., 12th N.Y. Inf., Spanish-Am. War, 1898. Chemist, Schieffelin & Co., 1889, vice-pres., 1903-06, pres., 1906-22, chmn. bd., 1922-29. Mem. London Chemical Soc., pres. Nat. Assn. Wholesale Druggists, 1910; chmn. Am. Friends of Czecho-Slovakia; president American Mission to Lepers; v.p. Am. Bible Soc. Trustee Hampton Inst. Tuskegee Inst.; director Me. Seacoast Mission. Col. 15th N.Y. Inf., 1918. Pres. Emeritus Huguenot Soc., Chmn. Emeritus Citizens Union. Clubs: Century, City, Church. Home: 620 Park Av., N.Y.C. Died Apr. 29, 1955.

SCHIFF, LEONARD ISAAC, physicist; b. Fall River, Mass., Mar. 29, 1915; s. Edward Ephraim and Matilda (Brodsky) S.; B.E., Ohio State U., 1933, M.S., 1934; Ph.D., Mass. Inst. Tech., 1937; m. Frances Margaret Ballard, Aug. 25, 1941; children—Ellen Margaret, Leonard Ballard. Research physicist Gen. Electric Co., summer 1937; Nat. Research Council fellow, research asso. U. Cal., Cal. Inst. Tech., 1937-40; instr. U. Pa., 1940-42, asst. prof., 1942-44, asso. prof., 1944-47, acting chmn. physics dept., 1942-45; research physicist Nat. Def. Research Com., Columbia, 1941-45, U. Cal., 1944-45; mem. anti-submarine warfare operation research group, 1943-45; staff Los Alamos Sci. Lab., N.M., 1945-46; asso. prof. Stanford, 1947-48, prof., 1948-71, exec. head physics dept., 1948-66; dir. Varian Assos., 1948-53; vis. prof. Ia. State Coll., 1952, U. Paris, 1956-57, Univ. Madras and Bombay (India), 1963; Guggenheim fellow, 1956-57; vis. com. physics dept. Mass. Inst. Tech., 1954-56, 68-71; cons. editor McGraw Hill Book Co., 1954-71; dir. Annual Reviews, Inc., 1969-71; Stewart lectr. U. Mo., 1955; Phillips lectr. Haverford, 1963; Tektronix Found. lectr. Ore., 1964. Vice president and director of the Varian Found., 1961-71, mem. phys. scis. program com. Alfred P. Sloan Found., 1961-66, chmn., 1965-66. Chmn. adv. com. physics div. Office Sci. Research, Air Research and Devel. Command USAF, 1955-65; sci. adv. group Office Aerospace Research, USAF, 1963-71; mem. consultative group Com. on Space Research, Internat. Council Sci. Unions, 1968-71; cons. ad hoc com. on phys. scis. NRC, 1968-70. Recipient Lamme medal Ohio State U., 1959; Oersted medal Am. Assn. Physics Tchrs., 1966; Dinkelspiel award Stanford U., 1966; award for outstanding contributions to research Office Aerospace Research, 1970. Mem. Internat. Conf. Theoretical Physics, Tokyo, also Kyoto, Japan, 1953. Fellow Am. Phys. Soc. (councillor 1953-57, chmn. nuclear physics div. 1967-68), Am. Acad. Arts and Scis., A.A.A.S., (mem. coun. 1966-69), California Acad. of Sci.; mem. Am. Assn. Physics Tchrs., Fedn. Am. Scientists (council del.), American Assn. Univ. Professors, National Acad. Sciences (mem. space science board 1965-70, chmn. sect. physics 1969-71), Sigma Xi, Tau Beta Phi. Club: Cosmos (Washington). Author: Quantum Mechanics, 3d edition, 1968. Author science research and review articles. Associate editor Review Sci. Instruments, 1943-45, Phys. Rev., 1945-47, 63-65, Physics Today, 1950-56, Rev. of Modern Physics, 1951-54, Ann. Rev. Nuclear Sci., 1952-63, Journal of Mathematical Physics, 1960-62. Home: Menlo Park CA Died Jan. 19, 1971; buried Alta Mesa Cemetery, Palo Alto CA

SCHINDLER, RUDOLF, physician; born Berlin, Germany, May 10, 1888; s. Richard I. and Martha (Simon) S.; student U. of Freiburg (Germany), 1905-07; M.D., U. of Berlin, 1912; m. Gabriele Winkler, 1922 (dec. 1964); children—Richard Rudolf, Peter (dec.), Wolfgang (dec.), Ursula (Mrs. James B. Gibson); m. 2d, Marie Koch. Came to U.S., 1934, naturalized, 1940. Asst. in path. dept. Hosp. Schwabing, Munich, Germany, 1913-14, asst. in med. dept., 1919-23; engaged in pvt. practice of medicine, specializing in gastroenterology, Munich, 1923-34, Chicago, 1934-43, Los Angeles since 1943; visiting prof. medicine, U. of Chicago, 1934-36, asso. clinical prof. medicine, 1936-37, asso. prof. medicine, 1937-43; attending gastroscopist Michael Reese Hosp., 1936-37; cons. gastroscopist Cook County Hosp., 1936-37; clinical prof. of medicine, Coll. Med. Evangelists, 1943-68; sr. attending staff mem. Los Angeles County Gen. Hosp. Consulting gastroenterologist, Veterans Administration, Midway Hosp., Los Angeles, Long Beach Veterans Hospital, Temple Hosp., Los Angeles. Served as military surgeon Bavarian Inf. Regt. and pathologist 6th German Army, 1914-18. Decorated Iron Cross; Bavarian Mil. Service Order with swords; German Cross for Trench Soldiers. Awarded gold medal, Am. Med. Assn., 1936. Author: Lehrbuch d. Gastroskopie, 1923; Nervensystem u. spontane Blutungen, 1927; Gastroscopy, 1937 (2d edit., 1950); Gastritis, 1947; numerous publications on stomach diseases. Invented rigid gastroscope, 1922; flexible gastroscope, 1932; optical diagnostic esophagoscope, 1948. Mem. Inst. Medicine Chicago, Am. Gastro-Enterological Assn., Internat. Gastro-Enterological Association, American Gastroscopic Society (1st. Pres.), A.A.A.S., A.M.A., Calif. Soc. Int. Med., Sigma Xi. Roman Catholic. Home: Los Angeles CA Died Sept. 1968.

SCHLAIKJER, ERICH MAREN, cons. geologist, engineer; b. Newton, O., Nov. 22, 1905; s. Erich and Clara (Ryser) S.; B.S., Harvard, 1929, M.A., Columbia, 1931, Ph.D., 1935; m. Jospehine Ayres, Apr. 28, 1951; children—Maren, Michael, Patrecia Jo. In charge, 10 geol. and paleontol. expedn., Gt. Plains Area of U.S. for Harvard U., 1925-34, Yukon Terr. Alaska Expdn. for Am. Museum of Nat. History, 1936, with Barnum Brown, Am. Museum-Sinclair Expdn., southwestern Wyo., 1937; Am. Museum-Sweet Expdns., Big Bend Area, Tex., 1939-40, Comml. Petroleum and Mining Geology, Rocky Mountain Area, 1946-49, Tutor of geology, Bklyn. Coll., 1932-34, instr., 1935-39, asst. prof., 1940-47, prof., 1948-50; pres. Lakota Petroleum Corp., 1950-67. Served in U.S. Air Force, 1st lt., 1942, active duty, advanced to lt. col., 1945. Awarded Bronze Star Medal, Army Commendation Ribbon, seven campaign stars to the Asiatic Pacific Theatre Ribbon. Awarded (with Barnum Brown) Cressy Morrison prize, N.Y. Acad. Sci., 1939. University fellow Columbia U. Fellow Geol. Soc. Am., Paleontol. Soc. Am., A.A.A.S.; mem. Am. Assn. Petroleum Geologists, Nat. Soc. Profl. Engrs., Am. Geophys. Union, Soc. for the Study of Evolution, Am. Inst. Profl. Geologists (charter), Sigma Xi. Clubs: Explorer's (dir., 1942-43, sec., 1947-49 and various coms.), Harvard (N.Y.C.); Petroleum, Columbine Country (Denver). Author articles on geology and paleontology profl. jours. Home: Littleton CO Died Nov. 5, 1972; buried Tower of Memories, Denver CO

SCHLENZ, HARRY EDWARD, civil engr.; b. Denver, Nov. 1, 1905; s. Edward and Viola G. (Harder) S.; B.S., U. Ill., 1927, M.S., 1929, C.E., 1933; m. Norma B. Addison, Aug. 4, 1942; children—Susan (Mrs. Robert L. Moran), Dianne, Deborah, Harry A. Research grad. asst. U. Ill. Engring. Expt. Sta., 1927-29, instr. water supply and sewage treatment, 1929-30; v.p., sales mgr. Pacific Flush Tank Co., 1930-54, pres., 1954-69, dir., 1933-69. Pres. Water Pollution Control Fedn. 1961-62, adv. com. to asst. sec. interior Frank DiLuzio, commr. Fed. Water Pollution Control Adminstrn. Trustee U. Ill. Athletic Assn., 1949-53, pres., 1953; trustee U. Ill., 1953-58. mem. Lake Geneva com. George Williams Coll. Recipient gold medal Camp Custer; William J. Orchard award for distinguished service to water pollution control field, 1968. Fellow Am. Soc. C.E.; mem. Ill. Soc. Engrs., Am. Pub. Works Assn., Am. Acad. San. Engrs., Water and Sewage Works Mfrs. Assn. (pres. 1957), Central States Water Pollution Control Assn., Sigma Xi, Alpha Kappa Lambda, Tau Beta Pi, Chi Epsilon, Scabbard and Blade. Clubs: Barrington Hills Country; Army and Navy (Chgo.); Engineers (N.Y.C.). Home: Barrington IL Died 1969.

SCHLERETH, C(HARLES) Q(UINBY), (slar'eth), mining engr.; b. Denver, Colo., July 10, 1884; s. Peter M. and Justina C. (Eberst) S.; E.M., Colo. State Sch. of Mines, 1906; m. Florence Louise Barrett, Jan. 12, 1915. Successively chemist, surveyor, engr., chief engr. Compania Minera de Penoles, Durango, Mexico, 1906-11; asst. mgr. Summit Copper Co., Globe, Ariz., 1911; examining engr. Penoles Exploration Co., Mexico, 1911-14; mgr. Bonanza Mines, Ltd., Nicaragua, 1914; asst. gen. supt. Ojuela Mines, Durango, Mexico, 1915, gen. supt., 1916-17; asst. gen. mgr. Mapimi Unit of Ojuela Mines, including lead smelter, arsenic plant, power plant and railway, 1917-18; gen. supt., subsidiaries of Am. Metal Co. (9 metal mines, 2 coal mines), Monterrey, Mexico, 1918-21; gen. mgr. San Francisco Mines of Mexico, Ltd., San Francisco del Oro, Mexico, 1921-23; cons. engr. San Francisco Mines of Mexico and gen. consulting practice, New York, 1923-24; gen. mgr. Potosi Mining Co. and Calera Mining Co., Chihuahua, Mexico, 1924-25; cons. practice Mexico, U.S., Wales, Greece, Venezuela, Australia, etc., since 1925. Mem. Am. Inst. Mining and Metall. Engrs., Mining and Metall. Soc. America, Colo. Mining Assn. Club: Denver. Home: 99 S. Downing St. Office: Equitable Bldg., Denver. Died Nov. 12, 1950.

SCHLESINGER, FRANK, (sles'in-jer), astronomer; b. New York, May 11, 1871; s. William Joseph and Mary (Wagner) S.; B.S., Coll. City of New York, 1890; M.A., Columbia, 1897, Ph.D., 1898; Sc.D., U. of Pittsburgh, 1920; Sc.D., Cambridge, 1925. In charge Internat. Latitude Obs., Ukiah, Calif., 1899-1903; astronomer Yerkes Obs., under auspices of Carnegie Instn., 1903-05; dir. Allegheny Obs. (U. of Pittsburgh), 1905-20; dir. Yale Univ. Obs., 1920-41; dir. emeritus since July 1, 1941. Fellow A.A.A.S. (past chmn. Sect. A), Am. Acad. Arts and Sciences; mem. Nat. Acad. Sciences, Am. Philos. Soc., Am. Astron. Soc. (past pres.), Internat. Astron. Union (past pres.), Phi Beta Kappa, Sigma Xi; hon. asso. Royal Astron. Soc. Can.; fgn. asso. Royal Astron. Soc. of London; hon. mem. Mexican Astron. Soc., Italian Soc. of Spectroscopists; corr. mem. French Acad. Sciences, French Bureau de Longitudes, Swedish Acad. Scis. Awarded Valz medal, French Acad. Sciences, 1926; gold medal, Royal Astron. Soc., 1927; Bruce gold medal, Astron. Soc. of Pacific, 1929; Officer Legion of Honor (France), 1935; Townshend medal, College of City of N.Y., 1935. Collaborating editor Astrophys. Journal. Author of 200 monographs in scientific journals on reduction of photographic plates, stellar parallaxes, variations of latitude, spectroscopic binaries. Home: Lyme, Conn. Died July 10, 1943.

SCHLING, MAX, horticulturist; b. Austria, Mar. 1, 1874; educated public and private schools and horticultural night school and college, Vienna; m. Louise Schling, June 5, 1904; children—Elizabeth, Max. Came to U.S., 1899, naturalized citizen, 1906. Began as retail florist, N.Y. City, 1901; now pres. Max Schling, Inc.; pres. Max Schling Seedsman, Inc. Chmn. Horticultural Assn., N.Y. Botanical Garden. Mem. Soc. Am. Florists and Ornamental Horticulturists, Rose Soc. Am., Am. Dahlia Soc., Orchid Soc. America, Canadian Gardeners Assn., Metropolitan Retail Florists, Hort. Soc. N.Y., Hort. Soc. Mass., Merchants Assn. New York, Fifth Ave. Assn. New York, Florists Telegraph Delivery Assn., Pi Alpha Xi (hon. mem. Alpha Chapter, Cornell U.); fellow Am. Hort. Legion of Honor (chmn.). Founder Max Schling's Students' Loan Fund, Cornell, 1926. Republican. Mason. Club: Westchester Country (Rye, N.Y.), Rotary. Home: 14 E. 75th St. Office: Savoy-Plaza, New York, N.Y. Died Feb. 12, 1943.

SCHLOTTERBECK, JULIUS OTTO, pharmacognosist; b. Ann Arbor, Mich., Sept. 1, 1865; s. Hermann William and Rosina Christina Schlotterbeck; Ph.C., U. of Mich., 1887, B.S., 1891; Ph.D., U. of Berne, Switzerland, 1896; m. Eda May Clark, Aug. 11, 1898. Asst. in pharmacognosy and pharmacy, 1888-90, in pharmacognosy, 1891-92, instr. pharmacognosy and botany, 1893-95, asst. prof., 1896-1904, jr. prof., 1904-07, prof., 1907—, dean Sch. Pharmacy, 1905—, U. of Mich. Discoverer of several new vegetable alkaloids. Mem. Com. Revision U.S. Pharmacopoeia, 1910—. Address: Ann Arbor, Mich. Died June 1, 1917.

SCHLUNDT, HERMAN, chemist; b. Two Rivers, Wis., July 16, 1869; s. Carl and Maria (Dryer) S.; B.S., U. of Wis., 1894, M.S., 1896, Ph.D., 1901; U. of Leipzig, 1899-1900; Cavendish Lab., 1921; m. Martha A. McMinn, July 27, 1899; children—Anna, Esther. Asst. in chemistry, U. of Wis., 1894-96; instr. physics and chemistry, high schs., Milwaukee, 1896-99; fellow in chemistry, U. of Wis., 1901-02; instr. chemistry, 1902-05, asst. prof. physical chemistry, 1905-07, prof., 1907—, U. of Mo. Mem. Wis. Acad. Sciences, Arts and Letters. Kiwanian. Home: Columbia, Mo. Died 1937.

SCHMIDT, CARL LOUIS AUGUST, coll. prof.; b. Brown County, S.D., Mar. 7, 1885; s. Gustav and Fridericke (Unverzagt) S.; B.S., U. of Calif., 1908, M.S., 1910, Ph.D., 1916; m. Esther May Skolfield, Apr. 11, 1914; children—Stanwood Skolfield, Alfred Carl, Esther Fredericka. Chemist gas company, San Francisco, 1908-09; expert chemist Referee Board, U.S. Dept. Agr., 1900-12; bacteriologist and chemist City of Berkeley, 1912-14; research asst. in physiology, U. of Calif., 1915-17, asst. prof. biochemistry, 1918-20, asso. prof., 1921-23, prof. since 1924, dean Coll. of Pharmacy, 1937-44; acting dean of Med. School, 1939; cons. tech. advisor Western Regional Research Lab. since 1941; cons. bio-chemist Southern Pacific Gen. Hosp.; mem. commn. A, com. on aviation medicine, com. on chemistry of proteins, Nat. Research Council. Awarded Carl Schurz fellowship, 1932. Mem. Am. Chem. Soc., Am. Soc. Biol. Chemists, Soc. Exptl. Biology and Medicine, Calif. Acad. of Medicine, Western Society of Naturalists, Kerr Medical Club, Pacific Coast R.R. Surgeons, Sigma Xi. Club: Faculty (U. of Calif.). Author: Fundamentals of Biochemistry (with F. W. Allen), 1938; The Chemistry of the Amino Acids and Proteins, 1938, 44. Mem. editorial com. Annual Review of Biochemistry since 1932; pres. Annual Reviews Inc. Mem. U.S. Pharmacopoeia revision com., 1940-50. Home: 2612 Piedmont Av. (4). Office: 1557 Life Sciences Bldg., Univ. of Calif., Berkeley, Calif. Died Feb. 23, 1946.

SCHMIDT, EDWARD CHARLES, mech. engr.; b. Jersey City, N.J., May 14, 1874; s. John Frederick and Katharine (Bisbord) S.; M.E., Stevens Inst. Tech., Hoboken, N.J., 1895; m. Violet Delille Jayne, June 15, 1904; 1 dau., Katharine. In employ of Kalbfleisch Chem. Co., New York and Buffalo, 1895-96; with C. W. Hunt Co., New York, 6 mos., 1896; in steam dept., as asst. to mech. engr., Edison Electric Illuminating Co., Brooklyn, 1897; with Am. Stoker Co., New York, 6 mos., 1898; instr. in machine design, later instr. and asst. prof. ry. engring. and experimental engring., U. of Ill., 1898-1903 (made many tests with 2 ry. dynamometer cars owned by U. of Ill., I.C. R.R. and C.,C.,C.&St.L. Ry.); asst. engr. Am. Hoist & Derrick Co., St. Paul, Minn., 1903-04; engr. of tests, Kerr Turbine Co., Wellsville, N.Y., 1904-06; asso. prof. and prof. ry. engring., U. of Ill., July 1, 1906-Apr. 12, 1919. Commd. maj., Ordnance Dept. U.S. Army, Aug. 11, 1917; served in N.Y. Dist. Ordnance Office, and on detached service in U.S. Fuel Adminstrn. and U.S. R.R. Adminstrn.; discharged, July 16, 1919. Mech. engr. North American Co., New York, 1919-21; prof. ry. engring. and head of dept., U. of Ill., 1921-40, prof. ry. engring. emeritus since Sept. 1, 1940. Mem. Am. Soc. M.E., mech. div. of Am. Ry. Assn., Western Ry. Club, Ry. Fuel and Traveling Engrs. Assn., Soc. Promotion Engring. Edn., Tau Beta Pi, Sigma Xi, etc. Club: University. Author of numerous articles, reports, etc., in the tech. press and trans. tech. socs. Home: 1 University Pl., Apt. 19C, New York, N.Y. Died Mar. 21, 1942.

SCHMIDT, HERBERT WILLIAM, physician, med. dir.; b. Red Wing, Minn., Feb. 23, 1904; s. Edward William and Inga (Einstensen) S.; B.A., St. Olaf Coll., 1926; M.D., U. Minn., 1932, M.S., 1938; m. Kathleen Campbell, Nov. 27, 1937; children—William Alexander, Jean Elizabeth, Judith Kathleen. Intern Mpls. Gen. Hosp., 1932-33; fellow Mayo Found., 1934-36, instr. to asso. prof., 1939-57, prof. medicine, 1957-64; cons. physician Mayo Clinic, 1936-48, head sect. medicine, 1948-62, sr. cons. internal medicine, 1962-64; med. dir. Minn. Mining and Mfg. Co., 1964-66. Bd. govs. Mayo Clinic, 1959-60; bd. regents St. Olaf Coll., 1960-65. Served from maj. to lt. col. M.C., AUS, 1943-46. Mem. A.M.A., Am., Internat. bronchoesophegol. assns., Am. Gastroscopic Soc., Am. Assn. Thoracic Surgery, Am. Thoracic Soc., Minn. Thoracic Soc. (pres. 1957), Central Soc. Clin. Research, Chest Club, Sigma Xi. Lutheran (bd. trustees). Contbr. articles to med. jours. Home: 713 Park Av., Mahtomedi, Minn. 55115. Office: 2501 Hudson Blvd., St. Paul. Died Apr. 6, 1966.

SCHMIDT, KARL P., zoölogist; b. Lake Forest, Ill., June 19, 1890; s. George Washington and Margaret Jane (Patterson) S.; student Lake Forest (Ill.) Coll., 1906-07; B.A., Cornell University, 1916; D.Sc. (honorary), Earlham College, 1952; married Margaret Rosanna Wightman, July 3, 1919; children—John Mungo, Robert George. Research asst. Am. Museum of Natural History, N.Y. City, 1916-22; curator of reptiles, Chicago Natural History Museum, 1922-40; chief curator of zoölogy, 1941-55; curator of zoology emeritus, 1955; member of the Cornell Geological Expedition to San Domingo, 1916; Survey of Puerto Rico, 1919; Marshall Field Central Am. Expdn., 1923; Marshall Field Brazilian Expdn., 1926; Crane Pacific Expdn., 1928-39; Mandel Guatemala Expdn., 1933-34; Magellanic Expdn., 1939. Served in U.S. Army, Camp Grant, and Camp Taylor, 1918. Mem. A.A.A.S., American Society Ichthyologists and Herpetologists (president 1942-46), American Society of Mammalogists, Biological Society Washington, Am. Acad. Arts and Sciences, National Academy of Sciences, Ecological Society of Am. Fellow of the John Simon Guggenheim Foundation, 1932. Democrat. Author: Homes and Habits of Wild Animals, 1934; Friendly Animals and Whence They Came, 1938; Field Book of Snakes (with D. D. Davis), 1941; Principles of Animal Ecology (co-author), 1949; Ecological Animal Geography (co-author), 1951; also many scientific papers on amphibians and reptiles and on animal distbrn. Sect. editor for reptiles of Biological Abstracts. Home: 1751 Cedar Rd., Homewood, Ill. Address: Chicago Natural History Museum, Chgo. 5. Died Sept. 26, 1957.

SCHMIDT, WALTER AUGUST, chem. engr.; b. Los Angeles, Aug. 26, 1883; s. August and Adelhaid (Ott) S.; B.S., U. Cal., 1906; m. Ethel Proudfoot, Oct. 17, 1910 (dec. Apr. 16, 1950); 1 son, Walter Malcolm; m. 2d, Louise Frick Hartwell, Sept. 6, 1952. With Western Precipitation Corp. (now a division of the Joy Manufacturing Co.), Los Angeles, 1908—, pres., gen. mgr., 1911-56, president and chairman of board, 1956-59, chairman of the board, 1959—, dir. parent co.; pres. Internat. Precipitation Company, 1911—, Precipitation Co. of Can., Ltd., 1935—. Mem. nat. adv. council to com. on patents Ho. of Reps. 76th, 77th Congresses. Mem. Am. Chem. Soc. (dir. 1931-36, 43-54), N.A.M. (Modern Pioneer award 1940), Am. Inst. Chem. Engrs., Electrochem. Soc., Am. Inst. Mining and Metall. Engrs., Am. Inst. E.E., A.A.A.S., Sigma Xi, Phi Lambda Upsilon. Contbr. sci. jours. Mem. adv. bd. Indsl. and Engring. Chemistry, 1920-49; bd. asso. editors Chem. Monographs, 1923-56. Patentee in field elec. precipitation process for purification of gases. Home: 716 N. Whittier Dr., Beverly Hills. Cal. Office: 1000 W. 9th St., Los Angeles 15. Died Sept. 14, 1962.

SCHMUCKER, SAMUEL CHRISTIAN, biologist; b. Allentown, Pa., Dec. 18, 1860; s. Beale Melancthon and Christiana Marie (Pretz) S.; A.B., Muhlenberg Coll., 1882, A.M., 1885, M.S., 1891; Sc.D., 1913; Ph.D., U. of Pa., 1893, hon. fellow in botany, same, 1899; m. Katherine Elizabeth Weaver, Dec. 29, 1885; children—Beale M., Dorothy M. Prof. natural science, Carthage (Ill.) Coll., 1883-84, Boys High Sch., Reading, Pa., 1884-89, State Normal Sch., Indiana, Pa., 1889-95; biology, State Teachers Coll., West Chester, 1895-1923, emeritus since 1923. Lecturer on biology, Phila. Cooking Sch., 1898-1902; dean of faculty and prof. zoology, Wagner Inst., Phila., since 1907; also popular lecturer to schools, teachers' gatherings and chautauquas. Mem. N.E.A. Episcopalian. Independent Republican. Author: The Study of Nature, 1907; Columbia Elementary Georgraphy, 1909; Under the Open Sky, 1910; The Meaning of Evolution, 1913; Man's Life on Earth, 1925; Heredity and Parenthood, 1929. Club: Rotary. Home: West Chester PA

SCHNABEL, TRUMAN GROSS, physician, educator; b. Georgetown, Pa., Feb. 7, 1886; s. Edwin Daniel and Emeline (Woodring) S.; A.B., Lehigh U., 1907; M.D., U. Pa., 1911; m. Hildegard Rohner, Oct. 21, 1916;children—Truman Gross, Elizabeth S. (Mrs. Chamblin). Intern Hosp. U. Pa., 1911-13; practice internal medicine, Phila., since 1913; tchr. med. sch. U. Pa., 1913-51, emeritus prof. medicine, 1951-71; former staff mem. Howard Hosp.; dir. out-patient dept. medicine Hosp. U. Pa.; cons. Phila. Gen., Presbyn., Rush, Kensington and Nazareth hosps. Mem. com. Am. Found. Studies in Govt. since 1934. Recipient of Strittmatter award, Philadelphia County Medical Society, 1960; also Shaffrey award from St. Joseph's College in 1963. Served as major M.C., Army of the U.S., 1917-19. Diplomate Am. Bd. Internal Medicine (chmn. 1949-50). Fellow A.C.P. (v.p. 1956-57), Phila. Coll. Physicians; mem. Am. (chmn. sect. internal medicine 1953), Pa. (speaker 1940-44), Phila. Co. (pres. 1953) med. socs., Am. Gastro Enterological Assn., Am. Clin. and Climatol. Assn., Phila. Pathol. Soc., S.R., Sigma Nu, Alpha Omega Alpha, Phi Alpha Sigma Sigma Xi. Author articles in med. jours. Home: Wynnewood PA Died Aug. 27, 1971.

SCHNEIDER, ALBERT, bacteriologist; b. Granville, Ill., Apr. 13, 1863; s. John and Elizabeth (Burcky) S.; M.D., Coll. of Phys. and Surg. Chicago, 1887; B.S., U. of Ill., 1894; M.S., U. of Minn., 1894; Ph.D., Columbia, 1897; m. Marie Louise Harrington, June 28, 1892; 1 dau., Cornelia Elizabeth. Instr. botany, U. of Minn., 1893; prof. pharmacognosy and bacteriology, Northwestern U. Sch. of Pharmacy, Chicago, 1897-1903; prof. pharmacognosy and bacteriology, 1903-19, materia-medica and therapeutics, 1904-06. U. of Calif.; dir. expt. sta. Spreckels Sugar Co., 1906-07; pharmacognosist, U.S. Dept. Agr., 1909-15; micro-analyst, Calif. State Food and Drug Lab., 1915-19; prof. pharmacognosy, Coll. Pharmacy of U. of Neb., 1919-21. Editor-in-chief of Pacific Pharmacist, 1910-15. Author: Primary Microscopy and Biology, 1890; A Text-book of General Lichenology, 1897; Guide to the Study of Lichens, 1898; Microscopy and Micro-Technique, 1899; Hints on Drawing for Students of Biology, 1899; General Vegetable Pharmacography, 1900; The Limitations of Learning, and Other Science Papers, 1900; Powdered Vegetable Drugs, 1920; Bird and Nature Study Chart Manual, 1903; Medicinal Plants of California, 1909; Drug Plant Culture in California, 1912; Pharmaceutical Bacteriology, 1920; Bacteriological Methods in Food and Drugs Laboratories, 1915; The Microbiology and Microanalysis of Foods, 1920; Microscope in Detective Work (rept., Office of Naval Intelligence), 1918; Laboratory Pharmacology and Toxicology, 1925. Translator: Westermaier's Compendium der Allgemeinen Botanik, 1896. Contbr. many papers to scientific jours. Mem. Internat. Jury of Awards, Panama P.I. Expn., 1915. Inventor of car ventilating system. Dean, School of Pharmacy, N. Pacific Coll., Portland, Ore., 1922—. Lecturer on crime investigation, U. Calif. summer sessions. Address: Portland, Ore. Died Oct. 27, 1928.

SCHNEIDER, CHARLES CONRAD, engr.; b. Apolda, Saxony, Apr. 24, 1843; s. Julius and Emilie (Bengel) S.; grad. Royal Sch. Tech., Chemnitz, 1864; m. Katharine Clyde Winters, Jan. 8, 1880. In machineshop practice in Germany, 1864-67; draughtsman Rogers Locomotive Works, Paterson, N.J., 1867-70; asst. engr. Mich. Bridge & Construction Co., Detroit, 1870-73, Erie Ry., New York, 1873-75; engaged on proposed Blackwell's Island Bridge across East River, New York, 1876; designer Del. Bridge Co., New York, 1876-78; civ. engr. in pvt. practice, New York, 1878-86, designing and superintending structural work for bridges and bldgs.; chief engr. bridge and constrn. dept., Pencoyd Iron Works, Phila., 1886-1900; v.p. Am. Bridge Co., in charge of engring., 1900-03; cons. engr., with splty. in bridges and structural steel work, 1903; mem. bd. of engineers, Quebec Bridge, 1911—. During period 1878-86 designed and constructed several long-span bridges, the most prominent being the Fraser River (Cantilever) Bridge, Can. Pac. Ry., 1882, and the Niagara Cantilever Bridge, 1883. Awarded Rowland prize, Am. Soc. C.E., 1886, for paper on constrn. of the Niagara Bridge. Norman medal, same, 1905, for paper on Structural Design of Buildings, and Norman medal, same, 1908, for paper on Movable Bridges; also, 1886, 1st prize on design for Washington Bridge across Harlem River, New York. Mem. Am. Society C.E. (dir. 1887, 1898-1900, v.p. 1902-03, pres. 1905). Author: General Specifications for Railroad Bridges, 1886; General Specifications for Highway Bridges, 1901; General Specifications for Structural Steel Work in Buildings, 1905. Home: Wissahickon, Phila. Died Jan. 8, 1916.

SCHNEIDER, EDWARD CHRISTIAN, biologist; b. Wapello, Ia., Aug. 21, 1874; s. John George and Augusta J. (Bauersfeld) S.; B.S., Tabor Coll., Ia., 1897; Ph.D., Yale, 1901; Sc.D., U. of Denver, 1914; M.P.E., International Y.M.C.A. Coll., 1923; Sc.D., Colorado Coll., 1932; m. Elsie M. Faurote, June 24, 1902; children—Edwin George, Marion Elsie (Mrs. R. E. Joyce). Instr. chemistry, 1897-99, prof. biology and physiol. chemistry, 1901-03, Tabor Coll.; prof. biology, 1903-07, head prof., 1907-19, Colo. Coll.; Daniel Ayres prof. biology, Wesleyan U., Conn., 1919-44, retired June 1944. John Jeffries award for contrbts. to aeromedicine Inst. Aeronautical Sciences, 1942. Member and sec. board control Conn. Agrl. Expt. Station, New Haven, Conn. Physiologist in charge of dept. Med. Research Lab., Air Service, U.S. Army, and later, officer in charge same to Aug. 1918; capt. Sanitary Corps, Dec. 1917, maj., June 1918; mem. Med. Research Bd. No. 1, A.E.F., Aug. 1918-Mar. 1919. Dir. physiology, Sch. of Aviation Medicine, Mitchel Field, L.I., N.Y., 1919-26; lt. col., S.R.C., 1920-30. Fellow A.A.A.S., Am. Phys. Edn. Assn.; mem. Am. Physiol. Soc., Am. Soc. Biol. Chemists, Am. Pub. Health Assn., Soc. Exptl. Biology and Medicine, Soc. Am. Bacteriologists, Sigma Xi, Phi Beta Kappa, Beta Theta Pi. Author: Physiology of Muscular Activity, 1933, revised edition, 1939 revised (with P. K. Karpovick), 1948. Part Author: Report of Pike's Peak Expdn., 1911; Manual of the Med. Research Laboratory, Air Service, publishing chiefly studies of the influence of high altitudes and low oxygen on mankind, aviation physiology, and effects of physical exercise and training. Home: 25 Gordon Pl., Middletown, Conn. Died Oct. 3, 1954.

SCHNEIDER, GEORGE, chemist, textile co. exec.; b. Bklyn., Mar. 28, 1897; s. Peter and Rose (Gelden) S.; grad. U. Buffalo, 1918; m. Gladys Bower, Jan. 1, 1919; 1 dau., Dorothy (Mrs. Henry Staehling); m. 2d, Hazel McIntyre, Sept. 4, 1956. Chemist, Celanese Corp. of Am., 1920-45, v.p., dir., 1945-50, sr. v.p., 1950-59, vice chmn., 1959-71; dir. Canadian Chem. Co., Celanese

Mexicana, Celanese Colombiana, Celanese Venezolana. Served as lt., C.W.S., U.S. Army, 1917-18. Fellow Am. Inst. Chemists; mem. Am. Inst. Chem. Engrs., Soc. Chem. Industry. Clubs: Chemists (N.Y.C.); Rock Spring (N.J.). Home: Short Hills NJ Died Nov. 1971.

SCHNEIDER, WALTER ARTHUR, physicist, educator; b. East London, S. Africa, Jan. 2, 1899; s. Richard and Frieda (Schroeder) S.; B.S., U.S. Africa, 1920; M.S., U. Mich., 1922, Ph.D., N.Y.U., 1927; E.E., Brooklyn Poly. Inst., 1936; m. Beatrice Haines, Aug. 8, 1925; 1 dau., Julia. Came to U.S., 1920, naturalized, 1932. Instrument tester Duquesne Light Co., Pittsburgh, 1920-21; asst. physics U. Mich., 1921-22; instr. Brooklyn Poly. Inst., 1929-35; instr. N.Y.U., 1922-27, asst. prof., 1927-29, asso. prof., 1929-46, prof. physics since 1947, dir. physics labs. since 1929; research photoelectricity, di-electric constants, nuclear physics. Civilian with A.E.C., 1942-46. Mem. Am. Phys. Soc., Am. Assn. Physics Tchrs., A.A.A.S., Sigma Xi, Sigma Pi Sigma. Author: Experimental Physics for Colleges (with L.B. Ham), 1932. Home: 68 Edgars Lane, Hastings on Hudson, N.Y. Office: 100 Washington Sq. E., N.Y.C. 3. Died Nov. 20, 1956.

SCHNELLER, GEORGE OTTO, inventor, mfr.; b. Nürnberg, Germany, Jan. 14, 1843; s. Henry and Elizabeth (Ruckert) S.; m. Clarissa Alling, May 1, 1873, 3 children. Came to U.S., 1860; cashier, accountant Osborne and Cheesman Co., brass manufactory, Ansonia, Conn.; returned to Germany, 1870, to U.S., 1872; obtained 4 patents on corset springs between 1872-73; bought spectacle factory, Shelton, Conn.; began mfr. brass corset eyelets; secured patents on die for making eyelets, eyelet machine, punch and die for eyelet machines, 1884; bought Osborne and Chessman business, 1882, reorganized it as Ansonia Osborne and Cheesman Co., began manufacture of brass goods under his patent rights; revolutionized corset industry of world by his inventions; founder, treas. Union Fabric Co., Ansonia; invented and patented hook and eye, bustle, machine for covering dress stays, button press, button-fastening device; active in building electric street ry. system between Derby, Ansonia and Shelton, Conn.; mem. Ansonia Bd. Edn.; represented Ansonia in lower house of Conn. Legislature, 1891-93. Died Ansonia, Oct. 20, 1895.

SCHOCH, EUGENE PAUL, chemist; b. Berlin, Germany, Oct. 16, 1871; s. Oscar and Jenny (Finck) S.; C.E., U. of Tex., 1894, A.M., 1896; Ph.D., U. of Chicago, 1902; m. Clara L. Gerhard, June 14, 1902; children—Arthur Gerhard, Margaret Magdalene, Eugene Paul. Fellow, U. of Tex., 1893-94, tutor chemistry, 1894-96, instr., 1897-1905, adj. professor, 1905-08, asso. prof., 1908-11, prof. phys. chemistry, 1911-40, prof. chem. engring. since 1938; dir. Bur. Indsl. Chemistry, 1928-42. Asso. editor Jour. of Physical Chem., 1909-23, Sch. Sc. and Mathematics (Chicago), 1905-10. Fellow A.A.A.S., Tex. Acad. Sc. (pres., 1908-09); mem. Am. Chem. Soc., Am. Inst. Chem. Engrs., Phi Beta Kappa, Sigma Nu. Democrat. Conglist. Author: (with W. A. Felsing) General Chemistry, 1938; also papers on research on reactions by electric discharges through gases, producing dry lump lignite, potassium sulfate from polyhalite, high strength gypsum plaster. Home: 2212 Nueces St., Austin TX

SCHODER, ERNEST WILLIAM, educator, hydraulic engr.; b. Dewey, Fidalgo Island, Wash., Aug. 17, 1879; s. Herman and Sophia (Huntemann) S.; B.S. and B.S. in Mining, U. of Washington, 1900; Ph.D., Cornell U., 1903; unmarried. In charge Hydraulic Lab., Cornell U., Sch. of Civil Engring., 1904; asst. prof. exper. hydraulics, Cornell U., 1904-19, prof. 1919-47, emeritus, 1947-68. Was hydraulic expert for U.S., State of N.Y., municipal and corporate interests; consultant for Army Engrs. on river models, 1937-38. Commd. capt. engrs., U.S. Army, Aug. 1917; instr. and engr. officer Camp Lee, Petersburg, Va.; asst. dir. of training, Camp Humphreys, Va.; spl. duty in Office of Chief of Engrs., Washington. Fellow A.A.A.S., Am. Soc. C.E.; mem. Soc. Am. Mil. Engrs., Phi Gamma Delta, Sigma Xi, Phi Beta Kappa. Author: Hydraulics Section, Marks' Mechanical Engrs'. Handbook (1st 4 edits.); Hydraulics (with F. M. Dawson), also author of papers on exptl. studies of pipes and wires in Trans. Am. Soc. C.E. and M.E. since 1902. Home: Seattle WA Died May 16, 1968; buried Lakeview Cemetery, Seattle WA

SCHOELLKOPF, JACOB F., mfr. aniline colors; b. Buffalo, N.Y., Feb. 27, 1858; s. Jacob F. and Christiana (Duerr) S.; prep. edn., St. Joseph's Coll., Buffalo; student poly. schs., Stuttgart and Munich, Germany, 1873-79; m. Wilma Spring, Mar. 31, 1882. Began in aniline business at Buffalo, 1880; inc., 1900, as Schoellkopf Aniline & Chem. Works, merged with Nat. Aniline & Chem. Co., Inc., 1917; retired from this company, Mar. 1918. Pioneer in aniline color industry in the U.S. Became connected, 1900 with Hydraulic Power Co., Niagara Falls, merged with Niagara Falls Power Co., 1917; chmn. bd. Schoellkopf, Hutton & Pomeroy, Buffalo. Trustee Univ. of Buffalo, Buffalo Foundation, Buffalo. Republican. Clubs: Buffalo, Buffalo Athletic, Wanakak Country. Home: Lake View, Erie County, N.Y. Office: 70 Niagara St., Buffalo, N.Y. Died Sep. 9, 1942.

SCHOELLKOPF, PAUL ARTHUR, (shawl'kof), pres. Niagara Falls Power Co.; b. Niagara Falls, N.Y., Mar. 7, 1884; s. Arthur and Jessie (Gluck) S.; B.A., Cornell U., 1906; m. Mattie Irwin Penn, Aug. 16, 1911; children—Jasmine, Paul A. Engaged with father in power development at Niagara Falls; president Niagara Falls Power Co. since 1919, director; chairman board and director Power City Trust Co., Buffalo Niagara & Eastern Power Corp.; president and dir. Gluck Realty Co., Lewiston Heights Co., Pine Av. Corp.; dir. Canadian Niagara Power Co., Ltd., Lower Niagara River Power & Water Supply Co., Lockport and Newfane Power & Water Supply Co., Niagara Junction Ry. Co., and numerous other cos. Mem. N.Y. State War Council. Dir. Falls Memorial Hosp., Y.M.C.A., Buffalo Museum Natural Science. Trustee Cornell Univ. Vice chmn. Niagara Frontier State Park Commn.; vice-pres. Niagara Frontier Authority. Mem. Niagara Falls Chamber of Commerce, Zeta Psi. Clubs: Niagara, Cornell, Bath, Niagara Falls Country; Buffalo, Country (Buffalo); Broad Street, Cornell (N.Y.). Home: Lewiston Hts., Niagara Falls. Office: Niagara Falls Power Co., Niagara Falls, N.Y. Died Sep. 30, 1947.

SCHOFIELD, ALBERT GEORGE, civil engr.; b. Berkeley, Cal., June 10, 1912; s. Albert Edward and Lena May (Lovie) S.; student San Jose State, 1929-31, Stanford, 1931-32, U. Cal., Fresno State; m. Eunice A. Bannon, May 21, 1935 (dec. Jan. 1969); children—Bonnie Elizabeth (Mrs. James McDaniel), Toni Jean (Mrs. Bruce A. Blackledge); m. 2d, Cuma Riggs, Feb. 1970. Engr., U.S. Bur. Pub. Rds., 1931, U.S. Forest Service, 1932-41, Lockheed Aircraft Corp., 1941-46, Pacific Gas & Electric Co., 1947-51; asso. hwy. engr. Cal. Div. Hwys., 1951-60; gen. practice civil engr., Fresno, 1960-70; pres., dir. A. G. Schofield, Inc.; part-time asst. prof. math., engring. Fresno State Coll. Mem. Am. Soc. C.E., Nat. Soc. Profl. Engrs. Home: Fresno CA Died May 6, 1970; buried Fresno Meml. Gardens Fresno CA

SCHOMMER, JOHN J(OSEPH), chem. engr.; b. Chicago, Jan. 29, 1884; s. Nicholas and Elizabeth (Kummer) S.; B.S., U. of Chicago, 1909, student (research in yeasts moulds and chemistry), 1909-10, B.S. in Chem. Engring., Armour Inst. Tech. (now Ill. Inst. Tech.), 1912, Master's degree in chemical engineering, 1918; m. Elsie Steffen, June 10, 1915 (died 1945); m. 2d, Jessie Hollecker Rogers. Prof. indsl. chemistry Ill. Inst. Tech. since 1933, dir. placement since 1938, now development officer Illinois Inst. Tech.; dir. Acme Planting Company, M. Steffens & Co. (both Chicago); cons. in chemistry and bacteriology; in law cases as expert and referee. Mem. Cook County Highway Authority; chmn. Ill. State Super Highway Commn.; State of Ill. occupational adviser for Selective Service System 4 yrs. Trustee Ill. Inst. Tech.; director Neoplastic Therapy Research Foundation. Awarded medal from Congress for work as Selective Service System occupational advisor, State of Ill., World War II. Fellow A.A.A.S.; mem. Am. Chem. Soc., Am. Inst. Chem. Engrs., Am. Soc. Engring. Edn., Ill. State Bacteriol. Soc. Republican. Roman Catholic. Clubs: University, Chemists, Farmer's (Chicago); Dairymen's Country (Boulder Jct., Wis.); Elmhurst Country, Executives (Chgo.). Home: 421 Melrose St., Chgo. 13. Died Jan. 11, 1960; buried Rosehill Cemetery, Chgo.

SCHONFELD, WILLIAM A., child psychiatrist; b. Nuremberg, Germany, Aug. 12, 1906; s. Martin and Helen (Spitzer) S.; brought to U.S., 1907; B.S., N.Y.U., 1928, M.D., 1931; m. Louise R. Rost, June 30, 1935; 1 son, William Rost. Intern Morrisania City Hosp., 1931-32, resident pediatrics and psychiatry, 1932-34; pediatric-psychiatry Bellevue Hosp. Psychiat. Inst., 1931, Mt. Sinai Hosp., 1942; pvt. practice, 1934-70; specialist in child and adolescent psychiatry; asst. attending psychiatrist, div. child psychiatry Presbyn. Hosp.; vis. pediatric-psychiatry, Morrisania City Hosp.; asst. clin. prof. child psychiatry Coll. Phys. and Surgs., Columbia; asso. attending Children Service, N.Y. Psychiat. Inst. & Hosp.; asso. clin. prof. pediatric-psychiatry, N.Y. Med. Coll., 1948-59. Chmn. Westchester's Multidisplinery Conf. Problems Adolescence, 1962-70. White House Conf. Children and Youth (tech. cons. 1950, 60, 70). Served as maj. M.C., AUS, 1942-46. Awarded Commendation Medal for Psychiatric Rehab. Diplomate Am. Bd. Pediatrics; Am. Bd. Psychiatry and Neurology in psychiatry; American Board Psychiatry and Neurology in child psychiatry. Fellow Am. Psychiat. Assn. (com. psychiatry childhood and adolescence and chairman of subcommittee on adolescence); mem. Westchester County Psychiat. Society (vice president 1956, 60), American Society for Adolescent Psychology (president since 1967-69), New York Academy Medicine, Soc. Research Child Devel., Am. Acad. Pediatrics (chairman of area Committee on Youth), Internat. Assn. Child Psychiatry, Am. Assn. U. Profs., Am. Ortho-Psychiat. Assn., Soc. Adolescent Psychiatry (pres. 1961-62), Westchester Mental Health Association (board directors, chairman committee on edn.). Mason (past master). Contbr. numerous articles devel. and psychiatry in adolescence to med. jours. Home: Mamaroneck NY Died Sept. 21, 1970.

SCHOONHOVEN, JOHN JAMES, biologist; b. McIntyre, N.Y., July 3, 1864; s. George W. and Maria (Mead) S.; A.B., St. Francis Coll., Brooklyn, 1893; A.M., Coll. of St. Francis Xavier, New York, 1894; L.I. Coll. Hosp., 1888-90; post-grad., philosophy, New York U., 1900-01; m. Helen E. Butterfield, June 16, 1897; 1 son, George Otis (dec.). Staff lecturer New York, Newark and Jersey City bds. of edn.; lecturer Brooklyn Inst. Arts and Sciences; apptd. spl. lecturer, instr. in edn. N.Y. Univ., 1930—. Specialist on subject of parasitism (animal parasites, entomogenous fungi and trypanosomiasis). Pres. dept. zoölogy, mem. council and fellow Brooklyn Inst. Arts and Sciences. Pres. Am. Assn. for Planting and Preservation of City Trees, 1910-12; del. 15th Internat. Congress on Hygiene and Demography; dir. Brooklyn Zoöl. Assn., 1915-25. Republican. Conglist. Contbr. articles to magazines and papers, scientific socs. Home: Brooklyn, N.Y. Died June 1936.

SCHOPF, JOHANN DAVID, physician, scientist; b. Wunsiedel, Germany, Mar. 8, 1752; studied medicine and natural sciences U. Erlangen (Germany), 1770-73, M.D., 1776. Served as surgeon in German regt. assigned to Brit. Army, N.Y., 1777-83; traveled throughout Eastern U.S. and Bahamas, 1783-84; pres. Ansbach Medicinal-Collegium, Prussia, 1795. Author: Beytrage zur Mineralogischen Kenntniss des Ostlichen Theils von Nordamerika und seiner Geburge (1st systematic work on Am. geology), 1787; Materia Medica Americana, Potissimum Regni Vegetabilis, 1787; Reise durch einige der mittlern and sudlichen vereinigten nordamerikanischen Staaten nach Ost-Florida und den Bahama-Inselen (his masterpiece), 2 vols., 1788; Historia Testiludinum, Iconibus Illustrata (Fasc. I-VI, Erlangen, 1792-1801;; wrote papers on Am. climate and diseases, also 1st papers ever written on Am. ichthyology, Am. frogs and turtles. Died Sept. 10, 1800.

SCHORGER, ARLIE WILLIAM, chemist; b. Republic, O., Sept. 6, 1884; s. John Valentine and Cora Ellen (Meyers) S.; Ph.B., Wooster (O.) Coll., 1906; M.A., Ohio State University, 1908; Ph.D., University of Wisconsin, 1916, D.Sc. (honorary), 1961; D.Sc. (honorary), Lawrence College, 1955; married William Davison, John Rodger. Asst. chemist Bur. Standards, Washington, 1908, Bur. Internal Revenue, 1909; research chemist U.S. Forest Service, 1909-17; dir. chem. research C. F. Burgess Labs., 1917-31; president of the Burgess Cellulose Company, Freeport, Illinois, 1931-50; professor wildlife management U. Wis., 1951-55, emeritus, 1955-72; dir. Research Products Corporation, Burgess Cellulose Company. Member of Wisconsin Conservation Commn., 1953-60. Recipient Brewster award, 1958. Fellow Am. Ornithol. Union; mem. Am. Chem. Soc., Nat. Audubon Soc. (dir. 1957-59), Am. Soc. Mammalogy, Cooper, Wilson, Wis. ornithol. socs., Wis. Hist. Soc., Wis. Archeol. Soc., Wis. Acad. Scis. (pres. 1942-43), Phi Beta Kappa, Sigma Xi, Delta Upsilon. Republican. Presbyn. Club: Madison. Author: Chemistry of Cellulose and Wood, 1926; The Passenger Pigeon, 1955; The Wild Turkey, 1966. Author articles on chemistry, ornithology. Holder numerous chem. patents. Home: Madison WI Died May 26, 1972.

SCHOTT, CHARLES ANTHONY, asst. U.S. Coast and Geodetic Survey; b. Mannheim, Baden, Germany, Aug. 7, 1826; grad. Polytechnic Sch., Carlsruhe, C.E., 1847. Came to U.S., 1848; entered U.S. Coast and Geodetic Survey, asst., 1856—. Mem. Govt. parties to observe total eclipse of the sun, Aug. 1869 (Springfield, Ill.), and Dec. 1870 (Cantania, Sicily); del. to Internat. Conf. on Terrestrial Magnetism, Bristol, Eng., 1898. Mem. Nat. Acad. of Sciences; Washington Acad. of Sciences. Author of many papers on hydrography, geodesy and particularly on terrestrial magnetism in reports of the Survey, and on tides, meteorology and physics of the globe in Smithsonian Instn. publs. between 1858 and 1881. Address: Washington, D.C. Died 1901.

SCHOUR, ISAAC, (shour), prof. of histology; b. Efingar, Russia, Jan. 11, 1900; s. Nachum and Leah (Passin) S.; brought to U.S., 1913, naturalized, 1918; B.S., U. of Chicago, 1921; D.D.S., U. of Ill., 1924, M.S., 1928; Ph.D., Univ. of Chicago, 1931; Sc.D., Washington Univ., St. Louis, Mo., 1941; m. Esther Kotin, June 14, 1925; children—Lionel, Gabrielle. Instr. in materia medica and therapeutics, U. of Ill., 1924-26, asst. prof. in histology, Coll. of Dentistry, U. of Ill., 1927-31, asso. prof., 1931-35, prof. of histology since 1935, head of dept. since 1937, asso. dean in charge of postgraduate studies, 1946-55, dean, Coll. of Dentistry, 1955—; dental cons. Hebrew U., Jerusalem, 1956—. Recipient Alpha Omega Nat. award, 1947; selected as one of 100 outstanding citizens of Chicago by Jesuit Centennial Committee, 1957. Diplomate Am. Bd. Oral Medicine. Mem. Am. Dental Assn., Internat. Assn. for Dental Research (pres. 1941-42), Chicago Inst. of Medicine, Am. Assn. of Anatomists, A.A.A.S., Soc. Exptl. Biology and Medicine, Phi Beta Kappa, Omicron Kappa Upsilon, Sigma Xi; hon. mem. Alpha Omega. Member Italian Medical Nutrition Mission, 1945. Jewish religion. Author: Atlas of the Mouth (with M. Massler), 1944; also Dentistry for Children (with J.C. Brauer, L.B. Higley and M. Massler), 1952, Oral and Facial Cancer (with B.G. Sarnat), 1950. Contbr. to professional mags. Editor: Noyes' Oral Histology and Embryology, 1953. Home: 625 W. Stratford Pl., Chgo. 13. Office: 808 S. Wood St., Chgo. 12. Died June 5, 1964.

SCHRADER, FRANK CHARLES, (shra'der), geologist; b. Sterling, Ill., Oct. 6, 1860; s. Christian C. and Angeline Marie (Piepo) S.; B.S., M.S., U. of Kan., 1891; A.B., Harvard, 1893, A.M., 1894; m. Kathrine Batwell, Nov. 19, 1919. Teacher of geology, Harvard, 1895-96; geologist U.S. Geol. Survey, 1896-1932; retired at age 72 on account age limit; since 1932 has done 5 years of scientific work; completed gratis the U.S. Geol. Survey report on mining dists. in the Carson Sink Region, Nev.; specialized in mining geology; has traveled widely on professional work in nearly all parts of Alaska and the U.S. Fellow Geol. Soc. Am.; mem. Am. Inst. Mining and Metall. Engrs., Nat. Geog. Soc., Am. Forestry Assn., Washington Acad. Sciences, A.A.A.S., Mining and Metall. Soc. America (mem. sub-com. on antimony), Soc. Econ. Geologists, Geol. and Mineral. societies, Washington Petrologists Club, Pick and Hammer Club, Mineral. Soc. of America. Clubs: Cosmos, Midriver. Contbr. to Reports U.S. Geol. Survey on ore deposits of Western States and Alaska; also articles to geog. mags. Has been chief examiner of mining properties and chief witness in important mining cases in the federal courts in many cities of U.S. Home: 20 Old Chester Rd., Bethesda, Md. Died Feb. 1944.

SCHRADER, FRANZ, zoölogist; b. Magdeburg, Germany, Mar. 11, 1891; s. Franz and Hedwig Dorothea (Rohde) S.; came to U.S., 1901; grad. Curtis High Sch., N.Y. City, 1910; B.S., Columbia, 1914, Ph.D., 1919; m. Sally Peris Hughes, Nov. 1, 1920. Scientific asst. U.S. Bur. Fisheries, 1915-16; asst. in zoölogy, Columbia, 1918-19; pathologist U.S. Bur. Fisheries, 1919-20; asso. in biology, Bryn Mawr. Coll., 1921-25, asso. prof., 1925-30; prof. zoölogy, Columbia U. since 1930 and head dept. zoölogy, 1937-40 and 1946-49, DaCosta prof., 1950-59, emeritus 1959—; vis. prof. Dept. Zool., Duke, 1959—. Trustee of the Marine Biol. Lab., Woods Hole, Mass., 1932-50. Mem. A.A.A.S. (v.p. 1947), Am. Soc. Zoölogists (president 1952), National Academy of Science, Am. Acad. Arts and Scis., Genetics Society, Nat. Resrch. Council. Author: The Sex Chromosomes, 1927, Mitosis, 1944. Also research and pub. papers on sex-determination, parthenogenesis and cytology. Asso. editor Jour. Morphology, 1933-36, Biol. Bull., 1938-50, 59—, Chromosoma, and Columbia Biol. Series, Jour. Biophysical and Biochemical Cytology. Address: Dept. of Zoology, Duke University, Durham, N.C. Died Mar. 22, 1962.

SCHREINER, OSWALD, chemist; b. Nassau, Germany, May 29, 1875; s. Louis and Susanne (Volkert) S.; grad. Baltimore Poly. Inst., 1892; Ph.G., U. of Md., 1894; Johns Hopkins, 1894-95; B.S., U. of Wis., 1897, M.S., 1899, Ph.D., 1902; m. Frances Rector, Oct. 11, 1902; children—Louis Rector, Oswald. U.S. Pharmacopeia research fellow, U. of Wis., 1895-96, asst. in pharm. technique, 1896-97, instr., 1897-1902, instr. phys. chemistry, 1902-03, expert phys. chemist, Bureau of Soils, U.S. Dept. Agr., summer 1902, chemist, 1903-06, chief Div. Soil Fertility Investigations, 1906-40; asst. to chief, Bur. of Plant Industry, 1940-44; collaborator since 1944; counseling professor chemistry, American University, 1914-34. United States delegate 1st International Congress of Soil Science, Washington, D.C., 1927, chmn. exec. com. same; U.S. del. 4th Pacific Science Congress, Java, 1929 and Congress Internat. Sugar Cane Technologists, Java, 1929; cons. del. Inter-Am. Conf. on Agr., 1930; U.S. del. 3d Internat. Congress Soil science, Oxford, Eng., 1935; del. 8th Am. Scientific Congress, Washington, 1939. Fellow A.A.A.S., Am. Society Agronomy; mem. American Chemical Society, American Soc. Biol. Chemists, Assn. of Agrl. Chemists (pres. 1928), Washington Acad. Science, Bot. Soc. America, Soil Sci. Soc. of America, Internat. Soil Sci. Soc., Internat. Sugar Cane Technologists, Sigma Xi, Phi Beta Kappa. Club: Cosmos. Author: The Sesquiterpenes, 1904; Colorimetric, Turbidity, and Titration Methods Used in Soil Investigations, 1906; The Chemistry of Soil Organic Matter, 1910, Lawn Soils, 1911; Nitrogenous Soil Constituents, 1913. Home: 21 Primrose St., Chevy Chase 15 MD

SCHRIEVER, WILLIAM, (shre'ver), physicist; b. Dakota City, Neb., Jan. 16, 1894; s. Fred and Elizabeth (Winkhaus) S.; A.B., Morningside Coll., Sioux City, Ia., 1916; M.S., Univ. Iowa, 1917, Ph.D., 1921; m. Lucille E. Weisenbach, Aug. 16, 1922; Children—William W., Elinor Marie. Asst. prof. physics, U. of Okla., 1919-24, asso. prof., 1924-27, prof. since 1927, chmn. dept. physics, 1942-52, dir. Sch. Eng. Physics, 1942-48; research fellow Am. Petroleum Inst., 1927-29. Served in sci. and research div., Signal Corps, U.S. Army in Airplane Radio Development, 1918. Fellow Am. Phys. Soc., A.A.A.S., Okla. Acad. of Sci. Dir. State Bureau of Standards since 1942. Mem. Soc. of Exploration Geophysicists, Am. Assn. Physics Teachers, Am. Geophys. Union, Sigma Xi (1st pres. Okla. chpt., 1930-31), Gamma Alpha, Sigma Gamma Epsilon, Sigma Pi Sigma. Author: Origin of The Carolina Boys; Magnetic Susceptibilities; Electric Currents Caused by Metallic Dental Fillings; Streaming of Potentials. Home: 910 Chautauqua Av., Norman, Okla. Died Nov. 20, 1958; buried Odd Fellow Cemetery, Norman, Okla.

SCHROEDER, ERNEST CHARLES, veterinarian; b. Baltimore, Apr. 3, 1865; s. Henry A. and Hermine (Wandscher) S.; ed. Baltimore City Coll., and Md. Agrl. Coll.; M.D.V., Harvard, 1887; specialized in scientific agr. and vet. medicine; m. Florence R. Brett, 1889; 1 son, Robert Brett. Attention devoted to experimental medicine. Contbr. to reports and bulls. U.S. Dept. Agr. concerning original investigations of various contagious and infectious diseases; also to various med. jours. Nat. del. Internat. Congress Tuberculosis, Rome, 1912. Home: Bethesda, Md. Deceased.

SCHUCHARDT, RUDOLPH FREDERICK, elec. engr.; b. Milwaukee, Wis., Dec. 14, 1875; s. Louis and Rose (Winkler) S.; B.S. and E.E., U. of Wis., 1897; m. Ada L. Briggs, June 6, 1906 (dec.); children—John William, Elizabeth Ann. With Janesville (Wis.) Electric Light & Power Co., 1897; engr. with Meysenberg & Badt, Chicago, 1897-98; entered employ of Commonwealth Edison Co. (then Chicago Edison Co.) as sub-station operator, June 1898, chief elec. engr., July 1909. Served as expert in Colorado Springs street lighting controversy, 1907; v.pres. and dir. Associated Engineers. Mem. administrative bd. and chmn. public affairs com. Am. Engring. Council. Fellow Am. Inst. Elec. Engrs., 1912 (pres. 1928-29); mem. Illuminating Engineering Soc. (chmn. Chicago sect., 1911-12), Nat. Electric Light Assn. (pres. Chicago sect., 1911-12; chmn. tech. nat. sect., 1922-23; chmn. power survey com.), Am. Acad. Polit. and Social Science, Western Soc. Engrs. (chmn. elec. sect., 1913), Chicago Elec. Assn. (pres. 1901). Awarded Chanute Medal, Western Soc. Engrs., 1907. Del. to World Engring. Congress, Japan, 1929. Congregationalist. Wrote booklet, "Panama and the Isthmian Canal," 1912; also papers read before Am. Inst. E.E. and other socs.; contbr. to tech. mags. Mem. Instn. of E.E. of Great Britain. Home: Glencoe, Ill. Died Oct. 25, 1932.

SCHUCHERT, CHARLES, paleontologist; b. Cincinnati, July 3, 1858; s. Philip and Agatha (Müller) S.; common sch. edn.; A.M. (hon.), Yale, 1904; LL.D., New York U., 1914; unmarried. Began as collector of fossils and made study of paleontology; asst. in paleontology to Mr. E. O. Ulrich, Newport, Ky., 1885-88, to Prof. James Hall, Albany, N.Y., 1888-91; geol. survey of Minn., 1891-92; preparator of fossils with Dr. Charles E. Beecher, Yale Univ., 1892-93; asst. paleontologist, U.S. Geol. Survey, 1893-94; asst. curator sect. paleontology, U.S. Nat. Mus., 1894-1904; prof. paleontology, Yale, prof. hist. geology, Sheffield Scientific Sch. and curator geol. collections, Peabody Mus., Yale, 1904-23 (emeritus). Mem. Nat. Acad. Sciences, Geol. Soc. Am. (pres. 1922), A.A.A.S. (v.p. sect. E, 1927). Author: Textbook of Historical Geological Paleogeography of North America; The Earth and Its Rhythms. Address: Peabody Musuem, New Haven, Conn. Died Nov. 20, 1942.

SCHULHOFF, HENRY BERNARD, army engr.; b. Keyport, N.J., Oct. 30, 1904; s. Adolph and Amalia (Feuerlicht) S.; B.S., Rutgers U., 1930, M.S., 1936; M. Esther Graham Bell, May 8, 1938; 1 son, Kenneth Bell. San. engr. Hdqrs. 1st U.S. Army Engrs., 1942-55; v.p. Lanning San. Engring. Co., 1955-58; san. engr. Hdqrs. 1st U.S. Army Engrs., 1958-61, Hdqrs. Eastern Transport Air Force, 1961-64; civil engr. (san.) Office of Post Engr., Ft. Dix. N.J., 1964-68. Fellow Am. Inst. Chemists; mem. Soc. Am. Mil. Engrs. Republican. Presbyn. Home: Yardville NJ Died Mar. 20, 1968.

SCHULMAN, JACK HENRY, scientist; b. Sao Paulo, Brazil, Nov. 22, 1904; s. Henry and Lucy Augusta (Heine) S.; student Haileybury Coll., Eng., 1918-21; diploma chem. engring., Swiss Fed. Engring. U., Zurich, 1926; Ph.D., Cambridge U., 1930, Sc.D., 1940; m. Frances Holt Logie, Sept. 9, 1950. Came to U.S., 1957. Asst. dir. research, dept. colloid sci., Cambridge U., 1937-50, fellow Trinity Hall, 1946-57, dir. Ernest Oppenheimer Lab., dept. colloid sci., 1949-57, readership in surface chemistry, 1950-57; Stanley Thompson prof. chem. metallurgy, Columbia, 1957—. Dir. Imperial Smelting Corp., London, 1951-57. Mgr. Royal Inst. of Gt. Britain, 1951-56; pres. sci. sect. World Meeting of Surface Activity, Paris, 1954, London, 1957. Decorated Officer Order Brit. Empire, 1945. Mem. Faraday Soc. (council 1949-58, v.p. 1954-56). Clubs: St. James; British University Ski (pres. 1940-57), Kandahar Ski (hon.), (London); Cambridge University Ski (pres. 1935-57), Hawk's (Cambridge). Home: 169 E. 69th St., N.Y.C. 10021. Died June 19, 1967.

SCHULTE, HERMANN VON WECHLLNGER, anatomist; b. Utica, N.Y., Aug. 9, 1876; s. Bernard and Julia Low (Nelson) S.; A.B., Trinity Coll., Conn., 1897; M.D., Coll. Phys. and Surg. (Columbia), 1902; summer course, U. of Berlin, 1905; m. Susan Augusta Embury, Sept. 11, 1907. Interne, Presbyn. Hosp., New York, 1902-04; successively instr. anatomy, asst. demonstrator, demonstrator, adj. prof., asst. prof., asso. prof., Coll. Phys. and Surg. (Columbia), 1904-16; prof. anatomy, 1916—, jr. dean, 1916-17, dean, 1917—, Creighton U. Sch. of Medicine, Omaha, Neb.; chief of staff, St. Joseph's Hosp.; pres. State Anatomical Bd. of Neb., 1916—; mem. Omaha Pub. Library Bd., 1927-30. Lt. col. Med. Res., comdg. Gen. Hosp. No. 55, 1922—. Mem. exec. com. Omaha Community Chest; trustee Soc. for Relief of Disabled; mem. bd. Omaha Social Settlement. Fellow A.A.A.S., New York Acad. Science, Neb. Acad. Science (pres. 1922). Mem. Am. Acad. Polit. and Social Science, Omaha Council Social Agencies (pres. 1925-29), Nebraska Conf. for Social Work (pres. 1928-29). Episcopalian. Home: Omaha, Neb. Died July 13, 1932.

SCHULTZ, ALFRED REGINALD, geologist; b. Tomah, Wis., Mar. 26, 1876; s. John Fredrick and Ida M. (Kirst) S.; B.S., U. of Wis., 1900; teacher mathematics and physics, high sch., Wausau, Wis., 1900-02; fellow U. of Chicago, 1904-05, Ph.D., 1905; m. Helene E. Burkhardt, Oct. 26, 1910; children—Irene Esther, Maxine Dorothy, John Burkhardt (dec.). Resident hydrologist, Wis., 1903; geologist in charge Leith exploration party, Ont., Can., 1904; became connected with U.S. Geol. Survey, 1905, has served as field asst., hydrologic aid, geologic aid, asst. geologist and geologist; mem. Coal Bd. (classification and valuation pub. coal lands), 1910; geologist Barber Asphalt Co. and Bermuda Oil Co., Venezuela and Trinidad, South America, 1910-11; chmn. Phosphate Board and Metall. Bd. Land Classification, U.S. Geol. Survey, 1912-16, geologist in charge mineral div. land classification, U.S. Geol. Survey, 1916-18; geologist, oil div. U.S. Fuel Adminstrn., 1918; mgr. Burkhardt Milling & Electric Power Co., 1918-42; pres. Willow River Power Co., 1922-42; pres. Afton Power Co., 1921-42; pres. Hudson Hotel Co., 1929-42; dir. First Nat. Bank; cons. geologist. Mem. Geol. Soc. America, A.A.A.S., Am. Foresty Assn., Sigma Xi, etc. Republican. Lutheran. Clubs: St. Paul (Minn.) Athletic; Commercial (Hudson, Wis.). Writer numerous papers and govt. bulls. on stratigraphic and economic geology, gold, soda, oil, coal, leucite, potash, phosphate, water supplies, etc. Home: 800 Vine St., Hudson, Wis. Died Sept. 30, 1943.

SCHULTZE, ARTHUR, university prof.; b. Germany, March 30, 1860; s. Gustav and Emma (Linemann) S.; ed. univs. of Leipzig, Berlin, and Kiel, Ph.D.; m. Christine Wichmann, of Germany, Oct., 1888. Instr. mathematics, Friedrich Werdersche Realschule, Berlin, 1887; asst. State Mining Bur., San Francisco, 1890; instr. mathematics, Hoboken (N.J.) Acad., 1892-97; principal-elect same, 1897; 2d asst., Boys' High Sch., New York, 1897-1902; head teacher mathematics, High Sch. of Commerce, New York, 1902-05; assistant prof. mathematics, New York Univ., 1905-1912. Examiner Coll. Entrance Exam. Bd., 1904-05-06. Inventor Dynamic Heater (patented 1896). Author: Propagation of Heat in a Homogeneous Rectangular Parallelopiped, 1887; Plane and Solid Geometry (with Dr. E.L. Sevenvak), 1901; Elementary Algebra, 1905; Advanced Algebra, 1906; Graphic Algebra, 1907; The Teaching of Mathematics in Secondary Schools, 1912. Fellow A.A.A.S. Home: Weehawken, N.J. Address: 952 Nene Jonas St., Rapperswil, Switzerland.

SCHUMACHER, ANTON HERBERT, indsl. engr.; b. Kansas City, Mo., May 3, 1908; s. Frank A. and Mary M. (Carey) S.; B.S., U. Kan., 1929; m. Winnifred E. Scholer, Aug. 30, 1929; 1 dau., Mary Winnifred (wife of Dr. D.M. Hawkins). Valuation engr. Mo. Pub. Service Commn., 1929-42; instr., prodn. engr., quality control engr. Pratt & Whitney Aircraft Corp. Mo., Kansas City, 1942-46; cost estimator J. F. Pritchard & Co., Kansas City, 1946-47; utilities engr., City of Kansas City, 1947-60; chief rate engr. Gas Service Co., Kansas City, Mo., 1960-68. Mem. Engrs. Club Kansas Cith, Native Sons Kansas City, Sigma Phi Epsilon. Club: Hillcrest Country. Home: Kansas City MO Died Aug. 12, 1968.

SCHUTTLER, PETER, wagonmaker; b. Wachenheim, Grand Duchy of Hesse Dormstadt, Germany, Dec. 22, 1812; m. Dorothy Gauch, 1838, 3 children including Peter. Came to U.S., 1834; worked in wagon shop, Buffalo, N.Y.; moved to Sandusky, O., 1838; established wagon shop, Chgo., 1843; in brewery bus. for short time; began mfg. buggies, carriages, harnesses, as well as wagons, 1849; Schuttler wagon. (stronger, lighter, larger capacity) helped displace old prairie schooner; traveled to Germany, 1855; owner finest mansion of the time of Chgo. Died Chgo., Jan. 16, 1865.

SCHUYLER, JAMES DIX, engr.; b. Ithaca, N.Y., May 11, 1848; s. Philip Church and Lucy M. (Dix) S.; ed. Friend's Coll., 1863-68; self-ed. after that; m. Mrs. Mary Ingalls Tuliper, July 1889. Engaged in ry. constrn. in Colo., 1869-73; removed to Calif., 1873; asst. state engr. Calif., 1878-82; chief engr. and supt. Sinaloa & Durango R.R., Mexico, 1882-84; built section of great sea-wall, San Francisco, 1884-85; built Sweetwater dam, 1887-88, and later the Hemet dam. Built water works in Denver, Portland, Ore., etc., and irrigation works in West. Cons. engr. in water-right litigation and water works constrn., from Hawaii to Ohio and from British Columbia to City of Mexico; also cons. hydraulic engr. Am. Beet Sugar Co. Engaged in bldg. large power plants in Calif. and Mex., and extensive works for irrigation and power development in Mex., Brazil, N.M., Colo., and other Western states; mem. of commn. of engrs. on Los Angeles City Aqueduct; cons. engr. to Territorial Govt. of Hawaii on constrn. of Nuuanu dam; to Monterey Water Works and Sewer Co., Ltd., Mex.; to Kobe Syndicate, on extensive power project in Japan, involving very high dam; to Mexican Light & Power Co., Ltd., on building of four large dams for power in Necaxa Valley, State of Puebla, Mex.; to Vancouver Power Co., Ltd., Vancouver, B.C., building dam at Coquitlam Lake. Mem. commn. of engrs. apptd. by President Roosevelt to accompany President-elect Taft to Panama, Jan. 1909, to finally decide type of canal.

Author: Reservoirs for Irrigation, Water Power and Domestic Water Supply, 1901. Contbr. to Engineering News and other scientific jours. Twice winner of Rowland prize, 1888 and 1896, for best papers of yr. read before Am. Soc. C.E. Home: Ocean Park, Calif. Died Sept. 13, 1912.

SCHWAB, MARTIN CONSTAN, cons. engr.; b. Baltimore, Md., 1880; s. Maurice and Laure (Constan) S.; (forebears settled Maryland 1780); preparatory education, Polytechnic Inst., Baltimore; grad. engring. course, John Hopkins, 1896; hon. Bach. Engring., extra-ordinem. same univ., 1926; m. Elizabeth Weisel, April 1904; children—Mrs. Katharine Boutet Scallan, Mrs. John E. B. Shaw. Assisted in electrification of B.&O. R.R., 1896; later apptd. cons. engr. for Md. Electric Co.; active in reconstruction of Baltimore after the fire; served as cons. engr. Soldiers' Home, Washington, D.C., and in design and construction of bldgs. in Washington, Phila. and New York, under firm name of Adams & Schwab; settled in Chicago and est. engring. business as Martin C. Schwab; served as cons. engr. for Sears, Roebuck & Co. since 1905 (installed first high speed vertical and horizontal assembly line; also first air-conditioned administration bldg. in U.S. with sealed windows, 1905); cons. engr. for electrification of drainage canal under Mayor Dunne's adminstrn.; cons. engr. Ill. State Bd. of Administration, 1913; identified with construction of the Bell Bldg., Mallers Bldg., Michigan Square Bldg., Adler Planetarium, Harris Trust & Savings Bank Bldg., Corn Exchange Nat. Bank, Hotel Sherman, Morrison Hotel, Mandel Bros., Rothschilds and the Lytton stores, 30 N. Michigan Av. Bldg., 333 N. Michigan Av. Bldg., WLS Broadcasting Station, Yellow Cab Bus properties; (all of Chicago), Gen. Am. Tank Car Corp., East Chicago, Ind., Union Station, Kansas City, Mo., Bamberger Dept. Store, Newark, N.J., Julia Lathrop Government Housing Project, Chicago. Patentee of various devices applied in large bldg. structures throughout the country. Has constructed bldgs. in approximately 150 cities in 43 states. Chmn. bd. Hosp. Liquids Corp., Chicago. Member of Friends of China, Rennaisance Club, Field Museum (governing life mem.), Chicago Art Institute, Oriental Inst. (U. of Chicago). Clubs: Engineering, Tavern, Lake Shore Country, Chicago Fishing (Chicago). Collector of etchings, early Chinese, Persian and Egyptian ceramics. Home: Ambassador East Hotel. Office: 333 N. Michigan Av., Chicago, Ill. Died Jan. 2, 1947.

SCHWAB, ROBERT SIDNEY, physician; b. St. Louis, Oct. 6, 1903; s. Sidney Isaac and Helen Dorothy (Stix) S.; A.B., Harvard, 1926, M.D., 1931; B.A., St. Johns Coll., Cambridge, 1928, M.A. Physiology, honors part II, Tripos, 1929; m. Dorothy Smith Miller, Aug. 26, 1932 (dec. May 1971); m. 2d, Joan Sheahan, Oct. 15, 1971. Intern medicine and neurology Boston City Hosp., 1931-34; resident neurology Mass. Gen. Hosp., Boston, 1935, established electroencephalographic lab., dir., neurologist, 1937-72; resident psychiatry Boston Psychopathic Hosp., 1936; asso. prof. neurology Harvard Med. Sch., now prof. emeritus; cons. neurologist Cape Cod Hosp., Mass. Eye and Ear Infirmary. Met. State Hosp., Br. Office Vets. Bur.; U.S. Naval Hosp., Chelsea, Mass. Mem. med. adv. bd. Parkinson's Disease Found.; chmn. med. adv. bd. Myasthenia Gravis Found. Am. Fulbright lectr. U. Munich, Germany, 1957. Served to comdr. USN, 1941-46. Diplomate Am. Bd. Neurology and Psychiatry. Fellow Am. Acad. Neurology; mem. Am. Neurol. Assn. (v.p.), Am. Psychol. Assn., Eastern Assn. Electroencephalographers (pres. 1946), Am. (sec. 1947-49, pres. 1950-51), Brit., French Italian electroencephalographic socs., Boston Soc. Neurology and Psychiatry, Assn. for Research in Nervous and Mental Disease, Internat. Fedn. Electroencephalographic Socs. (v.p.), Ergonomics Research Soc. Eng. Clubs: Cambridge Cruising (Eng.); Harvard (Boston). Author: Electroencephalography in General Practice, 1951. Editor: Electroencephalography and Clin. Neurophysiology. Contbr. articles to profl. jours. Home: Boston MA Died Apr. 6, 1972; buried Mt. Wollaston Cemetery, Quincy MA

SCHWAIN, FRANK ROBERT, chem. engr.; b. Cin., Feb. 5, 1913; s. Frank and Viola (Rosenfelder) S.; Ch.E., U. Cin., 1935; m. Georgia Vogele, Oct. 15, 1938; children—Gayle Frances, David George. Plant chemist Nat. Dairy, Cin., 1931-36; cereal chemist Kroger Food Found., Cin., 1936-40, chemist in charge cereal lab. and pilot bakery, 1940-43; quality control chemist Kroger Co., Columbus, O., 1943-47; in charge bakery research, exptl. bakery of bulk products service dept., Procter & Gamble Ivorydale, O. 1947—, now mgr. bulk food tech. services. Registered profl. engr., Ohio. Mem. Am. Assn. Cereal Chemists (nat. sec. 1946-53, nat. pres. 1954, William F. Geddes Meml. award 1966), Cin. Sect. Assn. Cereal Chemists (sec.-treas., vice chmn., chmn.), Am. Soc. Bakery Engrs., Am. Commons Club (nat. treas.), Alpha Chi Sigma. Roman Catholic. K.C. (3 deg., 4 deg.). Author articles, (series) biscuit and cracker flour tech. Cereal Chemistry, 1944, 45-46. Dept. editor Cereal Sci. Today. Home: 811 Finney Trail, Cin. 45224. Office: Procter & Gamble Co., M.A. & R. Bldg., Ivorydale, O. Died June 7, 1967.

SCHWAMB, PETER, engineer; b. Arlington, Mass., February 13, 1858; s. of Peter and Clara (Beucher) S.; S.B. in Mech. Engring., Mass. Inst. Tech., 1878, post-grad. student same, 1878-89; m. Amy E. Bailey, of Arlington, June 7, 1893. Draughtsman Howe Scale Co., Rutland, Vt., 1879-80, Hinkley Locomotive Co., Bosotn, 1880-83; instr. mech. engring., 1883-84, asst. prof. mechanism, 1884-88, asso. prof., 1888-96, prof., 1896-1901, prof. machine design, 1901-11, and 1883-1911 in charge dept. mechanical arts, Mass. Inst. Tech. Treas. The Theodore Schwamb Co., Arlington, since 1897. Member school com., 1897-1900, water commr., 1896-1903, chmn. bd. pub. works, 1904-07, Arlington. Republican. Fellow Am. Acad. Arts and Sciences; mem. Am. Soc. M.E., Boston Soc. C.E. Clubs: Technology, Engineers, Arlington Boat. Author: Elements of Mechanism (with Prof. A.L. Merrill), 1904. Address: Arlington, Mass.

SCHWARTZ, ISAAC HILLSON, physician; b. Somerville, Mass., Mar. 25, 1912; s. Edward Elias and Ida (Hillson) S.; M.D., U. Basle (Switzerland); m. Caroline Lewis Mekelburg, Oct. 17, 1937; children—Miriam (Mrs. Michael Jay Salkind), Jane, Jonathan. Pediatric house officer Boston City Hosp., 1940-41; intern St. Lukes Hosp., New Bedford, Mass., 1941-42, chief pediatric dept., chief electronencephlography, until 1970; resident in pediatrics U.S. Naval Hosp., Phila.; postgrad. in neuropsychiatry Hosp. of U. Pa.; pediatrician New Bedford Child and Family Service; med. dir. Dartmouth (Mass.) Well-Child Clinic, New Bedford Cerebral Palsy Unit; alternate electroencephlographer Truesdales Hosp., Fall River, Mass.; med. officer New Bedford Health Dept.; mem. neurology dept. seizure unit Boston Children's Med. Center. Corporator, New Bedford Five Cents Savs. Bank. Bd. dirs. Opportunity Center. Served to comdr., M.C., USNR, 1942-46. PTO. Diplomate Am. Bd. Pediatrics. Fellow Am. Acad. Pediatrics; mem. A.M.A., Am. Acad. Child Psychiatry, New Eng. Pediatric Soc., Mass. Med. Soc., Pi Lambda Phi. Democrat. Jewish religion. Research on electroencephalography. Home: Dartmouth MA Died Mar. 20, 1970; buried Tifereth Israel Cemetery, New Bedford MA

SCHWARTZ, LOUIS, physician, surgeon; b. N.Y.C., July 4, 1883; s. Jacob and Lena (Jonap) S.; A.B., Central High Sch. of Phila., 1901; M.D., Jefferson Med. Coll., 1905; m. Marguerite O. Adler, Apr. 30, 1907; 1 son, Anthony Max. Acting asst. surgeon USPHS, N.Y., 1906-11, asst. surgeon, 1911-15, past asst. surgeon, 1915-20, surgeon, 1920-31, sr. surgeon, 1931-37, med. dir., chief dermatoses sect. Indsl. Hygiene Div., 1937-47; ret. July 1947; cons. dermathology sec. USPHS. Asso. clin. prof. dermatology and syphilology N.Y. U. Coll. Medicine; adj. prof. dermatology Georgetown U. Sch. Medicine; cons. dermatology and condr. courses in occupational dermatoses. Cons. to U.S. Naval Med. Research Lab., Bethesda, Md., Army Indsl. Hygiene Lab., Balt. during World War II. Diplomate Am. Acad. Dermatology and Syphilology. Fellow A.M.A. (mem. com. on occupational dermatoses of sect. on dermatology and syphilology), Am. Pub. Health Assn. (chmn. com. on indsl. skin irritants), hon. fellow Am. Coll. Allergists; mem. N.Y. Acad. Medicine, Assn. Mil. Surgeons, Balt.-Washington Dermatol. Soc. Jewish religion. Adviser editorial bd. Jour. Investigative Dermatology. Co-author: Cosmetics and Dermatitis, 1946; Occupational Diseases of the Skin (2d edit. 1947). Author articles on occupational dermatoses and related subjects to various publs. Address: 915 19th St., N.W., Washington 6. Died Feb. 1963.

SCHWARZ, EDWARD R(OBINSON), educator; b. Lawrence, Mass., Mar. 4, 1899; s. Franz Herman and Susan Emily (Robinson) S.; S.B., Mass. Inst. Tech., 1923; M.S. (hon.), Lowell Textile Inst., 1950; m. Dorothy Alice Bourque, Dec. 27, 1926; children—Edward H., Hope Robinson (Mrs. Kenneth E. Cox), Dorothy Gretchen (Mrs. Robert W. Perkins). Prof. textile tech. Mass. Inst. Tech., 1937—, head textile div., 1940—. Pres. Mass. Safety Council, 1940-43, now dir.; cons. mil. planning div., research and development br. O.Q.M.G., 1942-45; coordinator safety engring. tng. E.S.M.W.T.P. Recipient Olney medal, Am. Assn. Textile Chemists and Colorists, 1947; H. deWitt Smith medal, Am. Soc. Testing Materials, 1951. Fellow Textile Inst., A.A.A.S., Textile Research Inst.; mem. Am. Inst. Physics, Am. Assn. Textile Technologists, Am. Soc. Quality Control, Fiber Society, National Fire Protection Association American Assn. Textile Chemists and Colorists, Sigma Xi, Tau Beta Pi. Congregationalist. Home: 63 Lovell Rd., Melrose 76, Mass. Office: Mass. Inst. of Tech., Cambridge 39, Mass. Died July 27, 1961.

SCHWARZMANN, HERMAN J., architect, engr.; b. Munich, Germany, 1843. Came to U.S., circa 1864, settled in Phila.; became asst. engr. on works in Fairmont Park, later chief engr. of design; architect-in-chief Centennial Expdn., Phila., 1876, identified especially with plans for Meml. Hall and Horticulture Bldg.; worked in assn. with Alfred Buchman, N.Y.C., from close of expdn. until 1890. Died Sept. 23, 1891.

SCHWATKA, FREDERICK, explorer; b. Galena, Ill., Sept. 29, 1849; s. Frederick Schwatka; attended Willamette (Ore.) U.; grad. U.S. Mil. Acad., 1871; M.D., Bellevue Hosp. Med. Coll., N.Y.C., 1876. Commd. 2d lt. 3d Cavalry, U.S. Army; admitted to Neb. bar, 1875; comdr. (with William Henry Gilder of N.Y. Herald) Arctic exploring expdn. sailing on ship Eothen from N.Y.C., 1878, they performed longest sledge journey then on record, 1879-80; resigned from U.S. Army, 1885; explored course of Yukon River; commanded Alaskan expdn. sponsored by N.Y. Times, 1886; established the fact that white men could exist and carry on useful scientific work in the Arctic. Author: Along Alaska's Great River, 1885; Nimrod in the North, 1885; The Children of the Cold, 1886; In the Land of Cave and Cliff Dweller, 1893. Died Portland, Ore., Nov. 2, 1892.

SCHWEINITZ, EMIL ALEXANDER DE, bacteriologist; b. Salem, N.C., Jan. 18, 1866; s. Bishop E. A. and Sophia A. (Herman) de S.; ed. at Nazareth Hall and Bethlehem, Pa.; grad. U. of N.C., 1882; Ph.D., Göttingen, Germany; M.D., Columbian U., Washington. Dir. biochemic lab., U.S. Dept. Agr.; dean and prof. Columbian Med. Sch. U.S. del. to 4th Internat. Congresses on Tuberculosis, Paris, 1898, and Berlin, 1899; U.S. del. to Internat. Med. Congress and Congress for Hygiene, Paris, 1900. Made many original investigations and published many papers on the products of bacteria, preparation of tuberculins, various antitoxins, the composition of bacilli, especially those of tuberculosis; the comparative virulence of tubercle bacilli and virulence of bovine tubercle bacilli for man; also on disinfectants and hygienic problems. Address: Washington, D.C. Died 1904.

SCHWEITZER, (JOHANN) PAUL, chemist; b. Berlin, Germany, Mar. 16, 1840; s. A. F. T. and Julia (Hoehne) S.; Ph.D., U. of Göttingen, 1869; LL.D., U. of Mo., 1897; m. Sarah Howard, June 18, 1870. Asst. to H. Rose, Berlin, 1863, Poly. Inst., Phila., 1865, Sch. of Mines (Columbia), 1866; prof. chemistry, 1872-94, prof. agrl. chemistry, 1874-1906, chemist, Expt. Sta., 1887-1906, U. of Mo. Gold medal Paris Expn., 1900. Author of numerous papers on chem. subjects in scientific jours. and Agrl. Sta. bulls. Address: Columbia, Mo. Died 1911.

SCHWIDETZKY, OSCAR, O. R., surg. instrument maker; b. Konitz, Polish Corridor, Dec. 31, 1874; s. August and Fredericke (Mohnke) S.; LL.D., Fairleigh Dickinson U., 1953; m. Anna Hasselhuhn, 1916. Came to U.S., 1900, naturalized, 1917. Apprentice to maker steel and surg. dental instruments, Berlin; worked with instrument makers, Berlin, Crefeld, also Aix-la-Chapelle; studied orthopedic work; importer surg. supplies, Germany, 1902-11; with Dr. Horace Greeley organized Greeley Lab., 1911-13; with Becton, Dickinson & Co., Rutherford, N.J., 1913—; originator numerous surg. instruments, including continuous caudal needle, syringes, Ace bandages, hypodermic needles for use in med. treatment, alleviation of pain; dir. South Bergen Savs. & Loan Assn., Wood Ridge, N.J. Hon. mem. Burge Tb Clinic, Phila. Mem. Assn. Med. Directors, Internat. Anesthesia Research Soc. (hon.), American Surgical Trade Assn. (hon.). Mem. Reformed Ch. Author articles, pamphlets on med. subjects. Home: 31 Lakeside Dr., Ramsey, N.J. Office: Becton, Dickinson and Co., Rutherford, N.J. Died Oct. 9, 1963.

SCHWINN, FREDERICK SIEVERS, civil engr.; b. Ft. Scott, Kan., June 20, 1889; s. Benjamin Franklin and Lillie (Sievers) S.; ed. Lewis Inst. and Armour Inst. Tech., Chicago; m. Beatrice Sanford Barnes, Dec. 25, 1912; children—Frederick Seamans, Elizabeth Caroline, David Sanford. Rodman, instrumentman and asst. engr. S.P. Co., Sacramento, 1908-13; asst. engr. and asst. supt. S.P. Lines, Lafayette, La., 1913-17; asst. div. supt. I.J.N. Ry., Palestine, Tex., 1917-18; engr. for receiver, 1918-20, chief engr. for receiver, 1920-22; chief engr. Internat. G.N. R.R. Co., Dec. 1, 1922-June 1, 1925; asst. chief engr. Gulf Coast Lines and Internat. G.N. R.R., 1925-27; asst. chief engr. M.P. Lines, 1927-56; engring. cons. and analyst, 1956-68. Registered professional engineer, civil. Member of American Railway Engineering Association (director 1941-45; v.p., 1947-48, pres. 1949), Am. Soc. Testing Materials, Soc. Am. Mil. Engrs., Am. Soc. C.E., Tex. Soc. Profl. Engrs., Houston Engring. and Scientific Soc. Republican. Episcopalian. Home: Houston TX Died Dec. 2, 1968; interred Meml. Mission Mausoleum, Forest Park's Calvary Cemetery Houston TX

SCHWITALLA, ALPHONSE MARY, clergyman, zoologist; b. Beuthen, Upper Silesta, Germany, Nov. 27, 1882; s. Peter J. and Pauline (Welzel) S.; came to U.S., 1885; A.B., St. Louis U., 1907, A.M., 1908; Ph.D. in Zoology, Johns Hopkins, 1921; LL.D., Tulane U., 1938; Sc.D., Lawrence Coll., 1939. Joined Jesuit Order, 1900; ordained priest Roman Cath. Ch., 1915; instr. chemistry St. Xavier Coll., Cin., 1907-10; instr. biology and physiology St. Louis U., 1910-12; instr. chemistry Rockhurst Coll., Kansas City, Mo., 1916-18; asso. prof. biology, St. Louis U., 1921-24, prof. biology, 1924-46, dean Sch. of Med., 1927, dean Sch. Nursing, 1928-40, regent, 1940-44, regent Sch. of Dentistry, 1924-44, Moderator Fedn. Cath. Physicians' Guilds, since 1945. Pres. Cath. Hosp. Assn. U.S. and Can., 1928-47, pres.

emeritus since 1947; past pres. North Central Assn. Colls. and Secondary Schs., 1936; hon. v.p. Am. Social Hygiene Assn., since 1947. Mem. sub-com. on Hosp. of Health and med. com. of Council on Nat. Def., Com. on Post-war Med. Service, A.M.A. since 1944; adv. com. on Pub. Edn. for Prevention of Venereal Disease, USPHS since 1943; adv. com. of the U.S. Cadet Nurse Corps, since 1943; exec. com. Adv. Council on Med. Ed.; adv. bd. on Health Services, A.R.C. since 1945; bd. dir. Nat. Soc. for Med. Research, 1946—; Asso. fellow A.M.A. (adv. com. Council on Med. Edn. and Hosps.); mem. Assn. Am. Med. Colls., Am. Council on Edn. (problems and plans com.), Internat. Hosp. Assn. (bd. dirs.), Am. Coll. Hosp. Adminstrs. (charter mem. and mem. com. on Edn.), Com. on Costs of Med. Care, Nat. Citizens Com. of the Community Moblzn. for Human Needs, Commn. on Instns. Higher Edn., North Central Assn., Mo. Social Hygiene Assn. (dir., pres. 1930-32), Nat. Soc. for Prevention Blindness (dir.), Mo. Soc. for Crippled Children (dir.), Am. Social Hygiene Assn. (dir.), Am. Assn. Med. Social Workers (adv. council), Nat. Orgn. for Pub. Health Nursing (adv. council), Am. Coll. Dentists (hon. fellow and mem. nat. research com.), others. Maj. Chaplains Res., U.S. Army, war chaplain, Kansas City, Mo., 1918-19. Mem. A.A.A.S., Ecol. Soc., St. Louis Acad. Sci., Am. Soc. Zoölogy, Anthrop. Soc. Am., Am. Sociol. Soc. Am. Soc. for Control Cancer, Am. Pub. Health Assn., Genetics Soc. Am., Mo. Acad. Sci., History of Sci. Soc., Mo. Med. Assn., So. Med. Assn., Phi Beta Kappa, Sigma Xi, Alpha Omega Alpha, Phi Nu, Phi Sigma, Theta Beta, K.C. Editor: Hospital Progress, 1928-47, Linacre Quar., 1945-48. Contbr. to Biology, Sociology, Med. Edn., Hosp. Adminstrn., Nursing Edn., various publs. Home: 221 N. Grand Av., St. Louis 3. Office: 1402 S. Grand Blvd., St. 4. Died May 1965.

SCIPIO, LYNN A., mech. engr., educator; b. White County, Ind., Oct. 20, 1876; s. Adolphus and Evaline (Mahiu) S.; A.B., Tri-State Coll., Angola, Ind., 1902; student Armour Inst. Tech., Chicago, 1903; B.S. in Mech. Engring., Purdue U., 1908; M.E., 1911, Ph.D., 1931; m. Margaret Booher, Aug. 27, 1908; 1 dau., Elizabeth E. Teacher, pub. schs., Ind. advancing to prin. and supt.; asst. prof. mech. engring., U. of Neb., 1908-12; dean Robert Coll. Engring. Sch., Constantinople, and cons. engr., 1912-20; dir. Am. Soc. Heating and Ventilating Engrs. Research Lab., U.S. Bur. Mines, Pittsburgh, 1920-21; dean Robert Coll. Engring. Sch., 1921-43; head engineer, War Production Board, 1943-44; industrial Rehabilitation Specialist for U.N.R.R.A., 1945-47; mem. Am. Soc. Mech. Engrs., Am. Soc. Heating and Ventilating Engrs., Nat. Research Council, Sigma Xi, Pi Tau Mu. Methodist. Mason. Author: English-Turkish Technical Dictionary, 1939; Elements of Machine Design, 1928. Home: 525 Hartford St., Worthington OH

SCOFIELD, CARL SCHURZ, agriculturist; b. Bloomington, Minn., Feb. 5, 1875; s. John Darius and Carolyn Samantha (Damon) S.; B.S.A., U. Minn., 1900; spl. course in chemistry of wheat Conservatoire des Arts et Métiers, Paris, 1901; m. Emma Theresa Scott, Sept. 8, 1903 (died Apr. 1935); children—Francis Collins, John Darius, Marcia Ann. With U.S. Dept. Agr., 1900-45, agriculturist in charge irrigation agr. 1905-45. Mem. Bot. Soc. Washington, Washington Acad. Scis., Am. Assn. Geographers, Am. Geophys. Union (chmn. sect. hydrology 1933-35). Club: Cosmos. Author various bulls. pub. by Bur. Plant Industry, U.S. Dept. Agr., also spl. reports and papers on quality of irrigation water. Home: 9301 Crandall Rd., Lanham, Md. 20801. Died Aug. 28, 1966; buried Atlantic, Me.

SCOTT, ARTHUR CURTIS, consulting engr.; b. Belmont, N.Y., Aug. 31, 1873; s. John Harrison and Mary A. (Kinney) S.; B.S. in M.E., R.I. State Coll., Kingston, R.I., 1895; post-grad. work, summers, Harvard, Brown, Cornell U., Mass. Inst. Tech., Clark U. and U. of Wis.; grad. student, U. of Wis., 1901-2, Ph.D., 1902; m. Alice Elizabeth Clarke, of Albany, N.Y., June 23, 1901. Instr. in physics, 1895-7, prof., 1897-01, prof. physics and elec. engring., 1902-3, R.I. State Coll.; prof. elec. engring., U. of Tex., 1903-11; consulting practice, 1911—; pres. Scott Consulting Engring. Co.; consulting engr., Austin, Tex., in rebuilding dam across Colo. River and hydro-electric installation, 1912, etc. Conglist. Mem. Am. Soc. Mech. Engrs., Am. Inst. Elec. Engrs., Soc. for Promotion of Engring. Edn.; hon. mem. Southwestern Elec. and Gas Assn. Home: 1420 Sanger Av. Office: 632 Wilson Bldg., Dallas TX

SCOTT, CHARLES FELTON, engineer; b. Athens County, Ohio, Sept. 19, 1864; s. William Henry and Sarah (Felton) S.; A.B., Ohio State U., 1885; post-grad. course 1 1/2 yrs., Johns Hopkins; A.M., Yale, 1911; Sc.D., U. of Pittsburgh; D.Eng., Stevens Inst. Tech., 1912, Brooklyn Poly. Inst., 1935; D.Sc., Ohio State U., 1937; LL.D., Rose Poly. Inst., 1939; m. Emily Clark, Oct. 15, 1895. With Westinghouse Electric & Mfg. Co., Pittsburgh, 1888-1911, prof. elec. engring., Yale, 1911-33 (emeritus). Pres. Nat. Council State Bds. Engring. Examiners, 1938-39. Pres. Engrs. Soc. Western Pa., 1902, Am. Inst. Elec. Engrs., 1902-03; chmn. bldg. com. Engring. Socs. Bldg. (gift of Andrew Carnegie), New York; mem. Soc. Promotion Engring. Edn. (pres. 1921-23; chmn. bd. investigation and coördination, 1922-33); mem. administrative bd. Am. Engring. Council, 1921-33; chmn. Engrs. Council for Professional Development, 1935-38, chmn. Com. on Professional Recognition since 1938; chmn. Conn. Bd. of Registration for Professional Engrs. and Land Surveyors since 1935. Awarded Edison medal by Am. Inst. Elec. Engrs.; Lamme medal by Soc. Promotion Engring. Edn. Mem. Am. Soc. Mech. Engrs., Am. Inst. Consulting Engrs., Sigma Xi, Tau Beta Pi, Phi Beta Kappa; hon. mem. Conn. Sec. Civil Engrs. Home: 19 Trumbull St., New Haven, Conn. Died Dec. 17, 1944.

SCOTT, EARL FRANCIS, mech. engr.; b. Marshall, Tex., Dec. 31, 1874; s. Francis Marion and Lucy Muncton (Duncan) S.; B.E., Vanderbilt, 1903, M.E., 1906; m. Nina Viola Elmer, Nov. 21, 1906; children—Elizabeth Elmer, Margueryte Elmer, Fred, William Elmer. Instr. in shop work, Vanderbilt U., 1897-1903; in the North and with consulting engrs., Miss., 1903-05; in employ A. M. Lockett & Co., New Orleans, 1905-08; in charge engring. dept. Gen. Fire Extinction Co., Atlanta, Ga., 1908-13; asst. mgr. Griscom Russell Co., Atlanta, 1913-14; pres. and mgr. Earl F. Scott & Co., contracting mech. engrs., Atlanta, 1914—. Mem. Bd. Mech. Engrs., City of Atlanta. Fellow Am. Soc. Mech. Engrs. (mgr. 1920-23, v.p. 1923-25). Episcopalian. Mason (32 deg., Shriner). Home: Atlanta, Ga. Died Dec. 18, 1940.

SCOTT, GEORGE GILMORE, biologist; b. Geneseo, N.Y., May 3, 1873; s. John Laughlin and Mary (Jameson) S.; A.B., Williams Coll., 1898; A.M., 1899; Ph.D., Columbia, 1913; m. Phebe Tomkins Persons, 1902;children—Robert Townley, Richard Persons. Associated with College of the City of New York since 1901, as tutor, instructor, assistant professor, asso. prof., prof., and since 1936, emeritus prof. of biology; investigator U.S. Bur. Fisheries, 1913, 14, 18; consultant in zoology, Rollins Coll.; mem. exec. com. Thomas R. Baker Museum, Rollins Coll. Fellow A.A.A.S., N.Y. Zool. Soc.; mem. Am. Soc. of Zoologist, Am. Soc. of Naturalists, Fla. Acad. Sciences (chmn. sect. of biol. sciences, 1939), Fla. Audubon Soc. (exec. com. 1944-45), Asso. Physicians of Long Island (hon.), Phi Beta Kappa, Club: University (Winter Park, Fla.; pres. 1941-42). Author: Science of Biology, 1930; Microscopic Anatomy of Vertebrates (with J. I. Kendall), 1935. Home: 460 Henkel Circle, Winter Park FL

SCOTT, ISAAC MACBURNEY, mfr.; b. Tuscarawas County, O., Feb. 19, 1866; s. Dr. Wm. Briar and Mary (Boyd) S.; ed. pub. schs., Morristown, O.; m. Fora B. Dickerson, Jan. 1, 1890; children—Hugh Briar, Henry Dickerson, Arthur MacBurney. Began with Aetna Iron & Nail Co., Bridgeport, O., 1883; sec. Beaver Tin Plate Co., Lisbon, O., 1894-98; sec. Aetna Standard Iron & Steel Co., Bridgeport, O., 1898-1900; auditor Am. Sheet Steel Co., N.Y. City, 1900-03; sec. La Belle Iron Works, Steubenville, O., 1903-04, pres., 1904-13; organized, 1913, Wheeling Sheet & Tin Plate Co., and built tin plate plant at Yorkville, O. (1st plant in world to successfully produce black-plate for tinning by cold-reducing process), merging with Wheeling Steel & Iron Co., 1914, and pres. latter, 1914-20; company merged, 1920, with La Belle Iron Works and Whitaker-Glessner Co., forming Wheeling Steel Corp., of which was pres. until Oct. 31, 1930; chmn. bd. Sharon Tube Co., Scott Lumber Co., Nat. Bank of W.Va.; pres. Buckeye Rolling Mill Co. Republican. Presbyterian. Clubs: Fort Henry (Wheeling); Duquesne (Pittsburgh); Ohio Soc. (N.Y.). Home: Stamm's Lane. Office: Wheeling Bank & Trust Bldg., Wheeling, W.Va. Died Apr. 27, 1942.

SCOTT, RUSSELL B(URTON), physicist; b. Ludlow, Ky., Apr. 17, 1902; s. Burton W. and Carrie May (Riggs) S.; B.S. cum laude, U. Ky., 1926, M.S., 1928; m. Leonora Downing, June 13, 1928; children—Marion Lee (Mrs. William F. Kenkel), Burton W. Instr. physics U. Ky., 1927-28; mem. staff Nat. Bur. Standards, 1928-67, chief cyrogenic engring. lab., Boulder, Colo., 1953-62, acting dir. Boulder labs., 1962-63, mgr., 1963-67. Mem. U.S. nat. com. Internat. Inst. Refrigeration, 1957-60, mem. ad hoc. com. establish U.S. membership, 1956-57, mem. commn. I, 1959-67. Fellow Am. Phys. Soc., A.A.A.S.; mem. Research Soc. Am. (pres. Boulder chpt. 1961), Phi Beta Kappa, Sigma Pi Sigma. Author: Cryogenic Engineering, 1959; also numerous articles. Am. editor, contbr.; Technology and Uses of Liquid Hydrogen, 1964, Am. editor Jour. Cyrogenics, 1960-67. Home: Boulder CO Died Sept. 24, 1967.

SCOTT, WALTER E(DWIN), JR., mining engr.; b. Black Hawk, Colo., Nov. 7, 1895; s. Walter Edwin and Annette (Gilhooley) S.; student Regis Prep. Sch.; B.S., Regis Coll.; m. Nora Beardsley Livingston, Dec. 19, 1925; 1 dau., Margaret Annette. Various engring. and exec. positions mining cos., Ariz., Cal., Colo., Ida., Mo., Nev., Can., and Alaska, 1917-37; cons. mining engr. pvt. office, Central City, Colo., 1937-50; city engr. City Central, 1938-48; co. engr. Gilpin Co., Colo., 1938-42; commr. mines State Colo., 1950-59, ret. 1959; chmn. Colo. Geol. Survey Bd. 1950—; sec.-treas., dir. Dumont Investment Co.; owner mining properties, Clear Creek and Gilpin cos., Colo. Chmn. Colo. Mineral Resources Bd., 1938-50; mem. Colo. Metal Mining Fund Bd., 1950. Registered profl. engr., Colo. Mem. Am. Inst. Mining and Metall. Engrs., Am. Mining Congress, Colo. Mining Assn. (past v.p.), Colo. Sci. Soc., Colo. Soc. Engrs. Mason (Shriner). Mining editor of the Register-Call, 1940—. Contbr. profl. jours. Home: Central City, Colo. Office: Museum Bldg., Denver 2. Died July 25, 1959; buried Bald Mountain Cemetery, Central City, Colo.

SCOTT, WENDELL G(ARRISON), physician; b. Boulder, Colo., July 19, 1905; s. Ira Dudley and Callie (Soper) S.; A.B., U. Colo., 1928, Sc.D. (honoris causa), 1954; M.D., Washington U., 1932; m. Ella Johnson, June 29, 1929; children—Horace Wendell, Ann (Mrs. Michel TerPogossian), Sarah Jane (Mrs. C. H. Wallace). Served his internship at the Barnes Hosp., St. Louis, 1933-34, asso. radiologist, 1938; instr. sch. medicine Washington U., St. Louis, 1934-38, asst. prof. radiology, 1938-40, asst. prof. clin. radiology, 1940-41, asso. professor, 1941-56, prof., 1956-72; mem. alumni rep., dir. Washington U., 1954-58. Cons. radiology Oak Ridge Inst. Nuclear Studies, 1955-62, mem. cancer control com. Nat. Cancer Inst. USPHS, 1958-60, 66-70, mem. nat. radiation adv. com., 1960-64; mem. dependents med. care adv. com. Dept. of Defense, 1958-67; mem. com. radiol. NRC., 1947-52, 54, chmn. 1955-64; cons. spl. med. adv. bd. Vets. Administration, 1952-57, chmn. 1954-56, area cons. radiol., 1957-72; cons. radiol., pathology, Armed Forces Inst. Pathology, 1953-58. Served as lt. to capt., med. corps USNR, 1942-46; rear adm. Med. R.C., 1958-65; res. consultant radiology Bur. Medicine and Surgery, Navy Dept., 1946-72; mem. adv. commn. cancer control br. U.S.P.H.S., Health, Edn., Welfare, Chmn. Genitourinary Task Force; mem. adv. bd. for conquest cancer U.S. Senate, 1970-71; mem. Nat. Cancer Adv. Bd., 1971-72, President's Nat. Cancer Adv. Bd. Dir. Am. Cancer Soc., 1957-72, pres., 1963-64. Recip. numerous awards, citations for sci. contbns. by med. socs. Diplomate Am. Bd. Radiology. Fellow Am. Coll. Radiology (chmn. commn. on pub. relations 1950-60, chancellor 1960-64, recipient gold medal 1965, chmn. com. mammography); mem. A.M.A. (chmn. section radiology 1958, del. 1966-72), Mo., So. med. assns., Detroit Medical Soc. (honorary), St. Louis Soc. Radiologists (pres. 1946-48), Am. Radium Soc. (v.p.), Am. Roentgen Ray Soc. (treas. 1947-56, pres. 1958-59), Radiol. Soc. N.A. (vice president 1944), U.S. Assn. Mil. Surgeons (exec. council 1946), Med. Cons. World War II, Tex., Rocky Mountain radiol. socs. (hon.), Washington U. Sch. Medicine Alumni Assn. (pres. 1954). Sociedad de Cancerologia de Guadalajara (hon.), also fraternities of Sigma Xi and Alpha Omega Alpha. Clubs: University, Bellerive Country, Racquet, St. Louis, Clayton, (St. Louis). Author articles medical journals. Editor: Genetics, Radiobiology, and Radiology (Charles C. Thomas), 1959; Planning Guide for Radiologic Installations; associate editor American Journal. Roentgenology and Radium Therapy, 1949-66. Editor Your Radiologist, 1956-68, Cancer, 1964-72. Home: St Louis MO Died May 4, 1972; buried Oak Grove Cemetery St Louis MO

SCOTT, WILLIAM BERRYMAN, geologist; b. Cincinnati, Feb. 12, 1858; s. Rev. William M. and Mary E. (Hodge) S., g.g.d. of Benjamin Franklin; A.B., Princeton 1877; Ph.D., Heidelberg, 1880; LL.D., U. of Pa., 1906; Sc.D., Harvard, 1909, Oxford U., 1912, Princeton, 1930; m. Alice A. Post, Dec. 15, 1883. Asst. in geology, Princeton U., 1883, prof. geology and paleontology, 1884-1930, now emeritus prof. Mem. Nat. Acad. Sciences, Am. Philos. Soc. (pres. 1918-25), Geol. Soc. America (pres. 1924-25). Awarded E. K. Kane medal, Geog. Soc. Phila.; Wollaston medal, Geol. Soc., London, 1910; F. V. Hayden medal, Acad. Nat. Sci., Phila., 1926; Elizabeth Clark Thompson gold medal, Nat. Acad. Sciences, 1931; R. A. Penrose gold medal, Nat. Acad. Sciences, 1944. Author: An Introduction to Geology, 1897, 3d edit., 1932; A History of Land Mammals in the Western Hemisphere, 1913, 2d Edit., 1937; The Mammalian Fauna of the White River Oligocens, 1935-41; Mammalian Fauna of the Duchesne River, 1945; The Theory of Evolution, 1917; Physiography, 1922; also about 60 monographs upon geol. and palaeontol. subjects. Editor and joint author of Reports Princeton University expdns. to Patagonia (9 vols.). Home: 7 Cleveland Lane, Princeton, N.J. Died Mar. 29, 1947.

SCOTT, WILLIAM EARL DODGE, naturalist; b. Brooklyn, N.Y., Apr. 22, 1852; s. Moses Warren (U.S.A.) and Juliet Ann (Cornell) S.; A.B., Harvard, 1873; m. Marian, d. James Johonot, June 22, 1877. Curator, Princeton, 1874-85, curator dept. ornithology, Princeton, 1897—. Did field work for Brit. Mus., Am. Mus. Natural History, Mus. of Comparative Zoölogy, etc. Author: Bird Studies, 1897; Story of a Bird Lover, 1902; Birds of Patagonia, Part I, 1903, Part II, 1910; also 60 tech. papers on birds in scientific jours., and popular articles in mags. Address: Princeton, N.J. Died 1910.

SCOVEL, SYLVESTER, engr. and promoter Cuban enterprises; b. Denny Station, Allegheny County, Pa., July 29, 1869; s. Rev. Sylvester F. and Caroline (Woodruff) S.; ed. pub. sch., Pittsburgh, and U. of Wooster, O.; grad. Mich. Mil. Acad., 1887; spent portions of 4 yrs. at U. of Mich., working between times; m. Frances, d. S. Carr Cabanné, Apr. 5, 1897. From 19 to 26 yrs. of age continuously time-keeper in blast furnace constrn., Tenn.; asst. supt. water works constrn., Ky.; mech. draughtsman, Pittsburgh; promoter, Chicago, and Cleveland, O., Oct. 5, 1895; sent to Cuba as war corr. Pittsburgh Dispatch and New York Herald; made prisoner, Havana, Jan. 1896; escaped; entered employ New York World; injured in field; lived with insurgents 11 months at different visits, ran Spanish mil. and police lines 20 times, going and coming from field; captured, Feb. 7, 1897, and imprisoned by Spaniards at Sancti Spiritus, Cuba; released by pressure of U.S. Govt., after legislatures of 13 States and U.S. senate had requested his release. Sent by The World to Turco-Greek war; then Spain; then to the Klondike; thence to Havana just before blowing up the "Maine"; then with U.S. navy and army until Am. occupation of Santiago and Spanish evacuation of Havana, Jan. 1, 1899; consulting engr. for U.S. mil. govt., Cuban customs service, 1899-1902. Address: Havana, Cuba. Died 1905.

SCOVELL, MELVILLE AMASA, chemist; b. Belvidere, N.J., Feb. 26, 1855; s. Nathan and Hannah (Aller) S.; B.S., U. of Ill., 1875, M.S., 1877, Ph.D.; m. Nannie D. Davis, Sept. 8, 1880. Instr. of chemistry, 1875-76, asst. prof., 1876-80, prof. agrl. chemistry, 1880-84, U. of Ill.; mgr. sugar factories, 1884; spl. agt. U.S. Dept. Agr., 1884-85; dir. Ky. Agrl. Expt. Sta., 1885-1910; dir. Agrl. Expt. Sta. and dir. Agrl. Coll., State U., 1910—. Pres. park commn. of Lexington, Ky.; mem. Ky. State Fair Com.; mem. U.S. Food Standard Com.; in charge pure food control, fertilizer control, concentrated feed control and seed control work of State of Ky. Invented a process of clarifying cane juices by superheating (with Henry A. Weber), a method now extensively used; also modification in the Kjedahl method where nitrates are present. Fellow A.A.A.S., Soc. Chem. Industry, London; mem. Am. Acad. Polit. and Social Science; past pres. Assn. Official Agrl. Chemists; past pres. Am. Assn. Agrl. Colls. and Expt. Stas. Address: Lexington, Ky. Died 1912.

SCOVILLE, WILBUR LINCOLN, pharmaceutical chemist; b. Bridgeport, Conn., January 22, 1865; s. Lemuel and Augusta C. (Fuller) S.; grad. Massachusetts College of Pharmacy, 1889; Ph.D. honoris causa, Phila. College of Pharmacy and Science, 1924; hon. Pharm.D., Massachusetts College of Pharmacy, 1927; hon. M.Sc., University of Michigan, 1928; hon. D.Sc. in Pharm., Columbia, 1929; m. Cora B. Upham, of Wollaston, Mass., Sept. 1, 1891; children—Amy Augusta (Mrs. Ralph D. Pearson), Ruth Upham (Mrs. T.G. Spriggs); m. 2d, Lillian W. Paine, of Detroit, Mich., Nov. 1919. Prof. pharmacy, Mass. Coll. Pharmacy, 1892-1904; research chemist, Parke, Davis ü Co., Detroit, 1907-34, head analytical dept., 1924-34; retired. Mem. com. revision of U.S. Pharmacopoeia, 1900-10 and 1920-40; mem. 2d, 3d and 5th, and chmn. 4th com. revision Nat. Formulary. Awarded Ebert prize in pharmacy, 1923; hon. mem. Rho Chi Soc., U. of Mich. Coll. of Pharmacy, 1927; hon. mem. Pa. State Pharm. Assn., 1927; hon. life mem. Mich. State Pharm. Assn., 1929. Awarded Remington honor medal, 1929. Author: Art of Compounding, 1895 (6 edits. to 1936). Editor New England Druggist, 1894-97, The Spatula, 1898-1903. Address: 10088 Crocuslawn, Detroit, Mich.

SCRIBNER, CHARLES EZRA, elec. engr.; b. Mt. Vernon, O., Feb. 16, 1858; s. Charles Harvey and Mary Elizabeth (Morehouse) S.; ed. Toledo High School; D.Engring., U. of Vt., 1920; m. Marietta Margaret Brown, Dec. 1, 1880 (died 1920); children—Charles Harvey, Margaret Belle, Mary Etta (dec.). Began with Western Electric Mfg. Co., Chicago, 1876, firm name changed, 1882, to Western Electric Co., connected with New York office, 1908-16, as chief engr. in charge of development and experimental work; retired. Took out between 400 and 500 U.S. patents (3d in elec. field in U.S.) and filed between 600 and 700 applications; prin. inventions relate to telephone switchboards. Awarded Gold Medal, Paris Expn., 1900. Fellow Am. Inst. E.E. (mgr. 1912-13, v.p. 1913-15). Republican. Mem. Evangelical Ch. Home: Jericho, Vt. Died June 25, 1926.

SCRIPTURE, EDWARD WHEELER, physician, psychologist; b. Mason, N.H., May 21, 1864; s. Orrin Murray and Mary F. (Wheeler) S.; A.B., Coll. City of New York, 1884, A.M., 1890; student at Berlin, Zürich; Ph.D., Leipzig, 1891; fellow Clark U., 1891; M.D., Munich, 1906; m. Leipzig, Germany, May Kirk (q.v.), Apr. 22, 1890. Dir. psychol. lab., Yale U., 1892-1902; investigator for the Carnegie Instn., 1902-06; asso. in psychiatry, Columbia Univ., 1909—. Discoverer of the law of "mediate association of ideas," of a method of measuring hallucinations and imaginations, and of a method of producing anaesthesia by electricity. Inventor of color-sight tester for detecting colorblind and color-weak employes in railroad and marine service, etc.; specially known for work on the voice. Awarded gold medal, Paris Expn., 1900; bronze medal, Buffalo Expn., 1901; Longstreth medal, Franklin Inst., 1902. Author: Thinking, Feeling, Doing, 1895; The New Psychology, 1897; Elements of Experimental Phonetics, 1901; Researchers in Experimental Phonetics, 1906; Stuttering and Lisping, 1912. Address: 236 W. 74th St., New York.

SCRUGGS, LOYD, inventor, mfr.; b. Willisburg, Ky., Mar. 11, 1875; s. Sabritt and Margaret Jane (DeBaun) S.; ed common schs. until 11; studied mechanics pvtly.; m. Edith B. Sims, Nov. 16, 1909. Pres. Copper Clad Malleable Range Co., prop. The Loyd Scruggs Co. Has taken out numerous patents covering improvements in cooking ranges, theatre ventilation, electric motors, electric razors, etc.; designer of apparatus for production of stage illusions, in collaboration with the late Howard Thurston, magician. Member Academy of Science of St. Louis, Mo. Member Christian (Disciples) Church. Clubs: Missouri Athletic, Contemporary Club. Contbr. on merchandising and business administration. Home: 7469 Washington Blvd. Office: Missouri Insurance Bldg., St Louis 1 MO

SCUDDER, JOHN MILTON, eclectic physician; b. Harrison, O., Sept. 8, 1829; s. John Scudder; grad. Eclectic Med. Inst., Cincinnati, 1856; m. Jane Hannah, Sept. 8, 1849; m. 2d, Mary Hannah, after 1861; at least 4 children. Prof. spl. and pathological anatomy Eclectic Med. Inst., 1857, dean, 1861, prof. diseases of women and children, 1858-60, prof. pathology and principles and practice of medicine, 1860-87, prof. hygiene and phys. diagnosis, 1887-94; edited Eclectic Med. Journal, 1861-94, Journal of Health, The Eclectic (literary journal); 1870-71. Author: Practical Treatise on the Diseases of Women, 1857; Materia Medica and Therapeutics, 1860; Eclectic Practise of Medicine, 1864; Domestic Medicine; or Home Book of Health, 20 editions, 1865; Principles of Medicine, 1867; Eclectic Practice in Diseases of Children, 1869; Familiar Treatise on Medicine, 1869; Specific Medication and Specific Medicines, 1870; Specific Diagnosis, 1874. Died Daytona, Fla., Feb. 17, 1894.

SCUDDER, SAMUEL HUBBARD, naturalist; b. Boston, Apr. 13, 1837; s. Charles and Sarah Lathrop (Coit) S.; A.B., Williams, 1857, A.M., 1860; B.S., Lawrence Scientific School (Harvard), 1862; Sc.D., Williams, 1890; LL.D., Western U. of Pa., 1890; m. Jeannie Blatchford, June 25, 1867. Assisted Louis Agassiz in Mus. Comparative Zoölogy, 1862-64; sec. Boston Soc. of Natural History, 1862-70, custodian, 1864-70, pres., 1880-87; asst. librarian, Harvard, 1879-82; palaeontologist of U.S. Geol. Survey, 1886-92. Mem. Nat. Acad. Sciences, 1877—; Am. Philos. Soc.; fellow Am. Acad. Arts and Sciences, A.A.A.S. (gen. sec., 1875). Author: A Century of Orthoptera, 1879; Catalogue of the Scientific Serials of All Countries, 1879; Butterflies, Their Structure, Changes and Life Histories, 1881; Nomenclator Zoölogicus, 1884; The Winnipeg Country, 1886; Butterflies of the Eastern United States and Canada, 1889; A Classed and Annotated Bibliography of Fossil Insects, 1890; The Fossil Insects of North America, 1890; Index to the Known Fossil Insects of the World, 1891; Tertiary Rhynchophorous Coleoptera of the United States, 1893; Brief Guide to the Common Butterflies, 1893; The Life of a Butterfly, 1893; Frail Children of the Air, 1895; Revision of the American Fossil Cockroaches, 1895; Guide to the Genera and Classification of N.A. Orthoptera, 1897; Revision of the Orthopteran Group, Melanopli, 1897; Everyday Butterflies, 1899; Catalogue of the Described Orthoptera of the United States and Canada, 1900; Adephagous and Clavicorn Coleoptera from the Tertiary Deposits at Florissant, Colo., 1900; Index to North Am. Orthoptera, Described in the 18th and 19th Centuries, 1901 (Boston Soc. Natural History). Address: Cambridge, Mass. Died 1911.

SCULLEN, ANTHONY JAMES, civil engr.; b. Little Falls, N.Y., Sept. 4, 1889; s. Thomas and Catherine (Fikely) S.; C.E., Rensselaer Poly. Inst., 1911; hon. D.Engr., Columbus U., 1930; m. Elizabeth Helen Moore, Dec. 31, 1912; children—Elizabeth Mary, Anthony James, Edward Joseph. Asst. city engr., Little Falls, N.Y., 1911-12; instr. civil engring., Catholic Univ., 1912-18, asso. prof., 1918-23, prof., 1923-70, dean, sch. engring. and architecture, 1937-70; chief engr., bldg. div., Dist. Columbia, 1924-34, consulting engr. since 1934. Papal decoration, Medale Benemarinte, 1938. Member Am. Soc. of C.E. K.C. Club: Cosmopolitan (Washington, D.C.). Home: Washington DC Died July 8, 1970; buried Gate of Heaven Cemetery, Silver Spring MD

SEAGRAVE, FRANK EVANS, astronomer; b. Providence, R.I., Mar. 29, 1860; s. George Augustus and Mary Greene (Evans) S.; ed. sch. of Rev. Charles H. Wheeler, 1869-74; Harvard Coll. Obs., 1875-77; M.A., Brown U., 1911; unmarried. During period 1878-1901 went on 3 total solar eclipse expdns. and observed visually and photographically many phenomena, such as the reversing layer, corona and prominence spectra; photographed transit of Venus, at Providence, R.I., Dec. 6, 1882; accomplished important work in relation to Halley's comet which appeared in 1909, 1910. Has made numerous observations of comets, and computations and observations of variable stars of different types to determine their periods and forms of their light curves; also orbits of comets, asteroids, the planet Pluto, etc. Owner and dir. of a new obs., N. Scituate, R.I. Died July 15, 1934.

SEAMAN, ARTHUR EDMUND, geologist; b. Casnovia, Mich., Dec. 29, 1858; s. George Washington and Sarah Melissa (Moore) S.; B.S., Mich. Coll. Mines, 1895, E.M., 1915; m. Mary Annette Brotherton, Nov. 11, 1885 (dec.); children—Wyllys Arthur, Mary Lucile. Connected with Mich. Coll. of Mines, 1889—, prof. geology, 1899—. Republican. Episcopalian. Mason. Home: Houghton, Mich. Died 1937.

SEAMAN, HENRY BOWMAN, engineer; b. New York, Jan. 20, 1861; s. Valentine H. and Rebecca (Cromwell) S.; B.S., Swarthmore Coll., 1881, C.E., 1884; m. Grace Dutton, Apr. 7, 1904; children—Ayres Cromwell, Henry Bowman. Admitted to N.Y. bar; in practice as civ. engr.; was asst. engr. Kings Co. Elevated Ry., Brooklyn; bridge engr. Erie Ry. system; resident engr. of constrn., N.Y.,N.H.&H. R.R. at Mt. Vernon, N.Y.; chief of engrs. Audit Co. of New York, 1898; engr. abolition of grade crossings, Syracuse, N.Y., 1898; chief engr. (for contractors) 4th Av. sect. Underground R.R., New York, 1900; reconstruction of bridges, N.Y.,N.H.&H. R.R., 1903; consulting engr. dept. bridges, New York; chief engr. Public Service Commn., New York; contractor's engr. for foundation and masonry Hell Gate Bridge, New York; supervising engr. shipbuilding plant, U.S.N.; chief engr. Steinway Tunnel Extension, Manhattan, New York. Home: Brooklyn, N.Y. Died Oct. 24, 1940.

SEARLE, ARTHUR, astronomer; b. London, Eng., Oct. 21, 1837; s. Thomas and Anne (Noble) S.; brother of George Mary S., came to U.S., 1840; A.B., Harvard, 1856, A.M., 1859; m. Emma Wesselhoeft, Jan. 1, 1873. After 12 yrs. in other places became asst. in Harvard Coll. Obs., 1869-83; asst. prof. of astronomy, 1883-87, Phillips prof., 1887-1912 (emeritus), Harvard U. Fellow Am. Acad. Arts and Sciences. Author: Outlines of Astronomy, 1874; Essays, I-XXX, 1910. Died Oct. 24, 1920.

SEARLE, GEORGE MARY, clergyman, astronomer; b. London, England, June 27, 1839; s. Thomas and Anne (Noble) S.; bro. of Arthur S.; came to U.S., 1840; A.B., Harvard, 1857, A.M., 1860; (hon. Ph.D., Catholic U., Washington, 1896). Asst. Dudley Obs., Albany, 1858-59; discovered the asteroid "Pandora"; with U.S. Coast Survey, 1859-62; asst. prof. U.S. Naval Acad., 1862-64; asst. Harvard, Obs., 1866-68. Converted to Roman Catholic faith, 1862; joined Paulists, March 1868; ordained priest, 1871; became teacher of science in Paulist Sem.; apptd. chief prof. mathematics, Catholic U., Washington, Oct. 1895. Superior gen. of the Paulist Fathers, 1904-09. Author: Elements of Geometry, 1877; Plain Facts for Fair Minds, 1895; How to Become a Catholic, 1906; The Truth About Christian Science, 1916. Retired. Died July 7, 1918.

SEARLE, HARRIET RICHARDSON (MRS. WILLIAM D. SEARLE), carcinologist; b. Washington; d. Charles F. E. and Charlotte Ann (Williamson) Richardson; A.B., Vassar, 1896, A.M., 1901; Ph.D., Columbian, 1903; m. William D. Searle, 1913. Collaborator Smithsonian Instn. Mem. Biol. Society, Washington, Washington Acad. Sciences; fellow A.A.A.S. Has contributed to Proceedings of United States National Museum and other publs.; monograph on the Isopods of North America, Bull. 54, U.S. Nat. Mus., 1905. Home: 1810 Wyoming Av., Washington DC

SEARLES, WILLIAM HENRY, engineer; b. Cincinnati O., June 4, 1837; s. Asbury M. and Rachel (Mitchell) S.; student Wesleyan Univ., 1856-57; C.E., Rensselaer Poly. Inst., 1860; m. Mary L. Doolittle, June 8, 1870. Prof. geodesy and road engring., Rensselaer Poly. Inst., 1862-64; locating and constructing rys. in Ohio, Mich., Pa., Ind., and N.Y., 1864-85; engr. N.Y. state canals, 1876-78; cons. engr. in gen. practice, 1880—. Author: Field Engineering, 1880; The Railroad Spiral, 1882. Home: Elyria, O. Died Apr. 25, 1921.

SEARS, FRED COLEMAN, pomologist; b. Lexington, Mass., May 11, 1866; s. Thomas Bartlett and Mary Katherine (Wellington) S.; B.S., Kan. Agrl. Coll., 1892, M.S., 1896; D.Sc., Kan. State Coll., 1937; m. Ruth T. Stokes, Oct. 19, 1897; children—Florence Hart and Elizabeth Kent (twins). Asst. horticulturist Kan. Expt. Sta., Manhattan, 1892-96; prof. horticulture Utah Agrl. Coll., 1897; dir. Nova Scotia Sch. of Horticulture, Wolfville, N.S., 1897-1904; prof. horticulture Nova Scotia Agrl. Coll., Truro, N.S., 1904-07; prof. pomology Mass. Agrl. Coll., 1907-36. Republican. Conglist. Mason. Author: Productive Orcharding, 1914; Productive Small Fruit Culture, 1920; Fruit-Growing Projects, 1928. Has spent each summer working with Sir Wilfred Grenfell, in Labrador, 1928-39. Home: Amherst, Mass. Died Oct. 1949.

SEARS, JULIAN D(UCKER), geologist; born Baltimore, Maryland, June 3, 1891; the son of Dr. Thomas Edward and Julia (Ducker) S.; A.B., Johns Hopkins, 1913, Ph.D., 1919; m. Elizabeth T. Lamdin, June 16, 1919 (dec. 1969); children—William Brewster, Richard Sherwood. Geologist, U.S. Geol. Survey, 1915-16. Sinclair Central Am. Oil Corp., 1917-18; rejoined staff, U.S. Geol. Survey, geologist, 1918-23, administrative geologist, 1924-48, staff geologist 1948-61. Recipient Distinguished Service medal Dept. Interior. Mem. Geol. Soc. of Am., Am. Assn. of Petroleum Geologists, Soc. of the Cincinnati of Md., Phi Gamma Delta, Phi Beta Kappa. Club: Kenwood Golf and Country (Bethesda, Md.). Contbr. numerous articles and reports to tech. jours. and U.S. Geol. Survey publs. Home: Chevy Chase MD Died May 1970.

SEARS, WALTER HERBERT, engineer; b. Plymouth, Mass., Dec. 8, 1847; s. Thomas Bartlett and Louisa (Churchill) S.; C.E., Mass. Inst. Tech., 1868; m. Ella M.

Blackmer, Nov. 18, 1897. As chief or prin. asst. engr. has built water works at Winchester, Beverly, Plymouth, Mass., Pawtucket, R.I., Newark, N.J., Rochester, N.Y., Stillwater, Minn.; also new water supply for New York, etc. Home: Plymouth, Mass. Died Oct. 7, 1911.

SEASTONE, CHARLES VICTOR, civil engr.; b. New Boston, Ill., Apr. 18, 1872; s. John August and Eva Sophia (Hillmore) S.; B.S., in Civ. Engring., U. of Ill., 1895; m. Susan Sarah Bouton, June 25, 1900; children—John Bouton, Charles Victor. Began in employ of U.S. Govt. on Mississippi River Survey, 1895; asst. dept. of theoretical and applied mechanics, U. of Illinois, 1898-1900; successively instr., asst. prof. and asso. prof. municipal and sanitary engring., Purdue U., 1900-07; cons. engr., Madison, Wis., 1907—; now asso. consultant Mead, Ward & Hunt, hydro-electric developments and power plants; pres. Madison Metropolitan Sewerage Commn. Republican. Home: Madison, Wis. Died Sept. 26, 1940.

SEATON, ROY ANDREW, educator, engineer; b. Glasco, Kan., Apr. 17, 1884; s. Oren Andrew and Sarah Elizabeth (Bartley) S.; B.S. in Mech. Engring., Kan. State Coll., 1904, M.S., 1910; studied U. of Wis., summer 1908; S.B. in Mech. Engring., Mass. Inst. Tech., 1911; Sc.D., honorary, Northeastern University, 1942; m. Gay Perry, June 26, 1913 (died Oct. 4, 1918); 1 son, James Newell; m. 2d, Elnora Wanamaker, June 14, 1921; children—Sarah Frances, Robert Wanamaker, Elnora Margaret, Roy Andrew, II. With Kan. State Coll. most of time, 1904-70, instr. asst. prof. of mathematics, 1904-06, instr. and asst. prof. mech. engring., 1906-10, prof. applied mechanics and machine design, 1910-20, dean school of engring. and architecture and director Engineering Experimental Station, 1920-49; prof. applied mechanics Kan. State Coll., 1949-70; on leave of absence as director of Engineering, Science and Management Defense Training, U.S. Office of Edn., 1940-42; acad. dir. Air Force Inst. Tech., Wright-Patterson AFB, O., 1953-57; designing draftsman steam turbine dept. Gen. Electric Co., 1911-12. Served as capt. engring. div. Ordnance Office, U.S. Army, Washington, D.C., designing arty. ammunition Jan.-Dec. 1918. Chmn. Kan. Registration Bd. for Professional Engrs., 1931-47; chmn. Kansas Bd. Engring. Examienrs since 1947; director Nat. Council of State Bds. of Engring. Examiners, 1935-37; rep. of Soc. for Promotion Engring. Edn. on Engrs. Council for Professional Development, 1937-42; mem. Com. on Professional Training, Engrs. Council for Professional Development, 1933-38. Mem. Am. Soc. Mech. Engrs. (past vice chmn. Mid-Continent sect.), Soc. for Promotion Engring. Edn. (pres. Neb.-Kan. Sect. 1923-24; mem. council 1926-29; v.p. 1930-31; pres. 1932-33; awarded Lamme medal, 1942), Kan. Engring. Soc. (v.p. and acting pres. 1929-30; pres. 1930-31), Engring. Sect. Assn. Land Grant Colls. and Univs. (sec. 1925-29; chmn. 1929-30), Am. Assn. U. Profs. (hon.), Phi Kappa Phi, Sigma Xi, Sigma Tau, Acacia. Mason. Clubs: Manhattan Country, Rotary. Author: Concrete Construction for Rural Communities, 1916; also bulletins, arts. in tech. press, etc. Editor Engring. Expt. Sta. Record Quarterly, 1925-29, Engring. Expt. Sta. Record Summary, 1929. Home: Manhattan KS Died May 23, 1970; buried Sunset Cemetery Manhattan KS

SEAVER, FRED JAY, mycologist; b. Webster County, Ia., Mar. 14, 1877; s. Joshua Marshall and Guhelma M. (Sturtevant) S.; B.S., Morningside Coll., Sioux City, Ia., 1902, Sc.D., 1931; M.S., State U. of Ia., 1904, Ph.D., 1912; student Columbia, 1906-07; m. Hortense Adelaide Schnebly, June 14, 1905 (died July 25, 1940); children—Bernice, Hortense Eloise (Mrs. Albert Cullen Hewitt, Jr.); m. 2d, Mrs. Finetta A. Fry Heller, Sept. 23, 1941; 1 stepson, Robert A. Heller. Instr. in biology, Iowa Wesleyan Coll., 1905-06, prof., 1906; asst. prof. botany, N.D. Agrl. Coll., mycologist to expt. station, 1907-08; dir. labs. N.Y. Bot. Gardens, 1908-11, curator 1912-43, head curator 1943-49, mem. board mgrs. 1947-49; ret.; asso. prof. biology Fla. Southern College, 1949-50. Received certificate of Accomplishment from State University of Iowa, 1947. Bot. explorations for New York Botanical Gardens in Bermuda, Trinidad and Puerto Rico for the government. Member Mycological Society America (editor Mycologia, official organ), Bot. Soc. America (chmn. mycol. sect., 1932), Nat. Geog. Soc., Torney Bot. Club (treas. 1921-22; v.p., 1943, pres. 1945), Sigma Xi; fellow A.A.A.S. Republican. Methodist. Author: The North American Cup-fungi (operaculates), 1928, supplemented edit., 1941; also many tech. papers. Home: Winter Park FL Died Dec. 21, 1970.

SEBENIUS, JOHN UNO, mining engr.; b. Sweden, Sept. 10, 1862; s. Carl William and Josephine Christine (Creutzer) S.; grad. Royal Tech. Inst. and Sch. of Mines, Stockholm, 1886; came to America, 1888; m. Susan May A. Manning, 1895 (died 1918); children—William Hobbs Manning, Carl Harald. Asst. supt. Witherbee, Sherman & Co., mines, Lake Champlain, N.Y., 1890-92; spl. exploration on Missabe Range, 1892-94; mining engr. for Rouchleau Ray Iron Co., 1894-98, for Lake Superior Consolidated Iron Mines, 1898, until U.S. Steel Corp. was formed, 1901; became mining engr. and supt. explorations and mineral lands on Missabe Range, for Oliver Iron Mining Co., 1901; gen. mining engr. for same company, 1905-30. Served as maj. on staff of Gov. John A. Johnson and as col. staffs Govs. Eberhardt, Hammond and Burnquist. Home: Duluth, Minn. Died Dec. 18, 1932.

SECOR, JOHN ALSTYNE, engineer; b. N.Y. City, June 28, 1847; s. Samuel and Caroline (Thompson) S.; ed. pub. schs., N.Y. City; m. Georgina E. Carpenter, of N.Y. City, June 22, 1877. Consulting engr., Advance-Rumely Co. A Pioneer in development of the farm tractor; designer of the oil-pull line, and inventor of Secor System of automatic multiple-unitary control by which the governor of an oil engine controls its speed, power, efficiency and quality of combustion, "solving the problem of using the heavy oil fuels in a throttling governed engine under varying loads." Mem. Am. Soc. Agrl. Engrs., Am. Soc. M.E. Republican. Methodist. Home: 1108 Indiana Av., LaPorte, Ind.

SEDDON, WILLIAM LITTLE, civil engr.; b. Stafford Co., Va., Oct. 14, 1862; s. John Seddon and Mary A. (Little) S.; student U. of Mo., 1880-81; m. Kate McD. Martin, Nov. 7, 1888; 1 dau., Mary Alexander. With Seaboard Airline Ry., 1898—, consecutively as instrument-man, resident engr. and asst. engr. until 1905, chief engr., 1905-13, asst. to pres., 1913-15; v.p. in charge of operation, 1915-18, gen. mgr., 1918-20, v.p. and cons. engr. Mar. 1, 1920—. Democrat. Presbyn. Home: Portsmouth, Va. Died July 10, 1937.

SEDGWICK, ALLAN E., (sej'wik), geologist, civil engr.; b. York, Neb., May 6, 1881; s. David Ernest and Jennie (Treat) S.; student U. of Neb., 1899-1902; Sch. of Mines, Columbia, 1902-05; B.S., in C.E., U. of Southern Calif., 1918, M.S., 1919; m. Jeannette Post, Sept. 5, 1906; children—Wallace Ernest, David Allan, Robert Post. Engr. Greenback (Ore.) Gold Mining Co., 1905-06; engr., constrn. hydro-electric plant and aerial tran. Tezuitlan Copper Co., La Aurora, Mexico, 1907-08; gen. mgr. Am. Engring. & Constrn. Co., Mexico City, Mex., 1908-10; gen. mgr. Me. & Neb. Mining & Smelting Co., Balsas, Guerro. Mex., 1910-12; designing engr., with Noonan & Richards, architects, Los Angeles, 1912-15; cons. engr., geology, mining, oil, water supply, elect. distribution, flood control, etc., Los Angeles, since 1915; asst. prof. geology, U. of Southern Calif., 1918-21, asso. prof., 1921-24, prof. and head dept., 1924-27, head dept. petroleum engring., 1927-29; cons. geologist, Dept. Water and Power, Los Angeles, City of Santa Barbara, Montecito County Water Dist.; chief engr. Seventh St. Light & Power Co. since 1918; consulting geologist Golden Gate Bridge & Highway Dist., San Francisco, since 1930. Instr. in hydrology, U.S., Coast Arty., 1918. Mem. Los Angeles County Commn. to investigate St. Francis Dam failure, 1928; mem. Los Angeles County Flood Control Commn., to investigate San Gabriel Dam site, 1929, to investigate Tejuna Dam site, 1930; chmn. Bd. of Consulting Engrs., and mem. Bd. of Edn., Los Angeles, 1933-35 (pres. 1934-35); cons. geologist Los Angeles County Flood Control Dist., 1934-35; cons. geologist Los Angeles Bur. of Water and Power, Mono Project, since 1931, Imperial Irrigation Dist. since 1940. Mem. Am. Soc. C.E., Seismol. Soc. America, Phi Kappa Psi. Republican. Presbyn. Died Nov. 16, 1941.

SEDGWICK, WILLIAM THOMPSON, biologist; b. West Hartford, Conn., Dec. 29, 1855; s. William and Anne Thompson (Barbour) S.; Ph.B., Sheffield Scientific Sch. (Yale), 1877; Ph.D., Johns Hopkins, 1881; (hon. Sc.D., Yale, 1909); m. Mary Katrine Rice, Dec. 29, 1881. Instr. physiol. chemistry, Sheffield Scientific Sch., 1878-79; fellow, and asso. biology, Johns Hopkins, 1879; asst. prof., asso. prof. and prof. biology, now prof. biology and public health, Mass. Inst. of Technology, 1883—. Biologist Mass. State Board of Health, 1888-96; curator Lowell Inst., Boston, 1897—; chmn. Pauper Instns.' Trustees, 1897-99, and (1899-1900) Instns.' Registrar, City of Boston. Trustee Simmons Coll., 1899—; pres. bd. dirs. Sharon Sanatorium, 1902—; mem. advisory bd. Hygienic Laboratory U.S. Public Health Service, 1902—. V.p. Boston Society Municipal Officers, 1898-1900; pres. Boston Civil Service Reform Assn., 1900, Mass. Civil Service Reform Assn., 1901, Soc. Am. Bacteriologist, 1900; fellow Am. Acad. Arts and Sciences, A.A.A.S. (v.p. 1905); mem. State Dept. Health of Mass., Internat. Health Bd., Rockefeller Foundation; chmn. Harvard Tech. Sch. of Pub. Health. Author: General Biology (joint author), 1886; Life and Letters of William Barton Rogers (asst. editor), 1896; Principles of Sanitary Science and Public Health, 1902; The Human Mechanism (joint author), 1906; A Short History of Science (joint author), 1917. Home: Boston, Mass. Died Jan. 26, 1921.

SEE, ELLIOT M., JR., astronaut; b. Dallas, July 23, 1927; s. Elliot See; B.S., U.S. Mcht. Marine Acad., 1949; M.Engring., U. Cal. at Los Angeles, 1962; m. Marilyn Jane Denahy; children—Sally, Carolyn, David. Former flight test engr., exptl. test pilot Gen. Electric Co.; now astronaut with duties including monitoring design and devel. elec. and sequential systems NASA Manned Spacecraft Center, Houston. Served as aviator USNR, 1953-56. Asso. fellow Am. Inst. Aeros. and Astronautics; mem. Soc. Exptl. Test Pilots. Office: NASA Manned Spacecraft Center, Houston 1. Died Feb. 28, 1966; buried Arlington Nat. Cemetery.

SEE, HORACE, naval architect; b. Philadelphia, July 17, 1835; s. Richard Colhoun and Margarita (Hilyard) S.; academic edn.; learned trade of machinist; supt. engr. William Cramp & Sons, Phila.; m. Ruth Ross Maffet, Feb. 20, 1879. Had much to do with introduction of triple-expansion engines into vessels of U.S. Navy; designed engines of cruisers Yorktown, Concord, Bennington, Philadelphia, Newark and Vesuvius; yachts, Atalanta, Corsair, Stranger, Peerless; steamer Monmouth; steamships, Mariposa, Queen of the Pacific, Caracas, Olivette; designed hull and machinery of steamships El Rio, El Valle, El Alba, Comus, Proteus, U.S. cruisers Yankee, Dixie, hosp. ship Solace; wrecking steamers Relief and Tasco, New York police launches, etc., into which many of his inventions were introduced, such as the hydropneumatic ash ejector, folding hatch cover, etc.; also inventor cylindrical mandrel for face bearings, which makes it possible to produce with certainty a true bearing and journal, double furnace water tube boiler, pneumatic siphon fire hydrant, etc. Superintends the constn., performance and maintenance of vessels and machinery; established at New York, 1889; consulting engr. Newport News Shipbuilding Co. and other corps. Private Gray Reserves early part of Civil War; corpl. 7th Regt. Pa. militia in Md., 1862; adj. 20th Regt. N.G. Pa. during July riots, 1877, and later capt. 1st Regt. N.G., Pa. Home: Glen Summit Springs, Pa. Died 1909.

SEE, THOMAS JEFFERSON JACKSON, astronomer, geometer; b. near Montgomery City, Mo., Feb. 19, 1866; s. Noah and Mary Ann (Sailor) S.; A.B., L.B., S.B., U. of Mo., 1889; A.M., Ph.D., U. of Berlin, 1892; m. Frances Graves, June 18, 1907. In charge observatory of U. of Mo., 1887-89; volunteer observer Royal Observatory, Berlin, 1891; organized and had charge dept. of astronomy, and aided in organization of Yerkes Observatory, U. of Chicago, 1893-96; astronomer Lowell Observatory in charge survey of Southern heavens, 1896-98; with 24-in. Clark refractor at Flagstaff, Ariz., and City of Mexico, examined about 200,000 fixed stars, in zone bet. 15 and 65 degrees south declination, which led to discovery and measurement of about 600 new double stars and remeasurement of some 1,400 double stars previously recognized by Sir John Herschel and other observers. Prof. mathematics, U.S. Navy, since 1899; in charge 26-in. equatorial telescope, U.S. Naval Observatory, 1899-1902; prof. mathematics, U.S. Naval Acad., 1902-03, Naval Observatory, Mare Island, Calif., since 1903; lecturer on sidereal astronomy, Lowell Inst., Boston, 1899. Commd. capt., 1913. Fellow or mem. numerous Am. and fgn. sci. socs. Sci. investigations cover wide math. and astron. range, with results proving, disproving or extending several major astron. theories, also cover exploration of new astron. features, and advancement of new theories. Author of books and papers, many pub. abroad as well as in U.S., relating to these various fields, 1893—; these writings include the following, giving summary description of treatise on wave-theory discovery of cause of gravitation and cosmical magnetism, modernizing Newton's Principia (1687) and Laplace's Mecanique Celeste (1790-1825): The Wave-Theory Outlined, 1938; Electrodynamic Waves, Currents, Magnets, 1938; Wave-Theory of Molecular Forces, 1939; Proofs of the Gravitational Waves, 1939; Nonsensical Theory of Expanding Universe Demolished, 1940; Several Profound Proofs of Waves in Nature Established, 1941; All the Disturbances of the Moon's Motion Fully Explained, 1942; Many New Tests of the Wave-Theory, 1943; Invariability of Sidereal Day (Royal Society Paper, Hill Lectures), 1949-50; Explosive Forces Investigated, also the Long Waves of Gravitation, 1946; Life of Laplace; Theory of Cosmical Magnetism, 1951-52, 53. Address: Vallejo, Cal. Died July 4, 1962; buried Montgomery City, Mo.

SEEGAL, DAVID, educator, clin. investigator; b. Chelsea, Mass., June 23, 1899; s. Morris and Rose (Beerman) S.; student Harvard, M.D., 1928; m. Emily Beatrice Carrier, July 8, 1925. Intern, asst. resident physician, resident physician Presbyn. Hosp. N.Y.C., 1928-32; asst. in medicine, instr. Columbia, 1930-35, asso. prof. medicine, 1942-47; dir. research, div. chronic diseases, Welfare Island, 1936-42; dir. research service 1st div. Goldwater Meml. Hosp., 1942-47, 51-64; prof. medicine L.I. Coll. Medicine, 1947-48; prof. medicine Columbia, 1951-64, prof. emeritus, 1964-72; prof. medicine State U. Med. Center, Bklyn., 1950-51, asso. attending physician, Presbyn. Hosp., 1945-47, 1952-56, attending physician, 1956-72; dir. med. service Maimonides Hosp., Bklyn., 1947-51. Cons. epidemic diseases U.S. Sec. War, 1942-45. Del., Nat. Conf. on Chronic Disease (chmn. com. on practice), Chgo., 1951; mem. N.Y. Com. on Study Hosp. Internships and Residencies; med. adv. com. Unitarian Service Com.; med. adv. council Masonic Found. Med. Research and Human Welfare, Assn. Am. Physicians, Assn. Am. Med. Colls. Recipient Army and Navy certificate of appreciation, 1948. Fellow A.M.A.; mem. Am. Soc. Clin. Investigation, Am. Assn. Immunologists, Soc. for Exptl. Biology and Medicine, Harvey Soc., A.A.A.S., Alpha Omega Alpha (mem. editorial bd. Pharos). Jewish religion. Club: Omega. Co-editor: Jour. Chronic Diseases, 1955. Contbr. chpt. on allgery (with E.B.C. Seegal) in Agents of Disease and Host Resistance (Frederick P. Gay), 1935; chpt. (study on hosp. internships and residencies in Trends in Medical Edn., 1947; chpt. Methuselah: Myth or Promise, in Frontiers in Medicine, 1950; contbr. articles to med. jours., poems to med., alumni, poetry mags. Mem. adv. bd. Familiar Medical Quotations; editorial adv. bd. Jour. Chronic

Diseases. Home: New York City NY Died July 24, 1972.

SEELYE, THEODORE EDWARD, cons. engr.; b. New Orleans, La., Nov. 7, 1887; s. Abram Booth and Mary (O'Connor) S.; spl. student, civil engring., U. of Mich., 1909-12; m. Georgia Reily Bailey, Nov. 6, 1922 (dec.); children—Caroline Reily (Mrs. Henry Cadwalader), James Bailey. With United States Engineer Department, 1906-09; hydraulic engr. Electric Bond & Share Co., 1913; div. engr. Water Supply Commn. of Pa., 1914-15; v.p. Gannett, Seelye & Fleming, Inc., 1916-32; director of Day & Zimmermann, Inc., 1933—; pres. North Pa. R.R. Co.; dir. Girard Trust Corn Exchange Bank, Delaware & Bound Brook R.R. Co., Fidelity Mut. Life Ins. Co. Served as captain and major, Engineers, U.S. Army, 1917-19, with 30th Division, War Damages Board of American Peace Commission and G5 General Staff. Mem. bd. mgrs., Phila. Zoological Society, Pa. Hosp. Mem. Am. Soc. C.E., Newcomen Soc., Soc. American Military Engineers, Engineers Soc. Pa. Clubs: Rittenhouse, Philadelphia (Philadelphia); State (Schuylkill, Pa.). Home: Morris Rd., Ambler, Pa. Office: 1700 Sansom St., Philadelphia 3. Died Mar. 7, 1963.

SEGUIN, EDOUARD, psychiatrist; b. Clamency, France, Jan. 20, 1812; s. T.O. Seguin; ed. Coll. of Auxerre, Lycee St. Louis, Paris, France; M.D. (hon.), Univ. City N.Y. (now N.Y.U.), 1861; m. 2d, Elsie Mead, 1880; at least 1 son, Edward Constant. Opened sch. for idiots in France, 1839; published chief work Traitement Moral, Hygiene et Education des Idiots, 1846; came to U.S., circa 1850; an organizer sch. for defectives, Randall's Island, N.Y.; published Idiocy and its Treatment by the Physiologic Method, 1866; interested in med. thermometry, Author: New Facts and Remarks Concerning Idiocy, 1869; Family Thermometry, 1873; The Clinical Thermoscope and Uniformity of Means of Observations, 1875; Medical Thermometry and Human Temperature, 1876. Died Mt. Vernon, N.Y., Oct. 28, 1880.

SEGUIN, EDWARD CONSTANT, neurologist; b. Paris, France, 1843; s. Edouard Seguin; grad. Coll. Physicians and Surgeons, N.Y.C., 1764; m. Margaret Amidon, 3 children. Came to U.S., 1850; served with M.C., U.S. Army, 1864-69, asst. surgeon, Little Rock, Ark., 1864-65, post surgeon in N.M., 1865-69; published paper on use of thermometer containing 1st temperature chart used in U.S., 1866; wrote papers on subcutaneous injection of quinine in malarial fevers in which he emphasized importance of a sterile hypodermic needle, 1867; studied mental and nervous diseases in Paris, 1869; contributed to the recognition of functional and organic nervous diseases; one of leading neurologists in U.S.; lectr. on diseases of nervous system Coll. Physicians and Surgeons, 1868-73, clin. prof., 1873-87; founder, pres. Am. Neurol. Assn., N.Y. Neurol. Soc.; advocated use of drugs in mental and spinal diseases, developed treatment these diseases involving use of iodies. Author: Opera Minora, 1884. Died Feb. 19, 1898.

SEIBELS, EDWIN GRANVILLE, (se'bl's), insurance executive; b. Columbia, S.C., Sept. 12, 1866; s. Edwin Whipple and Marie Jane (Smith) S.; A.B. with distinction in Mechanics and Engineering, U. of S.C., 1885; LL.D., Newberry Coll., 1942; D.C.L., University of S.C., 1944; m. Rosamond Kershaw, Jan. 31, 1917. Left school at 14 to become page in S.C. Senate; later reporter, Columbia Register; paid way through coll. by working in ins. office of E. W. Seibels & Son, became partner, 1886; general adjuster fire losses, 1892-97; manager Southern Department, Glens Falls Ins. Co., 1898. Later Royal Exchange Assurance Corp., Colonial Fire Underwriters, Franklin Nat. Ins. Co., South Carolina Ins. Co., Glens Falls Indemnity and Niagara Fire Ins. Co. (America Fore Group) were added to dept., and named changed to Seibels, Bruce & Co., Managers, of which he is chmn. of bd. Organized and apptd. mgr., 1919, of Cotton Fire & Marine Underwriters, writing cotton insurance throughout world; retired from management, 1944. Mem. S.C. Ho. of Reps., 1909-10; organized South Carolina Insurance Co., 1910, pres. and dir., 1910-46, chmn. bd. since 1946. Chmn. bd. trustees U. of South Carolina, 1932-47. Alumni mem. Phi Beta Kappa; mem. Omicron Delta Kappa Delta Sigma Pi, Blue Key honor fraternities. Invented vertical filing system, 1898, now in general use throughout world; original case deposited in Smithsonian Instn., Washington, D.C. June 1941. Received Am. Legion (S.C Dept.) Distinguished Public Service Award, 1945. Home: 1332 Pickens St., Columbia, S.C. Died Dec. 21, 1954; buried Trinity Church Yard, Columbia.

SEIDNER, HOWARD MAYO, physician; b. Chgo., July 23, 1921; s. Maurice P. and Bertha (Reisman) S.; B.S., Northwestern U., 1941; M.D., U. Ill., 1944; m. Rosalind S. Pearlman, Apr. 4, 1953; children—Ruth, Linda, Ann. Intern, Michael Reese Hosp., 1944-45, resident, 1945-47; practice medicine specializing in obstetrics and gynecology, Chgo., 1947-68; chief dept. obstetrics and gynecology Bethany Hosp., Chgo., 1956-68; obsete. cons. Chicago Board of Health, 1955-68. Diplomate Am. Bd. Obstetrics and Gynecology. Fellow Am. Coll. Obstetrics and Gynecology; mem. World, Am., Pan Am. med. assns., American Soc. Abdominal Surgeons, Ill., Chgo. med. socs., Ill. Soc. Med. Research, Am. Geriatrics Soc., Am. Writers Assn., Royal Society Health (Great Britain). Contributed articles in field to med. jours. Research in method of stabilizing aspirin in aqueous solution. Home: Evanston IL Died May 31, 1968.

SEIFERT, MATHIAS JOSEPH, physician, surgeon; b. Chicago, Ill., Mar. 2, 1866; s. Anthony V. and Margaret (Kannen) S.; Catholic Normal Sch., St. Francis, Wis., 1885, Bryant & Stratton Business Coll., 1886, Normal Dept. of Chicago Musical Coll., 1887; M.D., University of Illinois, 1901; clinics in 12 countries of Europe and U.S.; m. Mary C. Karst, Feb. 8, 1888; children—Earl (dec.), Myra, Marie. Teacher, choir director, church organist, Chicago, 1885-1896; organizer and pres., Western Musical Acad., 1888-96; intern and extern Marion Sims Hosp., 1899-1905; instr. gynecology, Chicago Polyclinic, 1900-05; asst. prof. physiology, U. of Ill. Coll. of Med., 1900-05; instr. senior medicine, 1901-05; dispensary staff, Alexian Bros. Hosp., 1901-06; adj. prof. operative surgery, U. of Ill. Med. Dept., 1904-09; prof. phys. diagnosis and anesthesiology, U. of Ill. Dental Dept., 1904-09; prof., head dept. surgery, Chicago Med. Sch., 1910-16; surgical staff St. Mary of Nazareth Hosp. since 1904, cons. surgeon since 1915; editorial staff Internat. Abstract of Surgery, Gynecology and Obstetrics since 1913; senior surgeon and pres. exec. staff Columbus Hosp. since 1915. Mem. Ill. governing com., Gorgas Memorial Inst. Fellow Am. Coll. Surgeons; mem. Chicago Med. Soc., Ill. State Med. Soc., Alpha Kappa Kappa, Miss. Valley Med. Editors Assn. (Ill. exec.). Catholic. Clubs: Native Chicagoan, Nippersink Country. Author: Eccyesis, with Prolonged Lactation; Case Report, 1920; Synthesis of Medical Terminology, 1925; Gynecology for Nurses, 1925; Cardio-Vascular Health Maxims, 1927; Olympian Rules, 1928. Contbr. to (books) Obstetrics, Gynecology and Abdominal Surgery, 1920; International Clinics, 1920; also numerous articles to med. jours. Made motion picture, "A High Posterior Gastro-Enterostomy," which he has exhibited since 1929. Radio speaker under auspices of Gorgas Memorial Inst. and Edn. Com. of the Ill. State Med. Society since 1926. Home: 585 Hawthorne Pl. Office: 30 Michigan Av., Chicago, Ill. Died Jan. 31, 1947; buried St. Boniface Cemetery, Chicago.

SEIFRIZ, WILLIAM, (si'frits), prof. of botany; b. Washington, Aug. 1, 1888; s. Paul and Anna (Schmidt) S.; B.S., Johns Hopkins, 1918, Ph.D., 1920; post-grad. study U. Geneva (Switzerland), Kings Coll. (London, Eng.), Kaiser Wilhelm Inst. (Germany), 1920-22; married. Instr. botany, U. of Mich., 1923-25; prof. botany, U. Pa., 1925—. Mem. Botanical Soc. Am., Ecological Soc., Am. Chem. Soc., A.A.A.S., Phi Beta Kappa, Sigma Xi. Asso. editor Protoplasma, Biodynamica, and Jour. Colloid Science; writer of books and sci. articles on protoplasm, physiology, colloid chemistry and plant geography. Home: 3543 Rhoads Av., Newtown Square, Pa. Address: University of Pa., Phila. Died July 13, 1955; buried Indiana, Pa.

SEITZ, CHARLES EDWARD, agrl. engr.; b. Reno, Nov. 6, 1890; s. Edward Lewis and Fannie Harvey (Leonard) S.; student U. Nev., 1911-12; asso. degree, Ont. Agrl. Coll., 1914; student Ia. State Coll., 1917, also corr. studies in engring., architecture, bus.; m. Nancy Dove Hughes, Jan. 23, 1918; children—Martha Leonard (Mrs. John David Wey), Charles Edward. Drainage engr. Va. Agrl. Extension Service, 1914-16, agrl. engr., 1916-19; asso. prof., head agrl. engring. dept. Va. Poly. Inst., 1919-22, prof., head dept., dir. extension, research and resident teaching, 1922-54, ret. Mem. Va. Planning Bd., 1930-38; chmn. Va. Com. on Relation of Electricity to Agr., 1924-34; chmn. Va. Farm Electric Council, 1945-52; pres., chmn. bd. dirs. Va. Tech. Athletic, Council, 1949-53; chmn. Va. Tech.-Blacksburg-Christianburg Water Authority, 1954-72. Served with 1st Va. Cav., Mexican Border Service, 1916-17, as cadet pilot, USAAF, 1917-18. Recipient Cyrus Hall McCormick Gold Medal, 1951; selected Man of the Year in Service to Agr., 1954. Fellow Am. Soc. Agrl. Engrs. (pres. 1932-33); mem. Soc. Promotion Engring. Edn., Sigma Alpha Epsilon, Epsilon, Sigma Phi, Alpha Zeta. Club: University (Blacksburg). Agrl. Engring. bldg. named Seitz Bldg. in his honor, Va. Polytech. Inst. Address: Blacksburg VA Died Aug. 20, 1972; buried Westview Cemetery, Blacksburg, VA

SEKERA, ZDENEK, educator; b. Tabor, Czechoslovakia, July 3, 1905; s. Emil and Marie (Zizkova) S.; B.A., M.A. in Math. and Physics, Masaryk U., Brno, Czechoslovakia, 1928; R.N.Dr. in Theoretical Physics, Charles U., Prague, Czechoslovakia, 1931, Ph.D. in Meteorology and Dynamic Oceanography, 1939; m. Gabriela Sterbova, Jan. 7, 1943; 1 son, Michael. Came to U.S., 1946, naturalized, 1953. Pvt. dozent meteorology Charles U., 1939, 45-47; sr. theoretical meteorologist U. Chgo., 1947-48; vis. asso. prof. U. Cal. at Los Angeles, 1948-49, mem. faculty, 1949-73, prof. meteorology, 1955-73, chmn. dept., 1962-67, mem. Inst. Geophysics, 1969-73. Cons. physics of planetary atmospheres to industry, 1957-73; mem. aerological commn. Internat. Meteorol. Orgn., 1945-49; mem. radiation commn. Internat. Assn. Meteorology and Atmospheric Physics, 1957-73. Recipient C.G. Rossby Research Medal Am. Meteorol. Soc., 1966. Guggenheim fellow, 1956, 61; NSF sr. post-doctoral fellow, 1957, 61. Mem. Am., Royal meteorol. socs., Am. Geophys. Union, Am. Optical Soc., A.A.A.S. Asso. editor Geophys. Research, 1968-70. Contbr. to Atmospheric Physics, 1969-73. Home: Los Angeles CA Died Jan. 1, 1973.

SELBY, AUGUSTINE DAWSON, botanist; b. in Athens Co., O., Sept. 2, 1859; s. Warren and Emily (Garretson) S.; B.S., Ohio State Univ., 1893; Washington U. and Shaw Sch. of Botany, 1899; Columbia, 1902-03; m. Libbie Glover, Dec. 15, 1883. Supt. schs., Huntington, W.Va., 1884-86; prin. high sch., Ironton, O., 1886-87, Garfield Sch., Columbus, O., 1887-89; teacher botany, Columbus High Sch., 1889-94; sec. Columbus Hort. Soc., 1888-94; botanist and chemist, Ohio Agrl. Expt. Sta., 1894-1902; botanist and chief of dept. of botany in same, 1902-23. Interested chiefly in diseases of plants and their remedies and in plant breeding; also commercial apple growing. Propr. Selby Heights Fruit Farm, Sharpsburg, O. Writer in reports, Ohio Agrl. Expt. Sta. (Wooster, O.), and in scientific jours. Dir. Ohio State Life Ins. Co. Mason. Home: Wooster, O. Died May 7, 1924.

SELDEN, GEORGE BALDWIN, inventor, lawyer; b. Clarkson, N.Y., Sept. 14, 1846; s. Henry Rogers and Laura Anne (Baldwin) S.; ed. U. Rochester, 1861-64, Yale, 1865-66, Sheffield Sci. Sch., 1867; m. Clara Drake Woodruff, Dec. 14, 1971 (dec. 1903), 2 sons, 2 daus.; m. 2d, Jean Shipley, Apr. 1909. Admitted to bar, 1871; joined father and uncle's law offices, specializing in patent law; studied road traction and power sources, particularly liquid and gas fuel engines; built unsuccessful kerosene-laughing gas combustion engine, 1875; patented machine for making barrel hoops, 1875; developed (on basis of George Brayton's internal combustion engine) 3-cylinder, gasoline combustion engine, 1877; designed automobile with engine, running gear, driving wheels, propellar-shaft, clutch, carriage body, 1879 (unpatented until 1895); sold patent rights on royalty basis to S.C. Whitney of Columbia Motor Co. and Electric Vehicle Co., 1899, received royalties from almost all automobile mfrs. until Otto type of engine came into common use, circa 1911; incurred heavy financial losses on his own mfg. ventures. Died Rochester, Jan. 17, 1922. *

SELIG, WILLIAM NICHOLAS, motion pictures; b. Chicago, Ill., Mar. 14, 1864; s. Francis Joseph and Antonia (Lunsky) S.; ed. pub. schs., Chicago; m. Mary H. Pinkham, Sept. 7, 1900. Early became interested in photography; actor and theatrical mgr., 1888-99; inventor of many appliances used in motion picture photography; in motion picture business since 1896; pres. Selig Polyscope Co., Chicago, also of Los Angeles, Calif., and London, Eng. First producer to make long hist. photodrama "Coming of Columbus," and first to introduce wild animals in dramatic action in photoplays. Finance expdns. of Prof. Frederick Starr to interior of Africa, Korea, Japan and Philippines; expdns. of Dr. E. B. McDowell to China, Africa and India; expdn. of Emmett O'Neill to the Amazon River, 1912. Presented medal, 1912, by Pope Pius X for "Coming of Columbus." Episcopalian. Mason. Clubs: Republican (New York); Chicago Athletic. Home: 112 N. Wilton Pl. Office: 6606 Sunset Blvd., Los Angeles, Calif. Died July 15, 1948.

SELLARDS, ELIAS HOWARD, geologist; b. Carter City, Ky., May 2, 1875; s. Wiley W. and Sarah (Menach) S.; B.A., University of Kansas, 1899, M.A., 1901; Ph.D., Yale University, 1903; married Anna Mary Alford, September 4, 1907; children—Helen Alford, Daphne Alford. Asst. Kansas State Geological Survey, 1900-01, Carnegie Museum, Pittsburgh, summer, 1903; instr. geology and mineralogy, Rutgers Coll., 1903-04; prof. geology and zoology, U. of Fla., 1904-07; state geologist of Fla., 1907-18; geologist, Bur. of Economic Geology, U. of Texas, 1918-22, chief geologist, 1922-25, associate director, 1925-32, director, 1932-45; director emeritus since 1945; director Texas Memorial Museum, Austin, since 1938; expert geologist Tex.-Okla. boundary dispute, 1921. Mem. first Conf. for Conservation of Natural Resources, Washington, 1908. Mem. Geol. Soc. of America (councillor 1938-40, 1943; v.p. 1943), Paleontological Society (president 1942), Society Econ. Paleontologists and Mineralogists (president 1938), Am. Assn. Petroleum Geologists, (hon. mem. since 1946). Author of reports and papers in Bulletin, Geol. Soc. of America, Am. Jour. of Science, Jour. of Geology, Kan. State Geol. Survey. State Geol. Survey of Fla. and Bur. of Economic Geology, U. of Tex. Home: 2525 Jarratt Av., Austin 21 TX

SELLERS, COLEMAN, consulting engr.; b. Phila., Jan. 28, 1827; s. Coleman and Sophonisba (Peale) S.; ed. private schools and Bolmar's Acad., West Chester, Pa.; E.D., Stevens Inst. of Technology; prof. engring. practice same, 1886—; Sc.D., Univ. of Pa., 1899; m. Cornelia, d. Horace Wells, of Cincinnati, Oct. 8, 1851. Chief engr. Niagara Falls Power Co., and chief mech. engr. Canadian Niagara Power Co. The engring. work of development of the power of Niagara Falls was undertaken under his advice and direction. Knight of the Royal Norwegian Order of St. Olaf. Mem. numerous scientific societies. Home: Philadelphia, Pa. Died 1907.

SELLERS, COLEMAN, JR., engineer; b. Cincinnati, Sept. 5, 1852; s. Coleman and Cornelia (Wells) S.; B.S., U. of Pa., 1873, M.S., 1876; spl. studies mech. engineering in works of Wm. Sellers & Co., Philadelphia; m. Helen Graham Jackson, June 3, 1880. Asst. mgr., 1886-1902, engr., 1902-19, and pres., 1919—, Wm. Sellers & Co., Inc. One of Pa. commrs. of navigation for River Delaware, 1907—. Pres. Phila. Chamber Commerce, 1908-12. Home: Philadelphia, Pa. Died Aug. 15, 1923.

SELLERS, HORACE WELLS, architect; b. Philadelphia, July 21, 1857; s. Coleman and Cornelia (Wells) S.; grad. Eastburn Acad., Phila., 1873; B.Sc., U. of Pa., 1877; m. Cora Wells, d. late Charles Wells, of Cincinnati, Nov. 22, 1899; children—Lester Hoadley, Charles Coleman, Jessie. Entered the office of Joseph M. Wilson (fellow A.I.A.), then engr. bridges and bldgs., Pa. R.R., 1877, and with Wilson Bros. & Co., engrs. and architects; engaged on architectural engring. and executive details connected with r.r., electric light and other developments and machine works, 1882-92; associated after 1892 with late Coleman Sellers who was pres. and chief engr. Niagara Falls Power Co., and in his gen. practice as consulting engr., at same time conducting individual architectural practice. Fellow A.I.A. (ex-dir.; pres. Philadelphia Chapter), Royal Soc. of Arts (Gt. Britain). Republican. Episcopalian; mem. Commn. on Ch. Architecture, Diocese of Pa. Home: Ardmore, Pa. Died Nov. 26, 1933.

SELLERS, MATTHEW BACON, aerodynamics; b. Baltimore, Mar. 29, 1869; s. Matthew Bacon and Annie L. (Lewis) S.; ed. pvt. schs. and under pvt. tutors, including 1 yr. in Göttingen, Germany, and 1 yr. in Evreux, France; LL.B., Harvard, 1892; spl. courses later, Lawrence Scientific Sch. (Harvard), and Drexel Inst., Phila.; m. Ethel Clark, June 18, 1918; children—Matthew B., John C. Research in aerodynamics, 1900—; in practice as cons. aeronautical engr.; apptd. by President Taft mem. Aerodynamic Lab. Com., 1912; mem. Navy Consulting Bd., Sept. 1915—. Dir. and mem. tech. bd. Aeronautical Soc. America. Inventor of lightest aeroplane in world, flying with least horsepower; first to determine lift and drift of arched surfaces by means of the "wind tunnel." Home: Ardsley-on-Hudson, N.Y. Died Apr. 5, 1932.

SELLERS, WILLIAM, mfr., mech. engr.; b. Delaware Co., Pa., Sept. 19, 1824; s. John and Elizabeth (Poole) S.; ed. private school; apprenticed to machinists' trade at 14; at 21 became foreman for Fairbanks, Bancroft & Co., Providence, R.I.; started in 1847 business now known as William Sellers & Co., incorporated, of which he is pres. and engr.; also pres. Edgemoor Iron Co., 1868—, and of Midvale Steel Co., 1873-87; dir. Phila., Wilmington & Baltimore R.R., 1865—; pres. Franklin Inst., 1864-67; park commr., Phila., 1867-72; mem. Nat. Acad. Sciences, from 1873; v.p. Centennial Bd. of Finance, for exhbn. of 1876. Chevalier Legion d'Honneur, 1889. Read paper before Franklin Inst., 1864, on "Screw Threads and Nuts," which has since become the standard for the U.S. and the form of thread for the continent of Europe. Home: Phila., and Edgemoor, Del. Died 1905.

SEMSCH, OTTO FRANCIS, architect, cons. engr.; b. Milwaukee, Wis., Sept. 26, 1872; s. Francis and Aurelia (Sieber) S.; student Tech. U., Karlsruhe, Germany, 1891-92, Tech. U., Charlottenburg-Berlin, Germany, 1892-94; m. Gertrude Luedeke (died Nov. 15, 1935); 1 dau., Gertrude May. Began as archtl. engr., 1894; designer of foundations, structural and mechanical engring. of Mills Hotel, Singer, Bourne, Scribner, Furness-Withy and Internat. Merchantile Marine office bldgs., New York, Gwynne Bldg., Cincinnati, O., First Nat. Bank, Conn. Mutual Life Ins. Bldg., Hartford, Conn., U.S. Naval Acad., Annapolis, Md., St. Luke's Hosp., New York, St. Margaret's Memorial Hosp., Pittsburgh, Pa., Naval Hosp., Washington, D.C.; architect Montclair (N.J.) Municipal Bldg.; designer of wind-bracing of the Singer Tower. Registered architect N.Y. and N.J.; licensed professional engr., N.Y. Mem. bd. of edn., Montclair, N.J.; mem. Soc. Am. Mil. Engrs. Republican. Congregationalist. Contbr. archtl. articles to jours. Home: 143 E. 39th St. Office: 111 E. 40th St., New York NY*

SENIOR, SAMUEL PALMER, civil engr.; b. Washington, D.C., July 5, 1874; s. Thomas Richard and Hannah Belle (Palmer) S.; C.E., Lehigh U., 1897; m. Blanche Regina Newman, Apr. 29, 1901; children—Samuel Palmer, Barbara. In engring. constrn. work since 1897, building dams, bridges, tunnels, deep foundations; built waterworks, Bridgeport; pres. Bridgeport Hydraulic Co., 1920-55, also chmn.; dir. Bridgeport Hosp.; director Bridgeport Gas Light Co., Conn. National Bank. Mem. Am. Soc. C.E., Conn. Soc. C.E., Am. Water Works Assn., N.E. Water Works Assn., Theta Delta Chi, Tau Beta Pi. Rep. Conglist. Clubs: University, Algonquin (Bridgeport). Home: 131 Sport Hill Rd., Easton, Conn. Office: 835 Main St., Bridgeport, Conn. Died Oct. 15, 1962.

SENNET, GEORGE BURRITT, ornithologist, mfr.; b. Sinclairville, N.Y., July 28, 1840; s. Pardon and Mary (Burritt) S.; m. Sarah Essex, 1 child. Mfr. oil-well machinery, Meadville, Pa., 1865-95, Youngstown, O., 1895-1900; mayor of Meadville, 1877-81; made ornithol. expdn. to Western Minn., 1867; made expdns. to Rio Grande region of Southern Tex., 1877, 78, 82; contbd. collection of birds to Am. Museum Natural History, N.Y.C., 1883; discovered 10 new species of birds; 4 birds named in his honor. Author articles "Notes on the Ornithology of the Lower Rio Grande, Texas, from Observations Made During the Season 1877," published in Bulletin of the U.S. Geol. and Geog. Survey of the Territories, Vol. IV, 1878; "Descriptions of a New Species and Two New Subspecies of Birds from Texas," published in Auk, 1888. Died Mar. 18, 1900.

SENSENEY, GEORGE EYSTER, (sens'ne), etcher; b. Wheeling, W.Va., Oct. 11, 1874; s. Charles Henry and Anna May (Eyster) S.; prep. edn., Linsley Inst., Wheeling; art edn., Corcoran Sch. of Art, Washington, D.C., and Julian Acad., Paris; pupil of Jean Paul Laurens and Benjamin Constant; m. Dorothy Lucile Stewart, Oct. 25, 1912; children—Virginia, George Leonard, William Stewart. Served as teacher of etching, Art Students League, N.Y. City; organizer New Sch. of Art, Chicago, 1916-17; asst. prof. design, Smith Coll., 1917-21; art dir. Am. Writing Paper Co., 1919-21; pres. Marvellum Co., mfrs. decorative papers, Holyoke, Mass., since 1921. Etcher. Represented in Library of Congress, Washington, D.C., Public Library, N.Y. City, South Kensington Museum, London, Eng. Dir. Holyoke League Arts and Crafts. Mem. Société des Graveurs Originale en Couleurs (Paris). Awarded silver medal, Panama-Pacific Expn., 1915. Inventor of process for printing textiles known as "Sentone Process." Democrat. Free Thinker. Club: Salmagundi (New York). Home: Ipswich, Mass. Office: Marvellum Co., Holyoke, Mass. Died Nov. 19, 1943.

SENSENICH, ROSCOE LLOYD, physician; b. Wakarusa, Ind., Nov. 20, 1882; s. Dr. Aaron Stauffer and Martha M. (Brubaker) S.; M.D., Rush Med. Coll., U. Chgo., 1905; m. Helen Frances Daugherty, Apr. 10, 1917; 1 dau., Helene Marjorie. Interne, Presbyn., St. Joseph hosps., Chgo.; practiced medicine, South Bend, Ind., since 1907; mem. med. staff Meml., St. Joseph hosps., South Bend; pres. bd. mgrs. St. Joseph County Tb Hosp. and South Bend Med. Found. (lab., research, edn.). Mem. adv. com. to div. of services for crippled children Ind. State Dept. Pub. Welfare, 1936-44; mem. fed. govt. com. on allocation med. personnel to armed forces and civilian population; mem. adv. com. to Selective Service, World War II; cons., mem. com. on phys. fitness FSA, 1944-45; mem. NRC, 1947-50; hon. cons. USN surgeon gen. Served as maj. M.C., U.S. Army, World War I. Diplomate Am. Bd. Internal Medicine. Fellow A.C.P.; mem. A.M.A. (chmn. bd. trustees, pres. 1948-49), Ind. (past pres.), St. Joseph County (pres. 1920) med. assns., Ind. State Tb Assn. (past pres.), Central Soc. for Clin. Research, Soc. Internal Medicine (Chgo.), Chgo. Inst. Medicine, Phi Rho Sigma, Alpha Omega Alpha. Clubs: University (Chgo.); Chain O'Lakes Country (South Bend). Contbr. research articles on undulant fever and studies in digestive disorders, also numerous articles on med. care to med. jours. and lay publs. Home: 128 S. Scott St., South Bend 46625. Office: 108 N. Main St., South Bend 5, Ind. Died Jan. 18, 1963; buried Riverview Cemetery, South Bend.

SEQUOYAH (later took name George Guess), inventor Indian syllabary; b. Loudon County, Tenn., 1770; s. Nicholas Gist; married, several children. Hunter, fur trader, silversmith with Cherokee Indians in Ga., until 1821; completed a table of 86 characters representing the sounds of the Cherokee language, 1821; taught thousands of Indians to read and write their own language; introduced system to Cherokees in Ark., 1822, moved with them to Okla., 1828; began publishing weekly paper in Cherokee, 1828; visited Washington (D.C.) as envoy for his tribe, 1828; granted life-time pension by Cherokee Nat. Council, 1843; Sequoia redwood trees in Cal. named for him; statue of him placed in Statuary Hall of Nat. Capitol by State of Okla. Died Tamaulipas, Mexico (probably), Aug. 1843.

SERRELL, EDWARD WELLMANN, civil and mil. engr.; b. abroad (but a citizen of U.S. by birthright), Nov. 5, 1826; academic edn.; m. Jane, d. Rev. Jesse Pound, Apr. 6, 1848 (died 1896); 2d, Marion Seaton Roorbach, Sept. 6, 1900 (died Nov. 1904). Began engring. profession under his father and elder brother. Was asst. engr. to commrs. of Erie R.R.; asst. to chief of Topog. Engrs., U.S.A.; asst. engr., 1848, Panama Survey; engr. Central R.R. of N.J.; chief engr. Niagara bridge, 1850; chief engr. St. John bridge, Hoosac tunnel and many other public works. In Civil War organized and comd. 1st regt. vol. engrs., U.S.A., becoming col. engrs.; chief engr. 10th corps, U.S.A.; chief engr. and chief of staff, Army of the James; chief engr. Dept. of the South, U.S.A.; was at capture of Fort Wagner; devised and built Swamp Angel batteries; was in 126 actions, becoming bvt. brig. gen. Made many useful inventions, in long wire, armor plate, impromptu gun carriages, electric coast defenses, iron viaducts, etc. Published many reports on railroads and canals. Is consulting engr. to several corps.; has projected an interoceanic canal from San Blas to Pearl Island Harbor. Consulting engr. Am. Isthmus Ship Canal Co. Home: West New Brighton, N.Y. Died 1906.

SESTINI, BENEDICT, clergyman, educator; b. Florence, Italy, Mar. 20, 1816; studied philosophy and theology Roman Coll. Entered Soc. of Jesus, Rome, Italy, 1836; asst. astronomer Roman Observatory until 1848; came to U.S., circa 1848; taught mathematics and natural scis. Georgetown U., Washington, D.D., 1848-69, continued research at univ. observatory; made studies of sun's surface, 1850-69; organized expdn. to Denver (Colo.) to observe total eclipse of sun, 1874, wrote account appearing in Am. Catholic Quarterly Review, 1878; planned and supervised constrn. Holy Trinity and St. Aloysius churches, Washington, also Jesuit Sem., Woodstock, Md., 1869-83; published Messenger of the Sacred Heart, (came to have widest circulation of any Catholic mag. in U.S.), 1866-85; taught higher mathematics Gonzaga Coll., Washington; taught astronomy and geology Jesuit Sem., Woodstock, 1869-85. Author: Memoria Sopra; Colori delle Stelle del Catalogo di Baily Osservati, 1845; Memoria Seconda Intorno ai Colori delle Stelle, 1847; A Treatise of Analytical Geometry, 1852; Astronomical Observations Made During the Year 1847 at the National Observatory, Washington, vol. III, 1853; A Treatise on Alegebra, 2 credits, 1855, 57; Elements of Geometry and Trigonometry, 1856; Manual of Geometrical and Infinitestimal Analysis, 1871; Theoretical Mechanics, 1873; Animal Physics, 1874; Principles of Cosmography, 1878. Died Frederick, Md., Jan. 12, 1890.

SETCHELL, WILLIAM ALBERT, botanist; b. Norwich, Conn., Apr. 15, 1864; s. George Case and Mary Ann (Davis) S.; A.B., Yale, 1887; A.M., Harvard, 1888, Ph.D., 1890; m. Clara Ball (Pearson) Caldwell, Dec. 15, 1920. Morgan fellow, Harvard, 1887-88, asst. in biology, 1888-91, instr. biology, Yale, 1891-95; prof. botany, U. of Calif., 1895-1934, now emeritus; instr. botany, Marine Biol. Lab., Woods Hole, Mass., 1890-95. Fellow Am. Acad. Arts and Sciences, A.A.A.S., Calif. Acad. Sciences, Torrey Bot. Club; mem. Nat. Acad. Sciences, Am. Philos. Soc., Washington Acad. Sciences, Bot. Soc. America, Am. Assn. Univ. profs., Calif. Bot. Club, Soc. Biogégraphie, Soc. Linn. de Lyons; asso. mem. New York Academy Science; honorary mem. Botanical Soc. Japan; fgn. mem. Linnaean Soc., London, Kunglig Vetenskaps och Vitterhets Samhället i Göteborg. Clubs: Bohemian (San Francisco); Athenian-Nile (Oakland, Calif.); Faculty (Berkeley). Author: Laboratory Practice for Beginners in Botany, 1897. Contbr. to bot. jours. Home: 2441 Haste St., Berkeley, Calif. Died April 5, 1943.

SEVER, GEORGE FRANCIS, engineer; b. Cambridge, Mass., July 30, 1866; s. Charles William and Mary C. (Webber) S.; ed. pvt. schs. and Cambridge High Sch.; studied elec. engineering, Mass. Inst. Tech.; (hon. M.S., Columbia, 1905); unmarried. In employ Thomson-Houston Electric Co., Lynn, Mass., 1887-89, Thomson Electric Welding Co., 1889-90; returned to Thomson-Houston Electric Co., 1890; asst. supt. Germania Electric Co., Marlboro, Mass.; engaged in ry. installation and constrn. for Thomson-Houston Electric Co., and its successor, Gen. Electric Co., 1892-93; instr. elec. engineering, 1893-1900, adj. prof., 1900-05, prof., 1905-1911, Columbia U. Established Montauk Point Signal Sta., serving Apr.-Aug., 1898, during Spanish War; hon. discharged from U.S.N., Aug. 1, 1899; consulting engr. Dept. Water Supply, Gas, and Electricity, New York, since Aug., 1902; supt. Dept. Elec. Exhibits, Buffalo Expn., 1900-01; mem. Internat. Jury of Awards, St. Louis Expn., 1904. Mem. Am. Inst. Elec. Engrs. (mgr. and ex-v.p.), A.A.A.S. Author: (with Fitzhugh Townsend) Laboratory and Factory Tests in Electrical Engineering, 1905. Extensive contbr. to elec. jours. Address: 7 W. 43d St., New York.

SEVERY, MELVIN LINWOOD, inventor; b. Melrose, Mass., Aug. 5, 1863; s. Solomon and Caroline Place (Babb) S.; ed. Walpole, Mass., to 3 yrs. high sch.; moved to Boston; grad. Monroe Coll. of Oratory, 1883; m. Wilhelmina Carlstrom, of Boston, Nov. 5, 1884 (died 1895); m. 2d, Elizabeth Ann Flint, of Plymouth, N.S., June 2, 1897 (died 1919). Began as inventor, 1882, and has taken out many patents; awarded John Scott medal of Franklin Institute, 1898, for invention known as the Severy process of printing; ex-pres. Severy Impression Process Co., Choralcelo Mfg. Co., Choralcelo Co.; dir. Solar Power Co., Automatic Tympan Co. (all founded in his inventions). Mem. Franklin Inst., Phila. Author: Fleur-de-lis and Other Stories; Materialization and Other Spiritual Phenomena from a Scientific Standpoint, 1897; The Darrow Enigma, 1904; The Mystery of June Thirteenth, 1905; Gillette's Social Redemption, 1907; Gillette's Industrial Solution, 1908. Sr. inventor of the choralcelo and the vocalcelo; sole inventor of the Vocalsevro. Home: 431 S. Berendo St., Los Angeles, Calif.

SEWALL, HENRY, M.D.; b. Winchester, Va., May 25, 1885; s. Thomas and Julia Elizabeth (Waters) S.; B.S., Wesleyan U., Conn., 1876; Ph.D., Johns Hopkins, 1879; hon. M.D., U. of Mich., 1888, Sc.D., 1912; M.D., U. of Denver, 1889; Sc.D., Wesleyan, 1926; U. of Colorado, 1927; m. Isabel Josephine Vickers, of Toronto, Ont., Sept. 21, 1887. Asst., fellow and asso. in biology, Johns Hopkins, 1876-81; prof. physiology, U. of Mich., 1882-89; prof. physiology, Denver and Cross Coll. of Medicine, 1890-1908; prof. medicine, 1911-17, prof. and lecturer in medicine, 1917-19, U. of Colo., prof.

medicine emeritus. Mem. Nat. Bd. Med. Examiners until 1919; secretary Colo. State Board of Health, 1893-99. Trudeau medalist, Nat. Tuberculosis Assn., 1930; Kober medalist, Assn. Am. Physicians, 1931. Author researches in physiology, published mostly in the Jour. of Physiology, 1877-90, and later in tuberculosis, immunology and clinical medicine. Home: Denver, Colo. Died July 8, 1936.

SEWALL, JAMES WINGATE, (se'wal), consulting forester; b. Old Town, Me., Feb. 12, 1884; s. James Wingate and Harriet Sterling (Moor) S.; A.B., Bowdoin Coll., 1906; m. Louise Belinda Gray, May 12, 1908—children—George Tingey, Mary Braley (Mrs. Richard C. Alden), Margaret Grazebrook, Joseph, Elizabeth Gray. Forester with David Pingree, Bangor, Me., and Salem, Mass., 1906-09; mem. firm Appleton & Sewall, cons. foresters, Bangor, Old Town and N.Y. City, 1910-12; practicing in own name since death of partner, 1912; has valued and mapped over 35 million acres of land in the United States, Canada and Newfoundland; acting forester in charge civilian conservation work for state camps, Me., 1933-36. Postmaster of Old Town, 1915-21, also various other pub. offices; Dem. candidate for Congress, 1922. Mem. Soc. Am. Foresters, Psi Upsilon, Phi Beta Kappa. Episcopalian. Mason. Elk. Club: Rotary. Home: Old Town, Me. Died July 20, 1946.

SEWARD, HERBERT LEE, educator, naval architect, marine engr., maritime cons.; b. Guilford, Conn., Apr. 17, 1885; s. Leonidas C. and Addie A. (Page) S.; Ph.B., Sheffield Sci. Sch. (Yale), 1906, M.E., Yale, 1908; m. Effie May Scranton, Aug. 4, 1909 (died Nov. 1958); children—Ruth, Marion, Dana (all dec.); m. 2d, Anna C. Bronson, Apr. 1959. Instr. mech. engring. Yale, 1908; prof., 1928; asst. to pres. Am. Bur. of Shipping, N.Y.C., 1929-32; mem. adv. com. U.S. Lines, Inc., Fuel Conservation com. U.S. Shipping Bd.; spl. expert and econ. adviser U.S. Maritime Commn.; maritime asst. to Sec. Commerce, 1937-38 (sabbatical leave Yale); cons. Electric Boat Co., Groton, Conn., others; sr. cons. Woods Hole Oceanographic Inst. Mem. OPM Com. on Shipyard Labor. Cons. to and expert for sec. navy in salvaging S.S. Normandie. Organized and operated as exec. officer USN Steam Engring. Sch., at Stevens Inst. Tech., Hoboken, N.J., World War I; served as 3d asst. engr. and asst. navigator S.S. Leviathan, and as comdg. officer U.S.S. Eagle 27; comdr. USNR, ret., naval aide, comdr. on staff of gov. Conn., 8 years. Licensed master of steam vessels, also licensed chief engr. (unlimited). Sec. of U.S. Dept. of Commerce Com. to Coördinate Marine Boiler Rules, 1929-36; tech. advisor to dir. U.S. Shipping Board Bur., U.S. Dept. Commerce; mem. tech. com. Am. Bur. Shipping. Dir. N.Y. Shipbldg. Corp., Camden, N.J., 2 yrs. Chmn. adv. bd., head dept. of Maritime Econs., USCG Acad. 16 yrs. Confidential cons. to Sec. Navy, World War II; asst. to State Dept. on radio aids nav., 1947; mem. tech. com. four experts study and report on collision of M.V. Stockholm and S.S. Andrea Doria. Chmn. Town Beach Erosion Bd., Old Saybrook. Fellow Am. Soc. M.E.; hon. v.p. Soc. Naval Architects and Marine Engrs.; mem. Am. Soc. Naval Engrs., Am. Soc. Engring. Edn., U.S. Power Squadrons, Propeller Club U.S., Sigma Xi (past pres. Yale chpt.), Tau Beta Pi, Phi Gamma Delta. Conglist. Mason. Clubs: Whitehall (N.Y.); Grad., Rotary (ex-pres.), Sojourners (New London); Army and Navy (Washington). Author: Constrn. of Diagrams for Engring. Formulas (text book), 1923; also articles in marine mags., tech. papers, bulls., rules for ship constrn., others. Editor-in-chief: Soc. N.A. and M.E. Text Books on Marine Engineering. Sole arbitrator Greek vs. Japanese and other internat. coml. cases. Home: P.O. Box 517, Sea Lane, Old Saybrook, Conn. 06475. Died July 1966.

SEYBERT, HENRY, mineralogist, philanthropist; b. Phila., Dec. 23, 1801; s. Adam and Maria Sarah (Pepper) S.; ed. Ecole des Mines, Paris, France. Discovered fluorine; mem. Am. Philos. Soc., 1822; contbr. numerous articles on mineralogy to Jour. Scis. and Art and other publs.; contbr. to various philanthropic projects, established chair of philosophy at U. Pa., bequeathed residue of estate to City of Phila. for assistance to poor children. Died Mar. 3, 1883.

SEYFERT, CARL KEENAN, (se fert), astronomer; b. Cleve., Feb. 11, 1911; s. Carl Reber and Rose Marion (Keenan) S.; B.S. magna cum laude, Harvard, 1933, M.A., 1934, Ph.D., 1936; m. Muriel Elizabeth Mussells, Oct. 12, 1935; children—Carl Keenan, Gail Carol. Astronomer McDonald Obs., U. Chgo. and U. Tex., 1936-40; Nat. Research Council fellow Mt. Wilson Obs., 1940-42; instr. and asst. prof. astronomy Case Inst. Tech., 1942-46; asso. prof. astronomy and physics, dir. Barnard Obs., Vanderbilt U., 1946-51, prof. astronomy and physics, dir. Arthur J. Dyer Obs., 1951—; Fulbright fellow, 1951. Conducted classified research ballistics problems for U.S. Army and Bell Telephone Lab., 1942-45; tchr. nav. for USGC and engring. for USN, Case Inst. Tech., 1942-46. Bd. dirs. Nashville Symphony Assn.; bd. dirs. Asso. Univs., Inc., Nashville Children's Museum, Univs. Research in Astronomy, advisory panel for astronomy National Science Foundation. Member Am. (council 1955-58), Royal astron. societies, Astron. Soc. Pacific, Internat. Astron. Union, Tenn. Acad. Sci. (pres. 1951-52, exec. com. 1947-55), Phi Beta Kappa, Sigma Xi. Rotarian. Home: Granny White Pike, Brentwood, Tenn. Died June 13, 1960.

SEYMOUR, ARTHUR BLISS, botanist; b. Moline, Ill., Jan. 3, 1859; s. Frank and Mary Elizabeth (Bliss) S.; B.S., U. of Ill., 1881, M.S., 1886; m. Anna Julia Conkling, May 6, 1886; children—Mary Elizabeth, Rosa Margaret, Frank Conkling, Edith Katharine. Botanist to Ill. State Lab. Natural History, 1879, 1881-83; pvt. asst. in Cryptogamic Herbarium and Gray Herbarium, Harvard Univ., 1883-85; instr. in charge bot. dept., U. of Wis., 1885-86; asst. in Cryptogamic Herbarium, Harvard, 1886—; teacher of cryptogamic botany, Radcliffe Coll., 1890-91, and summer classes, 1890, 92. Fellow Am. Acad. Arts and Sciences, and A.A.A.S. Compiler: A Provisional Host-Index of the Fungi of the United States (with W. G. Farlow), 1888-91; Host Index of the Fungi of North America, 1929. Editor and publisher (with F. S. Earle) Economic Fungi and Economic Fungi Supplement. Home: Belmont, Mass. Died Mar. 31, 1933.

SEYMOUR, JAMES ALWARD, mfr.; b. Auburn, N.Y., Oct. 11, 1864; s. James, Jr., and Mary Osborne (Lodewick) S.; Ph.B., Sheffield Scientific Sch. (Yale), 1885, M.E., 1890; m. Marion Melita Smith, Apr. 11, 1894; children—Jane Chedell (Mrs. Paul W. Hills), Mary Melita (Mrs. Pennington Sefton), James Sayre. Associated with John E. McIntosh, 1886, founding McIntosh, Seymour & Co., mfrs. of steam engines, Auburn, N.Y., and employing 700 persons; firm incorporated, 1911, as McIntosh & Seymour Co., of which was pres.; business sold, 1913, to McIntosh & Seymour Corp., mfrs. of diesel engines, of which became pres. and later chmn. bd. and cons. engr. until 1922, retired (dir. until 1936). Mem. Seymour (Public) Library Assn., Auburn City Hosp. Assn. Hon. mem. Am. Soc. M.E.; asso. mem. Am. Soc. Naval Engrs. Republican. Clubs: University, Yale (New York); Graduate (New Haven); Owasco Country Club (Auburn). Address: 64 South St., Auburn, N.Y. Died June 28, 1943.

SHAAD, GEORGE CARL, electrical engr.; b. Stratford, N.Y., May 5, 1878; s. George and Christina (Ernst) S.; B.S. in Elec. Engring., Pa. State Coll., 1900, E.E., 1905; m. Merthyr Tydvil Evans, Sept. 1, 1906; children—Margaret Louise (dec.), George Carl (dec.), Dorothy, Paul, George Ernst, David. With Gen. Electric Co., Schenectady, N.Y., 1900-02; instr. elec. engring., 1902-04, asst. prof., 1904-06, U. of Wis.; with Bur. of Standards, Washington, summer, 1905; asst. prof. elec. engring., 1906-07, asso. prof., 1907-09, Mass. Inst. Tech.; prof. elec. engring., U. of Kan., 1909—, and acting dean School of Engineering, 1917-18, dean of Sch. Engring. and Architecture, 1927; also cons. engr. Fellow Am. Inst. Electrical Engrs. Died July 9, 1936.

SHAFFER, PHILIP ANDERSON, biol. chemist; b. Martinsburg, W.Va., Sept. 20, 1881; s. Joseph H. and Hannah (Anderson) S.; A.B., West Virginia U., 1900; Ph.D., Harvard U., 1904; hon. D.Sc., U. of Rochester, 1939, Washington University, St. Louis, 1953; married Nan Jefferson Evans, June 30, 1904; children—Jane Jefferson, Nancy Elizabeth (dec.), Philip A. Research biol. chemist, McLean Hosp., Waverly, Mass., 1900-03; asst. and instr., chem. pathology, Cornell U. Med. Coll., N.Y. City, 1904-10; prof. biol. chemistry and head of dept., Washington U. Med. Sch., St. Louis, 1910-46, dean Med. Sch. same univ., 1915-19 and 1937-46, Distinguished Service Prof. biochemistry, 1946-52, professor emeritus Washington U. since 1951. Served as major Sanitary Corps, United States Army, A.E.F., 1917-19. Fellow Am. Assn. Advancement of Science; mem. Nat. Acad. Sciences, Am. Soc. Biol. Chemists (sec. 1913-15; pres. 1923-24), Am. Philosophical Soc., Phi Beta Kappa, Sigma Xi, Phi Kappa Psi, Alpha Tau Omega. Democrat. Home: 5466 Clemens Av., St. Louis, Mo. Died Dec. 4, 1960.

SHAFFER, RAY OSBORN, civil engr.; b. Lafayette, Ill., Jan. 25, 1904; s. James M. and Mary (Forbes) S.; C.E., Bradley U. and Rose Poly. Inst.; m. Mimi E. Mahaffey, Oct. 26, 1940; 1 son, James M. Chmn. bd. Fire Control Engring. Co., Mayfair Industries, Ft. Worth; sr. partner Tex. Rail Joint Co.; past chmn. bd. Reed Roller Bit Company, Houston; member board directors Continental Oil Co., Ft. Worth Union Depot Co., Ft. Worth Savs. & Loan Co., Halliburton Co. Dir. A.R.C., 1955-56, Jr. Achievement of Ft. Worth, United Fund of Tarrant County, 1955-56, Ft. Worth Boys' Choir. Dir. Texas Fund, Inc., Houston, 1954-56, Ft. Worth Hosp. Assn. Mem. Am., Ind. (dir.) petroleum assns., Petroleum Equipment Suppliers Assn. Mem. Christian Ch. (dir.). Club: Fort Worth (dir.). Address: P.O. Box 191, Ft. Worth 76101. Died Nov. 7, 1964; buried Greenwood Meml. Cemetery, Ft. Worth.

SHAFFNER, TALIAFERRO PRESTON, inventor; b. Smithfield, Va., 1818. Admitted to bar, circa 1840; asso. of Samuel F. B. Morse in constrn. of early telegraph lines, supervised constrn. of line from Louisville to New Orleans, 1851, also line from St. Louis to Jefferson; a promoter N. Atlantic cable enterprise, 1856-58; recieved 12 patents for methods of blasting with nitro-glycerine. Author: Telegraph Manual, 1859; The Secession War in America, 1862; Odd Fellowship, 1875. Died Troy, N.Y., Dec. 11, 1881; buried Troy.

SHAFTESBURY, ARCHIE D(AVIS), biologist; b. Pawnee County, Kan., Feb. 9, 1893; s. Calvin Pendleton and Martha Ann (Davis) S.; A.B., Southwestern Coll., Winfield, Kan., 1920; Ph.D., Johns Hopkins, 1934; m. Catharine Cox, June 15, 1940. Asst. in biology Johns Hopkins, 1920-24; research asst. bee culture lab. Dept. of Agr., Washington, summers 1921-23; prof. comparative anatomy Mt. Vernon Coll., Baltimore, 1924; asst. prof. zoology Woman's Coll., U. N.C., 1924-27, asso. prof., 1927-45, dir. marine lab., 1935—, prof., 1945-59, ret.; acting head biol. dept. Lenoir Rhyne Coll., 1959-62; vis. prof. biol. Greensboro (N.C.) Coll., 1962-65; lectr. High Point (N.C.) Coll., 1928; instr. Davidson (N.C.) Coll., 1944. Served with 353d Inf., 89th Div., A.E.F., U.S. Army, 1918-19. Mem. Am. Ornithologists Union, Am. Soc. Zoologists, Am. Genetic Assn., Wilson Ornithol. Club, Cooper Ornithol. Club, N.C. Acad. Sci. (v.p. 1947), Assn. Southeastern Biologists, Carolina Bird Club (pres. 1941; editor 1944-51), Sigma Xi. Methodist. Club: Kiwanis (Greensboro). Home: 315 Tate St., Greensboro, N.C. Died Apr. 9, 1967; buried Forest Lawn-Cemetery, Greensboro, N.C.

SHALER, NATHANIEL SOUTHGATE, dean Lawrence Scientific School and prof. geology, Harvard; b. Newport, Ky., Feb. 20, 1841; grad. Lawrence Scientific School, Harvard, 1862, Sc.D., 1865; served 2 yrs. as arty. officer in Union army during Civil war; instr. zoölogy and geology, Lawrence Scientific School, 1868-72; prof. palaeontology, 1868-87, then prof. geology Harvard; dir. Ky. geol. survey, 1873-80, devoting part of each year to that work; from 1884 geologist in charge Atlantic div., U.S. Geol. Survey; mem. Nat. Acad. Sciences, etc. Author: A First Book in Geology; Kentucky, a Pioneer Commonwealth; The Nature of Intellectual Property; The Story of Our Continent; The Interpretation of Nature; Illustrations of the Earth's Surface; Sea and Land; The United States of America: a Study of the American Commonwealth; Fossil Brachiopods of the Ohio Valley; American Highways; Features of Coasts and Oceans; Domesticated Animals: their Relation to Man; The Individual: Study of Life and Death, 1900; The Neighbor, 1904; The Citizen, 1903; etc. Died 1906.

SHAMBAUGH, GEORGE ELMER, M.D.; b. in Clinton Co., Ia., Nov. 15, 1869; s. John and Eva Ann (Ressler) S.; Ph.B., State U. of Ia., 1892; M.D., U. of Pa., 1895; studied U. of Berlin, 1895-96, U. of Vienna, 1896-97; m. Edith Capps, of Jacksonville, Ill., May 2, 1901. Specialist in diseases of the ear, nose and throat; prof. otolaryngology and head of dept., Rush Med. Coll., 1916-35; clinical prof. emeritus since 1935; instr. anatomy of the ear, nose and throat, U. of Chicago, 1900-35; otologist and laryngologist Presbyn. Hosp., 1902-35. Fellow Am. Otol. Society (ex-pres.), Am. Laryngol. Assn. (ex-pres.); mem. A.M.A., Chicago Med. Soc., Chicago Laryngological and Otological Soc. (ex-pres.). Awarded Lenval prize (international prize in otology) for research on the internal ear, 1912. Club: University. Contbr. to Journal of the Am. Med. Assn., Annals of Otology, Rhinology and Laryngology, Laryngoscope; editor Archives of Otolaryngology, 1923-37; has written chapters on the ear and nasal sinuses for several textbooks. Home: 5625 University Av. Office: Peoples Gas Bldg., Chicago IL

SHANAHAN, JOHN DANIEL, crop technologist; b. Buffalo, N.Y., Oct. 24, 1864; s. Daniel W. and Mary L. (Ulrich) S.; ed. pub. schs. of Buffalo; m. Minnie F. Hair, of Rochester, N.Y., Feb. 1, 1906. With grain inspn. dept. Buffalo Chamber of Commerce, 1887-98, chief of dept., 1898-1906; crop technologist in charge of div. of grain standardization, Bur. of Plant Industry, U.S. Dept. of Agr., Oct. 1, 1906-Dec. 1, 1910. Gained wide reputation by advocating reforms in grain classification and inspn.; first to publicly suggest standardization of class and grades of grains by the federal govt., 1902; mem. Grain and Warehouse Commn., State of Wis., July 1905-Apr. 1, 1906. Spent winter, 1910-11, in British India investigating oilseeds and manufacture; spent winter, 1912-13, on the west coast of Africa investigating the oil palm and palm oil industry; in grain business, Duluth, Minn., 1914-16; on staff Food Administration Grain Corpn., New York, 1917-19; field asst. to U.S. wheat dir., and leader of expedition traveled through all countries of Europe, except Russia, making survey of growing grain crops, 1919; market expert and wheat buyer for Niagara Falls Milling Co., 1919-30; grain expert, The Grain Stabilization Corpn., since 1930. Home: 784 Chestnut Hill Rd., East Aurora, N.Y.

SHANKLAND, EDWARD CLAPP, civil engr.; b. Pittsburgh, Pa., Aug. 2, 1854; s. Edward Russell and Emeline F. (Clapp) S.; pub. sch. edn.; C.E., Rensselaer Poly. Inst., 1878; (hon. M.A., Cornell Coll., Ia., 1904); m. Harriet Graham, July 19, 1881. Engaged on U.S. improvement of Mo. and Miss. rivers, 1878-83; bridge work, Canton, O., 1883-89; designing steel work for bldgs., 1889—; engr. for Burnham & Root, architects, 1889-94; engr. of constrn. and chief engr. of works, Chicago Expn., 1891-93; mem. D. H. Burnham & Co., 1894-98, of E. C. & R. M. Shankland, 1898—. Mem. Harbor Subway Commn., Chicago, 1911-16. Home: Chicago, Ill. Died June 3, 1924.

SHANKS, ROYAL E(ASTMAN), botanist; b. Ada, O., Nov. 11, 1912; s. William Carleton and Essie Fern (Eastman) S.; A.B., Ohio Northern U., 1933; M. Sc., Ohio State U., 1937, Ph.D., 1938; m. Betty Jane Morris, Jan. 3, 1935; children—Harriet Morris, Emily Morris. High sch. prin., tchr. North Bloomfield, O., 1933-36; grad. asst. botany Ohio State U., 1936-39, instr., 1939; instr. botany U. Tenn., 1940, asst. prof., 1940-41, asso. prof., 1946-48, prof., 1948—; prof. Austin Peay State Coll., 1941-46. Agt. barberry eradication U.S. Dept. Agr., summers 1936, 38; asst. Ohio Wildlife Research Sta., 1937; plant ecologist N.Y. State Mus., 1938-42; prof. Mountain Lake Biol. Sta., 1950, 53; bd. mgrs. Highlands Biol. Sta., 1954—; vegetation studies No. Alaska. Arctic Inst. N.A., summers 1955-59. Mem. A.A.A.S., Bot. Soc. Am., Ecol. Soc. Am., So. Appalachian Bot. Club (pres. 1951, 58), Brit. Ecol. Soc., Assn. Southeastern Biologists (president 1961-62), American Geophys. Union, Soc. Am. Foresters, Tenn. Acad. Sci. (exec. com. 1951-52), Sigma Xi, (pres. Tenn. chpt. 1951-52), Gamma Sigma Delta, Phi Epsilon Phi. Presbyn. Home: 319 Hermitage Rd., Knoxville, Tenn. 37920. Died Aug. 4, 1962; buried Foreigner's Cemetery, San Jose, Costa Rica.

SHANNON, SPENCER SWEET, mining cons.; b. Saxton, Pa., Nov. 14, 1893; s. William Wellington Ent and Elsie Jane (Sweet) S.; A.B., Univ. Pa., 1917, A.M., 1920; student in mining, Lehigh Univ., 1919-20; m. Katherine Wallace, Sept. 25, 1925; children—Spencer Sweet, Patricia (Mrs. Edward C. Booth). Engaged in coal and metal mining and consulting, 1920-42; vice president and director of the Carbon Coal & Coke Co., Boston, 1921; partner The Shannon Co., Dudley, Pa., 1921-44; cons. work in mining, as owner Shannon Co., Bedford, Pa., 1945-49; dir. 1st Nat. Bank of Saxton, Pa., 1st Nat. Bank of Huntington, Pa. Asst. chief metals and minerals br. Bd. Econ. Warfare, 1942; chief metals div., Fgn. Econ. Adminstrn., 1943; dir. materials office. Nat. Security Resources Bd., 1949-51; spl. asst. to the adminstr. R.F.C., 1951-52; mem. U.S. Tin Mission Malaya, 1951; cons. AEC, R.F.C., Nat. Sec. Resources Bd., 1952-53; mem. Sec. Interior Survey Team Bur. Mines, 1953-54; cons. asst. Sec. of the Interior for Mineral Resources, 1955; director of the office Minerals Mobilization, 1955—. Trustee Lycoming College, Bedford County Memorial Hospital. Served as 1st lt., U.S. Army, 1917-19. Recipient Distinguished Service award, U.S. Dept. Interior, 1960. Mem. Am. Inst. Mining, Metall. and Petroleum Engineers, Mining and Metall. Soc. Am., Am. Legion. Phi Beta Kappa, Psi Upsilon. Clubs: University (Washington); Mask and Wig (Phila.); Huntington Country; Bedford (Pa.) Springs Golf. Home: "Limeledge," Bedford, Pa. Office: Bedford, Pa. Died Jan. 8, 1964.

SHANTZ, HOMER LEROY, botanist; b. Kent County, Mich., Jan. 24, 1876; s. Abraham K. and Mary E. (Ankney) S.; B.Sc., Colo. Coll., Colorado Springs, Colo., 1901, Sc.D., 1926; Ph.D., U. of Nebraska, 1905; m. Lucia Moore Soper, Dec. 25, 1901; children—Homer LeRoy, Benjamin Soper. Inst. botany and zoölogy, Colorado Coll., 1901, 02; instr. botany, U. of Neb., 1903, 04, U. of Mo., 1905, 06; prof. botany and bacteriology, U. of La., 1907; spl. agt. and collaborator, alkali and drought resistant plant investigations, Bur. Plant Industry, U.S. Dept. Agr., summers, 1906, 07, expert, 1908, 09; plant physiologist same, 1910-20, sr. physiologist in charge physiol. and fermentation investigations, 1921-23, physiologist in charge plant geography in its relation to plant industry, 1924-26; prof. botany and head of dept., U. of Ill., 1926-28; pres. U. of Arizona, 1928-36; chief division of wildlife management, Forest Service, U.S. Dept. of Agriculture, 1936-1944; annuitant collaborator U.S. Dept. Agr., 1945—, prof. botany, U. Ariz., 1956, principal investigator Arizona African Expedition, 1956-57. Special lecturer on plant geography, Graduate Sch. Geography, Clark U., 1922-26. Mem. Ariz. State Bd. of Edn., State Bd. of Vocational Edn.; Ariz. State chmn. Rhodes Scholarship Com.; chmn. State Planning Bd. of Ariz. Fellow Am. Soc. Agronomy, Royal Soc. of Arts; mem. Phytog. Soc. Sweden, hon. pres., 7th Internat. Bot. Congress, Stockholm, 1950, also Paris, 1954. Mem. Botanical Soc., Washington, Assn. Am. Geographers, Ecol. Soc. Am., Soc. Plant Physiol. (Charles Reid Barnes life mem.), Wildlife Soc., Soc. pro Fauna et Flora Fennica, Internat. African Inst., Sigma Xi, Phi Kappa Phi (nat. pres., 1935-39), Theta Xi, Theta Alpha Phi, Alpha Zeta, Phi Beta Kappa, Blue Key, Phi Mu Alpha. Congregationalist. Clubs: Explorers (New York City); Federal, Cosmos (Washington, D.C.) Contributor many articles to jours. and publs. of the U.S. Govt., dealing chiefly with wildlife management, plant physiology and with natural vegetation and its value as an indicator of the agrl. capabilities of land, and the plant geography of N.A., S.A. and Africa; agrl. regions of Africa and management of wild animals on the national forests. Spl. detail to determine natural plant resources and crop producing possibilities of large portions of Africa and Latin America for use of Am. Commn. to Negotiate Peace, 1918-19; spl. detail as agrl. explorer with Smithsonian Instn. Africa Expdn., 1919-20; spl. detail as mem. Ednl. Commn. to East Africa under auspices of Phelps Stokes Fund and Internat. Ednl. Bd., 1924. Address: 454 Paseo del Descanso, Santa Barbara, Cal. Died June 23, 1958.

SHAPLEIGH, WALDRON, chemist; b. in Philadelphia, Jan. 25, 1848; s. Marshall S. and Elizabeth M. (Blandy) S.; ed. Episcopal Acad., Phila.; grad. Lehigh Univ., 1871; student chemistry, Paris and Vienna; m. Mary H. DuPuy, Dec. 23, 1880. Asst. prof. chemistry, Lehigh Univ., 1868-72; studied in Europe, 1872-74; supt. Kings Co. Refining Co., 1874-83; chemist Welsbach Light Co., 1887—; commr. from Pa. to Vienna Expn., 1873; judge awards World's Columbian Expn., 1893. Home: Philadelphia, Pa. Died 1901.

SHAPLEY, HARLOW, astronomer; b. Nashville, Mo., Nov. 2, 1885; s. Willis Harlow and Sarah (Stowell) S.; A.B., U. Mo., 1910, A.M., 1911, LL.D., 1927; Ph.D., Princeton, 1913, Sc.D., 1933; Sc.D., U. Pitts., 1931, U. Pa., 1932, Brown U., Harvard 1933, U. Toronto (Can.), 1935, N.Y. U., U. Copenhagen, 1946, U. Delhi, U. Hawaii, 1947, U. Ireland, 1959, St. Lawrence U., 1963; D.D., U. Chgo., 1969; LL.D., Oglethorpe U., 1931; Dr. Honoris causa, U. Michocan (Mex.), U. Mexico, 1951; Litt.D., Bates Coll., 1942; m. Martha Betz, Apr. 15, 1914; children—Mildred (Mrs. Ralph Matthews), Willis, Alan Lloyd, Carl. Astronomer, Mount Wilson Obs., Cal., 1914-21; dir. obs. Harvard, 1921-52, Paine prof. astronomy, 1922-56, emeritus, 1956-72; Wm. A. Neilsen research prof. Smith Coll., 1956-57; Phi Beta Kappa resident lectr. various Am. Colls., 1957-58. Lectr., Lowell Inst., 1922; exchange lectr. Belgian univs., 1926; Halley lectr., Oxford, 1928; Harry Todd lectr. State of Mass., 1929; lectr. Jayne Found., Phila., 1930; Darwin lectr. Royal Astron. Soc., 1934; lectr. several fgn. univs., 1951-72. Life mem. corp. Mass. Inst. Tech. Researches in photometry, cosmogony. Trustee Worcester Found. Exptl. Biology, pres., 1942-48; trustee Sci. Service, Institut Reserche Scientifique D'Afrique Central (Africa), Woods Hole Oceanographic Inst. Recipient numerous sci. awards including Pope Pius XI prize, 1941; Calcutta Sci. Soc. Medal, 1947; Gold medal Indian Assn. for Cultivation Sci., 1947; Order of Aztec Eagle (Mexico), Crux de Honor (Puebla). Fellow Am. Acad. Arts and Sci. (pres. 1939-44); mem. A.A.A.S. (pres. 1949), Indian (hon.), Nat. acad. scis., various other fgn. sci. assns., exec. officer of several. Author: The Inner Metagalaxy, 1957; Of Stars and Men, 1958; The View from a Distant Star, 1964; Beyond the Observatory; Through Rugged Ways to the Stars, 1969. Address: Cambridge MA Died Oct. 1972.

SHARP, BENJAMIN, zoölogist; b. Germantown, Phila., Nov. 1, 1858; s. Benjamin and Hannah Ballinger (Leedom) S.; ed. Swarthmore Coll., 1871-76; M.D., U. of Pa., 1879, Ph.D., 1880; Ph.D., Univ. of Würzburg, 1883; univs. of Berlin and Leipzig, and Zoöl. Sta., Naples, 1879-83; m. Virginia May Guild, Sept. 15, 1881. Prof. invertebrate zoölogy, Acad. Natural Sciences, Phila., 1883, U. of Pa., 1884-86; life mem. and corr. sec., 1890-1901, Acad. Natural Sciences, Phila., for which made expdns., collecting in Caribbee Islands in winter, 1888-89; to H.I., collecting archaeol. and zoöl. specimens summer of 1893; also in Arctic, 1895, on U.S. revenue cutter "Bear," in Alaska and Siberia. Had charge zoölogy in First Arctic Expedition, Lt. R. E. Peary, 1891. Vice-pres. Nantucket Hist. Assn. Mem. Soc. of Friends. Lecturer. Rep. in Gen. Court of Mass. for Nantucket, 1910-13. Home: Nantucket Island, Mass. Died Jan. 24, 1915.

SHARP, CLAYTON HALSEY, physicist, elec. engr.; b. Seneca, Falls, N.Y., Dec. 5, 1869; s. James B. and Martha (Halsey) S.; prep. edn., Mynderse Acad., Seneca Falls, N.Y.; A.B., Hamilton Coll., 1890; Ph.D., Cornell U., 1895; hon. D.Sc., Hamilton Coll., 1941; spl. work, U. Leipzig, 1899-1900; m. Kathleen Hamilton, Malloch, Oct. 27, 1900; children—Dorothy Malloch (Mrs. William Folterman, Jr.), Kathleen Halsey (Mrs. Walker Harden), Marjorie Hamilton (Mrs. William Caldwell), Eleanor Bruen, Mary Elizabeth (Mrs. Robert L. Simpson). Instr. in physics, Cornell U., 1895-1900; test officer for Elec. Testing Labs., N.Y.C., 1901-14, v.p., 1914-33; cons. in light and electricity; also patented various instruments for elec. and photometric measurements. Del. to meetings of Internat. Electrotech. Commn., Turin, 1911, Berlin, 1913, Geneva, 1922, London, 1924, The Hague, 1925, N.Y., 1926, Bellagio and Rome, 1927, Stockholm, 1930, Scheveningen and Brussels, 1935, Torquay-London, 1938, pres. U.S. Nat. Com. of same, 1924-39, hon. pres., 1930—; del. to meetings of the Internat. Commn. on Illumination, Berlin, 1913, Geneva, 1924, Bellagio, 1927, Saranac, 1928, Germany, 1935, and pres. U.S. Nat. Com. of same, 1914-28, v.p., 1928. Fellow Am. Phys. Soc., A.A.A.S., Am. Inst. E.E.; mem. Illuminating Engring. Soc. (pres. 1907-08), Société Française des Electriciens, Alpha Delta Phi, Phi Beta Kappa, Sigma Xi. Republican. Contbr. many technical papers. Home-Office: 294 Fisher Av., White Plains, N.Y. Deceased.

SHARP, EDWARD RAYMOND, aeronautical engr.; b. Hampton, Va., Mar. 9, 1894; s. Edward Turner and Lilly Pearl (Oldfield) S.; student law Coll. William and Mary; D.Sc. (hon.), Case Inst. Tech., 1948; E.D. (honorary), Fenn College, Cleve., 1958; m. Florence Aileen Gordon, Apr. 19, 1919 (dec. Apr. 23, 1932); 1 son Edward Gordon; m. 2d Elvira Bona, Mar. 2, 1935; children—Elinor Ray, Robert Richard Raymond. Admitted to Va. bar, 1924; staff Langley Aeronautical Lab., Nat. Adv. Com. Aeronautics, Langley Field, Va., 1922-25, administrative officer, 1925-40; administrative officer Ames Aeronautical Lab., Moffett Field, Cal., 1940; mgr. Lewis Flight Propulsion Lab., Cleveland, 1941-47, dir. since 1947. Dir., Lewis Research Center, NASA, to 1961. Mem. exec. com. A.R.C.; member of Mayor's advisory com. on Lakefront and Harbor Development; com. on aviation, Cleveland; exec. com. nat. air races. Trustee Cleveland Air Found. Served U.S.N., 1914-19, ret. as lt. comdr. 1940. Recipient Medal for Merit from Pres. Truman, 1947; distinguished service award, Cleve. Tech. Socs. Council, 1958. Fellow Can. Aero. Institute, Aeronautical Science (president, 1957), Academy Model Aeronautics (honorary), Royal Aeronautical Society, Canadian Aeronautical Institute; member Cleveland C. of C., Am. Ordnance Assn., Soc. Automotive Engrs., Newcomen Soc. Eng., A.A.A.S., S.A.R., Navy League of U.S. Presbyn. Home: 17877 Lake Rd., Lakewood 7, O. Office: 21000 Brookpark Rd., Cleve. 35. Died July 24, 1961.

SHARPE, FRANCIS ROBERT, mathematician; b. Warrington, Eng., Jan. 23, 1870; s. Alfred and Mary (Webb) S.; A.B., Cambridge U., 1892; Manchester U., 1900-01; Ph.D., Cornell U., 1907; m. Jeannette Welch, Sept. 1900; children—Elfreda J., Frances M., Edith J. Lecturer in mathematics, Queen's U., Kingston, Can., 1901-04; instr. mathematics, 1905-10, asst. prof., 1910-19, prof. 1919-38, emeritus prof. since 1938, Cornell U. Naturalized citizen of U.S., 1910. Mem. Am. Math. Soc., Sigma Xi. Republican. Presbyterian. Contbr. hydrodynamics and algebraic geometry. Home: Central Av., Ocean City, N.J. Died May 18, 1948.

SHARPE, PHILIP BURDETTE, author, firearms technician; b. Portland, Me., May 16, 1903; s. Elias Lorenzo and Jennie Mabelmaylor (Clark) S.; B.C.S., Portland U., 1924; m. Lotta Marguerite Burby, Oct. 12, 1928 (div. 1936); m. 2d, Ethel Marie Harmon, July 6, 1940 (div. 1954); children—Phyllis Eileen, Phillip B.; m. 3d, Marguerite Sharpe, Jan. 21, 1955. Entered business career as feature writer with Portland (Me.) Sunday Telegram, 1919-25; reporter Evening News, Portland, 1927-31; free-lance mag. writer since 1921, specializing in subject of firearms since 1919; formerly firearms editor Mich. Sportsman, Outdoors, Nat. Sportsman, Hunting & Fishing; firearms technician and cons. since 1930; owner The Philip B. Sharpe Research Labs., Fairfield, Pa., and Emmitsburg, Md., 1947—; pres., treasurer of Sharpe and Hart Associates, Inc. (Md., Pa., Cal.). President Emmitsburg Civic Association, Incorporated, Emmittsburg Community Fund. Served as capt., ordnance, U.S. Army, 1942-46; chief small arms historian Office Chief Ordnance, 1942-44; proof officer Fgn. Materiel (research and development sect.), Aberdeen Proving Ground, 1944; chief small arms unit, Ordnance Tech. Intelligence Enemy Equipment, E.T.O., 1945. Member National Rifle Association of Am. (mem. tech. div. staff, 1950-55), Vets. Fgn. Wars, Am. Legion, Am. Ordnance Assn., Nat. Skeet Assn., U.S. Revolver Assn., Outdoor Writers Assn. Am. Clubs: Lions Internat., Automobile of France (hon.). Author: This Handloading Game, 1934; The Complete Guide to Handloading, 1937; The Rifle in America, 1938. Designer (with Col. Douglass B. Wesson) The Smith & Wesson .357 magnum revolver and cartridge; 7 x 61 Sharpe & Hart cartridge, 1949-54. Home: Fairfield, Pa. Office: Emmitsburg, Md. Died Jan. 24, 1961; buried Arlington Nat. Cemetery.

SHARPLES, STEPHEN PASCHALL, chemist; b. West Chester, Pa., Apr. 21, 1842; s. Philip P. and Mary A. (Paschall) S.; S.B., Lawrence Scientific Sch. (Harvard), 1866; (hon. M.S., Pa. State Coll., 1915); m. Abbie M. Hall, June 16, 1870 (died 1914). Prof. chemistry, Boston Dental Coll., 1875-93; cons. chemist, 1872—. Insp. and assayer of liquors for Mass., 1885-1902; was expert on census, 1880; a judge of awards, Chicago Exposition, 1893. Fellow Am. Acad. Arts and Sciences, A.A.A.S., Soc. of Industrial Chemistry, Eng. Editor: Genealogical Magazine. Author: Chemical Tables, 1866. Joint editor: History of the Kimball Family, 1897; editor Records of the Church of Christ in Cambridge, 1906; etc. Home: Cambridge, Mass. Died Aug. 21, 1923.

SHATTUCK, CHARLES HOUSTON, forester, botanist; b. Vandalia, Mo., Nov. 21, 1867; s. Warren Charles and Matilda Catherine (Houston) S.; B.S., Campbell Coll., Holton, Kan., 1894, M.S., 1898; Ph.D., U. of Chicago, 1908; studied Woods Hole, Mass., and Biltmore (N.C.) Sch. of Forestry; m. Maud Elizabeth Stackhouse, Aug. 15, 1895. Prof. physical sciences, 1895-98, prof. biology and geology, 1898-1903, v.p., 1897-1903, Campbell Coll.; prof. natural history, Washburn Coll., Topeka, Kan., 1904-07; research and teaching fellow, U. of Chicago, 1908; instr. in botany, Woods Hole, Mass., summer, 1908; prof. botany and forestry, Clemson Coll., S.C., 1908-09; prof. forestry and bot. morphology, 1909-17, dean Coll. Letters and Sciences, 1914-17, U. of Idaho; also forester, U. of Idaho Expt. Sta., 1909-17, and with U.S. Forest Service, summers 1910-17; prof. forestry in charge grazing U. of Calif., 1917—. Republican. Methodist. Home: Berkeley, Calif. Died 1931.

SHATTUCK, GEORGE BURBANK, geologist; b. Lowell, Mass., 1869; s. Horace B. and Mary L. (Comins) S.; B.S., Amherst, 1892; Ph.D., Johns Hopkins, 1897; m.

Annie B. Gibson, 1896. Asst., asso. and asso. prof. geology, Johns Hopkins, 1897-1905; prof. geology, Vassar Coll., 1906—. Home: Poughkeepsie, N.Y. Died 1934.

SHATTUCK, GEORGE CHEEVER, physician; b. Boston, Mass., Oct. 12, 1879; s. Frederick Cheever and Elizabeth Perkins (Lee) S.; Noble and Greenough School, 1892-97; A.B., Harvard University, 1901, honorary A.M., 1919; M.D., Harvard University Medical Sch., 1905; med. study in Vienna, 1907-08; m. Virginia Grigsby Chandler (Peabody), July 9, 1932; step-sons, Francis W. Peabody, Grigsby C. Peabody. physician to out-patients, later assistant visiting physician Mass. Gen. Hosp., 1912-21; mem. Am. Red Cross Commn. to Serbia (combating typhus fever), 1915; maj. med. service, Harvard Surgical Unit, B.E.F., 1916; temp. hon. major, Royal Army Med. Corps, Harvard Unit, 1917-19; gen. med. sec. League of Red Cross Societies, Geneva, 1919-21; mem. visiting staff Boston City Hosp., 1921-41; attending specialist in tropical medicine, U.S. Marine Hosp., Brighton, Mass., 1923; mem. Hamilton Rice 7th Expedition to Amazon, 1924-25; consultant tropical diseases, Mass. General Hosp. since 1928; mem. faculty Museum of Comparative Zoology, Harvard, 1933-62; clinical prof. tropical medicine, Harvard School of Public Health, 1938-47; emeritus; consultant tropical diseases Boston City Hosp., from 1941; consultant to secretary of war on tropical medicine, 1941-44; cons. in tropical diseases, Peter Bent Brigham Hospital, Boston, emeritus, also V.A., West Roxbury, Mass., 1945-52, V.A. Boston and Farmingham since 1952; adviser to Resources Div., Office of Quartermaster Gen., War Dept., 1942. Pres. Boston Health League, Inc., 1939-49; pres. Mass. Central Health Council, 1938-48; chmn. Health Council United Community Services, Boston, 1950-53; pres. Brookline Citizens Committee, 1941. Awarded Serbia Order of St. Sava of III Class, 1918; Distinguished Service Order (Great Britain), 1919; Theobold Smith Medal, Am. Acad. Tropical Medicine, 1954; Orden Nacional de Merito Commendador, Carlos J. Findlay, Cuba, 1950; Orden Nacional do Cruzeiro do Sul, Oficial, Brazil, 1958; Prof. Honorario, Universidad de San Carlos, Guatemala, 1956; Richard Pearson Strong medal Am. Found. Tropical Medicine; bronze medal New England Wild Flower Soc., 1965. Mem. Mass. Med. Soc., Am. Pub. Health Assn., A.A.A.S., Am. Acad. Arts and Scis., Am. Acad. Tropical Medicine (pres. 1947-48), Am. Society Tropical Medicine, Royal Soc. Tropical Medicine and Hygiene (local sec. for U.S., 1939-49), Nature Conservancy (gov. 1956-62, Mass. rep. 1957-70; hon. mem.), Pan. Am. Soc. New Eng. (gov. 1941-65). Mem. Hon. Pub. Health Soc., Sigma Xi, Delta Omega, Beta Chapter. Author: Principles of Medical Treatment, 6th rev. edit., 1926; The Peninsula of Yucatan, 1933; Medical Survey of the Republic of Guatemala, 1938; Handbook of Health for Overseas Service (with Wm. Jason Mixter), 2d rev. edit., 1943; Diseases of the Tropic, 1950; A Memoir of Frederick Cheever Shattuck, M.D., 1967. Home: Brookline MA Died June 12, 1972.

SHATTUCK, GEORGE CHEYNE, physician, philanthropist; b. Templeton, Mass., July 17, 1783; s. Dr. Benjamin and Lucy (Barron) S.; A.B., Dartmouth, 1803, M.B., 1806, M.D. (hon.), 1812, LL.D. (hon.). 1853; M.D., U. Pa., 1807; m. Dliza Cheever Davis, Oct. 3, 1811; m. 2d, Amelia H. Bigelow, Aug. 17, 1835; 6 children including George Cheyne. Leading physician in Boston from 1807; consulting physician to City of Boston for short period; pres. Mass. Med. Soc., 1836-40; pres. Am. Statis. Assn., 1845-51; contbd. toward building of astron. observatory Dartmouth Coll.; contbd. funds to Harvard (endowment now Chattuck Professorship of Path. Anatomy, Harvard Med. Sch.); gave grant to Mass. Med. Soc. for foundation of Shattuck lectures; financially assisted John James Audubon with Birds of America, 1827-38; founder Shattuck Sch., Faribault, Minn.; won Boylston med. prize 2 years in succession for essay series published in Boston, 1808; mem. N.H. Med. Soc., Am. Acad. Arts and Scis. Author: A Dissertation on the Uncertainty of the Healing Art, 1829; Died Boston, Mar., 18, 1854.

SHATTUCK, LEMUEL, statistician, genealogist; b. Ashby, Mass., Oct. 15, 1793; s. John and Betsy (Miles) S.; m. Clarissa Baxter, Dec. 1, 1825, 5 children. Organizer 1st Sunday Sch. in Mich., circa 1820; mcht., Concord Mass., 1823-34; mem. Concord Sch. Com., reorganized schs., introduced annual sch. reports; mem. Mass. Legislature, 1838; publisher and bookseller, Boston, 1836-39; a founder Am. Statis. Assn., 1839, New Eng. Historic Geneal. Soc., circa 1840; influenced passage of law requiring system of registration of births, marriages and deaths, 1842; active mem. Boston Common Council, 1837-41, induced Council to take census in 1845; chmn. commn. to make san. survey of Mass., 1849, wrote its Report, 1850, resulting in creation of Mass. Bd. of Health. Author: A History of the Town of Concord, 1835; Memorials of the Descendants of William Shattuck, 1855. Died Boston, Jan. 17, 1859.

SHAVER, GEORGE FREDERICK, engineer; b. Ripley, Chautauqua Co., N.Y., Nov. 4, 1855; s. David and Julia E. S.; ed. at high sch.; in employ L.,S. & M.S. Ry., 1875-79; invented improved mech. telephone, self-righting and self-bailing lifeboat; automatic mail catcher; automatic screw driver, etc.; pres. Pocahontas Coal & Timber Co.; v.-p. and gen. mgr. Shaver Corpn., 1887-93; v.-p. Blue Jacket Consolidated Copper Co.; v.-p. Lackawanna, Catskill Mountain & Boston Ry. since 1893, Central Am. Steamship Co., 1893-95; pres. Wyckoff Bros., Inc., builders of steam and sailing yachts, Clinton, Conn., 1903; pres., 1905-06, dept. mgr. 1906-09, Larkin Co., Buffalo; pres. Pyrene Mfg. Co., New York, 1910-11; now pres. and chief engr. Hydragas Corpn., and inventor of "Hydragas," a chemical revolutionizing combustion of gasoline and operation of automobiles. Now mech. engr. motive power dept. Interboro Rapid Transit Co., New York. Dist. inspn. supervisor, Ordnance Dept. U.S.A., 1917-18. Commodore Yonkers Corinthian Yacht Club, 1892-93; owner many steam and sailing yachts. Clubs: New York Athletic, Magnetic, Old Timers' Telegraph, Brooklyn Engineers. Office: 40 Wall St., New York, N.Y.

SHAW, EUGENE WESLEY, geologist; b. Delaware, O., July 29, 1881; s. William Bigelow and Irene (Gardner) S.; B.S., Ohio Wesleyan U., 1905, D.Sc., 1927; U. of Chicago, 1905-07; m. Abbie Potter Haylett, Oct. 18, 1907. With U.S. Geol. Survey most of time, 1907-21; consulting geologist, 1921-29; chief geologist Iraq Petroleum Co., London, 1929—. Has made extensive investigations for oil corporations in various countries; in charge of natural gas valuation, U.S. Treasury Dept., 1918-19; chief of sub-sect. of sedimentation, U.S. Geol. survey, 1919-20. Has devoted attention principally to estimation of underground reserves of oil and natural gas, appraisal of oil and gas properties, developed and prospective; behavior of streams as involved in certain law suits and problems of river improvements; investigation of geologic history of mountain ranges, coasts and deltas of N. and S. America, Europe, Asia and Africa; studies of geophysics of the great sedimentary basins. Mem. various professional societies. Methodist. Author: Coal, Oil and Gas of Foxburg Quadrangle, Pa. (U.S. Geological Survey), 1909; Mud Lumps at Mouth of the Mississippi River, 1912; Natural Gas of North Texas, 1916; Oil Fields of Allen County, Ky., 1919; also about 100 other publs. Explored and mapped 100,000 sq. miles along east base of Andes, S. America. Home: Chevy Chase, Md. Died Oct. 7, 1935.

SHAW, FREDERICK WILLIAM, prof. bacteriology; b. Halifax, Eng., Dec. 14, 1882; s. Rowland and Ellen (Stansfield) S.; M.D., U. of Kan., 1906; B.Sc., U. of Mo., 1921, M.Sc., 1921; m. Elizabeth Martin, Nov. 10, 1909; 1 dau., Elizabeth. Came to U.S., 1887, naturalized, 1897. Intern Bethany Hosp., Kansas City, Kan., 1906-07; govt. service as physician, 1907-16; physician Mo. State Sanatorium, 1916-17; asso. prof. hygiene, U. of Mo. Sch. of Mines, 1919-22, prof., 1922-24; asso. prof. bacteriology, Med. Coll. of Va., 1924-29, prof. bacteriology and parasitology since 1929. Maj. Med. Corps, U.S. Army, 1917-18. Richmond Acad. Medicine, Va. Med. Soc., A.M.A., Socio Fundador, Sanatorio Belem, Porto Alegre, Brazil. Phi Beta Pi, Sigma Zeta. Clubs: Deep Run Hunt (Richmond, Va.); Army and Navy (Washington, D.C.) Collborator: Approved Laboratory Technic. Contbr. to Physicians Library, Practice of Allergy, also to med. jours. Home: 2312 Stuart Av., Richmond, Va.; (summer) Rolla, Mo. Died May 29, 1945.

SHAW, HENRY, founder Mo. Bot. Garden; b. Sheffield, Eng., July 24, 1800; s. Joseph and Sarah (Hoole) S. Settled in St. Louis, 1819; owned hardware and cutlery business until retirement, 1840; established Mo. Botanical Garden (instn. for systematic study of plants), St. Louis, 1857, opened garden to public circa 1860, established trust for its maintenance; established one of best bot. libraries, also one of largest herbariums in U.S.; endowed Henry Shaw Sch. of Botany at Washington U., St. Louis. Died St. Louis, Aug. 25, 1889; buried Mo. Bot. Garden.

SHAW, HOBART DOANE, civil engr.; b. Carrollton, Miss., Sept. 21, 1879; s. Hobart Doane and Adline (Hemphill) S.; B.S., Miss. Agrl. and Mech. Coll., 1903 (chosen by Alumni Assn. as orator, 1913); m. Olive Brown, Oct. 29, 1907; children—Hobart Doane, Josephine (Mrs. R. C. Dancy), Olive Abbott (Mrs. D. E. Post), Agnes, Philip Walker, Elizabeth Adair (Mrs. R. B. Webb), Emily Rose. Cons. engr. City of Gulfport. Commr. Gen. Assembly Presbyn. Ch., Atlanta, 1913; Augusta, Ga., 1936. Mem. Am. Shore and Beach Preservation Assn., Gulfport C. of C. Democrat. Mason (32 deg.). Rotarian. Designer, supr. world's longest concrete sea wall, located on Mississippi gulf coast. Author spl. articles and tech. reports. Home: Gulfport, Miss. 39501. Died Aug. 26, 1960.

SHAW, HOWARD BURTON, elec. engr.; b. Winslow, Me., Aug. 5, 1869; s. Henry Harrison and Mary E. (Hawes) S.; A.B., Univ. of N.C., 1890, B.C.E., 1891; A.M., Harvard, 1894; m. Gertrude Matthews, June 10, 1900 (dec.); children—Howard Burton, George Matthews; m. 2d, Eleanora Pratt. Sept. 6, 1930. Instructor in mathematics, 1889-90, math. surveying and drawing, 1891-93, U. of N.C.; asst. elec. laboratory, Lawrence Scientific Sch. (Harvard), 1894-96; asst. prof. elec. engring., 1896-99, prof., 1899-1913, dean Sch. Engring., 1907-13, dir. engring., Expt. Sta., 1909-13, U. of Mo. Commr. Mo. Pub. Service Commn., 1913-17; ednl. dir. Doherty Training Schs., New York, Denver, Toledo, Bartlesville, 1917-22; dir. Engring. Expt. Sta., N.C. State Coll., 1923-32, prof. indsl. engring. since 1932. Mem. Soc. Promotion Engring. Edn., N.C. Soc. of Engrs., Phi Beta Kappa, Sigma Xi, Zeta Psi, Tau Beta Pi, Phi Kappa Phi; asso. mem. Am. Institute E.E., Society for the Advancement of Management. Mem. highway economics dept. of the Highway Research Board. Democrat. Episcopalian. Author: Dynamo Laboratory Manual, Vol. 1, 1906, Vol. 2, 1910. Home: 1507 Ambleside Drive, Raleigh, N.C. Died Dec. 15, 1943.

SHAW, JOSHUA, artist, inventor; b. Bellingborough, Lincolnshire, Eng., circa 1777. Sign painter, Manchester, Eng.; became known as painter of portraits, flowers, still life, landscapes, cattlepieces; began exhibiting at Royal Acad., London, 1802; came to Am., 1817, settled in Phila.; travelled through South making sketches and taking subscriptions for series of Am. views, engraved and published, 1819-20; a founder Artists' Fund Soc.; exhibited frequently in Phila., N.Y.C., Boston and Balt.; made several important improvements in firearms for which he later received awards from U.S. and Russian govts.; moved to Bordentown, N.J., circa 1843; stricken with paralysis, 1853. Died Burlington, N.J., Sept. 8, 1860.

SHAW, THOMAS, inventor; b. Phila., May 5, 1838; s. James and Catherine (Snyder) S.; m. Matilda Garber, 1 dau. Apprenticed to machinist, Phila.; patented a gas meter (1st invention), 1858; patented a press mold for glass, gas stove, sewing machine, 1859; supt. Cyclops Machine Works, Phila., circa 1860; supt. Midvale Steel Works, 1867; produced many inventions including a centrifugal shot making machine, a steam power hammer, spring-lock nut washer, 1867-70; established factory for mfg. his inventions, Phila., 1871; patented some 200 devices including pressure gauges, pile drivers, hydraulic pumps, a device to detect and measure presence of noxious gases in mines (adopted by several European govts.), 1871-1901. Died Hammonton, N.J., Jan. 19, 1901; buried Phila.

SHEA, DANIEL WILLIAM, physicist; b. Portsmouth, N.H., Nov. 27, 1859; s. of Timothy and Margaret (McCarthy) S.; A.B., Harvard, 1886, A.M., 1888; Ph.D., Friedrich Wilhelm's Universität, Berlin, 1892; unmarried. Mem. N.H. Ho. of Rep., 1886-88; asst. in physics, Harvard, 1889, 1892; asst. prof. physics, 1892-94, prof., 1894-95, U. of Illinois; prof. physics, 1895—, dir. School of Technology, 1897-1906, dean Faculty of Sciences, 1906-09 and 1911-15, Catholic U. of America. Fellow A.A.A.S., Am. Phys. Society. Democrat. Author: Instruction Sheets for Experiments in Physics, 1913, revised edit., 1921. Home: Greenland, N.H. Died Oct. 1930.

SHEAFER, ARTHUR WHITCOMB, (sha'fer), mining engr.; b. Pottsville, Pa., Sept. 16, 1856; s. Peter Wenrich and Harriet Newell (Whitcomb) S.; B.S., U. of Pa., 1877, post-grad. work, 1 yr.; m. Mary Cope Russel, Apr. 20, 1904. Asst. geologist, 2d geol. survey of Pa., 1878-81; in gen. practice as mining engr. Mem. Am. Inst. Mining Engrs., A.A.A.S., N. of England Inst. of Mining Engrs., Engrs. Club of Phila., Am. Acad. Polit. and Social Science, Acad. Natural Sciences of Phila. Clubs: University (Philadelphia); Univ. of Pa. Club (New York). Home: Pottsville, Pa. Died Sept. 1, 1943.

SHEAR, CORNELIUS LOTT, plant pathologist; b. Coeymans Hollow, N.Y., Mar. 26, 1865; s. Henry Lansing and Mary (Speenburg) S.; grad. N.Y. State Normal Sch., Albany, 1888; B.S., U. Neb., 1897, A.M., 1901; Ph.D., George Washington U., 1906; studied plant pathology and mycology, Munich, Berlin, Leiden and London; m. Avis Morrison Sherwood, Dec. 25, 1890; children—Sherwood William, Deming Jonas, Mary Beatrice, George Myron, Dorothy Margaret, Cornelius Barrett. Spl. field agt. Div. Agrostology, summers, 1895-97; asst. agrostologist, 1898-1901, asst. pathologist, 1901-02, pathologist, 1902-23, sr. pathologist, 1923-25, prin. pathologist in charge office of mycology and disease survey, 1925-35; ret., apptd. collaborator, 1935, U.S. Dept. Agr. Editor Asa Gray Bull., 1898-1900; asso. editor Plant World, 1900-05; one of editors Phytopathology, 1911-15; asso. editor Mycologia since 1909; edited revision of plant pathol. and mycol. terms in Century Dictionary. Fellow A.A.A.S.; mem. Bot. Soc. Am., Am. Soc. Naturalists, Assn. Internationale des Botanistes, Am. Phytopathol. Soc. (sec.-treas.), Bot. Soc. Washington, Washington Acad. Scis., Sigma Xi. U.S. ofcl. del. Pasteur Centennial Celebration, Paris, 1923; del. to Internat. Bot. Congress, Cambridge, Eng., 1930. Pres. Am. Mycol. Soc., 1933; v.p. sect. mycology and bacteriology Internat. Bot. Congress since 1935. Author: (with Clements) "Key, to the Genera of Fungi" and many mycol., path. papers. Home: 1707 N. 6th St., Monroe, La. 71201. Office: Bureau Plant Industry, Beltsville, Md. Died Feb. 2, 1956; buried Columbia Gardens Cemetery, Falls Church, Va.

SHEARER, JOHN SANFORD, physicist; b. New York, Oct. 20, 1865; B.S., Cornell, 1893, Ph.D., 1900; m. Minnie Lee, June 20, 1888. Instr. physics, 1893-1902, asst. prof., 1902-09, Cornell; prof. physics, Columbia, 1909-10, Cornell, 1910—. Pres. Cornell Coöperative Soc. Commd. maj., Sanitary Corps N.A., 1917, lt. col., 1918; consultant in roentgenology, A.E.F.,

France. Republican. Conglist. Author: Notes and Questions on Physics, 1900; Lecture Outlines and Notes, 1906. Joint author: U.S.A. X-Ray Manual. Asso. editor Am. Jour. of Roentgenology. Home: Ithaca, N.Y. Died May 1922.

SHECUT, JOHN LINNAEUS EDWARD WHITRIDGE, physician; b. Beaufort, S.C., Dec. 4, 1770; s. Abraham and Marie (Barbary) S.; M.D., Coll. of Phila., 1791; m. Sarah Cannon, Jan. 26, 1792; m. 2d, Susanna Ballard, Feb. 7, 1805; 9 children. An early experimenter with use of electricity in treatment of yellow fever and crippled limbs, suggested that yellow fever was in part caused by lack of electricity in atmosphere; discouraged bloodletting and use of mercury as drug; organizer Antiquarian Soc. of Charleston (S.C.), 1813, incorporated as Literary and Philos. Soc. of S.C., 1814. Author: Flora Carolinaeensis (most thorough work on botany of S.C. then available), 1806. Died Charleston, June 1, 1836.

SHEDD, J(OEL) HERBERT, engineer; b. Pepperell, Mass., May 31, 1834; s. Joel and Eliza (Edson) S.; ed. Bridgewater Acad.; took 3 yrs.' course civ. engring. in a Boston office; (hon. A.M., Brown U., 1894); m. Julia A. Clark, Aug. 26, 1856 (died 1897); 2d, Sarah Marble, June 29, 1905. Practiced civ. engring. at Boston, 1856-69, Providence, 1869—. Has served on numerous commns. of Mass. and R.I. on river and harbor improvement. As engr. for the city of Providence, designed and built Providence water works, costing $4,500,000, the sewerage system, costing $5,500,000, and other large engring. works; chmn. State Bd. of Harbor Commrs. since its organization, 1876; engr. for many large water power developments; commr. for State of R.I. to Paris Expn., 1878. Mem. advisory com. Brown U. Home: Providence, R.I. Died Nov. 27, 1915.

SHEDD, SOLON, geologist; b. Illinois, May 25, 1860; s. Frank and Emily L. (Olin) S.; grad. Ore. State Normal Sch., Monmouth, Ore., 1889; A.B., Stanford U., 1896, A.M., 1907, Ph.D., 1910; m. Jeannette Wimberly, June 4, 1907. Teacher natural sciences, Ore. State Normal Sch., Monmouth, Ore., 1890-94; prof. geology and mineralogy, Wash. State Coll., 1896-1925; asst. state geologist, Wash. Geol. Survey, 1909-13, state geologist, 1921-25; curator Branner Memorial Geol. Library, Stanford U., since 1925. Acting asso. prof. geology, Stanford U., summer and autumn quaters, 1921, and actg. prof. same, summer quarter, 1922. Fellow Geol. Soc. America; mem. Am. Inst. Mining and Metall. Engrs., Scismol. Soc. America, A.A.A.S., Am. Ceramic Soc. Author of reports on iron ores, building and ornamental stones, clays, cement materials, etc., of Wash., bibliography of the geology and mineral resources of Calif. Home: Stanford University, Calif. Died Mar. 4, 1941.

SHEDD, THOMAS CLARK, prof, structural engring.; b. Worcester, Mass., July 2, 1890; s. Edward Whitten and Jessie (Dexter) S.; student U. of Va., 1908-09; B.S., Brown U., 1913; M.S., U. of Ill., 1932, C.E., 1925; m. Mary Margaret Campbell, Oct. 26, 1916; children—Thomas Clark, Milton Campbell, Harriet Martha. Instr. Brown U., Providence, R.I., 1913-15; Instr. Lehigh U., Bethlehem, Pa., 1917-18; with U. of Illinois, 1922—, professor structural engineering, until 1958, professor emeritus, 1958—; with Phoenix Bridge Co., Phoenixville, Pa., 1915-17, 18-22; Waddell & Hardesty, cons. engrs., N.Y.C., occasionally, 1926-41. Member Ill. Structural Engineers. Examining Com. (chmn.), Profl. Engrs. Examining Com. (chmn. 1945-48). Mem. Nat. Council State Bds. Engring. Examiners, Nat., Ill. socs. professional engrs., International Assn. Bridge and Structural Engineers, Am. Soc. C.E. (dist. dir.), American Ry. Engring. Assn., Am. Concrete Inst., American Soc. for Engring. Edn., Ill. Engring. Council (pres, 1941), Sigma Xi, Tau Beta Pi, Chi Epsilon, Phi Kappa Phi. Republican. Conglist. Club: Exchange (Urbana). Author: Theory of Simple Structures (with Jamieson Vawter), 1931; 2d edition, 1940; Structural Design in Steel, 1934. Home: 706 W. California. Office: Civil Engring. Dept., U. of Ill., Urbana, Ill. Died July 11, 1959; buried Roselawn Cemetery, Champaign, Ill.

SHEEHAN, DONAL, univ. med. dean; b. Carlisle, Eng., Aug. 2, 1907; s. Patrick and Eliza (Leeming) S.; B.Sc., U. of Manchester, Eng., 1926, M.B., Ch.B., 1929, M.Sc., M.D., 1932, D.Sc., 1936; m. Ruth Chapman, 1935 (dec.); children—Kevin, Terry, Peter. Came to U.S., 1937. Demonstrator in anatomy U. of Manchester, 1930-32; fellow in med., Vienna, Breslau, Amsterdam, 1932-33, McGill U. and Yale, 1933-35; lecturer in neuro-anatomy, U. of Manchester, 1935-37; prof. anatomy and dir. anatomical laboratories N.Y. Univ., 1937-48, acting dean coll. medicine, 1943-46, gen. dir. Commonwealth Fund, 1947-48, prof. anatomy, 1948-63, prof. of med. edn., 1963—, chmn. dept. anatomy 1948—; chmn. scientific com. N.Y.U.-Bellevue Med. Center, 1948-51, asso. dir. 1951-53, acting dir., 1953-55, dep. dir., 1955—, also dean coll. of medicine and of the post-graduate medical sch., 1955-60. Awarded Dickinson fellowship, 1932-33, Rockefeller fellowship, 1933-35. Mem. Anat. Soc. Great Britain, Physiol. Soc. Great Britain, Am. Physiol. Soc., Am. Neurological Assn., Am. Anat. Soc. Office: 550 First Av., N.Y.C. 16. Died July 18, 1964.

SHEEHAN, WINFIELD R., motion picture producer; b. Buffalo, N.Y., Sept. 24, 1883; s. Jeremiah F. and Angeline M. (Hens) S.; ed. St. Canisius Coll., Buffalo, 1897-1902 (studies interrupted by Spanish-Am. War); m. Maria Jeritza, Aug. 12, 1935. Reporter Buffalo Courier, 1901, New York World and New York Evening World, 1902-09; sec. to fire commr., N.Y. City, 1910, to police commr., 1911-14; organized studios of Fox Film Corp., Hollywood, Calif., 1914; organized Am., European and other foreign distribution branches and newsreel for same, 1914-21, v.p. and gen. mgr. of the corp. and studios, Hollywood, Calif., resigned 1935; produced "In Old Arizona," the first feature picture with sound on films; actively identified with development of sound recording on films; also produced "What Price Glory," "Seventh Heaven," "Four Sons," "State Fair," "Cavalcade," "Captain Eddie," 1944, and about 130 talking and musical motion pictures. Democrat. Catholic. Home. Hidden Valley, Camarillo, Calif. Died July 25, 1945.

SHEFFER, HENRY MAURICE, logician; b. Russia, Sept. 1, 1883; A.B., Harvard, 1905, A.M., 1907, Ph.D., 1908. Taught at Harvard, becoming prof. emeritus, 1952; although his early work in logic was highly acclaimed, especially by Bertrand Russell, he early became almost secretive in his work, published little; his work in founds. of maths., relational logic and gen. theory of notational relativity was very influential, especially his reduction of functional notation to one symbol (Sheffer stroke). Fellow A.A.A.S.; mem. Am. Philos. Assn., Assn. Symbolic Logic, Am. Math. Soc. Address: 1737 Cambridge St., Cambridge, Mass. Died Mar. 17, 1964. *

SHEININ, JOHN J(ACOBI), former coll pres.; b. Bobruysk, Russia, Mar. 21 1900; s. Jacob and Chernia (Rosenhaus) S.; naturalized citizen; B.S., U. Ala., 1928; M.S., Northwestern, 1929. Ph.D., 1932, M.B., 1932, M.D., 1933; Sc.D. (hon.), The Chicago Med. Sch., 1949; m. Ruth Aaron, Sept. 3, 1932; 1 son, James Charles. Instr., dept. anatomy, U. Ala., 1925-27; fellow in anatomy, dept. anatomy, med. sch., Northwestern University, 1927-32; prof. anatomy, The Chicago Med. Sch., 1932-66, prof. emeritus, 1967-72, chmn. dept. anatomy, 1932-57, dean, 1935-62, pres., 1950-66, pres. emeritus, 1967-72. Recipient Gold medal award Phi Lambda Kappa, 1952; Merit award Northwestern U., 1956; Horatio Alger award Am. Schs. and Colls. Assn., 1957; Jesuit Centennial citation, 1957; Edn. award Immigrants' Protective League, 1958; Founders' Day award Loyola U., 1962; Service to Youth award YMCA, 1964; Achievement award Phi Epsilon Pi, 1966; Merit award U.S. Navy and 9th Naval Dist., 1966; named to Hall Fame, City Chgo., 1967, Wisdom Hall Fame, 1970. Fellow Institute of Medicine of Chgo., Am. Acad. Gen. Practice, Am. Geriatrics Soc., Royal Soc. Health; mem. Assn. Am. Med. Colleges (emeritus), American Assn. Anatomists, Soc. for Exptl. Biology and Medicine, A.A.A.S., Am. Assn. U. Profs., Ill. Acad. Sci., Ill. Med. Soc., A.M.A., Fedn. State Bds., Chicago Med. Soc., Phi Delta Epsilon, Sigma Xi, Phi Epsilon Pi, Alpha Omega Alpha. Jewish religion. Clubs: Executives, Standard. Contbr. articles med. jours. Home: Chicago IL Died Jan. 9, 1972; buried Memorial Park Cemetery Skokie IL

SHELDON, HAROLD HORTON, research and devel. engr., coll. ofcl.; b. Brockville, Ont., Can., Apr. 13, 1893; s. Harvey and Mary Christian (Lageau) S.; A.B., Queen's University, Kingston, Ontario, 1916, A.M., 1917; Ph.D., U. Chgo., 1920, E.E., Poly. Inst. Bklyn., 1934; m. Bettye F. Walcott. Came to United States 1917, naturalized, 1924. Research associate, University of Chicago, 1918-19; instructor in physics, University of Michigan, 1920-22; asst. prof. physics, New York U., 1922-24, asso. prof., 1924-26, prof. of physics, 1927-41, administrative asst. in charge of science education, division of general education, 1936-41; head of dept. of research and development, Auto Ordnance Corp., 1942-43; independent research and development engineer, 1943-44; Research Prof. Engring., Univ. of Miami, 1946-48, prof. of indsl. engring., 1948-52, coordinator of research in engring. and phys. scis., 1950-52, dean div. of research and industry, 1952-53; exec. v.p. American Electric Fusion Corp., 1953-54; cons. Orgn. European Econ. Cooperation, Paris, France, 1954-56; cons. Office Saline Water U.S. Dept. Interior, 1956—, chmn. physics dept., 1956—; professor Roosevelt U., Chgo., 1956, trustee, 1960—, vice pres. and acting dean of faculties, 1962—; sci. editor New York Herald-Tribune, 1927-31; member editorial advisory board Current History, 1937. Mem. Mayor's Com. for Smoke Control, N.Y. City, also N.Y. and N.J. Smoke Control Bd., 1929; hon. past pres. Am. Inst. City of New York, mng. trustee, 1938-1941; chmn. of training committee Manhattan Council of Boy Scouts, 1938-42. Fellow A.A.A.S., Acoustical Soc. America; mem. Am. Physical Soc., Am. Soc. Engring. Edn., Am. Inst. E.E., Am. Soc. Mechanical Engineers, New York Electrical Society (pres. 1930-31), Sigma Xi, Gamma Alpha. Clubs: Engineers of New York, Physics (Chgo.); Newcomen Soc. Author: Physics for Colleges, 1927; Television, 1928; An Outline of Science (2 vols.), 1929; Space, Time and Relativity, 1931; also Light Waves and Their Uses (ednl. motion picture), 1937; Fuels, Heat Distribution, Thermodynamics, 1938; Physics for Home Study, 1947; editor-in-chief, "The Progress of Science," 1940-41. Inventor of colorscope for electrical color matching of textiles, co-discover of actino electric effect; discoverer of selective adsorption in charcoals; pioneer in Neon tube designs, and in cold cathode rectifiers. Address: 510 Sheridan Rd., Evanston, Ill. Died Dec. 23, 1964.

SHELDON, JOHN LEWIS, botanist, bacteriologist; b. Voluntown, Conn., Nov. 10, 1865; s. Samuel H. and Lucy A. (Lewis) S.; B.Sc., Ohio Northern U., 1895, M.Sc., 1899; B.Sc., U. Neb., 1899, A.M., 1901, Ph.D., 1903; m. Clara Adams Felming, Aug. 21, 1907; 1 son, Earl Fleming. Tchr. pub. schs., Conn., 1885-90, 1895-97; instr. Mt. Hermon (Mass.) Sch., 1892-94; instr. botany, prep. sch. U. Neb., 1898-99; acting head dept. biology, Neb. State Nornal Sch., 1899-1900; instr. botany, U. Neb., 1901-03; prof. bacteriology, W.Va. U., and bacteriologist, Agrl. Expt. Sta., 1903-07; prof. botany and bacteriology, 1907-13, rof. botany, 1913-19, W.Va. University. Fellow A.A.A.S., Bot. Soc. Am.; mem. Am. Phytopathol. Soc., Sullivant oss Soc., Am. Genetic Assn., Sigma Xi, Phi Beta Kappa, Theta Kappa Psi. Republican. Contbr. to bot. and agrl. publs.; investigator in plant pathology. Home: 308 Grandview Av., Morgantown, W.Va. Died Jan. 15, 1947; buried Central Village, Conn.

SHELDON, RALPH EDWARD, anatomist; b. Lisle, N.Y., Mar. 28, 1883; s. Herbert Clayton and Rosalia (Reed) S.; A.B., Cornell U., 1904, A.M., 1905; S.M., Harvard, 1907; Ph.D., U. of Chicago, 1908; m. Emily Evans, Aug. 13, 1908. Asst., U.S. Forest Service, summers, 1902, 1903; scholar in neurology, 1904-05, Goldwin Smith fellow in neurology, 1905-06, asst. in zoölogy, summers, 1904-07, Cornell U.; Edward Austin fellow, Harvard, 1906-07; asst. in anatomy, 1907-09, asso., 1909, U. of Chicago; scientific asst. and investigator, U.S. Bur. Fisheries, Woods Hole, Mass., summers, 1908, 1910; asst. prof. anatomy, 1909-12, asso. prof., 1912-14, prof. and head of dept., 1914—, U. of Pittsburgh. Home: Pittsburgh, Pa. Died July 9, 1918.

SHELDON, SAMUEL, electrical engr.; b. Middlebury, Vt., Mar. 8, 1862; s. Harmon Alexander and Mary (Bass) S.; A.B., Middlebury Coll., 1883, A.M., 1886; Ph.D., U. of Würzburg, 1888; asst. to Kohlrausch, distinguished physicist, with whom he was associated in his celebrated determination of the ohm; (D.Sc., U. of Pennsylvania, 1906; D.Sc., Middlebury Coll., 1911); m. Frances Warner Putnam, June 18, 1891. Asst. in physics, Harvard, 1888-89; prof. physics and elec. engring., Poly. Inst. of Brooklyn, 1889—; pres. dept. electricity Brooklyn Inst. Arts and Sciences; consulting engr. and frequently called to give expert testimony in state and federal cts.; expert of Swiss Dept. of Justice and Police, 1903—; sec. sect. B, Internat. Elec. Congress, 1904; mem. Internat. Elec. Jury of Awards, St. Louis Expn., 1904. Fellow A.A.A.S., Brooklyn Inst. Arts and Sciences; hon. fellow Am. Electro-Therapeutic Assn. Dir. John Fritz Medal Assn. (pres. 1910-11). Author: Dynamo Electric Machinery, 1900-03; Alternating Current Machines (joint author), 1902; Electric Traction and Transmission Engineering (joint author), 1911; Physics Laboratory Experiments (joint author). Home: Brooklyn, N.Y. Died Sept. 4, 1920.

SHELFORD, VICTOR E(RNEST), zoologist; b. Chemung, N.Y., Sept. 22, 1877; s. Alexander Hamilton and Sarah Ellen (Rumsey) S.; student W. Va. University, 1899-1901; University of Chicago, 1901-07, S.B., 1903, Ph.D., 1907; m. Mary Mabel Brown, June 12, 1907 (deceased August 17, 1940); children—Lois F. (Mrs. E. H. Bennett), John V. Teacher, pub. schs., Chemung County, N.Y., 1895-97; tutor in zoology, W.Va. U., 1901; asst. and inst. dept. of zoology, U. of Chicago, 1903-14; research work in European museums, 1908; in charge marine ecology, Puget Sound Biol. Sta., alternate summers, 1914-30, editorial bd. publs., 1921-30; asst. and asso. prof. zoology, U. of Ill., 1914-27, prof. 1927-46, acting head of dept., 1939-40; chmn. of dept., 1940-41, prof. emeritus, 1946; biologist in charge Research Labs., Ill. State Natural History Survey, 1914-29. Chmn. Nat. Research Council Com. on Grassland, 1932-39, mem. com. on Wild Life, 1931-35; founder, Grassland Research Foundation, 1939, pres., 1958, chmn. scientific adv. bd., 1959-68, Ecologists' Union (now Nature Conservancy), 1946; lecturer Purdue University Science Institute, 1935, Stone Laboratory, Ohio State University, 1937. Recipient Nash Conservation Award, 1953. Fellow Entomol. Society America, A.A.A.S.; member American Society Zoologist, Ecol. Society America (1st pres. 1916, chmn. com. on preserves 1917-19, sr. chmn. 1921-23 and 1930-36, editorial bd. Ecology 1920-28, chmn. com. for study of communities, 1931-37), Philadelphia Acad. Natural Scis. (corr.), Soc. Liminology and Oceanography, Am. Soc. Naturalists, National Association American Geographers, Illinois Academy of Sciences, Sociedad Mexicana de Historia Natural, Phi Beta Kappa, Sigma Xi, Phi Sigma. Author: Animal Communities in Temperate America, 1913; Laboratory and Field Ecology, 1929; Animal Ecology and Taxonomy (with Allee and Park), 1937; Bio-Ecology (F. E. Clements), 1939. Compiler: Naturalist's Guide to the Americas, 1925. Contbr. scientific jours. and publs. Home: Urbana IL Died Dec. 27, 1968.

SHELTON, E(BERLE) KOST, internist, endocrinologist; b. Bloomfield, Ia., May 19, 1888; s. Eberle Kost and Katherine (Hayes) S.; student U. of Denver, 1907-09; M.D., U. of Colo., 1912, Sc.D., 1944; post grad. student various endocrine clinics, 1927-30; m. Margaret Norine, Feb. 25, 1914; 1 son, Paul Kingsley. Resident physician, City and County Hosp., Denver, Colo., 1911-13; in gen. practice, 1913; internist, Denver and Antonito, Colo., 1914-26, Santa Barbara, Calif., 1930-40, Los Angeles, Calif., since 1938; asso. clin. prof. medicine, U. of Southern Calif., 1931-51; clin. prof. medicine, U. Cal., Los Angeles since 1951. sr. attending physician Harbor Gen. Hospital, since 1951; dir. endocrine clinic and mem. attending staff of hosp., Los Angeles Gen. Hosp.; mem. cons. staff St. Johns Hosp., Santa Monica, Calif. Diplomate Am. Bd. Internal Medicine. Fellow Am. Coll. Physicians; mem. Am. Med. Assn., Am. Therapeutic Soc., A.A.A.S., Assn. Study Internal Secretions, Los Angeles and Hollywood acads. medicine; Am. Soc. Research in Psychosomatic Problems, Alpha Kappa Kappa. Author of pituitary chapter, vol. VIII, Tice's Practice of Medicine, and editor of endocrine volume, 1935. Author brochures on problems of internal medicine and endocrinology; contbr. to med. text books. Home: 760 North Beverly Glen. Office: 921 Westwood Blvd., Los Angeles 24. Died Feb. 22, 1955.

SHENEHON, FRANCIS CLINTON, hydraulic engr.; b. Brooklyn, N.Y., Dec. 20, 1861; s. Ellsworth S. and Ella (Dalley) S.; B.C.E., U. of Minn., 1895, C.E., 1900; m. Kate Bird Cross, May 14, 1891. Engr. U.S. War Dept., on building of New Ft. Brady, Sault Ste. Marie, Mich., 1890-91; on building of ship lock and canal, and channelization of St. Mary's River, 1891-98; on Lake Survey, at Buffalo, Ogdensburg and Detroit, 1898-1909; dean Coll. of Engring., U. of Minn., and consulting engr., 1909-17; engring. practice, May 1917—. Consulting engr. Sanitary District Chicago for regulating works in St. Clair, Niagara and St. Lawrence rivers up to 1924; for Northern States Power Co., for water power development in Miss. and St. Croix rivers; engr. v.p. Byllesby Engring. & Management Corp., Chicago, 1923-24; consulting hydraulic engr. Author of Preservation of Niagara Falls, and The St. Lawrence Waterway to the Sea, and other tech. papers. Studied water power development in Norway, Sweden, Germany and Switzerland, 1927. Home: Minneapolis, Minn. Died Oct. 3, 1939.

SHEPARD, CHARLES UPHAM, mineralogist; b. Little Compton, R.I., June 29, 1804; s. Rev. Mase and Deborah (Haskins) S.; grad. Amherst Coll., 1824, LL.D. (hon.), 1857; M.D. (hon.), Dartmouth, 1836; m. Harriet Taylor, Sept. 23, 1831, 3 children. Lectr. botany Yale, 1830-31, lectr. natural history, 1833-47; in charge of Brewster Scientific Inst., New Haven, Conn., 1831-33; prof. chemistry S.C. Med. Coll., 1834-60, 65-69; lectr. natural history Amherst Coll., 1844-77; visited all known mineral localities East of Mississippi River; discovered phosphate of lime, 1865; his collection of meteorites largest in America by 1886; wrote 40 papers for Am. Journ. of Science and Arts; mem. Imperial Soc. of Natural Science (St. Petersburg, Russia), Royal Soc. of Gottingen (Germany), Soc. of Natural Science (Vienna). Author textbook: Treatise on Mineralogy, 1832, (2d part 1835). Died Charleston, S.C., May 1, 1886.

SHEPARD, EDWARD MARTIN, geologist; b. West Winsted, Conn., May 15, 1854; s. Samuel and Mary Isabella (Dennis) Shepard; Williams Coll., class of '78, A.M., 1881; Sc.D., Waynesburg Coll., Pa., 1902; LL.D., Drury Coll., Springfield, Mo., 1923; m. Harriett Elma Ohlen, June 28, 1881. Prof. natural science, Waynesburg Coll., 1878; prof. biology and geology, 1879-1908, acting pres., 1893-94, dean, 1903-08, Drury Coll. Spl. asst. Mo. Geol. Survey, 1894-95; state geologist, 1901; field asst. dept. hydrology, U.S. Geol. Survey, 1903-07. Mem. bd. mgrs., 1893-1911 and 1913—, v.p., 1903-06, sec., 1919—, Mo. Bur. of Geology and Mines. Mem. 10th Internat. Congress of Geologists, City of Mexico, 1906. Mem. numerous geog. and hist. societies. Mem. Springfield Park Bd., 1919-23, Springfield Chamber of Commerce; mem. bd. of mgrs. Springfield Children's Home. Author: Systematic Mineral Record, 1883. Conglist. Democrat. Died Apr. 28, 1934.

SHEPARD, FRANK EDWARD, mechanical engr.; b. Ashland, N.H., Nov. 29, 1865; s. Allan Bruce and Martha Maria (Dana) S.; B.S. in M.E., Mass. Inst. of Tech., 1887; m. Rebekah Clark-Shepard, of Denver, Apr. 2, 1901; children—David A., Jean, Richard C. In employ of Boston & Albany locomotive shops, 1887; asst. U.S. insp. steam vessels, Boston, 1888-89; mem. Thomas, Shepard & Searing, mech. and elec. engrs., 1890, Shepard & Searing, 1890-95; mech. engr. Denver Engineering Works, 1895-97, pres., 1897-1923; supt. U.S. Mint, Denver, Colo., since 1923. Mem. Denver Art Commn., Denver Smoke Abatement Commn. Mem. Am. Soc. M.E., Colo. Scientific Soc., Am. Inst. Mining and Metall. Engrs., Phi Gamma Delta; hon. mem. Tau Beta Pi. Clubs: University, Mile High. Home: 1330 Columbine St. Office: U.S. Mint, Denver, Colo.

SHEPARD, JAMES HENRY, chemist; b. Lyons, Mich., Apr. 14, 1850; s. Daniel Ensign and Lydia Maria (Pendell) S.; student Albion (Mich.) Coll., through sophomore yr.; B.S., U. of Mich., 1875; post-grad. study, same, 1881; m. Clara R. Durand, June 28, 1888. Supt. schs., Holly, Marquette, and Saline, Mich., 1875-80; instr. natural science, Ypsilanti (Mich.) High Sch., 1882-88; prof. chemistry, S.D. Agrl. Coll., and chemist Agrl. Expt. Sta. of S.D., 1888—. V.p. S.D. Agrl. Coll., 1890-1900; dir. Expt. Sta. of S.D., 1895-1901; chemist S.D. Pure Food Commn., 1901—. Republican. Presbyn. K.T. Author: Shepard's Elements of Chemistry, 1885; same (briefer course), 1890; Notes on Chemistry, 1886. Home: Brookings, S.D. Deceased.

SHEPARDSON, GEORGE DEFREES, engineer; b. Cheviot, O., Nov. 20, 1864; s. Daniel (D.D.) and Eliza (Smart) S.; A.B., Denison Univ., 1885, A.M., 1888; M.E., Cornell U., 1899; D.Sc., Harvard, 1912; m. Harriet B. King, 1892; 1 dau., Mary King. Prof. elec. engring., U. of Minn., 1891—. Mem. jury of awards, Buffalo Expn., 1901, St. Louis Expn., 1904. Author: Electrical Catechism, 1901, 1908; Electric Train Lighting, 1901; Theory of Telephone Apparatus, 1917; Elements of Electrical Engineering, 1924; An Engineer's Religion, 1926. Home: Minneapolis, Minn. Died May 26, 1926.

SHEPHERD, ERNEST STANLEY, chemist; b. Remington, Ind., Mar. 30, 1879; s. William and Harriette Ellen (Lockwood) S.; student Ind. U., 1897-1900; A.B., Cornell, 1902; private asst. to Prof. Bancroft, at Cornell, June-Sept. 1902; asst. in electrochemistry, Cornell, Sept.-Nov. 1902; resigned to take up research on Carnegie grant, under Prof. Bancroft, 1902-04; physical chemist, Geophys. Lab., Washington in charge research on lime-aluminasilica series of minerals, 1904-46, ret.; chemistry of volcanic phenomena. Member Am. Chem. Soc., Sigma Xi, etc. Club: Cosmos. Writer of numerous papers on alloys, minerals and chemistry of volcanic phenomena pub. in Journal of Physical Chemistry, Journal of Science, etc. Address: 426 Willard Av., Chevy Chase 15, Md. Died Sept. 29, 1949.

SHEPPARD, SAMUEL EDWARD, research chemist; b. Hither Green, Kent, Eng., July 29, 1882; s. Samuel and Emily Mary (Taplin) S.; B.Sc., 1st class honors in chemistry, University Coll., London, 1903; D.Sc., 1906; 1851 Exhbn. scholar, same univ., 1907; studied Marburg U., Sorbonne, Paris, and Cambridge, Eng.; m. Eveline Lucy Ground, Nov. 27, 1912; 1 son, Samuel Roger. Photographic research practice, Eng., 1910-11; chemist with Eastman Kodak Co., Rochester, N.Y., since 1912; asst. supt., in charge depts. of inorganic and physical chemistry of Research Lab., 1920, and asst. dir. of research since 1923. Carried out chem. development of colloidal fuels with Submarine Defense, 1917-19. Awarded Progress medal, Royal Photographic Soc., 1928; Adelsköld medal, Photog. Soc. of Stockholm, 1929; William H. Nichols medal, Am. Chem. Soc., 1930. Honorary fellow Photographic Society of America. Fellow Soc. Motion Picture Engrs., Chem. Soc., London; hon. fellow Royal Photographic Soc.; mem. Am. Chem. Soc., Am. Electrochem. Soc., American Standards Assn. (committee on photographic standards). Member Angelican Church. Author: Photochemistry, 1914; Gelatin in Photography, Vol. I, 1923. Part Author: Investigations on the Theory of the Photographic Process, 1907; Silver Bromide Grain of Photographic Emulsions, 1921; Photography as a Scientific Implement, 1923. Contbr. numerous papers on chem. topics. Developed process of electrodeposition of rubber. Hurter and Driffield Memorial lecturer, Royal Photographic Soc., 1928. Home: 183 Monteroy Road, Brighton, Rochester, N.Y. Died Sept. 29, 1948.

SHERBAKOFF, CONSTANTINE DMITRIEV, plant pathologist; b. Ekaterinaslav, Russia, May 24, 1878; s. Dmitri Ivanov and Anna Alexandrovna (Stolarova) S.; student Sch. of Agr., Kherson, Russia, 1895-1900, Sch. of Forestry, St. Petersburg, 1901-07; B.S.A., Cornell U., 1911, Ph.D., 1915; m. May Gibson, Nov. 11, 1916; 1 son, Paul Constantine. Came to U.S., 1907, naturalized 1919. Asso. plant pathologist Agrl. Expt. Sta., U. Fla., 1914-20; head dept. plant pathology Agrl. Expt. Sta., U. Tenn., 1920-50. Mem. Am. Phytopath. Soc., Am. Mycol. Soc., A.A.A.S., Sigma Xi. Contbr. tech. publs.; writer many bulls. in relation to work at exptl. stas., for Cornell, Fla. and Tenn. univs. Home: 203 8th Av., Fountain City, Tenn. Died Aug. 13, 1965; buried Lynnhurst Cemetery, Knoxville, Tenn.

SHERIDAN, LAWRENCE VINNEDGE, landscape architect, consultant on city and regional planning; b. Frankfort, Ind., July 8, 1887; s. Harry C. and Margaret (Vinnedge) S.; B.S. in C.E., Purdue U., 1909, C.E., 1912; student Harvard Sch. of Landscape Architecture, 1916-17; m. Grace Emmel, Dec. 15, 1919; children—Roger Williams, Roderick Kessler, Harry C. II, Philip. Transitman, insp., chief insp., Bd. of Park Commrs., Indianapolis, 1911-14; Bureau Municipal Research, N.Y., 1914-16; planner Camp Pike, Ark., 1917; engr. Dallas Property Owners Assn., 1919-21; exec. sec. City Plan Commn., Indianapolis, 1921-23; private practice in landscape architecture and city planning since 1923; pres. Met. Planners, Inc., 1953-56, planning counselor, 1956-72; tchr. history of landscape architecture Purdue U.; cons. planning and zoning USAF, 1955-72; cons. landscape architect for Purdue U., Crown Hill Cemetery, Indpls.; cons. to Ind. and Ky. State Planning Bds., 1934-37; regional counselor Nat. Resources Planning Bd. for Ind., Ill., Ohio, Wis., Mich., Ky., and W.Va., 1937-41; redesigned Camp Robinson, Ark., on site of Camp Pike, 1940; camp development or site plans for Ft. Eustis, Va., Billings Gen. Hosp., Ft. Benjamin Harrison, Ind., Camp Chaffee, Ark., and Camp Atterbury, Ind., 1940-41. Served as 2d lt., F.A., A.E.F., 1918-19; commd. 2d lt. Coast Arty. Reserve, 1923, and advanced to grade of lt. col., Construction Div., Q.M. General's Office, 1941; Deputy Service Command Engr., 9th Service Command, 1942-45; colonel, Corps Engrs., Army U.S., August 1942-46; resumed practice city and regional planning, and landscape architecture. Recipient of the Distinguished Service award by the American Institute of Planners, 1957. Fellow American Society of Landscape Architects, American Soc. of Civil Engineers (life); mem. American Inst. of Planners (pres. 1940), Ind. Engring. Soc. (past pres.), Indiana Society of Pioneers, Sigma Phi Epsilon. Christian Scientist. Club: Service (Indpls.). Home: Indianapolis IN Died Jan. 26, 1972.

SHERMAN, ALTHEA ROSINA, ornithologist; b. Farmersburg Twp., Clayton County, Ia., Oct. 10, 1853; d. Mark Bachelor and Sibyl Melissa (Clark) Sherman; student Upper Ia. U., Fayette, Ia., 1865-66; A.B., Oberlin, 1875, A.M., 1882; studied Art Inst. Chicago, Art Students' League, New York. Teacher pub. schs., 1875-78; instr. drawing and painting, Carleton Coll., Northfield, Minn., 1882-87; supervisor drawing, city schs., Tacoma, Wash., 1892-95. Conglist. Mem. A.A.A.S., Am. Ornithologists Union, Nat. Asssn. Audubon Socs., Cooper and Wilson ornithol. clubs, Am. Museum Natural History, Am. Soc. Mammalogists, Am. Genetic Assn., Biol. Soc. Washington, Ia. Acad. Science, State Hist. Soc. Ia., Miss. Valley Hist. Assn., Soc. of Mayflower Descendents. Has published many articles in ornithol. mags. on life histories of birds. Home: National, via McGregor, Ia. Died Apr. 16, 1943.

SHERMAN, CHRISTOPHER ELIAS, civil engr.; b. Columbus, O., Dec. 28, 1869; s. Sylvester Morrill and Lemyra Ann (Shoemaker) S.; grad. Columbus (O.) Central High Sch., 1887; 4 yrs. in civ. engring. (3 years in the field), Ohio State Univ., C.E., 1894; m. Elonora Bruning, June 22, 1897. In college and in gen. engring. work, 1888-94, chief draftsman, Ohio Geol. Survey, 1892; chief draftsman U.S. Barge Canal Survey, in Ohio, 1895-96; asst. prof. and prof. civ. engring., Ohio State U., from Sept. 1896, 1st U.S. asst. engr. 4th Army Corps, 1898; U.S. asst. engr. in Yellowstone Park, summers, 1899, 1900; rep. of govs. of Ohio in State Topographic Survey, 1902-36; also consulting work for State of Ohio; Ohio-Michigan boundary commr., 1915. Chief engineer Scioto-Sandusky Conservancy, 1935, pres. bd. dirs., 1937. Republican. Conglist. Author: Theory and Practice of Lettering, 1895; Preliminary Report on Topographic Survey of Ohio, 1904; A Commemorative Bulletin, 1910; Progress Report on Ohio Topographic Survey, 1910; The Ohio Water Problem, 1915; Final Report, Ohio Topographic Survey, Vols. 1 to 4, 1916 to 1933; Ohio Stream Flow, 1932; Land of Kingdom Come, 1936. Died May 6, 1940.

SHERMAN, FRANKLIN, zoölogist, entomologist; b. Ash Grove, Va., November 2, 1877; s. Franklin and Caroline (Alvord) S.; ed. Maryland College of Agriculture (now University of Maryland), 1893-97, and Cornell U., 1899-1900 (B.S. in Agr., 1900); hon. M.S., Md. Agrl. Coll., 1912; m. Grace Berry, May 12, 1903; children—Franklin, Josephine (dec.), Dallas Berry, Joseph Edgar, Grace Caroline. Entomologist N.C. State Dept. Agr., 1900-05, 1906-25; prof. zoölogy and entomology, Ont. (Can.) Agrl. Coll., 1905-06; head dept. zoölogy and entomology, Clemson Agrl. Coll. of S.C., entomologist S.C. Expt. Sta. and state entomologist since 1925. Fellow A.A.A.S.; mem. Am. Assn. Econ. Entomologists (ex-pres.), N.C. Acad. Science (ex-pres.), S.C. Acad Science (ex-pres.), Sigma Xi, Gamma Alpha. Democrat. Methodist. Mason. Club: Tri-state Country (Walhalla, S.C.). Author of bulletins of depts. of agr. and expt. stations. Contbr. to jours. Home: Clemson, S.C. Died June 23, 1947.

SHERMAN, HENRY CLAPP, chemist; b. Ash Grove, Va., Oct. 16, 1875; s. Franklin and Caroline (Alvord) S.; B.S., Md. Agrl. Coll., 1893; A.M., Columbia, 1896, Ph.D., 1897, D.Sc. (hon.), 1929; m. Cora Aldrich Bowen, Sept. 9, 1903 (dec.); children—Phoebe (dec.), Henry Alvord, William Bowen, Caroline Clapp Sherman Lanford. Asst. in chemistry Md. Agrl. Coll., 1893-95; fellow in chemistry Columbia, 1895-97, asst., 1897-98, lecturer, 1899-1901, instr., 1901-05, adj. prof. analytical chemistry, 1905-07, prof. organic analysis, 1907-11, prof. food chemistry, 1911-24, Mitchill prof. chemistry, 1924—, exec. officer, dept. of chemistry, 1919-39. Asst. in nutrition investigations U.S. Dept. Agr., 1898-99; research asso. Carnegie Instn., 1912-29, 33—. Mem. com. on food and nutrition Nat. Research Council, 1920-28, 40—, chmn. subcom. on human nutrition, 1924-28. Chmn. com. on nutritional problems Am. Pub. Health Assn., 1919-33; pres. Am. Inst. of Nutrition, 1931-33, 1939-40; collaborator U.S. Nutrition Lab., 1940—; chief Bur. of Human Nutrition, Dept. Agr., 1943-44. Fellow A.A.A.S.; mem. Am. Chem. Soc. (v.p. 1907-08), Am. Soc. Biol. Chemists (pres. 1926), Soc. Exptl. Biology and Medicine, Nat. Acad. Science; hon. mem. Harvey Soc. Major and mem.

Am. Red Cross mission to Russia, 1917. Medalist Am. Inst. of Chemists, 1933; Nichols medalist Am. Chem. Soc., 1934, Borden Award Am. Inst. Nutrition; Franklin medalist and made hon. mem. Franklin Inst., 1946; Chandler medalist Columbia, 1949. Author: Methods of Organic Analysis, 1905, 12; Chemistry of Food and Nutrition, 1911, 8th rev. edit., 1952; Food Products, 4th edit., 1948; The Vitamins (with S. L. Smith), 1922, 2d edit., 1931; Food and Health, 1934 (rev., 1947); Essentials of Nutrition (with C. S. Lanford), 3d edit., 1951; Introduction to Foods and Nutrition (with C. S. Lanford), 1943; The Science of Nutrition, 1943; Foods; Their Values and Management, 1946; Calcium and Phosphorus, 1947; The Nutritional Improvement of Life, 1950. Home: care Mrs. Oscar Lanford, Elmbrook Farm, Castleton-on-Hudson, N.Y. Died Oct. 7, 1955.

SHERMAN, JAMES MORGAN, bacteriologist; b. Ash Grove, Va., May 6, 1890; s. Franklin and Caroline (Alvord) S.; B.S., N. Carolina State Coll. of Agr. and Engring., 1911; M.S., U. of Wis., 1912, Ph.D., 1916; honorary D.Agr., University of North Carolina, 1948; m. Gertrude Hendricks, August 3, 1916 (died July 24, 1918); 1 dau., Gertrude Hendricks; m. 2d, Katherine Keiper, June 20, 1928; children—Richard Hinsdale, Thomas Fairchild. Asst. in bacteriology, U. of Wis., 1912-14; asst. prof. bacteriology, Pa. State College, 1914-17; also bacteriologist Pa. Agrl. Expt. Sta.; bacteriologist U.S. Dept. Agriculture, 1917-23; prof. bacteriology, 1923—, head Dept. Dairy Industry, Cornell Univ., 1923-55. Editor-in-Chief, Journal of Bacteriology, 1944-51; editorial com. Ann. Review of Microbiology, 1945-55. Member A.A.A.S., Soc. Am. Bacteriologists (pres. 1937), Am. Chem. Society, Society for Experimental Biology and Medicine, Am. Dairy Science Assn. (pres. 1930), Sigma Xi, Phi Kappa Phi, Kappa Sigma, Gamma Alpha, Alpha Zeta. Club: Cosmos (Washington, D.C.). Home: 223 Willard Way, Ithaca, N.Y. Died Nov. 5, 1956.

SHERMAN, WILLIAM BOWEN, physician, educator; b. Providence, Oct. 17, 1907; s. Henry Clapp and Cora Aldrich (Bowen) S.; A.B., Columbia, 1926, A.M., 1927, M.D., 1931; m. Catherine B. McKecknie, Sept. 20, 1941; children—Phoebe, Martha (dec.), John William. Intern Presbyn. Hosp., N.Y. City, 1931-33, asst. physician, 1936-47, asst. attending physician, 1947-55, associate attending physician, 1955-71; assistant resident physician, assistant medicine Johns Hopkins Hosp., 1933-35; clin. asst. Roosevelt Hosp., N.Y. City, 1936-41, asst. attending physician, 1941-46, attending physician, 1947-71, director of the Institute of Allergy, 1960-71; asst. medicine Columbia, 1936-47, associate, 1947-50, assistant clinical professor, 1950-52, asso. clin. prof. since 1952; pvt. practice medicine, N.Y.C. since 1935; cons. Halloran V.A. Hosp., 1948-51, Area Office, V.A. since 1946; civilian cons. to Surgeon Gen. of Army, 1947-71, cons. USPHS, 1956-71, National Advisory Council of Allergy and Infectious Diseases, 1959-63. Chmn. organizing com. 4th Internat. Congress Allergology, 1961; hon. pres. 6th Internat. Congress on Allergology, 1967; chairman board Allergy Found. Am., 1967-71; exec. com. Am. Found. Allergic Diseases. Served as capt. to lieutenant colonel, U.S. Army, 1942-46. Recipient Robert Chobot award, 1964; Distinguished Service award Am. Acad. Allergy, 1965. Diplomate in allergy Am. Bd. Internal Medicine (chairman of sub specialty board of allergy 1957). Fellow A.C.P., Am. Acad. Allergy (pres. 1957-58), N.Y. Acad. Med.; mem. Soc. Exptl. Biol. and Med., Am. Clin. and Climatol. Assn., American Medical Association, N.Y. Acad. Sci., Phi Beta Kappa, Phi Gamma Delta. Clubs: Century Association, University (N.Y.C.). Author: Hypersensitivity Mechanics and Management, 1968; asthma sect. Musser's Internal Medicine, 1951, sect. allergy in Sodeman's Pathologic Physiology, 1950; Allergy in Pediatric Practice (with W. K. Kessler), 1957; sects. on asthma and hay fever in Cecil-Loeb Textbook of Medicine, 1963; sect. on atopic diseases in Santer and Alexander's Immunologic Diseases, 1965; tech. papers med. jours. Editor Jour. of Allergy, 1950-56. Home: New York City NY Died Mar. 1, 1971; buried Sleepy Hollow Cemetery, Tarrytown NY

SHERRILL, MILES STANDISH, chemist; b. Louisville, Aug. 2, 1877; s. Benjamin Mason and Sarah Lilla (Miles) S.; B.S., Mass. Inst. Tech., 1899; studied U. Leipzig, 1900-01; Ph.D., U. Breslau, 1903; m. chemistry Mass. Inst. Tech., 1899-1900, instr., 1903-05, instr. theoretical chemistry, 1905-07, asst. prof., 1907-12, asso. prof., 1912-24, prof., 1924-44, prof. emeritus, 1944—; spl. lectr. Harvard, 1928-30, Wellesley, 1944-45, Boston Coll., 1948-49. Research chemist, explosive sect., engring. div. Ordnance Dept., U.S. Army, Washington, 1918. Fellow Am. Acad. Arts and Scis.; mem. Am. Chem. Soc., A.A.A.S., Am. Assn. U. Profs. Author: A Course of Study of Chemical Principles (with A. A. Noyes), 1921, rev. edit. 1938; Laboratory Experiments in Physico-Chemical Principles, 1923. Home: 82 Ivy St., Brookline 46, Mass. Died Nov. 1965.

SHERWIN, RALPH SIDNEY, chemist; b. Waseca, Minn., Sept. 21, 1876; s. Sidney Orville and Mary Adelaide (Shedd) S.; B.S., U. Okla., 1903; m. Elizabeth Christine Schattgen, Jan. 29, 1908; children—Margaret Elizabeth (Mrs. E. R. Sargent), Ralph Sidney, Charlotte Esther (Mrs. R. M. Toon). With Aluminum Co. Am., 1905-40, process control prodn. alumina, etc., 1932-40; with Reynolds Metals Co., Sheffield, Ala., since 1940, v.p. charge alumina research, 1945, now vice pres. alumina process development, investigation bauxite deposits, aluminum prodn., Europe, 6 yrs.; dir. Reynolds Mining Corp., Reynolds Research Inst. Recipient Certificate Appreciation, Sec. Army, 1951. Mem. Am. Chem. Soc., Am. Inst. Chem. Engrs., Am. Inst. Mining Engrs. (chmn. aluminum and magnesium com. 1950-52). Home: 910 Catalina Pl. Office: Reynold Metals Co., Box 109, Corpus Christi, Tex. Died July 2, 1957.

SHERWOOD, ANDREW, geologist; b. Mansfield, Pa., July 16, 1848; s. Albert and Julia A. (Clark) S.; desc. in 8th generation from Thomas S., the pioneer (b. in Eng., 1586, died, Fairfield, Conn., 1655); ed. State Normal Sch. and old U. of Chicago; m. Jennie L. Knapp, Apr. 17, 1872; children—Anna Leona, Hugh Miller, Mrs. Mattie Julia Beach, Mrs. Lola Inez Williams, Mrs. Jennie Elizabeth Marvin. With J. S. Newberry one year on the geol. survey of Ohio; in charge of field work under James Hall, 5 yrs., on geol. survey of N.Y.; asst. state geologist under J. P. Lesley, 5 yrs. on the 2d geol. survey of Pa.; in charge Pa. mineral exhibit, Chicago Expn., 1893; leader of expdn. to headwaters of the Yukon, 1898; apptd. U.S. dep. mineral surveyor for Ore., Ida. and Ariz., 1900. Prohibition candidate for Congress, 1894. Baptist. Author of geol. works and maps published by the state. Home: Portland, Ore. Died Oct. 31, 1933.

SHERWOOD, NOBLE PIERCE, bacteriologist; born Greenfield, Indiana, Mar. 24, 1882; s. Edwin Orlando and Elizabeth Elvira (Alexander) S.; grad. Kan. City (Mo.) Manual Training High Sch., 1901; B.S. in Engring., U. of Kan., 1905, M.A., 1911, grad. work Pasteur Inst. (U. of Mich.), 1911; studied U. of Chicago, summers 1912, 14; Ph.D., U. of Kan., 1921; B.M., U. of Minn., 1923, M.D., 1924; m. Mary Edith Kepner, June 30, 1910 (dec. Dec. 1958); children—Noble, Margaret, Edwin. Engring. experiences with A.,T.&S.F. and Kansas City Southern rys.; instr. in science, Trego County High Sch., 1908-10; with U. of Kan. since 1910, successively as asst. instr. in botany and bacteriology, 1910-11, instr. bacteriology, 1911-14, asst. prof., 1914-16, asso. prof., 1916-18, prof. bacteriology and immunology, 1918-52, prof. emeritus, 1952—, chmn. dept., 1917-49; vis. prof. microbiology, U. Cal. field staff at U. Indonesia, 1955-57; collaborator on research project Air Force, 1955—; exchange prof. Washington U. Sch. Med., 1918; asst. dept. med., U. Minn., 1922-23; lectr. on history of medicine; consultant bacteriologist Kansas State Bd. Health, 1911-21; past pathologist Lawrence Meml. Hosp.; cons. Watkins Meml. Hosp.; spl. cons. USPHS, 1938; mem. Kansas State Planning Board, 1938-42; chmn. Kan. State Lab. Adv. Commn., 1947-52. Teaching and doing rsrch. of sterilization of bandages for War Dept. at Washington U., 1918; organizer and director S.A.T.C. Hosp., Univ. of Kan., fall of 1918, and taught mil. hygiene and med. bacteriology. Chairman of the Douglas County Cancer Clinic. Recipient Citation from U. Indonesia Sch. of Med. Fellow A.M.A., Am. Coll. Allergists (hon.), Am. Acad. Microbiologists, A.C.P., A.A.A.S., Kansas City Academy of Medicine; member of Royal Soc. Health, Association of American Bacteriologists, Am. Assn. Pathologists and Bacteriologists, Am. Assn. Immunologists, N.Y. Acad. Science, Kan. Pathological Society, Society of History of Medicine, American Association of University Professors, Kan. State Med. Lab. Assn. (pres. 1924), Kansas State and Douglas County med. socs., Sigma Xi, Alpha Omega Alpha, Phi Sigma, Phi Beta Pi, Acacia. Diplomat Am. Bd. Pathology. Rep. Presbyn. Mason. Clubs: University, Faculty. Author: Lab. Manual of Bacteriology, 1941, rev. 1949; Immunology, 1951; also articles profl. jours. Home: 1801 Indiana St., Lawrence, Kan. Died Feb. 21, 1961.

SHEWHART, WALTER ANDREW, research statistician; b. New Canton, Ill., Mar. 18, 1891; s. Anton and Esta (Barney) S.; A.B., U. Ill., 1913, A.M., 1914; Whiting fellow U. Cal., 1915-16, Ph.D., 1917; D.Sc. (hon.), Indian Statis. Inst., Calcutta, 1962; m. Edna Hart, Aug. 4, 1914. Engr., Western Electric Co., 1918-25; mem. tech. staff Bell Telephone Labs., since 1925; specializing in application statistics in engring. and standardization, and theory and practice of control of quality of product; lectr. applied statistics Stevens Inst. Tech., 1930, U. London, 1932, U.S. Dept. Agr. Grad. Sch., 1938, Presidency Coll. Calcutta, 1948; cons. ammunition specifications War Dept., 1935-44; cons. editor on statistics John Wiley & Sons, N.Y.C., 1943—; hon. prof. statis. quality control Rutgers U., 1954; adviser on quality control program Govt. India, 1954. Mem. vis. com. dept. social relations Harvard. U.S. del. Gen Assembly, Inter-Am. Statis. Inst., 1947. Mem. adv. coun., dept. math. Princeton, 1941-48; mem. NRC, 1944-46, com. on applied math. statistics since 1943; chmn. subcom. on engring. applications of statistics; mem. adv. com. Inst. for Research in Mgmt. Indsl. Prodn., Columbia. Recipient Holley medal, A.S.M.E., 1954. Fellow Inst. Math. Statistics (v.p. 1936, pres. 1937, 44, mem. editorial bd. 1938-50), N.Y. Acad. Scis., Econometric Soc., A.A.A.S. (council 1942-49), Internat. Statis. Inst., Am. Statis. Assn. (pres. 1945); Royal Econ. Soc., Royal Statis. Soc.; mem. Am. Soc. for Quality Control (hon.), Am. Math. Soc., Math. Assn. Am., Am. Phys. Soc. Psychometric Soc., Acoustical Soc. Am., Sigma Xi, Kappa Delta Pi, Sigma Phi Epsilon. Rep. Methodist. Author: Economic Control of Quality of Manufactured Product, 1931; Statistical Method from the Viewpoint of Quality Control, 1939. Contbr. to sci., tech. articles. Home: 158 Lake Dr., Mountain Lakes, N.J. Office: Bell Telephone Labs., Murray Hill, N.J. Died Mar. 11, 1967.

SHIDY, LELAND PERRY, tidal expert; b. St. Louis, Mo., July 27, 1851; s. William and Mary T. (Bowers) S.; grad. Mo. State Normal Sch., 1871; attended Mo. State U., 1870-73, left senior class without graduation; received degree of analyt. chemist, Columbian U., 1887; m. Margaret Warren, Sept. 21, 1911. Tidal computer in Coast Survey Office, May 27, 1873-Nov. 18, 1897; chief of Tidal Div., U.S. Coast Survey, Nov. 19, 1897-Oct. 15, 1915, when Tidal Div. became sect. of Div. of Hydrography and Topography; retired, 1930. Introduced methods of saving labor in tidal computations; had annual volume of tide tables extended to the world, 1896; has published various annual reports; biographies of R. S. Avery and F. M. Little; results of tide observations at Nassau, New Providence Island, Bahamas; results of tide observations at Spitzbergen; "Present State of Our Knowledge of Tides," etc. Home: Stockton, Calif. Died Oct. 2, 1935.

SHIMEK, BOHUMIL, botanist; b. nr. Shueyville, Ia., June 25, 1861; s. Francis Joseph and Maria Theresa (Tit) S.; C.E., State U. of La., 1883, M.S., 1902; hon. Ph.D., U. of Prague, 1919; m. Anna E. Konvalinka, June 23, 1886 (died 1922); children—Ella, Bertha (Mrs. P. J. Hanzlik), Anna (Mrs. M. O. Hanzlik), Vlasta (Mrs. George Krepelka), Frank; m. 2d, Marguerite Meerdink, Mar. 6, 1924. Teacher sciences, in secondary schs. of Ia., 1883-88; instr. zoölogy, U. of Neb., 1888-90; instr. botany, 1890-93, asst. prof., 1893-1903, prof. physiol. botany, 1903-14, prof. botany and head of dept., 1914-19, research prof., 1919—, State U. of Ia. Lecturer (exchange prof.) U. of Prague, 2d semester, 1913-14; spl. asst. Ia. Geol. Survey, 1908—. Served at various times as dir. Ia. Lakeside Lab. Hon. chmn. geol. sect. Scientific Congress, Prague, 1914; fellow A.A.A.S. (v.p. sect. E, 1911), Geol. Soc. America, Ia. Acad. Sciences (pres.). Author of about 160 scientific papers. Home: Iowa City, Ia. Deceased.

SHIMER, HERVEY WOODBURN, paleontologist; b. Martins Creek, Pa., Apr. 17, 1872; s. John Calvin and Maria Rebecca (Engler) S.; student Gettysburg (Pa.) Coll., 1891-93, Sc.D. (hon.), 1916; A.B., Lafayette Coll., 1899, A.M., 1901; Ph.D., Columbia, 1904; student Harvard, 1904-05; m. Florence French Henry, June 1, 1904; children—John Asa, Mary Henry. Tutor modern langs. Lafayette Coll., 1899-1901; asst. paleontologist Columbia, 1901-03; instr. paleontology Mass. Inst. Tech., 1903-08, asst. prof., 1908-12, asso. prof., 1912-22, prof., 1922-42, prof. emeritus, 1942—. Fellow A.A.A.S., Am. Acad. Arts and Sci., Geol. Soc. Am.; mem. Boston Soc. Natural History, Washington Acad. Sci., Sigma Xi. Author: Evolution and Man, 1929; An Introduction to the Study of Fossils, rev. edit. 1933; Index Fossils of North America (with R.R. Shrock), 1944. Contbr. articles mags. Home: 42 Cottage St., Hingham, Mass. Died Dec. 13, 1965.

SHIMER, PORTER WILLIAM, chemist, metallurgist; b. Shimerville, Pa., Mar. 13, 1857; s. Peter A. and Ellen (Werkheiser) S.; E.M., Lafayette Coll., 1878, Ph.D., 1899; m. Elizabeth Sandt, Oct. 12, 1880; children—Katharine (Mrs. J. Willard Paff), William Robert, Edward Bernard, Margaret (Mrs. Paul Hoffman). Propr. chem. and metall. lab., Easton, Pa., 1885—; pres. Shimer Chem. Co., 1924—; in analytical, consulting and investigation work; lecturer iron and steel, Lafayette Coll., 1894-1902. Discovered titanium carbide; awarded John Scott medal, Franklin Inst., 1901, for invention of combustion crucible. Mem. Int. Steel Standards Com. Author of papers on new methods and apparatus used in analytical chemistry; application of chemistry to metall. and other problems. Inventor of a new process for case-hardening iron and steel, molten baths for steel treating, chaplet alloy used in iron founding, etc. Home: Easton, Pa. Died Dec. 7, 1938.

SHIRAS, GEORGE, 3D, (shi'ras), lawyer and biologist; b. Allegheny, Pa., Jan. 1, 1859; s. George Jr. and Lillie E. (Kennedy) S.; A.B., Cornell, 1881; LL.B., Yale Univ., 1883; Sc.D., Trinity Coll., 1918; m. Frances P. White, Oct. 31, 1885 (died Sept. 16, 1938); children—Ellen Kennedy (Mrs. Frank J. Russell), George Peter (dec.). Admitted to bar State of Pa., 1883; asso. in practice with his father until appmt. of latter to U.S. Supreme bench, 1892; mem. Shiras & Dickey, Pittsburgh, until 1904. Mem. Pa. Ho. of Rep., 1889-90; elected to the 58th Congress (1903-05), as an avowed Republican, on an independent ticket; writer since 1905, upon biol. subjects and legal questions connected with federal jurisprudence; pres. Kawbawgam Hotel Co. (Mich.). Noted as amateur photographer of wild animals; student of natural history; invented methods for taking pictures of wild animals at night by flashlight; promoter of legislation for protection of wild animals and birds. Author of bills putting under federal control migratory birds and migratory fish, the former becoming a law Mar. 4, 1913. Awarded gold medal at Paris Expn., 1900, and grand prize at St. Louis World Fair, 1904, for photographs of wild animals. V.p. Am. Game Protective

Assn. since 1912; mem. advisory bd. Migratory Bird Treaty Regulations, Department of Agriculture, since 1914; trustee Nat. Geog. Society since 1908. Clubs: Boone and Crockett, Explorers' (New York); Chevy Chase (Md.); Cosmos (Washington); Rotary of Marquette, Mich. (hon.). Presented a club house to Marquette Fedn. of Women's Clubs, and a municipal swimming pool and extensive lake shore frontage (now Shiras Park), City of Marquette. Donor with Mrs. Shiras of trust fund called the Shiras Inst., incorporated 1938, for recreational and cultural benefits of Marquette and vicinity. Author: Hunting Wild Life with Camera and Flashlight, 2 vols., 1935, 2d edit., 1936. Home: 460 E. Ridge St., Marquette, Mich. Died Mar. 24, 1942.

SHIVE, JOHN W(ESLEY), plant physiologist; born Halifax, Pa., Feb. 13, 1877; s. Daniel Aaron and Jane (Shoop) S.; Ph.B., Dickenson, 1906, A.M., 1907; Ph.D., Johns Hopkins, 1915; Sc.D., Rutgers, 1946; m. Kate Northrop, Aug. 27, 1907; children—John Northrop, Scott Lee. Asst. desert bot. lab., Carnegie Inst., summer 1913; plant physiologist, expt. sta., Rutgers U., 1915; asso. prof. plant physiol., 1921-23, prof. since 1923, emeritus prof. since 1946; collaborator U.S. Dept. of Ag. Regional Lab., 1939-46; asso. editor Soil Science, Bull. Torey Bot. Club. Fellow A.A.A.S., 1921 (rep. in council, 1944); mem. Bot. Soc. Am., Soc. Exp. Biol., Am. Chem. Soc., Am. Soc. Plant Physiologists (pres. 1939-40, Stephen Hales Prize Award, 1938). Mem. Royal Academy Agr. of Sweden, 1939. Mem. Sigma Xi, Phi Beta Kappa, Gamma Alpha. Contbr. articles to prof. jours. Home: 1 Rutgers St., New Brunswick NJ

SHOCK, WILLIAM HENRY, engineer-in-chief U. S. navy; retired June 15, 1883; b. Baltimore, June 15, 1821; entered navy as 3d asst. engr., Jan. 18, 1845; served in Mexican war; promoted 2d asst. engr., July 10, 1847; 1st asst. engr., Oct. 31, 1848; chief engr., March 11, 1851; superintended construction of machinery of various naval steamers, the marine engines at West Point, N. Y.; pres. examining bd. engrs., 1860-62; supt. building river monitors at St. Louis, 1862-63; fleet engr. under Admiral Farragut at Mobile and later under Admiral Thatcher, 1863-65; engr.-in-chief of navy, 1877-83; invented and patented numerous improvements in guns, steam devices, and a relieving cushion for wire rigging. Author: Steam Boilers: Their Design, Construction and Management. Address: 1404 15th St., Washington.

SHOEMAKER, DANIEL NAYLOR, plant breeder; b. Fair Haven, O., Nov. 16, 1869; s. Abraham and Mary (Kindley) S.; B.S., Earlham Coll., Richmond, Ind., 1894; teacher, Fair Haven High Sch., 1895-99; student Cold Springs Harbor Summer Sch., 1899, 1900; fellow in botany and asst. in zoology, Johns Hopkins, 1902-03, Ph.D., 1903; m. Frances E. Hartley, of Baltimore, July 15, 1903; 1 dau., Dorothy. Teacher, Welch Neck High Sch., Hartville, S.C., 1902-03, at same time engaging in cotton breeding work; became connected with U.S. Dept. of Agr., 1904; stationed at Waco, and engaged in cotton breeding, 1904-07; in charge cotton breeding investigation, 1907-10; plant breeder, hort. investigations, 1910-31 (retired). Mem. Bot. Soc. Washington (pres. 1925-26), Washington Acad. Sciences, Phi Beta Kappa. Mem. Soc. of Friends. Home: 6800 Eastern Av., Takoma Park DC

SHOHAT, JAMES ALEXANDER, (sho'hat), prof. mathematics; b. Brest-Litovsk, Russia, Nov. 18, 1886; s. Abraham Joseph and Esther (Goldberg) S.; grad. U. of Petrograd, 1910, fellow, 1912-16, Magister of Pure Mathematics (Ph.D.), 1922; m. Nadiashda Galli, Jan. 17, 1922. Came to U.S., 1923, naturalized, 1929. Instr. mathematics, Polytechnic Institute, Petrograd, 1913-17; instr. same, Mining Inst. of Petrograd, 1916-17; prof. mathematics, Ural U., Ekatherineburg, Russia, 1917-21, Pedagogical Inst. of Petrograd, 1921-23; asst. in mathematics, U. of Chicago, 1923-24; asst. prof. mathematics, U. of Mich., 1924-29; research in mathematics, Institut Henri Poincaré, Paris, 1930; asst. prof. mathematics, U. of Pa., 1931-35, associate professor, 1935-42, professor since 1942. Fellow Institute of Math. Statistics, A.A.A.S.; member American Math. Soc., Math. Assn. America, Sigma Xi. Mem. Orthodox Greek Ch. Home: 600 S. Eagle Rd., Upper Darby P.O., Pa. Died Oct. 8, 1944; buried in Arlington National Cemetery.

SHOLES, CHRISTOPHER LATHAM, editor, inventor; b. Mooresbury, Pa., Feb. 14, 1819; s. Orrin Sholes; m. Mary Jane McKinney, Feb. 4, 1841, 10 children. Editor, Wis. Enquirer, 1840, Southport (later Kenosha, Wis.) Telegraph, 1841-45; postmaster Southport, 1845; mem. Wis. Senate, 2 terms, Wis. Assembly, 1 term; editor Milw. News, 1860, then Milw. Sentinel; collector Port of Milw., circa 1862; patentee (with Samuel Soule) paging machine, 1964; patentee improvement on numbering machine, 1867; patentee (with Glidden and Soule) typewriter, 1868; patentee improvements, 1871, sold patents to Remington Arms Co., 1873. Died Milw., Feb. 17, 1890.

SHOOK, GLENN ALFRED, prof. physics; b. Osgood, Ind., July 16, 1882; s. Alfred Smith and Olive (Gould) S.; student Moores Hill (Ind.) College; A.B., U. of Wis., 1907; Ph.D., U. of Ill., 1914; m. Nellie Switzer, Nov. 15, 1911; 1 dau., Elizabeth Louise. Instr. physics, Purdue U., 1907-11, U. of Ill., 1911-14, U. of Mich., 1914-15, Williams Coll., 1915-18; prof. physics, Wheaton Coll., Norton, Mass., 1918-48, emeritus. Fellow Royal Soc. Arts, A.A.A.S.; mem. Am. Assn. Variable Star Observers, Am. Astron. Soc., Math. Soc. Am., Optical Soc. Am., Sigma Xi. Bahá'í. Author: (with others) Practical Pyrometry, 1917; Mysticism, Sciences and Revelation, (pub. Eng.), 1953. Pioneer worker in mobile color and applied optics. Lecturer. Home: Eliot, Me. Died Aug. 26, 1954; buried Eliot.

SHOPE, RICHARD EDWIN, physician; b. Des Moines, Dec. 25, 1901; s. Charles Cornelius and Mary (Hast) S.; M.D., State U. Ia., 1924; hon. M.S., Yale, 1936; hon. V.M.D., U. Utrecht, 1951; D.Sc. (hon.), Rutgers U., 1954; V.M.D., Justus-Liebig U., 1957; Sc.D., U. Chgo., 1958, U. Pa., 1959, State U. Ia., 1963; m. Helen Madden Ellis, July 28, 1925; children—Richard Edwin, Jr., Robert Ellis, Nancy Helen, Thomas Charles. Instr. pharmacology and materia medica State U. Ia., 1924-25; research at Rockefeller Inst. for Med. research, Princeton, N.J., 1925-49; Merck Inst. for Therapeutic Research, Rahway, N.J., 1949-52; mem., prof. Rockefeller Inst. Med. Research, N.Y.C., 1952—. Served with USNR, 1943-46. Received Anna Fuller Meml. Prize, 1952; Sigma Xi Semi-Centennial prize, 1936; Alverenga prize, 1937, John Phillips Meml. award, 1937; John Scott award, 1943; Legion of Merit, 1946; Albert D. Lasker award, 1957; Bertner Found. award, 1959; Howard Taylor Ricketts Meml. award, 1963; N.Y. Acad. Med. medal, 1965; Honor Iowan award Buena Vista College, 1966. Mem. Am. Acad. Arts and Scis., Am. Epidemiological Soc., Nat. Acad. Scis., Assn. Am. Physicians (Kober medal 1957), Am. Philos. Soc., Harvey Soc., Soc. Exptl. Pathol., Soc. Exptl. Biol. and Med., A.A.A.S., Royal Soc. Med. (Eng.), Sigma Xi. Presbyn. Mason. Club: Century Assn. (N.Y.C.). Home: Ridge Rd., Kingston, N.J. Office: Rockefeller Inst., 66th St. and York Av., N.Y.C. 21. Died Oct. 2, 1966.

SHORT, CHARLES WILKINS, physician, educator, botanist; b. "Greenfield," Woodford County, Ky., Oct. 6, 1794; s. Peyton and Maria (or Mary) (Symmes) S.; grad. Translyvania U., 1810; M.D., U. Pa., 1815; m. Mary Henry Churchill, Nov. 1815, 6 children. Prof. medicine and med. botany Transylvania U., 1825-38; initiated publication (with Dr. John Cooke) Translyvania Jour. Medicine and Associate Scis., 1828; with Robert Peter and H.A. Griswold wrote "A Catalogue of the Native Phaenogamous Plants and Ferns of Kentucky," 1833, prepared and distributed 25,000 specimens among correspondents in Europe and America within 5 years; prof. medicine Med. Inst. of Louisville (Ky.), 1838-48; valuable herbarium of over 15,000 species now belongs to Nat. Acad. Natural Scis., Phila. Died "Hayfield," nr. Louisville, Mar. 7, 1863; buried Cave Hill Cemetary, Ky.

SHORT, SIDNEY HOWE, inventor; b. Columbus, O., Oct. 8, 1858; s. John and Elizabeth (Cowen) S.; grad. Ohio State U., 1880; m. Mary Morrison, July 26, 1881, 4 children. Prof. physics and chemistry U. Colo., also v.p. univ., 1880; patented several electric traction inventions, 1880-85; joined U.S. Electrical Co., Denver, Colo., 1885, developed improved electric arc-lighting, new electric motor for streetcars; formed (with Charles Brush) Short Electric Ry. Co. for mfg. electric railroad equipment, Cleve., O., 1889, sold co. to Gen. Electric Co., 1892; joined Walker Mfg. Co., Cleve., 1893, made further improvements in electric traction equipment; obtained around 500 patents on elec. inventions, gained internat. reputation for knowledge in elec. ry. operation; went to Eng. to arrange for production of his inventions in electric ry. field, 1898; became tech. supt. English Electric Mfg. Co., Ltd., 1900. Died in Eng., Oct. 21, 1902.

SHOUDY, LOYAL AMBROSE, surgeon; b. Ellensburg, Wash., Sept. 23, 1880; s. John Alden and Mary Ellen (Stewart) S.; A.B., U. Wash., 1904; M.D., U. Pa., 1909; unmarried. Engaged in practice as surgeon, 1910—; intern German Hosp., Phila. (now Lankenau), 1910-13; physician in charge Mary Drexel Childrens Hosp., 1913-14, Phila.; chief surgeon Bethlehem Steel Co., 1914-18, chief med. service, 1918-45, med. dir., 1945—; cons. surgeon St. Lukes Hosps., Bethlehem, Pa. Chmn. com. on indsl. health Am. Iron and Steel Inst.; dir. Nat. Safety Council; pres. Bethlehem area Boy Scouts of America; mem. Health Adv. Council, U.S. C. of C.; Med. Adv. Group, N.A.M. Fellow A.C.S. (mem. fracture com); mem. Am. Assn. Indsl. Physicians and Surgeons (pres.), A.M.A., Am. Public Health Assn., Conf. Bd. of Indsl. Physicians, Pa. Med. Soc., Phi Gamma Delta, Phi Alpha Sigma. Clubs: University (past pres.). Rotary (hon.), Saucon Valley Country, Bethlehem (Bethlehem). Alumnus Summa Laude Dignatus, U. of Wash., 1943. Author numerous articles on traumatic and indsl. surgery, research on heat sickness and problems of indsl. hygiene. Home: Spring Valley Rd. Office: Bethlehem Steel Co., 701 E. 3d St., Bethlehem, Pa. Died Aug. 30, 1950; buried Ellensburg, Wash.

SHREVE, FORREST, botanist; b. Easton, Md., July 1878; s. Henry and Helen Garrison (Coates) S.; A.B., Johns Hopkins, 1901, Ph.D., 1905; m. Edith Coffin Bellamy, June 1909; 1 dau., Margaret Bellamy. Asst. prof. botany Goucher Coll., Balt., 1906-08; mem. staff Div. Plant Biology, Carnegie Instn., Washington, 1908-43, in charge Desert Lab., Tucson, 1926-39; mng. editor The Plant World, 1911-19. Fellow A.A.A.S. (pres. southwest div., 1928-29); mem. Ecol. Soc. Am. (pres. 1922), Bot. Soc. America, Torrey Bot. Club, Cal. Bot. Soc., Western Soc. Naturalists, Assn. Am. Geographers (v.p. 1940), Assn. Pacific Coast Geographers (pres. 1942), Soc. Am. Foresters, Tucson Nat. Hist. Soc. (pres. 1932-33), Phi Beta Kappa, Sigma Xi (pres. Ariz. chpt. 1932-33). Author: Plant Life of Maryland (with others), 1910; A Montane Rain-Forest, 1914; Vegetation of a Desert Mountain Range, 1915; The Cactus and Its Home, 1931; also numerous papers in sci. jours. Joint author: Distribution of Vegetation in the United States, 1921. Editor: Naturalists Guide to the Americas, 1926. Home: 297 N. Main St., Tucson. Died July 19, 1950.

SHULER, ELLIS W(ILLIAM), (shoo'ler), geologist; b. Comers Rock, Grayson County, Va., Oct. 15, 1881; s. James Alexander Hamilton and Amanda (Harrington) Shuler; B.A., Emory and Henry College, 1903, LL.D., 1943; M.A., Vanderbilt University, 1907; M.A., Harvard University, 1914, Ph.D., 1915; married Leona Berry Smith, Dec. 31, 1907; 1 son, Ellis William. Assistant in biology, Vanderbilt U., 1908; professor biology and geology, Poly. Coll., Ft. Worth, Tex., 1908-13; fellow Harvard, 1913-14; asst. in geology, Harvard, 1914-15; asso. prof. geology, Southern Methodist U., 1915-17, prof. since 1918, also dean Grad. Sch. since 1926. Mem. Shaler Memorial Expdn. to S. Appalachians, 1916; acting geologist Tex. Bur. Econ. Geology, 1917; geologist Tex. Oil Co., 1918. Fellow Geol. Soc. America, A.A.A.S., Texas Acad. Science; member of the American Association of Geographers, American Association Petroleum Geologists, Sigma Xi, Phi Beta Kappa. Democrat. Methodist. Author: Rocks and Rivers of America, 1945. Contbr. various tech. bulls., also articles in Am. Jour. Science, Scientific American, etc. Home: 3429 Haynie Av., Dallas. Died Jan. 1, 1954; buried Restland Meml. Cemetery.

SHULL, A(ARON) FRANKLIN, zoölogist; b. Miami County, O., Aug. 1, 1881; s. Harrison and Catharine (Ryman) S.; student Cornell U., summer 1906; A.B., U. Mich., 1908; Ph.D., Columbia, 1911; m. Margaret Jeffrey Buckley, Dec. 23, 1911; children—William Buckley (dec.), Catharine Ryman (dec.), Elizabeth Buckley (Mrs. Elizabeth Russell), Franklin Buckley. Entomol. Mich. Biol. Survey, summer, 1908; instr. zoology, 1911, asst. prof., 1912, asso. prof., 1914, prof. since 1921, U. Mich.; vis. prof. U. Cal.; summer 1938. Fellow A.A.A.S., Entomol. Soc. Am.; mem. Am. Soc. Zoölogists, Am. Soc. Naturalists (sec. 1920-26, v.p. 1929, pres. 1934), Genetics Soc., Soc. for Study Evolution, Am. Genetic Assn., Mich. Acad. Sci. (pres. 1921-22), Sigma Xi, Gamma Alpha. Henry Russel lectr., 1951. Author: Heredity, 1926; Evolution, 1936. Co-author: Laboratory Directions in Principles of Animal Biology, 1919; Principles of Animal Biology, 1920. Contbr. numerous articles on sex determination, heredity, mechanism of devel., evolution. Home: 431 Highland Rd., Ann Arbor, Mich. Died Nov. 7, 1961; buried Forest Hill Cemetery, Ann Arbor.

SHULL, GEORGE HARRISON, botanist; b. Clark County, O., Apr. 15, 1874; s. Harrison and Catharine (Ryman) S.; B.S., Antioch Coll., 1901; LL.D., 1940, Ph.D. (botany and zoölogy), U. of Chicago, 1904; Sc.D., Lawrence Coll., 1940, Ia. State Coll. Agr. and Mechanics Arts, Ames, 1942; m. Ella Amanda Hollar, July 8, 1906; 1 dau., Elizabeth Ellen (dec.); m. 2d, Mary J. Nicholl, Aug. 26, 1909; children—John Coulter, Georgia Mary, Frederick Whitney, David Macaulay, Barbara Weaver, Harrison. Bot. asst. U.S. Nat. Museum, 1902; bot. expert U.S. Bur. Plant Industry, 1902-04; asst. plant physiology, U. of Chicago, 1903-04; botanical investigator, Sta. for Exptl. Evolution, Carnegie Instn. of Washington, Cold Spring Harbor, L.I., 1904-15; prof. botany and genetics, Princeton University, 1915-42, emeritus, 1942—; visiting lecturer in genetics, Rutgers University, 1929-30, L. L. Kellogg memorial lecturer, 1931; lectr. in Heterosis Conf., Iowa State Coll., 1950. Member of Princeton Borough Bd. of Education, 1928-44, vice-pres. 1934-36, pres., 1936-44; pres. Mercer County Assn. Boards of Edn., 1934-37; Princeton Old Guard, 1944; member Food Panel of Princeton War Price and Rationing Board, 1944-45. Fellow A.A.A.S.; corresponding member Deutsche Botanische Gesellschaft; corr. mem. Academy Science, Vienna; hon. mem. Gesellschaft fur Pflanzenzüchtung in Wien; hon. mem. John Torrey Club of Princeton; mem. Deutsche Gesellschaft für Vererbungswissenschaft, Société Linnéenne de Lyon, Institut Internat. d'Anthropologie (Paris), Am. Assn. Univ. Profs., Torrey Bot. Club (pres. 1947), Bot. Soc. of Am., Am. Soc. Naturalists (v.p. 1911, pres. 1917), Ecol. Soc. America, Am. Genetic Assn. (chmn. plant sect. 1912, advisory com. 1922—), Eugenics Research Assn. Eugenics Soc. America, Genetics Soc. America, Sigma Xi (1st pres. Princeton chapter, 1932-33), Am. Geog. Soc., Am. Soc. Plant Physiology, Washington Acad. Sciences, Am. Philos. Soc. Hon. pres. Antioch Alumni Assn., 1940—; chmn. Island Beach (N.J.) Nat. Monument Committee, 1945-50. Awarded gold medal by DeKalb Agrl. Assn., 1940, for the invention of hybrid corn. Citation for distinguished service to agr. by New Jersey Bd. of Agr., 1945; John Scott medal and premium, 1946; Marcellus Hartley Medal, Nat., Acad. Science, 1949; mem. Hall of Fame Am. Mechanics Mag. Golden Jubilee, 1952.

Lecturer and author of papers on variation, heridity and plant-breeding. Founder and mng. editor of "Genetics" (mag), 1916-25, asso. editor, 1925—; vice-pres. Genetics, Inc., 1940—; first editor genetics sect. of Bot. Abstracts, 1918-22. Home: 60 Jefferson Rd., Princeton, N.J. Died Sept. 28, 1954; buried I O O F Cemetery, Santa Rosa, Cal.

SHULL, J(AMES) MARION, artist-botanist; b. Clark County, O., Jan. 23, 1872; s. Harrison and Catharine (Ryman) S.; ed. pub. schs., business coll., and through brief attendance at Valparaiso U. and Art Students' League, New York; m. Addie Virginia Moore, Dec. 20, 1906 (died April 2, 1937); children—Virginia Moore, Francis Marion; m. Mary Ethel Lerch, of Penn Yan, N.Y., April, 1947. Student and instr. Antioch Coll., Yellow Springs, O., 1896-98; supervisor music and drawing, Boise, Ida., 1898-99; teacher pub. schools, Ohio. and Commercial artist, Memphis, Tenn., 1899-1906; in U.S. Post Office Dept., 1906-07; dendrological artist U.S. Forest Service, Washington, D.C., 1907-09; bot. artist Bur. Plant Industry, 1909-25, asso. botantist, 1925-42, now retired. Has made over 1700 water color drawings and many in black and white for Dept. of Agr.; widely known as breeder of new varieties of iris and hemerocallis. Mem. A.A.A.S., Am. Hort. Soc., Bot. Soc. Washington, Am. Iris Soc. (silver medal), Nat. Carillon Assn. Distinguished Service medal of The Am. Iris Soc., 1944. Club: Arts. Author: Rainbow Fragments—A Garden Book of the Iris, 1931. Contbr. articles and illustrations to mags. Home: 207 Raymond St., Chevy Chase 15, Md. Died Sept. 1, 1948.

SHUNK, WILLIAM FINDLAY, civ. engr.; b. Harrisburg, Pa., Sept. 6, 1830; s. Francis R. and Jane (Findlay) S.; ed. pub. schs., Harrisburg, Harrisburg Acad., and Dickinson Coll.; midshipman, U.S.N., 1846-50; m. Gertrude Wyeth, Apr. 7, 1852. In Pa. R.R. service, 1851-56; in U.S. Coast Survey, 1856; asst. engr. Lewisburg & Spruce Creek R.R., 1856-57; clerk in State Dept., Washington, 1861-65; Rock Island U.S. Govt. surveys, 1865-66; asst. engr. Dutchess & Columbia R.R., 1867; chief engr. Conn. Western R.R., 1868-74; chief engr. Met. Elevated R.R., New York, during construction and of Manhattan Elevated R.R. after construction of roads, 1876-82; chief engr. S.Pa. R.R., 1882-85; chief engr. Kings Co. Elevated R.R., Brooklyn, 1887-89; engr. in charge Intercontinental R.R. Surveys, 1890-92; chief engr. Guayaquil & Quito R.R., Ecuador, 1898-1902; retired. Author: Shunk on Railway Curves, 1854; The Field Engineer (15 edits.), 1879-1903. Home: Harrisburg, Pa. Died 1907.

SHURLY, BURT RUSSELL, laryngologist, otologist; b. Chicago, Ill., July 4, 1871; s. Col. Edmund R. P. and Augusta (Godwin) S.; B.S., U. of Wis., 1894; M.D., Detroit Coll. of Medicine, 1895; post-grad. course, U. of Vienna; m. Viola Palms, June 28, 1905; children—Marie G., Beatrice A., Burt Russell, Edmund R. P., Fredricka P. Practiced, Detroit, since 1895; prof. laryngology and medicine, Detroit Coll. Med.; cons. laryngologist Harper Hosp.; chief of staff Shurly Hosp.; laryngologist and otologist Woman's Hosp.; pres. Detroit Tuberculosis Sanatorium. Actg. asst. surgeon U.S. Army and U.S. Navy, Spanish-Am. War; passed asst. surgeon, chief surgeon Mich. Naval Brig.; lieut. col. M.R.C.; med. dir. comdg. Detroit Coll. of Medicine and Surgery Base Hosp. No. 36, service in France, 1917-19; col. Med. R.C. Mem. Bd. of Edn., Detroit (pres.). Fellow Am. Coll. Surgeons, Am. Coll. Physicians, Am. Acad. Medicine; mem. A.M.A., Mich. State Med. Soc., Am. Laryngol. Assn. (pres. 1935), Am. Otol. Soc., Am. Climatol. and Clin. Assn. (ex-pres.), Am. Acad. of Ophthalmology and Otolaryngology (ex-pres.), Am. Assn. Rhinology, Laryngology and Otology, American Rhinol., Laryngol. and Otol. Assn. (ex-pres.); v.p. Am. Board of Otolaryngology. Republican. Episcopalian. Mason. Member Loyal Legion, Am. Legion, Military Order World War (former surgeon-general; comdr. Detroit Chapter). Clubs: Detroit, Detroit Athletic, University, Intercollegiate Alumni, Country, Grosse Pointe, Grosse Ile Country, Prismatic, Grist Mill. Mem Order of Purple Heart. Home: 1027 Seminole Av. Office: 62 Adams Av. W., Detroit MI*

SHUTE, NEVIL (NEVIL SHUTE NORWAY), author, airplane engr.; b. Ealling, Middlesex, Eng., Jan. 17, 1899; s. Arthur Hamilton Norway; student Shrewsbury Sch., 1913-16, Balliol. Coll., Oxford U., 1921-22 (B.A. in Engring.). Began career as aeronautical designer and engr. with De Havilland Aircraft Co., 1922-24; chief calculator with Airship Guarantee Co., 1924-28, dep. chief engr., 1928-30; mng. dir. Airspeed Ltd., airplanes, 1930-38; first novels pub. 1926; writing only since 1938. Served as pvt. Suffolk Regt. (inf.), 1918; lt. comdr. Royal Naval Vol. Reserve, 1940-44, Fellow Royal Aero. Soc. Mem. Church of England. Clubs: Oxford and Cambridge (London); also various yacht clubs. Author: Lonely Road, 1930; Kindling, 1938; Ordeal, 1939; Old Captivity, 1940; Landfall, A Channel Story, 1941; Pied Piper, 1942; Pastoral, 1943; Most Secret, 1945; The Chequer Board, 1947; No Highway, 1948; The Legacy, 1950; Round the Bend, 1951; The Far Country, 1952; In the Wet, 1953; Slide Rule, 1954; The Breaking Wave, 1955; Beyond the Black Stump, 1956; On the Beach, 1957; The Rainbow and the Rose, 1958. Home: Langwarrin, Victoria, Australia. Died Jan. 12, 1960.

SIBERT, WILLIAM LUTHER, army officer; b. Gadsden, Ala., Oct. 12, 1860; s. William J. and Marietta (Ward) S.; U. of Ala., 1878-80; grad. U.S. Mil. Acad., 1884; m. Mary Margaret Cummings, Sept. 1887; children—William Olin, Franklin Cummings, Harold Ward, Edwin Luther, Martin David, Mary Elizabeth; m. 2d, Evelyn Clyne Bairnsfather, of Edinburgh, Scotland, June 8, 1922. Apptd. 2d lt. engrs., June 15, 1884; grad. Engr. Sch. of Application, 1887; 1st lt., Apr. 7, 1888; capt., Mar. 31, 1896; maj., Apr. 23, 1904; lt. col., 1909; brig. gen. U.S.A. and extended the thanks of Congress by act approved Mar. 4, 1915; maj. gen., June 28, 1917; retired, Apr. 4, 1920. Asst. engr. river work in Ky., 1887-92; in constrn. ship channel connecting Great Lakes, 1892-94; in charge engring. river and harbor dist. (Ark.), 1894-98; instr. civ. engring., Engr. Sch. of Application, 1898-99; chief engr. 8th Army Corps, and chief engr. and gen. mgr. Manila & Dagupan R.R., 1899-1900; in charge engring. river and harbor dists. (hdqrs. Louisville and Pittsburgh), 1900-07; mem. Isthmian Canal Commn., Mar. 1907-Apr. 1914. Built the Gatun Locks and Dam, Panama Canal, the west breakwater, Colon Harbor, and excavated channel from Gatun to Atlantic Ocean. Under the joint auspices of the Am. Nat. Red. Cross and the Chinese Govt., served as chmn. bd. engrs. on flood prevention problem, Huai River Valley, China, June-Oct. 1914. Assigned as comdr. 1st Div., Am. troops in France, under Maj. Gen. Pershing, June 1917; comdr. Southeastern Dept., at Charleston, S.C., Jan.-May 1918; dir. Chem. Warfare Service, U.S.A., which he organized, May 1918-Feb. 1920. Chmn., chief engr. Ala. State Docks Commn., Nov. 26, 1923—; chmn. bd. engrs. and geologists apptd. July 1928, with approval of President of the U.S., to report on economic and engineering feasibility of Boulder Dam. Pres. Am. Assn. of Port Authorities, 1929-30. D.S.M. (U.S.); Comdr. Legion of Honor (French). Home: Bowling Green, Ky. Died Oct. 16, 1935.

SIBLEY, FREDERICK HUBBARD, prof. mech. engineering; b. Oxford, Mass.; s. Sumner and Maria F. (Miller) S.; Ph.B., Brown U., 1898; student nigh schs., Mass. Inst. Tech.; M.E., Case Sch. Applied Science, 1905; m. Annabelle Pearson, June 10, 1909; children—Alden Kingsland, Julia Pierson. Apprenticeship machine shop and surveyor's office; draftsman and asst. engr., Westinghouse Elec. Mfg. Co., and N.Y.C. & H.R. R.R., 1899-1903; instr. and asst. prof. mech. engring., Case Sch. Applied Science, Cleveland, O., 1903-08; prof. mech. engring., U. of Ala., 1908-12; asso. prof., later prof. mech. engring. and head of the dept., U. of Kan., 1912-20; dean Coll. of Engring., U. of Nev., 1920—. Mem. various engring. societies, etc. Unitarian. Author; Elementary Mechanical Drawing (with W. D. Browning), 1905; A. Text Book of Pure Mechanism, 1914; Engineering Thermo-dynamics, 1930; Manchaug—A Historical Novel, 1936. Research work on flow of stream through nozzles, mfr. of synthetic gasoline, strength of steel at high temperatures. Home: Reno, Nev. Died Apr. 2, 1941.

SIBLEY, ROBERT, engineer, editor; b. Round Mountain, Ala., Mar. 28, 1881; s. Robert Pendleton and Susie (Bolling) S.; B.Sc., Coll. of Mechanics, U. of Calif., 1903, E.E., 1922; grad. work under Harris J. Ryan and Dexter S. Kimball, Stanford, 1930; m. Catharine Stone, Sept. 8, 1904 (died May 29, 1942); 1 daughter, Catharine Sibley Oakes; m. 2d, Carol Rhodes Johnston, December 6, 1943. Chief electrical engineer, Mariposa Commercial & Mining Company, Jan.-Sept. 1903; professor mechanical engineering, U. of Mont., 1903-04, mech. and elec. engring., 1904-07, dean Sch. of Engring., 1903-07; in practice in Mont., as consultant for Chicago, Milwaukee & St. Paul, Bunker Hill and Sullivan mines and other corps., 1907-11; asso. prof. mech. engring., 1911-12, prof. until July 1, 1915, U. of Calif. Pacific Coast editor Electrical World and Electrical Merchandising and editor Journal Electricity, 1919-22; editor Journal of Electricity and Western Industry and pres. McGraw-Hill Co. of Calif., 1919-22; Pacific Coast consultant, McGraw-Hill Co. since 1923. Exec. mgr. Calif. Alumni Assn. since 1923; pres. Fidelity Acceptance Corp. since 1927; dir. Am. Alumni Council since 1939 (pres. 1942-44), chmn. bd. dirs. Bank of Berkeley since 1944. Chmn. bd. dirs. East Bay Regional Parks since 1948. Del World Power Conf., London, 1924. Fellow Am. Inst. Elec. Engrs., A.S.M.E; mem Delta Upsilon, Phi Beta Kappa, Sigma Xi, Tau Beta Pi, Golden Bear Soc. Mason (K.T., Shriner). Clubs: Bohemian, Commonwealth, Engineers (San Francisco); Faculty (U. of Calif.); Claremont Country (Oakland). Author: A Primer of Applied Thermodynamics: Elements of Fuel Oil and Steam Engineering (with C. H. Delany), 1918; Research Statistics on Undeveloped Water Power Resources of the U.S.; America's Answer to the Russian Challenge, 1931. Editor: Romance of the University of California, 1928, 33; Golden Book of California, 1936; Folio of California Wildflowers, 1939; Folio of The Seasons of California, 1940; Folio Birds of California, 1944, (Co-author with Carol Sibley) A Treasury of Tradition, Lore and Laughter, 1952. Home: 1777 Leroy. Office: 2333 Shaftuck Av., Berkeley 4, Cal. Died July 22, 1958.

SICKELS, FREDERICK ELLSWORTH, inventor; b. Gloucester County, N.J., Sept. 20, 1819; s. John and Hester (Ellsworth) S.; m. Ranane Shreeves, 5 children. Perfected 1st successful drop cut-off for steam engines devised in U.S., 1841, patented, 1842; patent pended for steam-steering apparatus, 1849-60; completed construction of a full-size steam-steering unit, 1854, succeeded in having equipment installed on steamer Augusta, 1858, secured no purchaser for invention; made trip to Eng., 1860-67, found no buyer there; thereafter became civil engineer; cons. engr. Nat. Water Works Co. of N.Y., 1890, chief engr. its operations at Kansas City, Mo., 1891. Died Mar. 8, 1895; buried Paterson, N.J.

SIDBURY, JAMES BUREN, physician; b. Holly Ridge, N.C., Mar. 2, 1886; s. Verlinza and Fannie (Williams) S.; A.B., Trinity Coll., N.C., 1908; A.M., M.D., Coll. Phys. and Surgeons, Columbia; 1912; m. Willie Daniel, Jan. 1, 1916; children—Julia Rowena, James Buren, Willie Daniel. Intern Roosevelt Hosp., N.Y.C., 1914, N.Y. Foundling Hosp., 1915; practice as children's specialist, Wilmington, N.C., 1915—; pediatrician James Walker Meml., Babies hosps. (both Wilmington); cons. pediatrist N.C. Trustee Duke, Babies' Hosp. Research Center. Endowed J. Buren Sidbury chair pediatrics Duke. Fellow A.C.P.; mem. Am. Acad. Pediatrics, Am. (past pres.), N.C. (past pres.), Fla. pediatric socs., N.C. Med. Soc. (pres. 1938), New Hanover County Med. Soc. (pres. 1927), Omicron Delta Kappa, Chi Zeta Chi. Rotarian. Home: 15 N. 5th St., Washington, D.C. Died Jan. 7, 1967.

SIEBEL, JOHN EWALD, chemist; b. Hofkamp bei Wermelskuchen, Germany, Sept. 18, 1845; s. Peter and Lisetta (Reininghaus) S.; A.B., Realgymnasium, Hagen, 1862; Ph.D., U. of Berlin, 1865; came to America, 1865; m. Anna Regina Schaeffer, 1870. Chief chemist Belcher's Sugar Refining Co., Chicago, 1866-67; established laboratory, 1868; analyt. and forensic chemist Cook Co. and chemist Bd. of Pub. Works and other city bds., 1869-73; prof. chemistry and physics, German High Sch., 1871; city gas insp. and acting city chemist, 1873-80; pub. and editor Am. Chem. Review, 1880-86; pub. and editor Original Communications of Zymotechnic Inst., 1890-1900; dir. Zymotechnic Inst. from incorporation, 1901, when Siebel's Brewing Acad. was added. Protestant. Author: Newton's Axiom Developed, 1868; Preparation of Dialized Iron, 1869; New Methods for Manufacture of Soda, 1874; New Methods for Manufacture of Phosphates, 1878; Compend of Mechanical Refrigeration, 1895, 9th edition, 1915; Thermo- and Electro-dynamics of Energy Conversion. Home: Chicago, Ill. Died Dec. 20, 1919.

SIEBENTHAL, CLAUDE ELLSWORTH, geologist; b. Vevay, Ind., Apr. 16, 1869; s. John Amie and Annie (McKay) S.; desc. of John Francis de Siebenthal, one of the Swiss founders of Vevay and Switzerland Co., Ind., 1801; student Ind. U., 1889-91, 1893-94; A.B., Stanford, 1892, A.M., 1893; fellow U. of Chicago, 1897-99, 1900-01; m. Myrtle Madden, Dec. 14, 1904. Asst. geologist Ark. Geol. Survey, 1889-93; instr. geology, Ind. U., 1891; asst. geologist Ind. Geol. Survey, 1896-99; instr. physiography and geology, Indianapolis Manual Training Sch., 1899-1900; asst. geologist, 1901-10, geologist, 1911—, U.S. Geol. Survey. Republican. Author: Joplin (Mo.) District Folio (with W. S. T. Smith), 1907; Geology and Water Resources of the San Luis Valley, Colo., 1910; Origin of the Zinc and Lead Deposits of the Joplin Region, 1915. Died Mar. 1, 1930.

SIEDER, OTTO F., constrn. engr.; b. Newark, N.J., Jan. 23, 1881; s. August and Sophia (Schalle) S.; B.S., Lafayette Coll., 1902, D.Sc., (hon.), 1952; m. Mary Elvina Gradwohl, Sept. 4, 1906 (dec.); children—Violet Mariot, Roswell Gilbert, Marion Janet (Mrs. Nils Ohlson); m. 2d, Viola Bicknell Lounsbury, Dec. 27, 1952. Design engr. Purdy & Henderson, N.Y.C., 1902-04; design engr., squad leader Am. Bridge Co., N.Y.C., 1904-06; design and constrn. engr. Westinghouse, Church, Kerr & Co., N.Y.C., 1906-09; fgn. rep. charge office Milliken Bros., Buenos Aires, 1909-12; chief engr. Levering & Garrigues Co., N.Y.C., 1912-21, v.p., chief engr., 1921-31; cons. engr. Marc Eidlitz & Sons, N.Y.C., 1931-33; pvt. practice, N.Y.C., also Maplewood, N.J., 1933-40; supervisor engring. and constrn. War Dept., Washington, 1940-42; chief Indsl. Constrn. Div., Office Chief of Engrs., Washington, 1942-45; exec. v.p., gen. mgr. The H. K. Ferguson Co., Cleve., 1945-53, pres., 1953-55, vice chmn. bd., 1955, retired; former chmn. bd. Central Pipe Fabrication & Supply Co. Chmn. adv. bd. Utilization Govt. Indsl. Plants, Washington. Pres. Bernardsville (N.J.) Civic Assn. Registered profl. engr., Ohio, Mich., N.Y. Mem. Nat. Constructors Assn., C. of C., Alpha Chi Rho. Presbyn. Club: Chagrin Valley Country (Cleve.). Home: Bernardsville NJ Died Oct. 17, 1969; buried Somerset Hills Meml. Park, Basking Ridge NJ

SIELAFF, GUSTAV JULIUS, geologist; b. Gold Hill, Nev., June 18, 1878; s. August Julius Emil and Alwine Augusta (Lietz) S.; B.S., Sch. of Mines, U. Nev., 1900; m. Villa May McDonald, Apr. 15, 1916; 1 dau., Alwine Lorraine. Miner and assayer, Virginia City, Nev., 1900-02; assayer and mill foreman, Abangarez Gold Fields, Costa Rica., 1902-03; gen. mgr. Boston Mines Co., Costa Rica, 1903-05; cons. engr., Reno, Nev., 1906-12; supt. Gongolona & Boston Mines, Costa Rica, 1912-13; gen. mgr. Abangarez Gold Fields, 1914-15;

with Southern Pacific Co., 1919-48, chief geologist, 1925-48. Served as capt. Engr. Corps, U.S.A., World War; capt. Chem. Warfare Service, 1919. Mem. Am. Inst. Mining and Metall. Engrs., Seismol. Soc. Am. Republican. Mason (K.T., Shriner). Club: Engineers (San Francisco). Home: 2045 University Av., Berkeley, Calif. Office: 65 Market St., San Francisco. Died Sept. 21, 1956.

SIGERFOOS, CHARLES PETER, (si'ger-foos), zoölogist; b. nr. Arcanum, O., May 4, 1865; s. George W. and Nancy (Shanck) S.; B.S., Ohio State U., 1889; Ph.D., Johns Hopkins, 1897; unmarried. Asst. in Ohio State U., 1889-91; instr. U. of Va., 1891-92, Johns Hopkins, 1895-97; asst. prof. animal biology, 1897-1900, prof. zoölogy, 1900-30, U. of Minn., now emeritus; was instr. embryology, Cold Spring Lab., summers, 1897-1902. Fellow A.A.A.S.; mem. Am. Soc. Naturalists, Am. Soc. Zoölogists, Phi Beta Kappa, Sigma Xi, Beta Theta Pi. Republican. Conglist. Clubs: Campus, Gown-in-Town. Address: Arcanum, Ohio. Died Nov. 26, 1944.

SIKORSKY, IGOR I., aero. engr.; b. Kiev., Russia, May 25, 1889; s. John S.; grad. Naval Coll., St. Petersburg, 1906; grad. Inst. Tech. Kiev, 1908; M.S. (hon.), Yale, 1935; hon. degrees Wesleyan and Lehigh U., Fla. So. Coll., R.I. State Coll., Northeastern U., U. Pa., U. Bridgeport (Conn.), Yale; D.Sc., Colby Coll., 1955, Trinity Coll., 1965, Fairfield U., 1966; m. Elizabeth A. Semion, Jan. 27, 1924; 1 dau., 4 sons. Came to U.S., 1919, naturalized, 1928. Designed and built flying machines on own account, 1908-11; with Russo-Baltic Railroad Car Works, 1912-18, as head of engring. dept. of its aviation factory; built and flew the first multimotored airplane, 1913; designed and built 75 large four-motored bombers used by Russian Army; went to France, 1918, and was commd. by French govt. to build the Sikorsky plane for mil. use, but prodn. cut short by armistice; organized Sikorsky Aero Engring. Corp., 1923, Sikorsky Mfg. Corp., 1925, and in 1928, Sikorsky Aviation Corp., United Aircraft Corp.; engring. mgr. Sikorsky Aircraft div. until 1957, ret., but continued as adviser and cons. Has developed several types of planes, among them the first 4-engine plane, 1913, 1st successful, long-range clippers, which pioneered transoceanic air service; developed first successful helicopter produced in Western Hemisphere, 1939. Recipient Potts medal Franklin Inst., 1933; hon. fellow Rochester Mus. Arts and Scis., 1943; hon. fellow Am. Helicopter Soc. 1944, Gen. W.E. Mitchell award, 1944; Copernican citation, 1943; Benjamin Franklin fellow Royal Soc. for Encouragement Arts, Manufactures and Commerce, London, 1960; First Fawcett Aviation award, 1944; Warner medal Am. Soc. M.E., 1944; Hawks Meml. Trophy, 1947; Gold medal Fed. Aeronautique Internat., 1947; Presdl. certificate Merit, 1948; Silver medal Royal Aero. Soc., Eng., 1949; Alexander Klemin award Am. Helicopter Soc., 1950; Collier Trophy, 1950; Daniel Gugenheim medal 1951; Nat. Def. Transp. award, 1952; Godfrey Lowell Cabot award N.E. Aero Club; one of 50 Americans chosen for Popular Mechanics Hall of Fame; John Scott medal City of Phila., 1955; James Watt Internat. gold medal (London, Eng.), 1955; United Aircraft Corp. established trophy in his honor, 1961; Engr. of Year, Conn. Soc. Profl. Engrs., 1962; Grover E. Bell award Am. Helicopter Soc., 1960; Cross of Chevalier Legion of Honor, France, 1960; Elmer A. Sperry award, 1964; Modern Pioneers Creative Industry medal N.A.M., 1965; award of honor Wisdom Soc., 1966; Hall of Fame award Internat. Aerospace Hall of Fame, 1966; Nat. Medal of Sci., 1967; Wright Brothers trophy, 1967; John Fritz medal, 1968, numerous other awards. Hon. fellow Royal Aero. Soc.; mem. Nat. Acad. Engring., Soc. Automotive Engrs., Am. Soc. M.E., Nat. Aero. Assn., Aero. C. of C., Am. Helicopter Soc., Am. Inst. Aeros. and Astronautics (Sylvanus A. Reed award 1942), Am. Soc. French Legion of Honor, Order of Daedalions, Soc. Exptl. Test Pilots, Aerospace Industries Assn. Am., Aircraft Owners and Pilots Assn., U.S. Naval Inst., Navy League U.S., Early Birds Aviation, Profl. Engrs. State Conn., Royal Soc. Arts (Eng.); Royal Aero. Soc. (Eng.). Mem. Russian Orthodox Ch. Clubs: OX5 of Am.; Quiet Birdmen; Wings; Nat. Aviation. Author: Winged Message of the Lord's Prayer, The Invisible Encounter. Address: Stratford CT Died Oct. 26, 1972; buried Stratford CT

SILBERSTEIN, LUDWIK, (sil'ber-stin), scientist; b. Warsaw, Poland, May 17, 1872; s. Samuel and Emily (Steinkalk) S.; grad. Gymnasium, Cracow, 1890; studied at Cracow, Heidelberg and Berlin U., Ph.D. in math. physics, Berlin, 1894; m. Rose Eisenman, June 29, 1905; children—George Paul, Hedwiga Renata, Hannah Emily. Asst. in physics, Lemberg, 1895-97; lecturer in math. physics, U. of Bologna, Italy, 1899-1904, U. of Rome since 1904; math. physicist at research lab., Eastman Kodak Co., 1920-29; cons. math. physicist since 1930. Lecturer on relativity and gravitation, Cornell, 1920, Toronto U. and Chicago U., 1921. Naturalized U.S. citizen since 1935. Mem. Am. Astron. Soc. Author: Vectorial Mechanics, 1913, 26; The Theory of Relativity, 1914, 24; Simplified Method of Tracing Rays Through Lenses, etc., 1918; Projective Vector Algebra, 1919; Elements of Electromagnetic Theory of Light, 1918; Elements of Vector Algebra, 1919; Theory of General Relativity and Gravitation, 1922; The Size of the Universe, 1930; Causality, 1933; also numerous papers on physics. Home: 129 Seneca Parkway, Rochester, N.Y. Died Jan. 17, 1948.

SILER, VINTON EARNEST, physician, educator; b. West Manchester, O., June 25, 1909; s. Raymond Henry and Mary Catherine (Brown) S.; B.A., Miami U., Oxford, O., 1931; B.M., U. Cin., 1934, M.D., 1935; m. Marjorie R. Hall, Sept. 12, 1941. Research asst. dept. pediatrics Research Found. U. Cin., 1931-34, instr. surgery, 1941-43, asst. prof., 1943-53, asso. prof., 1953-61, prof., 1961-71; intern Cin. Gen. Hosp., 1934-35, asst. resident in surgery, 1935-37, 38-40, resident in surgery, 1940-41, attending surgeon gen. surg. div., clinician out-patient dispensary, 1948-71, dir. Surg. Chem. Lab., 1941-71, founder, dir. hand clinic, until 1971; asst. resident in surgery U. Cal. Med. Sch., at San Francisco, 1937-38; attending surgeon Children's Hosp of U. Cin., 1948-71, Christian R. Holmes Hosp., 1948-71, Jewish Hosp., 1945-71; cons. surgeon Bethesda Hosp., 1943-71, VA Hosp., 1942-71; dir. laser surgery U. Cin. Med Center, 1965-71. Mem. exec. council Cin. Area council Boy Scouts Am.; chmn. devel. council Miami U., 1955-60, trustee, 1957-66. Recipient Alumni award Miami U., 1961. Diplomate Am. Bd. Surgery. Fellow Am. Assn. for Surgery of Trauma, Soc. for Surgery Alimentary Tract; mem. A.M.A., Am., Ohio, Mont Reid (pres. 1962), Cin. surg. socs., Internat. Soc. Surgery, A.C.S., Pan-Pacific, Western, Central surg. assns., Halsted Soc., Soc. Univ. Surgeons, Am. Soc. for Surgery Hand (pres. 1968-69), A.A.A.S., Ohio Med. Assn., Cin. Acad. Medicine, N.Y. Acad. Scis., Am. Soc. U. Profs., Hist. and Philos. Soc. Ohio, Endowment Fund Assn. U. Cin., Rookwood Philos. and Lit. Soc. Cin., Cin. Rose Soc. (pres. 1959-60), Phi Beta Kappa, Sigma Xi, Alpha Omega Alpha (pres. Cin. chpt. 1964-71), Pi Kappa Epsilon, Phi Sigma, Nu Sigma Nu, Theta Chi. Clubs: Commercial, Commonwealth (pres. 1959-60), Torch, Cincinnati Country, Camargo, Queen City, Faculty, University (Cin.); Recess; Stumps Boat. Contbr. articles to med. jours. Home: Cincinnati OH Died Oct. 27, 1971; buried Spring Grove Meml. Mausoleum, Cincinnati OH

SILLEN, LARS GUNNAR, chemist, educator; b. Stockholm, Sweden, July 11, 1916; s. Oskar and Brita (Gentele) S.; fil kand, U. Stockholm, 1934, fil mag. 1936, fil lic (Ph.D.), 1937, fil dr. 1940; m. Birgit Bjernekull, Apr. 9, 1939; children—Gunnar, Bo, Birgitta, Lars. Asso. prof. chemistry Stockholm U., 1941-48; prof. inorganic chemistry Chalmers' Inst. Tech., Goteborg, 1948-50; prof. inorganic chemistry Royal Inst. Tech., Stockholm, 1950-70, dean chemistry dept., 1956-60; Arthur D. Little vis. prof. chemistry Massachusettes Institute Technology, spring 1957; visiting professor geochemistry U. Cal., San Diego, 1966; Hill Foundation visiting prof. U. of Minnesota, 1967; vis. prof. U. Central Venezuela, 1968. Consultant Swedish Research Inst. National Defence, 1942-68; president commn. equilibrium data analytical sect., Internat. Union Pure and Applied Chemistry, 1953-59; chmn. exec. com. 7th Internat. Conf. Coordination Chemistry, Stockholm-Uppsala, 1962. Mem. vis. com. Woods Hole Oceanographic Instrn., 1962-65. Member Swedish Chem. Soc. (bd.), Swedenborg Inst., Swedish Numismatic Soc., Swedish Motordrivers Temperance Soc., Royal Swedish Acad. Scis., Royal Swedish Acad. Engring. Scis., Deutsche Akademie der Naturforscher Leopoldina. Author: (with others) Problems in Physical Chemistry, 1952; Stability Constants, Vol. I, 1956, Vol. II, 1957, 2d edit., 1964. Editor Svensk Kemisk Tidskrift, 1955-62. Mem. adv. bd. Acta Chem Scand, others. Home: Djursholm Sweden Died July 23, 1970.

SILLIMAN, BENJAMIN, educator, scientist; b. Trumbull, Conn., Aug, 8, 1779; s. Gold Selleck and Mary (Fish) S.; grad. Yale, 1796; M.D. (hon.), Bowdoin Coll., 1818; LL.D. (hon.), Middlebury (Vt.) Coll., 1826; m. Harriet Trumbull, Sept. 17, 1809; m. 2d, Sarah (McClellan) Webb, Sept. 17, 1851; 9 children including Benjamin. Admitted to Conn. bar, 1802; prof. chemistry, natural history Yale, 1802-53, gave 1st course of exptl. lectures ever given at Yale, 1804, large responsible for Yale's acquisition of George Gibbs' mineral collection, began full course illustrated lectures in mineralogy, geology, 1813, instrumental in establishment Yale Med. Sch. (opened 1813), became prof. chemistry, induced Yale corp. to establish Dept. of Philosophy and the Arts, 1847, became prof. emeritus, 1853; founder, propr., 1st editor Am. Jour. of Science and Arts, 1818; experimented with Votiac current produced by powerful deflagrator (which he had developed with improvements along lines of one made earlier by Robert Hare), early 1800's; delivered series of geol. lectures before Boston Soc. Natural History, 1835 (acquiring reputation as lectr.); mem. Am. Philos. Soc., 1805; 1st pres. Assn. Am. Geologists, 1840; an original mem. Nat. Acad. Sciences, 1863. Author: Elements of Chemistry, 1830-31. Editor: Elements of Experimental Chemistry (of William Henry), 1814. Died New Haven, Conn., Nov. 24, 1864.

SILLIMAN, BENJAMIN, JR., chemist, educator; b. New Haven, Conn., Dec. 4, 1816; s. Benjamin and Harriet (Trumbull) S.; grad. Yale, 1837; m. Susan Huldah Forbes, May 14, 1840, 7 children. Became asso. editor Am. Jour. of Science and Arts, 1838, editor, 1845-85; prof. practical chemistry Yale, 1846-53, founder Sch. Applied Chemistry in new Dept. of Philosophy and the Arts (later Sheffield Scientific Sch.), asso., 1847-69, prof. chemistry Yale Med. Sch. and Yale Coll., 1853-85; an original incorporator Nat. Acad. Scis., 1863; demonstrated that petroleum was essentially a mixture of hydrocarbons different in character from vegetable and animal oils and that it could be separated by distillation and simple means of purification into a series of distillates; identified what were to become major uses of petroleum for next 50 years, outlined principal methods of purifying those products; in charge chem. dept. World's Fair, N.Y.C., 1853. Author: First Principles of Chemistry, 1847; First Principles of Natural Philosophy, 1858. First Principles of Physics, 1859; Died New Haven, Jan. 14, 1885.

SILVER, THOMAS, inventor; b. Greenwich, Cumberland County, N.J., June 17, 1813; m. Miss Bird, at least 1 child. Patentee governor for marine engines, 1855, governor installed on U.S. mail steamships, 1856, patented in Eng., 1857, adopted by French Navy, adopted by Brit. Navy, 1864; inventor hoisting apparatus, completely enclosed oil lamp; mem. Franklin Inst., Phila., 1855. Died N.Y.C., Apr. 12, 1888.

SILVERMAN, ALEXANDER, chemist; b. Pittsburgh, Pa., May 2, 1881; s. Philip and Hannah (Schamberg) S.; Ph.B., Western U. of Pa. (now U. of Pittsburgh), 1902, M.S., 1907, hon. Sc.D., 1930; A.B., Cornell U., 1905; hon. Sc.D., Alfred U., 1936; m. Elrose Reizenstein, Dec. 16, 1908. Chemist, Macbeth-Evans Glass Co., Pittsburgh, 1902-04; instr. chemistry, U. of Pittsburgh, 1905-09, asst. prof., 1909-12, professor inorganic chemistry, 1912-51, head department of chemistry, 1918-51, head, prof. emeritus since 1952. United States del. to International Union of Chemistry, Liege, Belgium, 1930; Madrid, Spain, 1934; Lucerne, Switzerland, 1936; Rome, Italy, 1938, London, England, 1947, Amsterdam, Holland, 1949, New York, 1951, Stockholm, Sweden, 1953, Zurich, Switzerland, 1955, Paris, France, 1957, Munich, Germany, 1959, mem. commission on inorganic nomenclature, 1947—, v.p., 1950-55, pres., 1955-59, hon. pres., 1959—. Mem. Div. Chemical and Chem. Tech., National Research Council, 1938-1941, 1947-50, 1958-60. Received Pitts. Award, Am. Chemical Society, 1940; Albert Victor Bleininger Award, Am. Ceramic Society, 1958. Registered professional engineer, Pa. Fellow American Ceramic Soc., A.A.A.S., Am. Inst. Chemists (national honorary member), American Inst. Ceramic Engrs., Soc. of Glass Technology (England); emeritus member Am. Chem. Soc.; mem. Pa. Ceramic Assn., Am. Assn. University Profs., Pa. Academy Sciences, Sigma Xi, Phi Lambda Upsilon (nat. hon. mem.), Pi Lambda Phi (nat. hon. mem.), Omicron Delta Kappa. Clubs: Authors (hon.), Chemists, Polygon (Pittsburgh); Cosmos (Washington). Contbr. over 200 articles tech. publs.; tech., popular lectr. on glass. Cons. on glass; researches have resulted in manufacture of important commercial glasses; inventor of devices for microscope illumination. Died Dec. 16, 1962.

SILVERMAN, LESLIE, educator, cons. engr.; b. Chgo., Apr. 27, 1914; s. Hyman and Kate (Bernstein) S.; B.S. in Mech. Engring. with high honors, U. Ill., 1936; M.S. in Mech. Engring., Rutgers U., 1938; S.M. in Engring. (Gordon McKay scholar 1937-38), Harvard, 1938, Sc.D., 1943; m. Eleanore Riffin, Aug. 10, 1941; children—Hugh Jerald, Juliet, Mary Linda, Leslie Riffin. Grad. asst. mech. engring. Rutgers U., 1936-37; faculty Harvard, 1938—, asso. prof. indsl. hygiene engring. at univ., 1948-58, prof. engring. in environmental hygiene, dir. radiol. hygiene program, 1958—, head dept. indsl. hygiene Sch. Pub. Health and Grad. Sch. Arts and Scis., 1961—; vis. lectr. Mass. Inst. Tech., U. Cin., U. Mich., Mich. State U. Cons. engr. AEC, Chem. Corps of U.S. Army, Internat. Atomic Energy Agy., uSPHS; mem. commn. toxicology and indsl. hygiene Internat. Union Pure and Applied Chemistry; research and engring. adv. panel of med. scis. Dept. Def., 1959-61; nat. adv. com. community air pollution USPHS, 1957-60; mem. adv. com. reactor safeguards AEC, 1958—, chmn., 1960; tech. adviser U.S. delegation Internat. Conf. Peaceful Uses of Atomic Energy, Geneva, Switzerland, 1955; AEC del. EURATOM meeting, Brussels, Belgium, 1960. Trustee Am. Acad. San. Engrs. Certified Health Physicist, 1960, Indsl. Hygienist, 1962. Registered profl. engr., Mass. Diplomate Am. Bd. San. Engring. (trustee intersoc. bd. 1962—). Mem. Am. Indsl. Hygiene Assn. (dir. 1957-60, pres. elect 1966), Am. Soc. M.E., A.A.A.S., Am. Inst. Chem. Engrs., Am. Nuclear Soc., Am. Soc. Testing Materials, Am. Meteorol. Soc., Am. Soc. Engring. Edn., Health Physics Soc. (dir. 1961-64), Air Pollution Control Assn. (Richard Beatty Mellon award 1966), Sigma Xi, Tau Beta Pi, Sigma Tau, Pi Mu Epsilon, Delta Omega, Pi Tau Sigma, Phi Epsilon Pi. Author: Industrial Air Sampling and Analysis, 1947; Handbook on Air Cleaning, 1952; also numerous articles. Editor monograph. Patentee in field. Home: County St., Dover, Mass. 02030. Office: 665 Huntington Av., Boston 02115. Died Mar. 4, 1966; buried Dover Cemetery.

SIMMONS, GEO(RGE) FINLAY, zoölogist; b. Sherman Tex., Oct. 25, 1895; s. David Edward and Virgilia Octavia (Finlay) S.; student Houston Law Sch., 1913-14, Rice Inst., Houston, 1915-16; B.A., U. Tex., 1921, M.A., 1922; Ph.D., U. Chgo., 1934; m. Armede Victoria Hatcher, Mar. 2, 1922; children—George Finlay II, Robert Macgregor. Was successively stenographer, sec., law clerk, 1913-15; feature writer

Houston Post, 1912-15; reporter Houston Chronicle, 1916; sec. of police, Houston, 1916-17; asst. in gen. zoölogy U. Tex., 1919, asst. in comparative anatomy, 1919-21, instr. in zoölogy, 1921-22; asst. editor, later editor-in-chief Longhorn Mag., U. Tex., 1919-22; naturalist, 1921, 22, and chief dep. commr. Tex. Game Fish and Oyster Commn., 1923; sci. leader Blossom South Atlantic Expdn. of Cleve. Mus. Natural History, also capt. 3-masted exploring schooner Blossom, 1923-26; curator of ornithology, same museum, 1926-29; nat. lectr. Alber and affiliated bureaus, 1928-31; lectr. biol. scis. Cleve. Coll. of Western Reserve U., 1927-31; research in zoölogy Hull Zoöl. Lab., U. Chgo., 1931-34, 42-43; asst. prof. zoology Mont. State U., 1934-35, prof., 1936-43, pres., 1936-41; Ridgay fellow in zoology U. Chgo., 1943, also Ency. Brit. fellow in zoology, 1943-44; asst. prof. anatomy Loyola U. Sch. Medicine, 1943-48, asso. prof., 1948—; zoology adviser Ency. Brit., 1944—. Served as private Red Cross Ambulance Co. and Ambulance Corps, U.S. Army and as sergt., hosp. sergt., 2d lt., detachment comdr. and adj. Base Hosp. 130, 1917-18. Mem. A.A.A.S., Am. Ornithologists' Union, Am. Soc. Mammalogists, Am. Soc. Ichthyologists and Herpetologists, Cooper and Wilson ornithol. clubs, Sigma Xi, Phi Beta Kappa, Sigma Delta Chi, Sigma Upsilon, Phi Sigma, Phi Beta Pi, Phi Kappa Psi; hon. mem. Burroughs Nature Club, Can. Camp Fire Club, Sociedade do Oceanographia é Piscicultura do Brazil. Club: Explorers (N.Y.C.). Author: Birds of the Austin Region, 1926. Contbr. to mags. Home: 5424 S. University Av., Chgo. 15. Died July 19, 1955.

SIMMS, JOSEPH, physiognomist; b. Plainfield Center, N.Y., Sept. 3, 1833; s. of Ephraim Fitch and Florinda Johnson (Norton) S.; ed. dist. schs. and acad.; Med. Dept., New York U., 1866-67; Coll. Phys. and Surg. (Columbia), 1868-69; M.D., Eclectic Med. College, New York, 1871; m. Jemima Sinclair, of Edinburgh, Scotland, Apr. 7, 1885. Pub. sch. teacher, 1850-54; began lecturing on physiognomy and other subjects, 1854; served in Union Army under Generals Sherman and Grant, 1861-63. Traveled extensively in all the continents; lectured in all principal cities of U.S., Great Britain and Australia, delivering extensive courses in larger centers; spent over 3 yrs. in the islands of the Pacific, and journeyed in America from Alaska to Patagonia, studying birds, fishes, animals and races of men; retired from lecture platform, 1884, after acquiring a fortune. Republican. Elected mem. Anthropol. Inst. Great Britain and Ireland, 1875. Mason. Author: Physiognomical and Physiological Chart, 1867; An Original and Illustrated Physiological and Physiognomical Chart, 1873, 4th edit., 1888; Nature's Revelations of Character, 1874, 10th edit., 1891; Practical and Scientific Physiognomy, 1884. Died Apr. 11, 1920.

SIMON, EDWARD PAUL, architect and engineer; born in Philadelphia, Pennsylvania, June 1, 1878; son of Fred Paul and Mary Ann (Miles) S.; grad. Central High School, Philadelphia, 1896, Drexel Inst., 1900; m. Edith M. Darby, Nov. 5, 1904; children—Marion Darby, Elizabeth Esten. Draftsman, Dull & Coates, architects and engrs., 1900-03; mem. firm Caldwell & Simon, 1903-06, Edward P. Simon, 1907-08, Simon & Bassett, 1908-19; pres. and treas. Simon & Simon, 1919-26, Office of Edward P. Simon since 1926. Principal works include: Manufacturers Club, Fidelity-Philadelphia Trust Bldg., Strawbridge & Clothier Store, Drexel Inst. Tech., Van Rensselaer Dormitory for Women, Curtis Hall of Engring. (all Phila.); Meade Memorial, Washington, D.C.; First Camden (N.J.) Nat. Bank & Trust Co. Bldg.; office bldg. of Baldwin Locomotive Works, Eddystone, Pa. Trustee Drexel Inst. (chmn. com. on bldgs. and grounds). Mem. Am. Inst. Architects, Archtl. League of N.Y., Am. Soc. Professional Engrs., Pa. and N.J. Soc. of Architects. Republican. Presbyterian. Mason. Clubs: T Square, Midday. Home: 1530 Locust St. Office: Fidelity-Philadelphia Trust Bldg., Philadelphia, Pa. Died May 19, 1949.

SIMON, WILLIAM, chemist; b. Eberstadt, Hessen, Germany, Feb. 20, 1844; s. Rev. William and Agnes (Briegleb) S.; ed. at Giessen, 1852-60; in a drug store, 1860-66; Ph.D., U. of Giessen, 1869; (hon. M.D., Coll. Phys. and Surg., Baltimore, 1880; (Sc.D., U. of Pennsylvania, 1915); asst. to Prof. H. Will, 1869-70; in Franco-Prussian War, 1870; came to U.S., 1870; opened 1st chem. lab. for instrn. at Baltimore, 1871; m. Paula Driver, May 13, 1873. Chemist to Baltimore Chrome Works, 1870-1907; prof. chemistry, Md., Coll. Pharmacy, 1872-1902, Coll. Phys. and Surg., Baltimore, 1880—, Baltimore Coll. Dental Surgery, 1888—. Pres. Md. Pharm. Assn., 1887-88; fellow, mem. or hon. mem. of many chem. and pharm. socs. Author: Manual of Chemistry, 1884, 10th edit., 1912. Home: Catonsville, Md. Died July 19, 1916.

SIMONDS, JAMES PERSONS, pathologist; b. Cleburne, Tex., Mar. 19, 1878; s. Richard Harrison and Mary (Persons) S.; A.B., Baylor U., 1901, LL.D., 1951; M.D., Rush Med. Coll., 1907; Dr. P.H., Harvard, 1914; Ph.D., U. Chgo., 1923; m. Minnie Pearl Jones, Jan. 26, 1909. Asst. city bacteriologist, St. Louis, 1907-08; dir. Lab. Pathology and Bacteriology, Ind. Bd. Health, 1908-12; prof. preventive medicine U. Tex., 1912-14; asso. prof. pathology Northwestern U. Med. Sch., 1914-22; prof., head dept., 1922-43, prof. pathology emeritus, since 1943; attending pathologist Cook County Hosp., 1918-46; pathologist Passavant Meml. Hosp., 1929-38; dir. lab. Alexian Bros. Hosp., 1926-58, Children's Meml. Hosp., 1944-49; sent to France, 1916, by Rockefeller Inst. to study gas gangrene; coroner's physician, Cook County, 1918-20. Mem. bd. govs. Internat. House, Chgo., 1932-49. Fellow Coll. Am. Pathol.; mem. Ill. Soc. Pathol. (pres. 1948), A.M.A. (chmn. sect. on pathol. and physiol. 1941), Ill. Med. Soc., Chgo. Med. Soc. (pres. 1941, trustee 1949-64), A.A.A.S., Inst. of Medicine Chgo. (pres., 1937), Am. Assn. Pathologists and Bacteriologists, Geog. Soc. Chgo. (dir., pres. 1937-39), Am. Soc. for Exptl. Pathology, Internat. Acad. Pathologists, Assn. Clin. Scientists (diploma of honor 1962), Phi Chi. Baptist. Clubs: University, Chaos, Chicago Literary. Author: Practical Sanitation, 1914; Studies on Bacillus Welchii, 1915; numerous papers on pathology and related subjects. Home: 2150 Lincoln Park W. Office: 1200 Belden Av., Chgo. Died Mar. 17, 1964.

SIMPSON, CHARLES TORREY, naturalist; b. Tiskilwa, Ill., June 3, 1846; s. Jabez and Matilda (Cook) S.; student zoölogy and botany; Sc.D., U. of Miami, Fla., 1927; m. Cornelia Couch (dec.); m. 2d, Flora G. Roper, Sept. 17, 1902. On scientific staff, U.S. Nat. Mus., 1889-1902; collaborator U.S. Dept. Agr., 1914—. Some time lecturer in Georgetown U. Author: Geographical Distribution of the Land and Freshwater Mollusks of the West Indies, 1895; Synopsis of the Naides or Pearly Freshwater Mussels, 1900; Report on the Mollusks of the Fish Hawk Expdn. to Puerto Rico, 1901; Descriptive Catalogue of the Pearly Freshwater Mussels, 1913; Native and Exotic Plants of Dade County, Florida, 1913; Ornamental Gardening in Florida, 1915; In Lower Florida Wilds, 1920; Out of Doors in Florida, 1923; Florida Tree Snails of the Genus Liguus, 1929. Awarded Meyer medal for plant introduction, 1932. Home: Miami, Fla. Died Dec. 17, 1932.

SIMPSON, FRANK EDWARD, dermatologist; b. Saco, Me., Sept. 7, 1869; s. Charles P. and Adelaide (Reade) S.; A.B., Bowdoin, 1890; M.D., Northwestern U. Med. Sch., 1896; post-grad. work, Paris, Berlin and Vienna; m. Beulah Lichty, Nov. 22, 1898 (dec.); m. 2d, Beryl Lucile Kanagy, 1922; children—Frank Edward, Hugh Mills, William Langdon. Intern Cook County Hosp.; practiced at Chicago since 1897; prof. skin and venereal diseases, Chicago Policlinic, 1912-22; clin. prof. dermatology, Northwestern U. Med. Sch., and attending dermatologist Cook County., Wesley and Policlinic hosps. Former pres. Am. Radium Soc.; mem. A.M.A., Chicago Med. Soc., Chicago Dermatol. Soc., Phi Beta Kappa, Psi Upsilon, Nu Sigma Nu. Republican. Methodist. Club: University. Author: Radium Therapy, 1922; Radium in Cancer and Other Diseases, 1926; Contbr. to Oxford Surgery, Lahrbuch der Strahlentherapie, and spl. articles on radium therapy and dermatology to foreign and Am. scientific books and jours. Home: 445 Barry Av., Chicago 14. Office: 50 E. Madison St., Chicago, Ill. Died Dec. 13, 1948; buried Graceland Cemetery, Chicago.

SIMPSON, HOWARD EDWIN, geologist; b. Clarence, Ia., July 9, 1874; s. Hiram Garrison and Frances Abigail (Carter) S.; Ph.B., Cornell Coll., Mt. Vernon, Ia., 1896, Sc.D., 1930; student Univ. of Chicago 3 summers; A.M., Harvard U., 1905; m. Carrie Esther Bonebrake, Dec. 30, 1903; children—Jessie Frances, Robert Bonebrake, Carolyn Cradock (dec.), Howard Edwin. Science teacher, later prin. high sch., Knoxville, Ia., 1897-1900; supt. schs., Columbus Jct., Ia., 1900-03; field and lab. asst., 1903-04, asst. in physiography and meteorology, 1904-05, Harvard; instr. and asso. prof. geology, Colby Coll., 1905-09; asst. prof. geology, 1909-14, asso. prof., 1914-19, prof. geographic geology, 1919—, head dept. geology and geography and state geologist, 1933—, U. of N.D. Visiting prof., U. of Chicago, summer 1918, U. of Southern Calif., summer 1920. Served as asst. U.S. Geol. Survey, various seasons, and as water geologist Can. Geol. Survey, summer 1929; water geologist, National Resources Board, 1934; spl. meteorol. observer, U.S. Weather Bur. Fellow Geol. Soc. of America, Assn. Am. Geographers, A.A.A.S., Am. Meteorol. Soc., Am. Geog. Society. Mem. Gen. Conf. M.E. Ch., 1920, 28, 32, 36; mem. World Service Commn., M.E. Ch.; mem. Nat. Council Y.M.C.A.; mem. bd. trustees Wesley Coll. Mem. N.D. State Geographic Bd. and N.D. State Planning Bd. Author or joint author of Geography of North Dakota; Underground Water Resources of Iowa; Ground Water Resources of N.D.; Conservation of Artesian Waters; A Method of Prospecting for Water; etc. Home: Grand Forks, N.D. Died Jan. 31, 1938.

SIMPSON, RICHARD LEE, dentist; b. Fincastle, Va., Apr. 21, 1873; s. John Charlton and Sarah Elizabeth (Backenstoe) S.; student Washington and Lee U., 1891-92; D.D.S., U. of Md., 1896, hon. A.M., 1907; m. Elma Walker, 1901; 1 adopted dau., Virginia Jaqueline (Mrs. Leslie Reid Jones). Practiced dentistry, Fincastle, Va., 1896-1904, Richmond, Va., since 1904; prof. of operative dentistry, crown and bridge work and dean of dept., Univ. Coll. of Medicine, Richmond, 1905-13; prof., dean dental dept., Med. Coll. Va., 1913-15, now emeritus prof. clin. practice. Mem. Va. State Bd. Dental Examiners, 1903-05. Fellow Am. Coll. Dentists; mem. Nat. Dental Assn., Va. Dental Assn. (ex-pres.), Richmond Dental Soc. (past pres.), Xi Psi Phi, Omicron Kappa Upsilon. Democrat. Presbyterian (elder). Mason. Club: Hermitage Golf (Richmond). Inventor of several dental appliances; has lectured and given clinics before state and nat. socs., also Internat. Dental Congress, St. Louis, 1904, and Chicago Centennial Dental Congress, 1933. Originated the securing of the Betty Davis Wood $1,200,000 endowment for the Med. Coll. of Va. Recipient of testimonial banquet and gold medallion from the Richmond Dental Soc., Sept. 24, 1938. Home: 2913 Hawthorne Av. Office: 301 E. Franklin St., Richmond VA

SIMPSON, SUTHERLAND, physiologist; b. Orkney Islands, Scotland, Feb. 3, 1863; s. Sutherland and Margaret (Taylor) S.; ed. Heriot-Watt Coll., Edinburgh, 1882-85; B.Sc., Edinburgh U., 1894, M.B., Ch.B., 1899, M.D. (gold medal), 1901, D.Sc., 1903; m. Catherine Graham Pettigrew Anderson, of Edinburgh, Aug. 6, 1908. Prof. and head dept. physiology and biochemistry, Cornell U., 1908—. F.R.S., Edinburgh. Author original research papers on central nervous system, animal heat and body temperature, secretory glands, bile secretion, etc. Home: Ithaca, N.Y. Died Mar. 3, 1926.

SIMS, CHARLES ABERCROMBIE, civil engr.; ry. contractor; b. Memphis, Tenn., June 5, 1866; s. Clifford Stanley and Mary Josephine (Abercrombie) S.; m. Julia Watkins, Apr. 21, 1897 (died Jan. 10, 1940). Filled various positions on Pennsylvania R.R. engring. Corps, 1882-86; asst. engr. in charge constrn. W.Va. Central R.R., 1886-87; asst. engr. in charge constrn. surveys, etc., Pa. R.R. Co., 1887-90. Was resident engr. in charge bldg. Pa. R.R. Co's stone arch bridge over Conemaugh River that stood flood of 1889 at Johnstown, Pa.; was contractor Pa. R.R. 4-track stone arch bridge over Delaware River at Trenton, N.J. Mem. Soc. of the Cincinnati, Loyal Legion. Episcopalian. Address: 10 S. 18th St., Philadelphia, Pa. Died May 15, 1942.

SIMS, JAMES MARION, gynecologist; b. Lancaster County, S.C., Jan. 25, 1813; s. John and Mahala (Mackey). S.; grad. S.C. Coll., 1832; studied Charleston Med. Sch., 1833; grad. Jefferson Med. Coll., 1835, LL.D. (hon.), 1881; m. Eliza Theresa Jones, Dec. 21, 1836, 9 children. Practiced medicine, Ala., 1835-50, performed unprecedented fistula operations with notable success, attracting wide attention; published history of vesicovaginal operations, on which he was recognized authority, 1852; founder Women's Hosp., N.Y.C., 1854; visitor to France and Eng. several times, 1861-82, consulting with gynecologists, lecturing, receiving honors in several nations; pres. A.M.A., 1876, Am. Gynecol. Soc., 1881; author several works including autobiography, published 1884. Died N.Y.C., Nov. 13, 1883.

SIMS, W(INFIELD) SCOTT, inventor; b. New York, Apr. 6, 1844; s. Capt. Lindsay D. and Catherine B.S.; grad. high sch., Newark, N.J.; served in 37th N.J. Regt. in Civil War; m. Lida Leek, June 11, 1867 (died 1888); 2d, Mrs. Josephine Courter French, June 24, 1891. Invented various devices in electro-magnets; constructed an electric motor for light work in 1872, weighing 45 pounds, and having a battery of 20 half-gallon Bunsen cells, by means of which he was enabled to propel an open boat 16 feet long, with 6 persons on board, at the rate of 4 miles an hour; was first to apply electricity for propulsion of torpedoes, his device of a torpedo being a submarine boat with a cylindrical hull of copper and with conical ends, furnished with screw propeller and a rudder, the power being electricity generated on shore or on shipboard, by means of which the torpedo is propelled, guided and exploded; subsequently he devised a boat with a speed of 22 miles an hour and to carry a 500-lb. charge of dynamite; also invented the wireless dirigible torpedo, of which sold 5 to Japanese Govt., 1907; invented the Sims-Dudley Dynamite Gun, used by Cuban insurgents, and by the "Rough Riders" at battle of Santiago; now designing a dynamite cruiser to carry 100 tons of high explosives, controlled by an operator on ship or shore; has also designed a dynamite gun for use with dirigible warships, and an aeroplane dynamite gun. Home: Newark, N.J. Died Jan. 7, 1918.

SINCLAIR, ANGUS, editor, engr.; b. in Scotland, 1841; s. Alexander and Margaret (McLeay) S.; ed. at Lawrencekirk, Scotland; spl. studies in chemistry State U. of Ia.; m. Margaret A. Moore, 1877. Engaged in editorial work, 1883—; editor Automobile Magazine, and of Railway Engineering. Writer on railway and automobile subjects. Author: Locomotive Engine Running, 1884; Combustion in Locomotive Fire Boxes, 1890; Combustion and Smoke Prevention, 1896; Burning Soft Coal Without Smoke, 1899; Firing Locomotives, 1901; Twentieth Century Locomotives; History of the Development of the Locomotive Engine, 1907; Railroad Men's Catechism, 1907, etc. Home: Milburn, N.J. Died Jan. 2, 1919.

SINDEBAND, MAURICE LEONARD, elec. engring. exec.; b. Russia, Apr. 14, 1887; s. Simon and Ida (Jabelow) S.; brought to U.S., 1890, derivative citizen; E.E., Columbia, 1907; m. Lyllian Levy, Feb. 26, 1914;

children—Seymour J., Allan L. Asst. elec. engr. N.Y.C. R.R.; v.p. Am. Electric Power Co. (formerly) Am. Gas & Electric Co., 1914-28, Am. Brown Boveri Electric Corp., 1929-32; receiver Insull Elec. Properties in Ohio; vice chmn. Ogden Corp., dir.; v.p., sec. dir. Mt. Olive & Staunton Coal Co.; director American Bosch Arma Corp., Syntex Corporation, S.A., Avondale Shipyards, Incorporated. Profl. engr., N.Y. Fellow Am. Inst. E.E. Inventor electric automatic train control, automatic reactor for power circuits, electronic voltage regulator for generators, carrier telephony system using high-voltage power conductors, method for prevention electric power arcs from damaging high-tension transmission lines. Home: New York City NY Died Dec. 5, 1971.

SINGER, ISAAC MERRIT, inventor, machinist; b. Oswego, N.Y., Oct. 27, 1811; m. Catherine Maria Haley, 1835; m. 2d, Isabella Summerville, 1865. Patented rock-drilling machine, 1839, wood and metal carving machine, 1849; received 1st patent on sewing machine (superior because it could do continuous stitching), 1851; organized sewing machine mfg. firm I.M. Singer & Co., 1851, reached commanding position in sewing machine industry by 1854, brought about pooling of patents in industry; received 20 patents for improvements on his machine, including continuous wheel feed and yielding presser foot, 1851-63; developed 1st practical domestic sewing machine brought into wide use; withdrew from active connection with co., 1863. Died Torquay, Eng., July 23, 1875.

SINGER, WILLARD EDISON, educator, physicist; b. Bexley, O., May 2, 1904; s. Simon A. and Grace G. (Cromwell) S.; A.B., Capital U., 1925; B.E.E., Ohio State U., 1926, M.A., 1927, Ph.D., 1951; m. Irene K. Vogel, Dec. 25, 1932. Grad. asst. Ohio State U., 1927-28, 1930-31; instr. physics Bowling Green State U., 1927-34, asst. prof., 1934-43, asso. prof., 1943-51, prof. since 1951, chmn. dept, 1947-1967. Mem. A.A.A.S., Am. Assn. Physics Tchrs., Am. Phys. Soc., Ohio Acad. Sci. Lutheran (mem. ofcl. bds.) Home: Bowling Green OH Died Mar. 18, 1972; buried Fish Cemetery near Bowling Green OH

SINGMASTER, JAMES ARTHUR, chemist, metallurgist; b. Schuylkill Haven, Pa., Aug. 7, 1878; s. John Alden and Caroline (Hoopes) S.; A.B., M.A., Gettysburg Coll., 1898; studied Lehigh U., 1899; m. Helen Jacks, 1903; 1 son, James Arthur. With N.J. Zinc Co., 1900-27; now cons. chem., metall. engr.; pres. Singmaster & Breyer, Inc.; dir. Dictaphone Corp. Inventor, patentee numerous improvements in manufacture of zinc and its products, artificial silk, method for delustering rayon; spl. recognition for contbn. to Atomic Bomb Project by War Dept. Mem. Am. Inst. Chem. Engrs., Mining and Metall. Soc. Am., Ceramics Soc., Am. Inst. Mining and Metall. Engrs., Am. Chem. Soc., Am. Zinc Inst., Soc. Chem. Industry (London), Phi Beta Kappa. Republican. Lutheran. Clubs: Chemists', Uptown. Home: 46 Durham Rd., Lawrence Park W., Bronxville, N.Y. Office: 420 Lexington Av., N.Y.C. Died Apr. 12, 1962; buried Macungie, Lehigh County, Pa.

SINNOTT, EDMUND WARE, botanist; b. Cambridge, Mass., Feb. 5, 1888; s. Charles Peter and Jessie Elvira (Smith) S.; A.B., Harvard, 1908, A.M., 1910, Ph.D., 1913; D.Sc., Northeastern U., 1948; Lehigh, 1950; m. Mabel H. Shaw, June 24, 1916; children—Edmund Ware, Mildred Shaw, Clara Richardson. Austin teaching fellow and asst. in botany, Harvard, 1908-10, 1911-12; Sheldon traveling fellow of Harvard, for bot. research in Australasia, 1910-11; instr. Harvard Forestry Sch. and Bussey Instn., 1913-15; prof. botany and genetics, Conn. Agricultural Coll., 1915-28; prof. botany. Barnard Coll., 1928-39; prof. botany, Columbia, 1939-40; Sterling prof. of botany Yale, 1940-56, emeritus, chmn. dept. botany, 1940-50, director Sheffield Scientific School and chmn. Div. of Science, 1945-56, dean Graduate Sch., Yale, 1950-56. Mem. Nat. Acad. Scis., Am. Philos. Soc., Am. Acad. Arts and Sciences. Fellow A.A.A.S. (v.p. 1935, pres. 1948), Bot. Soc. of America (pres. 1937), Am. Soc. Naturalists (pres. 1945), New England Botanical Club, Torrey Bot. Club (pres. 1931-34). Phi Beta Kappa, Sigma Xi. McNair Lecturer U. of N.C., 1949. Club: Graduates (New Haven). Author: Botany Principles and Problems; (with L. C. Dunn and Th. Dobzhansky) Principles of Genetics; Cell and Psyche; Two Roads to Truth, 1953; The Biology of the Spirit, 1955; Matter, Mind and Man, 1957; Plant Morphogenesis, 1960; and various papers on antomy, morphogenesis and inheritance in the higher plants. Home: 459 Prospect St., New Haven. Died Jan. 6, 1968.

SIPLE, PAUL ALLMAN, explorer, author, geographer; b. Montpelier, O., Dec. 18, 1908; s. Clyde L. and Fannie Hope (Allman) Siple; B.S., Allegheny College, 1932, D.Sc. (honorary), 1942; Ph.D. (Geography), Clark U., 1939; D.Sc., U. Mass., 1958, Boston U., 1958, Clark U., 1958, Bowling Green State U., 1959, Kent State Coll., 1968; hon. grad. Phila. Textile Inst., 1946; LL.D., Gannon Coll., 1958; married Ruth I. Johannesmeyer, Dec. 1936; children—Ann Byrd, Jane Paulette (Mrs. Wertime), Mary Cathrin (Mrs. Remmington). Youngest mem. Admiral Byrd's Antarctic Expdn., chosen after tests among 600,000 Boy Scouts of America; in charge of biol. and zool. work of expdn., bringing back specimens of penguins, seals for Am. Museum of Natural History, 1928-30, head of biological dept. Adm. Byrd's 2d expdn., 1933-35, and mem. Byrd's personal staff; in charge erecting and equipping the base in which Byrd lived alone 4 1/2 mos. in 1934; leader Marie Byrd sledging party into newly discovered land; toured Europe, Asia Minor and N. Africa, off the beaten paths, 1932-33; geographer Div. Territories and Island Possessions, Dept. of Interior, assigned to U.S. Antarctic Expdn. as leader of West Base, Little America, 1939-41; geographer and tech. supervisor of supplies and equipment; on furlough, 1941, from U.S. Antarc. Expdn. and employed by the War Dept. as a civilian expert on design of cold climate clothing and equipment; head research and map projects for U.S. Antarctic Service, 1941-42; commd. capt. Q.M. Corps, AUS, July 1942; discharged as lt. col., Aug. 1946. Mil. Geographer, sci. adviser Office Chief of Research and Devel., Dept. Army Gen. Staff, 1946-63, leader winter environmental teams, 1951-53; sci. attache for Australia, New Zealand, Am. embassy, Canberra, Australia, 1963-66; spl. sci. adviser U.S. Army Research Office, Arlington, Va., 1967-68. Sr. war dept. rep. Navy Antarctic Expdn. Highjump, 1946-47; dep. to Admiral Byrd, U.S. Antarctic Programs, sci. adviser Operation Deep Freeze I, 1955-56; sci. leader U.S. IGY Amundsen-Scott South Pole Sta., 1956-57; mem. numerous arctic, sci. coms. Mem. nat. council and camping com. of Boy Scouts of Am. Awarded Congl. medals, 1930, 37, 46; Heckel sci. prize, Hatfield award, 1931, Legion of Merit Award, 1946; exceptional civilian service award, Dept. Army, 1957; David Livingstone Centenary medal, Am. Geog. Soc., 1958; Hubbard medal, Nat. Geog. Soc., 1958; Distinguished Civilian Service award, Dept. Def., 1958; Patron's medal, Royal Geog. Soc. 1958; Hans Egede medal, Royal Danish Geographical Society, 1960, numerous other medals and awards; Mt. Siple and Siple Island named for him by New Zealand govt. Fellow Arctic Institute of America, American Geographic Society; mem. Antarctican Soc. (past pres.), Australian Antarctic Club, A.A.A.S., Am. Polar Soc. (1st pres.), Assn. Am. Geographers (v.p. 1958, pres. 1959), Am. Geophys. Union, International Geophysical Year (U.S. com.), Vets. Fgn. Wars (hon.), Clark University Geography Society numerous other arctic and sci. socs., Phi Beta Kappa, Sigma Xi, Alpha Chi Rho, Omicron Delta Kappa, Phi Beta Phi, Alpha Phi Omega. Methodist. Clubs: Exchange (Erie, Pa.); Kiwanis (Bloomington, Ill.); Explorers. Lecturer. Author: A Boy Scout with Byrd, 1931, Exploring at Home, 1932; Scout to Explorer, 1936; The Second Byrd Antarctic Expedition—Botany Report, 1938; Adaptations of the Explorer to the Climate of Antarctica, 1939; 90 deg. South, 1959. Originator Wind-Chill Index; co-designer principles leading to devel. thermal boot; researcher design climate controlled housing; patentee in field. Home: Arlington VA Died Nov. 25, 1968; buried Nat. Meml. Park, Falls Church VA

SIRRINE, JOSEPH EMORY, industrial engring.; b. Americus, Ga., Dec. 9, 1872; s. George William and Sarah Euodias (Rylander) S.; Greenville Mil. Inst., 1883-86; B.S., Furman, 1890; hon. M.E., Clemson (S.C.) Agricultural College, 1928; LL.D., Presbyterian College, 1941; m. Jane Pinckney Henry, Nov. 8, 1898. Gen. engr. work, 1890-95; southern mgr. Lockwood, Green & Co., Greenville, S.C., 1895-1902; organizer, 1902, and since head of J. E. Sirrine & Co., designers of industrial and power plants, steam and hydro-electric; chairman board of directors Brandon Mills (Greenville, S.C.), vice president Dunean Mills, Industrial Cotton Mills, Chiquola Mfg. Co. all in S.C.; director Arcade Cotton Mills, Aragon Baldwin Mills, Watts Mills, Wallace Mills, Judson Mills, Piedmont Mfg. Co., The Florence Mills, Piedmont Plush Mills, F. W. Poe Mfg. Co., Union Bleachery, First Nat. Bank, Liberty Life Ins. Co., Greenville News-Piedmont Co. (all in Greenville), Ware Shoals Mfg. Co., Graniteville Mfg. Co., Woodside Cotton Mills, Easley Cotton Mills (all of S.C.), Marion Mfg. Co. (N.C.), Camperdown Mill, Norris Cotton Mills, Riverdale Mills, Inman Mills, Union-Buffalo Mills (all of South Carolina), J. P. Stephens & Co. (N.Y.). Life trustee Clemson College. Mem. American Soc. C.E., Am. Soc. Mech. Engrs., Am. Inst. E.E. Ind. Democrat. Episcopalian. Mason. Clubs: Greenville Country; Biltmore Forest Country (N.C.); Merchants (New York). Home: 210 Pettigrue St. Office: 215 S. Main St., Greenville SC*

SISCO, FRANK THAYER, metallurgist, research dir.; b. Lawrence, Kan., Apr. 14, 1889; s. William Cook and Emma Louise (Thayer) S.; student U. Ill., 1908-11; m. Anneliese Gruenhaldt Rudorff, Nov. 5, 1932. Chemist, melting apprentice Ill. Steel Co., Chgo., 1912-15; chief chemist, asst. supt. Hess Steel Corp., Balt., 1916-21; engr. tests Am. Steel and Wire Co., Waukegan, Ill., 1922-23; chief metallurgist USAAF, Wright Field, Dayton, O., 1923-30; dir. alloys of iron research Engring. Found., N.Y.C., 1930-63; cons. metallurgist, 1963—; pres. Engring. Index, Inc., N.Y.C., 1957-62, dir., 1957—; mem. exec. com. engring. div. NRC, 1960-63. Bd. dirs. Engring. Societies Library, 1948-62, chmn., 1957-58. Sr. mem. Am. Inst. Mining and Metall. Engrs. (chmn. iron and steel div. 1940, sec. metals div. 1941-45; Conf. award 1947); life mem. Am. Soc. Metals (bd. dirs. 1929-30, chmn. classification com., documentation com. 1948-62; Distinguished Service award 1948, Certificate Appreciation 1962); mem. Am. Soc. Testing Materials, British Iron and Steel Inst., British Inst. Metals, Metal Sci. Club N.Y., Theta Delta Chi. Republican. Presbyn. Author: Technical Analysis of Steel, 1923; Manufacture of Electric Furnace Steel, 1925; Metallurgy in Aircraft Production, 1925; Constitution of Steel and Cast Iron, 1930; Alloys of Iron and Carbon, 1937; Modern Metallurgy for Engineers, 2d edit., 1948; also numerous tech. papers. Metall. editor 16 sci. monographs, 1930-63. Home: 320 E. 42d St., N.Y.C. 17. Office: 345 E. 47th St., N.Y.C. 17. Died Jan. 12, 1965.

SISSON, SEPTIMUS, comparative anatomist; b. Gateshead, Eng., Oct. 2, 1865; s. George and Mary (Arnott) S.; came to America, 1882; S.B., U. of Chicago, 1898; V.S., Ont. (Can.) Vet. Coll., 1891; Univ. of Berlin, 1905-06; (D.V.Sc., U. of Toronto, 1921); m. Katherine Oldham, Oct. 5, 1892. Prof. comparative anatomy, Ohio State University, Sept., 1901—. Author: A Text-Book of Veterinary Anatomy, 1910; A Veterinary Dissection Guide, Part I, 1911; The Anatomy of the Domestic Animals, 1914. Translator: Ellenberger, Baum und Dittrich's Anatomie der Tiere für Künstler, 1906. Prin. contribution to anatom. knowledge consists of first descriptions of natural form and topography of the plastic organs and viscera of the chief domestic animals as determined by fixation in situ by means of intravascular injection of formalin or other hardening fluid. Unitarian. Home: Columbus, O. Deceased.

SIZER, NELSON, phrenologist; b. Chester, Mass., May 27, 1812; s. Fletcher and Lydia (Bassett) S.; m. 2d, Sarah Remington, Mar. 12, 1843; 3 children. Lectr. in South and East, 1839-49; became examiner in phrenological cabinet of Orson Fowler and Samuel Wells, N.Y.C., 1849; editor Am. Phrenological Jour., 1859-63; pres. Am. Inst. Phrenology, 1866. Author: Heads and Faces, and How to Study Them, 1885; How to Study Strangers by Temperament, Face, and Head, 1895; Forty Years in Phrenology, 1882. Died Bklyn., Oct. 18, 1897.

SKIFTER, HECTOR RANDOLPH, corp. exec.; b. Austin, Minn., Mar. 4, 1901; s. Jens A. and Anna (Welken) S.; B.A., St. Olaf Coll., 1922, D.Sc., 1945; m. Naomi Jeannette Hansen, Dec. 26, 1929 (dec. 1961); 1 dau., Janet; m. 2d, Helene Boyd du Toit, Nov. 30, 1963. Chief engr. Western Radio Engring. Co., St. Paul, 1929-33; cons. engr. radio stas. WEAV, WEBC, KDAL, WMIN, KSTP, 1933-42; asso. dir. Airborne Instruments lab., 1942-45, pres., 1945-59; cons. to asst. sec. def. research and devel., 1957-60, asst. dir. def. research and engring. Dept. Def., Washington, 1959-60; pres. airborne instruments lab. div., v.p. corp. Cutler-Hammer, Inc., 1960—; chmn. bd. Research Analysis Corp., Washington; dir. Rabinow Engring. Co., Washington. Am. Research & Devel. Corp. Cons. Air Nav. Devel. Bd., 1949—; chmn. com. air nav. Research and Devel. Bd., 1950-55; sci. adv. com. Dept. Ordnance, U.S. Army, 1955—; mem. Nat. Def. Research Com., 1942-45; cons. Pres.'s Sci. Adv. Com., NASA. Trustee Nassau Hosp., Hofstra Coll., Hempstead, N.Y. Recipient Distinguished Outstanding Civilian Service award, 1964. Fellow I.R.E.; mem. Inst. Nav., Profl. Group Engring. Mgmt. (program chmn. N.Y. chpt. 1955-56). Clubs: Cosmos Wings, University (Washington). Home: 24 Bonnie Heights Rd., Manhasset, L.I., N.Y. Office: Airborne Instruments Lab., Deer Park, L.I., N.Y. Died July 25, 1964; buried Knolls Cemetery, Manhasset.

SKILLMAN, THOMAS JULIEN, civil engr.; b. Trenton, N.J., Nov. 6, 1876; s. Luther S. and Mary B. S.; C.E., Princeton, 1898; m. Louise E. Jenkinson, Oct. 26, 1904; children—Margaret B., Thomas J., Richard J., Charlotte L. Began as rodman Pa. R.R., Mar. 1, 1899, and continued with same rd. successively as transitman, 1902; asst. supervisor, 1902-05; supervisor, 1905-13; div. engr., N.Y., Phila. & Norfolk R.R., 1913-14, West Jersey & Seashore R.R., 1914-17, Pa. R.R., 1917-19; prin. asst. engr., Eastern Pa. Div., Pa. R.R., 1919-20; chief engr. maintenance of way, Northwestern Region, and later Western Region, Pa. R.R., Chicago, 1920-26; asst. chief engr. of constrn., Western Region, Pa. R.R., Chicago, 1926; chief engr. Long Island R.R., July 1926-Feb. 1927; chief engr. Pa. R.R., Phila., 1927-36, chief engr., consultant, Oct. 1, 1936—. Republican. Presbyn. Home: Ardmore, Pa. Died Sept. 24, 1939.

SKINNER, AARON NICHOLS, astronomer; b. Boston, Aug. 10, 1845; s. Benjamin Hill and Mercy (Burgess) S.; student Beloit Coll., 1867-68; spl. course in astronomy, U. of Chicago, 1867-70; m. Sarah Elizabeth Gibbs, Feb. 9, 1874. Asst. at Dearborn Obs., Chicago, 1867-70; asst. astronomer U.S. Naval Obs., Washington, 1870-98; prof. mathematics, U.S.N., 1898—; astronomer in charge of 9-inch Transit Circle, U.S. Naval Obs., 1893-1902; in charge 26-inch equatorial, 1902, 1903; div. of equatorials, 1903—. In 1894-95 determined places of 8,824 stars in zone 14 degrees to 18 degrees south declination as a contbn. to the great Star Catalogue of Astronomische Gesellschaft, from 23 degrees south declination to 80 degrees north declination. Discoverer of 4 variable stars; active participant in all the meridian circle work of Naval Obs., 1871—chief U.S. Naval Obs. expdn. to Sumatra to observe total solar eclipse of May 17, 1901; retired from active service with rank of comdr. U.S.N., 1907. Fellow A.A.A.S., Astronomische Gesellschaft, Astron. and

Astrophys. Soc. of America. Author: Washington Zone Observations; Katalog der Astronomische Gesellschaft Zone 14 degrees bis 18 degrees (Leipzig), 1908. Home: Washington, D.C. Died Aug. 14, 1919.

SKINNER, CHARLES EDWARD, elec. engr.; b. Redfield, Perry County, O., May 30, 1865; s. Thomas Peter and Harriet Newell (Brown) S.; M.E., Ohio State Univ., 1890, D.Eng., 1935; hon. Sc.D., Ohio Univ., 1927; m. Harriet Gladys McVay (B.Ph. and B. Ped., Ohio U., 1889), Apr. 25, 1893; children—Dorothy Harriet, Anna Florence, Charles Edward, Bertha Gladys, Thomas McVay. With Columbus Cash Register Co., June-Aug. 1890; with the Westinghouse Elec. & Mfg. Co., 1890-1933; successively, insulation testing and design, and iron and steel testing, to 1902; engr. insulation div. (phys., chem., elec. labs.), 1902-06; engr. research div., 1906-20; mgr. research dept., 1920-21; asst. dir. engring., 1922-33; elec. engr. Fort Monmouth Signal Lab., U.S. Army, Apr. 1943-45. Mem. Nat. Research Council (exec. com.), 1917-18, engring. div. since 1921, engring council, 1918-20; chmn. Am. Engring. Standards Com., 1925-27; mem. Federated Am. Eng. Soc. and Am. Engring. Council since 1923; chmn. Am. delegation Internat. Electrotech. Commn., Brussels, 1920, Geneva, 1922; del. same, London, 1924, Hague, 1925, Amsterdam, 1926, Bellagio, 1927; del. World's Power Conf., London, 1924; spl. rep. of Am. Inst. Elec. Engrs. at Conf. on Elec. Standards bet. Can., Gt. Britain and U.S., London, Mar. 1915; chmn. orgn. com. Internat. Standards Assn., Apr. 1926, rep. for further orgn., London, Sept. 1926, U.S. mem. council since 1931. Fellow Am. Inst. E.E. (v.p. and mem. exec. com. 1919-20, standards com. since 1910; pres. 1931-32); hon. mem. Am. Inst. Elec. Engrs., May 1945; mem. Am. Physical Soc., A.A.A.S., Am. Soc. Testing Materials, Am. Petroleum Inst., Am. Electrochem. Soc., Engring. Soc., Western Pa., Pittsburgh Acad. Science and Art, Pittsburgh Philos. Soc., Franklin Inst., Beta Theta Pi, Sigma Psi, Tau Beta Pi, Sigma Tau. Mem. John Fritz Medal Bd. of Award, 1931-34, Edison Medal Com., 1929-32. Awarded Lamme gold medal, Ohio State U., 1931. Presbyterian. Iwadare Foundation lecturer, Japan, 1934. Contbr. to tech. press and engring. socs. Home: Ziba's House, Route 1, Athens, O. Died May 12, 1950.

SKINNER, CHARLES EDWARD, biologist; b. Brainerd, Minn., Mar. 18, 1897; s. Howard Terrill and Ann (Norrish) S.; B.S., State Coll. of Wash., 1921, M.S., 1923; Ph.D., Rutgers U., 1925; m. Helen Bushnell, May 27, 1933; 1 dau., Helen Anne. Research asst., Rutgers U., 1923-25; postdoctorate research fellow, Rothamsted Station, Eng., 1925-26; instr., U. of Minn., 1926-34, asst. prof., 1934-42, asso. prof., 1942-48; chmn. dept. of bacteriology, State Coll. of Wash. since 1948. Mem. Soc. of Am. Bacteriologists (mem. council, 1946-48), Mycol. Soc. of Am., Phi Beta Pi, Sigma Xi, Gamma Alpha, Phi Kappa Phi, Sigma Alpha Omicron. Democrat. Episcopalian. Club: Kiwanis. Mem. com. med. and vet. mycopathology Internat. Assn. Microbiologists. Author: Henricis Molds Yeasts and Actinomycetes (with Emmons and Tsuchiya), 1947. Contbr. articles and book revs. in tech. bacteriol. jours. Home: 1913 Monroe St., Pullman, Wash. Died May 10, 1958; buried Pullman, Wash.

SKINNER, CHARLES WILBUR, irrigation specialist; b. Troy, O., July 12, 1864; s. Elias and Martha Jane (Orbison) S.; ed. country schs.; m. Elena M. Dougherty; June 18, 1895; children—Ella (Mrs. Philip Clark Hanford), Charles Robert, Edna Kate, Henry Vance. Began as market gardener, 1874; constructed rude system of overhead field irrigation lines in order to save crops during period of drought, 1896; worked on improvements and perfected systems first placed on sale, 1904; founder of Skinner Irrigation Co., Troy, O., 1904; established firm of C. W. Skinner & Co., Newfield, N.J., 1912. Republican. Presbyterian. Home: Newfield, N.J. Deceased.

SKINNER, CLARENCE AURELIUS, physicist; b. Loudoun Co., Va., Jan. 6, 1871; s. John Thomas and Susanne (Tinsman) S.; B.Sc., U. of Neb., 1893, grad. student and fellow in physics, 1893-96; U. of Berlin, 1896-99, Ph.D., 1899; m. Christabel Ditchburn, 1916; 1 son, John William. Demonstrator physics, 1899-1901, adj. prof., 1901-03, asst. prof., 1903-06, prof. and head dept. physics, 1906-19, U. of Neb. Chief, optical div. U.S. Bur. of Standards, 1919—. Baptist. Mem. Am. Phys. Soc. Home: Kensington MD

SKINNER, CLARENCE EDWARD, physician; b. New Haven, Conn., June 8, 1868; s. William Joseph and Cecelia Eliza (Hoggan) S.; ed. Russell's Mil. Acad.; M.D., Yale, 1891; (LL.D., Rutherford Coll., 1900); m. Edith Hart Hotchkiss, of New Haven, Dec. 31, 1896. Has practiced at New Haven since 1891; began experiments with dry hot air in treatment of diseases, 1897; X-rays in treatment of Cancer, 1900; prof. thermaerotherapy, New York Sch. of Physical Therapeutics, 1901; editor dept. of thermaerotherapy, Journal of Advanced Therapeutics, 1901-04; editor-in-chief Archives of Physiological Therapy, 1904-06; organized Newhope Pvt. Sanitarium, New Haven, 1900; organized Elm City Pvt. Hosp., New Haven, 1908, and 3 yrs. phys.-in-charge, sec. and dir.; organized, 1912, and since phys.-in-charge, pres. and treas., Doctor Skinner's Sanatorium, New Haven. Episcopalian. Associate fellow N.Y. Acad. Medicine; mem. A.M.A., Am. Electro-Therapeutic Assn. (sec., 1902-05), Am., Röutgen Ray Soc. (v.-p., 19053, Conn. State, and New Haven Co. Med. Socs., New Haven Hist. Society. Awarded Diplome d' Honneur by Internat. Congress of Physiol. Therapy, Liege, Belgium, 1905. Clubs: Quinnipiac, Economic, New Haven Yacht. Author: Therapeutics of Dry Hot Air, 1902. Extensive contbr. to med. jours. Office: 67 York Sq., New Haven, Conn.

SKINNER, FRANK WOODWARD, engineer; b. Brownville, N.Y., June 6, 1858; s. Horace and Harriet Emery S.; B.C.E., Cornell, 1879; m. Rachel Sumner, of Buffalo, N.Y., Sept. 7, 1881. Asst. engr. Pittsburgh Bridge Co., on reconstruction of Niagara R.R. suspension bridge; with Delaware Bridge Co.; bridge engr. N.J. Steel & Iron Co.; resident engr. Dominion Bridge Co., Montreal; engr. of bridges, St. Paul & N.P. R.R. Co., building large bridges across St. John's and Mississippi rivers; practicing as consulting and expert constructional engr. since 1886, Asso. editor The Engineering Record; since 1898, non-resident lecturer in charge of course in field engring., Coll. of Civil Engring., Cornell U.; lecturer on field engring., McGill U., Yale, Harvard, Mass. Inst. Tech., etc. Inventor of many important improvements in sheet piles, foundation construction, and reinforced concrete bldg. design and constrn. Mem. Am. Soc. C.E.; hon. mem. Conn. Civ. Engrs.' and Surveyors' Assn. Author: Types and Details of Bridge Construction, 1906. Contbr. to mags. and tech. publs. Home: Tompkinsville, S.I., N.Y. Office: 114 Liberty St., New York.

SKINNER, HALCYON, inventor; b. Mantua, O., Mar. 6, 1824; s. Joseph and Susan (Eggleston) S.; m. Eliza Pierce, 2 sons and 3 daus.; m. 2d, Adelaide Cropsey. Designed hand loom to weave figured carpet, 1850; constructed and patented power loom to weave tufted carpet, 1856; invented power loom to weave ingrain carpets; patented power loom for weaving moquette carpets, 1877. Died Nov. 28, 1900.

SKINNER, HENRY, entomologist; b. Philadelphia, Mar. 27, 1861; s. William S. and Sarah (Irvin) S.; B.S., U. of Pa., 1881, M.D., 1884; Sc.D., U. of Pittsburgh; m. Celia Angela Beck, July 14, 1886; children—Marion (Mrs. Harvey Wilson Madara), William Henry. Associated with Dr. William Goodell in practice of medicine, 1884-1900; devoted entire attention to entomology from 1900; state entomologist of Pennsylvania; prof. entomology, Pa. Hort. Soc.; in charge entomol. dept. and chmn. publn. com. and mem. council, Acad. Natural Sciences, Phila.; v.p. Acad. Natural Sciences of Phila.; mem. various scientific societies. Editor Entomological News, 1890-1911. Mem. com. on nomenclature, Internat. Zoöl. Congress. Home: Narberth, Pa. Died May 29, 1926.

SKINNER, JOHN HARRISON, animal husbandman; b. Romney, Ind., Mar. 10, 1874; s. William and Mary (Alexander) S.; B.S., in Agr., Purdue, 1897; D.Agr. (hon.), Mich. State Coll., Lansing, 1935; m. Mary Edna Throckmorton, Sept. 3, 1903; children—John H., Mary Elizabeth, William E., Robert E. Instr. animal husbandry, U. of Ill., 1901-02; chief of dept. animal husbandry, Purdue Univ., 1902-28, became dean Sch. of Agr., 1907, dir. agrl. expt. sta. and extension dept., 1928-39 (retired; now dean and dir. emeritus). Mem. Animal Nutrition Soc., Am. Genetic Assn., Soc. Promotion Agrl. Science, Ind. Livestock Breeders' Assn., Ind. Corn Growers' Assn., Sigma Xi, Alpha Zeta. Republican. Presbyterian. Mason. Address: West Lafayette, Ind. Died Apr. 28, 1942.

SKINNER, LEWIS BAILEY, engr.; b. Cincinnati, O., July 8, 1874; s. John Calvin and Mary Jane (Bailey) S.; student Case Sch. Applied Science, Cleveland, O.; B.S., Colo. Sch. of Mines, 1895; m. Olive Anne Webb, Aug. 23, 1898. Metallurgist Standard Smelting & Refining Co., Durango, Colo., 1895-96; research chemist Anaconda (Mont.) Copper Mining Co., 1896-98; supt. chemically pure depts. Western Chem. Mfg. Co., Denver, 1898-1900; supt. U.S. Reduction &Refining Co., Colorado Springs, Colo., 1900-03; gen. supt. Portland Mill, Colorado Springs, 1903; treas. and gen. supt. Western Chem. Mfg. Co., 1903-10, v.p. and gen. mgr., 1910-20, now pres. and dir.; mgr. research dept. Midwest Refining Co., 1920-21; now cons. chem. and metall. engr., Denver, Colo. Inventor Skinner roasting furnace, muriatic and salt cake furnace, reverberatory volatilization process for complex zinc ores, process and apparatus for treating phosphate rock. Trustee Colo. Sch. Mines, 1919-23 (ex-pres. bd.). Mem. Am. Inst. Mining and Metall. Engrs., Colo. Scientific Soc. (ex-pres), Am. Chem. Soc.; Colo. Chemists Assn. (pres. 1935). Republican. Conglist. Mason (32 deg., K.T., Shriner). Clubs: Teknik, Denver Country, Denver Motor. Home: 1705 Franklin St., Denver CO*

SKINNER, WILLIAM WOOLFORD, chemist; b. Baltimore, Md., Mar. 28, 1874; s. Levin Phillips and Mary (Willis) S.; B.S., Md. Agr. Coll., 1895, M.S., Columbian U., 1897, Sc.D. (hon.), U. of Md.; m. Georgia Mitchell, Aug. 24, 1899; 1 child, Jean. Chemist, U. of Md., 1895-99; asst. chemist Agr. Exp. Sta., U. of Ariz., 1899-1902; asso. chemist, U. of Ariz., 1902-04; asst. chemist Bur. of Chemistry, U.S. Dept. of Agr., 1904-14; chief Water & Beverage Lab., Bur. of Chemistry, 1914-21; asst. chief Bur. of Chemistry, 1921-27; asst. chief chem. and tech. res., Bur. of Chemistry and Soils, 1927-35, asst. chief, 1935-39; asso. chief Bur. of Agrl. Chemistry and Engring., 1939-42; chief Bur. of Agrl. and Indsl. Chem., 1942-44; director Nat. Tech. Advisory Inst., since 1944. Member and chairman Board of Regents, U. of Md., 1916-42; chmn. Md. State Board Agr., 1935-42. Fellow A.A.A.S.; mem. Am. Chem. Soc., Assn. Official Agrl. Chemists (pres.), Washington Chem. Soc. (pres.), Kappa Alpha, Alpha Chi Sigma, Sigma Xi. Mason. Club: Cosmos (Washington, D.C.). Editor: Book of Methods. Joint author: Food Sanitation and Health, Chemistry in Industry, numerous technical bulletins and papers. Home: 6 Knowles Av., Kensington, Md. Office: Union Trust Bldg., Washington

SLACK, CHARLES MORSE, physicist; b. Marietta, O., Dec. 4, 1901; s. William Henry and Enid (Warner) S.; B.S., U. of Ga., 1922; M.A., Columbia U., 1923, Ph.D., 1926; m. Evelyn Francis, May 31, 1926; children—Charles William, Winifred Evelyn, Warner Vincent. Instr. in physics, Columbia U., 1926-27; research physicist, lamp div. Westinghouse Electric Corp., Bloomfield, N.J., 1927-43, asst. dir. research, 1943-46, dir., 1946-49, tech. dir. atomic power div., Pitts., 1949-50, asst. mgr., 1950, dir. engring. and research, lamp div., 1953. Mem. A.A.A.S., Am. Inst. E.E., Am. Phys. Soc. Author papers on X-rays and electronics. Home: Upper Montclair NJ Died Dec. 1971.

SLADE, CHARLES BLOUNT, physician; b. Columbus, Ga., May 15, 1874; s. James J. and Leila (Bonner) S.; ed. U. of Ga., 1891-92; M.D., Bellevue Hosp. Med. Coll., 1896; m. Constance A. Thill, Sept. 12, 1901. Interne Bellevue Hosp., 1896-98; traveled in Mexico and Europe, 1898-1900; gen. practice in New York since 1900, except 18 mos., 1902-04, in Mexico organizing med. service of Mut. Life Ins. Co. of New York; chief of clinic and instr. in physical diagnosis, Univ. and Bellevue Hosp. Med. Coll., 1905-14; physician N.Y. City Dept. of Health, 1906-33; cons. physician to Municipal Sanatorium, N.Y. Pres. Soc. Alumni of Bellevue Hosp., 1920; mem. N.Y. State Med. Soc., etc. Officer Reserve Corps, U.S. Army, 1917-18. Author: Physical Examination and Diagnostic Anatomy, 1910; The Establishment and Conduct of a Tuberculosis Sanatorium, 1917; also numerous monographs on medicine and pub. health. Home-Office: Greenwood Park, Greenwood Lake, N.Y. Died Aug. 23, 1942.

SLATE, FREDERICK, physicist; b. London, Eng., Jan. 21, 1852; B.S., Poly. Inst. of Brooklyn, 1871; studied univs. of Berlin and Strassburg, 1877-79; LL.D., U. of Calif., 1925; m. Ella H. DeWolfe, 1884. Instr. chemistry, 1874-77, prof. physics, 1891-1918, U. of Calif. (emeritus). Author: Principles of Mechanics, 1900; Elementary Physics, 1902; Fundamental Equations of Dynamics, 1918. Home: Berkeley, Calif. Died Feb. 26, 1930.

SLATER, WILLIAM KERSHAW, scientist, writer; b. Oldham, Eng., Oct. 19, 1893; s. James and Mary Ann (Kershaw) S.; B.Sc. with 1st honours in Chemistry, Manchester U., 1914, D.Sc., 1926; D.Sc. (hon.), Belfast U., 1952; m. Hilda Whittenbury, Apr. 6, 1921; children—James Keith, Evelyn Whittenbury (Mrs. Kendall Cork), John Michael. Lectr. chemistry Manchester U., 1917-20; Beit Med. Research fellow Univ. Coll., London, 1923-28; dir. research Dartington Hall, Devon, Eng., 1928-42; sr. advisory officer Ministry Agr., 1943-49; sec. Agrl. Research Council, 1949-60; cons., lectr., writer, 1961-70. Member scientific CENTO; vice president of the United Nationa Conference Application Science and Tech. for Benefit Less Developed Areas. Chmn. projects com. Freedom from Hunger Campaign. Decorated knight Order British Empire. Fellow Royal Inst. Chemistry (pres. 1961-63), Royal Soc.; mem. Brit. Assn. (hon. sec. 1962-66). Author: Man Must Eat, 1963. Address: Pulborough Sussex England Died Apr. 19, 1970.

SLAUGHTER, DANELY PHILIP, surgeon; b. Paris, Ill., June 1, 1911; s. Albert W. and Mary Golden (Danely) S.; B.S., U. Ill., Urbana, 1932, M.D., Chgo., 1936; m. Mary Elizabeth Whitney, Jan. 7, 1938; children—John W., Mary Golden. Served internship at Research and Educational Hospitals, Chgo., 1935-36, resident internal medicine, 1937 resident gen. surgery, 1937-39, attending surgeon, dir. Tumor Clinic, 1942-70; asst. resident Meml. Hosp., N.Y.C., 1939, fellow Nat. Cancer Inst., 1940-41, resident surgery, 1941-42; practice medicine specializing in gen. surgery, oncology, Chgo., 1942-70; clin. prof. surgery Coll. Medicine U. Ill., 1952-70; chief dept. surgery, dir. Tumor Clinic St. Francis Hosp., Evanston, Ill., 1946-70; attending surgeon Presbyn-St. Lukes Hosp., Chgo., 1942-70; mem. cancer control com. NIH, 1950-55; mem. com. cancer therapy and diagnosis NRC, 1951-56; mem. clin. studies panel on adjuvant chemotherapy of cancer, mem. sub-com. on breast cancer protocol Nat. Cancer Inst., 1950-55. Recipient Distinguished Service award Ill. div. Am. Cancer Soc., 1964; Danely Philip Slaughter ann. lecture established in his honor, 1969. Diplomate Am. Bd. Surgery. Mem. A.M.A., Chgo. Med. Soc., Chgo. Surg. Soc., A.C.S. (past com. chmn.), Soc. Head and Neck Surgeons (past pres.), James Ewing Soc. (past pres.), Am., Central surg. assns., Internat. Soc. Surgeons, Soc. U. Surgeons, Am. Thyroid Assn., Pan Am. Med. Assn., Am. Cancer Soc. (past pres., vice chmn. bd. dirs. Ill. div.), Inst. Medicine, Sigma Xi, Alpha Omega Alpha, Nu Sigma Nu, Sigma Chi. Clubs: University (Chgo.), Westmoreland Country (Wilmette, Ill.). Contbr. articles med. jours., chpts. to books. Home: Northfield IL Died Apr. 11, 1970.

SLAWSON, CHESTER BAKER, mineralogist; b. Greenville, Mich., Apr. 12, 1898; s. William Warren and Kate (Carney) S.; B.S., U. of Mich., 1919, A.M., 1920, Ph.D., 1925; m. Ethel R. Fralick, June 14, 1926; children—William Francis, Mary Elizabeth. Instr., U. of Mich., 1920-21; with Am. Book Co., 1922-23; geologist Mich. Geol. Survey, 1924-25; instr., U. of Mich., 1925-31; asst. prof., 1931-39, acad. counselor, 1937-46; asso. prof. mineralogy, 1939-46, prof. mineralogy since 1946; consultant U.S. Bur. Mines, 1951—. Chmn. materials adv. bd. synthetic diamonds committee National Acad. Sci., 1956-59. Honorary vice president of Gemmological Assn. of Australia. Chmn. Advisory Committee on Industrial Diamonds, and Supervisor of Research, War Metallurgy Com., Nat. Research Council, 1943-44. Served as pvt., F.A.C.O.T.S., Camp Taylor, Ky., 1918. Trustee Cranbrook Inst. of Science, Bloomfield Hills, Mich. Independent Democrat. Conglist. Fellow Am. Mineral Soc., Geol. Soc. Amer.; mem. Phi Beta Kappa, Sigma Xi, Phi Kappa Phi. Author: Gems and Gem Materials (with E. H. Kraus), 5th ed., 1947. Contbr. tech. articles to Am. Mineralogist. Home: 2201 Winchell Dr., Ann Arbor, Mich. 48104. Died Mar. 12, 1964; buried Northport, Mich.

SLEPIAN, JOSEPH, research engr.; b. Boston, Mass., Feb. 11, 1891; s. Barnett and Anne (Bantick) S.; A.B., Harvard, 1911, A.M., 1912, Ph.D., 1913; grad. study Gottingen, Germany, 1913-14, Sorbonne, Paris, 1914; D. Engring., Case Inst. Tech., 1949; D.Sc., Leeds, England, 1955; m. Rose Grace Myerson, Nov. 11, 1918; children—Robert Myer, David. Instr. mathematics, Cornell U., 1914-15; engr. Westinghouse Electric & Mfg. Co., East Pittsburgh, 1918-56, former asso. dir. research; developed auto-valve lightning arrester to protect cross country transmission lines, generating stas. and substas., the de-ion principle of de-energizing destructive arc of interrupted electric circuit and control of huge currents in electric arcs with current in pencil lead; inventor of Ignitron mercury arc retifier. Mem. Nat. Academy of Sciences, Am. Inst. E.E., Am. Phys. Soc., Am. Electrochem. Soc., Am. Math. Soc., Phi Beta Kappa. John Scott medal, 1932, Westinghouse Order of Merit; Lamme, Edison medals by Am. Inst. E.E. Author: Conduction of Electricity in Gases; also numerous technical papers. Home: Pittsburgh PA Died Dec. 19, 1969.

SLICHTER, CHARLES SUMNER, (slik'ter), univ. dean; b. St. Paul, Minn., Apr. 16, 1864; s. Jacob B. and Catherine (Huber) S.; B.S., Northwestern U., 1885, M.S., 1887, Sc.D., 1916; m. Mary L. Byrne, Dec. 23, 1890; children—Sumner Huber, Louis Byrne, Allen McKinnon, Donald Charles. Instr., U. of Wis, 1886, asst. prof. mathematics, 1889, prof. applied mathematics since 1892, also dean of the Grad. Sch., emeritus, 1934. Cons. engr. U.S. Geol. Survey; engr. in charge of investigation of movements of underground waters, U.S. Reclamation Service. Mem. Wis. Acad. Sciences, Arts and Letters (pres. 1900-03), Am. Math. Soc., Math. Assn. America, Am. Geophys. Union, Sigma Xi, Phi Beta Kappa, Gamma Alpha. Author: Theoretical Investigations on Underground Waters, 1898; Motions of Underground Waters, 1902; Field Measurements of the Motions of Groundwaters, 1904; Science in a Tavern, 1938; also gen. math. textbooks and many U.S. Geol. Survey reports on underground waters published by U. S. Geol. Survey. Episcopalian. Contbr. to tech. jours. Address: R.F.D. 1, Madison 4, Wis. Died Oct. 4, 1946.

SLICHTER, WALTER IRVINE, electrician; b. St. Paul, Minn., May 7, 1873; s. Henry Clay and Lettie (Irvine) S.; Coll. City of New York, 2 yrs.; in Europe 2 yrs.; E.E., Columbia, 1896; m. Mabel Ostrom, 1903; 1 dau., Margaret. Entered employ Gen. Electric Co., Schenectady, 1896; asst. to Dr. Charles Proteus Steinmetz, 1897-1904; mem. ry. dept. of co., 1904-09, and asst. to v.p. and chief engr. and mem. staff consulting engrs., 1909-10; prof. elec. engring. and head dept., Columbia U., 1910-41, professor emeritus since 1941. Republican. Episcopalian. Fellow Am. Inst. Elec. Engrs. (v.p. 1922-24; treas. since 1930); fellow Am. Soc. Mech. Engrs., Engring. Foundation (chmn. engring. library bd.), N.Y. Acad. Science, Am. Assn. Advancement of Sciences; member Society for Promotion of Engineering Education, Sigma Xi, Theta Delta Chi and Tau Beta Pi fraternities, etc. Club: Columbia University (New York). Author: Principles Underlying the Design of Electrical Machinery, 1926; also writer of technical articles read before engineering societies. Associate editor American Handbook of Elec. Engring., Am. Pocketbook of Mining Engring., Internat. Ency. Civilian dir. U.S. Air Service Sch. for Radio Officers, Columbia U., 1917-18. Address: care Dept. Electrical Engineering, Columbia Univ., Morningside Heights, New York 27 NY

SLIFER, HIRAM JOSEPH, civil engr.; b. Colmar, Pa., Oct. 12, 1857; s. John and Lydia (Huttel) S.; grad. in course of mining and civ. engring., Polytechnic Coll. of Pa., 1876; m. Mary A. Beatty, Oct. 11, 1882. Engaged as rodman, leveler, and transitman, Mexican Nat. Constrn. Co., 1879-82; asst. engr. Phila. div. Pa. R.R., 1882-91; prin. asst. engr. Milwaukee, West Shore & Western Ry., 1891-93; div. engr. Ashland div., C.&N.W. Ry., at Kaukauna, Wis., 1893-97; successively div. engr., engr. of 2d track in Iowa, and supt. Ia. div., same rd., 1897-1902; gen. supt. eastern dist., C.,R.I.&P. R.R., 1902-03, central dist., 1903-05; steam ry. expert and business mgr. constrn. dept., J. G. White & Co., New York, 1905-07; gen. mgr. Panama R.R. & S.S. Lines, at Colon, Panama, 1907-09; gen. mgr. C.G.W. Ry., 1909-12. Mason. Commd. lt. col. 21st Engrs. and with A.E.F. in France. Home: Chicago, Ill. Died Feb. 3, 1919.

SLIPHER, VESTO MELVIN, astronomer; b. on farm, Clinton County, Ind., Nov. 11, 1875; s. David Clark and Hannah (App) S.; A.B., Ind. U., 1901; A.M., 1903, Ph.D., 1909, LL.D., 1929; hon. Sc.D., U. of Ariz., 1923, U. of Toronto, Canada, 1935; m. Emma Rosalie Munger, Jan. 1, 1904; children—Marcia Frances, David Clark. Astromer, Lowell Obs., 1901-15, asst. dir., 1915-17, dir. 1917-52; in charge Lowell solar eclipse expdn. to Syracuse, Kan., June 1918, and to Ensenada, Mexico, 1923. Awarded the Lalande prize and gold medal, Paris Acad. Sciences, 1919; Henry Draper gold medal of Nat. Acad. Sciences for discoveries in astron. physics, 1932; gold medal of Royal Astron. Soc., 1933, George Darwin lecturer, same society, 1933; awarded the Catherine Wolfe Bruce gold by Astronomical Soc. of the Pacific, 1935. Mem. Nat. Acad. of Sciences, Am. Philos. Soc.; asso. Royal Astron. Soc. (London); fellow Am. Acad. Arts and Sciences, A.A.A.S. (v.p. 1933); mem. Internat. Astron. Union, Am. Astron. Soc. (v.p. 1931), Societe Astronomique de France, Phi Beta Kappa, Sigma Xi fraternities. Extensive investigations in astronomical spectroscopy; studies on the rotations and atmosphere of the planets; directed search that led to finding Lowell's trans-Neptunian planet—the new planet, Pluto. Discovered the rapid rotation and enormous space velocities of the nebulae, which furnished the observational basis for the expansion of the universe theory, that has grown out of Einstein's theory; high velocities of the star clusters; the cosmic radiations of the night sky; etc. Contributed numerous papers to astronom. publs. on the planets, nebulae, clusters, comets, stars and aurora. Address: Flagstaff AZDied Nov. 8, 1969.*

SLOAN, ALFRED PRITCHARD, JR., hon. chmn. bd. Gen. Motors Corp.; b. New Haven, May 23, 1875; s. Alfred Pritchard and Katherine (Mead) S.; B. Sc., Mass. Inst. Tech., 1895; LL.D., Princeton, 1947, Syracuse U., 1955, Wabash Coll., Columbia, Dartmouth, 1957, Williams Coll., U. Notre Dame, 1958, U. Pitts., 1959; D.C.S., N.Y.U.; D.Sc., Duke, Colgate U., 1962; L.H.D., Oberlin Coll., 1958; m. Irene Jackson. Pres., gen. mgr. Hyatt Roller Bearing Co., 15 yrs.; pres. United Motors Corp. 3 yrs.; pres. Gen. Motors Corp. 14 yrs., chmn. bd., 1937-56, now hon. chmn. bd. Trustee Sloan-Kettering Inst. for Cancer Research, So. Research Inst.; gov. Menninger Found.; chmn. Alfred P. Sloan Found. Clubs: University, Union, Metropolitan, Knickerbocker (N.Y.C.); Turf and Field (Belmont Park, L.I.). Author: My Years with General Motors, 1964. Home: 820 Fifth Av., N.Y.C. Office: 45 Rockefeller Plaza, N.Y.C. 20. Died Feb. 17, 1966; buried St. John's Meml. Cemetery, Cold Spring Harbor, N.Y.

SLOANE, T(HOMAS) O'CONOR, scientific expert; b. New York, Nov. 24, 1851; s. Christian S. and Eliza M. (O'Conor) S.; A.B., St. Francis Xavier Coll., 1869, A.M., 1873, LL.D., 1912; E.M., Columbia, 1872, Ph.D., 1876; m. Isabel X. Mitchel, Sept. 18, 1877; 1 son, T(homas) O'Conor; m. 2d, Alice M. Eyre, of Dublin, Ireland, Apr. 16, 1884; children—Charles O'Conor, John Eyre, Alice Mary. Prof. natural sciences, Seton Hall Coll., S. Orange, N.J., 1888-89; has given many scientific lectures and acted as expert in many lawsuits about patents. Invented Self-Recording Photometer, first instrument that ever recorded mechanically on an index card the illuminating power of gas. Described in 1877 new process for determining sulphur in illuminating gas, which was found on exhaustive trial to be scientifically accurate. Has been on editorial staff of Plumber and Sanitary Engineer, Scientific American, Youth's Companion, Everyday Engring., Practical Electrics, and mng. editor The Experimenter; editor Amazing Stories. Mem. adv. bd. N.Y. Electrical Sch. Mem. State Bd. Edn., N.J., 1905-11. Author: Home Experiments in Science, 1888; Rubber Hand Stamps and the Manipulation of India Rubber, 1891; Arithmetic of Electricity, 1891; Electricity Simplified, 1891; Standard Electrical Dictionary, 1892; Electric Toy Making for Amateurs, 1892; How to Become a Successful Electrician, 1894; Liquid Air and the Liquefaction of Gases, 1899; The Electrician's Handy Book, 1905; Elementary Electrical Calculations, 1909; Motion Picture Projection, 1921; Rapid Arithmetic, 1922. Compiler: Facts Worth Knowing, 1890. Translator: Electric Light (Alglave & Boulard), 1884; Jörgensen's Life of St. Francis of Assisi. Home: South Orange, N.J. Died Aug. 7, 1940.

SLOCUM, FREDERICK, (slo'kum), astronomer; b. Fairhaven, Mass., Feb. 6, 1873; s. Frederick and Lydia Ann (Jones) S.; A.B., Brown U., 1895, A.M., 1896, Ph.D., 1898, Sc.D., 1938; m. Carrie E. Tripp, June 29, 1899 (died 1942). Began as instructor in mathematics, 1895-1900, assistant professor astronomy, 1900-09, and acting director Ladd Observatory, 1904-05, Brown University; at Royal Astrophysical Observatory, Potsdam, Germany, 1908-09; lecturer on mathematics, New York U., summer of 1908; research asst., summer of 1907; instr. in astrophysics, 1909-11, asst. prof. astronomy, 1911-14, Yerkes Obs., U. of Chicago; prof. astronomy and dir. Van Vleck Obs., Wesleyan U., Conn., 1914-18 and since 1920; prof. nautical science, Brown U., 1918-20. Instr. navigation for U.S. Shipping Bd., 1917-18. Research asso. Carnegie Inst., Washington, 1920; prof. astronomy, Columbia U., summer 1923. Conglist. (Unitarian). Fellow Royal Astron. Soc., A.A.A.S. (ex-v.p. sect. D.); mem. Am. Acad. Arts and Sciences, Astronomische Gesellschaft, Société Astronomique de France, Am. Astron. Soc. (ex-v.p.), Internat. Astron. Union, Nat. Research Council (1934-37), Phi Beta Kappa, Sigma Xi, Phi Delta Theta. Author: Stellar Parallaxes From Photographs Made With the 20-inch Refractor of Van Vleck Observatory (with C. L. Stearns and B. W. Sitterly), 1938. Contbr. to Astrophysical Journal and other publs., chiefly as to observations on the sun and to determination of stellar distances. Home: 74 Wyllys Av., Middletown, Conn. Died Dec. 4, 1944.

SLOCUM, SAMUEL, inventor, mfr.; b. Cononicut Island, Jamestown Twp., Newport County, R.I. Mar. 4, 1792; s. Peleg and Anne (Dyer) S.; m. Susan Stanton, 1817, 3 surviving children. Perfected, patented machine to make wrought-iron nails, London, 1835; invented, patented machine for making pins with solid heads, 1835; established pin mfg. firm Slocum & Jillson, Poughkeepsie, N.Y., by 1840, operated firm till 1846; patented machine for sticking pins on paper, 1841, developed in partnership with John Ireland House, 1841, sold his interest to Am. Pin. Co., 1846; received extension and reissue of his patented machine for sticking pins on paper, 1855. Died Pawtucket, R.I., Jan. 26, 1861.

SLOCUM, STEPHEN ELMER, cons. engineer; b. Glenville, N.Y., June 5, 1875; s. William Warren and Mary E. (Conde) S.; B.E., Union Coll., N.Y., 1897; scholar and fellow, Clark U., 1897-1900. Ph.D. in mathematics and physics, 1900; m. Anna Jeannette Ware, June 25, 1902; children—Dorothy Jeannette, Walter Ware, Marianna Conde, Stephen Elmer. Instr. in civ. engring., U. of Cincinnati, 1900-01, in applied mathematics, 1901-04, asst. prof., 1904-05; asst. prof. mathematics, U. of Ill., 1905-06; prof. applied mathematics, U. of Cincinnati, 1906-20; cons. engr., Phila. and Ardmore, Pa., since 1920; specialist in marine propulsion and in noise and vibration engring. Former mem. Am. Soc. C.E.; mem. Am. Soc. Naval Engrs. (hon. life), S.R. Awarded gold medal by Am. Soc. Naval Engineers, 1927, for original research in modern hydrodynamics. Presbyn. elder since 1905. Author: Strength of Materials, 1906, 11; Theory and Practice of Mechanics, 1913; Resistance of Materials, 1914; Hydraulics, 1915; Beggars of the Sea (hist. novel), 1928; Noise and Vibration Engineering, 1931; also many monographs and articles in scientific, popular and Marine publs. Address: 244 E. Montgomery Av., Ardmore PA

SLYE, MAUD, pathologist; b. Mpls., Feb. 8, 1879; d. James Alvin and Florence Alden (Wheeler) Slyde; A.B., Brown U., 1899, Sc.D., 1937; post-grad. work U. Chgo., fellow, 1908-11. Prof. psychology and pedagogy R.I. State Normal Sch., 1899-1905; mem. staff Sprague Meml. Inst., Chgo., 1911-43; instr. pathology U. Chgo., 1919-22, asst. prof., 1922-26, asso. prof., 1926-45, prof. emeritus, 1945—. Research on mice many years to determine the nature of cancer, the relation of heredity to cancer, the laws governing malignancy and its localization, and age at which it will occur. Recipient gold medal A.M.A., 1914; Rickets prize, 1915; gold medal North Am. Radiol. Soc., 1922. Mem. Assn. Cancer Research (past v.p.), Chicago Inst. Medicine, A.A.A.S., A.M.A., Am. Assn. Sci. Workers, N.Y., Ill. acads. sci.; hon. mem. Seattle Acad. of Surgery, So. Cal. Med. Soc., Phi Beta Kappa, Sigma Xi, Sigma Delta Epsilon, Delta Kappa Gamma. Author: 42 brochures on cancer; also Songs and Solaces (poems), 1934; I in the Wind (poems), 1936. Home: 5822 Drexel Av., Chgo. Died Sept. 17, 1954; buried Oak Woods Cemetery, Chgo.

SMADEL, JOSEPH EDWIN, research physician; born Vincennes, Ind., Jan. 10, 1907; s. Joseph William and Clara (Green) S.; A.B., U. of Pa., 1928; M.D., Washington U., 1931; M.S. (hon.), Yale, 1950; D.Sc., Jefferson Med. Coll., 1955, U. Md., 1962; m. Elisabeth Moore, July 1, 1936. Intern Barnes Hosp., St. Louis, 1932-33; asst. pathology Washington U., 1931-32, asst. medicine, 1933-34; staff asst. Hosp. of Rockefeller Inst. for Med. Research, 1934-36, asso., 1936-42, asso. mem., 1942-46 (leave of absence for mil. duty, 1942-46); staff Army Med. Service Grad. Sch., Washington, 1946-56, chief, dept. virus and rickettsial diseases, 1946-56, tech. director research (communicable and parasitic diseases) 1950-56; vis. lectr. virology U. Md., 1950-54; visiting prof. rickettsial diseases U. Pa. Sch. Med., 1950-56;

asso. dir. Nat. Insts. Health, Bethesda, Md., 1956-60, chief laboratory of virology and rickettsiology Division of Biologics Standards, 1960—. Entered M.C., A.U.S. as captain, 1942; discharged as lt. colonel, 1946. Awarded United States of America Typhus Commn. medal, 1946, Gordon Wilson medal, 1949; Exceptional Civilian Service award, 1950; Howard Taylor Ricketts medal, 1953; Alumni citation Washington University, 1956; James D. Bruce Memorial award and Stitt award, 1959; Albert Lasker award for clinical research, 1962. Dir. commn. immunization, Armed Forces Epidemiological Board, 1947-52, dir. Commn. Hemorrhagic Fever, 1952-54, director Commission Rickettsial Diseases, 1958-60; mem. virus and rickettsial study sect. USPHS, 1946-51. Mem. com. on virus research and epidemiology and research fellowship in virology Nat. Found. Infantile Paralysis, 1948—. Fellow Am. Public Health Assn., A.A.A.S., N.Y. Acad. Sci.; member American Epidemiol. Soc., Am. Soc. Exptl. Pathology, Am. Soc. Clin. Investigation, Am. Soc. Pathologists and Bacteriologists, Soc. Exptl. Biol. and Medicine, Soc. Am. Bacteriologists, Harvey Soc., Am. Assn. Immunologists (president 1958), New York Academy of Medicine, American Association of Physicians, National Academy Science, Am. Soc. Tropical Medicine and Hygiene (mem. council 1957-61). Home: 1440 Hemlock St. N.W., Washington 20012. Office: Nat. Insts. Health, Bethesda, Md. Died July 21, 1963; buried Vincennes, Ind.

SMALL, JOHN KUNKEL, botanist; b. Harrisburg, Pa., Jan. 31, 1869; s. George H. and Catharine K. S.; A.B., Franklin and Marshall Coll., 1892, Sc.D., 1912; Ph.D., Columbia Univ., 1895; m. Elizabeth Wheeler, 1896; children—George Kunkel, Kathryn Wheeler, Elizabeth, John Wheeler. Curator, Herbarium of Columbia U., 1895-99; spl. agt. Ga. Geol. Survey, 1895; curator, Herbarium of New York Bot. Garden, 1898-1906, head curator, 1906-32, chief research asso. and curator, 1932—. Author: A Monograph of the North American Species of the Genus Polygonum, 1895; Flora of the Southeastern States, 1903, 2d edition, 1913; Flora of Miami, 1913; Flora of Lancaster County, 1913; Florida Trees, 1913; Flora of the Florida Keys, 1913; Shrubs of Florida, 1913; Ferns of Tropical Florida, 1918; Ferns of Royal Palm Hammock, 1918; From Eden to Sahara—Florida's Tragedy, 1929; Ferns of Florida, 1932; Manual of Southeastern Flora, 1932; Ferns of Vicinity of New York (illustrated), 1935. Interested in bot. exploration of southeastern U.S., the interpretation and classification of its flora and its phytogeography, with special reference to its native palms, irises, flowering epiphytes, cacti, and ferns. Home: New York, N.Y. Died Jan. 20, 1938.

SMALLWOOD, WILLIAM MARTIN, coll. prof.; b. Warsaw, N.Y., Apr. 30, 1873; s. William Waltrous and Eloise (Martin) S.; A.B., Syracuse U., 1896, A.M., 1897; Ph.D., Harvard Univ., 1902; honorary Sc.D., Syracuse University, 1943; m. Mabel Sarah Coon, Sept. 6, 1899. Instr. biology, Syracuse U., 1896-98; prof. biology and geology, Allegheny (Pa.) College, 1898-1902; asst. prof. zoölogy, Syracuse Univ., 1903-07, prof. comparative anatomy, 1907, and head department zoölogy, 1921-43, professor emeritus comparative anatomy since 1943. Fellow A.A.A.S., mem. N.Y. State Science Teachers' Assn. (pres., 1909), Am. Zoöl. Soc., Phi Beta Kappa, Sigma Xi, Phi Kappa Psi. Republican. Methodist. Author: Syllabus of Lectures on Animal Biology, 1908; Textbook on Biology, 1913, 6th edit., 1930; Practical Biology, 1916; Biology for High Schools, 1920; Man—the Animal, 1921, 27; The New Biology, 1924; New General Biology, 1929; New Biology, 1934; Natural History and the American Mind (with Mabel C. Smallwood), 1941. Contbr. to scientific jours. Awarded the Arents Medal, June 1939. Home: 525 Euclid Ave., Syracuse 10, N.Y. Died Nov. 20, 1949.

SMART, JOHN STUART, JR., metall. engr.; b. Des Moines, Mar. 24, 1913; s. John Stuart and Blanche (Senft) S.; B.S. in Chem. Engring., U. Mich., 1934; m. Lily Hindley, Mar. 6, 1937; children—John S., William F., Susan L. Metallurgist, Ford Motor Co., 1934-35, Detroit Lubricator Co., 1935-36; with Am. Smelting & Refining Co., N.Y.C., 1936-69, asst. to v.p., dir. research, 1953-56, asst. dir. research, 1956-58, gen. sales mgr., 1958-69; president Asarco Intermetallics, Incorporated. Mem. bd. United Engring. Trustees, 1962-69, treas., 1965-69; bd. Engring. Found., 1962-69. Recipient Mathewson medal Am. Inst. Mining and Metall Engrs., 1948. Mem. Internat. Lead-Zinc Research Organization, Inc. (vice pres. 1966-69), Am. Inst. Mining and Metall. and Petroleum Engrs. (v.p. 1961-62; pres. Metall. Soc. 1961), Am. Soc. Metals, Research Soc. Am., Metall. Soc. (pres. 1961), Lead Industries Assn. (v.p. 1962-63), Am. Zinc Inst. (dir. 1960-69, v.p. 1965), Mining and Metall. Soc. Am., Delta Upsilon. Episcopalian. Clubs: Bankers Am., Mining (N.Y.C.). Home: Westfield NJ Died Dec. 7, 1969.

SMART, RICHARD ADDISON, mech. eng'r; b. Fort Wayne, Ind., Nov. 18, 1872; s. Hon. James H. and Mary H. (Swan) S.; ed. pub. schs., Indianapolis; grad. Purdue Univ., M.E., 1892; m. La Fayette, Ind., June 12, 1901, Elsie Douglas Moore. Asso. prof. experimental eng'ring, Purdue Univ., 1899-1901; experimental eng'r for B. F. Sturtevant Co., Boston, 1901-3; now asst. to supt. of production, Westinghouse Electric & Mfg. Co., Pittsburg. Mem. Am. Soc. Mech. Eng'rs; asso. mem. Am. Ry. Master Mechanics' Assn. Author: Handbook of Engineering Laboratory Practice, 1898 W9. Address: Westinghouse Electric & Mfg. Co., East Pittsburg PA

SMILLIE, THOMAS W., photographer; b. Edinburgh, Scotland, Apr. 14, 1843; s. James and Elizabeth (Dhu) S.; ed. pvt. schs. and acads. Edinburgh and Washington; 3 yrs.' lab. course in chemistry. Hon. custodian and chief photographer U.S. Nat. Museum. Inventor of process of photographing on wood for engraving and other photographic processes and apparatus. Mem. jury of awards, Buffalo Expn. Fellow Royal Photog. Soc.; mem. A.A.A.S., Philos. Soc. Washington, Am. Acad. Polit. and Social Science; hon. mem. Académie Parisienne du Inventions; diploma Académie Nationale de Agricole. Home: 1808 R St. Office: U.S. Nat. Mus., Washington.

SMITH, ALBERT WILLIAM, chemist; b. Newark, O., Oct. 4, 1862; s. George H. and Mary (Sanborn) S.; Ph.C., U. of Mich., 1885; B.S., Case Sch. Applied Science, Cleveland, 1887; Ph.D., U. of Zürich, 1891; m. Mary Wilkinson, of Cleveland, June 5, 1890. Prof. metallurgy and chemistry, Case School Applied Science, 1891-1907, prof. metallurgy and head of dept. metall. engring., 1907-11, prof. chemistry and head of dept., 1911-27. Fellow A.A.A.S., Chem. Soc. London; mem. Am. Chem. Soc. (councillor), Franklin Inst., Am. Inst. Mining and Metall. Engrs., Am. Electrochem. Soc., Soc. Promotion Engring. Edn., Am. Inst. Chem. Engrs., Soc. Chem. Industry, French Soc. Industrial Chemists, Deutsche Chemische Gesellschaft, Phi Chi, Tau Beta Psi, Sigma Xi, Alpha Chi Zeta. Presbyterian. Clubs: University, Union. Contbr. to tech. papers. Home: Cleveland, O. Died Mar. 4, 1927.

SMITH, ALBERT WILLIAM, engineer, educator; b. Westmoreland, Oneida County, N.Y., Aug. 30, 1856; s. William and Caroline Georgiana (Strong) S.; B.M.E., Cornell, 1878, M.M.E., 1886; m. Ruby Green Bell, Aug. 16, 1905; children—Alpheus, Dorothy (Mrs. Harold Raynolds), Ruth Althea (Mrs. Robert P. Ludlum). Asst. prof. mech. engring., Sibley Coll., Cornell U., 1887-91; prof. machine design, U. of Wis., 1891-92; prof. mech. engring., Stanford U., 1892-1904; dir. Sibley Coll., Cornell U., 1904-15, dean, 1915-21, and acting pres. Cornell U., 1920-21 (retired). Mem. Am. Soc. M.E. Author: Elementary Machine Design, 1895; Materials of Machines, 1902, 14; John Edson Sweet, A Biography, 1923; A Biography of Walter Craig Kerr, 1927; A Biography of Ezra Cornell, 1934; Poems, 1934; A Spring Time Odyssey on the Shores of Southern Seas, 1939; Facing Life, 1939. Editor: The Bells of Cornell, 1930; Poems of Cornell, 1941. Home: 13 East Av., Ithaca, N.Y. Died Aug. 16, 1942.

SMITH, ALEXANDER, chemist; b. Edinburgh, Scotland, Sept. 11, 1865; s. Alexander W. and Isabella (Carter) S.; B.Sc., U. of Edinburgh, 1886; Ph.D., U. of Münich, 1889; LL.D., U. of Edinburgh, Scotland, 1919; m. Sara Bowles, Feb. 16, 1905. Asst. in chemistry, U. of Edinburgh, 1889-90; prof. chemistry and mineralogy, Wabash Coll., 1890-94; asst. prof. chemistry, 1894-98, asso. prof., 1898-1903, prof. and dir. of gen. and physical chemistry, 1903-11, dean Jr. Colls., 1900-11, U. of Chicago; prof. and head of dept. chemistry, Columbia U., N.Y., 1911-July 1, 1921. Author: Lassar-Cohn Laboratory Manual of Organic Chemistry (translated), 1895; Laboratory Outline of General Chemistry, 1899 (transl. into German, Russian, Italian, Portuguese); The Teaching of Chemistry and Physics (with E. H. Hall), 1902; Introduction to General Inorganic Chemistry, 1906 (transl. into German, Russian, Italian, Portuguese); General Chemistry for Colleges, 1908; Text-Book of Elementary Chemistry, 1914; Intermediate Chemistry, 1919. Home: Edinburgh, Scotland. Died Sept. 9, 1922.

SMITH, ALLEN S(TRATTON), chem. engr.; b. Oglesby, Ill., Feb. 10, 1906; s. Birney Merencie and May Belle (Stratton) S.; B.S., U. Minn., 1926, Ch.E., 1935; M.S., U. Louisville, 1931; Ph.D., U. Mich., 1940; m. Wilma James Davis, Jan. 9, 1928; children—Phyllis Stratton, Althea Maye. With Atmospheric Nitrogen Corp., Syracuse, N.Y., 1927-31, chem. engr. U.S. Bur. of Mines, Amarillo, Tex., 1931-36, asso. phys. chemist U. Mich., 1936-38, teaching fellow; Blaw-Knox div. Blaw-Knox Co., Pitts., 1938-46, research dir. U. Notre Dame, prof. chem. engring., cons. chem. engr. since 1946. Mem. Am. Chem. Soc. (chmn. St. Joseph Valley Sect. 1948-49), Am. Inst. Chem. Engr., Am. Assn. Univ. Profs., Sigma Xi, Phi Lambda Upsilon. Republican. Methodist. Club: Engineers (South Bend). Contbr. articles on separation processes (patented). Home: 1215 Woodlawn Blvd., South Bend, Ind. 46616. Office: U. of Notre Dame, Dept. Chemical Engring., Notre Dame, Ind. Died July 10, 1966; buried Highland Cemetery, South Bend, Ind.

SMITH, ANNIE MORRILL, botanist, genealogist; b. Brooklyn, Feb. 13, 1856; d. Henry Edwin (M.D.) and Cynthia (Langdon) Morrill; ed. Packer Collegiate Inst., Brooklyn; m. Hugh M. Smith, M.D., of Cayuga Co., N.Y., June 9, 1880 (died, 1897). Propr., 1899—, sole editor, 1900-10, The Bryologist, a bi-monthly jour. devoted to study of N. Am. mosses, hepatics and lichens. Member Brooklyn Inst. of Arts and Sciences, Sullivant Moss Soc., Brooklyn Botanic Garden, D.A.R.; fellow A.A.A.S. Conglist. Club: Bronxville Colony N.E. Women. Now devoting time to genealogy. Author: Morrill Kindred in America (2 vols.); Ancestors of Henry Montgomery Smith and Catherine Forshee. Home: 64 Sagamore Rd., Bronxville, N.Y.

SMITH, ARCHIBALD CARY, naval architect; b. New York, N.Y., Sept. 4, 1837; s. Rev. E. Dunlap and Jane B. (Cary) S.; ed. Univ. Grammar Sch., New York. Learned boat building trade under Robert Fish; built, 1860, the "Comet," which was champion for several yrs. Studied marine painting under Maurice F. H. de Haas, and painted pictures of many noted yachts. Built the Vindex, an iron yacht of novel design, which attracted much attention; abandoned painting and has since been engaged in designing and altering yachts and other boats, including: Schooners—Intrepid, Norma, Fortuna, Whim, Iroquois, Yampa, Lasca, Ariel, Oriole, Harbinger, Katrina, Elsemarie, Amorita, Carlotta, Helene, Vigil, Uncas, Clorita, Tekla, Laurus, Winona; sloops and yawls—Vindex, Madcap, Mischief (defended America's cup, 1887), Indolent, Meteor, Gorilla, Banshee, Cinderella, Montecito, Katona, Julnar, Polly, Vela, Sapho, Edith, Rover, Sakana, Priscilla, Myeera; steamboats—Richard Peck, City of Lowell, Chester W. Chapin, Refuge, Free Lance, pilot-boat New York, Espadon. Died 1911.

SMITH, CHARLES EDWARD, univ. dean; b. St. Joseph, Mo., Sept. 7, 1904; s. Charles Madison and Mabel Ellen (Kates) S.; student Sacramento Jr. Coll., 1923-25; A.B., Stanford, 1927, M.D., 1931; D.P.H., U. Toronto, 1934; m. Elizabeth Laidlaw, June 14, 1930; children—Edward Laidlaw, Charles Laidlaw. House officer, Alameda County Highland Hospital, 1931-32; instructor department pub. health and preventive medicine, Stanford U. Sch. Medicine, 1932-34, asst. prof., 1934-37, asso. prof., 1937-42, prof., 1942-49, prof., chmn. dept. U. Cal. Sch. Pub. Health since 1949; dean since 1951; spl. cons. to Surgeon Gen. USPHS, 1946-56, cons. communicable disease center USPHS, 1952-54; fellow internat. health div., Rockefeller Found., 1933-34; asso. Rockefeller Found. in Study of Teaching of Preventive Medicine and Pub. Health in N.Am. and Europe, 1936-37. Mem. Cal. State Bd. Health, 1940— (pres. 1944-64); cons. Surgeon Gen. 6th U.S. Army, Letterman Gen. Hosp., to sec. of war for epidemic diseases, 1941-46. Cons. to Sec. of War, then Sec. of Army, 1947-55; now cons. Surgeon Gen. Army, hon. cons. Surgeon Gen. Navy, nat. cons. Surgeon Gen. Air Force; dir. Armed Forces Epidemiological Bd. environmental hygiene commn., 1954-55, mem. commn. acute respiratory disease, member of central board. Bd. dirs. Florence Crittenton Home, San Francisco. Recipient Bronfman prize Am. Pub. Health Assn. Mem. A.M.A., Am. Pub. Health Assn. (past mem. exec. bd., chmn. com. profl. edn., mem. tech. devel. bd.), Nat. Adv. Health Council, Nat. Commn. Community Health Services, San Francisco Social Hygiene and Health Assn. (pres.), Am. Epidemiological Soc., Soc. Am. Bacteriologists, Am. Fedn. Clin. Research, Phi Beta Kappa, Sigma Xi, Alpha Omega Alpha, Alpha Kappa Kappa, Theta Chi. Mem. editorial bd. California Medicine. Contributor to tech. jours. Home: 12 W. Clay Park, San Francisco 21. Office: University of California School of Public Health, Berkeley 4, Cal. Died Apr. 1967.

SMITH, CHARLES GROVER, physicist; born Waco, Tex., Oct. 27, 1888; s. Sam Houston and Bell (McGaughy) S.; A.B., U. of Tex., 1911; Ph.D. in physics, Harvard, 1936; m. Aurelia Mayer Vick, Sept. 29, 1919; children—William Vick, Mary Elizabeth, Helen Aurelia. Research engr. Am.-Radio & Research Corp., Medford, Mass., 1919-22; research engr. Raytheon Mfg. Co. 1922-59 (a founder and dir. 1922-28); dir. Cambridge Labs., 1926-28, Thenos Corp., 1933-38. Mem. A.A.A.S., Am. Phys. Soc., Am. Inst. Elec. Engrs., Sigma Xi. Research in field of gaseous conduction; holds patents on rectifiers, oscillators, gaseous lamps, control devices. Home: Medford MA Died June 1969.

SMITH, CHARLES HOWARD, engr.; b. Portland, Ore., Sept. 4, 1884; s. Charles Jackson and Elizabeth (McMillan) S.; desc. Richard Smith who came to Mass. with Rogers Williams, 1636; grad. Seattle High Sch., 1901; student Phillips Andover Acad., 1901-02, Yale Sci. Sch., 1902-04; m. Jane Swindell, Sept. 28, 1909; children—Frances Townley (Mrs. Orville Anderson Tyler), Charles Jackson, Robert Fulton, Betsy Jane (Mrs. Jacques Bramhall, Jr.). Engr. Western Coal & Mining Co., St. Louis, 1905; v.p. Davis Coal & Coke Co., Balt., Pitts. Terminal Ry. & Coal Co., Western Coal & Mining Co., Consol. Coal Co., St. Louis; asst. to pres. Western Rd. R.R., 1907-11; v.p., gen. mgr. Durham Coal & Iron Co., 1911-12; expert mining engr., New York, 1913—; cons. engr. Clinchfield Coal Corp., 1913; asso. with Blair & Co., bankers, New York, 1914-21; pres. Internat. Coal Products Corp., Clinchfield Carbocoal Corp., Gen. Oil Gas Corp., Bregeat Corp. of Am., Am. & Automotive Gas Producers Corp., 1915-21; as cons. engr., 1921-27; chmn. bd. Gen. Waterworks & R.R. coal properties, C.&E.I. R.R., Utah Fuel Co., C., M.&St.P. Ry., etc.; organized Chenery & Smith, cons. engr., 1921-27; chmn. bd. Gen. Waterworkd & Elec. Co., 1928-29; pres. Charles H. Smith & Co., Engrs.; cons. engr. Utility Mgmt. Corp.,

1937-38; cons. engr. Federal Water Service Co.; pres. Middle States Natural Gas Co., So. Shipbuilding and Dry Dock Corp., 1941, Nat. Armor Co., 1942-43, The Charles H. Smith Co., Engrs., 1944; v.p. South Am. Coal & Iron Co.; pres. Big Inch Gas, Inc. & Big Inch Oil, Inc. which merged Jan 1947 with Big Inch Gas and Oil Corp. During Worlad War I did spl. work for Ordnance Dept., Us. Army, U.S. Fuel Adminstrn., War Indsl. Bd. Inventor of process for converting bituminous coal into a smokeless fuel, also effecting recovery of by-products. Mem. Am. Mining Congress, Am. Inst. Mining and Metall. Engrs., (asso.), Army Ordnance Assn. Republican. Episcopalian. Clubs: Yale (N.Y.); Short Hills (N.J.). Home: 9 Ferncliff Terrace, Short Hills, N.J. Office: 20 Broad St., N.Y.C. 4. Died Dec. 16, 1950.

SMITH, CHARLES SHALER, bridge engr.; b. Pitts., Jan. 16, 1836; s. Frederick Rose and Mary Anne (Shaler) S.; m. Mary Gordon Gairdner, May 23, 1865, several children. Asst. engr. Louisville & Nashville R.R., 1855, resident engr. on Memphis br., 1856, supr. track and bridge constrn. for Memphis div., 1859; chief engr. of bldgs. and bridges Wilmington, Charlotte & Rutherford R.R. (N.C.), 1860-61; served as capt. engrs. Confederate Army in Civil War, built powder mill in Augusta dist.; partner (with Benjamin H. and Charles H. Latrobe) in Balt. Bridge Co., 1866; built series of iron trestles on Louisville, Cincinnati & Lexington R.R. and Elizabethtown & Paducah R.R.; 1st to use metal viaducts; built Ky. River Bridge for Cincinnati So. R.R. (his most notable structure), 1876-77; cantilever became dominant type for long-span constrn. as result of his work; most eminent bridge engr. in Am. Author: Comparative Analysis of the Fink, Murphy, Bollman and Triangular Trusses (treatise), 1865; Wind Pressure Upon Bridges (paper), 1881. Died St. Louis, Dec. 19, 1886.

SMITH, CLARENCE BEAMAN, agriculturist; b. Howardsville, Mich., Sept. 21, 1870; s. Alonzo and Harriett (Maybee) S.; B.S., Mich. Agrl. Coll., 1894, M.S., 1895, D.Sc., 1917; univs. Halle and Bonn, Germany, 1898-99; m. Lottie Lee Smith, of Lansing, Mich., Oct. 2, 1901; children—Helen, Herbert, Beaman, Roger, Huron, June. With U.S. Dept. of Agr. since 1896; hort. editor, Experiment Station Record, 1897-1906; agriculturist in the office of Farm Management, 1906-12; in charge farm management field studies and demonstrations, 1912-14; chief of Office Extension Work North and West, 1915-21; chief, Office Extension Work, U.S. Dept. Agr., 1921-38; retired. Democrat. Protestant. Author: Farmer's Cyclopedia of Agriculture (with E. V. Wilcox), 1904; Farmer's Cyclopedia of Livestock (with same), 1907; The Agricultural Extension System of the U.S. (with M. C. Wilson), 1930. Home: 1 Montgomery Av., Takoma Park DC (summers) Atlanta MI

SMITH, CLINTON DE WITT, agriculturist; b. Trumansburg, N.Y., Mar. 7, 1854; s. Reuben S. and Clarissa G. (Pease) S.; B.S., Cornell, 1873, M.S., 1875; m. Anna Cora Smith, June 16, 1892. Prize capt. cadets, Cornell, 1873; comdt. Star Mil. Inst., New York, 1879; practiced law, Trumansburg, 1888-90; asst. agriculturist, Cornell U., 1890. Ark. Expt. Sta., 1891; dir. expt. sta. and prof. dairy husbandry, U. of Minn., 1891-93; prof. agr. and dir. expt. sta., 1893-1900, dir. expt. sta. and dean of special courses, 1900-08, Mich. Agrl. Coll.; pres. Escola Agricola ("Luiz de Queiroz"), Piracicaba, Sao Paulo, Brazil, 1908-13; in extension work, Cornell U., 1913—. Owner and mgr. of farm. Apptd. dean of Coll. of Agr., U. of Ill., 1897; elected pres. N.M. Agrl. Coll., 1902. Originated spl. courses and built dairy bldgs., both at U. of Minn. and Mich. Agrl. Coll. Baptist. Republican. Mem. teaching staff, Extension Div. Cornell U., and farmer at Trumansburg, N.Y. Home: Trumansburg, N.Y. Died Aug. 4, 1916.

SMITH, DAVID EUGENE, mathematician; b. Cortland, N.Y., Jan. 21, 1860; s. Hon. Abram P. and Mary E. (Bronson) S.; Ph.D., Syracuse U., 1881, Ph.M., 1884, Ph.D., 1887, LL.D., 1905; Master of Pedagogics, Mich. State Normal Coll., 1898; student in Europe at various times, also 1907-08; D Sc., Columbia University, 1929; L.H.D., Yeshiva Coll., 1936; m. Fanny Taylor, Jan. 19, 1887; m. 2d, Eva May Luse, November 5, 1940. Practiced law at Cortland, 1881-84; taught mathematics, State Normal Sch., Cortland, 1884-91; prof. mathematics, Mich. State Normal Coll., 1891-98; prin. N.Y. State Normal Sch., Brockport, 1898-1901; prof. mathematics, Teachers Coll. (Columbia), 1901-26 (emeritus). Librarian, 1902-20, v.p., 1922, and asso. editor Bull. of Am. Math. Soc., 1902-20; math. editor New Internat. Ency., 1902-16, Monroe's Cyclo. of Education, 1911-13, New Practical Reference Library, 1912, Ency. Britannica, 1927, Nat. Ency., 1933; asso. editor Am. Mathematical Monthly since 1916, Scripta Mathematica since 1932. Vice-pres. Internat. Commn. on the Teaching of Mathematics, 1908-20, pres., 1928-32, hon. pres. since 1932. Fellow Mediaeval Acad. America, A.A.A.S.; mem. Math. Assn. America (pres. 1920-21), History and Science Soc. (pres. 1927), Am. Math. Soc., Deutsche Math. Verein, Phi Beta Kappa, Psi Upsilon, Pi Nu Epsilon, etc.; hon. mem. Calcutta Math. Soc. Trustee Lingnan U., China. Decorated Gold Star, Order of Elmi, by Persian Govt., 1933. Author: History of Modern Mathematics, 1896; Teaching of Elementary Mathematics, 1900; Rara Arithmetica, 1907; Teaching of Arithmetic, 1909, 13; Teaching of Geometry, 1911; Hindu-Arabic Numerals (with L. C. Karpinski), 1911; History of Japanese Mathematics, 1912; Union List of Mathematical Periodicals (with C. E. Seely), 1918; Number Stories of Long Ago, 1919; The Sumario Compendioso of Juan Diez, 1920; Our Indebtedness to Greece and Rome in Mathematics, 1922; Essentials of Geometry, 1923; Historical-Mathematical Paris, 1924; Mathematics Gothica, 1925; History of Mathematics (2 vols.), 1924, 25; Progress of Arithmetic in 25 years, 1924; Progress of Algebra in 25 years, 1925; Computing Jetons, 1924; Teaching of Junior High School Mathematics (with W. D. Reeve), 1927; Le Comput Manuel de Magister Anianus, 1928; Source Book in Mathematics, 1929; History of American Mathematics Before 1900 (with J. Ginsburg), 1934; The Rubáiyát of Omar Khayyám (metrical version), 1933; Poetry of Mathematics and Other Essays, 1934; Numbers and Numerals (with J. Ginsburg), 1937; The Wonderful Wonders of 1, 2, 3, 1937; also over 40 math. textbooks and many articles in various journals. Translator: Descartes's La Géométrie, 1925. Editor: A Portfolio of Portraits of Eminent Mathematicians, Part I, 1905, Part II, 1906, high school edit., 1907; DeMorgan's Budget of Paradoxes (2 vols.), 1915; Portraits of Eminent Mathematicians, Portfolio I, 1936, Portfolio II, 1937; Firdausi Celebration, 1936. Extensive traveler; book collector. Address: 501 W. 120th St., New York, N.Y. Died July 29, 1944.

SMITH, DUDLEY CROFFORD, physician, educator; b. Lafayette Springs, Miss., Dec. 15, 1892; s. Dr. John General Marion and Carra (Powell) S.; B.S., U. of Miss., 1914; M.D., U. of Va., 1916; m. Lake Morrow, June 28, 1921; children—Dudley Crofford, Powell Morrow, Marjorie (Mrs. Hamilton Smithey). Intern, resident U. of Va. Hosp.; instr. medicine U. of Va., 1916-17, founded dept. dermatology and syphilology, 1924, prof., 1934-50; special consultant U.S.P.H.S. since 1933; investigator studying and standardizing syphilis treatment with penicillin in collaboration with Nat. Research Council and U.S.P.H.S., 1943-1949. Diplomate Am. Bd. Dermatology and Syphilology (founder). Mem. A.M.A. (chmn. sect. dermatology and syphilogy 1950), Am. Dermatol. Assn. (v.p. 1943-45), Am. Acad. Dermatology and Syphilology, Sigma Xi, Kappa Sigma, Alpha Omega Alpha, Phi Beta Pi, Omicron Delta Kappa, Raven Soc., Tilka Soc. Democrat. Baptist. Elk. Mason. Clubs: Rotary, Colonnade, Farmington. Author articles epidemology of syphilis and dermatology profl. jours. Home: 30 University Circle, Charlottesville, Va. Died Aug. 30, 1950; buried University Cemetery, Charlottesville.

SMITH, EARLE CLEMENT, metallurgist; b. New Brighton, Pa., Jan. 20, 1891; s. Perry Alexander and Sula (McLean) S.; E.M., Ohio State U., 1913, grad. student mineralogy, 1914; student Columbia, 1916; D.Sc., Case Inst. Tech., 1937, Ohio State U., 1958; m. Agnes Mellon, Sept. 4, 1919; children—Eleanor (Mrs. John M. Fox), William, Margery, David (dec.), Stephen. Furnace helper U.S. Steel Corp., Gary, Ind., 1914, metallurgist, 1915; instr. metallography O. State U., 1916; with Republic Steel Corp. and predecessor firms, 1919—, chief metallurgist 1932—, dir. of research, 1956—. Mem. of the American Steel Mission to Great Britain, 1942; mem. Am. Steel and Iron Ore Mining delegation to Soviet Union, 1958; member adv. council science and engring. U. Notre Dame; minerals and metals adv. bd. Nat. Acad. Scis. Metallurgist aircraft prodn., U. S. Army, 1917-18; mem. technical advisory com., Nat. Bur. Standards. Awarded Lamme medal Ohio State U. Mem. Acad. Polit. Sci., A.A.A.S., Am. Chem. Soc., Am. Foundry Soc., Am. Inst. Mining and Metall. Engrs. (Howe lectr. 1935), Am. Iron and Steel Inst. (medallist), Am. Soc. Engring. Edn., Am. Soc. Metals (Campbell lectr. 1950; Gold medallist), Am. Soc. Quality Control, Am. Soc. Testing Materials, Am. Welding Soc., Assn. Iron and Steel Engrs., Inst. Metals (Britain), Iron and Steel Inst. (Britain), Profl. Engrs. Soc., West of Scotland Iron and Steel Inst., Verien Deutscher Eisenhuttenleute, Soc. Auto Engineers, Sigma Xi. Roman Catholic. Club: Union (Cleve.). Office: Republic Steel, Cleve. 15. Died May 20, 1960; buried New Brighton, Pa.

SMITH, ED SINCLAIR, engr.; b. Angola, Ind., Mar. 28, 1897; s. Ed Sinclair and Helen (Kingsley) S.; B.Sc., U. Cal. at Berkeley, 1919, M.E., 1932; m. Adah Grace Fiske, July 1, 1929; children—Karyl (Mrs. Cesar Beltran), Helen (Mrs. Richard William Henley), Claire Elizabeth (Mrs. Earl D. Watterson), Ruth Proctor. Engaged as test engineer Richmond refinery Standard Oil Co. of Cal., 1919-21; design, hydraulic engr. Builders Iron Foundry, Providence, 1923-36; patent engr., registered patent agt. C. F. Tagliabue Mfg. Co., Bklyn., 1936-42; research engr., patent liaison engr. Bendix Aviation Corp., Teterboro, N.J., 1942-48; ballistician, ordnance engr. Ballistic Research Labs., Aberdeen Proving Ground, Md., 1948—. Designer, builder naval ammunition hoists, designer hydraulic replacements Pearl Harbor Drydock, World War II. Registered Patent Agt., 1939. Fellow A.S.M.E. (jr. award 1930, instruments and regulators div. award 1954); mem. Instrument Society of Am., New Jersey Patent Law Association, Am. Ordnance Association, American Legion, Sigma Xi. Author: Automatic Control Engring., 1944; Binomial, Normal and Poisson Probabilities, 1953. Author sci., tech. articles. Patentee fluid meters, automatic controls. Home: Box 279, R.F.D. 2, Bel Air, Md. Office: Ballistic Research Laboratories, Aberdeen Proving Ground, Md. Died Dec. 31, 1960; buried Arlington Nat. Cemetery.

SMITH, EDGAR FAHS, chemist, educator; b. York, Pa., May 23, 1856; s. Gibson and Susan (Fahs) S.; B.S., Pa. Coll., 1874; A.M., Ph.D., Göttingen, 1876; hon. degrees from various colls. and univs.; m. Margie A. Gruel, 1879. Instr. chemistry, U. of Pa., 1876-81; prof. chemistry, Muhlenberg Coll., 1881-83, Wittenberg Coll., 1883-88; prof. chemistry, 1888-1920; v.provost, 1899-1911, provost, 1911-20, U. of Pa.; pres. electoral course for Pa., 1925. Mem. Jury of Awards, Chicago Expn., 1893; mem. U.S. Assay Commn., 1895, 1901-05; adviser in chemistry, Carnegie Inst., 1902; trustee Carnegie Foundation, 1914-20; pres. Wistar Inst., Phila., 1911-22. Mem. Electoral Coll., Pa. (1915), Com. Pub. Safety, Commn. for Revision of Constn. of Pa. (1919), Coll. and Univ. Council (1911-20), State Council Edn. (1920-22); research asso. Carnegie Inst. (1915, 18). Apptd. by President Harding to bd. of tech. advisers, Disarmament Conf., 1921. Officer Legion of Honor of France, 1932. Awarded Elliott Cresson medal, Franklin Inst., 1914, Chandler medal, Columbia U., 1922. Mem. Nat. Acad. Sciences, Am. Philos. Soc. (pres. 1902-06), Am. Chem. Soc. (pres. 1898, 1921, 22). Author (or editor): Classen's Quantitive Analysis, 1878; Clinical Analysis of Urine (with John Marshall), 1881; Richter's Inorganic Chemistry (5th edit.), 1900; Smith & Keller's Chemical Experimentation, 1902; Richter's Organic Chemistry, 1900; Smith's Electro-Chemical Analysis, 1911; Oettel's Practical Exercises in Electro-Chemistry, 1897; Oettel's Electro-Chemical Experiments, 1897; Elements of Chemistry, 1919; Shorter Course Chemical Experiments, 1913; Theories of Chemistry, 1913; Elements of Electrochemistry, 1913; also numerous books and pamphlets relating to the history of chemistry in America, and investigations in inorganic chemistry, including the determination of atomic weights. Address: Philadelphia, Pa. Died May 3, 1928.

SMITH, EDWIN, astronomer, geodesist; b. New York, Apr. 13, 1851; s. Edwin and Adelia O. (McIntyre) S.; ed. Coll. City of New York to jr. yr., class of '71; self-study in astronomy and geodesy; m. Lucy S. Black, Nov. 17, 1885. Entered U.S. Coast and Geod. Survey, 1870, asst., 1874; astronomer in charge party to observe transit of Venus at Chatham Islands, S. Pacific, 1874; same, Auckland, New Zealand, 1882; next determined force of gravity at Auckland, N.Z., Sydney, New South Wales, Singapore, Tokio, Japan, San Francisco and Washington with the 3 Kater pendulums belonging to the Royal Soc. of England, which had been used in the Great Indian Survey; in charge instrument div. U.S. Coast and Geod. Survey, 1879-94, during which time also carried on observations for variation of latitude at Rockville, Md., in cooperation with the work of the Internat. Geod. Assn. Left Coast and Geod. Survey, 1895, and was with the N.Y. State Land Survey till end of 1897, when was again apptd. asst. Coast and Geod. Survey. In 1899 established Internat. Geod. Assn. Latitude Obs. at Gaithersburg, Md., and made observations for variation of latitude from Oct. 1899, to Jan., 1901; engaged on astron., magnetic, and geodetic work of the survey, 1901—. Wrote several papers pub. as appendices to Coast and Geodetic Service Reps. Address: Rockville, Md. Died Dec. 2, 1912.

SMITH, E(LIAS) A(NTHON) CAPPELEN, metall. engr.; b. Trondhjem, Norway, Nov. 6, 1873; s. Elias Anthon and Anna T. (Rovig) S.; grad. Tech. Coll., Trondhjem, Norway, 1893; m. Mary Ellen Condon (died 1927); m. 2d, Carmen Arlegui. Asst. chemist Armour & Co., Chicago, 1893-95; chemist Chicago Copper Refining Co., 1895-96; supt. of electrolytic copper refinery, Anaconda Copper Mining Co., Mont., 1896-1900; metall. engr. in charge metall. operations, Baltimore Copper Smelting & Rolling Co., 1901-10; cons. metall. engr. Am. Smelting & Refining Co., New York, 1910-12; cons. metall. engr. Guggenheim Bros. of New York, Chile Exploration Co., Braden Copper Co., 1912-25; mem. Guggenheim Bros., since 1925; v.p. and dir. Peirce-Smith Converter Co. (holder of patent on his method of coppper converting) since 1908; pres. and dir. Minerec Corp.; dir. Chilean Nitrate Sales Corp., Anglo-Chilean Nitrate Corp., Lautaro Nitrate Co., Ltd., Cia. Salitrera Anglo Chilena, Pacific Tin Corp. Trustee Am. Scandinavian Foundation, New York. Awarded gold medal of Mining and Metall. Soc. of America for distinguished service in art of hydrometallurgy, 1920; decorated Knight Comdr., 1st class, Order of St. Olaf by King of Norway, 1925; Commendador, Order Al Merito, 1943 (highest civilian decoration of government of Chile). Member Mining and Metallurgical Society America, Am. Inst. Mining and Metallurgical Engineers, Royal Norwegian Scientific Society. Clubs: Piping Rock, Bankers; Embassy (London); Nordmands-Forbundet, Norske Selskab (Norway). Inventor of extraction method in use of Chuquicamata plant of Chile Explortation Co., Chile; originator of Guggenheim method of extracting nitrate from caliche. Office: 120 Broadway, New York, N.Y. Died June 25, 1949.

SMITH, ELLIOTT, astronomer; b. Blue Earth County, Minn., Jan. 19, 1875; s. Frank Y. and Harriet Amanda (Cornish) S.; A.B., U. of Minn., 1903; student U. of

Calif., 1905-06; Ph.D., U. of Cincinnati, 1910; m. Louise Josephine Strautman, Nov. 28, 1908; children—Harriet Louise (Mrs. Paul Herget), Stephen E. Asst. in astronomy, U. of Minn., Licks Obs., 1903-05; fellow, U. of Calif., 1905-06; asst. in obs., Univ. of Cincinnati, 1907-10; asst. prof. astronomy, U. of Cincinnati, 1910-20, associate, 1920-36, prof. since 1936, prof. and dir. of obs. since 1940. Served as pvt. Co. D, 12th Minn. Vol. Inf., U.S. Army, Spanish-Am. War. Mem. A.A.A.S., Am. Astron. Soc., Astron. Soc. of the Pacific, Ohio Soc., Sons of the Am. Revolution, Phi Beta Kappa, Sigma Xi. Presbyterian. Clubs: Schoolmasters, Torch (Cincinnati). Author: Catalog of Proper Motion Stars (with others), 1916, 1930; A Catalog of 4,683 Stars Observed by Elliott Smith, 1922; The Luminosity of Meteors and Comets, 1940. Home: 3264 Observatory Av., Cincinnati, O. Died Sep. 29, 1943.

SMITH, ELMER DENNISON, florist; b. Detroit, Nov. 20, 1854; s. Nathan and Helen Antonette (Green) S.; ed. pub. schs. and 1 yr. at Evans Business Coll., Adrian, Mich.; Master of Horticulture (hon.), Mich. State Coll., 1927; m. Carrie Lee Bailey, Nov. 30, 1886. Began as florist, Adrian, 1876; originated 493 varieties of chrysanthemums. Mem. S.A.R., Phi Alpha Xi (hon.). Republican. Author: Smith's Chrysanthemum Manual. Home: 957 W. Maumee St., Adrian, Mich. Died Nov. 11, 1939.

SMITH, ERASTUS GILBERT, chemist; b. S. Hadley, Mass., Apr. 30, 1855; s. Byron and Nancy (Dwight) S.; A.B., Amherst, 1877, A.M., 1880; Ph.D., U. of Göttingen, 1883; LL.D., Beloit, 1921; m. Elizabeth Mayher, Dec. 26, 1883; children—Gilbert M., Philip M., Elizabeth, Rebecca, Eleanor (dec.). Prof. chemistry, 1881-1921, prof. emeritus, 1921, dean, 1903-04, Beloit Coll. Mayor of Beloit, 1887-89, 1890-91, 1924-26; pres. Beloit Savings Bank, 1913-21, chmn. bd., 1929—. Mem. Wis. Assembly three terms, 1927-1932. Fellow A.A.A.S. Mem. Wis. Acad. Sciences, Arts and Letters. State consul Modern Woodmen, 1922-29. Author: Determination of the Rock-forming Minerals, 1885; Manual of Qualitative Analysis; also various chem. monographs. Home: Beloit, Wis. Died June 19, 1937.

SMITH, ERMINNIE ADELLE PLATT, geologist, ethnologist; b. Marcellus, N.Y., Apr. 26, 1836; d. Joseph Platt; grad. Troy (N.Y.) Female Sem., 1853; m. Simeon H. Smith, 4 children. Mem. staff Bur. of Am. Ethnology of Smithsonian Instn., Washington, D.C., 1880, studied culture of Iroquois Indians, 1880-82, compiled Iroquois-English Dictionary; wrote Myths of the Iroquois, published by Bur. of Ethnology, 1883; 1st woman elected fellow N.Y. Acad. Scis.; mem. A.A.A.S.; reflected deep interest in geology and botany; founder, 1st pres. Aesthetic Soc. of N.J. Died Jersey City, N.J., June 9, 1886.

SMITH, ERNEST ELLSWORTH, M.D., chemist; b. New Haven, Conn., Dec. 20, 1867; s. Henry Ellsworth and Ellen Louise (Shares) S.; Ph.B., Sheffield Scientific Sch. (Yale), 1888, Ph.D., 1891; M.D., Bellevue Hosp. Med. Coll. (New York U.), 1898; m. Lillian I. Church, 1890; 1 son, Harold Ellsworth. Asst. in physiol. chemistry, Yale, 1888-91; research asso. Dr. C. A. Herter's pvt. labs., New York, 1891-95; prof. physiology and organic and biol. chemistry, Fordham U. Med. Sch., New York, 1906-11. Specialist in experimental medicine and clin. pathology. Fellow N.Y. Acad. Medicine, N.Y. Acad. Sciences (pres. 1918, 19), A.A.A.S. Author of Aluminum Compounds in Food; also many papers and monographs on chem. and med. subjects. Home: Richmond Hill, N.Y. Deceased.

SMITH, ERWIN F., plant pathologist; b. Gilbert's Mills, N.Y., Jan. 21, 1854; s. R. K. and Louisa (Frink) S.; B.S., in biology, U. of Mich., 1886, Sc.D., 1889; Sc.D., U. Wis., 1914; LL.D., U. Mich., 1922; m. Charlotte M. Buffett, Apr. 13, 1893 (died 1906); m. 2d, Ruth Annette Warren, Feb. 21, 1914. Expert pathologist U.S. Dept. of Agr., 1899—; later in charge lab. of plant pathology, Bur. of Plant Industry. Asso. editor Centralblatt für Bacteriologie (2 Abt., first 25 vols.); contbr. to Standard Dictionary (1st edit.). Trustee Marine Biol. Lab., Woods Hole, Mass. (3 terms). Certificate of honor, A.M.A., 1913, for cancer in plants. Mem. Council Nat. Defense. Mem. Nat. Acad. Sciences (chmn. bot. sect. 3 yrs.), Am. Philos. Soc.; fellow Am. Acad. Arts and Sciences, A.A.A.S. (pres. Sect. G, 1906); pres. Soc. Plant Morphology and Physiology, 1902, Soc. Am. Bacteriologists, 1906, Bot. Soc. America, 1910, Am. Phytopathol. Soc., 1916. An incorporator of Nat. Carillon Assn. Author: Bacteria in Relation to Plant Diseases, Vol. I, 1905, Vol. II, 1911, Vol. III, 1914; various papers on general botany, mycology, sanitary science and bacteriology; For Her Friends and Mine (sonnets, issued pvtly), 1915; Pasteur—the history of a Mind (transl. with Florence Hedges), 1920; An Introduction to Bacterial Diseases of Plants, 1920. Home: Washington, D.C. Died Apr. 6, 1927.

SMITH, EUGENE, engineer, zoölogist; b. New York, N.Y., Nov. 25, 1860; ed. pub. and high schs., Jersey City, and by pvt. instrn.; m. Sept. 1888. City surveyor and engr., Hoboken, N.J. Author: The Home Aquarium, 1902; also papers on The Fishes of the Fresh and Brackish Waters in the Vicinity of New York City, 1897, and The Turtles and Lizards in Proceedings Linnaean Society, New York. Address: Hoboken, N.J. Died Dec. 25, 1912.

SMITH EUGENE ALLEN, geologist; b. Autauga County, Ala., Oct. 27, 1841; s. Dr. Samuel P. and Adelaide Julia (Allen) S.; A.B., U. of Ala., 1862; Ph.D., Heidelberg, 1868; attended one semester in Berlin, one in Göttingen, 1865-66, and two in Heidelberg, 1866-68; LL.D., U. of Miss., 1899, U. of Ala., 1906; m. Jennie H., d. of Chancellor Landon C. Garland, of U. of Ala., July 10, 1872. Second lt. Co. K. 33d Ala., C.S.A., 1862; capt. and instr. tactics, 1862-65, prof. geology and mineralogy, 1871-74, chemistry, geology and natural history, 1874-78, chemistry, mineralogy and geology, 1878-90, mineralogy and geology, 1890—, U. of Ala. State geologist of Ala., 1873—. Hon. commr. to Paris Expn., 1878; spl. agt. on cotton culture, 10th Census, 1880; mem. Am. Com. Internat. Geol. Congress, 1884-89; mem. jury of awards, expns. at Atlanta, 1895, Nashville, 1897, St. Louis, 1904. Fellow A.A.A.S. (chairman Sect. E, 1904), Geol. Soc. America (council, 1892-95, 2d v.p. 1906, pres. 1913). Mem. State Highway Commn., 1911-23. Home: University, Ala. Died Sept. 7, 1927.

SMITH, F. JANNEY, physician; b. Baltimore, Md., Nov. 18, 1888; s. Dr. B. and Frances Gist (Hopkins) S.; A.B., Johns Hopkins, 1909, M.D., 1913; special course Rockefeller Inst., 1917; m. Jeanie Wilmer Smart, Feb. 14, 1917 (dec.); children—Martha Janney (Mrs. Charles A. McGowan), Virginia Carter, F. Janney (deceased), Robert Gibbons; m. 2d, Colleen F. Forney, May 22, 1948; children—Steven, Holly. Medical House office, Johns Hopkins Hospital, 1913-14; assistant resident physician and instructor in medicine in Johns Hopkins Medical School, 1914-15; first resident physician Henry Ford Hospital at its opening in 1915, physician in charge of cardio-respiratory division, 1919-66, senior consultant in cardiology, 1953-66; private practice of cardiology, 1959-66. Diplomate American Board of Internal Medicine, 1937. 1st lt., captain, M.C., U.S. Army, 1917-19. Fellow American Coll. of Physicians; mem. Am. Clin. and Climatol. Assn., Central Soc. for Clin. Research, Am. Trudeau Soc., Mich. Trudeau Soc., Am. Heart Assn., Wayne County Med. Soc., A.M.A., Johns Hopkins Med. and Surg. Assn., Pithotomy Club, Phi Gamma Delta, Phi Beta Kappa, Alpha Omega Alpha. Clubs: Detroit Boat; Country (Grosse Pointe, Michigan); Witenagemote. Contbr. numerous articles to med. jours. Home: Grosse Pointe Farms MI Died Nov. 9, 1966; buried Woodlawn Cemetery Detroit MI

SMITH, FERRIS, surgeon; b. Pontiac, Mich., Oct. 25, 1883; s. Samuel W. and Alida E. (DeLand) S.; A.B., U. Mich., 1908, M.D., 1910; post-grad. Vienna and Berlin; m. Florence Bannister, June 25, 1913. Began practice at Ann Arbor, 1910; settled in Grand Rapids, Mich., 1913; capt. Royal Med. Corps, Eng., Mar. 1917; facial plastic surgeon Queens Hosp., Eng., World War; prof. plastic surgery Internat. Clinic, Paris, 1923; surgeon Blodgett Meml. Hosp., Grand Rapids. Fellow A.C.S. (gov.); Internat. College of Dentists (hon.); mem. Founders Group Am. Bd. Plastic Surgery, A.M.A., Mich. Med. Soc., Oral and Plastic Surg. Soc. (pres.), Am. Soc. of Plastic and Reconstructive Surgery, Alpha Omega Alpha, Sigma Psi, Delta Tau Delta, Nu Sigma Nu. Co-author: Manual of Plastic and Maxillo-Facial Surgery, Army Med. Corps. Author: Plastic and Reconstructive Surgery, 1950. Home: 639 Plymouth Rd. S.E. Office: Blodgett Med. Bldg., Grand Rapids 6, Mich. Died Sept. 18, 1957; buried Restlawn Meml. Park.

SMITH, FRANCIS ORMAND JONATHAN, congressman, lawyer; b. Brentwood, N.H., Nov. 23, 1806; attended Phillips Exeter (N.H.) Acad.; studied law. Admitted to bar, practiced in Portland, Me., 1826; div. advocate 5th Div. Circuit Ct.-Martial in Me., 1829-34; mem. Me. Ho. of Reps., 1831, 63-64, pres. Me. State, 1833; mem. U.S. Ho. of Reps. (Democrat) from Me. 23d-25th congresses, 1833-39; assisted Morse in perfecting and introducing electric telegraph. Died Deering (later Woodfords), Me., Oct. 14, 1876; buried on his estate Forest Home; reinterred Evergreen Cemetery, Portland.

SMITH, FRANK, zoölogist; b. Winneconne, Wis., Feb. 18, 1857; s. Samuel Franklin and Aurelia (Shepard) S.; Ph.B., Hillsdale Coll., Mich., 1885 (D.Sc., 1923); A.M., Harvard, 1893; m. Edith M. Fox, Sept. 8, 1887 (died 1888); 1 son, Donald Fisk (dec.); m. 2d, Isadora Stamats, July 12, 1890. Prof. chemistry and biology, Hillsdale Coll., 1886-92; instr. in biology, Trinity Coll., Hartford, Conn., 1892-93, instr. in zoölogy, 1893-96, asst. prof., 1896-1900, asso. prof., 1900-13, professor zoölogy, 1913-26 (emeritus), U. of Ill. Fellow A.A.A.S. Unitarian. Contbr. chiefly to morphology and taxonomy of land and fresh water annelids, of fresh water sponges, and on migration of birds. Home: Hillsdale, Mich. Died Feb. 3, 1942.

SMITH, FRANK MARSHALL, mining engr.; b. Phila., Pa., Aug. 16, 1866; s. William Marshall and Mary Alice (Beath) S.; grad. High Sch., 1884; E.M., Sch. of Mines (Columbia), 1889; m. Clara Thatcher Everhart, June 21, 1893; children—Aldridge Everhart, Dorothy Alice (Mrs. Irving T. Atwater), Marjorie Helen (wife of Augustus D. Sanders, U.S.A.). With U.S. Geological Survey, 1889-90; assayer and asst. supt. Colo. Smelting Co., Pueblo, Colo., 1891-93; supt., later mgr., United Smelting and Refining Co., Great Falls, Mont., 1893-1901; asst. mgr. Utah dept., Am. Smelting & Refining Co., 1901-02; asst. mgr. E. Helena Plant, same company, 1902-05, mgr., 1905-19; asst. dir., Bunker Hill Smelter, Kellogg, Ida., 1919-20; dir. 1920-35; pres. Northwest Lead Co. (Seattle, Wash.), 1930-35; dir. Spokane Gas & Fuel Co.; cons. metall. engr. Treadwell Yukon Co., 1930. Mem. Am. Inst. Mining and Metall. Engrs. (chmn. Mont. sect., 1915; v.p., 1923-26; chmn. Columbia sect., 1927), Mont. Soc. Engrs. (pres. 1910), Am. Silver Producers Assn. (v.p. 1924—), Associated Engrs. of Spokane (pres. 1925), Northwest Mining Assn. (pres. 1929), Am. Mining Congress (chmn. Western div. 1929). Pres. Spokane Community Welfare Federation, 1929-30. Republican. Mason. Home: Spokane, Wash. Died June 1, 1937.

SMITH, GEORGE EDSON PHILIP, civil engr.; b. Lyndonville, Vt., Dec. 29, 1873; s. Franklin Horatio and Hattie Lovisa (Powers) S.; B.S. in C.E., Univ. of Vt., 1897, C.E., 1899, Dr.Engring. from same, 1929; studied U. of Wis., 1910-11; m. Maude North, Oct. 1, 1904; 1 son, George Edson Philip. Instr. civil engring., Univ. of Vermont, 1897-1900; professor civil engineering, University of Arizona, 1900-06, prof. irrigation engring. since 1906. Consulting engr. Agrl. Products Corp., 1916-19; also served as Ariz. land planning consultant, Nat. Resources Bd., 1934-35; mem. Tucson City Planning Commn., 1937-46. Introduced caisson well; wrote water code for Ariz.; assisted in development of pump irrigation; researcher in soil temperature control; irrigation econs.; etc. Fellow A.A.A.S.; life member American Geophysical Union; mem. Am. Soc. C.E. (formerly pres. Ariz. sect.), Am. Assn. Engrs., Am. Soc. Agrl. Engrs. (ex-chmn. Pacific Coast Sect.), Western Irrigation and Drainage Research Assn., Sigma Xi, Kappa Sigma, Phi Beta Kappa, Phi Kappa Phi, Phi Beta Kappa Assos. Conglist. Mason (K.T., Shriner). Author of papers and bulletins pertaining irrigation and ground water supplies in the Southwest, and to engring. and polit. problems of Colorado River and to relation of ground water supplies to the physiography. Home: 1195 Speedway, Tucson AZ

SMITH, GEORGE OTIS, geologist; b. Hodgdon, Me., Feb. 22, 1871; s. Joseph O. and Emma (Mayo) S.; A.B., Colby Coll., 1893, A.M., 1896, LL.D., 1920; Ph.D., Johns Hopkins 1896; Sc.D., Case Sch. Applied Sci., 1914, Colo. Sch. Mines, 1928; m. Grace M. Coburn, Nov. 18, 1896 (died Mar. 3, 1931); children—Charles Coburn (dec.), Joseph Coburn, Mrs. Helen Coburn Fawcett, Elizabeth Coburn (dec.), Louise Coburn. Engaged in geol. work in Mich., Utah, Washington, and in N.E., 1893-1906; asst. geologist and geologist, 1896-1907, dir. U.S. Geol. Survey, 1907-30, except 1922-23 while mem. U.S. Coal Commn.; chmn. Federal Power Commn., Dec. 1930-Nov. 1933; dir. Central Me. Power Co. Chmn. board of trustees, Colby Coll.; pres. board of trustees Redington Memorial Hosp. and Bloomfield Acad. Fellow Geol. Soc. America, A.A.A.S.; mem. Coal Mining Inst. America (hon.), Am. Inst. Mining and Metall. Engrs. (ex-pres.), Am. Forestry Assn., Wash. Acad. Sciences, Mining and Metall. Soc. America, Am. Assn. Petroleum Geologists, Nat. Geog. Soc. (trustee), Delta Kappa Epsilon, Phi Beta Kappa, etc. Author of reports on areal, economic, petrographic and physiographic geology in pubs. U.S. Geol. Survey, also papers and addresses on economics of mineral and power resources and administration of scientific work by govt.; editor and co-author of Strategy of Minerals, 1919. Baptist. Republican. Clubs: Cosmos, Press. Home: 2 Coburn Av., Skowhegan, Me. Died Jan. 10, 1944.

SMITH, GUSTAVUS WOODSON, army officer, engr.; b. Georgetown, Scott County, Ky., Mar. 1822; s. Byrd and Sarah Hatcher (Woodson) S.; grad. U.S. Mil. Acad., 1842; m. Lucretia Bassett, Oct. 3, 1844. Instr. civil, mil. engring. U.S. Mil. Acad., 1844-46; brevetted 1st lt., then capt., maj. U.S. Army for services at Vera Cruz, Cerro Gordo, Contreras, Churubusco, Mexico City, 1846-48; asst. prof. engring, U.S. Mil. Acad., 1848-54; designated by Treasury Dept. to supervise repairs to the Mint, and constrn. Marine Hosp., New Orleans, 1855; chief engr. Trenton Iron Works, 1856-58; street commr., N.Y.C., 1858-61; commd. maj. gen. 2d Corps, Confederate Provisional Army, 1861; commanded a wing of Army of No. Va. until conclusion Peninsular Campaign; commanded sector from right of Lee's theatre of operations on the Rappahannock to Cape Fear River with hdqrs. Richmond, 1862; sec. of war Confederate States Am., 1862; resigned commn. as maj. gen. Confederate Army, 1862; commd. maj. gen. to command 1st Div., Ga. Militia, 1864, assigned a sector in Dept. of S.C., Ga., Fla.; surrendered 1865; gen. mgr. Southwestern Iron Co., Chattanooga, Tenn., 1866-70; 1st ins. commr., Ky., 1870-75. Author: Notes on Life Insurance, 1870; Confederate War Papers, 1884; The Battle of Seven Pines, 1891. Died N.Y.C., June 24, 1896.

SMITH, HAMILTON, mining engr.; b. Louisville, Ky., July 5, 1840; s. Hamilton and Martha (Hall) S.; m. Mrs. Charles Congreve. Became head of engring. dept. at coal mine owned by father, Cannelton, Ind., circa 1858; supervised coal mines in Ky. and Ind., 1860's; became chief engr. Triunfo mine, Lower Cal., 1869; chief engr. mine in Nevada County, Cal., pioneered use of hydraulic power; supr. Rothschild mine, El Callao, in Venezuela, 1881-85; founder (with Edmund de Crano) Exploration Co., Ltd., London, Eng., 1886, developed many mines around the world; promoted Am. mining ventures in Eng., founded Fraser & Chalmers (mining machinery co.); consultant on orgn. of many mines; moved to N.Y., 1896, continued as consultant. Author: Treatise on Hydraulics, 1886; published article on costs of gold mining in Engring. and Mining Journal, 1886. Died Durham, N.H., July 4, 1900.

SMITH, HAROLD BABBITT, elec. engr.; b. Barre, Mass., May 23, 1869; s. Samuel Francis and Julia Asenath (Babbitt) S.; M.E., Cornell U., 1891; postgrad. student Cornell, 1891-93; m. Laura Bertha Smith, June 15, 1894; m. 2d, Persis H. Smith, September 28, 1911; children—P. Nancy, Margaret S., Richard S. Prof. elec. engring., U. of Ark., 1892; head designer and elec. engr. Elektron Mfg. Co., Springfield, Mass., 1893; prof. elec. engring., Purdue U. (dir. Sch. of Elec. Engring.), 1893-96; prof. elec. engring. and dir. dept. elec. engring., Worcester Poly. Inst., 1896—; elec. engr., designer, cons. engr., Westinghouse Electric & Mfg. Co., Pittsburgh, 1905—. Fellow Am. Inst. E.E. (dir. 1920-24; v.p. 1924-26; pres. 1929-30), A.A.A.S. Chmn. Internat. Group Jury of Awards in elec. engring., St. Louis Expn., 1904. Asso. mem. Naval Consulting Bd. U.S. and cons. engr. with spl. bd. of U.S. Navy on anti-submarine devices, 1917-19; mem. Am. Engring. Council, 1930-32. Writer of many monographs and contributions to transactions of socs. and engring. publs. Study and travel through Europe, Africa, India, China, Japan, etc., 1911-13. Address: Worcester, Mass. Died 1932.

SMITH, HARRY WORCESTER, sportsman, financier, inventor; b. Worcester, Mass., Nov. 5, 1865; s. Charles Worcester and Josephine (Lord) S.; ed. Worcester Poly. Ins., Mass. Inst. Tech., Chemnitz (Germany) Weaving Sch., Glasgow Sch. of Design, Bradford (Eng.) Tech. Sch.; m. Mildred Crompton, Oct. 19, 1892. Inventor of more than 40 patents pertaining to automatic weaving and design; consolidated the Crompton-Thayer and Crompton-Knowles cos., 1907, the combination making the largest loom works in the world; effected sale of the Queen Dyeing Co., of Providence, R.I., to the U.S. Finishing Co., of N.Y. City, for $2,000,000, in 1909; sold Thomas G. Plant shoe factory, at Jamaica Plains, Mass., and all his patents on shoe machinery, to U.S. Shoe Machinery Co. of America for $6,000,000, in 1910; consolidated the F. E. Reed and Prentice Bros., machine tool mfrs., the Reed Foundry, Reed-Curtis Screw Co. and the Crompton Associates plants into the Reed-Prentice Co., 1912. Mem. Worcester Park Commn. 7 yrs. Founder Masters of Foxhounds Assn. America, 1907; master of the Grafton Hounds; ex-master of Piedmont and Loudoun hunts, Virginia, and Westmeath, Ireland. Republican. Brought champion greyhounds of Eng. to America, 1885; won Fox Terrier Club grand challenge cup twice; won $10,000 champion Steeplechase of America, riding own horse, The Cad, Calvert Steeplechase, Baltimore, 1900, 1st and 2d $8,000 Grand National Steeplechase, Sheepshead Bay, etc.; won the Grafton-Middlesex American-English Internat. Foxhound match for $2,000 stake and plate, in Virginia, 1905; won, owner up, the Aiken and Camden, South Carolina, Hunter Trials, 1929, 30, 31. Established present Am. Foxhound standard. Judge of horse and hound shows, matches and tests in U.S. and Can.; founded the Frank Forester Soc. of America; collected funds and dedicated the memorial to Henry William Herbert ("Frank Forester"), at Warwick, Orange County, N.Y. Wrote: A Sporting Tour Through Ireland, England, Wales and France; The True American Foxhound; Fox Hunting in America; The Cubbing Season; Amateur Sunday Games; The Pulse of the People; also introductory chapters and published the Warwick Valley edit. of The Warwick Woodlands, 1921; wrote the foreword to the limited edit. of Trouting Along the Catasauqua, by Frank Forester, privately printed for The Angler's Club of New York, 1927; the foreword to the Hitchcock edit. of the works of Somerville and Ross; the foreword to Cooking in Old Creole Days, by Celestine Eustis, 1928; Steeplechasing in America, for the 14th edit. of the Ency. Britannica; Steeplechasing in America for "Racing at Home and Abroad," London, 1929; Life and Sport in Aiken and Those Who Made It, 1935; A Sporting Family of the Old South, 1937. Reviewer of books on racing and hunting. Mem. Engineers Club (New York). Home: Worcester, Mass. Died Apr. 5, 1945.

SMITH, HENRY MONMOUTH, chemist, educator; b. Middletown, Conn., Aug. 31, 1868; s. Samuel George and Sarah Melville (Hunt) S.; B.A., Wesleyan U., Conn., 1891, M.A., 1894; Ph.D., Heidelberg, Germany, 1898; m. Mary Louise O'Brien, May 8, 1909. Asst. chemist Storrs Expt. Sta., Conn. Agrl. Coll., 1891-92, Conn. Expt. Sta., 1892-93; spl. agt. nutrition investigations U.S. Dept. Agr., 1893-95; asso. prof. phys. sci. Hampden-Sidney (Va.) Coll., 1898-99; instr. chemistry Syracuse, 1899-1900, asso. prof., 1900-02, prof., 1902-13; research asso. Nutrition Lab., Carnegie Instn., Washington, 1913-20; prof. chemistry Mass. Inst. Tech., 1920-32. Mem. Am. Chem. Soc., A.A.A.S., Am. Acad. Arts and Sciences, Phi Beta Kappa, Sigma Xi, Alpha Chi Sigma, Beta Theta Pi. Republican. Unitarian. Club: University. Author: Human Vitality and Efficiency Under Prolonged Restricted Diet (with others), 1919; Gaseous Exchange and Physiological Requirements for Level and Grade Walking, 1922 (both bulls.), Carnegie Instn.; Torchbeares of Chemitry, 1948. Home: 25 Cotswold Rd., Brookline 46, Mass. Died Apr. 12, 1950; buried Forest Hills Cemetery, Boston.

SMITH, HERBERT HUNTINGTON, naturalist; b. Manlius, N.Y., Jan. 21, 1851; s. Charles and Julia Maria (Huntington) S.; studied Cornell U., 1868-72; m. Amelia Woolworth Smith, Oct. 5, 1880. Best known as collector of natural history specimens; traveled in Brazil, 1871, 1873-77, 1881-86, Mexico, 1889, W.I., 1890-95, Colombia, 1898-1901. In Mexico employed for the Biologia Centrali-Americana, in W.I. for W. Indian Com. of the Royal Soc. and Brit. Assn. Collections (at least 500,000 specimens) are in nearly every large museum in the world. Collaborated in Century Dictionary, Century Cyclo. of Names and Johnson's Cyclo. Curator Carnegie Museum, Pittsburgh, 1896-98, and connected with that instn., 1902; curator, Ala. Mus. of Natural History, 1910—. Author: Brazil—the Amazons and the Coast, 1880; De Rio de Janeiro á Cuyabá, 1886 (in Portuguese). Published His Majesty's Sloop Diamond Rock, over the pen-name, H. S. Huntington, 1904. Address: University, Ala. Died Mar. 22, 1919.

SMITH, HOMER WILLIAM, author, prof. physiology; b. Denver, Colo., Jan. 2, 1895; s. Albert C. and Margaret E. (Jones) S.; A.B., U. of Denver, 1917; Sc.D., Johns Hopkins, 1921; (hon.) M.S., Yale U., 1937; m. Carlotta Smith, Sept. 17, 1921 (div.); m. 2d, Margaret Wilson, Mar. 19, 1949 (dec.); 1 son, Homer Wilson. Research pharmacologist Hygienic Lab., D.C., 1919; research chemist Eli Lilly & Co., 1921-23; nat. research fellow in physiology, Harvard Med. Sch., 1923-25; prof. physiology, U. of Va., 1925-28, Guggenheim fellow in physiology, 1928, 30; prof. physiol., dir. physiol. labs., N.Y. U. Coll. Medicine, since 1928, Belfield lecturer, Chicago, 1938; Porter lecturer, Kansas City, 1939; Harvey lecturer, New York, 1940; Welch lecturer, New York, 1942; Herzstein lecturer, San Francisco, 1947, Rothschild lectr., N.Y.C., 1948, Millikan lectr., Nashville, 1948, Barlow lectr., Los Angeles, 1949, Sommer lectr., Portland, 1950, McGuire lectr., Richmond, 1950, Martland lectr., Newark, 1951, Freiberg lectr., Cin., 1952, Sherwood lectr., Lawrence, Kan., Musser lecturer, 1952, Ballenger lectr., Havana; Aaron Brown lectr., Phila., Bernard lecturer, Winston-Salem, 1953; also numerous other named lectureships; visiting professor Yale Med. Sch., 1936, Bowman Gray, 1953; Walker Ames prof. U. Washington, 1955; vis. prof. Rockefeller Inst., 1957; Graves vis. prof. U. Ind., 1958; research fellow N.Y. Acad. Medicine. Member med. fellowship bd. Nat. Research Council; chmn. NRC-AEC Post-doctoral Fellowship Bd. in Med. Sciences, 1947-52; division member National Defense Research Com., 1942-46. Served as lt., Chemical Warfare Service, World War, 1917-18. Recipient Lasker award, 1948, President Medal for Merit, 1948, Passano Award, 1954. Member Am. Acad. Scis. National Academy Sciences, Am. Physiol. Soc., Am. Soc. Biol. Chemists, Assn. Am. Physicians, Am. Soc. Icthyologists and Herpetologists, Soc. for Exptl. Biology and Medicine. Mount Desert Island Biological Laboratory (president), Bermuda Laboratory for Biological Research (trustee); mem. Harvey Soc., Phi Beta Kappa, Alpha Omega Alpha. Author: Kamongo, 1932; The End of Illusion, 1935; The Physiology of the Kidney, 1937; Lectures on the Kidney, 1943; The Kidney: Structure and Function in Health and Disease, 1951; Man and His Gods, 1952; From Fish to Philosopher, 1953; Principles of Renal Physiology, 1956. Asst. editor (physiology) Chem. Abstracts until 1946; associate editor Journal of Cellular and Comparative Physiology. Home: 242 E. 19th St., N.Y.C. Died Mar. 25, 1962; buried Rhea Springs, Tenn.

SMITH, HORACE, inventor, mfr.; b. Cheshire, Mass., Oct. 28, 1808; s. Silas and Phoebe Smith; m. Eliza Foster, 1836; m. 2d, Mrs. Eliza Hebbard Jepson, 1872; m. 3d, Mary Lucretia Hebbard, 1887. Self-employed gun mfr., 1846-49, improved breech-loading rifle, obtained 1st patent, 1851; formed partnership with Daniel Wesson to manufacture repeating rifle, Norwich, Mass., 1853, secured patent, 1854, sold business to Volcanic Arms Co., 1855; invented and patented (with Wesson) central-fire metallic cartridge, 1854, reestablished partnership (with Smith as exec. head 1857-73) to produce the new firearm and cartridge, Springfield, Mass., 1857, produced 1st revolvers, 1857, granted patents, 1859, 60 (revolver used by U.S. mil. authorities), built new plant, 1860; exhibited products at Internat. Expn., Paris, France, 1867, sold guns to many European nations; sold interst in co. to Wesson, 1873; pres. Chicopee Nat. bank, 1893. Died Jan. 15, 1893.

SMITH, HOWARD DWIGHT, architect; b. Dayton, O., Feb. 21, 1886; s. Andrew Jackson and Nancy Evelyn (Moore) S.; C.E. in Architecture, Ohio State U., 1907; B.Arch., Columbia, 1910, Perkins traveling fellow, 1910-11; m. Myrna Theresa Cott, Jan. 24, 1912; children—Marjorie Cott (Mrs. Marion Virgil Packard), Robert Jackson, Howard Dwight, Myrna Hazel (Mrs. Dale Dan Dupler, Jr.), and Priscilla Ruth (Mrs. Eugene C. D'Angelo); m. 2d, Mary Thompson Gramlich, Jan. 17, 1936. Engaged as architectural draftsman in Columbus, O., Washington, D.C., New York City, 1906-14; supervising architect, residence div., Office of John Russell Pope, 1914-18; prof. architecture, Ohio State U., 1918-21 and since 1929; architect Columbus, O., Bd. of Edn., 1921-29; univ. architect Ohio State U., 1929-56, ret.; Fulbright lectr. Alexandria U., Egypt, 1955-56; architectural advisor, Am. Commn. Living War Memorials, since, 1943. Principal bldgs. include Ohio Stadium (received Exhibition Gold Medal, Am. Inst. Architects, 1921); Columbus, O., City Hall and West High Sch.; 25 schs. in central Ohio; Marietta, O., City Hall; Springfield, O., Masonic Temple; 50 bldgs. for Ohio State U.; Upper Arlington, O., Elementary Sch. (received Exhibition Gold Medal, Ohio Soc. Architects, 1941). Fellow Am. Inst. Architects; mem. Sigma Xi, Tau Sigma Delta, Sigma Alpha Epsilon. Mason (32 deg.), Rotarian. Clubs: Faculty, Kit Kat (Columbus, O.). Home: 280 Village Dr., Columbus 14, O. Died Apr. 27, 1958; buried Green Lawn Cemetery, Columbus, O.

SMITH, HUBERT WINSTON, educator; born Tex., May 18, 1907; s. Thomas and Myrtle (Hawkins) S.; A.B., U. Tex., 1927, M.B.A., 1931; student U. Edinburgh, 1936-38; LL.B., Harvard (Faculty scholarship), 1930, M.D. (Henry Cabot Jackson fellow 1939-41), 1941; m. Catherine Hall McKinley, Aug. 26, 1936; children—Charles McKinley, Alan Winston, Stephen Hall, James Jackson. Asso. Price Waterhouse & Co., accts., Boston, 1928-29; admitted to Tex. bar, 1930; asso. Thompson, Knight, Baker & Harris, Dallas, 1930-34; partner Smith & Carter, 1934-36; prof. law Jefferson U., eves. 1930-35; demonstrator anatomy, med. sch. U. Edinburgh, 1936-37; Research fellow Rockefeller Found., asso. med.-legal research, law and med. schs. Harvard, 1941-44, prof. legal medicine U. Ill., 1945-49; research prof. law and medicine, prof. law and legal medicine, dir. law-sci. program Tulane U., 1949-52; lecturer legal medicine, med. school La. State U., 1951-52; professor law, sch. law, prof. legal medicine, sch. medicine (Galveston), and dir. law-sci. inst. U. Tex., 1952-67; chancellor of Law-Science Acad., 1967-71; dir. inter-profl. studies Coll. Law U. Okla., Norman, also cons. prof. dept. psychiatry and behavioral scis., U. Okla. Med. Center, Oklahoma City, 1968-71; lectr. legal aspects of psychiatry Menninger Clinic and Found. Member Nat. Bd. Med. Examiners. Cons. legal medicine V.A. Hosp., Houston; sometime cons. forensic psychiatry U.S. Pub. Health Hosp., Ft. Worth and V.A. Hosp., Gulfport, Tex. Mem. Coroner's Commn., Orleans Parish. Nat. adv. Am. Assn. Psychiatric Treatment Criminal Offenders; founder Law-Sci. Movement, Law-Sci. Short Course for trial lawyers; chmn. com. mental states and law La. State Inst., 1951-52. Mem. White House Conf. Problems Children and Youth, 1951; mem. com. on reform of Law of Evidence (Tex.); com. on cooperation of Tex. State Bar with med. profession. Served as lt. officer charge legal med. br. Bur. Medicine and Surgery, U.S.N., 1944-45. Awarded Sir Wright Smith prize in med. botany, 1937; Foster award, med. sch. Harvard, 1938; Milton award in sci. research, 1942-43; Gold medal, citation Law-Science Academy, 1959. Research fellow Rockefeller Found., 1941-44; fellow and chancellor Law Sci. Acad. Am.; pres. Law Sci. Found. Am. Mem. Nat. Bd. Med. Examiners. Fellow Internat.Academy Trial Lawyers and the New York Academy of Medicine; member Am. Soc. Science, Research, Mass. Soc. C.P.A. (hon.), Law-Sci. Acad. Am., Law-Sci. Found. Am. (pres.), Scribes, Phi Beta Kappa, Beta Alpha Psi, Beta Gamma Sigma, Order of Coif, Phi Delta Phi. Episcopalian. Author numerous monographs and articles in medico-legal field. Editor: National Symposia on Scientific Proof and Relations of Law and Medicine, 1941, 46; asso. editor Jour. Criminal Law and Criminology, 1946-60. Editor-in-chief, coordinator, contbr. Symposium on Law and Science, 1969. Home: Norman OK Died July 9, 1971; buried Sparkman-Hillcrest Meml. Park, Dallas TX

SMITH, HURON H(ERBERT), curator of botany; b. Danville, Ind., July 26, 1883; s. Wesley Orrison and Emma Lavina (McCurdy) S.; grad. high sch., Winchester, Ind., June 1902; B.S., De Pauw U., 1905; studied Cornell U., 1905-07; m. Ethel Auretta Clark, June 15, 1910; 1 dau., La Vaughn Chenewah. Asst. curator of botany, Field Mus., Chicago, worked on a dictionary, and collected N. Am. Dendrographic Display, 1907-17; curator of botany, Milwaukee Pub. Mus.; spl. research and publs. in ethnobotany of Wis. Indian tribes. Physical and ednl. sec. Y.M.C.A., World War I; troop transport sec. U.S. to France. Fellow A.A.A.S.; mem. Wis. Acad. Science, Arts and Letters. Sixth recipient of Increase A. Lapham medal, Wis. Archaeol. Soc. Republican. Methodist. Author: Ethnobotany of Menomini Indians, 1924; Ethnobotany of Meskwaki Indians, 1927; Ethnobotany of Ojibwe Indians; Mushrooms of Milwaukee Region; also year books Milwaukee Pub. Mus. and many articles in mags. Lecturer. Home: Milwaukee, Wis. Died 1933.

SMITH, JAMES PERRIN, paleontologist; b. Cokesbury, S.C., Nov. 27, 1864; s. Rev. James Francis and Julia (Forster) S.; A.B., Wofford Coll., S.C., 1884; A.M., Vanderbilt U., Tenn., 1886; Ph.D., Univ. of Göttingen, Germany, 1892; LL.D., Wofford Coll., S.C., 1916; m. Frances Norris Rand, Aug. 19, 1896; children—Forster Rand, Mary Norris, Howard Carlisle, Charles Kirtland. Prof. paleontology, Stanford U., 1892—; geologist U.S. Geol. Survey, 1895—. Democrat. Protestant. Author numerous monographs on scientific topics. Address: Palo Alto, Calif. Died Jan. 1, 1931.

SMITH, JESSE MERRICK, engineer; b. Newark, O., Oct. 30, 1848; s. Henry and Lucinda (Salisbury) S.; ed. Philo Patterson's Sch., Detrojt, Mich., Rensselaer Poly. Inst., Troy, N.Y., 1865-68, École Centrale des Arts et Manufactures, Paris, 1869-72, M.E., 1872; m. Ella A. Moore, Feb. 5, 1879 (deceased); m. 2d, Annie Coffin, Nov. 26, 1903 (deceased); m. 3d, Mabel A. MacKinney, June 24, 1916. Engaged in building iron blast furnaces, and in coal mines in Hocking Valley, O., 1874-80; cons. engr., Detroit, designing spl. machinery and mfg. and elec. power plants, and expert in patent litigation, 1880-98; cons. engr. and expert in patent litigation in New York, 1898-1914. Address: New York, N.Y. Died Apr. 1, 1927.

SMITH, JOHN AUGUSTINE, physician, coll. pres.; b. Westmoreland County, Va., Aug. 29, 1782; s. Rev. Thomas and Mary (Smith) S.; grad. Coll. William and Mary, 1800; studied St. Thomas Hosp., London, 1808-09; m. Letitia Lee, 1809, 9 children. Mem. 1st faculty Coll. Physicians and Surgeons, N.Y.C., lectr. on anatomy, 1807, prof. anatomy, surgery, 1808, prof. anatomy, surgery, physiology, 1811, 1825-31, pres. coll., 1831-43; pres. Coll. William and Mary, 1814-25, attempted unsuccessfully to move coll. to Richmond. Author: Prelections on Some of the More Important Subjects Connected with Moral and Physical Science, 1853. Editor: Medical and Physiological Jour., 1809; co-editor N.Y. Med. and Physical Jour., 1828. Died N.Y.C., Feb. 9, 1865.

SMITH, JOHN BERNHARDT, entomologist; b. New York, Nov. 21, 1858; s. John and Elizabeth S.; pub. sch. edn.; hon. Sc.D., Rutgers, 1891; m. Marie von Meske, June 22, 1886. Admitted to bar, 1879; spl. agt. Entomol. Div., U.S. Dept. Agr., 1884; asst. curator U.S. Nat. Mus., 1886; state entomologist of N.J., 1898; prof. entomology, Rutgers Coll., and entomologist N.J. Agrl. Coll. Expt. Sta., 1889—. In charge of N.J. State campaign against the mosquito pest, with an appropriation of $350,000. Fellow A.A.A.S. Editor Bulletin Brooklyn Entomol. Soc. and Entomologia Americana, to 1890; contbr. of several hundred articles to govt. and tech. publications. Author: Economic Entomology for the Farmer and Fruit-Grower, and for Use as a Text Book in Agricultural Schools and Colleges, 1896; Our Insect Friends and Enemies, 1909. Address: New Brunswick, N.J. Died Mar. 12, 1912.

SMITH, JOHN HAMMOND, prof. civil engring.; b. Wellsville, O., Oct. 14, 1867; s. John William and Almira (Hart) S.; E.E., Western U. of Pa. (now U. of Pittsburgh), 1898; post-grad. work, Cornell U., summer of 1900; m. Anna D. Coleman, July 3, 1901 (died 1906); children—Anna Virginia, Lillian Isabella; m. 2d, Gertrude M. Smith, June 23, 1909 (died 1918); m. 3d, Helen C. Dalrymple, June 25, 1919; children—Helen Ilene, Evelyn Almira, Martha Louise. With Julian Kennedy, Riter-Conley Mfg. Co., Am. Bridge Co. and Concrete Products Co., Pittsburgh, 1896-1910; supt. shops and instr., 1898-1900, prof. drawing, 1900-09, prof. civ. engring., 1909—, U. of Pittsburgh. Republican. Presbyn. Contbr. many papers on engring. and photo-sculpture. Inventor of new photo-sculpturing process and instruments for testing materials. Home: Pittsburgh, Pa. Died 1932.

SMITH, JOHN LAWRENCE, chemist, med. scientist; b. Charleston, S.C., Dec. 17, 1818; s. Benjamin Smith; attended U. Va., 1835-37; M.D., Med. Coll. of S.C., 1840; m. Sarah Julia Guthrie, June 24, 1852. With Dr. S. D. Sinkler founded So. Jour. of Medicine and Pharmacy (later became Charleston Med. Jour. and Review), 1846; adviser on cotton culture to Turkish govt., circa 1847, investigated their mineral resources and discovered emery and coal deposits, 1847-50; these observations were useful in discovery of several emery deposits in U.S.; prof. chemistry U. Va., 1852; prof. med: chemistry, toxicology U. Louisville (Ky.), 1854-66; his collection of meteoric stones (one of finest in Am.) sold to Harvard; pres. Louisville Gas Works; founder, liberal benefactor Baptist Orphanage of Louisville; pres. A.A.A.S., 1872; mem. Nat. Acad. Sciences. Author: (collected papers) Mineralogy and Chemistry; Original Researches, 1873. Died Louisville, Ky., Oct. 12, 1883; buried Cave Hill Cemetery, Louisville.

SMITH, J(OHN) WARREN, meteorologist; b. Grafton, N.H., Sept. 21, 1863; s. John R. and Mary E. (Wadleigh) S.; B.S., N.H. Coll. Agr. and Mechanic Arts, 1888, M.S., 1900; Lawrence Scientific Sch. (Harvard), 1891-92; grad. Summer Sch. of Agr., Ohio State U., 1902; married twice; children—(by 1st marriage) Ruth Eaton, Russell Wellington; (by 2d marriage) Audrey. Began with U.S. Weather Bur., 1888; dir. N.E. sect., 1890-96, Mont. sect., 1896-97, Ohio sect., 1898-1900; dist. forecaster at St. Louis, 1909-10; prof. meteorology and dir. Ohio sect., 1910-15; also prof. meteorol. science, Ohio State U., 1910-15; apptd. chief of div. agrl. meteorology, Weather Bur., Washington, 1916. Pres. Ohio Acad. Science, 1914-15. Author: Agricultural Meteorology, a Study in Weather and Crops (Rural Text Book Series), 1920. Home: Columbus, O. Died Jan. 21, 1940.

SMITH, J(ONAS) WALDO, civil engr.; b. Lincoln, Mass., Mar. 9, 1861; s. Francis and Abigail Prescott (Baker) S.; Phillips Acad., Andover, Mass.; C.E., Mass. Inst. Tech., 1887; D.Engring., Stevens Inst. Tech., 1918; D.Sc., Columbia, 1918. Chief engr. water works of his home town at 17; asst. in office of Essex Co., Lawrence, 1881-83; asst., summers, Holyoke Water Power Co., 1884, 85, and 1887-90; joined staff of Clemens Herschel, 1890; res. engr. E. Jersey Water Co., looking after constrn. of 4 reservoirs and dams on Pequannock watershed, 1890-92; prin. asst. engr., same co., in charge Passaic Water Co., Paterson, and also engr. Montclair Water Co. and Acquackanonk Water Co., of Passaic, 1892-1900; chief engr. E. Jersey Water Co., 1900-1903; chief engr. aqueduct commrs. of New York, 1903-05; completed constrn. of new Croton dam (largest masonry dam in the world); chief engr. Bd. of Water Supply of New York, 1905-22, cons. engr., 1922; cons. engr., Moffat Tunnel Commn., Denver, Boston and Providence Water Supplies, etc. Awarded John Fritz medal, 1918, "for achievement as engineer in providing the City of New York with a water supply"; Washington Award of Western Soc. Engrs., 1925. Conglist. Home: New York, N.Y. Died Oct. 14, 1933.

SMITH, LEON E(LKANAH), univ. prof.; b. Kemper, Ill., June 16, 1894; s. Jacob Elkanah and Elizabeth Edith (Smith) S.; B.S., Ottawa (Kan.) Univ., 1919; student, Univ. of Chicago, 1919-20; Ph.D., Univ. of Pa., 1926; m. Anna Louise Kuhn, June 7, 1922; children—Margaret (Mrs. Donald J. Bowers), Robert Donald. Teacher, dist. sch., Labette Co., Kan., 1912-13; prin., Lincoln Sch., Cherryvale, Kan., 1915-16; instr. physics, Univ. of Pa., 1920-28; Henry Chisholm prof. physics and dept. head, Denison U. Granville, O., 1928-54, senior professor, 1954-59, department chairman, 1957-59, emeritus professor of physics, 1959—; summer vis. prof. U. Conn., 1953, Ohio Wesleyan, 1957, 58. Superintendent Baptist Ch. Sch., Granville, 1932-50; mem. Granville Scout Troop com., since 1939, chmn., since 1945. Trustee, Pub. Affairs, since 1942 (pres. of bd. since 1946). Served with Kan. Nat. Guard, field arty., 1917-19. Recipient Silver Beaver award Boy Scouts, 1954. Fellow A.A.A.S., Ohio Acad. Sci., (v.p., sect. F, 1938-39); mem. Am. Phys. Soc., Acoustical Soc. of Am., Am. Assn. Physics Teachers, Ohio sect., Am. Phys. Soc. (sec.-treas., since 1942), Am. Inst. Physics, Am. Legion, Sigma Xi. Baptist. Mason (Acacia frat.). Club: Ohio Physics (pres., 1936-37). Asso. editor of Physics News, 1930-31. Research in radioactivity and luminescense. Home: 226 S. Main St., Granville, Ohio 43023. Died Jan. 22, 1961; buried Denison U. Cemetery, Granville.

SMITH, LLOYD DEWITT, designing engr.; b. Howell, Mich., Aug. 14, 1873; s. George Augustus and Henrietta Elizabeth (Savery) S.; ed. pub. schs. of Detroit, Mich.; m. Bessie King, Jan. 31, 1900 (divorced 1903); children—Lloyd Harold (dec.), Kenneth Homer; m. 2d Mabel E. Gale, May 8, 1915. Designing engineer, Murphy Iron Works, Detroit, 1893-1907; pres. Smith Chandelier Co.; established own bus. under name of Smith Chandelier Co., Detroit, Mich., 1907, ret. 1920. Mem. Gen. Soc. Mayflower Des. (dep. gov. gen.), S.A.R. (vice pres. general Nat. Soc., 1946-48), Soc. War of 1812 (pres. Mich. chapter 1946), Detroit Hist. Soc. Episcopalian. Mason (32 deg.), Home: 731 Grand Marais Blvd., Grosse Pointe 30 MI

SMITH, LLOYD RAYMOND, mfr.; b. Chicago, Ill., Aug. 21, 1883; s. Arthur Oliver and Edith (Nichols) S.; prep. edn., West Division High Sch., Milwaukee; student U. of Wis., LL.D., 1930; m. Agnes Gram, Jan. 30, 1915; children—Robert Lewis (dec.), June Ellyn, Lloyd Bruce, Suzanne, Dana Lou, Arthur Oliver. Began with The A. O. Smith Corp., mfrs. of automobile frames, etc., 1905, became pres. 1913, now chmn. bd., gen. mgr. and dir. Mem. advisory com. Milwaukee County Community Fund, Milwaukee Children's Hosp. Mem. Sigma Chi. Republican. Clubs: Milwaukee, Milwaukee Country. Developer of automatic plant for mass production of automobile frames (10,000 frames per day with force of 120 men); automatic steel pipe plant, having capacity of 32 miles of steel pipe per day; also the Smith-welding process. Home: 2220 N. Terrace Av. Office: The A. O. Smith Corp., Milwaukee, Wis. Died Dec. 23, 1944. *

SMITH, LOUIE HENRIE, chief in charge publications of Ill. Soil Survey; b. Crystal Lake, Ill., Apr. 15, 1872; s. Charles Watson and Ann (Robinson) S.; B.S., U. of Illinois, 1897, M.S., 1899; Ph.D., U. of Halle, Germany, 1907; m. Bessie I. Morgan, June 18, 1914. Assistant chemist, 1899-1903, chief asst. chemist, 1903-05, Ill. Agrl. Expt. Station (U. of Ill.); asst. prof. plant breeding, U. of Ill., 1905-11, prof., 1911-20, chief in charge of publications of Soil Survey since 1920, and acting head agronomy dept., 1913-14, 1918-19, emeritus prof. since 1940. Mem. Am. Chem. Soc., A.A.A.S., Am. Genetic Assn., Am. Soc. Agronomy, Ill. Acad. Science, Sigma Xi, Gamma Alpha, Phi Lambda Epsilon, Alpha Zeta, Gamma Sigma Delta. Universalist. Author of bulls. and other scientific contbns. along the lines of plant breeding and soil survey. Address: Rural Route No. 2 Urbana IL*

SMITH, MARION GERTRUDE, med. research; b. New Brighton, Pa.; d. Perry Alexander and Sula Gertrude (McLean) Smith; B.S., Ohio State, 1920, student grad. sch., 1922-24; unmarried. Undergrad. instr. dept. chemistry, Ohio State Univ., 1917-20, grad. instr., 1922-24; research asst., dept. biophysics, Harvard Med. Sch., 1924-26; research asst. (medicine), Rush Med. Coll., Univ. Chicago, 1928; medicine, clin. phys. therapy research dept., Gen. Electric X-Ray Corp., Chicago, 1926-28. Mem. Am. Bd. of Physical Medicine (asst. sec., treas. since 1947), Am. Soc. Physical Medicine (adv. mem., asst. sec. treas. since 1947), Am. Congress of Physical Medicine (exec. sec. since 1930), Am. Registry of Physical Therapy Technicians (treas. and registrar since 1935); executive secretary Baruch Committee, Phys. Medicine and Rehabilitation, since 1949. Member National Council on Family Relations. Member Theta Phi Alpha. Republican. Roman Catholic. Clubs: Zonta (bd. dirs., 1944-45), Illinois Club of Catholic Women. Home: 1455 E. 56th St., Chicago 37. Office: 30 Michigan Av., Chgo. 2. Died Aug. 19, 1951.

SMITH, NATHAN, physician, surgeon, educator, founder med. schs.; b. Rehoboth, Mass., Sept. 30, 1762; s. John and Elizabeth (Ide) Hills S.; M.B., Harvard, 1790, M.D. (hon.), 1811; M.D. (hon.), Dartmouth, 1801; m. Elizabeth Chase, Jan. 1791; m. 2d, Sarah Hall Chase, Sept. 1794; 10 children including Nathan Ryno. Practiced medicine in Cornish, N.H., 1787-96; prompted establishment of professorship of medicine at Dartmouth, 1798, prof., 1798-1814; pres. Vt. State Med. Soc., 1811; prof. Yale, 1813-29, through his personal efforts Conn. Legislature appropriated $20,000 to Yale Med. Sch. and development of bot. garden; performed successful ovariotomy, 1821; wrote Practical Essay on Typhous Fever, 1824; edited American Medical Review, 1824-26. Died New Haven, Conn., Jan. 26, 1829.

SMITH, NATHAN RYNO, surgeon, educator; b. Cornish, N.H., May 21, 1797; s. Dr. Nathan and Sarah Hall (Chase) S.; A.B., Yale, 1817, M.D., 1823; postgrad. U. Pa. Med. Sch., 1825, 26; m. Juliette Octavia Penniman, 1824; 8 children including Alan Penniman. Established med. sch. at U. Vt., circa 1824, with aid of his father; prof. anatomy, physiology, 1824-36; tchr. anatomy, mem. 1st faculty Jefferson Med. Coll., 1826-27; with father and others edited Am. Med. Review, circa 1825-26; founder Phila. Monthly Jour. of Medicine and Surgery, 1827, editor, 1827-28; prof. anatomy U. Md., 1827, prof. surgery, 1829-38, 40-70, prof. emeritus, 1870-77; founder, editor Balt. Monthly Jour. Medicine and Surgery, 1830; published Surgical Anatomy of the Arteries, 1832; constructed the anterior splint; prof. surgery Transylvania U., Lexington, Ky., 1838-40. Died Balt., July 3, 1877.

SMITH, NICOL HAMILTON, chemist; b. Phila., Pa., Apr. 20, 1899; s. Frank G. and Jeannie M. (McPherson) S.; B.S., U. of Pa., 1923, M.S., 1924, Ph.D., 1927; m. Agnes Morton, December 31, 1927; 1 dau., Isabelle M. Instr. U. of Pa., 1924-27; chief chemist Solidon Products, Inc., Phila., 1927-32; with Franklin Inst. Phila., 1932-70, asso. dir., 1932-50, exec. director labs., 1950-53, dir., 1953-70. Sr. tech. aide, N.D.R.C., 1942-44. Presdl. Certificate of Merit, World War II. Mem. Am. Chem. Soc., Am. Physical Soc., Phi Beta Kappa, Sigma Xi, Tau Beta Pi. Mason. Home: Huntingdon Valley PA Died Aug. 21, 1970.

SMITH, NORMAN MURRAY, educational adminstrator; born Williston, S.C., November 16, 1883; son Dr. Winchester C. and Eugenia Kanapau (Murray) S.; graduate U.S. Naval Academy, 1906; C.E., Rensselaer Poly. Inst., 1909; grad. Naval War Coll., 1926; hon. Dr. Eng. Rensselaer Poly. Inst., 1939; m. Genevieve Thompson, June 11, 1921. Around the world as midshipman on U.S.S. Colorado, transferred as jr. lieut. Civ. Engr. Corps, Apr. 20, 1907; promoted through grades to rear adm., Dec. 3, 1933; chief of Bur. of Yards and Docks and chief civil engr. of the Navy, 1933-38. Engaged on constrn. and maintenance of Training Sta. (Great Lakes, Ill.), Navy Yards of Puget Sound and Mare Island; built naval base, Pearl Harbor, 1914-17; built plants, hospitals, dredged harbors and developed waterfronts in 6th and 11th Naval Dists., World War I; duty in naval dists. and Bur. Yards and Docks, at San Diego, Norfolk, Washington, and Boston, 1913-33; built air sta. and all naval establishments within San Diego Naval Base, 1918-23; adminstr. Works Progress Adminstrn., 1935-38; retired Dec., 1937; returned to active duty with Naval Constrn. Battalions, Camp Parks, Calif., 1942; ret., 1945; pres. Univ. of South Carolina, 1946-52. Mem. Am. Soc. C.E., Am. Mil. Engineers, Nat. Soc. Professional Engrs., Mil. Order of the Carabao, Theta Xi. Democrat. Mason, K.T. Clubs: Athenian (Oakland, Calif.); Union (Boston); Arlington (Portland, Ore.); Army and Navy, Army-Navy Country (Washington); Chevy Chase, Cuyamaca (San Diego, Calif.). Home: Williston SC Died Nov. 1968.

SMITH, OBERLIN, engineer; b. Cincinnati, O., Mar. 22, 1840; s. George R. and Salome (Kemp) S.; ed. W. Jersey Acad., Bridgeton, N.J., 1859, Poly. Inst., Phila., etc.; studied engring.; m. Charlotte Hill, Dec. 25, 1876; children—Winifred Hill, Percival Hill. Started, 1863, business which became Ferracute Machine Co.; invented and designed its standard products. Awarded about 70 patents upon mech. inventions. N.J. commr. to Pan-Am. Expn., 1901. Author: Press Working of

Metals, 1896; The Material, Why Not Immortal?, 1920. Contbr. to engring. jours. and procs. Took active interest in Anti-Slavery cause, later in Y.M.C.A. and woman suffrage. Home: Bridgeton, N.J. Died July 18, 1926.

SMITH, PAUL KENNETH, educator; b. Brashear, Mo., Sept. 10, 1908; s. William Robert and Virginia (Johnston) S.; A.B., Westminster Coll., 1930; Ph.D., Yale, 1934; m. Elizabeth Robison Baker, Sept. 12, 1931; children—Robert Kenneth Robison, Katharine Virginia Rice, James Calvin Henderson. Asst. chemistry Westminster Coll., 1926-30; asst. physiol. chemistry, Yale, 1932-34, research fellow pharmacology, 1934-36, instr., 1936-38, asst. prof., 1938-41, chief pharmacology and biochemistry, sch. aviation med., 1942-46; prof. pharmacology and head dept. school medicine George Washington U. since 1946. Consultant therapeutics, University, D.C. General hosps. Served as capt. to colonel, USAF, 1941-46; mobilization assignment (colonel). Office Director Research, U.S.A.F. Delegate International Chemistry Union, London, 1947. Fellow New York Academy Sciences; member American Assn. Cancer Research, Am. Chem. Soc., Soc. Exptl. Biol. Med., Am. Soc. Biol. Chemists, Am. Soc. Pharmacol. Exptl. Therapeutics (councilor 1955-58), A.A.A.S., Aero-Medical Assn. Washington Acad. Medicine, Sigma Xi (chpt. pres. 1950-51), Phi Chi. Club: Cosmos. Author articles on pharmacology, biochemistry, radiobiology and chemotherapy. Home: 4323 Murdock Mill Rd., Washington 16. Office: 1335 H St., Washington 5. Died Oct. 6, 1960; buried Arlington Nat. Cemetery.

SMITH, PERCEY FRANKLYN, mathematician; b. Nyack, N.Y., Aug. 21, 1867; s. James and Maria Jane (Demarest) S.; Ph.B., Yale, 1888, Ph.D., 1891; univs. of Göttingen, Berlin, Paris, 1894-96; m. Julia C. Lum, Dec. 23, 1890; m. 2d, Ethel Harned Gauvran, Nov. 11, 1922. Instr. mathematics, 1888-94, asst. prof., 1895-1900, prof., 1900-36, now emeritus, Sheffield Scientific Sch. Mem. Conn. Acad. Arts and Sciences, Am. Math. Soc. Author: Elements of Differential and Integral Calculus (edith with W. A. Granville), 1904, new edit. (with W. R. Longley), 1934; Elements of Analytic Geometry (with A. S. Gale), 1905; Introduction to Analytic Geometry (with same), 1905; Theoretical Mechanics (with W. R. Longley), 1910; Elementary Analysis (with W. A. Granville), 1910; New Analytic Geometry, revised edit. (with A. S. Gale and J. H. Neelley), 1928. Address: 250 Edgehill Rd., New Haven, Conn. Died June 3, 1956.

SMITH, PHILIP E., anatomist; b. De Smet, S.D., Jan. 1, 1884; s. John E. and Elmira (Stratton) S.; B.S., Pomona Coll., 1908; M.S., Cornell U., 1910, Ph.D., 1912; Sc.D., Princeton, 1948, Pomona Coll., 1950, Columbia, 1954; m. Irene Patchett, 1913; children—Frederika Patchett, Philip Bartlett. Asst. instr. in anatomy Cornell U., 1910-11, instr., 1911-12; instr. in anatomy, U. Cal., 1912-17, asst. prof., 1917-21, asso. prof., 1921-26; asso. prof. anatomy, Stanford, 1926-27; prof. anatomy, Columbia, 1927-52, prof. emeritus, 1952-70; research associate Stanford University, 1956-70. Recipient Charles Mickle fellowship, 1940, E. R. Squibb award, 1942. Mem. Am. Assn. Anatomist (pres. 1940-42), Am. Physiol. Soc., Soc. Exptl. Biology and Medicine (pres. 1937-38), Assn. Study Endocrina Glands (pres. 1939-40), Harvey Soc. (pres. 1938-40), French Legion of Honor, Nat. Acad. Sci., Sigma Xi. Democrat. Co-author Bailey's Histology. Home: Florence MA Died Dec. 1970.

SMITH, PHILIP SIDNEY, geologist; b. Medford, Mass., July 28, 1877; s. Sidney L. and Kate (Butler) S.; A.B., Harvard, 1899, A.M., 1900, Ph.D., 1904; m. Lenore W. Kinney, Nov. 26, 1900; children—Sidney Butler, Katharine, Constance Smith Thurrell. Asst. and instr. in geology and physiography Harvard, 1900-06; with U.S. Geol. Survey, 1906-46, successively asst. geologist, geologist, adminstrv. geologist, acting dir., and chief Alaska geologist, retired 1946; engr. Fed. Emergency Adminstrn. of Public Works for Alaska, 1933-34. Chmn. U.S. delegation 17th Internat. Geol. Congress, U.S.S.R., 1937. Fellow Geol. Soc. America, A.A.A.S., Assn. Am. Geographers, Soc. Econ. Geologists, Soc. Am. Mil. Engrs., Am. Geog. Society; mem. Nat. Geographic Soc. (life), Washington Acad. Sciences, Geol. Soc. Washington, Am. Inst. Mining and Metall. Engrs., Am. Polar Soc., Am. Geophys. Union, Soc. Profl. Geographers, Loyal Legion, Nat. Council of American-Soviet Friendship, Inc. (sci. com.), Arctic Inst. of North America. Clubs: Delta Upsilon, Cosmos, Harvard (Washington); Travellers (Harvard); Explorers (New York). Writer various reports on areal, economic and physiographic geology, in publs. U.S. Geol. Survey and tech. jours. Home: 3249 Newark St., Washington; (summer) Philip Smith Landing, Wolfeboro, N.H. Died May 10, 1949; buried Wolfeboro.

SMITH, PHILLIPS WALLER, mfr. aircraft and missile components; b. St. Paul, June 28, 1906; s. Albert Horace and Marie Ada (Cholvin) S.; student St. John's Mil. Acad., 1921-23; B.S., U.S. Mil. Acad., 1930; M.S., Mass. Inst. Tech., 1935; M.B.A., Harvard, 1940; m. Veronica Bernadette McVeigh, June 12, 1930; children—Ann (wife Dr. Henrik A. Hartmann), Veronica (Mrs. George P. Koss), Sandra Jane, Phillips Waller. Commd. 2d lt. U.S. Army, 1930, advanced through grades to col., 1947, USAF, 1947-55, brig. gen., 1950-53, maj. gen., 1953-55, now ret.; exec. v.p. Bowser, Inc., Chgo., 1955-56; pres. Jack & Heintz, Inc., Cleve., 1960—. Decorated D.S.M., Legion of Merit with cluster. Mem. Old Boys Assn. St. John's Mil. Acad. (nat. pres. 1958-59), U.S. Mil. Forum. Club: Chgo. Athletic Assn. Home: 13605 Shaker Blvd., Cleve. 20. Office: 17600 Broadway, Cleve. 1. Deceased.

SMITH, RALPH ELIOT, plant pathologist; b. Boston, Mass., Jan. 9, 1874; s. Obed F. and Emily M. (Simpson) S.; B.S., Mass. Agrl. Coll., 1894; U. of Munich, Germany, 1898; m. Jessie A. Carroll, of Wilmington, O., June 28, 1896; 1 son, William Carroll (dec.). Instr. in botany, 1894-96, asst. prof., 1896-1903, Mass. Agrl. Coll.; asst. prof. plant pathology, 1903-08, asso. prof., 1908-11, prof. since July 1, 1911, U. of Calif. Republican. Mem. Am. Phytopathol. Soc., Societe Mycologique de France, A.A.A.S., Phi Sigma Kappa, Alpha Zeta, Sigma Chi, Phi Sigma. Club: Faculty (U. of Calif.) Home: 2721 Hillegass Av., Berkeley CA

SMITH, ROBERT, architect.; patriot; b. probably in Glasgow, Scotland, 1722; 3 children. Came to U.S.; mem. Carpenters Co., Phila.; built Nassau Hall, Princeton U., 1754, progenitor of a school of Am. college architecture; designed St. Peter's Ch., Phila., 1758; mem. Pa. Com. of Correspondence, 1774, originated plan to block Delaware River; Phila.'s most eminent architect; became mem. Am. Philos. Soc., 1768. Died Feb. 11, 1777.

SMITH, R(OBERT) BLACKWELL, JR., educator, pharmacologist; b. Petersburg, Va., Nov. 2, 1915; s. Robert Blackwell and Mary Lavinia (Ridout) S.; S.B., Med. Coll. of Va., 1937; S.M., U. of Fla., 1938; Ph.D., University of Chicago, 1941; LL.D., Hampden Sydney College, 1966; m. to Esther Bergliot Ostrem, Sept. 6, 1942; children—Peter Blackwell, Susan (Mrs. George Cabell III), Nan. Grad. scholar U. of Fla., 1937-38; univ. fellow in pharmacol., U. of Chgo., 1938-41; pharmacol., div. pharm., U.S. Food and Drug Adminstrn., Washington, 1941-45, acting chief, 1945; lectr. to full prof. pharmacology Med. Coll. Va., 1945-57, dean sch. of pharmacy 1947-56, asst. pres., 1954-56, pres., 1956-68; 1st provost Med. Coll. Va., health scis. div. Va. Commonwealth U., 1968-69, prof. pharmacology, 1969-71; cons. pharmacol., 1947-71; nat. cons. pharmacology surg. gen. USAF, 1956-62. Dir., treas. U. Center in Va., 1960-71. Mem. com. food protection NRC, 1950-71; chmn. pres.'s coun. Va. State Instns. of Higher Edn. 1959-62; chmn. joint WHO-FOA expert com. on food additives, Geneva, 1957; member WHO expert adv. panel on health lab. methods, 1958-71. Mem. Am. Soc. for Pharmacol. and Exptl. Therapeutics, A.A.A.S., Sigma Xi, Phi Kappa Phi, Rho Chi. Democrat. Baptist. Researcher in toxicology and biol. assay. Clubs: Torch, Commonwealth. Rotary; Country. Home: Richmond VA Died Oct 8, 1971.

SMITH, ROY HARMON, mfr.; b. Staunton, Va., Feb. 19, 1879; s. James Wickliffe and Laura Eudora (Staples) S.; grad. Miller Manual Labor Sch., Va., 1895; student R.I. Sch. of Design 2 yrs.; M.E., Brown University, Providence, R.I., 1901, LL.D. (hon.), 1956; special course in metallurgy under Prof. Boylston of Case Sch. of Applied Science, 1922-23; D.Eng. (hon.), Kent (Ohio) State U., 1954; m. Jessie Duncan Munro, Apr. 4, 1904; children—Laura Jessie, Martha Barret, Alexander Munro, Roy Harmon. Teacher R.I. Sch. of Design, 1900, 01; designer of automatic machinery 4 yrs.; mech. engr. with Am. Bridge Co., Pencoyd, Pa., 1903; asst. supt. Russell Burdsall & Ward Bolt & Nut Co., Portchester, N.Y., 1904; chief draftsman Waterbury Farrel Foundry & Machine Co., automatic machinery dept., 1905-07; gen. supt. Nat. Screw & Tack Co., Cleveland, 1907-14; sec., treas., gen. mgr. Falls Rivet Co., Kent, O., 1914-22; v.p., dir. operations Lamson & Sessions Co., mfrs. bolts, nuts, rivets, cotter pins and automobile specials, 1922-38, pres., 1938-51, chmn. bd. 1951-61, now hon. chmn. bd. Trustee sinking fund of the City of Kent, 1922-23; vice mayor and president City Council, Kent, 1924-25, mayor, 1930-31; chmn. Charter Commn. of Kent. Maj. Ordnance Dept. U.S. Army, 1917-18; citation "for work of exceptional value to the Government." Tech. consultant, rank of col., serving with Foreign Economic Adminstrn. Europe, June-Aug. 1945. Fellow Am. Soc. Mechanical Engrs.; mem. Soc. Automotive Engrs., Am. Soc. Testing Materials, Am. Soc. for Steel Treating, A.A.A.S., Cleveland Engrs.' Soc., Am. Legion (post comdr. 1932), Ohio Soc. of New York, Sigma Xi. Recipient of 20 U.S. patents. Democrat. Conglist. Mason, Elk. Clubs: Union, University (Cleveland); Rotary, Wranglers, Twin Lakes Country (Kent, O.); Portage Country (Akron, O.). Appeal agent Draft Bd. 2, Kent, O. Home: Kent, O. Address: Lamson & Sessions Co., Cleveland, O. Died Nov. 9, 1963; buried Kent, O.

SMITH, SIDNEY IRVING, biologist; b. Norway, Me., Feb. 18, 1843; s. Elliot and Lavinia H. (Barton) S.; Ph.B., Sheffield Scientific Sch. (Yale), 1867; A.M., Yale, 1887; m. Eugenia P. Barber, June 29, 1882. Asst. in zoölogy, 1867-75, prof. comparative anatomy, 1875-1906, prof. emeritus, 1906—, Sheffield Scientific Sch. (Yale). Had charge of deep water dredging in Lake Superior for U.S. Lake Survey, 1871; and for U.S. Coast Survey about St. George's banks, 1872; asso. with biol. work, U.S. Fish Commn., for many yrs. Mem. Nat. Acad. Sciences, 1884—. Author of numerous papers, especially in marine zoölogy. Blind for several years. Address: New Haven, Conn. Died May 17, 1926.

SMITH, T. GUILFORD, engineer; b. Phila., Aug. 27, 1839; s. Pemberton and Margaretta E. (Zell) S.; A.B., Central High Sch., Phila., 1858, A.M., 1863; C.E., Rensselaer Poly. Inst., 1861; LL.D., Hobart, 1899, Alfred, 1903; hon. Phi Beta Kappa, Hobart, 1894; regent U. State of N.Y., 1890— (life office); m. Mary Stewart Ives, July 14, 1864. Civil engr. Phila. & Reading R.R., 1861-65; gen. mgr. Phila. Sugar Refinery, 1866-69; sec. Union Iron Co., Buffalo, 1873-78; sales agt. Phila. & Reading Coal & Iron Co., 1878-92; sales agt. Carnegie Steel Co., 1889-1911. Pres. Buffalo Library and Buffalo Fine Arts Acad.; pres. Charity Organization Soc. of Buffalo, 1888—; pres. Buffalo Soc. Natural Sciences; dir. Am. Soc. C.E., 1894-96; del. 11th Internat. Congress Medicine and Surgery, Rome, 1894; chmn. fine arts com. Buffalo Expn., 1901. Regent U. State of N.Y., 1890—. Mem. Am. Acad. Polit. and Social Science. Home: Buffalo, N.Y. Died Feb. 20, 1912.

SMITH, THEOBALD, Am. pathologist; b. Albany, N.Y., July 31, 1859; s. Philip and Theresa (Kexel) S.; Ph.B., Cornell, 1881; M.D., Albany Med. Coll., 1883; hon. degrees Harvard U. Chgo., Yale, Princeton, other univs.; m. Lillian H. Egleston, May 17, 1888; children—Dorothea Egleston, Lilian Hillyer (Mrs. Robert F. Foerster), Philip Hillyer. Dir. pathol. lab., Bur. Animal Industry, Dept. Agr., 1884-95; dir. pathol. lab. Mass. Bd. Health, 1895-1915. Prof. bacteriology Columbian (now George Washington) U., 1886-95; prof. comparative pathology Harvard, 1896-1915; dir. dept. of animal pathology Rockefeller Inst. for Med. Research, 1915-29; Harvard exchange prof. to Berlin, 1911-12; pres. Internat. Union Against Tb, 1926, Congress of Am. Physicians and Surgeons, 1928. Recipient Mary Kingsley, Kober, Flattery, Trudeau, Sedgwick, Holland Soc. and Gerhard medals; Copley medal of Royal Soc. of Gt. Britain. Fellow Am. Acad. Arts and Scis., Soc. Tropical Medicine and Hygiene (hon. London), Path. Soc. Gt. Britain and Ireland; mem. French Acad. Scis. Fellow Royal Soc., 1932. Contbr. numerous med. jours. on nature and causation of infectious and parasitic diseases. Discovered (with F. L. Kilborne) causative agt. of Tex. cattle fever, Pyrosoma bigeminum, 1893, proved disease is transmitted by cattle tick Boöphilus bovis; credited with 1st clear distinction between human and bovine tubercle bacilli, 1898; successfully used neutral toxin-anti-toxin mixtures for immunization against diphtheria, by 1909. Died Dec. 10, 1934.

SMITH, VINCENT WEAVER, engr.; b. McSherrystown, Pa., Oct. 25, 1892; s. Charles Dominic and Clara Amelia (Weaver) S.; B.S. in Chemistry, Pa. State U., 1914, M.S. in Chemistry, 1915; m. Gertrude Agnes Reilly, Apr. 7, 1921; children—Joan (dec.), Martha (Mrs. Dean Widner), Vincent Weaver, Elmore Charles (dec.). Teaching fellow chemistry Pa. State U., 1914-15; asst. chemist U.S. Navy, 1915; asst. chief chemist British Chem. Co., Ltd., 1915-17; chief chemist College Point plant British Am. Chem. Co., 1917, chief chemist and asst. supt. Ridgefield Park (N.J.) plant, 1917-18; engr. Harbor Sales & Mfg. Co., 1918-21; works mgr. and engr. Atlantic Tar & Chem. Works, 1921-26; engr. The Superheater Co., 1926-31; asst. to pres., head oil dept. The Lummus Co., N.Y.C., 1931-35; v.p. Broderick Co., Muncie, Ind., 1935-39; project dir., asst. to v.p., the Lummus Co., 1939-49, v.p. charge engring., 1949-55, v.p. charge contracts for co. and subsidiaries 1955—. First lt., U.S. Army, 1917. Fellow, dir. Am. Soc. M.E. Patentee in field. Home: 3 Midland Gardens, Bronxville, N.Y. 10708. Office: 385 Madison Av., N.Y.C. 10017. Died Apr. 10, 1964.

SMITH, WARREN DU PRÉ, geologist; b. Leipzig, Germany, May 12, 1880; s. Prof. Charles Forster and Anna Leland (Du Pré) S.; brought to U.S. in infancy; B.S., U. Wis., 1902, Ph.D., 1908; M.A., Stanford, 1904; fellow U. Chgo., 1904-05; m. Phoebe Ellison, July 14, 1910 (dec.); children—James Francis, Warren Ellison, Phoebe Hall. Field asst. Wis. Geol. and Natural History Survey, 1900-02; geologist U.S. Govt. Mining Bur., Manila, 1905-06, Div. of Mines, Bur. of Science, 1906-07; chief Div. of Mines, P.I., 1907-14; pres. Philippine Soc. Engrs., 1912; head dept. of geology U. Ore., 1914-47, ret. 1947; chief div. mines Bur. of Science, Philippine Govt., 1920, 21 (leave of absence from U. of Ore.); cons. geologist on Owyhee Dam, Ore., U.S. Bur. of Reclamation, 1927; ranger-naturalist Crater Lake Nat. Park, 1934, 35. U.S. del. Internat. Geol. Congress, Toronto, 1913; del 1st Pan-Pacific Sci. Conf., Honolulu, 1920; mem. Governor's Spl. Mining Com., Ore., 1935; mem. Philippine com. Pacific Sci. Bd. Fellow Geol. Soc. America (pres. Cordilleran sect. 1925), Pacific Geog. Soc., Ore. Tchrs. Assn. (pres. geog. council 1933), Ore. Mining Congress (pres. 1934), Ore. Acad. Sci. (pres.-elect. 1948), Phi Beta Kappa, Sigma Xi, Sigma Alpha Epsilon. Rotarian. Author: Geology and Mineral Resources of the Philippine Islands; Scenic Treasure House of Oregon, 1941; also about 50 articles and monographs on spl. phases of Philippine and Malayan geology and papers on Ore. and Pacific geology and geography. Editor: Physical and Economic Geography of Oregon, 1940. Home: 1941 University St., Eugene, Ore. Died July 18, 1950; buried Resthaven Meml. Park, Eugene.

SMITH, WILLIAM FARRAR, mil. and civil engr.; b. St. Albans, Vt., Feb. 17, 1824; s. Ashbel and Sarah (Butler) S.; apptd. to West Point, 1841; grad. in topog. engrs., 1845; m. Sarah Ward, Apr. 24, 1861. Served on survey of Upper Lakes, 1845-46; dept. mathematics, West Point, 1847-48; surveys in Texas, 1849-50, and of Mexican boundary, 1850-51; of Florida ship canal, 1853, and other engr. duties, 1861. Served under Gen. Butler to June 20, 1861; col. 3d Vt. vols., July 23, 1861, in defense of Washington; brig. gen. U.S. vols., Aug. 13, 1861; comd. div. in Army of Potomac in siege of Yorktown, battles of Lee's Mills, Williamsburgh, Golding's farm, Malvern Hill, Crampton's Gap, Antietam, etc.; comd. 6th corps at Fredericksburg, 1862; 9th corps, Mar. 17, 1863; comd. div. of N.Y. and Pa. militia at Gettysburg; chief engr. of army of the Cumberland, Oct. 3, 1863; planned and executed capture of Brown's Ferry, Tenn., Oct. 27, 1863, opening shorter line of communication for supplies; chief engr. div. of Miss., Nov. 16, 1863; planned battle of Missionary Ridge. Threw a bridge 1,500 feet long across the Tennessee River for Sherman's army. In command 18th army corps, Apr. 1864; in battles of Drury's Bluff and Cold Harbor; assaulted and carried line of fortifications at Petersburg, June 15, 1864, etc. Resigned as maj. gen. vols., Nov. 4, 1865; resigned from army, Mar. 7, 1867. Pres. Internat. Ocean Telegraph Co., 1865-73; pres. New York Bd. of Police, 1877; civil engr., 1881—. Author: From Chattanooga to Petersburg, under Generals Grant and Butler. Address: Philadelphia, Pa. Died 1903.

SMITH, WILLIAM GRISWOLD, prof. engring.; b. Toledo, O., July 18, 1869; s. William Henry Harrison and Julia Welles (Griswold) S.; Yale, 1887-89; M.E., Cornell U., 1892; m. Marion Evans Twiss, June 23, 1904; children—Madeleine Marion, Janet Griswold. Bicycle mfr., Toledo, O., 1894-99; instr. mech. engring., U. of N.D., 1902-04; asso. prof. mech. engring., Armour Inst. Tech., 1905-20; prof. engring., Northwestern U., 1920-30; prof. emeritus Northwestern Tech. Inst. since 1939; spl. lecturer, Defense Training Inst. New York, 1941-43; spl. lecturer descriptive geometry and industrial management, U. of Calif., 1923-24. Mem. Delta Kappa Epsilon, Sigma Xi. Republican. Methodist. Club: University. Author: Practical Descriptive Geometry, 1912; Engineering Kinematics, 1923; Motor Tour of British Isles, 1930; Engineering Drafting, 1934. Home: 161 Beechwood, Packanack Lake, N.J. Died Dec. 25, 1943.

SMITH, WILLIAM SOOY, civil engr.; b. Tarlton, O., July 22, 1830; s. Sooy and Ann (Hedges) S.; A.B., Ohio U., 1849, later A.M.; grad. U.S. Mil. Acad., 1853; m. Elizabeth Haven; m. 2d, Josephine Hartwell, 1884; father of Charles Sooysmith. Apptd. 2d lt. 3d Arty. U.S.A.; promoted 2d lt. 3d Arty. U.S.A., and stationed in N.M.; resigned; went to Chicago, 1854, entered engring. service of I.C. R.R. Co.; soon afterward apptd. asst. engr. to Col. Graham, U.S. engr. in charge of improvements of Lake Michigan harbors, but resigned because of dangerous illness; conducted select sch. at Buffalo, 1855-57; practiced as civ. engr., 1857-59; chief engr. of co. building iron bridge across Savannah River for Savannah & Charleston R.R. Co., 1860-61; served as lt. col., col. and brig. gen. U.S.A., Apr. 1861-Sept. 1864, when resigned because totally disabled by inflammatory rheumatism. When sufficiently recovered resumed practice as civ. engr. at Chicago. Did much difficult work as engr. and contractor for U.S. Govt. and ry. cos., including reconstruction of Waugoshanee Light House at western entrance of Straits of Mackinac; built 1st all-steel ry. bridge in world (Glasgow, Mo.), and sub-structures of 6 other bridges, by pneumatic process, which developed and greatly improved; with son, Charles Sooysmith, introduced into this country freezing process for difficult subaqueous work, and sank 2 shafts through quick-sands and boulders, to depth of 100 feet, which could not have been put down by any other known method. Completely changed methods of constructing foundations for heavy buildings in Chicago, carrying the loads down through mud and soft earth to hard bottom, 50 feet or more, by means of piles cut off below water surface, and where these could not be driven without endangering foundations of adjacent buildings, by sinking columns of concrete to hard bottom and resting the bldgs. on them; aided in development of plans of high steel bldgs. in Chicago and throughout world; leader in urging Govt. to create bd. to test Am. metals and mem. of that bd. during the 3 yrs. of its existence. Invented the 1st pneumatic caisson ever built; designed new system of fireproof building. Address: Medford, Ore. Died Mar. 4, 1916.

SMITHSON, JAMES, scientist; b. France, 1765; s. Hugh and Elizabeth Keate (Macie) S.; grad. Pembroke Coll., Oxford (Eng.) U., 1786; never married. Became mem. Royal Soc., 1787; devoted his life to study of chemistry and mineralogy; Smithsonite (carbonate of zinc) named for him; never visited U.S.; made his will, 1826, leaving his estate to a nephew, with the provision that if the nephew should die childless, the estate would go "to the United States of America, to found at Washington, under the name of the Smithsonian Institution, an Establishment for the increase and diffusion of knowledge among men." Died Genoa, Italy, June 26, 1829; buried Genoa, reinterred main entrance of Smithsonian Instn.

SMOCK, JOHN CONOVER, geologist; b. Holmdel, Monmouth County, N.J., Sept. 21, 1842; s. Isaac G. and Ellen (Conover) S.; A.B., Rutgers, 1862; studied Bergakademie, and U. of Berlin, 1869-70; Ph.D., Lafayette, 1882; LL.D., Rutgers, 1902; m. Katherine E. Beekman, Oct. 15, 1874 (died 1922). Tutor in chemistry, 1865-67, prof. elec. mining and metallurgy, 1867, also prof., 1871-85, Rutgers; asst. on geol. survey of N.J., 1864-85; asst. in charge N.Y. State Mus., 1885-90; state geologist of N.J., 1890-1901; mem. bd. mgrs. N.J. Geol. Survey, 1901-15. Fellow A.A.A.S. Home: Hudson, N.Y. Died Apr. 21, 1926.

SMOOT, CHARLES HEAD, mech. engr.; b. Ilion, N.Y., Dec. 6, 1878; s. William Sidney and Mary Bunker (Head) S.; ed. Harvard and U. of Calif.; m. Katherine Elizabeth Ryan, Oct. 12, 1910; children—Mary Katherine, Charles Head, William Sydney. Engaged as mech. engr. in Calif., 1900; engr. and dir. Rateau Steam Regenerator Co., 1908-22; same, Rateau, Battu, Smoot Co., 1911-23; pres. Smoot Engring. Corp., 1923—. Republican. Home: Maplewood, N.J. Died Jan. 6, 1933.

SMULL, THOMAS JEFFERSON, JR., engr.; b. Mackeyville, Pa., Sept. 22, 1875; s. Thomas J. and Harriet (Sybil) S.; student at Central State Normal Sch., Lock Haven, Pa., 1892-94, 97; student Susquehanna U., Pa., 1900-01; C.E., Ohio Northern U., 1904, Arch., 1906; student U. of Mich. (one semester), Lafayette Coll. (one semester), 1904-05; Eng.D., Oglethorpe U., 1921; m. Cora Anita Kemp, Oct. 4, 1906; children—Miriam May, Thomas Kemp. Dean Coll. of Engring. Ohio Northern U., 1905-17, exec. sec., 1917-29, bus. mgr., 1929-42; materials engr. Dept. of Hwys., State of Ohio, 1942-55. City engr., Ada, 1906-23, also consulting practice, mem. Bd. Examiners State Civil Service Commn., 1914-16; appraisal engr. State Utilities Commn., Ohio, 1915; sr. mem. Smull and Unger, architects, 1912-30. Chmn. and chief examiner Bd. of Registration for Profl. Engrs. and Surveyors, State of Ohio. Mem. Ohio Soc. Univ. Business Officers (pres. 1941), Ohio Athletic Conf. (pres. 1943), Ohio Soc. Profl. Engrs. (pres. 1918), Soc. Promotion Engring. Edn., Nat. Soc. Profl. Engrs., Phi Gamma Delta. Republican. Presbyn. (elder). Mason. Lectr. on engring. topics. Mem. Ohio Waterways Commn. and Great Lakes Tidewater Assn., 1923-31. Mem. Scioto Conservancy Bd. since 1924. Clubs: Kiwanis (lt. gov. O. dist. 1929), Lost Creek Country. Home: 301 S. Main St., Ada, O. 45810. Died Feb. 15, 1962; buried Woodlawn Cemetery, Ada.

SMYTH, CHARLES HENRY, JR., geologist; b. Oswego, N.Y., Mar. 31, 1866; s. Charles Henry and Alice (DeWolf) S.; Ph.B., Columbia, 1888, Ph.D., 1890; U. of Heidelberg, 1890-91; m. Ruth A. Phelps, July 30, 1891; children—Charles Phelps, Henry DeWolf. Prof. geology and mineralogy, Hamilton Coll., 1891-1905; prof. geology, Princeton U., 1905-34, emeritus, 1934. Fellow Geol. Soc. of America, A.A.A.S. Author of many papers on pre-Cambrian geology, petrology, ore deposits, etc. Address: Princeton, N.J. Died Apr. 4, 1937.

SMYTH, ELLISON ADGER, biologist; b. Summerton, Clarendon County, S.C., Oct. 26, 1863; s. James Adger and Annie R. (Briggs) S.; A.B., Princeton, 1884, A.M., 1887; law dept., Columbia, 1884-85; U. of Va., 1887; LL.D., U. of Ala., 1906; m. Grace C. Allan, Dec. 29, 1897; children—Thomas, Amey Allan, Ellison A., Grace Allan, James Adger. Adj. prof. biology, U. of S.C., 1889-91; prof. biology, Va. Poly. Inst., 1891-1925 (retired), also dean of faculty, 1902-06. Democrat. Presbyn. (elder). Author of various papers on entomology in Entomol. News; bird notes in "The Auk"; biography and estimate of works of John Bennett, in Library of Southern Literature. Address: Salem, Va. Died Aug. 19, 1941.

SMYTH, HENRY FIELD, (smith), hygienist; b. Phila., Pa., Nov. 1, 1875; s. Isaac Scott and Catherine Comegys (Mason) S.; prep. edn., Germantown Acad.; certificate in biology. Univ. of Pa., 1893, M.D., 1897, Doctor of Public Health, 1912; studied University Vienna, 1899-1900; married Alice E. Brackett 1902 (deceased 1929); children—Henry Field, Catherine Mason (Mrs. Wilson Brazer); m. 2d, Clara F. Ellis, Oct. 1931. Resident physician Phila. Home for Incurables, July-Dec. 1897, Germantown Hosp., 1898; gen. practice until 1911; pub. health student, U. of Pa., 1911-12, Wood fellow in hygiene, 1912-13, Scott fellow in hygiene, 1913-14; mem. faculty, U. of Pa., 1914—, successively instr. in bacteriology and hygiene, asst. prof. same, asst. professor industrial hygiene, 1921-39, professor of industrial hygiene, 1939-41, emeritus professor, 1942—; acting director Laboratory of Hygiene, 1917-19, director pro tem., 1932-39; dir. of Symth Laboratories, Phila., 1941-45; consultation and investigation of public and industrial health problems. Member Pa. Commn. on School Ventilation, Pa. Commn. on Occupational Disease Compensation. Passed asst. surgeon U.S.P.H. Res., World War; duty in industrial hygiene control, 1917-19. Fellow A.M.A., American Public Health Association (governing council 15 yrs.), Am. Coll. Physicians, Am. Assn. Indsl. Phys. and Surgeons (former dir.); mem. Sigma Xi. Methodist. Pioneer indsl. hygiene research, work in anthrax and carbon tetrachloride toxicity. Author: (with Walter Lord Obold) Industrial Microbiology, 1930. Contbr. scientific articles. Home and Office: Box 232, Pocasset, Mass. Died Oct. 15, 1954; buried Ivy Hill Cemetery, Mt. Airy, Phila.

SMYTH, HENRY LLOYD, univ. prof.; b. near St. Mary's, Ontario, Jan. 11, 1862; s. Rev. Thomas Henry and Charlotte (Hughes) S.; A.B., Harvard, 1883, C.E., 1885; m. Margarita Pumpelly, Nov. 8, 1894; children—Mrs. Charlotte P. Russell (dec.), Mrs. Pauline P. Fraser-Campbell, Henry Lloyd, Barbara E. Instr. geol. surveying, 1893-95, asst. prof. of mining, 1895-1900, prof. mining and metallurgy, Harvard, 1900-24, dir. mining and metall. labs., emeritus since 1924. Fellow Am. Acad. Arts and Sciences, Geol. Soc. Am.; mem. Am. Inst. Mining Engrs., Mining and Metall. Soc. Am. Clubs: Century, Harvard (New York); St. Botolph, Oakley, Harvard (Boston). Author various monographs, and contbr. to procs. of scientific socs. and jours. Home: Belmont St., Watertown, Mass. Died Apr. 2, 1944.

SMYTH, WILLIAM HENRY, engineer; b. Birkenhead, Cheshire, Eng., May 16, 1855; s. Henry and Ann Jane (Finglass) S.; ed. Yorkshire Coll. of Tech., Leeds, followed by apprenticeship with Kitson & Co., Leeds; draftsman with Asquith & Co., Leeds, 1874-76; came to U.S.; in gen. practice as cons. engr., 1879—; m. Helen Pauline Bradshaw, 1884. Inventor of many machines and devices, including a drag-saw, 1879; many machines for making, soldering, testing and heading cans, 1889-1903; mech. movement, 1890; pneumatic apparatus, 1896; hydraulic and chain bucket dredger, 1898; air compressor valve, 1899; art of utilizing heat energy, 1900; internally fired engine, 1900; ore roasting furnace, mech. stoker, valve, etc., 1901; printing press, 1902; deep well pump, 1903; also inventor of system of raising water by direct explosion on its surface, later universally known as the direct explosion pump; segmental cargo boat for war use, 1917; power drive-chain, 1920; roller-hinge for heavy-duty chain, 1921; track-layer chain, 1922; resilient-track tractor, 1922; high-speed tractor, 1922; track-layer track-assembly, 1923; two-point-support wheel-base track-layer, 1923; convertible tractor, 1924; combined track-layer and round-wheel tractor, 1925; friction-drive track-layer, 1928; military tractor, 1929; convertible noiseless track-layer tractor, 1932; convertible tractor, 1932; new system of highspeed non-stop, railroad transportation, 1933. Life fellow Royal Econ. Soc. (London); fellow Am. Geog. Soc.; mem. Am. Acad. Polit. and Social Science. Author: Is the Inventive Faculty a Myth, 1895; Technocracy—National Industrial Management, 1917; Federation of Nations, 1922; The Story of the Stadium, 1923; Concerning Irascible Strong, 1926; Did Man and Woman Descend from Different Animals? A New Theory of the Origin of the Sexes, 1927; Coming Events, "Social Credit" Criticized, The Truth About Technocracy, 1933; National Master Code—Industrial Constitution for National Industrial Management, 1934; Women in Industry, 1934; Money and Currency, 1935; Problem of Crime, 1938; also many essays on economics and social science. Home: Berkeley, Calif. Died Feb. 18, 1940.

SNEED, WILLIAM LENT, orthopedic surgeon; b. Nashville, Tenn., Mar. 21, 1881; s. William Lent and Mary Lucy (Waller) S.; student Nashville Bible Coll., 1904-06; M.D., Vanderbilt Med. Sch., 1910; m. Marion E. Stokes, June 19, 1920; children—William Lent, Constance Blake, Pamela Ann Waller. Instr. in anatomy, Vanderbilt U., 1910-11; became attending surgeon orthopedic dept., Hosp. for Ruptured and Crippled, New York, 1912; now cons. surgeon Hosp. for Ruptured and Crippled and Meadow Brook Hosp. (Hempstead, L.I.); instr. in applied anatomy, Cornell U. Med. Coll., since 1917; cons. orthopedic surgeon Nassau County, French and North Shore Community hosps. Lt. Med. Corps, World War. Fellow Am. Coll. Surgeons; mem. A.M.A.; Acad. of Medicine, N.Y. Southern Soc., Tenn. Soc. of N.Y. Democrat. Clubs: Cornell, Racquet and Tennis (New York); Golf. Author: Orthopedics in Childhood, 1931. Home: 570 Park Av. Office: 654 Madison Av., New York, N.Y. Died Dec. 7, 1941.

SNELLING, WALTER OTHEMAN, chemist, inventor; b. Washington, D.C., Dec. 13, 1880; s. Walter Comonfort and Alice Lee (Hornor) S.; B.S. in Chemistry, Columbian (now George Washington) U., 1904; B.S. in Science, Harvard, 1905; M.S., Yale, 1906; Ph.D., George Washington U., 1907; Sc.D. (honorary), Lehigh University, 1963; m. Marjorie Gahring Snelling, an adopted dau., May 5, 1919; children—William Augustus, Robert Fulton, Constance Charlotte, Richard Arkwright, Marilyn Verna (adopted), Charles Darwin, Thomas Edison, Priscilla Cottrell, Walter Preston. Began in ednl. and scientific work, U.S. Bureau of Mines, 1907-12, consulting chemist, same, Jan.-Sept., 1912; consultant to Atomic Energy Commission. Inventor of waterproof detonator, continuous high-pressure oil-cracking process, sand-test method of testing detonators and explosives, densimeter used in testing dynamite, improved centrifuge test for explosives, a liquid gas (L.P.G.) made from waste natural gas (left Government service to develop this and other patents). Granted more than 200 patents covering inventions in fields of chemical products and explosives. Director research, Trojan Powder Co. 1917-54. Gave many inventions to U.S. Govt. without reserve (estimated that the waterproof detonator saved Govt. more than $500,000 a yr. in Panama Canal work). Recipient Edward Longstreth Medal, Franklin Inst., 1962. Republican. Member American Institute Mining and Metall. Engineers, American Chem. Society, American Electrochem. Society, Army Ordnance Association, Society of Am. Military Engineers, Engineers Club of the Lehigh Valley, Franklin Inst., etc. Club: Chemists' (New York). Author of about 50 scientific papers pub. by Bur. of Mines and scientific socs. Home: 1509 Linden St., Allentown, Pa. 18102. Died Sept. 10, 1965.

SNIDER, LUTHER CROCKER, (sni'der), geologist; b. Mt. Summit, Ind., Sept. 13, 1882; s. John and Lou (Leath) S.; student Rose Poly. Inst., 1903-04, U. of Okla., 1910-11; A.B., Ind. U., 1908, A.M., 1909; Ph.D., U. of Chicago, 1915; m. Ruth Gladys Marshall, Mar. 31, 1907; children—Hester Bernice, John Luther. Teacher common and high schs., 1901-03 and 1904-06; chemist, field geologist and asst. dir. Okla. Geol. Survey, 1909-15; field geologist Pierce Oil Corp., Tulsa, Okla., 1915-16, Cosden Oil & Gas Co., 1916-17; asst. chief and chief geologist Empire Gas & Fuel Co., Bartlesville, Okla., 1917-25; cons. geologist Henry L. Doherty & Co., 1925-35; same, Cities Service Co., 1935-40; prof. of geology, U. of Texas, since 1941. Fellow A.A.A.S., Geol. Soc. America, Soc. Econ. Geology; mem. Am. Assn of Petroleum Geologists (editor 1933-37; pres. 1940), Sigma Xi, Phi Beta Kappa (alumnus). Republican. Methodist. Mason. Author: Petroleum and Natural Gas in Oklahoma, 1913; Oil and Gas in the Mid-Continent Fields, 1920; Earth History, 1932; also various bulls. of Okla. Geol. Survey, 1910-16. Contbr. to scientific mags. Home: 1300 Northwood Rd., Austin 21, Tex. Deid May 24, 1947; buried Mount Summit, Ind.

SNODGRASS, ROBERT EVANS, entomologist; b. St. Louis, Mo., July 5, 1875; s. James Cathcart and Annie Elizabeth (Evans) S.; ed. Stanford U.; m. Ruth Mae Hansford, Sept. 18, 1924; children—Ruth Maye, Eleanor Hansford. Began teaching at Wash. State Coll., 1901; with Bur. of Entomology and Plant Quarantine, U.S. Dept. Agr., since 1918. Mem. Entomol. Soc. America, Washington Entomol. Soc.; hon. mem. Royal Entomol. Soc. of London, Societe Entomologique de Belgique, New York Entomol. Society, Societe Entomologique de France. Author: Anatomy and Physiology of the Honeybee, 1925; Insects, Their Ways and Means of Living, 1930; Principles of Insect Morphology, 1935; also technical papers on anatomy, metamorphosis and feeding apparatus of insects. Home: 3706 13th St. N.W., Washington DC

SNOOK, H(OMER) CLYDE, (snook), electrophysicist; b. Antwerp, O., Mar. 25, 1878; s. Wilson Hunt and Nancy Jane (Graves), S.; A.B., Ohio Wesleyan U., 1900, M.S., 1910, Sc.D. from same university, 1926; A.M., Allegheny Coll., Meadville, Pa., 1902; post-grad. work, U. of Pa., 1904-08; m. May Eusebia McKee, June 24, 1903. Prof. physics and chemistry, High Sch., Ohio Soldiers and Sailors Orphans' Home, Xenia, O., 1900-01; asst. prof. chemistry, Allegheny Coll., 1901-02; wireless telegraph expert, with Queen & Co., Phila., Pa., 1902-03; pres. Roentgen Mfg. Co., Phila., 1903-13, Snook-Roentgen Mfg. Co., Phila., 1913-16; v.p. Victor Electric Corp., Chicago, 1916-18; elec. engr. with Western Elec. Co., 1918-25; elec. engr. with Bell Telephone Labs., 1925-27; cons. engr. since 1927. Fellow Am. Inst. E.E., Am. Physical Soc.; mem. Am. Roentgen Ray Soc., Phila., Roentgen Society, Phi Beta Kappa, Phi Delta Theta. Awarded Edward Longstreth medal, Franklin Inst., 1919; gold medal, Radiol. Soc. of North America, 1923; hon. fellowship and gold medal, Am. Coll. Radiology, 1928. Chmn. noise elimination com. Nat. Safety Council, 1930. Presbyterian. Mason. Inventor X-ray transformer; numerous patented developments in X-rays, radio, the communication art, metallurgy and optics. Home: 45 Woodland Av., Summit, N.J. Died Sep. 22, 1942.

SNOW, BENJAMIN WARNER, physicist; b. Henry, Ill., Aug. 15, 1860; s. Norman G. and Charlotte D. (Warner) S.; B.S., Cornell, 1885; U. of Göttingen, 1887; U. of Strassburg, 1888; U. of Berlin, 1890-92, Ph.D., 1892; m. Agnes Campbell Butler, Sept. 22, 1896 (dec.). Fellow in physics, Cornell U., 1885-86; instr. physics, Ohio State U., 1886-87, Cornell, 1888-90; prof. physics, Ind. U., 1892-93, U. of Wis., 1893-1926 (retired). Fellow A.A.A.S. (sec. Sect. B, 1894). Home: Madison, Wis. Deceased.

SNOW, FRANKLIN AUGUSTUS, civil engr., retired; b. Providence, R.I., Feb. 10, 1856; s. Stephen W. and Harriet R. (Fisher) S.; ed. pub. schs., Providence, R.I.; m. Grace Darling, Feb. 23, 1887; children—Irene, Beatrice. Began as civil engr. at Providence, R.I., 1873; followed civil engring. for 9 yrs. in Brazil, Central Am. and Colo.; studied rys. of Peru and Chile, 1885; made surveys for the first steam railroad in Salvador, C.A., and helped to build same; chief engr. for the Dutch contractors for excavating the Culebra Cut, Panama Canal, also for Am. Contracting & Dredging Co., at Colon, Panama Canal, 1885, 86, during the time of Ferdinand de Lesseps; returned to U.S., 1886, and engaged in gen. contracting, building waterworks and sewerage systems; contractor since 1901 for underground conduit systems for Edison Electric Illuminating Co., of Boston, Fall River Electric Light Co., Cambridge Electric Light Co., and New Bedford Electric Light Co. Fellow Royal Geog. Soc., London; mem. Am. Soc. C.E., Boston Soc. C.E., Soc. Mayflower Descendants, Boston C. of C. Clubs: Engineers, University, Algonquin, Boston Art, Brae Burn Country, Boston Athletic. Home: 199 Dean Rd., Brookline, Mass. Died March 19, 1942.

SNYDER, BAIRD, III, civ. engr.; b. Lansford, Pa.; s. Baird and Jennie Craig (Romig) S.; student Cornell U., Yale; grad. Mass. Inst. Tech., 1924; m. Beatrice B. Short, Nov. 14, 1936; children—Baird, IV, Collins. Engr. ry. and anthracite mining, 1918-25; asst. supt., Lawrence Colliery, Madera Hill Coal Co., Frackville, Pa., 1925; pres. and gen. mgr., Snyder Engring. Co., 1926-35; chief engr., U.S. Farm Security Adminstrn., 1937-39; dep. adminstr., Wage and Hour Div., U.S. Dept. Labor, 1939-42; became asst. (dep.) adminstr., Federal Works Agency, 1942. Mem. Sigma Phi. Episcopalian. Home: 8 Blackstone Rd., Westmoreland Hills, Md. Office: 6137 Federal Works Agency Bldg., Washington, D.C. Died May 18, 1946.

SNYDER, JOHN OTTERBEIN, zoology; b. Butler, Ind., Aug. 14, 1867; s. James D. and Maria Adeline (Kiser) S.; A.B., Stanford U., 1897, A.M., 1899; m. Frances Arle Hamilton, June 2, 1901; children—Evelyn Hamilton, Cedric Otterbein. Asst. U.S. Fish Commn. large part of time, 1907-16; naturalist on U.S. Albatross, deep sea investigations, 1902, 06; expert ichthyologist U.S. Nat. Museum, 1914; fisheries expert Calif. Div. of Fish and Game, 1909-30; dir. U.S. Bur. of Fisheries Marine Lab., Woods Hole, Mass., 1926; exec. head dept. of zoology, Stanford U., 1926-32, emeritus prof. since 1932; in charge Bur. of Fish Conservation Division of Fish and Game of Calif., 1931-37. Fellow A.A.A.S., Calif. Acad. Science; mem. Sigma Xi, Cooper Ornithol. Club. Author of numerous papers and monographs on the geog. distribution and speciation of fishes of West America, Mexico, Hawaii, Japan and Okinawa; also Life History of Salmon. Home: Stanford University CA

SNYDER, MONROE B(ENJAMIN), astronomer; b. at Quakertown, Pa., Mar. 13, 1848; s. Amos Hinkle and Mary Ann (Plank) S.; prep. edn. Bucks County Normal and Classical Sch. and prep. dept. Pa. Coll.; Pa. Coll., 1866-68 and 1870; B.A., U. of Mich., 1872, M.A., 1875; m. Martha Julia Sheain, July 6, 1875 (died 1879); m. 2d, Susan Chaplin Berry, June 14, 1882. Instr. astronomy and mathematics, 1873-80, prof., 1880—, head of dept. of mathematics, 1896—, in charge obs., 1873-97, dir. Phila. Obs., 1897—, Central High Sch., Phila. Pres. bd. examiners elec. exhbn. Franklin Inst., 1884; mem. and sec. U.S. Elec. Commn., 1884; sec. Nat. Conf. Electricians, 1884. First to propose and plan Nat. Bur. of Standards in address, Sept. 10, 1884, before Nat. Conf. of Electricians, which, with the comments thereon by Sir William Thomson (Lord Kelvin), was reprinted for the 56th Congress, 1900, establishing the bureau. Planned Phila. Obs. equipment, 1897-1905, which was almost wholly destroyed by fire, Mar. 9, 1905, and was later partially restored. Fellow Royal Astron. Soc., A.A.A.S. Contbr. astron. articles on edn., and papers on astronomy in scientific jours. Announced, Jan. 20, 1905, discovery of the cosmic force, radioaction, due to the explosive transformation of the elements at critical physical conditions in the stars; discovered, 1909, stellar and terrestrial evidence of the serial explosive transformation of the atoms in the rare gas group; discovered, 1917, relation between atomic number and atomic mass of the elements which led by Aug. 3, 1918, to the complete, definitive proof that all atoms are explosive compounds of hydrogen, and to its expression in "The Fundamental Periodic Table of the Chemical Elements," which gives the true atomic number and true atomic mass of every known and unknown element and records the incidental discovery of the new rare gas, astron. Address: Philadelphia, Pa. Died 1932.

SNYDER, VIRGIL, coll. prof.; b. Dixon, Ia., Nov. 9, 1869; s. Ephraim and Elisa Jane (Randall) S.; B.Sc., Iowa State Coll., 1889; Cornell U., 1890-92; Ph.D., U. of Göttingen, 1894, studied same, 1899, 1903, Italy 3 yrs.; Heckscher fellow, Italy, 1921-22 and 1928-29; hon. doctorate, U. of Padua, 1922; m. Margarete Giesinger, Dec. 28, 1894; children—Herbert, Norman. Instr. mathematics, Cornell U., 1895-1903, asst. prof., 1903-10, prof., 1910-38, now emeritus. Visiting prof. mathematics, Brown Univ., 1942-43, Rollins College, Winter Park, Florida, 1943-44. Mem. National Research Council, 1926-29. Republican. Conglist. Mem. Am. Mathematical Society (editor Bulletin, 1903-21; mem. committee on publication, 1907-21; review editor since 1938; president, 1927-28), Deutscher Mathematiker-Verein, Circolo Matematico di Palermo, Sigma Xi, Gamma Alpha; fellow Am. Acad. Arts and Sciences, 1919. Club: Tennis Club. Author: Differential Calculus (with James McMahon, q.v.), 1898; Differential and Integral Calculus, 1902; Elementary Text-book on the Calculus, 1912; Analytic Geometry of Space, 1913; Topics in Algebraic Geometry, 1928, Supplement, 1935. Editor: Plane Geometry, 1910; Solid Geometry, 1912; also semi-centennial publs. of Am. Math. Soc., 1938. Home: 214 University Av., Ithaca, N.Y. Died Jan. 4, 1950.

SODDY, FREDERICK, physicist; b. Eastbourne, Eng., Sept. 2, 1877; s. Benjamin and Hannah (Green) S.; student Eastbourne Coll., 1893-94; B.A., Oxford, 1898; M.A., 1910; LL.D., Glasgow; m. Winifred Moller Beilby, Mar. 3, 1908 (dec. Aug. 17, 1936). Demonstrator chemistry McGill U., Montreal, Can., 1900-02; established atomic disintegration of radioactive elements and existence of atomic energy (with late physics prof. Ernest Rutherford); proved spectroscopically the prodn. of helium from radium (with Sir W. Ramsay), 1903-04; London U. extension lectr., Western Australia, 1904; lectr. phys. chemistry, radioactivity, U. Glasgow, 1904-14; prof. chemistry U. Aberdeen, 1914-19, Oxford, 1919-36; ret. 1936. Responsible for conception of isotopes and the displacement law of radioactive change which is at the root of nuclear physics. Awarded Nobel Laureate in chemistry, 1921, Cannizzaro prize by Acad. de Lincei, Rome, 1923. Author: Science and Life, 1920; Interpretation of the Atom, 1932. Applied phys. laws of conservation to econs. and writer on new econs.: Wealth, Virtual Wealth and Debt. 1926: Store of Atomic Energy, 1949. Address: 39 Overhill Dr., Brighton 6, Eng. Died Sept. 22, 1956.

SOHON, FREDERICK WYATT, seismologist; b. South Bethlehem, Pa., June 3, 1894; s. Michael Druck and Sarah Harrisonia (Marsteller) S.; Chem.E., Columbia, 1915; student St. Andrew-on-Hudson, Poughkeepsie, 1916-20; A.B., Woodstock (Md.) Coll., 1922, A.M., 1923; student Ignatuiskolleg, Valkenburg, Holland, 1924-28; Ph.D., Goergetown U., 1933. Entered Society of Jesus, 1916; ordained priest R.C. Ch., Holland, 1927. Instr. in mathematics, Coll. of Holy Cross, Worcester, Mass., 1915-16; prof. of chemistry and dir. seismic station, Fordham U., 1923-24; prof. of astronomy and asst. dir. Georgetown Astron. Observatory, 1928-30; dir. Seismol. Observatory, Georgetown U., from 1930, head of dept. and prof. of math. physics, from 1932, dean of Grad. Sch., 1934-36. Mem. A.A.A.S., Math. Assn. America, Am. Math. Soc., Am. Geophys. Union, Seismol. Soc. Am., Astronomische Gesellschaft, Washington Philos. Soc., Phi Lambda Upsilon, Tau Beta Pi, Sigma Xi. Democrat. Mem. K. of C. Author: Theoretical Seismology, Part I, 1936, Part II, 1932; The Stereographic Projection, 1941. Contbr. to professional jours. Died July 1972.

SOLEY, MAYO HALLTON, physician, dean; b. Malden, Mass., Apr. 14, 1907; s. Walter Hamilton and Grace Eliza (Mayo) S.; B.S., Bowdoin Coll., 1929; M.D., Harvard, 1933; spl. grad. student U. of Cal. Med. Sch., 1935; m. Karoline Boeker Jump, Feb. 19, 1938; children—Mayo Robert, Charles Hamilton, Jane Elizabeth. Intern Mass. Gen. Hosp., 1933-35; research asst. U. Cal., 1935-37, instr. physiology, medicine, pharmacology, 1937-39, asst. prof. medicine and pharmacy, 1939-42; asst. vis. physician U. Cal. Hosp., 1937-48, San Francisco Hosp., 1938-48, cons. pharmacologist, 1942-44; asst. prof. medicine, lecturer on pharmacology (chmn. div. pharmacology) and toxicology U. Cal., 1942-44, asso. prof., 1942-47, prof., 1947-48, asst. dean, 1944-48; dean, dir. med. services and research prof. medicine State U. Ia. Coll. Medicine, 1948—; cons. pharmacologist Langley Porter Clinic, 1943-44, attending physician, endocrine and metabolic, 1943-48; cons. Letterman Gen. Hosp., San Francisco, 1947-48, Vets. Hosp., Des Moines, Ia., 1948—. Mem. A.M.A., Am. Heart Assn. Assn. for Study Internal Secretions (councilor, 1948-51), Am. Soc. for Clin. Investigation, A.A.A.S., Am. Physiol. Soc., Soc. for Exptl. Biology and Medicine, Cal. Acad. Medicine, Am. Goiter Assn., Am. Fedn. for Clin. Research, Western Soc. for Clin. Research (pres. 1947-48), Assn. Am. Physicians, Sigma Xi. Contbr. numerous articles to med. jours. Specialist in internal medicine and diseases of the thyroid. Home: 1036 Woodlawn, Iowa City, Ia. Died June 21, 1949; buried Mountain View Cemetery, Oakland, Cal.

SOLLITT, SUMNER S(HANNON), engr., builder; b. Chgo., July 24, 1902; s. Sumner and Grace (Shannon) S.; B.S., Dartmouth, 1923; m. Louise Marshall, June 24, 1925 (div. 1949); children—Sumner Marshall, Sally Shannon, Arthur Marshall; m. 2d, Bettye Herb Nye, Nov. 30, 1949; 1 dau., Betsy Martin, (stepchildren) Judy Nye, Nancy Nye, Sally Nye. With Sumner Sollitt Co., Chgo., 1923—, pres., 1930-55, chmn., 1955—; pres. Sumner Sollitt Co. of Tex., Sumner S. Sollitt Constrn. Co., Sollitt Overseas Constrn. Co., Country Stores, Inc.; owner of Floraman Development Company. Member Phi Sigma Kappa. Republican. Presbyn. Clubs: Skokie, Builders, Chicago Yacht, University, South Haven Yacht, Lake Shore, Pullman (Chgo.); Dartmouth (N.Y.C.); Club Nautico (San Juan, P.R.); Saddle and Cycle. Pioneered atomic energy power plants. Home: 2430 Lakeview Av. Office: 307 N. Michigan Av., Chgo. 1. Died Apr. 2, 1964; buried Meml. Park Cemetery, Evanston, Ill.

SOLLMANN, TORALD HERMANN, med. educator; b. Coburg, Germany, Feb. 10, 1874; s. August and Adelheid (Eckardt) S.; ed. Gymnasium, Coburg, 1884-87, spl. studies, 1887-93; student pharmacy, chemistry and medicine, Paris, 1893-94; M.D., Western Res. U., 1896; special studies, Strassburg, summer 1899;

hon. D.Sc., Ohio State U., 1934; LL.D., Western Res. U., 1943; M. Alice M. Sersall, June 1902; 1 dau., Mary Alice. Demonstrator in physiology, 1895-99, lectr. in pharmacology, 1898-1901, asst. prof. pharmacology and materia medica, 1901-04, prof., 1904-44, dean, 1928-44, Western Res. Med. Sch., emeritus, 1944-65. Chmn. council on pharmacy and chemistry, A.M.A.; cons. in pharmacology, USPHS, 1935. Fellow Am. Acad. Arts and Scis., Am. Coll. Physicians; mem. Sigma Xi, Alpha Omega Alpha. Author: Textbook of Pharmacology with Some Allied Sciences (2d edit.), 1906; (with R. A. Hatcher) Textbook of Materia Medica, 1904; Manual of Pharmacology (7th edition), 1948, Laboratory Guide; Actions of Drugs, 1917; (with P. J. Hanzlik) Introduction to Experimental Pharmacology, 1928; Fundamentals of Experimental Pharmacology (with P. J. Hanzlik), 1939. Contbr. to med. and scientific periodicals. Home: 14327 Superior St., Cleveland Heights 18. Office: 2109 Adelbert Rd., Cleveland 6, O. Died Feb. 11, 1965.

SOMMER, ALVIN HENRY, metall. engr.; b. Peoria, Ill., Feb. 24, 1900; s. John and Lizzie (Schmutz) S.; student Bradley Acad., Bradley U.; m. Lina Stuber, Dec. 23, 1926; children—Miriam Louise, William Alvin, Jay Monroe. With Keystone Steel & Wire Co., Peoria, Ill., 1926—, supt. Steel Mills., 1935-52, dir., 1940-66, v.p., gen. supt. 1952-64; dir. Mid-State Steel & Wire Co., Crawfordsville, Ind. Exec. bd., pres. Ill. Heart Assn.; past mem. bd. Greater Peoria Heart Assn., past chmn. Greater Peoria Heart Drive. Chmn. Twelve Oaks Home Soc., Peoria. Mem. Am. Inst. Mining Metall. and Petroleum Engrs. (past chmn. nat. open hearth com.), Am., Brit. iron and steel insts., Ill., Peoria chambers commerce, Sigma Chi. Author papers on steelmaking, open hearth furnace design. Home: 205 N. Kickapoo Terrace. Office: 7000 S. Adams St., Peoria, Ill. 61609. Died Naples, Fla., Jan. 12, 1966; buried Parkview Cemetery, Peoria, Ill.

SOMMER, LUTHER ALLEN, pres. The Sommer & Adams Co.; b. Springfield, Ill., Nov. 3, 1878; s. William C. and Mary A. (Pierik) S.; ed. Armour Inst. Tech., Chicago, 1896-1900; m. Zoe M. Cobb, 1901; 1 dau., Mildred D. Employed in mfr. printing machinery, 1894, in mfg. scientific instruments, 1899; constrn. experimental apparatus, Armour Inst., 1900-04; instr. Armour Inst. Tech., 1904-07; engaged in mfg. automobile engines; pres. The Sommer & Adams Co., mfrs. special machinery, tools, fixtures, etc. Past pres. Nat. Tool and Die Mfrs. Assn.; former pres. Cleveland Tool, Die and Machine Shops Assn. Mem. Cleveland Chamber of Commerce, also Ohio Chamber of Commerce. Mem. Am. Tool Engineers Soc. Mason. Club: Mid-Day. Home: 3009 Lincoln Blvd. Office: 18511 Euclid Av., Cleveland, O. Died Mar. 2, 1946.

SONDERN, FREDERIC EWALD, pathologist; b. Stuttgart, Germany, Mar. 30, 1867; s. Charles F. and Augusta (Bever) S.; brought to U.S., 1871; ed. under tutors; M.D., Coll. Physicians and Surgeons (Columbia), 1889; m. Elsa M. Ottmann, Apr. 30, 1895. Began practice at N.Y. City, 1889; former pres. N.Y. Post-Grad. Med. Sch. and Hosp. Member Am. Assn. Pathologists and Bacteriologists, N.Y. Pathol. Soc., N.Y. Acad. Medicine. Republican. Episcopalian. Club: University. Home: 180 W. 58th St., New York City*

SONNE, FRED THEODORE, mfg. and engring. co. exec., inventor; b. Chgo., Feb. 9, 1899; s. William Washington and Freida Wilhelmina (Muscher) S.; ed. pub. schs., also home study; m. Eleanor Ruesch, Dec. 26, 1927 (dec. Oct. 1956); m. 2d, Itoko Kamewari, Mar. 23, 1960; stepchildren—Yasahara, Hiroko, Seiji. Engaged in aviation barnstorming, 1919-23; co-founder, 1923, Chgo. Aerial Survey Co., photography and mapping, v.p. until 1954; pres. Chgo. Aerial Industries, 1954-60, vice chmn. bd., 1960-62, chmn. bd., 1962-65. Mem. Am. Soc. of Photogrametry, Inst. Aero. Scis., Soc. Air Affairs, Exptl. Aircraft Assn., Antique Airplane Assn., Quiet Birdmen, 0X5 Club. Inventor continuous strip aerial camera, 1939. Home: 2755 Lawson Rd., Northbrook, Ill. Office: 550 W. Northwest Hwy., Barrington, Ill. Died Oct. 8, 1965.

SOOYSMITH, CHARLES, civil engr.; b. Buffalo, N.Y., July 20, 1856; s. William Sooy and Elizabeth (Haven) Smith; C.E., Rensselaer Poly. Inst., 1876; studied at Polytechnicum, Dresden, and other places in Europe, 1876-78; m. Pauline Olmstead, Dec. 17, 1887. Asst. supt. maintenance dept. A.,T.&S.F. R.R., 1879-80; pres. Sooysmith & Co., contracting engrs., 1884-1900, builders of many important subaqueous engring. works. Introduced into U.S. so-called freezing process for excavating, and took out many patents covering its application to building of subaqueous tunnels. Inaugurated pneumatic caisson method for foundations of large buildings; served as expert in connection with underground works, notably with Underground Rapid Transit R.R. in New York; mem. Met. Sewerage Commn. of New York. Home: New York, N.Y. Died June 1, 1916.

SOPER, GEORGE ALBERT, consulting engr.; b. New York, N.Y., Feb. 3, 1870; s. George A. and Georgianna Lydia (Bucknam) S.; B.S., Renssalaer Poly. Inst., Troy, N.Y., 1895; A.M., Columbia, 1898, Ph.D., 1899; m. M. Virginia McLeod, July 18, 1895; m. 2d, Eloise Liddon, Dothan, July 12, 1923. Began as civ. engr. with Boston Water Works; later engr. Cumberland Mfg. Co., builders of filtration works in many cities; engr. in charge sanitary work, rehabilitation of Galveston, Tex., after storm of 1900; sanitary engr. N.Y. City Health Dept., 1902; expert N.Y. State Health Dept. in charge of suppression of typhoid epidemic at Ithaca, N.Y., 1904, and subsequently for many other cities; discoverer of typhoid carrier, "Typhoid Mary," 1904; expert of Rapid Transit Commn., N.Y. City, in charge of investigation of subway air conditions, making over 5,000 analyses, etc., 1906, and recommending plan of ventilation subsequently adopted; mem. Met. Sewerage Commn. of N.Y. City, 1906-14 and pres. and dir. of its scientific work, 1908-14, resulting in comprehensive plan and policy of sewage disposal for N.Y. City; chmn. Internat. Bd. Engrs. on water supply and sewage disposal of Chicago, 1914-15; mng. dir. Am. Soc. for Control of Cancer, 1923-28; consulting engr. since 1928; consultant U.S. Housing Authority, 1939-1944. Del. 1st Internat. Conf. on Pub. Cleansing, London, 1931, 2d Conf., Frankfort-on-Main, 1935. Maj. Sanitary Corps, Medical Dept., U.S. Army, 1918-19. Fellow A.A.A.S.; mem. Am. Soc. C.E., Am. Pub. Health Assn., Delta Phi, Sigma Xi; hon. fellow Royal Sanitary Inst. Gt. Britain. Episcopalian. Club: Century. Author: The Air and Ventilation of Subways, 1908; Modern Methods of Street Cleaning, 1909; also numerous published scientific articles and published addresses. Home: Hampton Bays, Long Island, N.Y. Office: 154 Nassau St., New York, N.Y. Died June 17, 1948.

SORENSEN, ROYAL WASSON, educator; b. Wabaunsee County, Kan., Apr. 25, 1882; s. Soren and Margaret E. (Wasson) S.; B.S. in Elec. Engring., U. Colo., 1905, E.E., 1928, D.Sc., 1938; m. Grace Milner, Apr. 26, 1906; children—Jennie Marguerite, Grace Helen, Royal Milner, Georgiania (dec.), Lewis Robert Asst. engr. Golden Illuminating Co., 1900; testman Gen. Electric Co., 1905-06, research and design engr. transformer dept., 1906-10, cons. engr., 1929-30; asso. prof. elec. engring. Cal. Inst. Tech. (formerly Throop Poly. Inst.), 1910-11, prof., 1911-50, chmn. faculty, 1938-39, spl. lectr., 1950-52, prof. emeritus elec. engring., 1952-65. Mem. sci. adv. group to Japan, Nat. Acad. 1947; cons. engr. Cole Electric Co., U.S. Electric Mfg. Co., Met. Water Dist. of So. Cal.; cons. Kelman Electric Co. Cal. Portland Cement Co., So. Cal. Edison Co. Planned and designed equipment 1,000,000 volt cascade transformer system and lab.; invented (with Dr. Robert A. Millikan) vacuum switch for high potential electric circuit, other invention; spl. radio instr. Signal Corps, S.A.T.C., mem. research com. for submarine detection, World War I; coordinator radio courses, supr. courses war tng. program for engring. sci. and mgmt. U.S. Office Edn., World War II; asso. dir. spl. studies group Columbia U. Div. War Research, 1943-45; mem. engring. div. NRC, 1942-45; mem. Cal. Bd. Registration for Profl. Engrs., 1947-55; exec. sec. Joint Research Council on Power Plant Air Pollution Control, 1956-65; rep. Am. Inst. E.E. to Centennial Verein Deutscher Ingeniere, Berlin, 1956; mem. Conf. Internationale des Grands Reseux Electriques a Haute Tension. Recipient most valuable engring. service scroll Engrs. and Architects of Los Angeles, 1944; award for outstanding achievement air pollution control Los Angeles County Bd. Supervisors, 1958. Fellow of I.E.E.E. (research com. 1923-30, chmn. 1941-43, v.p. 1933-35, dir., 1937-40, pres. 1940-41, pres. mem. bd. 1941-43; hon. mem.); mem. Air Pollution Control Assn., Nat. Soc. Profl. Engrs., Am. Soc. Engring. Edn. (mem. mission for tech. coll. study in India 1958-59), Pasadena Tb Soc. (v.p.), Los Angeles, Pasadena chambers commerce, Royal W. Sorensen Fellows (hon. pres.), Soc. Promotion Engring. Edn. (gov. bd. 1938-40, v.p. 1938-39, chmn. com. grad. study 1942-43), Engring. Council of Founder Socs. So. Cal., A.A.A.S., Am. Assn. U. Profs., Pasadena YMCA (pres. 1933-39), Japan Institute of Electrical Engineers (hon.), Sigma Xi, Eta Kappa Nu (hon.), Tau Beta Pi. Republican. Baptist. Mason. Clubs: Joint Tech. (Los Angeles); Engineers, Twilight (Pasadena); Rotary. Author: tech. articles, papers. Home: 1715 Homet Rd., Pasadena, Cal. 91106. Died Oct. 27, 1965; buried Vista del Monte Cemetery.

SOSMAN, MERRILL C(LARY), (sos'man) roentgenologist; b. Chillicothe, O., June 23, 1890; s. Francis Asbury and Mollie (Browning) S.; A.B., U. Wis., 1913; M.D., Johns Hopkins, 1917; M.A. (hon.), Harvard, 1949; m. Arline Clark Adams, June 27, 1918; children—John Leland, Barbara Clark. Resident physician, U.S. Soldiers Home Hosp., Washington, 1917; grad. student, Mass. Gen. sp., Boston, 1921-22; became roentgenologist in chief, Peter Bent Brigham Hosp., Boston, 1922, now chmn. emeritus; cons. roentgenologist Childrens Hosp., Psychopathic Hosp., N. E. Peabody Home for Crippled Children (Boston), Cape Cod Hosp. (Hyannis). Instr. in roentgenology, Harvard Med. Sch., 1922-28, asst. prof., 1928-40, clin. prof., 1940-44, clin. prof. radiology, 1944-48, became prof. of radiology 1948, now prof. emeritus; now cons. radiology, Mass. Gen. Hosp. Served as 1st lt. Med. Corps, U.S. Army, 1917; capt., 1918-22. Recipient gold medal, Radiol. Soc. of Am. Diplomate Am. Bd. Radiology. Fellow A.A.A.S.; mem. A.M.A., N.E. Roentgen Ray Soc. (past pres.; George W. Holmes lectr., 1947), Radiol. Soc. N.A., Am. Roentgen Ray Soc. (past pres.; Caldwell lectr. 1947), Harvey Cushing Soc. (past pres.), Am. Coll. Radiology, Mexican Soc. Radiol. and Phys. Therapy (hon.), Venezuela Radiol. Soc., Am. Acad. Arts Scis., Sigma Xi., A.O.A. Mason. Clubs: Harvard (Boston); Country (Brookline). Contbr. of numerous articles on diagnosis and treatment of diseases or tumors by X-ray to sci. publs. Home: 24 Lee Rd., Chestnut Hill 67, Mass. Office: 721 Huntington Av., Boston 15. Died Mar. 28, 1959; buried Chillicothe, O.

SOSMAN, ROBERT BROWNING, chemist; b. Chillicothe, O., Mar. 17, 1881; s. Francis A. and Mary R. (Browning) S.; B.Sc., Ohio State U., 1903, hon. Sc.D., 1938; S.B., Mass. Inst. Tech., 1904, Ph.D., 1907; Sc.D., Alfred U., 1953, U. Toledo, 1954; m. Sarah Gibson Noble, September 30, 1911; children—Robert Noble, George Gibson, Esther Browning, Edward Carey. In lab. of A. D. Little, Boston, 1906-08; physicist, asst. dir., Geophysical Lab., Carnegie Inst., 1908-28; phys. chemist, asst. dir. Research Lab., U.S. Steel Corp., 1928-47; prof., Dept. Ceramics, Rutgers University, 1947-62. Consulting chemist, Ordnance Dept., U.S. Army, 1918; lecturer on geophysics, Mass. Inst. Tech., 1925-26; nat. councilor, Ohio State University Research Foundation, 1937-45. Chmn. com. C-8 on refractories, Am. Soc. Testing Materials, 1948-56. Mem. Am. Chem. Soc., Am. Phys. Soc., Am. Ceramic Soc. (pres. 1937, Orton Meml. lectr., hon. mem. 1952, Bleininger Award, 1953, Purdy Award, 1957, Jeppson award 1960), Am. Assn. U. Profs., Am. Geophys. Union, Am. Inst. Mining and Metall. Engrs. (Howe Meml. Lectr., 1948), Geol. Soc. Am., N.Y., N.J. mineral. clubs, Brit. (hon.), German ceramic socs., Appalachian Mt. Club (chairman N.Y. chpt., 1942-44), Sigma Xi; past president, Philos. Society Washington (1920), Washington Academy Sciences (1928). Club: Delta Upsilon. Author of The Properties of Silica, 1927; Pyrometry of Solids and Surfaces, 1940; and papers in scientific periodicals on high-temperature thermometry, refractories, and mineral chemistry and physics. Home: Westfield NJ Died Oct. 30, 1967.

SOULE, CAROLINE GRAY, (Miss), entomologist; b. Springfield, Mass., 1855; d. Augustus Lord (justice Supreme Court, Mass.) and Maria Goodwin (Gray) S.; granddaughter Gideon Lane Soule, LL. D., former prin. Phillips Exeter Acad.; ed. pvt. schs., Springfield and New York. Formerly mem. Woman's Edn. Assn., Boston, and Brookline Edn. Soc.; one of heads of div., English Literature Dept., Soc. for Promotion of Study at Home, and librarian of Ladies' Commn. on Books for Sunday Sch. and Other Libraries (a work of the Unitarian Assn.), but has given them all up on account of uncertain health. Mem. Boston Soc. Natural History. Unitarian. Author: (with Ida M. Eliot), Caterpillars and Their Moths, 1902 C2. Contbr. life-histories of Lepidoptera in "Psyche," articles on Nature-study in The Outlook, Education and other ednl. jours., and stories in Lend-a-Hand, and The Look-Out. Address: Brookline, Mass.

SOULE, MALCOLM HERMAN, (sul), bacteriologist; b. Allegany, N.Y., Dec. 5, 1896; s. Charles M. and Ida May (Ervin) S.; B.S., U. of Mich., 1921, M.S., 1922, D.Sc., 1924, LL.D., St. Bonaventures Coll., 1928; m. Alma Dengler, Sept. 7, 1926; children—Mary Alma, Margaret Laura. Instr. analytical chemistry, U. of Mich., 1919-20; instr. bacteriology, Sch. of Medicine, 1923-25, asst. prof., 1925-28, asso. prof., 1928-31, prof. since 1931, chmn., dept., and Hygienic Lab. since 1935; visiting prof., U. of Chicago, 1931; visiting prof., School Tropical Medicine, Puerto Rico, 1931; leprosy investigation, Leonard Wood Memorial, P.I., 1933-34, chairman Medical Advisory Board since 1944; consultant to director division health and sanitation, Coordinator of Inter-American Affairs since 1942. Del. of U.S. Govt. to 2d Internat. Congress Microbiology, London, 1936, Internat. Congress for Leprosy, Cairo, 1938; 3d Internat. Congress Tropical Medicine and Malaria, Amsterdam, 1938, 9th Pan-Am. Conf. on Health and Sanitation, Rio de Janeiro, 1942, 2d Pan-Am. Conf. on Leprosy, Rio de Janeiro, 1946, Internat. Congress of Cytology, Stockholm, 1947; 4th Congress Microbiology, Copenhagen, 1947; 5th Congress, Leprosy, Havana, 1948, 5th Internat. Congress Microbiology, Rio de Janeiro, 1950; adviser to dir. Leprosy Service and Malaria, Brazil, 1950; mem. med. ednl. mission to Japan, auspices SCAP, Unitarian Services Com., 1951. Member Com. Internat. Affairs, Nat. Research Council. Representative International Biol. Society on UNESCO. Fellow A.A.A.S. (mem. exec. com. since 1947); mem. Am. Assn. Pathologists and Bacteriologists (pres. 1947), Am. Acad. Tropical Medicine (council mem. since 1937), Am. Assn. Pathologists and Bacteriologists (on council since 1940), Am. Assn. Immunologists, Am. Chem. Soc., Am. Micros. Assn., Am. Pub. Health Assn. (fellow), Am. Soc. Exptl. Pathology, Am. Soc. Tropical Medicine (v.p. 1941), Bot. Soc. of America, Internat. Leprosy Assn., Path. So. Great Britain and Ireland, Soc. Exptl. Biology and Medicine, Soc. Am. Bacteriologists, corr. mem. Sociedad Medico-Quirurgica del Guayas, corr. mem. Societe de Pathologie Exotique; hon. mem. Brazilian Leprosy Association; mem. editorial bds., Science; American Jour. Pathology; American Jour. Tropical Med.; mem. Alpha Chi Sigma, Alpha Omega Alpha, Gamma Alpha, Nu Sigma Nu, Phi Kappa Phi, Phi Lambda Upsilon, Phi Sigma, Sigma Xi. Awarded gold medal by A.M.A., 1930. Protestant. Contbr. scientific articles on microbic respiration, microbic dissociation, goitre, undulant fever, leprosy, poliomyelitis, relapsing fever, tropical medicine. Home: 2110 Hill St., Ann Arbor, Mich. Died Aug. 3, 1951.

SOUTHALL, JAMES POWELL COCKE, educator; b. Norfolk, Va., Apr. 4, 1871; s. James Cocke and Eliza Frances (Sharp) S.; student McGuire's Sch., Richmond, Va.; Richmond Coll., Va., B.A., U. Va., 1891, M.A., 1893; fellow Johns Hopkins, 1898; m. Jeannie Oliver Abbot, Dec. 23, 1899 (dec. 1951); children—James Cocke (dec.), William Richardson Abbot. Tchr. McGuire's Sch., 1890-91; instr. in physics, U. Va., 1891-93; prof. physics and math. Miller Manual Tng. Sch. Albemarle, Va., 1893-98; Prendergast prof. physics, Hobart Coll., Geneva, N.Y., 1899-1901; prof. physics, Ala. Poly. Inst., 1901-14; asst. prof. physics, Columbia U., 1914-17, asso. prof., 1917-22, prof., 1922-40, prof. emeritus of physics, 1940-62. Mem. faculty, U. Cal., summer 1917. Fellow Phys. Soc., A.A.A.S., Optical Soc. (London); mem. Franklin Inst. Optical Soc. Am. (pres. 1921; asso. editor jour.), Va. Hist. Soc. (mem. exec. com. from 1940), Sigma Xi, Delta Kappa Epsilon, Tilka Soc., Phi Beta Kappa, Epsilon Psi Epsilon, Raven Soc. U. Va. (Alumnus Award 1941); hon. mem. Philos. Soc. U. Va. Mem. com. on physiol. optics of Nat. Research Council, 1921; mem. Soc. of The Virginians of N.Y.C. (vice gov. 1932-33; gov. 1933-35). Author: Principles and Methods of Geometrical Optics, Especially as Applied to the Theory of Optical Instruments, 1910; Mirrors, Prisms and Lenses, 1918 (rev. edit. 1923, 3d enlarged edit. 1933); Introduction to Physiological Optics, 1937; In the Days of My Youth; The Abbots of Old Bellevue; also numerous scientific papers, essays and addresses and geneal. contbns. to Va. Mag. of History and Biography and William and Mary Coll. Quarterly. Editor-in-chief Am. edit. of Helmhaltz's Physiological Optics; translator of Helmholtz's Physiological Optics (1924-25). Died Aug. 22, 1962; buried Charlottesville, Va.

SOUTHER, HENRY, consulting engr.; b. Boston, Mass., Sept. 11, 1865; s. Henry and Mary (Wheeler) S.; grad. Mass. Inst. Tech., 1887; m. Elizabeth Sherman, Mass., Sept. 11, 1888. Engr. with Pa. Steel Co., 1888-93, Pope Mfg. Co., Hartford, Conn., 1893-99; in con. practice, Phila., 1899—; pres. Henry Souther Engring. Co., metallurgists and engrs.; v.p. Standard Roller Bearing Co. and Ferro Machine & Foundry Co., Cleveland. Water commr., Hartford, Conn., 1899-1907. Republican. Address: Cleveland, O. Deceased.

SOUTHGATE, GEORGE THOMPSON, cons. engr.; b. Nashville, Tenn., June 26, 1886; s. William Wall and Martha Carrie (Thompson) S.; student Vanderbilt U., 1904-05, U. of Mo., 1905-06; B.S. in E.E., Mass. Inst. of Tech., 1910; m. May Collins, 1917. Field elec. engr. Ford, Bacon & Davis, New York, 1910-13; sponsor engr. Electric Bond & Share Co., New York, 1913-18; research engr. Am. Cyanamid Co., developing elec. phosphoric smelting, 1918-22; cons. engr. Swann Chem. Co., Grasselli Chem. Co., Electro-Metall. Co., developing Elec. furnace processes, 1922-29; research engr. Union Carbide & Carbon Research Labs., Inc., 1929-34; cons. engr., New York, 1934-43; chief engr. Vanadium Corp. of America since 1943. Fellow Royal Soc. of Arts; mem. Am. Inst. Elec. Engrs., Electrochemical Society, American Society for Metals. Democrat. Episcopalian. Inventor combustion-electric process of smelting and vibratorily commutated electric power conversion. Home: 1303 Shady Av., Pittsburgh 17, Pa. Office: Vanadium Corp. of America, Bridgeville, Pa. Died Nov. 8, 1946.

SOUTHWORTH, GEORGE CLARK, research engr., b. Little Cooley, Pa., Aug. 24, 1890; s. Freedom and Mary (Fleek) S.; B.S., Grove City Coll., 1914, M.S., 1916, Ph.D., Yale, 1923, D.Sc. (hon.), Grove City Coll., 1931; m. Lowene Smith, Aug. 14, 1913; children—Margaret Eleanor (Mrs. Arthur G. Pulis), George Howard. Asso. physicist, U.S. Bur. of Standards, 1917-18; instr., asst. prof. physics, Yale, 1918-23; radio research engineer, American Telephone & Telegraph Company, Bell Telephone Laboratory, 1923-55, radio consultant, from 1955. Recipient Medal of Honor, I.R.E., 1963. Fellow A.A.A.S., American Phys. Society, Inst. Radio Engrs.; member Sigma Xi. Awarded Morris Liebmann prize (I.R.E.) 1938, Levy medal (Franklin Inst.), 1946, Ballantine medal (Franklin Inst.) 1947. Republican. Presbyterian. Author: Principles and Applications of Wave-guide Transmission; Forty Years of Radio Research. Contributor of various articles relating to short electromagnetic waves and their application to problems in television and radar. Home: Chatham NJ Died July 6, 1972; buried Little Cooley PA

SPAETH, REYNOLD ALBRECHT, physiologist; b. Phila., Pa., Nov. 22, 1886; s. Adolph and Harriet Reynolds (Krauth) S.; B.S., Haverford, 1909; M.A., Harvard, 1911, Ph.D., 1913; student Smithsonian Table, Naples, 1914; m. Edith Eleanor Taussig, Aug. 18, 1913. Fellow, Harvard, 1909-13; Sheldon fellow, Kiel and Naples, 1913-14; instr. biology, Clark Coll., 1914-15; instr. biology, Yale, 1915-17, in embryology, 1918; asst. in Hygienic Lab., U.S.P.H.S., 1918; also in physiology, 1918-23, asso. prof., 1923—, Sch. of Hygiene and Pub. Health of Johns Hopkins U. Instr. embryology, Woods Hole, Mass., 1915-16, in physiology, 1920—; consultant in personnel and industrial hygiene. Awarded Walker prize, Boston Soc. Natural History, 1913. Fellow A.A.A.S. Home: Baltimore, Md. Died June 26, 1925.

SPAIN, WILL COOK, physician; b. Murfreesboro, Tenn., Aug. 10, 1891; s. Thomas and Annie May (Cook) S.; A.B., U. of Mich., 1914; M.D., Vanderbilt U., 1918; m. Grace Jones, Oct. 12, 1921; children—Joann (Mrs. Arthur Rasmussen), Janet (Mrs. William Spoor). Interne, N.Y. Post-Grad. Hosp., 1918-19, resident physician, 1919; attending physician, N.Y. Hosp., allergy clinic, 1919-29; instr. in immunology, Cornell U. Med. Sch., 1922-24, instr. clin. pediatrics, Cornell U., 1933-35; attending physician and dir., dept. of allergy, N.Y. Post-Graduate Hosp., Columbia U., 1924-48; prof. clin. medicine, N.Y. Post-Grad. Med. Sch., Columbia, 1930-48; chief pediatric allergy clinic, N.Y. Hosp., 1933-35; vis. physician, 1st Div. Welfare Hosp., 1940-41; asst. prof. clin. medicine, N.Y. Med. Coll., 1940-42; attending physician and dir. dept. allergy, U. Hosp., 1948—, prof. clin. medicine, N.Y.U. Post-Grad. Med. Sch., 1948—; vis. physician, 4th Med. Div., Bellevue Hosp., 1949—; cons. in allergy, Mather Meml. Hospital, 1930-53. Served as 1st lt., Med. Res. Corp. 1914. Fellow A.M.A., Am. Coll. Physicians, N.Y. Acad. Medicine, Med. Soc. of State N.Y., Med. Soc. Co. of N.Y.; mem. Soc. for the Study of Asthma and Allied Conditions (sec.-treas. 1924-45), Am. Acad. of Allergy (sec. 1944, v.p. 1946, president 1947); Am. Acad. of Allergy (chmn. com. on edn., 1946-49), N.Y. Allergy Soc. (a founder), A.A.A.S., Am. Bd. Internal Medicine (mem. adv. bd. for allergy 1947-53), Pan Am. Med. Assn. (pres. sect. allergy, 1952-54), N.Y. Post-Grad. Hosp. Alumni Assn., Am. Assn. Immunologists, Phi Chi, Alpha Omega Alpha. Mem. editorial bd. Jour. of Allergy, 1953—. Home: 570 Park Av., N.Y.C. 21. Office: 141 E. 55th St., N.Y.C. 22. Died May 12, 1956; buried Woodlawn Cemetery, N.Y.C.

SPALDING, LYMAN, physician, surgeon; b. Cornish, N.H., June 5, 1775; s. Dyer and Elizabeth (Parkhurst) S.; grad. at Charlestown, Mass., 1794; M.B., Harvard, 1797, M.D. (hon.); M.B., M.D. (hon.), Dartmouth; m. Elizabeth Coves, Oct. 9, 1802, 5 children. A founder Dartmouth Med. Sch., 1798, lectr. chemistry and materia medica, 1797-99; Portsmouth, N.H.; practiced medicine, Portsmouth, N.H., 1799-1812, also contract for U.S. Army troops in harbor; founded med. society which became Eastern Dist. br. of N.H. Med. Soc., 1802; lectured on chemistry and surgery at acad., Fairfield, N.Y., 1810-17 (became Coll. Physicians and Surgeons of Western Dist. N.Y., 1813), pres., 1813-17; practiced in N.Y.C., 1817-21; studied yellow fever, vaccination, hydrophobia; founded U.S. Pharmacopoeia; trustee N.Y.C., Coll. Author: Reflections on Fever, 1817. Died Portsmouth, Oct. 21, 1821.

SPALDING, THOMAS, planter, congressman; b. Frederica, St. Simon's Island, Ga., Mar. 26, 1776; s. James and Margery (McIntosh) S.; m. Sarah Leake, Nov. 5, 1795, 16 children. Admitted to Ga. bar, 1795; mem. Ga. Constl. Conv., 1798; mem. Ga. Legislature from Glynn County, 1794; mem. Ga. Senate; Mem. U.S. Ho. of Reps. from Ga., 9th Congress, Dec. 24, 1805-06; sent to Bermuda to investigate claims of Am. citizens against Gt. Britain for destruction of property, 1815; rep. from Ga. on Ga.-Fla. Boundary Commn., 1826; mem. Milledgeville (Ga.) Anti-Tariff Conv., 1832; pres. Ga. Conv. (concerned with slavery and secession), 1850; supported Compromise of 1850; pioneer of sea island cotton in South; 1st to grow sugar cane and manufacture sugar in Ga.; wrote "A Sketch of the Life of General James Oglethrope" published in Collections of the Georgia Historical Society, Vol. I, 1840. Died Darien, Ga., Jan. 5, 1851; buried St. Andrews Cemetery of Christ Church, Frederica.

SPALDING, VOLNEY MORGAN, botanist; b. E. Bloomfield, N.Y., Jan. 29, 1849; s. Frederick Austin and Almira (Shaw) S.; A.B., U. of Mich., 1873; Ph.D., U. of Leipzig, 1894; m. Harriet Hubbard, Sept. 7, 1876; m. 2d, Effie Almira Southworth, Jan. 1, 1896. Instr. zoölogy and botany, 1876-79, asst. prof. botany, 1879-81, acting prof., 1881-86, prof., 1886-1904, U. of Mich.; engaged in research at the Desert Bot. Lab. at Tucson, Ariz., of the Carnegie Instn., 1904-09. Member Mich. Acad. Sciences (pres. 1897-98). Author: Guide to the Study of Common Plants, and Introduction to Botany, 1895; Monograph on the White Pine, 1897; Biological Relations of Desert Shrubs, 1907; Distribution and Movements of Desert Plants, 1909; various papers in Annals of Botany, Science, American Naturalist, Therapeutic Gazette and other periodicals. Retired on Carnegie Foundation, Jan. 1, 1910. Address: Loma Linda, Calif. Died Nov. 12, 1918.

SPANGLER, HENRY WILSON, engineer; b. at Carlisle, Pa., Jan. 18, 1858; s. John Kerr and Margaret Ann (Wilson) S.; grad. U.S. Naval Acad., 1878; hon. M.S., Univ. of Pa., 1896, Sc.D., 1906; m. Nannie Jane Foreman, Dec. 1, 1881. Engr. U.S.N., 1878-89 and 1898; asst. prof. mech. engring., 1881-84 and 1887-89, prof., 1889—, U. of Pa. Mem. advisory council Engring. Congress, Chicago Expn., 1893; mem. Jury of Awards, Buffalo Expn., 1901. Author: Valce Gears; Notes on Thermodynamics; Graphics. Co-Author: Elements of Steam Engineering. Address: Philadelphia, Pa. Died Mar. 18, 1912.

SPARROW, CARROLL MASON, physicist; b. Baltimore, Md., Jan. 10, 1880; s. Leonard Kip and Anne Elizabeth Temple (Magill) S.; A.B., Johns Hopkins, 1908, Ph.D., 1911; m. Lettice Latané, Dec. 14, 1912. With U.S. Coast and Geodetic Survey, 1901-07; adj. prof. physics, U. of Va., 1911-17, asso. prof., 1917-20, prof., 1920—. Served as capt. Air Service (science and research div.), U.S.A., July 31, 1918-Sept. 3, 1919. Fellow Am. Physical Soc., A.A.A.S. Democrat. Contbr. to scientific jours., mainly on spectroscopy. Asso. editor Physical Rev., 1920-23; asso. editor Virginia Quarterly Rev. Home: University, Va. Died Aug. 30, 1941.

SPEER, J(AMES) RAMSEY, retired mfr.; b. Pittsburgh, Pa., July 23, 1870; s. John Z. and Katharine (McKnight) S.; B.S., Mass. Inst. Tech., 1893; m. Jeannette Lowrie Childs, 1898; children—Gertrude Childs, James Ramsey. Began with Shoenberger Steel Co., 1893, gen. mgr., 1898, v.p. and gen. mgr. for Am. Steel & Wire Co., purchasers of same, 1899-1900; v.p. S. Jarvis Adams Co., Midland, Pa., 1899-1911, pres., 1911-19, chmn. board, 1921; and organizer and pres. until 1904, Brownsvile Glass Co., an organizer, 1905, v.p. until 1911, Midland Steel Co.; pres. Mackintosh-Hemphill Co., mfrs. rolling mill machinery, Pittsburgh, 1924-29; pres. Easton Publishing Co.-The Easton Star-Democrat; director Easton (Md.) National Bank, Director, officer for alien property custodian, World War I, of Bayer Company, Hayden Chemical Works, Berlin Aniline Works, Kalli Color and Chemical Company. A founder and former trustee Arnold School. Democrat. Episcopalian. Clubs: Tred Avon Yacht; Talbot Country, Chesapeake Bay Yacht. Author: Chronology of Iron and Steel, 1920. Inventor of Adamite, a high carbon nickel-chrome steel alloy, also of molybdenum nickel chrome steel alloy, and of improvements in mechanical glass, etc. Joint inventor of electric ingot stripper. Home: "Wilderness," Trappe, Talbot County, Md. Office: care W. C. Rice, William Penn Hotel, Pittsburgh, Pa. Died Oct. 1, 1944.

SPEIR, SAMUEL FLEET, physician; b. Bklyn., Apr. 9, 1838; s. Robert and Hannah (Fleet) S.; attended Bklyn. Poly. Inst.; grad. med. dept. N.Y.U., 1860; m. Frances S. Hegeman, 1869, 3 children. Attended European clinics, mainly in Paris, 1860-62; publicized plaster of Paris splint, later used by mil. authorities in battlefields of Civil War; given 2 boats by Sanitary Commn. to care for wounded of Army of Potomac, 1862; went to Europe for postgrad. study in ophthalmology and otology, 1865; leading figure in med. profession in Bklyn.; mem. surg. staff Bklyn. Eye and Ear Infirmary and Bklyn. Dispensary; physician curator and microscopist Bklyn. City Hosp.; demonstrator of anatomy L.I. Coll. Hosp., 1864-65; awarded Gold medal for paper "On the Pathology of Jaundice," by A.M.A., 1865; invented artery constrictor; mem. county and state med. socs., A.M.A., N.Y. Path. Soc.; fellow N.Y. Acad. Medicine. Author: The Use of the Microscope in the Differential Diagnosis of Morbid Growths, 1871. Died Bklyn., Dec. 19, 1895.

SPENCER, ARTHUR COE, geologist; b. Carmel, N.Y., Sept. 27, 1871; s. Stephen Olin and Carrie (Adams) S.; B.S., Case Sch. Applied Science, Cleveland, 1892; Ph.D., Johns Hopkins, 1896; m. Betty Lublin, Mar. 19, 1902; children—Katharin, Oscar Lublin. Asst. geologist on geol. survey of Iowa in coal regions, 1893-94; geologist U.S. Geol. Survey, 1896-1939; retired, Oct. 1939. Worked upon geology of Rocky Mountains, San Juan Region, Colo., 1896-1900, geology of Copper River Region, Alaska, 1900-01; geol. studies in Cuba, under auspices U.S. Army, 1901-02; Pre-Cambrian and economic geology in Southern Wyo., 1902-03; Juneau gold belt, Alaska, 1903; Pre-Cambrian geology and ore deposits, N.J., 1904-07; Tex., 1908-09; copper deposits at Ely, Nev., 1909. Investigation of lands in Appalachian and White Mountains to determine if federal control of lands will promote navigability of dependent streams as prescribed under Weeks Act of 1911; studies relating to ore deposits of Wyo, Colo., N.M., Alaska and New Eng.; retired from Govt. service, 1939. Home: 3250 Highland Place, Washington 8 DC

SPENCER, FRANK ROBERT, physician and surgeon; b. Burlington, Ia., June 12, 1879; s. Dr. Robert Spencer and Alice (Kendall) S.; A.B., U. Mich., 1900, M.D., 1902; m. Edith Clayton, Apr. 5, 1911; children—Donald Clayton, John Robert. Began as physician and surgeon, 1902; asst., Med. Faculty, U. Mich., 1902-04; mem. Med. Faculty, U. Colo., 1905—; now prof. emeritus otolaryngology. Served as capt., Med. Corps, U.S. Army during World War I. Pres. Colo. State Bd. of Med. Examiners, 1924-26. Fellow Am. Coll. Surgeons, Am. Otol. Soc., Am. Laryngol. Assn. (pres. 1947), Am. Laryngol., Rhinol. and Otol. Soc., Am. Acad. of Ophthalmology and Otolaryngology (pres. 1941; mem. sect. on instrn., 1923-26), Sect. of Laryngology, Otology and Rhinology of A..A. (chmn. of sect., 1928). Charter mem. Am. Bd. of Otolaryngology; mem. Colo. Otolaryngol. Soc. (past pres.). Colo. State Med. Soc. (past pres.), Denver Clin. and Pathol. Soc. (asso.), Sigma Xi, Phi Gamma Delta, Nu Sigma Nu (former mem. exec. grand council). Republican. Episcopalian. Clubs: Boulder Rotary (past pres.). Author of textbook on Laryngeal Tuberculosis; also author more than 75 articles in med. jours.; contbr. to textbook on nose, throat and ear and their diseases;

also to Ency. of Medicine. Formerly mem. editorial bd. of Laryngoscope, St. Louis. Home: 427 Pine St. Office: Physicians Bldg., 2111 14th St., Boulder, Colo. Died 1957.

SPENCER, GUILFORD LAWSON, chemist; b. Lafayette, Ind., Dec. 21, 1858; s. Israel and Helen Virginia (Shipley) S.; B.S., Purdue U., 1879 (D.Sc., 1893), M.S., U. of Mich., 1882; m. Emma Louise Fiske, Sept. 11, 1888. Chief chemist, Magnolia Plantation, 1884-93, Chaparra Sugar Co., 1903, Nicaragua Sugar Estates, Ltd., 1898-1905, Cuban-American Sugar Co., 1906—. Author: A Handbook for Cane-Sugar Manufacturers and Their Chemists, 1899 (Spanish edit. 1917); A Handbook for Beet Sugar Chemists, 1897. Home: Herricks, Me. Died Mar. 23, 1925.

SPENCER, HERBERT, philosopher; b. Derby, Eng., Apr. 27, 1820; son of William G. Spencer. Engr., London & Birmingham R.R., 1837-46; an editor Economist, 1848-53; attempted to synthesize scientific knowledge of his day, especially concept of evolution, and systematically apply it to all fields of human endeavor; advocate of polit. laissez-faire, believed that struggle for existence in polit. sense would lead to survival of fittest, i.e., best form of govt.; his philosophy was widely accepted in Am. Author: Principles of Psychology, 1855; Synthetic Philosophy (including Principles of Biology, Principles of Sociology, Principles of Ethics), 10 vols., 1860-96. Died Dec. 8, 1903.

SPENCER, J. W. (JOSEPH WILLIAM WINTHROP), geologist; b. Dundas, Ont., Can., Mar. 26, 1851; s. Joseph and Eliza Eleanor (Coe) S.; B.A.Sc., McGill U., Montreal, 1874; A.M., Ph.D., Univ. of Göttingen, 1877; LL.D., from U. of Ala., 1913, from U. of Manitoba, 1919; m. Katherine Sinclair Thomson, 1896. Science master, Collegiate Inst., Hamilton, Ont., 1877-80; prof. geology and chemistry, King's Coll., 1880-82; prof. geology, U. of Mo., 1882-87; state geologist of Ga., 1888-93; geologist, W.I., 1894-1904; spl. commr. Geol. Survey Can., 1905-08. First to show the Great Lake basins due to stream (not glacial) erosion, and to discover buried channels between them; also to describe and name their four great glacial ancestors (Lakes Warren, Algonquin, Lundy, and Iroquois); by scientific measurements, was first to investigate physical changes and determine age of Niagara Falls (39,0004,000 yrs.); demonstrated present stability of lake region, after measuring late maximum deformation and its direction; correlating these earth movements with anomalies of gravity and submarine canyons off the coast, demonstrated recent great changes of level of land and sea. "Founder of the scientific history of the Great Lakes; discoverer of the evolution of the Falls of Niagara; founder of the science of submarine valleys"; founder Mus. Historic Geology, U. of Manitoba. Author reports on Georgia, Reconstruction of the Antillean Continent, Evolution of the Falls of Niagara, History of the Great Lakes, Age of the Shores of Lake Ontario and the Modern St. Lawrence River, and many papers in scientific jours. relating to above subjects. Fellow Geol. Soc. London, Geol. Soc. America, A.A.A.S. Address: Washington, D.C. Died Oct. 9, 1921. *

SPENCER, PAUL, elec. engr.; b. East Orange, N.J., Mar. 19, 1866; s. George Gilman and Caroline (Arnold) S.; A.B., Yale, 1887; M.E., Stevens Inst. Tech., 1891; m. Frances Margaret Durbin, Apr. 25, 1894; children—Frederick Gilman, Frances Margaret (Mrs. Archibald G. Roberson), Caroline (dec.). With Field Engring. Co. of New York, 1891-94, Stanley Elec. Mfg. Co., Pittsfield, Mass., 1894-97; gen. supt. People's Light & Power Co., Newark, N.J., 1897-1900; elec. engr. with United Gas Improvement Co., Phila., 1900—. Republican. Unitarian. Home: Philadelphia, Pa. Died Aug. 9, 1927.

SPENCER, PERCY LEBARON, inventor, radio engr.; b. Howland, Me., July 9, 1894; s. Jasper G. and Myrtle B. (Keene) S.; student Naval Wireless and Elec. Sch., Bklyn.; D.Sc., U. Mass., 1950; D.Sc., Nasson College, 1959, Univ. Me., 1961, Calvin Coolidge Coll. Liberal Arts, 1962; m. Louise Larsen, June 6, 1921 (died Feb. 10, 1956); children—John L., James H., Goerge R.; m. 2d, Lillian Ottenheimer, Nov. 18, 1960. Supt. operations Am. Radio and Research Corp., supt. Wireless Specialty Co., 1915-18; mgr. field engring. Submarine Signal Co., 1920-25; dir. development and engring. Raytheon Mgr. Co., Waltham, Mass., 1925-40, mgr., chief engr. microwave and power tube div., 1940-55, sr. v.p., director, 1955-65, director, consultant, until 1970; assisted in development photocell and gaseous rectifier tubes, mercury pool type tubes for welding, also subminiature tubes. Trustee Coburn Classical Inst., Waterville, Me. Served as radio electrician USN, 1912-15, radio aide Charlestown Navy Yard, 1918-20. Recipient Naval Ordnance award for exceptional service Bur. Ordnance, U.S. Navy, 1942, certificate commendation for outstanding service, 1947, distinguished pub. service medal, 1949. Fellow Am. Acad. Arts and Scis., Inst. Radio Engrs.; asso. mem. U.S. Naval Inst. Holder 100 patents on electronic tube processes. Home: Waban MA Died Sept. 7, 1970; buried Newton Cemetery Newton MA

SPENCER, PITMAN CLEMENS, surgeon; b. Charlotte County, Va., July 28, 1793; s. Gideon and Catherine (Clements or Clemens) S.; M.D., U. Pa., 1818; studied surgery, anatomy in London (Eng.) and Paris (France), 1827-30. Performed 1st lithotomy, 1833; published 1st article, "Case of Uninary Calculus successfully treated by Lithotrity," in Am. Jour. Med. Sciences, 1833; pres. Petersburg (Va.) Med. Faculty, 1851; v.p. Med. Soc. Va., 1855. Author: Results of Fifteen Operations for Lithotomy, 1850. Died Petersburg, Jan. 15, 1860.

SPENCER, ROBERT CLOSSON, architect, inventor; b. Milwaukee, Wis., Apr. 13, 1864; s. Robert C. and Ellen W. (Whiton) S.; B.M.E., U. of Wis., 1886; Rotch traveling scholarship in architecture (of Boston), 1891-93; m. Ernestine Elliott, Nov. 28, 1889 (died Nov. 1942); children—Marian L. (Mrs. John W. Smith), Ernestine M., Charles E. Entered archtl. work in Boston; came to Chicago, 1893; mem. Spencer & Powers, 1905-23; practiced alone in Chicago, 1923-28; associate professor architecture, Okla. A. and M. Coll., 1928-30; member faculty Sch. of Architecture and Allied Arts, U. of Fla., 1930-34. Designer of Oak Park (Ill.) High Sch. and many country houses; painted murals of 8 Fla. colonial houses for Federal Govt. and U. of Fla., 1935-38. Fellow Am. Inst. Architects; mem. Sigma Chi. Wrote article on Fla. architecture for Am. Guide, 1934-35. Inventor of widely used building appliances. Address: R.R. 4, Box 502, Tucson AZ*

SPENZER, JOHN GEORGE, chemist, M.D.; b. Cleveland, O., Sept. 6, 1864; s. Peter Ignatius and Mary Theresa (Molloy) S.; student Cleveland High Sch., 1879; M.D., Western Reserve U., 1884; grad. student Adelbert Coll. (Western Reserve U.), 1884-87; Ph.D., U. of Strassburg, 1893; m. Minnie Elizabeth Kittelberger, June 15, 1898; children—John Calvin, Caroline. Assistant in chemistry, medical dept., Western Reserve U., 1880-84; research chem. student, Columbus, O., 1888-91; engaged in research in med. chemistry and pharmacology, Strassburg, Alsace, Germany, 1893-94; practical sch. medicine, Paris, France, 1894, instr. pharmacology, Western Reserve Med. Sch., and prof. chemistry, Dental Sch., 1894-96; med. chem. research, U. of Berne, Switzerland, 1895; prof. gen. and med. chemistry and pharmacology, Cleveland Coll. Phys. and Surg. (med. dept. Ohio Wesleyan U.), 1896-1910; prof. chemistry, legal chemistry and medical jurisprudence, Western Reserve U., 1910-17. Fellow Chemical Soc., Eng.; mem. Berlin Chem. Soc., Philomatic Soc., Alsace-Lorraine; fellow A.A.A.S. Author: The Principles of Pharmacology, with Practical Exercises, 1899. Home: Cleveland, O. Died 1932.

SPERR, FREDERICK WILLIAM, mining engr.; b. Jefferson, O., June 5, 1856; s. Michael and Christine (Benighoff) S.; ed. Madison Sem., O., 1873-75; Ohio State U., 1879-81 and 1882-83; m. Julia S. Loomis, Aug. 10, 1884; children—Frederick William, Julian Dana, Percy Loomis, Donald (dec.), Harold George, Raymond, Bertram (dec.). Spl. agt. 10th Census, on bldg. stone investigation, 1881-82; engineer for Mining Stock Trust Co., Ariz., 1883-84, and supt. its successor, the Garden Springs Mining Corp., 1885-88; asst. prof. mining engring., Ohio State U., 1888-94; prof. civ. and mining engring., Mich. Coll. of Mines, 1894-1926; mining research, Mich. Coll. of Mining and Tech., 1926—. Consulting engr. and mining expert, 1888—, in mining states of the West, also Mexico, Ont. and B.C. Republican. Baptist. Author: Notes on Mine Surveying, 1895; Notes on Mine Accounting, 1895; Notes on Mining Engineering, 1895; Classification of Methods of Mining, 1917; revisions of same, also contbr. on tech. and ednl. topics. Home: Houghton, Mich. Died Nov. 19, 1929.

SPERRY, ELMER AMBROSE, elec. engr.; b. Cortland, N.Y., Oct. 12, 1860; s. Stephen Decatur and Mary (Burst) S.; student State Normal and Training Sch., Cortland, N.Y., 1876-79; Cornell U., 1879-80; E.D., Stevens, 1921, Lehigh, 1927; Sc.D., Northwestern, 1925; m. Zula A., d. Edward Goodman, June 28, 1887; children—Mrs. Helen Marguerite Lea, Edward Goodman, Lawrence Burst (dec.), Elmer Ambrose. Founder, 1880, Sperry Electric Co., Chicago, mfrs. arc lamps, dynamos, etc.; founder Sperry Electric Ry. Co., mfrs. cars, Cleveland, O. (sold to Gen. Electric Co., New York, 1894); inventor of gyro-compass, aeroplane and ship stabilizers, highest intensity searchlight (1 1/2 billion candle power), compound internal combustion engine, fire control apparatus, gyro track recorder, transverse fissure detector, and numerous special devices, principally for the U.S. Navy; pres. Sperry Gyroscope Co., Brooklyn, 1910-26, chmn. bd., 1926-29; pres. Sperry Development Co., Inc.; mfg. own inventions, 1910. Erected 350-foot electric beacon on Lake Michigan in 1883; also invented 1st electric chain mining machine, 1888; devised detinning and electrochem. processes and machinery for making fuse wires; designed electric automobile; held over 400 patents issued in U.S. and Europe. Member Naval Consulting Board, 1915— (chmn. coms. on aeronautics, mines and torpedoes, aids to navigation). Awards: First prize, Aero Club of France, 1914; Franklin medal, Philadelphia, 1914; grand prize for gyro-compass and gyroscopes, San Francisco Expn., 1915; Collier trophy, 1915, for drift set, 1916; Scientific Am. medal, Am. Mus. of Safety; also awarded John Fritz medal in 1927, Holley medal, 1927; Franklin Inst. medal, 1929; Am. Iron and Steel Inst. medal, 1930. Decorated by Czar Nicholas of Russia for navigation equipment; decorated by Emperor of Japan with Order of Rising Sun, and Order of Sacred Treasure. Mem. Am. Inst. E.E. (a founder), Am. Electrochem. Soc. (a founder), Nat. Acad. Science, Nat. Research Council (chmn. div. engring. and industrial research, 1928-30); chmn. Am. Com. World Engring. Congress, Tokyo, 1929. Author numerous papers and addresses. Died June 16, 1930.

SPICER, CLARENCE WINFRED, mech. engr.; b. West Hallock (now Edelstein), Ill., Nov. 30, 1875; s. John Green and Cornelia (Babcock) S.; student Alfred (N.Y.) U., 1891-94, D.Sc., 1935; student Cornell U., 1900-04; m. Anna Olive Burdick, Dec. 1, 1896; children—Harold Willis, Robert Thurston, John Reed, Wilfred Clarence. Inventor Spicer universal joint, 1902; owner and mfr. Spicer Universal Joints, 1904-05; pres. Spicer Universal Joint Mfg. Co., Plainfield, N.J., 1905-10; pres. Spicer Mfg. Co., Plainfield, 1910-14; pres. Spicer Mfg. Corp., 1914-15, v.p., 1915—, at Toledo, 1930—. Trustee Alfred U. Republican. Baptist. Contbr. articles to engring. jours. Home: Toledo, O. Died Nov. 21, 1939.

SPIES, ALBERT, engineer, editor; b. New York, July 20, 1862; s. Peter and Elise (Schuessler) S.; M.E., Stevens Inst. Tech., 1881; m. Gretchen Antonia Weisker, Dec. 23, 1895. In engring. practice and tech. journalism, 1881—; editor The Electrical Record, Jan. 1907—; dir. the Pulsometer Steam Pump Co., New York. Editor: The Life and Inventions of Edison; The Harnessing of Niagara, 1895; also many papers on tech. subjects. Home: Jersey City Heights, N.J. Died 1910.

SPIES, TOM DOUGLAS, physician, educator; b. Revenna, Tex., Sept. 21, 1902; s. John Earl and Mary (Love) S.; A.B., U. Tex., 1923; M.D., Harvard, 1927; Sc.D. (hon.), U. of South (Sewanee, Tenn.), 1944. Intern in pathology, Peter Bent Brigham Hosp., Boston, 1928-29; 1st asst. to Dr. F. B. Mallory, Boston City Hosp., 1929-30; intern Lakeside Hosp., Cleve., 1930-31; teaching fellow Western Reserve U., 1931-32, instr. in medicine, 1932-34, senior instr. medicine, 1934-35; asst. prof. medicine, U. Cin. Coll. of Medicine, 1935-36, asso. prof. medicine, 1936-47; vis. prof. medicine U. Ala., 1941—; prof. nutrition and metabolism, chmn. dept., Northwestern U. Med. Sch., 1947—; dir. Nutrition Clinic, Hillman Hosp., Birmingham, Ala., 1936—. Apptd. to Food and Nutrition Bd., Nat. Research Council, 1943; apptd. cons. to Sec. of War on Tropical Medicine Army Med. Sch., Washington, 1945. Recipient John Phillips Meml. award, Am. Coll. Physicians, 1939; Scientific award, Am. Pharmaceutical Mfrs. Assn., 1941; awarded So. Med. Assn. Research medal, 1943; Distinguished Achievement award Modern Medicine mag., 1957; Distinguished Service award of A.M.A., 1957; Oscar B. Hunter Meml. award in Therapeutics, American Therapeutic Society, 1959. Certified by American Board of Internal Medicine. Fellow Am. Coll. Physicians, Royal Soc. Tropical Medicine and Hygiene (Eng.); mem. A.M.A., A.A.A.S., Am. Assn. Pathologists and Bacteriologists, Am. Inst. Nutrition, Am. Soc. Clin. Investigation, Am. Soc. Exptl. Pathology, Assn. Am. Physicians, Am. Soc. Tropical Medicine, Central Soc. Clin. Research, Research Club, Soc. Exptl. Biology and Medicine, So. Med. Assn., Sigma Xi, Phi Beta Kappa. Co-author (with Dr. R. R. Williams) Vitamin B1 and Its Use in Medicine, 1938; also numerous scientific articles to med jours. Address: Hillman Hospital, Birmingham, Ala. Died Feb. 28, 1960.

SPILSBURY, EDMUND GYBBON, engineer; b. London, Eng., 1845; grad. U. of Louvain, Belgium, 1862; married. Asst. engr. Eschweiler Co., Stolberg, large miners and smelters of lead and zinc ores, 1862; engaged in important works in Europe until 1870; in U.S., 1870—; mng. dir. Trenton Iron Co., 1888-97; head E. G. Spilsbury Engring. Co., New York. V.p., 1893, pres., 1896, Am. Inst. Mining Engrs. Author of numerous technical papers. Home: Brooklyn, N.Y. Died May 28, 1920.

SPINDLER, GAROLD RALPH, educator, engr.; born Terra Alta, W.Va., Nov. 27, 1902; s. Charles Fiat and Nettie Ellathea (Metheny) S.; B.S., W.Va. Univ., 1932, E.M., 1940; m. Elizabeth Winwood Carroll, Dec. 21, 1946; children—Rebecca Winwood, Garold Ralph, James Andrew. Partner-supt., Spindler Coal Co., Kingwood and Spindler Construction Co., Kingwood, 1921-29; construction engr. and foreman Tri-State Engring. Co., Waynesburg, Pa., 1932-34; instr., mining extension dept., W.Va. Univ., Morgantown, W.Va., 1935-38, asst. dir. mining extension, 1939-41, asst. dir. Sch. of Mines, 1941-43. dir. Sch. of Mines and prof. mining engring., June-Aug. 1944, and since July 1948, dean of School of Mines, 1959—; consulting mining engineer, British Ministry of Fuel and Power, London, England, and lecturer on mine mechanization, U. of Sheffield (Eng.), 1943-44; chief W.Va. Dept. Mines, Charleston, 1944-46, chmn. bd. of review, 1958, chmn. Mine Inspectors Examination Board, 1958; European tech. adviser, Joy Manufacturing Co. (Pittsburgh) at Brussels, Belgium, 1946-48. Mem. Am. Inst. Mining and Metall. Engrs., Instn. of Mining Engrs. (London), Midland Inst. of Mining Engrs. (Sheffield, Eng.),

Newcomen Soc. Eng., Soc. for Promotion Engring., W.Va. Coal Mining Inst. (sec.-treas.), Sigma Xi, Tau Beta Pi, Sigma Gamma Epsilon, Phi Kappa Sigma. Elk. Club: Kiwanis. Author: Mine Mechanization, 1946. Home: 412 Elm St. Office: Mineral Industries Bldg., Morgantown, W.Va. Died Feb. 20, 1961; buried Beverly Hills Meml. Gardens, Morgantown.

SPIRO, CHARLES, inventor; b. N.Y. City, Jan. 1, 1850; s. Joseph and Louise S.; LL.B., Washington U., 1874, New York U., 1875; m. Grace Smadbeck, June 9, 1880. Practiced law, 1875-84; designed a matrix-making machine, 1879; pub. new system of phonography, dispensing with shaded lines, 1880; patented the "Columbia" typewriter, 1885, with feature of variable spacing; later the "Bar-lock" typewriter, with writing constantly in view; other inventions, including the "Visigraph" typewriter; patented watch, telegraphic and automatic machinery for various purposes; pres. C. Spiro Mfg. Co. Author: Spiro's Simple, Swift Shorthand, 1880. Home: Dobbs Ferry, N.Y. Died Dec. 17, 1933.

SPITZ, ARMAND N(EUSTADTER), author, inventor, astronomer; b. Phila., July 7, 1904; s. Louis and Rose (Neustadter) S.; student U. Pa., 1922-24, U. Cin., 1924-25; D.Sc., Otterbein Coll., 1956; m. Grace C. Scholz, Sept. 27, 1958; children by previous marriage Verne Carlin, Armand Lawrence. Editor, pub. Haverford Twp. News, 1928-36; pres. Spitz Pub. Co., 1928-35; asst. astronomer Haverford Coll. Obs., 1935-42; radio, TV lectr., 1935-71; staff Franklin Inst., 1936-55, editor The Inst. News, 1936-43, head dept. meteorology, 1940-47, asst. dir. pub. relations, 1941-43, lectr. Fels Planetarium, 1942-54, dir. edn., 1943-51; instr. astronomy Friends Central Sch., 1937-41; vis. cons. Dept. Edn., P.R., 1945; pres. Spitz Labs., 1949-53, dir., 1953-61, coordinator visual satellite observations Smithsonian Astro-physical Obs., 1956-61; spl. cons. Nat. Sci. Found., 1956-60; president Astro Murals, Incorporated, 1962-71. Asso. editor Review Popular Astronomy, 1958-71. Founder, former pres. Haverford Twp. Free Library; mem. intercultural com. World Affairs Council Phila.; mem. Phila. Sci. Council pres. 1948-52. Recipient silver medal Astron. Soc. Mexico, 1954; gold medal LaSalle Coll., Havana, Cuba, 1955. Fellow A.A.A.S. (council); mem. Am. Astron. Soc., Astron. League (award 1954), Am. Assn. Mus. Mem. Soc. Friends (trustee). Club: Cosmos (Washington). Author: The Pinpoint Planetarium, 1940; A Start in Meteorology, 1941; Dictionary of Astronomy and Astronautics, 1958; Weather, 1967; also mag. articles. Home: Fairfax VA Died Apr. 14, 1971.

SPITZKA, EDWARD ANTHONY, physician; b. New York, June 17, 1876; s. of Edward Charles and Catherine (Watzek) S.; ed. Coll. City of New York; M.D., Coll. Phys. and Surg. (Columbia), 1902; m. Alice Eberspacher, June 20, 1906. Demonstrator anatomy, 1904-06, prof. gen. anatomy, 1906-14, Jefferson Med. Coll.; dir. Daniel Baugh Inst. of Anatomy, Phila., 1911-14; pvt. practice, nervous and mental diseases, New York, 1914—. Performed autopsy and examined brain of Czolgosz, assassin of President McKinley, and attended many electrocutions, recording detailed observations upon electric death, anat. variations, etc., of criminals; studied brains of many eminent men and of various races; mem. Commn. on Resuscitation from Electric Shock. Fellow A.A.A.S.; mem. Com. on 1st Aid Treatment of Surg., Med. and Gas Poisoning Cases, Internat. Assn. Fire Engrs. Mem. Vets. 7th Regt. N.G.N.Y. Editor 18th Am. edition of Gray's Anatomy. Commd. capt., Med. R.C., June 1, 1917; assigned command of Field Hosp., Co. 341, 311th Sanitary Train, 86th Div., Camp Grant, Ill.; maj., Dec. 13, 1917; assigned as comdr. 311th Field Hosp. Sect.; lt. col. Med. Corps, Aug. 9, 1918; assigned as comdr. 311th Sanitary Train; overseas duty Sept. 16, 1918-Jan. 19, 1919; hon. discharged, Jan. 28, 1919; lt. col. Med. R.C., Nov. 7, 1919. Certified by U.S. Civil Service Commn. as spl. expert, med. referee, 1921; medical referee, neuro-psychiatric sect., U.S. Veterans' Bur., Washington, Mar. 1-Aug. 25, 1921; chief med. rating sect., U.S. Veterans' Bur., New York Office, Aug. 26, 1921—. Home: Mt. Vernon, N.Y. Died Sept. 5, 1922.

SPOEHR, HERMAN AUGUSTUS, (spor), chemist; b. Chicago, Ill. , June 18, 1885; s. Charles A. and Frida (Baeuerlen) S.; S.B., U. of Chicago, 1906, Ph.D., 1909, D.Sc., 1929; studied U. of Berlin, 1907, U. of Paris, 1908; m. Florence Mann, Dec. 17, 1910; children—Alexander, Hortense. Swift fellow, U. of Chicago, 1909; asso. in chemistry, same, 1910; became staff mem. Lab. Plant Physiology, Carnegie Instn., Washington, 1910, asst. dir. Coastal Lab. of same, 1926-27, chmn. div. of plant biology, 1928-20; acting prof. chemistry, Stanford, summer 1924; director natural sciences Rockefeller Foundation, 1930-31; chmn. div. plant biology Carnegie Inst., 1932-47, chmn. emeritus, 1947—. Consultant to Sec. of State, 1950-51. Mem. Am. Chem. Soc., Bot. Soc. of Am., A.A.A.S., Am. Academy of Arts and Sciences, Am. Philos. Soc., Am. Soc. Naturalists, Am. Soc. Plant Physiologists, hon. mem. Deutsche Botanische Gesellschaft, Linnean Soc., London. Club: Bohemian. Author of "Photosynthesis," and of numerous papers on photosynthesis and chemistry of carbohydrate metabolism. Home: 464 Coleride Av., Palo Alto, Calif. Address: Carnegie Institution, Stanford, Cal. Died June 21, 1954.

SPOFFORD, W(OLCOTT) E(DWARD), naval architect and shipbuilder; b. near Alex, Va., Sept. 17, 1895; s. Edward Coggeshall and Lydia (Riley) S.; grad. Univ. Prep. Sch., Washington, 1916; student Webb Inst. Naval Architecture and Marine Engring., N.Y. City, 1916-17, 1919-20, Franklin Inst., Phila., 1920-21; also spl. univ. courses; m. Dorothy Lincoln Hale, Apr. 20, 1922; 1 dau., Elizabeth Ann (Mrs. John Hyatt). Draftsman, Internat. Mercantile Marine, N.Y. City, 1921; draftsman United States Lines, N.Y. City, 1921-22, designer, 1922-23; vice pres. and naval architect Henry C. Grebe & Co., naval architects and yacht brokers, Chicago, 1924-25; designer, cost estimator and constructor, merchant and naval vessels Newport News (Va.) Shipbldg. & Dry Dock Co., 1926-31; asso. naval architect, Navy Yard, N.Y. City, 1931-37; naval architect U.S. Maritime Commn., Washington, 1937-39, regional dir. constrn. Great Lakes Area, Chicago, 1942-44, tech. consultant U.S. Maritime Commn., 1944-45, asst. to vice chmn., 1945-46, liaison officer Bur. Res. Fleet, 1946-48, chmn. claims review bd. Maritime Commn., Washington, 1948-50; supt. U.S. Maritime Adminstrn. Res. Fleet, Olympia, Wash., 1950-56; naval architect Puget Sound Naval Shipyard, Bremerton, 1957, ret.; now engring. aide bridge division Wash. Hwy. Dept.; naval architect and asst. chief engineer Consolidated Steel Corp., Los Angeles, 1939-42. Am. observer Internat. Conf. on standardization of screw threads, Ottawa, Can., 1945; marine cons. loaned to Internat. Training Adminstrn., Inc., for training 22 Chinese naval ensigns in technique of Am. shipbldg., 1946; Am. del. to Internat. Conf. on safety of life at sea, London, 1948. Enlisted in U.S. Army, 1917; commd. 2d lt., 1918; comdg. officer 114th Inf., N.J.N.G., 1920-21. Mem. Soc. Naval Architects and Marine Engineers, American Soc. Naval Engrs., Am. Legion, Webb Inst. Naval Architecture and Marine Engring. Alumni Assn. (sec.-treas. 1933-35). Profl. engr., Texas, Wash. Contbr. articles to maritime tech. mags. Died Oct. 18, 1961; buried Arlington Nat. Cemetery.

SPRAGUE, AUSTIN VELOROUS MLITON, inventor; b. Rochester, N.Y., May 28, 1840; s. Foster S.; ed. pub. schs. and Myron G. Peck's Acad., Rochester; has pursued spl. studies in law, medicine and engring.; m. Emily E., d. H. B. Sherman, M.D., 1864 (she died 1867); 2d, Mary E., d. Andrew Curtis, of Charlton, Saratoga, N.Y., 1869. Learned trade in shops of father who was hardware mcht. and mfr. of kitchen utensils, house heating and ventilating devices. Went to oil fields of Pa., 1865, and engaged in various enterprises, improving methods of oil production. Because of many boiler explosions caused by use of brackish water, conceived and executed plan for raising water of Allegheny River to overcome elevation of 740 feet in 2 1/2 miles, to a reservoir, whence it flowed by gravity to feed several hundred boilers with fresh water. Inventor of household articles, improvements in laundry machinery; especially notable for inventions of disinfectors, sterilizers and apparatus for thermaerotherapy; introduced steam for disinfection of textile fabrics, etc., 1889; steam under pressure for sterilization of surgical dressings, instruments, etc., 1890 (now in gen. use); began experiments with dry hot air for therapeutical purposes, 1891 (now largely used). Inventor of the "Sprague Aseptisier." Address: 2314 Broadway, New York.

SPRAGUE, FRANK JULIAN, engineer, inventor; b. Milford, Conn., July 25, 1857; s. David Cummings and Frances Julia (King) S.; grad. U.S. Naval Acad., 1878; D.Eng., Stevens Inst., 1921; D.Sc., Columbia, 1922; LL.D., U. of Pa., 1924; m. Mary Keatinge, 1885; 1 son, Frank D'Esmonde; m. 2d, Harriet Chapman Jones, Oct. 11, 1899; children—Robert Chapman, Julian King, Frances Althea. Mem. of jury, Crystal Palace Expn., London, England, 1882, and had charge of tests of dynamo-electric machines, gas engines and electric lights, as reported to Navy Dept.; elec. studies and experiments at Stevens Inst., Brooklyn Navy Yard and U.S. Torpedo Sta., Newport; resigned, 1883, to devote attention to elec. work; asst. for a time to Thomas A. Edison; founded, 1884, Sprague Electric Ry. & Motor Co., which, using his constant speed elec. motor, was first to engage in gen. mfr. and introduction of industrial elec. motors (endorsed by Edison Electric Light Co. 1885); developed pilot control of indsl. and other motors; pioneer in ry. electrification; equipped first modern trolley ry. in U.S. at Richmond, Va., 1887, later in Florence, Italy, Halle, Germany, and more than 100 rys. in 2 yrs.; developed A.C. induction smelting furnace, also high speed and house automatic elec. elevators and installed Central London equipment; invented method of operating two elevators on same rails in a common shaft, and acceleration control of car safeties; invented multiple-unit system of elec. train control, now in general use, and also system of regeneration used on mountain elec. rys. and on high speed elec. elevators; promoted high tension, direct current elec. ry. system; developed system of automatic signal and brake train control to enforce obedience to signals; etc.; engaged for yrs. in promoting underground rapid transit; pres. Sprague Development Corp., Sprague Safety Control & Signal Corp.; cons. engr. Sprague, Westinghouse, Otis and Gen. Electric cos.; mem. Terminal Electrical Commn. N.Y.C. & H.R. R.R. As cons. engr. S.P. Co. made studies for electrification of Sierra Nevada sect. of that system; selected as mem. U.S. Naval Consulting Bd. by Am. Inst. E.E. and the Inventors' Guild, and engaged during World War I in development of fuses and air and depth bombs. Trustee Sch. Applied Design for Women. Fellow and past pres. Am. Inst. E.E., New York Elec. Soc., Am. Inst. Consulting Engrs., Inventors' Guild. Awarded gold medal, Paris Expn., 1889, for elec. ry. development; Elliott Cresson medal, Franklin Inst., 1904, for multi-unit system; grand prize for "invention and development in electric rys.," St. Louis Expn., 1904; Edison gold medal "for meritorious achievement in electrical science, engineering and art," 1910; Franklin medal, 1921, "for fundamental inventions and achievements in elec. engring." Author of various scientific papers on electricity. On 75th birthday was designated as "Father of Electric Traction"; also, in 1934, a bronze portrait bust of him was presented to Am. Inst. E.E. Home: New York, N.Y. Died Oct. 25, 1934.

SPRAGUE, HOWARD B., physician; b. Swampscott, Mass., Nov. 3, 1895; s. Henry Breed and Laura Loring (Brown) S.; A.B., Harvard, 1918, M.D., 1922; m. Lucy Sprague, June 14, 1919 (dec. Mar. 7, 1958); children—Priscilla Bulfinch Goldthwait, Elizabeth Howard Manson (M.D.), Howard B., Jr.; m. 2d, Marian B. Norton, Sept. 19, 1958. Intern Mass. Gen. Hosp., Boston, Mass., 1922-24, cardiac residency, 1924-25, asso. physician, 1931-53, physician, 1953-56, bd. consultants, 1956-67, hon. physician, 1967-71; physician specializing in diseases of heart, Boston, from 1925; former chief of staff House Good Samaritan; lectr. medicine Harvard Med. Sch., 1956-59; mem. nat. adv. heart council USPHS, 1954-59; sr. cons. in internal med. to U.S. Naval Hosp., Chelsea, Mass.; area chief in cardiology, New England area, Vets. Adminstrn., 1946-58. Served with Medical Corps, United States Naval Reserve, on active duty, 1941-45; promoted comdr., 1942, capt., 1943; on overseas service in Pacific, 17 mos. Decorated Asiatic-Pacific Theater Medal, Naval Reserve Medal (10 yrs. Service), Am. Theatre World War II Victory medal; gold-heart award of American Heart Assn., 1954; gold medal Am. Coll. Cardiology, 1965; Theodore and Susan Cummings humanitarian award, 1967. Trustee, treasurer Boston Med. Library, 1946-58, president, from 1958; mem. bd. directors Inter-Am. Soc. Cardiology, from 1946 (v.p. 1952); treas. Internat. Cardiology Found., from 1964. Diplomate Am. Bd. Internal Medicine (Cardiology). Fellow Am. College of Physicians, American College of Cardiology; honorary mem. Mex., Chilean socs. of cardiology, Med. Soc. Santiago, Chile, med. faculty U. Chile; mem. Assn. Am. Physicians, Beacon Soc. Boston vice president 1952; president 1953-55), S.A.R., Soc. Colonial Wars, Harvard Alumni Assn. (dir. 1962-64), Bostonian Society, Am. Heart Assn. (sec. 1937-47, pres. 1950-51), Mass., N.E. Heart Assn. (pres. 1941-48), Mass. Med. Society, Am. Med. Assn., Am. Clin. and Climatol. Assn., Internat. Acad. Pathology, N.E. Cardiovascular Soc. (exec. com.), Internat. Soc. Cardiology, Phi Beta Kappa, Alpha Omega Alpha. Clubs: Harvard (Boston and N.Y.); Country (Brookline); Anglers (N.Y.C.); Cruising of Am. Contbr. numerous papers on diseases of circulation to med. publs. Home: Duxbury MA Died Nov. 4, 1971; buried Pine Grove Cemetery Lynn MA

SPRATLING, WILLIAM, architect, silversmith, writer; b. Sonyear, N.Y., Sept. 22, 1900; s. William Philip and Anna (Gorton) S.; student sculpture, Beaux Art Inst., N.Y.C., 1919; student Auburn U., 1971-21, L.H.D. (hon.), 1962. Asso. prof. architecture Tulane U., 1921-29; lectr. Nat. U. Mexico, 1927-29; propr. silversmith industry, Taxco, Mexico, 1930—; collector, writer preHispanic art, 1931—; designer, hand-mfr. silver, 1930—; donated collection ancient Vera Cruz day sculpture to Nat. U. Mexico, 1960; formulated plan for indigenous arts prodn. for Alaska for Dept. Interior, 1949. Recipient Gran prix for silversmithing, Brussells, 1960. Mem. A.I.A., Pi Kappa Alpha. Author: Sherwood Anderson and Other Famous Creoles (with William Faulkner), 1926; Old Plantation Houses of Louisiana, 1927; Little Mexico, 1931; More Human Than Divine, 1960; The Frescoes of Diego Rivera, 1931; A Small Mexican World, 1964; also numerous articles mags., newspapers. Address: Apdo. 48, Taxco, Guerrero, Mexico. Died Aug. 1967.

SPRATLING, WILLIAM PHILIP, physician; b. Chambers Co., Ala., Oct. 13, 1863; s. William Philip and Mary Ann S.; 1 term at State Poly. Inst., Auburn, Ala., and 1 term Moors' Business Coll., Atlanta, Ga.; med. student Vanderbilt U., 1 yr.; M.D., Coll. Phys. and Surg., Baltimore, 1886; m. Annie Gorton, of Brooklyn, Dec. 11, 1901. Entered U.S. Marine Hosp. Service, 1887, as med. interne; next became asst. phys. N.J. State Hosp. for Insane, Morristown, N.Y., for 5 yrs.; practiced medicine at New York 2 1/2 yrs., as specialist in nervous and mental diseases; medical supt. Craig Colony for Epileptics, the first instn. of its kind to be built in the world, 1894-1908. Ex-pres. Nat. Assn. for Study of Epilepsy; mem. N.Y. Acad. Medicine, Am. Medico-Psychol. Assn. Methodist. Independent in politics. Author: Epilepsy and Its Treatment, 1904; also various scientific publs. in pamphlet form. Address: Lafayette, Alabama.

SPRING, LA VERNE WARD, chemist, metallurgist; b. Coldwater, Mich., Sept. 22, 1876; s. Emerson and Lucinda (Ward) S.; A.B., U. of Mich., 1901; m. Emelyn J. Atkinson, Aug. 1905; children—Robert Ward, Dorothy Jane. Chemist, Ill. Steel Co., South Chicago, Ill., 1899-1900, Wolverine Portland Cement Co., Coldwater, Mich., 1901; again with Ill. Steel Co., 1901-03; chemist, Crane Co., Chicago, 1903-15, and chief chemist and metallurgist. Author: Non-Technical Chats on Iron and Steel, 1917; also various articles on chem. and physical testing and metallurgy. Home: Chicago, Ill. Died Mar. 23, 1932.

SPRING, LAURENCE ELLSWORTH, pres. tech. inst.; b. Orangeville, N.Y., June 1, 1898; s. Burt Ellsworth and Helen (Nesbitt) S.; student Colgate U., 1915-17, U.S. Mil. Acad., 1918; B.S., Syracuse U., 1924; Ed.M., U. Buffalo, 1954; m. Emma Lovina Colfax, Aug. 25, 1925; children—Jean Elizabeth (Mrs. Thomas E. Sheavly) and Mary Lou (Mrs. James V. Worrall) (twins). Instr., asst. prin. Seneca Vocationa High Sch., Buffalo, 1925-40; supr. N.Y. State Dept. Edn., 1941-45, asst. prof. tchr. tng., 1945-46; dean Erie County Tech. Inst., Buffalo, 1946-54, pres., 1954—. Chmn. N.Y. State Apprenticeship Council; mem.-at-large Buffalo area council Boy Scouts Am. Trustee N.Y. Nuclear Research Center, Buffalo, ednl. TV sta. WNED-TV, Buffalo. Served with U.S. Army, 1917-18. Mem. Buffalo C. of C., Am. Tech. Edn. Assn. (pres. 1959), N.Y. State Jr. Coll. Assn. (pres. 1962-63), Engring. Soc. Buffalo, Phi Delta Kappa, Alpha Tau Omega, Phi Kappa Phi, Delta Sigma Rho, Beta Gamma Sigma, Alpha Kappa Psi. Mem. Community Ch. Clubs: Rotary (past v.p.), Torch (past dir.) (Buffalo). Home: 20 Hancock Terrace, Snyder, N.Y. 14226. Died Oct. 26, 1963.

SPRINGER, ALFRED, chemist; b. Cincinnati, O., Feb. 12, 1854; s. Lemuel and Antonie (Fries) S.; pub. and high schs., Cincinnati; A.M., Ph.D., U. of Heidelberg, Germany, 1872; Dr. Natural Science, Ruperto Carola U., Heidelberg, Germany, 1931; m. Eda Elsas, Dec. 30, 1879; children—Elsa (Mrs. Christian Meyer), Alfred. Sole owner Alex. Fries & Bro., mfg. chemists, Cincinnati, 1873, until retired, 1936. Fellow A.A.A.S. (gen. sec., 1884; v.p., 1892); mem. Am. Chem. Soc.; corr. mem. Brit. Assn. for Advancement of Science. Awarded John Scott Legacy premium and medal, Franklin Inst., 1891. Has written many papers on chem. and phys. subjects. Co-inventor of the torsion balance, also patentee of same and of aluminum soundboards for mus. instruments. Home: Belvedere Apts., Avondale, Cincinnati. Office: 312 E. 2d St., Cincinnati, O. Died Feb. 24, 1946. *

SPRINGER, FRANK, paleontologist; b. Wapello, Ia., June 17, 1848; s. Francis and Nancy R. S.; ed. State U. of Ia.; m. Josephine M. Bishop, Oct. 10, 1876; children—Laura (Mrs. John J. K. Caskie), Helen (Mrs. John F. Fairbairn), Eva, Ada (Mrs. Warren B. Davis), Edward Thomas, Henry Strong (dec.), Lew Wallace. Admitted to the bar, 1869; also member bar of U.S. Supreme Court; mem. Legislative Council, N.M., 1901; pres. bd. trustees Maxwell Land Grant Co.; regent Museum of New Mexico. Author: Revision of the Palaeocrinoidea, 1879-86 (Phila. Acad. Natural Science); North American Crinoidea Camerata, 1897; Uintacrinus, its Structure and Relations, 1901; Cleiocrinus, 1905; New American Fossil Crinoids, 1911; Scyphocrinus, 1917; Mysticocrinus, 1918; Pentacrinus from East Indies, 1918; Crinoidea Flexibilia, 1920; Dolatocrinus, 1921; Crinoids from Northern Canada, 1921; Balanocrinus from Mexico, 1922; Family Catillocrinidae, 1923; Tertiary Crinoid from West Indies, 1924; The genus Holopus, 1924; Pentacrinus in Alaska, 1925; Apiocrinus in America, 1925; Unusual Forms Fossil Crinoids, 1926. Home: East Las Vegas, N.M. Died Sept. 22, 1927.

SPRINGER, FRANKLIN WESLEY, electrical engr.; b. Anoka, Minn., Jan. 18, 1870; s. Wesley John and Mary Elizabeth (Norris) S.; B.E.E., U. of Minn., 1893, E.E., 1898; studied factories and engring. schs. abroad, 1900; engring. schs. of Berlin and Paris, 1910-11; m. Grace Hamilton Pierce, Dec. 31, 1912; 1 dau., Suzanne. Asst. prof. elec. engring., 1900-07, prof., 1907—, U. of Minn., also acting head of the dept., 1925-28. Has taken out several patents on elec. and automobile devices. Fellow Am. Inst. E.E. (v.p. 1921-22). Republican. Methodist. Home: Minneapolis, Minn. Died Jan. 23, 1933.

SPRONG, SEVERN D., elec. engr.; b. East Greenbush, Rensselaer County, N.Y., Oct. 27, 1873; s. Willard D. and Pauline A. (Melius) S.; ed. pub. and private schs. and under tutelage; m. Margaret A. McMullen, Oct. 21, 1897; 1 dau., Katharine W. Supt. elec. dept., Consolidated Gas Co. of N.J., Long Branch, N.J., 1898-1901; chief engr. Central Electric Co., Metuchen, N.J., 1901-02; asst. chief elec. engr., N.Y. Edison Co., 1902-07; asst. elec. engr. United Electric Light & Power Co., New York, 1907-10; chief elec. engr., J. G. White Co., New York, 1910-12; elec. engr. Brooklyn Edison Co., 1912-22; v.p. Orange County Pub. Service Corp., 1922; pres. Engring. Products Corp. since 1924. Republican. Conglist. Fellow Am. Inst. E.E. (v.p. 1912-13); mem. Am. Soc. M.E., N.Y. Elec. Soc., A.A.A.S. Clubs: Engineers' (New York), Lawyers, Montauk Home: Monroe, N.Y. Office: 39 Cortlandt St., New York, N.Y. *

SPRUANCE, WILLIAM CORBIT, electrical engr.; b. Wilmington, Del., Sept. 26, 1873; s. William Corbit and Maria Louisa (Spotswood) S.; grad. Friends' Sch., Wilmington, 1890; Princeton Univ., 1894, E.E., 1895; m. Alice Moore Lea, May 4, 1907. Cons. practice until 1903; with duPont Co., 1903—, except mil. service; v.p. and dir. E. I. du Pont de Nemours & Co. Commd. maj. Ordnance R.C., U.S.A., Dec. 1917; lt. col. N.A., Jan. 1918; col. U.S.A., Oct. 1918; served as chief of explosives and loading div. Ordnance Dept.; mem. commodity sect. on explosives War Industries Bd. and com. on explosives investigation Nat. Research Council; hon. discharged, Feb. 1919. Awarded D.S.M. (U.S.), 1919. Republican. Presbyn. Home: Wilmington, Del. Died Jan. 9, 1935.

SPRUNT, ALEXANDER, JR., ornithologist; b. Rock Hill, S.C., Jan. 16, 1898; s. Alexander and Nell Richardson (Peck) S.; student Porter Mil. Acad., Charleston, S.C., 1910-11, Smith Sch., Charleston, S.C., 1912-13, Davidson (N.C.) Coll., 1914-18, Charleston Coll., 1954; D.Sc., Davidson Coll.; m. Margaret Malcolmson Vardell, Oct. 27, 1920; children—Alexander IV, Jean Vardell. Curator ornithology Charleston (S.C.) Mus., 1924-30, hon. curator, 1930-73; supr. So. sanctuaries, Nat. Audubon Soc., 1935-40, So. rep. Nat. Audubon Soc., N.Y., 1940-73, also lectr. Served with USN 1918. Fellow Am. Ornithologists Union. Author: Dwellers of the Silences, 1935; Birds of South Carolina, 1949; Album Southern Birds, 1953; Florida Birdlife, 1954; North American Birds of Prey, 1955; Carolina Low Country; (with others) Warblers of America, 1957. Contbr. nature articles and stories to popular mags., also sci. articles on ornithology to tech. jours. Address: Charleston SC Died Jan. 3, 1973; buried Magnolia Cemetery, Charleston SC

SPURR, JOSIAH EDWARD, geologist; b. Gloucester, Mass., Oct. 1, 1870; s. Alfred and Oratia E. (Snow) S.; A.B., Harvard, 1893, A.M., 1894; m. Sophie C. Burchard, Jan. 18, 1899; children—Edward Burchard, John Constantine, William Alfred, Robert Anton, Stephen Hopkins. Mining engr. and geologist to Sultan of Turkey, Apr. 1901-May 1902; geologist, U.S. Geol. Survey, 1902-06; chief geol. dept. Am. Smelting & Refining Co., Am. Smelters Securities Co., Guggenheim Exploration Co., 1906-08; Spurr & Cox (Inc.), cons. specialists in mining, 1908-11; v.p. in charge of mining, Tonopah Mining Co. of Nevada, 1911-17; mem. com. of mineral imports, U.S. Shipping and War Trade bds., 1917-18; exec. war minerals investigations, chief metal mining engineer, Bureau of Mines; chief engr., War Mineral Relief, 1918-19; editor Engineering and Mining Journal, 1919-27; prof. of geology, Rollins Coll., 1930-32. Mem. Mining and Metall. Soc. America (pres. 1921), Am. Inst. of Mining and Metall. Engineers, Soc. Econ. Geologists (pres. 1923), Geol. Soc. America, Am. Geog. Soc., Soc. Mayflower Descendants, Society of Colonial Wars. Author: The Iron-Bearing Rocks of the Mesabi Range in Minnesota (Minn. Geol. and Nat. Hist. Survey), 1894; Through the Yukon Gold Diggings, 1900; Geology Applied to Mining, 1904; The Ore Magmas, 1923; Geology Applied to Selenology, 1944; Features of the Moon, 1945; Lunar Catastrophic History, 1947; The Shrunken Moon, 1949; also various monographs and reports on economic geology, etc. Editor: Political and Commercial Geology, 1921. Mt. Spurr peak in Alaska named by U.S. Geol. Survey in honor of his explorations in Alaska, 1896, 98. Home: 324 Henkel Circle, Winter Park, Fla.; also Alstead, N.H. Died Jan. 12, 1950.

SPURZHEIM, JOHANN KASPAR, phrenologist; b. nr. Trier, Germany, Dec. 31, 1776; studied medicine, Vienna, Austria. Student of Franz Joseph Gall (founder of what came to be phrenology), 1800-05, became Gall's asst., 1805; travelled from Vienna to France, Eng. and later Am. in effort to spread Gall's doctrines, 1813; 1st to coin term phrenology; gave names to some mental faculties and parts of skull which are still in use today; lived and worked in U.S., circa 1813-32; believed that skull had 37 "powers" corresponding to 37 "organs." Author: (with Gall) Anatomie et Physiologie du Systéme Nerveux en Genéral, et du Cerveau en Particulier, avec Observations sur la Possibilité de Reconnaitre Plusiers Dispositions Intellectuelles et Morales de l'Homme et des Animaux par la Configuration de Leurs Têtes, 2 vols., 1810-19; The Physiognomical System of Gall and Spurzheim, 1815. Died Boston, Nov. 10, 1832.

SQUIBB, EDWARD ROBINSON, pharmacist, chemist, physician; b. Wilmington, Del., July 4, 1819; s. James R. and Catherine H. (Bonsal) S.; studied pharmacy under Warder Morris, Phila., 1837, under J. H. Sprague, Phila., 1837-42; M.D., Jefferson Med. Coll., 1845; m. Caroline F. Lownds, Oct. 7, 1852, 3 children. Commd. asst. surgeon U.S. Navy, 1847; med. officer in ships Perry, Erie, Cumberland, 1847-51; assigned to duty Bklyn. Naval Hosp., 1851; authorized by Navy Dept. to establish his own lab. for manufacture pharmaceuticals and chemicals, 1852; resigned U.S. Navy, 1853, became mfg. co-partner in firm Thomas E. Jenkins & Co. (known as Louisville Chem. Works), Louisville, Ky.; established chem. and pharm. lab. under name Edward R. Squibb, M.D., Bklyn., 1858, severely injured when lab. burned, 1858, later rebuilt factory, admitted his 2 sons as co-partners, 1892, changed name to E. R. Squibb & Sons; contbr. many articles to Am. Journal of Pharmacy. Died Bklyn., Oct. 25, 1900.

SQUIER, GEORGE OWEN, army officer; b. Dryden, Mich., Mar. 21, 1865; s. Almon Justice and Emily (Gardner) S.; grad. U.S. Mil. Acad., 1887; fellow, Johns Hopkins, 1902-03 and 1903-04, Ph.D., 1903; hon. D.Sc. from Dartmouth College, 1922; unmarried. Apptd. 2d lieut. 3d Artillery, June 12, 1887; 1st lt., June 30, 1893; capt. signal officer vols., May 20, 1898; lt. col. signal officer vols., July 18, 1898; hon. disch. from vols., Dec. 7, 1898; 1st lt. signal corps U.S.A., Feb. 23, 1899; capt. signal officer vols., Apr. 17, 1899; hon. disch. from vols., June 30, 1901; capt., signal corps U.S.A., Feb. 2, 1901; maj., Mar. 2, 1903. Comd. U.S. Cable-ship Burnside, 1900-02, during laying of Philippine cable-telegraph system. U.S. mil. attaché at London, Eng., 1912; commd. lt. col. Signal Corps, Mar. 17, 1913; brig. gen., chief signal officer U.S.A., Feb. 14, 1917; maj. gen., Oct. 6, 1917; in charge of army air service, May 20, 1916-May 20, 1918. Mem. nat. council Boy Scouts of America. D.S.M. (U.S.); Knight Comdr. St. Michael and St. George (Great Britain); Commander Order of the Crown (Italy); Commander Legion of Honor (France). Elliott Cresson gold medal, Franklin medal. Researches: Electrochemical effects due to magnetization; the polarizing photochronograph; the sine wave systems of telegraphy and ocean cabling; the absorption of electro-magnetic waves by living vegetable organisms; multiplex telephony and telegraphy; tree telephony and telegraphy, multiplex telephony and telegraphy, over open circuit bare wires laid in the earth or sea. Inventor of the monophone for broadcasting over telephone wires and over power wires, also wired wireless, 1910; inventor of "Quickaid," a first aid kit for Army and Red Cross use. War Department rep. and technical adviser to Am. delegation at Internat. Conf. on Elec. Communications, Washington, 1920; rep. dept. of State at sessions of Provisional Tech. com. of Internat. Conf. on Elec. Communications, Paris, 1921; designated an expert asst. to Am. Commrs. at Conf. on Limitation of Armament, Washington, 1921; ex-officio mem., representing War Dept., of U.S. Nat. Com. Internat. Electrotech. Commn. Founder, 1918, of "A Country Club for Country People, " Dryden, Mich. Died Mar. 24, 1934.

SQUIRE, EDWARD JACOB, civil engr.; b. Watertown, N.Y., Dec. 29, 1886; s. George P. and Mina (Geiger) S.; student Bulkeley Sch., New London, Conn.; C.E., Poly. Inst., 1910; M.S., N.Y. U., 1917; m. Eleanore Schneider, June 19, 1915; children—June (Mrs. Blase), Eleanore (Mrs. Bezer). Instr. civil engring., Bklyn. Poly. Inst., 1910-17, asst. prof., 1917-24, asso. prof., 1924-27, prof. structural engring. since 1927, head dept. civil engring., 1938-56, prof. emeritus; cons. engr.; v.p. Lockwood Kessler & Bartlett, Inc., Syosset; lectr. structures, Evening Div. Engring., N.Y. U., 1932-38; expert examiner N.Y. City Civil Service Commn. since 1928. Licensed profl. engr., N.Y., N.J., Conn., Pa., Ida., Minn. Decorated Chevalier de la Croix de Lorraine; Order of Scientific merit of Humanist Inst. of France; Knight Comdr. Star Order of Gold Cross of Cyprus and Jerusalem. Mem. Am. Society C.E., Am. Soc. Eng. Edn., N.Y. Acad. Sci. (fellow); Soc. Am. Mil. Engrs., New Eng. Soc., A.A.A.S. (fellow); Pi Kappa Phi, Tau Beta Pi, Sigma Xi, Chi Epsilon. Club: Brooklyn. Author: Elements of Graphic Statics; also tech. articles, book reviews. Home: 15 Silver Av., Huntington Station, N.Y. Office: 1 Aerial Way, Syosset, N.Y. Died Sept. 28, 1967.

STABLER, HERMAN, (stab'ler), civil engr.; b. Brighton, Md., Feb. 3, 1879; s. George Lea and Annie Dickinson (Cotton) S.; B.S., Earlham Coll., 1899; spl. course in engring., Columbian (now George Washington) U., Washington, 1902-03; m. Bertha R. Buhler, Nov. 1, 1905. Instr. mathematics and engring., Nat. Corr. Inst., Washington, 1899-1903; hydraulic and sanitary engr. with the U.S. Geol. Survey and U.S. Reclamation Service, 1903-22; chief of land classification br. U.S. Geol. Survey, 1922-25 and of conservation br. since 1925. Mem. Am. Soc. C.E. (dir., 1935-37), Am. Inst. Mining and Metall. Engrs., Washington Soc. of Engineers, Geol. Society of Washington, Washington Acad. Sciences, Am. Geog. Soc. Mem. Friends Ch. Mason. Clubs: Cosmos, Columbia Country. Author of numerous bulls. and papers relating to disposal of wastes of mfg. establishments and recovery of products therefrom; pollution of streams; composition of stream waters; development of ground waters; rate of erosion; silt accumulations; water power; industrial uses of water, etc. Home: 2700 Connecticut Av. Address: Cosmos Club, Washington, D.C. Died Nov. 24, 1942.

STABLER, JAMES PLEASANTS, electrician; b. Sandy Spring, Md., June 12, 1839; s. of James P. (eminent engr.); and Sarah (Briggs) S.; common school edn.; m. 1870, Alice, d. George E. Brooke, of Montgomery Co., Md. Early developed mech. abilities; patented inventions in classes of agrl. implements, steam engring. and electricity. Entered U. S. Agrl. Dept., 1866; became chief clerk statistical div., 1877; resigned, 1882, to engage in electrical pursuits; now foreman instrument shop C. of P. Telephone Co. Address: Washington.

STABLER, LAIRD JOSEPH, chemist; b. Bethany, O., Aug. 27, 1865; s. Daniel F. and Rachel A. (Le Sourd) S.; Ph.C., U. of Mich., 1885; B.S., Purdue U., 1890, M.S., 1892; Sc.D., U. of Southern Calif., 1916; m. Maude Jones, Aug. 27, 1890. Prof. industrial chemistry and dean Coll. of Pharmacy, U. of Southern Calif., 1894—. Dir. Bd. of Health, Los Angeles, 6 yrs.; trustee Pub. Library, 4 yrs. Republican. Methodist. Specialized in chemistry of petroleum oils. Died Nov. 26, 1939.

STACK, FREDERIC WILLIAM, naturalist; b. Poughkeepsie, N.Y., Nov. 21, 1871; s. George N. and Serena Martin (Macneil) S.; ed. pub. schs. and under pvt. tutelage of Prof. William B. Dwight, of Vassar Coll.; m. Cornelia Mollison Rockfellow, of Plainfield, N.J., Dec. 29, 1898. Mgr. dept. of publication mfr., Doubleday, Page & Co., since 1904. Served for 5 yrs. as pvt., 2d sergt. and sec. 15th Separate Co., N.G.S.N.Y.; formerly field collector for Mus. Natural History of Vassar Coll., and for mus. of the scientific sect. of Vassar Bros. Inst. Corr. mem. Delaware Valley Ornithol. Club; asso. mem. Am. Ornithologists' Union. Republican. Presbyn. K.T. Mason. Author: Wild Flowers Every Child Should Know, 1909. Extensive contbr. to mags. on nat. history and hort. subjects. Home: New Rochelle NY Office: 133 E. 16th St., New York NY

STACK, JOHN, engineer; b. Lowell, Mass., Sept. 13, 1906; s. Michael and Margaret (Connors) S.; B.S., Mass. Inst. Tech., 1928; m. Helen Sturtevant, Dec. 8, 1928; children—Martha (Mrs. John E. Sim), John Peter. Research, development, high-speed aerodynamics, 1928—; with Langley Aero Lab., NACA, beginning as research engr., successively sect. head, div. chief, then asst. dir.; mem. research adv. com. high speed aerodynamics, fluid mechanics, propellers, compressors; v.p. and dir. engring. Republic Aviation Corp., 1962-65; v.p. engring. Fairchild Hiller Co., from 1965; Wright Bros. lectr. Inst. Aero. Scis., 1944; Sci. Adv. Com. Tech. Adv. Panel Aero., Dept. Def.; vis. com. dept. mathematics Mass. Inst. Tech., 1954-56. Director Citizens & Marine Bank, Newport News, Va., Antilles Air Boats, Inc., St. Croix, V.I., Mac Aviation Corp., Ronkonkoma, L.I., United Virginia Bank/Citizens & Marine (Hampton, Va.). Recipient Science and Research award Air Forces Assn., 1948; awarded Collier trophy (with L. D. Bell, C. E. Yeager) for pioneer supersonic flight manned aircraft, 1948, for transonic wind tunnel development, 1952; awarded medal Soc. Engrs. Sweden, 1951, Wright Bros. Meml. Trophy, 1962. Fellow Royal Aero. Soc. Great Britian, Am. Inst. Aeros. and Astronautics (hon. mem.; recipient Sylvanus Albert Reid award 1953); hon. fellow Inst. Aerospace Scis.; mem. Air Force Assn. U.S. (hon.), Nat. Rifle Assn. Author sci. articles. Mem. editorial com. Jour. Aero. Scis. Home: Yorktown VA Died June 18, 1972; buried Grace Episcopal Churchyard, Yorktown VA

STADLER, LEWIS JOHN, (stad'ler), geneticist; b. St. Louis, Mo., July 6, 1896; s. Henry L. and Josephine (Ehrman) S.; B.S.A., U. of Fla., 1917; A.M., U. of Mo., 1918, Ph.D., 1922; grad. work Cornell U., 1919, 26, Harvard, 1925-26; m. Cornelia Field Tuckerman, Dec. 18, 1919; children—Maury Tuckerman, Henry Lewis, David Ross, John Brandeis, Eliot Tuckerman, Joan. Asst. prof. U. of Mo., 1922-25, asso. prof., 1925-36, prof., 1936—; vis. prof. Calif. Inst. Tech. 1940, Yale, 1950. Nat. Research fellow in biology, Harvard, 1925-26; sr. geneticist U.S. Dept. Agr., 1929-36, prin. geneticist, 1936-40, agent, 1940—. Mem. sci. adv. com. Selective Service System; Atomic Energy Commission, Postdoctoral Fellowship Board. Served as 2d lt. F.A., U.S. Army, 1918. Mem. A.A.A.S., Bot. Soc. America, Am. Soc. Agronomy, Genetics Soc. America (pres. 1938), Am. Soc. Naturalists (pres. 1953), Am. Acad. Arts and Scis., Nat. Acad. Scis., Am. Philos. Soc., Sigma Xi (pres.); nat. lectureship, Sigma Xi, 1938, Frank A. Spragg Memorial Lectureship, Mich. State College, 1939. Mem. editorial bd. Exptl. Biology Monographs, Advances in Genetics, American Naturalist, Univ. of Mo. Studies and Genetics. Home: 308 Thilly Av., Columbia, Mo. Died May 12, 1954.

STAFFORD, ORIN FLETCHER, chemist; b. Hillsboro, O., Feb. 7, 1873; s. E. and Sarah (Kurtz) S.; A.B., U. of Kan., 1900, A.M., 1902; U. of Berlin, 1908-09; m. Mary E. Straub, Dec. 24, 1903; children—Howard Straub, Miriam, John Edward. Asst. prof. chemistry, U. of Ore., 1902-06, prof., 1906—, also head of dept. and later dean of science and of Lower Division. On leave of absence, 1918-22, to develop autogenous process for wood carbonization applicable to use of waste woods; consulting practice. Home: Eugene, Ore. Died Sept. 17, 1941.

STAFSETH, H(ENRIK) J(OAKIM), coll. prof.; born Aalesund, Norway, Nov. 8, 1890; s. Knut Elias and Marie (Langset) S.; came to U.S., 1911, naturalized, 1918; student high sch. and gymnasium in Norway, 1904-11; B.S., N.D. State Agrl. Coll., 1915; D.V.M., Mich. State Coll., 1917, M.S., 1930, Ph.D., 1935; m. Inger Nordhem, Apr. 4, 1917; 1 son, Henrik Ekroll. Instr. and research asst. in bacteriology, Mich. State Coll., 1917-20, asst. prof. and research asst. in bacteriol., 1921-25, asso. prof. and research asso., 1926-30, prof. bacteriol. since 1930, head dept. bacteriol., bacteriologist, Mich. Agrl. Expt. Sta., dir. med. technol. and dir. div. biol. scis. Sch. Sci. and Arts, from 1948; cons. vet. edn. So. Regional Edn. Bd., 1949-52, U. Pa., 1956-57; dir. W. K. Kellogg Gull Lake biol. sta.; dist. veterinarian, Midtre Sondmor, Norway, Feb. 1910-July 1921; exchange prof. Royal Hungarian Vet. College, 1925-26; visited veterinary and other colls. and research labs., England, Norway, Sweden, Denmark, Germany, Austria, Switzerland, 1925-26; tech. adviser on poultry diseases to Dept. Agr. of Mexico, Nov. 1-Dec. 20, 1933. Chief veterinarian for U.N.R.R.A., China, Sept. 1945-Sept. 1946 (instrumental in establishing 1st modern vet. coll. in China at Lanchow, Kansu Province, summer 1946. Served in U.S. Army, 1917-19; discharged rank of 1st lt. Recipient Mich. State U. distinguished service award, 1955. Fellow Poultry Sci. Assn., Am. Pub. Health Assn., A.A.A.S.; mem. Royal Soc. Promotion Health, Am. Acad. Microbiologists, Am. and Michigan State Vet. Med. Assns., U.S. Live Stock San. Assn., Conf. Research Workers in Animal Diseases of N. Am., Soc. Am. Bacteriol., Am. Scandinavian Found., Mich. Acad. Science, American Legion, Military Order, Veterans of Foreign Wars, Sigma Xi, Sigma Chi, Alpha Psi, Phi Sigma, Phi Kappa Phi. Mem. People's Ch. (chmn. bd. trustees; chmn. Christian Student Foundation). Mason (K.T.), Kiwanian. Club: Walnut Hills Golf. Author: Laboratory Guide in Immunology and Lab. Guide in Pathogenic Bacteriology, 1942; Microbiology (with Ward Giltner), 1916; Diseases of Poultry (with Biester & Schwarte), 1948. Contbr. articles in profl. jours. Home: East Lansing MI Died Dec. 1, 1968.

STAGER, ANSON, telegraph pioneer, army officer; b. Ontario County, N.Y., Apr. 20, 1825; m. Rebecca Sprague, Nov. 14, 1847, 3 children. Worked in office Rochester (N.Y.) Daily Advertiser owned by Henry O'Reilly, 1841, bookkeeper by 1845; studied telegraphy in spare time; apptd. telegraph operator at Lancaster (Pa.) office, 1847 (after O'Reilly had contracted with Samuel F. B. Morse to build telegraph from Phila. to Middle West, circa 1845); mgr., Pitts. office, 1847; mgr. operating dept. of Pitts., Cincinnati & Louisville Telegraph Co., 1847-51; apptd. gen. supt. N.Y. & Mississippi Valley Printing Telegraph Co., 1852-56; gen. supt. Western Union Telegraph Co., 1856-61, assigned to rearrange many telegraph lines and establish good relations with railroads, established hdqrs. at Cleve.; commd. capt. and asst. q.m. gen. U.S. Army, 1861, placed in Washington (D.C.) as chief U.S. mil. telegraphs; promoted col., assigned as a.d.c. to Gen. Henry W. Halleck at War Dept., 1862; brevetted brig. gen. for meritorious services, 1865, discharged, 1866; became supt. Central div. Western Union Telegraph Co. with hdqrs at Cleve., later at Chgo., v.p. until 1881; pres. Western Edison Electric Light Co. from its formation until 1885. Died Chgo., Mar. 26, 1885.

STAHL, K(ARL) F(RIEDRICH), chemist; b. Zwiefalten, Wurttemberg, Germany, Mar. 14, 1855; s. Johann Jacob and Luise (Kurz) S.; student Inst. of Tech., Stuttgart, 1872-75; U. of Tübingen, 1875-76, D.Sc., 1876, renewed 1926; m. Emma Onyx Johnson, Aug. 8, 1881 (died Nov. 1924); 1 dau., Minneola Luise. Came to U.S., 1876, naturalized, 1888. Chemist Charles Lennig & Co., Phila., 1876-80, Northwestern Fertilizer Co., Chicago, 1880-82; supt. Nat. Fertilizer Co., Nashville, Tenn., 1882-84, Johnstown (Pa.) Chem. Works, 1884-90, James Irwin & Co., Pittsburgh, 1890-1899; supt. Pittsburgh works, Gen. Chem. Co., 1899-1913; research chemist Gen. Chem. Co. and cons. chemist since 1914. Fellow A.A.A.S.; mem. Am. Chem. Soc. (chmn. Pittsburg sect., 1916, emeritus 1933), Engr. Soc. of Western Pa. (dir. 1895; chmn. chem. sect. 1902), Nat. Assn. German-Am. Technologists (pres. 4 terms, hon. mem. 1937), Verein Deutscher Chemiker, Soc. Chem. Industry (England). Republican. Lutheran. Home: 839 Chislett St., Pittsburgh 6, Pa. Died Aug. 26, 1946.

STALDER, JACKSON R., mech. engr.; b. Oakland, Cal., Dec. 12, 1915; s. John Reed and Maude (Wells) S.; B.S., U. Cal. at Berkeley, 1941; m. Virginia Hall, July 22, 1950; children—Suellen, Barbara Lynn, Kenneth Reed. Aero. research scientist NACA, 1941-58; exec. with Vidya, Inc., 1958-65; chief scientist USAF Flight Dynamics Lab., 1965-67; tech. asst. to dir. NASA, Ames Lab., 1967-68; pres. KOWL, Inc., Bijou, Cal., 1963-68, Beavercreek Farms (Ore.), 1964-68. Fellow Am. Inst. Aeros. and Astronautics (asso.); mem. Sigma Xi. Home: Palo Alto CA Died Sept. 10, 1968.

STALDER, WALTER, cons. petroleum geologist; b. Oakland, Calif., Apr. 6, 1881; s. Joseph and Mary Amy (Birner) S.; B.S., U. of Calif., 1904, M.S., 1907; unmarried. Chemist, San Francisco Chem. Co., 1904-07; petroleum geologist since 1907; with M.L. Requa and Nev. Petroleum Co., 1909-11; land valuation, Union Oil Co. of Calif., 1911, when and where fundamentals of present decline curve method of estimating oil reserves originated; Nevada Petroleum Co., 1911-13; chief geologist on valuation, Independent Oil Producers, 1914-15; cons. practice since 1916. Mem. Am. Assn. Petroleum Geologists, Am. Inst. Mining and Metallurgical Engineers (chairman San Francisco section 1945), Am. Chem. Soc., A.A.A.S., Seismol. Soc. America, Calif. Acad. Sciences. Episcopalian. Mason (Shriner). Clubs: Engineers, Commonwealth Club of Calif. (chmn. mineral resources sect. 1922-29). Recommended and brought in Marysville Buttes Gas Field (1st real commercial discovery in Northern Calif.). Contbr. on early Calif. oilfield history and its geology. Home: 1812 12th Av., Oakland, Calif. Office: Crocker Bldg., San Francisco. Died March 15, 1949.

STALEY, ALLEN CONKLING, engineer; b. Miami County, O., Oct. 1, 1885; s. Wilmer Conkling and Grace Anna (Forgy) S.; prep. student Lawrenceville (N.J.), Groff (N.Y.C.); Ph.B., Yale, 1908, M.E., 1914; m. Helen M. Kinnear, July 7, 1908 (dec.); children—Allen Conkling, William K., Mary E. (Mrs. Fred A. Jennings); m. 2d, Alta E. Harris, Apr. 17, 1954. Steam expert Carnegie Steel Co., 1908-12; mem. faculty Yale Engring. Sch. and cons. engr., 1912-15; supr. power United Paperboard Co., 1915-18; engr. Stanley Motor Carriage Co., and Standard Engring. Co., 1918-21; prof. automative engring., Purdue U., 1921-26; cons. engr. N.W. Engring. Co., Dulany Trust, 1926-31; research engr. Chrysler Corp., also v.p., dir. Airtemp. div., dean Chrysler Inst. Engring., 1931-50; engring. cons., 1950-55. Mem. (or former mem.) Nat. Adv. Com. Aeronautics, Am. Soc. M.E., Am. Ordnance Assn., Soc. Automotive Engrs., Engring. Society of Detroit (dir.), Sigma Xi. Club: La Jolla Beach and Tennis. Pioneered domestic oil burners for homes. Author tech. papers; patentee in field. Died Dec. 2, 1960.

STALEY, CADY, engineer; b. Minaville, N.Y., Dec. 12, 1840; s. Harmanus and Eveline (Darrow) S.; A.B., Union Coll., 1865, C.E., 1866, Ph.D., 1874 (LL.D., 1888, Ohio Wesleyan, 1888); m. Kate Holcomb, of Waterford, N.Y., Dec. 23, 1869. One of the engrs. in building the Central Pacific R.R.; prof. civ. engring., 1868-86, dean of faculty, 1876-86, Union Coll.; pres. Case Sch. Applied Science, Cleveland, 1886-1902; traveling. Mem. Am. Soc. C.E. Author: The Separate System of Sewerage (with G. S. Pierson). Address: Case School of Applied Science, Cleveland, Ohio.

STAMM, EDWARD P(HILIP), forest consultant; b. Pitts., Sept. 26, 1892; s. Christian and Anna (Maeder) S.; B.S., Ohio No. U., 1919; m. Harriet Alcoke, Nov. 1, 1919; children—Edward A., Paul W., Donald S. Log supt. Pacific Lumber Co., Scotia, Cal., 1919-25; cons. logging engr., Eureka, Cal., 1925-26; log mgr. Crown Zellerbach Corp., Portland, Ore., 1926-53, v.p., 1953-57; dir. Wahkiakum County Bank, Cathlamet, Wash., 1928—, v.p., 1936-42; forest cons. Trustee Lewis and Clark Coll., Found. Am. Resource Mgmt. Forest Genetics Found. Served as lt. arty., U.S. Army, 1916-19. Mem. Am. (dir., pres.), Indsl. (chmn. 1947-50) forestry assns., Am. Assn. Engrs., Pacific Logging Congress (pres. 1935, dir. 1936-48). Republican. Presbyn. Mason. Club: Portland City, Rotary. Contbr. articles trade jours. Home: 3630 32d Pl., Portland 12, Ore. Died Dec. 6, 1964; buried Lincoln Meml. Park, Portland

STAMPS, THOMAS DODSON, univ. ofcl.; b. Kingsbury, Tex., July 23, 1893; s. Asa and Elizabeth (Willeford) S.; A.B., U. of Tex., 1912; B.S., U.S. Mil. Acad., 1917; B.S., Mass. Inst. Tech., 1921; m. Lois Baker, Oct. 4, 1919; children—Dorothy, Ann. Commd. 2d lt. U.S. Army, 1917, advanced through grades to brig. gen., 1956; with Corps Engrs., 1917-38, commanded engr. troops, World War I, constrn. engr., Miss. River, Ill. waterway; Am. Embassy project, Tokyo, Japan, 1930-31; coll. prof., head dept. mil. art and engring., U.S. Mil. Acad., 1938-56, dean of the academy, 1956-57; ret., 1957; dir. mil. studies U. Md., 1957—. Mem. Soc. Am. Mil. Engrs., Assn. U.S. Army, Am. Mil. Inst. Club: Army and Navy (Washington). Co-editor: A Short Military History of World War I; A Military History of World War II. Contbr. articles various jours. Home: 5409 Ridgefield Rd., Washington 20016. Office: U. Md., College Park, Md. Died Apr. 12, 1964; buried U.S. Mil. Acad. Cemetery, West Point, N.Y.

STANGLAND, BENJAMIN F., mechanical engr.; b. Noble Co., Ind., Jan. 20, 1848; s. Andrew and Susan (Cary) S.; ed. pub. schs. and Brockport (N.Y.) Acad.; m. Emily S. Bridgeman, of Orleans Co., N.Y., 1876. In employ of The Fairbanks Co., Chicago, 1873-77; with Howard & Morse, New York, since 1879; has designed many ventilating plants in New York and other cities and has installed many plants in large bldgs. of New York. Mem. Am. Soc. Mech. Engrs., 1892; charter mem. Am. Soc. Heating and Ventilating Engrs. Democrat. Methodist. Homes: 157 W. 123d St., New York; (summer), Morton, Orleans Co., N.Y. Office: 45 Fulton St., New York.

STANISLAUS, I(GNATIUS) V(ALERIUS) STANLEY, chemist; b. at South Bend, Ind., 1870; s. M. Sylvester and Rosalie (Strans) S.; ed. Gynasium of Gnesen, Germany, 5 yrs.; Ph.C., U. of Ill., 1895; studied organic chemistry, Polytechnicum of Zurich, Switzerland, 1905-6; B.Sc., Univ. of Notre Dame, Ind., 1901; Dr. of Pharmacy, Brooklyn Coll. of Pharmacy, 1903; student, Brooklyn Poly. Inst., 1904; Ph.D., U. of Providence, O., 1907; studied at Harvard, 1907; M.A., Ursinus Coll., 1910; m. Lillian B. Smith, of Brooklyn, Oct. 17, 1903. Asso. chemist for Vanderhoof & Co., South Bend, Ind., 1888-93; dean dept. pharmacy and prof. industrial chemistry, U. of Notre Dame, 1896-1901; chemist for Osborn-Colwell Co., later De Ronde & Osborn Paint Co., New York, 1901-3; chief chemist for Hegeman & Co. Corpn., 1903-5; teacher pharmacy, Brooklyn College of Pharmacy, 1904; dean

Medico-Chirurg. Coll. of Pharmacy, Phila., since July 1, 1906. Has done original work and investigation in chemistry of odorous principles and volatile oils and resins. Asso. editor, The Apothecary, Boston, since 1903. Mem. Am. Chem. Soc., Am., Pharm. Assn., Ind. Acad. Science, Phi Chi, Kappa Psi. Mason. Author: Systematic Qualitative Analyses, Inorganic and Organic, 1905; Text-Book on Pharmacy, 1907; Pharmaceutic Chemistry, 1908; Laboratory Guide Applied Pharmacy, 1909. Home: Landsdowne PA Office: 1715 Cherry St., Philadelphia PA

STANLEY, FRANCIS EDGAR, inventor, mfr.; b. Kingfield, Me., June 1, 1849; s. Solomon and Apphia (French) S.; grad. Farmington State Normal and Tng. Sch., 1871; m. Augusta Walker, Jan. 1, 1870, 3 children. Lived in Lewiston, Me., 1874-83, became a leading portrait photographer; organizer (with his brother Freelan) Stanley Dry Plate Co., 1883, sold firm to Eastman Kodak Co., 1905; produced 1st successful steam-operated automobile in New Eng., 1897; began quantity constrn. of car, 1898, but sold patent rights and business to J. B. Walker; repurchased patents (with his brother), organized Stanley Motor Carriage Co. (which produced famous Stanley Steamer), 1902, pres., 1902-12. Author: Theories Worth Having, published 1919. Died July 31, 1918.

STANLEY, FRANK ARTHUR, mechanical engr., author, editor; b. Providence, July 3, 1874; s. James White and Mary Adelaide (Bowen) S.; ed. pub. schs., S. Coventry, Conn., and spl. courses; m. 2d, Eleanor E. King, Aug. 21, 1917. Engaged in machine work as operator, apprentice, machinist, toolmaker, and as engineer and shop exec. in Am. and European plants, 1888-99 (apprenticeship served with Smith & Winchester, South Windham, Conn., 1892-94); designer with Fellows Gear Shaper Co., Springfield, Vt., 1899; with Ingersoll-Sergeant Rock Drill Co., Easton, Pa., 1900-01; on editorial staff Am. Machinist, 1902-14, western editor, 1910-14, editorial rep., 1914-19; factory mgr. Marchant Calculating Machine Co., 1919; editor Western Machinery World, 1921-22; editor Western Machinery and Steel World, San Francisco, 1932-46. Author: (with Fred H. Colvin) American Machinists Handbook, 1908; (with same) The Hill Kink Books (10 in series), 1908; (with C. L. Goodrich) Accurate Tool Work, 1908; (with same) Automatic Screw Machines, 1909; (with Fred. H. Colvin) Machine Shop Primer, 1910; (with same) American Machinists Grinding Book, 1912; Punches and Dies, 1919; Drawing Room Practice, 1921; Railroad Shop Practice, 1921; Tool and Gage Work, 1923; Poincons et Matrices (transl. by Maurice Varinois), 1923; (with Fred H. Colvin) Machine Tools and Their Operation, vols. 1 and 2, 1923; Turning and Boring Practice, 1936; Drilling and Surfacing Practice, 1936; Gear Cutting Practice, 1937; Grinding Practice, 1937; Running a Machine Shop, 1941. Specialized, 1915-18, on descriptive articles of railroad shop, navy yard and gun shop operation; also Navy repairs under war time conditions. Contbr. articles on sugar plantation and engineering methods in Hawaiian Islands, and construction operations on the Panama Canal, etc. Home and business address: Auburn, Cal. Died Jan. 26, 1960; buried East Lawn Cemetery, Sacramento.

STANLEY, FREELAN O., inventor; b. Kingfield, Me., June 1, 1849; s. Solomon and Apphia (French) S.; ed. Hebron Acad. and Bowdoin Coll.; m. Flora Tileston, 1876. Inventor, 1883 (with twin brother Francis E. (deceased), of Stanley dry plate, which revolutionized photography, also of Stanley steam automobile, 1897; a builder of car that made fastest mile record (up to that time) in the world (28 1/5 seconds) at Ormond Beach, 1906, and 2 miles in 59 3/4 seconds; a founder of Stanley Motor Co.; has developed plan for mfg. violins on a large scale, on scientific basis. Propr. Stanley Hotel, Estes Park, Colo. Writer and lecturer. Republican. Unitarian. Home: Newton, Mass. Died Oct. 2, 1940.

STANLEY, ROBERT CROOKS, mechanical and mining engr.; b. Little Falls, N.J., Aug. 1, 1876; s. Thomas and Ada (Crooks) S.; M.E., Stevens Inst. of Tech., 1899; E.M., Sch. of Mines (Columbia), 1901; Sc.D., Columbia, 1939; D.Eng., Stevens Inst. Tech., 1935; D.Eng., Rensselaer Poly. Inst., 1940; Doctor of Laws, Queen's U. (Kingston, Ont.), 1949; m. Alma Guyon Timolat, June 14, 1912; children—Doris (Mrs. Reuel E. Warriner), Robert Crooks, Jr. Has been with the International Nickel Co. since 1901, gen. supt., 1912-18, 1st v.p., 1918-22, pres., 1922; chmn. bd. dirs., chmn. exec. com. and mem. adv. com., Internat. Nickel Co. of Can., Ltd.; chmn. bd. and dir. The Internat. Nickel Co., Inc.; dir. and mem. finance com. U.S. Steel Corp.; mem. advisory com. The Mond Nickel Co., Ltd. (England); dir. Chase Nat. Bank (mem. exec., fgn., examination coms.), Canadian Pacific Ry. Co., Amalgamated Metal Corp., Henry Gardner & Co. (London), Centre d'Information du Nickel (France). Special trustee for life, Stevens Institute Tech. Mem. Nat. Foreign Trade Council, Am. Inst. Mining and Metallurgical Engineers, Am. Iron and Steel Inst., Am. Mining Congress, Mining and Metallurgical Soc. Am., Chamber of Commerce, State of New York, Institute of Metals (London), British Empire Chamber Commerce in U.S., Canadian Inst. Mining and Metallurgy, Council of Princeton U. Internat. Summer Sch. of Geology and Natural Resources, St. George's Soc. of New York, Copper Development Assn., London (councillor), Nat. Industrial Conf. Board, Inc., Academy of Political Science, Army Ordnance Assn., Canadian Soc. of New York, Newcomen Society of England. Comdr. Order of Leopold conferred by King Leopold at Brussels, Belgium, Apr. 14, 1937. Received Thomas Egleston medal from Columbia Engring. Schools Alumni Assn., 1939; First Charles F. Rand Foundation gold medal awarded by Am. Inst. Mining and Metall. Engrs., 1941; Gold Medal for Advancement of Research awarded by American Soc. for Metals, 1944; Alumni Award Medallion of Alumni Assn. of Stevens Inst., 1946; His Majesty's Medal for Service in the Cause of Freedom (Eng.), 1947; Platinum Medal of Inst. of Metals, London, 1948. Clubs: City Midday, Mining, Union, New York Yacht, Boca Raton, Richmond County Country; Mount Royal (Montreal); Toronto Club: St. James (London). Home: Country Club Grounds, Dongan Hills, Staten Island, N.Y. Office: 67 Wall St., N.Y. City 5. Died Feb. 12, 1951.

STANLEY, WENDELL M(EREDITH), bio-chemist; b. Ridgeville, Ind., Aug. 16, 1904; s. James G. and Claire (Plessinger) S.; B.S., Earlham Coll., Richmond, Ind., 1926, hon. Sc.D., 1938; M.S., U. of Ill., 1927, Ph.D., 1929; Sc.D., 1959; Sc.D., Harvard, Yale, 1938, Princeton, 1947, U. Pitts., 1962, U. Penn., 1964, Gustavaus Adolphus College, 1963, University of Toledo, 1968, Butler U., 1968; LL.D., U. Cal., 1946, Indiana U., 1951, Jewish Theol. Sem., 1953, Mills Coll., 1960; Dr. honoris causa, U. Paris, 1947; m. Marian Staples Jay, June 15, 1929; children—Wendell, Marjorie (Mrs. Robert J. Albo), Dorothy (Mrs. Roger Erickson), Janet E. Research asso. and instr. in chemistry, U. of Ill., 1929; Nat. Research fellow, Munich, Germany, 1930-31; with Rockefeller Inst. for Med. Research since 1931, mem., 1940-48; Hitchcock prof. U. Cal., 1940, chmn. dept. biochemistry, 1948-53; prof. biochemistry, dir. virus lab. Univ. Cal. at Berkeley, 1948-69, professor, chmn. dept. viorology, 1958-64, professor of molecular biology, 1964-71. Vanuxem lectr. Princeton, 1942; Messenger lectr. Cornell, 1942; Silliman lectr. Yale, 1947. Trustee Mills Coll., 1951-58. Mem. expert adv. panel on virus diseases WHO, 1951-71; nat. adv. cancer council USPHS, 1952-56; chairman section biochemistry National Academy Sciences, 1955-58; dir.-at-large Am. Cancer Soc., 1955-61; mem. bd. scientific counselors National Cancer Inst., 1957-61, chmn. 1957-58; adv. com. to dir. Nat. Insts. Health, 1966-71; spl. adv. com. to sec. Dept. Health, Edn. and Welfare; pres. 10th Internat. Cancer Congress, Houston, 1970. Fellow N.Y. Acad. Scis.; mem. Japan Acad. (hon.), Am. Assn. Immunologists. Am. Philos. Soc., Am. Chem. Soc., Am. Phytopathological Society, Harvey Soc. (hon.), Am. Soc. Biol. Chemists (mem. council 1951-54), A.A.A.S., Sigma Xi, Alpha Omega Alpha, Gamma Alpha, Phi Lambda Upsilon (hon.), Alpha Chi Sigma, Phi Kappa Phi. Awarded A.A.A.S. prize, 1936; Isaac Idler prize by Med. Sch. of Harvard, 1938; Rosenberger medal by U. of Chicago, 1938; John Scott medal, certificate, and premium by the City of Phila., 1938; gold medal of Am. Inst. of the City of New York, 1941; Copernican Citation by the Copernican Quadricentennial Nat. Com., 1943; Nichols Medal of the N.Y. Sect. of American Chem. Society, 1946; Nobel Prize in Chemistry, 1946; Gibbs Medal of Chicago Sect. of Am. Chem. Soc., 1947; Franklin Medal of Franklin Inst., 1948; Presdl. Certificate of Merit, 1948; Modern Medicine award, 1958; Am. Cancer Soc. award, 1959; nat. award Am. Cancer Soc. 1963; Sci. Achievement award A.M.A., 1966; Wendell M. Stanley Hall named in his honor by U. Cal. decorated 2d class Order Rising Sun (Japan), Contbr. to sci. jours. Home: Berkeley CA Died June 15, 1971; buried Berkeley CA

STANLEY, WILLIAM, electrical engr. inventor; b. Brooklyn Nov. 22, 1858; s. William and Elizabeth A. (Parsons) S.; ed. Williston Sem., Easthampton, Mass., and short time at Yale, class of '81, self-ed. in elec. science; m. Lila C. Wetmore, Dec. 22, 1884. Chief engr. Westinghouse Electric Co., 1885-88, Stanley Elec. Mfg. Co., 1890-95, Stanley Instrument Co., 1898-1903. Inventor alternating-current system of long distance light and power transmission. Home: Great Barrington, Mass. Died May 14, 1916.

STANTON, JOHN, mining engr.; b. Bristol, Eng., Feb. 25, 1830; s. John and Joan (Locke) S.; came with parents to Pa., 1835; studied engring. took active management of his father's iron mines at Dover, N.J.; m. Elizabeth R. McMillan, Dec. 24, 1857. Engaged in copper mining, 1852-61, in Md., Va. and Tenn.; mines in Tenn. confiscated by Confederate govt.; later developed copper mines in Lake Superior region and in Ariz., in which he is still largely interested, being pres. and mgr. of several cos. One of founders and 1st pres. N.Y. Mining Stock Exchange. Home: New York, N.Y. Died 1906.

STANTON, ROBERT BREWSTER, engineer; b. Woodville, Miss., Aug. 5, 1846; s. Robert Livingston (D.D.) and Anna Maria (Stone) S.; A.B., Miami U., 1871, A.M., 1878; (hon. A.M., U. of Wooster, 1885); m. Jean Oliver Moore, Dec. 1, 1881. Resident engr. Cincinnati Southern R.R., 1874-80; div. engr. U.P. Ry., 1880-84, and built noted "Georgetown Loop" ry., 1882-83; consulting civ. and mining engr., 1884—. Made ry. survey as chief engr. through Grand Cañon of the Colorado, 1889-90; engr. of various mines in U.S., Can., Mex., West and East Indies, Cuba; explorations for gold in island of Sumatra, Dutch East Indies, 1904. Author: The Cañons of the Colorado River of the West for Railway Purposes, 1892; The Great Land-Slides on the Canadian Pacific Ry. in British Columbia, 1898. Home: New York, N.Y. Died Feb. 23, 1922.

STANTON, TIMOTHY WILLIAM, geologist, paleontologist; b. Monroe County, Ill., Sept. 21, 1860; s. William and Mary A. (Blanchard) S.; B.S., U. of Colo., 1883, M.S., 1895, D.Sc., 1924; Johns Hopkins, 1888-89; Ph.D., Columbia (now George Washington) U., 1897; m. Grace M. Patten, Oct. 12, 1898; children—Grace, Elizabeth, Josephine. Asst. state librarian of Colo., 1885-88; asst. paleontologist, 1889-1900, paleontologist, 1900-03, geologist in charge paleontology, 1903-30, acting chief geologist, 1931, chief, 1932-35, U.S. Geol. Survey; retired. Instructor paleontology and stratigraphic geology, 1894-1905, asst. prof. paleontology, 1906-10, George Washington U. Fellow Geol. Soc. Am. (v.p. 1921), Paleontol. Soc. America (pres. 1921), A.A.A.S.; mem. Washington Acad. Sciences, Phi Beta Kappa, Delta Tau Delta. Republican. Methodist. Club: Cosmos. Has published numerous reports and papers on paleontology and stratigraphic geology. Home: 1017 N. Noyes Dr., Silver Spring, Md. Died Dec. 4, 1953.

STARBUCK, RAYMOND DONALD, ry. official; b. Ft. Ann, N.Y., July 26, 1878; s. George Starbuck and Meribah (Moore) S.; student Cornell U., 1896-1900; m. Ann M. McCauley, Jan. 2, 1902; children—John P., William H., Ann. Began as asst. engr. M.C.R.R., 1903, and continued as div. engr., 1904-05, asst. chief engr., 1905-12; spl. engr. to asst. v.p. N.Y.C. Lines, 1912-13, to v.p., 1913-15, to pres., 1915-16; asst. to v.p. same rd., 1916-17; asst. gen. mgr. lines west of Buffalo, same rd., 1917-18; asst. federal mgr. same, 1918-19; asst. regional dir. Eastern region, under U.S. R.R. Adminstrn., 1919-20; asst. v.p. N.Y.C. R.R. 1920-24, v.p., 1924-32, exec. v.p. N.Y.C. System, 1932-47, ret. Mem. Am. Ry. Engring. Assn. Republican. Clubs: Chicago (Chicago); Union League, Traffic (New York); Siwanoy Country. Home: Bronxville, N.Y. Died Aug. 16, 1965.

STARK, ORTON K(IRKWOOD), bacteriologist, educator; b. Cromwell, Ind., Sept. 21, 1898; s. Samuel Byron and Mary Elizabeth (Hart) S.; A.B., DePauw U., 1922; Ph.D., U. Ill., 1926; m. Mary Virginia Milligan, Sept. 10, 1926; children—Virginia Ruth (Mrs. Richard E. Sherrell), Edward William. Asso. prof. biology La. State Normal, Natchitoches, 1926-27; asst. prof. botany U. Wyo., 1927-29; asst. prof., then asso. prof. botany Miami U., 1929-44, prof., from 1944, chmn. dept., 1956-62. Served as pvt. U.S. Army, World War I. Mem. Soc. Am. Bacteriologists (pres. Ohio br. 1948), A.A.A.S., Am. Acad. Microbiology, N.Y. Acad. Scis., Am. Pub. Health Assn., Royal Soc. Health (Eng.), Sigma Xi, Phi Sigma. Contbr. research articles profl. jours. Home: Oxford OH Died Sept. 5, 1968; buried Oxford OH

STARKS, WILLIAM HENRY LORD, M. D., M. E. clergyman; b. Canaan, N. Y., Sept. 17, 1826; grad. Castleton Med. Coll., 1853; post-grad. course Coll. Phys. & Surg., New York, 1854; marine surgeon 1 yr.; entered practice in New York; vice-prin. and prof. mathematics and languages, Ft. Plain Female Coll., 1855; received diploma and Phi Beta Kappa honor, Union Coll., 1857; entered ministry M. E. Ch. and joined Troy Conf., 1857; pastor of many leading chs.; still a supernumerary mem. of that body and med. examiner of Conf. Life Ins. Assn.; widely known as med. lecturer; specialist in chronic diseases, surgeon, oculist and aurist; conducts saritarium at Ocean Grove, N. J. Address: Palmer, Mass.

STARLING, WILLIAM, chief engr. Mississippi levee dist.; b. Columbus, O., Jan. 25, 1839; grad. New York Univ., 1856 (A.M., C.E.). Served in Union army in Civil war. Member Loyal Legion; Am. Soc. Civil Engrs.; Instn. of Civil Engrs. of Great Britain; etc. Prominent Mason—past grand high priest; past grand comdr. Knights Templar; present grand master Masons in Mississippi. Unmarried. Author: The Improvement of the Mississippi River; Some Notes on the Holland Dikes; The Discharge of the Mississippi River; The Floods of the Mississippi River; etc. Home: Greenville, Miss. Died 1900.

STARRETT, MILTON GERRY, (star'et), engineer; b. Francestown, N.H., Jan. 24, 1861; s. James H. and Theresa (Morgan) S.; prep. edn. Francestown Acad.; C.E., Tufts Coll., 1886, Sc.D., 1905; m. Ruth Eastman Morrill, Dec. 28, 1893. Instr. mathematics, Tufts Coll., 1886-89; asst. engr. West End St. Ry. Co., Boston, 1889-91; chief engr. Brooklyn City R.R. Co., 1891-96; asst. chief engr., 1896-99, chief engr., 1899-1906, Met. St. Ry. Co. and its successors; consulting engr. until 1935; now retired. Mem. Am. Soc. C.E., A.A.A.S., New Eng. Assn. of New York. Home: New Canaan, Conn. Died Sep. 18, 1942.

STARRETT, THEODORE, constr. fireproof bldgs.; b. Lawrence, Kan., Jan. 21, 1865; s. William Aiken and Helen (Ekin) S.; ed. U. of Kan., Lake Forest U., class of 1884, but did not complete course (A.B., 1903). Became engr., 1886, for Burnham & Root, Chicago architects (who designed Chicago Expn.); builders and engineer, 1889—; built over 150 fireproof buildings, of which more than 100 are skyscrapers and monumental buildings, at Chicago, New York, Buffalo, Cleveland, Columbus, Boston, Princeton, Phila., Pittsburgh, Washington, Baltimore, San Francisco, Winnipeg, including the Washington Terminal, and the Pa. Sta. at Columbus; leader in the establishment of the constrn. co. idea; founder of the Thompson-Starrett Co. and pres., 8 yrs.; resigned to engage in constrn. work in individual capacity. Home: Prospect Plains, N.J. Died Oct. 9, 1917.

STARRETT, WILLIAM AIKEN, architect, engr.; b. Lawrence, Kan., June 14, 1877; s. William A. and Helen (Ekin) S.; ed. U. of Mich., 1893-95, B.S. in C.E., 1917; m. Eloise Gedney, June 14, 1900; children—Helen Ruth, David. A founder, 1901, and v.p. Thompson-Starrett Co., gen. contractors, New York, continuing until 1913; mem. Starrett & Van Vleck, Mar. 1913-Jan. 1, 1918. Mem. Plattsburg Training Camp, 1916; engr. corps training work, winter 1916-17; chmn. emergency constrn. com. of Council Nat. Defense, in charge govt. bldg. program, including constrn. cantonments, May 1, 1917; commd. capt., Engr. R.C., May 2, 1917, maj., June 13, 1917, col. Q.M.C., Mar. 18, 1918; hon. disch., Mar. 22, 1919. Col., U.S.A., R.C. V.p. George A. Fuller Co., gen. contractors, New York, 1919-21; with brothers, Paul and Ralph, founded Starrett Bros., Inc., Builders, New York, 1922, of which is v.p.; pres. The Starrett Corp. Introduced into Japan several modern steel frame buildings, 1919-21, specially designed to resist earthquake. Mayor of Madison, N.J., 1919-21. Author: Skyscrapers and the Men Who Build Them, 1929. Home: Madison, N.J. Died Mar. 26, 1932.

STARRING, FREDERICK A(UGUSTUS), civil and mining engr., lawyer, soldier; b. Buffalo, N.Y., May 24, 1834; s. Capt. Sylvenus Seaman and Adeline (Williams) S.; ed. Buffalo, Paris, Heidelberg, Vienna and grad. Harvard, class of 1865-66; admitted to bar, 1859; m. Louise Perle Whitehouse, July 21, 1889. Engr. on Ill. Central, location surveys and boundary line surveys, Tex. & Ind. Ter., etc. Sec. Cairo & Fulton R.R. Co. of Ark. and Mo., 1859-61. Served Civil war, maj. 46th Ill. inf., maj., 2d Ill. light arty., col. 72d Ill. inf. (Chicago Bd. of Trade regt.); brig. gen. comdg. 1st, 2d and 3d brigades, Army of Tenn., and maj. gen. and provost marshal gen., dept. of the Gulf. U.S. diplomatic and consular agt. Europe and other foreign countries, 1869-83. Home: New York, N.Y. Died 1904.

STATHAS, PERICLES PETER, elec. engr.; financial and mgmt. cons.; b. Tropaia, Greece, Apr. 7, 1898; s. Peter and Crissa (Constan) S.; student Milw. Sch. Engring., 1917-20; B.S., Marquette U., 1923, E.E., 1929; m. Mary Pegis, June 26, 1927; children—Diane, Thalia, Charles. Came to U.S., 1912, naturalized, 1920. Field engr, system engr. Wis. Electric Power Co., 1923-29, sr. engr. management staff, 1929-35; joined Duff & Phelps, pub. utility analysts and cons., 1936, partner, 1938, sr. partner, 1946-57; pres., dir. Duff & Phelps, Inc., 1958-60, chmn., chief exec. officer, dir., 1961-73; chmn., chief exec. Pa. & So. Gas Co.; chmn. bd. Southwest Gas Corp., Duff, Anderson & Clark, Inc., 1966-73; v.p. dir. Southeastern Mich. Gas Co.; dir., exec. com. Central La. Electric Co., Inc.; dir. Middle South Utilities, Inc., Selected Am. Shares, Inc., Piedmont Natural Gas Co., Inc., Pub. Service Co. N.M., Pubco Petroleum Corp.; also financial analyst. Trustee Northwestern Mil. and Naval Acad. Recipient McGraw Engring. award and Henry L. Doherty medal Edison Electric Inst., 1932; Distinguished Engring. Alumnus, Marquette U., 1967. Registered profl. engr., Wis., Ill. Mem. Am. Finance Assn., I.E.E.E., Am. Water Works Assn., So. Gas Assn., Pub. Utility Securities Club Chgo., Investment Analysts Soc., Western Soc. Engrs., Newcomen Soc., Eta Kappa Nu, Tau Beta Pi. Mason. Clubs: Union League, Attic, Executives, Exmoor, Chicago (Chgo.); Wall Street (N.Y.C.); Family (San Francisco); Harbor View, Author, lectr. pub. utilities papers. Expert witness pub. utility regulatory matters. Home: Lake Forest IL Died Feb. 22, 1973.

STAUDINGER, HERMANN, chemist; b. Germany, 1881; ed. univs. of Halle, Munich and Darmstadt; hon. degrees; Dr. Ing., T. Karlsruhe, 1950; Dr. Rer. Nat., U. Mainz, 1951; Dr. (C), U. Salamaca, 1954; Dr. Chem., U. Turin, 1954; Dr. Sci. Tech., Eidgenös Tech. Hochschule Zurich, 1955; Dr. h.c., Strassburg University, 1959. Lecturer chemistry Strassburg University, 1907-08; prof. Karlsruhe Tech. High Sch., 1908-12; prof. Fed. Tech. High Sch., Zurich, 1912-26, U. Freiburg im Breisgau, 1926-56, now prof. emeritus. Mem. Gottingen, Heidelberg, Halle, Munich acads. scis., Frankfurt, Zurich phys. societies, Royal Physiograph. Soc. Lund, also member Institut de France. Recipient of Leblanc medal from the French Chemical Society, 1931, Cannizzaro prize, Rome, Italy, 1933; The Nobel chemistry prize, 1953. Author: Die Ketene, 1912; Tabellen fur allgemeine und anorganische Chemie, 1935; Die hochmolekularen organischen Verbindungen, 1932; Organisch qualitative Analyse, 1939; Organische Kolloidchemie, 1941; Vom Aufstand der technischen Sklaven, 1974; Makromolekulare Chemie and Biologie, 1947; Arbeitserinnerungen, 1961. Address: Lugostrasse 14, Freiburg im Breisgau, Germany. Died Sept. 8, 1965.

STAUFFER, CLINTON RAYMOND, (stawf'fer), geologist; b. Polo, Ill., Oct, 2, 1875; s. Peter and Mary J. (Grise) S.; B.Sc., Ohio State U., 1903, M.A., 1906; Ph.D., U. of Chicago, 1909; m. Eva Grace Webb, Aug. 29, 1911; 1 son, Robert Clinton. Began as a principal of a high school, 1903-05; instructor in geology, Ohio State University, 1906-07; fellow in geology, University of Chicago, 1907-09; instr. geology, Western Reserve U., 1909-10; asst. prof. geology, Queen's U., Kingston, Can., 1910-11; asso. prof. geology, Western Res. U., 1911-14; asso. prof. geology, U. of Minn., 1914-17, prof., 1917-44; prof. emeritus, 1944; visiting prof. Division of Geol. Scis., Calif. Inst. of Tech., 1947-48, research associate, 1949-55. Geologist, Geol. Survey of Ohio, 1906-10, 1913-17, Geological Survey of Can., 1910-13, The Greenwood Company, 1919-21, Minn. Geol. Survey, 1922-44. United States Geol. Survey, 1944-45. Recipient of the Orton award Ohio State University, 1957, Columbus Limestone award, 1957. Fellow A.A.A.S., Geol. Soc. America, Ohio Acad. Science, Paleontol. Soc.; mem. Am. Assn. Petroleum Geologists, Assn. of Econ. Paleontologists and Mineralogists, Am. Inst. Mining and Metall. Engrs., Internat. Congress Geologists (1913), Am. Assn. Univ. Professors, Minn. Acad. Science, Sigma Xi, Sigma Gamma Epsilon, Acacia. Conglist. Mason. Author: The Middle Devonian of Ohio (Geol. survey of Ohio), 1909; Devonian of Southwestern Ontario (Can. Geol. Survey), 1915; Devonian of Minnesota, 1922; The Devonian of California; Conodonts, 1930; Text-Book of Geology, 1932, revised edit., 1939; Ordovician Polychaeta, 1933; Limestones of Minnesota, 1933; Shakopee fauna, 1936; Conodonts of the Olentangy Shale, 1938; The St. Croixian Series, 1939; Conodonts from the Devonian of Minnesota, 1940; Paleozoic and Related Rocks of Southeastern Minnesota, 1942; Pleistocene Mammals of Minnesota, 1945; The Genus Microcyclus, 1952. Also various other papers on geol. subjects. Home: 2247 Loma Vista St., Pasadena 7, Cal. Died July 11, 1960.

STAUFFER, DAVID MCNEELY, engineer; b. Mount Joy, Pa., March 24, 1845; s. Jacob and Mary Anna (McNeely) S.; left Franklin and Marshall Coll. without graduating, for war (hon. Litt.D., 1903)); m. Florence Scribner, Apr. 19, 1892. Served in U.S.N. in Civil War; comd. U.S.S. "Alexandria" in Mississippi River Fleet, 1865; civil engr. in railroad work, bridge and tunnel building, 1865-82; editor, and one of proprs. Engineering News, 1882-1906; retired. Mem. of Palisades Interstate Park Commn. under apptmt. from govs. of New York and N.J. Author: Modern Tunnel Construction, 1906; American Engravers on Copper and Steel, 1907. Home: Yonkers, N.Y. Died Feb. 5, 1913.

STAUFFER, HERBERT MILTON, physician; educator; b. Phila., Apr. 26, 1914; s. Milton F. and Anna (Hood) S.; M.D., Temple U., 1939, M.Sc., 1945; m. Joan Dunbar; 1 son, Scott. Intern, Temple U. Hosp., Phila., 1939-41, fellow in radiology, 1941-43; roentgenologist Univ. Hosp., Mpls., 1946-49; asst. prof. radiology U. Minn., Mpls., 1946-49; asso. prof. radiology Temple U., 1949-52, prof., 1952-70, head dept. radiology, 1957-70. Mem. radiation study sect. NIH, 1959-62, mem. internat. fellowship rev. panel, 1964-67, mem. diagnostic radiology tng. com., 1967-68; program USPHS. Bd. govs., mem. profl. edn. com. Heart Assn. Southeastern Pa., 1968-70. Served to lt., M.C., USNR, 1943-46. Diplomate Am. Bd. Radiology. Fellow Am. Coll. Radiology; mem. Assn. Univ. Radiologists (pres. 1963-64), Radiol. Soc. N.Am. (program com. 1964-66, dir. 1967-69, chmn. bd. dirs. 1970, pres.-elect. 1970), Am. (chmn. exec. council 1966, 2d v.p. 1969), Phila. (pres. 1969) roentgen ray socs., Phila. Tb and Respiratory Disease Assn. (dir. case detection com. Tb control adv. com. 1968-70). Contbr. numerous articles to med. jours., also chpts. to books. Home: Philadelphia PA Died Dec. 18, 1970.

STAUNTON, WILLIAM FIELD, (stawn'tun), mining engr.; b. Toledo, O., Dec. 23, 1860; s. William Field and Mary De Wolf (Gray) S.; prep. edn., Charlier Inst., N.Y. City; E.M., Columbia, 1882; m. Mary Fulton Neal, Mar. 23, 1892; children—William Field, Neal (dec.), Maria Gage. Supt. Tombstone (Ariz.) Mill & Mining Co., 1884-94; mgr. Congress (Ariz.) Gold Co., 1894-1910; vice-pres. and gen. mgr. Tombstone Consol. Mines Co., 1901-10, Imperial Copper Co., Southern Ariz. Smelting Co., Ariz. Southern R.R. Co., 1904-10; cons. mining engr., chiefly in oil and copper, Los Angeles, Calif., since 1910. Formerly mem. Ariz. Mining Code Commn. Mem. Am. Inst. Mining and Metall. Engrs., Mining and Metall. Soc. America, S.R., Tau Beta Pi. Republican. Episcopalian. Clubs: California, Engineers. Home: 512 S. Harvard Blvd. Office: I. W. Hellman Bldg., Los Angeles, Calif. Died Feb. 12, 1917. *

STAYTON, EDWARD M(OSES), civil engr.; b. Independence, Mo., Sept. 4, 1874; s. Thomas and Louisa Matilda (Corn) S.; grad. Independence High Sch., 1891; student in engring. U. of Mo., 1892-94; m. Bitha Estella Compton, July 26, 1898; 1 son, George Edward. Civil engr. engaged in railroad location and const. in Southwest and in Honduras, 1895-1911; locating and building highway and interurban railways in Kansas City area, 1911-17; building highways in Clay County, 1919-20; mem. bd. control Kansas City Street Ry., Co., 1920-26; design and constrn. Blue River sewer, Kansas City, 1925-27; cons. engr., Jackson County highways, 1928-33; street railway commr., Kansas City, Mo., 1926-40. Served as capt., 1910-14, major, 1914-17, Mo. Nat. Guard; maj. and lt. col. engrs., U.S. Army, with A.E.F., 1917-19; col. engrs. Mo. Nat. Guard, 1920-33, brig. gen., 1933-37, maj. gen., 1938, Mem. Nat. Defense Com. Mem. U.S. Chamber Commerece 1940-42. Awarded D.S.M. of Society of American Military Engineers; also Missouri Distinguished Service Medal; Master Conservationist Award of Mo. Conservation Commission 1946. Past State Comdr. Am. Legion; dir. Am. Legion Endowment Corp., 1929-42, pres., 1937-41. Delegate to Missouri Constl. Convention, 1943-44. Chmn. Mo. Statewide Forestry Com., 1946-50. Mem. Am. Soc. of Civil Engrs., Soc. of Country, Engineers (Kansas City). Home: 637 Proc-Am. Mil. Engrs., Mo. Acad. Science. Democrat. Mason (32 deg., Shriner). Clubs: Kansas City, Military ter Pl., Independence, Mo. Died Mar. 2, 1954; buried Woodlawn Cemetery, Independence.

STEACIE, EDGAR WILLIAM RICHARD, (sta'si), physical chemist; b. Westmount, Que., Dec. 25, 1900; s. Richard and Alice Kate (McWood) S.; student Royal Mil. Coll., 1919-20, D.Sc., 1960; B.Sc., McGill University, Montreal, Can., 1923, M.Sc., 1924, Ph.D., 1926, LL.D. (hon.), 1953; fellow Physikalisch-Chemisches Institut, Frankfurt and Leipzig, Germany, also King's Coll., U. London, 1934-35; D.Sc. (hon.), McMaster U., 1946, U. N.B., 1950, Laval U., 1952, Manitoba U., 1954, U. Toronto, 1954, Ottawa U., 1956, U. of B.C., St. Francis Xavier U., St. Lawrence U., 1957; LL.D., Queen's University, Dalhousie Univ., 1952, University of Western Ontario, 1958; Dr. de l'U. Montreal, 1956; D.Sc. (honorary), Oxford University, 1960; married Dorothy Catalina Day, 1925; children—Diana Jeanette (Mrs. W. A. Magill), John Richard Brian. Demonstrator chemistry McGill U., 1923-25, lectr. chemistry, 1928-30, asst. prof. chemistry, 1930-37, asso. prof., 1937-39; dir. div. chemistry Nat. Research Council, 1939-52, v.p., 1950-52, pres. since 1952; dep. dir. Brit.-Canadian atomic energy project, 1944-46. Decorated Order Brit. Empire, 1946; awarded gold medal, Profl. Inst. Pub. Service of Can., 1949, Bennett Commonwealth prize, Royal Society of Arts, 1960. Chairman of the board of governors Carleton U.; dir. Canadian Patents and Development, Ltd., Canadian Standards Association; mem. adv. com. for sci. U. Ottawa; rep. NATO (sci. com., 1958; member Internat. Adv. Committee UNESCO, 1958. Fellow royal socs. London, Can. (hon. sec. 1940-42, president 1954-55), Chem. Soc. London (hon.); mem. Chemical Institute Can. (pres. 1949-50), Internat. Union Pure and Applied Chemistry (v.p. 1951-53), Canadian Standards Assn. (dir.), Chem. Soc. London, Am. Chem. Soc., Faraday Soc. (pres. 1959), Polish Chem. Soc. (hon.), Nat. Acad. Scis. U.S. (fgn. asso.), Acad. Scis. of USSR (fgn. mem.). Author: Introduction to Physical Chemistry (with Dr. Maass), 1926; Atomic and Free Radical Reactions, 1946; Free Radical Mechanisms, 1946. Asso. editor: Can. Jour. Chemistry, 1954—. Member editorial adv. board, International Council of Scientific Unions, 1958. Contributor articles professional publs. Home: 275 Hillcrest Road, Rockcliffe Park, Ottawa. Office: Nat. Research Bldg., Sussex St., Ottawa 2, Ont., Can. Died Aug. 28, 1962.

STEARNS, CARL LEO, astronomer; b. Westbrook, Me., Sept. 14, 1892; s. Albert Joseph and Cora May (Weymouth) S.; A.B., Wesleyan U., Middletown, Conn., 1917; Ph.D., Yale, 1923; m. Mildred Parkhurst Booth, Aug. 9, 1923 (dec. 1966); children—Robert Leo, Elva Parkhurst (Mrs. Creeger), Doris Elizabeth (Mrs. Swain); m. 2d, Eddie McCormick. Asst. Dudley Observatory, Albany, N.Y., 1917-18; instr. in mathematics, Wesleyan U., 1918-19, instr. in astronomy, 1919-20; research asst., Yale Observatory, 1920-25; research asso. in astronomy, Van Vleck Obs., Wesleyan U., 1925-42, later dir. obs. asso. prof. astronomy 1942-44, prof. from 1944, instr. in nav. Naval Flight Prep. Sch., Wesleyan U., 1943; visiting instructor Trinity College, Hartford, Conn., 1940-41. Awarded Donohoe Comet medal by Astron. Soc. of the Pacific, 1927; Stearns comet named in his honor. Fellow Royal Astron. Soc., A.A.A.S.; mem. Am. Astron. Soc., Internat. Astron. Union, Middletown Sci. Assn. (past pres.), Phi Beta Kappa, Sigma Xi. Author: Stellar Parallaxes from Photographs Made with the 20-inch Refractor of the Van Vleck Observatory (with F. Slocum and B. W. Sitterly), 1938. Contbr. articles on stellar distances, solar eclipses, solar parallax, etc. to Astron. Jour. Home: Middletown CT Died Nov. 28, 1972; buried Indian Hill Cemetery.

STEARNS, FREDERIC PIKE, engineer; b. Calais, Me., Nov. 11, 1851; s. William Henry Clark and Mary Hobbs (Hill) S.; prep. edn. Calais High Sch.; (hon. A.M., Harvard, 1905; D.Sc., U. of Pa., 1906); m. Addie C. Richardson, June 21, 1876. In city surveyor's office, Boston, 1869-72; investigation, constrn. and maintenance additional water supply for Boston, 1872-80; constrn. and maintenance Boston main drainage works, 1880-86; chief engr. Mass. State Bd. of Health, 1886-95; mem. bd. of sanitary engrs. to devise system of sewerage for D.C., 1889-90; chief engr. Mass. Met. Water Works, 1895-1907; consulting engr. Charles River Basin Commn., 1903-10, Bd. of Water Supply, New York, 1905-14; mem. board of cons. engrs. for

Panama Canal, 1905-06; mem. bd. to devise system of sewage disposal for Baltimore, 1905-06; mem. bd. to examine and report on water supply for Los Angeles, 1906; mem. bd. consulting engrs. accompanying Sec. of War William H. Taft, to Panama, 1907 and 1909; mem. bd. to report on additional water supply for Baltimore, 1908-09; mem. bd. to report on water supply for Winnipeg, 1913; consulting engr. new water supply for Providence, 1914—. Fellow Am. Acad. Arts and Sciences. Home: Boston, Mass. Died Dec. 1919.

STEARNS, ROBERT EDWARDS CARTER, biologist; b. Boston, Feb. 1, 1827; s. Charles and Sarah (Carter) S.; pub. sch. edn., Boston; m. Mary Ann Libby, Mar. 28, 1850 (died 1879). Business training in a Boston bank; investigated coal fields of Southern Ind., 1850; paymaster and resident clerk for several Boston copper mining cos. at Keeweenaw Point, Lake Superior, 1854; went to San Francisco, 1858; in printing and publishing business and on editorial staff "The Pacific," deputy clerk Supreme Court, Calif., 1862-63; sec. Bd. State Harbor commrs., 1963-68; in east, 1868-70; made natural history collections in Fla., 1869; sec. Bd. Regents, Univ. of Calif., 1874-82; Ph.D. Univ. of Calif., 1881; adj. curator dept. mollusks, U.S. Nat. Mus., 1884; also paleontologist U.S. Geol. Survey until 1892; resigned; from 1892 hon. asso. zoölogy, U.S. Nat. Museum. Mem. numerous scientific societies. Home: Los Angeles, Calif. Died 1909.

STECKEL, ABRAM PETERS, engr., retired; b. Myersdale, Pa., Apr. 1, 1879; s. Lewis Daniel and Barbara (Peters) S.; E.E., Lehigh U., 1899; hon. Eng.D., for "contributions to art and science of steel mfrs." Lehigh University, 1941; married Mabel Rushworth, Sept. 1, 1908 (died 1926); children—Frederick Rushworth, Barbara Ann (Mrs. Thomas Taylor White). Began as engineer, 1900; engaged pvt. research, 1921-26; founded Cold Metal Process Company, Youngstown, O., 1926, retired, 1933. Received Modern Pioneer award by National Assn. of Manufacturers. Unitarian. Club: Saturn (Buffalo). Developed Steckel processes for hot rolling and cold rolling metals; in 1903, in collaboration with Stephen Piek, first handled bulk pig iron with electro magnet and crane, proof of such priority pub. by Bethlehem Steel Co., 1950. In 1942 presented to Lehigh County Hist. Soc. home of great-great-grandfather, Peter Steckel, built in 1756, and provided for restoration and endowment as a Pa. Dutch museum. In 1944 purchased and presented to same Hist. Soc., the home of George Taylor, a signer of the Declaration of Independence; located Catasauqua, Pa.; built 1768. Address: 433 Crandall Av., Youngstown, O. Died Aug. 19, 1954; buried Jamestown, N.Y.

STEDDOM, RICE PRICE, sanitarian; b. Lebanon, O., Dec. 23, 1864; s. Isaac Kelley and Narcissa (Price) S.; ed. dist. schs.; V.S., Ont. Vet. Coll., 1886. Was in the employ of Springer & Willard, horse importers, Okaloosa, Ia., 1886-89; on ranch in Colo. 2 yrs., then in gen. practice, in employ of Springer & Willard, at Galesburg, Ill., 1891-97; with Bur. of Animal Industry, U.S. Dept. of Agr., since 1897; federal meat inspn. duty, at Kansas City, Mo., 1897-98; quarantine work in Tex. and Calif., 1898-99 spl. investigation of live stock diseases in Porto Rico 1899; organizer, and in charge of quarantine and transportation of southern cattle, east of Miss. River 1900-02; on duty in connection with eradication of foot and mouth disease in New Eng., 1902-03, and in charge at Boston, 1903-04; transferred to Washington, D.C., May 1904; apptd. asst. chief of Inspn. Div., Bur. of Animal Industry, 1905; chief of div., 1906; chief of Federal Meat Inspection Service, 1912-35, retired, Jan. 1, 1935. Mem. Friends Ch. Home: Summit Farm, R.D. 3, Lebanon OH

STEDMAN, JOHN MOORE, biologist; b. Brockport, N.Y., Nov. 2, 1864; s. George Lemon and Mary (Moore) S.; B.S., Cornell, 1888; m. Edith Van Aiken, July 1, 1888; children—Barbara Mary, Lulu Rachel. Instr. entomology and invertebrate zoölogy, and 1st asst. entomologist, expt. sta., Cornell, 1888-90; biologist U.S. Dept. Agr., Washington, 1890-91; prof. biology, Trinity Coll., Durham, N.C., 1891-93; prof. biology and biologist, expt. sta., State Agrl. and Mech. Coll., Auburn, Ala., 1893-95; prof. entomology, U. of Mo., and entomologist expt. sta., 1895-1909; specialist in agrl. edn. extension, U.S. Dept. Agr., 1909-34. Mem. Am. Assn. Econ. Entomologists, Entomol. Soc., Washington, Entomol. Soc. of America, A.A.A.S., Sigma Xi. Has published many papers on biol. and entomol. subjects. Home: 48 Mountainview St., Springfield, Mass. Died Nov. 6, 1949.

STEELE, HENRY MAYNADIER, civ. engr.; b. Baltimore, Md., Sept. 26, 1865; s. Isaac Nevett and Rosa (Nelson) S.; ed. pvt. sch., acad. and Mass. Inst. Technology; m. Margaret Hollins McKim, Feb. 6, 1894. Asst. engr. B.&O. R.R., 1886-87; prin. asst. engr. Erie R.R., 1887-92; southern agt. Hall Signal Co., Baltimore, 1893; cons. engr., Asheville, N.C., 1894-97; chief engr., Central of Ga. Ry., 1897-1906; chief civ. engr. J. G. White & Co., July 1906—. Home: Woodmere, L.I. Died 1909.

STEELE, JOHN DUTTON, thoracic surgeon; b. Phila., Jan. 28, 1905; s. John Dutton and Edith (Williamson) S.; B.A., Williams Coll., 1926; M.D., U. Pa., 1932; M.S. in Surgery, U. Mich., 1937; m. Betsy Owen, July 2, 1936; children—Christopher, Polly (Mrs. W. Albert Munson), Wendy (Mrs. Harold Teasdale), Jenny (Mrs. Robert Allen). Intern Bryn Mawr (Pa.) Hosp., 1932-33; resident Internat. Grenfell Assn., St. Anthony, Newfoundland, 1933-35; resident thoracic surgery Univ. Hosp., Ann Arbor, Mich., 1935-37; pvt. practice thoracic surgery, Milw., 1938-55; chief surg. service Muirlale Sanatorium, Milw., 1938-55; asst. clin. prof. surgery Marquette U. Sch. Medicine, 1938-55; mem. faculty U. Cal. at Los Angeles Med. Sch., from 1957, clin. prof. surgery, from 1961; chief surg. service VA Hosp., San Fernando, Cal., 1955-67, cons. thoracic surgeon, from 1967; consulting thoracic surgeon Wadsworth VA Hosp., Los Angeles, Olive View Hospital, (Los Angeles). Diplomate Am. Bd. Thoracic Surgery (founder mem.). Fellow A.C.S.; mem. Am. Assn. Thoracic Surgery (sr.), A.M.A., Am. Thoracic Soc. (v.p. 1946-47, sec. 1950-53, pres. 1954-55, councilor 1962-65), Nat. Tb Assn. (dir. 1950-55, v.p. 1953-54; Trudeau medal 1962), Wis. Anti-Tb Assn. (dir. 1944-55) Cal. Thoracic Soc., Soc. Thoracic Surgeons (founder mem.). Author: The Solitary Pulmonary Nodule, 1964. Editor: (with others) The Surgical Management of Pulmonary Tuberculosis, Parasitic Diseases of the Chest, 1964; (with others) The Treatment of Mycotic and Alexander Monograph Series, 1957-65; The Annals of Thoracic Surgery, from 1965, Contbr. articles to med. jours. Home: Northridge CA Deceased.

STEELE, JOHN MURRAY, cardio-vascular specialist; b. Newport, R.I., June 7, 1900; s. John Murray and Gertrude (Brooks) S.; student Marstons U. Sch. for Boys, Balt., 1910-17; A.B., Harvard, 1921; M.D., Johns Hopkins, 1925; m. Sylvia Moulton Ward, July 1, 1932; children—John Murray, Charles Nevett, Lucy Ann. Resident Billings Hosp., also instr. U. Chgo., 1928-29; asst. in medicine Rockefeller Inst. Hosp., 1929-35; asso., 1935-39; prof. N.Y.U., 1939-69; dir. N.Y.U. research service Goldwater Meml. Hosp. Welfare Assn., N.Y.C., from 1948. Cons. to Montreal Hosps. for chronic disease care. Mem. Welfare Council, N.Y.C., from 1938. Served as pvt. U.S.M.C., 1918; comdr. M.C., U.S.N.R., 1942-46; Research Inst. Nat. Naval Med. Center, Bethesda, Md. Mem. Am. Soc. Clin. Investigation, Am. Heart Assn., Am. Physiol. Soc., Harvey Soc., Century Assn., A.A.A.S., Democrat. Editor: Vol. VI: Methods in Medical Research, 1942. Research in chronic diseases. Home: New York City NY Died Oct. 13, 1969.

STEENBOCK, HARRY, (sten'bok), biochemistry; b. Charlestown, Wis., Aug. 16, 1886; s. Henry and Christine (Oesau) S.; B.S., U. of Wis., 1908, M.S., 1910, Ph.D., 1916, Sc.D., 1938; grad. study Yale, 1912, U. of Berlin, 1913; Sc.D. (hon.), Lawrence Coll., 1947; m. Evelyn Carol Van Donk, March 6, 1948. Asst. in agricultural chemistry. U. Wis., 1908-10, Instr., 1910-16, asst. prof., 1916-17, asso. prof., 1917-20, prof., 1920-38, prof. biochemistry since 1938; fellow A.A.A.S.: mem. Am. Inst. of Nutrition, Am. Chem. Sec., Am. Soc. Biol. Chemists, Wis. Acad. Science, Royal German Acad. of Science (Halle), Sigma Xi, Alpha Zeta, Gamma Alpha, Phi Lambda Upsilon, Alpha Chi Sigma, Phi Sigma Kappa, Phi Beta Kappa. Republican. Clubs: University, Chaos, Black Hawk Country. Writer on human and animal nutrition with special attention to vitamins, mineral elements, and the effect of irradiation. Founder Wis. Alumni Research Found. Patentee ultra violet irradiation of food and synthesis of vitamin D. Home: 2117 W. Lawn Av., Madison, Wis. Died Dec. 25, 1967.

STEERE, JOSEPH BEAL, scientist; b. Lenawee Co., Mich., Feb. 9, 1842; s. William Millhouse and Elizabeth (Beal) S.; A.B., Univ. of Mich., 1868, LL.B., 1870 (hon. Ph.D., 1875); m. Helen Buzzard, Sept. 30, 1879. Made a scientific trip around the world by way of Brazil, up the Amazon, across the Andes, China, etc., 1870-75; instr., and asst. prof. zoölogy, 1876-79, prof., 1879-93, U. of Mich.; engaged in farming and study, 1893—. Led party of students to Amazon, 1879, to Philippines, 1887-88; on 3d trip to Amazon, 1901, collecting specimens for Smithsonian Instn. and Buffalo Expn. Author: Fifty New Species of Philippine Birds. Home: Ann Arbor, Mich. Died Dec. 7, 1940.

STEERS, GEORGE, naval architect; b. Washington, D.C., July 20, 1820; s. Henry Steer, never married; Built fast pilot schooner Mary Taylor (radically new design), 1849; managed boatyard Hathorn & Steers on Williamsburg side East River, N.Y.C., 1845-49; built (with brother James) many fast vessels including steamship Adriatic, warship Niagara (helped lay 1st transatlantic cable), 1849; built pleasure craft, most famous was the America, sailed in race around Isle of Wight, 1851, revolutionized yacht design in U.S. and fgn. countries. Died Great Neck, L.I. N.Y., Sept. 25, 1856.

STEFANSSON, VILHJALMUR, (stef'ans-sun), Arctic explorer; b. Arnes, Manitoba, Can., Nov. 3, 1879; s. Johann and Ingibjörg (Johannesdottir) S.; prep. dept. and State U. of N.D.; A.B., State U. of Ia., 1903; Harvard U. Div. Sch., 1903-04; Harvard Grad. Sch., 1904-06; LL.D., U. of Mich., 1921, U. of Ia., 1922, U. of N.D., 1930, University of Manitoba, 1937, University of Pittsburgh, 1938; A.M. Harvard University, 1923; Ph.D., Univ. of Iceland, 1930; L.H.D., Fla. So., 1945, Dartmouth, 1959; m. Mrs. Evelyn Baird, April 10, 1941. Trip to Iceland, 1904; archaeology expedition to Iceland under auspices Peabody Museum of Harvard U., 1905; ethnol. expdn. to Eskimo of Mackenzie delta under auspices Harvard U., and Toronto U., 1906-07 (18 mos.); 2d expdn., 1908-12 (53 mos. under auspices Am. Museum Natural History, New York, and Govt. of Can.); spent winter, 1908-09, Colville delta, N. coast of Alaska; winter, 1909-10, 11-12, Cape Parry; winter, 1910-11, Coronation Gulf and Victoria Island. Comdr. Canadian Arctic Expdn., 1913-18, exploring land and seas in Canadian and Alaskan sectors of the Arctic region; Arctic consultant, Northern Studies Program, 1947—. Mem. History of Science Society (pres. 1945), Assn. Am. Geographers (v.p. 1945). Contbr. popular and scientific magazines and to technical publications; adviser on northern operations, Pan-American Airways, 1932-45. Author numerous books 1913—, later ones include: Arctic Manual, 1941; Greenland, 1942; The Fat of the Land, 1956; Northwest to Fortune, 1958; Discovery: the autobiography of Vilhjalmur Stefansson. Editor tech. and source books including: Great Adventures and Explorations, 1947; New Compass of the World, 1949. Decorated Knighthood of the Order of the Falcon (Iceland); medallist of the American, National, Philadelphia, Chicago, London, Paris and Berlin geog. societies, Explorers Club of N.Y.; Silver Buffalo Award, Boy Scouts Am.; hon. fellow many learned socs. Clubs: Canadian, Century, Explorers, Harvard (New York); Faculty (Cambridge, Mass.); Cosmos (Washington); Athenaeum (London); Graduates (Hanover, N.H.). Author: Northwest to Fortune, 1958; Cancer: Disease of Civilization, 1960. Address: Dartmouth Coll., Hanover, N.H. Died Aug. 26, 1962; buried Pine Knoll Cemetery, Hanover.

STEGEMAN, GEBHARD (ste'ge-man), physical chemistry; b. Holland, Mich., June 14, 1890; s. John and Hannah (Kamps) S.; A.B., Hope Coll., Holland, Mich., 1913; A.M., Ohio State U., 1915, Ph.D., 1917; m. Mildred Smith, June 11, 1932. Instr. in chemistry, U. of Wash., 1917-18; asst. prof. of chemistry, U. of Pittsburgh, 1919-24, prof. since 1924; official investigator for the N.D.R.C., 1942-45. Served as chemist with Chemical Warfare Service, U.S. Army, 1918-19. Mem. Am. Chem. Soc., Alpha Chi Sigma, Sigma Xi. Republican. Mem. Dutch Reformed Ch. Club: Shannopin Country (Pittsburgh). Contbr. to Am. Chem. Soc. Jour., Jour. Phys. Chem. Home: 6 Oxford Rd., Ben Avon Heights, Pittsburgh 2. Died Sept. 5, 1949.

STEIDTMANN, WALDO E(DUARD), (stit'man), botanist; b. Prairie du Sac, Wis., Apr. 27, 1896; s. Charles Frederick and Bertha (Schoenberg S.; Rural Teachers Certificate, Wis. State Teachers College, (Whitewater, 1916; A.B., U. of Wis., 1923; M.S., U. of Mich., 1929, Ph.D., 1935; m. Evelyn Katherine Dressel, Sept. 8, 1930; children—Sally Ann, James Richard. Country sch. teacher, Wis., 1916-17; instr. in botany, Marquette U., Milwaukee, 1923-32; instr. in biology, Wis. State Teachers Coll., La Crosse, 1936; mem. faculty Bowling Green (O.) State U., 1936—, prof. of biology and chmn. biology dept., 1947—. Served in C.A. Corps, 1918-19, overseas in France. Fellow Ohio Acad. Sci. (chmn. plant sci. sect., 1943-44); mem. A.A.A.S., Bot. Soc. of Am., Sigma Xi, Phi Sigma Alpha Tau Omega, Omicron Delta Kappa. Mason. Club: Kiwanis. Research papers in paleobotany. Home: 4 Orchard Circle, Bowling Green, O. Died June 21, 1955; buried Oak Grove Cemetery, Bowling Green, O.

STEIGER, GEORGE, (sti'ger), chemist; b. Columbia, Pa., May 27, 1869; s. Benjamin F. and Martha L. (Young) S.; B.S., Columbian (now George Washington) U., 1890, M.S., 1892; unmarried. Chemist, U.S. Geol. Survey 1892, chief chemist, 1916-30, chemist, 1930-39, retired; now continuing work through facilities of the Geol. Survey. Mem. Am. Chem. Soc., Am. Inst. Mining Engrs., Geol. Soc., Washington, Mineral Soc., Wash. Acad. Scs.; S.A.R.; fellow A.A.A.S. Club: Cosmos. Has published various papers, mostly on original research on the constitution of certain silicates and methods of chem. analysis. Home: The Portner, Washington, D.C. Died Apr. 18, 1944. *

STEINBERG, SAMUEL SIDNEY, civil engr., educator; b. N.Y.C., Sept. 18, 1891; s. Harris and Anne (Smith) S.; B. Engring., Cooper Union Inst. Tech. N.Y., 1910, C.E., 1913; m. Kathryn Helene Dox, Dec. 18, 1916; children—Douglas Sidney, Edward Harris. Constrn. engr. N.Y. Highway Dept., 1910-13; asst. engr. Tela R.R. (United Fruit Co.), Honduras, C.A., 1913-14; jr. engr. Public Service Commn., New York, 1914; asst. engr. N.Y. State Highway Dept., 1915-18; road expert U.S. Govt. constrn., 1918, and asst. State highway engr. of S.C., 1918; asst. prof. civil engring. U. of Md., 1918-20, prof., head dept., 1920-56; dean, coll. engring., 1936-56; cons. sch. of engring. U. P.R., 1952—; dir. engineering expt. station, 1936-41; pres. Inst. Technológico de Aeronáutica, Sao José dos Campos, Sao Paulo, Brazil, 1956—; hon. prof. of numerous Latin Am. univs.; mem. com. on highways, Md. State Planning Commn.; chmn. advisory bd., Md. Bureau of Control Surveys and Maps; chmn., Md. Com. on Water Pollution, 1945-47; vice chmn. Md. Traffic Safety Commn., 1941-49, chmn., 1949; chmn. Md.

Water Resources Commn., 1940-41; chmn. Md. State Bd. Registration for Professional Engrs. and Land Surveyors, 1949-56; cons. and adviser numerous orgns., assns. and govtl. agencies on engring. matters. Spl. mission, U.S. Dept. of State, to make survey of engring. edn. in Latin Am., 1945, 48; mem. editorial adv. com., Journal Current Engr. Research. Mem. and hon. mem. numerous nat. and fgn. profl. socs., has served as chmn. cons. and officer several assns. Recipient Award of Merit, U. Fla., 1954. Episcopalian (vestryman). Clubs: Rotary (College Park); Engineers (Baltimore). Editor Annual Proceedings of Am. Road Builders Assn., 1937, 38, 40; editor Engring. Expt. Sta. Record, 1943-44, contbr. to tech. tours. Home: College Park, Md. Died Feb. 1968.

STEINHAUS, ARTHUR H., physiologist; b. Chicago, Ill., Oct. 4, 1897; s. Henry D. and Rosa (Daehler) S.; B.P.E., George Williams Coll., 1921, M.P.E., 1926; S.B., U. of Chicago, 1920, M.S., 1925, Ph.D., 1928; m. Eva Kunzmann, June 23, 1921; 1 son, Robert Arthur. Instructor biological sciences, George Williams Coll., 1920-28, prof. physiology, 1928-63, Oscar G. Mayer Distinguished Service prof., 1963-65, dir. div. health and phys. edn., 1953-62, dean coll., 1954-62, dean emeritus; Distinguished Service prof. physiology Chgo. Coll. Osteopathy, 1965-66; vis. professor Michigan State University, East Lansing, Michigan, 1966-70; chief Dir. Phys. Edn. and Health Activities, United States Office of Education, F.S.A., 1944; on leave as spl. adviser, The Robinson Foundation, Inc., Section on Health Edn., New York, 1945-46; lecturer biology Baptist Missionary Training School, 1935-45; visiting prof. U. of Calif. summers 1937, 39, 41, U. of Colo., 1942, Univ. Wis., 1943, Univ. Sask., 1946, U. Ore., 1950, 60 U. So. Cal., 1965; lectr. Internat. Congress Physical Edn., Internat. Sport Students' Congress in connection with XI Olympic Games, Berlin, 1936, 3d World Congress Phys. Edn., Istanbul, 1953, 1st Internat. Congress Phys. Edn. U.S., 1954; guest lectr. South African Assn. for Phys. Edn. and Recreation, 1965; cons. South African Fedn. for Youth and Sport, 1968. Consultant to Secretary of Navy on physical fitness and physical rehabilitation, during World War II. Fellow John Simon Guggenheim Memorial Foundation for study in Europe, 1931-32, Fulbright lectr. Germany, 1955, Japan, 1962-63. Recipient of Roberts-Gulick award, 1940, William G. Anderson Merit award, 1951; Honor award Am. College Sports Medicine, 1965; citation U. Toledo Div. Health, Phys. Edn. and Recreation, 1969. Fellow Am. Academy Physical Education (sec.-treas. 1936-41; v.p. 1941-42, pres. 1943-45), Am. Association Health, Physical Education and Recreation (pres. Midwest dist. 1955, Luther Halsey Gulick award 1969), Am. Pub. Health Assn., Am. School Health Assn., Am. Coll. Sports Medicine; membre appeles Fedn. Internat. Medico Sportive; mem. Fedn. Internat. Edn. Physique (v.p.), Ill. Assn. Health, Phys. Edn., Recreation (pres. 1948-49), Am. Physiol. Soc., Phys. Edn. Soc. New Zealand (v.p. 1963), South African Assn. for Phys. Edn. and Recreation (hon. v.p. 1967), Delta Psi Kappa (patron), Phi Epsilon Kappa (hon.), Kappa Delta Pi, Sigma Xi, Pi Gamma Mu. Baptist. Author: Tobacco and Health, 1939; The Romance of Service, 1940; How to Keep Fit and Like It, 1957; More Firepower for Health Education, 1945; Lectures on the Physiology of Exercise, 1948; Toward an Understanding of Health and Physical Education, 1963. Co-author Methods of Research in Health, Physical Education, and Recreation, 1959. Contbr. to Am. Journal Physiology, Jornal of Health and Phys. Edn., numerous other health jours. Home: East Lansing MI Died Feb. 8, 1970; buried Graceland Cemetery Chicago IL

STEINHAUS, EDWARD A(RTHUR), scientist, educator; b. Max, N.D., Nov. 7, 1914; s. Arthur Alfred and Alice (Rhinehart) S.; B.S., N.D. State Univ., 1936, Sc.D., 1962; Ph.D., Ohio State U., 1939; m. Mabry Clark, June 14, 1940; children—Margaret, Timothy Clark, Cynthia Alice. Asst. bacteriology Ohio State U., 1936-39; Muellhaupt scholar, 1939-40; asst. bacteriologist Rocky Mountain Lab., USPHS, 1940-41, asso. bacteriologist, 1942-44; asst. prof. bacteriology and insect pathology U. Cal., Berkeley 1944-49, insect pathologist Expt. Sta., 1945-63, organizer, dir. Lab. Insect Pathology, 1945-60, asso. prof. insect pathology, 1949-54, prof., 1954-63, vice chmn. dept. biological control, 1957-58, chairman of department insect pathol., 1960-63, prof., dean biol. scis., U. Calif. Irvine, Cal., 1963-68, dir. Center Pathobiology, 1968-69. Member United States Army Bullis Fever Commn., 1943-44; cons. NRC, 1951, Pacific Sci. Bd., 1951-69, USPHS, 1955-64; v.p. bacteriological sect. Internat. Congress Microbiology, 1950; mem. Internat. Com. Comparative Pathology, 1965-69; invertebrate cons. com. NRC, 1962-69; member NAS-NRC Com. Comparative Pathology, 1963-69; exec. com. Internat. Congress Insect Pathology, 1962-69. Guggenheim fellow, 1960-61. Fellow Entomol. Society America (president 1962-63, A.A.A.S., Am. Acad. of Microbiology; mem. Nat. Acad. Scis., Soc. Invertebrate Pathology (pres. 1967-68), Soc. Exptl. Pathology, Council of Biol. Editors, Soc. Am. Bacteriologists, Soc. Gen. Microbiology, Am. Soc. Protozoologists, Am. Inst. Biol. Scis. (governing bd.), Soc. Sci. and Tech., India, Entomol. Soc. USSR, Sigma Xi. Conglist. Author: Insect Microbiology, 1946; Principles of Insect Pathology, 1949. Editor Ann. Rev. Entomology, 1955-62, Jour. Invertebrate Pathology, 1959-69, Insect Pathology, an Advanced Treatise, 1962; mem. editorial bd. Jour. Econ. Entomology, Virology, U.C. Entomology Series; asso. editor Bergey's Manual of Determinative Bacteriology; editorial bd. Life Sciences. Author sci. papers. Home: Newport Beach CA Died Oct. 20, 1969; buried Corona del Mar CA

STEINMAN, DAVID BARNARD, bridge engr.; b. N.Y.C., June 11, 1886; s. Louis Kelvin and Eva (Scollard) S.; B.S. summa cum laude, Coll. City of N.Y., 1906, D.Sc., 1947; C.E., Columbia, 1909, A.M., 1909, Ph.D., 1911, D.Sc., 1953; E.D., Manhattan Coll., also Rensselaer Poly. Inst., 1953, Mich. Coll. Mining and Tech., 1954, U. Mich., 1956; D.Sc., Ohio Northern U., Sequoia U., U. Ghent, Minerva Academy Advanced Studies (Italy), 1953, Haute Academie Latine Internationale (France), 1953, Bradley Univ., 1956; D.C.E., Univ. of Bologna (Italy), 1953; Dr. Higher Learning (Vidya Ratna), Shri Bhuvaneshwari Pith. Kathiawad. India, 1953; LL.D., Alfred U., 1953, Tampa U., 1957; L.H.D., Florida Southern Coll., 1957, St. Lawrence U., 1958; Litt.D., Loyola U., 1957; m. Irene Hoffman, June 9, 1915; children—John Francis, Alberta, David. Engring. work until 1910; prof. civil engring. U. Ida., also practiced as cons., 1910-14; spl. asst. to Gustav Lindenthal on design and constrn. important bridges, 1914-17; prof. in charge civil and mech. engring. Coll. City of N.Y., 1917-20; in practice as cons., 1920—; designing or cons. engr. numerous notable bridges in U.S. and on four other continents, 1922—, Kingston Bridge, 1952-56, Mackinac Bridge, 1953-57, also Sky-Ride and Observation Towers, Century of Progress Expn., Chgo., 1933, mil. bridges for U.S. govt., 1941-53; engaged in reconstrn. Bklyn. Bridge, 1948-54; v.p. Tioga-Nichols Bridge Co., Smithboro Bridge Co.; dir. Independence Bridge Co., Interboro Bridge Co., Richmond-Hopewell Bridge Co.; Recipient honors, awards, prizes, U.S. and abroad, among latest: Goethals Medal, Soc. Am. Mil. Engrs., Chevalier Legion of Honor, Grand Cordon de l'Etoile du Bien et du Merite, Chevalier Ordre du Merite Scientifique, Croix d'Honneur Legion Franco-Belge, Knight Comdr. (with star) Order of Gold Cross of Mil. Chapter of Cyprus and Jerusalem, William Procter prize Sci. Research Soc. Am., Norman medal (second time), Croes medal, Rowland prize Am. Soc. C.E. Founder, pres. David B. Steinman Found. Vice pres. bd. trustees Ecole des Hautes Etudes, N.Y.C. Registered profl. engr. 20 states and fgn. countries. Fellow or mem. Am. and fgn. profl. and sci. socs. and assns., including Royal Soc. Arts, Soc. des Ingenieurs Professionels de France. Clubs: Columbia University, Engineers, City College, Brooklyn Engineers (N.Y.C.); Ends of the Earth; Millions of Sydney (hon.) (Australia). Author books relating to field, 1911—; latest: How Bridges Have Increased Man's Mobility, 1952; Famous Bridges of the World, 1953; Mackinac Straits Bridge, 1954; Suspension Bridges: The Aerodynamic Problem and Its Solution, 1954; Miracle Bridge at Mackinac, 1957; Bridges and Their Builders, revised edition, 1957. Contributor Encyclopedia Brit., Ency. Americana, Colliers Ency. Inventor in field. Home: 305 Riverside Dr. Office: 117 Liberty St., N.Y.C. Died Aug. 22, 1960; buried Ferncliff, Hartsdale, N.Y.

STEINMETZ, CHARLES PROTEUS, elec. engr., b. Breslau, Germany, Apr. 9, 1865; s. Carl Heinrich and Caroline (Neubert) S.; ed. Breslau, Berlin, Zürich, Switzerland; A.M., Harvard, 1902; Ph.D., Union U., N.Y., 1903. Came to U.S., 1889. Cons. engr. Gen. Electric Co., 1893-1923; prof. electrophysics Union Univ., 1902-23. Pres. Am. Inst. E.E., 1901-02, also Illuminating Engring., Soc., Nat. Assn. Corp. Schs. Author: Theory and Calculation of Alternating-Current Phenomena, 1897, 5th edition, 1916; Theoretical Elements of Electrical Engineering, 4th edit., 1915; Theory and Calculation of Transient Electric Phenomena and Oscillations, 1909, 3d edit., 1919; General lectures on Electrical Engineering, 5th edit., 1917; Radiation, Light and Illumination, 1909, 2d edit., 1911; Engineering Mathematics, 1910, 3d edit., 1917; Electric Discharges, Waves and Impulses, 1911; America and the New Epoch, 1916; Theory and Calculation of Electric Circuits, 1917; Theory and Calculation of Electrical Apparatus, 1917. Also math. papers and investigations and numerous papers on theoretical exptl. investigations in elec. engring. Established basic laws of magnetic hysteresis, 1891; 1st to use complex notation for alternating current problems, 1893; contbd. to electric machine design, electric traction, lightning protection, street lightning; patentee over 100 inventions; inventor improved generators, motors; research on theory and calculation of alternating current phenomena; devised lighting arresters for high power transmission lines. Died Oct. 26, 1923.

STEINMETZ, JOSEPH ALLISON, mechanical engr.; b. Phila., Pa., Mar. 22, 1870; s. John and Frances Morris (Janney) S.; prep. edn., Phila. Central High Sch.; student Lehigh U., 1900; m. Oma Frances Fields, 1903; children—Joseph Janney, Frances Margaret. Assisted Prof. Langley in producing spl. steel parts, early airplane engines, 1900; sr. mem. Janney-Steinmetz & Co., seamless steel containers, 1893—; president "Globar" Corp.; Phila. asso. Am. Car & Foundry Co.; designed and patented numerous devices for aerial and submarine warfare; engr. of land reclamation, Greenwich League Island Area, 1912-18; located Hog Island for war shipyard; founder and dir. Sch. of Aircraft Building, Phila., 1917-18. Mem. Submarine Defense Assn., New York, 1917-19, World War; spl. service overseas for War Industries Survey, 1918-19; mem. engring. div. Nat. Research Council, 1918; lt. col. U.S. ord. (Res.), 1919. Registered engr., Pa. Trustee Fairmount Park Art Assn. Member of numerous societies. Donor of annual medal for safety in aeronautics, by Soc. Engrs. of Phila. Home: Germantown, Pa. Died July 11, 1928.

STEINWAY, CHRISTIAN FRIEDRICH THEODORE, piano mfr.; b. Seesen, Germany, Nov. 6, 1825; s. Henry Engelhard and Juliane (Thiemer) S.; attended Jacobsohn Coll., Seesen; m. Johanna Luederman, Oct. 10, 1852. Partner piano mfg. firm Germany, used scientific principles to build pianos to meet demand of masters, 1852-65; came to N.Y.C., 1865, took charge constrn. factory dept. Steinway & Sons, investigated, tested relative qualities of various woods, continued study of chemistry to determine best ingredients of glue, varnish, oils, experimented in metallurgy to find proper alloy for casting iron plates strong enough for heavy strain, remained in N.Y.C., 1865-70, asso. with Am. firm until 1889. Died Brunswick, Germany, Mar. 26, 1889.

STEINWAY, HENRY ENGELHARD, (original name Steinweg legally changed 1864), piano mfr.; b. Wolfshagen, Duchy of Brunswick, North Germany, Feb. 15, 1797; m. Juliane Thiemer, Feb. 1825; children—Christian Friedrich Theodore, Doretta, Charles, Henry, Wilhelmina, William, Albert. Served in Napoleonic War, 1815; became organ maker, 1818; organist, village ch., Seesen, Germany, 1818-20; made his 1st piano, circa 1825; recipient Gold medal for piano manufacture Brunswick Fair, 1839; came to U.S., 1851; founder piano mfg. firm Steinway & Sons, 1853, gradually expanded bus. into various kinds of pianos, recieved numerous awards; built Steinway Hall, N.Y.C., 1867. Died N.Y.C., Feb. 7, 1871.

STEINWAY, WILLIAM, piano mfr.; b. Seesen, Germany, Mar. 5, 1835; s. Henry Engelhard and Juliane (Thiemer) S.; ed. Jacobsohn Coll., Seesen; m. Johanna Roos, Apr. 23, 1861; m. 2d, Elizabeth Raupt, Aug. 16, 1880; 5 children. Came with family to U.S., 1851; apprentice in piano mfg. William Nunns & Co., 1851-53; joined father's firm, 1853, took over mgmt., 1865, pres. Steinway & Sons, Inc., 1876-96; influential in opening Steinway Hall, N.Y.C., 1867, London, Eng., 1876; subsidized various concert artists in Am.; conducted aggressive advt. campaign to sell pianos; established factory, Hamburg, Germany, 1880; 1st chmn. Rapid Transit Commn. which planned 1st subway in N.Y.C.; founder Town of Steinway (L.I., N.Y.). Died N.Y.C., Nov. 30, 1896.

STEJNEGER, LEONHARD, (stin'e-ger), naturalist; b. Bergen, Norway, Oct. 30, 1851; s. P. Stamer and Ingeborg C. (Hess) S.; grad. R. Frederic's U., Christiania, 1875 (Cand. jur.); Dr. Philosophy, hon. cuasa, same univ., 1930; m. Marie Reiners, Mar. 22, 1892; 1 dau., Inga. Came to U.S., 1881; on a natural history expdn. to Bering Island and Kamchatka, 1882-83, collecting for U.S. Nat. Museum, asst. curator of birds, 1884-89, curator reptiles since 1889, head curator of biology since June 1, 1911. Revisited Commander Islands, 1895, for Fish Commn. to study fur-seal question, 1896-97, as mem. U.S. Fur Seal Commn., and again in 1922 for Dept. of Commerce. Del. from Smithsonian Instn. to Zoöl. Congress 7 times, 1901-35, to Internat. Ornithologists Congress, 1905; studied museum administration and finances in Europe, 1901, 04, 05, 13. Life mem. Bergen Museum; mem. Nat. Acad. Sciences, Acads. Sciences, Christiania and Washington; fellow Am. Ornithologists Union, A.A.A.S.; fgn. mem. Zoöl. Soc., London, Ornithol. Soc. Bavaria, Acad. Natural Sciences Phila.; mem. Biological Soc. Washington (pres. 1907, 08), Am. Soc. Ichthyol. and Herpetol. (ex-pres.), Com. on Nomenclature and of Permanent Com. of Internat. Zoöl. Congress, Assn. Am. Geographers, Sigma Xi; hon. mem. Calif. Acad. Sciences, British Ornithol. Union, Am. Soc. of Mammalogists, German Ornithol. Soc. Decorated Knight 1st class Royal Norwegian Order of St. Olav, 1906, Comdr., 1939. Walker Grand Prize, Boston Soc. Nat. Hist. Author: Norsk Ornitologisk Ekskursjonsfauna, 1873; Norsk Mastozoologisk Ekskursjonsfauna, 1874; Results of Ornithological Explorations in the Commander Islands and in Kamchatka, 1885; Standard Natural History, Vol. IV, Birds (greater part), 1885; Report of the Rookeries of the Commander Islands, Season of 1897, 1897; The Asiatic Fur-Seal Islands and Fur-Seal, Industry, 1898; The Relations of Norway and Sweden, 1900; The Herpetology of Porto Rico, 1904; The Herpetology of Japan and Adjacent Territory, 1907; The Origin of the So-called Atlantic Animals and Plants of Western Norway, 1907; Georg Wilhelm Steller, pioneer of Alaskan Natural History, 1936, also many monographs and contbns. on zoöl. subjects. Club: Cosmos. Address: Smithsonian Instn., Washington, D.C. Died Feb. 28, 1943.

STEPHENSON, JOHN, mfr.; b. County Armagn, Ireland, July 4, 1809; s. James and Grace (Stuart) S.; attended Wesleyan Sem.; m. Julia A. Tiemann, 1833, 3 children. Opened shop for repair of all kinds vehicles,

1831, conceived, built 1st omnibus or horse-car made in N.Y.C.; employed to build horse-drawn car for new N.Y. & Harlem R.R. (1st car for 1st street railway in world), 1831; largest street-car builder in world, made horse cars, cable, electric, open cars; 1st patent granted, 1833; factory produced carriages and pontoons for U.S. Govt. during Civil War. Died New Rochelle, N.Y., July 31, 1893; buried Beechwood Cemetery, New Rochelle.

STEPHENSON, S(EYMOUR) TOWN, physicist; born San Jose, Calif., Nov. 28, 1910; s. Rufus Town and Mary Eliza (Baldwin) Stephenson; B.A., DePauw Univ., 1930, D.Sc. (honorary), 1951; Ph.D., Yale, University, 1933; married Mildred May McFall, Sept. 7, 1933; children—David Town, John Rufus, Robert Bruce, Mary Elizabeth. Teaching fellow DePauw U., 1929-30, Yale, 1931-32; mem. faculty Wash. State Univ., 1933-42, 47—, prof., chmn. div. phys. Sciences, 1947-52, professor, dean faculty, 1950-64, academic vice president, 1964. Nat. Defense Research com. of U.S. O.S.R.D., 1942-45; spl. consultant U.S. Navy Radio and Sound Lab., 1945. Mem. Wash. State Weather Modification Bd. Recipient Certificate of Appreciation from War and Navy Depts., 1948. Fellow Am. Phys. Soc.; mem. Soc. Sigma Xi, Phi Beta Kappa, Delta Tau Delta. Methodist. Contbr. articles and abstracts on x-ray spectroscopy. Home: 1814 D St., Pullman, Wash. 99163. Died Dec. 15, 1964; buried City Cemetery, Pullman.

STERKI, VICTOR, zoölogist; b. Solothurn, Switzerland, Sept. 27, 1846; s. Anton and Magdalena (Müller) S.; acad. edn.; med. student, Berne and Münich, 1868-73; M.D., U. of Berne, 1873, post-grad. study, 1878; m. Mary Lanz, of Huttwyl, Switzerland, Feb. 2, 1875. Came to U.S., Sept. 13, 1883; spl. student of mollusca and protozoa; asst. curator of mollusca, Carnegie Mus., Pittsburgh, Apr. 1, 1910—. Home: New Philadelphia, O. Died Jan. 25, 1933.

STERLING, GUY, civil engr.; b. Cleveland, May 1, 1860; s. Theodore and Charlotte (Higgins) S.; Kenyon Coll., Gambier, O., 1877-78; C.E., Cornell U., 1887; spl. work in elec. engring., Lewis Inst., Chicago, 1904; m. Harriot Brewer, Sept. 4, 1890. In wholesale and retail carpet business with Sterling & Co., Cleveland, 1878-83; asst. engr. maintenance of way, Denver, 1887-88, topog. engineer surveys in northeastern Calif., 1888-89, U.P. Ry.; topographer U.S. Geol. Survey, on Clear Lake, Calif., and Snake River (Ida.) irrigation surveys, 1889; asst. engr. in charge constrn. Phyllis Canal, Ida., 1890; asst. chief engr. Sunnyside Canal, nr. Yakima, Wash., 1890-91; chief engineer Cowiche and Wide Hollow irrigation dist. nr. Yakima, Wash., 1891-92; again asst. chief engr. Sunnyside Canal, 1892-94; constrn. pvt. irrigation projects nr. N. Yakima, 1894-95; chief engr. Priest Rapids Project, on Columbia River north of Pasco, Wash., 1895; in practice in Utah and other states, Aug. 1895—, principally hydraulic engring., examinations and reports for eastern investors, supervision of constrn., etc. Republican. Episcopalian. Chmn. com. on research and invention Utah Council Defense, 1917-18. Inventor and patentee of processes for extracting potash from mother liquor salts and from silicates including wyomingite. Home: Salt Lake City, Utah. Deceased.

STERN, KURT GUENTER, biochemist; b. Tilsit, Germany, Sept. 19, 1904; s. John Kasper and Sonia (Goldberg) S.; student Werner-Siemens Realgymnasium, Berlin, 1912-23; Ph.D., Friedrich-Wilhelms U., 1930; m. Else E. Jacobi, Dec. 24, 1931; 1 son, Rudolph George. Came to U.S., 1935, naturalized, 1946. Carl Duisberg Found. fellow, Rockefeller Inst., N.Y. City, 1930-31; scientific guest Courtauld Inst. Biochemistry, London, 1933-35; vis. lectr., Brown Coxe Research fellow, Yale, 1935-38; research asst. prof. Yale, 1938-42; chief research chemist Overly Biochem. Research Found., N.Y. City, 1942-44; adjunct prof. biochem. Poly. Inst., Bklyn., 1944—. Cons. U.S. AEC Research Project, Montefiore Hosp., N.Y.C. Research cons. to med. indsl. orgns. Recipient Pasteur Medal, Soc. Chem. Biol. Paris, 1952. Fellow Am. Institute of Chemists, New York Academy of Scis.; mem. Am. Chem. Soc., American Soc. Biol. Chemists, Am. Assn. Cancer Research Harvey Society. Author: General Enzyme Chemistry (with J. B. S. Haldane), 1932; Biological Oxidation (with C. Oppenheimer), 1939; Protoplasm, Ency. Britannica (with R. Chambers), 1948. Contbr. articles to reference books, rev. and exptl. pubs. in field biochemistry. Home: 17 E. 96th St., N.Y.C. 28. Office: Polytech. Inst., Bklyn. Died Feb. 3, 1956.

STERNBERG, CHARLES HAZELIUS, naturalist; b. Middleburg, N.Y., June 15, 1850; s. Levi (D.D.) and Margaret Levering (Miller) S.; ed. Hartwick Sem. (N.Y.), Ia. Lutheran Coll. (Albion), Kan. State Agrl. Coll.; hon. A.M., Midland Coll., Atchison, Kan., 1911; m. Anna Musgrove Reynolds, July 7, 1880; children—George Fryer, Charles Mottram, Maud (dec.), Levi. In charge of parties collecting fossils for late Professor E. D. Cope, 1876-79 and 1894, 96, 97; in charge for late Prof. Agassiz, 1881, 1882; for late Prof. O. C. Marsh of Yale, 1884, and of expdns. for Munich (Bavaria) Paleontol. Mus., 1892, 95, 1901, 02, 05, etc. Was in charge collecting party for Geol. Survey of Can., and vertebrate paleontol. lab. at Victoria Memorial Mus., Ottawa, Can., and head collector and preparator of vertebrate fossils, Victoria Memorial Museum, Geol. Survey of Can. until 1916, resigned; conducting own lab., Lawrence, Kan., since 1917. Discovered 2 nearly complete skeletons 32 ft. long, Red Deer River, Alberta, 1916; also large skeleton Dimetrodon Permian of Tex., 1916, in Nat. Mus.; conducted expdn. to the Permian of Tex. and Kan. Chalk, 1918, to the Kansas Chalk and to Texas, in 1919; found four skeletons of Mosasaurs, 2 Pterodactyls, 3 of the great fish, a fine skeleton of Equus Scotti; explored the San Juan Basin, N.M., 1921-23; discovered new genera of ceratopsians and duckbilled dinosaurs and many turtles. Fellow A.A.A.S.; mem. Kan. Acad. Science (life), Soc. Am. Vertebrate Paleontologists. Republican. Lutheran. Author: The Life of a Fossil Hunter, 1909; Hunting Dinosaurs on Red River, 1916. Home: 603 Claxton Blvd., Toronto, Canada. Died July 20, 1943.

STERNE, THEODORE EUGENE, physicist; b. N.Y.C., Nov. 23, 1907; s. Eugene Washington and Dora (Kohn) S.; B.Sc., Princeton, 1928; Ph.D., Trinity Coll., Cambridge U., 1931; NRC fellow physics, Harvard and Mass. Inst. of Tech., 1931-33; M.A., Harvard, 1956; m. Grace Isabel DeRoo, Aug. 5, 1932; children—Theodore Drummond, John Robert; m. 2d Lois Cremins Isenberg, on Nov. 28, 1964. Research asso. Harvard Obs., 1933-34, astronomer, 1934-41, lecturer astrophysics, tutor Harvard, 1934-41, Simon Newcomb professor astrophysics, 1956-59; chief ballistician Ballistic Research Labs., Aberdeen Proving Ground, Md., 1946-56, chief spl. prob. br., 1941-45, comptng. lab., 1945-47, 52-53, term. ballistic lab., 1946-52, sci. adviser to dir., 1953-56; cons. operations research office Johns Hopkins, 1954-59; staff mem. Research Analysis Corp., 1961-65, Inst. Def. Analyses, Arlington, Va., 1965-70. Asso. director Astrophys. Obs., Smithsonian Instn., 1956-59; staff member of Johns Hopkins University Operations Research Office, Bethesda, Maryland, 1959-61, acting chief Air Def. division, 1960-61. Served from first lieut. to lieut. col., F.A., Ordnance Corps, AUS, 1941-46; col. Res. Fellow Am. Acad. Arts and Scis., A.A.A.S., Am. Physics Soc., Royal Astron. Soc.; mem. Am. Astron. Soc., Astron. Society of Pacific Operations Research Society of America, Cat Fanciers of Washington (pres. 1966-67), also Phi Beta Kappa, Sigma Xi. Club: Cosmos (Washington). Author: Introduction to Celestial Mechanics, 1960. Contbr. articles sci. jours., govt. publs. Home: Chevy Chase MD Died Feb. 6, 1970; buried Arlington Nat. Cemetery, Arlington VA

STETEFELDT, CARL AUGUST, metallurgist; b. Holzhausen, Gotha, Germany, Sept. 28, 1838; s. August Heinrich Christian and Friederika Christiane (Credner) S.; grad. U. Gottingen (Germany), 1862; m. Dec. 31, 1872. Came to U.S., 1863; asst. to Charles A. Joy (prof. chemistry Columbia), N.Y.C.; asst. to cons. firm Aedlberg & Raymond, 1864; partner (with John H. Bialt) assay office and cons. bus., Austin, Nev., 1865; builder 1st lead blast furnace in dist. of Eureka (Nev.); designer Stetefeldt furnace (a metall. advance in processing sulphide ores containing gold and silver by chlorination process); v.p. Am. Inst. Mining Engrs., contbr. to inst.'s Transactions. Author: The Lexivication of Silver-ores with Hyposulphite Solutions, 1888. Died Oakland, Cal., Mar. 17, 1896.

STETSON, HARLAN TRUE, astronomer, geo-physicist; b. Haverhill, Massachusetts, June 28, 1885; s. Henry Allen and Jennie Sarah (Rowe) S.; Ph.B., Brown University, 1908; Sc.M., Dartmouth College, 1910; Ph.D., U. of Chicago, 1915; married Florence May Brigham, on September 4, 1912 (deceased February 19, 1956); children—Helen May, Florence L., Harold Brigham (dec.). Asst. in physics, Dartmouth, 1908-10, instr., 1911-13; research asst. Yerkes Obs., summer 1909; instr. physics and astronomy, Middlebury Coll., summers 1912-13; instr. astronomy, Northwestern U., Dearborn Obs., 1913-14; studied at Yerkes Obs. and U. of Chicago, 1914-15; instr. physics, Northwestern U., 1916; instr. astronomy, Harvard, 1916-20, asst. prof., 1920-29; prof. astronomy, head dept. and dir. Perkins Obs., Ohio Wesleyan U., 1929-34. Harvard exchange prof. to Carleton, Knox and Pomona colls., 1929. Research asso. in geophysics, Harvard, 1933-36, research asso., Mass. Inst. Technology, 1936-49; established Laboratory for Cosmic Terrestrial Research, Needham, Mass., 1940. Served as instr. in navigation, recruiting service, U.S. Shipping Bd., 1917. Temp. asst., Smithsonian Instn., 1927, James Arthur lecturer, 1938. Mem. eclipse expdns., Cal., 1923, Norway, 1927; head of eclipse expdns., Conn., 1925, Sumatra, 1926, Malaya, 1929, Me., 1932. Fellow A.A.A.S. (exec. com. sect. D 1929-40; sec. sect. on astronomy, 1932-40, chairman of committee on grants 1944-48), American Academy of Arts and Sciences, Royal Astron. Soc.; mem. fgn., nat. and local scientific socs., active in com. work of socs., officer and dir. Clubs: Harvard (Boston); Engineers, Town Hall (New York City); Cruising Club of America; Cosmos (Washington). Author or co-author books relating to field including: Man and the Stars, 1930; Earth, Radio and the Stars, 1934; Sunspots and Their Effects, 1937; Sunspots in Action, 1947. Has specialized in photometric researches; eclipse phenomena, application of physical methods to astronomical problems; investigations of latitude variation, sun spot and radio correlations, variation in longitude, lunar effect on radio transmission, earthtides and earthquakes, cosmic-terrestrial relations. Contbr. articles Americana Ency. Address: 541 Lido Dr., Ft. Lauderdale Fla. Died Sept. 16, 1964.

STETSON, HENRY CROSBY, geologist; b. Cambridge, Mass., Oct. 10, 1900; s. Henry Crosby and Eleanor Morland (Gray) S.; A.B., Harvard, 1923, A.M., 1926; m. Edith Williams Reid, Oct. 15, 1927; children—Robert Gray, Thomas Reid, Edith Lincoln. Asst. in geology Harvard, 1924-25, asst. in meteorology, 1925-26, asst. curator paleontology Mus. Comparative Zoology, 1927-34, research asso. paleontology 1934-42, 42-43, research fellow in oceanography, 1943-46, asso. curator oceanography, 1946-48, research oceanographer, 1948—, lectr. geology, 1950—; research asso. Oceanographic Instn., Woods Hole, Mass., 1931-41, submarine geologist, 1941—; Alexander Agassiz fellow in oceanography, 194-42, in oceanography and zoology, 1946—; civilian with OSRD, 1944. Mem. Am. Acad. Arts and Scis., Geol. Soc. Am., A.A.A.S., Am. Geophys. Union, Am. Assn. Petroleum Geologists, Soc Econ. Paleontologists and Mineralogists. Author numerous publs. in field. Home: Belmont, Mass. Died Dec. 3, 1955; buried Mt. Auburn Cemetery, Cambridge, Mass.

STETTEN, DEWITT, surgeon; b. New York, N.Y., Jan. 22, 1881; s. Joseph and Bella (Rosenthal) S.; M.D. Coll. Physicians and Surgeons (Columbia), 1901; house staff German hosp., New York, 1901-03; studied Vienna, Prague and Breslau, 1904-05; m. Magdalen Ernst, Apr. 23, 1906; children—Margaret (Mrs. Maximilien Vanka), DeWitt, Jr.; m. 2d, Alice Mayer, May 5, 1930. Asst. and attdg. surgeon, German Dispensary, New York, 1905-11; anesthetist, German Hospital, New York, 1905-08; asso. surgeon German Hospital, later Lenox Hill Hospital, New York, 1908-21, actg. attending surgeon, 1921; attending surgeon Lenox Hill Hospital, 1922-46; Beth Israel Hospital, New York, 1930-33; cons. surgeon, Lenox Hill Hospital since 1946; instr. clin. surgery, Coll. Phys. and Surg., 1909-18; clin. prof. surgery, New York University Coll. of Medicine, 1931-46. Member Hospital Corps, 1st Batt., N.Y. Naval Milita, 1898-1902; 1st lt. M.R.C., U.S. Army, 1915-17, capt. 1917-18, maj. M.C., U.S. Army, 1918-19. With Neurol. Sch., U. of Pa., Sept.-Dec. 1917; asst. chief and acting chief of surg. service U.S. Army Gen. Hosp. No. 1, Williamsbridge, N.Y., Jan.-Oct. 1918; chief of surg. service U.S. Army Embarkation Hosp. No. 4, New York, 1918-19; acting comdg. officer same, Feb. 13-22, 1919. Fellow Am. Coll. Surgeons, A.M.A., New York Acad. Medicine, N.A.D., Am. Geog. Soc.; mem. Nat. Audubon Soc., Internat. Soc. of Gastro-Enterology, Am. Gastro-Enterol. Assn., Am. Assn. Thoracic Surgery, Nat. Tuberculosis Assn., Am. Cancer Soc., Assn. Military Surgeons of U.S., A.A.A.S., Acad. Polit. Sci., Fgn. Policy Assn., Med. Soc. State of N.Y., Med. Soc. County of New York (pres. 1929, trustee, 1932-35, chmn. bd. 1935), New York Surg. Soc., N.Y. Soc. for Thoracic Surgery, N.Y. Gastro-Enterological Assn., N.Y. Pathol. Soc., Military Order of the World Wars, Am. Legion, etc. Pres. bd. trustees Blood Transfusion Assn. of New York; mem. and sec. bd. dirs. United Med. Service, Diplomate founders group Am. Bd. of Surgery. Club: Dachshund Club of America. Contbr. more than 90 papers on surgical subjects. Address: 850 Park Av., New York 21, N.Y.; (summer) White Bridge Farm, Rushland, Bucks County, Pa. Died Nov. 10, 1951.

STETTNER, LUDWIG WILHELMIN, corp. exec.; b. Lowenstein, Germany, Sept. 1, 1887; s. Wilhelm and Wilhelmine (Sinzig) S.; student Schs., Lowenstein and Heilbronn; m. Martha Seger, Mar. 27, 1915; 1 son, Frederick Ludwig. Came to U.S., 1911, naturalized, 1918. Pres., chmn. Victor Equipment Co., San Francisco; pres. J. C. Menzies & Co., L & B Welding Equipment, Inc.; chmn. bd. Santa Cruz Aggegates. Rotarian. Inventor welding and cutting machine, high pressure regulators. Home: 179 Estates Dr., Piedmont, Cal. 94611. Office: 844 Folsom St., San Francisco 7. Died Apr. 16, 1964; buried Mountain View Cemetery.

STEVENS, EDWIN AUGUSTUS, engr., inventor; b. Hoboken, N.J., July 28, 1795; s. John and Rachel (Cox) S.; m. Mary B. Picton, 1836; m. 2d, Martha Bayard Dod, Aug. 22, 1854; 9 children including Mary Picton Stevens Garnett. Invented, patented (with Robert L. Stevens) a plow, 1821; took charge Union Stage-Coach Line (operated between N.Y.C. and Phila.), 1825, purchased it with his brothers, 1827; mgr. Camden & Amboy R.R. Transp. Co. (1st railroad in N.J.), 1830-65; invented, patented (with brother Robert "closed fire room" system of forced draft, 1842, 1st applied on Robert's steamboat North America; interested in naval vessels, applied to Navy Dept., received permission to build an armored vessel designed by Robert, 1842; The Stevens Battery was begun in 1852, never finished; founder Stevens Inst. Tech., Hoboken. Died Paris, France, Aug. 7, 1868.

STEVENS, EDWIN AUGUSTUS, engineer; b. Philadelphia, Mar. 14, 1858; s. Edwin Augustus (engr. and founder Stevens Inst. Tech.) and Martha Bayard (Dod) S.; A.B., Princeton, 1879; (D.Eng., Stevens Inst. Tech.); m. Emily Contee Lewis, Oct. 28, 1879. Pres. Hoboken Land Improvement Co.; trustee Stevens Inst.; has held various local offices; was col. 2d Regt., N.J. N.G.; pres. Dem. Soc. of State of N.J.; Dem. candidate for presdl. elector, 1888, 1892, 1904. Pres. N.J. Commrs. of the Palisades Interstate Park; state commr. pub. roads, 1911—. Designed the 1st screw ferryboat. Life mem. and v.p. Am. Soc. Mech. Engrs.; v.p. Soc. Naval Architects and Marine Engrs. Home: Bernardsville, N.J. Died Mar. 8, 1918.

STEVENS, EVERETT DUNCAN, elec. engr.; b. Goldsboro, N.C., Feb. 13, 1920; s. David Edgar and Stella (Benton) S.; student Wake Forest Coll., 1936-37, Mercer U., 1946; B.S., N.C. State U., 1950; m. Alma Ruth Jones, Nov. 28, 1940; children—Terell Everett, Nancy Lee. Equipment technician Western Electric Co., Raleigh, Charlotte N.C. and Charleston, S.C., 1938-43; indsl. sales mgr. Carolina Power & Light Co., Raleigh. Engring cons. to pvt. cons. firms. Vice chmn. Indsl. Sales Com., Southeastern Elec. Exchange, Indsl. Group, Edison Electric Inst. Mayor, Vetville, N.C., 1948-50. Mem. Rex. Hosp. Found. Served with USNR, 1944-45; ETO. Registered profl. engr., N.C. Mem. N.C. Soc. Engrs. (past pres., dir.), Profl. Engrs., N.C., Nat. Soc. Profl. Engrs., Raleigh C. of C., N.C. State U. Alumni Assn. (dir. 1966-69, pres. Wake County chpt. 1959). Democrat. Methodist (edn. commn.). Kiwanian. Club: Raleigh Engineers, Raleigh City, MacGregor Downs County. Research elec. power applications in industry. Home: Raleigh NC Died Jan. 17, 1969; buried Raleigh Meml. Park Raleigh NC

STEVENS, GEORGE THOMAS, physician; b. Essex Co., N.Y., July 25, 1832; s. Rev. Chauncey Coe and Lucinda (Hoadley) S.; ed. in N.Y. State; M.D., Castleton (Vt.) Med. Coll., 1857; (Ph.D., Union Coll., 1877); m. Harriet W. Wadhams, 1861. Commd. surgeon 77th N.Y. Vols., 1861; served in campaigns of Army of the Potomac, operating surgeon for his div. 2 1/2 yrs., and for a time med. insp. 6th Army Corps; prof. physiology and diseases of the eye, Union U., 1870-5; in practice in New York, 1880—. Highest prize from Royal Acad. of Medicine of Belgium for treatise on Functional Diseases of the Nervous System, 1883. Author: A Treatise on the Motor Apparatus of the Eyes, 1905; A Series of Studies of Nervous Diseases, 1911. Home: New York, N.Y. Died Jan. 30, 1921.

STEVENS, HOWARD EVELETH, civil engr.; b. Bluehill, Me., Mar. 8, 1874; B.C.E., U. of Me., 1897. With N.P. Ry. since 1904, successively inspr., draftsman, asst. engr., bridge engr., and chief engr., now v.p. in charge of operation and maintenance. Home: 725 Linwood Place. Office: Fifth and Jackson Sts., St Paul MN*

STEVENS, JOHN, engr., inventor; b. N.Y.C., 1749; s. John and Elizabeth (Alexander) S.; grad. Columbia, 1768; m. Rachel Cox, Oct. 17, 1782, at least 7 children including John Cox, Robert Livingston, Edwin Augustus, Mary, Harriet. Studied law, 1768-71, apptd. an atty., N.Y.C., 1771; served from capt. to col., obtaining loans for Continental Army during Revolutionary War; loan commr. for Hunterdon County (N.J.); treas. N.J., 1776-79; surveyor gen. Eastern div. N.J., 1782-83; instrumental in framing 1st patent laws, 1790; became cons. engr. for Manhattan Co. (organized to furnish adequate water supply to N.Y.C.), circa 1800; became pres. Bergen Turnpike Co., 1802; received patent for multitubular boiler, 1803; his steamboat Little Juliana (operated by twin screw propellers) put into use on Hudson River, 1804; attempted to operate regular line of steamboats on Hudson between N.Y.C. and Albany and on other inland rivers, prevented by lawsuits; sent the Phoenix (1st sea-going steamboat in world) to Phila., 1809; built the Juliana, began regular ferry service, 1811; obtained 1st Am. railroad authorization from N.J. Assembly in 1815; authorized by Pa. Legislature to build Pa. R.R., 1823; designed, built exptl. locomotive on his estate in Hoboken, N.J. (1st Am.-made steam locomotive though never used for actual service), 1825; proposed a vehicular tunnel under the Hudson as well as an elevated railroad system for N.Y.C. Died Hoboken, Mar. 6, 1838.

STEVENS, JOHN AMOS, consulting engr.; b. Galva, Ill., Sept. 16, 1868; s. George M. and Georgeanna (Ames) S.; direct desc. of John Alden of the Mayflower; student U. of Mich., 1891-92; m. Luella E. Holland, Oct. 6, 1896; children—Holland A., Richard A. Apprentice in shops of Mitts & Merrill, Saginaw, 3 yrs., later engr. on lake and ocean steamers; chief engr. Merrimac Mfg. Co., Lowell, 1896-1909; cons. practice, 1909—; treas. Stevens Products Co., Lowell. Mem. High Sch. Building Commn., Lowell; granted 13 patents on water tube boilers and 11 patents on shock absorbing devices; co-inventor Stevens-Pratt boiler. Chmn. com., apptd. 1911, by Am. Soc. Mech. Engrs., which prepared the standard boiler code; was mem. original Mass. Bd. of Boiler Rules; standardization engr. U.S. Shipping Bd. Emergency Fleet Corp., World War. Donor of John A. Stevens Trust Fund, Am. Soc. Mech. Engrs., for encouraging inventions in conservation of fuels and in generation of light, heat and power; presented with medal by Nat. Assn. Cotton Mfrs., 1917, for paper on "Evolution of the Steam Turbine in the Textile Industry." Home: Lowell, Mass. Died Nov. 18, 1929.

STEVENS, JOHN F., civil engr.; b. W. Gardiner, Me., Apr. 25, 1853; s. John and Harriet S.; LL.D., Bates College, Lewiston, Me., 1922; D.E., U. of N.C., U. of Mich., Poly. Inst. Brooklyn; m. Harriet T. O'Brien, of Dallas, Tex., Jan. 6, 1877. Assistant engineer City of Minneapolis, 1874-76; chief engineer Sabine Pass & North-Western Railway, 1876-79; assistant engineer D. & R. G. Ry., 1879-80, C., M. & St. P. Ry., 1880-82; div. engr. Canadian Pacific Ry., 1882-86; asst. engr. C., M. & St. P. Ry., 1886; prin. asst. engr. Duluth, South Shore & Atlantic Ry., 1887-89; asst. engr. Spokane Falls & Northern Ry., 1889; prin. asst. engr., 1889-93, asst. chief engr., 1893-95, chief engr., 1895-1902, gen. mgr., 1902-03, G.N. Ry.; chief engr., 1903-04, 2d v.p., 1904-05, C.,R.I. & P. Ry. Co.; chief engr. Panama Canal, 1905-Apr. 1, 1907; chmn. Isthmian Canal Commn., Feb.-Mar. 1907; v.p. N.Y.,N.H.&H. R.R., in charge operation, Aug. 1, 1907-09; pres. Spokane, Portland & Seattle Ry., Ore. Electric Ry., Oregon Trunk Ry., Pacific & Eastern Ry., 1909-11. Head of Am. Ry. Mission to Russia, 1917-18; pres. Inter-Allied Tech. Bd., supervising Siberian rys., 1919-23. Dir. B.&O.R.R.Co. Hon. mem. Am. Soc. C.E. (pres. 1927), N.C. Soc. of Engrs.; mem. Pacific Soc. Engrs., Chinese-Am. Assn. Engrs., Engineers Club of Phila. Awarded Fritz medal for "great achievements," 1925; gold medal, Franklin Inst.; Hoover medal, Am. Soc. C.E., 1939. Address: Southern Pines, N.C.

STEVENS, J(OHN) FRANKLIN, consulting engr.; b. Philadelphia, Pa., Jan. 1, 1870; s. John Stewart and Sarah Franklin (Bacon) S.; B.Sc., U. of Pa., 1890, M.E., 1891; m. Jessie M. Speace, Nov. 28, 1902. Engr. and mem. John S. Stevens & Sons, 1891-93; sec. and treas. LaRoche Electric Works, 1893-95; pres. Keystone Elec. Instrument Co., 1894-1911; v.p. Am. Meter Co., 1896-1900; mem. Stewart & Stevens Iron Works, 1902-13; consulting practice, 1911—. Vice chmn. conservation bd. and dist. chmn. for Southeast Pa. of power and conservation divs. of Federal Fuel Administration, 1918-19. Frequent lecturer and contbr. to engring. jours. Fellow Am. Inst. E.E. (mgr. 1912-15, v.p. 1915-17, chmn. finance com., etc.). Holder of 6 patents on elec. measuring instruments; dir. Cambria Mining & Mfg. Co., 1920—. Traveled and studied engring. practice and econ. conditions in Orient and Africa, 1921-25. Home: Philadelphia, Pa. Died Dec. 1933.

STEVENS, NEIL EVERETT, plant pathologist; b. Portland, Me., Apr. 6, 1887, s. Thomas Jefferson and Hattie (Mantle) S.; B.A., Bates Coll., 1908; Ph.D., Yale, 1911; m. Maude Bradford, Aug. 31, 1914; children—Russell Bradford, Carl Mantle II, Mary Christine. Inst. botany, Kan. State Coll., 1911-12; pathologist Bur. Plant Industry, U.S. Dept. Agr., 1912-28, sr. pathologist 1928-36; adjunct prof. at George Washington U., 1931-36; prof. of botany, U. of Ill., 1936-47, professor of plant pathology since 1947; senior specialist, Wisconsin Dept. of Agr., summers 1937-44; sec. and dir. Arlington and Fairfax Building and Loan Assn., 1933-35. Delegate Internat. Botanical Congress, 1930 and 1935. Mem. Am. Phytopathol. Soc. (v.p. 1933; pres. 1934), Bot. Soc. of Washington (sec. 1927; pres. 1931), A.A.A.S. (council 1947-50; v.p. and chmn. Sect. G, 1939), Mycol. Soc. of America (council 1932; v.p. 1944), Botanical Soc. of Am. (v.p. 1940, pres., 1946), Nat. Research Council (mem. exec. com. dir. of biology and agriculture, 1944), Sigma Xi, Phi Beta Kappa. Club: University (Urbana). Advisory editor of The Botanical Rev. since 1935. Writer of government bulletins and tech. papers on diseases of plants and the history of botany. Address: University of Illinois, Urbana, Ill. Died June 26, 1949; buried Clements Cemetery, Urbana, Ill.

STEVENS, ROBERT LIVINGSTON, engr., shipbuilder, inventor; b. Hoboken, N.J., Oct. 18, 1787; s. John and Rachel (Cox) s.; never married. Aided his father in building ferryboat Juliana, (inaugurating world's 1st steam-ferry system), 1811; leader in profession of naval architecture; designed, built at least 20 steamboats and ferries; introduced a forced-draft firing system under boilers, the split paddle wheel, "hog-framing" for boats, the present type of ferry slip; an organizer Camden & Amboy R.R. & Transp. Co., 1830, elected pres., chief engr.; designed the Trail and "hook-headed spike," circa 1830; began 1st steam railway service in N.J.; developed a percussion shell for naval use which could be fired from a cannon during War of 1812; interested in use of armor on ships of war; designed, built several craft including yacht Maria (fastest sailing vessel of her day), 1850. Died Hoboken, Apr. 20, 1856.

STEVENS, ROLLIN HOWARD, physician; b. Blenheim, Ont., Can., Jan. 7, 1868; s. Nathan Howard and Ada Jane (Burk) S.; Toronto U., 1 yr.; M.D., Homoe. Coll., U. of Mich., 1889; Coll. Physicians and Surgeons, Ont., Can., 1889; house surgeon, Grace Hosp., Detroit, 1889-91; spl. course Stanford, 1892; m. Mary Ella Thompson (A.B., M.D.), Mar. 16, 1892; children—Margaret (dec.), Frances Eleanor (Mrs. M. C. Davis). In gen. practice, Detroit, 1892-1903; went to Copenhagen, Denmark, 1903, to study the Finsen light and its use in lupus and other skin diseases, under Prof. Finsen; then went to Berlin, Vienna and Hamburg and studied diseases of the skin and the Roentgen ray; practice limited to dermatology and radiology since 1904; visited Paris for study, 1909; successively pathologist, surgeon and gynecologist, 1892-1904, dermatologist and Roentgenologist, since 1904, Grace Hosp.; lecturer on dermatology, Homoe. Coll. of U. of Mich., 1904-09; asst. clin. prof. Roentgenology, Detroit Coll. of Medicine, 1910-14, and asso. clin. prof. dermatology since 1925; extramural lecturer in post-grad. medicine, University of Mich., 1929; dir. and sec. Radiol. Research Inst.; founder Detroit Inst. of Cancer Research, Inc., pres. 1943-46 (Rollin Howard Stevens Research Laboratory, Memorial in his honor). Dir. Board of Commerce, Detroit, 1913; founder, 1900, and ex-president Detroit Mycological Club, later Detroit Inst. Science; founder and pres. Mich. Soc. for Social Hygiene; sec.-treas. Boys' Home and D'Arcambal Assn. Fellow A.M.A., Am. Coll. Physicians, Am. Coll. Radiology (pres. 1931), Radiol. Society N. America (pres. 1923); mem. Am. Roentgen Ray Soc., Wayne County Med. Soc., Mich. State Med. Soc., Am. Radium Soc. (pres. 1933-34), Am. Bd. Radiology, Detroit Roentgen Ray and Radium Soc. (pres. 1926-27), Detroit Dermatol. Soc. (pres. 1926-27), British Inst. Radiology, Mich. Assn. of Roentgenologists, Am. Malacological Society, Am. Assn. for Study of Neoplastic Diseases (v.p., 1939, Laymen's League (Unitarian), Foreign Policy Assn.; hon. mem. Chicago Roentgen Ray Soc. Mason. Clubs: Rotary, Detroit Yacht, Michigan Union of Ann Arbor (life), Torch. Extensive contributor on med. topics. Home: 47 Pingree Av. Office: David Whitney Bldg., Detroit 26, Mich. Died May 17, 1946.

STEVENS, S(TANLEY) SMITH, psychophysicist; educator; b. Ogden, Utah, Nov. 4, 1906; s. Stanley S. and Adeline (Smith) S.; Student U. Utah, 1927-29; A.B., Stanford, 1931; Ph.D., Harvard, 1933; m. Maxine Leonard, Mar. 28, 1930 (dec.); 1 son, Peter Smith; m. 2d, Geraldine Stone, Apr. 11, 1963. Asst. in psychology Harvard, 1932-34, nat. research fellow Med. Sch., 1934-35, research fellow in physics, 1935-36, faculty, 1936-73, prof., 1946-62, prof. psychophysics, 1962-73, dir. psychoacoustic lab., 1944-62, lab. psychophysics, 1962-73, psychol. labs., 1949-62. Sect. mem. NDRC, 1942-45; expert cons. Research and Devel. Bd., 1946-52; chmn. NRC Div. Anthropology and Psychology, 1949-52; mem. sensory diseases study sect. NIH, 1956-58; mem. Nat. Acad. Scis. NRC Physiol. Psychology Fellowship Bd., 1954-58; mem. space sci. bd. Nat. Acad. Sci., 1958-60. Recipient Beltone Inst. award for distinguished accomplishment, 1966; Rayleigh gold medal Brit. Acoustical Soc., 1972. Fellow Acoustical Soc. Am. (exec. council 1946-49), Am. Psychol. Assn. (Sci. award 1960); mem. Am. Philos. Soc., Nat. Acad. Sci., Soc. Exptl. Psychologists (Howard Crosby Warren medal 1943), Am. Physiol. Soc., Eastern Psychol. Assn. (past pres.), Psychonomic Soc. (governing bd. 1960-61), A.A.A.S. (v.p. sect. I 1955), Am. Acad. Arts and Scis., Philosophy Sci. Assn. (governing bd. 1957-59), Optical Soc. Am., Soc. for Neurosci., Am. Inst. Physics, Phi Beta Kappa, Sigma Xi, Pi Kappa Alpha. Mem. Ch. of Jesus Christ of Latter-day Saints. Author: (with Hallowell Davis) Hearing, Its Psychology and Physiology, 1938; (with W.H. Sheldon, W.B. Tucker) The Varieties of Human Physique, 1940; (with W.H. Sheldon) Varieties of Temperament, 1942; (with F. Warshofsky) Sound and Hearing, 1965; The Story of Psychophysics, 1974. Editor: Handbook of Experimental Psychology, 1951. Contbr. articles to various publs. Home: Cambridge MA Died Jan. 18, 1973.

STEVENS, TERRILL D(RYDEN), forester; b. Los Angeles, Mar. 27, 1903; s. Roy and Mary Lavina (Dryden) S.; student U. So. Cal., 1922; B.S.F., Mont. State U., 1936; Ph.D., Yale, 1940; m. Ada Sewell, May 13, 1932; 1 dau., Nancy May. Protective asst. Forest Service, U.S. Dept. Agr., Porterville, Cal., 1922, Pasadena, Cal., 1930-33; asst. prof. range management, Colo. State Coll., 1936-37; prof. and research prof. forestry, Mich. State Coll., 1941-47; head forestry dept., Ala. Polytech. Inst., 1947-50, cons. forester, 1945-50; head forestry dept. Mich. State U., East Lansing, Mich., 1950-65, prof. forestry, 1965—. Visited Germany under E.T.A. Project on forestry genetics adv. work, 1954, Taiwan under Mich. State U.'s contract AID, 1964. Mem. adv. com. Auburn Research Found. Sec., Mich. bd. registration foresters, 1955-57, chmn., 1957-58, 61-62. Elected Hon. State Farmer, Future Farmers Am., 1960. Fellow A.A.A.S.; mem. Soil Conservation Soc., Mich. Acad. of Scis., Ala. Acad. Sci. (chmn. research com.), Soc. Am. Foresters (chmn. Wis.-Mich. sect.), Ala. Forestry Council, Forest Farmers Assn., Sigma Xi, Phi Kappa Phi, Xi Sigma Pi, Gamma Sigma Delta. Episcopalian. Home: 3703 Waverly Hills Rd., Lansing, Mich. 48917. Died May 24, 1966; buried Deepdale Meml. Park, Lansing.

STEVENS, WALTER LE CONTE, physicist; b. Gordon Co., Ga., June 17, 1847; s. Dr. Josiah P. and Anna (Le Conte) S.; A.B., U. of S.C., 1868; hon. Ph.D., U. of Ga., 1882; Strassburg, Berlin, Zürich, 1890-92; m. Virginia Lee Letcher, d. war gov. of Va., Aug. 29, 1900. Prof. chemistry, Oglethorpe Coll., Atlanta, Ga., 1870-72; instr. physical science, Chatham Acad., Savannah, Ga., 1873-76, Cooper Inst., New York, 1879-82; prof. mathematics and physics, Packer Collegiate Inst., Brooklyn, 1882-90; prof. physics, Rensselaer Poly. Inst., 1892-98, Washington and Lee U., 1898-1922; retired and made prof. emeritus, 1922. Fellow A.A.A.S., N.Y. Acad. Sciences, Brooklyn Inst. Arts and Sciences, Royal Micros. Soc., London. Author: Revision of Steele's Physics, 1886. Home: Lexington, Va. Died Dec. 29, 1927.

STEVENS, WILLIAM CHASE, botanist; b. Princeton, Ill., Feb. 21, 1861; s. James Thomas and Elizabeth (Flint) S.; A.B., U. Kan., 1885, M.S., 1893; Harvard Summer Sch., 1890, Woods Hole Biol. Lab., 1890, U. Bonn, 1897; m. Ada E. Pugh, July 11, 1888. Prof. botany, U. Kan., 1899—. Fellow Bot. Soc. Am.; mem. Am. Soc. Naturalists, A.A.A.S., Sigma Xi. Author: Introduction to Botany, 1902; Histological Botany and Micro-technic, 1897; Plant Anatomy, 1915. Address: Lawrence, Kan. Deceased.

STEVENSON, ALEXANDER RUSSELL, JR., engring.; b. Schenectady, N.Y., May 28, 1893; s. Rev. A. Russell and Mary M. (Kennedy) S.; C.E., Princeton, 1914; M.S., Union Coll., Schenectady, N.Y., 1915, Ph.D., 1917; m. Helene Elink-Schuurman, May 5, 1934; children—Mary Kennedy, Alexander Russell III, Agathe Elink-Schuurman. With Gen. Electric Co., Schenectady, N.Y., 1917 and since 1919, in research laboratory, 1917, in power and mining engring. dept., specializing in application of synchronous elec. machinery connected to reciprocating apparatus, 1919-23, mem. staff of vice pres. in charge of engring. 1923; assisted Dr. Robert E. Doherty in starting advanced course in engring. in Gen. Electric Co., 1923, in complete charge of this ednl. program since 1930. Served in World War I, 1917-18; officer in charge testing, Langley Field, U.S.; in charge radio and elec. sect. Air Service, France; in charge flying and testing, Army Exptl. Field, France. Mem. spl. subcom. on jet propulsion Nat. Advisory Com. for Aeronautics, 1941-44; mem. Civilian Advisory Council, Mil. Training Div., Ordnance Dept., since 1942; advisory mem. N.Y. State Aviation Council, Inc. Pres. bd. trustees Brown Sch., Schenectady, N.Y. Past pres. Am. Soc. Refrigerating Engrs., Private Flyer's Assn. Fellow Am. Inst. E.E., Am. Soc. M.E. (vice president); mem. Engineer's Council for Professional Development, Soc. Promotion Engring. Edn. (chmn. com. on relations with industry), Phi Beta Kappa, Sigma Xi. Republican. Presbyterian. Contbr. of numerous scientific articles to technical publs. Home: 6 Union St. Office: General Electric Co., I River Rd., Schenectady 5, N.Y. Died Aug. 28, 1946.

STEVENSON, JOHN JAMES, geologist; b. New York, N.Y., Oct. 10, 1841; s. Rev. Andrew and Ann Mary (Willson) S.; A.B., New York U., 1863, A.M., 1866, Ph.D., 1867; (LL.D., Princeton, 1893, Washington and Jefferson, 1902); m. Mary A. Macgowan, Apr. 13, 1865 (died 1871); m. 2d, Mary C. Ewing, Jan. 1, 1879. Prof. chemistry and natural history, W.Va. U., 1869-71; prof. geology, 1871-82, chemistry and physics, 1882-89, geology and biology, 1889-94, geology, 1894-1909, emeritus prof., 1909, New York U. Aid on Ohio Geol. Survey, 1871-72, 74; geologist U.S. Geog. Survey, west of 100th Meridian, 1873, 74, 78, 79, 2d Geol. Survey of Pa., 1875-78, 1881-82. Corr. or hon. mem. geol. socs. of Russia, Hungary, Belgium, Vienna, Edinburgh, Liverpool, Australasia, acads. of Halle, Dresden, Moscow, Padua, Palermo, Pisa, London; del. Internat. Geol. Cong., 1903 (v.p. for U.S.). Author: Geology of a Portion of Colorado, 1875; Report on Greene and Washington Districts, Pa., 1876; Report on Fayette and Westmoreland Districts, Pa., 1877-78; Geological Examinations in Southern Colorado and Northern New Mexico, 1881; Geology of Bedford and Fulton Counties, Pa., 1882. Died Aug. 10, 1924.

STEVENSON, SARA YORKE, archaeologist; b. Paris, France, Feb. 19, 1847; d. Edward and Sarah (Hanna) Yorke; ed. in Paris to 1862; lived in Mexico; (Sc.D., U. of Pa.—the 1st hon. degree that instn. ever conferred on a woman); m. Cornelius Stevenson, June 30, 1870. Sec. Am. Exploration Soc., 1897, dept. archaeology, U. of Pa., 1894 (pres. 1904); pres. Acorn Club, Phila., 1894, Depository and Phila. Exchange for Woman's Work, 1895; pres. Pa. branch Aechaeol. Inst. America, 1899-1903; trustee Phila. Museums, 1894-1901; mem. and v.p. jury for ethnology, Chicago Expn., 1893; asst. curator Pa. Museum, 1908—. Mem. Citizens' Advisory Com. (1st woman called by the mayor), 1897, to consult on municipal loan of $12,000,000; pres. Civic Club of Phila., 1894-1900, v.p. 1900-07, again pres., 1913, and honorary pres., 1914—; pres. Pa. Equal Suffrage Soc., 1909. Went to Rome, 1897, on spl. mission for dept. of archaeology and palaeontology, U. of Pa., and 1898 to Egypt for the Am. Exploration Soc. and the City of Phila. in connection with archaeol. work in the Nile Valley. (First woman lecturer on Harvard calendar (Peabody Mus.), 1894.) Pres. Contemporary Club, 1913-14. V.chmn. emergency aid com. and chmn. French War Relief Com. of Phila., 1914—. Awarded academic palms by French Govt., as Officier d'Instruction Publique, 1916, for services. Author: Maximilian in Mexico. Lit. editor Public Ledger, 1908—. Chmn. women's com. of 100, United Rep. Campaign Com. for Mayor of Phila. (Moore), 1919. Home: Philadelphia, Pa. Died Nov. 14, 1921.

STEWART, COLIN C(AMPBELL), prof. physiology; b. Owen Sound, Ont., Can., Aug. 15, 1873; s. Rev. Colin Campbell and Elizabeth (McOuat) S.; A.B., U. of Toronto, 1894; scholarship in physiology, Clark U., 1894-95, fellow in physiology, 1895-97; Ph.D., 1897; m. Zoe E. Smiley, July 26, 1898; children—Dorothy Robson, Colin Campbell III. Summer sch. instr., Clark U., 1895, 97; asst. in physiology, Harvard Med. Sch., 1897-98; tutor in physiology, Coll. Phys. and Surgeons (Columbia), 1898-1900; demonstrator, U. of Pa., 1900-03, asst. prof. physiology, 1903-04, instr. summer sch., 1902; asso. prof. physiology, Dartmouth Med. Sch., 1904-07, prof. since 1907, also sec., 1913-24, acting dean, 1925-27; Brown prof. physiology, Dartmouth Coll., since 1908. Fellow A.A.A.S.; mem. Am. Physiol. Soc., A.M.A., N.H. Med. Soc. (hon.), N.H. Surg. Club (hon.), N.H. Acad. Science, Am. Museum of Natural History, Mt. Washington Observatory, Am. Soc. of Zoölogists, Am. Forestry Assn., Phi Alpha Sigma, Sigma Xi, Gamma Alpha. Home: Hanover, N.H. Died Jan. 22, 1944.

STEWART, DE LISLE, astronomer; b. Wabasha, Minn., Mar. 16, 1870; s. John and Malvina (Davis) S.; B.Litt., Carleton Coll., Northfield, Minn., 1891, Ph.D., 1895; m. Mary E. Hannemann, March 16, 1896; children—Catharine (dec.), John De Lisle, Philip Bruce, Louis Hannemann, Mary Elizabeth (Mrs. William Girdner). Teacher district school, Fertile, Minnesota, 1891-92; assistant Goodsell Observatory R.R. Time Signals, 1893-95; assistant Arequipa br. Harvard Coll. Obs., 1896-1902; instr. in astronomy, U. of Cincinnati, 1903-08; asst. in Cincinnati Obs., same univ., 1903-10, also observer Internat. Latitude Service, 1905-10. Makes a specialty of astronomical photography. Fellow A.A.A.S.; organizer, 1911, and pres. Cincinnati Astron. Society. Devoted much time to preservation of H. H. Richardson's Romanesque arches of former Cincinnati Chamber of Commerce Bldg. and use in the building of a photographic observatory, construction of which began July 1935, under Louisa M. Colclesser bequest. Conglist. Author: Richardson, the Architect, 1914. Home: Cleves, Ohio. Died Feb. 8, 1941.

STEWART, DUNCAN, educator; b. Detroit, Oct. 2, 1905; s. Duncan and Stella (Woodbridge) S.; B.S., U. Mich., 1928, Ph.D., 1933; Sc.M., Brown U., 1930; m. Graziella Furkart, Dec. 28, 1937; children—Duncan VIII, Arzelie, Stella. Instr. geology Carleton Coll., 1933-35, asst. prof., 1939-41, prof., 1945-62, chmn. dept., 1945-69, Charles L. Denison prof. geology, 1962-69; instr. Michigan State Coll., 1935-39, asst. prof., 1939; asst. prof. Lehigh U., 1941-43, asso. prof., 1943-45; cons. Lehigh Portland Cement Co., Penn-Dixie Cement Corp., Mo. Portland Cement Co., 1944-59, Ash Gorve Lime and Portland Cement Co., 1961, Wilson Nuttall Raimond Engrs., Inc., Costa Rica, 1964-69. Cons. U.S. Army in Alaska, 1960. Researcher, IGY under Hill Foundation, Scott Polar Research Inst., Cambridge U., Eng., 1956. Recipient grants for Antarctic petrography Sigma Xi, 1935-36, Geol. Soc. Am., 1935-36, Mich. State Grant Patent Fund, 1937-38, Geol. Soc. Am., 1952-53, Louis W. and Maud Hill Family Found., 1956; recipient Congressional medal, 1968; Stewart Hills in West Antarctica named in his honor. Fellow Geol. Soc. Am., Mineral. Soc. Am., American Association for Advancement of Sci.; mem. Soc. Econ. Paleontologists and Mineralogists (asso.), Minn., Pa. Acads. sci., Mich. Acads. Sci., Mich. Acad. Sci. Arts and Letters, Arctic Inst. Am. (charter asso.), Sci. Research Soc. Am., Rochester Earth Sci. Soc. (hon.), Am. Geophys. Union, Yorkshire Geol. Soc. (Eng.). Home: Northfield MN Died Nov. 5, 1969; buried Detroit MI

STEWART, FRED CARLTON, plant pathologist; b. French Creek, N.Y., Feb. 13, 1868; s. Almeron L. and Charlotte E. (Hubbard) S.; B.Sc., Ia. State Coll., 1892, M.Sc., 1894; grad. work, Harvard, Cornell U., U. of Munich; m. Alene Chestek, Nov. 20, 1895; children—Harland Hubbard, Ralph Walton, Hermine, Charlotte Amelia, Mayalene. Mycologist, N.Y. Agrl. Expt. Sta., 1894-98, botanist, 1898-1919, chief in research (botany), 1920-36; also prof. botany, N.Y. State Coll. of Agr., Cornell, 1920-36, emeritus prof. since 1936. Emeritus life mem. A.A.A.S. Author of numerous expt. sta. bulls. on plant diseases. Home: Geneva, N.Y. Died Apr. 24, 1946.

STEWART, GEORGE, ecologist; b. Tooele, Utah, Nov. 7, 1888; s. William and Ellen (Speirs) S.; A.B., U. of Utah, 1907; B.S., Utah Agrl. Coll., 1913; M.S., Cornell U., 1918; Shevlin fellow U. of Minn., 1924-25, Ph.D., 1926; m. Wynona Barber, Sept. 5, 1918; 1 dau., Betty Ann. Instr. in agronomy, Utah Agr. Coll., 1913-16, asst. prof., 1917-18, asso. prof., 1918-19, prof., 1919-30; became sr. ecologist branch of research U.S. Forest Service, 1930; supervisor Utah State Agrl. Coll.-Fgn. Operations Administration Contract for Agr., Iran, 1954-56; professor botany and agronomy Brigham Young U., 1956—. With U.S. Dept. Agr., 1951-53. Member Agricultural Commission to Iran (7 year plan), 1949. Chairman Scout committee Church of Latter Day Saints, 1942-48; member Ogden area Scouts council. Recipient Superior Service award, U.S. Department Agr.; Service award, Utah Acad. Science, 1951. Member American Soc. Agronomy, Am. Geog. Soc., Am. Genetic Assn., A.A.A.S., Soc. Am. Foresters, Am. Ecol. Soc., Sigma Xi, Gamma Sigma Delta, Phi Kappa Phi, Alpha Zeta. Mormon (Gen. M.I.A. Board). Author: Alfalfa Growing in U.S. and Canada, 1926. Co-Author: Principles of Agronomy, 1915; second edition of same completely revised, 1930; Development of Collective Enterprise, 1943. Co-editor: Western Agriculture, 1918. Student of crops, soils, and irrigation of intermountain-region, and their social development and of important features in wheat genetics and new varieties, sugar-beet breeding; varieties of vegetation on desert, semi-desert, and foothill ranges, grazing on public lands, reseeding range lands and range conservation. Contbr. to professional jours. Asso. editor: Journal of Forestry, 1939-46. Home: 23 W. 400 North, Orem, Utah. Died Oct. 27, 1957; buried Orem.

STEWART, GEORGE WALTER, physicist; b. St. Louis, Feb. 22, 1876; s. Oliver Mills and Eleanor (Bell) S.; A.B., DePauw U., 1898, Sc.D. (hon.), 1928; Ph.D., Cornell, 1901; Sc.D. (hon.), U. Pittsburgh, 1931; Sc.D., (hon.), Kalamazoo Coll., 1949; m. Dr. Zella M. White, July 7, 1904. Asst. in physics, Cornell, 1899-1901, instr., 1901-03; asst. prof. charge dept. physics, U. of N.D., 1903-04, prof. physics, 1904-09; prof. physics and head dept., U. of Ia., 1909-46, prof. physics (retired), 1946; acting dean, Graduate Coll., State U., 1921-22. Fellow A.A.A.S., Am. Acad. Arts and Scis., Ia. Acad. Sci., Am. Phys. Soc. (pres. 1949) Am. Acoustic Soc.; mem. Soc. for Promotion Engring. Edn., Am. Optical Soc., Nat. Acad. Scis., Am. Assn. Physics Tchrs. (Oersted medalist 1942), Phi Beta Kappa, Sigma Xi (pres. 1930-32), Phi Kappa Phi, Phi Kappa Sigma, Phi Kappa Psi. Author: introductory Acoustics, 1933; Theoretical Acoustics (with R. B. Lindsay), 1930. Contbr. to current research in physics, upon radiation, archtl. acoustics, sound diffraction, liquid structure. Home: 1010 Woodlawn, Iowa City, Ia. Died Aug. 16, 1956.

STEWART, JAMES CHRISTIAN, engring. contractor; b. Kingston, Ont., Can., Sept. 16, 1865; s. James and Martha (Lyall) S.; brought to U.S. in childhood; ed. pub. and high schs.; student prep. sch. of Washington U., St. Louis; m. Amelia Cora Breden, Sept. 27, 1885 (died Oct. 3, 1934); children—Alexandra (Mrs. William Woods Plankington), Fanniebelle (Mrs. C. P. Ellis, Jr.), James Breden (dec.). Began in employ of Todd & Stanley, St. Louis, 1885; entered contracting business as v.p. with father and brother, as James Stewart & Co., Inc., 1892-1920, pres. with hdqrs. in N.Y. City, since 1920; rebuilt Galveston (Tex.) waterfront after storm of 1899; built British Westinghouse Works at Manchester, Savoy Hotel in London; reconstructed Mersey Tunnel, Liverpool, and a large part of the London underground ry. systems; designed first woven cable submarine mats at mouths of Thames and Humber rivers; built N.Y. Central office bldg., 60 Wall Tower (3d tallest bldg. in world), Interstate Commerce and Dept. of Labor bldgs., Washington, D.C., State Capitol bldgs. at Salt Lake, Utah; also (during World War) a shipyard and many govt. bldgs. in the U.S. and France; dredged 65 miles of N.Y. Barge Canal; etc. Chairman of board James Stewart & Co. of N.J., James Stewart & Co., Inc., of N.Y., Canadian Stewart Co., Ltd.; dir. Stewart Realty Co., Stewart Land Co. of Pittsburgh, Continental Baking Corp. Mem. The Pilgrims. Decorated Grand Comdr. Officers of the Crown (Italy), 1925. Democrat. Presbyn. Clubs: N.Y. Yacht, N.Y. Athletic, Appawamis Country. Home: 79 E. 79th St., Office: 200 Park Av., New York, N.Y. Died Jan. 17, 1942.

STEWART, JOHN QUINCY, physicist, generalist; born at Harrisburg, Pennsylvania, on September 10, 1894; s. John Quincy and Mary Caroline (Liebendorfer) S.; B.S., Princeton U., 1915, Ph.D., 1919; m. Lillian V., d. John Howell Westcott, June 17, 1925; 1 son, John Westcott. Engineer dept. of development and research, Am. Telephone & Telegraph Co., New York, investigating speech and hearing, 1919-21; designed the first "electrical voice"; with dept. of astronomy, Princeton University, 1921-63, asso. prof. astron. physics, 1927-63; prof. metaphysics of sci. Prescott Coll., 1966-72. Organized small party which successfully observed longest modern total solar eclipse, from S.S. Steelmaker in the Pacific, June 8, 1937; duration was more than seven minutes. Served with 29th Engrs., A.E.F. (sound ranging), 1918-19. Fellow American Physical Society, Am. Geog. Soc. (hon.); member Am. Astron. Soc., American Assn. Univ. Profs. (nat. 1st v.p., 1940-41), Phi Beta Kappa, Sigma Xi. Clubs: Princeton (New York); Nassau (Princeton); Randolph Mountain. Presbyterian. Author: Astronomy (with H. N. Russell and R. S. Dugan), 1927, 1938; Navigation (with N. L. Pierce), 1944; Coasts, Waves, and Weather, 1945. Contributor research results in physics, astronomy, nav., meteorol., demography; organized studies in social physics, metaphysics. Home: Sedona AZ Died Mar. 19, 1972; buried Sedone AZ

STEWART, JOHN TRUESDALE, civil engr.; b. Loda, Ill., Jan. 13, 1868; s. William R. and Nancy (Barr) S.; B.S., in C.E., U. of Ill., 1893, C.E., 1909; m. Ida Belle Wilson, Jan. 1, 1900. In pvt. practice to 1897; field asst., topographic corps, U.S. Geol. Survey, 1898-1903; drainage engr., U.S. Dept. Agr., 1904-08; prof. and chief div. of agrl. engring., U. of Minn., 1908-17. Cadet officer U. of Ill.; bvt. capt. Ill. N.G., 1893; organized and drilled company for Spanish-Am. War, 1898, but not called into service; maj., Engrs. U.S.R., on active duty, May 26, 1917; lt. col. engrs., Oct. 18, 1918; hon. disch., Oct. 13, 1919; lt. col. E.O.R.C., Jan. 31, 1920, col. Jan. 14, 1924. In charge of ednl. activities in schools and colleges for Portland Cement Assn., Jan. 1921-Mar. 1922; consulting engr., drainage and wet land development, Apr. 1922—. Presbyn. Senior author of Engineering on the Farm. Home: St. Paul, Minn. Died June 9, 1928.

STEWART, MORRIS ALBION, coll. dean; b. Bath, Me., Apr. 8, 1902; s. Bertram R. and Lila (Robinson) S.; B.S., University of New Hampshire, 1924, LL.D., 1958; M.S., Cornell University, 1926; Ph.D., 1929; m. Marjorie Cathryn McFarlin, June 25, 1934; children—Donald Rogers, Michael Osborne. Jr. biologist U.S. Biol. Survey, 1924-26; instr. biology U. Rochester, 1926-27, The Rice Inst., 1927-35; cons. orthopedics Jefferson Davis Hosp., Houston, 1932-34, cons. pathologist, 1934-36; cons. charge research and bacteriology Meth. Hosp., 1932-35; from asst. prof. to prof. parasitology U. Cal. at Berkeley 1935—, asst. and asso. dean graduate division, 1945-55, dean, 1956—; honorary professor of parasitology Instituto Oriental de Biologia, Santa Cruz de la Sierra, Bolivia, 1944, consultant parasitologist Corporation Boliviana de Fomento, 1944. Dir. Internat. House, Newman Club, Herrick Hosp. Clinics, Berkeley, Internat. Hospitality Center, Coop. Research Found., San Francisco; adv. ednl. com. Conselho Nacional de Pesquisas, Brazil; member bd. gov. Internat. Science Foundation. Decorated Cavaliere, Order of Merit (Italy); Officer, The Royal Order of North Star (Sweden). Fellow A.A.A.S., Entomol. Soc. Am., Tex. Acad. Sci., Houston Acad. Medicine (hon.); mem. Am. Soc. Tropical Medicine, Tex. (past pres.), Pacific Coast (past v.p., pres.) entomol. socs., Soc. Am. Bacteriologists, Am. Pub. Health Assn., Entomol. Soc. Washington, Am. Acad. Polit. and Social Sci., Am. Soc. Parasitologists, Inst. Internat. Edn. (adv. com.), International House Association (chairman exec. com. bd. trustees N.Y.), International Science Foundation (treas., gov.), Sigma Xi, Phi Sigma, Delta Omega. Republican. Episcopalian. Clubs: Faculty (Berkeley); Vicious Circle, Leonardo da Vinci society (San Francisco). Home: 2673 Hilgard Av., Berkeley 9, Cal. Died Oct. 16, 1961.

STEWART, OSCAR MILTON, univ. prof.; b. Neosho, Mo., Nov. 3, 1869; s. Oliver Mills and Eleanor (Bell) S.; Ph.B., DePauw Univ., 1892, D.Sc., 1928; Ph.D., Cornell Univ., 1897; m. M. Estelle Williams, June 23, 1899 (dec.); 1 son, Lawrence Williams (dec.). Prof. physics and chemistry, Baker U., 1892-94; fellow, 1895-96, asst. in physics, 1896-98, instr. physics, 1898-1901, Cornell Univ.; asst. prof., U. of Missouri, 1901-05, prof., 1905-40, emeritus prof. physics since 1940. Fellow A.A.A.S., Am. Physical Soc.; mem. Soc. Promotion Engring. Edn., Am. Assn. Physics Teachers, Am. Assn. Univ. Prof., Phi Kappa Psi, Phi Beta Kappa, Sigma Xi, Tau Beta Pi. Author of numerous research articles in Physical Rev. since 1897, also a text book of coll. physics and joint author of a textbook of physics for secondary schs. Home: 211 Westmount Av., Columbia, Mo. *

STEWART, PHILO PENFIELD, missionary, coll. ofcl., inventor; b. Sherman, Conn., July 6, 1798; s. Philo and Sarah (Penfield) S.; m. Eliza Capen, 1878. Apptd. asst. missionary among Choctaws at Mayhew, Miss. by Am. Bd. Commrs. for Fgn. Missions, 1821; with John J. Shipherd evolved a plan of combination community and sch. whereby students could defray all their expenses by working, 1832, founder Oberlin (O.) Coll. (opened 1833), treas., gen. mgr., 1833-36; patented Oberlin Stove, 1834, began mfg. stoves, Troy, N.Y.; proceeds of stove patents went to aid Oberlin Coll. Lived Troy, N.Y. Died Oberlin, Dec. 13, 1868.

STICKNEY, SAMUEL CROSBY, engineer; b. at Stillwater, Minn., Nov. 19, 1865; s. Alpheus Beede (q.v.) and Kate W. H. (Hall) S.; C.E., Mass. Inst. Tech., 1886; married. Entered ry. service, 1886, as locating engr., Chicago, St. Paul & Kansas City Ry. (now C.G.W. Ry.), since which he was supt. constrn., engr. maintenance of way, asst. to pres., gen. mgr. and v.-p. and gen. mgr. Chicago Great Western Ry., until Mar., 1909; resigned to engage in pvt. business. Home: White Bear Lake, Minn. Office: 50 Church St., New York.

STIEGLITZ, ALFRED, (steg'lits), photographer, editor; b. Hoboken, N.J., Jan. 1, 1864; s. Edward and Hedwig (Werner) S.; ed. private and pub. schs. and City Coll., New York, 1879-81; studied mech. engring., 1881-84, photo-chemistry and photography, 1884-88, Berlin Polytechnic; chemistry, U. of Berlin, 1889-90; m. Emmeline Obermeyer, Nov. 16, 1893; 1 dau., Katherine Stearns; m. 2d, Georgia O'Keeffe, Dec. 11, 1924. Returned to New York, 1890; in photo-engraving business 3 yrs., experimenting in 3-color work, etc.; retired in 1895; editor Am. Amateur Photographer, 1892-96; founded, 1897, mgr. and editor, 1897-1903, Camera Notes (photog jour.); editor and pub. Camera Work (photog. quarterly) since Jan. 1, 1903. Hon. fellow Royal Photog. Soc., London, Vienna Camera Club (Austria); hon. mem. L'Effort (Brussels, Belgium), Photog. Club (Vienna, Austria), Photog. Soc., Hamburg, Germany, Am. Photog. Soc., Phila. Photog. Soc., Chicago Soc.; hon. v.p. Soc. of American Painters and Sculptors; dir. and founder Photo-Secession (nat. orgn. of pictorial photographers); founder of Little Galleries of the Photo-Secession (eventually known as "291"); famed for introducing modern Am. and European Art, 1905-17; founder, 1925, dir. Intimate Gallery; founder, 1929, Am. Place. With his series of "Equivalents" has demonstrated photography as an objectified philosophy. Has won over 150 medals for photography, Paris, London, Vienna, Berlin, Calcutta, New York, etc.; received, as dir. of the Photo-Secession, at Turin International Art Exhibition, the King of Italy's special prize for collection of Am. work exhibited. Has written photographic and scientific articles to tech. and art jours. the world over. Co-editor of "291" (monthly, devoted to development of art, literature and music). Awarded Progress medal, 1924, of Royal Photographic Soc. of London. Home: Lake George, N.Y. Died July 13, 1946.

STIEGLITZ, JULIUS (OSCAR), chemist; b. Hoboken, N.J., May 26, 1867; s. Edward and Hedwig (Werner) S.; brother of Alfred S.; grad. Real-gymnasium, Karlsruhe, Germany, 1886; A.M., Ph.D., U. of Berlin, 1889; (hon. D.Sc., Clark University, 1909; Ch.D., University of Pittsburgh, 1916); m. Anna Stieffel, of Karlsruhe, Germany, Aug. 27, 1891 (died 1933); m. 2d, Mary M. Rising, Aug. 30, 1934. With U. of Chicago, 1892—, prof. chemistry, 1905-33, prof. emeritus; dir. analytical chemistry, 1909-15, dir. univ. labs., 1912-24, chmn. chemistry dept., 1915-33. Hitchcock lecturer, U. of Calif., 1909; Dohme lecturer, Johns Hopkins, 1924; Fenton lecturer, U. of Buffalo, 1933. Fellow Am. Acad. Arts and Sciences, Washington Acad. of Sciences, A.A.A.S. (v.p.). Member Internat. Commn. Annual Tables Constants, 1915-21. Mem. div. of chemistry, Nat. Research Council, 1917-19 (chmn. com. synthetic drugs, 1917-19; v. chmn. div. of chemistry, 1919-21); spl. expert Public Health Service, 1918—. Willard Gibbs medal, 1923. Home: Chicago, Ill. Died Jan. 10, 1937.

STILES, CHARLES WARDELL, zoölogist; b. Spring Valley, N.Y., May 15, 1867; s. Rev. Samuel Martin and Elizabeth (White) S.; ed. Wesleyan U., Conn., 1885-86; Collège de France, 1886-87; U. of Berlin, 1887-89, U. of Leipzig, 1889-90; Trieste Zoöl. Sta., 1891; Pasteur Inst. and Collège de France, 1891; A.M., Ph.D., Leipzig, 1890; hon. M.S., 1896, D.Sc., 1906, Wesleyan U.; LL.D., U. of N.C., 1912; hon. M.D., Richmond, Va., Coll., 1913; D.Sc., Yale, 1915; m. Virginia, d. of Hon. Lewis Baker, June 1897. Zoölogist, 1891-92, consulting zoölogist, 1902-04, Bur. Animal Industry, U.S. Dept. Agr.; prof. of zoölogy, U.S.P.H.S., 1902-30; asst. surgeon general (res.), U.S.P.H.S., 1919-30, medical dir. same, 1930-31; prof. medical zoölogy, Georgetown U., 1892-1906; spl. lecturer on same, Army Med. Sch., 1894-1902, Johns Hopkins, 1897-1937, Navy Med. Sch., 1902—; hon. custodian helminthological collections, U.S. Nat. Mus., 1893-1931; sec. advisory com. Smithsonian Table at Naples Zoöl. Sta., 1894—. U.S. Govt. del. Internat. Zoöl. Congresses, Leyden, 1895, Cambridge, 1898, Berlin, 1901, Berne, 1904, Boston, 1907, Gratz, 1910, Monaco, 1913, Budapest, Hungary, 1927, Padua, 1930; sec., 1898-1936, Internat. Commn. on Zoöl. Nomenclature; sec., 1910-27, Internat. Commn. on Med. Zoölogy; detailed as agrl. and scientific attaché U.S. Embassy, Berlin, Germany, 1898-99; scientific sec. Rockefeller commn. for eradication of hookworm disease, 1909-14. Associate Smithsonian, 1931—; prof. zoölogy, Rollins College (winter faculty), 1931-38. Mem. many Am. and European scientific and medical societies; elected, 1892, successor to Joseph Leidy as foreign corr. Société de Biologie, France; elected 1896, fgn. corr. Académie de Médecine, France; 1899, corr. mem. Zoöl. Soc., London. Author: Trichinosis in Germany, 1901; Index Catalogue of Medical and Veterinary Zoölogy from 1902 (continuing publ.); The Cattle Ticks (Ixodoidea) of the United States, 1902; Emergency Report on Surra, 1902; Report on Hookworm Disease (Uncinariasis) in the United States, 1903; Illustrated Keys to Trematode and Cestode Parasites of Man; Trematoda, 1908; Taxonomic Value of Stigmal Plates in Ixodoidea, 1910; Watsonius Watsoni, 1910; Cestoda, 1912; Nematoda, 1920; Studies on Intestinal Parasites (especially Amoebae) in Man, 1923; Key-Catalogue of the Protozoa Worms, Crustacea, Arachnoids, and Insects of Man, Primates, Chiroptera, Insectivora, Carnivora, 1925-32; Early History of the Hookworm Campaign in Our Own Southern U.S., 1939. Home: Washington, D.C. Died Jan. 24, 1941.

STILES, PERCY GOLDTHWAIT, physiologist; b. Newtonville, Mass., July 1, 1875; s. Edmund Ely and Elmina Catherine (Kendall) S.; S.B., Mass. Inst. Tech., 1897; Ph.D., Johns Hopkins, 1902; m. Caroline Leonora Holden, Sept. 6, 1904. Instr. physiology, Bellevue Hosp. Med. Coll., New York, 1902-03; later instr. physiology, Mass. Inst. Tech., and instr. and prof., Simmons Coll., Boston; asst. prof. physiology, Harvard. Fellow Am. Acad. Arts and Sciences. Conglist. Author: Nutritional Physiology, 1912. Home: Newtonville, Mass. Died 1936.

STILL, ALFRED, elec. engr.; b. Gloucestershire, Eng., Jan. 28, 1869; s. Edmund Alexander and Julie Emma (Ott) S.; student College de Dieppe, France, 1879-85; grad. Finsbury Tech. Coll., London, 1889; m. Melita F.L. Gilbert, Sept. 17, 1902; children—Edmund Neville, Reginald Gilbert, Arthur John, Richard Waller. Designer of elec. machinery Edison & Swan Co., Manchester, Eng., 1890-99; chief engr. and mng. dir. Cowans, Ltd., Manchester, 1899-1911; chief elec. engr. Lake Superior Corp., Ont., Can., 1911-13; prof. elec. engring., Purdue Univ., 1913-34, retired. Fellow Am. Inst. Elec. Engrs.; mem. Institn. of Elec. Engineers (British), Eta Kappa Nu, Sigma Xi, Tau Beta Pi. Author: Polyphase Currents, 1906; Overhead Electric Power Transmission, 1913; Principles of Electrical Design, 1916; Electric Power Transmission, 1927; Principles of Transformer Design, 1919; Elements of Electrical Design, 1932; Soul of Amber, 1944; Soul of Lodestone, 1946; Communication Through the Ages, 1946. Contbr. on tech. and engring. subjects. Home: 6038 34th Av. N.E., Seattle 5 WA

STILLMAN, JOHN MAXSON, chemist; b. New York, Apr. 14, 1852; s. Dr. Jacob Davis Babcock and Caroline B. (Maxson) S.; Ph.B., U. of Calif., 1874, Ph.D., 1885 (LL.D., 1916); m. Emma Rodolph, June 1878. Asst. in chemistry, U. of Calif., 1873-75; student in chemistry, Strassburg and Würzburg, 1875-76; instr. organic and gen. chemistry, U. of Calif., 1876-82; chemist Boston and Am. Sugar Refining cos., 1882-91; prof. chemistry, 1891-1917, v.p., 1913-17, emeritus, 1917, Leland Stanford Jr. U. Asst. ednl. dir. S.A.T.C., 1918. Author: Paracelsus, as Physician, Chemist and Reformer, 1920. Died Dec. 13, 1923.

STILLMAN, THOMAS BLISS, chem. engr.; b. Plainfield, N.J., May 24, 1852; s. Dr. Charles H. and Mary Elizabeth (Starr) S.; B.S., Rutgers Coll., 1873, M.Sc., 1876; Ph.D., Stevens Inst. Tech., 1883; grad. Fresenius Lab., Weisbaden, Germany, 1877; m. Emma Louise Pomplitz, Nov. 3, 1881. Instr. analyt. chemistry, 1874-76, and 1881-86, prof. analyt. chemistry, 1886-1903, prof. engring. chemistry, 1903-09, Stevens Inst. Tech.; retired upon Carnegie Pension Fund, 1909. Apptd. state insp. of oils, N.J., 1884; examiner in chemistry Municipal Civil Service, N.Y., 1911—. City chemist, Jersey City, and Bayonne, N.J.; chemist to Medical Milk Commn., Newark. Editor The Stevens Institute Indicator, 1895. Author: Engineering Chemistry, 1897, 1901, 05, 10. Home: Hoboken, N.J. Died Aug. 10, 1915.

STILLWELL, LEWIS, BUCKLEY, electrical engr.; b. Scranton, Pa., Mar. 12, 1863; s. Richard and Margaret (Snyder) S.; student Wesleyan U., Conn., 1882-84; E.E., Lehigh U., 1885, M.S., 1907, D.Sc., 1914; Sc.D., Wesleyan, 1907; m. Mary Elizabeth Thurston, Apr. 19, 1892; 1 son, Richard. Asst. electrician, Westinghouse Elec. & Mfg. Co., 1886-90; chief elec. engr., same, 1890-97; elec. dir. Niagara Falls Power Co., 1897-1900; in practice as cons. elec. engr., New York, 1900—; cons. engr. Manhattan Elev. Ry. Co. (electrification of elevated lines in N.Y. City), 1899-1906; elec. dir. Rapid Transit Subway Constr. Co., 1900-09; cons. engr. Hudson Cos., 1905-13; mem. Erie R.R. elec. commn., 1906; cons. engr. United Rys. & Elec. Co. of Baltimore, 1906-20, Interborough Rapid Transit Co., 1909-20, N.Y.,N.H.&H. R.R. Co. (Hoosac Tunnel electrification), 1910-11, N.Y., Westchester & Boston Ry. Co., 1911-15, Lehigh Navigation Elec. Co., 1912-18; consulting engr. Holland Vehicular Tunnels, 1924-27; cons. engr. Port of New York Authority, 1927—. Life trustee, Princeton U., 1918—; mem. bd. dirs. Chamber of Commerce, U.S.A., 1921-23. Home: Princeton, N.J. Died Jan. 19, 1941.

STIMPSON, WILLIAM, naturalist, conchologist; b. Roxbury, Mass., Feb. 14, 1832; s. Herbert H. and Mary (Brewster) S.; attended Boston Latin Sch., 1848; studied under Louis Agassiz; M.D., Columbia, 1860; m. Annie Gordon, July 28, 1864, 3 children. First naturalist to employ deep sea dredging in work; apptd. to North Pacific Exploring Expdn., 1852-56, began classification of immense amount of data gathered during those years, with hdqrs. in Smithsonian Instn., Washington, D.C., 1856; results published in Smithsonian Miscellaneous Collections, Vol. XLIX, 1907; became dir. Chgo. Acad. Sciences, 1865, gathered collections and great manuscripts from naturalists all over the world; became youngest mem. Nat. Acad. Sciences, 1868; never recovered from loss of bldg. and its treasures when Chgo. Acad. Sciences was destroyed by great Chgo. Fire of 1871, Author (written in Latin): A Revision and Synonymy of the Mestaceous Mollusks of New England, 1851; Notes on North American Crustacea, 1859. Died Ilchester, Md., May 26, 1872.

STIMSON, ARTHUR MARSTON, public health officer; b. Rome, N.Y., Nov. 30, 1876; s. William Hamilton and Anna Braddock (Gallup) S.; M.D., Long Island Coll. Hosp., 1898; m. Sarah Boyd, Dec. 9, 1903;children—Elspeth (dec.), Jean, William Hamilton, Allan Braddock. Commd. asst. surgeon Pub. Health Service of U.S., July 1902; passed asst. surgeon, Aug. 1907; surgeon, Aug. 1914; asst. dir. Hygienic Lab., Washington, D.C.; detail sanitation officer U.S. Navy, 1917-19; asst. surg. gen., Pub. Health Service, 1922, med. dir., 1930; directing studies of heart disease at Nat. Inst. of Health, Washington, D.C., 1931-42; retired. Mem. Am. Public Health Assn., A.M.A. Author: Facts and Problems of Rabies; also brief history of bacteriological investigations in Public Health Service, Communicable Diseases, and other public health writings. Home: 414 Raymond St., Chevy Chase 15 MD

STINE, CHARLES MILTON ALTLAND, chemist; b. Norwich, Conn., Oct. 18, 1882; s. Milton Henry and Mary Jane (Altland) S.; A.B., Gettysburg (Pa.) Coll., 1901; B.S., 1903, A.M., 1904, M.S., 1905, Sc.D., 1926; Ph.D., Johns Hopkins, 1907; LL.D., Cumberland U., 1932, Temple U., 1941; Sc.D., U. Del., 1947; m. Martha E. Molly, Feb. 3, 1912; children—Mary Elizabeth (Mrs. F. Samuel Wilcox, Jr.), Barbara Ann (Mrs. J. Seth H. Cruice). Became prof. chemistry Md. Coll. for Women, 1904; fellow Johns Hopkins, 1906-07; joined staff E. I.

du Pont de Nemours & Co. (Eastern Lab.), July 1, 1907, in charge organic chem. work, 1909-16; trans. to Wilmington office as head organic div., 1917, made asst. dir. chem. dept., 1919, chem. dir. May 1, 1924-30, v.p. and dir. since 1930, mem. exec. com. 1930-45, retired 1945. Cons. to Chem. Warfare Service since 1942; mem. adv. com., dept. of chem. engring., Princeton U.; mem. bd. trustees The Delaware Hosp., Wilmington, Del.; chmn. bd. trustees Gettysburg Coll.; mem. bd. trustees Tower Hill Sch., Wilmington, U. Del.; mem. exec. com. bd. trustees U. Del.; dir. Acad. Natural Sciences of Phila. Perkin Medalist of Soc. of Chem. Industry, 1940. Mem. Directors of Industrial Research Assn., Am. Chem. Soc. (councillor; mem. com. to cooperate with C. W. S.), Am. Inst. Chem. Engrs. (councillor and pres. 1947), Franklin Inst. (life), Phi Beta Kappa, Gamma Alpha, Tau Beta Pi. Hon. mem. Soc. Chem. Industry, Princeton Engring. Assn., Chem. Engring. Soc. of South Africa, Chem. Engring. Soc. Australia. Clubs: Wilmington Country, du Pont Country (Wilmnigton); Chemical (Johns Hopkins U.); Wilmington (Del.); Everglades (Palm Beach, Fla.). Developer numerous processes and products, many patented, in connection with high explosives, propellent powder, dyes, artificial leather, varnishes, paints, and other inorganic and organic chem. processes and products. Home: 1100 Greenhill Av. Address: E. I. du Pont de Nemours & Co., Wilmington, Del. Died May 28, 1954.

STINSON, JOHN TURNER, agriculturist; b. Pierceton, Ind., Sept. 5, 1865; s. Archibald D. and Elizabeth (Doke) S.; B.S., Ia. State Coll. Agr. and Mech. Arts, 1890; m. Roberta Trott, Aug. 15, 1894; children—Rebecca (wife of Dr. Ben M. Bull), Benjamin A., Ruth Elizabeth (Mrs. G.W. Billmyer, Jr.), John T. Horticulturist, Ark. Agrl. Expt. Sta., Fayetteville, 1891-1900; prof. horticulture, U. of Ark., 1895-1900; dir. Mo. State Fruit Expt. Sta., Mountain Grove, 1900-03; supt. pomology, in charge fruit exhibits, La. Purchase Expn., St. Louis, Mo., 1903-04; agrl. agt., Mo.P. R.R. Co., 1906-07; sec. Mo. State Fair, 1908-16; with extension forces, U. of Mo., 1917; sec. Am. Swine Growers Assn., 1918; sec. Southeast Mo. Agrl. Bur., 1919-21; dir. agrl. development, Mo. P.R.R. Co., St. Louis, 1921-45. Member Kappa Alpha. Democrat. Mem. Christian (Disciples) Ch. Mason. Home: 6820 Delmar Blvd. Office: Missouri Pacific Bldg., St Louis MO

STIRTON, RUBEN ARTHUR, paleontologist; b. Muscotah, Kan., Aug. 20, 1901; s. John and Cora (Brock) S.; A.B., U. Kan., 1925; A.M., U. Cal., 1931, Ph.D., 1940; m. Lillian M. Miller, Dec. 23, 1927; 1 son, John Arthur. Mammalogist, Donald R. Dickey expdns. to El Salvador, Central Am., 1925-27; curator fossil mammals, mus. paleontologist U. Cal. at Berkeley, 1928—, lectr. paleontology, 1941-45, asso. prof. paleontology, 1945-51, prof. paleontology, 1951—, chmn. dept., 1949-55, dir. mus., 1949—; hon. curator mammal collection, U. Cal. at Los Angeles, 1941—; fellow Guggenheim Meml. Found., 1944-45, Fulbright scholar, 1953; prof. Miller Inst. basic research in sci., 1958-60. Mem. Geol. Soc. Am., Cal. Acad. Sci., Soc. Certebrate Paleontologists, Paleontology Soc., Am. Soc. Mammalogists, Soc. Study Evolution, Soc. Systematic Zoology. Home: 3611 Powell Dr., Lafayette, Cal. Office: U. Cal., Berkeley 4, Cal. Died June 14, 1966; buried Chapel of Memories, Oakland, Cal.

STOCKARD, CHARLES RUPERT, biologist, anatomist; b. Washington Co., Miss., Feb. 27, 1879; s. Dr. Richard Rupert and Ella Hyde (Fowlkes) S.; B.Sc., Miss. Agrl. and Mech. Coll., 1899, M.S., 1901; Ph.D., Columbia, 1906; M.D., U. of Würzburg, 1922; Sc.D., Univ. of Cincinnati, 1920; studied Carnegie Inst. Lab. for Tropical Biology, Dry Tortugas, Fla.; Naples Zoöl. Sta.; also visited chief zoöl. and anat. labs. of Europe; m. Mercedes Müller, of Munich, Germany, Aug. 14, 1912; children—Marie Louise, Richard Robert. Commandant and acting prof. mil. science and tactics, Miss. Agrl. and Mech. Coll., 1898-1900, Jefferson Mil. Coll., 1900-03; asst. in zoöl. dept., Columbia, 1905, 06; asst. in embryology and histology, 1906-08, instr. of comparative morphology, 1908-09, asst. prof. embryology and exptl. morphology, 1909-11, prof. anatomy, June 1911—, Cornell Med. Coll.; also investigator for Huntington Fund for Cancer Research, 1908—; pres. board Rockefeller Inst. Medical Research; DeLamar lecturer, Johns Hopkins, 1925, Harrington lecturer, U. of Buffalo, 1926, Beaumont Foundation lecturer, Detroit, 1927, Lane lecturer, Stanford, 1930, Potter Memorial lecturer, Jefferson Medical College, 1934; trustee Marine Biol. Lab., Woods Hole, Long Island Biol. Assn., Bermuda Sta. for Biol. Research. Mng. editor Am. Jour. of Anatomy; editor Jour. Experimental Zoölogy, Am. Anatomical Memoirs. Fellow A.A.A.S. (v.p. 1933), N.Y. Zoöl. Soc., N.Y. Acad. Medicine. Author: Origin of Blood, 1915; Hormones and Structural Development, 1927; The Physical Basis of Personality, 1931. Home: New York, N.Y. Died Apr. 7, 1939.

STOCKBRIDGE, HORACE EDWARD, agrl. chemist; b. Hadley, Mass., May 19, 1857; s. Levi and Joanna (Smith) S.; B.S., Mass. Agrl. Coll., 1878; student Boston U., and U. of Göttingen; Ph.D., Göttingen, 1884; m. Belle Lamar, Mar. 30, 1885; children—Basil Levi, Abigail Montague, Derry Lamar, John Sylvester. Asso. prof. chemistry, Mass. Agrl. Coll., 1884-85; prof. chemistry and geology, Imperial Coll. of Agr. and Engring., Japan, 1885-89; chief chemist Japanese Govt., 1887-89; dir. Ind. Expt. Sta., 1889; pres. N.D. Agrl. Coll., and dir. N.D. Expt. Sta., 1890-94; prof. agr., Fla. Agrl. Coll. and dir. State Agrl. Institutes of Florida, 1897-1906; editor Southern Ruralist, Atlanta, propr. Walnut Vale Farm. Mem. Nat. Bd. of Farm. Orgns., Am. Acad. Polit. and Social Science, pres. Farmers' Nat. Congress, 1916-17; mem. Nat. Agricultural War Conference. Writer of reports and mag. articles on agrl. and scientific subjects. Treas., Ga. State Rep. campaigns, 1920-24. Author: Rocks and Soils, 1888, 95, 1902; Land Teaching, 1910. Editor Southern Farm and Dairy. Address: Atlanta, Ga. Died Oct. 30, 1930.

STOCKDALE, PARIS B., geologist; b. Frankfort, Ind., Aug. 30, 1896; s. James Frank and Laura Jane (Myers) S.; A.B., Indiana U., 1919, A.M., 1921, Ph.D., 1930; grad. student, U. of Chicago, 1924-25; m. Faith Lee, June 14, 1923; 1 son, James Edgar. With Roxana Petroleum Corp., summer 1918; asst. instr. geology, Williams Coll., 1920-21; instr. geology, Ohio State U., 1921-29, asst. prof., 1929-33, asso. prof., 1933-41, instr. meteorology, Civilian Pilot Training Ground Sch., 1939-41; grad. asst., geology, U. of Chicago, 1924-25, with Ind. Geol. Survey, summers, 1925-29, Ohio Geol. Survey, summer 1930; engaged in misc. cons. work since 1930; spl. consultant Tenn. Valley Authority, 1941-44; prof. geology and head dept. geology and geography, U. of Tenn., 1941-61; vis. prof. Columbia University, summer, 1948. Mem. sub-com. on Mississipian Stratigraphy, Nat. Research Council, 1933-48; consultant A.E.C. at Oak Ridge, Tenn., 1948-58. Fellow A.A.A.S., Geol. Soc. Am., Paleontol. Soc. America, Ind. Acad. Science, Ohio Acad. Science (to 1941; vice pres., 1929-30), Tenn. Acad. Science (v.p., 1945-46, pres., 1946-47); mem. Geochemical Society, Assn. Am. Geographers, Nat. Archery Assn. (pres. 1941-43), Assn. Geology Tchrs., Phi Beta Kappa, Sigma Xi, Rotary (Knoxville, Tenn.). Author articles and chapters on stratigraphy and other geol. subjects in tech. and sci. jours. and Ency. Britannica. Mem. edit. bd., Geol. Soc. America, 1945-47. Specializes in stratigraphic and structural geology. Home: 7101 Sherwood Dr., Knoxville, Tenn. 37919. Died Mar. 18, 1962; buried Highland Meml. Cemetery, Knoxville.

STOCKWELL, JOHN NELSON, astronomical mathematician; b. Northampton, Mass., Apr. 10, 1832; s. William and Clarissa (Whittemore) S.; ed. common schs., Brecksville, O.; hon. A.M., 1862, Ph.D., 1876, Western Reserve; m. Sarah Healy, Dec. 6, 1855. Known for original investigations in astronomy. Author: Memoir on the Secular Variations of the Planetary Orbits, in Smithsonian Contributions to Knowledge, 1872; Stock and Interest Tables, 1873; Theory of the Moon's Motion, 1881; Eclipse Cycles, 1901; Sheet Tax Tables, 1903; Theory of Planetary Perturbations, and the Cosmogony of Laplace, 1904; Ocean Tides, with elaborate tables for their computation, 1919. Contbr. Am. and foreign scientific jours. Fellow Am. Acad. Arts and Sciences, A.A.A.S. Address: Cleveland, O. Died May 18, 1920.

STODDARD, JOHN TAPPAN, chemist; b. at Northampton, Mass., Oct. 20, 1852; s. William H. and Helen (Humphrey) S.; A.B., Amherst, 1874; student chemistry and physics, 1875-76; A.M., Ph.D., Göttingen, 1877; m. Mary Grover Leavitt, June 26, 1879; father of William Leavitt S. Asst. prin. Northampton High Sch., 1874-75; prof. physics and mathematics, 1878-81, chemistry and physics, 1881-97, chemistry, 1897—, Smith Coll. Author: Outline of Qualitative Analysis, 1883; Lecture Notes on General Chemistry (2 vols.), 1884, 1885; Quantitative Experiments in General Chemistry, 1908; Introduction to General Chemistry, 1910; The Science of Billiards, 1913; An Introduction to Organic Chemistry, 1914. Contbr. scientific articles and revs. to cyclos. and mags. Address: Northampton, Mass. Died Dec. 8, 1919.

STODDARD, JOSHUA C., inventor; b. Pawlet, Vt., Aug. 26, 1814; s. Nathan Ashbel and Ruth (Judson) S.; m. Lucy Maria Hersey, Jan. 23, 1845, at least 2 children. Worked on father's farm for long period, interested primarily in bee culture, honey prodn.; inventor improvements and variants on horse-drawn hay rake, recieved 16 patents; his most famous invention was steam calliope, patented 1855; organized Am. Steam Music Co., Worcester, Mass., 1855, forced out of co. by 1860; many calliopes placed on side-wheelers, other river vessels of day; received no financial benefit from most of inventions; patented a fruit-paring machine, 1901. Died Springfield, Mass., Apr. 3, 1902.

STODDARD, THOMAS A., physician, surgeon; b. Halifax, N. S., Aug. 22, 1857; s. Thomas and Elizabeth S.; ed. Dalhousie Coll., Halifax, N. S., 1877-78; grad. Mich. Univ., M. D., 1886; m. Halifax, Oct. 3, 1883, Minnie E. Lautz. Studied in Berlin under August Martin; London, under Bantock; practice limited to obstetrics and diseases of women and abdominal surgery. M. R. C. S., London; L. R. C. P., London; mem. British Med. Soc., Provincial Med. Soc. of Nova Scotia, Colo. State Med., Pueblo Co. Med., Southern Colo. Med., Pueblo Med. and Surg., Western Surg. and Gynecol. socs., and Pan-Am. Med. Congress. Has practiced in Pueblo since 1892. Extensive contributor to proc. of sceintific socs. and med. journals on obstetrics, genecology and abdominal surgery. Address: Pueblo, Colo.

STODDART, L(AURENCE) A., coll. prof., research ecologist; b. Trinidad, Colo., July 17, 1909; s. Laurence D. and Hilda (Green) S.; B.S., Colo. Agrl. Coll., 1931, M.S., 1932; Ph.D., U. of Neb., 1934; m. Ruth Young, May 28, 1932; children—Hilda Ruth, Elizabeth Ann, Laurence Charles. Teaching fellow Colo. Agrl. Coll., 1931-32; range agent U.S. Soil Conservation Serv., 1934-35; with Utah State University and Utah Expt. Sta., 1935-45, prof. and head dept. of range management, acting dean of forestry, 1942-43, 46-68; prof. and head of range mgt. dept. Tex. Agrl. and Mechanical Coll., 1945-46; chairman of the range and pasture com. Nat. Research Council 1949-62. Mem. Am. Soc. Range Mgmt. (nat. pres. 1952), Alpha Zeta, Sigma Xi, Xi Sigma Pi, Phi Kappa Phi. Republican. Episcopalian. Author: Range Management, 1943, rev. 1954; Technical Writing, 1938; rev., 1948. Contbr. articles to prof. jours.; author bulls. on range management, plant ecology, drought resistance, livestock mgt., soil conservation, animal nutrition, big game mgt. Mem. editorial staff Ecology, 1938-42; asso. editor Jour. of Forestry, 1946-50; mem. editorial bd. Jour. of Range Mgmt., 1948-50. Home: Logan UT Died July 17, interred Logan City Cemetery Logan UT

STOEK, HARRY HARKNESS, mining engr.; b. Washington, D.C., Jan. 16, 1866; s. Jacob F. and Susan (Lear) S.; B.S., Lehigh U., 1887, E.M., 1888; m. Miriam Ricketts, Dec. 20, 1894. Asst. engr. Susquehanna Coal Co., Wilkes-Barre, 1888-90; instr. in mining, metallurgy and geology, Lehigh U., 1890-93; asst. prof. mining engring., Pa. State Coll., 1893-97; editor Mines and Minerals, Scranton, Pa., 1897-1909; prof. mining engring. and head of dept., U. of Ill., 1909—. Sec. Ill. Mine Rescue Commn.; mem. Ill. Mining Investigation Commn. Republican. Episcopalian. Author: The Anthracite Coal Field, 1900; Economic History of Anthracite; Subsidence in Mining; Education of Mine Employees; The Storage of Coal. Also various bulletins. Address: Urbana, Ill. Died Mar. 1, 1923.

STOKES, JOSEPH, JR., physician; b. Moorestown, N.J., Feb. 22, 1896; s. Joseph and Mary (Emlen) S.; student Haverford Coll., 1912-16, Sc.D. (honorary), 1952; M.D., U. Pa., 1920; Med. Sc.D. (honorary), 1963; m. to Frances D. Eikitnon, Mar. 24, 1921; children—Jean Frances, Joseph, III, Donald E., Eleanor. Instr. U. of Pa. Med. Sch., 1923-24, instr. pediatrics, 1924-28, asso. pediatrics, 1928-31, Wm. H. Bennett asst. prof., 1931-33, asst. prof. pediatrics, 1933-36, asso. prof., 1936-38, William H. Bennett prof. pediatrics, 1939-62, emeritus professor; asso. physician in chief, Children's Hospital, 1936-38, physician in chief, 1939-63; dir. pediatric service, Abington Hospital, 1930-39; chief pediatric service, Hosp. of U. of Pa., 1939-62; director medical education Burlington County Meml. Hosp.; consultant Merck & Company. Hon. consul gen. Phila. for Govt. of Japan, 1967-72. Dir. Commd. Measles and Mumps Bd. for the Investigation and Control of Epidemic Diseases; cons. to surgeon gen., U.S. Army; consultant to secretary of war; mem. subcom. on maternity care and child health Office Fgn. Relief and Rehabilitation, U.S. State Dept.; mem. U.S. com. U.N. International Children's Emergency Fund; mem. bd. dirs. Phila. World Affairs Council; mem. commission on liver diseases, Armed Forces Epidemiological Bd.; mem. com. on blood and blood derivatives, NRC, mem. subcom. on plasma; nat. com. 1960 White House Conf. Children and Youth. Mem. expert adv. panel of the WHO; chmn. commn. on plasma fractionation Protein Foundation, Recipient Medal of Freedom; James E. Bruce medal, A.C.P., 1962; John Howland medal, Am. Pediatric Soc., 1962; Gordon Wilson medal Am. Clin. and Climatol Association. Made nutrition survey of unoccupied France for Am. Friends Service Committee, 1940. Director Pocono Lake Preserve; co-chairman joint committee on public health and preventive medicine, Coll. of Physicians and Philadelphia County Medical Society; mem. medical advisory bd., Visiting Nurse Soc.; mem. Sydeham Coterie, Interurban Clinical Club. Mem. bd. dirs., Philadelphia Child Guidance Clinic, Phila. Child Health Soc. Was co-chmn. for Pa. Am. Acad. Pediatrics. Trustee Woods Schs., Haverford Coll., Children's Seashore House. Fellow Philadelphia Coll. Physicians (council); mem. Wistar Association, A.M.A. (mem. council Pharmary and Chemistry), Am. Philos. Soc., Am. Pediatric Soc. (pres. 1958-59), Assn. Am. Physicians, Soc. Am. Microbiologists, Phila. County Med. Soc., Soc. Pediatric Research (one of founders), John Morgan Soc., Triangle Soc. of Haverford Coll., Sigma Xi, Phi Beta Kappa, Alpha Omega Alpha, Alpha Mu Pi Omega, Phi Kappa Sigma. Republican. Mem. Society of Friends. Contbr. articles to med. jours. Home: Chestnut Hill PA Died Mar. 9, 1972; buried nr. Moorestown NJ

STOLLER, MORTON JOSEPH, elec. engr., govt. ofcl.; b. N.Y.C., May 23, 1917; s. Samuel Bernard and Anna Estelle (Selman) S.; B. Elec. Engring., Coll. City N.Y., 1938; M. Elec. Engring., U. Va., 1949-52; m. Ruth Klarberg, Oct. 3, 1939; children—Peter J. and Robert N. (twins), Nancy E. With NASA, and predecessor, 1939—, head radio control and telemetering sect., 1946-47, asst. chief instrument research div., 1947-58, chief space sci. projects. Office Space Flight Devel.,

1958-60, asst. dir. satellite and sounding rocket programs, 1960-61, dep. dir. Office Applications, 1961-62, acting dir., 1962, dir., 1962—. Mem. working group telemetering Research and Devel. Bd., 1946-50, chmn. working group precision tracking radar, 1948-50; mem. pane unmanned spacecraft Aero. and Astronautics Coordinating Bd., 1960—, chmn., 1961—. Mem. Am. Inst. E.E., I.R.E., Am. Geophys. Union, Assn. Computing Machinery. Home: 6212 Bannockburn Dr., Bethesda, Md. 20034. Office: 400 Maryland Av. S.W., Washington 25. Died June 13, 1963.

STOLTZ, ROBERT BEAR, (stolts), prof. dairy technology; b. Bradford, O., Mar. 6, 1890; s. James Franklin and Ida (Bear) S.; B.S., Ohio State U., 1912; student U. of Wis., summers 1915, 16; m. Marie Cassel, June 12, 1912; children—Philip Cassel, Bonnie Marie, Susan Ann, Roberta Mary. Instr. in diarying, Ohio State U., 1912-14, asst. prof., 1914-23, prof., 1923-29, chmn. and prof. dairy technology since 1929; studied dairy conditions in New Zealand and Australia, 1937. Sec.-treas. Ohio Swiss Cheese Assn. 1918-45; sec. Nat. Cheese Assn., 1920-23, treas. 1923-25; sec. Columbus Milk Dist. Assn., 1933-45. Mem. Am. Dairy Science Assn. (pres. 1934, sec.-treas. since 1936), Acacia, Delta Theta Sigma, Gamma Sigma Delta. Republican. Mem. Community Church. Mason (33 deg., Scottish Rite). Officer in Gen. Grand Council of R. & S.M. of U.S. America. Home: 1971 Concord Rd., Columbus 12, O. Died Oct. 2, 1948; buried at Columbus, O.

STONE, ANDREW JACKSON, zoölogist; b. in Linn Co., Mo., Feb. 15, 1859; s. Granville H. and Mary C. S.; ed., in acad., Keokuk, Ia.; m. Alice K. Hoyt, of San Francisco, Nov. 19, 1905. Has traveled in almost all parts of Arctic and sub-Arctic America; sledged the extreme Arctic coast throughout entire winter, making over 3,000 miles, almost twice the distance made in one winter by any previous sledger. Is making spl. study of animal life of Far North. Has added to the list of species of large mammals of N. America: Rangifer osborni, Rangifer stonei, Rangifer granti, Ovis stonei Ursus merriami, Ovis dalli Kenai; also other animals. Address: Am. Museum of Natural History, New York.

STONE, CHARLES AUGUSTUS, elec. engr., financier; b. Newton, Mass., Jan. 16, 1867; s. Charles H. and Mary Augusta (Green) S.; S.B., Mass. Inst. Tech., 1888; hon. A.M., Harvard, 1914; m. Mary A. Leonard, June 2, 1902; children—Charles Augustus, Margaret, Whitney, Janet Elizabeth. With Edwin S. Webster organized, 1889, firm of Stone & Webster, engrs. and mgrs. public service cos.; investigated and reported on operations of pub. utility cos.; soon assumed management of such cos. for pvt. owners; later undertook engring. work and constrn. of street rys., electric light and power plants, hydro-electric plants and gas and indsl. properties, among them the power sta. of Mississippi River Power Co., at Keokuk, Ia., and transmission line to St. Louis. Firm constructed cantonment at San Antonio, Tex., enlarge U.S. Arsenal at Rock Island, Ill., built ordnance base for A.E.F. in France, besides engaging in other war constrn. work. Pres. Am. Internat. Corp., 1916-23, and aided in revival of Pacific Mail Steamship service, acquisition and development of N.Y. Shipbuilding Co., constrn. of Hog Island Shipyard and building of ships for Emergency Fleet Corp., besides large engring. and constrn. developments in S. America and elsewhere. Chmn. bd. Stone & Webster, Inc.; dir. Fed. Res. Bank of N.Y., 1919-23; dir. Stone & Webster Engring. Co., Union Pacific R.R. Co., Stone & Webster and Blodget, Incorporated, Research Corp., Stone & Webster Service Corp. Mem. corp., Mass. Inst. Tech. Home: New York, N.Y. Died Feb. 25, 1941.

STONE, CHARLES POMEROY, army officer, engr.; b. Greenfield, Mass., Sept. 30, 1824; s. Dr. Alpheus Fletcher and Fanny Lincoln (Cushing) S.; grad. U.S. Mil. Acad., 1845; m. Maria Louisa Clary, 1853; m. 2d, Annie Granier Stone, 1863; 6 children. Served as 1st lt. U.S. Army in Mexican War, 1846; resigned commn., 1856; commd. col. D.C. Volunteers, 1861, col. 14th Inf., U.S. Army, 1861, brig. gen. U.S. Volunteers, 1861; unjustly blamed for death of ex-senator Baker (col. in command at Battle of Ball's Bluff 1861) arrested 1862, imprisoned in Ft. Lafayette, released, 1862; served at Ft. Hudson and in Red River campaign; mustered out of volunteer commn., commd. col. U.S. Army; assigned to Army of Potomac, resigned, 1864; eng., supt. Dover Mining Co., Goochland County, Va., 1865-69; served in Egyptian army, 1870-83, chief of staff, lt. gen.; chief engr. Fla. Ship Canal Co., 1883-84; constructing engr. for foundations of Statue of Liberty. Died N.Y.C., Jan. 24, 1887; buried West Point, N.Y.

STONE, CHARLES WATERMAN, engr.; b. Providence, R.I., Dec. 24, 1874; s. Waterman and Emily Clark (Steere) S.; ed. U. of Kan., 3 1/2 yrs.; m. Harriet Anna Westinghouse, Sept. 4, 1902. Began with Franklin Electric Co., Kansas City, Mo., 1894; with W. S. Hill Electric Co., New Bedford, Mass., 1896-98, and Hancock Equipment Co., Boston, 1899; with Gen. Electric Co., Schenectady, N.Y., Aug. 1, 1899—, first draughting dept., later cons. engr., in charge of cons. dept., later mgr. central sta. dept., then cons. engr.; pres. Pioneer Thresher Co., Inc. Fellow Am. Inst. E.E. Republican. Episcopalian. Contbr. numerous papers to engring. assns. and lectured at various times before Engrs. Sch., Washington, D.C., Columbia U., etc. Home: Schenectady, N.Y. Died Feb. 3, 1938.

STONE, GEORGE EDWARD, botanist; b. Leicester, Mass., Sept. 6, 1860; s. Samuel Lamb and Sophia S. (McCrea) S.; B.S., Mass. Agrl. Coll., 1886; Mass. Inst. Tech., 1885-88; Ph.D., Leipzig, 1893; m. Mary Edward, d. Prof. Henry James Clark, Jan. 26, 1899. Botanist from youth; prof. botany, Mass. Agrl. Coll., 1893-1916, and plant physiologist, Mass. Agrl. Expt. Sta., 1895-1916; botanist to Mass. Bd. Agr. Fellow A.A.A.S. Home: Amherst, Mass. Died May 28, 1941.

STONE, GEORGE HAPGOOD, mining geologist; b. New York, Nov. 22, 1841; s. Rev. David and Louise (Ingalls) S.; A.B., Wesleyan U., 1868, A.M., 1871; m. Mary E. Clarke, June 18, 1871; m. 2d, Mary H. Hill, Nov. 20, 1876. Taught at Lima, 1869-72, Kent's Hill, Me., 1874-81; prof. geology, Colo. Coll., 1881-88; asst. geologist U.S. Geol. Survey. Author of monograph on glacial geology of Me. for U.S. Geol. Survey; and other geol. papers; also a work on monetary science, entitled "World Money," 1909. Inventor of a universal surveying instrument, and apparatus for the care of the helplessly ill. Address: Colorado Springs, Colo. Died Feb. 20, 1917.

STONE, HORACE GREELEY, lawyer; b. Kalamazoo County, Mich., Feb. 23, 1852; s. Horace A. and Hannah M. (Robbins) S.; grad. Kalamazoo High Sch., 1868. Employed in wholesale notion house, Kalamazoo, 1868-77, meanwhile studying law in office of U.S. Senator J. C. Burrows; removed to Chicago, and engaged in various pursuits until admitted to bar, 1878; atty. Chicago & W.I. Ry., 1878-81; pres. 1st Nat. Bank,Grand Forks, N.D., 1881-83; asst. receiver Northwestern Mfg. & Car Co., 1884-87; atty. in many corp. causes, among them the suit between 3 rys. involving 600,000 acres of land in northern Minn.; suit involving control of Duluth, Messabe & Northern R.R. and iron mines; Russell Sage suit for land grant in Minnesota; attorney for A. H. Wilder et al., St. Paul, defendants in $3,000,000 stock and double-liability suits; iron ore washing patent cases involving $40,000,000; chief counsel for Captain Oberlin M. Carter, U.S. Army, in suits to recover $500,000 by U.S. Govt.; atty. Ward will case; Detroit and Pewabic Mining Co. cases in Upper Mich.; suits involving laws seeking to break up department stores; foreclosure of "Alley L"; etc. Returned to Chicago, 1895; mem. Gurley, Stone & Wood, 1895-1906, practiced alone, 1906—. Inventor glass device preventing damage from freezing of water in engines, etc., method by which soft coal in two hours is divided into coke, by-products and gas worth over 3 times the value of the coal; methods of saving the iron ore and heat in blast furnace gas; also a spring tooth harrow, tractor wheel, auto spring wheel, concentrator for separating iron ore from sand, etc. Republican. Accompanied William H. Taft as his chief asst. throughout the entire presdl. campaign of 1908. Presbyn. Home: Chicago, Ill. Died Apr. 10, 1923.

STONE, JOHN STONE, electrical engr.; b. Dover, Va., Sept. 24, 1869; s. Gen. Charles Pomeroy and Jeannie (Stone) S.; ed. Columbia Grammar Sch., New York, 1884-86; Sch. of Mines (Columbia), 1886-88; Johns Hopkins, 1888-90; m. Sibyl Wilbur, Nov. 28, 1918. Experimentalist in laboratory, Am. Bell Telephone Co., 1890-99; gen. consulting elec. engr., 1899-1920; spl. lecturer on elec. oscillations, Mass. Inst. Tech., for a number of years; dir., v.p., and chief engr. from incorporation, 1902-08, pres. ane chief engr. June 10, 1908-10, Stone Telegraph & Telephone Co. (mfg. and leasing wireless telegraph apparatus). Has been granted over 135 U.S. patents for inventions relating to improvements in telephony and telegraphy. Read papers before Internat. Elec. Congress, St. Louis, in 1904, and Canadian Soc. Civ. Engrs., Montreal, 1905, before Soc. Wireless Tel. Engrs., 1908, 09, 10, before Wireless Inst., 1909, before Inst. of Radio Engrs., 1914-15; contbr. numerous papers on elec. subjects to scientific and technical press. Fellow Am. Acad. Arts and Sciences, A.A.A.S., Inst. of Radio Engrs. (v.p. 1913-14, pres. 1914-15, dir. 1912-18); organizer, vice chmn. Radio Engrs. Com. on National Defense; del. Internat. Elec. Congress, 1904, 2d Pan-Am. Scientific Congress, 1917; mem. advisory com. Am. Defense Society; pres. Soc. of Wireless Telegraph Engineers, 1906-09; member Franklin Institute, Alpha Delta Phi; asso. mem. Am. Inst. E.E. Awarded Edward Longstreth Medal for paper on "The Practical Aspects of the Propagation of High Frequency Waves Along Wires," by the Franklin Inst., 1913; medal of honor of Inst. of Radio Engrs. "for distinguished service in radio communication," 1923. Asso. Engr. at large dept. of development and research of Am. Tel. & Tel. Co., 1920-35. Clubs: Army and Navy (Washington); Radio Club America (hon.). Address: 1636 Torrence St., San Diego, Calif. Died May 20, 1943.

STONE, ORMOND, astronomer; b. Pekin, Ill., Jan. 11, 1847; s. Rev. Elijah and Sophia (Creighton) S.; U. of Chicago, 1866-70, A.M., 1875; m. Catharine Flagler, May 31, 1871 (died 1914); m. 2d, Mary Florence Brennan, June 9, 1915. Asst. U.S. Naval Obs., Washington, 1870-75; dir. Cincinnati Obs., 1875-82; prof. astronomy, U. of Va., and dir. Leander McCormick Obs., 1882-1912; retired on the Carnegie Foundation. Made noteworthy observations of double and variable stars, nebulae, satellites of Saturn, etc. Observed total eclipse of sun, Ia., 1869; in charge U.S. Naval Obs. eclipse expdn. to Colo., 1878, McCormick Obs. eclipse expdn. to S.C., 1900. Founder and editor Annals of Mathematics. Emeritus mem. A.A.A.S. (v.p. 1888); mem. Internat. Congress Arts and Sciences, St. Louis, 1904 (chmn. sect. astrometry); v.p. Va. State Teachers' Assn., 1902-12. Mem. and sec. Bd. Visitors to U.S.N. Obs., Washington, D.C., 1901-03. Contbr. to match. and astron. jours. Home: Clifton Station, Va. Died Jan. 17, 1933.

STONE, PHILIP CARLTON, educator, entomologist; b. Athol, Mass., Dec. 24, 1911; s. Harry Sylvester and Bernice May (Piedalue) S.; B.S., U. Mass., 1935, M.S., 1936; Ph.D., U. Ill., 1942; m. Ruth Evelyn Slabaugh, June 15, 1940; children—John Wyman, Helen Virginia, Paul Richardson, Charlotte Ruth. Lab. asst. entomology U. Ill., 1937-40; mem. faculty U. Mo., 1940-42, 46-68, prof. entomology, 1954-68, chmn. dept., 1954-68; cons. in field, 1950-68. Served to capt. AUS, 1943-46. Recipient citation research vacuum fumigation of lice U.S. Army, 1945. Fellow A.A.A.S.; mem. Entomol. Soc. Am. (pres. N.C. br. 1968), Kan. Entomol. Soc. (pres. 1967), Columbia Audubon Soc. (pres. 1968), Mo. Beekeepers Assn., Bee Research Assn., Mo. Pest Control Assn. (hon.), Sigma Xi, Phi Simga Kappa, Gamma Sigma Delta (Superior Teaching Achievement award 1965). Unitarian. Kiwanian. Author research papers. Home: Columbia MO Died Nov. 7, 1968.

STONE, RALPH WALTER, geologist; b. Camden, N.Y., Nov. 17, 1876; s. Walter Chester and Sarah Cornelia (Hosley) S.; Ph.B., Hamilton Coll., Clinton, N.Y., 1899; A.B., Harvard, 1900, A.M., 1901; hon. D.Sc., Lebanon Valley Coll., 1938; m. Mary Edna Bull, Nov. 16, 1910; children—Mary Elizabeth (Mrs. W. C. Everhart), Samuel Bull (killed in action N. Africa, Nov. 8, 1942). Geologist, U.S. Geol. Survey, 1901-21; contributing 50 repts. on geol. and mineral resources; asst. state geologist Pa. Topographic and Geol. Survey, 1922-46; state geologist, 1946; retired. Geologist on municipal water supply dam, Bogota, Colombia, 1930. Mem. Com. of Awards San Francisco Expn., 1915. Mem. Geol. Soc. Am., Geol. cal Soc. (past pres.), Harrisburg Natural History Soc. Alpha Delta Phi, Sigma Xi, Torch Club. Editor, Pa. Acad. Sci., 1926-39, pres., 1939-40. Author of Pa. State publs. on molding sands, feldspar, caves, building stones, also 250 articles in tech. and other periodicals. Home: 3115 N. Front St., Harrisburg, Pa. Died May 4, 1964.

STONE, ROBERT SPENCER, consultant radiologist; b. Chatham, Ont., Can., June 5, 1895; s. Spencer and Flora Maude (Campbell) S.; B.A., University of Toronto, 1919, M.A., 1922, M.B., 1924, M.D., 1928, LL.D. (hon.), Univ. of California, 1966; m. Willena Rose Crawford, June 24, 1924; children—Robert Spencer, Margaret Ishbol (Mrs. Richard Hager). Intern Grace Hosp., Detroit, 1924-25, asst. radiologist, 1925-28; asst. anatomy Peking (China) Med. Sch., 1919-21; asso. Rollin H. Stevens, Detroit, 1925-28; instr. radiology U. Cal., 1928-29, asst. prof., 1929-32, asso. prof., 1932-38, prof., 1938-62, now emeritus, chmn. dept. radiology, 1940-43, 46-62, dir. radiol. lab., 1951-64, now emeritus; asso. project dir. for health Metall. Project (atom bomb), U. Chgo., 1942-46, also vis. prof. roentgenology. Mem. Nat. Adv. Cancer Council, 1946-48; cons. U.S.P.H.S., 1949; mem. Nat. Com. Radiation Protection from 1946, Internat. Commn. Radiol. Protection 1953-65; mem. com. growth Nat. Research Council, 1952-56; past mem. radiol. safety adv. com. Cal. State Diaster Council. Recipient Medal for Merit for wartime activities, 1946, Gold Medal, Radiol. Soc. of N.A., 1946, Carman lectr., 1952, Janeway Medal, Am. Radium Soc., 1947, Medal for cancer control, Am. Cancer Soc., 1953, Gold Medal, Am. College of Radiology, 1959; citation and medallion United States AEC, 1964. Diplomate Am. Board of Radiology. Fellow Am. Coll. Radiology; mem. A.M.A., Radiol. Soc. N.A. (past pres.), Am. Roentgen Ray Soc., Cal. Acad. Medicine; hon. mem. Soc. de Cancerologica de Guadalajara, Coll. Physicians of Phila., Phila. Roentgen Ray Soc., Royal Soc. Medicine (London, Eng.). Author articles profl. jours. Editor: Industrial Medicine on the Plutonium Project, Vol. 20, Series 4, National Nuclear Energy Series. Home: San Francisco CA Died Dec. 16, 1966.

STONE, WARREN, physician; b. Saint Albans, Vt., Feb. 3, 1808; s. Peter and Jerusha (Stone) S.; M.D., Berkshire Med. Instn., Pittsfield, Mass., 1831; m. Malvina D. Johnson, 1843, at least 3 children including Warren. Asst. surgeon Charity Hosp., New Orleans, La., 1834, resident surgeon, 1835-39, vis. surgeon, 1839-72; cons. physician Hotel Dieu; founder (with Dr. William E. Kennedy) Maison de Sante (one of earliest pvt. hosps. in Am.), 1839; mem. staff Med. Coll. La. (now Tulane U.), 1834-72, prof., 1839-72; served as officer Confederate Army, Civil War, apptd. surgeon-gen. La.; 1st to resect part of a rib to secure permanent drainage in cases of empyema; made 1st successful cure for traumatic vertebral aneurism, 1850; responsible for 1st cure of an aneurism of 2d portion subclavian artery; made 1st use silver wire for ligation of the external iliac. Contbr. articles to New Orleans

Med. and Surg. Jour., co-editor, 1857-59. Died New Orleans, Dec. 6, 1872.

STONER, DAYTON, (ston'er), zoölogist; b. North Liberty, Ia., Nov. 26, 1883; s. Marcus and Nancy (Koser) S.; A.B., U. of Iowa, 1907, M.S., 1909, Ph.D., 1919; m. Lillian Rebecca Christianson, Aug. 3, 1912. Began as asst. in museum U. of Iowa, 1908-12, instr. in zoölogy, 1912-16, asso. in zoölogy, 1916-22, asst. prof., 1922-28; instr. ornithology and entomology U. Mich. Biol. Sta., summers, 1919-20; temp. field asst. U.S. Bur. Entomology, winters 1928-31; field ornithologist Roosevelt Wild Life Forest Exptl. Sta., summers 1928-32; state zoölogist N.Y. State Museum Albany since 1932. Conducted ornithol., entomol. and mammalol. field work in Ia., Colo., Mich., Fiji Islands, New Zealand, West Indies, Fla., New York and Vancouver Island. Fellow A.A.A.S., Ia. Acad. Science; mem. Am. Ornithol. Union, Am. Soc. Mammalogists, Wilson Ornithol. Club, Eastern Bird Band Assn., Wildlife Soc., Ia. Ornithol. Union, Sigma Xi. Author: Rodents of Iowa, 1918; Scutelleroidea of Iowa, 1920; Ornithology of Oneida Lake Region, 1932; Studies on The Bank Swallow, 1936; Wildlife Casualties on the Highways, 1936; Ten Years' Returns from Banded Bank Swallows, 1937; Temperature, Growth and Other Studies on the Eastern Phoebe, 1939; also other papers on birds, mammals, insects. Home: 399 State St. Address: N.Y. State Museum, Albany, N.Y. Died May 8, 1944.

STONER, GEORGE HIRAM, engring. exec.; b. Mt. Pleasant, Pa., Oct. 22, 1917; s. Howard M. and Bernice (Grimm) S.; B.S. in Chemistry, Westminster Coll., New Wilmington, Pa., 1938, D.Sc., 1969; postgrad. Mass. Inst. Tech., Columbia; m. Yvonne Bebie, Sept. 26, 1942; children—Renee, Peter, Michael, David. With Standard Oil Co. Ind., 1940-41; with Boeing Co. 1941-69, asst. v.p., gen. mgr. divisional planning pilotless aircraft div., 1955-58, mgr. advance projects proposal team, 1958-62, mgr. Dyna-Soar program, 1956-61, Saturn program, 1961-63, became v.p., 1962, assignment manager of aerospace division, 1964-66, vice pres., general mgr. space division, 1966-67, group v.p. aerospace, from 1967, sr. v.p. until 1971, also dir. Leader survey to review guided missiles in Europe, 1951; spl. work B-29 design, ground to air missile, B-47 bomber, Bonarc missile. Recipient Distinguished Service medal NASA, 1971. Fellow Am. Inst. Aero. and Astronautics; Am. Inst. Chemists; mem. New York Acad. Scis. (life), New Orleans C. of C. Clubs: Nat. Rocket (bd. govs.) (Washington); Internat. House, Round Table (New Orleans). Home: Mercer Island WA Died Feb. 18, 1971.

STOOKEY, BYRON, neurol. surgeon; b. Belleville, Ill., Jan. 4, 1887; s. Dr. Lyman Polk and Louise (Brumbaugh) S.; A.B., U. So. Cal., 1908; A.M., Harvard, 1909, M.D., 1913; D.Sc. Columbia U., 1959; studied univs. of Geneva, 1905-06; Vienna and Berlin, 1913-14; m. Helen Phelps Hoyt, May 11, 1929; children—John Hoyt, Lyman Brumbaugh, Byron. Began practice at Los Angeles, 1915; instr. neurology Columbia, 1919-20, asso. neurology, 1921-26, asso. prof. neurology and neurol. surgery, 1927-29, asso. prof. neurol. surgery, 1930-36, prof., 1937-38, attending surgeon, dir. neurol. surgery, 1938, prof. clin. neuro-surgery, 1939-52, emeritus prof., 1952—; dir. dept. neurol. surgery N.Y. Postgrad. Med. Sch. and Hosp., 1928-37; asst. prof. clin. surgery Cornell, 1929-35; attending neurol. surgeon N.Y. Neurol. Inst.; cons. neurol. surgeon, Meml. Hosp., Middlesex Gen. Hosp., Nassau. Hosp., Mineola, N.Y., New Rochelle Hosp., Sharon (Conn.) Hosp., Norwalk (Conn.) Gen. Hosp.; asso. cons. neurol. surg., St. Luke's. Trustee Sharon Hosp. Served as capt. Royal Army M.C., 1915-16; maj. USMC, 1917-19. Fellow A.A.A.S., A.C.S.; mem. Am. Surg. Assn., Am. Neurol. Soc., Assn. for Research in Nervous and Mental Diseases, Soc. Neurol. Surgeons (pres. 1939-40), N.Y. Acad. Medicine, N.Y. Surg. Soc., N.Y. Neurol. Soc. (pres. 1944-45), S.A.R., Sigma Chi, Nu Sigma Nu. Clubs: Harvard, University (N.Y.C.). Author: The Surgical and Mechanical Treatment of Peripheral Nerves, 1922; (with Joseph Ransohoff) Trigeminal Neuralgia, 1959; A History of Colonial Medical Education in the Province of New York with Its Subsequent Development (1767-1830), 1962; also numerous papers and publs. relating to field. Address: 455 E. 57th St., N.Y.C. 10022. Died Oct. 20, 1966; buried Green Mount Cemetery, Belleville.

STOOKEY, LYMAN BRUMBAUGH, physiologist, pathologist; b. Belleville, Ill., July 30, 1878; s. Dr. Lyman Polk and Louise (Brumbaugh) S.; A.B., Yale, 1900, Ph.D., 1902; U. of Strassburg, 1904-05; m. Margaret Powell, Dec. 31, 1903. Asso. in physiology, N.Y. State Path. Inst., 1902-04; prof. physiology, U. of Southern Calif., 1905—; pathologist to Clara Barton Hosp., 1906-18; med. adviser U.S. selective service, Los Angeles, World War I. Am. contbr. to Internat. Year Book of Chemical Physiology and Pathology, 1905—; published many researches in physiol. and pathol. chemistry in Am. and European jours. Fellow A.A.A.S., Am. Inst. Chemists, asso. fellow A.M.A. Democrat. Mason. Home: Los Angeles, Calif. Died Feb. 13, 1940.

STORER, DAVID HUMPHREYS, obstetrician, naturalist; b. Portland, Me., Mar. 26, 1804; s. Woodbury and Margaret (Boyd) S.; grad. Bowdoin, 1822; grad. Harvard Med. Sch., 1825; m. Abby Jane Brewer, 5 children including Horatio Robinson, Francis Humphreys. Joined Boston Soc. Natural History, 1830; lectured Harvard Med. Sch., prof. obstetrics and med. jurisprudence, 1854-68, dean, 1854-68; through his efforts over 10,000 volumes of med. works collected for Boston Public Library; collected coins; apptd. to com. for natural history survey of Mass.; mem. staff Mass. Gen. Hosp., 1849-58; founder Obstet. Soc. of Boston; gave discourse An Address on Medical Jurisprudence: Its Claims to Greater Regard from the Student and the Physician before Mass. Med. Soc., 1851; collected and described Mollusca of Mass.; issued translation of L. C. Kiener's work on shells General Species and Iconography of Recent Shells, Comprising the Massena Museum, the Collection of Lamarck, the Collection of the Museum of Natural History and the Recent Discoveries of Travelers, 1837; expanded volume into A History of Fishes in Massachusetts, 1867; other writings include: Report on the Ichthyology and Herpetology of Massachusetts, 1839; Synopsis of the Fishes of North America, 1846. Died Boston, Sept. 10, 1891.

STORER, NORMAN WILSON, elec. engr.; b. Orangeville, O., Jan. 11, 1868; s. Simon Brewster and Lemira (Jones) S.; M.E., Ohio State U., 1891; m. Elizabeth W. Perry, June 14, 1899 (dec. Jan. 14, 1908); children—Norman Wyman, Elizabeth Perry, Morris Brewster, Florence Treadwell; m. 2d, Ruth Esther Beyer, Dec. 7, 1911. Designer direct current generators, motors Westinghouse Electric & Mfg. Co., 1891, successively charge design elec. ry. apparatus, cons. ry. engr., specializing elec. transportation problems, development electric locomotives, electrification of steam rys. until 1936. Awarded Lamme medal Am. Inst. E.E. Fellow Am. Inst. E.E.; mem. Unitarian Layman's League. Home: 6818 Reynolds St., Pitts. Office: Care of American Institute Electrical Engineers, 33 W. 39th St., N.Y.C. Died June 5, 1947.

STORM, HANS OTTO, radio engr., author; b. Bloomington, Calif., July 26, 1895; s. Joachim Otto and Marie (Rehwoldt) S.; A.B. in Engring., Leland Stanford Jr. U., 1920; m. Grace Cleone Camp, May 21, 1921. Radio engr. in radio telegraphy with Federal Telegraph Co., Palo Alto, Calif., 1920-21; with San Francisco Water Dept., 1922-24; radio telegraphy Mackay Radio, 1925-30, All-American Cables, Nicaragua and Peru, 1931-32, Mackay Radio, 1932-34; design and installation of radio equipment Globe Wireless, Ltd., San Francisco, since 1935. Asso. mem. Inst. Radio Engrs. Author: Full Measure, 1929; Pitty the Tyrant, 1937 (gold medal Commonwealth Club of Calif.); Made in U.S.A., 1939; Count Ten, 1940. Short story, "The Two Deaths of Kaspar Rausch," appeared in O'Brien's Best Stories, 1940. Home: 1539 Greenwich St. Office: 311 California St., San Francisco, Calif. Died Dec. 11, 1942.

STORRS, HARRY ASAHEL, electrical engr.; b. Boston, Jan. 13, 1861; s. Asahel S. and Mahala (Parsons) S.; C.E., U. of Vermont, 1882; post-grad. Columbia, 1893-94; m. Alice E. Stillman, June 14, 1888;children—Nellie Stillman (Mrs. Rea W. Smith), Katherine Fay (Mrs. Wallace Henrich); m. 2d, Grace L. Cockle, June 11, 1914. In ry. work in Ohio and W.Va., 1882-83; supt. water works, Burlington, Vt., 1883-84; on topographic work in Va., 1884-85; with Western Electric Co., New York and Chicago, 1885-87, and laid cables from Nantucket to mainland and from Cape Charles to Cape Henry for signal corps, etc.; chief engr. for Pomona Land & Water Co., Calif., 1887; laid govt. cable across mouth of Columbia River for Western Electric Co., 1888; asst. prof. civ. engring., 1890-92, prof. elec. engring., 1892-99, U. of Vt.; also acting as cons. elec. and hydraulic engr. on elec. plants in Vt.; in summer of 1893 did instrumental work on survey of St. Lawrence River under U.S. Engr. Corps; in 1897 on constrn. work on sea coast fortifications, including elec. installations, and during summer of 1898 on same and was also chief electrician of harbor mines during Spanish-Am. War; elec. engr. under War Dept., designing and installing elec. plants, and also on river and harbor improvements, 1899-1903; elec. engr. U.S. Reclamation Service, 1903-09; cons. engr., chiefly hydro-electric power and pumping plants for irrigation, Denver, 1909-11, and reclamation of La. marsh lands by drainage, 1911-14, office, Chicago; constructing and operating irrigation systems and deep well pumping plants, Ariz., 1915-16; mgr. Yolo Water & Power Co., Woodland, Calif., 1917; hydrographic studies, Sacramento River basin, 1918-19; consulting engr., irrigation and hydro-electric projects, San Francisco, 1920-23; chief engr., Modesto (Calif.) Irrigation Dist., 1923-25; sr. insp. East Bay Municipal Utility Dist., 1925-39; elec. and mech. inspr. Possum Kingdom Dam and Power House, Brazos River Conservation and Reclamation Dist., 1939-40; cons. engr., Berkeley, Calif., since 1940. Address: 2115 Cedar St., Berkeley 7 CA

STORY, WILLIAM EDWARD, mathematician; b. Boston, Mass., Apr. 29, 1850; s. Isaac and Elizabeth Bowen (Woodberry) S.; A.B., Harvard, 1871; univs. of Berlin and Leipzig, 1871-75, Ph.D., Leipzig, 1875; m. Mary D. Harrison, June 20, 1878; 1 son, William Edward. Tutor mathematics, Harvard, 1875-76; asso., asst. prof., and asso. prof. mathematics, Johns Hopkins, 1876-89; prof. mathematics, Clark U., 1889-1921, emeritus, 1921. Editor in charge Am. Jour. Mathematics, 1878-82; editor Mathematical Review. Fellow Am. Acad. Arts and Sciences. Contbr. papers to Am. Jour. Mathematics, Proceedings London Math. Society, Mathematische Annalen, Proceedings Am. Acad., Transactions Am. Math. Soc., Math. Review; philos. mag. (London, Edinburgh and Dublin), Zeitschrift für Physikalische Chemie (Leipzig). Address: Worcester, Mass. Died Apr. 10, 1930.

STOSE, GEORGE WILLIS, geologist; b. Chgo., Oct. 5, 1869; s. Charles and Caroline (Sigwalt) S.; B.S. in Civil Engring., Mass. Inst. Tech., 1893, grad. study in geology, 1893-94; m. Sarah V. Kyte, Dec. 2, 1896 (dec. Aug. 1937); children—Harold Frederick, Charles Willis; m. 2d, Anna I. Jonas, Sept. 30, 1938. Instr. in geology Mass. Inst. Tech., summer 1893; field asst., U.S. Geol. Survey, 1894, asst. geologist, 1895-1900, geologist, editor geol. maps, 1900—, ret., 1943. Conducted maganese ore investigations, World War. Mem. A.A.A.S., Geol. Soc. Am., Geol. Soc., Washington (pres.), Washington Acad. Scis., (v.p.), Petworth Citizens Assn. (Founder; ex-sec.). Republican. Mem. Christian (Disciples) Ch. Writer of reports on geology of regions in Pa., Md., Va., N.C. and Colo.; compiled and directed publ. of geologic map of U.S. and of several states, for Fed. and State govts., Compiled and published geologic maps of North and South America for Geol. Soc. Am., 1943-47. Home: 2308 S. Nash St., Arlington, Va. 22202. Office: U.S. Geol. Survey, Washington. Died Jan. 30, 1960.

STOTT, HENRY GORDON, engineer; b. Orkney Islands, Scotland, 1866; s. Rev. David and Elizabeth Jane (Dibblee) S.; ed. Watson Coll. Sch., Edinburgh; Coll. Science and Arts, Glasgow, and Glasgow and W. of Scotland Tech. Coll.; m. Anna Mitchell, July 23, 1894. Worked with electric light co. at Glasgow, 1884; asst. electrician to Anglo-Am. Telegraph & Cable Co., 1885-89; devoted much time to exptl. work; asst. engr. Brush Electric Engring. Co.'s light plant, Bournemouth, Eng., 1889-90; electric works at Madrid, Spain, 1890-91; engr. with Buffalo Gen. Electric Co., 1891-1901; supt. motive power Interborough Rapid Transit Co., New York, 1901—, and New York Rys. Co., 1912—. Wrote many engring. papers. Home: New Rochelle, N.Y. Died Jan. 15, 1917.

STOTZ, EDWARD, JR., archtl. engr.; b. Pitts., Apr. 23, 1896; s. Edward and Arminda B. (Irwin) S.; C.E., Lehigh U., 1919; m. Doris Davidson, Oct. 5, 1929; children—Karen, Alice. Engaged in gen. practice as archtl. engr., 1919-36; partner Charles M. & Edward Stotz, Jr., Pitts., 1963—. Mem. Engrs. Soc. Western Pa. Republican. United Presbyterian. Home: 126 W. Prospect Av., Pitts. 15205. Office: 801 Bessemer Bldg., Pitts. 22. Died Dec. 29, 1964; buried Highwood Cemetery, Pitts.

STOUGHTON, BRADLEY, metall. engr.; b. New York, N.Y., Dec. 6, 1873; s. Coll. Charles Bradley (LL.D.) and Ada Ripley (Hooper) S.; Ph.B., Sheffield Scientific School, 1893; B.S., Mass. Inst. Tech., 1896; D.Eng., Lehigh U. 1943; m. Grace A. Van Everen, Jan. 4, 1899 (died Jan. 15, 1905); 1 son, Philip V.; m. 2d, L. Merwin, d. E. P. and Anna P. (Sands) Roe, Nov. 1, 1911; children— Sandroe, Rosamond, Leila Roosevelt. Teacher, Mass. Inst. Tech., 1896; asst. to Prof. H. M. Howe, Columbia U., 1897; metallurgist Ill. Steel Co., S. Chicago, Ill., 1898-99; chief of cost statis. div. Am. Steel & Wire Co., Cleveland, 1900; mgr. Bessemer steel dept., Benjamin Atha & Co., Newark, N.J., 1901; in business as consulting engr., 1902. Instr. adj. prof. and acting head dept. of metallurgy, Sch. of Mines, Columbia U., 1902-08; prof. metallurgy, Lehigh U., 1923—; also dean of Coll. of Engring. until 1939; chief heat treating equipment unit, Tools Section, WPB, 1941-45, acting head foundry equipment sect., 1944-45; London rep. tech. indsl. intelligence com. Fgn. Econ. Assn., July-Sept. 1945. Mem. bd. dir. Lukens Steel Co. Mem. Gen. Engring. Co., Nat. Council of Defense, 1918-19; head of metallurgical division, later v.-chmn. engring. div., Nat. Research Council; mem. welding com., Emergency Fleet Corp., 1918-20. Mem. Am. Inst. Mining and Metall. Engrs. (sec. 1913-21; chmn. iron and steel com., 1922-23), Am. Electrochem. Soc. (chmn. electrothermic div. 1922; pres. 1931), Yale Engring. Assn. (pres. 1922-24), Am. Iron and Steel Inst., Iron and Steel Inst. (Eng.), Am. Soc. for Metals (treas., 1938-39; pres. 1941), Am. Soc. for Testing Materials, Engrs. Club of Lehigh Valley (pres. 1928-29), corr. mem. Canadian Inst. Mining and Metallurgy; hon. mem. Yale Engring. Assn. Inventor converter for making steel castings, and a process for oil melting in cupolas. Club: Cosmos (Washington, D.C.). Author: The Metallurgy of Iron and Steel, 1908; Engineering Metallurgy (with Allison Butts), 1926. Made the field study and wrote technical report used by President Harding in his successful campaign to secure the 8-hour day in the U.S. steel industry, 1922. Awarded Grasselli medal by Soc. of Chem. Industry, 1929. In 1939 Lehigh Valley Chapter of Am. Soc. for Metals established Annual Stoughton Night, and in 1943, the Bradley Stoughton Award for outstanding contbn. to Metall. by a member of Lehigh Valley Chapter. Home: Bethlehem, Pa. Died Dec. 29, 1959.

STOUT, ARLOW BURDETTE, botanist; b. Jackson Center, O., Mar. 10, 1876; s. Hezekiah Milton and Harriet (Bond) S.; grad. State Normal Sch., Whitewater, Wis., 1903; A.B., U. Wis., 1909; Ph.D., Columbia, 1913; m. Zelda Judd Howe, June 22, 1909; children—Elizabeth Bond (Mrs. Herman Rausch), Arlow Burdette (dec.). Instr. botany U. Wis., 1909-11; dir. labs., N.Y. Bot. Garden, 1911-38, curator edn. and labs., 1938-47, emeritus. Recipient Roland medal from Mass. Hort. Soc., William Herbert medal from Am. Amarylis Soc.; Gold medal from Hort. Soc. N.Y.; Bertram Farr award, Am. Hemerocallis Soc.; Distinguished Service award, N.Y. Botanical Gardens. Fellow A.A.A.S., N.Y. Acad. Scis.; mem. Soc. Am. Naturalists, Am. Hemerocallis Society, Baraboo Wis. Hist. Soc., Bot. Soc. Am. Torrey Bot. Club, Am. Soc. Hort. Sci., Am. Amaryllis Soc., Am. Genetic Assn., Genetics Soc. Am., Ohio State Hist. and Archaeol. Soc., Wis. Archaeol. Soc., Hort Soc. N.Y. (hon. life mem.), Pa. Hort. Soc., Royal Hort. Soc., Phi Beta Kappa, Sigma Xi. Spl. fields sci. research, genetics, plant breeding, cytology, sterilities in flowering plants. Home: 4 Grove St., Pleasantville, N.Y. Office: N.Y. Botanical Garden, N.Y.C. Died Oct. 12, 1957; buried Kensico Cemetery, Valhalla, N.Y.

STOUT, ARTHUR PURDY, surgical pathologist; b. N.Y.C., Nov. 30, 1885; s. Joseph Suydam and Julia Frances (Purdy) S.; B.A., Yale U., 1907; M.D., Columbia U., 1912; m. Jean Stoddart, June 22, 1914 (dec. 1955); dau., Julia. Instr. surgery Columbia U., 1914-21, asst. prof., 1921-28, asso. prof., 1928-47, prof., 1947-51, ret., 1951; prof. pathology, 1950-54, professor surgery emeritus 1954; attending surgical pathologist Presbyterian Hosp., retired 1951, now consultant pathologist; attending pathologist Delafield Hosp., 1950-54, now consulting pathologist; consulting pathologist St. Luke's Hospital, 1949—; consulting pathologist Hospital for Special Surgery, 1936—, New York Arthopaedic Hosp. since 1931, Hackensack Hosp. since 1928, Roosevelt Hosp. since 1939, Mather Hospital (Port Jefferson, L.I.) since 1943, Rip van Winkle Clinic (Hudson, N.Y.) since 1947, White Plains Hosp. since 1947, Englewood Hosp. since 1947, Halloran Hosp., Vets. Adminstrn., 1946-51, Huntington Hosp., 1961—, Woman's Hosp. N.Y.C., 1948—, Lenox Hill Hosp., N.Y., 1958—, chmn. oncology, sub-com.; cons. path. Presbyn. Hosp., St. Luke's Hosp., N.Y.C., Walter Reed Hosp., Washington, N.Y.C. Health Dept. Cancer Adv. Com., East Orange V.A. Hosp., 1952—, Rosewell Park Meml. Inst., Buffalo, 1957—. Director of N.Y.C. Cancer Com.; member of the consultation bd. Army Medical Museum; civil cons. to surgeon gen. Army. Served as 1st lt., M.C., A.E.F., 1918-19. Recipient Am. Cancer Soc. Medal, 1951; Janeway Medal, Am. Radium Soc., 1952; Clement Cleveland award, N.Y.C. Cancer Com., 1953; James Ewing Soc. medal, 1957; alumni medal Coll. Physicians and Surgeons, Columbia, 1964. Fellow N.Y. Acad. Med., Royal Geog. Soc., A.C.S. (hon.), Am. Soc. Clin. Pathols. (honorary); hon. mem. Soc. Mexican Estudios Oncologicos, Mexican Acad. of Medicine, Mexican Association of Pathologists; member A.M.A., N.Y. Cancer Soc., Inter-Soc. Cytology Council, World Med. Assn., Soc. Anatomique Paris (asso.), N.Y. Soc. Pathologists, Harvey Soc., A.A.A.S., Nat. Research Council (chmn. sub-com. on oncology, member committee on pathology), Am. Assn. Cancer Research, N.Y. Academy of Sciences, N.Y. Pathological Society, (corr.) Sociedad Argentina de Anatomia Normal y Patologica, Alberta Society of Pathology (honorary), Society Belge d'Anatomie Pathologique (honoray mem.). Republican. Club: Halsted. Author: Human Cancer, 1932. Contributor numerous articles to med. jours. Asso. editor of Cancer, Postgraduate Medicine; adv. editor: Radiology; Jour. Nat. Cancer Inst., Modern Sci., Excerpta Medica. Home: 157 E. 72d St., N.Y.C. 10021. Office: 630 W. 168th St., N.Y.C. 10032. Died Dec. 1967.

STOUT, LAWRENCE EDWARD, educator; b. Seymour, Ind., Mar. 30, 1898; s. Edward Wagner and Rosalie (Lewis) S.; A.B., DePauw U., 1919; M.S., Ohio State U., 1921, Ph.D., 1923, Chem. E., 1934; m. Catherine Mary Frasch, Sept. 8, 1925; children—Lawrence E., Catherine (Mrs. R. H. Vanderpearl). Asst. prof. chemistry Miami U., Oxford, O., 1923-27; asso. prof. chemistry Washington U., St. Louis, 1927-34, asso. prof. chem. engring., 1934-38, prof., from 1938, head dept. chem. engring., 1940-63, dean sch. engring., 1948-55; dir. Sever Inst. Tech., 1948-55; cons. chemical engineer, 1923-66. Alderman, Clayton, Mo., 1950-57. Mem. Am. Chem. Soc., Am. Inst. Chem. Engrs., Am. Soc. Engring. Edn., Mo. Soc. Profl. Engrs., Sigma Xi, Tau Beta Pi, Phi Lambda Upsilon. Presbyn. Mason. Clubs: Rotary, University (St. Louis). Author articles profl. jours. Home: Clayton MO Died Dec. 30, 1966.

STOUT, OSCAR VAN PELT, civil engr.; b. Jerseyville, Ill., Nov. 14, 1865; s. John P. and Jane (McIntyre) S.; B.C.E., 1888, C.E., 1897, U. of Neb., hon. D.Eng., 1932; m. Edith Forbes, Oct. 23, 1890; children—Richard Forbes, Donald John, Oscar Charles, Marian Edith (Mrs. J. J. Wikkerink), Harris Pinkerton, Burt Elihu. With engr. depts. U.P.,C., B.&Q. and M.P. rys., 1886-90; city engr., Beatrice, Neb., 1890, 91; various grades from instr. to head prof. civ. engring., 1891-1920, also dean Coll. of Engring., 1912-20, U. of Neb.; in business, 1920-21; employed on coöperative irrigation investigations, U.S. Dept. Agr. and State of Calif., 1922—. Resident hydrographer, Neb. and adjoining states, U.S. Geol. Survey, 1894-1903; irrigation expert and engr. U.S. Dept. Agr., 1902-13; engr. Neb. State Bd. Agr.; irrigation engr., Neb. Agrl. Expt. Sta. Hon. mem. Am. Soc. Agrl. Engrs. (1st McCormick medalist 1932). Commd. maj. Engr. R.C., 1917; active service, Dec. 28, 1917-Feb. 1, 1919. Home: Berkeley, Calif. Died Aug. 4, 1935.

STOUT, WILLIAM BUSHNELL, aero. engr.; b. Quincy, Ill., Mar. 16, 1880; s. Rev. James Frank and Mary L. (Bushnell) S.; ed. Hamline U., St. Paul, 1899-1900; U. Minn., 1901-02; m. Alma E. Raymond, June 16, 1906; 1 dau., Wilma Frances. Tech. and aviation editor Chgo. Tribune, 1912; joined staff of Motor Age and Automobile; founded Aerial Age; moved to Detroit, 1914, as chief engr. Scirpps-Booth Co., advt. mgr., 1915, gen. sales mgr., 1916; apptd. chief engr. aircraft div., Packard Motor Co., 1917; during development of Liberty engine. Apptd. tech. adv. to Aircraft Bd., Washington, D.C.; built for bd. the first internally braced cantilever airplane in Am., veneer and wood constrn.; founded Stout Engring. Labs. and built 1st Am. comml. monoplane, known as Batwing, flown at Selfridge field, 1919; undertook contract, 1920, for first metal plane built in U.S., an all metal torpedo plane for U.S. Navy, flown by Eddie Stinson, Selfridge field, 1922; formed, 1922, Stout Metal Airplane Co., to build comml. metal planes. Built air sedan, three seater cabin plane, all metal, and later Liberty engine eight passenger transport; sold Stout Metal Airplane Co. to Ford Motor Co., 1925, and served as v.p., gen. mgr. during development of Ford tri-motored transport plane from the original single engine transport. Started Stout Air Services, 1926, operating first exclusive passenger airplanes in U.S., Detroit to Grand Rapids; on development of tri-motors, transferred line, Detroit to Cleve., 1927, and added the Detroit to Chgo. route; Stout Air Lines sold, 1929, to United Aircraft and Transport Co., N.Y.; Stout Engring. Labs. revived, 1929, for research and development work in aeros. Built and developed all-metal Sky Car, new type airplane for pvt. owner use; designed and built under a contract with The Pullman Car and Mfg. Corp., a highspeed "Railplane" as a basis of change in r.r. passenger work; recently developed new fibreglas automobile with engine in rear, at Graham-Paige Motors Corp., Willow Run, Mich. Commr. Mich. Aero. Commn. Dir. Nat. Aero. Assn. Past pres. Soc. Automotive Engrs., Inst. Aero. Scis.; mem. Detroit Aviation Soc. Clubs: Detroit Athletic, Orchard Lake Country. Home: 1331 W. Edgemont Av. Office: 2211 S. 19th Av., Phoenix. Died Mar. 20, 1956; buried Phoenix.

STOW, MICOLLIUS NOEL, phys. and surg.; b. Jesup, Ga., Nov. 15, 1915; s. M. N. and Georgia (Bright) S.; M.D., Emory U., 1939; D.M.S., Columbia, 1945; m. Pauline Synder, Nov. 16, 1940; children—Edward Noel, Joyce Pauline. Rotating intern West Balt. Gen. Hosp., 1939-40; resident, ophthalmologist Balt. Eye, Ear and Throat Hosp., 1940-41, otolaryngologist, 1941-42; resident ophthalmology Inst. Ophthalmology, Columbia-Presbyn. Med. Center, 1942-44; clin. instr. ophthalmology George Washington Sch. Medicine, asso. ophthalmologist George Washington U. Hosp., cons. ophthalmologist, chief eye clinic Warwick Cancer Clinic; asso. ophthalmologist D.C. Gen. Hosp.; attending surgeon Children's Hosp.; head eye cancer clinic, ophthalmologist tumor bd. Washington Hosp. Center, also sr. surgeon dept. ophthalmology; civilian cons. research ophthalmic pathology Army Inst. Pathology; civilian cons. ophthalmic research Walter Reed Army Hosp. and Postgrad. Med. Sch.; cons. ophthalmology USPHS, Nat. Insts. Health. Diplomate Am. Bd. Ophthalmology. Fellow A.M.A., Am. Acad. Ophthalmology and Otolaryngology; mem. D.C. Med. Soc., Ophthalmic Pathology Club, Washington Ophthal. Soc., Phi Chi. Democrat. Methodist. Author articles. Home: 4859 Rockwood Parkway, Washington 16. Office: 1746 K St. N.W., Washington.

STOWELL, CHARLES FREDERICK, engineer; b. Owego, N.Y., Feb. 28, 1853; s. Thomas Pollard and Henrietta (Fowler) S.; student Rochester Free Acad.; C.E., Rensselaer Poly. Inst., Troy, N.Y., 1879; m. Emily A. Blossom, Oct. 10, 1882; children—Grace Elizabeth, Thomas Charles. Engaged in practice, 1879; bridge engr. to Bd. of R.R. Commrs., State of N.Y., 1883-91; bridge engr. to Bd. of R.R. Commrs., Vt., 1901-07; designing and cons. engr. on bridges. Democrat. Author: Report on Strains in Railroad Bridges, State of New York, 1891. Home: Albany, N.Y. Died Aug. 31, 1933.

STOWELL, LOUISE MARIA REED, microscopist; b. Grand Blanc, Mich., Dec. 23, 1850; d. Seth (D.D.) and Harriet (Russell) Reed; B.S., U. of Mich., 1876, M.S., 1877; taught micros. botany U. of Mich., 1877-89; m. Charles Henry Stowell (q.v.), July 10, 1878. Apptd. by President mem. bd. trustees Girls' Reform Sch., D.C., 1891; mem. bd. trustees pub. schs. of D.C., 1893. Author: Microscopical Structure of Wheat; Microscopic Diagnosis (with C. H. Stowell). Engaged as writer and editor in scientific work. Address: 99 Fairmount St., Lowell, Mass.

STRAHAN, CHARLES MORTON, civil engr.; b. Goochland County, Va., May 9, 1864; s. Charles and Jane Cave (Morton) S.; C.M.E., U. of Georgia, 1883; hon. D.Sc., 1915; studied Cornell U., summer, 1894; studied architecture, Columbia, and abroad; m. Margaret Amelia Basinger, Oct. 31, 1894; 1 dau., Mary. Tutor, instr. and adj. prof. chemistry, U. of Ga., 1883-90, prof. civil engring., 1890-1934, prof. emeritus, actg. prof. mathematics, since 1934; also cons. engr. Mem. Water Works Commn., Athens, Ga., 1892-94; county surveyor Clarke County, Ga., 1890-1908, county engr., since 1908; mem. Court House Commn., Athens; mem. City Bd. of Health; chmn. Ga. State Highway Bd., 1919-21, dir. of research, same, 1921-28; mem. Bd. of Rd. Commrs., Clarke County, Ga., 1930; mem. com. on design of roads of Nat. Research Council. Democrat. Episcopalian. Carter mem. Ga. Acad. Science, 1921; mem. Am. Soc. C.E., Am. Assn. State Highway Officials, Kappa Alpha. Author of Research on Top Soil, Sand-Clay, and Semi-Gravel Roads, 1921, reissued in fuller form by U.S. Bur. Pub. Roads, in Sept. number of "Good Roads," 1929. Home: Athens, Ga. Died Dec. 28, 1947.

STRAIN, ISAAC G., naval officer, explorer; b. Roxbury, Pa., Mar. 4, 1821; s. Robert and Eliza (Geddes) S.; attended naval sch., Phila., 1842-43. Became midshipman U.S. Navy, 1837; served in W.I. and S.Am., 1837-42; on leave of absence, 1843-44, led expdn. partially financed by Acad. Natural Scis. of Phila. to Brazil; served in frigate Constitution in East Indies, 1844; served in ship Ohio during Mexican War, 1848; crossed S.Am. from Valparaiso to Buenos Aires, 1848-49; served to Mexican boundary commn. of Dept. of Interior, 1850; led exploration of Isthmus of Darien to evaluate route for possible canal, 1853; joined Lt. O. H. Berryman's expdn. in ship Arctic to investigate possibility of laying submarine cable between U.S. and Gt. Britain, 1856. Author: Cordillera and Pampa, Mountain and Plain, 1853; A Paper on the History and Propsects of Interoceanic Communication by the American Isthmus, 1856. Died May 14, 1857.

STRANDJORD, NELS MAGNE, radiologist, educator; b. Grenora, N.D., Aug. 18, 1920; s. Selmer J. and Eunice (Langeland) S.; B.A., Luther Coll., 1942; M.D., U. Chgo., 1946; m. Margaret E. Fry, Sept. 10, 1944; children—David Christian, Sarah Eunice, Mark Charles, Daniel Theodore. Intern, Ancker Hosp., St. Paul, 1946-47; gen. practice medicine, Virginia, Minn., 1948-51; resident U. Chgo., 1955-57, instr. radiology, 1958-59, asst. prof., 1959-61, asso. prof., 1961-65; prof., chmn. dept. radiology U. Kan., Kansas City, 1965-67; asso. prof. radiology U. Chgo., 1967-68. Vis. prof. Nat. Def. Med Center, Taipei, Taiwan, 1960-61; mem. physicians team Care-Medico and Department of State, Algiers, 1962; Project Vietnam, 1966. Served to captain in Medical corps, AUS, 1951-54. Recipient James A. McClintock award for outstanding teaching U. Chgo., 1960. Picker scholar in radiol. research, 1959-62. Diplomate Am. Bd. Radiology. Mem. Am. Coll. Radiology, Assn. U. Radiologists, Chgo. Roentgen Soc., Sigma Xi. Contbr. profl. jours. Home: Chicago IL Died Sept. 11, 1968; buried Belview MN

STRATTON, GEORGE MALCOLM, psychologist; b. Oakland, Calif., Sept. 26, 1865; s. James T. and Cornelia A. (Smith) S.; A.B., U. of Calif., 1888; A.M., Yale, 1890; A.M., Ph.D., Leipzig, 1896; m. Alice Elenore Miller, May 17, 1894; children—Elenore (Mrs. Robert Fliess), Malcolm, Florence (Mrs. A. Reinke). Fellow in philosophy, 1891-93; instr. philosophy, 1893-96, University of Calif.; mem. Instit für Experimentelle Psychologie, Leipzig, 1894-96; instr., asst. prof. and asso. prof. psychology, 1896-1904, dir. psychol. lab., 1899-1904, U. of Calif.; prof. experimental psychology, Johns Hopkins, 1904-08; prof. psychology, U. of Calif., 1908-35, prof. emeritus psychology since 1935. Captain Aviation, United States Army, 1917; major head of psychology section Medical Research Laboratory, Mineola, Long Island, 1918. President American Psychology Association, 1908; mem. Nat. Research Council, 1921-24; chmn. anthrop. and psychol. div., same, 1925-26; mem. Nat. Acad. of Sciences; hon. mem. Nat. Inst. Psychology; corresponding mem. Am. Inst. of Czechoslovakia. Taylor lecturer, Yale Univ., 1920; lectured in various univs. of U.S., Europe and Orient. Chmn. Round Table Confs., Inst. of Politics, Williamstown, 1931, and at Riverside, Mills College, and elsewhere. Author: Experimental Psychology and Its Bearing upon Culture, 1903; Psychology of the Religious Life, 1911; Theophrastus and the Greek Physiological Psychology Before Aristotle, 1917; Developing Mental Power, 1922; Anger, Its Religious and Moral Significance, 1923; Social Psychology of International Conduct, 1929; International Delusions, 1936; (with J. W. Buckham) George Holmes Howison, Philosopher and Teacher, 1934; Man, Creator or Destroyer, 1952; also contributions to various psychological journals upon perception of change, eye movements, the aesthetics of visual form, railway accidents and the color sense, race, nations, and international action. Home: 2809 Hillegass Av., Berkeley, Cal. Died Oct., 1957.

STRATTON, SAMUEL WESLEY, physicist; b. Litchfield, Ill., July 18, 1861; s. Samuel and Mary B. (Webster) S.; B.S., U. of Ill., 1884, D.Eng., 1903; D.Sc., Western U. of Pa. (now U. of Pittsburgh), 1903,

Cambridge, 1909, Yale, 1919; LL.D., Harvard, 1923; Ph.D., Rensselaer Poly. Inst., 1924; unmarried. Instr. mathematics, asst. prof., and prof. physics and elec. engring., U. of Ill., 1885-92; successively asst. prof., asso. prof. and prof. physics, U. of Chicago, 1892-1901; dir. Nat. Bur. of Standards, Washington, 1901-23; pres. Mass. Inst. of Tech., 1923—. Ensign, lt. jr. grade, lt. and lt. comdr. Ill. Naval Militia, 1895-1901; lt. U.S.N., during Spanish-Am. War, May-Nov. 1898; comdr. comdg. D.C. Naval Militia, 1904-12. Mem. Internat. Com. on Weights and Measures, Am. Inst. Elec. Engrs., Nat. Acad. Sciences, Nat. Advisory Com. for Aeronautics. Chevalier Legion of Honor, 1909, Officer, 1928. Home: Cambridge, Mass. Died Oct. 18, 1931.

STRAUB, LORENZ GEORGE, (stroub), engr. and educator; b. Kansas City, Mo., June 7, 1901; s. Joseph Valentine and Marie (Weth) S.; B.S. in C.E., U. of Ill., 1923 (won final honors and engring. scholarship), M.S. in Structural Engring., 1924, Ph.D., 1927, C.E., 1930; student Tech. U., Free City of Danzig, 1927, Tech. U., Karlsruhe, Germany, 1927-28, Tech. U., Berlin, 1928; unmarried. Began as civil engr., 1919; research, U. of Ill., 1923-24, engring. fellow, 1925-27; reports, design and investigation of hydraulic engring. structures, Burns-McDonnell Engring. Co., 1924-25; 1st Freeman traveling fellow of Am. Soc. C.E. in Europe, 1927-29; head spl. studies dept., U.S. Engr. Dept., Kansas City Dist., 1929-30; in practice as consulting engineer, Minneapolis, Minn., since 1929; associate professor, dept. mathematics and mechanics, U. of Minn., 1930-34, prof. hydraulics since 1935 (on leave of absence, 1942-45); special consultant Nat. Resources Bd., 1934, 36; administrative asst., Inst. of Tech., U. of Minn., 1936-38; dir. St. Anthony Falls Hydraulic Lab. since 1938. With Nat. Defense Research Committee 1941-44; head department civil engring., U. of Minn., 1945—; mem. Research and Development Bd., 1948-53. Received Navy award for Distinguished Service in Ordnance Development, 1947; President's certificate of appreciation for wartime services, 1949; Officer d'Academie, 1949; Order of Palms, 1950 (France); recipient Research award Am. Soc. C.E., 1958; Norman medal American Soc. Civil Engrs., 1961. Fellow A.A.A.S., member nat., state and local profl. engring. socs., of which active on many coms., chmn. of several as well as officer of parent assn.; cons., adv. or mem. several govtl. engring. agencies. Clubs: Engineers, Minneapolis Professional Men's, Campus of Univ. of Minn. (Minneapolis); Cosmos (Washington, D.C.). Author several items including many articles profl. jours.; translator two books. Address: Mississippi River at 3d Av. S.E., Mpls., 14. Died Oct. 29, 1963; buried Calvary Cemetery, Kansas City, Mo.

STRAUB, WALTER F., mfg. chemist; b. Chgo., May 11, 1897; s. John Phillip and Barbara (Ringle) S.; B.S., U. Ill., 1918; m. Anne Wiebolt, June 14, 1919; children—Anita (Mrs. William W. Darrow), Suzanne (Mrs. R.T. Peterson), John William. Pres., gen. mgr. W.F. Straub & Co., Chgo., since 1919; dir. Libby, McNeill & Libby, Hules & Hunter Company, Wiebolt Stores, Incorporated; dir. Diversey Corp.; introduced pure honey, previously sold as a pharmaceutical produce to food industry. President, dir. Wiebolt Foundation. Engaged in essential chemical research on products for military forces during World War I; dir. food rationing, 1943-44; cons. to Chief Q.M., E.T.O., 1945; cons. to adminstrn. on food matters since 1944. Dir. Emergency Food Program, Dept. of Agr., 1946, Wiebolt Found. (a philanthropic corp.), Growth Industry Shares. Vice pres. director Cook County Sch. Nursing. Member Sigma Xi. Episcopalian. Clubs: The Chicago, Univ. (Chgo.); Indian Hill (Wilmette, Ill.). Home: 771 Sheridan, Winnetka, Ill. Office: 5518 Northwest Highway, Chgo. Died July 12, 1964; buried Churchyard, Christ Ch., Winnetka, Ill.

STRAUSS, JOSEPH BAERMANN, engineer; b. Cincinnati, O., Jan. 9, 1870; s. Raphael and Lena (Baermann) S.; ed. grammar and high schs., Cincinnati; C.E., U. of Cincinnati, 1892, D.Sc., 1930; m. May Van, June 9, 1895; children—Ralph V., Richard K. Draftsman N.J. Steel & Iron Co., Trenton, N.J., 1892-94; instr. Coll. of Engring., U. of Cincinnati, 1894-95; detailer, insp., estimator and designer Lassig Bridge & Iron Co., Chicago, 1895-97; designer and squad boss Sanitary Dist. of Chicago, 1897-99; prin. asst. engr. in charge of office of Ralph Modjeski, Chicago, 1899-1902; cons. engr. in pvt. practice, 1902-04; pres. and chief engr. The Strauss Engineering Corp., cons. engrs., 1904—. Made a specialty of original design and movable and long span bridge design; built nearly 500 bridges in U.S., Can. and abroad; originated the 5 types of the Strauss trunnion bascule bridge which became a world standard, and 2 types of Strauss lift bridge; designed and built the Aeroscope at the San Francisco Expn., and the portable searchlight outfits employed by the U.S. and Russian govts. during the World War I; invented and perfected the yielding barrier used in bridges and for grade crossing protection; designed and built a series of reinforced concrete freight cars as a war emergency measure; invented and built the bascule-door hangar and many other bridge and mechanical devices employed in the arts; apptd. chief engr., 1929, for the Golden Gate Bridge, at San Francisco, Calif., the longest single-span bridge in the world, main span 4,200 feet, total length 9,200 feet; co-designer of Montreal-South Shore Bridge for Harbour Commn., Montreal, 2 miles long; designer and engr. Columbia River Bridge at Longview, Wash., second longest cantilever built; designing engr. for the bascule span of the Arlington Memorial Bridge across Potomac River at Washington, D.C.; cons. engr. to Port of New York Authority on George Washington Memorial Bridge, second-longest single span in the world, across Hudson River, at 178th St., New York, also the 1,650-ft. Bayonne Arch. Originator of movement for better citizenship through medium of citizenship training; founder of Citizen-Training Corps. Address: San Francisco, Calif. Died May 16, 1938.

STRAUSS, MAURICE J., dermatologist; born New Haven, Conn., Jan. 3, 1893; s. Jacob and Theresia (Herrman) S.; A.B., Yale, 1914; M.D., Columbia, 1917; m. Carolyn Ullman, June 12, 1923; 1 son, John Steinert. Interne Bellevue Hosp., N.Y. City, 1917-18; pvt. practice of medicine, City of New Haven, 1919—; specialist in dermatology, 1929—; clin. asst. in dermatology and syphilology New York Post-Grad. Hosp. and Med. Sch., 1917-29, asso. attending dermatologist to dispensary, 1929-32; asst. clin. prof. dermatology, Yale U. Sch. of Medicine, 1932-36, asso. clin. prof., 1936-43, clin. prof. of dermatology, 1943-55, emeritus, 1955—; asst. attending physician New Haven Hosp. and Dispensary, 1932-37, attending physician, 1937—; dir. New Haven Venereal Disease Clinic, 1920-45; attending dermatologist Grace Hosp., 1928—, Hosp. of Saint Raphael, 1931—; cons. dermatologist Laurel Heights Sanitorium Shelton, Conn.; consultant in dermatology and syphilology Norwich (Conn.) State Hosp., Newington (Conn.) V.A. Hosp., New Britain (Conn.) Hosp., and consultant in dermatology, Griffin Hosp., Derby, Conn. Diplomate Am. Bd. Dermatology and Syphilology, 1933. Fellow in dermatology and syphilology of N.Y. Acad. of Medicine; mem. A.M.A., Soc. for Investigative Dermatology, Am. Acad. of Dermatology and Syphilology, Am. Acad. of Compensation Medicine; N.E. Dermatol. Soc., Atlantic Dermatologic Conf., Conn. State Med. Soc., Sigma Xi, Phi Beta Kappa. Clubs: Faculty (Yale). Home: 18 Everit St., New Haven 11. Office: 43 Trumbull St., New Haven 10. Died Feb. 2, 1958; buried New Haven.

STRECKER, HERMAN, sculptor, lepidopterist; b. Phila., March 24, 1836; s. Ferdinand H. and Anna (Kern) S.; ed. pub. schs.; removed to Reading, 1847, Ph.D., Franklin and Marshall Coll.; began granite and marble work when 12 yrs. old; acquired great skill as sculptor and designer; designed Soldiers' Monument at Reading and numerous other works; spent all spare time in study of zoölogy, mineralogy, archaeology and botany; specially well known for his works on butterflies and his collection of over 370,000 of those insects. Author: Lepidoptera, Rhopaloceres and Heteroceres, Indigenous and Exotic, 1872-77; Butterflies and Moths of North America, 1878; etc. Address: Reading, Pa. Died 1901.

STREERUWITZ, WILLIAM H., RITTER VON, civil and mining engr., etc.; b. Mics, Bohemia, July, 1833; grad., B. Sc., Univ. of Prague; came to U. S., 1863; asst. city engr., Pittsburg, Pa., 1863-72; prof. civil and mechanical engring. Western Univ. of Pa., 1863-73; civil and mechanical engr., Pittsburg, 1873-76, Houston, Tex., 1876-88; since then State geologist for Western Texas. Member Am. Assn. Adv. Science, and many scientific societies; has written many reports on mineral resources of Texas, as well as essays in English, German and French on many technical subjects. Address: Austin, Tex.

STREETER, GEORGE LINIUS, (stret'er), anatomist; b. Johnstown, N.Y., Jan. 12, 1873; s. George Austin and Hannah Green (Anthony) S.; A.B., Union Coll., New York, 1895, D.Sc., 1930; A.M., M.D., Columbia Univ., 1899; D.Sc., Trinity College, Dublin, 1928; LL.D., U. of Michigan, 1935; m. Julia Allen Smith, Apr. 9, 1910; children—Sarah Frances, George Allen, Mary Raymond. Asst. and instr. anatomy, Johns Hopkins 1902-06; asst. prof. anatomy, Wistar Inst. Anatomy, Phila., 1906-07; prof. anatomy and dir. anat. lab., U. of Mich., 1907-14; research asso. Carnegie Instn. of Washington, 1914-18, dir. dept. of embryology, 1918-40, chmn. division animal biology, 1935-40, research asso. since 1940. Trustee Samuel Ready School, Baltimore. Fellow Royal Society (Edinburgh). Mem. American Philos, Soc. of Philadelphia, American Soc. Naturalists, National Acad. Sciences, Am. Assn. Anatomists, Am. Soc. Zoologists, Inst. Internat. d'Embryologie; fgn. mem. Zoöl. Soc. London; hon. mem. Anat. Soc. Gr. Britain and Ireland. Home: 3707 St. Paul St., Baltimore 18, Md. Died July 27, 1948.

STRICKLAND, WILLIAM, architect, engr.; b. Phila., circa 1787; s. John Strickland. Designed Masonic Temple (his 1st major bldg.), Phila. (so-called Gothic), 1810, also Custom House (1st in U.S.), Phila., 1819, Bank of U.S., 1824, Mchts. Exchange, Phila., 1834, New Chestnut St. Theatre, Phila., U.S. Mint, 1829; leading architect in Greek revival mode in Am. architecture; reconnaissance engr. Chesapeake and Del. Canal, 1824, engr. Pa. State Canal; designed, built Delaware Breakwater, begun 1829; made survey for a railroad between Wilmington, Del. and Susquehanna River, 1835; became mem. Am. Philos. Soc., 1820; engraved a number of plates for Port Folio and Architecture Mag., dealing chiefly with scenes and episodes of War of 1812. Author: Tomb of Washington at Mount Vernon (report), 1840. Died Nashville, Tenn., Apr. 6, 1854; buried beneath Tenn. Capitol, Nashville.

STRINGFELLOW, HENRY MARTYN, horticulturist, b. Winchester, Va., Jan. 21, 1839; s. Horace and Harriet Louisa (Strother) S.; A.M., William and Mary Coll., Va., 1858; Theol. Sem., Alexandria, Va., 1859-61; m. Alice Johnston, Dec. 15, 1863. Voted against secession, 1861; enlisted in C.S.A. as pvt., June 1861; participated in campaign at Yorktown, Va., and around Richmond, 1862; went to Tex. with Gen. Magruder, fall of 1862; was in battle of Galveston, and capt. in ordnance dept. at close of war. Pioneer in discovering value of gulf coast of Tex. for raising fruit and vegetables; planted first pear orchard on coast, 1882; planted first Satsuma oranges in Tex., 1884; in nursery business until 1895, later devoting attention to experiments in horticulture; moved to Fayetteville, Ark., 1909, and set out the first English walnut grove of 500 trees, in the state. Democrat. Spiritualist. Author: The New Horticulture, 1896. Address: Fayetteville, Ark. Died June 17, 1912.

STROBEL, CHARLES LOUIS, engineer; b. Cincinnati, O., Oct. 6, 1852; s. Carl and Ida Louise (Merker) S.; C.E., Royal Inst. Tech., Stuttgart, Germany, 1873; m. Henrietta Baxter, Dec. 2, 1890 (died 1905); children—Charles Louis, Marion (Mrs. James Herbert Mitchell); m. 2d, Mary Wilkins, July 30, 1910. Began as draftsman in r.r. office in Cincinnati, 1873; asst. engr. Cincinnati Southern Ry., 1874-78; chief engr. and v.p. Keystone Bridge Co., Pittsburgh, 1878-85, also cons. engr. to Carnegie, Phipps & Co., Ltd., and, as such, brought out and edited the co.'s handbook for engrs. and architects, designing new standard sections for steel beams and introducing Z-bar column. Rep. of Keystone Bridge Co. and Carnegie firms in Chicago, 1885-93, at the same time cons. engr., and taking a leading place in the development of skeleton steel constrn. for Chicago office bldgs.; designed large bridges over the Mo., Miss., Ohio and other rivers; in independent business as contracting engr., 1893—, incorporated, 1905, as Strobel Steel Constrn. Co.; retired 1926. Home: Chicago, Ill. Died Apr. 4, 1936.

STROMBERG, GUSTAF (BENJAMIN), astronomer; b. Gothenburg, Sweden, Dec. 16, 1882; s. Bengt Johan Gustaf Lorentz and Johanna Elisabeth (Noehrman) S.; prep. edn., Real Sch., Gothenburg, 1892-1902; student U. Kiel, Germany, 1904-05; Candidate of Philosophy, U. Stockholm (Stockholms Högskola), 1915, Licentiate of Philosophy, 1915; Ph.D., U. Lund, Sweden, 1916; m. Helga Sofia Henning (pen name Sister Benediction), May 11, 1914. Came to U.S., 1916, naturalized, 1922. Instr. in astronomy, U. Stockholm, 1906-13; asst., Stockholm Obs., 1906-13; astronomer Mt. Wilson Obs., 1917-46. Sci. research work for U.S. Navy and Air Force 1943-45. Mem. Am. Astron. Soc., A.A.A.S., Internat. Astron. Union, Royal Astron. Soc., Eng. Am. Phys. Soc., Royal Soc. Scis. Sweden, Sigma Xi. Club: University. Author of sci. papers most of which deal with statis. astronomy, stellar motions, the intrinsic brightness of the stars, and the philosophy of science. Listed among citizens of foreign birth who have made outstanding contributions to American culture in the Wall of Fame at the N.Y. World's Fair, 1940. Author: The Soul of the Universe, 1940; The Searchers, 1947; A Scientist's View of Man, Mind, and the Universe, 1966. Home: 1383 N. Marengo Av., Pasadena, Cal. 91103. Died Jan. 30, 1962; buried Pasadena Mausoleum.

STRONG, CHARLES LYMAN, mining engr.; b. Stockbridge, Vt., Aug. 15, 1826; s. David Ellsworth and Harriet (Fay) S.; m. Harriet Williams Russell, Feb. 26, 1863, at least 4 children. Went to San Francisco as agt. Wells & Co. of N.Y. to establish bank, 1850; partner firm Le Count & Strong, booksellers, publishers of The Pioneer (literary periodical in Cal.), 1852; 1st supt. Gould & Curry Mine (part of Comstock Lode), Virginia City, Nev., 1860, built plant for reduction of ore, successful as dir. mining operations, fought encroachments on company mining properties; retired to San Gabriel Valley, Cal., 1864; interested in various mining ventures in Cal. and Nev. Committed suicide, Feb. 9, 1883.

STRONG, EDWIN ATSON, physicist; b. Otisco, Onondaga Co., N.Y., Jan. 3, 1834; s. Phineas and Fanny (Pomeroy) S.; A.B., Union Coll., 1858, A.M., 1865; m. Harriet Jane Pomeroy, of Auburn, N.Y., Aug. 8, 1861 (she died Dec. 19, 1888). Prin. Grand Rapids (Mich.) High Sch., 1858-62; supt. pub. schs., Grand Rapids, 1862-71; head science dept., Oswego (N.Y.) Normal Sch., 1871-73; prin. Grand Rapids High Sch., 1873-75; head dept. physics, State Normal Coll., Ypsilanti, Mich., since 1885. For 18 yrs. curator mus. and many terms pres. Kent Scientific Inst. of Grand Rapids; mem. Mich. State Bd. Health, 1880. Charter mem. Mich. Acad. Science; mem. A.A.A.S., N.E.A. (dir. 1892-94); pres. Mich. Teachers' Assn., Mich. Schoolmaster's Club, Mich. Assn. High Sch. Prins. Congregationalist. Republican. Writer of numerous pamphlets on scientific and ednl. subjects, laboratory manuals 2 numbers of List of Fossils of the Lower Carboniferous of Kent Co., Mich., etc. Address: 127 Normal St., Ypsilanti, Mich.

STRONG, FREDERICK FINCH, M.D., inventor; b. Aurora, N.Y., June 6, 1872; s. Thomas Campbell (D.D.) and Mary Arabella (Finch) S.; grad. high sch., Ithaca, N.Y.; student Cornell U., 1889-93, Univ. of Berlin, 1893-94. Boston U. Med. Sch., 1895-97; M.D., Tufts Coll. Medical School, 1898; 1st Am. pupil of Dr. Paul Ehrlich, Berlin; m. Ethel Ellen Haley, Sept. 27, 1916. Instr. in clin. hematology, Tufts Coll. Med. Sch., 1898, lecturer in electrotherapeutics, 1898-1908; in gen. practice of medicine, Boston, 1898-1908; research in paper-pulp, St. Petersburg, Fla. (granted 4 patents on pulp process), 1910-13; in practice of medicine, St. Petersburg, 1913-15; lecture tour of U.S., 1917-18; began practice at Hollywood, 1919; becoming dir. Strong Therapeutic Inst., 1928; dean research dept. Arcanum Corp., Los Angeles; regent Life Research Foundation. Mem. Am. Medical Editors and Authors Assn., Pacific Physiotheraphy Assn. Mason. Republican. Theosophist. Author: Modern Electrotherapeutics, 1906; High-Frequency Currents, 1908; Science of a Living Universe, Vital Normalization, Dance of the Octaves (scenario), 1939; (fiction) The Life Condenser, 1938; Prisoners of Space, 1940; (poetry) Book of Villanelles; Book of Sonnets; Echoes. Composer: "Valse Petite," "Minuet in C," "Barcarole," "Sanscrit Chant," "Love in the Waves." Contbr. to N.E. Masonic Jour., Med. Herald, Archives of Medicine and Surgery and Archives of Radiology. Inventor of 1st Tesla-Thompson therapeutic high-frequency apparatus, cold quartz mercury ultra violet apparatus, cold ray monochromatic system, ultra-short wave for cure of high bood pressure, Photosonic Synchronizer, Photosonic Harmony System, Silent Music Therapy, Life Condenser for food preservation. Home: and Office: 6129 Fountain Av., Hollywood 28 CA

STRONG, LEE A(BRAM), plant pest control; b. Russell, Ia., June 17, 1886; s. Hez G. and Julia B. (Ashby) S.; ed. public schools, Nehawka, Neb.; hon. D.Sc., Louisiana State U., 1938; m. Edith M. Colton, Mar. 2, 1921; children—Madeleine Virginia, Lee A., Helen Tesora. Hort. insp., Los Angeles County, Calif., 1910-12; plant quarantine insp., Calif. State Dept. Agr., July 1912-18; served with 537th Engrs., U.S.A., Mar. 1918-July 1919, 12 mos. in France; with Calif. State Dept. Agr., 1919-23; in charge port inspection work, Federal Hort. Bd., U.S. Dept. Agr., 1923-25; asst. dir. Calif. State Dept. Agr., 1925-29; chief of plant quarantine and control administrn. and chmn. plant quarantine bd., U.S. Dept. Agr., Dec. 1929-June 30, 1932; chief Bur. of Plant Quarantine to Sept. 30, 1933; chief Bur. of Entomology, 1933-34; chief Bur. Entomology and Plant Quarantine, July 1934—; chmn. Nat. Plant Bd., 1924-29. Republican. Mason. Home: Chevy Chase, Md. Died June 2, 1941.

STRONG, REUBEN MYRON, anatomist, educator; b. West Allis, Wis., Oct. 8, 1872; s. Myron W. and Mary A. (Leonard) S.; A.B., Oberlin, 1897; A.M., Harvard, 1899, Ph.D., 1901; investigator at Senckenbergische Neurol. Inst., Frankfort, Germany, 1909, and at Naples Zoöl. Sta., 1910, also various summers at Marine Biol. Labs., Woods Hole, Mass.; m. Ethel Freeman, June 20, 1907; 1 dau., Madelaine Freeman. Instr. biology, Haverford (Pa.) Coll., 1902-03; Carnegie research asst., 1903-04, asso. in zoölogy, 1904-07, instructor, 1907-14, U. Chgo.; prof. anatomy, U. Miss., 1914-16; asso. prof. anatomy, 1916-17, prof. microscopic anatomy, 1917-18, prof. anatomy, 1918, Vanderbilt U. Med. Sch.; prof. anatomy, head of dept. Loyola U. Sch. Medicine, 1918-46, prof., chmn. emeritus, 1946—. Research asso. in anatomy Chgo. Natural History Mus., 1946—. Prof. zoölogy U. Mich. Summer Biol. Sta., 1916, 17. Recipient citation as 1 of 100 outstanding Chgo. citizens, 1957. Fellow A.A.A.S.; mem. Am. Assn. Anatomists (exec. com., 1916-19), Am. Soc. Zoölogists, Am. Ornithologists Union, Wilson Ornithol. Soc. (pres. 1894-1901, 20, 21; hon. mem.), Nature Conservatory (hon.), Chgo. Ornithol. (hon.), Friends of Our Native Landscape (hon.), Inst. Medicine Chgo. (mem. bd. govs. 1936-40), Nat. Parks Assn., Wilderness Soc., Chgo. Neurol. Soc. Conservation Council Chgo. (chmn. 1937—), Ill. Audubon Soc. (pres. 1941-51, now hon. pres.), Sigma Xi, Phi Beta Pi. Clubs: Chaos, Quadrangle. Author: A Bibliography of Birds, 4 vols. Contbr. articles, results of research in neurology, comparative anatomy, osteology, animal coloration, integumental structures, ossification, heredity, senses and behavior of birds, to sci. jours. Home: 5716 Stony Island Av., Chgo. 37. Died Aug. 11, 1964; buried Wauwatosa, Wis.

STRONG, THEODORE, mathematician; b. South Hadley, Mass., July 26, 1790; s. Joseph and Sophia (Woodbridge) S.; grad. Yale, 1812; m. Lucy Dix, Sept. 23, 1818, 2 sons, 5 daus. Tutor mathematics Hamilton Coll., Clinton, N.Y., 1812-16, prof. mathematics and natural sci., 1816-27; prof. mathematics Rutgers Coll., 1827-61, prof. emeritus, 1861-69; fellow Am. Acad. Arts and Scis., 1832, Am. Philos. Soc., 1844; an incorporator Nat. Acad. Scis., 1863. Author: Treatise on Elementary and Higher Algebra, 1859; Treatise on Differential and Integral Calculus, 1869; contbr. to Gill's Math. Miscellany; Sillman's Am. Journal of Sci.; Runkle's Math. Monthly. Died Feb. 1, 1869.

STRONG, WILLIAM WALKER,physicist; b. Good Hope, Cumberland County, Pa., May 16, 1883; s. William Harrison and Maria (Garretson) S.; B.S. with honors, Dickinson Coll., 1905; Ph.D., Johns Hopkins, 1908; m. Mary Alberta Kirk, June 17, 1916; children—Walker Albert, Margaret Kirk. Fellow by courtesy, Johns Hopkins, 1908; research asst. Carnegie Inst., Washington, D.C., 1908-11, also asst. Johns Hopkins, 1909-11; fellow Mellon Inst. Pitts., 1911-13, also prof. elec. theory, U. Pitts., pres. Scientific Instrument & Elec. Machine Co., 1912; instr. Carnegie Inst., Pittsburgh, 1914; physicist for Research Corp., 1915, 19; cons. practice. Developed a fume mask for diphenylchlorasin and other poisonous fumes during World War I. Discovered effect of magnetic psychoanalysis, 1921. Sec. Soldiers and Sailors Memorial Park Commn., 1936-49. Fellow A.A.A.S., Am. Phys. Soc.; Tax Justice League of Pa. (v.p). Democrat. Methodist. Mem. Phi Beta Kappa. Mason. Author: The Absorption Spectra of Solutions (Carnegie Instn.), 2 parts, 1910, 11; The New Science of Fundamental Physics, 1918; The New Philosophy of Modern Science, 1920; also vols. I, II, III, IV of collected papers from phys. and chem. jours.; Immortality in the Light of Modern Thought, 1923; Ourselves and Our Sciences, 1930. Discovered Phoenician letters and words incised on stones in Pa., 1941. Has extended American Phoenician to 400 words. Home: Mechanicsburg, Pa. Died Oct. 25, 1955.

STROSACKER, CHARLES JOHN, chem. engr.; b. Valley City, O., Nov. 15, 1882; s. William George and Caroline Fredricka (Frank) S.; student Baldwin U., 1902-03; B.S., Case Sch. Applied Sci., 1906, D.Eng., 1941; D.Sc., Baldwin-Wallace Coll., 1949. Chem. engr. Ontario Nickel Co., Worthington, Ont., 1906-08; chem. engr. Dow Chem. Co., 1908-09, supt. prodn., 1909-15, production manager, 1915—, v.p., 1941—, director, 1931—. Trustee Baldwin Wallace Coll. Mem. Am. Chem. Soc., Sigma Xi. Republican. Presbyn. Mason. Clubs: Midland Country, Rotary (Midland); Benmark (Roscommon County, Mich.); Saginaw Valley (Mich.) Torch. Home: 907 W. Park Dr. Office: Dow Chemical Co., Midland, Mich. Died Mar. 27, 1963; buried Midland Cemetery.

STROUP, THOMAS ANDREW, mining engr.; b. Lewistown, Mo., Dec. 2, 1885; s. John Knox and Eliza (Weaver) S.; B.S., Sch. of Mines (U. of Mo.), 1912; spl. work, Armour Inst. Tech., and McGill U., Montreal, Can.; unmarried. Mech. engr. with Jeffrey Mfg. Co., Columbus, O., 1912-15; mining engr., Tenn. Copper Co., 1915-16, Utah Copper Co., 1916-18; mining engr. and supt. of mines, Utah Fuel Co., 1918-25; now cons. engineer W.Va. Coal & Coke Corp., Ohio River Co. Engaged in exploration and production of rare minerals, Utah and Nev., World War. Mem. Am. Inst. Mining and Metall. Engrs., Rocky Mountain Coal Mining Inst., Tau Beta Pi. Democrat. Unitarian. Mason. Club: University. Contbr. on coal mining and labor problems. Home: 710 N. 4th St., Quincy, Ill. Died Aug. 27, 1943.

STRUTHERS, JOSEPH, b. New York, Nov. 13, 1865; s. Joseph and Anne E. (Galloway) S.; Coll. City of New York, 1880-81; Ph.B. in Chemistry, School of Mines (Columbia), 1885; Ph.D., Columbia, 1895; unmarried. On staff of instrs., Dept. of Metall., Columbia, 1895-1900, hon. lecturer in metall., 1900-02; organized and conducted first summer sch. in practical metall. of Columbia U., at Butte, Mont., 1896. Field asst. U.S. Geol. Survey, 1901, 1902. Spl. agt. U.S. Census, 1903; sec. Div. Mining Engring., St. Louis Expn., 1904; chmn. Jury Mines and Metallurgy Sect., Jamestown Expn., 1907; del. Am. Inst. Mining Engrs. to Governors' Conf. on Conservation of Nat. Resources, Washington, D.C., 1908. Asst. editor, 1903-06, asst. sec., editor and asst. treas., 1906-11, sec., editor and asst. treas., 1911-13, Am. Inst. Mining Engrs.; v.p. Johnson Electric Smelting Co., New York, 1914-15; treas. Federal Export Corp., Fed. Shipping Co., 1916; supervising engr. of tests, Ordnance Dept., U.S.A., N.Y. Dist., 1918-20. Sec., trustee Engrs. Club, New York, 1909—; treas., dir., United Engring. Soc., 1910—; treas. Engring. Foundation, 1916—; asst. treas. Mil. Engring. Com., New York, 1917. Author: Quiz Compend of Chemistry and Physics, 1890. Editor: Mineral Industry, Vols. VIII-XI, 1901-04; Bulletin Am. Inst. Mining Engrs., Nos. 1-75, 1905-13; Transactions Am. Inst. Mining Engrs., Vols. XXXVII-XLIII, 1907-13. Home: New York, N.Y. Died Feb. 18, 1923.

STRUVE, OTTO, (stroo've), astronomer; b. Kharkov, Russia, Aug. 12, 1897; s. Ludwig and Elisabeth (Grohmann) S.; student Michael Artillery Sch., Petrograd, Russia, 1916-17; Diploma of First Rank, U. of Kharkov, 1919; Ph.D., U. Chgo., 1923; hon. Sc.D., Case Sch. Applied Sci., 1939, U. Pa., 1956; Ph.D., (hon.), Copenhagen, 1946, U. Mexico, 1951; D.Sc. (hon.), Liege U., 1949; Wesleyan U., 1960; D. Phil., Kiel U., 1960; married Mary Lanning, May 21, 1925. Came to America, 1921, naturalized, 1927. Asst. in astronomy, Yerkes Obs., 1921-23, instr., 1924-27, asst. prof., 1927-30, asso. prof., 1930-32, asst. dir., 1931-32, dir. 1932-47, chmn. and hon. dir., 1947-50; prof. astrophysics, U. of Chicago, 1932-47, Andrew MacLeish Distinguished Service prof., 1946-50; dir. McDonald Observatory of University of Texas, 1932-47, honorary director, 1947-50, chairman astronomy dept., 1947-49; professor of astrophysics, chmn. dept. dir. Leuschner Obs. U. Calif. at Berkeley 1950-59; director National Rario Astronomy Obs., 1959—; editor: The Astrophysical Journal, 1932-47; fellow International Education Board, Mt. Wilson Observatory, 1926; Guggenheim Foundation fellow, Cambridge (England) U., 1928. Trustee Associated Universities of N.Y., 1957-59, Associated Universities Incorporated of N.Y., 1959. Served as lt. in Imperial Russian Army, 1916-17; lt. White Russian Army, 1919-21. Fellow A.A.A.S.; mem. Nat. Acad. of Sciences, Am. Philos. Soc., Am. Astron. Soc. (pres., 1946), Astron. Soc. of Pacific (pres. 1951), Am. Phys. Soc., Wis., Cal. acads. sci., Am. Acad. Arts and Sci., Sigma Xi, Internat. Astron. Union (pres., 1952-55), Amsterdam, Stockholm and Oslo Acads., Uppsala Soc. Scis., Society Astr. de France, Astr. Gesellschaft; corr. mem. Société Royale des Sciences de Liége, Acad. Sci., Copenhagen, Haarlem (Holland) Soc. of Sciences; fgn. asso. mem. Royal Astron. Soc. (Eng.); fgn. mem. Royal Soc. London, Edinburgh; hon. mem. Royal Astr. Soc. Can. Decorated Chevalier, Comdr. Order of Crown (Belgium); Gold Medal, Royal Astr. Soc. (London), 1944; Bruce Gold Medal, San Francisco, 1948; Draper Gold Medal, Nat. Acad. Sci., 1950; Rittenhouse Medal, Phila., 1954; Janssengold medal Paris Acad. Sci., 1955; Bruce Blair award, 1956. Address: 853 Station Pl., Berkeley 7, Cal. Died Apr. 6, 1963.

STUART, CHARLES BEEBE, engr.; b. Chittenango Springs, N.Y., June 4, 1814; s. Henry Y. and Deborah S.; m. Sarah Breese, July 2, 1836; m. 2d, Frances Welles, Apr. 17, 1841; 3 children. Chief engr. N.Y. & Erie R.R., 1840; chief engr. of a railroad line between Batavia and Rochester, N.Y., 1842; surveyor of Rochester; dir. Am. and Canadian bridge cos., 1847; contracted with Charles Ellet, Jr. for constrn. of railroad and carriage bridge over Niagara River; engr. and surveyor N.Y. State, 1849; in charge of Bklyn. drydocks for U.S. Govt., 1849; engr.-in-chief U.S. Navy, 1850-53; wrote specifications for Cal. floating drydocks; pres. Ia. Land Co., circa 1856, participated in laying out Clinton (Ia.); cons. engr. for projected railroad in Tex., 1860; raised Col. Stuart's Independent Regt., N.Y. Inf., 1861; served with Army of Potomac on fortification constrn. Author: Lives and Works of Civil and Military Engineers of America, 1871. Died Geneva, N.Y., Jan. 4, 1881.

STUART, CHARLES EDWARD, (stu'art), consulting engr.; b. Alexandria, Va., Aug. 29, 1881; s. Judge Charles Edward and Ruth (Yeaton) S.; E.E., Va. Mil. Inst., 1901; engring. course, Westinghouse Electric & Mfg. Co.; m. Dorothy Sanders, Apr. 16, 1911; children—Dorothy Du Val, Elizabeth Charles, Patricia. Principal Ashland, Va., High School, 1901-02. With Westinghouse Electric & Mfg. Co., Pittsburgh, Pa., 1902-11; sr. partner and pres. Stuart, James & Cooke, New York, since 1911; cons. engr. to Govt. of Russia in relation to the projection of new mines and rehabilitation of old in coal, iron and copper; report to Russian Govt., 1931, on the subject of rationalization, 1926-32; exec. vice-pres. of Export-Import Bank, Washington, D.C., 1934-36; has carried out many assignments in U.S., Great Britain and European Continent. Served as chief of Power Conservation, Bureau, U.S. Fuel Adminstrn., World War; also mem. of Nat. Production Com. for fuel administration and asso. mem. Power Com. and of War Industries Bd. Following conferences with leading govt. officials and industrial authorities, made several reports on internat. trade and export credits for State and Commerce Depts., 1935; visited Europe summer of 1936 as mem. of Com. of Inquiry into Cooperative Enterprise sent abroad by the President. Dir. Am.-Russian Chamber of Commerce; governing mem. Nat. Fgn. Trade Council. Mem. Am. Inst. E.E., Am. Institute Mining and Metall. Engrs. Clubs: New York Athletic, Virginians, Southern Society of New York; Whitehall, New York; Oakland Golf, Long Island, Duquesne, Pittsburgh. Contbr. tech. and economic articles to U.S. and foreign mags. Office: 52 William St., New York, N.Y.; and Hibbs Bldg., Washington, D.C. Died June 20, 1943.

STUART, FRANCIS LEE, engr.; b. Camden, S.C., Dec. 3, 1866; s. Barnwell Rhett and Emma Croome (Lee) S.; ed. Emerson Inst., Washington; m. Anne Morson Rives, Mar. 18, 1901; children—Anne M., Emma L., Elizabeth S., Rives. Asst. engr. B.&O. R.R., 1892; div. engr. Nicaragua Canal Commn., 1898, Isthmian Canal Commn., 1900; dist. engr., 1901-03, engr. of surveys, 1903-04, B.&O. R.R.; chief engr. Erie R.R., 1905-11; chief engr., B.&O. R.R., 1911-15; pvt. practice cons. engr., 1915—. Chmn. terminal port facilities com., War Industries Bd., and mem. depot bd., War Dept., 1917; chmn. budget com. U.S. R.R. Adminstrn., 1918; cons. engr. Cunard project, N.Y. Harbor and Hydro-Electric Power Commn. project, Niagara Falls, 1920; engring. expert Port Development Commn., Baltimore, 1921; vice-chmn. tech. bd., N.Y. Port Authority, 1921; mem. Transit Advisory Bd., Phila., 1923; cons. engr. Greater Harbor Com. of 200, Los Angeles, Calif., 1924-25; mem. Chicago Bd. of Review, lake lowering controversy; mem. com. on Regulation of Gt. Lakes and com. on Lake to Gulf Transportation; mem. Giant Power Survey Bd. of Pa., 1924; cons. engr. Hudson River Bridge, New York; cons. engr. Com. of R.R. Executives, Port of New York. Home: Essex Fells, N.J. Died Jan. 15, 1935.

STUART, JAMES LYALL, civil engr.; b. St. Louis, Apr. 17, 1872; s. John Lyall and Mary Emma (Batchelder) S.; C.E., Washington U.; student U. Chgo.; m. Emma Catherine McKeen, Nov. 11, 1903;

children—Emily McKeen, James Lyall. Milwright, erecting machinery and equipment in grain elevators; engr., asst. supt. constrn., closing of crevass on mouth of Mississippi River; established office James Stewart & Co., Pitts., 1900, erected plants for Westinghouse interests, 1900-06; pvt. practice engring., 1906—; designed and erected cement plant Chgo. Portland Cement Co., Ogilvie, Ill.; supervised bldg. additions to locks Mongahala River; erected office bldgs., churches, hosps., indsl. plants, Pitts., Cleve., Detroit, other areas; projects include Cleve. City Hall, Hilton Village for Newport News Shipbuilding & Dry Dock Co. at Edgewood Arsenal, Allegheny Gen. Hosp. Bldg., Gulf Bldg., Pitts., bldgs. Carnegie Tech. and U. Pitts., Nat. Gallery of Art, Washington, Pitts. Plate Glass Co., Ford City and Crystal City, Mo. Trustee Berea Coll. Mem. S.A.R., Am. Soc. C.E., Phi Delta Theta. Presbyn. Mason. Clubs: Edgeworth (Sewickley, Pa.); Eastern Point Yacht (Gloucester). Home: 515 Cochrane St., Sewickley, Pa. Office: Duquesne Club, Sixth Av., Pitts. Died Dec. 3, 1961; buried St. Louis.

STUDEBAKER, CLEMENT, mfr.; b. Gettysburg, Pa., Mar. 12, 1831; s. John S., wagon maker; moved to Ashland, O., 1836; learned blacksmith trade with father; went to South Bend, Ind., 1850; taught school one winter; engaged in smithing and wagon business with brother Henry, 1852; business grew until one of the largest vehicle factories in the world; business was incorporated, 1868; pres. of co., 1868—. Del. to several Rep. Nat. Convs.; commr. to Paris Expn.; pres. Ind. Commn. to World's Columbian Expn.; mem. Pan-Am. Congress; pres. Chautauqua Assembly of N.Y. Address: South Bend, Ind. Died 1901.

STUDEBAKER, JOHN MOHLER, mfr.; b. Gettysburg, Pa., Oct. 10, 1833; s. John and Rebecca (Mohler) S.; removed to Ashland County, O., 1835; ed. dist. sch.; m. Mary Jane Stull, Jan. 2, 1860. Removed with father's family to S. Bend, 1851; in spring of 1852 entered employ of John Cotton, wagonmaker, of S. Bend. Made woodwork of a wagon, in winter of 1852, for which his brothers, Henry and Clem, made ironwork; gave this wagon to a company organized to go to Calif. to pay for his share of the company's expenses; party disbanded at Hangtown, Calif., Aug. 31, 1853; worked for H. L. Hines, a blacksmith, and was later his partner; returned to S. Bend, 1858; bought his brother Henry's interest in firm of Studebaker Bros., which then became C. & J. M. Studebaker (with brother Clem); they later admitted two other brothers, P. E. and Jacob F., building up Studebaker Bros. Mfg. Co., of which became pres., company operating largest vehicle works in the world. Address: South Bend, Ind. Died Mar. 16, 1917.

STUHLMAN, OTTO, JR., educator; b. Germany, Nov. 12, 1884; s. Otto and Elizabeth (Hensmann) S.; A.B., U. Cin., 1907; A.M., U. Ill., 1909; Ph.D. (Class of 1860 Exptl. Sci. fellow), 1911; m. Cecil Craighead Wilbur, June 4, 1913 (dec. Mar. 1960); m. 2d, Florence Lester, Aug. 22, 1962. Instr. Stevens Inst. Tech., Hoboken, N.J., 1911-12, U. Pa., 1912-17, asst. prof. U. Ia., 1917-19, W.Va. U., 1919-20; asso. prof. U. N.C., 1920-24, prof. physics, 1924—, exec. head dept., 1929-35. Received Poteat Award, N.C. Acad. Sci., 1947; Rep. Am. Phys. Soc. on Nat. Research Council, 1930-32. Fellow Am. Phys. Soc. (pres. S.E. sect. 1939), A.A.A.S.; mem. N.C. Acad. Sci., Elisha Mitchell Sci. Soc. (pres. 1923; asso. editor, 1929-33), Sigma Xi, Sigma Phi Sigma. Presbyterian. Author: An Introduction to Biophysics, 1943. Contbr. International Critical Tables, 1926; Medical Physics, 1949. Abstractor, Biol. Abstracts, 1949. Research in photoelectric effects, electronics, biophysics. Home: Chapel Hill, N.C. Died Dec. 8, 1965; buried Chapel Hill Cemetery.

STULL, RAY THOMAS, ceramic engr.; b. Elkland, Pa., Mar. 12, 1875; s. David W. and Mary (Thomas) S.; E.M. in Ceramics, Ohio State U., 1902; m. Lena Taylor, of Mansfield, Pa., Apr. 15, 1903. Chemist Am. Terra Cotta & Ceramic Co., Terra Cotta, Ill., 1902-4; supt. Mt. Savage Enamel Brick Works, 1904-6; supt. Steiger Terra Cotta & Pottery Works, 1907; with department of ceramics engring., U. of Ill., 1907-15, becoming acting dir.; ceramic engr. Dunn Wire-Cut Lug Brick Co., at Conneaut, O., 1915-17; chief ceramist U.S. Bur. of Mines since Sept. 1, 1917, also supt. Ceramic Expt. Sta. of same. Mem. Am. Ceramic Soc. (ex-pres.), Sigma Xi, Alpha Chi Sigma, Acacia. Mason. Home: 114 W. 10th Av., Columbus OH

STUNTZ, STEPHEN CONRAD, botanist; b. Clarno, Wis., Apr. 4, 1875; s. Albert Conrad and Lydia Ann (Sturtevant) S.; B.S., U. of Wis., 1899, grad. student, 1899-1902; m. Lena Grayson FitzHugh, June 4, 1907. Library asst., U. of Wis., 1895-1902; cataloguer and classifier, Library of Congress, 1902-08; bibliographer, Bur. of Soils, 1908-10; botanist, office of Foreign Seed and Plant Introduction, 1910—. Conducted geneal. and hist. research in State Hist. Soc. Library at Madison, 1897-1902. Presbyn. Author: The Second Mrs. Jim, 1904; Mrs. Jim and Mrs. Jimmie, 1905; The Soil of Our Hills, 1915. Writer under pseudonym Stephen Conrad. Home: Vienna, Va. Died Feb. 2, 1918.

STURGIS, WILLIAM CODMAN, botanist; b. Boston, Mass., Nov. 15, 1862; s. Russell and Susan Codman (Welles) S.; A.B., Harvard, 1884, A.M., 1887, Ph.D., 1889; m. Carolyn Hall, Apr. 4, 1889. Asst. in Cryptogamic Lab., Harvard, 1888-89; vegetable pathologist Conn. Agrl. Expt. Sta., 1891-1901; lecturer Yale Sch. of Forestry, 1899-1901, Colo. Coll., 1904-17; ednl. sec. Bd. of Missions P.E. Ch., New York, 1917 to 1927; lecturer, Coll. of Preachers, Washington, D.C., 1928-31; warden St. Martin's House, Bernardsville, N.J., 1934-37. Fellow A.A.A.S.; mem. Am. Forestry Assn., N.E. Bot. Club, Boston Soc. Natural History, Alpha Delta Phi, Delta Kappa Epsilon. Home: Annisquam, Mass. Died Sep. 30, 1942.

STURTEVANT, ALFRED HENRY, zoologist; b. Jacksonville, Ill., Nov. 21, 1891; s. Alfred H. and Harriet E. (Morse) S.; A.B., Columbia, 1912, Ph.D., 1914; Sc.D., Princeton, 1947, U. Pa., 1949, Yale, 1951; m. Phoebe Curtis Reed, Apr. 22, 1922; children—William C., Harriet M. (Mrs. Howard E. Shapiro), Alfred H. Employed as research assistant Carnegie Instn., Washington, 1915-28; prof. genetics, Cal. Inst. Tech., 1928-47, Thomas H. Morgan prof. biology, 1947-62, now emeritus; visiting professor Univ. Washington, 1960, University of Texas, 1962, Princeton University, 1963, University Wisconsin, 1964, U. Ore., 1966, U. Cal. at Santa Cruz, 1966; visiting Carnegie prof., Birmingham, 1932, Leeds and Durham, 1933; vis. lectr. Harvard, 1940. Recipient Kimber medal Nat. Academy Sci., 1957; John J. Carty medal Nat. Acad. Scis., 1965, National Medal of Science, 1968. Fellow Am. Assn. Advancement Sci. (pres. Pacific div. 1953-54); mem. Am. Soc. Zoologist (president 1934), Nat. Acad. Scis., Genetic Soc. Am. (pres. 1944), Am. Philos. Soc., British (hon.), Japanese genetical socs. Author: A History of Genetics, 1965. Address: Pasadena CA Died Apr. 6, 1970; buried Woods Hole MA

STURTEVANT, BENJAMIN FRANKLIN, inventor, mfr.; b. Martins Stream, Me., Jan. 18, 1833; s. Seth and Hulda (Besse) S.; m. Phoebe Chamberlaine, 1852, 2 children. Inventor shoe pegging machine, 1857-59, obtained 5 patents for improvements, retained no rights; inventor pegwood lathe, 1860-63, retained only patent rights to shoe pegs; founder pegwood factory, Conway, N.H. (with proceeds of sale of patents); patentee rotary exhaust fan, 1867, built factory for manufacture (largest of kind in world), Jamaica Plains, Mass., 1878; liberal contbr. to ednl. instns. including Colby U., Vt. Acad. Died Jamaica Plains, Apr. 17, 1890.

STURTEVANT, CARLETON WILLIAM, civil engr.; b. Ruggles, O., Jan. 25, 1864; s. Samuel Carter and Adelaide Elizabeth (Taylor) S.; C.E. and Mil. Engineer, University of Missouri, 1884; LL.D., same university, 1929; m. Rosalie Lightcap Denio, of Vicksburg, Miss., Sept. 3, 1902; children—Marguerite, Julian Flad. Civil engr., 1884-1919, cons. engr., 1919-36; supt. for various contracting firms, engaged in dredging work on ship canal, Mobile, Ala., Tampa, Fla., Pascagoula River, Miss.; on diversion canal, Vicksburg, N.Y. State Barge Canal, Panama Canal; river control, Mississippi River, Missouri River, Magdalena River, Colombia, S.A. Served as capt. U.S. Vol. Engrs., Spanish-Am. War; lt. col. and col. U.S. Engrs., World War. Apptd. civilian mem. Mississippi River Flood Control Bd., by President Coolidge, May 16, 1928. Mem. Am. Soc. C.E., Soc. Am. Mil. Engrs., Am. Legion. Republican. Retired. Home: 1598 Sussex Rd. N.E., Atlanta, Ga.

STURTEVANT, EDWARD LEWIS, agrl. scientist; b. Boston, Jan. 23, 1842; s. Lewis W. and Mary (Leggett) S.; grad. Bowdoin Coll., 1863; grad. Harvard Med. Sch., 1866; m. Mary Mann, Mar. 9, 1864; m. 2d, Hattie Mann, Oct. 22, 1883; 5 children including Grace. Commd. lt., Co. G, 24th Me. Volunteers, 1861, later capt.; with brother purchased and began devel. of Waushakum Farm, South Framingham, Mass., 1867; conducted numerous agrl. expts., particularly interested in physiology of milk and milk secretion (gained acceptance for his research); editor or co-editor Scientific Farmer, 1876-79; erected 1st lysimeter in Am. at Waushakum Farm; studied history of edible plants; 1st dir. N.Y. Agrl. Expt. Station at Geneva, 1882; leader movement for expt. stas. Author: (with brother Joseph) The Dairy Cow: A Monograph on the Ayrshire Breed, 1875; North American Ayrshire Register, 4 vols., 1875-80; Sturtevant's Notes on Edible Plants (edited by U. P. Hedrick), 1919. Died South Framingham, July 30, 1898.

SUDWORTH, GEORGE BISHOP, dendrologist; b. Kingston, Wis., Aug. 31, 1864; s. Bishop Birch and Mary Elizabeth S.; A.B., U. of Mich., 1885; m. Frances Gertrude Kingsbury, Feb. 24, 1897. Instr. botany, Mich. Agrl. Coll., 1885-86; botanist in Div. of Forestry, U.S. Dept. of Agr., 1886-95; dendrologist, div. and bur. of forestry, 1895-1904; chief of dendrology, Forest Service, Dept. of Agr., 1904—. Author: Forest Flora of the Rocky Mountain Region; Forest Flora of Washington, D.C.; Forest and Ornamental Trees of Savannah (Ga.) City Park; Forest Flora of Tennessee; Nomenclature of Arborescent Flora of the United States; Trees of the United States Important in Forestry; Check List of North American Forest Trees with Geographical Distribution; Collecting Tree Seeds and Raising Forest Trees; Forest Resources of Western Colorado Timber Reserves; The Forest Nursery; The Forests of Allegany Co., Md.; Forest Resources of the Northern California Timber Reserves; Forest Conditions of the Sierra Timber Reserve; Forest Trees of the Pacific Slope; Forest Trees of the Rocky Mountain Region. Home: Washington, D.C. Died May 10, 1927.

SULLIVAN, EUGENE CORNELIUS, chemist; b. Elgin, Ill., Jan. 23, 1872; s. Thomas E. and Mary A. (Richards) S.; B.S. in Chemistry, U. of Mich., 1894, hon. Sc.D., 1933; studied Göttingen Univ., 1896, Leipzig Univ., 1896-99, Ph.D., 1899; m. Ada Bisbee, July 16, 1902; children—Eldon Bisbee, Dorothy (Mrs. S. Lytton Scott), Genevieve (Mrs. James Robertson); married second, Gladys Lindsay, December 27, 1949. Instr. in analyt. chemistry, U. of Mich., 1899-1903; with Chem. Lab. U.S. Geol. Survey, 1903-08; with Corning Glass Works since 1908, successively chief chemist, lab. dir., v.p. in charge mfg., pres. and hon. chmn. and dir. research; organized laboratory which produced "Pyrex" laboratory and household ware and various spl. glasses, also indsl. silicones; hon. chmn. and dir. Dow Corning Corp.; hon. chmn. bd., dir., member executive committee Corning Glassworks; vice president and director Corhart Refractories Company; dir. Dow-Corning Ltd., London, Owens-Corning Fiberglas Corp., Pittsburgh Corning Corp., Cristalerias Rigolleau, Buenos Aires, Argentina, L'Electro-Refractaire, Paris, France. Mem. Nat. Research Council, 1939-42; Soc. Indsl. des Silicones, Paris. Director Corning Glass Works Foundation; member and trustee Corning Museum of Glass. Fellow of the Am. Ceramic Soc.; mem. Am. Chem. Soc. (editorial adv. bd.), and other scientific socs.; hon. fellow Soc. Glass Technology (Eng.). Received jointly with W. C. Taylor, Potts medal of Franklin Inst., 1928; Perkin medallist, 1929. Democrat. Conglist. Clubs: Chemists (New York); Genesee Valley; Corning, Elmira, Rochester Country; Indsl. Research Dirs., Electrical Manufacturers. Author of papers on inorganic and physical chemistry, mineral and geol. chemistry, and glass. Home: Corning, N.Y. Died May 12, 1962.

SULLIVAN, FRANCIS PAUL, architect; b. Washington, D.C., June 25, 1885; s. Thomas Joseph and Mary Katherine (Connolly) S.; A.B., Georgetown U., Washington, D.C., 1904; student George Washington U., 1905-09; m. Villette Anderson, June 28, 1911; 1 dau., Mannevillette. Engaged in practice of architecture, Washington, 1926—. partner with Delos H. Smith and Joseph Whitfield Burnum, 1956—; cons. architect for work on U.S. Capitol, House and Senate office bldg.; asso. architect with David Lynn (architect of the Capitol) and Harbison Hough, Livingston and Larson (cons.) to design reconstrn. of House and Senate Chambers. Principal works: Afghanistan Embassy, Children's Country Home, East Wing Senate Office Bldg., residence of Chief Justice Harlan F. Stone, Canadian Embassy; U.S. Legation, Tirana, Albania (in collaboration with Nathan C. Wyeth); Carrollsburg Housing Project Nat. Sports Center. Served as 1st lt., Ordnance Reserve, 1918-19; capt., Ordnance Dept., U.S. Army, 1919-20, Finance Dept., 1920-22; in charge of audit of war contracts, rep. of sec. of War in settlements with aluminum industry; comptroller, Post Office Dept., 1922-26. Nat. exec. officer Historic American Buildings Survey, 1934. Mem. constrn. code com. N.R.A., 1933. Fellow A.I.A. (2d v.p., 1935-36; chmn. com. Nat. Capital, 1930-42; chmn. com. pub. works, 1936-38; chmn. com. inter-professional relations, 1938-40; pres. Wash., D.C., chapter, 1933), Am. Geog. Soc.; mem. Soc. Archtl. Historians, Thornton Soc., Columbia Hist. Soc., Am. Planning and Civic Assn. (mem. com. of 100 on Nat. Capital), Phi Sigma Kappa. Del. Internat. Congress of Architects, Paris, 1937. Clubs: Cosmos, University (Washington). Author: The Portion of a Champion, 1916; also numerours articles relating to architecture, art criticism and city planning pub. in mags. and newspapers. Home: 3320 Rowland Pl., Washington 8. Office: 808 17th St., Washington 6. Died Feb. 3, 1958; buried Arlington Nat. Cemetery.

SULLIVAN, HARRY STACK, psychiatrist; b. Norwich, N.Y., Feb. 21, 1892; s. Timothy J. and Ella M. (Stack) S. Graduated Chicago College of Medicine and Surgery 1917 and became industrial surgeon; mil. service World War I as 1st lt., jr. mem. Board of Examiners for Medical Corps; asst. med. officer, 8th Dist. Hdqtrs. of Rehabilitation Div., Federal Board for Vocational Ed.; U.S. Veterans liaison officer; on staff St. Elizabeth's Hosp., Washington, D.C.; Dir. of Clinical Rsch. Sheppard and Enoch Pratt Hosp., Baltimore, Md.; primarily concerned with schizophrenia, psychological rehabilitation, place for psychiatry among social sciences; promoted est. of standing committee on relations of psychiatry and social sciences, American Psychiatric Assoc.; assoc. prof. of psychiatry, U. of Md. Med. Sch.; entered private practice in N.Y.C. 1931; Pres. William Alanson White Psychiatric Found.; co-ed. Psychiatry: J. of Biology and Pathology of Interpersonal Relations; 1940 consultant in psychiatry to Selective Service System; med. advisor, personnel sect., War Dept. General Staff; publications in American J. of Psychiatry, Psychoanalytic Review. Died Jan. 15, 1949.

SULLIVAN, MICHAEL XAVIER, biochemist, educator; b. Fall River, Mass., Oct. 25, 1875; s. John W. and Mary (Holland) S.; A.B. magna cum laude, Harvard, 1899; A.M., Brown U., 1902, Ph.D., 1903; m. Rachel Brock, July 28, 1919; 1 dau., Nancy Ruth. Asst.

chemist Harvard, 1899-1900; instr. biochemistry Brown U., 1907; fertility expert Bur. Soils, U.S. Dept. Agr., 1907-15; biochemist, USPHS, 1915-31; dir. chemo-med. research inst. Georgetown U., 1931-36, dir., research prof. Grad. Sch. Chemistry, head dept. chemistry Grad. Sch. 1936-54, emeritus, 1954—. Fellow A.A.A.S.; mem. Soc. Exptl. Biology and Medicine, Am. Soc. Biol. Chemists, Am. Bacteriology Soc., Am. Chem. Soc. (councillor), Washington Acad. Sci., Phi Sigma Kappa, Phi Kappa, Alpha Chi Sigma, Sigma Xi, Gold Key. Democrat. Catholic. Club: Cosmos (Washington). Author 190 articles field biochemistry, relation chemistry to health and disease. Originator highly specific tests for important biol. constituents. Research on chemistry of cancer: Tumor destroying compounds. Tests for radio-active intermediates of food matter, cons. Home: 3100 Ellicott St. N.W., Washington. Died May 3, 1963; buried Carolltown, Ga.

SULLIVANT, WILLIAM STARLING, botanist; b. Columbus, O., Jan. 15, 1803; s. Lucas and Sarah (Starling) S.; studied Ohio U.; grad. Yale, 1823; LL.D. (hon.), Kenyon Coll., 1864; m. Jane Marshall, Apr. 7, 1824; m. 2d, Elisa Griscom Wheeler, Nov. 29, 1834; m. 3d, Caroline Sutton, Sept. 1, 1851; 13 children including Thomas Starling. Compiler, A Catalogue of Plants, Native and Naturalized, in the Vicinity of Columbus, Ohio, 1840; contbr. 2 important sects. to 2d edit. Gray's Manual, 1856, republished separately as The Musci and Hepaticae of the Unites States East of the Mississippi River, 1856; greatest work: Icones Muscorum, 1864 (supplement 1874); distinguished as American's foremost bryologist; commemorated by genus Sullivantia which he discovered in Ohio mem. Am. Acad. Arts and Scis., 1845. Died Columbus, Apr. 30, 1873.

SULLY, JOHN MURCHISON, mining engr.; b. Dedham, Mass., July 5, 1868; s. John and Agnes Eliza (Murchison) S.; B.S., Mass. Inst. Tech., 1888; m. Beulah K. Lilly, 1892; children—Kenneth M., Gertrude Agnes, Ruth; m. 2d, Marjorie L. Bloom, Dec. 10, 1924; children—James Allan, John Murchison. With Boston & Mont. Consol. Silver & Gold Mining Co., 1888; asst. supt. Bergen Pt. Chem. Works, Bayonne, N.J., 1888-90; with Nier & Hartford, engrs., Chattanooga, 1890-92, Hebert & Co., Chattanooga, 1892-93; engr. and supt. Chickamauga Coal & Iron Co., 1894-1900; in charge mines, at Joplin, Mo., 1900-01, Hites Cove Mining Co., Mariposa, Calif., 1901-02; exam. mines, Calif. and Mex., 1902-03; asst. supt. Woodstock Iron Co., Anniston, Ala., 1903-04; with Hermosa Copper Co., Hanover, N.M., 1904; made examination and report on properties of Santa Rita (N.M.) Mining Co., 1905-06; examining Mexican properties, 1906-08; cons. engr. and engr. in charge Santa Rita (N.M.) Mining Co., 1908-09; with Chino Copper Co., 1909-24; gen. mgr. same and Ray Consolidated Copper Co., 1924-26; gen. mgr. Chino Mines, N.M. Div., and Nev. Consol. Copper Co.; v.p. and mng. dir. Gallup (N.M.) American Coal Co. Mem. N.M. Council of Defense, World War I. Regent N.M. State Sch. of Mines. Republican. Conglist. Mason, K.P., Elk. Home: Santa Rita, N.M. Died July 15, 1933.

SUMMERS, HENRY ELIJAH, zoologist; b. at Rochester, N.Y., Aug. 18, 1863; s. Theodore A. and Mary A. (Minnis) S.; B.S., Cornell, 1886; fellow Cornell, 1886-88. Asso. prof. biology, U. of Tenn. and consulting entomologist, Tenn. Agrl. Expt. Sta., 1888-91; asso. prof. human physiology and vertebrate anatomy, U. of Ill., 1893-98; biol. work abroad and in connection with Chicago Expn., 1891-93; prof. zoology, Ia. State Coll. Agr. and Mech. Arts, since 1898; entomologist Expt. Sta. and state entomologist for Ia. Writer on entomol. subjects. Fellow and mem. council A.A.A.S. (gen. sec. 1912); past treas. and past pres. Ia. Acad. Sciences; past sec. and past v.p. Am. Assn. Econ. Entomologists; mem. Entomol. Soc. America, Am. Micros. Soc., Entomol. Soc. Washington. Granted leave of absence, 1916—. Winter Address: Sarasota, Fla. Address: Ames, Ia.

SUMMERS, LELAND LAFLIN, consulting engr.; b. Cleves, O., Mar. 6, 1871; s. Charles H. and Emma (Porter) S.; grad. high sch., Highland Park, Ill.; m. Eve H. Brodlique, Apr. 4, 1899; children—Lesley E. (dec.), Llewelyn L. B. Asst. engr. Western Union Telegraph Co., 1889-92; electrician Postal Telegraph Cable Co., Western Div., 1892-94; cons. practice, Chicago, 1894-1914; tech. advisor on munitions purchases, to J. P. Morgan & Co., 1915-17; advisor munitions to U.S. Govt., 1917-18; head of firm L. L. Summers & Co. Mem. War Industries Bd., Washington, D.C., 1917-18; tech. advisor same, and chmn. War Industries Bd. in Europe; tech. advisor Am. Commn. to Negotiate Peace, Paris, France, 1917-18; Am. mem. Inter-Allied Munitions Council, Paris. Decorated Officier Légion d'Honneur (French); Officer Crown of Italy; Commander Order of the Crown (Belgian); D.S.M. Home: Whitestone, N.Y. Died Mar. 10, 1927.

SUMNER, FRANCIS BERTODY, zoölogist; b. Pomfret, Conn., Aug. 1, 1874; s. Arthur and Mary Augusta (Upton) S.; B.S., U. of Minn., 1894; Ph.D., Columbia, 1901; m. Margaret Elizabeth Clark, Sept. 10, 1903; children—Florence Anne, Elizabeth Caroline, Herbert Clark. Tutor and instr. natural history, Coll. City of New York, 1899-1906; dir. biol. lab., U.S. Bur. Fisheries, Woods Hole, Mass., 1903-11; naturalist, U.S. Bur. Fisheries steamer "Albatross," 1911-13; asst. prof. biology, Scripps Inst. for Biol. Research (later Inst. of Oceanography), U. of Calif., 1913-19, asso. prof., 1919-26, prof. since 1926, acting dir., 1923-24; research asso. Carnegie Instn., Washington, D.C., 1927-30. Fellow A.A.A.S. (chmn. sect. R, 1938), Calif. Acad. of Sciences, San Diego Natural History Soc.; mem. Am. Soc. Zoölogists, Am. Soc. Naturalists, Western Soc. Naturalists (pres. 1921-22), Am. Soc. Mammalogists, Ecol. Soc. America, Am. Genetic Assn., Am. Soc. Ichthyologists and Herpetologists, Nat. Acad. of Sciences, (corr.) Phila. Acad. of Sciences, Am. Philos. Soc., Soc. for Exptl. Biology and Medicine, Phi Beta Kappa, Sigma Xi. Author papers on embryology and physiology of fishes, marine ecology, geographic variation, heredity and evolution. Address: Scripps Institution, La Jolla, Calif. Died Sep. 6, 1945.

SUMNER, JAMES BATCHELLER, Am. biochemist; b. Canton, Mass., Nov: 19, 1887; s. Charles and Elizabeth Rand (Kelly) S.; prep. edn., Roxbury (Mass.) Latin Sch., 1900-06; A.B., Harvard, 1910; A.M., 1913, Ph.D., 1914; grad. study U. of Brussels, 1921-22; m. Bertha Louise Ricketts, July 20, 1915 (divorced); children—Roberta Rand, Nathaniel (dec.), Prudence Avery, James Cosby Ricketts, Frederick Overton Burnley; m. 2d, Agnes Paulina Lundkirst, 1931 (div.); m. 3d, Mary Beyer, 1943; children—John Increase, Samuel B. (dec.). Acting prof. chemistry, Mt. Allison College, Sackville, N.B., Can., 1911; research asst. Worcester (Mass.) Poly. Inst., 1911-Jan. 1912; asst. prof. bio-chemistry, Cornell U., 1914-29, prof., 1929—, director of Lab. of Enzyme Chemistry, 1947-55; fellow Commn. for Relief in Belgian Ednl. Foundation, 1921-22; Guggenheim fellow, 1937. Awarded Scheele medal at Stockholm, Sweden, 1937; (with Stanley and Northrop) Nobel Prize in Chemistry, 1946. Mem. Am. Soc. Biol. Chemists, A.A.A.S., Soc. Exptl. Biology and Medicine, Nat. Acad. Science, Am. Acad. Arts and Sciences, Sigma Xi. Author: Textbook of Biological Chemistry, 1927; Laboratory Experiments in Biological Chemistry; Chemistry and Methods of Enzymes, 1943. Co-editor: The Enzymes, Chemistry and Mechanism of Action, 1950-52. Research on enzymes; 1st to isolate and crystallize an enzyme and show it to be protein, 1926; stimulated research in enzymes and viruses. Died Buffalo, N.Y., Aug. 12, 1955.

SUNDBACK, G., engr., mfg. exec.; b. Jonkoping, Sweden, Apr. 24, 1880; s. Otto and Kristina (Klasdotter) S.; M.E.E., Bingen am Rhein, 1903; Allegheny Coll., 1937; m. Marguerite Frances Titus, 1916; children—Ruth Margit, Paul Philip, Richard Robert, Eric Henry. Naturalized citizen. Pres., chief engr. Lightning Fastener Co. Ltd., St. Catharines, Ont., Can.; dir. Talon Inc., Meadville, Pa. Developed and constructed first slide fastener, Talon, and machinery for its prodn. Home: 502 Chestnut St. Office: 950 Grove St., Meadville, Pa. Died June 21, 1954; buried Greendale Cemetery, Meadville.

SUPLEE, HENRY HARRISON, engineer; b. Phila., Pa., Oct. 23, 1856; s. Nathan R. and Maria Isabella (Harrison) S.; B.S., U. of Pa., 1876; m. Catherine Elizabeth Colwell, Apr. 24, 1901 (died Mar. 30, 1924). In engring. work, 1876-87; editor of Mechanics, 1887-1890; with Yale & Towne Mfg. Co., 1890-95; travel and study in Europe, 1896; tech. editor Engineering Magazine, New York and London, 1897-1906; editor Engineering Index, 1897-1905; editorial contbr. to the Forum; editor Cassier's Magazine, 1906-12; cons. engr. and spl. tech. investigator. With U.S. War and Navy Depts., Washington, D.C., 1914-18, specializing in mil. aviation and motors; research work in Europe, hdqrs. London and Paris, since 1920. Mem. Am. Soc. M.E., Société des Ing. Civils de France; del. Internat. Engring. Congress, and Internat. Automobile Congress, Paris, 1900; del. to Congrés Houille Blanche à Grenoblee, 1925. Author: The Mechanical Engineer's Reference Book, 1907; The Gas Turbine, 1910. Translator: The Constructor, a Handbook of Machine Design (from the German of F. Reuleaux), 1893; Mathematics Self Taught (from the German of H. B. Lübsen. Has taken out many patents relating to aeroplanes, submarines, power generation and transmission. Address: 97 Boulevard Malesherbes, Paris, France. *

SURE, BARNETT, biol. chemist; b. Vilkomir, Russia, Feb. 7, 1892; s. Harry and Dina (Jochelson) S.; student pub. schs., Russia and Union of S. Africa; student Milw. Normal Sch., 1913-14, Johns Hopkins Sch. Hygiene, 1917-18; B.S., U. Wis., 1916, M.S., 1917, Ph.D., 1920; m. Ethel Estes, Dec. 21, 1924; 1 dau., Charmian. Came to U.S., 1908, naturalized, 1915. Asst. in agrl. chemistry, U. Wis., 1916-17; asst. in biochemistry, Sch. Hygiene and Pub. Health, Balt., 1917-18; scholar, asst. in agrl. chemistry U. Wis., 1918-20; asst. prof., dept. agrl. chem. U. Ark., 1920-21, asso. prof., 1921-27, prof., head dept., 1927—. Mem. Am. Soc. Biology Chemists, Soc. Exptl. Biology and Medicine, Am. Inst. Nutrition, Sigma Xi. Author: Vitamins in Health and Disease, 1933; The Little Things in Life—Vitamins, Hormones, and Other Minute Essentials for Health, 1937. Editor: The Vitamins (symposium), 1932. Co-author: Wohl's Dietotherapy, 1945; Modern Nutrition in Health and Disease, 1955. Contbr. papers to chem., med. and nutritional jours. Independent discoverer of vitamin E. Home: Fayetteville, Ark. Died June 1960.

SURFACE, FRANK MACY, biologist, economist; b. Eaton, O., Apr. 22, 1882; s. Charles W. and Alwilda (Macy) S.; B.A., Ohio State U., 1904, M.A., 1905; Ph.D., U. Pa., 1907. Harrison fellow, 1905-07; studied Royal Agrl. Coll., Copenhagen, Denmark, 1911; m. Anna Bunger, Aug. 5, 1905; children—Nan Alwilda, Moses Andrew (dec.), Martha Lillian, Paul Macy, Dorothy May. Asso. biologist Me. Agrl. Expt. Sta., 1907-10; biologist Ky. Agrl. Expt. Sta., 1910-13, Me. Agrl. Expt. Sta., 1913-17; asst. chief (later acting chief) Statis. Div. U.S. Food Adminstrn., 1917-18; food statistician Am. Commn. to Negotiate Peace, Paris, 1919; chief statistician Am. Relief Adminstrn., Paris and London, 1919-20; economist Bur., Washington Herald, 1920-21; spl. agt. Bur. U.S. Grain Corp., 1920; dir. Trade and Finance Census, as founder, and editor of Survey of Current Bus., 1921-23; spl. agt. Bur. Fgn. and Domestic Commerce, in charge of survey of world trade in agrl. products, 1923-24; economist U.S. Grain Corp. (in liquidation), 1924-26; asst. dir. in charge Domestic Commerce, Bur. Foreign and Domestic Commerce, 1926-33; acting prof. marketing Grad. Sch. Bus., Stanford, 1929-30; dir. sales research Standard Oil Co. N.J., 1933-44, exec. asst. to pres., 1945-47, cons. to bd. dirs., 1947—. Fellow A.A.A.S., Am. Statis. Assn.; mem. Am. Soc. Naturalists, Am. Econ. Assn., Am. Farm Econ. Assn., Am. Marketing Soc. (pres. 1935), Am. Acad. Polit. and Social Sci., Phi Eta, Phi Kappa Phi, Alpha Zeta, Sigma Xi. Club: Cosmos. Author: American Pork Production in the World War; The Grain Trade during the World War; American Food in the World War and the Reconstruction Period. Co-author: Marketing; also author or co-author of over 60 articles in sci. jours. Home: 1 W. 72d St. Office: 30 Rockefeller Plaza, N.Y.C. Died Aug. 30, 1965; buried Hillcrest Cemetery, Gainesville, Fla.

SURFACE, HARVEY ADAM, zoologist; b. nr. Waynesville, O., July 25, 1867; s. Daniel and Maria Josephine (Thomas) S.; B.S., Ohio State U., 1891, M.S., 1892; post-grad. work U. of Ill., 1893-94, Cornell, 1896-98; (D.Sc., Franklin and Marshall College, 1907); m. Ida May Bleasdale, of Cleveland, May 30, 1894. Prof. natural history, Univ. of the Pacific, 1894-96; spl. teacher, ornithology and nature study, Teachers' Summer Insts.; fellow and teacher, Cornell, 1897-98; supervisor of nature study, Ithaca, N.Y., 1898-1900; scientific asst. U.S. Fish Commn., 1900; served as prof. zoology, State Coll. of Pa., economic zoologist of State of Pa., and ornithologist Pa. State Bd. Agr. Mem. Am. Soc. Naturalists, Am. Ornithologists' Union, Audubon Soc., etc. Address: Harrisburg, Pa.

SUTRO, ADOLPH HEINRICH JOSEPH, mayor San Francisco, mining engr.; b. Aix-la-Chapelle, Prussia, Apr. 29, 1830; m. Leah Harris, 1856, 6 children. Came to Am., 1850; went to San Francisco, 1851; went to Nev., 1860, established quartz-reducing mill at East Dayton; originated scheme for driving a tunnel 10 feet high, 12 feet wide and some 3 miles long with lateral branches, nr. Comstock, Nev.; formed Sutro Tunnel Co., chartered by Nev. Legislature, 1865; granted (with assos.) right of way through public lands penetrated by tunnel by U.S. Congress, 1866 (tunnel completed, 1878); invested tunnel profits in real estate in San Francisco City and County; mayor of San Francisco (Populist), 1894-96; left library of over 200,000 rare volumes, half destroyed in fire, 1906, remainder now in San Francisco Public Library. Died San Francisco, Aug. 8, 1898.

SUTTLE, ANDREW DILLARD, agronomist, geneticist; b. Louisville, Miss., June 22, 1890; s. Thomas I. and Sallie (Fulton) S.; B.S., Miss. State Coll., 1915, M.S., 1920; M.S., Cornell, 1921, Ph.D., 1924; m. Ruth Heckerman, June 20, 1925; 1 son, Andrew Dillard. Prof. agronomy, Miss. State seed analyst Miss. State Coll., 1915-17, instr., 1924, prof. agronomy, 1924—; instr. A. and M. Coll. Tex., 1917, asst. prof., 1919-20; student asst. Cornell, 1919-24; flax investigation expt. sta. U.S. Dept. Agr., Lansing, Mich., plant breeder (flax), 1924; Miss. State seed analyst, 1936—; operator personal farm, seed corn and dairying, nr. State Coll., Miss., 1936—. Recipient Certificate of Meritorious Service awarded by Seedmen's Assn., 1946. Pres., Miss. Seedsmen's Assn., 1950-51. Mem. A.A.A.S., Assn. Ofcl. Seed Analysts, Farm Bur. Assn., Am. Legion, Sigma Xi, Alpha Zeta (pres. Miss. br.), Pi Gamma Mu. Democrat. Presbyn. Address: State College, Miss. Died Nov. 7, 1964; buried Meml. Gardens, Oktibbeha County, Miss.

SUTTON, CHARLES WOOD, civil engr.; b. nr. Smyrna, Del., Jan. 26, 1877; s. Thomas Layton and Sara Edwards (Weaver) S.; B.S., U. of Washington, 1898; post-grad. work in engring. and economics, U. of Pa., 1902, and department of economics and public law, Columbia U., 1914. Civil and hydraulic engring, practice with Seattle & Internat. Ry., U.S. Geol. Survey, U.S. Reclamation Service, and Corps of Engrs. of Mines of Peru, 1898-1908; chief engr. Peruvian Irrigation Service and consulting engr. Peruvian Dept. of Agr., 1908-14; consulting engr. Bd. Water Supply City of Lima, Peru, 1913-14; consulting engr., New York and Lima, 1914-19; consulting and constructing engr., Dept. of Irrigation Works, Peruvian Govt., 1919—. Mem. Am. Soc. C.E., Peruvian Soc. Engrs., Peruvian Geog. Soc. Clubs: Phoenix, National, Union (Lima). Address: Apartado 152, Lima Peru*

SUTTON, FRANK, geographer; b. Indiana, Pa., May 14, 1859; s. Peter and Jane (Mechling) S.; student State Normal Sch., Indiana, Pa.; C.E., Pa. Mil. Coll., 1879, M.C.E., 1912; unmarried. In railroad constrn. and location, 1879-86; with U.S. Geol. Survey since 1887, as topographer to 1905 and geographer since 1906. Mem. Am. Soc. C.E., Washington Soc. C.E., Geol. Soc. Washington, A.A.A.S. Clubs: Cosmos, Chevy Chase. Maj. Engr. O.R.C., 25th, 29th and 604th Engrs., 1917-18. Address: Cosmos Club, Washington, D.C.

SUTTON, LEE EDWARDS, JR., pediatrist; b. Richmond, Va., Dec. 9, 1891; s. Lee Edwards and Ella (Wagner) S.; B.S., Va. Poly. Inst., 1914; student Johns Hopkins Sch. Medicine, 1914-16; M.D., Harvard, 1921; postgrad. study, Vienna, 1923-24; m. Ruth Rogan McClellan, Feb. 8, 1930; children—Lee Edwards III, Jonathan McClellan. Acting resident pathologist Roosevelt Hosp., N.Y., 1916-18; pathologist influenze commn. Boston City Hosp., 1919, intern, 1919-22, asst. physician, 1922-28; asst. in pediatrics, Harvard Med. Sch., 1926-28; asso. in pediatrics, Med. Coll. Va., 1928-30, asst. prof., 1930-32, asso. prof., 1932-38, prof., 1938—, acting dean Sch. of Med., 1929-32, dean, 1932-42; pediatrist in chief Hosp. Div., Med. Coll. Va., also Crippled Children's Hosp. Mem. bd. dirs. Children's Meml. Clinic, Richmond (pres. 1933-35). Fellow Am. Acad. Pediatrics, A.C.P.; mem. A.M.A., Va. Med. Soc., Va. Acad. Sci., Richmond Acad. Medicine, So. Med. Soc., Va., Richmond pediatrics socs., Va. Hist. Soc., Mental Hygiene Soc. Va., Pithotomy, Alpha Omega Alpha. Democrat. Presbyn. Clubs: Rotary, New York Southern, Commonwealth. Home: 605 N. Davis Av. Address: 1200 E. Broad St., Richmond, Va. Died June 24, 1964; buried Hollywood Cemetery, Richmond.

SUTTON, LOUIS VALVELLE, utilities exec.; b. Richmond, Va., Aug. 6, 1889; s. Lee Edwards and Ella (Wagner) S.; student Petersburg (Va.) Acad., 1904-06; B.S. in elec. engring., Va. Poly. Inst., 1910; D.Eng. (hon.), N.C. State Coll., Raleigh, 1944; m. Cantey McDowell Venable, Apr. 30, 1912; children—Louis Valvelle, Sarah Tomlinson. Apprentice engr. test course, Gen. Electric Co., Lynn, Mass., 1910-12; successively statistician, asst. engr., div. mgr., commercial mgr., asst. to gen. mgr. Carolina Power & Light Co., Raleigh, N.C., 1912-24; asst. gen. mgr. Ark. Central Power Co., Little Rock, 1924-27; v.p., gen. mgr., dir. Miss. Power & Light Co., Jackson, 1927-33; pres., Carolina Power & Light Co., 1933-63, gen. mgr., 1933-49, dir., 1933-69, chmn. bd., chief exec. officer, 1949-69; v.p., dir. Carolinas Va. Nuclear Power Assos., Inc., Parr Shoals, S.C.; president and dir. of Capitan Corp., Raleigh. Vice pres., dir., past pres. Bus. Found., U. N.C.; dir. Research Triangle Found. N.C. Recipient award for engring. achievement, N.C. Soc. Engrs., 1953; Distinguished Alumnus award Va. Poly. Inst., 1961. Mem. Va. Poly. Inst. Alumni Assn. (past v.p., dir.), I.E.E.E., N.A.M. (past dir.), Southeastern Electric Exchange (dir., past pres.), Nat. Assn. Elec. Cos. (dir., past chmn.), Newcomen Soc., Soc. the Cincinnati (hon.), Edison Electric Inst. (past pres., director), National Electric Heating Association (director), Tau Beta Pi, Phi Kappa Phi, Omicron Delta Kappa. Episcopalian. Clubs: Rotary, Carolina Country, Sphinx, Milburnie (Raleigh); Cape Fear (Wilmington); Mountain City (Asheville); Coral Bay (Morehead City); Country of N.C. (Southern Pines). Home: Raleigh NC Died Jan. 1970.

SWAIN, GEORGE FILLMORE, civil engr.; b. San Francisco, Mar. 2, 1857; s. Robert Bunker and Clara Ann (Fillmore) S.; B.S., Mass. Inst. Tech., 1877; Royal Poly. Sch., Berlin, 1877-80; LL.D., New York U., 1907, U. of Calif., 1918; m. Katharine Kendrick Wheeler, July 7, 1891 (died 1901); 1 dau., Barbara; m. 2d, Mary Hayden Lord, Jan. 23, 1904 (died 1914); 1 dau., Clara; m. 3d, Mary Augusta Rand, Aug. 21, 1914; step-daughter, Alice Rand. Hydraulic expert 10th U.S. Census, 1880-84; Hayward prof. civ. engring., Mass. Inst. Tech., 1887-1909; prof. civ. engring., Harvard Engring. Sch., 1909-29 (emeritus). Cons. engineer Mass. R.R. Commn., 1887-1914; mem. 1894-1918, chmn, 1913-18, Boston Transit Commn. Mem. of many commns., and engr. for many structures and other works; made appraisal of assets and liabilities of N.Y.,N.H.&H. R.R. for state commn., 1910; also valuations of N.Y. Central, Chicago elevated, Canadian railroads and other rys. Mem. delegation of Am. engrs. to France, 1918, and mem. Franco-Am. Engring. Commn., 1919. Fellow Am. Acad. Arts and Sciences. Author: Notes on Hydraulics, 1885, 90; Conservation of Water by Storage, 1915; How to Study, 1917; The Young Man and Civil Engineering, 1922; Strength of Materials, 1924; Fundamental Properties of Materials, 1924; Stresses, Graphical Statics and Masonry, 1927; also articles on hydraulic and structural subjects. First recipient of Lamme medal, 1928. Home: Brookline, Mass. Died July 1, 1931.

SWAIN, ROBERT ECKLES, chemist; b. Hollister, Cal., Jan. 5, 1875; s. Thomas Henry and Leila Belle (Gilbert) S.; A.B., Stanford, 1899; M.S., Yale, 1901, Ph.D., 1904; studied Strassburg, Germany, 1901-02, Heidelberg, 1902; LL.D., Coll. Pacific, 1929; m. Harriet King Cuthbertson, Aug. 22, 1900 (dec.); children—Dorothy Muriel (Mrs. Ralph Begien, Jr.), Robert Cuthbertson; m. 2d, Juanita Elena Jaffe, May 1947. Instr. chemistry Stanford, 1900, asst. prof., 1902, asso. prof., 1907, prof. 1912-40, exec. head dept., 1917-40, acting pres., 1929-33, prof. emeritus, 1940—; gen. chmn. 50th Anniversary Commemoration, 1939-41. Spl. agt. U.S. Dept. Justice, in smelter smoke investigations, 1909-11; expert chemist with Referee Bd. Cons. Sci. Experts, U.S. Dept. Agr., 1910-12. Fellow A.A.A.S., London Chem. Soc., Cal. Acad. Scis.; mem. Am. Assn. Biol. Chemists, Am. Chem. Soc. (mem. nat. com. on teaching of chemistry 1934-35; com. on profl. status of chemists 1935-36; com. on profl. tng. chemists, 1936-41, chmn. 1939-41; dir., 1937-46), Alpha Omega Alpha (hon.), Sigma Xi, Phi Beta Kappa, Phi Lambda Upsilon, Alpha Chi Sigma. Commr., U.S. Fed. Court in settlement smelter smoke litigation, Salt Lake Valley, 1920-21. Chandler medal, Columbia, 1923; vis. lectr. U. Ariz., 1925; chmn. bd. overseers Cal. Coll. in China, 1931-33, pres. bd. trustees, 1933-46; trustee Inst. Forest Genetics, Placerville, Cal.; chmn. div. chem. edn., chmn. Cal. sect. Am. Chem. Soc., 1934-35; mem. U.S. delegation Internat. Union Pure and Applied Chemistry, Cambridge, Eng., 1923, The Hague, 1928, Madrid, 1934, Lucerne, 1936, Rome, 1938 (v.p. 1938—); mem. Internat. Commn. Biochem. Nomenclature, 1934; chmn. Com. Biochem. Nomenclature, NRC; mem. Commonwealth Club Cal. (chmn. com. on strategic war materials, 1941-43; bd. govs. 1943-45; chmn. exec. com. 1944); hon. v.p. China Council. Sci. adviser to internat. tribunal on Trail Smelter case, Can., U.S., 1937-38; tech. cons., 1938-41; prodn. cons. WPB, 1944; bd. dirs., Hoover Inst. and Library, Stanford, 1938-46, mem. adv. bd., 1946—. Mem. Citizens Com. on Reorgn. Fed. Govt., 1949—. Decorated Chevalier Legion of Honor (France). Mem. National Council of Nat. Econ. League. Republican. Methodist. Clubs: Bohemian (San Francisco); Rio Del Mar Golf and Country. Home: 634 Mirada Av., Stanford, Cal. Died May 31, 1961.

SWALLOW, GEORGE CLINTON, geologist; b. Buckfield, Me., Nov. 9, 1817; grad. Bowdoin Coll., 1843; A.M., M.D., Mo. Med. Coll.; LL.D., U. of Bo.; lecturer on botany, Bowdoin, 1843; prin. Hampden (Mo.) Acad., 1848; prof. geology and chemistry U. of Mo., 1852; State geologist, Mo., 1852; led movement for agrl. dept. in U. of Mo., established 1859, and taught its first class; prof. geology and dean Agrl. Coll., U. of Mo., 1870; now retired. Was State geologist of Kan., 1865. In 1858 announced discovery of permian rocks in Kansas (the first in America); helped build first silver furnace at Argenta, Mont., and first silver mill at Philipsburg, Mont.; apptd. inspector of mines by Gov. Lesley of Mont. Died 1900.

SWAN, CLIFFORD MELVILLE, cons. engr.; b. Boston, Mass., Aug. 6, 1877; s. Reuben Samuel and Emma Augusta (Melville) S.; S.B., Mass. Inst. Tech., 1899; A.M., Harvard, 1908; unmarried. Instr. physics, Mass. Inst. Tech., 1902-11; associated with Prof. W. C. Sabine in pioneer development of science of archtl. acoustics, 1911-18; chief acoustical engr. Johns-Manville Co., 1911-27, dir. co., 1926-27; cons. engr. in acoustics since 1918; cons. bd. of design N.Y. World's Fair, 1939. Past chmn. Nat. Interfraternity Conference Fellow Acoustical Society America; member Harvard Engring. Soc., N.Y. Geneal. and Biog. Society, Soc. Colonial Wars, Soc. Mayflower Descendants, New England Hist.-Geneal. Soc., Delta Epsilon (dir., past pres.). Republican. Episcopalian. Clubs: Century, University, Harvard, (New York); Harvard (Boston); Bohemian (San Francisco). Contbr. articles on archtl. acoustics to Am. Architect, Archtl. Forum, Jour. of Am. Inst. Architects, Architectural Record and other mags. Office: 271 Madison Av., N.Y.C. 16. Deceased.

SWAN, JOHN MUMFORD, physician; b. Newport, R.I., Jan. 23, 1870; s. John Mumford and Annie Frances Greene (Taggert) S.; grad. Rogers High Sch., Newport, 1887; M.D., U. Pa., 1893; m. Sara Halyday Raymond, Dec. 16, 1896 (died Oct. 13, 1949). Demonstrator osteology and asst. demonstrator anatomy, U. Pa., 1895-1904; instr. clin. pathology and instr. tropical medicine, Phila., Polyclinic and Coll. for Grades. in Medicine, 1904-10; asso. prof. clin. medicine, Medico-Chirurg. Col. of Phila., 1909-10; med. dir. The Glen Springs, Watkins, N.Y., 1910-12. Commd. 1st lt. Med. Res. Corps, AUS, Dec. 9, 1915; maj., Apr. 9, 1917; lt. col., Aug. 20, 1918; comdg. officer Base Hosp. 19, July 1918 to demobilization, May 1919; active service at Vichy, France; chief med. service Base Hosp., Camp Devens, Mass., May-Aug. 1919; discharged Aug. 18, 1919. Citation from comdg. gen. A.E.F., Apr. 1919, "for especially meritorious and conspicuous service at Base Hosp. 19." Field rep. A.R.C., Dominican Republic and Haiti, 1919-20. Col., Med. Res., U.S. Army, May 1923; col. Auxiliary Res., U.S. Army, Jan. 1934. Awarded Purple Heart. Fellow A.C.P., Coll. Physicians Phila.; mem. Am. Climatol. and Clin. Assn., Am. Acad. Polit. and Social Sci., A.M.A., Am. Cancer Soc. (state sec. N.Y. State Div.), Mil. Order Fgn. Wars, Assn. Mil. Surgeons of U.S. Am. Legion Post No. 194 (comdr. 1942), Am. Soc. Tropical Medicine (pres. 1921). Author: A Manual of Human Anatomy, Arranged for Second Year Students, 1898; A Manual of Human Anatomy, Arranged for First Year Students, 1900; Prescription Writing and Formulary, 1910. Address: 457 Park Av., Rochester 7, N.Y. Died Nov. 22, 1949; buried Arlington Nat. Cemetery.

SWAN, JOHN NESBIT, chemist; b. New Jefferson, O., Oct. 14, 1862; s. Thomas and Jane (Hadden) S.; A.B., Westminster Coll., Pa., 1886; Ph.D., Johns Hopkins U., 1893; m. Jane Duffield, Mar. 19, 1890; children—Stewart Duffield, Thomas Hadden, William Orr. Teacher in Burlington, Ia., 1886-87; in Tarkio Coll., 1887-88, Westminster Coll., 1889-91, Monmouth Coll., 1893-1915 (acting pres. 1902-03); head of dept. of chemistry, U. of Miss., 1915—. Fellow by courtesy, Johns Hopkins, 1930-31; research asso., Westminster Coll., Pa., 1931-32. Chmn. North Miss. Development Assn. Home: University, Miss. Died June 8, 1937.

SWANBERG, HAROLD, educator; b. Phila., July 13, 1891; s. William H. and Lillian (Goerz) S.; B.S., Loyola U, 1916, Md., 1916; Harvard, summer 1924; certificate, U. Vienna, 1931; ScD., Carthage (Ill.) Coll., 1963; m. Zoe Johnson, Dec. 10, 1919 (div. 1933); 1 son, William Harold; m. 2d Mildred Wilber Spiva, Feb. 10, 1934; 1 dau., Nancy Gail; step-children—JoAnn Spiva, Mary Spiva. Practice of medicine, 1916-61; resident St. Luke's Hosp., Chgo., also instr. anatomy sch. medicine Loyola U., 1917; radiologist, dir. Quincy X-Ray & Radium Labs., 1919-61, sec., mng. editor. Recipient Distinguished Service award, Miss. Valley Med. Soc., 1946, Am. Med. Writers Assn., 1952; Golden Deeds award, Quincy Exchange Club, 1962. Served as radiologist, lt. to maj. med. R.C., U.S. Army, 1917-19, 24-29. Fellow Am. Pub. Health Assn., A.C.P., A.A.A.S. Am. Geriatrics Soc., Soc. Academic Achievement; mem. A.M.A., Miss. Valley Med. Soc. (founder, sec. 1935-61), Am. Med. Writers' Assn. (founder, sec. 1940-60, hon. pres.), Radiol. Soc. N.A., Am. Roentgen Ray Soc., Society for Academic Achievement (founder, sec.-teeas. from 1959), Adams County (past sec., editor, pres., del.), Ill. (past chmn sect. radiology, secs. conf.) med. socs., Chgo. Am. Assn. Ret. Persons (past chpt. pres., v.p., del.), Quincy C. of C., Nat. Edn. Assn. U.S. Council Basic Edn., Med. Assn. Vienna, Hist. Soc. Quincy and Adams County, Am. Legion. Clubs: Art, Kiwanis (past president). Author: The Intervertebral Foramen, 1914; The Intervertebral Foramina in Man, 1915; Radiologic Maxims, 1932; History of American Medical Writer's Assn., 1965; also articles and editorials radiologic and ednl. subjects. Founder and editor Quincy Med. Bull., 1924-30, Miss. Valley Med. Jour., 1924-60; editor; Academic Achievement, from 1959; founder Swanberg Med. Found. 1943, Swanberg Kiwanis Found., 1948, Swanberg Collegiate Education Foundation, 1956. Member of the Golden Key Soc. (U. Vienna). Home: Quincy IL Died June 27, 1970; buried Quincy IL

SWANN, RALPH CLAY, educator, chemist; b. Barboursville, W.Va., May 17, 1912; s. Robert Ambrose and Mary Inez (Hatfield) S.; B.S. in Chemistry, Morris Harvey Coll., 1932; Ph.D. in Organic Chemistry, Mass. Inst. Tech., 1944; m. Winifred Phoebe Marvin, Aug. 16, 1941; children—Wendy, Judith, Ralph Clay. Research chemist Standard Ultramarine Co., Huntington, W.Va., 1933-38; group leader, sr. chemist Pure Oil Co., 1941-45; dir. research Am. Mineral Spirits Co., 1945-47, Bon Ami Co., 1947-51; pvt. cons., 1951-52; asst. dir. Ordnance Missile Labs., Redstone Arsenal, Huntsville, Ala., 1953-58, tech. dir., 1958-61; prof. chemistry, head dept. N.C. State Coll. of U. N.C. at Raleigh, 1961—. Mem. Gov. N.C. Sci. Adv. Com. Mem. Am. Chem. Soc., Assn. U.S. Army, Am. Ordnance Assn., Sigma Xi. Home: 2109 St. James Rd., Raleigh, N.C. 27607. Died Jan. 3, 1967.

SWANN, WILLIAM FRANCIS GRAY, physicist; b. Ironbridge, Shropshire, Eng., Aug. 29, 1884; s. William Francis and Anne (Evans) S.; student Brighton (Eng.) Tech. Coll., 1900-03, Royal Coll. of Science (London), Univ. Coll., Kings Coll., City and Guilds of London Inst., 1903-07; B.Sc., London, 1905, D.Sc., 1910; asso. Royal Coll. of Science, 1906; hon. M.A., Yale, 1924; hon. D.Sc., Swarthmore Coll., 1929; hon. F.T.C.L., London, 1936; Litt.D. (hon.), Temple U., 1954; m. Sarah Frances Mabel Thompson, Aug. 14, 1909; (dec. 1954); children—Willian Francis, Charles Paul, Sylvia; m. 2d, Helene Laura Diedrichs, Dec. 23, 1955. Came to U.S. 1913. Chief Phys. div. Dept. Terrestrial Magnetism, Carnegie Instn. Washington, 1913-18; mem. faculties U. Minn., U. Chgo., Yale, 1918-27, dir. Sloane Lab., 1924-27, also chmn. advisory research com. Bartol Research Foundation of Franklin Inst., 1924-27, dir. same, 1927-59, dir. emeritus, 1959—, sr. staff advisor Franklin Inst. Labs. for Research and Development, 1945—. Fellow Imperial College of Science and Technology (London, Eng.), Phys. Soc., London, Am. Physical Soc. (v.p. 1929, 30; pres. 1931-33); mem., sometime officer numerous profl. assns. Mem. bd. dirs. Phila. Musical Academy, chmn. 1951-58. Recipient Elliott Cresson Gold Medal, Franklin Inst., 1960. Episcopalian. Clubs: Cosmos (Washington, D.C.); Explorers, Yale (New York City); Great Chebeaque Golf (Maine); Rolling Green Golf (Springfield, Pa.); Phila. Art Alliance (Phila.). Author or co-author three books; contbr. profl. jours., mags. Home: 609 Ogden Av. Address: Bartol Research Foundation, Whittier Pl., Swarthmore, Pa. 19081. Died Jan. 29, 1962; buried Cheb- eaque Island, Me.

SWART, WALTER GOODWIN, mining engr.; b. Fredonia, N.Y., Feb. 19, 1868; s. Eddy F. and Sarah H. (Bradish) S.; ed. Auburn (N.Y.) High Sch., Cornell U. and U. of Denver (non-grad.); E.M., Colorado Sch. of

Mines, 1917; m. Clara C. Chollar, Sept. 5, 1894; children—Richard Houghton, Ellen Orinda (wife of Dr. H. R. Smithies), John Alvah. With Ark. Valley Smelter, Leadville, Colo., 1890-92, and various mining companies; operated laboratory on own account in Denver, 1895-99; with Blake Mining and Milling Co., developing ore separating apparatus, 1899-1907; mgr. separating dept., Am. Zinc, Lead & Smelting Co., Denver; now v.p. and gen. mgr. Mesabi Iron Co., Babbitt, Minn., consulting engineer Ill. Zinc Co., Hayden, Stone & Co. and others. Mem. Am. Inst. Mining Engrs., Mining and Metall. Soc. America, Am. Iron and Steel Inst., Duluth Engrs. Club (first pres.), Engrs. Club of Northern Minn., Teknik Club of Denver, San Francisco Engring. Club, etc. Mason (32 deg.). Republican. Home: 1712 High St., Alameda, Calif. Died Apr. 17, 1946. *

SWARTZ, CHARLES KEPHART, geologist; b. Baltimore, Jan. 3, 1861; s. Joel and Adelia (Rosecrans) S.; A.B., Johns Hopkins, 1888, Ph.D., 1904; U. of Heidelberg, 1889; fellow, Clark U., Mass., 1889-90; B.D., Oberlin Theol. Sem., 1892; m. Elizabeth A. Howard, Dec. 12, 1892; children—Joel Howard, William Hamilton, Frank McKim, Howard Currier, Charles Dana. Instr. geology, Johns Hopkins U., 1904-05, asso., 1905-06, asso. prof. geology and peleontology, 1907-10, collegiate prof. geology, 1910-31, emeritus prof. since 1931. Fellow Geol. Soc. of Am., A.A.A.S. Pres. Paleontological Soc., 1935; v.p. Geol. Soc. of America, 1936. Home: 2601 Lyndhurst Av., Baltimore 16, Md. Died Nov. 28, 1949.

SWASEY, ALBERT LORING, (swa'ze), naval architect; b. Auburndale, Mass., Sept. 14, 1876; s. Albert Edgar and Ella Cecelia (Wilson) S.; ed. Bristol Acad., Taunton, Mass., 1882-94, Mass. Inst. Tech. (naval architecture), 1894-98; m. Dorothy Lovering, Nov. 26, 1907; children—David Loring, John Loring. Draftsman hull depts., Newport News Shipbuilding Co., 1898, Cramp's Shipbuilding Co., 1899, N.Y. Shipbuilding Co., Camden, N.J., 1900-05; mem. firm Swasey, Raymond & Page, yacht designers, Boston, 1898-1917; v.p. Herreshoff Mfg. Co., Bristol, R.I., 1917-23; mem. firm Burgess, Swasey & Paine, naval architecture and yacht design, Boston, 1923-27; v.p. Henry Gielow Corp., naval architecture and yacht design, N.Y. City, 1927-32; marine insurance broker and agent, Boston Ins. Co., 1915-40. Comd. lt. comdr. Constrn. Corps, U.S., N.R.F., Apr. 2, 1917, comdr., 1919, capt., July 3, 1938; served as supt. constrn. U.S. Navy, N.Y. City, Bureau Constrn. and Repairs, Washington, D.C., mem. Appraisal Bd. for Curtiss Engr. Corpn., mem. sec. of Navy's Bd. of Review, 1917-21; mem. President's Bd. of Commandeering Merchant and Private Vessels, 1917-18; designed submarine chasers and patrol boats; member Sec. of Navy's Bd. of Appraisal of Merchant and Private Vessels, 1917-18; retired Sept. 14, 1940; recalled to active duty, Dec. 31, 1940; promoted to Commodore, 1944, retired 1945. Decorated Silver Star for services in designing and building submarine chasers, Legion of Merit. Dir. Taunton Boys Club; regional dir. Mass. Sea Scouts Am. Mem. U.S.N.R. Assn. (v.p. Mass. U.S.N.R. Assn.), Delta Psi. Episcopalian (Junior Warden). Clubs: Exchange (Boston); St. Anthony (New York City); Army and Navy, Metropolitan, Chevy Chase (Washington, D.C.); Segreganseet Country (Taunton, Mass.); Edgartown (Mass.) Yacht, Edgartown Reading Room. Contbr. to mags. Home: 146 High St., Taunton, Mass. Died Jan. 7, 1956.

SWEET, JOSHUA EDWIN, prof. surgical research; b. Unadilla, N.Y., Aug. 9, 1876; s. Joshua J. and Emeline G. (Allen) S.; prep. edn., Unadilla Acad.; A.B., Hamilton Coll., 1897, A.M., 1900, hon. Sc.D., 1922; M.D., U. of Giessen, Germany, 1901; studied at Pasteur Inst., Paris, 1901; m. Greta McCauley, June 22, 1904 (died Jan. 2, 1942); 1 dau., Ruth; m. 2d, Florence West, June 6, 1942. With Univ. of Pa., 1906-26, prof. surg. research, 1917-26; prof. research, Cornell U. Med. Coll., 1926-41, emeritus 1941. Lt. col. with A.E.F. in France, as consultant in surg. research, 1917-19; m. staff Base Hosp. No. 10. Fellow Am. Coll. Surgeons; mem. A.M.A., N.Y. State and N.Y. County med. socs., Am. Soc. Ecptl. Pathology, Am. Physiol. Soc., Harvey Soc., Society of Exptl. Biology and Medicine, N.Y. Acad. Medicine, N.Y. Surg. Soc., Phila. Acad. Surgery, Surg. Research Soc., Theta Nu Epsilon, Delta Kappa Epsilon, Phi Beta Kappa, Sigma Xi, Alpha Omega, Phi Alpha Sigma. Republican. Presbyterian. Awarded Alveranga prize for essay, "The Surgery of the Pancreas," 1915; delivered annual oration, Phila. Acad. Surgery, 1916; Mütter lecture, "The Gallbladder, Its Past, Present and Future," 1923. Contbr. 75 papers to med. lit. Home: Unadilla, N.Y. Died Apr. 8, 1957; buried Evergreen Hill Cemetery, Unadilla.

SWEET, LOUIS DENNISON, agriculturist; b. Barry, Ill., May 4, 1863; s. John L. and Ella (Peck) S.; ed. pub. schs.; m. Jennie Mulliken, Aug. 27, 1889; 1 son, Stuart Louis. Cowboy, South Park, Colo., 1880-84; ry. operator agt., 1885-87; county treas., Pitkin County, Colo., 1889-94; gen. mgr. Ry. Supply Co., Denver, Colo., 1894-1900; v.p. Manifold Co., N.Y. City, 1900-04; farming in Colo., 1904—. Mem. com. which organized Colo. for war work, 1917; with U.S. Food Administration, Washington, 1917-Nov. 11, 1918, U.S. Dept. Agr. until Nov. 1919; mem. War Finance Agency for Colo. Pres. Potato Assn. America, 1914-18; pres. Colo. State Forestry Assn., Denver Civic and Commercial Assn.; mem. exec. com. Agr. and Live Stock Bur. Republican. Conglist. Mason. Home: Denver, Colo. Deceased.

SWEZEY, GOODWIN DELOSS, astronomer; b. Rockford, Ill., Jan. 10, 1851; s. Lewis Samuel and Sarah (Cook) S.; A.B., Beloit (Wis.) Coll., 1873, A.M., 1876; Yale Div. Sch., 1873-74, 1875-76; B.D., Andover (Mass.) Theol. Sem., 1880; studied summer schs. of U. of Ill. and Ind. U.; m. Mary Frances Hill, Aug. 7, 1884 (died 1891); children—Mrs. Minnie Elmendorf, Emma Josephine, Marien Francis. Instr. natural sciences, Beloit Coll., 1874-75, 1876-79; prof., Doane College, Crete, Neb. 1886-94; meteorologist, Neb. State Bd. Agr., 1891-1900; prof. astron. and meteorology, U. of Neb., 1896—. Dir. Neb. Weather Service, 1884-96; meteorologist, U.S. Expt. Sta., Lincoln, 1894-1906. Author: New Elementary Agriculture (with others), 1903; Practical Exercises in Astronomy, 1904; Boys' Book of Astronomy, 1929. Home: Lincoln, Neb. Died July 10, 1934.

SWIFT, HOMER FORDYCE, physician; b. Paines Hollow, N.Y., May 5, 1881; s. Charles Fayette and Nancy Maria (Fordyce) S.; Adrian (Mich.) Coll., 1898-1900; Ph.B., Western Res., 1902, student med. dept., 1902-04; M.D., U. and Bellevue Hosp. Med. Coll., 1906; D.Sc., N.Y. U., 1931; received the medallion of Meritorious Service award by Alumni Fedn. N.Y.U., 1933; m. Emma Fordyce MacRae, Apr. 24, 1922; step-dau., Alice MacRae (Mrs. Lester Kissel). Interne Presbyn. Hosp., N.Y., 1906-08; asst. in pathology and dermatology, U. and Bellevue Hosp. Med. Coll., 1908-10; asst. res. physician, Rockefeller Hosp., 1910-12, res. physician, 1912-14; asso. prof. medicine, Columbia, 1914-17; same (on leave), Cornell Med. Coll., 1917-19; asso. mem., Rockefeller Inst., 1919-22, mem., 1922-46, Emeritus mem., 1946—; physician Hosp. of Rockefeller Inst. Med. Research, 1942-46, emeritus mem., 1946—. Mem. Council N.Y.U., 1942-46. Mem. bd. dirs. Russell Sage Inst. Pathology 1923-48; Kober lectr. Georgetown U. Med. Sch., 1949. With A.E.F. in France, May 1917-Apr. 1919, attached to B.E.F., May 1917-May 1918; mem. A.R.C. Trench Fever Commn., also cons. in medicine 1st Army Corps 3d Army (Army of Occupation), A.E.F.; discharged as col. med. corps, World War I. cons. to sec. of war, 1942-46. Spl. investigator OSRD study of streptococci 1942-45. Has specialized in treatment of syphilis of the central nervous system, and in study of rheumatic fever, streptococcus infections and trench fever. Chmn. gen. adv. com. for the cardiac program, N.Y. State Dept. Health, 1941—. Chmn. Am. Council Rheumatic Fever, 1945-46. Mem. A.M.A., N.Y. State Med. Soc., Assn. Am. Physicians, Am. Soc. Clin Investigation (pres. 1928), N.Y. Acad. Medicine, Soc. Am. Bacteriologists, Am. Soc. Immunology, Harvey Soc. (pres. 1925-26), Alpha Tau Omega, Nu Sigma Nu, Theta Nu Epsilon, Alpha Omega Alpha; fellow A.A.A.S. Club: Century. Collaborator: Trench Fever (report of commn. A.R.C. Research Com.), 1918. Contbr. to Forchheimer's Therapeusis of Internal Diseases, Practical Treatment (Musser and Kelly), Nelson's Loose-Leaf Medicine, Oxford Loose-Leaf Medicine, Text-Book of Medicine (Cecil); Bacterial and Mycotic Infections of Men (Dubos), also numerous articles med. jours. Home: 888 Park Av. Office: Rockefeller Institute Hospital, 66th St. and York Av., N.Y.C. 21. Died Sept. 24, 1953.

SWIFT, JOSEPH GARDNER, army officer, engr.; b. Nantucket, Mass., Dec. 31, 1783; s. Dr. Foster and Deborah (Delano) S.; grad. U.S. Mil. Acad. (1st graduating class), 1802; m. Louisa Walker, June 6, 1805, 1 son. Served as cadet in corps of artillerists and engrs., Newport, R.I., 1800, trans. to U.S. Mil. Acad., 1801; commd. 1st. lt. Engr. Corps, U.S. Army, 1805, capt., 1806, maj., 1808, lt. col., 1812, became col. and chief engr., 1812; served with Gen. Wilkinson during abortive invasion of Can., 1813, brevetted brig. gen., 1814; charge constrn. of fortifications N.Y.C., 1814; supt. U.S. Mil. Acad., 1816-18; resigned commn., 1818; surveyor Port of N.Y., 1818-26; chief engr. various railroads including Balt. & Susquehanna, New Orleans & Lake Pontchartrain, 1826; civil engr. in U.S. Govt. service, in charge harbor improvement on Gt. Lakes, 1829-45; 1st Am. engr. trained wholly in U.S. Died Geneva, N.Y., July 23, 1865.

SWIFT, LEWIS, astronomer; b. at Clarkson, N.Y., Feb. 29, 1820; s. Gen. Lewis and Anna (Forbs) S.; ed. Clarkson Acad.; hon. Ph.D., U. of Rochester, 1880; twice married. About 1854 took up study of astronomy, and made a 3-in. refractor, which was accidentally broken; bought a 4 1/2-in. refractor with which he discovered numerous comets; became dir. Warner Obs., Rochester, N.Y., 1882; subsequently of Lowe Obs. Discovered many comets and nebulae, and received medals and prizes from leading Am. and foreign socs. Before the completion of the Warner Obs. the people of Rochester presented Dr. Swift with a 16-in. refractor costing $11,000, with which he discovered 900 nebulae there and over 300 at Echo Mountain, Calif., and in both places a dozen comets. In 1878, during the total solar eclipse, at Denver, discovered two intra-Mercurial planets; received 3 gold, 1 silver, and 4 bronze medals and $1,150 cash for astron. discoveries. Fellow Royal Astron. Soc. of England, 1879. Author: Simple Lessons in Astronomy, 1888. Died Jan. 5, 1913.

SWIFT, WILLARD EVERETT, envelope mfr.; b. Worcester, Mass., Oct. 16, 1879; s. Henry Daniel and Emma Colburn (Fuller) S.; grad. Haverford (Pa.) Coll., 1903; m. Alice Metcalfe, June 15, 1904; children—Chrystella Alice, Willard Everett, Arthur Henry, Began in mill dept. U.S. Envelope Co., 1903, now pres. and chmn. 'exec. com.; mem. bd. of dirs. Worcester Mfrs. Mutual Ins. Co. Mem. exec. com. Associated Industries of Mass. Trustee Moses Brown Sch., Providence, R.I., Independent Industrial Schs., Worcester, Hahnemann Hosp., Worcester. Republican. Mem. Soc. of Friends. Member Newcomen Soc. of England (American Branch). Clubs: Worcester, Economic, Worcester Country. Originator of many labor saving devices and machines used in envelope mfr. Home: 5 Massachusetts Av. Office: 75 Grove St., Worcester, Mass. Died Jan. 14, 1947.

SWIFT, WILLIAM HENRY, army officer, engr.; b. Taunton, Mass., Nov. 6, 1800; s. Dr. Foster and Deborah (Delano) S.; grad. U.S. Mil. Acad.; m. Mary Stuart, 1825; m. 2d, Hannah Howard, 1844; Commd. 2d lt. arty. U.S. Army, 1st lt., 1824; worked on coastal improvements on surveys for Chesapeake and Ohio Canal for a projected canal across Fla. peninsula; brevetted capt., 1832, also asst. topog. engr.; commd. capt., 1838; prin. asst. in Topog. Bur., Washington, D.C., 1843-49; responsible for constrn. of 1st skeleton iron tower lighthouse in U.S., Black Rock Harbor, Conn., resigned Commn., 1849; became pres. Phila., Wilmington & Balt. R.R., also Mass. Western R.R.; pres. bd. trustees Ill. & Mich. Canal, 1845-71; published report on Chesapeake & Ohio Canal, 1846. Died N.Y.C., Apr. 7, 1879.

SWIGART, CHARLES H., civil engr.; b. Tiffin, O., July 23, 1864; s. Aaron and Abby (Whidden) S.; Heidelberg Coll., Tiffin, one term; Ohio State U., Columbus, O., about 2 yrs.; m. Pearl Battenfield, of McClure, O., Jan. 10, 1895. Began as rodman, B. & M. Railway, 1887; passed through various positions to asst. roadmaster; removed to Wash., and in charge heavy r.r. and dock constrn., G.N. Ry., 1902-05; investigated Sunnyside canal system for U.S. Reclamation Service, 1906; resident engr. maintenance of way, G.N. Ry., at Seattle, Wash., 1907; again joined U.S. Reclamation Service; with Yakima Project, 1907-09, supervising engr. Wash. Div., 1909—. Conglist. Address: 106 S. 10th Av., North Yakima, Wash.

SWINGLE, WALTER T(ENNYSON), botanist, agriculturist; b. Canaan, Wayne County, Pa., Jan. 8, 1871; s. John Fletcher and Mary (Astley) S.; received early schooling at home; B.Sc., Kan. State Agrl. Co., 1890, M.Sc., 1896; U. of Bonn, 1895-96; U. of Leipzig, 1898; D.Sc., Kan. State Agrl. Coll., 1922; m. Lucie Romstaedt, June 8, 1901 (died 1910); m. 2d, Maude Kellerman, Oct. 2, 1915; children—John William, Stella (Mrs. Stanley F. Reed), Frank Anthony, Mary (Mrs. Francis L. Albert, Junior). Asst. boanist Kan. Agrl. Exptl. Sta., 1888; U.S. Dept. Agr., Bur. Plant Industry, 1891-41; collaborator since 1941; cons. tropical botany, U. of Miami, Coral Gables, Fla., since 1941; organizing large scale preparation of serial microtome sections herbarium and fresh material economic plants. Investigated for Dept. Agr. the agriculture and botany of France, Algeria, Morocco, Italy, Spain, Greece, The Balkans, Asia Minor, China, Japan, Philippines, Mexico. Introduced the fig insect into Calif., 1899, thereby rendering possible culture of Smyrna type figs; first successful shipment standard varieties of date palms from Algeria into Calif. and Arizona, 1900, in charge establishment commercial culture of date palm, 1900-34; owns and operates an experimental date garden of Indio, California; helped to establish Egyptian cotton in Arizona; originated by hybridization in Fla., citranges, limequats, tangelos and other new citrus fruits; discovered neophyosis (rejuvenescence of old citrus varieties from nucellar buds seedlings, thereby eliminating all virus infections). First proved existence of centrosomes in plants; originated name and theory of metaxenia for direct effect of pollen on dates, 1928. Introduced many new corp plants alkaloid-yielding species of Ephedra and high-yeilding strains of tropical tung (abrasin). Awarded Meyer medal, 1948; Barbour medal, 1950. Fellow and life member A.A.A.S.; orig. member Washington Academy Sciences, Wash. Acad. Medicine (past v.p.); mem. Acad. Natural Science (Phila.); Am. Bot. Soc., Soc. Nat. d'Acelimination de France; corr. mem. Academie d'Agriculture de France; corr. mem. Academie d'Agriculture of France; honorary life member National Geographical Society. Del. of U.S. Government and Nat. Research Council to 3d Pan-Pacific Science Congress, Tokyo, Japan, 1926. Visited Brazil, Apr.-June 1939, on invitation of Minister of Foreign Affairs, to advise regarding culture of cinchona, tung (abrasin), rubber and other tropical crops for export to U.S. Author numerous papers on botany (some 25 on citrus and related genera), culminating in a complete synopsis of orance subfamily, The Botany of Citrus and Its Wild Relatives, 1943; conducting search for new rootstocks immune to Tristeza, fatal disease of Citrus. Studied economic plants of China, supervised extensive translations from Chinese literature on them; assisted the Librarian of Congress in building up the largest collection of Chinese books outside the Orient; wrote annual reports on same, 1915-35; named hon. cons. in development Orientalia Coll., 1947. Club: Cosmos. Author: Our Agricultural Debt to Asia, 1945. Home: 4753 Reservoir Rd. N.W., Washington. Died Jan. 19, 1952.

SWOPE, GERARD, elec. engr.; b. St. Louis, Mo., Dec. 1, 1872; B.S. in E.E., Mass. Inst. Tech., 1895; hon. D.Sc., Rutgers, 1923, Union Coll., 1924; LL.D., Colgate U., 1927; Dr. Engring., Stevens Inst. Technology, 1929; D.Sc., Washington U., 1932; m. Mary Dayton Hill, 1901; LL.D. (hon.), Dartmouth, 1952; children—Henrietta H., Isaac G., Gerard, David, John. Began as helper Gen. Electric Co., 1893; entered employ Western Electric Co., 1895, mgr. in St. Louis, 1899-1906; trans. to Chicago, 1906, to N.Y. as gen. sales mgr., 1908, and elected v.p. and dir., 1913; elected pres. Internat. Gen. Electric Co., Jan. 1919, chmn. 1922-33, now hon. chmn., pres. General Electric Co., 1922-39, retired, 1939, hon. pres. and dir., 1940-42 and, 1944—(re-elected pres. 1942-44). Dir. National City Bank, also many foreign corps. First pres. and now mem. bd. of govs. of Nat. Elec. Mfrs. Assn.; mem. first Playground Commn. of St. Louis, 1901-03; chmn. of first public Bath Commn., St. Louis, 1903-06; chmn. N.Y.C. Housing Authority, 1940-42; asst. to sec. of treasury, 1942. Mem. gen. staff U.S. Army, World War I, served as asst. dir. purchase, storage and traffic. Mem. Indsl. Adv. Bd. of N. R.A. (Washington), 1933; first chmn. Bus. Adv. and Planning Council for Dept. of Commerce, 1933; chmn. Coal Arbitration, Bd., 1933; mem. first Nat. Labor Board, 1933; mem. President's Adv. Counil on Economic Security, 1934; mem. Adv. Council on Social Security, 1937-38; chmn. Indsl. Relations Commn. to Great Britain and Sweden, 1938; life mem. corp. and mem. exec. com. Mass. Inst. Tech.; mem. vis. com. Dept. of Astronomy, Harvard, 1927—; former pres. and now dir., Greenwich House (New York); alternate mem. Nat. Defense Mediation Bd., 1941. Chmn. 8th Am. Red Cross Roll Call, 1924; chmn. Nat. Mobilization for Human Needs, 1935-36, gater hon. pres. community chests and councils; organizer and chmn., Com. to Study Budget of Relief Appeals for fgn. countries, 1942; an organizer, mem. exec. com., chmn. and chairman budget com., Nat. War Fund; chmn. Nat. Health and Welfare Retirement Association. F. Am. Inst. Elec. Engrs.; mem. Council on Foreign Relations and various scientific socs.; hon. mem. Tau Beta Pi, 1932. Awarded D.S.M. (for work on procurement program for U.S. Army, 1918), Chevalier Legion of Honor (French); Order of Rising Sun (Japanese). Awarded Gold Medal of Nat. Inst. Social Sciences, 1932; Gold Medal and purse for signal contributions to elec. manufacturing industry, 1932; Hoover medal, 1942, for pub. service in social, civic and humanitarian fields. Clubs: Technology (New York); Mohawk (Schenectady). Author: Stabilization of Industry (often referred to as "Swope Plan"), 1931; Futility of Conquest in Europe, 1943; Some Aspects of Corporate Management. Contbr. papers and articles on unemployment and economic subjects. Home: The Croft, Ossining, N.Y. Office: 570 Lexington Av., N.Y.C. Died Nov. 20, 1957.

SYDENSTRICKER, VIRGIL PRESTON, physician, educator; b. Hamilton, Mo., July 15, 1889; s. Hiram and Alma (Willis) S.; B.A., Washington and Lee U., 1910, M.A., 1911; M.D., Johns Hopkins, 1915; m. Olive Thompson, May 27, 1920; 1 dau., Anne Willis (Mrs. Joel M. Le Sueur). Intern, asst. resident physician Johns Hopkins Hosp., 1915-17; prof. medicine Med. Coll. Ga., 1923—. Mem. nutrition com. NRC, 1940-45; cons. Surgeon Gen. of Army, 1940—; adviser Brit. Ministry of Health, 1942-43, nutrition div. WHO, 1950; head European nutrition sect. UNNRA, 1944-45; mem. internat. health div. Rockefeller Found., 1942-43. Served from 1st lt. to capt., M.C., U.S. Army, 1917-19. Recipient King's Medal for Service, Eng., 1946, citation, U.S. War Dept., 1945, Brit. Govt., 1945, Dutch Govt., 1945. Master A.C.P.; fellow A.A.A.S.; mem. Assn. Am. Physicians, Soc. Exptl. Biology and Medicine, Am. Nutrition Inst., Royal Soc. Medicine (Gt. Britain). Home: 2223 Overton Rd., Augusta, Ga. Died Dec. 12, 1964; buried Augusta.

SYLVESTER, JAMES JOSEPH, mathematician, educator; b. London, Eng., Sept. 3, 1814; s. Abraham Joseph; grad. St. John's Coll., Cambridge (Eng.) U., 1831 (barred from degree by Jewish faith, but awarded B.A. and M.A. after Test Act of 1872); B.A., M.A., U. Dublin (Ireland), 1841; never married. Prof. natural philosophy U. Coll., London, 1837-41; prof. mathematics U. Va., 1841-42; returned to London in 1844, did actuarial work, 1844-56; called to the bar, Eng., 1850; prof. mathematics Johns Hopkins U., Balt., 1876-83; a leader in advancing math. research in U.S.; 1st editor Am. Jour. Mathematics, 1878-84; Savilian prof. geometry Oxford (Eng.) U., 1883-97. Author: The Collected Mathematical Papers of James Joseph Sylvester, 4 vols., 1904-12 (edited by H.F. Baker); The Laws of Verse, 1870; translations of Horace, German poets. Died Oxford, Mar. 15, 1897.

SYMMERS, DOUGLAS, (sim'mers), pathologist; b. Columbia, S.C., Sept. 17, 1879; s. George and Jessie (McKay) S.; student U. of S.C. and Univ. Tutorial Coll., London, Eng.; M.D., Jefferson Med. Coll., Phila., 1901; unmarried. Instr. pathology, Bellevue Med. Coll., New York, 1907, Cornell Med. Coll., 1908-11; asst. pathologist, New York Hosp., 1908-13; prof. pathology, Bellevue Med. Coll., 1911-18; dir. labs. Bellevue and Allied Hosps., 1918-29; gen. dir. labs., Dept. of Hosps., N.Y. City, since 2929; cons. pathologist Englewood and Beekman St. hosps. Mem. N.Y. Pathol. Soc. (pres. 2 terms), Assn. Am. Pathologists and Bacteriologists, International Med. Museums, Sigma Alpha Epsilon; fellow New York Academy of Medicine. Episcopalian. Editor Ziegler's General Pathology (5th Am. edit.), 1921. Contbr. about 80 papers on research work. Home: 140 E. 28th St. Address: Bellevue Hospital, N.Y.C. Died Apr. 19, 1952.

SYMONS, THOMAS BADDELEY, dean agr.; b. Easton, Md., Sept. 2, 1880; s. Robert and Susan (Baddeley) S.; B.S., Md. Agrl. Coll., 1902, M.S., 1905, D.Agr., 1918; m. Susie La Roche, Apr. 10, 1907; children—Helen (Mrs. Innis LaRoche Jenkins), Isabel (Mrs. Owen Godwin), Josephine (Mrs. James Robert Troth). Asst. entomologist, Md. Agrl. Coll., 1902-04, state entomologist, 1904-14, dean sch. of Horticulture, 1913-14; dir. of extension, U. of Md. from 1914, acting dean Coll. of Agr., 1937-39, dean, 1939-50, pres. pro tem U. Md., 1953-54; pub. relations dir. Suburban Trust Co., 1950-70, also dir.; dir. Prince Georges Bank & Trust Co. Mem. A.A.A.S., Md. State Hort. Soc., Md. Agrl. Soc., Kappa Alpha, Epsilon Sigma Phi. Democrat. Episcopalian. Club: Rotary. Home: College Park MD Died July 4, 1970; buried St. John's Cemetery Beltsville MD

SYMONS, THOMAS WILLIAM, colonel U.S.A.; b. Keesville, N.Y., Feb. 7, 1849; s. Thomas and Syrena (Eaton) S.; grad. U.S. Mil. Acad., 1874; m. Letitia V. Robinson, Oct. 12, 1884. In service on civ. and mil. engring. works in Washington, D.C., Ore., Calif., Nev., Wash., Ida., Mont., and the Great Lakes until retired from mil. service, 1898, to devote attention to work of bldg. the New York state canals. Built the largest breakwater in the world, at Buffalo, N.Y.; had charge of U.S. light houses from Detroit, Mich., to Ogdensburg, N.Y.; was supt. pub. bldgs. and grounds and mil. aide to the President; mem. Canal Advisory Bd. and consulting engr. on canals State of N.Y. Author: The Columbia River, 1882; A Ship Canal from the Great Lakes to the Sea (engring. report), 1897. Home: Washington, D.C. Died Nov. 22, 1920.

SYNG, PHILIP, silversmith; b. Cork, Ireland, Sept. 29, 1703; s. Philip and Abigail (Murdock) S.; m. Elizabeth Warner, Feb. 5, 1729/30; 21 children including Philip. Came to Annapolis, Md., 1714; opened shop in Phila., circa 1720; most famous silver work was inkstand made for Pa. Assembly, 1752 (used at signing both Declaration of Independence and U.S. Constn.; mem. Benjamin Franklin's Junto and one of few serious experimenters with Franklin in electricity in 1740's; invented a machine which aided in generation of electricity, by 1747; mem. Am. Philos. Soc., treas., 1769-71; a grantee charter for Phila. Library Co. a founding trustee Coll. and Acad. of Phila. (later part U. Pa.); warden Phila., 1753, treas., 1759-69; mem. Pa. Provincial Commn. of Appeals, 1765; signer Non-Importation Agreement, 1765. Died Phila., May 8, 1789.

SYVERTON, JEROME T., physician, educator; b. Courtenay, N.D., Mar. 29, 1907; s. John and Thea (Nelson) S.; A.B., U. of N.D., 1927, B.S., 1928; M.D., Harvard, 1931; m. Mildred Sloulin, June 26, 1932; children—Jane, Gail, Laurie. Instr. in bacteriology, Univ. N.D., 1928; interne and asst. resident in medicine, Duke Univ. Hosp., 1931-32; asst. pathology and bacteriology, Rockefeller Inst. Med. Research, 1932-34; vis. asso. prof. pathology and bacteriology, Vanderbilt Univ., April-Oct., 1942; in str. bacteriology, Univ. of Rochester Sch. Medicine and Dentistry, 1934-37, asst. prof., 1937-39, asso. prof., 1939-47; prof. microbiol. and head dept., La. State U., Sch. Medicine, 1947-48; prof. and head of department of bacteriology U. of Minnesota since 1948. Mem. microbiol. panel Office of Naval Research, 1946-50; cons. surgeon gen. USPHS, 1950—, as mem. virus, rickettsial and microbiology study sects., 1950-55, National Adv. Allergy and Infectious Diseases Council, 1957-61, adv. panel on viruses and cancer Nat. Cancer Council, 1959—; mem. scientific advisory board consultants Armed Forces Institute Pathology, 1960—. Served in Med. Corps, U.S.N.R., 1941-47; active duty April 1944-Jan. 1946 with appointment as vis. investigator Hosp. Rockefeller Inst., Apr.-Nov., 1944; fgn. duty Naval Med. Research Unit 2 in Pacific theater to Jan., 1946. Recipient Lilly award for Research in Bacteriology and Immunology, 1938; Commonwealth Fund Award in Support of Creative Work, 1957. Diplomate Nat. Bd. Med. Examiners. Mem. A.M.A., American Academy of Microbiology, also Society Am. Bacteriologists, Soc. Clin. Investigation, Soc. Exptl. Pathology, Am. Assn. Immunol.; Am. Soc. Tropical Med., Am. Epidemiol. Soc., Tissue Culture Association Central Society Clinical Research, New York Academy of Science, A.A.A.S., Minnesota Med. Assn., Am. Soc. Cancer Research, Soc. Exptl. Biology and Medicine, American Assn. Pathologists and Bacteriologists (exec. council 1959—), Am. Soc. Cell Biology, Harvey Society (N.Y.), Alpha Omega Alpha, Sigma Xi. Presbyn. Clubs: Campus (U. Minn.); Harvard (Minn.); Lafayette. Author: scientific articles in field of infectious disease for profl. jours. Mem. editorial bd. Bacteriological Reviews, Cancer Research, Proceedings of Soc. for Exptl. Biology and Medicine. Home: Woodbridge Rd., Route 1, Box 18, Wayzata, Minn. Office: 1060 Mayo Meml. Bldg., U. of Minn., Mpls. 14. Died Jan. 28, 1961.

SYVERTSEN (VON WEDEL JARLSBERG), ROLF CHRISTIAN, medical dean; b. Taunton, Mass., Mar. 22, 1896; s. Ole Christian and Ellen Gertrude (Badger) Syvertsen von Wedel-Jarlsberg; B.S., Dartmouth, 1921; student Dartmouth Med. Sch., 1920-23, Mary Hitchcock Meml. Hosp., 1935-36; M.D., Rush Med. Coll., 1936; m. Margaret Huntly Gordon, Mar. 10, 1935; children—Rosalind Gordon, Margaret Gordon, Caroline Gordon, Astrid Gordon. Asst. in biology Dartmouth, 1919-21, instr., 1921-22, instr. in evolution, 1922-23; instr. in anatomy Dartmouth Med. Sch., 1923-32, asst. prof., 1923-38, prof. since 1938, asst. dean, 1942-45, dean since 1945, sec., 1923-42; research work Mary Hitchcock Meml. Hosp., 1935-36, mem. bd. trustees since 1945. Mem. health com. New Hampshire Citizens Council. Served with U.S. Army, 1917-19. Mem. A.A.A.S.; Dartmouth Scientific Assn., Grafton Co. Med. Soc., N.H. Med. Soc., N.H. Hist. Soc., Soc. for Advancement of Scandinavian Studies. Norwegian-Am. Hist. Assn., Alpha Tau Omega. Alpha Kappa Kappa, Alpha Omega Alpha. Republican. Episcopalian. Clubs: Dartmouth Outing (dir. Winter Carnival 1925-26; trustee since 1947). The Graduate, Appalachian Mountain. Home: Great Hollow Farm, Hanover, N.H. Died Jan. 29, 1960.

SZILARD, LEO, (ze-lärd), physicist; b. Budapest, Feb. 11, 1898; s. Louis and Thekla (Vidor) S.; student engring., Budapest Inst. of Tech.; Dr. Phil., U. of Berlin, 1922; m. Gertrud Weiss, 1951. Came to U.S., 1937, naturalized, 1943. Mem. teaching staff, U. of Berlin, 1925-32; research work in nuclear physics, St. Bartholomew's Hosp., London and Clarendon Lab., Oxford, Eng., 1934-38; worked on atomic energy, Columbia, 1939-42; chief Physicist, Metall. Lab., U. of Chgo., 1942-46, prof. U. Chgo.; resident fellow Salk Inst. Biol. studies, La Jolla, California, 1964—. Recipient Atoms for Peace award, 1960. Fellow Am. Phys. Soc. With Enrico Fermi, devised chain reaction system composed of uranium and graphite, used in setting up chain reaction, U. of Chicago, 1942, also used at Hanford in mfr. of plutonium. Mem. staff Enrico Fermi Inst. Office: Salk Inst. Biol. Studies, La Jolla, Cal. Died May 30, 1964.

TACKETT, JOHN ROBERT, physician; b. Richland, Holmes Co., Miss., Dec. 18, 1868; s. Dr. John and Elizabeth Anne Tackett; ed. Richland, Miss., public schools, Univ. of Miss., 1884-86 (through junior yr.); grad. Tulane Univ., La., M.D., 1889; post-graduate studies New York Policlinic; m. Columbus, Miss., Oct. 16, 1902, Juanita H. Ayres. Sec. Miss. State Med. Assn., mem. Am. Med. Assn., Miss. Valley Med. Assn.; Lauderdale Co. Med. Assn.; asst. supt. East Miss. Insane Asylum, 1894-97; commr. to Havana, Cuba, to investigate yellow fever for the State bd. of health, 1897; acting asst. surgeon U.S.A., 1898; stationed in yellow fever hosp. across Santiago Harbor, Santiago de Cuba; served in Cuba and Porto Rico during Spanish Am. war; co. health officer Lauderdale Co.; Democrat. Elected mem. Miss. State Bd. Health, Apr., 1903. Address: Meridian, Miss.

TAFF, JOSEPH ALEXANDER, geologist; b. Ten Mile, Tenn., Nov. 20, 1862; s. Albert G. and Tirzah A. T.; student U. of Ark., 1886-88; B.S., U. of Tex., 1894; m. Mary M. Leverett, Dec. 24, 1891; children—Elizabeth Simonds, Charles Leverett, Mary Willis, Joseph Whitham, Rosa LeRoche. Mem. Ark. and Tex. geol. surveys, 1888-94; geologist on U.S. Geol. Survey, 1894-1909; geologists S.P. Co., 1909-25, cons. geologist, 1925-32; chief geologist, Associated Oil Co., 1921-29; cons. geologist, 1929-37; retired, 1937. Mem. Geol. Soc. America (hon.), Geol. Soc. Washington, A.A.A.S., Am. Inst. Mining Engrs., Seismol. Soc. America, Nat. Geog. Soc., Calif. Acad. Science, Am. Assn. of Petroleum Geologists (hon.), Sigma Xi. Author of papers, folios and bulletins in publs. of Tex., and U.S. geol. surveys and in jours. of tech. socs. on gen. and econ. geology of coal, oil, asphalt and cement resources in 11 states. Home: 628 Cowper St., Palo Alto, Calif. Deceased.

TAFT, LEVI RAWSON, horticulturist; b. Mendon, Worcester Co., Mass., Aug. 22, 1859; s. Austin Augustus and Helen Maria (Mather) T.; B.S., Mass. Agrl. Coll., 1882; U. of Mo., 1886-87; m. Ella S. Maynard, of Northboro, Mass., June 10, 1884. Asst. prof. horticulture, Mass., Agrl. College, 1882-85; prof. horticulture, U. of Mo., 1885-88; prof. horticulture and horticulturist Expt. Sta., Mich. Agrl. Coll., 1888-1902; supt. farmers' insts. and state insp. nurseries and orchards, Mich., 1902—; pres. Eveline Fruit & Land Co.; v.p. Mich. Knitting Co.; dir. Hammond Pub. Co., Cuban Fruit & Sugar Co. (all of Lansing, Mich.). Republican. Unitarian. Mem. American Pomol. Assn. (treas.), corr. mem. Hort. Soc. of France; Officer de Mérite Horticole, France. Author: Greenhouse Construction, 1891; Greenhouse Management, 1895. Collaborator for Garden Making, 1898, and for The Practical Farmer and Gardener, 1902; contbr. to Bailey's Cyclopedia of Horticulture and Bailey's Cyclopedia of Agriculture. Address: E. Lansing, Michigan.

TAFT, ROBERT, prof. chemistry; b. of Am. parents, Tokyo, Japan, Mar. 24, 1894; s. George Wheaton and Jessie (Humpstone) T.; brought to U.S., 1897; A.B., Grand Island (Neb.) Coll., 1916; M.S., U. Ia., 1919; Ph.D., U. Kan., 1925; m. Josephine Miller, Neb., July 24, 1916; children—Robert, Dorothy. Instr. chemistry Grand Island Coll., 1916-17, Gilbert (Minn.) High Sch., 1917-18, U. Ia., 1918-19, Ottawa (Kan.) U., 1919-22; mem. faculty U. Kan., 1922—, asso. prof. physical chemistry, 1930-37, prof., 1937—. Mem. Am. Assn. U. Profs., Kan. Acad. Science (past pres.), Kan. State Hist. Soc. (past pres.). An authority on Am. historical photographs and pictures; lectr. Chmn. Kan. Territorial Centennial Commn., 1952-54. Author: Photography and the American Scene, 1938; Across the Years on Mount Oread, 1941; Pictorial Record of the Old West, 1946; Fifty Years in Bailey Chemical Laboratory, 1950; Artists and Illustrators of the Old West (Bryan Caldwell Smith award), 1953; The Years on Mount Oread, 1955. Editor of Transactions Kan. Acad. of Science, 1941. Contbr. articles to tech. jours. Home: 1713 Louisiana St., Lawrence, Kan. Died Sept. 22, 1955.

TAFT, ROBERT BURBIDGE, radiology; b. Charleston, S.C., Sept. 20, 1899; s. Augustus Robert (M.D.) and Mary Walter (Witsell) T.; student Porter Mil. Acad., Charleston, 1910-17; B.S., Coll. of Charleston, 1923, M.A., 1934; M.D., Med. Coll. State of S.C., 1923; post-grad. study, U. of Mich. and U. of Vienna, Austria, 1929; m. Mary Joyce Steedman, Oct. 6, 1926; 1 dau., Joyce Shannon. Interne Bellevue Hosp., N.Y. City, 1923-24; asst. in radiology to father until his death, 1927, since in pvt. practice; radiologist Baker sanatorium (Charleston); prof. and dir. dept. of radiology Medical Coll. State of S.C., also director of the radioisotope laboratory. Mem. bd. cons. Oak Ridge Inst. Nuclear Studies. Served in U.S. Army, Plattsburg, N.Y., 1918, World War; classed as essential civilian physician World War II. Mem. bd. commrs. Charleston Mus. Licensed as comml. pilot. Awarded silver medal of Am. Roentgen Ray Soc. for research exhibit, 1936, certificate of merit, 1938, 44, silver medal, 1942; Jefferson Medal of South Carolina Academy of Science, 1929. Member A.M.A., Medical Society State of S.C., S.C. State Medical Association, American Roentgen Ray Society (former chairman committee for use and rental of radium; former chmn. com. on safety and standards); American College Radiology (former councillor South Carolina), Radiology Society of North America (2d v.p.; com. on standardization of x-ray measurements; counselor for S.C.), Am. Phys. Soc., S.C. X-Ray Society, S.C. Acad. of Science (former mem. exec. council), Kappa Alpha, Phi Chi. Author: Radium Lost and Found, 1938, 2d edit., 1946. Author numerous articles summarizing his research work and discoveries. Tech. editor Am. Jour. Roentgenology. Home: 135 S. Battery, Charleston 21. Office: 103 Rutledge Av., Charleston 16, S.C. Died Apr. 16, 1951.

TAGLIABUE, GIUSEPPE, inventor, instrument maker; b. Como, Italy, Aug. 10, 1812; s. Caesar Tagliabue; m. 2d, Adelaide Arniboldi; 6 children. Began mfg. thermometers, N.Y.C, 1829; became one of most prominent and successful instrument makers of U.S., 1831-78; produced variety of new hydrometers; hydrometer for proving of whiskey officially adopted by U.S. Revenue Bur.; perfected and patented several instruments including mercurial barometers and apparatus for testing iron and coal, 1859-71; known for precision of instruments. Died Mt. Vernon, N.Y., May 7, 1873.

TAINTER, CHARLES SUMNER, inventor; b. Watertown, Mass., Apr. 25, 1854; s. George and Abigail (Sanger) T.; pub. sch. edn.; m. Lila R. Munro, June 22, 1886; m. 2d, Laura Fontaine Onderdonk, Apr. 7, 1928. Inventor of the graphophone, also of the dictaphone; associate inventor of the radiophone, an instrument for transmitting sounds to a distance through the agency of light; member of the U.S. expedition sent to the South Pacific to observe transit of Venus, 1874. Awarded gold medal at Electrical Exhbn., Paris, 1881, for inventions in connection with the radiophone; Officier de l'Instruction Publique, France, for invention of graphophone, 1889; John Scott medal, 1900, by City of Phila., for the invention of the graphophone; gold medal, 1915, at Panama P.I. Expn. for work in connection development of the talking machine. Home: San Diego, Calif. Died Apr. 20, 1940.

TAKAMINE, JOKICHI, chemist; b. Takaoka, Japan, Nov. 3, 1854; s. Dr. Seichi and Yuki T.; grad. in chem. engring., Engring. Coll., Imperial U. of Tokyo, 1879; Japanese Govt. student, U. of Glasgow and Andersonian U., Glasgow, 3 yrs., 1879-81; (Dr. Chem. Engring., Imperial U. of Japan, 1899, Dr. Pharm., 1906); m. Caroline Hitch, 1885. Head chemist Imperial Dept. Agr. and Commerce, Tokyo, 1881-84; Imperial Japanese commr. to Cotton Centennial Expn., New Orleans, 1884-85; organized and erected 1st superphosphate works at Tokyo, 1887; came to America, 1890, and applied new process of conversion and fermentation to practical use resulting in production of diastatic enzyme ("Takadiastase"), now largely used as a starch digestant; established research lab. in New York and originated a process for isolating the active principle of the suprarenal glands, the product being known as ("adrenalin"); cons. chemist. Decorated by Emperor of Japan with 4th Order of the Rising Sun, 1915; apptd. by Emperor mem. Royal Acad. Sciences, Japan, 1913. Home: Passaic, N.J. Died July 22, 1922.

TALBOT, ARTHUR NEWELL, engineer; b. Cortland, Ill., Oct. 21, 1857; s. Charles A. and Harriet (Newell) T.; B.S., U. of Ill., 1881, C.E., 1885, LL.D., 1931; Sc.D., U. of Pa., 1915; D.Eng., U. of Mich., 1916; m. Virginia Mann Hammet, June 7, 1886 (died Dec. 4, 1919); children—Kenneth Hammet, Mrs. Mildred Virginia Gilkey, Mrs. Rachel Harriet Westergaard, Mrs. Dorothy Newell Goodell. Engring. work on rys., roads, bridges, bldgs. and municipal pub. wks. since 1881; asst. prof. engring. and mathematics, U. of Ill., 1885-90, prof. municipal and sanitary engring. and in charge theoretical and applied mechanics, 1890-1926, now prof. emeritus; made many investigations on properties of steel, brick, concrete, reinforced concrete, etc., and on bldgs. in connection with U. of Ill. Engring. Exptl. Sta. and as consultant, also investigations of water purification, sewage treatment and hydraulic questions; dir. investigation conducted by Am. Soc. C.E. and Am. Ry. Engring. Assn. to determine stresses in railroad track since 1914. Mem. Am. Soc. C.E. (pres. 1918; hon. mem. 1925), Soc. for Promotion Engring. Edn. (pres. 1910-11), Am. Soc. Testing Materials (pres. 1913-14; hon. mem. 1923), Am. Water Works Assn. (hon. mem. 1930), Western Soc. Engrs. (Washington award, 1924; hon. mem. 1927), Am. Public Works Assn., Am. Ry. Engring. Assn. (dir. 1915-18, 1928-31; hon. mem. 1933), Am. Soc. Mech. Engrs., New Eng. Water Works Assn., A.A.A.S. (v.p. 1928), Am. Concrete Inst. (Turner medal, 1928; hon. mem. 1932), Instn. Civ. Engrs. (London); hon. mem. Instn. Structural Engrs. (London); mem. bd. visitors U.S. Naval Acad., 1918-21; etc. Awarded Henderson medal, Franklin Institute, 1931; Lamme medal, Soc. for Promotion Engring. Edn., 1932; John Fritz medal of the Founder Societies, 1937. Clubs:

TALBOT, HENRY PAUL, chemist; b. Boston, May 15, 1864; s. Zephaniah and Eliza Frances T.; B.S., Mass. Inst. Tech., 1885; Ph.D., Leipzig, 1890; Sc.D., Dartmouth, 1921; m. Frances E. Dukehart, June 17, 1891; 1 son, Paul Dukehart (dec.). Asst., 1885-87, instr. 1887-88 and 1890-92, asst. prof., 1892-95, asso. prof., 1895-98, prof. analyt. chemistry, 1898-1902, prof. inorganic chemistry, in charge dept. chemistry and chemical engring., 1902-20, in charge dept. chemistry, 1920-22, chmn. faculty, 1919-21, chmn. administrative com., 1920-23, dean students, 1921—, Mass. Inst. Tech. Lecturer Wellesley Coll., 1892-94. Mem. Advisory Bd. U.S. Bur. Mines (gas defense), 1917. Fellow Am. Acad. Arts and Sciences, A.A.A.S. Author: Introductory Course of Quantitative Chemical Analysis, 1897; Bibliography of the Analytical Chemistry of Manganese, 1902; The Electrolytic Dissociation Theory (with A. A. Blanchard), 1905. Home: West Newton, Mass. Died June 18, 1927.

TALBOT, M(URRELL) W(ILLIAMS), forester, ecologist; b. Appleton City, Mo., Aug. 18, 1889; s. LeRoy Hitt and Lettie E. (Williams) T.; B.S., U. Mo., 1913; postgrad. U.S. Dept. Agr. Grad. Sch., 1931; m. Zenaida Merriam, Oct. 27, 1928; children—Lee Merriam, Zenaida (Mrs. William Penn Mott III). Various positions U.S. Forest Service and Bur. Plant Industry, 1913-31; sr. ecologist charge range research Pacific S.W. Forest & Range Expt. Sta., Berkeley, Cal., 1931-55, acting dir., 1941-45, also dir., 1946-55, cons., 1955-72; cons. Govt. Spain, Pack Found., Salt River Basin, Ariz., State Cal.; collaborator U.S. Department of Agriculture. Member Alameda County Grand Jury. Served to 2d lt. F.A., U.S. Army, 1918. Recipient Spl. Meritorious award U.S. Dept. Agr., 1945, Alumnus of year citation Merit U. Mo., 1959. Fellow A.A.A.S.; mem. Am. Soc. Range Mgmt. (pres. 1963), Soc. Am. Foresters, Ecol. Soc. Am., Wilderness Soc., Alpha Zeta, Xi Sigma Pi. Republican. Conglist. Mason (32 deg.). Clubs: Faculty University California, Outlook (Berkeley); Commonwealth (San Francisco); Hillside (Berkeley). Author articles in field. Home: Berkeley CA Died Jan. 12, 1972.

TALCOTT, ANDREW, army officer, engr.; b. Glastonbury, Conn., Apr. 20, 1797; s. George and Abigail (Goodrich) T.; grad. U.S. Mil. Acad., 1818; m. Catherine Thompson, Apr. 1826; m. 2d, Harriet Randolph Hackley, Apr. 11, 1832; 11 children. Brevetted 2d lt. U.S. Army, 1818; 1st lt. Engr. Corps, 1820, capt., 1830; engr., aide-de-camp to Gen. Henry Atkinson in establishment of posts on Upper Missouri and Yellowstone rivers, 1820-21; chief engr. Ft. Delaware, Del., 1824-25; supt. constrn. canal through Dismal Swamp in Va., 1826-28; supervised constrn. Ft. Monroe, Ft. Calhoun, Hampton Roads, Va., 1828-34; astronomer for determining boundaries between Ohio and Mich., 1828-35; chief engr. in charge of Western div. N.Y. & Erie R.R., 1836-37; supt. improvement of delta of Mississippi River, 1837-39; chief engr. Richmond & Danville R.R., 1848-55; astronomer, surveyor for making the northern boundary of Ia., 1852-53; chief engr. Ohio & Miss. R.R. from Cincinnati and St. Louis, 1856-57; located, constructed railroad from Vera Cruz to Mexico City, 1857-60, 61-67; mgr. Sonora Exploring & Mining Co., chief engr. State of Va., 1860-61; elected chief engr. Va., 1861; devised method of determining terrestrial latitudes through the observation of stars near the zenith; mem. Am. Philos. Soc. Died Richmond, Va., Apr. 22, 1883.

TALCOTT, EDWARD N. KIRK, civil and mech. engr.; b. Cuba, N.Y., June 10, 1840; s. William H. and Harriet N. T.; grad. Univ. City of New York, 1859. Private 7th N.Y. Nat. Guard, 1861-62; in 1st regt. N.Y. engrs., U.S. vols., 1862-65 (2d lit., 1st lt., capt.). Asst. Thomas Iron Works, Pa., 1865-66; supt. other large iron mfg. enterprises, 1866-76; supt. Ill. Mil. Acad., 1876-90; consulting civ. and mech. engr.; m. Antoinette M. Watkins;, May 23, 1867; m. 2d, Lillian Baird, Nov. 26, 1884. Home: Goshen, N.Y. Died 1901.

TALIAFERRO, HENRY BECKWITH, (tol'i-ver), govt. ofcl.; b. Washington, July 15, 1904; s. Henry Addison and Sarah (Ashlin) T.; B.S., U.S. Naval Acad., 1928; m. Dorothy Tower Butts, June 7, 1928. Served as seaman 2d class to ensign, U.S.N., 1923-30, comdr., 1942-47, ret. as capt., 1947; design and test engr. Gen. Electric Co., 1930-31; staff of v.p. and chief engr. Potomac Electric Power Co., 1931-35; elec. engr. El Segondo and Richmond Refineries, Standard Oil Co. of Cal., 1935-37; elec. engr. constrn. and operation govt. of D.C., 1937-39; elec. engr. substa. and transmission line constrn. Bonneville Power Adminstr., 1939-41, asst. to adminstr., Washington, 1941-42; elec. engr., power mgr. U.S. Bur. Reclamation, Sacramento, 1947-51, asst. dir. power utilization, Washington, 1951-52, dir., 1952-56; dir. of power utilization Power Authority State of N.Y., 1956—. Decorated Legion of Merit, Commendation Ribbon, Unit Citation, Victory Medal. Registered profl. engr., Cal. Mem. Am. Inst. E.E., C.I.G.R.E. Club: Commonwealth. Home: The Westchester, 4000 Cathedral Av., N.W., Washington. Office: Coliseum Tower, 10 Columbus Circle, N.Y.C. 19. Died Nov. 5, 1958; buried Arlington Nat. Cemetery, Arlington, Va.

TALIAFERRO, NICHOLAS LLOYD, (tol'i-ver), coll. prof.; b. Augusta, Ky., Oct. 6, 1890; s. Nicholas Curtis and Julia Perine (Lloyd) T.; B.S., U. of Calif., 1913, Ph.D., 1920; m. Ann Freeman Watson, Jan. 2, 1937; children—Nicholas (by first marriage), Anthony Watson. Geologist, Standard Oil Co. of N.Y., in China, 1913-16; jr. engr., U.S. Bureau Mines, 1917; instr. geology, U. of Calif., 1918-20, asso. prof., 1926-36, prof. since 1936, chmn. dept. since 1937; chief geologist, Ventura Consol., 1922-26. Fellow Geol. Soc. America, Mem. Seismol. Soc. America, Beta Theta Pi, Theta Tau, Tau Beta Pi, Sigma Xi. Protestant. Republican. Club: Faculty. Home: 160 Alderwood Rd., Walnut Creek, Calif. Died Nov. 16, 1961; buried Mountain View Cemetery, Oakland, Cal.

TALLMADGE, GUY KASTEN, physician, educator; b. Milw., Apr. 27, 1901; s. Samuel W. and Alma (Kasten) T.; A.B., U. Wis., 1923, A.M., 1924, Ph.D., 1936; M.D., U. Pa., 1926; m. Alice C. La Boule, Apr. 9, 1929; 1 son, Guy Kasten. Intern, Columbia Hosp., Milw., 1926-27, resident, 1927-28; practice medicine, specializing in internal medicine, Milw., 1928—; asso. med. staff Columbia Hosp., 1928—; asst. prof. anatomy Marquette U., 1931-48, prof. history medicine, 1948—, dir. dept. history medicine, 1954—, univ. com. fine arts, 1956—, univ. com. acad. honors, 1956—; lectr. U. Lisbon, U. Rome, Chulalonghorn U., Bangkok, Thailand, others. Field capt. Milw. United Charities, 1952; participant Marquette U. Endowment, 1954—. Mem. Am. Assn. Anatomists, Am. Assn. History Medicine (council), A.A.A.S., Internat. Acad. History Sci., Internat. Soc. History Medicine, History Sci. Soc., N.Y. Acad. Scis., Luso-Hispano-Americana Soc. History Sci. Club: University. Author: Basic Biology of Man, 1953. Contbr. articles to profl. jours., symposial vols., also Am. Coll. Dictionary. Home: 4314 N. Stowell Av., Milw. 11. Office: 924 E. Wells St., Milw. 2. Died Sept. 17, 1966.

TALMAGE, JAMES EDWARD, geologist, theologian; b. Hungerford, Berkshire, Eng., Sept. 21, 1862; s. James J. and Susannah (Preater) T.; emigrated, 1876, family having embraced faith of Latter-Day Saints; Brigham Young Acad., Provo, Utah, 1876-82; Lehigh U., 1882-83; Johns Hopkins, 1883-84; B.S., Lehigh, 1891; Ph.D., Ill. Wesleyan U., 1896; hon. D.Sc. and Didactics, Ch. of Jesus Christ of Latter-Day Saints, 1890; hon. D.Sc., Lehigh, 1912; LL.D., Brigham Young U. and U. of Utah, 1922; m. Mary May Booth, June 14, 1888; children—Sterling Booth, Paul Booth, Zella (dec.), Elsie, James Karl, Lucile, Helen May, John Russell. Prof. chemistry and geology, Brigham Young Acad., 1884-88; pres. Latter-Day Saints Coll., Salt Lake City, 1888-93; pres. U. of Utah, 1894-97; resigned presidency, 1897, retaining chair of geology; resigned professorship, July 1907. Ordained one of twelve apostles Ch. of Jesus Christ of Latter-Day Saints, Dec. 1911. Del. from Royal Soc. of Edinburgh to Internat. Geol. Congress, St. Petersburg, 1897. Author: First Book of Nature, 1888; Domestic Science, 1891; The Articles of Faith, 1899; The Book of Mormon, an Account of Its Origin, etc., 1899; Tables for Blowpipe Determination of Minerals, 1899; The Great Salt Lake, Present and Past, 1900; The Story of Mormonism, 1907; The Great Apostasy, 1909; The House of the Lord, 1912; The Philosophy of Mormonism, 1914; Jesus the Christ, 1915; The Vitality of Mormonism, 1919. Home: Salt Lake City, Utah. Died July 27, 1933.

TALMAN, CHARLES FITZHUGH, meteorologist, writer; b. Detroit, Aug. 31, 1874; s. late Robert Fitzhugh and Jessica (Mack) T.; ed. Detroit pub. schs., Kalamazoo (Mich.) Coll. and pvt. tutors; m. Grace F., d. Lt. Comdr. B. L. Edes, U.S.N., Nov. 16, 1909;

children—Constance Elizabeth Marjorie (wife of Mario Rodriguez), Benjamin Long Edes. With U.S. Weather Bur., Oct. 1896—; in charge meteorol. stas. in S. America and W.I., 1898-99; librarian, 1908-35, meteorol. consultant, July 1, 1935—, jr. prof. meteorology, 1912-14, prof. meteorology, 1914-22, meteorologist, 1922—, U.S. Weather Bureau. Fellow Am. Meteorol. Soc., A.A.A.S. Specialist in meteorology for Standard Dictionary, 1910-11; writer for Science Service, 1921—. Author: Meteorology, the Science of the Atmosphere, 1922 (republished as Our Weather, 1925); The Realm of the Air, 1931, republished as A Book about the Weather, 1935. Home: Washington, D.C. Died July 24, 1936.

TANNER, BENJAMIN, engraver; b. N.Y.C., Mar. 25, 1775; m. Mary Bioren, Sept. 6, 1806. Apprenticed to engraver Peter C. Verger, N.Y.C., 1790-96; moved to Phila., set up own engraving shop, 1799-1811; worked with brother Henry Schenck Tanner in map engraving, Phila., 1811-17; established bank note engraving bus. with Francis Kearny and Cornelius Tiebout, 1817-18, organized gen. engraving co. with same partners, 1818-24; he (or his brother) devised way in which check blank could be engraved so that it could not be altered without detection, 1828; engaged mainly in engraving check and note blanks under trade name "Stereograph," 1835-45; went to Balt. to receive treatment for abcess on brain, 1845; engravings include: Perry's Victory, Capture of the Macedonian, Surrender of Cornwallis. Died Balt., Nov. 14, 1848.

TANNER, FRED WILBUR, bacteriologist; b. Buffalo, Feb. 15, 1888; s. Wellington Boughton and Emma Melvina (Olds) T.; B.S., Wesleyan U., 1912, D.Sc., 1943; M.S., U. Ill., 1914, Ph.D., 1916; m. Hope Stuart Montgomery, June 10, 1916 (died 1935); children—Fred Wilbur, Wells Montgomery, Stuart Wellington, Hope Montgomery (dec.); m. 2d, Louise Milliken Pickens, Dec. 27, 1936. Bacteriologist Ill. State Water Survey, 1912-15; with U. Ill., 1915—, prof. bacteriology, 1923—, head dept. bacteriology to 1948; bacteriologist, branch lab. Ill. Dept. Health. Mem. Am. Chem. Soc., Soc. Am. Bacteriologists, Soc. Exptl. Biology and Medicine, Inst. Food Technologists (pres. 1945-46), Internat. Assn. Milk Sanitarians, Alpha Chi Rho, Alpha Chi Sigma, Phi Sigma, Sigma Xi, Pi Gamma Mu; fellow A.A.A.S., Am. Pub. Health Assn.; asso. fellow A.M.A. Repulbcan. Clubs: University, Rotary. Author: Bacteriology and Mycology of Foods, 1919; The Yeats (Guilliermond-Tanner), 1920; Bacteriology, 1929; Practical Bacteriology, 1929; The Microbiology of Foods, 1944; Food-Borne Infections and Intoxications, 1933, also numerous contbr. to sci. jours. Contbr. Ecy. Britannica. Editor-in-Chief of Food Research. Home: 921 Lincoln Circle, Winter Park, Fla. Died Feb. 24, 1957.

TAPPAN, FRANK GIRARD, educator; b. Mt. Pleasant, Ia., Sept. 20, 1882; s. David Stanton (D.D.) and Anna Louise (Grand-Girard) T.; student Miami U., Oxford, O., 1901-03; B.A., cum laude, Washington and Jefferson Coll., 1904, M.A., 1909; M.E., Cornell U., 1907; m. Mary Pearl Jenks, Aug. 17, 1911; children—Mary Oella, Helen Nina, Ruth Julia, Frances Lois, Frank Girard. Instr. in elec. engring. Cornell U., 1907-17; asso. prof. elec. engring., U. Okla., 1917, prof., 1918—, also dir. Sch. Elec. Engring. 1918-47, acting dean Coll. Engring., 1935-36, Boyd prof. elec. engring., 1947—. Ednl. supr. S.A.T.C., U. Okla., in charge radio, 1917, 18. Fellow Am. Inst. E.E.; mem. Soc. Promotion Engring. Edn., Sigma Tau, Tau Beta Pi, Eta Kappa Nu, Beta Theta Pi. Progressive Republican. Presbyn. Clubs: University Faculty, Lions. Home: Rest Home, Houston. Died Mar. 19, 1962; buried Odd Fellow Cemetery, Norman.

TAQUINO, GEORGE JAMES, (tak-ke-nô), surgeon; b. New Orleans, La., Oct. 19, 1884; s. Thomas P. and Victoria Marie (Guyot) T.; M.D., Tulane University, 1911; D.Sc. (hon.), Loyola University, 1942; married Alice Savich, Mar. 1, 1919; 1 son, George James. Intern Ear, Nose and Throat Hosp., New Orleans, 1911-13; clin. asst. dept. otolaryngology post grad., Tulane, 1913; asst. prof., Tulane, 1915-21; asso. with Dr. Robt. C. Lynch, 1912-22; asst. visiting surgeon Charity Hosp., 1921-26; visiting surgeon, 1926-30, sr. visiting surgeon since 1930; prof. clin. otolaryngology, La. State U., 1931-36, dir. and prof. dept. oto-rhinolaryngology since 1936; prof. bronchoscopy and esophagoscopy La. State U. Med. Center; cons. bronschopist, U.S. Marine Hosp., New Orleans. Served as 1st lt., Gen. Hosp. No. 14, World War. Fellow Am. Acad. of Ophthalmology and Otolaryngology, American Laryngol., Rhinol. and Otological Society, Am. Broncho-Esophagological Society, A.M.A., Am. Coll. of Surgeons, Southeastern Surg. Congress, Internat. Coll. of Surgeons; mem. Orleans Parish, La. State and Southern med. assns., New Orleans Eye, Ear, Nose and Throat Club, Am. Bd. of Otolaryngology, Am. Assn. Mil. Surgeons, Mil. Order World War, Round Table University Club, La. State U. Sch. of Medicine Faculty Club (pres.), Blue Key. Catholic. Clubs: Lions, Metairie Golf. L'Union Francais. Home: 18 Fontainbleau Drive. Office: 1313 Nat. Bank of Commerce Bldg., New Orleans 12. Died Aug. 29, 1953.

TARBOUX, JOSEPH G(ALLUCHAT), educator, engr.; b. Juiz de Fora, Brazil, Aug. 15, 1898; s. John William and Sue Frances (Kirkland) T. (Am. Citizens); B.S., Clemson (S.C.) Coll., 1918; E.E., Cornell, 1923, M.E.E., 1926; Ph.D., 1937; m. Isabelle Nicholas, June 12, 1923; children—John William, Emily Joyce. Instr. Clemson Coll., 1918-19; mem. faculty Cornell, 1919-29, prof. elec. engring., 1946-52; prof. elec. engring. U. Mich. since 1952; professor and head dept. elec. engring. U. Tenn., 1929-46; employed with Fla. Power Co., Ala. Power Co., Pub. Service Co. of N.J., Westinghouse Elec. Corp., Gen. Elec. Co.; cons. since 1929. Fellow Am. Inst. E.E. chmn. com. on education, 1946; Hoover medal bd. of award, 1947-53, v.p. dist. 1, 1950-52); mem. Am. Soc. Engring. Edn. Nat. Soc. Profl. Engrs., Inst. Radio Engrs., Engring. Soc. Detroit, Eta Kappa Nu, Sigma Xi, Tau Beta Pi, Phi Kappa Phi. Contbr. to Collier's Engring. Ency., Standard Handbook for Elec. Engrs., various periodicals, publs. Home: 580 Riverview Dr., Ann Arbor, Mich. Died Feb. 6, 1959; buried Knoxville, Tenn.

TARR, WILLIAM ARTHUR, geologist; b. New Cambria, Mo., Mar. 29, 1881; s. John W. and Ida Elizabeth (Hill) T.; B.S., Oklahoma A. and M. College, 1904, hon. D.Sc., 1927; B.S. in Mining Engring., U. of Arizona, 1908; Ph.D., Univ. of Chicago, 1916; m. Coralynn Gertrude Neumann, Apr. 30, 1905. Instr. in geology and mining, U. of Ariz., 1908-09; research asst., U. of Chicago, 1909-11; instr. geology and mineralogy, 1911-13, asst. prof., 1913-17, asso. prof., 1917-19, prof., 1919—, U. of Missouri. Democrat. Conglist. Author: Introductory Economic Geology, 1930; Introduction to Geology, 1935. Home: Columbia, Mo. Died July 28, 1939.

TASKER, CYRIL, engr.; b. Manchester, Eng., Jan. 8, 1899; s. Percy William and Annie E. (Flint) T.; B.S. Tech., Univ. of Manchester, Coll. of Tech. (Foundation scholar), 1921, M.S. Tech., 1923; m. Ada Ruth Brooks, June 19, 1929. Came to U.S., Oct. 1943. With dept. of scientific and indsl. research, Fuel Research Bd., London, Eng., 1924-30; office in charge N. Staffordshire Coal Survey, 1926-30; sr. research fellow Ontario Research Foundation, Toronto, Can., 1930-43; dir. of research Am. Soc. of Heating and Ventilating Engrs., Cleveland, O., since 1943. Served as lt. spl. brigade, Corps of Royal Engrs., 1917-19. Fellow Inst. of Fuel, London; member Inst. of Heating and Ventilating Engrs., London, Eng., Am. Soc. Heating and Ventilating Engrs. (mem. com. on research, 1936-43; mem. council, 1941-43, pres. Ontario chapter, 1941). Presbyterian. Am. corr. Heating and Ventilating Engr. and Journal of Air Conditioning, London, Eng., since 1939. Contbr. many articles on Am. practice, developments and research in field of heating and ventilating. Home: 3538 Edison Rd., Cleveland 21. Office: 7218 Euclid Av., Cleve. 3. Died May 27, 1953; buried Highland Cemetery, Urn Garden, Cleve.

TASSIN, WIRT, chemist, metallurgist; b. Ft. Whipple, Va., Aug. 11, 1869; s. Col. A. G. and Mary (Tilley) T.; grad. Cornell and Harvard; m. Mary Scott Moran, Aug. 15, 1895. Engaged in applied chemistry, then became spl. agt. U.S. Geol. Survey at Chicago Expn.; chemist and asst. curator, div. of mineralogy, U.S. Nat. Mus., 1893-1909; consulting metallurgist and chem. engr., May 1909—. Home: Washington, D.C. Died Nov. 2, 1915.

TATE, JOHN TORRENCE, physicist; b. Lenox, Adams County, Ia., July 28, 1889; s. Samuel Aaron and Minnie Maria (Ralston) T.; B.Sc., U. of Neb., 1910, M.A., 1912, hon. D.Sc., 1938; Ph.D., U. of Berlin, 1914; hon. D.Sc., Case Sch. of Applied Science, 1945; m. Lois Beatrice Fossler, Dec. 28, 1917 (dec.); 1 son, John Torrence; m. 2d, Madeline Margarite Mitchell, June 30, 1945. Instr. physics, U. of Neb., 1914-15, asst. prof., 1915-16; instr. physics, U. of Minn., 1916-17, asst. prof., 1917-18, asso. prof., 1919-21, prof., 1921-37, dean Coll. Science Lit. and Arts, 1937-43, prof. physics since 1943. Served as 1st lt. signal corps, U.S. Army, 1917-18; chief div. 6, Nat. Defense Research Com., 1941-45. Fellow Carnegie Inst. of Washington. Mem. Am. Phys. Soc. (mng. editor since 1926, pres. 1939); Am. Inst. Physics (governing bd., since 1932, chmn. 1936-39), Nat. Acad. Science, Am. Optical Soc., Am. Philos. Soc., Acoustical Soc. of America, American Assn. Physics Teachers, Sigma Xi, Phi Beta Kappa. Protestant. Clubs: Cosmos, Century Assn. Editor: Physical Review, Review of Modern Physics. Address: 518 Southeast 7th St., Minneapolis. Died May 27, 1950.

TATHAM, WILLIAM, civil engr., geographer; b. Hutton-in-the-Forest, Cumberland, Eng., Apr. 13, 1752; s. Rev. Sandford and Miss (Marsden) T. Clk., Watauga Assn., drafted petition of inhabitants on Western waters for incorporation into govt. of N.C., 1776; with Col. John Todd prepared History of the Western Country, 1780; clk. Va. Council of State, circa 1783; admitted to N.C. bar, 1784; del. N.C. Gen. Assembly, 1787; lt. col. N.C. Militia, circa 1787; contbr. to various publs. engring. and agrl. subjects, London, circa 1796-1805; supt. constrn. Wapping Docks on Thames River, London, 1801; surveyed coast from Cape Fear to Cape Hatteras, 1805-circa 1810; 1st to define functions of nat. library for U.S.; draftsman, geographer Dept. of State, Washington, circa 1810-circa 1815. Author: Memorial on the Civil and Military Government of the Tennessee Colony, 1790; Remarks on Inland Canals, 1798; Political Economy of Inland Navigation, Irrigation, and Drainage, 1799. Died Richmond, Va., Feb. 22, 1819.

TATLOCK, JOHN, astronomer; b. Williamstown, Mass., Mar. 12, 1860; s. Rev. John (D.D.) and Lucy Beman (Whitman) T.; B.A., Williams, 1882, M.A., 1885; m. Kate Chamberlin, Mar. 2, 1886. Asso. astronomer, U. of Wis., 1883-84; prof. astronomy, Beloit Coll., Wis., 1884-85; asst. actuary Mut. Life Ins. Co. of New York, 1889-1905; pres. Washington Life Ins. Co., 1905-08; pres. Westchester Av. Bank, New York, 1910-17. Fellow Royal Astron. Soc., London, New York Acad. Sciences (treas.); asso. Inst. of Actuaries, London. Presbyn. Home: New York, N.Y. Died Jan. 3, 1926.

TAUBENHAUS, JACOB JOSEPH, plant pathologist; b. Saffed, Palestine, Oct. 20, 1884; s. Meyer and Bet Sheba T.; grad. Nat. Farm Sch., Doylestown, Pa., 1904; B.S. Cornell U., 1908, M.S., 1909; Ph.D., U. of Pa., 1913; m. Esther Hirchenson, 1910; children—Leon Yahir, Ruth Ziporah. Asso. plant pathologist Delaware Coll., Newark, 1909-16; chief of div. of plant pathology and physiology, Tex. Agrl. Expt. Sta., 1916—; in charge cotton root rot investigations in Texas. Russell lecturer, Mass. Hort. Soc., 1916. Mason. Author: Culture and Diseases of Sweet Pea, 1917: Diseases of Truck Crops, 1918; Diseases of Greenhouse Crops, 1920; Diseases of the Sweet Potato, 1923; Culture and Diseases of the Onion in America, 1924. Home: College Station, Tex. Died 1937.

TAUSSIG, ALBERT ERNST (tou'sig), physician; b. St. Louis, May 6, 1871; s. Joseph S. and Mary L. (Cuno) T.; A.B., Harvard, 1891; M.D., Washington U. Med. Sch., St. Louis, 1894; m. Harriet Palmer Learned, 1903; children—Joseph Bondi, Barrett Learned, Lucelia Wakefield, Mary Cuno, Lenore Parker. Asso. prof. medicine, Washington U. Med. Sch., 1913-31; prof. of clinical medicine since 1931; physician to Barnes and Jewish hospitals. Mem. Assn. Am. Physicians, A.M.A., Mo. State Med. Assn. Democrat. Unitarian. Club: University. Home: 5038 Washington Av. Office: 4500 Olive St., St. Louis, Mo. Died Jan. 16, 1944.

TAUSSIG, FREDERICK JOSEPH, gynecologist; b. Brooklyn, N.Y., Oct. 26, 1872; s. Joseph S. and Mary L. (Cuno) T.; A.B., Harvard, 1893; M.D., Washington U., 1898; m. Florence Gottschalk, May 4, 1907; children—Mary Bolland (Mrs. L. Benoist Tompkins), Frederick. Served as interne and assistant supt. St. Louis Female Hospital, 1898-1901; intern Imperial and Royal Elizabeth Hosp., Vienna, Austria, 1902-03; practiced in St. Louis since 1902; clin. prof. of gynecology and prof. of clin. obstetrics, Washington U. Med. Sch. since 1911; gynecologist Barnard Free Skin and Cancer, Jewish and St. Louis City hosps.; obstetrician St. Louis Maternity Hosp. Fellow Am. Coll. Surgeons; mem. Am. Gyneol. Soc. (pres. 1936-37), Am. Assn. for Cancer Research, Am. Soc. for Control of Cancer (dir. 1938), A.M.A., St. Louis Med. Soc., Central Assn. Obstetricians and Gynecologists (pres. 1932-33), St. Louis Surg. Club. Member of Ethical Society. Clubs: Harvard, University Club. Author: Diseases of the Vulva, 1923; Abortion, Spontaneous and Induced, Medical and Social Aspects, 1935. Contbr. Nelson's Loose-Leaf Surgery, Lewis' Practice of Surgery, Curtis' Obstetrics and Gynecology, 1929-33, Christopher Surgery, Davis' Obstetrics and Gynecology, Brenneman's Pediatrics, Pack's Treatment for Cancer and Allied Diseases. Home: 50 Westmoreland Pl. Office: 3720 Washington Av., St. Louis, Mo. Died Aug. 21, 1943.

TAYLOR, ALBERT DAVIS, landscape architect, town planner, civil engineer; born Carlise, Massachusetts, July 8, 1883; son of Nathaniel and Ellen (Davis) Taylor; B.S., Massachusetts State College, 1905, LL.D., 1945; A.B., Boston Coll., 1905; M.S., Cornell University, 1906; Sc.D., Oregon State College, 1940; m. Genevieve Brainerd, June 16, 1917; 1 son, Charles Brainerd. Instructor in landscape architecture, Cornell University, 1906-08; began practice at Boston, 1908; at Cleveland, Ohio, and Orlando, Florida, since 1915; non-resident professor landscape architecture, Ohio State U., 1916-24; lecturer, U. of Mich., since 1938; contbg. editor Landscape Architecture Magazine. Consulting landscape architect, U.S. Forest Service. Landscape architect for Harding, Spanish War, and Roosevelt Warm Springs Memorials, Pentagon Bldg. Site, and Boys Town, and many other pub. and pvt. developments; town planner U.S. Housing Corp., 1917-18; collaborator for the U.S. Nat. Arboretum; consultant for various U.S. Marine hospitals, for War Dept. and for Housing Div.; chief consultant in site planning, War Dept., 1941; site planner for Fla. State Capital development. Mem. landscape architecture jury, Am. Acad. in Rome, Cleveland City Plan Commn., 1928-43; pres. Am. Soc. Landscape Architects, 1935-41 (chmn. committee on bicentennial commn.; ex-pres. O.-Mich. chapter); trustee Lake Forest Foundation Sch., Cambridge Sch. Landscape Architecture. Mem. Am. Inst. Park Execs., City Planning Inst., American Society of Civil Engineers, Phi Kappa Phi, Gamma Alpha, Alpha Sigma Phi. Unitarian. Clubs: Hermit, Cleveland Skating. Author: Shade Trees, Their Care and Preservation, 1908; Plants for Landscape Planting, 1916; Complete Garden, 1920; Landscape Construction

Notes, 1928; Problems of Landscape Architecture in the National Forests, 1936; Camp Stoves and Fireplaces, 1937; Landscape Details, 1939. Home: 2178 S. Overlook Rd., Cleveland Heights, O. Office: 7016 Euclid Av., Cleveland. Died Jan. 8, 1951; buried Riverside Cemetery. Cleve.

TAYLOR, ALBERT HOYT, physicist, radio engr.; b. Chgo., Jan. 1, 1879; s. Albert H. and Harriet (Getschell) T.; B.S., Northwestern U., 1902; Ph.D., Goettingen U., Germany, 1909; D.Sc. (hon.), U. N.D., 1953; m. Sarah E. Hickman, Aug. 9, 1911; children—Albert H., Barbara M., Harriet, Margaret A. Instr., later asst. prof. physics U. Wis., 1903-08; prof., head physics dept. U. N.D., 1909-17; commd. lt. USNR, 1917, advanced through grades to comdr., 1922, supt. radio div. naval research lab., 1923-45, pioneer research in devel. radar, ret. 1948. Awarded medal of honor by I.R.E., 1941, John Scot medal and premium, 1942, medal for merit by U.S. Pres., 1944. Fellow I.R.E. (pres.), Am. Phys. Soc., A.A.A.S., Am. Inst. E.E.; mem. Naval Inst., Sigma Xi. Club: University. Home: 691 W. 12th St., Claremont, Cal. Died Dec. 11, 1961; buried Arlington Nat. Cemetery, Washington.

TAYLOR, CHARLOTTE DE BERNIER SCARBROUGH, entomologist, writer; b. Savannah, Ga., 1806; d. William and Julia (Bernard) Scarborough; ed. Madam Benzes' Sch., N.Y.C.; m. James Taylor, Apr. 27, 1829; 3 children. Published her most important articles in Harper's New Monthly Mag., during 1850's, showing her clear understanding of agrl. significance of entomology, called attention to econ. necessity for systematic destruction of wheat parasites, Dec. 1859, predicted revival of silk-raising industry in U.S., May 1860, published study on anatomy and natural history of spiders, Sept. 1860; wrote Microscopic Views of the Insect World for N.Y. Am. Agriculturist, 1858-59, 60; other works include Homestead, 1859, The Unwelcome Guest of Insects, The Soundings. Died Isle of Man, Nov. 26, 1861.

TAYLOR, EDWARD RANDOLPH, chemist; b. Brasher Falls, N.Y., July 1, 1844; s. Thomas R. and Julia E. (Taft) T.; B.S., Lawrence Scientific School (Harvard), 1868; m. Mrs. Carrie A. Williams, Oct. 8, 1873. Prof. chemistry and toxicology, Homoe. Hosp. Coll., Cleveland, 1869-73; chemist, Cleveland Rolling Mill Co., 1869-76; pres. Taylor Chem. Co., Penn Yan, N.Y., founded, 1876. Trustee Keuka Coll., Keuka Park, N.Y. Republican. Presbyn. Awarded Elliott Cresson gold medal, Franklin Inst., 1907. Del. Internat. Congress Applied Chemistry, Berlin, 1903, Rome, 1906, London, 1909. Home: Penn Yan, N.Y. Died May 28, 1917.

TAYLOR, EDWY LYCURGUS, pub. utilities; b. Albany, N.Y., Sept. 8, 1879; s. Edwy Lycurgus and Elizabeth Ellison (Taylor) T.; Ph.B., Yale, 1901, C.E., 1904; m. Helen Very Curtis, Dec. 9, 1911; children—John, William Curtis, Helen Angeline. Asst. instr. Yale, 1901-03, instr., 1904-06; asst. prof., U. of Kan., 1903-04; with engring. dept. N.Y., N.H.,&H. R.R., 1906; with N.Y.C. R.R., 1906-12, maintenance of way dept., 1906-08, asst. engr. electric div., 1908-11, asst. engr. in office of designing engr., 1911-12; with N.Y.,N.H.&H. R.R., 1912-18, 1919-30, asst. engr. 1912-14, contract agt., 1914-18, 1919-25, asst. to v.p., 1925-29, asst. to exec. v.p., 1929-30; asst. to treas. Conn. Savings Bank, New Haven, Jan.-May 1931; mem. Conn. Pub. Utilities Commn., 1931-41, chmn., 1934, 35 and 38; corporator Conn. Savings Bank. Trustees for Receiving Donations for Support of the Bishop of Conn.; col. on Governor's staff, 1931-38. Served as 1st lt. engrs., U.S. Army, with A.E.F., 1918-19; capt. Engrs. Res. Corps, 1920-24, maj., 1924-39, lt. col. since 1939. Mem. Soc. Am. Mil. Engrs., Am. Soc. Civil Engrs., Conn. Sect. Am. Soc. Civil Engrs., Conn Soc. Civil Engrs. (hon.), Am. Legion, Mil. Order of the World War, Res. Officers Assn., Nat. Assn. of R.R. and Utilities Commrs., Am. Ry. Engring. Assn., Am. Water Works Assn., Am. Gas Assn., New England Regional Planning Commn. (advisory com.), New Haven Colony Hist. Soc., Sigma Xi, Berzelius Soc. (Yale). Democrat. Episcopalian (warden). Clubs: New Haven Lawn, Graduate (New Haven); Yale (N.Y. City); Hartford (Hartford); Army and Navy (Washington, D.C.); Camden Yacht, Megunticook Golf (Camden, Me.). Home: 165 Everit St., New Haven, Conn. Deceased.

TAYLOR, FRANK BURSLEY, geologist; b. Ft. Wayne, Ind., Nov. 23, 1860; s. Robert Stewart and Fanny (Wright) T.; grad. high sch., 1881; attended Harvard as a spl. student without entering for degree; m. Minnetta A. Ketchum, of Mackinac Island, Mich., Apr. 24, 1899. Since 1892 has published numerous papers relating to history of the Great Lakes and Niagara Falls, and to the glacial and post-glacial geology of the lake region, both in U.S. and Can.; employed in Mich. Geol. Survey, 1900, in U.S. Geol. Survey, Glacial Div., 1900-16, Canadian Geological Survey, 1908-09. Author: (with E. M. Kindle) Niagara Folio, folio No. 190, U.S. Geol. Survey, 1913; (with F. Leverett) Pleistocene of Indiana and Michigan and History of Great Lakes, monograph No. 53, U.S. Geol. Survey, 1915; also papers on origin of mountains, continents and oceans, 1910, and since 1923. Fellow A.A.A.S., Geol. Soc. America, Am. Acad. Arts and Sciences, Mich. Acad. Sciences. Address: 420 Downing Av., Ft. Wayne, Ind.

TAYLOR, FREDERIC WILLIAM, agriculturist; b. Weeping Water, Neb., Apr. 13, 1860; S. William and Sophronia (Isbell) T.; educated high sch. and by private instruction; m. Stella Arnold, 1885 (died July 9, 1891); children—Jettie Arnold (Mrs. J. H. Gray), Herbert Solomon, Mary Stella (wife of Capt. R. M. Lhamon, U.S. Navy); m. 2d, Marion Treat, 1898; children—William Treat, George Frederic. Received training in horticulture under his father, a nurseryman; later employed in leading nurseries. Prof. horticulture, U. of Neb., 1891-93; sec. U.S. Agrl. Expt. Sta., Lincoln, Neb., 1894-95; sec. Neb. State Hort. Soc., 1892-95; supt. Neb. fruit exhibit, Chicago Expn., 1893; supt. agr. and horticulture, Omaha Expn., 1898; supt. horticulture and dir. of concessions, Buffalo Expn., 1901; chief, depts. agr. and horticulture St. Louis Expn., 1904; dir. of agr., P.I., 1911-14; dir. general of agr. of El Salvador, C.A., 1923-27; v.p. Am. Rubber Producers, Inc., since 1927. Fellow Royal Geog. Soc., etc.; mem. A.A.A.S., S.A.R. Clubs: Circumnavigators (New York); University (Los Angeles). Officer Legion of Honor, France; Knight of the Order of Jesus Christ, Portugal; Order of the Rising Sun, Japan; Order of the Crown, Italy. Wrote monographs: The Apples, 1894; Small Fruits, 1895, and other reports Neb. State Hort. Soc.; also contbns. to mags. Has traveled widely, including two trips around the world. In 1897 introduced from Russia a number of cereals, of which the variety of oats, Kherson, has been widely distributed and is grown extensively in the West. Made ascent of Mt. Popocatepetl, 17,780 ft., 1894. Republican. Conglist. During war was agrl. adviser to Draft Bd. for Southern dist. Ariz. Home: 3939 W. 7th St., Los Angeles, Calif. Died Jan. 12, 1944.

TAYLOR, FREDERICK WINSLOW, engineer; b. Germantown, Phila., Pa., Mar. 20, 1856; s. Franklin and Emily (Winslow) T.; prepared for Harvard at Phillips Exeter Acad., 1874; left because of impaired eyesight; M.E., Stevens Inst. Tech., 1883; (Sc.D., U. of Pa., 1906; LL.D., Hobart Coll., 1912); m. Louise M. Spooner, May 3, 1884. Entered employ Midvale Steel Co., Phila., 1878, and was successively gang boss, asst. foreman, foreman of machine shop, master mechanic, chief draftsman, and chief engr. to 1889; left 1889 to begin work of organizing management of mfg. establishments of various kinds, in shop, office, accounting and sales dept.; has organized many kinds, including the Bethlehem Steel Co., Cramp's Shipbuilding Co., Midvale Steel Co. Inventor of Taylor-White process of treating modern high-speed tools, for which received personal gold medal from Paris Expn., 1900, and Elliot Cresson gold medal of Franklin Inst. Has received about 100 patents for various inventions. Unitarian. Author: Concrete, Plain and Reinforced (with S. E. Thompson), 1905; Art of Cutting Metals, 1906; Concrete Costs (with S. E. Thompson), 1911; The Principles of Scientific Management, 1911; Shop Management, 1911. Won double championship of U.S., at Newport, 1881, in lawn tennis. Home: Philadelphia, Pa. Died Mar. 21, 1915.

TAYLOR, HARDEN FRANKLIN, sci. cons.; b. West Plains, Mo., July 15, 1890; s. Robert Marion and Nettie Clay (Laffoon) T.; A.B., Trinity Coll. (now Duke), 1913, D.Sc. (hon.), 1936; m. Ella Wolstenholme, July 3, 1919 (dec.); m. 2d, Eloise Aley, Sept. 10, 1963. Asst. to profl. biology Duke, 1911-13; high sch. teacher, Tarboro, N.C., 1913-14, prin., 1914-15; sci. asst. Marine Biol. Lab., U.S. Bur. Fisheries, summers, 1911-14, sci. asst. div. sci. inquiry, Washington, 1915-18, chief technologist, 1918-22, chief div. fishery industries, 1922-23; dir. research Atlantic Coast Fisheries Co., 1923-25, v.p. for sci. research, 1925-30, dir., 1927-44, mgmt. com., 1929-30, pres., 1930-44; sci. cons., 1944; cons., mem. exec. com. Inst. Fisheries Research, U. N.C., 1947-60; sci. dir. N.C. Shrimp Survey, 1947-50; cons. Oceanographic Inst., Fla. State U., 1951. Del., World Engring. Congress, Tokyo, 1929, Internat. Congress Refrigeration, The Hague, Netherlands, 1926; mem. Pacific Sci. Congress (com. on fish tech.); fishery adv. com. U.S. Dept. Commerce, 1936-38 (chmn. subcom. on research, 1939); mem. Internat. Institut du Froid, Commission III, London meeting, 1938; mem. adv. council Refrigeration Research Found.; chmn., fisheries sec. div. biology and agr. NRC; mem. ad hoc com. on fisheries FAO, UN, 1945; exec. dir. Survey of Marine Fisheries of N.C., U. N.C.; dir. Nortex Oil & Gas Corp. Recipient Wildlife Soc. award, 1952. Fellow A.A.A.S., Am. Inst. Chemists, N.Y. Acad. Scis. (trustee, treas., pres. 1946-48); mem. Am. Chem. Soc., Am. Inst. N.Y.C. (trustee, pres. 1951), Princeton Engring. Assn., Am. Soc. Limnology & Oceanography, Newcomen Soc., Phi Beta Kappa Alumni Assn. N.Y. (pres. 1965—), Alpha Chi Sigma, Phi Beta Kappa, Omicron Delta Kappa, Sigma Upsilon. Methodist. Clubs: Fortnightly (pres. 1928-30, 44-46) (N.Y.); Quill. Contbr. sci. articles to govt. publs. and other jours., and revs. Holder U.S. and fgn. patents in field. Home: 50 E. 58th St., N.Y.C. 22. Office: 115 Broadway, N.Y.C. 6. Died Feb. 4, 1966.

TAYLOR, HARRY, army officer; b. Tilton, N.H., June 26, 1862; s. John Franklin and Lydia T.; grad. U.S. Mil. Acad., 1884, Engr. Sch. of Application, 1887; m. Adele Austin Yates, Oct. 30, 1901. Commd. 2d lt. engrs., June 15, 1884; promoted through grades to maj. gen., June 19, 1924. Engr. duties on Columbia River, and river and harbor works in Ore. and Wash., 1891-96, in charge defense works, Puget Sound, Wash., 1896-1900; in Philippines, 1903; commd. 3d Batln. Engrs., in P.I., 1904; engr. officer Dept. of Luzon, 1903-04; fortification constrn., 1904-05; in charge defenses of eastern entrance L.I. Sound and various improvements, 1906-11; asst. to chief of engrs., War Dept., 1911-16; in charge river and harbor works New York Harbor, Hudson River and Lake Champlain, dept. engr. Eastern Dept., Governors Island, 1916-17; chief engr. A.E.F. in France, May 1917-Sept. 1918; apptd. asst. chief of engrs. U.S.A., Sept. 1918, and chief of engrs., June 1924; retired 1926. Awarded D.S.M. (U.S.); Comdr. Legion of Honor (French). Episcopalian. Home: Washington, D.C. Died Jan. 28, 1930.

TAYLOR, H(ARVEY) BIRCHARD, M.E., exec. and engr.; b. Phila., Pa., Nov. 17, 1882; s. Charles Tracy and Sophie (Davis) T.; grad. Northeast Manual Training Sch., Phila., 1901; spl. courses Towne Scientific Sch. (U. of Pa.), class of 1905 (class pres. sr. yr.; center, Varsity football team, 1903); m. Florence Bodine, 1908; children—Helen Louise (Mrs. George B. Clothier), Charles Tracy II; m. 2d, Mrs. John McEntee Bowman, 1934; step-children—Clarissa Anne Bowman (Mrs. Ward Sullivan), John McEntee Bowman, Jr. Began with I.P. Morris Co., subsidiary of Wm. Cramp & Sons Ship & Engine Building Co. of Pa., 1905, draftsman, designer and engineer in manufacture high power hydraulic turbine machinery; apptd. asst. hydraulic engr., 1907, hydraulic engr. in charge, 1911; in charge design and mfr. turbine machinery for developments at Niagara, Keokuk, Muscle Shoals, Conowingo in U.S., and Ceders Rapids, Shawinigan and Niagara in Canada. Asst. to pres. Cramp Co., 1915, v.p. and dir., 1917-27; pres. Cramp-Morris Industrials, Inc., Federal Steel Foundry Co., I.P. Morris & De La Vergne, Inc., Pelton Water Wheel Co., Cramp Brass & Iron Foundries Co., 1927-31; exec. v.p. Baldwin-Southwark Corp., 1931-32; exec. mgr. The Phila. Authority, 1939-40; v.p., dir. Cramp Shipbuilding Co., 1940-46; chmn., pres. Phila. Lascala Opera Co., 1946-48; mem. adv. bd. Admiral Farragut Acad. Past trustee U. of Pa., 1934-44; Gen. Alumni Soc. of U. of Pa. (ex-p.). Mem. Phila. Bourse (dir.), Guild of Bracket lecturers of Princeton U. Fellow Am. Soc. Mech. Engineers (v.p. 1924-25); Mem. Am. Inst. E.E., Am. Soc. C.E., Naval Architects and Marine Engrs., Franklin Inst., Atlantic Coast Shipbuilders Assn. (pres. 1920), Navy League of U.S. (ex-pres.), Sandlot Sports Assn. (dir.), Bicentennial Com. U. of Pa. (exec. dir.), Newcomen Soc. of England, Beta Theta Pi, Sphinx Sr. Soc. (U. of Pa.), Soc. Colonial Wars, Colonial Soc. of Pa., S.R., Descendants Knights of Garter, Colonial Society Royal Descent (pres.). Republican. Presbyterian. Clubs: Union League, Rittenhouse, Merion Cricket, Engineers (Phila.). Home: The Barclay, Rittenhouse Sq. East, Philadelphia, Pa. Died Dec. 29, 1959.

TAYLOR, JAMES H., univ. prof.; b. Sharon, Pa., Feb. 21, 1893; s. James and Cornelia (Jackson) T.; B.S., U. of Nebraska, 1916; A.M., Princeton, 1920; Ph.D., U. of Chicago, 1924; m. Ethel Victoria Graham, Dec. 24, 1919; children—Richard Jackson, Lawrence Martin. Instr. in mathematics, U. of Nebraska, 1920-22; Nat. Research fellow, Princeton, 1924-25; asst. prof. mathematics, Lehigh U., 1925-26, U. of Wis., 1926-29; prof. mathematics George Washington U., Washington, D.C., 1929-72. Served as 2d lt., 351st Inf., 88th Div., U.S. Army, 1917-18, 1st lt., 1918-19. Mem. Math. Assn. America, Am. Math. Society, Washington Academy of Sciences, Phi Beta Kappa, Sigma Xi. Mason. Club: Cosmos (Washington). Author: Vector Analysis, 1939. Home: Avlon Rockville MD Died Mar. 30, 1972.

TAYLOR, JOHN BELLAMY, elec. engr.; b. Brookline, Mass., Aug. 20, 1875; s. Washington Irving and Ann Maria (Bellamy) T.; B.S. in elec. engring., Mass. Inst. Tech., 1897; m. Marcia Estabrook Jones, June 10, 1903. Began with N.E. Tel. & Tel. Co., 1897; with Gen. Electric Co., Boston, 1899-1902, Schenectady, 1902-13; cons. practice, N.Y., 1913-17; became cons. engr., Gen. Electric Co., Schenectady, 1917; retired. Work has been principally on problems of generation, transmission and transformation of electricity; specialized on inductive interferences to telephone and telegraph systems, acoustics, mus. instruments, and photomicrography. Lectr., contbr. to tech. mags. Mem. Am. Inst. E.E. (v.p), Am. Phys. Soc., Am. Electrochem. Soc., Illuminating Engring. Soc., Soc. Engrs. of Eastern N.Y. Clubs: Mohawk, Mohawk Golf (Schenectady); Engineers, Technology (N.Y.). Home: 1279 Lowell Rd., Schenectady. Died Dec. 1963.
*

TAYLOR, LLOYD WILLIAM, prof. physics; b. Pittsfield, Me., Jan. 4, 1893; s. Levi William and Carrie Elnora (Brown) T.; B.S., Grinnell (Ia.) Coll., 1914; Ph.D., U. of Chicago, 1922; m. Esther Elenora Bliss, Dec. 11, 1917; children—Ruth Mildred, Edwin Floriman. Prin. high sch., Grandview, Ia., 1914-15; instr. in physics and mathematics, Grinnell Coll., 1915-17; asst. in physics, U. of Chicago, 1919-22, instr. in physics, 1922-24; prof. physics and head of dept., Oberlin (O.) Coll., since 1924. Served as 2d, later 1st lt. C.A.C., U.S. Army, 1917-19. Mem. A.A.A.S., Am. Physical Soc., Ohio Acad. Science, Am. Assn. Physics Teachers (pres. 1943-44), Am. Inst. Physics (mem. governing bd., 1944-48), Optical Soc. of America, Gamma Alpha, Phi Beta Kappa, Sigma Xi.

Congregationalist. Author: College Manual of Optics, 1924; General Physics for the Laboratory (with W. W. Watson and C. E. Howe), 1926, revised, 1943; A Numerical Drill Book on Physics, 1926; Physics: the Pioneer Science, 1941; Fundamental Physics, 1943. Contbr. tech. articles in professional mags. Address: Oberlin College, Oberlin, O. Died Aug. 8, 1948; buried Grinnell, Ia.

TAYLOR, NORMAN, botanist; b. Hereford, England, May 18, 1883; s. James Durham and Mary Ann (Preece) T.; student Cornell U., 1901-02; D.Sc. (honorary), Washington College, 1958. Came to U.S., 1889, naturalized, 1896. Asst. curator N.Y. Botanical Garden, Bronx Park, 1905-11; curator of plants Brooklyn Botanic Garden, 1911-29; botany, horticulture and forestry editor, Webster's New Internat. Dictionary, 2d edition; editor of The Garden Dictionary, Houghton, Mifflin Co., 1933-36; director of Cinchona Products Inst., Inc., 1937-50; advisor Cinchona Instituut, Amsterdam, 1951-53; plant exploring expdns. to Bahamas, Haiti, Cuba, Santo Domingo, Puerto Rico, Yucatan, Guatemala, Bolivia, Peru, Ecuador and Brazil. Awarded Massachusetts Horticultural Society gold medal, 1936, Distinguished Service Award, N.Y. Bot. Garden, 1961, Liberty Hyde Bailey gold medal Am. Hort. Soc., 1963. Fellow New York Academy of Sciences, A.A.A.S.; associate fellow N.Y. Acad. Medicine; mem. Massachusetts Horticultural Soc., Torrey Botanical Club. Episcopalian. Clubs: Century, Players, Explorers (N.Y.C.); Cosmos (Washington). Author: Botany, Science of Plant Life, 1924; Guide to the Wild Flowers, 1928; Cinehona in Java, 1945; Taylor's Encyclopedia of Gardening, 1948; Flight From Reality, 1949; The Permanent Garden, and Color in the Garden, 1953; Fragrance in the Garden, Herbs in the Garden, 1954; Fruits in the Garden, The Everblooming Garden, 1955; Wild Flower Gardening, 1956; Guide to Garden Flowers, 1957; Taylor's Garden Guide, 1957; The Ageless Relicts, 1962; 1001 Questions Answered About Flowers, 1963; Narcotics: Nature's Dangerous Gifts, 1963; Guide to Garden Shrubs and Trees, 1965; Plant Drugs that Changed the World, 1965. Contbr. mags., Ency. Brit. and Book of Knowledge. Home: Princess Anne MD Died Nov. 5, 1967; interred New Episcopal Cemetery Princess Anne MD

TAYLOR, OLIVER GUY, civil engr.; b. Boone County, Ind., Oct. 28, 1883; s. Charles Andrew and Margaret Ann (Kern) T.; B.S., in C.E., Purdue U., 1909; m. Marjorie Edwina Macdougall, May 15, 1915. Topographer U.S. Geol. Survey, 1900-13, 1914-17, 1919-20; civil engr., Republic of Argentine, 1914; park engr., Yosemite Nat. Park, 1920-30; civil engr. charge engring. Eastern Nat. Park Areas, 1930-37; chief engr. Nat. Park Service, 1937-43, regional dir. 1943-44, supr. concessions, 1944—. Served as 2d lt., 1st lt. and capt., Engrs., U.S. Army, with A.E.F., 1917-18. Mem. Soc. Civil Engrs. Mason. Club: Cosmos (Washington). Home: 6313 Georgia St., Chevy Chase, Md. Office: National Park Service, Washington 25. Died Aug. 26, 1950; buried Arlington Nat. Cemetery.

TAYLOR, RICHARD COWLING, geologist; b. Suffolk, Eng., Jan. 18, 1789; s. Samuel Taylor; apprenticed to a land surveyor, Gloucestershire, Eng., 1805-11; studied with William Smith in Am.; m. Emily Ervington, 1820, at least 4 children. Surveyed in various parts of Eng., 1811-13; engaged in ordnance survey of Eng., 1826-27; sailed to U.S., 1830; engaged in survey of Blossburg (Pa.) coal region; explored many mineral deposits, went as far as copper mines in Cuba and gold fields in Panama; expert on stratification of deposits. Author: Index Monasticus, or the Abbeys and Other Monasteries. . . Formerly Established in the Diocese of Norwich and the Ancient Kingdom of East Anglia, 1820; On the Geology of East Norfolk, 1827; Statistics of Coal, 1848. Died Phila., Oct. 27, 1851.

TAYLOR, SAMUEL ALFRED, engr.; b. N. Versailles Twp., Allegheny County, Pa., Oct. 24, 1863; s. Charles Thomas and Elizabeth J. (Maxwell) T.; C.E., Western U. Pa. (now U. Pitts.), 1887; Sc.D., U. Pitts., 1919; m. Anna J. Gilmore, May 17, 1893; 1 dau., Mary Elizabeth (Mrs. W.O. Lytle). Chief draughtsman structural iron dept., Carnegie Steel Co., 1887-88; asst. engr. of constrn., Pa. R.R., 1888-93; in pvt. practice, 1893-1905, cons. engr., 1905—; dean Sch. Mines, U. Pitts., 1910, 12. Tech. adv. to U.S. fuel adminstr., 1917-19. Trustee U. Pitts., Western Pa. Sch. for the Deaf. Mem. Am. Mining Congress (pres. 1912), Am. Soc. C.E., Am. Inst. Mining and Metall. Engrs. (pres., 1926), Internat. Soc. Geologists, A.A.A.S., Engrs. Soc. Western Pa. (pres. 1913-14), Coal Mining Inst. Am. (pres. 1911), etc. Club: Duquesne (Pittsburgh). Author various papers publs. of tech. assns. Home: 617 Whitney Av., Wilkinsburg, Pa. Died Aug. 20, 1950.

TAYLOR, S(AMUEL) N(EWTON), physicist; b. Farmingdale, N.Y., Apr. 24, 1858; s. Francis James and Ann (Newton) T.; Ph.B., Wesleyan U., Conn., 1887; fellow in physics, Clark U., Worcester, Mass., 1893-96, Ph.D., 1896; studied German univs., 1902-03; m. Mabel Wright Burr, Dec. 27, 1887; 1 dau., Mabel Burr. Expert electrician with Gen. Electric Co., 1887-93; instr. physics, Purdue U., 1896-99; asso. prof. physics, Syracuse U., 1899-1903; prof. physics and elec. engring., Univ. of Pittsburgh, 1903-08; in charge of astron. time service, Allegheny Obs., 1904-05; prof. elec. engring., U. of Cincinnati, 1908-11; became prof. physics, Goucher Coll., Baltimore, Sept. 18, 1911, now emeritus. Hon. fellow A.A.A.S., 1917; mem. Am. Inst. E.E., Soc. Promotion Engring. Edn., Alpha Delta Phi, Mystical Seven. Contbr. papers on elec. and tech. subjects. Methodist. Home: 2514 Maryland Av., Baltimore MD

TAYLOR, THOMAS ULVAN, engineer; b. Parker Co., Tex., Jan. 2, 1858; s. John Henry and Louisa (Allison) T.; ed. Sam Houston Normal, Huntsville, Tex., 1879-80; C.E., U. of Va., 1883; M.C.E., Cornell U., 1895; m. Maria Montgomery (Daisy) Moon, of Albemarle Co., Va., July 17, 1888; children—Summerfield M., Mrs. Julia Houston. Prof. physics and mathematics, Miller Inst., Albemarle County, 1883; prof. civ. engring. since 1888, dean engring. dept. since 1906, U. of Tex. Mem. Am. Math. Soc., Am. Soc. C.E. Author: Prismoidal Formulae, 1898; The Austin Dam, 1900; Plane and Spherical Trigonometry (with Prof. Charles Puryear), 1902; Irrigation Systems in Texas, 1902; Backbone of Perspective, 1901; Surveyor's Hand Book, 1904; Water Powers of Texas, 1905; Underground Waters of Texas Coastal Plain, 1907; Silting of Reservoirs, 1930. Mem. bd. engrs. Fort Worth water supply; mem. bd. engrs. to select engrs. for Dallas-Oak Cliff viaduct; mem. bd. of engrs. Dallas water supply, 1910; engr. for Travis Co., Tex., to select engrs. for reinforced concrete bridge; chmn. Cost Review Bds. to report on proper cost of U.S. Reclamation projects at Carlsbad, N.M., Rio Grande above and below El Paso, Tex., and Salt River at Phoenix, Ariz. Cons. engr. water supply Abilene, 1917; cons. engr. City of Dallas on whole aspect of city water supply, 1921; chmn. gov.'s engring. council of Tex.; consulting engr. City of Austin on water supply, 1923, and on water power, 1925; cons. engr. on water supply for Wichita Falls, Tex., 1925, 26. Home: 2215 San Antonio St., Austin, Tex.

TAYLOR, WILLIAM ALTON, pomologist; b. Chelsea, Mich., June 23, 1863; s. Rev. James Franklin and Mary Ann Lewis (Porter) T.; B.S., Mich. State Coll., 1888, D.Sc., 1913; m. Helen C. Patterson, Dec. 15, 1891 (died Aug. 29, 1921); children—Porter Ross, Ritchie Patterson; m. 2d, Marie Patton Cisco, June 6, 1923; 1 son, William Cisco. Mgr. fruit farm and nursery, Douglas, Mich., 1888-1891; asst. pomologist, U.S. Dept. of Agr., 1891-1901; pomologist in charge of field investigations, 1901-10 (agricultural exploration Canal Zone, 1909), and assistant chief Bur. Plant Industry, U.S. Dept. Agr., 1910-13; chief of Bureau Plant Industry, 1913-33, collaborator since 1934. Expert in horticulture U.S. Commn. to Paris Expn., 1900 (mem. Internat. jury on fruit trees and fruit); mem. Internat. Jury Dept. of Horticulture, St. Louis Expn., 1904. Mem. Agrl. Commn. to Europe, 1918. Chevalier du Mérite Agricole, 1900; silver medal, Societe Nationale d'Horticulture de France, 1900, silver medal, Societe des Agriculteurs de France, 1918; gold medal, Mass. Hort. Soc., 1939. Fellow A.A.A.S.; mem. Am. Pomol. Soc. (sec. 1897-1903, v.p. 1934-35), Bot. Soc. Washington (pres. 1910), Am. Soc. for Hort. Science (pres. 1908-09), Agrl. Hist. Soc., Biol. Soc. Washington. Presbyterian. Club: Federal. Author numerous papers and addresses before hort. and pomol. socs., bulletins and papers U.S. Dept. Agr. Home: Lake Ridge Farm, R.D. 2, Fennville, Mich.; (winter) 30 Berkley Place, Columbus 1, O. Died Feb. 8, 1949.

TAYLOR, WILLIAM DANA, engineer; b. Montgomery, Ala., Jan. 22, 1859; s. William Thomas and Mary (Hubbard) T.; B.E., Ala. Poly. Inst., 1881, C.E., 1885; grad. student in mathematics, Johns Hopkins; summer work, Cornell U., 1894, U. of Chicago, 1896; m. Annie L. MacIntyre, Feb. 1897. Civil engr. on Mexican Central R.R., 1882-83; taught in acads. at Eclectic and Evergreen, Ala., 1883-84 and 1885-86; chief engr. rys. in Ala., 1886-91; prof. engring., La. State U., 1891-98; apptd., July 1898, capt. 3d U.S.V. engrs.; became chief engr. St. Louis, Peoria & Northern R.R., Nov. 1898, and in 1902, chief engr. Knoxville, LaFollette & Jellico R.R., of Louisville & Nashville System; prof. ry. engring., U. of Wis., 1901-06; expert engr. to Wis. State Bd. of Assessment, 1903-06; chief engr. C.&A. R.R., Feb. 1, 1906—, Toledo, St. Louis & Western Ry., Oct. 1907—, Minneapolis & St. Louis, and Ia. Central rys., Oct. 1909—. Presbyn. Republican. Home: Chicago, Ill. Died 1911.

TAYLOR, WILLIAM MODE, manufacturer, engr.; b. Indianapolis, June 29, 1865; s. Franklin and Phebe (Mode) T.; student Purdue U., 1881-82; B.S. in Mech. Engr., Mass. Inst. Tech., 1886; m. Mary Shepard Allen, Feb. 16, 1893; children—Dudley F., Frederic W., Eleanor. Entered employ of Chandler & Taylor Co., mfrs. engines, boilers and machinery, Indianapolis, 1886, pres., 1897-1926; partner Maluminum Co., mfrs. of foundry fluxes, 1931-44. Mem. Indianapolis Sch. Bd., 1902-17 (pres. 1914); chmn. bldg. com. Indianapolis City Library, 1916-17; mem. Library and Historical Bd., State of Ind., 1925-33 (pres. 1926-27); mem. Ind. State Library Building Commn., 1929-31 (chmn. legislative com. to secure funds, 1929). Mem. Am. Soc. Mech. Engrs., Ind. Hist. Soc., Ind. Engring. Council, Sigma Chi. Club: Dramatic. Home: 124 W. 41st St., Indianapolis 8, Ind. Died Apr. 24, 1947.

TEAGUE, CHARLES C., agriculturalist; b. Caribou, Me., June 11, 1873; s. Milton D. and Clara (Collins) T.; LL.D., U. Calif., 1924, U. of Me., 1931; m. Harriet McKevett, Nov. 10, 1897; children—Alice (Mrs. John H. Cox), Milton M., Charles M. Pres. Teague-McKevett Co., Santa Paula, Calif., since 1908, Limoneria Co. since 1917, Santa Paul Water Works Ltd., since 1917, Farmers Irrigation Co. since 1917, Thermal Belt Water Co. since 1917, Calif. Orchard Co., King City, Calif., since 1919, Fruit Growers Supply Co., Los Angeles, since 1920, McKevett Corp., Santa Paul, 1927-33; v.p. Security-First Nat. Bank of Los Angeles since 1928, dir.; v.p. Salinas Land Co., King City, since 1923; pres. Rancho La Cuesta, Ltd., Santa Paula, 1930—; pres. Teague-McKevett Assn., Santa Paula, 1934—, Soledad (Cal.) Ranch Co. since 1936, Calif. Fruit Growers Exchange since 1920; Agrl. Council of Calif. (hon. pres., life mem., exec. com., 1919-45); Santa Clara Water Conservation Dist., Santa Paula, since 1927; mem. Fed. Farm Bd., 1929-31; v.p. Am. Inst. Cooperation, 1933-44; pres. Nat. Council Farmer Coop., 1942-43. Cons. prof. cooperating marketing Grad. Sch. of Bus., Stanford, 1935-40. Pres. Calif. Walnut Growers Assn., 1912-42 (now pres. emeritus), Calif. State C. of C., 1932-34. Regent U. of Calif. at Berkeley since 1930. Received silver plaque from dir. of Calif. Fruit Growers Exchange in appreciation for 25 yrs. service, 1945. Universalist. Mason. Clubs: California, University (Los Angeles); Saticoy Country (Saticoy, Calif.). Author: Fifty Years a Rancher, 1944. Home: 724 McKevett Dr., Santa Paula, Calif. Died March 20, 1950.

TEAGUE, WALTER DORWIN, industrial designer; b. Decatur, Ind., Dec. 18, 1883; s. Rev. Martin Addison and Hester Anne (Towell) T.; grad. Pendleton (Ind.) High Sch., 1902; student Art Students League, New York, 1903-07; m. Cecil Fehon; children—Walter Dorwin, Cecily Fehon (Mrs. Richard H. Crowe), R. Lewis; m. 2d, Ruth Mills Holmes, Aug. 31, 1937. Began as artist, 1907, designing advertising, books, magazine illustrations; entered industrial designing, 1926; cons. on design to Eastman Kodak Co., A. B. Dick Co., Boeing Airplane Co., others; mem. bd. design N.Y. World's Fair, 1939; designed bldgs. and exhibits of Eastman Kodak, Consol. Edison, Nat. Cash Register, Ford Motor Co., U.S. Steel, duPont de Nemours & Co. for N.Y. World's Fair, 1939; designed bldgs. and exhibits of Ford at San Diego, 1935, Dallas, 1936, Miami, 1937; Texas Co., Dallas, 1936; exhibits Ford, duPont and U.S. Steel, San Francisco, 1939. Senior partner Walter Dorwin Teague Associates. Has designed automobiles, service stations, railway equipment, plane interiors, cameras, household and heating appliances, business machines, machine tools, offices, show rooms, furniture, dept. stores, periodicals, etc. Executed 130 research and development assignments for Bur. Ord., U.S. Navy, 1942-47, receiving Nav. Ord. Development Award, 1946. Lecturer N.Y.U., U. of Minn., M.I.T., Harvard, Columbia, Magill U., U. of Toronto, Pres. Am. Inst. of Graphic Arts. Recipient Ann. award Am. Soc. Indsl. Designers, 1957; Ann. award Phila. Mus. Coll. Arts, 1958. Officer of Order of Merit of Republic of Italy, 1959. Fellow Soc. Industrial Designers (1st pres.), Royal Soc. Arts, Hon. Royal Designer to Industry. Received Am. Design award, 1939; Nat. Advt. award, 1941. Author: Design This Day—The Technique of Order in the Machine Age, 1940; (with Ruth Teague) You Can't Ignore Murder (a mystery), 1942; Land of Plenty, A Summary of Possibilities, 1947; Flour for Man's Bread, A History of Milling, 1952 (with John Storck). Home: River Farm, Annandale, N.J. Died Dec. 5, 1960.

TEDESCHE, LEON G(REENFIELD), (te-des'ke), bacteriologist; b. Cincinnati, O., Sept. 28, 1878; s. Alexander and Jennie (Greenfield) Tedesche (originally Tedeschi); A.B., University of Cincinnati, 1902, M.D., 1905; unmarried; adopted daughter, Ensign Lucile Elinor Morgan (Mrs. W.P. Steward). Began as assistant bacteriologist to trustees Commissioners Water Works Filtration Experts, 1898-99; experimental work, Louisville, Kentucky, Hornellsville, New York, Chicago Drainage Canal Suit for St. Louis at Grafton, Ill., 1900; instr. pathology, bacteriology and histology, 1902-04, 1906-07, 1913-14, prof. histology and pathology, 1917-18, Cincinnati Veterinary College; asst. bacteriologist, 1902-05, asst. in electrotherapeutics, 1906-07, Med. Coll. of Ohio, Cincinnati; scientific asst. of sec. Smithsonian Instn., 1907; bacteriologist, filtration plant of Cincinnati Water Works, 1907-10; chemist and bacteriologist, Milk Commn. of Cincinnati Acad. Medicine, 1910-12; in charge water sterilization of Hamilton, O., 1913, flood Disaster with State Med. Corps.; prof. physiology, later prof. bacteriology and pathology, Eclectic Med. Coll., 1914-29; prof. physiology, Cincinnati Coll. Dental Surgery, 1917-20; lecturer theoretical pharmacy, Cincinnati Coll. Pharmacy, 1921-24. Volunteer Med. Service Corps, Nov. 9, 1918, essential teacher Surgeon Gen's. office; capt. Med. R.C. (ret.). Instr. A.R.C. First Aid Service for Boy Scout leaders, 1929—; asso. dir. Indsl. Emergency Hosp., 1924-30; dir. West End Indsl. Dispensary, 1939—. Mem. exec. council, U. Cin. Alumni Assn. Mem. Med. Corps, O. Nat. Guard, 1907-17; chmn. health and safety com. Cin. Council Boy Scouts Am., West dist. chmn. troop com., also merit badge counselor Wabash Court of honor; received Silver Beaver award, 1943. Fellow A.M.A., A.A.A.S.;

mem. Am. Soc. Social Hygiene, Internat. Philatelic Assn. (sec., treas.), Ohio State Med. Assn., Hamilton County (O.) Acad. Medicine, Am. Pub. Health Assn., Assn. Mil. Surgeons U.S., Daniel Drake Research Soc., Pioneer Philatelic Phalanx (hon. life), Soc. Philatelic Americans (life), Tau Alpha Epsilon, Pi Gamma Mu, Am. Philatelic Soc. (life; bd. of v.p. 1927-29), Com. of 100, U. Cin. Alumni Assn., Am. Nature Assn. V.p. Liberal Art Alumni, B'nai B'rith. Mason (32 deg., Shriner), Grotto. Patron O.E.S., 1905, 29, 42, 45-46; past asso. pres. Matrons and Patrons Assn., 20th Dist. O., 1939-40; 68 Club (trustee). Rep. Masonic Library. Clubs: Cincinnati Military, Cincinnati Auto; Collectors (New York). Republican. Home: 1016 Valley Lane, Avondale 29 and 2401 Tigertail Av., Miami 33, Fla. Office: 2201 Gest St., Cin. 4. Died Apr. 29, 1956.

TEEPLE, JOHN EDGAR, cons. chemist; b. Kempton, Ill., Jan. 4, 1874; s. William Harvey and Abby M. (Hinckley) T.; B.S., Valparaiso (Ind.) U., 1893, A.B., 1894; B.S., Cornell U., 1899, Ph.D., 1903; m. Lina Pease, Aug. 17, 1897; children—John Hazen, Charlotte Marion, Granger Odell. Instr. in chemistry and physics, Fremont (Neb.) Coll., 1894-98; instr. in organic and physiol. chemistry, Cornell U., 1899-1904; dir. Industrial Labs., N.Y. City, 1904-08; cons. chemist and chem. engr., N.Y. City, 1908—; interim prof. chemistry and chem. engring., Columbia, 1917; cons. chem. engr. Am. Potash & Chem. Corp., Darco Corp. Asso. editor Chem. Markets. Awarded Perkin medal, 1927. Author: The Industrial Development of Searles Lake Brines, 1929; Maya Astronomy, 1930. Home: Montclair, N.J. Died Mar. 1931.

TEETERS, WILBER JOHN, educator; b. Alliance, O., Oct. 10, 1866; s. Williamson and Dorcas E. (Johnson) T.; B.S., Mt. Union Coll., Alliance, 1893, M.S., 1897; Ph.C., U. of Mich., 1895; m. Anna Hollister, June 6, 1895 (died July 25, 1909); m. 2d, Sara Hayden Harrison, June 23, 1912 (died July 25, 1921); children—Wilber Otis, Wilber J.; m. 3d, Hazel R. Reynolds, Sept. 2, 1925 (died Nov. 1, 1930). Demonstrator of chemistry, Med. Coll., State U. of Iowa, 1895-1903; asso. prof. pharmacy, State U. of Ia., 1903-04, dean Coll. of Pharmacy, 1904-37; dean emeritus and prof. of pharmacy since 1937; mayor of Iowa City, 1943-47. Fellow A.A.A.S., American Pharm. Association; mem. Am. Conf. Pharm. Faculties (past sec., past pres.), Alpha Phi Omega, Gamma Alpha, Sigma Alpha Epsilon, Phi Delta Chi, Beta Phi Sigma, Rho Chi, Dolphin, Alpha Chi Sigma. Republican. Methodist. Mason (K.T., 32 deg.). Clubs: Country, Kiwanis. Home: Iowa City IA

TEE-VAN, JOHN, zoologist; b. Bklyn., July 6, 1897; s. Patrick J. and Wilhemina (Wehnke) Tee-V.; student N.Y.U., D.Sc., Reusselaer Polytechnic Institute, 1955; m. Helen Therese Damrosch, July 17, 1923. Asst. dept. tropical research N.Y. Zool. Soc., 1917-24, gen. asst., 1925-30, gen. asso., 1931-41; exec. sec. N.Y. Zool. Park, 1942-52, dir., 1952-56, gen. dir., 1956-62, now emeritus; cons. to San Francisco Park Commission, 1945. Mem. Museums Council, N.Y.C., chmn. 1945-48. Fellow N.Y. Acad. Sci. (councilor 1949-51, rec. sec. 1952-53, president, 1954), New York Zoological Soc. (gold medal 1962), Am. Inst. Park Executives; mem. Am. Soc. Ichthyologists and Herpetologists (v.p. 1951-52). Clubs: Century Assn., Explorers (first v.p. 1949-50, pres. 1951-52). Pacific Sailfish (Panama), Boone and Crockett, The Coffee House. Author: Fishes of Port-au-Prince Bay, Haiti (with William Beebe), 1928; Field Book of the Shore Fishes of Bermuda (with William Beebe), 1933. Editor-in-chief: Fishes of the Western North Atlantic (2 vols.), 1948, 54. Home: Sherman, Conn. 06784. Office: N.Y. Zool. Park, N.Y.C. 10460. Died Nov. 1967.

TEFFT, WILLIAM WOLCOTT, cons. engineer; b. Milbank, S.D., Feb. 28, 1882; s. Levant C. and Ada M. (Wolcott) T.; B.S. in C.E., U. of Mich., 1907, Dr. Engring., 1930; m. Ethel L. Foote, Oct. 8, 1910; children—Richard F. (dec.), Robert F. Asst., civ. engring. dept., U. of Mich., 1907; in charge field surveys, later resident engr., Cooke Dam, Au Sable River, Mich., Kalamazoo Steam Plant, and Grand Rapids, Mich., for Commonwealth Power Co., 1908-11; mem. Fargo Engring. Co., 1911-19, in charge report and economics dept., 1915-19; with Hodenpyl, Hardy & Co., Jackson, Mich., Feb. 1919 to 1928; cons. civil and hydraulic engr., Consumers Power Co., 1919-24, v.p., 1922—; v.p., chief engr. Commonwealth Power Corp., 1924-28; chief engr. Central Ill. Light Co., Southern Ind. Gas & Electric Co., Ohio Edison Co., Ill. Power Co., Ill. Electric Power Co., Northern Ohio Power & Light Co., Tenn. Electric Power Co., 1924-28; cons. engr., 1928—; pres. Gen. Power Corp.; v.p. Fargo Engring. Co. Mem. Am. com., World Power Conf. Pres. bd. trustees Albion (Mich.) Coll.; pres. Methodist Foundation of Mich., 1931; chmn. finance com. Mich. George Washington Bicentennial Commn., 1932. Republican. Methodist. Elk. Home: Jackson, Mich. Died June 24, 1932.

TEHON, LEO ROY, (ta'h'n), botanist; b. Dumont, S.D., June 21, 1895; s. Patrick John and Bertha (Whittier) T.; student Fremont (Neb.) Normal Sch., 1909, Gregg Sch., Chicago, 1913; A.B., U. of Wyo., 1916; M.A., U. of Ill., 1920; Ph.D., 1934; m. Mary Viola Bruner, Apr. 13, 1918; children—Stephen Whittier, Atha Lee. Asst. in botany, U. of Wyo., 1915-16, U. of Ill., 1916-17, 1924-25; teacher of botany, Arsenal Tech. Sch., Indianapolis, Ind., 1917-18; asst. plant pathologist U.S. Dept. Agr., Ill. State leader in barberry eradication, 1919-20, 1921-22; collaborator, U.S. Dept. Agr. Plant Disease Survey, 1921—; with Mount Arbor Nurseries, Shenandoah, Ia., 1920-21; botanist in charge bot. sect. Ill. State Natural History Survey, 1921-35, head of sect. of applied botany and plant pathology, 1935—; acting chief, 1945-47; prof. plant pathology, U. of Ill., Nov. 1947—; cons. pathologist Davey Tree Expert Co., 1934-42; mem. advisory com. Ill. State Weed Control, 1937-39, of Ill. Seed and Weed Council, 1939—; mem. Nat. Oak Wilt Technical Com., 1949—. Served in U.S. Army, 1918-19. Mem. Central States Forestry Congress, 1933. Pres. Arrowhead Council Boy Scouts of America, 1944-45. Fellow A.A.A.S.; scientific mem. Nat. Shade Tree Conf. (member executive com., 1944—); Midwestern Shade Tree Conf. (mem. exec. commn., 1946—); charter mem. Mycol. Soc. of Am.; mem. Bot. Soc. Am., Torrey Botanical Club, Ecol. Soc. of Am., Am. Phytopathol. Soc., Am. Biol. Soc., Am. Forestry Assn., Ill. State Acad. Sci. (sec., 1943-46, pres., 1946-47), Ill. State Nurserymen's Assn. (hon.), Am. Legion, Phi Beta Kappa, Sigma Xi. Clubs: Am. Coll. Quill (hon.); Exchange (local president, 1932); member national committee on junior exchange 1932-33. Author: The Native and Naturalized Trees of Illinois (with Robert B. Miller); Fieldbook of Native Illinois Shrubs; Drug Plants of Illinois. Contbr. numerous technical monographs, bulletions, reports and articles on botany, plant pathology and mycology; also author of several non-technical pamphlets including "Rout the Weeds!", "Pleasure with Plants" and Ill. Plants Poisonous to Livestock; conductor of column "Diseases of Trees" in Am. Nurseryman magazine, 1940-44. Translator: Targioni-Tozzetti's Alimurgia. Member editorial board Phytopathology, 1945-47. Home: 1003 S. Busey St. Office: Natural Resources Bldg., Urbana, Ill. Died Oct. 17, 1954.

TEILHARD DE CHARDIN, PIERRE, philosopher, paleontologist; b. Auvergne, France, May 1, 1881; s. Emmanuel T. de C.; student religion Jesuit sch., Villefranche, later in Sussex, Eng.; student geology in Paris; Sc.D., U. Paris, 1922. Taught sci., Cairo, Egypt; ordained priest Soc. of Jesus, Roman Cath. Ch., 1912; worked under Marcellin Boule, Inst. Human Paleontology, Mus. Natural History, Paris; prof. geology Catholic Inst. Paris; made several sci. expdns. to Far East, taking part in discovery skull of Peking man; named dir. Lab. Advanced Studies in Geology and Paleontology, Paris, 1938; in China during World War II; returned to Paris, 1946, was forbidden by superiors to publish philosophy or put forward his candidature for professorship in Coll. de France; elected Membre de l'Institut; moved to U.S., 1951, conducted anthrop. projects for Wenner Gren Found., N.Y.C. Dir. research Centre National de la Recherche Scientifique. Served as stretcher bearer, World War I. Named officer Legion of Honor. Corr. mem. Acad. des Sciences. Contbd. to Western understanding of paleontology and geology of Far East; his philosophy (pub. posthumously) fuses sci. and religion in analyzing the evolution, phenomenon and future of man. Author books including: Building the Earth; Phenomenon of Man, 1959; Divine Milieu, 1960; Letters from a Traveller, 1962; Future of Man, 1964; Hymn of the Universe, 1965; Making of a Mind, 1965. Died after a stroke, N.Y.C., Apr. 10, 1955. *

TEMPLIN, RICHARD LAURENCE, civil and mech. engr.; b. Minneapolis, Kan., Jan. 20, 1893; s. Grant and Maude (Davis) T.; B.S., in C.E., U. Kan., 1915, M.E., 1926; M.S., U. Ill., 1917; m. Mabel Jane Harper, June 20, 1919; children—Richard Laurence, Gordon Harper. Began as rodman, A.T.&S.F. Ry., 1915; research fellow in engring. Expt. Sta., U. Ill., 1915-17; structural engring. detailer for Kansas City Terminal Ry., summer 1916; asst. engr. physicist U.S. Bur. Standards, Washington, chief engr. tests Aluminum Co. Am., 1919—, asst. dir. research, 1942—; spl. cons. to U.S. Navy on fatigue test machines. Awarded Edward Longstreth medal, Franklin Inst., 1940. Mem. sub-coms. NASA, 1931—. Mem. Am. Soc. for Testing Materials (Charles B. Dudley medal 1934) v.p. 1946-48; pres.; dir. 1949-52), Am. Soc. C.E. (Thomas Fitch Rowland prize 1936), Am. Soc. for Metals, Am. Soc. M.E., Am. Soc. for Testing Materials (hon.), Am. Inst. Mining, Metall. and Petroleum Engrs., Soc. for Exptl. Stress Analysis, Acacia, Tau Beta Pi, Sigma Xi. Republican. Episcopalian (vestryman St. Andrews' Ch. 1920-49). Mason. Club: University (Pitts.). Author: H. W. Gillett Memorial Lecture, 1954; other sci. papers. Contbr. tech. articles to mags. Home: 354 Riverview Drive, New Kensington, Pa. 15069. Died Apr. 7, 1965; buried Highland Cemetery, Mpls.

TENBROECK, CARL, bacteriologist; b. Parsons, Kan., Sept. 5, 1885; s. Andrew and Carrie (Aldrich) T.; A.B., U. Ill., 1908; M.D., Harvard, 1913; m. Janet Rinaker, Apr. 28, 1917; children—Carlon (dec.), Jane, Nancy. Asso., Rockefeller Inst. for Med. Research, 1914-20, mem. dept. animal pathology, 1927-51, emeritus, 1951—, dir., 1929-51; asso. prof. bacteriology, Peking (China) Union Med. Coll., 1920-23, prof., head dept. pathology, 1923-27. Cons. to Sec. of War, 1942-46. Served as 1st lt. M.C., U.S. Army, 1917-18. Recipient Medal of Freedom. Mem. A.A.A.S., Am. Soc. Immunologists, Soc. Exptl. Biology and Medicine. Research on animal diseases. Address: Bar Harbor, Me. Died Nov. 1966.

TENNENT, DAVID HILT, biologist; b. Janesville, Wis., May 28, 1873; s. Thomas and Mary (Hilt) T.; B.S., Olivet (Mich.) Coll., 1900; Ph.D., Johns Hopkins, 1904; m. Esther Margaret Maddux, Apr. 8, 1909; 1 son, David Maddux. Acting prof. biology and physics, Randolph-Macon Coll., Va., 1903; lecturer in biology, 1904-05, asso., 1905-06, asso. prof., 1906-12, prof., 1912-38, research prof., 1938—, Bryn Mawr Coll. Dir. instrn. in dept. of embryology, Marine Biol. Lab., Woods Hole, Mass., 1920-22; visiting prof. biology, Keio Univ., Tokyo, 1930-31; exec. officer Tortugas Marine Biol. Lab. Carnegie Instn. of Washington, 1937-40. Investigations in marine biology at Marine Biol. Lab., Woods Hole, Mass., Cold Spring Harbor, L.I., Bur. Fisheries Lab., Beaufort, N.C., Hopkins Marine Sta., Pacific Grove, Calif., Carnegie Inst. Washington, at Dry Tortugas, Fla., Jamaica, Naples Sta., Torres Strait, Australia, Japan. Home: Bryn Mawr, Pa. Died Jan. 14, 1941.

TENNENT, JOHN, physician; b. Eng., circa 1700; m. Dorothy Paul, 1730; m. 2d, Mrs. Hanger, Nov. 8, 1741. Came to Am., 1725; developed treatment for pleurisy using rattlesnake root, 1735; returned to Eng., 1739, met with little success in securing recognition for rattlesnake root medicine (which he claimed would cure pleurisy, gout, rheumatism, dropsy, nervous disorders). Author: Essay on the Pleurisy, 1736; Detection of a Conspiracy . . . The Singular Case of John Tennent, published by him in London (defense of his career), 1743; Every Man His Own Doctor, advocated use of medicines grown in Am., 2d edit., 1724. Died circa 1760.

TENNY, LLOYD STANLEY, agricultural expert; b. Hilton, N.Y., Dec. 24, 1876; s. Delos P. and Fannie Elizabeth (Lee) T.; grad. State Normal Sch., Brockport, N.Y., 1896; A.B., U. of Rochester, 1902; scholarship for research, Marine Biol. Lab., Woods Hole, Mass., 1902; studied, Cornell, 1908; m. Abby Warn, June 1, 1907; children—Fannybelle Lee, Stanley Warn, Lloyd Stanley. With Cornell U., 1911-13, advancing to prof. of extension; 1st state leader of county agrl. agts. in N.Y. State and assisted in establishing the first country farm bureaus; in charge service and regulatory work and asst. chief Bur. Agrl. Economics, U.S. Dept. Agr., 1921-26; chief of Bur. Agrl. Economics, 1926-28; v.p. Calif. Vineyardists Assn., 1928-29; pres. Federal Fruit Stabilization Corp. of Calif., Apr.-Nov. 1929; gen. mgr. Chicago Mercantile Exchange since Nov. 1929. Mem. Advisory Com. War Finance Corp., 1921. Treas. 7th World Poultry Congress, Cleveland, O., 1939. Republican. Baptist. Clubs: Alpha Delta Phi (New York); Cosmos (Washington); Electric (Chicago). Author of articles in mags. and published addresses. Address: Chicago Mercantile Exchange, 110 N. Franklin St., Chicago IL*

TERMAN, LEWIS MADISON, (tûr'man), psychologist; b. Johnson County, Ind., Jan. 15, 1877; s. James William and Martha Parthenia (Cutsinger) T.; A.B., Central Normal Coll., Danville, 1898; A.B., Ind. U., 1902, A.M., 1903, LL.D., 1929; fellow in psychology and edn., Clark U., 1903-05, Ph.D., 1905; LL.D., U. Cal., 1945, U. So. Cal., 1949; Sc.D., U. Pa., 1946; m. Anna Belle Minton, Sept. 18, 1899; children—Frederick Emmons, Helen Clare. Prin. high schs., Smiths Valley, Ind., 1898-1901, San Bernardino, Cal., 1905-06; prof. psychology and pedagogy, State Normal Sch., Los Angeles, 1906-10; asst. prof. edn., Stanford, 1910-12, asso. prof., 1912-16, prof., 1916—, exec. head dept. psychology, 1922-42, prof. emeritus, 1942—. Mem. com. Psychol. Exam. Recruits, Com. on Classification of Personnel, U.S. Army, 1918-19; served as maj. in div. of psychology, Surgeon General's Office, Washington. Fellow A.A.A.S., Brit. Psychol. Soc., Ednl. Inst. Scotland (hon.); mem. Am. Psychol. Assn. (pres. 1923), N.E.A., Am. Sch. Hygiene Assn. (pres. 1917), Nat. Soc. Study Edn., Nat. Acad. Scis., Phi Beta Kappa, Sigma Xi. Mem. bd. 5 psychologists appts. to revise Army mental test methods for use in schs.; author of researches on gifted children. Republican. Author: The Teacher's Health, 1913; The Hygiene of the School Child, 1914; (with Dr. E.B. Hoag) Health Work in the Schools, 1914; The Measurement of Intelligence, 1916; The Stanford Revision of the Binet-Simon Intelligence Scale, 1916; The Intelligence of School Children, 1919; The Terman Group Test, 1920; (with T.L. Kelley and G.M. Ruch) The Stanford Achievement Test, 1923; (with others) Genetic Studies of Genius, Vol. I, 1925, Vol. II (with Catharine M. Cox), 1926, Vol. III (with Barbara Burks and Dortha Jensen), 1930; Children's Reading (with Margaret Lima), 1925; Sex and Personality (with Catharine Cox Miles), 1936; Measuring Intelligence (with Maud A. Merrill), 1937; Marital Happiness, 1938; The Terman-McNemar Test of Mental Ability (with Q. McNemar), 1942; The Gifted Child Grows Up (with Melita Oden), 1947; The Gifted Group at Mid-Life (with Melita Oden), 1959. Editor The Measurement and Adjustment Series; asso. editor Brit. Jour. Ednl. Psychology; Jour. Genetic Psychology; Genetic Psychology Monographs. Address: 761 Dolores St., Stanford University, Stanford, Cal. Died Dec. 21, 1956.

TERRY, ELI, inventor, clock mfr.; b. East Windsor, Conn., Apr. 13, 1772; s. Samuel and Huldah (Burnham) T.; m. Eunice Warner, Mar. 12, 1795; m. 2d, Harriet Ann (Pond) Peck, Oct. 1840; 11 children. Worked for numerous clockmakers in Conn., 1786-92; made his 1st clock, 1792; built 1st clock factory in Am., manufactured 10 to 20 clocks at a time by means of water power, 1800; established (with Seth Thomas and Silas Hoadley) firm Terry, Thomas & Hoadley, 1807; established his own business at Plymouth Hollow, 1810; devised "Pillarcroll top case" clock, 1814; patented about 10 improvements in clocks. Died Plymouth, Conn., Feb. 26, 1852.

TERRY, MARSHALL ORLANDO, physician; b. Watervliet Center, N.Y., June 21, 1848; s. William Henry and Sally (Burke) T.; scientific edn.; grad. Cleveland Homoe. Hosp. Coll., 1872; 2 yrs. in New York at Ophthalmic and Aural Inst., Manhattan Eye and Ear Infirmary and New York Eye and Ear Infirmary; special instrn. under Heitzmann in microscopy, at Bellevue in physical diagnosis and surgery; also in England; m. Mrs. A. M. McGregor, 1905 (died 1912); m. 2d, Mrs. A. R. Merritt. Practiced, 1872—. Apptd. by Gov. Cornell surgeon with rank of maj. N.G.N.Y., 1880; apptd. by Gov. Morton surgeon gen., rank of brig. gen., Jan. 1, 1895, reapptd. by Gov. Black, Jan. 1, 1897; apptd. by President Cleveland U.S. pension exam. surgeon and was pres. bd. 4 yrs.; declined position of chief surgeon of div. during Spanish-Am. War, offered by President McKinley, because of duties as surgeon gen. N.Y. Surgeon-in-chief Utica Homoe. Hosp., 1895-1905; formerly mem. surg. staff Gen. Hosp., and surgeon-in-chief Commercial Travelers' Mut. Accident Assn. America. Invented Terry stretcher and field case, adopted by State of N.Y., as were ambulance and regimental chest; discovered spread of typhoid due largely to flies. Decorated by Oneida Co. War Com. "in recognition of patriotic services during war between U.S. and Spain." Hon. mem. Coronado (Calif.) Camp No. 59, United Spanish War Vets Hon. pres. bd. trustees Am. Legion Post 6, San Diego, Calif.; member Association Army of U.S. Republican. Episcopalian. Author: The Soldier's Medical Friend (for gift to allied troops). Home: Coronado, Calif. Died Oct. 11, 1933.

TERRY, NATHANIEL MATSON, physicist; b. Lyme, Conn., Apr. 6, 1844; s. Rev. James Pease and Catharine A. (Matson) T.; A.B., Amherst, 1867, A.M., 1870; Ph.D., U. of Göttingen, 1871; hon. A.M., Yale, 1873; LL.D., Amherst, 1917; m. Frances A. Griswold, Nov. 6, 1878 (died 1915); children—Frances Griswold (wife of A. K. Atkins, U.S.N.), Nathaniel Matson, Louisa Mather. Prof. physics, U.S. Naval Acad., 1872-1917, head of dept. of physics and chemistry, 1886-1913. Commd. prof. mathematics U.S.N., 1913, and ordered to duty in connection with post-grad. course at U.S. Naval Acad.; retired with rank of commodore, U.S.N., 1917. Mem. bd. control Naval Inst., 22 years; trans. to retired list U.S. naval officers, 1917. Mem. exec. com. Navy Athletic Assn., 10 yrs.; hon. mem. U.S. Naval Acad. Graduates' Assn.; pres. First Ecclesiastical Soc. of Old Lyme. Home: Lyme, Conn. Died Oct. 12, 1938.

TERRY, ROBERT JAMES, anatomist; b. St. Louis, Jan. 24, 1871; s. John Henry and Elizabeth Helen (Todd) T.; Cornell U., 1890-92; M.D., Mo. Med. Coll., 1895; A.B., Washington U., St. Louis, 1901; studied in Edinburgh, 1898, Freiburg, 1903; Austin teaching fellow Harvard, 1906-07; m. Grace Valle Speck, Nov. 24, 1897; children—Celeste Speck (Mrs. Howard M. Forbes), Dr. Robert Todd, Charles Speck. Prof. anatomy Washington U., 1903-41. Dean, Officers Sch. Oral and Plastic Surgery, U.S. Army, 1917-18. Collaborator in establishing migratory bird treaty between U.S. and Gt. Britain. Fellow A.A.A.S. (chmn. sec. H, 1927), Inst. Am. Geneal.; mem. Am. Assn. Anatomists, Anat. Soc. Gt. Britain, St. Louis Med. Soc., St. Louis Acad. Scis. (pres. 1935, 36), Am. Anthrop. Assn., Am. Assn. Phys. Anthropology (pres. 1939-41), Soc. Research Child Devel., Am. Assn. U. Profs., Eugenics Research Assn., Am. Genetic Assn., Am. Ornithol. Union, Audubon Soc. Mo., Mo. Hist. Soc. (trustee), Soc. Mayflower Descs., S.R., Zeta Psi, Phi Beta Kappa, Sigma Xi, Alpha Omega Alpha. Democrat. Unitarian. Clubs: University, Cornell, Harvard, Town and Gown, St. Louis Naturalists, St. Louis Audubon Society (founder). Author: Introduction to Study of Human Anatomy, 1929. Contbr. Morris' Human Anatomy, also original research papers on human and comparative anatomy, anthropology, wild life conservation. Home: St. Louis 3. Died Apr. 18, 1966; buried St. Louis.

TERRY, THEODORE BRAINARD, agriculturist; b. at Lafayette, N.Y., Jan. 2, 1843; s. Rev. Parshall and Fannie Buel (Howell) T.; ed. Painesville (O.) Acad., and Western Reserve Coll., Hudson, O.; m. Eleanor M. Tillotson, Mar. 1, 1865. Bought a poor farm in 1870, made a success of it and for 27 yrs. has been in demand as lecturer at farmers' insts., and writer; has worked in 17 states. Pres. Hudson Telephone Co. Author: A B C of Potato Culture; A B C of Strawberry Culture; Our Farming; How to Keep Well and Live Long, 1909. Associate editor Practical Farmer, Phila. Home: Hudson, O. Died Jan. 1, 1916.

TERRY, WALLACE IRVING, surgeon; b. Sacramento, Calif., Nov. 26, 1868; s. Wallace Emmet and Laura Abigail (Morrill) T.; B.S., U. of Calif., 1890, M.D., 1892; univs. of Berlin and Paris, 1894-96; m. Mary Frances Dudley, Apr. 19, 1898; children—Elizabeth Dudley (Mrs. Robertson Ward), Wallace Irving. Interne, St. Luke's Hosp., San Francisco, 1892-93; city physician, Sacramento, 1893; asst. in surgery, U. of Calif., 1899-1903, instr., 1903-07, asst. prof., 1907-12, prof., 1912-32, clin. prof., 1932-39; clinical prof. emeritus since 1939. Fellow Am. Surgical Assn., Am. Coll. Surgeons, Pacific Coast Surg. Assn.; mem. Zeta Psi, Nu Sigma Nu, Alpha Omega Alpha, Sigma Xi; hon. mem. San Francisco County Med. Soc. Republican. Episcopalian. Mason. Club: Pacific Union. Home: 2712 Broadway, San Francisco 15 CA

TERZAGHI, KARL, cons. engr., educator; b. Prag, Austria, Oct. 2, 1883; s. Anton and Amalia (Eberle) T.; M.E., Technische Hochschule, Graz, Austria, 1904, D.Tech., 1911; Doctor honoris causa, U. Istanbul, U. Mexico, Eidgen Poly. Zurich; Eng.D. (hon.), Lehigh U.; Sc.D., Trinity Coll., Dublin, Ireland; E.D., Technische Universitöot, W. Berlin, Germany, 1958; Eng. D. Norges Tekniske Hogskole, Trondheim, 1960; m. Ruth Allen Doggett, June 2, 1930; children—Eric Anthony, Margaret. Came to U.S., 1912, naturalized, 1943. Jr. engr. Adolf Baron Pittel, Vienna, 1905-06; designing engr., supt. construction in Austria, Croatia, Russia, U.S., 1906-14; prof. foundation engring. Ecole impériale d'Ingénieurs, Constantinople, Turkey, 1916-18, Am. Robert Coll., Constantinople, 1918-25; prof. soil mechanics and found. engring. Mass. Inst. Tech., also cons. in N. and Central Am., 1925-29; prof. Technische Hochschule, Vienna, also cons. in Europe, Asia and Africa, 1929-38; hon. pres. Internat. Conf. Soil Mechanics and Found. Engring., Cambridge, Mass., 1957—; guest lectr. in U.S., 1936; cons. in U.S., 1939—; prof. civil engring. Harvard U., emeritus, 1956—; vis. lectr. research cons., U. Ill. Cons. work U.S., S.Am., India, Eng., France, North & Central Africa; pres. Internat. Conf. Soil Mech. Found. Eng., Rotterdam, 1948, Zurich, 1953. Recipient Normal medal Am. Soc. C.E., 1930, 42, 47; FitzGerald medal, Clemens Herschel prize Boston Soc. Civil Engrs., 1926, 28, 43; Brown Medal, Franklin Soc., Phila.; James Forrest lectr. Inst. Civil Engrs., London, 1939, James Alfred Ewing Medal, 1960. Mem. Am. Soc. C.E. (hon.), Boston Soc. Civil Engrs. (hon.), Inst. Civil Engrs. (London), Am. Acad. Arts and Scis., Sigma Xi. Author: Erdbaumechanik, 1925; Ingenieurgeologie, 1929; Theorie der Setzung von Tonschichten, 1936; Theoretical Soil Mechanics, 1943; Soil Mechanics in Engineering Practice, 1948; From Theory to Practice in Soilmechanics, 1960. Address: 3 Robinson Circle, Winchester, Mass. Died Oct. 25, 1963; buried South Waterford, Me.

TESLA, NIKOLA (tes'la), electrician; b. Smiljan, Lika (border of Austria-Hungary), July 9, 1856; s. of Greek clergyman and orator, and of Georgina Mandic, who was an inventor, as was her father; ed. 1 yr. at elementary sch., 4 yrs. at Lower Realschule, Gospic, Lika, and 3 yrs. at Higher Realschule, Carlstadt, Croatia, graduating 1873; student 4 yrs. at Polytechnic Sch., Gratz, in mathematics, physics and mechanics; afterward 2 yrs. in philos. studies at U. of Prague, Bohemia; hon. M.A., Yale, 1894; LL.D., Columbia, 1894; D.Sc., Vienna Polytechnic. Began practical career at Budapest, Hungary, 1881, where made his first electrical invention—a telephone repeater—and conceived idea of his rotating magnetic field; later engaged in various branches of engring. and manufacture. Since 1884 resident of U.S., becoming naturalized citizen. Invevtor and discoverer: System of arc lighting, 1886; Tesla motor and system of alternating current power transmission, 1888; system of elec. conversion and distribution by oscillatory discharges, 1889; generators of high frequency currents, and effects of these, 1890 Tesla coil, or transformer, 1891; system of wireless transmission of intelligence, 1893; mech. oscillators and generators of elec. oscillations, 1894-95; researches and discoveries in radiations, material streams and emanations, 1896-98; high-potential magnifying transmitter, 1897; system of transmission of power without wires, 1897-1905; Tesla's steam and gasturbine and pump; etc. Chiefly engaged, since 1903, in development of system of telegraphy and telephony, and designing plant for transmission of power without wires, to be erected at Niagara. Address: The New Yorker Hotel, New York, N.Y. Died Jan. 7, 1943. *

TEWKSBURY, WILLIAM DAVIS, physician; b. Hutchinson, Kan., May 7, 1885; s. William Brainard and Minnie (Davis) T.; M.D., George Washington U. Med. Sch., 1908; m. Susan Tidball West, Feb. 25, 1911; children—Jane West, Helen Davis. Began practice at Washington, 1908; resident physician Tuberculosis Hosp., 1908-09; physician in charge Catawba Sanatorium, Va., 1909-11; medical supt. Tuberculosis Hosp., 1911-20; clin. prof. medicine, George Washington U. Med. Sch., since 1915; physician in charge Health Dept. Tuberculosis Clinic, 1915-21; asso. prof. medicine, Georgetown Med. Sch., 1917-19. Mem. Vol. Med. Service Corps. Fellow A.M.A., Am. Coll. Physicians; mem. Am. College of Chest Physicians, Hypocrates Galen Med. Society, Med. Soc. D.C., Tuberculosis Association D.C. (dir.), Sigma Alpha Epsilon, Phi Chi. Episcopalian. Club: Chevy Chase. Contributor of papers on pulmonary disease to Journal of A.M.A., Am. Review of Tuberculosis, Va. Medical Semi-Monthly, etc. Original work in use of artificial pneumothorax in treatment of acute pulmonary abscesses, 1916. Home: 101 E. Lenox St., Chevy Chase, Md. Office: Washington Medical Bldg., Washington. Died Dec. 28, 1956.

TEXTOR, GORDON EDMUND, army engr.; b. Kasota, Minn., July 9, 1902; s. Charles E. and Louise (Offenloch) T.; B.A., B.M.S., U.S. Mil. Acad., 1924; C.E., Cornell, 1928; married; children—Mary Louise, Gretchen Elizabeth. Served in U.S. Army, Corps of Engrs., 1928—, advancing to brig. gen., 1945; dir. projects, W.P.A., 1937-39; dir. constrn. and facilitation bur. W.P.B., 1942-43; gen. officer, War Dept. Gen. Staff, 1943-45. Address: 314 Mansion Drive, Alexandria, Va. Died Mar. 30, 1955.

THACHER, ARTHUR, mining engr.; b. Newtonville, Mass., May 8, 1857; s. Thomas and Catherine (Worcester) T.; E.M., C.E., Columbia, 1877; m. Carrie Greene, June 19, 1890; children—Theodora, Arthur Worcester. Has engaged in mining in Mex., Ariz., Colo. and Ida.; adj. prof. metallurgy, Washington U., 1891; pres. and gen. mgr. Central Lead Co., 1892-1905; consulting engr. Am. Smelting Securities Co., 1906; Western mgr. of mines N.J. Zinc Co., 1906—. Home: St. Louis, Mo. Died July 2, 1934.

THACHER, EDWIN, engineer; b. DeKalb, N.Y., Oct. 12, 1839; s. Seymour and Elizabeth (Smith) T.; C.E., Rensselaer Poly. Inst., 1863; m. Anna E. Bartholomew, Apr. 22, 1872. Chief engr. Keystone Bridge Co., 1881-87; cons. engr. for bridges and bridge contractor; mem. Concrete-Steel Engring. Co. Inventor and patentee Thacher's cylindrical slide rule, improved duplex slide rule, steel bridge trusses, combination bridge trusses, system of concrete-steel arches, steel super-structure for concrete-steel bridges, bar for reënforcing concrete, and system for concrete-steel floors. Home: New York, N.Y. Died Sept. 21, 1920.

THANNHAUSER, SIEGFRIED JOSEF, physician, educator; born Munich, Germany, June 28, 1885; son Josef and Lotte (Langermann) T.; ed. Luitpold Gymnasium, Munich, 1895-1904; M.D., U. of Munich, 1909, Ph.D., 1913, M.D. (hon.), 1955; M.D. (hon.), U. Freiburg, U. Dusseldorf; m. Franziska Reiner, 1918. Came to U.S., 1934, naturalized 1940. Asso. prof. medicine Univ. of Munich, 1910-24, professor, University Heidelberg, 1924-27; professor medicine Academy Dusseldorf, 1927-30, University of Freiburg, 1930-34; clin. prof. medicine Tufts College 1934-48, emeritus; consultant physician Joseph H. Pratt Diagnostic Hospital, 1938—. Recipient of the Mueller medal, 1958. Fellow American Academy Arts and Sciences; member A.M.A., Massachusetts Medical Soc., Assn. Am.-Phys., Am. Heart Assn., Am. Chem. Soc., A.A.A.S., Am. Diabetes Assn., Am. Soc. Biol. Chemists, Assn. Study Internal Secretions, hon. mem. Spanish Acad. Medicine since 1934, Bulgarian Assn. Medicine since 1936. Democrat. Jewish. Author: Metabolism and Metabolic Diseases, 1934; Lipidoses: Diseases of the Cellular Lipid Metabolism, 1950, rev. 1958; sect. respiratory diseases, joints and bone diseases to internal medicine textbook. Contbr. to med. jours. Office: 30 Bennet St., Boston, Mass. Home: 93 Ivy St., Brookline, Mass. Died Dec. 18, 1962; buried Lakeview Cemetery, Wolfboro, N.H.

THARALDSEN, CONRAD ENGERUD (tär'äld-sen), prof. anatomy; b. Battle Lake, Minn., May 20, 1884; s. Iver and Caroline Emelie (Engerud) T.; B.S., St. Olaf Coll., Northfield, Minn., 1907; post-grad. work, Harvard, Columbia, U. of Wis. and Marine Biol. Lab., Woods Hole, Mass.; M.A., Columbia, 1918, Ph.D., 1925; m. 2d, Ethel M. Smith, 1927; children—Margaret Emelie, Constance Ethel. Instr. biology, Blaine High Sch., Superior, Wis., 1907-09; head of biology dept., State Normal Sch., Mayville, N.D., 1909-17; prof. zoölogy, Northwestern U., 1919-27; prof. anatomy and head of dept., New York Homeo, Med. Coll. (now New York Med. Coll.) since 1927, chmn. Grad. Edn. Div. Inventor micro-vivisection appartus and other biol. research appliances. Mem. bd. mgrs. of Collegiate Div. of Y.M.C.A. Fellow A.A.A.S., N. Y. Acad. Science; mem. Am. Assn. Univ. Profs., Soc. Exptl. Biology and Medicine, History of Science Soc., Sigma Xi.; hon. mem. New York Acad. Pathol. Science (pres. 1937-40), Am. Assn. Anatomists. Investigator and contbr. on zoöl. topics. Home: 51 Biltmore Av., Crestwood, N.Y. Office: 1 E. 105th St., New York, N.Y. Died May 20, 1944.

THARP, BENJAMIN C(ARROLL), univ. prof.; b. Pankey, Tex., Nov. 16, 1885; s. Edwin Harris and Angelina Victoria (McJunkin) T.; Diploma, Sam Houston Normal Inst., Huntsville, Tex., 1910; A.B., U. of Tex., 1914, A.M., 1915, Ph.D., 1925; m. Norris Ophelia Wallis, Sept. 16, 1914; children—Benjamin Carroll, George Edwin. History teacher, Rockdale (Tex.) High Sch., 1910-11; plant pathologist, Tex. State Dept. Agr., 1915-17; asso. prof. biology, Sam Houston State Teachers Coll., 1917-19; instr. botany University of Texas, 1919-20, assistant prof., 1920-25, asso. prof., 1925-33, prof. botany, 1933-56, emeritus, 1956—, asst. dean Coll. Arts and Scis., 1928-34, dir. Herbarium, 1943-56, dir. emeritus, 1956—. Mem. parks bd. City Austin, 1938-52. Fellow A.A.A.S., mem. Bot. Soc., Am.

Ecol. Soc. (past v.p.), Am. Soc. Plant Taxonomists, Torr. Bot. Club, Am. Assn. U. Profs., Tex. Acad. Sci. (past pres.), Tex. Interscholastic League (mem. exec. com. since 1922), Phi Beta Kappa, Sigma Xi. Mason (33 deg. Scottish rite, Shriner). Author: Tex. Range Grasses, 1952. Democrat. Baptist. Club: Kiwanis. Home: 506 Bellevue Pl., Austin 21, Texas. Died Nov. 29, 1964.

THAXTER, ROLAND, botanist; b. Newton, Mass., Aug. 28, 1858; s. Levi L. and Celia (Leighton) T.; A.B., Harvard, 1882, Ph.D., and A.M., 1888; m. Mabel Gray Freeman, June 8, 1887; children—Charles Eliot (dec.), Katharine, Elizabeth, Edmund Lincoln. Asst. in biology, Harvard, 1886-88; mycologist, Conn. Agrl. Expt. Sta., 1888-1891; asst. prof. cryptogamic botany, 1891-1901, prof., 1901-19, prof. emeritus, 1919—, Harvard. Fellow Am. Acad. Arts and Sciences, A.A.A.S. Contbr. scientific publs. Home: Kittery Point, Me. Died 1932.

THAYER, BENJAMIN BOWDITCH, mining engr.; b. San Francisco, Calif., Oct. 20, 1862; s. Benjamin Bowditch and Lucy W. (Phipps) T.; Ph.B., Lawrence Scientific Sch. (Harvard), 1885; m. Marie C. Renouard, Jan. 29, 1890. Began in employ Anaconda Copper Mining Co., 1885, of which was pres., 1908, until its absorption, 1915, by the Amalgamated Copper Co.; pres. Raritan Copper Works, Anaconda Sales Co., Electrolytic Zinc Process Co., Santiago Mining Co.; v.p. Anaconda Copper Mining Co., Internat. Smelting Co., Potrerillos Ry. Co., Andes Copper Mining Co., Chile Copper Co., Chile Exploration Co. Mem. Naval Cons. Board, 1915 (chmn.). Republican. Home: New York, N.Y. Died Feb. 22, 1933.

THAYER, JOHN ELIOT, ornithologist; b. Boston, Mass., Apr. 3, 1862; s. Nathaniel and Cornelia (Van Rensselaer) T.; (mother a dau. of Stephen Van Rensselaer, of Albany, the last Patroon); A.B., Harvard, 1885, hon. A.M., 1910; m. Evelyn Duncan Forbes, June 22, 1886; children—John E., Evelyn, Nora Forbes, Natalie, Duncan Forbes. Trustee of the Clinton Savings Bank. Chmn. selectmen Town of Lancaster; mem. staff of Gov. William E. Russell, 3 yrs. Mem. board Am. Unitarian Assn. He built a museum in town of Lancaster, which is open to the public and has one of the most complete collections of N.Am. birds in the world. Fellow Am. Acad. Arts and Sciences. Home: Lancaster, Mass. Died July 22, 1933.

THAYER, SYLVANUS, mil. engr., educator; b. Braintree, Mass., June 9, 1785; s. Nathaniel and orcas (Faxon) T.; attended Dartmouth, 1807, L.. (hon.), 1846; grad. U.S. Mil. Acad., 1808; LL.D. (hon.), St. John's Coll., Kenyon Coll., 1846, Harvard, 1857. Commd. 2d lt. Corps Engrs., U.S. Army, 1808; served on Canadian frontier and Norfolk (Va.) during War of 1812; commd. capt., 1813; brevetted maj., 1815; apptd. supt. U.S. Mil. Acad., West Point, N.Y., 1817-33; commd. maj., 1828, col., 1833; engr. in charge constrn. of certifications at Boston Harbor and improvement harbors on New Eng. coast, 1833-63; profl. ty in Europe, 1843-46; brevetted brig. gen., 1862; retired from army, 1863; established and dowed Thayer Sch. Engring., Dartmouth Coll., 1867. Author: Papers on Practical Engineering, 1844. died South Braintree, Sept. 7, 1872; buried West Point.

THAYER, WILLIAM SYDNEY, M.D.; b. Milton, Mass., June 23, 1864; s. James B. and Sophia B. (Ripley) T.; A.B., Harvard, 1885 (Phi Beta Kappa; pres. 1929), M.D., 1889; LL.D., Washington Coll., Chestertown, Md., 1907, Edinburgh U., 1927, McGill U., 1929; hon. Dr. U. of Paris, 1928; Sc.D. from U. of Chicago; m. Susan Chisolm, d. late Benjamin Huger Read, of Charleston, S.C., Sept. 3, 1901. Visiting phys. Johns Hopkins Hosp.; prof. emeritus of medicine, Johns Hopkins U. (Phi Beta Kappa). Mem. Bd. Overseers, Harvard, two terms; mem. Bd. Trustees. Carnegie Inst. of Washington, 1929. Fellow Am. Acad. Arts and Sciences; mem. numerous Am. and fgn. societies. Maj. and dep. commr. Am. Red Cross Mission to Russia, June 1917-Jan. 1918; maj. col. and brig. gen. Med. Corps, U.S.A., and chief consultant med. services, A.E.F., in France, Mar. 1918-Jan. 1919; became brig. gen. Medical Sect. O.R.C., U.S.A.; brig. gen. Auxiliary, U.S.A., 1929. Awarded distinction badge, Red Cross of Russia, 1918; D.S.M. (U.S.), 1919; Comdr. Legion of Honor, France, 1928; Bright medalist, Guy's Hosp., London, 1927. Author: Lectures on the Malarial Fevers, 1897; (with Dr. Hewetson) The Malarial Fevers of Baltimore (Johns Hopkins Hosp. Reports), 1895; Studies on Bacterial Endocarditis (pub. by same), 1925; America—1917, and Other Verse, 1926. Home: Baltimore, Md. Died Dec. 10, 1932.

THEILER, MAX, research physician; b. Pretoria, South Africa, Jan. 30, 1899; s. Arnold and Emma (Jegge) T.; student U. Capetown 1917-18; L.R.C.P., Mem. Royal Coll. Surgeons, St. Thomas' Hosp., 1922; D.T.M. and H., London Sch. Tropical Medicine, 1922; m. Lillian Graham, Feb. 18, 1928; 1 dau., Elizabeth. Came to U.S. 1922. Asst., Instr. dept. tropical medicine, med. sch. Harvard, 1929-30; staff mem. Rockefeller Found., N.Y.C., 1930-72, dir. div. medicine and pub. health labs., 1951-64; prof. Yale Sch. Medicine, 1964-67, prof. emeritus epidemiology and microbiology, 1967-72, lectr.; extensive research on yellow fever, on mouse encephalomyelitis and viruses isolated in tropics, 1940-72. Recipient Chalmers' medal, 1939; Flattery medal, 1945; Lasker award, 1949; Nobel prize in physiology and medicine for devel. vacine against yellow fever, 1951. Mem. Am. Soc. Tropical Medicine, Harvey Soc., Royal Soc. Tropical Medicine and Hygiene. Author chpts. in med. books; also numerous. sci. articles. Home: New Haven CT Died Aug. 11, 1972.

THEIS, EDWIN RAYMOND, (tis), educator, chemist; b. Newport, Ky., July 8, 1896; s. Edwin David and Ida Eliza (Holbrook) T.; Ch.E., U. of Cincinnati, 1921, Ph.D., 1926; m. Martha Celestine Pauling, July 2, 1921; children—Edwin Raymond, Richard Carl. Engaged as research asso. and dir. chem. research Dept. Leather Research, U. of Cincinnati, 1921-27; chem. engr., Frederick Stearns & Co., Detroit, Mich., 1927; asst. prof. chem. engring., Lehigh U., Bethlehem, Pa., 1927-30, asso. prof., 1930-38, prof. chem. engring. 1938-45; research prof. chemistry, dir. Div. Leather Technology, Institute of Research, Lehigh University since 1945; has served as consultant to leather and allied industries since 1927; mem. spl. U.S. Govt. com. sent to China and Japan for inspection imported skins, summer 1937; ECA point 4 program Holland, 1950. Served as 2d lt. inf., United States Army, 1918-19; 1st lt. Ordnance Reserve, 1926-31, capt. since 1931. Fellow American Institute of Chemists; Am. Chem. Soc., Tech. Assn. of Fur Industry, Tau Beta Pi, Sigma Xi, Delta Sigma Phi. Republican. Hon. life mem. American Leather Chemists Assn. Co-author: Chemistry of Leather Manufacture (mono- Methodist. Clubs: Lions International, Chemists'. graph). Awarded Moffatt medal by Tanners Council of America, 1943. Invited lecturer to Soc. of Internat. Leather Trades Chemists and to Faraday Soc., London, England, Sept. 1946. Home: 1021 Raymond Av., Bethlehem, Pa. Died Apr. 25, 1953.

THEIS, FRANK VICTOR, surgeon; b. Chgo., Feb. 25, 1899; s. Victor and Anna (Blonn) T.; B.S., U. Chicago, 1920, M.D., 1923; Francis Hardy fellow in surgery, Rush Med. Coll., 1926-28; post grad., U. Vienna, 1928-29; m. Hazel H. Ericsson, Dec. 9, 1931; children—Henry Ericsson. Peter Frank. Intern Cook Co. Hosp., Chgo., 1924-25. attending surgeon 1946—; prof surgery Cook County Grad. School Medicine; resident Presbyn.-St. Lukes Hosp., 1926-28, asso. attending surgeon, from 1943; surg. staff St. Joseph's Hosp., 1929-38; cons. surgeon Norweglan Am. Hosp.; pvt. practice surgery since 1929; asso. prof. surgery Rush Med. Coll., U. Ill. since 1941. Bd. dirs. Senior Centers Metropolitan Chgo. Served as comdr. M.C., U.S.N.R., since 1942. Diplomate Am. Bd. Surgery. Fellow A.C.S.; mem. Ill. State, Chgo. med. socs, Inst. medicine Chgo., Am. Heart Assn., Soc. Vascular surgeons, A.M.A., Chgo. Surg. Soc., Chgo. Inst. Medicine, Internat. Cardiovascular Soc., Central Surg. Soc., Am. Diabetic Assn., Pan Am. Med. Assn., Chgo. Council American Scandinavian Found., Internat. Surg. Soc., N.Y. Acad. Scis., Sigma Chi. Republican. Episcopalian. Clubs: Executives, University (Chgo.). Home: Chicago IL Died Mar. 12, 1972; buried Rosehill Cemetery, Chicago IL

THELEEN, DAVID E., naval officer; b. Kenosha, Wis., Nov. 6, 1875; s. Charles G.T.; grad. U.S. Naval Acad., 1897; m. Mary C. Persons, of Auburn, Ala., June 2, 1903. Promoted ensign, July 1, 1899; lt. jr. grade, July 1, 1902; lt., Aug. 10, 1903; lt. comdr., July 1, 1909; comdr., Aug. 29, 1916; capt. (temporary), Feb. 1, 1918. Served on Massachusetts during Spanish-Am. War, 1898; on surveying cruises in West Indies 3 yrs. and with Atlantic Training Squadron 3 yrs.; duty at Naval Proving Gound, Indian Head, Md., and two times at Naval Gun Factory, Navy Yard, Washington, D.C.; comdr. U.S.S. Glacier in U.S. Pacific Fleet, at outbreak of World War; served in Brazil and off East Coast S. America; duty Navy Yard, Washington, D.C., Sept. 1917-19; assigned as comdr. U.S.S. St. Louis, Oct. 8, 1919. Has specialized in ordnance work and engring. Mem. Am. Soc. Naval Engrs., Naval Inst. Republican. Baptist. Mason. Clubs: Army and Navy (Washington, D.C., and Manila). Address: Navy Dept., Washington DC

THOM, CHARLES, (tom), botanist and mycologist; b. Minonk, Ill., Nov. 11, 1872; s. Angus Sutherland and Louisa Electa (Herrick) T.; A.B., Lake Forest Coll.. 1895, A.M., 1897. D.Sc. (hon.), 1936; Ph.D., U. Mo., 1899; grad. study Cornell U., 1902-04; Marine Biol. Lab., summer, 1897; m. Ethel Winifred Slater, Dec. 20, 1906 (dec. Oct. 1942); children—Beatrice (dec.), Charles Richard; m. 2d, Charlotte J. Bayles, Sept. 1944. Sci. tchr. Danville (Ill.) High Sch., 1895-96; instr. biology and botany, asst. prof. botany U. Mo., 1897-1902; asst. in botany Cornell U., 1902-04; mycologist in cheese investigations, dairy div. Bur. Animal Industry, U.S. Dept. of Agr., charge coöperative work in soft and fancy cheesemaking. Agrl. Expt. Sta., Storrs, Conn., 1904-13, Washington, 1913-14; in charge microbiol. lab. Bur. of Chemistry, 1914-27, of soil microbiology, Bur. Chemistry and Soils, 1927-34; with Bureau of Plant Industry, 1934-42, retired Nov. 30, 1942; collaborator U.S. Dept. Agr.; cons. mycologist; lectr. soil microbiology U. Md., 1929-38. Fellow A.A.A.A.; mem. Acad. Medicine (charter), Nat. Acad. Sciences, Washington Acad. Sci. (pres. 1937), Bot. Soc. Am., Am. Naturalists, Internat. Society Soil Sci. Soc. Am. Bacteriologists (pres. 1940), Am. Phytopathological Soc., Sigma Xi, Phi Beta Kappa. Club: Cosmos. Author: The Penicillia, 1930. Co-author: The Book of Cheese; Hygienic Fundamentals of Food Handling; Manual of the Aspergilli, Manual of the Penicillia. Contbr. govt. bulls. Address: Bayles Hill, Port Jefferson, N.Y. Died May 24, 1956; buried Storrs, Conn.

THOMAS, AMOS RUSSELL, homoeopathic physician, educator; b. Watertown, N.Y., Oct. 3, 1826; s. Azariah and Sarah (Avery) T.; grad. Syracuse Med. Coll., Feb. 1854; attended Pa. Med. U.; m. Elizabeth M. Bacon, Sept. 26, 1847, 2 children. Prof. anatomy Pa. Med. U., 1856-66; lectr. artistic anatomy Phila. Acad. Fine Arts, 1856-70; surgeon during Civil War, Washington, D.C.; prof. anatomy Hahnemann Med. Coll. of Phila., 1867-95, dean, 1874-95; editor Am. Jour. Homoeopathic Materia Medica, 1871-76; pres. Homoeopathic Med. Soc. of Pa., 1887. Author: A Practical Guide for Making Post-Mortem Examinations and for the Study of Morbid Anatomy, 1873; History of Anatomy, 1893. Died Phila., Oct. 31, 1895.

THOMAS, BENJAMIN FRANKLIN, physicist; b. Palmyra, O., Oct. 14, 1850; s. David D. and Eleanor (Evans) T.; B.S., Ripon Coll., 1874, M.S., 1877; Ph.D., Stevens Inst., Hoboken, N.J., 1880; grad. student Stevens Inst., and Mass. Inst. Tech., 1878-79; research asst. (with Prof. A. M. Mayer) Stevens Inst., 1879-80; m. Caroline P. Smith, Apr. 13, 1881. Farmer (in charge instrn. of Indians in outdoor work), Ft. Berthold (Dak.) Indian Reservation, 1875-76; instr. physics and mathematics, Carleton Coll., Northfield, Minn., 1876-79; prof. physics, U. of Mo., 1880-85; prof. physics, Ohio State U., 1885—; ex-officio state sealer of weights and measures, 1890—. Mem. bd. examiners Phila. Elec. Expn., 1884, jury of awards, Dept. Electricity, Chicago Expn., 1893; has made investigations in rapidly varying phenomena in elec. circuits, and in photometry (papers, A.A.A.S., and Am. Inst. Elec. Engrs.). Episcopalian. Republican. Home: Columbus, O. Died 1911.

THOMAS, CARL CLAPP, engineer; b. Detroit, Mich., July 14, 1872; s. George Roscoe and Caroline Melissa (Clapp) T.; Leland Stanford Jr. U., 1891-94; M.E., Sibley Coll. (Cornell U.), 1895; m. Katharine L. Nash, July 14, 1899; children—Dorothy Grace (dec.), Alfred Randall, Roscoe. Draftsman, asst. engr., chief engr. Globe Iron Works Co., Cleveland, 1895-99; chief draftsman marine dept. Md. Steel Co., 1899-1901; prof. marine engring. and naval architecture, New York U., 1901-03; asst. prof. mech. engring., U. of Calif., 1903-04; prof. marine engring., Cornell, 1904-08; prof. steam engring., U. of Wis., 1908-13; prof. mech. engring. John Hopkins, 1913-20; western rep. and vice pres. Dwight P. Robinson & Co., Inc., 1920—; city director of Pasadena, Calif., 1921-24; associate in engineering research, Calif. Institute Tech. Member Nat. Guard of Calif., 1889-92. Mgr. machinery fabrication of Am. Internat. Shipbuilding Corp., Phila. (on leave from Johns Hopkins), 1917-19. Author: Steam Turbines, 1906. Inventor of the Thomas electric gas meters, steam calorimeters and separators. Home: Pasadena, Calif. Died June 5, 1938.

THOMAS, CHARLES RANDOLPH, JR., editor, engineer; b. Beaufort, N.C., Mar. 29, 1888; s. Charles Randolph and Laura Pasteur (Davis) T.; B.S., in C.E., U. of N.C., 1912; spl. student U. of Wis., Columbia, Pa. State Coll., and Northwestern U.; m. Clara Norwood MacNeill, 1915 (died 1919); children—Charles Randolph, III, Francis Pasteur; m. 2d, Elzada Mackie, June 29, 1927. Engring. work with U.S. Bur. Pub. Roads and state highway depts.; mem. engring. research staff, Pa. State Coll.; asso. prof. civil engring., N.C. State Coll.; in charge sect. of review of results, U.S. Forest Products Lab.; successively asso. editor Engineering and Contracting, editorial dir. Successful Methods, editor, mgr. Professional Engineer, editor, pub. Reclamation and Farm Engineering until 1926; mng. editor and editor Highway Engr. and Contractor since 1926. Mem. Am. Soc. C.E., Kappa Sigma. Episcopalian. Club: University (Evanston, Ill.). Author: (technical bulletins) Highway Culverts and Bridges in North Carolina (with T. F. Hickerson), 1913; Tests of Vertical Pressure Through Earth (with R. B. Fehr), 1914; Highway Maintenance in North Carolina (with D. H. Winslow), 1917; also articles in Nation's Business, Saturday Evening Post, Engineering News-Record, etc. Compiler: Publicity Methods for Engineers, 1922. Home: Kedzie St., Evanston, Ill. Office: 53 W. Jackson Blvd., Chicago. Died March 8, 1931.

THOMAS, CYRUS, entomologist; b. Kingsport, Tenn., July 27, 1825; s. Stephen and Maria (Rogan) T.; ed. village schs. and acad.; admitted to bar, 1851, and practiced until 1865; m. Dorothy Logan, sister of Gen. John A. Logan, of Murphysboro, Ill., June 13, 1850; m. 2d, Miss L. V. Davis, Apr. 20, 1865. County clerk Jackson Co., Ill., 1850-53; minister Evang. Luth. Ch., 1865-69; asst. on U.S. Geol. and Geog. surveys of Territories, under Ferdinand V. Hayden, 1869-73; prof. natural sciences, Southern Ill. Normal U., 1873-75; state entomologist of Ill., 1874-76; mem. U.S. Entomol. Commn., 1876-77; archeologist U.S. Bur. of Ethnology, 1882—. Author: Synopsis of the Acrididae of North America; Noxious and Beneficial Insects of Illinois (5 vols. reports as state entomologist); Aid to the Study of

Maya Codices; The Cherokees and Shawnees in Pre-Columbian Times; Mound Explorations of Bureau of American Ethnology; Prehistoric Works East of the Rocky Mountains; Introduction to American Archaeology; Numeral Systems of the Mexican and Central American Tribes; The Mayan Calendar Systems; Indians of North America in Historic Times; Prehistoric North America; Languages of Mexico and Central America. Died 1910.

THOMAS, DAVID, iron mfr.; b. Glamorganshire, South Wales, Nov. 3, 1794; s. David and Jane Thomas; m. Elizabeth Hopkins, 5 children. Gen. supt. Yniscedwyn Iron Works, 1817; went to Scotland to observe hotblast methods being employed, circa 1836, returned with permission to use this process, work started immediately on constrn. furnace, blown, 1837; hired by Lehigh Coal & Navigation Co. of Pa. to construct and operate similar furnaces on Lehigh River, circa 1838; arrived in Allentown, Pa., 1839; organized Lehigh Crane Iron Co. (1st furnace produced good foundry anthracite iron, 1840, 1st anthracite-iron mfg. facility to be permanently successful from both engring. and comml. standpoint, included higher and larger furnaces, better and more powerful blast machinery); organized (with several others) Thomas Iron Co., Hokendauqua, Pa., 1854; pres. Catasaugua & Fogelsville R.R., 1st pres. Am. Inst. Mining Engrs. Died Catasauqua, Pa., June 20, 1882.

THOMAS, FLAVEL SHURTLEFF, physician, author; b. Hanson, Mass., Sept. 7, 1852; s. Isaac and Abby (Shurtleff) T.; ed. Phillips Acad., Andover Mass.; M.D., Harvard, 1874; Cornell U.; M.A., Shurtleff Coll., 1876; Boston U., Ill. Wesleyan U., Mass. Inst., Tech.; V.S., Montreal Veterinary Coll., 1879; B.Sc., Syracuse U., 1885, M.Sc., 1886; D.V.Sc., McGill U., 1890; (LL.D., Shurtleff, 1892; diploma, Dec. 1, 1907, as one of Authors' League of Am. Health League of the A.A.A.S.); m. Caroline Moore Smith, July 9, 1879. Has devoted much time to zoölogy, comparative medicine, preventive medicine and univ. edn., administration, and degrees; town phys., sch. phys., insp. of animals, phys. to Gordon Rest, and to Maquan Sanatorium. One of editors of Standard Dictionary of the English Language. Author: A Dictionary of University Degrees; also of the work on univ. degrees and education in the Standard Dictionary. Mason. Home: South Hanson, Mass. Died Nov. 26, 1922.

THOMAS, FRANKLIN, civil engr.; b. Red Oak, Ia., May 19, 1885; s. Rev. Thomas D. and Eleanor (Jones) T.; B.E., University of Iowa, 1908, C.E., 1913; studied McGill University, Montreal, Can., 1908-09; Doctor of Engring., U. of Southern Calif., 1949; m. Marie Elizabeth Planck, Sept. 20, 1910; children—William Planck, Richard Erik, Edward Albert (dec.), John Robert (dec.), Eleanor May (Mrs. Lee R. Champion), Margaret (dec.), Katherine (Mrs. Donald G. Langille). Chainman C.B.&O. Ry., 1903-04; with the Mines Power Co., Cobalt, Ontario, Canada, 1909-10; instructor dept. of engring. U. of Mich., 1910-12; with Ala. Power Co., made designs for developments at Lock 18, Coosa River and Muscle Shoals, Tenn. River, 1912-13; prof. civ. engring., Calif. Inst. of Tech. since 1913, also chmn. administrative com. of faculty, 1917, and 1920-21 during absence of president and following his resignation, chairman division engring. 1926-44, Dean of students since 1944. Assistant Engineer U.S. Reclamation Service, while on leave, 1919. Has served as consultant on municipal projects. Commd. 1st lt. Engr. R.C., U.S. Army, 1918. Member and vice chmn. Bd. Dirs. City of Pasadena, 1921-27; pres. Chamber Commerce, Pasadena, 1927; pres. Pasadena Community Chest, 1928; pres. Pasadena Civic Orchestra Assn., 1929-31; mem. bd. Metropolitan Water Dist. of Southern Calif. since 1928, vice chmn. 1929-48; chmn. Colo. River Bd. of Calif. since 1948. Awarded gold medal (Arthur Noble award) for 1939 by City of Pasadena for notable service in promoting welfare of the city. Mem. Am. Soc. C.E. (v.p. 1944-45; pres. 1949; pres. Los Angeles sect. 1924). Am. Soc. for Engring. Edn., American Water Works Association, Sigma Tau, Sigma Xi, Tau Beta Pi. Republican. Conglist. Clubs: Twilight, New Century (Pasadena), Kiwanis. Home: 685 S. El Molino Av., Pasadena 5, Cal. Died Aug. 27, 1953.

THOMAS, GERALD BURISON, aircraft co. exec.; b. Greensboro, Ala., May 29, 1927; s. Parker B. and Cora L. (Talbott) T.; B.S. in Aero. Engring., Miss. State U., 1948; M.S. in Aero. Engring., Ga. Inst. Tech., 1949; m. Dorothy Ann Top, Jan. 7, 1951; children—Bryan T., Sherry, Todd. With Douglas Aircraft Co., 1949-72, supr. advanced design performance, 1959-60, rep. in N.Y.C., 1960-64, dir. sales devel., 1964, v.p. domestic comml. sales, 1964-71, v.p. comml. sales 1971-72. Served with USNR, 1945-46. Mem. Am. Inst. Aero. and Astronautics, Soc. Automotive Engrs., Newcomen Soc. N.Am. Clubs: Cloud, Wings (N.Y.C.); Long Beach Yacht. Home: Long Beach CA Died Aug. 26, 1972; buried Sunnyside Meml. Park, Long Beach CA

THOMAS, HENRY M., neurologist; b. Baltimore, Md., May 25, 1861; s. Dr. James Carey and Mary (Whitall) T.; brother of M. Carey T.; Haverford Coll., 1878-79; Johns Hopkins, 1879-82; M.D., U. of Md., 1885; studied abroad, 1886; (hon. A.M., Johns Hopkins, 1902); m. Josephine Gibson Carey, Oct. 10, 1889. Clin. prof. neurology, Johns Hopkins, 1896—; neurologist Johns Hopkins Hosp. and Dispensary, 1896—. Home: Baltimore, Md. Died June 21, 1925.

THOMAS, HENRY M., JR., physician; b. Balt., Dec. 30, 1891; s. Henry M. and Josephine Gibson (Carey) T.; B.S., Haverford Coll., 1912; M.D., Johns Hopkins, 1916; m. Caroline Cunningham Bedell, June 23, 1934; children—Henry M., Eleanor Carey, Mary Whitall. House officer Mass. Gen. Hosp., 1916-17; resident physician Boston City Hosp., 1919-20; asst. resident Johns Hopkins Hosp., 1920, resident physician 1921, vis. physician, 1925—; instr. Johns Hopkins Med. Sch., 1921-32, asso. in medicine, 1932-39, asso. prof. medicine, 1939—; pvt. practice, internal medicine, Balt., 1922—. Served as 1st lt. Med. Res. Corps, 1917-18; col., med. cons., U.S. Army, Southwest P.T.O., 1943-45. Decorated Legion of Merit. Bd. mgrs., Haverford Coll.; trustee Calvert Sch., 1946-49; Bd. mental hygiene State of Md., 1932-36. Diplomate Am. Bd. Internal Medicine (sec. 1951, vice chmn. 1953). Fellow A.C.P. (master, v.p.); mem. Assn. Am. Physicians (sec. 1947-52), Soc. U.S. Med. Consultants in World War II (pres.), A.M.A., Am. Clin. and Climatol. Assn. (pres. 1955), Johns Hopkins Med. and Surg. Assn. (pres. 1963-64), Phi Beta Kappa. Democrat. Mem. Soc. Friends. Contbr. to med. jours. on various forms of infectious diseases, metabolic and endocrine diseases and schistosomiasis japonica. Home: 314 Overhill Rd., Balt. 21210. Office: 1201 N. Calvert St., Balt. 21202. Died June 28, 1966; buried Loudon Park Cemetery, Balt.

THOMAS, HORACE DAVIS, educator, geologist; b. Laramie, Wyo., Mar. 25, 1905; s. William C. and Dulcie (Davis) T.; A.B., U. Wyo., 1926, M.A., 1928; Ph.D., Columbia, 1935; m. Maxine Nelson, Aug. 29, 1942; one son, Tom Nelson (adopted). Graduate assistant University Wyoming, 1926-27, instr. field geology summer camp, 1929-30, instr. geology, 1931-34, asst. prof., 1934-38, asso. prof., 1938-44, prof. since 1944; grad. asst. Columbia, 1929-30, research asst., 1930-31; geologist Geol. Survey Wyo., 1933-41, state geol., dir., since 1941; com. stratigraphy Nat. Research Council since 1935; cons. geologist Union Oil Co. Cal., 1936-37, 39-41, U.P. R.R., summer 1938; collaborator seismology U.S. Coast and Geodetic Survey since 1941; mem. Wyo. Oil and Gas Conservation Commn., 1951—, American Commn. on Stratigraphic Nomenclature, 1954-56. Mem. pub. relations com. Am. Geol. Inst., 1950; subcom. on development mineral resources Columbia Basin Interagy. Com., 1950-58. Named distinguished lectr. Am. Assn. Petroleum Geologists, 1949; recipient Matson award Am. Assn. Petroleum Geologists, 1962. Fellow Geol. Soc. Am. (asso. editor), Paleontological Soc.; mem. Assn. Am. State Geologists, Am. Assn. Petroleum Geologists (v.p. 1954-55), Wyo. Geol. Assn. (hon.), Rocky Mtn. Assn. Geologists, Phi Beta Kappa, Sigma Xi. Contbr. tech. articles profl. publs. Office: U. Wyo., Larmie, Wyo. Died May 14, 1967; buried Greenhill Cemetery, Laramie.

THOMAS, ISAAC, congressman, lawyer; b. Sevierville, Tenn., Nov. 4, 1784; studied law. Admitted to bar, 1808, began practice law in Winchester, Tenn.; mem. U.S. Ho. of Reps. (Democrat) from Tenn., 14th Congress, 1815-17; moved to Alexandria, La., 1819, practiced law, became one of the largest landowners and slaveholders in La.; 1st man to introduce cultivation sugar cane Central La.; also mcht., operator sawmills, steamboats; served as brig. gen. La. Militia; mem. La. Senate, 1823-27; moved to Cal., 1849, returned to Alexandria. Died Alexandria, Feb. 2, 1859; buried Flint lot, Rapides Cemetery, Pineville, La.

THOMAS, JAMES, M.D.; b. March 3, 1843; ed. common schools, Covington, Ky., 1853-59; Miami Univ., 1859-63; grad. Univ. of Pa., 1866, Med. Coll. of Ohio, 1867 (A.M., LL.D., Miami Univ.); m. Aug., 1890, to Virginia Joy. Prof. theory and practice of medicine, med. dept., Cincinnati Univ.; frequent contributor to medical journals and magazines. Author: Lectures on Physiology; Theory and Practice of Medicine (text-book); volume on Heart Disease in "Twentieth Century Practice;" Exiled for Lèse Majesté; etc. Editor The Clinic, 1871-78. Address: Cincinnati.

THOMAS, JOHN JACOBS, pomologist, writer; b. Ledyard, N.Y., Jan. 8, 1810; s. David and Hannah (Jacobs) T. Owned nurseries successively at Palmyra, Macedon and Union Springs, N.Y.; became asst. editor Genesee Farmer, 1838; an editor New Genesee Farmer and Gardener's Jour., 1840-41; asso. editor Country Gentleman, 1853-94; organized Am. Pomol. Congress, 1855; classified fruits according to various characteristics; wrote The American Fruit Culturist (became textbook in horticulture), 1849, Farm Implements and Machinery, 1854; editor 9 volumes entitled Rural Affairs, 1869-81. Died Feb. 22, 1895.

THOMAS, JOHN JENKS, neurologist; b. Columbus, O., Sept. 6, 1861; s. Alfred and Martha A. (Hoge) T.; A.B., Williams, 1886; M.D. and A.M., Harvard, 1890; studied univs. of Heidelberg, Berlin and Vienna; m. Frances Pickering, d. Rear Admiral John G. Walker, Oct. 21, 1899; children—John G. W., Henry Pickering, Alfred Rebecca Pickering. Dist. phys. and phys. to Boston Dispensary, 1892-97; asst. phys. for nervous system, Boston City Hosp., 1893-1906, phys. same, 1906-25, and consulting physician to same from 1925; asst. neurologist, Children's Hosp., 1893-1913, neurologist, 1913-19, and consulting neurologist to same, 1919—; pathologist, Boston Insane Hosp., 1898-1903; instr. in neurology, 1902-06, asst. prof., 1906-12, prof., 1912-16, prof. emeritus, 1916—, Tufts Coll. Med. Sch.; asso. in neurology, Harvard Grad. Sch. of Medicine; consulting neurologist to Quincy City, Infants' hosps. Served with Harvard Unit at English Base Hosp., 1915, as lt. col. comdg. med. div.; maj. Med. Corps, A.E.F., 1918-19; with Base Hosp. 7, and as consultant in neuro-psychiatry. Joint author: Modern Treatment of Nervous and Mental Diseases; Cerebral Paralyses of Children, in Nelson's Loose Leaf Medicine; "Malingering," in Peterson, Haynes and Webster's Legal Medicine and Psychology. Home: Boston, Mass. Died July 17, 1935.

THOMAS, KIRBY, mining engineer; b. Wisconsin; ed. U. of Wisconsin; married. Iron and copper explorations, Lake Superior region and Can., prior to 1906; examination and valuation mining properties in western states, 1906-09; in Mexico, 1909-10; asso. editor Engineering and Mining Journal, New York, 1910-11. Extensive work in Brazil and Mexico, 1915-17; consulting practice. Home: New York, N.Y. Died June 22, 1931.

THOMAS, PERCY H(OLBROOK), elec. engr.; b. Boston, Mar. 31, 1872; s. James Francis and Lurinda Brown (Holbrook) T.; B.S. in Elec. Engring., Mass. Inst. Tech., 1893; m. Isabelle Mary Patten, 1900. With engring. dept., Westinghouse Electric & Mfg. Co., Pitts., 1893-1902; chief engr. Cooper-Hewitt Electric Co., 1903-07, and consulting engr., 1907-16; consulting elec. engr. Guggenheim Bros., 1916-23; practicing on own account, 1928-34; chief of power requirements div. of Nat. Power Survey of Fed. Power Commn., 1934-37; regional dir. Atlantic office Fed. Power Commn., 1937-41; with Office of Chief Engr., Washington, D.C., 1941-49, ret. Patentee. Fellow American Inst. E.E.; mem. Am. Soc. M.E., Delta Upsilon. Unitarian. Home: 3051 Idaho Av. Office: Federal Power Commn., Washington, D.C. Died Mar. 1957.

THOMAS, SAMUEL MORGAN, electrical engr.; b. Searcy, Ark., Dec. 12, 1903; s. George Crawford and Annie (Tapscott) T.; B.S., Ga. Sch. Tech., 1926; m. Bebe Wharton, June 21, 1930; 1 son, Samuel Morgan. Employed by Allis Chalmers Mfg. Co., Milw., 1926-31; elec. engr. Corps Engrs., U.S. Army, 1931-40; commd. capt. Signal Corps, Army U.S., 1940 and advanced through grades to brig. gen.; signal dir., Persian Gulf Comd., Teheran, Iran, U.S. Army, 1942-45, chief of staff, 1945; dir. communications and postal service, U.S. Control Group Council, Berlin, Germany, 1945; brig. gen., Signal Corps. Res., 1947; asst. chief engr., RCA Communications, Inc., 1947; v.p., 1947-51; spl. asst. to sec. of army, 1952; v.p. Hazeltine Electronics Corp. 1954-62, sr. v.p. Hazeltine Dir. Internat. div., 1962-73. Decorated Legion of Merit with oak leaf cluster, Bronze Star, Order of Kutuzov (Russia); Order British Empire. Mem. Phi Kappa Phi, Tau Beta Pi, Alpha Tau Omega. Clubs: Greenwich Country; Army and Navy (Washington). Home: Greenwich CT Died Jan. 4, 1973; buried Arlington Nat. Cemetery, Washington DC

THOMAS, SETH, pioneer clock mfr.; b. Wolcott, Conn., Aug. 19, 1785; s. James and Martha (Barnes) T.; m. Philena Tuttler, Apr. 20, 1808; m. 2d, Laura Andrews, Apr. 14, 1811; 6 children, including Seth. Manufactured clocks in partnerships with Eli Terry and Silas Hoadley, 1807-12; purchased mfg. rights to Terry's clock, 1814, built highly successful business, incorporated as Seth Thomas Clock Co., 1853; the factory portion of Plymouth (Conn.) became new town called Thomaston in his honor. Died Plymouth, Jan. 29, 1859.

THOMAS, STANLEY JUDSON, bacteriologist; b. Scranton, Pa., Feb. 10, 1889; s. Daniel Judson and Adelaide (Keller) T.; B.S., Lafayette Coll., Easton, Pa., 1912; M.S., Lehigh, 1913, M.A., 1916; Ph.D., U. of Pa., 1928; m. Katharine March, Apr. 7, 1914. Asst. in biology, Lehigh, 1912-13, instr. in biology, 1913-16; research bacteriologist, H. K. Mulford Co., 1916-18, asso. dir. Mulford Labs., 1918-23; asso. prof. bacteriology, Lehigh, 1923-29, prof. since 1929, head dept. of biology since 1937. Major Sanitary R.C., U.S. Army, discharged. Chmn. Bethlehem Civilian Defense Council. Fellow A.A.A.S.; mem. Soc. Am. Bacteriologists, Am. Social Hygiene Assn., American Public Health Association, American Legion, Sigma Xi, Alpha Chi Rho, Alpha Epsilon Delta. Republican. Clubs: Rotary, Bethlehem, Saucon Valley Country. Author: Bacteriology, 1925; Laboratory Manual in Bacteriology, 1930. Co-author (with R. C. Bull): Notes on Personal Hygiene, 1925; Freshman Hygiene, 1926; Social Hygiene, 1938; Bacteria (with T. H. Grainger) 1952 Contbr. to bacteriol. publs. Home: 30 W. Market St., Bethlehem, Pa. 18018. Died Oct. 15, 1960.

THOMPSON, ALBERT F(AYETTE), mech. engr.; b. Clarence, Mo., June 19, 1888; s. Miles and Helen Marr (Wallace) T.; Navy tng. course Stevens Inst. Tech., 1919; m. Lillian Elizabeth Holzbaur, May 1, 1915. Chief engr. Armour & Co., S. St. Paul plant, 1919-21, Independence (Mo.) power plant, 1922-24, Montgomery Ward power plant, Kansas City, 1924-42;

mech. engr. Neb. Def. Corp., hdqrs., Fremont, 1942-43; nat. sec., Nat. Assn. Power Engrs., Inc., Chgo., 1943, nat. pres., 1932-33, dir., 1936-43, nat. sec., 1943-49, sec.-treas., 1949-54; chief engr., bldg. supt. Chatham County Meml. Hosp., 1954-65. Commd. ensign, U.S. N.A.R.F., 1919, active duty, 1919-23, inactive list, 1923-31. Mason (Scottish Rite, Shriner). Home: 6 Col. Estill Dr., Savannah, Ga. 31406. Died Dec. 19, 1965; buried Mt. Moriah, Kansas City, Mo.

THOMPSON, ALMON HARRIS, geographer; b. Stoddard, N.H., Sept. 24, 1839; s. Lucas and Mary (Sawyer) T.; ed. Southboro, Mass., 1848-56, and Wheaton, Ill., Coll., 1857-61 (scientific course); m. Ellen L. Powell, July 8, 1862. Soldier Civil war, 1st lt. 139th Ill. vol. inf.; supt. schools, Lacon, Ill., 1865-67, Bloomington, Ill., 1867-68; acting curator Ill. Natural History Soc., 1869-70; topographic engr., 1870—. Engaged in exploration Colo. River of the West, in charge of geog. work, with Maj. J. W. Powell, 1870-78; geographer U.S. Geol. Survey, 1882—; in charge geog. work of U.S. Geol. Survey, west of Mississippi River, 1884-95; field and office work, U.S. Geol. Survey, 1896-1903; in charge exhibits U.S. Geol. Survey, La. Purchase Expn., 1904. Address: Washington, D.C. Died 1906.

THOMPSON, BENJAMIN (COUNT RUMFORD), physicist; b. Woburn, Mass., Mar. 26, 1753; s. Benjamin and Ruth (Simonds) T.; attended grammar sch., apprenticed as storekeeper and importer, Salem, Mass., 1770; attended lectures Harvard; m. Sarah Walker Rolfe, Nov. 1772; 1 dau., Sarah; m. 2d, Marie Anne Pierrette Paulze Lavoisier, Oct. 24, 1805 (separated 1809). Taught sch., Rumford (now Concord), N.H., 1771; decided on mil. career, became commd. maj. 2d Provincial Regt., N.H., 1773; went to Eng. as loyalist refugee, 1776; apptd. sec. Province of Ga., 1776; under-sec. of state Am. Dept., 1780-81; apptd. lt. col. Brit. Army for Sevice in Am., Charleston, S.C., 1781; commdr. Queen's Rangers, Brit. Legion, King's Dragoons, Long Island, N.Y., 1782; returned to Eng., 1783; apptd. col. by King George III; col. and aide-de-camp to Charles Theodore of Salzbach, Elector of Bavaria and Palatine and performed services as initiating army reforms, philanthropic work for poor, 1784-98; maj. gen., head War Dept. Bavaria, from 1788; supr. constrn. of Eng. garden, Munich, Germany, 1789; introduced steam engine into Palatinate at Mannheim, 1791; prevented (at request of regency) French and Austrian armies from entering neutral city of Munich, 1796; apptd. head police dept., Bavaria, 1796; retuned to London, 1798, retired from Bavarian Service, 1798; made proposals, 1799, which resulted in incorporation of Royal Instn., London, 1800; planned orgn. of Bavarian Acad. Arts and Scis., Munich, 1801; travelled to Paris, 1801. Fellow Royal Soc., 1779 (Copley medal, 1792, first Rumford medal, 1802); mem. French Acad. Scis., 1802, Munich, Berlin, Mannheim acads. Best known for his cannon expts. showing heat to be a mode of motion, thereby disproving prevalent notion of heat as fluid material substance (caloric); tried to calculate mech. equivalent of heat; performed expts. to show there is no change of weight accompanying heating or cooling of bodies (thus fluid caloric, if it existed, must be weightless); conducted expts. to determine the most advantageous constrn. of firearms, also explosive force of gunpowder, and velocities of bullets; pioneer in establishing workshop and soup kitchen as efficient and humane means of helping poor; investigated warmth provided by natural and artificial clothing; discovered remedy for smoky chimneys; improved constrn. of fireplaces, chimneys, and cooking appliances; pioneer of central steam and hot water heating, and efficient prodn. of heat and its controlled conveyance for heating of large halls and rooms; made expts. to determine thermal conductivity of liquids; invented shadow photometer, water compensation calorimeter, and passage thermometer; improved Argand lamp; endowed Rumford professorship, Harvard, also Rumford medal of Royal Soc. and Am. Acad. Arts and Scis., 1796. Died Auteuil, nr. Paris, France, Aug. 21, 1814.

THOMPSON, CHARLES OLIVER, engr., educator; b. East Windsor Hill, Conn., Sept. 25, 1836; s. Rev. William and Eliza (Butler) T.; B.A., Dartmouth, 1858, Ph.D. (hon.), 1870; m. Maria Goodrich, May 14, 1862, 3 children. Prin., Peacham Acad., circa 1858-64, Cotting High Sch., Arlington, Mass., 1864-68, Worcester County Free Inst. of Indsl. Science (later Worcester Poly. Inst.), 1868; made European trip, 1868, resulted in innovations in Am. tech. edn. such as mech. arts course equipped with workshop; one of 1st to introduce shop practice in engring. teaching; organizer, 1st pres. Rose Poly. Inst., Terre Haute, Ind., 1883-85; mem. A.A.A.S. Author: Hints Toward a Profession of Teaching, 1867; Manual Training in the Public School. Died Terre Haute, Mar. 17, 1885.

THOMPSON, C(LARENCE) BERTRAND, biochemist; b. Denver, Colorado, April 12, 1882; son of James Beauregard and Medora Gertrude (Reed) Thompson; LL.B., U. of So. Cal., 1900; A.B., Harvard, 1908, A.M., 1909; postgrad. U. Cal. at Berkeley, 1940-44; m. Maravene Kennedy, 1906 (divorced 1922); m. 2d, Lisbet Heimann, 1926. Mem. faculty, Grad. School of Business Administration, Harvard, 1911-16, also serving apprenticeship Taylor System of Business Management, 1912-15; counsel for Am., French, German and Italian concerns; research associate Instituto de Fisiologia, Facultad de Medicina. Montevideo. Decorated Legion d' Honneur (France). Member Am. Chemical Society, Sociedad de Biologia de Uruguay. Clubs: Rosburghe (San Francisco); Typophiles (New York City). Am. Association (Montevideo). Author: The Churches and the Wage Earners, 1909; How to Find Factory Costs, 1915; Theory and Practice of Scientific Management, 1917; Le Systeme Taylor (also in Polish) 1919; Methodes Americaines de Prix de Revient, 1920; (with others) La Reorganisation des Usines (2 vols.), 1926; articles in economic, engring. and chem. periodicals. Compiler and part author of Scientific Management, 1914, and editor of several vols. of translations of Am. business classics into French. Research on cancer. Home: Montevideo Uruguay Died Jan. 9, 1969; buried British Cemetery, Montevideo, Uruguay

THOMPSON, DAVID, explorer, geographer, fur trader; b. London, Eng., Apr. 30, 1770; s. David and Ann (Thompson) T.; attended Oxford (Eng.) U.; m. Charlotte Small, June 1799, 13 children. Came to Am., circa 1784; apprenticed to Hudson's Bay Co.; with Hudson's Bay Co. and N.W. Co. making records of all travels for 25 years, served in Western Can., 1789-1812; discovered new route to Lake Athabasca; discovered Turtle Lake, claimed source of Mississippi River, Apr. 27, 1798; marked crossing 49, by Red River; surveyed No. source of Mississippi River and course of St. Louis River to Lake Superior, 1798; discovered Columbia River, 1807, surveyed Columbia River from source to mouth, 1811; in charge Brit. Commn. to mark boundary of U.S. and Can. from St. Lawrence River West to Lake of the Woods, 1816-26. David Thompson's Narrative of his Explorations in Western America published in vol. XII of Champlain Soc. Publications, 1916. Died Longueil, Montreal, Que., Can., Feb. 10, 1857; buried Mt. Royal Cemetery, Montreal.

THOMPSON, FRED LAWRENCE, civil engr.; b. nr. Grendview, Edgar County, Ill., Feb. 1, 1872; s. Edward Taylor and Mima J. (McDonald) T.; B.S. in C.E., U. of Ill., 1896; m. Maude Nellie Martin, Nov. 21, 1900; children—Donna, Ruth. Entered engring. corps. I.C. R.R. as chainman, 1896; rodman, 1896-99, asst. engr., 1899-1903, roadmaster, 1903-07, asst. engr. of bridges, 1907-10, engr. of bridges and buildings, 1910-13, was engineer of construction, 1913-14, asst. chief engr., 1914-18, chief engr., 1918-25, v.p. since Feb. 1, 1925, all with I.C. R.R. Mem. Western Soc. Engrs., Am. Ry. Engring. Assn. Republican. Methodist. Clubs: Engineers, South Shore Country. Home: 6906 Constance Av. Office: Central Station, Chicago IL*

THOMPSON, GILBERT, topographer U.S. Geological Survey; b. Blackstone, Mass., Mar. 21, 1839; s. William Venner and Harriet (Gilbert) T.; ed. common sch.; m. Mary Frances Reed McNeil, Sept. 28, 1869. Printer by trade; soldier, U.S. engr. battalion, Nov. 22, 1861, to Nov. 21, 1864; asst. engr. headquarters Army of Potomac, 1864-65 on Western explorations and surveys, etc., 1866—; comd. engr. battalion, D.C. militia, 1890-98; historian Veteran U.S. Engrs. Assn. Address: Washington, D.C. Died 1909.

THOMPSON, GUSTAVE WHYTE, chemist; b. Brooklyn, N.Y., July 27, 1865; s. John and Lucy (Whyte) T.; Dr. Sc., Armour Inst. of Technology, 1927; m. Alice C. Wilmarth, Apr. 1897. Chief chemist Nat. Lead Co., 1892-1938, dir., 1916-40; dir. of Titanium Pigment Company. Fellow A.A.A.S.; mem. Am. Chem. Soc., Soc. Chem. Industry, Am. Inst. Chem. Engrs. (ex-pres.), Am. Soc. for Testing Materials (v.p. 1926, pres. 1928), Internat. Assn. for Testing Materials. Clubs: Chemists. Home: 39 Plaza St., Brooklyn, N.Y. Died Apr. 22, 1942.

THOMPSON, HEBER SAMUEL, engr.; b. Pottsville, Pa., Aug. 14, 1840; s. Samuel and Elizabeth (Cunningham) T.; A.B., Yale, 1861, A.M., 1871; studied mining engring. in pvt. offices; m. Sarah E. Beck, Jan. 23, 1866. Enlisted pvt., Apr. 16, 1861, "First Defenders," 1st troops of war of secession to enter Washington (Apr. 18, 1861); later served, 1861-65; lt. and capt. 7th Pa. Cav.; engr. and agt. Girard Estate, Mar. 16, 1874—. Pres. bd. trustees State Hosp. for Injured, anthracite coal region, Pa., Ashland, Pa. ("Miners" Hosp."); apptd. under act of assembly, by gov. of Pa., on "Coal Waste Common."—pub. report, 1893. Address: Pottsville, Pa. Died 1911.

THOMPSON, HUGH LINDSAY, cons. engr.; b. Thistle, Md., Dec. 8, 1863; s. Robert Hughes and Margaret Helen (Bone) T.; student Knapp's Acad., Baltimore, 1877-80; m. Caroline Goss, Oct. 17, 1900; children—Caroline Goss, Helen Lindsay (widow of Rev. Arthur F. McKenny). Began as mech. draftsman's apprentice Robt. Poole & Son Co., 1880, draftsman, engr. and designer of engines, boilers, machinery, etc., 1880-93; asst. supt. Waterbury Farrel Foundry & Machine Co., 1893-96; cons. engr., Waterbury, since 1897; cons. and administrative engr., Scovil Mfg. Co., Waterbury, 1900-46; invented improvements in design and arrangement of rolling mills and in annealing furnaces; designed and installed various brass and copper rolling mills in New Eng. and the Middle West; director Citizens and Mfrs. National Bank, Waterbury. Member executive committee Waterbury Com. on Additional Water Supply. Mem. Mattatuck Hist. Soc. Council, Am. Soc. M.E. Republican. Conglist. Clubs: Waterbury, Country (Waterbury). Home: 129 Pine St., Waterbury, Conn. Died Feb. 14, 1949.

THOMPSON, JAMES STRATTON, educator; b. Bedford, Ia., Nov. 13, 1899; s. Seth Edward and Adelaide (Stratton) T.; Sc.B., U. Chgo., 1922, Ph.D., 1930; studied U. Munich, Germany, summer 1930; m. Mildred Bergren, June 26, 1926; 1 son, James Stratton. Began asst. in physics, Armour Inst. Tech. (now Ill. Inst. Tech.), Chgo., 1924, successively instr., asst. prof., asso. prof., prof. physics, 1934—, also chmn. dept. physics; physicist Simpson-Breed Radium Inst., 1927—. Served as 2d lt. Heavy Arty., O.R.C., 1919-24. Fellow A.A.A.S. Mem. Am. Phys. Soc., Am. Assn. Physics Tchrs., Chgo. Physics Club (pres. 1943), Am. Soc. Engring. Edn., Swedish Engrs. Soc., Am. Assn. U. Profs., Sigma Alpha Epsilon, Sigma Xi. Presbyn. Contbr. tech. articles. Home: 5540 Kenwood Av. Office: 3300 Federal St., Chgo. Died Aug. 5, 1951.

THOMPSON, JOHN FAIRFIELD, industrialist; born at Portland, Me., Mar. 8, 1881; s. Frank E. and Mary J. (Clarke) T.; B.S., Sch. of Mines, Columbia, 1903, Ph.D., 1906; D.Sc. (honorary), Columbia University, 1950; LL.D., Queen's U., 1954, Bowdoin Coll., 1959; married Elizabeth Fisher Wheeler, October 10, 1911; children—John Fairfield, Barbara Warren (Mrs. Ralph R. Birdsall). Assistant in metallurgy, School of Mines, Columbia, 1903-06; associated with The International Nickel Company in a number of technical and executive positions from 1906, exec. v.p. and dir., 1935-49, pres., dir., 1949-52, chmn. bd., dir. since 1951. Exec. v.p. and dir., Internat. Nickel Co. of Can., Ltd., 1936-49, pres., dir., 1949-52, chmn. bd., dir., from 1951; mem. bd. dirs. Whitehead Metal Products Co., Inc., Texas Gulf Sulphur Company, Am. Bank Note Co., Am. Metal Climax, Inc., Bank of N.Y. Trustee Packer Collegiate Institute, Nat. Safety Council. Recipient Instn. Mining and Metallurgy Gold medal, London, 1957. Honorable mem. Inst. of Metals (Eng.). Mem. American Society for Metals, Am. Inst. Mining, Metall., and Petroleum Engrs. (Rand Meml. medal 1958), Mining and Metall. Soc. American (past pres.). Am. Soc. Testing Materials. Unitarian. Clubs; City Midday, Columbia University (New York), University, Down Town Assn., (New York); New Canaan (Conn.) Country. Thomas Egleston Medal from Columbia Engring Schs. Alumni Assn., 1944; Comdr. Order White Rose (Finland). Home: New Canaan CT Died July 1968.

THOMPSON, JOHN TALIAFERRO, army officer, mech. engr., inventor; b. Newport, Ky., Dec. 31, 1860; s. Lt. Col. James and Julia Maria (Taliaferro) T.; student Ind. U., 1876-77; grad. U.S. Mil. Acad., 1882; torpedo course, U.S. Engrs.' Sch., 1884; grad. U.S. Arty. Sch., 1890; LL.D., Ind. U., 1922; m. Juliet Estelle, d. Judge M. B. and Almira Lewis Hagans, July 27, 1882; 1 son, Lt. Col. Marcellus Hagans. Commd. 2d lt. arty., June 13, 1882; promoted through grades to col., Oct. 30, 1913; retired, Nov. 2, 1914; brig. gen. ordnance, O.R.C., Army of U.S., 1924. Served various garrisons, Naval Gun Factory, Nat. Armory, etc.; lt. col. U.S. Vols., Tampa, Fla., 1898, and in Cuba; connected with development of service small arms; charged by War Dept. with preparation of war plans of Ordnance Dept., 1908-14, lecturer Army War Coll, 1908-14—; cons. engr., New York, 1914-17; in charge design and mfr. of all small arms and cartridge for U.S., Apr. 16, 1917-18. Brig. gen. (temp.), Aug. 1918; advisory engr. to chief of ordnance; dir. of ordnance training; dir. of arsenals. Awarded D.S.M., 1919, "For exceptionally meritorious and conspicuous service," as chief of small arms div.; later pres. John T. Thompson Corp., New York. Episcopalian. Writer of various tech. pamphlets and articles. Inventor of firearms, machinery and airplane devices. Home: Great Neck, L.I., N.Y. Died June 21, 1940.

THOMPSON, JOSEPH OSGOOD, physicist; b. Weymouth, Mass., July 29, 1863; s. Samuel and Mary Ann (Eaton) T.; student Thayer Acad., S. Braintree, Mass., 1878-79; B.A., Amherst Coll., 1884; Ph.D., U. of Strassburg, Germany, 1891; courtesy fellow, Yale, 1920; m. Lulu Lester Burbank, May 22, 1912; children—Rebecca Burbank, Samuel Mountfort. Teacher of science, Park Coll., Parkville, Mo., 1884-86; asst. in physics, Amherst Coll., 1886-87, instr. in mathematics, 1887-89; instr. in physics, Haverford (Pa.) Coll., 1891-94; asso. prof. physics, Amherst Coll., 1894-1918, prof., 1918-28, emeritus prof., 1928—. Fellow A.A.A.S., Am. Physical Soc.; mem. Phi Beta Kappa. Republican. Conglist. Club: Faculty. Established law of elastic lengthening in metals. Home: 209 Lincoln Av., Amherst, Mass. Died Dec. 12, 1953.

THOMPSON, MILTON JOHN, aeronautical engr.; b. Grand Rapids, Mich., July 28, 1904; s. Schuyler D and Jennie L. (Albertson) T.; B.S., U. of Mich., 1925, M.S., 1926; Sc.D., Warsaw Polytech. Inst. (Guggenheim fellow in aerodynamics, 1928-30) 1930; m. Helen B. Frank, Aug. 22, 1931; children—Richard D., Barbara J. Instr. engring. math., U. of Mich., 1926-28, asst. prof., aero. engring., 1930-37, asso. prof., 1937-41; prof. aeronautics dept. mech. engring. U. Tex., 1941-42, prof. dept. aero. engring., 1942-71, chmn., 1942-66; asso. dir. Def. Research Lab., from 1945; cons.

aero engr., 1930-71; v.p. Haneman Assos., Inc., consultants, 1961-71. Recipient grants NSF, Ford. Found. and NATO for research at U. Gottingen, Imperial Coll. and Cambridge U., Liverpool U., 1967-68. Registered professional engineer, Texas. Fellow Am. Society M.E. (aviation sect., gen. com.); member American Institute of Aeronautics and Astronautics, A.A.A.S., Am. Astronautical Society, American Society of Engring. Edn., Phi Kappa Phi, Sigma Gamma Tau, Sigma Xi, Tau Beta Pi, Pi Tau Sigma. Mem. aerodynamics panel, Navy Bur. Ordnance Bumblebee Guided Missile project, 1945-65; mem. panel target drones Guided Missile Com. Research and Development Bd., 1950-52; mem. panel on boundary layers Navy Bur. Ordnance Com. on Aero-ballistics, 1949-52, chmn. panel on drag., 1953-55. Club: Exchange. Author: The Theory of Single Burbling (with C. Witoszynski), Vol. III, division F. of Aerodynamic Theory, ed. by W.F. Durand, 1943; Fluid Mechanics (with R.A. Dodge), 1935. Contbr. articles on aerodynamics and aero. engring; classified reports on aero. research for aircraft industry and mil. aero. agys. Home: Austin TX Died July 23, 1971; buried Austin Meml. Cemetery, Austin TX

THOMPSON, RALPH LEROY, pathologist; b. Lisbon, Me., Nov. 15, 1873; s. Haley P. and Mehitable (Smith) T.; A.B., Bates Coll., Lewiston, Me., 1896, A.M., 1901; M.D., Harvard, 1900; grad. student, U. of Berlin; fellow Rockefeller Inst., 1902-03; m. Elizabeth Scammell Schuyler, May 28, 1918. Pathol. house officer and 2d and 1st asst. in pathology, Boston City Hosp., 1901-05; asst. prof. pathology, St. Louis U., 1905-07, prof. since 1907, now prof. emeritus; dir. Nat. Pathol. Lab., St. Louis, also hosp. commr., 1933-41, 1st lt. U.S. Army Med. R. C., 1910-15; pathologist, 23d Gen. Hosp., B.E.F., Etaples, France, summer 1915. Editor Mo. State Med. Jour., 1942-47, editor emeritus, 1947. Mem. Am. Assn. Pathologists and Bacteriologists, Am. Assn. Cancer Research, A.M.A. Clubs: University, Artists Guild. Author: Glimpses of Medical Europe, 1908; Surgery and Pathology of the Thyroid and Parathyroid Glands (with Albert J. Ochsner), 1910; also papers and articles in med. jours., chiefly on immunity, infectious diseases and parathyroid glandules. Home: 4406 McPherson Av. 8. Office: 607 N. Grand, St Louis 3 MO

THOMPSON, RALPH SEYMOUR, engineer; b. Edwards Co., Ill., 1847; s. Samuel and Katherine (Ronalds) T.; reared on farm; ed. at home; m. Margaret I. Weed, of Wayne Co., Ill., Oct. 15, 1872. At 18 established village drug store; started a newspaper; sold out and went to Cincinnati, 1873; moved to Springfield, O., 1876, to Columbus, O., 1909; gen. mgr. Ideal Heating Co. Became lecturer State Grange of Ohio; prominent in temperance work; started The New Era as Prohibition paper, 1884; state chmn. Prohibition party, Ohio, 1885; has been Prohibition candidate for U.S. senator and Congress; later candidate for Congress on Nat. ticket; originated "broad gauge" movement in Prohibition party, which he left in 1896 on defeat of that movement; organizer of Union Reform party, 1898. Home: 111 Chittenden Av. Office: 165-167 W. Main St., Columbus, Ohio.

THOMPSON, ROBERT ANDREW, cons. engr.; b. New Waverly, Walker County, Tex., July 11, 1869; s. Andrew Jackson and Mary (Gillespie) T.; B.S. in C.E., U. of Tex., 1892, M.A., 1893, C.E., 1900; m. Evelyne Dickson, Cleburne, Tex., Dec. 21, 1897; children—Frances, Robert, Elizabeth, Eleanor, Evelyne, Frederick, Lucy. Instr. civ. engring., U. of Tex., 1893-94 and 1897-98; chief engr. R.R. Commn. of Tex., 1898-1908; chief engr. Wichita Falls & Northwestern R.R., 1908-11; chief engr. R.R. Commn. of Calif., 1911-13; mem. engring. bd. (R.R. valuation) Interstate Commerce Commn., 1913-21; chief engr. and gen. mgr. Wichita County (Tex.) Water Im. Dist. No. 1, 1921-23; chief engr. (with J. C. Nagle) on constrn. Garza Dam for Dallas, Tex., 1923-27; mem. firm Thompson & Butler, cons. engrs., San Francisco, 1925-26; chief engr. Tex. Highway Dept., Austin, Tex., 1927-28; cons. highway engr. Dallas Chamber Commerce, 1928-33, 1934-38; cons. engr. Brown County (Tex.) Water Improvement Dist. Reservoir Dam, 1930-33; state engr. for Tex., Fed. Emergency Adminstrn. of Public Works, 1933-34. Democrat. Presbyn. Address: Ft. Worth, Tex. Died May 30, 1941.

THOMPSON, SAMUEL RANKIN, scientist, coll. dean; b. South Shenango, Pa., Apr. 17, 1833; s. William and Mary (Latta) T.; B.A., Westminster Coll., New Wilmington, Pa., 1863, M.A., 1881; m. Lucy Gilmour, 1859, 1 dau. Began teaching in Clarion County, Pa.; taught sch. in Neb., 1848-56 (except 1854-55); supt. Crawford County (Pa.) Schs., 1860-65; prof. natural scis., vice prin. State Normal Sch., Ellenboro, Pa., 1865-67; prin. Pottsville (Pa.) High Sch., 1868; organized state normal sch. at Marshall Coll., Huntington, W. Va., 1869-71; became prof. agr. U. Neb., 1871, 1st dean Coll. of Agr., 1872-75; prin. Neb State Normal Sch., Peru, 1876-77, prof. agr. and didactics, 1882-84; returned to Westminster Coll. as prof. physics, 1884-96. Died New Wilmington, Oct. 28, 1896.

THOMPSON, SANFORD ELEAZER, engineer; b. Ogdensburg, N.Y., Feb. 13, 1867; s. Eleazer and Harriet Newell (Sanford) T.; Adelphi Acad., Brooklyn, and Danbury (Conn.) and Medway (Mass.) high schs.; S.B. in Civ. Engring., Mass. Inst. Tech., 1889; m. Stella Antoinette Converse, 1900 (dec.); children—Katharine Converse (dec.), Marion Sanford (Mrs. Ward Beckwith), David Sanford Taylor (dec.), Dr. Dorothy Dewhurst; married 2d, Frances Lord Marsh, Mar. 1947. Engaged in civil and management engring. since 1889; now pres. The Thompson & Lichtner Co., Inc., engrs. in management, industrial research and constrn.; president The Thompson Co., Inc., of New York, Lt. col., Ordnance Dept., U.S. Army, chief of progress sect., Office Chief of Ordnance, 1917-19. Apptd. by Herbert Hoover, mem. com. on elimination of waste in industry of Federated Am. Engring. Soc., 1921; apptd. by President Harding, mem. econ. advisory bd. to the Unemployment Conf., 1921; chmn. bd. of arbitration Rochester (N.Y.) shoe industry, 1921; apptd. by Sec. Hoover to study methods of stabilizing production and distribution (pub. as chapter of "Business Cycles and Unemployment"), 1922; apptd. by U.S. Coal Commn. as engr. to investigate underground management in bituminous coal mines, 1923; apptd. by Boston Chamber of Commerce to make report on boot and shoe industry in New Eng., 1924, also report on metal trades industry of New Eng., 1925; supervised New Eng. Council surveys of shoes, knit goods and textiles, 1926; prepared outline for distribution survey for Twentieth Century Fund, Inc., 1930; mem. waste com. of Nat. Construction Conf., 1931; represented various U.S. technical societies at 38th Oxford Management Conf., England, 1938; expert consultant to sec. of war, 1941-42. Trustee Chaplain David Sanford Fund. Fellow Am. Inst. of Management, Am. Soc. M.E., life mem. Am. Soc. C.E., Soc. for the Advancement of Management, Am. Management Assn.; mem. American Soc. Testing Materials, Boston Soc. C.E., Taylor Soc. (ex-pres.); honorary member American Concrete Inst., Institut Naukowej Orfanizacji (Warsaw, Poland). Clubs: Brae Burn Country, Appalachian Mountain. Author: Treatise on Concrete, Plain and Reinforced (with Frederick W. Taylor), 1905; Concrete Costs (with same), 1912; Reinforced Concrete Bridges (with Frederick W. Taylor and Edward Smulski), 1939. Writer of papers on scientific management and constrn. for tech. socs. Home: Newton Highlands, Mass. Office: Park Square Bldg., Boston, Mass.; and 8 Alton Pl., Brookline, Mass. Died Feb. 1, 1949.

THOMPSON, THEOS JARDIN, scientist, nuclear engr.; b. Lincoln, Neb., Aug. 30, 1918; s. Theos Jefferson and Mabel E. (Dow) T.; A.B., U. Neb., 1941, M.A., 1942, Doctor of Science (honorary), 1964; Ph.D. in Nuclear Physics, University of Cal. at Berkeley, 1952; m. Dorothy Sibley, Feb. 14, 1947; children—Jeff, Edward, Robert, Elizabeth. Physicist U. Cal. Radiation Lab., 1948-52, lectr. physics, Berkeley, 1949-52; staff Los Alamos Sci. Lab., 1952-55, reactor design and constrn.; asso. prof. nuclear engring. Mass. Inst. Tech., 1955-58, prof., 1958—, dir. nuclear reactor for design, constrn. and operation; cons. Mem. AEC adv. com. reactor safeguards, 1959-66, chmn., 1960; co-editor AEC project Safety Information for Technology of Reactors, 1962-70; commr. AEC, 1969-70. Served from 2d lt. to maj., C.W.S., AUS, 1942-46. Recipient E.O. Lawrence Meml. award, Atomic Energy Commn., 1964; Guggenheim Found. fellow, 1963-64. Fellow American Nuclear Soc. (director); mem. Am. Academy of Arts and Sciences, American Phys. Soc., Phi Beta Kappa, Sigma Xi. Home: Winchester MA Died Nov. 25, 1970; buried Lincoln NB

THOMPSON, THOMAS GORDON, educator; b. Rosebank, N.Y., Nov. 28, 1888; s. John Haslam and Mary Elizabeth (Langdon) T.; grad. Bklyn. Comml. High Sch., 1906; B.A., Clark U., Worcester, Mass., 1914; M.S., U. Wash., 1915, Ph.D., 1918; m. Hariert Galbraith, June 27, 1922 (dec.); children—Thomas, John Souter, Harriet; m. 2d, Isabel Harris Costigan, July 14, 1954; children (adopted)—Charles Harris, Gary Howard. Lab asst. Am. Brass Co., 1906-11; asst. chemist Am. Steel & Wire Co., 1911; teaching fellow U. Wash., 1914-17, instr. chemistry, 1919, asst., asso., prof., 1919-51, dir. oceanographic labs., 1930-51, prof. oceanography, 1951—, mil. leave of absence, 1942-46. Pvt., Inf., 1st lt. Ordinance, capt. CWS, 1917-19; maj. CWS Res. 1924-42, active service as lt. col. 1942-45, col. 1945—; dir. War Dept. Civilian Protection Sch., Seattle, 1942-43; Chem. Warfare Bd., 1943-44; tech. dir. San Jose Project, Panama, 1944-45. Ret. col. AUS, 1946. Rep., Am. Geophys. Union to Internat. Geodetic and Geophys. Union, Stockholm, 1930, Lisbon, 1933, Edinburgh, 1936, Washington, 1939; chmn. internat. com. on Pacific Sci. Congress, 1936-53; chmn. com. on oceanography NRC, 1935-41; mem. oceanographic panel Research and Devel. Bd., 1947-51. Awarded Agassiz Gold medal, Nat. Acad. Scis., 1948; Carnegie Scholar Brit. Iron and Steel Inst., 1915; Rockfellow Found. travel grantee, 1930; 1st State of Wash. Distinguished Service Citation 1960. Fellow Cal. Acad. Scis.; mem. Nat. Acad. Scis., Am. Chem. Soc. (chmn. Puget Sound sect. 1922-25), A.A.A.S. (pres. Pacific Div., 1946-47), Am. Geophysics Union, Oceanographic Sec. (pres. 1935-38), Am. Geog. Soc., Alpha Delta Phi, Sigma Xi, Phi Lambda Upsilon. Club: Cosmos. Author: numerous sci. papers reporting results of original research. Home: 4002 Burke Av. N., Seattle, also McConnell Island, Deer Harbor, Wash. Died Aug. 10, 1961; buried McConnell Island.

THOMPSON, WILLARD OWEN, physician; b. Fredericton, N.B., Can., Feb. 17, 1899; s. Samuel Stirling and Mary (Owen) T.; B.A., Dalhousie U., Halifax, N.S., 1919; M.D., Harvard, 1923; m. Phebe K. Christianson, June 21, 1923; children—Willard Owen, Frederic Christianson, Nancy Kirsten, Donald McRae. Came to U.S. 1920, naturalized, 1937. Engaged in practice of medicine since 1925; interne Boston (Mass.) City Hosp., 1923-25; research fellow in medicine Harvard Med. Sch., 1925-28. Henry P. Walcott fellow, 1928-29; fellow Nat. Research Council, 1926-28; grad. asst. in medicine Mass. Gen. Hosp., 1925, research fellow in medicine, 1926-29, in charge metabolism lab., 1926-29; asst. in chemistry, Harvard, 1927; asst. clin. prof. medicine, Rush Med. Coll., U. of Chicago, 1929-35, asso. clin. prof. 1935-41; asso. prof. medicine, U. of Ill. Coll. of Medicine, 1941-43, prof. medicine, 1943-45, clin. prof. medicine since 1945; research asso. in pathology, Cook County Hosp., 1934-40; asso. attending physician, Presbyn. Hosp., Chicago, 1930-46; attending physician, Grant Hosp., Chicago, since 1947; attending physician, sr. staff, Henrotin Hosp., Chicago, since 1947; attending physician, U. of Ill. Research and Ednl. Hosps., 1945—. Mem. exec. forum Chgo. Assn. of Commerce and Industry. Certified by Am. Bd. Internal Medicine, 1937; diplomate, Nat. Bd. Med. Examiners, 1925. Fellow A.C.P., A.M.A., Am. Geriatrics Soc. (pres.) Soc. for Research in Child Development; mem. Assn. Am. Physicians, Am. Soc. Clin. Investigation, Central Soc. Clin. Research, Endocrine Society (vice pres.), Soc. for Exptl. Biology and Medicine, Am. Goiter Assn. (president), A.A.A.S., Am. Assn. History Medicine, American Diabetes Assn., Am. Soc. Research in Psychosomatic Problems, Am. Therapeutic Soc. (v.p.) Gerentol. Soc., Am. Soc. for Study of Sterility, Am. Heart Assn., World Med. Assn., Am. Med. Writers' Assn., Am. Genetic Assn. Am. Acad. Compensation Medicine, Chicago Med. Service (bd. trustees), Association American Medical Colleges, Institute Medicine of Chicago, Chicago Soc. Internal Med., Soc. Med. History of Chicago, Chicago Med. Soc. (pres.), Asso. Diplomates of Nat. Bd. Med. Examiners (pres.), Miss. Valley Med. Soc. (recipient distinguished Service award, 1952; president, trustee executive com.), Ill. State Acad. Sci., Ill. State Med. Soc., Sigma Xi, Pi Kappa Epsilon. Republican. Presbyterian. Clubs: University, Racquet, Harvard (v.p. for Chicago). Contbr. numerous articles to med. jours. and textbooks. Mng. editor Jour. Clin. Endocrinology and Metabolism; editor Journal of Am. Geriatrics Soc., American Lectures in Endocrinology; asso. editor Am. Practitioner; editorial bd. Miss. Valley Med. Journal; adv. editorial bd. Jour. Am. Acad. Gen. Practitioners. Home: 1430 Lake Shore Dr., Chgo. 10. Office: 700 N. Michigan Av., Chgo. 11. Died Mar. 23, 1954; buried Rosehill Cemetery, Chgo.

THOMPSON, WILLIAM FRANCIS, fisheries scientist; b. St. Cloud, Minn., Apr. 3, 1888; s. Pirrie and Janet (Crooks) T.; student U. Wash., 1906-09; A.B., Stanford, 1911, Ph.D., 1930; m. Julia Bell Shands, Sept. 26, 1915; children—William Francis, Janet Douglas (Mrs. Howard E. Rothenbuhler), Betsy Elliott (Mrs. James Senechal), John Shands. Sci. asst. to David Starr Jordan, Stanford, 1909-15, asst. in zoölogy, Stanford, 1910-11; scientist Cal. Fish and Game Commn., 1911-12, Provincial Fisheries Dept., B.C. Can., 1913-17; dir. Cal. State Fisheries Lab., 1917-24, Internat. Fisheries Commn., 1924-37, Internat. Pacific Salmon Fisheries Commn., 1937-43; cons. various orgns., 1943—; prof. fisheries U. Wash., 1930-47, dir. Sch. Fisheries, 1934-47; dir. Fisheries Research Inst., 1947-58, also research prof. Sch. Fisheries; cons. for history of Pacific Salmon and lit. retrieval Fish and Wildlife Service, also for John Day Dam on Columbia River, U.S. Engrs., 1958-65. Mem. biology and research com. Internat. N. Pacific Fisheries Commn. U.S. mem. 5th Pacific Sci. Congress. Fellow Cal. Acad. Scis.; mem. Am. Assn. Ichthyologists and Herpetologists (pres. western div.), A.A.A.S., Am. Inst. Fishery Research Biologists (pres. 1957—), Western Soc. Naturalists, Am. Fisheries, Soc. (hon.), Pacific Fisheries Biologists, Ecol. Soc. Am., Sigma Xi. Author sci. publs. Home: 3621 43d Av. N.E., Seattle 98105. Died Nov. 7, 1965; buried Saxon Cemetery, Acme, Wash.

THOMPSON, ZADOCK, historian, naturalist, mathematician; b. Bridgewater, Vt., May 23, 1796; s Capt. Barnabas and Sarah (Fuller) T.; grad. U. Vt., 1823; m. Phebe Boyce, Sept. 2, 1824, 2 children. Published an almanac, 1819; gazeteer of Vt., 1824; tutor U. Vt., 1825-33, prof. chemistry and natural history, 1851; wrote The Youths' Assistant in Practical Arithmetick (his only lucrative venture), 1825; edited mag. Iris, 1828, also Green Mountain Repository, 1832; taught in Can., 1833-37; ordained deacon Protestant Episcopal Ch., 1835; tchr. Vt. Episcopal Inst., Burlington, 1837; state naturalist Vt., 1853. Author: History of the State of Vermont, from Its Earliest Settlement to the Close of The Year 1832, 1833; Geography and History of Lower Canada, 1835; Natural, Civil, and Statistical History of Vermont (most important work), 1841-43; Geography and Geology of Vermont, 1848. Died Burlington, Jan. 9, 1856.

THOMS, HERBERT, physician, teacher; b. Waterbury, Conn., Jan. 5, 1885; s. William Peter and Adeline Delia (Hart) T.; M.D., Yale Univ., 1910; post grad. student John Hopkins Univ., 1914-15; m. Edith May Comstock, Aug. 21, 1912; 1 dau., Margaret Alison. Intern, Backus Hosp., Norwich, Conn., Memorial Hospital, New London, Conn., 1910-11; asst. resident Sloane Hosp. For Women, 1912; became prof. obstetrics and gynecology, chmn. dept. Yale Univ. Sch. Medicine, 1947, prof. emeritus; curator Yale Medical School Library; member of the staff of Grace-New Haven Hosp., Meriden Hosp., New Britain Hosp., Hungerford Hosp., Norwalk Hosp., Stamford Hosp., Backus Hosp., Milford Hosp. Exhibited art work at Phila. Art Alliance, 1932, Am. Soc. Etchers, 1933, Old Lyme Art Assn, Salmagundi Club, others. Chmn. med. adv. com. Conn. Planned Parenthood League, 1961. Awarded Lasker Award, 1953, Yale medal, 1961. Mem. Am. Med. Assn., American Gynecological Society. Clubs: Acom. Beaumont Medical, Elizabethan. Author: The Estimation of Pelvic Capacity, 1940; The Obstetric Pelvis, 1935; Chapters in American Obstetrics, 1933; Classical Contributions to Obstetrics and Gynecology, 1935; Training for Childbirth, 1950; Understanding Natural Childbirth, 1950; Pelvimetry, 1956; The Doctors Jared of Connecticut, 1958; The Docters of Yale College, 1701-1815, 1960; Our Obstetric Heritage, 1960; Samuel Seabury, Priest and Physician, Bishop of Connecticut, 1963; Jared Eliot, Minister, Doctor, Scientist and His Connecticut, 1967; Yale Men and Landmarks in Old Connecticut, 1967. Home: Stony Creek CT Died Oct. 27, 1972; buried Stony Creek CT

THOMSON, ELIHU, electrician; b. Manchester, Eng., Mar. 29, 1853; s. Daniel and Mary A. (Rhodes) T.; A.B., Central High Sch., Phila., 1870, A.M., 1875; hon. A.M., Yale, 1890; Ph.D., Tufts, 1894; Sc.D., Harvard, 1909; LL.D., U. of Pa., 1924; D.Sc., Victoria Univ., Manchester, England, 1924; m. Mary L. Peck, May 1, 1884 (died 1916); children—Stuart (dec.), Roland D., Malcolm, Donald T.; m. 2d, Clarissa Hovey, 1923. Prof. chemistry and mechanics, Central High Sch., Phila., 1870-80; 1880—, electrician for Thomson-Houston and General Electric cos., which operate under his inventions, more than 700 patents having been obtained; inventor of electric welding, which bears his name, and many other important inventions in electric lighting, power; dir. Thomson Lab. of Gen. Electric Co., Lynn, Mass. Pres. Internat. Elec. Congress and chamber of official delegates thereto, St. Louis, 1904; pres. Internat. Electrotech. Commn., 1908-11. Fellow Am. Acad. Arts and Sciences (v.p.); mem. Nat. Acad. Sciences. Awarded Grand Prix in Paris, 1889 and 1900, for elec. inventions; decorated, 1889, by French Govt., Chavalier and Officer Legion of Honor, for elec. research and inventions; grand prize, St. Louis, 1904, for elec. work; Rumford medal, 1902; awarded 1st Edison medal, Am. Inst. E.E., 1910; Elliott Cresson medal, John Fritz medal, and Hughes medal of Royal Soc., London, 1916; Kelvin medal, 1924; the Franklin medal, by the Franklin Inst., 1925; Faraday medal, by Instn. of Elec. Engrs., Gt. Britain, 1927; also twice awarded the John Scott Legacy medal and premium, by City of Phila., and medals, Trans. Miss. Expn., Omaha, and Columbian Expn., Chicago; also Grashof Medal awarded by the Verein Deutscher Ingenieure of Germany, Mar. 29, 1935. Trustee and pres. Peabody Mus., Salem, Mass.; mem. Corp. Mass. Inst. Tech. and its acting pres., 1920-22; v.p. Am. Philos. Soc. Mem. Nat. Research Council. Contbr. to tech. jours. Home: Swampscott, Mass. Died Mar. 13, 1937.

THOMSON, FRANCIS A(NDREW), mining engr., educator; b. London, Eng., Dec. 21, 1879; s. John Alexander and Frances Springett (Wyatt) T.; E.M., Colo. Sch. Mines, 1904, M.S., 1914, D.Sc., 1923; studied Royal Sch. Mines, London, Ecole des Mines, Paris; m. Josephine H. Bruckman, Aug. 16, 1906 (died June 5, 1927); children—Andrew Halleck, Richard Wyatt; m. 2d, Edna L. Michaelsen, July 16, 1928; 1 dau., Jean Louise. Prospector, miner and assayer, Western States and Can., 1895-98; asst. engr. Northwest Smelting & Refining Co., B.C., 1902-03; cons. engr., supt. properties, Colo. and Nev., 1904-07; head dept. mining engring., State Coll. Wash., 1907-17; dean Sch. Mines, U. Ida., 1917-28; dir. Ida. State Bur. Mines and Geology, 1919-28; pres. Mont. Sch. Mines, and dir. State Bur. Mines and Geology, 1928-50, ret.; cons. engr. U.S. Bur. Mines, 1919-28. Mem. Am. Inst. Mining and Metall. Engrs., Mining and Metall. Soc. Am., Am. Mining Congress (bd. govs.), Soc. Promotion Engring. Edn., Mont. Soc. Engrs., Sigma Nu, Sigma Xi, Sigma Tau, Sigma Gamma Epsilon. Episcopalian. Author: Stamp Milling and Cyaniding, 1915. Contbr. numerous articles tech. mining press U.S. and Can. Address: South 1704 Cedar, Spokane. Died Jan. 11, 1951.

THOMSON, JAMES E. M., orthopaedic surgeon; b. Los Angeles, Calif., Aug. 17, 1889; s. Rev. Edward and Ella M. (Tarr) T.; student Evanston (Ill.) Acad., 1909, Northwestern U., 1909; A.B., Arlington Heights Coll., Fort Worth, Tex., 1913; European travel and study, 1910; M.D., Rush Med. Coll., 1915; D.Sc. (hon.), Ohio Wesleyan U., 1957; married Helen Virginia Yoke, June 21, 1916; children—Helen Jean, James E. M. Intern and resident, Crippled Children's Home and Hosp., Chgo., 1915-16; practice of orthopaedic surg., Lincoln, Neb., since 1916; dep. supt. of health, City of Lincoln, 1935-48; charge of arthritics and orthopaedic clinic, City Health Dept., 1932-48; surgeon and examiner for Rock Island Railroad Co., Northwestern P.R., Burlington Railroad; chief department bone and joint surgery Bryan Memorial Hosp.; honorary orthopedic surgeon Lincoln Gen. and St. Elizabeth hosps.; cons., chief orthopedic service VA Hospital; cons. Neb. State Hosp., VA Hosp., Grand Island; chmn. Neb. Bd. Health, 1952—; civilian consultant to United States Air Force; special lecturer several univs., symposia and assn. meetings; asso. clin. prof. orthopaedics University of Nebraska College of Medicine. Red Cross Base Hospital, 49, France, World War I; contributor research finding relating to local shock, Nat. Research Council. World War II. Chairman of Neb. State bd. of Health, 1952—. Recipient numerous awards and honors, latest being: Order of White Lion, 1946; Centennary distinguished citizen award in professions City of Lincoln, 1959. Diplomate American Board Orthopedic Surgery. Fellow A.C.S., International College Surgeons (vice president 1948); honorary mem. numerous fgn. profl. socs.; mem. Am. Acad. Orthopaedic Surgeons (pres. 1947), Am. Orthopaedic Assn., Clin. Orthopaedic Soc. (pres. 1937), Am. Ry. Surgeons Assn. (pres. 1948), Internat. Soc. Orthopaedics and Traumatology, State Med. Assn. Neb. (past pres.), other national state and local medical and scientific socs., has served as officer of several. Democrat. Methodist. Mason (32 deg., Shriner). Club: University (past pres.). Editor: Peace and War Orthopaedic Surgery, 1943; Reconstruction Surgery of the Extremities, 1944; Regional Orthopaedic Surgery and Fundamental Orthopaedic Problems, 1946; Fundamentals in Orthopedic Surgery, 1947. Contbr. med. jours. Home: Box 577, Rancho Santa Fe, Cal. 92067. Died May 24, 1962; buried Wyuka Cemetery, Lincoln, Neb.

THOMSON, JAMES WILLIAM, chief engr. U.S.N.; b. Wilmington, Del., Nov. 10, 1836; s. James William and Sarah (Peters) T.; acad. edn.; m. Laura N. Troth, Oct. 7, 1862. Apptd. 3d asst. engr. U.S.N., June 26, 1856; 1st asst. engr., Aug. 2, 1859; chief engr., Feb. 2, 1862; retired, June 26, 1896; advanced to rank of rear admiral retired, June 29, 1906, for services during Civil War. Served on various vessels and at various stations during Civil and Spanish wars; mem. bd. Naval Acad., Oct.-Nov. 1875, bd. of inspection, Nov. 5, 1875-Aug. 1, 1876, bd. of examiners, May 12-May 31, 1881, examining bd., Phila., 1885-87. Home: Moorestown, N.J. Died Mar. 17, 1914.

THOMSON, REGINALD HEBER, engr.; b. Hanover, Ind., Mar. 20, 1856; s. Samuel Harrison and M. Sophronia (Clifton) T.; A.B., Hanover (Ind.) Coll., 1877, A.M., Ph.D., 1903; m. Sarah Adeline Laughlin, Aug. 29, 1883; children—James Harrison, Marion Wing, Reginald Heber, Frances Clifton. Instr. mathematics, Healdsburg (Cal.) Inst. and Alexander Acad., 1879-81; with F.H. Whitworth, civ. and mining engr., Seattle, and his partner, 1882-86; city surveyor, Seattle, 1884-86; locating engr. mountain div. Seattle, Lake Shore & Eastern R.R., 1886-88, res. engr. at Spokane, 1888-89; designed G.N. Ry. track encircling butte above Scenic, 1889; mining engr. at Seattle, 1889-92; city engr., 1892-1911; chmn. Bd. Pub. Works, 1896-1908, 1900-11. In charge design and constrn. Seattle municipal improvement, 1892-1912, requiring expenditure of over $42,000,000, including gravity water system conveying water from mountain stream, 28 miles distant, etc.; cons. engr. Water Bd., city of Portland, Ore.; mem. Wash. Armory Commn., 1905, 1906; mem. adv. bd. to gov. of Wash., 1909-11; cons. engr. city of Tacoma, city of Prince Rupert, B.C.; chief engr. Seattle Port Commn., 1911-12; cons. engr. Prov. of Brit. Columbia, 1912-15; spl. engr. Rogue River Valley Canal Co., 1921-23. Mem. Seattle City Council, 1916-22; spl. engr. hydro-electric power constrn., Eugene, Ore., 1922-24; charge water development, City of Bellingham, 1927-33, city engr., Seattle, 1930-31; cons. engr., City of Wenatchee Met. Water System, 1933, Inter-County River Improvement, 1937, engr. State of Wash. Pontoon Bridge Commn. Pres. bd. mgrs. U. Wash. Y.M.C.A., 1905-15. Pres. Pacific N.W. Soc. Civ. Engrs., 1902, 1903, Wash. Good Roads Assn., 1910-11; hon. mem. Am. Soc. C.E., Engring. Inst. Can., W. Coast Mineral Assn., Beta Theta Pi. Club: Arctic. Address: 2404 42d Av. N., Seattle 2. Died Jan. 7, 1949; buried Lake View Cemetery, Seattle.

THOMSON, SAMUEL, physician; b. Alstead, N.H., Feb. 9, 1769; s. John and Hannah (Cobb) T.; m. Susan Allen, July 7, 1790, 8 children. Began farming, experimented with herb cures, eventually devoted full time to med. practice, circa 1790; his use of medical roots "Thomsonian System" involved him in many law suits, once charged with murder; believed that all ills were based on cold and treated with heat producers; treatment consisted of labelia herb followed by Cayenne pepper and vapor bath, patented, 1813, revised, 1823; short-lived journals advocating system were Botanic Sentinel, 1835-40, Thomsonian Recorder (later called Botanic-Medical Recorder), lasted until 1852. Author: A Brief Sketch of the Causes and Treatment of Disease, 1821; Materia Medica and Family Physician; New Guide to Health: or Botanic Family Physician, 1822. Died Boston, Oct. 4, 1843.

THOMSON, T. KENNARD, cons. engr.; b. Buffalo, Apr. 25, 1864; s. William Alexander and Lavinia Day (Newcomb) T.; grad. U. Toronto, 1886 (head of class), C.E., 1892, D.Sc., 1913; m. Mary Julia Harvey, 1888; children—Annis Eveleen, M.D., Mary Marjory, M.D., A. Kennard, W. Glencairn (capt. U.S.N.), H. Stranraer. Large experience in bridge, r.r., deep found. work; chief engr. Arthur McMullen & Co., Found. contrs., 9 yrs.; retained for found. work Comml. Cable Bldg., Mut. Life Bldg., U.S. Express Bldg., 41-story Singer Bldg., Zinn Bldg., Govt. Assay Bldg., Municipal Bldg., Bankers Trust. Seaboard Nat. Bank, N.Y., First Nat. Bank of Jersey City and over forty other bldgs. Has taken out several tunnel and lighthouse patents. Mem. bd. cons. engrs. for Barge Canal (enlargement of old Erie Canal), 1911-14. Built over two hundred bridges; designed bridges to be built over the Niagara River to celegrate the victory of World War; originator of Manhattan extension and belt line ry., also 2,000,000 h.p. Niagara River and St. Lawrence River power development, and made valuation and appraisals; appraised 110 bldgs., Manhattan, 1937; has done much work connection subway constrn.; proposed solution Miss. River problem; proposed Internat. Forest Park from Lake Superior to Pacific Coast to be 20 miles wide in width by 1500 miles long. Founder, life mem. U. Toronto Engring. Soc., 1884; life mem. Am. Soc. C.E. (dir. 1911-14), Am. Soc. M.E., Engring. Inst. Can., Niagara Hist. Soc., N.Y. Profl. Engrs., Past and Present Officers of Am. Soc. C.E.; mem. St. Andrews Soc. N.Y., etc. Republican. Episcopalian. Clubs: Engineers; hon. life mem. Canadian Club of New York (pres. 1912-14) and U. of Toronto Club of New York (ex-pres.). Mason. Proposed elevated streets for Manhattan, airplane landing for Manhattan, 1919. Has written over 200 papers on engring. subjects. Received medal for walking from Dr. John H. Finley, 1936; has walked 15 miles a day every April. Office: 32 W. 40th St., N.Y.C. Died July 1, 1952.

THOMSON, WILLIAM, physician, surgeon; b. Chambersburg, Pa., Jan. 28, 1833; ed. Chambersburg Acad. and by pvt. tutors; grad. Jefferson Med. Coll., 1855; practiced at Merion, nr. Phila., 1855-61; entered regular army, 1861, as asst. surgeon; served at hdqrs. Army of Potomac, 1862; surgeon in charge Douglass Hosp., 1863; became med. insp., Dept. of Washington, 1864; received 2 bvts.; was sent to La. after the war; passed 2d exam. but resigned from the army, Feb. 25, 1866; practicing at Phila., 1866—. As an army surgeon introduced local application of carbolic acid as disinfectant in treatment of wounds; also introduced several reforms in med. and surg. field service. Specialist in ophthalmic surgery; filled many professional and hosp. positions and wrote much on his specialty. 25 yrs. teacher (later emeritus prof. ophthalmology), Jefferson Med. Coll.; cons. surgeon of Wills Eye Hosp. With Dr. W. F. Norris made 1st successful photographic negatives with microscope, in 1864, at Douglass Hosp. Address: Philadelphia, Pa. Died 1907.

THOREAU, HENRY DAVID, writer; b. Concord, Mass., July 12, 1817; s. John and Cynthia (Dunbar) T.; grad. Harvard, 1837. Opened pvt sch. with brother John, 1838; gave 1st of nearly annual lectures to Concord Lyceum, 1838; lived at home of Ralph Waldo Emerson, 1841-43, 47-49; edited The Dial during Emerson's absence, 1843; tutor in home of William Emerson on S.I., N.Y., 1843-44; resided at Walden Pond, arrested for failure to pay poll tax, 1845; wrote journals which formed basis of Walden; lived in family home in Concord, 1849-62; published Walden (his only organized work), 1854; his life at Walden Pond was an experiment designed to prove that a meaningful existence was possible apart from industrialism and materialism of New Eng.; set his own conscience above laws of govt. thus incurring charge of anarchism; philosophy of his essay on civil disobedience (classic statement of individualism in conflict with State) present in Walden; descriptions of nature contained in this and other works established him as naturalist (though not as a scientist); though not a reformer, deeply concerned with problem of slavery, spoke vigorously in defense of John Brown, 1859; Thoreau was part of extremely close-knit family and participated in pencil mfg. conducted in family home; his influence on later Am. literature has been ascribed to his pithy and forceful style which employed vivid imagery; mem. Transcendentalist Club (including Amos Bronson Alcott, J.F. Clarke, Margaret Fuller, F.H. Hodge); distrusted group action and relied upon his own definitions of morality believing in human perfectibility; his skill in writing made him foremost interpreter of Am. flora and fauna; wrote A Week on the Concord and Merrimac Rivers (notable for literary criticism and nature studies), 1849; from his journals describing trips to Me., Cape Cod, and Can., 1848-53, there were published posthumously: Excursions, 1863; The Maine Woods, 1864; Cape Cod, 1865; A Yankee in Canada, 1866; Letters to Various Persons, edited by R.W. Emerson, 1865; Early Spring in Massachusetts, 1881, Summer, 1884, Winter, 1888, Autumn, 1892, selections from journals edited by H.G.O. Blake; Poems of Nature, edited by Salt and Sanborn, 1895; Walden edition of Writings of Henry David Thoreau, 20 vols., 1906, contains all journals except Apr. 1843-July 1845. Died Concord, Mass., May 6, 1862; buried New Burying Ground, Concord, reinterred Sleepy Hollow Cemetery.

THOREK, MAX, (tôr'ek), surgeon; b. Hungary, Mar. 10, 1880; s. Isaac and Sarah (Mahler) T.; prep. edn., Budapest, Hungary; came to U.S., 1900; M.D., Rush Med. Coll. (U. of Chicago); 1904; hon. LL.D., Lincoln Memorial U., Sc.D., Wesleyan Coll.; Honoris Causa, U. Istanbul, Turkey, 1954; married Fannie Unger, April 16, 1905; 1 son, Philip (M.D.). Practiced at Chgo., 1904—; asst. in gynecology to late Prof. Henry Banga, for 5 yrs.; prof. clin. surgery, Loyola U., 3 yrs.; chief surgeon to Am. Hosp., Chicago; prof. of clinical surgery, Cook County Grad. Sch. of Medicine; attending surgeon Cook County Hosp., cons. surgeon Municipal Tuberculosis Sanitarium; Cusing lecturer McGill U., Montreal, 1954. Fellow A.M.A., Internat. College Surgeons (life; internat. founder and permanent sec. general; editor in chief of jour.), Nat. Acad. Medicine (Colombia, S.A.), Nat. Gastroenterol. Soc., Internat. Coll. Anesthetists, Royal Soc. of Arts, Royal Photographic Soc. of Gt. Britain, Am. Coll. Gastroenterology; hon. fellow Royal Surg. Society (Sofia, Bulgaria), Internat. Society of Gastroenterologists; hon. member Belgian Society Gastroenterology; corr. fellow Peruvian Surg. Society; mem. Ill. State and Chicago med. socs.; mem. Orden del Sol, Republic of Peru; member American Eugenics Society, Rush Medical Coll. Alumni (life), Mark Twain Society (life); Chicago Historical Soc., Mississippi Valley Medical Society (charter mem.), Internat. Hospital Association, Internat. Soc. of Gastroenterology, Internat. Anesthetic Research Soc., Am. Soc. French Legion of Honor, DePaul Art League, Pi Gamma Mu (Life); hon. mem. Terre Haute Acad. Medicine; corr. academician Nat. Acad. Sciences of Mexico, Surg. Acad. of Mexico; corr. mem. Soc. des Chirurgiens (Paris), Soc. Scientifique Française de Chirurgie Reparatrice, Russian Endocrinol. Assn. (Moscow), Soc. of Neurology and Endocrinology (Jassy, Roumania), Sociedad das Sciences Medicas (Lisbon), Brazilian Coll. Surgeons; asso. corr. mem. Royal Acad. Medicine (Turin, Italy); hon. corr. mem. Egyptian Med. Assn. (Cairo, Egypt); past pres. American Physicians Art Assn.; Collaborator Rassegna Internazionale di Clinica Terapia, Milano, Italy; U.S. del. Internat. Congress Hepatic Insufficiences, Vichy, France, 1927. Decorated Knight of Legion of Honor (France); Knight Order of Crown of Italy; comdr. Order of St. Alexander (Sofia, Bulgaria); Medal of Honor (Republic of Venezuela); distinguished citizens medal from Vets. of Fgn. Wars of U.S.; Aztec Eagle, Mexican Govt., Gold Medalist Phi Lambda Kappa, 1951; Comdr. Cruzeiro do Sul (Brazil); Grand Officer Order of Merit (Argentina); Comdr. Nat. Order of Merit Carlos J. Finlay, Cuba. Club: Chicago Alumni. Author: The Human Testis and Its Diseases, 1924; Surgical Errors and Safeguards, 1931, 4th editions, 1943; Modern Surgical Technic (3 vols.), 1941; Plastic Surgery of the Breast Abdominal Wall, 1942; A Surgeon's World, 1944. Translator: Surgery of the Brain and Spinal Cord (by Fedor Krause), 1912. Cons. editor: Arquivos de Cirurgia Clinica e Experimental, Sao Paolo, Brazil. Contbr. to surg. lit. Guest lecturer in surgery, Washington U., 1940. Founder Photographic Society of America. Home: 3920 Lake Shore Drive. Office: American Hospital, 850 Irving Park Rd., Chgo. 13. Died Jan. 25, 1960.

THORKELSON, HALSTEN JOSEPH, mechanical engr.; b. Racine, Wis., Jan. 18, 1875; s. Mathias and Mary (Eggen) T.; B.S., U. of Wis., 1898, M.E., 1901; m. Mary Schuyler Carver, June 14, 1900; children—Mary Elizabeth, Florence Carver, Martha Seymour, Halsten John. Laborer, clk. and draftsman in mfg. establishment 7 yrs.; asst. supt. J. I. Case Plow Works, Racine, Wis., 1901-02; instr. steam engring., asst. prof., asso. prof. and prof., Coll. of Engring., U. of Wis., 1902-14; acting business mgr. and business mgr., U. of Wis., 1914-21; with Gen. Edn. Bd., New York, 1921-28; with Kohler Co., Kohler, Wis., 1928-43, becoming vice pres. and dir.; dir. Security Nat. Bank, Sheboygan, Wis.; retired Dec. 1943. Mem. Wis. Acad. Arts, Letters and Science; fellow A.A.A.S. Mason. Presbyterian. Clubs: Madison, University. Author: Air Compression and Transmission, 1913. Address: University Club, 803 State St., Madison 5 WI

THORNBER, JOHN JAMES, botanist; b. Rantoul, Ill., Feb. 8, 1872; s. James and Ann (Strickland) T.; B.S., S.D. Agrl. Coll., Brookings, 1895; B.S., U. of Neb., 1897, A.M., 1901; m. Harriet Ann Brown, June 26, 1897; 1 son, John Stickland; m. 2d, Miriam Rainier Harris, July 11, 1932. Prof. botany, U. of Ariz., and botanist Ariz. Agrl. Expt. Sta., 1901-43, also dir. Ariz. Agrl. Expt. Sta., 1921-28, and dean Ariz. Coll. of Agr., Tucson, 1922-28. Sabbatical leave to study in Smithsonian Instn. and Asa Gray Herbarium, 1911-12. Fellow A.A.A.S.; mem. Bot. Soc. America, Washington Acad. Sciences, Torrey Bot. Club, Sigma Xi, Phi Kappa Phi. Lambda Gamma Delta (hon. agrl. judging fraternity), Pi Gamma Mu. Mem. Presbyterian ch. Mason (32 deg., Shriner). Author: (with Margaret Armstrong) Field Book of Western Wild Flowers, 1915; (with Frances Bonker) Sage of the Desert and Other Cacti, 1930; (with same) The Fantastic Clan—The Cactus Family, 1931. Writer bulls. and articles on plants and plant life in Ariz. Built up herbarium of 100,000 sheets in the U. of Ariz.; has devoted much time to study of restoration of depleted grazing areas in Southwest, and to the introduction of trees and shrubs adapted to an arid, semitropical climate. Home: 2041 E. 2d St., Tucson AZ

THORNBURG, CHARLES LEWIS (thorn'burg), mathematician; b. Barboursville, W.Va., Apr. 17, 1859; s. James Lewis and Virginia Frances (Handley) T.; grad. Marshall Coll., Huntington, W.Va., 1876; B.S., Vanderbilt, 1881, B.E., 1882 C.E., 1882, C.E., 1883, Ph.D., 1884; LL.D., Lehigh, 1925; m. Mary Eulalia Green, Nov. 4, 1886; children—Eulalie, Charles Garland, Chesley Covington, Lewis, Marion, Richard Beaumont, Lucille Leighton, Frances Green. Fellow in mathematics, 1881-82, grad. in mathematics, 1882-84, instr. engring. dept., 1884-86, Vanderbilt; adj. prof. in engring. dept. and astronomy, 1886-95, prof. mathematics and astronomy, 1895-1925, sec. of faculty, 1900-23, Lehigh U., now prof. emeritus. Fellow A.A.A.S.; mem. Am. Math. Soc., Soc. Promotion Engring. Edn., Beta Theta Pi, Phi Beta Kappa, Tau Beta Pi. Democrat. Methodist. Author: Calculus Notes, 1906; (brochure) Elementary Differential Equations, 1914. Home: 238 E. Market St., Bethlehem, Pa. Died Oct. 14, 1944. *

THORNDIKE, EDWARD LEE, psychologist; b. Williamsburg, Mass., Aug. 31, 1874; s. Edward R. and Abby B. (Ladd) T.; A.B., Wesleyan U., Conn., 1895; A.B., Harvard, 1896, A.M., 1897, LL.D., 1933; Ph.D., Columbia U., 1898, Sc.D., 1929; Sc.D., Wesleyan and LL.D., Iowa, 1923; Sc.D., U. of Chicago, 1932; LL.D., Edinburgh, 1936; Sc.D., Athens, 1937; m. Elizabeth Moulton, Aug. 29, 1900; children—Elizabeth Frances, Virginia (dec.), Edward Moulton, Robert Ladd, Alan Moulton. Instr. edn. and teaching, Western Reserve U., 1898-99; instr. genetic psychology, Teachers Coll., Columbia, 1899-1901, adj. prof. ednl. psychology, 1901-04, prof., 1904-40, emeritus prof. since 1941; Wm. James lecturer, Harvard University, 1942-43. Fellow A.A.A.S. (president, 1934), N.Y. Acad. Sciences; mem. Nat. Acad. Science, Am. Philos. Soc., Am. Psychol. Assn., Am. Acad. of Arts and Sciences; hon. mem. Brit. Psychol. Assn. Clubs: Century (New York); Cosmos (Washington). Author: Educational Psychology, 1903; Mental and Social Measurements, 1904; Elements of Psychology, 1905; Principles of Teaching, 1905; Animal Intelligence, 1911; The Original Nature of Man, 1913; The Psychology of Learning, 1914; Psychology of Arithmetic, 1922; Psychology of Algebra, 1923; The Measurement of Intelligence, 1926; Fundamentals of Learning, 1932; Your City, 1939; Human Nature and the other books, monographs and articles on psychological Social Order, 1940; Man and His Works, 1943; also various and educational subjects. Home: Montrose, N.Y. Died Aug. 9, 1949.

THORNE, CHARLES EMBREE, agriculturist; b. Greene County, O., Oct. 4, 1846; s. Elijah and Mary (Charles) T.; ed. Mich. Agrl. Coll., summer, 1866; Antioch Coll., 1868-69, 1869-70; hon. M. Agr., Ohio State U., 1890; hon. D.Sc., Coll. of Wooster, 1926; m. Viola J. Hine, May 10, 1871 (died 1924); children—Bertram Hine (dec.), Mrs. Bessie Mary Brooks, Charles Brooks. Raised on farm, Greene County; farm mgr. Ohio State U., 1877-81; asso. editor Farm and Fireside, Springfield, O., 1882-88; dir. 1887-1921; chief in soil fertility, 1888-1925, cons. chief, 1925—, Ohio Agrl. Expt. Sta. Pres. Am. Soc. Agronomy, 1914-15 (fellow 1925); pres. Assn. Am. Agrl. Colls. and Expt. Stas., 1915-16, Soc. Promotion Agrl. Science, 1915-16; pres. Wayne Bldg. & Loan Co., 1905—. Author: Farm Manures, 1913; Maintenance of Soil Fertility, 1931. Home: Wooster, O. Died Feb. 29, 1936.

THORNTHWAITE, CHARLES WARREN, consulting climatologist; b. Bay City, Mich., Mar 7, 1899; s. Ernest William and Mildred (Hudson T.; A.B., Central Mich. Teachers Coll., 1922; student U. of Mich., summers 1923, 24; Ph.D., U. Cal., 1929; D.Sc., Central Mich. U., 1963; m. Denzil Arlene Slentz July 29, 1925 (dec. 1962); children—Elizabeth (Mrs. Joseph Higgins), Dorothy Ann (Mrs. Robert Kupelian), Sally (Mrs. Dean Evans Fazenbaker). Teaching fellow, U. of Cal., 1924-27; geographer, Kentucky Geol. Survey, 1926-30; assistant professor geography, U. of Okla., 1927-35; geographer, U. of Pa., 1934-35; chief, clim. div., Soil Conservation Service, Washington, D.C., 1935-46; prof. of climatology U. of Md., 1944-47; consultant Mexican Irrigation Commn., 1944-46; consulting climatologist, since 1946; prof. of climatology, Johns Hopkins U., 1947-55, dir. Lab. of Climatology, 1948—; adjunct prof. climatology Drexel Institute Tech., 1954-59; professor climatology University of Chicago, 1956—; president C. W. Thornthwaite Associates. United States mem. UNESCO adv. com. on Arid Zone Research, 1956-60. Cons. U.S. Army, 1952. Pres. Commn. for climatology World Meteorological orgn., 1951-57. Hon. fellow Am. Geog. Soc. (Cullum medal 1958). Mem. Am. Geophs. Union (v.p. sect. of meteorology, 1938-41, pres., 1941-44). Am. Meteorol. Soc., Assn. Am. Geographers, Ecol. Soc. of Am., Sigma Xi. Clubs: Cosmos (Washington); Johns Hopkins (Balt.). Contbr. over 100 papers and monographs in sci. and tech. jours. Originator of the Thornthwaite classification of climate, 1931. Home: Elmer, N.J. Office: Laboratory of Climatology, Centerton, N.J. Died June 11, 1963.

THORNTON, GUSTAVUS BROWN, physician, sanitarian; b. Bowling Green, Va., Feb. 22, 1835; s. James Bankhead and Mariana T. Thornton; ed. Richmond Coll., 1852-56; M.D., U. Med. Coll. (New York U.), 1860. Asst. surgeon C.S.A., 1861-62; chief surgeon of div., Army of the Tenn., 1862-65; asst. phys., 1866-68, phys.-in-charge, 1868-79, Memphis City Hosp. (covering yellow fever epidemics, 1873 and 1878); pres. Memphis bd. of health, 1879-89 and 1893-98, and founder of the new City Hosp., 1897, and had charge of the famous sanitary reformation of Memphis; reapptd., 1893; local surgeon I.C. R.R. Co., Southern R.R. Co., Union R.R. Co. (Belt Line), etc. Pres. Med. Soc. of Tenn., 1881-82; officer Am. Pub. Health Assn.; pres. Assn. of Med. Officers of the Army and Navy of the Confederacy, 1910. Author: Yellow Fever, Pathology and Treatment, 1878; Six Years' Sanitation in Memphis; and essays and official reports. Address: Memphis, Tenn. Died May 13, 1914.

THORNTON, WALTER EDWIN, physician; b. Bloomington, Ind., June 30, 1878; s. Felix G. and Clementine (Uland) T.; M.D., Ind. U., 1901; m. Juanina Marie Young, Oct. 25, 1913; children—Georgiana, Edythe Cale (Mrs. L. Moffitt Cecil). Gen. practice of medicine, Montpelier, 1901-13; Blackford County coroner, 1906, 1908, 1910; med. dir. Ind. Nat. Life Ins. Co., Indianapolis, 1914-21; asst. med. dir. The Lincoln Nat. Life Ins. Co., Fort Wayne, Ind., 1921-23, medical dir., 1923-24, 2d v.p., 1934, med. dir., 1923-49, dir., 1930—. Awarded 50 year certificate of merit State Med. Soc. Ind. for distinguished service in the profession, 1951. Fellow A.M.A.; mem. Ind. and Allen County med. socs., Sigma Nu. Mason (32 deg., Jester). Home: 601 Oakdale Dr., Fort Wayne 6, Ind. Died Oct. 27, 1960.

THORNTON, WILLIAM, architect, inventor, pub. ofcl.; b. Jost van Dyke, Virgin Islands, May 20, 1759; s. William and Dorcas Downing (Zeagens) T.; attended U. Edinburgh (Scotland), 1781-84; M.D., Aberdeen (Scotland) U., 1784; m. Anna Maria Brodeau, Oct. 13, 1790. Arrived in N.Y.C., 1787, became U.S. citizen in Del., 1788; earned prize for design of Library Co. of Phila., 1789; asso. with John Fitch in experimenting with paddle-driven steamboats, 1778-90, advanced much of cost; won competition for design of Nat. Capitol, Washington, D.C., 1792, received post as commr. City of Washington, 1794-1802, supervised constrn. Capitol until replaced by Latrobe, 1803; North Wing constructed in accordance with Thornton's ideas, constrn. of South Wing conformed with it, 1800; his idea of great central rotunda also adhered to by later architects of bldg.; supervised constrn. of George Washington's 2 houses in Washington, D.C., 1798-99; built the Octagon for John Tayloe, 1798-1800 (standing in 1935 and had been hdqrs. A.I.A.); made sketches for 2 bldgs. at U. Va., one of which (Pavillion VII) was built; clk. in charge patents State Dept., 1802-28, saved Patent Office from destruction during capture of Washington by British, 1814. Died Washington, Mar. 28, 1828; buried Congressional Cemetery, Washington.

THORP, CLARK ELWIN, chem. engr.; b. Cleve., Aug. 15, 1914; s. Ayers Clark and Ada (Mercy) T.; B.Sc., Fenn Coll., Cleve., 1935; m. Amelia Greenawalt, Aug. 14, 1937; 1 son, Clark Elwin. Research engr. Fullers Earth Co., Cleve., 1936-37; dir. research Ozo-Ray Process Corp., Chgo., 1937-41; suprv. chem. engring. Armour Research Found., Chgo., 1941-44, mgr. chemistry and chem. engring. research, 1950-58; president Fiber Products Research Center, Inc., Beaver Falls, New York, 1958-68. Mem. Am. Inst. Chem. Engrs., Tech. Assn. Paper and Pulp Industry, Am. Assn. Research Dirs., Am. Inst. of Chemists (chairman), Am. Ordnance Assn., Electrochem. Soc., Am. Soc. Testing Materials, Am. Mgmt. Assn., Ill. Acad. Sci., Paper Industry Mgmt. Assn., Sigma Xi, Sigma Chi Alpha. Contbr. profl. publs. Patentee in field. Address: Beaver Falls NY Died Aug. 15, 1968; buried Crown Hill Cemetery, Twinsburg OH

THORP, FRANK HALL, chemist; b. Bloomington, Ill., Feb. 25, 1864; s. Edward and Mary R. (Hall) T.; B.S., Mass. Inst. Tech., 1889; Ph.D., U. of Heidelberg, Germany, 1893; m. Kate Lunger, of Davenport, Ia., June 30, 1891. Asst. in chemistry, 1889-91, instr., 1894-1900, asst. prof. industrial chemistry, 1901-16, Mass. Inst. Tech. Asso. editor Jour. Industrial and Engring. Chemistry, 1908-09. Home: 200 Mt. Vernon St., West Roxbury, Mass.

THORP, JOHN, machinist, inventor; b. Rehoboth, Mass., 1784; s. Reubin and Hannah (Bucklin) T.; m. Eliza A. Williams, Aug. 18, 1817. Received 1st patent for hand water loom, 1812, renewed, 1843, 2d patent for power loom, 1816; received 3 patents for improvements in spinning and twisting cotton (called "ring spinning;" basic method of continuous spinning still used), 1828; patent for netting machine, 1828; received 4 patents including narrow fabric loom (possibly 1st gang loom operated by power), 1829; established as machine builder, Providence, R.I., later North Wrenthan, Mass., 1830's. Died Nov. 15, 1848.

THORSON, GUNNAR AXEL WRIGHT, marine biologist, ebducator; b. Copenhagen, Denmark, Dec. 31, 1906; s. Charles U. and Astrid (Gjertsen) T.; M.Sc., Copenhagen U., 1930, Ph.D., 1936; m. Ellen Johanne

Gudrun Jorgensen, Dec. 23, 1940; children—Ole, Bodil (Mrs. Soren Larsen). Curator, Copenhagen Zool. Mus. 1934-57; lectr. marine biology Copenhagen U., 1946-57, prof., 1957-70; dir. Elsinore Marine Biol. Lab. (Denmark), 1958-70; pres. Nordic Council for Marine Biology, 1960. Mem. adv. bds., marine insts. Miami, Paris, Naples, Eilat. Decorated knight Order Dannebrog, officer Siamese White Elephant; recipient Danish Merit medal, 1935, Danish Sci. prize, 1947. Mem. Royal Danish Acad. Sci.; corr. or hon. mem. sci. socs. Finland, France, Italy, Norway, Spain, Sweden, U.K., U.S. Author: Reproduction and Larval Development of Danish Marine Bottom Invertebrates, 1946; Bottom Communities, 1957; Light as a Ecological Factor in Dispersal and Settlement of Marine Larvae 1964; Some Factors Influencing the Recruitment and Establishment of Marine Communities. Contbr. profl. jours. Home: Elsinore Denmark Died Jan. 25, 1971; buried Frederiksberg Old Cemetery, Copenhagen Denmark

THROCKMORTON, TOM BENTLEY, neurologist and psychiatrist; born at Derby, Ia., Jan. 20, 1885; son of Tom Morford and Mary Ann (Bentley) T.; graduate high school Chariton, Ia., 1902; B.Sc., Simpson College, 1907, D.Sc., 1960; M.D., Jefferson Medical College, Philadelphia, 1909; post-graduate study, Philadelphia, 1915, also at Harvard Med. Sch., 1921; m. Edna Jeniza Dudley, Jan. 21, 1911; children—Tom Dercum, Robert Bentley, Hobart Hare (air pilot U.S. Naval Reserve, killed in Aleutians), and James Priestley. Began practice in Phila., 1909; interne Phila. Orthopedic Hosp. Infirmary for Nervous Diseases, 1910-11; asst. physician Cherokee (Ia.) State Hosp. for Insane, July 1911-12; practiced in Des Moines since 1912; specialist in neurology and psychiatry. Served on Draft Bd. for Polk County, Ia., World War. Mem. Inter-State Post-Grad. Med. Assn. of N.A. (trustee 1929, secretary 1932-52), A.M.A. (chmn. sect. on nervous and mental diseases 1940-41), Polk County Med. Soc. (pres. 1952), Ia. State Med. Soc. (sec. 1916-30), Central Neuropsychiatric Assn., Am. Coll. Physicians (ex-governor for Iowa), honorary mem. of the Chicago Medical Society and of the Chicago Neurol. Soc., Iowa Neuro-psychiatric Soc., Am. Acad. Neurology, Alpha Omega Alpha. Rep. Meth. Mason (grand master, Grand Lodge, Ia., 1936-37; hon. 33 deg.). Author: (brochure) True Masonic Teachings; History of Medicine in Lucas County. Contbr. to med. jours., 1910—. Home: 919 45th St., Des Moines 50312. Office: 1407 Woodland Av., Des Moines, Ia. Died July 4, 1961; buried Masonic Cemetery, Des Moines.

THURBER, CHARLES, inventor, mfr., educator; b. East Brookfield, Mass., Jan. 2, 1803; s. Rev. Laban and Abigail (Thayer) T.; A.B., A.M., Brown U., 1827; m. Lucinda Allen, 1827; m. 2d, Caroline Esty. 1852; 2 daus. Tchr., Milford, (Mass.) Acad., 1827-31; prin. Latin Grammar Sch., Worcester, Mass., 1831-39; in partnership with brother-in-law Ethan Allen to manufacture firearms, Worcester, 1836-56; granted patent for hand printing machine which preceded typewriter, 1843; received 2d patent for a "mechinical chirographer" (a writing machine), 1845; county commr. in Mass., 1842-44; mem. Mass. Senate, 1852-53; trustee Brown U., 1853-86; ret. from bus., 1856. Died Nashua, N.H., Nov. 7, 1886.

THURBER, GEORGE, botanist, horticulturist, author, editor; b. Providence, R.I., Sept. 2, 1821; s. Jacob and Alice Ann (Martin) T.; attended Union Classical and Engring. Sch., Providence; M.D., N.Y. Med. Coll., 1859. Partner in a pharmacy, stimulated his interest in chemistry; lectured on chemistry with Franklin Soc., Providence; botantist, q.m., commissary on survey of boundary between U.S. and Mexico, 1850; with U.S. Assay Office, N.Y.C., 1853-56; lectr. botany Coll. of Pharmacy, N.Y., 1856-61, 65-66; lectr. Cooper Union; prof. botany and horticulture Mich. State Agrl. Coll. (later Mich. State Coll.), 1859-63; editor Agriculturist, N.Y.C., 1863-85; specialized in study of Am. grasses; pres. Torrey Bot. Club, 1873-80; life mem. Am. Pomol. Soc.; became corr. mem. Royal Hort. Soc. of London, 1886. Author: American Weeds and Useful Plants (a revision of William Darlington's Agricultural Botany, published 1847), 1859. Died Passaic, N.J., Apr. 2, 1890.

THURNAUER, GUSTAV (tûrn'ou-er), chemist; b. San Francisco, Calif., Jan. 30, 1867; s. William and Minna (Bruell) T.; ed. Realschule, Bayreuth, Germany, 1877-83; Industrieschule, Nuremberg, 1884-86; A.M., Ph.D., U. of Berlin, 1890; m. Therese Mayer-Weismann, May 21, 1907. Asst. chemist Gewerbemuseum, Nuremberg, 1890-92; chemist Fairfield (Conn.) Chem. Works, 1893; chemist Chicago & Aurora Smelting & Refining Works, 1894-99; sec. and treas. Aurora Metal Co., mfrs. bearing metals, metallic packing for locomotives and aluminum-bronze diecastings, 1899-1912, vice-president and treasurer, 1912-1934, president, 1934-40, chairman board since 1941. Mem. Aurora Public Library, 1905-43; treas. Anti-Tuberculosis Soc., 1911-39; dir. Pub. Health Assn. since 1919; first pres. Aurora Social Service Fedn. (now Aurora Community Chest), 1922, 23, dir. budget com. 1923-43 (past chmn.). Mem. Am. Chem. Soc. (v.p. Chicago sect., 1901, 09; councilor, 1908), Aurora Chamber Commerce. Elk. Clubs: Chemists, Ill. Athletic (Chicago). Contbr. articles pertaining to metals and alloys, etc. Home: 563 Downer Pl. Address: Aurora Metal Co., Aurora, Ill. Died 1947.

THURSTON, ROBERT HENRY, univ. prof., engr., author; b. Providence, R.I., Oct. 25, 1839; s. Robert L. and Harriet (Taylor) T.; grad. Brown U., C.E. and Ph.B., 1859, A.M., 1869; LL.D., 1889; Dr.Engring., Stevens Inst. Tech., 1885; trained in his father's shops until 1861; in U.S.N., 1861-72, asst. engr. and engr. in charge of vessels; at U.S. Naval Acad., Annapolis, acting asst. prof. natural philosophy, 1865-71; prof. mech. engring., Stevens Inst. of Tech., 1871-85; dir. Sibley Coll., Cornell U. and prof. mech. engring., 1885—; m. Susan Taylor Gladding, Oct. 1865 (died 1878); m. 2d, Leonora Boughton, Aug. 4, 1880. First pres. (two terms, 1880-83) Am. Soc. Mech. Engrs.; 3 times v.p. A.A.A.S., 1877-78 and 1884; v.p. Am. Inst. Mining Engrs., 1878-79; inventor of testing machines, engine governors and other devices; U.S. commr. to Vienna Expn., 1873, Paris, 1889; served on many U.S. and State commns. Author: Friction and Lubrication; Materials of Engineering, 3 vols., 1884; Manual of the Steam-Engine, 2 vols., 1890, 1901; Materials of Construction, 1884; Stationary Steam Engines, 1885; Friction and Lost Work in Machinery and Mill Work, 1885; Manual of the Steam Boiler, 1888; Handbook of Engine and Boiler Trials, 1889; Motive Power of Heat (from French of Carnot), 1890; Heat as a Form of Energy, 1890; Life of Robert Fulton, 1891; History of the Steam Engine, 1878, 1901. Also about 300 professional and scientific papers. Is an editor of Science and of Johnson's and Appleton's Cyclopaedias. Address: Ithaca, N.Y. Died 1903.

THURSTON, ROBERT LAWTON, mfr. steam engines; b. Portsmouth, R.I., Dec. 13, 1800; s. Peleg and Ruth (Lawton) T.; m. Eliza Stratton, 1827; m. 2d, Harriet Taylor, Jan. 5, 1839; 3 children including Robert Henry. Built with John Babcock, Sr.) an exptl. steam engine and "safety tubular boiler" of Babcock's invention, 1821, placed them in small boat designed for use at Slade's Ferry, nr. Fall River, Mass.; completed 2 steamboats, The Babcock, the Rushlight for the Providence-N.Y.C. run, 1826, 28; became partner (with John Babcock, Jr.) Providence Steam Engine Co. (R.I.) (1st co. of its kind in New Eng., 3d in U.S.), 1830, disaster forced reorgn. as Thurston, Green and Co., 1845, purchased and incorporated the "drop cut off" for steam engines, became 1st mfrs. in Am. to build a standard form of expansion steam engine, 1846; retired, 1863. Died Providence, Jan. 13, 1874.

THURSTONE, LOUIS LEON, (thûr'ston), prof. psychology; b. Chicago, Ill., May 29, 1887; s. Conrad and Sophie (Stroth) T.; M.E., Cornell U., 1912; Ph.D., U. of Chicago, 1917; Ph.D. (hon.), U. Gothenburg, Sweden, 1954; m. Thelma Gwinn, July 17, 1924; children—Robert Leon, Conrad Gwinn, Fredrick Louis. Prof. of psychology, Carnegie Inst. Tech., 1915-23, University of Chicago since 1924; psychologist Inst. for Govt. Research, Washington, D.C., 1923-24, Charles F. Grey distinguished service prof., 1938; now research prof. and dir. psychometric lab. U. of N.C.; vis. prof. of Frankfurt, Germany, 1948; vis. prof. University of Stolkholm, Sweden, 1954. Author of trade tests for occupational classification in U.S. Army, World War I; mem. com. on classification of mil. personnel, Adj. Gen.'s Office, World War II. Editor of intelligence tests of Am. Council on Edn. Recipient Centennial Award Northwestern U., 1951. Fellow A.A.A.S.; hon. fellow British Psychol. Society, Swedish Psychol. Soc.; mem. Am. Philosophical Society, Am. Psychological Assn. (member council; pres. 1932-33), Soc. Promotion Engring. Edn. (council), Nat. Acad. Sciences, Academy of Arts and Sciences, Sigma Xi, Eta Kappa Nu, Phi Delta Kappa, Acacia. Mason. Clubs: Quadrangle. Literary (Chgo.); Cosmos (Washington). Author: The Learning Curve Equation, 1918; The Nature of Intelligence, 1924; Fundamentals of Statistics, 1924; The Measurement of Attitude, 1929; The Vectors of Mind, 1935; Primary Mental Abilities, 1938; (with Thelma Gwinn Thurstone) Factorial Studies of Intelligence, 1941; A Factorial Study of Perception, 1944; Multiple Factor Analysis, 1947. Home: 400 Laurel Hill Rd., Chapel Hill, N.C. Died Sept. 29, 1955.

THWING, CHARLES BURTON, physicist; b. Theresa, N.Y., Mar. 9, 1860; s. Charles Grandison and Harriet (Corbin) T.; A.B., Northwestern U., 1888, A.M., 1890; A.M., Ph.D., U. of Bonn, 1894; m. Lucy Blakeslee White, at Cazenovia, N.Y., Aug. 3, 1893; children—Myra, John Burton, Philip Lenard, Alice Cushing. Instr. physics, Northwestern U. Acad., 1888-93, U. of Wis., 1894-96; prof. physics, Knox Coll., 1896-1901, Syracuse U., 1901-05; research work, Western Reserve U., 1905-06; mfr. pyrometers since Nov., 1906, also mfr. paper testing apparatus; pres. Thwing-Albert Instrument Co. Has made several inventions in electricity and metallurgy. Author: Exercises in Physical Measurement (with Louis Winslow Austin), 1896; An Elementary Physics, 1900. Contbr. to scientific jours. Home: 45 W. Tulpehocken St. Office: 3339 Lancaster Av., Phila., Pa.

TIBBETTS, FREDERICK HORACE, civ. and cons. engr.; b. Oshkosh, Wis., Apr. 28, 1882; s. Horace Albert and Amanda (Arnold) T.; grad. Commercial Dept., U. of Pacific, 1901, B.S., Coll. of Liberal Arts, 1903, M.S., 1905; B.S., U. of Calif., 1904, M.S., 1906; m. Flora Macdonald; 1 son, Reginald. Began practice civ. engring., San Francisco, Calif., 1905; asst. instr., later asst. prof. civ. engring., U. of Calif., 1906-11; mem. Haviland & Tibbetts, civ. engrs., later Haviland, Dozier & Tibbetts Constrn. Co., 1909-17; civ. and cons. engr., San Francisco, 1917—; chief engr. Nev. Irrigation Dist., Sacramento River West Side Levee Dist., Linden Irrigation Dist., Knights Landing Drainage Dist., Anchorage Light & Power Co., Reclamation dists. 108 and 2047; cons. engr. Pershing County and Roosevelt water conservation dists. of Nev. and Ariz., Santa Clara Valley Water Conservation District. Republican. Methodist. Mason. Home: Berkeley, Calif. Died Aug. 2, 1938.

TIFFANY, (LEWIS) HANFORD, educator; b. Lawrenceville, Ill., July 20, 1894; s. Charles Edward and Mary Frances (Hull) T.; grad. Eastern Ill. State Tchrs. Coll., 1915, Ph.D. (hon.), 1949; B.S., U. Chgo., 1920; M.S., Ohio State U., 1921, Ph.D., 1923; m. Loel Zehner, Sept. 10, 1921. Began as tchr. in pub. schs., 1912; instr. botany, O. State U., 1920-25, asst. prof., 1925-28, asso. prof., 1928-32, prof., 1932-37; prof. botany, chmn. dept. botany Northwestern U., 1937-49, William Deering prof. botany, 1945-62, William Deering prof. botany emeritus, 1962—; hon. asso. in cryptogamic botany, Chgo. Natural History Mus., 1944—; hon. life mem. Centro Italiano de Studi Anglo-Franco-Americani, 1946—; prof. algology, Stone Lab., summers 1928-36; bus. mgr., Ohio Jour. Sci., 1920-30. Mem. Ill. Bd. Natural Resources and Conservation, vice chmn., sec.; v.p. phycology sect. 8th Internat. Bot. Congress, Paris, 1954. Served as 2d lt. F.A., U.S. Army, 1918. Patron, Smithsonian Inst. Fellow A.A.A.S., Ohio Acad. Sci.; mem. Am. Soc. Naturalists, Bot. Soc. Am., Ecol. Soc. Am., Am. Microscopic Soc. (pres. 1934), Limnol. Soc. Am. (pres. 1939), Am. Soc. Plant Physiology, Am. Soc. Plant Taxonomy, Chgo. Acad. Scis. (bd. govs. 1941—; hon. life mem.), Ill. Acad. Sci., Phycological Soc. Am. (pres. 1949), Cowles Bot. Soc., Sigma Xi, Gamma Alpha. Republican. Clubs: University (Evanston); Chaos (Chgo.). Author: The Oedogoniaceae, 1930; Work Book in General Botany (with E. N. Transeau and H. C. Sampson), 1934; Algae, the Grass of Many Waters, 1938; Text Book of Botany (with E. N. Transeau H. C. Sampson), 1940; The Study of Plants, 1944; chpt. on ecology in Manual of Phycology, 1951; The Algae of Illinois (with M. E. Britton), 1952; Life (with G. G. Simpson and C. Pittendrigh), 1957. Editor: Culturing of Algae (with J. Brunel, G. W. Prescott), 1951. Mem. editorial bd. Ecology, 1950-52. Contbr. to sci. jours. Home: Route 3, Lawrenceville, Ill. Office: Northwestern U., Evanston, Ill. Died Mar. 13, 1965; buried Derr Cemetery, Lawrenceville.

TIFFANY, ROSS KERR, cons. engr.; b. Union, Ia., June 11, 1879; s. Walter John and Harriet Emily (Kerr) T.; B.C.E., Cornell Coll., Mt. Vernon, Ia., 1901, C.E., 1905; m. Ella Eichar, July 3, 1903; children—Ross K., June. Maintenance engr., later chief engr. and mgr. for pvt. corp., Yakima Project, Wash., 1901-10; supt. and project mgr. Yakima Project, U.S. Reclamation Service, 1910-20; mgr. Spokane Valley Irrigation System, and cons. engr. on irrigation and drainage, 1920-25; state hydraulic engr., Wash., 1925-29; cons. engr. on hydroelectric power and irrigation. Mem. U.S. Com. on Conservation and Adminstrn. of Pub. Domain, 1929-30; exec. officer Wash. State Planning Council, 1934—. Conglist. Mason. Home: Olympia, Wash. Died June 1, 1939.

TILDEN, CHARLES JOSEPH, civil engr.; b. Brookline, Mass., Oct. 3, 1873; s. George Thomas and Alice Olmstead (Butler) T.; S.B. in Civ. Engring., Harvard, 1896; hon. M.A., Yale, 1919; m. Mabel Katherine Myers, Oct. 14, 1902 (died Mar. 8, 1940); children—Elinor (Mrs. H.G. Hitchcock), Carol (Mrs. D.L. Morris); m. 2d, Linda Palmer Littlejohn of Sydney, Australia, Apr. 6, 1942. Assistant instructor engring., Harvard University, from 1896 to 1897; assistant engineer New York Rapid Transit Commn., 1897-1903; instr. civ. engring., Cornell U., 1903-05; instr., asst. prof. and jr. prof. civ. engring., U. of Mich., 1905-11, prof. and head dept. of engring. mechanics, 1911-13; prof. civ. engring., Johns Hopkins, 1913-19; Strathcona prof. engring. mechanics, Yale, 1919-40, emeritus, 1940—, and fellow of Branford Coll., 1933—. Mem. Conn. Highway Safety Commission, 1936-42. Capt. Engr. O.R.C. 1917-37. With Signal Corps, U.S. Army, 1942-44. Mem. Am. Soc. C.E.; fellow A.A.A.S.; mem. Sigma Xi, Phi Beta Kappa, Omicron Delta Kappa; hon. mem. Tau Beta Pi. Author of various articles in mags., etc. Clubs: Harvard (New York); Graduate (New Haven). Home: Westport, Conn. Office: Strathcona Hall, Yale Univ., New Haven, Conn. Died Nov. 15, 1959.

TILDEN, JOSEPHINE ELIZABETH, botanist; b. Davenport, Ia.; d. Henry and Elizabeth Aldrich (Field) Tilden; B.S., U. Minn., 1895, M.S., 1896. Prof. botany, U. Minn., to 1938; studied and collected algae in Yellowstone Park, western United States and Canada, Hawaiian Islands, Society Islands, New Zealand, Australia, Japan, and Minnesota Seaside Station, summers 1901-07, Puget Sound Biol. Sta., summer 1918. Delegate to 1st Pan-Pacific Sci. Conf., Honolulu, 1920; 2d Pan-Pacific Congress, Melbourne, Sydney, Australia, 1923; 3d Congress, Tokyo, Japan, 1926; 1st Pan-Pacific Food Conservation Congress, Honolulu,

1924. Author: (or editor) American Algae, 1894—; Postelsia (the year-book of the Minn. Seaside Sta., 2 vols.), 1902, 1906; South Pacific Algae, 1909—; Myxophyceae of North America, 1910; South Pacific Plants, 1912—; Index Algarum Universalis, 1915—; Bibliography of Pacific Ocean Algae, 1920; Our Richest Source of Vitamins, 1928; A Classification of the Algae, 1933; Standardization of Method of Drawing Algae for Publication, 1934; South Pacific Plants, second series, 1934-35; The Algae and Their Life Relations, 1935-37. Made trip around world with ten grad. students, collecting algae in Australia and New Zealand, 1934, 35. Fellow A.A.A.S., Am. Geog. Soc.; mem. Bot. Soc. Am., Am. Soc. Naturalists, Am. Microscopical Soc., Nat. Geog. Soc., Bull Torrey Botany Club, Fla. Acad. Science, Sigma Xi. Home: Golden Bough Colony, Hesperides, Lake Wales, Fla. Deceased.

TILESTON, WILDER, prof. medicine; b. Concord, Mass., Jan. 22, 1875; s. John Boies and Mary Wilder (Foote) T.; A.B., Harvard, 1895, M.D., 1899; post-grad. work, Vienna and Gratz, Austria; m. Clare Williams, Nov. 18, 1903 (died 1905); m. 2d, Ethel Walker, d. of Rev. Newman Smyth, June 20, 1912; children—Wilder (dec.), Thomas Newman, Anne, David Edsall (dec.), Peter Ayer. Intern, Mass. Gen. Hosp., Boston, 1899-1900; practiced in Boston, 1902-09; asst. in clin. chemistry, Harvard Med. Sch., 1902-03, in clin. medicine, 1906-08; dir. Harvard Summer Sch. of Medicine, 1909; asst. visiting physician, Long Island Hosp., Boston, 1902-09; consulting physician, Mass. Charitable Eye and Ear Infirmary, 1905-09; asst. prof. medicine, Yale Med. Sch., 1909-19, and clin. prof. of med. since Sept. 1919, emeritus, 1943; cons. phys. Meriden Hosp., Griffin Hosp. (Derby), New Haven Hosp., Grace Hosp., Middlesex Hosp., Norwalk Hosp., chief of staff, Grace Hosp., 1926-29. Lecturer in medicine, Yale Med. Sch., 1943-46. Mem. Assn. American Physicians, Am. Med. Assn. (sec. sect. on practice of medicine, 1909-11, chmn. 1912), Am. Soc. Clin. Investigation (sec. 1910-12), Conn. State Med. Soc. (sec. 1912-13), Interurban Clinical Club. Republican. Unitarian. Club: Graduate. Home: 15 Edgehill Road. Office: 442 Temple St., New Haven CT

TILGHMAN, RICHARD ALBERT, chemist; b. Phila., May 24, 1824; s. Benjamin and Anna Maria (McMurtrie) T.; B.A., U. Pa., 1841; studied chemistry under James C. Booth, Phila.; m. Susan Price Toland, 1860, 5 children. Wrote and delivered paper On the Decomposing Power of Water at High Temperatures (1st systematic study of hydration) before Am. Philos. Soc., 1847; developed process of hydrolysis for extracting acid from animal fat; produced caustic soda through hydrolysis; developed processes for mfg. potassium dichromate, paper pulp, and for producing gas from coal; sold discoveries to various industries in U.S. and Eng.; developed sandblast process for forming articles made of hard, brittle materials; dir. George Richards & Co., Ltd., mfrs. machine tools, also Tilghman Sand Blast Co., nr. Manchester, Eng. Died Mar. 24, 1899.

TILLMAN, SAMUEL ESCUE, army officer; b. near Shelbyville, Tenn., Oct. 2, 1847; s. Lewis and Mary Catherine (Davidson) T.; grad. U.S. Mil. Acad., 1869; hon. M.A., Yale, 1906; m. Clara Williams, Apr. 20, 1887; 1 dau., Mrs. Katharine Tillman Martin. Second lt. 4th Arty., June 15, 1869; on frontier duty in Kan., 1869-70; asst. prof., 1870-73, and 1879-80, prof. chemistry, mineralogy and geology, with rank of col., 1880-1911, U.S. Mil. Acad.; retired by operation of law, Oct. 2, 1911; recalled to active service, June 6, 1917, and assigned to duty as supt. U.S. Mil. Acad. until June 12, 1919; brig. gen. U.S. Army retired, Mar. 4, 1919. D.S.M., June 11, 1919 "for especially meritorious and conspicuous services as supt. U.S. Mil. Acad. during the period of the emergency." Asst. astronomer U.S. Transit of Venus Expdn., Tasmania, 1874-75; instr. in mechanics, U.S. Mil. Acad., 1875-76; asst. engr. on the U.S. (Wheeler) explorations west of the 100th meridian, 1873-74 and 1876-79. Author: Essential Principles of Chemistry, 1884; Elementary Lessons in Heat, 1889; Elementary Mineralogy, 1894; Descriptive General Chemistry, 1899; Important Minerals and Rocks, 1900. Address: Century Assn., 7 W. 43d St., New York, N.Y. Died June 24, 1942.

TILLOTSON, EDWIN WARD, chemist; b. Farmington, Conn., Feb. 28, 1884; s. Edwin Ward and Mary Lewis (Root) T.; B.A., Yale, 1906; Loomis fellow, 1907-08, Silliman fellow, 1908-09, Ph.D., 1909; m. Lida Charles LeSuer, July 24, 1913; children—Mary Katherine (Mrs. Eugene L. Combs), Edwin Ward. Research fellow dept. indsl. research U. Kan., 1909-13; asst. dir. Mellon Inst. Indsl. Research, U. Pitts., 1913-51, dir. research, 1951—; specialist in chemistry and tech. glass and ceramics and indsl. research mgmt. Awarded Albert V. Bleininger medal Am. Ceramic Soc., 1949. Mem. Am. Chem. Soc. (chmn. Pitts. sect., 1920), Am. Ceramic Soc. (sec. glass div., 1919-21; v.p. 1922; pres. 1925; fellow, 1931), Am. Optical Soc., Soc. Glass Tech., Soc. Rheology, Sigma Xi, Alpha Chi Sigma, Phi Lambda Upsilon. Club: University. Republican. Mason. Home: 505 S. Murtland Av., Pitts. 15208. Died May 19, 1965; buried Allegheny Cemetery, Pitts.

TILLSON, GEORGE WILLIAM, engineer; b. Thomaston, Me., Dec. 18, 1852; s. Perez and Harriet (Collins) T.; C.E., Bowdoin College, 1877, Sc.D., 1910; m. Mary E. Abbott, Oct. 5, 1887; 1 dau., Madalene Abbott. Asst. engr. in charge sewer constrn., Memphis, Tenn., 1880; made plans and constructed sewer system, Kalamazoo, Mich., 1880-81; in charge paving and sewer constrn., Omaha, Neb., 1881-87; city engr., 1887-92; asst. engr. in charge pavements, 1895-1902, Brooklyn; chief engr. Bur. of Highways, Borough of Brooklyn, 1902-07; chief engr. Bur. of Highways, Borough of Manhattan, New York City, 1907-11; cons. engr. Dept. of Pub. Works, Borough of Brooklyn, N.Y., May 1, 1911-July 1918; actg. commr. of pub. works, Borough of Brooklyn, 1913-14; pres. bd. dirs. La Grange Pub. Library, 1936—. Mem. Commn. of engrs. of Am. Soc. C.E., to visit France, 1918, to confer with a French congress for reconstruction work after the war. Author: Street Pavements and Paving Materials, 1900. Also 4 sections of American Highway Engineers' Pocket Book. Contbr. several papers on paving subjects to Proceedings Am. Soc. Municipal Improvements, and to engineering periodicals. Home: La Grange, Ill. Died May 13, 1940.

TILNEY, FREDERICK, neurologist; b. Brooklyn, N.Y., June 4, 1875; s. Thomas J. and Katharine (Hutchinson) T.; A.B., Yale, 1897; M.D., Long Island Coll. Hosp., 1903; Ph.D., Columbia, 1912; m. Camilla Hurley, June 15, 1903. Practiced in N.Y. City, 1905—; prof. neurology, Coll. Phys. and Surg. (Columbia), 1914—; med. dir. New York Neurol. Inst.; attending neurologist and consultant to Roosevelt, Presbyn., Brooklyn, Methodist Episcopal, Kings County, Coney Island and Greenwich hosps. Mem. bd. visitors N.Y. State Training Sch. for Boys (Warwick). Fellow Am. Philos. Soc., N.Y. Zoöl. Soc., N.Y. Acad. Science. Republican. Home: New York, N.Y. Died Aug. 7, 1938.

TILTON, EDWARD LIPPINCOTT, architect, archaeologist; b. New York, Oct. 19, 1861; s. Benjamin W. and Mary (Baker) T.; Chappaqua Mountain Inst.; École des Beaux Arts, Paris, 1887-90; m. Mary Eastman Bigelow, June 5, 1901. In practice as architect, 1891—; also archaeologist; in Greece, 1895-96, for Archaeol. Inst. America, to restore site of Hera (Argive Heraeum). Fellow Am. Inst. of Architects. Awarded gold medal, Paris Expn., 1900; gold medal, Am. Inst. Architects, 1925; medals—Buffalo Expn., 1901, St. Louis Expn., 1904. Wrote chapters: "Greece, Architecture of," in Dictionary of Architecture (Russell Sturgis), 1901; "Architecture of the Argive Heraeum," in The Argive Heraeum, 1902. Home: Scarsdale, N.Y. Died Jan. 5, 1933.

TILTON, JAMES, congressman; b. Kent County, Del., June 1, 1745; M.B., Coll. of Phila. (now U. Pa.), 1768, M.D., 1771. Served as surgeon Del. Regt., Continental Army, 1776; in charge of mil. hosps. at Princeton, Trenton (N.J.), New Windsor (Md.), 1777-80 (to improve san. conditions built "hosp. huts" for each 6 patients); promoted sr. hosp. physician, surgeon, 1780; operated hosp. at Williamsburg, Va. during Yorktown campaign; mem. Continental Congress, also Del. Ho. of Reps., 1783-85; govt. commr. loans, Del., 1785-1801; physician and surgeon-gen. U.S. Army, 1813-15, made tour inspection along No. frontier instituting widespread san. reforms. Author: Economical Observations on Military Hospitals: and the Prevention and Cure of Diseases Incident to an Army, 1813; Regulations for the Medical Department, 1814. Died nr. Wilmington, Del., May 14, 1822; buried Wilmington and Brandywine Cemetery.

TIMBY, THEODORE RUGGLES, inventor, author; b. Dover, Dutchess County, N.Y., Apr. 5, 1819; s. George W. and Sarah Johnson T., of Pittsfield, Mass.; ed. pub. schs.; hon. degrees; A.M., Madison U., 1867; S.D., U. of Troy, O., 1882; LL.D., Iowa Wesleyan U., 1891; m. Charlotte M. Ware, 1844. Invented floating dry-dock, 1836; invented, 1841, the revolving turret used on the Monitor, and battleships; invented practical method of raising sunken vessels, 1841, the Am. turbine waterwheel or motor, 1844, and in 1857, the first commercially portable 33-inch mercurial barometer. From 1861 to 1891, invented and patented, at home and abroad, a system of coast defenses known as follows: The sighting and firing of heavy guns by electricity; the tower and shield; the cordon across the channel; the planetary and subterranean systems, with 15 other modifications of the turret system; invented and patented improvements in pneumatic and hydraulic power; also a new prin. in Turbine water-wheels or motors. In 1890 the N.Y. legislature, by unanimous concurrent resolution, and the judges of N.Y. Supreme Ct. and Ct. of Appeals, by petition, asked Congress to give him nat. recognition. Author: Beyond; Stellar Worlds; Lighted Lore for Gentle Folk. Address: Brooklyn, N.Y. Died 1909.

TIMKEN, HENRY, inventor, mfr.; b. nr. Bremen, Germany, Aug. 16, 1831; s. Jacob Timken; m. Fredericka Heinzelmann, 1855, 5 children. Came to U.S., 1841; apprentice and journeyman wagon maker, 1847-55; owner-operator carriage factory, St. Louis, 1855-60, 65-87, 94-97; prospected for gold nr. Pike's Peak, 1860; served as capt. 13th Regt., Mo. Militia, 1861-64; patented carriage Spring (Timken Spring), 1877, tapered roller bearing, 1898; organized Timken Roller Bearing Axle Co., Canton, O.; pres. Carriage Builders Nat. Assn., 1896-97. Died San Diego, Cal., March 16, 1909.

TIMME, WALTER, (tim'me), physician; b. New York, N.Y., Feb. 24, 1874; s. Frederick and Emma (Wirth) T.; B.S., Coll. of City of New York, 1893; M.D., Columbia, 1897; grad. student, U. of Berlin, 1912-13; m. Ida Helen Haar, June 27, 1901; m. second Anne C. Auwell, July 28, 1951. Began as physician, 1897; was chief of clinic, Vanderbilt Clinic, N.Y.; sr. attending neurologist, mil. dir. neuroendocrine dept. and consultant in endocrinology, Neurol. Inst. of New York; prof. clin. neurology, Columbia. Fellow N.Y. Acad. Medicine; founder member Assn. for Research in Nervous and Mental Diseases (pres.); mem. Assn. for Study Internal Secretions (pres.), N.Y. Endocrine Soc. (pres.), Am. Neurol. Assn., Assn. of Alumni Coll. of City of N.Y. (pres.), Phi Beta Kappa, Phi Delta Theta, Phi Beta Kappa Associates. Townsend Harris Medal 1948. Clubs: Columbia University, City College, Marshall Chess (New York); Highland Country (Garrison, N.Y.). Author: Lectures in Endocrinology, 1923. Contbr. to volumes of Assn. for Research in Nervous and Mental Diseases; also to med. jours. Home: Cold Spring, N.Y. Died Feb. 12, 1956; buried Timme Mausoleum, Cold Spring.

TIMMERMAN, ARTHUR HENRY, electrical engineer; b. New York, N.Y., May 1, 1871; s. John Henry and Celia (Lussen) T.; B.S., Coll. City of N.Y., 1891; M.E. in elec. engring., Cornell U., 1892. M.M.E., 1893; m. Mary E. Pearson, July 25, 1894; 1 son, Arthur Pearson; married 2d, Rooney G. Ousley, June 21, 1941. Instr. in physics, Washington University, St. Louis, 1893-94; prof. physics and elec. engring., Sch. of Mines and Metallurgy (U. of Mo.), Rolla, Mo., 1894-99; engr., 1899, chief engr., 1908-19, v.p. and chief engr., 1919-26, v.p. in charge engring. and mfg. since 1926, also dir., Wagner Electric Corp., St. Louis; dir. Wagner Brake Service Co., Ltd., Industry mem. St. Louis Regional Labor Bd., 1933-34. Mem. Liberty Truck Design Com. Second v.p., 1936-38, 1st v.p., 1938-40, pres., 1940-42, Nat. Metal Trades Assn. (mem. exec. com. 1936-44); pres., 1940-42, mem. exec. com. 1936-44); pres., 1940-42, mem. council, 1936-46, Acad. of Science of St. Louis; mem. exec. com., 1942-45, mem. council, 1937-45, Asso. Industries of Missouri. Mem. exec. com. St. Louis Safety Council, 1939-41; mem. indsl. com. Y.M.C.A., 1939-42. Fellow Am. Inst. E.E.; mem. Soc. Automotive Engrs., Nat. Electric Light Assn., Nat. Elec. Mgrs. Assn., St. Louis Acad. Science, Electric Power Club (pres. 1923-25), Phi Gamma Delta, Sigma Xi. Republican. Clubs: Engineers, Cornell, Bellerive Country (St. Louis). Home: 40 Ridgetop, Richmond Heights 17, Mo. Office: 6400 Plymouth Av., St Louis MO

TIMOSHENKO, STEPHEN, univ. prof., author; b. near Kiev, Russia, Dec. 23, 1878; s. Prokop and Jozefina (Sarnavskaja) T.; grad. Inst. of Engrs. of Ways of Communication, Russia, 1901; D.Sc., Lehigh U., 1936; D.Eng., Michigan University, 1938; D.Eng., l'Ecole Polytechnique, Zurich, 1948, Technische Hochschule, Munchen, 1948, University of Zagreb, 1956; LL.D., University of Glasgow, 1951; married Alexander Archangelskaja, March 3, 1902;children—Anna (Mrs. F. Hetzelt), Gregor, Marine (Mrs. J. N. Goodier). Came to United States, 1922, naturalized, 1927. Instructor Inst. of Engr. of Ways of Communication, 1902-03; asst. prof. Polytechnical Inst., St. Petersburg, Russia, 1903-06; prof. Polytechnical Inst., Kiev, 1906-11, Electrotechnical and Polytechnical Inst., St. Petersburg, 1912-17, Polytechnical Inst., Zagreb, Yugoslavia, 1920-22; research engr. Westinghouse Electric and Mfg. Co., Pittsburgh, 1923-27; prof. of engring. mechanics, U. of Mich., 1927-36; prof. of theoretical and applied mechanics Stanford, 1936-44, emeritus. Corr. mem. Acad. Sciences (Russia), Acad. Tech. Sciences (Poland). Corr. mem. French Acad. Sciences since 1939. Mem. American Philos. Soc., 1939; mem. Nat. Acad. Sciences, 1940. Foreign mem. Royal Soc. of London, since 1944, Accademia Nationale del Lincei, Rome, since 1948. Mem. Greek Orthodox Ch. Author or co-author books relating to field since 1925; also articles in profl. jours. Home: Wuppertal-Elbenfeld Germany Died May 30, 1972.

TINGLE, JOHN BISHOP, chemist, educator; b. Sheffield, Eng., Nov. 12, 1866; s. Alfred and Mary Elizabeth (Bishop) T.; ed. pvt. sch., Sheffield Royal Grammar Sch.; Owens Coll., Manchester, Eng., 1884-87; Ph.D., U. Munich, 1899; married. Teacher of chemistry, 1889—; came to U.S., 1896; professor chemistry, Ill. Coll., Sept. 1901-04. Asst. in charge organic chemical laboratory, Johns Hopkins U., and sub-editor Am. Chem. Journal, Sept., 1904—. Fellow Chem. Soc., England, German Chem. Soc., Am. Chem. Soc., A.A.A.S. Translated and enlarged: General Organic Chemistry (E. Hjelt), 1890, Spectrum Analysis (J. Landauer), 1898, Determination of Radicles in Carbon Compounds (H. Meyer), 1899, 2d edit., 1903, Application of Some General Reactions to Investigations in Organic Chemistry (Lassar-Cohn), 1904. Address: Johns Hopkins University, Baltimore. Died 1918.

TIPTON, ROYCE JAY, civil engr.; b. Litchfield, Ill., Mar. 23, 1893; s. Basil Foster and Sarah (Calvert) T.; student U. Colo., 1915-17, C.E. (hon.), 1940; m. Natalie Knight, Aug. 25, 1919 (dec. Oct. 1961); children—John Knight, Robert Royce, Natalie Jean (Mrs. Thomas Milaskey); m. 2d, Jincy Hunt, July 30, 1962. Pvt. practice civil engring., Monte Vista, Colo., 1922-28, Denver, 1933—; designing engr. Rio Mante Project, Mexico, 1928; spl. engr. interstate water problems and water resources studies Colo. Engr.'s Office, 1929-33; assisted negotiation interstate compacts Upper Colo. River, Pecos River, Costella Creek and Rio Grande, also negotiation Mexican Water Treaty, 1944, Indus Water Treaty, 1960; mem. bd. cons. Pecos River Joint Investigations, 1939-42, Nat. Resources Planning Bd., 1935-42, canal linings U.S. Bur. Reclamation, 1948; mem. task force water resources and power 2d Hoover Commn., 1953-55; cons. Colo. Water Conservation Bd., 1937-58, Colo. Planning Commn., 1933-37, Climax Molybdenum Co., 1935-52; tech. adviser Internat. Boundary and Water Commn., U.S. and Mexico, 1938—; architect-engr. War Dept. projects, World War II. Served to 2d lt., C.E., U.S. Army, World War I; AEF in France and Germany. Recipient Norlin medal U. Colo., 1958. Mem. Am. Geophys. Union, Soc. Am. Mil. Engrs., Colo. Engring. Council (Gold Medal award 1963), Colo. Soc. Engrs., Am. Soc. C.E. (v.p. 1965-67), Internat. Commn. Irrigation and Drainage (v.p. 1964-67), Internat. Commn. Large Dams, Colo. Hist. Soc., Am. Legion, Alpha Sigma Phi, Tau Beta Pi, Chi Epsilon. Mason. Clubs: Denver Athletic, Denver, University (Denver); Metropolitan (Washington). Home: 4570 E. Yale Av., Denver 80222. Office: 831 14th St., Denver 80202. Died Dec. 1967.

TISELIUS, ARNE (WILHELM KAURIN), biochemist; b. Stockholm, Sweden, Aug. 10, 1902; s. Hans J. and Rosa (Kaurin) R.; Dr. phil., U. Upsala, 1931; student Princeton, 1934-35; Dr. honoris causa, univs. of Paris, Bologna, Glasgow, Madrid and Cambridge, Caroline Inst., Stockholm, U. Oxford, Oslo U., U. Lyon, U. Cal., Berkeley, Gustavus Adolphus College; m. Ingrid Margareta Dalen, Nov. 26, 1930; children—Eva, Per. Research asst. in phys. chemistry U. Upsala, 1925, became asst. prof., 1930, prof. biochemistry, 1938-68. Mem. nat. sci. research com. Atomic Energy Research Com., Com. for Reformation of the Univs., Med. Research Council of Sweden, 1944-47; president Swedish Natural Science Research Council, 1946-50; vice president Nobel Foundation, 1947-60, pres., 1960-64, chmn. chemistry com.; head Nobel Inst. of Swedish Royal Acad. Scis.; mem. sci. adv. council Swedish Govt.; pres. Internat. Union Pure and Applied Chemistry, 1951-55. Awarded Nobel Prize in chemistry, 1948. Hon. fellow Royal Inst. Chemistry London; hon. member French Chem. Soc., Swedish Society Physicians, Harvey Soc. N.Y., N.Y. Acad. Scis., N.Y. Acad. Medicine, Royal Inst. Great Britain, Chem. Soc. London, Internat. Assn. Allergists Zurich, Real Sociedad Espanola de Fisica y Quimica Madrid, Soc. Sci. Helsingfors, Consejo Super. de Investigaciones Scientificas Madrid, Am. Acad. Arts and Sci., Royal Dutch, Swiss chem. socs., National Acad. Scis. India; fgn. mem. Royal Soc. and Soc. Chem. Industry London, American Philosophical Society; corresponding member Society Philomat. Paris, Academie des Ciencias de Lisboa, Acad. des Sciences, Paris; mem. Pontificia Sci. Acad. of Vatican, Royal Swedish Acad. Sci., Nobel Com. Chemistry, Royal Acad. Engring. Scis., Royal Soc. Sci. Upsala, Royal Soc. Scis. and Letters Gothenburg, Nat. Acad. Scis. Washington, Royal Danish Sci. Soc., Copenhagen and Accademia Nazionale De quaranta Roma, Polish Acad. Sci., Warsaw, Rumanian Acad. Scis. (hon.); fgn. mem. Czeckoslovak Acad. Sci.; hon. mem. Soc. Electropheresis, Tokyo, Indian Inst. Scis. Liberal. Luth. Home: Upsala Sweden Died Oct. 29, 1971.

TITCOMB, HARVEY BURGESS, ry. pres.; b. Indianapolis, Ind., Dec. 10, 1871; s. Daniel and Emma (Brown) T.; prep. edn., high sch., Indianapolis; student Cogswell Poly. Coll., San Francisco, Calif.; m. Mabel Havens, of San Francisco, Aug. 25, 1900; 1 dau., Mildred Havens. Began with S.P. Co., 1889, successively telegraph operator, draftsman, asst. engr. and roadmaster Western div., to 1900, roadmaster and asst. engr., 1900-05, div. engr., 1905-08, dist. engr. Los Angeles and San Francisco, 1908-17, supt. Stockton div., 1917-18; v.p. and gen. mgr. Pacific Electric Ry. Co., Los Angeles, 1918-21; pres. S.P. R.R. Co. of Mexico, 1921-33, retired. Address: 600 N. June St., Los Angeles CA

TITCOMB, JOHN WHEELOCK, fish culturist; b. Farmington, N.H., Feb. 24, 1860; s. George Alfred and Mary Elizabeth Lemist (Lancaster) T.; grad. Phillips Exeter Acad., 1880; passed examination for Harvard with honors; m. Martha Ross, Dec. 22, 1896; children—Elizabeth, Jonathan Ross. In employ of Howe Scale Co., 1880-93, asst. supt., 1888-93; chmn. Vt. Fish and Game Commn., 1891-1902; chief of Div. of Fish Culture, U.S. Bur. of Fisheries, 1902-09; state fish and game commr. of Vt., 1910-16, also pvt. sec. to Theodore N. Vail; state fish culturist, New York, 1916-21; supt. Conn. State Bd. of Fisheries and Game, 1922—. Employed by Argentine Govt., 1903-04, to explore waters of the country; built first hatchery in S.A., and introduced several species of salmonidae, trout, etc. Republican. Conglist. Mason. Home: Bloomfield, Conn. Died Jan. 26, 1932.

TITTMANN, OTTO HILGARD, geodesist; b. Belleville, Ill., Aug. 20, 1850; s. Edward and Rosa (Hilgard) T.; ed. pub. schools, St. Louis, 1859-66; D.Sc., Stevens Inst. and Washington U., 1915; LL.D., George Washington U., 1915; m. Kate Trowbridge Wilkins, 1880; 1 son, Charles Trowbrige. With Coast and Geodetic Survey, 1867—; asst. astronomer Transit of Venus Expdn. to Japan, 1874; in charge various surveying expdns. E. and W. coast of U.S.; in charge of weights and measures, 1889-93; sent to Paris, 1890, to bring to U.S. the Nat. standard metre and to inspect weights and measures offices, London, Paris and Berlin; U.S. del. to Internat. Geodetic Conf., Berlin, 1895. Mem. Permanent Commn. Internat. Geodetic Assn., 1900; asst. in charge U.S. Coast and Geod. Survey Office, 1895-99, asst. supt., 1899-1900, supt., 1900-Mar. 1915. Apptd. to represent U.S. in demarkation of boundary between Alaska and Canada under modus vivendi of Oct. 1899; U.S. commr. Alaska Boundary, 1904, and of Northern Boundaries, excepting Great Lakes, under Treaty of 1908, resigned 1915. Fellow Philos. Soc. Washington (pres. 1899); mem. Am. Philos. Soc.; pres. Nat. Geog. Soc., 1915-19, Washington Acad. Sciences, 1913. Contbr. to publs. of Survey, also geod. and meteorological articles in various jours. Home: Leesburg, Va. Died Aug. 21, 1938.

TITUS, PAUL, obstetrician, gynecologist; b. Batavia, N.Y., May 6, 1885; s. Rev. John Wentworth and Elma Margaret (Titus) Sanborn; adopted by maternal grandparents, Rev. and Mrs. Wicks Smith Titus; M.D., Yale, 1908; m. Mary Cushing. Asst. Universitäts Frauenklinik, Heidelberg, Germany, 1908-10; asst. in obstetrics, Johns Hopkins Hosp., Baltimore, 1910-11; resident obstetrician and gynecologist, Magee Hosp., Pittsburgh, 1911-12; now obstetrician and gynecologist, St. Margaret Memorial Hosp.; cons. obstetrician and gynecologist, Shadyside Hosp. Sec.-treas. and dir. Am. Bd. of Obstetrics and Gynecology; sec.-treas. Adv. Bd. for Med. Specialists, 1933-41, v.p., 1943-45, pres., 1945-47; mem. adv. editorial bd., Am. Jour. Obstetrics and Gynecology; directing editor, Directory of Medical Specialists, 1937-47. Pres. the Assn. of Yale Alumni in Med., 1942-43. Special agt. for Naval Intelligence, and Mil. Intelligence Sect., War Dept., 1915-19. Consultant to surg. gen., U.S. Army, 1943-44; lt. comdr. to capt., M.C., U.S.N.R., attached to Professional Div., Bur. Med. and Surg., Navy Dept., Washington, 1944-45 and 1946; mem. Reserve Consultants Adv. Bd., Bur. Medicine and Surgery, Navy Dept., since 1946; mem. Armed Forces Medical Adv. Com., 1948-50. Awarded Navy Commendation Ribbon. Fellow Am. Coll. Surgeons, A.M.A., Am. Assn. of Obstetricians, Gynecologists and Abdominal Surgeons (exec. council 1929-35, and 1939-45; pres. 1937-38), Am. Gynecol. Soc. (v.p. 1948-49); mem. Med. Soc. State of Pa., Pittsburgh Acad. Medicine (pres. 1929-30), Allegheny County Med. Soc., Soc. Royale, Belge de Gynécologie et d'Obstetrique, Phi Gamma Delta, Nu-Sigma Nu. Awarded Commanders Cross, Order of Merit, Hungary, 1938. Author: Management of Obstetric Difficulties, 1937, 2d edit., 1940, 3d edit., 1945, 4th edit., 1950; Diseases of Women for the General Practitioner, 1937; Atlas of Obstetric Technic, 1943, 2d edit., 1949. Home: Schenley Apts., 5th Av. Office: Highland Bldg., Pittsburgh 6. Died June 28, 1951.

TOBOLSKY, ARTHUR VICTOR, educator; b. N.Y.C., May 16, 1919; s. William H. and Ruth (Lemanowitz) T.; B.A. (Albert Asher Green Meml. prize, John Dash Van Buren, Jr. prize math. 1940), Columbia, 1940; Ph.D. in Physics and Chemistry, Princeton, 1944; m. Dorothy Epstein, Jan. 18, 1943; children—Margo Linda, William Harris, Steven Bennett. Faculty Princeton, 1944-72, Eugene Higgins prof. chemistry, 1960-65, Russel Wellman Moore prof. chemistry, 1965-72; sci. cons. chem. companies; asso. editor Am. Scientist, 1958-72; research asso. Textile Research Inst., 1960-72; cons. editor John Wiley and Sons., 1960-72. Recipient Gold Medal award Soc. Plastics Engrs., 1970. Fellow Am. Phys. Soc. (Ford prize 1968); mem. Soc. Rheology (Bingham medal 1956), Am. Chem. Soc. (Witco award 1972), Sigma Xi. Author: Physical Chemistry of High Polymeric in Polymer chemistry Systems, 1950; Organic Peroxides, 1954; Properties and Structures of Polymers, 1960; Polymeric Sulfur and Related Polymers, 1965; Polymer Science and Materials, 1971; Synthetic Polymers, 1973; also numerous articles. Home: Princeton NJ Died Sept. 7, 1972.

TOCH, MAXIMILIAN (tok), chemist; b. New York, N.Y., July 17, 1864; s. Moses and Caroline (Levy) T.; spl. course in chemistry, New York U., 1882, LL.B., 1886; post grad. special course, Columbia U., 1896; Chem. E., Cooper Union; D.Sc., Peking Univ., 1924; m. Hermine E. Levy, Oct. 14, 1891; children—Elaine, Constance, Alam, Maxine. Lecturer on organic chemistry, Columbia, 1905-06; municipal lecturer on paint, Coll. City of New York, 1909; adj. prof. industrial chemistry, Cooper Union, 1919-24; hon. prof. chem. engring. and industrial chemistry, U. of Peking and Nat. Inst. Technology, China, 1924; prof. chemistry of artistic painting, Nat. Acad. Design, New York, 1924-36; pres. and chief chemist Toch Bros., Inc.; chmn. bd. Standard Varnish Works, mfrs. paints, varnishes, enamels and chemicals. Fellow A.A.A.S., Micros. Soc. of New York, Royal Photographic Soc., Chem. Soc. of London, Am. Inst. Chemists (pres.); mem. Am. Chem. Soc., Soc. Chem. Industry, Am. Inst. Chemical Engineers, Hon. member American Institute of Chemists. Society of American Magicians. In charge of camouflage, United States, World War I, and originator of Toch system of camouflage. Clubs: Chemists' (ex-pres.), Camera (New York); Cosmos (Washington). Author: Materials for Permanent Painting, 1911; How to Paint Permanent Pictures, 1921; Chemistry and Technology of Paints, 3d edit., 1925; Protection and Decoration of Concrete, 1930; Paint, Painting and Restoration, 1931, 2d edition, 1945. Home: 50 Central Park West, New York, N.Y. Office: 2600 Richmond Terrace, Staten Island, N.Y. Died May 26, 1946.

TODD, ALBERT MAY, chemist, polit. economist; b. farm nr. Nottawa, St. Joseph County, Mich., June 3, 1850; s. Alfred and Mary Ann (Hovey) T.; grad high sch., Sturgis, Mich.; student Northwestern U., traveled in foreign countries studying their institutions and govts.; m. Augusta M. Allman, Jan. 23, 1878; children—William Alfred, Albert John, Ethel May (Mrs. Edwin Le Grand Woodhams), Paul Harold, Allman. Organizer A. M. Todd & Co., 1889, retiring 1929 as pres. Todd Foundation, "for enlargement of happiness of mankind." Prohibition nominee for governor of Mich., 1894; mem. Congress, 1897-99. Pres. Pub. Ownership League of America from its foundation, 1916-22; mem. Am. Acad. Polit. and Social Science, Am. Proportional Representation League, Mich. Acad. of Science, Arts and Letters, Coöperative League America, Am. Civil Liberties Union, League for Industrial Democracy, Nat. Child Labor Com. Actively interested in progressive government; spent 14 months (1912-13) in foreign countries studying applied democracy—chiefly pub. ownership of pub. utilities, and coöperation; advocate of pub. ownership. Founded three art museums and library of 10,000 rare books and illuminated MSS. Author: Municipal Ownership in Europe and America, 1918; The Relation of Public Ownership to Social Justice and Democracy, 1920. Home: Kalamazoo, Mich. Died Oct. 1931.

TODD, DAVID, astronomer; b. Lake Ridge, N.Y., Mar. 19, 1855; s. Sereno Edwards and Rhoda (Peck) T.; A.B., Amherst, 1875, A.M., 1878; Ph.D., Washington and Jefferson Coll., 1888; m. Mabel Loomis, Mar. 5, 1879; 1 dau., Millicent (wife of Dr. W. V. Bingham). Asst. U.S. Transit of Venus Commn., 1875-78; chief U.S. Naval Observatory eclipse parties in Tex., 1878; chief asst. on U.S. Nautical Almanac, 1878-81; prof. astronomy and nav. and dir. of obs., Amherst Coll., 1881-1920; prof. emeritus (Carnegie Foundation), 1920. Astronomer in charge Lick Obs. observations, transit of Venus, 1882; prof. astronomy and higher mathematics, Smith Coll., 1882-87; astronomer in charge Am. eclipse expdn. to Japan, 1887; chief U.S. scientific expdn. to W. Africa, 1889-90; chief Amherst eclipse expdn. to Japan, 1896, to Tripoli, Barbary, 1900, to Dutch E. Indies, 1901, Tripoli, 1905, Russia, 1914, Florida, 1918, South America, 1919, and in 1925 (Mitchel Field, L.I.) securing, in coöperation with U.S. Army Air Service, first photograph of the solar corona from an aeroplane; chief of the Lowell Mars expedition to the Andes, 1907. Fellow A.A.A.S., Astron. Soc. America, Royal Soc. Arts. London. Imperial Saki cup from Mikado of Japan for services to Japanese education. Author: A New Astronomy, 1897; Stars and Telescopes, 1899; Népszerü Csilla gászat (Popular Astronomy in Hungarian, Budapest), 1901; Lessons in Astronomy, 1902; Astronomy To-Day, 1924; also articles in mags. and revs. Editor: Columbian Knowledge Series (3 vols.), 1893-95. Designed and erected new observatories at Smith Coll., Northampton, 1886-87, and at Amherst Col., 1903-05. Address: New York, N.Y. Died June 1, 1939.

TODD, ELI, physician; b. New Haven, Conn., July 22, 1769; s. Michael and Mary (Rowe) T.; grad. Yale, 1787; studied medicine; m. Rhoda Hill, Aug. 9, 1796; m. 2d, Catherine Hill, Nov. 1828. Treated epidemic of "spotted fever", Farmington, Conn., 1808; practiced medicine in Hartford, Conn., 1820; mem. Conn. Med. Soc., v.p., 1823, pres., 1827-28; investigated conditions in insane asylums and became interested in treatment of mentally ill, 1812; a founder Soc. for Relief of Insane, 1822; a founder Conn. Retreat for Insane, Hartford, 1824, 1st supt., 1824-33, used trained personnel, recognized alcoholism as a mental disease. Author med. articles. Died Hartford, Nov. 17, 1833.

TODD, JAMES EDWARD, geologist; b. Clarksfield, O., Feb. 11, 1846; s. Rev. John and Martha (Atkins) T.; A.B. Oberlin, 1867, A.M., 1870; Union Theol. Sem., 1867-69; Oberlin Theol. Sem., 1869-70; studied at Sheffield Scientific Sch., Yale, 1870-71; Harvard Summer Sch. of Geology, 1875; m. Lillie J. Carpenter, June 15, 1876. Pvt. Co. K, 150th Ohio Inf., 100 days, 1864; on U.S. Fish Commn., 1871-73; prof. natural science, Tabor Coll., 1871-92; adj. prof. natural science, Beloit (Wis.) Coll., 1881-83; prof. geology and mineralogy, 1892-1903, acting pres., 1897-98, U. of S.D.; asst. prof. geology and mineralogy, U. of Kan., 1907—. Asst. geologist and spl. asst. U.S. Geol. Survey, 1881-1909, on Mo. Geol. Survey, 1891-92, Minn. Geol. Survey, 1892-93; state geologist of S.D., 1893-1903. Fellow A.A.A.S., Geol. Soc. America. Conglist.

Progressive. Author of papers and pamphlets on geol. subjects. Address: Lawrence, Kan. Died 1922.

TODD, SERENO EDWARDS, agriculturist, editor; b. ompkins County, N.Y., June 3, 1820; s. Josiah and ucretia (Ingersoll) T.; m. Rhoda Peck, June 19, 1844; m. 2d, Dora Amanda Peterson, Mar. 19, 1887; 2 children including Prof. David Peck. Contbr. Country Gentleman, 1860; agrl. adviser to Gov. onzo B. Cornell of N.Y.; asso. editor Am. Agriculturist, 1865; in charge of agrl. dept. of N.Y. Times, 1866; editor home dept. of N.Y. Observer; editorial iter Hearth and Home; agrl. editor N.Y. Tribune; ited Practical Farmer; patented power ditching machine, 1872. Author: The Yound Farmer's Manual, vol. 1, 1860, vol. 2, 1867; The American Wheat lturist, 1868. Died Orange, N.J., Dec. 26, 1898.

TODD, T(HOMAS) WINGATE, anatomist; b. Sheffield, Eng., Jan. 15, 1885; s. James and Katharine (Wingate) T.; M.B., and Ch.B., Manchester U. and London Hosp., 1907; m. Eleanor Pearson, Nov. 9, 1912; children—Arthur Wingate, Donald Pearson, Eleanor Margaret. Jr. and sr. demonstrator anatomy, Manchester U., 1907-08; house surgeon Royal Infirmary, 1909; lecturer on anatomy and clin. anatomy, U. of Manchester, 1910; prof. anatomy, Western Reserve U., 1912—. Dir. Hamann Mus. Comparative Anthropology and Anatomy; chmn. Brush Foundation; dir. research, Development Health Inquiry of the Asso. Foundations, Cleveland. Fellow of the Royal College of Surgeons (England), 1911; mem. Am. Assn. Anatomists, Soc. Anatomists Great Britain and Ireland, Am. Anthropol. Assn.; fellow Galton Soc. Home: Cleveland Heights, O. Died Dec. 28, 1938.

TODD, WALTER EDMOND CLYDE, ornithologist; b. Smithfield, O., Sept. 6, 1874; s. William and Isabella (Hunter) T.; ed. Beaver (Pa.) High Sch., 1887-91; m. Leila E. Eason, Dec. 9, 1907 (died 1927). Asst. in Div. of Econ. Ornithology and Mammalogy (later Bur. of Biol. Survey), U.S. Dept. of Agr., 1891-99; curator of ornithology, Carnegie Museum, Pittsburgh, 1899-1944; curator emeritus, 1945-67. Fellow American Ornithologists' Union; member of the Biological Society of Washington. Methodist. Conducted numerous scientific expdns. to the east coast of Hudson Bay and to the coast and interior of Labrador, 1901-45. Awarded Brewster medal (with M.A. Carriker), 1925, by Am. Ornithol. Union, "for meritorious work on ornithology." Author: Birds of Western Pennsylvania, 1940. Contbr. numerous papers, mostly on neo-tropical birds. Home: Beaver PA Died June 1967.

TOFTOY, HOLGER NELSON, army officer; b. Marseilles, Ill., Oct. 31, 1902; s. Nils and Thea (Thorsen) T.; student U. Wis., 1920-22; B.S., U.S. Mil. Acad., 1926; student Army-Navy Staff Coll., 1942-43; LL.D., Athens Coll., 1955; m. Hazel Eunice Schweikert, Dec. 28, 1926; children—Doris (Mrs. George K. Williams), Charles Nelson. Commd. 2d lt. U.S. Army, 1926, advanced through grades to maj. gen., 1952; instr. U.S. Mil. Acad., 1930-35; chief research and devel. and indsl. divs. Submarine Mine Depot, 1938-44; chief ordnance tech. intelligence teams ETO, 1944-45; chief rocket br. research and development div. Office Chief Ordnance, 1945-52; dir. Ordnance Missile Labs., 1952-54; comdg. gen. Redstone Arsenal, 1954-58; dep. comdr. U.S. Army Missile Comd., 1958; comdg. gen. Aberdeen Proving Ground, Md., 1958—. Nat. com. mem. Aero. Bd., 1945-47; guided missile com. Research and Devel. Bd., 1947-52; mem. tech. com. Nat. Adv. Com. Aeros. Decorated Legion of Merit, Bronze Star (U.S.); Croix de Guerre with palm (France); D.S.M., 1958. Recipient James H. Wyld award for outstanding application of rocket power, Am. Rocket Soc. Fellow Am. Rocket Soc.; mem. Am. Ordnance Assn., Am. Legion, Mil. Order World Wars. Clubs; Rotary (Huntsville); Toastmaster (Redstone). Address, Aberdeen Proving Ground, Md. Died 1967.

TOLAND, HUGH HUGER, surgeon, coll. pres.; b. Guilder's Creek, S.C., Apr. 16, 1806; s. John and Mary (Boyd) T.; grad. (1st in class) Transylvania U., Lexington, Ky., 1828; m. Mary Goodwin, 1833; m. 2d, Mary Avery, 1844; m. 3d, Mrs. Mary B. (Morrison) Gridley, 1860; 3 children. Performed successful operations for relief of clubfoot and strabimus (using lithotomy forceps), Columbia, S.C., 1833; went to Cal., 1852; chief surgeon Marine Hosp., San Francisco, 1853; staff mem. county hosp.; founder Toland Med. Coll., San Francisco, 1864, pres., prof. surgery, 1864-80, gave all facilities of sch. to U. Cal., 1873; wrote 71 articles, many published in Pacific Medical and Surgical Jour.; wrote textbook on surgery; noted for work on bladder stones, plastic surgery. Died S.C., Feb. 27, 1880.

TOLLMIEN, WALTER GUSTAV, scientist; b. Berlin, Germany, Oct. 13, 1900; s. Gustav and Amalia (Alschausky) T.; student U. Berlin, 1919-21; Dr. phil., U. Gottingen, 1924, Dr. phil. habil., 1935; Dr. rer. nat. h.c. Tech. U., Clausthal Mining Acad. 1965; m. Sigrid Kosch, Mar. 18, 1948; children—Uwe, Renate (Mrs. Schultheis), Cordula, Franziska, Sibylle. Asst., Kaiser-Wilhelm-Institut for Stromungsforschung, 1924-30, sect. leader, 1934-37; research fellow Cal. Inst. Tech., 1930-33; privatdozent for applied mathematics and mechanics, Gottingen, 1936-37; prof. Technical U., Dresden, 1937-45; dir. Outside Institutes Gottingen, 1945-46; sci. Royal Aircraft Establishment, Farnborough, 1946-47; prof. U. Gottingen, 1947-68; dir. Max-Planck-Institut fur Stromungsforschung. Permanent mem. organizing com. Internat. Congresses on Applied Mechanics. Mem. A.A.A.S., Gottingen Acad. Sci. Contbr. numerous articles on honorary layer theory, turbulance theory, gas-dynamics, dynamic meterology, other fields to profl. publs. Home: Gottingen Germany Died Nov. 25, 1968.

TOLMAN, CHARLES PRESCOTT, cons. engr.; b. Boston; s. Charles Francis and Ann Eliza (Randall) T.; B.S., Mass. Inst. Tech., 1902; m. Hazel Buckingham Kelley, July 30, 1910, (dec.); children—Lee, Hazel Buckingham (dec.). Engr. during student years, 1900-02; asst. chief engr., Nat. Electric Co., Milw., 1902, chief engr. 1903-05; in practice as cons. engr., 1905-07; crief engr., Nat. Lead Co., N.Y.C., 1907, chmn. mfg. com., 1908-22; cons. chem., mech., elec. engr. and patent expert 1922—. Head cons. Office of Production Research and Development, W.P.B. Cons. engr. for Nat. Soc. Prevention Blindness 1941-49, in charge indsl. program of society and of nat. program for conservation and utilization of eyesight in industry for soc. in cooperation with W.P.B., U.S.P.H.S., War Manpower Commn. and U.S. Dept. Labor; pres. Nat. Safety Council, 1920-21. Dir. glaucoma project Ophthal. Found., Inc.; dir. tech. research and development, Am. Found. Blind, Inc. Fellow Am. Soc. M.E.; life mem. Am. Inst. E.E., cons. to com. on occupational vision, Am. Optometric Assn.; mem. Inst. Chem. Engrs., Am. Pub. Health Assn., A.A.A.S., Illuminating Engring. Soc. (com. on lighting study projects), Pan-Am. Assn. Ophthalmology. Asso. mem. joint com. on indsl. ophthal. A.M.A. and Am. Acad. Ophthalmology and Otolaryngology. Clubs: Engineers, Cosmos (Washington). Contbr. book reviews Am. Econ. Rev., also articles to mags. Inventor ophthalmic instruments; developer audio visual ednl. techniques using films and note texts. Author texts and instrnl. films. Home: 83-09 Talbot St., Kew Gardens 15, N.Y. Died Nov. 25, 1961.

TOLMAN, CYRUS FISHER, JR., geologist; b. Chicago, June 2, 1873; s. Rev. Cyrus F. and Mary (Bronson) T.; B.S., U. of Chicago, 1896; grad. student and fellow in geology, same, 1896-99; m. Hannah Martha Van Steen, Aug. 22, 1900. Spl. asst. geologist, U.S. Geol. Survey, 1896; cons. geologist and mining engr. since 1899; prof. geology, U. of Ariz., 1905-06, prof. geology and mining, 1906-12; territorial geologist of Ariz., 1910-12; asso. prof. econ. geology, Stanford U., 1912-19, and prof. since 1919. Mem. 1st Ill. Vols., Spanish-Am. War, 1898, service in Cuba. Fellow Geol. Soc. Am.; mem. Am. Inst. Mining Engrs., Seismol. Soc. Am. (v.p.). Author: The Graphic Solution of Fault Problems, 1911. Contbr. on geol. processes of semi-arid regions, geology of Ariz. and Calif., ore deposits, ground water, oil (especially origin of oil), the geology of dam foundations and reservoir sites, etc. Home: Stanford University, Calif. Died Oct. 13, 1942.

TOLMAN, EDWARD CHACE, psychologist; b. West Newton, Mass., Apr. 14, 1886; s. James P. and Mary (Chace) T.; S.B., Mass. Inst. Tech., 1911; A.M., Harvard, 1912, Ph.D., 1915; Sc.D., Yale, 1951; McGill U., 1954; LL.D., U. Cal., 1959; m. Kathleen Drew, Aug. 30, 1915; children—Deborath (Mrs. J. G. Whitney), Mary (Mrs. Thomas John Kent), Edward. Began as instr. psychol., Northwestern U., 1915; instr. psychology, U. of Calif., 1918-20, asst. prof., 1920-23, associate professor, 1923-28, professor, 1928-54, professor emeritus, same univ., 1954—. Fellow A.A.A.S., Brit. Psychol. Soc. (hon.); mem. Am. Acad. Arts and Scis., Am. Psychol. Assn. (mem. council 1931-34; pres. 1937; bd. dirs. 1945-47), Nat. Acad. Scis., Am. Philosophical Soc., Western Psychological Assn., Society for Psychological Study of Social Issues (council 1938-40; chmn. 1940), Sigma Xi, Phi Beta Kappa. Author: Purposive Behavior in Animals and Men, 1932. Co-author: Comparative Psychology, 1934; Drives Toward War, 1942. Contbr. scientific articles to periodicals. Home: 1038 Middlefield Rd. Berkeley 8, Cal. Died Nov. 19, 1959.

TOLMAN, RICHARD CHACE (tol'man), physicist; b. West Newton, Mass., Mar. 4, 1881; s. James Pike and Mary (Chace) T.; S.B., Mass. Institute of Technology, 1903, Ph.D., 1910; Sc.D., Princeton University, 1942; studied at Charlottenburg and Crefeld, Germany, 1903-04; m. Ruth Sherman, Aug. 5, 1924. Instr. in theoretical chemistry, 1907-09, research asso. in physical chemistry, 1909-10, M.I.T.; instr. physical chemistry, U. of Mich., 1910-11; asst. prof. same, U. of Cincinnati, 1911-12, U. of Calif., 1912-16; prof. physical chemistry, U. of Ill., 1916-18; chief dispersoid sect. Chem. Warfare Service, rank maj., 1918; asso. dir., 1919-20, and dir., 1920-22, Fixed Nitrogen Research Lab., War Dept.; prof. physical chemistry and mathematical physics and dean of the Grad. Sch., Calif. Inst. Tech., since 1922. Vice chmn. Nat. Defense Research Com., 1940. Sci. adv. to U.S. rep., U.N. Atomic Energy Comn., 1946. Fellow Am. Acad. Arts and Sciences, A.A.A.S.; mem. Am. Chem. Soc., Nat. Acad. Sciences, Am. Philos. Soc., Am. Physical Soc., Washington Acad. Sciences. Author: The Theory of the Relativity of Motion, 1917; Statistical Mechanics with Applications to Physics and Chemistry, 1927; Relativity, Thermodynamics and Cosmology, 1934; The Principles of Statistical Mechanics, 1938; Investigations on theory of colloids, theory of relativity, theory of similitude, mass of the electron, nature of the fundamental quantities of physics, partition of energy, behavior of smokes, electric discharge in gases, reactions of nitrogen compounds, rate of chem. reaction, specific heat and entropy of gases, quantum theory, statistical mechanics, relativisitc thermo-dynamics, cosmology, etc. Address: Calif. Institute of Technology, Pasadena, Calif. Died Sep. 5, 1948.

TOLTZ, MAX, cons. engr.; b. Koeslin, Germany, Sept. 2, 1857; s. Hermann and Malvine (Beilfuss) T.; C.E., Royal Acad. Science and Engring., Berlin, Germany, 1887; D.Eng., Ramsey Inst. Tech., 1924; m. L. Elizabeth Argue, 1919. Came to U.S., 1882, naturalized, 1892. Began as draftsman, G.N. Ry., 1882, successively asst. engr., bridge engr., acting chief engr. and mech. engr. in charge motive power dept. until 1904; cons. engr. C.P. Ry., Butte, Anaconda & Pacific Ry., N.P. R.R., Erie R.R., G.N. Ry., 1904-07; cons. engr. in pvt. practice, 1907—. Mem. Minn. N.G. 23 yrs., advancing to maj., engrs.; supervising engr. constrn. div., U.S.A., 1917-18. Republican. Home: St. Paul, Minn. Died Jan. 12, 1932.

TOMPKINS, CHARLES HOOK, constructing engr.; b. Baltimore, Md., Nov. 30, 1883; s. Edward H. and Louise O. (Chappell) Tompkins; student Lehigh U., 1903-04, George Washington University, 1905-06 (hon. D.Eng., 1946); married Lida R. Tompkins, Nov. 30, 1906 (dec.), children—Francis M., Louise C. (Mrs. Andrew Parker), Emma H. (Mrs. Malcolm Matheson, Jr.), Charles H., Jr. Engineer with U.S. Corps Engrs., 1904, E. Saxton, Ry. constr., 1905, D.C. Govt., 1906, Ohio Elec. Ry. Co., 1907-08, Capital Traction Co., 1909, Smithsonian Inst., 1910; constr. engineer under own name, 1911-21; pres. of Chas. H. Tompkins Co., construction engrs., since 1922; builders of many defense projects including Bainbridge Naval Training Sta.; Ft. Belvoir Cantonment and Engr. Bd. bldgs.; Allegheny Ordnance Plant; White Oaks Naval Ordnance Lab.; in Washington, many notable structures such as Dalecarlia Filtration Plant; Garfinckel Dept. Store; Tower Bldg.; World War Red Cross Mem.; District of Columbia National Guard Armory; D.C. Scottish Rite Temple; groups of buildings for Georgetown, George Washington, and American Universities, National Inst. Health, Naval Research Lab., United States Court House, and many others; inventor Concrete Distributing System; pres. and dir. H St. Bldg. Corp.; former chmn. bd. Old Dutch Refining Co.; former pres., dir. Wis. Petroleum Terminals Corp.; dir., mem. exec. com. Woodward & Lothrop; dir., mem. exec. com. Riggs Nat. Bank; gov. and p.p. Washington Bldg. Congress; trustee George Washington U.; mem. bus. adv. com. Am. U.; mem. bd. directors Gallaudet Coll., Washington; mem. exec. com. Fed. City Council; mem. adv. bd. YMCA; mem. Commrs. Planning Adv. Com. Dist. of Columbia; mem. Commn. 100 Fed. City; hon. permanent mem. bd. Children's Hosp.; dir. Centennial Engineering, 1952; mem. council Corcoran Gallery of Art; dir. D.C. adv. bd. A.A.A.; past pres. D.C. chapter, A.G.C.; past pres. Master Bldrs. Assn.; dir. D.C. chapter, A.R.C.; dir. Wash. Boys Club; life mem. Am. Soc. Civil Engrs. mem. Soc. Am. Military Engrs. (dir., past pres. Washington post). Wash. Bd. Trade (econ. development com.), Wash. Soc. Engrs., Theta Delta Chi (trustee ednl. found.) Sigma Tau, Omicron Delta Kappa. Mason (32 deg., Shriner). Episcopalian. Clubs: Cosmos (member board) Metropolitan. Chevy Chase; Eastern Point Yacht (Gloucester, Mass.); Casanova (Va.) Hunt Lehigh, Rotary. Alfalfa. Home: 3055 Whitehaven St., N.W. Office: 907 16th St., Washington 6. Died Dec. 12, 1956; buried Rock Creek Cemetery, Washington.

TOMPKINS, CHRISTOPHER, physician; b. at Richmond, Va., Sept. 7, 1847; s. Col. Christopher Q. and Ellen (Wilkins) T.; Ph.B., Coll. of William and Mary, Williamsburg, Va., 1868; U. of Va., 1 yr.; M.D., Med. Coll. of Va., 1870; m. Bessie McCaw, Nov. 1, 1877. In med. practice at Richmond, 1871—; prof. anatomy, 1880-84, obstetrics, 1884-99, emeritus, 1899—, dean, 1893-13, Med. Coll. of Va. Phys. to Smallpox Hosp., Richmond, 2 yrs.; maj. and surgeon 4th Battalion Arty., Va. Militia. Mem. A.M.A., Southern Surg. and Gynecol. Assn., Southern Med. Coll. Assn. (ex-v.p.), Med. Soc. Va. (a founder, hon. mem.), etc. Democrat. Episcopalian. Home: 116 E. Franklin St., Richmond, Va.

TOMPKINS, DANIEL A., engineer; b. Edgefield County, S.C., Oct. 12, 1852; s. DeWitt Clinton and Hannah Virginia (Smyly) T.; S.C. Coll.; C.E. Rensselaer Poly. Inst., 1873; unmarried. Learned machinist's trade in Bessemer steel works of John A. Griswold & Co., Troy, N.Y., and 10 yrs. with Bethlehem Iron Works, Pa., under John Fritz, as machinist, draftsman, head draftsman and asst. to master machinist; master machinist Crystal Plate Glass Works and Crystal Ry. Co., Crystal City, Mo., 1880-82, building large addition to plant; at Charlotte, N.C., 1882—, as contracting engr., constructing many cottonsed oil mills and refineries, cotton mills, elec. light works, acid phosphate works, etc.; pres. D. A. Tompkins Co., mfrs., engrs. and contractors; pres. High Shoals and Atherton cotton mills, etc. Pres. Underwriters Fire Ins. Co. of

Greensboro, N.C.; dir. Equitable Assurance Soc. of the U.S. Mem. U.S. Industrial Commn. Author: Cotton Mill, Processes and Calculations; Cotton Mill Commercial Features; Cotton and Cotton Oil; American Commerce, Its Expansion; Cotton Values in Textile Fabrics; History of Mecklenburg County, North Carolina; and many pamphlets. Address: Charlotte, N.C. Died Oct. 18, 1914.

TONDORF, FRANCIS ANTHONY, seismologist; b. Boston, Mass., July 17, 1870; s. Joseph and Louise (Musler) T.; A.B., Woodstock (Md.) Coll., 1895; Ph.D., Georgetown U., 1914; unmarried. Asst. Georgetown U. Obs., later chief Georgetown U., Seismol. Obs. Fellow A.A.A.S., Royal Astronomical Soc. Catholic. Author various brochures, and articles in scientific jours. Known for researches in epicentres and microseisms. Address: Washington, D.C. Died Nov. 29, 1929.

TONER, JOSEPH MEREDITH, physician; b. Pitts., Apr. 30, 1825; s. Meredith and Ann (Layton) T.; attended Western U. Pa., Pitts., Mt. St. Mary's Coll., Emmitsburg, Md.; attended Jefferson Med. Coll., 1849-50, M.D., 1853; M.D., Vt. Med. Coll., Woodstock, 1850; never married. Began practice of medicine, Washington, D.C., 1855; a founder St. Joseph's Orphan Asylum, physician; physician St. Vincent's Female Orphan Asylum, St. Ann's Infant Asylum; pres. A.M.A., 1873, Am. Pub. Health Assn., 1874; donated 27,000 volumes to Library of Congress, 1882; made subject index for all Am. med. jours. up to 1870; began library for A.M.A., 1868, later removed to Newberry Library, Chgo.; a founder Columbia Hist. Soc., 1894; Author: Internal Instinct, 1864; The Medical Men of the Revolution, 1876; Address on Medical Biography, 1876; Editor: Washington's Rules of Civility and Decent Behavior, 1888; Journal of Colonel George Washington . . . in 1754, published 1893. Died Cresson, Pa., July 30, 1896; buried family plot, Derry, Pa.

TORBERT, JOHN BRYANT, topographic and geologic draftsman; b. Washington, D.C., May 8, 1867; s. John Peyton and Elizabeth (Bryant) T.; high sch. edn., Washington; LL.B., Columbian (now George Washington) U., 1888, LL.M., 1889; m. Florence Kalbfus, Nov. 19, 1890; children—Florence, John Peyton, Mrs. Elizabeth Bryant Mertz, Helen May (dec.). Admitted to bar, 1889; draftsman U.S. Geol. Survey, 1886-93, in topographer's office, Post-Office Dept., 1893-1908, U.S. Geol. Survey, 1908—. Identified with 8th Internat. Geog. Congress, Washington, D.C., 1904. Hist. cartographer, Jamestown Expn., 1907. Scientific illustrator U.S. Geol. Survey. Contbr. articles, maps and drawings to mags. and scientific publs., besides illustrating the works of others. Diploma of Highest Excellence, Turin Expn., 1911. Mem. D.C. Liberty Loan Com.; four-minute man; dist. food administrator, 1917-19. Address: Cleveland Park, D.C. Deceased.

TORCHIO, PHILIP, electrical engineer; born Vercana (Como), Italy, Aug. 2, 1868; s. Filippo and Luisa (Prandi) T.; B.A., U. of Pavia, 1890; M.E. and E.E., Royal Polytechnic, Milan, 1893; m. Angela de Nova, 1893; children—Anna Luisa, T. Desmond, Philip, Brady, Angela. Draftsman and chief draftsman, Sprague Electric Elevator Co., New York, 1893-95; with New York Edison Co., Inc., as engr. of economics, 1895-1901, engr. of distribution, 1901-05, chief elec. engr., 1905-24, v.p., 1924-31, sr. v.p., 1931-36, and with merged company, The Consol. Edison Co., as v.p. till 1938; cons. engr., 1905-28; dir. N.Y. & Queens Electric Light & Power Co. and other allied companies, 1931-38; retired, 1938; chmn. bd., pres. and dir. Bank of Naples Trust Co. of N.Y. Important work in development of electricity in stream and hydraulic stations and unification of systems of transmission and distribution over large territories; originated improvements in apparatus, cables, storage batteries, and electric control. Mayor of Bronxville, 1929-31. Mem. New York City Mayor's Defense Com., 1941. Past pres. N.Y. Elec. Soc.; fellow Am. Inst. E.E. Presented numerous papers and results of original researches before tech. socs. and internat. congresses at St. Louis Turin and Pan-American Congress, Washington; also lectured at Columbia, Yale, Johns Hopkins. Grand Officer Crown of Italy. Awarded Edison medal by Am. Inst. Elec. Engrs., 1939. Home: Bronxville, N.Y. Died Jan. 14, 1942.

TORGERSEN, HAROLD, engr., univ. dean; b. Bklyn., Jan. 2, 1910; s. Anton and Marie (Evensen) T.; B.S., in Elect. Engring., N.Y.U., 1929; student U. Wis., 1932, Columbia, 1933-34; M.S., Harvard, 1939. Test engr. Gen. Electric Co., 1929-30; instr. elec. engring. N.Y.U., 1930-39, supr. power plant, 1935-36, asst. prof., 1939-46, asso. prof., 1946-53, asst. dean evening div. engring., 1946-52, asst. dean engring., 1952-56, prof. elec. engring., 1953-57, asso. dean engring., 1956-57; dean engring. prof. elec. engring. U. Conn., 1957—. Served from lt. (j.g.) to comdr. USNR, 1941-46. Fellow Am. Inst. E.E.; mem. Am. Soc. Engring. Edn., Inst. Radio Engrs., Conn. Soc. Civil Engrs., Harvard Engring. Soc., S.I. Hist. Soc., Perstare et Praestare, Tau Beta Pi, Eta Kappa Nu, Pi Tau Sigma. Clubs: Harvard (N.Y.C.); Nordmanns Forbundet. Home: 24 Whitney Rd., Storrs, Conn. Died Nov. 5, 1961.

TORIAN, OSCAR NOEL, pediatrician; b. Evansville, Ind., Oct. 6, 1875; s. Augustine Garnett and Anna Shelby (Boswell) T.; A.B., U. of the South, 1896; M.D., U. of Pa., 1900; m. Sarah Hodgson, Sept. 19, 1907; children—Anna Garnett, Telfair Hodgson (dec.), John Potter (dec.). Interne King's County Brooklyn) Hosp., 1900-01; asst. in pediatrics, 1908, asso. and then clin. prof., 1915-20, prof. pediatrics, 1920-41, emeritus prof., 1941-71, Ind. U. Sch. Medicine; staff physician Riley, Meth. (mem. bd.) and St. Vincent's hosps.; mem. Ind. Com. Child Health and Maternal Welfare (chairman of pediatric section); pediatrician of Emerald-Hodgson Hospital, Sewanee, Tenn., since 1941, Licentiate American Bd. of Pediatrics. Former trustee U. of the South (mem. bd. regents). Mem. A.M.A., Central States Pediatrics Soc., Am. Acad. Pediatrics (chmn. Ind. com.), Ind. Pediatric Soc. (pres. 1938), Tenn. State Med. Soc., Franklin County Med. Soc., Phi Rho Sigma, Omicron Delta Kappa, Sigma Xi, Phi Delta Theta. Democrat. Episcopalian. Clubs: E.Q.B., Sewanee Golf. Home: Sewanee TN Died Mar. 29, 1971; buried Sewanee TN

TORKELSON, MARTIN WILHELM, civil engr.; b. Jackson County, Wis., Oct. 27, 1878; s. Iver and Martine (Anderson) T.; B.S. in C.E., U. Wis., 1904, C.E., 1916; m. Cornelia R. Herried, Dec. 24, 1907; children—William Edward, Christine Martha, Ivar John. Ry. work in Ky., Tenn. and Va. 4 yrs.; bridge engr. Wis. Hwy. Dept., 1908, later sec. and asst. state hwy. engr.; resigned, 1927, to specialize as cons. in municipal engring.; dir. regional planning, 1929-55, also state hwy. engr. 1931, 32, now cons. to state chief engr.; exec. officer Wis. State Planning Bd., 1932-56; exec. sec. Natural Resources com. State Agys., Wis. since 1951; works progress adminstr. for Wis., 1936-38; sec. Wis. State Council Nat. Def., 1940-43. Prepared 1st hwy. bridge standard plans used by Wis. Hwy. Dept. and one of first in U.S. Recipient Distinguished Service citation U. Wis. Coll. Engring., 1959. Mem. Am. Soc. C.E. Lutheran. Mason. Home: 4157 Manitou Way, Madison, Wis. Died Apr. 2, 1963; buried Forest Hill Cemetery, Madison.

TORREY, JOHN, botanist, chemist, educator; b. N.Y.C., Aug. 15, 1796; s. Capt. William and Margaret (Nichols) T.; M.D., Coll. Physicians and Surgeons, N.Y.C., 1818; A.M. (hon.), Yale, 1823; LL.D. (hon.), Amherst Coll., 1845; m. Eliza Shaw, Apr. 20, 1824, at least 4 children. Catalogued plants growing near N.Y.C., 1817; gave spl. attention to plants of Northeastern U.S.; as result of govt. sponsored expedition (1820), reported on plants collected by David Bates Douglass near source of Mississippi River, 1820; apptd. prof. chemistry, mineralogy and geology U.S. Mil. Acad., 1824-27; prof. chemistry Coll. Physicians and Surgeons, 1827-55, prof. emeritus until 1873; prof. chemistry and natural history Coll. of N.J. (now Princeton), 1830-54; worked with Asa Gray on Flora of North America, 1838-43; apptd. N.Y. State botanist, 1836; wrote reports of exploring expdns. of Frémont, Marcy and others, circa 1836-58; elected fgn. mem. Linnean Soc. of London, 1839; mem. Am. Acad. Arts and Scis., 1841; U.S. assayer, 1853-73; Torrey's Peak (Colo.) named for him; plants named in his honor include Torreya Taxifolia, Torreya California, Torreya Nucifera, Torreya Grandis. Author: Flora of Northern and Middle Sections of the United States, 1823; A Compendium of the Flora of the Northern and Middle States, 1826; Flora of the State of New York, 2 vols., 1843. Died N.Y.C., Mar. 10, 1873.

TOTTEN, CHARLES ADIEL LEWIS, inventor, author; b. New London, Conn., Feb. 3, 1851; s. Gen. James and Julia H. (Thatcher) T.; grad. Trinity Coll., Hartford, 1869, A.M., 1885; grad. West Point, 1873; m. Eda, d. Maj. Lewis Smith, U.S.A.; m. 2d, Mary, d. Matthew Bunker, of Garden City, L.I. Commissioned 2d lt., 4th Arty., 1873; 1st lt., Nov. 1, 1874; prof. mil. science and tactics Mass. Agrl. Coll., 1875-78; afterward served in west, including Bannock War, 1878, and Chircahua campaign; prof. mil. science and tactics, Cathedral Sch., St. Paul, N.Y., 1883-86, and at Yale, 1889-92; resigned to devote attention to Biblical investigations. Publisher of Our Race (devoted to his theories of the Second Advent, and the identify of the Anglo-Saxon race with the ten lost tribes of Israel). Inventor and patentee of "Strategos" (military game), and other inventions. Author: Important Questions in Metrology, 1887; Strategos, 1881; Lost Israel Found in the Anglo-Saxons, 1890; Joshua's Long Day and the Dial of Ahaz, 1891; The Kings Daughters, 1891; The Coming Crusade, 1897; some 300 books and brochures; all published by Our Race Pub. Co., New Haven. Home: Milford, Conn. Died 1908.

TOTTEN, GEORGE MUIRSON, civil engr.; b. New Haven, Conn., May 28, 1809; s. Gilbert and Mary (Rice) T.; grad. Norwich (Vt.) Mil. Acad., 1827; m. Harriet Seely, July 12, 1835, at least 2 children. Asst. engr. on Farmington Canal, 1827, on Juniata Canal, Pa., 1828-31, on Delaware and Raritan Canal, N.J., 1831-35; assisted in constrn. railroad fron Reading to Port Clinton, Pa., 1835, also railroads in Va., Pa., N.C.; with Pa. Sunbury and Danville R.R., 1837-40, Gaston & Raleigh R.R. (N.C.), 1840-43; received 1st S.Am. commn. as chief engr. to build Canal del Dique, Columbia, 1843; joined Panama R.R. as engr.-in-chief, 1850, remained on Isthmus of Panama, 25 years; engr. on railroads in Venezuela; cons. engr. on 1st Panama Canal project, circa 1879-83; mem. Am. Philos. Soc., 1851. Died N.Y.C., May 17, 1884.

TOTTEN, JOSEPH GILBERT, army officer, engr.; b. New Haven, Conn., Aug. 23, 1788; s. Peter and Grace (Mansfield) T.; grad. U.S. Mil. Acad., 1805; A.M. (hon.), Brown U., 1829; m. Catlyna Pearson, 1816, 7 children. Commd. 2d lt. engrs. U.S. Army, 1805, 1st. lt., 1810, capt., 1812; asst. engr. harbor defenses N.Y.C., 1808, spl. supr. Ft. Clinton, Castle Garden, N.Y.; asst. in defenses of New Haven, New London (Conn.), Sag Harbor; chief engr. U.S. Army on Niagara frontier, 1812; brevetted maj., 1813, lt. col., 1814; engaged in coastal fortifications, 1815-38; promoted maj., 1818, lt. col., 1828, col., 1838; chief engr. U.S. Army, insp. U.S. Mil. Acad., 1838-64; served with Gen. Winfield Scott as chief engr. and mem. so-called Little Cabinet; orginated successful plan of operations at Battle of Veracruz during Mexican War; brevetted brig. gen., 1847; mem. Lighthouse Bd., 1851-58, 60-64; instrumental in putting into use system of lighting by Fresnel lenses; commd. brig. gen. U.S. Army, 1863; supr. defensive works around Washington, D.C.; mem. bd. to regulate and fix heavy ordnance, 1861-62; brevetted maj. gen. by U.S. Congress, 1864; published Essays on Hydraulic and Common Mortars and on Lime-Burning, 1838; corporator Nat. Acad. Scis., 1863; studied conchology, 2 shells (gemma and succinca tottenii) named for him; Ft. Totten (N.Y.C. Harbor) named for him. Died Washington, D.C., Apr. 22, 1864.

TOUMEY, JAMES WILLIAM, forester; b. Lawrence, Mich., Apr. 17, 1865; s. Dennis and Mary (Buckley) T.; B.S., Mich. Agrl. Coll., 1889, M.S., 1895; spl. student, Harvard, 1893; hon. M.A., Yale U., 1907; hon. Sc.D., Syracuse, 1920; hon. F.D., Michigan State Coll., 1927; m. Constantia Hayes Blake, June 17, 1897; 1 son, James William; m. 2d, Nannie Byrne Trowbridge, Sept. 1908. Asst. dept. botany, Mich. Agrl. Coll., 1890-91; prof. biology, U. of Ariz., 1891-98; dir. Ariz. Agrl. Expt. Sta., 1897-98; supt. of tree planting, Div. of Forestry, U.S. Dept. of Agr., 1898-1900; asst. prof. forestry, 1900-03, prof. forestry, 1903-09, prof. silviculture, 1909, dean Sch. Forestry, 1910-22, prof. silviculture, 1922—, Yale. Author: Seeding and Planting in the Practice of Forestry; Foundations of Silviculture upon an Ecological Basis; bulls. and articles on bot. and forestry subjects. Home: New Haven, Conn. Died May 6, 1932.

TOUPS, ROLAND LEON, sugar co. exec.; b. Thibodaux, La., July 25, 1911; s. Leonidas M. and Maude (Peltier) T.; B.S. in Mech. Engring., Ga. Inst. Tech., 1933; m. Gertrude Daigle, Sept. 27, 1935;children—Roland Michael and Leon Henry (twins), Henry Etta. With Godchaux Sugars, Inc., New Orleans, 1933-42; with South Coast Corp., New Orleans, 1945-69, v.p., gen. mgr., 1953-64, pres., 1964-69; dir. Raceland Bank & Trust Co. (La.), La. Agrl. Credit Corp., New Orleans, Gulf South Financial Advisers, Inc., Thibodaux. Past chmn. St. John and Terrebonne parishes Boy Scouts Am., past mem. exec. bd. New Orleans area; past pres. St. Francis Boys Sch. Fathers Club. Houma, La. Served to lt. col. AUS, 1942-45. Named King Sucrose XXVII for La. Sugar Cane Festival, 1968. Registered profl. engr., La. Mem. Sugar Industry Technicians, Am. Sugar Cane Tech. Assn. (past pres.), La. Engring. Soc., Nat. Soc. Profl. Engrs., Houma-Terrebonne C. of C. (bd. dirs.), Lambda Chi Alpha, Pi Tau Sigma, Scabbard and Blade. Home: Houma LA Died May 9, 1969; interred St. Francis de Sales Mausoleum Houma LA

TOUR, REUBEN S(IMKIN), (toor), chem. engr.; b. Troy, N.Y., Aug. 20, 1889; s. James and Sophia (Simkin) T.; B.S., U. of Mich., 1910, M.S.E., 1915, Ch.E., 1927; m. Margaret Meyer, 1914; 1 son. Robert Louis. Asst. supt., Consolidated Gas Co., N.Y. City, 1911-13; asst. prof. gas engring., U. of Calif., 1913-17; capt. Ordnance Dept., U.S. Army, chief of tech. dept. U.S. Nitrate Plant No. 1, Muscle Shoals, Ala., 1917-19; chem. engr. nitrate div. Ordnance Dept., U.S. Army, 1919-21; prof. chem. engring. and head of dept., U. of Cincinnati, since 1921; cons. chem. engr. (industrial gases). Lt. col. Ordnance O.R.C., to 1942. Mem. Am. Inst. Chemical Engrs., Am. Soc. Engineering Educ., A.A.A.S., Am. Assn. Univ. Profs., Sigma Xi, Tau Beta Pi, Phi Lambda Upsilon. Mason. Contributor of articles on nitrogen fixation and chemical engineering. Address: University of Cincinnati, Cin. 21. Died Aug. 1, 1952.

TOWER, GEORGE WARREN, JR., geologist; b. Cambridge, Mass., Oct. 27, 1871; s. George W. and Abby A.T.; A.B., Harvard, 1894, A.M., 1895; m. Clara Burchard, Jan. 5, 1898; children—William Burchard, George Warren, Elizabeth A., Jessica C. U.S. geologist 4 yrs.; wrote reports on mining dists. of Butte, Mont., Tintic, Utah, Rico, Colo., and Black Hills, S.D.; geologist and consulting engr.; consulting mining engring. Staff of Guggenheim Bros., 1918-37; gen. consultation work in mining and geology, 1937-38. Home: Denver, Colo. Died Sept. 13, 1939.

TOWER, OLIN FREEMAN, chemist; b. Brooklyn, Mar. 19, 1872; s. Freeman Pratt and Julia Ann (Cleveland) T.; A.B., Wesleyan U., Conn., 1892, A.M., 1893; Ph.D., U. of Leipzig, 1895; m. Elizabeth Williams, June 1899. Asst. in chemistry, Wesleyan U.; 1893-94; 1896-98, instr. chemistry, Adelbert Coll. of Western

Reserve U., 1898-1901, asst. prof., 1901-07, Hurlbut prof. chemistry, 1907-42, prof. emeritus since 1942. Fellow A.A.A.S.; mem. London Chem. Soc., Am. Chem. Soc., Phi Beta Kappa, Sigma Xi, Phi Nu Theta (Wesleyan). Author: The Conducitivity of Liquids, 1905; Qualitative Analysis, 1909. Contbr. to various chem. jours. Home: Sylvan Drive, Mt. Dora, Fla. Died Dec. 21, 1945.

TOWER, RALPH WINFRED, curator; b. Amherst, Mass., May 24, 1870; s. Francis Emory and Ella Sophia (Shepardson) T.; student Colby U., 1888-90; Brown U., 1890-93, and 1894-95, A.B., 1892, A.M., 1893, Ph.D., 1903; student U. of Leipzig, 1893-94, med. dept. Harvard U. (John Ware Memorial Fellowship), 1900-01; m. Bessie Belle West, 1893. Demonstrator of anatomy, 1894-95, instr. chem. physiology, 1895-98, asst. prof., 1898-1901, asso. prof., 1901-03, Brown U. Curator of physiology, 1903-12. Curator anatomy and physiology, 1912-21, curator comparative physiology, 1921—, Am. Museum Natural History, Librarian, 1904—, recording secretary and editor, 1917—, New York Acad. of Sciences; also librarian N.Y. Micros. Soc. and Linnaean Soc. of N.Y.; asst. Biol. Lab., U.S. Fish Commn., Woods Hole, Mass., 1898-1903; expert spl. agent U.S. Census of Fisheries, 1908. Pres. trustees Rochelle Public Library. Fellow A.A.A.S., New York Academy of Sciences; corr. mem. Sociedad Cubana de Historia Natural. Author: Laboratory Guide to the Dissection of the Cat (with Frederic Poole Gorham), 1895; Laboratory Course in Chemical Physiology, 1897; also numerous scientific papers. Hon. curator Natural History Libraries, Columbia U., 1913—. Home: Rochelle Park, New Rochelle, N.Y. Died Jan. 26, 1926.

TOWER, WILLIAM LAWRENCE, zoologist; b. Halifax, Mass., Dec. 22, 1872; s. Lorenzo Augustus and Mary Sheldon (Thompson) T.; Lawrence Scientific Sch. (Harvard), 1893-96; Grad. Sch., Harvard, 1898-1900; S.B., U. of Chicago, 1902; m. Lucia Kieve, of Bloomington, Ill., Aug. 21, 1898. Prof. zoology, Antioch Coll., 1900—; asst. in embryology, 1901-3, asso., 1903-4, instr., 1904-7, asst. prof., 1907-11, asso. prof., 1911—, U. of Chicago. Fellow A.A.A.S.; mem. Am. Soc. Zoologists, Am. Soc. Naturalists, etc. Republican. Club: Quadrangle. Home: 5461 Lexington Av., Chicago IL

TOWL, FORREST MILTON, (tol), civil engr., corp. pres.; b. Parma, Cuyahoga County, O., Jan. 14, 1863; s. Theodore M. and Sarah L. (Ackley) T.; C.E., Cornell U., 1886, M.C.E., 1935; m. Mary Elizabeth Dean, Dec. 18, 1888; children—Theodore Clinton, Sarah Dean, Forrest Milton (dec.). Engaged in surveys of pipe lines, summers, 1879-86; asst., later chief engr. Nat. Transit Co., 1886-1902; mgr. pipe line dept. Pacific Coast Oil Co. (now Standard Oil Co. of Calif.), 1902-03, designed and built first long hot oil pipe line from Bakersfield to San Francisco Bay; gen. supt. trunk pipe lines controlled by Standard Oil Co., 1903-06; consulting engr. Standard Oil Co., 1906-11; pres., 1911-32, chmn. bd. since Jan. 1, 1932, Southern Pipe Line Co., Eureka Pipe Line Co., South West Pa. Pipe Lines, Cumberland Pipe Line Co.; engaged in research work, at Cornell U., in pipe line flow of fluids since Sept. 1934; has had charge of building over 7,000 miles of pipe line. Mem. fuel and fuel handling sub-com. U.S. Navy; consulted with U.S. Navy and British Admiralty on pipe line across Scotland to supply allied navies with fuel oil and recuited to U.S. Navy unit which built this 36 mile 8-in. pipe line in 60 days, 1918. Hon. lecturer on mech. engring., Columbia U., 1911. Mem. Am. Soc. C.E., Am. Soc. M.E., Am. Inst. Mining and Metall. Engrs., Cornell Engring. Assn., Chi Psi, Chi Epsilon; fellow A.A.A.S. Republican. Mem. Dutch Ref. Ch. Wrote: The Pipe Line Flow Factor, 1934; The Pipe Line Flow Constant 0.0283 (in press). Home: Dering Harbor, N.Y., and 45 Montgomery Pl., Brooklyn, N.Y. Office: 30 Rockefeller Plaza, New York, N.Y. Died Jan. 3, 1946.

TOWLE, NORMAN LINCOLN, (tol), educator; b. Fall River, Mass., Nov. 24, 1895; s. Wesley Albert and Nettie Francis (Batcheller) T.; B.M.C., Durfee High Sch., Fall River, Mass.; B.S., Worcester Polytech. Inst., 1917, E.E., 1920; m. Mildred E. Hess, Oct. 1948. Engr. Westinghouse Elec. & Mfg. Co., 1916-19; instr., dept. elec. engring., Ia. State College, 1919-20; instr., asst. prof., dept. elec. engring., Cooper Union Sch. Engring., 1920-32, prof. in charge, 1932-48, dean, school of engineering since 1948. Licensed prof. engr, N.Y. State. Mem. Nat. Soc. Profl. Engrs., Am. Soc. E.E., Nat. Geog. Soc., A.A.A.S, N.E.A., Am. Inst. E.E., Sigma Xi, Tau Beta Pi, Sigma Alpha Epsilon. Republican. Conglist. Home: 40 Marion Road, Upper Montclair, N.J. Office: The Cooper Union, Cooper Square, N.Y. City 3. Died May 15, 1963; buried Hershey Cemetery, Kinzers, Pa.

TOWNE, HENRY ROBINSON, manufacturer, engr.; b. Phila., Aug. 28, 1844; s. John Henry and Maria (Tevis) T.; student U. of Pa., 1861-62; hon. A.M., 1887; m. Cora E. White, 1868 (died 1917). Began active career in 1862, as draughtsman, Port Richmond Iron Works, owned by the firm of I. P. Morris, Towne & Co., for nearly 2 yrs., and in 1863 was put in charge of Govt. work in the shops for repairs of gunboat Massachusetts; in 1864-66 was in charge of erecting engines in monitors Monadnock and Agamenticus and similar work, until war closed. After war became spl. student of engring. with Robert Briggs, and took spl. course in physics at the Sorbonne, Paris; afterward connected with shops of William Sellers & Co., Phila. Became associated, in summer 1868, with Linus Yale in mfr. of locks and after Mr. Yale's death, Dec. 1868, became pres. Yale & Towne Mfg. Co., Stamford, Conn., until 1915; later chmn. bd.; chmn. bd. Morris Plan Co. N.Y. Life mem. Am. Soc. M.E. (v.p. 1884-86, pres. 1888-89); pres. Merchants' Assn. of New York, 1908-13. Author: Towne on Cranes, 1883; Locks and Builders' Hardware, 1905. Home: New York, N.Y. Died Oct. 15, 1924.

TOWNE, JOHN HENRY, engineer, philanthropist; b. Pitts., Feb. 20, 1818; s. John and Sarah (Robinson) T.; m. Maria R. Tevis, 1843, 3 children including Henry Robinson. Received engineering tng. with firm Merrick & Agnew, Phila., jr. partner, 1836-49; engaged in private engring. projects after 1849, particularly building gas works; v.p. North Pa. R.R. Co., 1856-58; became partner I.P. Morris and Co., 1861 (company owned Port Richmond Iron Works); produced engines for Monitor, Monadnock and other vessels during Civil War; built engines for federal mint and blowing machinery for manufacture anthracite iron; company's reputation based on its ability to construct large and heavy machinery; dir. Phila. and Reading R.R. Co., 1862-64; benefactor U. Pa. Hosp., Pa. Acad. Fine Arts, Acad. Natural Sciences of Phila.; trustee U. Pa. to which he bequeathed residuary estate, Towne Scientific Sch. created in his memory. Died Paris, France, Apr. 6, 1875.

TOWNER, ZEALOUS BATES, army officer, engr.; b. Cohasset, Mass., Jan. 12, 1819; s. Nichols and Ann (Bates) T.; grad. U.S. Mil. Acad., 1841. Engaged in mil. constrn. duty U.S. Army, 1841-46; served in Mexican War, 1847-48; brevetted maj. for gallantry, 1847; in charge of San Francisco defenses, 1855-58; commanded Ft. Barrancas (Fla.), 1861; brevetted lt. col. U.S. Army, commd. brig. gen. U.S. Volunteers for defense of ft. against Confederate Army; served in battles of Cedar Mountain and 2d Bull Run, severely wounded, out of field service for 1 year; brevetted col. and brig. gen. U.S. Army, 1862; supt. U.S. Mil. Acad., 1864; in charge of field defense, Nashville, Tenn., 1864; insp. gen. fortifications Dept. of Miss.; brevetted maj. gen. U.S. Volunteers and maj. gen. U.S. Army, 1865; ret., 1883. Died Cohasset, Mar. 20, 1900.

TOWNLEY, CALVERT, electrical engr.; b. Cincinnati, Oct. 18, 1864; s. John Ackerman and Carrie A. (Calvert) T.; Ph.B., Sheffield Scientific Sch., 1886, M.E., 1888; m. Edith W. Case, Sept. 18, 1889; children—Clifford Calvert, Donald Case; m. 2d, Mabel McCormaick Steele, Dec. 30, 1911. Connected with Westinghouse Electric & Mfg. Co., 1887-1904 and 1911—; was v.p. of about 30 utility corps. controlled by N.Y.,N.H.&H. R.R. Co., 1904-11, also consulting elec. engr. for electrification out of New York; asst. to pres. Westinghouse Elec. & Mfg. Co. until 1932, retired. Fellow Am. Inst. E.E. (past pres.). Republican. Conglist. Home: New York, N.Y. Deceased.

TOWNLEY, SIDNEY DEAN, astonomer; b. Waukesha, Wis., Apr. 10, 1867; s. Robert and Mary (Wilkinson) T.; B.S., U. of Wis., 1890, M.S., 1892; Sc.D., U. of Mich., 1897; studied universities Calif., Berlin and Munich; m. Frances Wright, July 1, 1895; children—Lucile, Isabel, Ruth (dec.), Frances Jane. Instr. astronomy, U. of Mich., 1893-98, U. of Calif., 1898-1903; astronomer in charge Internat. Latitude Obs., Ukiah, Calif., 1903-07; lecturer in astronomy, U. of Calif., 1904-07; asst. prof. applied mathematics, Stanford U., 1907-09, asso. prof., 1909-18, prof., 1918-29, prof. astronomy and geodesy since 1929; visiting lecturer in astronomy, Harvard, 1925-26. Mem. Calif. Acad. Sciences, A.A.A.S., Am. Astron. Soc., Astron. Soc. Pacific, Seismol. Soc. America (sec.-treas. 1910-30; pres. 1935), Sigma Xi, Phi Beta Kappa. Author: Descriptive Catalog of Earthquakes of the Pacific Coast of the United States, 1769-1928 (with Maxwell W. Allen), 1939; Diary of a Student of the University of Wisconsin, 1886-1892, 1940; also about 100 articles in astron. and seismol. jours.; editor of Bull. of Seismol. Soc. America, 1911-35; former editor publs. of Astron. Soc. Pacific. Address: Stanford University, Calif. Died Mar. 16, 1946. *

TOWNSEND, CHARLES HASKINS, zoölogist; b. Parnassus, Pa., Sept. 29, 1859; s. Rev. D. W. and Elizabeth (Kier) T.; ed. pub. schs.; hon. Sc.D., Washington and Jefferson Coll., 1909. Asst. U.S. Fish Commn. in Salmon propagation in Calif., 1883; naturalist U.S.S. Corwin, Arctic Expdn., 1885; resident naturalist, U.S.S. Albatross, deep-sea investigations in Atlantic and Pacific, 1886-96; actg. dir. Am. Museum Natural History, 1910; dir. investigations U.S.S. Albatross, Gulf of Calif., 1911; mem. Bering Sea Fur Seal Commn., 1896; chief of fisheries div. U.S. Fish Commn., 1897-1902; fishery expert, Russo-Am. arbitration at The Hague, 1902; dir. New York Aquarium, 1902-37. Mem. Am. Fisheries Soc. (pres. 1912-13); fellow New York Acad. Sciences, N.Y. Zoöl. Soc.; mem. council Oceanographic Inst., Paris, since 1923. Club: Century. Author 100 documents on the fisheries, fur seal industries, deep-sea exploration and gen. zoölogy. Address: 3985 Douglas Road, Coconut Grove, Fla. Died Jan. 28, 1944.

TOWNSEND, CHARLES H(ENRY) T(YLER), biologist, physicist; b. Oberlin, O., Dec. 5, 1863; s. Nathan Haskin and Helen Jeannette (Tyler) T.; Columbian (now George Washington) U. Sch. of Medicine, 1887-91; B.S., George Washington U., 1908, Ph.D., 1914; m. Caroline W. Hess, Sept. 10, 1889 (died 1901); children—Karl Hess, Leland (dec.), Helen Tyler (dec.); m. 2d, Margaret C. Dyer, June 1, 1908; children—Charles Henry Tyler, Edward Dyer, Nathaniel Ostend, Mary Louise. Asst. entomologist, U.S. Dept. Agr., 1888-91; prof. entomology, zoölogy, and physiology, N.M. Agrl. Coll., and entomologist, Expt. Sta., 1891-93; curator Museum, Inst. Jamaica, 1893-94; field agt. div. entomology, U.S. Dept. Agr., 1894-98; again with N.M. Agrl. Coll. Expt. Sta., 1898-99; prof. biol., etc., Batangas Provincial Sch., P.I., 1904-06; expert, Gipsy Moth Lab., Bur. Entomology, U.S. Dept. Agr., 1907-09; govt. entomologist and dir. entom. stations, Peru, 1909-14; entom. asst., Bur. Entomology, U.S. Dept. Agr., 1914-19; hon. custodian muscoid diptera, U.S. Nat. Museum, 1914-25; chief entomologist, State of São Paulo, Brazil, 1919-22; ant expert in Brazil for Am. Cyanamid Co., 1923; dir. Cotton Plagues Lab., Piura, Peru, 1923-24; cotton plagues expert, Chamber Commerce and Agr., Iquitos, Peru, 1925; chief Inst. Parasitologia Agricola, Lima, Peru, 1926; chief entomologist Estacion Experimental Agricola S.N.A., Lima, 1927-29; head firm Charles Townsend & Filhos, São Paulo, since 1929; cons. entomologist Cia. Ford Industrial do Brasil, Rio Tapajós, Pará, since 1932. Author: Manual of Myiology (12 parts); also about 1000 titles on muscoid flies, cotton plagues, med. entomology, biogeography, ecology and physics. Pioneer work on American cotton weevils; discovered mode of transmission of disease, verruga, in Peruvian Andes; first analysed insect environments; demonstrated Cephenemyia as the swiftest organism; established about 1000 valid muscoid genera; explained gravity; recorded exact atomic weights; determined exact velocity of light; defined cosmic units of length, time and mass; explained moon's origin and earth's axial inclination; set Pleistocene duration and man in America at two million years. Home: Fazenda Casagrande Velha. Itaquaquecetuba, São Paulo, Brazil S.A. Died Mar. 17, 1944.

TOWNSEND, CHARLES ORRIN, pathologist; b. Washtenaw County, Mich., Jan. 16, 1863; s. Orrin Russell and Phebe Ellen (DeMill) T.; grad. Mich. State Normal Sch., 1884; B.S., U. of Mich., 1888, M.S., 1891; Ph.D., U. of Leipzig, 1897, specializing in botany and plant physiology; m. Mary Louise Taylor, Mich., Feb. 3, 1891; 1 dau., Martha Ellenor. Prof. natural science, St. John's Coll., Annapolis, Md., 1888-91, Wesleyan Coll., Macon, Ga., 1891-95; instr. botany, Barnard Coll., New York, 1897-98; prof. botany Md. Agrl. Coll. and state plant pathologist for Md., 1898-1901; in charge of sugar beet investigations, 1901-09, sugar plant investigations, 1909-10, collaborator, 1910-12, U.S. Dept. of Agr.; consulting agrlist., U.S. Sugar & Land Co., Garden City, Kan., 1910-12; plant pathologist, 1912-14, pathologist in charge of sugar beet investigation, 1914-17, of sugar plant investigations, 1917-23, U.S. Dept. of Agr.; spl. expert sugar div., 1923-25, chief, 1925-34, U.S. Tariff Commn.; retired. Author of bulls. relating to diseases and production of sugar beets and other plants. Home: Woodside, L.I., N.Y. Died June 2, 1937.

TOWNSEND, CHARLES WENDELL, ornithologist, author; b. Boston, Nov. 10, 1859; s. Thomas Davis and Frances Barnard (Smith) T.; A.B., Harvard, 1881, M.D., 1885; m. Gertrude Flint, Sept. 28, 1891 (died 1917); children—Gertrude, Margaret (Mrs. Hale Sutherland), Frances (Mrs. Wendell Taber), Charles; m. 2d, Sarah G. Flint, July 2, 1919 (died 1924). Visiting phys. Sea Shore Home, Boston, Mass., 1887-90; asst. in obstetrics, Harvard Med. Sch., 1887-97; phys. to out-patients dept. Children's Hosp., 1887-1903, Boston Lying-in Hosp., 1887-98, Mass. Gen. Hosp., 1891-1909; visiting phys., Floating Hosp., 1907-09. Author: The Birds of Essex County, Mass., 1905; Along the Labrador Coast, 1907; Birds of Labrador (joint author), 1907; A Labrador Spring, 1910; Captain Cartwright and His Labrador Journal, 1911; Sand Dunes and Salt Marshes, 1913; In Audubon's Labrador, 1918; Supplement to Birds of Essex Co., 1920; Beach Grass, 1923; From Panama to Patagonia, 1931; also chapter on birds in Grenfell's book on Labrador. Home: Ipswich, Mass. Died Apr. 3, 1934.

TOWNSEND, EDGAR JEROME, coll. prof.; b. Litchfield, Hillsdale County, Mich., Feb. 22, 1864; s. Warren and Henriette (Crocker) T.; Ph.B., Albion (Mich.) Coll., 1890, LL.D., 1915; Ph.M., U. of Mich., 1891; U. of Chicago, summers 1894, 95; A.M., Ph.D., U. of Göttingen, Germany, 1900; m. Phebe Belle Miller, June 24, 1891; children—Mrs. G.L. Alexander, Jerome T. (dec.). Prin. pub. schs., Reading, Mich., 1887-88; county examiner schs., Hillsdale County, Mich., 1887-90; teacher mathematics, Chicago Manual Training School, 1891-93; asst. prof. mathematics, U. of Ill., 1893-95, asso. prof., 1895-1905, prof., 1905, dean Coll. of Science, 1905-13 (now retired). Fellow A.A.A.S.; mem. Am. Math. Soc. (Council, 1905-08), Delta Tau Delta, Sigma Xi, Phi Beta Kappa. Conglist. Author: Functions of a Complex Variable, 1915; Functions of Real Variables, 1929. Co-author: First Course in Calculus, 1910; Essentials of Calculus, 1910; Essentials of Calculus, 1910; A Layman's View of the

Bible, 1954. Translator of: Foundation of Geometry (from the German of Hilbert), 1902. Editor of American Mathematical Series. Contbr. to math. and ednl. jours. Home: 510 John St., Champaign, Ill. Died July 8, 1955; buried Rose Lawn, Champaign.

TOWNSEND, FRANCIS EVERETT, physician; b. Fairbury, Ill., Jan. 13, 1867; s. George Warren and Sarah Jane (Harper) T.; student rural schs. Livingston County, Ill., 1875-85; grad. Franklin (Neb.) Acad., 1893; M.D., U. Neb., 1903; LL.D., Met. U. Los Angeles, 1950; m. Mrs. Minnie Bogue, Oct. 30, 1906; children—Robert Craig, Marlyn (Mrs. Lester Pennock, dec.). Practiced in S.D., Wyo. and Mont., hdqrs. Belle Fourche, S.D., 1903-19, Long Beach, Cal., 1919-31; served as asst. health officer City of Long Beach; physician to indigent; originator and pres. Townsend Plan, Inc. (monthly pensions, based on a 3 percent gross income tax above $250 mo. exemption, to U.S. citizens over 60 yrs. of age, to include all totally and permanently disabled persons between 18 and 60 yrs. of age, with certain restrictions); pres. Townsend Nat. Weekly, Inc., United Pub. Co.; also pres. and trustee Townsend Found. Served as 1st lt. M.C., World War, 1918. Awarded Wilson Service medal; winner Life Begins at Eighty contest, M.B.S., 1949. Author autobiography, New Horizons; also pamphlets, articles on pension plan. Home: 227 N. New Hampshire St., Los Angeles. Office: 6875 Broadway, Cleve. 5. Died Sept. 1960.

TOWNSEND, JOHN KIRK, ornithologist; b. Phila., Aug. 10, 1809; s. Charles and Priscilla (Kirk) T.; m. Charlotte Holmes, 1 child. Joined overland expdn. to Ore., 1835, to H.I., 1835; surgeon Ft. Vancouver, 1835-36; assembled valuable collection of birds and mammals; new birds from Ore. country described by him in Jour. of Acad. of Natural Scis. of Phila.; conceived idea of preparing work on birds of U.S., published one part of Ornithology of the United States of North America, 1840; Townsend's Bunting is named for him; birds from his collection were painted for last volume of Audubon's Birds of America, 1844, his mammals described and painted by Audubon and John Bachman in Viviparous Quadrupeds of North America; secured and mounted birds for Nat. Inst., Washington, D.C., 1842; studied dentistry, Phils., 1845; elected mem. Acad. Natural Sciences of Phila., 1833, life mem. 1850. Author: Narrative to a Journey Across the Rocky Mountains to the Columbia River, 1839. Died Washington, D.C., Feb. 6, 1851.

TOZZER, ARTHUR CLARENCE, constrn. engr.; b. Lynn, Mass., July 18, 1879; s. Samuel Clarence and Caroline Blanchard (Marston) T.; B.S., Dartmouth, 1902, C.E., 1903; m. Dorothy LaCroix, June 1, 1916; children—Edith, Caroline, Dorothy; m. 2d, Isabel Kellers, Sept. 28, 1937; stepson, James McW. Kellers. Assistant engr. with Henry F. Bryant, Brookline, Mass., 1903; with Foundation Co., N.Y. City, East River Tunnel, Pa. R.R. Tunnel, S. Pearson & Son, 1904-05; supt. Turner Constrn. Co., 1905-13, gen. supt., 1913-18, exec. mgr. (in charge constrn. $28,000,000 U.S. Army Supply Base, Brooklyn), 1918-19, v.p. since 1919, dir. dir. since 1925; ex-pres., dir. Asso. Gen. Contractors of America, Inc.; dir. Turner Rostock Corp., Overseer Thayer Sch. of Civ. Engring. (Dartmouth). Mem. Am. Soc. C.E., Am. Concrete Inst., Archtl. League N.Y. City, Chi Phi. Republican. Club: Dartmouth (New York). Contbr. to tech. press. Home: 47 Brookline Rd., Scarsdale, N.Y. Office: 420 Lexington Av., New York, N.Y. Died Sep. 9, 1942.

TRACY, JOHN CLAYTON, civil engr.; b. Willimantic, Conn., Nov. 3, 1869; s. John Theodore and Annie (Downer) T.; Ph.B., Sheffield Sci. Sch. (Yale), 1890, C.E., 1892; m. Elizabeth Mary Blakeslee, Oct. 23, 1894 (died Mar. 30, 1934); children—John Blakeslee, Philip Louis (dec.), Thomas North, Delia Elizabeth. Instr., Yale U., 1891-1902, asst. prof. structural engring., 1902-15, prof., May-Nov. 1915, prof. civil engring., 1915-36, emeritus, 1936—. Pres. New Haven C. of C., 1925-26, New Haven Taxpayers, Inc., 1936-37. Mem. Am. Soc. C.E., Soc. Promotion Engring. Edn., Conn. Soc. C.E., Sigma Xi, Tau Beta Pi. Author: An Introductory Course in Mechanical Drawing, 1898; Plane Surveying, 1907; Exercises in Surveying, 1909; Aesthetic Elements in Engineering Design; Some Experiments in Reading Leveling Rods and Stadia Rods, 1908; Bridge Design, 1900; Descriptive Geometry, 1913. Dir. New Haven War Bur. Conn. State Council Def., Jan. 1918-May 1919. Gov. N.E. Kiwanis Dist., 1923. Author: Stresses Statically Determined, 1929; The Enrichment of Experience in the Development of the Teacher, 1932; Contemporary Science and Personal Faith, 1934; Commonplace Mysteries, 1943; Surveying—Theory and Practice, 1947. Address: 345 Winthrop Av., New Haven. Died Nov. 1, 1955.

TRACY, SAMUEL MILLS, botanist; b. Hartford, Vt., Apr. 30, 1847; s. Samuel and Emeline (Newton) T.; B.S., Mich. State Agrl. Coll., 1868, M.S., 1871; spl. work in botany, Harvard, 1885; m. Martha A. Terry, July 23, 1874 (died 1904). Prof. botany and horticulture, U. of Mo., 1877-87; dir. Miss. Agrl. Expt. Sta., 1887-97; special agent, 1897-1914 and agronomist, 1914—, U.S. Dept. Agriculture. Pvt. Co. A, 41st Regt. Wis. Vols., Civil War. Episcopalian. Pres. State Hort. Soc. of Mo., 1886; pres. Soc. for Promotion Agrl. Science, 1910-11. Author: Flora of Missouri, 1886; Flora of the Southern United States, 1899. Home: Laurel, Miss. Died Sept. 5, 1920.

TRACY, WILLIAM W., horticulturist; b. Hudson, O., May 21, 1845; B.S., Mich. State Agrl. Coll., East Lansing, Mich., 1867, M.S., 1870 (hon. Sc.D., 1907). Prof. horticulture, Mich. State Agrl. Coll., 1870-72; supt. testing gardens, U.S. Dept. Agr., 1902—. Home: Washington, D.C. Died Mar. 1, 1932.

TRAEGER, CORNELIUS HORACE, physician; b. St. Louis, Aug. 14, 1896; s. Victor and Selma (Goetz) T.; B.A., Columbia, 1923, M.D., 1927; m. Janet Reisner, July 8, 1962; 1 son, Charles. Intern, Roosevelt Hosp., N.Y.C., 1927-29, clin. asst., 1929-31, cons. attending physician internal medicine and arthritis, chief arthritis clinic, 1940-64, cons., 1964-68; co-chief rheumatic diseases Hosp. Spl. Surgery, N.Y.C., 1930-64, chief emeritus, 1964-68; asst. prof. clin. medicine Cornell U., 1954-64; exec. med. dir. N.Y. Infirmary, 1962-64. Med. dir. Nat. Multiple Sclerosis Soc., 1948-55; mem. adv. council NIH Neurol. Diseases and Blindness, 1950-54, NIH Arthritis and Metabolic Diseases, 1962-66, regional med. programs for heart, cancer and stroke, 1965-68; spl. cons. to Surgeon Gen., USPHS, 1954-57, 62-68. Bd. govs. Arthritis Found., also N.Y. chpt. Recipient Floyd B. Odlum award, 1965. Fellow American College Physicians (life), N.Y. Acad. Medicine, N.Y. Acad. Sci., Am. Acad. Neurology; mem. WHO, Am. Rheumatism Assn., Arthritis and Rheumatism Foundation (all co-founder). Am. Geriatric Soc., Assn. Am. Med. Colls., A.M.A., N.Y. State, N.Y. County med. socs., A.A.A.S., Am. Pub. Health Assn., Assn. Mil. Surgeons, Assn. Am. Physicians and Surgeons, Assn. Research Nervous and Mental Diseases. Contbr. articles to med. jours. Home: New York City NY Died Sept. 24, 1968.

TRAINER, DAVID WOOLSEY, JR., educator; b. Huntington, N.Y., Aug. 6, 1899; s. David W. and Emma B. (Jones) T.; B.S., Dartmouth, 1921; M.S., Northwestern U., 1923; Ph.D., Cornell U., 1926; m. Elizabeth Richmond Moyer, Aug. 18, 1926; children—Mary Elizabeth (Mrs. Joseph E. Crandell, Jr.), Ann Woolsey (Mrs. William D. Mayer). Asst. geology Northwestern U., 1921-23; asst., then instr. geology Cornell U., 1921-31; mem. faculty Colgate U., 1931—, prof. geology, 1950—. Fellow Geol. Soc. Am.; mem. mineral, socs. Am., Can. Home: 42 University Av., Hamilton, N.Y. 13346. Died July 11, 1965; buried Colgate U. Cemetery.

TRANSEAU, EDGAR NELSON, botanist; b. Williamsport, Pa., October 21, 1875; s. Samuel and Martha Edith (Zimmerman) T.; A.B., Franklin and Marshall Coll., Lancaster, Pa., 1897; studied Marine Lab., Brooklyn Inst. Arts and Sciences, summer 1899; Univ. of Chicago, 1900-01; Ph.D., U. of Michigan, 1904; honorary Sc.D., Franklin and Marshall College, 1941, Ohio State University, 1949; married Gertrude Hastings (M.D.), August 23, 1906; 1 daughter, Elizabeth Hastings (Mrs. August Mahr). Prof. biology, Alma Coll., 1904-06; investigator Sta. for Experimental Evolution, at Cold Spring Harbor, L.I., N.Y., 1906-07; prof. botany, State Teachers Coll., Charleston, Ill., 1907-15; prof. plant physiology and ecology, Ohio State Univ., 1915-46, chairman of department, 1918-46, retired; plant ecologist in Europe, for U.S. Bur. Entomology, 1927; collaborator Central States Forestry Expt. Station, 1929-32. Fellow A.A.A.S.; mem. Botanical Soc. of America (pres. 1940), Assn. Am. Geographers, Ecol. Soc. America (pres. 1924), Phycological Society of America (president 1951), American Geographic Soc., Ohio Acad. Sciences (pres. 1924) Phi Beta Kappa, Sigma Xi, Phi Kappa Sigma. Author: Science of Plant Life, 1919; General Botany, 1923; (with H. C. Sampson) Laboratory Manual in General Botany, 1923; (with Sampson and Tiffany) Work Book in General Botany, 1934; Textbook of Botany (with Sampson and Tiffany), 1939; The Zygnemataceae, 1951. Contbr. to bot. jours. Home: 2079 W. 5th Av., Columbus OH

TRAPHAGEN, FRANK WEISS, chemist, metallurgist; b. Eaton, O., July 20, 1861; s. Henry Laurens and Martha M. (Weiss) T.; Ph.B., Sch. of Mines (Columbia), 1882, Ph.D., 1883; m. Hattie M. Van Horn, Apr. 25, 1883; children—Gertrude Luciene (Mrs. Floyd M. Belleau), Elizabeth Lynde (Mrs. Robert P. Shollenberger). Instr. chemistry and physics, Staunton (Va.) Mil. Acad., 1884; prof. chemistry, Coll. of Mont. and Mont. Sch. of Mines, Deer Lodge, Mont., 1887-93; assayer and metallurgist, Champion Mining Co., 1888-92; in charge of Mont. Mining Exhibit, Chicago Expn., 1893; prof. chemistry, Mont. State Coll., and chemist Mont. Expt. Sta., Bozeman Mont., 1893-1903; prof. metallurgy and assaying, Colo. Sch. of Mines, 1903-16; pres. and gen. mgr. Colo. Metal Mining & Reduction Co., Georgetown 1916-17; prof. metallurgy, S.D. Sch. of Mines, Rapid City, 1917-21; metallurgist and mgr. White Hills Mining Co., 1922-24; research chemist Standard Metal & Chemical Corp., Denver, Colo., 1925, mgr. and tech. director, 1926-28; vice-pres. Sewage Treatment Corp. of Chicago. First pres. Western Assn. Tech. Chemists and Metallurgists. Cons. metallurgist, 1927—. Home: Loudonville, N.Y. Died Jan. 21, 1941.

TRASK, JOHN WILLIAM, physician; b. Bay City, Mich., Feb. 18, 1877; s. William Henry and Ellen Grey (McKim) T.; M.D., U. Mich., 1901; m. Fleta Lawrence, Aug. 23, 1902; children—Elsie Margaret, Ethel Lawrence, John Lawrence. Apptd. asst. surgeon USPHS, 1902; passed asst. surgeon, 1907; asst. surgeon gen., 1909-18; surgeon, 1918; promoted med. dir., 1930. Served at Detroit, Ft. Stanton (N.M.), Washington; charge of U.S. Marine hosps., Buffalo, Balt., Chgo., Boston, also fgn. quarantine and immigration inspection, Charleston, S.C. Editor Pub. Health Reports and charge Div. San Reports and Statistics, USPHS, 1909-18; med. dir. U.S. Employees' Compensation Commn., 1918-22. Mem. sub-coms. on tb and statistics Com. Hygiene and Sanitation of Gen. Med. Bd. and sub-com. on information and statistics of Com. Labor of Council Nat. Def., 1917-18; commr. pub. health, City of Pittsfield, Mass., Apr. 1942-June 1946. Fellow A.C.P.; mem. A.M.A., Am. Pub. Health Assn. (chmn. sect. vital statistics, 1915-18), Mass. Med. Soc., Phi Rho Sigma. Author: A Digest of the Laws and Regulations of the Various States Relating to the Reporting of Cases of Sickness, 1911; Vital Statistics, 1914; Physiology, Hygiene and Sanitation and Primer of Personal Hygiene (text books), 1923; also chpts. various med. books and articles med. jours., principally on vital statistics, tb, malaria, milk as a factory in the spread of disease; geographic distribution of disease, etc. Address: 30 Sampson Pkwy., Pittsfield, Mass. Died Jan. 6, 1951.

TRATMAN, EDWARD ERNEST RUSSELL, editor; b. Bristol, Eng.; ed. private schs., studied engring. as asst. under Edward Wilson, London, and in ry. and other practice; came to U.S., 1884; m. Florence R. Kirkwood, 1897. Was special agt. U.S. Govt. to report on metal and wooden ry. ties. For many years was editor Engineering News-Record. Mem. Am. Soc. C.E., Am. Inst. Mining Engrs., Am. Ry. Engring. Assn., Internat. Tramways Union, etc. Received Norman medal, Am. Soc. C.E., for paper on English Railway Track, 1888. Contbr. numerous papers on ry. engring., article, "Railways," Johnson's Universal Cyclopaedia, etc. Author: Railway Track and Track Work, 1908-25; Specifications and Standards for Public Works Engineering, 1933; Railway Car-Ferries, 1936-40. Reports on Metal and Wooden Railway Ties and Preservation of Ties, 1890, 1894. Home: Wheaton IL

TRAUGOTT, ALBERT MASER, (traw'got), civil engr.; b. Rochester, N.Y., July 31, 1882; s. Frederick George and Maria (Meier) T.; prep. edn., Rochester Free Acad. and Mechanics Inst., Rochester; student Purdue, 1899-1902; m. Myrtle Perkins, Nov. 6, 1920 (deceased July 17, 1942); children—Mary Perkins (Mrs. Townsend Brown). Myrtle Patricia (Mrs. John F. Rixev). Chainman Buffalo, Rochester & Pittsburgh Ry., 1898, Delaware, Lackawanna & West, R.R., 1900; successively rodman, draftsman, instrumentman, Virginian Ry., 1903-07, resident engr., locating engr. and div. engr., 1908-18, acting chief engr., 1919, asst. chief engineer, 1920-26, chief engineer, 1927-47, retired 1947—. Mem. Rodmasters and Maintenance of Way Association. American Society Civil Engineers, Am. Railway Engring. Assn., Sigma Alpha Epsilon. Mason (Shriner). Clubs: Hampton Roads Engineers, Princess Anne Country. Norfolk Yacht and Country. German. Home: 1516 Blandford Circle, Lochhaven, Norfolk 5, Va. Died Jan. 1, 1954; buried Forest Lawn Cemetery, Norfolk.

TRAUTWINE, JOHN CRESSON, engr.; b. Phila., Mar. 30, 1810; s. William and Sarah (Wilkinson) T.; m. Eliza Ritter, circa 1838, at least 2 children. Civil engr. assisting in erection public buildings including U.S. Mint; asst. engr. Phila., Wilmington & Balt. R.R., 1835; chief engr. Hiwassee R.R., 1836; worked on constrn. of Canal del Dique, New Granada (now Columbia), S.A., 1844-49; went to Isthmus of Panama to make surveys for Panama R.R., 1849-51; in Panama to seek inter-oceanic canal route (reported no possibility of canal), 1852; surveyed Lackawanna & Lanesboro R.R., 1856; surveyed route for interoceanic railway in Honduras, 1857; planned system of docks for Montreal, 1858; planned harbor for Big Glace Bay, N.S., Can., 1864; consultant on various engring. problems. Author: Engineers' Pocket Book, 1871. Died Phila., Sept. 14, 1883.

TRAUTWINE, JOHN CRESSON, JR., engineer; b. Philadelphia, Mar. 17, 1850; s. John Cresson and Eliza (Ritter) T.; ed. pvt. schs., Phila., 1855-65; studied civ. engring. with father; m. Lucy L. Smith, May 23, 1872. Chief Bur. of Water, Phila., 1895-99. Advocated waste-restriction by use of watermeters and purification by means of filters. Life mem. Franklin Inst., Phila.; mem. and past pres. Engrs. Club, Philadelphia. Editor and propr. from 1888 of father's Civil Engineer's Pocket Book, 1872. Home: Philadelphia, Pa. Died July 4, 1924.

TREADWELL, AARON LOUIS (tred'wel), biologist; b. Redding, Conn., Dec. 23, 1866; s. Aaron and Lois (Mead) T.; B.S., Wesleyan U., Middletown, Conn., 1888, M.S., 1890, hon. D.Sc., 1938; fellow, 1897-98, Ph.D., 1899, U. of Chicago; m. Sarah Hill, June 15, 1892 (died May 25, 1938); children—Lois (Mrs. Beardsley Ruml), Merlin (dec.), Alvin Hill (dec.), Arthur Burr, Louis Mead (dec.). Asst. in natural history, Wesleyan U., 1888-91; prof. biology and geology, Miami U., Oxford, O., 1891-1900; prof. biology, Vassar Coll.,

1900-14, prof. of zoölogy, 1914-37, emeritus since 1937, Instr. Marine Biol. Lab., Woods Hole, Mass., 1898-1906, 13. Cold Spring Harbor, L.I., 1907; hon. curator annulates, American Museum of Natural History, N.Y., 1909-18, research associate in same since 1918; mem. research staff, N.Y. Zoöl. Soc., 1930, 31. Fellow A.A.A.S.; mem. Am. Soc. Zoölogists (v.p. 1921), Am. Soc. Naturalists (sec. 1912), Phi Beta Kappa, Chi Psi. Writer of biology and zoölogy articles in New Internat. Ency. Year Book, since 1907, and various papers in zoöl. jours. With Carnegie Instn. expdns. through West Indies, Fiji and Samoa. Address: Vassar Coll., Poughkeepsie, N.Y.; (summer) Redding, Conn., P.O. R.D. 2, Danbury, Conn. Died June 24, 1947. *

TREADWELL, DANIEL, inventor, educator; b. Ipswich, Mass., Oct. 10, 1791; s. Capt. Jabez and Elizabeth (Dodge) T.; studied medicine with Dr. John Ware, 10 years; A.M. (hon.), Harvard, 1829; m. Adeline Lincoln, Oct. 6, 1831, no children. Silversmith, circa 1807-11; built a screw-making machine, circa 1812, put into operation, Saugus, Mass., circa 1813; elected fellow Am. Acad. Arts and Scis., 1823, recording sec., 1833-39, v.p., 1852-63; an editor Boston Jour. of Philosophy and Arts, 1823-26; invented a means of printing on both sides of a paper without shifting the sheet; super-intended constn. water system for Boston, 1825; mem. 2 commns. to investigate practicability of a water supply for Boston, 1825, 37; patented 1st power press in U.S., 1826, 1st used in newspaper work by Boston Daily Advertiser, 1829; received 4 patents on a machine for spinning hemp, 1831-35; Runford prof. on the applications of science Harvard, 1834-45; organized the Steel Cannon Co. to manufacture for U.S. Govt., 1842. Author: The Relation of Science to the Useful Arts, 1855. Died Cambridge, Mass., Feb. 27, 1872.

TREADWELL, GEORGE A., metallurgist, miner; b. Me.; ed. pub. schs., followed by courses in geology and metallurgy at Yale. Went to Calif. and Ariz.; became, 1878, supt. of the Vulture mine, Ariz., and built an 80-stamp mill, then the largest in the world; went to Europe, 1884, lecturer Dexter Sch. of Mines, London, 1884-7; in Ariz., 1887; discovered the copper deposits in the Verde country; now pres. George A. Treadwell Mining Co. Residence: The Waldord-Astoria. Office: 27 William St., New York NY

TREADWELL, NANCY CLAAR, obstetrician and gynecologist; born Chgo., March 27, 1924; d. Elmer A. and Evelyn Janet (Smith) Claar; B.A., Smith Coll., 1944; B.S., U. Ill., 1948, M.D., 1950; m. Warren S. Treadwell, Dec. 25, 1947; children—Susan Millard, Jennifer Anne, Alan Clay. Intern Henrotin Hosp., 1950-51 resident, 1951-52, preceptorship Dr. Joseph B. Teton, 1952-56, asso. attending obstetricia and gynecologist, 1953-58; attending obstetrician and gynecologist Louis A. Weiss Meml. Hosp., 1959-63; courtesy staff obstetrics and gynecology, Lutheran Gen. Hospital 1962-63, associate attending cons. in obstetrics and gynecology, 1963-70; clin. asst. U. Ill. Coll. Medicine, 1954-60, clin. instr., 1960-70; pvt. practice medicine specializing in obstetrics and gynecology 1956-70. Diplomate Am. Bd. Obstetrics and Gynecology, Nat. Board Med. Examiners. Fellow A.C.S., Am. Coll. Obstetricians and Gynecologists, Chicago Gynecol. Soc., International Coll. Surgeons (asso. fellow); member of American Com. on Maternal Welfare, Am. Soc. Study Sterility, Am. Med. Women's Assn., Ill., Chgo. med. socs., A.M.A., Alpha Epsilon Iota, Alpha Omega Alpha. Conglist. Author articles in field. Home: Wilmette IL Died Dec. 15, 1970.

TREAT, MARY, naturalist; b. (Davis) Tompkins Co., N.Y., Sept. 7, 1830; d. of Methodist minister; ed. in common schs.; m. Dr. Joseph Treat, 1863. Author: Home Studies in Nature; Chapters on Ants; Insects Injurious to Vegetation; My Garden Pets; Through a Microscope (with Samuel Wells); also wrote on flora of N.J. for "Garden and Forest." Home: Vineland, N.J. Deceased.

TREES, MERLE JAY, civil engineer; born on farm near Mayview, Ill., June 14, 1883; s. George Washington and Jennie Myrtle (Ray) T.; B.S., U. of Ill., 1907, C.E., 1911; m. Emily Lavinia Nichols, Jan. 2, 1909; children—Katherine, George Spencer. With Chicago Bridge & Iron Co., Oct. 1908—, beginning as estimator, apptd. gen. sales mgr., 1911, dir., 1913, v.p., 1918, exec. v.p., 1942, chmn. bd. 1945, dir. Guardite Corp., International Harvester Co., Am. Lumber & Treating Co., John I. Hay Co., Northern Trust Co., A.T.&S.F. Ry., Horton Steel Works, Ltd., Chgo. Bridge & Iron Wks., Ltd., Sociedad Chibridge de Construcoes Ltd. Has served as pres. bd. dirs. United Charities of Chicago, Chicago Commonwealth Club, U. of Ill. Alumni Assn., Nat. Ry. Appliance Assn.; mem. executive com. Chicago Community Trust; mem. Cancer Research Committee Univ. Chgo.; mem. bd. trustees, U. of Ill. (past pres.), 12 years; mem. bd. trustees Art Inst. of Chicago, 4th Presbyn Ch. Life mem. Chicago Hist. Soc., Art Inst. Chicago, Field Museum of Natural History. Mem. Am. Soc. Civil Engrs., Western Soc. Engrs., Steel Plate Fabricators Assn. (past pres.), U. of Ill. Alumni Assn. (past pres.), Nat. Ry. Appliance Assn. (past pres.), Am. Iron and Steel Inst., Phi Delta Theta. Republican. Mason. Clubs: Chicago, Commercial (past pres.) Commonwealth, University, Illini, Wayfarers, Casino, Economic, Ind. Soc. of Chgo., Glenview (Chgo.). Home: 1500 Lake Shore Dr. Office: 322 S. Michigan Blvd., Chgo. Died Aug. 6, 1954.

TRELEASE, SAM FARLOW, (tre-les'), plant physiololgist; born in St. Louis, Missouri, July 3, 1892; the son of William and Julia Maria (Johnson) T.; A.B., Washington University, 1914; Ph.D., Johns Hopkins, 1917; m. Mrs. Helen Mary Cato Ashton, July 11, 1922. Asst. in plant physiology, Johns Hopkins, 1916-17, instr., 1920-23; asst. prof., U. of Philippines, 1917-19, asso. prof., 1919-20; asst. prof., U. of Louisville, 1923-25; asso. prof., Columbia, 1925-28, prof. botany, 1929-36, Torrey prof. botany since 1937, exec. officer of dept. since 1930. Mem. bd. mgrs. New York Bot. Garden. Fellow Am. Assn. Advancement Science (asst. sec. 1921-23; sec. council 1921-30; program editor 1923-30; sec. sect. G 1925-36), Bot. Soc. America (sec. 1932; editor Am. Jour. Bot., 1933-39; v.p. 1941), Am. Soc. of Plant Physiologists, Torrey Bot. Club, Soc. Bot. de France, Gamma Alpha, Sigma Xi. Author: Laboratory Exercises in Agricultural Botany, 1919; How to Write Scientific and Technical Papers, 1957; Selenium (with O. A. Beath), 1949. Contbr. various papers on bot. subjects. Home: 520 W. 114th St., N.Y.C. 25. Died Feb. 1, 1958; buried St. Louis.

TRELEASE, WILLIAM, botanist; b. Mt. Vernon, N.Y., Feb. 22, 1857; s. Samuel R. and Mary (Gandall) T.; B.S., Cornell, 1880; Sc.D., Harvard, 1884; LL.D., U. of Wis., 1902, U. of Mo., 1903, Washington U., 1907; m. Julia M. Johnson, July 19, 1882; children—Frank Johnson, Marjorie (dec.), Sam Farlow, Sidney Briggs, William. In charge Summer Sch., Botany, Harvard, 1883-84; lecturer botany, Johns Hopkins, 1884; instr. botany, U. of Wis., 1881-83, prof., 1883-85; prof. botany, Washington U., 1885-1913; dir. Mo. Bot. Garden, 1889-1912; prof. botany, U. of Ill., 1913-26, emeritus since 1926. Mem. Ill. State Board Natural Resources and Conservation since 1917. Chmn. Am. board editors Botanisches Centralblatt, 1900-21. Fellow Am. Acad. Arts and Sciences (1892), A.A.A.S.; mem. Nat. Acad. Sciences (1902), Am. Philos. Soc. (1903), etc., directeur (pres.) Académie Internationale de Géographie Botanique, 1896; 1st pres. Bot. Soc. America, 1894-95 and 1918; pres. Am. Soc. Naturalists, 1903, Cambridge Entomol. Club, 1889, Engelman Bot. Club, 1898-99 (hon. pres. since 1900); sec. Wis. Hort. Soc., 1882-85, Acad. Science St. Louis, 1896 (president 1909-11). Club: Round Table (St. Louis). Mem. of Delta Upsilon, Sigma Xi, Phi Beta Kappa, Pi Gamma Mu. Edited (with Asa Gray) Botanical Works of the late George Engelmann. Translated Poulsen's Botanical Micro-Chemistry and Salomonsen's Bacteriological Technology. Author: Agave in the West Indies, 1913; The Genus Phoradendron, 1916; Plant Materials of Decorative Gardening, 1917, 21, 26, 30; Winter Botany, 1918, 25, 30; The American Oaks, 1925; also many papers and reports on botany and entomology. Commemorated in many plant names and in Mount Trelease (12,500 ft. high), at head of Clear Creek, Colo., at first ascent to Loveland Pass. Home: 804 S. Lincoln Av., Urbana, Ill. Died Jan. 1, 1945.

TREVES, NORMAN, surgeon; b. Crawfordsville, Ind., Jan. 2, 1894; s. Max and Ida (Kahn) T.; A.B., Wabash Coll., 1915, A.M., 1916, Sc.D., 1953; M.D., Johns Hopkins, 1920; m. Rebecca Bacharach, July 26, 1932. Intern, asst., resident surgeon Hosp. for Women of Md., Balt., 1920-23; resident surgeon Meml. Hosp., N.Y.C., 1923-25, asso. surgeon, 1936-52, attending surgeon, 1952-60; asso. prof. clin. surgery Cornell University, 1953-60, asso. prof. clin. surgery emeritus; consulting surgeon tumor clinic Meadowbrook Hosp., Hempstead, N.Y., clin. dir. 1944-56; cons. breast service Strang Clinic, Meml. Center, 1952-60; asso. Sloan-Kettering Inst., 1953-57, clinician, 1957-60. Trustee Wabash College. Recipient Frank Billings gold medal A.M.A., 1940. Cancer Society medal, 1951. Recipient James Ewing Society Gold Medal, 1959. Diplomate Am. Bd. Radiology, Am. Bd. Surgery (founders group). Fellow N.Y. Acad. Medicine, A.C.S.; mem. A.M.A., Am. Cancer Research and Control Socs., Am. Radium Soc., Assn. Study Neoplastic Diseases, A.A.A.S., New York Academy of Sciences, Am. Geriatrics Soc., Harvey Society, James Ewing Society, Johns Hopkins Surgical Society, Phi Beta Kappa; affiliate of the Royal Society of Medicine. Mason (39 deg.). Contbr. articles medical jours. Home: 30 Sutton Pl., N.Y.C. 22. Office: 445 E. 67th St., N.Y.C. 21. Died May 17, 1964; buried Ferncliff, Scarsdale, N.Y.

TRIBUS, LOUIS LINCOLN, civil and sanitary engr.; b. Northampton, Mass., May 26, 1865; s. Louis and Harriet Jeannette (Kingsley) T.; B.S. and C.E., New York U., 1885, M.S., 1888; m. Letitia Hall McCampbell, Oct. 3, 1899; children—Lucien Hall, Theron Kingley. With Samuel R. Bullock & Co., water works constructors, 1885-87; with Charles B. Brush, consulting engr., 1887-93; instr. and asst. prof. engring., New York U., 1887-90; in pvt. practice, 1894—; mem. Tribus & Massa; in charge of pub. improvements, Borough of Richmond, City of New York, 1902-13. Engr. mem. and sec. N.Y. Bay Pollution Commn., 1903-06. Republican. Home: Richmond, New York, N.Y. Died Nov. 9, 1930.

TRILLEY, JOSEPH, rear admiral U.S.N.; b. in Ireland, Sept. 25, 1838; s. Samuel and Ann T.; ed. Phila., and Baltimore; studied engring. Md. Inst. Sch. of Design; m. Blanche Haynes, Apr. 25, 1868. Apptd. 3d asst. engr. U.S.N., Aug. 11, 1860; 2d asst. engr., July 1862; 1st asst. engr., July 1864; chief engr., Feb. 1871; capt. in the line, Mar. 1899; rear admiral, Sept. 25, 1899, and retired same date. During Civil War took part in engagements at Fort Sumter, burning of Norfolk Navy Yard, Acquia Creek, Hatteras Inlet, Hilton Head, Fernandina, Port Hudson, Donaldsonville, Mobile Bay and several other minor engagements. Served on the West Indian, European (and, as fleet engr.) on the China and Pacific stas.; also as chief engr. of the Portsmouth and Mare Island Navy Yards. Died 1911.

TRIMBLE, ISAAC RIDGEWAY, army officer, engr.; b. Culpeper County, Va., May 15, 1802; s. John Trimble; grad. U.S. Mil. Acad., 1822; m. Maria Presstman; m. 2d, Ann Presstman; 2 children. Served with U.S. Army, until 1832; asst. engr. Boston & Providence R.R., 1832-35; successively chief engr. Balt. Susquehanna R.R., Phila., Wilmington & Balt. R.R., Phila. & Balt. Central, 1835-59; gen. supt. Balt. & Potomac R.R., 1859-61; burned bridges to obstruct movement of Union troops to Washington, D.C., 1861; col. of engrs. in Va., 1861; commd. brig. gen. Confederate Army, 1861; constructed defences of Norfolk, Va.; constructed batteries on Potomac to prevent passage of U.S. vessels, 1861; commanded a brigade in Army of No. Va., 1862; took part in Stonewall Jackson's operations in Shenandoah Valley, 1862; participated in Seven Days' battles, nr. Richmond, 1862; captured Union depot of supplies at Manassas Station, 1862; as maj. gen. led division at Battle of Chancellorsville, 1863; had command of troops in Shenandoah Valley, June 1863, campaigned as far north as Carlisle, Pa.; assigned command of a division of Hill's Corps at Battle of Gettysburg, 1863, lost leg on 3d day of battle; prisoner, 1863-65. Died Balt., Jan. 2, 1888.

TRINKS, WILLIBALD, mech. engr.; b. Berlin, Germany, Dec. 10, 1874; s. Wilhelm and Bertha (Obst) T.; grad. with honors, Charlottenburg Poly., 1897; m. 2d, Edith Moore, Aug. 8, 1910 (dec.); 1 son, Harold Rodney (dec.); m. 3d, Ruth Eudora Bittner, June 13, 1938. Came to U.S., 1899; chief mech. engr. William Tod Co., Youngstown, O., 1902-05; prof. mech. engring., Carnegie Inst. Tech., Pittsburgh, 1905-43; consulting and research on ammunition, 1942-46; cons. engineer Jones & Laughlin Steel Co., 1920-49. Member Am. Soc. M.E., Engrs. Soc. of Western Pa., Assn. of Iron and Steel Engrs., Society for Metals, Am. Iron and Steel Inst. Author: Governors, and the Governing of Prime Movers, 1919; Industrial Furnaces, Vol. I, 1923, 3d edit., 1934, Vol. II, 1925, 2 edit., 1942; Roll Pass Design (3 vols), 1933. Home: R.D. 1, Ohiopyle PA

TRIPLER, CHARLES E., physicist, inventor; b. New York, 1849; ed. New York; made spl. study of physical sciences and phenomena; established private physical laboratory; carried on various expts. in electricity and mechanics and later in the study of gases; greatest achievement is the manufacture of "liquid air," which he has experimentally applied to the operation of an engine with remarkable results, this product being obtained by compression of atmospheric air at a temperature of over 300 degrees below zero. Address: 40 W. 77th St., New York.

TRIPP, WILLIAM HENRY, JR., naval architect; b. N.Y.C., Sept. 22, 1919; s. William Henry and Ethel Mary (Moran) T.; grad. Dwight Prep. Sch., N.Y.C., 1939; m. Alice Shelly Williamson, Sept. 14, 1944; 1 son, William Henry III. Propr. W. H. Tripp & Co., Port Washington, N.Y., from 1954; designer specialized comml. craft, sail and power yachts, racing and cruising sail boats. Served to lt. (j.g.) USCGR, 1942-46; PTO. Mem. Soc. Yacht Brokers and Designers. Clubs: N.Y. Yacht; Manhasset Bay Yacht. Office: Port Washington LI NY Died Oct. 13, 1971; cremated.

TROLAND, LEONARD THOMPSON, research engr.; b. Norwich, Conn., Apr. 26, 1889; s. Edwin and Adelaide Elizabeth (O'Brien) T.; B.S., Mass. Inst. Tech., 1912; A.M., Harvard, 1914, Ph.D., 1915; Bowdoin prize in chemistry, 1914; Sheldon traveling fellow, 1915-16; m. Florence Rogers Crockford, 1924. Research in physiol. optics, Nela Research Lab., Gen. Electric Co., Cleveland, 1915-16; with Harvard, 1916—, asst. prof. psychology, 1922-29; lecturer on psychology, 1929—. Engr. with Kalmus, Comstock & Westcott, Inc., 1918-25; research for Technicolor Motion Picture Corp., manufacturers colored motion pictures, 1918-25, dir. of research and process control, 1925—; co-inventor, and responsible for development of manufacturing methods of Technicolor process for motion pictures in natural colors. Employed by U.S.N. during World War I, in development of submarine listening devices; mem. sub. com. of Nat. Research Council on vision and aviation psychology, during the war, also com. on physiol. optics. Fellow Am. Physical Soc., Acoustical Soc. America. Methodist. Author: (with Daniel F. Comstock) The Nature of Matter and Electricity, 1917; The Present Status of Visual Science, 1922; The Mystery of Mind, 1925; The Fundamentals of Human Motivation, 1928; The Principles of Psychophysiology (4 vols.), 1929-32; also numerous tech. papers. Home: Cambridge, Mass. Died May 27, 1932.

TROOST, GERARD, mineralogist; b. Bois-le-Duc, Holland, Mar. 15, 1776; s. Everhard Joseph and Anna Cornelia (van Haeck) T.; M.D., U. Leyden; Master in Pharmacy, U. Amsterdam, 1801; pupil of Rene Haiiy in mineralogy, crystallography; m. Margaret Tage, Jan. 14, 1811; m. 2d, Mrs. O'Reilly; 2 children. Collected minerals for Cabinet of King of Holland, 1807-09; apptd. mem. Dutch scientific commn. to Java, 1809; corr. mem. Museum of Natural History of France, Paris; arrived in Phila., 1810; established a pharm. and chem. lab., Phila., 1812-17; prof. mineralogy Phila. Museum, 1821; prof. pharm. and gen. chemistry Phila. Coll. Pharmacy, 1821-22; prof. mineralogy, chemistry U. Nashville (Tenn.), 1828-50; state geologist Tenn., 1831-50; his meteorite collection now at Yale; mem. Am. Philos. Soc., Geol. Soc. Pa.; did important research on fossil crinoids in Tenn., results published, 1909. Died Nashville, Aug. 14, 1850.

TROTZ, J(OHAN) O(TTO) EMMANUEL, engr.; b. Hammersta, Sweden, Mar. 6, 1860; s. Sir Carl Otto and Lady Ebba Maria Augusta (née Baroness Löwen) T.; grad. in mining and metallurgy, Royal High Sch. of Mines, 1883; in research work for Assn. Swedish Iron Masters, 1884; came to U.S., 1887; m. Selma P. Ahlström, June 7, 1890. Chemist, insp. of material, gen. supt. and metall. engr., attached to office of pres. of U.S. Steel Corp., 1887-1904; cons. and expert engr., and designer and supt. of erection of steel plant and rolling mills of John A. Roebling's Sons Co., Trenton, N.J., 1904-08; pres. and gen. mgr. Kockums Jernverks Aktb., Sweden, 1910—; dir. Aktb. Svenska Handelsbanken, etc. Knight Order of Vasa, by King Oscar of Sweden, 1907; Address: Svanevik, nr. Ronneby, Sweden. Died July 18, 1925.

TROWBRIDGE, ARTHUR CARLETON, geologist; b. Glasgow, Mo., March 4, 1885; s. Samuel Hoyt and Julia Almira (Goodhue) T.; B.S., U. of Chicago, 1907; Ph.D., 1911; m. Sue Estelle Bussey, Aug. 29, 1911; children—Charles Lambert, Carolyn Frances. Asst. in geology, U. of Chicago, 1907-09, instr., 1909-11; prof., U. of Ia., since 1911, head dept., since 1934; dir. and state geologist, Ia. Geol. Survey, 1934-47; field asst. Ill. Geol. Survey, 1907, geologist, 1910; asst. U.S. Geol. Survey, 1913-20, geologist, 1920-24, asso. geologist, 1924-32; geologist Turkish Petroleum Co., Ltd., in Iraq, 1925-26; cons. geologist Nine Foot Channel Bd. Miss. River, 1928-30. With Army Y.M.C.A., Camp Dodge, Ia., 1917-18, N.Y. City, 1918-19. Fellow Geol. Soc. America (v.p. 1943). Mem. A.A.A.S., Ia. Acad. Science (pres. 1937), Nat. Research Council (chmn. com. sedimentation, 1932-35), Sigma Xi, Phi Kappa Sigma. Republican. Methodist. Club: Triangle (Ia. City). Author books relating to field; editor other publs. Home: Iowa City IA Died Nov. 16, 1971.

TROWBRIDGE, AUGUSTUS, physicist; b. New York, Jan. 2, 1870; s. George Alfred and Cornelia Polhemus (Robertson) T.; Phillips Acad., 1886-87; Columbia U., 1890-93, D.Sc., 1929; A.M., Ph.D., U. of Berlin, 1898; m. Sarah Esther Fulton, Sept. 20, 1893. Instr. physics, U. of Mich., 1898-1900; asst. prof. physics, 1900-03, prof. 1903-06, U. of Wis.; later prof. physics, Princeton; dean of Grad. Sch. Princeton, 1928—. Mem. Internat. Congress Applied Chemistry, Berlin, 1903; sec. Physics Sect., Internat. Congress Arts and Sciences, St. Louis, 1904. Trustee Princeton U. Press. Commd. maj., Engr. R.C., 1917; intelligence dept., attached to Gen. Pershing's staff at hdqrs. A.E.F. in France; lt. col., 1918; discharged, 1919. D.S.M. and D.S.O.; Officer Legion of Honor (France); Knight of Order of St. Olav (Norway). Republican. Member National Acad. Sciences (chmn. div. physics, 1921); chmn. div. physical sciences and mem. research fellowship bd., Nat. Research Council, 1920-21, and mem. research fellowship bd. in physics and chemistry, 1920-25; European dir. for Science Internat. Edn. Bd.; fellow A.A.A.S. Address: Princeton, N.J. Died Mar. 14, 1934.

TROWBRIDGE, CHARLES CHRISTOPHER, physicist; b. Astoria, L.I., N.Y., Apr. 26, 1870; s. Gen. William Petit and Lucy (Parkman) T.; B.S., Trinity Coll., Conn., 1892, M.S., 1903, Sc.D., 1908; unmarried. Asst. in physics, 1892-96, tutor, 1896-1903, instr., 1903-13, asst. prof., 1913—, Columbia. Fellow A.A.A.S. Contbr. to scientific jours. Home: New York, N.Y. Died June 3, 1918.

TROWBRIDGE, EDWARD DWIGHT, engr., author; b. of Am. missionary parentage, Marash, Turkey, Oct. 1, 1870; s. Rev. Tillman C. (D.D., LL.D.) and Margaret (Riggs) T.; student U. of Mich., 1887-88; m. Flora Lindsay, Nov. 9, 1897. With Am. Telephone & Telegraph Co., at Detroit and Cleveland, 1892-99; supt. Erie Telegraph & Telephone Co., 1899-1901; gen. mgr. Mich. Telephone Co., Detroit, 1901-05; connected with Pearson Engring Corp., London, Eng., successively as asst. gen. mgr. Rio Janeiro Tramway, Light & Power Co., 1906-09, gen. mgr. Mexican Light & Power Co., 1910-11, and as v.p. Ebro Irrigation & Power Co., 1911-15; pres. The Apartments Co. of Detroit. Served during war period on Draft Bd. and on Civil Bd. for Examinations for Commns. in N.A. Republican. Episcopalian. Author: Mexico Today and Tomorrow, 1919. Home: Detroit, Mich. Died Nov. 24, 1929.

TROWBRIDGE, JOHN, physicist; b. Boston, 1843; s. John Howe and Adeline T.; S.B., Lawrence Scientific Sch. (Harvard), 1865, S.D., 1873; m. Mary Louise Thayer, 1875. Tutor Harvard, 1866-69; asst. prof. physics, Mass. Inst. Tech., 1869-70; asst. prof. physics, 1870-80, prof., 1880-88, Rumford prof. applied science, 1888—, dir. Jefferson Physical Lab., 1884—, Harvard. Asso. editor Am. Jour. of Science. Mem. Internat. Congress of Electricians, Paris, 1883; del. U.S. Congress of Electricians, Phila., 1884. Mem. Nat. Acad. Sciences, Am. Acad. Arts and Sciences (pres.). Author: The New Physics, 1884; The Electrical Boy, 1891; Three Boys on an Electrical Boat, 1894; What Is Electricity?, 1896; The Resolute Mr. Pansy, 1897; Philip's Experiments in Electrical Science, 1898. Address: Cambridge, Mass. Died Feb. 18, 1923.

TROWBRIDGE, WILLIAM PETTIT, engineer, scientist, educator; b. Troy, N.Y., May 25, 1828; s. Stephen Van Rensselaer and Elizabeth (Conkling) T.; grad. U.S. Mil. Acad., 1848; A.M. (hon.), Rochester U., 1856, Yale, 1870; Ph.D. (hon.), Princeton, 1879; LL.D. (hon.), Trinity Coll., 1883, U. Mich., 1887; m. Lucy Parkman, Apr. 21, 1857, 6 surviving children. Asst. prof. chemistry U.S. Mil. Acad., 1847-48; commd. 2d lt. Corps Topog. Engrs., U.S. Army, 1848; served on Atlantic coastal survey, 1849; commd. 1st lt., 1854; prof. mathematics U. Mich., 1856-57; asst. supr. Coast Survey; selected to install self-registering instrument of permanent magnetic observatory established at Key West, 1860; executed hydrographic survey of Narragansett Bay, 1860, established navy yard; in charge of army engr. agy. for supplying materials for fortifications and for constructing engring. equipage for armies in field, N.Y.C., 1861; superintending engr. of constrn. at fort, Willets Point, N.Y., 1861; v.p., gen. mgr. Novelty Iron Works, N.Y.C., 1865-71; prof. dynamic engring. Yale, 1871-77; prof. engring. Columbia, 1877-92; mem. New Haven (Conn.) Board Harbor Commrs.; councilor N.Y. Acad. Sciences, 1878-84, v.p., 1885-89; prominent mem. A.A.A.S.; mem. Nat. Acad. Sciences. Died New Haven, Aug. 12, 1892.

TROXELL, EDWARD LEFFINGWELL, geologist; b. Deshler, Neb., Apr. 15, 1884; s. Jacob and Evelyn Virginia (Leffingwell) T.; prep. edn., Collegiate Inst., Salt Lake City, Utah; A.B., Northwestern U., 1908, A.M., 1911; Ph.D., Yale, 1914; student Sorbonne, Paris, 1919; m. Jane Allen Campbell, Oct. 17, 1917. Research asst., Yale, 1919, research asso. in paleontology, 1920; asst. prof. geology, 1920-25, prof. since 1925, Trinity Coll., dean of Coll., 1925-28; dir. State Geol. and Natural History Survey since 1940; Red Cross first aid instr., 1941; member State Defense Minerals Resources Committee. Joined First O.T.C., Fort Sheridan, Ill., 1917; commd. capt. inf., Aug. 15, 1917; at Camp Custer, Aug. 1917-July 1918; overseas, July 1918-July 1919; with 82d and 86th Divs., Argonne Forest. Fellow Geol. Soc. America, Am. Geog. Soc., Am. Assn. for Advancement of Science, Paleontol. Soc.; mem. Assn. of Am. State Geologists (exec. com.; pres. 1947-48), Am. Soc. Mammalogists, Am. Assn. Univ. Profs., Phila. Acad. Natural Sciences, Sigma Xi, Pi Gamma Mu (vice chancellor), Alpha Delta Phi, Book and Bond of Yale. Congregationalist. Clubs: Hartford Engineers, Twentieth Century, Hartford Golf. Field trips and exploration in the West, specimens now in many museums; important discoveries in fossil reptiles, birds and mammals. Contbr. plans in flood control and engring.; Gildersleeve Canal, etc. Author of about 80 papers, mostly on paleontology, geology and education, in Am. Jour. Science, Scientific Monthly, Yale Alumni Weekly, etc. Inventor. Home: West Hartford CT Died Sept. 21, 1972.

TROY, JOHN HENRY, horticulturist; b. Mt. Hissarlik, Co. Kildare, Ireland, Apr. 29, 1856; ed. pub. schs.; m. Margaret Muir Wylie (now dec.); 1 son, William Wylie. Gardener apprenticeship in Ireland and Eng.; attached to Queen Victoria Gardens, Windsor, Eng.; foreman in gardens of Duke of Westminster, Eaton Hall, Cheshire, Eng., 1878-84; rose specialist and landscape plantsman. Came to U.S., 1885; chmn. Bd. Commrs. of Parks, Docks and Harbors, New Rochelle, N.Y., 1910-16; city councilman, New Rochelle, N.Y., 1910-12; pres. New Rochelle Housing Corpn.; dir. New Rochelle Trust Co., Peoples Bank for Savings. Mem. Hort. Soc. of N.Y. (life), C. of C., New York Florists' Club (ex-pres.), Soc. Am. Florists and Ornamental Horticulturists (life). Mason (K.T.). Clubs: City (New York); Rotary (New Rochelle). Home: 257 Mayflower Av., New Rochelle, N.Y. Died Mar. 24, 1931; buried Beechwood Cemetery, New Rochelle, N.Y.

TRUDEAU, EDWARD LIVINGSTON, physician; b. New York, Oct. 5, 1848; s. Dr. James and Cephise (Berger) T.; M.D., Coll. Phys. and Surg. (Columbia), 1871; hon. M.S., Columbia, 1899; LL.D., McGill U., Can., 1904; LL.D., U. of Pa., 1913; m. Charlotte G. Beare, June 29, 1871. Began practice in New York, 1872 but ill health forced him to go to the Adirondack Mountains, where became resident; founded, 1884, Adirondack Cottage Sanitarium for treatment of incipient consumption in working men and women, first of its kind in America; founded, 1894, Saranac Lab. for study of tuberculosis, first research lab. for the purpose in America. Address: Saranac Lake, N.Y. Died Nov. 15, 1915.

TRUE, FREDERICK WILLIAM, zoölogist; b. Middletown, Conn., July 8, 1858; s. Rev. Charles Kittredge and Elizabeth Bassett (Hyde) T.; brother of Alfred Charles T.; B.S., New York U., 1878, M.S., 1881, LL.D., 1897; m. Louise E., d. D. Webster Prentiss, M.D., Feb. 16, 1887. Joined Govt. service, 1878; expert spl. agt. 10th census (on Fisheries), 1879; custodian of collections of U.S. Fish Commn. at Berlin Fisheries Exhbn., 1880; librarian, 1881-83, curator of mammals, 1883-92, exec. curator, 1892-99, head curator dept. biology, 1897-1911, U.S. Nat. Mus.; asst. sec., Smithsonian Instn., in charge of library and exchanges, June 1911—. Rep. of Smithsonian Instn. and Nat. Mus. at expns., at Nashville, 1897, Omaha, 1898, Buffalo, 1901, St. Louis, 1904, and Portland (Ore.), 1905, and at Internat. Fisheries Congress, 1908; U.S. delegate 7th Internat. Zoöl. Congress, 1907. Fellow A.A.A.S. Made a spl. study of whales. Author: Review of the Family Delphinidae (or the dolphins), 1889; The Whalebone Whales of the Western North Atlantic (Smithsonian Contbns. to Knowledge, Vol. 33), 1904; An Account of the Beaked Whales of the Family Ziphiidae (Bull. U.S. Nat. Mus., No. 73), 1910; also numerous short papers on cetaceans and other mammals. Home: Washington, D.C. Died June 25, 1914.

TRUE, GORDON HAINES, animal husbandman; b. Baraboo, Wis., Dec. 14, 1868; s. John Mathias and Mary Anne (Beede) T.; B.S., U. of Wis., 1894; m. Elizabeth Spayd Stubbs, Oct. 3, 1904; children—Elizabeth Ella, Gordon Haines, Eunice Miriam. Instr. in dairy husbandry, Mich. Agrl. Coll., 1894-98; prof. animal husbandry, U. of Ariz., 1898-1902; prof. agr. and animal husbandry, 1902-13, dir. Agrl. Expt. Sta., 1912-13, U. of Nev.; prof. animal husbandry, U. of Calif., July 1, 1913—. Mem. Nev. State Bd. Agr., 1912-13; state quarantine officer, Nev., 1913. Republican. Conglist. Fellow A.A.A.S. Mason. Chmn. live stock commn. U.S. Food Administrn. for Calif., 1918; sec. and mgr. Calif. Internat. Live Stock Show, 1919. Home: Berkeley, Calif. Died June 4, 1928.

TRUE, RODNEY HOWARD, botanist, physiologist; b. Greenfield, Wis., Oct. 14, 1866; s. John M. and Mary Annie (Beede) T.; B.S., U. of Wis., 1890, univ. fellow in botany, 1890-92, M.S., 1892; student botany under Pfeffer, at Leipzig, 1893-95, Ph.D., 1895; m. Katharine McAssey, July 1, 1896 (dec.); 1 son, Rodney Philip; m. 2d, Martha A. Griffith, Dec. 22, 1927. Taught common schs. in Wis. 2 yrs.; prin. Wis. Acad., Madison, 1892-93; instr. pharmacognosy, 1895-96, asst. prof. pharmacognosy, 1896-99, U. of Wis.; lectured at Harvard, winter, 1899-1900, and asst. Radcliffe Coll.; lecturer in botany, Harvard, 1900-01; plant physiologist, U.S. Dept. Agr., 1901-20, in charge physiol. investigations; prof. botany and dir. Botanic Garden, U. of Pa., 1920-37, emeritus prof. of botany, 1937—; dir. Morris Arboretum, U. of Pa., 1933—. Mem. gen. com. for revision of 9th U.S. Pharmacopoeia; adv. council of Allegheny Forest Expt. Sta., 1934—, chmn., 1936—. Fellow A.A.A.S. (sec. com. one hundred on scientific research, 1925, mem. council, 1926). Episcopalian. Contbr. of papers on original research to Annals of Botany, Botanisches Centralblatt, and other scientific jours. and govt. bulls. Home: Philadelphia, Pa. Died Apr. 8, 1940.

TRUELL, ROHN, physicist; b. Washington, Apr. 6, 1913; s. Karl O. and Anna M. (Rohn) T.; B.S. in Engring. Physics, Lehigh U., 1935; postgrad. Columbia, 1936-38; Ph.D., Cornell U., 1941; m. Marjory Ann Schminck, Sept. 12, 1942; children—Ann Rohn, Marcia Lee. With RCA, 1935-38, RCA Labs., Princeton, 1941-44; staff Stromberg Carlson, 1944-46; asst. prof. Brown U., 1946-48, asso. prof., 1948-51, prof., 1951-68, chmn. div. applied mathematics, dir. metals research lab., chairman phys. science council. Member of the board of trustees Roger Williams Hosp. Guggenheim fellow, 1959-60. Fellow Am. Phys. Soc.; mem. I.E.E.E., (sr.), Am. Math. Soc. Author: Ultrasonic Methods in Solid State Physics, 1969. Home: Providence RI Died Jan. 10, 1968; buried Nashua NH

TRUITT, RALPH PURNELL, physician; b. Snow Hill, Md., Aug. 4, 1885; s. George Worthington and Gertrude Duncan (Purnell) T.; grad. high sch., Snow Hill, student Washington Coll., Chestertown, Md.; M.D., U. of Maryland, 1910; m. Eleanor McConnell, Sept. 2, 1920 (died 1946); 1 son, James McConnell. Intern University Hospital, Baltimore, 1909-10; jr. assistant physician N.J. State Hospital, Trenton, 1910-12; psychiatrist in chief City Hosp. (insane department), Baltimore, Maryland, 1912; assistant resident Psychiatrist Johns Hopkins Hosp., 1913-14; clin. dir. La. State Hosp., Jackson, La., 1915; sr. physician N.J. State Hosp., 1916-17; lt., capt. and maj. Med. Corps, U.S. Army, 1917-19; med. dir. Ill. Soc. for Mental Hygiene and asst. prof. neurology and psychiatry, U. of Ill. Med. Dept., 1919-23; dir. Child Guidance Clinic Demonstration under auspices Nat. Com. for Mental Hygiene, Los Angeles, Calif., 1924; dir. Div. on Prevention of Delinquency, Commonwealth Fund Program, New York, 1925-27; asso. prof. psychiatry and dir. psychiatric clinic, U. of Md., 1927-46, prof. clin. psychiatry and chief of psychiatric service, 1946-50, chairman of the department of psychiatry, 1948-50. Mem. Am. Psychiat. Assn., Am. Orthopsychiatric Assn. (pres.

1935-36), Phi Sigma Kappa. Home: Stevensville MD Died June 20, 1966.

TRULLINGER, R(OBERT) W(ILLIAM), (trul'in-ger), sci. research administr.; b. Farragut, Ia., Feb. 25, 1889; s. William Barton and Lucy Martha (Butler) T.; B.S., Ia. State Coll., 1910, A.E., 1925; Engr. D. (hon.), Rutgers U., 1941; m. Pearl Maude Jordan, Jan. 24, 1913; 1 dau., Virginia (Mrs. Roy C. Dawson). Gen. practice civil engring., Clarinda, Ia., and Omaha, Neb., 1910-12; specialist in agrl. engring., Office Expt. Sta., U.S. Dept. Agr., Washinton, 1912-17, expt sta. adminstr., 1919-38, asst. chief, 1938-46, chief Office of Expt. Stas. and asst. research administr., since 1946. Served as 1st lt., then capt., U.S. Army, 1917-19; assigned research in arty. ammunition. Awarded John Deere gold medal by Am. Soc. Agrl. Engrs., for distinguished achievement in application of sci. and art to soil, 1941; U.S. Department Agriculture Gold Medal Award, 1951. Fellow Am. Soc. Agrl. Engrs. (pres. 1931); mem. Nat. Research Council, Western Irrigation and Drainage Research Assn. (hon.), Tau Beta Pi, Phi Kappa Phi, Sigma Alpha Epsilon. Mason. Episcopalian. Contbr. articles and bulls. on various aspects of agrl. research and its adminstrn. Home: 7120 Colesville Rd., Hyattsville, Md. Office: Office Experiment Sta., U.S. Dept. Agriculture, Washington 25. Died Nov. 8, 1955; buried Arlington Nat. Cemetery.

TRUMBULL, GURDON, artist, ornithologist; b. Stonington, Conn., May 5, 1841; s. Gurdon and Sarah A. (Swan) T.; studied in Hartford and New York; made many notable paintings of fish; of recent years devoted to study of birds. Author: Names and Portraits of Birds Which Interest Gunners, with descriptions, 1888. Wrote notable paper on The American Woodcock (Philohela minor) in Forest and Stream, Dec. 11, 1890, containing 1st record of a bird's power to curve the upper mandible. Address: Hartford, Conn. Died 1903.

TRUMP, EDWARD NEEDLES, engineer; b. at Phila., Pa., Nov. 9, 1857; s. Charles Newbold and Helen M. (Needles) T.; student Cornell U., 1876-78; m. Katharine M. Croasdale, of Phila., Oct. 10, 1883. Learned machinist's trade, built and operated beet sugar works at Wilmington, Del., 1879-82; first engr. employed by Solvay Process Co., 1882, mfg. first soda-ash made in U.S.; gen. mgr. same co., 1893-1913, v.p. and chmn. tech. com., 1913-30; pres. Salina Realty Security Co.; v.p. Trump Corp., cons. chem. engrs.; treas., cons. engr., Sanitary Metal Cap Corp.; trustee Onondaga Co. Savings Bank. Administrative engr. U.S. Fuel Administration, for State of N.Y., 1918. Commr. Central N.Y. State Park Commn.; mem. Syracuse Grade Crossing Commn. Mem. Am. Soc. M.E. (v.p. 1905-07), Technology Club (Syracuse). Republican. Mem. Society of Friends (Quaker). Home: 1912 W. Genesee St. Office: 725 E. Water St., Syracuse, N.Y.

TRUMPLER, ROBERT JULIUS, astronomer; b. Zurich, Switzerland, Oct. 2, 1886; s. Wilhelm Ernst and Luise (Hurter) T.; grad. Gymnasium, Zürich, 1905, student U. of Zürich, 1906-08; student U. Göttingen, Germany, 1908-11, Ph.D., 1910; m. Augusta C. O. De La Harpe, Aug. 5, 1916; children—Cecile Eliane Ramona, Marguerite Caroline Jacqueline, Elizabeth Julie Helen, Robert Hamilton, Alfred Oswald. Astronomer of Swiss Geodetic Survey, 1911-15; came to U.S., 1915, and served as asst. in determination of stellar parallaxes, Allegheny Obs., Pitts., until 1919; Martin Kellogg fellow, Lick Obs., Mt. Hamilton, Calif., 1919-20, asst. astronomer (studies of Mars and star clusters), 1920-26, asso. astronomer, 1926-29, astronomer, 1929-38; prof. astronomy, Berkeley dept., U. Cal., 1938-51, ret. Mem. Am. Astron. Soc., Astron. Soc. of Pacific, Int. Astron. Union, Nat. Acad. of Sciences, Astronomische Gesellschaft, Royal Astron. Soc., Société Astronomique de France hon. mem. Société Helvétique Sc. Nat., Sigma Xi. Unitarian. Author: Statistical Astronomy (with H. F. Weaver), 1953. Made exptl. test confirming Einstein's theory, at Wallal, Australia, 1922, a determination of light absorption in Galactic System, 1930. Address: 620 Bay View Dr., Box 1750, Aptos, Cal. Died Sept. 10, 1956; buried Berkeley, Cal.

TRYON, GEORGE WASHINGTON, conchologist; b. Phila., May 20, 1838; s. Edward K. and Adeline (Savidt) T. Manufactured and sold firearms and hunting equipment; mem. Acad. Natural Scis. of Phila., 1859, largely responsible for erection of new bldg., an organizer conchological sect., 1866, donated his private collection over 10,000 species, curator, 1869-76, conservator conchological sect., 1875-88; wrote paper "On the Mollusca of Harper's Ferry, Virginia," 1861; wrote more than 70 papers on land, freshwater and marine mollusks; edited, published Am. Jour. of Conchology, 1865-72; wrote Manual of Conchology, Structural and Systematic, with Illustrations of the Species (chief work), 1st vol., 1879, 3 vols. published 1888, continued by Dr. Henry A. Pilsbry; wrote comic opera Amy Cassonet or the Elopement, 1875; went to Europe, 1874, 77; wrote accounted of earlier trip The Amateur Abroad, 1875; published Structural and Systematic Conchology, 3 vols., 1882-84. Died Feb. 5, 1888.

TUCKER, CARLTON EVERETT, educator; b. Whitman, Mass., Nov. 13, 1896; s. Amasa C. and Lizzie M. (Reed) T.; S.B., Mass. Inst. Tech., Harvard, 1918; m. Louise Porter, Aug. 12, 1922; children—Caroline Louise (Mrs. Wilson H. Seward), Nancy Elisabeth (Mrs. George E. McLaughlin). Asst., Mass. Inst. Tech., 1918-19, instr., 1919-24, asst. prof. elec. engring., 1924-30, asso. prof., 1930-38, became prof., 1938, now prof. emeritus, student placement officer, 1943-53, dir. radar sch., 1943-49, exec. officer dept. elec. engring., 1942—; cons. telephone systems. Mem. sch. com., Whitman, Mass., 1928-47, chmn., 1930-38. Follow I.E.E.E.; mem. Am. Soc. Engring. Edn. (chmn. New Eng. sect. 1946-49), Tau Beta Pi, Eta Kappa Nu. Republican. Conglist. Author: (with C. W. Ricker) Electrical Engineering Laboratory Experiments, 1922 (4th edit. 1940); sect. 19 Electrical Measurements in General Engineering Handbook (C. E. O'Rourke), 2nd. edit. 1940. Home: 64 Fullerton Av., Whitman, Mass. 02382. Office: 77 Massachusetts Av., Cambridge 39, Mass. Died Jan. 17, 1966; buried Colebrook Cemetery, Whitman, Mass.

TUCKER, HARRY, highway engr.; b. Amherst County, Va., Feb. 7, 1890; s. Cornelius Sale and Sallie (Stickley) T.; A.B., and B.S., Washington and Lee U., 1910, C.E., 1923; m. Mary Lillian Briggs, May 5, 1918 (died Aug. 24, 1930); children—Harry, Robert Briggs. Admitted to N.C. bar, 1914; instr. in civil engring., N.C. State Coll. of Agr. and Engring., 1910-16, prof. of highway engring. since 1920, dir. Engring. Expt. Sta. since 1932; cons. engr. and tech. expert in civil engring., highway transportation and safety. Served with 105th Engrs., U.S. Army, with A.E.F., advancing from pvt. to capt., 1917-19. Mem. N.C. Utilities Commn. Mem. Am. Society Civil Engrs., Inst. of Traffic Engrs., N.C. Bar Assn., Sigma Phi Epsilon, Theta Tau, Phi Kappa Phi. Ind. Democrat. Presbyterian. Author: The History of the 105th Engineer Regiment (with W. P. Sullivan), 1919; Highway Accidents in North Carolina and Guides to Safety, 1935; Manual in the Testing of Materials, 1935; Highway Economics (with M. C. Leager). Contbr. many articles on highway transportation, accidents, etc., to jours. Home: 20 Logan Court, Raleigh, N.C. Died Mar. 18, 1942.

TUCKER, RICHARD HAWLEY, astronomer, retired; b. Wiscasset, Me., Oct. 29, 1859; s. Capt. R. H. and Mary (Armstrong) T.; C.E., Lehigh U., 1879, Sc.D., 1922; m. Ruth Standen, Apr. 29, 1914; children—Mary Ronald, Jane Standen. Astron. work, Dudley Obs., 4 yrs.; instr. mathematics and astronomy, Lehigh U., 1883-84; at Argentine Nat. Obs., Cordoba, 9 yrs.; at Lick Obs., 1893-1908; dir. So. Obs., Carnegie Instn., San Luis, Argentine, S.A., 1908-11, Lick Obs., 1911-26. Mem. Albany Inst., Astron. Soc. Pacific, A.A.A.S., Astronomische Gesellschaft, Soc. Astronomique de France, Am. Seismol. Soc., Am. Philos. Soc. Author: Vol. IV, 1900, Vol. VI, 1903, Vol. X, 1907, Vol. XV, 1925, Lick Obs. publs.; contbr. astron. jours., etc. Address: 1525 Waverly St., Palo Alto, Cal. Died Mar. 31, 1952; buried Wiscasset, Me.

TUCKER, WILLIAM CONQUEST, sanitary engr.; b. New York, Oct. 4, 1863; s. Stephen Davis and Sarah Ann (Conquest) T.; ed. Wilson & Kellogg Sch., New York; Ph.B., Sheffield Scientific Sch. (Yale) 1888, C.E., 1890; m. Englewood, N.J., Oct. 28, 1893, Mabel Clarkson Reid. Entered office of Albert L. Webster, sanitary engr., 1889, where remained until 1900, since in pvt. practice. Lecturer house sanitation, Yale. Contbr. to tech. jours. on sanitary engring. topics. Mem. Royal Sanitary Inst. of Great Britain, Am. Pub. Health Assn., A.A.A.S., Municipal Art Soc., Gen. Soc. of Mechanics and Tradesmen, Theta Xi. Episcopalian. Republican. Clubs: University, Yale, Englewood. Sanitary engring. expert, housing div. U.S. Shipping Bd. Emergency Fleet Corp. Office: 501 5th Av., New York, N.Y. *

TUCKER, WILLIS GAYLORD, chemist; b. Albany, N.Y., Oct. 31, 1849; s. Luther and Margaret Lucinda Smith (Burr) T.; brother of Gilbert Milligan T.; ed. Albany Acad.; M.D., Albany Med. Coll., 1870; hon. Ph.D., Union, 1882; Ph.G., Albany Coll. of Pharmacy, 1882; m. May Newman, Sept. 17, 1879. Prof. chemistry and toxicology, 1876-1915, registrar, 1882-1914, and dean faculty, 1914-15, Albany Med. Coll.; prof. chemistry, 1881-1918, dean faculty, 1883-1918, hon. dean, 1918—, Albany Coll. of Pharmacy. Fellow A.A.A.S. Home: Albany, N.Y. Died 1922.

TUCKERMAN, EDWARD, botanist, educator; b. Boston, Dec. 7, 1817; s. Edward and Sophia (May) T.; B.A., Union Coll., 1837, M.A., 1843; grad. Harvard Law Sch., 1839, B.A., Harvard, 1847, grad. Harvard Div. Sch., 1852; m. Sarah Eliza Sigourney Cushing, May 17, 1854. Curator coll. museum Union Coll., 1842-43; lectr. in history Amherst (Mass.) Coll., 1854-58, prof. botany, 1858-86; contbd. articles to N.Y. Churchman on biog., hist. and theol. topics; in 1842 described Oakesia (a new genus of flowering plants from New Eng.); authority in field of Am. lichenology; 1st to explore mountains of New Eng. for lichens; mem. Nat. Acad. Scis., 1868. Author: Enumeratio Methodica Caricum Quarundam, issued privately, 1843; Enumeration of North American Lichens, 1845, also supplement, "Synopsis of the Lichens of New England, the Other Northern States, and British America;" Lichens of California, Oregon, and the Rocky Mountains, 1866; General Lichenum: An Arrangement of North American Lichens (probably his greatest work) 1872; Catalogue of Plants Growing without Cultivation within Thirty Miles of Amherst College, issued privately, 1875; A Synopsis of North American Lichens, Part I, 1882. Died Amherst, Mar. 15, 1886.

TUCKERMAN, FREDERICK, anatomist; b. Greenfield, Mass., May 7, 1857; s. Frederick G. and Hannah L. (Jones) T.; B.S., Mass. Agrl. Coll. and Boston U., 1878; M.D., Harvard, 1882; student London and Berlin, 1882-83, Berlin, London and Heidelberg, 1892-94; A.M., Ph.D., Heidelberg, 1894; m. Alice G. Cooper, Sept. 6, 1881; children—Margaret, Frederica. Lecturer anatomy and physiology, Mass. Agrl. Coll., 1883-86; fellow Clark U., Worcester, 1889-90. Fellow A.A.A.S. Edited Diaries and Letters of Samuel Cooper, 1901-03; (with others) Life of Charles Anthony Goessmann, 1917. Author: Amherst Academy, a New England School of the Past, 1929; also various papers on vertebrate anatomy and embryology. Address: Amherst, Mass. Died 1929.

TUCKERMAN, L(OUIS) B(RYANT), engineer, physicist, cons.; b. West Williamsfield, Ashtabula Co., O., Sept. 26, 1879; s. Louis Bryant and Mary Ellen (Hopkins) T.; prep. edn., Central High Sch. (Cleve.) and New Lyme (O.) Inst.; A.B., Adelbert Coll. (Western Reserve U.), 1901; grad. student in physics, Univ. of Nebraska, 1901-02; student in physics, U. of Berlin, 1904-06; Ph.D., Johns Hopkins, 1921; m. Una Venable, June 20, 1911; children—Mary V. McCoy, Louis Bryant. Asst. in physics, Ohio State U., 1902-04; instr. physics, U. of Neb., 1906-07, adj. prof., 1907-08, asso. prof., 1908-16, prof. theoretical physics, 1916-19; with Nat. Bur. of Standards since 1919, asst. chief div. of mechanics and sound since 1925. Chmn. Bur. of Standards Ednl. Com. since 1921. Head of radio div. S.A.T.C., U. of Neb., World War. Mem. spl. com. on design of Airship ZR1 (Shenandoah), 1922-23; of Army semi-rigid Airship RS-1, 1923-25; mem. advisory com. on stratosphere flight Nat. Geog. Soc. and U.S. Army Air Corps since 1934; mem. sub-com. on structural loads and methods of structural analysis, Nat. Advisory Com. for Aeronautics, 1927-39, mem. of com. on aircraft structures 1939-44; mem. div. of physical sciences, Nat. Research Council, 1933-39, mem. com. on selection and training of aircraft pilots since 1939. Awarded Department of Commerce Gold medal, 1949. Mem. A.A.A.S., Am. Phys. Soc., Optical Soc. of America (sec. 1929-39), Inst. of the Aeronautical Sciences, Am. Soc. for Testing Materials (Edgar Marburg lecturer 1935), Washington Acad. Sciences (corr. sec. 1927-31; manager 1931-33, pres. 1934), Philos. Soc. Washington (pres. 1932), Acad. of Medicine of Washington, D.C., Deutsche Physikalische Gesellschaft, Deutsche Gesellschaft für Technische Physik, Phi Beta Kappa, Sigma Xi, Pi Gamma Mu. Awarded John Price Wetherill medal of Franklin Inst., 1935. Dohme lecturer Johns Hopkins, 1937; Edward Orton Jr. Memorial lecture, 1942. Clubs: Cosmos, Federal, Tourbillon. Contributor to scientific and tech. press. Invented fabric tension meter, Tuckerman optical lever system. Tuckerman optical strain gage. Retired Oct. 1, 1949. Address: Cosmos Club, Washington 5, Died Feb. 4, 1962.

TUDOR, FREDERIC, ice mcht.; b. Boston, Sept. 4, 1783; s. Col. William and Delia (Jarvis) T.; m. Euphemia Fenno, Jan. 2, 1834, 6 children. Sent (with brother) cargo of ice to Martinique, 1804, vessel arrived in Saint-Pierre, 1806; established bus. in Havana, Cuba and Charleston, S.C., New Orleans by 1821; learned how to ship ice with least possible loss, devised structure which kept ice in warm climates, succeeded in making use of ice accepted in cities; sent 1st cargo to Calcutta, India, 1833; increased shipping from 130 tons in 1806 to 146,000 tons in 1856; designed new type of hull for sailing vessels; developed graphite mine Sturbridge, Mass.; created Maolis Gardens (probably 1st amusement park in U.S.), Nahant, Mass. Known as ice king. Died Boston, Feb. 6, 1864.

TUDOR, RALPH ARNOLD, ex-govt. ofcl.; engr.; b. Colorado Springs, Colo., Mar. 19, 1902; s. E. A. and Ida J. (Herzog) T.; B.S., U.S. Mil. Acad., 1923; C.E., Cornell U.; m. Mary Lucile Taylor, 1925; 1 dau., Jean Ellen. Commd. 2d lt., C.E., U.S. Army, 1923, served to 1st lt., 1929, resigned; bridge engr. San Francisco-Oakland bridge, 1929-37, prin. engr., 1939-40; assistant executive officer and chief engineer of Golden Gate International Exposition, 1937-38; lieutenant col., later colonel, Corps of Engrs., U.S. Army, 1941-42; dist. engr., Portland, 1943-45; chief engr. Morrison-Knudsen, engrs., China, 1946; v.p. Morrison-Knudsen Internat. Co., San Francisco, 1947—; president of Tudor Engring. Co., specializing in road and bridge construction, San Francisco, 1947—, also civil engring. projects. Under sec. of Interior, 1953-54. Decorated Legion of Merit. Fellow Am. Soc. Civil Engrs.; mem. Am. Soc. M.E., Assn. Grads. West Point (trustee). Presbyn. Clubs: Engineers (San Francisco); Commonwealth (Cal.). Home: 140 Selby Lane, Atherton. Cal. Office: 595 Mission St., San Francisco 5. Died Nov. 12, 1963; buried U.S. Mil. Acad., West Point, N.Y.

TUKEY, HAROLD BRADFORD, horticulturist; b. Berwyn, Ill., Sept. 30, 1896; s. James Bradford and Armenia (Mehrhof) T.; B.S., U. of Ill., 1918, M.S., 1920; Ph.D., U. of Chicago, 1932; D.H.C. (honorary), Hanover, Germany, 1957; m. Margaret Davenport, November 23, 1918 (deceased February 7, 1930); children—Loren Davenport, Lois (Mrs. W. D. Baker, Jr.), Ronald Bradford; married 2d, Ruth Ann Schweigert, Nov. 23, 1932; children—Harold Bradford, Ann. Asst. horticulturist N.Y. State Agrl. Expt. Station, 1920-23; horticulturist in charge Hudson Valley Fruit Investigations, 1923-27; chief in research (horticulture), N.Y. State Agricultural Experimental Station, professor pomology, Cornell University, 1927-45. Head dept. of horticulture, Mich. State U., 1945-62, now prof. emeritus; U.S. tech. adv. Internat. Conf. on Atomic Energy, 1955. Commd. 1st lt. F.A., U.S. Army, 1918, serving W.W. Awarded Jackson Dawson Medal, 1948, Marshall P. Wilder medal 1956, N. J. Colman award, 1956, citation Am. Hort. Council, 1957; Gold medal of Honor, 1967; Liberty Hyde Bailey medal, 1967. Fellow A.A.A.S., Royal Hort. Soc. (Eng.), Am. Inst. Biol. Scis. (organizing bd. 1946-47, v.p.); mem. Am. Pomol. Soc. (bd. mgrs. 1925-28; exec. bd., 1925-48; pres. 1950-52; chairman Wilder Medal Award 1942-56, 59-62), Internat. Soc. Horticultural Sci. (pres. 1962-66), Am. Soc. Hort. Sci. (sec.-treas. 1927-46; pres. 1946; editor proc., 1927-50), Bot. Soc. Am., Am. Society Plant Physiologists, American Society Naturalists, Society Growth and Development, Soc. Nationale d'Horticulture de France (hon.), Mass. Hort. Soc., Michigan Horticultural Soc. American Horticultural Society, Phi Kappa Phi, Pi Alpha Xi, Theta Chi, Sigma Xi, Alpha Zeta. Republican. Presbyterian. Rotarian. Author: (books) The Pears of New York (with others), 1921; The Pear and Its Culture, 1929; Plant Regulators in Agrl., 1954; Dwarfed Fruit Trees, 1964. Contbr. to jours., agrl. press, and bulls. expt. sta. Mem. editorial and exec. staff Rural New Yorker, 1923-64; asso. editor Am. Fruit Grower. Contbr. Fruit Year Book (Eng.). Delivered Amos Meml. Lectr. (Eng.), 1952. Del. Internat. Hort. Congress, London, 1952, Scheveningen, 1955, Brussels, 1962, U.S., 1966, pres. XVIIth, 1966. Home: Woodland MI Died Nov. 1971.

TULLER, JOHN JAY, neurologist; b. Newark, O., Dec. 26, 1861; s. Emory R. and Jane (Powers) T.; M.D., Hahnemann Med. Coll. and Hosp., Phila., 1892; post-grad. work, Germany, Austria and France, 1895-97; m. Katherine Maibauer, of Ardmore, Pa., June 10, 1916. Began practice at Phila., 1892; clin. instr. neurology, 1900-04, demonstrator neuro-histology and lecturer on insanity, 1904-05, prof. neuro-histology and mental diseases, 1905-10, prof. neurology, 1910-11, prof. neurology and psychiatry since 1912, Hahnemann Med. Coll. and Hosp., now emeritus, also head of dept. Neurologsit Hahnemann Hosp., Women's Homoe. Hosp., Children's Homoe. Hosp.; mem. bd. dirs. Children's Homoe. Hosp., Phila.; trustee Homoe. State Hosp. for the Insane, Allentown, Pa. Mem. Am. Inst. Homoeopathy, Pa. State and Phila. Co. homoe. socs., Clinico-Path. Soc., Phila. Med. and Surg. Soc., etc. Clubs: Union League, Phila. Country, Overbrook Golf. Home: 4248 Chestnut St. Office: 2104 Walnut St., Philadelphia, Pa.

TUOHY, EDWARD BOYCE, (too'e), physician; b. Duluth, Minn., March 17, 1908; s. Edward Leo and Ida Mary (Boyce) T.; B.S., U. of Minn., 1925-29; M.D., U. of Pa., 1929-32; M.S. in Anesthesiology, Mayo Foundation Grad. Med. School, U. of Minn., 1933-36; m. Dorothy A. Johnson, April 11, 1934; children—Barbara, Michael, Patrick. Fellowship in anesthesiology, Mayo Foundation; Mayo Clinic staff, 1935, consultant 1935-47; prof. of anesthesiology, Georgetown Med. Center 1947-51; prof. surgery (anesthesiology) U. So. Cal. 1953; pvt. practice anesthethesiology. Mem. Reserve Corps. U.S. Army; active duty, May 1942; disch. rank maj., 1945; cons. USAF, 1954-56. Diplomate Am. Bd. Anesthesiology (mem. bd. 1950-56, del. A.M.A. 1951-55). Mem. Am. Soc. Anesthesiology for Pharmacology and Exptl. Therapeutics (pres. 1947), A.A.A.S., Sigma Xi, Nu Sigma Nu, Chi Psi. Roman Catholic. Contbr. chapters to Surgery and Dental Science and Dental Art by Dean Lewis; also over 100 articles to jours. Address: 2485 Sherwood Rd., San Marino, Cal. Died Jan. 12, 1959; buried Calvary Cemetery, Los Angeles.

TUPPER, CLAUDE A., cons. engr.; b. Chicago, Ill., May 26, 1877; s. Charles A. and Louise V. (Aikens) Tupper; spl. courses in engring., U. of Wis.; m. Caroline A. Davis, June 3, 1905; children—Preston E. (dec.), Leslie C., Ellis C., Jane Elizabeth. Field engring. and mil. campaigns various countries, particularly of the Orient, until 1905; with Allis-Chalmers Mfg. Co., Milwaukee, 1905-12; sec. Penton Pub. Co., Cleveland, O., 1912-14; pres. Internat. Trade Press, Inc., Chicago, 1914-30; cons. engr., 1930—. Republican. Baptist. Home: Oak Park, Ill. Died Apr. 8, 1937.

TURCK, FENTON BENEDICT, cons. engr.; b. Chgo., May 4, 1902; s. Fenton Benedict and Avis Loveland (Paine) T.; B.S., Sheffield Sci. Sch., Yale, 1923; m. Claire Schenck, 1925 (div. 1940); 1 dau., Lorraine; m. 2d, Eleanor Plenge, 1945; children—Fenton Benedict III, Nancy. With Am. Radiator & Standard Sanitary Corp., 1923-39, v.p., 1929-39; pres. F. B. Turck & Co., Inc., cons. engrs., from 1938. Am. del. to Internat. Congress, Paris, 1946; mem. Distbn. Hall Fame, Boston Conf. Distbn. Trustee Fla. Ocean Scis. Inst., Inc., Deerfield Beach. Decorated Officer Order of Orange Nassau (Netherlands); recipient citation for engring. contbn. to distbn. Am. Soc. M.E., 1953. Profl. engr., N.Y. Fellow Am. Soc. M.E.; mem. Am. Inst. Cons. Engrs., Holland Soc., Nat. Soc. Profl. Engineers, National Institute of Social Sciences, Newcomen Society, S.A.R., Soc. Colonial Wars. Clubs: University, Elizabethan, Metropolitan Opera (New York, City). Author: Applying Engineering Principles to Distribution; Scientific Methods of Distribution; The American Explosion; Changes in Distribution Economics; Distribution of Diversified New Products; Ideas, Inertia and Achievement; also papers on indsl. operations. Established Turck Lectures on Distbn., Yale, 1951. Home: New York City NY Died Sept. 19, 1970.

TURCK, FENTON BENEDICT, physician; b. Milwaukee, Aug. 25, 1857; s. J. Byron and Sarah A. (Ashby) T.; prep. edn. Markham Acad., Milwaukee; M.D., Chicago Med. Coll. (Med. Dept. Northwestern U.), 1891; m. Avis L. Paine, June 10, 1897; children—Katherine Paine, Fenton Benedict. House surgeon, Alexian Bros. Hosp., Chicago, 1891-92; prof. internal medicine, Post-Grad. Med. Sch., 1893; lecturer Jefferson Med. Coll., Phila., 1896, Coll. Phys. and Surg., Chicago, 1901-02, U. of Rome, Italy, 1906. Admitted Feb. 21, 1913, to practice in N.Y. without examination by Bd. of Regents Univ. State of N.Y., "because of having attained a position of eminence and authority in his profession"; dir. Research Lab. Turck Foundation. Capt. Reserve M.C., U.S.A. Fellow New York Acad. Medicine. Del. Internat. Med Congress 5 times between 1894 and 1913. Devised instruments, including gyromele for exploration and scientific research in the alimentary tract, 1893; original research on gastritis, peptic ulcer, traumatic shock, etc.; studies in immunity on the shock phenomena and related living processes; investigations on Cytost-Anticytost reaction in cell division, regeneration and metabolism in plants and animals. Author of "Experimental Studies in Biology," and numerous original scientific publs. Home: New York, N.Y. Died Nov. 16, 1932.

TURLEY, JAY (tûr'le), engineer; b. Beaver City, Utah, Apr. 16, 1877; s. Omner and Louisa Ann (Woodhouse) T.; both born west of Rocky Mts.; ran away from home at 17 to attend sch.; matriculated in Ore. State Agrl. Coll., 1895; but did not grad.; spl. advanced studies in U. of Tex. and George Washington U.; m. Urna Bradford Hickox, Sept. 7, 1904 (divorced Apr. 28, 1921). Apptd. U.S. dep. surveyor for Ida., 1899, for N.M., 1900-06; formulating extensive irrigation projects in Rio San Juan, N.M., since 1901; made original draft of irrigation laws for State of N.M., 1903-05; cons. engr. for N.M., in suit against Tex. over boundary along Rio Grande, 1913-16, 1921, 25; admitted to practice law, N.M., 1916, D.C., and Supreme Court of U.S., 1921. Mem. Idaho Nat. Guard, 1894-98; capt. engrs., U.S. Army, 1917-19, serving with 316th Engrs., 91st Div., and with 116th Engrs., 41st Div., A.E.F., also spl. staff and liaison service; retired as capt. Engrs., May 20, 1929. Republican. Mason (32 deg.). Opposed, 1925, bldg. of St. Francis Dam, near Los Angeles, Calif., which burst in 1928; reported, 1928, on "astral collision," at Crater Mound, Ariz., contending that it caused fissures forming Grand Canyon of the Colorado; reported, 1929, geological and other conditions for building high dam above Grand Canyon, instead of below at Boulder site; on spl. scientific research and writing up data since 1931; working on case of old Spanish grant community ditches of central N.M. in connection with suit before Supreme Court since 1934 and on development of water supply sources near Albuquerque, N.M. Home: near Albuquerque, N.M. Address: P.O. Box 161, Albuquerque, N.M. Died Sep. 17, 1942.

TURNBULL, J(OHN) GORDON, engr.; b. San Francisco, Nov. 8, 1891; s. Alexander and Margaret (Noakes) T.; specialized tng. engring. U. Louvain, 1907-10; m. Susan Aycock, 1938; children—John Gordon, Alexander, Susan Gay. Draftsman, San Francisco, 1911-13; engr., Portland, Ore., 1913-15; partner W. A. Kramer Co., Portland, and co-adventurer Hans Pederson Co., Seattle, constn. Nisqually Dam, Tacoma Power Plant and transmission lines, Lake Washington Canal Locks, 1915-17; cons. archtl., indsl. engr. for Ford, G.M., Paige, Dodge, Hudson & Packard Motor cos., Curtis-Wright, Chance-Vought Airplane cos., Pratt-Whitney Engine Co., and others, 1918-37; cons. engr. G.M. Corp. (Detroit Diesel, Allison Engine, Electro-Motive plants), 1938-41; pres., chmn. bd., chief cons. J. Gordon Turnbull, Inc., 1941—, designing and supervising constrn. synthetic rubber plants including, Rubber Res. Corp.; tire plants including, Goodyear, U.S. Rubber, Kelly Springfield; aircraft plants including, N.A. Aviation, Lockheed, Goodyear); aluminum reduction and extrusion plants including, Reynolds Metals Co.; def. installations including, Canol Project comprising airfields, highways, pipelines, refineries and dockage: airfields at Ferry Island Groups, Honolulu to New Guinea; master plans U.S.A.F. bases, U.S.A., Eng., and Japan; and other engring. projects for U.S. C.E., AEC, Air Force; headed spl. engring. mission to Europe for U.S. State Dept., Army, Navy and Air Force, 1948. Mem. Am. Soc. C.E. Clubs: Rainier (Seattle); Union (Cleve.). Home: 11499 Bellagio Rd., Los Angeles. Died Apr. 1, 1953; buried Glen Haven Meml. Park, San Fernando, Cal.

TURNBULL, WILLIAM, army officer, engr.; b. Phila., 1800; s. William and Mary (Nisbet) T.; grad. U.S. Mil. Acad., 1819; m. Jane Graham Ramsay, 1826, 10 children, including Charles N. Commd. 2d lt. on topog. duty Corps Arty., U.S. Army, 1819-31, 1st lt., 1823; capt. Topog. Engrs. on survey of railroad route in Miss., 1831-32; assigned to constrn. of Potomac Aqueduct across Potomac River at Georgetown, D.C., 1832-43 (one of 1st important Am. engring. works); published Report on the Construction of the Piers of the Aqueduct of the Alexandria Canal across the Potomac River at Georgetown, District of Columbia, 1836, 2d report, 1838; chief topog. engr. on staff of Gen. Winfield Scott, participated in operations from siege of Vera Cruz to capture of Mexico City; brevetted lt. col. for services in battles of Contreras, Churubusco, col. for Battle of Chapultepec; superintending engr. of constrn. custom house, New Orleans, 1848-49; surveyed Whales Back Rock, Portsmouth, N.H. (for a lighthouse site), examined practicability of bridging Susquehanna River at Havre de Grace, 1850-52; mem. bd. to examine feasibility of additional canal around the Falls of the Ohio, 1853-56; engaged in lighthouse constrn., Oswego, N.Y., 1853-55. Died Dec. 9, 1857.

TURNEAURE, FREDERICK EUGENE, (tûr-nûr'), engineer; b. Freeport, Ill., July 30, 1866; s. Giles and Clarissa (May) T.; C.E., Cornell, 1889; studied engring. abroad, 1895-96; Dr. Engring., U. of Ill., 1905; m. Mary D. Stewart, Aug. 25, 1891 (died 1916); 1 son, Frederick Stewart. Instr. Washington U., 1890-92; prof. bridge and sanitary engring., U. of Wis., 1892-1902, acting dean Coll. Engring., 1902-03, dean and prof. engring., 1903-37, dean emeritus since 1937. Mem. ex officio Wis. State Highway Commn., 1911-29; city engr. Madison, 1900-02. Mem. A.A.A.S., Soc. for Promotion Engring. Edn. (pres. 1908-09). Western Soc. Engrs., Am. Ry. Engring. Assn., Am. Soc. of Civil Engineers (hon.), American Concrete Institute, American Society Testing Materials. Author: Theory and Practice of Modern Framed Structures (with J. B. Johnson and C. W. Bryan), 1893; Public Water Supplies (with Dr. H. L. Russell), 1900; Principles of Reinforced Concrete Construction (with Edward Rose Maurer), 1907. Investigations on stresses in bridges under moving train loads, also on strength of steel columns, Trans. Am. Soc. Civ. Engrs., 1899, 1927, 31; Bulletins of Am. Ry. Engring. Assn., 1910-17. Home: 166 Prospect Av., Madison, Wis. Died Mar. 31, 1951.

TURNER, CLAUDE ALLEN PORTER, consulting engr.; b. Lincoln, R.I., July 4, 1869; s. John M. and Elizabeth (Darling) T.; C.E., Lehigh U., 1890; m. Mary E. Burns, June 6, 1894 (died 1941); children—Margaret E. H., William M.; m. 2d, Kathleen Flavin, 1943. With N.Y. and N.E. Ry., 1890-91, Edgemore Bridge Co., of Wilmington, Del., 1891; asst. engr. Columbus Bridge Co., 1892; draftsman Pittsburgh Bridge Co., 1893, Berlin Bridge Co., 1894-95; asst. engr. Pottsville Iron & Steel Co., 1896, Gillette-Herzog Co., Minneapolis, Minn., 1897-1900; engr. western contracting dept. Am. Bridge Co., Minneapolis, 1901; consulting practice, Minneapolis, since 1901; took over bus. founded by Theo. A. Wegener in 1941; cons. bridge engr. for Soo Line R.R., 15 yrs. prior to World War; also cons. engr. for tunnel under Bunker Hill, St. Paul; designed structure and power plant of Electric Steel Elevator, Minneapolis, and dam for Manistique (Mich.) Pulp & Paper Co. Originator and patentee of flat slab "mushroom system" of floor constrn. and spiral mushroom floor constrn., a type embodied in hundreds of buildings and many important bridges. Designer of Missouri River Bridge between Bismarck and Mandan, N.D.; series of arches over St. Croix River for the Soo Line; series of concrete arches over the Minnesota River at Ft. Snelling; development of the theory of ultimate economy in steel frame trusses. Author: Elasticity, Structure and Strength of Materials (Part I develops the exact stress mechanism of beams, shafts and plates for the first time and contains an introduction to the theory of thermo-elasticity which is so developed in Part III that physical properties of materials are coordinated with atomic weights and numbers, melting and vaporization temperatures, specific heat and density; chem. mechanics is developed in Part III so that the heat of formation of reversible chem. compounds of all classes may be calculated by thermal theory, coordinating with melting and vaporization temperatures. Physical problems, the permanence of solar heat, nature of gravity and electrical energy are accounted for by thermo-elasticity which explains in detail the molecular vibration of heat energy); Natural Philosophy of the Science of Physics, Chemistry and Engineering, 1947; Educational and Industrial Problems With Intermolecular Forces Analyzed in Engring., Physics and Chemistry, 1948; A Research in Natural Phenomena, 1951; Revision of Thermal Mechanics, 1952. Home: 1007 Delaware Av. Address: 964 N. High St., Columbus, O. Died Jan. 10, 1955.

TURNER, DANIEL LAWRENCE, civ. eng'r; b. Portsmouth, Va., Oct. 25, 1869; s. Daniel James and Mary Elizabeth (Lawrence) T.; early ed'n Norfolk (Va.) Acad.; grad. Rensselaer Poly. Inst., C.E., 1891; m. at Norfolk, Va., Feb. 3, 1896, Eva Barcine Denby. Asst. in mathematics, Rensselaer Poly. Inst., 1892-3; in active practice as civ. eng'r in Conn., N.Y. State and New York City since 1893; instr. in surveying and hydraulics, and in charge Harvard Eng'ring Camp, Harvard Univ., 1893-1903; asst. eng'r in charge of stations Rapid Transit R. R. Comm'n, New York. Mem. Am. Soc. Civ. Eng'rs. Author: Sketch and Note Book for Stadia Work, E15. Residence: 220 W. 107th St. Office: Rapid Transit R. R. Commission, 320 Broadway, New York NY

TURNER, HAROLD, bus. exec., engr.; b. Bealton, Ont., Jan. 29, 1902; s. Hugh and Nellie Adell (Taylor) T.; B.A.Sc., University Toronto, 1924; married Anna Louise Coyne, August 5, 1926; children—Patricia (Mrs. David H. Wiltsie), Stephen, Margaret. Came to U.S., 1924, naturalized, 1940. Engr., Gen. Electric Co., Schenectady, N.Y., 1924-26; asst. to elec. engr. Am. Gas & Electric Co. and Am. Gas & Electric Service Corp., 1926-33, asst. to chief engr., 1933-34, asst. to v.p. and chief engr., 1934-41; asst. gen. mgr. Ohio Power Co., Canton, 1941-46, v.p., general mgr., 1946-54; exec. v.p. operating, dir. American Electric Power Service Corp. (formerly Am. Gas & Electric Service Corp.), 1954—; v.p. Beech Bottom Power Co., Central Appalachian Coal Co., Central Ohio Coal Co.; dir. Captina Operating Company, West Virginia Power Company; v.p., dir. Appalachian Electric Power Co., Central Coal Company, Central Operating Co., Franklin Real Estate Co., Ind. & Mich. Electric Co., Kanawha Valley Power Co., Ky. Power Co., Kingsport Utilities, Inc., Ohio Power Co., Radford Limestone Co., Wheeling Electric Co. Pres. Ohio Electric Inst., 1950-52. Profl. engr. O. and N.Y. Mem. Am. Inst. E.E., Am. Soc. Mil. Engrs., Nat., Ohio socs. profl. engrs., Ohio Soc. N.Y. Mem. Dutch Reformed Ch. Mason (Shriner). Clubs: Railroad Machinery, Harbor View (N.Y.C.); St. Andrew's Golf (Hastings-on-Hudson, N.Y.). Author tech. papers. Office: 2 Broadway, N.Y.C. 4. Died Oct. 24, 1960.

TURNER, HENRY H., physician; b. Harrisburg, Ill., Aug. 28, 1892; s. John William and Alice (Rose) T.; student St. Louis U., 1914-15, Sch. of Medicine, 1915-18; M.D., U. of Louisville 1921; m. Frances Bulkley, June 28, 1923; children—Marian Frances, Alice Ann. Asst. in medicine U. Louisville, 1921-24; instr. U. Okla. Sch. Medicine, 1924-28, asst. prof. medicine, 1928-29, asso., clin. prof. 1939-69, clin. prof. medicine emeritus, 1969-70, asso. dean, 1948-49; pvt. practice internal med., 1925-70; resident in medicine Louisville Hosp., 1922-24; vis. physician Okla. State U. Hosp., State Crippled Children's Hosp., St. Anthony's Hosp., Okla., 1924-70; cons. endocrinologist University and Children's Hosp., 1924-70; chief metabolic clinic out-patient dept., Univ. Hosp., 1924-70; sec.-treas., Endocrine Soc., 1941 (v.p. 1937-38, council 1938-41). Seale Harris award So. Med. Assn., 1961. Schering Scholar, 1959. Diplomate Am. Bd. Internatl Medicine. Fellow A.C.P.; mem. Am., So. (v.p. 1938-39, trustee 1962-63) med. assns., Soc. Nuclear Medicine (pres. 1959-60), Am. Therapeutic Soc. (pres. 1939-40), Central Soc. Clin. Research, Okla. Med. Assn. (pres. 1940-41). Oklahoma County Med. Soc., Endocrine Soc. (sec.-treas. 1941-66, pres. 1967-68), Oklahoma City Acad. Medicine (sec. 1937, pres. 1938). Clubs: Doctor's Dinner, Lotus, Tower. Contbr. articles to med. jours. and books. Home: Oklahoma City OK Died Aug. 4, 1970.

TURNER, HENRY WARD, geologist, mining engr.; b. Silver Lake, Susquehanna County, Pa., Aug. 22, 1857; s. Edwin Morgan and Martha L. (Ellis) T.; student Cornell U., 1874-76 and 1882; Leipzig, 1879-80; B.S., Columbian (now George Washington) U., 1895; m. Caroline Wadsworth, Apr. 18, 1892. Mem. U.S. Geol. Survey, 1882-1900; pvt. practice, 1901—. Author: The Origin of Yosemite Valley, 1900; several geol. folios of Calif., papers on geology of Calif. and other regions in annual reports geol. survey and in geol. and mining jours. Address: Ross, Calif. Died Nov. 25, 1937.

TURNER, JOSEPH AUGUSTINE, agriculturist; b. Hollins, Va., Nov. 21, 1875; s. Joseph Augustine and Leila Virginia (Cocke) T.; ed. Richmond (Va.) Coll., 1892-94, U. of Va., 1894-97, Eastman Business Coll., summer 1899; m. Mary VanFossen Masters, Feb. 16, 1904; children—Mary VanFossen, Joseph Augustine, Susanna Pleasants. Teacher Alleghany Inst., 1897-98; with Hollins Coll., 1898—; gen. mgr. and mem. bd. of govs., 1901-32, bus. mgr. and sec. Hollins Coll. Corp., 1932—. Mem. bd. visitors Virginia Agrl. and Mech. Coll. and Poly. Inst., 1912-19. Awarded certificate Va. Agrl. and Mech. Coll. and Poly. Inst. "for promoting development of agriculture." Democrat. Baptist. Contbr. to farm jours. Speaker on education, agriculture, Va. history, etc. Died Oct. 21, 1937.

TURNER, LEWIS M., college dean; b. Heyworth Ill., Sept. 7, 1898; s. Frank and Harriet (Cogswell) T.; student U. of Michigan, 1919-21; B.S., U. of Illinois, 1923, M.S., 1925; Ph.D., U. of Chicago, 1931; m. Eunice Josephine Brown, July 11, 1925; children—Frederick Brown, Lewis MacDonald. Teacher science, Heyworth (Ill.) High Sch., 1923-24; fellow, dept. botany, U. of Ill., 1924-25, U.S. Dept. Agr., summer 1925; head dept. biology, Blackburn Coll., 1925-29; teaching fellow U. of Chicago, 1929-31; asst. prof. forestry, U. of Arkansas, 1931-36; asso. conservationist, U.S. Forest Service, 1937-38, forester, 1938-39, sr. forester, 1939-43, asst. chief, div. forest influences, branch of research, 1941-43; dean College Forest Range and Wildlife Management, Utah State University, Logan, Utah, 1943—; U.S. Operations Mission to Iran to establish Nat. Forestry School, 1954, 58. National Forester 1949—. Served with U.S. Army, 1918-19; 2d. lt., Organized Reserves, 1926-31. Fellow A.A.A.S.; senior member Soc. Am. Foresters (chairman program com. national meeting, 1958); mem. Ecol. Soc. America, Bot. Society Am. Am. Assn. Univ. Profs., Am. Forestry Assn., Ill. and Utah acads. sciences, Kiwanis Internat., N.E.A., Am. Soc. Range Mgrs., Am. Council Forestry Sch. Execs., Am., Utah edn. assns., Sigma Xi, Phi Delta Kappa, Phi Kappa Phi, Xi Sigma Pi. Mason. Author: Articles, bulls. and booklets. Based on original research to sci. publs. Home: 228 N. 4th East St., Logan, Utah. Died Nov. 4, 1960.

TURNER, ROSCOE, aviator; b. Corinth, Miss., Sept. 29, 1895; s. Robert Lee and Aquilla (Derryberry) T.; ed. pub. schs., business coll.; m. Carline Stovall, Sept. 29, 1924; m. 2d, Margaret Madonna Miller, Dec. 1946. Chmn. bd. Roscoe Turner Aero Corp.; cons. House Com. Science and Astronautics, 1960, 63, Barnstorming flyer and stunt performer, 1919-27; operated pioneer comml. air field, Richmond, Va., 1927-28; operated world's pioneer high speed air line, 1929-30; holder cross country speed records Nat. Air Races, as winner Bendix Race, 11 hrs. 30 mins. N.Y. to Los Angeles, 1933 (record still standing in 1938); Nat. Air Races as winner Thompson Trophy Race, 1934, 38, 39; finished 2d. Speed Div., Internat. Air Race from London to Melbourne, 1934. Awarded Harmon Trophy by Ligue Internationale des Aviateurs as America's premier aviator for 1932. Served Air Service. World War; disch. 1st lt., 1919. Decorated Distinguished Flying Cross, 1952; recipient Paul Tissandier Diploma, Federation Aeronautique Internationale, (Austria), 1956; Beechcraft Man of Year award, 1960; Spl. Recognition award Ind. Aviation Trades Assn., 1960; Silver Wings award, 1964; Distinguished Citizen award Ind. dept. Am. Legion, 1969; Distinguished Nat. Vets. award Combined Vets. Orgns., 1969; honored with Col. Roscoe Turner Day in City of Indpls., 1969; Roscoe Turner Musuem established in his honor. Formerly col. gov.'s staff of Nev. Nat. Guard, Miss. Nat. Guard, on staff gov. of Cal.; now colonel in Civil Air Patrol. Honorary mem. Los Angeles Police Dept.; Sheriff's Staff, Los Angeles; capt. Aero Police, St. Joseph, Mo.; C. of C. Pitts.; Jr. C. of C., Dayton, O.; New York Detective Endowment Assn. Mem. Quiet Birdmen, Nat. Aeronautic Assn., Racing Pilots Assn. of Nat. Aeronautic Assn., Ind. Soc. of Chgo., Nat. Pilots Assns., Conquistadores Del. Celo. Am. Legion, Ligue Internationale des Aviateurs, Texas Rangers, Ind., Indpls. chambers commerce, Civil Air Patrol, Civil Air Patrol Nat. Aerospace Edn. Assn., Am. Inst. Aeros. and Astronautics, Air Force Assn., Nat. Aviation Traders Assn., Nat. Defense Transp. Assn., Inst. Aero. Scis., Soc. Automotive Engrs., Sigma Alpha Tau, other orgns. Mason (Shriner); mem. Order Eastern Star. Clubs: Flying (Columbus, O.), Kiwanis (Cleve.); Lions (Anderson, S.C.). Home: Indianapolis IN Died June 23, 1970; interred Crown Hill Cemetary Mausoleum, Indianapolis IN

TURNER, SCOTT, mining; b. Lansing, Mich., July 31, 1880; s. James Munroe and Sophie Porter (Scott) T.; A.B., U. of Mich., 1902, D.Eng., 1930; B.S. and E.M., Mich. Coll. Mines, 1904, D.Eng., 1932; Sc.D., Colorado School of Mines, 1930; D.Sc., Kenyon Coll., 1940; m. Amy Prudden, June 25, 1919. Mining engr., Ida. and Ore., 1902, Ariz., 1904, Calif., Panama, Nev. and Colo., 1905; examining engr., Nev., 1906; mining engr., Ida., 1906; asso. editor Mining Scientific Press, 1907; mining engr., Alaska, Wash., 1908; mine geologist, Calif. and Pacific Coast, 1909-10; mine examiner, Europe, 1911; mine mgr., Norway and Spitzbergen, 1912-16; mining engr., Peru, Chile, Bolivia, 1916-17; cons. engr., Can., 1919-25; dir. U.S. Bur. Mines, 1926-34; v.p. and dir. various mining cos., consultant in mining. Mem. Nat. Research Council, tech. com. and Div. Fed. Relations; mem. Nuclear, orgn. and geophys. coms. of Internat. Geol. Congress; mem. research com. Engring. Foundation; Holmes Safety Assn. (past pres.); mem. Geol. Soc. of Am.; mem. Council and Bd., World Power Conf.; mem. tech. adv. com. Fed. Oil Conservation Bd., 1926-34. Sole U.S. del. to Empire Mining Congress, Can., 1928. Apptd. by Dept. of Justice as mem. U.S. Anaconda Smelter Smoke Commn., 1926; apptd. by sec. of state as U.S. del. to World Engring. Congress, Tokyo, 1929; to World Power Conf., Berlin, 1930; to Internat. Congress of Mining, Liege, Belgium, 1930; Apptd. by secy. of treas. to U.S. Assay Commission and other important Fed. posts. Past chmn. Nat. Interfrat. Conf.; chmn. Hoover Medal Bd. of Award; dir. Belgian-Am. Ednl. Foundation; mem. Nat. Technol. Adv. Com. apptd. by sec. of war. Recipient Hoover medal (engring.), 1957. Served as lieutenant (s.g.) USNRF, 1917-19. Mem. Am. Inst. Mining, Metall. and Petroleum Engrs. (past pres.), Am. Inst. of Cunsulting Engrs. (pres.), Mining and Metall. Soc. Am., Canadian Inst. Mining and Metallurgy, Lake Superior Mining Inst., hon. mem. Am. Zinc Inst., Coal Mining Inst. of Am., Am. Rifle Assn., S.A.R., Tau Beta Pi, Psi Upsilon (nat. pres.). Republican. Mason. Clubs: Leash; Hammonasset Fishing; Burning Tree, Chevy Chase, Cosmos, Met. (Washington); Round Hill, Milbrook Gun (pres.), Engineers, River Hills Fishing (Conn.); Turtle Lake (Mich.); University, Century Assn., Mining, Explorers; Camp Fire of Am.; Boone and Crockett; Preston Mountain Club, Incorporated, Verbank Hunting and Fishing, Economic, A.R.A. Assn. (New York). Home: Greenwich CT Died July 30, 1972; buried Mt. Hope Cemetery, Lansing MI

TURNER, WALTER VICTOR, engineer, inventor; b. Epping Forest, Essex County, Eng., Apr. 3, 1866; s. George and Beatrice (Brandon) T.; ed. Textile Tech. Sch., Wakefield, Yorkshire, Eng.; m. Beatrice Woolford, Nov. 1887. Came to U.S., 1888; sec. and mgr. Lake Ranch Cattle Co., Raton, N.M., 1893; with A.,T.&S.F. R.R., 1897, and same yr. developed first patent; with Westinghouse Air Brake Co., 1903—, apptd. mech. engr., 1907, chief engr., 1910, asst. mgr., 1915, mgr. of engring., 1916. His elec., mech. and pneumatic inventions covered by over 400 U.S. patents, and in use on most of rys. of world and in many large indsl. plants; awarded Longstreth medal, 1911, Elliott Cresson medal, 1912; testimonial as the leading air brake expert, by Air Brake Assn., Richmond, Va., 1912. Fellow Royal Soc. of Arts (Eng.). Republican. Methodist. Author: Train Control—Its Development and Effect on Transportation Capacity (2 vols.), 1918. Home: Wilkinsburg, Pa. Died Jan. 9, 1919.

TURNER, WILLIAM DE GARMO, chem. engring.; b. Sioux City, Ia., Sept. 25, 1889; s. William De Garmo and Jessie Gertrude (Skinner) T.; Ph.B., Morgan Park (Ill.) Acad., 1905; B.S., U. Chgo., 1909, Ph.D., 1917; m. Alice N. Tyler, Oct. 17, 1914; children—William De Garmo, John Salisbury (dec.). Expert, Bur. Chemistry, Dept. Agr., 1909-10; comml. analyst Armour & Co.. 1910-14; asst. in dept. chemistry U. Chgo., 1914-15, asso., 1915-17, asst. prof. chemistry, Mo. Sch. Mines, U. Mo., 1917-18, prof., head dept., 1918-29; in charge Bakelite research Columbia U., 1927-45, prof. chem. engrnig., 1929-46; cons. chem. engr.; tech. engr. for Bermuda Water Works; tech. dir. Airkem, Inc., 1945-58, emeritus, in residence, 1958—. Fellow A.A.A.S., Am. Inst. Chemists (nat. councilor); mem. Am. Inst. Chem. Engrs., Am. Pub. Health Assn., Soc. Chem. Industry, Am. Waterworks Assn., Am. Chem. Soc., Sigma Xi, Phi Kappa Phi; hon. mem. Lambda Chi, Theta Tau, Pi Gamma Mu, Phi Lambda Upsilon, Hon. Cum Laude Soc. Mason (K.T.). Club: Chemists. Author papers, also chpts. in books. Address: 241 E. 44th St., N.Y.C. 17. Died 1960.

TUSKA, GUSTAVE ROBISHER, cons. engr.; b. N.Y. City, July 15, 1869; s. Adolph and Elsie (Robisher) T.; B.Sc., Coll. City of N.Y., 1888, M.Sc., 1891; C.E., Sch. of Mines (Columbia), 1891; m. Isabel Pappenheim, Nov. 24, 1902. Asst. engr. Link Engring. Co., 1891-92; bridge engr., L.I. R.R. Co., 1892-93; lecturer on bridge design and masonry constrn., Columbia, 1893-97; resident engr., Knoxville, Cumberland Gap and Louisville R.R. Co., 1894-95; engr. to Health Dept., N.Y. City, 1894-96; resident engr. Central N.Y. and Western R.R., 1896; chief engr. Panama R.R. and superintending engr. Panama S.S. Co., 1896-99; pres. and chief engr. Am. Process Co., in charge constrn. plants handling waste products, 1899-1925; pres. and chief engr. Atlantic Constrn. Co., 1899-1907; lecturer on municipal engring., Columbia, 1915-17. Consultant on municipal engring. work, City of New York, St. Louis, Chicago, Buffalo, Washington, D.C., and water power plants, railroads and piers, N.H., Va., N.Y., etc.; pres. Internat. Engineering Corp., 1923—. Maj. engrs. U.S.A., Sept. 24, 1917-July 28, 1919, at Camp Lee and Camp Humphrey's, Va., on staff of chief of engrs. U.S.A., and at office of Dir. Gen. Mil. Rys., Washington; lt. col. engrs., Res., U.S.A., 1923. Mem. steel com. War Industries Bd., Washington, 1918; mem. Mexican Com., U.S. Govt., 1919; del. 2d Pan-Am. Congress, Washington, 1920, to 3d Pan-Am. Congress, 1927. Fellow A.A.A.S.; mem. Nat. Inst. Social Sciences, Am. Acad. Polit. and Social Science; trustee Allied Patriotic Socs. Home: New York, N.Y. Died May 28, 1931.

TUTTLE, ALBERT HENRY, biologist; b. Cuyahoga Falls, O., Nov. 19, 1844; s. Henry Blakeslee and Emeline (Reed) T.; B.Sc., State Coll. of Pa., 1868, M.Sc., 1872, hon. A.M., 1918; m. Kate Austin Seeley, Aug. 7, 1873; children—William Buckhout, Clara Mary (Mrs. W. Ramsey Probasco), Anna Seeley (Mrs. W. Harry Heck, dec.). Prof. natural sciences, State Normal Sch., Platteville, Wis., 1868-70; instr. microscopy, Harvard, 1870-72; commr. from Ohio to Vienna Expn., 1873; prof. zoölogy and comparative anatomy, Ohio State U., 1874-88; prof. biology, U. of Va., 1888-1913; retired upon Carnegie Foundation. Fellow A.A.A.S. (v.p. sect. microscopy, 1882), Royal Micros. Soc., London. Author occasional papers on scientific and ednl. subjects. Address: University, Va. Deceased.

TUTTLE, ARTHUR LEMUEL, mining engr.; b. Salt Lake City, Oct. 30, 1870; s. Rt. Rev. Daniel S. and Harriet M. (Foote) T.; E.M., Washington U., 1893; m. Mary E. Hackley, Oct. 8, 1896; 1 son, Arthur Lemuel. Instr. mining dept., Washington U., 1893-94; ore buyer and mine supt. La Gran Fundicion Nacional Mexicana, Mexico, 1894-97; supt. Conrey Placer Mining Co., Virginia City, Mont., 1897-98; supt., mgr. Catherine Lead Co., Fredrickton, Mo., and Columbia Lead Co., Flat River, Mo., 1899-1902; gen. supt. Jimulco Mining Co., and Continental Mining Co., Mexico, 1902-16; asst. mgr. and gen. mgr. Tenn. Copper Co., Copperhill, Tenn., 1916-19; consulting engr. Tenn. Copper Chem.

Co., N.Y.C., 1919-23; engr. and resident mgr. in Mexico of Gen. Development Co., 1923-26; practicing at Danville, 1926—. Mem. Am. Inst. Mining and Metall. Engrs. Republican. Episcopalian. Address: 212 N. 3d St., Danville, Ky. Died Jan. 21, 1958.

TUTTLE, ARTHUR SMITH, cons. engr.; b. Burlington, Conn., Mar. 26, 1865; s. Theron and Jennie E. (Beach) T.; C.E., New York U., 1885; D.Eng., Rensselaer Poly Inst., 1942; m. Helen Aldridge Smith, June 1, 1892; children—Marguerite, Walter Aldridge, Laurence C. Assistant engineer, Brooklyn Water Works, 1884-1901; chief engineer investigation for proposed irrigation and water power development, Bishop Estate, Honolulu, 1901-02; prin. asst. and deputy chief engr. Bd. Estimate and Apportionment, City of N.Y., 1902-20, chief engineer, 1921-28, consulting engineer, 1928-33; consulting engr. Citizen Budget Commission, 1933; New York state engineer Federal Emergency Administration of Pub. Works, Aug. 1933-36, state dir., 1936-37; federal project engr. or acting project engr. Triboro Bridge, Lincoln Tunnel and Queens Midtown Tunnel, 1933-37; mem. N.Y. City Adminstrn. for Work and Home Relief, Apr.-Aug. 1933; private practice and cons. engr. for WPA, 1937-41; dir. N.Y. City, Fed. Public Works Reserve, 1941-42; mem. Tuttle, Seelye, Place & Raymond, cons. engrs., 1941-44; consulting engr. and chmn. Tuttle-Haller Cos. since 1944; (engineering, inspection, testing); inventor water meter for large mains. Twice cited for distinguished service by Mayor La Guardia, 1937-39. Honorary member American Society C.E. (formerly president, v.p., treasurer and director); former member and ex-chairman John Fritz Medal Board. of Award; mem. United Engring. Trustees (past v.p.), Am. Inst. Cons. Engrs. (past mem. council), Municipal Engrs. of N.Y. City (ex-pres.), Regional Plan Assn., Am. Shore and Beach Preservation Assn. (dir.), Sound View Assn. (dir.), N.Y. Univ. Alumni Fedn. (ex-pres.), New York Univ. Council, Phi Beta Kappa, Tau Beta Pi, Delta Phi; former mem. Engring. Foundation. Clubs: Engineers of New York (dir., ex-pres.); Cosmos (Washington); St. Georges Golf and Country; Municipal of Brooklyn (ex-pres.), Pleiades (ex-pres.), Brooklyn Engineers. Author of many articles for tech. press and engring. socs. Mem. advisory bd. of editorial staff, Sewage Works Engring. Home: 24 Monroe Pl., Brooklyn, N.Y. (winter) and Stony Brook, L.I., N.Y. Office: 801 Second Av., New York, N.Y. Died May 19, 1949.

TUTTLE, CHARLES WESLEY, astronomer, lawyer; b. Newfield, Mass., Nov. 1, 1829; s. Moses and Mary (Merrow) T.; attended Harvard Law Sch., 1854, A.M. (hon.), 1854; Ph.D. (hon.), Dartmouth, 1880; m. Mary Louisa Park, Jan. 31, 1872. Asst., Harvard Observatory, 1850; made his most important contbn. to astronomy by explaining Saturn's "dusky" ring, 1850; discovered a comet, 1853; computed cometary orbits and ephemirides; participated in eclipse expdn. to summit of Mt. Washington, 1854; admitted to Mass. bar, 1856; practiced, Boston, 1856; admitted to practice in U.S. circuit cts., 1858, U.S. Supreme Ct., 1861; took testimony for use before Ct. of Ala. Claims, 1874; made hist. and antiquarian studies of Me. and N.H. Author: Captain John Mason (edited by J. W. Dean), published posthumously, 1887; also numerous articles published in New Eng. Hist. and Geneal. Register, Proceedings of Mass. Hist. Soc., Notes and Queries. Died July 17, 1881.

TUTTLE, DAVID KITCHELL, chemist; b. at Whippany, Morris County, N.Y., Sept. 19, 1835; s. Silas and Lorania (Baker) T.; student New York U., 1851-53; B.S. summa cum laude, Lawrence Scientific Sch. (Harvard), 1955; Ph.D., Georgia Augusta U., Göttingen, 1857 (hon. diploma Jubilee 50th yr.); m. Ellen White Humes, April 7, 1864 (dec.). Asst. prof. chemistry, U. of Va., 1857-61; in pvt. business as tech. chemist, 1861-86; melter and refiner Carson City Mint., 1886-88, Phila. Mint, 1888—. Mem. Am. Acad. Polit. and Social Science. Author: Qualitative Analysis (Tuttle and Chandler). Contbr. to tech. jours. and reports. Home: Philadelphia, Pa. Died Apr. 8, 1915.

TUTTLE, MORTON CHASE, constrn. engr.; b. Milford, N.H., June 29, 1875; s. Charles Bell and Cornelia (Chase) T.; B.S., Dartmouth Coll., 1897, A.M., 1925; m. Alice Kidder, June 4, 1907. Gen. mgr. Aberthaw Constrn. Co., Boston, 1896-1923; pres. Morton C. Tuttle Co., engrs., Boston, since 1923; dir. State Street Trust Co. Mem. emergency constrn. com., War Industries Bd., later mgr. supply production div., later consol. supply div., Emergency Fleet Corp., World War. Republican. Conglist. Clubs: Brae Burn Country (Boston); Country (Brookline); Army and Navy (Washington). Home: Newton Centre, Mass. Office: Park Square Bldg., Boston. Died July 19, 1957.

TWEEDY, FRANK, topographical engr.; b. N.Y. City, June 12, 1854; s. Oliver Burr and Maria (Lord) T.; C.E., Union Coll., Schenectady, N.Y., 1875; m. Emma Adelaide Hydn, Dec. 20, 1888. Engr. on N.Y. State Adirondack survey, 1875-79; sanitary engr. under late George E. Waring, Jr., Newport, R.I., 1880-81; asst. topographer on Northern Transcontinental Survey, 1882-83; topographer, 1884-1915, then topog. engr., U.S. Geol. Survey; retired from govt. service. Author: Flora of the Yellowstone; also short stories. Home: Washington, D.C. Died 1937.

TWENHOFEL, WILLIAM HENRY, (twen'hof-el), geologist; b. Covington, Ky., Apr. 16, 1875; s. Ernst August Herman Julius and Helena (Steuwer) T.; B.A., Nat. Normal U., Lebanon, O., 1904; B.A., Yale, 1908, M.A., 1910, Ph.D., 1912; m. Virgie Mae Stephens, Sept. 10, 1899; children—Lillian Helena, Helen Vivian, William Stephens. Tchr. village and country schs., Ky., 1896-1902; tchr. sci. and mathematics, E. Tex. Normal Coll., Commerce, Tex., 1904-07; asst. and asso. prof. geology, U. Kan., 1910-16; state geologist of Kan., 1915-16; asso. prof. geology, 1916-21, U. Wis., prof., 1921—, chmn. dept., 1940—, ret., 1945. Prof., summer session, Stanford U., 1930. Chmn. Com. on Sedimentation, Nat. Research Council, 1923-31, chmn. Div. Geology and Geography, 1931-34, chmn. com. on Paleocology, 1934-37, geol. work in Kan., St. Lawrence, Baltic regions, Upper Miss. Valley. Mem. Geol. Soc. Am., Paleontol. Soc. Am. (pres. 1930), A.A.A.S., Wis. Acad. Sci., Am. Assn. Petroleum Geologists, Soc. Econ. Paleontologists and Mineralogists (pres. 1935); chmn. research com., 1938—, Rotary Internat., Sigma Gamma Epsilon, Sigma Xi, Phi Beta Kappa, Phi Kappa Phi, Sigma Alpha Epsilon. Conglist. Contbr. on sedimentation, stratigraphy and paleontology. Home: Rt. 3, Woodsmere, Orlando, Fla. Died Jan. 4, 1957; buried Orlando.

TWINING, ALEXANDER CATLIN, engr., astronomer, inventor; b. New Haven, Conn., July 5, 1801; s. Stephen and Almira (Catlin) T.; B.A., Yale, 1820, M.A., 1822; attended Andover Theol. Sem., 1823; studied civil engring. U.S. Mil. Acad., 1833; m. Harriet Kinsley, Mar. 2, 1829, at least 6 children. Tutor, Yale, 1823-24; observed star shower of Nov. 1833; formulated theory of cosmic origin of meteors (that shooting stars are bodies coming into air from external space); railroad engr. for Hartford & New Haven R.R. Co., 1834-39; prof. mathematics and natural philosophy Middlebury (Vt.) Coll., 1839-49; inventor method of mfg. ice (one of earliest applications of absorption process for mfg. ice on comml. scale), patented 1853. Died New Haven, Nov. 22, 1884.

TWITCHELL, AMOS, surgeon; b. Dublin, N.H., Apr. 11, 1781; s. Samuel and Alice (Willson) T.; A.B., Dartmouth, 1802, A.M., B.M., 1805, M.D., 1811; studied medicine under Nathan Smith; m. Elizabeth Goodhue, 1815. Leading surgeon in Northern New Eng.; one of 1st in U.S. to perform extensive amputations for malignant disease, operations for stones in bladder and ovarian tumors, tracheotomy, trephining of long bones for suppuration; performed 1st tying off of carotid artery in U.S., 1807; overseer Dartmouth, 1816; pres. N.H. Med. Soc., 1829-30; mem. A.M.A., Coll. Physicians of Phila., Nat. Instn. for Promotion of Science, 1841. Died Keene, N.H., May 26, 1850.

TWITTY, VICTOR CHANDLER, biologist; b. near Loogootee, Ind., Nov. 5, 1901; s. John MacMahon and Emma (Chandler) T.; B.S., Butler U., 1925; Ph.D., Yale, 1929; Nat. Research Council fellow, Kaiser Wilhelm Inst., Berlin, 1931-32; m. Florence Eveleth, Aug. 3, 1934; children—John, Eveleth (deceased), Sarah Ellen (dec.), Edith Anne. Instr. zool. Yale, 1929-31; asst. prof. zool. Stanford, 1932-35, asso. prof., 1935-36, prof., 1936-63, Herzstein prof., 1963—, exec. head dept. biol. scis., 1939-63; instr. Marine Biol. Lab., Woods Hole, summer 1930; lectr. zoology U. of Mich. summer 1941. Civilian with Office Scientific Research and Development, 1942-44; panel mem. com. on growth Nat. Research Council, 1947-50; mem. adv. com. on gen. biology Office of Naval Research, 1950. Fellow American Academy of Arts and Sciences; member Soc. Study of Growth and Development (pres. 1955), American Society Zoologists (pres. 1959), Western Society Naturalists (president, 1960), Institute Internationale D'Embryologie, Nat. Acad. Scis., Internat. Soc. Cell Biology. Author articles in profl. jours. Home: 714 Alvarado Row, Stanford, Cal. Died Mar. 22, 1967; buried Alta Mesa Cemetery.

TYLER, JOHN MASON, biologist; b. Amherst, Mass., May 18, 1851; s. Prof. William Seymour and Amelia Ogden (Whiting) T.; A.B., Amherst, 1873, A.M., 1876; Union Theol. Sem., 1874-76; univs. of Göttingen and Leipzig, 1876-79; hon. Ph.D., Colgate, 1888; m. Elizabeth Smith, July 12, 1883; children—Mason Whiting (dec.), Elizabeth Stearns (dec.). Instr. biology, 1879-81, zoölogy and botany, 1881-82, Stone prof. biology, 1882, emeritus, 1917, Amherst Coll. Author: Whence and Whither of Man, 1897; Growth and Education, 1907; Man in the Light of Evolution, 1908; New Stone Age, 1921; Coming of Man, 1923. Home: Amherst, Mass. Died Apr. 12, 1929.

TYLER, STANLEY A(LLEN), educator; b. Aztalan, Wis., Feb. 28, 1906; s. Willis Elmer and Lois Margret (Hunnel) T.; A.B., U. Wis., 1928, M.A., 1929, Ph.D., 1935; married Myrtle Simonsen, September 8, 1930 (died May 14, 1958); children—John, Robert; married 2d, Gail A. Kelling, November 28, 1959. Instructor N.D. State Agricultural College, 1930-31, asst. prof. geology, 1931-32; instr. geology U. Wis., 1935-37, asst. prof., 1937-45, asso. prof., 1945-46, prof., 1946—, chmn. dept., 1950-55; cons. geologist Jones and Laughlin Steel Corp., 1937-53. Fellow Geol. Soc. Am.; mem. Geochemical Soc., Soc. Econ. Geologists. Author articles in sci. jours.; contbr. book chpts. Home: 726 Huron Hill, Madison, Wis. Died Jan. 11, 1963; buried Aztalan.

TYLER, STEPHEN LESLIE, engr.; b. New Haven, Sept. 25, 1889; s. Frank P. and Stella M. T.; Ph.B., Yale, 1911; m. Adele DuCret, July 23, 1921 (dec.); m. 2d, Hazel C. Sack, Jan. 28, 1928; children—Stephen Leslie, William F. Test dept. N.Y., N.H.&H. R.R., New Haven, 1912-13; Thermal Syndicate Ltd., Bklyn., 1913-37; sec., exec. sec. Am. Inst. Chem. Engrs., 1937-54, ret.; sec. engring. edn. com. Engrs. Council for Profl. Devel. Mem. Am. Chem. Soc., Tau Beta Pi. Club: Chemists. Patentee absorption and condensing apparatus, 1923. Home: 5 Columbia Dr., Somerville, N.J. Office: 29 W. 39th St., N.Y.C. 18. Died Apr. 3, 1966; buried Evergreen Cemetery, New Haven.

TYRRELL, HENRY GRATTAN (tyr'rel), cons. engr.; b. Weston, Ont., Can.; s. William and Elizabeth (Burr) T.; grad. school Practical Science, Toronto; C.E., University of Toronto, 1894; married Alicia Bryant, January 1, 1890 (died January 1906); children—George, Bryant, Alicia; m. 2d, Mary Maude Knox, Nov. 7, 1907; 1 son, H. Grattan Knox. On exploration surveys in western Canada discovering large coal deposits, and railroad construction, Quebec and Maine, 4 yrs.; design and constrn. bridges and bldgs., 1888-1904, including designs and plans for all bridges, viaducts on railway line Lake Superior to Hudson Bay; spl. engr. bridges and bldgs., Harriman Rys., 1906-08; cons. engineer since 1908; prop. Tyrrell Engring. Co.; gave services to U.S. Govt., World War, in designing, building and valuation of war plants. Has been connected with constrn. of many notable bridges and other structures in U.S. and foreign countries; reported on rebuilding the twice-destroyed line of ry. through Rainbow Canyon between Salt Lake City and Los Angeles; designed improved type of ry. crossing gates; also types of regulating gates for canals and waterways; plans for St. Clair Memorial Bridge, and high level crossings of rivers at Detroit, Montreal, Norfolk, Va., Sidney, Australia, etc.; spanning 20 miles of Chesapeake Bay, from Baltimore to Eastern Shore; crossing Irish Channel from Ireland to Scotland by means of bridge and tunnel; prepared standard designs and estimated costs for bridges of ordinary span, steel and concrete, and published original charts and formulae for weight and cost, now in general use; since World War I and through World War II, to present date, has prepared engineering reports for construction (U.S. and foreign) together with writing and other engineering work, to the approximate value of $3,000,000,000. Awarded medal and diploma by Colonial and Indian Exhibition (London). Built hospital buildings in New Eng. for U.S. Govt. Mem. Soc. Promotion Engring. Edn., Am. Assn. Engrs., A.A.A.S. Clubs: Canadian (Washington); Engineers, Civitan. Author: Mill Building Construction, 1900; Concrete Bridges and Culverts, 1909; Mill Buildings, 1910; History of Bridge Engineering, 1911; Artistic Bridge Design; Engineering, of Shops and Factories; Movable Bridges; Structural Engring. Manual, etc.; and several non-tech. writings, nearly all being pioneer works on the subjects. Assisted by his wife in publication of his books (see Women of America, London). Extensive contbr. to engring. and scientific jours. of Am. and Europe. Proprietor Grattan Tyrrell Co., Baltimore. Home: "Grattanwood," Catonsville, Md. Office: 100 Eutaw St., Baltimore, Md. Died Feb. 4, 1948; buried in Loudon Park Cemetery, Baltimore.

TYSSOWSKI, JOHN, (ti-sou'ske) business exec., engr.; b. Washington, Jan. 19, 1887; s. Thaddeus Matthew and Alice Walton (Green) T.; B.S., mining, U. Calif., 1908; m. Catherine Woodward, Oct. 9, 1915. Various positions in mining, 1908-14; asst. to gen. mgr., Childs Co., 1914-16, gen. mgr. and treas. Bennett Day Importing Co., 1922-28; pres. Copper Deoxidation Corp., 1928-38; dir. Woodward & Lothrop, dept. store, Washington, since 1919, v.p., 1942-46, chmn. exec. com., 1946-48, chmn. bd. dirs. 1948-57, chairman of the executive committee; 1957—; farmer, Cobbler Mt. Farms, Delaplane, Virginia 1941—. Mem. exec. com., v.p. Atlantic Rural Exposition. Richmond. Mem. board visitors, Va. Polytech. Inst. Served with Squadron A, Cav., Nat. Guard N.Y., on Mexican border, 1916-17; commd. capt. U.S. Army Res.; active duty 1917-19; discharged as lt. col.; col. U.S. Res. Corps; inactive status for phys. disability, 1941; now col. Hon. Reserve. Mem. Va. Hereford Breeders Assn., Inc. (past president), American Institute of Mining Metallurgical and Petroleum Engineers, also mem. Mining and Metal. Soc. Am., Phi Delta Theta, Tau Beta Pi. Author numerous tech. articles in tech. and live stock jours. Home: Cobbler Mt. Farms, Delaplane, Va. Office: Woodward & Lothrop, Washington 13 Died Nov. 24, 1960.

UDDEN, JOHAN AUGUST, geologist; b. Lekasa, Sweden, Mar. 19, 1859; s. Andrew Larson and Inga Lena (Andersdotter) U.; immigrated to Carver, Minn., 1861; A.B., Augustana Coll., Rock Island, Ill., 1881, hon. Ph.D., 1900, LL.D., 1929; Sc.D., Bethany Coll., Lindsborg, Kan., 1921, Tex. Christian U., 1923; m. Johanna Kristina Davis, 1882; children—Antonia Thilda, Jon Andreas, Anton David, Svante Mauritz. Taught at Bethany Coll., Lindsborg, Kan., 1881-88; studied U. of Minn. part of 1886; Oscar II prof. geology and natural history, Augustana Coll., 1888-1911; geologist, Bureau of Econ. Geol. and Technology, 1911-15, dir. 1915—, U. of Tex. Spl. asst. Ia. Geol. Survey, 1899-1903; asst. geologist, U. of Tex. Mineral Survey, 1903-04; geologist, Ill. Geol. Survey, 1906-11; spl. agt. U.S. Geol. Survey, 1908-14. Knighted by King of Sweden, 1911 (Riddare af nordstjerneorden). Fellow Geol. Soc. America, A.A.A.S., Am. Inst. Mining and Metall. Engrs.; member American Association of Petroleum Geologists; del. 12th Internat. Geol. Congress, Toronto, 1913. Author: The Mechanical Composition of Wind Deposits; An Old Indian Village, 1900; The Mechanical Composition of Clastic Sediments; The Texas Meteor of October 1, 1917; Aids to the Identification of Geological Formations; and many other papers on geol. subjects. First to discover potash in the Permian of Tex. and first suggested the likelihood of finding petroleum on the State Univ. lands in W. Tex. Home: Austin, Tex. Died Jan. 5, 1932.

UEHLING, EDWARD A., (u'ling), mech. engr.; b. Richwood, Dodge County, Wis., June 3, 1849; s. Frederick and Anna Margareth (Krug) U.; Northwestern U., Watertown, Wis., winters, 1871, 1872; M.E., Stevens Inst. Tech., 1877 (hon. D.Eng.); m. Jeannette Mertz, Dec. 25, 1881; children—Fritz Frederic, Gretchen (dec.), Edward. Began as asst. to Dr. Thurston, Stevens Inst. Tech., 1877-78; on ry. survey and draftsman, Douglas Furnace Co., Sharpsville, Pa., to 1880; operated commercial lab., Sharpsville, 1880-83; chief chemist Bethlehem Iron Co., Pa., 1883-85; supt. Sharpsville Furnace Co., 1885-87; supt. blast furnaces, Bethlehem Iron Co., 1887-90, Sloss Iron & Steel Co., 1890-95; started Uehling Instrument Co., mfrs. recording instruments, pres., 1896-1919. Inventor pneumatic pyrometer (the pioneer autographic recording pyrometer), Uehling pig iron casting machine (now in use in all large iron-making plants), a recorder which continuously records per cent of carbon dioxide in flue gas, and about 25 other inventions. Introduced pig casting machine in prin. European countries. Recipient Stevens Inst. Notable Achievement Medallion, 1951. Fellow Am. Soc. M.E.; mem. Am. Inst. Mining and Metall. Engrs., Engineers' Soc. of Milwaukee, Delta Tau Delta, Tau Beta Pi. Contributor many papers to tech. publs. and socs. Author: Heat Loss Analysis. Home: 2360 S. 81st St., West Allis, Wis. Died Dec. 21, 1952.

UHLER, HORACE SCUDDER, (yool'er), physicist; b. Balt., Aug. 5, 1872; s. Philip Reese and Sophia (Werdebaugh) U.; B.A., Johns Hopkins, 1894, Ph.D., 1905; M.A., Yale, 1937; m. Beatrice Drummond Ward, Nov. 24, 1897 (died Nov. 10, 1920); m. 2d, Minnie Ida Fleischer, July 12, 1922. Instr. Acad. of Northwestern U., 1896-97; dir. Lab. of U. Sch., Balt., 1897-1902; Carnegie asst. in physical chemistry, Johns Hopkins, 1905; instr. physics, 1906-09, asst. prof., 1909-22, asso. prof., 1922-25, Yale; dir. dept. physics, Gettysburg Coll., 1925; asso. prof. physics, Yale, 1926-37, prof., 1937-41, spl. lectr. physics, 1941-43, prof. emeritus, 1941—. 1st lt. R.O.T.C.; tchr. firing data, S.A.T.C., at Yale, 1 yr. Fellow A.A.A.S., Am. Phys. Soc.; mem. Am. Math. Soc., Am. Math. Assn., Optical Soc. Am., Phi Beta Kappa, Sigma Xi; life mem. Société Française de Physique. Disproved Thiele's Theory of band spectra and established a fundamental formula in prism theory. Formerly asso. editor Am. Jour. Sci., Phys. Review, Am. Math. Monthly, Jour. Optical Soc. Am. Author: Atlas of Absorption Spectra, 1907. Contbr. variosus papers on geometrical optics, spectroscopy, X-rays and pure mathematics. Translator of Haas' Die Welt der Atome, 1927, also of his contributions to vol. 2 of Special Commentary on the Work of J. W. Gibbs, Table of 1/n! to 475 Decimals, 137-place Logarithmic Tables, and Exact Values of the First 300 Factorials. Home: 12 Hawthorne Av., Hamden 14, Conn. Died Dec. 6, 1956.

UHLER, PHILIP REESE, scientist; b. Baltimore, June 3, 1835; s. George Washington and Anne Maria (Reese) U.; ed. at D. Jones' Latin School and under pvt. tutors; LL.D., New York U., 1900; m. Sophia Werdebaugh, 1869 (died 1883); m. 2d, Pearl Daniels, Apr. 29, 1886. Spent nearly 3 yrs. at Harvard as librarian and asst. to Prof. Louis Agassiz, in his mus. of comparative zoölogy; explored parts of Island of Hayti for him; became connected with Peabody Library, Baltimore, 1862, later librarian, devising new methods adopted in its catalogue. Pres. Md. Acad. Sciences; asso. in natural sciences, Johns Hopkins U.; fellow A.A.A.S. Author of numerous papers on geology, entomology, archaeology and libraries. Home: Baltimore, Md. Died Oct. 21, 1913.

UHLMANN, ERICH MYRON, physician; b. Bad Driburg, Germany, Apr. 21, 1901; s. Gerson and Rose (Franck) U.; ed. univs. and med. schs., Bonn, Leipzig, Kiel and Hamburg; M.D., U. Heidelberg; m. Ilse E. Abraham, Sept. 14, 1925; children—Gary J., Frank W., Ralph P. Came to U.S., 1938, naturalizd. 1943. Intern univ. hosps., Frankfurt, Germany, 1923-24, resident, 1924-25, chief radiation therapy, 1925-30; director of radiation therapy University of Freiburg, 1933, assistant professor, 1930-36; also research associate Institute Tuberculosis and High Climate, Davos, Switzerland, 1933, also Finsen Inst. and Radium Sta., Copenhagen, Denmark, 1933-34; med. dir. Inst. Radiology and Biophysics, Istanbul, Turkey, 1934-37; research asst. Inst. Phys. Foundations of Medicine, U. Frankfurt, 1928-30, Curie Inst., Paris, France, 1934, Radiumhemmet, Stockholm, Sweden, 1934; director tumor clinic Michael Reese Hospital and Medical Center, Chicago, Illinois, 1938—; consultant of VA Hospital, Hines, 1962; professor University Freiburg, 1945; Commonwealth prof. U. Louisville, 1948; asst. prof. Northwestern U. Med. Sch., 1954. Mem. A.M.A., A.A.A.S., Am. Cancer Soc. (dir.), Radiol. Soc. N.A., Am. Roentgen Ray Soc., Am. Coll. Radiology, Colegio Interamericano de Radiologia, Ill., Chgo. med. socs., Chgo. Roentgen Soc. Author: Indicationen und Methodik Der Strahlenbhdlg, 1930. Co-editor: Encyclopedia of Medical Radiology, 1963; member editorial board Der Radiologe, 1961. Home: 910 N. Lake Shore Dr., Chgo. 11. Office: 2839 S. Ellis Av., Chgo. 16. Died Sept. 14, 1964.

ULREY, ALBERT BRENNUS, biologist; b. N. Manchester, Ind., Dec. 31, 1860; s. Samuel S. and Phebe (Miller) U.; grad. Ind. State Normal Sch., 1885; studied Woods Hole, Mass., summer, 1892; A.B., Ind. U., 1892, A.M., 1894; student Rush Medical Coll., Chgo., 1900-1. Instr. zoölogy, Ind. U., 1892-4; prof. biology, Manchester Coll., 1895-9, U. Southern Cal., since 1901; prof. biology, Summer Sch. of Biology, Warsaw, Ind., 1895; instr. histogenesis, biol. sta. Ind. U., summers, 1896-97. Mem. A.A.A.S., Southern Cal. Acad. of Sciences (chmn. Biol. Sect). Author of several zoöl. publs. Address: 1435 W. 23d St., Los Angeles, Cal. Died Dec. 21, 1932.

ULRICH, EDWARD OSCAR (ul'rik), paleontologist; b. Cincinnati, O., Feb. 1, 185?; s. Charles and Julia (Schnell) U.; studied German Wallace Coll., Berea, O.; hon. A.M., 1886, D.Sc., 1892; studied Ohio Med. Coll.; m. Albertine Zuest, June 29, 1886; m. 2d, Lydia Sennhauser, June 20, 1933. Curator geology, Cincinnati Soc. Natural History, 1877-81; paleontologist to geol. surveys of Ill., Minn. and Ohio, 1885-96; geologist U.S. Geol. Survey since 1897. Asso. in paleontology, U.S. Nat. Museum, 1914-32, retired; asso. editor Am. Geologist for 10 years. Author: American Paleozoic Bryozoa, 1884 (Cincinnati Soc. Natural History); American Paleozoic Sponges and Paleozoic Bryozoa (Vol. VIII, Ill. Geol. Survey), 1890; monographs in Vol. III, Geol. Survey of Minn., on the Lower Silurian Bryozoa, Lamellibranchiata, Ostracoda and Gastropoda of Minn. (2 parts), 1893-97; Geology of the Lead, Zinc and Fluor Spar District of Western Ky., 1904; Revision of Paleozoic Systems, 1911; The Ordovician-Silurian Boundary, 1914; Formations of the Chester Series, 1917; Correlation by Displacements of the Strandline, 1916; Major Causes of Land and Sea Oscillations, 1922; Silurian Formations of the Appalachian Region, 1923; Monograph of Silurian Ostracoda and New Classification of Paleozoic Ostracoda, 1923; Formations and Breaks between Paleozoic Systems in Wisconsin, 1924; Classification of the Conodonta, 1925; Relative Values of Criteria Used in Defining Paleozoic System, 1927; Mongraph of the Telephidae, 1929; Monograph Dikellocephalidae, Parts 1 and 2, 1932. Contbns. to textbooks and journals on paleontol. and stratigraphic themes. Mem. Nat. Acad. Sciences, Washington Acad. Sciences; fellow Geol. Soc. America, Paleontol. Soc.; foreign mem. Geol. Society London; corr. member Geol. Society of Sweden, Senkenberg, Naturforsch. Gesells.; corr. Phila. Acad. Science, 1932. Awarded Mary Clark Thompson medal, 1930. Penrose medal, 1932. Home: 611 Butternut St., Takoma Park, D.C. Office: U.S. National Museum, Washington, D.C. Died Feb. 22, 1944.

UMBERGER, HARRY JOHN CHARLES, (um'ber-ger), agriculturist; b. Hymer, Kan., Sept. 27, 1881; s. Martin David and Sarah Stephania Ernestine (Hartert) U.; B.S., Kan. State Coll., 1905; m. Rachel M. Kolck, June 12, 1909; children—Grace Kolck (Mrs. Ralph Marshall), John David, Pauline Ernestine (Mrs. John C. Pierce, Jr.); m. 2d, Marguerite V. Harper, Aug. 11, 1934. Scientific assistant Bureau of Soils, United States Dept. of Agriculture, 1906, Bureau of Plant Industry, U.S. Dept. of Agr., 1907-11; established and supt. Expt. Sta., Moro, Ore., 1909-11; asst. in charge cooperative experiments, Kan. State Coll., 1911-12; farmer, Chase County, Kan., 1912-15; demonstration supervisor and asst. county agt. leader, Div. of Extension, Kan. State Coll., 1915-17, county agt. leader, 1917-19, acting dean, 1919, dean since July 1, 1919. Dir. Kan. Crop Improvement Assn., 1909-20; sec. Kan. State Farm Bur., 1919-20; chmn. radio com. Land Grant Coll. Assn., 1929-40 and 1943; v.p. Nat. Com. on Edn. by Radio since 1929; mem. Kan. Agrl. advisory Council, 1933; chmn. Regional Advisory Com. on Land Use Practices in Southern Great Plains Area, 1935-44; mem. Southern Great Plains Regional Agrl. Council, 1940-42; mem. Upper Ark. River Drainage Basin com. Nat. Resources Planing Bd., 1941, Lower Mo. Drainage Basin Com., 1942; mem. State adv. com. United Service Orgns., 1942; vice-pres. American Country Life Assn., 1937; chmn. extension sub-sect., Land Grant Coll. Assn., 1924; mem. com. on extension organization and policy, Land Grant College Assn., 1938-41; chairman, Northern Great Plains Council, 1946. Mem. Manhattan Chamber of Commerce. Mem. Kan. Hist. Soc., Farm House Fraternity, Phi Kappa Phi, Alpha Zeta, Gamma Sigma Delta, Epsilon Sigma Phi (com. on academic standing, 1939; vice-grand dir. nat. frat., 1944-45; grand dir., 1946-47). Democrat. Mason. Club: Rotary (Manhattan). Contbr. articles on "Farming and You" in Kansas newspapers. Awarded certificate for Distinguished Service Ruby, also Ruby for distinguished work in extension at National Epsilon Sigma Phi meeting, 1942. Home: 1412 Leavenworth St., Manhattan, Kan. Died Oct. 1, 1951.

UMPLEBY, JOSEPH B(ERTRAM), consulting geologist; b. Graysville, O., Nov. 20, 1883; s. George Stuart and Izina (Cole) U., student Ohio Wesleyan U., 1903-05; A.B., U. of Wash., 1908; M.S., U. of Chicago, 1909, Ph.D., magna cum laude, 1910; m. Bertha Irene Gray, Dec. 30, 1907; children—Virginia Cole (Mrs. Paul D. Lutey); Joseph (dec.), Berta Bartlett (Mrs. James B. Cresap), Stuart Standish. Mem. U.S. Geol. Survey, 1908-19, asst. chief metalliferous sect., 1914-18, in charge sect. foreign mineral deposits, 1918-19; in charge mimeral investigations Am. Com. to Negotiate Peace, Paris, 1918-19; geologist Wash. Geol. Survey, 1909-11; acting asso. prof. geology, U. of Calif., 1915-16; prof. geology and dir. Sch. of Engring. Geology, U. of Okla., 1919-24; pres. Petroleum Reclamation Co. and Goldelline Oil Corp., 1924-28; independent oil operator since 1928; asst. deputy Coordinator of Solid Fuels, in charge of Pacific Coast Area, 1942-43. Fellow A.A.A.S.; mem. Am. Inst. Mining and Metall. Engrs. (chmn. petroleum div. 1929; dir. 1931-35, chmn. North Pacific Section 1941-42, chmn. Reorganization Com. Petroleum Div., 1945-46, service award 1949), Geol. Soc. Am., Soc. Econ. Geology, Am. Assn. Petroleum Geologists, Wash. Geol. Soc., Okla. and Wash. acads. science, Delta Upsilon, Sigma Xi, Sigma Gamma Epsilon. Republican. Presbyn. Mason (Shriner). Author numerous publs. on gen. geology, mining geology, engring., and petroleum subjects. Home: 6214 Park Lane, Dallas 25. Died July 1967.

UNDERHILL, CHARLES REGINALD, electrical engr.; b. Chappaqua, N.Y., Nov. 2, 1874; s. Joshua Bowron and Elizabeth (Green) U.; desc. of Capt. John U.; on account of deafness did not attend college; largely self-ed., specializing through corr. and textbooks, in mathematics, physics, and engring.; m. Ella Howell Johnson, Apr. 6, 1898; children—Charles Reginald, Marguerite Allaire. Employed in inspection dept. Western Electric Co., N.Y. City, 1892-1900; chief elec. engr. Varley Duplex Magnet Co., Jersey City, N.J., and Providence, R.I., 1900-04; consulting elec. engr., N.Y. City, 1904-09; editor and tech. writer, Westinghouse Electric & Mfg. Co., Pittsburgh, 1909-10; chief engr., Am. Electric Fuse Co., Muskegon, Mich., 1910-11; chief elec. engr., Acme Wire Co., New Haven, Conn., 1911-21; cons. elec. engr., 1921-26; with Wappler Elec. Co., Inc., L.I. City, 1926-29, developing surg. and other high frequency machines. Has made extensive researches in the actions of electromagnets, the results of which have been published largely in Electrical World and Trans. Am. Inst. Elec. Engrs. Lectured on "Electromagnets," in leading colleges and univs. of U.S. Inventor of wireless telegraph printing system and other telegraphic and signaling devices. Commd. capt., Aviation Sect., Signal R. C., 1917; officer in charge radio tests in flight, Langley Field, on flying status; transferred to Air Service, 1918; served as radio officer, Sch. for Aerial Observers, Langley Field, also as radio stats. officer, Air Service Mil. Aeronautics. Fellow A.I.E.E., A.A.A.S.; mem. Mil. Order World War, Am. Legion, National Society Puritan Descendants, Pi Gamma Mu. Democrat. Author: The Electromagnet, 1903; Wireless Telegraphy and Telephony (with W. W. Massie), 1908; Solenoids, Electromagnets and Electromagnetic Windings, 1910; Magnets, 1924; Coils and Magnet Wire, 1925; Power Factor Wastes, 1926; Electrons at Work, 1933. Contbr. to Standard Handbook for Electrical Engineers since 1913. Discovered connections between elec. resistivity and heat content of metals. Address: Lower Bank, N.J. Died Oct. 3, 1950.

UNDERHILL, JAMES, mining engr.; b. N.Y.C., Apr. 9, 1871; s. James and Louise Fuller (Johnson) U grad. Phillips Exeter Acad., 1890; B.A., Harvard, 1894; M.A., U. Colo., 1905, Ph.D., 1906; m. Lucy Caroline Stoller, Dec. 18, 1899. Cons. practice Idaho Springs, Colo., 1896—; asso. prof. mining. Colo. Sch. Mines, 1919-46; ret. Geologist, Colo. Geol. Survey, 1907-08; mem. State Bd. Examiners Engrs., 1924—. County food adminstr. Clear Creek Co., Colo., World War I. Capt., Engrs. O.R.C., 1923—. Mem. Am. Inst. Mining and Metall. Engrs., Theta Tau, Tau Beta Pi, Kappa Sigma, Scabbard & Blade. Mason (Shriner). Author: Mineral Land Surveying, 1906. Home: Idaho Springs, Colo. Died Apr. 22, 1954.

UNDERWOOD, JOHN COX, engr.; b. Georgetown, D.C., Sept. 12, 1840; s. Judge Joseph Rogers (of Ky.) and Elizabeth Threlkeld (Cox) U.; C.E., Rensselaer Poly. Inst., Troy, N.Y., 1862; hon. A.M., Center Coll., Ky., 1876; m. Drue A. Duncan, May 16, 1867. Officer in C.S.A., Civil War, reaching rank of lt. col.; prisoner in Fort Warren nearly a year; mayor of Bowling Green, Ky., 1870-72; city, county and cons. state engr., 1866-75; lt. gov. of Ky., 1875-79. Conservative Democrat. Grand Sire and Generalissimo, I.O.O.F. of World, 1888-90; lt. gen. Patriarchs Militant, 1885-93; maj. gen. United Confederate Vets., and erected monument over Confederate dead at Chicago, 1891-95. Chronol. and geneal. historian. Address: Covington, Ky. Died Oct. 26, 1913.

UNDERWOOD, LUCIEN MARCUS, botanist; b. New Woodstock, N.Y., Oct. 26, 1853; s. John Lincklaen and Jane H. (Smith) U.; lived on farm in boyhood; grad. Syracuse U., 1877, Ph.D.; m. Marie Antoinette Spurr, Aug. 10, 1881. Taught in various colls. in Ill., 1879-83; Syracuse U., 1883-91; De Pauw U., Ind., 1891-95, Ala. Polytechnic Inst., 1895-96, prof. botany, Columbia, 1896—. Author: Descriptive Catalogue of North American Hepaticae, 1884; Moulds, Mildews and Mushrooms, 1899; Our Native Ferns and Their Allies, 1900; Our Native Ferns and How to Study Them, 1901. Address: New York, N.Y. Died 1907.

UNDERWOOD, WILLIAM LYMAN, naturalist, lecturer; b. Belmont, Mass., Mar. 4, 1864; s. William James and Esther Crafts (Mead) U.; pub. sch. edn.; m. Ida Cushing, Nov. 16, 1887 (died 1922); 1 son, William James; m. 2d, Elizabeth Farley Kelly, Sept. 8, 1923. Left sch., 1880, to enter father's business, William Underwood Co., mfrs. canned goods, established 1822, of which became dir. Began lecturing in Boston and vicinity, 1896; lecturer in biol. dept. Mass. Inst. Tech., 1900—; writer and lecturer on bacteriology as applied to canned and preserving industries, mosquitoes and their extermination, the Gypsy and Brown Tail Moth problems; also on wild life in field and forest. Fellow A.A.A.S., Am. Acad. Arts and Sciences, Unitarian. Author: Wild Brother; Wilderness Adventures. Home: Belmont, Mass. Died Jan. 28, 1929.

UPDEGRAFF, MILTON, astronomer; b. Decorah, Ia., Feb. 20, 1861; s. William B. and Lydia Maria (Shear) U.; B.S. and B.C.E., U. of Wis., 1884, M.S., 1886; m. Alice M. Lamb, Sept. 8, 1887; children—Helen, Mabel, Ruth. Aid, U.S. Coast and Geod. Survey, 1882-83; asst. astronomer in Washburn Obs., U. of Wis., 1884-87; astronomo segundo Observatorio Nacional, Cordoba, Argentine Republic, 1887-90; prof. astronomy, U. of Mo., 1890-99; prof. mathematics, U.S.N., June 1899—; astronomer U.S. Naval Obs., Washington, 1899-1902; instr. U.S. Naval Acad., 1902-07; dir. Nautical Almanac, Washington, 1907-10; also in charge 6-inch Transit Circle U.S. Naval Obs., 1908-10. In charge U.S. Naval Obs. eclipse party at Barnesville and Griffin, Ga., May 1900; in charge geod. and other scientific work, Survey of Am. Samoa, 1913-14; on court martial and other duty, Navy Yard, Mare Island, Calif., 1915-17; in charge of meteorol. observations at Whipple Barracks, Prescott, Ariz., 1918-20. Placed on retired list U.S.N. with rank of comdr., July 1920. Fellow A.A.A.S. Elector New York U. Hall of Fame, 1925, 30, 35. Home: Prescott, Ariz. Died Sept. 12, 1938.

UPHAM, CHARLES MELVILLE, civil engr.; b. Stoughton, Mass., Mar. 6, 1886; s. Melville M. and Ann Caroline (Curran) U.; B.S., Tufts Coll., 1908, M.S., 1925; C.E., U. of N.C., 1924; m. Ina E. Hutchinson, 1912; children—Charles Melville, John Exley. Engr. with Charles River (Mass.) Basin Commn., 1908-09; resident engr. Mass. State Highway Commn., 1909-12; testing engr., Coleman du Pont Rd., Del., 1912-15, chief engr., 1915-17; chief engr. Del. State Highway Commn., 1917-21; county engr. Sussex County, Del., 1917; chief engr. N.C. State Highway Commn., 1921-26; cons. engr. Republic of Mexico, 1925, 26, later cons. engr. one third of Central Highway in Cuba, highway department Republic of Honduras, 1956-58, Royal Thailand highway dept., 1957—, Kerman Development Corporation, of Iran, 1958—, engineer-director Am. Road Builders Assn., 1926-51; chairman D.C. Motor Vehicle Parking Agency; Charles M. Upham Assos., cons. engrs., Washington. Cons. engr. on Pa. Turnpike Commn.; cons. engr. Federal Highway Commn. of Mexico, and Compania Cubana de Contratistas, Havana; consulting engineer, highways of Egypt; consulting engineer Md. State Roads Commn., 1936-39; cons. engr. and v.p., Eno Foundation, Saugatuck, Conn. Received the Bartlett Award for Highway Work, 1946. Mem. joint secretariat Construction League of U.S., 1935; U.S. del. to Permanent Internat. Road Congress, The Hague, 1938. Mem. Advisory Planning Commn. for Dist. of Columbia. Decorated Aquila Azteca (Mexico), 1952. Fellow Inst. of Highway Engrs. (London): mem. Am. Soc. Civil Engrs. (life), Am. Society for Testing Materials, Highway Research Board, National Research Council, L'Association Internationale Permanente des Congres de la Route, La Asociacion de Ingenieros y Arquitectos de Mexico, Pan-Am. Soc., Nat. Acad. Science (dir. highway research bd. of Nat. Research Council 1923-26) Washington Board of Trade, Washington Society of Engineers, Geneva Society Mayflower Descendants, S.A.R., John Alden Society. Clubs: Shrine, Engineers, Cosmos, Tufts, 100,000 Mile. Assisted in organizing Ordnance Companies, AUS, 1942. Address: 615 2d Av. S., Mpls. Died Nov. 1966.

UPHAM, ROY, physician; b. Dartmouth, Mass., Mar. 16, 1879; s. Joseph Kellog and Sarah Condon (Davis) U.; M.D., N.Y. Med. Coll., 1901; grad. study N.Y. Post Grad. Hosp., 1912, N.Y. Polyclinic Med. Sch., 1913, Ryks Hosp., Copenhagen, 1912, Vienna (one month each), 1922, 23, 24, 26, 28, 30, St. Marks Hosp., London, 1933, 34, Kasr-el-Aini Hosp., Cairo, Egypt, 1934; m. Edna Norma Tingley, Aug. 16, 1916. Intern Hahnemann Hosp., N.Y. City, 1901-03; practice in N.Y. City since 1903, specializing in gastroenterology since 1910; asst. attending surgeon Cumberland Hosp., New York, 1908-14; attending gastroenterologist, Cumberland Hosp., 1904-26, Carson Peck Hosp., 1921-26, Prospect Heights Hosp., 1910-26; attending physician and head of gastroenterology sect. Met. Hosp.; cons. gastroenterologist Jamaica, New York Ophthalmic, Flower-Fifth Av. hosps.; chief of gastro-intestinal clinic, outpatient dept. Met. Hosp., Flower-Fifth Av. Hosp.; cons. gastroenterologist Evang. Luth. Hosp., Brooklyn; asso. N.Y. Med. Coll., 1903—, successively demonstrator histology, lectr. gastroenterology, assistant and associate professor, professor of clinical medicine, 1953—, chief of gastroenterology section since 1935; hon. mem. staff Utrecht Homeo. Hosp., Utrecht, Holland, 1946. Diplomate Am. Bd. Internal Medicine (sub-splty. gastroenterology), Internat. Bd. Surgery. Fellow Am. Acad. Proctology (hon.), A.C.S. Internat. Coll. Surgeons; mem. Am. College Gastroenterology (sec.-gen.), Am. Med. Assn., Acad. Pathol. Science, Nat. Gastroenterological Assn. (sec. gen.), Am. Med. Assn. of Vienna (life), N.Y. Academy. Medicine, N.Y. State Med. Soc., N.Y. Co. Med. Soc., N.Y. State, N.Y. Co. and Kings Co. Homeo. med. socs.; hon. mem. Monroe Co. and Albany Co. homeo. med. socs., Gen Homeo. Society Germany, Italian Gastroenterological Assn.; Internat. Homeo. League (hon. pres.); mem. (hon.) Argentine Homeo. Med. Soc., British Homeo. Assn. (hon. v.p.). Club: Lotos. Mason (32 deg., Shriner). Contbr. articles to med. jours. Address: 45 E. 74th St., N.Y.C. 21. Died 1956.

UPHAM, WARREN, geologist, archaeologist; b. Amherst, N.H., Mar. 8, 1850; s. Jacob and Sarah (Hayward) U.; A.B., Dartmouth, 1871, A.M., 1894, D.Sc., 1906; m. Addie M. Bixby, Oct. 22, 1885; 1 dau., Pearl (dec.). Asst. geol. survey of N.H., 1875-78; on geol. survey of Minn., 1879-85; on U.S. Geol. Survey, 1885-95; sec. and librarian of Minn. Hist. Soc., St. Paul, 1895-1914, and archaeologist, 1914—. Fellow A.A.A.S. Author: The Glacial Lake Agassiz, 1895; Greenland Icefields and Life in the North Atlantic, with a New Discussion of the Causes of the Ice Age (with Prof. G. F. Wright), 1896; Minnesota in Three Centuries, Vol. I, 1908; Catalogue of the Flora of Minnesota, 1884; Minnesota Geographic Names, 1920; Congregational Work of Minnesota, 1832-1920; Stages of the Ice Age, 1922; Chapters of Minnesota and Its People, 1924; also many geol. reports and papers in scientific and hist. mags., chiefly relating to glacial subjects and Minn. history. Editor: Minn. Hist. etc. Collections, vols. 8-17, 1898-1920, contributing papers on Groseilliers and Radisson, the First White Men in Minnesota, and the Progress of Discovery of the Mississippi River. Address: St. Paul, Minn. Died Jan. 29, 1934.

UPSON, FRED WILBERT, educator; b. Byron, Ill., Feb. 2, 1883; s. Richard Empey and Mary (Johnston) U.; B.S., U. of Neb., 1907, A.M., 1908; Ph.D., U. of Chicago, 1910; m. Georgia Field, June 16, 1915; 1 son, John Field. Instr. in chemistry, U. of Cincinnati, 1910-12; research instr. in chemistry, U. of Chicago, 1912-13; prof. agrl. chemistry, U. of Neb., 1913-18, prof. chemistry and chmn. dept. of chemistry, 1918-39, dean of Graduate School, 1929-39, dean and prof. emeritus since 1939. Fellow A.A.A.S.; mem. Am. Chem. Soc., Am. Assn. Univ. Profs., Sigma Xi. Republican. Protestant. Author of numerous articles in chemistry, chiefly in the fields of carbohydrate chemistry and of chem. mechanism. Home: 4642 Bancroft Av., Lincoln, Neb. Died Feb. 10, 1942.

UPSON, MAXWELL MAYHEW, engr.; b. Milwaukee, Wis., Apr. 22, 1876; s. Edwin M. and Kittie (Parsons) U.; A.B., U. of N. Dakota, 1896, Dr. Engring., 1931; M.E. Cornell U., 1899; m. Mary Shepard Barrett, Apr. 28, 1915; (died Dec. 14, 1963); 1 dau., Jeanette. With Westinghouse, Church, Kerr & Co., N.Y. City, advancing to mng. engr., 1899-1905; asst. to pres. and chief engr. Hockanum Mills Co., Conn., 1905-07; gen. mgr., chief engr., v.p. Raymond Internat., Inc., 1907-31, pres. 1931-46; chmn. bd., 1946-60, hon. chmn. bd., 1960-69. Mem. Com. Econ. Devel. Holds many patents on methods of bldg. and placing concrete piles and bldg. of retaining walls, seawalls and off-shore oil derrick founds. Vice pres. Boys Clubs Am.; trustee emeritus Cornell U., Awarded Edward Longstreth medal by Franklin Inst., 1940 also; pres.dl. councilor. recipient Nat. Golden Keystone award Boys Clubs Am., 1964. Member of the American Concrete Inst. (pres. 1926-28), Am. Soc. C.E., A.S. M.E., Am. Soc. for Testing Materials, Pan Am. Soc. Republican Presbyn. Clubs: University, Bankers, Cornell University of New York, Knickerbocker Country; Yeamans Hall (Charleston, S.C.). Co-author; American Individual Enterprise System. Home: Englewood NJ Died May 1, 1969.

UPSON, RALPH HAZLETT, aeronautical engr.; b. New York, N.Y., June 21, 1888; s. William F. and Grace (Hazlett) U.; M.E., Stevens Inst. Tech., 1910, hon. Aeronaut. Engr.; m. Frances Talbot Allen, May 19, 1915; children—Frank Allen, Julia Ann, Nancy, Brent Talbot. Research in aerodynamics and airship engring., 1908-12; won Internat. Balloon Race, 1913; won Am. nat. balloon race, 1913, 19, 21; chief engr. aeronautical dept. Goodyear Tire & Rubber Co., 1914-20, producing most of the Am. balloons and airships used during World War I. Flew first U.S. Navy coast patrol airship, Chicago to Akron, in demonstration flight, 1917; rep. U.S. Navy design mission in Europe, 1918-19. Chmn. lighter-than-air div. Aeronautical Safety Code Commn. of Bur. of Standards, 1922-24; chief engr. Aircraft Development Corp., 1922-27; designer ZMC-2, first successful metal-clad airship, 1929; engaged in airplane development with Aeromarine-Klemm Corporation, and other companies, 1928-42; chief aeronautical engineer with H. J. Heinz Co., 1942-44; applied aircraft design methods to other vehicles, including pioneer streamlined train of Union Pacific R.R., 1933; research specialist and lecturer, N.Y.U., 1944-46; prof. aero. engring. Univ. Minn., 1946-56, prof. emeritus, 1956-68; research specialist Aerospace div. Boeing Co., 1956-64. Fellow Am. Institute of Aeronautics and Astronautics, Royal Aeronautical Society (Gt. Britain); member of Soc. Automotive Engrs. Co-Author: Free and Captive Balloons. Contbr. papers on airplane and airship design. Holder of pilot certificates for balloon, airship and airplane. Recipient of award "for outstanding service rendered aeronautics," by Am. Soc. Mech. Engrs., 1929; awarded Wright Brothers medal, Soc. of Automotive Engrs., for contribution to wing design, 1930. Home: Seattle WA Died Aug. 13, 1968.

UPSON, WALTER LYMAN, prof. elec. engring.; b. Cleveland, O., July 3, 1877; s. Joseph Edwin and Cornelia Maria (Lyman) U.; B.S., Princeton, 1899, E.E., 1902, M.S., 1903; University Coll., London, Eng., 1906-07; M.E.E., Harvard, 1908; m. Anna Leigh Richardson, Aug. 20, 1906; children—Joseph Edwin II, David Richardson. Began teaching at Princeton U., 1904; asst. prof. elec. engring., Ohio State U., 1908-10; prof. elec. engring., U. of Vt., 1910-12; asst. prof. elec. engring., 1912-14, asso. prof., 1914-20, Union U.; prof. elec. engring., Washington U., 1920-42; consulting engineer, Torrington Manufacturing Company, Torrington, Conn. Vice pres. Litchfield Water Co.; v.p. Progress, Inc. Founder St. Louis Museum Science and Industry; v.p. Wolcott and Litchfield Lending Library. Fellow A.A.A.S.; mem. Am. Inst. E.E., Sigma Xi, Tau Beta Pi. Repub. Conglist. Clubs: Sanctum, Princeton (New York). Author: (with E. J. Berg) Electrical Engineering, 1916; Electrical Engineering Studies, 1931. Contbr. numerous scientific and ednl. papers. Inventor of air impellers. Home: Litchfield CT

UPTON, CLIFFORD BREWSTER, (up'tun), univ. prof.; b. Detroit, May 10, 1877; s. Albert B. and Esther A. (Johnstone) U.; grad. Mich. State Normal Coll., Ypsilanti, Mich., 1898; A.B., U. Mich., 1902; A.M., Columbia, 1907; student U. Göttingen, 1907, U. Paris, 1908-10; m. Siegried Maia Hansen, Sept. 14, 1905. Instr. Arthur Hill High Sch., Saginaw, Mich., 1898-1900; instr. mathematics, Mich. State Normal Coll., Ypsilanti, Mich., 1901; instr., head dept. mathematics, Horace Mann High Sch., Tchrs. Coll., Columbia, 1902-10; instr. mathematics, Tchrs. Coll., Columbia, 1907, asst. prof., 1910, asso. prof., 1917, prof., 1927-42, prof. emeritus, 1942—, sec. Tchrs. Coll., 1911-19, and provost, 1919-24. Mem. Internat. Commn. Teaching Mathematics, Am. Math. Soc., Math. Assn. Am., Nat. Council Tchrs. Mathematics, Assn. Symbolic Logic. Dir. Am. Book Co. Author: Modern Calculating Machinery, 1907; Standardized Tests in Mathematics for Secondary Schools, 1923; Studies in the Teaching of Arithmetic, 1927; The Strayer-Upton Arithmetics (with G. D. Strayer), 1928; The Strayer-Upton Junior High School Mathematics (with same), 1929; Modern Algebra, 1930; A Series of 8 Arithmetic Workbooks for Elementary Schools, 1932, 39; Number Primer, 1933; First Days with Numbers, 1946; Practical Arithmetics (with G. D. Strayer), 1934; Practical Junior Mathematics (with same), 1935; Practical Algebra, 1936; Social Utility Arithmetics, 1937, 1951; Adventures in Arithmetic, 8 volumes, 1938-40; Air Navigation Workbook (with Lt. A. D. Bradley, U.S.N.R.), 1943; Short Course in Arithmetic, 1953; Arithmetics, Grades 3 to 8 (with K. G. Fuller), 1945-47, 1957; Junior Mathematics, 2 books, 1951; Arithmetic Workshop, Books 1 to 8 (with M. Uhlinger) 1949-51. Contbr. yearbooks of Nat. Council Tchrs. Mathematics. Home: 501 W. 120th St., N.Y.C. Died Sept. 25, 1957.

UPTON, WINSLOW, astronomer; b. Salem, Mass., Oct. 12, 1853; s. James and Sarah Sophia (Ropes) U.; A.B., Brown, 1875; A.M., U. of Cincinnati, for grad. course in astronomy, 1877; Sc.D. Brown, 1906; m. Cornelia A., d. Wm. H. Babcock, Feb. 8, 1882. Asst. Harvard Obs., 1877-79; asst. engr. U.S. Lake Survey, 1879-80; computer U.S. Naval Obs., 1880-81; computer and asst. prof. U.S. Signal Service, 1881-83; prof. astronomy, 1883—, dean, 1900-01, Brown U. Mem. U.S. Eclipse expdns., 1878, 1883, and of 4 pvt. eclipse expdns., 1887, 1889, 1900, 1905; dir. Ladd Obs., 1891—; absent on leave from Brown, attached to Southern Sta. of Harvard Obs. at Arequipa, Peru, 1896-97. Author: Star Atlas (for schools) 1896; etc. Address: Providence, R.I. Died Jan. 8, 1914.

UREN, LESTER CHARLES, (u-ren), prof. petroleum engring.; b. Grass Valley, Calif., Sept. 1, 1888; s. Charles Edwin and Margaret Adelia (Jameson) U.; Calif. Sch. of Mech. Arts, San Francisco, 1905-07; B.S., U. of Calif., 1911; m. Ethel Eveleth, Dec. 28, 1912; 1 son, Donald Eveleth. Asst. in mining, U. Cal., 1912-15, successively instr. mining, assistant prof. petroleum engring., asso. prof., prof., 1925-54, emeritus, 1954—, acting dean College of Mining, 1940-41; director Army Air Force

Meteorology Training Program and coordinator Navy Training Programs; University of California, 1942-45; chairman, division mineral technology, 1946-49. Engineer United States Fuel Administration, World War I. Cons. petroleum engr., U.S. Bur. Mines, also various oil cos. Capt. C.W.S., AEF, 1918-19. Mem. Am. Inst. Mining, Metall. and Petroleum Engrs., Am. Assn. Petroleum Geologists, Am. Petroleum Inst., Sigma Xi, Tau Beta Pi, Theta Tau. Republican. Clubs: Faculty, Kiwanis. Author: A Textbook of Petroleum Production Engineering, 1924; A Decimal Index of Petroleum Technology, 1952; Oil-Field Development, 1956; Oil-Field Exploitation, 1953; Petroleum Production Economics, 1950. Contbr. technical papers and articles on petroleum technology. Died Aug. 21, 1960; buried Berkeley, Cal.

URQUHART, LEONARD CHURCH, (ûr'kit), structural engr.; b. Cleve., Oct. 24, 1886; s. William and Belle (Church) U.; student Western Reserve U., 1903-05; C.E., Cornell U., 1909; m. Jane Dalziel McKelway, June 10, 1915 (div. 1936); children—Edmond Ragland, Leonard Church, Junior (deceased); married second, Augusta Packard Graff, June 25, 1936; one daughter, Sylvia. Engr. Nickel Plate R.R., Cleve., 1909; with Cornell U., 1911-46 (on leave 1941-46), as instr., asst. prof., prof. structural engring. 1925—; prof. civil engring. Drexel Inst., Phila., 1925, prof. engring. U. Hawaii, 1940, with engring. branch constrn. div. O.Q.M.G., Washington, 1941; now consulting engr. Porter, Urquhart, McCreary & O'Brien (Newark, Los Angeles, Sacramento, San Francisco). Served as 2d lt., engineers, July 1918-Mar. 1919, World War I; col. Engrs. Corps, Chief, Engring. Div., Office Chief Engrs., Washington, D.C., World War II. Decorated Legion of Merit. Mem. Am. Soc. Civil Engrs., Am. Concrete Inst., Beta Theta Pi, Phi Kappa Phi. Republican. Baptist. Author: Design of Concrete Structures, 1923, 6th edit., 1958; Stresses in Simple Structures, 1926, 2d edit., 1932; Design of Steel Structures, 1930. Editor in chief of Civil Engineering Handbook, 1934, 4th edit. 1959; Elementary Structural Engineering, 1941. Home: 94 Knollwood Rd., Short Hills, N.J. Office: 415 Frelinghuysen Av., Newark. Died Mar. 1960.

USINGER, ROBERT L(ESLIE), educator, entomologist; b. Ft. Bragg, Cal., Oct. 24, 1912 s. Henry Clay and Edith (Johnson) U.; B.S., U. Cal. at Berkeley, 1935, Ph.D., 1939; m. Martha Boone Putnam, June 24, 1938; children—Roberta Christine (Mrs. Ronald Manuto), Richard Putnam. With Bishop Museum, Honolulu, 1935-36, Cal. Acad. Scis., 1936-39; faculty U. Cal. at Berkeley, 1939-68, entomologist in expt. sta., 1953-68, prof. entomology, 1953-68, chmn. div. entomology and acarology, 1963-68. NIH spl. research fellow Brit. Mus. National History, 1948-49; chmn. Pacific sci. bd. NRC-Nat. Acad. Sci., 1961-63, participant bd.'s Coral Atoll study, Marshall Islands, 1950, Laysan expdn. 1961; chmn. biology div. Pacific Sci. Congress, Honolulu, 1961; mem. comite permanent Internat. Congresses Entomology and Internat. Union Biol. Scis., 1953-68; dir. Galapagos Internat. Sci. project, 1964; participant Congo expdn. Institut pour la Recherche Scientifique en Afrique centrale, 1959. Served to maj. sanitarian, USPHS, 1943-46. Decorated Gold medal King Frederick of Denmark, 1956; medal and award of merit Govt. of Ecuador, 1964; named hon. citizen Guayaquil, Ecuador, 1964. Fellow Royal Entomol. Soc. London, Linnean Soc. London; mem. Entomol. Soc. Am. (pres. 1966), Pacific Coast Entomol. Soc. (pres. 1952), Soc. Systematic Zoology (pres. 1967). Author: Elements of Zoology, 2d edit., 1961; General Zoology, 4th edit. 1965; Methods and Principles of Systematic Zoology, 1953; Classification of Aradidae, 1959; Aquatic Insects of California, 1956; Sierra Nevada Natural History, 1964; Life in Rivers and Streams, 1967; Autobiography of an Entomologist, 1972. Editor Pan-Pacific Entomologist, 1939-49. Home: Berkeley CA Died Oct. 1, 1968; buried Mountain View Cemetery, Oakland CA

VAIL, ALFRED LEWIS, mfr.; b. Morristown, N.J., Sept. 25, 1807; s. Stephen and Bethiah (Young) V.; grad. U. City N.Y., 1836; m. Jane Elizabeth Cummings, July 23, 1839; m. 2d Amanda Eno, Dec. 17, 1855; 3 children. Bought an interest in Samuel F. B. Morse's telegraph, 1837, agreed to manufacture complete set of telegraphic instruments and to finance U.S. and fgn. patents; made 1st public exhbn. of telegraph, N.Y.C., 1838; demonstrated telegraph before Franklin Inst., Phila., also U.S. Congress, 1838; Phila. rep. Speedwell Iron Works of Morristown, 1839-43; became Morse's chief asst. after Congress provided funds for exptl. telegraph line between Washington, D.C. and Balt., 1843; received test message "What hath God wrought!" at Balt., 1844; supt. telegraph lines at Phila., 1844-48. Author: The American Electro Magnetic Telegraph, 1845. Died Morristown, Jan. 18, 1859.

VAIL, CHARLES DAVIS, civil engr.; b. Lone Tree, Ill., Sept. 11, 1868; s. Richard R. and Catherine (Brokaw) V.; B.S., U. of Ill., 1891, C.E., 1936; m. Jessie Poden, Sept. 7, 1893; children—Richard R. (dec.), Allan P., Kenyon C., Charles C. (dec.), Vera M. (Mrs. Willis Winslow). Civil engr. for U.P. R.R., O.S.L. R.R. and others, 1891-93; water works and irrigation engring. in Mont., Idaho, Nev. and Colo., 1895-1917; engr. Pub. Utility Corp. of Colo., 1917-23; mgr. improvements and parks, city of Denver, 1923-30; state highway engr. of Colo. since 1930. Mem. Am. Soc. C.E., Colo. Soc. of Engrs., Am. Assn. of State Highway Officials (v.p.). Democrat. Mason (32 deg., Shriner), Elk. Clubs: Denver Athletic, Rotary, Democratic (pres.). Home: 547 S. Corona St. Office: State Office Bldg., Denver, Colo. Died Jan. 1945. *

VAILLANT, GEORGE CLAPP (val'yant), archeologist; b. Boston, Mass., Apr. 5, 1901; s. George Wightman and Alice Vanlora (Clapp) V.; student Phillips Acad., Andover, Mass., 1916-18; A.B., Harvard, 1922, A.M., 1925, Ph.D., 1927; m. Mary Suzannah Beck, Mar. 10, 1930; children—Joanna Beck, George Eman, Henry Winchester. Mem. archaeol. expdn. to Me., 1919; field asst. archeol. expdns. in N.M. and Ariz., 1921, 22, 25, to Egypt, 1923-24, to Yucatan, 1926; in charge Valley of Mexico excavations of Am. Museum Natural History, N.Y. City, 1928-36; tutor in anthropology, Harvard, 1924-25; asst. curator Am. Museum Natural History, 1927-30, asso. curator of Mexican archeology, 1930-41, hon. curator 1941-44; dir. Univ. Museum. U. of Pa., since 1941; cultural attache, U.S. Foreign Service Auxiliary, Lima, Peru, 1943-44; appmt. asst. professor, Yale Univ., 1938-40; lecturer, New York Univ., 1938-39, Columbia Univ., 1930-40, 1941-42, Am.-Philosophical Soc., 1941-43; prof. anthropology, Univ. of Pa., since 1944, hon. prof. Museum of Mexico, since 1938. Served in U.S. Marine Corps, part of 1918. Mem. Am. Ethnol. Soc., Am. Anthrop. Assn., Soc. for Am. Archeology, Soc. de Americanistes de Paris, Soc. Antonio Alzate, Inst. for Andean Research. Mem. joint com. on Latin-Am. Studies, Pan-Am. Assn. (Phila.), Inter-Am. Soc. Anthropology and Geography. Mem. adv. com. on Art, State Dept.; trustee, Archaeological Inst. of Am.; co-trustee grad. studies, Div. Fine Arts, Univ. of Pa. Clubs: Harvard, Century Assn. (New York); Franklin Inn, Rittenhouse (Phila.). Author: (all anthropolgical papers of Am. Museum Nat. History), Excavations at Zacatenco (vol. 32, no. 1), 1930: Excavations at Ticoman (vol. 2, no. 2), 1931; (with S. B. Vaillant) Excavations at Gualupita Val. 35, no. 1), 1934; Excavations at El Arbolillo (vol. 35, no. 2), 1935; Early Cultures of the Valley of Mexico (vol. 35, no. 3); (with R. E. Merwin) Ruins of Holmul, Guatemala, 1932; Indian Arts in North America, 1939; Aztecs of Mexico, 1941. Contbr. articles and reviews. Home: Old Orchard Farm, New Centerville, Devon, Pa. Address: University Museum, University of Pa., Philadelphia, Pa. Died May 13, 1945.

VALUE, BEVERLY REID, civil engr.; b. Montgomery, Ala., Apr. 7, 1863; s. Jesse Reine and Edith (Bailey) V.; E.M., Sch. of Mines (Columbia), 1884; m. Rebecca Roe Morris, Oct. 1886. Exec. engr., New Croton Dam, N.Y., during constrn., 1886-91; div. engr. Rapid Transit Commn. during constrn. of subways, 1900-03; chief engr. Elec. Development Co. during constrn. large hydro-electric plant, Niagara River, 1903-06; constrn. engr. McCall's Ferry Power Co., during constrn. large hydro-electric plant, Susquehanna River, 1906-08; v.p., dir. Interlake Engring. Co., Kerbaugh-Empire Co., Empire Engring. Co., Geo. W. Rogers & Co.; v.p. Bellwood Engring Co. Episcopalian. Home: New York, N.Y. Died June 10, 1920.

VAN ALSTYNE HENRY ARTHUR, engineer; b. N. Chatham, Columbia Co., N.Y., Oct. 9, 1869; s. Charles G. and Rachel Landon (Huyck) V.; ed. Nassau (N.Y.) Acad., Marshall Sem., Easton, N.Y.; C.E., Union U., 1893; m. Bertha Stone Neher of Rochester, N.Y., Oct. 11, 1899. Engr. in charge constrn. pub. works, 1893-4; asst. engr. in state engr.'s dept., N.Y., 1894-7; supt. constrn. and engr. for Furnaceville Iron Co. in connection with improvement of state canals, Western div., 1897, and on completion of work, with Union Bridge Co. at Athens, Pa., until 1899, when re-entered state engr.'s dept., N.Y., as asst. engr. Eastern div.; later promoted 1st asst., then to resident engr., and in 1901 to div. engr. Eastern div.; state engr., N.Y., 1904-7; v.-p. Acme Engring. & Contracting Co.; pres. Sterling Iron & Ry. Co. Republican. Clubs: Unconditional Republican, Ft. Orange. Home: 149 Echo Av., New Rochelle NY Office: 475 5th Av., New York NY

VAN ANTWERP, EUGENE IGNATIUS, civil engr., mayor; b. Detroit, July 26, 1889; s. Eugene Charles and Cecilia Mary (Renaud) Van A.; ed. U. Detroit; m. Mary Frances McDevitt, June 21, 1911; children—Mary Dolores, Pauline Annetta (Mrs. Robert Denton), Frances Lauretta (Mrs. Julius Aloysius Jaeger), Eugene Ignatius, Francis Joseph, Anthony Gore, Joan Cecilia (Mrs. John Francis Shannon, Jr.), Agnes Carolyn, George Bernard, Rita Dacia, Daniel Janse. Instr., Gonzaga Coll., Spokane, Wash., from 1910 to 1911; constrn. dept. Mich. Central R.R., 1912-13; engring. dept., Grand Trunk Ry., 1913-17, land and tax dept., 1919-26; chief engr. Nat. Survey Service, Detroit, 1926-28; private practice since 1928. Registered profl. engr. and land surveyor, State of Mich. Served as 1st lt. 16th Engrs., U.S. Army, 1917-18; with A.E.F.; capt. staff of chief engrs., Washington, 1918; capt. Engrs., Mich. N.G., 1919-24; maj. 310th Engrs., Reserve, 1924-36. Mem. City Council of Detroit, 1932-47, 50-62; mayor of Detroit, 1948-49; past chmn. Bd. Suprs., Wayne County, Mich.; past chmn. ways and means com. Detroit City Council; trustee Mich. Municipal League; first chmn. Detroit Met. Airport Authority. Mem. V.F.W. (comdr.-in-chief 1938-39; trustee Nat. Security Fund), S.A.R., Holland Soc. of N.Y., Am. Legion, D.A.V., Mil. Order of World War, Engring. Soc. Detroit, Am. Soc. C.E., Mich. Engring. Soc., Mich. Soc. Registered Land Surveyors; hon. pres. Canadian Corps Assn.; hon. mem. French Vets. of Mich. Democrat. Roman Catholic. Elk, K. C. (4 deg.), Knight of St. John (4 deg.), Knight of Equity; Ky. Col.; mem. Ancient Order Hibernians. Home: 16845 Muirland Av. Office: 103 City Hall, Detroit. Died Aug. 5, 1962; buried Holy Sepulchre Cemetery, Detroit.

VAN BARNEVELD, CHARLES EDWIN, mining engr.; b. Doetinchem, Netherlands, Nov. 26, 1874; s. Arnout S. D. and Louisa (deLacy) Van B.; ed. Holland, France, Eng. and Can.; M.Sc. and E.M., McGill Univ., Montreal, 1895; m. Mary Caroline Howard, Dec. 7, 1897; children—Frances Louise, John Howard, Elizabeth Grace, Mary Alice. Assayer in N.M., 1895; supt. Enterprise Mine, Ariz., 1896; engr. and chemist, Globe, Ariz., 1896-97; cons. engr., Mexico, 1897-99; asso. prof. mining, 1899-1900, head of mining dept., 1901-13, U. of Minn.; chief Dept. Mines and Metallurgy, Panama, P.I. Expn., 1913-15; prof. mining, U. of Calif., 1915-16; supt. Southwestern Expt. Sta., U.S. Bur. of Mines, Tucson, Ariz., 1917-21; supt. Miss. Valley Expt. Sta., U.S. Bur. of Mines, St. Louis, 1922-24; consulting practice. Has served as cons. mining engr. and reported on many mining projects since 1900. Mem. Am. Inst. Mining and Metall. Engrs. Author: Iron Mining in Minnesota, 1912; Leaching Nonsulphide Copper Ores with Sulphur Dioxide, 1923; Mechanical Underground Loading in Metal Mines, 1924. Home: Chatsworth, Calif. Died Sep. 1942.

VAN BEUREN, FREDERICK THEODORE, JR. (van-bu'ren), surgeon; b. New York, N.Y., Feb. 10, 1876; s. Frederick T. and Elizabeth A. (Potter) Van B.; A.B., Yale, 1898; M.D., Coll. Phys. and Surg. (Columbia), 1902; m. Jessica T. Mohlman, May 26, 1906; children—Frederick T. III, Jessica, Michael M. II, John M. Asso. in anatomy, 1905-13, asso. in surgery, 1920, asst. professor, 1922, asso. prof. clin. surgery since 1929, asso. dean, 1921-34, Coll. of Physicians and Surgeons (Columbia); pres. Morristown (N.J.) Memorial Hosp. since 1933; asst. attending surgeon, Lincoln Hosp., 1910-13, Roosevelt Hosp., 1913-21; attending surgeon Lincoln Hosp., 1910-13, Roosevelt Hosp., 1913-21; attending surgeon Volunteer Hosp., 1915-17, Sloan Hosp. for Women, 1920-38, asso. visiting surgeon Presbyn. Hosp. Mem. Squadron A., Nat. Guard N.Y., 1899-1910, resigned as capt.; 1st lt. M.R.C., U.S. Army, 1910-18; capt. and maj. M.C., U.S. Army, 1918-19; with A.E.F., July 1918-Feb. 1919; hon. disch. Feb. 2, 1919; maj. M.R.C., U.S. Army, 1920-35. Fellow Am. Coll. Surgeons, Am. Surg. Assn., Am. Foundation of Surgery; mem. A.M.A., New York Surg. Soc., Acad. Medicine, Alpha Delta Phi, Wolf's Head. Republican. Presbyterian. Clubs: Century (New York); Morris Country Golf; Yeamans Hall. Home: Morristown, N.J. Office: 65 5th Av., New York, N.Y. Died Mar 13, 1943.

VAN BUREN, JOHN DASH, civil engr.; b. New York, Aug. 8, 1838; s. Col. John D. and Elvira L. (Aymar) V.; studied Lawrence Scientific School, Harvard; grad. Rensselaer Polytechnic Inst., 1860; m. 1875, Elizabeth Ludlow Jones, New York. Asst. engr. Croton aqueduct, New York, 1860-61; entered engr. corps U.S. navy; served in Gulf of Mexico and at Bureau of Steam Engring. under Commodore Isherwood; took part in James River campaign, 1862; on duty as asst. prof. natural philosophy and engring., 4 yrs., U.S. Naval Acad.; commissioned 1st asst. engr. (lt.), Jan. 1, 1865; resigned commn. 1868; in charge construction, dept. docks, New York, under Gen. McClellan; on Tilden commn. to investigate New York canals, 1875; State engr. and surveyor of New York, 1876-77; author numerous tech. papers; mem. N.Y. Bar, Am. Soc. Civil Engrs., Naval Architects and Marine Engrs.; mem. Loyal Legion, Holland Soc., St. Nicholas Soc., Soc. Naval Engrs. Address: New Brighton, New York.

VAN CLEAVE, HARLEY JONES, (van-klev'), zoölogy; b. at Knoxville, Ill., Oct. 5, 1886; s. Jasper McMurtry and Mary (Jones) Van C.; B.S., Knox Coll., Galesburg, Ill., 1909; M.S., U. of Ill., 1910, Ph.D., 1913; m. Bernice Ford, Aug. 1, 1914; children—Mrs. Dorothy Lincicome, Philip Ford. Began as instr. zoölogy, U. of Ill., 1913, asso. 1916-19, asst. prof., 1919-22, asso. prof., 1922-29, prof., 1929-48, research prof., 1948-52, emeritus, 1952—, acting head zoölogy, chmn. div. biol. scis., 1938-39; mem. staff Ill. State Normal U., summers, 1913-15, Puget Sound Marine Sta., summer, 1916; asst. U.S. Bur. Fisheries, summers, 1919, 21; field naturalist Roosevelt Wild Life Expt. Sta., Syracuse, N.Y., 1929-34. Mem. staff Cold Spring Harbor Biol. Lab., summer 1936; Isles of Shoals Zoöl. Lab., summer 1939. Received Knox Coll. first Alumni Achievement award, 1938. Fellow A.A.A.S. (council 1925-31, 1944), mem. Am. Micros. Soc. (ex-pres.), Am. Soc. Zoölogists, Am. Soc. Parisitologists (past v.p.; pres. 1947), American Fisheries Society, Am. Soc. Naturalists, Ecol. Soc. of America, Illinois State Academy of Science (pres. 1928), Limnol. Soc. of America, Wild Life Society, Helminthological Soc. of Washington, Am. Assn. University Profs. (pres. Ill. chapter 1932-33), Sigma Xi (pres. of Illinois chapter 1924), Phi Beta Kappa (president Illinois chapter, 1942-43), Kappa Delta Pi, Phi Sigma, Beta Beta Beta, Phi Kappa Phi, Gamma Alpha, Alpha Kappa Lambda. Conglist. Club: University. Author: Invertebrate Zoölogy, 1924; A Textbook in General Zoölogy (with Linville and Kelly), 1929; Laboratory Directions for an Elementary Course in General Zoölogy (8th edit.), 1930; Biological Principles in General Zoölogy (with Linville and Kelly), 1930. Editor Trans. Am. Micros. Soc., vols. 44-50, 1925-31. Mem. editorial bd. Ill. Biological Monographs. Biological Abstracts, Bios, American Mid. Nat. Contbr. numerous articles in mags. Home: 713 W. Indiana Av., Urbana, Ill. Died Jan. 2, 1953.

VANCOUVER, GEORGE, naval officer; b. Eng., 1758; never married. Entered Brit. Navy, 1771; accompanied Capt. James Cook on his 2d and 3d voyages, 1772-74, 76-80; assigned to exploring project in ship Discovery, Jan. 1790 (project abandoned because of Nootka Sound controversy); given command of ship Courageux; promoted comdr., Dec. 1790, placed in charge of ship Discovery and sent to N.W. coast of Am. to regain territory taken over by Spanish, also to survey coast North to latitude 30 deg. and to search for Northwest passage; set sail, Apr. 1791, went by way of Cape of Good Hope to Australia, then to New Zealand (which he explored), Tahiti and Hawaii; sighted West coast of Am., Apr. 18, 1792; carefully surveyed coast North to latitude 52 deg. 18'; discovered Gulf of Georgia, circumnavigated Vancouver Island (named for him); visited Hawaiian Islands again Feb.-Mar. 1793, then returned for further explorations of Am. coast; surveyed coast North to 56 deg. latitude and South to 35 deg.N, Apr. 1793; returned to Hawaiian Islands, accepted their submission to Gt. Britain (annexation never ratified); then surveyed Am. coast North of San Francisco, also So. part of Lower Cal. and Galapagos Islands; returned to Eng., Oct. 1795. Died Petersham, Surrey, Eng., May 10, 1798.

VAN DE GRAAFF, ROBERT JEMISON, physicist; born Tuscaloosa, Ala., Dec. 20. 1901; s. Adrian Sebastian and Minnie Cherokee (Hargrove) Van de G; B.S., U. of Ala., 1922, M.S., 1923, hon. D.Sc., 1941; student Sorbonne, 1924-25; B.Sc., Oxford, 1926; Ph.D., 1928; hon. degree Fla. State U., U. Utrecht; m. Catherine Boyden, April 12, 1936 (dec. Dec. 1972); children—John Hargrove, William Boyden. Rhodes scholar, 1925-28; Internat. Edn. Bd. fellow, Oxford, 1928-29; Nat. Research fellow, Princeton, 1929-31; Research associate, Mass. Inst. Tech., 1931-34; asso. prof., 1934-60; dir. OSRD radiographic project, 1941-46; dir. High Voltage Engring. Corporation 1946-67, mem. exec. com. 1957-67; chief scientist. Awarded Elliott Cresson medal, Duddell medal, Dudley medal; Naval Ordnance Devel. award, 1946. Fellow Am. Phys. Soc. (Bonnerprize 1966); mem. Am. Acad. Arts and Scis., Sigma XI, Tau Beta Pi, Delta Kappa Epsilon. Home: Lexington MA Died Jan. 16, 1967; buried Beverly MA

VAN DEMAN, HENRY ELIAS, pomologist; b. Ross Co., O., Nov. 3, 1845; s. Joseph and Elizabeth Sylvia (Case) V.; ed. pub. schs. and S. Salem Acad.; pvt. 1st Ohio vols., 1863-65; m. Anna McCormick, Dec. 28, 1876. Prof. botany and practical horticulture, Kan. State Agrl. Coll., 1878-79; chief and founder div. of pomology, U.S. Dept. Agr., 1886-93. Associate editor of Green's Fruit Grower, Rochester, New York, and Southern Fruit Grower, Chattanooga, Tenn. Pres. Am. Nut and Fruit Co. Author: Tropical and Semi-Tropical Fruits in America, 1887. Home: Washington, D.C. Died Apr. 28, 1915.

VAN DEN BROEK, JAN A., engr., educator; b. Middleharnis, Holland, Mar. 6, 1885; s. Christian Jan Hagen and Peternella (Van den Broek); B.S., U. Kan., 1911; Ph.D., U. Mich. (Carnegie scholar), 1918; m. Wendelina Pot, Dec. 1920; m. 2d, Helen Margaret Olbrych, June 12, 1929. Came to U.S., 1905, naturalized, 1924. Surveyor, Colo. Bell Telephone Co., 1910-11, also Caribou Willow River Ry., B.C.; detailer Boston Bridge Works, 1911-12; designer bridge dept. C.P. Ry., 1913-14; faculty mem. U. Mich. since 1914, prof. engring. mechanics since 1926. Awarded Norman medal, Am. Soc. C.E., 1941. Mem. Am. Soc. C.E., Engring. Inst. Can., Am. Soc. Engring. Edn. Author: Elastic Energy Theory, 1942; Theory of Limit Design, 1945; articles in Am. and fgn. profl. jours. Home: 785 Arlington Blvd., Ann Arbor. Died Apr. 20, 1959; buried Arborcrest, Ann Arbor.

VAN DEPOELE, CHARLES JOSEPH, scientist, inventor; b. Lichtervelde, Belgium, Apr. 27, 1846; s. Peter John and Maria (Algoed) Van D.; attended Imperial Lyceum, Lille, France; m. Ada Van Hoogstraten, Nov. 23, 1870, 7 children including Romaine Adeline. Came to U.S., settled in Detroit, 1869; became mfr. ch. furniture; exhibited arc lights, 1870; demonstrated feasibility of electric transp. by both overhead and underground conductors, 1874; worked on vibratory regulation for arc lights, demonstrated improved lights publicly, 1879; formed Van Depoele Electric Light Co., Inc. as Van Depoele Electric Light Co. of Chgo., 1881, Van Depoele Electric Mfg. Co., 1884; made 1st practical demonstration in world of a spring pressed under-running trolley at Chgo. Inter-State Indsl. Expn., 1883; successful with both the underground and overhead circuits in Toronto, Ont., Can., 1884, 85; overhead system in operation in South Bend, Ind., 1885, adopted in Minneapolis, Minn., Montgomery, Ala., 1885-86; eight lines installed in U.S., Can., 1886; sold electric railway patents to Thomson-Houston Electric Co., Lynn, Mass., 1888; sold Van Depoele Electric Mfg. Co., 1889; made 444 patent applications, granted 249 in his name including; little "Giant" generator, 1880, 1st patent on electric rys., 1883, 1st on overhead conductor, 1885, patent for carbon contract brushes in electric motors, 1888, coal mining machine, 1891; experimented with electric refrigeration, 1886; made photographs in color, 1889-90. Died Lynn, Mar. 18, 1892; buried St. Mary's Cemetery, Lynn.

VAN DER GRACHT, W. A. J. M. VAN WATERSCHOOT, geologist; b. Amsterdam, Holland, May 15, 1873; s. W. S. J. van Waterschoot and M. C. A. J. van der Does de Willebois V.; prep. edn., Katwyk Coll., Holland; student Stonyhurst Coll., Eng., 1892; LL.D., Amsterdam U., 1899; M.E., Sch. of Mines, Freiberg, 1904; hon. Sc.D., Colo. Sch. of Mines, 1924; m. Baroness J. F. R. G. M. Hammer-Purgstall, of Styria, Austria, May 22, 1901; children—Idesbald W. P. J. M., Arthur B. T. J. M. Walter J. J. M. (dec.), Marie-Gisele M. J. Began practice at The Hague, 1904; dir. Netherlands Geol. Survey, 1905-17; explored mineral resources of Holland for the Govt. and discovered extensive deposits of coal and rock salt; drafted safety regulations for coal mines in Holland, and acted as adviser and explorer in various countries for mining and petroleum corpns.; came to U.S., 1915; pres. Roxana Petroleum Co. (Royal Dutch-Shell), 1917-21; v.p. Md. Oil Co. Mem. Am. Assn. Petroleum Geologist, Am. Inst. Mining Engrs., Geol. Soc. Belgium, Geol. Soc. Holland (ex-pres.), Internat. Geol. Congress; fellow Geol. Soc. London. Decorated Knight Order of the Lion of the Netherlands; Comariere Segreto by Popes Leo XIII, Pius X and Pius XI. Catholic. Author: The Deeper Geology of the Netherlands and Adjacent Regions, 1910; also numerous Netherland Govt. repts. and papers in periodicals of Netherlands, Germany and America. Home: Ponca City OK

VANDERHOOF, DOUGLAS, physician; b. Bklyn., Dec. 31, 1879; s. Hervey Brundage and Emma Frances (Douglas) VanderH.; B.L., Dartmouth, 1901 (hon. A.M., 1907); M.D., Johns Hopkins, 1905; m. London, Julie Marriott Osterloh, Aug. 17, 1910 (dec. Feb. 1924); m. 2d, Mrs. Nancy Selden Habliston, June 22, 1926. Resident physician, Johns Hopkins Hosp., 1905-06; began practice at Richmond, 1906; adj. prof. medicine, Med. Coll. of Va., 1906-14, prof. 1914-29; mem. exec. com., Bd. of Visitors, Med. Coll. of Va., 1929, and chmn., 1936-53; former specialist in internal medicine; retired from practice, 1936. Dir. State-Planters Bank and Trust Co. Enlisted in Vol. Med. Service Corps, U.S. Army, 1918, and served as mem. sec. Med. Adv. Bd., Richmond. Trustee Richmond Community Fund, 1930-53 (pres. 1933, 34; dir. budget, 1935-48); dir. Community Chests and Councils, N.Y., 1936-38; mem. Richmond panel arbitrators, N.Y. Stock Exchange; mem. adv. bd. Va. Home for Incurables; dir. Va. Mus. Fine Arts. Dir., mem. exec. com. Richmond chpt. A.R.C. and Brit. War Relief Soc., 1940-45. Precinct chmn. Richmond Office of Civilian Defense; mem. Nat. Employment Com.; physician Henrico County bd. Selective Service System, 1941-46. Mem. Selec. Service Appeal Bd. State of Va., since 1948. Trustee St. John's Church Found., trustee Church Schools in Diocese of Va. Life mem. Va. Hist. Soc. Mem. Assn. Am. Physicians, A.M.A., Am. Therapeutic Soc. (pres. 1918-19), So. Med. Assn., Tri-State Med. Assn., Med. Soc. Va., Richmond Acad. Medicine, Holland Soc. of N.Y., Phi Beta Kappa, Theta Delta Chi, Casque and Gauntlet (Dartmouth), Pithotomy Club (Johns Hopkins), Sons of Revolution in State of Va. Democrat. Episcopalian (vestryman, sr. warden). Clubs: Commonwealth, Richmond German, Country (Va.). Contbr. numerous articles to med. jours. Home: 5501 Cary Street Rd., Richmond 26, Va. Died Oct. 31, 1957.

VANDERKLEED, CHARLES EDWIN, chemist; b. Lafayette, Ind., Apr. 24, 1878; s. Charles and Elizabeth (Van Aalst) V.; Ph.G., Purdue U., Lafayette, Ind., 1895, Ph.C., 1896, B.Sc., 1899, A.C., 1901, D.Sc., 1934; Pharm.D., Medico-Chirurg. Coll., Phila., 1908; Ph.M., Phila. Coll. of Pharm. and Science, 1929; m. Edith Parks, Sept. 18, 1901 (died 1937); children—Lois Lee (Mrs. H. L. Haws) (dec.), Eugene Parks (dec.); m. 2d, Carolyn G. Bailey, Jan. 20, 1939. Asst. chemistry, Purdue, 1896-1901; chem. expert, Ind. courts, 1899-1901; analyt. chemist, Sharp & Dohme, Baltimore, 1901-02; dir. chem. labs., H.K. Mulford Co., Phila., 1902-17; prof. pharm. chemistry, Medico-Chirurg. Coll., Phila. 1908-14, prof. analytical chemistry, 1914-16; lectr. chem. control, Phila. Coll. Pharmacy, 1916-28, trustee lectr. pharm. control, drug legislation, 1948-56; chemist Hercules Powder Co., 1918-19; sec. dir. Cellulose Silk Co. Am. 1920-22; supt. of Robert McNeil Lab., Phila., 1920-33; v.p. and scientific dir. McNeil Labs., Inc.; now retired. Cons. Nat. Security Resources Bd. Procter Medal award of Phila. Drug Exchange, 1948. Fellow American Institute Chemists; member revision com., U.S. Pharmacopoeia, 1910-20; mem. Am. Chem. Soc., Am. Pharm. Assn., A.A.A.S., Nat. Inst. Social Scis., Phi Zeta Delta, Beta Phi Sigma, Rho Chi, Kappa Psi. Clubs: Tavistock Country, Collingswood. Author: Course in Quantitative Chemical Analysis (with Julius W. Sturmer), 1898; Course in Qualitative Inorganic Chemistry (with Arthur L. Green), 1903; sect. on Strychnos Alkaloids in Allen's Commercial Organic Analysis, 1912. Extensive contbr. to chemical and pharm. jours. Home: 200 Harvard Av., Collingswood, N.J. Died Feb. 4, 1962.

VAN DEVENTER, JOHN HERBERT, (van'dê-ven-ter), engr., editor; b. Paramus, N.J., Apr. 24, 1881; s. Rev. John Cornelius and Eliza Jane (King) Van D.; M.E., Sibley Coll. (Cornell), 1903; m. Isabelle M. Stone, Feb. 23, 1905; children—John Herbert, Mrs. Helen Law, Mrs. Mary Sweeney, Henry Cornelius, George Mather, Mrs. Jane Godley, Mrs. June Rickard, Peter, Arthur. Supt. prodn., cost manager Goulds Mfg. Co., Seneca Falls, N.Y., 1905-07; gen. supt., factory mgr. Buffalo Forge Co., 1907-14; asso. editor Am. Machinist, 1915, editor in chief, 1917-20; editor Indsl. Management, The Engring. Mag., Industry Illustrated, 1921-26; pres. Engring. Mag. Co., N.Y.C., 1921-26; cons. editor McGraw-Hill Pub. Co., 1927-28; editor The Iron Age, 1930-46, pres., editorial dir., 1939-46; v.p. Chilton Co. until Nov. 1946; dir. information Com. for Econ. Development, 1947-49, trustee, 1945-54. Chmn. bus. papers industry, 1943-46; ret. 1950. Called to Washington, Sept. 1917, to assist in organizing Ordnance Dept.; maj., U.S. Army, 1917-18. Organized Army Ordnance Assn., 1919; chmn. N.Y. Bus. Pubs. Assn., 1923-24, pres., 1924-25. Guest of Brit. govt. on tour of United Kingdom war plants, 1944. Republican. Roman Catholic. Presented paper on Mass Prodn. at World Engring. Congress, Tokyo, Japan, 1929. Home: R.F.D., Brewster, N.Y. Died Mar. 5, 1956.

VAN DIEST, EDMOND CORNELIS, (van-dest'), cons. engr.; b. Buitenzorg, Java, Aug. 13, 1865; s. Pieter Hendrik and Josine (Gude) van D.; came to U.S., 1871, naturalized, 1888; E.M., Colo. State Sch. Mines, 1886; hon. Dr. Mining Engring., 1936; m. Anna Louise Meyer, May 4, 1890; children—Alice Elfrieda, Annette Josine (Mrs. Ralph E. Weldie), Eloise Margaret (Mrs. David M. Skilling, Jr.). Engr. charge Monument Valley Park and Glen Eyrie, Colo., 1903-19; mgr. Costilla Estates, 1886-1906; pres. Western Pub. Service Co., 1909-26, Gen. Service Corp., 1927—; pres. Rito Seco Gold Mines Co., Colo. Concrete Co., Hygienic Service Co. Mem. Bus. Adv. Planning Council for Dept. Commerce until July 1936; trustee Colo. Coll. Mem. Am. Inst. Mining and Metall. Engrs., Colo. Engrs. Soc., Alpha Kappa Psi. Republican. Episcopalian. Elk. Club: El Paso. Home: 1730 N. Cascade Av. Office: Mining Exchange Bldg., Colorado Springs, Colo. Died Aug. 1, 1950; buried Evergreen Cemetery, Colorado Springs.

VAN DYCK, CORNELIUS VAN ALEN, Arabic scholar, med. missionary; b. Kinderhook, N.Y., Aug. 13, 1818; s. Henry L. and Catherine (Van Alen) Van D.; grad. Jefferson Med. Coll., Phila., 1839; m. Julia Abbott, Dec. 23, 1842, at least 4 children including W. T. Van Dyck. Missionary, Am. Bd. Commrs. for Fgn. Missions, Syria, 1840, Beirut, 1841; studied Arabic; moved to 'Abeih in the Lebanon with Dr. William Thompson, June 1843, conducted high school for boys; prepared Arabic textbooks on geography, navigation, natural history, algebra, geometry, plane and spherical trigonometry; ordained by the mission, 1846; transferred to Sidon, headquarters for extensive medical practice and preaching tours, 1849-57; completed translation of Bible into Arabic (begun by Eli Smith, 1848), 1865; returned to U.S., 1865; tchr. Hebrew, Union Theol. Sem., 1865-67; returned to Beirut, 1867, editor journal al-Nashrah; prof. pathology in med. dept. Syrian Protestant Coll., prof. astronomy dept. arts and scis., dir. astron. and meteorol. observatory; had medical practice; wrote Arabic texts on pathology, chemistry, internal medicine, phys. diagnosis and astronomy; resigned professorship, 1883; practiced in Hosp. of St. George, Beirut, 1883-93; had important part in modern renaissance of Arabic literature. Died Beirut, Nov. 13, 1895.

VAN DYCK, FRANCIS CUYLER, physicist; b. Coxsackie, N.Y., June 3, 1844; s. Jacob Cuyler and Mary Frances (Bogardus) V.; freshman yr., Williams Coll., 1861; A.B., Rutgers, 1865, A.M., 1868; Ph.D., Union College, N.Y., 1888; (hon. Sc.D., Rutgers Coll., 1910, and LL.D., same 1915); m. Rebecca Jane Van Bergen, Dec. 27, 1871 (died 1879); m. 2d, Sarah Mercereau Van Nuis, Sept. 15, 1897. Tutor, 1866-70, prof. chemistry, 1870-78, physics, 1878-1917, dean, 1901-13, Rutgers Coll. Retired on Carnegie Foundation as prof. emeritus, June 1917. Home: New Brunswick, N.J. Died Apr. 12, 1927.

VAN DYKE, EDWIN COOPER, prof. entomology; b. Oakland, Calif., Apr. 7, 1869; s. Walter and Rowena (Cooper) Van D.; B.S., U. of Calif., 1893; M.D., Cooper Med. Coll. (now Stanford U.), 1895; m. Mary Ames, June 7, 1915. In practice of medicine, San Francisco, 1895-1913; instr. in entomology, U. of Calif., 1913-15, asst. prof. entomology, 1915-21, asso. prof., 1921-27, prof., 1927-39, prof. emeritus since 1939; hon. curator entomology Calif. Academy Science. Fellow A.A.A.S., Entomol. Soc. Am. Mem. Pacific Const. Entomol. Soc. (ex-pres.), Calif. Acad. Science (hon. curator). Beta Theta Pi, Phi Rho Sigma, Sigma Xi; corr. mem. Am. Entomol. Soc. Republican. Address: Calif. Acad. of Science, San Francisco CA

VAN DYKE, HARRY BENJAMIN, university prof.; b. Des Moines, Ia., Jan. 31, 1895; s. Benjamin and Louise V. (Boody) van D.; B.S., Univ. of Chicago, 1918, Ph.D., 1921; M.D., Rush Medical College, 1923; m. Elizabeth E. Allan, Apr. 14, 1920; children—Jane Elizabeth (Mrs. John H. Felber), Arthur Cushny (dec.). National Research Council fellow, Edinburgh, 1924-25, Brussels, 1925, Freiburg in Breisgau, 1925-26; associate professor of pharmacology, University of Chicago, 1926-30, prof., 1930-32; prof. Peiping Union Med. Coll., 1932-38; head div. pharmacology, The Squibb Inst. for Med. Research, 1938-44; David Hosack prof. pharmacology, Coll. Physicians and Surgeons, Columbia University, 1944-63, professor emeritus, 1963-71; vis. prof. pharmacology, Taiwan, 1963-64, U. Malaya, Kuala Lumpur, 1965-67. Recipient Sir Henry Dale medal Brit. Soc. Endocrinology, 1970. Fellow N.Y. Acad. Med.; mem. Am. Soc. Pharmacol. and Experimental Therapeutics (president 1962), A.A.A.S., A.M.A., Am. Physiol. Soc., Am. Soc. Pharmacology and Exptl. Therapeutics, Assn. Am. Physicians, Assn. Study Internal Secretions, Biochem. Soc. (Gt. Britain), Harvey Soc., Soc. Exptl. Biology and Medicine, Sigma Xi, Alpha Omega Alpha, Alpha Kappa Kappa. Editor, Journal Pharmacology and Experimental Therapeutics, 1950-53. Author of two books on the pituitary body; also contributor sci. articles to various publications. Home: Englewood NJ Died Feb. 14, 1971.

VAN DYKE, KARL SKILLMAN, physicist; b. Bklyn., Dec. 8, 1892; s. Frank H. and Charlotte May (Atwater) Van Dyke; B.S., Wesleyan U., Middletown, Conn., 1916, M.S., 1917; Ph.D., U. Chgo., 1921; m. Lua Stewart Docking, Oct. 26, 1917; children—Karl Skillman, Mary Louise (Mrs. Alan Moulton Thorndike), Florence Atwater (Mrs. John David Anderson), Muriel Mansfield (Mrs. Alden Watrous Wilcox). Grad. student and asst. in physics, Wesleyan U., 1916-17; engr., devel. and research dept., Am. Tel. & Tel. Co., 1917-19; grad. student and mem. teaching staff, dept. of physics U. Chgo., 1919-21; asst. prof. physics, Wesleyan U., 1921-25, asso. prof., 1925-28, prof. since 1928, on leave of absence, 1941-45, ret., 1960. Asst. dir., div. defense research, U. Cal., 1941-42, asso. dir., 1942; expert consultant, coordinator for quartz crystals, chief physicist, Office Chief Signal Officer, U.S. Army, 1942-44; dir. research Long Branch Signal Lab., Signal Corps Ground Signal Agency, 1944-45. Fellow A.A.A.S., Am. Phys. Soc., Inst. Radio Engrs.; mem. Acoustic Soc. Am., Am. Assn. Univ. Profs., Assn. Physics Teachers, Phi Beta Kappa, Sigma Xi, Phi Nu Theta. Author: Sound Recording Equipment for School (with Richard L. Brown), 1940, School Recording Techniques, 1941. Contbr. sci. and tech. articles to Physical Review and Proceedings of I.R.E. Home: 41 Lawn Av., Middletown 06457. Office: Scott Laboratory, Middletown, Conn. Died Oct. 5, 1966; buried Mt. Hebron Cemetery, Upper Montclair, N.J.

VAN DYKE, THEODORE STRONG, irrigation engr.; b. New Brunswick, N.J., July 19, 1842; grad. Princeton Coll., 1863 (A.M.). Practiced law 9 yrs.; health failed and he has since devoted attention to out-door pursuits. Mem. assembly of Mnin., 1872. Writer for press on irrigation, field sports and out-of-doors subjects. Author: The Still Hunter; Rifle, Rod and Gun in Claifornia; Southern California; Millionaires of a Day; Game Birds at Home:—all F2. Address: Daggett, Calif.

VAN ES, LEUNIS, animal pathologist; b. Melissant, Netherlands, Oct. 3, 1868; s. Jacob and Maatje (Zaayer) Van E.; grad. Govt. Sch. of Agr., Wageningen, Netherlands, 1886; Vet. Surgeon, Ont. (Can.) Vet. Coll., 1893; M.D., Med. Coll. Ala., 1898; Sc.D., U. Pa., 1935; m. Alice E. Wilson, July 11, 1894; children—Jacob, Maatje (wife of Dr. W. C. Zulauf), Marie (Mrs. Charles Rumbolz). Came to U.S., 1889, naturalized citizen, 1899. In practice of vet. surgery, 1893-1903; demonstrator in bacteriology and microscopic anatomy, Med. Coll. Ala., 1898-1903; prof. vet. science, N.D. Agrl. Coll., 1903-18; also chief state veterinarian, N.D., 1903-07, dir. N.D. Serum Inst., 1909-18, and acting dir. N.D. Agrl. Expt. Sta., 1918; prof. animal pathology and hygiene, U. Neb., since 1918. Mem. Am. Vet. Med. Assn., A.A.A.S., U.S. Live Stock Sanitary Assn. (pres. 1927), Nat. Assn. Study and Preventive of Tuberculosis, Am. Pub. Health Assn., Soc. Netherlands' Scholars in N. America, Conf. of Research Workers in Animal Diseases of N. America. Sigma Xi, Gamma Sigma Delta, Alpha Zeta, Phi Zeta. Author: Principles of Animal Hygiene and Preventive Veterinary Medicine, 1932. Contbr. many articles on animal diseases and rural hygiene to agrl. jours. expt. sta. publs., etc. Address: 3335 W Street, Lincoln, Neb. Died 1956.

VAN EVERA, BENJAMIN DOUGLASS, educator; b. Davenport, Ia., May 28, 1901; s. Charles and Henrietta (Kepler) Van E.; B.S., Coe Coll., 1923, Sc.D. (hon.), 1952; M.S., Ia. State Coll., 1925; Ph.D., State U. Ia., 1937; m. Margaret Lorimer, Sept. 12, 1925. With George Washington U., 1925-70, successively instr. chemistry, asst. prof., exec. officer chemistry dept., asst. prof., prof., 1938-70; adminstrv. dir. Allegany Ballistics Lab., 1942-46, coordinator sci. activities, 1946-57, dean for sponsored research, 1957-66. Survey for India Government of fertilizer plants with Nat. Research Council and Tech. Cooperation Adminstrn., 1952. Mem. Am. Chem. Soc., Chem. Soc. Washington (pres. 1949), Am. Assn. U. Profs., A.A.A.S., Am. Soc. Engring. Edn., Washington Acad. Scis. (pres. 1962-63), Am. Inst. Chemists (honor award 1956), Sigma Xi, Alpha Chi Sigma (profl. service award 1965), Phi Lambda Upsilon, Omicron Delta Kappa. Club: Cosmos (Washington). Asso. editor Jour. Chem. Edn., 1949-55. Home: Falls Church VA Died Apr. 9, 1970; buried Summit Cemetery, Davenport IA

VAN FLEET, WALTER, horticulturist; b. Piermont, N.Y., June 18, 1857; s. Solomon and Elvira (Du Bois) V.; common and pvt. schs.; M.D., Hahnemann Med. Coll., Phila., 1880; post-grad. work, Jefferson Med. Coll., Phila., 1887; m. Sarah C. Heilman, Aug. 7, 1883. Practiced medicine, central Pa., 1880-92; hort. editor Rural New Yorker, New York, 1890-1910, and v.p. Rural Pub. Co., 1902-10; expert plant breeder and physiologist, Bur. of Plant Industry, U.S. Dept. of Agr., 1910—; in charge U.S. Plant Introduction Garden, Chico, Calif., 1910-11. Has devoted large part of time to plant breeding, 1872—; widely recognized as leader in development of gladioli, garden roses and chestnuts. Author: Bird Portraits, 1888; The Gladiolus (with M. Crawford), 1911; (brochures) Vegetable Breeding, 1907, Breeding Hardy Roses, 1907, Hybridizing Gladiolus Species, 1909. Awarded George Robert White medal of honor for eminent services in horticulture, 1918, by Mass. Hort. Soc. Home: Glendale, Md. Died Jan. 22, 1922.

VAN HAZEL, WILLARD, surgeon; b. Grand Rapids, Mich., Aug. 30, 1896; s. Barend and Neltje (Kriekaard) Van H.; A.B., Hope Coll., Holland, Mich., 1920; M.D., Rush Med. Coll., U. of Chicago, 1924; m. Grace M. Mersen, Aug. 30, 1929; 1 son, Willard. Practiced surgery in Chicago since 1927; clin. prof. surgery, U. of Ill. Med. Sch.; surgeon, Research Educational Hosp., U. of Ill., since 1927; senior surgeon Presbyn. St. Luke's Hosp. Served as lt. Field Arty., U.S. Army World War I. Diplomate Am. Bd. Thoracic Surgery. Fellow Am. Coll. Surgeons; mem. Chicago Surg. Soc., Am. Thoracic Society, Chicago Institute of Medicine, American Association for Thoracic Surgery, Am. Coll. Chest Physicians, Am. Bd. Surgery (founders' group), Midwest Chest Club (founders' group). Clubs: University; Statler. Home: 1448 Lake Shore Dr., Chgo. 10. Office: 224 S. Michigan Av., Chgo. Died Aug. 24, 1961.

VAN HORN, FRANK ROBERTSON, geologist, mineralogist; b. Johnsonburg, N.J., Feb. 1872; s. George W. and Ellen J. (Robertson) V.; State Model Sch., Trenton, 1886-88; B.S., Rutgers, 1892, M.S., 1893, D.Sc., 1919; U. of Heidelberg, 1893-97, Ph.D., 1897; m. Myra Van Horn, June 8, 1898; children—Kent R., Hilda L. Instr. in mineralogy, Rutgers, 1892-93; instr. in geology and mineralogy, 1897-99, asst. prof., 1899-1902, prof., 1902—, Case Sch. Applied Science, Cleveland. Fellow Geol. Soc. America (librarian 1913-18), Mineral Soc. America (sec. 1923—), A.A.A.S. Progressive. Presbyn. Author: Lecture Notes on Systematic Zoölogy, 1902; Lecture Notes on General and Special Mineralogy, 1903; Geology and Mineral Resources of the Cleveland District, Ohio, 1931. Home: Cleveland Heights, O. Died Aug. 1, 1933.

VAN HORN, ROBERT BOWMAN, engring., educator; b. Nova, O., July 1, 1893; s. Francis J. (D.D.) and Amy Bell (Richards) Van H.; B.S. in Civil Engring., Univ. of Washington, 1916, C.E., 1926; m. Sydnia Caldan, Feb. 20, 1926. Sanitary inspector, U.S. Pub. Health Service 1916; acting instr. in civil engring., U. of Washington, 1920; designing and maintenance engr., U.S. Reclamation Service, Yakima, Wash., 1920-25; instr., Coll. of Engring., U. of Washington, 1925-28, asst. prof., 1928-34, asso. prof., 1934-38, prof. hydraulic engring. and head dept. civil engring. 1938-62, prof. emeritus, 1962-72; cons. hydraulic and sanitary engr.; with state highway dept. summer 1926; in irrigating engring. U.S. Bureau Reclamation (Wash.) summers 1927-29; asst. engr. designs and constrn. U.S. Nat. Park Service, Mount Rainier Nat. Park, summers 1930-33. Served as 1st lt., 20th Engrs., U.S. Army, 1917-19; with A.E.F., France, 1918-19. Mem. Am. Soc. C.E., Soc. Am. Mil. Engrs., Soc. Promotion Engring. Edn., Tau Beta Pi, Sigma Xi, Phi Kappa Sigma. Editor: Hydraulic Tables, 1933. Author: Cost Estimation of Irrigation Works, 1926; Sanitary Engineering Laboratory Manual, 1931; A Short Course in Plane Surveying, 1934; Discharge of Commercial Cippoletti Weirs, 1936. Home: Seattle WA Died May 5, 1972; buried Fox Island WA

VAN INGEN, GILBERT, geologist, paleontologist; b. Poughkeepsie, N.Y., July 30, 1869; s. Henry and Josephine (Koelman) V.; student Cornell U., 1886-88, Yale, 1892-93; m. Harriet Galusha, Sept. 3, 1903. Asst. geologist, U.S. Geol. Survey, 1889-91; asst. paleontologist, Cornell U., 1891-92; at Columbia, 1893-95, curator geology, 1895-1901; spl. asst. paleontologist, N.Y. State, 1901-03; asst. geologist and curator invertebrate paleontology, 1903-08, asst. prof. geology, 1908-19, associate prof. of geology, 1919—, Princeton University. Dir. Princeton geol. expdns. to Newfoundland, 1912, 13, 14. Pres. Acad. Bd. U.S. School of Mil. Aeronautics at Princeton U., 1917-Feb. 1919. Fellow N.Y. Acad. Sciences, Geol. Soc. of America, Paleontological Society of America. Editor depts. geology and paleontology, New Internat. Ency., 1901-02. Home: Princeton, N.J. Died July 7, 1925.

VAN KEUREN, ALEXANDER HAMILTON, naval officer; b. Howell, Mich., Mar. 9, 1881; s. James Irvin and Fanny Ann (Morgan) Van K.; ed. U. of Mich., 1898-99, U.S. Naval Acad., 1899-1903 (B.S.), Mass. Inst. Tech., 1905-08 (M.S.), Naval War Coll., 1925-26; m. Helen Cuthbert Molten, June 19, 1911; children—Alexander Hamilton, Frances Cuthbert (Mrs. H. G. Pestalozzi). Commd. ensign, U.S. Navy, 1905, advanced through grades to rear adm., 1939; served on the U.S.S. Wisconsin, Oregon, Villalobos, Asiatic Station, 1903-05; duty at Navy Yards, East and West Coasts, 1908-16. Bur. Constrn. and Repair, design div., 1916-20, East and West Coasts, 1920-25; staff Naval War Coll., Newport, R.I., 1926-27; head design div., Navy Dept., Bur. Constrn. and Repair, 1927-36, also tech. adviser London Naval Conf., 1930, Gen. Disarmament Conf., Geneva, 1932; superintending constructor for U.S. Navy, N.Y. Shipbuilding Co., Camden, N.J., 1936-37; mgr. indsl. dept. Navy Yard, Phila., 1937-39; chief constructor and chief Bur. Constrn. and Repair, U.S. Navy (rank read adm. Constrn. Corps), 1939-40; asst. chief Bureau of Ships, 1940-42; Chief Bureau of Ships, 1942; dir. Naval Research Laboratory, Anacostia Sta., 1942-45; Navy Dept. 1945-46; permanent rank of rear adm., 1941, ret., 1946. Mem. Soc. Naval Architects and Marine Engrs., Sigma Chi. Mem. Sojourners. Episcopalian. Club: Chevy Chase (Md.). Home: Washington. Died July 1966.

VAN LEER, BLAKE RAGSDALE, (van-ler'), college pres.; b. Mangum, Tex., now Okla., Aug. 16, 1893; s. Maurice Langhorne and Mary (Tarleton) Van L.; B.S., in Elec. Engring., Purdue U., 1915, M.E., 1922; M.S. in Mech. Engring., U. of Calif., 1920; student U. of Caen, France, Feb.-June 1919, U. of Munich, Germany, 1927-28; Sc.D. (hon.) Washington and Jefferson U., 1943; D. Engring. (hon.), Purdue U., 1944; m. Ella Wall, Sept. 6, 1924; children—Blake Wayne, Maryly (Mrs. Jordan Brown Peck), Samuel Wall. Instructor and assistant professor hydraulics, University of California, 1915-28; engineer with S.P. Ry. Co., Byron-Jackson Pump Co., 1922-26; asst. sec. Am. Engring. Council, 1928-32; dean engring., U. of Fla., 1932-37, consolidated colls. of engring. of U. of N.C. and N.C. State Coll., Raleigh, N.C., 1937-44; pres. Ga. Inst. Tech., since July 1, 1944; Florida representative U.S. Coast and Geodetic Survey, 1933-35; tech. adviser Fla. Emergency Relief Adminstrn., 1934-35; tech. adviser Fla. State Planning Bd., 1934-37; water consultant Nat. Resources Com., 1936; vice-pres. Fla. State Bd. Engr. Examiners, 1937. Mem. United States Commn. for UNESCO, 1945-49. Served as 1st lt. Co. F, 316th Engr. Corps, U.S. Army, with A.E.F., 1917-19; maj. Engrs. Res. Corps, 1928-42; lt. col. Army of U.S., May 17, 1942-Oct. 1943, col. Gen. Staff Corps, Oct. 1943-July 1944; chief facilities branch Army Specialized Training Division. Former member N.C. Defense Council; regional advisor, engineering, science and management. Defense Training, Virginia, North Carolina, South Carolina. Chmn. Ga. State Ports Authority, 1945-49. Pres. S.E. Conf. Intercollegiate Athletics, 1949; v.p. National Collegiate Athletics Assn., 1948-49. Registered professional engineer, Fla., N.C. and Ga. Awarded Croix de Guerre (France); awarded Freeman traveling scholarship for study of hydraulics in Europe by Am. S.M.E., 1927-28. Fellow and Life Mem. A.S.M.E. Mem. Am. Society of Engring. Edn. (mem. council 1933-36; pres. S.E. sect. 1939-40), Soc. Am. Mil. Engrs., Fla. Engring. Soc. (v.p. 1937-38), N.C. Soc. of Engrs., Ga. Engring. Soc., Ga. Soc. Professional Engrs., Atlanta; Pine Burr, Newcomen Soc., Am. Legion, Tau Beta Pi, Sigma Tau, Sigma Xi, Alpha Tau Omega, Eta Kappa Nu, Omicron Delta Kappa, Scabbard and Blade; honorary member of A.I.A. Democrat. Episcopalian. Mason (32 deg.). Clubs: Cosmos, Army and Navy Country (Washington); Atlanta Rotary Internat., Capital City (Atlanta). Contbr. of articles on hydraulics to engring. jours. Home: 292 10th St., N.W., Atlanta. Died Jan. 23, 1956; buried Marietta Nat. Cemetery.

VAN MAANEN, ADRIAAN (van-mä'nen), astronomer; b. Sneek, Holland, Mar. 31, 1884; s. Johan Willem Gerbrand and Catharina Adriana (Visser) Van M.; B.A., U. of Utrecht, 1906, M.A., 1909, Sc.D., 1911; U. of Groningen, 1909-10; came to U.S., 1911; unmarried. Volunteer asst., Yerkes Obs., Williams Bay, Wis., 1911-12; astronomer, Mt. Wilson Obs., since 1912. Has specialized in study of parallaxes and proper motions of stars and nebulae; gen. magnetic field of the sun. Mem. Astron. Soc. America, Astron. Soc. Pacific, Internat. Astron. Union, Soc. Astron. de France, Astr. Gesellschaft, Royal Astr. Soc., Amsterdam Acad., Utrecht Soc., Sigma Xi, etc. Clubs: Valley Hunt (Pasadena, Calif); Student Fund of Pasadena. Home: Terrace Villa No. 4, Pasadena 2, Calif. Died Jan. 26, 1946.

VAN NORDEN, RUDOLPH WARNER, cons. engr.; b. St. Albans, Vt.; s. Charles and Anna Hubbell (Mygatt) Van Norden; student Cornell University, 1892-94; A.B. in Mech. Engring., Stanford, 1896; m. Rowena Fay Jackson, Oct. 12, 1904 (died Jan. 11, 1929). Began as asst. engr. with Central Calif. Electric Co. (merged into Pacific Gas & Electric Co. 1905), Sacramento, 1896, div. supt., 1905-06; cons. engr., San Francisco, Calif., since 1906; tech. adviser to U.S. Sec. of Interior on Boulder Dam questions, 1929-30; cons. engr., U.S. Bur.

of Reclamation. Chief statistician San Francisco Traffic Survey, 1937; asso. engr. Federal Power Commn., 1938; tech. engr. Fed. Pub. Works Adminstrn., 1938-39; cons. electrical engr., 9th Corps Area, Zone Construction, Quartermaster Corps, U.S. Army, 1941. Has been cons. engr. State of Calif., Dept. of Pub. Works of San Francisco, Oakland, Stockton Modesto, Susanville, Sacramento, Santa Cruz, various cos., irrigation dists. and individuals; supervising engr.; locomotive fueling plant (oil), So. Pacific relocation, Shasta Dam Central Valleys project, Calif., 1942. Tech. engr. on design and constrn. of low-head hydro-elec. powerplant for Truckee-Carson Irrigation Dist., Nev., 1946-47. Designed 30 hydro-elec. power plants and supervised constrn. of 8 of these; designed over 50 high dams; owner of patent on multicone type of dams, also on electric-magnetic reduction gear for ship propulsion; has frequently appeared as expert witness. Rated Head Engr. by U.S. Civil Service, 1942. Mem. of Court of Honor, San Francisco area, Boy Scouts of America. Fellow and life mem., Am. Inst. E.E.; life mem., Am. Soc. C.E.; mem. Kappa Alpha (Southern). Democrat. Mason. Club: Engineers. Address: 1500 Sutter St., San Francisco CA

VAN ORNUM, JOHN LANE, (van-ôr'num), civil engineer; b. Hartford, Vt., May 14, 1864; s. Adoniram Judson and Sarah Josephine (Lane) Van O.; B.S. in C.E., U. of Wis., 1888, C.E., 1891; m. Carrie Beattie Scott, July 25, 1894; children—Thurwood, Judson (dec.). Municipal engring. work, Milwaukee, Wis., July-Nov. 1888; surveyor and inspector U.S. harbor works, Ga. and Fla. coasts, 1888-90; asst. engr. Milwaukee, Lake Shore & Western R.R., in Mich. and Wis., May-Oct. 1890; U.S. asst. engr. on river surveys, etc., in Ga. and Tenn., 1890-91; chief topographer Mexican Boundary Survey, 1891-94; instr. civ. engring., Washington U., 1894-97; traveled in Europe, 1897-98; capt. and maj. 3d U.S. Vol. Engrs., Spanish-Am. War, 1898-99, assisting in elemination of yellow fever in Cienfuegos, Cuba, etc.; prof. civ. engring., Washington U., 1899-1934, emeritus prof. since 1934. Fellow A.A.A.S.; mem. Am. Soc. Civil Engrs., Am. Soc. Testing Materials, Internat. Assn. Navigation Congresses (life mem.), Soc. for Promotion Engring. Edn., Engineers Club St. Louis (past pres.), Mil. Order Foreign Wars, Sigma Xi, Tau Beta Pi (hon. mem.), Beta Theta Pi, etc. Presbyterian. Author: The Regulation of Rivers, 1914; also many articles in tech. mags. as result of original research, etc. Home: 126 Linden Av., Clayton, Mo. Died Nov. 6, 1943.

VAN PELT, JOHN VREDENBURGH, architect; b. New Orleans, Feb. 24, 1874; s. John Vredenburgh and Emma Louisa (Fields) Van P.; ed. Germantown, Phila., and Paris, France; art and tech. edn. at Eole des Arts Décoratifs, Atelier Droillard-Thierry-Deglane, and École des Beaux Arts; (1st Am. to obtain values for diploma; awarded Architect Diplomé par le Gouvernement, 1895); postgrad. (Beaux Arts), 1895-97, 1903-04; m. Betsey A. Southworth, Mar. 20, 1902; children—Betsey V.P. Smith, Margaret V.P. Vilas, John V. Asst. prof. architecture in charge of design, Cornell U., 1897-1900; traveled in Germany, Italy, Sicily, England, etc., 1900-02; prof. design and dean of Coll. Architecture, 1902-04; practicing as architect, N.Y., since 1904. Exhibited Paris Salon (sect. Architecture), 1895-96 (sect. Painting), 1898. At Beaux Arts received 1st medal in plan, 1896, later two 2d medals for planning, medals in esquisse, 1896 and 1903, a medal for modeling, and in 1904 Prix St. Agnan Boucher (1,000 francs) for pupil of École des Beaux Arts holding greatest number of values of all graduates. Holds grand medal Société Centrale des Architectes (Foundation Destors), for 1897, and grand medal Société des Architectes Diplomés, 1896-97. Asso. dir. Atelier of Columbia U., 1904-13; prof. of design, U. Pa., 1914-17; in charge Columbia U. extension studios in architecture, 1923-27; lectr. on theory of composition, Columbia. Architect of Joan of Arc Monument, N.Y., Gennadeion Library, Athens, Greece (partner W. S. Thompson); Ch. of St. John Nepomuk; Ch., Sch. and Rectory of the Guardian Angels, N.Y.; rectory extension and basement ch. Sanctuary, Ch. of Annunciation, for Bishop John J. Dunn, N.Y.; Patchogue (N.Y.) Post Office, for U.S. Treasury Dept.; Brookhaven Town Hall; Contemporary Arts Bldg. (with F. A. Ackerman and Joshua Lowenfish), N.Y. World's Fair, Otisville Sanatorium for N.Y.C.; Standard Oil and Griswold Bldgs. of Loomis Sanatorium and, from 1922 to 1946, was architect of Union Health Center Clinics of Dressmakers' Union, I.L.G.W.U.; placed on Roster of Approved Architects for Hosp. Work by Hosp. Assn. Public Schools: Piermont; Sparkill; Orangeburg, N.J. Sect. Patchogue C. of C., 1933-41. Fellow and mem. emeritus A.I.A.; life mem. Société des Architectes Diplomes; life mem. Museum City of N.Y., trustee 1926-39; (chmn. com. on architecture, 1936-40); sec. art commn., State of N.Y.; mem. emeritus of Beaux Arts Soc.; mem. S.A.R. Holland Soc., Century Assn. of N.Y., Fine Arts Fedn. N.Y. (sec. 1924-33), Kappa Alpha. Presbyn. Author: Essentials of Composition as Applied to Art, 1902, revised edition, 1913; 3 Pencil Points Books; Monograph of W. K. Vanderbilt House; also numerous mag. articles. Home: Roe Blvd. West. Office: Patchogue, L.I., N.Y. Died May 30, 1962.

VAN SICLEN, MATTHEW, mining engr.; b. N.Y. City, Nov. 8, 1880; s. George West and Sarah Jane (Gregory) Van S.; grad. Cornwall Heights Sch., Cornwall-on-Hudson, N.Y., 1898; B.A., Amherst, 1902, M.A., 1905; E.M., Sch. of Mines (Columbia), 1906; m. Alice V. Petar, May 4, 1936. Surveyor Tenn. Copper Co., 1905; with various mines in Chihuahua, Zacatecas, Durango, Hidalgo, Sonora, Mexico, 1907-12, advancing to gen. supt.; supt. of exploration (oil shale), at Rosevale, N.B., 1913; leaser in Northwest Ark., 1914; operator zinc and lead mines, Webb City, Mo., 1915-17; lt. Air Service, U.S. Army, 1917-18; Pa. anthracite, 1919; examining engr., War Minerals Rlief Commn., 1919-21; asst. chief mining engr., U.S. Bur. Mines, Washington, D.C., 1921-24; engr. in charge Div. of Mining Research, same, 1924-26; del. U.S. Govt. to XIVth Internat. Geol. Congress, Madrid, Spain, 1926; inspected metal and coal mines and mining methods in Europe, 1926; cons. mining engr., 1927-33, 1935-37; mining engr. to Turkish Govt., 1933-35; chief engr., coal economics div., U.S. Bur. Mines, 1937—. Episcopalian. Home: Arlington, Va. Died Mar. 3, 1941.

VAN SLYKE, DONALD D., biol. chemist; b. Pike, N.Y., Mar. 29, 1883; s. Lucius L. and Lucy (Dexter) Van S.; A.B., U. of Michigan, 1905; Ph.D., 1907, Sc.D., 1935; studied U. of Berlin, 1911; Sc.D., Yale, 1925; M.D., U. of Oslo, 1938; Sc.D., Northwestern University, 1940, University Chicago, 1941, University of London, 1951; M.D. (honorary), University of Amsterdam, 1962; m. Rena Mosher, June 24, 1907 (dec.); children—Elsa, Karl Keller; m. 2d, Else von Bardenfleth Brock Aug. 1948. Research chemist, Rockefeller Inst., since 1907; chief chemist at hosp. for same, 1914-48, emeritus; asst. dir. in chge. research in biology and medicine, Brookhaven Nat. Lab., 1948-51, research chemist, 1951-71; counselor Eli Lilly Research Grants, 1951-56; visiting professor at Peking Medical Sch., China, 1922. Pres. Am. Bureau for Med. Aid to China, John Phillips Meml. Award Am. Coll. Physicians, 1954, 57, Donald D. Van Slyke award Am. Soc. Clin. Chemistry, 1957; Franklin medal 1965. Mem. of American Chem. Soc., Biol. Chemists (pres. 1921-22), Harvey Soc. (pres. 1927-28), N.Y. Acad. Medicine, Assn. Am. Physicians, Nat. Acad. Science, Acad. Science of India (honorary), Royal Danish Academy of Science and Letters, Brit. Physiol. Soc. (hon.), Swedish Royal Acad. Science, Accademia Medica Lombarda (hon.), Societa Italiana di Biologia Sperimentale (hon.), Societe de Biologie Chimique (France), Societe de Pathologie Renale, Sigma Xi, Beta Theta Pi; hon. member Renal Association (London), Physiological Society (Britain), Am. Philos. Soc. Contbr. articles American and foreign jours., chiefly concerning chemistry of proteins and protein derivatives and their role in physiology and pathology, enzyme action, blood chemistry, and the metabolic conditions of diabetes and nephritis. Author: Factors affecting distribution of electrolytes, water, and gases in the animal body; Micromanometric Analyses. published in 1961; co-author (with J. P. Peters) Quantitative Clinical Chemistry; (with C. Lundsgaard) Cyanosis; (with E. Stillman and others) The Course of Bright's Disease. Awarded Conne medal, Assn. Am. Physicians, 1937; Willard Gibbs medal, 1939; Kober medal, 1942; Mickle fellowship for contbns. to medicine, 1936; Order of Jade (China); Am. Chem. Soc. award, 1953; Scientific Achievement award, A.M.A., 1962; Cresson medal Franklin Inst., 1965; Nat. Medal of Sci., 1965. Home: Port Jefferson NY Died May 4, 1971; buried Glenwood Cemetery, Geneva NY

VAN SLYKE, LUCIUS LINCOLN, chemist; b. Centerville, N.Y., Jan. 6, 1859; s. William J. and Katherine (Keller) V.; A.B., U. of Mich., 1879, A.M., 1881, Ph.D., 1882; student and fellow by courtesy in chem. lab., Johns Hopkins, 1889-90; m. Lucy W., d. Rev. R. H. Dexter, June 15, 1882 (died 1885); children—Donald Dexter, Carl Osborne (dec.); m. 2d, Julia Hanford, d. Dr. Francis Upson, Apr. 5, 1888 (died 1924); 1 son, Lawrence Prescott; m. 3d, Mrs. Hedwig Sheul, June 2, 1926. Asst. chem. lab., U. of Mich., 1882-85; prof. chemistry, Oahu Coll., Honolulu, and govt. chemist, H.I., 1885-88; lecturer on gen. chemistry, U. of Mich., 1888-89; chief research chemist, New York Agrl. Experiment Station, 1890-1929, also prof. dairy chemistry, N.Y. State Coll. Agr., Cornell Univ., 1920-29 (emeritus). Fellow A.A.A.S.; pres. Assn. Official Agrl. Chemists, 1900, N.Y. State Dairymen's Assn., 1897. Author: Modern Methods of Testing Milk and Milk Products, 1906; Science and Practice of Cheese Making (with C. A. Publow); Fertilizers and Crops, 1911; Cheese (with W. V. Price), 1927. Home: Geneva, N.Y. Died Sept. 30, 1931.

VAN SPLUNTER, JOHN MARCUS, engr.; b. Grand Rapids, Mich., July 2, 1881; s. James and Nellie (Van Dam) Van S.; B.S., U. Mich., 1904. Engring. dept. Sargent & Lundy, cons. engrs., Chgo., 1904-06; sales, constrn. engr. Stanley G. I. Electric Co., Pittsfield, Mass., 1906-08; sales engr. Gen. Electric Co., Chgo., 1908-12; chief engr. Elec. Engrs. Equipment Co., Chgo., 1912-14; sec., elec. engr. Gen. Devices & Fittings Co., Chgo., 1914-24, pres., sec., Grand Rapids, 1924—. Pres., owner Grand Rapids Baseball Club; pres. Olympic Athletic Club. Served as lt. comdr. USN, 1917-19. Mem. Am. Inst. E.E. Home: 930 Lafayette Av. S.E., Grand Rapids 7. Office: 1450 Buchanan Av. S.W., Grand Rapids 2, Mich. Died 1957.

VANUXEM, LARDNER, geologist; b. Phila., July 23, 1792; s. Jame and Rebecca (Clarke) V.; grad. École des Mines, Paris, France, 1819; m. Elizabeth Newbold, 1830. Prof. chemistry and mineralogy S.C. Coll. (now U. S.C.), 1819-27, made geol. surveys of N.C., S.C.; made geol. surveys of N.Y., Ohio, Ky., Tenn., Va., 1827-30; bought farm nr. Bristol, Pa., 1830; assigned to 3d and 4th dists. for geol. surveys of N.Y., 1836-42; mem. group which established 1st uniform geol. nomenclature; founder Assn. Am. Geologists and Naturalists (now A.A.A.S.), 1840. Died Bristol, Jan. 25, 1848.

VAN VALZAH, ROBERT, (van-val'zä), prof. medicine; b. Spring Mills, Pa., Nov. 1, 1882; s. Frank H. and Jane R. Van V.; A.B., Princeton, 1904; M.D., U. of Pa., 1908; m. Aglae Keen, Aug. 24, 1912; children—Robert, Algae Louise. Chief resident physician University Hosp., Phila., 1909; instr. clin. medicine, University of Wisconsin, 1910, asst. prof., 1911, asso. prof., 1913, prof. since 1918. Chmn. Med. Advisory Bd. No. 13, Selective Service, U.S. Army, 1917. Fellow Am. Coll. of Physicians; mem. A.M.A., Phi Alpha Sigma, Alpha Omega Alpha. Home: Goby, Va. Address: 1300 University Av., Madison, Wis. Died Nov. 23, 1946.

VAN VLECK, EDWARD BURR, (van-vlek'), mathematician; b. Middletown, Conn., June 7, 1863; s. John Monroe and Ellen Maria (Burr) Van. V.; A.B., Wesleyan U., Conn., 1884, A.M., 1887; grad. student mathematics and physics, 1885-87, fellow, 1886-87, Johns Hopkins; student mathematics, U. of Göttingen, 1890-93, Ph.D., 1893; LL.D., Clark U., 1909, Wesleyan U., 1925; Dr. of Mathematics and Physics, U. of Groningen, 300th Anniversary, 1914; Sc.D., U. of Chicago, 1916; m. Hester Laurence Raymond, July 3, 1893; 1 son, John Hasbrouck. Instr. mathematics, Wesleyan U., 1887-90; instr. mathematics, U. of Wis., 1893-95; asso. prof. mathematics, Wesleyan U., 1895-98, prof., 1898-1906; prof. mathematics, U. of Wis., 1906-29, prof. emeritus since 1929. Mem. Nat. Research Council, 1921-24. Mem. Nat. Acad. Sciences, Am. Math. Soc. (v.p., 1909, pres., 1913-15), Deutsche Matematiker-Vereiningung, Société Mathématique de France, Circolo Matematico di Palermo; fellow A.A.A.S. (v.p. Sect. A, 1912); mem. Phi Beta Kappa, Nat. Arts Club (New York). Asso. editor, 1902-05, editor 1905-10, Trans. Am. Math. Soc., and del. of soc. to Abel Centenary, Christiania, Norway, 1902. Sec. Local Draft Bd., Madison, Wis., 1917-18. Officier de l'Instruction Publique (France). Author: Theory of Divergent Series and Algebraic Continued Fractions, 1903; also monographs in math. jours. Home: 519 N. Pinckney St., Madison, Wis. Died June 2, 1943.

VAN VLECK, JOHN MONROE, mathematician, astronomer; b. Stone Ridge, N.Y., March 4, 1833; s. Peter and Ann (Hasbrouck) V.; A.B., Wesleyan Univ., 1850; (LL.D., Northwestern Univ., 1876, Wesleyan, 1900); m. Ellen Maria Burr, May 2, 1854 (died 1899); father of Edward Burr V. Teacher Greenwich (R.I.) Acad., 1850; asst. in Nautical Almanac Office, Cambridge, Mass., 1851-53; adj. prof. mathematics, 1853-57, prof. mathematics and astronomy, 1858-1904 (emeritus), v.p., 1890-1903, acting pres., 1872-73, 1887-89, 1896-97, Wesleyan Univ. Mem. U.S. solar eclipse expdn. at Mt. Pleasant, Ia., 1869; del. Meth. Ecumenical Confs., London, 1881, Washington, 1891, London, 1901. Prepared astron. tables in Am. Ephemeris and Nautical Almanac, 1855-96. Home: Middletown, Conn. Died Nov. 4, 1912.

VAN WAGENEN, JAMES HUBERT, civil engr.; b. Adams Co., Ia., Nov. 8, 1881; s. Isaac and Margaret (McClintic) V.; Knox Coll., Galesburg, Ill., 1901-03; B.S. in C.E., U. of Mo., 1908; m. Lois Jean Andrews, Dec. 27, 1914; children—Elizabeth, Marcia Anne. Appraisal and valuation engr. with Interstate Telegraph & Telephone Co., in Ill., 1908; pvt. engring. practice in Ia., 1908-09; topographic engr. with U.S. Geol. Survey in N.D., 1909; asst. engr. Ill. Highway Commn., 1909-10; with Internat. Boundary Commn., May 1910—; engr. in charge field parties, Mont., N.D. and Minn. until 1915; chief engr. U.S. Sect. of Commn., 1915—, in charge work of commn. on line between Alaska and Can. and U.S. and Can.; apptd. U.S. commr. on Internat. Boundary Commn. U.S.—Alaska and Can., May 3, 1929. Mem. Bd. Surveys and Maps of Fed. Govt., apptd. chmn. 1921, of com. Am. Engring. Council to investigate devices for stabilizing business as part of the work of the "Conference on Unemployment" called by President Harding, Sept. 1921. Inventor of radio and automotive devices. Mem. Iowa N.G., 1900-06. Home: Washington, D.C. Died May 17, 1935.

VAN WINKLE, EDGAR BEACH, engineer; b. New York, N.Y., Mar. 4, 1842; s. Edgar Simeon and Hannah (Beach) V.; A.B., Union College, 1860, C.E., 1861; m. Elizabeth, d. Judge William Mitchell, June 7, 1876 (died 1894); m. 2d, Mary Flower, d. William Speiden, of New York, June 3, 1899. Employed on Croton water works extension, 1861-62; pvt. and 1st lt., 1862, capt., 1865, U.S.V.; served on staffs of Gens. Viele, Gilmore and Hatch in Civil War. Elected Companion (1st class) Mil. Order Loyal Legion, 1866; recorder N.Y. Commandery, same, 1886; mem. Commandery-in-Chief, same. Col. and division engr., 1st Div. N.G.S.N.Y., 1876-83. As civil engr. employed on sewerage system, New York; also by Erie R.R., Shepaug Valley R.R.; chief engr. Dept. Public Parks, New York, 1878-84. Home: New York, and Litchfield, Conn. Died Apr. 27, 1920.

VARIAN, RUSSELL HARRISON, physicist; b. Washington, Apr. 24, 1898; s. John Osborne and Agnes (Dixon) V.; A.B., Stanford, 1925, M.A., 1927; D.Eng. (hon.), Poly. Inst. Bklyn., 1943; m. Dorothy Hill, 1947; children—George Russell, Charles John, Susan Aileen. Research physicist Humble Oil & Refining Co., 1929, Farnsworth Television Co., 1930-33; pvt. research 1934-35; research asso. Standford, 1937-40, 46—; research engr. Sperry Gyroscope Co., 1940-46; pres. Varian Associates, mfrs. ultra-high frequency microwave tubes, 1948-56, chmn. bd. 1956—. Awarded John Price Wetherill medal, Franklin Inst., 1950. Fellow Inst. Radio Engrs., Cal. Acad. Sci., Am. Phys. Soc., A.A.A.S.; mem. Sigma Xi. Inventor klystron radio tube for prodn. waves in range of one to a few centimeters; patentee approximately 100 devices in microwave, applied physics field. Home: 10114 Crescent Rd., Cupertino. Office: 611 Hansen Way, Palo Alto, Cal. Died July 28, 1959.

VARNEY, WILLIAM HENRY, naval officer; b. Wolfsborough, N.H., Apr. 19, 1838; s. Henry Weed and Ruth Basset (Buffum) V.; ed. Boston pub. schs.; studied naval architecture, and was designer of merchant vessels; m. Boston, Jan. 1, 1863, Mary Elizabeth Hoffman, of Port Huron, Mich., Apptd. asst. naval constr. U.S.N., July 29, 1869; promoted naval constr., Mar. 12, 1875; retired Apr. 19, 1900. Served at various navy yards, and as superintending constr. of several vessels, mem. Bd. of Inspection and Survey, etc. Author: Ship Builders' Manual, 1877 01. Home: 712 N. Carey St., Baltimore.

VARNEY, WILLIAM WESLEY, engr., lawyer; b. Boston, Mass., Sept. 17, 1864; s. William Henry (capt. U.S. Navy) and Mary E. (Hoffman) V.; mech. engring. course, Mass. Inst. Tech., 1883-86; LL.B., U. of Md., 1893; m. Edith McDonnal, Sept. 6, 1899; children—William Henry, John Hoffman. Draftsman, superintending constructor's office, U.S. Navy, Cramp's Shipyard, Phila., 1886-89; draftsman in charge superintending constructor's office, U.S. Navy, Baltimore, 1889-92; admitted to bar, federal and state, 1893; cons. engineer, Baltimore, 1893-99; city commissioner, Baltimore, 1899-1900; also city engr., pres. Bd. Pub. Works and mem. Water Bd.; cons. engr., Baltimore City, 1903-17, harbor engr., 1917-18; also in practice as patent lawyer since 1895. Mem. Am. Soc. M.E. (Am. Engring. Council 1925-27), Am. Soc. C.E., Soc. Naval Architects and Marine Engrs. Mem. Christian (Disciples) Ch. Odd Fellow; Grand Master I.O.O.F. of Md., 1910. Club: Maryland Yacht. Pioneer in television; field application for 2 patents, Jan. 1892, on method of elec. transmission of optical impressions, and transmission of moving pictures in natural colors from life as well as from films. Home: 6017 Bellona Av., Baltimore, Md. Died July 30, 1943.

VASEY, GEORGE, botanist; b. Scarborough, Yorkshire, Eng., Feb. 28, 1822; brought to N.Y., 1823; attended Oneida (N.Y.) Inst., Berkshire Med. Inst., Pittsfield, Mass.; m. Miss Scott, 1846; m. 2d, Mrs. (Barber) Cameron, 1867; at least 6 children. Practiced medicine, Dexter, N.Y., 1846-48, Elgin and Ringwood, Ill., 1848-66; collected, classified and studied prarie flora; organizer, 1st pres. Ill. Natural History Soc., 1866; accompanied Maj. John Wesley Powell on Colo. bot. expdn., 1868; curator natural history mus. Ill. State Normal U., 1869; became co-editor Am. Entomologist and Botanist, 1870; botanist U.S. Dept. of Agr., 1872, also in charge U.S. Nat. Herbarium. Author: Catalogue of the Forest Trees of the United States Which Usually Attain a Height of Sixteen Feet or More, 1870; Agricultural Grasses of the United States, 1884; Grasses of the Southwest, 1890-91; Grasses of the Pacific Slope, 1892-93. Died Washington, D.C., Mar 4, 1893.

VASS, ALONZO FREDERICK, govt. ofcl.; b. Glasco, Kan., Oct. 26, 1888; s. Thomas and Louisa (Clark) V.; B.S., Kan. State Agrl. Coll., 1909; student U. of Kan., 1910; M.S., U. of Wis., 1911; Ph.D., Cornell U., 1926; m. Helen Clare McGarrity, July 18, 1927; children—Thomas Clark, Linda Lee. Instr. Ore. State Agrl. Coll., 1912-13, asst. prof., 1914-15, grad. student and asst., Cornell U., 1915-17; asso. prof. U. of Wyo., 1917-20, prof. and head dept. of agronomy ad agrl. econ., 1920-58, prof. emeritus; cons. Bur. of Reclamation, U.S. Department of Interior, 1958—; chmn. com. Nat. Forum of Labor, Agrl. and Industry, 1944-50, research coms. of 11 Western States for making crop and livestock adjustments, 1935; rep. Nat. Livestock Assn. and Beef Com. before Congl. and Deptl. Hearings, 1941-45. Mem. Am. Acad. Polit. and Social Sci., Can. Agr. Econ. Assn., Wyo. Stockgrowers Assn. (hon. life mem.), Am. Soc. Agronomy, Am. Farm Econ. Assn. (past v.p.), Western Farm Econ. Assn. (past v.p.), Internat. Assn. Agrl. Econ., Colo. Acad. Science, U.S. Chamber of Commerce (national resources com.), Nat. Reclamation Assn. (land limitations com.), International Congress Soil Science (mem. organizing com.), Sigma Xi, Phi Kappa Phi, Alpha Zeta, Phi Delta Theta, Blue Key. Club: Rotary. Author of articles: Methods for Determining Value of Grazing Lands, 1940; Production Costs and Fair Prices for Wool and Lambs, 1901-45, and many others. Home: 1116 Ivinson St., Laramie, Wyo. Office: Bur. Reclamation, Dept. of Interior, Washington 25. Died Aug. 15, 1960; buried Green Hill Cemetery, Laramie.

VAUGHAN, DANIEL, educator, mathematician; b. Glenomara, Ireland, 1818; s. John Vaughan. Came to U.S., 1840; tutor to Col. Stamp, Bourbon County, Ky., 1842; prof. Greek coll. in Bardstown, Ky., 1845-50; moved to Cincinnati, 1850; lectr. chemistry Eclectic Med. Inst., 1850; mem. A.A.A.S., 1851; lectured widely on astronomy and other scientific topics; prof. chemistry Cincinnati Coll. Medicine and surgery, 1860-72; contributed frequently to Proceedings of A.A.A.S. Author: Destiny of the Solar System, 1854. Died Apr. 6, 1879.

VAUGHAN, GUY W., pres. Curtiss-Wright Corp.; b. Bayshore, L.I., N.Y., Aug. 15, 1884; s. Gustavus and Elmira (Tilden Goetchius) V.; grad. New Rochelle High Sch., 1898; m. Helen Knapp, Oct. 8, 1908; 1 son, Guy. Began with Desberon Motor Co., New Rochelle (N.Y.), 1898; designed and developed the Vaughan automobile, 1909; drove the Decauville racer which won the Gordon Bennett race, 1902, and made other records; became cons. engr. Babcock Electric Works, Buffalo, N.Y., and Olds Motor Works, Lansing, Mich., 1912; asso. with F. B. Stearns Co. as asst. to pres. and exptl. engr. to assit in devel. of Knight car; was made quality mgr. Wright-Martin Aircraft Co., later factory mgr. for same co.; was v.p. and gen. mgr. Van Blerck Motor Co., Monroe, Mich.; later pres. and gen. mgr. Standard Steel & Bearings Co., Phila.; connected with Wright Aeronautical Corp. since 1924, v.p. and gen. mgr. until 1930, pres. and gen. mgr., 1930-35, pres. 1935-46, chmn. bd., 1935-49, pres. Curtiss-Wright Corp. Comdr. U.S. Naval Res. Dir. Aircraft Industries Am.; chmn. of bd. L.G.S. Spring Clutch Corp., Indpls, Victor Animatograph Corp., Davenport, Ia.; Marquette Metal Products Co., Cleve.; dir. Manufacturers Trust Co., N.Y.; dir. and mem. exec. com. Western Elec. Co., N.Y. Mem. Inst. Aero. Scis., Naval Reserve Officers Assn. Clubs: Engineers (New York); Army-Navy (Washington). Address: 720 Pelham Rd., New Rochelle, N.Y. Died Nov. 21, 1966.

VAUGHAN, HAROLD STEARNS, surgeon; b. Burlington, N.S., Can., Oct. 7, 1876; s. William Stearns and Clara Jane (McCulloch) S.; came to U.S., 1889; D.D.S., U. of Pa., 1899; M.D., College Physicians and surgeons, Columbia, 1904; Doctor of Scienc, Acadia Univ., 1948; married Sara M. Campbell, May 24, 1905; 1 son, Harold Campbell (dec.). Practiced N.Y.C. since 1905; specializes in plastic maxillo-facial surgery; attending surgeon N.Y. Post Grad. Hosp. 1919-47, ret.; cons. surgeon of Southampton, Manhattan Eye, Ear and Throat, N.Y. U. Bellevue Med. Center hosps.; former prof. clin. surgery, New York Post-Grad Medical School (Columbia). Formerly trustee Joseph Purcell Research Memorial. Fellow American College Surgeons; mem. Am. Society of Plastic and Reconstructive Surgery, Am. Bd. Plastic Surgery (founder group), A.M.A., American Association Plastic Surgeons, N.Y. Acad. Medicine, New York Laryngological Society. Republican. Presbyterian. Clubs: Century; also Ardsley Country. Author: An Abstract of Literature on Mouth Infections, 1924; Mouth Infections and Their Relation to Systemic Diseases, Vol. I, 1930, Vol. II, 1933; The Surgery of Cleft Lip, Cleft Palate and Associated Nasal Deformities, 1939. Contbr. on maxillo-facial plastic surgery, including the surgical correction of harelip and cleft palate. Providing Harold Campbell Vaughan Meml. Library at Arcadia U. in N.S. Home: Irvington-on-Hudson NY Deceased.

VAUGHAN, HARRY BRIGGS, JR., cons. engr.; b. Norfolk, Va., July 24, 1888; s. Henry B. and Josie C. (Cannon) V.; B.S. in Civil Engring., Virginia Poly. Inst., 1911, C.E., 1912; grad. Engr. Sch., 1924, Command and Gen. Staff Sch., 1930; m. Marion R. Evans, Feb. 7, 1921; children—Marion Evans (Mrs. William C. Clement), Harry B., David. Engaged in municipal engring., 1912-17, commd. lt., Engr. Corps, U.S. Army, 1917, advanced through grades to maj. gen.; retired 1946. Decorated D.S.M., Legion of Merit. Silver Star, Purple Heart; Companion of the Bath (Eng.); Comdr. of The Couronne (Belgium); Croix de Guerre with Palm (France). Mem. Am. Soc. C.E., Soc. Naval Architects and Marine Engrs., Soc. Mil. Engrs. Clubs: Army and Navy (Washington); Union League, Engineers (Philadelphia); Army Constituency (Fort Leavenworth). Home: Ithan, Pa. Died Mar. 1964.

VAUGHAN, T(HOMAS) WAYLAND, geologist, oceanographer; b. Jonesville, Tex., Sept. 20, 1870; s. Dr. Samuel Floyd and Annie R. (Hope) V.; B.S., Tulane U., 1889, D.Sc., 1944; A.B., Harvard, 1893, A.M., 1894, Ph.D., 1903; LL.D., U. of B.C., 1933, U. of California, 1936; studied mus. in Europe; married Dorothy Q. Upham, March 22, 1909 (deceased, August 18, 1949); one daughter, Caroline Ely (Mrs. James H. Fortune, Jr.). Engaged in geologic and paleontologic researches, with U.S. Geol. Survey, 1894-1923; geologist in charge Coastal Plain investigations, 1907-23, sr. geologist 1924-28, prin. scientist, 1928-39; retired. Custodian of Madreporarian corals, U.S. Nat. Museum, 1903-23; asso. in marine sediments, 1924-42, in paleontology since 1942; dir. Scripps Inst. of U. of Calif., La Jolla, 1924-36, dir. emeritus since 1936. Specialist on tertiary geology, fossil and recent corals, larger Foraminifera, and marine sediments. Decorated Order of Rising Sun, 3d class, Japan, 1940; awarded Agassiz medal for research in oceanography, Nat. Acad. of Science, 1935; Mary Clark Thompson medal for geology and paleontology, 1945; Penrose Medal, Geol. Soc. of America, 1946. Fellow Am. Academy Arts and Sci., Am. Philos. Soc., Calif. Acad. Sciences, A.A.A.S. (pres. Pacific div. 1930-31), Geol. Soc. America (1st v.p. 1938, pres. 1939), Assn. Am. Geographers, Paleontol. Soc. (pres. 1923), Washington Acad. Science (pres. 1923); San Diego Soc. Natural History (pres. 1926); mem. Nat. Acad. Sciences, Am. Geophys. Union (chmn. oceanography sect. 1926-28), Geol. Soc. of Washington (pres. 1915); Oceanographic Soc. of the Pacific (pres. 1935-36); Philos. Soc. Tex.; corr. mem. Zoölogical Soc. of London, Acad. Natural Sciences Philadelphia, Konk. Nat. Ver. Nederl.-Ind., Soc. Geograf., Cuba, fgn. mem. Linnean Soc., fgn. fellow Geol. Soc., London; hon. mem. Geological Soc., Peru. U.S. del. 1st Pan-Pacific Science Conf., Honolulu, 1920 (chairman sect. geology); del. U.S., Nat. Acad. Sciences, etc., to 2d Pan-Pacific Science Congress, Melbourne and Sydney, Australia, 1923; 3d Pan-Pacific Science Congress, Japan, 1926; 4th Pacific Science Congress, Java, 1929, 5th Congress, Victoria and Vancouver, 1933; mem. div. geology and geography, Nat. Research Council, 1919-26; chmn. Internat. Com. Oceanography of Pacific, Pacific Science Assn., 1926-35; chmn. sect. geol. sciences, 8th Am. Sci. Congress, Washington, 1940. Clubs: Cosmos (Washington); Faculty (Berkeley). Author: The Eocene and Lower Oligocene Coral Faunas of the United States (Monograph 39, U.S. Geol. Survey); Recent Madreporaria of Hawaiian Islands and Laysan (Bull. 59, U.S. Nat. Museum); Contributions to the Geology and Paleontology of the Canal Zone, Panama (Bull. 103, U.S. Nat. Mus.); Geologic Reconnaissance of the Dominican Republic; International Aspects of Oceanography; and more than 300 other scientific papers. Made trip around world, 1932-33, to study provisions for oceanographic research for Nat. Acad. Science. Home: 3333 P St. 7. Office: U.S. National Museum, Washington 25. Died Jan. 16, 1952.

VAUGHAN, VICTOR CLARENCE, scientist; b. Mt. Airy, Mo., Oct. 27, 1851; s. John and Adeline (Dameron) V.; B.S., Mt. Pleasant Coll., Mo., 1872; M.S., U. of Mich., 1875, Ph.D., 1876, M.D., 1878, LL.D., 1900; hon. Sc.D., U. of Western Pa., 1897; LL.D., Central Coll., 1910; Jefferson Med. Coll., Phila., 1915, U. of Mo., 1923; m. Dora Catherine Taylor, August 21, 1877; children—Victor C. (dec.), John Walter, Herbert Hunter, Henry Frieze, Warren Taylor. Assistant in chem. lab., 1875-83, lecturer med. chemistry, 1879-80, asst. prof., 1880-83, prof. physiol. and pathol. chemistry and asso. prof. therapeutics and materia medica, 1883-87, prof. hygiene and physiol. chemistry, and dir. Hygienic Lab., 1887-1909, dean dept. medicine and surgery, 1891-1921, U. of Mich. in Santiago campaign, 1898, as maj. and surgeon 63d Mich. Vol. Inf.; apptd. div. surgeon, 1898; recommended by President for bvt. of lt. col.; col., M.C. U.S.A., in charge of communicable diseases, 1917-18. Chmn. div. of med. sciences, Nat. Research Council; member Typhoid Commn. Awarded D.S.M. Pres. Assn. Am. Physicians, 1908-09; pres. A.M.A., 1914-15. Knight Legion of Honor, France, 1923. Author: Osteology and Myology of the Domestic Fowl, 1876; Text-book of Physiological Chemistry (3 edits.), 1879-83; Ptomaines and Leucomaines and Cellular Toxins (with Dr. Novy); Protein Split Products (with Victor C. Vaughan, Jr., and J. Walter Vaughan), 1913; (with Henry F. Vaughan and George T. Palmer) Epidemiology and Public Health, 3 vols.; A Doctor's Memories. Mng. editor Jour. Lab. and Clin. Medicine, 1915-23. Home: Detroit, Mich. Died Nov. 21, 1929.

VAUGHAN, WARREN TAYLOR, physician; b. Ann Arbor, Mich., Feb. 22, 1893; s. Victor Clarence and Dora Catherine (Taylor) V.; student Lancy, Switzerland, 1908-09; A.B., U. of Mich., 1913, M.D., 1916, hon. M.S., 1941; m. Emma Elizabeth Heath, June 21, 1917; children—Victor Clarence III, Warren Taylor, John Heath, David DuPuy. House officer, Peter Bent Brigham Hosp., Boston, Mass., 1916-17; asst. in preventive medicine and hygiene, Harvard Med. Sch., 1919-20; in practice internal medicine, specializing in allergy, Richmond, Va., since 1920; dir. Vaughan-Graham Clinic. Served as 1st lt., advancing through grades to lt. col. Med. Corps, U.S. Army, 1917-19; chief of med. service, Camp Hosp. 41, A.E.F. Mem. advisory com. to Committee on Costs of Medical Care; mem. com. on aerobiology and food habits of Natural Research Council; mem. Research Council on Problems of Alcohol (dir.); chmn. com. on medicaments and pharmaceuticals, American Academy of Allergy. Fellow A.A.A.S. (council since 1938); mem. Medical Society of Virginia (vice-pres. 1931-32), Southern Medical Assn., A.M.A., Am. Society Clin. Pathologists, Am. Assn. Study Allergy (sec.-treas. 1928-38, pres. 1939), Soc. for Study Asthma and Allied Conditions (pres. 1938-39), Am. Rheumatism Assn., Soc. of Investigative Dermatology, Internat. Soc. Gastroenterology, Inst. of Practice of Medicine, Barcelona, Spain (hon.), Soc. Study Allergy, Argentina (hon.), Va. Acad. Science (chmn. biol. sect., 1931), Huguenot Soc., Beta Theta Pi, Phi Rho Sigma, Sigma Xi, Alpha Omega Alpha. Formerly mem. Assn. Am.

Phys., Am. Coll. Physicians. Episcopalian. Clubs: Commonwealth, Harvard Club of Va. (pres. 1940-41). Author: Influenza, An Epidemiologic Study, 1921; Allergy and Applied Immunology, 1931; Practice of Allergy, 1930; Primer of Allergy, 1939; Strange Malady, 1941. Editor in chief Journal Laboratory and Clinical Medicine; asso. editor Jour. of Allergy; mem. editorial bd. Am. Jour. Digestive Diseases, Am. Journal Clin. Pathology; formerly mem. editorial bd. Review of Gastro-enterology, Am. Jour. Syphilis and collaborating editor Folia Clinica Chimica et Microscopica (Bologna, Italy). Contributor of over 150 articles to current med. lit.; also contbr. to Ency. Americana and Oxford Medicine. Office: 201 W. Franklin St., Richmond, Va. Died Apr. 2, 1944.

VAUGHN, FRANCIS ARTHUR, consulting engr.; b. Prairie du Chien, Wis., Dec. 6, 1871; s. Orion Squiers and Margaret (Howell) V.; B.S. in E.E., U. of Wis., 1895; m. Lucile K. Phillips, Jan. 11, 1897; children—Shirley Louise, Janice Margaret. With Milwaukee Electric Ry. & Light Co., 1896-1910; mem. Vaughn & Meyer, 1910-13 and 1916-21; pres. F. A. Vaughn, Inc., 1921-24. Firm consulting engr. State Bd. of Control of Wis., 1910-16, of Minn., 1916-20; consulting engr. City and Co. of Milwaukee on st. lighting, 1913 and 1921, 22; radio mgr., Radiocast Sta., WSOE, Milwaukee; vice-pres. Sch. Engring. and pres. Coll. Elec. Engring., Milwaukee. Lecturer U. of Pa., 1916. Fellow Am. Inst. E.E.; mem. numerous professional societies. Republican. Editor: Electrical Meterman's Handbook, 1912. Home: Milwaukee, Wis. Died Jan. 23, 1934.

VEASEY, CLARENCE ARCHIBALD, (vez'ê), ophthalmologist; b. Pocomoke City, Md., Aug. 9, 1869; s. Thomas Jefferson and Marietta (Richards) V.; student Western Md. Coll., Westminster, 1885-87, A.M., 1896; M.D., Jefferson Md. Coll., Phila., 1890; interne Jefferson Med. Coll. Hosp., 1890-91; student European hosps., 1891; m. Gertrude Mabel Clogg, June 20, 1894; children—Clarence, Archibald (M.D.), Winona Gertrude. In practice at Phila., 1890-08, at Spokane, Wash., 1908—. Clinical asst. Wills Eye Hosp., 1891-92; asst. demonstrator surgery, Jefferson Med. Coll., 1891-92; consulting ophthalmologist, Phila. Lying-in-Charity Hosp., 1892-1908; clin. asst. ophthal. dept. Jefferson Med. Coll. Hosp., 1892-94; chief clin. asst., and asst. ophthal. surgeon, 1894-1905, demonstrator diseases of the eye, 1897-1903, asst. prof. ophthalmology, 1905-08, Jefferson Med. Coll.; asst. ophthalmologist, Jefferson Med. Coll. Hosp., 1905-08; instr. operative ophthalmology, Phila. Polyclinic, 1894-95; adj. prof. diseases of the eye, Phila. Polyclinic, 1895-1900; ophthalmic surgeon M.E. Hosp., Phila., 1901-08. Retired. Member of American Ophthal. Society, Am. Acad. Ophthalmology and Oto-Laryngology, Pacific Coast Oto-Ophthalmol. Soc. (pres. 1916-17), Spokane Acad. Ophthal. and Otolaryn. (pres. 1943-44), Western Ophthalmol. Soc., Assn. for Research in Ophthalmology, A.M.A., Wash. State Med. Soc., Spokane County Med. Soc.; fellow Coll. Physicians of Phila., Am. Acad. Medicine, Am. Coll. of Surgeons; hon. mem. Alpha Kappa Kappa (Epsilon). Clubs: Spokane City University. Author: Ophthalmic Operations as Practiced on Animals' Eyes, 1896; A Manual of Diseases of the Eye, 1903; also many essays and monographs on affections of the eye. Home: 1118 W. 9th Av., Spokane 4, Wash. Died Aug. 11, 1957; buried Spokane.

VEATCH, ARTHUR CLIFFORD, geologist; b. Evansville, Ind., Oct. 26, 1878; s. Harry and Mary Kate (Babcock) V.; Ind. U., 1896-97, Cornell U., 1898 and 1900-01, U. of Wis., 1905; m. Caroline Hornbrook Evans, Apr. 16, 1902. Asst. geologist, La. Geol. Survey, 1898-1900; asst. in charge areal and stratigraphic geology, Cornell Sch. of Field Geology, 1900-01; petroleum geologist, Beaumont, Tex., 1901-02; prof. geology, La. State U., and geologist La. Geol. Survey, 1902; asst. in charge underground water investigations, La., Ark. and L.I., 1902-04; asst. geologist, 1904-06, geologist, 1906-10, U.S. Geol. Survey; chief geologist Gen. Asphalt Co., Trinidad and Venezuela, 1910-11; scientific adviser U.S. Dept. Justice, 1912, 1930-31; in charge oil exploration, fgn. dept., S. Pearson & Son, Ltd., London, 1913-19; cons. petroleum technologist, U.S. Bur. Mines, 1919—; in charge exploration dept. Sinclair Consol. Oil Corp., 1919-28; cons. petroleum geologist, 1928—. Investigated mining laws of Australia and New Zealand, as spl. commr., apptd. by President Roosevelt, 1907-08; organizer and chmn. oil, coal, mineral and water power bds., U.S. Geol. Survey, 1908-10. Mem. numerous professional societies. Republican. Presbyterian. Author: Quito to Bogota, 1917; Evolution of the Congo Basin, 1935. Home: Port Washington, L.I. Died Dec. 25, 1938.

VEBLEN, OSWALD, mathematician; b. Decorah, Ia., June 24, 1880; s. Andrew A. and Kirsti (Hougen) V.; A.B., U. Ia., 1898; A.B., Harvard, 1900; Ph.D., U. Chgo., 1903, D.Sc., 1941; hon. D.Sc., Oxford, 1929; hon. Ph.D., U. Oslo, 1929, Hamburg, 1933; LL.D., Glasgow U., 1951; m. Elizabeth M. D. Richardson, 1908. Asso. in math. U. Chgo., 1903-05; preceptor in math. Princeton, 1905-10, prof., 1910-32, prof. Inst. for Advanced Study, Princeton, 1932-50, prof. emeritus since 1950. Pres. Internat. Congress Mathematicians held at Harvard, 1950. Capt. and maj. Ordnace Dept., U.S. Army, 1917-19. Chmn. phys. scis. NRC, 1923-34; Fellow Am. Acad. Arts and Sciences, Am. Phys. Soc., A.A.A.S.; mem. Nat. Acad. Sciences, Am. Philos. Soc., Am. Math. Soc. (pres. 1923-24), Math. Assn. Am.; hon. mem. London Math. Soc., Circolo Mathematico di Palermo, Société Mathematique de France (hon. mem. bureau); fgn. corr., Academia Nacional de Ciencias Exactas, Lima, Peru; hon. fellow, Royal Soc., Edinburgh; mem. Royal Irish Acad. (Dept. Sci.); fgn. mem. Royal Danish Acad. of Sciences; Polish Acad. Scis. and Letters, Accademia dei Lincei; Knight, 1st Class, Royal Order of St. Olav (Norway). Army-Navy Certificate of Merit, 1948. Author: Infinitesimal Analysis (with N. J. Lennes), 1907; Projective Geometry (Vol. I, with J. W. Young), 1910, Vol. II, 1918, Cambridge Colloquium Lectures on Analysis-Situs, 1922; Invariants of Quadratic Differential Forms, 1927; Foundations of Differential Geometry (with J. H. C. Whitehead), 1932; Projektive Relativitätstheorie, 1933; Geometry of Complex Domains (with Wallace Givens), 1936. Home: 452 Herrontown Rd., Princeton, N.J. Died Aug. 10, 1960; cremated.

VEEDER, CURTIS HUSSEY, inventor, mfr.; b. Allegheny, Pa., Jan. 31, 1862; s. Herman and Hannah (Adair) V.; grad. Lehigh Univ., 1886, M.E. and Dr. Engring., 1839; m. Louise G. Stutz, Sept. 19, 1908; children—Josephine Adair (Mrs. Donald H. Andrews), Dorothy Irwin (Mrs. Charles E. Tilton). Draftsman Pope Manufacturing Co., bicycle mfrs., July-Oct. 1886; chief draftsman, mech. dept., Calumet & Hecla Mining Co., Calumet, Mich., 1886-89; draftsman and engr., Thomson-Houston Elec. Co., Lynn, Mass., 1889-93; draftsman, Hartford Cycle Co., 1894-95; pres. Veeder Manufacturing Co., Hartford, Conn., 1895-1928; dir. Veeder-Root, Inc., Automatic Signal Corp. Prin. inventions and patents: bicycle saddles, 1880, 82; cyclometer for bicycles, 1894; automatic casting machine and spl. alloys, 1896, 98; liquid tachometer, 1901. Mem. Am. Soc. Mech. Engrs., A.A.A.S., Am. Geog. Soc., Army Ordnance Assn., Franklin Inst., Am. Astron. Soc., Am. Forestry Assn., Soc. Automotive Engrs., Holland Soc. New York, Sigma Xi. Republican. Clubs: University, Hartford, Appalachian Mountain, Auto (Hartford); University (New York); Laurentides Fish and Game (Quebec). Home: 1 Elizabeth St., Hartford, Conn. Died Dec. 27, 1943.

VEEDER, MAJOR ALBERT, physician; b. Ashtabula, O., Nov. 10, 1848; s. Gerrit and Martha (Williams) V.; A.B., Union Coll., N.Y., 1870, later A.M.; M.D., U. of Buffalo, 1883; m. Mary E. Wood, Sept. 5, 1871. Prin. Ives Sem., Antwerp, N.Y., 1875-78; practiced medicine, Lyons, N.Y., 1883—. Fellow A.A.A.S.; mem. Internat. Conf. of Charities and Corrections. Published many papers on public water supply, garbage disposal, the relative importance of flies and water supply in spreading disease; made study of the relation of pack ice in the great lakes of N. America to the glacial period; made extended investigation of electro-magnetic phenomena of solar origin, especially with reference to the causation of the aurora, and the production of certain weather conditions. Home: Lyons, N.Y. Died Nov. 16, 1915.

VEITCH, FLETCHER PEARRE, (vech), chemist; b. Baltimore, Md., May 22, 1868; s. Fletcher Roberts and Caroline Virginia (Pearre) V.; B.S., Md. Agrl. Coll., 1891, D.Sc., 1914; M.S., George Washington U., 1899; m. Laura T. Boyle, May 12, 1896. Asst., Md. Agrl. Expt. Sta., 1891-92; chemist with W. S. Powell & Co., Baltimore, 1892-93; asst. chemist, Md. Agrl. Coll., 1894-99; asst. soil physicist, Md. Agrl. Expt. Sta., 1899-1901; with Dept. Agr., Washington, since 1901; asst. chemist, Bur. of Soils, 1901-02; same, Bur. of Chemistry, 1902-04; chief of Leather and Paper Lab., 1904-14; chemist in charge same, 1914-27; chemist in charge division industrial farm products, Bureau Chemistry and Soils, 1927-35; chief naval stores division Food and Drug Adminstrn. and naval stores research division Bureau Chemistry and Soils, 1935-38. Fellow A.A.A.S.; mem. Am. Chem. Soc., Am. Leather Chemists' Assn. (ex-pres.), Society Leather Trades Chemists, Am. Soc. Testing Materials (chmn. naval stores com.), Assn. Agrl. Chemists (pres. 1922). Democrat. Author of 275 bulletins and articles on soils, fertilizers, tanning materials, leathers, turpentine, wood products, paper and paper making materials. Mem. com. on leather of Nat. Research Council, 1917-18, div. research extension, 1919-24; chmn. com. on paper specifications to joint com. on printing, 1913-36; mem. paper tech. com. Federal Specifications Bd., 1923-36; v. chmn. div. leather and gelatine, Am. Chem. Soc., 1923. Home: College Park, Md. Died Oct. 14, 1943.

VEKSLER, VLADIMIR I., physicist; b. 1908. Inventor autophasing principle; developed proton synchrophasotron; dir. High Energy Lab., Dubna Joint Inst. Nuclear Research, 1955—. Recipient Stalin prize, 1953, Lenin prize, 1959; Atoms for Peace award, 1963. Mem. Soviet Acad. Scis. Address: Joint Inst. Nuclear Research, Head Post Office, Box 79, Moscow, USSR. Died Sept. 22, 1966. *

VENABLE, WILLIAM MAYO, engineer; b. Cincinnati, O., Feb. 14, 1871; s. William Henry and Mary Ann (Vater) V.; B.S., U. of Cincinnati, 1892, M.S. (electricity), 1893, C.E., 1909; m. Jessie Genevieve Tuckerman, Dec. 26, 1901; children—Henry, John Ellinwood, Emerson. Mgr. Nat. Contracting Co., sect. A, East Boston Tunnel, and portion of New Orleans drainage system, 1900-04; mgr. Municipal Engring. Co. and Sanitary Engring. Co. of New York, 1904-06; div. engr. Fla. East Coast R.R. building Long Key Viaduct, 1906-08; in charge of sewer work for Ferro-Concrete Constrn. Co., 1908-09; mgr. Blackstaff Engring. Co., Louisville, 1909-10; engr. Blaw-Knox Co., Pittsburgh, since 1912. Mem. Am. Soc. C.E., A.A.A.S., Optical Society Am.; American Astronomical Society; vice president American Rights League, 1916. Author: The Second Regiment of United States Volunteer Engineers, 1899; Interior Wiring, 1900; Garbage Crematories in America, 1906; Methods and Devices for the Bacterial Purification of Sewage, 1908; The Sub-Atoms, 1933; The Spectrum of Hydrogen, 1942; The Interpretation of Spectra, 1948; Hydrogen in Chemical Atoms, 1950. Also has written various engineering papers and contributions to knowledge of color and of the structure of hydrogen and of helium; pamphlets on spectra, 1951 and 1952. Home: 6111 Fifth Av., Pitts. 32. Died June 3, 1955; buried Spring Garden Cemetery, Cin.

VERHOEFF, FREDERICK HERMAN, ophthalmologist; b. Louisville, Ky., July 9, 1874; s. Herman and Mary Jane (Parker) V.; Ph.B., Yale, 1895; M.D., Johns Hopkins, 1899; LL.D., 1953; A.M., Harvard, 1902; study ophthalmology, in Europe, 1902-03; Margaret F. Lougee, Sept. 17, 1902; children—Mary Josephine (dec.), Margaret. Externe Johns Hopkins Hospital, 1899-1900; asst. surgeon Baltimore Eye, Ear and Throat Charity Hosp., 1899-1900; asst. in pathology, Harvard Med. Sch., 1900-02; asst. ophthalmic surgeon Carney Hosp., Boston, 1902-06; pathologist, Mass. Charitable Eye and Ear Infirmary, 1900-31, asst. ophthalmic surgeon, 1905-13, ophthalmic surgeon, 1913-32, chief of research, 1925-32, cons. chief of ophthalmology since 1932; instr. in ophthalmic pathology, Harvard Med. School, 1907-16, asst. prof. of ophthalmic research 1916-21, asst. prof. ophthalmology, 1921-24, prof. ophthalmic research, 1924-40, emeritus since 1940; scientific dir. Howe Lab. of Ophthalmology, 1931-32, dir. 1932-40. Maj. Med. Corps, U.S. Army, 1918-19. Fellow Am. Acad. Arts and Sciences, A.A.A.S., Am. Coll. Surgeons; mem. Am. Ophthal. Soc. (awarded Howe medal 1932; pres. 1937). A.M.A. (chmn. sect. on ophthalmology, 1932; awarded Knapp medal 1922, ophthalmic research medal, 1930). Awarded Leslie Dana Medal, 1947. Clubs: Harvard, Yale, Longwood Cricket, Algonquin, Eastern Yacht. Home: 61 Monmouth St., Brookline 16 MA Office: 395 Commonwealth Av., Boston 15 MA

VERMEULE, CORNELIUS CLARKSON, civil engr.; b. New Brunswick, N.J., Sept. 5, 1858; s. Adrian and Maria (Veghte) V.; B.Sc., Rutgers Coll., 1878, M.S., C.E., 1880; m. Carolyn Carpenter Reed, June 7, 1888; children—Cornelius Clarkson, Warren Carpenter. In charge topog. survey, State of N.J., 1878-88, and continued until 1918 as consulting engr. State Geol. Survey; in gen. practice at New York since 1888, as consulting or construction engr. for many cities and pvt. corps., in the Untied States and Cuba, also to Cuban government; organized York Cliffs (Me.) Improvement Co., 1892; obtained action by U.S. Govt., 1908, in rehabilitation of the sanitation of Cienfuegos, Cuba, at cost of $3,000,000, the work having been interrupted by political disturbances; engr. in charge of dismantling and reconstruction of Morris Canal for State of N.J. Mem. N.J. Hist. Society, N.J. Sanitary Assn., Am. Water Works Assn., Am. Soc. Civil Engrs., Holland Soc., New York Geneal. and Biographical Soc., New England Soc. of New York. Presbyterian. Has written various monographs upon topography, water supply, etc.; author of map of Manhattan Island as it existed in 1776, and of several hist. monographs. Home: E. Orange, N.J. Office: 38 Park Row, New York, N.Y. Died Feb. 1, 1950.

VERNER, SAMUEL PHILLIPS, explorer; b. in S.C., 1873; grad. Univ. of S.C.; hon. fellow, Yale. Was supt. Stillman Inst., Tuskaloosa, Ala.; took 3 expd'ns to Central Africa; as comm'r La. Purchase Exposition brought the first group of Pygmies for anthrop. exhibit; discovered new mountains, lakes and territory in the Southern Congo. Dir. Am. Congo Concessions which he persuaded the King of Belgium to grant; collected ethnol. specimens for Smithsonian Inst'n. and bot. specimens for Mo. Bot. Garden. Contb'r to mags. Author: Pioneering in Africa; The Cape to Cairo Railway; The Baluba Language; The Pygmies; etc. Address: Kasai River, Congo Free State, and 358 W. 57th St., New York NY

VERNON, CLARENCE CLARK, chemist, educator; b. Milo, Ia., Apr. 28, 1896; s. Marion T. and Martha Jane (Clark) V.; B.S., Ia. State at Ames, 1921, M.S., 1924, Ph.D., 1928; m. Anna Bernice Brooks, Sept. 20, 1922; 1 dau., Mary Bernice. Grad. asst., Ia. State Coll., 1921-22, instr., 1924-26, sr. instr., 1926-28; asst. prof. organic chemistry, Univ. of Louisville (Ky.), 1928-36, asso. prof. 1936-42, asso. prof. and acting head chemistry dept., 1942-46, prof. and head chemistry dept. since 1946. Served U.S. Navy, 1917-19; active duty U.S.S. Pa., 1918-19; civilian instr. in charge of chemistry, V-12 training program, U.S.N., Univ. of Louisville, 1942-45; served as regional mem. adv. com.

Am. Chem. Soc., War Prodn. Bd., 1942-45. Mem. Am. Chem. Soc. (local chmn. 1936, mem. exec. com., etc.; asst. in compiling nat. organic chemistry exams. since 1940); Ky. Acad. Sci. (chmn. chemistry sect., 1944-45), Phi Lambda Upsilon, Theta Chi Delta (grand regional vice pres.), Alpha Epsilon Delta (faculty adviser). Contbr. articles on organic chem. to nat. and fgn. chemistry jours. Home: 17 Avon Rd., Louisville, Ky. Died Sept. 20, 1948.

VERNON, SAMUEL, silversmith; b. Narragansett, R.I., Dec. 6, 1683; s. Daniel and Ann Hutchinson (Dyre) V.; m. Elizabeth Fleet, Apr. 10, 1707, 8 children including William. Silversmith in R.I., work represented in collections in Victoria and Albert Museum, London, Eng.; signed work with mark of heart containing initials in Roman capitals over a fleur-de-lis; engraved plates for 1st indented bills of credit of 1st bank established by Colony of R.I. and Providence Plantations, 1715; asst. in R.I. Gen. Ct., 1729-37; judge Superior Ct. of Judicature. Died Dec. 5, 1737.

VERRILL, ADDISON EMERY, zoölogist, geologist; b. Greenwood, Me., Feb. 9, 1839; s. George Washington and Lucy (Hilborn) V.; S.B., Harvard, 1862; hon. A.M., Yale, 1867; m. Flora L., d. Elliot Smith, of Norway, Me., June 15, 1865; children—George Elliot, Evalina Flora (dec.), Alpheus Hyatt, Edith Barton, Clarence Sidney (dec.), Lucy Lavinia. Asst. in Museum Comparative Zoölogy, 1860-64, prof. zoölogy, 1864-1907, emeritus prof. 1907, curator Zoöl. Mus., 1865-1920, instr. geology Sheffield Scientific School, 1870-94, Yale. Curator Boston Soc. Natural History, 1864-74; prof. comparative anatomy and entomology, U. of Wis., 1868-70; asso. editor Am. Jour. of Science, 1869-1920; asst. in charge of scientific explorations by the U.S. Fish Commn., 1871-87. Mem. Nat. Acad. Sciences; pres. Conn. Acad. Arts and Sciences; fellow Am. Acad. Arts and Sciences. Made valuable original investigations in relation to the invertebrata of the entire Atlantic and Pacific coasts of N. America, and especially of the deep-sea fauna, and on the marine faunae of Bermuda, W. Indies, Brazil, H.I. and Panama; wrote over 350 papers on zoöl. and geol. subjects. Contributed all the zoöl. matter to Webster's Internat. Dictionary, 1890, and Supplement, 1900. Author: Report upon the Invertebrate Animals of Vineyard Sound and Adjacent Waters, 1873; The Bermuda Islands, 1903; Zoölogy of the Bermuda Islands, Vol. I, 1903; Geology and Paleontology of the Bermudas, 1906; Coral Reefs of the Bermudas, 1907; Monograph of the Shallow Water Starfishes of the North Pacific Coast, 1914; Report on West Indian Starfishes, 1915; Reports on Alcyonaria and Actinaria of Canadian Arctic Expedition, 1921; Crustacea of Bermuda, 3 parts, 1923; Alcyonaria of the Blake Expedition, 1925. Died Dec. 10, 1926.

VER STEEG, KARL, (ver-steg'), geologist; b. Pella, Ia., Mar. 10, 1891; s. Nicholas and Marguerite (Van der Zyl) Ver S.; B.S., Central Coll., Pella, Ia., 1914; M.S., U. of Chicago, 1926; Ph.D., Columbia, 1930; Honorary D.Sc., Central College, Pella, Ia., 1946; m. Helena Martha Erdman, May 31, 1919. Began as instr. in science, Pella High Sch., 1914; served as principal, instr. in science, and as dir. of athletics in high schs.; instr. in geology and geography, U. of Ida., 1920-21; prof. geology and head of dept., Wis. Sch. of Mines, Platteville, Wis., 1921-23; prof. geology, Coll. of Wooster, 1923-26, prof. and head dept. since 1926, dir. civil pilot training program, 1940-41; special lecturer in meteorology and geography, Army pre-flight training program, Mich. School of Mines and Technology, Houghton, Michigan, summer, 1943; consulting geologist for various corporations and industries, consulting geologist for Texas Co., summer 1944. Served as director of athletics, Army Y.M.C.A., Camp Dodge, 1918. Mem. industrial water supply and conservation and flood control sub-coms., Ohio Chamber of Commerce ground water table com., 1940-41. Mem. National Affairs Committee of U.S. Chamber Commerce, of Western Ohio Bd. Trade, 1943-45. Fellow Geol. Soc. America, A.A.A.S., Ohio Acad. Sci. (past v.p.); mem. Ohio Athletic Conf. (v.p. 1945-47, pres. 1947-49), N.Y. Acad. Arts and Sciences; Seismological Soc. Am., Am. Assn. of U. Professors, Am. Soc. Professional Geographers, Nat. Aeronautic Assn., Ohio Forestry Assn., Sigma Xi. Republican. Presbyn. Mason. Author: (monograph) Wind Gaps and Water Gaps of the Northern Appalachians, Their Characteristics and Significance, 1930; co-author, Water Supplies of Ohio, Bulletin, 44, Ohio Geological Survey; also writer of publications on the buried topography of Ohio and parks of Ohio, jointing in the coal beds of Ohio, structural geology of Ohio, and contbr. scientific articles and reviews to jours. Home: 1105 Quinby Av., Wooster, O. Died Oct. 10, 1952; buried Pella, Ia.

VERY, FRANK WASHINGTON, astronomer; b. Salem, Mass., Feb. 12, 1852; s. Washington and Martha Needham (Leach) V.; S.B. (in chemistry), Mass. Inst. Tech., 1873; m. Portia Mary Vickers, Apr. 11, 1893; children—Alice Needham (Mrs. Edmund R. Brown), Marjorie Vickers, Arthur Oldfield, Eleonora Virginia, Ronald Winthrop. Instr., physical lab., Mass. Inst. Tech., 1877; astronomer at Allegheny (Pa.) Obs., 1878-95; adj. prof. astronomy and instr. in geology, Western U. of Pa., 1890-95; acting dir. Ladd Obs. and prof. astronomy, Brown U., 1896-97, completing, at own expense, research on Atmospheric Radiation, published as bull. "G" by U.S. Weather Bur., 1900; spl. agt. U.S. Weather Bur., 1900; dir. Westwood Astrophys. Obs., 1906—. For 10 yrs. Prof. Langley's prin. asst.; made many original investigations. Swedenborgian. Fellow A.A.A.S.; mem. Am. Astron. Soc.; hon. mem. Acad. Arts and Sciences, Utrecht, Holland. Frequent contbr. to leading scientific mags. and to publs. of the New Ch. Demonstrated that the solar constant exceeds 3.5 c.g. min.; proof of light absorption by a medium filling all space, and theory of origin of matter; proof that the white nebulae are galaxies; confirmation of author's previous announcement of existence of water vapor and oxygen in the atmosphere of Mars, showing amount of oxygen to be about half of that in the earth's atmosphere; also zonal distribution of water vapor on Mars, etc. Invented instrument for making accurate quantitative measurements of intensities of Fraunhofer lines in the solar spectrum. Home: Westwood, Mass. Died Nov. 24, 1927.

VESPUCCI, AMERIGO, navigator; b. Florence, Italy, Mar. 9, 1451; son of Nastogio Vespucci. Employed by comml. house of Medici, for a time; accompanied Alonso de Ojeda on expdn., 1499-1500, separated from Ojeda, and he alone discovered and explored mouth of Amazon River, then sailed along coast of No. South America; entered service of Portugal, 1501; made voyage on which he discovered mouth of Rio De La Plata, explored 6,000 miles of S.Am. coastline, 1501-02; on this trip calculated new method of determining longitude, also calculated earth's equatorial circumference (only 50 miles short of correct figure); also proved that S.Am. was separate continent, not part of Asia; name America (in his honor) was 1st applied to New World by Martin Waldseemüller in Cosmographiae introductio, 1507. Died of malaria, Seville, Spain, Feb. 22, 1512.

VEST, WALTER EDWARD, physician; b. Floyd County, Va., Jan. 20, 1882; s. William Madison and Mary Susan (Boone) V.; A.B., Coll. William and Mary, 1902, M.A. (honorary), 1958; M.D., Medical College of Virginia, 1909, D.Sc. (honorary), 1939; m. Saddie Pearl Blankinship, May 26, 1910; 1 son, Walter Edward. Interne, Memorial Hosp., Richmond, Va., 1909-10; gen. practice at Meherrin, Va., 1910-15, Huntington, since 1916; practice limited to diagnosis and treatment of med. conditions; consultant C.&O. Ry. Co., Chesapeake & Ohio Hosp., U.S. Veterans Hospital; attending physician St. Mary's and Cabell Huntington Hosps. Chief med. service, base hosp. Camp Wadsworth, S.C., 1918-19. Past pres. State Med. Licensing Bd. W.Va. Fellow A.M.A. (ex-mem. Ho. of Dels., Council Constitutions and Bylaws), American Coll. Physicians, Am. Coll. Chest Physicians; mem. Southern Med. Assn. (ex-chmn. council; chmn. sect. gastro-enterology 1935; pres. 1939), W.Va. State Med. Assn. (pres. 1930), Cabell Co. Med. Soc. (pres. 1936), W.Va. Hosp. Assn. (pres. 1932), Assn. of Surgeons of the C.&O. Ry. (pres. 1936), Am. Thoracic Society, W.Va. Tuberculosis Assn. (ex-pres.), Am. Therapeutic Soc. (pres. 1943), Am. Geriatrics Soc. (pres. 1946), Alumni Assn. Coll. of William and Mary (ex-pres.), Alumni Soc., Med. Coll. of Va. (pres. 1931), Fedn. Med. Licensing Bds. U.S. (past pres.), Alpha Omega Alpha, Phi Beta Kappa, Phi Beta Pi. Dem. Meth. Mason (Shriner). Kiwanian. Editor W.Va. Medical Jour. Contbr. to Ky. Medical Jour., Southern Med. Jour., Internat. Jour. Surgery, Social Science; Journal of A.M.A., Geriatrics. Home: 1115 9th Av. Office: First Huntington National Bank Bldg., Huntington, West Virginia. Died Jan. 28, 1962.

VESTINE, ERNEST HARRY, physicist; b. Mpls., May 9, 1906; s. Olaf Algot and Frida Christina (Lund) V.; B.S., U. Alberta, 1931; grad. study U. Toronto, 1933; Ph.D., Diploma Imperial Coll., Imperial Coll. Sci. and Tech., U. London, 1937; m. Lois Ann Reid, May 20, 1943; 1 son Henry Charles. Leader expdn. Internat. Polar Year, to Meanook, Can., 1932-33; staff mem., dept. terrestrial magnetism Carnegie Instn. of Washington, 1938-57; phys. scientist Rand Corp., Santa Monica, Cal., 1957-68; expert cons. Office Sec. of Def. to 1954, also to applied physics lab. John Hopkins. Chmn. internat. com. on world magnetic survey of International Union Geodesy and Geophysics; cons. Dept. Commerce, National Aeronautics Space Administration, 1959-68; professor meterology, U. California at Los Angeles director data coordination office. International Geophysical Year, National Acad. Scis., 1956; member Com. on Polar Research; member com. on aurora and airglow IGY; mem. committee on particles and fields Space Science Bd. Recipient John A. Fleming Gold Medal award, 1967. Member American Physical Society, Am. Geophysical Union, (chmn. com. Cosmic and Terrestrial Relationships, 1957, pres. sect. geomagnetism and aeronomy 1965-68), International Union Geodesy and Geophysics (secretary-general world magnetic survey bd.), Nat. (chmn. panel on world magnetic survey), Washington acads. scis. Author: Description of the Earth's Main Magnetic Field, 1947; Description and Analysis of the Geomagnetic Field, 1948; The Earth and its Atmosphere, 1957. Home: Pacific Palisades CA Died July 18, 1968.

VIALL, ETHAN, (vil), editor, cons. engr.; b. Kalamazoo, Mich., Aug. 17, 1873; s. Ethan and Mary Ophelia (Conklin) V.; high sch., tech. edn., Bloomington, and Chicago, Ill.; m. Evia Mae Sickles, Dec. 26, 1898 (dec.); children—Alda Sickles (dec.), Mrs. Eloise Brittingham, Mrs. Verda Isabelle Dell; m. Fern L. Parks, Jan. 28, 1939. Mech. apprenticeship, Chgo., 1893-98; foreman, supt. and mgr. various machine shops until 1908; began writing as corr. Am. Machinist, Machinery. Power, Am. Blacksmith; asso. editor Machinery, 1909-11; asso. editor, Am. Machinist, 1911-13, western editor, 1913-17, mng. editor, 1917-19, and editor-in-chief, 1919-21; gen. mgr. T. W. Minton & Co., 1921-22; special corr. Am. Machinist, and feature writer, 1922-26; editor Motor Service Magazine, Chicago, 1927-30, field editor since 1937. Is regarded as an authority on fine tool and die work, broaching and automatic machinery. Mem. Am. Soc. M.E., Am. Inst. Elec. Engrs., A.A.A.S., Franklin Inst. Soc. Automotive Engrs., Am. Soc. Testing Materials, Am. Steel Treaters Soc., Am. Assn. Business Paper Editors. Clubs: Engineers, Motor (Cincinnati); Commonwealth (New York). Republican. Mason (32 deg., K.T., Shriner), Odd Fellow, Woodmen of the World (thrice consul comdr., Cincinnati). Author: United States Artillery Ammunition, 1917; (with others) Manufacture of Artillery Ammunition, 1916; United States Rifles and Machine Guns, 1917; Broaches and Broaching, 1917; Welding and Cutting, 1920; Electric Welding, 1921; Gas-Torch and Thermit Welding, 1921; Grinders and Grinding, 1924; Mechanical Forging, 1924; also articles on Machine Tools, Thermit and Thermit Welding, Gas-Torch Welding, etc., for 12th and 13th edits. Ency. Britannica; also numerous tech. articles. Home: Knox, Ind. Died Dec. 15, 1949; buried Crown Hill Cemetery, Knox.

VICK, ROBERT ELLSWORTH, engr.; b. Caroleen, N.C., June 16, 1914; s. Robert Willard and Elizabeth (Brown) V.; B.S., N.C. State U., 1937; m. Catherine Lasater Rollins, Sept. 3, 1938; children—Mary Catherine (Mrs. Thomas Marvin Vick III), Barbara Lois (Mrs. George Larry Ketchum, Jr.), Robert Ellsworth, Jr. Jr. engring. draftsman N.C. Budget Bur., 1937-57; cons. engr. div. property control and constrn. N.C. Dept. Adminstrn., Raleigh, 1957-59, chief standards engr., engring. and standards sect. Div. Purchase and Contract, 1959-69. Served with USAAF, 1942-46. Registered profl. engr., N.C. Mem. Profl. Engrs. of N.C. (past pres.). Presbyn. Home: Raleigh NC Died Sept. 3, 1967.

VICTOR, ALEXANDER F., inventor, industrialist; b. Bollnäs, Sweden, June 20, 1878; s. Johan Alfred and Amelia Sofia (Klaar) Victor; educated in Sweden. Came to U.S., 1901, naturalized 1919. Pioneer exhibitor motion pictures, India and other oriental countries, 1895-96; invented electric washing machine, 1908; chairman of board Victor Animatograph Corp., Davenport, Ia., 1910—; president Alexander F. Victor Enterprises; introduced pioneer world standard for motion pictures; created safety standard 1918, permitting use of motion pictures in edn., industry, home, used effectively in training U.S. Armed Forces, World War II; pioneer inventor 16 millimeter cameras and projectors, 1923, continuous optical reduction printer permitting addition of sound, 1930; designing and mfg. spl. devices for U.S. and British govt. since 1939. Mem. Soc. Motion Picture Engrs., Am. Soc. Swedish Engrs., Swedish C. of C., French Legion of Honor, Edison Pioneers. Clubs: Players (N.Y.C.); Adventurers (Chgo.); Town, Country (Davenport, Ia.); Savage (London). Contbr. articles to tech. jours. Address: Box 266, Carmel-by-the-Sea, Cal. Died Mar. 29, 1961.

VIEHOEVER, ARNO, coll. prof.; b. Wiesbaden, Germany, Nov. 3, 1885; s. Joseph and Franciska (Maldaner) V.; Pharmaceutical Chemistry degree, University of Marburg, 1908, Food Chemistry degree, 1912; Ph.D., 1913; Pharmaceutical D. (honorary), 1938; m. Mabel E. Johnson, Nov. 21, 1915; children—Arnold Joseph, Ellen Margaret, Kent. Asst. and instructor, Bot. Pharmacognostical Inst., Marburg, 1909-13; pharmacognosist and chemist in charge Pharmacognosy Lab., Bur. of Chemistry, U.S. Dept. Agr., Washington, 1913-23; prof. in charge dept. biology and pharmacognosy, Phila. Coll. Pharmacy and Science, 1923-34, research prof. and dir. biol. and biochemical research laboratory 1934-38, also curator, dir. micros. labs. and expt. gardens; research director Hyper Humus Co., Newton, N.J., Lincoln Labs., Ill., Phenolphthalein Research Inst., N.Y.C.; scientific adviser to Ministry of Economic Affairs. Dept. of Science, Bangkok, Thailand, also prof. Chulalongkorn U., 1939-42; assistant Chief, U.S. Economic Mission to Siam, 1945-46; editor Bulletin Thailand Research Society, 1940-42; advisor to Office of Coordinator of Inter-Am. Affairs, Div. of Food Supplies to office Food Programs, Fgn. Econ. Adminstrn., 1942-45; chief, European Med. and Food investigations, O.T.S. Comm., 1946-48; chief research br., vet. div. Army Med. Dept. Research, 1948-50; chief pharmacol., biochem. and nutritional br., med. div. Office Sci. Information, CIA, 1950-57; mng. dir. Viehoever & Campbell, waste cons., 1965-68; owner Abbey Real Estate, 1963-69. Composer of songs and marches. Naturalized citizen of U.S., 1919. Recipient Ebert prize Am. Pharm. Assn., 1917; Local Outstanding Citizen award, 1964, Civic Congress Spl. Citation, 1966; meml. in Children's Hosp., Washington, 1969. Pres., Broad Creek Citizens Assn., 1920-23. Chmn., U.S.

Pharmcopoeia Com., Bur. Chemistry, 1914-23. First registered profl. engr. in biochem. engring., Md. Fellow A.A.A.S.; mem. American Chemical Society, American Pharmacy Association (chmn. sci. sect.), Philadelphia Academy of Science, Franklin Inst. Bot. Society, Brazil Society of Nutrition (hon.); French Soc. Chemical Industry (honorary), Thailand Pharm. Soc., Thailand Research Soc.; honorary member Kappa Psi; mem. Sigma Xi. Referee Daphnia Methods of Assn. of Agrl. Chemists. Rotarian. Author: (petry) Jublance, 1969. Contbr. numerous articles to profl. jours. Home: Oxon Hill MD Died Dec. 11, 1969.

VIELÉ, EGBERT LUDOVICKUS, soldier, engr., author; b. Waterford, N.Y., June 17, 1825; grad. West Point, 1847; served in Mexican war; also in Indian campaigns on Western frontier; resigned as lt., Oct. 26, 1850. Settled in practice in New York as civil engr.; State engr. of N.J., 1854-56; apptd. chief engr., 1856, of Central Park, New York, and prepared original plan which was adopted for the park; engr. Prospect Park, Brooklyn, 1860, but resigned on 1st call for vols., 1861, and comd. force that opened Potomac River to Washington; capt. engrs. 7th N.Y. regt.; commd. brig. gen. vols., Aug. 17, 1861. 2d in command of Port Royal expdn.; comd. at capture of Ft. Pulaski; planned and executed march on Norfolk, Va., mil. gov. Norfolk, May to Oct. 1863; resigned and resumed practice; engr. of many pub. works; commr. of parks, 1883, and pres. dept. parks, 1884; mem. Congress, 1885-87. Democrat. V.p. Am. Geog. Soc.; appeared before Com. of British House of Lords on subject of municipal administrn., 1896. Author: Handbook for Active Service; Topographical Atlas of City of New York; etc. Died 1902.

VIGNEC, ALFRED J., physician; b. N.Y. City, Apr. 4, 1905; s. Auguste and Marie (Eigeldinger) V.; B.S., N.Y.U., 1928; M.D., Yale, 1934; m. Wilhelmina Vissers, 1943 (deceased 1952); children—Alfred A., Ann L. (both adopted); married second, Elsie E. Essmuller, 1954; one son, Paul Alfred. Interne, L.I. Coll. Hosp., Brooklyn, 1934-35, resident, 1935-37; research fellow Yale, 1937-39; instr. pediatrics, L.I. Coll. of Medicine, 1939-41; med. dir., pediatrician-in-chief, N.Y. Foundling Hospital since 1944; dir. pediatrics St. Vincent's Hosp., N.Y. City, since 1947; instr. pediatrics Cornell Med. Sch., and asst. pediatrician, N.Y. Hosp., 1944-47; asso. pediatrician St. Clare's Hosp., N.Y. City, 1944-47; clin. prof. pediatrics N.Y.U.-Bellevue Med. Center; cons. pediatrician, N.Y. State Rehabilitation Hosp., West Haverstraw, N.Y., St. Joseph's Hosp., Yonkers, N.Y., St. Agnes Hosp., White Plains, N.Y., St. Clares Hosp., and Misercordia Hospital, New York City; associate pediatrician, University Hospital (Post-Grad.), N.Y.C.; medical dir. Kennedy Child Study Centre, N.Y.C. Mem. pediatric adv. com. Commr. of Health N.Y.C., premature adv. com. Dept. of Health, N.Y.C.; Medical Advisory Board for Dependent Children, N.Y. City Dept. of Welfare. Capt., M.C., U.S. Army, 1942-43. Decorated papal Knight Order of Holy Sepulchre. Fellow Am. Acad. of Pediatrics, A.M.A., N.Y. Acad. Medicine; mem. N.Y. Co. Med. Soc. (mem. milk commn., com. on infant mortality); honorary member of Sigma Xi. Roman Catholic. Clubs: Yale (N.Y.C.) Strathmore-Vanderbilt Country. Contributor articles on poliomyelitis infant nutrition to technical and profl. jours. Home: 119 Mill Spring Rd., Manhasset, N.Y. Office: 39-A, Gramercy Park, N.Y.C. 10. Died Feb. 4, 1962; buried Woodland Cemetery, S.I., N.Y.

VILBRANDT, FRANK CARL, (vil'brant), chem. engr.; b. Fostoria, O., Aug. 12, 1893; s. Ferdinand Albert and Henrietta (Papenfus) V.; A.B., Ohio State U., 1915, A.M., 1916, Ph.D., 1919, Chem.E., 1935; m. Magdalene J. Ohm, Sept. 7, 1916 (dec.); children—Charles Franklin, Ruth Eloise (dec.), Mariellyn Ohm, Janet Ann. Jr. chemist U.S. Bur. Standards, Washington, D.C., 1916-17; instr. industrial chemistry, Ohio State U., 1917-21; asso. prof. industrial chemistry, U. of N.C., 1921-27, prof., 1927-30; prof. chem. engring., Ia. State Coll., and chem. engr. Ia. Engring. Expt. Sta., 1930-35; prof. chem. engring. Virginia, Polytechnic Institute, Blacksburg, Va., 1935—; councilor Oak Ridge Institute of Nuclear Studies; chem. engr. Tallassee Power Co., Badin, N.C., 1923-26; chem. engr. Va. Engring. Expt. Sta. since 1935; consultant and plant manager, Division of War Research, 1944; consultant on cotton-mill, insulation-lumber, waste-gas, chemurgic and industrial waste problems; designer and supt. Butane Processing Plant, Good Hope, La., summers 1932-33; chief Bur. Fisheries, Exptl. Sta., Brunswick, Ga., 1928; profession expert, 3d Service Command; plant mgr., S.A.M. Labs., Manhattan Project, 1944. Mem. Adv. Council on Va. Econ., com. industry, 1950-53. Mem. Am. Institute Chemical Engineers, American Society Engring. Edn., Am. Chem. Soc. (chmn. Blue Ridge sect.), A.A.A.S., Va. Soc. Professional Engrs., Va. Acad. of Sci., Tau Beta Pi, Phi Beta Kappa, Alpha Chi Sigma, Sigma Xi, Phi Kappa Phi, Phi Lambda Upsilon, Omega Chi Epsilon, Golden Triangle. Lutheran. Author: Chemical Engineering Plant Design, 1934, 42, 49, 59. Contbr. to govt. bulletins and scientific jours. Died Jan. 5, 1960; buried Oak Harbor, O.

VINCENT, JESSE GURNEY, mech. engr.; b. Charleston, Ark., Feb. 10, 1880; s. Joseph M. and Nellie (Gurney) V.; ed. public schs. and I.C.S.; hon. M. Engring., U. Mich., 1929; m. Clarinda Blood, Oct. 2, 1902 (died 1943); m. 2d, Rachel M. Hawes. Machinist and toolmaker, St. Louis, 1898-1902; supt. inventions Burroughs Adding Machine Co., Detroit, 1903-10; chief engr. Hudson Motor Car Co., 1910-12; v.p. engring., Packard Motor Car Co. since 1912. Commd. maj. U.S. Signal Corps, 1917; lt. col., 1918; col. S.O.R.C., 1919. Built exptl. sta. at McCook Field, later in charge airplane engr. dept., Dayton, O.; apptd. chief Airplane Engring. Div., Bur. Aircraft Prodn., 1918, title of chief of engring.; mem. Joint Army and Navy Tech. Aircraft Bd., 1918; co-designer of Liberty Aircraft Engine. Dir. Am. Standards Assn. to rep. Auto Mfrs. Assn. Mem. Soc. Automotive Engrs., Am. Soc. M.E. Clubs: Detroit Athletic, Detroit Automobile, Detroit Country. Home: 415 Burns Dr., Detroit 14. Died Apr. 1962.

VINES, FRED DANIEL, elec. engr.; b. South Portland, Me., Dec. 8, 1902; s. Daniel Ambrose and Susan (Dyer) V.; B.S., Northeastern U., 1924; m. Bertha M. Gross, Nov. 9, 1951; children—Betty L. (by previous marriage), Richard W., William F. Student test engr. Gen. Electric Co., 1924-26; erection engr. Bucyrus-Erie Co., 1926-33, sales dept., 1933-48, central sales mgr., Chgo., 1948-50; asst. chief engr. M. A. Hanna Co., Cleve., 1950-53, chief engr., 1953—; v.p. Hanna Mining Co., Cleve. Home: 22114 Cottonwood Dr., Rocky River 16, O. Office: 1300 Leader Bldg., Cleve. 14. Died Apr. 3, 1965.

VINSON, ALBERT EARL, chemist; b. Dayton, O., Oct. 30, 1873; s. Samuel H. and Mary (Mull) V.; B.S., Ohio State U., 1901; Ph.D., Gottingen U., 1904; studied univs. of Chicago and Wis., also at Sorbonne, Paris, 1910; m. Louisa M. Albert, June 10, 1897 (dec.); m. 2d, Blanche Morrison, Apr. 20, 1940. Asst. in agrl. chemistry, Ohio State U., 1896-1901, instr., 1901-02; asso. chemist, Ariz. Expt. Sta., 1905-07, later chemist, also prof. agrl. chemistry, U. of Ariz., till 1924; chemist Service Technique du Departement de l'Agriculture, Port-au-Prince, Haiti, 1924-31. Fellow A.A.A.S.; mem. Western Soc. for Soil Management and Plant Nutrition (pres. 1923-24). Sigma Xi, Phi Kappa Phi. Methodist. Mason (32 deg.). Author of numerous bulletins on agrl. topics and articles in tech. mags.; has made extensive physiol. studies on ripening of the date; also studies on alkali soils and on the behavior of dry soils when wetted. Home: 811 E. Prince Rd., Tucson AZ

VINSONHALER, FRANK, (vin'sun-hä-ler), ophthalmologist; b. Graham, Mo., Apr. 14, 1864; s. George and Sarah (Rea) V.; Northwestern Normal Sch., Oregon, Mo., M.D., Coll. Physicians and Surgeons, Columbia, 1885; student extraordinary U. of Vienna, 1892; Royal Ophthalmic Hosp., London, England; LL.D., U. of Ark., 1929; m. Wrennetta Beidelman, Feb. 9, 1898; children—Marion Wilmer, Frances Rea, George. In practice at Little Rock since 1893; prof. ophthalmology, U. of Ark., since 1893, also dean Med. Sch.; retired. Commd. maj., Med. R.C., 1917; lt. col., 1919; comd. Base Hosp. 109, Vichy, France. Colonel U.S.R. Fellow Am. Coll. Surgeons; pres. Ark. Med. Soc., 1900-01. Awarded medal Columbia Univ., 1935. Mem. Phi Beta Kappa. Home: 500 E. 9th St., Little Rock, Ark. Died Sep. 1, 1942.

VINTON, FRANCIS LAURENS, army officer, engr.; b. Fort Preble, Me., June 1, 1835; s. John Rogers and Lucretia (Parker) V.; grad. U.S. Mil. Acad., 1856; attended Ecole des Mines, France, 1856-60. Instr. mech. drawing Cooper Union, N.Y.C., 1860; led expdn. to explore mineral resources of Honduras, 1861; commd. capt. 16th U.S. Inf., 1861, raised 43d N.Y. Volunteers, commd. col. 1861 served in various battles Va. peninsular campaign, 1862, commanded brigade in VI Corps, Army of the Potomac, 1862, wounded in Battle of Fredericksburg, 1862; commd brig. gen. U.S. Volunteers, 1863, resigned commn., 1863; prof. civil, mining engring. Sch. Mines, Columbia, 1864-77; cons. mining engr., Denver, Colo., 1877-79; Colo. corr. Engring. and Mining Jour. of N.Y. Died Leadville, Colo., Oct. 6, 1879.

VISHER, STEPHEN SARGENT, geographer; b. Chicago, Ill., Dec. 15, 1887; s. Rev. John and Julia (Sargent) V.; B.S., U. of Chicago, 1909, M.S., 1910, Ph.D., 1914; M.A. U. of S.D., 1912; fellow U. of Chicago and Yale; m. Martha Bolks, June 20, 1914 (deceased 1949); children—Ruth (Mrs. D. A. Smalley), John Edwin, Paul Sargent, Mary (Mrs. R. L. Mayer); m. 2d, Halene Hatcher, Mar. 21, 1951; 1 dau. Peggy Mildred. Instructor geology, Univ. of S.D., 1910-13; prof. geography, State Coll. Moorhead, Minn., 1915-18; land classifier U.S. Geol. Survey, 1918-19; prof. geography Ind. U. since 1919; prof. summers, U. Colo., 1925, Cornell U., 1926, 27, 30, U. of Pa., 1928, U. of Brit. Columbia, 1937, 40; research professor U. of Indiana, 1957-58; acting associate geographer, U.S. Dept. of State, 1931-32. Mem. U. of Chicago ecological expdn. to Alaska, 1907; sci. asst. Carnegie Instn., Desert Lab., Ariz., 1909; geographer and asst. state geologist S.D. Geol. Survey, 1909, 1910-14; scientist in soil survey, U.S. Bur. Soils; with U.S. Soil Conservation Service, summer, 1936; geographer Ind. Geol. Survey, 1919-46. Investigations in West Indies, 1915; in Spain, Italy, Britain, 1920; mem. Yale Indiana Expdn. South Seas, Australia, Far East, 1921-22. Awarded Distinguished Alumnus citation, U. Chicago, 1943; Distinguished Service to Geography award, Nat. Council Geography Teachers, 1948; Outstanding Achievement award Association of American Geographers, 1959. Honorary life member National Geographic Society, 1945. Fellow Geol. Soc. Am., A.A.A.S., Am. Meteorol. Soc., Royal Meteorol. Soc., Ind. Acad. Sci. (pres. 1950), Assn. Am. Geographers (vice pres. 1933), Geographic Assn. (British), Phi Beta Kappa, Sigma Xi. Author: Geography of South Dakota, 1918; Climatic Changes, Their Nature and Causes (with E. Huntington), 1922; Economic Geography of Indiana, 1923; Laws of Climate, 1924; Tropical Cyclones of the Pacific and Their Effects, 1925; Geographic Supplement to New Century Dictionary, 1927; Geography of American Notables, 1928; Climate of Kentucky, 1930; Economic Geography of Europe (with W. O. Blanchard), 1931; Our Natural Resources and Their Conservation (co-author), 1936, 39, 65; Aids to Students of Conservation, 1937; Principles of Economic Geography (with E. Huntington), 1940; Climate of Indiana, 1944; Introduction to Global Geography (with G. T. Renner and others), 1944; Scientists Starred 1903-43 in American Men of Science, 1947; Indiana Scientists, 1951; Climatic Atlas of the U.S., 1954, 66; also reports, articles. Co-author: Conservation of Natural Resources, 1950, rev. edit., 1965; Geography in the Twentieth Century, 1951; Regional Geography of the Midwest (with Garland and others), 1955. Home: Bloomington IN Died Oct. 25, 1967.

VISSCHER, J(OHN) PAUL, prof. biology; b. Holland, Mich., Sept. 19, 1895; s. Johannes W. and Everdena (Bolks) V.; A.B., Hope Coll., Holland, Mich., 1917; A.M., Johns Hopkins, 1920, Ph.D., 1924; m. Grace Yeomans, June 14, 1921; children—Marideen Julia, Paul Hummison. Instr. zoölogy, Washington U., St. Louis, 1920-22; spl. investigator, U.S. Bur. Fisheries, 1920-25; asst. prof. biology, Western Res. U., 1924-26, asso. prof., 1926-31, prof., 1931—, chmn. div. biology 1937-45; instr. Marine Biology Lab., Woods Hole, Mass., summer 1919-23. On leave absence as consultant, Chmn. Div., Naval Research Lab., Washington, 1945-46. Served as lt., Chem. Warfare Service, U.S. Army, 1917-18; spl. investigator, div. constrn. and repair, U.S. Navy, 1935-36. Bruce fellow, Johns Hopkins, 1918-19. Trustee Cleve. Mus. Natural History, Cleve. Bird Club. Fellow Ohio Acad. Sci. A.A.A.S.; mem. Zoölogy Soc. Am., Cleve. Regional Sci. Tchrs. Assn., Am. Soc. Naturalists, Ornithol. Union. Clubs: Wild Flower and Conservation (pres.), Professional Men's (past pres.) (Cleveland). Author: Nature and Extent of Fouling of Ships' Bottoms, 1928. Home: 2859 Scarborough Rd., Cleveland Heights, O. Office: 2080 Adelbert Rd., Cleve. Died Feb. 11, 1950; buried Pilgrim Home Cemetery, Holland, Mich.

VIVIAN, ALFRED, agricultural educator; b. Mineral Point, Wis., Mar. 14, 1867; s. John H. and Amelia (Stansmore) V.; Ph.G., U. of Wis., 1894; m. Frances H. Chandler, of Galena, Ill., Apr. 21, 1898. Instr. in pharmacy, 1894-95, asst. in agrl. chemistry, 1895-97, U. of Wis.; instr. in agrl. chemistry and asst. chemist, U. of Wis. Expt. Sta., 1897-1902; asso. prof. agrl. chemistry, 1902-05, prof. since 1905, dean Coll. of Agr. since 1915, Ohio State U. Pres. Ohio State Bd. of Edn., 1917-21. Author: First Principles of Soil Fertility; Everyday Chemistry. Mem. A.A.A.S., Am. Soc. Agronomy, Sigma Xi, Rotary Club, etc. Episcopalian. Home: 1778 N. High St., Columbus, O.

VIZCAINO, SEBASTIAN, mcht., explorer; b. Huelva, Spain, circa 1550; s. Antonio Vizcaino; married before 1589, 1 child. Went to Mexico, 1585; interested in China trade; organizer, condr. of company for exploration of Gulf of Cal., 1593; sailed from Acapulco with 3 ships, 230 men, 1596; explored outer coast of Cal. as far as Cape Mendocino, 1602, hoped to find supposed Strait of Anian, discovered Monterey Bay, made maps of coast (1st scientific exploration of West Coast, did much to disprove myth of the Northwest passage) 1602; recommended establishing port at Monterey, pleaded case before Council of Indies, in Spain, received royal decree, establishing port under his command, 1607, plan later abandoned; in command of expdn. to discover islands Rica de Oro and Rica de Plata, 1611, established nonexistence of the islands, made unsuccessful attempt to promote relations with Japan, returned to Mexico, 1614; enlisted a force in New Spanish provence of Avalos to defend coast against Dutch attack, 1615. Died Madrid, Spain, 1628.

VOGELBACK, WILLIAM EDWARD, cons. engr., business exec.; b. N.Y. City, June 9, 1893; s. Louis and Antonia (Hanosey) V.; ed. civil and elec. engring. various tech. schs., N.Y.; M.B.A., U. Chicago; m. Parthenia Carmichael, concert pianiste, Dec. 25, 1920. Mem. engring. staff Sanderson & Porter, 1914-17, asst. Chgo. mgr., 1920-24; ind. cons. engr. 1924—; pres. So. States Power Co., 1926, Standard Tel. Co., 1927-28, Boise (Ida) Water Co., 1927-28, Am. Engring. & Management Corp., 1927-42, Am. States Pub. Service Co. (also pres. or chmn. of its 34 subsidiaries and affiliates), 1928-33, and several other corps.; pres. and chmn. bd. Union Gas & Electric Co., 1944—. Mem. U. of Ill. Citizens Com.; mem. governing bd., trustee Library of Internat. Relations. Cons. engineer, aircraft, W.P.B., Washington, 1942; central field commissioner, Pacific and China, Dept. of State, 1946. Served with 1st Ill. Cav., Mex. Border, 1916; attended Plattsburg (Arty.), 1917, Sch. Mil. Aeronautics (O.S.U.); commd.

in Signal Corps (Aviation), 1918. Mem. bd. assos. Northwestern U.; citizens bd. U. Chgo.; mem. bd. Salvation Army, Chgo. Mem. Am. Inst. E.E., Soc. Am. Mil. Engrs., Ill. and Nat. socs. profl engrs, Beta Gamma Sigma. Profl. engr., N.Y., Ill. Clubs: Racquet, Chicago, Tavern, Chicago Golf; Metropolitan (N.Y.C.). Author: Magnets Light, in Library and Sci. Series, 1933 (editor). Designed and pub. Series Pictorial Maps of various countries; also Panorama Western Theatre of War in Europe, 1940. Home: 232 E. Walton Pl. Office: 230 N. Michigan Av., Chgo. Died Apr. 17, 1960.

VOGT, WILLIAM, ecologist; born Mineola, N.Y., May 15, 1902; s. William and Frances Bell, (Doughty) V.; A.B., St. Stephens (now Bard) Coll., New York, 1925; Sc.D., Bard College, 1953; m. Johanna von Goeckingk, Dec. 26, 1959. Assistant editor N.Y. Acad. Sciences, 1930-32; curator Jones Beach State Bird Sanctuary, 1932-35; editor Bird-Lore Magazine, and field naturalist and lecturer for Nat. Assn. Audubon Socs., 1935-39; cons. ornithologist, Compania Administradora del Guano, Lima, Peru, 1939-42; studied in Chile on fellowship of Com. for Inter-American Artistic and Cultural Relations, 1942; expert consultant, War Dept., 1942; asso. director, Div. of Science and Education. Office Coordinator Inter-Am. Affairs, 1942-43; chief Conservation Sect., Pan.-American Union, 1943-49; national director Planned Parenthood Federation of America, 1951-61; sec. Conservation Foundation, N.Y.C., 1964-68; del. to the International Planned Parenthood Conf., Bombay, India, 1952, Stockholm, 1953, Tokyo, 1955; Delhi, 1959. Recipient field research prize Linnaean Soc. N.Y., 1938, Mary Soper Pope medal, 1949. Lasker Foundation award 1951. Member A.A.A.S. American Ornithologists Union, N.Y. Zoological Soc. (Fellow), Am. Pub. Health Assn., Linnaean Society of New York (former pres. and sec.), Ecological Soc. Am., Soc. Gen. Semantics, Am. Geog. Society, Sociedad Geografica de Lima, Sociedad Mexicana de Historia Natural also Population Association U.S. Clubs: Century Assn.; Cosmos (Washington). Author: Audubon's Birds of America, 1937; El Hombre y la Tierra, 1944; Road to Survival, 1948; People! 1960. Contbr. articles and scientific papers to natural history and general mags. Home: New York City NY Died July 12, 1968; cremated.

VOLLMER, JOHN PHILLIP, capitalist; b. Birkenfeld, Würtemberg, Germany, Jan. 25, 1847; s. Otto Phillip and Elizabeth (Fix) V.; removed to Ind. in boyhood; ed. Northwestern Christian (now Butler) U. and Prof. Richter's Sch. of Tech., Indianapolis; m. Sallie Elizabeth Barber, Sept. 27, 1870. Engaged in banking, merchandising, milling, mfg., farming (owning about 300 farms), etc.; mem. firms of John P. Vollmer & Co., E. Baumeister & Co., Vollmer & Scott. Pres. First Nat. Bank, Lewiston, Ida., First Nat. Bank, Genesee, Ida., Vollmer-Clearwater Co., First Bank, Asotin, Wash., Sweetwater Ditch Co., Lewiston Milling Co., Bank & Trust Co., Vollmar, Ida.; propr. Asotin (Wash.) Flouring Mills Co.; First Nat. Bank, Grangeville, Ida.; interested in Cash Hardware Co., Lewiston, Scott Mercantile Co., Vollmer, Ida.; pres. Kendrick Warehouse & Milling Co.; v.p., dir. Nez Perce & Eastern R.R. Co. of Ida. Built first telegraph line in northern Ida., 1876; built and operated first practical Bell Telephone line on Pacific Coast, 1878. Republican. Mem. of Telephone Pioneers of America. Assisted Mark Twain by furnishing materials for "Innocents Abroad," "Life on the Mississippi," and "Captain Stormfield," while en route with him from New York to San Francisco via the Isthmus of Panama, in March and April 1868. Home: Lewiston, Ida. Died May 7, 1917.

VON BEKESY, GEORG, physicist; b. Budapest, Hungary, June 3, 1899; s. Alexander and Paula (Mazaly) von B.; student U. Berne, 1916-20; Ph.D., U. Budapest, 1923; M.D. (hon.), Wilhelm U., Munster, Germany, 1955; M.D. (hon.), Univ. Berne, Switzerland, 1959; M.D. (hon.) U. Padua, Italy, 1962; D.Sc., Gustavus Adolphus Coll., 1963; D.Sc., U. Pa., 1965, Nat. U. Cordoba, 1968, U. Buenos Aires, 1968, U. Hawaii, 1969. With research lab. Hungarian Tel. System, 1923-46, Central Lab., Siemens & Halske A.G., Berlin, Germany, 1926-27; privatdozent U. Budapest, 1932-39, ausserordentlicher prof., 1939-40, ordentlicher prof., 1940-46; Karolinski Inst., Stockholm, Sweden, 1946-47; research lectr. Psycho-Acoustic Lab., Harvard, 1947-49, sr. research fellow psycho-physics, 1949-66; prof. of sensory sci. U. of Hawaii, 1966-72. Recipient Denker prize in otology, 1931, Guyot Prize for speech and otology, Groningen U., 1939, Leibnitz Medal, Akademic der Wissenchaften, Berlin, 1937, Acad. Award, Academy of Sci., Budapest, 1946, Shambaugh prize in otology, 1950, Howard Crosby Warren medal, Soc. Exptl. Psychologists, 1955, gold medal Am. Otol. Soc., 1957; achievement award Deafness Research Found., 1961; Nobel prize for medicine for research on how the human ear hears, 1961. Fellow of the Acoustical Society of America; mem. American Acad. Arts and Scis.; hon. mem. Am. Otol. Soc., Nat. Acad. Scis., several fgn. sci. socs. Contbr. sci. publs. Address: Honolulu HI Died June 13, 1972.

VON EGLOFFSTEIN, FREDERICK W., army officer; b. Aldorf, Bavaria, May 18, 1824. Served in army; came to U.S. (N.Y.), engaged engraver Samuel Sartain to work with him on new engraving process involving photography and glass screens covered with an opaque varnish; served as col. N.Y. Volunteers during Civil War; wounded in N.C., ret. as brig. gen. Died N.Y.C., 1885.

VON ENDE, CARL LEOPOLD, chemist; b. Burlington, Ia., July 2, 1870; s. Charles Ende (b. Carl Conrad von Ende) and Thusnelda (Leopold) E.; B.S. State U. of Ia., 1893, M.S., 1894; Ph.D., U. of Göttingen, Germany, 1899; m. Alice Ankeney, July 28, 1904; children—Eunice Ankeney, Carl Ankeney. Demonstrator in chemistry, State U. of Ia., 1894-95; science teacher, high sch., Burlington, Ia., 1895-96; instr. in chemistry, 1896-97, 1899-1905, asst. prof., 1905-07, State U. of Ia.; research asso., Research Lab. Physical Chemistry, Mass. Inst. Tech., 1907-08; prof. chemistry and head of dept., U. of Ida., 1908—; sabbatical leave at Univ. Coll. of Wales, Aberystwyth, 1928. Fellow A.A.A.S. Democrat. Translator: Dolezalek's Theory of the Lead Accumulator, 1904; Abegg's Electrolytic Dissociation Theory, 1907. Contbr. articles describing results of researches in physical and inorganic chemistry. Home: Moscow, Ida. Died Oct. 9, 1934.

VON KARMAN, THEODORE, aeronautical engr.; b. Budapest, Hungary, May 11, 1881; s. Prof. Maurice and Helen (Konn) de Kármán; M.E., Royal Tech. U., Budapest, 1902; Ph.D., U. of Göttingen, Germany, 1908; hon. D.Eng., Tech., U. Berlin, 1929, U. Liege, Belgium, 1947, Princeton, 1947, Columbia, 1948, Yale, 1951, Hebrew Inst. Tech., Israel, 1952, Technische Hochschule, Aachen, 1953; D.Sc., Univ. Brussels, 1937, U. d'Aix, Marseille, 1948, U. Lille, 1953, U. Istanbul, 1953; Dr. Applied Scis., Technische U., Berlin, 1953; LL.D., U. Cal., 1942; Dokfor Honoris Causa, Istanbul Tech. U., 1955, U. Sevilla, Spain, 1958, U. Braunschweig, 1960, Politecnico d. Torino, 1960, U. Athens, 1961; D.Sc., Northwestern, 1956, U. So. Cal., 1958, New York University, 1960, Brown University, 1960. Came to U. S., 1930, naturalized citizen, 1936. Research engr. Ganz & Co., Germany, 1902; assistant prof. Royal Tech. U., Budapest, 1903-06; privat docent, U. Göttingen, 1909-12; dir. Aero. Inst., U. of Aachen, 1912-29; cons. Junkers Airplane Works, also Luftschiffbau Zepplin, Germany, 1924-28; research asso. Cal. Inst. Tech., 1928-30, dir. Guggenheim Aero. Labs., 1930-49, dir. jet. propulsion lab., 1942-45; founder, chief cons., Aerojet Engring. Corp., now Aerojet-General Corp., 1942—; chmn. adv. group for Aero. Research and Development NATO. 1951—; chmn. scientific advisory board to chief of staff USAF, 1944-55; cons. numerous cos. and govtl. agencies on aero. items, 1930—; has held named lectureships in several univs. and confs. Wright Brothers lectr. Inst. Aeronautical Sciences, 1946. Awarded Am. Soc. of Mechanical Engineers medal, 1941; Sylvanus Reed award of Inst. Aeronautical Sciences, 1942; Medal for Merit, 1946; John Fritz Medal, 1948; Kelvin Gold Medal, 1950; officer Legion of Honor, 1947; also among others, Astronautics Award, Am. Rocket Soc., 1954. Wright Bros. Memorial Trophy, 1954, Daniel Guggenheim medal, 1955, Vincent Bendix award, 1957, Timoshenko medal, 1958; Lamme award, 1960; Robert H. Goddard Meml. award, 1960; Karl Friederich Gauss medal, 1960; Christopher Columbus gold medal, Genova, Italy, 1960. Hon. fellow Inst. Aeronautical Sciences, Royal Aeronaut. Soc.; fellow Am. Rocket Soc., Am. Acad. Arts and Scis., Am. Physical Soc.; mem. Nat. Acad. Scis. (Rome), Royal Soc. London, Academy of Sciences (Paris, France), 1946, Academy of Sciences (Torino, Italy), American Society M.E., Nat. Acad. Science, American Philos. Society, Academmia dei Lincei, Spanish Academy Sciences, A.A.A.S., Am. Soc. Civil Engrs., Franklin Inst., Am. Geophysical Society, Sigma Xi. Nominated by Pope Pius XII, Pontifical Acad. Sciences. Editor of books on aerodynamics in German lang. Author: (with J. M. Burgers) General Aero-dynamic Theory (2 vols), 1924; (with M. A. Biot) Mathematical Methods in Engineering (with M. A. Biot), 1940; Aerodynamics, 1954. Contbr. scientific articles to jours. Developed 1st theory of supersonic drag (called Kármán Vortex Trail), 1935; pioneer in devel. high speed aircraft and missiles; initiated research that developed 1st plane to break sound barrier; designed supersonic wind tunnels; research in math. analysis thermodynamics, aerodynamics, hydrodynamics. Died Aachen, Germany, May 6, 1963.

VON LAUE, MAX, educator, physicist; b. Pfaffendorf bei Koblenz, Germany, Oct. 9, 1879; student Protestant Gymnasium, Strassburg, 1893-98, Univs. Strassburg, Göttingen, Munich, 1898-1903; Dr. deg., U. Berlin, 1903; m. Magdalene Degen. Oct. 6, 1910; children—Theodor Hermann, Hildegard Minna (Mrs. Kurt Lemcke). Privat dozent U. Berlin, 1906-09, U. Munich, 1909-12; extraordinary prof. U. Zurich, 1912-14; prof. U. Frankfurt am Main, 1914, U. Berlin, 1919-43; acting dir. Kaiser-Wilhelm-Inst. Physics, 1921—, Max-Planck-Inst. Physics, 1943-51; dir. Fritz-Haber-Inst. of the Max-Planck-Gesellschaft, Berlin-Dahlem, 1951-59, emeritierter director (director emeritus), 1959—. Recipient Nobel prize in physics for discovery X-ray interferences, 1914; Planck-Medaille, 1932. Orden Pour le mérite für Künste and Wissenscaft, 1952; Grosses Verdienstkreuz mit stern der Bundesrepublik, 1953; Offizierskreuz der Ehrenlegion der französischen Republik, 1957. Mem. academies of science; New York, Vienna, Washington, Rome and numerous others. Author: Relativitätstheorie. I, 1911, 11 1921; Rögenstrathinterferenzen, 1941; Materiewellen und ihre Interferezen, 1943; Geschichte der Physik, 1947; Theorie der Supraleitung, 1947. Home: Berlin-Dahlem, Faradayweg 8. Office: Berlin-Dahlem, Faradayweg 4-6, West-Berlin, Germany. Died Apr. 24, 1960; buried Stadtfriedhof in Göttingen.

VON MISES, RICHARD, (me'zes), scientist; b. Austria, April 19, 1883; son Arthur Edler and Adele (Landau) von M.; Dr. tech., Tech. Univ. of Vienna, 1907; Dr. honoris causa, U. Brussels, 1935, Tech. U. Vienna, 1951, U. Istanbul, Turkey, 1952; M.A. honoris causa, Harvard Univ., 1945. Lecturer on mechanics, Tech. Univ. of Brno, 1908-09; asso. prof. of applied mathematics, Univ. of Strasbourg, 1909-18, Univ. of Frankfurt, 1918-19; prof. of strength of materials, Tech. Univ. of Dresden, 1919-20; prof., dir. of inst. of applied mathematics, Univ. of Berlin, 1920-33; prof. mathematics, U. Istanbul (Turkey), 1933-39; prof. of applied mathematics, Harvard Univ. since 1939, Gordon McKay prof. of aerodynamics and applied mathematics, 1944-53; founder and editor Zeitschrift für Angewandte Mathematik und Mechanik, 1920-33; editor Differential und Integralgleichungen der Mechanik und Physik (with Philipp Frank), 1925-30. Served with Austro-Hungarian Air Force, 1914-18; built 600 horsepower plane of the Austrain Army, 1915. Fellow Am. Acad. of Arts and Sciences, Inst. of the Aeronautical Scis., Inst. Math. Statistics, and numerous other hon. socs. Author: Elemente der technischen Hydromechanik, 1914; Fluglehre, 1918; Wahrscheinlichkeit, Statistik und Wahrheit, 1928; Wahrscheinlichkeits-Rechnung und ihre Anwendungen, 1931; Kleines Lehrbuch des Positivismus, 1939; Theory of Flight, 1945; also numerous scientific papers, 1905-53. Editor: (bibliography) Rilke in English, 1946; 3 collections of writings in Rainer Maria Rilke (pvtly. printed); Advances in Applied Mechanics, Vols. I-III. Home: 10 Chauncy St., Cambridge 38, Mass. Died July 14, 1953.

VON NEUMANN, JOHN, mathematician; b. Budapest, Hungary, Dec. 28, 1903; s. Max and Margaret (Kann) V.; student Berlin U., 1921-23, Zurich Inst., 1923-25; Ph.D., Budapest, 1926; D.Sc. Princeton, 1947, U. Pa., Harvard, 1950, Case Inst. Tech., U. Istanbul, 1952, U. Md., 1952, Munich Inst. Polytechnics, 1953, Columbia U., 1954; m. Mariette Kovesi, Jan. 1, 1930; 1 dau., Marina; m. 2d, Klara Dan, Dec. 18, 1938. Privatdozent mathematics, Berlin U., 1927; visiting prof. mathematical physics, Princeton U., 1930, prof., 1931-33, prof. Institute for Advanced Study, 1933. Mem. and consultant various Army, Navy, O.S.R.D., AEC, Committees, 1940—; appointed to membership AEC, October, 1954. Received Medal for Merit and Distinguished Civilian Service award, 1947; Medal of Freedom, 1956, Albert Einstein award, 1956, Enrico Fermi award, 1956. Fellow Am. Physical Society; mem. Am. Math. Soc. (pres. 1951-53), American Mathematical Association, National Academy of Scis., Am. Philos. Soc., Am. Acad. Arts and Scis.; corr. mem. Royal Dutch Acad. Scis. (The Hague), Istituto Lombardo (Milan, Italy); associate mem. Academia Nacional de Ciencias Exactas, Lima, Peru. Mem. Sigma Xi. Author: Mathematical Foundation of Quantum Mechanics, 1931; (with O. Morgenstern) The Theory of Games and Economic Behavior, 1944. Contbr. articles on math. subjects. Editor Annals of Mathematics (Princeton). Co-editor Compositio Mathematica (Amsterdam, Holland). Developed game theory, 1928; showed how game theory could be applied to social scis., esp. econs.; showed math. equivalence of Schrödinger's wave mechanics and Heisenberg's matrix mechanics, 1944; contbn. to operator and set theories, math. logic and theory continuous groups, periodic functions, ergodic theorem, computer theory and design. Died Washington, Feb. 8, 1957.

VON PAGENHARDT, MAXIMILIAN HUGO, (fon-pä'gen-härt), cons. engr.; b. Stuttgart, Germany, June 20, 1884; s. Baron Robert and Princess Alexandria (zu Ysenburg-Budingen-Waechtersbach) von P.; B.A., Royal Sch. of Cadets, Berlin, 1904; grad. as lt., Student Sch. of Ensigns, Potsdam, 1905; lt. inf., 120th Regt., "Kaiser Wilhelm II," Ulm; naval architect, Royal Polytechnicum, Charlottenburg, 1910; m. Marie Dupuy Adams, May 25, 1918; 1 son, Maximilian F. Robert. Came to U.S., 1910, naturalized, 1932. Naval architect for Miss. Valley Transportation Co., St. Louis, 1910-11, for Kansas City-Mo. River Transportation Co., 1912-17; naval architect and cons. engr., St. Louis, 1917-23, designing fleet for U.S. Dept. of War for Miss. River, for Magdalena River (Colombia, S.America), for Standard Oil Co., for Panuco River (Mexico), for Cities Service Co., etc.; founder, 1924, and now pres. of M. H. Pagenhardt & Co., engrs., designers and constructors of power plants, Washington, D.C.; registered professional engr. Commonwealth of Pa. Mem. Am. Soc. Mech. Engrs. Evang. Luthern. Contbr. tech. articles on marine engring. to tech. jours. Home: 2415 Foxhall Rd., Washington, D.C. Died Oct. 25, 1943.

VON PHUL, WILLIAM, (von-pool), consulting engr.; b. New Orleans, La., July 20, 1871; s. William and Mary McDougall (Williams) P.; B.S., Tulane U., 1891, M.E., 1893, Dr.Engring., 1931; Marie Alzire Cade, Nov. 19, 1895; children—William, Mrs. A. A. Uebelacker, Mrs. W. T. Smith, Mrs. R. M. Ollinger, Mrs. Charles G. Ollinger, Jr. Engr. with Edison Electric Co., New Orleans, La., until 1902; with Sargent & Lundy, Chicago, Ill., 1902, and was in charge of construction of works, later of operation, Cincinnati Gas and Electric Co.; joined staff of Ford, Bacon & Davis, New York, 1905, in operation of pub. utilities in New Orleans, Memphis, Nashville, Birmingham, Little Rock and Houston; mem. same firm, 1912-45; with his partners designed and built the cotton warehouses for Bd. of Commrs. of Port of New Orleans; v.p. Am. Cities Co., 1911-13; v.p., gen. mgr. United Railroads of San Francisco, 1916, pres., 1919; pres., gen. mgr. Market St. Ry. Co., San Francisco, 1919-22; dir. United Rys. Inv. Co., Calif. Ry. & Power Co.; pres. and dir. Ford, Bacon & Davis, Inc., engrs., New York, 1922-42, chmn. exec. com. and dir. 1942-43; formerly dir. Ford, Bacon & Davis Construction Corp., Interstate Natural Gas. Co., Inc., Easy Washing Machine Corp., L.C. Smith & Corona Typewriter, Inc., Lackawanna & Wyo. Val. R.R. Co., Lackawanna & Wyoming Valley Power Co., Laurel Line Transportation Co. Fellow A.A.A.S.; mem. Am. Soc. Municipal Engrs., Am. Soc. C.E., Am. Soc. M.E., La. Engring. Soc., Am. Acad. Polit. and Social Science, S.A.R., Sons of the Revolution, Kappa Alpha. Republican. Catholic. Clubs: Boston (New Orleans); City Midday (New York), 82 Willows Av., Larchmont, N.Y. Died Apr. 17, 1949.

VON RUCK, KARL, physician; b. Stuttgart, Germany, July 10, 1849; s. George and Clara von R.; B.S., Stuttgart, 1867; M.D., U. of Tübingen, 1877; M.D., U. of Mich., 1879; studied U. of Berlin, 1882; m. Delia Moore, Dec. 25, 1872. Founder, and med. dir. Winyah Sanatorium, Asheville, N.C., 1888-1910; cons. phys., 1910—; founder Von Ruck Research Lab. for Tuberculosis, Asheville, 1895, and in charge, 1895—(this laboratory for original investigations only). Discoverer of vaccine for the prevention and cure of tuberculosis. Contbr. to Am. and European jours. and revs. on subject of tuberculosis. Author: Studies in Prophylactic and Therapeutic Immunization against Tuberculosis (with his son), 1916. Home: Asheville, N.C. Died Nov. 6, 1922.

VON SCHON, HANS AUGUST EVALD CONRAD, civil engr.; b. in Prussia, June 25, 1851; s. Alexander and Lousie (Wilde) von S.; grad. Royal Prussian Acad., Berlin, Germany, 1869; m. Ida Jennings, of Morrow, Ohio, June 22, 1887. Came to America, 1872; in gen. civ. engring., until 1891; with U.S. Engr. Corps, 1891-97; chief engr. Lake Superior Power Co., Sault Ste. Marie, Mich., 1897-1902; consulting practice, Hydro-Electric Engring., 1902—. Managing editor and owner The Water Chronicle (monthly publ.), Detroit. Served in Prussian Army, 1869-71; in Franco-Prussian War, 1870-71, as 2d lt., 3d Rhenish Inf., 29th Regt.; decorated with Iron Cross. Progressive. Lutheran. Mem. Am. Soc. C.E., 1902, Western Soc. Engrs., Mich. Engring. Soc., etc. Author: Hydro-Electric Practice, 1908. Home: 50 Tuxedo Av. Office: Wayne Co. Bank Bldg., Detroit.

VON SCHRENK, HERMANN, (von-shrenk), timber engr.; b. College Point, L.I., N.Y., March 12, 1873; s. Prof. Joseph and Anna (Bandtke) V.; B.S., Cornell, 1893; A.M., Harvard, 1894; Ph.D., Washington U., 1898; m. Mary Jane Kimball, Feb. 22, 1909. Instr. plant diseases, Shaw Sch. Botany, Washington U., 1896-1903; pathologist charge Miss. Valley Lab., Bur. Plant Industry, U.S. Dept. Agr. 1898-1907, charges investigations on timber diseases and timber preservation; spl. agt., chief div. forest products, Bur. Forestry, 1901-05; lectr. diseases of trees and timber preservation, Yale Forest Sch., 1902-09; lectr. plant pathology, U. Wis., 1909. Cons. timber engr., R.I., Frisco and C.&E.I. rys., 1907-12; Kansas City So., 1907—, D.,L.&W. Ry., 1909-19; Lehigh Valley Ry., 1909-11; N.Y.C.&H.R. R.R., Lake Shore, Big Four, 1910-26; Mo. Pac., 1912—, M., K.&T., 1915—; N.Y., N.H.&H. R.R., 1921-30; Boston & Me., 1923-25; Wabash R.R., 1920—; N.Y. Central Lines, 1926—; Eric Railroad, 1927-46; St.L. S.W. Railroad, 1917—; T.&P.R.R., 1920—; St. Louis & San Francisco Lines 1946—; Nickel Plate Ry., 1916-43; Fla. E. Coast Ry., 1941-43; engr. Nat. Lumber Mfrs. Assn., 1914-18. Chmn. Mo. State Forest Commn., 1908-12; lectr. timber preservation, Baltimore Forest Sch., 1906-14; pathologist, Mo. Bot. Garden, 1907—. Sec. Am. bd. editors Botanisches Centralblatt, 1908-14, engaged in investigations of diseases of fruit trees and forest trees, and timber preservation. Author: The Decay of Timber and Methods for Preventing It, 1902; Seasoning of Timber, 1903; Diseases of Hardwood Trees, 1909; Protection of Ties Against Mechanical Wear, 1930; also papers on kindred subjects. Mem. sub-com. forest products s.w. region, U.S.R.R. Adminstrn., 1919-20. Del. Internat. R.R. Congress, Madrid, 1930. Home: 289 St. Denis St., Florissant, Mo. Office: Tower Grove and Flad Avs., St. Louis. Died Jan. 30, 1953; buried Florissant, Mo.

VON SCHWEINITZ, LEWIS DAVID, clergyman, botanist; b. Bethlehem, Pa., Feb. 13, 1780; s. Baron Hans Christian Alexander and Anna Dorothea Elizabeth (de Watteville) von S.; entered Moravian Theol. Sem., Niesky, Silesia, Germany, 1798; m. Louisa Amelia Ledoux, 4 children including Edmund Alexander de Schweinitz. Tchr., Moravian Theol. Sem., Niesky, 1800-07; pastor, Gnadenberg, Germany, 1807-14, Gnadou, Saxony, 1807-12; gen. agt. Moravian Ch., Salem, N.C., 1812-21, adminstr. No. province, 1821-34; 1st to describe fungi in N.C. and Pa.; discovered over 1,000 new species; wrote Fungi of Lusatia, 1805, Fungi of North Caroline, 1818, a pamphlet describing 76 Hepaticae, 1821, a monograph on genus Viola, naming 5 new species which he submitted to Am. Jour. of Science, 1821, Narrative of an Expedition to the Source of St. Peter's River, 1824; published his greatest work A Synopsis of North American Fungi, 1831, contained description of 3,098 species belonging to 246 genera (of which he discovered 1,203 species and 7 genera) Schweinitzia Ororata (North Atlantic plant) named in his honor. Died Bethlehem, Feb. 8, 1834; buried Moravian Cemetery, Bethlehem.

VOORHEES, EDWARD BURNETT, agrl. chemist; b. Mine Brook, Somerset County, N.J., June 22, 1856; s. John and Sarah (Dilley) V.; A.B., Rutgers Coll., 1881, A.M., 1884; D.Sc., U. of Vt., 1900; m. Anna E. Amerman, Oct. 18, 1883. Asst. to prof. chemistry, Wesleyan U., 1881-82; asst. chemist, 1882-88, chemist, 1888-93, dir., 1893, N.J. Agrl. Expt. Sta.; dir. N.J. Agrl. College Expt. Sta., 1896. Prof. agr., Rutgers Coll., 1890—; supt. N.J. Agrl. Coll. Farm, 1896—; agt. U.S. Dept. Agr. for irrigation in N.J., 1896—; pres. bd. dirs. N.J. Weather Bur., 1893; v.p., 1893-1901, pres., 1901—, N.J. State Bd. Agr. Received Nichols Research Medal for best paper containing results of chem. research reported to Am. Chem. Soc. Jour. in 1902—for paper on Dentrification. Mem. Ref. Ch. in America. Republican. Author: First Principles of Agriculture, 1895; Fertilizers, 1898; Forage Crops, 1907; also many bulls. and mag. articles on agrl. topics. Lecturer before farmers' insts., bds. of agr., dairy and breeders' assns., and hort. socs. in all Eastern States. Home: New Brunswick, N.J. Died 1911.

VOORHEES, JAMES D., physician; b. at Morristown, N.J., May 21, 1869; s. of George E. and Mary G. V.; grad. Princeton, 1890; A.M., 1893; Coll. Phys. and Surg., Columbia University, 1893. Resident physician Prby'n Hospital, 1894-6; New York Foundling Hosp., 1896-7; Sloane Maternity Hosp., 1897-1900; instr. in obstetrics from 1897, Coll. Physicians and Surgeons; secretary faculty Coll. Phys. and Surg., 1901-1905. Republican. Presby'n. Contb'r to med. jours. Address: 106 E. 60th St., New York NY‡

VOORHEES, LOUIS A(UGUSTUS), chemist; b. New Brunswick, N.J., Mar. 6, 1865; s. Charles Holbert (M.D.) and Charlotte (Bournonville) V.; A.B., Rutgers Coll., 1885, A.M., 1888; m. May Wilcox, Oct. 24, 1900. Began with N.J. State Agrl. Expt. Sta., 1885, and advanced to chief chemist, 1895; resigned and opened own lab., 1905; chemist to Dept. of Health, City of New Brunswick, since 1920. A pioneer in various agrl. investigations, 1885-1905. Charter mem. Inst. of Food Technologists; mem. A.A.A.S., Am. Chem. Soc., Am. Pub. Health Assn., Assn. Official Agrl. Chemists, Am. Dairy Science Assn., Internat. Assn. of Milk Sanitarians, N.J. Health Officers Assn., N.J. Health and Sanitary Assn., Inst. Food Technologists, New Brunswick Scientific Soc., S.A.R., Sons of Union Vets., Phi Beta Kappa. Democrat. Mason, Elk. Home: 357 George St. Office: City Hall, New Brunswick, N.J. Died Aug. 14, 1945.

VOORHEES, SAMUEL STOCKTON, chemical engr.; b. Springfield, O., Jan. 15, 1867; s. John Hunn and Elizabeth Aston (Warder) V.; student scientific course, Lehigh U., Pa., class of 1888 (non-grad.); spl. course in chemistry, Columbian (now George Washington U.), Washington, D.C.; m. Laura Toucey Kase, July 10, 1895. Asst. chemist Cambria Iron Co. and Pa. R.R., Altoona, Pa., 1887-96; chemist in charge for Southern Ry., Washington, 1896-99, N.Y.C.&H.R. R.R., 1899-1901; engr. of tests, U.S. supervising architect's office, 1901-08; engr. of tests, U.S. Geol. Survey, technol. work, 1908-10; engr. chemist U.S. Bur. Standards, July 1910—. Episcopalian. Author various repts. of tech. committees of scientific socs. Home: Washington, D.C. Died Sept. 23, 1921.

VOORHEES, STEPHEN FRANCIS, (voor'ez), architect; b. Rocky Hill, N.J., Feb. 15, 1878; s. Charles Hagaman and Mary Frances (Skillman) V.; prep. edn., State Model Sch., Trenton, N.J.; C.E., Princeton, 1900; hon. Dr. Engring., Princeton, 1937. Rensselaer Poly. Inst., 1939; A.F.D. (hon.), N.Y.U., 1939; m. Mabel Aleda Buys, Oct. 15, 1907 (dec.). Civil engr. with William P. Field, Newark, N.J., 1900-02; civil engr. and supt. constrn. with Eidlitz & McKenzie, 1902-10; mem. firm McKenzie, Voorhees & Gmelin, 1910-26, Voorhees, Gmelin & Walker, 1926-39, Voorhees, Walker, Foley & Smith, 1939-55, Voorhees, Walker, Smith & Smith, 1955-59; consultant architectural firm Voorhees, Walker. Smith, Smith & Haines, New York City, 1959-64; cons. Smith, Smith, Haines, Lundberg & Waehller, 1964—; supervising architect Princeton, 1930-49; dir. Marine Midland Trust Co. Rockland Co., Bank N.Y. Principal works: New York Telephone Headquarters Bldg., Western Union Telegraph Bldg., One Wall St. Building (all New York, N.Y.), Bell Telephone Laboratories, Murray Hill, N.J., Prudential Ins. Co. of Am. Headquarters Building, Newark, N.J.; chmn. Board of Design New York World's Fair, 1936-40. Served as corpl. U.S. Vol. Engrs., Spanish-Am. War, 1898-99; maj. Sanitary Corps, U.S. Army, 1917-19; cons. W.P.B., 1940-42. Charter trustee Princeton U., 1943-48, trustee emeritus since 1948. Trustee Stevens Inst. of Tech., Met. Museum of Art, N.Y.C. Fellow Am. Inst. Architects (past pres.), New York chapter, A.I.A. (past pres.); mem. Am. Soc. C.E., Am. Soc. M.E., Princeton Archtl. Assn. (past pres.), Princeton Engring. Assn. (past pres.), Archtl. League N.Y. N.Y. C. of C., Commerce and Industry Assn. of New York, Holland Soc., Royal Inst. British Architects (hon. correspondent). Republican. Elder Dutch Reformed Ch. Clubs: University, Princeton, Union League, Century Association, Rockland Country (New York). Home: Voorhis Point, Nyack, N.Y. Office: 101 Park Av., New York 17, N.Y. Died Jan. 23, 1965.

VORHIES, CHARLES TAYLOR, (vor'hez), prof. zoölogy; b. Lockridge, Ia., Sept. 7, 1879; s. Daniel and Rachel Elizabeth (Taylor) V.; B.S., Ia. Wesleyan Coll., Mt. Pleasant, 1902; Ph.D., U. of Wis., 1908; m. Marie Isabel Tuttle, Sept. 7, 1901 (died 1928); 1 son, Charles Tuttle; m. 2d, Georgia Ann Clark, July 29, 1929. Instr. biology, Ia. Wesleyan Coll., 1902-04; asst. in zoölogy, U. of Wis., 1904-08; prof. zoölogy and botany, U. of Utah, 1908-15, actg. dean Med. Sch., 1911-13; instr. in entomology, Cornell U., summer, 1915; asst. prof. biology, U. of Ariz., 1915-16, prof. zoölogy, 1916-18, prof. entomology, 1918-33, prof. zoölogy, and econ. zoölogist since 1933; actg. dean of agr., actg. pres. and administrative adviser at various times. Fellow A.A.A.S. (pres. S.W. div. 1933); asso. Am. Ornithologists Union; mem. Ecological Soc. America (pres. 1939), Am. Soc. Mammalogists, Cooper Ornith. Club, Wildlife Soc., Am. Soc. Ichtyologists and Herpetologists, Ariz. Wildlife Federation (sec'y-treas. 1939-), Sigma Xi, Phi Kappa Phi, Phi Delta Theta. Methodist. Author numerous bulls., also articles in scientific books and mags. Has done outstanding research work on rodents of the range and desert. Home: 1424 E. Fifth St., Tucson, Ariz. Died March 10, 1949.

VOTEY, JOSIAH WILLIAM, civil engr.; b. Ovid, N.Y., July 23, 1860; s. Charles Augustus and Fanny Graves (Anderson) V.; grad. Vermont Acad., 1881; C.E., U. of Vt., 1884, D.Sc., 1911; also D.Sc., U. of Me., 1922; m. Emma Luella Lane, Mar. 25, 1886; children—Florence, Ruth, Dorothy, Constance, Instr. civ. engrings., 1884-89, asst. prof., 1889-90, asso. prof., 1890-93, prof., 1893—, dean Coll. Engring., 1901—, U. of Vt. Cons. civ. and sanitary engr.; city engr., Burlington, 1887; mem. Vt. State Highway Commn., 1892-96; mem. Bd. of St. Commrs., Burlington, 1902-05; mem. Bd. Water Commrs., Burlington, 1908-09; sanitary engr., Vt. Bd. of Health, 1908—. Fellow A.A.A.S. Home: Burlington, Vt. Died Sept. 16, 1931.

VOUGHT, CHANCE MILTON, aircraft designer, mgr.; b. N.Y.C., Feb. 26, 1890; s. George and Annie (Colley) V.; attended N.Y. U., U. Pa.; m. Ena Lewis, Dec. 4, 1920, 2 children. Learned how to fly from Wright Bros., 1910; cons. engr. for Aero Club of Ill., 1912; editor Aero and Hydro mag., 1914; designed trainer used by British in World War I, 1914; chief engr. Wright Co., Dayton, O., 1916, built Vought-Wright Model V mil. biplane; organized (with financing by B. B. Lewis) Lewis & Vought Corp., 1917; produced Vought VE-7, 1919; merged with Pratt & Whitney and Boeing airplane cos. to form United Aircraft & Transport Corp., 1929. Died Southampton, L.I., N.Y. July 25, 1930.

VUILLEUMIER, ERNEST ALBERT, (ve'um-ya), prof. chemistry; b. New City, Rockland County, N.Y., Mar. 1, 1894; s. Charles and Matilda (Barny) V.; B.S. in Chemistry, U. of Pa., 1914; grad. student, same, 1915-16; Ph.D., U. of Berne, Switzerland, 1918; m. Frances E. Smith, Dec. 27, 1924. Analytical and control chemist, Powers-Weightman-Rosengarten Co., Phila., 1914-15; instr. chemistry, Drexel Inst., Phila., 1915-16; Rosengarten traveling scholarship, U. of Pa., at Berne, 1916-18; research chemist Powers-Weightman-Rosengarten Co., 1919-20; became head dept. chemistry, Dickinson Coll., 1920-58, dean of the junior class, 1927-28, the freshman class, 1928-33, acting dean of the college, 1933-35, dean 1935-47, also C. Scott Althouse prof. chemistry, 1951—. With A.E.F. in France, 1918-19. Acting Swiss consul, Pa., N.J., and Del., summer 1923. Fellow Am. Inst. Chemists, A.A.A.S.; mem. Am. Chemical Society (chmn. S.E. Pa. section 1951-52), American Electrochem. Society, Verein für Chemiker der Universitaet Berne, Pa. Acad. of Science (pres. 1941-42), Phi Beta Kappa, Omicron Delta Kappa. Republican. Methodist. Author of articles presenting investigations in electrodeposition, analysis of alcoholic liquids, etc. Inventor Dickinson alcohometer and Dickinson solids-hydrometer; co-inventor of contractometer for study of peeling of nickelplating. Address: Dickinson College, Carlisle, Pa. Died Oct. 6, 1958; buried Halifax, Pa.

WACHSMUTH, CHARLES, paleontologist; b. Hanover, Germany, Sept. 13, 1829; s. Christian Wachsmuth; m. Bernandina Lorenz, 1855. Came to N.Y.C. as agt. merc. house in Hamburg, 1852; went to Burlington, Ia., 1854; gathered large collection of rare crinoids and established spl. library on the subject which attracted attention of scientists; Louis Agassiz purchased the material for Mus. of Comparative Zoology, Cambridge, Mass., 1873; went with Agassiz to Cambridge, worked with him, until 1873; engaged in study of N.Am. crinoids (with Frank Springer), after 1873. Author: (with Springer) North American Crinoidea Camerata (monograph) 1897. Died Burlington, Feb. 7, 1896; buried Aspen Grove Cemetery, Burlington.

WACK, OTIS, engr.; b. Lansdale, Pa., Dec. 11, 1880; s. David and Susan (Fetterolf) W.; degree in C.E., LaFayette Coll., Easton, Pa., 1906; m. Bessie Wier Manee, June 25, 1910; children—Edwin Otis, Virginia Annabell (Mrs. M. A. Heagy), Elaine Manee (Mrs. C. M. Maffie). Engring. in and around N.Y.C., 1906-13; work mgr., v.p. Wentworth Gypsum Co., Gypsum Packet Co., Newport Plaster Mining and Mfg. Co., Hillsboro Plaster Mining Co. (Canadian subsidiaries J. B. King and Co.), 1913-24; operating mgr. in Can., U.S. Gypsum Co., 1924-36; chief engr., 1936-46, v.p., 1946—. Mem. Engring. Socs. Can. and N.S. Mason (K.T., Shriner), Rotarian. Home: 3039 Payne St., Evanston, Ill. Office: United States Gypsum Co., 300 W. Adams St., Chgo. Died Feb. 21, 1951.

WADDELL, CHARLES EDWARD, (wa-del'), consulting engr.; b. Hillsboro, N.C., May 1, 1877; s. Francis Nash and Ann Ivy (Miller) W.; ed. Bingham Mil. Sch., N.C., and in shops of Gen. Electric Co.; Sc.D., N.C. State Coll. Agr. and Engring., 1925; m. Eleanor Sheppard Belknap, Apr. 19, 1904; children—Eleanor B. (Mrs. George M. Stephens), Charles E. Built various steam and hydraulic plants along the eastern seaboard; cons. engr. to George W. Vanderbilt, for "Biltmore" (designed and built majority of engring. works at Biltmore); designer, and builder of N.C. Elec. Power Co.'s system, 1903-23; cons. engr. United Electric Securities Co., Boston, 1912; consulting engr. on State water powers for the City of Medellin, Colombia, South America, 1927. Cons. engr. to power sect. Council of Nat. Defense, in surveying and analyzing the power resources of the Southern States for war emergency, 1917; engr. to Q.-M. Dept., U.S. Army, for constrn. of gen. hosps. No. 12 and No. 19, 1918; dir. of conservation for the State of N.C., U.S. Fuel Administration. Chmn. and mem. N.C. Board Engring. Examiners, 1921-26; mem. N.C. Ship and Water Transportation Commn., 1923-24; commr. Biltmore Forest, 1923-27; pres. Biltmore Hosp., 1920-23; cons. engr. City of Asheville, 1925-27; cons. engr. to N.C. Corp. Commn. in readjustment of utility rates, 1932-34. Cons. engr. Tenn. Valley Authority, 1936-38, and for City of Asheville, N.C., 1940; for Ecusta Paper Corp., Pisgah Forest, N.C., since 1941; for Am. Enka Corp., 1943-44. Fellow American Institute Electrical Engrs. (chmn. N.C. sect. i936); mem. Am. Soc. C.E. (pres. N.C. sect. 1923-24; hon. mem. N.C. sect. 1943), Am. Soc. M.E., N.C. Soc. Engrs. (pres. 1928; hon. mem. 1942). Clubs: Asheville Civitan (president 1923), Pen and Plate (president 1916), Biltmore Forest Country (gov. 1922-30). Episcopalian. Home: Biltmore, N.C. Office: Asheville, N.C. Died Apr. 20, 1945.

WADDELL, JOHN ALEXANDER LOW, cons. engineer; b. Port Hope, Can., Jan. 15, 1854; s. Robert Needham and Angeline Esther (Jones) W.; prep edn., Trinity Coll. Sch., Port Hope; C.E., Rensselaer Poly. Inst., 1875; B.Applied Science (ad eundem gradum), and M.Engring., McGill U., 1882, D.Sc., 1904; LL.D., Univ. of Mo., 1904; D.E., U. of Neb., 1911; Kogakuhakushi (D.Eng.), Imperial U. of Japan, 1915; D.Litt, University of Puerto Rico, 1934; m. Ada Everett, July 13, 1882 (died 1934); children—Needham Everett (dec.), Leonard, Ethel. Engring. work, C.P. Ry., 1876-77; asst. prof. rational and tech. mechanics, Rensselaer Poly. Inst., 1878-80; chief engr. Raymond & Campbell, bridge builders, Council Bluffs, Ia., 1881-82; prof. civ. engring., Imperial U. of Japan, 1882-86; cons. bridge engr., Kansas City and New York, 1887—; mem. Waddell & Hardesty. Knight Comdr. Order of the Rising Sun (Japan), 1888; Knight First Class Order of Société de Bienfaisance of Grand Duchess Olga of Russia (for services as prin. engr. Trans-Alaska-Siberian Ry. project); 2d Class Order of Sacred Treasure of Japan; 2d Class Order of Chia Ho (China); Cavalier of Crown of Italy; awarded 1st Clausen gold medal, Am. Assn. Engrs., 1931. Engr. bridges in U.S.A., Canada, Mexico, Cuba, Japan, China, New Zealand, Russia, also bridges for over 25 important cities of U.S., and Can. and for numerous ry. bridges in U.S., Can. and Mexico; mainly occupied in the engring. of toll highway bridges, city bridges, and movable bridges; originator, 1889, of modern vertical-lift-bridge, of which has designed and engineered more than 100 moving spans. Retained by Chinese Govt. (Peking), 1921, as mem. jury of award in competition for new Yellow River bridge for Peking-Hankow Ry. and also to estimate upon some $20,000,000 worth of bridges; cons. engr. and tech. adviser to Ministry of Railways, Nat. Govt. of China (Nanking), 1929, hon. tech. adviser in U.S., 1929—. Author: Specifications for Steel Bridges, 1900; Engineering Specifications and Contracts, 1907; Nickel Steel for Bridges (Norman medal, 1909, of Am. Soc. C.E.); The Possibilities in Bridge Construction by the Use of High Alloy Steels (Norman medal, 1915); Alloy Steels for Bridge-Work; Bridge Engineering (2 vols.), 1916; Economics of Steel Arch Bridges (Norman medal, 1918); Economics of Bridgework, 1921; Principal Professional Papers (22 papers, edited by John L. Harrington), 1905; Memoirs and Addresses of Two Decades (75 papers, edited by Frank W. Skinner), 1928. Joint editor, with John L. Harrington, of Addresses to Engineering Students, 1911. Apptd. by Am. Assn. Engrs. mem. com. of 3 to compile book on Vocational Guidance in Engring. Lines. Home: New York, N.Y. Died Mar. 3, 1938.

WADE, JOSEPH SANFORD, biologist, writer; b. Cumberland Co., Ky., July 20, 1880; s. James Ballanger and Nancy (Beck) W.; student Fairmount College, Wichita, Kan., 1905-06; U. of Chicago, 1923-25; unmarried. Lit. and hist. research work, 1906-13; field and lab. research work, cereal and forage insect investigations Central Great Plains, U.S. Dept. Agr., 1913-17; adminstrv. and research work, with same, at Washington, 1917-50; collaborator, 1950—; specialist in American entomol. bibliography; has made spl. studies of immature stages of North Am. Coleoptera and in the history of biology. Fellow A.A.A.S., Entomological Society Am.; mem. Entomol. Soc. Wash. (pres. 1934), Biol. Soc. Wash. (corr. sec. 1933-43; v.p. 1943-46; pres., 1946-47); Kan. Acad. Science, Am. Ornithologists Union, Washington Acad. Scis., Am. Fedn. Arts, Thoreau Soc. Presbyn. Clubs: Cosmos (Washington); Athenaeum (Boston); Filson (Louisville). Author technical government publs. and many articles in scienti&c and lit. mags. Deceased.

WADLEIGH, FRANCIS RAWLE, consulting engineer; b. Muncy, Pa., October 25, 1864; s. Albra W. and Emily (Rawle) W.; A.B., Princeton, 1883; m. Mariana Rogers, Petersburg, Va., Mar. 24, 1898; children—Francis Rawle, Eleanor Floyd, Mariana Rogers. Began as shop apprentice Pa. R.R., 1883; locomotive fireman, 1884-88; various capacities with N.&W. Ry., 1888-97; with Castner, Curran & Bullitt, 1897-1908; asst. to pres., engring. work, Chesapeake & Ohio Coal & Coke Co., 1908-13; consulting practice, Norfolk, Va., and Phila., Pa., 1913-17; chief engr. Internat. Coal Products Corp., 1917-18; export sales mgr. and cons. engr., Weston Dodson & Co., New York, 1919-21; asst. to pres. Tuttle Corp., 1921. War service with Supply Div., Emergency Fleet Corp., on staff Central Bur. Planning Statistics, and mem. Conservation Bd., State of Pa.; with U.S. Govt. as chief of Coal Div., Dept. of Commerce, and commercial engr. U.S. Bur. of Mines, 1921-22; asst. to federal fuel distributor, 1922-23; federal fuel distributor, Jan. 1-Sept. 22, 1923; chief of coal div. U.S. Dept. Commerce, and commercial engr. U.S. Bur. of Mines, to Dec. 25, 1923; resigned but retained as consultant Dept. Commerce and consulting engr. Bur. Mines; v.p. Tuttle Coal Corp., Paragon-Elkhorn Collieries Co., Tuttle Corp., also v.p. and gen. mgr. Super-Fuel Corp. of New York, and dir. Pittsburgh Terminal Coal Corp., 1924-25; consulting engr., coal and coke, 1925-30; pres. The Wadleigh Bur., Inc., Washington, D.C., 1930-31; apptd. spl. agt. U.S. Bur. Foreign and Domestic Commerce, May 1931; cons. engr., U.S. Dept. Interior in Alaska, June 1931-Feb. 1932; now engaged in consulting work on coal. Mem. Am. Soc. M.E., Am. Soc. Testing Materials, Inst. Mining and Metall. Engrs., Am. Chem. Soc., Franklin Inst. Republican. Episcopalian. Club: Cosmos (Washington). Author: A Coal Manual, 1921. Address: Southern Bldg., Washington, D.C.: also care Alaska Railroad, Anchorage, Alaska.

WADSWORTH, FRANK LAWTON OLCOTT, engineer, inventor; b. Wellington, Ohio, 1867; s. Francis Sage W.; grad. E.M. (mining engr.), Ohio State U., 1888, B.Sc., 1889, M.E. (mech. engr.), 1889; Clark U., 1889-92; m. Laura Poole, Sept. 1893; m. 2d, Mildred Schinneller, July 1914. Del. from Smithsonian Instn. to Internat. Bur. Weights and Meas., Paris, to assist in establishing absolute length of standard meter, 1892; sr. asst. in charge Astrophysical Obs., Washington, 1892-94; asst. prof. physics, U. of Chicago, 1894-96; asst. prof. astrophysics, 1896-97, asso. prof., 1897-98, Yerkes Obs.; dir. Allegheny Obs., 1900-04; spl. engr. and expert work, Pittsburgh and Washington, 1898-99; consulting expert to the John A. Brashear Co., 1901-04; gen. mgr. Pressed Prism Plate Glass Co., 1904-05; chief engr. Am. Window Glass Co., 1905-08; consulting engr., 1908—. Pres. Miller Non-Corrosive Metal Co., 1909—; dir. Pressed Prism Plate Glass Co., 1904-13. Pres. bd. visitors Ohio State U. Asst. editor Astrophys. Jour.; asso. editor Harper & Bros. Scientific Memoirs. Has served on numerous public service coms. and commns., and has published over 100 papers and reports in scientific publs., and soc. proceedings. Patentee of over 250 inventions relating to manufacture of glass, steel, electric lights, railway appliances, machine tools, engring. instruments, wire working machinery, appliances, tires, etc. Originator and designer vertical tower telescope, curved plate camera, fixed deviation spectroscope, polar reflecting heliostat, precision interferometers, and other novel forms of physical and astrophysical instruments; author of the hexaplex system of golf course design, and papers on economic subjects. Has testified as tech. expert in upwards of 200 patent suits in U.S. and Canadian courts. Home: Pittsburgh, Pa. Died Apr. 11, 1936.

WADSWORTH, MARSHMAN EDWARD, geologist; b. Livermore Falls, Me., May 6, 1847; s. Joseph and Nancy F. (Eaton) W.; A.B., Bowdoin Coll., 1869, A.M., 1872; A.B., Harvard U., 1874, A.M., Ph.D., 1879; U. of Heidelberg, 1884-85; M.D., Nat. Med. Coll., 1894; (E.M., Pa. State Coll., 1917; Sc.D., U. of Pittsburgh, 1919). Principal and supt. schools in Maine, N.H., Minn. and Wis., 1863-73; prof. chemistry, Boston Dental Coll., 1873-74; instr. mathematics and mineralogy, Harvard, 1874-77; asst. in geology, Mus. Comparative Zoölogy, Harvard, 1877-87; prof. mineralogy and geology, Colby, 1885-87; asst. geologist, Minn. Geol. Survey, 1886-87; dir., prof. mining geology and petrography, 1887-97, pres. 1897-99, Mich. Coll. of Mines; state geologist of Mich., 1888-93; geologist and mining expert, Keweenawan Assn., 1898-1903; prof. mining and geology, and dean Sch. of Mines and Metallurgy, 1901-08, Pa. State Coll.; dean Sch. of Mines and prof. mining geol., 1907-12, emeritus dean and prof., and curator of mineral, and petrographical collections, 1912—, U. of Pittsburgh. Geologist Pa. State Bd. Agr., 1902-05. A pioneer in microscopic petrography (taught 1st course in U.S.), in meteorites, pre-cambrian geol., etc. Mason. Author: Geology of the Iron and Copper Districts of Lake Superior, 1880; Lithological Studies, 1884; Report of the Mich. Geol. Survey, 1893; The Azoic System (with the late Josiah Dwight Whitney), 1884; Crystallography, 1909; Michigan College of Mines in the Nineteenth Century, 1916. Home: Pittsburgh, Pa. Died Apr. 21, 1921.

WAGER, ALAN TURNER, physicist, educator; b. Veteran, N.Y., Oct. 27, 1904; s. Benjamin Marsh and Grace (Turner) W.; B.S., Hobart Coll., Geneva, N.Y., 1926; M.A., Cornell U., 1931; Ph.D., U. Chgo., 1948; m. Eula Snyder, Aug. 15, 1940. Master, Donaldson Sch. Boys, Ilchester, Md., 1926-30; instr. physics Hobart Coll., 1930-36; part-time instr. math. and phys. scis. Oak Park (Ill.) Jr. Coll., 1937-38, Central YMCA Coll., Chgo., 1937-38, Armour Inst. Tech., 1938-39, George Williams Coll., Chgo., 1938-41; asst. prof., then asso. prof. physics Birmingham-So. Coll., 1942-49; prof. physics Ariz. State U., Tempe, 1949—, chmn. dept., 1957-63; research asso. Oak Ridge Nat. Lab., summer 1953, Argonne Nat. Lab., summer 1956. Dir. Central Ariz. Regional Sci. Fair, 1954-55; dir. In-Service Inst. Secondary Tchrs., NSF, 1958-59, 62—, dir. Acad. Year Inst. Secondary Tchrs., 1959-60, 62—, Summ Inst. Secondary Tchrs., 1960, 63, dir. Undergrad. Research Participation Program, 1960, asso. program dir. Acad. Year Insts., 1960-61, cons., 1961—; cons. Sci. Services, Inc., 1962-63. Fellow A.A.A.S. (pres. Southwestern and Rocky Mountain div., 1960-61); mem. Ariz. Acad. Sci. (pres. 1956-57, treas. 1959-63; hon. mem.), Ariz. Sci. Tchrs. Assn., Am. Inst. Physics, Am. Physics Soc., Nat. Sci. Tchrs. Assn., Am. Assn. U. Profs., Phi Beta Kappa, Tau Kappa Epsilon, Phi Kappa Phi. Club: Internat. Torch, Phoenix Executives. Home: 335 E. Palmcroft Dr., Tempe, Ariz. 85281. Died May 7, 1966.

WAGNER, CHARLES GRAY, physician; b. Minden, N.Y., Oct. 10, 1856; s. Edward and Alida E. W.; B.S., Cornell U., 1880; M.D., Coll. Phys. and Surg. (Columbia), 1882; m. Mrs. Elizabeth Bennett, Nov. 2, 1903. House phys. and surgeon, Presbyn. Hosp., N.Y. City, 1882-84; asst. phys., Utica State Hosp., 1884-92; med. supt. Binghamton (N.Y.) State Hosp., 1892—. Lecturer on insanity, Sage Sch. of Philosophy (Cornell U.), 1896-1900 inclusive; expert witness in many important trials. Asso. editor Am. Jour. Insanity, 1884-92. Trustee Cornell U., 1896-1906. Republican. Episcopalian. Died Nov. 6, 1923.

WAGNER, FRANK CASPAR, engineer; b. Ann Arbor, Mich., Oct. 5, 1864; s. William and Priscilla (Meller) W.; A.M., U. of Mich., 1884, B.S., 1885; D.Sc., Rose Polytechnic Inst., 1924; Dr.Engring., Univ. of Mich., 1927; m. Mabel E. Peck, June 16, 1892; children—Helen Ward (Mrs. J. L. McCloud), Frank Caspar, Priscilla Meller (Mrs. Fred B. Johnson), Willys Peck, Barbara, Constance (dec.). Engring. work with Thomson-Houston Electric Co., 1886-89; asst. prof. mech. engring., U. of Mich., 1890-96; asso. prof. steam engring., 1896-1904, prof. steam and elec. engring. 1904-20, prof. mech. engring., 1920-23, pres., 1923—, Rose Poly. Institute. Administrative engr. for Ind. of U.S. Fuel Administration, 1918. Author: Notes on Applied Electricity, 1903. Home: Terre Haute, Ind. Died Nov. 21, 1928.

WAGNER, HERMAN ALEXANDER, cons. engr.; born Grahamstown, N.Z., Apr. 17, 1864; s. William Alexander and Helen Rose (Cameron) W.; M.E., Freiberg (Saxony) Mining Acad., 1888; Ph.D., U. Heidelberg, Germany, 1889; unmarried. Came to U.S., 1901, naturalized, 1906. Metallurgist, Dowlais Steel Coal & Iron Co., Cardiff, Wales, 1889-90; mgr. Barney Barnato Bros., Johannesburg, S. Africa (gold mining), 1890-99; cons. engr F. A. Heinze, Butte, Mont., 1901-04; mining engr. globe exploration, London, Eng., 1904-06; cons. mining and metall. engr. since 1907, N.Y. City, 1907-12, Mayer, Ariz., 1912-15, Chicago since 1926; pres., gen. mgr. Gray Eagle Reduction Co., since 1916; pres. Arminius Land & Cattle Co., since 1919, Mayer Ore Purchasing Co. since 1920; dir. Mayer State Bank. Field cornet Boer War, 1899-1901. Fellow A.A.A.S.; mem. Am. Assn. Engrs. (past pres.), Inst. Mining and Metall. Engrs., Inst. E.E., Am. Soc. for Engring. Edn., Soc. Am. Mil. Engrs., Electrochem. Soc., Chicago Tech. Socs. Council (dir., 1946-51). Co-author: Technologists Stake in the Wagner Act; Technologists Stake in the Taft-Hartley Act; Principles of Professional Conduct in Engineering (The Annals of Am. Acad. Polit. and Social Science), 1955. Contbr. articles on the "Deadline at Forty", prof. engrs. welfare, mediation in engring. publs. Acting as mediator and arbitrator in prof. engrs. disputes. Inventor processes for treatment of refractory ores, prodn. of electrolytic zinc, copper; process for the electrolytic desposition of rubber. Office: 8 Michigan Av., Chicago 3. Died Apr. 10, 1960; buried Forest Homes, Des Plaines, Ill.

WAGNER, MARTIN, architect; b. Koenigsberg, Prussia, Germany, Nov. 5, 1885; s. Carl and Johanna (Hardt) W.; Diploma as engr., Technische Hochschule, Dresden, Germany, 1910; Dr. Engring. Technische Hochschule, Berlin, 1915; m. Gertrud Sandow, April 29, 1911; children—Irmgard Wagner Schüle, Bernhard, Sabine. Began as town planner of the City of Berlin-Weissensee, 1910; with City of Hamburg, 1910-12; chmn. bldg. dept., City of Wilhelmshaven, 1911-14; chief of planning bur., City of Berlin, 1914-18, chmn. bldg. dept., 1926-33; organizer German Bldg. Guilds, 1920-26; prof. housing, regional planning, Harvard, 1938-50, prof. emeritus 1950—. Served as pvt., Germany Army, during World War I. Received Iron Cross, 1918. Fellow Am. Acad. Arts and Sciences. Mem. Prussian Acad. of Arts, 1931. Author: Städtische Freiflächenpolitik, 1916; Amerikanische Bauwirtschaft, 1925; Städtebauliche Probleme in Amerikanischen Städten, 1929; Das Wachsende Haus, 1932; Wirtschaftlicher Städtebau, 1951. Also author articles. Home: 33 Bowdoin St., Cambridge, Mass. Died May 28, 1957; buried Mt. Auburn Cemetery, Cambridge.

WAGNER, SAMUEL TOBIAS, civil engr.; b. Philadelphia, Pa., Aug. 30, 1861; s. John and Sarah A. (Wood) W.; B.Sc., U. of Pa., 1881 (sr. civ. engr. prize), C.E., 1884; m. Mary Clara Reeves Scull, Nov. 13, 1888; children—Mary, John Jr., William Worrell, Thomas Rowan. With Phoenix Iron Co., Phoenixville, Pa., as draftsman, insp., asst. master mechanic and supt. of shops, 1881-93; asst. engr. in charge of Pa. Av. Subway and Tunnel, Bur. of Surveys, Phila., 1894-1900; asst. engr. in charge of improvement and filtration of water supply, same, 1900-02; asst. engr. in charge of abolishment of grade-crossings, Phila. & Reading R.R. Co., 1902-15, chief engr., April 15, 1915-Jan. 1, 1927; cons. engineer, 1927—. Trustee Wagner Free Inst. of Science, and prof. engring., same, 1892—(pres. bd.); mem. Pa. State Bd. for Registration Professional Engrs. Republican. Episcopalian. Home: Germantown, Phila., Pa. Died Aug. 7, 1931.

WAGNER, WEBSTER, mfr.; b. Palatine Bridge, N.Y., Oct. 2, 1817; s. John and Elizabeth (Strayer) W.; m. Susan Davis, 5 children. Station mgr., freight agt. N.Y. Central R.R., Palatine Bridge, 1843-circa 1858; designed a sleeping car; with financial help of Commodore Vanderbilt completed 4 sleeping-cars put into operation on N.Y. Central R.R., 1858; organized N.Y. Central Sleeping Car Co. at Palatine Bridge to manufacture cars for exclusive use on N.Y. Central R.R., (reorganized as Wagner Palace Car Co. mfg. sleeping and drawing-room cars, 1865); contracted with George M. Pullman to make Pullman's newly patented folding upper berth and hinged back and seat cushions for the lower berth with understanding that Wagner Co. would use them only on N.Y. Central R.R., 1870; received contract to run cars over Mich. Central R.R. (made connection for Vanderbilt lines between N.Y.C. and Chgo.), 1875, as a result of this breach of contract Pullman Co. brought an infringement suit against Wagner's co. for $1,000,000 (suit still in process at his death); mem. N.Y. Assembly from Montgomery County, 1870; mem. N.Y. Senate from 18th Dist., 1871-72; del. to Republican Nat. Conv., Chgo., 1880. Died in train collision at Spuyten Duyvil, N.Y., Jan. 13, 1882.

WAGNER, WILLIAM, naturalist, philanthropist; b. Phila., Jan. 15, 1796; s. John and Mary Ritz (Baker) W.; grad. Phila. Acad., 1808; m. Caroline Say, Jan. 1, 1824; m. 2d, Louisa Binney, Mar. 1841. Asst. supercargo in Stephen Girard's ship Helvetius to Far East, 1816-18, during voyage gathered a large collection of minerals, shells, plants, and organic remains which became basis of Wagner Free Inst. of Science; arranged museum for his collection at his home; obtained permission to use part of Commrs. Hall in Dist. of Spring Garden (dist. absorbed into Phila. 1854), 1847, received permission from city govt. for continued use of bldgs., established Wagner Free Inst. of Science, granted charter by Pa. Legislature, 1855, empowered to confer degrees; read paper before Acad. Natural Sci., Phila., published in Journal 1839; name applied to several fossil specimens (which he described for 1st time). Died Phila., Jan. 17, 1885; buried in tomb in Wagner Free Inst. of Science.

WAHL, WILLIAM HENRY, scientific journalist, metall. and electro-chemist; b. Philadelphia, Pa., Dec. 14, 1848; s. John H. and Caroline R. W.; ed. public schools, Philadelphia and Dickinson Coll., A.B., 1867; Ph.D., Univ. Heidelberg, Germany, 1869; special courses in chemistry, geology, mineralogy; m. Julia Lowther, Seafield, Co. Mayo, Ireland, Sept. 9, 1874. Resident Sec. Franklin Inst., 1870-74, and from 1882; instr. science Episcopal Acad., Phila., 1871-73; prof. physics and physical geography Central High School, 1873-74. Editor Polytechnic Review, Phila., 1876-78; asso. editor Engineering and Mining Journal, New York, 1878-80; editor Manufacturer and Builder, New York, 1880-95; editor Journal Franklin Institute, 1870-74 and from 1882. Author: Techno-chemical Receipt Book (with Wm. T. Brannt), 1885; Handbook of Assaying (Wedding) translated, with additions, from German; Iconographic Encyclopaedia, Vol. V, Constructive Arts, Phila., 1893; Historical Sketch of the Franklin Institute, 1894. Home: Philadelphia, Pa. Died 1909.

WAIDNER, CHARLES WILLIAM, physicist; b. Baltimore, Md., Mar. 6, 1873; E.E., Johns Hopkins, 1892, A.B., 1896, Ph.D., 1898. Asst. in physics, Johns Hopkins, 1898-99; instr. physics, Williams Coll., 1899-1901; ab. asst., 1901-04, asso. physicist, 1904-10, physicist, 1910—, Bur. Standards, Washington, D.C. Died Mar. 11, 1922.

WAILES, BENJAMIN LEONARD COVINGTON, naturalist, planter; b. Columbia County, Ga., Aug. 1, 1797; s. Levin and Eleanor (Davis) W.; attended Jefferson Coll., Washington, Miss. Territory; m. Rebecca Covington, Mar. 30, 1820, 10 children. Surveyor and clk., land offices in Miss. Territory, 1814-20; asst. to Choctaw agt., attended treaty confs. of 1818 and 1820 with Choctaws; register of land office, Washington, Miss., 1826-35; managed small plantation at Washington, 2 others in Warren County; collected specimans of soil, rocks, fossils, shells, plant and animal life; helped build collections at Jefferson Coll., U. Miss. and at Miss. capitol; supplied information and specimans of natural history of region to other scientists and Smithsonian Instn.; asst. prof. agriculture and geol. scis. U. Miss.; performed field work for projected survey of Miss.; founder, 1st pres. Miss. Hist. Soc.; trustee Jefferson Coll., 40 years, pres. bd. at time of death; mem. Miss. Legislature, 1825, 26. Author: Report on the Agriculture and Geology of Mississippi, 1854. Died Nov. 16, 1862.

WAINDLE, ROGER F(RANCIS), engr.; b. Madison, Wis., May 6, 1909; s. Francis J. and Mary (Riordan) W.; B.S. in mech. engring., Ill. Inst. Tech., 1932; m. Helen Irene Keane, June 15, 1940; children—Mary Kathryn, Roger John, Frank K. Successively marine engr., sales engr., sales mgr., chief engr., ordnance engr;, mgr., gen. mgr. Cannon-Muskegon (Mich.) Corp., v.p., gen. mgr., dir., 1951-63; general mgr. indsl. products div. Elgin Nat. Watch Co. since 1944; gen. mgr. Alloy Casting Co., Champaign, Ill., 1944-63; pres. Wai Met Engineering Co., 1953-63; chmn. bd., pres. Ziebart Process Co., 1963-73; vice pres., dir. Blake-Waindle Corp., West Newton, Mass.; research dir. Nugent Sand Co.; dir. Standard Sand Co. Chief tank-automotive prodn. War Dept., Chgo. Ordnance Dist., A.S.F., 1942-44; adv. non-metallic minerals Munitions Bd. Registered profl. engr., Mich., Ill. Mem. Am. Soc. Tool Engrs. (nat. dir., v.p.), Am. Ordnance Assn. (dir., past chmn. instrument bearings nat. com., member nat. coms. gage industry), Indsl. Diamond Assn. Am. (past nat. chmn. diamond abrasives), Am. Soc. for Metals, Engring. Soc. Det., Newcomen Soc. Am., Triangle, Tau Beta Pi, Pi Tau Sigma. Clubs: Columbia Yacht (Chgo.); Muskegon (Mich.) Country. Author articles tech. jours. Home: Chicago IL Died Apr. 15, 1973.

WAIT, CHARLES EDMUND, chemist; b. Little Rock, Ark., Nov. 3, 1849; s. William B. and Martha L. (Reardon) W.; C.E., M.E., B.S., U. of Va., 1874; Ph.D., U. of Mo., 1888. Dir. Sch. of Mines of Mo., 1877-88; prof. chemistry, U. of Tenn., 1888—. Fellow Chem. Soc. of London, A.A.A.S. Author of bulletins on nutrition and numerous chem. papers. Home: Knoxville, Tenn. Died 1923.

WAIT, HENRY HEILEMAN, engineer, inventor; b. Chicago, Ill., Oct. 27, 1869; s. Horatio Loomis and Chara Conant (Long) W.; grad. Chicago Manual Training Sch., 1886; B.S. in E.E., Mass. Inst. Tech., 1891; m. Edna, d. Edward A. and Kate Davidson Kimball, May 24, 1913; children—Edward Kimball, Horatio Henry, Nathaniel Sears. In employ of Economic Elec. Mfg. Co., Boston, 1891-92; with Western Electric Co., Chicago, 1892-1905; pres. Rateau Turbine Co. Specially active in evolution and improvement of dynamos, both of bipolar and multipolar types, including type L, Western Electric multipolar direct-current generators; patentee of a varipolar motor or dynamo and a semi-automatic machine for winding small armatures, spools, etc., as well as for improvements on arc lamps; inventor and patentee Wait turbo-generator; designer and builder Wait "Bulldog" steam turbines, Wait "Bulldog" dynamos. Lieut. Illinois Naval Reserves. Republican. Home: Chesterton, Ind. Died Nov. 16, 1931.

WAIT, JOHN CASSAN, lawyer, civ. engr.; b. Norwich, N.Y., June 4, 1860; s. Andrew Marcellus and Ambrosia Jane (Sergent) W.; ed. common schs. and Norwich Acad. to 1878; apprentice in planing mill, 1878; received, 1878, competitive state scholarship to Cornell U.; C.E., Cornell, 1882, Master C.E., 1891; M.S., Norwich U., 1887; LL.B., Harvard U., 1891; m. Ginerva Caroline Westlake, June 1886; children—Luella Ambrosia (dec.), Annar Marie, Justin Federal, Constance Elaine. Instr. and asst. prof. in Harvard, 1887-94; engr. in charge N.Y. State canals, $9,000,000 improvement, 1896-97; asst. corp. counsel, City of New York, 1900-04. Independent Democrat. Asso. editor Railroad Gazette, 1894-95. Capt. arty., Vt. N.G., 1886-87. Author: Engineering and Architectural Jurisprudence, 1897; Law of Operations Preliminary to Construction in Engineering and Architecture, 1900; Law of Contracts, 1901; Descendants of Thomas Wait of Portsmouth, R.I., 1904; Genealogical and Biographical History of the Wait(e) families of New England. Pioneer as author and in practice of engring. and architectural jurisprudence, representing large constrn. and mfg. interests. Home: New York, N.Y. Deceased.

WAIT, WILLIAM B., educator, inventor; b. Amsterdam, N.Y., Mar. 25, 1839; s. Christopher B. and Betsey Grinnell (Bell) W.; grad. Albany Normal Coll., 1859; admitted N.Y. bar, 1862; m. Phebe J. Babcock, 1863. Prin. N.Y. Instn. for Blind, 1863-1905, emeritus prin., 1905—. Inventor Kleidograph, machine for writing New York Point system, Stereograph, machine for embossing same on metal plates for printing; power presses, for printing on both sides of the leaf from embossed plates, and improved method of binding embossed books. Trustee Am. Coll. of Musicians, Soc. for Providing Evang. Religious Lit. for the Blind. Author: The New York Tangible Point System of Literature, 1866; The New York Tangible Point System of Music for the Blind, 1872; Normal Course of Piano Technic, 1887; Harmonic Notation, 1888. Home: New York, N.Y. Died Oct. 25, 1916.

WAITE, HENRY MATSON, civil engr.; b. Toledo, O., May 15, 1869; s. Henry Selden and Ione (Brown) W.; grad. Toledo High Sch.; student Mass. Inst. of Tech., LL.D., Univ. of Miami; Dr. of Engring., Univ. of Cincinnati; m. Mary Mason Brown, Apr. 15, 1914. With C.,C.,C.&St.L. Ry. as transitman, 1890-92, engr. maintenance of way, 1892-93; div. engr. C.,N.O.&T.P. Ry., 1893; bridge engr., roadmaster and supt. Cincinnati div., same rd., 1899-1905, supt. Chattanooga div., 1905-07; supt. Seaboard Air Line Ry., 1907-09; v.p. and chief engr. Clinchfield Coal Corp., Dante, Va., 1909-12; chief engr. City of Cincinnati, 1912-14; city mgr., Dayton, 1914-18; v.p. and chief engr., Lord Constrn. Co., N.Y., 1919-20; pres. Lord Dry Dock Corp., N.Y., 1920; in private practice at N.Y., 1920-27; chief engr. Cincinnati Union Terminal Co., 1927-1933; dep. adminstrn. of Public Works, July 1933-Sept., 1934; dir. Regional Dept. of Economic Security, Cincnnati, since Sept. 1934; private practice cons. engr. since 1937; chmn. Chicago Subway Commn., Public Works Adminstrn.; chmn. public works com. Nat. Resources Com. Col. of engrs. Transportation Corps, U.S.A., with A.E.F., 1918-19; served as chief engr. Trans. Corps, asst. dep. gen. of transportation, 2d Army, in Advance Zone, and as a.d.g. Trans., 3d Army in Germany; one of members of Am. Bridgehead Commn. at Coblenz before arrival of Am. Army; asst. to officer in charge civ. affairs at advanced G.H.Q. at Treves, Germany. Mem. Am. Soc. C.E., Am. Inst. Mining and Metall. Engrs., Am. Ry. Engring. Assn. Awarded D.S.M. (U.S.); Officer Légion d'Honneur (French). Club: Engineers. Home: 3515 Cornell Place, Cincinnati. Died Sept. 1, 1944.

WAITE, HERBERT HAROLD, bacteriology; b. Leverett, Mass., July 4, 1868; A.B., Amherst, 1892, A.M., 1903; M.D., U. of Mich., 1901; m. Constance Elizabeth Webber, June 20, 1901 (died 1906); children—Wallace Leonard, Alice Webber; m. 2d, Mary Henderson Ames, April 8, 1908 (died 1911); children—Constance Elizabeth, Herbert Ames. Instr. in bacteriology, U. of Mich., 1896-1901; asst. prof. bacteriology and pathology, 1902-05, asso. prof., 1905-07, prof., 1907—, U. of Neb. Contract surgeon, U.S.A., Oct. 12, 1918-Jan. 9, 1919; maj. Med. Res. Corps, U.S.A. Delegate from Neb. to 15th Internat. Congress of Hygiene and Demography. Author: Disease Prevention, 1920. Home: Lincoln, Neb. Deceased.

WAITE, J(OHN) HERBERT, ophthalmologist; b. Bellefonte, Pa., Nov. 24, 1889; s. John Sitman and Mary Lucetta (Bottorf) W.; student Pa. State Coll., 1907-08; Sc.B., in Biology, Bucknell University, 1911, Sc.M., 1919, Sc.D. (honorary), 1936; M.D., Harvard U. Med. Sch., 1916; m. Marion S. Kennedy, Feb. 4, 1916 (died 1917); children—(twins) John H. and Joanne (wife Dr. David H. Scott); m. 2d, Florence E. Long, Sept. 20, 1919; 1 dau., Elinor (Mrs. Bruce A. MacDonald). In Far East service, Rockefeller Foundation, 1916-19; interne, resident, teaching fellow in ophthalmology, Mass. Eye and Ear Infirmary, 1920-24; instr. in ophthalmology, Harvard, 1925-29, asst. prof., 1930-34, clin. prof. and head of dept., 1934-40, lecturer in ophthalmology since 1941; ophthalmic chief of staff Mass. Eye and Ear Infirmary, 1931-41, cons. surgeon in ophthalmology since 1941; consultant in ophthalmology Peter Bent Brigham, Children's and Infants', N.E. Deaconess, N.E. Baptist, N.E. Peabody Home for Crippled Children, Winchester, and other hospitals. Fellow Mass. Med. Soc.; fellow Boston Med. Library; mem. Am. Med.

Assn., A.A.A.S., Am. Ophthalmol. Society, N.E. Ophthalmol. Society; associate Guild of Boston Artists; mem. Phi Beta Kappa, Phi Gamma Delta, Nu Sigma Nu. Mem. editorial bd. Archives of Ophthalmology, 1929-42; mem. bd. hon. consultants Army Med. Library, 1946. Contbr. to Dictionary of Am. Biography. Home: 1731 Beacon St., Brookline, Mass. Office: 7 Bay State Rd., Boston. Died Feb. 23, 1957.

WAITE, MERTON BENWAY, plant pathologist; b. Oregon, Ill., Jan. 23, 1865; s. E. J. and Elizabeth (Benway) W.; B.S., U. of Ill., 1887; D.Agr., Univ. of Md., 1919. Asst. pathologist, U.S. Dept. Agr., 1888-1901, pathologist in charge of fruit disease investigations, 1901. Mem. Bot. Soc. America, Am. Phytopath. Soc., etc. Author: Pollination of Pear Flowers; Pear Blight and Its Remedy; and other bot. papers. Home: 1447 Euclid Av. N.W., Washington. Died June 5, 1945.

WAKEFIELD, ARTHUR PAUL, physician; b. North Bloomfield, O., Oct. 5, 1878; s. Edmund Burritt and Martha (Sheldon) W.; Ph.B., Hiram (O.) Coll., 1900; M.D., Rush Med. Coll. (U. of Chicago), 1904; A.M., Bethany (W.Va.) Coll., 1907; Rockefeller Foundation fellow, Sch. Tropical Medicine, Harvard, 1917; resident Boston City Hosp., Westfield (Mass.) Sanatorium; m. Olive Catharine Lindsay, June 14, 1904; children—Vachel Lindsay, Mary Churchill (dec.), Catharine Frazee, Martha Isabel. Began practice at Springfield, 1904; med. missionary, China, 1905-27, at Nanking, 1905, in charge hosp., Luchowfu, 1912-19, in charge student health work, Boone U., Wuchang, 1919-27 (aided in saving univ. property when Wuchang was seized by soviet-nationalist army, 1927); chief of Chadwick Clinics (state child tuberculosis clinics), Mass., 1928-33; supt. Central Me. Sanatorium, Fairfield, Me., 1932-36; supervisor State Clinics for Crippled Children, Mass. Dept. of Pub. Health, since 1936. Decorated by Chinese Nat. Red Cross for flood relief work on Yangtze and reconstruction Yangtze dyke at Wuhu. Episcopalian. Mason. Home: 75 Richardson Road, Belmont, Mass. Address: Dept. of Pub. Health, State House, Boston, Mass. Died Feb. 6, 1942.

WAKEMAN, SETH, med. cons., b. Batavia, N.Y., May 18, 1893; s. Wm. Sprague and Jennie (DeBow) W.; A.B., Hobart Coll., 1916, A.M., 1917; Ph.D., Cornell, 1922; m. Marion Delamater Freeman, May 29, 1926, 1 son, Seth Freeman; m. 2d, Mary Perley Storer, Nov. 18, 1961. Instr. edn. Cornell, 1919-22, asst. prof., 1922-25; prof. education Smith Coll., Northampton, Mass., 1925-57, dir. exptl. schs., 1945-46; asso. Robert Boggs, Assos., cons. med. affairs, 1956-61; in charge medicine and med. edn. Samuel H. Kress Found., N.Y.C., 1949-51. Asst. adminstr. Services to Armed Forces A.R.C., 1943-45, cons., 1946-47. Bd. trustees Martha's Vineyard Hosp.; bd. dirs. Martha's Vineyard Community Services, Edgartown Boys Club; chmn. Martha's Vineyard chpt. A.R.C. Served with psychology div., U.S. Army, 1918-19, A.R.C., 1919. Fellow A.A.A.S.; mem. Phi Delta Kappa, Phi Kappa Phi. Clubs: Edgartown Yacht, Edgartown Golf, Reading Room (Edgartown). Contbr. sci. jours. Home: Martha's Vineyard MA Died Feb. 8, 1968; buried Chilmark MA

WALBRIDGE, GEORGE HICKS, exec. engineer; b. Bennington, Vt., Aug. 22, 1869; s. James Hicks and Delia M. (Perry) W.; M.E., Cornell, 1890; m. Mary Gilley Taylor, Oct. 17, 1900; 1 dau., Elizabeth Stebbins, V.p. J. G. White & Co., engrs., 1890-1902; gen. engring. practice, 1902-07; pres. Colo. Power Co., in charge constrn. and management hydro-electric plants, 1907-11; with Bonbright & Co., investment bankers, 1911-20, v.p. from 1914; asso. with L. P. Hammond, management, pub. utilities and industrials, 1920-24; chmn. bd. Royalties Management Corp. Republican. Home: New York, N.Y. Died Aug. 5, 1936.

WALCOTT, CHARLES DOOLITTLE, scientist; b. New York Mills, N.Y., Mar. 31, 1850; s. Charles D. and Mary (Lane) W.; ed. pub. schs., Utica, N.Y., LL.D., Hamilton, 1898, U. Chicago, 1901, Johns Hopkins, 1902, U. of Pa., 1903, Yale, 1910, St. Andrews, 1911, Pittsburgh, 1912; Sc.D., U. of Cambridge, Eng., 1909, Harvard, 1913; Ph.D., Royal Fredericks U., Christiania, 1911; m. Helena B. Stevens, June 22, 1888 (died 1911); children—Charles D. (dec.), Helen B. (Mrs. Cole B. Younger), Sidney S., Stuart B. (dec.); m. 2d, Mary Morris Vaux, June 30, 1914. Early showed a predilection for geologic research; became asst. in N.Y. State Survey, 1876; asst. geologist U.S. Geol. Survey, 1879, the Cambrian rocks and faunas of the U.S. being his especial subjects of inquiry; presented his Cambrian researches before Internat. Geol. Congress, London, 1888. Paleontologist in charge invertebrate paleontology, 1888-93, geologist in general charge geology and paleontology, 1893-94, and dir., 1894-97, U.S. Geol. Survey; hon. curator dept. paleontology, 1892-97, and 1898—; at head of Nat. Mus., Jan. 1897-July 1898, with title of acting asst. sec. Smithsonian Instn., and from Jan. 1907, sec. same; sec. Carnegie Instn., Washington, 1902-05, also vice chmn. bd. trustees and, 1917-22, chmn. exec. com. of same; dir. U.S. Reclamation Service, 1905-07; dir. Research Corporation, N.Y. City. Fellow Christiania Scientific Soc., Am. Acad. Arts and Sciences, Geol. Soc. America (pres. 1901), Geol. Soc. London (Bigsby medal, and Wollaston medal, 1918), Imperial Soc. Naturalists (Moscow), Royal Geog. Soc. (London), Acad. Science Inst. Bologna; Gaudry medal, Soc. Géol., France; foreign asso. French Acad. Sciences; Hayden medal, Acad. Natural Sciences Phila.; Mary Clark Thompson medal, Nat. Acad. Sciences, 1921; pres. Washington Soc. Archaeol. Inst. America, 1915-18; mem. Royal Swedish Acad. Sciences, 1920, Trail Riders Canadian Rockies (pres. 1924—). Chairman Nat. Advisory Com. for Aeronautics, apptd. by Pres. Wilson; vice chmn. Nat. Research Council (chmn. govt. relations com.). Author: The Trilobite; Paleontology of the Eureka District; The Cambrian Faunas of North America; The Fauna of the Lower Cambrian or Olenellus Zone; Pre-Cambrian Fossiliferous Formations; Correlation Papers; Cambrian Geology and Paleontology; Cambrian Brachipoda; The Cambrian Faunas of China; The Cambrian and Its Problems in the Cordilleran Region; Pre-Cambrian Algonkian Algal Flora; Discovery of Algonkian Bacteria; Evidences of Primitive Life; Appendages of Trilobites. Home: Washington, D.C. Died Feb. 9, 1927.

WALDEN, PERCY TALBOT, prof. chemistry; b. Brooklyn, N.Y., June 29, 1869; s. Daniel Treadwell and Caroline Amelia (Williams) W.; Ph.B., Sheffield Scientific Sch. (Yale), 1892; Ph.D., Yale, 1896; studied univs. of Leipzig and Munich; m. Sarah Scovill Whittelsey, June 22, 1905; children—Sarah Scovill, Joseph Whittelsey. Asst. in chemistry, 1892-94, instr., 1894-99, asst. prof., 1900-19, prof. 1919-37, Yale, also chmn. freshmen chemistry faculty, acting dean of freshmen, 1924-25, dean of freshmen, 1925-37, dean and prof. emeritus since 1937, was also chmn. bd. of admissions. Chief examiner in chemistry and chmn. chem. commn. for College Entrance Exam. Bd. since 1918. Mem. Am. Chem. Soc., A.A.A.S., Aurelian Soc., Sigma Psi, Chi Phi. Episcopalian. Club: Graduate. Contbr. to professional jours. Home: 210 St. Ronan St., New Haven, Conn. Died Apr. 14, 1943.

WALDO, FRANK, meteorologist, engineer; b. Cincinnati, Nov. 4, 1857; s. Frederic Augustus and Frances (Leonard) W.; brother of Leonard W.; B.S., Marietta Coll., 1878, Ph.D., 1889; Harvard U., 1880-84; m. Sarah M. Jaques, Sept. 13, 1881. Asst. in Harvard Obs., 1878-81; computer and prof. U.S. Signal Service, 1881-87; instr. astronomy, Harvard Annex (now Radcliffe Coll.), 1880-81; in U.S. Govt. service, in Europe, 1882-83; instr. meteorology, Corcoran Sch. of Science, Columbian U., 1884-85. Spl. agt. U.S. Weather Bur., 1890. Cattle ranching, 1896-1902; editorial work, 1902-07; expert in industrial edn. Mass. Commn. on Industrial Edn., Mass. State Bd. of Edn., 1907-11; improvement and building engring., 1914—; served as prof. of meteorology U.S.N., aviation detachment, Mass. Inst. Tech., 1917-18. Mem. staff Nat. Industrial Conf. Board. Author: Modern Meteorology, London, 1893; Elementary Meteorology, for Schools and Colleges, 1896. Co-editor: Blinds' George Eliot, 1904. Home: Belmont, Mass. Died May 7, 1920.

WALDO, LEONARD, metallurgical and elec. engr.; b. Cincinnati, May 4, 1853; s. Dr. Frederic Augustus and Frances (Leonard) W.; brother of Frank W.; B.S., Marietta College, 1872, A.M., 1877; studied Columbia School of Mines; Sc.D., Harvard, 1879; (hon. A.M., Yale, 1880); m. Dora Fullerton, 1875 (dec.); m. 2d, Ada Louise Purdy, 1887. Asst. astronomer U.S. Transit of Venus expdn. to Tasmania, 1874; asst. in Harvard Obs., 1875-80; astronomer in charge horological bur., Yale Obs., 1879-88. Consultant for U.S. Steel Corp., etc., in steel research; consulting engr. War Dept. in production of shells and illuminants in World War. Inventor of magnesium production process. Mem. fatigue of metals com. of Nat. Research Council; medallist Royal Soc. Arts; sometime chmn. library bd. United Engring. Soc. Home: Plainfield, N.J. Died Jan. 25, 1929.

WALDRON, CLARE BAILEY, horticulturist; b. Ravenna, O., Dec. 6, 1865; s. David S. and Louisa (Root) W.; B.S., Mich. Agrl. Coll., 1887, post-grad. study, 1887-89; D.Agr., North Dakota Agrl. Coll., 1939; m. Lois Hooper, Dec. 24, 1891. Instr. botany, Michigan Agrl. Coll., 1888-89; prof. horticulture and forestry, N.D. Agrl. College, since 1890, dean of agr. since 1915. Mem. jury awards, St. Louis Expn., 1904; chairman jury awards, Portland (Oregon) Expn., 1905. Park commr., Fargo, N.D., since 1910; mem. N.D. Conservation Commn.; pres. Tri-State Grain and Stock Growers Assn.; chmn. agrl. com. State Council Defense. Fellow A.A.A.S.; mem. N.D. Acad. Science (pres. 1910). Development specialist in vocational edn., U.S. Army, 1920-21. Address: 1404 12th Av. N., Fargo, N.D. Died Mar. 6, 1947. *

WALDSEEMÜLLER, MARTIN, cartographer; b. Freiburg, Germany, circa 1470; studied theology U. Freiburg. Became interested in cartography and geography as a youth; published map of world, Universalis cosmographia (contains 1st mention of name America, shows S.Am. as island) and Cosmographiae introductio (contains explanation of use of name America, suggests this name for New World), 1507 (a 1st edit. now in N.Y. Public Library); published Latin translation of 4 voyages of Amerigo Vespucci; produced Carta itineraria Europae (1st printed wall map of Europe), 1511; helped prepare 1513 edit. of Ptolemy's Geography (considered 1st modern atlas); apptd. canon of St. Dié, Lorraine, France, 1514; produced Carta marina navigatoria, 1516; often signed his maps with Greek spelling of his name, Illacomilus. Died St. Dié, circa 1522.

WALDSTEIN, MARTIN E., chemist; b. New York, Oct. 18, 1854; s. Henry and Sophie W.; brother of Louis and Charles W. (both q.v.); Columbia Sch. of Mines, 1870-73; Ph.D., Heidelberg, 1875; m. Emma Freund, of New York, July 11, 1880. Pres. Maas & Waldstein Co., mfg. chemists, also dir. Maas & Waldstein Extract Co. Has written various chem. articles. Home: Tunbridge Wells, Eng.

WALKER, ALFRED, dentist; b. New York, N.Y., May 22, 1876; s. Alfred and Jane (Finnegan) W.; D.D.S., New York Coll. of Dentistry, 1897; m. Elizabeth Muir, Jan. 24, 1912; children—Alfred, John Muir. Practiced in N.Y. City since 1897; formerly mem. Bd. of Dental Examiners, State of N.Y.; prof. emeritus of pulp canal therapy, New York Univ. Coll. of Dentistry. Served as pvt. 7th Regt., Nat. Guard N.Y., 1901-11; 1st lt. and capt. 107th Inf., Nat. Guard N.Y., 1918-23; lt. comdr. U.S. Naval Res. (hon. retired list). Hon. trustee Boys' Club. Pres. dental sect. Pan Am. Med. Assn. Recipient of N.Y. U. Alumni Federation Medallion, 1935. Pierre Fauchard Medal Award, 1940. Fellow Am. Coll. Dentists, N.Y. Acad. Dentistry, Internat. Coll. Dentists; mem. Am. Dental Assn. (life), Dental Soc. State N.Y. (pres. i930-31, life mem.), 1st Dist. Dental Soc. (pres. life mem.), Florida State Dental Society, Miami Dental Society, F.A.A.A.S., New York Academy Sciences, Psi Omega, Omicron Kappa Upsilon. Democrat. Author of numerous papers and repts. on dental subjects. Co-author, vol. on Dental Practice Management; co-author, vol. on Oral Diagnosis and Treatment. Home: 2131 Biarritz Drive. Office: 420 Lincoln Rd., Miami Beach, Fla. Died Oct. 16, 1948.

WALKER, ARTHUR LUCIAN, metallurgist; b. New York, N.Y., Jan. 14, 1863; s. Thomas George and Lucy (Holbrook) W.; student Charlier Inst., New York; Morris Acad., Morristown, N.J.; E.M., Columbia, 1883. Chemist, Old Dominion Copper Co., Ariz., 1883-85, engr., 1885-87; gen. supt., 1887-93; mgr. Baltimore Electrolytic Refining Co., 1893-99; mgr. Perth Amboy (N.J.) plant of Am. Smelting & Refining Co., 1899-1906; dir. same, 1906-07; prof. metallurgy, Columbia, 1908-29. Spl. lecturer in metallurgy, Post-Grad. Sch., U.S. Naval Acad., 1912, new engring. sch., Harvard, 1919. Invented, 1898, the Walker mech. casting machine which revolutionized methods used for casting refined copper into shapes and obviated hard labor; invented new system, 1902, for tank room arrangement in electrolytic copper refining plants; designed many copper casting installations and/or electrolytic refining tank rooms for plants in the U.S., Can., S. America, Australia, Russia and Africa; cons. metallurgist-at-large for ordnance, War Dept., 1917-18. Received Egleston Medal from Columbia U. for distinguished engring. achievements, 1939. Mem. Am. Inst. Mining and Metall. Engrs., Mining and Metall. Soc. America, Sigma Xi, Tau Beta Pi. Clubs: Century, Columbia Univ., Psi Upsilon, Mining; Richmond County Country. Contbr. articles to mining, metall. and hist. jours. Address: Whippany, N.J. Died Sept. 30, 1952; buried Woodlawn Cemetery, N.Y.C.

WALKER, CHARLES CLEMENT, engr.; b. Highgate, London, Eng., Aug. 25, 1877; s. William Thomas and Claudia Ann (Smith) W.; student London U. Coll., 1892-95; m. Eileen Kenneth Hood, Sept. 2, 1916. Apprenticeship John Abbot & Co., Newcastle-on-Tyne, 1895-98; articled to J. J. Taylor, 1899-1904; various civil engring. positions rys., water supply, drainage, 1915; chief technician Aircraft Mfg. Co., 1915-20; chief engr., dir. De Havilland Aircraft Co., Ltd. since 1920. Asso. mem. Inst. C.E. Home: Foresters, Stanmore Common, Middlesex. Office: Hatfield Aerodrome, Hatfield Hertfordshire England

WALKER, DAVID HAROLD, otolaryngologist; b. Pitts., Aug. 7, 1873; s. David H. and Anna B. Walker; M.D., Harvard, 1898; m. Adeline G. Perry, July 5, 1898; children—Hester (Mrs. M. H. Taylor), Eleanor (Mrs. Francis Weille), Doris (Mrs. R. G. Pritchard). Practiced in Boston, 1901—; Le Compte prof. otology emeritus, Harvard Med. Sch.; cons. aural surgeon, mem. bd. mgrs. Mass. Charitable Eye and Ear Infirmary (Boston); cons. otologist Mass. Gen., Children's hosps., New Eng. Hosp. for Women and Children. Chmn. bd. trustees Research Fund Am. Otological Soc. Mem. A.M.A., Mass. Med. Soc., Am. Laryngol., Otol. and Rhinol. Soc., Am. Otol. Soc., N.E. Otol. and Laryngol. Soc. Republican. Episcopalian. Club: Harvard. Home: Tree Tops, Peterborough, N.H. 03458. Office: 5 Bay State Rd., Boston 15, Mass. Died Jan. 13, 1963.

WALKER, HARRY BRUCE, agrl. engr.; b. Macomb, Ill., Apr. 13, 1884; s. Henry Boyd and Margaret Alcinda (Yeast) W.; preparatory edn., Highland Park (Ia.) Coll.; B.S. in C.E., Ia. State Coll., 1910, C.E., 1920; post-grad., Kan. State Coll., 1925; LL.D. U. Cal., 1954; m. Coralie Harris Walker, Sept. 11, 1912; children—Mary Margaret, Boyd Wallace. Topographer C.,B.&Q.R.R., 1906-07; asst. drainage engr. Humboldt County, Ia., 1909, 10; with Kan. State Agrl. Coll., drainage and irrigation engr., 1910-17, extension engr., 1919-21, head dept. agrl. engring., and agrl. engr., Engring. Expt.

Sta., 1921-28; state irrigation engr., Kan., 1913-17; engr. Kan. Water Commn., 1917-26; dir. research mech. farm equipment, U.S. Dept. Agr., 1927-28; with U. Cal., head of dept. agrl. engring., agrl. engr., Agrl. Expt. Sta., 1928-47, prof. agrl. engring., 1947-51, prof. emeritus, 1951—, agrl. engr. in Expt. Sta., 1947—; cons. agrl. engr., 1951—. Capt. engrs., U.S. Army, 1917-19; asst. div. engr. 78th Div., A.E.F., 13 mos.; in St. Mihiel and Meuse-Argonne offensives. Awarded John Deere medal for distinguished achievement in application of sci. and art to soil, by Am. Soc. Agrl. Engrs., 1939. Fellow Am. Soc. Agrl. Engrs. (acting pres., 1924-25; pres., 1942-43), A.A.A.S., mem. Am. Soc. C.E., Am. Soc. Engring. Edn., Am. Soc. Sugar Beet Technologist (v.p. 1942-43), Sigma Xi, Sigma Tau, Tau Beta Pi, Phi Kappa Phi, Alpha Zeta, Gamma Sigma Delta, Delta Tau Delta. Del. World Engring. Congress, Tokio, 1929. Republican. Presbyn. Author pamphlets, bulls., etc. Club: Commonwealth (San Francisco). Home: 54 College Park, Davis, Cal. Died July 27, 1957.

WALKER, JAMES EVERETT, physician, surgeon; b. Nunda, N.Y., May 21, 1854; s. Henry L. and Susan (Perry) W.; ed. State Normal Sch., Genesco, N.Y.; M.D., Cincinnati Medical Coll., 1876; post-grad. work in New York, London, and Vienna; unmarried. In gen. practice until 1892, then, after post-grad. work in Europe; engaged in Steuben Sanitarium, of which he is supt., v.p. and part owner. Medical examiner Essex State Hosp. for Incipient Tuberculosis. Director Bank of Steuben, Hornell, N.Y. Mem. A.M.A., N.Y., State Med. Assn. Steuben Co. Med. Assn., Hornellsville Med. and Surg. Assn.; mem. Internat. Med. Congress, Rome, 1894; hon. mem. many other med. socs.; ex-pres. Keuka Med. and Surg. Assn. Extensive traveler, having been throughout the world studying methods relating to his profession. Address: Hornell, N.Y.

WALKER, JAMES WILSON GRIMES, civil engr.; b. Salem, Mass., Sept. 22, 1868; s. Rear-Adm. John Grimes (U.S. Navy) and Rebecca White (Pickering) W.; prep. edn. St. Paul's Sch., Concord, N.H., Neuchatel, Switzerland, Pont Levoy, France, and Heidelberg, Germany; civil engring. Mass. Inst. Tech.; Nina Chinn, Feb. 24, 1897; children—Elizabeth Grimes (Mrs. John Williams Davis), John Grahame, Robert Serrell Wood, Herbert Wood. Employed gen. engring. work, bridge constrn., ry. location, constrn. and mgmt., 1890-97; charge surveys by Nicaragua Canal Commn., between Lake Nicaragua and Pacific Ocean, 1898; commd. civil engr. USN, 1898; resigned 1912. Mem. Am. Soc. C.E., N.H. Soc. Cin., Acad. Polit. Sci., Naval Hist. Found. Author: Ocean to Ocean, an Account, Personal and Historical, of Nicaragua and Its People, 1902. Address: Brownfield, Me. Died Nov. 2, 1950; buried Mt. Auburn Cemetery, Cambridge, Mass.

WALKER, JOHN BALDWIN, surgeon; b. Lodi, N.J., Jan. 16, 1860; s. Avery Skinner and Rosanna (Baldwin) W.; A.B., Harvard, 1884, M.D., 1888; post-grao. work in Vienna, Munich, Paris, London and Berlin, 1890-93; Sc.D., Amherst Coll.; m. Mai Elmendorf Hackstaff, June 22, 1910. House surgeon, Boston City Hosp., 1888-89; instr. in surgery, N.Y. Polyclinic Med. Sch. and Hosp., 1894-97; asst. surgeon, 1894-1902, asso. surgeon, 1902-09, instr. operative surgery, 1897-1910, prof. clin. surgery since 1910, Coll. Phys. and Surg. (Columbia); consulting surgeon Manhattan State and Bellevue hosps., Hosp. for the Ruptured and Crippled. V.p. Eugene A. Hoffman Estate. Mem. A.M.A., Am. Coll. Surgeons, Am. Surg. Assn., Med. Soc. State of N.Y., New York County Med. Soc., New York Surg. Soc., New York Acad. Medicine, Société Internationale de Chirurgie, New England Soc., S.R., Soc. Colonial Wars, Am. Bible Soc. Trustee Bard Coll., City Mission. Home for Old Men and Aged Couples. Republican. Episcopalian. Clubs: Century, University, Union, Harvard, Church, Army and Navy, Holland Lodge. Author: Vol. IX—Hernia—in Twentieth Century Practice of Medicine. Contbr. papers upon operative treatment of fractures in Trans. Am. Surg. Assn. and in various other surg. publs. Col. Med. R.C., 1917; commanding officer Base Hosp. 116, A.E.F. Awarded D.S.M. Home: 117 E. 72d St., New York, N.Y. Died Apr. 13, 1942.

WALKER, JOSEPH ALBERT, test pilot; b. Washington, Pa., Feb. 20, 1921; s. Thomas Jefferson and Pauline Sharp (Smith) W.; B.A. in Physics, Washington and Jefferson Coll., 1942, D.Aero. Scis. (hon.), 1962; m. Grace McClary, Apr. 16, 1949; children—Thomas Daniel, James Paul, Joseph Brian, Elizabeth Ann. With NASA, 1945—; project pilot on D-558, X-IE, X-3, X-5, X-15; research on F-100, F-101, F-102, F-104, B-47; 1st flight on 15, 1960, since then 25 more; attained speed 4104 Miles per hour, 1962, altitude 348,700 feet, 1963; flight tested Lunar Landing Research Vehicle. Mem. Adv. Commn. Aviation, County Los Angeles. Served to capt. USAAF, 1942-45. Decorated D.F.C., Air medal with 7 oak leaf clusters; recipient Robert J. Collier trophy, 1961, Harmon Internat. trophy for aviators, 1961, Kincheloe award, 1961, Octave Chanite award, 1961, pilot of year award Nat. Pilots Assn., 1963, Henry De Lavaulx prix Fedn. Aero. Internat., 1963. Charter mem. Sox. Exptl. Test Pilots (v.p. 1963-64); mem. Aero-Space Profls., Phi Gamma Delta. Home: 1309 West Av. L-4, Lancaster, Cal. 93534. Office: care NASA, Edwards AFB, Cal. Died June 8, 1966.

WALKER, J(OSEPH) FREDERIC, chemist; b. Perth Amboy, N.J., Dec. 7, 1903; s. Joseph F. and Mary (Hall) W.; B.S., Mass. Inst. Tech., 1925, M.S. (du Pont fellow 1926-27), 1928, Ph.D., 1929; m. Lois E. Lefler, Aug. 22, 1929; children—Lois M. (Mrs. John W. Wagner), Frederic R., Alan H. Research chemist Roessler & Hasslacher Chem. Co., Perth Amboy, 1927-30; with E. I. du Pont de Nemours & Co., Inc., 1930-64, research supr. electrochems. dept., Perth Amboy, 1945-50, Niagara Falls, N.Y., 1950-55, patent agt. patent sect., Niagara Falls, 1955-60, spl. assignment Exptl. Sta. Wilmington, Del., 1961-64; cons., Haddam, Conn., 1964-69; editorial asst. Choice, A.L.A., Middleton, Conn., 1965-69. Amateur artist, exhibiting at Studio Group Niagara Falls, 1950-69, Essex Art Assos., 1958-69. Recipient James E. Reid award for oil painting Western N.Y. Exhibit, Buffalo, 1959; Jacob F. Schoellkopf medal award Am. Chem. Soc., 1957. Licensed U.S. patent agt. Mem. Am. Chem. Soc. (chmn. Western N.Y. 1943-44), Am. Inst. Chemists (chmn. Niagara chpt. 1960-61, chmn. Del. chpt. 1962-63, chmn. com. ethics and status 1964-67), Conn. Patent Law Assn. Episcopalian (lay reader). Author Am. Chem. Soc. monograph, also articles in encys. World authority on formaldehyde chemistry. Address: Haddam CT Died Jan. 8, 1969.

WALKER, MARY E., physician; b. Oswego, N.Y., Nov. 26, 1832; d. Alvah and Vesta (Whitcomb) W.; ed. under parents (both teachers); M.D., Syracuse Med. Coll., 1855. Began practice in Columbus, O.; later settled in Rome, N.Y.; asst. surgeon, U.S. Army, Civil War, rank of 1st lt. (first woman commissioned to serve on surg. staff of any army in time of war). Awarded Congressional Medal of Honor "for bravery and valuable services in the field." Advocate of equal suffrage, dress reform, etc. Spiritualist. Home: Washington, D.C. Died Feb. 21, 1919.

WALKER, MERIWETHER LEWIS, army officer; b. Lynchburg, Va., Sept. 30, 1869; s. Thomas Lindsay (M.D.) and Catherine Maria (Dabney) W.; grad. U.S. Mil. Acad. 1893; grad. U.S. Engr. Sch., 1896, Army War Coll., 1920; m. Edith, d. Gen. A. B. Carey, Sept. 28, 1904; 1 dau., Cary Dabney (Mrs. R. B. Luckey). Commissioned additional 2d lt. Corps of Engineers, June 12, 1893; promoted through regular grades to col., July 1, 1920; col. and brig. gen. N.A., World War. Dir. Army Field Engr. Sch., 1912-14; prof. practical mil. engring., U.S. Mil. Acad., 1914-16; chief engr. Punitive Expdn. into Mexico, 1916-17; went to France as chief engr. 41st Div., Nov. 1917; prin. asst. to chief engr. A.E.F., Jan.-July 1918; dir. Motor Transport Corps, A.E.F., Aug. 1918-Aug. 1919; instr. Army War Coll., 1919-20; comdr. U.S. Engr. Sch., 1920-21; engr. of maintenance, Panama Canal, 1921-24; apptd. gov. Panama Canal, Oct. 16, 1924; promoted to brigadier general, July 1, 1927; comdg. 18th Brig., U.S. Army, Boston, Oct. 16, 1928-Aug. 16, 1933; retired, Sept. 30, 1933. Decorated D.S.M. (U.S.); Officer Legion of Honor (French). Episcopalian. Home: Vineyard Haven, Mass. Died July 29, 1947.

WALKER, PERLEY F., mech. engr.; b. Embden, Me., Apr. 28, 1875; s. Cephas and Martha Ann (Washburn) W.; B.M.E., U. of Me., 1896, M.E., 1900; M.M.E., Cornell U., 1901; m. Charlotte Edith Crowell, Dec. 22, 1902. Instr. mech. engring., U. of Me., 1896-1900; draftsman in estimating and design, Newport News (Va.) Shipbuilding Co., 1901-02; prof. mech. engring., U. of Me., 1902-05; prof. mech. engring., 1905—, dean Sch. of Engring., and prof. industrial engring., 1913—, U. of Kan.; consulting engr. petroleum and power engring lines, reporting on industrial development possibilities. Entered mil. service, May 14, 1917; commd. maj. 314th Engrs., Aug. 15, 1917; lt. col. 109th Engrs., Oct. 9, 1917; col. engrs., and apptd. comdr. 219th Regt., Aug. 9, 1918; hon. discharged, Feb. 21, 1919; col. engr. sect. O.R.C. Aug. 13, 1919; comdr. 314th Engr. Reserves. Republican. Conglist. Author: Management Engineering, 1923. Co-author of Industrial Coal, on results of coal storage investigations, 1924. Home: Lawrence, Kan. Died Oct. 16, 1927.

WALKER, REUBEN LINDSAY, army officer, civil engr.; b. Logan, Va., May 29, 1827; s. Meriwether Lewis and Maria (Lindsay) W.; grad. Va. Mil. Inst., 1845; m. Maria Eskridge, 1848; m. 2d, Sally Elam, 1857; 8 children. Commd. capt. in Confederate Army in Civil War, 1861; maj. chief arty., A.P. Hill's div., 1862, connected with Hill's command throughout war, promoted col., chief of arty. when Hill became comdr. III Army Corps; brig. gen: arty., 1865; supt. Marine and Selma R.R., 1872-74; employed by Richmond & Danville R.R., 1876-77; supt. Richmond (Va.) street railways; constrn. engr. Richmond & Alleghany R.R.; superintended building of women's dept. Va. State Penitentiary; supt: constrn. Tex. State Capitol, 1884. Died on his farm at fork of Rivanna and James rivers, Va. June 7, 1890.

WALKER, RUTH IRENE, educator; b. Dansville, Mich., Aug. 2, 1896; d. Frank M. and Mary Jane (Evans) Walker; A.B., U. Mich., 1920; M.S., U. Wis., 1924, Ph.D., 1926; Am. Assn. U. Women fellow, Radcliffe Coll., Harvard, 1937-38. Asst. botany U. Mich., 1919-20; instr. high sch., Mishawaka, Ind., 1920-21; instr. N.C. Coll. for Women, 1921-23; asst. botany U. Wis., 1923-26, instr. botany, 1926-31; instr. botany U. Wis., Milw., 1931-32, asst. prof., 1932-38, asso. prof., 1938-46, prof., 1946—. Fellow A.A.A.S.; mem. Bot. Soc. Am., Am. Assn. U. Profs., Wis. Acad. Sci., Arts and Letters, Torrey Bot. Club, Am. Assn. U. Women, Sigma Xi, Sigma Delta Epsilon, Delta Kappa Gamma, Alpha Xi Delta. Episcopalian. Contbr. articles bot. jours. Home: 1330 N. Prospect Av., Milw. 2. Died Dec. 16, 1962.

WALKER, SAMUEL J., railway equipment cons.; b. Chicago, Feb. 23, 1895; s. Dr. Samuel J. and Bertha E. (Smith) W.; A.B., Yale, 1917; m. Elizabeth Ware, Apr. 16, 1921; 1 son, Malcolm M. Began business career as industrial engr. Joseph T. Ryerson & Son, Chicago, following World War I; became asst. to pres. Chicago Ry. Equipment Co., 1941, exec. v.p., 1946, pres., July 1947-61; chmn., 1956-63, ret.; now cons. Served with U.S. Army, World War I. Home: 303 Bluff Edge Dr., Lake Forest, Ill. Died Nov. 11, 1964; buried Graceland Cemetery, Chgo.

WALKER, SCOTT WELLS, univ. dean; b. Galena, Kan., Apr. 2, 1909; s. Charles William and Cora Lucy (Andrews) W.; student Kan. State Coll., 1927-29; B.S. in Chem. Engring., U. Ark., 1937; M.S. in Chem. Engring., Mass. Inst. Tech., 1940, Sc.D., 1942; grad. Advanced Mgmt. Program, Harvard, 1953; m. Jane Caldwell, June 9, 1945; children—William B., James D., John C. From grad. asst. to asst. prof. chem. engring. Mass. Inst. Tech., 1937-46; chemist Eagle-Picher Co., 1932-37; chief chem. engring. div. chem. warfare development lab. Mass. Inst. Tech., 1942-46; dir. process research Pan Am. Petroleum Corp., 1946-53, asst. mgr. research dept., 1953-60; dean petroleum scis. and engring. U. Tulsa, 1960—. Registered profl. engr., Okla. Mem. Am. Inst. Chem. Engrs., Am. Chem. Soc., Am. Inst. M.E., Am. Soc. Engring. Edn., Okla. Acad. Sci., Okla. Soc. Profl. Engrs., Sigma Xi, Tau Beta Pi, Alpha Chi Sigma. Home: 3443 S. Florence Pl., Tulsa 5. Died May 30, 1965.

WALKER, SEARS COOK, mathematician, astronomer; b. Wilmington, Mass., Mar. 23, 1805; s. Benjamin and Susanna (Cook) W.; grad. Harvard, 1825. Became actuary Pa. Co. for Ins. on Lives and Granting Annuities, 1836; founded one of 1st astron. observatories in connection with Phila. High Sch., 1837; prepared parallactic tables which reduced time required to compute phases of occultation, 1834; mem. staff U.S. Naval Observatory, Washington, D.C., 1845, discovered that planet Neptune was identical with star seen twice by Lalande in 1795, which had been referred to as star Number 26266, 1847; in charge of computations of geog. longitude in U.S. Coast Survey, 1847-53; originated telegraphing of transits of stars; developed registry of time observations known as Am. method. Published articles on astron. subjects. Died Cincinnati, Jan. 30, 1853.

WALKER, STANTON, engr.; b. Vevay, Ind., Mar. 18, 1894; s. Harvey Edwin and Emma Deane (Williamson) W.; B.S., Univ. of Ill., 1917; m. Amelia Bertha Ramseyer, Aug. 12, 1916; children—John Stanton Robert, Richard David. Asso. research and research engr. for Portland Cement Assn., Structural Materials Research Lab., Lewis Inst., Chicago, 1917-26; dir. of engring. Nat. Sand and Gravel Assn., Washington 1926-62, emeritus, 1962-71, also dir. assn.'s Research Found., U. Md.; dir. engring. Nat. Ready Mixed Concrete Assn., 1930-62; emeritus 1962-71, also dir. Assn.'s Research Found. U. Md.; lectr. materials dept. civil engring. U. Md.; cons. or concrete and mineral aggregates; cons. engr. Nat. Indsl. Sand Assn., 1935-62. Recipient Roy W. Crum award, Highway Research Bd., 1956. Mem. Am. Soc. C.E. (hon.), Am. Soc. Testing Materials (mem exec. com. 1952-53, dir. 1951-54; recipient Award of Merit 1951, and Frank E. Richart award 1957 Sanford E. Thompson award 1960, Turner medal 1961; hon. mem.), Am. Concrete Inst. (mem. bd. 1940-50, pres. 1947, hon. mem.), Hwy. Research Bd. (exec. com. 1941-49, chmn. 1944-45), Am. Inst. Mining and Metall. Engrs. Contbr. articles dealing with research in concrete and mineral aggregates in tech. pubs. and in transactions and proc. profl. socs. Home: Blacksburg VA Died July 1971.

WALKER, THOMAS BARLOW, lumberman; b. Xenia, O., Feb. 1, 1840; s. Platt Bayless and Anstis Keziah (Barlow) W.; ed. Baldwin U., Berea, O., now Baldwin-Wallace Coll. (LL.D.); m. Harriet G. Hulet; children—Gilbert Marshall, Julia (Mrs. Ernest F. Smith), Leon Barlow (dec.), Fletcher Loring, Willis Jay, Clinton Llewellyn, Archie Dean. Taught school, and later became a traveling salesman. Went to Minneapolis, 1862; was engaged on government surveys and later on survey for St. Paul & Duluth R.R. Large operator in Minn. timber lands and lumbering operations in the pine timber of Minn.; has extensive interests in Calif. white and sugar pine. Projector and builder of St. Louis Park, suburb, and the trolley line to it. Owned extensive property in Minneapolis; built central city market and the wholesale commn. district which placed Minneapolis in the front rank as a wholesale and retail market. Originator and builder Minneapolis Pub. Library; pres. library bd., annually elected for 34 yrs.; was responsible for the building up of Acad. of Science and its museum of science and art; presented to the city important collections of art, including over 500 oil paintings, 300 miniatures, and over 7,000 art objects, consisting of pottery, porcelain, jades, ancient glass, necklaces, crystals, etc., mostly from the tombs, ruins and temples of Syria, Egypt, Greece, Persia and Babylonia. Advocate of practical methods of conserving the forests for perpetual use. Home: Minneapolis, Minn. Died Aug. 28, 1928.

WALKER, WILLIAM HULTZ, chemical engr.; b. Pittsburgh, Pa., Apr. 7, 1869; s. David H. and Anna (Blair) W.; B.S., Pa. State Coll., 1890; A.M., Ph.D., U. of Göttingen, 1892; Sc.D., U. of Pittsburgh, 1915; m. Isabelle Luther, Sept. 15, 1896. Prof. industrial chemistry, now chem. engring., Mass. Inst. Tech., 1894-1921; lecturer on industrial chemistry, Harvard, 1905-08; cons. chem. engr., 1900—; mem. Little & Walker, 1900-05; dir. research lab. applied chemistry, Chem. Products Co. Professional work has been principally in the production of art glass, the mfr. of sterling silver, the chemistry of cellulose and its industrial applications and uses, the cause and prevention of the corrision of iron and steel, and the technology of petroleum. Has invented and introduced numerous industrial processes of value. Commd. lt. col. N.A., 1917; chief of chem. service sect.; promoted col. U.S.A., in charge Gas Offense Div. Chem. Warfare Service; comdr. officer Edgewood Arsenal. Fellow Am. Acad. Arts and Sciences, Am. Iron and Steel Inst., Am. Electrochem. Soc. (pres. 1910-11), Am. Chem. Soc. (pres. Eastern Sect. 1904), Am. Soc. for Testing Materials, Soc. Chem. Industry (London). Awarded Nichols medal, 1908. Presbyn. Awarded D.S.M., 1919. Home: Pasadena, Calif. Died July 9, 1934.

WALL, EDWARD EVERETT, civil engr.; b. Cambridge, Saline County, Mo., Aug. 15, 1860; s. John and Mary Brown (Gault) W.; C.E., U. of Mo., 1884, LL.D., 1935; m. Jessie Towne, Feb. 20, 1901. Engaged in ry. surveys and constrn., in Kan., Mo. and Neb., 1885-88; U.S. asst. engr. on secondary triangulation of upper Mo. River, 1889; municipal engring. and contracting, St. Louis, 1890-95; engr. in charge of sewer constrn. and reconstruction, St. Louis, 1895-1903, continuing as prin. asst. engr., Water Dept. 1903-06, asst. water commr., 1906-11, water commr., rebuilding and modernizing Water Works, 1911-25; dir. pub. utilities, 1925-26 and 1933-41; cons. engr., 1926-33. Designed supplementary water works for St. Louis to cost $25,000,000; designed and began construction new lighting system to cost $8,000,000. Mem. Am. Soc. Civil Engrs. (dir. 1918-20; v.p. 1921-22; hon. mem. since Oct. 1938), Am. Water Works Assn. (hon. mem. since 1936), St. Louis Inst. Cons. Engrs. (v.p. 1927; pres. 1933), St. Louis Acad. of Science, Engineers Club (pres. 1909; hon. mem. since 1940), Beta Theta Pi, Tau Beta Pi. Awarded Thomas Fitch Rowland prize, 1908, by Am. Soc. C.E., for best paper of the year. Mason. Clubs: Noonday, Circle. Author: Engineers, Engineering and Some Vagaries, 1931; Literary Productions of Two Engineers, 1940. Address: 5361 Pershing Av., St. Louis, Mo. Died June 26, 1944.

WALL, HUBERT STANLEY, mathematician, educator,; b. nr. Rockwell City, Ia., Dec. 2, 1902; s. Samuel H. and Gratia (Wright) W.; B.A., Cornell Coll., 1924, M.A., 1924, D.Sc. (hon.), 1970; Ph.D., U. Wis., 1927, postgrad. Inst. Advanced Study, 1937-38; m. Mary Kate Parker, Oct. 18, 1947. Fellow U. Wis., Madison, 1924-26, asst., 1926-27; instr. math. Northwestern U., 1927-30, asst. prof., 1930-36, asso. prof., 1936-43, prof., 1943-44; lectr. Ill. Inst. Tech., Chgo., 1944-45, prof., 1945-46; prof. U. Tex., Austin, 1946-70, prof. emeritus, 1970-73. Mem. Am. Math. Soc. Author: Analytic Theory of Continued Fractions, 1948; Creative Mathematics, 1963. Contbr. articles to profl. jours. Home: Austin TX Died Sept. 12, 1971; buried Rockwell City IA

WALL, WILLIAM GUY, consulting engr.; b. Baltimore, Md., Aug. 7, 1876; s. William Edward and Mary Catherine (Dade) W.; grad. in Civ. Engring., Va. Mil. Inst., 1894; B.S., Mass. Inst. Tech., 1896; m. Minnie Tyndall, 1909 (died 1931); m. 2d, Helen Wessel, 1934. Practiced at Indianapolis, 1900—; founder, v.p. and chief engr. Nat. Motor Car Co.; cons. engr. for several prominent automobile companies. Maj. and lt. col., U.S.A., World War; col. Res. Secretary, Am. Legion Endowment Fund Corp. Democrat. Episcopalian. Home: Indianapolis, Ind. Died Jan. 16, 1941.

WALLACE, CHARLES FREDERICK, mfg. co. exec., inventor; b. Kansas City, Mo., July 1, 1885; s. Charles Stewart and Nellie (Galehouse) W.; student U. Mich., 1905-06; D.Sc. (hon.), Monmouth Coll., 1960; m. Florence Murray, Aug. 27, 1914; children—Jane Murray Wallace (Mrs. Niblack Thorne), Barbara Stewart (Mrs. Joseph C. Cornwall), Elizabeth Glover (Mrs. Paul E. Sharts). Co-founder Wallace & Tiernan, Inc., Belleville, N.J., 1911, v.p., 1913-53, sec., 1913-53, vice chmn. bd., 1953—. Patentee chlorination processes, water sterilization, indsl. chlorination, automatic controls, cooling and dispensing beer, clocks, flashing signals, radio beacon signals, science of telemetering, pressure sensitive instruments, weather instruments, steam sterilizer, indsl. bleach panel. Trustee ELJABAR Found., Florence Murray Wallace Fund. Co-recipient Edward Longstretch medal Franklin Inst., 1922; recipient Modern Pioneer award N.A.M., 1940. Republican. Conglist. Club: Little Egg Harbor Yacht (Beach Haven). Home: 629 Tremont Av., Westfield, N.J.; also 104 Belvoir Av., Beach Haven, N.J. Office: 25 Main St., Belleville 9, N.J. Died June 3, 1964; buried Fairview Cemetery, Westfield, N.J.

WALLACE, JOHN FINDLEY, civil engr; b. Fall River, Mass., Sept. 10, 1852; s. David A. and Martha (Findley) W.; student monmouth (Ill.) Coll.; C.E., U. of Wooster, 1882; (LL.D., Monmouth Coll., 1904; Sc.D., Armour Inst., Chicago); m. Sarah E. Ulmer. Assistant U.S. engineer on upper Mississippi River and improvements of Rock Island Rapids, 1871-76; co. surveyor and city engr., 1876-78; chief engr. and supt. Peoria & Farmington R.R., 1878-81, Central Ia. Ry., in Ill., 1881-83; constrn. engr. and master of transportation Central Ia. Ry., 1883-86; bridge engr. A.,T.&S.F. R.R., 1886-89; resident engr. Chicago, Madison & Northern R.R., 1889-91; with I.C. R.R., 1891-1904, as engr. of constrn., 1891-92, chief engr., 1892-97, asst. to 2d v.p., 1897-1900, asst. gen. mgr., 1900-01, gen. mgr., 1901-04; 1st Am. chief engr. Panama Canal, 1904; Isthmian Canal commr. and v.p. and gen. mgr. Panama R.R. & Steamship Co., 1905; pres. and chmn. bd. dirs. Westinghouse, Church, Kerr & Company, 1906-17. Designed and constructed World's Fair terminals, Chicago, 1892; also new pass. terminals for C.&N.W. R.R., Chicago; conducted extensive surveys and examinations and created the initial orgn. for Panama Canal, etc.; chmn. Chicago Ry. Terminal Commn.; adviser and consultant to large corps. Independent. Presbyn. Home: New York, N.Y. Died July 3, 1921.

WALLACE, ROBERT CHARLES, exec. director Arctic Institute of N.A.; b. Orkney, Scotland, June 15, 1881; s. James and Mary (Swanney) W.; M.A., Edinburgh U., 1901, B.Sc., 1907, D.Sc., 1912; Ph.D., Gottingen U., 1909; student St. Andrews U., 1909-10; hon. LL.D., Univ. of Manitoba, 1928, Queen's Univ., 1930, Univ. of Toronto, 1933, Univ. of Saskatchewan, 1936, McMaster Univ., 1936, McGill Univ., 1938. U. of Western Ont., 1938, Temple U., 1940, St. Lawrence U., 1942, Harvard, 1944, U. Buffalo, 1946, U. Edinburgh, 1947, U. Ottawa, 1948, U. N.B., 1950, U. Alberta, 1951; D.Sc., Mich. Coll. Mining and Tech., 1942, Queen's U., Belfast, 1949; Laval U., 1951; D.C.L., Bishop's U., 1945, Oxford U., 1948; m. Elizabeth Harcus Smith, May 7, 1912; children—Ronald Stuart (deceased), Sheila Craigie (Mrs. David Woodsworth), Brenda Swanney (Mrs. Hiley Addington), Elspeth Harcus (Mrs. Charles Baugh). Lecturer in charge of dept. geology and mineralogy, U. of Manitoba, Winnipeg, 1910-12, prof., 1912-28; pres., U. of Alberta, 1928-36; prin. and vice chancellor, Queen's Univ., 1936-51; pres. Research Council of Ontario, 1948-51; executive director Arctic Institute of North America. Commissioner for Mines and Natural Resources, 1926-28; commr. Northern Manitoba, hdqrs. at The Pas, 1918-21. Mem. bd. of trustees, Carnegie Foundation Advancement of Teaching, 1938-51. Chmn. Nat. Adv. Com. for Children from Overseas 1941-46; mem. Commn. for Investigation of Cancer Remedies in Ont., mem. Com. on Reconstrn.; chmn. sub-com. Conservation and Development of Nat. Resources, 1940-43; former chmn. Ont. Research Commn. Fellow Royal Soc. of Canada (pres. 1940-41), Geological Soc. of London, Soc. Economic Geologists, Geological Soc. of Am., Mineralogical Soc. of Am.; mem. Canadian Inst. Mining and Metallurgy (pres. 1924-25), Manitoba Edn. Assn. (pres. 1925-26), Assn. Canadian Clubs (pres. 1930-31); hon. mem. Engring. Inst. of Can. Companion of St. Michael and St. George, 1944. Club: Rotary (Canada). Member United Church of Can. Author: The Burwash Lectures, A Liberal Education in a Modern World, 1932; Religion, Science and the Modern World, 1952; also tech. papers. Address: 4 Centre St., Kingston, Ont., Can. Died Jan. 29, 1955; buried Cataraqui Cemetery, Kingston.

WALLACE, R(OBERT) JAMES, photo-physicist; b. Galashiels, Scotland, Nov. 15, 1868; s. Robert and Elizabeth (Pringle) W.; ed. various pub. and normal schs. in Edinburgh and Kelso, Scotland, and later grad. from scientific and art depts., The Royal Instn., Edinburgh; m. Jessie Gardner Robertson, of Chicago, Sept. 24, 1891. Ed. as artist and pursued that profession in Edinburgh; came to U.S., 1888, and continued as illustrator and designer; acquired practical knowledge of all Am. and European photo-engraving and reproductive printing processes, to 1894. Art editor David C. Cook Pub. Co., 1894-99; in 1894 equipped pvt. laboratory for photo-physical investigations, having first taken up this study as an amateur while in Edinburgh about 1886; 1903 at the Yerkes Obs. as photo-physicist; instr. in photo-physics, Yerkes Obs. (U. of Chicago), 1906; dir. research lab. of G. Cramer Dry Plate Co., St. Louis, 1909-17; tech. dir. Central Dry Plate Co., St. Louis, Sept. 1, 1917—. Fellow Royal Astron. Soc. (London); asso. American Physical Soc.; fellow A.A.A.S. Episcopalian. Author: Isochromatism, 1901; Color Photography, 1902; More About Isochromatism, 1903; also numerous papers on original research in photographic sensitometry, pub. in Astrophysical Journal, Popular Astronomy, etc. *

WALLACE, STUART ALLEN, physician, educator; b. Metcalfe, Ont., Can., Dec. 1, 1898; s. David W. and Esther (Eastman) W.; M.D., C.M., Queen's U., 1922. Came to U.S., 1923, naturalized, 1949. Intern, Hamilton Gen. Hosp., Ont., Can., 1922-23; with N.Y. Lying-In Hosp., 1923; mem. staff Manchester-Meml. Hosp., 1923-25; grad. work pathology Tulane Med. Sch., 1925-27; mem. staff Baylor U. Hosp., 1927-33; mem. faculty Baylor U. Coll. Medicine, 1936—, prof., 1943—, chmn. dept. pathology, 1943-61; cons. pathology Hermann Hosp., Tex. Children's Hosp., Meth. Hosp., St. Luke's Episcopal Hosp., VA Hosp., Jefferson Davis Hosp. (all Houston). Recipient Dean Fowler award Queens U., 1921, Silver Beaver award, 1953, award of merit Am. Med. Edn. Found. Fellow Am. Coll. Pathologists; mem. Am. Soc. Clin. Pathologists, Am. Assn. Pathologists and Bacteriologists, A.M.A. Prebyn. Address: Houston. Died Oct. 13, 1965.

WALLACE, WILLIAM MCLEAN, physician; b. Montclair, N.J., Jan. 12, 1912; s. Albert Howard and Ethel (McLean) W.; A.B., U. Pa., 1934, M.D., 1938; m. Patricia Raymond, July 2, 1949; children—William, Andrew, Jane, Harriet, Patricia. Intern Robert Packer Hosp., Sayre, Pennsylvania, 1938-39; NRC fellow Harvard, 1939-41, Rockefeller Found. fellow, 1946-48, asst. prof. pediatrics, med. sch., 1948-51; intern, resident Children's Hosp., Boston, 1941-42; prof. pediatrics Western Res. U. Sch. Medicine, 1951-68; dir. pediatrics Univ. Hosp., Cleve., 1951-68. Mem. human embryology and devel. study sect. NIH. Served from 1st lt. to maj. M.C., AUS, 1941-45. Decorated Silver Star, Bronze Star, Purple Heart. Diplomate Am. Bd. Pediatrics. Mem. A.M.A., Am. Soc. Clin. Investigation, Soc. Pediatric Research, Am. Pediatric Soc., American Institute Nutrition, Am. Assn. Advancement Sci., Am. Acad. Pediatrics, Home: Cleveland Heights OH Died Nov. 9, 1968; cremated.

WALLAU, HERMAN L., elec. engr.; born Brooklyn, N.Y., Jan. 26, 1877; s. George Jacques and Marie Lucile (Neuville) W.; B.S., Brooklyn Poly. Institute, 1896 (valedictorian), E.E. from same inst., 1897; m. Irene Louise Owers, Dec. 3, 1902; children—Irene Owers, Lucille Marian. With elec. engring. div. Brooklyn Rapid Transit Co., 1897-98, line constrn. same, 1898-99; draftsman Goodson Graphotype Co., Apr.-Aug. 1899; multiple unit equipment insp., Brooklyn Rapid Transit Co., Sept.-Dec. 1899; with Elec. Launch Co., Jan.-Oct. 1900, Westinghouse Electic & Mfg. Co., 1900-01; with Cleveland Electrical Illuminating Co., Oct. 1901-Jan. 1942; became chief electrical engr., 1907, designing elec. features of its Lake Shore, Avon and Ashtabula stations; dir. installation first 66,000 volt underground transmission circuits in U.S.; retired Jan. 1942. Fellow Am. Inst. E.E.; mem. Edison Electric Inst., Assn. Edison Illuminating Cos. Episcopalian. Home: 3051 E. Derbyshire Rd., Cleveland Heights 18 OH

WALLER, ELWYN, chemist; b. New York, N.Y., Mar. 22, 1846; s. Joseph Fernando and Martha (Brookes) W.; brother of Frank W.; A.B., Harvard, 1867, A.M., 1870; E.M., Columbia Sch. of Mines, 1870, Ph.D., 1875; m. Ella White, July 15, 1880 (died 1887); m. 2d, Margaret V. Dorsey, Dec. 2, 1888 (died 1906); m. 3d, Frances Dorsey, Nov. 28, 1907 (died 1908). Asst. instr., 1871-77, instr., 1877-85, prof. analytical chemistry, 1885-93, Columbia Sch. Mines. Mineralogist San Domingo Expdn., Jan. to Apr. 1871; health inspector and chemist, New York Health Dept., 1872-85. Edited, completed and revised Quantitative Analysis, by F. A. Cairns, 1880, 1896. Home: Morristown, N.J. Died July 6, 1919.

WALLIS, EVERETT STANLEY, univ. prof.; b. Waitsfield, Vt., Dec. 17, 1899; s. George Wilbur and Georgia Adelle (Bragg) W.; B.S., U. Vt., 1921, M.S., 1922, D.Sc., 1962; A.M., Princeton, 1924, Ph.D., 1925; D.Sc. honoris causa, Middlebury College, 1949; LL.D., Temple U., 1961; D.Sc., University Vt., 1962; m. Mary Fletcher Northrop, June 26, 1926; 1 son, Peter Bent Brigham Northrop (dec.). Part-time instr. in chemistry, Univ. of Vt., 1921; part-time instr., Princeton, 1922-23, University Scholar, 1923-24, Charlotte Elizabeth Proctor fellow, 1924-25; asst. prof. chemistry, St. Johns Coll., Annapolis, Md., 1925-26, asso. prof. and head dept. of chemistry, 1926-30, asst. prof. chemistry, Princeton, 1930-35, asso. prof., 1935-40, A. Barton Hepburn prof. of organic chemistry, 1940—; M.D. Anderson vis. prof. chemistry U. Houston, 1962-63; vis. prof. biochemistry Baylor Coll. Medicine, 1962—; cons. Merck & Co., Inc., Rahway, N.J., 1933-65. Special adviser to Q.M. Gen., Army, on flame proofing wearing apparel, Vermont Civil Defense. Served as acting corpl. Co. D, S.A.T.C., U. of Vt., 1918. Received award from commanding officer, 2d Service Command, for services rendered in World War II, Certificate of Ward, OSRD, 1945, National Cystic Fibrosis Award (Texas), 1962. Trustee of the Proctor Foundation, Princeton University (Episcopal). Senior warden Trinity Church, Princeton, 1942; mem. bd. of missions Episcopal Ch., Diocese of N.J. Member Cathedral Foundation (Episcopal.) Diocese of N.J. Fellow A.A.A.S., New York Academy of Science; mem. American Chemical Society, American Inst. Chemists, Phi Beta Kappa, Sigma Xi, Alpha Tau Omega. Clubs: Nassau, Rotary (Princeton, New Jersey). Contbr. to Advanced Treatise on Organic Chemistry Gilman; Organic Reactions Vol. III Adams; also contbr. many papers to jours. of learned socs. Home: 115 Broadmead. Office: Frick Chemical Laboratory, Princeton University, Princeton, N.J. Died July 10, 1965; buried Waitsfield, Vt.

WALLIS, WILLIAM FISHER, magnetician; b. Baltimore, Md., June 5, 1874; s. William Hawkins and Maria Isabella (Griffith) W.; grad. Baltimore City Coll., 1893; A.B., Johns Hopkins, 1896; B.S., Mass. Inst. Tech., 1913; m. Mary Alberta Sigelen, Dec. 25, 1920; 1 son, Richard Fisher. Magnetic observer, U.S. Coast and Geodetic Survey, 1900-10; magnetician, Dept. Terrestrial Magnetism, Carnegie Instn., Washington, D.C., 1913-39; retired. Recalled to active duty by the Dept. Terrestrial Magnetism to assist in the Department's war service. Retired again Dec. 1946. Magnetic survey work in U.S., Europe, Africa, Hawaii, Australia and S. America. Mem. Philos. Soc. Washington, etc. Home: 5219 42d St. N.W., Washington 15 DC

WALSH, BENJAMIN DANN, entomologist; b. Clapton, London, Eng., Sept. 21, 1808; s. Benjamin Walsh; B.A., Trinity Coll., Cambridge (Eng.) U., 1831, M.A. (hon.), 1834; m. Rebecca Finn, 1837. Came to U.S., 1838; pioneer in demonstrating that Am. farmers aided multiplication of insects by improper planting of crops, also pioneered introduction of fgn. parasites and natural enemies of imported insect pests; founder and editor (with Charles V. Riley) Am. Entomologist, 1868; state entomologist Ill., published his only ofcl. report in Transactions of the Ill. State Hort. Soc., 1867. Author: The Comedies of Aristophanes, Translated into Corresponding English Metres, published in Blackwood's Mag., 1837; contbr. agrl. articles to Proceedings of Boston Soc. of Natural History, also Transactions of Am. Entomol. Soc. Died Rock Island, Ill., Nov. 18, 1869.

WALSH, JAMES JOSEPH, physician; b. Archbald, Pa., Apr. 12, 1865; s. Martin J. and Bridget (Golden) W.; A.B., Fordham Coll., N.Y., 1884, A.M., 1885, Ph.D., 1889; M.D., U. of Pa., 1895; univs. of Paris, Vienna, Berlin, 1895-98; LL.D., Georgetown U., 1912; Litt.D., Catholic U. of America, 1915; Sc.D., Notre Dame, 1909; D.E., U. of San Francisco, 1930; m. Julia H. Freed, 1915; children—James J., Jr., Moira. In practice at New York since 1898; prof. physiol. psychology, Cathedral Coll., New York, since 1906; cons. physician Gabriels Sanatorium. Fellow N.Y. Acad. Med.; mem. A.M.A.; N.Y. State and N.Y. County med. socs., A.A.A.S.; life mem. N.Y. Hist. Soc., Nat. Arts Club. Catholic. Knight Comdr. Papal Order of St. Gregory; Knight of Malta. Democrat. Author: Makers of Modern Medicine, 1907; Catholic Churchmen in Science (3 volumes), 1917; The Popes and Science, 3d edition, 1916; The Thirteenth, Greatest of Centuries, 10th edit., 1937; Old Time Makers of Medicine, 1911; Education, How Old the New, 1910; Modern Progress and History, 1912; The Century of Columbus, 1914; History of Medicine in New York (5 vols.), 1919; Medieval Medicine, 1920; Health Through Will Power, 1920; Religion and Health, 1920, Success in a New Era, 1919; What Civilization Owes to Italy, 1923; Cures, 1923; Psychotherapy, 1912. World's Debt to the Catholic Church, 1924; Safeguarding Children's Nerves (with Dr. John Foote), 1924; Eating and Health, 1925; Spiritualism a Fake (contains also Spiritualism a Fact, by Hereward Carrington), 1925; Our American Cardinals, 1926; The World's Debt to the Irish, 1926; These Splendid Priests, 1926; These Splendid Sisters, 1926; Laughter and Health, 1927; The Church and Healing, 1928; History of Nursing, 1929; Priests and Long Life, 1927; Mother Alphonsa, 1930; Sex Instruction, 1931; A Golden Treasury of Medieval Literature, 1931; American Jesuits, 1934; Education of the Founding Fathers of the Republic, 1935; High Points of Medieval Culture, 1937. Co-author: Essays in Pastoral Medicine, Makers of Electricity. Trustee Catholic Summer Sch. of America. Address: 344 W. 72d St., New York, N.Y. Died Feb. 28, 1942.

WALSH, THOMAS F., mine owner and mining engr.; b. County of Tipperary, Ireland, 1851; ed. in public schools; learned millwright's trade; emigrated to U.S. at age of 19, and settled in Colo.; m. Carrie B. Reed, 1879. Engaged in mining business, made close study of geology, mineralogy, metallurgy, the deposition of ore bodies and the development and treatment of ores, and was instrumental in introducing new methods of treatment. Developed, equipped and is large owner in the Camp Bird mines, Ouray, Colo. One of Nat. Commrs. to Paris Expn., 1900. Home: Washington, D.C. Died 1910.

WALSON, CHARLES MOORE, army officer; b. Delaware, Aug. 24, 1883; s. George W. and Minnie S. (Collins) W.; M.D., Jefferson Med. Coll., Phila., 1906; grad. Army Med. Sch., 1912; m. Bonnie Miller, June 2, 1915; children—Charles W. (officer U.S. Army), Elizabeth W. (wife of Lt. Col. George W. Bixby). Commd. 1st lt., Med. Corps, U.S. Army, 1912, and advanced through the grades to brig. gen., 1945; surgeon, Expeditionary Forces, Vera Cruz, Mexico, 1914; during World War I served successively at Honolulu and Schofield Barracks, T.H.; camp surgeon, Camp Lewis, Wash.; div. surgeon, 15th Div., Camp Logan, Houston, Tex.; comdg. officer, Gen. Hosp. 33, Fort Logan H. Roots, Little Rock, Ark.; asst. to chief surgeon, A.E.F., France; at station hosp. Am. Forces in Germany, Coblenz, Germany; hosp. inspector and exec. officer, Walter Reed Gen. Hosp., 1922-26; asst. to corps area surgeon, 7th Corps Area Surgeon's Office, Omaha, Neb., 1926-31; surgeon, Station Hosp., Fort Benjamin Harrison, Ind., 1931-35; in Surgeon Gen.'s Office, Washington, D.C., 1935-39; asst. to corps area surgeon, II Corps Area, 1939, corps area surgeon, 1940-42; Service Command surgeon Aug. 1942-June 1946, surgeon of 1st Army since consolidation of 1st and 2d Service Commands. With St. Joseph Infirmary, Fort Worth, Texas, 1906-07, St. John's Hospital, St. Louis, Mo., 1907-08; asst. to clinical professor surgery, St. Louis U., 1908-11; assts. to city health officer, St. Louis, 1909-11; lecturer on vital statistics Creighton U., 1926-30, on tropical medicine, Indiana U. Med. Sch., 1930-34. Adminstr. Am. Red Cross Blood Program, Greater N.Y., 1947-51, Washington, 1951—. Decorated Mexican Service, Victory, Army Occupation of Germany medals, Am. Defense Ribbon, Am. Theater Campaign Medal, Victory Medal World War II, Legion of Merit, Army Commendation Ribbon. Fellow Am. Coll. Surgeons; mem. A.M.A., Assn. Mil. Surgeons of U.S.A., Am. Hosp. Assn., Phi Rho Sigma. Mason. Club: Army-Navy Country (Washington). Home: Washington, D.C. Died May 14, 1959.

WALSTER, HARLOW LESLIE, dean of agr.; b. Troy Twp., Sauk County, Wis., Apr. 20, 1883; s. George Albert and Mary Etta (Stelzman) W.; B.S.A., U. of Wis., 1908; A.M., Harvard, 1913; Ph.D., U. of Chicago, 1918; m. Ada Georgene Meadows, June 15, 1921; 1 dau., Eunice Mary. Instr. in soils, U. of Wis., 1908-15, asst. prof., 1916-19; agronomist N.D. Agrl. Expt. Sta., Fargo, N.D., 1919-34; dean, div. of agr., N.D. Agrl. Coll., Fargo, 1924—, dir. agrl. extension service, 1934-37, dir. Agrl. Expt. Sta. 1934-37 and 1939—; consultant to Bureau of Reclamation, U.S. Dept. of Interior, 1944—; v.p. Fargo Sch. of Religious Edn., N.D. Agrl. Coll. Fellow A.A.A.S.; mem. Am. Soc. Agonomy, Am. and Internat. Society Soil Science, American Agricultural Historical Society, N.D. Academy of Science, Phi Beta Kappa, Phi Kappa Phi, Alpha Zeta, Phi Lambda Upsilon, Gamma Alpha, Alpha Gamma Rho. Conglist. Mason. Clubs: Lions, Commons (Fargo). Author: Soils and Soil Fertility (with A. R. Whitson), 1912. Author of many agrl. expt. station bulletins. Home: 1130 4th St. N., Fargo, N.D. Died Oct. 7, 1957; buried Mount Pleasant Cemetery, Lodi, Wis.

WALTER, HERBERT EUGENE, biologist; b. Burke, Vt., Apr. 19, 1867; s. Augustus Porter and Betsey Ann (Brockway) W.; A.B., Bates Coll., 1892; A.M., Brown U., 1893; studied several summers, Woods Hole, Mass., 1892-1905, U. of Freiburg, Germany, 1894, 1903, Ph.D., Harvard, 1906; Sc.D., Middlebury (Vt.) Coll., 1934; Sc.D., Bates Coll., 1939; m. Alice E. Hall, Aug. 25, 1896. Instr. biology, Chicago High Sch., 1894-1904; asst. prof. comparative anaotmy, Brown U., 1906-13, asso. prof., 1913-23, prof., 1923-37, emeritus since 1937; instr. field zoölogy, Cold Spring Harbor, N.Y., 1906-17, asst. dir., 1917-26. Fellow A.A.A.S.; mem. Am. Soc. Naturalists, Am. Soc. Zoölogists, Am. Genetics Assn. Eugenics Research Assn., Am. Museum Natural History, Sigma Xi, Phi Beta Kappa, Am. Ornithologists Union. Republican. Unitarian. Author: The Birds of Androscoggin County, 1891; The Reactions of Planarians to Light, 1907; Genetics, 1913 (3d rev. 1938); The Human Skeleton, 1918; Biology of the Vertebrates, 1928 (revised 1939); One Innocent Abroad, 1913; also studies of Animal Life (with Worrallo Whitney and F. Colby Lucas), 1900; Wild Birds in City Parks (with wife), 1901 (many editions and revisions); Biology: The Story of Living Things (with George William Hunter and George William Hunter III), 1937. Home: 67 Oriole Av., Providence, R.I. Died Oct. 1, 1945.

WALTER, RAYMOND F(OWLER), civil and irrigation engr.; b. Chicago, Ill., Oct. 31, 1873; s. John Huffman and Susie (Garlock) W.; B.S. in Engring., Colorado State Coll., 1893, M.S. in Civ. and Irrigation Engring., 1929; m. Lilliam Leon Phillips, Nov. 26, 1896; children—Dorothy Lilliam (Mrs. George Harger), Donald Scott. Project engr., in charge constrn. Belle Fourche (S.D.) irrigation project, 1903-08; supervising engr., in charge constrn., Bur. Reclamation, U.S. Dept. Interior, on projects in Colo., Wyo., Neb., Kan., Okla., S.D., 1908-15, chief engr. for same bur., all Western States, 1924—; also chief engr. Boulder Dam and Boulder Canyon Project, 1929—, Grand Coulee Dam and Columbia Basin project and 20 other reclamation and power projects, 1933—. Presbyn. Mason, K.P. Home: Denver, Colo. Died June 30, 1940.

WALTER, THOMAS, botanist; b. Hampshire, Eng., circa 1740; m. Anne Lesesne, Mar. 26, 1769; m. 2d, Ann Peyre, Mar. 20, 1777, 2 daus.; m. 3d, Dorothy Cooper, after 1780, 1 dau. Collected herbarium, presented to Linnean Soc. of London, 1849, acquired by Brit. Mus. Natural History, 1863; tried to introduce (with John Fraser) a native Carolina grass, Agrostis perennans, into gen. cultivation in Eng. Author: Flora Caroliniana (sole record of work, describing approximately 1,000 species of flowering plants representing 435 genera, from specimins collected with Fraser in S.C.). Died Jan. 17, 1789; buried in small bot. garden on plantation on bank of Santee River, S.C.

WALTERS, FRANCIS MARION, JR., metallurgist; born Monticello, Ind., Apr. 25, 1888; s. Francis M. and Jennie Elizabeth (Horning) W.; A.B., U. of Mo., 1911, A. M., 1914, Ph.D., 1920; m. Roma Crow, Nov. 16, 1916; children—Jane (dec.), Francis Marion, III, John Linton, Thomas Charles. In charge of dept. of physics U. of Mont., 1915-16; instr. in physics, Central H.S. and Jr. Coll., St. Joseph, Mo., 1916-18; asst. physicist Bur. of Standards, Washington, 1918-20, asso., 1920-21; prof. physics, St. John's Univ., Shanghai, China, 1921-22; asso. physicist, Bur. of Standards, 1922-24; dir. Bur. of Metall. Research, 1924-32; physicist Metals Research Lab., Carnegie Inst. Tech., 1932-34; research engr. Youngstown Sheet & Tube Co., 1935-38; cons. metallurgist, 1938-39; metallurgist, Naval Research Lab., 1939-40, sr. metallurgist and acting supt., div. of phys. metallurgy, since 1940, prin. metallurgist, 1942, head physicist and supt. div. of physical metallurgy, 1943-46; asso. div. leader chemistry metallurgy div., Los Alamos Sci. Lab. since 1946. Awarded Henry Marion Howe medal, Am. Soc. for Steel Treating, 1932; Navy Distinguished Service Award, 1946. Fellow Am. Phys. Society; member Washington Philosophical Society, Am. Inst. of Mining and Metall. Engrs., Am. Soc. for metals Iron and Steel Inst., Gamma Alpha, Sigma Xi, Phi Beta Kappa. Presbyterian. Research in spectroscopy, photography, metallurgy. Home: 4911 Trinity Dr., Los Alamos, N.M. Died April 18, 1953; buried Warrensburg, Mo.

WALTERS, GEORGE ALEXANDER, inventor; b. Canfield, Ont., Can., Nov. 11, 1872; s. John Comstock and Margaret (MacDonald) W.; brought to U.S., naturalized, 1898; LL.B., Detroit Coll. of Law, 1912; m. Ethelwyn Taylor, Nov. 28, 1900 (dec. 1945); children—Margaret (Mrs. Herbert Noxon), George (died Nov., 1946). Editor Kingsville (Ont.) Reporter, 1891-97; representative Sun Life Insurance Co., China, 1901-03; vice consul general, Central China, Hankow, 1903-05; editorial and feature writer Detroit News, Detroit Journal, Detroit Free Press, 1905-12; admitted to Mich. bar, 1912; dep. police commr. Detroit, 1912-22; v.p. Great Lakes Land Co., 1930-34; office mgr. Lawrence Aero. Corp., Linden, N.J., 1940-44; personnel mgr. Gen. Motors Corp., Linden, 1944-45. Invented, developed stop and go traffic signal; writer Negligent Homicide Act; pioneer in establishment accident investigation bur., safety zones, safety edn. programs for schools and public. Sheriff, Wayne County, Mich., 1922-26; councilman, Detroit, 1926-30. Served with Mich. Inf. Vol., Spanish-Am. War, 1898. Mem. Delta Theta Phi. Republican. Presbyn. (deacon). Mason (Shriner, 32 deg.). Clubs: Detroit Yacht, Detroit Rotary; St. Clair River Country. Home: 58 E. 79th St., N.Y.C. 21. Died Jan. 1, 1960.

WALTHER, HENRY WELLMAN EMILE, urologist; b. New Orleans, La., Sept. 7, 1888; s. Otto and Georgiana (Brown) W.; M.D., Tulane U. of La., Sch. of Medicine, 1910; m. Lilian Helen Cormier, Mar. 12, 1912 (now dec.); 1 dau., Lilian Helen (Mrs. Alfred F. Page, Jr.); m. 2d, Mrs. Elsie Cottrell Landram, Sept. 21, 1941. Interne, U.S. Marine Hospital, New Orleans, 1910; practiced New Orleans since 1910; former prof. urology, Tulane U., Loyola U. of the South, and La. State U.; chief urologist, Southern Bapt. Hosp.; former sr. visiting urologist Charity Hosp.; cons. urologist, U.S. Marine Hosp., 1918-22; urologist to Illinois Central Ry. Hosp., 1918-22; attending urologist, Hotel Dieu. V.p. 2d Pan-Am. Med. Congress. Asst. surgeon U.S. Pub. Health Service during World War I; consulting urologist Medical Advisory Board, Selective Service System, World War II. Member Board of New Orleans City Park Commrs. Pres. New Orleans Graduate Medical Assembly, 1945. Fellow Am. Coll. Surgeons, Am. Bd. Urology (Founders Group), fellow Am. Urol. Assn. (co-founder and pres. Southeastern Branch 1936), Southeastern Surg. Congress; mem. Am. Med. Assn. (in house of del. 1930-36; chmn. sect. on urology 1937), Am. Neisserian Soc., Southern Med. Assn. (chmn. sect. on urology 1923), La. State Med. Soc. (chmn. sect. on urology 1927), Orleans Parish Med. Soc. (treas. 1917-18), La. Urol. Soc. (co-founder and pres. 1941), New Orleans Social Hygiene Soc. (co-founder and pres. 1933-35); corr. member German Urol. Soc.; mem. Art Assn. of New Orleans (pres. 1930-34), Isaac Delgado Museum of Art (vice-pres.), Friends of the Howard-Tilton Memorial Library of Tulane U. (co-founder and pres. 1941), Japan Soc. of New Orleans (v.p. 1928-34), Bibliog. Soc. of America, Phi Beta Pi (supreme southern praetor 1909, editor of Quarterly 1910-12, supreme vice archon 1913), Pi Gamma Mu. Democrat. Methodist. Clubs: Armor and Arms (New York); New Orleans Country; Southern Yacht; Grolier (New York); Arts and Crafts (New Orleans). Member Lafcadio Hearn Society, Shakespeare Society, La., Soc. Print Connoisseurs, Hist. Soc. Library (Bibliotheca Waltheriana) presented to Tulane Univ. in 1941. Contbr. of many articles to the urol. lit. Inventor of numerous instruments used in urol. surgery. Home: 424 Pine St. Office: Whitney Bank Bldg., New Orleans 12, La. Died Jan. 6, 1945.

WALTMAN, WILLIAM DEWITT, mining engr.; b. Kendallville, Ind., Feb. 8, 1875; s. Martin Van Buren and Catherine (Aller) W.; E.M., Colo. Sch. of Mines, Golden, Colo., 1899; m. Eula C. Hamilton, Mar. 24, 1927; 1 son, Wm. DeWitt, Jr. Began as mining engr., Cripple Creek, Colo., 1900; editor of Hills Manual of Cripple Creek Mines, 1901; prin. asst. city engr., Colorado Springs, 1901-04; supt. mining, Panama Canal, 1905-06; supt. constrn., Culebra and Porto Bello divs., Panama Canal, 1906-09; chief engr. Costilla Estates Development Co., San Acacio, Colo., 1910-11;

gen. mgr. Fanco Wyo. Oil Co., 1912-19; corp. pres. petroleum Producing Cos., U.S. and Mexico, 1919-25; pres. dir. and gen. mgr. in charge of U.S. operations of Franco Wyoming Oil Co., 1926—; pres. and dir. Franco Western Oil Co., Franco Central Oil Co., Franco Wyoming Securities Corp., McElroy Ranch Company, Arzaco, Inc., Oil Producers Agency Calif.; ret., 1951. Capt. U.S. Army, Chem. Warfare Reserve. Mem. Am. Soc. Civil Engrs. (life), Am. Assn. Petroleum Geologists, Am. Inst. Mining and Metall. Engrs., Society of American Military Engineers, American Petroleum Inst., Am. Numismatic Soc., Colo. Soc. Engrs., Calavo Growers Assn. Past pres. bd. of trustees, Colo. Sch. of Mines. Awarded Roosevelt Panama medal, Medal of Individual Merit and Honor, Colo. Sch. of Mines (first medal ever granted by this institution), 1942. Republican. Methodist. Mason. Clubs: California, Jonathan (Los Angeles). Home: 325 S. Plymouth Blvd., Los Angeles 5. Died Feb. 14, 1955; buried Colorado Springs, Colo.

WALTON, ARTHUR CALVIN, educator; b. Meadville, Pa., Oct. 16, 1892; s. Calvin Levi and Minnie Belle (Stevens) W.; B.A., Northwestern U., 1914, M.A., 1915; student Harvard, 1915-17; Ph.D., U. of Ill., 1923; student U. of Colo., summer, 1926; m. Isyl Spiker, July 30, 1919; children—James Calvin, Robert Leslie, Richard Earl. Instr. biology, North Central Coll., Naperville, Ill., 1917-18, asst. prof., 1919-21, prof., 1921-22 and 1923-24; prof. biology, Knox Coll., Galesburg, 1924-25, chmn. dept. biology, 1925-54, prof. geology and geography, chmn. dept., 1954-67, Wallace C. Abbott, prof., 1940-67; civilian instr. med. arts and geography, Army Air Forces Tech. Training Comd., Knox Coll., 1943-46; mem. summer faculty U. of Ill., 1924, 25, 27; mem. summer faculty U. of Colo., 1928-33; visiting asso., Brit. Museum Natural History, London, Eng., 1932; mem. zoology staff U.S.P.H.S., Washington, D.C., 1939-40, summer 1941. Served with San. Service, A.E.F., 1918-19. Mem. Corp. of Bermuda (B.W.I.) Biol. Sta. Fellow A.A.A.S.; mem. Am. Soc. Zoology, Am. Soc. Parasitologists (pres.), Am. Soc. Systematic Zoology, Am. Micros. Soc., Ill. Acad. Sci., Phi Beta Kappa, Sigma Xi. Republican. Presbyn. Co-author: Introduction to Nematology, 1940. Contbr. numerous articles on parasitology and cytology to scientific jours. Home: Galesburg IL Died Apr. 23, 1967.

WALTON, JAMES HENRY, chemist; b. Deer Isle, Me., Feb. 26, 1878; s. James Hume and Florence Strode (Hewlett) W.; B.S., Mass. Inst. Tech., 1899; Austin traveling fellow from M.I.T., 1901-03; Ph.D., U. of Heidelberg, Germany, 1903; m. Dorothy Brockway Dana, Apr. 20, 1918; children—Marcia Dana, Judith Dana. Asst. in chemistry, U. of Ill., 1899-1900, Mass. Inst. Tech., 1900-01; instr. chemistry, 1903-06, asso., 1906-07, U. of Ill.; asst. prof. chemistry, 1907-12, asso. prof., 1912-19, prof. since 1919, U. of Wis. Commd. capt. Sanitary Corps, Sept. 20, 1917; maj. engrs., May 3, 1918; in charge training in gas defense in U.S., Sept. 1917-July 1918; 1st army gas officer, A.E.F., Aug. 1918-Jan. 1919; hon. disch., Jan. 25, 1919; lt. col. C.W. Res., May 8, 1926-May 8, 1931. Mem. Am. Chem. Soc. (ex-pres. Wis. sect.), Zeta Psi, Sigma Xi, Alpha Chi Sigma, Phi Lambda Upsilon, Scabbard and Blade. Unitarian. Club: University. Author: (with A. T. Lincoln) Elementary Quantitative Chemical Analysis, 1907; (with L. Kahlenberg) Qualitative Chemical Analysis, 1911; (with F. C. Krauskopf) A Laboratory Manual of General Chemistry, 1921; (with C. H. Sorum) Introduction to Qualitative Analysis, 1937; An Introduction to General Chemistry (with F. C. Krauskopf), 1943; numerous papers in scientific jours. Collaborated with Lt. Col. S. J. M. Auld, of Brit. Mil. Mission in preparation of 4 monographs on gas warfare, used in training troops in U.S. and in A.E.F. Home: 2122 Vs Av., Madison, Wis. Died June 6, 1947.

WALTON, LUCIUS LEEDOM, pharmacist; b. Clinton, N.J., July 8, 1865; s. Thomas Cooper and Jane Eliza (Fly) W.; grad. Clinton (N.J.) Classical Inst. and Dickinson Sem., Williamsport, Pa.; Ph.G., Phila. Coll. Pharmacy, 1888, Pharm.M., honoris causa, 1912; Pharm.D., honoris causa, U. of Pittsburgh, 1912; m. Cora Olive Brooks, Nov. 1890; children—Beatrice Brooks (Mrs. Louis Saulbach), Brooks Lamar, Caroline Scott (Mrs. J. Lowell Budinger). Mem. L. L. Walton & Co., druggists, Williamsport, 1892—. Mem. Pa. State Bd. Pharmacy, 1906— (sec. 1909-26; pres., 1931—). Methodist. Home: Williamsport, Pa. Died Dec. 26, 1935.

WALTON, NORTON HALL, chem. engr.; b. Phila., Nov. 26, 1910; s. William Berkheimer and Emma Jane (Hall) W.; B.S. U. Pa., 1932; m. Ruth Anne Bowen, Oct. 12, 1934 (div.); 1 son, William Alfred; m. 2d, Margarete Wilson, Nov. 1967. Asst. supt. chemicals Atlantic Refining Co., Phila., 1933-60; operating supt., asst. to plant mgr. Sun Olin Chem. Co., Claymont, Del., 1960-66, marketing tech. asst., 1966-67, manager commercial development, 1967-69. Registered profl. engr., Pa., Del. Mem. Nat. Soc. Profl. Engrs., Am. Inst. Chem. Engrs., Am. Chem. Soc. Engring. and Tech. Socs. Council Delaware Valley (chmn. 1960-61), Phila. Sci. Council (pres. 1960-63), Phila. Engrs. Club, Alpha Chi Sigma, Sigma Zeta. Republican. Episcopalian. Home: Springfield PA Died Sept. 12, 1969; buried Boehm's Cemetery Blue Bell PA

WALTON, WILLIAM RANDOLPH, entomologist; b. Bklyn., Sept. 23, 1873; s. Walter and Susan (MacArdell) W.; ed. pub. schs. and Stevenson Sch. Art, Pitts., 1904-05 (prize student); m. Mary Agnes Becher, June 9, 1904; children—Walter F., M. Margaret, Wm. R., Henry V., John M. Telegraph operator Erie R.R., 1890; later with engring. depts. various rys., N.Y. and Pa., and with engring. firms until 1906; specialist, artist, Pa. State Div. Econ. Zoölogy, Harrisburg, Pa., 1906-10; with Bur. Entomology, U.S. Dept. Agr., 1910—, entomologist charge cereal and forage insect investigations, 1917-23, sr. entomologist, 1923-43, now ret. Specializes in dipterology, families of Syrphidae, Asilidae, and Tachinidae. Fellow Entomol. Soc. Am., A.A.A.S.; mem. Entomol. Soc. Washington, Am. Assn. Econ. Entomol. Author illus. papers on taxonomy of Muscoidean and other flies, including illustrated glossary of terms used in describing them; publs. on insects affecting cereal and forage crops, also many articles on fresh-water fishing and lure making. Home: 4323 Madison St., Hyattsville, Md. Died Oct. 20, 1952.

WANK, ROLAND ANTHONY, architect; b. Budapest, Hungary, Oct. 2, 1898; attended Royal Polytechnicum, Budapest, 1917-19, Tech. U., Brunn, Czechoslovakia, 1919-21; also studied Coll. of Beaux-Arts and Sch. of Applied Arts, Budapest; LL.D., Fairleigh Dickinson University, 1959; m. Piroska Szabo, Dec. 2, 1922; children—Peter John, Andrew George. Came to U.S., 1924, naturalized, 1930. Chief architect, European engring. and constrn. orgns., 1921-24; asso. with George Springsten, Fellheimer and Wagner firms, 1924-33; chief designer, Grand St. Apts., N.Y. City (A.I.A. gold medal), Cincinnati Union Terminal (A.I.A. gold medal); head architect, Tenn. Valley Authority, 1933-44; chief architect, Greenhills (Ohio) Resettlement Adminstrn.; chief cons. architect, Rural Electrification Adminstrn.; designer engring. structures, towns, pub., semi-pub. and coop. bldgs. Chief designer, Albert Kahn Asso. Architects & Engr., Inc. 1944-45; mem. firm Wank, Adams & Slavin, architects and engrs., 1945-70, sr. partner, 1958-70; archtl. cons. UN Hdqrs. Commn., 1946. Past mem. Planning Bd., City of New Rochelle, N.Y. Fellow A.I.A.; member American Inst. Planners, Nat. Association Planning Officials, Nat. Planning Assn., Nat. Assn. of Housing Officials. Contbr. articles to mags; spl. lectures at Harvard and M.I.T.; critic at Princeton. Home: New Rochelle NY Died Apr. 22, 1970.

WANTLAND, WAYNE W(ARDE), univ. prof.; born Sheridan, Ill., Sept. 5, 1905; s. Hosmer Vorhees and Elma Maude (Burgess) W.; student North Central Coll., Naperville, Ill., 1923-24, Northern Ill. State Teachers Coll., DeKalb, 1924-25 and summers of 1925, 1926 and 1927; B.S., Northwestern U., Evanston, Ill., 1930, M.A., 1932, Ph.D. 1935; m. Edna Marie Lohmeyer, Aug. 19, 1928 (deceased September 11, 1963); 1 son, William Stanley; m. second, Evelyn Kendrick Kinney, Apr. 29, 1964. Principal of Newark (Ill.) High Sch., 1925-27, supt., 1927-29; asst. in zoology, Northwestern U., 1930-34, instr., 1934-37; prof. biology, DePaul U., Chicago, 1935-37; instructor zoology, Eastern Ill. State Teachers Coll., Charleston, Ill., 1937-38; dir. biol. sci., Stephens Coll., Columbia, Mo., 1938-42; fellow Am. Council on Edn., U. of Chicago, 1940-41; prof. and head dept. of biology, Ill. Wesleyan U., Bloomington, 1944-45, dean of men, 1944-45, chmn. div. natural sciences, 1945-71, and George C. and Ella Beach Lewis prof. of biology, 1947-71, dir. Cancer Research Program, 1948-51, dir. Biol. Research Lab., 1951-71, dir. U.S. Pub. Health Research on mouth protozoa, 1956-64, also bd. dirs. Ill. Wesleyan U. Served as lt. administration and malariology, USN, 1942-44. Fellow A.A.A.S.; mem. Internat. Assn. Dental Research, Am. Soc. Zoologists, Am. Inst. Biol. Scis., Am. Soc. Parasitologists, Am. Cancer Soc., Ill. Acad. Sci., N.E.A., Research Soc. Am., Soc. Protozoologists, Am. Legion, Sigma Xi, Phi Kappa Phi. Republican. Methodist. Mason. Club: College Alumni (Bloomington). Contbr. profl. jours. Home: Bloomington IL Died Mar. 4, 1971; buried Bloomington IL

WARBURG, OTTO HEINRICH, scientist, biology; b. Freiburg, Baden, Oct. 8, 1883; s. Emil Warburg and Elizabeth Gertner; Dr. der Chemie, Berlin, 1906; Dr. der Medizin, Heidelberg U., 1911. Dir. Max Planck Inst. Zellphysiologie, Berlin-Dahlem, 1933-70. Served with Prussian Horse Guards, 1914-18. Decorated Ordre pour le Merite, Great Cross Star and Shoulder Ribbon, Bunderrepublik; recipient Nobel prize for medicine, 1931. Fgn. mem. Royal Soc. Author: Freedom of West Berlin, 1963. Address: Berlin-Dahlem Germany Died Aug. 1970.

WARD, ALGER LUMAN, chemical cons.; b. Easthampton, Mass., May 4, 1890; s. Oscar and Ella Jeanette (Alexander) W.; grad. Williston Acad., Easthampton, 1910; B.S. in chemistry, Syracuse U., 1914, M.S., 1915, Sc.D., 1941; m. Emma Undritz, June 5, 1915. Research chemist for E. I. du Pont de Nemours & Co., 1915-20, discovering processes for synthesis of acetic acid, acetone, alky anilines, ethylene glycol and glycerine, covered by basic Am. and foreign patents; research chemist for United Gas Improvement Co., Phila., 1920-34; mgr. chem. labs. United Gas Improvement Co., 1934-35; principal work in physical properties, separation and polymerization of hydrocarbons; cause and prevention of formation of liquid-phase and vapor-phase gums in gas distribtuion systems (basic Am., fgn. patents); metal corrosion; dir. Research Laboratory, Pa. Industrial Chemical Corporation, 1946-55; principal work in synthetic resins, plasticizers for synthetic rubber, binders for asphaltic floor tile. Discovered and exponent (with S. S. Kurtz, Jr.) the Refractivity Intercept. Awarded Louis E. Levy medal Franklin Inst. 1938. Mem. Franklin Inst., Am. Chem. Soc., Soc. of Chem. Industry, Sigma Beta, Alpha Chi Sigma. Republican. Episcopalian (vestryman St. Clement's Ch., Phila.). Co-author: Styrene, 1951; Styrene Monomer, Ency. Chemical Technology, 1954. Contbr. to and honorary associate editor of The Science of Petroleum, 1938. Contributor numerous articles to profl. jours. Home: Bala-Cynwyd PA Died Jan. 19, 1969; buried West Laurel Hill Cemetery, Bala-Cynwyd PA

WARD, ARCHIBALD ROBINSON, bacteriologist; b. Ithaca, N.Y., Sept. 12, 1875; s. Albert Riley and Henrietta (Robinson) W.; B.S.A., Cornell U. Coll. of Agr., 1898; D.V.M., N.Y. State Vet. Coll. (Cornell), 1901; m. Flora Lillian Pinkham, May 21, 1914 (died 1915); m. 2d, Augusta Wolfe Russell, July 25, 1917 (died 1945); 1 daughter, Alice Russell. Assistant in dairy bacteriology, Cornell University College of Agriculture, 1898-1901; with University of Calif., 1901-10 (except 1 yr.), in many capacities, including instr. and asst. prof. vet. science, dir. State Hygienic Lab., asst. prof. bacteriology, research in infectious diseases of animals, of man, etc.; leave of absence, 1909-10, at Hygienic Lab. of U.S. Pub. Health and Marine Hosp. Service; in P.I., 1910-14, serving as chief veterinarian Bur. of Agr., dean Coll. Vet. Science and prof. preventive vet. medicine of U. of Philippines, also pres. Vet. Examining Bd. of P.I.; sr. pathologist and acting chief Pathol. Div. Bur. of Animal Industry, U.S. Dept. Agr., June 15, 1914, title sr. pathologist, 1918; prof. bacteriology and pathology in charge of Biol. Lab., Md. State Coll. Agr., 1918; asst. chief dairy research bur. of The Mathews Co., Detroit, Mich., 1923-32; operating dairy testing laboratory and milk quality control service since 1932; consultant, dairy research bur., The Mathews Co., Detroit, 1940-45. Pres. P.I. Vet. Med. Assn., 1913-14; mem. Soc. Am. Bacteriologists (charter mem., pres. Mich. br. 1936-38), Am. Vet. Med. Assn., Am. Pub. Health Assn., Kappa Sigma, Sigma Xi; hon. member Alpha Zeta (California Chapter). Club: Faculty (Berkeley). Author: Pure Milk and the Public Health, 1909; Diseases of Domesticated Birds (with B. J. Gallagher), 1919. Contbr. articles on bacteriology of milk, city milk supply, diseases of fowls, diseases of cattle (more particularly rinderpest), etc. Home: 1986 Waverly Av., Detroit 6 MI*

WARD, CHARLES HOWELL, osteologist; b. Rochester, N.Y., Oct. 28, 1862; s. Henry Augustus and Phoebe Ann (Howell) W.; ed. Alfred U. and U. of Rochester; m. Anna T. Cheek, 1920 (dec.); 1 son, Roswell H.; m. 2d, Gertrude L. Green, Sept. 1925. In charge dept. human anatomy, Ward's Natural Science Establishment, Rochester, 1891-99; mgr. Anatomical Lab. of Chas H. Ward, 1899-1926, pres. of same, inc., since 1926; has for many years devoted his time to the collecting and preparation anatomical specimens for ednl. purposes. Mem. A.A.A.S.; hon. mem. Rochester Dental Soc., 7th Dist. N.Y. Dental Soc.; fellow Rochester Acad. Science. Home: 598 Monroe Av. Office: 205 Main St. W., Rochester, N.Y. Died Jan. 18, 1943.

WARD, DELANCEY WALTON, chem. engr.; b. New York, July 8, 1866; grad. School of Mines, Columbia Coll., 1888 (Ph.D., Columbia, 1895); m. 1898, Samantha Newhouse Nostrand, Whitestone, N.Y. Hon. asst. chemistry Columbia School of Mines, 1888-90; asst. in organic chemistry, 1890-94; prof. dental chemistry and metallurgy New York Dental School since 1894; mem. New York Acad. Sciences, Am. Chem. Soc., French Chem. Soc., Paris, etc. Author: Chemistry and Physics ("Students' Quiz" series); etc. Address: Flushing, N.Y.

WARD, DUREN J(AMES) H(ENDERSON), b. Dorchester, Ontario, Can., June 17, 1851; s. Samuel and Eunice (Varnum) W.; A.B., Hillsdale (Mich.) Coll., 1878, B.D., 1884; A.M., Harvard University, 1883; fellow in Europe, 1885-87; Ph.D., University of Leipzig, 1887; m. Zuba A. Corss, of Memphis, Mich., Aug. 18, 1875 (died Oct. 1, 1889); m. 2d, Lizzie Adams Cheney, of Cambridge, Mass., Dec. 31, 1890 (died Aug. 31, 1933). Principal of New Lyme Acad., Ashtabula Co., O., 1879-82; librarian, Harvard Divinity School, and lecturer on philosophy and anthropology, Harvard University, 1887-89; supt. Workingman's Sch., New York, 1889-91; lecturer, writer, 1891-94; asst. pastor Unitarian Ch., Baltimore, 1894-95; pastor Unitarian Church, Dover, N.H., 1895-98; professor English, Kansas State Agrl. Coll., Manhattan, 1899-1900; pastor Iowa City, Ia., 1900-06, Ft. Collins, Colo., 1906-08; editor and pub. Up The Divide (liberal mag.), Denver, 1909-14; also editor The World for Workers; dir. College Work for Busy Folk (psychology, character analysis, vocational adjustment), 1914—. Pres. Free Speech League of Denver, 1914-16. Red Cross organizer, govt. translator, 1917. Fellow Am. Assn. for Advancement of Science. Club: Ben Franklin. Author: Psychologicla Origin of Religion, 1887; Government

Ownership in 100 Countries, 1895; Historico-Ethnical Classification of Human Races, 1904; Classification of Religions, 1908; Outline of Anthropology, 1913; The Modern God, 1916; History of Modern Sciences (18 Continued articles in "Up The Divide"); A Personality Invoice, 1920; A Receivership for Civilization, 1922; Education, 1923; Origin and Evolution of Christmas and New Year, 1923; Darwin and Evolution, 1924; Crime—Its Biology and Psychology, 1924; World Peace, 1924; Biography of God from Fetichism to Monism, 1925; Origin of Mind, 1925; Letters to Future Ages, Nos. I, II, 1925; Evolution of Marriage, 1925; Fundamentalism and Modernism—A Seaside Episode, 1925; Ward-Varnum Genealogy, 1926; Dorchester (Ont.) Early Settlers, 1927; Philosophical Attitudes—A Historical Epitome, 1927; The Golden Rule in the Light of History and Science, 1931; The Minister's Course of Study, 1931; The Calendar—A Solution, 1932; Family Record Book, 1932; Soliloquy over 80 Years, 1932; Humna Names, 1933; The Human Sciences, 1934; About Future Life, 1935; Established Far-Reaching Foundation for Preserving Records to Future Ages, 1935; Prospectus of The Temple to Civilization, 1940. Address: 958 Acoma St., Denver, Colo.

WARD, FREEMAN, geologist; b. Yankton, S.D., Aug. 9, 1879; s. Joseph and Sarah Frances (Wood) W.; Yankton Coll., 1898-1901, Sc.D., 1934; A.B., Yale U., 1903, Ph.D., 1908; m. Daisy Lee Eyerly, 1906; 1 dau., Sarah Wood. Asst. instr. and asst. prof. geology, Yale, 1903-15; prof. geology and head of dept., U. of S.D., also state geologist, 1915-26; prof. geology and head of dept., Lafayette Coll., since 1926. Field work Conn. State Survey, Pa. State Survey and U.S. Geol. Survey, various summers. Mem. A.A.A.S., Geol. Soc. America, Am. Assn. Petroleum Geologists, Am. Assn. Univ. Profs., Sigma Xi. Republican. Conglist. Home: 40 McCartney St., Easton, Pa. Died Sept. 14, 1943.

WARD, GEORGE CLINTON, engr.; b. White Plains, N.Y., Jan. 9, 1863; s. James and Elizabeth (Ennis) W.; grad. Phillips Acad., Andover, Mass., 1882; D.Eng., U. of Southern Calif., 1927; Sc.D., Oberlin, 1928; m. Katherine L. Schweinsberg, Sept. 15, 1886; 1 dau., Louise Whipple (Mrs. E. Frank Watkins). Began with engr. corps on construction New York, West Shore & Buffalo R.R., 1882; preliminary surveys, location and constrn. as asst. and chief engr. on various railroads, 1884-1902; in charge water works properties in Ohio, 1902-05; v.p. and gen. mgr. Huntington Land & Improvement Co., 1905-12; v.p. Pacific Light & Power Corp., 1912-17; v.p. Southern Calif. Edison Co., 1917—, later exec. v.p. Home: South Pasadena, Calif. Died Sept. 11, 1933.

WARD, GEORGE GRAY, gynecologist; b. London, Eng., Aug. 15, 1868; s. George Gray and Marianne (Smith) W.; brought to America, 1874; ed. Bklyn. Collegiate and Poly. Inst., Holbrook Mil. Acad. (Ossining, N.Y.); M.D., L.I. Coll. Hosp., 1891; studied U. Berlin, 1892-93, also London and Paris; m. Edith Wigham, June 23, 1898. Prof. diseases of women, N.Y., Post-Grad. Med. Sch., 1905-16, sec. faculty, 1910-16; prof. obstetrics and gynecology, Cornell U. Med. Coll., 1916-34, emeritus; chief surgeon Woman's Hosp., 1918-38, emeritus; prof. clin. obstetrics and gynecology, Columbia; formerly attending gynecologist, Bellevue Hosp.; con. gynecologist, N.Y. Post-Grad. Hosp., N.Y. Hosp., Monmouth Meml. Hosp., Lawrence Hosp., Home for Incurables, Booth Meml. Hosp. Mem. 7th Regiment, Nat. Guard, N.Y., 8 yrs.; capt., asst. surgeon, 12th Regt., 1895-98; maj. surgeon, 1898-1902; maj. surgeon 12th Regt. Inf., N.Y. Vols., Spanish-Am. War. Founder, fellow A.C.S.; fellow Am. Gynecology Soc. (ex-pres.), N.Y. Acad. Medicine; hon. fellow Edinburgh Obstet. Soc., Royal Coll. Obstetricians and Gynecologists, Royal Med. Soc. Budapest; hon. mem. British Congress Obstetrics and Gynecology; mem. A.M.A. (chmn. sect. obstetrics and gynecology), Med. Soc. State N.Y., N.Y. County Med. Soc. (ex-pres.), N.Y. Obstet. Soc. (ex-pres.), Hosp. Grads.' Club (ex-pres.), Phi Alpha Sigma, Alpha Omega Alpha, Mil. Order Fgn. Wars, Naval and Mil. Order Spanish-Am. War. Rep. Episcopalian. Clubs: Union, Century, Riding, Racquet (New York); Rumson Country; Army and Navy (Washington), Travellers (Paris). Co-author: Gynecology in Operative Therapeusis, 1915; Kelly's Gynecology, 1928; Lewis Practice of Surgery, 1928; Curtis Obstetrics and Gynecology, 1933; Davis Gynecology and Obstetrics, 1933; and numerous monographs on gynecology and obstetrics. Home: 1175 Park Av. Office: 101 E. 80th St., N.Y.C. Died Dec. 21, 1950; buried Greenwood, Bklyn.

WARD, HENRY AUGUSTUS, naturalist; b. Rochester, N.Y., Mar. 9, 1834; s. Henry Meigs and Eliza (Chapin) W.; ed. Middlebury Acad.; also, 1851-52, at Williams Coll., A.M., Williams; LL.D., Rochester U. Asst. to Prof. Louis Agassiz, Harvard Scientific Sch., 1854; studied at Paris, and traveled through Europe and the Orient, 1855-59; m. Phoebe A. Howell, Nov. 1860 (died 1890); m. 2d, Mrs. Lydia Avery Coonley, Mar. 18, 1897. Prof. natural sciences, Rochester U., 1860-65; mgr., gold mines in Mont. and in S.C., 1866-69; traveled, 1870-1900, in all countries, making large and valuable cabinets of mineralogy and geology (known as "Ward Cabinets") which are distributed to univs., colls., etc., throughout U.S. Founded at Rochester Ward's Natural Science Establishment, where cabinets are compiled; acting naturalist of U.S. Expdn. to Santo Domingo, 1871. Fellow A.A.A.S. Author: Notices of the Megatherium Cuvieri; Description of the Most Celebrated Fossil Animals in Royal Museums of Europe. Home: Chicago, Ill. Died 1906.

WARD, HENRY BALDWIN, zoölogist; b. Troy, N.Y., Mar 4, 1865; s. Richard Halsted and Charlotte Allen (Baldwin) W.; A.B., Williams Coll., 1885; postgrad. studies, univs. of Göttingen, Freiburg (Baden) Leipzig; A.M., Ph.D., Harvard, 1892; Sc.D., U. of Cincinnati, 1920, William Coll., 1921; LL.D., U. of Ore., 1932, U. of Neb., 1935; m. Harriet Blair, Sept. 11, 1894; children—Mrs. Cecilia Tanton, Charlotte Baldwin. Teacher of science, Troy High Sch., 1885-88; instr. morphology, U. of Mich., 1892-93; asso. prof. zoölogy, 1893-98, prof., 1899-1909, dean Coll. of Medicine, 1902-09, U. of Neb.; prof. zoölogy, U. of Ill., 1909-33, emeritus prof. of zoölogy since 1933; mem. Ill. State Bd. Mus. Advisers (sec. since 1937). In charge biol. work Mich. Fish Commn. on Lake Mich., 1894; asso. biol. survey Great Lakes, U.S. Fish Commn., since 1898; asso. editor Am. Naturalist, and of Reference Handbook of the Medical Sciences. Sec. Am. Micros. Soc., 1898-1904, pres. 1905; fellow A.A.A.S. (sec. sect. F, 1900, sec. council, 1901, gen. sec., 1902, v.p., 1905, permanent sec., 1933-37, del. to Brit. Assn. of Science Oxford, 1928); pres. Am. Soc. Zoölogists, 1912-14; pres. Am. Fisheries Soc., 1913; chmn. Nat. Wildlife Fed. Com. on Conservation Edn. since 1938; trustee Science Service, Inc., Washington; member American Med. Editors and Authors Assn., Zoöl. Soc. France, German Zoöl. Soc.; foreign mem. Imperial Soc. (Russian) for Acclimatization of Animals and Plants, Acad. Sciences of Czechoslovakia; foreign corr. mem. Venezuela Acad. Medicine; corr. mem. Royal Acad. Agr. Turin; pres. Neb. Acad. Science, 1901, Assn. Am. Med. Colls., 1908; first pres. Am. Soc. Parasitologists, 1925; mem. permanent com. on Internat. Zoöl. Congresses; gen. sec. Sigma Xi, 1895-1922, pres., 1922-24; nat. pres. Izaak Walton League America, 1928-30, mem. nat. exec. com. since 1925; mem. Delta Phi, Phi Beta Kappa, Sigma Xi, Alpha Omega Alpha. Clubs: University (Chicago); University (Urbana, Ill.); Cosmos (Washington, D.C.). Author: Quarter Century Record and History of Sigma Xi, 1913; Freshwater Biology, 1917; Parasites of the Human Eye, 1918; Introduction and Spread of the Fish Tapeworm in the United States, 1930; Foundations of Conservation Education, 1941; Medical Zoology in America's First Century, 1946. Contbr. of various monographs and papers on biol. subjects, especially animal parasites and relations of animals to disease; also articles on biology and stream pollution to Outdoor America, etc. Founder and editor Journal of Parasitology, 1914 (18 vols.). Address: Urbana, Ill. Died Nov. 30, 1945.

WARD, HENRY LEVI, naturalist; b. York, Livingston County, N.Y., Oct. 8, 1863; s. Henry Augustus and Phoebe Ann (Howell) W.; ed. pub. schs. and Free Acad., Rochester, N.Y., and U. of Rochester (spl.), 1883-84; m. Elva Mary Selby, Nov. 21, 1891; children—Margaret and Alice Greenleaf (twins, dec.), Marian Elizabeth (Mrs. Paul H. Gillan), Henry Selby. Collector of natural history specimens in West Indian Islands and S. America, 1879, on Calif. coast, 1883; anatomist Ward's Natural Science Establishment, Rochester, 1884-86; mem. Mexican govt. expdn. in search of the West Indian seal, 1886; osteologist of the Geog. and Exploring Commn., of the Mexican Govt., 1887-91; also mem. Mexican Commn. to Paris Expn., 1889; dir. and mgr., 1891-1902, v.p., 1901-02, Ward's Natural Science Establishment, Rochester; dir. Pub. Mus. of City of Milwaukee, 1902-20; rancher, Bellingham, Wash., 1921; dir. Kent Scientific Mus., Grand Rapids, Mich., 1922-32; dir. Neville Pub. Mus., Green Bay, Wis., 1933-41. Editor Ward's Natural Science Bulletin, 1884-86; contbr. to scientific press and publs. of various scientific assns.; pres., Wis. Acad. Sciences, Arts and Letters, 1916-18; past v.p. Wis. Nat. Hist. Soc.; charter mem. Am. Assn. Museums (pres. 1913); Wis. Archaeol. Soc., Wis. Hist. Soc., Brown County Hist. Soc., Chi Psi; fellow A.A.A.S. Received silver and bronze medals as collaborator, Paris Expn., 1889; diploma as collaborator Chicago World's Fair, 1893; gold medal, Ill. Acad. Science, 1941. Home: 1345 C St., Lincoln, Neb. Died Dec. 17, 1943. *

WARD, HENRY TIBBELS, chem. engr., educator; b. Chatsworth, Ia., July 25, 1897; s. George Ernest and Helen (Tibbels) W.; grad. Shattuck Sch., Faribault, Minn., 1916; B.S., U. Mich., 1921, Ph.D., 1931; M.S., U. Wyo., 1929; m. L. Babcock, June, 1922; children—Helen Elizabeth (wife Dr. Calvin B. Kitchen), Henry Horace; m. 2d, Grace Job, Jan. 15, 1944. Instr. chem. dept. U. Wyo., 1927-29; research asso. U. Mich., 1929-31; asso. prof. chem. engring. Mont. State Coll., 1931-36, Drexel Inst. Tech., 1936-47; prof., head chem. engring. U. Ark., 1947-48, Kan. State Coll., 1948—; on leave, research engr. Argonne Nat. Lab., 1954-55; cons. fuels paint, water treating. Mem. Am. Inst. Chem. Engrs., Am. Chem. Soc., Am. Soc. Engring. Edn., Nat. Soc. Profl. Engrs., Am. Nuclear Soc., Kan. Engring. Soc. Office: Dept. Chem. Engring., Kan. State Coll., Manhattan, Kan. Died Apr. 6, 1960; buried Graceland Cemetery, Sioux City, Ia.

WARD, LESTER FRANK, geologist; b. Joliet, Ill., June 18, 1841; A.B., Columbian (now George Washington) U., 1869, LL.B., 1871, A.M., 1873, LL.D., 1897. Served in Civil War; in U.S. Treasury Dept., 1865-72; asst. geologist, 1881-88, geologist, 1888, U.S. Geol. Survey. Specially known for researches in paleobotany; later extensive contbr. to the literature of sociology. Mem. Am. Acad. Polit. and Social Science; fellow A.A.A.S. Author: Guide to the Flora of Washington and Vicinity, 1881; Dynamic Sociology, 1883; Sketch of Paleobotany, 1885; Synopsis of the Flora of the Laramie Group, 1886; Types of the Laramie Flora, 1887; Geographical Distribution of Fossil Plants, 1888; Psychic Factors of Civilization; Psychological Basis of Social Economics; Political Ethics of Spencer; Principles of Sociology; Outlines of Sociology, 1898; Sociology and Economics, 1899; Pure Sociology, 1903; Text-book of Sociology (with James Quayle Dealey), 1905. Home: Providence, R.I. Died April 18, 1913.

WARD, MARCUS LLEWELLYN, dental educator; b. Howell, Mich., Aug. 5, 1875; s. Albert F. and Sarah (Kirkland) W.; D.D.S., U. Mich., 1902, D.D.Sc., 1905; m. Millie J. Carpenter, May 31, 1899. Instr. operative technics and operative dentistry U. Mich Sch. Dentistry, 1903-05, lectr. operative principles, 1905-08, prof., 1908-12, prof. dental physics and chemistry, 1912-19, prof. dental metallurgy, and crown and bridgework, 1919-34, dean faculty, 1916-34, Jonathan Taft prof. dentistry, 1934-45, prof. emeritus dentistry, dean emeritus Sch. Dentistry, 1945—. Recipient Newell Sill Jenkins Meml. medal, 1938, William Jarvie Fellowship medal, 1941, Callahan Mem. award, 1942, John N. Crouse Meml. award, 1943. Fellow Am. Coll. Dentists; mem. Internat. Assn. for Dental Research, A.A.A.S., Am. Assn. U. Profs., Am. Assn. for Adult Edn., N.Y. Acad. Dentistry, Mich. Acad. Sci. and Letters, Sigma Xi, Phi Kappa Phi, Omicron Kappa Upsilon, Delta Sigma Delta; hon. mem. Conn. State, Ohio State dental socs.; pres. Mich. State Dental Soc., 1912, Am. Dental Assn., 1939, Am. Assn. Dental Schs., 1925. Republican. Conglist. Club: University. Editor, contbr. American Textbook of Operative Dentistry, 1920-45. Home: 1308 Cambridge Rd., Ann Arbor, Mich. Died Sept. 9, 1963.

WARD, RICHARD HALSTED, biologist, microscopist; b. Bloomfield, N.J., June 17, 1837; s. Israel Currie and Almeda (Hanks) W.; A.B., Williams, 1858, A.M., 1861; M.D., College Phys. and Surg. (Columbia), 1862; m. Charlotte Allen Baldwin, June 10, 1862; father of Henry Baldwin W. Acting asst. surgeon in Civil War; practicing medicine at Troy, N.Y., 1863—. Instr. botany, 1867, prof. and lecturer on histology and microscopy, 1869-92, Rensselaer Poly. Inst.; gov., 1st v.p. and chmn. med. bd. Marshall Infirmary and Sanitarium, 1868—. Distinguished for original research in econ. botany and microscopy; witness as microscopist in murder and forgery trials, etc. Mem. for U.S. of hon. com. of patrons Internat. Expn. of Microscopy, Antwerp, 1891; del. at several meetings of Internat. Med. Congress and Brit. Assn. Adv. Sci. Fellow Royal Micros. Soc., A.A.A.S., Am. Acad. Medicine; pres. Nat. Micros. Congress, Indianapolis, 1878, Am. Micros. Soc. 1879 (hon. mem. 1896), Am. Postal Micros. Club, 1895, Troy Scientific Assn., 1870; hon. mem. Société Belge de Microscopie. Writer of numerous monographs and contributions on micros. subjects. Address: Troy, N.Y. Died Oct. 28, 1917.

WARD, ROBERT DE COURCY, climatologist; b. Boston, Nov. 29, 1867; s. Henry Veazey and Anna Saltonstall (Merrill) W.; A.B., Harvard, 1889, A.M., 1893; m. Emma Lane, Apr. 28, 1897; children—Henry DeCourcy, Robert Saltonstall, Anna Saltonstall Magruder, Emma Lane. Asst. in physical geography, 1890-94, asst. in meteorology, 1894-95, instr., 1895-96, instr. climatology, 1896-1900, asst. prof., 1900-10, prof., 1910—, Harvard; exchange prof., Western colleges, 1927. Editor Am. Meteorol. Jour., 1892-96, contbg. editor Geog. Review. Member Shaler Memorial Expdn. to Brazil, 1908. Fellow Am. Acad. Arts and Sciences, Royal Meteorol. Soc., London, Assn. Am. Geographers (pres. 1917), Am. Meteorol. Soc. (pres. 1920, 21), Am. Assn. Advancement of Science; mem. Harvard Travellers Club (gold medalist, 1926); one of founders, 1894, Immigration Restriction League. Episcopalian. Author: Practical Exercises in Elementary Meteorology, 1899; Climate Considered Especially in Relation to Man, 1908; The Climates of the United States, 1925. Translator: Hann's Handbuch der Klimatologie, Vol. I, 1903. Contbr. to scientific jours., and to 11th, 12th and 13th editions Ency. Britannica. Home: Cambridge, Mass. Died Nov. 12, 1931.

WARD, WILLARD PARKER, mining engr.; b. New York, Oct. 12, 1845; s. Lebbeus B. and Abby Dwight (Partridge) W.; A.B., Columbia, 1865, A.M., 1871; studied in mining schs., Clausthal, and Berlin, 1865-69; Ph.D., N.Y. U., 1875; m. Ruby, d. John Erskine, U.S. judge, Dist. of Ga., Oct. 23, 1872. Engaged in professional work, 1869—; 1st maker of ferromanganese in U.S. (1874). Engaged in gold and silver-mining in Far West, 1883—. Home: Savannah, Ga. Died Jan. 17, 1928.

WARDER, JOHN ASTON, physician, horticulturist, forester; b. Phila., Jan. 19, 1812; s. Jeremiah and Ann (Aston) W.; grad. Jefferson Med. Coll., 1836; m. Elizabeth Haines, 1836, at least 4 children. Practiced medicine, Cincinnati, 1837-55; mem. Western Acad. Natural Scis., Cincinnati Soc. Natural History; pres. Ohio Hort. Soc. many years; sec., v.p. Am. Pomol. Soc.; edited Western Horticultural Review, 1850-53; 1st described Catalpa Speciosa; contbd. articles on systematic pomology and fruit culture to publs. including Am. Jour. of Horticulture; an author "Report of the Flax and Hemp Commission;" edited Vineyard Culture (DuBreuil), 1867; mem. Ohio Bd. Agr., 1871-76; pres. Am. Forestry Assn., 1875-82; an organizer Am. Forestry Congress; did much to foster landscape gardening and beautification of parks and cemeteries. Author: Hedges and Evergreens: A Complete Manual for the Cultivation, Pruning, and Management of All Plants Suitable for American Hedging, 1858; American Pomology: Apples, 1867; Report of the Commissioner (ofcl. report on forests and forestry), vol. 1, 1876. Died July 14, 1883.

WARDER, ROBERT BOWNE, chemist; b. Cincinnati, March 28, 1848; s. John A. and Elizabeth Bowne W.; grad. Earlham Coll., Richmond, Ind., 1866, A.M., 1873; grad. Lawrence Scientific Sch., Harvard, B.S. (in chemistry), 1874; also studied in Germany, 1874-75; prof. U. of Cincinnati, 1875-79, Haverford Coll., 1879-80, Purdue U., Ind. (and State chemist), 1883-87; prof. physics and chemistry, Harvard U., 1887—; m. Gulielma M. Dorland, Mar. 25, 1884. Fellow A.A.A.S. (v.p. for chemistry, 1890). Author of various papers on physical chemistry. Died 1905.

WARDWELL, FRANK CARLTON, civil engr.; b. Conneaut, O., Aug. 30, 1887; s. Jonn B. and Anna J. (Wilcox) W.; B.S., Ohio State U., 1911, C.E., 1920; m. Nettie E. Peirsol, Aug. 23, 1912 (dec. Mar. 1952); 1 son, Frank P.; m. 2d, Grace Andress Grant, Nov. 18, 1958. Draftsman to asst. chief engr. various R.R.'s, 1912-24; engr. hydroelec. project Stone & Webster, 1925-35, chief engr., project mgr., 1941-50, cons. devel. Canadian iron ore fields, 1951-54; cost engr., sr. accountant, asst. project mgr. power projects TVA, 1936-40; cons. 1200 mile r.r. rebldg. Govt. of Mexico, 1955-59; exec. v.p., dir. Wardwell, Inc., Retail Mdse., Ft. Meade, Fla., 1960-68. Mem. panel Nat. Safety Council, 1947-50. Registered profl. engr., Ind. Fellow Am. Soc. C.E. Contbr. articles in field to profl. jours. Address: Winter Haven FL Died Jan. 22, 1968.

WARE, JOHN, physician, educator; b. Hingham, Mass., Dec. 19, 1795; s. Rev. Henry and Mary (Clark) W.; grad. Harvard, 1813, M.D., 1816; m. Helen Lincoln, Apr. 22, 1822; m. 2d, Mary Green Chandler, Feb. 25, 1862; 8 children including Maj. Robert. Began practice medicine, Boston, 1814; an editor Boston Jour. of Philosophy and the Arts, 1823-26; co-editor Boston Med. and Surg. Jour., 1828; Hersey prof. theory and practice of physic Harvard Med. Sch., 1836-64; a founder Boston Soc. Med. Improvement, 1839; pres. Mass. Med. Soc., 1848-52. Author: (novel) Charles Ashton, 1823; (essay) Remarks on the History and Treatment of Delerium Tremens, 1831; Memoir of the Life of Henry Ware, Jr. (chief literary effort), 1846; Discourses on Medical Education and on the Medical Profession, 1847; Hints to Young Men, 1850; On Hemoptysis as a Symptom, 1860; Philosophy of Natural History, 1860. Editor: Philosophy of Natural History (William Snellie), 1824; Natural Theology (William Paley), 1829. Died Apr. 29, 1864.

WARE, LEWIS SHARPE, engr., editor; b. Phila., June 18, 1851; s. Lewis S. and Elizabeth W. (Roberts) W.; Hill Sch., Pottstown, Pa.; grad. Ecole Centrale, Paris, 1875; unmarried. A leader in establishing sugar-beet industry in U.S.; sent several tons of beet seed to U.S., 1874; which was gratuitously distributed among farmers east and west; investigated world's sugar production, visiting all sugar producing countries; wrote articles protesting against expensive and futile sorghum experiments of U.S. Dept. Agr., and in favor of the sugar beet. Sent to Paris Expn., 1889; apptd. by U.S. Govt., 1900, mem. Internat. Jury, Paris Expn., to represent cane and beet sugar Industries of U.S., Cuba and Hawaii; U.S. commr. gen. Internat. Expn., Liege, Belgium, 1905. Chevalier Mérite Agricole, 1893, Officier, 1904; Chevalier de la Légion d'Honneur, 1901, Officier, 1906; Officer Ordre de Leopold; Commandeur Etoile Noire; Commandeur of Cambodge; Officier de l'Instruction Publique; Grand Officier Nichan Iftikhar. Editor The Sugar Beet (monthly jour.); contbr. to many jours. on sugar question; presented exhaustive paper on The Sugar Beet Industry at Nat. Tariff Conv., New York, 1881. Author: The Sugar Beet, 1880; Study of the Various Sources of Sugar, 1881; Production, Requirements and Selection of Sugar Beet Seed, 1896; Sugar Beet Seed, 1898; Cattle Feeding with Sugar Beets, Sugar, Molasses, etc., 1902; Beet Sugar, Manufacturing and Refining (2 vols.), 1907. Died Nov. 20, 1918.

WARFIELD, HARRY RIDGELY, JR., engineer, research dir.; b. Morgantown, W.Va., Aug. 17, 1904; s. Harry Ridgely and Susan Elizabeth (Sadtler) W.; B.Engring., Johns Hopkins, 1928; m. Juliet Linn Reaney, June 17, 1932 (dec. Apr. 1968); children—Harry Ridgely III, Susan Linn; m. 2d, Helen Gardner Howard, Oct. 31, 1968. With works mgmt. course Westinghouse Electric Co., 1928; application engr. Silica Gel Corp., 1930; dist. engr. Frigidaire div. Gen. Motors Corp., 1932; partner Fonda and Warfield, cons. engrs., 1938-41; mem. Inst. Coop. Research, Johns Hopkins, 1947-69, research engr., 1948-50, asst. dir., 1950-53, dir., 1953-69. Mem. Md. N.G., 1931-53; served from 2d lt. to col. F.A., AUS, 1941-45, ETO. Decorated ETO Service Medal with Assault Arrowhead, Normandy, No. France, Rhineland and Central Germany battle stars, Legion of Merit, B.S.M. (U.S.); Legion of Honor, Croix de Guerre with palm (France); Order of Leopold, Croix de Guerre with palm (Belgium). Mem. Soc. Colonial Wars, Alpha Delta Phi. Tau Beta Pi, Omicron Delta Kappa. Episcopalian (exec. council Diocese Md. 1951-57). Home: Baltimore MD Died Oct. 3, 1969.

WARING, GEORGE EDWIN, agriculturist, san. engr.; b. Poundridge, N.Y., July 4, 1833; s. George Edwin and Sarah (Burger) W.; m. Euphemia Blunt, Feb. 22, 1855; m. 2d, Virginia Clark, Dec. 27, 1865; m. 3d, Mrs. Louise E. Yates, July 20, 1898; at least 1 dau. Lectr. on scientific agr. to farmers in Me. and Vt., 1854-55; managed Horace Greeley's farm, Chappaqua, N.Y., 1855-57; drainage engr. Central Park, N.Y.C., 1857-61; maj. Garibaldi Guards, U.S. Army, 1861, raised 6 cos.; commd. col. 4th Mo. Cavalry, U.S. Volunteers, 1862; installed system of sewers, Memphis, Tenn., 1878; spl. agt. for 10th Census 1879; street cleaning commr. of N.Y.C., 1895-98; went to Havana to report to U.S. Govt. steps necessary to rid Havana of yellow fever, 1898, contracted disease. Author: The Elements of Agriculture, 1854; The Handybook of Husbandry: A Guide for Farmers, Young and Old, 1870; The Sanitary Drainage of Houses and Towns, 1876; The Sewerage of Memphis, London, 1881; Street Cleaning and the Disposal of a City's Wastes, 1897. Died of yellow fever, N.Y.C., Oct. 29, 1898.

WARING, JAMES JOHNSTON, physician; b. Savannah, Ga., Aug. 11, 1883; Lawrenceville (N.J.) Sch., 1899-1901; Ph.B., Sheffield Scientific Sch. (Yale), 1904; student med. dept., Johns Hopkins, 1904-07; M.D., University of Colorado, 1913, D.Sc. (honorary), 1956; married to Ruth Porter, June 15, 1921; children—Ruth Porter, Anne Johnston. In practice at Denver since 1913; instr. in medicine, U. of Colo., 1928-29, asst. prof., 1930-32, prof. of medicine, 1932-52, prof. emeritus, 1952—; now president board trustees Webb Inst. for Med. Research. Chairman Am. Bd. Internal Medicine, 1946. Recipient Alfred Stengel Memorial award, A.C.P., 1949, Trudeau medal, Nat. Tb Association, 1953. Master Am. Coll. Physicians; mem. A.M.A., Nat. Tuberculosis Assn. (dir.; mem. exec. com. 1929-30, 1932-33; pres. 1935-36), Colo. Med. Assn., Med. Soc. City and County of Denver (past pres., dir. medical library), Denver Public Health Council, Am. Clin. and Climatol. Assn. (pres. 1941), Delta Phi, Nu Sigma Nu, Alpha Omega Alpha, Sigma Psi. Episcopalian. Clubs: Denver Country, University (Denver). Contbr. med. jours. Home: 2125 Hawthorne Pl., Denver 6. Died June 2, 1962; buried Denver.

WARNER, ALTON G., M.D.; b. Dundee, Yates Co., N.Y., May 7, 1858; s. Jacob K. and Mary (Platt) W.; Hudson River Inst.; M.D., New York Homoe. Med. Coll., 1883; m. Fanny Bailey, of Watkins, N.Y., Aug. 12, 1885; children—Stuart D., Mrs. Genevieve Cummings, Mrs. Irene Ayers, Alan G. Began practice in Brooklyn, 1887; now retired; oculist and aurist, Cumberland St. Hosp. since 1889; consulting oculist and aurist Prospect Heights and Jamaica hosps. Republican. Conglist. Fellow Am. Coll. Surgeons; mem. Am. Inst. Homeoopathy, Homoe. Med. Soc. State of N.Y., also County of Kings (ex-pres.), Am. Homoe. Ophthal, Otol., and Laryngol. Soc., Brooklyn Med. Club, Sons of Revolution, etc. Address: 88 Morningside Drive, New York N.Y.

WARNER, C(HARLES) A(LBERT), cons. (petroleum); b. Jefferson, New York, April 27, 1894; son of Michael Silas and Anna B. (Dyckman) W.; A.B., Cornell University, Ithaca, New York, 1920; m. Jean R. Davis, Oct. 28, 1942. Field geologist, Empire Gas & Fuel Co., Okla. and Kan., 1917-19; dist. geologist, Emerald Oil Co., Lawton, Okla., 1919-20, Empire Gas & Fuel Co., Okmulgee, Okla., 1920-21; midcontinent dist. mgr. Houston Oil Co. of Tex., Okmulgee and Tulsa, Okla., 1921-32; mid-continent dist. mgr. and petroleum engr., Houston, 1932-34, mgr. land and lease department, Houston, 1932-50, director, 1941-44, v.p., director, 1944-51, v.p., secretary, dir., 1951-56; secretary Houston Pipe Line Company, Southwestern Settlement and Development Co., 1951-56; cons. (petroleum), 1956-68. Member Independent Petroleum Association, Texas Midcontinent Oil and Gas Association, American Association Petroleum Geol., Am. Inst. Mining and Metall. Engrs. (chmn. petroleum div. 1943), Am. Petroleum Inst., Houston Geol. Soc., Nat. Oil Scouts and Landmens Assn., Houston Landmens Assn., Tex. Gulf Coast Historical Association (trustee), also member Texas Surveyors Association. Clubs: Austin (Austin); Houston (Houston, Texas); Beeville (Tex.) Country. Author: Field Mapping for the Oil Geologist, 1921; Texas Oil and Gas since 1543, 1939; contbr. articles on oil industry to various publs. Home: Houston TX Died Nov. 6, 1968.

WARNER, EDWARD (PEARSON), engr., internat. ofcl.; b. Pittsburgh, Nov. 9, 1894; s. R. L. and Anne (Pearson) W.; B.A., Harvard, 1916, B.S., 1917; B.S., Mass. Inst. Tech., 1917, M.S., 1919; hon. D.Sc., Norwich Univ., 1938; m. Joan, d. of William H. Potter, Feb. 13, 1931; children—Sandra, Barry. Instr. aeronautical engring., Mass Inst. Tech., 1917-18; aero. engr. U.S. Army, 1918; chief physicist Nat. Advisory Com. for Aeronautics, 1919-20; tech. attaché N.A.C.A. in Europe, 1920; asso. prof. aeronautical engineering, Mass. Inst. Tech., 1920-24, prof. aeronautical engineering, 1924-26; asst. sec. Navy for aeronautics, 1926-29; editor of Aviation, 1929-34; vice chmn. Fed. Aviation Commn., 1934-35; cons. engr., 1935-38; mem. Civil Aeronautics Board, 1939-45; (v. chmn. 1943-45); resigned 1945; pres. Interim Council of Provisional Internat. Civil Aviation Orgn., 1945-47; pres. council Internat. Civil Aviation Orgn., 1947-57. Lend-lease staff, U.S. Embassy, London, Mar.-June 1941. Mem. N.A.C.A., 1929-45 (chmn. com. on aerodynamics and operating problems). Decorated Comdr. Mil. Order of Christ (Portugal); Order of Francisco de Miranda (Venezuela); Order of Cedars (Lebanon); Knight comdr. Order of Falcon (Iceland); Comdr. Legion of Honour (France); Order of Duarte, Sanchez and Mella (Dominican Republic); Comdr. Order Crown (Belgium); Grand Officer Order Aero. Merit (Brazil); Order Sacred Treasure (Japan); Comdr. Royal Order of St. Olav (Norway); Comdr. Order Al Merito (Italy); Comdr. Dannebrog (Denmark); recipient Wright Bros. medal Soc. Auto. Engrs., 1932; Daniel Guggenheim medal for achievement in aeronautics, 1950; FAI Gold Medal, 1952; Flight Safety Found. award, 1956; Wright Bros. Meml. Trophy, 1956. Hon. fellow Canadian Aero. Inst., Aeronautical Soc. of India, Institute Aero-Sciences, Royal Aeronautical Society; mem. Am. Soc. Mech. Engrs., Soc. Automotive Engrs. (pres. 1930), International Society of Aviation Writers (honorary). Clubs: Harvard (Boston); Royal Aero. and Anthenaeum (London); Cosmos (Washington); Harvard, Wings (New York City); University (Montreal). Author: Aerostatics, 1926; Airplane Design—Aerodynamics (awarded medal of Aero Club de France as leading work in aviation of year), 1927; Aviation Handbook, 1931; Airplane Design-Performance, 1936. Wilbur Wright Lectr., Royal Aeronautical Soc., 1943. Address: Duxbury, Mass. Died July 12, 1958.

WARNER, JAMES CARTWRIGHT, industralist; b. Gallatin, Tenn., Aug. 20, 1830; s. Jacob L. and Elizabeth (Cartwright) W.; m. Mary Williams, Nov. 3, 1852, 8 children. Established hardware business, Chattanooga, Tenn., 1852; mayor Chattanooga, 1 term; mem. Tenn. Gen. Assembly, 1861; sec. Tenn. Coal, R.R. Co., 1868-74; spent 25 years in developing mineral resources of South; purchased Rising Fawn iron property in Ga.; pres. Tenn. Coal, Iron & R.R. Co., 1874-98; noted for his revival and modernization of charcoal iron industry in Middle Tenn.; organized Warner Iron Co. composed of Nashville (Tenn.) capitalists, 1880, pres., 1880-89; 50-ton hotblast Warner Furnace set new precedent in charcoal iron industry by its efficient operation; built charcoal by-product plant. Died July 21, 1895.

WARNER, ROBERT WILBERFORCE, univ. prof.; b. Freeport, Ill., Aug. 20, 1889; s. George Wilberforce and Ida Mary (Buckley) W.; A.B., Washburn Coll., 1911; B.S. in elec. engring., U. of Kan., 1918, E.E., 1928; D.Sc., Washburn Coll., 1941; m. Miriam Tregemba, Dec. 27, 1923; 1 dau., Virginia Elizabeth. Jr. engr. H. L. Doherty & Co., Denver, 1919-20; asst. to chief engr. Topeka Edison Co., 1920-21; instr. in elec. engring., U. of Kan., 1921-22, U. of Wis., 1922-23; engr. Gen. Electric Co., Schenectady, N.Y., 1923-24, Kansas City Power & Light Co., 1924-28; asst. prof. of elec. engring., U. of Kan., 1928-29, asso. prof., 1929-33, prof., 1933-38; exchange prof. of elec. engring., Mass. Inst. Tech., 1935-36, head of dept., 1936-38; prof. of elec. engring. and chmn. of dept. U. of Tex., 1938-45, prof. since 1945. Served in Ordnance, Dept., U.S. Army, May-Dec. 1918. Fellow Am. Inst. E.E. (v.p. 1944-46); mem. Am. Soc. Engring. Edn., Theta Tau, Tau Beta Pi, Sigma Xi, Eta Kappa Nu. Presbyn. Contbr. to tech. jours. Home: 902 W. 23d St., Austin, Tex. Died Sept. 18, 1961; buried Austin Meml. Park.

WARNER, THOR, geologist; b. near Gottenburg, Sweden, Sept. 15, 1883; s. John Jacob Anderson and Lizzie (Johnson) W.; prep. edn. in Europe; studied evening schs., also U. of Calif., 1922-23; unmarried. With U.S. Steel Corp., Negaune, Mich., until 1903; mem. discovery party of Cobalt, Can., 1903-04; jr. mem. Leighton & Warner, Haileybury, Ont., Can., 1909-12; comdr. Canadian Sub-Arctic Expdn., 1914-15; comdr. geol. expdn. to headwaters of Amazon River, 1919-20; cons. geologist, specializing on petroleum, Los Angeles, Calif., 1920—. Vol. with assigned rank as 2d lt. Engr. Corps, U.S. Army, World War. Mem. Am. Inst. Mining and Metall. Engrs., Seismol. Soc. America, Am. Anthrop. Assn. Democrat. Author: Earth's Story of Evolution, 1920; The Siege of Lopeno, 1954. Contbr. to Am. Anthropologist, Art and Archaeology, etc. Discoverer Rio Puerco ruins, an ancient city (500 rooms), at Rio Puerco, N.M., 1925. Home: St. Anthony Hotel, San Antonio. Died Jan. 20, 1956; buried San Jose Burial Park, San Antonio.

WARREN, BENJAMIN S., sanitarian; b. Clayton, Ala., Nov. 9, 1871; s. Monroe (M.D.) and Mary Frances (Lawson) W.; prep edn., Clayton (Ala.) Male Acad.; student Atlanta Med. Cool., 1889-90; M.D., Tulane, 1891; post-grad. work Polyclinic Sch., New York, 1893; m. Lee Ella Underwood, July 18, 1894; children——Monroe, R. Bates, Lee Ella, Hugh, Benj. S., Ruth. Practiced at Clayton, 1894-99; apptd. asst. surgeon U.S.P.H.S., June 22, 1900; passed asst. surgeon, July 11, 1905; surgeon, Dec. 1, 1912; asst. surgeon gen., Feb. 1, 1918; med. dir. Dist. No. 2, July 15, 1922; med. dir., July 1930. Prof. of hygiene, med. dept. of St. Louis U., 1909-11; sanitary adviser U.S. Commn. on Industrial Relations, 1913-15; med. dir. U.S. Employees Compensation Commn., 1917. Took active part in health legislation enacted by Congress, 1902, 12, 22; investigated health ins. systems and formulated a plan for coördinating such systems with existing health agencies. Democrat. Mason. Author of various Govt. bulls. and articles relating to open air schs., health ins., relation of wages to public health, etc. Home: Chevy Chase, Md. Died May 19, 1935.

WARREN, CHARLES HYDE, mineralogist; b. Watertown, Conn., Sept. 27, 1876; s. Charles Alanson and Frances Maria (Hyde) W.; Ph.B., Sheffield Sci. Sch. (Yale), 1896, Ph.D., 1899; m. Charlotte Wardner Lamson, June 17, 1903; children—Richard, Allen Johnson, William Lamson. Asst. in chemistry and mineralogy, Sheffield Sci. Sch., 1896-99, instr., 1899-1900; instr., asst., asso. prof. mineralogy, Mass. Inst. Tech., 1900-12, prof., 1912-22; dean Sheffield Sci. School, Yale, and prof. mineralogy, 1922-45; master Trumbull Coll. of Yale U., 1938-45; ret. June 1945. Fellow Geol. Soc. Am., Am. Acad. Arts and Scis.; mem. Am. Philos. Soc. Author: Manual of Determinative Mineralogy, 1910. Contbr. Am. and German tech. jours. Home: Litchfield, Conn. Died Aug. 16, 1950; buried Watertown, Conn.

WARREN, CYRUS MOORS, chemist, mfr.; b. Fox Hill, West Dedham, Mass., Jan. 15, 1824; s. Jesse and Betsey (Jackson) W.; B.S., Lawrence Scientific Sch., 1855; studied chemistry, Paris, France and Heidelberg, Germany; m. Lydia Ross, Sept. 12, 1849, 7 children. Partner (with brother Samuel) tarred roofing mfg. co., Cincinnati, 1847; established laboratory, Boston, 1863, developed improved process of fractional condensation, studied complex mixture of hydrocarbons in Pa. petroleum, invented process of purifying Trinidad asphalt; founder, pres., treas. Warren Chem. Mfg. Co., Boston, Warren-Scharf Asphalt Paving Co., N.Y.C.; prof. organic chemistry Mass. Inst. Tech., 1866-68; left bequests for promotion of science to Harvard and Am. Acad. Arts and Scis. Contbr. 13 papers to publs. including Poggendorff's Annalender Physik, Am. Jour. of Sci., Proceedings and Memoirs of Am. Acad. Arts and Scis. Died Manchester, Vt., Aug. 13, 1891.

WARREN, EDWARD ROYAL, naturalist; b. Waltham, Mass., Oct. 17, 1860; s. Royal Sibley and Susan Elizabeth (Bates) W.; S.B., Mass. Inst. Tech., 1881; Colorado Coll., 1881-83, D.Sc., 1939; m. Oct. 11, 1916, Maude Smith Bard; children—Ruth Elizabeth, Margaret Bates. Assaying and surveying, Gunnison County, Colo., 1882-92, surveying and mining engring., Cripple Creek, 1892-96; natural history work, specializing in mammalogy and ornithology, Colorado Springs, since, 1902. Formerly hon. dir. Museum of Colorado Coll.; collaborator and field naturalist, Roosevelt Wild Life Expt. Sta., 1921-28. Mem. Am. Ornithologists Union, Cooper Ornithol. Club, Wilson Ornithol. Club, Colorado Audubon Soc., Biol. Soc. Washington, Am. Soc. Mammalogists; fellow of A.A.A.S. Unitarian. Author: The Mammals of Colorado, 1910; The Beaver—It Work and Its Ways, 1927; also contbr. The Beaver in Yellowstone Nat. Park and Notes on the Beaver in Estes Park, in Roosevelt Wild Life Annals. Address: 1511 Wood Av., Colorado Springs, Colo. Died Apr. 20, 1942.

WARREN, GOUVERNEUR KEMBLE, army officer, engr.; b. Cold Spring, N.Y., Jan. 8, 1830; s. Sylvanus Warren; grad. U.S. Mil. Acad., 1850; m. Emily Forbes Chase, June 17, 1863, 2 children. Brevetted 2d lt. Corps Topog. Engrs., 1850, commd. 2d lt., 1854, 1st lt., 1856; engaged in making map and reconnaissances of Dakota Territory, 1856-59; asst. prof mathematics U.S. Mil. Acad., 1859-61; lt. col. 5th N.Y. Volunteers, 1861; col. of a regt. of engrs. U.S. Army, 1861, capt., 1861; brevetted lt. col. for service in Battle of Gaine's Mill, 1862; brig. gen. U.S. Volunteers, 1862; chief topographic engr. Army of Potomac, 1863; brevetted col. U.S. Army for services in Battle of Gettysburg; commd. maj., 1864, brevetted maj. gen., 1865; resigned volunteer commn. 1865, re-entered Corps Engrs., U.S. Army; superintending engr. of surveys and improvements of upper Mississippi River; commd. lt. col. Corps Engrs., 1879; mem. Am. Philos. Soc., Nat. Acad. Sciences. Author: An Account of the Operations of the Fifth Army Corps, 1866; Report on Bridging the Mississippi River between St. Paul, Minnesota and St. Louis, Missouri, 1878. Died Newport, R.I., Aug. 8, 1882.

WARREN, HENRY ELLIS, inventor, corp. exec.; b. Boston, May 21, 1872; s. Henry and Adelaide Louise (Ellis) W.; S.B., Mass. Inst. Tech., 1894; D.Sc., Rutgers, 1950; m. Edith B. Smith, Jan. 19, 1907. Elec. engr., Saginaw Valley Traction Co., Mich., 1897-1902; supt., engr. Lombard Governor Co., Boston and Ashland, Mass., 1902-20, pres. 1937—; pres. Warren Telechron Co. (formerly Warren Clock Co.), 1914-43; cons. engr. Gen. Electric Co., 1919-40. Awarded Wetherill Medal by Franklin Inst., 1935. Chmn. Ashland (Mass.) selectmen, 1907-09, water commrs., 1910-17, Ashland Town Forest Com., 1937—. Trustee Middlesex County Extension Service in Agr. and Home Econs., 1936-45, pres., 1945-53; trustee Framingham Union Hosp. Chmn. Summer Inst. Social Progress, Wellesley, 1938-47, vice-chmn., 1948—. Trustee Algonquin Council Boy Scouts Am., Salvation Army. Fellow (life) Am. Inst. E.E. (Lamme medalist, 1935). Contbr. of papers to engring. publs. Home: 531 Chestnut St., Ashland, Mass. Died Sept. 21, 1957; buried Mount Auburn Cemetery.

WARREN, JAMES GOOLD, army officer; b. at Buffalo, Sept. 12, 1958; s. Joseph and Jane Vail (Goold) W.; grad. U.S. Mil. Acad., 1881; m. Sarah Clifton Wheeler, of West Point, N.Y., July 6, 1881 (died May 4, 1901). Commd. additional 2d lt. engrs., June 11, 1881; 2d, lt., Apr. 5, 1882; 1st lt., Mar. 26, 1883; capt., Apr. 12, 1894; maj., May 3, 1901; lt.-col., Nov. 15, 1907; col., Feb. 27, 1912. Service with engr. troops at Engr. Sch. and U.S. Mil. Acad.; in charge of constrn. of fortification and river and harbor works at various points; now div. engr. Lakes Div., in charge divs. of water for power purposes at Niagara Falls. Mem. Am. Soc. C.E., Western Soc. Engrs., Mil. Service Instn. U.S. Episcopalian. Clubs: Army and Navy (Washington and New York), Buffalo, Saturn, University (Buffalo). Office: Federal Bldg., Buffalo, N.Y.

WARREN, JOHN, surgeon; b. Roxbury, Mass., July 27, 1753; s. Joseph and Mary (Stevens) W.; grad. Harvard, 1771, M.D. (hon.), 1786; m. Abigail Collins, Nov. 4, 1777, 17 children including John Collins, Edward. Surgeon, Col. Pickering's Regt.; Mass. Militia, 1773; took active part in Boston Tea Party, 1773; sr. surgeon hosp. at Cambridge, Mass., 1775; went to N.Y., surgeon gen. hosp. on L.I., 1776; established hosp. for innoculation when smallpox prevalent, Boston, 1778; gave pvt. course of anatomical lectures at mil. hosp., Boston, 1780-81; an organizer Boston Med. Soc., 1780; established 1st school of medicine connected with Harvard, 1782, became prof. anatomy and surgery, 1783; pioneer in abdominal operations, amputation at shoulder joint; prominent in dealing with yellow fever epidemic, Boston, 1798; grand master Mass. Lodges Free and Accepted Masons, 1783-84; a founder, pres. Mass. Humane Soc.; mem. Agrl. Soc., Am. Acad. Arts and Scis. Author: A View of the Mercurial Practice in Febrile Diseases, 1813. Died Boston, Apr. 4, 1815.

WARREN, JOHN COLLINS, surgeon, educator; b. Boston, Aug. 1, 1778; s John and Abigail (Collins) W.; grad. (valedictorian) Harvard, 1797, M.D. (hon.) 1819; studied medicine under his father in Europe, 1799-1802; m. Susan Powell, Nov. 17, 1803; m. 2d, Anne Winthrop, Oct. 1843; 6 children. Pres., Hasty Pudding Club, Harvard; partner in father's med. office, 1802; an original mem. Anthology Club; helped prepare Pharmacopeia for Mass. Med. Soc., 1808; adjunct prof. anatomy and surgery Harvard Med. Sch., 1809-15, full prof., 1815-47, prof. emeritus, 1847, dean, 1816-19; surgeon Mass. Gen. Hosp., 1821; a founder New Eng. Jour. of Medicine and Surgery, 1821; 1st surgeon in U.S. to operate for strangulated hernia; connected with 1st demonstration of ether anesthesia, 1846; active in temperance reform, 1827-56; pres. Mass. Temperance Soc., 1827-56; contributed $10,000 in his will to temperance cause; active mem. Mass. Agr. Soc.; pres. Boston Soc. Natural History; left many paleontol. and geol. specimens to Harvard Med. Sch., formed Warren Museum. Author: A Comparative View of the Sensorial and Nervous Systems in Men and Animals, 1822; Surgical Observations on Tumours with Cases and Operation, 1837; Physical Education and the Preservation of Health, 1845; Etherization; with Surgical Remarks, 1848; The Mastodon Giganteus of North America, 1852, 55; The Preservation of Health, 1854. Died Boston, May 4, 1856.

WARREN, JOSIAH, philosopher, inventor; b. Boston, circa 1798. Orchestra leader, tchr. of music, Cincinnati, circa 1818; granted patent for lardburning lamp, 1821; established lamp factory, Cincinnati; resident, participant in Robert Owen's community, New Harmony, Ind., 1825-27; formulated theory having basic principle of "sovereignty of the individual" and "cost the limit of price"; invented speed press, 1830, not patended; started jour. The Peaceful Revolutionist, 1833; made own press type molds and stereotype plates; invented and perfected cylinder press self-inking and fed from continuous roll of paper, 1837-40; established 3 towns based on concept of mutualism, eliminating any hierarchy in community (1st: Village of Equity, Ohio, 1834, 2d: Utopia, 1846, 3d and most famous: Modern Times, L.I., N.Y., 1850-62); at various times operated "equity stores" in which he neither received profit nor loss; founder of philos. anarchism in Am. Author: Equitable Commerce, 1846; Written Music Remodeled, and Invested with the Simplicity of an Exact Science, 1860; True Civilization an Immediate Necessity, 1863; True Civilization: a Subject of Vital and Serious Interest to all People, 1875. Died Charlestown, Mass., Apr. 14, 1874; interred Mt. Auburn Cemetery, Cambridge, Mass.

WARREN, LILLIE EGINTON, educator; b. at Newtonville, Mass., Jan. 25, 1859; ed. 12th St. Sch., New York, and pvt. teachers; unmarried. Teacher of articulation to children born deaf, 1879-93; since 1893 teacher of expression reading by her own method, patented and known as Warren Method of Expression, by which persons who are growing deaf are taught to understand spoken speech by the external movements of the face; makes a specialty of curing defective speech. Prin. Warren Sch. of Expression-Reading and Articulation, New York, and branch schs. in Boston, Phila. and Washington, and of the Warren Correspondence Sch. Also prin. Warren Schools in Europe—Warren Method applied to German, French and Italian. Author: Defective Speech and Deafness, 1895. Address: 123 E. 29th St., New York, and Via Pompeo Mogno 1, Rome, Italy.

WARREN, MINTON M(ACHADO), cons. engr.; b. Salem, Mass., Aug. 7, 1888; s. Minton and Salome A. (Machado) W.; desc. in 10th generation from Richard Warren of the Mayflower, 1620; prep. edn., Browne and Nichols Sch., Cambridge, Mass.; A.B. cum laude, Harvard, 1910, M.C.E., 1912; m. Sarah Ripley Robbins, Sept. 17, 1927; children—Minton, William Bradford. Began engring. service under Hugh L. Cooper, on dam across Miss. River at Keokuk, Ia.; with Stone & Webster, constrn. engrs., 10 yrs., in design, constrn. and management; after World War I, served as chief engr. Technicolor Motion Picture Corp., also starting prodn. of several indsl. plants, in New England and Calif.; organized Aero Supply Co., mfrs. of hardware and fittings for airplane cos., in 1925; went to England, 1928, arranged for manufacture of the De Havilland Moth plane in the U.S. and was apptd. pres. of co. in U.S. and in charge of factory in Lowell, Mass.; v.p., mgr. and dir. Curtiss-Wright airplane mfg. plant at St. Louis, later sec. Curtiss-Wright Corp., Wright Aeronautical Corp., etc., until 1931; cons. practice N.Y. City and Boston since 1920; dir. research, Van Alstyne, Noel & Co., N.Y.; pres. and dir. Aeronautical Securities, Inc.; dir. Hercules Steel Products Corp. Commd. 1st lt. engrs., U.S. Army, Aug. 1917, capt., Aug. 1918; with 26th Div. in France; organized the first Am. topographical sect. participated in actions at Chemin-des-Dames, Chauteau Thierry, St. Mihiel, and Meuse-Argonne, at Verdun. Known for original research work in "water hammer," and discovery of formulas in hydraulics now largely adopted. Mem. Am. Soc. C.E., Harvard Engring. Soc. (pres. 1941-42), Soc. Mayflower Descendants. Republican. Episcopalian. Clubs: Harvard, City Midday Church Club (New York); Harvard (Boston). Home: 55 E. 86th St. Died Nov. 4, 1947.

WARREN, RUSSELL, architect, engr.; b. Tiverton, R.I., Aug. 5, 1783; s. Gamaliel and Ruth (Jenckes) W.; m. Sarah Gladding, Mar. 10, 1805; m. 2d, Lydia Gladding, 1817; no children. Served as maj. Bristol (R.I.) Militia; diversified archtl. achievements included churches, banks, public bldgs., residences; constructed bridge over Great Pedee River, S.C.; most notable works are Athenaeum and Arcade, Providence, R.I., Unitarian Ch., Free Public Library, Bedford, Mass.; architect stone mansion of John Avery Parker (most significant work), 1834; leader Greek revival movement in U.S. Died Providence, Nov. 16, 1860.

WARREN, WILLIAM HOMER, chemist; b. Charleston, S.C., Nov. 4, 1866; s. George William and Harriet (Strong) W.; A.B., Harvard, 1889, A.M., 1891, Ph.D., 1892; studied U. of Heidelberg, 1905, 06; m. Lucy Ellen Sargeant, of East Saugus, Mass., Dec. 20, 1894; children—Katharine, Priscilla, Juliet. Chemist, E. R. Squibb & Sons, Brooklyn, N.Y., 1892-96, New York Quinine & Chem. Works, Brooklyn, 1896-97; prof. chemistry, Washington U. Med. Sch., St. Louis, 1898-1911, sec. faculty, 1901-08, dean 1908-10; asst. prof. chemistry, Clark Coll., Worcester, Mass., 1911-12; univ. docent, Clark U., 1911-12; prof. chemistry, Wheaton Coll., Norton, Mass., 1912-17; chemist Peerless Color Co., 1919-22, Noil Color and Chem. Works, 1922-25; prof. chemistry, Clark U., since 1925. Commd. capt., Q.M.R.C., and on active duty at Camp Hancock, Augusta, Ga., and Washington, D.C., 1917-18; capt. Chem. Warfare Service, with A.E.F. in France; with Am. Commn. to Negotiate Peace, Paris. Mem. Am. Chem. Soc., Am. Inst. Chemists, Mil. Order World War, Deutsche Chemische Gesellschaft, Phi Beta Kappa. Translator: Autenrieth's Auffindung der Gifte, 1905. Home: 166 Woodland St., Worcester, Mass.

WARRINER, LEWIS LEGRAND, mgmt. and engring. cons.; b. N.Y.C., Aug. 30, 1898; s. Lewis Smith and Elida Belle (Steen) W.; M.E., Pratt Inst. Sci. and Tech., 1917; m. Ruth Louise Thomas, Mar. 23, 1919; children—Homer Legrand, Carlton Thomas. exec. Prodn. supt., chief engr., gen. mgr. Fairbanks Morse Co., Beloit, Wis., 1917-30; v.p. charge mfg. and engring. Master Electric Co., Dayton, O., 1930-33, v.p., gen. mgr., 1936-41, pres., gen. mgr., 1941-56; mgr. research and engring. A.O. Smith Corp., Milw., 1933-34; pres., gen. mgr. Summitville Consol. Mines, Denver, 1935-36; chmn. bd., chmn. exec. com. Cooper-Bessemer Corp., Mt. Vernon, O.; chmn exec. com., mgmt. cons. Huffman Mfg. Co., Dayton, O.; dir. Winters Nat. Bank & Trust

Co., Dayton, Cooper-Bessemer Corporation, Huffman Manufacturing Co., Sta-Rite Products, Inco., Delavan, Wis., Monarch Machine Tool Co., Sidney, O., Wheel Craft, Inc. (Azusa, Cal.). Served with AS, U.S. Army, 1918-19; AEF. Republican. Baptist. Mason. Home: 207 Hadley Av., Dayton 19. Office: P.O. Box 2277, Dayton 29, O. Died Jan. 19, 1965; buried Meml. Park Cemetery, Dayton.

WARTHIN, ALDRED SCOTT, pathologist; b. Greensburg, Ind., Oct. 21, 1866; s. Edward Mason and Eliza Margaret (Weist) W.; A.B., Indiana U., 1888, LL.D., 1928; A.M., U. of Mich., 1890, M.D., 1891, Ph.D., 1893; music diploma (teacher), Cincinnati Conservatory of Music, 1887; post-grad. work in medicine, Vienna and Freiburg; m. Dr. Katharine Angell, June 27, 1900; children—Margaret, Aldred Scott, Virginia, Thomas Angell. Asst. in internal medicine, 1891-92, demonstrator internal medicine, 1892-95, demonstrator pathology, 1896, instr., 1897, asst. prof., 1899, junior prof., 1902, prof. and dir. pathol. lab., 1903—, med. dept. U. of Mich. Pres. Am. Assn. Pathologists and Bacteriologists, 1908; pres. Internat. Assn. Med. Museums, 1910-13, mem. council for U.S., 1914-17, v.p. Am. Sect., 1914, editor of Bulletin, 1913-19, Annals of Clinical Medicine, 1924—; mem. Assn. Am. Physicians (council 1921-28; v.p., 1926-27; pres. 1927-28), Society Exptl. Medicine and Biology, Am. Assn. for Cancer Research (pres. 1927-28), Internat. Med. Hist. Soc. (vice-pres., 1929-30), Am. Heart Assn., Chicago Medical Hist. Soc., Assn. Exptl. Pathology (v.p. 1922-23, pres. 1924, del. to Nat. Research Council 1925-28); pres. Mich. Assn. Prevention and Relief of Tuberculosis, 1908-09, Michigan Social Hygiene Assn., 1917-18; sec. Ann Arbor Anti-Tuberculosis Assn. Author: Practical Pathology, 1896, 1911. Editor and translator of 10th edit. Ziegler's General Pathology, 1903; editor dept. Pathology, 2d and 3d edits., Wood's Reference Hand-Book of the Medical Sciences; Text-Book fo General Pathology, 1914; Medical Aspects of Mustard Gas Poisoning, 1919; Old Age—The Major Involution, 1929; The Creed of a Biologist, 1930. Wrote over 1,000 articles in medical journals and textbooks; contbns. from the Pathological Laboratory of U. of Mich., 14 vols., 1896-1927. Most important researches on anatomy and pathology of the haemolymph glands, and the pathology of diseases of the blood and blood-forming organs, cardiac syphilis, latent syphilis, tuberculosis, and toxic action of mustard gas, fat embolism, action of X-rays, heart in diphtheria, thymus, heredity in cancer, pathology of goiter. Russell lecturer at U. of Mich., 1929. Home: Ann Arbor, Mich. Died May 23, 1931.

WARWICK, C. LAURENCE, civil engr.; b. Phila., Pa., July 29, 1889; s. Charles F. and Emily N. (Meyers) W.; B.S., U. of Pa., 1909, C.E., 1926; m. Mary E. Orem, Jan. 25, 1915; children—C. Laurence, Robert O., Mary Elizabeth. Instr. and asst. prof. structural engring., civil engring. dept. U. of Pa., 1909-19; editorial asst. Am. Soc. for Testing Materials, 1909-17, assistant secretary, 1917-19, sec.-treasurer, 1919-45, executive secretary since 1945. Consultant and chief specifications branch (later, materials branch), conservation div. War Production Bd., 1941 to Sept. 1943, consultant to dir. conservation div. and chief specifications staff Sept. 1943 to June 1944, engaged in conserving critical materials; adminstr. nat. emergency steel specifications project War Prodn. Bd., 1941 to 1944. Commr. Radnor Twp., Del. Co., since 1937. F. of A.A.A.S., assoc. mem. Am. Soc. C.E.; mem. A.S.T.M., A.S.M., Sigma Xi Soc., hon. mem. Sigma Tau. Republican. Presbyterian. Clubs: Engrs. (Phila.), St. David's Golf Home: 418 Woodland Av., Wayne, Pa. Office: 1916 Race St., Phila. 3. Died Apr. 23, 1952; buried Valley Forge Gardens, King of Prussia, Pa.

WASHBURN, EDWARD ROGER, educator, chemist; b. Big Rapids, Mich., Sept. 22, 1899; s. Edward Rush and Myrtilla (Rogers) W.; B.S., U. Mich., 1922, M.S., 1923, Ph.D., 1926; m. Dorothy May Adams, Aug. 23, 1926; children—Dorothy Elaine (wife of Dr. Robert Dudley Olney), Edward Roger, Robert Henry, Carolyn May. With dept. chemistry U. Neb., 1926-67, successively instr., asst. prof., asso. prof., 1926-41, prof., 1941-67, chmn. dept. chemistry, 1955-64. Served with USNRF, 1918; with Chem. Warfare Res., U.S. Army, 1927-37. Mem. Am. Chem. Soc., A.A.A.S., Am. Assn. U. Profs., Neb. Acad. Sci., Sigma Xi, Phi Lambda Upsilon, Alpha Chi Sigma. Author sci. articles on solubility, surface tension, monomolecular films. Home: Lincoln NE Died Aug. 31, 1967; buried Wyuka Cemetery Lincoln NB

WASHBURN, EDWARD WIGHT, chemist; b. Beatrice, Neb., May 10, 1881; s. William Gilmor and Flora Ella (Wight) W.; U. of Neb., 1899-1901; B.S., Mass. Inst. Tech., 1905, Ph.D., 1908; m. Sophie Wilhelmina de Veer, June 10, 1910; children—William de Veer, Janet, Roger D., Barbara. Research asso. in phys. chemistry, Mass. Inst. Tech., 1906-08; asso. in chemistry, 1908-10, asst. prof., 1910-13, prof. phys. chemistry, 1913-16, prof. ceramic chemistry and head of dept. of ceramic engring., 1916-22, U. of Ill.; editor Internat. Critical Tables (phys. chem. and engring. constants), 1922-30; chief chemist U.S. Bur. Standards, 1926—. Vice-chmn. and actg. chmn., 1918-19, chmn. 1922-23, div. chemistry Nat. Research Council; del. Internat. Chem. Union, London, 1919, Lyons, 1922, Cambridge, 1923, and Internat. Research Council, Brussels, 1919 and 1922; Am. commr. Internat. commn. annual tables phys. and chem. constants, 1921-29; chmn. Internat. Commn. on Physico-Chemical Standards; mem. Internat. Com. Thermochemistry, 1929—. Fellow A.A.A.S. (chmn. Sect. C 1923-24), Royal Soc. Arts, Am. Ceramic Soc. (editor Jour. 1920-22). Author: Introduction to the Principles of Physical Chemistry, 1915 (French translation by Noyes and Weiss, Payot et Cie, Paris, 1925), etc. Died Feb. 6, 1934.

WASHBURN, FRANK SHERMAN, engr.; b. Centralia, Ill., Dec. 8, 1860; s. Elmer and Elizabeth Jane (Knight) W.; C.E., Cornell, 1883; post-grad. work in history and polit. science, 1885; m. Irene May Russell, Dec. 3, 1890. Engr. of bridges, C.&N.W. R.R., 1885-88; supt. and mgr. Union Stock Yard & Transit Co., Chicago, 1889; contracting and cons. engr. at N.Y. City, 1890-1900; Southern enterprises, 1900-1910; pres. Am. Cyanamid Co., chemicals (New York), Air Nitrates Corp. (New York), Goodham Mfg. Co. (Chicago). In charge engring., constrn. and operation of 3 govt. plants for converting air into nitrates, during World War I. Presbyn. Home: Rye, N.Y. Died Oct. 9, 1922.

WASHBURN, FREDERIC LEONARD, biologist; b. Brookline, Mass., Apr. 12, 1860; s. Nehemiah and Martha (Parmelee) W.; A.B., Harvard U., 1882, grad. student, 1888-89, A.M., 1895, Johns Hopkins, 1886-87; m. Frances L. Wilcox, Dec. 27, 1887; children—Martha Wilcox (Mrs. C. D. Allin), Alice Julia (Mrs. Phillips Byfield). Instr. zoölogy, U. of Mich., 1887-88; prof. zoölogy, Ore. Agrl. Coll. and entomologist to Expt. Sta., 1889-95; prof. biology, U. of Ore., 1895-1902; state biologist Ore., 1899-1902; prof. entomology, 1902-18, prof. economic vertebrate zoölogy, 1918—, U. of Minn.; State entomologist of Minn., 1902-18. Home: Minneapolis, Minn. Died Oct. 15, 1927.

WASHBURN, ICHABOD, mfr., philanthropist; b. Kingston, Mass., Aug. 11, 1798; s. Ichabod and Sylvia (Bradford) W.; m. Ann Brown, Oct. 6, 1823; m. 2d, Elizabeth Cheever, 1859; at least 1 dau. Entered partnership with W.H. Howard to manufacture lead pipe and machinery used in prodn. of woolen goods, 1821; partner Washburn & Goddard, mfrs. machinery for carding and spinning wool, 1823-24; devised wire drawblock; manufactured wire, Worcester, Mass., 1834-68, firm name I. Washburn & Moen after 1859; made steel piano wire, 1850; introduced galvanized iron telegraph wire; developed 1st continuous method of tempering and hardening metal, 1856; benefactor Lincoln (now Washburn) Coll. (Kan.); trustee, benefactor Worcester County Free Inst. of Indsl. Sci. Died Worcester, Dec. 30, 1868.

WASHBURN, JOHN HOSEA, agriculturist; b. Bridgewater, Mass., June 5, 1859; s. Hosea and Wealthy (Packard) W.; B.S., Mass. Agrl. Coll., 1878; post-grad. in chemistry, Brown U., 1880-81, Mass. Agrl. Coll., 1881-83, U. of Göttingen, 1885, 1887-89, A.M., Ph.D., 1889; m. Martha W. Merrow, May 26, 1887. Teacher in common and high schs., 1878-81; prof. chemistry, Storrs (Conn.) Agrl. Sch., 1883-87; pres. and prof. agrl. chemistry, R.I. Coll. of Agr. and Mech. Arts, 1889-1902; dir. Nat. Farm Sch., Bucks County, Pa., 1892-Mar. 1, 1917. Republican. Mem. New Church (Swedenborgian). Died Aug. 3, 1932.

WASHINGTON, HENRY STEPHENS, petrologist; b. Newark, N.J., Jan. 15, 1867; s. George and Eleanor P. (Stephens) W.; A.B., Yale, 1886; A.M., 1888; Ph.D., Leipzieg, 1893; post-grad. studies, Yale, Leipzig, and Am. Sch. Classical Studies (Athens); m. Martha Rose Beckwith, Oct. 25, 1893. Asst. in physics, Yale, 1886-88; excavations in Greece, 1889-94; asst. in mineralogy, Yale, 1895-96; geol., volc., petrol. investigations in Greece, Asia Minor, Italy, Spain, Brazil, Hawaiian Islands, and U.S., and chem. study of igneous rocks and minerals; cons. mining geologist, 1906-12; bd. mgrs. Geol. Survey N.J., 1909-14; with Geophysical Lab., Carnegie Instn. of Washington, 1912—. Chem. asso. and scientific attaché Am. Embassy, Rome, 1918-19; vice chmn. sect. volcanology, Internat. Geophys. Union; chmn. Am. Geophys. Union, 1927-29. Decorated Cavalier Order Crown of Italy. Author: Chemical Analyses of Igneous Rocks, 1903, 1917; Manual of the Chemical Analysis of Igneous Rocks, 1904; The Roman Comagmatic Region, 1906. Joint Author: Quantitative Classification of Igneous Rocks, 1903. Contbr. of articles on petrol., mineral. and archaeol. subjects in scientific jours., 1887—. Died Jan. 7, 1934.

WASON, CHARLES WILLIAM, elec. engr.; b. Cleveland, Apr. 20, 1854; mech. engring. course, Cornell U., 1872-76; m. Jettie Morrill, 1882; m. 2d, Margaret Wright; m. 3d, Mabel Breckenridge. Established as elec. engr. in Cleveland, becoming distinguished as expert on application of electricity to propulsion; largely interested in street ry. co.'s stocks. Home: Cleveland, Ohio. Died Apr. 15, 1918.

WASON, LEONARD CHASE, engineer; b. Brookline, Mass., Aug. 5, 1868; s. Elbridge and Mary I. (Chase) W.; B.S. (in elec. engring.), Mass. Inst. Tech., 1891; m. Harriet C. Willis, Oct. 8, 1896; children—Elbridge, Alfred Boyd, Raymond, Lawrence Willis; m. 2d, Annie B. Redlon, June 24, 1916. Pres., 1895—. Aberthaw Co., specializing in reinforced concrete, and built numerous bridges, mills, residences, the Harvard Stadium, and the largest concrete standpipe for water in the world; dir. Fed. Mutual Liability Ins. Co., Fed. Mutual Fire Ins. Co.; mem. advisory bd. Lumbermen's Mut. Casualty Co. of Chicago. Pres. Am. Concrete Inst. Republican. Author: Engineer's Handbook of Reinforced Concrete, 1905. Awarded Phebe Hobson Fowler prize, Am. Soc. C.E., 1929, "for meritorious achievement in engineering." Home: Brookline, Mass. Died Apr. 30, 1937.

WASSERMANN, FRIEDRICH, anatomist; b. Munich, Germany, Aug. 13, 1884; s. Franz and Amalie (Fechheimer) W.; M.D., U. Munich, 1910; Ph.D. (honorary), University of Frankfurt, 1958; M.D. (honorary). University of Giessen, 1959; m. Margaret Schmidgall, M.D., Feb. 3, 1917; children—Gertrude (Mrs. Fetcher) Franz Walter. Came to U.S., 1937, naturalized, 1943. Privatdozent anatomy U. Munich, 1914, teaching and research work in anatomy, histology and cytology, 1919-30, prof. anatomy and head dept. histology and embryology, 1931-36; prof. of anatomy U. Chicago, 1937-49; sr. biologist Argonne Nat. Lab., Chicago, 1949-69; visiting prof. anatomy Western Reserve University, 1942, U. Heidelberg, Germany, 1952, University of Frankfurt, Germany, 1954, Albert Einstein College of Medicine, N.Y., 1955, 57. Mem. med. mission Unitarian Serv. Com. to Germany, 1948. Served as med. officer, German Army, 1914-18. Decorated Comdr. Cross of Order of Merit (Germany). Mem. Am. Soc. Zoologists, Internat. Soc. for Cell Biology, Internat. Soc. Dental Research, Am. Association Anatomists, Anatomische Gesellschaft (hon.), Soc. Exptl. Biology and Medicine, Society of Growth, A.A.A.S., Chicago Ethical Soc., Deutsche Akademie der Naturforscher Leopoldina, Sigma Xi. Clubs: Quadrangel (Chgo.). Author: Growth and reproduction of the living matter, 1929. Home: Downers Grove IL Died June 16, 1969; buried Waldfriedhof, Stuttgart Germany

WASSON, THERON, geologist; b. nr. Springville, N.Y., Apr. 23, 1887; s. George Fuller and Hattie Bevins (Smith) W.; student Griffith Inst., Springville, N.Y., 1905; B.S., Carnegie Inst. Tech., 1910; student Columbia, 1919-20; m. Isabel D. Bassett, June 11, 1920 (div. May 1953); children—Elizabeth (Mrs. E.A. Bergstrom), Edward B., Anne (Mrs. Gregory Harney); m. 2d, Ann M. Hand, June 3, 1959. Assistant surveys coal mines, railroads, oil and gas fields, pipe lines, New York, Pa., N.J., Cal., 1903-15; designer hydraulic fill Lake Almanor Dam. Gt. Western Power Co., San Francisco, 1913; water engr. Geol Survey State of N.J., Trenton, 1916; field geologist Twin State Oil Co., Tulsa, also topographer U.S. Geol. Survey, 1917; chief geologist Am. Oil Engring. Corp., Ft. Worth, 1920; with Leonard Exploration Co., N.Y., explorations east of the Andes in Ecuador, 1921; chief geologist The Pure Oil Co., Chgo., 1922-52, sr. geologist, advisor exec. com., 1952-54, consulting geologist. 1954-70. Advisory committee constrn. geol. exhibits Chgo. Century Progress, 1932-33; credited with discovery new oil fields of So. Ill., 1937; adv. council department geological engring. Princeton, 1941-55; radio program Adventures in Ecuador. Adventurers Club, Chgo., 1947; exec. com. oil exhibits Chgo. Mus. Sci. and Industry, 1947-58; del, UN Sci. Conf. on Conservation and Utilization of Resources, Lake Success, 1949; vis. geol. advisor Naval Petroleum Res. No. 4, Point Barrow, Alaska, 1950. Served as 2d lt. 117th and 1st Engrs., U.S. Army, 1917-19; city engr. Sinzig on Rhine, Germany, 1919. Recipient Award of Merit Carnegie Inst. Tech., 1951, certificate appreciation, Am. Petroleum Inst., 1955. Registered engr., Ill. Fellow Geol. Soc. Am.; mem. Am. Petroleum Inst. (adv. com. research occurrence and recovery of petroleum 1940-50), A.A.A.S., Western Soc. Engineers, American Geog. Society, American Association of Petroleum Geologists (honorary), Society of Econ. Geologists (vice pres. 1954), Am. Geophys. Union. Am. Inst. Mining and Metall. Engrs., Rainbow Div. Vets., Am. Geol Inst. (founder), Ill. Soc. Mayflower Descs., Tau Beta Pi. Unitarian. Mem. Order of the Top of the World. Clubs: Adventurers (Chgo.); Sierra (San Francisco); Petroleum (Denver). Author: Explorations in Eastern Ecuador, 1923; Geological Explorations East of the Andes in Ecuador, 1927; Geology of Cabin Creek Field, West Virginia, 1927; The First Geological Studies in the Eastern Region of Ecuador in a zone between Baeza-Coca and Canelos-Macas, 1937; Los Primeros Estudios Geologicos del Oriente, 1937; Geology of the Creole Oil Field, Gulf of Mexico, 1948; also ann. reports, oil and gas devel., various states, 1932-47. Editor of Mineral Map of Europe, 1940. Home: North Riverside IL Died Aug. 6, 1970; buried Maplewood Cemetery, Springville NY

WASSON, WILLIAM WALTER, physician, radiologist; b. Chrisman, Ill., Aug. 19, 1884; s. William Alexander and Matilda Ann (Layne) W.; diploma Northwestern U. Acad., 1904; student U. Ill., Urbana, 1904-06; A.B., U. Colo., 1908, M.D., 1910; m. Katharine L. Crouch, Sept. 24, 1908; children—Richard Van Cleave and Madolin Layne (Mrs. Richard Des Jardins) (twins). Asso. electrotherapeutics, Dr. E.H. Robertston, Boulder, Colo., 1910-13; practice of radiology, Boulder, 1910-16, Denver, 1916-68; asso. Dr. John Samuel Bouslog, 1918-68; established x-ray depts. St. Anthony's Hosp., Children's Hosp., Denver; co-founder, mem. bd. control Solmene Winter Found., 1922-68, dir., 1922-27; adv. com. Radiol. Research Inst.; radiology cons. Presbyn., Children's, St. Luke's hosps., Denver. Mem. com. on growth and development White House Conf. Child Health and Protection, 1929-32; radiologist to med. adv. bd. Rocky Mountain Region, World War II. recipient gold medal for studies in chest disease, Radiol. Soc. N.A., 1926, for distinguished service Am. Coll. Radiology, 1958; recipient Norlin award, University Colorado, 1960. Fellow A.M.A. (chairman sect. on radiology 1947-48), Am. Coll. Radiology (charter 1923; v.p. 1932-33, chancellor 1923-30, 42-47), Clin. and Pathological Soc. of Denver; mem. Western Roentgen Ray Soc. (dist. counsellor 1919), Radiol. Soc. N.A. (exec. com. 1920, past counselor, pres. 1941-42), Am. Roentgen Ray Soc. (v.p. 1947), Am. Radiol. Soc., Child Research Council (co-founder, mem. bd. control 1927-34, dir. 1927-30), Colo., Denver County med. socs., Colo., Rocky Mountain radiol. socs., Sigma Xi, Delta Upsilon, Pi Beta Phi. Clubs: Denver Country. Author: The Auxiliary Heart, 1954. Contbr. articles med. jours. Former profl. pitcher Western Baseball League. Home: Golden CO Died Apr. 14, 1968; buried Fair Mount Cemetery.

WATERFALL, HARRY WILLIAM, prof. mech. engring.; b. Boston, Mass., June 6, 1887; s. Harry and Helena (Hood) W.; S.B., Mass. Inst. Tech., 1911; m. Marie Ross Sinclair, Aug. 25, 1915. Asst. in mech. engring., Mass. Inst. Tech., 1911-12; asst. to chief engr. Cramp Shipbuilding Co., 1912-13; instr. in machine design U. of Ill., 1913-17; mech. engr. The Angus Co., Ltd., Calcutta, India, 1917-19; asst. prof. mech. engring. U. of Ill., 1919-20; asso. prof. mech. engring. Johns Hopkins U., 1920-29; sec. and mech. engr. Kwong Yuen & Co., Inc., New York, N.Y., 1929-35; special lecturer in engring. thermodynamics, New York U., 1935-36; asso. prof., later prof. and head dept. of mech. engring. Louisiana State U., since 1936. Awarded Franklin Medal (Boston), 1907; scholarship awards Mass. Inst. Tech., 1908, 1909, 1910. Mem. Am. Soc. M.E., American Soc. for Engring. Edn., La. Teachers Assn., La. Engring. Soc., Sigma Xi, Tau Beta Pi. Home: 416 E. State St., Baton Rouge 13, La. Died Mar. 1947.

WATERHOUSE, BENJAMIN, physician; b. Newport, R.I., Mar. 4, 1754; s. Timothy and Hannah (Proud) W.; apprenticed to Dr. John Halliburton, surgeon, 1770; med. student at Edinburgh, 1775; grad. U. Leyden, 1780; attended med. dept. of Harvard, 1783; m. Elizabeth Oliver, June 1, 1788; m. 2d, Louisa Lee, Sept. 19, 1819; 6 children. Prof. theory and practice of physic, med. dept. of Harvard, 1783-1812 (forced to resign); pioneer Am. vaccinator; received from England vaccine for small pox in form of infected threads, immediately used it on his son, 1800; vaccinated others with cowpox with good results; sent vaccine to Pres. Jefferson (who had about 200 persons vaccinated with it), 1802; wrote many newspaper articles on vaccination; lectured on natural history, mineralogy and botany at R.I. Coll. (now Brown U.), 1784-86, at Cambridge, Mass., from 1788; drew up plans for Humane Soc. of Commonwealth of Mass., 1785; med. supt. of all mil. posts in New Eng., 1813-20; editor John B. Wyeth's Oregon (published to deter Western emigrations), 1833. Author: A Synopsis of a Course of Lectures on the Theory and Practice of Medicine, 1786; A Prospect of Exterminating the Small Pox (his 1st report on smallpox), 1800. Cautions to Young Persons Concerning Health . . . Shewing the Evil Tendency of the Use of Tobacco . . . with Observations on the Use of Ardent and Vinous Spirits, 1805; The Botanist, 1811; A Circular Letter, from Dr. Benjamin Waterhouse, to the Surgeons of the Different Post, 1817. Died at home, Cambridge, Oct. 2, 1846; buried Mt. Auburn Cemetery, Cambridge.

WATERHOUSE, GEORGE BOOKER, metallurgical engr.; b. Sheffield, Eng., May 25, 1883; s. Joseph J. and Mary E. (Booker) W.; B.Met., U. of Sheffield, 1901; post-grad. work same univ., 1901-03; Ph.D., Columbia U., 1907; Dr. Metallurgy, U. of Sheffield, 1937; D.Eng., Nova Scotia Technical College, 1949; married Eleanor F. Wood, June 29, 1909 (died Dec. 16, 1935); m. Germaine S. Souverain, June 15, 1938. Came to U.S., 1903, naturalized citizen, 1910. With Lackawanna Steel Co., as metallographist, metallurgist and metall. and insp. engr., until 1922; prof. metallurgy, Mass. Inst. Tech., 1922-45; was prof. emeritus; cons. practice; mem. research adv. bd. Westinghouse Electric & Mfg. Co.; dir. Belmont Trust Co.; mem. Corp. Belmont Savings Bank; cons. engr. U.S. Bur. Mines. Served as mem. 74th Regt. N.Y. Nat. Gd., hon. discharged as 1st lt., May 1919. Mem. Am. Iron and Steel Inst., Am. Inst. Mining and Metall. Engrs. (chmn. iron and steel div. 1929; dir. 1933-1939), Am. Soc. for Testing Materials, Am. Soc. for Metals (trustee since 1934, pres. 1937-38), Am. Foundrymen's Assn., Sigma Xi, Scabbard and Blade, also Iron and Steel Institute and Cleveland Institute Engineers (all of Great Britain); chairman metallurgical advisory committee U.S. Bureau Standards, 1920-43; chmn., dir. research, iron alloys com. of Engineering Foundation, 1929-42; spl. staff consultant Office Prodn. Management, June 1941-Dec. 1941, steel div. of War Prodn. Bd., Dec. 1941-Aug. 1942, Office Lend-Lease Adminstrn. since Aug. 1942, Office Fgn. Econ. Adminstrn., Dec. 1943-May 1945. Mem. Belmont (Mass.) Sch. Com. (chmn. 1934, 36, 37). Republican. Mason. Contbr. numerous scientific papers and articles; export witness in suits relating to iron and steel. Home: 16 Fairmont St., Belmont 78, Mass. Died May 10, 1952; buried Bergen (N.Y.) Cemetery.

WATERMAN, ALAN TOWER, physicist; b. Cornwall-on-Hudson, N.Y., June 4, 1892; son Frank Alan and Florence (Tower) W.; A.B., Princeton, 1913, A.M., 1914, Ph.D., 1916; Doctor of Science (hon.). Tufts Coll., 1952, Northeastern U., 1953, U. Vt., 1955; LL.D., Cornell Coll., 1956, American University, University of Chattanooga, 1958; Sc.D., Bowdoin Coll., U. of Arizona, 1958; LL.D., U. Mich., 1959, U. Cin., 1959, U. Cal. at Berkeley, 1960, Ill. Inst. Tech., Mich. State U., 1962, Rockefeller Inst., 1963, Denison U., 1964; Sc.D., U. Notre Dame, U. Akron, 1960, U. So. Cal., Kenyon College, Norwich U., Poly. Inst. Bklyn., Loyola U., 1962, U. of Pitts., 1963; m. Mary Mallon, Aug. 1917; children—Alan Tower, Neil John, Barbara (Mrs. Joseph R. Carney), Anne (Mrs. William C. Cooley), Guy van Vorst. Instr. U. Cincinnati, 1916-17; instructor physics, Yale, 1919-22, assist. prof. of physics, 1923-30; National Research fellow, physics, King's Coll., London, 1927-28; asso. prof. of physics Yale univ., 1931-48; dep. chief and chief scientist Office Naval Research, Navy Dept., 1946-51; dir. NSF, 1951-63, cons., 1963—. Trustee of Atoms for Peace Awards; cons. President's Sci. Advisory Com.; mem. Nat. Aeros. & Space Council, 1958-59; mem. Fed. Council for Sci. and Tech., 1958-63, Def. Sci. Bd., 1956-63; mem. Distinguished Civilian Service Awards, Board, 1957-60; chmn. Interdependental com. on science Research and Development, 1958. Pvt. to first lt., Science and Research div. Signal Corps, U.S. Army, 1917-19; served as vice chmn. div. D, Nat. Research Defense Com., 1942-43; dep. chief office of field service, OSRD, 1943-45, chief, 1945. Chief reader, physics, coll. entrance examination board, 1935-41, chief examiner, physics, 1937-49. Recipient 1st ann. Capt. Robert Dexter Conrad award, 1957; Pub. Welfare medal Nat. Acad. Scis., 1960, Procter Prize, Sch. Research Soc. Am., 1960; Presdl. Medal of Freedom. Fellow A.A.A.S. (pres. 1963, chmn. bd. 1964), American Physical Soc., Am. Assn. Physics Tchrs.; mem. Am. Inst. E.E., Washington Acad. Sci., Philos. Soc. Washington, Washington Acad. of Medicine, Am. Assn. Univ. Profs. Scientific Research Soc. of America, Phi Beta Kappa, Sigma Xi. Clubs: Graduates, (New Haven), Cosmos (Wash.). Medal for Merit, 1948. Editor: Combat Scientists, 1947. Mem. editorial bd., Am. Jour. of Sci., 1934-42. Contbr. sci. papers to The Phys. Rev., Am. Jour. of Sci., Philos. Mag., Proc. Royal Soc. Home: 5306 Carvel Rd., Westmoreland Hills, Washington 16. Died Nov. 1967.

WATERMAN, EARLE LYTTON, univ. prof.; b. Glover, Vt., Sept. 1, 1885; s. Darwin Samuel and Nora (Willey) W.; B.S. in C.E., U. Vt., 1907, C.E., 1913; m. Florence Votey, Dec. 21, 1910; 1 dau., Anne. Successively asst. instr., asst. prof., asso. prof. hydraulic and san. engring., Pa. State Coll., 1907-19; asso. prof. pub. health, extension div., U. Ia., 1919-22; asso. prof. san. engring., Coll. Engring., 1922-25, prof., 1925—; head Dept. Civil Engring., 1944; asst. state engr., Mich. State Dept. Health, 1916-17; in pub. health engring. and cons., summers 1923-40; state san. engr., Vt. Dept. Pub. Health, summers 1931-40. Served as lt., capt., San. Corps, U.S. Army, 1918-19. Chmn. City Plan Commn., Iowa City, 1930—; pres. Social Service League, Iowa City, 1925-29. Recipient Fuller Award, 1945. Mem. Am. Soc. C.E. (mem. exec. com. san. engring. div., 1936-40; chmn. 1940; former pres. Ia. sect.), Am. Water Works Assn. (dir. 1938-41; sec. Mo. Valley sect., 1929-45), Am. Pub. Health Assn., Soc. Promotion Engring. Edn., Ia. Engring. Soc. (former pres.), Ia. Wastes Disposal Assn. (past pres.), Federated Sewage Works Assn. (dir. bd. control), Boulder Soc., Triangle, Sigma Xi, Chi Epsilon, Tau Beta Pi, Phi Delta Theta. Episcopalian. Republican. Clubs: Engineers; Mt. View Country (Greensboro, Vt.). Home: 24 Heat's Bridge Rd. Concord, Mass. Office: Eliot-Pearson Sch., Tufts, Mass. Died July 30, 1951.

WATERMAN, FRANK ALLAN, physicist; b. Oswego, N.Y., July 9, 1865; s. David Allen and Eliza Dunning (Van Vorst) W.; A.B., Princeton U., 1888, Ph.D., 1896; m. Florence Tower, Aug. 19, 1891; children—Alan Tower, Lesley (Mrs. Edward Kramer Funkhouser), Ransom. Instr. physics, 1891-92, prof., 1892-93, Purdue U., Lafayette, Ind.; instr. physics, Princeton U., 1893-97; prof. physics, Smith Coll., Northampton, Mass., 1897-1933, prof. emeritus since 1933. Fellow A.A.A.S., Am. Phys. Soc.; member Societe Francaise de Physique, Sigma Xi. Author: Laboratory Experiments in Physics, 1892. Contbr. to scientific jours. and revs. Address: Northampton MA

WATERMAN, LEWIS EDSON, inventor, mfr.; b. Decatur, N.Y., Nov. 20, 1837; s. Elisha and Amanda (Perry) W.; m. Sarah Ann Roberts, June 29, 1858; m. 2d, Sarah Ellen Varney, Oct. 3, 1872; at least 3 children. Moved to Ill., 1853; engaged in various jobs as tchr., lockseller, carpenter; began selling life insurance, 1862; Boston rep. Aetna Life Ins. Co., 1864-70; perfected type of fountain pen, 1st patent issued, 1884 (his improvement over other types was in ink-feeding device); organized, operated Ideal Pen Co., 1884-87, reorganized and incorporated as L. E. Waterman Co., 1887, pres., mgr., 1887-1901, continued to improve pen throughout these years. Died Bklyn., May 1, 1901; buried Forest Hill Cemetery, Boston.

WATERMAN, SIGISMUND, M.D.; b. Bruck, Bavaria, Feb. 22, 1819; ed. in Erlangen, Bavaria; grad. in medicine, Yale, 1848; practiced in New York; from 1857 for about 30 years was police surgeon; consulting physician and later medical director, Home for Aged and Infirm Hebrews, New York; specialist, writer and lecturer on use of the spectroscope in medicine; has also written many papers on other medical subjects. Address: 165 E. 60th St., New York.

WATERMAN, WARREN GOOKIN, prof. botany; b. Southport, Conn., Sept. 3, 1872; s. Edwin Southworth and Martica (Gookin) W.; A.B., Yale, 1892, A.M., 1907; Ph.D., U. Chgo., 1917; m. Anna Sarah Mueller, June 14, 1898 (died Feb. 23, 1944); children—Warren G., Alice Southworth, John French. Instr. natural sci., Fisk U., Nashville, 1896-1902, prof. geology, 1903-11; asst. prof. biology, Knox Coll., Galesburg, Ill., 1912-15; asst. prof. botany, 1917-23; asso. prof., 1923-33, prof., 1933-37, Northwestern U., chmn. dept., 1928-37, ret.; formerly fellow A.A.A.S.; formerly mem. Bot. Soc. Am., Ecol. Soc. Am., Ill. State Acad. Sci. (ex-pres.), Ill. Bd. Mus. Advs., Conservation Council Chgo., Sigma Xi, Mich. Acad. Sci., U. Clubs of Chgo. and Evanston. Republican. Conglist. Author: Plant Communities (mimeograph edit.), 1924; also articles on plant communities, especially in bog and dune habitats. Home: R.F.D., Frankfort, Mich. Died Nov. 1952.

WATERS, CAMPBELL EASTER, chemist, botanist; b. Baltimore County, Md., Sept. 14, 1872; s. Charles E. and Anne M. (Easter) W.; A.B., Johns Hopkins, 1895, Ph.D., 1899; m. Mary Snedeker, Apr. 16, 1907; children—Charles Emory, Elizabeth (Mrs. Allan H. Graeff). Professor of chemistry and physics, Connecticut Agricultural College, 1900-01; assistant in chemistry, Johns Hopkins, 1901-04; asst. chemist, Nat. Bureau Standards, 1904, asso. chemist, May 1, 1909, chemist, 1919-42, asst. chief chem. Aug. 1937-Sept. 1942; retired. Fellow A.A.A.S.; mem. Am. Chem. Soc., Md. Hist. Soc., Va. Hist. Soc., Chem. Soc. of Washington, Washington Academy Sciences, Wild Flower Preservation Society; hon. and charter mem. Am. Fern Soc. Democrat. Author: Ferns, 1903. Contbr. to Am. Chem. Jour., Jour. Am. Chem. Soc., Industrial Engring. Chemistry, Nat. Bur. of Standards publs.; also on bot. topics, especially ferns, to the Fern Bulletin, Rhodora, and the Plant World. Home: 5812 Chevy Chase Parkway, Washington 15 DC

WATERS, LEWIS WILLIAM, chemist; b. Orange, Mass., Oct. 3, 1888; s. William Wadsworth and Anna Amelia (Stone) W.; grad. Orange High Sch., 1906; B.S., Mass. Inst. Tech., 1910; m. Hazel E. Rugen, Apr. 4, 1915; children—Sally Eleanor, Lewis William. Instr. in food analysis, Mass. Inst. Tech., 1910-11; chemist Campbell Soup Co., 1911-14; asst. to Prof. W. T. Sedgwick, Mass. Inst. Tech., 1914; in charge research lab. United Fruit Co., Port Limon, Costa Rica, 1914-17; in charge biol. research dept. Expt. Sta., E. I. Du Pont de Nemours, Wilmington, Del., 1917-20; mgr. research dept., Minute Tapioca Co., 1920-27; asst. to exec. v.p. Gen. Foods Corp., 1927-30, v.p. in charge of research and development, 1930-43, v.p. in charge scientific relations since 1943. Lecturer N.Y. Univ. Consultant to scientific com. War Prodn. Bd.; mem. adv. com. on research and development Office of Q.M. Gen.; mem. tech. adv. com. Nutrition Foundation, Inc. Mem. A.A.A.S., Am. Chem. Soc. (councillor since 1937), Am. Pub. Health Assn., Nat. Assn. Mfrs. (com. scientific research 1939-41), Nat. Research Council, Inst. Food Technologists (councillor), Soc. Chem. Industry (councillor), Am. Acad. Sociol. and Polit. Sciences, Am. Inst. of Chemists. Clubs: Chemists (N.Y.); Oriental (Mamaroneck, N.Y.). Contbr. to periodicals. Home: 80 Hartsdale Rd., White Plains, N.Y. Office: 250 Park Av., New York, N.Y. Died Mar. 31, 1944.

WATERS, WILLIAM LAURENCE, engr.; b. London, Eng.; s. Rev. William and Ellen (Turnbull) W.; Central Technical College (London University), C.E. and M.E., 1898; m. Hilda Johnston, Milwaukee, Wis., 1906; 1 dau., Carolinda; m. 2d, Mildred M. Warner, Baltimore, 1942. With L. & S. Ry., London, Eng., 1898-1901; chief engr., Nat. Brake & Electric Co., Milwaukee, 1901-05; consulting engr., Westinghouse Air Brake and Canadian Westinghouse and Westinghouse Electric & Mfg. cos., Pittsburgh, 1905-13; consulting engr. in pvt. practice, N.Y. City and Montreal, Can., since 1913; partner in Bury & Waters, consulting engrs., New York and London, Eng., with Sir George Bury (formerly sr. v.p. Canadian Pacific Ry.). Episcopalian. Mem. Am. Inst. E.E., Am. Soc. M.E., Am. Soc. C.E., Engr. Inst. of Can. Clubs: University (Milwaukee and Pittsburgh); Bankers, Economic, Sleepy Hollow Country (New York). Home: 3 Westview Av., White Plains, N.Y. Died 1956.

WATKINS, DALE BAXTER, physician, teratologist; b. Chinook, Mont., June 9, 1914; s. Dale Baxter and Elsie (Laughton) W.; M.D., U. Minn., 1943; m. Celia Justina Cross, Oct. 15, 1944; children—Wendy Ann, Dale Baxter III, Diane Grace. Commd. ensign M.C. USNR, 1943, advanced through grades to capt. M.C. USN, 1957; grad. tng. in medicine USN Hosp.,

Bethesda, Md., 1946, San Diego, 1947-49, Oakland, 1950-51; tng. in dermatology USN Hosp., Phila. U., 1955-58; research Walter Reed Army Med. Center, Washington, 1951-52; head medicine USN Hosp., Pensacola, Fla., 1952-53; chief, outpatient clinics, allergy Tripler Army Hosp., Honolulu, 1953-55; chief dermatology USN Hosp., Key West, Fla., 1958-63; ret., 1964; dir. Cross Inst. Teratology, Honolulu, 1964-71. Teaching fellow Hahnemann Med. Sch., Phila., 1955-57. Active Key West Players, 1958-63, Community Concert Assn., Key West, 1958-63. Fellow Am. Acad. Dermatology; mem. A.C.P., A.A.A.S., A.M.A., Am. Geriatric Soc., Am. Soc. Tropical Medicine and Hygiene Am. Genetic Assn., Soc. for Study Evolution, Soc. Investigative Dermatologists, Am. Inst. Biol. Sci., Am. Fedn. for Clin. Research, Internat. Soc. Tropical Dermatologists, Internat. Leprosy Assn., U.S. Naval Inst., Assn. Mil. Surgeons, Assn. Mil. Dermatologists, Ret. Officers Assn. Researcher in field, 1964-71. Address: Honolulu HI Died Feb. 7, 1971; buried Arlington Nat. Cemetery.

WATKINS, J(AMES) STEPHEN, engr.; b. London, Ky., Nov. 14, 1892; s. Nathaniel and Dorcas (Chestnut) W.; student Sue Bennett Coll., London, Ky., 1907-12; B.S. in Civil Engring., U. Ky., 1930, C.E., 1938, LL.D., 1964; m. Martha Willis, June 21, 1923; 1 dau., Martha L. (Mrs. Barrett McVey Morris), County highway engr. Laurel County, Ky., 1916-17; engr. Briar Hill Steel Works, also Goodyear Tire & Rubber Co., 1919; hwy. engr. Ky. State Hwy. Dept., 1919-29. chief engr., 1927-29; chief engr., constrn. supt. Codell Co., 1930-32; pres. Watkins & Assos., Inc., 1962-66, chmn. bd., 1966-67; partner Wilson, Bell & Watkins, architects, engrs., 1941-45, Gillig, Watkins & Wilson, 1950-55, Balke & Watkins, Cons. engrs., 1952-55; sr. partner Watkins, Burrows & Assos., architects and engrs.; pres. East High Corp. of Lexington (Ky.); commr. hwys. Commonwealth Ky., 1943-48; dir. Security Trust Co. (Lexington). Vice pres. Ky. Mountain Laurel Festival, 1954-55; hwy. study com. Commn. on Intergovtl. Relations, 1954-55; mem. Ky. Adv. Commn. Div. Library Extension; bd. Fayette County chpt. Am. Cancer Soc. Pres. Ky. Med. Found.; trustee U. Ky., Coll. of Bible, Lexington; sponsor's com. Bellarmine Coll.; mem. Ky. State Fair Bd., 1956; chmn. exec. com. Ky. Sesquicentennial Commn.; dir. Ky. Constl. Edn. Found.; mem., bd. dirs. Ky. Spindletop Research Center; pres. Ky. Better Rds. Council. Served as 2d lieut. U.S. Army, 1918. Named Ky. Engr. of Year by Ky. Soc. Profl. Engrs., 1955. Member Kentucky C. of C. (director, past pres.), Am. Society C.E., American Road Builders Association (director), American Inst., Cons. Engrs., Am. Soc. Testing Materials, Am. Water Works Assn., Internat. Soc. Soils Mechanics and Foundation Engring., Newcomen Soc. Eng. in N.A., Ky. Soc. Profl. Engrs. (past pres.), Civil War Round Table, Sigma Nu. Member of the Christian Church. Clubs: Filson (Louisville); Lexington, Idle Hour Country, Lexington Country, Rotary, Kentucky Mountain (Lexington). Conbtr. tech. profl. jours. Home: Lexington KY Died Nov. 2, 1967.

WATSON, EARNEST CHARLES, physicist; born Sullivan, Ill., June 18, 1892; s. Charles Grant and Alice Bell (Smith) W.; Ph.B., Lafayette Coll., Easton, Pa., 1914; postgrad. U. Chgo., 1914-17; Sc.D., Lafayette Coll., 1958; m. Elsa Jane Werner, October 6, 1954. Asst. in physics Univ. of Chicago, 1914-17; asst. prof. of physics, Calif. Inst. Tech., 1919-20, associate professor, 1920-30, professor, 1930-62, emeritus, 1962-70, dean faculty, 1945-60 chairman faculty board, chmn. div. Physics, Mathematics and Astronomy, 1946-49, acting pres., 1956-57; cons. Ford Found. S. and S.E. Asia Program, 1964-70. Sci. attache to Am. Embassy New Delhi, India, 1960-62; del. to various confs. Served in U.S.N.R.F., 1917-1919; member Division 3, National Defense Research Committee, 1941-44. Official Investigator, OSRD Contract OEMsr-418 (research and development work on artillery rockets, torpedoes, atomic bomb and other ordnance devices), 1941-45. Chmn. library adv. bd. City Pasadena, 1956-60. Fellow Am. Phys. Soc., A.A.A.S.; mem. Am. Assn. Physics Teachers, History of Science Soc., Am. Assn. Univ. Profs., Fgn. Policy Assn., Indian Internat. Centre, Phi Beta Kappa, Sigma Xi, Tau Beta Pi, Gamma Alpha. Clubs: Athenaeum. Author: Mechanics, Molecular Physics, Heat and Sound, 1937. Contbr. sci. jours. Home: Santa Barbara CA Died Dec. 5, 1970.

WATSON, ELKANAH, businessman, agriculturist; b. Plymouth, Mass., Jan. 22, 1758; s. Elkanah and Patience (Marston) W.; m. Rachel Smith, Mar. 3, 1789, 5 children. Employed by Brown family, R.I. mchts., 1773-79, went to S.C. to invest funds for his employers, 1777; partner (with M. Cossoul) in mcht. firm, 1779-84; embarked for France to carry money and dispatches to Benjamin Franklin, 1779; made spl. study of inland waterways of Holland; organized Bank of Albany (N.Y.); promoted 2 canal cos., also stage line from Albany to Schenectady, N.Y.; lobbied successfully for charter which authorized a company to build canal around Niagara Falls; secured charter for N.Y. State Bank; staged cattle show which preceded incorporation of Berkshire Agrl. Soc. (which sponsored 1st county fair in U.S., 1810). Author: A Tour of Holland. . ., 1790; History of Agricultural Societies on the Modern Berkshire System, 1820; History of the Rise and Progress, and Existing Condition of the Western Canals in the State of New York, 1820; Men and Times of the Revolution; or Memoirs of Elkanah Watson, published 1856. Died Port Kent, Essex County, N.Y., Dec. 5, 1842.

WATSON, EMILE EMDON, consulting actuary; b. nr. Miami, Saline County, Mo., Feb. 7, 1885; s. Benjamin Frank and Sarah Ellen (Hawk) W.; B.A., William Jewell Coll., 1908, M.A., 1909; grad. work, Univ. of Chicago, 1909-11; LL.D., Florida Southern Coll., 1945; L.H.D. (honorary), Philathea College, London, Ontario, 1946; Litt. D. (honorary), St. Andrews University, 1954; Ph.D. (honorary), Chatham Hill Coll.; married Melisse Baye Wadlington, Aug. 16, 1911; children—Benjamin Wayne, Emile Enoch, William Wallace, Sallie Melisse, Gwendolyn Rita. Began as statistician, Chicago, 1910; moved to Columbus, O., 1911; actuarial work for states of N.Y., Md., W.Va., Ohio, Illinois, N.D., Ore., Idaho, also Ill. Mfrs. Mut. Casualty Assn., Associated Industries of Mo. and a large number of employers' assns. and industrial corps. Cons. actuary to Bur. War Risk, U.S. Treasury Dept., and adviser to com. on ins., War Dept., World War I; upon invitation of the gov. of Puerto Rico has made 4 actuarial surveys of the island, 1926, 1931, 1935 and 1951, consultant actuary to Puerto Rico Workmen's Compensation Plan, 1935-41; cons. actuary State Ins. Fund of Puerto Rico, 1952—; governmental actuarial survey for Hawaii, 1954; survey for Brazil, 1954. Assisted the War Department in connection with Ohio war industries; mem. Ohio Production for Victory Committee; advisory services on absenteeism and loss of man power during World War II. General chairman for Ohio, 1st birthday ball for President Franklin D. Roosevelt, January 30, 1934, director organization of National Committee of 2d birthday ball for the President, Jan. 30, 1935, also mem. Nat. Com.; chmn. Survey of Infantile Paralysis for Warm Springs Foundation, 1934-35; made personal study of social ins. plans of leading countries of Europe, 1935; cons. New York Unemployment Insurance Plan, 1935. Received Citation for Special Achievement, William Jewell Coll., 1945, Silver Medallion of Merit, Am. Internat. Acad. N.Y.C., 1954; Diploma & Medallion, Found. Internat. Elroy Elfaro of Panama, 1955. Fellow Consular Law Soc. N.Y.; mem. Am. Soc. Internat. Law, National Social Sci. Honor Society, Am. Internat. Acad. (acad. council and senate), Am. Sociological Society, Acad. Political Science, Ohio Society of New York, Lambda Chi Alpha; associate member International Assn. of Industrial Accident Bds. and Commns., Royal Society of St. George, London, Pi Gamma Mu. Mason. Clubs: Columbus Rotary, Columbus Athletic, Scioto County, Business Men's (Columbus); Cincinnati. Rl. est. in Florida, Ohio and Canada. New Adminstrn. bldg. at Fla. Southern Coll. dedicated in his honor. Author: Is Civilization Gaining or Losing Ground, 1948; Compulsory Military Training, 1945; Dynamic Power of Educational Training, 1949; Can Man Use This Earth, 1949; The Human Value World, 1950; Godless Stalinism—Whose Will Shall Be Done?, 1951; meditations of Joseph Stalin, 1952; An Actuarial Analysis of Man. Home: 1801 Roxbury Rd., Upper Arlington. Office: LeVeque-Lincoln Tower, Columbus, O. Died Jan. 31, 1958.

WATSON, FLOYD ROWE, physicist; b. Lawrence, Kan., Apr. 23, 1872; s. Norman Allen and Helen Altana (Hitchcock) W.; grad. State Normal Sch., Los Angeles, Calif., 1893; B.S., U. of Calif., 1899; Ph.D., Cornell U., 1902; m. Estelle Jane Barden, Aug. 14, 1902; children—Norman Allen, Robert Barden. Asst. in physics, U. of Calif., 1897-99; fellow in physics, U. of Calif. and Cornell U., 1899-1902; instr. in physics, U. of Ill., 1902-04, asst. prof., 1904-15, asso. prof., 1915-17, prof. experimental physics, 1917-40, prof. of physics, emeritus since 1940. Fellow A.A.A.S., Am. Physical Soc., Acoustical Society of America, Sigma Xi. Methodist. Expert in acoustics. Home: 1504 Milan Av., South Pasadena CA

WATSON, JAMES CRAIG, astronomer; b. Fingal, Ont., Can., Jan. 28, 1838; s. William and Rebecca (Bacon) W.; grad. U. Mich., 1857; Ph.D. (hon.), U. Leipsig (Germany), Yale; LL.D. (hon.), Columbia; m. Annette Waite, May 1860, no children. Came to U.S., 1850; mastered theoretical and practical astronomy studying under Francis Brunnow; while still a student, ground, polished and mounted 4" achromatic objective; published 15 astron. papers before age 21; prof. astronomy in charge of observatory U. Mich., 1859, prof. physics, 1860-63, prof. astronomy, dir. observatory, 1863-79; discovered asteroid Eurynome (1st of his 22 astron. discoveries), 1863; participated in eclipse expdns. to Ia., 1869, Sicily, 1870, Wyo., 1878; in charge of expdn. to observe transit of Venus in China, 1874; dir. Washburn Observatory, U. Wis., Madison, 1879-80; mem. Nat. Acad. of Scis., 1868, Royal Acad. of Scis. in Italy, Am. Philos. Soc.; recipient Lalande prize French Acad. of Scis., 1870; named knight comdr. of Imperial Order of Medjidich of Turkey and Egypt, 1875; contbr. papers to Am. Journal of Sci., Gould's Astron. Journal, Brunnow's Astron. Notices and Astronomische Nachrichten. Author: Popular Treatise on Comets, 1861; Theoretical Astronomy (became textbook in U.S., Germany, France, Eng.), 1868; Tables for the Calculation of Simple or Compound Interest, 1878. Died Madison, Wis., Nov. 22, 1880.

WATSON, JOHN B(ROADUS), psychologist; b. Greenville, S.C., Jan. 9, 1878; s. Pickens Butler and Emma K. (Roe) W.; A.M., Furman U., 1900; grad. student in psychology U. Chgo., 1900-03. Ph.D., 1903; LL.D., Furman U., 1919; m. Mary Ickes, Oct. 1, 1904; children—Mary I., John I.; m. 2d, Rosalie Rayner, Dec. 31, 1920; children—William Rayner, James Broadus. Prin. Batesburg Inst., 1899-1900; asst. in exptl. psychology U. Chgo., 1903-04, instr., 1904-08; prof. exptl. and comparative psychology, dir. psychol. lab., Johns Hopkins, 1908-20; became v.p. J. Walter Thompson Co., N.Y., 1924; v.p. William Esty & Co., N.Y., 1936-46. Editor Psychol. Rev., 1908-15, Jour. Exptl. Psychology, 1915-27. Commd. maj. Aviation Sect., Signal Corps, U.S.R., 1917; on duty, Washington, Mineola, and with A.E.F. Fellow Am. Acad. Arts and Scis.; mem. Am. Psychol. Assn. (pres. 1915), Am. Physiol. Soc., Sigma Xi, Phi Beta Kappa. Author: Animal Education, 1903; Behavior, 1914; Homing and Related Activities of Birds, 1915; Suggestions of Modern Science Concerning Education, 1917; Psychology from the Standpoint of the Behaviorist, 1919; Behaviorism, 1925. Ways of Behaviorism, 1928; Psychological Care of Infant and Child, 1928. Contbr. on neurology, animal and infant psychology; founded behaviorist sch. of psychology opposing introspective sch.; formulated stimulus-response pattern as basic unit of behavior; accepted Pavlov's conditioned response concept; from his research, concluded that there are 3 unlearned responses in newborn infants—love, fear, rage; stressed that psychology should be empirical study of what man observedly does and not study of conscious and unconscious mind. Died N.Y.C., Sept. 25, 1958.

WATSON, SERENO, botanist; b. East Windsor Hill, Conn., Dec. 1, 1826; s. Henry and Julia (Reed) W.; grad. Yale, 1847, began study of chemistry and mineralogy Sheffield Scientific Sch., 1866; Ph.D. (hon.), Ia. Coll., 1878; never married. Permitted to join Clarence King exploration party in Cal. as volunteer aid, 1867, commissioned to collect plants and secure data regarding them; asst. Gray Herbarium, Cambridge, Mass., 1873, curator, 1874-92, revised Gray's Manual of Botany, 1889. Author: Botany, 1871; Botany of California, 1st vol., 1876, 2d vol., 1880; Bibliographical Index to North American Botany, 1878; Manual of the Mosses of North America, 1884. Died Cambridge, Mass., Mar. 9, 1892; buried Harvard Lot at Mt. Auburn Cemetery, Cambridge.

WATSON, THOMAS AUGUSTUS, electrician; b. Salem, Mass., Jan. 18, 1854; s. Thomas R. and Mary (Phipps) W.; ed. pub. schs., Salem and spl. course, geology, Mass. Inst. Tech.; hon., A.M., Union Coll., 1919; D.Eng., Stevens Inst. Tech., 1921; D.Sc., U. of N.H., 1929; m. Elizabeth S. Kimball, Sept. 5, 1882. Mfr. elec. apparatus, 1871-74; asso. with Prof. Alexander Graham Bell in experiments in the electric telephone, 1874-78; supt. Bell Telephone Co., 1878-81; mem. shipbuilding firm of F. O. Wellington & Co., 1884-1900; pres. Fore River Ship & Engine Co., 1900-03; retired from active business, 1903. Mem. sch. com., Braintree, Mass., 1891-1908 (chmn. 1891-98). Fellow Am. Inst. Elec. Engrs. Home: Boston, Mass. Died Dec. 13, 1934.

WATSON, THOMAS LEONARD, geologist; b. Chatham, Va., Sept. 5, 1871; s. Fletcher B. and Pattie Booker (Tredway) W.; B.Sc., Va. Agrl. and Mech. Coll. (now Va. Poly. Inst.), 1890, M.Sc., 1893; grad. student U. of Va., 1891; Ph.D., Cornell U., 1897; m. Adelaide Stephenson, Feb. 8, 1899. Instr. geology and mineralogy, Va. Agrl. and Mech. Coll., 1892-95; asst. chemist, Va. Expt. Sta., 1890-95; mem. Cornell U. party of geologists on 6th Peary Arctic expdn. to N. Greenland, 1896; pvt. research worker on rock decay, U.S. Nat. Mus., 1897-98; asst. state geologist of Ga., 1898-1901; prof. geology, Denison U., 1901-04; geologist, Ga. Geol. Survey, 1902, N.C. Geol. Survey, 1903; field asst., U.S. Geol. Survey, 1903-08; prof. geology, Va. Poly. Inst., 1904-07; prof. economic geology, 1907—, head prof. schools of geology, 1910—, U. of Va. State geologist and dir. Va. Geol. Survey, 1908—. Mem. sub-com. of Nat. Research Council; asso. mem. from Am. Inst. Mining Engrs. of War Minerals Com.; mem. Com. of 100 on Scientific Research; mem. exec. com. Nat. Conservation Congress. Fellow Geol. Soc. America (coulcilor, 1915-17), A.A.A.S., Mineral. Soc. America (councilor 1922—; chmn. com. on nomenclature and classification of minerals), Soc. Econ. Geologists. Co-author of Ries and Watson's Engineering Geology; Elements of Engineering Geology; contbr. numerous articles and books on theoretic and economic geology in various geol. publs. and reports of state and federal surveys. Died Nov. 10, 1924.

WATSON, WILLIAM, sec. Am. Acad. Arts and Sciences, 1884—; b. Nantucket, Mass., Jan. 19, 1834; s. William and Mary (Macy) W.; S.B., engring. (Boyden prize in mathematics), Harvard, 1857, S.B., mathematics, 1858; instr. differential and integral calculus, scientific sch., Harvard, 1857-59; Ph.D., U. of Jena, 1862; partial course École Nationale des Ponts et Chaussées, Paris, France; m. Margaret, d. Augustus H. Fiskc, 1873. Univ. lecturer, Harvard, 1863-64; collected, 1860-63, information in Europe on tech. edn., which was made basis of scheme of organization, 1864, of Mass. Inst. Tech., in which was prof. mech. engring. and descriptive geometry, 1865-73. U.S. commr. to

Vienna Expn., 1873; mem. Internat. Jury, Paris Expn., 1878; hon. pres. Paris Congress Architects and v.p. Internat. Congress of Hygiene, 1878; hon. pres. engring. sect. French Assn. Adv. Science, 1878, 81, 83, 89; v.p. International Congress of Construction, 1889; sec. World's Columbian Water Commerce Congress, 1893. Fellow Am. Acad. Arts and Sciences, A.A.A.S. Author: Technical Education, 1872; Descriptive Geometry, 1873; Civil Engineering, Architecture and Public Works at the Vienna International Exhibition, 1875; On the Protection of Life from Casualties in the Use of Machinery, 1880; Courses in Shades and Shadows, 1889; The Civil Engineering, Architecture and Public Works at the Paris Exposition of 1889, 1891; The International Water Transportation Congress, Chicago, 1893, 1894; also many tech. papers. Died Sept. 30, 1915.

WATSON, WILLIAM FRANKLIN, scientist, traveler; b. N.B., Can., May 11, 1861; s. George Corey and Isabella (Byron) W.; A.B., Colby Coll., 1887, A.M., 1890, Sc.D., 1924; student univs. of Pa. and Chicago; m. Clara Norwood, June 24, 1889 (died Aug. 30, 1935); children—Ethel Drysdale (Mrs. Arthur L. Collins), Lucia Norwood (Mrs. Norman C. Mendes); m. 2d, Anette M. Phelan, Oct. 14, 1938. Prof. of chemistry, Furman U., Greenville, S.C., 1887-1912, of biology, 1898-1912, curator of museum, 1902-1912, sec. of faculty, 1904-11, lecturer, 1911-14. Mem. commn. apptd. by Nat. Civ. Fedn. to inspect ednl. instns. of Great Britain; lecturer on scientific subjects and travel. Experimenter in photographing with lenses from the eyes of insects and higher animals; originator of new methods in photo-micrography. Received medal of Charleston Expn., 1902, for invention of a method for concentration of monazite sand. Mem. Am. Microscopical Soc. (v.p., 1906), Navy League of U.S., Am. Nature Study Soc., Internat. Lyceum Assn., Am. Health League (advisory com), Ga. Acad. Science, Phi Delta Theta, Atlantic Union of London, London Teachers Assn., Royal Soc. of Arts, London, Société Linnéenne de Lyon, France; fellow A.A.A.S., Science League America. K.P. Clubs: Club of Thirty-nine of Greenville, S.C. (pres.), British Empire Club of London (hon.). Author: Children of the Sun (poems), 1887; Textbook on Experimental Chemistry, 1901; Laboratory Courses in Chemistry, 1895. Contbr. to periodicals, London, Paris, Madrid, and in U.S. Made tour of the world, 1912-13. Lecturer for Dept. of Edn., New York City, 1914-15. Address: 1539 3d Av., Bradenton, Fla. Died Mar. 22, 1953.

WATSON, WILLIAM HENRY, physician; b. Providence, R.I., Nov. 8, 1829; only s. Hon. William Robinson and Mary Ann (Earle) W.; A.B., Brown, 1852; M.D., Homoe. Med. Coll. of Pa., 1854; studied at U. of Pa., and Pa. Hosp., Phila.; hon. A.M., Brown, 1855; hon. M.D. from Bd. Regents, U. State of N.Y., 1878; LL.D., Hobart Coll., 1901, "in recognition of long and faithful service in the development of the higher educational system of the State, especially those parts of it pertaining to the study of medicine"; m. Sarah T. Carlile, May 1, 1854 (died 1881); m. 2d, Mrs. Julia M. Williams, Dec. 16, 1891. Regent U. State of N.Y., 1881-1904. Inspired and procured passage of act fixing ednl. qualifications essential in beginning study of medicine; influential in extending term of study for practice of medicine from 3 yrs. to 4; decisively influential in determining basis of admission to practice in the three legalized branches of the med. profession through jurisdiction of independent court appointed by state. A founder and trustee Middletown State Hosp.; U.S. pension examining surgeon, 1875-81; surgeon gen. State of N.Y., with rank of brig. gen., 1880. Examiner in diagnosis and pathology in 1st N.Y. Bd. of State Med. Examiners apptd. under act of 1872. Mem. Advisory Bd. on Tuberculosis, N.Y. State Dept. Health. Sr. warden Grace Ch., Utica, Del. General Conv., P.E. Ch., 1889, 1904, 07; representative of U. of State of N.Y. at "Abel Fest" of Royal U. of Christiania, and at tercentenary of Bodleian Library, Oxford, 1902. Author of Medical Education and Medical Licensing (address at 23d Convocation U. State of N.Y.), 1885; Memorial Address on U.S. Senator Francis Kernan; also various addresses on med. subjects. Died Jan. 1913.

WATT, DAVID ALEXANDER, engineer; b. at Maidstone, Eng., Dec., 1865; s. David Gilkison and Jane (Powell) W.; ed. Maidstone, 1874-79, Clapton Coll., London and London Inst. 1879-85 (grad.); m. Josephine Abercrombie, of Memphis, Tenn., July, 1906. Engaged in design and erection of bridges and structural ironwork for about 6 yrs., and on canalisation by fixed and movable dams of rivers in the Ohio Valley, Tex., Wis., and elsewhere. Spl. N.Y. del. Internat. Congress of Navigation, Milan, Italy, 1905. Investigated waterways of Europe for the State Engr. Dept., 1905; now in charge of river improvements for new barge canal system of N.Y. State; U.S. asst. engr. Mem. Am. Soc. C.E., Soc. Engrs. Eastern N.Y. Author: The Improvement of Rivers (with B. F. Thomas), 1903. Contbr. on engring. topics. Address: Barge Canal Office, Albany, N.Y.

WATTERS, WILLIAM HENRY, (wot'terz), physician; b. Mechanic Falls, Me., June 23, 1876; s. William and Judith (Nichols) W.; A.B., McGill U., 1897; M.D., Boston U., 1900, M.A., 1907, Ph.D., 1909; m. Gertrude Hepburn, 1904; children—Preston Hepburn, Doris Nichols. Practiced, Boston, 1900—; prof. pathology, Boston U., 1903-25, prof. preventive medicine, 1925-35; emeritus prof. preventive medicine 1936—; asso. dept. legal medicine, Harvard Med. Sch.; founder med. dir. Boston-Miami Clinic, Coconut Grove, Miami, Fla.; asso. med. examiner Suffolk County. Republican. Fellow A.C.P.; mem. A.M.A., Am. Assn. Pathologists and Bacteriologists, Am. Assn. Clin. Pathologists, Mass. Med. Soc., Mass. Medico-Legal Soc. (pres. 1929-30), Mass. Surg. and Gynecol. Soc., Internat. Assn. Med. Museums. Mason. Clubs: Highland (West Roxbury); Com. of One Hundred (Miami Beach); Century (Coral Gables, Fla.); Harvard (Boston). Home: Coconut Grove, Miami, Fla. Died Oct. 11, 1949; buried Searsport, Me.

WATTIS, EDMUND ORSON, ry. contractor; b. Uintah, Utah, Mar. 6, 1855; s. Edmund and Mary Jane (Corey) W.; ed. pub. schs.; m. Martha Ann Bybee, June 25, 1879; children—Leland Ray, Mattie C. (Mrs. Wm. Henry Harris), Edmund Earl (dec.), Ethel Marie (Mrs. Wm. Rice Kimball), Marguerite E. (Mrs. Emil Joseph Hanke), Edna Orson (wife of Ezekiel Ricker Dumke, M.D.), Paul Lyman, Ruth. In railroad constrn. work from early youth; a dir. and in charge constrn. work Utah Constrn. Co., 1911—, v.p., 1911—, also chmn. bd.; an organizer, 1931, later pres. Six Companies, Inc., builders of Hoover Dam; pres. Lake View Mining Co.; v.p. Utah Rapid Transit Co.; dir. Lion Coal Co. Prin works; W.P. R.R. from Salt Lake City to Oroville, Calif.; U.P. from Salt Lake City to Calif. state line; 100-mile extension of S.P. R.R. of Mexico; new constrn. and re-location for U.P. R.R., S.P. Co., D.&R.G. R.R., involving building over 200 tunnels; also builder of many concrete and earth dams for power and irrigation purposes, including O'Shaughnessy Dam, for water and power supply of San Francisco and Am. Falls Dam, Ida., for U.S. Dept. Interior, 2 of largest dams in world. Republican. Mason. Home: Ogden, Utah, Feb. 3, 1934.

WATTS, ARTHUR S., ceramic engr.; b. Zanesville, O., Mar. 27, 1876; s. Arthur H. and Reliance M. (Holton) W.; B.S., Ohio State U., 1901; Ceramic Engr. (professional), Ohio State U., 1928; studied Technische Hochschule, Charlottenburg, Germany, 1909-10; m. Olive May Graham, July 26, 1917; children—Arthur Graham, Richard Lee. With Locke Insulator Co., Victor N.Y., 1901, Bell Pottery Co., Findlay, O., 1902-03, New Lexington (O.) Insulator Co., 1904, Locke Insulator Co., Victor, 1905-08; quarry technologist, U.S. Bur. of Mines, 1911-13; prof. ceramic engineering, Ohio State University, 1914-46, prof. emeritus, 1946. Member American Ceramic Society, American Society for Testing Materials, Sigma Xi, Tau Beta Pi. Mason (K.T., Shriner). Baptist. Author: Feldspars and Kaolins of the South Appalachians (U.S. Bureau Mines), 1913; Feldspars of the New England and North Appalachian States (U.S. Bur. Mines), 1916; The Selection of Dinnerware for the Home, 1930. Home: 172 16th Av., Columbus OH*

WATTS, FREDERICK, agriculturist, govt. ofcl.; b. Carlisle, Pa., May 9, 1801; s. David and Julian (Miller) W.; attended Dickinson Coll.; m. Eliza Cranston, Sept. 1827; m. 2d, Henrietta Edge, Mar. 1835; 9 children. Practiced law, Carlisle; sec. bd. control Dickinson Coll., 1824-28, mem. bd., 1828-33, 41-44; reported cases of Western dist. Pa. Supreme Ct., 1829-45; pres. Cumberland Valley R.R. Co., 1845-71; judge 9th Pa. Jud. Dist., 1849-52; experimented with farm bldgs. and equipment, breeds of livestock, encouraged agrl. fairs; pres. Pa. State Agrl. Soc., Cumberland County Agrl. Soc.; successful in putting through Legislature a charter for Farmers' High Sch. which developed into Pa. State Coll., 1854, 1st pres. bd. trustees; U.S. commr. of agr., 1871, div. of microscopy established during his term, started what later became forestry div. of Dept. Agr. Died Carlisle, Aug. 17, 1889; buried Carlisle.

WATTS, LYLE FORD, forester; b. Cerro Gordo County, Ia., Nov. 18, 1890; s. James A. and Mary Jane (Liggett) W.; B.Sc. in forestry, Ia. State Coll., 1913, M.F., 1928, D.Agr. (hon.), 1948; m. Nell Bowman, Dec. 5, 1915; children—Gordon Lyle, Arline June. Forest asst. U.S. Forest Service, 1913, forest examiner, 1917, asst. forest supr., 1918, supr. Weiser Nat. Forest, 1920, supr., Ida. Nat. Forest, 1922, forest insp., 1926; dean Sch. Forestry, Utah State Agrl. Coll., 1928; U.S. Forest Service, 1929—, sr. silviculturist, Intermountain Forest and Range Expt. Sta., 1929-30; dir., North Rocky Mountain Forest and Range Expt. Sta., 1931-36; regional forester, N. Central Region (comprising Ind., Ill., Ia., Mich., Mo., N.D., O. and Wis.), 1936-39, regional forester, N. Pacific Region (Wash. and Ore.), 1939-42; chief, U.S. Forest Service. Decorated Officer of Merite Agricolae, French, 1947. Mem. Soc. Am. Foresters, Am. Forestry Assn., A.A.A.S., Izaak Walton League, Alpha Zeta, Phi Kappa Phi. Presbyn. Mason. Club: Cosmos. Contbr. numerous sci. articles to tech. jours. and reports Dept. Agr. Home: Washington. Office: U.S. Forest Service, Dept. Agr., Washington. Died June 5, 1962.

WATTS, RALPH L., horticulturist; b. Kerrmoor, Clearfield County, Pa., June 5, 1869; s. Martin Overholser and Marian Elizabeth (Hoyt) W.; B.S. in Agr., Pa. State Coll., 1890, M.S., 1899; D.Agr., Syracuse U., 1916; D.Sc.; R.I. State Coll., 1931; m. Hattie Searle, Jan. 1, 1895 (died 1940); children—Gilbert Searle, Curtis McClure, Grace Elizabeth; m. 2d, Bertha P. Myers, June 11, 1941. Horticulturist Tenn. Expt. Sta., 1890-99; lecturer farmers institutes, 1899-1908; prof. horticulture, Pa. State Coll., 1908-12, dean and dir. Sch. of Agr. and Expt. Sta., 1912-39, dean emeritus since Jan. 1, 1939. Mem. Soc. for Hort. Science, Vegetable Growers Assn. America (ex-pres.), A.A.A.S.; pres. Pa. State Conservation Council. Presbyterian. Mem. Phi Kappa Phi, Gamma Sigma Delta, Alpha Zeta, Delta Theta Sigma, Sigma Pi. Author: Vegetable Gardening (coll. textbook), 1912; The Vegetable Garden; Vegetable Forcing, 1917; Vegetable Growing Projects, 1921; Growing Vegetables, 1923; Rural Pennsylvania, 1925; The Vegetable Growing Business (with Gilbert S. Watts), 1939. Address: 225 E. Foster Av., State College, Pa. Died July 2, 1949.

WATTS, WILLIAM LORD, mining engr.; b. Edmonton, nr. London, England, Sept. 24, 1850; s. William M. and Eleanor (Lord) W.; studied mineralogy under Prof. Tennant, and geology under Prof. Wiltshire, King's Coll., London; pvt. student British Mus., and chemistry and metallurgy under Prof. Patrick, of U. of Kan.; diploma in metallurgy and assaying, Univ. of Kan., 1883; m. Mary Riordan, of Chicago, Sept. 22, 1880 (died 1895); 2d, Euphemia T. Stirling, of Australia, 1910. Headed an exploring expdn. to Iceland, 1875; asst. to Prof. Patrick, 1881-83; chemist and assayer, Organ Mountain Mining and Smelting Co., N.M., 1883-85; in gen. practice, San Francisco, 1885-88; asst. in the field, 1889-99, state expert in mining, 1899-1901, Cal. Mining Bur.; since in pvt. practice; mem. firm Overholser and Marian Elizabeth (Hoyt) W.; B.S. in Agr., Pennsylvania State Coll., 1890, M.S., 1899; (D.Agr., Syracuse Univ., 1916); m. Hattie Searle of Knoxville, Tenn., Jan. 1, 1895. Horticulturist Tenn. Expt. Sta., 1890-99; lecturer farmers' institutes, 1899-1908; prof. horticulture, 1908-12, dean and dir. Sch. of Agr. and Expt. Sta., Nov. 1, 1912—, Pa. State Coll. Mem. Soc. for Hort. Science, Vegetable Growers' Assn. America (ex-pres.). Presbyn. Author: Vegetable Gardening (coll. text book), 1912; The Vegetable Garden; Vegetable Forcing, 1917; also numerous bulls.; contbr. to agrl. press. Address: 215 Foster Av., State College, Pa.

WAUGH, JOHN MCMASTER, (waw), physician; b. Tarkio, Mo., June 8, 1905; s. Clifton M., M.D. and Mamie (McMaster) W.; A.B., Tarkio Coll., 1927; also recipient Doctor of Humanities (honorary); M.D., Rush Med. Coll., 1932; M.S., U. Minn., 1935; m. Amy Logan, July 18, 1935; children—Anne Lenora, Mary Jean, John Logan, Amy Martha. Intern Presbyn. Hosp., Chgo., 1931-32; fellow surgery Mayo Found. Grad. Sch., 1932-35, 1st asst., asst. surgeon, 1935-37, head sect. gen. surgery, 1937—, prof. surgery, 1950—; chief of gen. surgery Mayo Clinic, 1957—. Mem. Conf. Com. Grad. Tng. Surgery, 1957-62; dir. YMCA. Dir. Tarkio Coll. Diplomate Am. Bd. Surgery (mem. bd. 1951-57). Fellow A.C.S. (bd. govs. 1953-59); mem. A.M.A., Soc. Clin. Surgery, Internat. Soc. Surgery, Am., Western surg. assns., Minn., Central surg. socs., Am. Gastro-Enterologic Assn., Sigma Xi. Presbyn. (mem. commn. on ecumenical mission and relations U.P. Ch. in U.S.A. 1958—). Home: 1023 Plummer Circle. Office: 200 First St. S.W., Rochester, Minn. Died Aug. 12, 1962; buried Tarkio, Mo.

WAUGH, KARL TINSLEY, psychologist; b. of Am. parents, Cawnpore, India, Nov. 30, 1879; s. James Walter (D.D.) and Jennie Mary (Tinsley) W.; B.A., Ohio Wesleyan U., 1900, M.A., 1901, LL.D., 1927; studied Columbia; M.A., Harvard, 1906, Ph.D., 1907; m. Emily L. Sprightley, Sept. 4, 1912; children—Eleanor Tinsley (Mrs. J.A. Hanley; now dec.), Charles MacCarthy. Professor of philosophy and mathematics, Claflin University, S.C., 1900-04; Weld fellow and asst. in philosophy to prof. William James, Harvard, 1906-07; associate in psychology, U. of Chicago, 1907-09; head dept. philosophy and psychology, Beloit Coll., 1909-18; dean and prof. psychology and philosophy, Berea (Ky.) Coll., Sept. 1919-23; dean Coll. Arts and Sciences, and prof. psychology, U. of Southern Calif., 1923-31; prof. psychology, chmn. div. psychology and edn., Long Island U., Brooklyn, N.Y. 1930-31; pres. Dickinson Coll., Carlisle, Pa., 1931-34; dean Charles Morris Price Sch., Phila., 1934-39; state dir. of student aid, Nat. Youth Adminstrn. for Pa., 1935-37; exec. dir. Fed. Cooperative Health Service during 1937; personnel officer, Dept. of Public Assistance of Pa., 1939-42; field rep., student war loans fund, U.S. Office of Edn., 1942-43. Supervisor, Vocational Advisement, U.S. Vets. Adminstrn. from 1944; conducted educational and psychological investigation in China and India, 1916-17; lecturer in psychology, Univ. of Colorado, 1909, 14, Northwestern Univ. 1921. Served as 1st lt., capt. and maj. U.S. Army, psychol. div., World War, Aug. 1917-Feb. 5, 1919; in Surgeon General's Office, Washington, D.C.; chief psychol. examiner at Camp Gordon, Ga., Camp McClellan, Ala., trans. to Ft. McPherson, Ga.; supervisor Fed. Bd. for Vocational Edn., 5th Dist., Feb.-Sept. 1919. Treated successfully, by suggestion, nervous disorder, hysterical blindness, stammering, shell shock, etc.; organized first university courses leading to motion picture careers, Los Angeles. Fellow A.A.A.S.; mem. Am. Psychol. Assn., Am. Acad. Polit. and Social Science, Ky. Acad. Science, Soc. Psychical Research, Engenics Research Assn., Western

Psychol. Assn., Psychol. Corp. (pres. Calif. br.), N.Y. Acad. of Sciences, Society for Adv. of Education, Sigma Xi, Phi Beta Kappa, Phi Delta Theta, Phi Kappa Phi, Pi Gamma Mu, Acacia, Omicron Delta Kappa. Methodist. Mason. Clubs; Poor Richard, Schoolmen's, Mendelssohn, Blackstonian, Executive Advancement. Author of articles: Vision in Animals, 1910; Mental Diagnosis of College Students, 1915; Comparative Mentality of Oriental and American Students, 1920; Rational Empiricism Views Teleology, 1927; The Liberal Arts College Faces the Present Age, 1932; Psychology in Modern Industry, 1934; Personal Hurdles (with J.W. Irwin), 1936; The Humanizing of Psychology; "Saturday Night Thoughts," contributed to newspaper columns. Specialist in the writings of Rudyard Kipling; editor poetry sect. Artland Mag. and California Southland, 1925-30. Home: Washington DC Died May 9, 1971.

WAUGH, WILLIAM HAMMOND, ex-army officer, civil engineer; b. Greenville, Pennsylvania, April 13, 1875; son John Harold and Ella Louise (Hammond) W.; educated Shattuck School, 1892-93; married Queen Scott Lawson, January 23, 1909; children—William Hammond (lieutenant colonel, C.A.C.), Dorothy Scott (Mrs. G. M. Watson). Began with Pecos Irrigation and Improvement Co., N.M., 1893; with Bessemer & Lake Erie Railroad, Greenville, Pa., 1895-98, locating engineer, same, 1903-04; contracting in Cuba, 1899-1902; chief engineer Shenango Traction Company, Greenville, Pennsylvania, 1904-07, Little Rock & Pine Bluff Traction Co., 1907-09; div. engr. Bur. Pub. Works, Manila, P.I., 1909-15; consulting practice, Riverside, Calif., 1915-17; pres. Alaska Road Commn., 1917-20, also acting district engr. Bur. Pub. Rds. and cons. engr., Ty. of Alaska, 1917-20. Corpl. Pa. Nat. Guard, 1897-98; corpl. 15th Pa. Vol. Inf., May-July 1898; 1st sergt. 3d Regt., U.S. Vol. Engrs., July 1898-April 1899; constructing engr. Q.-M. Dept. U.S. Army, Apr.-Oct. 1899; capt. Engr. Corps, Calif., 1916-June 1917; capt. engrs. U.S. Reserve, June 1917-June 1918; maj. engrs. U.S. Army, 1918-20; capt. Corps of Engrs., 1920-36, maj., 1936-39, retired; real estate dealer since 1940. Mem. Am. Soc. C.E., S.A.R. Republican. Episcopalian. Mason. Home: 345 Elmhurst Av., San Antonio TX

WAY, SYLVESTER BEDELL, public utilities; b. Phila., Pa., Aug. 29, 1874; s. Wilson Bedell and Ellen Lord (Dewey) W.; graduated as special electric engineer, Drexel Institute, Philadelphia, 1896, Sc.D., hon. 1942; m. Lillie Elmyra Bauer, November 28, 1899; 1 dau., Helen Emma. Draftsman and erecting engr., Electric Storage Battery Co., Phila., 1896-98; chief electrician, Imperial Electric Light, Heat & Power Co., St. Louis, 1898, until its consolidation, 1902, with other cos. forming the Union Electric Light & Power Co., with which continued until 1911; with Milwaukee Electric Ry. & Light Co. (now Wis. Electric Power Co.) since 1911, first as asst. gen. mgr., and vice pres. and general manager, 1914-25, pres. since Oct. 23, 1925; chmn. bd. Milwaukee Electric Ry. & Transport Co. since 1938; pres. Wis. Gas & Electric Co. (Racine), Milwaukee Light, Heat & Traction Co., Wisconsin-Michigan Power Co.; dir. First Wisconsin National Bank, First Wisconsin Trust Co. Patentee various devices for equipment of electric and street ry. service. Fellow Am. Institute E.E. Republican. Baptist. Mason. Clubs: Milwaukee. Home: Hotel Schroeder. Office: Public Service Bldg., Milwaukee, Wis. Died Sep. 20, 1946.

WAYNE, ARTHUR TREZEVANT, ornithologist; b. Blackville, S.C., January 1, 1863; s. Daniel G. (capt. C.S.A.) and Harriett Julia L. (Wrad) W.; grad. Charleston High Sch., 1880; m. Maria L., D. Philip Edward Porcher, of Mt. Pleasant, S.C., June 6, 1889. Engaged in ornithol. researches since 1878; rediscovered in S.C., Seaninson's Warbler, 1884 (nest and eggs taken, 1885), Bachman's Warbler, 1901 (nest and eggs taken, 1906); and Wayne's Warbler (Dendroica vhens waynei); added tropical species to S.C. fauna; represented in ornithol. nomenclature by Wayne's Clapper Rail (Rallus crepitans waynei). Honorary curator division of birds, Charleston Mus.; mem. Am. Ornithologists' Union, Nat. Geog. Soc.; life mem. S.C. Audubon Soc. Author: Birds of South Carolina, 1910. Contbr. 190 tech. papers on birds in scientific jours. Has added to the avifauna of S.C., 44 species of birds. Mem. Huguenot Soc. of S.C. Home: Mt. Pleasant, S.C.

WEAD, CHARLES KASSON, physicist, patent examiner; b. Malone, N.Y., Sept. 1, 1848; s. Samuel Clark and Mary E. (Kasson) W.; A.B., U. of Vt., 1871; studied at Berlin, 1875-76; m. Sarah W., d. Rev. Calvin Pease, pres. of U. of Vt., Aug. 13, 1879 (died 1889). Acting prof. physics, U. of Mich., 1877-85; in elec. business at Hartford, Conn., 1887-90; examiner U.S. Patent Office, 1892-1921. Fellow A.A.A.S. Author: Notes on Sound and Light, 1879; Aims and Methods of the Teaching of Physics, 1883; Musical Scales (in Rep. U.S. Nat. Mus.), 1900; also sundry papers in Silliman's Journal, Science, Proceedings A.A.A.S., and mags., especially on acoustical subjects. Died Apr. 2, 1925.

WEAGANT, ROY ALEXANDER, (we'gant), elec. engr., inventor; b. Morrisburg, Ont., Can., Mar. 29, 1881, s. William Henry and Annie Gouin (McMartin) W.; g.g.s. John Gunter Weagant, of Baltimore, Md., about 1794 or 95, who later moved to Can.; brought to Derby Line, Vt., 1884, and became citizen of U.S. by marriage of mother, after father's death, to native-born American; student Stanstead Coll., 2 yrs.; B.S., McGill, 1905; m. Isobel Louise Reichling, Dec. 8, 1906; 1 son, Carl Ludwig (dec.). Began with Montreal Light, Heat & Power Co., 1906, Westinghouse Electric & Mfg. Co., Pittsburgh, Pa., 1907, De Laval Steam Turbine Co., Trenton, N.J., 1908, Nat. Electric Signaling Co., 1908-13, chief engr. Marconi Wireless Telegraph Co., 1915-20, and cons. engr. of its successor, Radio Corp. of America, 1920-24; became v.p. and chief engr. De Forest Radio Co., 1924; now consultant, patent expert, Radio Corp. America. Perfected invention solving static problem in wireless telegraphy, 1919, reducing amount of power previously required by one-half and doing away with tall steel towers (awarded the Morriw-Liebman prize for this work). Charter mem. and fellow Inst. Radio Engrs.; mem. New York Elec. Soc. Republican. Episcopalian. Home: Douglaston, N.Y. Died Aug. 23, 1942.

WEAR, D. WALKER, mfr.; b. St. Louis, July 8, 1879; s. David W. and Laura (Beaty) W.; ed. pub. schs., St. Louis, and high sch., Washington; m. Angeline Hotchkiss, 1911; children—David Walker, III, Carolyn Hotchkiss, Joan Francis. Began with various ry. constrn. cos., Mo., Ark., Tex.; with Armour & Harriman, automatic telephone and subways, Chgo., 1907-09; with Am. Manganese Steel Co., bldg. plants in Chicago Heights, Ill., and New Castle, Del., 1904-07; supt. constrn. East Chicago Co., bldg. canal and turning basin, Indiana Harbor, Ind., 1909-10; filling in land, Whiting, Ind., 1911-12; with N.Y. Central and Hudson River R.R., constrn. at Gibson, Ind., 1913-15; exec. with H. H. Rogers Estates, operating pub. utilities, N.Y.C., 1915-16; dir. Empire Airlines; pres. Stow mfg. Co., Binghamton, N.Y., 1916-38. Served as mil. aide to Gov. Smith of N.Y., also on staff of Gen. Dyer and mem. Adj. General's Staff, World War I; mem. N.G. of Mo. Mem. N.Y. State Athletic Commn., 1920—, now sr. mem. Dir. Orgn. Nat. Found. for Infantile Paralysis; dir. Psychiat. Found.; asst. nat. chmn. Com. for Celebration President's Birthday for several years. Democrat. Mason (33 deg., Scottish Rite). Episcopalian. Clubs: Binghamton, Binghamton County, Bankers of Am. (N.Y.). Home: 23 West End Av., Binghamton, N.Y.; also 1 Fifth Av., N.Y.C. Office: 120 Broadway, N.Y.C. Died 3, 1960; buried Floral Park, Binghampton.

WEATHERBY, CHARLES ALFRED, botanist; b. Hartford, Conn., Dec. 25, 1875; s. Charles Nathaniel and Grace Weld (Young) W.; A.B., 1897, A.M., 1898, Harvard U.; m. Una Lenora Foster, May 16, 1917. Associated with Gray Herbarium, Harvard U., since 1908, senator curator, 1937-40, research associate since 1940. Mem. Am. Acad., A.A.A.S., Bot. Soc. of Am., Am. Society Plant Taxonomists (president 1945), Am. Fern Soc. (sec., 1914-18; pres. 1943-44), Soc. Bibliography of Nat. Hist. (London), Brit. Pteridol. Soc. (hon.), New England Bot. Club, Conn. Bot. Soc. (v.p., 1910-29). Mem. Internat. Com. on Nomenclature of Vascular Plants since 1935; v.p. sect. on nomenclature of Internat. Congress, 1949. Editor Fern Journal, 1915-40; asso. editor Rhodora since 1929, Brittonia since 1943. Home: 27 Raymond St., Cambridge 40, Mass. Died June 21, 1949.

WEATHERBY, LEROY SAMUEL, chemistry; b. Baldwin, Kan., Mar. 29, 1880; s. Samuel S. and Delia (Stearns) W.; A.B., U. of Kan., 1906, A.M., 1908; Ph.D., U. of Chicago, 1911; m. Frances Johnson, Sept. 6, 1911; 1 dau., Virginia. Began as teacher pub. schs., 1897; instr. physics and chemistry, Baker U., Baldwin, Kan., 1906-08; asst. prof. chemistry, Okla. Agrl. and Mech. Coll., 1908-09; teaching fellow and instr. in chemistry, U. of Chicago, 1909-11; with U. of Southern Calif. since 1911, prof. chemistry since 1913; exchange prof. Northwestern U., summers, 1924 and 1936; lecturer in chemistry, Columbia, 1st semester, 1924-25; exchange prof. U. of Wash., summer, 1927, George Washington U., summer, 1938, U. of Pittsburgh, summer, 1941. Mem. Am. Chem. Soc., Am. Inst. Food Tech., Sigma Xi, Phi Kappa Phi, Phi Lambda Upsilon, Alpha Epsilon Delta. Methodist. Contbr. on research in organic chemistry and nutrition. Home: 1209 W. 37th Drive. 7. Address: U. of So. Calif., Los Angeles, Calif. Died Oct. 21, 1946.

WEAVER, CLARENCE EUGENE, civil engr.; b. Newark, N.J., Jan. 7, 1877; s. William Albert and Sarah Bowen (Matteson) W.; Ph.B. in C.E., Yale, 1899 (1st honors); m. Marie Dickey, Jan. 7, 1903; children—Maxwell Dickey, Sarah Bowen. Asst. engr. Mexican Internat. R.R., 1899-1906; res. engr. Sonora Ry., Mexico, 1906-09; engr. maintenance of way, S.P. R.R. of Mexico, 1909-11; roadmaster I.C. R.R., 1911-13, dist. engr., 1913-16; engr. maintenance of way, Central of Ga. Ry., 1916-26, chief engr., 1926—, asst. gen. mgr., 1931-33, gen. mgr., 1933—; southern regional dir. for fed. coördinator of transportation, 1933-36. Mason. Home: Savannah, Ga. Died Nov. 28, 1938.

WEAVER, GEORGE HOWITT, physician; b. Sussex, Wis., Oct. 22, 1866; s. William and Mary (Howitt) W.; ed. Carroll Coll., 1882-85, Univ. of Wooster, 1885-86; M.D., Rush Med. Coll., Chicago, 1889; m. Carolyn Earle, June 1901. Prof. pathology, Women's Med. Coll. of Northwestern Univ., 1893-97; asst. prof. pathology, Rush Med. Coll. (U. of Chicago), since 1899; asst. pathologist, Memorial Inst. for Infectious Diseases, Chicago, since 1902; attending physician children's and contagious diseases, Cook County (Ill.) Hosp., 1905-13; became attending physician Durand Hosp., 1913; became prof. pathology, Rush Med. Coll., now prof. emeritus. Mem. Assn. Am. Physicians, Am. Assn. Pathologists and Bacteriologists, A.M.A., Ill. and Chicago med. socs., Chicago Pathol. Soc. Home: Wilmette, Ill. Died Apr. 19, 1947.

WEAVER, HARRY OTIS, lawyer, agriculturist; b. Marshall Twp., Louisa County, Ia., Apr. 20, 1866; s. Erastus and Mary Elizabeth (Marshall) W.; Ph.B., State U. of Ia., 1892, LL.B., 1893; m. Alma A. Neuse, Oct. 6, 1896; 1 son, William Otis. Practiced at Wapello, 1893—. Mem. Rep. State Central Com. 12 yrs. (chmn. 1898-1902); collector internal revenue 4th Dist. of Ia., by apptmt. of President Roosevelt, 1902-13; mem. Ia. Ho. of Reps., 1894-1900 (assisted in revising drainage laws); chmn. Ia. delegation to Rep. Nat. Conv., Chicago, 1920. In charge agrl. dept. Ia. State Fair. Odd Fellow, K.P., Woodman, Elk. Home: Wapello, Ia. Died June 1933.

WEAVER, MYRON MCDONALD, physician, educator; b. Detroit, Oct. 19, 1901; s. Joseph Marion and Mary Belle (Blanchard) W.; A.B., Wheaton Coll., 1924; M.S., U. Chgo., 1926; Ph.D., 1929; M.D., Rush Med. Coll., 1932; m. Edna Glenola McMillen, Mar. 27, 1927; children—Myron McMillen, Margaret Ann. Teaching asst. U. Chgo., 1925-26; asst. prof. physiology U. W.Va., 1926-28; asst. prof. physiology and pharmacology Loyola U. Med. Sch., 1929-30; intern Presbyn. Hosp. Chgo., 1931-32; asso. prof. health and phys. edn., dir. Student Health Service, Carlton Coll., 1932-34; dir. research relations Eli Lilly & Co., Indpls., 1934-41; prof. health and hygiene Knox Coll., Galesburg, Ill., 1941-42; attending physician Galesburg Cottage Hosp., 1941-42; asso. prof. medicine and pub. health U. Minn., 1942-49, asst. dean Med. Sch., 1944-49, attending physician Univ. Hosps., 1947-49; attending physician Mpls. Gen. Hosp., 1945-49; dean, prof. faculty medicine U. B.C. (Can.), Vancouver, 1949-56; sr. attending physician Vancouver Gen. Hosp., 1949-56, also trustee; attending physician Children's Hosp., Vancouver, 1950-56; cons. St. Paul's Hosp., Vancouver, 1950-56; prof. health, coll. physician, dir. Health Service, Union Coll., Schenectady, 1956—; attending physician Albany Hosp., 1957, Ellis Meml. Hosp., Schenectady, 1957—; clin. prof. medicine Albany Med. Coll., 1957—. Mem. President's Commn. on Health Am. People, 1952; Canadian rep. 1st World Conf. on Med. Edn., London, 1953; treasury bd. appointee to survey Canadian Pension Commn. and Treatment Service, Dept. Vets. Affairs, 1955. Dir. B.C. Cancer Found., Minn. Med. Service (Blue Shield). Served with USMC, 1920-22; capt. 1st med. bdn. Minn. N.G., 1943-45. Diplomate Am. Bd. Internal Medicine, 1947; certified specialist internal medicine Royal Coll. Phys. and Surg. Can., 1950. Fellow A.C.P., Royal Coll. Phys. and Surg. of Can., A.M.A.; mem. Nat. Research Council Can., Canadian Med. Assn. (chmn. med. edn. com. 1953-56), Am. Heart Assn., Am. Diabetes Assn., Am. Pub. Health Assn., A.A.A.S., Physiotherapists Assn. Can. (v.p. 1952-56), B.C. Soc. Internal Medicine, B.C. Acad. Sci., North Pacific Soc. Internal Medicine, Osler Soc. Vancouver, Vancouver Med. Assn., Sigma Xi, Alpha Omega Alpha. Home: 1152 Morningside Av., Schenectady 9. Died Dec. 25, 1963.

WEAVER, RUFUS B., anatomist; b. Gettysburg, Pa., Jan. 10, 1841; A.B., Pa. Coll., Gettysburg, 1862, A.M., 1865; M.D., Pa. Med. U., 1865, Hahnemann Med. Coll., Phila., 1891; Sc.D.; m. Madeleine Louise Bender, Dec. 21, 1869. Successively apptd. demonstrator of anatomy, 1869, lecturer on regional anatomy, 1876-96, prof. applied anatomy, 1896—, Hahnemann Med. Coll. Dissected and mounted, 1888, the entire cerebro-spinal nervous system of a human body, the only specimen of its kind. Home: Phila., Pa. Died July 15, 1936.

WEAVER, WILLIAM DIXON, engr.; b. Greensburg, Pa., Aug. 30, 1857; ed. Ky. U., 1875-76; grad. U.S. Naval Acad. (cadet-engr.), 1880; studied in elec. lab. of The Sorbonne, Paris, and Sch. of Elec. Engring., London, 1884, LL.D., U. of Kentucky, 1919; m. Mildred Niebuhr, 1900. Went on first Greeley relief expdn., 1883; resigned from navy, 1892; vol. chief engr., U.S.S. Glacier during Spanish-Am. War. Editor Elec. World, 1893-96, and 1899-1912; founded Am. Electrician and editor 1896-99. U.S. Govt. del. Internat. Elec. Congress, Paris, 1900; treas. and bus. mgr. Internat. Elec. Congress, St. Louis, 1904. Declined appmt. on Naval Advisory Bd., 1915. Mem. Am. Inst. Elec. Engrs. (mgr. 6 yrs.). Officier de l'Instruction Publique (France). Home: Charlottesville, Va. Died Nov. 2, 1919.

WEBB, FRANK ELBRIDGE, industrial engr., pub. works contractor; b. Calaveras County, Calif., Sept. 1, 1869; s. Elbridge and Annie E. (Settle); desc. of Mayflower ancestry; grad. Lincoln High Sch., San Francisco; studied law under John H. Dickinson, San Francisco; m. Elsa White Reid, Apr. 1928. Joined Nat. Guard of Calif., 1884; recruited regt. for Spanish-Am. War, but was sent on spl. mission around the world as confidential representative of President of U.S.; later served in Q.M. Dept. of the Army; engaged in handling gen. govt. supplies; with John A. Bensel, engr., 1906-16; made study of engring.; assisted in organization Plattsburg training camps; purchased supplies for French, English and Belgians in earlier years of World War, also assisted in organization for Am. defense; actively identified with construction of ships and loading plants on Eastern Seaboard, after U.S. entered World War; name carried on confidential list of War Dept. under rank of col.; connected with bridge building on Pacific Coast in Calif. since 1923; engr. for Chelsea docks and canals for State of N.Y. Mem. S.A.R. Decorated Knight Comdr. of the Holy Sepulchre; Knight Comdr. of Crown of Charlemagne. Candidate of Farmer-Labor Party for President of U.S., 1928; nominated for Presidency by same party in spring of 1932, declined; nominated for Presidency by Liberty Party, July 4, 1932. Presbyterian. Home: Washington, D.C.; also San Francisco, Calif. Address: 815 15th St. N.W., Washington, D.C. Died June 15, 1949.

WEBB, J(OHN) BURKITT, engineer; b. Phila., Nov. 22, 1841; s. Charles Rose and Eliza Ann (Greaves) W.; C.E., U. of Mich., 1871; studied mathematics and physics at univs. of Heidelberg, Göttingen, Berlin, and Paris, 1878-81; m. Mary Emlenie, d. Hon. John M. Gregory, 1st pres. of U. of Ill., Apr. 19, 1876. Prof. civ. engring., U. of Ill., 1871-79; prof. applied mathematics, Cornell U., 1880-85; prof. mathematics and mechanics, Stevens Inst. Tech., 1885—; now consulting engr. Judge at Internat. Elec. Exhbn., 1884; juror at St. Louis Expn., 1904. Inventor of the Floating Dynamometer, Viscous Dynamometer, and Dynamophone for the measurement of power, and other scientific apparatus. Fellow A.A.A.S.; mem. Circolo Matematico di Palermo, Am. Math. Soc., Am. Soc. Mech. Engrs. Retired on Carnegie Foundation, 1907. Author of many scientific papers. Home: Glen Ridge, N.Y. Address: Hoboken, N.J.

WEBB, WALTER LORING, engineer; b. Rye, N.Y., June 25, 1863; s. Edward Dexter and Emily (Loder) W.; B.C.E., Cornell U., 1884, C.E., 1889; m. Mary Tremaine Hubbard, Sept. 1, 1886. Instr. civ. engring., Cornell, 1888-92; asst. prof. civ. engring., U. of Pa., 1893-1901; cons. engr., 1901—. Author: Shades, Shadow and Perspective; Problems in the Use and Adjustment of Engineering Instruments, 1907; Railroad Construction, 1931; Economics of Railroad Construction, 1912, transl. into the Russian, 1921. Contbr. sect. 3 (railroads) to Am. Civil Engineers' Pocket Book; also contbr. to engineering and scientific periodicals. Maj. of engrs., U.S.A., 1917-20, in France as chief engr. of renting requisitions and claims service, in charge of valuations. Mason. Awarded Fuertes graduate gold medal by Cornell U., 1932, in recognition of 9th edit., "Railroad Construction." Home: Lansdowne, Pa. Died Jan. 24, 1941.

WEBB, WILLIAM HENRY, shipbuilder; b. New York, June 19, 1816 (son of a shipbuilder); learned shipbuilding; at 20, under sub-contract from his father, built the packet-ship "Oxford," of the Black Ball Line; partner in Webb & Allen, shipbuilders, 1840-43; in same bus. alone, 1843-68; built over 150 large vessels; devised a new model for navy vessels which the U.S. and afterward French govt. refused, but Russian govt. accepted; upon this built and launched, 1858, The General Admiral, 7,000 tons displacement, screw frigate for Russia; later built two frigates for Italian govt. King Victor Emanuel conferring upon him order of Saints Maurice and Lazarus; also built the Dunderberg, later named Rochambeau for French govt., long the fastest armored vessel afloat; after retiring from shipbuilding conducted several steamship lines; three times declined nomination for mayor of New York; 14 years pres. N.Y. City Council of Municipal Reform; built and endowed Webb's Acad. and Home for Ship-builders, Fordham Heights, Westchester County, N.Y. Died 1899.

WEBBER, HERBERT JOHN, plant physiologist; b. Lawton, Mich., Dec. 27, 1865; s. John Milton and Rebecca Anna (Bradt) W.; B.S., U. of Neb., 1889, M.A., 1890; Ph.D., Washington U., 1901; hon. D.Agr., U. of Neb., 1913; hon. L.L.D., University of California, 1943; m. Lucene Anna Hardin, September 8, 1890; children—Mrs. Eugene Francis Morrison, Mrs. Fera Ellen Shear, Herbert Earl, John Milton. Instr. botany, U. of Neb., 1889-90; instr. botany, Shaw Sch. of Botany, Washington U., St. Louis, 1891-92; investigator of orange diseases in Fla. for U.S. Dept. Agr., 1893-97; investigator plant breeding, Washington, 1897-98; in charge of plant breeding investigations, U.S. Dept. Agr., 1899-1907; prof. exptl. plant biology, Cornell U., 1907-08; acting dir., 1909-10, prof. plant breeding, 1910-12, N.Y. State Coll. of Agr.; dir. Citrus Expt. Sta., dean Grad. Sch. of Tropical Agr. and prof. plant breeding, 1912-18, U. of Calif.; dir. Agrl. Expt. Sta. and prof. plant breeding, U. of Calif., 1919-20; gen. mgr., Pedigreed Seed Co., Hartsville, S.C., 1920-21; prof. subtropical horticulture, and dir. citrus expt. sta., 1921-29, prof. subtropical horticulture, 1929-36, acting dean College Agr., 1923-24, U. of Calif., new prof. emeritus. Representative of U.S. Dept. of Agr. at Internat. Conf., London, on hybridization and cross-breeding, July 1899. Spl. commr. to study and report on citrus industry and organization of agricultural education and research dept. of agr., Union of South Africa, 1924-25. Medalist, Avocado Assn., 1938. Fellow and emeritus life mem. A.A.A.S.; mem. Am. Bot. Soc., American Genetic Assn., Ecol. Soc. America, Am. Soc. Hort. Science, Fla. State Horticultural Soc. (hon.), Nat. Council Boy Scouts of America, Sigma Xi, Alpha Zeta, Kappa Delta Rho. Mason. Contbr. to various reports, bulletins, and many other papers on plant breeding, anatomy, horticulture and diseases. Editor: The Citrus Industry: History, Botany and Breeding, Vol. I (U. of Calif. Press), 1943. Address: Citrus Experiment Sta., Riverside, Calif. Died Jan. 18, 1946.

WEBBER, SAMUEL GILBERT, physician; b. Boston, July 24, 1838; s. Aaron D. and Maria (Gilbert) W.; A.B., Harvard, 1860, M.D., 1865; studied in Vienna, 1866-67; m. Nancy Sturtevant, of Boston, Apr. 13, 1864. Asst. surgeon U.S.N., 1862-65; settled in Boston, 1865; pathologist Boston City Hosp., 1869-72; phys. dept. nervous diseases, Boston Dispensary, 1873-78; visiting phys. dept. of nervous and renal diseases, Boston City Hospital, 1877-85; supt., 1885-91, and since then consulting phys. to Adams Nervine Asylum; clin. instr. nervous diseases, Harvard Med. Sch., 1875-85; prof. neurology, Tufts Coll. Med. School, 1893-1902. Mem. Mass. Med. Soc., Boston Soc. Med. Improvement, Boston Soc. Neurology and Psychiatry, Boston Med. Library Assn., Am. Neurol. Assn., A.A.A.S., Nat. Geog. Soc., S.A.R.; hon. mem. A.B.C.F.M.; life mem. Boston YMCA, Mass. Home Missionary Soc.; mem. Boston Congregational Club. Author, Cerebro-Spinal Meningitis (Boylston prize essay), 1866; Treatise on Nervous Diseases, 1885; Genealogy of the Southworth Family, 1905; also 100 articles in med. jours. Home: Boston; (summer) Sagamore Beach, Mass.

WEBER, ARTHUR WILLIAM, engr., mfg. exec.; b. Bklyn., May 17, 1910; s. William A. and Alice E. (Fisher) W.; B.S. in M.E., Yale, 1933; M.S. in Bus. Adminstrn., Mass. Inst. Tech., 1941; m. Margaret Jensen, Sept. 4, 1937; children—William A., Roger A., James S., John M. Lab. engring. asst. Nat. Sugar Refining Co., 1933-34; tech. trainlee Am. Thread Co., 1934-35; with Corning Glass Works (N.Y.), 1935-68, beginnining as mech. engr. research lab., successively mech. engr., Charleroi, Pa. and Central Falls, R.I., asst. plant mgr., Wellsboro, Pa., asst. to gen. mgr., Charleroi, gen. mgr., Charleroi, mgr. mfg. consumer products div., asst. to dir. mfg. and engring., chief mech. engr., dir. engring., 1935-57, dir. engring. and mfg. staffs, 1957-68, v.p., 1957-61, vice pres. and dir. mfg. services, 1961-66, v.p., dir. facilities div., 1966-68. President, dir. Three Rivers Development Foundation, 1966. Adv. com. engring. Bucknell, also Carnegie Tech. Alfred P. Sloan fellow, 1941. Registered profl. engr. N.Y., N.J. Fellow Am. Soc. M.E. (v.p. 1957-59); chmn. bd. edn.); mem. Engrs. Council Professional Development (pres. 1967-68, dir.), Am. Soc. Engring. Education, Am. Ceramic Soc., Nat., N.Y. State socs. profl. engrs., New York State Bd. of Examiners Professional Engineers (chairman 1967-68), Newcomen Society of North Am., Yale Engring. Assn. (v.p.), Sigma Xi, Tau Beta Pi, Phi Gamma Delta. Episcopalian (vestry, warden). Clubs: Engineers, Yale (N.Y.C.); Rotary (Corning). Home: Corning NY Died Sept. 14, 1968.

WEBER, GUSTAV C. E., M.D.; b. Bonn, Prussia, May 26, 1828; studied at Univ. of Bonn until revolution of 1848 caused him to come to U.S.; settled as farmer near St. Louis, Mo. Later completed studies at Vienna, Amsterdam and Paris; practiced medicine in New York, 1853; and later in Cleveland, O.; prof. surgery, Cleveland Med. Coll., 1856-63; surgeon-gen. Ohio, 1861; organized system for better medical care of troops in field; founded, 1864, Charity Hospital Med. Coll., in which he became prof. clinical surgery and dean of faculty; retained chair after the coll. became med. dept. of Univ. of Wooster; returned to Germany. Address: Nuremburg, Bavaria, Germany.

WEBER, HARRY M(ATHEW), physician, radiologist; b. Lewistown, Mont., June 30, 1899; s. Matt and Anna Barbara (Nickol) W.; student St. John's U., 1918-21; B.S., U. Minn., 1924, M.B., 1925, M.D., 1926; m. Kathleen Osborn, Feb. 16, 1937; children—Harry Osborn, Frederic William, George Osborn. Intern St. Joseph's Hosp., 1925, Ancker Hosp., 1926 (both St. Paul); fellow radiology U. Minn. Mayo Found., 1927-30, successively instructor, assistant and asso. professor, professor radiology, 1952—; head section of roentgenology at Mayo Clinic and affiliated hosps., since 1951. Served as lt. comdr., M.C., U.S.N.R., 1942. 1st award for sci. exhibit by 5th Internat. Congress of Radiology, 1937. Fellow Am. Coll. Radiology; mem. A.M.A., Olmsted-Houston-Fillmore-Dodge Co. Med. Soc., So. Minn. Med. Assn., Minn. Radiol. Soc., Detroit Roentgen Ray Soc. (hon.), St. Louis Med. Soc. (hon.), Am. Roentgen Ray Society (president 1953-54, dir. section instruction 1948-56), Rocky Mountain Radiol. Soc., Radiological Society of North America, Am. Gastroenterol. Assn., Assn. Resident and Ex-Resident Physicians of Mayo Clinic, Sociedad de Radiolgia y Fisioterapia (hon., Havana, Cuba), Sigma Xi, Phi Rho Sigma. Roman Catholic. Author numerous med. papers and treatises. Home: 1219 7th St. S.W. Office: 200 1st St. S.W., Rochester, Minn. Died Oct. 6, 1958; buried Calvary Cemetery, Rochester, Minn.

WEBER, HENRY ADAM, chemist; b. Clinton Tp., Franklin Co., O., July 12, 1845; s. Frederick and Caroline (Tascher) W.; student Otterbein U., 1861-63, Poly. Sch., Kaiserslautern, 1863-66 (grad.); U. of Munich, 1866-68; (Ph.D., Ohio State U., 1879); m. Rosa Ober, of Columbus, O., Dec. 29, 1870. Asst. chemist Ohio Geol. Survey, 1869-74; prof. chemistry, U. of Ill., 1874-82; mfr. sugar from sorghum, 1882-84; prof. agrl. chemistry, Ohio State U., since 1884. Chemist to State Bd. Agr., Ill., also Ill. State Bd. Health, 1874-82; state chemist and chief chemist, Ohio State Dairy and Food Commn., 1884-97. Fellow A.A.A.S.; mem. Am. Chem. Soc., Am. Soc. Microscopists, Assn. Official Agrl. Chemists, Ohio Acad. Science; mem. Internat. Congress of Applied Chemistry. Author: Select Course in Qualitative Analysis, 4 edits., 1875-91; contbr. to Journal American Chemical Society. Address: 1342 Forsythe Av., Columbus, O.

WEBER, JOHN, mech. engr.; b. Pitts., Oct. 20, 1885; s. John and Emma Wilson (Beitler) W.; M.E., U. Pitts., 1909; D.Sc.; m. Blanche J. Martin, Mar. 21, 1912; children—John Martin, James Harold, Dorothy Ellen. With U. Pitts., 1909—, except during war period, successively research asst., instr. in mech. engring., asst. prof., asso. prof., prof. and head of dept., 1922-25, bus. mgr., supervising engr. constructional work, 1926-36, sec. of univ., 1936—. Served as capt. engrs., World War; mem. Vehicle Standardization Bd., also Automotive Products Com., War Industries Bd. Mem. Delta Tau Delta, Omicron Delta Kappa, Sigma Tau, Scabbard and Blade. Republican. Mem. United Presbyn. Ch. Club: University (Pitts.). Home: 1317 Dennison St., Pitts. 15217. Died Mar. 1, 1966.

WEBNER, FRANK ERASTUS, industrial engr.; b. Chicago, Ill., Dec. 9, 1865; s. John Theodore and Mary Ann (Ceperly) W.; student Armour Inst. Tech.; C.P.A., U. of Ill., 1904; m. Mary Rachel Simpson, of Chicago, June 6, 1889; children—Harold John Theodore, William Gordon. Paymaster C.&N.W. Ry., Chicago, 1888-90; began "system" work, 1890; business economist, with Stephen T. Williams, 1895-1900; head of Frank E. Webner & Co., industrial engrs., since 1902; civil asst. Naval Compensation Bd., Washington, since 1917; spl. expert on valuation, U.S. Tariff Commn., since 1931; pres. Webner Devices, Inc.; partner (with son) Pine Manor Farm. Mem. 1st Inf. Ill. N.G. 14 yrs. Mem. Am. Soc. Mech. Engrs., Soc. Industrial Engrs., Am. Soc. C.P.A., S.R. Republican. Conglist. Mason (32 deg., K.T., Shriner). Clubs: Cosmos, Harvard, Nat. Press (Washington, D.C.). Author: Factory Costs, 1911; Factory Accounting, 1916; Factory Overhead, 1922. Inventor various mechanical devices. Home: 4450 Reservoir Rd. Office: 600 F St., Washington, D.C.

WEBSTER, ARTHUR GORDON, physicist; b. Brookline, Mass., Nov. 28, 1863; s. William Edward and Mary Shannon (Davis) W.; A.B., Harvard, 1885; studied Berlin, Paris, Stockholm, 1886-90; Ph.D., U. of Berlin, 1890; D.Sc., Tufts, 1905; LL.D., Hobart, 1908; m. Elizabeth Munroe Townsend, Oct. 8, 1889. Instr. mathematics, Harvard, 1885-86; docent in physics, 1890-92, asst. prof., 1892-1900, prof. and dir. of phys. lab., 1900—, Clark U. Awarded Thomson prize (5,000 francs), Paris, 1895, for exptl. research on the Period of Electrical Oscillations. Fellow A.A.A.S., Am. Acad. Arts and Sciences, Am. Inst. E.E., Inst. Radio Engrs. Del. U.S. Govt. to Internat. Radiotelegraphic Conf., London, 1912. Mem. U.S. Naval Consulting Bd., 1915—, Nat. Research Council, 1917—. Author: A Mathematical Treatise on the Theory of Electricity and Magnetism, 1897; Dynamics of Particles, and of Rigid, Elastic and Fluid Bodies, 1904; Lowell Institute Lectures on Electricity and Ether, 1897; Harrison Lectures on Sound, U. of Pa., 1911; also many papers on physics, chiefly on mat. physics, mechanics, sound, electricity and ballistics. Home: Worcester, Mass. Died May 15, 1923.

WEBSTER, EDWIN HARRISON, dairy expert; b. Yates Center, Kan., Feb. 25, 1871; s. Rufus Durkee and Harriett (Edwards) W.; B.S., Kan. State Agrl. Coll., Manhattan, 1896, M.S., 1901; B.S. Agr., Ia. State Coll., Ames, 1901; m. Eleanor Florence Fryhofer, of Randolph, Kan., Apr. 10, 1900. Asst. in dairying, Ia. State Coll., 1900-1; asst. prof. dairying, 1901-2, prof., 1902-3, Kan. State Agrl. Coll.; scientific expert in dairying, Dept. Agr., 1903-4; chief, dairy div., Bur. Animal Industry, Dept. Agr., 1905-8; dean agr. and dir. Expt. Sta., Kan. State Agrl. Coll., 1908-12; asso. editor Hoard's Dairyman, Ft. Atkinson, Wis., 1912-13; asst. gen. mgr. Cal. Central Creameries, 1915-19; dairy engr., 1920—. Mem. Nat. Dairy Instrs'. Assn., A.A.A.S. Republican. Methodist. Mason. Office: Wholesale Terminal Bldg., Los Angeles CA

WEBSTER, EDWIN SIBLEY, engr.; b. Boston, Aug. 26, 1867; s. Frank G. and Mary (Messinger) W.; B.S., Mass. Inst. Tech., 1888; LL.D., Northeastern U.; m. June de Peyster Hovey, June 1, 1893. Organizer with Charles A. Stone, 1889, firm of Stone & Webster (later Stone & Webster, Inc.), engrs. and mgrs. pub. service cos.; ret. as chmn. bd. 1946; dir. traction, light, power and other cos., Life Mem. Corp. Mass. Inst. Tech.; mem. exec. com. Mass. Inst. Tech.; trustee Mus. Fine Arts. Mem. Am. Inst. E.E. Unitarian. Clubs: Somerset, Union, St. Botolph, Engineers, University, Down Town (Boston); Eastern Yacht; The Country (Brookline).

Home: Chestnut Hill, Mass. Office: 49 Federal St., Boston. Died May 10, 1950.

WEBSTER, FRANCIS MARION, entomologist; b. Lebanon, N.H., Aug. 8, 1849; s. J. S. and Betsey A. (Riddle) W.; M.S., U. of Ohio, 1893; m. Maria A. Potter, Aug. 21, 1870. Asst. state entomologist of Ill., 1882-84; spl. agt. U.S. Dept. Agr., 1884-92; entomologist Ohio Agrl. Expt. Sta., 1891-1902; asst. on biol. survey of Ill., 1903-04; in charge cereal and forage-crop insect investigations, U.S. Dept. Agr. Prof. econ. entomology, Purdue U., 1885-88, and cons. entomologist to Ind. Expt. Sta., 1888-91. Sent on mission to Melbourne (Australia) Internat. Expn., by U.S. Depts. of State and Agr., 1888, visiting other portions of Australia, Tasmania, and New Zealand, in interests of agr., returning 1889; engaged during part of years, 1886-90, in problems of suppression of buffalo gnat in valley of Lower Misssissippi River. Fellow A.A.A.S., Ind. Acad. Science. Contbr. reports and papers to govt. and state publs., Am. and foreign. Home: Kensington, Md. Died Jan. 3, 1916.

WEBSTER, FREDERIC SMITH, naturalist; b. Hudsno, N.Y., Dec. 23, 1849; s. William Wallace and Anna Elizabeth (Ketelhuyn) W.; ed. pub. schs., bus. coll., Cooper Inst., New York, and pvt. tutors; m. Hattie Hicks Gilbert, of Rochester, N.Y., Sept. 6, 1882. Studied ornithology, taxidermy and collecting; made collections in Tex. and Mexico, Fla. and British Islands, 1876; entered Ward's Natural Science Establishment, Rochester, N.Y., 1877, where was employed 7 yrs. preparing zool. specimens; moved to Washington, 1883, and engaged on contracts for Smithsonian Instn. and Nat. Mus.; moved to New York, 1892, organized firm of Sowdon & Webster, mfg. furriers and preparators; later mgr. Webster Studio, and for 10 yrs. preparator-in-chief Carnegie Mus., Pittsburgh; resident dir. of Pittsburgh Newsboys' Home three years; instr. Emma Farm Camp for Children, Harmony, Pa., 2 yrs.; animal expert for motion picture studios. Was 1st pres. and 1st v.p. Soc. of Am. Taxidermists. Was sec. 1st expn. Am. Sportsmen's Assn. (Madison Sq. Gardens, N.Y.). First v.p. Acad. Science and Art of Pittsburgh, also gen. sec. for 7 yrs. Treas. western branch Pa. Child Labor Assn.; guardian Andrew Carnegie Naturalists' Club of Boys; city ornithologist of Pittsburgh by appmt. of mayor, 1913-15. Dir. Worthington Soc. for Study of Bird Life, Shawnee, Del.; mem. Pittsburgh Mural Efficiency Commn.; mem. Pittsburgh Divic Commn. (dir.), Civic Club of Allegheny Co. (dir.), Lewis and Clark Club; dir. Ketelhuyn Studio Sch. of Nature. Frequently called upon as lecturer on general natural history. Home: 555 N. Harvard Blvd., Hollywood, Cal.

WEBSTER, GEORGE SMEDLEY, civil engr.; b. Phila., Oct. 19, 1855; s. John Hambleton and Lydia (Smedley) W.; B.S., U. of Pa., 1875 (Sc.D., 1910); m. Mary Heston Anderson, Dec. 5, 1883; 1 son, Maurice A. Webster. Mem. engring. corps, Centennial Expn., Phila., 1875-76; asst. engr., U.S. Coast and Geod. Survey, 1877; asst. engr. City of Phila., 1877-92, prin. asst. engr. and acting chief engr., 1892-93, chief engr., 1893-1916 and 1920-21, Engring. Dept., City of Phila.; dir. Dept. of Wharves, Docks and Ferries, Phila., 1916-20; mem. bd. engrs. Del. River Bridge Joint Commn., Jan. 1, 1921—; mem. Pa. State Sanitary Water Board, 1927—. Mem. Am. Soc. C.E. (pres. 1921), Am. Soc. Testing Materials (pres. 1920), Franklin Inst., Engring. Alumni Assn. U. of Pa. (pres. 1912), Municipal Engineers' Soc. (pres. 1914). Mem. Nat. Research Council, Nat. Conf. on City Planning; pres. bd. mgrs. Friends Hosp. Tech. v.p. Regional Planning Fedn. of Phila. Tri-State Dist. Home: Frankford, Pa. Died Jan. 23, 1931.

WEBSTER, JOSEPH DANA, engr., army officer; b. Hampton, N.H., Aug. 25, 1811; s. Josiah and Elizabeth (Wright) W.; grad. Dartmouth, 1832; m. Miss Wright, 1844, at least 3 children. Entered govt. service as civil engr., 1835; commd. 2d lt. Topog. Engrs., U.S. Army, 1838, 1st lt., 1849, capt., 1853; resigned, 1854; engaged in mfg. farming implements, Chgo.; mem. Chgo. Sewerage Commn., 1855; maj., paymaster in U.S. Volunteers, 1861; commd. col. 1st Ill. Light Arty.; chief of staff under U. S. Grant, in charge of all mil. rys. in Grant's area; commd. brig. gen. U.S. Volunteers, 1862 chief of staff under Gen. William T. Sherman a Battle of Nashville; brevetted maj. gen. volunteers 1865; resigned commn., 1865; assessor internal revenue, 1869-72; asst. treasurer U.S., 1872-75; collector internal revenue, 1875-76. Died Chgo., Mar. 12, 1876.

WEBSTER, LESLIE TILLOTSON, med. research; b. New York, N.Y., July 23, 1894; s. Oliver C. and Florence A. (Tillotson) W.; B.A., Amherst, 1915, D.Sc., 1935; M.D., Johns Hopkins, 1919; m. Emily Johnston de Forest II, Jan. 5, 1924; children—Leslie Tillotson, Henry de Forest, John Crosby Brown, Emily Ann. Asst. resident pathologist, Johns Hopkins Hosp., and asst. in dept. of pathology, Johns Hopkins Med. Sch., 1919-20; with Rockefeller Institute for Medical Research since 1920, asso. mem. 1927-34, mem. since 1934. Mem. Soc. for Exptl. Biology and Medicine, Am. Soc. for Exptl. Pathology, Am. Epidemiol. Soc., Am. Assn. Pathologists and Bacteriologists, Soc. Am. Bacteriologists, Harvey Soc., A.A.A.S., Am. Pub. Health Assn., Alpha Delta Phi, Phi Beta Kappa, Alpha Omega Alpha fraternities. Congregationalist. Clubs: Cruising Club of America, Ausable Club. Author of paper treating of exptl. epidemiology, spread of epidemics, poliomyelitis, encephalitis, rabies, resistance to infectious diseases, etc. Home: 17 Dolma Rd., Scarsdale, N.Y. Address: Rockefeller Institute for Medical Research, 66th St. and York Av., New York, N.Y. Died July 12, 1943.

WEBSTER, WILLIAM, business exec.; b. Bel Air, Md., Dec. 6, 1900; s. Richard Henry and Harriet Archer (Williams) W.; grad. U.S. Naval Acad., 1920; B.S. and M.S., Mass. Inst. of Tech., 1923; D.Sc., Tufts Coll., 1950, Lowell Technol. Institute, 1961; LL.D., Bates College, 1950; D.S. in B.A., Bryant Coll., 1965; D. in C.S., Suffolk U., 1970; m. Eleanore Blodgett, April 21, 1924 (dec. April 1961); 1 son, Richard; m. 2d, Vollie Sanderson, November 29, 1963. Asst. to gen. mgr. New Eng. Power Assn., Boston, 1928-33, asst. to pres., 1933-35, asst. dist. mgr., 1935-42; pres. Narragansett Electric Co., Providence, past pres. United Electric Rys. Co.; vice pres. New Eng. Power Assn. and pres. Mass. Utilities Assos., 1942; exec. v.p., dir. N.E. Electric System, 1950-59, pres., 1959-63, chmn., chief executive, 1963-70; chmn., dir. Yankee Atomic Electric Company; v.p., dir. Vt. Yankee Nuclear Power Company, Maihe Yankee Atomic Co.; dir. Conn. Yankee Atomic Power Co., Huyck Corp., Arthur D. Little, Inc., State St. Bank & Trust, Mitre Corp., Fed. Res. Bank Boston; trustee Band Corp.; mgmt. cons. OPA, 1942-45; with Nat. Defense Research Com., 1943-46; appointed chairman Research and Development Board of U.S. Dept. of Defense, 1950; deputy sec. defense for atomic energy, chmn. mil. liaison com. Dir., v.p. Am. Inst. Counselling and Personnel Research; mem. gen. adv. com. AEC; dir. chmn. New Eng. Council; mem. NACA, 1950-51; mem. Sci. Adv. Bd., 1951-52, Army Sci. Adv. Panel, 1951-58; v.p., dir. Atomic Indsl. Forum; trustee Fund Peacetime Atomic Development; dir. Edison Electric Inst., Am. Transit Assn.; mem. Hudson Inst. Trustee Moses Brown Sch., 1940. Bates Coll., 1945, Sci. Engring. Inst., Woods Hole Oceanographic Institute, Baystate Sci. Found.; chairman advisory committee of Woodrow Wilson School, Princeton, 1959-66; life mem. corp. Mass. Inst. Tech. Served USN, 1917-28, naval constructor, 1922-28. Patriotic Civilian Service award; Exceptional Civilian Service award; New Eng. award Outstanding Engr., 1964, citation Atomic Energy Commission, 1967; John Fritz medal Am. Soc. M.E., 1971. Fellow Am. Academy of Arts and Scis.; mem. Am. Nuclear Soc. (charter mem.), Soc. Naval Architects and Marine Engrs., U.S.N. Acad. Grads. Assn., Delta Psi. Clubs: The Algonquin (Boston); Army and Navy, Cosmos (Washington). Home: Boston MA Died May 17, 1972; interred Bel Air MD

WEBSTER, WILLIAM REUBEN, engr.; b. Oyster Bay, N.Y., Apr. 30, 1868; s. William Reuben and Helen C. (Stephenson) W.; M.E., Cornell U., 1890; m. Susan W. Hinckley, Oct. 8, 1892; children—Eleanor (Mrs. Pendleton Marshall), William Reuben. Began as sales engr., Westinghouse, Church, Kerr & Co., 1890; engr., Aluminum Brass & Bronze Co., Bridgeport, Conn., 1892-93; supt. Bridgeport Copper Co., 1893-97; successively dept. supt., gen. supt., v.p., Bridgeport Brass Co., 1897-1936, dir. and chmn. bd. since 1930; trustee Bridgeport Peoples Savings Bank; dir. Bridgeport-City Trust Co. Mem. Bd. of Edn., Bridgeport, 1913-22. Fellow Am. Soc. Mech. Engrs., Am. Inst. Mining and Metall. Engrs., Am. Soc. for Testing Materials, Royal Society of Arts, Inst. of Metals (Gt. Britain), Theta Delta Chi, Soc. Colonial Wars. Republican. Episcopalian; sr. warden St. John's Ch. (Bridgeport). Clubs: University, Brooklawn Country (Bridgeport); Cornell Club of N.Y.; Lake Placid Club. Home: 208 Brooklawn Av. Office: Bridgeport Brass Co., Bridgeport, Conn. Died Apr. 28, 1945.

WEDDELL, DONALD J., author, scientist, educator, adminstr.; b. Sault Ste. Marie, Mich., Sept. 25, 1903; s. John Wesley and Katherine Isabelle (Metzgar) W.; B.S. in Forestry, Mich. State Coll., 1928, M.S. 1932; m. Winifred Mildred Tornblom, Mar. 23, 1932; children—Mary, Caroline, James. Forester Goodman (Wis.) Lumber Co., 1928-32; nurseryman Fla. Forest Service, Tallahassee, 1932-34; asst. prof. forestry Ala. Poly. Inst., Auburn, 1934-39; acting dir. div. forestry Dept. Natural Resources, Atlanta, 1939; dean sch. forestry U. Ga., 1939—. Mem. Soc. Am. Foresters (sr. mem., chmn. S.E. sect. 1940), Assn. So. Agrl. Workers (chmn. 1948-49), Ga. Forestry Council (sec. 1940, 54, 55), Ga. Forestry Assn. (v.p. 1940), So. Assn. Sci. and Industry (exec. com. 1944-46), Forest Farmers Assn. (dir. 1951-54), Phi Kappa Phi, Omicron Delta Kappa, Xi Sigma Pi, Phi Sigma, Phi Kappa Tau, Blue Key. Clubs: Gridiron, Kiwanis (past pres. Athens, lt. gov. 7th dist., chmn. internat. com. on agr. and conservation). Author articles in profl. jours., bulls. and mags. Home: 270 Cloverhurst Av., Athens, Ga. Died May 31, 1956; buried Evergreen Meml. Park, Athens.

WEDDERBURN, JOSEPH HENRY MACLAGAN, mathematician; b. Forfar, Scotland, Feb. 26, 1882; s. Alexander Stormonth Maclagan and Anne (Ogilvie) W.; M.A., Edinburgh U., 1903, D.Sc., 1908; studied Leipzig, Berlin and U. of Chicago; unmarried. Asst. in mathematics, Edinburgh U., 1905-09; asst. prof. mathematics, Princeton University, 1909-21, associate professor, 1921-28, professor, 1928-45, professor emeritus since 1945. Captain Seaforth Highlanders and capt. Royal Engrs., British Army, 1914-19. Fellow A.A.A.S., Royal Soc. (London), Royal Soc. (Edinburgh); mem. Am. Math. Soc., Circolo Matematico di Palermo. Presbyterian. Author: Lectures on Matrices, 1934. Contbr. on scientific topics. Home: 134 Mercer St., Princeton, N.J. Died Oct. 3, 1948.

WEED, CLARENCE MOORES, naturalist; b. Toledo, O., Oct. 5, 1864; s. Jeremiah Evarts and Sarah J. (Moores) W.; B.S., Mich. Agrl. Coll., 1883, M.S., 1884; Sc.D., Ohio State U., 1890; m. Adah Lilian Aber, 1888; children—Helen Irene, Walter Aber, Margaret Aber. Entomologist and botanist, Ohio Expt. Sta., 1888-91; prof. zoölogy and entomology, 1891-1904, entomologist in Expt. Sta., 1891-1904, N.H. Coll. Agr. and Mech. Arts; instr., 1904-22, prin., 1922-32, pres. 1932-35. State Teachers Coll., Lowell, Mass.; secretary and manager Moses Greeley Parker Lectures, beginning 1922. Was regional dir. U.S. School Garden Army, 1918-20. Author: Insects and Insecticides, 1891; Fungi and Fungicides, 1894; Ten New England Blossoms and Their Insect Visitors, 1895; Spraying Corps, 1895; Life-Histories of American Insects, 1897; Stories of Insect Life, 1898; Seed-Travelers, 1898; Insect World, 1899; The Flower Beautiful, 1903; Birds in Their Relations to Man (with N. Dearborn), 1903; Laboratory Guide in Zoölogy (with C. W. Crossman), 1902; The Nature Calendar Series, 1902-03; Stories of Bird Life (compiler), 1903; Wild Flower Families, 1908; Our Trees—How to Know Them, 1908; The School Garden Book (with Philip Emerson), 1909; Farm Friends and Farm Foes, 1910; Seeing Nature First, 1913; Crop Production (with W. E. Riley), 1914; Butterflies Worth Knowing, 1917; Manual of School-Supervised Gardening, 1920; Over and Over Stories (with Margaret Weed), 1929; Insect Ways, 1930. Address: 854 Andover St., Lowell, Mass. Died July 20, 1947.

WEED, LEWIS HILL, anatomist; born Cleveland, O., Nov. 15, 1886; s. Charles Henry and Mary Frances (Lewis) W.; A.B. Yale, 1908, A.M., 1909, M.D., John Hopkins, 1912; Sc.D., U. of Rochester, 1929; Univ. of Pennsylvania, 1942. Washington Univ. (St. Louis), Lafayette Coll., 1944, U. of Western Ont., 1947; LL.D., Duke, 1938, Tufts College, 1943, Tulane University, 1944, Birmingham U., England, 1947; unmarried. Fellow in charge of Laboratory of Surgical Research, Harvard Medical School, 1912-13; Arthur Tracy Cabot fellow, same school, 1913-14; instructor, asso. and asso. prof. anatomy, Johns Hopkins U., 1914-19, professor, 1919-47, dean medical faculty, 1923-29, director School of Medicine 1929-46. Served as capt., Med. Corps, U.S. Army, Aug. 1917-May 1919; was mil. dir. Army Neuro-Surg. Lab. at Johns Hopkins Med. Sch. Research asso. Carnegie Instn. of Washington, 1922-35. Trustee Inst. for Advanced Study since 1930; trustee Carnegie Instn. of Washington since 1935; mem. Med. Fellowship Board, Nat. Research Council, 1935-39, chairman Division of Medical Sciences, same, 1939-49; successor fellow Yale Corp. Mem. Health and Med. Com., Council of Nat. Defense, 1940-41; mem. and v. chmn. Com. on Med. Research, Office of Scientific Research and Development, 1941-47. Chmn. med. and health advisory com. Am. Red Cross, 1943-44, chmn. advisory bd. for The Health Services, 1945-47. Mem. bd. of honorary consultants Army Med. Library since 1944. Mem. Am. Assn. Anatomists, A.A.A.S., Am. Physiol. Soc., Am. Philosophical Soc. Author of monographs and original articles on anatom. and neurology subjects. Research in experimental neurlogy. Clubs: Cosmos (Washington); Century Assn. (New York). Received Medal for Merit, 1946; Order British Empire. Home: 720 Centre Av., Reading, Pa. Died Dec. 21, 1952; buried Cleve.

WEED, WALTER HARVEY, geologist; b. St. Louis, May 1, 1862; s. Samuel Richards and Nellie S. (Jones) W.; E.M., Columbia Univ. Sch. of Mines, 1883; m. Helena C. Hill, 1896; children—Mrs. Eleanor Sharp, Walter Harvey, Mary Hill (Mrs. Mary W. Stephenson); m. 2d, Alma Stencel, 1913; 1 dau., Almita Patricia. Was on geol. survey of Yellowstone Park, 1883-89; discovered that colors of hot springs and geyser deposits are due to algae living in hot waters, and that the deposits are formed by algae life; discovered Death Gulch, Yellowstone Park, where elk, bears, etc., are killed by carbon dioxide gas of extinct hot spring. Also made valuable discoveries while engaged in gen. geol. exploration of Mont., 1889-98, mapping over 10,000 square miles, the results appearing as geologic folios of Geol. Survey of U.S.; in recent yrs. devoted mainly to economic geology, visiting mining centers of U.S., Can., Cuba, Hayti, Cent. Am. and Mexico; first to publish theory of secondary enrichment of ore deposits, 1899; spl. study and geologic exams. in Can. and British Columbia, 1906-07; with Adolph Lewisohn (Gen. Development Co.), 1906-09; in pvt. practice as Weed & Probert, 1910-12, since alone. Geologist U.S. Geol. Survey, 1883-1906; geologist N.C. Geol. Survey, 1901-06. Spl. commr. and expert on copper, and mem. Internat. Jury of Awards (mining), St. Louis Expn., 1904. Spl. editorial corr. Engineering and Mining Journal, New York, 1908; spl. corr. Mining and Scientific Press, San Francisco, 1910-12. Mem. Pan-Am. Scientific Congress, 1916. Fellow Geol. Soc Am.; mem. Am. Inst. Mining Engrs. Club: Engineers' (New York). Author: Enrichment of Gold and Silver Veins, 1900; The Nature of Ore Deposits (Beck-Weed),

2 vols., 1905; Classificiation of Ore Deposits, 1906; Copper Mines of the World, 1907; Geology of Castle Mountain (U.S. Geol. Survey); Geology of Butte, Montana, 1914. Also in part, Genesis of Ore Deposits, 1901 (publ. Am. Inst. Mining Engrs.), and similar title, "Emmons" vol., 1913. Has written numerous papers on geol. subjects, particularly with reference to mineral deposits in U.S. and Mexico. Editor and pub. The Copper Handbook (Vols. XI-XVI), later The Mines Handbook (successor), until 1925. Home: Scarsdale, N.Y. Died Sept. 5, 1944.

WEEKS, JOSEPH DAME, tech. journalist, statistician; b. Lowell, Mass., Dec. 3, 1840; s. Jonathan and Mary (Dame) W.; grad. Wesleyan U., 1869; m. Mattie J. Fowler, Feb. 28, 1871. Served with U.S. Christian Commn., 1863-65; editor Am. Manufacturer, 1872-76 (consolidated with Iron World in Pitts., 1874), obtained control, continued as editor, 1886-96; instrumental in fixing iron prices; responsible for 1st wage scale offered to Amalgamated Assn. Iron and Steel Workers; conducted experiments that led to 1st use of gas in puddling furnace; made survey iron ores of James River Valley, Va.; pres. Am. Assn. Mining Engrs., 1895; spl. agt. for Census of 1880; wrote volume on wages in mfg. industries with supplementary reports on trade soc. strikes and lockouts for Census of 1890; prepared articles on mining petroleum gas and manganese and manufacture refined petroleum coke and gas; employed by dept. mineral resources U.S. Geol. Survey, 1885-95; judge awards dept. mines and mining World's Columbian Expn., 1893; chmn. Pa. Tax Conf. Commn., 1896. Author: History of the Knights of Pythias, 1871; Report on the Practical Operation of Arbitration and Conciliation . . . in England, 1879; Industrial Conciliation and Arbitration in New York, Ohio and Pennsylvania, 1881; Labor Differences and Their Settlement, 1886. Died Pitts., Dec. 26, 1896.

WEEKS, STEPHEN HOLMES, surgeon; b. Cornish, Me., Oct. 6, 1835; s. John and Mehitable (Holmes) W.; Fryeburg Acad., Me.; M.D., U. of Pa., 1864; hon. A.M., Bowdoin, 1889; LL.D., Amherst, 1905; m. Mary A. Richmond, 1864. Prof. anatomy, 1877-81, surgery, 1881-1905, Med. Sch. of Me. (Bowdoin); surgeon Me. Gen. Hosp., 1874-98, cons. surgeon, 1898—; first to make and use drainage tubes from arteries of animals. Mem. Internat. Med. Congress, Berlin, 1895, 1899, 1906; fellow Am. Surg. Assn., Am. Acad. Medicine. Republican. Congregationalist. Contbr. to med. press. Died 1909.

WEEMS, JULIUS BUEL, chemist; b. Baltimore, Aug. 27, 1865; s. Edwin Dawson and Rosetta L. (Norman) W.; grad. Md. Agrl. Coll., 1888; Johns Hopkins, 1889-90 and 1890-91; fellow in chemistry, Clark U., 1892-93 and 1893-94, Ph.D., 1894; m. Lila C. Fletcher, June 26, 1895; children—Rachel Fletcher, George Macduff, Carolyn Virginia, Julius Buel. Prof. agrl. chemistry and chemist Expt. Sta., Ia. State Coll., 1895-1904; consul. and analytical chemist, 1904-11; investigating farm life problems, 1911-15; chief chemist, Dept. of Agr., Va., July 15, 1915—. Fellow A.A.A.S. Contbr. or many papers on agr., agrl. edn., water and sewage. Home: Ashland, Va. Died Jan. 25, 1930.

WEESE, A(SA) O(RRIN), (wes), zoölogist; b. Hutchinson, Minn., Nov. 7, 1885; s. Peter Chester and Alice Martha (Van Buskirk) W.; B.A., Univ. of Minn., 1909; M.A., U. of Ill., 1917, Ph.D., 1922; m. Josephine Mousley, June 2, 1915. Prof. biology, U. of N.M., 1911-22; prof. biology, James Millikin U., 1922-24; prof. zoölogy, University of Oklahoma since 1924, dean Graduate College, 1946-47, David Ross Boyd professor zoology since 1948; professor ecology, Rocky Mountain Biological Lab., since 1928; pres. bd., 1938-54; ecologist, Okla. Biol. Survey since 1928, also editor of its publications. Mem. Nat. Research Council Com. on Ecology of Grasslands, 1933-50; mem. Grasslands Research Found. (pres. 1941-47; v.p.). Fellow A.A.A.S.; mem. Ecol. Soc. of America (sec. 1920-30; pres. 1931), British Ecol. Soc., Am. Soc. Zoölogists, Wildlife Soc., Okla. Acad. Science (pres. 1931, permanent sec. since 1946), The Nature Conservancy, Sigma Xi, Phi Kappa Phi, Phi Sigma. Episcopalian. Contbr. to scientific publs. Home: 809 W. Brooks St. Address: Univ. of Okla., Norman, Okla. Deceased.

WEGMANN, EDWARD, engr.; b. Rio de Janiero, Brazil, Nov. 27, 1850; s. L. Edward and Mary W. (Sand) W.; ed. Zürich, Switzerland, 1859-68, Brooklyn Poly. Inst., 1867-68; C.E., New York U., 1871; m. Charlotte H. Drummond, May 6, 1901. Engaged in ry. constrn., 1871-84; on constrn. new water works for New York, 1884-1910; cons. engr., Dept. of Water Supply, Gas and Electricity, New York, 1910-14, in private practice as consulting engineer, 1914—. Author: The Designs and Construction of Masonry Dams, 1888; The Water Works of the City of New York (1658-1895), 1896; The Design and Construction of Dams, 1899; Conveyance and Distribution of Water, 1918. Home: Yonkers, N.Y. Died Jan. 3, 1935.

WEICKER, THEODORE, pharmacist, b. Darmstadt, Germany, June 6, 1861; s. Ludwig Martin and Elisabeth (Momberger) W.; grad. Real-Gymnasium, Darmstadt, 1878; Ph.G. and Ph.C., Columbia, 1911; Ph.M. honoris causa, Philadelphia, Coll. of Pharmacy and Science; m. Florence Palmer, Jan. 21, 1901; children—Theodore, Lowell Palmer, Frederick E., Florence Palmer. Came to U.S., 1885, naturalized, 1890. Began career as apprentice to E. Merck, Darmstadt, 1878; U.S. rep. Merck interests, 1887-90; partner Merck & Co., 1890, sold interests in firm, 1904; with Lowell M. Palmer bought controlling interest in E. R. Squibb & Sons (mfg. chemists), dir., 1905—, chmn. bd.; mem. bd. dirs. Squibb Plan, Inc.; dir. Lentheric, Inc., Squibb Properties Corp. Trustee Columbia U. Coll. of Pharmacy, 1917—; life mem. Columbia U. Coll. of Pharmacy, 1900—. Mem. Riverside Ch. (non-sectarian). Home: Greenwich, Conn. Died Aug. 7, 1940.

WEIDMAN, SAMUEL, geologist; b. Reedsburg, Wis., Oct. 11, 1870; s. Alexander and Eleanor (McIlvaine) W.; desc. of Martin Weidman who emigrated from Germany and settled in Pa., 1733; B.S., U. of Wis., 1894; fellow in geology, same, 1895-96; fellow in geology, U. of Chicago, 1896-97; Ph.D., U. of Wis., 1898; m. Adda J. Westenhaver, Nov. 22, 1899; children—Samuel Henry, John McIlvaine, Robert Hulburt. Field asst. U.S. Geol. Survey in Lake Superior region, 1894-96; asst. geologist, 1897-99, geologist, 1899-1917, Wis. Geol. and Natural History Survey; prof. geology, University of Oklahoma, 1919-43, emeritus professor since September 1943. Democrat. Unitarian. Fellow Geol. Soc. America, A.A.A.S., Assn. American Geographers; mem. Am. Inst. Mining and Metall. Engrs., Am. Assn. Petroleum Geologists, Okla. Acad. of Science (pres. 1924), Sigma Xi. Author: Soils and Agriculture of North Central Wis., 1903, 2d edit., 1908; The Baraboo Iron-Bearing District, 1904; The Geology of North Central Wis., 1907; Soil Survey of Northwestern Wis., 1911; Soil Survey of Marinette County, Wis., 1911; The Water Supplies of Wisconsin, 1916; Miami-Picher Zinc-Lead District, 1932. Home: 512 Lahoma Av., Norman, Okla. Died Sept. 22, 1945.

WEIGEL, ALBERT CHARLES, engring. exec.; b. Knoxville, Tenn., July 13, 1887; s. John Henry and Mary (Rothe) W.; B.S., U. Tenn., 1908; m. Ethel Mary Schofield, July 30, 1912; children—Albert S., John Henry. Began with Walsh & Weidner Boiler Co., 1908, v.p., dir., 1920-28; joined Combustion Engring.-Superheater, Inc., N.Y.C., 1928, v.p., 1940—. Vice pres. Water Commn., East Orange, N.J. Fellow Am. Soc. M.E.; mem. Am. Boiler Mfrs. Assn. and Affiliated Industries (pres.), Am. Welding Soc. (pres.), Am. Soc. Metals, Newcomen Soc., Soc. Naval Architects and Marine Engrs. Home: 5916 Shore Acres Dr., Badenton, Fla. Office: 200 Madison Av., N.Y.C. 16. Died May 30, 1964; buried Manasota Meml. Park, Oneco, Fla.

WEILAND, CHRISTIAN FREDERICK VAN LEEUWEN, (wi-land), elec. engr.; b. Rotterdam, Netherlands, Feb. 19, 1887; s. Johannes and Clazina Johanna (van Leeuwen) W.; student Acad. of Creative Arts and Tech. Sciences, and Tech. Crafts Sch., The Hague, 1902-05; E.E., Rhenish Engring. Coll., Bingen, Germany, 1910; married Alida Jeanne Jacoba Briedé, March 13, 1913; 1 son, Johannes; m. 3d, Elise Cunningham, November 22, 1942. Came to U.S., 1924, naturalized, 1936. Began as machinist apprentice, 1905; successively engr. testing lab. Garbe Lahmeyer Co., Aix-la-Chapelle, Engr. Algemeene Electriciteits My, Amsterdam; engr. in charge lit. and advertising dept. "Heemaf," Holland, chief engr. in charge sales dept. Machine Works, Breda, Holland; held various engring. positions in U.S., 1924-29, foreign lang. and tech. editor Engineering Index, Inc., 1929-40; chief elec. engr. Todd Shipyards Corp., 1940-43; now chief elec. engr. Slocum & Fuller, New York. Mem. Am. Inst. Elec. Engrs. Protestant. Club: Netherland. Author of tech. publs. published in Europe. Home: 3875 Waldo Av., Riverside, N.Y.C. 63. Died Jan. 13, 1953.

WEIMER, BERNAL ROBINSON, retired educator; b. Port Royal, Pa., Dec. 4, 1894; s. George McCullough and Ada Ruth (Robinson) W.; A.B., A.M., W. Va. U.; Ph.D., U. Chgo., 1927; m. Margaret Grace Robinson, Aug. 31, 1918; children—John Robinson, Margaret Brown, George Alexander. Supervising prin. schs., Mifflintown, Pa., 1918-21; prof. biology Bethany Coll., 1921-70, distinguished prof. biology, 1966-70, chmn. sci. and math. group, 1931-70, dean faculty, 1936-70, acting pres., 1952-57; instr. zoology W.Va. U., summers 1924, 32, U. Chgo., summer 1927. Served with inf., M.C., U.S. Army, World War I. Fellow A.A.A.S.; mem. Am. Soc. Zoologists, Am. Assn. Biology Tchrs., W.Va. Acad. Sci., W.Va. Biol. Survey, Phi Beta Kappa, Sigma Xi, Beta Beta Beta (nat. pres.). Democrat. Mem. Disciples of Christ Ch. Mason. Author: (with P. D. Strausbaugh) General Biology, 1938; A Manual for Biology Laboratory, 1938; Elements of Biology, 1944; (verse) Nature Smiles, 1940; (with E. M. Core) A New Manual for Biology Laboratory, 1944; Man and the Animal World, 1951; Of Things Bi-iilogical, 1957. Contbr. articles sci. and gen. mags. and jours. Address: Bethany WV Died July 20, 1970.

WEINBERG, TOBIAS, physician; b. Balt., Mar. 3, 1910; s. David and Yetta (Goodman) W.; B.A., Johns Hopkins, 1930, M.D., 1933; m. Rhoda Perlo, July 14, 1940; 1 son, David Jonathan. Intern, asst. resident in medicine Balt. City Hosps., 1933-36; fellow, asst. in pathology Mt. Sinai Hosp., N.Y.C., 1936-40; pathologist-in-chief, dir. labs. Sinai Hosp., Balt., 1940-69; asso. prof. pathology Dental Sch. U. Md., 1952-59, Med. Sch., 1954-69, Johns Hopkins Med. Sch., 1961-69; pathologist Johns Hopkins Hosp.; cons. pathologist Springfield State Hosp., Lutheran Hosp., Kernan's Hosp. Diplomate Am. Bd. Pathology. Fellow A.C.P., Am. Soc. Clin. Pathologists, Coll. Am. Pathologists; mem. A.M.A., Internat. Acad. Pathology, Md. Soc. Pathologists, Med. and Chir. Faculty of Md., Am. Assn. for Neoplastic Diseases, Am. Assn. Pathologists and Bacteriologists, Sigma Xi. Home: Pikesville MD Died Nov. 21, 1969.

WEINERMAN, EDWIN RICHARD, physician, educator; b. Hartford, Conn., July 17, 1917; s. David Tolner and Anna (Schwartz) W.; A.B., Yale, 1938; M.D., Georgetown U., 1942; M.P.H., Harvard, 1948; m. Shirley Basch, Dec. 23, 1940; children—Jeffrey Alan, Diane Lee. Med. house officer Beth Israel Hosp., Harvard and Tufts Services, Boston, 1942-43; resident communicable diseases Charles V. Chapin Hosp., Providence, 1942; resident internal medicine Drew Field Regional Hosp., Fla., 1943-44; spl. resident internal medicine San Francisco VA Hosp. U. Cal. Service, 1952-53; practice medicine, specializing in internal medicine, Berkeley, Cal. 1953-62; asst. chief med. officer health services div. FSA, Washington, 1946-47; asso. in med. care adminstrn. div. pub. health methods USPHS, 1947; asso. prof. med. econs., head div. med. care adminstrn. Sch. Pub. Health, U. Cal., 1948-50; med. dir. Permanente Health Plan, Oakland, Cal., 1950-51; med. dir. Herrick Meml. Hosp. Clinics, Berkeley, 1952-62; physician-in-charge Rheumatic Fever Clinic, Richmond, Contra Costa County Health Dept., 1953-62; dir. ambulatory services Yale-New Haven Hosp., Yale-New Haven Med. Center, 1962-66; prof. medicine and pub. health (med. care) Yale Sch. Medicine, 1962-70; cons., Group Health Corp. Puget Sound, Seattle, 1949; Am. fellow WHO, summer 1950; med. cons. San Francisco Labor Council, 1952; cons. med. group practice President's Commn. on Health Needs of Nation, 1952; med. plan adviser Sheet Metal Industry Welfare Fund, Oakland, 1956-62; med. cons Community Health Assn., Santa Rosa, Cal., 1961-62; cons. United Automobile Workers and Am. Motors Co., Milw., 1961, Office Econ. Opportunity, 1964-65; mem. adv. bd., cons. dept. univ. health Yale, 1964-70; cons. med. adv. com. Commn. on Delivery Personal Health Services, N.Y.C., 1966-70; mem. adv. com. on Medicaid, Conn. Dept. Welfare, 1967-70. Served to capt., M.C., AUS, 1943-46. Sr. faculty award Commonwealth Fund, 1967. Diplomate Nat. Bd. Med. Examiners, Am. Bd. Preventive Medicine. Fellow A.M.A., Am. Pub. Health Assn. (com. chmn.); mem. Conn., New Haven med. assns., Conn. Pub. Health Assn., Assn. Tchrs. Preventive Medicine, Am. Heart Assn., Internat. Acad. Legal Medicine and Social Medicine, Group Health Assn. Am., Am., Conn. hosp. assns., Assn. Am. Med. Colls., Royal Soc. Health (Gt. Britain), Nat. Rehab. Assn., Delta Omega (past nat. pres.). Contbr. articles profl. jours. Home: Hamden CT Died Feb. 20, 1970.

WEINIG, ARTHUR JOHN, metall. engr.; b. Durango, Colo., June 10, 1883; s. Kilian and Mary (Hartkorn) W.; student U. Colo., 1903-04; E. Met., Colo. Sch. Mines, 1908; m. Mary LeGill, July 3, 1913; children—Louise Margaret (Mrs. Wayne Spear), Catherine Marion, Arthur John. Smelter sampler and engr., 1908-11; foreman, mill supt., gen. supt. Liberty Bell Gold Mining Co., Telluride, Colo., 1911-21; metallurgist Metals Exploration Co., 1921-23; dir. exptl. plant Colo. Sch. Mines, 1923-49; cons. metall. engr. for a number of large mining and chem. corps., 1921—; inventor processes for manganese and potash ores and cement materials; many apparatus inventions on flotation and cyanidation and equipment. Awarded gold medal Colo. Engring. Council 1 and Colo. Sch. Mines medal For Excellence, 1944. Mem. Am. Inst. Mining and Metall. Engrs., A.A.A.S., Mining and Metall. Soc. Am., Torrey Bot. Club. Episcopalian. Mason; mem. Eastern Star. Author: Functional Size Analyses of Ore Grids, 1929; (with Irving A. Palmer) Trend of Flotation, 1933; (with C. B. Carpenter) Trend of Flotation, 1937. Contbr. articles to mining and metall. jours. Home: 509 14th St., Golden, Colo. Died Sept. 23, 1966; buried Crown Hill Cemetery.

WEINMANN, JOSEPH PETER, pathologist; b. Neu Bistritz, Czechoslovakia, May 13, 1896; s. Ludwig and Theresa (Bandler) W.; M.D., U. Vienna, 1923; m. Regina Altstadt, Dec. 31, 1940; 1 dau., Katherine. Came to U. S., 1938, naturalized, 1944. Instr. U. Vienna, 1921-23, research asso. oral histology, 1923-38; research fellow Coll. Dentistry U. Ill., 1938-39; asst. prof. research Columbia, 1939-40: asst. prof. oral pathology and research, Loyola U. Dental Sch., Chgo., 1940-46; asso. prof. histology Coll. Dentistry U. Ill., 1946-49, prof. pathology, head div. oral pathology, 1949—. Recipient Chaim prize 1st Dist. Dental Soc., 1941. Diplomate Am. Acad. Oral Pathology (past pres.), Fellow A.A.A.S.; mem. Chgo. Soc. Pathology, Internat. Assn. Dental Research, Sigma Xi. Author: (with Dr. Harry Sicher) Bone and Bones, 2d edit., 1955; (with Dr. M. Diamond) Human Enamel, 1940. Home: 1089 Ridgewood Dr., Highland Park, Ill. Office: 808 S. Wood St., Chgo. 12. Died May 1960.

WEINSTEIN, ALEXANDER, (win'stin), consulting industrial engr.; b. New York, N.Y. Oct. 8, 1891; s. David and Frieda (Chester) W.; student Columbia,

1922-28; unmarried. Industrial engr. Pacific Novelty Co. (Dupont Viscoloid Co.), 1918-20, Gem Safety Razor Co., 1924-26, Colombia Bank, 1920-24; cons. industrial engr. Hamersley Mfg. Co., 1926-34, Gilman Paper Co., 1934-35; apptd. by Federal Court as receiver Kelly Springfield Tire Co., 1935; apptd. by N.J. Chancery Court receiver Kelly Springfield Cos., 1935; sec. and treas. Kelly Springfield Tire Co., 1935; apptd. by Federal Court trustee Warner-Quinlan Co., 1936; cons. engr. for Preferred Stockholders Com. of Standard Gas & Electric Co., 1935-36. Served as lt. Sanitary Corps, U.S. Army, 1918-19. Rep. of industry on City Industrial Relations Bd.; mediator and arbitrator representing public on N.Y. St. Bd. of Mediation. Research asso., dept. of industrial engring., Columbia; dir. Hebrew Ednl. Soc. Fellow A.A.A.S.; mem. Am. Soc. Mech. Engrs., Nat. Soc. Professional Engrs., N.Y. State Soc. Professional Engrs., Tech. Assn. Paper and Pulp Industry, Acad. Polit. Science, Economic Research Round Table of Bankers Club, Soc. for Advancement of Management (advisory bd.), Soc. Industrial Engrs. (nat. treas.). Hebrew religion. Clubs: Bankers, Faculty of Columbia University, Economic, Sheepskin, Beethoven Soc. Philharmonic Soc. (New York); Inwood Country (L.I.). Contbr. to jours. Home: 1221 Hilldale Av., Los Angeles, Calif. Office: 120 Broadway, New York, N.Y. Died Feb. 19, 1947; buried in Mt. Zion Cemetery, Maspeth, L.I., N.Y.

WEINZIRL, ADOLPH, hygienist; b. Albuquerque, N.M., Feb. 3, 1900; s. John and Jacquetta (Lee) W.; B.S., U. of Ore., 1922; M.D., U. of Ore., 1925; M.P.H., Johns Hopkins, 1932; m. Elizabeth H. Halberstadt, June 17, 1925; children—Barbara Jean (Mrs. Robert E. Symonds), Elizabeth Jacquetta (Mrs. William R. Johnston), Henrietta Lee Weinzirl (Mrs. Durward L. Boyles). Served as deputy commr. of health, City of Seattle, 1926; epidemiologist, Baltimore City Health Dept., 1932; city health officer, Portland, Ore., 1937; prof. pub. health and preventive medicine, U. of Ore. Med. Sch. since 1941, chmn. dept., 1947—; director E. C. Brown Trust Div. Social Hygiene Edn., 1941-48. Served as pvt. U.S. Army, 1918; chief, Emergency Med. Service, Portland and Multnomah County Civilian Defense Council, 1941-45. Fellow Am. Pub. Health Assn., A.M.A.; mem. A.A.A.S., Delta Omega, Alpha Omega Alpha. Home: 3416 S.W. 12th Av. Office: 3181 S.W. Sam Jackson Park Rd., Portland 1, Ore. Died June 10, 1967; buried Rose City Cemetery, Portland.

WEIR, PAUL, mining engr.; b. Punxsatawney, Pa., Dec. 3, 1894; s. Charles Steele and Carrie M. (Bell) W.; student Indiana (Pa.) State U., 1913-14; B.S., Pa. State U., 1919, E.M., 1949; m. Lura Hickox, Sept. 28, 1921 (dec. 1963); children—Charles Richard, John Paul, Mary Frances; m. 2d, Venetta Lewis, Oct. 5, 1963. Instr. mining Case Inst. Tech., 1919-20; chief engr., later gen. supt., v.p. Bell and Zoller Coal Co., Chgo., 1920-37; cons. mining engr., 1937-72; founder Paul Weir Co., mining engrs., 1937, successively pres., chmn. bd., now cons. Mem. U.S. Coal Mission to U.K., Trustee Sch. Ozarks. Recipient Erskine Ramsay Gold medal award Am. Inst. M.E., 1950; medal, Distinguished Alumni award Pa. State U., 1954. Hon. mem. Inst. Mining Engrs. (U.K.); mem. Am. Inst. Mining, Metall. and Petroleum Engrs. (life), Am. Mining Congress, Ill. Mining Inst. (life), Coal Mining Inst. Am., Rocky Mountain Mining Inst., Alpha Tau Omega, Tau Beta Pi. Republican. Presbyn. Mason. Clubs: Tower (Chgo.); Missouri Athletic (St. Louis); Duquesne (Pitts.). Address: Lookout MO Died Oct. 26, 1972.

WEIR, W(ILLIAM) VICTOR, (wer), engr., pub. utilities exec.; b. Warren, Ind., July 18, 1902; s. David Hamilton and Anna Florence (Beard) W.; B.S., Washington U., 1923; m. Marion Susan Wilson, June 30, 1928; children—Joan (Mrs. W. J. Stradal, Jr.), Peter, Thomas. Jr. engr. West St. Louis Water & Light Co., 1923-26; engr. St. Louis County Water Co., 1926-27, asst. mgr., 1927-33, chief engr. and supt., 1933-45, v.p., supt., 1945-46, pres., gen. mgr. since 1946; supt. of Mo. Water Co., 1943-45, v.p., gen. mgr., 1945-46, pres., gen. mgr. since 1946; pres. No. Ill. Water Corp., Ill. Water Service Co., L.I. Water Corp., Gary-Hobart Water Corp. Chmn. St. Louis Met. Plan Assn., 1956-59. Registered engr., Mo. Recipient honors Am. Water Works Assn.: Diven Memorial medal, 1940, Fuller Meml. award, 1943, Goodell prize, 1950. Mem. Am. Water Works Assn. (v.p. 1949, pres., 1950; chmn., plant management and operation division, 1937; chmn., finance and accounting division, 1943; chmn. Mo. Valley sect., 1944; dir. 1946-52; mem. coms.), American Society C.E., Missouri Society Profl. Engrs. Mo. Assn. Pub. Utilities, Mo. Water and Sewerage Conf. (past chmn.), Sigma Xi, Tau Beta Pi, Phi Delta Theta. Clubs: Engineers'. Contributor to water supply journals, manuals and periodicals. Home: Mosley Rd., Creve Coeur, Mo. Office: 8390 Delmar Blvd., University City, St. Louis 24. Died Nov. 19, 1959.

WEISER, HARRY BOYER, (wī'ser), prof. chemistry coll. dean; b. Greencastle, O.. Sept. 5, 1887; s. Calvin Walace and Mary (Boyer) W.; B.A., Ohio State U., 1911, M.A., 1912; Ph.D., Cornell, 1914; m. Hazel Eleanor McKean, Sept. 18, 1915; children—Dorothy Boyer (Mrs. W. W. Seale, Jr.), Marjorie McKean (Mrs. H. T. Witherspoon, Jr.). Instr. chemistry, U. Tenn., 1914-15; instr. chemistry, Rice Inst., Houston, 1915-18, asst. prof., 1918-19, prof., 1919—, dean 1933—. Capt. Chem. Warfare Service, 1918; chief of Catalytic Unit, Research Div.; chmn. com. on chemistry of colloids div. of chemistry and chemical technology, NRC, 1925-1943. Fellow Am. Acad. Arts and Sciences, A.A.A.S., Am. Inst. Chemists; mem. Am. Chem. Soc. (sec. div. of physical and inorganic chemistry, 1925, chmn. 1926; chmn. div. of colloid chemistry, 1927; chmn. colloid symposium committee, 1934-46); mem. The Faraday Society, Phi Beta Kappa, Sigma Xi, Phi Lambda Upsilon, Alpha Chi Sigma fraternities. Democrat. Presbyn. Mason. Author: The Hydrous Oxides, 1926; The Colloidal Salts, 1928; Inorganic Colloid Chemistry—Volume I, The Colloidal Elements, 1933, Vol. II, The Hydrous Oxides and Hydroxides, 1935; Vol. III, The Colloidal Salts, 1938; Colloid Chemistry, 1939. Also numerous articles on photo-chemistry and colloid chemistry. Editor Colloid Symposium Monograph; asso. editor Jour. of Physical Chemistry, 1927-28, 31-32, 36-37, 45-46; editor Colloid Chemistry, Jour. of Phys. and Colloid Chemistry, 1947—. Home: 1320 Milford, Houston, Texas. Died Sept. 27, 1950; buried Forest Park Cemetery, Houston.

WEISS, JOHN MORRIS, (wis), chemical engr.; b. Phila., Pa., Mar. 11, 1885; s. Julius and Frances (Henlein) W.; grad. Central High Sch., Phila., 1901; B.S., U. of Pa., 1905; m. Bertie Heine, May 18, 1909 (died Aug. 17, 1937); children—Robert Paul, Francis Benjamin; m. 2d, Madeleine Kroeplin, May 11, 1938. Research chemist Barrett Co., Frankford, Pa., 1905-06, chief chemist, 1907-11; chief chemist, Barrett Co., New York, 1911-17; mgr. research dept., 1917-21, dir. of development, 1921-22; pres. and treas. Weiss & Downs, Inc., New York, 1923-44. Partner John M. Weiss and Co., consulting chemical engineers, since 1943. First v.p. and dir. Calorider Corp., Stamford, Conn., since 1937. Registered engineer in N.Y. and N.J. Mem. Pa. Nat. Guard Engrs. Corps, 1909; consultant Army-Navy Munitions Bd., 1941-42. Awarded Howard N. Potts gold medal by Franklin Inst., 1922; Acad. of Polit. Science, Am. Gas Assn., Chemical Com., 1921-31. Fellow Am. Inst. Chemists (ex-pres. N.Y. sect., chmn. ethics com., 1924-26; chmn. com. on economic welfare 1946-47), A.A.A.S.; member American Chemical Society (chmn. N.Y. sect. 1934; chmn. Nichols medal jury, 1935, 38), American Institute Chemical Engineers (chmn. regional com. on legislation, 1933-54, rep. on engr. council for professional development, 1933-35, rep. N.C.S.B.E.E., adv. bd., com. on Nat. Bur. Engr. Reg., 1933-54); mem. com. control of nitrogen in Germany. Nat. Engr. Council, 1945; mem. Am. Soc. Testing Materials (chmn. com. D 8, 1932-44, publications com. 1933-39, chmn. com. D 16, 1940-46), Assn. Cons. Chems. and Chem. Engrs. (dir. 1929-34 and 1945-48), Franklin Institute (science and arts committee since 1911), General Alumni Society of U. Pa., Fed., N.Y. Co. grand jury assns., Nat. Research Council (insulation com.), Nat. Safety Council, Nat. Soc. Profl. Engrs., N.Y. State Soc. Professional Engrs. (dir. 1931-33), N.J. State Soc. Professional Engrs., Commercial Chemical Development Association, Society of Chemical Industry (London), Chemists Club, Sigma Xi. Mem. adv. bd. Ind. Ed., Chem. and Engring. News, I.E.C., 1944-50. Republican. Author: The Technical Organization—its Development and Administration, 1924. Contributor to scientific journals; special writer for Wall St. Jour. Patentee. Home: 155 E. 38th St., N.Y.C. 16. Office: 50 E. 41st St., N.Y.C. 17. Died June 6, 1963.

WEISS, SAMUEL, physician, med. research cons.; b. May 6, 1885; s. Jacob and Nina (Weinberger) W.; M.D., L.I. Coll. Hosp., 1907, Sc.D., 1947; m. Ella M. Margareten, Jan. 11, 1914; children—Daniel, Jerome, Bernard. Prof. medicine (digestive diseases), Essex Coll. Medicine and Surgery, Newark; staff exec., dir. dept. gastroenterology N.Y. Polyclinic Med. Sch. and Hosp.; now emeritus prof. gastroenterology N.Y. Polyclinic Med Sch.; cons. gastroenterologist Polyclinic Hosp.; cons. gastroenterologist Jewish Meml. Hosp., N.Y.; cons. gastroenterology Grand Central, Long Beach hosps. Surgeon (R), USPHS (ret.). Decorated Legion of Honor (France). Hon. fellow Belgian Gastroent. Assn., gastroent. assns. Paris and Rome; Internat. Acad. Proctology, Med. Sci. Club, Phila., N.Y. Acad. Sci., Royal Acad. Health (Eng.). Diplomate Am. Bd. Internal Medicine (G.E.). Fellow A.C.P., A.A.A.S., N.Y. Acad. Gastroenterology, Am. Coll. Gastroenterology (founder, trustee), Am. Pub. Health Assn., Nat., Internat. gastroent. assns., World Congress Gastroenterology, Am. Soc. Clin. Radiology (exec. com.); mem. Am., N.Y. State, N.Y. County med. assns., Am. Med. Writers Assn. (adv. com.), Internat. Congress Internal Medicine, Fifty Year Club Am. Medicine, Assn. Mil. Surgeons, Assn. Res. Officers USPHS (R), Biol. Photog. Assn., Royal Photog. Soc. Eng., Soc. Advancement Gastroenterology (founder), Am. Soc. French Legion Honor, Jewish Acad. Arts and Scis. (v.p.), Internat. Med. Club, (life mem.) Phi Delta Epsilon. Mason (32 deg., Shriner). Club: Physicians' Square. Author: Diseases of the Liver, Gallbladder and Pancreas, 1935; The Acute Medical Syndrome and Emergencies, 1939; Clinical Lectures of the Gallbladder and Bile Ducts, 1944; contbr. numerous articles to med. jours. Editor Am. Jour. Gastroenterology; Rev. Gastroenterology, 1934—; Functional Diseases of the Pancreas and Liver, 1937. Office: 435 E. 79th St., N.Y.C. 10021. Died Apr. 5, 1966.

WEITZEL, GODFREY, army officer, engr.; b. Cincinnati, Nov. 1, 1835; s. Louis and Susan Weitzel; grad. U.S. Mil. Acad., 1855; m. 2d, Louisa Bogen, circa 1864; at least 1 child. Brevetted 2d lt. engrs. U.S. Army, 1855, commd. 2d lt., 1856, 1st lt., 1860; served in fortification of New Orleans, 1855-59; asst. prof. engring. U.S. Mil. Acad., 1859-61; with an engr. co. on expdn. to Ft. Pickens (Fla.) to save it for Union, 1861; chief engr. fortifications of Cincinnati, 1861; chief engr. under Gen. Benjamin Butler in expdn. against New Orleans, 1862; asst. mil. comdr. New Orleans; commd. brig. gen. U.S. Volunteers, 1862; capt. Engr. Corps, U.S. Army, 1863, brevetted maj. and lt. col. for gallantry at battles of Thibodeaux and Port Hudson; chief engr. Second Div., XVIII Army Corps, 1864; brevetted maj. gen. volunteers; brevetted col. regular army for gallantry at capture of Fort Harrison (Va.); maj. gen. volunteers, 1864; brevetted brig. general, major general, U.S. Army for service in final operations against Richmond (Va.), 1865; commanded Rio Grande Dist., 1865; mustered out of U.S. Volunteers, 1866, returned to duty with Corps Engrs., promoted maj., 1866; asso. with constrn. of ship canals at falls of Ohio River, and Sault Sainte Marie (Mich.), lighthouse at Stannard's Rock in Lake Superior; commd. lt. col., 1882. Died Phila., Mar. 19, 1884.

WEIZMANN, CHALM, (vitz'män ki'im), Zionist leader, scientist; b. Motol, Prov. of Grodno, Russia, Nov. 27, 1874; s. Reb Oiser and Rachel (Czerminsky) W.; ed. Pinsk High Sch. and U. of Berlin; D.Sc., U. of Freiburg, 1900; Sc.D., U. of Manchester, 1909, LL.D., 1919; m. Dr. Vera Chatzmann, 1906; children—Benjamin, Michael (dec.). Became naturalized Brit. subject, 1910; adjured Brit. citizenship on establishment of new State of Israel, of which is now citizen. Lecturer in organic chemistry U. of Geneva, 1901-04; became reader in biochemistry U. of Manchester; dir. Brit. Admiralty Labs., 1916-19, Elected president of the state of Israel, 1949; chairman 1st Zionist Commn., recognized by Brit. Govt. as adv. body to Brit. authorities in all Jewish questions, 1918; pres. World Zionist Orgn., 1921-29, Extended Jewish Agency for Palestine, 1929-31, 1935-46; obtained League of Nations ratification of mandate for Palestine, which also provided for severance of Trans-Jordan from Palestine area; pres. English Zionist Fedn., 1931-48; presided at World Zionist Congress, London, Aug. 1945; head Jewish delegation at meeting of U.N. Special Com. on Palestine, Lake Success, N.Y., Oct. 1947; chmn. bd. Hebrew U., Jerusalem, since 1932; dir. Daniel Sieff Research Inst., Rehovoth; elected pres. provisional govt. of new State of Israel, 1948. Author: Trial and Error (autobiography), 1949. Address: Hakirya, Israel. Died Nov. 9, 1952. *

WELBORN, CURTIS R., fire prevention engr.; b. Ellisville, Miss., Jan. 10, 1894; s. Jefferson Lee and Lurline (Watson) W.; B.S. in Elec. Engring., Miss. State Coll., 1920; m. Ethel Len Privett, Aug. 17, 1920; 2 children. With Underwriters' Labs., Inc., Chicago, 1920-59, pres., 1948-59. Served as capt., A Co., 346th Regt., 87th Div., World War I. Mem. University Club, Tau Beta Pi. Home: Winnetka IL Died Apr. 1973.

WELCH, ASHBEL, civil engr.; b. Nelson, Madison County, N.Y., Dec. 4, 1809; s. Ashbel and Margaret (Dorrance) W.; m. Mary Hannah Seabrook, Oct. 25, 1834, at least 4 children. Became asso. with Del. & Raritan Canal, Trenton, N.J., 1830, chief engr., in charge of all engring. work, 1835, designed and built wooden lock, Bordentown, N.J., 1847; builder Belvidere Del. R.R.; a designer steamship Princeton; examined coal and iron properties in Va.; designer and builder Chesapeake & Del. Canal, 1853; v.p. Camden & Amboy R.R., 1862, presented plan for telegraphic safety signals, 1865; pres. United Cos. of N.J., in charge all adminstrv. matters, 1867-71; active in improvement of railroad rolling stock; mem. Am. Soc. C.E., v.p., 1880, pres., 1882. Died Lambertville, N.J., Sept. 25, 1882.

WELCH, WILLIAM ADDAMS, park and cons. engr.; b. Cynthiana, Ky., Aug. 20, 1868; s. Ashbel Standard and Priscilla (Addams) W.; ed. high sch., Colorado Springs, Colo., Colorado Coll. (C.E. 1882), U. of Va. (M.E. 1886); m. Camille Beall, 1902; children—Jessie Elizabeth (Mrs. I. H. McAnally), William Addams. Engr. in railway location and constrn., in Eastern, Southern and Western states, Alaska, Mexico, and S. America; also engr. in reclamation, hydroelectric and harbor developments until 1900; gen. mgr. and chief engr. Palisades Interstate Park Commission, N.Y., since 1900; cons. engr. Bear Mountain Hudson River Bridge Corp. Served as chief engr. spruce production div., rank of maj., Air Service Production Div., U.S. Army, during World War; received commendation of chief of Air Service. Mem. Council Boy Scouts America (awarded the Silver Buffalo, also the Pugsley Medal, gold); dir. Nat. Council of State Parks; hon. pres. Appalachian Trail Conf. Mem. Am. Road Builders Assn., Am. Inst. Park Execs., Am. Soc. C.E., Adirondack Mountain Club, Audubon Soc., Nat. Park Soc., Am. Game and Protective Assn. Episcopalian. Clubs: Engineers, Camp Fire, Explorers (New York); Cosmos (Washington). Address: Bear Mountain, N.Y. Died May 4, 1941. *

WELCH, WILLIAM HENRY, pathologist; b. Norfolk, Conn., Apr. 8, 1850; s. William Wickham and Emeline (Collin) W.; A.B., Yale, 1870; M.D., Coll. Phys. and

Surg. (Columbia), 1875; univs. of Strassburg, Leipzig, Breslau and Berlin, 1876-78, 1884-85; hon. M.D., U. of Pa., 1894; LL.D., Western Reserve, 1894, Yale, 1896, Harvard, 1900, Toronto, 1903, Columbia, 1904, Jefferson Med. Coll., 1907, Princeton, 1910, Washington U., 1915, U. Chicago, 1916, U. of Southern Calif., 1930, Univ. State of N.Y., 1930; Sc.D., Cambridge, 1923, Western Reserve, 1929, U. of Pa., 1930; Doct., Strassburg, 1923. Prof. pathol. and anatomy and gen. pathology, Bellevue Hosp. Med. Coll., 1879-84; Baxley prof. pathology, 1884-1916, dean, med. faculty, 1893-98, dir. School of Hygiene and Public Health, 1916-26, professor history of medicine, 1926-30, emeritus, 1931, Johns Hopkins; pathologist Johns Hopkins Hosp., 1889-1916. Pres. Med. State Bd. Health, 1898-1922, and mem. to 1929; pres. bd. dirs. Rockefeller Inst. for Med. Research, 1901—; mem. Internat. Health Bd. and China Med. Bd. of Rockefeller Foundation; trustee of Carnegie Instn., 1906—. Huxley lecturer, Charing Cross Hosp. Med. Sch., London, 1902. Pres. Med. and Chirurg. Faculty of Md., 1891-92, Congress of Am. Phys. and Surg., 1897, Assn. Am. Physicians, 1901, A.A.A.S., 1906-07, A.M.A., 1910-11, Nat. Tuberculosis Assn., 1910-11 (hon. pres.), Nat. Acad. Sciences, 1913-16, Am. Social Hygiene Assn., 1916-19, Nat. Com. Mental Hygiene (hon. pres.), History of Science Society, 1931; fellow Am. Acad. Arts and Sciences, Coll. of Physicians, Phila.; hon. fellow Royal Soc. Medicine, Royal Sanitary Inst., London, Royal Coll. of Phys., Edinburgh, Soc. Med. Officers of Health (Eng.). Commd. maj., Med. R.C., U.S.A., July 16, 1917; lt. col., Feb. 20, 1918; col., July 24, 1918; hon. discharged, Dec. 31, 1918; col. Med. Sect. O.R.C., U.S.A., Feb. 24, 1919; brig. gen. O.R.C., Dec. 23, 1921. Awarded D.S.M. (U.S.); Order of Rising Sun (Japan), 3d Class; Comdr. Order of St. Olav (Norway), 2d Class; Order of Mercy (Kingdom of Serbs, Croats and Slovenes); Officer Legion of Honor (France); gold medal, Nat. Inst. Social Sciences; medal of honor, U. of Vienna; Kober medal, 1927; Harbin gold medal, 1931. Author: General Pathology of Fever, 1888; The Biology of Bacteria, Infection and Immunity, 1894; Bacteriology of Surgical Infections, 1895; Trombosis and Embolism, 1899; also numerous papers on pathol. and bacteriol. subjects, and addresses. Home: Baltimore, Md. Died Apr. 30, 1934.

WELCH, WILLIAM MCNAIR, petroleum engr. and executive; b. Oil City, Pa., Aug. 23, 1874; s. John Collins and Eliza Jane (McNair) W.; M.E., Stevens Inst. Tech., 1898; m. Nina Oliver Thompson, of N.Y. City, Apr. 24, 1901; children—Marjorie Thompson, Elizabeth Hunter, Helen Collins, Wm. McN. Engring. work connected with natural gas industry until 1912; chief engr. Mexican Eagle Oil Co. (S. Pearson & Sons), Tampico, Mex., 1912-14; petroleum and natural gas engr., U.S. Bur. Mines, Washington, D.C., 1914-16; v.p. and gen. mgr. Tidal Refining Co., Okla., and Tidal-Western Oil Corpn., Texas, 1916-24; pres. White Oak Refining Company, Beaver Refining Co., Ltd.; retired from petroleum industry, 1928; engaged in grapefruit and orange growing, etc., since 1928; with Texas Railroad Commission, oil and natural gas department, engring. div., since 1935; preparing a statis. and hist. review of the natural gas industry in Texas. Pres. Assn. Natural Gasoline Mfrs., 1921-23; dir. Am. Petroleum Inst., Western Petroleum Refiners' Assn., Internat. Petroleum Expn. and Congress, 1924. Episcopalian. Mason (32 deg.). Home: Austin TX

WELCH, WILLIAM WICKHAM, physician, congressman; b. Norfold, Conn., Dec. 10, 1818; s. Benjamin and Elizabeth (Loveland) W.; M.D., Yale Med. Sch., 1839; m. Emeline Colin, Nov. 7, 1845; m. 2d, Emily Sedgwick, May 2, 1866; 2 children including William Henry. Practiced medicine, Norfolk; interested in treatment of hydrophobia and venomous reptile bites; mem. Conn. Ho. of Reps., 1848-50, 69, 81, Conn. Senate, 1851-52; mem. U.S. Ho. of Reps. (Am. Party) from Conn., 34th Congress, 1855-57; pres. Norfolk Leather Co.; an incorporator Conn.-Western R.R., Norfolk Savs. Bank. Died Norfolk, July 30, 1892; buried Norfolk Cemetery.

WELD, LAENAS GIFFORD, univ. dean; b. Sherwood, Mich., Dec. 30, 1862; s. Le Roy Tryon and Nancy Rose (Dougherty) W.; Northwestern U., 1878-80; B.S., State U. of Iowa, 1883, A.M., 1886, LL.D., 1912; studied aborad, 1897; m. Harriet Magdalene Doane, June 24, 1887. Teacher mathematics, Burlington (Ia.) High Sch., 1884-86; asst. prof. 1886-87, acting prof., 1887-89, prof. mathematics and astronomy and head dept., 1889-1911, dean Graduate Coll., 1900-07, dir. Sch. of Applied Sciences, 1903-05, dean Coll. Liberal Arts, 1907-10, State U. of Ia. State supt. weights and measures for Ia., 1888-1911; dir. Pullman (Ill.) Free School of Manual Training, Sept. 1, 1911—. Fellow A.A.A.S. (sec. Sect. A, 1904-09). Congregationalist. Author: Theory of Determinants; Determinants. Home: Pullman, Ill. Died Nov. 28, 1919.

WELKER, PHILIP ALBERT, civil engr.; b. Toledo, O., June 1, 1857; s. Philip and Maria (Pauly) W.; C.E., Cornell U., 1878; m. Maude B. Loud, Mar. 17, 1885 (died 1890); 1 dau., Maude Antoinette (Mrs. Howard R. Willis); m. 2d, Gertrude M. Lanahan, June 29, 1904; 1 son, Philip Lanahan. In city engrs.' office, Toledo, O., 1878-79; with U.S. Coast and Geod. Survey, 1879—, operating in nearly every part of U.S. and Alaska, P.R., Isthmus of Panama and P.I.; with Alaskan Boundary Survey, 1893-95; in comd. U.S. steamer Bache, hydrographic surveys, Atlantic Coast, 1898-1910; rep. U.S. Govt. on commn. of engrs. for locating and determining ownership of Ft. Myers Mil. Rd., Va., 1910; dir. coast surveys, P.I., 1911-14, also sec. Philippine Com. on Geog. Names, and mem. Harbor Lines Commn. of P.I.; asst. in charge of office, 1914-17, engr. in charge of office, U.S. Coast and Geodetic Survey, June 1917-June 1920, retired, June 1, 1921. Pres. Welker Supply Co., Cleveland, O. Mason. Home: Washington, D.C. Died Dec. 24, 1926.

WELKER, WILLIAM HENRY, teacher, investigator; b. Red Hill, Pa., Aug. 20, 1879; s. William Alexander and Angelina (Wile) W.; A.C., Lehigh U., 1904; Ph.D., Columbia, 1908; Sc.D., Franklin and Marshall College, 1942; m. Evie M. Hutchinson, June 1904 (dec. June 3, 1950); 1 dau., Dr. Dorothy Hutchinson (Mrs. Joseph Greengood); m. 2d, Grace Day, Dec. 1953. Asst. in biol. chemistry, Columbia, 1904-07; pathol. assistant in obstetrics, Sloane Maternity Hosp., New York, 1906-07; demonstrator physiol. chemistry, U. Pa., 1907-10; chemist to German Hosp., New York, 1910; asso. in biol. chemistry, 1910-11, asst. prof., 1911-12, Columbia; asst. prof. physiol. chemistry, U. Ill. Coll. Medicine, 1913, asso. prof. 1919-21, prof., 1921-31, prof., head of dept., 1931-47, emeritus; mem. grad. teaching faculty, U. Ill., 1916—, mem. exec. faculty, Graduate Sch., 1946—. Fellow A.A.A.S.; charter mem. Am. Soc. Biol. Chemists; mem. Radium Inst. America, Soc. Exptl. Biology and Medicine, Harvey Soc., Tau Beta Pi, Sigma Xi, Alpha Omega Alpha; fellow Inst. of Medicine Chicago (v.p. 1947); asso. fellow A.M.A.; mem. Am. Pub. Health Assn., Ill. Acad. Science, Internat. Assn. for Dental Research, Am. Congress on Internal Medicine; F.A.C.P.; affiliated mem. of the Chicago Allergy Society. Gibbs prize, $2,000, N.Y. Academy Medicine, 1907 (with Dr. Dittman) for essay on nephritis. Contbr. to scientific jours. Home: 534 N. Elmwood Av., Oak Park, Ill. Died July 7, 1956; buried East Greenville, Pa.

WELLER, CARL VERNON, pathologist; b. St. Johns, Mich., Feb. 17, 1887; s. Martin and Emma (Pulfrey) W.; A.B., Albion (Mich.) Coll., 1908; M.D., U. Mich., 1913, M.S., 1916, D.Sc., Albion College, 1956 (honorary); graduated study in pathology, Vienna, Austria, 1925; m. Elsie Huckle, June 26, 1913; children—Thomas Huckle, John Martin. Mem. faculty, U. Mich., 1911—, instr. pathology, 1911-16, asst. prof., 1916-21, asso. prof., 1921-24, prof., 1924—, asst. dir. pathol. labs., 1924-31, dir., 1931-37, chmn. dept. of pathology, 1938—, also mem. exec. com. Med. Sch., 1934-37, 1946-49. Mem. sci. adv. bd. Armed Forces Inst. Pathology, 1950—. Fellow Am. Geriatrics Soc., A.C.P.; member N.Y. Acad. Scis., Nat. Research Council (com. on pathol. 1947-50), Am. Assn. Cancer Research, Am. Assn. Pathologists and Bacteriologists (ex-pres.), A.M.A., Assn. Am. Physicians (emeritus), Fedn. of Am. Socs. for Exptl. Biology, Internat. Assn. Geographic Pathology, Internat. Assn. Med. History (Am. sect.), Internat. Assn. Med. Museums (ex-pres. Am.-Canadian sect.), Am. Cancer Soc. (mem. edn. com. 1946-47), Sociedad Argentina de Argentina de Anatomia Normal y Patologica, Mich. Pathological Soc. (ex-pres.), U. Mich. Research Club (ex-pres.), Soc. Experimental Biology and Medicine, American Soc. for Exptl. Pathology (ex-pres.), Galens, Alpha Omega Alpha, Sigma Xi (Mich. ex-pres.), Phi Sigma, Gamma Alpha, Nu Sigma Nu. Author: (with A. S. Warthin) Medical Aspects of Mustard Gas Poisoning, 1919; Hemolymph Node Chapter in Handbook of Hematology, 1938. Editor: Contributions to Medical Science, 1927; Annals Internal Medicine, 1931-33; Am. Jour. Path., 1941—. Mem. editorial bd. of Physiol. Reviews, 1941-44. Contbr. many articles to med. jours. Home: 1130 Fair Oaks Parkway, Ann Arbor, Mich. Died Dec. 10, 1956.

WELLER, STUART, geologist; b. Maine, Broome County, N.Y., Dec. 26, 1870; s. James and Henrietta (Marean) W.; B.S., Cornell U., 1894; Ph.D., Yale U., 1901; m. Harriet A. Marvin, Sept. 23, 1897; children—James Marvin, Chester Marean, Allen Stuart. Asst. Mo. Geol. Survey, 1890, U.S. Geol. Survey, 1891; mus. asst. in charge palaeontology, 1892-93, asst. in geology, 1893-94, Cornell U.; asst. in palaeontology, and grad. student, Yale, 1894-95; palaeontologist N.J. Geol. Survey, 1899-1907; asst. geologist, 1901-06, geologist, 1906—, U.S. Geol. Survey; geologist Ill. Geol. Survey, 1906—; asst., 1895-97, asso. 1897-1900, instr., 1900-01, asst. prof. palaeontologic geology, 1901-08, asso. prof., 1908-15, prof., 1915—, U. of Chicago; asst. geologist, Geol. Survey of Ky., 1920—. Author of reports and many papers on palaeontol. and geol. subjects. Home: Chicago, Ill. Died Aug. 5, 1927.

WELLINGTON, ARTHUR MELLEN, civil engr., editor; b. Waltham, Mass., Dec. 20, 1847; s. Oliver Hastings and Charlotte (Kent) W.; m. Agnes Bates, 1878. Surveyor Bklyn. Park Dept., circa 1867; joined Buffalo, N.Y. & Phila. R.R., 1870, became prin. asst. engr.; locating engr. Mich. Central R.R., 1873; engr. in charge of Toledo, Can. So. & Detroit R.R.; prin. asst. engr. N.Y., Pa. & Ohio R.R., 1878; engr. in charge of location, surveys Mexican Nat. Ry., 1881-84, later asst. gen. mgr.; part owner, an editor Engring. News, 1887; mem. bd. engrs. Nicaragua Canal, 1890; adviser to Mass. Legislature on street rys. in Boston. Author: Methods for the Computation from Diagrams of Preliminary and Final Estimates of Railway Earthwork, 1874; The Economic Theory of the Location of Railways, 1877. Died May 16, 1895.

WELLINGTON, CHARLES, chemist; b. Limerick, Me., May 4, 1853; s. Horace and Helen Elizabeth (Locke) W.; grad. Mass. Agr. Coll., 1873; student U. of Va., 1876-77, Leipzig, 1882-83, Berlin, 1883 (summer), Paris, 1883 (winter), Göttingen, 1883-85, Ph.D., Göttingen, 1885; m. Grace Martin Huntingdon, July 28, 1887. Asst. chemist U.S. Dept. Agr., 1877-82; prof. chemistry, Mass. Agr. Coll., 1885-1923. Republican. Contbr. various articles in reports, bulls. and jours., chiefly on chem. subjects. Home: Amherst, Mass. Died Nov. 15, 1926.

WELLMAN, CREIGHTON, physician; b. near Kansas City, Mo., Jan. 3, 1873; s. Wheeler Montgomery and Nellie Jane (Blake) W.; Central High Sch., Kansas City; M.D., Med. Dept., U. of Kan., Kansas City, 1894; clin. study Rush and Cook County hosps., Chicago; natural science and social science, Chicago; clin. pathology, London (Eng.) hosps.; tropical medicine and hygiene, London Sch. of Tropical Medicine, diploma, 1904; Charite and Nat. Mus., Berlin; British Mus.; Smithsonian Instn.; m. Kathryn Edna Willis, of Buffalo, N.Y., July 20, 1908. Interne City Hosp., Kansas City, 1894-5; practiced Bihe Dist., later Bailundo Dist., Portuguese West Africa, with several periods of study in Europe, 1898-1907; scientific exploration line of Lobito-Katanga Ry., 1907; prof. tropical medicine Oakland (Cal.) Coll. of Medicine, 1909-11; instr. summer sch. U. of Cal., 1911; prof. tropical medicine, hygiene and preventive medicine, head of dept. and dir. labs., 1911-12, dean Sch. of Hygiene and Tropical Medicine, 1913-15, Tulane U. Editor Am. Jouranl of Tropical Diseases and Preventive Medicine, 1913-15. Democrat. Fellow and Am. sec. Soc. Tropical Medicine and Hygiene, London; fellow Entomol. Soc., London; mem. Societe de Medicine et d'Hygiene Tropicales de Paris, Am. Soc. Tropical Medicine (v.-p.), Am. Climatol. Assn., Am. Micros. Soc. (pres.), Washington Helminthological Soc., Societe Entomologique de France, Societe Entomologique de Belgique, Deutsches Entomologisches Gesellschaft, Schweizes Entomologisches Gesellschaft, Societas Entomologica Zurich, Pacific Coast Entomol. Soc., Acad. Natural Sciences, Phila., New Orleans Acad. Sciences (curator), etc.; mem. permanent com. for Internat. Entomol. Congresses. Mem. Nu Sigma Nu and Stars and Bars Senior Med. Scholarship Soc., Tulane (pres.). Club: Boston. Wrote one vol. on insects, in series, "Fauna of British India," 1912; contbr. to Forcheimer's Therapeusis of Internal Diseases, 1913. Has published over 150 papers in English, Latin, German, French and Portuguese on scientific and med. subjects. Home: 2231 Prytania St., New Orleans LA

WELLMAN, SAMUEL THOMAS, engr.; b. Wareham, Mass., Feb. 5, 1847; s. Samuel Knowlton and Mary Love (Bessee) W.; ed. pub. schs., Nashua, N.H., and 1 yr. Norwich (Vt.) U., C.E., 1904; m. Julia Almina Ballard, Sept. 3, 1868. Chief engr. and supt. Otis Iron & Steel Co., Cleveland, 1873-89; pres. Wellman Steel Co., 1890-95, Wellman, Seaver Engring Co., 1896, then of Wellman, Seaver, Morgan Co., becoming chmn. Corpl. Co. F, 1st N.H. Heavy Arty., 1864-65. Pres. Am. Soc. Mech. Engrs. Congregationalist. Republican. Home: Cleveland, O. Died July 11, 1919.

WELLS, BULKELEY, mining engr.; b. Chicago, Ill., Mar. 10, 1872; s. Samuel Edgar and Mary Agnes (Bulkeley) W.; A.B., Harvard, 1894; m. Grace Daniels Livermore, Oct. 16, 1895; m. 2d, Mrs. Virginia Schmidt, Jan. 19, 1923. In machine shops of Amoskeag Mfg. Co., Manchester, N.H., 1894-95; with B.&A. R.R., 1895-96; mining business, 1896—. Identified with Smuggler Union Mining Co. and various other mining corps., Colo. Served as officer Colo. N.G. many yrs., retiring, 1917, with rank of brig. gen.; with Mil. Intelligence Sect., War Dept., Washington, World War I. Mason, Elk. Died May 1931.

WELLS, CHARLES EDWIN, engr.; b. N. Adams, Mass., Apr. 27, 1858; s. Daniel M. and Mary M. (Sly) W.; B.S., Worcester Poly. Inst., 1880; m. Katherine Belden, Feb. 19, 1891; children—Katherine Zeruah (Mrs. Leon R. Whipple), Marcus Belden (dec.), Sarah Frances, Margaret Adams. Asst. engr. Troy & Greenfield R.R. and Hoosac Tunnel, Mass., 1880-85, C.,B.&N. R.R., 1886; div. engr. Chicago, Santa Fé & Calif., R.R., 1887-88; locating engr. Sault Ste. Marie & Southwestern Ry., 1888; asst. engr. C.&N.W. Ry., 1889-90; engr. and supt. constrn. MacArthur Bros. Co., Chicago, 1891-93; pvt. practice, Davenport, Ia., 1894; supt. water works, Galesburg, Ill., Apr.-Aug. 1895; div. engr. Met. Water and Sewerage Bd. of Mass., 1895-1903; engr. reservoir dept., same, 1903-04; supervising engr. U.S. Reclamation Service for Southern Wyo., Neb. and S.D., 1905-07; div. engr. Bd. Water Supply City of N.Y., 1907-17. Resident engr. constrn. of U.S. Embarkation Camp, Merritt, N.J., 1917; supervising plant engr. U.S. Shipping Bd., constrn. of concrete shipyard plant, San Diego, Calif., 1918-19; cons. engr., 1919—. Home: North Adams, Mass. Died Aug. 4, 1940.

WELLS, CHARLES RAYMOND, dentist; b. Phila., Oct. 30, 1895; s. Dwight Sidney and Lillian Ida (Myers) W.; D.D.S., Northwestern U., 1918; D.Sc., Georgetown U., 1943; m. Clara Lillian Horn, Aug. 9, 1919; children—Steacy Raymond, Catherine Lillian (Mrs. John Mitchell Hoskiewicz). Pvt. practice dentistry, Bklyn., 1925—. Lt. on active duty with USN, 1918-25; entered at lt. comdr. Dental Corps, USNR, 1934; called to active duty as chief dental officer, also asst. chief med. div., Nat. Hdqrs. SSS, Washington, 1941; promoted comdr., 1942, capt., 1943, sr. dental officer; Naval Sta., Bklyn., and U.S. Naval Hosp., St. Albans, 1945; promoted to rear adm. USNR, 1954, ret. 1956; cons. Bur. Medicine and Surgery of Navy, 1955-57; impartial specialist Workmen's Compensation Bd. N.Y. State, 1956—; mem. dental adv. com. Dept. Welfare, N.Y.C., 1963—. Mem. Task Force, Med. Adv. Bd., Sec. Def., 1949-50. Dir. oral surg. Queens Gen. Hosp., Horace Harding Hosp., N.Y., now cons. dentistry Decorated Victory (World War I), Am. Def., Naval Res., Am. Theater, World War II, Selective Service, Legion of Merit medals. Recipient award of merit, Northwestern U., 1934, Pierre Fauchard medal, Pierre Fauchard Acad. (dental), 1943, Jarvie Fellowship award, medal, Dental Soc. N.Y., 1955. Diplomate N.Y. Bd. Oral Surgery. Fellow L.I. Acad. Odontology (ed. 1953), N.Y. Acad. Dentistry, Internat. Coll. Dentists (pres. 1941), Am. Coll. Dentists; mem. Am. Arbitration Assns. (nat. panel arbitrators), 2d Dist. (N.Y.), N.Y., Bklyn., Vt. state (hon.), Detroit (hon.), Costa Rica (hon.) State dental socs., Am. Dental Assn. (pres. 1944), S.R., Psi Omega, Am. Legion, Navy League; hon. mem. Omicron Kappa Upsilon. Methodist. Mason. Contbr. articles to profl. publs. Home: 86-56 Clio St., Hollis, N.Y. Office: 1 DeKalb Av., Bklyn. Died Dec. 9, 1966.

WELLS, GEORGE MILLER, cons. engr.; b. New Brunswick, Can., July 4, 1879; s. Asael James and Apphia (Moore) W.; student U. of Wash., 1893-96, Mich. Coll. of Mines, 1901, non-resident extension course, U. of Chicago, 1902-03; m. Elizabeth Gibson Bradley, July 7, 1909; children—George Calhoun, Thomas Moore. Jr. civil engr., sea coast defenses, U.S. Engr. Corps, 1902-04; asst. engr. in charge surveys, Panama Canal, Atlantic Coast to continental divide, 1904-06, office engr. in charge Atlantic div. designs, 1908-13, resident engr. in charge municipal division and bldg. div., 1913-16; partner Geo. W. Goethals Co., cons. engrs., 1916-23; pres. Solvay Process Co., Semet Solvay Co., Atmospheric Nitrogen Co., Brunner-Mond Co. of Can.; vice pres. Allied Chem. and Dye Corp., 1923-32; pres. Union Sulphur Co., 1932-45; in private practice, 1945—; dir. and mem. exec. com. Va. Carolina Chem. Corp., Congoleum Nairn Corp.; dir. Daystrom, Inc., Heyden Chem. Corp. Mem. Am. Soc. C.E. Rep. Episcopalian. Clubs: Recess, Union League (New York); Upper Montclair (N.J.) Country. Home: 152 Clarewill Av., Upper Montclair, N.J. Office: 67 Wall St., N.Y.C. Died May 3, 1957; buried Newton, Mass.

WELLS, (GRANT) CARVETH, explorer, author, lecturer; b. Barnes, Surrey, Eng., Jan. 21, 1887; s. Thomas Grant Wells, of Bermuda, and Anna Carkeet, of Cornwall; Civil and Mech. Engineer, London U., 1909; m. 2d, Zetta Robart, Mar. 7, 1932; 1 dau., Francis Virginia. Engineer on the original survey of Grand Trunk Pacific Railway, Canada; later assistant professor civil engineering, London Univ.; sent to Malay Peninsula by British Govt. and lived in the jungle for 6 yrs. surveying route for East Coast Ry., and making study of flora, fauna and people of the peninsula; came to U.S., 1918, taking out naturalization papers; made expdn. to Arctic Lapland for Swedish Govt. and Am. Museum Natural History; traveled in Morocco, Syria, Palestine, Egypt, China, Japan, Manchukuo, India; Chicago del. to Centenary of Royal Geog. Soc., London; leader of Massee expdn. to Mountains of the Moon (Ruwenzori) for Chicago Geog. Soc.; leader of Milwaukee Museum expdn. to Kenya and Tanganyika, and of Massee expdn. to Caribbean Sea; leader Chicago Geog. Soc. Expdn. to Russia Caucasus Mts. and Mt. Ararat, 1932, expdn. to Panama and Mexico, 1935; expdn. to Hokkaido, Japan, study of Hairy Ainus; also returned to Malay Jungle, auspices Nat. Geog. Soc., Chicago Geog. Soc., Nat. Travel Club, 1939; expedition to Kashmir, Pakistan and India, 1950. Has lectured widely in the U.S., Great Britain, Norway and Sweden; civilian orientation lecturer to soldiers about to go abroad, U.S. War Dept., 1942 and 1943. Pioneer radio television broadcaster; producer of motion pictures, "Hell Below Zero," "Cockeyed Animal World," "Russia Today," "Lapland." Fellow American Geog. Soc., Royal Geog. Soc.; asso. mem. Instn. Civ. Engrs. (Eng.); elected patron Chicago Geog. Soc., 1930. Mem. Ch. of England. Clubs: Ends of the Earth, Explorers, Nat. Arts, Circumnavigators, Authors, Adventurers, Faculty Club of Columbia U., Dutch Treat (New York); Old Pauline, British Commonwealth. Royal Socs. Club (London); Penang (Straits Settlements); Mandalay (Southampton, Bermuda); Explorers (N.Y.). Author: Field Engrs. Handbook, 1913; Six Years in the Malay Jungle, 1925; A Jungleman and His Animals, 1925; Let's Do the Mediterranean, 1928; In Coldest Africa, 1929; Adventure, 1931; Kapoot, 1933; Exploring the World, 1934; Bermuda in Three Colors, 1935; Pana-mexico, 1937; Around the World with Bobby and Betty, 1939; North of Singapore, 1940; Raff, The Jungle Bird, 1941; Introducing Africa, 1943; Raffles The Bird Who Thinks He's A Person, 1945. Home: "Mandalay," Southampton, Bermuda. Address: Explorers Club, N.Y. City; also "Mandalay," Southhampton, Bermuda. Died Feb., 1957.

WELLS, H(ARRY) EDWARD, chemist; b. Hudson Falls, N.Y., Jan. 4, 1874; s. Thomas E. and Charlotte A. (Cornell) W.; B.S., Middlebury Coll., 1894, A.M., 1895; Ph.D., U. of Leipzig, 1897; m. Violet Harper, Apr. 2, 1910; children—Harry Edward, Durbin Harper, McDonald Harper. Food investigation, with W. O. Atwater, 1898-1900; instr. chemistry, Wesleyan U., Conn., 1899-1901; asso. prof. and prof. chemistry, Allegheny Coll., 1902-07; prof. chemistry, Washington and Jefferson Coll., 1907-18; instr. chemistry, Harvard, 1919-20; also atomic weight research; prof. chemistry, Smith Coll., since 1920; chemist Pratt & Whitney Div., United Aircraft, 1942-45. Captain C.W.S., 1918. Fellow A.A.A.S.; mem. Am. Chem. Soc., Delta Kappa Epsilon. Republican. Congregationalist. Home: 58 Paradise Road, Northampton, Mass. Died May 24, 1947; buried Sleepy Hollow Cemetery, Tarrytown, N.Y.

WELLS, H(ARRY) GIDEON, pathologist; b. New Haven, Conn., July 21, 1875; s. Romanta and Emma Townsend (Tuttle) W.; Ph.B., Sheffield Scientific Sch. (Yale), 1895; A.M., Lake Forest (Ill.) U., 1897; M.D. Rush Med. Coll., Chicago, 1898; Ph.D., U. of Chicago, 1903; interne Cook County Hosp., 1898-99; studied in Berlin, 1904-05; A.M., Yale, 1912; m. Bertha Robbins, Apr. 2, 1902. Asso. in pathology, U. of Chicago, 1901-02, instr., 1903-04, asst. prof., 1904-09, asso. prof., 1909-13, prof. since 1913, professor emeritus since 1940, dean in medical work, 1904-14; director of medical research, Otho S. A. Sprague Memorial Institute, Chicago, since 1911. Member American Red Cross Commission to Rumania, 1917-19; commissioned lt. col. Mem. Assn. American Physicians, Cancer Research Soc., A.M.A., Chicago Pathol. Soc., Am. Assn. Pathologists and Bacteriologists, A.A.A.S., Soc. Biol. Chemistry, Nat. Acad. Sciences, 1925. Author: Chemical Pathology, 1907; Chemistry of Tuberculosis, 1923; Chemical Aspects of Immunity, 1925, 29. Contbr. numerous articles to med. and biol. jours. Address: University of Chicago, Chicago, Ill. Died Apr. 26, 1943.

WELLS, HORACE, dentist, anesthetist; b. Hartford, Vt., Jan. 21, 1815; s. Horace and Betsy (Heath) W.; m. Elizabeth Wales, July 4, 1838, 1 child. Opened dentistry office, Hartford, Conn., 1836; became interested in narcotic effects of nitrous oxide inhalation, circa 1840; suggested its use as means of deadening pain in tooth extraction; had tooth extracted without pain, 1844; claimed to have used ether in extractions, and believed it might be used in major operations (also wrongly believed nitrous oxide superior to ether); 1st printed statement of his claims to discovery of anesthesia appeared in Hartford Courant, 1846, taught dentistry to William T.G. Morton. Author: An Essay on Teeth; Comprising a Brief Description of Their Formation, Diseases and Proper Treatment, 1838; A History of the Discovery of the Application of Nitrous Oxide Gas, Ether, and Other Vapors, to Surgical Operations, 1847. Committed suicide largely because of discouragements in profl. life, Jan. 24, 1848.

WELLS, HORACE LEMUEL, chemist; b. New Britain, Conn., Oct. 5, 1855; s. Levi Sedgwick and Harriet (Francis) W.; Ph.B., Sheffield Scientific Sch. (Yale), 1877, A.M., 1896; Sc.D., U. of Pa., 1906; m. Sarah Lord Griffin, Oct. 7, 1896. Asst. prof. chemistry, 1888-93., prof. analyt. chemistry and metallurgy, 1893-1923, emeritus, 1923, Yale. Original investigations in inorganic chemistry. Mem. Nat. Acad. Sciences, Am. Chem. Soc. Author: Laboratory Guide in Qualitative Analysis; Studied from the Chemical Laboratory of the Sheffield Scientific School, 1901; Chemical Calculations, 1903; Text-book of Chemical Arithmetic, 1905. Translator: Fresenius' Qualitative Analysis. Home: New Haven, Conn. Died Dec. 19, 1924.

WELLS, JAMES SIMPSON CHESTER, engr.; b. Brooklyn, Sept. 13, 1851; s. James S. and Elizabeth (Walker) W.; Ph.B., Sch. of Mines (Columbia), 1875, Ph.D., 1877; m. Alice Jacobson, Feb. 1, 1883; 1 dau., Mrs. Josephine Greene. Instr. analytical chemistry, 1875-1905, adj. prof., 1905-09, Columbia; on leave of absence in the West, 1905-07, engaged in metall. work; resigned July 1, 1909, to devote entire time to mining and metall. engring. Author: Inorganic Qualitative Analysis. Contbr. on analytical and metall. chemistry to chem. and engring. jours. Joined Canadian Expeditionary Force, 1915, as capt. engrs.; transferred to field arty., 1916, and for a year in active service at the front in France, and in reserve in Eng. until 1918. Home: Dobbs Ferry, N.Y. Died Oct. 29, 1931.

WELLS, ROGER CLARK, chemist; b. Peterboro, N.Y., Oct. 24, 1877; s. Byron Wells and Lucy (Clark) W.; A.B., Harvard, 1901, Ph.D., 1904; m. Etta May Card, Feb. 24, 1914; children—Arthur Byron, Roger Clark. Asst. in chemistry, Harvard, 1902-04, working on atomic weights of sodium and chlorine with T. W. Richards, also instructor, 1904-05; instructor physical chemistry, Univ. of Pennsylvania, 1905-07; research chemist, Gen. Electric Co., 1907-08; physical chemist, U.S. Geol. Survey, 1908-30, mineral resource specialist on sodium compounds, 1917-20, chief chemist since 1930. Examined potash deposits in Chile, 1916; del. 1st Pan-Pacific Scientific Congress, Honolulu, 1920. Mem. Chem. Soc. of Washington (pres. 1921), Am. Chem. Soc., Washington Acad. Sciences, Geol. Soc. Washington (pres. 1937), Am. Inst. Mining and Metal. Engrs., Am. Geophys. Union, Sigma Xi, Phi Delta Theta; fellow Am. Mineral Soc., A.A.A.S., Geol. Soc. America. Clubs: Cosmos, Harvard. Author: Electric Activity in Ore Deposits, Analyses of Rock and Minerals (U.S. Geol. Survey); Determination of the Common and Rare Alkalis in Mineral Analysis (with R. E. Stevens); over 100 other govt. publs. and scientific papers. Home: 5607 Chevy Chase Parkway. Office: Geological Survey, Washington, D.C. Died Apr. 19, 1944.

WELLS, SAMUEL ROBERTS, phrenologist; b. West Hartford, Conn., Apr. 4, 1820; s. Russell Wells; studied phrenology under Lorenzo and Orson Fowler; m. Charlotte Fowler, Oct. 13, 1844. Mem. publishing firm O.S. & L.N. Fowler (became Fowler & Wells 1844), sole propr., circa 1846; advocate of physiognomy as means of reading and guiding human character; taught utility of shorthand; advocated improved agrl. methods including proper soil cultivation, crop rotation, irrigation, draining, subsoiling, proper fencing and selection of implements; a founder (with his wife) inst. of phrenology, managed famous phrenological cabinet, N.Y.C., 1850-62. Died N.Y.C., Apr. 13, 1875.

WELLS, THEODORE D(ONALD), naval architect; b. Hudson Falls, N.Y., Oct. 22, 1875; s. Thomas E. and Charlotte A. (Cornell) W.; B.S., Middlebury (Vt.) Coll., 1898; post-grad. work, U. of Glasgow (Scotland), 1902; m. Anna Miner Fletcher, Oct. 9, 1901; children—Fletcher, Theodora Fletcher. Began as mem. firm Herreshoff & Wells, N.Y. City, 1902; mem. firm Wintringham & Wells, 1903-07, alone, 1907-17 and since 1919; mgr. Tebo Yacht Basin Co., 1913-16. Mem. Constrn. Corps, U.S.A., 1917-19. Mem. Soc. Naval Architects and Marine Engrs., Inst. Naval Architects (London), Am. Legion, Delta Kappa Epsilon. Republican. Episcopalian. Mason. Club: Whitehall. Designer of many pvt. yachts, etc. Home: 33 St. Austin's Pl., W. New Brighton, SI NY*

WELLS, WILLIAM CHARLES, physician; b. Charleston, S.C., May 24, 1757; s. Robert and Mary Wells; M.D., U. Edinburgh, 1780; never married. Fled to Eng. at outbreak of Am. Revolution; surgeon with Scotting regt. in mercenary service with Dutch in Europe, 1779; returned to Am., 1781; returned to Eng., 1784, practiced medicine, London, 1794-1817; licentiate Royal Coll. of Physicians, 1788; mem. Royal Soc., 1793; a pioneer in recognizing principle of natural selection; claimed to have been 1st to experiment with use of belladonna for the eyes; wrote essay on single vision with two eyes, also essay on nature and quality of dew. Died London, Sept. 18, 1817; buried parish ch. St. Brides', London.

WELSH, ASHTON LEROY, physician; b. N. Bend. O., July 27, 1906; s. Carl and Belle (Zapf) W.; B.S., U. Cin., 1928, M.D., 1930; M.S., U. Minn., 1946; m. Evelyn Cogswell, May 2, 1955. Fellow sect. dermatology and syphilology Mayo Clinic, Rochester, Minn., 1931-34, 1st asst. dept., 1934-36; pvt. practice specializing in dermatology, Cin., 1936—; sr. staff dept. dermatology Christ Hosp., 1940—; co-dir. Bethesda Hosp., 1942—; cons. dermatologist Children's Hosp.; attending dermatologist, clinician dept. dermatology out-patient dispensary, also attending dermatologist dermatol. service and clinician, Cin. Gen. Hosp.; asso. attending staff Good Samaritan Hosp., Jewish Hosp.; dir. Benet Lab. Topical Research, Cin., 1948—; cons. Hill Top Research Inst., Miamiville, O., 1951—; faculty U. Cin. Coll. Medicine, 1936—, asst. prof. dermatology, 1947-62, associate clinical professor dermatology, 1962—. Part owner Carlson Assos., Buckeye Music Co., Sunfran Music Co., Harry Bare Music Co. Mem. Am. Acad. Dermatology and Syphilology (past bd. dirs.), Am. Dermatol. Assn., Central States, Cin., Minn. (hon.), Swedish (corr.), Noah Worcester (trustee 1960-61, pres. 1961-62), dermatol. socs., Soc. Investigative Dermatology, A.M.A., N. Central Clin. Soc., Acad. Medicine Cin., Ohio Med. Soc., Soc. Dermatology Mexico (asso.), Alumni Found. Mayo Found., Hist. and Philos. Soc. Ohio, N.Y. Acad. Sci., Internat. Soc. Tropical Dermatology, Sigma Xi, Alpha Kappa Kappa (trustee alumnae assn. 1945—), Alpha Omega Alpha. Clubs: Cincinnati, Queen City (Cin.); Hermitage (Newtown, O.); University (Chgo.). Author: Dermatological Formulary: A Guide for Medical Students and Resident Physicians in Dermatology, 1st edit., 1951, 2d edit., 1952; Differential Diagnosis of Leukoplakia, Leokokeratosis and Cancer in the Mouth, 1955; The Dermatologists Handbook, 1957; Psychotherapeutic Drugs, 1958; The Fixed Eruption—A Possible Hazard of Modern Drug Therapy, 1961; Side Effects of Anti-Obesity Drugs, 1961; also numerous articles med. jours. Home: Netherland Hilton Hotel, Cin. 2. Office: Carew Tower, Cin. 2. Died Aug. 25, 1963; buried Maple Grove Cemetery, Cleves, O.

WELSH, LILIAN, M.D.; b. Columbia, Pa., Mar. 6, 1858; d. Thomas and Nancy Eunice (Young) W.; grad. Millersville (Pa.) State Normal Sch., 1875; M.D. Woman's Med. Coll. of Pa., 1889; U. of Zurich, 1889-90; LL.D., Goucher, 1924. Began teaching in pub.

schs., Pa., 1875; in practice of medicine at Baltimore, 1891—; prof. physiology and hygiene, Goucher Coll., 1894-1924, prof. emeritus, physiology and hygiene since 1924; mem. A.M.A., Med. and Chirurg. Faculty of Md., A.A.A.S., Assn. for Promoting Scientific Research by Women, Baltimore Assn. for Promotion Univ. Edn. of Women, Am. Assn. University Profs., etc. Clubs: College, City. Home: The Charles, Baltimore, Md.

WELTE, CARL MICHAEL, mfr., inventor, musician; b. Norwich Town, Conn., Aug. 8, 1872; s. Emil and Emma M. (Foerstner) W.; student various pianists, 1886-90, City Coll. N.Y., 1888-92, Packard Bus. Sch., 1893-94; m. Annie Morgan, Nov. 12, 1903. Joined grandfather's firm M. Wolte & Sons (mfrs. mus. instruments), 1894, mem. firm, 1901-32. Trustee estate of Phillipina Young, Emma M. Welte, Annie E. Morgan, Empire Tin Mining Co. of Nome, Alaska. Inventor pneumatic valve action, 1900, driving control, 1917, control mechanically, 1918, playing control mus. instruments, 1919. Democrat. Lutheran. Mason. Home: 34 E. Town St., Norwich Town, Conn. Died Mar. 25, 1955.

WELTMER, SIDNEY ABRAM, mental scientist; b. Wooster, O., July 7, 1858; s. Abraham and Catharine (Hull) W.; removed to Mo. at 7 yrs. of age; principally self-ed.; studied medicine 4 yrs. under Dr. J. W. Brent, of Tipton, Mo.; m. Mary Genoa Stone, Oct. 8, 1879. Licensed to preach in Bapt. Ch. at 19 but soon gave up ministry; taught sch. in Mo. until 1896; founded, and pres., Akinsville (Mo.) Normal Sch., 1885-89; organized Sedalia Pub. Library, and librarian, 1893-95; made extensive experiments in hypnotic phenomena, leading to study of suggestion in cure of disease; founded Weltmer Inst., Nevada, Mo., 1896, which became Weltmer Inst. of Suggestive Therapeutics Co. (Inc.), of which pres.; pres. (life) Weltmer Foundation. Mason, Elk, Odd Fellow. Author: Regeneration, 1898; Self Protection, 1898; Real Man, 1901; New Voice of Christianity, 1902; Hypnotism, 1908; Therapeutic Suggestion, 1908; also Suggestion Simplified; Intuition; Is Prayer Ever Answered? Who Is a Christian? Eternal Now; The Undying Character of Thought; Mystery Revealed; Self-Reliance; Telepathy; Complete Clinical Texts on Suggestive Therapeutics and Applied Psychology, 1908; Day Dreams, 1916; The Healing Hand, 1918; etc. Home: Nevada, Mo. Died Dec. 5, 1930.

WENDELL, GEORGE VINCENT, prof. physics; b. Plainfield, N.J., Aug. 16, 1871; s. George W. and Mary E. (Frazee) W.; S.B., Mass. Inst. Tech., 1892; A.M., and Ph.D., U. of Leipzig, 1898; U. of Berlin, 1898-99; m. Mary P. Hitchcock, July 29, 1902. Asst. in physics, 1892-93, instr., 1893-1901, asst. prof., 1901-04, asso. prof., 1904-07, Mass. Inst. Tech.; prof. physics and head of dept., Stevens Inst. Tech., 1907-10; prof. physics, Columbia, July 1, 1910—. Established dept. of physics, Simmons Coll., Boston, 1902, and at Boston U., 1906. Home: New York, N.Y. Died Mar. 15, 1922.

WENDELL, OLIVER CLINTON, astronomer; b. Dover, N.H., May 7, 1845; s. Oliver Ellsworth and Vienna (Willey) W.; grad. Dover High Sch., 1862, Franklin Acad., 1864; A.B., Bates Coll., 1868, A.M., 1871, D.Sc., 1907; m. Sarah Butler, July 11, 1870. Asst. in Harvard Obs., 1868-69; civ. and hydraulic engr., 1869-79; asst. in Harvard Obs., 1879-98, asst. prof., 1898—. Fellow Am. Acad. Arts and Sciences, A.A.A.S. Republican. Author of observations and reductions in various vols. Obs. Annals; also calculator of many orbits and ephemerides, and writer of papers of scientific, prose and poetic character. Home: Cambridge, Mass. Died Nov. 6, 1912.

WENDT, EDWIN FREDERICK, (went), consulting engr.; b. New Brighton (Pittsburgh), Pa., May 12, 1869; s. Christian Ihmsen (M.D) and Agnes (Scott) W.; g.g.s. Frederick Wendt, glass mfr. Pittsburgh, 1800, and of David Scott, q.m. Army of Gen. Anthony Wayne, 1792; A.B. Geneva (Pa.) Coll. (valedictorian), 1888, D.Sc., 1913. Began engring. work on Pittsburgh & Lake Erie R.R. (N.Y. Central Lines), 1888, successively rodman, transitman, inspector, locating engr. and resident engr.; asst. (chief) engr. in charge of engring. parties, maintenance of way, constrn. and contract work, 1898-1913 (road reconstructed during his service, developed from single track to 4-track road); engr. in charge constrn. Lake Erie & Eastern R.R. (Youngstown, O.), 1911-13; mem. N.Y. Central Lines Engring. Com., 1907-13; mem. Govt. Commn. which inspected Alaska R.R. (500 mi.) under constrn., 1917, and the coal deposits available for development; mem. engring. bd., Interstate Commerce Commn., 1913-21; also chief engr. in charge Eastern dist., Bur. of Valuation, investigated 600 R.R.s and prepared estimate of cost values and depreciation; cons. engr. since 1921; in general practice particularly the valuation, appraisal and cost analysis of railroads and public utilities. Admitted to practice before Interstate Commerce Commn., 1929. Mem. bd. trustees Geneva Coll. (10 yrs.), Beaver Falls, Pa. Charter mem. Am. Ry. Engring. Assn. (pres. 1913-14; member committee accounts, signals and waterways). Member American Society C.E. (chairman executive committee engineering economics division, 1935. 36, 37; mem. com. on valuation procedure), Am. Inst. Cons. Engrs. (pres. 1936-37), Engrs. Soc. of Western Pa., Washington Soc. of Engrs. (pres. 1918), A.A.A.S., Signal Sect. of A.A.R., Ry. Club of Pittsburgh, Am. Economic Assn., Washington Acad. Sciences, Historical Soc. of Western Pa. United Presbyterian. Clubs: Cosmos (Washington); University (Pittsburgh). Author numerous reports and articles on engring., transportation, depreciation and valuation. Home: 5860 Solway St., Pittsburgh 17, Pa. and 1470 3rd Av., New Brighton, Pa. Office: Union Trust Bldg., Pitts. Died Sept. 30, 1952.

WENIGER, WILLIBALD, physicist, coll. prof.; born Milwaukee, Wis., June 20, 1884; s. Heinrich Wilhelm and Carolina (Taubert) W.; A.B., U. of Wis., 1905, A.M., 1906, Ph.D., 1908; m. Myrtle Elizabeth Knepper, May 13, 1918 (died April 23, 1950); 1 son, George Edward. Teacher of algebra and physics, Wis. Acad., Madison, Wis., 1903-05; computer Washburn Obs., Madison, 1904-06; asst. and fellow in physics, Univ. of Wis., 1906-08; head dept. physics, Ore. State Coll., 1908-14, and 1920-49, asst. dean, Grad. Sch., 1933-47, dean, 1947-49; prof. physics, University of Alaska, College, Alaska, 1951-55; head of the department of physics and elec. engineering, 1952-55; acting dir. agr., engring., forestry, Idaho State College, 2d semester 1956-57; physicist, Nela Research Lab. Gen. Elec. Co., East Cleveland, O., 1914-20. Fellow Am. Phys. Soc., A.A.A.S.; mem. Optical Soc. of Am., Illuminating Engring. Soc., Am. Assn. Physics Teachers, Ore. Acad. Sci., Phi Beta Kappa, Sigma Xi, Phi Kappa Phi, Sigma Pi Sigma. Republican. Episcopalian. Mason (Shriner). Author: Fundamentals of Physics, 1940. Contbr. articles to physics jours. Address: 1010 N. 29 St., Corvallis, Ore. Died Mar. 13, 1959; buried Masonic Cemetery, Corvallis, Ore.

WENNER, FRANK, (wen'er), physicist; b. Garrison, Ia., Jan. 18, 1873; s. Christian and Margaret (Cokely) W.; B.S., Knox Coll., Galesbury, Ill., 1899, Sc.D., 1942; student U. Wis., 1900-02; Ph.D., U. Pa., 1909; m. Lottie Louisa Ward, Jan. 1, 1903. Instr. physics, Ia. State Coll., 1902-05, U. of Pa., 1905-07; with Nat. Bureau of Standards, 1907-43, 51-54; cons. physicist Carnegie Inst. of Washington, 1943-46, and of Rubicon Co., Phila., 1943-51. Mem. panel of com. on Geophysics. Research and Development Bd., National Mil. Establishment, 1947-48. Fellow Am. Inst. E.E., Am. Phys. Soc., Washington (pres. 1937), Am. Geophysical Union, Sigma Xi. Delegate to 4th and 7th General Assembly of the International Geodetic and Geophysical Union; del. 2d Pan-American Science Congress. Mason (32 deg., Shriner). Clubs: Cosmos, Federal. Author of numerous papers on galvanometers and electric resistance measurements; researches on the theory of seismometers having electromagnetic magnification and electromagnetic damping; control for guns on airplane (World War I); the distribution of current in systems of linear electrical conductors; potentiometers; fundamental or absolute measurement of electrical resistance; apparatus for study of ground movements within the destructive area of major earthquakes; land and sea mines, their detection in offensive operations and use in defense operations (World War II). Home: 5614 32d St., Washington. Died Feb. 7, 1954; buried Evergreen Cemetery, Vinton, Ia.

WENRICH, CALVIN NAFTZINGER, physicist; b. Bernville, Pa., Nov. 21, 1873; s. Isaac S. and Emalina (Naftzinger) W.; B.E., Keystone State Normal Sch., Kutztown, Pa., 1896, M.E., 1898; A.B., Franklin and Marshall Coll., 1902, A.M., 1904; Ph.D., U. of Pa., 1910; m. Ivah Patterson, Dec. 21, 1910. Teacher pub. schs., Pa., 3 yrs.; teacher physics and mathematics, Franklin and Marshall Acad., 1900-04, 1906-07; prof. physics, Carthage (Ill.) Coll., 1904-06; instr. physics, U. of Pa., 1907-08, fellow in physics, 1908-10; instr. physics, U. of Pittsburgh, 1910, asst. prof., 1912, prof. and head of dept., 1914-20, research physicist, Armstrong Cork Co., 1920-42; now retired. Trustee Franklin and Marshall Coll. Mem. Am. Phys. Soc., A.A.A.S., Sigma Xi. Republican. Home: Country Club Drive, Battle Creek MI

WENTE, EDWARD CHRISTOPHER, physicist; b. Denver, Ia., Jan. 2, 1889; s. Christian William and Sophia (Biesterfeld) W.; B.A., U. of Mich., 1911; M.A., Lake Forest (Ill.) U., 1912; B.S. in E.E., Mass. Inst. Tech., 1914; Ph.D., Yale, 1918; m. Sophia Mary Brockman, Sept. 17, 1924; children—Edward Frank, Henry Christian. Asst. in physics and mathematics, Lake Forest (Ill.) Coll., 1911-12; with engring. dept. Western Electric Co., New York, 1914-16 and 1918-25; mem. tech. staff, Bell Telephone Labs., 1925-54, ret., acoustical research engr., 1927-33, research physicist 1933-48, research cons., 1949-54. Research optics, acoustics, telephony, recording. Recipient Biennial Gold Medal award, Acoustical Soc. Am., 1959. Fellow Am. Phys. Soc., A.A.A.S., Acoustical Soc. (pres. 1942-43); mem. Soc. of Motion Picture Engrs., Sigma Xi, Gamma Alpha. Awarded Wetherill medal, by Franklin Inst., 1931; 1st recipient of Progress medal, 1935, of Soc. of Motion Picture Engrs., for "outstanding achievement in motion picture technology"; Award of Merit plaque, Acad. Motion Picture Arts and Scis., 1936; Modern Pioneer award, Am. Mfrs. Association, 1940. Lutheran. Inventions: Condenser and moving coil microphones; loud speakers; light valves used in picture transmission and in sound recording for motion pictures; acoustical instruments. Contbr. to scientific jours. Home: Summit NJ Died June 9, 1972; buried Fairview Cemetery Westfield NJ

WENTWORTH, EDWARD NORRIS, livestock historian, specialist; b. Dover, N.H., Jan. 11, 1887; s. Elmer Marston and Elizabeth Tilton (Towne) W.; B.S., in Agr., Ia. State Coll. Agr. and Mechanic Arts, 1907, M.S., 1909; grad. study Cornell U. and Harvard; m. Alma B. McCulla, June 14, 1911; children—Edward Norris (dec.), Raymond Howard (dec.). Asst., asso. prof. animal husbandry, Iowa State Coll. Agr. and Mech. Arts, 1907-13; asso. editor Breeder's Gazette, also prof. zoötechny, Chicago Vet. Coll., 1913-14; prof. animal breeding, Kan. State Agrl. Coll., 1914-17; public relations dept., Armour and Co., Chgo., 1919-20, Bur. of Agrl. Research und Economics, 1920-23; ir. Armour's Livestock Bur., 1923-54, retired 1954; lectr. U. Chgo., 1923-31. Served as capt. F.A., U.S. Army, and mil. dir. Coll. Agr., A.E.F. Univ., Beaune, France, World War I; col., Honorary Reserve; mem. advisory com. to Q.M. General. Mem. Am. Farm Economics Assn., Am. Genetic Assn., Am. Soc. Animal Production, A.A.A.S., Am. Soc. Naturalists, Am. Econ. Assn., Am. Statis. Assn., S.A.R., Soc. of Piscataqua Pioneers, Am. Legion, Mil. Order World Wars (past commander in chief), Miss. Valley Hist. Assn., Reserve Officers' Assn. U.S., Sigma Alpha Epsilon, Alpha Zeta, Alpha Psi, Sigma Delta Chi, Phi Kappa Psi. Decorated Officer du Merite Agricole (French). Republican. Clubs: University, Saddle and Sirloin, Army and Navy Club, Army and Navy (Washington, D.C.); Town and Country Equestrian Assn. (pres.). Author: Portrait Gallery of Saddle and Sirloin Club, 1920; America's Sheep Trails, 1948. Co-author: Progressive Beef Cattle Raising, 1920; Progressive Hog Raising, 1922; Marketing Live Stock and Meats, 1924; Progressive Sheep Raising, 1925; Cattle Breeding, 1925. Co-author with Charles W. Towne, Shepherds' Empire, 1945; Pig's Progress, 1949. Home: R.R. 3, Box 285, Chesterton, Ind. Address: Armour and Co., Chgo. Died Apr. 21, 1959.

WENTWORTH, GEORGE ALBERT, mathematician, author; b. Wakefield, N.H., July 31, 1835; s. Edmund and Eliza (Lang) W.; prep. Phillips Exeter Acad.; grad. Harvard, 1858; m. Emily J. Hatch, Aug. 8, 1864. Prof. mathematics, Phillips Exeter Acad., 1858-91. Author: Wentworth Series of Mathematical Works (about 40 works on arithmetic, algebra, geometry, trigonometry); also (with G. A. Hill) of Wentworth & Hill Series of exercise books in algebra, arithmetic and geometry; also physics. Died 1906.

WERKMAN, CHESTER HAMLIN, (werk'man), bacteriologist; b. Fort Wayne, Ind., June 17, 1893; s. John Carl and Ada Alice (Groves) W.; B.S., Purdue U., 1919; Ph.D., Ia. State College, 1923; D.Sc. (causa honoris), Purdue University 1944; m. Cecile A. Baker, Oct. 11, 1913; 1 son, Robert Theodore. Asst. bacteriologist, U. of Ida., 1920-21; instr. and asst. chief bacteriology sect., Ia. State Coll., 1921-24, asst. prof. bacteriology, 1925-28, associate professor, 1928-33, prof., 1933—, head of department, 1942-57; asst. prof. bacteriology, Mass. State Coll., Amherst, 1924-25. Recipient Pasteur Award, 1951. Mem. Am. Assn. for Advancement of Sci., Soc. Am. Bacteriologists, Am. Chem. Soc., Biochemical Soc. (Gt. Britain), Iowa Academy of Science, National Academy of Sciences, Society for Experimental Biology and Medicine, Am. Soc. Biol. Chemists, American Association of Univ. Professors, Internat. Soc. Microbiology, vice Pres. of Section, 1936-39. Sigma Xi, Kappa Delta Pi, Phi Lambda Upsilon, Phi Kappa Phi, Theta Chi. Mason. Author: (with E. I. Fulmer) Chemical Action of Micro-organisms on Non-Nitrogenous Organic Substrates, 1930; also numerous scientific articles on physiology of bacteria. Asst. editor Enzymologia. Author and editor Bacterial Physiology. Home: 522 Ash Av., Ames, Ia. 50010. Died Sept. 10, 1962; buried Ames, Ia.

WERNWAG, LEWIS, bridge builder, civil engr.; b. Riedlingen, Wurttemberg, Germany, Dec. 4, 1769; children include Lewis, William. Came to Am., 1786; built 29 bridges during career, including bridge across Neshaminy Creek (his 1st bridge), 1810, drawbridge across Frankford Creek, Bridgeburg, Pa., 1811, bridge across Schuylkill River at Upper Ferry, later Fairmount sect. (Coossus of Fairmount, 340 feet span. largest in Am. at time), 1812; built bridge across Delaware River near New Hope, Pa. (6 arch spans of 175 feet, 2 wagon ways, 2 footways), 1813; planned Fairmount waterworks and dam, Phila.; moved to onowingo Md., built bridge over Susquehanna River and sawmill for preparing his timber; built railroad bridge for B. & O. R.R., 1830. Died Harpers Ferry, Va. (now W.Va.), Aug. 12, 1843.

WERTMAN, KENNETH FRANKLIN, educator; b. Pitts., Apr. 25, 1913; s. Thomas and Isabelle (Dunlap) W.; B.S., U. Pitts., 1938, M.S., 1940, Ph.D., 1946; m. Ruth McMoil, July 3, 1938; children—Kenith Louise, James Thomas, Kenneth Franklin. Engaged in virus and rickettsial disease research, diagnostic methods epidemic typhus, murine typhus, Rocky Mountain spotted fever, fievre boutonneuse, 1941-45; research vitamin deficiency, susceptibility to infection U. Pitts., 1946-56, prof. bacteriology, 1951-56; prof. microbiology, head dept. U. Ariz., 1956—. Mem. Ariz.

Bd. Examiners Basic Scis., 1956—. Mem. Tucson Com. Fgn. Relations Bd. dirs. Ariz. Heart Assn. Served to capt., San. Corps, AUS, 1941-45. Diplomate Am. Bd. of Microbiology, Charter fellow Am. Acad. of Microbiology; mem. Am. Soc. Microbiology, Am. Assn. Immunologists, Soc. Exptl. Biology and Medicine, Electron Microscope Soc. Am., Sigma Xi. Author reports. Home: 2233 E. Waverly St., Tucson. Died Mar. 30, 1967; buried East Lawn, Tucson.

WESCOTT, ORVILLE DE WITT, physician; b. Gladbrook, Ia., July 21, 1871; s. Delos Gary and Mary Ruana (Dibble) W.; B.S., Cornell Coll., Ia., 1900; M.D., Rush Med. Coll., Chicago, 1904; m. Sue May Gailey, Alexandria, La., Oct. 8, 1910. Interne Muskoka Cottage Sanatorium for Consumptives, Gravenhurst, Ont., 1904-5; asst. phys., Agnes Memorial Sanatorium, Denver, 1905-9; in pvt. practice, specializing in diseases of chest, throat and nose, 1909—. Sec. Colo. State Assn. for Prevention and Control of Tuberculosis, 1908, dir., 1908-9-10; awarded gold medal for ednl. leaflet at Internat. Congress on Tuberculosis, Washington, D.C., 1908; mem. Nat. Assn. for Study and Prevention of Tuberculosis, A.M.A., Denver Med. Science Club, etc. Mem. Ia. Vol. Inf., Apr.-Nov., 1898, Spanish-Am. War; mem. Colo. N.G., 1910; commd. maj. and regtl. surgeon to 157th Inf., 40th Div., N.G., Camp Kearny, Cal., 1917. Republican. Mason (32 deg., Shriner). Clubs: University, Denver Athletic, Lakewood Country. Home: 2219 Ivy St., Denver CO

WEST, ARTHUR, mechanical engr.; b. Milwaukee, Wis., Mar. 25, 1867; s. Hubbell and Helen (Roberts) W.; M.E., U. of Wis., 1887; m. Alice Florence Tourtellot, Dec. 22, 1900. Engr. Edward P. Allis Co., Milwaukee, 1887-98, asst. to chief engr., 1898-1900; asst. chief engr. Allis-Chalmers Co., Milwaukee, 1900-04, also mgr. pumping engine dept., 1901-04; chief engr. Westinghouse Machine Co., Pittsburgh, 1904-08, v.p., 1906-08; mgr. power dept., Bethlehem Steel Co., 1908-27. Consulting mechanical engineer New York, Board of Water Supply, 1903-08; lecturer Johns Hopkins, Lehigh Univ. and U.S. Naval Academy, 1909-27. Mem. Am. Soc. Mech. Engrs. (v.p. 1905-07), Inventor's Guild (New York), Chi Psi. Republican. Club: Lake Placid (mem. council). Home: Lake Placid Club, Essex County, N.Y. Address: First Nat. Bank and Trust Co., Bethelehem PA

WEST, EDWARD AUGUSTUS, exec. engr.; b. Wiarton, Ont., Can., Nov. 5, 1882 (parents U.S. citizens); s. Henry Gilder and Annie Alice (Masters) W.; student Bromfield-Pearson Engring. Sch., Tufts Coll. 1905-09; Lowell Sch. for Indsl. Foremen, Mass. Inst. of Tech., 1907-09; m. Charlotte Barton, Mar. 1907; children—Barton Gilder, Franklin Griffith, Edward Wilford; m. 2d, Marion Maxwell Kirkland, Apr. 27, 1923. Constr. engr. Portland (Ore.) R.R., Light & Power Co.. 1909-12, efficiency engr., 1912-16; chief engr. Denver Tramway Co., 1916, gen. supt., 1918-25; vice-pres., gen. mgr. and dir. Utah Light & Traction Co., 1925-36; exec. v.p., dir. Fla. Power & Light Co., Miami, 1936-37; v.p. Miami Water Co.; v.p. Miami Beach R.R.; v.p., gen. mgr. Consumers Water Co.; exec. v.p. Denver & Rio Grande Western R.R. Co.; pres. Rio Grande Motorway, Larsen Transport Co.; pres. Salt Lake City Union Depot & R.R. Co., Denver Union Terminal R.R.; dir. Pueblo Union Depot & R.R. Co., Denver Market & Produce Terminal, Denver Nat. Bank. Served as chief petty officer, U.S. Navy, 1901-04, and ensign, U.S. Naval Res., 1912-16. Mem. C. of C., Timpanogas (Salt Lake City), Newcomen Soc., Soc. Military Engrs., Theta Delta Chi, Spanish Am. War Vets. Clubs: Denver, Denver Athletic, Press, Country, Civic (Denver), Country, Alta (Salt Lake City). Contbr. to professional jours. Originator of modern trolley coach and application of the rear engine principle to mass transportation vehicles. Address: 1919 Yalecrest St., Salt Lake City. Died Feb. 22, 1955.

WEST, ERDMAN, educator; b. Glenside, Pa., Jan. 6, 1894; s. Frank and Elizabeth Sargeant (Bell) W.; B.S. in Botany, Pa. State Coll., 1917; M.S., U. Fla., 1931; m. Ruth Lambert, Nov. 18, 1916. Instr. botany Pa. State Coll., 1918; asst. nursery insp. N.J. Dept. Agr., 1918-20, chief nursery insp., 1920-25; asst. in plant pathology Fla. Agrl. Expt. Sta., State Plant Bd. Fla., 1925-27, mycologist, 1927-45, botanist mycologist, 1945—, prof. botany Coll. of Agr., U. Fla., 1946-64. Mem. A.A.A.S., Am. Phytopath. Soc., Torrey Bot. Club, Mycol. Soc. Am., Fla. Acad. Sci., Am. Fern Soc., Fla. State Hort. Soc., Appalachian Bot. Soc., Soil Sci. Soc. Fla., Sigma Xi, Phi Kappa Phi, Phi Sigma. Episcopalian. Author: The Native Trees of Florida (with Lillian E. Arnold), 1946; The Native Shrubs and Woody Vines of Florida (in prep.); also numerous articles on Fla. plants and fungi in various sci. and popular jours. and mags. Home: 220 N.W. 12th Terrace, Gainesville 32601. Office: Florida Agricultural Expt. Sta., Gainesville, Fla. Died Aug. 26, 1965; buried Hillcrest Meml. Park, Gainesville.

WEST, JAMES HARTWELL, hort. cons.; b. Perry, O., Sept. 5, 1897; s. Thomas B. and Emma (Champion) W.; student Ohio State U., 1916-18; m. Theda C. Child, June 15, 1921; 1 dau., Barbara Jean (wife of Dr. Bernard T. Lomas). Owner, mgr. T. B. West & Son Nursery, Perry, O., 1936—; chmn. Peoples Broadcasting Corp.; dir. Peoples Devel. Co., Mut. Income Found., Inc., Peoples Mortgage Co., Approved Finance Co., Am. Nat. Foods, Inc., Nat. Casualty Co., Detroit. Chmn., Lake County chpt. A.R.C., 1949-51; dir. Lake County YMCA, 1930-40. Mem. Lake County Nurserymen's Assn., Lake County Nurserymen's Assn., Lake County Farm Bur., Ohio Farm Bur. Fedn. (trustee 1942-49, v.p. 1945-49), Alpha Gamma Rho. Methodist (dist. lay leader N.E. Ohio Conf. 1952-56). Home: 3650 W. Main St., Perry, O. 44081. Died July 20, 1966.

WESTBROOK, LAWRENCE, research and development engineer, govt. ofcl.; b. Belton, Texas, August, 23, 1889; s. Joel Whittsett and Margaret (Whitington) W.; student U. Tex., 1906-08; m. Martha Wooton, Mar. 22, 1937; children—Joel, Lawrence, Hirma. Dir. Tex. Relief Com., 1933-34; asst. adminstr. Fed. Emergency Relief Assn., 1934; dir. Nat. Rural Rehabilitation Progm., Drought Relief, rural settlements Matanuska, Alaska, Dyess, Ark., Pine Valley, Ga., and others, 1935; asst. adminstr. Work Projects Administrn., 1935-36, chmn. adv. bd., 1937-39, asst. commr., 1940; dir. mutual home ownership div. Fed. Works Agy., 1940-41. Cons. Rheinisch-Westfaeliches Inst. Fuer Wirtschaftforschung of Essen. Asst. chmn. Dem. Nat. Com. 1952. Pres. U.S. Joint Purchasing Bd., S. Pacific area; dir. Mil. Econ. Mission to New Zealand, 1942-43; mem. spl. planning div. Gen. Staff War Dept., 1944-45; mem. U.S. nat. commn. UNESCO, 1961—. Served from lieut. to maj., Signal Corps, U.S. Army, 1917-19; col., Army Services Forces, 1942. Decorated hon. officer mil. br. Order of Brit. Empire, 1946. Mem. Sigma Alpha Epsilon. Episcopalian. Clubs: Army and Navy, Nat. Press (Washington). Home: 1912 Jade Dr., San Angelo, Tex. Died Jan. 24, 1964; buried Ft. Sam Houston Mil. Acad., San Antonio.

WESTERGAARD, HARALD MALCOLM, (wes'ter-gard), prof. civil engring.; b. Copenhagen, Denmark, Oct. 9, 1888; s. Harald Ludvig and Thora Alvilda (Koch) W.; B.S. in C.E., Royal Tech. Coll., Copenhagen, 1911; U. of Gottingen, spring, 1913; Technische Hochschule, Munich, spring 1914, Dr. Ing., 1925; Ph.D., U. Ill., 1916; Dr. Techn., Royal Tech. Coll., 1929; D.Sc., Lehigh, 1930; m. Rachel Talbot, Sept. 15, 1925; children—Mary Talbot, Peter Talbot. Naturalized U.S. citizen 1920. In engineering work, chiefly reinforced concrete design, Copenhagen, Hamburg, London, 1911-14; fellow Am.-Scandinavian Foundation, 1914-15; instr. in theoretical and applied mechanics, U. Ill., 1916-19, asso., 1919-21, asst. prof., 1921-24, asso. prof., 1924-27, prof., 1927-36; Gordon McKay prof. of civil engring., Harvard, 1936—, dean of Grad. Sch. of Engring., Harvard, 1937-46. With U.S. Bur. of Pub. Roads, summers, 1923, 26, 28, 29 and 32, U. of Mich., summers, 1931, 32, 34 and 36; sr. mathematician, U.S. Bur. of Reclamation, on Boulder Dam, 1929-30, cons. engr. on same, 1930-32; cons. structural engr., Bureau of Yards and Docks, Navy Dept., 1935-37; cons. U.S. Army, airfield pavements. Lt. comdr., Civil Engr. Corps., U.S.N.R., 1936-39, comdr., 1939, capt., 1946; on active duty, intermittently, 1942-46; mem. Bureau of Yards and Docks mission to Japan, 1945. Consultant to Panama Canal, 1946-47. Trustee Am. Scandinavian Found., 1938—. Fellow Am. Acad. Arts and Scis.; mem. Am. Soc. M.E., Am. Soc. E.E., Am. Concrete Inst., Am. Soc. Engring. Edn., Danish Instn. Engrs., Dansk Selskab for Bygningstatik, Am. Philos. Soc., Phi Beta Kappa, Tau Beta Pi, Sigma Xi. Awarded Wason medal, Am. Concrete Inst., 1922, J. J. R. Croes medal, Am. Soc. Civil Engrs., 1934. Recipient Thomas Fitch Rowland prize, 1950. Clubs: Harvard Faculty (Cambridge); Harvard (Boston); Harvard (N.Y.); Cosmos (Washington, D.C.). Contbr. papers to tech. jours. and publs. of tech. socs. Home: 33 Pinehurst Road, Belmont 78, Mass. Address: Pierce Hall, Harvard University, Cambridge 38, Mass. Died June 22, 1950; buried Belmont, Mass.

WESTERVELT, WILLIAM YOUNG, mining engr.; b. Jersey City Heights, N.J., July 30, 1872; s. Richard Henry and Mary (Welsh) W.; E.M., Sch. Mines Columbia, 1894; m. Mary Westervelt Young, Sept. 12, 1900 (died 1926); m. 2d, Henrie Whiting Mellwaine, July 27, 1929. Chemist, surveyor, engr. and supt. mines, Ducktown Sulphur, Copper & Iron Co., 1894-98, cons. 1898—, responsible for development of Ducktown Co.'s mines to 1923; cons. engr. Anglo-Am. Copper Co., of London, 1905, and developed the Ray (Ariz.) property to the point of sale to present owners; apptd. consulting engr. Grasseli Chem. Co., of Cleveland, O., 1909, developed and organized its New Market (Tenn.) zinc property, Butte and Superior Mines, Butte, Mont.; apptd. consulting engr. Wilkes-Barre Dredging Co., 1914, organized the gold property of the co. at Folsom, Calif.; prepared report on pyrites resources of the world, 1916; selected, 1917, by Am. Inst. Mining Engrs. and the Mining and Metall. Soc. American mem. War Minerals Com., Washington, D.C., was chmn. of com.; organizer and pres. Copper Pyrites Corp., of Ducktown Mining Dist., Tenn., 1919; in 1927 purchased control of Ducktown Chemical & Iron Co. for Ducktown Pyrites Corp. Head consultant on mining Office of Dep. Dir. Gen., Industry Div., War Production Bd., 1942-44. Author of various articles on mining in tech. journals and of section on Mine Examinations, Valuations, and Reports, in Peele's Mining Engineer's Handbook. Fellow A.A.A.S., Royal Soc. of Arts (London, England); mem. Am. Inst. Mining and Metall. Engrs., Mining and Metall. Soc. America (v.p. 1920-22), Electrochem. Soc., Am. Mining Congress, Holland Soc., others. Clubs: Century, Columbia University (New York); Arts (Washington); Royal Societies (London). Presbyterian. Home: 4103 N. State St. (30). Office: Lamar Life Bldg., Jackson 2, Miss. Died Oct. 8, 1958.

WESTFALL, W(ILHELMUS) D(AVID) A(LLEN), univ. prof., mathematician; b. Montague, N.J., Jan. 27, 1879; s. Wilhelmus and Hanna Jane (Everett) W.; A.B., Yale, 1901; Ph.D., Goettingen U., 1905; m. Frederica Kees, Mar. 24, 1904 (dec. Jan. 22, 1917); 1 dau., Frederica (Mrs. Leon Barkman) m. 2d, Ruth Rollins, Dec. 22, 1921; children—David, Ellen. Instr. U. Mo., 1905-08, asst. prof., 1908-14, asso. prof., 1914-21, prof., 1921—. Home: 11 S. Glenwood, Columbia, Mo. Died Apr. 18, 1951.

WESTGATE, LEWIS GARDNER, geologist; b. Phenix, R.I., Oct. 8, 1868; s. George Lewis and Sarah Elizabeth (Gardner) W.; A.B., Wesleyan U., Conn., 1890; A.B., Harvard University, 1891, A.M., from same, 1892, Ph.D., from same, 1896; Sc.D., Wesleyan University, 1940; m. Martha Josephine Beach, Sept. 5, 1893. Asst. in geology, Harvard, 1891-92, Wesleyan U., 1892-93; teacher of science, Evanston Twp. (Ill.) High Sch., 1893-1900; prof. geology, Ohio Wesleyan U., 1900-39, emeritus since 1939; asst. geologist, U.S. Geol. Survey, 1912-19, asso. geologist, 1919-35. Fellow Geol. Soc. America (v.p. 1926), Mineral Soc. America, Ohio Acad. Science (pres. 1910-11); mem. Psi Upsilon, Omicron Delta Kappa, Phi Beta Kappa, Sigma Xi. Democrat. Methodist. Author of numerous geol. articles. Home: 124 Oak Hill Av., Delaware, O. Died March 30, 1948.

WESTINGHOUSE, GEORGE, inventor, mfr.; b. Central Bridge, N.Y., Oct. 6, 1846; s. George and Emeline (Vedder) W.; removed to Schenectady, 1856; ed. pub. and high schs. and later to sophomore yr. Union Coll.; hon. Ph.D., Union, 1890; Dr. Engring., Königliche Technische Hochschule, Berlin, 1906; spent much time in father's machine shop, inventing at 15 a rotary engine; m. Marguerite Erskine Walker, Aug. 8, 1867. Mem. 12th N.G.S.N.Y. and 16th N.Y. Cav., Union Army, June 1863-Nov. 1864; asst. engr. U.S.N., Dec. 1864-Aug. 1865. Invented a device for replacing derailed steam cars, 1865; patented his invention of the air brake, 1868; applied pneumatic devices to switching and signaling, greatly increasing efficiency; also utilized electricity in this connection, and became interested in development of electric machinery; acquired Gaulard & Gibbs patents, 1885, and introduced the alternating current system of elec. distribution for light and power; made many elec. inventions; backed Tesla financially and with shop facilities in developing the induction motor, which made possible utilization of alternating current for power purposes; built the first 10 great dynamos for Niagara, the dynamos for the elevated and subway roads in New York, and for the Met. Ry., London. Devised a complete system for controlling natural gas and conveying it through pipe lines for long distances, thereby established the practicability of utilizing natural gas as fuel in homes, mills and factories; took a foremost part in developing gas engines, and in adapting steam turbines to electric driving. Founded works at Wilmerding, East Pittsburgh, Swissvale, and Trafford City, Pa.; Hamilton, Can.; Manchester, and London, Eng.; Havre, France; Hanover, Germany; St. Petersburg, Russia; Vienna, Austria; Vado, Italy; pres. of 30 corps.; trustee Equitable Life Assurance Soc. of U.S., June 10, 1905-Jan. 1911. Decorated Legion of Honor, France, Royal Crown, Italy, and Leopold of Belgium; 2d recipient of John Fritz medal. Hon. mem. Am. Soc. Mech. Engrs. (pres., 1909-10), Nat. Electric Light Assn. Died Mar. 12, 1914.

WESTINGHOUSE, HENRY HERMAN, mech. engr.; b. Central Bridge, N.Y., Nov. 16, 1853; s. George and Emeline (Vedder) W.; grad. Union High Sch., Schenectady, N.Y., 1870; student mech. engring., Cornell, 1871-72; m. Clara Louise Saltmarsh, June 20, 1875. Continuously with Westinghouse Air Brake Co., 1873—, chmn. bd., also of Canadian Westinghouse Co., Ltd.; dir. Westinghouse Electric & Mfg. Co., Westinghouse Brake & Saxby Signal Co., Ltd. (London); pres. Compagnie des Freins Westinghouse, Paris. Invented Westinghouse single-acting steam engine, 1883; founder Westinghouse, Church, Kerr & Co., engrs., New York, 1885. Mem. Am. Soc. Mech. Engrs., Am. Acad. Polit. and Social Science; fellow A.A.A.S. Trustee Cornell U. Republican. Protestant. Died Nov. 18, 1933.

WESTON, CHARLES VALENTINE, civil engr.; b. Kalamazoo, Mich., Feb. 14, 1857; s. John and Catherine (Clark) W.; ed. pub. schs., Kalamazoo; m. Catherine Dyer, Nov. 12, 1889 (died 1914); children—Charles Edward (dec.), Florence E.; m. 2d, Olga Thimm, Jan. 10, 1917. Entered employ Tex. Trunk Ry. Co. as transitman in surveying corps.; asst. engr. M.,K.&T. R.R. in Tex., 1880-81, Kansas City, Springfield & Memphis Ry., 1881-82; asst. engr. C.&N.-W. Ry., 1882-84; asst. engr. Kansas City, Clinton & Springfield Ry., 1884-86; div. engr. in charge constrn. Gulf, Colo. & Santa Fe R.R., 1886-88. Located in Chicago, 1888; in charge constrn. of intake crib and water-supply tunnel under Lake Michigan for city of Lake View, and after annexation of that municipality to Chicago, 1889, completed work for the greater city. In charge constrn. of tunnel for W. Chicago St. Ry., 1890-94; chief engr. of Northwestern Elevated R.R. Co., Lake St. Elevated Ry. Co., Union Elevated, etc.; with brother George, in firm of Weston Bros., cons. and constructing engrs., 1901-03; built various electric rys. in Ill. and Mich.; chief engr., 1903-07, pres. and gen. mgr., 1908-11, South Side Elevated R.R. Co., Chicago; later in practice as cons. engr.; operating mgr. Market St. Elevated Rys., Phila., 1918-20; cons. engr. Chicago Surface Lines, 1920—; mem. Bd. of Supervising Engrs. Chicago Traction. Home: Chicago, Ill. Died Jan. 27, 1933.

WESTON, EDMUND BROWNELL, engr.; b. Duxbury, Mass., Mar. 25, 1850; s. Hon. Gershom Bradford and Deborah (Brownell) W.; ed. pub. schs., Partridge Acad. (Duxbury), Highland Mil. Acad. (Worcester, Mass.), and pvt. instrn.; unmarried. Student in office chief eng. Providence water works 1871-74, asst. engr., 1874-77; engr. in charge Providence water dept., 1877-97; resigned to engaged in gen. practice. Conducted filtration experiments, 1893-94, for city of Providence, which demonstrated efficiency of mech. filtration for purification of municipal water supplies; designed filtration systems for many cities of U.S., Austria, India, Egypt, Germany, Japan, France, Finland, China, Korea, Siam, Italy, Ceylon. Pres. and gen. mgr. Jewell Export Filter Co. Devoted much time to original research relative to hydraulics and water purification, and traveled abroad extensively, making spl. study of water purification, water supply and sanitary engring. Author: Weston's Friction of Water in Pipes, 1878. Home: Providence, R.I. Died Dec. 8, 1916.

WESTON, EDWARD, electrician; b. England, May 9, 1850; ed. there and studied medicine; LL.D., McGill U., Can., 1903; Sc.D., Stevens Inst. Tech., 1904, Princeton, 1910; LL.D., U. of Pa., 1924. Came to U.S., 1870, and became chemist to Am. Nickel Plating Co.; introduced improvements in nickel plating; later invented several dynamo-electric machines, and established in Newark, 1875, the first factory in America devoted exclusively to that class of machines; consol. business, 1881, with U.S. Electric Lighting Co., of which was electrician until 1888; formed Weston Elec. Instrument Co., Waverly Park, Newark, N.J., 1888, to mfr. the Weston measuring instruments; v.p. same co., 1888-1905, pres. 1905, later chmn. bd. Charter mem. Am. Inst. E.E. (pres., 1888). Fellow A.A.A.S. Awarded Franklin medal, 1924. Home: Montclair, N.J. Died Aug. 20, 1936.

WESTON, ROBERT SPURR, cons. engr.; b. Concord, N.H., Aug. 1, 1869; s. Lon and Martha Burtch (Greenman) W.; B.Sc., Amherst Coll., 1891; A.M., 1894; student Mass. Inst. Tech., 1894-96, U. of Berlin (winter) 1896-97; m. Josephine Fitz-Randolph, Dec. 21, 1909; children—Elizabeth (died. 1932), Joseph Fitz-Randolph. Asst. chemist, Louisville Water Co., 1895, 1896-98, Superior Water, Light & Power Co., 1898-99; with George W. Fuller, civil engr., New York, 1899; in private practice, 1899-1912; mem. Weston & Sampson since 1912; served states, cities, towns and corps. in connection with water supply, water purification, stream pollution, sewerage, sewage and industrial waste treatment; asst. prof. public health engring., Mass. Inst. Tech., 1913-16. Cons. engr. U.S. Shipping Bd., U.S. Housing Corp. and U.S. Army Engring. Corps. Mem. Am. Inst. Cons. Engrs. (former v.p.), Am. Soc. Civil Engrs., Am. Inst. Chem. Engrs. (ex-pres.), Am. Water Works Assn. (hon. life mem.), New England Water Works (ex-pres. and hon. mem.), Am. Pub. Works Assn., Am. Chem. Soc., Am. Pub. Health Assn., Howard Benevolent Soc. (v.p.). Independent Republican. Congregationalist. Clubs: Boston City, Rotary (ex-pres.). Expert witness in important cases such as Chicago Drainage Canal, N.Y. vs. N.J., Delaware River Case, and Conn. vs. Mass. Author of tech. papers; joint author "Water Works Handbook." Home: 501 Boylston St., Brookline, Mass. Office: 14 Beacon St., Boston, Mass. Died July 29, 1943.

WESTON, THEODORE, engineer; b. Sandy Hill, N.Y., Oct. 9, 1832; s. Frederick and Elizabeth (Hart) W.; A.B., Yale, 1853; m. Sarah Chauncey Winthrop (died 1864); m. 2d, Catharine Boudinot Stimson. Engaged on surveys and constrn. Genesee Valley R.R., 1853-55; asst. engr. N.Y. State canals, 1855-57; prin. asst. engr. surveys and constrn., etc., Brooklyn Water Works, 1857-60; engr. in charge sewage and drainage, City of New York, 1861-70; supt., engr., trustee and architect Equitable Life Assurance Soc. of U.S., 1870-82; architect of Met. Mus. of Art, 1884-90, and other works. Republican. Incorporator, sec. and trustee, Met. Mus. of Art, New York. Author: Report upon Water Supply for Brooklyn, 1861. Wrote: Water Works of Rome, The Crayon, New York, 1864. Home: New York, N.Y. Died May 6, 1919.

WESTON, WILLIAM, civil engr.; b. nr. Oxford, Eng., circa 1752. Engr. of stone bridge across Trent River at Gainsborough, Eng., 1790, also turnpike rd.; contracted with Schuylkill & Susquehanna Navigation Co., Pa. to engr. its canal, served 2 years; arrived in U.S., early 1793; examined and reported on locks under constrn. at Gt. Falls of the Potomac, 1795; engr. for Western Island Lock Navigation Co., N.Y., 1796, 97; pioneer in design and constrn. of locks and canals; sources of future water for N.Y.C., 1799; designer piers for Permanent Bridge across the Schuylkill River in Phila., also deep coffer dam in connection with bridge; returned to Eng., 1800. Author: An Historial Account of the Rise, Progress and Present State of the Canal Navigation in Pennsylvania, 1795. Died London, Eng., Aug. 29, 1833.

WETHERILL, CHARLES MAYER, chemist; b. Phila., Nov. 4, 1825; s. Charles and Margaretta (Mayer) W.; grad. U. Pa., 1845; M.A., Ph.D., U. Giessen, 1848; M.D. (hon.), N.Y. Med. Coll., 1853; m. Mary Benbridge, Aug. 12, 1856. Conducted chem. lab. for pvt. instrn. and analysis, Phila., 1848-53; elected to Am. Philos. Soc., 1851; published treatise The Manufacture of Vinegar, 1860; apptd. chemist U.S. Dept. Agr., 1862; published Report on the Chemical Analysis of Grapes (1st scientific bulletin issued by Dept. of Agr.), 1862; chemist Smithsonian Instn., Washington, 1863-66, conducted investigation of ventilation of new House and Senate chambers in U.S. Capitol extensions; prof. chemistry Lehigh U., Bethlehem, Pa., 1866-71. Author: Syllabus of Lectures on Chemical Physics, 1867; Lecture Notes on Chemistry, 1868. Died Bethlehem, Mar. 5, 1871.

WETHERILL, SAMUEL, inventor, zinc co. exec., army officer; b. Phila., May 27, 1821; s. John Price and Maria Kane (Lawrence) W.; grad. U. Pa., 1845; m. Sarah Maria Chatton, Jan. 1, 1844; m. 2d, Thyrza A. James, Oct. 19, 1870; 10 children. Joined firm Wetherill & Brother, 1845, operated white lead and chem. works; employed by N.J. Zinc Co., 1850; inventor process for deriving white oxide of zinc direct from the ore, 1852; founder Lehigh Zinc Co., 1853; developer process for manufacture of metallic zinc and rolled zinc sheets, 1857, commd. capt. 11th Pa. Cavalry, 1861, maj., 1861, honorably discharged, 1864; brevetted lt. col., 1865. Died Oxford, Md., June 24, 1890.

WETZLER, JOSEPH, engineer; b. Hoboken, N.J., Dec. 6, 1863; s. Albert and Anna (Neumann) W.; M.E., Stevens Inst. Tech., 1882; m. Pauline Gerson, Oct. 30, 1895. Editor Electric World, 1885-90, Electric Engineer, 1890-99; founded, 1898, and from then pres. Electric Engineer Inst. of Correspondence Instrn. Sec. and dir. Hebrew Tech. Institute. Home: New York, N.Y. Died 1911.

WEXLER, HARRY, meteorologist, govt. ofcl.; born Fall River, Mass., Mar. 15, 1911; s. Samuel and Mamie (Starr) W.; S.B., Harvard, 1932; D.Sc., Mass. Inst. Tech., 1939; m. Hannah Paipert, Dec. 3, 1934; children—Susan Carol, Libby. Meteorologist U.S. Weather Bur., 1934-40, 41-42, chief sci. services, 1946-55; asst. prof. meteorology University Chicago, 1940-41; dir. meteorol. research, U.S. Weather Bureau, 1955—; chief scientist U.S. Expdn. to Antarctic for International Geophys. Year, 1955-58; chairman meteorol. panel of Nat. Acad. of Science, com. to study biological effects of atomic radiation; mem. Nat. Acad. of Sci. space sci. bd., com. polar research, also chmn. com. meteorological aspects of satellites, U.S. nat. com. IGY. Served as capt. to lt. col. Weather Service, A.A.F., 1942-46, lt. col. Res. Recipient Robert M. Losey award for outstanding services to aeronautics, Inst. Aeronautical Sci., 1945; Exceptional Service award, Dept. of Air Force, 1956, Dept. Commerce, 1958; Distinguished Pub. Service award, U.S. Navy, 1960; Nat. Civil Service League award, 1961. Fellow A.A.A.S., American Astronautical Society, also the American Acad. Arts and Scis.; mem. Am. Meteorol. Soc., Am. Geophys. Union, Royal Meteorol. Soc. Gt. Britain, Am. Vets. Com. Author sci. articles. Home: 204 S. Lee St., Falls Church, Va. Office: U.S. Weather Bureau, Washington 25. Died Aug. 11, 1962.

WEYL, CHARLES, engr.; b. Phila., May 22, 1896; s. Maurice N. and Carrie (Stein) W.; student Germantown Acad.; B.S., U. Pa., 1917, M.S., 1927; m. Elinor Gittelson, Apr. 28, 1920; children—Elinor Jean, Doris Anne; m. 2d, Helen Roberts, Dec. 4, 1948; children—Charles Frederick, Mary Caroline. Engring. design, adminstrn. various firms; dir. Moore Sch. X-Ray Lab., 1925-45, prof. elec. engring. Moore Sch. Elec. Engring., U. Pa., 1937-50, asso. prof. radiol. physics Grad. School Medicine, 1942-50; director IRC, Inc., 1929-67, pres., 1953-59, chmn., 1959-67; former chmn. Edward Stern & Co., Inc. Served as ensign, USNR, World War I; Naval Expt. Sta., New London, Conn., also submarine detection duty, 1918-19. Recipient Centennial citation, Schools of Engineering, University of Pennsylvania, 1955. Member of the Franklin Institute (Longstreth medal 1930), I.E.E.E., also A.A.A.S., Sigma Xi. Author: Apparatus and Technique for Roentgenography of the Chest (with S. Reid Warren, Jr.), 1935. Co-author: Radiologic Physics, rev. edit., 1951. Contbr. articles profl. publs., fiction mags. Home: Rydal PA Died Aug. 23, 1967.

WEYL, HERMANN, (vil), mathematics; b. Elmshorn, Germany, Nov. 9, 1885; s. Ludwig and Anna (Dieck) W.; ed. univ. of Munich and Göttingen; Ph.D., Göttingen, 1908; hon. Dr. Philosophy, University of Oslo, 1929; hon. Dr. Technology, Hochschule, Stuttgart, 1929; D.Sc., University of Pennsylvania, 1940, Columbia, 1954; Dr. Math. (honoary), Tech. Hochschule, Zürich, 1945; Dr., Université de Paris, 1952; married Helene Joseph, Sept. 1, 1913 (dec.); children—Fritz Joachim, Michael; m. 2d Ellen Baer Lohnstein, Jan. 7, 1950. Privatdozent U. of Götteingen, 1910-13; professor mathematics Tech. Hochschule, Zürich, 1913-30; Jones research prof. in mathematical physics, Princeton, 1928-29; prof. mathematics, U. of Göttingen, 1930-33; prof. mathematics Inst. for Advanced Study, Princeton, since Dec. 1, 1933. Mem. National Academy, American Academy Arts and Sciences, American Philosophical Society, American Math. Society, and mem. or hon. mem. various European socs. including Royal Soc. of London, Pontificial Acad. of Sciences. Award Lobatschefsky prize, Kazan, 1925. Research work in differential equations, topology, relativity, theory, infinitesimal geometry, group theory, philosophy of mathematics, etc. Author of 8 books pub. in Europe, and 7 books pub. in U.S.—The Open World, 1932; Mind and Nature, 1934; The Classical Groups, 1939; Algebraic Theory of Numbers, 1940; Meromorphic Functions and Analytic Curves, 1943; Philosophy of Mathematics and Natural Sci., 1949; Symmetry, 1952; also articles in mags. Address: 284 Mesces St., Princeton, N.J. Died Dec. 8, 1955.

WEYMOUTH, AUBREY, civil engr.; b. Richmond, Va., Nov. 18, 1872; s. Edgar Jenkins and Medora (Strode) W.; C.E., Lehigh Univ., 1894, D.Eng., 1935; m. Alice White, Apr. 27, 1901; children—Medora (Mrs. A. Hawley Peterson), Martha (Mrs. Russell H. Moock). Practiced engring., 1894—; with Post & McCord, New York, 1897—, becoming vice-pres. and chief engineer. Trustee Lehigh Univ. Home: Flushing, N.Y. Died July 27, 1939.

WEYMOUTH, CLARENCE RAYMOND, (wa'muth), mechanical engr.; b. Oakland, Calif., Nov. 14, 1876; s. Tobias Delmont and Laura Nevada (Wells) W.; B.S., U. of Calif., 1898; unmarried. Asst. to prof. of mech. engring., U. of Calif., 1898-99; with Charles C. Moore & Co. Engrs., San Francisco, 1898-1925, serving as chief engr. and dir. (resigned). Chmn. com. on engring. and inventions, Calif. State Council of Defense, during latter part of World War I. Inventor of Moore automatic fuel oil system for controlling oil-fired boilers; designer of many steam-electric power plants in Inter-mountain and Pacific Coast states. Mem. Tau Beta Pi (hon. mem.), Sigma Psi; mem. Internat. Engring. Congress, 1915 (com. of management). Club: University. Contbr. papers on plant design, etc., to Trans. Am. Soc. Mech. Engrs. Home: Hotel Fairmont, San Francisco 6. Died Feb. 12, 1949.

WEYMOUTH, FRANK ELWIN, civil engr.; b. Medford, Me., June 2, 1874; s. Andrew Jackson and Charlotte Prudence (Powers) W.; C.E., U. of Me., 1896, E.D., 1934; m. Mary Maude Lane, Dec. 3, 1900; m. 2d, Barbara Turner, Nov. 10, 1938. Sewer and water works constrn., Boston and Malden, Mass., 1896-99; asst. city engr. Winnipeg, Man., 1899; with Isthmian Canal Commn. in Nicaragua, C.A., and Washington, 1899-1901; resident engr. Guayaquil & Quito Ry. Co., Ecuador, 1901-02; with U.S. Reclamation Service, 1902-24, on surveys and investigations in Mont. and N.D., 1902-04; project engr. in charge of Lower Yellowstone project in eastern Mont., 1905-08; supervising engr. in charge of Ida. Dist., including Snake River drainage in Wyo., Idaho and eastern Ore., covering irrigation of more than 400,000 acres of land, and storage dams at Jackson Lake, Wyo., and on upper branches of Snake and Boisé rivers, including building of the Arrowrock dam, 1909-15; chief of constrn., U.S. Reclamation Service, in charge all work (except legal) in the West, 1916-20, chief engr., Apr. 1920-Oct. 1924; pres. Brock & Weymouth engrs., Nov. 1924-June 1926; chief engr. J. G. White Engring. Corp., S. en C., Mexico, 1926-29; chief engr. of Water Works, City of Los Angeles, Mar. 1929-Dec. 1930; chief engr. Metropolitan Water Dist. of Southern Calif., constructing Colorado River Aqueduct, July 1929-Jan. 1932, gen. mgr. and chief engr., 1932—. Home: San Marino, Calif. Died July 22, 1941.

WEYMOUTH, THOMAS ROTE, gas engr.; b. Lock Haven, Pa., Mar. 16, 1876; s. George and Effie Pamelia (Rote) W.; S.B. in E.E., Mass. Inst. Tech., 1897; m. Josephine Goettel Loomis, Apr. 8, 1913; 1 step-son, William Goettel Loomis. Draftsman, Met. St. Ry. Co., N.Y.C., 1898; elec. engr., Internat. Hydraulic Co. (subsidiary of Emerson McMillin Co.), 1898-1903; asst. chief engr., Nat. Transit Co., Oil City, Pa., 1903-11; chief engr., United Natural Gas Co., Oil City, Pa., and Pa. Gas Co., Warren, Pa., 1911-23; pres. Iroquois Gas Corpn., Iroquois Building Corpn., Peoples Gas Light & Coke Co., 1923-28; pres. Am. Natural Gas Corpn., Okla. Natural Gas Corpn., Okla. Natural Building Co., Texokan Oil Corpn., Western Natural Gas Corpn., 1928-30; v.p. in charge of operations, Columbia Gas & Electric Corpn. and subsidiaries 1930-41, retired 1941. Formerly pres. Bd. Edn., Oil City, Pa. Mem. Am. Soc. M.E., Am. Gas Assn., Delta Upsilon, Royal Arcanum. Republican. Presbyn. Clubs: Saturn, Country (Buffalo). Author of Weymouth Formula for measuring flow of gas in pipe lines; inventor fluid measuring devices; contbr. on professional subjects. Address: 930 Park Av., N.Y.C. Died Sept. 23, 1958.

WEYSSE, ARTHUR WISSWALD, biologist; b. Machias, Me., Nov. 16, 1867; s. Jacob and Margaret (Larrabee) W.; A.B., Harvard, 1891, A.M., 1892, Ph.D., 1894; studied Leipzig, Berlin, Paris, Naples, Harvard U. Med. Sch. and London; registered physician, Mass.,

1905; M.D., Basel, Switzerland, 1907; unmarried. Asst. in botany and zoology, Harvard, and Radcliffe Coll., 1892-94; instr. zoology, Mass. Inst. Tech., 1896-1907; prof. exptl. physiology, Boston U. Sch. of Medicine, 1899-1924, also prof. biology, Boston U. since 1904; lecturer on venereal disease, Boston U. Sch. of Medicine, 1915-24; acting dean Grad. Sch. of Boston U., 1917-22; and dean, 1922-33, prof. emeritus since 1939. Fellow Am. Academy Arts and Sciences, A.A.A.S.; mem. Am. Soc. Zoologists, Am. Soc. Naturalists, Am. Assn. Anatomists, Am. Genetic Assn., Am. Social Hygiene Assn., Mass. Soc. for Social Hygiene, Boston Soc. Med. Sciences, Boston Soc. Natural History, Boston Med. Library. Republican. Episcopalian. Mason (32 deg., K.T.). Clubs: Harvard, Boston. Author: Human Histology, 1898; Textbook of Zoology, 1904; Medico-Legal Moral Offenses, 1911; also numerous original papers on anatomy, embryology, physiology. Home: 291 Mishawum Road, Woburn MA

WHEELER, ALBERT HARRY, mathematician; b. Leominster, Mass., Jan. 18, 1873; s. Albert Alpheus and Ella Louise (Gibson) W., B.S., Worchester (Mass.) Poly. Inst., 1894; A.M., Clark U., 1921; m. Helen Marion Bonzey, Aug. 19, 1901; 1 dau., Helen Marjorie (Mrs. Paul E. Haney). Teacher of mathematics, English High Sch., Worcester, 1896-1916, North High Sch., Worcester, Mass., since 1916; retired, 1943; lecturer in mathematics, Brown Univ., 1924-26, Wellesley Coll., 1926-28; lecturer on math. subjects at ednl. meetings since 1905; prof. affiliate in mathematics, Clark U., 1943-44. Mem. American Math. Soc., Math. Assn. America, Assn. Teachers of Mathematics of New England. Republican. Mason. Author: First Course in Algebra, 1907; Examples in Algebra, 1914. Engaged in research on theory and construction of polyhedra; has collection of math. models which have been exhibited to univs. and math. socs. Home: 44 Beverly Rd., Worcester 5 MA

WHEELER, C(HARLES) GILBERT, chemist; b. London, Canada, July 23, 1836; s. William and Caroline M. W.; B.S., Harvard, 1858; studied in German univs.; m. Sarah Jenkins, May 10, 1863. Asst. state geologist of Mo., 1859-61; U.S. consul to Nuremberg, 1862-67; traveled in Europe and N. Africa, 1867-68; prof. chemistry, U. of Chicago and Chicago Med. Coll., 1868; frequent visits to Mexico and Central America examining mines for Am. capitalists, 1868-1900; invented "Babcock" chem. fire extinguisher, 1869; scientific expert for Bell Telephone Co. and other cos. in patent and other litigation; reads 11 and speaks 7 modern langs. State commr. from Ill. to Vienna Expn., 1873; pres. Chicago Coll. Pharmacy, 1882; geologist and interpreter in commn. to examine route Nicaragua Canal, 1899. Consul at Chicago for Republic of Panama. Author: Natural History Charts; Catalogue Polyglottus; Determinative Mineralogy; Chemistry of Building Materials; Medical Chemistry. Home: Chicago, Ill. Died 1912.

WHEELER, EBENEZER SMITH, engineer; b. Wayne Co., Pa., Aug. 27, 1839; s. Ransom and Adeline W.; C.E., U. of Mich., 1867 (hon. M.S., 1897); m. Clara P. Fuller. U.S. asst. engr., 1867—; was engr. in constrn. of Saint Ste. Marie locks; chief engr. Nicaragua Canal Commn. of 1887. Home: Detroit, Mich. Died Jan. 5, 1913.

WHEELER, GEORGE MONTAGUE, soldier, engr.; b. Grafton, Mass., Oct. 9, 1842; grad. West Point, 1866; assigned to engrs.; promoted 1st lt., Mar. 7, 1867; at head of Geog. Survey of U.S. west of 100th Meridian, as supt. engr., 1869-79; supervised the reports of that expdn.; promoted capt., 1879, and later maj. and retired, owing to illness, June 15, 1888; of late years has practiced as civ. engr.; mem. Am. Soc. Civ. Engrs. since 1894. Address: 930 16th St., N.W., Washington.

WHEELER, HENRY LORD, chemist; b. Chicago, Sept. 14, 1867; s. George Henry and Alice I. (Lord) W.; Ph.B., Yale, 1890, Ph.D., 1893; U. of Munich, 1893-94, U. of Chicago, 1894-95; m. Eva F. Swarthout, Mar. 16, 1906. Asst. in chemistry, 1890-95, instr. organic chemistry, 1895-99, asst. prof., 1899-1908, prof., 1908—, Yale. Home: New Haven, Conn. Died 1914.

WHEELER, HOMER JAY, agrl. chemist; b. Bolton, Mass., Sept. 2, 1861; s. Jesse Brown and Martha Ann (Sykes) W.; B.S., Mass. Agrl. Coll., also from Boston, Univ., 1883; A.M., Ph.D., U. of Göttingen, 1889; Sc.D., Brown Univ., 1911; D.Sc., Mass. State Coll., 1933; m. at Brooklyn, Frieda H. F. Ruprecht, May 15, 1891; children—Carl Otto Jordan, William Edwin, Roland Arthur. Asst. chemist, Mass. Agrl. Expt. Sta., 1883-87; chief chemist, R.I. Agrl. Expt. Sta., 1889-1905; dir. and agronomist, agrl. expt. sta., Sept. 1, 1901-12, acting pres., 1902-03, prof. geology, 1893-1912, and agrl. chemistry, 1903-07, R.I. State Coll.; resigned as dir. agrl. expt. sta., 1912; chief agronomist The Am. Agrl. Chem. Co., until Dec. 1931. Ex-pres. Assn. Official Agrl. Chemists U.S.; mem. Am. Chem. Soc., A.A.A.S., Am. Geog. Soc., Am. Soc. Agronomy (ex-pres.). Author: Manures and Fertilizers; Citrus Culture in Florida; Citrus Culture in California; also numerous bulletins, and reports of R.I. Agrl. Expt. Station, and miscellaneous publns. Chairman, during World War I, of sub-com. on soils and fertilizers of Nat. Research Council. Home: 386 N. Fullerton Av., Upper Montclair, N.J. Died Nov. 18, 1945.

WHEELER, LESLIE ALLEN, agrl. cons.; b. Ventura, Ia., Dec. 20, 1899; s. Frank and Lottie (Rankin) W.; A.B., Pomona Coll., Claremont, Calif., 1921; M.B.A., Harvard, 1923; m. Louise Price, Nov. 17, 1927. Spl. agt. U.S. Dept. of Commerce, 1923-26; asso., sr. and prin. agrl. economist and chief of the Foreign Agrl. Service, Bur. of Agrl. Econ., U.S. Dept. of Agr., 1926-39, dir. of the Office of Foreign Agrl. Relations 1939-48; apptd. fgn. service officer (class 1) and sec. in diplomatic service, 1948; assigned Dept. of State, 1948; minister-counselor of Embassy, Mexico City, 1948-50; vice chmn., exec. com., Food and Agriculture orgn. of U.N.; chmn. Internat. Wheat Council; chmn. International Cotton Advisory Com., 1942-48; director Interim office for technical collaboration, 1950; cons. Internat. Fedn. Agricultural Producers, 1951-68; chief econ. advisory mission, Iran; del. to numerous internat. confs. Member American Farm Economic Assn. Club: Cosmos (Washington, D.C.). Contbr. articles on internat. trade in agrl. products to jours. Home: Chevy Chase MD Died Apr. 26, 1968.

WHEELER, NATHANIEL, inventor, mfr.; b. Watertown, Conn., Sept. 7, 1820; s. David and Sarah (De Forest) W.; m. Huldah Bradley, Nov. 7, 1842; m. 2d, Mary E. Crissey, Aug. 3, 1858; at least 14 children. Engaged in carriage building in father's shop, 1841-46; formed partnership Warren, Wheeler and Woodruff, mfrs. metalware, Watertown, 1848; assumed control mfg. Allen B. Wilson's sewing machine, engaged Wilson to superintend factory, 1850, reorganized co. under name Wheeler and Wilson Mfg. Co., 1851-53, moved factory to Bridgeport, Conn., 1856, served as pres. until 1893; invented, patented wood-filling compound, 1876-78, ventilating system for houses and railroad cars, 1883; dir. N.Y., N.H. & H. R.R.; served in Conn. Legislature, 1866, 68, 70, 72-74. Died Bridgeport, Conn., Dec. 31, 1893.

WHEELER, RUTH, physiol. chemist; b. Plains, Pa., Aug. 5, 1877; d. Jared Ward and Martha Jane (Evans) Wheeler; A.B., Vassar, 1899; Ph.D., Yale, 1913. Served as teacher science and German, high sch., Pa., and N.Y.; teacher chemistry, Pratt Inst., Brooklyn, 1905-11; instr. dietetics and nutrition, U. of Ill., 1912-13, asst. prof., 1913-15, asso. prof., 1915-16; dir. home economics dept., Goucher Coll., 1918-21; prof. and head dept. of nutrition, Coll. of Medicine, and chief dietitian, Univ. Hosps., State U. of Ia., 1921-26; professor nutrition and physiology, Vassar Coll., 1926-44; retired July 1944; prof. emeritus physiology, Vassar Coll., since 1944; also chmn. div. of euthenics and dir. summer Institute of Euthenics (Vassar), 1929-42; consultant in nutrition, department of medicine, Presbyterian Hospital (Columbia University, 1926-30. Chairman of Advisory committee on nutrition, American Red Cross, 1917-32; formerly member editorial bd. Jour. Home Economics, Am. Dietetic Assn. Fellow Am. Assn. for the Advancement of Science; mem. Am. Dietetics Assn. (pres. 1924-26), Am. Soc. Biol. Chemists, Sigma Xi. Episcopalian. Author: (with Helen Wheeler) Talks to Nurses on Dietetics and Dietotherapy, 1926; American Red Cross Textbook on Food and Nutrition, 1927. Contbr. articles on nutrition and nutrition education. Address: Vassar College, Poughkeepsie, N.Y. Died Sept. 29, 1948.

WHEELER, SCHUYLER SKAATS, engineer; b. New York, May 17, 1860; s. James Edwin and Annie (Skaats) W.; ed. Columbia Grammar Sch. and Columbia Coll.; D.Sc., Hobart, 1894; hon. M.Sc., Columbia, 1912; m. Ella Adams Peterson, Apr. 1891; m. 2d, Amy Sutton, Oct. 1898. Left Coll., 1881, to become asst. electrician Jablochkoff Elec. Light Co., until 1882; next with U.S. Elec. Lighting Co.; soon after became one of Edison's engring. staff in charge of work at the first sta. at time of its starting, 1883, when incandescent light was introduced. Contributed many of the devices adopted; later erected sta. apparatus at Fall River, Mass., and Newburgh, N.Y. Became electrician Herzog Teleseme Co.; electrician and mgr. C. & C. Electric Motor Co., 1886, first concern established for regular mfr. of electric motors. Organized firm of Crocker & Wheeler, 1888; pres. of Crocker-Wheeler Co., Ampere, N.J., mfrs. elec. equipment, 1889—. Prominent in development of the electric motor and especially in direct application of electricity to driving tools. Elec. expert of Bd. of Elec. Control New York, 1888-95. Inventor of numerous elec. and mech. devices, especially in the early days, such as electric elevator, electric fire engine, series multiple motor control, paralleling of dynamos, etc. Received the John Scott medal of Franklin Inst., 1904, for invention of electric buzz fan, 1886. Brought to this country the Latimer Clark library, the largest collection of rare elec. books in existence (catalogued, 2 vols. illus., as the "Wheeler Gift") and presented it to Am. Inst. Elec. Engrs., 1901, which led to erection of United Engring. Soc. Bldg. in N.Y., which he organized; author of code of professional ethics for engrs. adopted by Am. Inst. Elec. Engrs., 1912. Author: Practical Management of Dynamos and Motors (with Prof. Francis B. Crocker), 1894. Home: Bernardsville, N.J. Died Apr. 20, 1923.

WHEELER, WILLIAM ARCHIE, agronomist, marketing specialist; b. Stockton, Minn., June 28, 1876; s. Charles and Sylvia M. (Allen) W.; B.Agr., U. of Minn., 1900, M.S., 1901; m. Harriet Maria Alden, June 3, 1901; children—Harold Alden, Helen, Margaret, Catherine, Harriet. Instr. bot., U. of Minn., 1898-1903; prof. bot. and head of dept., S.D. State Coll., 1903-07; sec. and mgr. Dak. Improved Seed Co., Mitchell, 1907-16; specialist in charge seed marketing, Bur. of Markets, U.S. Dept. Agr., 1916-19; in charge marketing information, same bur., 1920-22; chief, hay, feed and seed div., Bur. of Agrl. Economics, 1922-39; became special consultant in seed and forage marketing; Agricultural Marketing Service, 1939; in charge of greatly expanded vegetable seed production program of U.S. and of supplying all United Nations and neutrals with seeds under Lend-Lease Adminstrn. during World War II, 1941-46; dir. agr. research, Field Seed Inst. of N.A., since 1946. Commd. by Sec. of Agr. Houston to investigate and report on seed conditions in Europe immediately following signing of Armistice, 1919-20; initiated and supervised the publ. by the U.S. Dept. Agr., The Seed Reporter, 1918-19, and The Market Reporter, 1920-21; initiated and developed the field of broadcasting of official federal and state crop and market reports to agrl. interests by radio, 1920-21; U.S. Dept. Agr. rep. on Nat. Radio Service Commn.; apptd. by Secretary Wallace and P.M. General Hays to investigate use of radio for broadcasting information, 1921-22; rep. of U.S. Dept. of Agr. on 1st, 2d, 3d and 4th Nat. Radio confs., 1922-25. V.p. Nat. Corn Assn., 1908-11; mem. Sigma Xi, Am. Soc. Agronomy. Republican. Unitarian. Author: Forage and Pasture Crops, 1950. Editor of Farm Clip Sheet for Nat. Farm & Garden Bur., Chicago. Home: 3041 Sedgwick St., Washington 8 DC

WHEELER, WILLIAM MORTON, zoölogist; b. Milwaukee, Mar. 19, 1865; s. Julius Morton and Caroline Georgiana (Anderson) W.; grad. German-Am. Normal Coll., Milwaukee, 1884; Ph.D., Clark U., 1892; occupant of Smithsonian table, Naples Zoöl. Sta., 1893; univs. Würzburg and Liége, 1893; Sc.D., U. of Chicago, 1916, Harvard, 1930, Columbia, 1933; LL.D., U. of Calif., 1928; m. Dora Bay Emerson, June 28, 1898. Curator Milwaukee Pub. Mus., 1887-90; fellow and asst. in morphology, Clark U., 1890-92; instr. embryology, 1892-97, asst. prof., 1897-99, U. of Chicago; prof. zoölogy, U. of Tex., 1899-1903; curator of invertebrate zoölogy, Am. Mus. Natural History, 1903-08; prof. entomology, Harvard, 1908—, dean of Bussey Inst. for Research in Applied Biology, 1915-29. Research asso. Am. Mus. Natural History. Fellow Am. Acad. Arts and Natural History, Am. Acad. Arts and Sciences, A.A.A.S., Washington Acad. Sciences, N.Y. Acad. Sciences. Awarded Elliott and Leidy medals. Author: Ants, Their Structure, Development and Behavior, 1910; Social Life Among the Insects, 1923; Demons of the Dust, a Study in Insect Behavior, 1930; also numerous zoöl. publs. Asso. editor Biological Bulletin, Jour. of Morphology, Jour. of Animal Behavior and Psyche. Home: Boston, Mass. Died Apr. 19, 1937.

WHEELOCK, CHARLES DELORMA, educator; born in Riverside, Calif., July 28, 1897; s. Arthur N. and Kate Dudley (Johnson) W.; B.S., U.S. Naval Acad., 1920; M.S., Mass. Inst. Tech., 1924; m. Beatrice Grace McLeish, June 6, 1922; children—Beatrice Jeanne (Mrs. Jeanne W. Lilly), Charles Arthur. Commd. ensign, U.S.N., 1920, and advanced through grades to rear adm., 1946; on duty in naval shipyards, 1924-34, at sea, 1934-36, in ship design, Bur. of Ships, 1936-43, head of design, 1943-44; prodn. officer, Mare Island, naval shipyard, 1944-46; prof. naval constrn., Mass. Inst. Tech., 1946; dep. and asst. chief, Bur. of Ships, Washington, 1946-51, insp. gen., 1951-53, ret.; research engr. Scripps Institution of Oceanography of U. Cal., LaJolla, Cal., 1953-58, prof. marine resources U. Cal., La Jolla, Cal., 1958—. Dir. Inst. Marine Resources. Mem. Soc. of Naval Architects and Marine Engrs. (v.p.). Episcopalian. Home: 8355 Paseo del Ocaso, La Jolla, Cal., and Carmel, Cal.

WHERRY, WILLIAM BUCHANAN, bacteriologist; b. of Am. parents at Lodeana, India, Dec. 24, 1875; s. Elwood Morris and Clara Maria (Buchanan) W.; A.B., Washington and Jefferson Coll., 1897; M.D., Rush Med. Coll., 1901; m. Marie Eleanor Nast, 1906; children—William Nast, Margaret Rutan. Asst. in bacteriology, U. of Chicago, 1901-02, asso., 1902-03; bacteriologist, U.S. Govt. labs., Manila, P.I., 1903-05; prof. bacteriology, Oakland (Calif.) Coll. Medicine, 1907; bacteriologist, Bd. of Health, San Francisco, and acting asst. surgeon on plague duty, U.S. Pub. Health Service, 1907-09; asst. prof. bacteriology, Ohio-Miami Med. Coll., U. of Cincinnati, 1909, asso. prof., 1910-13; prof. bacteriology and hygiene, Med. Coll., U. of Cincinnati, 1914—; visiting prof., Sch. of Hygiene, Manila, 1929-30. Served on med. advisory bd., Cincinnati, 1917. Mem. Nat. Advisory Health Council, U.S. Pub. Health Service. Contbr. to Jour. Infectious Diseases, etc. Home: Cincinnati, O. Died Nov. 1, 1936.

WHETZEL, HERBERT HICE, (hwet'zel), plant pathologist; b. Avilla, Ind., Sept. 5, 1877; s. Joseph Conrad and Gertrude (Eckles) W.; B.A., Wabash Coll., 1902, M.A., 1906; Cornell Univ., 1902-06; hon. D.Sc., U. of Puerto Rico, in 1926; hon. D.Sc., Wabash College, 1931; m. Lucy Ethel Baker, May 17, 1904;

children—Lucy Gertrude, Joseph Conrad; m. 2d, Bertha A. Baker, June 10, 1914. Assistant in botany, Cornell, 1902-04, instr., 1904-05; asst. prof. botany, 1906-07, asst. prof. plant pathology, 1907-09, prof. since 1909, N.Y. College Agr. (Cornell Univ.); also head of dept. plant pathology, Cornell U., 1906-22. Chmn. war emergency bd. of Am. Plant Pathologists, 1918. Mycol. explorations in Puerto Rico, Venezuela and Bermuda. Fellow A.A.A.S.; mem. Am. Phytopathol. Soc., Bot. Soc. America, Mycol. Soc. America, British Mycol. Soc., Canadian Phytopathol. Soc., Phi Delta Theta, Phi Beta Kappa, Gamma Alpha, Sigma Xi, Phi Kappa Phi, Alpha Zeta. Democrat. Club: Rotary. Author: Laboratory Outline in Plant Pathology, 1916, 25; (with L. R. Hesler) Manual of Fruit Diseases, 1917; An Outline of the History of Phytopathology, 1918. Home: Forest Home, Ithaca, N.Y. Died. Nov. 30, 1944.

WHINERY, SAMUEL, engr.; b. nr. Salem, O., Nov. 20, 1845; common sch. edn.; m. Elizabeth A. Crawford, Nov. 10, 1875; father of Charles Crawford W. Engaged in location and constrn. of railroads and other engring. work, 1868-86, including 2 yrs., 1878-80, as U.S. asst. engr. on improvement of Tenn. River at Mussel Shoals, and other govt. works; location, constrn. and operation N.O.&N.E. R.R., 1881-84, during which employed 1st telephone in ry. constrn. and train dispatching; constrn. of incline ry. up Lookout Mountain, Chattanooga, Tenn., etc.; v.p., gen. mgr. and pres. Warren-Scharf Asphalt Paving Co., 1887-1901, and designed and built 1st self-propelling st. concrete mixer and 1st ry. asphalt paving plant; cons. civ. engr., New York, Mar. 15, 1901—. Cons. engr. Finance Commn. of Boston, 1907-08, Commn. on City Expenditures, Chicago, to pres. Borough of Manhattan, 1905, etc.; chmn. state commn. to reappraise railroads and canals of N.J. Mem. reserve examining bd. of Bur. of Yards and Docks, Navy Dept., 1918. Author: Municipal Public Works, 1903; Specifications for Pavements and Roads. Contbr. numerous papers on engring. subjects to socs. and mags. Home: East Orange, N.J. Died Jan. 14, 1925.

WHIPPLE, AMIEL WEEKS, topog. engr., army officer; b. Greenwich, Mass., 1816; s. David and Abigail (Pepper) W.; grad. U.S. Mil. Acad., 1841; m. Eleanor Sherburne, Sept. 12, 1843. Mem. survey team established to settle Northeastern boundary of U.S., 1844-49; surveyed boundary between Mexico an U.S., 1849-53; surveyed route for railroad line to Pacific Ocean, 1853-56; supervised operation designed to open Gt. Lakes for large craft, 1856-61; chief topog. engr. at Battle of Bull Run, 1860; commd. maj. U.S. Army, 1861; promoted brig. gen. U.S. Volunteers, 1862; wounded 2d day of fighting at Battle of Chancellorsville, 1863; promoted maj. gen. U.S. Volunteers before his death. Died Washington, D.C., May 7, 1863.

WHIPPLE, GEORGE CHANDLER, engineer; b. New Boston, N.H., Mar. 2, 1866; s. Joseph K. and Sarah Adeline (Chandler) W.; S.B., Mass. Inst. Tech., 1889; m. Mary E. Rayner, June 29, 1893. Biologist Boston Water Works; later dir. Mt. Prospect Lab., dept. of water supply, gas and electricity, New York City; mem. firm of Hazen and Whipple, cons. engrs., New York. Prof. sanitary engring., Harvard U., 1911—, Mass. Inst. of Tech., 1914-16. Mem. council Mass. State Dept. of Health, 1914-23; sr. sanitary engr. (reserve) U.S. Pub. Health Assn., 1919—; chief of dept. of sanitation, League of Red Cross Socs., 1919-20. Major, and mem. Am. Red Cross mission to Russia, 1917. Fellow Am. Acad. Arts and Sciences, A.A.A.S. Author: Microscopy of Drinking Water, 1889, 1905; Value of Pure Water, 1907; Typhoid Fever, 1908; State Sanitation, 1917; Vital Statistics, 1919. Home: Cambridge, Mass. Died Nov. 27, 1924.

WHIPPLE, RALPH W(HEATON), geologist; b. Phila., Oct. 5, 1890; s. Fenner E. and Anna Elizabeth (Murray) W.; grad. Dean Acad., Franklin, Mass., 1910; B.S., Amherst Coll., 1914, A.M., 1917; student U. Paris (Sorbonne), 1929; m. Marjorie Davis, June 19, 1919; children—Ann, James Wheaton. Asst. in geology Amherst Coll., 1914-17; instr. in geology Marietta (O.) Coll., 1919-20, asst. prof., 1920-23, prof., 1923-25, Ebenezer Baldwin Andrews prof. natural scis. and curator of museum, 1925—. Served with U.S. Ambulance Service, French Army, 1917-19; with Civilian Defense, also AC cadet tng. Marietta Coll., 1942-43. Decorated Croix de Guerre (France). Mem. A.A.A.S., Ohio Acad. Sci., Geol. Soc. Am., Sigma Delta Rho. Republican. Unitarian. Contbr. to sci. jours. Home: 214 1/2 Fifth St., Marietta, O. Died Dec. 3, 1954.

WHIPPLE, SQUIRE, civil engr., inventor; b. Hardwick, Mass., Sept. 16, 1804; s. James and Electa (Johnson) W.; A.B., Union Coll., 1830; m. Anna Case, 1837. Resident engr. div. N.Y. & Erie R.R., 1836-37; invented lock for weighing boats, 1840; invented truss of trapezoidal form used in bridges, 1846, used truss design in 1st long railroad bridge span on Rensselaer & Saratoga line, 1853; built drawbridge with left span over Erie Canal, Utica N.Y., 1872 hon. mem. Am. Soc. Civil Engrs. Author: A Work on Bridge Building (his chief contbn. to bridge engring.), 1847; The Doctrine of Central Forces, 1866. Died Albany, N.Y., Mar. 15, 1888.

WHISTLER, GEORGE WASHINGTON, civil engr., army officer; b. Fort Wayne, Ind., May 19, 1800; s. John and Ann (Bishop) W.; grad. U.S. Mil. Acad., 1819; m. Mary Roberdeau Swift; m. 2d, Anna Mathilda McNeill, Nov. 3, 1831; 8 children including Deborah Dleano (Dasha), George William, James Abbott McNeill (painter Whistler's Mother), William Gibbs McNeill. Commd. 2d lt. arty. U.S. Army, assigned to topog. duty, 1819-21; asst. drawing tchr. U.S. Mil. Acad., 1821-22; surveyed internat. boundary between Lake Superior and Lake of the Woods; served in cabinet of U.S. Pres. as commr. to make surveys, plans, estimates, 1826-28, assigned to locate Balt. and Susquehanna R.R., then Paterson and Hudson R.R., circa 1829; resigned from U.S. Army as 1st lt., 1833; supr. Providence & Stonington R.R., 1837; cons. engr. Western R.R. of Mass., chief engr., 1840-42; began work in Russia, 1842, supr. constrn. of fortifications and docks at Cronstadt, ran bridge over Neva River (both in Russia). Decorated Order of St. Anne by Emperor of Russia, 1847. Died St. Petersburg, Russia, Apr. 7, 1848; buried Stonington, Conn.

WHITAKER, HERBERT COLEMAN, mathematician; b. Cape May, N.J., Oct. 31, 1862; s. Franklin and Lydia Leaming (Ross) W.; B.S., U. of Pa., 1885, M.E., 1886, Ph.D., 1896; m. Agnes Tweed, Dec. 22, 1887. Prof. mathematics in the high schools of Phila., 1887—, later head dept. of mathematics, South Phila. High Sch. Inventor. Author: Elements of Trigonometry (with tables), 1898. Extensive contbr. to math. jours., also on genealogy. Died Nov. 17, 1921.

WHITAKER, MILTON C., chem. engr.; b. Frazeysburg, O., Dec. 16, 1870; s. Reuben B. and Jennie (Magruder) W.; B.S., U. of Colo., 1898, M.S., 1900, LL.D., 1913; D.Chem. Engring., U. of Pittsburgh, 1915; m. Mabel Martin, July 9, 1900; children—John M., Robert M.; m. 2d, Frances Strader Culver, June 16, 1934. Instr. in chemistry, U. of Colo., 1898. Columbia, 1902; chemist, 1903, gen. supt., 1903-10, Welsbach Co.; prof. chem. engring., Columbia U., 1911-17; v.p. U.S. Industrial Alcohol Co., 1917-27; pres. U.S. Industrial Chem. Co., 1917-27; cons. practice in New York City, 1927-30; v.p., dir. Am. Cyanamid Co., 1930-47, cons., 1947—; dir. Ruberoid Co.; editor Jour. of Industrial and Engring. Chemistry, 1911-16. Awarded Perkin medal "for distinguished services to applied chemistry," 1923; medal for Excellence, Columbia, 1950; Chandler medal, Columbia, 1951. Mem. Am. Institute Chemical Engrs. (pres. 1914), Am. Inst. Chemists, Am. Chem. Soc., Soc. Chem. Industry, A.A.A.S., Chemists' Club, Delta Tau Delta, Phi Beta Kappa, Sigma Psi, Tau Beta Pi. Clubs: Chemists, Rockefeller Center Luncheon. Home: North East. Cecil County, Md. Office: 30 Rockefeller Plaza, N.Y.C. Died Apr. 2, 1963; buried St. Mary Anne's Episcopal Ch., North East, Cecil County, Md.

WHITAKER, ORVIL R(OBERT), mining engr.; b. Frazesburg, O., Oct. 21, 1875; s. Reuben Barker and Jennie (Magruder) W.; M.E., Colo. Sch. of Mines, 1898; m. Mina Killgore, June 14, 1905; children—Mary, Charles Killgore (dec.), Orvil Robert, George Barker. Assayer and chemist Silver Lake Mines, Colo., 1898-99; supt. of mines H. C. Harrison properties, Mexico, 1900; asst. mgr. and engr. Silver Lake Mines, 1901-02; engr. Anaconda Copper Mining Co., Butte, Mont., 1902; foreman War Eagle Mines, Rossland, B.C., Canada, 1903; supt. of mines New York and Honduras Rosario Mining Co., Honduras, C.A., 1903-04; examining engr. Guggenheim Exploration Co., 1905; gen. supt. mines Compania Minera de Penoles, Mapimi, Duranzo, Mexico, 1906-11; gen. cons. and operating practice since 1912; cons. engr. Molybdenum Corp. of America, Howe Sound Co., Molybdenum Gold Mining Co., Aspen Leases, Humphreys Gold Corp.; has made extensive examinations for various large companies; conducted investigation of ore smelting contracts for State of Colo., 1918, Province of British Columbia, Canada, 1919. Mem. Am. Inst. Mining and Mining Engrs., Mining and Metall. Soc. of America, Colo. Soc. Engrs. Club: University (Denver). Home: 1819 Gaylord St. Office: Equitable Bldg., Denver CO*

WHITE, ALFRED HOLMES, chem. engr.; b. Peoria, Ill., Apr. 29, 1873; s. Samuel Holmes and Jennie (McLaren) W.; student McGill U., 1889-90; A.B., U. Mich., 1893, B.S., 1904; grad. study Polytechnicum, Zurich, Switzerland, 1896-97; Sc.D., Northwestern, 1942; Eng.D. (hon.) U. Detroit, 1948; m. Rebecca Mason Downey, July 28, 1903; children—Alfred McLaren (dec.), Mary Julian. Asst. chemistry U. Ill., 1893-96; instr. chem. tech., U. Ch., 1897-1904, asst. prof. U. Mich., 1904-07, prof. chem. engring., 1907-43, prof. emeritus, 1943—, head dept. chem. engring., 1914, chmn. dept. chem. and metall. engring., 1938-42; cons. engr. U.S. Bur. Mines, 1907-20. Served from capt. to lt. col. Ordnance Dept., U.S. Army, 1917-19; chief research sect., asso. chief nitrate div., 1917-19; lt. col., Ordnance R.C., 1919, col., 1925; cons. chem. engr., Ordnance Dept., U.S. Army, 1919-22. Mem. Am. Gas Assn., Am. Inst. Chem. Engrs. (pres. 1929-31), Am. Soc. Testing Materials, Am. Chem. Soc., Soc. Promotion Engring. Edn. (pres. 1941-42), Phi Beta Kappa, Sigma Xi, Tau Beta Pi, Phi Lambda Upsilon, Alpha Chi Sigma, Phi Sigma Kappa. Republican. Unitarian. Clubs: Chemists (N.Y.C.); Cosmos (Washington); Rotary (Ann Arbor). Author: Technical Gas and Fuel Analysis, 1913; Engineering Materials, 1939. Contbr. tech. jours. Home: 120 E. 30th St., N.Y.C. Died Aug. 25, 1953.

WHITE, ARTHUR FAIRCHILD, analyst, statistician; b. Manhattan, Kan., Apr. 13, 1895; s. Francis H. and Anna D. (Fairchild) W.; A.B., Pomona (Calif.) Coll., 1916; m. Irene Leek, Oct. 19, 1918 (dec.); children—Arthur, Raymond, Donald, George; m. 2d, Mrs. Harriet Callis Frankman. Executive dept. statistician of Southern Pacific Co., San Fraicisco, 1918-33; pioneered in development of comparable transportation statistics for railways, water lines, bus and truck lines and coördination of railway with highway service, on staff of federal coördinator of transportation, Washington, D.C., 1933-35—in charge of collecting, analyzing and publishing statistics of railway, waterway, highway, airway and pipe-line traffic, service and costs; a leading govt. witness at Interstate Commerce Commn. hearings for investigations of railway passenger fares, 1935—; head cost analyst and asst. dir. Interstate Commerce Commn., Apr. 1935—. Home: Bethesda, Md. Died May 1, 1940.

WHITE, CANVASS, civil engr.; b. Whitesboro, N.Y., Sept. 8, 1790; s. Hugh and Tryphena (Lawrence) W.; m. Louisa Loomis, 1821, 3 children. Shipped as supercargo on mcht. vessel for Russia, 1811; returned, 1814, served as enlisted man during War of 1812; made extended trip to examine canal constrn. in Gt. Britain, 1817; patented waterproof cement, 1820; worked on Eastern sect. Erie Canal, 1816-25, supr. Glens Falls feeder; chief engr. Union Canal of Pa., 1825; cons. engr. Schuylkill Navigation Co., locks at Windsor (on Connecticut River), Farmington Canal; chief engr. Delaware & Raritan Canal (N.J.), Lehigh (Pa.) Canal. Died St. Augustine, Fla., Dec. 18, 1834.

WHITE, CHARLES ABIATHAR, geologist; b. North Dighton, Mass., Jan. 26, 1826; s. Abiathar and Nancy (Corey) W.; ed. there and Burlington, Ia.; M.D., Rush Med. Coll., Chicago, 1864; (hon. A.M., Ia. Coll., 1866; LL.D., State U. of Ia., 1893); m. Charlotte R. Pilkington, Sept. 28, 1848. State geologist of Ia., 1866-70; prof. natural history, State U. of Ia., 1867-73, Bowdoin Coll., Me., 1873-75; geologist and palaeontologist to various U.S. Govt. surveys, 1874-92. Honorarily connected with Smithsonian Instn. and U.S. Nat. Mus., 1895—. Author: Manual of Physical Geography of Iowa, 1873; Report on Invert. Fossils (Geog. and Geol. Expl.) and Surveys West of 100th Meridian, 1875; Bibliography of North American Invertebrate Palaeontology, 1878; Contribçôes á Palaeontolgia do Brazil, 1887; The Relation of Biology to Geological Investigation, 1894. Address: Washington. Died 1910.

WHITE, CHARLES EDGAR, mathematician; b. Trafalgar, Ind., Oct. 25, 1868; s. James Newton and Nancy Jane (Lane) W.; Central Normal Coll., Danville, Ind.; A.B., Ind. U., Bloomington, Ind., 1896, M.A., 1907; Vanderbilt U., 1908, 1909; m. Lillie E. Wright, of Bloomington, Ind., July 20, 1898. Principal high schs., Somerset, Garrette, Providence and Sheridan, Ind., and teacher mathematics, High Sch., Mishawaka, Ind., to 1906; instr. in mathematics, Vanderbilt U., 1908, 1909; prof. mathematics, W. Va. Wesleyan Coll., since 1909. Democrat. Methodist. Author: Theory of the Irreducible Cases of Equations, 1913. Address: Buckhannon, West Virginia.

WHITE, CHARLES HENRY, geologist; b. Yadkin County, N.C., Aug. 13, 1865; s. William and Sarah Catherine (Nicholson) W.; Licentiate of Instrn. diploma, Peabody Coll., 1887; student Vanderbilt U., 1887-88; S.B., U. N.C., 1894; S.B., Harvard, 1897, A.M., 1902; m. Josephine Pope, June 5, 1890 (died Jan. 4, 1919); m. 2d, Sarah Elizabeth MacDonald, June 4, 1920 (dec. Aug. 20, 1946); m. 3d, Marjorie Mills, Feb. 23, 1950. Asst. prof. mining and metallurgy Harvard, 1905-15, prof., 1915-17, chmn. dept., 1909-14; cons. geologist San Francisco, 1917—; has travelled in many countries for engring. and mining cos., mainly in search of copper mines. Commd. capt. Ordnance R.C., U.S. Army, and assigned to Watertown Arsenal, Feb. 14, 1918; discharged, Jan. 11, 1919; commd., Feb. 24, 1919, capt. Engrs. R.C. for 7 yrs. Mem. Am. Inst. Mining and Metall. Engrs., Soc. Econ. Geologists, Le Conte Geol. Club, Acad. Polit. Science, Calif. Acad. Sciences, Seismol. Soc. of Am., Harvard Engring. Soc., Phi Beta Kappa. Fellow Am. Geog. Soc., Royal Geog. Soc. Club: Commonwealth. Author: Methods in Metallurgical Analysis, 1915, 2d edit., 1920; Structural Geology, with Special Reference to Economic Deposits (with B. Stoces), 1936. Contbr. to tech. and scientific jours. Address: 3440 Clay St., San Francisco 18. Died Mar. 17, 1952; buried Cypress Lawn Cemetery, San Franciso.

WHITE, CHARLES JAMES, physician; b. Boston, Dec. 26, 1868; s. James Clarke and Martha Anna (Ellis) W.; A.B., Harvard, 1890, M.D., 1893; studied medicine in Paris, Vienna, London, Bonn, Berlin, Breslau and Prague, 1893-95; m. Olivia Alger Richardson, June 29, 1893; children—James C. (M.D.), Ellen Phelps (Mrs. Charles C. Cabot), Richardson. Asst. phys. diseases of skin Mass. Gen. Hosp., 1895-1903, physician, 1903-25, chief dermatol. dept., 1925-27, became mem. bd. consultation, 1927, hon. physician, 1939; asst. in dermatology Harvard Med. Sch., 1898-1902, instr., 1902-11, asst. prof., 1911-16, prof., 1916-27, now prof.

emeritus. Chmn. adv. bd. Com. Mass. Hosp. for Lepers; cons. dermatologist Boston Insane, Infants' and N.E. Deaconess hosps., Mass. Charitable Eye and Ear Infirmary, Editorial bd. Archive Dermatology and Syphilology. Republican. Trustee First Church of Boston. Hon. fellow London Dermatol. Soc.; hon. mem. Am. Dermatol. Assn. (sec., treas. 1902-05, pres. 1915-16), Am. Acad. Dermatology and Syphilology, N.E. Soc. Dermatology and Syphilology (sec. 1910-12); mem. Mass. Med. Soc. (chmn. dermatol. sect. 1935), A.M.A. (chmn. dermatol. sect. 1910-12), A.A.A.S., Am. Assn. for Cancer Research, Boston Med. Library Assn.; corr. hon. mem. dermatol. sect. of Brit. Royal Soc. Medicine; corr. mem. Brit. Assn. Dermatology and Syphilogy; corr. fgn. mem. Soc. Franc. de Dermatologie et de Syphiligraph-Danish Dermotol. Soc., Vienna Dermatol. Soc. Contbr. to med. jours. Home: 259 Marlborough St., Boston. Died 1964.

WHITE, CHARLES JOYCE, mathematician; b. Cambridge, Mass., Jan. 5, 1839; s. Thomas and Sarah (Russell) Joyce (name of White added by act of legislature, 1846); A.B., Harvard, 1859, A.M., 1862; unmarried. Pvt. tutor, 1859-61; asst. prof. and prof., 1861-70, first mathematics, and later astronomy and navigation, U.S. Naval Acad.; asst. prof. mathematics, 1870-85, prof., 1885-94, prof. emeritus, 1911—, Harvard; registrar faculty, Harvard Coll., 1875-88. Author: Elements of Theoretical and Descriptive Astronomy, 7 editions, 1869-1901. Died Feb. 12, 1917.

WHITE, DAVID, geologist; b. Palmyra, N.Y., July 1, 1862; s. Asa Kendrick and Elvira (Foster) W.; B.S., Cornell, 1886; D.Sc., U. of Cincinnati and U. of Rochester, 1924, Williams Coll., 1925; m. Mary Elizabeth Houghton, Feb. 2, 1888. With U.S. Geol. Survey, 1886—, now sr. geologist; also curator in paleobotany, Smithsonian Institution, 1903—; associate of Carnegie Institution. Mem. Am. Acad. Arts and Sciences; mem. various scientific societies. Home: Washington, D.C. Died Feb. 7, 1935.

WHITE, EDWARD HIGGINS II, astronaut; b. San Antonio, Nov. 14, 1930; s. Edward Higgins and Mary (Haller) W.; B.S., U.S. Mil. Acad., 1952; M.S. in Aero. Engring., U. Mich., 1959, Dr. Astronautics (hon.), 1965; grad. Air Force Test Pilot Sch., 1959; m. Patricia Eileen Finegan, Jan. 31, 1963; children—Edward, Bonnie Lynn. Commd. 2d lt. USAF, 1952, advanced through grades to lt. col., 1965; flight tng., Fla. and Tex., 1952-54; assigned fighter squadron in Germany, 1954-57; exptl. test pilot fighter div. aero. systems div., Wright Patterson AFB, O., 1960-66; became astronaut NASA, Oct. 1962; apptd. sr. pilot Apollo I; made 4 day orbital flight in Gemini-Titan 4, June 3, 1965; became first Am. to walk in space, first to propel self in space with maneuvering unit during extra vehicular activity. Active Scouting activities, Little League. Recipient Gen. Thomas D. White Space Trophy, 1966. Mem. Soc. Exptl. Test Pilots, Sigma Delta Psi, Tau Beta Pi; asso. mem. Inst. Aero. Scis. Home: Seabook, Tex. Office: Manned Spacecraft Center, NASA, Houston. Died Jan. 27, 1967.

WHITE, GEORGE FREDERIC, chemist; b. Melrose, Mass., June 15, 1885; s. George and Elizabeth (Dyer) W.; S.B., Mass. Inst. Tech., 1906; Ph.D., Johns Hopkins, 1910; m. Emma Clarke, Oct. 22, 1913; children—George Frederic, Virginia Clarke. Asst. in analytic and organic chemistry, Mass. Inst. Tech., 1906-08; fellow Johns Hopkins, 1909-10; asso. prof. chemistry, Richmond Coll., 1910-12; instr. organic chemistry, 1912-13, asst. prof., 1913-18, asso. prof., 1918-20, prof., 1920-25, Clark U.; dir. scientific dept. Baner & Black, Chicago, 1925—. Research chemist, U.S. Bur. of Fisheries, 1910-16, U.S. Pub. Health Service, 1916-18, Worcester City Hosp., 1919; prof. summer session, Coll. of William and Mary, 1923. Author: Laboratory Manual of Inorganic Chemistry, 1911; Qualitative Chemical Analysis, 1916. Episcopalian. Home: Evanston, Ill. Died Sept. 1929.

WHITE, GEORGE STARR, physician, surgeon; b. Danbury, Conn., July 13, 1866; s. William Starr and Mary Elizabeth (Nichols) W.; ed. under pvt. tutors; Yale U.; studied medicine with preceptors, 1881-85; "drugless" practician till 1904; Cornell U. of Med. Coll., 1904-06 (med. teaching); M.D., New York Homoe. Med. Coll. and Flower Hosp., 1908; Ph.D., Nat. Eclectic Inst., Inc., Pa., 1918; LL.D., Oscaloosa Coll., 1919; N.D., D.C., Ph.C., Los Angeles College of chiropractic, 1921; D.O., Vetus Academia Physio Medica, Inc., Pa., 1921. Inventor and designer of wire-working machinery and elec. machines, also physicians' and surgeons' apparatus; discoverer of magnetic meridian and color method of diagnosing disease; discovered new methods for making milk foods and largely interested in their mfr., 1895-1913. Lecturer on bio-dynamo-chromatics, diagnosis and modern physical therapeutics. Fellow Inc. Soc. of Science, Letters and Art (London), Am. Electro-Therapeutic Assn.; mem. Nat. and Central socs. physical therapeutics, Nat. Assn. Audubon Socs., Vol. Med. Service Corps U.S.A., etc. Unitarian. Mason. Author: Guide Book to Infant Feeding, 1908; Fermented Milk in Health and Disease, 1908; Lecture Course on Diagnosis and Physical Therapeutics, 1915 (7th edit., 1918); Prostatic Disease and Impotency, 1919; Think, 1920; Youth, 1921; The Natural Way, 17th edit., 1922; also many papers on med. subjects. Address: 327 S. Alvarado St., Los Angeles, Calif.

WHITE, HENRY CLAY, chemist; b. Baltimore, Md., Dec. 30, 1848; s. Levi S. and Louisa (Brown) W.; B.S., C.E. and M.E., U. of Va., 1870, Ph.D., 1875; hon. Ph.D., U. of Ga., 1877; D.C.L., U. of South, 1904; LL.D., Ill., 1905, Columbia, 1908, Ga., 1922; Sc.D.; Mich., 1907; m. Ella Frances, d. Leonard F. Roberts, of Chester Co., Pa., Dec. 19, 1872 (died 1913). Prof. chemistry, Md. Inst., 1870-71; science lecturer, Peabody Inst., Baltimore, 1871; prof. chemistry, St. John's Coll., Annapolis, Md., 1871-72, prof. chemistry, U. of Ga., 1872—. Pres. Ga. State Coll. Agr. and Mech. Arts (U. of Ga.), 1890-1907; state chemist of Ga., 1880-90; chief chemist Ga. Expt. Sta., 1888-1914. Pres. Assn. Official Chemists of U.S., 1881-82, Assn. Am. Agrl. Coll. and Expt. Stas., 1897-98 (chmn. exec. com., 1901-07); fellow Chem. Soc., London, 1880, A.A.A.S. Author: Elementary Geology of Tennessee (with Wm. Gibbs McAdoo), 1873; Complete Chemistry of the Cotton Plant, 1874; Lectures and Addresses (2 vols.), 1885-91; Manuring of Cotton, 1896. Collaborator U.S. Dept. Agr. Cotton Investigations, 1895-96; dietary studies, 1903-05. Home: Athens, Ga. Died Nov. 30, 1927.

WHITE, ISRAEL C., geologist; b. Monongalia County, W.Va., Nov. 1, 1848; s. Michael and Mary A. (Russell) W.; A.M., W.Va. U., 1872; Columbia, 1876-77; Ph.D., U. Ark., 1880; LL.D., W.Va. U., 1919; D.Sc., U. of Pittsburgh, 1921; m. Mary M. Moorhead, Dec. 4, 1878; m. 2d, Mrs. Julia Wildman, Feb. 12, 1925. Asst. geologist, 2d geol. survey, Pa., 1875-84, and author of 8 reports of same; asst. geologist, U.S. Geol. Survey, 1884-88; prof. geology, W.Va. U., 1877-92; resigned to take charge of a large petroleum business; state geologist of W.Va., 1897—; cons. geologist B.&O. R.R. Co. and Hope Natural Gas Co., 1916—. Chief, Brazilian Coal Commn., 1904-06. Specialist in coal, petroleum and natural gas; made discoveries in connection with those products. Treas. Geol. Soc. America, 1892-1907 (pres. 1920); pres. Am. Assn. Petroleum Geologists, 1919-20; v.p. A.A.A.S., 1896-97; del. Internat. Geol. Congress, St. Petersburg, 1897, Paris, 1900; one of the speakers at the White House Conf. of Governors, May 13-15, 1908. Mem. Nat. Advisory Bd. apptd. by President Roosevelt, 1906; mem. federal trade com. Chamber Commerce U.S.A. Trustee Kiwanis International, 1923-25. Home: Morgantown, W.Va. Died Nov. 25, 1927.

WHITE, JAMES GILBERT, capitalist, engr., contractor; b. Milroy, Pa., Aug. 29, 1861; s. Rev. J. W. and Mary Miller (Beaver) W.; A.B., Pa. State College, 1882, A.M., 1884; Ph.D., Cornell Univ., 1885; m. Maud Mullon, Dec. 15, 1886; 1 son, James Dugald. Instr. physics in charge of dept., U. of Neb., 1885-87; pres. Western Engring Co., 1887-90; with Edison United Mfg. Co., 1890; in business as contractor, engr. and investment banker since 1890; established J. G. White & Co., Ltd., London, 1900. Mem. Am. Inst. E.E., Am. Soc. C.E., Pa. Soc., New York Elec. Soc., The Pilgrims, S.R. Home: Greenwich, Conn. Office: 37 Wall St., New York, N.Y. Died June 2, 1942.

WHITE, (JOHN) BEAVER, engineer; b. Milroy, Pa., June 10, 1874; s. Rev. John W. and Mary Miller (Beaver) W.; B.S. in M.E., Pa. State Coll., 1894; M.E. in E.E., Cornell, 1899; m. in Buckinghamshire, Eng., Harriet H. Stevens, of Lewiston, Idaho, June 9, 1904 (died Mar. 25, 1928); children—Harriet, Clarissa, Joan, Louise; m. 2d, Margery Thompson Sperry, of London, Eng., July 25, 1934. Began with J. G. White & Company, engineers and builders, Baltimore, Md., 1894; gen. mgr. and engr. Eastchester Electric Co., Mt. Vernon, N.Y., 1896-98; practiced at Salisbury and Winston-Salem, N.C., 1899-1900; constructing electric light and power and street ry., San Juan, P.R., 1900-01; in Mandalay, Burma, and Hyderabad and Bombay, India, 1901-02; in charge street ry. constrn. in many cities in England, for J. G. White & Co., Ltd., 1902-04; financial dir. same company, in London, Eng., 1904-09; established firm Beaver White & Co., London, 1909; dir. Internat. Light & Power Co., Home and Foreign Securities Company. Member of American Relief Committee, London, 1914-15; dir. Commn. for Relief in Belgium, in charge purchase and shipping, London, 1914-15, in America, 1915-16; was mem. Advisory Com. for Belgian Relief; assisted in preliminary work of U.S. Food Administration; representative of U.S. Food Administrator on Exports Administrative Bd.; mem. War Trade Bd., representing the food administrator, Oct. 1917-Feb. 1919. Chmn. Am. delegation to Internat. Communications Conf., Paris, 1925; apptd. by President Coolidge del. to Internat. Radio Conf., Washington, 1927; apptd. by President Hoover as mem. Annual Assay Commn., 1933. Officer Order of the Crown, Belgium, 1919. Studying economic conditions in Eng., France and Germany. Home: Villa Nova PA Office: Land Title Bldg., Philadelphia PA

WHITE, JOHN BLAKE, physician; b. Charleston, S.C., Oct. 9, 1850; ed. Phillips Exeter Acad., class of 1869; entered Harvard, class of 1873, but left in junior yr. to commence study of medicine; M.D., Coll. Phys. and Surg. (Columbia), 1874; m. Margaret Stuyvesant, d. late George E. B. Jackson, of Portland, Me., Oct. 25, 1877. House surgeon Brooklyn City Hosp., 1875; sanitary insp., New York, 10 yrs.; visiting phys. to Charity Hosp. 12 yrs., and held other hosp. positions; lecturer Post-Grad. Med. Coll. 2 yrs.; authority on diseases of the chest. Mem. numerous med. socs., author many papers. Address: 1013 Madison Av., New York.

WHITE, JOHN DEHAVEN, dentist; b. New Holland, Pa., Aug. 19, 1815; s. John and Sarah (DeHaven) W.; studied medicine and dentistry, 1836, grad. Jefferson Med. Coll., 1844; m. Mary Elizabeth Meredith, 1836, 11 children. Carpenter's apprentice, 1833-36; practiced dentistry, Phila., 1837-93; an organizer Pa. Assn. Dental Surgeons, 1845, pres., 1857; mem. Am. Soc. Dental Surgeons, 1850; an organizer Phila. Coll. Dental Surgery, 1852, prof. anatomy and physiology, 1854-56; editor-in-chief Dental News Letter, 1853-59; an editor Dental Cosmos, 1859-65; v.p. Am. Dental Conv., 1861. Author: Mary Blaine and Hazel Dell and Miscellaneous Poems, (volume of poetry) 1870. Died Masonic Home, Phila., Dec. 25, 1895.

WHITE, JOSEPH AUGUSTUS, prof. ophthalmology; b. Baltimore, Md., Apr. 19, 1848; s. Ambrose M. and Mary (Hurley) W.; A.B., A.M., Mt. St. Mary's Coll., Md., 1867, LL.D., 1929; M.D., U. of Md., 1869; post-grad. study College of Phys. and Surg. (Columbia), and at London, Paris, Freiburg, Heidelberg, Berlin, until 1872; m. Sophie Berney, December 27, 1877 (died September 1901). Began practice at Baltimore, 1872, moved to Richmond, 1880; specializes in diseases of eye, ear, throat and nose; prof. ophthalmology, Med. Coll. of Va., since 1893. Mem. Va. Council of Defense, World War. Mem. A.M.A., Med. Soc. of Va., Am. Ophthal. Soc., Am. Otol. Soc., Am. Laryngol., Rhinol. and Otel. Soc., Nat. Inst. Social Sciences, S.A.R., Pi Mu. Democrat. Catholic. Clubs: Westmoreland, Commonwealth, Country. Author of numerous addresses before med. socs. and articles in med. publs. Home: 3020 Hanes Av., Richmond, Va. *

WHITE, JOSEPH HILL, sanitarian; b. Milledgeville, Ga., May 4, 1859; s. Edward J. and M.A. (Hill) W.; pvt. and high schs.; M.D., Coll. Phys. and Surg., Baltimore, 1883; m. Emily H. Humber, Jan. 8, 1885; children—Emily H. (Mrs. R.A. Herring), Mary Roberta, Josephine H., Joseph H. Entered U.S. Marine Hosp. Service (since changed to U.S. Pub. Health Service), Oct. 2, 1884; passed asst. surgeon, Oct. 1887; surgeon, Aug. 1898; detailed to asst. surg.-gen., in charge of service quarantine div., 1899-1903; senior surgeon, 1915; asst. surgeon gen., 1920; first chmn. National Leprosy Commn. Lecturer on hygiene and tropical diseases, University of Alabama, 1903-05. Sanitary work as quarantine officer, 1885-91; in charge of smallpox epidemic in Southern Ga., 1891; sanitary rep. of U.S. at Hamburg during cholera epidemic, 1893; inspecting quarantine officer from Norfolk to Jacksonville, 1894; in charge smallpox epidemic, Key West, Fla., 1896, yellow fever epidemics in La. and Miss., 1897-98; inspected the troops returning from Cuba, 1898; eliminated the yellow fever out-break at Soldiers' Home, Hampton, 1899; disinfected San Francisco after plague, 1900; given full control by nat., state and city authorities to stamp out yellow fever epidemic, New Orleans, 1905 (epidemic fully started—wiped out before frost, for first time in history of yellow fever); dir. for Latin-America, Internat. Health Commn., 1914. On request of sec. of war was detailed to war service, July 1917, and served through the war as gen. insp. of anti-malarial work for army; commd. col., May 1918; eradicated epidemic of yellow fever in Guatemala, Sept. 1918; chief general inspector U.S.P.H.S., February 1919-23. Vice director International Sanitary Bureau, 1920-25, retired; member Yellow Fever Council since 1921. Lecturer on public health, U. of Tenn. Summer School, 1915-19, and Peabody Coll., Nashville, Tenn. Decorated Grand Officer of Order of Quetzai by Govt. of Guatemala for distinguished service with commendation by the president personally, Jan. 1943. Chmn. Section of Hygiene and Sanitary Science A.M.A., 1909; pres. Am. Soc. Tropical Medicine, 1911; hon. mem. Orleans Parish Med. Soc.; U.S. del. 6th Internat. Sanitary Conf., Montevideo, 1920. Pioneer proponent of total eradication yellow fever and director yellow fever campaigns for International Health Board in all Latin-America, 1921-27. Clubs: Mobile Round Table (hon. life); Egyptians (Memphis); Cosmos (Washington). Author of many papers on sanitary science. Contbr. to Nelson's System of Medicine, 1927-29. Home: 2955 Newark St., Washington DC

WHITE, J(OSEPH) WARREN, orthopedic surgeon; b. Boston, Mass., Mar. 2, 1892; s. Dr. Herbert Warren and Elizabeth (Dudley) W.; grad. Roxbury (Mass.) Latin Sch., 1909; A.B., Harvard, 1913, M.D., 1917 m. Helen Angell, Aug. 18, 1917; children—Joseph Warren, Gilbert Angell. Interne Quiriqua Hosp. Guatemala 1915; became assistant surgeon, United States Navy, May 1917; served at sea, 1917-19; then student orthopedic surgery for 18 months; charge orthopedic service Chelsea Naval Hosp., 1921-23; resigned from U.S. Navy, 1923; private practice as orthopedic surgeon, Boston, 1923-24; orthopedic staff, Mass. Gen. Hospital, 1921-24; chief surgeon Shriners Hospital for Crippled Children, Honolulu, 1924-27; chief surgeon Shriners Hosp., Greenville, S.C., 1927-49. Orthopedic surg. local base hosp. unit, U.S.P.H.S. Res. Chmn. tech. adv. com., div. for crippled children, State Bd. of Health, 1936-46; cons. orthopedic surgeon Oliver Gen. Hosp.,

Augusta, Ga., 1946-49, Tripler Gen. Hosp., Honolulu, 1949—; world med. tour lectr. New Delhi and Barcelona, 1957; teaching mission to Japan, cons. Surg. Gen. Army, 1948; cons. orthopedic surg. Territorial Bd. of Health since 1949. Hale Mohalu (Hosp. for Lepers), 1949-54; chief orthopedic service Kuakino Hosp. (Japanese); chief orthopedic sect. Straub Clinic; mem. advisory bd., chief fracture service Queens Hosp., Honolulu. Instr. orthopedic surg. Harvard, 1921-24, Duke U., 1945-49. Trustee Furman U., 1938-49. Licentiate Am. Bd. Orthopedic Surgery since 1935. (mem. bd. 1948-50); mem. Am. (pres. 1954-55), Western (pres. 1954-55) orthopedic assns., Pan Pacific Surgical Association (trustee), American Academy Orthopedic Surgeons, A.M.A. (chmn. Orthopedic Section, 1947), S.C. State Med. Soc. (v.p. 1942-43), So. Med. Assn. (councilor S.C. 1943-48), A.C.S. (pres. local chpt. 1955-56; chmn. com. on trauma 1953—), La Societe Internationale de Chirurgia Orthopedique, Hawaii Terr. Med. Assn., Orthopedic Forum Am. Assn. R.R. Surgeons. Mason (Shriner; Jester). Clubs: Rotary, Elks, Outrigger, Aesculapian, Adventurers, Pacific. Kahala Yacht. Contbr. med. jours. Home: Diamond Head Apts., 2969 Kalakaua Av., Honolulu 96815. Office: 1020 Kapiolani, Honolulu. Died Sept. 12, 1959; buried Greenville, S.C.

WHITE, LAZARUS, civil engr.; b. Rochester, N.Y., Feb. 26, 1874; s. Max A. and Ann (Lewine) W.; student N.Y.U., 1892-93; C.E., Columbia, 1897; m. Marie Emelin, June 23, 1904; children—Felicia Marie (wife of Dr. Hans Peter Gossman), Edward Emelin, Robert Emelin. Inspector U.S. Engrs. Key West, Fla., 1897-98; rodman Pa. R.R., Jersey City, 1898-1900; asst. engr. Rapid Transit Commn., N.Y., 1900-06; div. engr. Bd. of Water Supply, New York, 1906-14; engr. Smith, Hauser & MacIsaac, 1914-19; pres. Spencer, White and Prentis, Inc., 1919-50, ret.; pres. Pleasantville Construction Co.; mem. exec. com. Dry Dock Associates. Recipient Egleston medal Columbia, 1941. Mem. Soc. for Ethical Culture, Am. Acad. Science, Am. Soc. for Testing Materials, Am. Soc. C.E. (dir.), Sigma Xi. Clubs: Engineers, Columbia University (N.Y.C.); Faculty (Harvard U.). Author: Catskill Water Supply of New York City, 1911. Co-author: (with E. A. Prentis) Modern Underpinning, 1917; Underpinning, 1929; Cofferdams, 1940. Contbr. to mags. Home: 28 Pryer Lane, Larchmont, N.Y. Died July 30, 1953; buried Mt. Pleasant Cemetery, Hawthorne, N.Y.

WHITE, OCTAVIUS AUGUSTUS, physician; b. Charleston, S.C., Feb. 8, 1826; s. John Blake and Anna O. (Driscoll) W.; grad. Coll. of Charleston, 1946, A.M., 1847, LL.D., 1890; grad. S.C. Med. Coll., 1848; m. Claudia R. Bellinger, 1849 (died 1852); m. 2d, Elizabeth Winthrop Chanler, 1855. Confederate surgeon during Civil War; yellow fever expert; served through numerous epidemics in Charleston, S.C.; at Wilmington, N.C., 1862; Savannah, Ga., 1876; etc. In practice in New York, 1865—; writer on med. and surg. subjects—especially yellow fever; invented numerous surg. instruments. Died 1903.

WHITE, PHILIP (RODNEY), research physiologist; b. Chgo., July 25, 1901; s. Henry K. and Mary J. (Pattee) W.; A.B., University of Montana, 1922, D.Sc. (hon.), 1956; student University of Wash., 1922-23, Ecole Normale d'Instituteurs, Valence, France, 1923-24; Ph.D., Johns Hopkins, 1928; guest investigator, U. Berlin, Germany, 1930-31; m. Caroline D. M. Smith, Nov. 22, 1935; children—Christopher John, Jonathan Peter (dec.). Asst. botany U. Mont., 1920-21; grad. asst. U. Wash., 1922-23; lectr. d'Anglais, Ecole Normale d'Instituteurs, Valence, France, 1923-24; microscopic technician Bur. Plant Industry, Dept. of Agr., 1925-26; research asst. botany and U. Fellow Johns Hopkins, 1924-26; Johns Hopkins Tropical Expdn., Jamaica, B.W.I., 1926; spl. investigator United Fruit Co., Jamaica, Panama, Costa Rica, 1926-28; asst. prof. botany and plant physiology U. Mo., 1928-29; Nat. Research Council fellow, Boyce Thompson Inst. for Plant Research, 1929-30; Rockefeller Found. fellow Pflanzenphysiologisches Inst., U. Berlin, 1930-31; fellow dept. animal and plant pathology, Rockefeller Inst. for Med. Research, Princeton, N.J., 1932-34, asst., 1934-38, asso., 1938-45; sr. mem., dir. div. gen. physiology Inst. for Cancer Research, Phila., 1945-51; research asso. Roscoe B. Jackson Meml. Lab., Bar Harbor, Me., 1951-56, sr. staff scientist, 1957-66. Summer lectr. Ia. State Coll., 1942; guest prof. Yale, 1947-48; in charge summer tissue culture program Mt. Desert Island Biol. Lab., 1947-53; exchange prof. University of Paris, 1958-59; Distinguished visiting prof. Pa. State University, in 1963; lecturer University Me., 1965-66, univs. Delhi, Poona, Bombav, Baroda, Calcutta. 1967-68. Recipient Centenary medal; Societe Bot. de France, 1954, Medal of Honor, U. of Liege, 1959; Philip White lectureship founded in his honor Indian Acad. Scis. Fellow Am. Acad. Arts and Scis., A.A.A.S. (Cleveland medal 1965); mem. Am. Soc. Plant Physiologists (Stephan Hales award, 1940). Internat. Soc. Cell Biology, Soc. Study Growth and Devel., Am. Bot. Soc., Internat. Society Plant Morphology, Am. Soc. Naturalists, Tissue Culture Assn. (pres. 1958-59). Soc. Gen. Physiologists, Scandinavian Society Plant Physiology. Societe Francais de Physiology Veget Sigma Xi. Sigma Upsilon. Phi Sigma. Author: A Handbook of Plant Tissue Culture, 1943; Micrurgical and Germ-Free Methods (with others). 1943: Cultivation of Animal and Plant Cells, 1954, rev. edit. 1963. Home: Bar Harbor ME Died Mar. 25, 1968; buried West Parish Cemetery, Winchester NH

WHITE, ROLLIN HENRY, mech. engr.; b. Cleve., July 11, 1872; s. Thomas Howard (founder White Sewing Machine Co.) and Almira Louise (Greenleaf) W.; M.E., Cronell U., 1894; m. Katharine Elizabeth King, Sept. 2, 1896; children—Katharine Elizabeth, William King, Rollin Henry. Began with White Sewing Machine Co., 1894; served as chief engr., v.p. White Motor Co.; organized Cleve. Tractor Co., 1916, pres., 1916-26, chmn. bd., 1926—. Awarded 2 gold medals for inventions. Home: Hobe Sound, Fla. Died Sept. 10, 1962; buried Lake View Cemetery, Cleve.

WHITE, SAMUEL STOCKTON, dentist; b. Hulmeville, Bucks County, Pa., June 19, 1822; s. William Rose and Mary (Stockton) W.; m. Sarah Jane Carey, Mar. 31, 1846, 7 children. Began practice of dentistry, 1843; began mfg. artificial teeth with firm Jones and White, Phila., circa 1845, branches established, N.Y.C., 1846, Boston, 1850, Chgo., 1858, largest co. in world for prodn. of porcelain teeth, for 75 years, also manufactured instruments, appliances, supplies for dentists, introduced new improved dental chairs, engines, appliances, instruments, materials for dental offices and laboratories; mem. Pa. Assn. Dental Surgeons; mem. exec. com. Am. Dental Conv., 1868. Died Paris, France, Dec. 30, 1879.

WHITE, WALTER PORTER, physical investigator; born Roxbury, Mass., Feb. 23, 1867; s. Frederick Oscar and Ruth Porter (Stockbridge) W.; A.B., Amherst, 1887; post-grad. work, Harvard, Mass. Inst. Tech., U. of Wis.; Ph.D., Cornell U., 1904; m. Christina I. Thomson, Aug. 14, 1901. Taught school, 1887-89, 1891-1901; engaged in investigations at Geophys. Lab., Washington, 1904-35. Member Philos. Society, Washington (pres. 1923), Am. Physical Soc. Author: The Modern Calorimeter, 1928; also numerous scientific papers. Address: 3210 Newark St., Washington. Died Feb. 7, 1946.

WHITE, WILLIAM CRAWFORD, surgeon; b. Hoboken, N.J., Aug. 20, 1886; s. William Henry and Mary (Lavell) W.; B.S., Wesleyan U., 1908, Sc.D., 1946; M.D., Columbia, 1912; m. Caroline Ruth Taylor, June 1, 1917; children—Thomas Taylor, Mary Lavell (Mrs. John Lawrence Fearey), Norval Crawford. Interne, Roosevelt Hosp., 1913-15, surgical pathologist, 1921-28, assistant attending surgeon, 1921-28, asso., 1928-40, chief 2d surgical division Roosevelt Hospital, 1940-52, consulting surgeon since 1952; attending surgeon Lincoln Hospital, 1920-25; consultant surgeon N.Y. Nursery and Childs. 1928-33, Tuxedo Memorial Hospital, 1930—, St. Luke's Hospital, Lincoln Hosp., Vassar Bros. Hosp., Poughkeepsie, N.Y., Meml. Hosp., Morristown, N.J., Norwalk (Conn.) Hosp.; instr. in surg., Coll. of Physicians and Surgeons, Columbia U., 1916-28, asst. clin. prof., 1938-42, clin. prof. of surgery, 1942-52. Served as capt., M.C., A.E.F., World War I, 1917-19. Trustee Wesleyan U., 1942—. A founder Am. Bd. of Surgery, 1937. Fellow Am. Coll. fo Surgeons; mem. N.Y. County Med. Soc. (pres., 1946-47), A.M.A., N.Y. Surg. Soc. (pres. 1943-45), Am. Surg. Assn. N.Y. Acad. Med. (v.p. 1950-53), Am. Cancer Soc. (dir. 1939-46), N.Y. Cancer Soc. (pres.), Phi Beta Kappa, Phi Nu Theta. Pres. Soc. Relief Widows and Orphans of Med. Men. 1938—. Clubs: Century, Clinical Research, Hospital Graduates. Republican. Presbyterian. Author: Cancer of the Breast, 1930. Contbr. many surgical papers to surg. and med. jours. Address: Boggs Hill Rd., Newtown, Conn. 06470. Died Nov. 22, 1962.

WHITE, WILLIAM LAWRENCE, botanist; b. Salina, Pa., May 29, 1908; B.S., Pa. State Coll., 1934; Ph.D., Cornell U., 1940; A.M. (hon.), Harvard, 1948. Asst. curator fungi Garlow Herbarium, Harvard, 1940-45; sr. mycologist, supv. mycol. lab., Q.M.C., Phila., 1946-48; dir. Farlow Library and Herbarium, also asso. prof. botany, Harvard, 1948—; cons. research and development labs. Q.M.C., U.S. Army, 1948—. Mem. Mycol. Soc. Am., Bot. Soc. Am. Home: 45 Hillcrest St., Arlington, Mass. Died July 30, 1952.

WHITE, WILLIAM MONROE, hydraulic engr.; b. 1871; student Univ. of Ala.; M.E., Tulane U., 1899, hon. D.Sc., 1930; unmarried. Engr. with New Orleans Drainage Bd., 1899-1902; hydraulic engr. and chief engr., I. P. Morris Dept. of Wm. Cramp & Sons Ship and Engine Bldg. Co., Phila., 1902-11; was in charge hydraulic work of the co., including design and building of large hydro-electric installations in N. America, including those at Niagara Falls; chief engr. and mgr. hydraulic dept. Allis-Chalmers Mfg. Co., Milwaukee, Wis., 1911-43; cons. engr. since Jan. 1943; pres. Milwaukee Art Inst., 1941-46. Mem. Am. Soc. M.E., Nat. Electric Light Assn., Am. Inst. E.E., Sigma Xi, Tau Beta Pi. Contbr. numerous articles in tech. jours. of U.S., Europe and Japan. Received from Nat. Assn. of Mfrs., award of "Modern Pioneer," 1938. Home: 2963 N. Summit Av. Address: First Wisconsin Nat. Bank, Milwaukee, Wis. Died Feb. 9, 1949.

WHITE, WILLIAM NATHANIEL, horticulturist, editor; b. Longridge, Conn., Nov. 28, 1819; s. Anson and Anna (Fitch) W.; grad. Hamilton Coll., N.Y., 1847; m. Rebecca Benedict, Aug. 28, 1848, 9 children. Moved to Terminus (now Atlanta), Ga. for health reasons, 1847, taught 30 pupils there; mgr. bookstore owned by W. C. Richards, Athens, Ga., 1848, owner, operator, 1849-67; became expert in horticulture and pomology; wrote for Atlanta Luminary Horticulturist, Gardener's Monthly; asst. editor newspaper Southern Cultivator, 1862, assumed full control, 1863, maintained paper throughout Civil War; mem. 9th Regt., Ga. State Guards, 1863-64. Author: Gardening for the South, 1856. Died July 14, 1867.

WHITEHEAD, JOHN BOSWELL, elec. engr.; b. Norfolk, Va., Aug. 18, 1872; s. Henry Colgate and Margaret Walke (Taylor) W.; EE., Johns Hopkins, 1893, A.B., 1898, Ph.D. 1902; m. Mary Ellen Colston, Apr. 14, 1903; children—Clara (dec.), Margaret Walke, Joan Boswell. Elec. engr. Westinghouse Electric & Mfg. Co., 1893-96, Niagara Falls (N.Y.) Power Co., 1896-97; instr. applied electricity Johns Hopkins, 1897-1900, asso., 1901-04, asso. prof., 1904-10, prof., 1910—, dean, 1919-38, dir. Sch. Engring., 1938-42, prof. emeritus, 1942—; exchange prof. to France, 1926-27. Lab. asst. U.S. Bur. Standards, 1902; research asst. Carnegie Instn. Washington, 1902-05. Edison medalist, 1941. Fellow Am. Inst. E.E. (pres. 1933-34); Am. Phys. Soc., A.A.A.S.; mem. Nat. Acad. Scis., Nat. Research Council, Société Française des Electriciens, (hon.), Phi Beta Kappa, Tau Beta Pi, Delta Phi, Commd. maj. Engr. R.C., 1917. Democrat. Episcopalian. Clubs: Maryland, Johns Hopkins. Author: Electric Operation of Steam Railways, 1909; Dielectric Theory and Insulation, 1927; Impregnated Paper Insulation, 1935; Electricity and Magnetism, 1939; also many researches in field of high voltage insulation. Home: 3100 St. Paul St., Balt. 18. Died Nov. 16, 1954.

WHITEHEAD, RICHARD HENRY, anatomist; b. Salisbury, N.C., July 27, 1865; s. Marcellus (M.D.) and Virginia (Coleman) W.; A.B., Wake Forest Coll., N.C., 1886; M.D., U. of Va., 1887; LL.D., U. of N.C., 1910; m. Virgilia Whitehead, June 4, 1891. Demonstrator anatomy, U. of Va., 1887-89; prof. anatomy and dean med. dept., U. of N.C., 1891-1905; prof. anatomy and dean of med. dept., U. of Va., 1905—. Author: Anatomy of the Brain, 1900. Contbr. of anat. and pathol. papers to med. jours. Died Feb. 6, 1916.

WHITEHOUSE, F(REDERIC) COPE, lawyer; b. Rochester, N.Y., Nov. 9, 1842; s. Rt. Rev. Henry John and Evelina Harriet (Bruen) W.; A.B. (highest honors), Columbia, 1861, A.M., 1863; studied in France, Germany and Italy; unmarried. Admitted to bar, 1871. Hon. mem. fellow and corr. mem. of many learned socs. in U.S., Europe and Egypt; made Comdr. of Osmanieh and Grand Officier Medjidieh on account of efforts for better regulation of the Nile. Discovered the depression in the Egyptian desert known as the Wadi Raiyan, 1882, and wrote many papers advocating it as a storage reservoir. Made extensive researches in Semitic traditions relating to the Canal of Joseph and the land of Goshen, which he identified with the Fayoum, submerged in the time of Herodotus and then known as Lake Moeris. Frequent contbr. on topics relating to astron., geol. and other scientific subjects, and on foreign banks and banking. Home: Newport, R.I. Died 1911.

WHITFIELD, J(AMES) EDWARD, chemist; b. Albany, N.Y., Sept. 27, 1859; s. Robert P. and Mary (Henry) W.; acad. edn.; Ph.D., Nat. Coll. Pharmacy, Washington, 1880; studied 4 yrs. at Rensselaer Poly. Inst., but was not grad.; m. Florence P. Morton, Dec. 25, 1885. With U.S. Geol. Survey, 1880-88; with firm of Booth, Garrett & Blair, analytical chemists and engrs., Phila., 1888—. Died Nov. 4, 1930.

WHITFIELD, ROBERT PARR, geologist; b. New Hartford, N.Y., May 27, 1828; s. William Fenton and Margaret (Parr) W.; mostly self-ed.; hon. A.M., Wesleyan, 1882. Worked for his father, a spindlemaker, until 1848, when he entered employ of Samuel Chubbuck, instrument-maker, Utica, becoming mgr., 1849-56. Spent spare time studying natural history and geology; asst. in palaeontology and geology. N.Y. State Natural History, 1856-76; U.S. Geol. Survey, 1872; teacher, 1872-75, and prof. geology, 1875-78, Rensselaer Poly. Inst., Troy, N.Y.; curator geol. dept., Am. Mus. Natural History, 1877—. Original fellow A.A.A.S.; fellow Geol. Soc. America. Author of Palaeontol. papers, U.S. Geol. Survey, Ohio Palaeontology, Palaeontology of New Jersey, 3 vols., etc. Contbr. on geol. subjects. Died 1910.

WHITFORD, ALFRED E(DWARD), dean; b. Milton, Rock County, Wis., Sept. 4, 1875; s. Albert and Chloe Eliza (Curtis) W.; B.A., Milton (Wis.) Coll., 1896; B.A., U. of Chicago, 1900; M.A., U. of Wis., 1911; hon. Sc.D., Alfred U., 1926; m. Mary Whitford, Aug. 15, 1900; children—Alfred Edward, Dorothy Euphemia (Mrs. Nelson C. Lerdahl); m. 2d, Ruth A. Rogers, Dec. 27, 1938. Teacher, Waupun (Wis.) High Sch., 1896-97; prin. public schools, Milton, 1897-99; prof. physics and asst. mathematics, Milton Coll., 1901-11, prof., mathematics and physics, 1911-23, prof. mathematics, 1923-30, registrar, 1903-21, acting pres., 1921-23, pres., 1923-30; lecturer mathematics, U. of Wis., 1930-32; prof. mathematics, Alfred (N.Y.) U. since 1932, dean Coll. Liberal Arts; 1934-46, dean emeritus since 1946. Mem. Math. Assn. America, Am. Assn. Univ. Profs.

Seventh Day Baptist. Home: 60 W. University St., Alfred NY

WHITFORD, EDWARD EVERETT, prof. mathematics; b. Brookfield, N.Y., Jan. 31, 1865; s. Calvin and Emeline (Burch) W.; A.B., Colgate, 1886, A.M., 1890; Ph.D., Columbia, 1912; m. Lilla E. York, July 31, 1890 (dec. May 1943); 1 son, Robert Calvin. Teacher, Colby Acad., New London, N.H., 1886-91, Keystone Acad., Factoryville, Pa., 1891-98; bank cashier, Brookfield, N.Y., 1898-1900; prin. high sch., Brookfield, 1900-02, Commercial High School, Brooklyn, 1902; prof. mathematics, College of the City of New York, 1905-35, prof. emeritus, 1935—. Served in Y.M.C.A. educational work, Eng. and Scotland, 1918, Army Ednl. Corps, France, 1919. Mem. Am. Math. Soc., Math. Association America, Delta Upsilon, Phi Beta Kappa. Republican. Seventh Day Baptist. Author: The Pell Equation, 1912. Home: Brookfield, N.Y. Died May 3, 1946.

WHITFORD, OSCAR F., civil engr.; b. Saratoga County, N.Y., July 15, 1833; s. Earl Hartwell and Asenath (Palmer) W.; grad. Union Coll., Schenectady, 1858, A.M. in course, 1861; post-graduate course in chemistry, same; vol. U.S.A., 4 months, 1862; prof. mathematics and civil engring., People's Coll., Havana, N.Y., 1864-66; practiced as civil engr. in U.S., Mexico and S. America, 1866—; engr. in charge of constrn. for the Ontario Power Co., of Niagara Falls. Unmarried. Author of professional pamphlets, reports and papers. Deceased.

WHITING, SARAH FRANCES, physicist, astronomer; b. Wyoming, N.Y., Aug. 23, 1847; d. Joel and Elizabeth Lee (Comstock) Whiting; A.B., Ingham Coll., LeRoy, N.Y., 1865; student Mass. Inst. Tech., 1876-79, U. of Berlin, 1889, Edinburgh, 1896-97; Sc.D., Tufts Coll., 1905. Prof. physics and phys. astronomy, Wellesley, 1879-1912; dir. Whitin Obs., 1904-16, prof. emeritus, 1916—. Fellow A.A.A.S. Conglist. Author: Daytime and Evening Exercises in Astronomy; also articles for astron. journals. Lecturer. Died 1927.

WHITING, WILLIAM ALONZO, prof. biology; b. Meadville, Pa., June 15, 1890; s. John Xenophon and Anna Hayward (Smith) W.; B.S., Allegheny Coll., 1914; Ph.D., Cornell U., 1921; m. Marion Bright, Sept. 11, 1918; children—John Irwin, Allan Bright. Instr. bacteriology, Cornell Univ., 1917-21; prof. biology, Birmingham-Southern College, 1922-55, also chmn. div. natural sciences. Fellow A.A.A.S.; mem. Alabama Academy of Science. Beta Beta Beta, Omicron Delta Kappa, Theta Chi Delta, Lambda Chi Alpha. Dem. Meth. Co-Author: Variations in Bacteria Counts from Milk as Affected by Media and Incubation Temperature, 1922. Author: The Relations between the Clumping of Bacteria and the Utensil Flora, 1924; Laboratory Manual in General Zoölogy, 1925; Flora of the Birmingham District, 1927; Laboratory Manual in General Biology, 1931. Home: 715 8th Av. W., Birmingham 4, Ala. Died Feb. 2, 1957; buried Elmwood Cemetery, Birmingham.

WHITLOCK, ELLIOTT HOWLAND, mech. engr.; b. Brooklyn, N.Y., May 5, 1867; s. Elisha Schanck and Sarah Jane (Elliott) W.; student Agrl. and Mech. Coll. of Texas, 1886; M.E. Stevens Inst. of Tech., Hoboken, N.J., 1890, hon. M.Sc., 1933; m. Mrs. Charles H. Wellman, Oct. 24, 1907. With motive power dept. Pa. R.R. at Columbus, O., 1890-91; prof. mech. engring., Agrl. and Mech. Coll. of S.D., 1891-92; constrn. and operation of gas plants and in commercial business, 1892-96; with Nat. Carbon Co., Cleveland, 1896-1914; cons. practice, 1914-17; owner Whitlock Mfg. Co.; gen. mgr. Am. Fire Clay and Products Co.; mem. bd. dirs. Wellman-Seaver-Morgan Co.; commr. Division of Smoke Inspection, Cleveland, 1925-30; research prof. smoke abatement, Stevens Inst. Tech., 1930-32. Commd. maj. Engrs. R.C., U.S. Army, Feb. 23, 1917; called to active duty, May 7, 1917; assigned to 24th Engr. Regt. (Shop and Supply); sailed for France, Feb. 16, 1918; with Service of Supply, 2d and 3d armies; promoted lt. col. 24th Engrs., Dec. 31, 1918, and returned to U.S. in comd. of regt., June 1, 1919; commd. col. 112th Engr. Regt., 37th Div., Ohio Nat. Guard, June 1928. Mem. Am. Soc. Mech. Engrs. (v.p.), Soc. Am. Mil. Engrs., Cleveland Engring. Soc. (ex-pres.), S.A.R. Presbyterian. Club: University (Cleveland). Home: 3813 Euclid Av., Cleveland 15

WHITLOCK, HERBERT PERCY, mineralogist; b. New York, 1868; s. Thomas and Caroline V. (Hull) W.; grad. Charlier Inst., New York, 1884; C.E., Columbia U. Sch. of Mines, 1889; m. Julia Jaques Gardner, 1904. Asst. in mineralogy, Columbia U., 1892-1901; asst. in mineralogy, N.Y. State Museum, 1901-04, mineralogist, 1904-16, state mineralogist, 1916-18; curator of mineralogy, Am. Museum Natural History, 1918-41, curator emeritus since 1941, dept. minerals and gems. Engaged in mineralogic and crystallographic research on mineral species, with special reference to calcite. Fellow Am. Acad. Arts and Sci., Mineral Soc. Am., Geological Soc. Am. N.Y. Acad. Science, hon. mem. N.Y. Mineralol. Club. Wrote Museum bulls.: Guide to Mineralogic Collection of the N.Y. State Museum, 1902; List of New York Mineral Localities, 1903; monograph on New York Calcite, 1910; List of New Crystal Forms of Minerals, 1910, 1922; The Story of the Minerals, 1925; The Story of the Gems, 1936; also many mineralogic contbns. Edited articles on minerals for Internat. Encyclopedia. Specialist on methods of public museum installation. Home: 103 Waverly Place. Office: Am. Museum of Natural History, New York, N.Y. Died Feb. 22, 1948.

WHITMAN, ARMITAGE, orthopedic surgeon; b. Boston, Mar. 13, 1887; s. Royal and Julia Lambard (Armitage) W.; ed. St. Mark's Sch., 1901-05; A.B., Harvard, 1909; M.D., Columbia U., 1912; m. Mary Lyman Sturgis, 1912 (div. 1933); children—Royal II, Robert Shaw Sturgis, Charlotte Armitage; m. 2d, Fraunziska Kaschewski, Sept. 4, 1933. Surg. interne Roosevelt Hosp., 1912-14; attending surgeon Ogdensburg (N.Y.) City Hosp., 1914, Hosp. for the Ruptured and Crippled, 1931-35; vis. surgeon N.Y. State Bd. Health, 1916-17; orthopedic surgeon Lincoln Hosp., Booth Meml. Hosp.; clin. prof. orthopedic surgery N.Y.U. Med. Sch.; asso. attending orthopedic surgeon U. Hosp.; cons. surgeon Hosp. for Ruptured and Crippled, N.Y. State Dept. Health and Tuxedo Meml., St. Joseph's, Mather Meml. hosps.; mem. med. adv. bd. Selective Service Act; awarded Congl. medal. Served as capt. M.C., U.S. Army, 1917-19; AEF. Awarded Victory medal with 7 bars. Diplomate Am. Bd. Orthopedic Surgeons. Fellow A.C.S., N.Y. Acad. Medicine; mem. Am. Orthopedic Assn., Am. Acad. Orthopedic Surgeons, Alpha Omega Alpha. Episcopalian. Club: Harvard (N.Y.). Author: From Head to Foot. Asst. lit. editor N.Y. State Jour. Medicine, 1946—. Contbr. to med. jours. Home: 433 E. 51st St., N.Y.C. 10022. Office: 71 Park Av., N.Y.C. Died Sept. 14, 1962; buried Arlington Nat. Cemetery, Washington.

WHITMAN, CHARLES OTIS, zoölogist; b. Woodstock, Me., Dec. 14, 1842; s. Joseph and Marcia W.; A.B., Bowdoin, 1868, A.M., 1871; Ph.D., Leipzig, 1878; fellow Johns Hopkins, 1879; LL.D., U. of Neb., 1894; Sc.D., Bowdoin, 1895; Doctor of Biology, Clark U., 1909; m. Emily Nunn, Aug. 15, 1884. Prof. zoölogy, Imperial U. of Japan, 1880-81, Naples Zoöl. Sta., 1882; asst. in zoölogy, Harvard, 1883-85; dir. Allis Lake Lab., 1886-89; prof. zoölogy, Clark U., 1889-92; prof. and head dept. zoölogy and curator Zoö. Mus., 1892—, U. of Chicago. Dir. Marine Biol. Lab., Woods Hole, Mass., 1888-1908. Editor Jour. of Morphology, 1887—, Biological Bulletin, 1897—. Biological Lectures, 1890-99. Home: Chicago, Ill. Died 1910.

WHITMAN, EZRA BAILEY, cons. engr.; b. Balt., Feb. 19, 1880; s. Ezra B. and Belle Cross (Slingluff) W.; student Balt. City Coll.; C.E., Cornell U., 1901; m. Fanny Glenn, Oct. 15, 1906; children—Fanny Glenn (Mrs. T. Brian Parsons), Ezra B., John Glenn. Mem. Williams & Whitman, N.Y., 1902-06; div. engr. on design and constrn. Balt. Sewage Disposal Plant, 1906-11; chief engr. Balt. Water Dept. (design and constrn. Filtration Plant and Loch Raven Dem), 1911-14; mem. Greiner & Whitman, 1914-16, Norton, Bird & Whitman, 1916-25; mem. Whitman, Requardt & Smith, engrs., 1925-44; mem. Whitman, Requardt and Assos., 1944—. Mem., chmn. Pub. Service Com. Md., 1921-27; mem. Engring. Bd. Rev. Chgo. in lake level controversy, 1924-25; chmn. Efficiency and Economy Commn., apptd. by mayor to reorganize city govt. Balt.; chmn. Efficiency and Economy Commn., Pitts.; chmn. Md. State Roads Commn., 1939-45. Maj. constrn. div. U.S. Army, 1917-19; constructing q.m. and utilities officer, Camp Mead, Md. Whitman, Requardt and Assoc. were architect-engineers for three Chem. Warfare Service plants at Edgewood, Md., Huntsville, Ala., Denver, 1941-44. Trustee emeritus Cornell. Fellow Am. Soc. M.E.; mem. Am. Inst. Cons. Engrs. (past pres.), Am. Soc. C.E. (dir., pres.), Am. Inst. E.E., Am., N.E. water works assns., Am. Pub. Health Assn., Sigma Xi, Tau Beta Pi, Delta Upsilon. Democrat. Episcopalian. Mason. Clubs: Maryland, Elkridge, Engineers', Merchants (Balt.); Cornell (N.Y.). Home: 139 W. Lanvale St. Office: 1304 St. Paul St., Balt. Died 1966.

WHITMAN, FRANK PERKINS, physicist; b. Troy, N.Y., July 29, 1853; s. William Warren and Caroline Keith (Perkins) W.; A.B., Brown U., 1874, A.M., 1877, hon. Sc.D., 1900; studied Johns Hopkins; m. Charlotte Webster Wheeler, May 26, 1881. Instr. in English and Classical Sch., Providence, 1874-78; prof. physics, Rensselaer Poly. Inst., Troy, 1880-86, Western Reserve U., 1886—. Fellow A.A.A.S. (v.p. 1898). Contbr. to scientific jours. Home: Cleveland, O. Died June 15, 1919.

WHITMORE, EUGENE R(ANDOLPH), pathologist, medical educator; b. Lancaster, Wis., June 18, 1874; s. Eugene and Rosena Catherine (Beers) W.; B.S., U. of Wis., 1896; M.D., Coll. Physicians and Surgeons, Chicago, 1899; intern Cook County Hosp., 1899-1901; post-grad. work, London School Tropical Medicine, 1905 (grad. with distinction), Vienna, 1906, Koch's Inst., Berlin, 1910-11; Dr.P.H., Johns Hopkins, 1921; Ph.D., Georgetown, 1929; m. Josephine W. Baker, Nov. 9, 1918. Apptd. asst. surgeon, rank of 1st lt., U.S. Army, June 29, 1901; capt. asst. surgeon, June 29, 1906, and capt. Med. Corps same date; maj., Jan. 1, 1910; lt. col., May 15, 1917; col., Nov. 30, 1917. Prof. pathology, Army Med. Sch., Washington, D.C., Sept. 1913-19, also prof. tropical medicine; curator Army Med. Museum, 1913-15; retired, Jan. 8, 1920. Prof. bacteriology and preventive medicine, George Washington U. Med. School, 1920-24; prof. parasitology and pathology, Georgetown U., 1924-46, emeritus; head div. tropical diseases, Doctors Hospital; dir. pathology labs., Casualty Hospital, Washington, D.C. Pathologist, Bureau of Science, Manila, P.I., 1908-10; sec. Sect. VIII (med. sciences and hygiene), 2d Pan-Am. Scientific Congress, Washington, 1915; pathologist Yellow Fever Commn. Internat. Health Bd., Rockefeller Foundation, S. Am., summer 1916. Sec. Am. Assn. for Study of Neoplastic Diseases. Diplomate Am. Bd. of Pathology; fellow Am. Coll. Physicians, A.M.A., A.A.A.S., Am. Soc. of Clin. Pathologists; mem. Washington Soc. of Pathologists, George Washington U. Med. Soc., Pan-Am. Med. Assn., Am. Assn. Pathologists and Bacteriologists, Am. Soc. Parasitologists, Southern Med. Assn., Nu Sigma Nu. Episcopalian. Clubs: Army and Navy, Cosmos, Army and Navy Country. Home: 2139 Wyoming Av. N.W. Office: 2139 Wyoming Av. N.W., Washington 8 DC

WHITMORE, FRANK CLIFFORD, prof. organic chemistry; b. N. Attleboro, Mass., Oct. 1, 1887; s. Frank Hale and Lena Avilla (Thomas) W.; A.B., Harvard, 1911, A.M., 1912, Ph.D., in organic chemistry, 1914; (hon.) Sc.D., Franklin & Marshall Coll., 1937, U. of Delaware, 1937, Allegheny College, 1938, Philadelphia College of Osteopathy, 1943; married Marion Gertrude Mason, June 22, 1914; children—Frank C., Mason, Harry Edison, Marion Mason II, Patricia Joan (dec.). Instr. organic chemistry, Williams, 1916-17, Rice Inst., Houston, Tex., 1917-18; asst. prof. organic chemistry, U. of Minn., 1918-20; prof. organic chem., 1920, acting head chem. dept., 1924-25, head, 1925-29, Northwestern U., dean Sch. of Chem. and Physics, Pa. State Coll. since 1929; research prof. of organic chemistry since 1937. Mem. advisory com. Chemical Warfare Service U.S. Army 1934-40. Mem. Nat. Research Council (chmn. div. chemistry and chmn. technology, 1927-28 and central petroleum com., 1928-31; com. survey of research in industry, 1939-40); Nat. Defense Research Com. (chmn. sect. B-2, 1941-42 mem. sect. 16.3). Chemical consultant Office Prodn. Management, 1941, Office Q.M. Gen., U.S. Army, since 1942; mem. referee bd., Chem. Div., War Prodn. Board 1942-45. Mem. visiting com. chem. dept., Mass. Inst. Tech. since 1939. Fellow A.A.A.S. (v.p. 1932; chmn. Section C; council 1941-44); mem. American Academy, American Chemical Society (councilor 1926-28; director 1928-39; pres. 1938), Am. Inst. Chem. Engrs., Am. Inst. of N.Y., Nat. Inst. of Social Sciences, Nat. Pioneer Award Com., N.A.M., 1939-40, Pa. Job Mobilization Com., 1939-40, Pa. Chem. Soc. (pres. 1942-45), Com. Survey of Research in Industry, 1939-40, Chem. Soc. London, Deutsche Chemische Gesell., Army Ordnance Assn., U.S. Inf. Assn., Soc. for Advancement of Edn., American Philos. Society, Franklin Institute, Newcomen Society, Sigma Tau, Alpha Sigma, Sigma Xi, Alpha Chi Sigma, Phi Lambda Upsilon, Phi Kappa Phi, Sigma Pi Sigma, Alpha Epsilon Delta, Phi Beta Kappa, Phi Eta Sigma. Awarded Wm. H. Nichols Medal, 1937; Willard Gibbs medal, 1945. Clubs: Chemists (Chicago); Chemists (New York); Cosmos (Washington, D.C.); Center Hills Country (State College Pa.). Author: Organic Compounds of Mercury, 1921; Organic Chemistry, 1937. Mem. editorial bd. Chemical Bulletin, 1923-28, Organic Synthesis, 1925— (editor in chief Vol. 7, 1927, Vol. 12, 1932). Home: State Coll., Pa. Died June 24, 1947.

WHITNALL, HAROLD ORVILLE, (hwit'nal), geologist; b. Morristown, N.J., Aug. 3, 1877; s. Thaddeus O. and Jessie (Minard) W.; Ph.B., Colgate, 1900, A.M., 1909; graduate study, Harvard, 1902-03; S.C.D., Bates College, 1939; S.C.D., Colgate Univ., 1944; m. Elizabeth Sherwood, Aug. 18, 1908; children—Thaddeus Orville, Helen S. (Mrs. Dale Gunn), Faith Esther. With Colgate University since 1903, instructor geology until 1909, assistant professor, 1909-12, asso. professor, 1912-21, prof. since 1921; also consulting practice; geologist for New York, Ontario & Western R.R. Asst. in geology, Harvard, summer 1908; field asst. N.Y. State, since 1943. Rep. presdl. elector, 37th N.Y. Dist., 1924; mem. Assembly State of N.Y., 1927-29; chmn. Republican Com. of Madison County, N.Y., since 1940. Treas. Colgate Univ. Alumni Corp. since 1919; holder of Alumni award for distinguished service to Colgate U. Fellow A.A.A.S.; mem. Am. Inst. Mining and Metall. Engrs., Am. Assn. Mammalogists, Soc. Meteoric Research, N.Y. State Hist. Soc., Delta Kappa Epsilon, Phi Beta Kappa, Sigma Gamma Epsilon. Mason. Baptist. Author: Dawn of Mankind, 1924; Dinosaurs and Their World, 1924; A Parade of Ancient Animals, 1936; Hunter of The Caverns, 1939. Contbr. to mags. and newspapers. Home: Hamilton, N.Y. Died May 18, 1945.

WHITNEY, ALFRED RUTGERS, constructing engr.; b. New York, N.Y., June 16, 1868; s. Alfred R. and Adeline Peers (Nesbitt) W.; M.E., Stevens Inst. Tech., 1890, E.D., 1921; unmarried. With Portage Iron Co., Duncansville, Pa., 1890-91; gen. mgr., later v.p. Puget Sound Wire Nail and Steel Co., Everett, Wash., 1891-94, also gen. mgr. and elec. engr. Everett R.R. and Electric Co. and cons. engr. Puget Sound Pulp and Paper Co., Everett & Monte Cristo R.R., 1891-94; rep. Carnegie Steel Co., in Japan, 1894; mem. firm A. R. Whitney, iron and steel mfrs. and contractors, New

York, 1894-96; organizer, 1896, A. R. Whitney, Jr. & Co., Inc., 1899, as The Whitney Co., of which was pres. and treas. until 1926, chmn. bd., 1926-29; retired from active business, 1929. Company constructors of Great Am. Ins. Co. Bldg., W. R. Grace & Co. Bldg., Iron Age Bldg., New York; Masonic Temple and Central Branch Y.M.C.A., Brooklyn; Stock Exchange Bldg., Baltimore; Wentworth Inst., Boston; Amherst (Mass.) Coll. Library; International Trust Co. Bldg., Denver; Smith Building, Seattle, Wash., etc. War corr. in Ethiopia, 1930. Dir. Morristown Trust Co. Mem. Squadron A, cav., N.Y. Nat. Guard, 1897; maj. staff Gov. Frank W. Higgins, 1905, and of Gov. John Alden Dix, 1911; brevet maj., 1911, successively capt. and regtl. adj., maj. and brigade adj. gen., 1912-16; aide to rear admiral Nathaniel R. Usher, 1913-17; aide Bur. of Naval Intelligence, World War. Mem. Am. Soc. C.E., New Eng. Soc., Am. Geog. Soc., S.R., Delta Tau Delta. Republican. Episcopalian. Clubs: Union League, University, Downton Assn., Metropolitan Opera, Piping Rock, New York Yacht, Seawanhaka-Corinthian Yacht, Cruising Club of America, Anglers' (New York); Traveler, Explorer, Angler, Yachtsman and Navigator. Writer on engring., travel, cruising, fishing, etc. Designer and builder of the "Ruffhouse," original of now universally accepted type of Fla. houseboat. Home: Morristown, N.J.; also 277 Park Av., New York 17, N.Y. Died Oct. 7, 1946.

WHITNEY, ASA, inventor, mfr.; b. Townsend, Mass., Dec. 1, 1791; s. Asa and Mary (Wallis) W.; m. Clarinda Williams, Aug. 22, 1816, at least 5 children. Small scale mfr. of axles for horse-erecting machinery on inclined planes, Albany and Schenectady, N.Y., also bldg. railroad cars for Mohawk and Hudson R.R., 1830-39; canal commr. N.Y. State, 1838-42; obtained patent for locomotive steam engine, 1840, 2 patents for cast-iron car wheel with corrugated center web, and for method of manufacturing same, 1847; organized (with 3 sons) Asa Whitney & Sons, Phila., 1847; received patent for improved process of annealing and cooling cast iron wheels, 1848; pres. Reading R.R., 1860-61; bequeathed $50,000 to U. Pa. to establish chair of dynamic engring., $12,500 to Franklin Inst., $20,000 to Old Men's Home, Died Phila., June 4, 1874.

WHITNEY, CHARLES SMITH, cons. engr.; b. Bradford, Pa., Nov. 4, 1892; s. Henry Parker and Myra (Allen) W.; C.E., Cornell, 1914, Master C.E., 1915; m. Gertrude Schuyler, June 19, 1920; children—James S., Lillian R., Charles A. Asst. engr. John Parkinson, architect, Los Angeles, 1916-17; chief engr. A. C. Eschweiler, architect, Milwaukee, 1919-20; chief engr., mgr. Hool & Johnson, engrs., Milwaukee office, 1920-22; cons. and designing engr. city planning, design and supervision bldgs., bridges, sewer and water systems, and numerous other municipal improvements, Milw., 1922—; chief architect, planning Camp McCoy, Wis., 1941; partner Ammann & Whitney, cons. engrs., N.Y.C., Milw., 1946—; designer or cons. numerous structures including hangars, expressways, bridges, theatres, office bldgs., hosps., chs., Am. Airlines, TWA hangers, Chgo., Onondago Meml. Auditorium, Syracuse, N.Y., Montgomery (Ala.) Livestock Coliseum, Pitts. Civic Light Opera Amphitheatre, Milw. expressway system, N.Y. Throughway, New Jersey, Connecticut and Ohio Turnpikes. Development of plastic theory reinforced concrete design, method of design of structures to resist atomic bombs and earthquakes, design air raid shelters. Served as Sgt., 25th C.E., U.S. Army, 1917-19; AEF. Awarded J. James R. Cross medal 1925, Am. Soc. C.E.; Fuertes Grad. medal, Cornell, 1925, 37; Wason medal, Am. Concrete Inst., 1932-53; Alfred E. Lindau award, Am. Concrete Inst., 1951; Ammann & Whitney recipients 1st ann. award. Concrete Reinforcing Steel Inst., 1949. Registered profl. engr., Wis., N.Y., Conn., Ohio, Mo., Cal., Tex., Colo., Mich., Fla.; structural engr. Ill. Mem. Am. Soc. C.E. (pres. Milw. sect. 1930), Am. Concrete Inst. (v.p. 1953-54, pres. 1955), Am. Inst. Cons. Engrs., Wis. Soc. Profl. Engrs., Am. Assn. Airport Execs. Inst. Aero. Scis., Internat. Assn. Bridge and Structural Engring., Soc. Exptl. Stress Analysis, Am. Ry. Engring. Assn., Am. Road Builders Assn., A.I.A., Sigma Xi, Tau Beta Pi. Clubs: University (Milw.); Engineers (N.Y.C.). Author: Bridges, 1929; Concrete Designers Manual. Numerous reports, articles tech. jours. Home: 2710 E. Bellevue Pl., Milw. 11. Offices: 724 E. Mason St., Milw. 2; 111 Eighth Av., N.Y.C. 11. Died Oct. 25, 1959; buried Forest Home Cemetery, Milwaukee.

WHITNEY, ELI, inventor; b. Westboro, Mass., Dec. 8, 1765; s. Eli and Elizabeth (Fay) W.; grad. Yale, 1792; m. Henrietta Frances Edwards, Jan. 6, 1817, 3 children. Made and repaired violins, manufactured nails in father's shop, 1780-82; designed cotton gin on Mrs. Nathaneal Greene's plantation in Ga., with one operator could clean 50 pounds of cotton daily, 1793; in partnership with Phineas Miller to patent and manufacture cotton gins, 1793; received patent for cotton gin, 1794, failed to benefit because of infringements and long litigation; U.S. exports in 1795 were 40 times greater than before invention of cotton gin; received U.S. Govt. contract for 10,000 muskets to be delivered in 2 years, 1798; devised system of manufacturing interchangeable gun parts; purchased mill site for factory for firearms prodn., nr. New Haven, Conn., site now known as Whitneyville; built 1st successful milling machine. Died New Haven, Jan. 8, 1825.

WHITNEY, GWIN ALLISON, engr.; b. Superior, Wis., June 4, 1893; s. William Allison and Esther (Gwin) W.; ed. Northwestern Mil. and Naval Acad., Highland Park, Ill., 1909-12, Cascadilla Prep. Sch., Ithaca, N.Y., 1912-13, Cornell U., 1913-14; m. Charlotte Wilson, Mar. 28, 1918; children—James Wilson, William Allison, Gwin Richard. Construction engr. Whitney Bros. Co., Superior, Wis., 1914-15; v.p. same, Duluth, Minn., 1915-18, pres., 1918-30; pres. Merritt-Chapman & Whitney Corp., 1930-32; v.p. Merritt-Chapman & Scott Corp., 1932-33, pres., 1933—; pres. and mng. dir. Merritt-Chapman-Lindsay, Ltd.; pres. and dir. Am. Constrn. Co., Whitney Corp. Home: New York, N.Y. Died Feb. 11, 1939.

WHITNEY, JOSIAH DWIGHT, geologist; b. Northampton, Mass., Nov. 23, 1819; s. Josiah Dwight and Sarah (Williston) W.; grad. Yale, 1839; m. Louisa (Goodard) Howe, June 1854, 1 dau. Read law, 1841; travelled and studied in France, Germany, Italy, 1842-45; worked survey of mineral lands of Northern peninsula of Mich., 1847-49; independent cons. expert in mining, 1849-54; Ia. State chemist and prof. mineralogy Ia. State U., 1855-58; mem. Ill. State Survey; geologist of Cal., 1860-74, began survey of state; promoted Cal. Acad. Science; commr. Yosemite; mem. Philos. Soc., Nat. Acad. Sciences; apptd. to Harvard faculty, 1865, opened Harvard Sch. Mines, 1868, Sturgis-Hooper prof. geology, 1875-96; returned briefly to Cal. to continue survey; elected to Geol. Soc. London. Author: Metallic Wealth of the United States, 1854; The Auriferous Gravela of the Sierra Nevada of California, 1880; Climatic Changes of Later Geological Times, 1882; Names and Places, 1888. Died Lake Sunapee, N.H., Aug. 19, 1896.

WHITNEY, MARY WATSON, astronomer; b. Waltham, Mass., Sept. 11, 1847; d. Samuel B. and Mary W. (Crehore) W.; A.B., Vassar Coll., 1868, A.M., 1872; studied at U. of Zürich, 1874-76. Became asst. to Prof. Maria Mitchell, 1881; prof. astronomy and dir. of obs., Vassar Coll., 1889-1910 (emeritus prof.). Many of her articles were pub. in Astronomical Journal and other astron. periodicals. Home: Waltham, Mass. Died Jan. 20, 1921.

WHITNEY, MILTON, soil expert; b. Baltimore, Aug. 2, 1860; common school edn.; spl. 3 yrs. course, chemistry, Johns Hopkins; m. Annie C. Langdon, June 30, 1891. Asst. chemist Conn. Agrl. Expt. Sta., 1883; supt. Experiment Farm of N.C. Expt. Sta., 1886-88; prof. agr., U. of S.C., and v. dir. of S.C. Expt. Sta., 1888-91; soil physicist, Md. Expt. Sta., 1891-94; chief Bur. Soils, U.S. Dept. Agr., 1894-1927. Author: Soil and Civilization. Home: Takoma Park, D.C. Died Nov. 11, 1927.

WHITNEY, PAUL CLINTON, hydrographic engr.; b. Washington, D.C., Aug. 28, 1882; s. Arthur Pierce and Margaret Jane (Milburn) W.; student George Washington U., 1900-03; m. Jeannette B. Prescott, Dec. 17, 1908; 1 daughter, Margaret Jeannette (Mrs. Margaret Adams); married 2d, Barbara Schmitt, Sept. 24, 1932. With United States Coast and Geodetic Survey, 1902—; commd. hydographic and geodetic engr., 1917; participated in and directed surveys, coasts of Alaska and Philippine Islands, and Pacific and Atlantic coasts, 1903-17; chief of Sect. of Coast Pilot, Washington, D.C., 1919-25; insp. San Francisco Field Sta., 1925-28; chief Div. of Tides and Currents, Washington, 1928-42, supervisor, S.E. District 1942-46. Magnetic observer on first magnetic cruise, Pacific Ocean, under auspices of Carnegie Instn., 1905. Served as lt. and lt. comdr. U.S. Navy, World War I; now capt. U.S. C. and G. S. (retired.). Mem. Washington Soc. Engrs., Philos. Soc. of Washington, Poetry Society of Virginia, American Geophysical Union A.A.A.S., Wash. Academy of Science. Author of various technical government publications, and articles on tides and ocean currents. Club: Cosmos. Home: 1306 Rockbridge Av., Norfolk, Va. Address: U.S. Coast and Geodetic Survey, Washington. Died June 9, 1954; buried Hillsboro, N.D.

WHITNEY, WILLIAM FISKE, anatomist; b. Boston, Mar. 26, 1850; A.B., Harvard, 1871, M.D., 1875; house officer Mass. Gen. Hosp., 1875; studied in Europe, 1875-88. Curator Warren Anat. Mus., Harvard, 1879—; sec. med. faculty, Harvard, 1883-90; prof. parasites and parasite diseases, Veterinary Sch., Harvard, 1891-1901. Home: Boston, Mass. Died Mar. 4, 1921.

WHITNEY, WILLIS RODNEY, chemist; b. Jamestown, N.Y., Aug. 22, 1868; s. John J. and Agnes (Reynolds) W.; S.B. Mass. Inst. Tech., 1890; Ph.D., Univ. of Leipzig, 1896; hon. Sc.D., Union U., 1919; Ch.D., U. of Pittsburgh, 1919; Sc.D., U. of Syracuse, 1926, U. of Mich., 1927; LL.D., Lehigh, 1929; m. Evelyn Jones, June 26, 1890; 1 dau., Mrs. Evelyn Schermerhorn. Asst. instr., asst. prof. to 1904, nonresident asso. prof., 1904-08, nonresident prof. theoretical chemistry since 1908, Mass. Inst. of Tech.; dir. Research Laboratory of General Electric Co., Schenectady, N.Y., 1900-28, v.p. in charge of research, 1928-41, now honorary vice-president General Electric Co. Hon. mem. American Steel Treaters' Soc., Franklin Inst.; mem. U.S. Naval Consulting Bd. since 1915; mem. advisory com. U.S. Bur. of Standards, 1925-30, Nat. Research Council. Trustee Albany Med. Coll., Union Coll.; mem. Corp. Mass. Inst. Tech. Willard Gibbs medal, Am. Chem. Soc., 1916; Chandler medal, Columbia U., 1920; Perkin medal, Am. Sect. of Soc. Chem. Industry, 1921; Franklin medal, 1931; Edison medal, 1935; Pub. Welfare medal, Nat. Acad. Sciences, 1938. Chevalier Legion d'Honneur (France), 1937; received John Fritz medal, 1943; medal of Industrial Research Institute, 1946. Member of National Academy of Sciences; fellow American Academy of Arts and Sciences, A.A.A.S., Am. Chem. Soc. (pres. 1910), Am. Electrochem. Soc. (pres. 1911), Am. Inst. Mining and Metall. Engrs., Am. Inst. E.E., Am. Philos. Soc., Am. Phys. Soc., etc. Presbyterian. Republican. Translator of M. Le Blanc's Electro-Chemistry, 1896. Home: Box 2684 Troy Rd., Schenectady. Died Jan. 9, 1958; buried Parkview Cemetery, Schenectady.

WHITTEMORE, AMOS, inventor, mfr.; b. Cambridge, Mass., Apr. 19, 1759; s. Thomas and Anna (Cutter) W.; m. Helen Weston, June 18, 1781, at least 12 children. After public sch. edn. apprenticed to gunsmith; mfr. brushes for carding cotton and wool, 1795, supt. mech. equipment in 3 factories; received patents for machine which cut nails, loom for weaving duck, form of mech. ship's log, 1796; patented machine which eliminated all hand labor in making cotton and wool cards, 1797, attempted unsuccessfully to introduce new machine into England, 1799-1800; in partnership (with brother William and Robert Williams) to make card-making machines and cards themselves, 1800-12; renewed patent, 1808, sold patent rights and machinery to a N.Y.C. co., 1812, ret. Died West Cambridge (now Arlington), Mass., Mar. 27, 1828.

WHITTEMORE, DON JUAN, engineer; b. Milton, Vt., Dec. 6, 1830; ed. Bakersfield Acad.; C.E., U. of Vt., 1884; Ph.D., 1884, LL.D., 1895, U. of Wis. Became engr., 1847, Vt. Central Ry., Great Western Ry. of Canada, Central Ry. of Ohio; chief asst. engr. LaCrosse & Milwaukee R.R., 1853-57; chief engr. Southern Minn. Ry.; chief asst. engr. Western Ry. of Cuba; chief asst. engr. La Crosse & Milwaukee, 1861-63; chief engr. C.,M.&St.P. Ry. Co., 1863-Dec. 6, 1910; became consulting engr. same rd. Pres. Am. Soc. C.E., 1884-85. Home: Milwaukee, Wis. Died July 16, 1916.

WHITTEMORE, HERBERT LUCIUS, mech. engr.; b. Milw., Oct. 1, 1876; s. Lucius Lorenzo and Charlotte Elizabeth (Hanson) W.; B.S. in Mech. Engring., U. Wis., 1903, M.E., 1910; m. Elizabeth Amanda Kittredge, Mar. 31, 1923; children—William Kittredge, Nancy. Asst. supt. Sullivan Machinery Co., Claremont, N.H., 1902-04; engr. A. P. Hanson Co., Berlin, Germany, 1905; prodn. engr. British Westinghouse Electric & Mfg. Co., Manchester, Eng., 1906; instr. engring. mechanics U. Ill., 1906-10; engr. of tests Watertown Arsenal, Mass., 1910-12; instr. mechanics Columbia, 1912-16; prof. mechanics U. Okla., 1916-17; chief engring. mechanics sect. Nat. Bur. Standards, Washington, ret. 1946. Recipient Morehead medal Internat. Acetylene Assn., 1927; Longstreth medal Franklin Inst., 1937. Mem. Am. Soc. M.E., Washington Acad. Sciences. Unitarian. Club: Cosmos (Washington). Author of many bulletins pub. by govt. Home: 3906 McKinley St. N.W., Washington. Died July 11, 1954.

WHITTEMORE, JOHN WEED, college dean; born Sioux City, Ia., Sept. 27, 1897; s. James Henry and Jennie Lois (Weed) W.; B.S., Ia. State Coll., 1921, degree of Ceramic Engineer Iowa State College, 1927; D.Sc. (honorary), Alfred University; married Clifford Kelly, August 30, 1926; children—Mary Ann (Mrs. R. P. Harman), Joan Weed (Mrs. J. C. South, Jr.). Began as superintendent Sioux City Brick & Tile Co., 1921-26; ceramic engr. Dept. of Conservation, State of La., 1926-29; asst. prof. ceramic engring., Louisiana State U., 1926-29; prof. ceramic engring. and head dept., Va. Poly. Inst., 1929-52, asso. dean of engring., 1943-52, dean engring. and architecture, 1952—, dir. Va. Engring. Experiment Sta.; with engring. dept. E. I. du Pont de Nemours & Co., 1951-52. Mem. O.T.S., F.A. Camp Zachary Taylor, 1919. Licensed Ceramic Engineer State of Virginia, also registered engineer District of Columbia. Cons. for Fgn. Econ. Adminstrn., 1946. Fellow American Ceramic Soc. (pres. 1948); mem. Inst. Ceramic Engrs. (pres. 1949), Am. Soc. Testing Materials, Am. Soc. for Engring. Education, Tau Beta Pi, Keramos, Sigma Nu, Sigma Xi, Omicron Delta Kappa. Democrat. Episcopalian. Mason. Club: University (Blacksburg). Author articles, paper and bulls. in field. Home: 900 Draper Rd., Blacksburg, Va. 24060. Died Apr. 13, 1963; buried Blacksburg, Va.

WHITTEN, JOHN CHARLES, horticulturist; b. Augusta, Me., Sept. 14, 1866; s. Albert and Viola W.; B.S., S.D., Agrl. Coll., 1892, M.S., 1899; studied Cornell U., part of 1892; Mo. Bot. Garden, 1893-94; Ph.D., U. of Halle, 1902; m. Nora Todd, Oct. 31, 1895. Instr. horticulture and horticulturist Expt. Station, Brookings, S.D., 1892; asst. in horticulture, Mo. Bot. Garden, St. Louis, 1893-94; prof. horticulture, U. of Mo., and horticulturist Mo. State Expt. Sta., 1894-1918; prof. pomology, Univ. of Calif., 1918—. Author repts. and bulls., also several hundred papers in hort. mags. Home: Berkeley, Calif. Died June 5, 1922.

WHITTIER, CHARLES COMFORT, cons. engr.; b. Somerset County, Me., Dec. 10, 1876; s. Philander Coburn and Laura Ann (Taylor) W.; B.C.E., Univ. of Me., 1899; m. Leonore Arlie Leuckel, Sept. 2, 1908; children—Charles Taylor, John Coburn. Asst. engr. maintenance of way, B.&M. R.R., Boston, 1899-1900; asst. engr., Southwestern R.R. of Ariz., Bisbee, Ariz., 1900-01; mining engr. with Robert W. Hunt Co., engrs., Chicago, 1901-07; chief engr. and asst. gen. mgr. Zeigler Coal Co., Ziegler, Ill., 1904-07; inspecting and reporting engr. Robert W. Hunt Co., 1907-13; gen. mgr. Robert W. Hunt Co., Ltd., Montreal, 1913-15; chief engr. and mng. dir. Field Mining & Milling Co., 1915-19; v.p. and cons. engr. Hunt Mining Co., 1919-23; cons. engr. with Robert W. Hunt Co., 1923-32; partner Nutrition Research Laboratories; was sec. Illinois Mineral Industries Com.; inventor of mineral materials, vitamins and foods. Specialist in value and use of industrial plants and processes, quality of mineral deposits and development of new and improved mineral commodities. Mem. Engring. Inst. Can., Am. Inst. Mining and Metall. Engrs. (dir. 1932-35), Western Soc. Engrs. (pres. 1934-35), Inst. of Food Technologists. Clubs: Chicago Engineers (ex-pres.), Union League. Home: 6758 Muirlands Drive, La Jolla, Calif. Office: 4210 Peterson Av., Chicago IL

WHITTLESEY, DERWENT (STAINTHORPE), (hwit'-l-si), geographer; b. Pecatonica, Ill., Nov. 11, 1890; s. Joseph Henry and Sophia Jane (Derwent) W.; Ph.B., U. of Chicago, 1914, M.A., 1915, Ph.D., 1920; hon. M.A., Harvard, 1942; D.Sc. (honorary), Beloit College, 1953. Acting assistant professor history, Denison U., 1915-16; successively instr., asst. prof. and asso. prof. geography, U. of Chicago, 1919-28; asst. prof. geography, Harvard, 1928-31, asso. prof., 1931-43, prof. since 1943; consultant to U.S. State, War and Navy Depts., and Office of Strategic Services, 1940-46; mem. panel Research and Dev. Bd. Dept. of Defense, 1948-53; com. chmn. div. geol. and geog. National Research Council, 1937-43, and 1948-53. Fulbright Research Scholar in Tropical Africa, 1951. Served as private, ordnance sergeant and 2d lt., U.S. Army, 1918-19. Hon. fellow and gold medalist. Chicago Geographic Society, fellow American Academy Arts and Sciences; member Assn. Am. Geographers (pres. 1944, hon. pres. 1954), Sigma Alpha Epsilon, Sigma Xi. Club: Harvard Faculty. Author: Major Geographic Regions of North America (with M. C. Stark), 1923; Introduction to Economic Geography (with W. D. Jones), 1925; The Earth and the State, 1939; German Strategy of World Conquest, 1942; Geografia Politicia, 1948; Environmental Foundations of European History, 1949; Wall Map of Agricultural Regions of the World, 1951; Regional Study with Special Reference to Geography, 1952. Contbr. to Geographic Aspects of International Relations, 1937; War as a Social Institution. 1941; Makers of Modern Strategy, 1943; Ten Eventful Years, 1947; Goode's School Atlas, 1949; Ency. Brit. World Atlas 1945, 51, and Ency. Brit. since 1946; American Geography: Inventory and Prospect, 1954; also to mags. Home: 20A Prescott St., Cambridge 38, Mass. Died Nov. 25, 1956; buried Twelve Mile Grove Cemetery, Seward, Ill.

WHYTE, CARL BARZELLOUS, engr., oil co. exec.; b. Springfield, Mo., Nov. 5, 1902; s. Walter Marcus and Blanche (Jackson) W.; B.S., Ga. Inst. Tech., 1925; m. Lelia Monk, Oct. 21, 1927; children—Carl Barzellous, Lelia Nan. Research, test engr., later asst. chief engr. La. Oil Refining Co., 1925-36; chief engr. refining div. Ark. Fuel Co., 1936-41; chief engr., gen. supt. Cities Service Def. Corp., 1941-43; chief engr. Cities Service Refining Corp., 1943-46; chief constrn. engr. Universal Oil Products Co., 1946-50; exec. v.p. Procon, Inc., 1950-52, pres., 1952-65, chmn. bd. dirs., chief exec. officer, 1965—; mng. dir. Procon (Gt. Britain), Ltd., Procon Pty. (Australia); president and dir. Vica Procon (Venezuela), Procofrance Promon (Brazil), Procon (Canada), Limited, Procon International, S.A., Fabricated Steel Products, Inc. Registered engr., Tex., Ill.; registered with Nat. Bur. Engring. Mem. Am. Soc. M.E., Am. Inst. E.E., A.I.M., Am. Petroleum Inst., Western Soc. Engrs., La. Engring. Soc., Nat. Constructors Assn. (past pres.), Res. Officers Assn., Chi Psi. Methodist. Clubs: Engineers, New York Athletic (N.Y.C.); Shreveport; Wing and Fin (Volo); Tam O'Shanter Country (Chgo.); American (London, Eng.). Home: 1502 Palmgren Dr., Glenview, Ill. Office: 1111 Mt. Prospect Rd., Des Plaines, Ill. Died May 1967.

WHYTE, FREDERICK WILLIAM CARRICK, (hwīt), mining engr.; b. Biggar, Scotland, July 27, 1863; s. Robert and Catharine (Carrick) W.; grad. High Sch., Stirling, 1878; mining course, night sch., Glasgow; m. Adeliza Crichton, Mar. 23, 1892; 1 son, Keith Carrick. Apprentice with Johnstones & Rankine, Glasgow, 1878-83; in Office of Pub. Works, Glasgow, 1883-85; asst. engr. Johnstones & Rankine, 1885-87; came to America, 1887; asst. and resident engr., work on location and constrn., in Mont., G.N. Ry., 1887-92; chief engr. constrn., Butte, Anaconda & Pacific Ry., 1892-94; engr. at Belt Coal Mines, for Anaconda Copper Mining Co., 1895-96, gen. mgr. coal dept., 1896-1936; cons. engr., 1936—; gen. mgr. Diamond Coal & Coke Co., 1899-1936. Mem. Am. Inst. Mining and Metall. Engrs., Mont. Soc. Engrs. Presbyn. Club: Anaconda Country. Home: Anaconda, Mont. Died Sept. 15, 1949.

WICKENDEN, WILLIAM ELGIN, engr., educator; b. Toledo, O., Dec. 24, 1882; s. Thomas Rogers and Ida (Consaul) W.; B.S., Denison U., 1904; U. of Wis., 1905-07; hon. Dr. Engr., Lafayette Coll., 1926, Worcester Poly. Inst., 1927, Case Sch. Applied Science, 1929, Rose Poly. Inst., 1936, Tulane U., 1939; hon. Sc.D., Denison Univ., 1928, Bucknell U., 1930; LL.D., Oberlin Coll., 1930, U. of Toledo, 1940; L.H.D., Otterbein U., 1933; m. Marion Susan Lamb, Sept. 2, 1908; children—Elizabeth, William Clarence. Instr., U. of Wis., 1905-09; asst. prof. elec. engring., Mass. Inst. Tech., 1909-14, asso. prof., 1914-18; personnel mgr. Western Electric Co., 1918-21; asst. v.p. Am. Telephone & Telegraph Co., 1921-23; dir. investigation, Soc. for Promotion Engring. Edn., 1923-29; pres. Case School of Applied Science since 1929. Regional supervisor personnel methods, S.A.T.C., 1918, World War. Chmn. Regional Labor Board for Northern Ohio, 1933, Ohio Highway Survey Commn., 1935-38. Chmn. Gen. Products Group, Office Production Management, 1941. Mem. Engrs. Council for Professional Development, 1933-38. Trustee Lake Erie Coll. Fellow A.A.A.S. (v.p. 1936), Am. Inst. E.E. (v.p. 1943); Am. Soc. M.E., Am. Acad. Polit. and Social Science, Soc. Promotion Engring. Edn. (pres. 1933; awarded Lamme medal 1935), Sigma Chi, Sigma Xi, Phi Beta Kappa, Tau Beta Pi, Theta Tau. Presbyterian. Author: Illumination and Photometry, 1909; Comparative Study of Engineering Education in the U.S. and in Europe, 1929. Home: 2530 Fairmount Blvd., Cleveland Heights, O. Address: Case School of Applied Science, Cleveland, O. Died Sep. 1, 1947.

WICKHAM, HENRY FREDERICK, entomologist; b. Shrewton, Wiltshire, England, Oct. 26, 1866; s. George and Sarah (Light) W.; student State U. of Iowa, 1887-91, M.S., 1895; m. Fanny Chastina Thompson, Sept. 10, 1891. Instr. and asso. prof., 1891-1903, prof. entomology, 1903—, State Univ. of Iowa. Has made numerous and extensive collecting trips to remote parts of continent, which have been made the basis of numerous published reports; specially known for his researches and articles on beetles. Fellow A.A.A.S., Ia. Acad. Sciences, Entomol. Soc. America. Home: Iowa City, Ia. Died Nov. 17, 1933.

WIDMANN, BERNARD PIERRE, radiologist; b. Johnstown, Pa., July 21, 1890; s. John and Magdalene (Graf) W.; student St. Francis Coll., Johnstown, Pa., 1909-11, St. Vincent's Coll., Latrobe, Pa., 1911-12; Medico Chirurgical Coll. of Medicine and Surgery, Phila., 1912-16; LL.D., St. Vincent's College; D.Sc., Hanahman Medical College, 1952, St. Joseph's College, 1958; married Mary Eileen Maher, Aug. 27, 1919 (died May 1937); children—Mary Eileen, Ann Stevens. Asst. prof. radiology, grad. sch. of medicine, U. of Pa., 1921-37, prof. since 1937, chairman in radiology in Graduate School since 1945; dir. X-ray dept., Philadelphia Gen. Hosp. since 1928, Fitzgerald-Mercy Hosp., Philadelphia, since 1928. Dir. Our Lady of Lourdes Hosp., Camden, N.J. Served as radiologist, Army X-ray Sch., Camp Greenleaf, 1918. Recip. Gold medal Am. Coll. Radiology, 1964. Gold medal, Strittmater award Philadelphia County Medical Society. Diplomate of the American Board of Radiology (pres. 1959-60, trustee). Mem. Phila. Radiol. Soc. (past president), American Radium Soc., American Roentgen Ray Society (president 1950), Radiologic Society N.A., American College Radiology (v.p. 1954), A.M.A., American Board of Radiology (president 1958, trustee since 1935), Sigma Xi, Phi Chi. Contributor over 150 papers on radiological subjects to professional publs. Home: Philadelphia PA Died Feb. 26, 1971; buried Holy Cross Cemetery, Yeadon PA

WIECHMANN, FERDINAND GERHARD, chemist; b. Brooklyn, N.Y., Nov. 12, 1858; s. Ernst Gustav and Anna Caecilie (Albers) W.; Ph.B. (in chemistry), Sch. of Mines, Columbia, 1881, Ph.D., 1882; m. Marie Helen Damrosch, Mar. 26, 1885. Instr. chemistry, Columbia, 1883-97; lecturer on chemistry, cons. research chemist, New York, 1883—. Author: Sugar Analysis, 1890, 3d edit., 1914; Lecture Notes on Theoretical Chemistry, 1893, 2d edition, 1895; Chemistry—Its Evolution and Achievements, 1899; Maid of Montauk (under pen-name Forest Monroe), 1902; Notes on Electrochemistry, 1906. Died Apr. 24, 1919.

WIEGAND, KARL MCKAY, (we-gand), botanist; b. Truxton, N.Y., June 2, 1873; s. John Christopher and Annie (McKay) W.; B.S., Cornell, 1894, Ph.D., 1898; m. Ella Maude Cipperly, Aug. 21, 1906. Asst. and instr. botany, Cornell U., 1894-1907; asso. prof. botany, Wellesley, 1907-13; prof. botany and head of dept., N.Y. State Coll. Agr., at Cornell U., 1913-41, prof. emeritus since Aug. 15, 1941. Fellow A.A.A.S.; mem. Bot. Soc. America, New Eng. Bot. Club, Sigma Xi, Phi Kappa Phi. Author of about 100 papers on bot. topics. Home: Upland Rd., Ithaca, N.Y. Died Mar. 12, 1942.

WIELAND, G(EORGE) R(EBER), paleontologist; b. Boalsburg, Pa., Jan. 24, 1865; s. Washington Frederick and Margaret (Reber) W.; B.S., Pa. State Coll., 1893; studied U. Göttingen, 1894; U. Pa., 1896-97; Yale U., 1899, Ph.D., 1900; m. Edla Kristina Andersson, 1891 (deceased); 1 son, Hans Leonard. Asso. Carnegie Inst.; asso. prof. paleobotany, Yale, Mem. Wilderness Soc. Author: Polar Climate in Time the Major Factor in the Evolution of Plants and Animals, 1903; Osteology of Protostega, 1906; Armored Dinosauria, 1911; La Flora Liasica de la Mixteca Alta (in the Spanish), 1914; American Fossil Cycads, Vol. I, 1906, Vol. II, 1916; New North American Cycadedoids, 1921; Antiquity of the Anglosperms, 1926; A New Cycad from the Mariposa Slates, 1929; Raumeria of the Zwinger of Dresden, 1934; The Cerro Cuadrado Petrified Forest, 1935; Cycadeoid Types of the Kansas Cletaceous, 1942; The Carpathian-Black Hills Cycadeoid parallel, 1941; Fossil Cyad National Monument, 1944; The Yale Cycadeoids, 1945; also Chemistry of Petrifaction; Ancient Flower and cone-bearing Plants; The World's two greatest Petrified Forests; Land Types of the Trinity Beds; Mesaverde Cycadeoids; Wood Opalization Origin of Angiosperms; Ancient Climates; Dinosaur Extinction, etc. Awarded Archcuke Rainer medal, Vienna, 1914; Bologna, 1907. Mem. N.Y. Acad. Sci.; hon. mem. Botanical Society of India, 1935. Proposed establishment "Fossil Cycad National Monument" of the Southern Black Hills, donating site of 320 acres including the world's finest flowering petrified forest, 1922; brought to light there, Nov. 1935, aided by the C.C.C. over one ton of in situ cycadeoids, proving a three-fold value—evolutionary, chemic, and stratigraphic. Discovered the giant fossil turtle Archelon in 1895, various paleontologic explorations in the West, Mexico and S. America. Democrat. Home: Anawan Rd., West Haven, Conn. Died Jan. 18, 1953.

WIENER, NORBERT, mathematician; b. Columbia, Mo., Nov. 26, 1894; s. Leo and Bertha (Kahn) W.; grad. Ayer (Mass.) High Sch., 1906; A.B., Tufts Coll., 1909; Harvard, 1909-10, 1911-13; Cornell, 1910-11; A.M., Harvard, 1912, Ph.D., 1913; studied Cambridge, England, 1913-14, 1914-15, Göttingen, 1914, Columbia U., 1915; m. Marguerite Engemann, Mar. 26, 1926; children—Barbara (Mrs. Gordon Raisbeck). and Margaret (Mrs. John T. Blake). Docentlecturer, Harvard, 1915-16; instr. U. of Me., 1916-17; staff writer Ency. Americana, Albany, N.Y., 1917-18; newspaper work Boston Herald, 1919; instr. in mathematics, Mass. Inst. Tech., 1919-24, asst. prof., 1924-28, asso. prof., 1928-32, prof. since 1932; visiting prof. Tsing Hna U., Peiping, China, 1935-36. Lectured, Cambridge, England, 1931-32; Fullbright lecturer at College de France, 1951; guest prof. Indian Statis. Inst., Calcutta, 1955-56, Bowdoin prize, Harvard, 1914; Bocher prize, Am. Math. Soc., 1933; Guggenheim fellow, Göttingen and Copenhagen, 1926. Civilian computer, later pvt., Aberdeen Proving Ground, Md., 1918-19. Mem. Am. Math. Soc. (v.p.), Nat. Acad. Sciences, London Math. Soc. Author: The Fourier Integral and Certain of Its Applications; Harmonic Analysis in Complex Domain; Cybernetics, 1948; The Human Use of Human Beings, 1950; Ex-Prodigy, 1953; I Am a Mathematician, 1956; Extrapolation, Interpolation, and Smoothing of Stationary Time Series with Engineering Applications, 1949; Nonlinear Problems in Random Theory, 1958; God and Golem, Inc.; also articles in field and on epistemology. Worked in theories of probability and potential, theory of postulates, founds. of math., Fourier integrals and transforms, relativity and quantum theory; worked out math. theory of Brownian movement, 1920; research on math. physiology, harmonic analysis, vector and differential spaces; interest in automatic computers, feedback and statistical analysis of communication flow led to his foundation of cybernetics (science of communication control). Died Stockholm, Sweden, Mar. 18, 1964.

WIENER, PAUL LESTER, city planner, architect; b. Leipzig, Germany, May 2, 1895; s. Julius and Helen (Goldmann) W.; grad. architect Royal Acad. Vienna; postgrad. Kunstgewerbe Acad. (Berlin); prof. honoris causa, Nat. U. San Carlos, Guatemala; m. Ingeborg A. E. Tenhaeff, July 13, 1948; children by previous marriage—Barbara Frank, Paul Lester. Came to U.S., 1913, naturalized, 1919. Co-founder Contempora, internat. art service, 1927; tech. adviser U.S. commn. Internat. Expn. in Paris, 1936-37; founder (with Jose Luis Sert), Town Planning Assos., N.Y.C., 1942; dir. tech. studies New Sch. Social Research, N.Y.C., 1943-45; cons. Office Prodn. Research and Devel., WPB, 1943-45; adj. prof. of urban planning Columbia, 1965-67; lectr. univs. U.S., France, Belgium, Netherlands, Chile, Brazil, Colombia, Peru, Cuba, Venezuela; U.S. specialist for Dept. of State, specialists div. Internat. Edn. Exchange Service; designer architecture and interior Am. Pavilion, Exposition Arts and Scis., Paris, 1937, also interior Brazilian Pavilion; Ecuadorian Pavilion, N.Y. World's Fair; sonsultant to government of Peru for founding of National Plan Office; cons. to government of Bahamas for planning of New Providence and Nassau; devel. pilot plan for numerous cities, Brazil, Colombia, Cuba, Peru, Venezuela; devel. plan for indsl. community, prefabricated and demountable housing project, Sydney, N.Y.; recent archtl. projects include pilot plan for urbanization of Island of Tierra Bomba, developed as an extension City of Cartagena, Colombia; cons. planner, designer Gateway Center devel., Mpls.; site planner, designer Downtown Community Devel., Syracuse, N.Y.; cons. planner, designer Washington Square Village residential devel., N.Y.C.; cons., planner designer for McCombs Bridge Urban Renewal project, N.Y.C.; master plan for Aspen, Colorado and Pitkin County, Colorado. Decorated chevalier Legion of Honor (France); Southern Cross (Brazil); recipient three grand prix for Pub. Architecture, Pvt.

Architecture, Interior Design, Internat. Jury Arts and Scis., Paris. 1937; prize (with P. Bezy, J. Stedman, Jr.) Wheaton Coll. Art Center; prize Museum Modern Art, N.Y.C., 1939. Mem. American Society of Planning Officials, Pan-Am. Soc. (affiliate member), American Institute of Planners; hon. mem. archtl. socs. of Brazil, Peru, Belgium, Mexico, Colombia. Works published in profl. publis., U.S., S.A., Europe. Home: 25 Washington Sq. N., N.Y.C. Office: 119 E. 18th St., N.Y.C. 3. Died. Nov. 1967.

WIGGANS, CLEO CLAUDE, prof. horticulture; b. Mercer County, Mo., Oct. 20, 1889; s. Joshua Sherman and Lucy Ann (Barnes) W.; B.S., Mo. Coll. Agr., 1912; A.M., U. of Mo., 1913, Ph.D., 1918; m. Martha Chinn, Sept. 29, 1918; children—Samuel Claude, Donald Sherman. Instr. horticulture, U. of Mo., 1913-18; research horticulturist, U. of Del., 1918-19; asso. prof. horticulture, U. of Neb., 1919-24, prof. and chmn. dept., 1924-67. Mem. Gamma Sigma Delta, Gamma Alpha, Farm House, Sigma Xi. Mem. Disciples of Christ. Mason. Author various research bulls. and articles. Home: Lincoln NE Died Feb. 28, 1967; buried Lincoln NB

WIGGERS, CARL JOHN, physiologist; b. Davenport, Ia., May 28, 1883; s. George and Margaret (Kuendel) W.; M.D., U. Mich., 1906; D.Sc., 1941; research student Physiol. Inst., Munich, 1911; hon. doctorate degrees Ludwig Maxmillian U. Munich, 1953, U. Brussels, 1956, U. Brazil, 1960; Dr. Sci., Ohio State U., 1958, Western Res. U., 1959; m. Minnie E. Berry, Aug. 17, 1907; children—Harold Carl, Raymond Paul. Instr. physiology U. Mich., 1906-11; instr. physiology Cornell U. Med. Coll., N.Y.C., 1911-13, asst. prof. physiology, 1913-18; prof., dir. dept. physiology Sch. of Medicine, Western Res. U., Cleveland, 1918-53, professor emeritus, 1953—; honorary professor of physiology Bunts Edn. Inst., Cleveland. Decorated Order of the Southern Cross (Brazil). Fellow A.C.P.; mem. Royal Belgian Acad. Med. (Gold medal award), American Physiol. Soc. (president 1949-50), Society for Pharmacology and Experimental Therapeutics, International Congress Physiology, Nat. Acad. Scis., Am. Coll. Cardiology, Am. Heart Assn. (v.p. 1947-48; Gold Heart award; Albert Lasker award 1955), Physiol. Soc. Gt. Britain, Soc. Argentina de Biol., Acad. Nac. de Medicina (Buenos Aires), Cleveland Acad. Medicine, Cleveland Medical Library, also member Harvey Soc. of N.Y., Sigma Xi, Alpha Omega Alpha; hon. mem. fgn. cardiol. socs., also of faculties U. Chile, Cath. U. Chile. Unitarian. Author books relating to field; latest: The Physiology of Shock, 1950; Circulatory Dynamics, 1952; Reminiscences and Adventures in Circulation Research, 1958. Contbr. other sci. publs. Home: 13800 Terrace Rd., East Cleveland, O. 44112. Office: 2020 E. 93d St., Cleve. 44116. Died Apr. 27, 1963; buried Lakeview Cemetery.

WIGGIN, TWING BROOKS, M.D.; b. Allegheny City, Pa., Jan. 8, 1865; s. Richard and Rebecca Howe (Johnson) W.; student Vanderbilt U., Nashville, Tenn., 1883; M.D., Coll. of Phys. and Surgeons, Chicago, 1886; post-grad. courses at New York Post-Grad. Sch., London, Vienna, and Johns Hopkins; m. Louise Adele Merrill, of Janesville, Wis., Nov. 23, 1887. Began practice in Chicago, 1886; prof. physiology, Am. Dental School, 1889-94; prof. physiology, 1894-1923, prof. principles and practice of medicine, 1923—, Northwestern Univ. Dental Sch.; prof. physiology, 1896-99, prof. microscopical and chemical diagnosis, 1899-1901, adjunct prof. practice of medicine and clin. medicine, since 1901, prof. physical diagnosis, 1908-14, Coll. of Phys. and Surg.; mem. asso. staff of phys. to Cook Co. Hosp. Mem. A.M.A., Chicago Med. Soc., Ill. State Med. Soc. Republican. Baptist. Clubs: Physicians, Beverly Country. Author: Outlines of Physiology; Lectures on Pathology; etc. Office: 30 N. Michigan Av., Chicago, Ill.

WIGGINS, WILLIAM D., civil engr.; b. Richmond, Ind., Apr. 28, 1873; s. Philamon and Henrietta (McCullough) W.; grad. Rose Poly. Inst., Terre Haute, Ind., 1895; m. Lula J. Daft, 1910; children—Jane Wiggins Spencer, William D., Jr. (USNR). Entered service of Pa. Lines West of Pitts., engring. dept., 1895, has held various positions including div. engr., div. supt., valuation engr., chief engr. maintenance of way, chief engr. Central region, acting v.p. engr., and chief engr. Pa. R.R., 1935-43, v.p. engring., 1943, retired. Mem. Am. Soc. C.E., Am. Ry. Engring. Assn. Republican. Episcopalian. Clubs: Union League, Merion Golf (Phila.). Home: Merion, Pa. Died June 12, 1949.

WIGGLESWORTH, EDWARD, dermatologist; b. Boston, Dec. 30, 1840; s. Edward and Henrietta May (Goddard) W.; grad. Harvard, 1861, M.D., 1865; studied dermatology in Europe, 1865-70; m. Mrs. Sarah (Willard) Frothingham, Apr. 4, 1882, 3 children. Served with Union Army during Civil War; founded and maintained Boston Dispensary for Skin Diseases, 1872-77; head dept. of skin diseases Boston City Hosp.; instr. dermatology Harvard Med. Sch.; pres. Am. Dermatol. Assn., 1885; active in introducing law to require registration of physicians in Mass.; founded Boston Med. Register. Died Boston, Jan. 23, 1896.

WIGGLESWORTH, EDWARD, gemologist; b. Boston, Mass., Nov. 3, 1885; s. Edward and Sarah (Willard) W.; A.B., Harvard, 1908, A.M., 1909, Ph.D., 1917; m. Sarah P. Rackemann, June 15, 1914; children—Edward, Thomas, Mary, Sarah, Jane, Anne. Asst. in geology, Harvard, 1910-16, also curator dept. of geology, 1909-17; curator mineralogy and geology, Boston Society Natural History, 1914-40, director, 1919-39, scientific director, 1939-40; hon. curator of gems since 1940; dir. Eastern Laboratory Gemological Inst. of America. Served as asst. to food administrator of Mass., World War. Mem. bd. dirs. and v.p. Farm and Trades Sch. Trustee Essex Agrl. Sch. Member Draft Appeal Bd., Essex County, A.A.A.S., Am. Mineral Soc., Am. Ornithologists Union, Am. Gem Society. Republican. Clubs: Union (Boston); Country of Brookline. Author: (with J. B. Woodworth) Geography and Geology of the Region, including Cape Cod, the Elizabeth Islands, Nantucket, Marthas Vineyard, No Man's Land and Block Island, 1934. Contributor to mags. Home: 7 Chestnut St. Address: 69 Newbury St., Boston, Mass. Died May 6, 1945. *

WIGHT, FRANK CLINTON, editor, engineer; b. Washington, D.C., Feb. 26, 1882; s. George Ambrose and Ida (Morgan) W.; student Columbian (now George Washington) U., 1899-1901; C.E., Cornell U., 1904; m. Julia Theodora Welles, Oct. 5, 1911; children—Barbara, John Welles, Shirley, Richard Morgan. With Library of Congress, 1898-1901; in employ surveyor's office, D.C., 1902, 03; asst. to engr. of bridges, D.C., 1904-07; asso. editor Engring. News, New York, 1907-12, mng. editor, 1912-17; with Engring. News-Record, 1917—, editor, 1924—. Mem. bd. dirs. Am. Construction Council; mem. Hoover Nat. Conf. on Street and Highway Safety, 1924-25; v.p. Nat. Conf. Bus. Papers Editors, 1926-26; chmn. Editorial Conf. N.Y. Bus. Publishers' Assn., 1925-26. Universalist. Contbr. to Am. Internat. Ency., Nelson's Loose-Leaf Ency., Am. Year Book. Home: Summit, N.J. Died Sept. 1927.

WILBAR, CHARLES LUTHER JR., physician; b. Phila., June 8, 1907; s. Charles Luther and Clara May (Schmidt) W.; A.B., U. Pa., 1928, M.D., 1932; D.Sc., Phila. Coll. of Pharmacy and Sci., 1966; m. Mildred Irene Robinson, Sept. 3, 1935; children—Irene May, Charlotte Ellen, Frederick Hanson. Gen. rotating intern Abington (Pa.) Meml. Hosp. 1932-33; resident pediatrics Mary Drexel Children's Hosp., Phila., 1943; resident medicine Queen's Hosp., Honolulu, H.I., 1935; dir. Ewa (H.I.) Health Project, research pub. health, nutrition and pediatrics, 1936-39; dir. bur. maternal and child health Bd. Health, Honolulu, 1939-41, pres. Bd. Health, 1943-53; pediatric tng. Children's Hosp., Cin., 1940-41; part-time faculty U. Hawaii, 1936-53; dep. sec. health, Pa., 1953-57, sec. health, 1957-67; lectr. Grad. Sch. Pub. Health U. Pitts., 1953-67; vis. prof. pub. health and preventive medicine U. Pa., 1958-67; asso. pub. health adminstrn. dept. Sch. Hygiene and Pub. Health, Johns Hopkins 1964-69; clin. prof. medicine W.Va. U. Sch. Medicine, 1967-69; director West Virginia Regional Medical Program for Heart, Cancer and Stroke, since 1967. Chairman of the Ohio River Valley Water Sanitary Commn., 1961-62, Interstate Commn. on the Potomac River Basin, 1963-65. Chairman of the Central Pennsylvania chapter of the National Multiple Sclerosis Soc., 1958-61; mem. board dirs. Nat. Multiple Sclerosis Soc., 1962-69; bd. dirs. Pa. Tb and Health Soc., 1958-67. Served from capt. to major Medical Corps, AUS, 1941-42. Recipient citation for distinguished service American Podiatry Association, 1966. Diplomate of American Board of Pediatrics, Am. Bd. Pub. Health and Preventive Medicine, Fellow Am. Pub. Health Assn.; mem. A.M.A., Assn. State and Provincial Health Authorities N.A. (pres. 1951-52), Assn. State and Territorial Health Officers (pres. 1962-63), National (dir. 1959-61), Pa. (v.p. 1959-61) health councils. Unitarian (pres. bd. trustees 1959-64). Club: Lions (pres. Honolulu 1952-53; dist. gov. Pa. 1957-58). Contbr. articles sci. jours. Home: Morgantown WV Died Jan. 22, 1969; inurned Arlington Cemetery Philadelphia PA

WILBUR, CRESSY LIVINGSTON, vital statistician; b.Hillsdale, Mich., Mar. 16, 1865; s. Rodney G. and Frances (Cressy) W.; Ph.B., Hillsdale Coll., 1886, Ph.M., 1889; student Dept. Medicine and Surgery, U. of Mich., 1888-89; M.D., Bellevue Hosp. Med. Coll. (New York U.), 1890; m. Blanche M. Mead, June 30, 1891, Chief Div. Vital Statistics, Mich., 1893-1905; med. referee (classification of causes of death) and expert spl. agent, in charge extension of registration area for U.S. Census Bur., 1901-06, chief statistician for vital statistics, July 1, 1906-July 31, 1914; dir. Div. of Vital Statistics, N.Y. State Dept. of Health, Apr. 7, 1914—. Special lecturer vital statistics, Medical Dept., U. of Mich., 1902-05. Official del. of Census Bur. to Internat. Congress on Tuberculosis, Washington, 1908 (v.p. Sect. VI); official del. of U.S. to Internat. Statis. Inst., Paris, 1909; 2d Decennial Internat. Commn. of Revision of Classification of Causes of Death, by French Govt., Paris, 1909 (v.p. and preparer of official English list); sec. Div. of Demography, Internat. Congress of Hygiene and Demography, Washington, 1912. Editor: Michigan Annual Registration Reports (Vital Statistics), 1891-1903; Michigan Monthly Bulletin of Vital Statistics; Bertillon Classification of Causes of Death (under auspices Am. Pub. Health Assn.), Lansing, 1899; Manual of International Classification of Causes of Death (U.S. Census, 1902, 1913); U.S. Census annual reports on Mortality Statistics, 1905-12, and numerous census pamphlets and bulls. Contbr. articles on vital statistics to med. and statis. publs. Home: Albany, N.Y. Died Aug. 9, 1928.

WILBY, FRANCIS BOWDITCH, army officer, engr.; b. Detroit, Apr. 24, 1883; s. Richard Clark and Margaret Ann (Ingersoll) W.; student Harvard, 1900-01; B.S., U.S. Mil. Acad., 1905; grad. Army Engr. Sch., 1908, Sch. of Line, Ft. Leavenworth, 1922, Gen. Staff Sch., 1923, Army War Coll., 1924; D.Engring. (hon.), Clarkson Coll., 1943; m. Dorothy Langfitt, May 25, 1911 (dec. 1948): 1 son, Langfitt; m. Olive Emerson Payne, July 2, 1949. Commd. 2d lt., Engrs., 1905; advanced through grades to maj. gen. (temp.), 1941; dist. engr., Memphis, 1928-31; chmn. Fed. Bd. Surveys and Maps, 1931-35; mem. bd. mgrs. Fed. Barge Lines, 1935-38; sr. mem. Beach Erosion Bd. Shore Protection Bd., 1938-39; chief staff, First Army, N.Y., 1939-41; supt. U.S. Mil. Acad., 1942-45; ret. with rank of maj. gen., 1946. Chmn., N.Y. State Power Authority. Mem. Miss. River Commn., 1935-38. Awarded D.S.M. (twice), Legion of Merit, various campaign medals (U.S.); Croix de Guerre (France). Mem. Soc. Am. Mil. Engrs., Am. Soc. C.E. Clubs: Army and Navy, Army-Navy Country (Washington). Office: Knappen Tippetts Abbett Engring. Co., 62 W. 47th St., N.Y.C. Died Nov. 1965.

WILCOX, DEWITT GILBERT, surgeon; b. Akron, O., Jan. 15, 1858; s. David Gilbert and Hannah (Whitney) W.; student Buchtel Coll., Akron; M.D., Cleveland Hosp. Med. Coll., 1880; post-grad. work, St. Bartholomew Hosp., London, Eng., 1882-83; New York Post-Grad. Sch., 1887; m. Jennie Green, 1883; children—Margaret (Mrs. John M. Colony), Helen (Mrs. Jacob H. Randolph), John Maxson (M.D.), DeWitt Gifford (killed in World War, 1918). Began practice at Akron, O., 1880; moved to Buffalo, N.Y., 1887; attending surgeon, Buffalo Homoe. Hosp., 1890-1908, Erie County Hosp., 1892-98; surgeon-in-chief of Lexington Heights Hosp., 1890-1909; prof. gynecology, Boston U. Sch. of Medicine, 1909-32. Retired after 59 years of service, June 15, 1939. Apptd. surgeon Mass. State Guard with rank of capt., by Gov. McCall; attached to Mass. State Base Hosp., Commonwealth Armory. Attending surgeon Newton Hosp., 1918-32; attending gynecologist Westboro State Hosp., 1920-32. Was the first to operate on criminal's brain, 1909, for purpose of effecting change in character, F.A.C.S.; mem. A.M.A., Am. Inst. Homoeopathy (pres. 1914), Phi Delta Theta; ex-pres. N.Y. State Homeoe. Soc. Ex-pres. Boston Bapt. Sociol. Union. Author: Health Hygiene, Happiness, 1910; Physical Awakening of the Boy, 1911. Home: 118 Homer St., Newton Center MA

WILCOX, EDWIN MEAD, botanist, b. Busti, N.Y., May 21, 1876; s. Abram F. and Sally Maria (Mead) W.; brother of Earley Vernon Wilcox; B.S., Ohio State U., 1896; A.M., Harvard, 1898, Ph.D., 1899; married; children—Elizabeth Sally, Christine Louise, Mead Nicholas. During 1899-1900 made trip around the world, studying tropical agr. Prof. botany and entomology, Okla. A. and M. Coll., 1900-01; prof. plant physiology and pathology, Ala. Poly. Inst., 1901-08; prof. plant pathology, U. of Neb., 1908-20; dir. Estacion Agronomica and Colegio de Agricultura, Santo Domingo, 1920-21; prof. biology, Transylvania Coll. Capt. O.R.C., Sanitary Corps, U.S.A. Fellow A.A.A.S. Mason. Episcopalian. Contbr. to bot. jours. of articles on original researches and bulls., Okla., Ala. and Neb. expt. stas. Died 1931.

WILCOX, HERBERT BUDINGTON, physician; b. Bklyn., July 1, 1874; s. George and Mary (Budington) W.; A.B., Yale, 1898; M.D., Columbia, 1902; m. Louise Geer, Nov. 23, 1905; children—Herbert Budington, Jarvis Geer, George Gunton, Mrs. Louise W. Knowlton. Interne St. Luke's Hosp., 1902-04; asso. in pediatrics Coll. Phys. and Surg., 1904-20, Carpentier prof. diseases of children, 1921-31, prof., 1931-39, prof. emeritus, 1939—; attending physician Children's Med. Div., Bellevue Hosp., 1909-20, dir., 1920-25; physician in chief Babies Hosp., 1925-31; cons. pediatrician Sloane Maternity, Presbyn., New Rochelle, Manhattan Eye, Ear and Throat, New York Neurological hosps. to 1940. Trustee Am. Child Health Assn.; dir. Normal Child Development Study, Babies Hosp., 1935-39, N.Y. Acad. of Medicine, 1939-46. Mem. Am. Pediatric Soc., A.M.A., N.Y. Quiz and Pathol. Assn., St. Luke's and Babies hosps. alumni socs. Republican. Conglist. Club: Century Assn. (N.Y.C.). Author: Infant and Child Feeding, 1928. Contbr. articles on child health to jours. Home: Orford, N.H. Died Feb. 1, 1955; buried Green Wood Cemetery, N.Y.C.

WILCOX, REYNOLD WEBB, M.D.; b. Madison, Conn., Mar. 29, 1856; s. Col. Vincent Meigs and Catherine Millicent (Webb) W.; B.A., Yale, 1878; M.D., Harvard, 1881; post-grad. med. study at Vienna, Heidelberg, Paris, Edinburgh, 1881-82; hon. M.A., Hobart, 1881; LL.D., Maryville, 1892; D.C.L., Wittenberg, 1915; m. Grace, d. Col. Floyd Clarkson, Dec. 12, 1917. Prof. medicine, New York Post-Grad. Med. Sch., 1884-1908; consultant in medicine, St. Mark's Hosp., 1910—; cons. physician, Ossining Hosp., 1910—, Eastern Long Island Hosp., 1913—; cons.

internist, N.J. State Hospital, 1917—. Major M.R.C., U.S.A., on duty as instr., Camp Greenleaf, Fort Oglethorpe, Ga., 1917; lt. col., 1924. Pres. Am. Therapeutic Soc., 1901-02, Am. Assn. Med. Jurisprudence, 1913-14, Am. Congress on Internal Medicine, 1915-17, Am. Coll. of Physicians, 1915-21, Harvard Med. Soc., 1894-95, Med. Assn. Greater City of N.Y., 1910-14, N.Y. Soc. Med. Jurisprudence, 1912-14, N.Y. div. Assn. of Med. Reserve Corps U.S.A., 1914-16; fellow A.A.A.S.; mem. Soc. American Wars (surgeon gen., 1915-27; comdr. N.Y. Comdry., 1919-20), Society Colonial Wars, S.R., War of 1812 (v.p. Pa. Soc. 1897-1925; v.p. gen. 1908-25; pres. gen. 1925). Author: System of Case Records, 1887; Materia Medica and Therapeutics, 1892 (12 edits.); Manual of Fever Nursing, 1904 (2 edits.); Treatment of Disease, 1907 (4 edits); also (genealogical) The Descendants of William Wilcoxson, Vincent Meigs and Richard Webb, 1893; Madison—Her Soldiers, 1890; and numerous med. and hist. papers. Home: Princeton, N.J. Died June 6, 1931.

WILCOX, STEPHEN, inventor, engr., mfr.; b. Westerly, R.I., Feb. 12, 1830; s. Stephen and Sophia (Vose) W.; m. Harriet Hoxie, 1865. Inventor, also patentee (with partner D.M. Stillman) safety water-tube boiler with inclined tubes, 1856; patentee steam generator based on principle of earlier boiler (designed with George Herman Babcock), 1867; founder firm Babcock, Wilcox and Co., 1867, pres., 1867-93; secured total of 47 patents. Died Bklyn., Nov. 27, 1893.

WILDER, BURT GREEN, educator and author; b. Boston, Mass., Aug. 11, 1841; s. David and Celia Colton (Burt) W.; B.S., in anatomia summa cum laude, Lawrence Scientific Sch. (Harvard), 1862, M.D., 1866; m. Sarah Cowell Nichols, June 9, 1868 (died 1904); m. 2d, Mary Field, June 11, 1906 (died 1922). In U.S.A., July 1862-Sept. 1865, as med. cadet, asst. surg. and surg. 55th Mass. Inf. (colored); asst. in comparative anatomy, Mus. Comparative Zoölogy, 1866-68; curator herpetology, Boston Soc. Nat. Hist., 1867-68; prof. neurol. and vertebrate zoölogy, Cornell U., Ithaca, N.Y., 1867-1910, emeritus, 1910—. Lecturer on comparative anatomy, Anderson (Agassiz) Summer Sch. of Natural History, 1873-74, and 1875, summer schs. at Peoria and Normal, Ill.; on physiology, Med. Sch. of Me., 1875-84, and U. of Mich., 1876; at Lowell Inst., 1866, 1871. Mem. advisory council Simplified Spelling Board; v.p. Non-Smokers Protective League. In 1863, nr. Charleston, S.C., reeled 150 yards of silk from a spider since identified as Nephila clavipes; in 1865 silk from these spiders was woven into ribbon on a steamloom; the account of their habits, in the Atlantic, Aug., 1866, was the only article ever illustrated by that mag. Devised the "Slip-system of notes," 1867, and the "Correspondence-slip,", 1884. Prepared nearly 2000 vertebrate brains, including 13 from educated persons. Advocated (since 1880) the simplification of anatomic nomenclature; the dissection of the cat as a pre-requisite of that of man, 1879; the objective study of the brain in primary schs. (1889), and (1905) beginning with the brain of the acanth shark; temperance as distinct from total abstinence (1869); and (1873) the use of chloroform in capital punishment. The first American "Festschrift" was the "Wilder Quarter-Century Book," comprising papers prepared for the occasion by 15 former pupils, presented at the 25th anniversary of the opening of Cornell University. Author: What Young People Should Know, 1874; Anatomical Technology (with S. A. Gage), 1882; Physiology Practicums; Emergencies, 1888; Health Notes for Students, 1890; The Brain of the Sheep, 1903; biographic articles on Jeffries Wyman, 1874, Louis Agassiz, 1907; Founder's Hymn, words and music, 1907; Fiat Justitia, internat. hymn for first Universal Races Congress, 1911, words and music; Old Ironsides, music, the words by O.W. Holmes, 1912, arranged by N. C. Page for full orchestra and as one of Ditson's School Songs, 1916; The Peacemaker, words by Joyce Kilmer; also several other songs, many scientific papers, mostly on the brain, numerous revs. and articles in mags. and in the Reference Handbook of Med. Sciences. Died Jan. 22, 1925.

WILDER, GERRIT PARMILE, horticulturist; b. Honolulu, Hawaii, Nov. 5, 1863; s. Samuel Gardner and Elizabeth Kinau (Judd) W.; student Oahu Coll., Honolulu; M.S., U. of Hawaii, 1923; m. Lillian Kimball, Nov. 7, 1887. Supt. Kahului Ry. Co., Maui, 1884-96, pres., 1896-98; pres. Estate S. G. Wilder, Ltd., 1898—; retired from active business to devote time to horticulture, 1898; U.S. dep. protector H.I. Bird Reservation, 1918—; asso. in botany Bernice P. Bishop Mus., Honolulu, 1924, and made 4 bot. expdns. to South Seas, West Indies, Ceylon, etc., introducing into Hawaii from these countries many tropical trees, plants, etc. Fellow Royal Soc. of Arts (London). Republican. Mason. Author: Fruits of the Hawaiian Islands, 1906, 11; Breadfruit of Tahiti, 1928; Flora of Rarotonga, 1931. Home: Honolulu, Hawaii. Died Sept. 29, 1935.

WILDER, HARRIS HAWTHORNE, zoölogist; b. Bangor, Me., Apr. 7, 1864; s. Solon (musical director) and Sarah Watkins (Smith) W.; A.B., Amherst, 1886; Ph.D., U. of Freiburg (Baden), 1891; m. Inez Luanne Whipple, July 26, 1906. Prof. zoölogy, Smith Coll., 1892—. Fellow Am. Acad. Arts and Sciences. Author: Invertebrate Zoölogy, 1894; Synopsis of Animal Classification, 1902; The History of the Human Body, 1910, 2d edit., 1923; Personal Identification (with B. Wentworth), 1918; Manual of Anthropometry, 1920; Man's Prehistoric Past, 1923; The Pedigree of the Human Race, 1925; also numerous papers on vertebrate anatomy and physical anthropology, especially on amphibians, diploteratoldgy and the epidermic markings of human and simian palms and soles. Home: Northampton, Mass. Died Feb. 1928.

WILDER, LAURENCE RUSSELL, elec. engr., mfr.; b. Oak Park, Ill., Nov. 22, 1887; s. John E. and Laura (Hurlbut) W.; Junior M.E., Lewis Inst., Chicago, 1905; spl. study Princeton, 1906-08, Purdue, 1910-12; m. Dorothée Richardson, Dec. 3, 1924. Built first large scale production small internal combustion engine, Aero Motor Co., Chicago, 1907-08; exec. mgr. Wilder Tanning Co., Waukegan, Ill., 1909-17; aircraft production, Washington, D.C., 1917-18; pres. Fansteel Products Co., North Chicago, mfrs. electric specialties, 1919-21; rep. in U.S. of Brown Boveri & Co., Ltd., Switzerland, 1922-24, acquiring Am. rights in latter yr.; organized Am. Brown Boveri Electric Corp., 1925, acquiring N.Y. Shipbuilding Corp. (Camden, N.J.), Condit Electrical Mfg. Corp. (Boston) and Moloney Electric Co. (St. Louis); pres. Am. Brown Boveri Electric Corp., 1925-27, chmn. advisory com. of the company's shipbuilding div., also chmn. bds. Moloney Electric Co., Condit Elec. Mfg. Corp., and Transoceanic Corp. of the U.S., and pres. Scintilla Magnetos Co., Inc., Sidney, N.Y. Republican. Presbyn. Built first Scintilla magnetos, later standard for aviation ignition, 1925. Home: New York, N.Y. Died Nov. 16, 1937.

WILDER, MARSHALL PINCKNEY, mcht., agriculturist; b. Rindge, N.H., Sept. 22, 1798; s. Samuel Locke and Anna (Sherwine) W.; m. Tryphosa Jewett, Dec. 31, 1870; m. 2d, Abigail Baker, Aug. 19, 1833; m. 3d, Julia Baker, Sept. 3, 1855; 14 children. Postmaster, Rindge, circa 1819, also taught vocal music; rep. Mass. Legislature, 1839; mem. Mass. Exec. Council, 1849; pres. Mass. Senate, 1850; capt. Ancient and Honorable Arty. Co., 1856; a founder Constl. Union Party of 1860; founder Mass. Inst. Tech., v.p., 1865-70, trustee, 1870-86; became mem. New Eng. Historic Geneal. Soc. 1850, pres., 1868-86; Mason (33 deg. mem. supreme council); planted nursery, Boston, 1832, began hort. expts.; developed "Wilder Rose"; pres. Mass. Hort. Soc., 1840-48; called a conv. of fruit growers, N.Y.C. which resulted in Am. Pomol. Soc., pres., 1848-86; instigated Mass. Central Bd. Agr. (composed of several socs.), 1851, pres.; pres. U.S. Agrl. Soc., 1852-58; prin. founder Mass. Agrl. Coll.; mem. U.S. Commn. to Paris Universal Expn., 1867; contbr. articles to agrl. jours. including Horticulturist, New Eng. Farmer, Country Gentleman, Genessee Farmer. Died Dec. 16, 1886.

WILDER, RUSSELL MORSE, physician, ret.; b. Cincinnati, O., Nov. 24, 1885; s. William Hamlin and Ella (Taylor) W.; grad. South Side Acad., Chgo., 1903; B.S., U. Chgo., 1907, Ph.D., 1912; M.D, Rush Med. Coll., 1912; grad. study U. of Chgo., 1913, Vienna, 1914; m. Lucy Elizabeth Beeler, Mar. 18, 1911; children—Russell Morse, Thomas Carroll. Instr. in anatomy and pathology, U. of Chgo., 1909-10; began practice at Chgo., 1912; resident Presbyn. Hosp., Chgo., 1915-17; instr. in medicine, Rush Med. Coll., 1915-17; mem. Mayo Clinic, 1919-29; asst. prof. medicine, Mayo Foundation, U. of Minn., 1919-22, asso. prof., 1922-29; prof. of med. and chmn. dept. of medicine, U. of Chgo., 1929-31; prof. med. and head dept. of med., Mayo Foundation, and mem. Mayo Clinic, Rochester, Minn., 1931-50; dir. Nat. Inst. Arthritis and Metabolic Diseases U.S. Pub. Health Service, 1951-53. Served as medical gas officer, A.E.F., 1918-19. Mem. Com. on Med., 1940-46, and chmn., 1940, also mem. Food and Nutrition Bd., 1940-50, and chmn., 1940-41—both of Nat. Research Council. Chief, Civilian Food Requirements Branch, Food Distribution Adminstrn., U.S. War Food Adminstrn., 1943. Recipient Howard Taylor Ricketts award, 1949; Joseph Goldberger award, 1954; Am. Bakers Assn. award, 1956. Member A.M.A. (mem. council on foods; Frank Billings Meml. lectr. 1950), A.C.P. (master 1957), Assn. Am. Physicians, Am. Soc. Clin. Investigation, Am. Physiol. Soc., Minn. Soc. of Internal Medicine, Chgo. Inst. Med., Inst. Nutrition, Am. Diabetes Assn. (pres. 1947), Minn., Washington acads. med. Central Interurban Clin. Club, Sigma Xi, Alpha Omega Alpha, Nu Sigma Nu, Delta Kappa Epsilon. Democrat. Episcopalian. Clubs: University. Author publs. relating to field, also collaborator on several med. books. Asso. editor profl. jours. Home: 705 Eighth Av. S.W. Address: Mayo Clinic, Rochester, Minn. Died Dec. 16, 1959.

WILDS, GEORGE JAMES, JR., plant breeder; b. Longtown, Fairfield County, S.C., Sept. 19, 1889; s. George James and Mary Leslie (Crawford) W.; A.B., U. of S.C., 1913, LL.D., 1946; A.M., Cornell U., 1917; D.Sc., Clemson Coll., 1937; m. Ruth Lawton, June 8, 1918; 1 son, George James III. Asst. plant breeder Coker's Pedigreed Seed Co., Hartsville, S.C., 1908-11, plant breeder, 1913-15, 17-19, dir. plant breeding since 1919, pres. and mng. dir., 1938-47, pres., treas. and mng. dir. since 1947. Awarded testimonial for distinguished service to agrl. development of S.C., Clemson College, 1932; medallion Assn. Southern Agricultural Workers, for years of distinguished service in Southern agr., 1947; Man of the Year in Service to S.C. Agr., Progressive Farmer Mag., 1947; American Legion Plaque for Distinguished Service to South Carolina, 1948. Member A.A.A.S., S.C. Academy Science, American Phytopathol. Soc., S.C. Seedsmens Assn. (pres. 1947), Darlington County Agriculture Soc. (pres. 1945-47), Southern Agricultural Workers Assn., Omicron Delta Kappa, Phi Beta Kappa, Sigma Xi. Democrat. Presbyterian (elder). Mason. Club: Rotary (Hartsville). Breeder of full length, wilt-resistant short staple cottons and upland long staple cottons; breeder of smut, cold and rust resistant oats, mildew and rust resistant wheat. Home: 1210 Home Av. Office: Coker's Pedigreed Seed Company, Hartsville, S.C. Died Oct. 26, 1951; buried Hartsville.

WILE, IRA SOLOMON, physician; b. Rochester, N.Y., Nov. 29, 1877; s. Solomon and Amelia (Meyer) W.; A.B. and B.S., U. of Rochester, 1898, M.S., 1908; M.D., U. of Pa., 1902; m. Saide E. Rigby, Sept. 27, 1905; children—Ira Rigby, Rigby, Alan Rigby, Mildred Rigby. Formerly lecturer in ednl. hygiene, New York U., and lecturer in dietetics and nutrition, dept. dental hygiene, Columbia; commr. of edn., N.Y. City, 1912-18. Mem. New York Milk Com.; a founder, N.Y. school lunch system, Manhattanville Nursery; founder Nat. Round Table for Speech Improvement, Assn. for Personality Training (pres. 1929-41); officer or dir. various philanthropic orgns. Editor Med. Review of Reviews, 1912-16; editor dept. surg. sociology, Am. Jour. Surgery, 1910-21; editor Med. Pickwick, 1921-22; asso. editor Am. Medicine, 1916-35; lecturer Am. Social Hygiene Assn., New School for Social Research, New York U., Coll. Phys. and Surg. (Columbia), Hunter Coll., Coll. City of New York, Brooklyn Coll.; asso. in pediatrics, Mt. Sinai Hosp. Mem. Nat. Com. for Mental Hygiene, Internat. Com. for Mental Hygiene. Fellow Am. Psychiatric Assn., Am. Pub. Health Assn., Am. Orthopsychiatric Assn. (pres. 1932), Am. Speech Correction Assn.; mem. A.A.A.S., Am., N.Y. State and County med. socs., Am. Acad. Polit. and Social Science, Am. Child Health Assn., Soc. for the Advancement of Education, Phi Beta Kappa. Republican. Jewish religion. Club: Civic (ex-pres.). Author: Blood Examinations in Surgery, 1908; Sex Education, 1912; The Challenge of Childhood, 1925; Marriage in the Modern Manner, 1929; Handedness—Right and Left; The Man Takes a Wife, 1937. Editor: Sex Life of the Unmarried Adult; Personality Development and Social Control in Terms of Constitution and Culture, 1939; The Challenge of Adolescence, 1939. Asso. editor Am. Jour. Orthopsychiatry; The Nervous Child. Home: 264 W. 73d St., New York, N.Y. Died Oct. 9, 1943.

WILE, UDO JULIUS, physician, educator; b. N.Y.C., Aug. 8, 1882; s. Julius and Hedwig (Haas) W.; B.A., Columbia, 1904; M.D., Johns Hopkins, 1907; LL.D., U. Mich., 1959; m. Katharine Eleanor Work, Aug. 31, 1916; children—Thomas Larimer, David Everett, Frank Sloan and Eleanor Katharine (twins). Prof. dermatology and syphilology, U. Mich. Med. Sch., 1912-47, emeritus, on mil. leave of absence, 1942. Established 1st u. hosp. clinic for tng. specialists in skin diseases and syphilis, 1912. Served as lt. M.R.C., U.S. Army, 1913-17; maj., M.C., 1917-19; san. insp. Base Hosp. 2, Bazoilles-sur-Meuse, France, 1917; built, organized and comdg. officer Am. R.C. Mil. Hosp. 4, Liverpool, Eng., 1917-18. Serving as chief med. cons., med. dir. USPHS, with rank of col. AUS, 1942—. Commandeur de la Sante Publique, French Govt., 1946. Pres. Bd. Health, Ann Arbor, 1925-35. Mem. Am. Dermatol. Assn. (pres. 1929-30), A.M.A. (sect. chmn.), Mich. State, Washtenaw County (pres. 1916) med. socs., U. Research Club, Chgo., Detroit dermatol. socs., Nu Sigma Nu, Sigma Xi, Phi Sigma, Alpha Omega Alpha; hon. mem. Soc. Francaise de Dermatologie et de Syphilographie and Danish Cos. same; hon. mem. Italian Soc. same; corr. mem. Argentine Dermatol. Soc.; hon. mem. Brit. Soc. Dermatology, Hunterian Soc.; corr. mem. Swedish Dermatol. Soc. Republican. Clubs: University (Ann Arbor); Tavern (Chgo.). Research on skin diseases, problems concerning germ of syphilis and the invasion of syphilis into the nervous system; discovered filterable viruses as the causes of two contagious skin diseases. Contbr. to profl. jours. Home: 2013 Carhart Av. Office: First National Bldg., Ann Arbor, Mich. Died June 7, 1965; buried Ann Arbor.

WILEY, ANDREW J., engr.; b. New Castle Co., Del., July 15, 1862; s. John and Mary (Hukill) W.; Ph.B., Del. Coll., Newark, 1882; unmarried. Engaged in surveys and constrn. Phila. and Baltimore br. B.&O. R.R. in Del. and Md., 1883; rodman and asst. engr. Ida. Mining & Irrigation Co., Boise Ida., 1883-86; asst. engr. constrn. U.P. R.R., Butte, Mont., 1886-88; chief asst. engr. Ida. Mining & Irrigation Co., on constrn. large irrigation system, 1888-92; chief engr. and mgr. Owhyee Land & Irrigation Co., Grand View, Idaho, constructing large irrigation system, 1892-98; chief engr. Swan Falls Power Plant, Boise, Ida., 1900-02; chief engr. Boise-Payette River Electric Power Co. and City of Cheyenne, Wyo., on constrn. of Granite Springs reservoir, 1902-04; chief engr. Barber Lumber Co., Boise, Ida., for constrn. of large dam and power plant on Boise River, 1904-05; cons. engr. Twin Falls North Side Land & Water Co., Twin Falls Oakley Land & Water Co., Twin Falls Salmon River Land & Water Co., 1906-14. Chief engr. Trade Dollar Consol. Mining Co.'s Swan Falls Power Plant Extension, 1909-11, Great Shoshone and Twin Falls Water Power Co., 1907-14, Southern Ida. Water

Power Co.'s Am. Falls Power Plant, 1911-14. Cons. and designing engr. Don Pedro dam and power plant for Turlock and Modesto irrigation dists., Calif., 1918-23; cons. engr. Kern River Water Storage Dist., San Joaquin River Water Storage Dist., Merced Irrigation Dist.'s Exchequer Dam and Power Plant, South San Joaquin and Oakdale Irrigation Dist.'s Melones Dam, 1924-27; cons. engr. on dam design, U.S. Dept. Interior, 1925—, also cons. engr. on Boulder Canyon Dam, 1929—; cons. engr. to Brit. Govt. in India, Oct, 1927-Feb. 1928. Home: Boise, Ida. Died Oct. 8, 1931.

WILEY, HARVEY WASHINGTON, chemist; b. Kent, Ind., Oct. 18, 1844; s. Preston P. and Lucinda Weir (Maxwell) W.; A.B., Hanover (Ind.) Coll., 1867, A.M., 1870; M.D., Ind. Med. Coll., 1871; B.S., Harvard, 1873; hon. Ph.D., Hanover, 1876, LL.D., 1898; LL.D., U. of Vt., 1911; D.Sc., Lafayette, 1912; m. Anna Campbell Kelton, Feb. 27, 1911; children—Harvey Washington, John Preston. Prof. Latin and Greek, Butler Coll., Indianapolis, 1868-70; teacher science, high sch., Indianapolis, 1871; prof. chemistry, Butler U., 1874; prof. chemistry, Purdue U., and state chemist of Ind., 1874-83; chief chemist, U.S. Dept. Agr., 1883-1912; prof. agrl. chemistry, George Washington U., 1899-1914; cons. prof. Brooklyn Poly. Inst., 1905. Mem. Jury of Awards, Paris Expn., 1900; U.S. del. 3d Internat. Congress Applied Chemistry, Vienna, 1898, 4th, Paris, 1900, 5th, Berlin, 1903, 6th, Rome, 1906, 7th, London, 1909 (chmn. Am. com.); hon. pres. First Internat. Congress Repression of Adulteration of Alimentary and Pharm. Products, Geneva, 1908; U.S. representative Soc. univ. de la Croix blanche de Génève; pres. U.S. Pharmacopoeial Conv., 1910-20; v.p., 1886, sec. council, 1890, gen. sec., 1891, A.A.A.S.; pres. Am. Chem. Soc., 1893-94, Am. Therapeutic Soc., 1911. Chevalier du Mérite Agricole (France), 1900; medal (first class), Physico-Chem. Acad. Italy, 1908; Chevalier Legion of Honor (France), 1909. Contbg. editor Good Housekeeping Mag., 1912—. Author: Songs of Agricultural Chemists', 1892; Principles and Practice of Agricultural Chemistry (3 vols.), 1894-97, 1909-11; Foods and Their Adulterations, 1907-11, 1917; 1001 Tests, 1914; The Lure of the Land, 1915; Not by Bread Alone, 1915; Beverages and Their Adulterations, 1919; Health Readers for Schools, 1919; History of a Crime Against the Food Law, 1929; also 60 Govt. bulletins and 225 scientific papers, etc. Died June 30, 1930.

WILEY, WALTER H(OWARD), engr.; b. Trenton, Ill., Jan. 27, 1862; s. Dr. Martin and Emma (Danforth) W.; grad. Colo. State Sch. of Mines, 1883; m. Laura Parshall, Sept. 17, 1884; 1 son, Dana. In practice as cons. mining engr., 1883—, throughout western portion of U.S., including Alaska, and in British Columbia and Mexico, S. America and Asia. Home: Glendora, Calif. Died May 16, 1931.

WILGUS, WILLIAM JOHN, engr.; b. Buffalo, N.Y., Nov. 20, 1865; s. Frank Augustus and Margaret Ann (Woodcock) W.; grad. Buffalo Central High Sch., 1883; pupil in civ. engring., Buffalo, 1883-85; hon. D.E., Stevens Inst. Tech., 1921, U. of Vt., 1927; m. May Reed, Mar. 1, 1892 (died Oct. 2, 1918); m. 2d, Gertrude Bernadette Tobin, June 16, 1919. Rodman, draftsman, resident engr., div. engr., constrn. Minn. & Northwestern R.R. and its successor the C.,St.P.& K.C. Ry. (now C.G.W. Ry.), 1885-91; locating engr. Duluth & Winnipeg R.R., and Duluth & Iron Range R.R. extension to Mesabe range and resident engr. in charge constrn. Chicago Union Transfer Ry., 1890-93; with N.Y.C.&H.R. R.R. during rehabilitation, as assistant engineer Rome, Watertown & Ogdensburg div., 1893-97, chief engr. Terminal Ry. of Buffalo, 1895-98, resident engr., Eastern div., 1897, chief asst. engr., 1898, engr. maintenance of way, 1898-99, chief engr. constrn., and maintenance of way, enlargement of terminals, bridges, etc., including Grand Central Sta., New York and Weehawken terminals, 1899-1903, v.p. in gen. charge of constrn., including new extensions, change of motive power from steam to electricity and other improvements in New York electric zone, and inception and creation of new Grand Central Terminal, Feb. 1903-Sept. 1907; chairman Buffalo Union Station Committee, 1907; chmn. advisory bd. of engrs. for constrn. of tunnel under Detroit River, Detroit, connecting M.C. R.R. and Canada Southern Ry., 1905-10. Private consulting practice, 1908-30; chmn. bd. cons. engrs. for building interstate vehicular tunnel of States of N.Y. and N.J. beneath North River, New York, 1919-22; cons. engr. proposed railroad tunnel under The Narrows for City of New York, 1921-22; cons. engr. N.Y. Transit Commn., 1923-24; same to Regional Plan of New York and its Environs; cons. to rys., industries, states and Fed. Government. During World War mem. mil. ry. commn. to England and France; dir. mil. rys. and deputy dir. gen. transportation, A.E.F., rank col. U.S. Army. Awarded D.S.M. (U.S.), Officer Legion of Honor (France), Conspicuous Service Cross, State of N.Y. Mem. Art Commn. City of New York, 1922-24; director Work Relief, N.Y., 1934-35; War Dept. advisor, World War II, 1941-42. Hon. mem. Am. Society C.E. (Rowland prize, 1909; Wellington prize, 1942; past director, past pres., Metropolitan section); member American Railway Engring. Assn., Am. Ry. Guild, Engrs. Soc. of St. Paul, Vt. Soc. Engrs., Vt. Hist. Soc., N.E. Soc., Art Commn. Associates (New York), Am. Hist. Assn., Soc. Mayflower Descendants, S.A.R., Inst. C.E. Great Britain (Telford gold medal, 1911); hon. mem. Am. Inst. Architects. Clubs: Century (New York); University (Winter Park, Florida). Author: Transporting the A.E.F. in Western Europe, 1931; The Railway Interrelations of the United States and Canada, 1937; The Grand Central Terminal in Perspective, 1940; Life of Captain Stewart Degan, A Character of the American Revolution, 1942; The Role of Transportation in the Development of Vermont, 1945; also papers and articles on engring. subjects and public affairs. Home: 203 Broad St., Claremont, N.H. Died Oct. 24, 1949.

WILHELM, RICHARD HERMAN, educator; b. N.Y. City, Jan. 10, 1909; s. Ernst Richard and Ida Emma (Krebs) W.; B.S., Columbia, 1931, Ch. E., 1932, Ph.D., 1935; m. Rachel Marjorie Hixson, June 19, 1937 (dec. Sept. 1964); children—Karen Elise, Joan Andrea, Richard David Washburn; m. 2d, Sarah Kollock Strayer, July 2, 1966. Faculty Princeton, 1934-68, prof. chem. engring., 1946-68, chmn. dept. engring., 1954-68, Henry Putnam Univ. prof., 1968; indsl. cons. Ofcl. investigator, Nat. Defense Research Com., 1941-43; cons. chem. warfare panel, Research and Development Bd., 1949-53. Recipient Profl. Progress award Am. Inst. Chem. Engrs., 1952, Warren K. Lewis award in chem. Engring. edn., 1966, William H. Walker award, 1951; Indsl. and Engring. Chem. award Am. Chem. Soc., 1966. Registered profl. engr., N.J. Fellow Am. Acad. Arts and Scis.; mem. Am. Inst. Chem. Engrs. (dir. 1956-59), Am. Chem. Soc., Am. Soc. Engring. Edn., Nat. Acad. Engring., Sigma Xi, Tau Beta Pi. Presbyn. Club: Nassau. Home: Princeton NJ Died Aug. 6, 1968.

WILHELMJ, CHARLES MARTEL, (wil-hel'me). med. educator b. East St. Louis, Dec. 17, 1896; son Charles Frederick and Emma Elizabeth (Martel) W.; B.S. and M.D., St. Louis U., 1922, M.S., 1923; m. Irene Bergen, Mar. 17, 1916; children—Charles Martel, Jean Marie. Teaching fellow in anatomy, St. Louis U., 1918-22, instr. in bacteriology and immunology, 1924-25; fellow in medicine, Mayo Foundation, 1925-27, asso. in div. exptl. surgery and pathology and mem. permanent staff, 1927-30; also instr. in physiology, U. of Minn. Sch. of Medicine, 1927-30; professor of physiology at Creighton University School of Medicine, since 1930, dean of the school of Medicine 1939-48, dir. research, 1948—; chmn. research com., mem. med. adv. bd. Vets. Hosp., Lincoln, Neb.; mem. research com. Vets. Hosp., Omaha, Neb. Past pres. Omaha Mid-West Clin. Soc., Omaha Douglas Co. Med. Soc.; mem. Am. Fedn. for Clin. Research, A.M.A., Am. Physiol. Soc. Exptl. Biology and Medicine, Am. Gastro-enterological Soc., Central Soc. for Clin. Research, Alumni Assn. Mayo Clinic, Am. Assn. History of Medicine, Omaha-Mid-West Clin. Soc., Neb. and Omaha med. socs., Alpha Omega Alpha, Sigma Xi, Phi Rho Sigma. Club: Omaha Athletic. Author of numerous articles on biol. chemistry, metabolism, physiology of digestion, med. history. Home: 1714 S. 91st Av., Omaha. Died Nov. 25, 1963.

WILKERSON, WILLIAM WESLEY, JR., physician; b. Nashville, Nov. 11, 1897; s. William Wesley and Emma Dunn (Hill) W.; M.D., Vanderbilt U., 1920; m. Fawn L. Parent, Oct. 30, 1924; children—William Wesley, Nancy Fawn (Mrs. Walter Joseph Diehl, Jr.), Emma Jane (Mrs. Thomas L. Yount, Jr.). Intern, Long Island City Hosp., 1920; resident Bellevue Hosp., N.Y.C., 1921-24; staff Vanderbilt U. Hosp., 1924—, Mid-State Bapt. Hosp., Nashville; asst. prof. otolaryngology Vanderbilt U.; practice medicine, 1924-56, specializing otolaryngology; founder, med. dir., pres. Bill Wilkerson Hearing and Speech Center, 1951-58, chmn. bd., 1958—. Chmn. Davidson County Zoning Com., 1938, Nashville Smoke Abatement Com., 1944, Tenn. State Tb Hosps.; med. adv. com. Tenn. Vocational Rehab. Service; mem. Gov.'s Com. for Handicapped. Dir. Tenn. Hearing and Speech Found.; bd. dirs. Cordell Hull Found. Served as pvt. U.S. Army, 1918. Diplomate Am. Bd. Otolaryngology, Fellow A.C.S.; mem. Am. Laryngol., Rhinol., Otol. Soc. (v.p. So. sect. 1950), Tenn. Med. Assn., Nashville Acad. Medicine (pres. 1949), Tenn. Acad. Ophthalmology and Otolaryngology (pres. 1944), Am. Laryngol. Assn., Am. Legion, Nashville C. of C. (dir. 1948). Presbyn. Club: Belle Meade Country. Home: Curtiswood Lane, Nashville 4. Office: Bill Wilkerson Hearing and Speech Center, 19th and Edgehill Sts., Nashville 12. Died Mar. 14, 1961.

WILKINS, SIR HUBERT, explorer, scientist, lecturer; b. South Australia, Oct. 31, 1888; s. Harry and Louisa (Smith) W.; ed. Australian State Sch. and Adelaide (S. Australia) Sch. of Mines and Industries; m. Suzanne Bennett, Aug. 1929. Employed as elec. engr. and meteorologist; cine photographer and theater manager, 8 years; second-in-command Stefansson's Canadian Arctic Expdn., 1914-17; navigator England Australia flight, 1919; second-in-command British Imperial Antarctic Expedition, 1919-20; naturalist Shackleton "Quest Expdn.," 1921-22; comdr. Australian Islands Expdn., 1922-25; comdr. Detroit Arctic Expdns., 1925-28, making 1st trans-arctic flight by airplane; comdr. Wilkins Hearst Expdns. to Antarctic, making pioneer flight in Antarctica, discovering 5 new islands, more than 500 miles of coast line and several large glaciers, 1928-30, Nautilus submarine expdn. to Arctic, making pioneer submarine trip under Arctic ice, 1931; mgr. Ellsworth expdns., Antarctica, 1932-39; comdr. Soviet search expdn. for Levanevsky, covering 170,000 sq. miles never before seen by man, 1937-38. Consultant to Mil. Planning Div., U.S. Army, 1942-54, cons. to U.S. Army Q.M. Research and Engring. Command, 1954-57, USN Office Sci. Research, 1946-47, Weather Bur., 1946-48. Councilor Arctic Institute of N.A., 1947. Served as capt., Australian Flying Corps, 1917-19; overseas in Aleutians, also service with Office Strategic Services, World War II. Created Knight Bachelor, 1928. Decorated Order St. Maurice and St. Lazarus (Italy); Mil. Cross with bar; numerous citations; recipient Founders Medal Royal Geog. Soc., Finley-Breeze-Morse medal Am. Geog. Soc., also gold medals from foreign geog. socs. and aero. socs. of France, Norway, Denmark, International League of Aviators; Explorers Club medals; 16 honor medals from various socs. Mem. Royal Meteorol. Soc., Royal Geog. Soc., Am. Meteorol. Soc., Geophys. Union, Ornithologists Union, A.A.A.S. Clubs: Explorers, Adventurers, Circumnavigators, Royal Socs., City (N.Y.). Author: Undiscovered Australia, 1925; Flying the Arctic, 1928; Under the North Pole, 1931; (with Harold M. Sherman) Thoughts Through Space, 1942. Contbr. to scientific jours., mags. and newspapers. Lecturer McGill Summer Sch. of Geography, 1947-48, Nat. Defense Coll., Can., 1948-50. Home: Walhalla, R.D. 4, Montrose, Pa. Office: 37 W. 53d St., N.Y.C. 19. Died Dec. 1, 1958.

WILKINS, LAWSON, physician; b. Balt., Mar. 6, 1894; s. Dr. George Lawson and Harriet I. (Schreiner) W.; A.B., Johns Hopkins, 1914, Md., 1918, postgrad. tng. pediatrics, 1919-21; postgrad. Yale, 1919-20; m. Lucile Mahool, June 9, 1926 (dec. June 1959); 1 dau., Elizabeth B. (Mrs. Philip B. McMaster); married 2d Catrina A. Francis, Apr. 24, 1961. Pvt. practice of pediatrics, Balt., 1921-46; asst. prof., then. asso. prof. pediatrics Johns Hopkins, 1921-46, research and teaching pediatric endocrinology, 1946-57 professor of pediatrics, 1957-59, professor of pediatrics emeritus, 1959—; acting pediatrician-in-chief Johns Hopkins Hosp., 1954-56, dir. div. pediatric endocrinology, 1936—. Served as 1st lt., M.C., U.S. Army, 1917-19; AEF in France; capt. M.C., Md. N.G., 1923-28. Recipient Borden award Am. Acad. Pediatrics, 1953; Francis Amory prize Am. Acad. Arts and Scis., 1955; Modern Medicine award, 1955; Koch award Endocrine Soc., 1961; Howland award, Am. Pediatric Society, 1963. Mem. A.M.A., Am. Pediatric Soc. (pres. 1961-62), Soc. Pediatric Research, Am. Acad. Pediatrics, Assn. Am. Physicians, Endocrine Soc. (pres. 1956-57); honorary member Swedish Endocrine Society, Royal Soc. Medicine (Eng.), Societe de la Pediatrie de Paris, La Sociedad Colombiana de Endocrinolgia, Sociedad de Pediatria de El Salvador. Sociedad de Pediatria de Uruguay. Author: The Diagnosis and Treatment of Endocrine Disorders in Childhood and Adolescence, rev. edit., 1957. Home: 501 Edgevale Rd., Balt. 10. Died Sept. 27, 1963; buried Druid Ridge Cemetery, Pikesville, Md.

WILKINS, THOMAS RUSSELL, prof. physics; born Toronto, Ont., Can., June 6, 1891; s. Thomas and Annie (Cornell) W.; B.A., McMaster U. (Can.), 1912; Ph.D., U. of Chicago, 1921; grad. study, Cambridge (Eng.), 1925-26; m. Olive Cross, June 17, 1913. Science master Woodstock Coll. (Can.), 1913-14; instr. physics, U. of Chicago, 1916-17; prof. physics, Brandon (Can.) Coll., 1918-25, U. of Rochester since 1925; dir. Inst. of Optics, Rochester, since 1928. Served as master signal electrician, U.S. Signal Corps, 1917-18. Mem. Am. Phys. Soc., Optical Soc. Am., A.A.A.S., Am. Assn. Univ. Profs., Am. Assn. Physics Teachers, Sigma Xi, Alpha Chi. Baptist. Club: Fortnightly. Editor (with others) Orientation Course in Natural Science 1938. Contbr. tech. articles on radioactivity, atomic physics, photographic research. Secured photographic recordings of cosmic rays and of successive disintegrations of radium atoms. Home: Rochester, N.Y. Died Dec. 10, 1940.

WILKINS, WALTER (EUGENE), physician; b. Columbia, S.C., July 9, 1908; s. Walter and Sallie (Bailey) W.; Ph.D. (biol. chem.), Vanderbilt U., 1933; M.D., 1938. Asst. biochemistry, Vanderbilt Sch. Medicine, 1929-31, instr., 1931-36; interne pediatrics Vanderbilt Hosp., 1938-39, Willard Parker Hosp., N.Y.C., 1939; dir. div. sch. health N.C. State Bd. Health, 1939-42; med. nutrition officer War Food Adminstrn., Washington, 1942-45; surgeon (res.) USPHS, sr. surgeon (res.) in charge Nutrition Sect., 1945; dir. nutrition investigations and services, Fla. State Bd. Health 1946-50; engaged in pvt. practice and research, 1950—. Fellow Am. Pub. Health Assn.; mem. Duval County, Fla. med. socs., A.M.A., So. Med. Assn., Am. Sch. Health Assn. (governing council 1940—, pres. 1946-47), Phi Beta Pi, Alpha Omega Alpha. Contbr. papers to sci. and med. jours. Inventor cup needle for taking blood samples for lab. tests. Home: 5139 Blackburn Rd. Office: 1905 Blanding Rd., Jacksonville, Fla. Died Mar. 2, 1953; buried Mars Hill, N.C.

WILKINS, WILLIAM GLYDE, engineer; b. Pittsburgh, Pa., Apr. 16, 1854; s. Alvin and Charlotte (Glyde) W.; C.E., Rensselaer Poly. Inst., 1879; m. Sarah A. Simmons, Dec. 29, 1880. On U.S. Govt. surveys of Miss. River, 1 yr.; asst. engr. of constrn. Pa. R.R., 7 yrs.; city engr. Allegheny, Pa., 2 yrs.; mem. of The W. G.

Wilkins Co., engrs. and architects, Pittsburgh, 1887—, during which time has been engineer for 18 complete coke plants aggregating 6,000 ovens, and 30 complete coal mining plants costing over $15,000,000. Member Pittsburgh Flood Commn. Republican. Presbyn. Home: Pittsburgh, Pa. Died Apr. 12, 1921.

WILKINSON, CHARLES FORE, JR., educator, physician; b. College Park, Ga., Mar. 30, 1912; s. Charles Fore and Martha Inez (Hardin) W.; B.S., Ga. Sch. Tech., 1932; grad. study U. N.C., 1932-33; M.D., Emory U., 1937; m. Frances Elizabeth Wallace, Apr. 22, 1939; children—Charles Fore, Martha Wallace, Robert Gage. Intern dept. internal medicine U. Mich. Hosp., 1937-38, asst. resident, 1938-39, resident, instr., Upjohn fellow clin. investigation, 1939-40; asst. prof. internal medicine, coordinator grad. med edn. U. Mich., 1946-49; civilian cons. internal medicine Percy Jones Gen. Hosp., Battle Creek, Mich., 1946-49; asso. dir. div. medicine W. K. Kellogg Found., Battle Creek, 1948-49; prof., chmn. department of medicine, post-grad. med. sch. N.Y.U. N.Y. City, since 1949; vis. physician, dir. 4th Med. N.Y.U. div. Bellevue Hosp., med. service U. Hosp., 1949—; cons. in internal medicine, Manhattan V.A. Hospital. Served as 1st lt. to col. with M.C., A.U.S., 1940-46. Diplomate Am. Bd. Internal Medicine. Fellow N.Y. Acad. Medicine, A.A.A.S., A.C.P.; mem. Harvey Soc., Am. Fedn. Clin. Research, Am. Genetic Assn., N.Y. Medico-Surgical Society, American Therapeutic Soc., Society for Experimental Biology and Medicine, American Society of Human Genetics, Am. Soc. Study of Arteriosclerosis, Am., N.Y. heart assns., Soc. Biol. Research, Sigma Xi. Author tech. and sci. articles med. jours. Home: 24 Ellery Lane, Westport, Conn. Office: New York University Post-Graduate Medical School, 550 First Av., N.Y.C. Died Sept. 29, 1959.

WILKINSON, DAVID, inventor, mfr.; b. Smithfield, R.I., Jan. 5, 1771; s. Oziel and Lydia (Smith) W.; m. Martha Sayles, 4 children. Obtained patent for machine for cutting screw threads which incorporated slide rest, 1798; established iron manufactory (with brother) known as David Wilkinson & Co., Pawtucket, R.I., circa 1800; perfected mill to bore cannon by water power (cannon revolved around the boring tool). Died Caledonia Springs, Ont:, Can., Feb. 3, 1852; buried Pawtucket.

WILKINSON, JEREMIAH, mfr., inventor; b. Cumberland, R.I., July 6, 1741; s. Jeremiah and Elizabeth Amey (Whipple) W.; m. Hope Mosier; m. 2d, Elizabeth Southwick; at least 6 children. Worked as blacksmith, silversmith, during youth; began mfg. hand cards for carding wool, circa 1772; developed machine for shaping iron wire used in wool cards; invented mill for grinding cornstalks; manufactured pins and needles; farmed in Cumberland Valley, throughout life. Died Jan. 29, 1831.

WILKINSON, WILLIAM DONALD, educator, geologist; b. Minot, N.D., Sept. 23, 1901; s. William A. and Ella (Walker) W.; B.A., U. Ore., 1923, Ph.D deg. 1932; student U. Cal. at Berkeley, 1923-24; m. Marguerite F. Hill, Jan. 16, 1926; 1 dau., Janet Lee (Mrs. James R. Snook). Instr., U. Ore., 1929-31; mem. faculty Ore. State U., 1931-69, prof. geology, 1945-69, chmn. dept., 1960-69. Served to capt. USAAF, 1942-45. Fellow A.A.A.S., Geol. Soc. Am.; mem. Am. Inst. Metall. and Mining Engrs., Am. Inst. Profl. Geologists (charter, 1st pres. Ore. chpt.), Ore. Acad. Sci., Sigma Xi, Phi Kappa Phi. Mason. Contbr. profl. jours. Home: Corvallis OR Died Jan. 3, 1969; buried Oaklawn Cemetery, Corvallis OR

WILKS, SAMUEL STANLEY, math. statistician; b. Little Elm, Tex., June 17, 1906; s. Chance C. and Bertha May (Gammon) W.; A.B., N. Tex. State Coll., 1926; M.A., U. Tex., 1928; Ph.D., U. Ia., 1931; m. Gena Orr, Sept. 1, 1931; 1 son, Stanley Neal. Nat. Research Council fellow mathematics Columbia, 1931-32, U. London and Cambridge U., 1932-33; instr. mathematics Princeton, 1933-36, asst. prof., 1936-38, asso. prof., 1938-44, prof. math. statistics since 1944, dir. statis. research group since 1944; Fulbright Research appointment Cambridge U., 1951. Trustee Russell Sage Found. Mem. Selective Service Sci. Advisory Committee, 1948-53; med. scientific advisory board Nat. Security Agency, 1953—; advisory committee div. statis. standards Bur. Budget since 1951; mem. Nat. Com. Math., 1951-54; spl. cons. Ednl. Testing Service; mem. U.S. nat. commn. for UNESCO, 1960-62. Recipient Presdl. Certificate of Merit; Centennial Alumni award U. Ia., 1947. Mem. NRC (phys. scis. div. 1947-49, math. div. 1951-57, chmn. 1958-60), Nat. Sci. Foundation (com. on math. and phys. sci. 1952-54), Social Sci. Research Council (bd. dirs.) American Philos. Soc., Am. Statis. Assn. (pres. 1950), Inst. Math. Statistics (pres. 1940), Internat. Statistical Inst., Am. Acad. Arts and Scis., A.A.A.S., Royal Statis. Society, Am. Math. Soc., Am. Math. Assn., Am. Soc. Quality Control, Am. Soc. for Human Genetics, Biometric Soc., Econometric Soc., Market Research Council, Psychometric Society, Lawrenceville Sch. Fathers Association (president 1949). Clubs: Cosmos (Washington); Nassau (Princeton, N.J.). Author: Statistical Inference, 1937; Mathematical Statistics, 1943; Elementary Statistical Analysis, 1948; about 40 research papers. Editor of Annals of Math. Statistics, 1938-49. Home: 1 Campbelton Circle, Princeton, N.J. Died Mar. 7, 1964; buried Little Elm, Tex.

WILLARD, CHESTER EZRA, indsl. engr.; b. Ionia, Mich., Mar. 4, 1886; s. Alonzo L. and Huldah Ann (Dixon) W.; grad. high sch., Ionia, 1905; B.S. in Commerce, Northwestern U., 1923, M.B.A., 1924; m. Mildred Elizabeth Scheidt, Mar. 31, 1906; children—Keith Russell (dec.), Kester Thomas, Kenneth Alonzo, Genevieve Pearl. Clk. in post office, Ionia, 1906-16; gen. agt. Roman Standard Life Ins. Co., 1916-17; instr. in business orgn. and marketing Northwestern U., 1923-25; asst. prof., 1926-29, asso. prof., 1929-42, dir. bus. relations Sch. of Commerce since 1941, prof. indsl. mgmt., 1942-52, prof. emeritus since 1952, coordinator, veterans' edn. since 1944; mgmt. engr. Swanson Ogilvie & McKenzie since 1952. Served as flyer, U.S. Army 1918-19. Mem. Am. Assn. Univ. Profs., Am. Marketing Assn., Inst. Indsl. Engrs. and Execs., Alpha Kappa Psi, Alpha Pi Zeta. Republican. Methodist. Clubs: University (Evanston); Northwestern University (Chgo.). Home: 723 Emerson St., Evanston, Ill. Office: 176 W. Adams St., Chgo. Died May 9, 1961.

WILLARD, DANIEL EVERETT, geologist; b. at Nile, N.Y., Aug. 22, 1862; s. DeWitt Clinton and Lavinia (Lanphear) W.; A.B., Alfred (N.Y.), 1888, A.M., 1890; U. of Chicago, 1892-95; m. Mary Emma Davis, of Nebraska City, Nev., Nov. 11, 1903. Teacher of science and prin., Albion (Wis.) Acad., 1888-91; prin. high sch., Pewaukee, Wis., 1891-92; prof. natural sciences, State Normal Sch., Mayville, N.D., 1895-1903; prof. geology, N.D. Agrl. Coll., 1903-10, also dir. State Agrl. and Geol. Survey; development agt. N.P. Ry. since 1910. Fellow A.A.A.S., Am. Geog. Soc. Episcopalian. Mason (32 deg.). Club: Commercial (St. Paul). Author: The Story of the Prairies, 1902; Geography of North Dakota, 1903; Soils of North Dakota, 1909; Soil Map of North Dakota, 1909. Office: Northern Pacific Bldg., St. Paul, Minn.

WILLARD, JOHN ARTEMAS, cons. engr.; b. Wrentham, Mass., Sept. 29, 1887; s. Artemas and Mary (Ballom) W.; B.S., Mass. Inst. Tech., 1909; m. Marion Inez Hall, Dec. 2, 1909; children—Virginia (Mrs. N. H. Wentworth), Elizabeth (Mrs. F. L. Cusumano), Marion (Mrs. Leslie M. Bell), John Artemas. Instr. Mass. Inst. Tech., 1909-10; foreman testing dept. Trenton Iron Works, 1910-11; draftsman, engr., gen. supt. Bemis Bros. Bag Co., 1911-22; staff engr. Cooley & Marvin Co., 1922-24; partner Bigelow, Kent, Willard & Co., cons. engrs., Boston and N.Y., 1924-57; v.p. Bigelow, Kent, Willard div. of H. B. Maynard & Co., Inc., 1957—; dir. Kaumagraph Co., Wilmington, Del., Century Electronics and Instruments Company. Tulsa. Member of the engineers advisory committee small war plants div. OPM; adv. com. to Chief Engrs. U.S. Army on utilitzation surplus indsl. facilities. Profl. engr., Mass., New York. Fellow Am. Soc. M.E.; mem. Assn. Cons. Mgmt. Engrs. (past pres.), Nat. Mgmt. Council (past chmn.), Soc. Advancement Mgmt. (dir., past treas.), Nat. Assn. Cost Accountants, Theta Chi. Mason. Clubs: Engineers (N.Y.C.; Boston); Arlington (Mass.) Rifle. Home: 10 Noyes St., Needham, Mass. 02192. Office: 136 Federal St., Boston; also 60 E. 42d St., N.Y.C. Died Mar. 14, 1963; buried Center Cemetery, Wrentham, Mass.

WILLARD, JULIUS TERRASS, chemist; b. nr. Wabaunsee, Kans., Apr. 9, 1862; s. Julius F. and Mary E. (Terrass) W.; B.S., Kan. State Coll. Agr. and Applied Science, 1883, M.S., 1886, D.Sc., 1908; Johns Hopkins, 1887-88; m. Lydia P. Gardiner, Aug. 6, 1884; 1 son, Charles Julius. Asst. in chemistry, Kan. State Coll. Agr. and Applied Science, 1883-87, asst. prof., 1891-96, asso. prof., 1896-97, prof. applied chemistry, 1897-1901, prof. chemistry, 1901-18, dean div. gen. science, 1909-39, v.p., 1918-36, college historian since 1936; asst. chemist Agrl. Expt. Sta., 1888-97, chemist, 1897-1918, dir., 1900-06, vice-dir., 1907-18. Fellow A.A.A.S.; mem. Am. Chem. Soc., Kan. Acad. Science, Nat. Edn. Assn., Kan. State Teachers Assn., Sigma Xi, Phi Kappa Phi, Alpha Zeta, Gamma Sigma Delta, Phi Lambda Upsilon, Acaci. Mason (32 deg.). Republican. Rotarian. Author: Organic Compounds of Every-day Life, 1894; History of the Kansas State College of Agriculture and Applied Science, 1940; also numerous Expt. Sta. publs. and hist. articles. Home: 1207 Houston St. Address: Kansas State College, Manhattan, Kan. Died July 26, 1950; buried Sunset Cemetery, Manhattan.

WILLARD, SIMON, clockmaker; b. Grafton, Mass.; Apr. 3, 1753; s. Benjamin and Sarah (Brooks) W.; m. Hannah Willard (his cousin), Nov. 29, 1776; m. 2d, Mary (Bird) Leeds, Jan. 23, 1788; 11 children. Apprenticed to clockmaker, Grafton, 1765, made 1st grandfather clock (better than his master's), 1766; established clock factory, Roxbury, Mass., circa 1777-78; patented Willard Patent Timepiece (came to be known as banjo clock), 1802; patented alarm clock, 1819; ret., 1839. Died Aug. 30, 1848.

WILLARD, THEODORE A., inventor, mfr.; b. Castle Rock, Minn., Dec. 10, 1862; s. Robert R. and Ester (Day) W.; ed. country sch.; m. Florence V. Voorhees, Dec. 3, 1914. Learned trade of mech. engr.; spent over 30 yrs. in inventing devices for storage batteries; awarded 65 patents; inventor of the Willard Storage Battery and ex-pres. Willard Storage Battery Co., hdqrs. in Cleveland, O., branches in principal countries of the world. Methodist. Dir. Amateur Cinema League of New York City. Clubs: Bell Air Bay, Los Angeles, Los Angeles Country; The Racquet (Palm Springs, Calif.); Cleveland; Adventurers (Los Angeles). Author: The City of the Sacred Well, 1926; Wizard of Zacna, 1929; Bride of the Rain God, 1930; The Lost Empires of the Itzaes and Mayas, 1932; Kukulcan, The Bearded Conqueror, 1941. Home: 617 N. Linden Drive, Beverly Hills, Calif.; (winter) "Casa Maya," Palm Springs, Calif. Office: 246 131st St., Cleveland, O. Died Feb. 3, 1943.

WILLARD, WILLIAM A(LBERT), biologist; b. Grinnell, Ia., Apr. 24, 1873; s. William Origin and Emma Elizabeth (Shaw) W.; A.B., Grinnell Coll., 1895; A.M., Tufts Coll., 1898; A.M., Harvard, 1899, Ph.D., 1910; m. Blanche Ellis Snider, July 2, 1907; children—William Raymond, Ruth Eleanor. Instr. biology, Grinnell Coll., 1895-97, acting head dept., 1901-02; instr., asst. prof. zoology, U. of Neb., 1902-10, prof. and head dept. embryology and histology, 1910-14, prof. anatomy, Coll. of Medicine, 1914-46, prof. emeritus since 1946; also directed research students in neuroanatomy in Grad. Coll.; mem. summer faculties, U. of Ill. and Northwestern U. Mem. Am. Assn. Anatomists, Am. Soc. Zool., Sigma Xi (pres. Neb. chap. 1936), Phi Beta Kappa, Nu Sigma Nu. Conglist. Home: 1029 Park Av., Omaha 5 NB Office: University of Nebraska College of Medicine, Omaha NB

WILLCOX, MARY ALICE, zoölogist; b. Kennebunk, Me., Apr. 24, 1856; d. William Henry (D.D., LL.D.) and Annie Holmes (Goodenow) Willcox; student State Normal Sch., Salem, Mass., 1875; student Mass. Inst. Tech., and Boston Soc. of Natural History, 1878-80, Newnham Coll., Eng., 1880-83; Ph.D., U. of Zürich, 1898. Teacher Frederick (Md.) Female Sem., 1875-76, Charlestown High Sch., Boston, 1876-78; prof. zoölogy, Wellesley Coll., 1883-1910, prof. emeritus, 1910. Mem. Boston Soc. Natural History, Sigma Xi, Mass. Audubon Soc., National Assn. Audubon Societies. Author: Pocket Guide to Common Land-Birds of New England, 1895; also various papers on Zoöl. subjects. Chmn. sub-com. on Americanization, Mass. Federation of Women's Clubs, 1914-19; dir. Newton League of Women Voters, 1940—; chmn. com. on interracial relations, 20th Century Assn., Boston, 1940-45. Home: Pocasset, Mass. Deceased.

WILLCOX, WALTER FRANCIS, univ. prof., statistician; b. Reading, Mass., Mar. 22, 1861; s. William Henry and Annie Holmes (Goodenow) W.; brother of Mary Alice Willcox; A.B., Amherst Coll., 1884, A.M., 1888; LL.B., Columbia, 1887, Ph.D., 1891; LL.D., Amherst Coll., 1906; m. Alice E. Work, Mar. 30, 1892 (dec. Sept. 1952); children—Bertram Francis, Mary Goodenow, Alanson Work, William Bradford. Prof. econs. and statistics, Cornell U., 1891-1931, emeritus, 1931; was dean Coll. Arts and Scis., 1902-07, faculty rep. on bd. trustees, 1916-20. Statis. expert for War Dept. upon Censuses of Cuba and P.R., 1899-1900; chief statistician 12th U.S. Census, 1899-1901; spl. agt. U.S. Census Bur., 1902-31; mem. Census Advisory Com. (representing Am. Econ. Assn. 1921-28; chmn. 1928-31); mem. N.Y. State Bd. Health, 1899-1902, cons. statistician, 1907-20. Mem. Am. Econ. Assn. since 1892 (sec. 1896-99; pres. 1915); mem. Am. Statis. Assn. since 1892 (pres. 1912; fellow since 1917); mem. Internat. Statis. Inst. since 1899 (v.p. 1923-47, pres. 1947, hon. pres. since 1947; hon. mem. since 1935), U.S. del. to its sessions, Berlin, 1903, London, 1905, Paris, 1909, Brussels 1923, Rome 1925, Warsaw 1929, Tokyo 1930, Madrid 1931, Mexico 1933, London 1934, Athens 1936, Prague 1938, Washington, 1947, New Delhi, India, 1951, Petropolis, Brazil, 1955, Stockholm (1957), vice chmn. exec. com., pres. sect. on demography Internat. Congress on Hygiene and Demography, Washington, 1912; mem. Am. Council Learned Socs. (rep. Am. Econ. Assn. 1925; exec. com. 1925-28; v. chmn. 1926-28); fellow Royal Statis. Soc. since 1897 (hon. since 1918); hon. mem. Statis. Soc. of Hungary, Czechoslovak Statis. Soc., Mexican Soc. Geography and Statistics; mem. World Statis. Congress (pres.), Social Science Research Council (rep. Am. Statis. Assn., 1925-26); mem. Psi Upsilon, Phi Beta Kappa, Sigma Xi. Clubs: Century, City (N.Y.); Cosmos (Washington). Author: The Divorce Problem—a Study in Statistics, 2d edit., 1897; supplementary Analysis and Derivative Tables, 12th Census, 1906; Introduction to the Vital Statistics of the United States (1900-1930), 1933; Studies in American Demography (with Bibliography), 1940. Home: Ithaca, N.Y. Died Oct. 1964.

WILLETS, DAVID GIFFORD, medical zoologist; b. Scullville, N.J., Dec. 28, 1873; s. John Hope and Elizabeth Gifford (Scull) W.; Ph.B., Wesleyan U., Conn., 1902; M.D., Med. Sch., George Washington U., 1907; m. Mary Esther Kirpatrick, of Colorado Springs, Colo., Feb. 6, 1913. Asst. in Zool. Lab., Hygienic Lab., U.S. Pub. Health and Marine Hosp. Service, Washington, 1903-7; pathologist, Ga. State Sanitarium, Milledgeville, Ga., 1908, 1909; asst. Biol. Lab., Bur. of Science, Manila, 1910-13; asst. prof. med. zoology, Coll. of Medicine and Surgery, U. of Philippines, 1910-13; asst. epidemiologist, U.S. Pub. Health Service, 1914—. Methodist. Mem. A.M.A., Ga. State Med. Assn.,

Southern Med. Assn., Helminthol. Soc. of Washington, Alpha Delta Phi, Phi Chi. Mason. Author of bulls. and articles on pellagra, intestinal parasites, conditions affecting pub. health in P.I., etc. Address: U.S. Public Health Service, Washington DC

WILLEY, HENRY, journalist, botanist; b. Geneseo, N.Y., July 19, 1824; s. Ogden Moseley and Abigail Belden (Chamberlain) W.; ed. Normal School, Bridgewater, Mass.; admitted to N.Y. bar, 1848; practiced law at Geneseo and later in Spencerport, N.Y.; went to Mass., 1851; taught for several yrs.; on editorial staff New Bedford Daily Evening Standard, July 1857 to Jan. 1, 1900. Spl. student and collector of N. Am. lichens. Author: Isaac Wiley, of New London, Conn., and His Descendants; Introduction to the study of Lichens; Synopsis of the Genus Arthonia; Enumeration of the Lichens of New Bedford, Mass. Home: Weymouth, Mass. Deceased.

WILLIAMS, ARTHUR, engineer; b. Norfolk, Va., Aug. 14, 1868; s. Rev. Christopher Stephen and Hannah Sanford (Rogers) W.; ed. pub. and pvt. schs., Hartford and New York; unmarried. Formerly vice-pres. New York Edison Company and other electrical orgns.; now dir. Metropolitan Life Ins. Co. Comdg. officer New York volunteer defense forces, mining New York Harbar during Spanish-Am. War. Fellow Am. Inst. E.E.; mem. numerous societies, civic orgns., etc. Trustee Village of Roslyn Harbor, L.I., and of French Inst. Chevalier Légion d'Honneur and Office de l'Instruction Publique conferred by French Republic; decorated by King of Spain, Knight Royal Order of Isabel the Catholic. Apptd. federal food adminstrn. for N.Y. City, Oct. 1917. Home: Roslyn, L.I. N.Y. Died Apr. 14, 1937.

WILLIAMS, CARLOS GRANT, agrl. experimentation b. Gustavus, O., Jan. 18, 1863; s. Carlos A. and Elmina (Moore) W.; ed. Gustavus Academy; hon. D.Sc., College of Wooster, O., 1931; m. Mayme A. Elder, Jan. 16, 1896; children—Margaret, Ruth, Robert. Agronomist, O. Agrl. Expt. Sta., 1903-21, dir. 1921-37; cons. agronomist since 1937. Contbg. editor Ohio Farmer since 1908; mem. Ohio Agrl. Commn., 1913-14; dir. Peoples Savings & Loan Co., Commercial Banking & Trust Co. (pres.). Mem. O. Council Defense, 1917-18; pres. Wayne County Red Cross, 1918. Fellow A.A.A.S. (vice-pres. 1931), Am. Soc. Agronomy (pres. 1925-26); mem. Soc. Promotion Agrl. Science, Grange. Conglist. Clubs: Century, Rotary. Originator 3 varieties of wheat. Author of 18 expt. sta. bulls. Contbr. to scientific jours. Home: 1004 N. Bever St., Wooster, Ohio. Died Oct. 4, 1946.

WILLIAMS, CHARLES BURGESS, agronomist; b. Shiloh, N.C., Dec. 23, 1871; s. Robert Jones and Susan (Burgess) W.; B.S., N.C. Agricultural and Mech. Coll., 1893, M.S., 1896; Johns Hopkins, 1896-97; m. Margaret Williams Moring, July 5, 1900. Asst. state chemist of N.C., Raleigh, 1899-1907; head of dept. of agronomy, N.C. Expt. Sta., 1906-24, 1926-40, dir. of the station, 1907-12, vice-dir., 1913-32; dean of agriculture, N.C. State Coll., 1917-24, prof. emeritus of agronomy; agronomist, Dept. of Agronomy, N.C. Agrl. and Mech. Coll. Mem. A.A.A.S., Am. Soc. Agr., N.C. Acad. Science, Phi Kappa Phi. Democrat. Missionary Baptist. Home: 1405 Hillsboro St., Raleigh, N.C. Died June 25, 1947.

WILLIAMS, CHARLES MALLORY, dermatologist; born Brooklyn, N.Y., Oct. 16, 1872; s. Charles Phelps and Fanny Elizabeth (Mallory) W.; A.B., Brooklyn Collegiate and Poly. Inst., 1890; Ph.B., Yale, 1892, post-grad. work, 1892-94; M.D., Coll. Physicians and Surgeons (Columbia U.), 1898; hon. D.Sc., U. of Vt., 1932; m. Margaret Dows Worcester, Feb. 25, 1904 (died March 30, 1941); children—Mary Low (wife of Dr. Macdonald Dick, of Duke U.), Margaret (wife of Billings B. Fairbrother); m. 2d, Edith Bramhall Cullis, Apr. 14, 1942. Intern Roosevelt Hosp., 1898-1900, Sloane Hospital 1900; specialized in dermatology since 1902; served in dispensaries Vanderbilt Clinic, North-Western Dispensary, and Bellevue Hospital, and New York Skin and Cancer Hospital; prof. dermatology, University of Vermont, 1913-30; attending physician New York Skin and Cancer Hospital, 1920-34, president med. bd. same, 1928-34; served as consulting dermatologist Memorial Hosp.; prof. clin. dermatology and syphilology, Post-Grad. Med. Sch. (Columbia), 1934-35; retired, 1935. Entered U.S. Army as 1st lt. M.C., 1917; advanced to lt. col., 1919; originated and put into practice segregation of venereal cases in separate battalion, in training camps; with 79th Div. in Meuse-Argonne; citation for services in World War I. Mem. A.M.A., Am. Dermatol. Assn. (pres. 1934-35; dir. 1935-39), New London County (Conn.) Medical Society, Medical Advisory Board (Connecticut), Society Colonial Wars, Century Assn. Republican. Episcopalian. Mason (32 deg.). Clubs: Yale (New York); Graduate, Beaumont Med. (New Haven); Wadawanuck Country (Stonington, Conn.). Contbr. on dermatology, especially in connection with fungus diseases. Home: Stonington, Conn. Died Nov. 12, 1951; buried Stonington, Conn.

WILLIAMS, CHARLES PAGE, hydraulic and irrigation engr.; b. Chillicothe, Mo., Feb. 3, 1866; s. Charles Andrew and Ann Catherine (Page) W.; B.S., Topog. Engr. and Prin. of Pedagogy, cum laude, U. Mo., 1890; m. Lena Leigh Johnson, Jan. 5, 1892; children—Ben Charles, Catherine Elizabeth (Mrs. Robert L. Templeton); m. 2d, Rose Conklin Klinzing, July 10, 1927. Instr. in mathematics, Mo. Mil. Acad., Mexico, Mo., 1890-91; topographer, U.S. War Dept., 1891-92; agt. St. Louis Bridge & Iron Works, 1893; draftsman, U.S. Engrs. Office, Sioux City, Ia., 1894; draftsman, St. Extension Dept., D.C., 1895-97; jr. engr. and supt. constrn. seacoast defs., Portland, Me., and New London, Conn., 1897-1903; with U.S. Reclamation Service, successively engr. design for irrigation works, Wyo. and Mont., mgr. Huntley Irrigation Project, Mont., asst. to supervising engr. northern div., mgr. Milk River and Sun River projects, Mont., and Shoshone Project, Wyo., asst. chief engr. and cons. engr., 1904-24; cons. engr. Hidalgo County (Tex.) Flood Control Com. and La Feria, Pharr-San Juan and El Jardin water improvement dists., 1924-26; cons. engr., Los Angeles, 1926-35; cons. engr. J. G. White, and Co., irrigation development, Baja, California, Mexico, 1927-28; cons. engr. Comisión Nacional de Irrigación of Mexico, water development, Baja California, Mexico, including Rodriguez Dam, highest dam of the Ambursen type in the world, 1928-35; cons. engr. in office that commission, Mexico City, 1936-38, engr. Ambursen Engring. Corp., N.Y., proj. engr. Possum Kingdom Dam and Power House, Brazos River Conservation and Reclamation District, Texas, 1938-40; resident engr. San Vicente Dam, City of San Diego, 1941-43; resident engr. Lake Loveland Project, Sweetwater Falls Dam, Alpine, Cal., 1943-45; cons. engr. Ambursen Engring. Corp., N.Y. and Houston, 1945-46; pvt. work. Mem. Am. Soc. C.E., S.A.R., Phi Delta Theta. Democrat. Mason (32 deg.). Address: 1269 Law St., San Diego 9, Cal. Died Dec. 28, 1955.

WILLIAMS, CLEMENT CLARENCE, engr., educator; b. Bryant, Ill., Feb. 21, 1882; s. Isaac Greenbury and Martha Ann (Davis) W.; B.S., Southern Ia. Normal Sch., 1900; B.S. in C.E., U. of Ill., 1907; C.E., U. of Colo., 1909; LL.D., Lafayette, 1935; Eng.D., Northeastern U., 1936; Eng.D., Bucknell U., 1937, Case Sch. Applied Science, 1939; Sc.D., Hannemann Med. Coll., 1938, Muhlenberg Coll., 1940; LL.D., Rutgers, 1941, Moravian Coll., 1941; m. Grace Josephine Black, Aug. 31, 1910 (died Feb. 3, 1917); m. 2d, Ora Louella Webb, June 8, 1921; children—Ora Louise, Ellen Webb, Clement Webb. Formerly engaged in railway, bridge, municipal and highway engring. work; instr., asst. prof. and acting prof. civil engring., U. of Colo., 1907-14; prof. ry. engring., U. of Kan., 1914-18, prof. civ. engring., 1918-22; prof. civil engring. and head of dept., U. of Ill., 1922-26; dean Coll. of Engring., U. of Ia., 1926-35; pres. Lehigh U. 1935-44; cons. in engring. and indsl. education since 1944. Supervising engineer War Dept., in construction of explosive plants, 1918-19; trustee Carnegie Foundation for Advancement of Teaching. Mem. Am. Soc. C.E., Am. Ry. Engring. Assn., Wis. Acad. Science, Am. Soc. for Engring. Edn. (pres. 1934-35), Pa. Soc. Coll. Presidents (pres. 1940-41), Tau Beta Pi, Sigma Xi, Sigma Tau; fellow A.A.A.S. Republican. Congregationalist. Author: Design of Railway Location, 1917; Design of Masonry Structures and Foundations, 1921; Building and Engineering Career, 1934; Foundations, 1934; also various bulls. and articles in engring. mags. Licensed professional engineer. Home: 129 N. Prospect Av., Madison 5, Wis. Died. Feb. 20, 1947.

WILLIAMS, CLIFTON CURTIS, JR., astronaut; b. Mobile, Sept. 26, 1932; s. Clifton Curtis and Gertrude (Medicus) W.; student Spring Hill Coll., 1949-51; B.M.E., Auburn U., 1954; m. Jane Elizabeth Lansche, July 1, 1964. Commd. 2d lt., USMC, 1954, advanced through grades to maj., 1963; naval aviator, 1956-60; test pilot Naval Air Test Center, Patuxent River, Md., 1960-63; astronaut Manned Space Flight Center, NASA, Houston, 1963-67. Home: Dickinson TX Died Oct. 5, 1967.

WILLIAMS, DANIEL H., physician; b. Hollidaysburg, Pa., Jan. 28, 1858; s. Daniel and Sarah Ann (Price) W.; grad. Janesville Classical Acad., 1878; M.D., Chicago Med. Coll., 1883; LL.D., Wilberforce U., 1908; m. Alice D. Johnson, Apr. 2, 1898. Surgeon to South Side Dispensary, Chicago, 1884-92; founded, 1891, and surgeon Provident Hosp.; phys., Protestant Orphan Asylum, 1884-93; surgeon-in-chief, Freedman's Hosp., Washington, 1893-98; asso. on staff, St. Luke's Hosp., Chicago. Mem. Ill. State Bd. of Health, 1889, reapptd., 1891. Fellow Am. Coll. Surgeons. Prof. clin. surgery, Meharry Med. Coll., Nashville, Tenn., 1899—. Credited with 1st successful closing of wound of heart and pericardium. Died Aug. 4, 1931.

WILLIAMS, EDWARD HIGGINSON, JR., engineer; b. Proctorsville, Vt., Sept. 30, 1849; s. Edward Higginson and Cornelia Bailey (Pratt) W.; Phillips Acad., Andover, 1865-68; A.B., Yale, 1872; B.S. in Chemistry, Lehigh, 1875, E.M., 1876; Sc.D., U. of Vt.; LL.D., Wheaton, 1899. Adrian, 1909; m. Jane Clarissa 1883; children—Olive Bemis (Mrs. Nathan Parke, II), Cornelia (Mrs. Charles W. Fowler), Elizabeth (Mrs. Seymour Ballard), Edward Higginson, III, Norman, Amory Leland, Wentworth, Laurens, Augustine. In engring. corps, Pa. R.R., 1872-73; in charge mining corps, anthracite region, 1876-79; supt. mines Montour Iron & Steel Co., 1879-80; asst. mining engr. Cambria Iron Co., 1880-81; prof. mining engring. and geology, 1881-1902, lecturer on mining and geology, 1902—, Lehigh U. Mem. Legion of Honor of Am. Inst. Mining and Metall. Engrs.; original fellow Geol. Soc. America; emeritus life fellow A.A.A.S. V.pres. Corp. Norman Williams Pub. Library, Woodstock, Vt., 1900—. Author: Manual of Lithology, 1886; 1896; Vigintennial Record of the Class of 1868, Phillips Academy, Andover, 1888; Early History of Woodstock, Vt., 1907. Editor: second edition, Atkinson's Gases Met Within Coal Mines, 1886; Coal and Metal Miners' Pocket Book, 1890; Robert Williams of Roxbury and Descendants, Four Generations, 1890. Contbr. to Science, Am. Jour. of Science, Jour. Am. Geol. Soc. and Proc. of Am. Philos. Soc., 1893-1920. Wrote: (brochure) Pennsylvania Glaciation, First Phase, 1917. Home: Woodstock, Vt. Died Nov. 2, 1933.

WILLIAMS, ELKANAH, ophtalmologist; b. Lawrence County, Ind., Dec. 19, 1822; s. Isaac and Amelia (Gibson) W.; grad. Ind. Asbury U. (now DePauw U.), 1847; M.D., U. Louisville, 1850; m. Sarah L. Farmer, Dec. 1847; m. 2d, Sarah B. McGrew, Apr. 7, 1857. Practiced medicine, Cincinnati, 1855, specialized in diseases of eye and ear (one of 1st in country to limit his practice to this specialty); established charity eye clinic similar to European instns. in connection with Miami Med. Coll., 1855; prof. ophthalmology and aural surgery Miami Med. Coll. (1st chair devoted to this specialty in U.S) 1865-68; one of 1st in Am. to make use of ophthalmoscope; published article "The Ophthalmoscope" in London Med. Times and Gazette, 1854; co-editor Cincinnati Lancet and Observer, 1867-73; mem. Am. Ophthal. Soc., pres., 1876; mem. Am. Otological Soc.; hon. mem. Ophthal. Soc. of Gt. Britain, 1884; mem. staff Cincinnati Hosp., 1862-73; asst. surgeon U.S. Marine Hosp., Cincinnati, during Civil War. Died Oct. 5, 1888.

WILLIAMS, EVERARD MOTT, educator, cons. engr.; b. New Haven, Feb. 2, 1915; s. Cecil H. and Phyllis H. (Mason) W.; B.S., Yale, 1936, Ph.D., 1939; m. Mary Stansel, Apr. 2, 1938; children—Thomas Granville, Nancy Reid, Susan Mott, Peter Biddle. Instr. elec. engring. Pa. State Coll., 1939-42; chief engr. devel. br. spl. projects lab. (USAAF) Wright Field, 1942-45; asso. prof. Carnegie-Mellon U., 1945-49, prof., 1949-72, head dept. elec. engring., 1952-69, George Westinghouse prof. engring., 1969-72, chmn. applied space scis. program, 1963-69; cons. engr., Pitts., 1945-72; expert cons. research and devel. bd. Dept. Def., 1949-51; sci. cons. USAF, 1951-53; cons. U.S. Army Signal Corps, 1953, U.S. Army Ordnance Corps, 1953-54; dir. research Method X Co., 1952-55; cons. Method X div. Firth Sterling, Inc., 1955-60; mem. scientific adv. com. Regional Indsl. Devel. Corp., 1962-72; cons. Def. Dept., 1955-72; research adv. com. on control, data processing and instrumentation NASA, 1963-64; adv. com. Diamond Ordnance Fuse Labs., U.S. Army Ordnance Corps, 1955-64; pres., chmn. bd. El-Gar Rehab, Inc., 1968-72; dir. Microwavel Systems, Inc., Narda Microwave Corp.; adv. com. Harry Diamond Labs. Mem. Edgewood (Pa.) Sch. Bd., 1961-65. Trustee C. C. Mellor Meml. Library, 1961-63. Recipient Pres.'s certificate merit outstanding service World War II; Eta Kappa Nu award as most outstanding young elec. engr. in U.S.A., 1946; Man of Yr. in Engring. award Pitts., 1957; Western Electric award for excellent instrn., 1971. Fellow I.E.E.E.; mem. Am. Soc. Engring. Edn. Club: Cosmos (Washington). Author: Careers in Electronics, 1955; Transmission Circuits, 1957; Electrical Engineering Problems, 1960; Solutions of OLDECC, 1968. Contbr. to bulls. and profl. jours. Home: Pittsburgh PA Died Oct. 24, 1972.

WILLIAMS, FRANCIS HENRY, M.D.; b. Uxbridge, Mass., Apr. 15, 1852; s. Henry Willard and Elizabeth (Dewe) W.; B.S., Mass. Inst. Tech., 1873; M.D., Harvard, 1877; European study, 1877-79; m. Anna Dunn Phillips, Sept. 25, 1891. Asst. U.S. Transit of Venus Expdn. to Japan, 1874; tour around world, 1874-75; practicing phys. at Boston, 1879—. Instr. in materia medica, 1884-85, materia medica and therapeutics, 1885-86, asst. prof. materia medica and therapeutics, 1886-88, asst. prof. therapeutics, 1888-91, Harvard Med. Sch.; visiting phys., 1896-1913, sr. phys., 1913—, Boston City Hosp. Life member Corp. of Mass. Inst. Tech. (mem. exec. com. its 1st 25 yrs.), 1882—. Fellow A.A.A.S., American Acad. Arts and Sciences; pres. Assn. Am. Physicians, 1917-18. Author: The Roentgen Rays in Medicine and Surgery, 1901-03. Initiated bacteriol. examinations in diphtheria, Boston City Hosp., 1892 (first in community to use antitoxin, 1894); developed original methods of treatment of various diseases with the beta rays from radium, especially diseased tonsils (instead of operation) and many diseases of the eye; first paper on subject (published Med. News Feb. 6, 1904) "Some Physical Properties and Medical Uses of Radium Salts," with report of forty-two cases treated with pure radium bromide. Devised clinical method of measuring the X-rays and the beta rays from radium. Home: Boston, Mass. Died June 22, 1926.

WILLIAMS, FRANK B(LAIR), mathematician; b. Warrensburg, Mo., Jan. 23, 1871; s. Oliver Davis and Margaret M. (Houx) W.; Warrensburg State Normal Sch. 3 yrs.; C.E., U. of Mo., 1890, M.S., 1893; Ph.D.,

Clark U., 1900; m. Elizabeth McCarthey, June 21, 1900. Survey work with Miss. River and Mo. River commn., 1890-92, and Miss. River Commn., summer 1900; U.S. asst. engr. in charge Tenn. River Survey, 1895-97; engring. work for N.Y. State Barge Canal and boundary lines, 1902-06; with Clark U., 1907—; prof. mathematics, 1908—. Y.M.C.A. sec. with A.E.F. in France, 1917-18. Fellow A.A.A.S. Conglist. Home: Worcester, Mass. Died 1933.

WILLIAMS, FRANK MARTIN, civil engr.; b. Durhamville, N.Y., Apr. 11, 1873; s. William and Ellen L. (Sterling) W.; A.B., Colgate U., 1895, D.Sc., 1915; LL.B., Syracuse U., 1897, hon. M.C.E., 1919; m. Lucy M. Sterling, June 4, 1907; children—Frank Martin (dec.), David Sterling. Admitted to N.Y. bar, 1897, but engaged in engring. and contracting, Oneida, 1897-1900; entered service State of N.Y., state engr.'s dept., 1900, and was promoted to resident engr.; state engr. and surveyor, term 1909-10; chmn. Barge Canal Terminal Commn., to investigate canal harbors in U.S. and abroad, 1910-11; chief engr. Coleman-duPont Rd. (highway), Del., 1911-12; same Portage County Improvement Assn., Ravenna, O., 1912-13; state engr. and surveyor of N.Y., 1914-23; pvt. practice, 1923—. Consultant for N.Y. State Bridge and Tunnel Commn. and N.J. Interstate Bridge and Tunnel Commn. on constrn. of vehicular tunnel under Hudson River from New York to Jersey City; cons. engr. on Hudson River Regulating District; chief engr. Water Service Commn., city of Oswego, N.Y.; cons. engr. Utica Gas & Electric Co., Cohoes Power and Light Corp., Niagara, Lockport & Ontario Power Co., Power Corp. of New York. Mem. State Council of Defense, 1917-18. Republican. Baptist. Mason, Elk. Home: Albany, N.Y. Died Feb. 20, 1930.

WILLIAMS, FRANKLIN G., educator; b. Bridgeport, Vt., May 17, 1893; s. Henry K. and Minnie A. (Grandey) W.; A.B., Middlebury Coll., 1913; A.M., Pa. State Coll., 1923; Ph.D., Cornell U., 1929; grad. student, U. Pa., 1932-33; m. Sarah H. Lewis, June 17, 1919; 1 dau., Ellen Lewis. Prin. high sch., Waitsfield, Vt., 1913-15; instr. De Veaux Sch., Niagara Falls, N.Y., 1915-17, Swarthmore (Pa.) Prep. Sch., 1917-18, Harrisburg (Pa.) Acad., 1918-19, Arnold Sch., Pitts., 1919-20, Pa. State Coll., 1920-27, Cornell U., 1927-29; prof. math. Susquehanna U., 1929-32; prof. math. Pa. Mil. Coll., also headmaster affiliated prep. sch., Chester, Pa., 1933-45; founder, headmaster Atlantic Air Acad., Rye Beach, N.H., 1945-50; tutor, math. cons., 1950—; ednl. cons. C. V. Starr & Co., N.Y.C., 1952—, dir. tng., 1953-62; ednl. cons. Starr Found., 1958—; lectr. mathematics, Columbia, 1953-55; instr. mathematics L.I. U., 1953-58, asso. prof., 1958-62, prof., 1962—; instr. mathematics Pratt Inst., 1955-63; part-time prof. mathematics Pa. State Coll. Optometry, 1933-43; lectr. math. Swarthmore Coll., 1942-44. Mem. Ins. Soc. N.Y., Math Assn. Am., Am. Math. Soc., education com. N.Y.C. C. of C. 1958-62. Mem. Sigma Xi, Kappa Delta Rho, Phi Mu Alpha, Phi Kappa Phi. Republican. Presbyn. Home: 175 Willoughby St., Bklyn. 1. Died May 20, 1963.

WILLIAMS, GARDNER FRED, mining engr.; b. Saginaw, Mich., Mar. 14, 1842; s. Alpheus Fuller and Ann Keyes (Simpson) W.; grad. Coll. of Calif. (now U. of Calif.), Oakland, 1865; studied Freiberg (Saxony) Mining and Acad., 3 yrs.; LL.D., U. of Calif., 1910; Dr.Engring., U. of Mich., 1917; m. Fanny Locke, Oct. 23, 1871 (died 1911); father of Alpheus Fuller W. Examined salt deposits of Carman Island, Mex., 1869; asst. assayer U.S. Mint, San Francisco, 1870; supt. and assayer Meadow Valley Co., Pioche, Nev., 1871-74; supt. and engr. various mines, Nev., Utah and Calif., and cons. engr. to New York capitalists, 1875-84; in charge of gold mines in Northern Transvaal, S. Africa, 1884-85; engr. for Exploration Co., Ltd., of London, in S.Africa, 1886-87; gen. mgr. De Beers Co., which later became DeBeers-Consol. Mines, Ltd., 1887-1905, organized by Cecil Rhodes, Alfred Beit and others, which produced 95 per cent of the diamond yield of the world. Author: The Diamond Mines of South Africa (2 vols.), revised edit., 1906; The Genesis of the Diamond, 1905. Died Aug. 23, 1922.

WILLIAMS, GARDNER STEWART, cons. engr.; b. Saginaw (W.S.), Mich., 1866; s. Stewart B. and Juliet M. (Ripley) W.; B.S., U. of Mich., 1889, C.E., 1899; m. Jessie B. Wright, 1893; children—Harriet Ripley (Mrs. John B. Waite), William Wright. Asst. engr. water works constrn., Bismarck, N.D., 1887; resident engr. water works constrn., Greenville, Mich., 1888, and Owosso, Mich., 1889; civ. engr. Bd. Water Commrs., Detroit, 1893-98; engr. in charge hydraulic lab., Cornell, 1899-1904; prof. civ., hydraulic and sanitary engring., U. of Mich., 1904-11; cons. engr., Sept. 24, 1911—, specializing in hydraulics and water power. Commd. major Engr. O.R.C., 1917. Mem. Internat. Waterways Commn., 1903-05; mem. Am. Engring. Council, 1920 (v.p. 1923-29). Author: (with Allen Hazen) Hydraulic Tables, 1905; "Hydraulics," in Am. Civ. Engrs.' Pocketbook. Home: Ann Arbor, Mich. Died Dec. 12, 1931.

WILLIAMS, GEORGE HUNTINGTON, mineralogist, petrologist, educator; b. Utica, N.Y., Jan. 28, 1856; s. Robert Stanton and Abigail (Doolittle) W.; B.A., Amherst Coll., 1878; Ph.D., U. Heidelburg (Germany), 1882; m. Mary Clifton Wood, Sept. 15, 1886, 3 children. Asso. in mineralogy Johns Hopkins, 1883-85, asso. prof. mineralogy, 1885-89, asso. prof. inorganic geology, 1889-91, prof. inorganic geology, 1891-94. Author: The Gabbros and Associated Hornblende Rocks Occurring in the Neighborhood of Baltimore, Md. (Bulletin 28 of U.S. Geol. Survey), 1886; Elements of Crystallography (textbook), 1899; The Greenstone Schist Areas of the Menominee and Marquette Regions of Michigan (most valuable publication; Bull. 62 of U.S. Geol. Survey), 1890. Died July 12, 1894.

WILLIAMS, HENRY EUGENE, Weather Bur. official; b. Bethel, Conn., Apr. 3, 1844; s. Ira and Almira (Stowe) W.; ed. public schs. and acad., Bethel; m. Theresa A. Riopelle, Oct. 15, 1876. Entered U.S. weather service (then a branch of the Signal Corps of the Army), Mar. 24, 1876; instr. in Sch. of Instrn., Fort Myer, 1881-85; chief of Forecast Div., 1895-98; chief clk. Weather Bur., 1898-1903; asst. chief, July 1, 1903-June 30, 1914; meterologist in charge Forecast Div., 1914—. Englisted in Co. C, 17th Conn. Inf., July 26, 1862; mustered out as 1st lt., Aug. 19, 1865. Trustee Universalist Gen. Conv., 1909-17. Mason. Wrote: Temperatures Injurious to Food Products in Storage and During Transportation (bull. 13), 1896. Home: Washington, D.C. Died 1930.

WILLIAMS, HENRY SHALER, geologist; b. Ithaca, N.Y., Mar. 6, 1847; s. Josiah B. and Mary H. (Hardy) W.; Ph.B., Yale, 1868, Ph.D., 1871; m. Harriet H. Wilcox, 1871. Asst. in paleontology, Yale, 1868-70; prof. natural science, Ky. Univ., 1871-72; asst. prof. geology, 1880-92; prof., 1892, Cornell U.; Silliman prof. geology, Yale, 1892-1904; prof. geology and head geol. dept. and director of museum, 1904-12, emeritus prof. geology, 1912—, Cornell U.; also in charge Devonian Lab. of U.S. Geol. Survey. Asso. editor Am. Jour. of Science and Jour. of Geology. Am. commr. Internat. Congress of Geology; fellow London Geol. Soc., Soc. Geology du Nord, Geol. Soc. America, A.A.A.S. Author: Geological Biology; Correlation Papers, Devonian and Carboniferous; On the Theory of Organic Variation; also numerous papers on Devonian geology and palaeontology. Home: Ithaca, N.Y. Died Aug. 1, 1918.

WILLIAMS, HENRY SMITH, physician, author; b. Durand, Ill., Mar. 4, 1863; s. Edward Jenner and Orrilla N. (Webster) W.; brother of Edward Huntington W.; A.B., State U. of Iowa, 1887; M.D., Chicago Med. Coll., 1884; in univs., hosps. and libraries of Berlin, Paris, London, etc., 1898-1902; LL.D., Western Reserve, 1903; m. Florence Whitney, Nov. 9, 1889; m. 2d, Marina M. Gardner, Feb. 12, 1925. Practiced since 1884; specialist in nervous and mental diseases; asst. physician and pathologist State Hospital for Insane, Independence, 1887; asst. physician Manhattan State Hospital, 1888, Bloomingdale Asylum, 1889; medical supt. Randall's Island Hospital, 1892. Lecturer Hartford School of Sociology, 1891-92. Author: Check List of Iowa Birds (with C. L. Keys), 1887 (Davenport Acad. Science); The Story of Nineteenth Century Science, 1900; The History of Art of Writing, 1902; A History of Science (5 vols.), 1904 (with E. H. Williams, M.D.); The Effect of Alcohol, 1909; The Science of Happiness, 1909; Every Day Science (14 vols.), 1909-10 (with E. H. Williams, M.D.); The Conquest of Nature, 1911; Mental Obliquities, Science and Civilization, 1912; The Wonders of Science in Modern Life (10 vols.), 1912; Miracles of Science, 1913; Adding Years to Your Life, 1914; Luther Burbank—His Life and Work, 1915; The Proteal Treatment of Cancer and Allied Conditions, 1916; Proteal Therapy, 1917; The Proteomorphic Theory and the New Medicine, 1918; The Witness of the Sun, 1920; The Phantom Auto, 1921; Practical Radio, 1922; Story of Modern Science, 1923; The Great Astronomers, 1930; The Literary Digest Book of Marvels, 1931; The Biography of Mother Earth, 1931; Survival of the Fittest, 1932; Why Die Before Your Time?, 1933; Drugs Against Men, 1935; Wonder Book of World Progress (10 vols.), 1935; Your Glands and You, 1936; The Dope Ring, 1937; Drug Addicts Are Human Beings, 1938; The Private Lives of Birds, 1939; Etching Is the Ideal Hobby, 1941. Editor: Historians' History of the World (25 vols.), 1904; Works of Luther Burbank (12 vols.), 1915. Specialist in haematology; originator of the Proteomorphic Theory of Immunization, 1914, and one of the originators of nonspecific protein therapy and of the hypodermic use of vegetable proteins, or proteals, in treatment of conditions of disturbed metabolism. In recent years active as painter and etcher. More than 400 of his pictures are reproduced, many in full color, in mags. and books since 1930. Address: 200 N. Av. 66, Los Angeles, Calif. Died July 4, 1943.

WILLIAMS, HENRY WILLARD, ophthalmologist; b. Boston, Dec. 11, 1821; s. Willard and Elizabeth (Osgood) W.; grad. Harvard Med. Sch., 1849; m. Elizabeth Dewe, 1848; m. 2d, Elizabeth Adeline Law, 1860; 6 children. Organized voluntary class of Harvard students for ophthalmology lectures, 1850; lectr. ophthalmology Harvard Med. Sch., 1866-71, 1st prof. ophthalmology, 1871-95; ophthal. surgeon Boston City Hosp., 1864-91; a founder Am. Ophthal. Soc., 1864, pres., 1868-75; wrote article on cataract operation for Boston Med. and Surg. Jour., 1850; pres. Mass. Med. Soc., 1880-82. Author: A Practical Guide to the Study of the Diseases of the Eye, 1862; Our Eyes, and How To Take Care of Them, 1871; The Diagnosis and Treatment of the Diseases of the Eye, 1881. Died Boston, June 13, 1895.

WILLIAMS, HERBERT UPHAM, pathologist; b. Buffalo, Nov. 28, 1866; s. Frank and Olive W.; lit. dept. U. of Mich., 1884-86; M.D., U. of Buffalo, 1889; M.D., U. of Pa., 1891; studied, Johns Hopkins, 1895, U. of Göttingen, 1899; m. Mary Carver, d. Col. William P. Stoddard, 1909. Apptd. prof. pathology and bacteriology, med. dept. U. of Buffalo, 1894, also served as dean of dept. Fellow A.A.A.S. Author: Manual of Bacteriology, 1898. Contbr. to Jour. Med. Research, Jour. Exptl. Medicine, Am. Jour. Pathology and Archives of Pathology, especially on the subject of human paleopathology, mummies the origin of syphilis. Home: Buffalo, N.Y. Died Dec. 8, 1938.

WILLIAMS, HORATIO BURT, physiologist; b. Utica, N.Y., Sept. 17, 1877; s. Horatio Olin and Julia Amanda (Pierce) W.; A.B., Syracuse U., 1900, M.D., 1905, Sc.D., 1925; m. Abbie Prentiss Schermerhorn, 1905 (died January 27, 1944). Interne New York Hospital House of Relief, 1905-06; engaged in medical practice, N.Y. City, 1907-11, asst. in physiology, Cornell U., Med. Sch., 1907-11; asso. in physiology, Columbia, 1915-16, asst. prof., 1916-22, Dalton prof. and executive officer of department, 1922-37, Dalton prof., 1937-42, professor emeritus since Sept. 17, 1942; consultant Greenwich (Conn.) Hosp.; dir. and tech. adviser Cambridge Instrument Co., Inc.; registered engr., Conn. Served as capt., Corps of Engrs., U.S. Army 1917-19; instr. Engr. Sch., U.S. Army, 1919; capt. Engr. Res. Corps, 1919-39. Mem. com. on safety, Am. Inst. E.E., Nat. Com. Radiation Protection, Am. Physiol. Soc. Am. Phys. Soc., Phys. Soc. of London, Optical Soc., Acoustical Soc. of America, Math. Society, A.M.A. (former mem. council phys. med.), New York Academy of Medicine, Society Am. Mil. Engrs., Am. Inst. Elec. Engrs., Am. Soc. Anesthetists (hon.), Nat. Soc. Professional Engrs., Conn. Soc. Professional Engrs., Society of Experimental Biology and Medicine, Saint Nicholas Soc. of N.Y., Psi Upsilon, Nu Sigma Nu, Sigma Xi (v.p. Columbia Chapter, 1939-40; pres. 1940-41), Alpha Omega Alpha. Republican. Clubs: Faculty, Engineers, University (N.Y. and Chgo); Cosmos (Washington). Contbr. sci. articles to publs. Home: Dingletown Rd., Greenwich, Conn.; (summer) Woodstock, N.Y. Died Nov. 1, 1955; buried St. Marks Ch. in the Bouwerie, N.Y.C.

WILLIAMS, JAMES LEON, research dentist; b. Embden, Me., Apr. 21, 1852; s. Calvin and Susan C. (Wells) W.; prep. edn., Oak Grove Sem., Vassalboro, Me.; D.D.S., Baltimore (Md.) Dental Coll.; L.D.S., Royal Coll. Surgeons of Ireland, 1889; m. Alice P. Robinson, of North Vassalboro, 1873; children—Lena (dec.), Eugenia B. (dec.), Percy N., Harry S. Began practice at North Vassalboro, 1871; moved to New York, 1885, to London, 1887; returned to U.S., 1915 and has since associated with Dentists' Supply Co., New York, in production of his invention, the Trubyte System of artificial teeth. Discovered that there are three distinct types of teeth in all races of men and that these three types are strongly marked in anthropoid apes, apparently proving a near relationship between man and the anthropoid apes. Fellow Am. Coll. Dentists, Am. Acad. Dental Science, New York Acad. Science, Royal Anthrop. Inst. of Great Britain and Ireland; mem. Internat. Assn. for Dental Research (ex-pres.), Psi Omega. Awarded 3 gold medals "for contributions to science and human welfare." Writer of Gray and the Elegy; The Land of Sleepy Hollow; The Home and Haunts of Shakespeare. Asso. editor Jour. for Dental Research. Presented to Am. Mus. Natural History, New York, a collection of pre-historic human skulls, the nucleus of the notable display on exhibition in "The Hall of Man." Home: 160 Riverside Drive, New York, N.Y., and Concord Haven, Solon, Me.

WILLIAMS, JESSE LYNCH, civil engr.; b. Westfield, N.C., May 6, 1807; s. Jesse and Sarah (Terrell) W.; m. Susan Creighton, Nov. 15, 1831. Held minor position in 1st survey of Miami & Erie Canal in Ohio (Cincinnati to Maumee Bay), 1828; mem. bd. engrs. using reservoirs rather than longfeeders from distant streams to supply summit level of canal with water; chief engr. Wabash Erie Canal, 1832; surveyed all other canals of Ind., 1835; engr.-in-chief all canal routes in Ind., 1836, all railroads and turnpikes, 1837; chief engr. Wabash & Erie Canal, 1847-76, Ft. Wayne Chgo. R.R., 1854-56; U.S. dir. U.P. Ry., 1864-69; apptd. receiver Grand Rapids & Ind. R.R., 1869; apptd. chief engr. in charge of completion of Cincinnati, Richmond & Ft. Wayne R.R., 1871; an original dir. Presbyn. Theol. Sem. of N.W. (later McCormick Theol. Sem.). Died Oct. 9, 1886.

WILLIAMS, JOHN H(ARRY), physicist; b. Asbestos Mines, P.Q., Can., July 7, 1908; s. Harry John and Josephine Leonore (Stockwell) W.; came to U.S., 1928, naturalized, 1942; A.B., U. of B.C., 1928, D.Sc., 1958; A.M., U. Cal., 1930, Ph.D., (Whiting fellow), 1931; NRC fellow U. Chgo., 1931-33; E.D., Pa. Mil. Coll., 1960; m. Vera Martin, 1928; children—Lloyd J., M. Ann, Susan M. Asst. prof. physics U. Minn., 1933-37, asso. prof., 1937-42; research scientist Los Alamos Lab., 1943-46; prof. physics U. Minn., 1946-58, 60—; dir.

Div. Research, U.S. AEC, 1958-60, commr., 1959-60. Mem. Nat. Acad. Scis., Am. Phys. Soc., Am. Assn. U. Profs., Sigma Xi, Phi Beta Kappa. Home: 23 Mid-Oaks Lane, St. Paul 55113. Died Apr. 18, 1966.

WILLIAMS, JOHN RALSTON, physician; b. Renfrew, Ont., Can., Dec. 27, 1874; s. John Foster and Mary S. (Crozier) W.; M.D., U. Mich., 1903; m. Ethel M. Rafter, Apr. 17, 1907; children—Elizabeth Rafter (Mrs. Albert F. Gallun, Jr.), John Ralston, Margaret Eleanor (Mrs. Richard J. Meyer), George Rafter. Served as asst. Spanish War Typhoid Fever Commn., 1903-04; sec. Milk Commn. of Medical Soc. of County of Monroe, N.Y., 1908-16 (in charge numerous investigations of municipal milk problems), also practicing as physician since 1904; cons. in medicine Highland Hosp.; cons. in medicine Strong-Meml. Hosp.; specialized in diseases of metabolism and made extensive researches in diabetes millitus. Commr. Rochester Municipal Mus. Fine Arts; pres. Rochester Mus. Arts and Scis.; mem. Nat. Alumni Council U. Mich. Mem. Nat., N.Y. State and Rochester coms. Council of Nat. Defense, 1917. Fellow A.M.A., A.C.P., Am. Soc. Clin. Investigation; mem. Rochester Hist. Soc. Republican. Mem. Am. Unitarian Assn. Clubs: University of Michigan, Torch, Interurban Medical, Oak Hill Country (Rochester). Author of numerous scientific articles on typhoid fever, economics of milk prodn. and distbn., domestic refrigeration, the devel. and use of insulin, problems of human nutrition, etc. Home-Office: 388 Monroe Av., Rochester, N.Y. 14607. Died Dec. 27, 1965.

WILLIAMS, JOHN TOWNSEND, engineer; b. Glen Cove, N.Y., May 16, 1852; s. John Townsend and Ida Ann (Coles) W.; g.s. Richard S.W., long pres. Market Nat. Bank; E.M., Ph.B., Columbia Sch. of Mines (Columbia University), 1873; m. Louise Ladew, of New York, Mar., 1874 (died Sept. 1915). Engaged 15 yrs. with mfg. enterprises as engr. and expert, and part owner. Engr. and architect Central Nat. Bank Bldg., Silk Exchange, and many other large bldgs. in New York, including one at Broadway and White St. and Lord's Court Bldg., of which he was the owner; more recently interested as engr. and owner of extensive mining, metall. and chem. works, also development, reorganization and financing such properties; pres. Va. Consol. Chem. Corp., and John T. Williams & Son, Inc. Home: New York Yacht Club. Office: 100 Broadway, New York.

WILLIAMS, JOSEPH WHITE, civil engr.; b. Milan, O., Oct. 20, 1879; s. Daniel Newton and Sophia E. (White) W.; grad. high sch., Milan, 1897; m. Eliza L. Hunt, Sept. 24, 1902; children—Joseph Hunt, Mary Elinor. On railroad location and constrn., N.M. and Calif., 1900-07; asst. chief engr. Northwestern Pacific R.R., 1907-14, chief engr. constrn., 1914-17, chief engr., 1919-21; chief engr. Western Pacific R.R., Aug. 1921—. Served as pvt. 52d Ia. Vol. Inf., Spanish-Am. War; again entered military service, in Apr. 1917; maj., lt. col. 18th Engrs., U.S.A., World War I; in France, Aug. 1917-Apr. 1919; col. engrs. O.R.C. Republican. Home: Ross, Calif. Died Feb. 3, 1941.

WILLIAMS, KENNETH POWERS, mathematician, historian, educator; b. Urbana, O., Aug. 25, 1887; s. John H. and Eva Augusta (Powers) W.; student Clark Coll., Worcester, Mass., 1905-06; A.B., Ind. U., 1908, A.M., 1909; Ph.D., Princeton, 1913; m. Ellen Laughlin Scott, Aug. 30, 1920. With Ind. U., 1909—, instr. mathematics until 1914, asst. prof., 1914-19, asso. prof., 1919-24, prof., 1924—, chmn. dept., 1937-44. Served as 1st lt. Indiana National Guard, Mexican Border, 1916; captain Field Artillery, United States Army, with A.E.F., 1917-19; maj. F.A., Ind. Nat. Guard, 1921-24, lt. col., 1924-31, col. and chief of staff, 38th Div., Nat. Guard, 1931-39, col., Q.M.C., comdg. 113th Q.M. Regt., and Q.M., 38th Div., in fed. service, 1941. Received Gold Medal Soc. of Libraries of N.Y.U., Diploma of Honor Lincoln Memorial U., and others. Fellow A.A.A.S.; mem. Am. Math. Soc., Math. Assn. Am. (mem. bd. govs., 1945-47, chmn. commn. on place of math. in secondary edn. 1934-40), Am. Astron. Soc., Société Astronomique de France, Am. Assn. Univ. Prof. (chmn. com. required courses in education 1931-35, council, 1946-48), Phi Beta Kappa, Sigma Xi, Scabbard and Blade. American Legion. Republican. Mason. Author: Dynamics of the Airplane, 1921; College Algebra, 1928; The Calculation of the Orbits of Asteroids and Comets, 1934; The Mathematical Theory of Finance, 1935, revised edit., 1947; Lincoln Finds a General, Vol. I, II, 1949, III, 1952; math. and astron. papers. Home: 702 E. 10th St., Bloomington, Ind. Died Sept. 25, 1958; buried Columbus, Ind.

WILLIAMS, NEIL HOOKER, prof. of physics; b. Almont, Mich., Oct. 23, 1870; s. Rev. Horace Robbins and Amelia (Robbins) U.; B.S., in elec. engring.; U. of Mich., 1893; M.S., 1895; Ph.D., 1912; m. Elizabeth McDonald, Aug. 8, 1899; children—Donald Hooker, Howard Robbins. Teacher, West Bay City (Mich.) High Sch., 1895-98, Central High Sch., Detroit, 1898-1901, Shortridge High Sch., Indpls., 1901-03; asst. prof. Rose Poly. Inst., Terra Haute, Ind., 1903-08; instr. of physics, U. Mich., 1908-12, asst. prof., 1912-16, asso. prof., 1916-19, prof., 1919-41, now prof. emeritus. Fellow A.A.A.S., Am. Phys. Soc.; mem. Inst. Radio Engring. Republican. Conglist. Author: General College Physics (with H. M. Randall and W. F. Colby), 1929, revised edit., 1937; Electron Tubes, 1935. Contbr. articles to scientific jours. Home: 1020 Olivia Av., Ann Arbor, Mich. Died Nov. 26, 1956.

WILLIAMS, O(SCAR) B(ROWN), univ. prof.; b. Kosse, Tex., Sept. 17, 1895; s. William Alfred and Matilda (Lowrey) W.; A.B., U. Tex., 1921, A.M., 1923; Ph.D., U. Cal., 1928; m. Frances Rowe, Dec. 14, 1923; children—Oscar Brown, Katherine Rowe. City water bacteriologist, Austin, Tex., 1921-23; instr. U. Tex., 1922-25, adjunct. prof., 1925-27, asso. prof., 1927-35, became prof. bacteriol. 1941, now chmn. dept. and athletic council; bacteriol. Research Lab., Nat. Canners Assn., Washington, 1935-41. Served in Med. Corps, U.S. Army, 1917-19; sgt. 1-c. Mem. subcom. on animal products Nat. Research Council. Mem. Soc. Am. Bacteriol. Inst. Food Technol., Am. Pub. Health Assn., A.A.A.S., Chi Phi, Phi Beta Kappa, Sigma Xi, Gamma Alpha, Phi Sigma, Alpha Epsilon Delta. Democrat. Methodist. Mem. editorial bd. Advances in Food Research, McGraw-Hill series in food technol. 1944—, Jour. of Bacteriology, 1951—. Home: 2509 Spring Lane, Austin 21, Tex. Died Sept. 23, 1959.

WILLIAMS, ROBERT PURCELL, JR., cons. engr.; b. Columbia, Ala., Feb. 25, 1908; s. Robert Purdy and Mamie Drake (Purcell) W.; B.S., Ga. Inst. Tech., 1931; M.S., Yale, 1933; m. Sylvia Ethel Lantz, Mar. 7, 1942. Engr. Ala. Public Service Commn., 1935-40; joined Rheem Mfg. Co., 1942, mgr. Washington office, 1943-52, v.p., 1952-57; founded Williams Engring. Co., 1957, pres., 1957—. Tech. advisor cartridge case com. NATO, 1952. Served as lt. Ordnance Corps, AUS, 1940-42. Mem. Am. Ordnance Assn., Am. Soc. Naval Engrs., Nat. Security Indsl. Association, Armed Forces Chem. Assn., Yale Engineering Association (vice president). Presbyterian (deacon). Clubs: Army and Navy, Congressional Country (Washington); Yale (N.Y.C. and Washington). Home: 1306 36th St., Washington 7. Office: 839 17th St., Washington 6. Died Feb. 14, 1958; buried Arlington Nat. Cemetery.

WILLIAMS, ROBERT R., chemist; b. Nellore, India, of Am. parents, Feb. 16, 1886; s. Robert Runnels and Alice Evelyn (Mills) W.; student Ottawa (Kan.) U., 1905; B.S., of Chicago, 1907; M.S., 1908, post grad. study, 1911-12; Sc.D., Ottawa U., 1935, Ohio Wesleyan U., 1938, U. Chgo., 1941, Colombia, 1942, Yale, 1942, Stevens Inst. Tech., 1940, U. Denver, 1952; LL.D., Washington U., 1956; m. Augusta C. Parrish, Mar. 27, 1912; children—Robert Reynolds, Elizabeth Alice, Jean Parrish, June Augusta. Began as teacher in Phillipines, 1908; chemist Bur. of Science, Manila, 1909-15, Bur. of Chemistry, Washington, 1915-18, Western Electric Co., 1919-24; chem. dir. Bell Telephone Labs., N.Y.C., 1925-45, dir. grants, Research Corp., 1945-51, asst. to pres., 1946-56, ret., past dir.; research asso. Tchrs. Coll. Columbia, Carnegie Inst., 1923-34. Engaged in C.W.S. and Air Service research, Washington, World War I. Chmn. Cereal Com., Food and Nutrition bd NRC, 1940-59. Founder Williams-Waterman Fund, Research Corp. Fellow A.A.A.S. Mem. Am. Chem. Soc., Soc. Exptl. Biology and Medicine, Soc. Biol. Chemistry, Am. Philosophical Soc., Nat. Acad. Sci., Am. Dietetic Assn. (hon.). Baptist. Inventor of processes for making submarine and textile insulation, etc. Structure and synthesis of Vitamin B1, enrichment of flour and bread. Contributor technical articles to magazines. Awarded Willard Gibbs medal, 1938; Elliott Cresson medal, 1940; designated Modern Pioneer by Nat. Assn. Mfrs., 1940; 8th Annual Award of Asso. Grocery Mfrs., 1941; John Scott medal of City of Phila., 1941; Charles Frederick Chandler medal Columbia U., 1942; Perkin Medal, 1947; Carlos Manual de Cespedes medal (Cuba), 1950; the Carlos Finlay medal (Cuba), 1953; Hart award Inst. of Food Technologists, 1964; Alumni medal U. Chgo., 1965. Co-author: (with T. D. Spies) Vitamin B1 and Its Use in Medicine; author: Williams-Waterman Fund, 1935-55, 1956; Toward Conquest of Beriberi, 1961. Home: 45 Woodland Av., Summit, N.J. 07901. Died Oct. 2, 1965; buried Fairmount Cemetery, Chatham, N.J.

WILLIAMS, ROSWELL CARTER, JR., entomologist; b. Brooklyn, N.Y., Aug. 21, 1869; s. Roswell Carter and Ellen Sophia (Woodford) W.; B.S., Adelphi Acad., Brooklyn, 1888; M.E., Cornell U., 1892; m. Margaret Hamilton, of Belfast, Ireland, Mar. 5, 1910; children—Roswell Carter III, Hamilton, Arthur Phelps, Charles Montgomery; m. 2d, Carrie Hamsher, of Barnesville, Pa., Feb. 28, 1929. Elec. engr. and contractor, at Phila., Pa., 1894-1918; research asso. Acad. Natural Sciences, Phila., since 1918, dir. R. C. Williams & Co., groceries, N.Y. City. Served as capt. Ordnance Dept., U.S.A., 1 yr., World War. Mem. Entomol. Soc. America (pres.), Kappa Alpha. Republican. Mason (32 deg.). Clubs: Manufacturers, Penn Athletic. Contbr. to Entomol. News, Trans. Am. Entomol. Soc. Home: 4537 Pine St. Office: Acad. Natural Sciences, Philadelphia PA

WILLIAMS, SIDNEY JAMES, engr.; b. Milwaukee, Wis., May 12, 1886; s. Gavin Perry and Fannie (West) W.; B.S., U. of Wis., 1908, C.E., 1915; m. Margaret Frankenburger, Sept. 6, 1909; children—Dorothy Ann, Barbara. Asst. engr. Utah Gas & Coke Co., Salt Lake City, Utah, 1906-07; supt. for R. B. Hartman, building contractor, Milwaukee, 1908-13; engr. Industrial Commn. of Wis., Madison, 1913-18; chief engr. Nat. Safety Council, Chicago, 1918-24, dir. of pub. safety div., 1924-43, gen. mgr., 1943-45, asst. to pres. since 1945. Dir. of safety Fed. Civil Works Administration, 1933-34; consultant to various federal agencies. Beecroft Memorial Lecturer, Society Automotive Engrs., 1950. Chairman safety and industrial health advisory board, Atomic Energy Commn., 1947—. Received C.I.T. Safety Foundation grand award for greatest contribution to pub. safety, 1938, Arthur Williams Memorial Award, 1954. Mem. Am. Soc. C.E., Inst. Traffic Engrs., Soc. Automotive Engrs., Alpha Delta Phi, Phi Beta Kappa, Tau Beta Pi. Conglist. Author: The Manual of Industrial Safety, 1927; (with W. W. Charters) Safety (high sch. text), 1940. Contbr. articles on safety, traffic, etc., and lecturer. Home: 2501 McDaniel Av., Evanston, Ill. Office: 425 N. Michigan Av., Chgo. 11. Died Aug. 5, 1956; buried Forest Home Cemetery, Milw.

WILLIAMS, STEPHEN RIGGS, zoologist; b. Kalgan, N. China, Aug. 22, 1870; s. Mark and Isabella Burgess (Riggs) W.; A.B., Oberlin Coll., 1892, A.M., 1893; A.M., Harvard, 1898, Ph.D., 1900; m. Mary Covington, of Brooklyn, N.Y. and Oxford, O., Sept. 14, 1904. Teacher high sch., Lima, O., 1894-96; asst. in zoology, Harvard, 1898-1900; asst. and instr., Cold Spring Harbor, L.I., summer sessions, 1900-04; prof., biology and geology, 1900-05, zoology since 1905, Miami U.; mem. staff, Lake Lab., Ohio State U., summer sessions, 1913-34. Mem. A.A.A.S., Am. Soc. Zoologists. Conglist. Contbr. Anatomy of the Texas Fever Tick, Specific Gravity of Fresh Water Organisms, etc. Home: Oxford OH

WILLIAMS, STEPHEN WEST, medical historian; b. Deerfield, Mass., Mar. 27, 1790; s. William Stoddard and Mary (Hoyt) W.; A.M. (hon.), Williams Coll., 1829, M.D. (hon.), 1842; M.D. (hon.), Berkshire Med. Instn., 1824; m. Harriet Godhue, Oct. 20, 1818. 4 children including Helen (Williams) Huntington. Explored hills of Western Mass. collecting herbarium of imdigenous medical plants; lectr. medical jurisprudence Berkshire Med. Instn., 1823-31; faculty Willoughby (O.) U., 1838-53; lectr. Dartmouth Med. Sch., 1838-41; added notes to A Compendium of Medical Practice (James Bedingfield), 1823; wrote papers for N.Y. Hist. Soc., similar assns.; contbr. biographies to American Medical Biography, published 1845. Author: Floral Calendar Kept at Deerfield, Mass., 1819; (lecture) A Catechism of Medical Jurisprudence, 1835. Died Laona, Ill., July 6, 1855.

WILLIAMS, VAN ZANDT, physicist; b. Providence, Mar. 29, 1916; s. Arthur Olney and Elizabeth (Gillespie) W.; A.B., Brown U., 1937; Ph.D., Princeton, 1941; m. Mary Parmelee Bridgeman, Sept. 20, 1941; children—Van Zandt, Richard Bridgeman. With Am. Cyanamid Research Labs., 1941-48, asst. dir. physics div., 1943-48; with Perkin-Elmer Corp., 1948-65, v.p. tech. devel., 1960-65; dir. Am. Inst. Physics, 1965—. Fellow Am. Phys. Soc.; mem. Am. Assn. Physics Tchrs., Optical Soc. Am. (pres. elect 1965), Am. Chem. Soc., N.Y. Acad. Scis., Soc. Applied Spectroscopy, Coblentz Soc., Phi Beta Kappa, Sigma Xi, Sigma Pi Sigma. Home: 4 Tower Rd., Riverside, Conn. 06878. Office: Am. Inst. Physics, 335 E. 45th St., N.Y.C. 10009. Died May 13, 1966; buried Woodstock, Conn.

WILLIAMS, WILLIAM HORACE, engring. exec.; b. Fort McIntosh, Laredo, Tex., June 18, 1882; s. Maj. William Morrow (U.S. Army) and Eugenie Lelia (Simon) W.; preparatory edn., high sch., Detroit, and Doane Acad., Granville, O.; student Denison U. to 1902; m. Ruby Ionia Mugnier, Dec. 30, 1908 (dec.); children—Elizabeth Ionia, William Horace, Eugenie Lorrance, Robert Milton; m. 2d, Viola Bloch, October 26, 1923; children—Robert Howard (dec.), John Wesley. On preliminary surveys, Pa. R.R., 1901-02; with U.S. Army engrs., on constrn. breakwaters, Lorain, O., in charge levees, New Orleans to Gulf of Mexico, 1903-04; resident engr. Christie & Lowe, civ. engrs., jetty constrn., Miss. River, 1905-07; mem. Doullut & Williams, 1908-21; sec.-treas. and gen. mgr. Doullut & Williams Shipbuilding Co., 1918-21; pres., gen. mgr. Doullut & Williams, Inc., 1921-24; became pres., gen. mgr. W. Horace Williams Co., Inc., 1925, pres., dir., 1933-40, pres., gen. mgr., 1950-51, chmn. bd., 1951—; mem. firm, gen. mgr. W. Horace Williams Co., 1940—; v.p. Merritt-Chapman & Scott Corp., 1931-32; pres., gen. mgr. Merritt-Chapman & Williams Corp., 1931-33; pres., dir. Baronne Howard Realty Co., Inc.; dir., mem. exec. com. Whitney Nat. Bank, New Orleans. Mem. La. Engring. Soc. (past pres.; life mem.), Am. Soc. C.E., Am. Soc. Mil. Engrs., Beta Theta Pi. Mason (Shriner). Clubs: Bankers (N.Y.), Internat. House (New Orleans); various carnival orgns. Home: Galabank-on-the Jourdan, Star Route, Bay St. Louis, Miss. Office: 833 Howard Av., New Orleans. Died Feb. 6, 1957; buried Metairie Cemetery, New Orleans.

WILLIAMS, WYNANT JAMES, prof. elec. engring.; b. Port Dover, Ont., Can., Mar. 9, 1884; s. Benjamin and Christine (Alexander) W.; student Heriot Watt Coll., Edinburgh, Scotland, 1899-1900; B.S. in Civil Engring., Rensselaer Poly. Inst., Troy, N.Y., 1905; student Technische Hochschule, Berlin, 1909-10; m. Alice Louise Carpenter, Dec. 28, 1912; children—Wynant James, Ruth Louise. Asst. in physics and elec. engring.

Rensselaer Poly. Inst., 1905-06, instr., 1906-13, asst. prof., 1913-34, prof., 1934-40, head of elec. engring. dept., 1940—. Mem. Am. Inst. E.E., Soc. Engrs. Eastern N.Y., A.A.A.S., Sigma Xi, Tau Beta Pi. Presbyn. Home: 40 Norwood Av., Albany, N.Y. Died May 1, 1950.

WILLIAMSON, CHARLES SPENCER, M.D.; b. Cincinnati, May 15, 1872; s. William F. and Mary Louise (Spencer) W.; M.S., U. of Cincinnati, 1893; M.D., Med. Coll. of Ohio, 1896; m. Josephine Gillette Stillwell, Oct. 15, 1903; children—Mary Josephine, Isabel Gillette, Elizabeth Spencer. Resident phys., Cincinnati Hosp., 1896-97; post-grad. study Leipzig, Berlin, Vienna and Paris, 1897-1900; removed to Chicago, 1901; adj. prof. medicine, 1901-03, prof. clin. medicine, 1903-12, Coll. Phys. and Surg.; asst. prof. diseases of stomach, 1901-07, prof., 1907—, Chicago Polyclinic; prof. medicine and clin. medicine, and head of dept. of internal medicine, U. of Ill. Coll. of Medicine, 1912, Lt. col. M.C. U.S.A., and dir. dept. sanitation, Ft. Riley, Kan., and Ft. Oglethorpe, Ga.; also dir. Sch. of Mil. Hygiene and Sanitation, Ft. Oglethorpe, Ga. Awarded gold medal by A.M.A. for exhibit of research work, 1918. Mem. Assn. Am. Physicians. Episcopalian. Editor: French's Practice of Medicine, 1910. Contbr. several monographs containing results of original research in Am. and European publs. Home: Chicago, Ill. Died Feb. 16, 1933.

WILLIAMSON, HUGH, congressman, scientist; b. West Nottingham, Pa., Dec. 5, 1735; s. John W. and Mary (Davison) W.; grad. Coll. of Phila. (now U. Pa.), 1757; studied medicine in Edinburgh, London, Utrecht, 1764; M.D., U. of Utrecht (Holland); hon. degree U. Leyden; m. Maria Apthorpe, Jan. 1789, 2 sons. Prof. mathematics Coll. of Phila.; became mem. Am. Philos. Soc., 1768; commd. to study orbits of Venus and Mercury, 1769; published An Essay on Comets; carried 1st news of Boston Tea Party to Eng.; authored The Plea of the Colonies (anonymous letter to Lord Mansfield), 1775; sailed for U.S., 1776; began merc. bus. in Charleston, S.C., moved to Edenton, N.C., traded with French W.I.; as physician to Gov. Caswell of N.C. sent to New Bern to inoculate troops against smallpox; surgeon-gen. N.C. troops; at Battle of Camden; mem. N.C. Ho. of Commons, 1782, 85; mem. Continental Congress, 1782-85, 87-89; apptd. to Annapolis Conv., 1786; del. U.S. Constl. Conv., 1787, worked for ratification by publishing Remarks on the New Plan of Government in a N.C. newspaper; del. Fayetteville Conv., 1789; agt. to settle N.C. accounts with fed. govt., 1788; mem. U.S. Ho. of Reps. from N.C., 1st-2d congresses, 1789-93; mem. Holland Soc. of Science, Soc. of Arts and Sci. of Utrecht; founder Lit. and Philos. Soc. of N.Y.; prominent mem. N.Y. Hist. Soc.; original trustee U. N.C.; trustee Coll. of Phys. and Surg., U. State of N.Y. Author: Historical Papers Published by the Trinity College Historical Society (pamphlet); Letters of Sylvius (published anonymously; opposed paper currency, advocated excise instead of land or poll tax); Of the Fascination of Serpents; Conjectures Respecting the Native Climate of Pestilence; Observations on Navigable Canals; Observations on the Climate in Different Parts of America (1811); The History of North Carolina, 2 vols., 1812. Died May 22, 1819.

WILLIAMSON, JOHN ERNEST, undersea exploration and photography; b. Liverpool, Eng., Dec. 8, 1881; s. Charles and Sarah (Smith) W.; came with parents to U.S., 1889; grad. high sch., Newport News, Va., 1896; m. Lilah Sylvia Freeland, Sept. 26, 1927; children—Sylvia, Annecke Jans. Mech. draftsman and pattern maker with Newport News Shipbuilding Co., etc., 1897-1908; newspaper cartoonist and photographer with Virginian-Pilot and Phila. Record, 1908-13; made first undersea photographs, Chesapeake Bay, Va., 1913, first undersea motion pictures, 1914, first undersea color pictures, 1924; producer of undersea photoplays, photographing undersea life by means of Williamson submarine tube, since 1913; condr. sci. expdns., Field Museum-Williamson Undersea Expdn. to Bahamas, 1929, Bahamas-Williamson Undersea Expdn., 1939. Has produced motion pictures, The Submarine Eye, Girl of the Sea, Wet Gold, Twenty Thousand Leagues Under the Sea, The White Heather, The Uninvited Guest Williamson Submarine Expedition, With Williamson Beneath the Sea, Wonders of the Sea. Hon. life mem. Am. Mus. Natural History; hon. mem. Aquarium Soc. N.Y. Club: Explorers. Author: Twenty Years Under the Sea. Co-author: Child of the Deep. Contbr. to Scientific American, N.Y. Times, Science and Invention, etc. Inventor of foldable transparent diving helmet. Founder world's first undersea postoffice, in Williamson Photosphere, Bahamas, 1939. Address: Explorers Club, N.Y.C. or P.O. Box 307, Nassau, Bahamas, B.W.I. Died July 1966.

WILLIAMSON, SYDNEY BACON, civil engr.; b. Lexington, Va., Apr. 15, 1865; s. Thomas Hoomes and Julia Anna (Lewis) W.; grad. Va. Mil. Inst., 1884; m. Helen C. Davis, May 20, 1890. Instr. mathematics, Kings Mountain (S.C.) Mil. Sch., 1884-86; with engring. depts. C.B. & Northern, St. Paul & Duluth, and N.P. rys., 1886-90; entered gen. engring., Montgomery, Ala., 1890; in employ U.S. Govt., on Tenn. River improvements, 1892-1900 (except during Spanish-Am. War), and at Newport, R.I., as asst. engr. on fortification work, 1900-04; in practice, New York, Baltimore and other cities, 1904-07; engr. in charge of Pacific Locks, and div. engr. Pacific Div., Panama Canal, 1907-12 (resigned); chief of constrn., U.S. Reclamation Service, Dec. 10, 1914-Jan. 1916 (resigned); apptd. cons. civil engr. for Guggenheim Brothers, 1916. Asso. with Gen. Geo. W. Goethals as cons. engr. for Port of Palm Beach, Fla.; apptd. by President of the U.S. mem. Interoceanic Canal Bd. to investigate and report on the Nicaragua Canal route and other possible canal routes for connecting the Atlantic and Pacific oceans; retired May 1, 1935. Mem. of exec. com. Chile Exploration Company, Braden Copper Company. Served as capt. U.S. Volunteer Engrs., Spanish-Am. War; detailed as asst. to Col. George W. Goethals, chief engr. 1st Army Corps. Commd. col. engrs., and comd. 55th Engrs. A.E.F.; in France as sect. engr., intermediate Sect. West, and of the Paris Dist. Awarded D.S.M. (U.S.). Episcopalian. Home: Lexington, Va. Died Jan. 13, 1939.

WILLIAMSON, THOM, chief engr. U.S.N.; b. Edenton, N.C., Aug. 5, 1833; s. William Price and Penelope Benbury (McDonald) W.; ed. Norfolk (Va.) Mil. Acad. and St. Mary's Coll., Baltimore, to 1850; m. Julia Price, Dec. 2, 1861. Apptd. 3d asst. engr. U.S.N., May 23, 1853; 2d asst. engr., June 27, 1855; 1st asst. engr., July 21, 1858; chief engr., Aug. 5, 1861; relative rank of capt., Jan. 30, 1889; retired on account of age, Aug. 5, 1895; chief engr. with rank of rear admiral, June 29, 1906. Offered a signed commn. as chief engr. in C.S.N. at outbreak of Civil War, but declined; sr. engr. officer with Admiral Farragut's fleet in fights at Fts. Morgan and Gaines and in operations in Mobile Bay; head of dept. of steam engring., U.S. Naval Acad., 1868-69; fleet engr. N. and S. Atlatnic and Pacific stas. and acted as supt. State, War and Navy Depts. Bldg. under successive spl. orders from Presidents Harrison and Cleveland; mem. bd. to examine plans for coaling ships at sea during Spanish-Am. War; on duty in Navy Dept., Oct. 19, 1901-June 6, 1912. Awarded medal and diploma for collaboration, by Paris Expn., 1900, and diploma for distinguished services, by Buffalo Expn., 1901. Home: Annapolis, Md. Died Mar. 1918.

WILLIS, BAILEY, geologist; b. Idlewild-on-Hudson, N.Y., May 31, 1857; s. Nathaniel Parker and Cornelia (Grinnell) W.; E.M., Columbia School Mines, 1878, C.E., 1879; hon. Ph.D., U. of Berlin, Germany, 1910; Sc.D., Columbia, 1929; m. Miss A. II. Grinnell, Mar. 4, 1882 (died 1896); 1 dau., Hope; m. 2d, Miss M. D. Baker, Apr. 21, 1898 (died March 21, 1941); children—Cornelius G., Robin, Margaret. Spl. expert iron ores, 10th Census, 1879-81; geologist Northern Transcontinental Survey, exploration for N.P. and allied cos., 1881-84; geologist U.S. Geol. Survey, 1884-1916; in charge Appalachian Div., New York to Ala., Cascade Range and Puget Sound Div., Wash., and editor Geologic Atlas of U.S.; asst. to dir. U.S. Geol. Survey, 1897-1902; geologist in charge of div. or areal and stratigraphic geology, 1900-02; geologist engaged in geol. explorations in China under auspices of Carnegie Instn. of Washington, 1903-04, gold medal, Société Géographique de France, 1910. Lecturer on geology, Johns Hopkins, 1895-1902, U. of Chicago, 1909; cons. geologist to minister pub. works, Argentina, 1911-15; prof. geology, Stanford U., Calif., 1915-22; emeritus, 1922. Chief of Latin Am. div. of Col. E. M. House "Inquiry," for Peace Conf., 1918. Seismologist, Carnegie Instn. of Washington expdns. to Chile, 1923, to Orient, Palestine, Cypus, 1927, East Africa, 1929, to Japan, Philippines, India, 1937. Consulting geol. engineer since 1922. Decorated Commander Order of Leopold II, 1933; Belgian Legion of Honor, 1936. Mem. Geol. Society of Am. (pres. 1928), Society Am. Geographers, Am. Philos. Soc., Am. Acad. Arts and Sciences, Seismol. Soc. America (pres. 1921-26), Am. Inst. Mining and Metall. Engrs., Soc. Econ. Geologists, Nat. Acad. Sciences, etc.; hon. mem. Royal Geog. Soc. (London); Société Géologique de Belgique; foreign corr. Geol. Soc. London; Wissenschaftliche Gesellschaft (Munich), Gesellsch. z. Erdkunde (Berlin). Penrose medalist, 1944. Clubs: Engineers, Commonwealth (San Francisco); Cosmos (Washington). Author: Mechanics of Appalachian Structure; Research in China; Geologic Structures; Living Africa; African Plateaus and Rift Valleys; Northern Patagonia; Earthquake Conditions in Chile; Earthquakes in the Holy Land; A Yanqui in Patagonia; Geol. Map of N. America; also numerous sci. articles. Home: 539 Lasuen. Address: Box 1365, Stanford University, Calif. Died Feb. 19, 1949.

WILLIS, CHARLES FRANCIS, mining engr., editor; b. Boston, Mass., Aug. 18, 1885; s. Frank Eugene and Elizabeth Ann (King) W.; S.B. in Mining Engring., Mass. Inst. Tech., 1906; E.M., N.M. Coll. of Mines, 1916; m. Helen Isabel Heckman, Feb. 20, 1908; children—Barbara Lee (Mrs. B. F. C. Miller), Anne Harrison (Mrs. James H. Quint), Manager of the Enterprise Mining Co., Cooney, N.M., 1906, Pelican Mining Co., Lake City, Colo., 1909; first dir. Ariz. Bur. Mines, Tucson, 1912; cons. supervisior dept. indsl. relations, Phelps Dodge Corp., Bisbee, Ariz., 1918; editor and pub. The Mining Journal, 1920-46 (Mining Jour. then consol. with Mining World); editorial writer Mining World since 1946. Was active in war work as state dir. 1st and 2d Y.M.C.A. drives, United War Work Drive, Armenian and Jewish Relief drives, Near East Relief; was mem. Ariz. Council of Defense and in charge war mineral production, World War I; cons. Metals Reserve Co., mem. Ariz. War Manpower Commn., industry panel. Mem. 10th Regional Labor Bd., Ariz., dir. Com. on Econ. Development, World War II. Chmn. bd. of govs., Ariz. Dept. of Mineral Resources; consultant, Metals Reserve Co.; state sec. Arizona Small Mine Operators Assn.; mem. Nat. Minerals Adv. Council (chmn. pub. lands com.); mem. nat. adv. council Small Bus. Adminstrn. Recipient Medallian of Honor, U. Ariz., 1960. Mem. Am. Inst. Mining and Metall. Engrs. (dir. Ariz. Sect.); Am. Mining Congress, (gov. Western div.), Am. Assn. Engrs. (ex-pres. Phoenix chpt.), Soc. Promotion Engring. Edn. Ariz. Newspapers Assn. (past sec.). Republican. Episcopalian. Clubs: Arizona, Phoenix, Kiwanis (former dist. gov. S.W. Dist.), Advertising (ex-pres.). Home: Phoenix AZ Died Dec. 10, 1968; buried Greenwood Meml. Park, Phoenix AZ

WILLIS, CLODIUS HARRIS, univ. prof.; b. Culpeper County, Va., Aug. 4, 1893; s. John Harrison and Sallie Hart (Harris) W.; B.S., U. Richmond, 1914, Sc.D., 1955; B.S.E. Johns Hopkins 1916, Ph.D., 1926; m. Katherine Vaughan, June 28, 1923; children—Julia Somerville, Sallie Hart, Katherine Lee, Clodius Harris. Instr. in physics, U. Richmond, 1916-17, acting prof., 1919-20, asso. prof. applied physics, 1920-21; in elec. constrn. work, Huntington. W.Va., 1921-22; prof. applied physics, U. Richmond, 1923-25; asst. prof. elec. engring., Princeton, 1926-29, asso. prof., 1929-36, Doty prof. elec. engring. since 1938. Served with U.S. Signal Corps during World War I; commd. 319th Field Signal Bn., 2d lt., France, 1918. Mem. Am. Inst. E.E., I.R.E., Am. Phys. Soc., A.A.A.S., Soc. Promotion Engring. Edn., Phi Beta Kappa, Sigma Xi, Tau Beta Pi, Pi Gamma Delta. Joint author: (with W. H. Chandler) Introductory Electrical Engineering, 1953. Home: 329 Harrison St., Princeton, N.J. Died Dec. 14, 1964; buried Princeton Cemetery.

WILLIS, HORACE HAROLD, textile consultant; b. Spartanburg, S.C., April 25, 1891; s. James Henry and Julia Ann (Finley) W.; B.S., Clemson Agrl. and Mech. Coll., 1917; m. Alice Moore, Dec. 23, 1922; 1 son, Ernest Moore. Employee Clifton Mfg. Co. intermittently 1903-17; Lt. World War I, 1917-19; instr. Clemson Coll., 1920; asst. state supervisor textile indsl. edn., State Dept. Edn., North Carolina, 1920-21; cotton specialist supervising tests in California, Ariz., and Tex., Bur. Plant Industry, U.S. Dept. Agr., 1921-24; in charge cotton spinning research, U.S. Dept. Agr., 1924-30; dir. Textile Sch., Clemson Coll., 1927-33; in charge flax spinning research, Textile Foundation, 1933; dean, Textile Sch., Clemson Coll., 1933-43; consultant cotton mfg. and labor relations, 1943-70. Mem. Southern Textile Assn., Arkwrights, Southeastern Econ. Council; S.C. Acad. Science, Am. Soc. Testing Materials, Blue Key, Phi Psi. Club: Kiwanis (Anderson, S.C.). Mason. Joint author series textile texts; contbr. to textile journals; writer of many spinning test reports and bulletins for U.S. Dept. Agr. Home: Clemson SC Died Aug. 11, 1970; buried Old Stone Cemetery Clemson SC

WILLISTON, ARTHUR LYMAN, engr., educator; b. Cambridge, Mass., Oct. 11, 1868; s. Lyman Richards and Anne E. (Gale) W.; S.B., Mass. Inst. Tech., 1889, grad. course, 1889-90; m. Irene L. Simmons, June 21, 1893 (died May 1, 1924); m. 2d, Mary de F. Denny, Dec. 9, 1925. Asst. to chief engr. C.C.C.&St.L. Ry., 1890-91; instr. steam engring. Mass. Inst. Tech., 1891-92; mech. engr. Lockwood & Greene, Boston, 1892-93; dir. dept. industrial arts and prof. engring., Ohio State U., 1893-98; dir. Sch. of Science and Technology, Pratt Inst., Brooklyn, 1898-1910; prin. Wentworth Inst., Boston, 1910-24; dir. ednl. and industrial survey, Norwood, Mass., 1925-27; ednl. research and asst. to dir. Am. Council on Edn., Washington, D.C., 1927-32; mem. Hawkes Com. on Personnel Research, 1929-32. Internat. examiner in steam engring. and machine design, Y.M.C.A., 1902-14; mem. expert advisory com. Carnegie Tech. Schs., Pittsburgh, 1902-05; educational expert for Reed College, Boston School Committee, 1908, also for superintendent of schools, New York City, 1908-09, for Wentworth Inst., 1908-10, Ohio Mechanics Inst., Cincinnati, 1917-18. Ednl. dir. New England edn. and spl. training com. U.S. War Dept., 1918-19; organizer and dir. for U.S. War Dept. of Boston Sch. of Occupational Therapy, 1918-19. Am. del. World Federation of Edn., Edinburgh, 1925, World Conf. on Adult Edn., Copenhagen, 1926. Mem. Exec. Comm. (N.E. Br.) Com. to Defend America by Aid to Allies, 1940-41; mem. Council and sec. Citizens Com. for a Nat. War Service Act, 1942-46; treas. Mass. Br. Citizens Com. for Universal Mil. Training of Young Men since 1946. Initiated and planned program of Experimental Unit in U.M.T. at Ft. Knox, Ky. for U.S. War Dept., 1947. Mem. Am. Soc. Mech. Engrs. (pres. Boston sect. 1916-17), A.A.A.S., Fedn. of Arts, N.E.A. (pres. vocational edn. and practical arts dept., 1912-14; pres. science dept., 1918-19). Soc. for Promotion Engring. Edn. (mem. council 1900-03 and 1904-07; sec. 1907-09; vice-pres. 1909-10), Nat. Soc. for Promotion Indsl. Edn. (exec. comm.; sec.-treas. N.Y. State Br.) Writer of numerous published articles and reports on industrial, engineering, and gen. edn. subjects. Author: Beyond the Horizon of Science, 1944. Address: 986 High St., Dedham MA

WILLISTON, SAMUEL WENDELL, palaeontologist; b. Boston, July 10, 1852; s. Samuel and Jane A. (Turner) W.; B.S., Kansas Agricultural Coll., 1872, A.M., 1875; M.D., Yale, 1880, Ph.D., 1885; hon. degree Sc.D., Yale, 1913; m. Annie I. Hathaway, Dec. 20, 1880. Asst. in palaeontology and osteology, 1876-85, demonstrator of anatomy, 1885-86, prof., 1886-90, Yale; prof. hist. geology and anatomy and dean Med. Sch., U. of Kan., 1890-1902; prof. palaeontology, U. of Chicago, 1902—. Asst. palaeontologist, U.S. Geol. Survey, 1882-85; asst. editor Science, 1885-86; health officer, New Haven, Conn., 1888-90; mem. Kan. State Bd. Health, 1898-1900, Bd. Med. Examiners, 1900-02. Mem. Nat. Acad. Sciences; fellow Am. Acad. Arts and Sciences. Author: Manual of North American Diptera, 1896, 1908; Reports University Geological Survey of Kansas, Vols. IV, VI, 1898, 1900; American Permian Vertebrates, 1911; Water Reptiles of the Past and Present, 1914; also about 250 scientific papers on entomology, zoölogy, sanitation, comparative anatomy and palaeontology, bulls., etc. Died. Aug. 30, 1918.

WILLOUGHBY, JULIUS EDGAR, civil engr.; b. Arkadelphia, Ala., Oct. 12, 1871; s. John P. and Mary Jane (Cosby) W.; B.C.E., 1892, and C.E., U. of Ala.; m. Mary Alice Byars, Oct. 17, 1895; children—William (dec.), Mary, Ruth. Began with L.&N. R.R., 1892, asst. chief engr. constrn., 1900, engr. of constrn. and chief engr. of certain L.&N. subsidiary lines, 1901-11; chief engr. Caribbean Constrn. Co. and of Nat. Ry. of Hayti, 1912; with Atlantic Coast Line since 1913, asst. chief engr. until 1916, chief engr., 1916-42, consulting engineer since 1942; also chief engineer Tampa Southern R.R. Company, Ft. Myers Southern R.R. Co., Charleston & Western Carolina Ry. Co. to 1942. Fellow A.A.A.S.; mem. Am. Soc. C.E., Am. Ry. Engring. Assn., N.C. Soc. Engrs. (hon.), Soc. Am. Mil. Engrs., Fla. Engr. Soc. Republican. Methodist. Club: Cape Fear. Has built and rebuilt more than 3,000 miles of ry. Address: Wilmington, N.C. Home: Blount Springs, Ala. Died Mar. 11, 1944.

WILLS, ALBERT POTTER, coll. prof.; b. Waltham, Mass., Feb. 25, 1873; s. William Russel and Lucretia (Potter) W.; B.E.E., Tufts Coll., 1894, Sc.D., 1911; Ph.D., Clark U., 1897; univs. of Göttingen and Berlin, 1898-99; m. Agnes Randall Brune, May 18, 1909 (died 1910); m. 2d, Gertrude Pardee Carter, June 10, 1920. Asso. in physics and applied mathematics, Bryn Mawr Coll., 1899-1902; physicist, Cooper Hewitt Lab., New York, 1902-03; instr. mechanics, 1903-05, adj. prof., 1905-09, prof. math. physics, 1909—, Columbia. Contbr. papers on magnetic susceptibility, magnetic shielding, magnetostriction, conduction of electricity in mercury vapor, and hydrodynamics. Home: New York, N.Y. Died Apr. 17, 1937.

WILLSON, GEORGE HAYWARD, meteorologist; b. Kent Co., Md., Feb. 23, 1858; s. George Hayward and Henrietta Eleanor (Brooke) W.; ed. Rock Hill Coll., Ellicott City, Md., 1874-76; m. Cynthia A. Parker, of Klamath Co., Ore., Aug. 25, 1885; children—George Hayward, Bernard Parker. Entered Signal Corps U.S.A., at Washington, 1880; transferred to Weather Bur., 1891; stationed various places in N.D., Mont., Ore., San Francisco, Seattle, Olympia; asst. forecaster, San Francisco, 1898-1913; in charge San Francisco office and S. Pacific Coast Forecast Dist., Sept. 1, 1913-June 30, 1917, also dir. Cal. Climatol. Service; asst. to the dist. forecaster in charge Pacific Coast. Dist., 1917-25, climatologist, 1926-32, retired. Club: Commercial. Home: 2340 Fulton St., San Francisco, Cal.

WILLSON, ROBERT WHEELER, astronomer; b. West Roxbury, Mass., July 20, 1853; s. Rev. Edmund B. and Martha A. (Buttrick) W.; A.B., Harvard, 1873; Ph.D., Würzburg, 1886; m. Annie Downing West, Dec. 14, 1881. Asst. Argentine Nat. Obs., 1873, Harvard Coll. Obs., 1874; tutor in physics, Harvard, 1875-81; asst. astronomer, Winchester Obs., Yale, 1881-84; instr. astronomy and physics, 1891-99, asst. prof., 1899, prof. astronomy, 1903, emeritus, 1919, Harvard. Fellow Am. Acad. Arts and Science, A.A.A.S., Am. Astron. Soc., Am. Geog. Society. Unitarian. Author: Laboratory Astronomy, 1905; Times of Sunrise and Sunset in the United States, 1908. Home: Cambridge, Mass. Died Nov. 1, 1922.

WILMOT, R(OYAL) J(AMES), horticulturist; b. Rochester, N.Y., Jan. 9, 1898; s. Louis George and Gertrude (Bennett) W.; B.S.A., U. Tenn., 1922; M.S.A., U. Fla., 1931; m. Gladys Gallaher, Nov. 14, 1922; 1 son, Royal James. With Agr. Exp. Sta., Gainesville, Fla., 1927—. Sec. Am. Camellia Soc., 1945—; editor Am. Camellia Yearbook, 1946-49. Served as 2d lt., F.A., U.S. Army, 1918. Mem. Fla. State Hort. Soc., Sigma Nu, Alpha Zeta, Phi Sigma, Phi Kappa Phi, Thyrsus. Democrat. Presbyterian. Club: Mens Garden (Gainesville, Fla.). Contbr. articles to profl. and sci. publs. Specialist in ornamental horticulture and fumigation research. Home: Box 2397, Gainesville, Fla. Died May 7, 1950.

WILMS, JOHN HENRY, surgeon; b. Cincinnati, O., Nov. 17, 1879; s. Frederic Henry and Fredericka (Kruse) W.; prep. edn., Cincinnati Business Coll. and Eisle's Scientific Acad.; student U. of Cincinnati; M.D., Pulte Med. Coll., Cincinnati, 1902; m. Louise Margaret Evatt, June 2, 1920; children—Janet (dec.), John Henry. In gen. practice of medicine and surgery, Cincinnati, 1902—; prof. anatomy, Pulte Med. Coll., 1905-10. Fellow Am. Coll. Surgeons. Mason. Reported med. cures for endocarditis, thyrotoxicosis, pancreatic diabetes, hypothyroid states. Discoverer of antidotal action of calcium sulphid in bichloride of mercury poisoning. Home: Cincinnati, O. Died Nov. 26, 1938.

WILSON, ALEXANDER, poet, ornithologist; b. Seed Hills of Paisley, Scotland, July 6, 1766; s. Alexander and Mary (McNab) W. Published volume Poems, 1790; came to Am., 1794; took over sch. at Gray's Ferry on Schuylkill River, Phila., 1802; asst. editor Abraham Ree's Cyclopaedia; wrote verse The Foresters, 1805; visited ornithological wilderness West of Alleghanies, 1810. Author: American Ornithology, 9 vols., 1808-14; also work published posthumously as Poems; Chiefly in the Scottish Dialect, by Alexander Wilson, Author of American Ornithology, with an Account of His Life and Writings, 1814. Died Aug. 23, 1813; buried Graveyard, Old Swedes Ch., Phila.

WILSON, ALLEN BENJAMIN, inventor; b. Willet, N.Y., Oct. 18, 1824; s. Benjamin and Frances (Wilson) W.; m. Harriet Brooks, 1850, at least 1 child. Journeyman cabinet maker in East and Middle West; conceived idea of sewing machine about same time as Elias Howe, 1847, prepared full-sized drawings; began constrn. 1st machine, 1849, secured U.S. Patent (a year after Howe's), 1850, sold all interests; designed rotary hook and bobbin to substitute for double-pointed shuttle, patented 1851; began mfg. sewing machines as partner Wheeler, Wilson & Co.; contrived stationary bobbin; patented four-motion feed (used on later sewing machines), 1854. Died Woodmont, Conn., Apr. 29, 1888, buried Waterbury, Conn.

WILSON, CHARLES ALFRED, civil engr.; b. in Cecil Co., Md., April 4, 1855; s. John Howard and Anna Catharine (Cheyney) W.; ed. Friends pvt. sch., Columbia, Pa., Friends High Sch., West Chester High Sch., Pa.; m. Carrie Ione Stevens, of Norwalk, O., Nov., 1883. Began ry. service as flagman, engr. corps Phila. & Reading R.R., 1869; held various engring. positions on different rys., 1869-79; resident engr. Hocking Valley Ry., 1879-80; prin. asst. engr. constrn., 1880-82, chief engineer, 1882-96, also gen. supt., 1893-95, Wheeling & Lake Erie Ry.; also chief engr. Cleveland & Marietta R.R., 1882-85; chief engineer C.,H.&D. Ry., 1896-1906. Mem. Am. Soc. C.E., Am. Ry. Engring. and Maintenance of Way Assn. Mason. Home: Wyoming, O. Office: 68 Carew Bldg., Cincinnati.

WILSON, CHARLES BRANCH, biologist; b. Exeter, Me., Oct. 20, 1861; s. Col. John B. and Samantha (Perkins) W.; A.B., Colby Coll., 1881, A.M., 1884, Sc.D., 1908; Ph.D., Johns Hopkins, 1910; grad. student and tutor in botany, Colby Coll., 1881-84; m. Lilla Belle Turner, July 22, 1885; children—Carroll Atwood, John Ellis. Pvt. tutor, 1884-91; prof. science, State Normal Sch., Gorham, Me., 1891-94; post-grad. student and asst. in biology, Johns Hopkins, 1894-96; prof. biology, 1896-97, head dept. science, 1897-1932, State Teachers Coll., Westfield. Author: Nature Study Outline for Graded Schools, 1898; Outlines for Laboratory Work in Science, 1900. Home: Westfield, Mass. Died Aug. 18, 1941.

WILSON, DAVID MATHIAS, prof. civil engring.; b. Belleville, Mich., Oct. 3, 1896; s. William Henry and Mary E. (Mathias) W.; B.S.C.E., U. Mich., 1920, C.E., 1937; m. Dorothy Hope Ream, Sept. 10, 1921; children—Shirley Margaret, John Collins. Instr. in math. U. Mich., 1918-20; asst. engr. Texas Co., Port Arthur, Tex., 1920; instr. in mechanics U. Wis., 1920-23, in structural engring. 1923-24; resident engr. Athens, Wis., 1924; asst. engr. Central Aguirre (P.R.) Sugar Co., 1924-29; appraisal engr. Pa. Salt Mfg. Co., Wyandotte, Mich., 1929; asst. prof. of civil engring. U. So. Cal., Los Angeles, 1929-31, asso. prof. civil engring., 1931-37; prof. civil engring., since 1937, head of gen. engring., 1930-47, head civil engring. dept., since 1945. Registered civil and structural engr., Cal., since 1931. Mem. Am. Soc. C.E. (treas., dir. Los Angeles sect. 1946-47), Am. Soc. Engring. Edn. (chmn. Pacific Southwest sect., 1933, mem. com. on sects. and brs. 1936, chmn. relations with industry com. 1954). Structural Engr. Assn. Cal. (dir. 1958-59, chmn. structural exam. com. 1960), Structural Engrs. Assn. So. Cal. (1st v.p. 1961, dir. 1960-61, pres.-elect 1962), Clements Library Assos. at U. Mich., Am. Assn. Univ. Profs., Am. Soc. Testing Materials (mem. dist. council, chmn. student awards com.), Am. Arbitration Assn. (nat. panel arbitrators), Internat. Assn. for Bridge and Structl. Engring., Phi Kappa Phi, Tau Beta Pi, Sigma Xi, Chi Epsilon; Sigma Phi Delta, Los Angeles Alumni of Tau Beta Pi (sec.-treas. 1934-36). Republican. Methodist. Author: Analysis of Statically Indeterminate Structures, 1934; Analysis of Rigid Frames by Superposition (article), Transactions (A.S.C.E., Vol. 110), 1945. Contbr. discussions in Transactions. Home: 4334 Palmero Blvd., Los Angeles 90008. Died Dec. 2, 1961; buried Forest Lawn Hollywood Hill, Los Angeles.

WILSON, EDMUND BEECHER, zoölogist; b. Geneva, Ill., Oct. 19, 1856; s. Judge Isaac C. and Caroline (Clark) W.; Ph.B., Yale, 1878; Ph.D., Johns Hopkins, 1881; univs. of Cambridge, and Leipzig, 1881-82; LL.D., Yale, 1901, U. of Chicago, 1901, Johns Hopkins, 1902; Sc.D., U. of Cambridge, 1909, Harvard, 1924; hon. M.D., U. of Leipzig, 1909; hon. Ph.D., U. of Lwów, 1926; D.H.C., U. of Louvain, 1927; Sc.D., Columbia, 1929; m. Anne Maynard Kidder, Dec. 27, 1904; 1 dau., Nancy. Lecturer on biology, Williams, 1883-84, Mass. Inst. Tech., 1884-85; asso. professor and prof. biology, Bryn Mawr, 1885-91; adj. prof. biology, 1891-94, prof. invertebrate zoölogy, 1894-97, prof. zoölogy, 1897-1909, Da Costa prof. zoölogy, 1909—, emeritus prof. in residence, 1928—, also dean of faculty of pure science, 1905-06, member Univ. Council, 1901-03, 1905-06, 1913-15, Columbia. Fellow Am. Acad. Arts and Sciences, A.A.A.S. (pres. 1913), N.Y. Acad. Sciences (pres. 1904); mem. numerous Am. and fgn. scientific societies. Author: General Biology (with W. T. Sedgwick), 1887; Atlas of Karyokinesis and Fertilization, 1895; The Cell in Development and Heredity, 1896, 1900, 1925; The Physical Basis of Life, 1923. Died Mar. 3, 1939.

WILSON, EDWIN BIDWELL, college prof., b. Hartford, Conn., Apr. 25, 1879; s. Edwin Horace and Jane Amelia (Bidwell) W.; A.B., Harvard, 1899; Ph.D., Yale, 1901; École Normale Superieur, Paris, 1902-03, also The Sorbonne and College de France, Paris; LL.D. (honorary), Wesleyan Univ., 1955; m. Ethel Sentner, July 5, 1911 (dec.); children—Enid, Doris. Instr. mathematics, Yale, 1900-06, asst. prof., 1906-07; asso. prof. mathematics, Mass. Inst. Tech., 1907-11, prof., 1911-17, prof. math. physics and head of the dept. of physics, 1917-22, mem. administrative com., 1920-22; prof. of vital statistics, Harvard Sch. of Public Health, Boston, Mass., 1922-45, emeritus since 1945. Stevenson lecturer on citizenship. Glasgow, Scotland, 1945-46. Consultant, Office of Naval Research, Boston, since 1948. Vice pres. Nat. Acad. Scis., 1949-53, editor of Proceedings, 1915—. President Social Science Research Council, 1929-31; former chmn. Am. Soc. for Control of Cancer. Hon. fellow Royal Statistical Soc. (London); mem. American Statistical Association (president 1929), Am. Acad. Arts and Sciences (pres. 1927-31), Am. Philosophical Society, also member Phi Beta Kappa, Sigma Xi; fgn. hon. mem. Math. Soc. Benares, India. Club: Harvard (Boston). Author: Gibbs Vector Analysis, 1901; Advanced Calculus, 1912; Aeronautics, 1920. Home: 42 Brington Rd., Brookline, Mass. Office: Office of Naval Research, 495 Summer St., Boston 10. Died Dec. 28, 1964.

WILSON, ERNEST DANA, coll. prof.; b. Harlan, Ia., Nov. 2, 1890; s. Charles Henry and Harriet Elizabeth (Dana) W.; B.S., U. of Neb., 1913; Ph.D., U. of Chicago, 1915; research associate physical chemistry Massachusetts Institute Technology, 1913-14; m. Avilda Downing Moore, Dec. 29, 1915; children—Robert Downing, Avilda Dana. Fellow Mellon Inst., Pittsburgh, Pa., 1916-18; chief engr., Graton & Knight Mfg. Co., Worcester, Mass., 1918-20; chief, comml. research, George Batten Co., N.Y. City, 1920-21; dept. head, Am. Cyanamid Co., N. Y. City, 1922-33; consultant, Barsky and Wilson, N.Y. City, 1934-36; pres., Zialite Corp., N.Y. City, since 1936; prof. chem. engring., and chemistry, and head dept., Worcester Poly. Inst., 1940—; dir. Zialite Corp. Mem., past chmn. Mass. State Board Registration Profl. Engrs. Fellow A.A.A.S., mem. Am. Inst. Chem. Engrs., Am. Soc. Engring. Edn., Am. Chem. Soc., Electrochem. Soc., Am. Soc. Profl. Engrs., Am. Assn. U. Professors, Society Chem. Industry (British), Pi Delta Epsilon, Sigma Xi, Tau Beta Pi, Gamma Alpha, Alpha Chi Sigma, Phi Gamma Delta. Baptist. Republican. Clubs: Engineers (Boston); Worcester (Mass.) Country. Home: 33 Flagg St. Office: Worcester Poly. Inst., Worcester 9, Mass. Died Oct. 19, 1958; buried Beechmont Cemetery, Centerville, Mass.

WILSON, ERNEST HENRY, botanist, author, traveler; b. Chipping Campden, Gloucestershire, Eng., Feb. 15, 1876; s. Henry and Annie (Curtis) W.; ed. Royal Coll. of Science, London; hon. M.A., Harvard, 1916; m. Ellen Ganderton, Edgbaston, Warwickshire, Eng., June 8, 1902; 1 dau., Muriel Primrose. Came to U.S., 1906; asst. dir. Arnold Arboretum, Harvard, 1919-27, keeper, 1927; traveled in China 11 yrs., 3 yrs. in Japanese Empire, also traveled in Australasia, India, South Africa, etc. Trustee Massachusetts Hort. Soc. Awarded Victoria medal of honor, George Robert White medal, Veitch memorial medal, Geoffrey St. Hilaire gold medal. Fellow Am. Acad. of Arts and Sciences. Author: Naturalist in West China, 1913; Cherries of Japan; Conifers and Taxads of Japan, 1915; Aristocrats of the Garden, 1916; The Romance of Our Trees, 1920; A Monograph of Azaleas (Wilson and Rehder), 1921; Lilies of Eastern Asia, 1925; America's Greatest Garden, 1925; Plant Hunting, 1927; More Aristocrats of the Garden, 1928; China, Mother of Gardens, 1929. Home: Jamaica Plain, Boston, Mass. Deceased.

WILSON, EUGENE BENJAMIN, engineer; b. New Haven, Conn., Nov. 27, 1857; s. Elisha and Julia (Benjamin) W.; ed. Sheffield Scientific Sch. (Yale), 1879; m. Corrinne Munson, Aug. 31, 1885; children—J. Beatrice, E. Munson, S. Casselberry. In anthracite mining, 1880-85; iron mining and smelting, 1885-90; bituminous coal mining, 1890-94; gold and silver mining, metallurgist and consulting engr., 1894-1900;

prin. sch. ore mining and metallurgy of Internat. Correspondence School, 1900-09. Author: Practical and Theoretical Mine Ventilation, 1884; Cyanide Processes, 1895; Chlorination Process, 1896; Hydraulic and Placer Mining, 1897; Ihlseng and Wilson's Manual of Mining, 1905. Editor Mines and Minerals, and Colliery Engineer, 1909-15. Home: Scranton, Pa. Died June 16, 1929.

WILSON, FRANK N., physician; b. Livonia, Mich., Nov. 19, 1890; s. Norman O. and Mary (Holtz) W.; B.S., U. of Mich., 1911, M.D., 1913; m. Juel A. Mahoney, Aug. 6, 1914; 1 dau., Julia Ann. Asst. in medicine, Univ. of Mich., 1913-14, instr. 1914-16, asso. prof., 1920-24, professor, 1924—; instructor, Washington University, 1916-20. Henry Russel lecturer, Univ. of Mich., 1939-40; Dr. honoris causa, Escola Paulista Medicina (Brazil); hon. mem. Faculta de Biologia y Ciencia Médicas de la U. de Chile; Soc. de Med. de Montevideo; Soc. Medicine de Sanitago de Chile; Uniao Cultural Brasil-Estados Unidos; corr. mem. Acad. Nacional de Med. do Brasil; Soc. Argentina de Cardiologia; hon. mem. Cardiac Soc., Great Britain and Ireland. Fellow Am. Coll. Physicians, A.A.A.S., A.M.A.; mem. Assn. Am. Physicians, Am. Soc. Exptl. Pathology, Soc. Exptl. Biology and Medicine, Am. Soc. Clin. Investigation, Central Soc. Clin. Research, Am. Heart Assn., Alpha Omega Alpha, Sigma Xi. Served as lt. and capt., Med. Corps, U.S. Army, 1917-19. Author 100 articles on electrocardiography; lectured in Brazil, Uruguay, Argentina, Chile, Peru. Address: Route 2, Stockbridge, Mich. Died Sept. 11, 1952.

WILSON, GEORGE FRANCIS, mfr., inventor; b. Uxbridge, Mass., Dec. 7, 1818; s. Benjamin and Mercy (Wilson) W.; m. Clarissa Bartlett, 1844, at least 5 children. Founded and conducted Chgo. Acad., 1844-48; went to Providence, R.I., 1848; partner (with Eben N. Hirsford) in George F. Wilson and Co., chem. mfrs., 1855, name changed to Rumford Chem. Co.; invented process of steel manufacture, a turning paper-pulp boiler, improvements in illuminating apparatus for lighthouses; mem. R.I. Ho. of Reps., 1860-62; mem. Providence Sch. Com., Providence Town Council; bequeathed $100,000 to Brown U., $50,000 to Dartmouth for scientific purposes. Died Jan. 19, 1883.

WILSON, HAROLD ALBERT, prof. physics; b. York, Eng., Dec. 1, 1874; s. Albert William and Ann (Gill) W.; M.Sc., Leeds U., Eng., 1897; univ. scholar London U., 1896-98; 1851 Exhbn. scholar, 1897-1900, D.Sc., London, 1900; studied U. Berlin, 1899; Allen scholar, U. Cambridge, 1900, Clark-Maxwell student, 1901-04, M.A., Cambridge, 1904; m. Marjorie Paterson-Smyth, Aug. 1, 1912; children—Kathleen, Joan, Jack, Stephen. Fellow of Trinity Coll., Cambridge, 1901-07; prof. physics, King's Coll., London, 1905-09; prof. physics, McGill U., Montreal, Can., 1909-12; prof. physics, Rice Inst., Houston, 1912-24; prof. natural philosophy, U. Glasgow, Scotland, 1924-25; prof. physics Rice Inst., 1925-47, prof. physics emeritus since 1947; prof. physics U. Chgo., summers 1922-23, 1928; cons. physicist Humble Oil & Refining Co. Episcopalian. Fellow Royal Soc. London; mem. Cambridge Philos. Soc., London Phys. Soc., Am. Phys. Soc.; fellow Am. Philos. Soc. Club: Rice Faculty. Tech. expert on anti-submarine devices at U.S. Naval Exptl. Sta., New London, Conn., 1917-19. Research physicist on atomic bomb, Office Scientific Research Devel., 1942-43. Author: The Electrical Properties of Flames, 1912; Experimental Physics, 1915; Modern Physics, 1928; Mysteries of the Atom, 1934; Electricity, 1941; also about 100 papers on physics. Address: Rice Institute, Houston 1. Died Oct. 13, 1964; cremated.

WILSON, HENRY HARRISON, engineer, constructor, editor; b. Jan. 15, 1882; native home, "Bonbrook," Cumberland Co., Va.; s. Henry Joseph and Lucy Harrison (Gay) W.; prep. edn., Seven Islands Acad., Buckingham Co., and high sch., Richmond, Va.; B.S. in C.E., Va. Poly. Inst., 1906, C.E. with highest honors, 1907; m. Lily, d. Gov. J. Hoge Tyler of Va., June 16, 1915; children—J. Hoge Tyler, Lily Norwood, Henry Harrison. Clk., Richmond, 1899-1904; instr. in civ. engring., Va. Poly. Inst., Jan.-June 1907; civ. engr., summer 1906 and 1907-08; engr. Winston & Co. on Ashokan dams, Catskill Aqueduct, Brown Sta., N.Y., 1909-11; partner Snead & Wilson, highway constrn., Cropseyville, N.Y., 1912-13; spl. partner Winston & Co. on highway and ry. constrn. and operation of crushed stone business, 1914-25; mng. asso. Winston Bros. Co. & Wilson (Minneapolis, Minn., and Harrisburg, Pa.), on bridge and other constrn. work, 1925-31; past pres. and chmn. bd. Associated Pa. Constructors, Harrisburg, 1924—; pres. and treas. Lime Bluff Co., 1930—; dir. All States Life Ins. Co., Peoples Bank of Radford. Author: Cost Keeping for Highway Construction, 1924. Editor Highway Builder. Delivered address on Benjamin Harrison "The Signer," at Capitol, Richmond, Va., Oct. 1931. Home: Harrisburg; also East Radford, Va. Died May 31, 1933.

WILSON, HENRY PARKE CUSTIS, gynecologist; b. Workington, Md., Mar. 5, 1827; s. Henry Parke Custis and Susan E. (Savage) W.; B.A., Coll. of N.J. (now Princeton), 1848; studied medicine U. Va.; grad. U. Md., 1851; m. Alicia Griffith, 1858, 5 children. Surgeon in charge Balt. City Almshouse Infirmary, 1857-58; cons. surgeon St. Agnes Hosp., 1879, Johns Hopkins Hosp., 1889; with William T. Howard founded Hosp. for Women of Md., 1882; 1st physician in Md. to remove uterine appendages by abdominal section, 2d in Md. to perform successful ovariotomy, 1866, 2d in world to remove ultrauterine tumor filling whole pelvis by marcellation; devised instruments for gynecol. surgery; pres. Med. and Chirurg. Faculty of Md., 1880-81; founder Balt. Obstet. and Gynecol. Soc., also Am. Gynecol. Soc., 1880-81; mem. Brit. Gynecol. Assn.; hon. fellow Edinburgh (Scotland) Obstet. Soc. Died Balt., Dec. 27, 1897.

WILSON, HENRY VAN PETERS, educator, biologist; b. Baltimore, Md., Feb. 16, 1863; s. Rev. Samuel A. and Sophia Anne (Stansbury) W.; A.B., Johns Hopkins, 1883, Ph.D., 1888; m. Edith Theresa Stickney, June 10, 1893 (dec.); children—Edith Stedman (Mrs. Thorndike Saville), Eleanora Stansbury (Mrs. Howell Peacock), Henry Van Peters. Asst. U.S. Fish Commn., 1889-91; prof. biology, 1891-1904, prof. zoölogy, 1914-17, Kenan prof. zoölogy, 1917—, University of N.C. Director U.S. Fisheries Laboratory, Beaufort, N.C., 1899-1902; southern exchange lecturer, 1915-16. Dohme lecturer, Johns Hopkins University, 1936. Original investigations on the embryology and regeneration of sponges, coelenterates, lower vertebrates; classification of sponges. Home: Chapel Hill, N.C. Died Jan. 4, 1939.

WILSON, HERBERT COUPER, astronomer; b. Lewiston, Minn., Oct. 24, 1858; s. Thomas and Ann W.; A.B., Carleton Coll., 1879, A.M., 1882; Ph.D., U. of Cincinnati, 1886; studied astronomy, Cincinnati Obs., 1880-81; m. Mary B. Nichols, Dec. 20, 1882 (died 1924); children—Ralph Elmer, Ruth Edna (Mrs. William H. Geer), Mary Helen (Mrs. George M. Constans), Lois Norma (Mrs. W. Harlan Pye); m. 2d, Florence E. Rice, Aug. 26, 1926. Assistant astronomer, 1881-82, astronomer in charge, 1882-84, assistant astronomer, 1884-86, Cincinnati Observatory; computer to U.S. Transit of Venus Commn. U.S. Naval Observatory, Washington, 1886-87; asst. prof. astronomy, 1887-1900, asso. prof. mathematics and astronomy, 1900-08, prof. and dir. Goodsell Obs., 1908-26, also dean faculty, 1906-10, Carleton Coll.; retired on Carnegie Foundation, 1926. Asso. editor, Astronomy and Astrophysics, 1892-94, Popular Astronomy, 1894-1909; editor Popular Astronomy, 1909-26. Asst. astronomer, Lick Obs., 1910-11, Harvard Obs., 1916, Mt. Wilson Obs., 1920-21. Devoted much attention to double and variable star observations and astronomical photography. Home: Northfield, Minn. Died March 9, 1940.

WILSON, HERBERT MICHAEL, engineer; b. Glasgow, Scotland, Aug. 23, 1860; s. Henry and Ellen (Yeates) W.; studied at Plainfield, N.J., and Cooper Union, New York; C.E., Columbia Sch. Mines, 1881; m. Elizabeth, d. Thom Williamson, Nov. 16, 1893. Ry. engr. in Mexico, 1881-82; on U.S. Geol. Survey as topographer, 1882-88, irrigation engr., 1889-91, as geographer, 1892-1906, chief engr. technologic branch, 1907-09, engr. in charge, U.S. Bur. of Mines, 1910-14; dir. dept. of inspection and safety, The Associated Ins. Cos., 1915-19; general manager of same, 1919—. Has lectured extensively on irrigation, geography, fuel testing, smoke abatement, mine fires and rescue, fireproof building construction, swamp reclamation, etc. Author: Manual of Irrigation Engineering, 1893; Topographic Surveying, 1899; American Civil Engineers' Pocket Buok. Home: Sewickley, Pa. Died Nov. 25, 1920.

WILSON, JAMES WALTER, biologist; b. Manchester, N.H., June 17, 1896; s. James Walter and Genieve Beatrice (Knight) W.; Ph.B., Brown U., 1918. Ph.D., 1921; Ed.D. (honorary), R.I. College of Edn., 1960; Sc.D. (hon.), Providence Coll., Coll. Holy Cross, 1963; m. Hope Burgess, June 22, 1922; 1 dau., Margaret (Mrs. R. Weed). Instr. in biology, Brown U., 1921-22; asst. prof., 1922-29, asso. prof., 1929-44, prof., 1944-45. Frank L. Day prof. of biology, 1945-69, professor emeritus of biology, chairman of the 1944-60; instructor of biol. lab., Cold Spring Harbor, N.Y., 1919-24; mem. Corp. R.I. Hosp., Corp. of Marine Biol. Lab., Woods Hole, Mass. Member President's Conf. on Heart and Cancer, 1961. Chmn. morphology and genetics study sect., U.S.P.H.S., 1949-54, mem. screening panel Cancer Chemotherapy Nat. Service Center, 1955-69, nat. adv. council health research facilities, 1956-61, Radiation Study Sect., 1955-56; nat. adv. cancer council, 1960-64; bd. scientific cons. Sloan-Kettering Inst., 1956-69; corp. mem. Miriam Hosp., R.I. Hosp.; mem. vis. com. Brookhaven Nat. Lab., 1949-55, chmn., 1950-55; advisory com. instl. grants Am. Cancer Soc. Mem. Com. Cons. Med. Research to Senate Appropriations Com., 1959-60; sec.-gen. XI Internat. Congress for Cell Biology, 1964. Fellow A.A.A.S., N.Y. Acad. Sci., Am. Acad. Arts, Scis.; mem. Am. Soc. Zool. (pres. 1953-54). Gerontological Soc., Am. Acad. Neurologists, Biometric Soc., Soc. for Cell Biology, Am. Physiol. Soc., Am. Assn. Anatomists, Histochem. Soc. (pres. 1953-54), Soc. Exptl. Biol., Medicine, Soc. Study of Development and Growth. Am. Microscopical Soc., Am. Soc. Cancer Research. History of Science Soc., Biol. Stain Commn., Genetics Soc. Am., Am. Soc. Naturalists, Am. Cancer Soc. (adv. com. personnel research 1956-59, research adv. council 1959-64), Phi Beta Kappa, Sigma Xi. Author articles sci. and med. jours. Home: Providence RI Died May 10, 1969; buried Swan Point Cemetery, Providence RI

WILSON, JAMES WILBUR, agriculturist; b. Traer, Iowa, Feb. 12, 1871; s. James and Esther (Wilbur) W.; B.S.A., Ia. State Coll., 1896, M.S.A., 1898; attended lectures at Georgetown U. Law Sch. and Nat. U. Law Sch., Washington, and received private instruction in law in office at Cedar Rapids, Ia.; LL.D., Univ. of S.Dak., 1922; m. Elsie Chappell, of Brookings, S.D., Apr. 18, 1906; children—James Wilson, Robert C., Thomas V. Asst. prof. agr., Ia. State Coll., 1897; pvt sec. to sec. of agr. Washington, 1897-1900; became dir. S.D. Expt. Sta. and prof. animal husbandry, S.D. Agrl. Coll., 1902, now emeritus. Sec.-treas. S.D. Improved Live Stock and Poultry Breeders' Assn. Mem. Internat. Jury of Awards, St. Louis Expn. Fellow A.A.A.S.; mem. Gamma Sigma Delta, Phi Kappa Phi. Republican. Mason (K.T., Shriner); mem. Grange. Author of numerous bulls. along agrl. lines, and articles in agrl. press. Home: Brookings SD*

WILSON, JOHN, civil engr.; b. Wisbeach, Cambridge, Eng., Jan. 23, 1841; s. John and Sarah (Fisher) W.; grad. Cooper's Hill Div. Engring. Coll., Staines, Eng., 1865; m. Eliza Ellen Barrow, Dec. 26, 1904. Civ. engr., Pub. Works Dept., India, 1869-82; came to U.S., 1882; constructing engr. on cable rys., Phila. St. Ry. Co., 1883-88; pvt. practice Pittsburgh, 1888-92, Texas, 1892-95; surveys in Mex., 2,000,000 acres, mostly in the Sierra Madre Mts.; built 1st electric ry. in El Paso, Tex., 1899; constrn. irrigation canals in W. Tex., 1904-06; v.p., chief engr. Barston Irrigation Co., 1906-13; mem. Bd. Water Engrs. of Tex., Sept. 1, 1913-19. Mason, Elk. Democrat. Episcopalian. Home: El Paso, Tex. Died June 28, 1921.

WILSON, JOHN ARTHUR, chemist; b. Chicago, Ill., Aug. 16, 1890; s. Ernest Clyde and Amy Florence (Christian) W.; student New York U., 1911-12, U. of Leeds, Eng., 1914-16; D.Sc., Lehigh U., 1929; m. Wynnaretta Cain, May 1, 1912; 1 dau., Wynnaretta. Began career as chemist, Edison Chem. Works, Silver Lake, N.J., 1911; chief chemist, A. F. Gallun & Sons Corp., Milwaukee, Wis., 1912-29; hon. research asst., Procter Internat. Research Lab., Leeds, Eng., 1915-16; cons. chemist, Milwaukee Sewerage Commn., 1920-30; spl. lecturer U. of Chicago, 1925, Columbia U., 1926; pres. Security Management Co., Milwaukee, 1926-29; pres. Internat. Security Management Co., Chicago, 1929-30; pres. Wis. Investment Co., 1930-38; pres. John Arthur Wilson, Inc., 1929-38; pres. Wilson Leather Co., Appleton, Milwaukee and N.Y. City, since 1933; tech. dir. Bona Allen, Inc., Buford, Ga., 1938-40; cons. chemist, N.Y. City since 1940. Noted for discoveries in tanning skins and treatment of leather and chemistry of leather manufacture; discovered system of chemically treating sewage sludges and disposal into fertilizer; invented process for making sheet leather; invented the new metaphosphate tannage; developed new concept of atomic structure. Coöperating expert Internat. Critical Tables; member Colloid Committee Nat. Research Council, 1920-26. Awarded Chandler medal, Columbia U., 1928, Nichols medal, N.Y. Sect. of Am. Chem. Soc., 1931. Dir. Procter Internat. Research Lab., U. of Leeds, Eng. Fellow A.A.A.S.; mem. Am. Chem. Soc. (v.p. 1921-27, chmn. Milwaukee sect., 1920, leather div., 1921-27), Am. Leather Chemists Assn. (pres. 1928-30), Internat. Society Leather Trades Chemists, Internationalen Vereines der Leder-Industrie-Chemiker, Société de Chimie Industrielle, Professional Men's Club of Milwaukee (pres. 1927-28), Sigma Xi. Republican. Episcopalian. Clubs: Athletic, Chemists Circle (pres. 1928), Ozaukee Country (pres. 1937-38), Yacht; Capital City (Atlanta). Author: The Chemistry of Leather Manufacture, 1923, 2d edit. Vol. I, 1928, Vol. II, 1929, Vol. III, 1941, also transl. into German, French and Russian; Viewing Leather Through the Eyes of Science, 1924; Colloid Chemistry as Applied to Activated Sludge, 1924; Sanitation, 1925; Analysis of Leather, 1931; Electronic Theory of Tanning, 1937; Modern Practice in Leather Manufacture, 1941; more than 200 articles in jours. of chem. and leather trades. etc. Home: 200 Cabrini Blvd. Address: 11 W. 42d St., New York, N.Y. Died Sep. 10, 1942.

WILSON, JOHN HENRY, engr.; b. Honolulu, T.H., Dec. 15, 1871; s. Charles Burnett and Evaline Maletta (Townsend) W.; ed. pub. and pvt. schs. in Hawaii; student Stanford, 1891-94; m. Jennie Kapahu, May 8, 1909. Joined engring. staff, Oahu Ry. & Land Co., Ltd., 1896; connected with Dept. Pub. Works under Republic of Hawaii, 1897; formed firm of Wilson and Whitehouse, civil engrs. (with L. M. Whitehouse), 1897; constructed internationally famous Pali Road, Lahaina (Maui) waterworks system, and numerous other works, partnership dissolved 1900; supt. hwys. Island of Maui and supt. streets Honolulu, 1908-11; engaged in pvt. practice; pres. Wilsonite Brick Co., Ltd., Honolulu. City engr. of Honolulu, 1919, mayor, 1920-23, 24-27, 29-30, 47-48, 49-54, postmaster, 1934-39, dir. Dept. Pub. Welfare, 1939-46. Dem. Nat. Committeeman for Hawaii, 1912-40. Charter member Engring. Assn. of Hawaii (1st pres. 1920-21); mem. Order of Kamehameha. Home: 1551-A Oili Rd. Address: City Hall, Honolulu 43, Hawaii. Died July 2, 1956.

WILSON, JOSEPH MILLER, civil engr., architect; b. Phoenixville, Pa., June 20, 1838; grad. Rensselaer Poly. Inst., C.E., 1858, (A.M., Univ. of Pa., 1877); m. 1869, Sarah Pettit. Asst. engr. Pa. R.R., 1860-63; resident engr. middle div., same, 1863-65; engr. bridges and buildings, 1865-86; asso. engr. and architect for designing and constructing main building and Machinery Hall, Centennial Expn., 1876; from 1876 in general practice in firm Wilson Bros. & Co.; mgr. Franklin Inst., 1868, pres., 1887-97. Fellow Am. Inst. Architects, A.A.A.S. Home: Philadelphia, Pa. Died 1902.

WILSON, LEONARD SELTZER, geophysicist, geographer; b. Detroit, July 10, 1909; s. Clyde E. and Esther S. (Seltzer) W.; A.B., U. Mich., 1932, M.S., 1933, Ph.D. (Earhart fellow 1934-35, U. fellow 1935-36), 1936; m. Mary W. Jarboe, Nov. 15, 1944; children—Leonard J., Susan M. Teaching fellow U. Mich., 1934-36; from instr. to prof. geography Carleton Coll., 1936-49; chief map intelligence br. Dept. State, 1945-46; map officer internat. sect. UN Conf. of Internat. Orgn., 1945; geog. adviser internat. sect. UN, 1945; chief geog. br. G-2, Far East Command, Supreme Comdr. Allied Powers, Tokyo, Japan, 1949-55; chief geophys. scis. br. Office Chief Research and Development, U.S. Army, 1955-60, chief Environmental Research Div., 1960-68; nat. leader sub-group T tech. cooperation Program United States Department of Defense, 1968-70, national leader ground mobility panel technical Coordination Program 1968-70. Head U.S. Army delegation to Quadripartite Ground Mobility Conf., 1959, 61, 63, 65; U.S. delegation NATO Long Range Study Group Naples, Italy, 1961; United States alternate mem. research coordination com. Am., Brit. Canadian, Australian Armies Weapons Standardization Orgn., 1956-63, U.S. mem. and chmn., from 1963; U.S. Army rep. Dept. Def. Forum Environmental Scis., 1964-65; sr. member environmental sciences The Army Research Council, 1964-65; chairman Army Committee Environment, from 1955, Army Com. for Internat. Geophys. Year, 1957-59, Army Coordinating Com.; del. U.S. Nat. Acad. Scis., 9th Pacific Sci. Congress, Bangkok, Thailand, 1958. Served lt. (j.g.) to lt. comdr. USNR, 1943-46; dep. chief map div. OSS, 1942-45 (as civilian 1942); chief map div. OSS, ETO, 1944. Decorated Bronze Star medal; recipient Army commendation medal, commendation certificate, meritorious civilian award, Army certificate meritorious achievement, also decoration for exceptional civilian service awarded posthumously. Fellow A.A.A.S., Sigma Xi.; mem. Menn. Council Geography Tchrs. (pres. 1946-47), Assn. Am. Geographers (treas. 1963-65; mem. finance com., mem. mil. geography com.), Am. Geog. Soc., Royal Geog. Soc. London, Tokyo Geog. Soc., S.A.R., Nat. (Am. Soc. com. 1959), Mich. Minn. acads. scis., Chi Gamma Phi, Theta Chi. Episcopalian. Asso. editor: Oxford Am. Atlas, 1951; editor, compiler: Terrestrial Globe, 1957. Author articles profl. jours. Home: Alexandria VA Died Dec. 6, 1970; buried Culpepper Nat. Cemetery Culpepper VA

WILSON, LOUIS BLANCHARD, pathologist; b. Pittsburgh, Pa., Dec. 22, 1866; s. Henry Harrison and Susan (Harbach) W.; M.D., U. of Minn., 1896, D.Sc., 1940; m. Mary Stapleton, Aug. 26, 1891 (died in 1920); children—Mrs. Alice Martin, Carroll Louis; m. 2d, Maud H. Hellish, Aug. 21, 1924 (died 1933); m. 3d, Grace G. McCormick, Jan. 2, 1935. Asst. prof. pathology and bacteriology, U. of Minn., 1896-1905; dir. Labs. of Mayo Clinic since 1905; prof. of pathology and dir. The Mayo Foundation for Medical Edn. and Research, U. of Minn., 1915-37; emeritus prof. pathology and dir., The Mayo Foundation, since 1937. Commd. Col. Medical R.C., U.S. Army, 1917. D.S.M. (U.S. Army), 1920. Mem. Assn. Am. Physicians, Am. Assn. Pathologists and Bacteriologists, Am. Anat. Soc., Am. Assn. Cancer Research, A.M.A. (council on edn. and hosps.), Assn. of Amcrican Med. Colleges (pres. 1931-33), Nat. Bd. of Med. Examiners, A.A.A.S., Adv. Bd. of Medical Specialties (pres. 1935-37), Minn. Hort. Society, Nat. Rifle Assn., Phi Beta Kappa, Sigma Xi (pres. 1932-33), Alpha Kappa Kappa, Alpha Omega Alpha. Unitarian. Clubs: University, Campus (Minneapolis); University, Commercial (Rochester). Contbr. various articles reprinted in "Collected Papers," by staff of Mayo Clinic, since 1910. Home: Rochester, Minn. Died Oct. 5, 1943.

WILSON, MURRAY ALDERSON, cons. engr.; b. Parmyra, Ia., Aug. 15, 1894; s. Charles Herbert and Harriet (Alderson) W.; A.B., Baker U., 1916; student U. Wis., summer 1919; B.S. in Civil Engring., Kan. State U., 1922, C.E., 1926, awarded Doctor of Science (honorary), 1963; L.H.D., Kansas Wesleyan U., 1953; m. Edith May Coffman, June 21, 1919; children—Mary Helen (Mrs. Donald Hayman), Dorothy (Mrs. Merrill H. Werts). Prin. high sch., Oswego, Kan., 1916-17; head dept. math. Neodesha (Kan.) High Sch., 1919-20; city engr., Hays, Kan., 1922-24; research engr. Bur. Pub. Roads, 1924-26; chief engr. Kan. Forestry, Fish and Game Commn., 1926-32; cons. engr., 1932-69; partner firm Paulette & Wilson, Salina, Kan., 1932-41; owner Wilson & Co., Salina, 1942-59, cons. to company, 1959-69; dir. Nat. Bank Am., Sunflower Prestress, Inc. (both Salina). Mem. Kan. Bd. Engring. Examiners, 1947-58; mem. Gov. Kan. Adv. Com. Flood Control, 1942-56; adv. com. for pvt. enterprise AID, 1966. Trustee Kan. Wesleyan U., 1945-69, chmn., 1948-53; mem. Kan. State U. Research Found. Recipient Distinguished Service award Baker U., 1954, Kan. State U., 1957. Served with U.S. Army, 1917-19. Registered profl. engr., Kan., N.M., Colo., Neb., Ga. Fellow Am. Soc. C.E. (pres. Kan. 1941); mem. Nat. Soc. Profl. Engrs. (pres. 1961, award for outstanding service to profession 1967), Kan. Engring. Soc. (pres. 1936, chmn. cons. sect. 1957-59), Kan. Sewage Works Assn. (pres. 1947), Am. Inst. Cons. Engrs., Am. Water Works Assn., Am. Road Builders Assn., Am. Pub. Works Assn., Water Pollution Control Assn., Am. Legion, Alpha Delta Sigma, Phi Kappa Phi, Sigma Tau, Zeta Chi. Methodist (del. world conf. 1961). Mason (33 deg., Shriner), Lion. Home: Salina KS Died Apr. 17, 1969; interred Williamsburg Mausoleum, Salina KS

WILSON, PHILIP ST. JULIEN, civil engr.; b. Powhatan Co., Va., May 30, 1867; s. Samuel M. and Sallie B. (Cocke) W.; prep. edn. Episcopal High Sch., Va.; C.E., Va. Mil. Inst., 1886; unmarried. Instr. mathematics and engring., at Suffolk, Va., 1887-91; asst. city engr., Richmond, Va., 1902-06; state highway commr. of Va., 1906-13; asst. dir. Bur. Pub. Roads, Washington, D.C., 1914-16; chief engr. Bur. Pub. Roads, U.S. Dept. Agr., 1916—. Served as capt. inf., Spanish-Am. War. Democrat. Episcopalian. Mason. Home: Washington, D.C. Died Sept. 17, 1936.

WILSON, ROBERT ERASTUS, chem. engr.; b. Beaver Falls, Pa., Mar. 19, 1893; s. William Hyatt and Madge (Cunningham) W.; Ph.B., magna cum laude, College of Wooster (Ohio), 1914, hon. Sc.D., 1931; B.S. in Chem. Engring., Mass. Inst. Tech., 1916; hon. Dr. Engring., Brooklyn Poly. Inst., 1940; LL.D. (hon.), Colby Coll., 1941, Northwestern U., 1947, Lake Forest Coll., 1952, William Jewell Coll., 1953, Hamline U., 1953; U. Akron, 1955, Washington U. Huron Coll., 1957, Colorado Coll., 1958, Am. U., 1961; L.H.D. (hon.), University of Tulsa, Okla., 1948. Shurtleff Coll., 1955; H.H.D. (honorary), Bradley U., 1954, Parsons College, 1955; Sc.D., Drexel Inst. Tech., 1955; Sc.D., Geneva Coll., Beaver Falls, Pa., 1963; m. Pearl M. Rockfellow, Dec. 22, 1916; children—Doris Mildred (Mrs. L. O. Blanchard, Jr.), Lois Marian (Mrs. Danial J. Miles), Janice Marjorie (Mrs. William E. George). Research asst., Research Lab. Gen. Elec. Co., 1916; research assoc., Research Lab. Applied Chemistry, Mass. Inst. Tech., 1916-17; cons. chem. engr., Bur. of Mines, Washington, D.C., 1917-18; capt. and maj. C.W.S., 1918-19, World War I, directing research div.; Mass. Inst. Tech. as dir. Research Lab. of Applied Chemistry, and asso. prof. chem. engring., 1919-22; asst. dir. research, Standard Oil Co. (Ind.), 1922-28; asst. to v.p. in charge mfg., 1929-30, dir., v.p. in charge research and development, 1931-34, chmn. bd. and chief exec. officer 1945-58, ret.; vice chairman Pan Am. Petroleum & Transport Co., 1935-37, pres., 1937-44; chmn. bd. and dir., 1945-54; chmn. American Oil Company, 1954-58; commr. U.S. AEC, 1960—. Mem. Corp. Mass. Inst. Tech.; trustee Carnegie Inst. of Washington, Coll. of Wooster (Ohio), Princeton (N.J.) Theological Seminary. Senior member of National Industrial Conference Board. Recipient Chemical Industry Medal, 1939; Perkin Medal, 1943; Cadman Meml. Medal, 1951; Northwestern U. Centennial Award, 1951; Washington Award, 1956; First Annual Pub. Information Award, Illinois Soc. C.P.A.'s, 1956. Mem. of 25 Year Club Petroleum Industry, Am. Philos. Soc., Royal Soc. Arts (Eng.), Am. Chem. Soc., Am. Inst. Chem. Engrs., Am. Petroleum Inst., Am. Soc. Testing Materials, Am. Nuclear Soc., Newcomen Soc. Eng., Nat. Acad. Scis., Phi Beta Kappa, Alpha Chi Sigma, Delta Sigma Rho. Republican. Presbyn. Clubs: Chicago, Commercial (Chgo.); Links (N.Y.C.); Glen View (Golf, Ill.); Burning Tree (Bethesda, Md.); Cosmos, Metropolitan, M.I.T. (Washington); Pacific-Union (San Francisco). Contbr. numerous articles profl. jours. Patentee in field. Home: 4000 Cathedral Av. N.W., Washington 20016. Office: Commr. U.S. AEC, Washington 25. Died Sept. 1, 1964; buried Wooster, O.

WILSON, ROBERT LEE, elec. and mech. engr.; b. Shelbyville, Ill., Jan. 29, 1871; s. William G. (M.D.) and Frances Anna (Lee) W.; student State U. Iowa, 1 yr.; B.S. in M.E., Rose Poly. Inst., 1892; postgrad. work in elec. engring., Johns Hopkins, 1894; m. Fanny Hampton Jeffers Kennard, Nov. 15, 1900; children—Robert L., Eloise Hampton. With Gen. Electric Co., Schenectady, N.Y., 1892; with Westinghouse Electric & Mfg. Co., 1894—, successively as engineer, supt., gen. supt., works mgr., asst. v.p. and gen. mgr., asst. to pres.; superintended original electrification of the Manhattan Elevated R.R. and New York Subway; built and installed equipment for electrification of N.Y., N.H.&H. R.R. and the St. Clair Tunnel of Grand Trunk R.R.—the first two important alternating current r.r. electrifications in the U.S.; directed mfg. operations of Westinghouse Electric & Mfg. Co. at East Pittsburgh, 1914-31, then consultant to same; retired 1938. Fellow Am. Inst. E.E.; mem. Engrs.' Soc. Western Pa., S.A.R. Republican. Methodist. Clubs: University, Edgewood Country (Pittsburgh); Engineers' (New York). One of the first to advocate workman representation in works councils (joint conf. coms.); frequent speaker upon industrial relations. Home: Bel Air, Md. Died Dec. 2, 1957.

WILSON, ROBERT NORTH, chemistry; b. Lenoir, N.C., Mar. 3, 1875; s. Jethro Reuben and Louisa Jane (Round) W.; student Guilford (N.C.) Coll., 1893-94; A.B., Haverford (Pa.) Coll., 1898; grad. study, Harvard, 1905-06, U. of Ill., 1922-23; M.S., U. of Fla., 1909; m. Saza Hendrick Peck, of Greensboro, N.C., Sept. 15, 1910; children—Robert North, Jane Bliss. Teacher in chemistry and physics, Guilford Coll., 1898-1908; soil chemist, Fla. Agrl. Expt. Sta., 1908-10; asst. prof. chemistry, Trinity Coll. (now Duke U.), 1910-16, prof. since 1916. Commr. Durham Council Boy Scouts America. Mem. Am. Chem. Soc., A.A.A.S., Soc. Promotion Engring. Edn., N.C. Acad. Science, Soc. Mayflower Descendants. Democrat. Methodist. Kiwanian. Home: 822 3d St., Durham NC

WILSON, THEODORE DELAVAN, naval engr. b. Bklyn., May 11, 1840; s. Charles and Ann Elizabeth (Cock) w.; m. Sarah Stults, before 1867, 4 children. Entered U.S. Navy as ship's carpenter, 1861, served in ship Cambridge, N. Atlantic Squadron, until 1863; asst. naval constructor Pensacola (Fla.) Navy Yard, then Phila., 1866; instr. in ship constrn. U.S. Naval Acad., 1869-73; invented bolt extractor, 1880; promoted naval conductor, 1873; mem. 1st Naval Adv. Bd. to formulate plans for new steel navy, 1881; chief bur. of constrn. and repair, 1882-93; supervised constrn. of 45 ships; 1st Am. mem. Brit. Instn. Naval Architects; 1st v.p. Soc. Naval Architects; 1st v.p. Soc. Naval Architects and Marine Engrs., 1893, contbr. article "The Steel Ships of United States Navy" to its Transactions, 1893. Author: An Outline of Shipbuilding, Theoretical and Practical (published as textbook at U.S. Naval Acad.), 1873; (pamphlet) The Center of Gravity of the U.S. Steamer Shawmut, 1874. Died Boston, June 29, 1896.

WILSON, WILBUR M., engring. research; b. West Liberty, Ia., July 6, 1881; s. Mathias and Ruth (Mosher) W.; B.M.E., Ia. State Coll., 1900, C.E., 1914; M.M.E., Cornell U., 1904; Dr. Engring., Ia. State Coll., 1942; m. Teresa May Stewart, June 28, 1905; children—Grace, Matt. Fellow Cornell, 1903-04; asst. prof., asso. prof. mech. engring., Ia. State Coll., 1904-07; pvt. practice, 1908-13; asst. prof. structural engring. U. Ill., 1913-17, asso. prof., 1919-20, research prof., 1921—. Observer, Bikini Atom Bomb Test, 1946. Student 1st O.T.C., 1917; capt. engrs. O.R.C., 1917; maj. N.A., 1918; served as regtl. supply officer 109th Engrs., testing engr. concrete ship sect. U.S. Shipping Bd. and in charge of building of concrete ships at Wilmington, N.C.; hon. disch., 1918; col. O.R.C. Mem. Am. Soc. C.E. (dir. 1946-47), Am. Soc. Engring. Edn., Am. Soc. Testing Materials, A.A.A.S., Am. Ry. Engring. Assn., Western Soc. Engrs., Am. Welding Soc., Internat. Assn. for Bridge and Structural Engring., Ill. Soc. of Engrs., Am. Concrete Inst., Sigma Xi, Theta Tau, Tau Beta Pi. Author of numerous bulls. pub. by U. of Ill. Engr. Expt. Sta. Awarded the Chanute medal (twice), Western Soc. Engrs.; J. James R. Croes medal, Am. Soc. C.E.; Wason medal, Am. Concrete Inst.; Anson Marston award, Ia. State Coll., 1949. Conglist. Home: 807 S. Busey Av. Office: 118 Talbot Lab., U. of I., Urbana, Ill. Died Nov. 28, 1958; buried Oak Ridge Cemetery, West Liberty, Ia.

WILSON, WILFORD MURRY, meteorologist; b. Espyville, Pa., Jan. 24, 1860; s. Cyrus and Katherine (Mason) W.; Allegheny (Pa.) Coll., 1881-85; M.D., Memphis Hosp. Med. Coll., 1895; m. Winifred M. Hatch, of Oregon, Ill., Apr. 9, 1892 (died Apr. 12, 1930); children—Wendell Hatch, Kenneth Mason. With Signal Corps U.S.A., and U.S. Weather Bur., 1885—. Lecturer in meteorology, 1906, instr., 1907-10, prof., 1910-25 (now emeritus), Cornell U.; engaged in meteorol. survey of sites for tuberculosis sanatoria for N.Y. State Dept. Health, 1931. Fellow Am. Meteorol. Soc.; mem. Phi Gamma Delta. Republican. Methodist. Mason (Shriner). Clubs: Town and Gown, Country. Home: St. Petersburg, Fla.

WILSON, WILLIAM B., biology; b. Jonesboro, Tenn., Mar. 7, 1866; s. George Washington and Elizabeth (Erwin) W.; B.S., Ottawa (Kan.) U., 1895, grad. study, 1896-97, M.S., 1898; grad. study, U. of Chicago, 1903, 07, 09, Puget Sound Marine Sta. (U. of Kan.), 1912; Sc.D., Hillsdale (Mich.) Coll., 1924; (hon.) LL.D., Ottawa Univ., Ottawa, Kan., 1937; m. Indie Clara Brinkerhoff, Apr. 11, 1893 (died Mar. 11, 1928); m. 2d, Alice Ida Gordon, Aug. 19, 1930. Prof. mathematics and natural science, Bacone (Okla.) Acad., 1895-96; prof. natural science, Bethel Coll., Russellville; Ky., 1897-1904; prof. biology, Ottawa U., since 1904, registrar, 1904-12, v.p., 1916-19, dean Coll. of Arts and Sciences, 1919-25, became dean and dir. summer sessions, 1924, and dean of men, 1934; prof. botany, summer sessions, Kansas U., 1915-19. Fellow A.A.A.S.; mem. Bot. Soc. America, Kan. Acad. Science (pres. 1929-30; exec. council 1930-31), Kan. Coll. Athletic Assn. (pres. 1923-30), Kan. Coll. Assn. (ex-pres.), Kan. State Teachers Assn. (chmn. coll. dept. 1926-28). Baptist. Clubs: Kiwanis, Schoolmasters, Country. Home: 748 Poplar St., Ottawa, Kan. Died Aug. 31, 1946.

WILTSEE, WILLIAM PHARO, civil engr.; b. Cin., May 30, 1878; s. Charles Spinning and Ida Belle (Hood) W.; ed. grammar and high schs.; m. Viola Bertha Day, Jan. 24, 1900 (died Aug. 1942); children—Virginia Agnes (Mrs. Walter L. Young), Donald Lee, Mary Lee (Mrs. Peyton R. Keller); m. 2d, Agnes Gray, Sept. 1,

1943. Rodman, transitman, draftsman, resident engr., etc., for various lines, 1895-1901; with Norfolk & Western Ry. Co., 1901—, successively draftsman, chief draftsman to engr. of br. lines, asst. engr. with engr. br. lines, 1903-12, asst. engr. maintenance and constrn., 1912-16, asst. engr. assigned to office of chief engr. on spl. maintenance of way matters, etc., 1916-22, prin. asst. engr., 1922, acting chief engr., 1923, chief engr., 1924-1949, ret. In charge of extensive tide-water improvements at Norfolk, Va., 1912-15, and improvements calling for large expenditures annually from 1925. Dir. First Fed. Savs. & Loan Assn. of Roanoke; past pres. Roanoke Hosp. Assn., Hosp. Service Assn. of Roanoke. Life mem. Am. Soc. Civil Engrs.; mem. Am. Soc. for Testing Materials, Am. Wood Preservers Assn., Roadmasters and Maintenance of Way Assn. (ex-pres.), Am. Ry. Engring. Assn. (v.p., dir., chmn. com. on track 1918-25, pres. 1933-34), Holland Soc. (New York). Episcopalian, K.P. Club: Cincinnati (Cin.). Home: 2818 Avenham Av., Roanoke, Va. Died Feb. 3, 1958; buried Evergreen Cemetery, Roanoke, Va.

WINANS, ROSS, railroad engr.; b. Sussex County, N.J., Oct. 17, 1796; s. William and Mary Winans; m. Julia De Kay, Jan. 22, 1820; m. 2d, Elizabeth K. West, 1854; 5 children including Julia, Thomas De Kay, William L. Sold horses to B. & O. R.R., Balt., 1828; invented model "rail wagon" with friction wheel; engr. B. & O. R.R., assisted Peter Cooper with Tom Thumb engine, 1829-30; mem. firm Gillingham & Winans, 1834-59, took charge of improving railroad machinery, B. & O. R.R. shops, Mt. Clare, Md.; planned 1st 8-wheel passenger car; credited with mounting car on 2 four-wheeled trucks; constructed locomotive Mud-Digger (used until 1844), 1842; retired from locomotive building, 1860; mem. Md. Legislature, 1861; Southern sympathizer in Civil War, twice arrested and paroled, 1861. Died Balt., Apr. 11, 1877.

WINANS, THOMAS DEKAY, engr., inventor; b. Vernon, N.J., Dec. 6, 1820; s. Ross and Julia (DeKay) W.; m. Celeste Revillon, Aug. 23, 1847, 4 children. Engr. with Harrison, Winans & Eastwick (firm organized to handle Russian railroad constrn. venture), went to Russia to take charge of mech. dept. of railroad from St. Petersburg to Moscow, 1843, contracted to equip railroad with locomotives and other rolling stock in 5 years, established shops at Alexandrovsky; returned to U.S. (left brother in charge in Russia), 1851, recalled to Russia for new constrn. contract, 1866; business interests taken over by Russian Govt. with payment of large bonus, 1868; dir. B. & O. R.R.; established soup station opposite his home during Civil War; devised (with his father) cigar-shaped hull for trans-Atlantic steamers, 1859; invented device which made organ as easy of touch as piano, invented glass feeding vessels for fish (adopted by Md. Fish Commn.); used undulation of waves to pump water of a spring to reservoir at top of his villa, Newport, R.I. Died Newport, June 10, 1878.

WINCHELL, ALEXANDER, educator, geologist; b. Town of Northeast, Dutchess County, N.Y., Dec. 31, 1824; s. Horace and Caroline (McAllister) W.; grad. Wesleyan U., Middletown, Conn., 1847, LL.D. (hon.), 1867; m. Julia F. Lines, Dec. 5, 1849, 6 children. Sch. tchr., South Lee, Mass., 1841-42, Pennington (N.J.) Male Sem., N.J., 1847-49; prof. natural history Amenia Sem., N.Y., 1849; in charge of acad., Newbern, Ala., 1850; opened Mesopotamia Female Sem., Eutaw, Ala., 1851; pres. Masonic U., Selma, Ala., 1853; prof. physics and engring. U. Mich., Ann Arbor, 1853-55, prof. geology, zoology and botany, 1855-73, prof. geology and paleontology, 1879-91; directed state geol. survey Mich., 1859-61, 69-71, located salt beds of Saginaw Valley; chancellor Syracuse (N.Y.) U., 1872-74; prof. geology and zoology Vanderbilt U., 1875-78; chmn. com. to organize Geol. Soc. of Am., pres., 1891. Author: Sketches of Creation, 1870; Preadamites, 1880; World Life, 1883; (textbook) Geological Studies, 1886; also published bibliography of over 250 titles. Died Ann Arbor, Mich., Feb. 19, 1891.

WINCHELL, HORACE VAUGHN, econ. geologist; b. Galesburg, Mich., Nov. 1, 1865; s. Newton Horace and Charlotte Sophia (Imus) W.; brother of Alexander Newton W.; B.S., U. of Michigan, 1889; m. Ida Belle Winchell, Jan. 15, 1890. Asst. state geologist, Minn., 1889-91; in charge explorations Minn. Iron Co., 1892-93; in gen. practice as econ. geologist and mining engr., 1893-97; geologist for Anaconda Copper Mining Co. and for other auxiliary corps. of the Amalgamated Copper Co., 1898-1906; cons. geologist Amalgamated Copper Co., 1906—; chief geologist G.N. Ry. Co., 1906-08; in general practice, 1908—. Asso. editor Zeitschrift für praktische Geologie of Berlin and Economic Geology. Author: (with Prof. N. H. Winchell) The Iron Ores of Minnesota, 1891. Home: Los Angeles, Calif. Died July 28, 1923.

WINCHELL, NEWTON HORACE, geologist, archeologist; b. North East, N.Y., Dec. 17, 1839; s. Horace and Caroline (McAllister) W.; brother of Samuel Robertson W.; A.B., U. of Mich., 1866, A.M., 1869; m. Charlotte Sophia Imus, Aug. 24, 1864; father of Horace Vaughn and Alexander Newton Winchell. Superintendent public schools, Adrian, Mich., 1866-69; asst. state geologist, Mich., 1869-70; asst. geol. survey, Ohio, 1870-72; state geologist of Minn., 1872-1900; prof. geology and mineralogy, U. of Minn., 1873-1900; archeologist, Minn. Historical Soc., May 1906—. Member U.S. Assay Commn., 1887, founder and editor, Am. Geologist, 1888-1905. Author: Catalogue of the Plants of the State of Michigan, 1861; Geology of Ohio and Minnesota, 1872-1900; The Iron Ores of Minnesota (with Horace V. Winchell), 1891; Elements of Optical Mineralogy (with Alex. N. Winchell), 1909; The Aborigines of Minnesota; The Paleoliths of Kansas; also papers in scientific jours. Home: Minneapolis, Minn. Died May 2, 1914.

WINDET, VICTOR, (win-det'), mech. engr.; b. Chicago, Ill., Aug. 12, 1867; s. Arthur W. and Eliza Vilette (Duncan) W.; B.Sc., Mass. Inst. Tech., 1889; m. Laura T. Barrett, Nov. 1894; children—Frances (dec.), Victor (dec.), Arthur, Charles B. Engr. with Chicago & Calumet Terminal R.R., 1889; mech., civ. and metall. engr. Ill. Steel Co., Chicago, 1889-1901; gen. contractor, heavy masonry, 1901-17; with Wellman Engring. Co., Cleveland, O., engr. gas producer div., 1917-27, mgr. div., 1928-32. Built two sulphuric acid plants in Wis. and steel furnaces at Watertown (Mass.) Arsenal for War Dept., World War; designed and built first concrete ore docks supported by submarine pilage and grillage, at South Chicago, for Ill. Steel Co. and Iroquois Iron Co. Republican. Presbyterian. Author: The Open Hearth, 1920; also engring., econ. and polit. contbns. to tech. and daily press. Home: 314 24th St. N., St. Petersburg, Fla. Died Apr. 10, 1945.

WINFIELD, JAMES MACFARLANE, physician; born Brooklyn, Jan. 28, 1901; s. James M. and Mabel (Dunning) W.; A.B., Princeton, 1922; M.D., U. of Pennsylvania, 1926; m. Katharine C. Wells; children—James Macfarlane, Katrina; m. 2d, Helen Curtiss, June 28, 1962. Intern U. Pa. Hosp., Phila., 1926-28, resident gynecology, 1928-29; instr. surgery U. Mich. Hosp., 1929-32, U. Pa. Med. Sch., 1933-37; asso. surgeon Delaware (Del.) Hosp., 1933-37; asso. prof. surgery Wayne U. Coll. Medicine, Detroit, 1937-46; asso. surgeon Receiving Hosp., Detroit, 1937-46; attending surgeon Flower and Fifth Avenue Hosps., N.Y. City, 1946-59; Valentine professor, chairman department of surgery N.Y. Med. Coll. 1946-59, dir. surgery, vis. surgeon Met. Hosp., 1946-59; attending surgeon St. Clair's and Doctors hosps., N.Y.C.; cons. surgeon Southampton Hosp.; asso. med. dir. New York City Transit Authority. Served as col., chief of surg. service, 36th Gen. Hosp., E.T.O., U.S. Army, 1943-45. Received Unit citation, four combat stars, Legion Merit. Diplomate Am. Bd. Surgery. Mem. Am. Surg. Assn., A.C.S., Societe Internationale de Chirurgie, Western Surg. Assn., Central Surg. Assn., A.A.A.S., N.Y. Acad. Scis., Am. Assn. for Surgery of Trauma, N.Y. Surg. Soc., Excelsior Surg. Club, N.Y. State Med. Soc., N.Y. County Med. Soc., Surgeons Club. Home: 1175 York Av., N.Y.C. 10021. Office: 123 E. 69th St., N.Y.C. 21. Died; buried Port Ewen Cemetery, New Paltz, N.Y.

WING, CHARLES BENJAMIN, civil engr.; b. Willow Brook (now Clinton Corners), N.Y., Jan. 18, 1864; s. Phineas Rice and Mary (Sands) W.; prep. edn. Poughkeepsie Mil. Inst.; C.E., Cornell U., 1886; fellow civ. engring., Cornell, 1886-87; m. Anna Maria Paddock, Sept. 18, 1888 (died Feb. 1905); children—Sumner Paddock, Winchester Paddock, Charles Benjamin, Robert Lewis; m. 2d, Mrs. Marian (Colt) Browne, Feb. 20, 1908; step children—Ashley Colt Browne, Mrs. Frances Browne Wenzel. Instr. civil engring., Cornell, 1886-90; asst. prof., 1890-91, prof. bridge and hydraulic engring., 1891-92, U. of Wis.; prof. structural engring., 1892-1929, emeritus since 1929, exec. head dept. civil engring., 1923-29, Stanford U.; vice chmn. and exec. officer Calif. State Redwood Park Commn., 1911-26; chief of Div. of Parks of State Dept. of Natural Resources of Calif., 1928-35; chief State Park Authority and engr. in charge of Federal coöperative projects in Calif. State Parks, 1935-36; cons. civil engr. since 1936. Major and lt. col. 23d Engineers, on ry. constrn. and highway work and with 1st Army in Argonne-Meuse, in France, April 1918-June 1919. Cons. engr. bridges, wireless towers and spl. structures, among which are the 1,000 ft. towers for the Shanghai, China, station of the Federal Telegraph Co. Councilman Palo Alto, 1909-29. Mem. Am. Soc. C.E., Pacific Assn. Cons. Engrs., Am. Soc. Testing Materials, Sigma Xi. Clubs: Commonwealth, Engineers (San Francisco). Author: Freehand Lettering for Working Drawings, 1893; Manual of Bridge Drafting (with C. H. Wright), 1896; also various papers in Trans. Am. Soc. C.E. and other tech. jours. Home and office: 345 Lincoln Av., Palo Alto, Calif. Died Aug. 22, 1945. Died Aug. 22, 1945.

WING, CHARLES HALLET, chemist; b. Boston, Mass., Aug. 4, 1836; s. Benjamin Franklin and Adeline (Hallet) W.; B.S., Harvard, 1870. Prof. chemistry, Cornell U., 1870, Mass. Inst. Tech., 1874-84. Fellow Am. Acad. Arts and Sciences, etc. Home: Brighton, Mass. Died Sept. 13, 1915.

WING, WILSON MUNFORD, physician; b. Washington, Nov. 15, 1908; s. David LaForest and Mary Blanche (Mumford) W.; M.D., Columbia, 1936; M.P.H., Johns Hopkins U., 1947; m. Elsa June Stockfisch, Nov. 2, 1940; children—David Lohr, Deborah Thom, Daniel Cushing. Intern, Babies Hosp., Presbyn. Med. Center, N.Y.C., 1936-37, asso. attending pediatrician Vanderbilt Clinic, 4 years; house physician in pediatrics Children's Hosp., Boston, 1938-39, asst. pediatrician, 1939-40; research fellow in allergy Roosevelt Hosp., N.Y.C., 1940-42; staff internat. health div. Rockefeller Found., Eng., 1947-48; asst. in pediatrics Harvard; asso. prof. pub. health adminstrn. Johns Hopkins U., Balt., 1948-56, 57; U.S. dir. High Inst. Pub. Health ICA, Alexandria, Egypt, 1956-58; cons. pub. health adminstrn. WHO, Rio de Janeiro, Brazil, 1958-59; health officer Western health dist. Balt. City Health Dept., 1960-64, Eastern health dist., 1964—. Served from capt. to lt. col., M.C., AUS, 1942-46. Diplomate Am. Bd. Preventive Medicine, Am. Bd. Pediatrics. Fellow A.A.A.S., Am. Pub. Health Assn. Home: Baltimore MD Died Jan. 31, 1971.

WINGATE, CHARLES FREDERICK, consulting sanitary engr.; b. New York, N.Y., March 5, 1848; s. Charles and Mary P. W.; ed. public schools and Cooper Inst. Engaged in mercantile business in early life, then in editorial work for 20 yrs.; for 5 yrs. New York corr. Springfield (Mass.) Republican, under signature "Carlfried." Founded the Twilight Club, 1883, and Twilight Park, in the Catskills, 1887. Author: Views and Interviews on Journalism; What Shall Our Boys Do for a Living?; Twilight Tracts; An Episode in Municipal Government (4 nos. N. Am. Rev.); etc. Home: Twilight Park, N.Y. Died 1909.

WINGE, OJVIND, geneticist; b. Aarhus, Denmark, May 19, 1886; s. Sigfred Victor and Petra (Rian) W.; M.S., U. Copenhagen, 1910; Ph.D., 1917; student univs. Stockholm, Paris, Chgo., 1910-11; D.Sc., Oxford Univ., Stockholm University; married Julie Begtrup Moller, May 8, 1913; 1 son, Capt. Per. Asst. physiol. dept. Carlsberg Laboratorium, Copenhagen, 1911-21; prof. genetics Royal Vet. and Agrl. Coll., 1921-33, also lectr. genetics U. Copenhagen, 1929-35; prof. physiology dept. Carlsberg Laboratorium, 1933-56; leader Exptl. Farm Nordgaarden, Herfolge, Denmark, 1938-62; Hitchcock prof. U. Cal., 1957. Recipient Scheele medal for biochemistry, Sweden, 1942, Danish Fermentation Industry prize, 1946, Emil Chr. Hansen medal, Denmark, 1958. Member Royal Danish Acad. (chmn. sect. sci. and mathematics 1946-62), Royal Soc.; hon. mem. No. Genetics Soc., genetics socs. Gt. Britain, Japan, Sweden; mem. acads. Helsinki, Stockholm, Lund, Oslo, Japan, Nat. Academy Sciences. Home: Frederiksberg Bredegade 7, Copenhagen. Office: Carlsberg Laboratorium, G1. Carlsborvej 8, Copenhagen, Denmark. Died Apr. 5, 1964; buried Vestre Kirkegaard, Copenhagen, Denmark.

WINKELMAN, NATHANIEL WILLIAM, neuropsychiatrist and neuropathologist; b. Phila., Pa., Oct. 28, 1891; s. Frank N. and Frieda (Cohen) W.; M.D., (with honor), U. of Pa., 1914; m. Lillie Gabel, Sept. 16, 1919; children—Nathaniel William (M.D.), Alean G. (dec. 1942). Interne, Allegheny Gen. Hosp., 1914-15; resident neuropsychiatrist, Pittsburgh City Hosp., 1915-18; post grad. study U. of Hamburg, Germany, 1925-26; apptd. to teaching staff, U. of Pa., 1919 advancing through grades to asst. prof. neurology, 1929; prof. neuropathology, U. of Pa., grad. sch. of medicine, 1927—; prof., head of dept. neurology, Temple U. Med. Sch., 1929-36; neurologist, Mt. Sinai Hosp., 1930-35; neurologist, Jewish Hosp. (now Albert Einstein Med. Center, No. div.), 1932—; visiting neurologist, Phila. Gen. Hosp., 1933-35; asso. editor in charge of neurology, Jour. of Syphilis and Neurology, 1933-38; dir., John L. Eckel Lab., U. of Pa., grad. sch. of medicine, 1936—; medical director Phila. Psychiatric Hospital, 1937-53, vice president medical affairs, 1953—; cons. St. Joseph Hosp., Reading, Pa., 1940—. U.S. Army Med Corps, neurologist to base hosp., 87, Toul, France, 1918-19. Established and directed dept. of neuropathology, Phila. Gen. Hosp., 1920-35. Awarded medal and diploma, Athens Med. and Surg. Soc., 1952. Diplomate Am. Bd. Psychiatry and Neurology. Fellow A.M.A., Am. Psychiat. Assn., Coll. of Physicians of Phila., Am. Academy of Neurology; life mem. N.Y. Acad of Science; mem. Phila. Neurological Soc. (past pres.), Phila. Pathological Soc., Phila. Psychiat., Soc., Am. Neurological Assn. (2d vice president 1944-45), Am. Assn. of Neuropathologist (past pres.), Assn. for Research in Nervous and Mental Diseases, Nat. Mental Hygiene Com. Pa. Chapter, Phila. Med. Soc., Pa. State Med. Soc., Pa. Psychiatric Soc., Med.-Surg. Acad. Athens, Sigma Xi. Author: Chronic Syphilitic Poliomyelitis, 1932; Progressive Pallidal Degeneration, 1932; Brain Trauma; Histopathology during the Early Stages, 1934; Residual Lesions in the Brain in Cases of Old Head Injury, 1936; Syphilis of the Spinal Cord, 1936; Cerebral Fat Embolism, 1942; Scarlatinal Encephalomyelitis, 1942; Neurohistologic Findings in Experimental Electric Shock Treatment, 1944; Observations on the Histopathology of Schizophrenia I. The Cortex, 1949; Neurologic Symptons Following Accidental Intraspinal Injection, 1951. Degeneration, 1932, called Winkelman's Disease. Address: 1911 Spruce St., Phila. 3. Died Feb. 13, 1956; buried Mt. Sinai Cemetery, Phila.

WINLOCK, JOSEPH, educator, astronomer; b. Shelby County, Ky., Feb. 6, 1826; s. Fielding and Nancy (Peyton) W.; grad. Shelby Coll., 1845; A.M. (hon.), Harvard, 1868; m. Mary Isabella Lane, Dec. 10, 1856, 6 children. Prof. mathematics and astronomy Shelby

Coll., Shelbyville, Ky., 1845-52; mem. staff Am. Ephermeris and Nautical Almanac, Cambridge, Mass., 1852-57, supt., 1858-59, circa 1862-66; prof. mathematics U.S. Naval Observatory, 1857; head dept. mathematics U.S. Naval Acad., 1859; Phillips prof. astronomy, also dir. observatory Harvard, 1866-75; 1st astronomer to obtain photograph of corona during solar eclipse, also 1st to adapt to photographic purposes telescope of long focus, fixed horizontally and used without eye piece; corporate mem. Nat. Acad. Scis.; mem. Am. Acad. Arts and Scis. Died Cambridge, June 11, 1875.

WINN, JOHN F., physician; b. Fluvanna Co., Va., Sept. 13, 1852; s. Dr. Philip James and Elizabeth Rebecca (Ballow) W.; student U. of Va.; M.D., same, 1875; post-grad. courses Jefferson Med. Coll., and Phila. Lying-In Hosp., 1879-80, Phila. Polyclinic, 1893-94. Practiced in his native county, 1875-81; since then at Richmond; m. Miss W. Rosalie Yeamans, of Hanover Co., Va., Sept. 2, 1897. Established, Dec., 1886, and owner and editor, 1886-1912, Richmond Journal of Practice; 1st corr. sec., Coll. of Phys. and Surg. (later Univ. Coll. of Medicine), 1893; 1st med. supt., Va. Hosp.; professor obstetrics, Univ. Coll. of Medicine; obstetrician to Va. Hosp.; supt. and consulting obstetrician, 17th Street, and of Brook Avenue Lying-In Dispensaries; prof. obstetrics and head of dept. Med. Coll. of Va., since 1913; obstetrician to Memorial Hosp. Mem. Richmond Acad. Medicine and Surgery; mem. (and for 22 yrs. corr. sec.) Med. Soc. of Va.; mem. A.M.A. Author: One Thousand Cases in Students' Out-Door Obstetric Practice; Treatment of Ante-Partum Eclampsia; The Present Status of Toxemia of Pregnancy; The Prophylactic Care of the Breasts; Indications for and Technique of Forceps Delivery; Concerning Diagnosis and Treatment of Toxeimas of Pregnancy; Cerebral Birth Traumas as interesting to the Obstetrician. Address: 5 W. Grace St., Richmond, Va.

WINSLOW, ARTHUR, mining engr. geologist; b. Salem, N.C., Aug. 5, 1860; s. Francis and Mary S. (Nelson) W.; lived during childhood in Boston; for 5 yrs. of boyhood at school in Stuttgart, Germany, and 1 yr. in France; B.S., Mass. Inst. Tech., 1881; m. Mary Livingston Devereux, May 19, 1887. Asst. geologist Pa. Geol. Survey, 1881-84; in pvt. practice in Va., and N.C., 1884-87; in charge of state geol. survey of coal fields of Ark., 1887-89; state geologist, Mo., 1889-94; practiced at St. Louis, 1894-95; in 1896 began acting as gen. mgr., cons. engr. and later pres. of the Liberty Bell Gold Mining Co. and of the U.S. and British Columbia Mining Co. Author of several state geol. reports and numerous articles and papers in scientific procs. and periodicals. Home: Boston, Mass. Died 1938.

WINSLOW, BENJAMIN EMANUEL, architect and engr.; b. Chicago, July 2, 1867; s. Christian Wilhelm and Christiane W.; ed. Richmond Co., Va., until 1878, Hauck's Latin og Real Skole, Copenhagen, Denmark, 1878-83, Sch. of Tech. Soc., Copenhagen, 1883-88, Royal Acad. Fine Arts, Copenhagen, 1889-91; unmarried. In practice of profession since Sept., 1891. Mem. Am. Soc. Civ. Engrs., Western Soc. Engrs., Ill. Chapter Am. Inst. Architects, Chicago Architectural Club. Author: The Winslow Tables—Diagrams for Calculating the Strength of Wood, Steel and Cast Iron Beams and Columns, 1900 E15; The Winslow Sliderule for Calculating the Strength of Wooden and Steel Beams, 1907 X1. Residence: 59 Alexander Pl. Office: 1615 Ashland, Chicago.

WINSLOW, CHARLES-EDWARD AMORY, sanitarian; b. Boston, Feb. 4, 1877; s. Erving and Catherine Mary (Reignolds) W.; B.S., Mass. Inst. Tech., 1898, M.S., 1899; A.M., Yale, 1915; Dr.P.H., N.Y.U. 1918; m. Anne Fuller Rogers, 1907; 1 dau., Anne. Asst. health officer, Montclair, N.J., 1898; spl. work in engrs. office, Mass. State Bd. Health, summers of 1899-1902; asst. 1900-01, instr. sanitary bacteriology, 1902-05, asst. prof. sanitary biology, 1905-10, Mass. Inst. Tech., and biologist-in-charge Sanitary Research Lab., same, 1903-10; asst. prof. bacteriology, U. of Chicago, winter term, 1910; asso. prof. biology, Coll. City of New York, 1910-14; curator of pub. health, Am. Museum Natural History, New York, 1910-22; dir. Div. Pub. Health Edn., N.Y. State Dept. Health, 1914-15; Anna M.R. Lauder prof. public health, Yale Medical School, 1915-45, professor emeritus since 1945; director John B. Pierce Laboratory of Hygiene, 1932-47. Senior sanitarian, U.S.P.H.S. (reserve); Rosenberg lecturer, University of California, 1941. Member board of scientific directors of Internat. Health Div., Rockefeller Foundation, 1929-30. Pres. Nat. Assn. Housing Officials, 1942-43. Received Sedgwick Memorial medal American Public Health Association, 1942; W. Paul Anderson medal, A.S.H.V.E., 1949; Léon Bernard medal, WHO, 1952; Lasker award 1952; Nat. Inst. Social Sci. Medal, 1941; Lemuel Shattuck Medal, Mass. Tb. Pub. Health Assn., 1951; Elizabeth S. Prentiss Award, 1945. Fellow Am. Public Health Assn. (ex-pres.), A.A.A.S. (ex-chmn. sect. K); hon. fellow Royal Soc. Health, Soc. Med. Officers Health (London); member of Conn. Society of Civil Engineers, Army Medical Library, also Society History of Medicine (Peru). Conn. Acad. of Arts and Sciences, Society of Exptl. Biology and Medicine, Soc. Am. Bacteriologists (ex-pres.), Am. Society Naturalists, New England Water Works Assn., American Soc. Heating and Ventilating Engrs. (president 1945), chairman New York State Commn. on Ventilation, 1917-23, 1926-31; mem. Am. Red Cross mission to Russia, July 1917; mem. Pub. Health Council Conn., 1917-51; editor-in-chief Journal Bacteriology, 1916-44; editor American Journal of Public Health, 1944-54. Gen. med. director League of Red Cross Socs., Geneva, 1921; expert assessor Health Committee, League of Nations, 1927-30; chmn. Housing Authority, New Haven, since 1938. Clubs: Century (N.Y. City); Graduate (New Haven). Author: Magda (translation Herman Sudermann's Heimath), 1896; Elements of Water Bacteriology (with S. C. Prescott), 1904; Elements of Industrial Microscopy, 1905; Systematic Relationships of the Coccaceae (with Anne Rogers Winslow), 1908; Sewage Disposal (with L. P. Kinnicutt and R. W. Pratt), 1910; Healthy Living, 1917; Health Survey of New Haven, Conn. (with J. C. Greenway and D. Greenberg), 1917; The Land of Health (with Grace T. Hallock), 1922; Nursing and Nursing Education in the United States (chmn.), 1923; Report of the New York State Commission on Ventilation (chmn.), 1923; The Evolution and Significance of the Modern Public Health Campaign, 1923; A Pioneer of Public Health—William Thompson Sedgwick (with E. O. Jordan and G. C. Whipple), 1924; The Laws of Health and How to Teach Them (with Pauline Brooks Williamson), 1925; Fresh Air and Ventilation, 1926; The New Healthy Living (with Mary L. Hahn), 1929; Life of Hermann M. Biggs, 1929; The Road to Health, 1929; Health on the Farm and in the Village, 1931; A City Set on a Hill, 1934; Health Under the "El" (with Savel Zimand), 1937; The Conquest of Epidemic Disease (Princeton U. Press), 1943; The Cost of Sickness and the Price of Health, 1951; Man and Epidemics, 1952. Home: 313 St. Ronan St., New Haven. Died Jan. 8, 1957.

WINSLOW, FREDERIC I., cons. engr.; b. New Bedford, Mass., Jan. 30, 1863; s. George William and Jane Lucretia (Southwick) W.; ed. pvt. and pub. schs. and under tutors; m. Myrtle Smith, June 15, 1892. Practiced at Boston, 1883-1919, as gen. hydraulic engr. and miscel. engring. work; in charge all new constrn. of Boston water system, 1911-16; U.S. supervising engr. constrn. Squantum Destroyer Plant, 1917-18, later div. engr. Sudbury dept., Met. Dist. Commn., Mass. Conglist. Died Feb. 21, 1924.

WINSOR, FRANK EDWARD, civil engr.; b. Providence, R.I., Nov. 16, 1870; s. George Henry and Lucy Jane (Draper) W.; Ph.B., Brown U., 1891, C.E., 1892, A.M., 1896, Sc.D., 1929; m. Catharine Holbrook Burton, Oct. 25, 1893; children—Lucy Burton (Mrs. Hugh B. Killough), Edward, Catharine (Mrs. Hazen H. Ayer). On constrn. of the Metropolitan Sewer System, Boston, 1891-95, design and constrn. of Metropolitan Water Works, 1895-1903; water supply investigations, N.Y. City, Feb.-Nov. 1903; designing engr. and dep. chief engr. Charles River Basin Commn., Boston, 1903-06; div. engr. and dept. engr. Catskill Water Works, for N.Y. City; in charge constrn. Kensico and Hillview reservoirs, 32 miles of Catskill Aqueduct, etc., 1906-15; chief engr. new water supply, Providence, 1915-26; chief engr. Met. Dist. Water Supply, under Met. Dist. Water Supply Commn., Boston, 1926—; cons. engr. Bd. of Water Supply, N.Y. City. Trustee Brown U. Mem. Am. Soc. C.E. (dir. 1922-24; v.p. 1930-31); fellow Am. Acad. of Arts and Sciences. Mason. Home: West Newton, Mass. Died Jan. 30, 1939.

WINSOR, PAUL, engineer; b. at Milton, Mass., June 12, 1863; s. Frederick W. and Ann Bent (Ware) W.; student Mass. Inst. Tech.; m. Jessie Baldwin, of Winchester, Mass., 1888. Served apprenticeship with Pa. R.R., and with Thompson-Houston Electric Co.; supt. constrn. with Keystone Constrn. Co., Pittsburgh, Pa., 1886-92; resident asst. gen. mgr. West End St. Ry. Co., Pittsburgh, 1892-96; gen. mgr. Southern Electric Co., Baltimore, 1896-1900; with Boston Elevated Ry. Co. since 1900, now chief engr. mech. and elec. engring. dept. Mem. Am. Elec. Ry. Engrs.' Assn. (ex-pres.), Am. Soc. Mech. Engrs., Am. Inst. Elec. Engrs., N.E. Street Ry. Club (ex-pres.). Unitarian. Clubs: Engineers', Technology (Boston); Engineers' (New York). Home: Weston, Mass. Office: 101 Milk St., Boston, Mass.

WINSTEIN, S(AUL), univ. prof.; b. Montreal, Canada, Oct. 8, 1912; s. Louis and Anne (Dick) W.; A.B., U. of Calif., 1934, A.M., 1935; Ph.D., Calif. Inst. Tech., 1938, post-doctorate fellow, 1938-39; Nat. Research fellow, Harvard, 1939-40; Docteur Honoris Causa, U. Montpellier, 1962; m. Sylvia V. Levin, Sept. 3, 1937; children—Bruce, Carolee. Came to U.S., 1923, naturalized, 1929. Instr., Ill. Inst. Tech., 1940-41; instr., U. of Cal., Los Angeles, 1941-42, asst. prof., 1942-46, asso. prof., 1946-47, prof., 1947-69. Max Tishler lectr., Harvard U., 1954, G. N. Lewis lectr., U. Cal., 1955, Baker Non-Resident lectr., Cornell U., Spring 1957. Received Am. Chem. Soc. award in pure chemistry, 1948; Richards medal American Chemical Society, 1962, James Flack Norris award in phys. organic chemistry, 1967; Cal. Scientist of Year award, 1962. Mem. Am. Acad. Arts and Scis., Bayerische Akademie der Wissenenschaften, National Academy of Sciences, America Chemical Society, Phi Beta Kappa, Sigma Xi, Phi Lambda Upsilon. Specializes in physical-organic chemistry and reaction mechanisms. Home: Los Angeles CA Died Nov. 23, 1969.

WINSTON, CHARLES HENRY, physicist; b. nr. Richmond, Va., Aug. 21, 1831; s. Peter and Ann Eliza (Woodward) W.; A.B., Hampden-Sidney Coll., 1854 (LL.D., 1883); A.M., U. of Va., 1857; m. Nannie Steger, of Amelia Co., Va., Mar. 18, 1858. Asst. prof. ancient langs., Hampden-Sidney Coll., 1854-55; prof. ancient langs., Transylvania U., Ky., 1857-58; pres. Richmond Female Inst. (now Woman's Coll.), 1859-73; prof. physics and astronomy, 1873-1908, emeritus prof. physics and prof. astronomy since 1908, Richmond (Va.) Coll. During Civil War in charge Confed. chem. works at Charlotte, N.C. Mem. Foreign Mission Bd. Southern Bapt. Conv. since 1859 (pres. 1895-1902). Has written and lectured much on religious, Sunday Sch. and scientific subjects, and worked in normal insts. generally as conductor (Va. and N.C.). Address: 2607 Hanover Av., Richmond, Va.

WINSTON, ISAAC, hydrographic and geodetic engr.; b. Tuscumbia, Ala., Sept. 7, 1853; s. Isaac and Olive B. (Michie) W.; grad. Va. Mil. Inst., 1873; engaged as farmer, 1873-76; m. Anna Maria Otis, Sept. 19, 1882. In govt. service under corps of engrs. U.S.A., on constrn. pub. works, 1876-78; in service U.S. Coast and Geod. Survey, 1878—; insp. in charge of Field Sta., N.Y. City. U.S. del. Internat. Geod. Assn., 13th Gen. Conf., 1900. Home: New York, N.Y. Died Dec. 7, 1923.

WINTERBOTHAM, JOSEPH, indsl. engr.; b. Joliet, Ill., Feb. 24, 1878; s. Joseph and Genevieve Fellows (Baldwin) W.; Yale, 1900; M.A. (hon.) Univ. of Vt., 1941; m. Eleanor Hall, 1902 (dec.); 1 dau., Louise (Mrs. George McKay Schieffelin); m. 2d, Harriot Lee, Mar. 1929. Industrial exec. and engr., now retired from a large part of business activities; formerly served as pres. Perth Amboy Terra Cotta Co., Mitchell-Lewis (now Nash) Motor Co., Muller Export Co.; formerly vice-pres. Paramount (now Bear Brand) Knitting Co., Racine Rubber Co.; formerly chmn. bd. Atlantic Terra Cotta Co.; dir. Bear Brand Knitting Co., J. H. Winterbotham & Sons, J. C. Pennoyer Co., Tenak Products, Inc., Pennoyer Merchants Transfer Co., Muller Export Co., Nash Motor Co. Perth Amboy Terra Cotta Co., New England Indsl. Development Co., Vt. Soy Bean Assn., Inc. Chmn. Vt. Agrl. and Indsl. Products Commns. since 1939. Supervisor of art and consultant Fleming Museum, U. of Vt., 5 yrs.; governing mem. and mem. spl. com. Art Inst. of Chicago. Mem. exec. bd. regional (Boston) Boy Scouts of America. State chmn. British Relief Soc. Trustee Old Ladies Home, Burlington, Vt. Chmn. housing administrn., planning bd., post war planning bd., Burlington, Vt. Chmn. Vermont Indsl. Agrl. Products Commn. Mem. exec. bd. Nat. Seaway Council, Washington, D.C. Clubs: University, Tavern, Arts, Casino (Chicago); Century Assn. (N.Y. City). Home: Burlington, Vt. (summer); Roosevelt Hotel, New Orleans, La. (winter). Office: 8 S. Dearborn St., Chgo. Died Apr. 19, 1954.

WINTERNITZ, MILTON CHARLES, (win'ter-nits), pathologist; b. Baltimore, Feb. 19, 1885; s. L. Carl and Jennie (Kittner) W.; A.B., Johns Hopkins U., 1903, M.D., 1907; M.A. (hon.), Yale, 1917, LL.D., 1952; m. Helen Watson, M.D., Mar. 20, 1913 (died Apr. 1930); children—Elizabeth Watson, Jane Kimball, Thomas Watson, Mary Watson, William Welch; m. 2d, Pauline Webster Whitney, Apr. 6, 1932. Fellow, asst. instr. and asso. prof. pathology, Johns Hopkins Med. Sch., 1907-17; asst. resident pathologist, Johns Hopkins Hosp., 1910-13, asso. pathologist, 1913-17; pathologist to City Hosp., Baltimore, 1910-17; prof. pathology and bacteriology, Yale, Sept. 1917-25, Anthony N. Brady prof. of pathology, 1925-50, prof. emeritus, 1950—; dean Yale Med. Sch., 1920-35; asso. dir. Inst. Human Relations, Yale, 1931-50. Mem. Commn. Orgn. Exec. Br. Govt., 1953-55. Mem. bd. Gaylor Farm Sanatorium, Grace-New Haven Community Hosp.; dir. bd. sci. advisers Jane Coffin Childs Meml. Fund for Med. Research, 1948—; chmn. Div. of Med. Scis., Nat. Research Council, Washington, 1950-53. Captain and major United States Medical Corps, 1918. Recipient Newell Sill Jenkins Meml. medal, 1932; King's Medal for Service in Cause of Freedom, 1948; Pres.' Certificate of Merit, 1948; Yale Medal, 1952. Fellow Royal Soc. Medicine, A.M.A., A.A.A.S.; mem. Am. Soc. Experimental Pathology, Assn. Bacteriologists and Pathologists, New Haven Medical Society, Society for Experimental Biology, National Com. for Mental Hygiene, Conn. Society for Mental Hygiene, New Haven Co. Med. Assn., Conn. Birth Control League. Clubs: Yale, N.Y. Graduates, New Haven Lawn; Cosmos. Author: The Pathology of Influenza, 1919; The Biology of Arteriosclerosis, 1937. Compiler: Collected Studies on the Pathology of War Gas Poisoning, 1919; Pathology of Vascular Disease. Home: 2126 Connecticut Av., Washington 8. Died Oct. 3, 1959.

WINTERSTEINER, OSKAR PAUL, chemist; b. Bruck a/d Mur. Austria, Nov. 15, 1898; s. Carl and Eva (Torkar) W.; Ph.D., U. Graz (Austria), 1921; D.Sc. (hon.), Western Res. U., 1968; m. Margaret Ralston Prest, Sept. 21, 1934; children—Peter, Susanne. Instr. med. chemistry and organic microanalysis U. of Graz, Austria, 1921-26; fellow Internat. Edn. Bd., Johns Hopkins Med. Sch., Rockefeller Inst., 1926-27; instr. pharmacology Johns Hopkins Med. Sch., 1927-29; asst. prof. biochemistry Coll. Phys. and Surgs., Columbia U., 1929-39, asso. prof., 1939-41; dir. div. organic chemistry, Squibb Inst. Med. Research, 1941-59, director biological chemistry, 1959-63, sci. adviser, 1961-63, cons., 1964-67, sr. sci. adviser, 1967-71; hon. prof. biochemistry Rutgers U., 1942-71, emeritus prof., 1968-71; cons. and mem. antibiotic study sect. National Inst. Health, 1946-49; member board of scientific advisers National Inst. Arthritis and Metabolic Diseases, 1957-59. Awarded Presdl. Certificate of Merit, 1948; Nichols medal, 1950. Mem. Nat. Acad. Scis., Am. Chem. Soc. (chmn. North Jersey sect. 1957), A.A.A.S., Harvey Soc., Soc. Exptl. Biology and Medicine, Swiss Chem. Soc., Sigma Xi. Editor: Proceedings Soc. Exptl. Biology and Medicine, 1938-43, 1948-50; mem. editorial bd. Jour. Biol. Chemistry, 1952-62, Jour. Am. Chem. Soc., 1959-68. Home: Graz Austria Died Aug. 15, 1971.

WINTHROP, JOHN, astronomer; b. Boston, Dec. 19, 1714; s. Adam and Anne (Wainwright) W.; A.B., Harvard, 1732, LL.D. (1st hon. LL.D. given by Harvard), 1773; LL.D. (hon.), U. Edinburgh (Scotland), 1771; m. Rebecca Townesend, July 1, 1746; m. 2d, Hannah (Fayerweather) Tolman, Mar. 24, 1756; several children including James. Hollis prof. mathematics and natural philosophy Harvard, 1738-79; did research in astronomy, published results in Philos. Transactions of the Royal Soc.; made series of sun-spot observations, Apr. 19-22, 1739 (1st set observations sun-spots in Mass. Colony); made study of transit of Mercury over sun, 1740, also reported transits, 1743, 69; established 1st lab. of exptl. physics in Am. at Harvard, 1746, demonstrated laws of mechanics, light, heat, movement of celestial bodies according to Newtonian system, introduced into math. curriculum elements of fluxions (now known as differential and integral calculs), 1751; reported on earthquake that shook New England, 1755; delivered lecture on return of Halley's Comet of 1682, 1759 (1st predicted return of a comet); made preparations for transits of Venus, 1761, 69, dir. 1st astron. expdn. sent by Harvard, to St. John's, (Newfoundland) for 1761 transit; elected fellow Royal Soc., 1766; mem. Am. Philos. Soc., 1769; a founder Am. Acad. Arts and Scis., 1769; 1st astronomer in Am. Author: Relation of a Voyage from Boston to Newfoundland for the Observation of the Transit of Venus, 1761; Two Lectures on the Parallax and Distance of the Sun, 1769. Died Cambridge, Mass., May 3, 1779; buried King's Chapel Burying ground, Boston.

WINTNER, AUREL, mathematician; b. Budapest, Hungary, Apr. 8, 1903; s. Edward and Charlotte (Hirschfeld) W.; student U. Vienna, U. Göttingen; Ph.D., U. Leipzig, 1929; m. Dr. Irmgard Hölder, Sept. 11, 1930; 1 son, Claude Edward. Came to U.S., 1930, naturalized, 1937. Mem. faculty Johns Hopkins, 1930—, prof. mathematics, 1946—. Rockefeller Found. fellow U. Rome, 1929, Copenhagen Obs., 1930; mem. Inst. for Advanced Study, Princeton, 1937-38; John Simon Guggenheim Meml. Found. fellow, 1941. Mem. Astronomische Gesellschaft, London Math. Soc., Edinburgh Mathematical Society, Palermo Mathematical Society. Author: Spektraltheorie der unendlichen Matrizen, 1929; Beweis des E. Strömgrenschen dynamischen Abschlussprinzips der periodischen Bahngruppen in restringierten Dreikörper-problem. Publikationer og mindre Meddelelser fra Köbenhavns Observatorium, 1931; Sortengenealogie, Hekubakomplex und Gruppenfortsetzung, 1931; Lectures on asymptotic distributions and infinite convolutions, 1938; Analytical Foundations of Celestial Mechanics, 1941; Eratosthenian Averages, 1943; Theory of Measure in Arithmetical Semi-groups, 1944; The Fourier transforms of probability distributions, 1947. Asst. editorial bd. of Mathematische Zeitschrift and of Jahrbuch über die Fortschritte der Mathematik, 1927-29; asso. editor Am. Jour. Mathematics, 1936-39, editor, 1943—, sec., 1954—; cons. editor Rendiconti Del Circolo Matematico Palermo, 1951—. Contbr. articles math. jours. Address, Johns Hopkins U., Balt. 18. Died Jan. 15, 1958.

WINTON, ALEXANDER, inventor, mfr.; b. Grangemouth, Scotland, June 20, 1860; s. Alexander and Helen (Fea) W.; common sch. edn.; m. Jeanie Muir MacGlashan, 1883 (died 1903); children—Helen F., James M., Agnes M., Jeanie, Cathrine, Alexander; m. 2d, La Belle MacGlashan, of Scotland, 1906; children—La Belle (dec.), Clarice; m. 4th, Mrs. Mary E. Avery, September 2, 1931. Established Winton Bicycle Co., Cleveland, 1890; began manufacture of motor cars, 1894; incorporator, 1897, and later pres. The Winton Co.; established Winton Marine Oil Engine Works, 1912. Mason. Home: Lakewood, O. Died June 22, 1932.

WINTON, ANDREW LINCOLN, chemist; b. Westport, Conn., Jan. 26, 1864; s. Andrew Leavenworth and Mary Esther (Gorham) W.; Ph.B., Yale, 1884, Ph.D., 1904; U. of Graz, 1904; m. Kate G. Barber, Dec. 16, 1911. Chemist, Conn. Agrl. Expt. Sta., 1884-90, in charge Analytical Lab., 1890-1907, instr. organic analysis, Yale, 1902-06; chief of Chicago Food and Drug Lab., U.S. Dept. of Agr., 1970-14. Pres. Assn. Official Agrl. Chemists of U.S., 1898; mem. Am. Chem. Soc., Sigma Xi, Phi Lambda Upsilon; hon. mem. Phila. Coll. of Pharmacy. Author: Microscopy of Vegetable Foods; Course in Food Analysis; (with wife) Structure and Composition of Foods (4 vols.), The Analysis of Foods. Collaborator: Moeller's Mikoskopie der Nahrungs—u. Genussmittel. Translator: Hanausek's Microscopy of Technical Products. Reviser: Leach's Food Inspection and Analysis. Contbr. papers on chem. and micros. analysis, adulteration of foods, etc., in Am. and foreign scientific jours. Home: Wilton, Conn. Died Oct. 17, 1946; buried Mountain Grove Cemetery, Bridgeport, Conn.

WINZLER, RICHARD JOHN, biochemist b. San Francisco, Sept. 29, 1914; s. Joseph and Esther (Hoppe) Brand; student San Mateo Jr. Coll., 1932-34; B.S., Stanford, 1936, Ph.D., 1938; m. Georgann E. Martin, June 17, 1939; children—Joan, Natalie, Lee. Sterling fellow physiology Yale, 1938-39; NRC fellow med. sci. Wenner-Grens Inst., Stockholm, Sweden, 1939-40, Cornell U. Med. Sch., 1940-41; research fellow Nat. Cancer Inst., Bethesda, Md., 1941-43; asst. prof. biochemistry U. So. Cal. Sch. Medicine, 1943-46, asso. prof., 1946-49, prof., 1949-52; vis research prof. physiol. chemistry U. Wis. Sch. Medicine, 1951; prof., head dept. biol. chemistry U. Ill. Coll. Medicine, 1952-65; prof., head dept. biochemistry State U. N.Y. at Buffalo, 1965-69; prof. chemistry Fla. State U., Tallahassee, 1969-72. Cons. in med. edn. Chiengmai U. Med. Sch., Thailand, 1962. Mem. Nat. Bd. Med. Examiners, 1954-64. Commonwealth Fund scholar U. Freiburg, 1959. Mem. Soc. Exptl. Biology and Medicine, Am. Chem. Soc., Am. Assn. Cancer Research, A.A.A.S., Am. Fedn. Clin. Research, Am. Soc. Cell Biology, Am. Assn. Clin. Chemists, Am. Soc. Biol. Chemists, Sigma Xi. Bd. editors Proc. Soc. Exptl. Biology and Medicine, 1953-58, Cancer Research, 1955-60. Home: Tallahassee FL Died Sept. 28, 1972.

WIRTSCHAFTER, ZOLTON TILLSON, (wert'shaf-ter) physician; b. Cleveland, O., Oct. 10, 1899; s. Adolph and Tillie (Gutman) W.; M.B., U. of Cincinnati, 1926, M.D., 1927; B.S., Case Sch. of Applied Science, 1921; married Reitza Dine, 1933; children—Jonathan, David. Med. consultant to Brotherhood of Locomotive Firemen and Enginemen 1932-42; sr. instr. Clin. Medicine, Western Reserve Univ. Med. Sch.; sr. vis. physician Mt. Sinai Hosp., Cleveland; chief, diabetic clinic, Mt. Sinai Hosp., Cleveland, 1939-42; sr. vis. physician, chief of diabetic clinic Cleveland City Hosp., 1939-42; med. consultant Veterans Adminstrn., Wadsworth Gen. Hosp., Sawtelle; asso. prof. of clin. medicine, U. of Southern Cal. Los Angeles, 1947-49; chief med. service V.A. Hosp., Portland, 1953-56, dir. research, 1956—; asso. prof. medicine U. Ore., 1957—. Served with A.U.S. as lt. col. Aero Med. Research Lab., Wright Field, 1942-46. Received 2 Army Commendation Ribbons. Diplomate Am. Bd. of Internal Medicine. Fellow A.C.P., Am. Pub. Health Assn.; mem. Am. Diabetic Assn. (gov.), A.A.A.S., A.M.A., Los Angeles Co. Med. Assn., Beverly Hills Med. Soc. Jewish Author: Diabetes Mellitus, 1941; Minerals in Nutrition, 1941, (with Morton Korenberg); Genesis of the Mouse Skeleton, 1960; (with Donald G. Walker). The Genesis of Rat Skeleton, 1957; also research articles in connective tissue diseases, nutritional diseases. Address: VA Hosp., Sam Jackson Park, Portland 7, Ore. Died Aug. 18, 1967; buried Portland.

WISE, JOHN, balloonist; b. Lancaster, Pa., Feb. 24, 1808; married, 1 child. Developed intense desire to study aerostatics as a youth; apprenticed to cabinet maker, 1831-35; made his 1st ascent in balloon, Phila., 1835; made one of 1st proposals to use balloons in tactical warfare during Mexican War; set distance record for balloon trip, traveling 804 miles from St. Louis to Henderson (N.Y.), 1859; failed in attempted balloon trip to Europe, landed in Canaan Conn., 1873; credited with inventing rip panel (safety device). Author: A System of Aeronautics, 1850; Through the Air, 1873. Drowned while ballooning over Lake Michigan, Sept. 29, 1879, body never recovered.

WISLOCKI, GEORGE BERNAYS, (wis-lok'i), anatomist; b. San Jose, Calif., Mar. 25, 1892; s. Stanislaus and Lily C. (Bernays) W.; A.B., Washington U., 1912, Sc.D. (hon.), 1951; M.D., Johns Hopkins, 1916; A.M., (hon.), Harvard U., 1942; m. Florence Clothier, Feb. 13, 1931; children—Louis Clothier, Johanna, George Stanislaus, Edith Ball. Anatomist, Johns Hopkins, 1916-31; Parkman prof. of anatomy, Harvard U., 1931-1941, James Stillman prof. of comparative anatomy since 1941, and Hersey professor of anatomy, 1947—, mem. faculty Mus. Comparative Zoology, 1952—. Served as 1st lieutenant U.S. Med. Corps, 1917-18. Mem. Harvard Infantile Paralysis Com., Ella Sachs Plotz Foundation, Elizabeth Thompson Science Fund; mem. Scientific Advisory Bd., Wistar Inst. of Anatomy and Biology, 1939-40. Trustee emeritus Forsyth Dental Infirmary. Fellow A.A.A.S., Zool. Society London (hon. fgn.); member Anatomical Soc. Great Britain and Ireland (honorary), National Academy of Sciences, American Academy Arts and Sciences, Am. Assn. Anatomists, Histochemical Society (president 1950-51), American Physiological Society, Am. Soc. Zoölogists, Institut internat. d'embryol., Phi Beta Kappa, Sigma Xi, Alpha Omega Alpha. Asso. editor Johns Hopkins Hosp. Bulletin, 1926-31; associate editor American Journal Anatomy, 1939-46, Journal of Histochemistry, 1953—; editor Am. Anatomical Memoirs. Author of papers on embryology, histology and endocrinology. Clubs: 14 W. Hamilton St. (Baltimore); Med. Exchange, Harvard (Boston). Home: 148 Hillside St., Milton, Mass. Office: Harvard Medical School, 25 Shattuck St., Boston. Died Oct. 22, 1956; buried Walnut Hill, Brookline, Mass.

WISNER, GEORGE MONROE, civil engr.; b. Detroit, Mich., Feb. 9, 1870; s. George Y. and Carrie (Palmer) W.; B.S. in C.E., U. of Mich., 1892; m. Edith K. Young, Feb. 5, 1902. In employ engring. dept. Sanitary Dist. of Chicago, July 7, 1892—; asst. engr. in charge Chicago River improvement, 1897-1901, asst. chief engr., 1901-07, chief engr., 1907-20, cons. engr., 1920—; engr. for settlement of rapid transit and subway problem of City of Chicago, 1929. Home: Chicago, Ill. Died Aug. 26, 1932.

WISNER, GEORGE Y., civil engr.; b. West Dresden, N.Y., July 11, 1841; s. William and Jane (Downey) W.; grad. U. of Mich., C.E., 1865; m. Carrie Palmer, Oct. 15, 1867. Engaged in Govt. surveys on Great Lakes and Mississippi river, 1865-80; on surveys of Mississippi, Des Plaines and Illinois rivers improvements, 1880-84; supt. constrn. 10th and 11th U.S. Light House dists., 1884-87; in private practice, 1887—; 1888-91, resident engr. South Pass Jetty Works, and chief engr. Brazos River Harbor Improvement; organized and directed, 1895-97, sanitary dept. Detroit Bd. of Health; mem. U.S. Deep Waterways Commn., 1897-1900; cons. engr. Montreal, Ottawa & Georgian Bay Canal Co., 1901—; cons. engr. for U.S. Reclamation Service, 1903—. Author: Geodetic Field Work, 1883; Brazos River Harbor Improvement, 1891; Worthless Government Engineering, 1892; Breakwaters, Sea-Walls and Jetties, 1893; Hydraulics of Rivers Having Alluvial Beds, 1896; Sewage Disposal, 1896; Regulation of Lake Levels, 1895-99; Report of Deep Waterway Commission, 1900; Canals from the Great Lakes to the Atlantic, 1900. Home: Detroit, Mich. Died 1906.

WISSLER, CLARK, (wis'ler), anthropologist; born, Wayne County, Ind., Sept. 18, 1870; s. Benjamin Franklin and Sylvania (Needler) W.; A.B., Ind. U., 1897, A.M., 1899; Ph.D., Columbia University, 1901; LL.D. from Indiana University, 1929; m. Etta Viola Gebhart, June 14, 1899; children—Stanley Gebhart, Mary Viola. Instr. edn., New York U., 1901-02; asst. in anthrpology, 1903-05; lecturer, 1905-09, Columbia; asst. in anthropology, 1903-06; curator, 1906-41, Am. Museum Natural History; professor anthropology, Yale, 1924-40. Division chmn. Nat. Research Council, 1920-21; consulting anthropologist Bishop Mus., Honolulu since 1920. Fellow N.Y. Acad. Sciences, Am. Ethnol. Soc., Am. Geog. Soc.; mem. Nat. Acad. Sciences, Sigma Xi, Phi Beta Kappa. Author: North American Indians of the Plains, 1912; Man and Culture, 1922; The Relation of Nature to Man in Aboriginal America, 1926; Social Anthropology, 1929; The American Indian, 1938; Indian Cavalcade, 1938; The Indian in the United States, 1940. Home: 15 W. 77th St., New York 24, N.Y. Died Aug. 25, 1947.

WISTAR, CASPAR, physician; b. Phila., Sept. 13, 1761; s. Richard and Sarah (Wyatt) W.; B.M., U. State of Pa., 1782; M.D., Edinburgh U., 1786; m. Isabella Marshall, May 15, 1788; m. 2d, Elizabeth Mifflin, Nov. 28, 1798; 3 children. Served 2 terms as pres. Royal Med. Soc. (student orgn.) at Edinburgh, also assisted in founding natural history soc.; elected jr. fellow Coll. Physicians of Phila. (organized 1787), 1787; prof. chemistry med. sch. Coll. of Phila., 1789; adjunct prof. anatomy, surgery and midwifery at new U. Pa., 1792, prof. anatomy and midwifery, 1808, prof. anatomy, 1810-18; mem. staffs Phila. Dispersary, Pa. Hosp., 1793-1810; elected mem. Am. Philos. Soc., 1787, curator, 1793, v.p., 1795, pres., 1815-18; served in yellow fever epidemic, 1793; founded soc. for promotion of vaccination, 1809; plant Wistaria named for him; his family gave his anatomical collection to U. Pa. for museum. Author: System of Anatomy (1st Am. textbook on subject), 2 vols., 1811; Eulogium on Doctor William Shippen, 1818. Died Phila., Jan. 22, 1818.

WITEBSKY, ERNEST, physician; b. Frankfurt, Germany, Sept. 3, 1901; s. Michael and Hermine (Neuberger) W.; student U. Frankfurt, 1920-25; M.D., U. Heidelberg, 1926; Dr. Med., h.c., University of Freiburg, 1958; married Ruth Mueller-Erkelenz, June 23, 1935; children—Frank G., Grace E. Came to U.S., 1934, naturalized, 1939. Asso. prof. bacteriology U. Buffalo, 1936-40, prof. bacteriology and immunology, 1940-54, distinguished prof., 1954-69, head dept. bacteriology and immunology, 1941-67, dir. Center for Immunology, 1967-69, acting dean Sch. Medicine, 1958-59, dean, 1959-60; bacteriologist, serologist Buffalo Gen. Hosp., 1936-68, dir. blood bank, 1941-67; cons. bacteriology VA Hosp., 1951-69. Diplomate clin. microbiology Am. Bd. Pathology. Fellow Am. Soc. Clin. Pathologists; mem. A.M.A., Am. Assn. Pathologists and Bacteriologists, Am. Assn. Immunologists, Soc. Am. Bacteriologists, Soc. Exptl. Biology and Medicine, Am. Assn. Blood Banks, International Society of Hematology, Royal Society of Medicine, Sigma Xi. Contributor of English, German, French, Am. med. jours. Home: Buffalo NY Died Dec. 7, 1969; buried Buffalo NY

WITHERS, WILLIAM ALPHONSO, chemist; b. River View, nr. Davidson, N.C., May 31, 1864; s. William B. and Sarah L. (Rutledge) W.; A.B., Davidson

Coll., N.C., 1883, A.M., 1885, Sc.D., 1917; student in chemistry, 1888-90, fellow, 1889-90, Cornell U.; m. Elizabeth Witherspoon Daniel, June 11, 1896 (died 1905); m. 2d, Jane Hinton Pescud, July 29, 1909. Asst. chemist, 1884-88, chemist, 1897-1921, acting dir., 1897-99, N.C. Agrl. Expt. Sta.; prof. chemistry, 1889—, v.p., 1916—, dir. Summer Sch., 1917—, N.C. State Coll. of Agr. and Engring. State chemist, 1897-98; state statis. agent U.S. Dept. of Agr., 1895-1902 and 1905-15. Mem. exec. com. Nat. Pure Food and Drug Congress, 1898, N.C. Agrl. Soc., 1898—; author of N.C. (pure food law, 1899; discoverer (with F. E. Carruth) of the toxic principle of cottonseed, 1915; chmn. com. on pure food legislation, Assn. Am. Agrl. Colls. and Expt. Stas., 1899-1903; pres. N.C. sect. Am. Chem. Soc., 1901-02; pres. Assn. Official Agrl. Chemists, 1909-10; sec. N.C. Coll. Assn.; fellow A.A.A.S.; dir. of Raleigh Y.M.C.A., 1914— (pres. 1920, 21, 22). Mem. N.C. Council Defense, 1917-18; mem. co. bd. food adminstrs., 1917-18; exec. com. local chapter Am. Red. Cross, 1917-18; chmn. Wake County Bd. of Edn., 1919—. Democrat. Presbyn.; exec. com. N.C. S.S. Assn., 1914— (pres. East Central region 1923-24). Grand Comdr. K.T. of N.C., 1896; Grand High Priest R.A.M., 1897. Author of bulls., articles, etc., mainly on nitrification, food adulteration, and cottonseed. Died June 20, 1924.

WITMER, FRANCIS POTTS, civil engr.; b. Phila., Pa., Apr. 2, 1873; s. Ambrose E. and Imogene B. (Potts) W.; A.B., Central High Sch., Phila., 1891; B.S., U. of Pa., 1893, C.E., 1894; m. Minnie Sears Barr, June 24, 1897; children—Dorothy Imogene (dec.), Francis Potts; instr. in civil engring., U. of Pa., 1894; draftsman and designer Phoenix Bridge Co., 1897-1900; engr. in charge bridge design, Am. Bridge Co., Phila. office, later New York office, 1901-13; structural engr. New York, Municipal Ry. Corp. (Brooklyn Rapid Transit System), 1913-20; cons. engr., associated with Howard C. Baird, New York, since 1920; dir. civil engring. dept.; prof. civil engring., U. of Pa., 1924-43; retired. Asso. with Mr. Baird in constrn. of Bear Mountain Bridge over Hudson River, 1922-24. Mem. Am. Soc. C.E., Am. Soc. for Testing Materials, Am. Concrete Inst., Soc. for Promotion Engring. Edn., Engineers Club (Phila.), Franklin Inst., Sigma Xi, Tau Beta Pi, Phi Beta Kappa. Republican. Episcopalian. Home: 738 Penna. Av., Prospect Park, Pa. Office: 95 Liberty St., New York NY

WITSCHI, EMIL, biologist; b. Bern, Switzerland, Feb. 18, 1890; s. Johann and Elisabeth (Blank) W.; student State Teachers Coll. and State U., Bern, Switzerland, 1905-11; Ph.D., U. of Munich, 1913; M.D. honoris causa, University Basel, 1960; Rockefeller Foundation fellow, Yale, 1926, U. of Chicago, 1926, U. of Calif., 1927; m. Ida Martha Muehlestein, July 10, 1914; children—Marianne, Hans Walter. Came to U.S., 1926, naturalized, 1933. Teacher zoology and comparative anatomy, U. of Basel, 1921-23, lecturer exptl. zoology, 1924-27; prof. zoology, embryology and endocrinology, State U. Ia., 1927-58, professor emeritus, 1958-71; guest prof. Univ. of Tubingen, Germany, 1948-49; vis. prof. U. Paris, 1959, Yale, 1961, Taiwan U., 1962, Basel University, 1963-67; program specialist for reproducation physiology Ford Foundation, 1962-67; sr. scientist, biomed. div. Population Council Rockefeller University, New York City, N.Y., 1967-71. Member permanent committee Internat. Congress of Zoologists, Jubile Scientifique Sorbonne, 1959. Fellow A.A.A.S., N.Y., Idaho academies sci., Internat. Inst. Embryology (Utrecht); mem. German Acad. Sci., Swiss Soc. Natural Scis., Am. Soc. Zoologists (pres. 1959, 60), Am. Assn. Anatomists, Endocrine Soc., Am. Genetics Soc., Soc. Exptl. Biology and Medicine, Am. Naturalists, Sigma Xi (tour lectr. 1960), Gamma Alpha; hon. mem. Societe Zoologique France, Societe d'Endocrinologie Paris others; corr. mem. Swiss Genetics Soc., others. Kiwanian. Author: Sex Deviations, Inversions and Parabiosis, 1932, 2d edit., 1939; Development of Vertebrates, 1956. Contbr. to Ency. Brit., 1957: also articles to scientific jours. Home: New York City NY Died June 9, 1971.

WITT, JOSHUA CHITWOOD, engr.; b. Connersville, Ind., Aug. 5, 1884; s. Isaac Snyder and Amanda (Chitwood) W.; A.B., Butler U., 1908; B.S., U. of Chicago, 1909; M.S., U. of Pittsburgh, 1912, Ph.D., 1915; M.E., Armour Institute Technology (now Illinois Institute Technology), Chicago, 1935; m. Florence Ruth Oldham, Dec. 5, 1918. Testing and research asst. Swift & Co., Chicago, 1908-10; mgr. testing dept. R. W. Hunt Co., Pittsburgh, 1910-15; chief of sect. Bur. of Science, Manila, P.I., 1915-17; tech. dir. Rizal Cement Co., Manila, 1917-19; asst. prof. U. of Pittsburgh, and cons. engr., 1919-20; dir. chem. research Portland Cement Assn., Chicago, 1920-23; dir. research Universal Atlas Cement Co., Chicago, 1924-39; tech. dir. Marquette Cement Mfg. Co., 1939-48; cons. engr., 1948-71. Cons. U.S. Bur. of Mines, 1922-23. Sect. editor Chemical Abstracts, 1924-71; cons. editor, Concrete, 1933-48. Fellow Am. Soc. M.E., A.A.A.S., Am. Soc. C.E., Am. Inst. Chem. Engrs.; mem. Am. Inst. of Consulting Engineers, American Chem. Soc., Am. Concrete Inst., Am. Soc. Testing Materials, Ill. Acad. Sci., Sigma Xi, Phi Delta Theta, Tau Beta Pi. Rep. Presbyn. Mason (32 deg., K.T., Shriner), Clubs: Adventures, Engineers (Chgo.). Author of Portland Cement Technology (also in Spanish), second edition in English, 1966; also numerous science and tech. papers. Patentee in cement. Home: Chicago IL Died Apr. 7, 1971; buried Liberty IN

WITTHAUS, RUDOLPH AUGUST, toxicologist; b. New York, Aug. 30, 1846; s. Rudolph A. and Marie A. (Dunbar) W.; A.B., Columbia, 1867, A.M., 1870; M.D., Univ. Med. Coll. (New York U.), 1875; studied Sorbonne and Collège de France, Paris, 1873-74; unmarried. Asso. prof. chemistry and physiology, New York U., 1876-78; prof. chemistry and toxicology, U. of Vt., 1878-98; prof. physiol. chemistry, 1882-86, chemistry and physics, 1886-98, Univ. Med. Coll.; prof. chemistry and toxicology, U. of Buffalo, 1882-88; prof. chemistry and physics, Cornell U. Med. College, 1898-1911, prof. emeritus, 1911—. Toxicol. expert in Carlyle Harris, Buchanan, Mayer, Fleming, Benham, Molineux and many other cases. Fellow A.A.A.S. Author: Essentials of Chemistry, 1879; General Medical Chemistry, 1881; Manual of Chemistry, 1879, 1908; Laboratory Guide in Urinalysis and Toxicology, 1886. Editor: Witthaus and Becker's Medical Jurisprudence (4 vols.), in which contributed introduction and Vol. 4 on Toxicology, 1894, 1906. Wrote Articles on Poisoning by Hydrocyanic Acid, Oxalic Acid, Opium and Strychnine, and on Ptomaines, Wood's Handbook of Medical Sciences; on homicide by morphine; detection of quinine; post-mortem imbibition of poisons; Researches Loomis Laboratory, etc. Home: New York, N.Y. Died Dec. 23, 1915.

WITTICH, FRED WILLIAM, physician; b. Carlisle, Pa., Feb. 3, 1885; s. Rev. Philip and Virginia (Klinger) W.; A.B., Pa. Coll., 1908, A.M., 1911; M.D., Johns Hopkins, 1913; m. 1st, Anna Jean Wetterau, 1916 (div. 1934); 1 son, Fred Wetterau; m. 2d, Viola Annette Lerum, Aug. 5, 1935; 1 son, F. William. Intern, Saranac Lake (N.Y.) Hosp., 1914-15; resident North Chicago Hosp., Chgo., 1915-16; pvt. practice medicine, Mpls., since 1918; specialist in allergy since 1937; asst. chief med. clinic Univ. Hosp., 1918-19; asso. in Tb, Mpls. Gen. Hosp., 1920-21; physician in charge chest clinic out patient dept., U. Minn., 1919-25; instr. medicine U. Minn., 1919-20, asst. prof., 1920-25, mem. faculty of extension course since 1948; mem. Glen Lake Sanatorium out-patient staff, 1934-46; staff mem. St. Barnabus Hosp. Participant USPHS interdepartmental conf. on air pollution, Washington, 1950. Sec.-treas., Am. Coll. Allergists, 1942-55, pres. emeritus and cons.; chmn. exec. com. Internat. Assn. Allergists, 1945-51; past pres. Internat. Assn. Allergology; mem. com. on honor 50th Anniversary of Discovery of Anaphylaxis, 1952. Recipient Pasteur Inst. silver medal for promoting internat. relations, 1946. Fellow A.M.A., Am. Coll. Allergists, Am. Coll. Chest Physicians, Am. Acad. Allergy, Internat. Assn. Allergists; mem. Am. Med. Writers Assn., Am. Geriatric Soc., Am. Assn. Immunologists, A.A.A.S., Am. Trudeau Soc., Nat. Tb Assn., Mpls. Acad. Medicine, Soc. Internal Medicine, Sigma Xi, Beta Beta Beta, Phi Gamma Delta, Phi Beta Pi; hon. mem. Argentinian, Brazilian, Colombian, Peruvian, Chilian, Swedish, Spanish, Cuban, French allergy socs., Brazilian Soc. History of Medicine, Argentinian Assn. Allergy and Applied Immunology. Republican. Meth. Author: Information for the Tuberculous, 1918; Allergy Laboratory and Diagnostic Procedures, 1951. Editor Review of Allergy and Applied Immunology. Editorial bd. Annals of Allergy. An editor in chief Internat. Archives of Allergy and Applied Immunology, 1949—, Folia Clinica Internacional. Contbr. on research to med. publs., textbooks. Home: 3230 Alabama Av., Mpls. 55416. Office: Marquette Bank Bldg., Mpls. 2. Died Feb. 3, 1965.

WITZEMANN, EDGAR JOHN, (wits'e-man), chemist; b. Decatur, Ill., July 13, 1884; s. Albert C. and Eliza (Düring) W.; A.B., James Millikin Univ., Decatur, Ill., 1907; A.M., Ohio State U., 1909, Ph.D., 1912; m. Lulu L. Laughlin, Aug. 30, 1910; 1 dau., Margaret Elisa. Fellow in chemistry, Ohio State U., 1907-09, instr., 1909-12; mem. Otho S. A. Sprague Memorial Inst. (U. of Chicago), 1912-25; research chemist Mayo Foundation, Rochester, Minn., 1925-27; asst. prof. physiol. chemistry, U. of Wis., 1927-35. asso. prof., 1935-47, prof., 1947. Research chemist Chem. Warfare, Washington, D.C., 1918. Fellow A.A.A.S.; mem. Am. Chem. Soc., Am. Soc. Biol. Chemists, Soc. Exptl. Biology and Medicine, Deutsche Chemisches Gesellschaft, Sigma Xi. Republican. Conglist. Author numerous research repts. in Am. chem. periodicals. Home: 1913 Regent St., Madison, Wis. Died Nov. 30, 1947; buried Decatur, Ill.

WOERMANN, JOHN WILLIAM, (wer'man), engr.; b. St. Louis, Mo., Jan. 18, 1868; s. Henry William and Catherine M. (Schwiering) W.; C.E., Washington U., 1890; m. Elizabeth Graff Honens, Oct. 15, 1891; children—Elsie (Mrs. W. E. Kling), Lillian (Mrs. R. L. Ward). Surveys and improvements for U.S. Govt. on Rock River, Chicago River, Mo. River, and Ill. and Miss. Canal (Hennepin Canal), 1890-1902; in charge of surveys, plans and estimates for 14-ft. waterway from Chicago to St. Louis, 1902-05; pvt. practice on bridge construction and water power development, 1905-08; made plans and estimates for 14-ft. waterway, St. Louis to Cairo, and for 9-ft. waterway, Chicago to St. Louis, 1908-09. U.S. asst. engr., Western Div. and Northwestern Div., U.S. Army, inspection of projects, plans, specifications, etc., for improvements on 35 rivers, harbors and canals in middle west, 1909-22; prin. asst. engr., Chicago District, 1922-29, senior and prin. engr. same office, 1929-39; now cons. engr. Mem. Am. Soc. C.E., Western Soc. of Engrs., Internat. Navigation Congress, Washington Univ. Assn.; pres. Alumni Assn. Washington U., 1916. Presbyterian. Mason. Clubs: Engineers (pres. 1915), City (St. Louis). Author of many papers and reports on lock and dam construction, navigation, water power, and flood control. Home: 1525 E. 65th St., Chicago, Ill. Died Dec. 9, 1942.

WOGLOM, WILLIAM HENRY, pathologist; b. Bklyn., Sept. 13, 1879; s. William Henry and Flora (Williams) W.; B.S., Columbia, 1921; M.D., Coll. Phys. and Surg., Columbia U., 1901; studied in London and Berlin, 1911-12; m. Emilie Marie Cordes, 1913; children—William H., Eleanor (Mrs. Victor Bary), Katherine (dec.); m. 2d, Edna. E. Good. Interne, St. Barnabas' Hosp., Newark, N.J., 1903, Lying-in Hosp., N.Y., 1904; asst. in pathology L.I. Coll. Hosp., 1907-08; pathologist, bacteriologist, Dept. Health, N.Y.C., 1908-09; asst. in cancer research Columbia U., 1909-12; asst. to dir. Imperial Cancer Research Fund, London, Eng., 1911-12; asst. prof. cancer research Inst. Cancer Research, Columbia U., 1912-17, asso. prof., 1917-46, prof. emeritus, 1946—. Mem. sci. adv. com. Internat. Cancer Research Found., 1941-46. Editor Jour. Cancer Research, 1917-22, Cancer Research (Jour.), 1942-46. Mem. A.M.A., Am. Assn. Cancer Research (pres. 1937), Path. Soc. (pres. 1924, 25), A.A.A.S., Soc. Exptl. Biology and Medicine, Holland Soc., etc. Royal Photog. Soc. Gt. Britain (asso.). Episcopalian. Author: The Study of Experimental Cancer—a Review, 1913; Discoverers for Medicine, 1949; also various monographs. Translator; The Commoner Diseases, Their Causes and Effects (from Jores' Anatomische Grundlagen wichtiger Krankheiten), 1915; The Riddle of Cancer (from Oberling's Le Probléme du Cancer), 1944; Secretary of Europe (by Golo Mann); The Problem of Knowledge (by Ernst Cassirer). Address: 621 Tilden Av., Teaneck, N.J. 07666. Died Aug. 8, 1953; buried Woodlawn Cemetery, N.Y.C.

WOHLENBERG, ERNEST T. F., cons. forestry; b. Lincoln, Neb., Sept. 9, 1889; s. Peter Jacob and Gretchen (Tychsen) W.; B.S., U. Neb., 1912, M.F., 1913; postgrad. forest econs. U. Cal. at Berkeley, 1933-35; m. Grace Shafer, Jan. 19, 1925 (dec.); dau., Joan Marie (Mrs. Joseph L. Eldredge). Forest examiner U.S. Forest Service, Ariz., N.M., 1913-17, prin. forester charge pvt. forestry, Western U.S., 1937-41; various positions lumber industry, Ore., Wash., 1919-22; valuation engr. lumber sect. U.S. Treasury Dept., Western half U.S., 1922-37; gen. mgr. Edward Hines Lumber Co., Burns, Ore., 1941-45; forest counsel Western Forestry and Conservation Assn., Portland, Ore., 1945-48; v.p., gen. mgr. Masonite Corp., 1948-54, retired; prof. indsl. forestry school of forestry Yale University, 1954-59, emeritus; consultant in forest industries, 1959—; adv. board Bank of Am., Ukiah; member board of directors Yokayo Land Co., Ukiah. First pres. Redwood Region Conservation Council, 1950-52, now dir. Trustee Found. for American Resource Management. Served as capt. 10th Engrs., A.E.F., 1917-19 Mem. Western Forestry and Conservation Assn. (pres.), Soc. Am. Mil. Engrs., Soc. Am. Foresters, Sigma Phi Epsilon. Episcopalian (vestry). Club: Faculty. Author articles on forestry. Address: P.O. Box 246, Ukiah, Cal. Died Sept. 11, 1963.

WOHLENBERG, WALTER JACOB, (wo'len-berg), prof. mech. engring.; b. Lincoln, Neb., Feb. 17, 1888; s. Peter Jacob and Gretchen (Tychsen) W.; B.S. in M.E., U. of Neb., 1910, hon. D.Engring., 1937; M.S., U. of Illinois, 1914; hon. M.A., Yale Univ., 1928; m. Charlotte Alvarita Spangler, June 24, 1918 (dec.); 1 dau., Barbara (dec.); m. 2d, Eleanor B. Hutchins, Sept. 6, 1950. Asst. prof. mechanical engring. U. Okla., 1914-16, U. of Mont., 1916-18; asst. prof. same, Yale, 1918-25, asso. prof., 1925-28, prof. since 1928, Sterling professor mech. engring. since 1930, dean sch. engring. 1948-55, researcher; chairman mechanical engineering dept., Yale, 1946; spl. lecturer on heat transfer by radiation, Purdue Univ., 1940; cons. engr. on steam generating equipment since 1920. Mem. Div. Engring. and Indsl. Research, Nat. Research Council, 1930-32. Fellow A.S.M.E. (life mem.; chmn. fuel test code com. 1930-45, spl. research com. on radiation in boiler furnaces, 1934-41; main com. power test codes; mem. com. on meetings and programs 1936-41, chmn. 1941; v.p. 1943-45; member main committee on furnace performance factors; sub-committee on heater in furnaces). Society for Promotion Engineering Education, Yale Engineering Assn., Sigma Xi, Sigma Tau. Clubs: Graduate (New Haven); Yale (New York). Widely known for theoretical work in heat transfer, leading to a rational basis for design of furnaces. Author of tech. papers. Home: 1220 Ridge Road, Hamden, Conn. Address: 400 Temple St., New Haven. Died Aug. 8, 1956.

WOLBACH, SIMEON BURT, pathologist; b. Grand Island, Neb., July 3, 1880; s. Samuel N. and Rosa (Stein) W.; student Lawrence Scientific Sch., Harvard, 1897-99; M.D., Harvard, 1903; m. Anna F. Wellington, 1914; children—William, John Gray, Edmund (dec.). Shattuck prof. emeritus pathol. anatomy, Harvard U. Med. Sch. since 1947; pathologist emeritus to Peter Bent Brigham, Children's, Infants' and Boston Lying-In hospitals, also Free Hosp. for Women, since 1947; dir. Div. Nutritional Research of The Children's Hosp. since 1947; cons. AEC Div. Biology and Medicine, Armed

Forces Institute of Pathology, Boston Lying-In Hosp., Free Hosp. for Women. Dir. League Red Cross Socs. Research Commn. on Typhus Fever to Poland, 1920. Recipient of the Howard Taylor Ricketts Award, 1950. Fellow American Academy of Arts and Sciences, Royal Society of Tropical Medicine and Hygiene; member Association of American Physicians, Society for Exptl. Pathology (ex-pres.), Am. Assn. Pathologists and Bacteriologists, Am. Assn. for Cancer Research (ex-pres.), Soc. Exptl. Biology and Medicine, National Academy of Sciences; American Academy of Tropical Medicine; corresponding mem. Société de Pathologie Exotique. Comdr. 3d class Order of Polonia Restituta. Hon. mem. Harvey Soc., Alpha Omega Alpha, Sigma Xi. Clubs: St. Botolph, Harvard, Harvard Travelers; Country (Brookline); Millwood Hunt. Author of medical papers, and monographs on Rocky Mountain spotted fever and typhus fever; Pathology of the Deficiency States. Home: Sudbury, Mass. Office: 300 Longwood Av., Boston 15. Died Mar. 19, 1954.

WOLCOTT, ROBERT HENRY, zoölogist; b. Alton, Ill., Oct. 11, 1868; s. Robert N. and Agnes (Swain) W.; B.L., U. of Mich.. 1890, B.S., 1892, M.D., 1893; M.A., U. of Neb., 1895; m. Clara Buckstaff, June 2, 1897; children—Robert Allen, Emily Agnes. Asst. in zoölogy, 1894-95, instr., 1895-98, adj. prof., 1898-1902, asst. prof., 1902-03, asso. prof., 1903-05, prof. anatomy, 1905-09, head prof. zoölogy, 1909—, acting dean Coll. Medicine, 1909-13, jr. dean, 1913-15, U. of Neb. On Mich. Fish Commn. biol. survey of waters of the state, 1893-94; engaged in faunal work in Neb. Fellow A.A.A.S. Contbr. to scientific jours. on ornithology, entomology, fresh water biology, fauna of Neb., and especially on Am. water-mites. Home: Lincoln, Neb. Died Jan. 23, 1934.

WOLD, PETER IRVING, (wold), prof. physics; b. South Dakota, Nov. 27, 1881; s. Ivor Peterson and Gurine (Gimse) W.; B.S., U. of Ore., 1901, E.E., 1903; studied George Washington U.; Ph.D., Cornell U., 1915; m. Mary Helen Helff, June 30, 1909; children—Ivor Peterson, Mary Elizabeth, John Schiller. Instr. in physics, U. of Ore., 1900-03; examiner of patents, U.S. Patent Office, Washington, D.C., 1903-05, 1908-10; instr. in physics, Cornell U., 1905-08; adviser on patent matters, U.S. Signal Corps, 1910; prof. physics, Am. Indemnity Coll., Peking, China, 1911-14; Andrew D. White fellow in physics, Cornell U., 1914-15; physicist and asst. to chief engr., Western Electric Co., New York, 1915-20; prof. physics and head of dept., Union Coll., Schenectady, N.Y., since 1920, chmn. div. of science, same, since 1940; sometime consultant Gen. Electric Co. Research Lab.; visiting prof. of science (on leave of absence) in China for China Med. Bd. of Rockefeller Foundation, 1923-24; dir. Civil Aeronautics Administration at Union College, 1939-40; physicist on special research (on leave of absence) U.S. Navy at Pearl Harbor, Honolulu, 1940-41; Navy liaison office, Rudiatim Lab., Cambridge, Mass., 1943. Former mem. exec. com. of Div. Physical Sciences of Nat. Research Council; pres. Schenectady Council of Boy Scouts of America, 1931-35, mem. Nat. Council since 1938; pres. N.Y. State Sect. of Am. Physical Soc., 1938-40. Fellow Am. Physical Soc.; mem. A.A.A.S., Optical Soc. of America, Am. Assn. of Physics Teachers, Sigma Xi, Phi Beta Kappa, Eta Kappa Nu, Gamma Alpha, Rotary Club. Elder Presbyn. Ch. Inventor in elec. field. Lecturer on Chinese life, edn. and history. Author: Kimball-Wold College Physics. Contbr. on scientific subjects. Navy liaison office, Rudiatim Laboratory, Cambridge, Mass. Address: Union College, Schenectady, N.Y. Died June 17, 1945.

WOLF, AUGUST STEPHEN, chemist Equitable Assurance Soc. since April 1, 1900; b. New York, April 2, 1869; s. Stephen and Marguerita W.; ed'n at Middletown, N.Y.; grad. New York Coll. of Pharmacy, Ph. G., 1889; m. Aug. 2, 1894, Henrietta Taylor, of Woodstock, Vt. Passed exam. in med. chemistry and toxicology, Bellevue Hosp. Med. Coll.; expert in urinary analysis. Mem. A.A.A.S., Soc. Chem. Industry. Residence: 540 W. 112th St. Office: 120 Broadway, New York NY

WOLF, CHARLES GEORGE LEWIS, chemist; b. London, Eng., Nov. 6, 1872; s. Joseph and Isobel (Davis) W.; A.B., Manitoba College, Can., 1890; C.M., M.D., McGill Univ., Montreal, 1894; studied chemistry at Cambridge and Wirzburg univs. and King's Coll., London, 1896-9; unmarried. Asst. prof. chemistry, Cornell Univ. Med. Coll., New York, since 1900. Author: Elements of Stereo-Chemistry (translation Hantzch's Stereochemie), 1901; Physiological Chemistry, 1902. Contbr. papers on chemical and med. subjects to jours. and chemical soc. transactions. Home: 128 Lexington Av., New York NY

WOLF, ROBERT BUNSEN, mech. engr.; b. Newark, Del., May 1, 1877; s. Theodore R. and Rose (Kohler) W.; B. Elec. Engring., Delaware Coll. (now U. of Del.), 1896, M.E., 1916; m. Harriette Couch, Sept. 18, 1901; children—Robert Bunsen, Theodore R., Ann, Margaret (Mrs. Frederick T. Wolverton). Employed in pulp and paper mills in N.Y. and N.E., 1896-99; in constrn. and maintenance dept. Internat. Paper Co.; later, supt. Piercefield Sulphite Pulp Mill; became asst. chief engr. Union Bag and Paper Co., 1900; designer and supervisor constrn., later becoming mill supt., Fenimore Sulphite Mill; mgr. Burgess Sulphite Fibre Co., Berlin, N.H., 1906-17; mgr. Spanish River Pulp and Paper Mills, Ltd., Sault Ste. Marie, Ont., 1917-18; organized R. B. Wolf Co., specializing in design, constrn. and operation of pulp and paper mills, 1919; pres. Pulp Bleaching Corp., N.Y.C., 1923; mgr. pulp div. Weyerhauser Timber Co., Longview, Washington, 1931-47; now indsl. cons. Served as staff asst. to v.p. U.S. Emergency Fleet Corp. 1918. Recipient Frederick W. Taylor Key, Soc. Advancement Management, 1946. Fellow Am. Soc. M.E.; mem. Tech. Assn. Pulp and Paper Industry (gold medalist 1942), Canadian Tech. Sect. Pulp and Paper Industry, Am. Pulp and Paper Mills Supts. Assn., A.A.A.S., U.S. Pulp Producers Assn. (dir.), Pacific Coast Assn. Pulp and Paper Mfrs. (vice pres.), Sigma Phi Epsilon, Tau Beta Pi. Mem. Engineers Club (N.Y.C.). Author of numerous tech. articles pub. in trade and profl. jours. Received patents covering method and apparatus for processes used in pulp and paper industry. Home: 84 Weed St., New Canaan, Conn. Died Nov. 10, 1954.

WOLFE, JAMES JACOB, biologist; b. Sandy Run, S.C., Sept. 14, 1875; s. John Archie and Frederica A. (Geiger) W.; A.B., Wofford Coll., Spartanburg, S.C., 1896; student U. of Chicago, 1900-02; Ph.D., Harvard, 1904; m. Cornelia Wilhelmina Lehrmann, June 28, 1904. Prin. schs., Fork, S.C., 1896-98, Marion, 1898-1900; prof. biology, Trinity Coll., Durham, N.C., 1904—; instr. Marine Biol. Lab., Woods Hole, Mass., summers, 1903-06; investigator Marine Biol. Lab., Beaufort, N.C., summers, 1910—. Trustee Watts Hosp., Durham. Democrat. Methodist. Died June 1920.

WOLFE, THOMAS KENNERLY, agronomist; b. Elkton, Va., July 14, 1892; s. Joseph Henry and Elizabeth (Coffman) W.; B.S., Va. Poly. Inst., Blacksburg, 1914, M.S., 1915; Ph.D., Cornell U., 1921; m. Helen Hughes, June 27, 1923. Asst. in agronomy, Va. Poly. Inst., 1914-15, instr. in agronomy, 1915-17, asso. prof. agronomy, 1917-23, prof., 1923-27; also asst. agronomist Va. Agrl. Expt. Sta., 1915-17, asso. agronomist, 1917-23, agronomist, 1923-27; editor Southern Planter, 1927-33; mgr. fertilizer service, later distribution service, Southern States Coop., since 1934. Asst. comdt. Va. Poly. Inst., 1914-16. Mem. Phi Kappa Phi, Sigma Xi. Democrat. Author: (with T. B. Hutcheson) The Production of Field Crops, 1924, rev. 1937, 48, 53. Contbr. bulls. Va. Expt. Sta. Discoverer of superiority of unhulled sweet clover seed over scarified seed. Home: Richmond VA Died 1972.

WOLFEL, PAUL LUDWIG, civil engr.; b. Dresden, Germany, Apr. 19, 1862; s. Frederick E. and Emma W.; ed. Polytechnikum, Dresden, 1880-85; asst. prof. Polytecknikum, Prague, 1885-87; came to U.S., 1888; m. 1893, Emma Brecht, Phila. Became asst. engr., B. & C. dept., Pencoyd Iron Works, June, 1888; asst. chief engr., same, 1891; engr. railroad dept., Am. Bridge Co., May, 1900; div. engr., eastern div., Am. Bridge Co., Oct., 1900; chief engr., Am. Bridge Co., May, 1901. Address: American Bridge Co., 15th and Chestnut Sts., Philadelphia.

WOLFF, FRANK ALFRED, physicist; b. Baltimore, Md., Apr. 8, 1871; s. Frank Andrew and Theresa (Haupt) W.; A.B., Johns Hopkins, 1890, Ph.D., 1893, fellow in physics and chemistry, 1892-93; studied U. of Leipzig, 1894; m. Lillian Marie Jones, Jan. 28, 1897; children—Frances H., Lyman H. Expert physicist Bur. of Soils, U.S. Dept. of Agr., 1894-96; prof. physics and elec. engring., Columbia (now George Washington) U., 1894-1908; in office Standard Weights and Measures, 1897-1901; asso. physicist, Bur. of Standards, 1901-17, physicist, 1917-24, prin. physicist, 1928, now prin. telephone engr.; detailed to Federal Communications Commn., 1935-37. Engaged since establishment of bureau in development of improved apparatus and methods of measurement, and in research on the internat. standards of resistance and electromotive force, and on the development of standards of service for telephone utilities. Especially active in economics and its relation to the stabilization of the purchasing power of the dollar; the analysis of governmental expenditures and revenues; the principles underlying public utility regulation and valuation, standardization, and municipal advancement; retired Apr. 1941. Chief dept. social economy, Panama P.I. Expn., 1913-14. Mem. Am. Inst. E.E. Home: 2957 Tilden, Washington DC*

WOLFF, HAROLD G., physician; b. New York City, May 26, 1898; s. Louis and Emma (Recknagel) W.; B.S., City Coll. of New York, 1918; M.D., Harvard, 1923, M.A., 1928; m. Isabel Bishop, August, 1934; one son, Remsen N. Resident, neurol. service, Bellevue Hosp., 1923-24; med. interne, Roosevelt Hosp., New York, 1924-26; asst. attending physician, Harvard Service, Boston City Hosp., 1926-28; asst., dept. of Neuropathology, Harvard Med. Sch., 1926-28; Nat. Reserach Council Fellow in neuropharmacology, with Otto Loewi, Graz, Austria, 1928-29; asst. dept. of psychiatry, Johns Hopkins Hosp., 1929-31; fgn. study, clinics and travel, 1931-32; Anne Parrish Titzel prof. medicine, Cornell Univ. Med. Coll.; attending physician N.Y. Hosp.; cons. neurologist, Westchester Div., White Plains; asso. attending psychiatrist, Payne Whitney psychiatric clinic, New York Hosp.; consultant in neurology, Vets. Adminstrn., U.S. Pub. Health Service, Nat. Research Council; mem. nat. adv. com. Vets. Adminstrn., Department of Army. Fellow Am. Coll. Physicians, A.A.A.S., A.M.A.; mem. Am. Physiol. Soc., Am. Psychiatric Assn., Am. Soc. for Clin. Investigation, Assn. for Research in Nervous and Mental Diseases, Harvey Soc., American (president), New York neurological associations, Association American Physicians, Harvey Cushing Society, Soc. Research Psychosomatic Medicine, Internat. League against Epilepsy, N.Y. Acad. of Sciences, Soc. for Exptl. Biology and Medicine, Am. Soc. for Pharmacology and Exptl. Therapeutics, Soc. for Investigation of Human Ecology (pres.), Sigma Xi, Alpha Omega Alpha. Author: Pain, 1943, 47, 58, Human Gastric Function, 1943, 1947; The Nose, An Experimental Study, etc., 1949; Headache and other Head Pain, 1948; Pain Sensations and Reactions, 1952; The Human Colon, 1952; Stress and Disease, 1953; Headache, 1953; Social Science in Medicine, 1954; Life Stress and Essential Hypertension, 1955. Editor: Life Stress and Bodily Disease, 1950; Investigations in Human Ecology, 1956, 57, 58, 59. Editor-in-chief A.M.A. Archives of Neurology; editor: Jour. Psychosomatic Research, Psychosomatic Medicine. Contbr. tech. articles and papers to jours. Home: 355 W. 246th St., Riverdale N.Y.C. 10471. Office: 525 E. 68th St., N.Y.C. 21. Died Feb. 21, 1962; buried Elmwood Cemetery, New Brunswick, N.J.

WOLFF, JOHN ELIOT, geologist; b. Montreal, Can., Nov. 21, 1857; s. Philippe and Hannah (Crocker) W.; A.B., Harvard, 1879, A.M., Ph.D., 1889; postgrad. student, Heidelberg, 1884-85; m. Ethel P. Loder, Oct. 20, 1887. Asst. geologist U.S. Geol. Survey, 1885-93; asst. in geology, 1881-82, instr., 1887-92, asst. prof. petrography, 1892-95, prof. petrography and mineralogy, and curator Mineral Mus., 1895-1923, emeritus, 1923, Harvard. Mem. Geol. Soc. America, Am. Acad. Arts and Sciences. Home: Pasadena, Calif. Died Aug. 9, 1940.

WOLFROM, MELVILLE L(AWRENCE), chemist; born Bellevue, O., Apr. 2, 1900; s. Frederick and Maria Louisa (Sutter) W.; A.B., Ohio State U., 1924; M.Sc., Northwestern, 1925, Ph.D., 1927; Guggenheim fellow, U. of Zurich, 1939; m. Agnes Louise Thompson, June 1, 1926; children—Frederick L., (dec.), Eva M., (Mrs. David Frank), Betty J. (Mrs. Chalmers G. Hixson, Jr.), Anne M. (Mrs. Wilson Fleming, Jr.), Carl T. Engaged as development chemist with National Carbon Company, Fremont, O., 1917-18; U.S. Gypsum Co., Gypsum, O. and Chicago, summers 1921-24; asst. instr. chemistry Northwestern, 1924-27; Nat. Research Council fellow in chemistry Nat. Bur. Standards, Rockefeller Inst. for Med. Research, Ohio State U., 1927-29, instr. in chemistry, 1929-30, asst. prof., 1930-36, asso prof., 1936-40, prof., 1940-69, head div. organic chemistry, 1948-60, research prof., 1960-65, Regents' prof., 1965-69. An ofcl. investigator Nat. Def. Research Com., 1940-45; chmn. symposium Internat. Union Biochemistry, Vienna, Austria, 1958. Served S.A.T.C., 1918. Recipient citation Government of Austria, 1959; Austin M. Patterson award for chem. documentation Dayton chpt. Am. Chem. Soc., 1967; Kenneth A. Spencer award Kansas City sect. Am. Chem. Soc., 1967; Wolfrom meml. issue Jour. Carbohydrate Research pub. in his honor, 1970. Mem. A.A.A.S., Am. Chem. Soc. (chmn. cellulose div. 1940, sugar div. 1948, chmn. carbohydrate romenclature com. carbohydrate div.), Am. Assn. Cereal Chemists, Nat. Acad. Scis., Am. Acad. Arts and Scis., Am. Soc. Biol. Chemists, Chem. Soc. (London), N.Y. Acad. Science, Ohio Acad. Sci., Technical Association Pulp and Paper Industry, Phi Beta Kappa, Sigma Xi, Phi Lambda Upsilon, Pi Mu Epsilon, Alpha Chi Sigma. Co-editor: Advances in Carbohydrate Chemistry, 1945-49, 52-69; editor Methods in Carbohydrate Chemistry; editor carbohydrates sect. Chem. Abstracts 1959-69; adv. bd. Chem. Abstracts Service, 1964-69. Author articles on organic chemistry of carbohydrates and natural products in chem. jours. Home: Columbus OH Died June 20, 1969; buried Bellevue OH

WOLL, FRITZ WILHELM, agrl. chemist; b. Bergen, Norway, May 23, 1865; s. Rev. Carsten L. and Mathilde Helen (Krum) W.; prep. edn. Realgymnasium, Christiania, Norway; B.S., Royal Frederik's U., Christiania, Norway, 1882, Ph.B., 1883; M.S., U. of Wis., 1886, Ph.D., 1904; m. Helene Walloe, May 16, 1891. Second asst. chemist, 1887, asst. chemist, 1890, chemist, 1897-1913, Wis. Agrl. Expt. Sta.; asst. prof., 1893-1904, asso. prof., 1904-06, prof. agrl. chemistry, 1906-13, U. of Wis.; prof. animal nutrition, U. of Calif., 1913—. Author: Agricultural Calendar, 1895; Dairy Calendar, 1895; A Book on Silage, 1895, 1900; A Handbook for Farmers and Dairymen, 1897, 1914; Testing Milk and Its Products (with Prof. E. H. Farrington), 1897, 1918; Productive Feeding of Farm Animals, 1915, 1916; Feed Manual and Note Book, 1917. Translator: Modern Dairy Practice (from Swedish of G. Grotenfelt), 1894, 1905. Extensive contbr. to tech. publs. and to agrl. and dairy papers. Fellow A.A.A.S.; mem. Wis. Acad. Sciences, Arts and Letters, Assn. Official Agrl. Chemists (pres. 1910-11). Mem. internat. Jury, Panama P.I. Expn., 1915. Home: Berkeley, Calif. Deceased.

WOOD, ARTHUR JULIUS, mech. engr.; b. Newark, N.J., Sept. 3, 1874; s. De Volson and Frances (Hartson) W.; grad. Steven's Sch., Hoboken, N.J., 1892; M.E., Stevens Inst. Tech., 1896; M.S., Pa. State Coll., 1916; m. Helen M. Kerr, July 26, 1904; 1 son, Reginald De Volson. Asso. editor Railroad Gazette, 1896-1900; instr. in mech. engring., Worcester Poly. Inst., 1900-02; prof. mech. and elec. engring., Del. Coll., 1902-04; with Pa. State Coll., 1904—; organizer, 1912, and in charge of courses in ry. mech. engring., same coll., also prof. mech. engring., 1918—, in charge Engring. Expt. Sta., 1918-22, head of dept., 1922—, adviser, 1922—; cons. engr. in refrigeration and heat engines. Fellow A.A.A.S.; mem. Am. Soc. Refrigerating Engrs. (v.p. 1926-28; pres. 1928-29). Republican. Presbyn. Author: Principles of Locomotive Operation, 1915, 25. Contbr. to Mechanical Engring.; Refrigerating Engring., Ry. Mech. Engr. Home: State College, Pa. Died Apr. 18, 1931.

WOOD, BERNARD AUGUSTINE, civil engr.; b. Tuscaloosa, Ala., Feb. 11, 1867; s. Sterling Alexander Martin and Lelia (Leftwich) W.; B.E., U. of Ala., 1887 (hon. C.E., 1917); m. Maebelle McEachin, of Tuscaloosa, Nov. 28, 1898 (now dec.); 1 son, Wm. W.; m. 2d, Lilla McCarley, of Okalona, Miss., Apr. 19, 1905 (now dec.); children—Bernard A., Mary Elizabeth; m. 3d, Katharine Le Noir Cox, of Columbus, Mississippi, February 1, 1927. Resident engineer, 1888, assistant engineer, 1889-90, L.N. R.R.; assistant engineer Internat. Boundary Survey, U.S. and Mexico, 1891-93, Nicaragua Canal Bd., 1895; mining engr., Colo., 1896; asst. and resident engr., 1897-1909, chief engr. since 1910, Mobile & Ohio R.R. Mem. Am. Ry. Engring. Assn., Kappa Alpha. Democrat. Catholic. Home: 4525 Lindell Blvd. Office: Fullerton Bldg., St. Louis, Mo. *

WOOD, CASEY ALBERT, ophthalmologist; b. of Am. parents, Wellington, Ont., Can., Nov. 21, 1856; s. Orrin Cottier and Rosa Sophia (Leggo) W.; ed. pvt. English and French schs.; grad. Ottawa (Can.) Collegiate Inst., 1874; C.M., M.D., Univ. Bishop's Coll., 1877, D.C.L., 1903; M.D., McGill U. 1906, LL.D., 1921; M.C.P.S., Ont., 1878; student N.Y. Eye and Ear Infirmary and Post-Grad. Med. Sch., 1886, also many European hosps., 1886-1914; m. Emma Shearer, Oct. 28, 1886. Clin. asst. Royal London Ophthal. Hosp. (Moorfields), 1888-89; asst. Wm. Lang Eye dept., Middlesex Hosp., London, 1889; house surgeon Central London Ophthal. Hosp., Gray's Inn Rd., 1889; asst. surgeon West London Ophthal. Hosp., 1889; went to Chicago, 1900; attending ophthal. surgeon Alexian Bros., Passavant Memorial and St. Luke's hosps. (later consultant); cons. surgeon (eye) Cook County and St. Anthony hosps.; prof. chemistry and pathology, Univ. Bishop's Coll., 1878-85; prof. ophthalmology, Chicago Post-Grad. Med. Sch., 1890-97; prof. clin. ophthalmology, Coll. Physicians and Surgeons, Chicago, 1898-1906; head prof. ophthalmology, Northwestern U., 1906-08, U. of Ill., 1909-13 (now emeritus). Hon. collaborator on birds, Smithsonian Instn., 1927; hon. lecturer on ornithology, Stanford U., 1928; research asso. Calif. Inst. Technology, 1932; retired from practice, 1917. Active service U.S. Army, as 1st lt., Nov. 1916-Feb. 1917, and later as maj.; head of exam. unit, at Chicago, of candidates for aviation and U.S. Signal Corps; in charge eye dept., Camp Sherman, O., Sept.-Dec. 1917; lt. col. on staff of surgeon gen., Washington, D.C., Dec. 1917-June 1919; now col. Med. Res. Corps, U.S. Army. Fellow Am. Acad. Medicine (pres. 1907), A.A.A.S., Mitglied d. ophthal. Gesellschaft (Germany), Am. Coll. Surgeons (foundation fellow), Acad. Medicine and of Medico-legal Soc. (Chicago), Am. Med. Assn. (chmn. sect. of ophthalmology 1889), Am. Acad. of Othalmology and Otology (pres. 1905-06), Am. Geog. Soc., Zoöl. Soc. of London (del. to Centenary); mem. Assn. Military Surgeons, Calif. Acad. Science, Am., British and Royal Austral. Ornithol. unions; hon. mem. Am. Numismatic Soc. (New York), N.Y. Charaka Club, Peregrine Club (Phila.); ex-pres. Chicago Ophthal. Soc. Editor in chief Annals of Ophthalmology, 1894-1901; chief editor Ophthal. Record, 1902-08; editorial staff Anales de Oftalmologia (Mexico), Med. Standard (Chicago) and Annals of Med. History (New York); editor Am. Journal of Ophthalmology, 1908-14; editor eye sect. Practical Med. Series, 1908-15; contbr. to various "systems" and textbooks, also author of many mag. articles on medical and natural history, including numerous transls. from German, French, Italian, Spanish, Latin and Arabic treatises. Traveled 15 yrs. in Europe, 1919-34, also in the Far East (3 yrs. in India and Ceylon), Oceania, S. America (with Dr. Wm. Beebe, 2 winters in British Guiana), and in West Indies for zoölogic and medico. hist.-research. Founder of Wood gold medal and of several spl. libraries at McGill Univ. Clubs: University (Chicago); Cosmos (Washington, D.C.); Authors (London); Athenaeum (Pasadena, California). Author: Lessons in Diagnosis and Treatment of Eye Diseases, 1895; Toxic Amblyopias, 1896; Commoner Diseases of the Eye (3d edit., 1907, with T. A. Woodruff); Primary Sarcoma of the Iris (with Brown Pusey), 1908; A System of Ophthalmic Therapeutics, 1909; A System of Ophthalmic Operations, 2 vols., 1911; American Encyclopedia of Ophthalmology, 17 vols., 1908-12; Fundus Oculi of Birds, 1917; A Physician's Anthology (with Fielding Garrison), 1920; Birds of Fiji (with Alexander Wetmore), 1927-28; Introduction to the Study of Vertebrate Zoölogy (with annotated catalogue), 1931. Transl. (with notes) Benevenutus Grassus, De Oculis (A.D., 1474), 1930; transl. Tadhkirat, Arabic Note-Book of an Oculist (1000 A.D.), 1930; annotated transl. Notebook of a Tenth Century Oculist, 1936; transl. (with notes) of a Twelfth Century Codex, the De Arte Venandi cum Avibus by Emperor Frederic II (with Marjorie Fyfe), 1940. Home: Caltec, 551 S. Hill Av., Pasadena, Calif. Address: Hotel del Coronado, Coronado, Calif. Died Jan. 26. 1942.

WOOD, CHARLES P., indsl. engr.; b. Warrenton, Va., Mar. 11, 1883; s. Daniel Pollard and Sallie (Parkinson) W.; M.E. in E.E., Cornell U., 1904; m. Frances Laura Fay, Jan. 8, 1923. Asst. supt., Buckeye Cotton Oil Co., Macon, Ga., 1904-08; Gibbs Gas Engring. Co., Atlanta, Ga., Standard Gas Power Co., N.Y., 1908-16; Empire Floor and Wall Tile Co., Metuchen, N.J.), 1916-17; trade commr., U.S. Dept. Commerce in France and Belgium, 1919-20; partner, Lockwood Greene Engrs., N.Y.C., from 1920; dir. in charge of party sent to Russia to advise textile industry, 1929; govt. rep., code authority Ry. Car Building, Industry Nat. Recovery Adminstrn., 1934; consultant, Div. Contract Distbn., O.P.M., 1941; National Resources Planning Bd., 1941-43. Founder of Levere Memorial Found. Unit chmn. Greater New York Fund, 1963. Served as 1st lieutenant, Engr., O.R.C., 1917, advanced to lt. colonel, C.W.S., 1918, World War I. Consultant Control Division, A.S.F. and Q.m. Gen. offices, 1942-45, World War II. Awarded Croix de Guerre, gold star. Licensed professional engineer, N.Y., Conn., Pa., Va. Mem. Am. Inst. Elec. Engrs. (life), American Institute of Consulting Engineers, Society of Colonial Wars, Vet. Corps Artillery (member council of administration), Am. Indsl. Development Council (hon. life) (chmn. 1935-36; mem. advisory bd.), Am. Soc. Military Engrs., Am. Ordnance Assn., Cornell Soc. Engrs., Nat. Bur. Engring. Registration, S.A.R., N.Y. Southern Soc., Virginians (governor 1951-52, honorary member 1963), Wilderness Society, Society American Wars, Society War of 1812, Mil Order Foreign Wars, World Wars, Am. Legion, Am. Defense Soc., Ypres League, Order of Lafayette, American Order of the French Croix de Guerre, Sigma Alpha Epsilon (mem. nat. bd. trustees). Clubs: University, Engineers, Cornell (N.Y.C.); Merion (Phila.); Army and Navy (Washington). Author: Industrial Machinery in France and Belgium; Factors Controlling Location of Various Types of Industry. Contbr. papers on indsl. and econ. subjects to profl. jours. Baptist. Past cons. editor Textile World. Contbr. article on Factory Construction and Planning Ency. Britannica, 1952. Made indsl. surveys of S.A.L. Ry., States of Okla., Me., Cities of Flint, Troy, Dallas, Okla. City, Okmulgee, Wilkes-barre, Decatur, Wilmington, Huntington, Gloucester, Hannibal (Mo.); report for Mo. State Dept. Resources and Development; report on cotton textile mfg. in Cal.; indsl. surveys Alexandria, Va., Wichita, Kan. Home: New York City NY Deceased.

WOOD, DE VOLSON, educator, inventor; b. Smyrna, N.Y., June 1, 1832; s. Julius and Amanda (Billings) W.; grad. Rensselaer Poly. Inst., Troy, N.Y., 1857; m. Cordera E. Crane, 1859; m. 2d, Frances Hartson, 1868; 7 children. Prof. civil engring. U. Mich., 1857-72; prof. mathematics and mechanics Stevens Inst., Hoboken, N.J., 1872-85, prof. engring., 1885-97; invented an air compressor, steam rock drill; mem. Am. Soc. C.E., Soc. Mech. Engrs., A.A.A.S. Died Hoboken, June 27, 1897.

WOOD, EDWARD STICKNEY, prof. chemistry, Harvard Med. School, 1876—; b. Cambridge, Mass., April 28, 1846; s. Alfred and Laura (Stickney) W.; grad. Harvard, 1867, M.D., 1871, A.M., 1872; studied physiol. and med. chemistry, Berlin and Vienna, 1872; m. Elizabeth Richardson, Dec. 24, 1883. Asst. prof. chemistry, Harvard Med. School, 1871-76, prof., 1876—; mem. med. commn. on Boston's Water Supply, 1874; mem. Com. of Revision and Publication, U.S. Pharmacopoeia, 1880; chemist Mass. Gen. Hosp., 1873—. Translator: Neubauer & Vogel's Analysis of Urine, 1879. Revised (with Dr. R. Amory) Vol. II, On Poisons, Wharton & Stillé's Medical Jurisprudence, 1884. Wrote articles: Examination of Blood and Other Stains, and Examination of Hair, in Wilthaus & Becker's Medical Jurisprudence, 1894; Arsenic as a Domestic Poison (Mass. Bd. Health, etc.), 1885; Report on Sanitary Qualities of the Sudbury, Mystic, Shawshine and Charles River Waters (part author), 1874. Home: Pocasset, Mass. Died 1905.

WOOD, ERIC FISHER, architect, engr., army officer; b. N.Y. City, Jan. 4, 1889; s. William B. (M.D.) and Frances (Fisher) W.; Ph.B., Sheffield Scientific Sch. (Yale), 1910; A.B., Yale, 1910; studied Columbia U. Sch. of Architecture, and École des Beaux Arts Paris; m. Vera de Ropp, Apr. 20, 1918; children—Eric Fisher (killed in action), Eleanor Morton (Mrs. Stanley M. Dye), Peter de Ropp, Alec Laughlin. Prop. Eric Fisher Wood & Co., architects and indsl. engrs.; with H. Hornbostel, won competition and selection as architects for Warren G. Harding Memorial at Marion, O. Attaché at the American Embassy, Paris, France, under Ambassador Herrick, 1914; officer Am. Ambulance Corps in France, 1915; maj. British Army, 1917, wounded at Battle of Arras; maj. U.S.N.A., Aug. 14, 1917, and asst. chief of staff, 83d Div.; lt. col. G.S. asst. chief of staff, 88th Div.; wounded in Meuse-Argonne; col. 107th U.S. Field Artillery, 1923; brig. gen., U.S. Army, Dec. 1940; on active duty, 1941-45; major general, 1949. Decorated Legion of Merit, Purple Heart with oak leaf; Knight-Officer of Polonia Restituta and White Lion (Bohemia); Croix de Guerre, 1918 and 1945, Comdr. Legion of Honor (France). V.p. National Security League, 1915-16; a founder Am. Legion, 1919, and elected its 1st nat. adj. past national, comdr.; mem. Beaux Arts Inst. Design, A.I.A. Chairman Pennsylvania Republican State Executive Committee, 1926-28; sec. Pa. Delegation to Republican National Convention, 1928. Clubs: Duquesne (Pittsburgh). Author: Note Book of an Attaché, 1915; The Writing on the Wall, 1916; The Note Book of an Intelligence Officer, 1918; Biography of Leonard Wood, 1920; Basic Manual Field Artillery, 1934; Troop Leading and Staff Procedure, 1941; also articles, Century Magazine. The Outlook, Saturday Evening Post. Home: R.D. 1, Bedford, Pa. Died Oct. 4, 1962; buried Arlington Nat. Cemetery, Washington.

WOOD, FRANCIS CARTER, pathologist; b. Columbus, O., Dec. 30, 1869; s. Henry Raynor and Annie (Carter) W.; B.S., Ohio State U., 1891; M.D., Coll. Physicians and Surgeons (Columbia), 1894; studied at Berlin, Vienna, 1896; B.S. (hon.), Tufts, 1925, Ohio State U., 1931; m. Edith Warren Sterling, 1901; children—Eleanor Carter, Edith Sterling, Mary Lydia, Francis Carter, Winifred Warren. Intern, 1894-96, pathologist, 1897—, attending physician St. Luke's Hosp., N.Y.C., 1909-38, cons. physician 1938—; dir. pathol. lab., 1910—, dir. radiotherapeutic dept., 1921—; asst. in clin. pathology, Coll. Physicians and Surgeons, Columbia, 1896-98, instr., 1898-1904, adj. prof., 1904-06, prof., dir. dept. clin. pathology, 1906-12; prof., dir. Inst. Cancer Research (founded by George Crocker), Columbia, 1912-40, now emeritus; v.p. Internat. Union Against Cancer, 1935—. Mem. Am. Assn. Pathologists and Bacteriologists, Soc. Exptl. Biology and Medicine, N.Y. Pathol. Soc., A.M.A., Am. Cancer Soc., Am. Assn. Cancer Research, Assn. Am. Physicians, Radiol. Soc. N.A., Beta Theta Pi, Sigma Xi, Phi Beta Kappa, Radiol. Soc. of the Scandinavian Countries (hon.). Mem. Legion of Honor (France); Begian Order of the Crown. Club: Century. Republican. Episcopalian. Author: Clinical Diagnosis, 1899; Chemical and Microscopical Diagnosis, 1905; Delafield and Prudden's Text-Book of Pathology, 16th edit., 1935; also numerous med. papers. Editor Am. Jour. of Cancer, 1930-41. Home: 110 Lydecker St., Englewood, N.J. Died Jan. 5, 1951; buried Brookside Cemetery, Englewood, N.J.

WOOD, FREDERICK WILLIAM, consulting engr.; b. Lowell, Mass., Mar. 16, 1857; s. William and Elizabeth French (Kidder) W.; B.S., Mass. Inst. Tech., 1877; m. Caroline Peabody Smith, Jan. 24, 1884; children—Frederick Brayton, Dorothy, Elizabeth (Mrs. Clarke Farwell Freeman), Helen, Caroline (Mrs. Carl Billings Willard), Richard Minot. Began with Pa. Steel Co. at Baldwin (now Steelton), Pa., 1877, gen. supt., 1884-89, gen. mgr., 1889-91, 2d v.p., 1893; pres. Md. Steel Co., 1891-1916; in charge of same after purchase by Bethlehem Steel Co., 1916-18; v.p. Am. Internat. Shipbuilding Corp., 1918-21; now chmn. bd. Eastern Rolling Mill Co.; dir. Consol. Gas, Electric Light & Power Co. of Baltimore, Savings Bank of Baltimore. Mem. Claims Commn. of U.S. Shipping Bd., Emergency Fleet Corp., 1921-23; term mem. of Corp. Mass. Inst. Tech., 1906-11; trustee Johns Hopkins U.; dir. Md. Inst. Mem. Am. Inst. Mining and Metall. Engrs., Am. Soc. M.E., Am. Soc. Naval Architects and Marine Engrs., Am. Iron and Steel Inst., A.A.A.S. Republican. Unitarian. Clubs: Maryland, Merchants (Baltimore); Engineers' (New York). Home: 2429 Keyworth Av., Baltimore, Md. Died Dec. 23, 1943.

WOOD, HENRY A(LEXANDER) WISE, inventor, writer; b. New York, Mar. 1, 1866; s. Fernando and Alice F. (Mills) W.; father mayor of New York 3 terms, mem. Congress 20 yrs.; ed. Media (Pa.) Acad.; m. Elizabeth Ogden Brower, 1891. Inventor the Autoplate, a machine for making printing plates for newspapers theretofore made by hand, for which was awarded in 1908 the Elliott Cresson gold medal by the Franklin Inst.; also other mechanisms for the printing art; announced, 1916, series of inventions doubling speed of newspaper printing press; announced, 1932, mechanism for replenishing paperrolls of newspaper presses at full speed. Pres. Wood Newspaper Machinery Corp. Founder Flying Mag. and editor, 1911-19. Mem. United States Naval Cons. Bd., 1915; chmn. of Conference Com. on Nat. Preparedness. First Pres. Am. Soc. Aeronautic Engrs.; v.p. Aero Club America, 1913-19; a founder, 1919, League for Preservation Am. Independence. Author: Fancies (verse), 1903; Book of Symbols, 1904; Money Hunger, 1908. Home: New York, N.Y. Died Apr. 9, 1939.

WOOD, HORATIO CHARLES, JR., physician, pharmacologist; b. Phila., Pa., Feb. 26, 1874; s. Horatio C. and Eliza H. (Longacre) W.; grad. William Penn Charter Sch., Phila., 1890; student lit. dept. U. of Pa. 2 yrs.; M.D., U. of Pa., 1896; research work, U. of Berne, 1897-98, U. of Turin, 1898; m. Alice L. Lovell, Dec. 19, 1899; children—Horatio C. III, Florence L. Demonstrator in pharmacodynamics, U. of Pa., 1898-1907; asso. prof. pharmacol., 1907-10; prof. pharmacol. and therapeutics, Medico-Chirurg. College, Phila., 1910-16; prof. same, U. of Pa., 1916-42; prof.

pharmacology, Phila. Coll. of Pharmacy and Science, 1921-50. Asst. visiting physician to Phila. General Hosp., 1904-08; mem. Com. on Revision of U.S. Pharmacopoeia, 1910-40; vice-pres. U.S. Pharmacopoeia Convention, 1941. Fellow A.A.A.S.; mem. Am. Soc. Pharmacology, Am. Pharm. Assn. Presbyterian. Editor: Therapeutics, Its Principles and Practice, 11th to 13th edits. (with father), 1899; United States Dispensatory, 20th edit., 1918, 21st edit., 1926, 22d edit., 1937, 23d edit., 1943. Author: A Text Book of Pharmacology, 1912. Home: 319 S. 41st St., Phila. Died Mar. 31, 1958; buried West Laurel Hill Cemetery, Phila.

WOOD, JAMES J., engineer, inventor; b. Kinsale, Ireland, Mar. 25, 1856; s. Paul H. and Elizabeth (Shine) W.; brought to U.S., 1864; grad. Evening High Sch., Brooklyn, N.Y., 1876; grad. as mech. engr. and draftsman, Poly. Inst. of Brooklyn, 1878; m. Nellie B. Scott, Jan. 20, 1916; children—Venie Elizabeth (Mrs. Joseph H. Appel), Alexander Paul, Elia May (Mrs. William S. Savage). Began in employ of Branford (Conn.) Lock Co. at age of 11, and at 16 designed a horizontal steam engine; with Brady Mfg. Co., Brooklyn, 1874-80, becoming supt. and chief engr.; partner Fuller-Wood Co., 1880-85; with Thomson-Houston and Gen. Electric cos. as inventor and cons. engr., 1885—. Inventor of "Wood" system, and "father" of the closed coil, constant current, high tension, self-regulating series arc dynamo; Brayton oil engine, installed in first Holland submarine; built first lamps for Sir Hiram Maxim; built machines for constructing main cables, original Brooklyn Bridge; holder of 240 patents covering elec. and mech. devices, including dynamo for flood lighting, first used on Statue of Liberty. Fellow Am. Inst. Elec. Engrs. Republican. Episcopalian. Home: Fort Wayne, Ind. Died Apr. 20, 1928.

WOOD, JAMES RUSHMORE, surgeon; b. Mamaroneck, L.I., N.Y., Sept. 14, 1816; s. Elkanah and Mary (Rushmore) W.; grad. Vt. Acad. Medicine, Castleton, 1834; m. Emma Rowe, 1853. Instr. anatomy Vt. Acad. Medicine, 1834; practiced medicine, N.Y.C., 1837; a founder Bellevue Hosp., N.Y.C., 1847, mem. bd.; an organizer Bellevue Hosp. Med. Coll., 1856, prof. operative surgery and surg. pathology, 1886, created 1st hosp. ambulance service in U.S., 1869; opened 1st tng. sch. for nurses in U.S. at Bellevue, 1873; pioneer in cure of aneurism by pressure; perfected bisector for rapid operation for vesical calculus; wrote paper "Early History of the Operation of Ligature of the Primitive Carotid Artery"; established one of largest collections of postmortem and pathological material in world; twice pres. N.Y. Path. Soc.; mem. N.Y. Acad. Medicine, N.Y. State, Mass. med. socs., mem. A.M.A., N.Y. Surg. Soc., Med. Jour. Assn. Died N.Y.C., May 4, 1882.

WOOD, JETHRO, inventor; b. Dartmouth, Mass. (or White Creek, N.Y.), Mar. 16, 1774; s. John and Dinah (Hussey or Starbuck) W.; m. Sylvia Howland, Jan. 1, 1793. Owned farm, Poplar Creek, Cayuga County, N.Y., 1800-34; obtained 1st patent for cast-iron plow, 1814; patented the Wood plow, featuring good balance, strength and interchangeable parts, 1819 (design and constrn. principles copied throughout North). Died Scipio, N.Y., Sept. 18, 1834.

WOOD, JOHN, author, cartographer; b. Scotland, 1775. Travelled in Switzerland, 1789; came to N.Y.C., 1800; tutor to Aaron Burr's daughter Theodosia; as pamphleteer supported Burr's polit. activities in such writings as "A Letter to Alexander Addison, Esq. . . . in Answer to His Rise and Progress of Revolution," 1801; after writing attack on Adams' adminstrn., Burr felt it so vicious that he sought to buy out edition, 1802, publication under title "The Suppressed History" led to separation of Burr and Wood; had short assn. with Frankfort (Ky.) Western World, 1806, opened publicity on activities of James Wilkinson and other Spanish agts.; settled in Richmond, Va., circa 1808; contracted with state of Va. to make accurate chart of each county and gen. map of state, 1819, work nearly finished by 1822. Author: A General View of the History of Switzerland, 1799; A Full Statement of the Trial and Acquittal of Aaron Burr, 1807. Died May 15, 1822.

WOOD, MONTRAVILLE (M.), lecturer, inventor; b. Leon, N.Y., Apr. 16, 1860; s. Cornelius S. and Elizabeth W. (Taylor) W.; ed. pub. schs. and Collegiate Inst., Jamestown, N.Y.; m. Carrie Frances Whittemore, Sept. 30, 1885. Chief insp. and mgr., Am. Bell Telephone Co., Jamestown, 1883; elec. engr. Pa. R.R., Erie, Pa., 1884-85; elec. engr. Erie County Light Co., Erie, Pa., 1885-89; dist. engr., Edison Electric Co., Portland, Ore., 1889, 1890; elec. engr. Ansonia Elec. Co., Chicago, 1891-93; with Stanley Elec. Co., Pittsfield, Mass., 1893-95; with Gen. Electric Co., Schenectady, N.Y., until 1906; continued research work in own lab. and lecturing before chautauquas and lyceums. Inventor two-button snap switch (electric) and many other devices. Holder nearly 100 patents many of which are in general use; inventor of the "torpedo with ears." First aerial postmaster apptd. in U.S. Served 18 months in secret service dept., 1917-18. Republican. Mason. Home: Berwyn, Ill. Died Jan. 6, 1923.

WOOD, PAUL MEYER, anesthesiology; b. Frankfort, Ind., June 8, 1894; s. John Anderson and Louise (Meyer) W.; student Notre Dame U., 1912-13; B.S., Columbia, 1917, M.D., 1922; m. Harriet Amelia Muller, Sept. 30, 1924; children—Beatrice Bird, Bruce Muller, Associate, Grenfell Med. Mission, Labrador, 1922; interne Roosevelt Hosp., N.Y. City, 1923-24; in. med. practice as anesthesiologist since 1925; anesthetist Union Hosp., Bronx,; cons. anesthetist for Peekskill (N.Y.), Bergen Pines, Paramus, N.J., Castle Pt. VA; N.Y. Infirmary, Lincoln, St. Vincent's, Misericordia, City, French and Midtown hosps. (N.Y.C.), Horton Meml. Hosp. (Middletown, New York), N.Y. State Reconstruction Hospital (W. Haverstraw, N.Y.) until 1944, Northern Westchester Hosp. (Mt. Kisco, N.Y.); attending anesthetist, Community, Roosevelt hospitals until 1946, N.Y. City; cons. anesthetist, Halloran Veterans' Hospital, Cornwall (N.Y.) Hospital; asst. attending anesthetist, Flower-Fifth Av. until 1956 and Lenox Hill hosps., N.Y. City; asst. clin. prof. N.Y. Med. Coll.; expert consultant to surgeon gen. of Army, 1946; cons. East Orange (New Jersey) V.A. Hospital, lecturer N.Y. Polyclinic Hosp. and Medical School. Recruited ambulance corps Number 10, Columbia U., 1917; served as 1st lt., comdg. sect. 557, U.S. Army Ambulance Service, Italy, 1918-19. Decorated Croce de Guerra (Italy). Awarded cup, Internat. Coll. Anes., 1938; First Distinguished Service Award, Am. Soc. Anes., 1945. Diplomate Am. Bd. Anesthesiology (sec.-treas. 1936-48, pres. 1948). Fellow N.Y. Acad. Med., Am. Soc. Anesthetists (sec.-treas., 1930-43), Am. Coll. Anesthetists, N.Y. Acad. Scis., Internat. Coll. Anesthetists; mem. Acad. Anesthesiology (historian 1959—), New York State Society for Medical Research, Sons Ind., Theta Xi, Phi Chi, mem., hon. mem. or hon. officer numerous profl. socs. Mason. Clubs: Columbia University, New York Athletic, Notre Dame University (New York City), Volkswagen Club of America. Editor: Directory American Society Anesthetists 1944. Contbr. numerous med. papers to profl. publs. Curator, Wood Library-Museum of Anesthesiology, Inc. 1950—. Address: 23 Cozzens Av., Highland Falls, N.Y. Died May 29, 1963.

WOOD, ROBERT WILLIAMS, physicist; b. Concord, Mass., May 2, 1868; s. Dr. Robert Williams and Lucy J. (Davis) W.; A.B., Harvard, 1891; student Johns Hopkins, 1891-92, U. Chgo., 1892-94, U. Berlin, 1894-96; LL.D., Clark U., 1909. U. Birmingham, 1913, U. Edinburgh, 1921; Ph.D., honoris causa, U. Berlin, 1931; D.Sc., honoris causa, Oxford U., 1948; m. Gertrude Ames, Apr. 19, 1892; children—Margaret, Robert Williams, Elizabeth, Bradford (dec.). Instr. physics U. Wis., 1897-99, asst. prof., 1899-1901; prof. exptl. physics, Johns Hopkins, 1901-38, prof. emeritus, 1938, later reappointed research professor. In 1898 originated method now in general use of thawing frozen street mains and service pipes by passing an electric current through them. Awarded John Scott Legacy premium and medal Franklin Inst., Phila., for color-photography; Rumford premium, a gold and a silver medal, by Am. Acad., 1909, for researches on theory of light; silver medal London Soc. Arts for color-photography process; gold medal for physics for 1918, Societa Italiana delle Scienze (delta dei XL). Rome; Ive's medal Optical Soc. of Am., 1933; Rumford gold medal Royal Soc., London, 1938; Henry Draper gold medal Nat. Acad. of Sci. for distinguished contbns. to astronomy, 1940. Served as cons. in development of atom bomb; with Manhattan group in New York during World War II; served at Aberdeen proving ground, and as cons. in Navy Experiments on shock waves under water. Commd. major, Signal O.R.C., Aug. 1917; with A.E.F.; developed methods for secret signaling. Fgn. mem. Royal Soc., London, Acad. Sci., Leningrad.; Royal Swedish Acad. (1932); hon. fellow Royal Micros. Soc., London, London Phys. Soc. (1933); hon. mem. London Optical Soc., Royal Instn., London, Am. Optical Soc. (1945); corr. mem. Königliche Akademie der Wissenschaften du Göttingen; fgn. asso. Academia dei Lincei, Rome; fellow Am. Acad. Arts and Sciences; mem. Nat. Acad. Sciences, Am. Philos. Soc., Am. Phys. Soc. (pres. 1935); hon. fgn. mem. Indian Assn. for Cultivation of Science, Calcutta, 1931. Author: Physical Optics, 1905, rev. edits., 1911, 34; Researches in Physical Optics, 2 vols.; (fiction) The Man Who Rocked the Earth, and the Moon-Maker (with Arthur Train), 1915. Illustrated nonsense verses, How to Tell the Birds from the Flowers and other wood-cuts. Researches in optics, spectroscopy, atomic and molecular radiation, supersonics improvements in diffraction gratings recorded in some 260 papers in European and Am. tech. jours. Complete bibliog. on all papers at end of William Seabrook's biography, "Dr. Wood," pub. 1941, translated into Russian by V. Vavilov, introduction by Sergei Vavilov, 1946. Home: 1023 St. Paul St., Balt. 2. Died Aug. 11, 1955; buried Concord, Mass.

WOOD, WALTER ABBOTT, congressman, inventor, mfr.; b. Mason, N.H., Oct. 23, 1815; s. Aaron and Rebecca (Wright) W.; m. Bessie A. Parsons, 1842; m. 2d, Elizabeth Warren Nichols, Sept. 2, 1868; 4 children. Partner with John White in mfg. plows, Hoosick Falls, N.Y., 1840's; with J. R. Parsons founded firm Wood and Parsons to build mowing and reaping machines, 1852, firm reorganized under name Walter A. Wood Mowing & Reaping Co., 1865, became pres.; received over 40 patents for improvements on machines; began to market products in Europe, 1856, later exhibited at fairs and expositions in U.S. and abroad; won over 1,000 prizes in exhibits all over world; decorated chevalier Legion of Honor following exhbn. of machines at Paris Expn. of 1867; decorated Imperial Order of Franz Joseph, Vienna, 1873; mem. U.S. Ho. of Reps. (Republican) from N.Y., 46th-47th congresses, 1879-83. Died Hoosick Falls, N.Y., Jan. 15, 1892; buried Maple Grove Cemetery, Hoosick Falls.

WOOD, WILLIAM BARRY, JR., physician; b. Milton, Mass., May 4, 1910; s. William Barry and Emily Niles (Lockwood) W.; A.B., Harvard, 1932; M.D., Johns Hopkins, 1936; m. Mary Lee Hutchins, July 2, 1932; children—William Barry III, Margaret, Peter, Jonathan, Jean. Medical house officer, Johns Hopkins Hosp., 1936-39; Nat. Research Council fellow in bacteriology, Harvard Med. Sch., 1939-40; asst., dept. of medicine, Johns Hopkins Med. Sch., 1937-39, associate, 1940-42; prof. medicine, Sch. of Medicine, Washington U., St. Louis, 1942-55; v.p. Johns Hopkins U. and Hosp., 1955-59; prof. microbiology Johns Hopkins School of Medicine, 1955-71, also director of department of microbiology, 1959-71. Member bd. trustees Rockefeller Found. Fellow A.C.P; mem. Am. Soc. Clin. Investigation (pres. 1952), Soc. Exptl. Biology and Med., Central Soc. Clin. Research (pres. 1952), Soc. Am. Bacteriologists, Assn. Am. Physicians (president 1962-63), National Academy of Sciences (member council 1962-65), Sigma Xi, Alpha Omega Alpha, Phi Beta Kappa. Home: Owings Mills MD Died Mar. 9, 1971.

WOODBRIDGE, DWIGHT EDWARDS, cons. engr.; b. Newton, Mass., July 19, 1865; s. Jonathan Edwards and Lydia (Judkins) W.; A.B., Carleton Coll., Northfield, Minn., 1887; m. Mary Munger, Oct. 6, 1890; children—Roger M., Mrs. Lydia W. Jamar. Began as mining engineer, Duluth Minn., 1898; late cons. engr. U.S. Bur. Mines in charge of all iron mining investigation. Pres. Ariz. Manganese Corp. Mem. Am. Inst. Mining and Metall. Engrs., Phi Kappa Psi. Mason (32 deg.). Home: 1735 Wallace Av. Office: Sellwood Bldg., Duluth, Minn. Died July 15, 1944. *

WOODBRIDGE, SAMUEL HOMER, engr.; b. Perth Amboy, N.J., Dec. 26, 1848; s. Stephen G. and Sarah (Fisher) W.; A.B., Williams, 1873; student Mass. Inst. Tech., 1876-79; m. Adele R. Taylor, June 25, 1891; children—Stephen Taylor (dec.), Philip Dudley (M.D.), Helen W. (Mrs. Albert H. Imlah). Asst. instr., 1882-84, instr., 1884-95, asst. prof., 1895-1900, asso. prof. heating and ventilation, 1900-14, Mass. Inst. Tech. Cons. and designing engr. for heating, ventilating and sanitary installation: U.S. Capitol, 1895-1911; Capitol Power plant, 1907-10 and 1923-25; Congressional bldgs., and Nat. Mus., 1904-10; Nat. Cathedral P.E. Ch., Washington, D.C.; Post-office bldg., Pa. R.R. Sta., New York, etc. Reported to Congress on economic value of central plant for power, lighting and heating for federal exec. bldgs., Washington, 1905; reported on sanitary condition of sch. houses of Boston, New York, Phila., Portland and Auburn, Me., Portsmouth and Concord, N.H., 1896-1908; served on expert commn. New York Ct. House, 1913-14. Pres. Sanitary Engring. Co. Chmn. com. on car sanitation Am. Pub. Health Assn. Organizer and dir. of 3-yr. nat. campaign which resulted in overthrow of La. Lottery after its removal to Tampa and Honduras. Chmn. bd. trustees Mass. State Hosp. for Dipsomaniacs; dir. N.E. Watch and Ward Soc. (v.p., 1925—). Mem. U.S. Naval League. Home: Brookline, Mass. Died June 4, 1926.

WOODBURY, CHARLES JEPTHA HILL, engr.; b. Lynn, Mass., May 4, 1851; s. J. Porter and Mary Adams (Hill) W.; prep. edn. pub. schs., Lynn; tech. edn. Mass. Inst. Tech.; hon. A.M., Tufts, 1893; Sc.D., Union, 1906, Dartmouth, 1908; m. Maria H. Brown, Nov. 26, 1878. Engr. Factory Mut. Ins. Co., 1878-94; asst. engr. Am. Bell Telephone Co., 1894-1908; cons. engr., 1908—. Non-resident lecturer Mass. Inst. Tech. and Cornell; chmn. Lynn Sch. Com., 1886-95. Awarded Alsacian medal, Société Industrielle de Mulhouse, 1883; John Scott medal, City of Phila., for meritorious elec. invention, 1885; Assn. medal, Nat. Assn. of Cotton Mfrs., 1910. Mem. Am. Soc. Civ. Engrs., Am. Soc. Mech. Engrs., Am. Inst. Elec. Engrs. Fellow A.A.A.S. Author: Fire Protection of Mills, 1882; Telephone Line Engineering; The Telephone System, 1899; Bibliography of the Cotton Manufacture, 1909; Wrote numerous monographs and papers on fire protection, polit. economy and engring. Home: Lynn, Mass. Died Mar. 20, 1916.

WOODHOUSE, JAMES, chemist, physician; b. Phila., Nov. 17, 1770; s. William and Anne (Martin) W.; B.A., U. State of Pa. (now U. Pa.), 1789, M.A., 1790, M.D., 1792; never married. Founder, Chem. Soc. of Phila., 1792; prof. chemistry U. Pa., 1795; experimented with prodn. of white starch and indsl. purification of camphor, 1804; undertook expts. on nitrous oxide gas, confirming its anaesthetic properties, 1806; proved superiority of anthracite over lituminous coal for indsl. use, 1808; known for work in chemistry of plants and in develop. of chem. analysis. Author: Observations on the Combinations of Acids, Bitters and Astringents, 1793; The Young Chemist's Pocket Companion (1st manual of chem. expts. for students), 1797; Experiments and Observations in the Vegetation of Plants, 1802; edited

Parkinson's Chemical Pocket Book, Phila., 1802. Died Phila., June 4, 1809.

WOODHOUSE, SAMUEL W., physician, ornithologist; asst. surgeon Med. Corps, U.S. Army; participated Pacific Railroad surveys; Woodhouse's jay named in his honor.

WOODMAN, ALPHEUS GRANT, chemist; b. at Kingston, Mass., Oct. 30, 1873; s. Dr. Aurin Payson and Emily (Grant) W.; B.S. in chemistry, Mass. Inst. Tech., 1897; m. Marion L. Cade, of Brighton, Mass., Aug. 4, 1902. Instr. chemistry, 1897-1907, asst. prof. of food analysis since 1907, Mass. Inst. Tech. Mem. Am. Chem. Soc., Soc. of Arts, Boston, A.A.A.S., Nat. Geog. Soc. Author: Air, Water and Food from a Sanitary Standpoint, 1900. Contbr. to chem. and photog. jours. Home: Watertown MA

WOODMAN, DURAND, cons. chemist; b. New York, 1859; s. George and Lucy M. (Durand) W.; grad. Stevens Inst. of Tech., B.S., 1880; Ph.D., 1888; course in organic chemistry, U. of Berlin, and in analytical laboratories of Fresenius, Wiesbaden, (diploma, 1890); m. Katherine Lincoln Bowles, 1893. Chemist, U.S. Electric Light Co., 1883-86; cons. chemist and analyst, 1890—. Chem. examiner of supplies for U.S. Light House Establishment, 3d dist., N.Y. Home: New York, N.Y. Died 1907.

WOODMAN, J(OSEPH) EDMUND, geologist; b. Newbury, Mass., July 4, 1873; s. Charles Henry and Mary Josephine (Poore) W.; S.B., Lawrence Scientific Sch. (Harvard), 1896; Harvard Grad. Sch., 1896-1902, A.M., 1900, S.D. 1902; m. Amy Baker Smith, Sept. 4, 1895; children—Malcolm White, Olive Amy W., Jean W. (dec.). Asst. in geology, Harvard, and instr. Radcliffe Coll., 1896-1902; instr. Harvard Summer Sch., 1897-1905; asst. prof. geology, 1902-05, prof., 1905-09, Dalhousie U., Halifax, N.S.; prof. geology and dir. Geol. Mus., New York U., 1909—. Geologist, Dept. of Mines, N.S., 1897-98; geologist in charge iron ore and limestone investigations in N.S., for Mines Branch, Can. Dept. Mines, 1906-13; mem. commn. on final revision plans and specifications for Catskill Water Supply Project, New York, 1910; cons. geologist to Bd. of Estimate, N.Y. City, 1922—. Republican. Presbyn. Fellow Geol. Soc. America, A.A.A.S., New York Acad. Sciences, Am. Geog. Soc. Author: Report on Iron Ores of Nova Scotia (Vol. I, Can. Dept. of Mines), 1909. Home: New York, N.Y. Died May 19, 1939.

WOODMAN, LAWRENCE EWALT, elec. engr.; b. Manhattan, Kan., June 27, 1904; s. Louis Hall and Augusta (Ewalt) W.; B.S. in Elec. Engring. Kan. State U., 1927; m. Grace Walsh, Nov. 2, 1935; children—Judith (Mrs. Charles R. Coons), James Walsh. Student engr. S.W. Bell Telephone Co., 1927; heating salesman Kansas City Fuel Oil Co., 1927-29; heating engr. Mo. Power & Light Co., 1929-32; owner, operator Woodman Engring Co., Jefferson City, Mo. Mem. Smoke Abatement Bd., Jefferson City, Greater Jefferson City Planning Commn.; mem. Jefferson City Symphony Orch., from 1929, pres., 1960-61. Bd. dirs. Jefferson City Community Concert Assn Mem. Nat., Mo. socs. profl. engrs., Refrigeration Service Engrs. Soc., Engrs. Club, Am. Soc. Heating Refrigeration and Airconditioning Engrs., Am. Soc. Refrigeration Engrs. Presbyn. Rotarian. Home: Jefferson City MO Deceased.

WOODROW, H(ARRY) R(AY), engr. and pub. utility exec.; b. Rock County, Minn., Apr. 15, 1887; s. Joseph Thomas and Della E. (Kennedy) W.; B.S., Drake U., 1909, LL.D., 1934, M.S., U. of Ill., 1911; m. Anna Louise Stillgebauer, 1912; children—Raymond J., Richard A. Asst. to chief elec. engr. N.Y. Edison Co., 1911-17, asst. chief elec. engr., 1917-20; elec. engr. Stone & Webster, 1920-22; gen. engr. Westinghouse Elec. & Mfg. Co., 1922; asst. elec. engr. Brooklyn Edison Co., 1922-26, elec. engr., 1926-32, v.p., 1932-37; v.p. Consolidated Edison Co. of N.Y., Inc., 1937—; dir. Brooklyn Edison Co.; trustee and treas. United Engring. Trustees, Inc. Fellow Am. Inst. Elec. Engrs. Presbyn. Home: Bronxville, N.Y. Died Aug. 12, 1940.

WOODROW, JAY W(ALTER), prof. physics; b. Rock Co., Minn., Apr. 3, 1884; s. Joseph Thomas and Della Erbain (Kennedy) W.; A.B., Drake U., Ia., 1907; B.A., Rhodes scholar from Ia., Oxford U., 1910; Ph.D., Yale, 1913; m. Flora Bernice Williams, June 23, 1915; 1 dau., Margaret Williams. Instr. physics, U. Ill., 1910-12; fellow in physics, Yale, 1912-13; research engr. Western Electric Co., N.Y.C., 1913-14; instr. physics, U. Colo., 1914-15, asst. prof., 1915-18, prof., 1918-21; prof. physics, Ia. State Coll. Agr. and Mechanic Arts, 1921—; Guggenheim fellow for study in Europe, 1927-28. Mem. Am. Phys. Soc., Soc. Promotion Engring. Edn., A.A.A.S., Phi Beta Kappa, Sigma Xi and Gamma Alpha. Mem. Christian (Disciples) Ch. Home: Ames, Ia. Deceased.

WOODRUFF, ELMER GRANT, cons. geologist; b. Bradford County, Pa., June 9, 1872; s. George W. and Katherine (De Reamer) W.; B.S., U. of Neb., 1901, M.S., 1904; m. Amy Grace Bucklin, Sept. 19, 1907 (died 1925); children—Vivian Grant, Edith Amy, Elaine Bucklin, Eva May; married 2d, Anna S. Wolfe, 1936. Austin fellow, Harvard University, 1906-07; with Neb. Geol. Survey, 1899-1904, U.S. Geol. Survey, 1904-14; chief geologist Tex. Oil Co., 1914-18, Okla. Producing & Refining Corp. since 1918; mem. Woodruff & Eches; geologist U.S. Army Engrs., Memphis, Tenn., 2 mos., 1935, Conchas Dam, Tucumcari, New Mex., 9 mos. to June, 1936, Memphis, Tenn. and Little Rock, Ark., Dists. since 1936. Served as lt. Third Neb. Vol. Infantry, Spanish-Am. War. Mem. Geol. Soc. America, Am. Assn. Petroleum Geologists, Tulsa Geol. Soc. (pres.), Sigma Xi. Mason. Author repts., also articles in tech. and trade jours. Home: 1611 S. Detroit St., Tulsa. Died June 25, 1952; buried Rose Hill Burial Park, Tulsa.

WOODRUFF, JOSEPH TALMAGE BATTIS, consulting engr.; b. Colorado Springs, Colo., June 30, 1894; s. Joseph Miller and Marie Antoinette (Talmage) W.; student Mass. Inst. Tech., 1914-17, Boston U., 1918; m. Dorothy Gray, June 12, 1920; children—Gordon Gray (dec.), Randolph Talmage, Rosamond Gray. City planning and zoning consultant for Springfield, Mass., 1921—; also same for various New England communities; planning engr. Regional Planning Fedn. of Phila. Tri-State Dist., 1929-31; chief Bur. of Planning, Greater Pa. Council, 1931-32; consultant Fairfield County (Conn.) Planning Assn., 1932—; consultant to Nat. Resources Com., Dist. No. 1, N.E. Regional Planning Commn., 1934—; asst. prof. regional planning, Mass. Inst. Tech. Served as pvt. 23d Engrs., U.S.A., World War. Mem. Nat. Conf. on City Planning; sec., treas. Am. City Planning Inst. Republican. Conglist. Home: Longmeadow, Mass. Died Dec. 18, 1937.

WOODRUFF, LORANDE LOSS, biologist; b. New York, N.Y., July 14, 1879; s. Charles Albert and Eloise Clara (Loss) W.; A.B., Columbia, 1901, A.M., 1902, Ph.D., 1905; (hon. M.A., Yale, 1915); m. Margaret Louise Mitchell, Dec. 21, 1905; children—Margaret Eloise (Mrs. T. C. Wilson), Dr. Lorande Mitchell. Asst. in biology, 1903-04, instr., 1904-07, Williams Coll.; instr. biology, 1907-09, asst. prof., 1909-15, prof., 1915-22, prof. of protozoölogy since 1922, Yale Univ.; dir. Osborn Zoöl. Lab., chmn. dept. of Zoölogy, and fellow of Branford Coll., Yale University, lecturer in zoölogy, 1905-07, embryology, 1907-14, Marine Biol. Lab., Woods Hole, Mass., trustee of same. Consulting physiologist, Chem. Warfar Service, U.S. Army, 1918. Chmn. of div. of biology and agr., Nat. Research Council, 1928-29; lecturer on protozoölogy, Univ. of Va., 1931, 36, 38, 40. Townsend Harris medal, Coll. City of N.Y., 1935. Fellow A.A.A.S.; mem. Nat. Acad. Sciences, Am. Soc. Zoölogists (sec.-treas., 1907-09, pres. 1942), Am. Physiol. Soc., Soc. for Exptl. Biology and Medicine, Am. Soc. Naturalists (v.p. 1923), Conn. Acad. Arts and Sciences, Am. Micros. Soc., Am. Assn. Univ. Profs. (chmn. Yale br. 1920-22), Sigma Xi (pres. Yale Chapter, 1915-16), Phi Beta Kappa, Alpha Delta Phi, Gamma Alpha; hon. mem. Sociedad Mexicana de Historia Natural. Republican. Conglist. Mason. Clubs: Graduate, Faculty. Author Foundations of Biology. 1922; 6fh edition, 1941; Animal Biologv. 1932. 2d edition. 1938: studies on life historv of Protozoa. chiefly based on pedigreed race of Paramecium of over 20,000 generations; Endomixis, its significance in Infusoria, History of Biology. Contributing author: Evolution of the Earth and Its Inhabitants, 1918; Development of the Sciences, 1923, 2d series, 1941; Organic Adaptation to Environment, 1924; Earth and Man, 1929; Protozoa in Biological Research, 1941; Biological Symposia, 1940, 1941. Asso. editor Jour. of Morphology, 1922-24, and 1932-34. Home: 146 Cottage St., New Haven, Conn.; (summer) Woods Hole, Mass. Died June 23, 1947; buried Woods Hole, Mass.

WOODRUFF, NATHAN H(AGGARD), biologist; b. Pleasant View, Tenn., Apr. 13, 1913; s. Samuel Thomas and Corrie Belle (Crosby) W.; B.A., Vanderbilt U., 1934; M.A., George Peabody Coll. Tchrs., 1935, Ph.D., 1939; m. Louise Daugherty, Dec. 19, 1937; children—Nathan H(aggard), Jana Louise, Susan Lee. Asst. prof. biology Tenn. Polytech. Inst., 1937-40; asst. prof. sci. Ball State Tchrs. Coll., 1940-43; prof. organic chemistry Westminster Coll., 1943-45; with AEC, 1946-65, dir. Office Research and Medicine, then asst. mgr. for operations, Oak Ridge operations, 1951-57, sci. rep. to Latin Am., Buenos Aires, 1957-59, dir. Office Health and Safety, Washington, 1959-61, dir. div. operational safety, 1961-65; sci. attache Am. embassy, Buenos Aires, Argentina, 1965—. AEC mem. working group Fed. Radiation Council, 1959-61; assisted U.S. sci. staff Inter-Am. Pres.' Conf., Uruguay, 1967. Fellow A.A.A.S.; mem. Tenn. Acad. Sci., Am. Nuclear Soc., Health Physics Soc., Pi Kappa Alpha, Omega Delta Kappa, Phi Delta Kappa. Baptist (trustee), Baptist (deacon). Author articles use and proper handling radioactive materials; sect. editor Biol. Abstracts, 1949-51. Home: 9911 Julliard Dr., Bethesda, Md. 20034. Office: Am. Embassy, Buenos Aires, Argentina, care State Dept. Mail Room, Washington. Died May 7, 1967; buried Adams, Tenn.

WOODRUFF, THEODORE TUTTLE, inventor, mfr.; b. Burrville, N.Y., Apr. 8, 1811; s. Simeon and Roxanna (Tuttle) W.; 1 child. Master car-builder for Terre Haute and Alton R.R., Alton, Ill., in 1840's; received 2 patents for sleeping-cars on trains, 1856; successfully demonstrated sleeping-car coach to Pa. R.R.; with brother began T. T. Woodruff and Co., small scale mfrs. of sleeping cars, Phila., 1858; received 2 additional patents for improvements of his car seat and couch, 1859-60; established Norris Iron Co., Norristown, Pa., circa 1870; received patents for process and apparatus for mfg. indigo, 1872, coffee hulling machine, 1872; ended bus. career in bankruptcy, 1875; received patents for later inventions, including steam plow, improved surveyor's compass, screw propellers to be used at side of vessel. Died Gloucester, N.J., May 2, 1892; buried Watertown, N.Y.

WOODS, ALAN CHURCHILL, ophthalmologist; b. Baltimore, Md., Aug. 20, 1889; s. Hiram and Laura (Hall) W.; prep. edn. Boys Latin Sch., Baltimore, 1900-06; A.B., Johns Hopkins, 1910, M.D., 1914; LL.D. (honorary), Hampden-Sydney, 1951; married Anne Powell Byrd, June 19, 1917; children—Alan Churchill, Anne Byrd, Jacquelin Ambler. House officer Peter Bent Brigham Hosp., Boston, 1914-15; fellow in research medicine and asst. in ophthalmology, U. of Pa., 1915-17; instr. in ophthalmology, Johns Hopkins Med. Sch., 1919-22, asso., 1922-26, asso. prof., 1926-34; acting prof. ophthalmology, 1934, dir. dept., 1937, prof., 1946-55, emeritus; ophthalmologist in chief Johns Hopkins Hosp., 1937-55, ophthalmologist in chief, 1955-60; visiting lectr., ophthalmology Harvard U., 1957. Member commission to review phys. standards for induction, 1944. Civilian consultant on ophthalmology to the surgeon general of the army, 1944. Member of com. on ophthalmology National Research Council, 1943, chmn., 1947, 58. Served as 1st lt. Med. Corps, U.S. Army, Mexican Punitive Expdn., 1916; capt. and maj., 1917-18; with A.E.F. Awarded A.M.A. Ophthal. Research Medal, 1948; Howe Research medal Am. Ophthal. Soc., 1953, Gonin medal, 1958. Hon. fellow Royal College of Surgeons (Edinburgh), 1950. Mem. Am. Ophthal. Society (president 1955), American Academy Ophthal. and Otolaryngol. (president 1947), Association American Immunologists, A.M.A., Ophthal. Soc. U.K. (honorary), Greek Ophthal. Soc. (hon.) Phi Kappa Psi, Sigma Xi. Presbyterian. Clubs: Maryland, Elkridge Hunt, Hamilton Street (Baltimore). Author: Allergy and Immunology in Ophthalmology, 1933; Endogenous Uveitis, 1956; Endogenous Inflammation of the Ureal Tract, 1961. Contbr. articles to ophthal. jours. Home: 103 Millbrook Rd., Balt. 18. Office: Johns Hopkins Hospital, Balt. 21205. Died Feb. 15, 1963.

WOODS, CHARLES DAYTON, agriculturist; b. Brooks, Me., Sept. 11, 1856; s. Henry J. and Maria N. (Colcord) W.; B.S., Wesleyan U., 1880; (Sc.D., U. of Me., 1905); m. Mary A. Morgan, June 1, 1882. Asst. in chemistry, Wesleyan U., 1880-83; teacher sciences, Wilbraham (Mass.) Acad., 1883-88; chemist and vice dir. Storrs (Conn.) Agrl. Expt. Sta., 1888-96; food expert U.S. Dept. Agr., 1894-1908; prof. agr., Univ. of Me., 1896-1903; dir. Me. Agrl. Expt. Sta., 1896-1920; consultant in agr., U.S. Dep., 1921; di,. of information, Mass. Dept. Agr., 1922—. Home Newton, Mass. Died Mar. 1925.

WOODS, FREDERICK ADAMS, biologist; b. Boston, Mass., Jan. 29, 1873; s. Solomon Adams and Catherine (Watts) W.; student Mass. Inst. Tech., 1890-94; M.D., Harvard, 1898; m. Ellen Payson, 1918; m. 2d, Baroness Marie Thérèse de Lebzeltern-Collenbach, of Austria and New York, 1924. Asst. in histology and embryology, 1898-1901, instr., 1901-02, Harvard Med. Sch.; lecturer biology, Mass. Inst. Tech., 1903-23. Fellow Am. Acad. Arts and Sciences; mem. Nat. Research Council, 1922; v.p. Internat. Congress for Studies Regarding Population Problems, Rome, 1931. Author: Mental and Moral Heredity in Royalty, 1906; The Influence of Monarchs, 1913; Is War Diminishing? (with Alexander Baltzly), 1915. Died Nov. 5, 1939.

WOODS, FREDERICK SHENSTONE, mathematician; b. Monson, Mass., Mar. 8, 1864; s. Frederick and Sarah H. (Shenstone) W.; A.B., Wesleyan U., Conn., 1885, A.M., 1888; Ph.D., U. Göttingen, 1894; m. Ethel M. Eager, June 20, 1899; children—Emily, Helen. Asst. in physics and astronomy, Wesleyan U., 1885-86; tchr. mathematics, Lima, N.Y., 1886-90; instr. mathematics, 1890-95, asst. prof., 1895-1903, asso. prof., 1903-06, prof. mathematics, 1906-34, Mass. Inst. Tech. emeritus prof., 1934—, hon. lecturer, 1934-35. Lectr. mathematics, Harvard, 1898-99; editor Annals of Mathematics, 1900-11. Mem. American Math. Soc., Math. Assn. of America, Psi Upsilon fraternity. Author: (with F. H. Bailey) Plane and Solid Analytic Geometry, 1897; (with E. B. Van Vleck and H. S. White) Boston Colloquium Lectures on Mathematics, 1905; (with F. H. Bailey) A Course in Mathematics for Students of Engineering and Applied Science, 1908; (with F. H. Bailey) Analytic Geometry and Calculus, 1917; Higher Geometry, 1922; (with F. H. Bailey) Elementary Calculus, 1922; Advanced Calculus, 1926. Editor: Journal of Mathematics and Physics. Home: 123 Sumner St., Newton Centre 59, Mass. Died Dec. 1, 1950.

WOODS, ROBERT PATTERSON, engr.; b. Buffalo N.Y., Mar. 4, 1870; s. Thomas Hamilton and Margaret Jane (Patterson) W.; grad. Buffalo Central High Sch., 1890; m. Bertha Dicken, Oct. 10, 1894; children—Dorothy (Mrs. Lester D. Castle), Robert Dicken (dec.), Helen (Mrs. Ansel N. Mitchell). With Henry L. Lyon, civ. engr., Buffalo, 1888-91, as asst. engr.; chief engr., Queen City Electric Ry., Marion, Ind., Mar.-Sept. 1891; city engr., Wabash, Ind.,

1891-1901, and during same period in private practice on water works, bridge work and sewer design; chief engr. constrn. Wabash River Traction line (19 miles), 1900, Indianapolis, Shelbyville, Southeastern Traction line (27 miles), 1901, Indianapolis & Northwestern Traction line (92 miles), 1902-04 Lebanon-Thornton Traction Co. (10 miles), 1905, Indianapolis & Western Ry. Co. traction lines (74 miles), 1906-08; irrigation projects in N.M., 1910-11; chief engr. construction electric roead Kansas City to St. Joseph, Mo., and Kansas City to Excelsior Springs, Mo. (80 miles), 1911-13; mem. bd. of control Kansas City Rys. Co., 1914-20; pres., gen. mgr. K.C.,C.,C.&St.J. Ry. Co., 1920-30, receiver 1930-36; pres. Consumers Tie Service Co.; practicing as cons. engr. Pres. Midwest Electric Ry. Assn. 1931-32; president Research Hospital, 1922, 23; director, 1917—; mem. and v. chmn. City Plan Commn., 1920-40; street railway commr. and dir. Kansas City Public Service Co., May 20, 1940—; local War Transportation adminstr., 1942-46. Awarded Collingwood prize American Society C.E., 1900, for paper on "Street Grades and Cross-Sections in Asphalt and Cement." Mem. Am. Soc. C.E. (pres. Kansas City sect. 1936), Ind. Engring. Soc. (twice pres.), Am. Wood Preservers Assn., Mo. Soc. of Professional Engrs., Kansas City C. of C. Presbyterian. Republican. Clubs: K.C. Engrs., Kansas City Club. Registered professional engr., Mo. Home: 5527 East Mission Dr., Kansas City 15, Mo. Office: 1627 Main St., Kansas City 8, Mo. Died May 20, 1958; buried Forest Hills Cemetery, Kansas City, Mo.

WOODSON, ROBERT EVERARD, JR., univ. prof., biologist; b. St. Louis, Apr. 28, 1904; s. Robert Everard and Ada Lee (Cowan) W.; A.B., Washington U., St. Louis, 1926, M.S., 1927, Ph.D., 1929; A.M., Harvard, 1928. Prof. botany Washington U., 1945—; curator of herbarium Mo. Botanical Garden, 1958—. Member Batan Soc. of Am., Am. Society Plant Taxonomists, St. Louis Academy of Science, American Geographical Society, Phi Beta Kappa, Sigma Xi. Democrat. Episcopalian. Author: articles on evolution, plant geog., taxonomy, floristics. Home: 14 Scarsdale, Richmond Heights, Mo. 63117. Office: Washington U., St. Louis 63105. Died Nov. 6, 1963.

WOODWARD, CLIFFORD DEWEY, elec. and mech. engineer; b. Norwalk, O., Apr. 21, 1878; s. Dewey Amus and Agnes Helen (Tod) W.; ed. pub. schs., Norwalk, Cleveland and Lorain, O.; m. Anna Oswald, May 24, 1900; 1 dau., Claudia Helen. Electrician, Boston & Mont. Consolidated Copper & Silver Mining Co., Great Falls, Mont., 1898-1900; chief electrician Highland Boy Gold Mining Co., Murray, Utah, 1900-02; same, Boston & Mont. Reduction Works, Great Falls, 1902-10; asst. master mechanic same works, 1910-16; asst. chief engr. Anaconda Copper Mining Co. Reduction Works, Great Falls, 1916-18; chief elec. engr. Anaconda Copper Mining Co., Butte, 1918-27, chief engr. since 1927. Asso. mem. Am. Inst. E.E., S. AR Republican. Mason (Shriner). Club: Butte Country. Home: 1034 Caledonia St., Butte, Mont. Died Oct. 26, 1949; buried Mt. Moriah Cemetery, Butte.

WOODWARD, JOSEPH JANVIER, physician; b. Phila., Oct. 30, 1833; s. Joseph Janvier and Elizabeth Graham (Cox) W.; M.D., U. Pa., 1853; married twice; m. 2d, Blanche Wendell; at least 1 son, Janvier. Began practice of medicine, Phila.; became asst. surgeon Med. Corps, U.S. Army, 1861, served at 1st Battle of Bull Run; transferred to Surgeon Gen.'s Hdqrs., Washington, D.C., with duties of planning hosp. constrn., performing surgery, keeping med. records, 1862-65; asst. to curator Army Med. Museum; in charge of med. part of Medical and Surgical History of the War of the Rebellion, 1870-88; promoted maj. U.S. Army, 1876; mem. Nat. Acad. Scis., A.A.A.S., Washington Philos. Soc.; pres A.M.A., 1881. Author various works including: Official Record of the Post-Mortem Examination of the Body of Pres. James A. Garfield, 1881. Died Wawa, Pa., Aug. 17, 1884.

WOODWORTH, JAY BAKCUS, geologist; b. Newfield, N.Y., Jan. 2, 1865; s. Rev. Allen Beach and Amanda (Smith) W.; B.S., in geology, Lawrence Scientific Sch. (Harvard), 1894. Instr. geology, 1893, asst. prof., 1901, asso. prof., 1912—, Harvard Univ.; mem. administrative bd., 1901-05, chmn. dept. geology and geography, 1904-08, Harvard Coll. In charge Harvard Seismog. Sta., 1908—; geol. survey of S.E. Mass. for Geol. Survey, 1915-17, 1918-19; geologist, U.S. Geol. Survey, 1918—. Mem. com. on geology and paleontology and chmn. sub-com. on use of seismographs in war, of Nat. Research Council, 1917-18. Fellow Geol. Soc. America (councillor, 1910-12, 1st v.p., 1921), Am. Acad. Arts and Sciences. Home: Cambridge, Mass. Died Aug. 4, 1925.

WOODWORTH, PHILIP BELL, engineer-attorney; b. Auburn, N.Y., Oct. 19, 1865; s. Thomas Bell and Mary Gertrude (Smith) W.; B.S., Mich. State Coll., 1886, Sc.D., 1920; M.E. in E.E., Cornell, 1890; U. of Berlin, 1891-92; m. Lucy M., d. of late Pres. Clute, of Mich. State Coll., and U. of Fla., 1893; children—Paul Merrylees, Robert Clute, Gertrude Elizabeth and Marion Merrylees (twins). Asst. prof. physics and engring., Mich. State Coll., 1892-99; prof. engring., later dean engring., Lewis Inst., Chicago, 1899-1917; served in war plans div., Gen. Staff U.S.A., 1917-21; pres. Rose Poly. Inst., Terre Haute, Ind., 1921-23. Mem. Rummler, Rummler & Woodworth, Chicago, 1907—. Mem. bar of Supreme Court of Indiana. Mason. Home: Glen Ellyn, Ill. Died June 7, 1937.

WOODWORTH, ROBERT SESSIONS, psychologist; b. Belchertown, Mass., Oct. 17, 1869; s. William Walter and Lydia Ames (Sessions) W.; A.B., Amherst Coll., 1891, Sc.D., 1951; A.B., Harvard, 1896, A.M., 1897; Ph.D., Columbia, 1899, Sc.D., 1929; LL.D., Lake Erie Coll., 1934; Sc.D., U. of N.C., 1946, U. of Pa., 1946; grad. study, univs. of Edinburgh, Liverpool, Bonn; m. Gabrielle Marie Schjöth, Apr. 23, 1903; children—Svenssen, Greta Sessions, William, Mary Virginia. Teacher sciences, Watertown (N.Y.) High Sch., 1891-93; instr. mathematics, Washburn Coll., Kan., 1893-95; asst. in physiology, Harvard Med. Sch., 1897-98; instr. physiology, Univ. and Bellevue Hosp. Med. Coll., N.Y.C., 1899-1902; demonstrator in physiology, U. of Liverpool, Eng., 1902-03; instr. psychology, Columbia U., 1903-05, adj. prof., 1905-09, prof., 1909-42, prof. emeritus, 1942—. Supt. of sections anthropometry and psychometry, St. Louis Expn., 1904. Recipient Gold Medal Am. Psychol. Found., 1956. Fellow A.A.A.S. (v.p. 1909, 1924), N.Y. Acad. Scis., British Psychol. Soc., Am. Acad. Arts and Scis.; mem. Am. Philos. Soc., Nat. Acad. Scis., Nat. Research Council (chmn. div. anthropology and psychology, 1924-25), Am. Psychol. Assn. (pres. 1914), Social Science Research Council (treas. 1927-29; pres. 1931-32), Psychol. Corp. (pres. 1929), Nat. Inst. Psychology, Theta Delta Chi. Author: Le Mouvement, 1903; Elements of Physiological Psychology (with George T. Ladd), 1911; The Care of the Body, 1912; Dynamic Psychology, 1918; Psychology, 1921, 5th edit. (with D. G. Marquis), 1947; Contemporary Schools of Psychology, 1931; Adjustment and Mastery, 1933; Experimental Psychology, 1938; Psychological Issues, 1939; Heredity and Environment, 1941; First Course in Psychology (with Mary R. Sheehan), 1944; Dynamies of Behavior, 1958; also Sci. papers in psychol. and physiol. jours. Editor: Archives of Psychology, 1906-45. Home: 400 West 119 St., N.Y.C. 27. Died July 4, 1962; buried Clinton, Conn.

WOODYATT, ROLLIN TURNER, (wood'yät), physician; b. Chgo., June 3, 1878; s. William Henry and Clara (Burnham) W.; grad. Chgo. Manual Tng. Sch., 1897; Cornell, 1897-98; M.D., Rush Med. Coll., 1902; B.S., U. Chgo., 1906; studied European labs., 1906-08; spl. work U. Chgo., 1908-09. Intern. Presbyn. Hosp., 1902-04, later attending physician; apptd. asso. prof. medicine, Rush Med. Coll., 1912; clin. prof., U. Chgo., chmn. dept. medicine, Rush Med. Coll.; now clin. prof. emeritus, U. Ill. Mem. A.M.A., Assn. Am. Phys. (pres. 1935), Am. Soc. Clin. Investigation (pres. 1916), Am. Soc. Biol. Chemists, Am. Chem. Soc., Sigma Xi, Sigma Chi, Phi Rho Sigma. Clubs: University, Cliff Dwellers, Tavern. Contbr. studies in metabolism and nutrition. Home: 237 E. Delawar Place. Office: 700 N. Michigan Av., Chgo. Died Dec. 17, 1953.

WOOLF, ALBERT EDWARD, chemist, inventor; b. New York, N.Y., Sept. 26, 1846; s. Edward W. (founder, 1837, of "Judy," first illustrated comic paper in U.S.); ed. Coll. City of New York; m. Rosamond Wienpfheimer, Sept., 1874. Introduced peroxide of hydrogen, to bleach grey and black ostrich feathers to white; also the first to use same as antiseptic; discovered the elec. decomposition of sea-water for sanitation, used in many large cities for treatment of drinking water, sewage and garbage, and adopted by the U.S. Govt. to combat yellow fever epidemic in Cuba; discovered antiseptic and med. properties of sea-water in combination with electric current. More recently discovered the treatment of garbage, sewage and refuse to fill in waste or marshy land, and for general land reclaiming; by this method is prevented the formation of noxious gases, by killing the germ of putrefaction, and propagating the germ which transforms the refuse into fertile soil. Practically demonstrated the value of the hypochlorites, so that Great Britain, France and U.S. Govt. have adopted their use in their navies and armies. Discovered cause of pyorrhoea (Riggs disease), etc. Modeled bronze medallion of Gen. Grant, which decorated the places where Grant's body lay in state (medallion now hangs in room at Mt. McGregor where Gen. Grant died). Home: New York, N.Y. Died Apr. 19, 1920.

WOOLFOLK, WILLIAM GORDON, cons. engr., corp. exec.; b. Columbus, Ga., Aug. 16, 1877; s. Joseph Washington and Josie (Wilkins) W.; student Sheffield Scientific Sch., Yale, 1899; m. Emma Ward, Apr. 29, 1909; 1 dau., Emma Ward. Practiced in Chicago, 1914—; pres. William G. Woolfolk & Co., 1919-30; president and chairman of executive committee Michigan Consolidated Gas Company, 1932—; chmn. Mich.-Wis. Pipe Line Co., Am. Natural Gas Co. Mem. Chi Phi. Democrat. Episcopalian. Mason (K.T.). Clubs: Chicago (Chicago); Detroit, Detroit Athletic, Bloomfield Hills Country, Grosse Point (Detroit); Yale, The Links, Recess (New York). Home: 415 Burns Drive, Detroit. Office: Michigan Consolidated Gas Co., Detroit, Mich.; Am. Natural Gas Co., N.Y.C. Died Apr. 20, 1954.

WOOLLEY, D(ILWORTH) WAYNE, scientist; b. Raymond, Alta., Can., July 20, 1914 (parents Am. citizens); s. Andrew Dilworth and Henrietta (Schonfeld) W.; B.S., U. Alta., 1935, LL.D., 1958; M.S., U. Wis., 1936, Ph.D., 1938; M.D. (hon.), U. Amsterdam, 1949; m. Janet McCarter, June 24, 1945. Research scientist, 1933—; fellow Rockefeller Inst. for Med. Research, 1939-43, asso., 1943-46, asso. mem., 1946-48, mem., 1948—. Mem. Nat. Acad. Scis., N.Y. Acad. Medicine, Soc. Biol. Chemists, Am. Inst. Nutrition, Am. Chem. Soc., Soc. Am. Bacteriologists, Soc. Exptl. Biology and Medicine, Harvey Soc., Am. Soc. Pharmacology. Author: A Study of Antimetabolites, 1952; The Biochemical Bases of Psychoses, 1962; also numerous articles. Office: Rockefeller Inst., 66th St. and York Av., N.Y.C. 21. Died July 23, 1966; buried Grantsville (Utah) Cemetery.

WOOLLEY, PAUL GERHARDT, pathologist; b. Paris, Ill., Apr. 7, 1875; s. John Granville and Mary Veronica (Gerhard) W.; B.S., U. of Chicago, 1896; M.D., Johns Hopkins, 1900; fellow in pathology, McGill Univ., 1901-02; m. Helen Bradford Thompson, Aug. 8, 1905; children—Eleanor F., Charlotte G. Resident house officer, Johns Hopkins Hosp., 1900-01; bacteriologist and pathologist, 1902-04, dir. serum lab., 1904-06, Bur. of Science, Manila, P.I.; dir. and pathologist, St. Paul's Hosp., Manila, 1905-06; dir. Siamese Govt. Serum Lab., 1906-07; chief insp. health, Bangkok, Siam, 1907-08; asso. prof. pathologic anatomy, U. of Neb., 1908-09; prof. pathology, U. of Cincinnati, 1909-18; dean Coll. of Medicine same, 1910-13. Commd. capt. M.R.C., 1917; maj. M.C., 1918; lt. col. M.R.C., 1919; instr. mil. hygiene, Camp Greenleaf, 1917-18; epidemiologist, Camps Greene and Devens, 1918-19; camp sanitary insp., asst. camp surgeon Camp Devens, 1918-19. Asso. prof. of pathology, Detroit Coll. Medicine and Surgery, 1920-23; dir. Nat. Pathol. Lab. of Mich., 1919-23; asso. dir. Detroit Clin. Lab., 1923-24; moved to Los Angeles, 1924; pathologist firm of Brem, Zeiler & Hammack, 1924-26; visiting pathologist Angelus, Lutheran, Good Samaritan and other hosps. and cons. pathologist Kern Gen. Hosp., 1924-26. Formerly dir. labs. and pathologist to Cincinnati Hosp.; pres. Hosp. Social Service Assn. of Cincinnati, 1911-14. Del. from Siam to Internat. Congress of Tuberculosis, 1908, and to Internat. Congress Hygiene and Demography, 1912. Decorated Officer of the Crown of Siam. Author: The Clinical History in Outline, 1914. Asso. editor Jour. Laboratory and Clinical Medicine. Home: Pasadena, Calif. Died 1932.

WOOLSON, HARRY THURBER, engring. consultant; b. Passaic, N.J., Sept. 20, 1876; s. George C. and Sarah Martin (Thurber) W.; ed. priv. sch., Stevens Prep. Sch.; M.E., Stevens Inst. of Tech., 1897; m. Bessie Van Iderstine, Aug. 19, 1903; children—L. Irving, George Thurber, Herbert C. Served as 2d class machinist, U.S. Navy, Spanish-Am. War. Draftsman with Nat. Meter Co. of Brooklyn, N.Y., 1903; later draftsman with Gas Engine & Power Co.; then draftsman advancing to chief engr. with Charles L. Seabury & Co., N.Y. City, 1899-1915; truck engr. Packard Motor Car Co., Detroit, 1915-16; engring. dept. Studebaker Corp., Detroit, 1916-20; with Willys Corp., Elizabeth, N.J., and Zeder-Skelton-Breer Engring. Co., Newark, N.J., 1921; with Chrysler Corp., Detroit, 1921-47, as chief engr. and later exec. engr., 1935-47, retired Jan. 1, 1947; pres. Chrysler Inst. of Engring., 1940-47. Mem. Com. on Internat. Screw Thread Unification. Has designed steam and gasoline marine machinery, developed automobile chassis, medium tanks and other war equipment. Awarded Stevens Inst. medal for accomplishments in engring., 1945; 2 citations from U.S. Army Ordnance Dept. Fellow Am. Soc. Mech. Engrs.; mem. Franklin Inst., Brit. Inst. Automotive Engrs., mem. (life) Soc. Automotive Engrs. v.p. 1928; councillor, 1932-36; pres., 1937; chmn. Detroit. Sect., 1934; mem. Ordnance adv. com.); mem. Engring. Soc. of Detroit, Tau Beta Pi. Clubs: Detroit Athletic, Detroit Golf, Ingleside Golf, (Detroit). Mason. Presbyterian. Home: 1780 Strathcona Drive, Detroit MI

WOOLSON, IRA HARVEY, mechanical engr.; b. Lewiston, N.Y., Aug. 11, 1856; s. Charles and Jane Ann (Yerington) Sharp W.; E.M., Columbia, 1885; m. Anita Mason, May 27, 1893. Asst. in assaying and drawing, 1886-90, instr. mech. engring., 1891-1903, adj. prof., 1903-08, adj. prof. civ. engring., 1908-10, Columbia U.; official investigator of building materials, N.Y. City, 1900-10; official del. from N.C. City to Internat. Fire Prevention Congress, London, 1903; consulting engr. Nat. Bd. of Fire Underwriters, 1910—; advisory engr. to bldg. materials div., War Industries Bd., 1918-19; chmn. Bldg. Code Com. of U.S. Dept. Commerce, 1921—. Prog. Republican. Author: Recommended Building Code, 1915; Code for Construction of Dwellings, 1918. Home: Summit, N.J. Died May 8, 1927.

WOOLSON, L. IRVING, engr.; b. N.Y.C., June 27, 1904; s. Harry T. and Bessie V. (Van Iderstine) W.; M.E., Cornell, 1926; m. Helen L. Chappell, June 23, 1928; children—James E., Helen L. (Mrs. William Plevich). With Yale & Town Mfg. Co., Stamford, Conn., 1926; mngr. Am. Smelting & Refining Co., Perth Amboy, N.J., 1926-28; with Chrysler Corp., Detroit,

1928—, v.p., 1953—, pres. De Soto div., 1952—. Dir. Detroit YMCA. Mem. Soc. Automotive Engrs. (chmn. Detroit sect. 1950-51). Tau Kappa Epsilon. Presbyn. Club: Cornell of Michigan. Home: 715 Glengary Rd., Birmingham, Mich. Office: 6000 Wyoming Av., Detroit 31. Died Mar. 4, 1966; buried Woodlawn Cemetery, Detroit.

WOOTEN, BENJAMIN ALLEN, (woo'ten), prof. physics; b. Jefferson, Ala., July 29, 1891; s. Benjamin Allen and Louise (Danelly) W.; B.S. in E.E., Ala. Poly. Inst., 1911; E.E., 1912; M.A., Columbia, 1915, Ph.D., 1917; m. Mary Samford, June 1, 1916; 1 son, Benjamin Allen. Instr. in elec. engring., Ala. Poly. Inst., 1913-15, asst. prof. physics, 1915-16, prof. physics, 1919-21; instr. physics, Coll. of City of N.Y., 1917-19; McCormick prof. physics, Washington and Lee U., 1922-28; research work at Yerkes Obs., summers 1926 and 1934; head of physics dept., U. of Ala., since 1928; research asso., Underwater Sound Lab., Harvard, 1944. Fellow American Association for the Advancement of Science; mem. Am. Phys. Society, Am. Geophys. Union, Assn. Physics Teachers, Am. Phys. Soc. (1939-40), Phi Beta Kappa, Tau Beta Pi, Sigma Xi, Alpha Tau Omega. Democrat. Episcopalian. Mason. Contbr. to mags. Home: 1505 10th St., Tuscaloosa, Ala. Died July 9, 1947.

WORCESTER, ALFRED (woos'ter), physician; born Waltham, Mass., June 22, 1855; s. Benjamin and Mary Clapp (Ruggles) W.; A.B., Harvard U., 1878, A.M., 1881, M.D., 1883; Sc.D., Tufts Coll., 1931; m. Elizabeth Joy Hill, Oct. 19, 1886. Practiced at Waltham, Mass., since 1883; trustee Mass. Hosp. for Consumptives, 1897-1901 (the first state sanatorium for tuberculous patients); founder Waltham Training Sch. for Nurses; chmn. Mass. Commission on Maternity Benefits, 1920. Prof. hygiene, Harvard, 1925-35, prof. emeritus since 1935; one of earliest surgeons to operate for appendicitis. Dep. commr. rank of maj., Am. Red Cross for Switzerland, June 1918-Feb. 1919. Mem. Mass. Med. Soc. (pres. 1919-21), Obstetrical Soc. of Boston, Harvard, Med. Alumni Assn. (ex-pres.). Decorated Officer Order Leopold II by King Albert of Belgium. Mugwump. Episcopalian. Author: Monthly Nursing, 1886; Small Hospitals, 1894; Nurses for Our Neighbors, 1913; Nurses and Nursing, 1927; Selected Medical Papers, American Red Cross Service in Switzerland; Hygiene for Freshman; Sex Hygiene; The Care of the Aged, the Dying and the Dead. Home: Waltham, Mass. Died Aug. 28, 1951.

WORCESTER, JOSEPH RUGGLES, (woos'ter), civil engr.; b. Waltham, Mass., May 9, 1860; s. Benjamin and Mary Clapp (Ruggles) W.; A.B., Harvard, 1882; m. Alice Jeannette Wheeler, Jan. 2, 1889; children—Alice M. (Mrs. C. D. Howe), Barbara (Mrs. C. T. Porter), Thomas, Ruth H. With Boston Bridge Works, most of time as chief engr., 1882-94; cons. practice, 1894-1906; sr. partner J. R. Worcester & Co., 1906-24. Trustee New Ch. Inst. Edn. Mem. Am. Soc. Civil Engrs., Am. Concrete Inst., Am. Soc. for Testing Materials, Am. Inst. Cons. Engrs., Am. Ry. Engring. Assn., Am. Acad. Arts and Sciences. Designed bridge over Connecticut River, at Bellows Falls, Vt.; bridge between Portland and South Portland, Me.; train shed of South Sta., Boston, etc. Swedenborgian. Home: Waltham. Mass. Office: 79 Milk St., Boston, Mass. Died May 9, 1943.

WORCESTER, P(HILIP) G(EORGE), geologist, univ. administr.; b. Thetford, Vt., May 5, 1884; s. George Steele and Ida Eldora (Kinney) W.; student, U. of Mich., 1904-06; A.B. U. of Colo., 1909, A.M., 1911; Ph.D., U. of Chicago, 1924; m. Mollie Brown, Aug. 29, 1911; children—Willis G., John B. (lst lieut., U.S.A.A.F., killed in service), Mary Ellen (Mrs. Geo. R. Lewis), Thomas K. Instr. geology U. of Colo., 1912-14, asst. prof., 1914-18, asso. prof. 1915-24, dean of men, 1920-30, prof., 1924-69, head dept., 1934-49, dean grad. sch., 1943-69; geologist Colo. Geol. Survey, 1912-27; geologist Canadian Exploration Co., summers, 1927-30; consulting geologist, since 1914. Moderator 1st Congl. Ch.; mem. Sch. Bd. Boulder Dist. No. 3, 1934-40; trustee Chicago Theol. Sem., 1922-24. Fellow Geol. Soc. Am., A.A.A.S.; mem. Sigma Xi, Phi Beta Kappa, Alpha Chi Sigma, Sigma Gamma Epsilon. Awarded Norlin Medal by U. of Colo. Alumni Assn., 1946. Republican. Conglist. Mason. Club: Internat. Rotary. Author: Textbook of Geomorphology (D. Van Nostrand Co.), 1939, revised edition, 1948; Molybdenum Deposits of Colo., 1918; Geology of Ward Dist. Colo., 1920. Home: Boulder CO Died 1969.

WORCESTER, WILLIS GEORGE, educator; b. Boulder, Colo., June 26, 1918; s. Philip George and Mollie (Brown) W.; B.S. in Elec. Engring., U. Colo., 1939, M.S. in Elec. Engring., Cal. Inst. Tech., 1940; Ph.D., Stanford; 1952; m. Mary Isobel Toy Greenway, June 7, 1940; children—Robert L., Willis George. Engr., Gen. Electric Co., 1941-46, mem. faculty U. Colo., 1946-63, prof. elec. engring., 1956-63, acting dean Grad. Sch., 1960-61; chmn. dept. elec. engring., 1961-63; dean engring, Va. Poly. Inst., 1963-70; engring. cons., 1948-70; specialist in planning research inst. Kabul (Afghanistan) U., summer 1960. Dir. Hathaway Instruments, Inc., 1960-62. Mem. Citizens Com. Edn. Handicapped Children, Boulder, 1957, Citizens Com. Water Supply Devel., Boulder, 1961. Registered profl. engr., Colo., Va. Sr. mem. I.E.E.E.; member of Sigma Xi, Tau Beta Pi, Eta Kappa Nu, Sigma Pi Sigma, Pi Mu Epsilon. Presbyn. (elder). Rotarian. Home: Blacksburg VA Died Feb. 10, 1970.

WORDEN, EDWARD CHAUNCEY, I, chemist; b. Ypsilanti, Mich., Apr. 17, 1875; s. Chauncey Perry and Elvira Mabel (Brainerd) W.; Ph.C., U. of Mich., 1896; B.S., New York U., 1907, M.A., 1909, D.Sc., 1921; m. Anna Wilhelmina Breitsman, Sept. 25, 1901; children—Marian Alice (Mrs. De Witt Bell), Edward Chauncey II, Anna Lois, Waite Warren, Loanna. Served as chemist as N.Y. Agrl. Expt. Station, Geneva, 1896-97; mem. Crane & Worden, chemists, New York, 1899-1900; chemist Celluloid Zapon Co., Springfield, N.J., 1900-02, Clark Thread Co., Newark, 1902-14, Worden Lab., Milburn, N.J., 1914—. Chmn. com. on airplane coatings, Nat. Research Council, 1916; edition Report 10382 and 13228 (5000 pages) "Aviation Chemistry, 1914-18," prepared for U.S. Army Air Service; chief of airplane wing coating sect., Bur. of Aeronautics, Washington, D.C., 1916-18, crossing Atlantic 14 times for U.S. Govt. Fellow Chem. Soc., London, and French Acad., Paris. Mason. Author: Nitrocellulose Industry, 2 vols., 1911; Cellulose Acetate, 1915; Technology of Cellulose Esters, Vol. I (3,709 pages), 1921; Chemical Patents Index (United States), 1915-1924, 5 vols., 1927; (with Edward C. Worden, II) Technical Dict. of Chemistry (containing over 400,000 separate headings in alphabetical arrangement). Asso. editor Kunstoffe, also of La Coutchoue et la Guttapercha. Home: Milburn, N.J. Died Sept. 22, 1940.

WORLEY, JOHN STEPHEN, cons. engr.; b. Jackson Co., Mo., Apr. 19, 1876; s. Albert Harrison and Mary Elizabeth (Campbell) W.; ed. Odessa (Mo.) Coll.; U. Mo., 1896-97; B.S., and M.S., U. Kan., 1904, C.E., 1922; m. Mayme Lee Baker, Dec. 22, 1897; 1 dau., Mary Louise Symons. Various positions in design and construction of pub. utility plants, steam and interurban rys. in Mo., Kan., Ark., Okla., Mich., Ohio and Ind., 1904-09; bur. of Valuation, 1913-20; federal receiver, exec. v.p. and gen. mgr. Habirshaw Electric Cable Co. and affiliated cos., 1921-27; cons. engr. City of Detroit, 1932-40; cons. engr. U.S. Engr. Corps., 1945-46; cons. engr. econ. and engring. problems cities, states, and Province of Ontario, with appearances before committees of Congress and state legislatures, 1922-53; prof. transportation engring. and curator Transportation Library, U. Mich., 1922-46. Lt. Col., Specialist Res., U.S. Army, Mem. Am. Soc. C.E., Am. Ry. Engring. Assn., Sigma Xi, Tau Beta Pi, Phi Kappa Phi, Sigma Chi, Scabbard and Blade. Methodist. Author of numerous articles and pamphlets on transportation and related subjects. Address: Engineering School, University of Michigan, Ann Arbor, Mich. Died May 25, 1956.

WORMLEY, THEODORE GEORGE, physician, toxicologist, educator; b. Wormleysburg, Pa., Apr. 1, 1826; s. David and Isabella (Foster) W.; attended Dickinson Coll., Carlisle, Pa., 1842-45, Ph.D. (hon.), 1870; M.D., Phila. Coll. Medicine, 1849; LL.D. (hon.), Marietta Coll., 1870; Ph.D. (hon.) Pa. Coll., 1877; m. Ann Eliza Gill. Prof. toxicology Capitol U., Columbus, O., 1852-73, Starling Med. Coll., 1852-77; gas commr. for State of Ohio, 1867-75; chemist Ohio Geog. Survey, 1869-74; editor Ohio Med. and Surg. Jour., 1862-64; delivered address on toxicology before Internat. Med. Congress, Phila., 1876; prof. chemistry and toxicology med. dept. U. Pa., 1877-97. Author: The Micro-Chemistry of Poisons, 1867. Died Phila., Jan. 3, 1897.

WORRALL, AMBROSE ALEXANDER, aerospace cons.; b. Barrow-in-Furness, Eng., Jan. 18, 1899; s. Alexander and Rebecca (Mattocks) W.; came to U.S., 1923, naturalized, 1930; certificate Barrow-in-Furness Sch., 1918; student St. Ignatius Coll., Cleve., 1923-24, Cleve. Coll., 1927-29; diploma Nat. Radio Inst., 1964; Ph.D. (hon.); m. Olga Nathalie Ripich, June 7, 1928; children—Ambrose Mattocks and Alexander Karanczay (twins) (Dec.). Aero. engr. Vickers Ltd., Barrow-in-Furness, 1920; dept. mgr. Martin Co., Balt., 1924-64; cons. Martin Marietta Corp., Balt., 1964-68, Westinghouse Electric Corp., Balt., 1968-69; v.p. K & W Enterprises, Inc., Balt., 1964-73, Markari Research Labs, Inc., Englewood, N.J., 1966-73; dir. Life Energies Research, Inc., N.Y.C., 1968-73. Mem. corp. bd. Springfield (Mass.) Coll., 1962-73. Served with Brit. Army, 1918-19. Mem. Wainwright Center Devel. Human Resources, Spiritual Frontiers Fellowship, Chs. Fellowship for Psychial and Spiritual Studies, Radionic-Magnetic Centre Orgn. Methodist (asso. dir. New Life Clinic 1950-73). Mason. Author: Essay on Prayer, 1952; Meditation and Contemplation, 1956; Silentium Altum, 1961; The Philosophy and Methodology of Spiritual Healing, 1961; Basic Principles of Spiritual Healing, 1963; The Gift of Healing, 1965; The Miracle Healers, 1968; Explore Your Psychic World, 1970; Your Power to Heal. Address: Baltimore MD Died Feb. 2, 1973; buried Dulaney Valley Meml. Gardens, Cockeysville MD

WORRALL, DAVID ELBRIDGE, (wor'äl), chemist; b. Westerley, R.I., Aug. 2, 1886; s. William Francis and Iona May (Paine) W.; B.S., R.I. State Coll., 1910; A.M., Harvard, 1911, Ph.D., 1919; grad. student U. of Graz, Austria, 1928; m. Harriet Taber Tucker, Nov. 28, 1914 (died Nov. 7, 1940); children—David Elbridge, Edward Tucker, Hilda. Chemist Guantanamo Sugar Co., Cuba, 1911-12; instr. chemistry, Smith Coll., 1914-17; asst. gas chemist Bur. of Mines, 1918-19; instr. chemistry, Harvard, 1919; asst. prof., chemistry, Tufts Coll., Medford, Mass., 1919-24, prof. since 1924; dir. of chem. laboratories since 1939; visiting lecturer, Radcliffe College, 1924-26. Served as 1st lt. Chem. Warfare Service, U.S. Army, 1918. Fellow A.A.A.S., Am. Acad. Arts and Sciences; mem. Am. Chem. Soc. (chmn. N.E. Sect. 1929-30); Am. Geog. Soc., Phi Beta Kappa (hon.), Alpha Chi Sigma, Theta Chi, Phi Kappa Phi. Unitarian. Republican. Author: Principles of Organic Chemistry, 1927. Contributor articles to Jour. Am. Chem. Soc. Home: 72 Badger Rd., Medford, Mass. Died Feb. 7, 1944.

WORTHEN, AMOS HENRY, geologist; b. Bradford, Vt., Oct. 31, 1813; s. Thomas and Susannah (Adams) W.; m. Sarah B. Kimball, Jan. 14, 1834, 7 children. Moved to Warsaw, Ill., 1836, entered dry-goods bus.; moved to Boston, 1842; ret. from business, became geologist assisting in Ill. Geol. Survey, 1844; became geologist Ia. Geol. Survey, 1855; apptd. state geologist Ill., 1858; described over 1600 species of fossils; particularly interested in classification of lower Carboniferous strata; mem. Am. Philos. Soc., Nat. Acad. Scis. Author: Geological Survey of Illinois, 8 vols., 1866-90. Died Warsaw, May 6, 1888.

WORTHEN, EDMUND LOUIS, soil technologist; b. Hancock County, Ill., Oct. 5, 1882; s. George Byron and Mary (Bedell) W.; B.S., U. Ill., 1904; M.S. in Agr., Cornell U., 1906; m. Xenia Woolman, Nov. 5, 1909; children—Rachel Daura, Albert Woolman, Elizabeth Jane. Asst. in agronomy U. Ill., 1904-06; scientist in soil survey U.S. Dept. Agr., 1906-09; in charge soil investigations, N.C. Dept. Agr., 1909-12; asst., later asso. prof. agronomy, Pa. State Coll., 1912-19; became prof. soil technology, Cornell, 1919, now emeritus. Fellow Am. Soc. Agronomy, A.A.A.S.; mem. Alpha Zeta, Gamma Sigma Delta. Unitarian. Author: Farm Soils. Home: Brooktondale, N.Y. Died Oct. 5, 1965.

WORTHING, ARCHIE GARFIELD, (wûr'thing), physicist; b. LeRoy, Wis., Feb. 6, 1881; s. Arthur James and Loella (McKnight) W.; grad. State Normal Sch., Oshkosh, Wis., 1900; B.A., U. of Wis., 1904; State U. of Ia., 1906-09; Ph.D., U. of Mich., 1911; m. Exie Lillian Witherbee, June 23, 1905; children—Marion Witherbee, Helen Witherbee, Robert Witherbee. Teacher grammar sch., Brandon, Wis., 1900-01; asst. in physics, U. of Wis., 1904-06; acting instr. physics, State U. of Ia., 1906-09; asso. physicist Physical Laboratory of National Lamp Works, Cleveland, Ohio, 1910-14; physicist Nela Research Laboratories, Cleveland, 1914-25; head of physics department Univ. of Pittsburgh, 1925-37, professor physics since 1925. Fellow Am. Phys. Soc.; mem. Optical Soc. Am. (vice-pres. 1939-41; pres. 1941-43), Am. Assn. Physics Teachers (vice-pres. 1940, pres. 1941), Am. Inst. Physics (member board govs. since 1941), Phi Beta Kappa, Sigma Xi, Sigma Pi Sigma. Unitarian. Co-author of books on scientific and tech. subjects and contbr. to scientific and tech. jours. Determined the true temperature scale of tungsten and other metals and their emissivities at incandescent temperatures. Home: 1372 N. Sheridan Av., Pittsburgh 6, Pa. Died July 30, 1949.

WORTHINGTON, CHARLES CAMPBELL, mech. engr., retired; b. Brooklyn, N.Y., Jan. 6, 1854; s. Henry Rossiter and Sara (Newton) W.; gen. engring. course, Columbia; m. Julia A. Hedden, 1879 (dec.); children—Julia Hedden (Mrs. Edmund Monroe Sawtelle), Henry Rossiter (dec.), Chas. Campbell (dec.), Edward Hedden, Reginald Stuart; m. 2d, Maude C. Rice, June 7, 1906; children—Sara Newton, Alice Rice. Owner and pres. Henry R. Worthington Corp., mfrs. steam pumps, 1875-1900 (retired); cons. and nominal pres. Worthington Mower Co., Stroudsburg, Pa. Inventor of Worthington high duty water works engine and hydraulic machinery now in use in principal countries of the world. Invented, 1913, and introduced the Worthington gang lawn mower, in general use on golf courses. Mem. Am. Soc. M.E. (ex-mem. council). Republican. Episcopalian. Clubs: Engineers', New York Athletic; Racquet and Tennis, Chevy Chase (Washington, D.C.). Home: Shawnee-on-Delaware, Pa. Died Oct. 21, 1944.

WORTHINGTON, HENRY ROSSITER, engr., inventor; b. N.Y.C., Dec. 17, 1817; s. Asa and Frances (Meadwocraft) W.; m. Laura I. Newton, Sept. 24, 1839, 4 children. Worked on problems of city water supply as hydraulic engr., N.Y.C., circa 1838; placed exptl. steam canal boat in operation, 1840; invented automatic feeding pump, patented, 1840; received patent for improvement in propelling of canal boats, 1844; 1st to build direct steam pump, 1845-55; built pump manufacturing plant in N.Y.C., 1859; developed duplex steam feed pump which was adopted widely in waterworks, 1859, also invented pump engine using no flywheel, and various machine tools; pres. Nason Mfg. Co., N.Y.; founder Am. Soc. M.E. Died Tarrytown, N.Y., Dec. 17, 1880.

WRAITH, WILLIAM, mining engr.; b. in Eng., Nov. 23, 1872; s. Samuel and Mary Jane (Hardy) W.; brought to U.S., 1882, naturalized, 1900; student U. of Ill., 1890-91; E.M., Mich. Coll. Mines and Tech.,

Houghton, 1894, D. Eng., 1938; m. Erma M. Davis, Jan. 12, 1897; children—William, Erma M. (Mrs. C.E. Carstens). Mine surveyor for fuel dept. A.,T.&S.F. Ry., 1894-97; construction engineer Boston & Mont. Co., Butte & Boston Co., Anaconda Copper Mining Co., 1897-1906; asst. supt. Washoe smelter of Anaconda Copper Mining Co., 1906-13; mgr. Internat. Smelting Co., Salt Lake City, 1913-18; now exec. vice-president Andes Copper Mining Co., Chile Copper Co., Chile Exploration Co., president Chile Steamship Co.; vice-president Greene Cananea Copper Co., Inspiration Consolidated Copper Co.; dir. Internat. Smelting & Refining Co. Mem. Am. Inst. Mining and Metall. Engrs., Am. Soc. Mech. Engrs. Clubs: Engineers, India House; Plandome (N.Y.) Golf; Manhasset Bay Yacht (Port Washington, N.Y.). Retired. Home: Lafayette Hotel, Long Beach 2 CA

WRATHER, WILLIAM EMBRY, (ra'ther), petroleum geologist; b. Brandenburg, Ky., Jan. 20, 1883; s. Richard Anslem and Glovy Washington (Munford) W.; Ph.B., U. of Chicago, 1907; grad. study 2 yrs.; D.Sc. So. Meth. U., U. of Ky., 1950, Mont. Sch. Mines, 1952; D.Eng., Colo. School of Mines, 1947; m. Alice Mildred Dolling, Dec. 30, 1910; children—Jane Farwell, Catherine Morgan. Petroleum geologist Gulf Production Co., Beaumont and Houston, Tex., 1908-16; consulting petroleum geologist, Dallas, Tex., 1916-42; asso. chief metals and minerals div. Board of Economics Warfare, Washington, D.C., 1942-43; dir. U.S. Geological Survey, 1943-56, retired. Spl. lecturer, depts. of geology, Univ. of Chicago, 1922, Univ. of Texas, 1927, Yale, 1930, Northwestern U., 1931, Southern Meth. U., 1935. Mem. scientific advisory com. Chicago World's Fair, 1933. Del. from Nat. Acad. Sciences and Nat. Research Council to Internat. Geol. Congress, Madrid, 1926; Pretoria, South Africa, 1929; mem. orgn. com. of 16th Internat. Geol. Congress, Washington, D.C., 1933; del. 17th Congress, Moscow, 1937, 19th Cong., Algiers, 1952; del. 3d World Petroleum Congress, Hague, 1951. Mem. Hist. Com. of Texas Centennial, 1936. Mem. Development Bd., U. of Tex., 1940-43. Awarded Alumni medal, 50th Anniversary, U. Chgo.; John Fritz Medal, 1954; Sidney Powers Memorial medal, 1956. Fellow Geological Society of American (council 1928-30, v.p. 1932, 1st v.p. 1936), A.A.A.S. (treas.; mem. exec. com. 1942-46); mem. Nat. Geog. Society (life trustee), American Association Petroleum Geologists (pres. 1922-23), Soc. Econ. Geologists (pres. 1934), Tex. Geog. Soc. (dir.; pres., 1940-42); Tex. Folk-Lore Soc., Tex. State Hist. Assn. (pres. 1932-39), Philos. Soc. of Tex., Am. Inst. Mining and Metall. Engrs. (pres. 1948-49; Anthony Lucas Medal, 1950), Seismological Soc. of America, Geol. Soc. Wash., Wash. Acad. Science, Mining & Metall. Soc., Sigma Nu, Phi Delta Phi. Unitarian. Clubs: Dallas Petroleum (Dallas); Cosmos (Washington, D.C.); Chevy Chase. Asso. editor Economic Geology. Home: 4710 Woodway Lane, Washington 20016. Died Nov. 28, 1963.

WRAY, JAMES GLENDENNING, elec. engr.; b. Janesville, Wis., May 19, 1872; s. James and Helen (Edgar) W.; B.S. in E.E., U. of Wis., 1893; m. Clara May Williams, Sept. 25, 1895; children—Florence Vivian (Mrs. A. H. Ward), Ernest Lee (dec.), Alice May (Mrs. J.A. Bailey), Ethel Lois (Mrs. Stanley D. Grace), Helen Norma (wife of J.D. Emrich, Jr.), James Glendenning, Jr., Clara Grace (Mrs. Alvin H. Mitchell). With Chicago Telephone Co., 1893, served as asst. chief engr., asst. supt. of maintenance, supt. of maintenance, electrician, supt. of equipment and chief engr., until 1916; chief engr. Wis. Telephone Co., Mich. State Telephone Co., Cleveland Telephone Co., and Central Union Telephone Co., 1911-16; chief engr. receivers of Central Union Telephone Co., 1914; pres. and dir. United Telephone Co., 1927-29, dir., 1930; v.p., dir. Standard Telephone Co., 1927-28; pres., dir. Southeastern Telephone Co., 1929-31; president Pa Wray Pickle Co., J.G. Wray & Co. Member Board of Education, Wilmette, Ill. (president 1917-19); member Bd. of Visitors, University of Wisconsin, 1909-12; former director Chicago Regional Plan Commn.; mem. Glencoe (Ill.) Plan Commn., 1929-30, Glencoe Park Bd. (v.p. since 1930). Fellow Am. Inst. E.E. (chmn. Chicago sect. 3 yrs.), A.A.A.S.; mem. Western Soc. Engrs., Ill. Acad. Sciences, Wis. Soc. of Chicago (secretary, treasurer and president), U. of Wisconsin Alumni Assn. (exec. com.). Formerly mem. Wis. Nat. Guard. Republican. Conglist.; former dir. Chicago City Missionary Soc. Mason (past master). Clubs: University, University of Wis. Club of Chicago (pres., sec. and treas.). Home: 625 Washington Av., Glencoe IL Office: Bankers Bldg., Chicago IL*

WRIGHT, ARTHUR WILLIAMS, physicist; b. Lebanon, Conn., Sept. 8, 1836; s. Jesse and Harriet (Williams) W.; A.B., Yale, 1859, Ph.D., 1861; admitted to bar, 1866, but did not practice; univs. of Heidelberg and Berlin, 1868-69; m. Susan Forbes, d. Prof. Benjamin Silliman, 2d, of Yale, Oct. 6, 1875. Assisted in preparing revised edit. Webster's Dictionary, 1862-63, and in 1890; tutor in Latin, 1863-66, in physics, 1866-68, Yale; instr. physics, Sheffield Scientific Sch. (Yale), 1867-68; prof. physics and chemistry, Williams Coll., 1869-72; prof. molecular physics and chemistry, 1871-87, prof. experimental physics, 1887-1906, prof. emeritus, 1906—, Yale University. In charge of Sloane Physical Laboratory, Yale, built from his plans under his supervision, 1883-1906. Consulting specialist, U.S. Signal Service, 1881-86. Was the first to observe the electric shadow in air; discovered and analyzed gases in stony meteorites; measured polarization of zodiacal light, also of light of moon, solar corona and comets; applied cathode discharge in vacuo to form metallic films for mirrors. Fellow Royal Astron. Soc. of Great Britain. Home: New Haven, Conn. Died Dec. 19, 1915.

WRIGHT, AUGUSTINE WASHINGTON, civil engr.; b. Chicago, Ill., May 29, 1847; s. John Stephen and Catharine Blackburn (Turner) W.; ed. pub. schs. and under pvt. tutors; m. Natalie Jordan, Jan. 1, 1890. Began in engring. dept. U.P. Ry., 1867; chief engr. and gen. supt. of various rys. until 1879; chief engr. and supt. constrn. North Chicago City Ry., 1879-86; mem. Wright & Meysenburg, consulting engineers, 1886—. Pres. Bd. Pub. Utilities of Los Angeles, 1914—. Republican. Author: American Street Railway Construction and Operation, 1888. Home: Los Angeles, Calif. Died Feb. 3, 1918.

WRIGHT, BENJAMIN, canal engr.; b. Wethersfield, Conn., Oct. 10, 1770; s. Ebenezer and Grace (Butler) W.; m. Philomela Waterman, Sept. 27, 1798, 9 children including Benjamin H. Land surveyor Oneida and Oswego counties (N.Y.), 1792-96; active in promoting canal bldg. to facilitate transport of farm produce, 1792; elected to N.Y. State Legislature, circa 1797; reported on canal route from Rome on Mohawk to Waterford on Hudson for state canal commission, 1811; apptd. county judge, 1813; in charge of bldg. middle sect. of Erie Canal, 1816, later in charge of constrn. Eastern sect., chief engr., until 1827; cons. engr. on several canal projects; chief engr. Chesapeake & Ohio Canal, 1828-31, St. Lawrence Canal, 1833; street commr. N.Y.C., 1833; made surveys for road from Havana to interior of Cuba, 1835-36. Died N.Y.C., Aug. 24, 1842.

WRIGHT, CHARLES, botanist; b. Wethersfield, Conn., Oct. 29, 1811; s. James and Mary (Goodrich) W.; grad. Yale, 1835; never married. Taught sch., Miss., also East Tex., 1835-44; tchr. Rutersville (Tex.) Coll., 1845; accompanied battalion of U.S. troops from San Antonio to El Paso, Tex., summer 1849, collected plants and sent many specimens to Asa Gray at Harvard; botanist on U.S.-Mexican boundary survey, 1851-52; became botanist of N. Pacific Exploring and Surveying Expdn., 1852; made collections of plants at Cape of Good Hope, Hong Kong, Loo Choo Islands, Japan, 1853-56; conducted bot. explorations of Cuba, 1856-67; curator herbarium, Cambridge, Mass., 1868. Died Wethersfield, Aug. 11, 1885.

WRIGHT, CHARLES HERBERT, civil engr.; b. Templeton, Mass., July 2, 1857; s. Edwin and Rebecca (Sprague) W.; grad. Worcester Poly. Inst., 1879; m. Emma L. Giffen, of Templeton, Mass., June 11, 1881. Engr. bridges, Iron Mountain R.R., 1882-84; engr. Edge Moor Bridge Works, 1887-98; chief engr. Brown Hoisting Machinery Co., since 1898. Mem. Am. Soc. C.E., Cleveland Engrs. Club. Club: Colonial. Author: Bridge Drafting, 1896; Plate Girder Draw Spans, 1898; The Designing of Draw Spans, 1898. Contbr. articles on bridge design and more recently, on ore and coal handling machinery on the Great Lakes to engring. jours. Home: The Colonial, Russell and Euclid Avs. Office: Brown Hoisting Machinery Co., Cleveland, O.

WRIGHT, FRANK JAMES, geologist; b. Bridgewater, Va., Nov. 22, 1888; s. Robert Joseph and Alice Mary (Sanger) W.; A.B., Bridgewater (Va.) Coll., 1908, LL.D., 1947; A.M., U. of Va., 1911; Ph.D., Columbia, 1918; m. Anna Catherine Zigler, Aug. 15, 1914; children—Robert James, Harold Douglas. Prof. geology, Bridgewater Coll., 1911-24, dean, 1921-24; prof. geology Denison U., 1924-49, emeritus; vis. asso. in physiography, Columbia, 1923-24, teacher, summers, 1918, 1920-26, 28, 30, 31, 36, 37, 38, 1940-43. Director Mutual Cold Storage, Incorporated, Broadway, Va., 1918-45. Mem. Virginia House of Delegates, 1916-20. Mem. bd. editors, Geol. Society of Am. 1943-46. Awarded Walker Memorial Prize by Boston Soc. Natural History, 1922; A. Cressy Morrison Prize in Natural Science by N.Y. Acad. of Sciences, 1931. Fellow Geol. Soc. America, A.A.A.S.; mem. Assn. of Am. Geographers, Ohio Acad. of Science (v.p. 1931, 38), Am. Assn. of Univ. Profs., Phi Gamma Delta, Phi Beta Kappa (pres. Denison chapter, 1935-38), Sigma Xi, Omicron Delta Kappa. Republican. Mem. Ch. of the Brethren. Author various bulletins and papers on geol. subjects, especially the Southern Appalachians. Home: Granville O. Died Sept. 5, 1954; buried Oak Lawn Cemetery, Bridgewater, Va.

WRIGHT, FRANK LLOYD, architect; b. Richland Center, Wis., June 8, 1869; s. William Russell Cary and Anna Lloyd (Jones) W.; student civil engring., U. of Wis., 1884-88; m. Catherine Lee; children—Lloyd, John, Catherine, David, Frances, Llewellyn; m. 2d, Miriam Noel; m. 3d, Olga Lazovich, Aug. 25, 1928; 1 dau., Iovanna. Began practice at Chicago, Ill., 1893; architect of Imperial Hotel, Tokio, Japan, and numerous other buildings of note; work characterized in America as "The New School of the Middle West" and in Europe as "The American Expression in Architecture." Phi Delta Theta; hon. mem. Academie Royale des Beaux Arts d'Anvers, 1927, Nat. Acad. of Cuba, 1927, Nat. Acad. of Brazil, 1932, Royal Inst. British Architects, 1941, Nat. Acad. Architects, Mexico, 1943, Nat. Acad. of Finland, 1946; hon. mem. Nat. Acad. and Society of Architects (Uruguay), 1942; extraordinary hon. mem. Akademie der Kunst (Royal Acad.), Berlin, 1929; hon. mem. Am. Inst. Decorators, Am. Nat. Inst. Arts and Letters; life member American Academy Arts and Letters. Honored guest of the Soviet Republic, 1937. Awarded Royal Gold Medal for Architecture by King George VI, 1941; Gold Medal of A.I.A., 1948. Hon. Doctor of Fine Arts, Princeton, 1947, M.A., Wesleyan U., 1939. Architect Imperial Household, Japan, 1914; high honors, Holland and Switzerland, 1921; Gold Medal by Am. Inst. Architects, 1949; Star of Solidarity (Italy). Clubs: Players (N.Y.); Tavern (Chicago). Author: An Interpretation of Japanese Prints, 1912; In the Cause of Architecture (essays), 1909-23; Experimenting with Human Lives, 1923; Ausgeführte Bauten und Entwürfe, 1909, Sonderheit, 1910; Wendingen, 1925 (last three pub. in Europe); Modern Architecture (Kahn lectures at Princeton), 1931; The Nature of Materials, 1932; An Autobiography—Frank Lloyd Wright, 1932, later revised, expanded and brought up to date, 1943; The Disappearing City, 1932; Architecture and Modern Life (with Baker Brownell); Frank Lloyd Wright on Architecture, 1894-1940 (edited by Frederick Gutheim); In the Nature of Materials (edited by Henry-Russell Hitchcock), 1941; When Democracy Builds, 1946; Genius and the Mobocracy, 1949. The founder and the conductor of the "The Taliesin Fellowship," a cultural experiment in the arts, by way of a non-profit organization entitled The Frank Lloyd Wright Foundation situated at "Taliesin" in Wis. (Apr.-Nov.) and Ariz. (Dec.-Mar.), about 40 apprentices participating. Editor of "Taliesin," Fellowship magazine, pub. 6 times a year; and The Taliesin Square Papers pub. from time to time at Taliesin. Home "Taliesin," Spring Green, Wis.; and "Taliesin West," Paradise Valley, Phoenix, Ariz. Died Apr. 9, 1959.

WRIGHT, FREDERICK EUGENE, geologist; b. Marquette, Mich., Oct. 16, 1877; s. Charles Eugene and Carolyn Alice (Dox) W.; grad. Ann Arbor High Sch., 1895; student Realgymnasium, Weimar, Germany, 1895-96; Ph.D., U. of Heidelberg, 1900; hon. Sc.D., U. of Mich., 1940; m. Kathleen Ethel Finley, June 16, 1909; children—Kathleen Margaret (dec.), Frederick Hamilton, Mary Helen, William Finley, Kenneth Aldro. Instr. petrology, Mich. Coll. of Mines, 1901-04; asst. state geologist of Mich., 1903-04; asst. geologist, 1904-05, geologist, 1906-17, U.S. Geol. Survey; petrologist Geophys. Lab., Carnegie Instn., Washington, 1906-44, ret. Commd. capt. Ordnance Res. Corps, 1917; maj. U.S. Army, 1918-19; lt. col., Ordn. Res. Corps, 1919, col., 1928; chief physicist, A.S.F., War Dept., Jan. 1942 to Jan. 1946. Awarded exceptional service medal, U.S. Army, 1945. Fellow Am. Acad. Arts and Sciences, Phys. Soc. London, A.A.A.S.; mem. Nat. Acad. Sciences (v.p. 1927-31; home sec. 1931-51), Mineral. & Geology (foreign member) socs., London, Am. Philos. Soc., Mineral. Society America (pres. 1941, Roebling Medal, 1952), Geological Society America, American. Phys. Soc. Optical Soc. America (pres. 1917-19), Astron. Soc. America, Washington Acad. Sciences, Am. Inst. Mining and Metall. Engrs., Army Ordnance Assn., Nat. Research Council, Am. Geophys. Union, Sigma Xi. Republican. Baptist. Clubs: Cosmos. Writer of papers of petrologic and phys. nature. Home: 2134 Wyoming Av., Washington 8. Office: 1530 P St., Washington 5. Died Aug. 25, 1953.

WRIGHT, HORATIO GOVERNEUR, army officer, engr.; b. Clinton, Conn., Mar. 5, 1820; s. Edward Wright; grad. U.S. Mil. Acad., 1841; m. Louise M. Bradford, Aug. 11, 1842, 2 children. Commd. 2d lt. Corps Engrs., U.S. Army, 1841, capt., 1855; asst. to chief engr., Washington, D.C., 1861, built defenses for Capitol; fought in Battle of Bull Run; chief engr. Port Royal expdn.; commd. brig. gen. U.S. Volunteers, 1861, maj. gen., 1864; chief engr. Dept. of Ohio, U.S. Army, 1862; fought in battles of Gettysburg, Mine Run, Wilderness; commanded VI Corps, U.S. Army, his troops were first to pierce Petersburg (Va.) defenses; commanded Dept. of Tex., 1865-66; returned to various constrn. assignments after Civil War; promoted brig. gen. U.S. Army, chief engrs., 1879; ret., 1884. Died Washington, July 2, 1899; buried Arlington (Va.) Nat. Cemetery.

WRIGHT, JAMES HOMER, pathologist; b. Pittsburgh, Apr. 8, 1869; s. Homer and Sarah L. (Gray) W.; A.B., Johns Hopkins, 1890; M.D., U. of Md., 1892; Thomas A. Scott fellow in hygiene, 1892-93, Harvard, A.M., 1895, hon. S.D., 1905; Sc.D., U. of Mo., 1907; m. Aagot Lunde, Dec. 25, 1901. Asst. in pathology, 1893-96, instr., 1896-1907, asst. prof., 1907—, Harvard; consulting pathologist, Mass. Gen. Hosp., 1925—. Author: (with Dr. F. B. Mallory) Pathological Technique (8 edits.), 1897. Home: Boston, Mass. Died Jan. 3, 1928.

WRIGHT, JESSIE, physician; b. Eccleshall, Eng., Sept. 5, 1900; d. James and Mary (Keightley) Wright; came to U.S., 1907, naturalized, 1924; B.Sc., U. Pitts., 1932, M.D., 1934. Intern Allegheny Gen. Hosp., Pitts., 1934-35; med. dir. D.T. Watson Sch. Physiatrics U. Pitts., 1935-67; chief staff D. T. Watson Home, affiliated U. Pitts., 1948-67; instr. orthopedics U. Pitts., 1936-51, asso. prof. phys. medicine and rehab., 1952-67; cons. U. Pitts. Med. Center Hosps., 1952-67, surgeon gen. USAF, 1950-53. Mem. nat. adv. com. Nat. Found., 1947-70, cons. to found. for ICA in Argentina, 1956; nat. clin. adv. com. United Cerebral Palsy Assn., 1954-67; rep. Nat. Soc. Crippled Childrens and Adults at Internat. Soc. Welfare Crippled, Amsterdam, Holland, 1954; moderator panel rehab. 3d Internat. Conf. Poliomyelitis, Rome, Italy, 1954, participant 4th Internat. Conf., Geneva, Switzerland, 1957. Trustee U. Pitts., 1961-67. Named Pitts. Woman of Year, 1950, Distinguished Dau. Pa., 1952. Mem. Am. Acad. Cerebral Palsy (pres. 1962), Am. Rheumatism Assn., Am. Acad. Phys. Medicine and Rehab., Internat. Soc. Rehabilitation Disabled, American Medical Writers Assn. Presbyn. (elder). Clubs: U. Pitts. Century, Civic, Zonta, 20th Century (Pitts.). Developed electrically controlled rocking bed for treatment respiratory paralysis, 1945. Contbr. articles med. Jours. Home: Pittsburgh PA Died Sept. 9, 1970.

WRIGHT, JOHN KIRTLAND, geographer; b. at Cambridge, Mass., Nov. 30, 1891; s. John Henry and Mary (Tappan) W.; grad. Browne and Nicholas Sch., 1909; A.B., Harvard, 1913, A.M., 1914, Ph.D., 1922; LL.D., Clark U., 1967; m. Katharine Wolcott McGiffert, Jan. 12, 1921; children—Austin McGiffert, Gertrude Huntington, Mary Wolcott. Instr. in history, Harvard, 1916-17; librarian Am. Geographical Soc., 1920-36, research editor, 1936-37, director, 1938-49, research asso., 1949-56, ret.; vis. prof. Dartmouth Coll., 1957, La. State U., 1968. Served as cpl., inf., U.S. Army, Sept. 1917-Feb. 1919, attached to hist. sect., G.H.Q., Chaumont, France, Aug.-Dec. 1918. Recipient Charles P. Daly Medal, Am. Geog. Soc., 1954. Patrons medal Royal Geog. Soc., 1955, Outstanding Achievement award Assn. Am. Geographers, 1956. Member Association of American Geographers (president 1946), History of Science Society, A.A.A.S. (v.p., 1943). Author: Aids to Geographical Research, 1923, rev. edit., 1947; The Geographical Lore of the Time of the Crusades, 1925, rev. edit., 1965; The Leardo Map of the World (1452 or 1453), 1928; The Geographical Basis of European History, 1928; Geography in the Making: The American Geographical Society, 1851-1951, 1952; Human Nature in Geography, 1966. Editor: Oriental Explorations and Studies (by Alois Musil), 6 vols., 1926-28; Atlas of the Historical Geography of the United States (by C. O. Paullin), 1932; New England's Prospect (by 27 authors), 1933, and other publs. of Am. Geog. Soc. Home: Lyne NH Died Mar. 24, 1969.

WRIGHT, JOSEPH JEFFERSON BURR, physician, army officer; b. Wilkes-Barre, Pa., Apr. 27, 1801; A.B., Washington (Pa.) Coll., 1821; attended U. Pa. Sch. of Medicine, 1825-26; m. Eliza Jones; 3 children including Joseph P. Served as asst. surgeon U.S. Army, 1833-40, in Seminole War, 1840-41, 43; with the Inf. in occupation of Tex., 1846; served in battles of Palo Alto and Resaca de la Palma during Mexican War; in charge of hosp., Matamoras; wrote report on cholera epidemic published in So. Med. reports, 1849; on field duty with troops in Kan., 1857, Utah expdn., 1858; served as med. dir. Dept. Ohio on Gen. George B. McClellan's staff, Civil War; in battles of Rich Mountain, Carrick's Ford (W.Va.); surgeon Cavalry Recruiting Depot, Carlisle, Pa., 1862-76; brevetted col., 1864; promoted brig. gen., 1865; contbd. case reports to surg. vol. Medical and Surgical History of War of Rebellion, 6 vols., 1870-88. Died Carlisle, May 14, 1878.

WRIGHT, ORVILLE, inventor; b. Dayton, O., Aug. 19, 1871; s. Milton and Susan Catharine (Koerner) W.; ed. pub. and high schs. to 1890; hon. B.S., Earlham Coll., Ind., 1909, LL.D., 1931; Dr. Tech. Sci., Royal Tech. Coll., Munich, 1909; LL.D., Oberlin, 1910, Harvard Univ., 1930, Huntington (Ind.) Coll., 1935; Sc.D., Trinity, 1915, Cincinnati, 1917, Ohio State U., 1930; M.A., Yale, 1919; Dr. Engring., Univ. of Michigan, 1924; D.Sc., Otterbein Coll., Westville, Ohio, 1947; Doctor of Engineering, University of Dayton, 1943; unmarried. With his late brother, Wilbur, was the first to fly with a heavier-than-air machine, Dec. 17, 1903, and with him the inventor of the system of control used in flying machines of today; dir. Wright Aeronautical Laboratory, Dayton, O. Awarded the Collier trophy, 1913, for development of the automatic stabilizer; gold medals: Aero Club of France, 1908; Aero Club of United Kingdom, 1908; Acad. of Sports of France, 1908; Aeronautical Soc. Gt. Britain, 1908; Congress of U.S., 1909; State of Ohio, 1909; City of Dayton, 1909; Aero Club America, 1909; French Acad. Sciences, 1909; Cross of Chevalier of Legion of Honor, French, 1909; Cross of Officer of Legion of Honor, 1924; Langley medal, Smithsonian Inst., 1910; Elliott Cresson medal, Franklin Inst., 1914; Albert medal. Royal Soc. Arts, 1917; The John Fritz medal, 1920; bronze medal, International Peace Society; The John Scott medal, 1925; Washington award, 1927; Distinguished Flying Cross awarded, Feb., 1929; Daniel Guggenheim medal, 1930; Franklin medal, 1933; Medal for Merit, 1947; hon. mem. Aero Club of Sarthe, France, Aeronautical Society, Great Britain, Aero Club of United Kingdom, Österreichischen Flugtechnischen Vereines, Vienna, Verein Deutscher Flugtechniker, Berlin, American Society Mech. Engrs., Aeronautical Soc. America, Nat. Aeronautic Assn. (gov. at large, 1929-39), Nat. Exchange Club, Ohio Society of New York, Inst. of Aeronautical Science, 1932, Franklin Inst., Nat. Fedn. Post Office Clerks, Inst. of Mech. Engrs., London, Air Line Pilots Assn., Inc.; hon. fellow Royal Aeronautical Soc.; mem. Nat. Inventors Council, Nat. Acad. Sciences, Nat. Museum Engring. and Industry (v.p., 1924), Nat. Adv. Com. for Aeronautics, A.A.A.S., Franklin Inst., S.A.E., Engineers' Club of Dayton (hon. life); hon. scout Boy Scouts America. Mem. Daniel Guggenheim Fund for Promotion of Aeronautics; chmn. advisory com., Daniel Guggenheim Sch. of Aeronautics, New York Univ.; hon. Aircraft Pilot Certificate No. 1, issued by Civil Aeronautics Authority, 1940. Home: Park and Harmon Avs. Office: 15 N. Broadway, Dayton, O. Died Jan. 30, 1948; buried Woodlawn Cemetery, Dayton.

WRIGHT, SYDNEY LONGSTRETH, educator, chemist; b. Germantown, Phila., Oct. 9 1896; s. William Redwood and Letitia Ellicott (Carpenter) W.; student Episcopal Acad. Phila.; B.S. (Princeton, 1918, A.M. (Sayre fellow), 1920, Ph.D. (Proctor fellow), 1928; Nat. Research Council fellow medicine U. Pa., 1928-30, fellow, 1930-32, 32-33; m. Catharine Wharton Morris, Feb. 28, 1925; children—Anna Wharton, William Redwood, Ellicott, Harrison Morris. Research chemist Barrett Co., Phila., 1919-21; chemist Ayer Clinic Lab., Pa. Hosp., 1923-28; instr. dept. research medicine U. Pa., 1931-34, instr. dept. physiol. chemistry, 1932-36; asso. dir. Franklin Inst., 1943-40, dir. membership, 1936-40 asst. to sec. 1939-40; dir. Library Co. of Phila., 1937-43; pres. Meadowbrook Sch., 1938-42; dir. Pa. Acad. Fine Arts 1939-59. Chmn. Cheltenham Twp. Def. Council, 1941-45. Trustee Wagner Free Inst. Sci. 1931-58, sec.; 1935-40, treas., 1940, vice pres., 1948-58; trustee Pa. Sch. Horticulture for Women Ambler, 1945-46; dir. Nat. Farm Sch., Doylestown, Pa., 1943-46; trustee of the Rhode Island Oceanarium. Served as private U.S. Army 1917-19. Mem. Franklin Inst. (Phila.), Am. Soc. Biol. Chemistry; Newport (R.I.) Hist., Soc. (dir. 1950-51, pres. since 1951), Keats-Shelley Assn. Am. (dir. 1949—). Am. Soc. Biol. Chemists. Clubs: Mid Ocean (Bermuda); Franklin Inn Univ. Barge (Phila.); Tower (Princeton); Saunderstown Yacht (dir. 1941-47); Royal Bermuda Yacht. Author: The Story of Franklin Institute, 1938. Editor of Bull. Wagner Free Inst. Pa., 1931-58. Home: Jamestown RI Died Oct. 8, 1970.

WRIGHT, THEODORE PAUL, aircraft engr.; b. Galesburg, Ill., May 25, 1895; s. Philip Green and Elizabeth Quincy (Sewall) W.; B.S., Lombard Coll., Galesburg, 1915, Mass. Inst. Tech., 1918; D.Sc., Knox Coll., Galesburg, 1937; m. Margaret McCarl, Dec. 4, 1918; children—Douglas Lyman, Theodore Paul. Began as naval insp. aircraft (in charge inspection NC Flying Boats which made pioneer Transatlantic crossing by air), 1918; exec. engr. Curtiss Aeroplane & Motor Co., 1921, asst. factory mgt., 1922, asst. chief engr., 1923-25, chief engr. airplane div., 1925-30, in charge orgn. which designed and produced Curtiss "Tanager" airplanes, winner Guggenheim Found. prize, Safe Aircraft Competition, 1929; gen. mgr., chief engr., airplane div. Curtiss Wright Corp., 1930-34, v.p., dir. the corp., 1930-41, dir. engring., chmn. engring., policy and planning com., 1934-41; vice president research Cornell University, 1948-60, acting president, 1951; pres. Cornell Aero. Lab., Inc., 1948-58, chmn. board, 1948-60, chmn. exec. com., 1960-70; pres. Asso. Univs., Inc., 1965-66; dir. Power Reactor Devel. Corp. Trustee Sloan Kettering Cancer Research Inst., 1948-60. Director of Fund for Peaceim Atomic Development, Cornell-Guggenheim Aviation Safety Center; chairman of bd. dirs. Cornell Research Found.; dir., governor Flight Safety Foundation. Served with the National Defense Advisory Council, Washington, 6 months, 1940; asst. chief, aircraft sect. OPM, 1940; dir. Aircraft Resources Control Office, also mem. Aircraft Prodn. Bd., 1942-44; tech. sec. Internat. Aviation Conv. (which established Internat. Civil Aviation Orgn.), Chgo., 1944; adminstr. Civil Aeronautics, 1944-48; dir. aircraft div. U.S. Strategic Bombing Survey, 1945; mem. NACA, 1941-53, chmn. aerodynamics sub com., 1941-53, vice chmn., 1953. Recipient medal, citation exceptional civilian service, 1944, Medal of Freedom, 1946 (both War Dept.), Daniel Guggenheim medal for aeronautics, 1945. Medal for Merit from the Pres., 1945. Hon. fellow Inst. Aerospace Sci. (founder council; pres. 1938), Royal Aero. Soc. London, Canadian Aero. and Space Institute; member of Soc. Automotive Engrs. (Wright Brothers medal 1930), Council Fgn. Relations, Sigma Xi, Sigma Nu, Tau Beta Pi. Democrat. Unitarian. Club: Cosmos (Washington). Author papers on aero. and ednl. subjects, presented in numerous speeches, also tech. contbns. to mags.; articles and speeches pub. in 3 vols., 1962. Delivered 33d Wilbur Wright lecture, Royal Aero. Soc., 1945. Home: Ithaca NY Died Aug. 21, 1970.

WRIGHT, WALTER HENRY, educator, dentist; born southwest Pa., Feb. 18, 1893; s. Elmer Henry and Martha (Dean) W.; D.D.S., U. Pittsburgh, 1917, B.S., 1931, M.S., 1932, Ph.D., 1934; m. Esther Emily Prugh, Mar. 31, 1916; 1 son, David Walter (U.S.N.). Practice of dentistry, Pittsburgh, 1935-46; lecturer anatomy, 1918-19; asst. prof. anatomy and clin. prosthesis, 1919-20; asso. prof. prosthetic dentistry, 1933-37, prof. of anatomy and prosthesis, 1938-June, 1946, U. Pittsburgh Sch. of Dentistry; prof. of prosthetic dentistry and dean N.Y.U. Coll. Dentistry since 1946; dental cons. to surgeon gen. U.S. Army, also cons. to Vets. Adminstrn. Served as dental consultant to surgeon gen. U.S. Army, World War II. Advisor Health Council Greater N.Y. Fellow Am. Coll. Dentists (past pres.); mem. Am. Dental Assn. (past chmn. prosthetic sect.), A.A.A.S., Am. Assn. Anatomists, Am. Acad. Cleft Palate Prosthesis (pres. 1946), Am. Assn. Univ. Profs., Am. Assn. Dental Schs. (chmn. plans and projects com.), Internat. Assn. for Dental Research, Nat. Soc. Denture Prosthesis (past pres.), Nat. Bd. Dental Examiners, Odontol. Soc. of Western Pa., Pa. State Dental Soc., N.Y. Acad. of Dentistry, Omicron Kappa Upsilon (past pres.), Omicron Delta Kappa, Sigma Xi, Phi Sigma, Delta Sigma Delta. Contbr. about 65 articles on the teaching and practice of dentistry, dental edn., research reports in dental jours. Past dir. Men's Glee Club, U. Pittsburgh. Home: 43 Fifth Av., N.Y.C. 3. Office: N.Y.U. Coll. of Dentistry, 209 E. 23d St., N.Y.C. 10. Died Dec. 31, 1951.

WRIGHT, WILBUR, aeronaut; b. nr. Millville, Ind., Apr. 16, 1867; s. Milton and Susan Catharine (Koerner) W.; brother of Orvile W.; ed. high schs., 4 yrs., Richmond, Ind., and Dayton, O.; (hon. B.S., Earlham College, Ind., 1909; LL.D., Oberlin College, Ohio, 1910); unmarried. From 1903, with his brother, Orville, devoted time to heavier-than-air flying machine, patented by Wright Bros. in leading countries of world. Has made numerous flights in U.S. and abroad; sold a machine to U.S. Govt. for $30,000. Awarded gold medal by French Academy Sciences, 1909; also many others. Mem. Aero Club of America. Home: Dayton, Ohio. Died May 30, 1912.

WRIGHT, WILLIAM HAMMOND, astronomer; b. San Francisco, Nov. 4, 1871; s. Selden Stuart and Joanna Maynard (Shaw) W.; B.S., U. Cal., 1893, grad. student, 1894-96, U. Chgo. (Yerkes Obs.), 1896-97; D.Sc., Northwestern U., 1929; m. Elna Warren Leib, Oct. 8, 1901. Asst. astronomer Lick Obs., 1897-1908, astronomer, 1908-44, emeritus, 1941—, dir., 1935-42, in charge obs.' expdn. to So. Hemisphere, 1903-06. Served as capt. Ordnance U.S. Army, 1918-19. Fgn. asso. Royal Astron. Soc. London; mem. Nat. Acad. Sci.; Am. Philos. Soc., Am. Astron. Soc. Contbr. astron. publs. Address: 60 N. Keeble Av., San Jose 26, Cal. Died May 16, 1959; buried Oak Hill Cemetery, San Jose, Cal.

WRIGHT, WILLIAM RYER, cons. engineer; b. N.Y. City, July 31, 1888; s. William Franklin, M.D., and Marie Louise (Ryer) W.; grad. Stevens School, Hoboken, N.J., 1907; E.M., Sch. of Mines (Columbia Univ.), 1911; m. Agnes R. Mackenzie, Feb. 18, 1913; children—Agnes Louise, William Ryer, Jr., Barbara Ashley. Began practice in N.Y. City, 1905; on Hudson Tunnel constrn., 1907; engr. with Braden Copper Co., 1911-12, Stafford & Wright, 1912-14, W. & W. F. Crockett, 1914-15, Aetna Explosives, Inc., 1916-17, Smith & Serrell, 1919-21; Chicago manager (partner) Ford, Bacon & Davis, Inc., consulting engrs., 1921-50 (retired from business activity with firm, July 1950, retaining connection as stockholder-partner); now in private practice as cons. engr.; State of Ill., since Nov. 1945. Served as 1st lt. Ordnance Dept., U.S. Army, 1917-19; formerly lt. col. Ordnance Reserve. Fellow, Am. Geographical Soc. Mem. Am. Institute Mining and Metallurgical Engineers (past dir.) Mining and Metall. Soc. of Am., Western Soc. Engineers, English-speaking Union, Acad. Polit. Science, S.R., Fraunces Tavern (N.Y. State), Army Ordnance Assn. (dir. Chicago Post), Delta Kappa Epsilon. Republican. Presbyterian. Mason. Clubs: University, Exmoor Country. Home: 1167 Lincoln Av. S., Highland Park, Ill. Died Nov. 27, 1952.

WULLING, FREDERICK JOHN, (wul'ing), pharmacologist; b. Brooklyn, N.Y., Dec. 24, 1866; s. John J. and Louise C. (Muns) W.; grad. business coll., 1884; grad. Columbia U. Coll. Pharmacy, 1887; Pharm.D., U. of Minn., 1894, LL.B., 1896, LL.M., 1898; hon. Pharm.M., Phila. Coll. Pharmacy, 1917; hon. Sc.D. Columbia U., 1929; ednl. trips to Eng., Germany, France, 1887, 89, 94, 97, 1911; m. Lucile Truth Gissel, 1897, 1 son, Emerson G. Prof. inorganic pharmaco-diagnosis, Brooklyn Coll. Pharmacy, 1891-92; dean of faculty and prof. pharmacology, Coll. of Pharmacy, 1892-1936, dir. medicinal plant garden, 1911-1936, U. of Minn. Retired with the title of Emeritus Dean, 1936. Asso. editor Pharm. Record, 1887-91. Trustee U.S. Pharmacopoeial Conv., 1920-30. Pres. Am. Conf. Pharm. Faculties, 1914-15; pres. Am. Pharm. Assn., 1916-17; fellow A.A.A.S.; emeritus mem. Am. Chem. Soc.; mem. Minn. State Pharmaceutical Assn. (honorary life president since 1943), Minn. Academy Sciences (chairman 1910-30), Minneapolis Soc. Fine Arts (dir.); hon. mem. N.J. State Pharm. Assn., Phi Delta Chi, Gamma Mu, Rho Chi, etc. Clubs: Automobile, Campus, Country, Dinner, Art, Lafayette, etc. Author: Evolution of Botany, 1891; Medical and Pharmaceutical Chemistry, 1894; Chemistry of the Carbon Compounds, 1900; A Course in Law, 1908; The Pharmacist's Relation to the Public, 1931; Charles F. Chandler: A Retrospect, 1944; Peter Wendover Bedford: A Retrospect, 1945; The First Four Melendy Memorial Lectures, 1946. Contbr. to various tech. and other jours. Wulling Hall, U. of Minn. bldg., named in his honor, 1942. Home: 3305 2d Av. S., Minneapolis 8, Minn.; (summer) Felstow, Excelsior, Minn. Died Oct. 21, 1947.

WUNDER, CLARENCE EDMOND, architect, engr.; b. Phila., Pa., Nov. 14, 1886; s. Otto and Katherine (Dirks) W.; ed. Central Manual Training Sch., Phila., and pvt. instrn.; m. Elizabeth I. Geissel, Oct. 18, 1910; children—Clarence Edmond, Katherine Elizabeth, Richard Paul. Draftsman with Kurt W. Peuckert, architect and engr., Phila., 1905-10; mem. Peuckert & Wunder, 1910-14, alone, 1914—; designer of Pennsylvania Hotel, Temple Univ. Stadium, Bonwit, Teller & Co.'s Store, George Allen Store, Cuneo Eastern Press, Inc., Keekler-Weyl Baking Co., etc. Mem. Am. Inst. Architects. Mason. Home: Ardmore, Pa. Died Oct. 19, 1940.

WURTS, ALEXANDER JAY, electrical engr.; b. Carbondale, Pa., Mar. 3, 1862; s. Charles Penberton and Lauro (Jay) W.; brother of John W.; Ph.B., Sheffield Scientific Sch. (Yale), 1883; M.E., Stevens Inst. Tech., 1884; studied electricity under Prof. Kohlrausch, Polytechnikum, Hanover, Germany, 1884-86; m. Jeanie Lowrie Childs, June 30, 1890 (died 1924); m. 2d, Elizabeth R. Wurts, 1927. On tech. staff Westinghouse Electric & Mfg. Co., 1887-98; mgr. Nernst Co., 1898-1904; gen. engr. Westinghouse Electric & Mfg. Co., 1904-05; prof. applied electricity and head of elec. dept., Carnegie Inst. Tech., 1905-21, prof. engineering research, same, 1921—; chmn. student welfare, 1924—. Discoverer of the five non-arcing metals. Awarded John Scott medal by City of Phila. through Franklin Inst. for inventions in lightning arresters. Home: Pittsburgh, Pa. Died 1932.

WÜRTTEMBERG, FRIEDRICH PAUL WILHELM, (Duke of Württemberg, Prince Paul), natural scientist; b. Germany, 1797; mil. edn. Abandoned mil. career to devote life to natural scis., 1817; made 1st of 5 trips to Am., traveling up Missouri River as guest of Am. Fur Co., 1822-24; pub. jour. of trip, Stuttgart, 1835; settled in Mergentheim, assembled charts, tables and sketches of his journeys; traveled in Am., circa 1850-58, made last trip, 1857-58. Died 1860.

WYATT, BERNARD LANGDON, (wi'at), internist; b. Tilton, N.H., Nov. 18, 1883; s. Walter Clement and Clara Rowena (Thorpe) W.; prep. edn., Tilton Sch., 1897-1901; M.D., N.Y.U., Bellevue Hosp. Med. Coll., 1905; post-grad. N.Y., 1915-17; Europe, 1917-21; m. Laura Wright, May 27, 1929 (dec.); m. 2d, Henry Etta Jones, Sept. 6, 1959. Began med. practice at Monterey, Mexico, 1905; medical officer of health, District of Abaco, Bahama Islands, 1912-15; associate director Rockefeller Commn. to France, 1917-21; pres. and dir. The Desert Sanatorium and Institute of Research, Tucson, Arizona, 1925-29; director The Wyatt Clinic, Tucson, 1929-41; former sr. partner of the Wyatt-Bensema Clinic and Research Labs.; cons. internal medicine. Past consultant health demonstrations, State Charities Aid Assn., N.Y.; former sec. tech. bd. and mem. advisory bd. Milbank Memorial Fund. Consultant to Motion Picture Relief Fund. Fellow Am. College Physicians, A.M.A., N.Y. Acad. Medicine; founder, mem. bd. dirs. and past pres. Am. Anti-Arthritis Assn.; mem. bd. dirs. Am. Acad. Applied Nutrition, 1946-49. Member Los Angeles Co. Medical Assn. (research found.), Hollywood Acad. Med., Cal., Los Angeles County medical socs., N.Y. University Alumni Assn. (mem. Alumni Hall Fund Com. and chmn. L.A. com. 1945-46), Am. Soc. French Legion of Honor. Chevalier Legion of Honor, Medaille de la reconnaissance française, 1st class (France); Medaille d'Honneur, Comite Nat. Contre la Tuberculose (France), 1937. Club: Pima Pistol (pres. 1943-46). Author med. books: Chronic Arthritis and Rheumatoid Affections, 1930; Diagnosis and Treatment of Chronic Arthritis and Fibrositis, 1933. Recipient Stacy medal and award Coll. Medicine, U. Cin., 1936. Contbr. on arthritis, nutrition, etc. Asso. editor: Acta Rheumatologica, 1930-33. Address: 3244 Mel Av., Las Vegas, Nev. Died June 22, 1961; buried Forest Lawn Meml. Park, Glendale, Cal.

WYER, SAMUEL S., cons. engr.; b. Wayne County, O., Feb. 18, 1879; s. David and Katherine (Eicher) W.; M.E., Ohio State U., 1903; m. Pauline L. Conover, June 16, 1904; children—Jean, Neal, Ramon; m. 2d, Eva Armstrong, Apr. 29, 1926. Practiced at Columbus, O., 1905—. Chief of Natural Gas Conservation, U.S. Fuel Adminstrn., during war period. Mem. Am. Soc. Mech. Engr., Am. Inst. Mining Engrs., A.A.A.S., Am. Gas Assn., Sigma Xi. Republican. Unitarian. Club: Athletic. Author: Producer Gas and Gas Producers, 1905; Catechism on Producer Gas, 1906; Gas Engines and Gas Producers (textbook), 1910; Regulation, Valuation and Depreciation of Public Utilities, 1913; Natural Gas—Its Production, Service and Conservation (Bull. 102, Smithsonian Instn.); The Smithsonian Instn.'s Study of Natural Resources Applied to Pa.'s Resources; Living Together in a Machine Civilization; reports on Niagara Falls, Power Possibilites at Muscle Shoals; Living-Together in a Power Age, also many reports on corp. problems. Retired temporarily and giving all time to research and pub. speaking on changing social order problems. Home: 1325 Cambridbe Blvd., Columbus, O. Died Nov. 30, 1955; buried Columbus, O.

WYMAN, WALTER, surgeon gen.; b. St. Louis, Mo., Aug. 17, 1848; s. Edward and Elizabeth (Hadley) W.; grad. City U. of St. Louis, 1866; A.B., Amherst, 1870, A.M., 1889; M.D., St. Louis Med. Coll., 1873; LL.D., Western U. of Pa., 1897, U. of Md., 1907. In Marine Hosp. Service, 1876—, serving successively at St. Louis, Cincinnati, Baltimore, New York, and Washington; gave spl. attention to physical conditions affecting seamen of merchant marine and was instrumental in having laws passed for their benefit; also brought to notice cruelties imposed on deck-hands on Western rivers and on crews of oyster vessels in Chesapeake Bay; established hosp. for latter; had charge of Govt. measures to ward off cholera, 1893. Supervising surgeon gen. U.S. Marine Hosp. Service, 1891-1902; surgeon gen. U.S. Pub. Health and Marine Hosp. Service, 1902—. Administrator Nat. quarantine law and establishments. Suggested and established first Govt. sanatorium for consumptives at Fort Stanton, N.M.; instrumental in securing enactment of laws relating to quarantine, quarters and food for seamen, govt. regulation of mfr. and sale of viruses, serums, toxins, etc., the establishment of a leprosy investigation sta. in Hawaii, the creation of a hygienic lab. at Washington, establishment of a bur. of pub. health. Author many pamphlets on public health. Mem. bd. of visitors Govt. Hosp. for Insane; chmn. Internat. Sanitary Bur. of Am. Republics; pres. Am. Pub. Health Assn., 1902-03, Assn. Mil. Surgeons, 1904-05; acting pres. Am. Nat. Red Cross, 1904; hon. fellow Am. Assn. Obstetricians and Gynecologists; sec. sect. pub. and internat. hygiene, 9th Internat. Med. Congress, Washington, 1887; chmn. com. internat. quarantine, Pan-Am. Med. Congress, Mex., 1896; chmn. sect. pub. health, Internat. Congress Arts and Sciences, St. Louis, 1904; pres. sect. state and municipal control, Internat. Congress on Tuberculosis, Washington, 1908; mem. many med. and other socs. Home: Washington, D.C. Died 1911.

WYNNE, THOMAS NEIL, mech. engr.; b. Indianapolis, Ind., June 24, 1980; s. Thomas Alfred and Mary Isabel (Neil) W.; prep. edn., Culver (Ind.) Naval Sch. and Indianapolis Manual Training High Sch.; student Cornell U., 1912; B.S. in Mech. Engring., U. of Wis., 1914, M.E., 1926; m. Hazel Black, Nov. 8, 1915; children—Catherine Jane, Mary Elizabeth, Thos. Neil, Martha Ann, John Watterson. With Indianapolis Light & Heat Co., 1914-26, becoming chief engr.; in business under title of Thos. N. Wynne & Associates, as pub. utility adviser and expert, since 1926; pres. Poll Mines, Inc., Metal Furnace Block Corp., Am. Public Service Corp., Wynnedale Constrn. Corp.; president, director, National Uniforms, Inc.; trustee Thomas A. Wynne Estate. Inventor and patentee Wynne Metal Furnace Block. Organized Town of Wynnedale, 1939, former trustee and pres. bd. (acting). Served as capt. Co. B, Ind. State Militia; organizer 113th Ind. Engrs., 1917; mgr. Chicago Dist. War Prodn. Bd., 1942. Fellow Am. Geog. Society; organizer Ind.-Ky. sect. Amateur Athletic Union (past pres.); mem. Am. Soc. M.E. (past pres. Ind. sect.), Am. Inst. E.E., Nat. Electric Light Assn., Ind. Engring. Society, Acad. Polit. Science, Nat. Aeronautical Soc., Ind. Electric Light Assn. (past pres.), Nat. Assn. Purchasing Agents (past pres. Ind. sect.). Republican. Episcopalian. Mason (32 deg., K.T., Shriner). Clubs: Hoosier Motor, Highland Golf, Optimist (hon. life mem. and past pres.). Author: Facts on Indiana Coal, 1926. Inventor various mech. appliances. Designer of subaqueous coal storage pit. Home: 2110 W. 42d St., Indpls. Died Jan. 30, 1953.

XANTUS, JÁNOS, ornithologist; b. Csokonya, Hungary, Oct. 5, 1825. Admitted to bar, Pest, Hungary, 1857; served in Hungarian War of Independence, 1848, captured by Austrians, 1849, escaped, 1850; came to U.S., 1851; topographer on Pacific R.R. expdn., 1852; mem. U.S. survey expdn. to find most feasible railroad route from Mississippi River to Pacific Ocean, 1855-57, collected bird specimens for Smithsonian Instn., discovered several new species; mem. U.S. expdn. to make meteorol. observation of Pacific Ocean, 1861, credited with discovering 89 islands and sand banks; his descriptions of newly-discovered Am. birds published in Vols. X-XII of Proceedings of Acad. of Natural Scis. Phila., 1859-61; apptd. U.S. consul to Manzanillo, Mexico, 1861; resumed permanent residence in Hungary, 1864; keeper of ethnographical div. Nat. Museum, Budapest, Hungary, until 1894. Author: Levelei Ejszakameukából (account of his travels), 1858; Utazás Kalifornia déli Részeibeu (dealt with So. Cal.). Died Budapest, Dec. 13, 1894.

YAGER, LOUIS, engineer; b. Germantown, Wis., July 12, 1877; s. Frederick R. and Mary (Eberlein) Y.; grad. high sch., Preston, Minn., 1895; C.E., U. of Minn., 1900; m. Hester Elizabeth Whiteley, of Brainerd, Minn., Aug. 14, 1902. Rodman and insp. N.P. Ry., 1900, asst. engr. on constrn., 1901-02, supervisor bridges and bldgs., at Minneapolis, 1902-07, asst. engr., St. Louis Bay Bridge reconstrn., Duluth, and constrn. Glendive (Mont.) East Line, 1907-10, div. engr., St. Paul, 1910-17, engr. maintenance of way, St. Paul, 1917-19; chief maintenance of way engr., U.S. R.R. Administration, Washington, D.C., 1919-20; engr., maintenance of way, N.P. Ry., St. Paul, 1920-22, asst. chief engr. since 1922. Mem. Am. Soc. C.E., Am. Ry. Engrs. Assn. (pres. 1929). Republican. Presbyn. Mason (32 deg.). Club: St. Paul Athletic. Home: 1156 Lincoln Av. Address: Northern Pacific Ry. Co., St Paul MN

YAGLOU, CONSTANTIN PRODROMOS, engr.; b. Constantinople, Turkey, Jan. 25, 1897; s. Prodromos and Helen (Petropoulos) Yagloglou; S.B. in Mech. Engring., Robert Coll., Sch. Engring., Constantinople, 1919; M.M.E., Cornell U., 1920; A.M., Harvard (hon.), 1947; m. Jane Louise Finn, June 14, 1927; 1 son, Edward. Came to U.S., 1919, naturalized, 1925. Research engr. Am. Soc. Heating & Ventilating Engrs. Research Lab., Pitts., 1921-25; instr. indsl. hygiene Harvard Sch. Pub. Health, 1925-27, asst. prof., 1927-38, asso. prof., 1938-47, prof., 1947—. Lt. comdr. USNR, 1940-50, comdr., 1950—. Mem. Am. Pub. Health Assn. (chmn. or mem. various coms.), Am. Soc. Heating and Air Conditioning Engrs. (chmn. or mem. various coms., Paul Anderson Gold medal 1958), A.A.A.S., Am. Indsl. Hygiene Assn., Delta Omega (pres. Beta chpt., 1947), Sigma Xi. Devel. effective index of warmth, hosp. air conditioning, arctic housing, arctic and tropic clothing, etc. Home: 10 Vernon Rd., Belmont, Mass. Died June 3, 1960.

YALE, LINUS, lock mfr.; b. Salisbury, N.Y., Apr. 4, 1821; s. Linus and Chlotilda (Hopson) Y.; m. Catherine Brooks, Sept. 14, 1844, 3 children. Entered lock mfg. bus., Shelburne Falls, Mass., 1851; introduced Monitor Bank Lock (1st combination bank lock), 1862, became consultant on bank locks; invented Cylinder Lock based on pin-tumbler mechanism (later adopted generally throughout U.S.); patented pin-tumbler lock, 1861, 65; partner (with Henry R. Towne) Yale Lock Mfg. Co., Stamford, Conn., 1868. Died N.Y.C., Dec. 25, 1868.

YANDELL, LUNSFORD PITTS, physician, paleontologist; b. nr. Hartsville, Tenn., July 4, 1805; s. Dr. Wilson and Elizabeth (Pitts) Y.; studied medicine under his father; attended Transylvania U., Lexington, Ky., 1822-23; grad. U. Md., Balt., 1825; m. Susan Juliet Wendal, Oct. 1825; m. 2d, Eliza Bland, Aug. 1861; 4 children. Practiced medicine, Murfreesboro, Tenn., 1826; moved to Nashville, Tenn., 1830; prof. chemistry and pharmacy Transylvania U., 1831-37; edited Transylvania Jour. of Medicine and Asso. Scis., Lexington, 1832-36; an organizer Louisville (Ky.) Med. Inst., 1837, prof. chemistry and materia medica, 1837-59, prof. physiology, after 1849; co-editor Western Jour. of Medicine and Surgery, 1840-55; taught in med. sch. Memphis, Tenn. until Civil War; joined Confederate Army as hosp. surgeon, 1861; entered ministry Presbyn. Ch., 1862, ordained pastor, Dancyville, Tenn., 1864, resigned, 1867; returned to med. practice, Louisville, 1867-78. Author: (with Dr. B. F. Shumard) Contributions to the Geology of Kentucky, 1847; author many articles in various periodicals concerned with medicine, geology, local history, education, and religion. Died Louisville, Feb. 4, 1878.

YANT, WILLIAM PARKS, (yant), chemist; b. East Sparta, O., Nov. 13, 1893; son of James Alpheus and Sarah Elizabeth (Parks) Y.; B.S., Wooster (Ohio) College, 1918, Sc.D., 1942; special course in chemistry, University of Pittsburgh; m. Elizabeth M. Grossman, July 29, 1933; children—William Parks, Gretchen Elizabeth, and Susan Jane. Instructor inorganic chemistry, Wooster Coll., 1919-20; jr. chemist Gas Lab., U.S. Bur. of Mines, Pittsburgh Expt. Sta., 1921, continuing successively as asst. chemist, chemist in charge of lab., supervising chemist of Health Lab. sect., supervising engr. U.S. Bur. Mines, Pittsburgh Expt. Sta. and chief chemist Health Div., U.S. Bur. of Mines, since 1936, dir. of research and development Mine Safety Appliances Co., Pittsburgh, Pa. Cons. U.S. Govt. and Armed Forces, Nat. Research Council, Office Sci. Research and Development; Mission to England, 1942; chmn. research com. Pres's Conf. on Indsl. Safety, 1949-54; chmn. steering com., equipment panel United States Conf. on Air Pollution, 1950. In Chem. Warfare Service, 1918; research on gas masks. Recipient Pittsburgh Award for Service in Chemistry, 1946. Member American Chem. Soc. (chmn. Pittsburgh sect., 1931, council, 1932-46), American Institute Mining and Metallurgical Engrs., Am. Public Health Assn. (chmn. indsl. hygiene section, 1942), Am. Soc. Safety Engineers (pres. 1950-51), Industrial Hygiene Found. (trustee); chmn. bd. trustees 1958—), Nat. Safety Council (vice president for industry 1952-53, member board directors); v.p. for research and member exec. com. of bd. 1959—), American Standards Assn., American Industrial Hygiene Association (pres. 1939; Cummings Meml. lectr. 1947), Ramazzini Soc., Phi Beta Kappa. Club: University (Pitts.). Contbr. many articles in govt. publs. and in tech. press, in the field of applied gas chemistry and engring., with particular reference to problems of health and safety from industrial gases, vapors and dusts; holder many patents. Home: R.D. 1, Box 278, Murrysville, Pa. Office: Mine Safety Appliances Co., J.T. Ryan Memorial Laboratory, 100 N. Braddock Av., Pitts. 15208. Died Jan. 29, 1963; buried East Sparta, O.

YATES, LORENZO GORDIN, naturalist; b. in England, Jan. 8, 1837; s. Richard Owen and Rosetta Mary Y.; ed. private schools; came to U.S., 1853; taught in common schools, Wis., 1854; sutdied medicine and dentistry; m. Eunice Amelia Lake, 1861 (died 1898). Was on staff Prof. J. D. Whitney in Geol. Survey of Calif.; specialist in ferns, general botany, conchology, mineralogy, palaeontology, N. Am. Indians; was in charge scientific dept. Froebel Inst., Los Angeles; catalogued collections and prepared "Guide" for Golden Gate Park Museum, San Francisco; pres. Santa Barbara Soc. of Natural History; hon. mem. S. Calif. Acad. of Sciences; fellow Linnaean Soc. of London;

Geol. Soc. of America. Author: California Digest of Masonic Law, 1867; Charm Stones, 1886; The Ferns of Ceylon, 1887; Notes on Hawaiian Ferns, 1887; The Channel Islands, 1890; The Mollusca of Santa Barbara County and New Shells from the Santa Barbara Channel, 1890; All Known Ferns; Aboriginal Weapons of California, 1900; Prehistoric California—Its Topography, Flora and Fauna, etc. (bull. S. Calif. Acad. Sciences), 1903. Died 1909.

YEAGER, ALBERT FRANKLIN, (ya'ger), horticulturist; b. Bazaar, Kan., Feb. 12, 1892; s. Charles D. and Mary T. (Schimpff) Y.; B.S., Kansas State Coll., 1912; M.S., Ore. State Coll., 1916; Ph.D., Ia. State Coll., 1936; m. Arline B. Stepanek, June 27, 1917; children—Mary (Mrs. L. F. Hough), Albert. Field agt. Pa. Chestnut Blight Commn., 1913-14; agr. instr. Crete (Neb.) High Sch., 1913-15; instr. horticulture Pa. State Coll., 1916-19; mem. faculty N.D. Agr. Coll., 1919-37, prof. horticulture, 1931-37; asst. prof. horticulture Mich. State Coll., 1937-39, prof. horticulture, horticulturist, chmn. dept. U. N.H., 1939-59; now emeritus asso. dir. Biol. Inst., 1946-48; horticulture consultant Beechnut Pkg. Co., 1948-56; consultant Office of Exptl. Stations, U.S. Dept. Agr., 1958—; cons. Watlee Burpee Seed Co. Awarded Certificate of Achievement, Vegetable Growers Assn. Am., 1953; Stevenson Meml. Gold Medal, Winnipeg, Can., 1954, Robertson Meml. gold medal, Brookings, S.D., 1956; Wilder medal American Pomological Society, 1957; Gold Seal award, Nat. Council State Garden Clubs, 1960. Fellow A.A.A.S., Am. Inst. Biol. Scis., Am. Acad. Arts and Scis.; member American Society of Horticultural Science (pres. 1950-51), American Society Plant Physiologists, Sigma Xi, Phi Kappa Phi, Alpha Zeta. Plant breeder, introduced 40 varieties of vegetables, fruits and flowers; 4 All Am. award medal winners. Author articles in various publs. Conglist. Home: 1645 Winkler Av., Ft. Myers, Fla. Died Nov. 4, 1961; buried Durham, N.H.

YEATES, WILLIAM SMITH, State geologist of Ga., and curator of the Georgia State Museum, 1893—; b. Murfreesboro, N.C., Dec. 15, 1856; s. Maj. Jesse J. and Virginia Scott Y.; B.A., Emory and Henry Coll., Va., 1878, M.A., 1881; m. Julia W., d. Maj. John W. Moore, C.S.A., of Ahoskie, N.C., Jan. 16, 1884. On U.S. Fish Commn. spring 1879; taught sch., 1879-80; employed in the Fisheries Div., 10th U.S. Census, 1880-81; aid, asst., acting curator and asst. curator, U.S. Nat. Museum, in charge collection of minerals and gems, 1881-93; prof. minerology, Corcoran Scientific School. Columbian Univ., Washington, 1884-93; prof. geology, same, 1890-93; exec. commr. for Ga., La. Purchase Expn., in charge of geology and forestry. Fellow Geol. Soc. of America; mem. many scientific socs. Home: Atlanta, Ga. Died 1908.

YEATMAN, POPE, mining engr.; b. St. Louis, Aug. 3, 1861; s. Thomas and Lucretia (Pope) Y.; M.E., Washington U., 1883; m. Georgie Claiborne Watkins, June 28, 1894 (dec. Jan. 1941); children—Jane Bell (Mrs. Ernest C. Savage), Georgina Pope, Pope. In mining in Mexico, Mo., N.M., Colo., 1883-95; mining engr. Consol. Gold Fields of S. Africa, Ltd., and mgr. Robinson Deep Gold Mining Co., Johannesburg, South Africa, 1895-99; also gen. mgr. Simmer and Jack Proprietary Gold Mining Co. Ltd., 1899; gen. mgr. and cons. engr. Randfontein Estates Gold Mining Co., Ltd., Transvaal, South Africa, 1899-1904; cons. engr. M. Guggenheim's Sons Co., and Guggenheim Exploration Co.; also cons. engr. Nev. Consol. Copper Co., Steptoe Valley Smelting & Mining Co., Chile Exploration Co., of Chile, Braden Copper Co., of Chile, 1906-16; ind. cons. practice since 1916. Vol. for service of U.S. in World War, Aug. 1917; cons. engr., later chief non-ferrous metals div. War Industries Bd., Washington, until Jan. 1919. Decorated D.S.M. Mem. Am. Inst. Mining Engrs., Am. Soc. C.E., Instn. Mining and Metallurgy (London), Engrs.' Society St. Louis, Mining and Metall. Soc. of America. Republican. Home: 520 East Gravers Lane, Chestnut Hill, Phila. Office: 70 Pine St., N.Y.C. 3. Died Dec. 5, 1953.

YERKES, ROBERT MEARNS, (yĕr'kez), psychobiologist; b. Breadysville, Pa., May 26, 1876; s. Silas Marshall and Susanna Addis (Carrell) Y.; A.B., Ursinus, 1897; A.B., Harvard, 1898, A.M., 1899, Ph.D., 1902; LL.D., Ursinus, 1923; D.Sc., Wesleyan U., 1923; hon. M.A., Yale, 1931; m. Ada Watterson, 1905; children—Roberta Watterson, David Norton. Began as teacher and investigator at Harvard, 1901, asst. prof. comparative psychology, 1908-17, psychologist to the Psychopathic Hosp., Boston, 1913-17; prof. psychology and dir. Psychol. Lab., U. of Minn., 1917-19 (absent on mil. duty); chmn. research information service, Nat. Research Council, 1919-24 (chmn. com. for research in problems of sex, 1921 47); prof. psychology, Inst. Psychology, Yale, 1924-29; prof. psychobiology, Yale 1929-44, emeritus, 1944—; organized and dir. Yale Labs. of Primate Biology, Orange Park, Fla., 1929-41, named Yerkes Labs. of Primate Biology, 1942. Chief, division of psychology, office Surg. Gen., A.U.S., 1917-18. Consulting services War Dept. and Nat. Research Council, World War II. Fellow Am. Acad. of Arts and Sciences, A.A.A.S.; mem. Nat. Acad. Sciences, Am. Philos. Soc., Am. Psychol. Assn. (pres., 1916-17), American Physiological Society, American Society Naturalists (pres. 1938), Soc. of Mammalogists. Club: Cosmos. Author: The Dancing Mouse, A Study in Animal Behavior, 1907; Introduction to Psychology, 1911; Methods of Studying Vision in Animals (with J. B. Watson), 1911; Outline of a Study of the Self (with D. W. La Rue), 1914; A Point Scale for Measuring Mental Ability (with R. S. Hardwick and J. W. Bridges), 1915; The Mental Life of Monkeys and Apes—A Study of Ideational Behavior, 1916; Psychological Examining in the U.S. Army (with others), 1921; Chimpanzee Intelligence and Its Vocal Expressions (with B. W. Learned), 1925; Almost Human, 1925; The Mind of a Gorilla, 1927; The Great Apes (with A. W. Yerkes), 1929; Chimpanzees: A Laboratory Colony, 1943; published papers chiefly on physiology of the nervous system, animal behavior, comparative psychology and mental measurement. Especially interested in psychobiological research, mental engineering, and problems of population. Home: 4 St. Ronan Terrace, New Haven. Died Feb. 3, 1956.

YODER, WORTH NICHOLAS, engr.; b. Wakarusa, Ind., Apr. 7, 1899; s. Nicholas B. and Clara (Longenecker) Y.; A.B., Asbury Coll., 1920; B.S. in Civil Engring., Purdue U., 1923; m. Eva May Merrill, June 4, 1921; children—Worth Nicholas, C. Merrill, Betty Lane (Mrs. Robert Fulwider). Engr., Indiana Service Corp., Ft. Wayne, 1923-27; constrn. engr. W.F. Schulz, Memphis, 1927-28; engr. Cin. Street Ry. Co., 1928-39; city mgr. City of Tipton (Ind.), 1939-48, City of Sturgis (Mich.), 1948-68, retired, 1968; spl. engr. City of Bloomington (Ind.), 1948; cons. engr., 1968-72. Served with U.S. Army, 1918; to maj. AUS, 1943-44; ETO. fellow Am. Soc. C.E.; mem. Internat. City Mgrs. Assn. (life), Mich. Community Health Assn. (dir.), Mich. Health Officers Assn., C. of C. Mason (Shriner). Home: Sturgis MI Died July 4, 1972.

YOUMANS, EDWARD LIVINGSTON, scientist, author; b. Caeymans, N.Y., Jan. 3, 1821; s. Vincent and Catherine (Scofield) Y.; M.D., U. Vt., circa 1851; m. Catherine (Newton) Lee, 1861. More than half blind most of life, aided by his sister, Eliza Ann; popular lectr. on science, 1851-68; became disciple of Herbert Spencer after reading his Principles of Psychology, 1856; called apostle of evolution; established Popular Science Monthly (later Scientific Monthly), N.Y.C., 1872. Author: A Classbook of Chemistry (became standard text), 1851; Hand-Book of Household Science, 1857. Editor: The Culture Demanded by Modern Life, 1867, Correlation and Conservation of Forces, 1864 (both collections of papers); The International Scientific Series, introduced with publ. of Forms of Water (Tyndall), 1872. Died N.Y.C., Jan. 18, 1887.

YOUNG, AARON, botanist, diplomat; b. Wiscasset, Me., Dec. 19, 1819; s. Aaron and Mary (Colburn) Y.; attended Bowdoin Coll., 1840-41, Jefferson Med. Coll., Phila., 1842-43. Asst. to Prof. Parker Cleaveland in natural history dept. Bowdoin Coll., 1840-41; sec. Bangor Natural History Soc., 1840's; state botanist Me., 1847-49, explored Mt. Kathadin and Castine Bay, published report on 1st surveys of Mt. Katahdin in Me. Farmer, Mar.-May, 1848; practiced medicine specializing in ear surgery, Auburn, Lewiston and Portland (Me.); founded, wrote and printed 3 small weekly newspapers, Farmer and Mechanic, Pansophist, Touchstone (all Farmington, Me.), 1852-54; published Franklin Journal of Aural Surgery and Rational Medicine, Farmington; Am. counsul to Rio Grande do Sul, Brazil, 1863-73; mem. Mass. Med. Soc., circa 1875. Author: A Flora of Maine, 1848. Died Jan. 13, 1898.

YOUNG, ABRAM VAN EPS, chemist; b. Sheboygan, Wis., June 5, 1853; s. Van Eps and Arlisle (Seaman) Y.; Ph.B., Ph.C., U. of Mich., 1875; fellow, Johns Hopkins, 1878-80; unmarried. Asst. in chemistry, U. of Mich., 1875-77, Harvard, 1884-85; prof. chemistry, Northwestern U., 1885—. Author: The Elementary Principles of Chemistry. Died Dec. 23, 1921.

YOUNG, ARCHER EVERETT, mathematician; b. Haddam Neck, Conn., Mar. 12, 1873; s. Hezekiah Russell and Sarah E. (Andrews) Y.; A.B., Wesleyan U., Conn., 1898; Ph.D., Princeton, 1903; m. Grace Louise Wiard, of New Britain, Conn., Sept. 1, 1903; children—Everett W., Mary Louse, James Russell, Marjorie Evelyn. Instr. Shadyside Acad., Pittsburgh, 1898-1901; prof. mathematics, Purdue U., Layayette, Ind., 1903-08; same, Miami U., Oxford, O., 1908-21, also dean, 1913-21; with Standard Oil interests, 1921—. Mem. Am. Math. Soc., Phi Beta Kappa, Alpha Delta Phi. Presbyn. Frequent contbr. to math. publs. Home: 1524 Asbury Pl., Pittsburgh PA

YOUNG, CHARLES AUGUSTUS, prof. astronomy, Princeton U., 1877-1905; b. Hanover, N.H., Dec. 15, 1834; grad. Dartmouth, 1853; Ph.D., U. of Pa., 1870, Hamilton Coll., New York, 1871; LL.D., Wesleyan, Conn., 1876, Columbia, 1887, Western Reserve, 1893, Dartmouth, 1903; m. Augusta S. Mixer, Aug. 26, 1857. Served as capt. Co. B, 85th Regiment, Ohio vols., 4 months, 1862. Prof. mathematics, natural philosophy and astronomy, Western Reserve Coll., 1857-66; prof. natural philosophy and astronomy, Dartmouth, 1866-77; then at Princeton until resigned, June, 1905. Mem. of Nat. Acad. Sciences and many other Am. and foreign learned socs. Specialist in solar physics; discoverer of the solar "reversing layer." Author: The Sun (in Internat. Scientific Series), 1882; A General Astronomy, 1889; Elements of Astronomy, 1890; Lessons in Astronomy, 1891; Manual of Astronomy, 1902; Uranography. Home: Hanover, N.H. Died 1908.

YOUNG, C(HARLES) GRIFFITH, engineer; b. at Bath, Steuben Co., N.Y., Nov. 1, 1866; s. of Charles Henry and Marion (Kellogg) Y.; ed. Haverling Acad.; m. Bessie Curtis Leonard, of New York, Oct. 21, 1890. With Schyler Electric & Mfg. Co., Hartford, and Middletown, Conn., 1886-87; gen. supt. Mt. Morris Electric Lighting Co., New York, 1887-92; gen. supt. constrn., constrn. mgr. White-Crosby Co. and the J. G. White, Am. and foreign corps., 1892-1909; independent practice with headquarters in New York, 1909-18; exec., war service com. of typewriter industry, 1918; pres. C. G. Young Co., Inc., consulting engrs. Has done much important engring. and constrn. work, original investigations and plans for consolidations and financing of pub. utilities and industrials, in many Am. cities and in Can., S. America, Central America, W.I., China, Japan, Philippines, New Zealand, Australia, Siberia and several European countries. Fellow Am. Inst. Elec. Engineers; member New York Electrical Society (pres.), Am. Soc. Civil Engrs., Pan-Am. Soc. Pan-Am. Chamber of Commerce, Steuben Soc.; member Council on Foreign Relations. Clubs: Engineers', Railroad, Circumnavigators, Adirondack League. Home: 981 Madison Av. Office: 14 Wall St., New York, N.Y.

YOUNG, FRANKLIN KNOWLES, author, inventor; b. Boston, Oct. 21, 1857; ed. there; inventor automatic breech-action for small arms and field artillery. Author: The Minor Tactics of Chess; The Major Tactics of Chess; The Grand Tactics of Chess; Chess Strategetics, Illustrated; Napoleon's Campaigns. Address: Press Club, Boston.

YOUNG, GEORGE A., veterinarian; b. Syracuse, Neb., Jan. 27, 1917; s. George A. and Genevieve (Cunningham) Y.; B.A., U. Neb., 1939; D.V.M., Cornell U., 1943; m. Anetta Ruth Wendeln, June 23, 1940; children—James Alan, Judy Ann, William Joe. From research asso. to asso prof. Hormel Inst., U. Minn., 1946-55; prof. dept. vet. sci. U. Neb., 1955-62, chmn. dept., 1956—, Bert Rodgers prof. vet. sci., 1962—; developed method for elimination and control chronic diseases of swine. Bd. dirs., past pres. N.E. Lincoln YMCA, 1957-63. Served from lt. to capt., Vet. Corps, AUS, 1943-46. Recipient Distinguished Service Research award Animal Health Inst., 1961; Distinguished Service award agr. Gamma Sigma Delta, 1961. Mem. Am. Acad. Microbiology, Am. Soc. Microbiology, Soc. Exptl. Biology and Medicine, Am. Vet. Med. Assn., Sigma Xi. Conglist. (bd. deacons). Author numerous sci. articles. Home: 6320 Madison Av., Lincoln, Neb. 68507. Died Apr. 17, 1964; buried Park Hill Cemetery, Syracuse, Neb.

YOUNG, GEORGE HUSBAND, research chemist; b. Meyersdale, Pa., May 14, 1909; s. Wayland Phillips and Edith (Husband) Y.; B.S., Pa. State Univ., 1932, M.S., 1934, Ph.D., 1936; m. Ann Lewis Reimel, Aug. 5, 1933 (div. 1951); 1 dau., Patricia Ann; m. 2d, Mary Elizabeth Schollenberger Lester, July 25, 1952 (dec. 1961); stepchildren—Susan Philips Lester, R. Holmes Lester, III. Engr. Western Electric Company, 1928-30, graduate assistant Institute of Paper Chemistry, Lawrence Coll., 1932; research chemist Anthracite Institute, 1933; fellow Mellon Institute for Industrial Research, 1935-36, senior fellow, 1936-44, exec. assistant to director, 1944-47, asst. dir., 1947-51, dir. research since 1952; director research Stoner-Mudge, Inc., 1938-44; cons. Office Assistant Sec. of Defense, Research and Development. Admitted to practice United States Patent Office, 1940; licensed professional engineer (Pennsylvania), 1945. Sec.-treas. American Coordinating Com. on Corrosion, vice chmn., 1944, chmn., 1945; civilian adviser on corrosion, U.S. Army and Navy Dept., since 1938; chairman of the advisory committee on endl. standards of Am. Bd. for Certification of Orthopedic Appliance and Limb Mfrs. Assn. Trustee Pa. State U., 1948-51. Fellow Am. Inst. Chemists, A.A.A.S.; mem. Newcomen Soc., Brit. Soc. Chem. Industry, Brit. Soc. Plastics Industry, Brit. Soc. Glass Tech., Am. Chem. Soc., Nat. Assn. Corrosion Engrs., Pitts. Patent Law Assn., Pa. Chem. Society (pres. 1950), Assn. Research Dirs., Soc. Naval Architects and Marine Engr., Ordnance Association. Clubs: Pittsburgh and New York Chemists; Cosmos (Washington); University; Republican. Mem. editorial bd. Corrosion Handbook. Contbr. Jour. Indsl. Chemistry and Engring., Jour. Am. Chem. Soc., Zeitschrift für Kristallographie, Record Chem. Progress, Science, Nature. Authority in fields of synthetic resins, protective coatings, corrosion technology, marine and anti-fouling paints. Received Naval Ordnance Development civilian award for work in these fields, World War II. Home: 533 Briar Cliff Rd., Pittsburgh 21. Office: 4400 Fifth Av., Pitts. 15213. Died Oct. 10, 1961; buried Somerset, Pa.

YOUNG, GEORGE JOSEPH, mining engr.; b. San Francisco, Oct. 3, 1876; s. Joseph and Mary (Wilburn) Y.; B.S., U. of Calif., 1899; m. Wayman A. Atterbury, June 24, 1912 (dec.); 1 child, Marion Wayman; m. 2d, Hulda Hanson, 1920. Asst. prof. metallurgy, U. of Nev., 1900-03, prof. mining and metallurgy, 1903-13; in charge of Mackay Sch. of Mines, U. of Nev., 1908-13;

prof. mining, U. of Minn., 1913-16; prof. metallurgy, Colo. Sch. of Mines, 1916-17; cons. mining and metall. engineer, San Francisco, since 1917. Was dir. of Cooperative Lab., potash investigations of Bur. of Soils, Dept. of Agriculture and Mackay School of Mines. Mem. Am. Inst. Mining and Metall. Engrs. Clubs: Engineers', Sierra. Author: Elements of Mining; The Working of Unstratified Mineral Deposits. Asst. editor Engineering and Mining Journal, 1918-19, asso. editor same, 1919-32, consulting editor since 1933. Lecturer in mining U. of Calif., 1946-48. Home: 5928 Keith Av., Oakland 18 CA

YOUNG, GILBERT AMOS, mechanical engr.; b. Owosso, Mich., June 24, 1872; s. Amos G. and Mary (Alling) Y.; B.S. in M.E., S.D. State Coll., 1894; B.S. in M.E., Purdue U., 1899, M.E., 1903; M.M.E., Harvard, 1910; m. Berdella J. Keith, June 25, 1902; 1 son, Ronald Keith. Instr. practical mechanics, S.D. State Coll., 1894-98; asst. Purdue U., 1899-1901, instr. in mech. engring., 1901-03, successively asst., asso. and full prof. mech. engring., 1903-09, head Sch. of Mech. Engring. and dir. of Mech. Engring. Labs. since 1911. Republican. Presbyterian. Mem. Am. Soc. Mech. Engrs., Soc. Automotive Engrs., Soc. Promotion Engring. Edn., Pi Tau Sigma, Tau Beta Pi, Phi Gamma Delta, etc. Author: Text Notes, Steam Turbines, Gas Engines, Thermodynamics. Co-author (with V. W. Young) Text book Elements of Thermodynamics. Writer on mech. engring. subjects. Home: Lafayette, Ind. Died June 27, 1943.

YOUNG, HERBERT A(LEXANDER), coll. dean; b. San Diego, Cal., Oct. 10, 1906; s. William Alexander and Aldie (Jennings) Y.; B.S., U. Cal., 1928, Ph.D., 1932; m. Maxine Bardsley, Aug. 12, 1929; 1 son, John C. Inst. chemistry U. Cal. at Berkeley, 1933-34, asst. prof. chemistry, Davis, Cal., 1934-40, asso. prof., 1940-46, chmn. div. chemistry, 1940-51, prof. since 1946, dean coll. letters and sci. since 1951; dir. chem. research, development Tenn. Eastman Co., Clinton Engr. Works, Oak Ridge, Tenn., 1943-45. Recipient Fulbright award, 1955-56, 62-63. Mem. Am. Chem. Society (v.p., president, mem. council Sacramento sect.). Contbr. articles profl. jours. Home: 726 Oak Av., Davis, Cal. Died Jan. 14, 1965.

YOUNG, HUGH HAMPTON, surgeon, b. San Antonio, Tex., Sept. 18, 1870; s. Gen. William Hugh and Frances Michie (Kemper) Y.; A.B., A.M., U. of Va., 1893, M.D., 1894; Johns Hopkins, 1894-95; D.Sc., Queen's U., Belfast, 1933; m. Bessy Mason Colston, June 4, 1901 (died May 21, 1928); children—Frances Kemper (Mrs. Wm. Francis Rienhoff), Frederick Colston, Helen Hampton (Mrs. Bennett Crain), Elizabeth Campbell (Mrs. Warren Russell Starr). Pathologist to Thomas Wilson Sanitarium, 1895; successively asst. resident surgeon, 1895-98, head of dept. urol. surgery, and asso. surgeon Johns Hopkins Hospital, and clinical professor urology, Johns Hopkins U. Pres. Md. State Lunacy Commn. Pres. Am. Assn. Genito-Urinary Surgeons, 1909, Am. Urol. Assn., 1909, Medico-Chirurgical Faculty of Maryland, 1912; dir. urology A.E.F., 1917; sr. consultant in same, A.E.F., 1918; col. Med. Corps U.S. Army. Chmn. Bd. of Mental Hygiene for Md.; chmn. Md. Aviation Commn.; v.p. Baltimore Museum of Art; pres. Lyric Theatre; pres. Baltimore Opera Club; chmn. Md. Commn. for New York World's Fair, 1939. Awarded Keyes medal, for contributions to Urology, 1936; Francis Amory Septennial Prize for outstanding work on cancer of the prostate, 1941. Mem. Internat. Assn. Congres Internationale d'Urologie (pres. 1927); corr. mem. Association Française d'Urologie, Deutsche Gesellschaft für Urologie, Sociedad de Cirujia de Buenos Aires, Societa Italiana di Urologia, R. Romanne Medicorum Academie Praeses, Chi Phi and Nu Sigma Nu fraternities; fellow Royal College Surgeons of Ireland; honorary fellow Royal Society of Medicine; fellow American College of Surgeons. Clubs: Maryland, Elkridge, Gibson Island, Baltimore Country, Johns Hopkins, Bachelors Cotillon. Author: Studies in Urological Surgery (Vol. XIII, Johns Hopkins Hosp. Repts.), 1906); Hypertrophy and Cancer of the Prostate (Vol. XIV, Johns Hopkins Reports), 1906; Young's Practice of Urology (2 vols.); Urological Roentgenology; Genital Abnormalities, Hermaphroditism and Related Adrenal Diseases; Hugh Young, A Surgeon's Autobiography, 1940. Founder and editor Jour. of Urology. Has contributed over 350 papers to Am. and foreign med. jours. Home: 100 W. Cold Spring Lane, Baltimore, Md. Died Aug. 23, 1945.

YOUNG, JOHN WESLEY, coll. prof.; b. Columbus, O., Nov. 17, 1879; s. William Henry and Marie Louise (Widenhorn) Y.; ed. Karlsruhe, Germany, and Columbus, O., 1885-89; Gymnasium Baden-Baden, Germany, 1889-95; Ph.B., Ohio State U., 1899, A.M., Cornell U., 1901, Ph.D., 1904; m. Mary Louise Aston, July 20, 1907; 1 dau., Mary Elizabeth. Instr. mathematics, Northwestern U., 1903-05; preceptor mathematics, Princeton, 1905-08; asst. prof. mathematics, U. of Ill., 1908-10; prof. and head of dept. of mathematics, U. of Kan., 1910-11; prof. mathematics, U. of Chicago, summer quarter, 1911; prof. of mathematics, Dartmouth Coll., 1911—. Chief examiner in geometry, Coll. Entrnace Exam. Board, 1915-17. Editor, Bulletin Am. Math. Soc., 1907-25. Was pres. Math. Assn., America and mem. many other socs.; chmn. Nat. Com. on Math Requirements, 1916-23. Author: Projective Geometry, Vol. 1 (with Oswald Veblen), 1910; Lectures on Fundamental Concepts of Algebra and Geometry, 1911 (Italian transl., 1919); Plane Geometry (with A. J. Schwartz), 1915, 2d edit., 1922; Elementary Mathematical Analysis (with F. M. Morgan), 1917; Plane Trigonometry (with F. M. Morgan), 1919; Projective Geometry, 1929; also papers in various math. jours. Editor, for the Houghton Mifflin Co., of a series of math. texts. War work, 1918, with ednl. bur. Y.M.C.A., N.Y. City, and with Com. on Edn. and Spl. Training, War Dept., Washington, D.C. Home: Hanover, N.H. Died Feb. 17, 1932.

YOUNG, LEWIS EMANUEL, cons. engr.; b. Topeka, Oct. 1, 1878; s. William O. and Martha (Lebegern) Y.; B.S., Pa. State Coll., 1900; E.M., Ia. State Coll., 1904; Ph.D., U. Ill., 1915; D.Engring., Mo. Sch. Mines, 1947, Colo. Sch. Mines, 1951; m. Mabel E. Webb, July 1, 1903 (dec.); children—Edwin Webb, Lewis Eugene (dec.); m. 2d, Elizabeth Whipple, Oct. 3, 1927. Instr. mining Ia. State Coll., 1900-03; prof. mining Colo. Sch. Mines, 1903-07; cons. engr., Denver, 1903-07; dir. Mo. Sch. Mines, 1907-13; spl. field work Ill. Geol. Survey, 1913-17; asst. prof. bus. adminstrn. U. Ill., 1915-18; mining engr. Union Colliery Co., St. Louis, 1918-22, gen. mgr., 1922-26; prodn. v.p. Pitts. Coal Co., 1927-39; cons. mining engr., Pitts., 1939. Mem. Am. Inst. Mining and Metall. Engrs. (dir. 1937-42, v.p. 1942-45, pres. 1949), Canadian Inst. Mining and Metallurgy, Mining and Metall. Soc. Am., Am. Mining Congress, Coal Mining Inst. Am., Inst. Mining Engrs. (Eng.), Sigma Xi, Tau Beta Pi, Kappa Delta Pi, Beta Gamma Sigma, Phi Kappa Phi. Mason (Shriner). Clubs: Duquesne (Pitts.); Mining (N.Y.C.); University. Home: Schenley Park Apts., Fifth Av., Pitts. 13. Office: Oliver Bldg., Pitts. 22. Died Dec. 27, 1953; buried Homewood Cemetery, Pitts.

YOUNG, ROBERT THOMPSON, zoologist; b. Phila., Pa., Feb. 14, 1874; s. James Thompson and Lucy Stoddard (Peet) Y.; B.S., U. of Pa., 1896; Ph.D., U. of Neb., 1906; m. Ellen Farrar Pierce, Mar. 22, 1907; 1 son, Robert Thompson. With U. of N.Dak., 1906-26, prof. zoology, 1914-26; prof. zoology, U. of Mont., 1927-34. Mem. Am. Soc. Zoologists, Sigma Xi. Spl. researches in cytology and cestodes, protective coloration of animals, biology of lakes. Author: Biology in America. Home: La Jolla CA

YOUNGER, JOHN ELLIOTT, engr., prof. engring.; b. Canyon, Tex., Mar. 7, 1892; s. James Beauregard and Mary Ella (Elliott) Y.; student West Tex. State Teachers Coll., 1911-12, U. of Tex., 1914-15; B.S., U. of Calif., 1923, M.S., 1924, Ph.D., 1925; m. Nancy Brunette Francis, June 3, 1919; children—John Francis, Nancy Ella. Prin. Abernathy (Tex.) High Sch., 1912-14; teacher Philippine Islands, 1914-17; teacher of mech. engring., U. of Calif., 1923-27; sr. aeronautical engr. U.S. Army Air Corps, 1927-29; prof. of mech. engring., U. of Calif., 1929-38; prof. mech. engring., head dept., U. of Md., 1938-47, since 1948; prof. Structures, Inst. Tecnológica de Aeronáutico, Brasil, 1947-48. Served as 2d lt., Res. mil. aviator, Air Serv., U.S.A., 1917-19. Stud. aeronautl. developments in round-the-world tour, 1936; lectured before Royal Aeronaut. Soc. of Great Britain, London, on high altitude flying, 1938. Recipient of Spirit of St. Louis Gold medal for contributions to science of aviation, 1941. Fellow Inst. Aeronautical Sciences; mem. A.S.M.E., Am. Soc. Engring. Edn., American Assn. of Univ. Profs., Sigma Xi, Tau Beta Pi. Author: Dynamics of Airplanes (with B. M. Woods), 1931; Airplane Construction and Repair, 1931; Structural Design of Metal Airplanes, 1935; Airplane Maintenance (with A. F. Bonnalie and N. F. Ward), 1937; Mechanics for Engineering Students, 1938; Mechanics of Aircraft Structures, 1942; Advanced Dynamics, 1958. Contbr. many papers to jours. of scientific socs. Home: 4124 Woodbery St., Hyattsville, Md. Office: U. of Md., Coll. Park, Md. Died Dec. 29, 1958; buried Arlington Nat. Cemetery.

YOUNGKEN, HEBER WILKINSON, (yung'ken), botanist, pharmacognosist; b. Richland Tp., Bucks County, Pa., Oct. 31, 1885; s. Charles Eugene and Marian W. (Wilkinson) Y.; Ph.G., Medico-Chirurg. Coll., Phila., 1905; med. student same, 1909-11; A.B., Bucknell U., Lewisburg, Pa., 1909, A.M., 1912; M.S., U. of Pa., 1914, Ph.D., 1915; hon. Ph.M., Phila. Coll. of Pharmacy, 1919; hon. Sc.D., Bucknell U., Pa., 1934; Pharm. D. (hon.), Mass. College of Pharmacy, 1956; m. Clara Maude Eastman, Sept. 12, 1911; children—Marion E., Heber W., Flora E., Eugene W. Demonstrator biology and pharmacognosy, 1909-11, instructor, 1911-12, assistant professor, 1912-14, adjunct professor, 1914-16, professor, 1916, Medico-Chirurgical College; assistant professor botany and pharmacognosy, Phila. Coll. of Pharmacy and Science, 1916-17, acting prof., 1917-18, prof., 1918-23; prof. biology, Ursinus Coll., 1918-19; prof. pharmacognosy and biology and chmn. dept. of materia medica, Mass. Coll. of Pharmacy, 1923-51, research prof. pharmacognosy and botany, 1951-57, emeritus prof. of pharmacognosy and botany, 1957—. Ebert medallist, 1925, 31; chmn. com. on pharm. botany and pharmacognosy, National Research Council, 1923-42; executive secretary of Section K, 4th International Botanical Congress, 1926; hon. fgn. mem. Acad. Pharm., Brazil; mem. sub-com. tests and standards and gen. tests Revision Com. U.S. Pharmacopoeia, mem. conv., 1920—; chmn. E. L. Newcomb Meml. awards com. Am. Found. Pharm. Edn. Fellow A.A.A.S.; mem. Am. Pharm. Assn. (chmn. scientific section 1921-22; sec. history section, 1934-35; chmn. history section 1935-36; chmn. com. Kilmer Prize, 1938-41; chmn. com. hort. nomenclature hon. pres. 1961), Am. Soc. Pharmacognosy, Herb. Soc. Am., Am. Soc. Plant Taxonomists, Internat. Soc. for Plant Taxonomy, Boston Druggists' Assn. (pres. 1934-36), Bot. Soc. America, New England Bot. Club, Josselyn Bot. Soc. of Maine, Vt. and N.H. State pharm. assns., Sigma Xi, Rho Chi, Phi Chi, Beta Phi Sigma, Kappa Psi (Grand Regent 1937-41); corr. mem. Phila. Bot. Club. Mason. Author books, also papers and monographs, relating to field. Editor sect. on pharmacognosy and pharm. botany Biol. Abstracts since 1927; asso. editor U.S. Dispensatory, 21st-25th edits., cons. pharmacognosist. Address: 17 Cox Rd., Winchester, Mass. Office: 179 Longwood Ave., Boston 15. Died July 20, 1963; buried Bloomsburg, Pa.

YOUNGS, J(OHN) W(ILLIAM) T(HEODORE), educator, mathematician; b. Bilaspur, India, Aug. 21, 1910 (parents Am. citizens); s. Cornelius Herman and Lulu Gertrude (Johnson) Suckau; student Philander Smith Sch., Naini Tal, India, 1922-28; B.S., Wheaton Coll., 1930; M.A., Ohio State U., 1931, Ph.D., 1934; m. Marguerite Davenport Strong, Sept. 3, 1938; children—John William Theodore, Christopher Emory Strong. Came to U.S., 1928. Master, Stony Brook Sch., 1934-37; instr. Ohio State U., 1937-41; instr. Purdue U., 1941-42, asst. prof., 1942-46; asso. prof. Ind. U., 1946-48, prof., 1948-65, chmn. dept. mathematics, dir. Grad. Inst. Mathematics and Mechanics, 1956-65; prof. math. Univ. Cal., Santa Cruz, 1965-70. Supt. Sandia Corp., 1951-52. Cons. OSRD, 1944, 8th Air Force, 1944-45, U.S. Strategic Bombing Survey, 1945, RAND Corp., 1948-70, Ramo-Wooldridge Corp., 1953-56; cons. Naval Research Laboratory, 1960-70. Trustee George Washington Carver Institute also Carver Research Foundation. Guggenheim fellow, 1946-47. Mem. NRC (chairman liaison com. division mathematics), Am. Math. Soc. (asso. sec. 1948-63), Institute for Defense Analyses, Mathematical Assn. Am., Sigma Xi. Editor Jour. Combinatorial Theory. Author articles on math. subjects. Home: Santa Cruz CA Died July 20, 1970; buried Youngs Meml. Cemetery, Oyster Bay NY

YOUTZ, LEWIS ADDISON, (utz), chemist; b. Canton, O., July 21, 1864; s. Reuben J. and Harriett (Miller) Y.; Ph.B., Simpson Coll., Indianola, Ia., 1890, Ph.M., 1893, M.S., 1902; Ph.D., Columbia, 1902; m. Eva I. Moore, Nov. 3, 1892. Science teacher high sch., Des Moines, Ia., 1891-93 asso. prof. chemistry; and biology, Simpson Coll., 1893-99; prof. science, Montana Wesleyan U., 1899-1900; prof. chemistry, Lawrence Coll., Appleton, Wis., 1902— and of Inst. Paper Chemistry, 1930—; former chemist, Riverside Paper and Fiber Co., Great Lakes Chem. Co., Pattern Paper Co. (all of Appleton). Mem. Am. Chem. Soc., Phi Kappa Psi, Phi Beta Kappa. Republican. Methodist. Author: Laboratory Outline of General Inorganic Chemistry, 1904. Home: 843 E. South St., Appleton, Wis. Died Nov. 19, 1947.

YOWELL, EVERETT IRVING, astronomer; b. Cin., Jan. 2, 1870; s. Richard Chase and Sarah Louisa (Lloyd) Y.; C.E., U. Cin., 1891, M.S., 1893, Ph.D., 1911; studied U. Göttingen, 1894-95; m. Elizabeth Cabell Carrington, May 30, 1912; children—John Lloyd, Mary Tucker, Everett Carrington, Elizabeth Morton. Instr. mathematics, U. Cin., 1891-94, 1895-97; asst. in Cin. Obs. (part of U. Cin.), 1897-1901, U.S. Naval Obs., 1901-06; instr. in mathematics, U.S. Naval Acad., 1906-09; 1st asst. Cin. Obs., 1909-30, acting dir., 1930-31, dir. and head dept. of astronomy, 1931-40, acting dir., 1943-46; v.p., chmn. math. sect., Ohio Acad. Sci., 1944-46. Fellow A.A.A.S. (v.p., chmn. astronomy sect., 1939); mem. Am. Astron. Soc., Am. Math. Soc., Math. Assn. Am., Nat. Inst. Social Scis., Sigma Alpha Epsilon, Sigma Xi. Mem. Naval Obs. eclipse party, 1900, 05; Internat. Latitude observer, 1910-16; in charge Cin. Obs. eclipse party, 1932. Ind. Republican. Author of various publs. of Cincinnati Observatory. Home: 3127 Griest Av., Cincinnati 8, O. Died Mar. 13, 1959.

YUDKIN, ARTHUR M(EYER), ophthalmologist; born at Ansonia, Connecticut, December 31, 1892; son of Michael and Minnie (Zandler) Y.; Ph.B., Yale University, 1914, M.D., 1917; married Adele I. Weissman, Jan. 25, 1920; children—Gerald S., Marvin H. Asst. resident physician, New Haven Hosp., 1917-18, interne ophthalmology, 1918; clin. asst. ophthalmology and laryngology, Yale Sch. of Medicine, 1918-21, clin. instr. ophthalmology, 1921-25, asst. clin. prof., 1925-28, asso. clin. prof., 1928-34, clin. prof. ophthalmology since 1934; attending surgeon ophthalmology, Grace-New Haven Community Hosp. Univ. Service, attending ophthalmologist St. Raphael Hosp.; cons. ophthalmologist Griffin Hosp., Derby, Conn., Bristol Hosp. and Meriden Hosp., also to Nat. Soc. for Prevention of Blindness. Major Med. Res. Corp, 1943. Mem. Am. Acad. Ophthal. and Otol., A.M.A. (sect. ophthalmology), Am. Ophthol. Soc., Assn. Resrch. in Ophthol., Nat. Soc. Prevention Blindness, Soc. Exptl. Biol. and Medicine, N.Y. Acad. Medicine, N.Y. Soc. Clin. Ophthol., A.A.A.S., Sigma

Xi, Sigma Alpha Mu. Clubs: Milford Yacht; Racebrook Country; Faculty (Yale). Co-editor: Practitioners Library of Medicine and Surgery, Vol. 11, 1939. Contbr. articles to med. jours. Home: Tallwood Rd., Woodbridge. Office: 257 Church St., New Haven 10, Conn. Died May 1957.

YUNCKER, TRUMAN GEORGE, educator; b. Carson City, Mich., Mar. 20, 1891; s. Albert and Lillian (Wilson) Y.; B.S., Mich. State Coll., 1914, D.Sc., 1941; A.M., U. Neb., 1915; Ph.D. (fellow 1918-19), U. Ill., 1919; m. Ethel Burnett Claflin, Oct. 23, 1915; children—Betty-Jane C., Barbara Ann. Asst. prof. botany DePauw U., 1919-20, prof. botany, chmn. dept., 1921-56, prof. emeritus, 1956—, curator herbarium, 1956—; bacteriologist U.S. Army Med. Sch., 1918; research European Herbaria, summer 1926; prof. botany U. So. Cal., summer 1931; Yale Bishop Museum fellow Bishop Mus., Honolulu, Hawaii, 1932-33, 39-40, asso. botanist, 1941—; bot. expdns. to Honduras, 1934, 36, 38, Samoa and Nine Island, 1939-40; vis. research prof. U. Ill., 1946-47. Guggenheim fellow, also Nat. Sci. Found. research grantee for study flora Tongan Islands, 1953; Fullbright fellow bot. research Jamaica, 1957-58; Nat. Sci. Found. grant, Brazilian plants, 1960. Fellow A.A.A.S., Ind. Acad. Science (pres. 1939); mem. Bot. Soc. Am. (treas. 1947-52, v.p. 1953; chmn. taxonomy sect. 1937; golden ann. certificate of merit 1956), Am. Soc. Naturalists, Am. Soc. Plant Taxonomists (pres. 1957), Torrey Bot. Club, Am. Legion, Sigma Xi, Phi Delta Theta, Scabbard and Blade. Republican. Methodist. Mason (32 deg., K.T.); mem. Order Eastern Star (grand patron Ind. 1931-32). Author: Flora of Tonga; also articles Ind. flora, Convolvulacaae, Revision of Genus Cuscuta, Revisions in Hawaiian, Fijian, Cuban, Polynesian and Micronesian Species of Peperomia; Piperaceae No. S.A., Argentina, Boliva, Chile, Trinidad, Tobago. Contbr. Flora of Honduras. Home: 620 Highwood Av., Greencastle, Ind. Died Jan. 8, 1964; buried Evergreen Cemetery, Jackson, Mich.

ZAHORSKY, JOHN, pediatrician; b. Mereny, Hungary, Oct. 13, 1871; came to U.S., 1872, naturalized by father's citizenship; s. John and Amalia (Gura) Z.; A.B., Steelville (Mo.) Inst., 1892; M.D., Mo. Med. Coll., St. Louis, 1895; post-grad. Johns Hopkins, 1899; m. Elizabeth Silverwood, June 27, 1900; children—Theodore S., Elizabeth (Mrs. Joseph W. Cushing). Began practice 1895; resident physician, Bethesda Hosp., 1896-98; editor St. Louis Courier Medicine, 1900-1905; lectr. pediatrics Washington U., 1900-05, clin. prof., 1905-11; chief Children's Clinic, Washington U. Hosp. Clinic, 1905-11; attending physician, St. Louis Children's Hosp., 1910-12; pediatricians St. Louis City Hosp., 1920-23, St. John's Hosp., 1920-27; prof. pediatrics St. Louis U., 1912-48, chmn. dept., 1928-33, named dir. dept., 1933, now emeritus; pediatrician-in-chief St. Mary's Group Hosp., 1924-48. Licentiate Am. Bd. Pediatrics, 1936: pres. bd. dirs. Bethesda Gen. Hosp. Received awards from St. Louis U. and St. Louis Pediatric Soc. Fellow A.C.P.; mem. A.M.A., So. Med. Assn., Acad. Pediatrics, St. Louis Med. Soc., Acad. Sci., Mo. Hort. Soc., Mo. Hist. Soc., Phi Beta Pi, Alpha Omega Alpha, Sigma Xi. Mason (32 deg., Scottish Rite), Modern Woodman, Ruling elder, Kingshighway Presbyn. Ch. Republican. Author: Baby Incubators, 1905; Golden Rules of Pediatrics, 1913; Synopsis Pediatrics, 6th edit., 1953; The Infant and Child, 1939; From the Hills, Autobiography, 1950; also about 125 med. articles. Home: Box 186, Steelville, Mo. 65565. Died Feb. 5, 1963; buried Steelville.

ZALINSKI, EDMUND LOUIS GRAY, soldier, inventor pneumatic dynamite torpedo gun; b. Kurnich, Prussia Poland, Dec. 13, 1849, came with parents to U.S. when 4 yrs. old; settled at Seneca Falls, N.Y.; ed. pub. schs., Seneca Falls, Syracuse High School, 1861-63; entered army as vol. a. d. c. on staff Gen. Nelson A. Miles, 1864, served till close of war April, 1865; promoted Feb. 1865, to 2d lt. in 2d New York heavy arty. for gallantry at battle of Hatcher's Run, Va. Mustered out of vol. service Sept. 1865; apptd. 2d lt., 5th U.S. Arty., Feb. 1866; 1st lt., Jan. 1867; capt., Dec. 1887. Prof. mil. science Mass. Inst. Technology, 1872-76; grad. United States Artillery School, Fort Monroe, Va., and School of Submarine Mining, Willett's Point, N.Y., 1880. From 1883 to 1889 devoted time to development and perfecting of pneumatic dynamite torpedo gun. Traveled under orders in Europe, 1889-90 to obtain mil. information. Invented an intrenching tool, a ramrod bayonet, a telescopic sight for arty. and a system of range and position finding for sea-coast and arty. firing; on garrison duty at San Francisco, Calif., 1892; retired, Feb. 1894; promoted maj., Apr. 25, 1904. Home: New York, N.Y. Died 1909.

ZAND, STEPHEN JOSEPH, aeronautical engr., experimental cons.; b. Lodz, Poland, Sept. 18, 1898; s. Julius and Florentine (Volberg) Z.; D.E., Fed. Inst. Tech., 1920; Aeronautical Engr., Ecole Superieure de'Aeronautique, 1925; grad. study Columbia, 1931, N.Y.U., 1940; m. Helen Stankiewicz, July 6, 1925; children—Elizabeth (Mrs. Kellerman), Michael Christopher. Airplane designer Curtiss-Wright Co. and Ford Motor Co., 1929; research engr. Pioneer Instrument Co., 1931; research engr., asst. to v.p. Sperry Gyroscope Co., 1932-47; tech. adv. French Air Ministry, 1935; v.p. in charge engring. Lord Mfg. Co., Erie, Pa., 1947-52; exptl. cons. Research and Development Bd., 1952—; vice pres. Unitec, Incorporated, Boston, 1957—. Served as tech. aid Comdg. Gen. A.S. Command, U.S. A.A.F., World War II; now cons. Research and Development Bd. Recipient Wright Bros. medal, 1931; Presdl. Medal of Merit; French Legion of Honor, Croix de Guerre (Belgium, France). Profl. engr., N.Y., Pa., Conn., Mass. Fellow Royal Aero. Soc. of Gt. Britain, Inst. Aero. Scis.; mem. Soc. Automotive Engrs. Author: Kapok—An Exhaustive Study of Kapok and its Qualities as Soundproofing Material, 1941; also tech. articles. Contbr., co-editor: Aeronautical Handbook, 1951. Inventor automatic control mechanisms and scanning devices for aircraft; holds patents in field. Address: 187 Hubbard St., Lenox, Mass. Died Jan. 23, 1963; buried St. Ann's Cemetery, Lenox, Mass.

ZECHMEISTER, LASZLO KAROLY ERNO, prof. organic chemistry; b. Gyor, Hungary, May 14, 1889; s. Charles and Irene (Mocsary) Z.; student Polytech. Inst., Zurich, Switzerland, 1907-11 (diploma in chemistry, 1911; Dr. Engring., 1913); married. Began as asst., Kaiser Wilhelm-Inst. fur Chemie, Berlin, 1912; instr. Danish Royal Vet. Acad., Copenhagen, 1921-23; prof. of chemistry and dir. chem. lab., Med. Sch., U. of Pecs, Hungary, 1923-40; prof. organic chemistry, Calif. Inst. Tech., Pasadena, Calif., 1940-59; Guggenheim fellow, 1949; Sigma Xi lecturer, 1948. Awarded Pasteur medal, Paris, 1935; Claude Bernard medal, Paris, 1947. Member Hungarian Acad. Science (received the great prize of this Acad. 1937), Roy Danish Acad. Sci. (foreign mem.), Jr. Am. Chem. Soc. Author: Textbook of Organic Chemistry, 1930, 1932; Carotinoide, 1934; Principles and Practice of Chromatography (by L. Z. and L. Cholnoky), 1941, 43; and about 200 research papers. Editor: Progress in the Chemistry of Organic Natural Products, 1938. Address: Pasadena CA Died Feb. 28, 1972.

ZEIT, F(REDERIC) ROBERT AENISHAENSLIN, pathologist; b. Gelterkinden, Switzerland, Mar. 13, 1864; s. Robert and Lina (Metzger) Aenishaenslin Z.; ed. pub. schs. of Cologne, Düsseldorf and Elberfeld, Germany, and gymnasium at Elberfeld; M.D., Western Reserve U., Cleveland, 1887; m. Hanna F. David, of Basel, Switzerland, May 5, 1888; children—Mrs. Gretchen Gardner, Mrs. Edith Buker, Mrs. Elsie McClellan. Practiced as physician and surgeon in state of Wis., 1887-97; collaborator and 1st asst. of Prof. Edwin Klebs, 1897-1900; prof. of bacteriology and of clinical pathology, 1900-01, prof. pathology, 1902—, Northwestern U. Med. Sch.; prof. pathology and bacteriology, Post-Grad. Med. School of Chicago, 1900-19; cons. pathologist of Wesley and Grant hosps. Founder Frederic Robert Zeit Mus. of Pathology, Northwestern U. Republican. Presbyterian. Home: Winnetka, Ill. Died Dec. 5, 1935.

ZELENY, ANTHONY, (zel'e-ni), physicist; b. Racine County, Wis., Apr. 20, 1870; s. Anthony Herbert and Josephine (Pítka) Z.; B.S., U. of Minn., 1892, M.S., 1893, Ph.D., 1907; U. of Chicago, 1900; Göttingen, 1912; Princeton, 1915-16; m. Mattie L. Day, June 8, 1897; children—Leslie Day, Lawrence. Instr. Physics, 1897-1906, asst. prof., 1906-09, prof., 1909-38, prof. emeritus since 1938, U. of Minn. Fellow A.A.A.S. (v.p. 1914), Am. Phys. Soc.; mem. Sigma Xi; foreign mem. Nat. Acad. Sciences of Czechoslovakia (Masarykova Akademie Práce). Author: A Manual of Physical Measurements (with H. A. Erikson), 1902; Elements of Electricity, 1930; also papers on elec. condensers, induction, galvanometers, thermocouples, low temperatures, etc. Home: 1933 E. River Terrace, Minneapolis 14, Minn. Died Dec. 15, 1947.

ZELENY, CHARLES, zoölogist; b. Hutchinson, Minn., Sept. 17, 1878; s. Anthony H. and Josephine (Pitka) Z.; B.S., U. of Minn., 1898, M.S., 1901; Columbia, 1901-02; Stazione Zoölogica, Naples, Italy, 1902-03; Ph.D., U. of Chicago, 1904; m. Ida Benedicta Ellingson, May 29, 1911; 1 son, Charles Ellingson. Prof. zoölogy Ind. U., 1904-09, U. of Ill., 1909—, also head of dept., 1933—. Author of papers in field of experimental zoölogy, especially experimental embryology, regeneration and genetics. Home: Urbana, Ill. Died Dec. 21, 1939.

ZELENY, JOHN, physicist; b. Racine, Wis., Mar. 26, 1872; s. Anthony Herbert and Josephine (Pitka) Z.; B.S., U. Minn., 1892, Ph.D., 1906; student U. of Berlin, 1897; A.B., U. of Cambridge, Eng., 1899; M.A., Yale, 1915; m. Carolyn S. Rogers, June 21, 1905 (died Dec. 13, 1936); children—Elizabeth Rogers, Henrietta Carolyn; m. 2d, Clara Rogers Dunn, Dec. 26, 1938. Instr. physics, U. Minn., 1892-96, asst. prof., 1896-1900, asso. prof., 1900-08, prof. and head dept., 1908-15, acting dean Grad. Sch., 1912-13; prof., chmn. dept. and dir. grad. studies in physics Yale, 1915-40, emeritus since 1940, lecturer, 1941-43. Mem. Am. Phys. Soc., Am. Philos. Soc., A.A.A.S., Am. Acad. Arts and Sciences, Am. Assn. U. Profs., Am. Assn. Physics Tchrs., Phi Beta Kappa, Sigma Xi, Berzelius, Aurelian. Club: New Haven Country. Writer of monographs and articles on subjects in physics, especially on elec. conduction through gases, and related topics. Home: 44 Cold Spring St., New Haven. Died June 19, 1951.

ZENTMAYER, JOSEPH, inventor; b. Mannheim, Germany, Mar. 27, 1826; m. Catherine Bluim, 1849. Forced to leave Germany for polit. reasons due to his part in revolution of 1848; instrument maker, Phila., 1853-87; invented photog. lens for microscope, 1865; awarded Elliott Cresson gold medal for his scientific inventions, 1874; received gold medal for his improvements of microscope at Centennial Expn., Phila., 1876, Paris Exhbn., 1878. Died Phila., Mar. 28, 1888.

ZENTMAYER, WILLIAM, physician; b. Phila., Pa., Oct. 28, 1864; s. Joseph and Catharine (Bluim) Z.; M.D., U. of Pa., 1886; unmarried. Professor diseases of the eye, Graduate School of Medicine, U. of Pa., now emeritus; cons. surgeon to Wills (Eye) Hospital, St. Mary's Hospital and Glen Mills School. Fellow A.M.A. (chmn. section ophthalmology, 1916-17), Coll. Physicians of Phila. (chmn. sect. on ophthalmology, 1909-10); mem. Am. Ophthal. Soc. (pres. 1926-27), Acad Ophthalmology and Oto-Laryngology, Acad. Nat. Sciences, Pa. Acad. Fine Arts, Ophthal. Soc. of United Kingdom (British), A.A.A.S.; pres. local Med. Alumni Soc. of U. of Pa., 1922-23; chmn. sect. on eye, ear, nose and throat, Med. Soc. of State of Pa., 1935-36. Asso. editor Archives of Ophthalmology. Dir. of Nat. Soc. for Prevention of Blindness. Guest of honor of section on ophthalmology Annual Meeting of A.M.A., 1941. Awarded the Leslie Dana Gold Medal, 1945, by the St. Louis Soc. for the Blind. Home: 265 Forrest Av., Merion, Pa. Office: 1930 Chestnut St., Philadelphia 3 PA

ZERBAN, FREDERICK WILLIAM, (zer'ban), chemist; b. Oppenheim-on-Rhine, Germany, Oct. 20, 1880; s. Alexander and Mathilde (Witterstaetter) Z.; prep. edn., Gymnasium, Darmstadt, Germany, 1893-99; Ph.D., U. of Munich, 1903; m. Helen Regan, Aug. 18, 1908. Came to U.S., 1904, naturalized citizen, 1920. Carnegie research asst., Coll. City of New York, 1904-06; chemist La. Sugar Expt. Sta., 1906-08; dir. Sugar Expt. Sta., Lima, Peru, 1908-09; sub-dir. Agrl. Expt. Sta., Tucuman, Argentina, 1909-10; research chemist, Porto Rico Sugar Planters Expt. Sta., Rio Piedras, 1911-12; mgr. agrl. office, Potash Syndicate, New Orleans, 1913-17; research chemist La. Sugar Expt. Sta., New Orleans, 1917-20; dir. research, Penick & Ford, Ltd., New Orleans, 1920-23; chemist in charge New York Sugar Trade Lab. since 1923. Fellow A.A.A.S., Am. Inst. Chemists, Am. Inst. Chemical Engineers; member American Chemical Society, Inst. Food Technologists, International Soc. Sugar Cane Technologists (pres.), Assn. des chimistes de sucrerie de France; corr. mem. Nat. Acad. Sciences of Peru; hon. fellow Sugar Technologists of India; honorary mem. of Sugar Technologists of Peru; mem. Internat. Sugar Commn. Republican. Club: Chemists. Author: System of Cane Sugar Factory Control. Co-author: Sugar Analysis. Contbr. to chem. and tech. sugar trade jours. Home: 50 Commonwealth Av., Boston 16. Office: 113 Pearl St., N.Y.C. 4. Died Aug. 31, 1956; buried Westport, Conn.

ZERNIKE, FRITS, physicist; b. Amsterdam, July 16, 1888; s. C. F. A. and Anne (Dieperink) Z.; Sc.D., U. Amsterdam, M.D., 1952; Sc.D., U. Poitiers, 1955; m. Dora van Bommel van Vloten, 1929; 2 children. Became asst. astron. lab. U. Groningen, 1913, lectr. theoretical physics, 1915, prof. theoretical and tech. physics and theoretical mechanics, phase contrast microscope and galvanometer. Deco-1920-58, ret.; vis. prof. Johns Hopkins, 1948; devel. Scis., Haarlem, 1912; Rumford medal Brit. Royal Royal cipient gold medal U. Groningen, 1908, Dutch Soc. rated Officer Legion of Honor (France), 1954; re Royal Soc. Contbr. articles learned jours., Holland, Royal Netherlands Acad. Scis.; hon. mem. Royal Micros. Soc. London, Optical Soc. Am.; fgn. mem. Soc., 1952; Nobel prize for physics, 1953. Mem. Germany, U.S., Great Britain, Died Mar. 1966.

ZIESING, AUGUST, civil engr.; b. Peru, Ill., Feb. 19, 1858; s. Dr. Henry and Katherine (Brennemann) Z.; B.S., U. of Ill., 1878 (C.E., 1905); m. Alice A. Hanna, Feb. 27, 1884; children—Mabel (dec.), Henry Hanna, Mrs. Margarette Rector, Mrs. Gertrude Kemper, Mrs. Katherine Van Cleave. In bridge designing and constrn. work, 1878-81, ry. engring., 1881-83; mgr. and engr. Lassig Bridge Works, 1883-97; consulting engr., specialty railway structures, 1897-1901; v.p. and western manager, 1901-05, pres., Sept. 1905-1927, Am. Bridge Co.; retired from active bus., April 1, 1927. Mem. Am. Soc. C.E., Western Soc. Engrs., Am. Ry. Engring. Assn. Republican. Clubs: University, Union League, Engineers' (Chicago). Home: 125 Beach Rd., Glencoe, Ill. Died Feb. 16, 1942.

ZIMMER, JOHN TODD, museum curator, ornithologist; b. Bridgeport, O., Feb. 28, 1889; s. Franklin Pierce and Ida Virginia (Todd) Z.; B.S., U. of Neb., 1910, M.A., 1911, D.Sc., 1943; m. Margaret Louise Thompson, 1917; children—Ida Elizabeth (Sprague), Lawrence Thompson. Field expert in entomology, Nebraska Expt. Sta., 1911-13; asst. entomologist, P.I. Bur. of Agr., 1913-16; agrl. expert Ter. Papua, 1917-21; asst. curator birds, Field Museum Natural History, 1922-30; associate curator birds of Western Hemisphere, Am. Museum Natural History, 1930-34, acting curator, 1935, executive curator,

1936-42, curator, 1942—, became chairman, 1954. Fellow of the American Ornithologists' Union (council 1937-38, 1939-41; com. check list since 1930; Brewster Award com., 1940-45, chmn., 1942-45; recipient Brewster Award Medal, 1952). Fellow A.A.A.S., New York Zoological Soc.; mem. Society Systematic Zoology, Society for Study of Evolution, American Society of Mammalogists, Biol. Society of Washington, Neb. Ornithol. Union (hon.), Sigma Xi. Clubs: University (White Plains); Explorers (N.Y.). Mem. John Burroughs Memorial Award Com. since 1942. Republican. Presbyn. Author: Catalogue of Edward E. Ayer Ornithological Library (2 vols.), 1926; Birds of Marshall Field Peruvian Expedition, 1930; Studies of Peruvian Birds, Nos. 1-52 (cont.), 1931—; various papers on tropical Am. birds, P. I. birds, birds and insects of Neb., etc. Editor The Auk, 1942-47. Home: 112 Ralph Av., White Plains, N.Y. Office: Am. Mus. Natural History, N.Y.C. Died Jan. 6, 1957.

ZIMMERLEY, HOWARD HENRY, agrl. research; b. Erie, Pa., Feb. 26, 1890; s. Henry and Elizabeth (Petrie) Z.; B.S., Pa. State Coll., 1912; Ph.D., U. of Md., 1931; grad. study, U. of Md., part time, 1927-31; D.Sc., Clemson Agrl. Coll., 1937; m. Viola Olivet White, Dec. 21, 1916. Instr. horticulture, Pa. State Coll., 1912; horticulturist Kreg Pecan Co., Albany, Ga., 1913-14; asst horticulturist, Va. Truck Experiment Station, 1916, county agrl. agent, Del., 1917-19; horticulturist Va. Truck Expt. Station, 1918-31; sr. horticulturist U.S. Dept. Agr., 1931-32; dir. Va. Truck Expt. Station since 1932. Fellow Am. Assn. Agrl. Science; mem. Am. Soc. Hort. Sciences, Am. Soc. Plant Physiologists, Phi Kappa Phi, Sigma Psi. Democrat. Presbyterian. Mason. Club: Norfolk Rotary. Address: P.O. Box 2160, Norfolk, Va. Died Oct. 15, 1944.

ZIMMERMAN, HARVEY J., statistician; b. Stoyestown, Somerset Co., Pa., Oct. 5, 1869; s. Joseph J. and Elizabeth (Specht) Z.; grad. Central Teachers College of Pa., 1891; LL.B., Georgetown U., 1905; m. Bessie Dear Wynkoop, of Loudon Co., Va., Jan. 12, 1910. Teacher pub. schs. of Pa. 6 yrs.; served with 5th Regt. Pa. Vol. Inf., Spanish-Am. War, 1898; apptd. clk. Census Office, May 24, 1900; advanced to chief administrative grade; chief statistician for cotton and oils div., in general charge of the several processes involved in the collection, compilation and publication of the periodical reports of cotton ginned, cotton consumed and on hand, activity in cotton spinning, cottonseed and cottonseed products, and animal and vegetable fats and oils. Mem. Am. Statis. Assn., S.A.R., Pa. German Soc. Republican. Mem. Ref. Ch. Mason (Shriner). Home: 1517 Varnum St. N.W., Washington DC

ZIMMERMAN, PERCY WHITE, plant physiologist; b. Manito, Ill., Feb. 23, 1884; s. Henry and Elizabeth Ann (Singley) Z.; student Eastern Ill. State Normal Coll., 1907-10; B.S. and M.S., U. of Chicago, 1916, Ph.D., 1925; m. Patti C. Martin, Aug. 16, 1911; children—Jack Lois (Mrs. Wm. Gerow), Robert Louis. Supt. sch., Westville, Ill., 1910-13; asst. in botany, U. of Chicago, 1916; asso. prof. botany, U. of Md., 1916-17, actg. dean div. plant industry, 1917-18, prof. botany and dean coll. agr., 1918-25, prof. botany and asso. dean on part time, 1925-27; plant physiologist on part time, Boyce Thompson Inst. for Plant Research, 1925-27, plant physiologist, 1927—. Fellow A.A.A.S.; mem. Am. Soc. for Hort. Science Botanical Soc. of America, Torrey Botany Club (pres. 1946), Am. Chem. Soc., Am. Soc. Naturalists, Internat. Mark Twain Soc. (hon.), Sigma Xi, Alpha Zeta, Phi Kappa Phi, Pi Alpha Xi (honorary). Awarded (with others) A Cressy Morrison prize in exptl. biology by N.Y. Acad. Sciences, 1932. Awarded with Dr. A. E. Hitchcock $1000 prize of A.A.A.S. for research on plant hormones, 1935; Vaughn award of Am. Soc. for Hort. Science, 1946. Republican. Protestant. Author: Plant Hormones, 1946; and many scientific publs. on physiology of plants, etc. Contbr. to bot. and hort. jours. Home: 18 Greystone Pl., Yonkers 3, N.Y. Died Aug. 14, 1958.

ZIMMERMANN, JOHN EDWARD, mech. engr.; b. Buenos Aires, Argentine Republic, Jan. 31, 1874; s. John C. and Anna C. (MacKinley) Z.; B.A., Nat. Coll. of Buenos Aires, 1894; studied U. of Buenos Aires and U. of Pa.; m. Sarah Ann Frazier, June 5, 1900; children—Harriet F. (Mrs. Gerald W. Caner), Anna Cecilia (Mrs. Kennth Van Strum), Helena (Mrs. Reinhardt Wilbolz), Audrey (Mrs. Geo. Davis Gammon), Jean (Mrs. Edward L. Marshall). Served as private and interpreter with First City Troop of Phila., Puerto Rican campaign, Spanish-Am. War. Superintendent Am. Pulley Co., Phila., 1899-1901, sec., 1901-07; formerly mem. Dodge & Day, now Day & Zimmermann, Inc., pres. until 1929; pres. United Gas Improvement Co., 1929, chmn. of the board since Dec. 27, 1940; dir. Phila. Electric Co., Am. Pulley Co., United Gas Improvement Co., Conn. Gas & Coke Securities Co., Phila. Steam Co., Pa. R.R. Trustee U. of Pa. Mem. Am. Soc. Mech. Engrs., Franklin Inst. Clubs: Racquet, Philadelphia, Midday, Rittenhouse, Sunnybrook Golf, Boca Raton, Corinthian Yacht. Home: 25 E. Summit St., Chestnut Hill. Office: 1401 Arch St., Philadelphia, Pa. Died May 30, 1943.

ZINN, AARON STANTON, civil engr.; b. Logansport, Ind., Aug. 26, 1862; s. George and Eliza Jane (Nutt) Z.; grad. high sch., Logansport, 1884; completed 3 yr. course civil engring., Rose Poly. Inst., Terre Haute, Ind., 1887; m. Mabel Gray Cooper, June 1897; 1 son, Kenyon Cooper. Began in employ I.C. R.R., at Dubuque, Ia., 1887; county surveyor Will Co., Ill., 1892-95; asst. engr. Penna. Lines and C.,R.I.&P. R.R., 1895-1906; resident engr. Central Div. of Panama Canal, 1906-14; cons. engr. Republic of Panama, 1914-17; practised in Los Angeles, Calif., 1923—. Republican. Episcopalian. Home: Los Angeles, Calif. Died May 7, 1936.

ZINSSER, HANS, bacteriologist; b. New York, Nov. 1878; s. August and Marie Theresia (Schmidt) Z.; A.B., Columbia U., 1899, A.M., 1903, and hon. D.Sc. in 1929; M.D., College of Phys. and Surg. (Columbia U.), 1903; hon. D.Sc., Western Reserve U., 1931, Lehigh U., 1933, Yale, 1939, Harvard, 1939; m. Ruby Handforth Kunz, June 1905. Interne, 1903-05, bacteriologist, 1905-06, Roosevelt Hospital; asst. bacteriologist Coll. Phys. and Surg., 1905-06, instr. bacteriology and hygiene, same, 1907-10; asst. pathologist St. Luke's Hosp., 1906-10; asso. prof. bacteriology, Stanford U., Calif., 1910-11, prof., 1911-13; prof. bacteriology, Columbia, 1913-23; prof. bacteriology and immunity, Harvard Med. Sch., Boston, 1923—. Bacteriologist Presbyn. Hosp., 1913-23; consulting bacteriologist Children's Hosp., 1924-34, chief bacteriol. service, same, 1934—, Infant's Hosp., 1935—; consulting bacteriologist Peter Bent Brigham Hosp., 1924—. Mem. Am. Red Cross Sanitary Commn. to Serbia, 1915. Maj., M.C., U.S. Army, 1917, later col. Med. Corps; served as sanitary insp. 1st Army Corps, and 2d Field Army A.E.F., and as asst. dir. labs. and infectious diseases, A.E.F.; sanitary commr. in Russia for League of Nations, health sect., summer 1923; exchange prof. to France, 1935. Trustee Mass. Gen. Hosp. Decorated D.S.M., French Legion of Honor, Serbian Order of St. Sava. Mem. Nat. Acad. Sciences, A.M.A., Am. Acad. Arts and Sciences, Am. Acad. Tropical Medicine, and many other med. socs. Author: Text-Book of Bacteriology, 1911; Infection and Resistance; Resistance to Infectious Diseases; Rats, Lice and History, 1935. Home: Boston, Mass. Died Sept. 4, 1940.

ZIRKLE, CONWAY, biologist; b. Richmond, Va., Oct. 28, 1895; s. Charles Milton and Mary Louise (Timberlake) Z.; B.S., U. of Va., 1921, M.S., 1921; Ph.D., Johns Hopkins, 1925; student U. of London, Eng., 1923, U. of Geneva, Switzerland, 1924; m. Helen Emily Kingsbury, Oct. 4, 1923. Instr. in biology, U. of Va., 1920-21; asst. in botony, Johns Hopkins U. 1921-24; Nat. Research Council fellow, Harvard, 1925-28, research associate, 1929-30; asso. prof. of botany, U. of Pa., 1930-37, prof., 1937-72. Served with U.S. Army Med. Corps. 1918-19. Fellow A.A.A.S. (v.p. sect. L 1951-52); mem. Bot. America, Am. Soc. Naturalists (mem. editorial board), History of Science Soc., Raven Soc. of Va., Phi Beta Kappa, Sigma Xi, Gamma Alpha. Author: The Beginnings of Plant Hybridization, 1935; Death of a Science in Russia, 1949; also numerous scientific papers and monographs. Member editorial board of Isis since 1934, of Bot. Reviews from 1944, Stain Technology from 1946. Secretary board of trustees Biol. Abstracts, 1939-44. Home: Secane PA Died Mar. 28, 1972.

ZON, RAPHAEL, forester; b. Simbirsk, Russia, Dec. 1, 1874; s. Gabriel and Eugenia (Berliner) Z.; B.A., Classical Gymnasium, Simbirsk, 1892; B.S., Imperial U., Kazan, 1896; Cornell U., 1901; m. Anna Puziriskaya, 1903; children—Leo, Henry. Came to U.S., 1897, naturalized, 1903. With Forest Service, U.S. Dept. Agr., 1901—; asst. until 1907, chief of forest investigations, 1907-22, dir. Lake States Forest Expt. Sta., 1922-45; prof. forestry U. Minn. Fellow Soc. Am. Foresters, Originated and developed forest research in U.S. Clubs: Campus (Mpls.); Cosmos (Washington). Author: Forest Resources of the World, 2 vols. (with W. N. Sparhawk), 1923; also numerous govt. bulls. and articles in mags. Home: 2237 Doswell Av., St. Paul 8. Died Oct. 29, 1956.